THE
HOLY BIBLE

CONTAINING THE

OLD AND NEW TESTAMENTS

Revised Standard Version

TRANSLATED FROM THE ORIGINAL LANGUAGES
BEING THE VERSION SET FORTH A.D. 1611
REVISED A.D. 1881–1885 AND A.D. 1901
COMPARED WITH THE MOST ANCIENT AUTHORITIES
AND REVISED A.D. 1946–1952
SECOND EDITION OF THE NEW TESTAMENT A.D. 1971

Reference Edition with Concordance and Maps

Introductions, Annotations, Topical Headings,
Marginal References, and Index
Prepared and Edited by

HAROLD LINDSELL, Ph.D., D.D.

CAMBRIDGE
UNIVERSITY PRESS

LIBRARY OF CONGRESS CATALOG CARD NUMBER: 64–17541

Printed in Canada
Published by the Zondervan Corporation
Grand Rapids, Michigan 49506, USA

LONG PRIMER PRONOUNCING TYPE
STUDY BIBLE EDITION

Bound at the University Press, Cambridge

ISBN 0 521 51105 4 Hardback

Preface

The Revised Standard Version of the Bible is an authorized revision of the American Standard Version, published in 1901, which was a revision of the King James Version, published in 1611.

The first English version of the Scriptures made by direct translation from the original Hebrew and Greek, and the first to be printed, was the work of William Tyndale. He met bitter opposition. He was accused of willfully perverting the meaning of the Scriptures, and his New Testaments were ordered to be burned as "untrue translations." He was finally betrayed into the hands of his enemies, and in October 1536, was publicly executed and burned at the stake.

Yet Tyndale's work became the foundation of subsequent English versions, notably those of Coverdale, 1535; Thomas Matthew (probably a pseudonym for John Rogers), 1537; the Great Bible, 1539; the Geneva Bible, 1560; and the Bishops' Bible, 1568. In 1582 a translation of the New Testament, made from the Latin Vulgate by Roman Catholic scholars, was published at Rheims.

The translators who made the King James Version took into account all of these preceding versions; and comparison shows that it owes something to each of them. It kept felicitous phrases and apt expressions, from whatever source, which had stood the test of public usage. It owed most, especially in the New Testament, to Tyndale.

The King James Version had to compete with the Geneva Bible in popular use; but in the end it prevailed, and for more than two and a half centuries no other authorized translation of the Bible into English was made. The King James Version became the "Authorized Version" of the English-speaking peoples.

The King James Version has with good reason been termed "the noblest monument of English prose." Its revisers in 1881 expressed admiration for "its simplicity, its dignity, its power, its happy turns of expression . . . the music of its cadences, and the felicities of its rhythm." It entered, as no other book has, into the making of the personal character and the public institutions of the English-speaking peoples. We owe to it an incalculable debt.

Yet the King James Version has grave defects. By the middle of the nineteenth century, the development of Biblical studies and the discovery of many manuscripts more ancient than those upon which the King James Version was based, made it manifest that these defects are so many and so serious as to call for revision of the English translation. The task was undertaken, by authority of the Church of England, in 1870. The English Revised Version of the Bible was published in 1881–1885; and the American Standard Version, its variant embodying the preferences of the American scholars associated in the work, was published in 1901.

Because of unhappy experience with unauthorized publications in the two decades between 1881 and 1901, which tampered with the text of the English Revised Version in the supposed interest of the American public, the American Standard Version was copyrighted, to protect the text from unauthorized changes. In 1928 this copyright was acquired by the International Council of Religious Education, and thus passed into the ownership of the churches of the United States and Canada which were associated in this Council through their boards of education and publication.

The Council appointed a committee of scholars to have charge of the text of the American Standard Version and to undertake inquiry as to whether further revision was necessary. For more than two years the Committee worked upon the problem of whether or not revision should be undertaken; and if so, what should be its nature and extent. In the end the decision was reached that there is need for a thorough revision of the version of 1901, which will stay as close to the Tyndale-King James tradition as it can in the light of our present knowledge of the Hebrew and Greek texts and

iii

their meaning on the one hand, and our present understanding of English on the other.

In 1937 the revision was authorized by vote of the Council, which directed that the resulting version should "embody the best results of modern scholarship as to the meaning of the Scriptures, and express this meaning in English diction which is designed for use in public and private worship and preserves those qualities which have given to the King James Version a supreme place in English literature."

Thirty-two scholars have served as members of the Committee charged with making the revision, and they have secured the review and counsel of an Advisory Board of fifty representatives of the cooperating denominations. The Committee has worked in two sections, one dealing with the Old Testament and one with the New Testament. Each section has submitted its work to the scrutiny of the members of the other section; and the charter of the Committee requires that all changes be agreed upon by a two-thirds vote of the total membership of the Committee. The Revised Standard Version of the New Testament was published in 1946. The publication of the Revised Standard Version of the Bible, containing the Old and New Testaments, was authorized by vote of the National Council of the Churches of Christ in the U.S.A. in 1951.

The problem of establishing the correct Hebrew and Aramaic text of the Old Testament is very different from the corresponding problem in the New Testament. For the New Testament we have a large number of Greek manuscripts, preserving many variant forms of the text. Some of them were made only two or three centuries later than the original composition of the books. For the Old Testament only late manuscripts survive, all (with the exception of the Dead Sea texts of Isaiah and Habakkuk and some fragments of other books) based on a standardized form of the text established many centuries after the books were written.

The present revision is based on the consonantal Hebrew and Aramaic text as fixed early in the Christian era and revised by Jewish scholars (the "Masoretes") of the sixth to ninth centuries. The vowel signs, which were added by the Masoretes, are accepted also in the main, but where a more probable and convincing reading can be obtained by assuming different vowels, this has been done. No notes are given in such cases, because the vowel points are less ancient and reliable than the consonants.

Departures from the consonantal text of the best manuscripts have been made only where it seems clear that errors in copying had been made before the text was standardized. Most of the corrections adopted are based on the ancient versions (translations into Greek, Aramaic, Syriac, and Latin), which were made before the time of the Masoretic revision and therefore reflect earlier forms of the text. In every such instance a footnote specifies the version or versions from which the correction has been derived, and also gives a translation of the Masoretic Text.

Sometimes it is evident that the text has suffered in transmission, but none of the versions provides a satisfactory restoration. Here we can only follow the best judgment of competent scholars as to the most probable reconstruction of the original text. Such corrections are indicated in the footnotes by the abbreviation *Cn*, and a translation of the Masoretic Text is added.

The discovery of the meaning of the text, once the best readings have been established, is aided by many new resources for understanding the original languages. Much progress has been made in the historical and comparative study of these languages. A vast quantity of writings in related Semitic languages, some of them only recently discovered, has greatly enlarged our knowledge of the vocabulary and grammar of Biblical Hebrew and Aramaic. Sometimes the present translation will be found to render a Hebrew word in a sense quite different from that of the traditional interpretation. It has not been felt necessary in such cases to attach a footnote, because no change in the text is involved and it may be assumed that the new rendering was not adopted without convincing evidence. The analysis of religious texts from the ancient Near East has made

clearer the significance of ideas and practices recorded in the Old Testament. Many difficulties and obscurities, of course, remain. Where the choice between two meanings is particularly difficult or doubtful, we have given an alternative rendering in a footnote. If in the judgment of the Committee the meaning of a passage is quite uncertain or obscure, either because of corruption in the text or because of the inadequacy of our present knowledge of the language, that fact is indicated by a note. It should not be assumed, however, that the Committee was entirely sure or unanimous concerning every rendering not so indicated. To record all minority views was obviously out of the question.

A major departure from the practice of the American Standard Version is the rendering of the Divine Name, the "Tetragrammaton." The American Standard Version used the term "Jehovah"; the King James Version had employed this in four places, but everywhere else, except in three cases where it was employed as part of a proper name, used the English word LORD (or in certain cases GOD) printed in capitals. The present revision returns to the procedure of the King James Version, which follows the precedent of the ancient Greek and Latin translators and the long established practice in the reading of the Hebrew scriptures in the synagogue. While it is almost if not quite certain that the Name was originally pronounced "Yahweh," this pronunciation was not indicated when the Masoretes added vowel signs to the consonantal Hebrew text. To the four consonants YHWH of the Name, which had come to be regarded as too sacred to be pronounced, they attached vowel signs indicating that in its place should be read the Hebrew word *Adonai* meaning "Lord" (or *Elohim* meaning "God"). The ancient Greek translators substituted the word *Kyrios* (Lord) for the Name. The Vulgate likewise used the Latin word *Dominus*. The form "Jehovah" is of late medieval origin; it is a combination of the consonants of the Divine Name and the vowels attached to it by the Masoretes but belonging to an entirely different word. The sound of Y is represented by J and the sound of W by V, as in Latin. For two reasons the Committee has returned to the more familiar usage of the King James Version: (1) the word "Jehovah" does not accurately represent any form of the Name ever used in Hebrew; and (2) the use of any proper name for the one and only God, as though there were other gods from whom He had to be distinguished, was discontinued in Judaism before the Christian era and is entirely inappropriate for the universal faith of the Christian Church.

The King James Version of the New Testament was based upon a Greek text that was marred by mistakes, containing the accumulated errors of fourteen centuries of manuscript copying. It was essentially the Greek text of the New Testament as edited by Beza, 1589, who closely followed that published by Erasmus, 1516–1535, which was based upon a few medieval manuscripts. The earliest and best of the eight manuscripts which Erasmus consulted was from the tenth century, and he made the least use of it because it differed most from the commonly received text; Beza had access to two manuscripts of great value, dating from the fifth and sixth centuries, but he made very little use of them because they differed from the text published by Erasmus.

We now possess many more ancient manuscripts of the New Testament, and are far better equipped to seek to recover the original wording of the Greek text. The evidence for the text of the books of the New Testament is better than for any other ancient book, both in the number of extant manuscripts and in the nearness of the date of some of these manuscripts to the date when the book was originally written.

The revisers in the 1870's had most of the evidence that we now have for the Greek text, though the most ancient of all extant manuscripts of the Greek New Testament were not discovered until 1931. But they lacked the resources which discoveries within the past eighty years have afforded for understanding the vocabulary, grammar and idioms of the Greek New Testament. An amazing body of Greek papyri has been unearthed in Egypt since the 1870's—private letters, official reports, wills, business ac-

counts, petitions, and other such trivial, everyday recordings of the activities of human beings. In 1895 appeared the first of Adolf Deissmann's studies of these ordinary materials. He proved that many words which had hitherto been assumed to belong to what was called "Biblical Greek" were current in the spoken vernacular of the first century A.D. The New Testament was written in the Koiné, the common Greek which was spoken and understood practically everywhere throughout the Roman Empire in the early centuries of the Christian era. This development in the study of New Testament Greek has come since the work on the English Revised Version and the American Standard Version was done, and at many points sheds new light upon the meaning of the Greek text.

A major reason for revision of the King James Version, which is valid for both the Old Testament and the New Testament, is the change since 1611 in English usage. Many forms of expression have become archaic, while still generally intelligible—the use of thou, thee, thy, thine and the verb endings -est and -edst, the verb endings -eth and -th, it came to pass that, whosoever, whatsoever, insomuch that, because that, for that, unto, howbeit, peradventure, holden, aforetime, must needs, would fain, behooved, to you-ward, etc. Other words are obsolete and no longer understood by the common reader. The greatest problem, however, is presented by the English words which are still in constant use but now convey a different meaning from that which they had in 1611 and in the King James Version. These words were once accurate translations of the Hebrew and Greek Scriptures; but now, having changed in meaning, they have become misleading. They no longer say what the King James translators meant them to say. Thus, the King James Version uses the word "let" in the sense of "hinder," "prevent" to mean "precede," "allow" in the sense of "approve," "communicate" for "share," "conversation" for "conduct," "comprehend" for "overcome," "ghost" for "spirit," "wealth" for "well-being," "allege" for "prove," "demand" for "ask," "take no thought" for "be not anxious," etc.

The Revised Standard Version of the Bible, containing the Old and New Testaments, was published on September 30, 1952, and has met with wide acceptance. This preface does not undertake to set forth in detail the lines along which the revision proceeded. That is done in pamphlets entitled *An Introduction to the Revised Standard Version of the Old Testament* and *An Introduction to the Revised Standard Version of the New Testament*, written by members of the Committee and designed to help the general public to understand the main principles which have guided this comprehensive revision of the King James and American Standard versions.

These principles were reaffirmed by the Committee in 1959 in connection with a study of criticisms and suggestions from various readers. As a result, a few changes were authorized for subsequent editions, most of them corrections of punctuation, capitalization, or footnotes. Some of them are changes of words or phrases made in the interest of consistency, clarity, or accuracy of translation.

The Revised Standard Version Bible Committee is a continuing body, holding its meetings at regular intervals. It has become both ecumenical and international, with active Protestant and Catholic members, who come from Great Britain, Canada, and the United States.

The Second Edition of the translation of the New Testament (1971) profits from textual and linguistic studies published since the Revised Standard Version New Testament was first issued in 1946. Many proposals for modification were submitted to the Committee by individuals and by two denominational committees. All of these were given careful attention by the Committee.

Two passages, the longer ending of Mark (16.9–20) and the account of the woman caught in adultery (Jn 7.53–8.11), are restored to the text, separated from it by a blank

space and accompanied by informative notes describing the various arrangements of the text in the ancient authorities. With new manuscript support, two passages, Luke 22.19b–20 and 24.51b, are restored to the text, and one passage, Luke 22.43–44, is placed in the note, as is a phrase in Luke 12.39. Notes are added which indicate significant variations, additions, or omissions in the ancient authorities (Mt 9.34; Mk 3.16; 7.4; Lk 24.32, 51, etc.). Among the new notes are those giving the equivalence of ancient coinage with the contemporary day's or year's wages of a laborer (Mt 18.24, 28; 20.2; etc.). Some of the revisions clarify the meaning through rephrasing or reordering the text (see Mk 5.42; Lk 22.29–30; Jn 10.33; 1 Cor 3.9; 2 Cor 5.19; Heb 13.13). Even when the changes appear to be largely matters of English style, they have the purpose of presenting to the reader more adequately the meaning of the text (see Mt 10.8; 12.1; 15.29; 17.20; Lk 7.36; 11.17; 12.40; Jn 16.9; Rom 10.16; 1 Cor 12.24; 2 Cor 2.3; 3.5,6; etc.).

The Revised Standard Version Bible seeks to preserve all that is best in the English Bible as it has been known and used through the years. It is intended for use in public and private worship, not merely for reading and instruction. We have resisted the temptation to use phrases that are merely current usage, and have sought to put the message of the Bible in simple, enduring words that are worthy to stand in the great Tyndale–King James tradition. We are glad to say, with the King James translators: "Truly (good Christian Reader) we never thought from the beginning, that we should need to make a new Translation, nor yet to make of a bad one a good one . . . but to make a good one better."

The Bible is more than a historical document to be preserved. And it is more than a classic of English literature to be cherished and admired. It is a record of God's dealing with men, of God's revelation of Himself and His will. It records the life and work of Him in whom the Word of God became flesh and dwelt among men. The Bible carries its full message, not to those who regard it simply as a heritage of the past or praise its literary style, but to those who read it that they may discern and understand God's Word to men. That Word must not be disguised in phrases that are no longer clear, or hidden under words that have changed or lost their meaning. It must stand forth in language that is direct and plain and meaningful to people today. It is our hope and our earnest prayer that this Revised Standard Version of the Bible may be used by God to speak to men in these momentous times, and to help them to understand and believe and obey His Word.

THE NAMES AND ORDER

OF THE

BOOKS OF THE OLD TESTAMENT

BOOKS OF THE NEW TESTAMENT

ABBREVIATIONS

In the notes to the books of the Old Testament, the following abbreviations are used: Ms for manuscript; Mss for manuscripts. Heb denotes the Hebrew of the consonantal Masoretic Text of the Old Testament; and MT denotes the Hebrew of the pointed Masoretic Text of the Old Testament.

The ancient versions of the Old Testament are indicated by:

Gk   Septuagint, Greek Version of Old Testament
Sam Samaritan Hebrew text of Old Testament
Syr Syriac Version of Old Testament
Tg   Targum
Vg   Vulgate, Latin Version of Old Testament

Cn indicates a correction made where the text has suffered in transmission and the versions provide no satisfactory restoration but the Committee agrees with the judgment of competent scholars as to the most probable reconstruction of the original text. The reader is referred to the Preface for a statement of policy concerning text and notes.

The following symbols are used in the Introductions, Annotations and marginal references of the EYRE & SPOTTISWOODE STUDY BIBLE:

f, ff: Indicates that the verse(s) which follow are to be read. For example, 1 Ki 15.5ff means verse 5 and those which follow.

cf: Means compare the verse in the text with the verse in the cross reference.

see: Indicates that the verse in the cross reference is the starting point of, or justification for, the verse in the text.

This edition of the Revised Standard Version of the Bible is pertinently cross-referenced. In many instances the references are not listed in the order in which they appear in the Bible, but instead are arranged in chronological sequence. For example, under Numbers 25.11 the first reference is Psalm 106.30 and the last reference is Deuteronomy 32.16,21. This occurs because the verse from the Psalm applies to the opening portion of verse 11, and the Deuteronomy entry is in direct relation to the closing part of that passage. With this system, the references follow logically in immediate connection.

Each reference has been placed as close to its corresponding verse in the text as it was mechanically possible to do so.

Parallel names that are spelled differently in the cross reference are indicated in italics.

ABBREVIATIONS

The following abbreviations for the books of the Bible are used in the RSV footnotes: (Where the abbreviations differ in the Introductions, Annotations, and cross references they are indicated in parentheses.)

OLD TESTAMENT

Gen	Genesis	Eccles (Ecc)	Ecclesiastes
Ex	Exodus	Song (Sol)	Song of Solomon
Lev	Leviticus	Is (Isa)	Isaiah
Num	Numbers	Jer	Jeremiah
Deut	Deuteronomy	Lam	Lamentations
Josh	Joshua	Ezek	Ezekiel
Judg	Judges	Dan	Daniel
Ruth	Ruth	Hos	Hosea
1 Sam	1 Samuel	Joel	Joel
2 Sam	2 Samuel	Amos	Amos
1 Kings (1 Ki)	1 Kings	Obad	Obadiah
2 Kings (2 Ki)	2 Kings	Jon	Jonah
1 Chron (1 Chr)	1 Chronicles	Mic	Micah
2 Chron (2 Chr)	2 Chronicles	Nahum (Nah)	Nahum
Ezra	Ezra	Hab	Habakkuk
Neh	Nehemiah	Zeph	Zephaniah
Esther (Est)	Esther	Hag	Haggai
Job	Job	Zech	Zechariah
Ps	Psalms	Mal	Malachi
Prov	Proverbs		

NEW TESTAMENT

Mt	Matthew	1 Tim	1 Timothy
Mk	Mark	2 Tim	2 Timothy
Lk	Luke	Tit	Titus
Jn	John	Philem	Philemon
Acts	Acts of the Apostles	Heb	Hebrews
Rom	Romans	Jas	James
1 Cor	1 Corinthians	1 Pet	1 Peter
2 Cor	2 Corinthians	2 Pet	2 Peter
Gal	Galatians	1 Jn	1 John
Eph	Ephesians	2 Jn	2 John
Phil	Philippians	3 Jn	3 John
Col	Colossians	Jude	Jude
1 Thess	1 Thessalonians	Rev	Revelation
2 Thess	2 Thessalonians		

TABLE OF PRONUNCIATION SYMBOLS

In this book, the less common proper names have been marked with pronunciation symbols. Accents have not generally been used with names of two syllables. Names of three or more syllables have, for the most part, only one accent. Where there are unusually lengthy compound names, two and occasionally three accents will be found, however, without indication of primary or secondary stress. A short hyphen (-) has been placed in compound names where a division may aid the reader. In those instances where a proper name occurs twice in the same verse, pronunciation symbols are supplied only once.

ā	*as in* gate		į	*as in* union
ă	*as in* bat		ō	*as in* note
a	*as in* father		ŏ	*as in* not
ą	*as in* care		o	*as in* sort
ȧ, ȧh, aȧ, aė	*as in* sofa		ȯ, oė	*as in* reason
ä, aë	*as in* senate		oē	*as in* amoeba
aē	*as in* mediaeval		oi	*as in* oil
aĕ	*as in* aesthetic		ū	*as in* use
āi	*as in* bait		u	*as in* rule
aī	*as in* aisle		ŭ	*as in* put
aō	*as in* note		ụ	*as in* secular
au	*as in* haul		ú	*as in* burn
aȳ	*as in* aye		ȳ	*as in* fly
ē	*as in* evil		y̌	*as in* hymn
ĕ	*as in* met		ẏ	*as in* myrtle
ë	*as in* England		y	*as in* you
ę	*as in* obey		cçh, çh	*as in* character
ė, ėh	*as in* her		ç	*as in* ocean
eē	*as in* beet		ç	*as in* cell
eë	*as in* been		Cṇ	'*c*' *silent as* '*k*' *in* know
eī	*as in* height		ḍ, dḍ	*as in* graduate
ēi	*as in* ceiling		ġ	*as in* gym
eu, ew	*as in* grew		Mṇ	'*m*' *silent as in* mnemonic
eū, e
̄w	*as in* few		Pṭ	'*p*' *silent as in* ptomaine
ī	*as in* bite		ṣ	*as in* has
ĭ	*as in* bit		ṣ	*as in* pleasure
ï	*as in* machine		ṭ	*as in* motion
į	*as in* firm		x̣	*as in* xylophone

THE OLD AND NEW TESTAMENT BOOKS ARRANGED IN ALPHABETICAL ORDER WITH THE PAGE NUMBERS ON WHICH THEY BEGIN

THE BOOKS IN THE NEW TESTAMENT ARE INDICATED BY ITALICS

Foreword

"The Bible can serve its function in the modern world only if it is understood."—from the preface to *The Ancestry of our English Bible,* Ira M. Price (Harper & Row). Such is the purpose of the EYRE & SPOTTISWOODE STUDY BIBLE.

This work is neither a dictionary of the Bible nor a commentary on the Scriptures, and is not intended as a substitute for such books. A volume of this size, devised for the average reader, cannot deal extensively in involved questions of text and translation differences, important as these are to the world of technical scholarship, and about which there are as many views as there are scholars. To have done this would have focused attention on a subject which would create more problems than could be solved without adding hundreds of pages to an already substantial volume. This indispensable work is published primarily for students, clergymen, and laymen who desire the Revised Standard Version with annotations helpful to an understanding of the text, and useful for personal devotional reading, pulpit exposition, and classroom study. The wide margins will allow for the reader's own notes in ball-point ink or pencil.

The EYRE & SPOTTISWOODE STUDY BIBLE is made up of seven parts, each having an integral relationship to the others. Serious study of all of the parts by the reader is strongly recommended, for only a thorough knowledge of the individual segments will bring the whole Bible into sharper focus, and lead to a greater appreciation and love for the inspired Word of God.

(1) *The Introductions:* Prefacing each book is a substantive introduction—a summation of authorship, background, and proper historical and religious setting and characteristics. A general outline in the introduction capsules the contents, substance, and import of the book.

(2) *The Text:* The text of the Revised Standard Version appears precisely as copyrighted, together with the translators' notes. Single column, wide measure setting provides maximum ease of reading and study.

(3) *The Topical Headings:* Non-theological and non-interpretive, the topical headings provide a reliable guide to the contents and teachings of each book without bringing other books of the Bible to bear upon it. This device, arranged within appropriate verses throughout the text and set by typographers long skilled in Bible production, is an invaluable aid to Bible students and enables the reader to grasp the structure of the book and the meaning of its message quickly.

(4) *The Marginal References:* The cross reference system is unique in that the references, instead of being listed in the order in which they appear in the Bible, are arranged in chronological sequence for immediate association. These appear at the outside of the text, either to the left or right, on facing pages, and as closely adjacent to the related verse as possible. The asterisks (*) next to many of the references indicate an apposite footnote at the bottom of the page, further illustrating the subject under discussion. Parallel names that are spelled differently in the cross references are set in italics here.

(5) *The Annotations:* In addition to the Revision Committee's footnotes, the EYRE & SPOTTISWOODE STUDY BIBLE has hundreds of

interpretive notes written from the standpoint of conservative
theological scholarship. These annotations furnish historical,
archaeological, biographical, and textual information. Some bear on
a given theme or subject, others suggest alternate readings; all bring
together related Scripture from various parts of the Bible. Major
doctrines of the Christian faith are frankly set forth, obscure
passages are brought to light, terms are defined, and parables are
clearly explained. The annotations also include specific biblical
references, making the material a useful tool for Church schools,
Bible classes, and religious workers. All of this explanatory material
appears at the bottom of the relevant pages, thereby eliminating any
loss of continuity while reading. It is also an indispensable feature
for students who do not have ready access to extensive biblical
reference works.

(6) *The Index:* Approximately 1700 entries, appropriately cross-
indexed, direct the reader to any subject in the footnote material.

(7) *The Concordance:* A significantly new, practical concordance
contains more than 2100 entries built around 300 key theological
terms and favorite passages. Biographical summaries give biblical
references to the main events in the lives of leading characters in
the Bible. Careful use of the index *and* the concordance together
will uncover many of the vast riches contained in the Scriptures.

—HAROLD LINDSELL

Pasadena, California
July, 1964

The
Old Testament

INTRODUCTION TO
THE FIRST BOOK OF MOSES
COMMONLY CALLED
GENESIS

Authorship and Background: Genesis, the title given by the Septuagint translators, means "origin," "beginning." The Hebrew title, *Bereshith*, meaning "In the beginning," is the first word of the Hebrew text. Genesis is the first book of the Pentateuch (a Greek term meaning "five books"), which has been traditionally attributed to Moses. All events recorded in Genesis antedate Moses and so it is likely that he made use of whatever oral and written sources were available to him. One source, for example, may be the unit 1.1—2.3 where God is called by His generic name *Elohim*, "God." The heading, "These are the generations of the heavens and the earth" (2.4) may reflect another unit of source material. In this section (2.4—3.24) God is also called *Yahweh*, His personal name, and so this part of the book is characterized by the compound title *Yahweh Elohim*, "LORD God."

According to Ex 17.14; 24.4–8; 34.27; Num 33.1, 2; Deut 31.9, 22, 24 Moses was instructed to record certain specific information. Moreover, other Old Testament books refer to "the law of Moses" (1 Ki 2.3); "the book of the law of Moses" (2 Ki 14.6); and "the book of Moses" (Ezra 6.18; Neh 13.1, etc.). The New Testament also refers to Moses and the Law of Moses (cf. Mt 19.8; Mk 1.44; 10.4, 5; Lk 5.14; 16.31; 20.37; Acts 3.22; 13.39; 15.5ff; 26.22; Rom 10.5, 19; 1 Cor 9.9; 2 Cor 3.15; Rev 15.3).

The account of the death of Moses (Deut 34) appears to have been added by a later writer. It is also quite possible that in the course of time some changes were made in the text, and notes were added for the purpose of clarifying terms and explaining certain expressions and historical situations. Thus, for example, the name of a city in the time of Moses is given as Dan (Gen 14.14), whereas we are told that prior to the events recorded in Judges 18 this place was known as Laish (ver 29).

Many scholars of the last two centuries have objected vigorously to the idea of the Mosaic authorship of the Pentateuch. Among the best known viewpoints to reject this authorship is the Documentary Hypothesis of Wellhausen, although some eminent liberal scholars of the twentieth century have challenged almost every one of the basic positions represented in this view. Numerous variations of the Documentary Hypothesis and of other theories are current today. It may be said that most of the scholars who adhere to the non-Mosaic school of thought hold to the four documents in the order J, E, D, and P. Scholars in the conservative tradition steadfastly regard the Pentateuch as essentially Mosaic and attribute its authorship to Moses, even though there have been later minor editorial insertions and changes. These same scholars hold that there is not

Introduction to Genesis

sufficient evidence to categorically undermine the common tradition of Mosaic authorship.

Characteristics: An understanding of the Book of Genesis is fundamental to an understanding of the whole Bible. In it is found an account of generation (ch 1, 2), degeneration (ch 3—11), and regeneration (ch 12—50). The story of redemption begins after Adam's sin and is carried forward progressively in the selection of Seth, the saving of the Noahic family, the choice of Abraham, then Isaac (not Ishmael), and Jacob (not Esau). The line of redemption continues through the twelve sons of Jacob (Israel). The favored son Joseph is the focus of attention in the closing chapters of Genesis. The account opens with early man in the Garden of Eden and ends with the sons of Israel in Egypt. Much of Genesis is biographical as the life stories of the leading characters are portrayed. No effort is made to gloss over the sins and shortcomings of the major characters, so that the biographies include stories of trickery, deception, false witness, incest, fornication, and murder. At the same time there are numerous instances of faith and obedience under trying and difficult circumstances. Heroism, sacrifice, devotion, and uprightness of heart may be found in all of its pages. God is revealed by different names such as *Elohim*, *Yahweh*, and *Yahweh Elohim*. Through the whole book the writer traces the plan and work of God in his specific redemptive program for the world. A leading characteristic of the book is the recurring use of the phrase *'elleh toledoth*, "these are the generations of," which provides the divisions of the general outline.

Genesis begins with a unique view of God which underlies the whole Bible and which marks off the Hebrew-Christian tradition from the other religions of the world as generically different and springing from a self-revelation of God to man.

Contents:

I. The generations of the heavens and the earth. 1.1—4.26: The beginning followed by the six days of creation which end with God's Sabbath rest. The creation of Adam and Eve, their temptation in the Garden, and their fall. The consequences of the fall, the promise of a redeemer, and the expulsion of Adam and Eve from the Garden. The birth of Cain and Abel and the murder of Abel by Cain, followed by the birth of Seth and the renewal of the seed of promise.

II. The generations of Adam. 5.1—6.8: The descendants of the godly line of Seth and their intermarriage with the sons of Cain, followed by the degeneration of the race.

III. The generations of Noah. 6.9—9.29: God's command to Noah to construct the ark. The gathering of the animals and the commencing of the flood. The subsiding of the water and the return of Noah and the animals to the land. The establishment of human government and the promise never to destroy the earth again by water. Noah's drunkenness and later blessing and cursing of his children.

IV. The generations of the sons of Noah. 10.1—11.9: The renewal of life on the earth after the flood through the sons of Noah, followed by spiritual degeneration. The confusion of tongues at the tower of Babel.

V. The generations of Shem. 11.10–26: The ancestry of Abram from Shem through Abram's father, Terah.

Introduction to Genesis

3

VI. The generations of Terah. 11.27—25.11: Abram's departure from Ur to Haran. His journey to Canaan and then to Egypt. His return to Canaan and the struggle between him and Lot. Lot's backsliding and deliverance from captivity by Abram. Abram's return from battle and payment of the tithe to Melchizedek. God's covenant with Abram and the promise of a son. Ishmael's birth to Hagar. God's renewal of His promise, the change of Abram's name to Abraham, and the covenant seal of circumcision. God's destruction of Sodom and Gomorrah, and the saving of Lot and his daughters. The birth of Isaac; Ishmael and Hagar cast out. Abraham's offering of Isaac on Mt. Moriah, and God's intervention. Sarah's death and burial. Rebekah the bride of Isaac. Abraham's marriage to Keturah and death.

VII. The generations of Ishmael. 25.12–18

VIII. The generations of Isaac. 25.19—35.29: Jacob and Esau born; the covenant confirmed to Isaac by God. Jacob's stolen blessing and flight to Laban's home to escape the wrath of Esau. The covenant confirmed to Jacob at Bethel. Jacob's marriages to Leah and Rachel. The birth of sons, the prosperity of Jacob, his trouble with Laban, and his flight. Jacob's wrestling with God at Jabbok; becoming Israel, a prince with God. The meeting with Esau. Dinah's defilement by Shechem; Jacob's sons destroy Shechem and his family. God speaks to Jacob again at Bethel. The birth of Benjamin and Rachel's death. Isaac's death.

IX. The generations of Esau. 36.1–43

X. The generations of Jacob. 37.1—50.26: Joseph's vision; his deliverance into slavery. Judah's sin against Tamar and shame. Joseph's prosperity in Egypt; loss of his position with Potiphar and sentence to prison. Pharaoh's dream and Joseph's interpretation; his elevation to power. The famine; the visit of Joseph's brethren to Egypt. Their bringing of Benjamin. Joseph identifies himself. Jacob's descent to Egypt. His sickness and death: the blessing of his children and Joseph's children prior to his death. Joseph's death; his body placed in a coffin in Egypt.

THE FIRST BOOK OF MOSES

COMMONLY CALLED

GENESIS

I. *The generations of the heavens and the earth 1.1–4.26*

*1.1
Jn 1.1,2;
Ps 8.3;
Isa 44.24;
42.5; 45.18
1.2
Jer 4.23;
Ps 104.30

A. *The beginning*

1 In the beginning God created*a* the heavens and the earth. 2 The earth was without form and void, and darkness was upon the face of the deep; and the Spirit*b* of God was moving over the face of the waters.

B. *The seven creative days*

1. *First day: light*

*1.3
Ps 33.6,9;
2 Cor 4.6
1.4
Isa 45.7
*1.5
Ps 74.16

3 And God said, "Let there be light"; and there was light. 4 And God saw that the light was good; and God separated the light from the darkness. 5 God called the light Day, and the darkness he called Night. And there was evening and there was morning, one day.

2. *Second day: firmament*

1.6
Jer 10.12
1.7
Prov 8.28;
Ps 148.4

6 And God said, "Let there be a firmament in the midst of the waters, and let it separate the waters from the waters." 7 And God made the firmament and separated the waters which were under the firmament from the waters which were above the firmament. And it was so. 8 And God called the firmament Heaven. And there was evening and there was morning, a second day.

a Or *When God began to create*   *b* Or *wind*

1.1 Monotheism, or the belief in one God, has been shown to be a characteristic of the earliest religions. This concept runs counter to the modern notion that the idea of God was gradually evolved from primitive animism to polytheism, and then finally to monotheism. The researches of Schmidt, Langdon, Petrie, and Zwemer strongly support primitive monotheism. The development of polytheism and lower views of God as a retrogression from monotheism may be explained by the advent of sin and the spiritual decline which necessarily ensued. In Rom 1.19–23 the Apostle Paul summarizes this tragic devolution from monotheism.

1.3 The Genesis account of creation is not the only extant record of beginnings, for many of the pagan cultures preserved creation legends. Along with their gross polytheism, the Babylonian and Assyrian creation stories in particular contain certain similarities to the Genesis account. For example, *the deep* (Hebrew *tehom*) of 1.2 refers to the subterranean ocean on which, according to all the peoples of ancient southwestern Asia, the earth rested. Babylonian creation epics mention two primeval monsters (pictured in art as dragons): Apsu, the fresh-water subterranean ocean, and his consort Tiamat (etymologically the same as *tehom*), the salt-water ocean surrounding the earth. The symbol of the sea dragon as a representation of chaos and evil over which God is victorious is clearly stated in Ps 74.13, 14; Isa 27.1. Another similarity is that the firmament or heavens, like an inverted bowl, separated the waters above from the earth. When *the windows of the heavens were opened* (7.11), then the waters above descended as rain. In 2.6 the Hebrew word *ed*, translated *mist*, probably derives from Sumerian *id*; "stream," "river;" which the Babylonians personified as the river god Id. Thus, the footnote "flood" (2.6) is closer to the original meaning of a stream. Notwithstanding these and many other similarities with ancient sources, there is a vast difference between the exalted monotheism of the Genesis record and the crude polytheism of the pagan myths. Truly, the inspired Genesis account evidences the work of the Spirit of God on the mind of the biblical writer.

1.5 There are differences of opinion whether the days of creation were twenty-four-hour solar days or long periods of time marked by a beginning and an ending. The word *day* is used both ways in Scripture. Since this is true, some are of the opinion that it is proper to conclude from a scientific viewpoint that the days were probably periods of time rather than twenty-four-hour days. *Day* in 2.4 cannot possibly mean a twenty-four-hour day, and it may be inferred from 2.7–23 that a considerable period of time was included in the sixth creative day (cf. 1.27 *male and female he created them*).

3. Third day: dry land and vegetation

9 And God said, "Let the waters under the heavens be gathered together into one place, and let the dry land appear." And it was so. 10 God called the dry land Earth, and the waters that were gathered together he called Seas. And God saw that it was good. 11And God said, "Let the earth put forth vegetation, plants yielding seed, and fruit trees bearing fruit in which is their seed, each according to its kind, upon the earth." And it was so. 12 The earth brought forth vegetation, plants yielding seed according to their own kinds, and trees bearing fruit in which is their seed, each according to its kind. And God saw that it was good. 13And there was evening and there was morning, a third day.

4. Fourth day: luminaries

14 And God said, "Let there be lights in the firmament of the heavens to separate the day from the night; and let them be for signs and for seasons and for days and years, 15 and let them be lights in the firmament of the heavens to give light upon the earth." And it was so. 16And God made the two great lights, the greater light to rule the day, and the lesser light to rule the night; he made the stars also. 17And God set them in the firmament of the heavens to give light upon the earth, 18 to rule over the day and over the night, and to separate the light from the darkness. And God saw that it was good. 19And there was evening and there was morning, a fourth day.

5. Fifth day: birds and fishes

20 And God said, "Let the waters bring forth swarms of living creatures, and let birds fly above the earth across the firmament of the heavens." 21 So God created the great sea monsters and every living creature that moves, with which the waters swarm, according to their kinds, and every winged bird according to its kind. And God saw that it was good. 22And God blessed them, saying, "Be fruitful and multiply and fill the waters in the seas, and let birds multiply on the earth." 23And there was evening and there was morning, a fifth day.

6. Sixth day: animals and man

24 And God said, "Let the earth bring forth living creatures according to their kinds: cattle and creeping things and beasts of the earth according to their kinds." And it was so. 25And God made the beasts of the earth according to their kinds and the cattle according to their kinds, and everything that creeps upon the ground according to its kind. And God saw that it was good. 26 Then God said, "Let us make man in our image, after our

1.9
Job 26.10;
Prov 8.29;
Jer 5.22;
2 Pet 3.5
1.10
Ps 33.7
1.11
Lk 6.44

1.14
Ps 74.16;
104.19

1.16
Ps 136.8,9;
Job 38.7

1.18
Jer 31.35

1.21
Ps 104.25,
26
1.22
Gen 8.17

*1.24

1.25
Jer 27.5
*1.26
Ps 100.3;
Acts 17.26,
28,29;
Col 3.10

1.24 *cattle*, a general term referring to domesticated animals, also including sheep and goats. *beasts of the earth*, wild animals.
1.26 *Let us make man.* Many interpret *us* to mean the Trinity (see note to Mt 28.19), but probably early readers understood the word as the plural of majesty, just as the plural *Elohim* (Hebrew) is used for God to denote his majesty and attributes. Another possible interpretation is the picture of God consulting with his angelic court, *the host of heaven* (1 Ki 22.19) or *the sons of God* (Job 1.6). *man* is the generic Hebrew term *adam*. The man Adam was a special creation made up of body and spirit. He was made in the moral and spiritual image of God, a free rational being. He possessed something of God's knowledge, righteousness, and true holiness (Col 3.10; Eph 4.24). All human life derives from Adam and Eve (Acts 17.26; Rom 5.12; 1 Cor 15.21, 22).

likeness; and let them have dominion over the fish of the sea, and over the birds of the air, and over the cattle, and over all the earth, and over every creeping thing that creeps upon the earth." 27 So God created man in his own image, in the image of God he created him; male and female he created them. 28And God blessed them, and God said to them, "Be fruitful and multiply, and fill the earth and subdue it; and have dominion over the fish of the sea and over the birds of the air and over every living thing that moves upon the earth." 29And God said, "Behold, I have given you every plant yielding seed which is upon the face of all the earth, and every tree with seed in its fruit; you shall have them for food. 30And to every beast of the earth, and to every bird of the air, and to everything that creeps on the earth, everything that has the breath of life, I have given every green plant for food." And it was so. 31And God saw everything that he had made, and behold, it was very good. And there was evening and there was morning, a sixth day.

1.27
1 Cor 11.7;
Gen 5.2;
Mt 19.4
1.28
Gen 9.1,7;
Lev 26.9
1.29
Ps 104.14,
15; 136.25
1.30
Ps 145.15;
Job 38.41
1.31
Ps 104.24

7. Seventh day: the Sabbath

2 Thus the heavens and the earth were finished, and all the host of them. 2And on the seventh day God finished his work which he had done, and he rested on the seventh day from all his work which he had done. 3 So God blessed the seventh day and hallowed it, because on it God rested from all his work which he had done in creation.

2.1
Ps 33.6
*2.2
Ex 20.11;
Heb 4.4
*2.3
Isa 58.13

C. The creation of man

1. Man made: placed in Eden

4 These are the generations of the heavens and the earth when they were created.

In the day that the LORD God made the earth and the heavens,

*2.4

2.2, 3a rested is a translation of the Hebrew word shabath, "to cease, rest." Thus, the seventh day was designated as Shabbath, the holy day of rest, which through the influence of the Septuagint came to be spelled Sabbath.

2.3b There was a divine order in creation which admits of no other explanation than a divine intelligence at work. To suppose that accident, apart from design, produced all this marvelously adjusted mechanism of the universe is far more difficult to accept than the biblical account that God devised and constructed it all out of His own marvelous wisdom. "The account of creation is unique in ancient literature. It undoubtedly reflects an advanced monotheistic point of view, with a sequence of creative phases so rational that modern science cannot improve on it, given the same language and the same range of ideas in which to state its conclusions. In fact, modern scientific cosmogonies show a disconcerting tendency to be short-lived and it may be seriously doubted whether science has yet caught up with the biblical story." W. F. Albright, THE OLD TESTAMENT AND ARCHAEOLOGY (Old Testament Commentary, edited by Alleman and Flack), p. 135.

2.4 The names for God are varied in the Old Testament. Not only are single names given but there are compound ones as well. Some contend that the use of different names in Genesis presupposes multiple authorship. Others hold that Moses may have drawn his material from different sources which used different names, or he may have used different names himself. (1) El, Eloah, and its plural Elohim (all of which are translated God and imply the Mighty One, the ruler over all the created universe); (2) Yahweh, the covenantal name of the God of Israel (often, although erroneously, rendered "Jehovah"), meaning "He is" (i.e., He is the covenant-keeping God to His people, according to Ex 3.14), or "He causes (all things) to be," the theme of the prophets and Psalmists (instead of reading the sacred name Yahweh, pious Israelites substituted the word Adonai, "Lord" so that Yahweh is translated LORD in KJV and RSV); (3) Adonai, meaning "Lord" (emphasizing God's sovereignty as King); (4) Elyon, signifying the Most High; and (5) Shaddai, the Almighty. Here in 2.4 the compound Yahweh Elohim (LORD God) is used, indicating that the mighty Creator of chapter 1 is the One who enters into covenant relations with mankind.

5 when no plant of the field was yet in the earth and no herb of the field had yet sprung up—for the LORD God had not caused it to rain upon the earth, and there was no man to till the ground; 6 but a mist*c* went up from the earth and watered the whole face of the ground—7 then the LORD God formed man of dust from the ground, and breathed into his nostrils the breath of life; and man became a living being. 8And the LORD God planted a garden in Eden, in the east; and there he put the man whom he had formed. 9And out of the ground the LORD God made to grow every tree that is pleasant to the sight and good for food, the tree of life also in the midst of the garden, and the tree of the knowledge of good and evil.

10 A river flowed out of Eden to water the garden, and there it divided and became four rivers. 11 The name of the first is Pīshŏn; it is the one which flows around the whole land of Hăv′ĭlăh, where there is gold; 12 and the gold of that land is good; bdellium and onyx stone are there. 13 The name of the second river is Gīhŏn; it is the one which flows around the whole land of Cŭsh. 14And the name of the third river is Tīgrĭs, which flows east of Assyria. And the fourth river is the Eūphrā′tēs.

2. *The forbidden tree*

15 The LORD God took the man and put him in the garden of Eden to till it and keep it. 16And the LORD God commanded the man, saying, "You may freely eat of every tree of the garden; 17 but of the tree of the knowledge of good and evil you shall not eat, for in the day that you eat of it you shall die."

3. *The creation of Eve*

18 Then the LORD God said, "It is not good that the man should be alone; I will make him a helper fit for him." 19 So out of the ground the LORD God formed every beast of the field and every bird of the air, and brought them to the man to see what he would call them; and whatever the man called every living creature, that was its name. 20 The man gave names to all cattle, and to the birds of the air, and to every beast of the field; but for the man there was not found a helper fit for him. 21 So the LORD God caused a deep sleep to fall upon the man, and while he slept took one of his ribs and closed up its place with flesh; 22 and the rib which the LORD God had taken from the man he made into a woman and

c Or *flood*

Cross-references

2.5 Gen 1.12; Job 38.26–28
2.7 Gen 3.19; Ps 103.14; Job 33.4; Acts 17.25; 1 Cor 15.45
★2.8 Isa 51.3; Gen 3.24; 4.16
2.9 Ezek 31.8; Gen 3.22; Rev 2.7; 22.2,14
2.12 Num 11.7
2.14 Dan 10.4 *Hiddekel-Tigris*
★2.17 Deut 30.15, 19,20; Rom 6.23; Jas 1.15
2.18 1 Cor 11.9
2.19 Gen 1.20, 24; Ps 8.6
2.21 1 Sam 26.12

2.8 The location of the Garden of Eden has never been precisely determined. Scripture locates it generally on the Tigris (designated in KJV by its ancient name Hiddekel) and Euphrates rivers where they were joined by the rivers Pishon and Gihon. The last two have never been identified. Tradition has located Eden south of Ur, at a site known as Eridu. British archaeologists excavated the ruins of Eridu in 1918–19. On the other hand, Albright thinks that Pishon and Gihon may have been the Blue and White Nile.
2.17 "Covenant of works." God made a covenant with Adam in the Garden. It was an agreement between the Creator and man, a free moral agent. Adam was given the privilege of eating of the fruit of the Garden except for the *tree of knowledge*. This prohibition was given to make it clear that Adam's responsibility was to offer God perfect obedience. Moreover he was warned of the consequences of disobedience if he should eat of the forbidden fruit. But Adam disobeyed and thus reaped death for himself and for the human race of which he was the federal head (Rom 5.12, 18). Every covenant has a seal. The seal of God's covenant with Adam was the tree of life. It was the outward sign. From that tree Adam was separated because of sin. And to that tree believers shall some day be restored because of redemption (3.24; Rev 22.2).

★2.23 Eph 5.30; 1 Cor 11.8	brought her to the man. 23 Then the man said,
★2.24 Mt 19.5; Mk 10,7,8; 1 Cor 6.16; Eph 5.31	
2.25 Gen 3.7,10, 11	

brought her to the man. 23 Then the man said,
"This at last is bone of my bones
    and flesh of my flesh;
she shall be called Woman,*d*
    because she was taken out of Man."*e*
24 Therefore a man leaves his father and his mother and cleaves to his wife, and they become one flesh. 25And the man and his wife were both naked, and were not ashamed.

D. The fall of Adam

1. The temptation and sin of Adam and Eve

★3.1 2 Cor 11.3; Rev 12.9; 20.2

3 Now the serpent was more subtle than any other wild creature that the LORD God had made. He said to the woman, "Did God say, 'You shall not eat of any tree of the garden'?" 2And the woman said to the serpent, "We may eat of the fruit of the trees of the garden; 3 but God said, 'You shall not eat of the fruit of the tree which is in the midst of the garden, neither shall you touch it, lest you die.' " 4 But the serpent said to the woman, "You will not die. 5 For God knows that when you eat of it your eyes will be opened, and you will be like God, knowing good and evil." 6 So when the woman saw that the tree was good for food, and that it was a delight to the eyes, and that the tree was to be desired to make one wise, she took of its fruit and ate; and she also gave

d Heb *ishshah* *e* Heb *ish*

2.23 *Woman* (Eve) was, like Adam, created by God in His own moral and spiritual image (1.27). She was taken from Adam's side (2.21, 22) to be a helpmate for him (2.18, 20). Woman was made for man (1 Cor 11.9), was subject to his authority (1 Cor 11.3), and was to be his glory (1 Cor 11.7). Sin had its beginnings through Eve, who was first deceived by Satan (3.1–6; 2 Cor 11.3; 1 Tim 2.14), although Adam freely chose to sin and thereby merited guilt and death.

2.24 The institution of marriage was established and ordained of God for the welfare and personal fulfilment of man and for the increase of the human race (1.28; 2.18; 9.1). This is God's plan as given in the Old Testament. The enlargement comes in the New Testament but this verse was the basis for Jesus' concept of marriage. The New Testament teaching includes the following: (1) marriage is lawful for all (1 Cor 7.2, 28; 1 Tim 5.14); (2) it is an honorable estate (Heb 13.4); (3) Christians should marry fellow Christians (2 Cor 6.14–18; 1 Cor 7.39); (4) marriage cannot be dissolved during the life of the partners except for biblical reasons (Mt 19.6ff; Rom 7.2, 3). (See also note to Deut 24.1 on divorce).

3.1 Verses 1–6 have in them all of the elements basic to any temptation which is likely to confront man. Doubting God, raising questions, pitting one's will against His, all have theological implications which one is apt to overlook when the story is read casually.

3.3 Adam's probation in the Garden of Eden was conditioned upon obedience. God warned Adam of the consequences of eating of the forbidden fruit. The sentence for disobedience was twofold: (1) spiritual death, by which Adam's nature was corrupted and he himself spiritually separated from God by his sin; (2) physical death, a penalty which was not immediately executed, but which made Adam mortal. According to the New Testament, both physical and spiritual death have been transmitted to the entire human race through Adam (Rom 5.12–14).

3.6 Adam sinned and fell. This all will admit. The vexing problem is whether the guilt of Adam was imputed to the whole human race. However theologians may differ, they agree that all men are sinners and need a Savior. Those who hold that Adam's guilt is imputed believe that infants are born not only sinners by natural inheritance but are also personally guilty and under condemnation. Infants who die are to be saved only by the free application of Christ's merits. Those who hold that infants are born sinful but without guilt attached also believe that when infants reach the age of accountability they choose to sin and thus need a Savior; but infants who die in infancy are saved by God's grace since they have incurred no personal guilt by overt acts of sin. The former view is known as "federal headship" since by God's *covenant* (in Latin, *foedus*) Adam was the covenantal representative of all his descendants.

3.6 Adam fell because of his disobedience (3.6–12; Rom 5.12–19). He was incited by Satan to do so (3.1–5; Rev 12.9) although he yielded to temptation by his own free will. Adam was banished from Eden, condemned to temporal death, and promised both labor and sorrow (3.14–24). God also imposed penal consequences which passed from Adam to his posterity and thus to all men.

some to her husband, and he ate. 7 Then the eyes of both were opened, and they knew that they were naked; and they sewed fig leaves together and made themselves aprons.

2. The judgment of God
a. The sin uncovered

8 And they heard the sound of the LORD God walking in the garden in the cool of the day, and the man and his wife hid themselves from the presence of the LORD God among the trees of the garden. 9 But the LORD God called to the man, and said to him, "Where are you?" 10And he said, "I heard the sound of thee in the garden, and I was afraid, because I was naked; and I hid myself." 11 He said, "Who told you that you were naked? Have you eaten of the tree of which I commanded you not to eat?" 12 The man said, "The woman whom thou gavest to be with me, she gave me fruit of the tree, and I ate." 13 Then the LORD God said to the woman, "What is this that you have done?" The woman said, "The serpent beguiled me, and I ate." 14 The LORD God said to the serpent,

3.8
Job 31.33;
Jer 23.24

3.10
1 Jn 3.20

3.12
Prov 28.13

3.13
2 Cor 11.3;
1 Tim 2.14

*3.14
Isa 65.25;
Mic 7.17

b. The curse on the serpent

"Because you have done this,
  cursed are you above all cattle,
  and above all wild animals;
upon your belly you shall go,
  and dust you shall eat
  all the days of your life.
15 I will put enmity between you and the woman,
  and between your seed and her seed;
he shall bruise your head,
  and you shall bruise his heel."

*3.15
Jn 8.44;
Acts 13.10;
1 Jn 3.8;
Isa 7.14;
Mt 1.23;
Rom 16.20;
Rev 12.7

c. The curse on Eve

16 To the woman he said,
"I will greatly multiply your pain in childbearing;
  in pain you shall bring forth children,
yet your desire shall be for your husband,
  and he shall rule over you."

3.16
Isa 13.8;
Gen 4.7;
1 Cor 11.3;
Eph 5.22

d. The curse on Adam

17 And to Adam he said,
"Because you have listened to the voice of your wife,
  and have eaten of the tree
of which I commanded you,
  'You shall not eat of it,'

3.17
1Sam15.23;
Gen 2.17;
Rom 8.20–
22

3.14 Following the fall of Adam, God laid down certain conditions which were to govern the life of man until the end of the age: (1) the serpent, the instrument in the temptation, was cursed; (2) a Redeemer was promised for mankind (ver 15); (3) the condition of womanhood was altered in two respects: (a) multiplied pain in childbirth and (b) a status of subjection to her husband; (4) the ground was cursed to bring forth thorns and thistles; (5) man was to earn his living by the sweat of his brow; (6) physical death was to be the lot of all men. (Also read verses 15–19.)

3.15 This is the first promise of a Redeemer. The conflict of the ages is predicted—a conflict between the seed of the woman and the seed of the serpent. The Redeemer will finally bring ruin to Satan and his seed although in the process Satan will bruise the Redeemer (as took place at Calvary). Isa 53.10 further reveals that Satan's maltreatment of Christ the Redeemer was in accord with the permissive will and all-wise plan of God the Father.

cursed is the ground because of you;
in toil you shall eat of it all the days of your life;
18 thorns and thistles it shall bring forth to you;
and you shall eat the plants of the field.
19 In the sweat of your face
you shall eat bread
till you return to the ground,
for out of it you were taken;
you are dust,
and to dust you shall return."

e. The expulsion from the garden

20 The man called his wife's name Eve,*f* because she was the mother of all living. 21And the LORD God made for Adam and for his wife garments of skins, and clothed them.

22 Then the LORD God said, "Behold, the man has become like one of us, knowing good and evil; and now, lest he put forth his hand and take also of the tree of life, and eat, and live for ever"—23 therefore the LORD God sent him forth from the garden of Eden, to till the ground from which he was taken. 24 He drove out the man; and at the east of the garden of Eden he placed the cherubim, and a flaming sword which turned every way, to guard the way to the tree of life.

E. Cain and his descendants

1. The offerings of Cain and Abel

4 Now Adam knew Eve his wife, and she conceived and bore Cain, saying, "I have gotten*g* a man with the help of the LORD." 2And again, she bore his brother Abel. Now Abel was a keeper of sheep, and Cain a tiller of the ground. 3 In the course of time Cain brought to the LORD an offering of the fruit of the ground, 4 and Abel brought of the firstlings of his flock and of their fat portions. And the LORD had regard for Abel and his offering, 5 but for Cain and his offering he had no regard. So Cain was very angry, and his countenance fell. 6 The LORD said to Cain, "Why are you angry, and why has your countenance fallen? 7 If you do well, will you not be accepted? And if you do not do well, sin is couching at the door; its desire is for you, but you must master it."

f The name in Hebrew resembles the word for *living* *g* Heb *qanah*, get

Cross references (margin):
*3.18 Ps 104.14; 3.19 Gen 2.7; Ps 90.3; 104.29; Ecc 12.7; *3.21; *3.22 Rev 22.2; 3.23 Gen 4.2; 3.24 Gen 2.8,9; 4.2 Lk 11.50,51; 4.3 Num 18.12; *4.4 Num 18.17; Lev 3.16; Heb 11.4; 4.5 Isa 3.9; Jude 11; *4.7

3.18 It is possible that thorns and thistles, tooth and claw, may have existed already outside of Eden. One need not suppose that death was not present in the animal kingdom long before the sin of man.
3.21 Garments in Scripture, when used symbolically, may represent the tattered rags of self-righteousness (Isa 64.6) which make a shabby cloak for our sins; the righteousness and excellencies of Christ imputed and imparted to the believer (Rev 3.18; 19.8).
3.22 The implication here is that the *tree of life* was now disallowed only because of knowledge gained through man's sin.
4.4 Abel offered an animal sacrifice; Cain offered the fruit of the ground. From the analogy of Scripture it may be concluded that the difference between the two sacrifices was not merely one of personal piety and faith. Evidently they had both been told of the necessity for a blood sacrifice as an expression of true faith. Abel therefore offered *a more acceptable sacrifice* (Heb 11.4). He became the first martyr (Mt 23.35) and is listed as a hero of the faith (Heb 11.4). His death is compared with that of Christ in Heb 12.24.
4.7 The same Hebrew word (*chattath*) is used for *sin* and *sin-offering*. In Mosaic usage the offerer placed his hand on the head of the victim, thus identifying himself with his sin-offering. Even so *For our sake he made him to be sin* (2 Cor 5.21) so that men could become righteous through faith in Him. (See also note to 1 Pet 2.24.)

2. Cain slays Abel: God's curse

8 Cain said to Abel his brother, "Let us go out to the field."[h] And when they were in the field, Cain rose up against his brother Abel, and killed him. 9 Then the LORD said to Cain, "Where is Abel your brother?" He said, "I do not know; am I my brother's keeper?" 10And the LORD said, "What have you done? The voice of your brother's blood is crying to me from the ground. 11And now you are cursed from the ground, which has opened its mouth to receive your brother's blood from your hand. 12 When you till the ground, it shall no longer yield to you its strength; you shall be a fugitive and a wanderer on the earth." 13 Cain said to the LORD, "My punishment is greater than I can bear. 14 Behold, thou hast driven me this day away from the ground; and from thy face I shall be hidden; and I shall be a fugitive and a wanderer on the earth, and whoever finds me will slay me." 15 Then the LORD said to him, "Not so![i] If any one slays Cain, vengeance shall be taken on him sevenfold." And the LORD put a mark on Cain, lest any who came upon him should kill him. 16 Then Cain went away from the presence of the LORD, and dwelt in the land of Nŏd,[j] east of Eden.

3. Cain's children

17 Cain knew his wife, and she conceived and bore Enoch; and he built a city, and called the name of the city after the name of his son, Enoch. 18 To Enoch was born Ī′răd; and Irad was the father of Mē-hū′jä-ėl, and Me-huja-el the father of Mē-thu′-shä-ėl, and Me-thusha-el the father of Lāmėch. 19And Lāmėch took two wives; the name of the one was Ādáh, and the name of the other Zĭlláh. 20Ādáh bore Jābál; he was the father of those who dwell in tents and have cattle. 21 His brother's name was Jubál; he was the father of all those who play the lyre and pipe. 22 Zĭlláh bore Tu′bál-cāin′; he was the forger of all instruments of bronze and iron. The sister of Tubal-cain was Nā′ámáh.

23 Lāmėch said to his wives:
"Adáh and Zĭlláh, hear my voice;
   you wives of Lamech, hearken to what I say:
I have slain a man for wounding me,
   a young man for striking me.
24 If Cain is avenged sevenfold,
   truly Lāmėch seventy-sevenfold."

F. The birth of Seth

25 And Adam knew his wife again, and she bore a son and

Marginal references:
4.8 Mt 23.35; 1 Jn 3.12
4.10 Heb 12.24; Rev 6.10
4.12 ver 14
4.14 Ps 51.11; Gen 9.6; Num 35.19, 21,27
4.15 Ps 79.12; Ezek 9.4,6
4.17 Ps 49.11
4.18 Gen 5.25, 28,30
*4.22
4.23 Ex 20.13; Lev 19.18; Deut 32.35; Lk 3.36; ver 18
4.24 ver 15
4.25 Gen 5.3; ver 8

h Sam Gk Syr Compare Vg: Heb lacks Let us go out to the field
i Gk Syr Vg: Heb Therefore j That is Wandering

4.22 For nearly three centuries the accepted chronology of the Bible was based upon the assumption that Adam commenced his career around 4004 B.C. This chronology was worked out by Archbishop Ussher in the 17th century. Recent scientific advances, including the carbon dating method, make the Ussher chronology impossible. Many scholars accept interpretations of the biblical text which allow for substantial chronological gaps in the genealogical lists of Gen 5, 11, thus allowing for an age of man much greater than that suggested by Ussher. Bronze did not become common until 3300–3000 B.C. and iron did not appear until 1500–1200 B.C. Tubal-cain, the 8th generation from Adam, according to this verse was the forger of all instruments of bronze and iron. This, along with scientific data, makes it evident that the biblical chronologies have tremendous gaps in them.

4.26
1 Ki 18.24;
Ps 116.17;
Joel 2.32;
Zeph 3.9;
1 Cor 1.2

called his name Sĕth, for she said, "God has appointed for me another child instead of Abel, for Cain slew him." 26 To Sĕth also a son was born, and he called his name Ēnŏsh. At that time men began to call upon the name of the LORD.

II. The generations of Adam 5.1–6.8

A. Adam and Seth

5.1
Gen 1.26;
Eph 4.24;
Col 3.10
5.2
Gen 1.27
5.3
Gen 4.25
5.5
Gen 3.19;
Heb 9.27

5 This is the book of the generations of Adam. When God created man, he made him in the likeness of God. 2 Male and female he created them, and he blessed them and named them Man when they were created. 3 When Adam had lived a hundred and thirty years, he became the father of a son in his own likeness, after his image, and named him Sĕth. 4 The days of Adam after he became the father of Sĕth were eight hundred years; and he had other sons and daughters. 5 Thus all the days that Adam lived were nine hundred and thirty years; and he died.

B. Seth and Enosh

5.6
Gen 4.26
5.7
Lk 3.38

6 When Sĕth had lived a hundred and five years, he became the father of Ēnŏsh. 7 Sĕth lived after the birth of Ēnŏsh eight hundred and seven years, and had other sons and daughters. 8 Thus all the days of Sĕth were nine hundred and twelve years; and he died.

C. Enosh and Kenan

5.11
1 Chr 1.1

9 When Ēnŏsh had lived ninety years, he became the father of Kēnȧn. 10 Ēnŏsh lived after the birth of Kēnȧn eight hundred and fifteen years, and had other sons and daughters. 11 Thus all the days of Ēnŏsh were nine hundred and five years; and he died.

D. Kenan and Mahalalel

5.12
1 Chr 1.2

12 When Kēnȧn had lived seventy years, he became the father of Mȧ-hā′lȧlĕl. 13 Kēnȧn lived after the birth of Mȧ-hā′lȧlĕl eight hundred and forty years, and had other sons and daughters. 14 Thus all the days of Kēnȧn were nine hundred and ten years; and he died.

E. Mahalalel and Jared

5.15
1 Chr 1.2

15 When Mȧ-hā′lȧlĕl had lived sixty-five years, he became the father of Jārĕd. 16 Mȧ-hā′lȧlĕl lived after the birth of Jārĕd eight hundred and thirty years, and had other sons and daughters. 17 Thus all the days of Mȧ-hā′lȧlĕl were eight hundred and ninety-five years; and he died.

F. Jared and Enoch

5.18
Jude 14,15

18 When Jārĕd had lived a hundred and sixty-two years he became the father of Enoch. 19 Jārĕd lived after the birth of Enoch eight hundred years, and had other sons and daughters. 20 Thus

all the days of Jārĕd were nine hundred and sixty-two years; and he died.

G. Enoch and Methuselah

21 When Enoch had lived sixty-five years, he became the father of Mĕthu'ṣĕláh. 22 Enoch walked with God after the birth of Mĕthu'ṣĕláh three hundred years, and had other sons and daughters. 23 Thus all the days of Enoch were three hundred and sixty-five years. 24 Enoch walked with God; and he was not, for God took him.

5.21
1 Chr 1.3;
Lk 3.37;
Jude 14

*5.24
2 Ki 2.11;
Heb 11.5

H. Methuselah and Lamech

25 When Mĕthu'ṣĕláh had lived a hundred and eighty-seven years, he became the father of Lāmĕçh. 26 Mĕthu'ṣĕláh lived after the birth of Lāmĕçh seven hundred and eighty-two years, and had other sons and daughters. 27 Thus all the days of Mĕthu'ṣĕláh were nine hundred and sixty-nine years; and he died.

5.26
Lk 3.36

*5.27

I. Lamech and Noah

28 When Lāmĕçh had lived a hundred and eighty-two years, he became the father of a son, 29 and called his name Noah, saying, "Out of the ground which the LORD has cursed this one shall bring us relief from our work and from the toil of our hands." 30 Lāmĕçh lived after the birth of Noah five hundred and ninety-five years, and had other sons and daughters. 31 Thus all the days of Lāmĕçh were seven hundred and seventy-seven years; and he died.

5.29
Gen 3.17–
19

J. Noah and his sons

32 After Noah was five hundred years old, Noah became the father of Shĕm, Ham, and Jāphĕth.

5.32
Gen 6.10;
10.21

K. The wickedness of men: the judgment of God

6 When men began to multiply on the face of the ground, and daughters were born to them, 2 the sons of God saw that the daughters of men were fair; and they took to wife such of them as they chose. 3 Then the LORD said, "My spirit shall not abide in

6.1
Gen 1.28
6.2
Deut 7.1–4
6.3
1 Pet 3.19;
Ps 78.39

5.24 Hebrews 11.5 reveals that Enoch was taken into heaven alive, never tasting physical death. This "translation" was a miracle. The only other instance of this kind in Scripture is that of Elijah (2 Ki 2.11).
5.27 Methuselah was the oldest person whose life is recorded in Scripture. There has been great debate over the question of longevity and three possible solutions have been proposed. One is that men actually lived nine hundred or more years because conditions in the antediluvian world were different and thus made longevity possible. Since the flood, the life span of man has been cut down. A second theory is that time must be reduced. There are Babylonian records which speak of men living 30,000 years. The theory of reduction ratio of time hardly appears feasible, however, and must be rejected. If, for ex-

ample, one were to divide the ages by ten then Methuselah's life span was close to one hundred years but his father (Enoch) would have been six and one-half years of age (Gen 5.21) when Methuselah was born. The third theory is that the biblical records deal with the families of the people mentioned and not their chronological ages. Thus it was the family of Methuselah and not the individual about which the author wrote. This view is complicated by the fact that Hebrews 11.5 speaks of Enoch as an individual and records his personal translation, not the translation of his family. Present medical forecasts predict greatly extended life spans for men, lending credence to the view that the patriarchal antediluvians may well have lived nine hundred or more years.

man for ever, for he is flesh, but his days shall be a hundred and
twenty years." 4 The Nĕph′ilim were on the earth in those days,
and also afterward, when the sons of God came in to the daughters
of men, and they bore children to them. These were the mighty
men that were of old, the men of renown.

5 The LORD saw that the wickedness of man was great in the
earth, and that every imagination of the thoughts of his heart was
only evil continually. 6And the LORD was sorry that he had made
man on the earth, and it grieved him to his heart. 7 So the LORD
said, "I will blot out man whom I have created from the face of
the ground, man and beast and creeping things and birds of the
air, for I am sorry that I have made them." 8 But Noah found
favor in the eyes of the LORD.

III. The generations of Noah 6.9–9.29

A. The command to build the ark

9 These are the generations of Noah. Noah was a righteous man,
blameless in his generation; Noah walked with God. 10And Noah
had three sons, Shĕm, Ham, and Jāphĕth.

11 Now the earth was corrupt in God's sight, and the earth was
filled with violence. 12And God saw the earth, and behold, it was
corrupt; for all flesh had corrupted their way upon the earth.
13And God said to Noah, "I have determined to make an end of
all flesh; for the earth is filled with violence through them; behold, I will destroy them with the earth. 14 Make yourself an ark
of gopher wood; make rooms in the ark, and cover it inside and
out with pitch. 15 This is how you are to make it: the length of the
ark three hundred cubits, its breadth fifty cubits, and its height
thirty cubits. 16 Make a roof*k* for the ark, and finish it to a cubit
above; and set the door of the ark in its side; make it with lower,
second, and third decks. 17 For behold, I will bring a flood of
waters upon the earth, to destroy all flesh in which is the breath

k Or *window*

6.4 The KJV reads "there were giants in the earth." Many have construed this to mean that angels (the sons of God) were joined in marriage to human beings and spawned a mixed race. The Nephilim were strong, violent, tyrannous men of great wickedness. But it is far more likely that *the sons of God* refer to those descendants of Seth who trusted in the LORD but whose children intermarried with women descended from Cain. The marriage union was not with angels then, but one consummated between the godly and ungodly families of men. Angels neither marry nor are given in marriage so that the verse hardly applies to them. On the other hand, Peter speaks of angels (2 Pet 2.4) and apparently referred to the Book of Enoch (20.2) where sons of God is interpreted "angels." It may be then that the explanation of the original meaning of 6.1–4 has been lost to us.

6.14 Noah's ark probably was about 450 feet long, 75 feet wide and was divided into three stories of about 15 feet each. The task of building the ark, gathering the animals, and

storing the food was tremendous. It may well have taken the labors of many more people than the immediate Noahic family. The ark itself was constructed of gopher wood and covered with pitch. How many animals it could have accommodated cannot be determined accurately although it has been estimated that there was room for 7000. In the New Testament the ark is regarded as a type of Christ who serves as a place of refuge for the redeemed (cf. 1 Pet 3.20, 21).

6.17 There are three views generally held about the extent of the flood: (1) it was geographically and ethnologically universal (all land was covered and all life died); (2) it was geographically local but ethnologically universal (not all land was covered but all life died); (3) it was geographically and ethnologically local (not all land was covered and not all life died). Extra-biblical evidence appears to be against a universal flood. The genealogies of chapter 10 make no reference to the Negroid and Mongoloid races, which leads one to suppose that these races were not included in the flood.

of life from under heaven; everything that is on the earth shall die.
18 But I will establish my covenant with you; and you shall come
into the ark, you, your sons, your wife, and your sons' wives with
you. 19And of every living thing of all flesh, you shall bring two
of every sort into the ark, to keep them alive with you; they shall
be male and female. 20 Of the birds according to their kinds, and
of the animals according to their kinds, of every creeping thing
of the ground according to its kind, two of every sort shall come in
to you, to keep them alive. 21Also take with you every sort of food
that is eaten, and store it up; and it shall serve as food for you and
for them." 22 Noah did this; he did all that God commanded him.

B. The command to fill the ark

7 Then the LORD said to Noah, "Go into the ark, you and all
your household, for I have seen that you are righteous before
me in this generation. 2 Take with you seven pairs of all clean
animals, the male and his mate; and a pair of the animals that are
not clean, the male and his mate; 3 and seven pairs of the birds of
the air also, male and female, to keep their kind alive upon the face
of all the earth. 4 For in seven days I will send rain upon the earth
forty days and forty nights; and every living thing that I have
made I will blot out from the face of the ground." 5And Noah did
all that the LORD had commanded him.

C. The flood

6 Noah was six hundred years old when the flood of waters came
upon the earth. 7And Noah and his sons and his wife and his sons'
wives with him went into the ark, to escape the waters of the
flood. 8 Of clean animals, and of animals that are not clean, and of
birds, and of everything that creeps on the ground, 9 two and two,
male and female, went into the ark with Noah, as God had commanded Noah. 10And after seven days the waters of the flood
came upon the earth.
11 In the six hundredth year of Noah's life, in the second
month, on the seventeenth day of the month, on that day all the
fountains of the great deep burst forth, and the windows of the
heavens were opened. 12And rain fell upon the earth forty days and
forty nights. 13 On the very same day Noah and his sons, Shĕm
and Ham and Jāphĕth, and Noah's wife and the three wives of his
sons with them entered the ark, 14 they and every beast according
to its kind, and all the cattle according to their kinds, and every
creeping thing that creeps on the earth according to its kind, and
every bird according to its kind, every bird of every sort. 15 They
went into the ark with Noah, two and two of all flesh in which
there was the breath of life. 16And they that entered, male and
female of all flesh, went in as God had commanded him; and the
LORD shut him in.
17 The flood continued forty days upon the earth; and the
waters increased, and bore up the ark, and it rose high above
the earth. 18 The waters prevailed and increased greatly upon the

6.18 Gen 7.1, 7,13; 1 Pet 3.20; 2 Pet 2.5
6.19 Gen 7.8, 9,15,16
6.20 Gen 7.9,15
6.22 Heb 11.7; Gen 7.5
7.1 Mt 24.38; Lk 17.26
7.2 Lev ch 11; 10.10; Ezek 44.23
7.7 Gen 6.22; ver 1
*7.11 Gen 8.2; Prov 8.28; Ezek 26.19
7.12 ver 4,17
7.13 ver 1,7; 6.18
7.15 Gen 6.20
7.16 ver 2,3
7.17 ver 4,12
7.18 Ps 104.26

7.11 *fountains of the great deep* is another reference to the subterranean ocean. Thus, the flood is explained as the convergence of the waters below and above the earth.

earth; and the ark floated on the face of the waters. [19]And the waters prevailed so mightily upon the earth that all the high mountains under the whole heaven were covered; [20] the waters prevailed above the mountains, covering them fifteen cubits deep. [21]And all flesh died that moved upon the earth, birds, cattle, beasts, all swarming creatures that swarm upon the earth, and every man; [22] everything on the dry land in whose nostrils was the breath of life died. [23] He blotted out every living thing that was upon the face of the ground, man and animals and creeping things and birds of the air; they were blotted out from the earth. Only Noah was left, and those that were with him in the ark. [24]And the waters prevailed upon the earth a hundred and fifty days.

D. The subsiding of the waters

8 But God remembered Noah and all the beasts and all the cattle that were with him in the ark. And God made a wind blow over the earth, and the waters subsided; [2] the fountains of the deep and the windows of the heavens were closed, the rain from the heavens was restrained, [3] and the waters receded from the earth continually. At the end of a hundred and fifty days the waters had abated; [4] and in the seventh month, on the seventeenth day of the month, the ark came to rest upon the mountains of Ar'arăt. [5]And the waters continued to abate until the tenth month; in the tenth month, on the first day of the month, the tops of the mountains were seen.

[6] At the end of forty days Noah opened the window of the ark which he had made, [7] and sent forth a raven; and it went to and fro until the waters were dried up from the earth. [8] Then he sent forth a dove from him, to see if the waters had subsided from the face of the ground; [9] but the dove found no place to set her foot, and she returned to him to the ark, for the waters were still on the face of the whole earth. So he put forth his hand and took her and brought her into the ark with him. [10] He waited another seven days, and again he sent forth the dove out of the ark; [11] and the dove came back to him in the evening, and lo, in her mouth a freshly plucked olive leaf; so Noah knew that the waters had subsided from the earth. [12] Then he waited another seven days, and sent forth the dove; and she did not return to him any more.

E. The return to dry land

[13] In the six hundred and first year, in the first month, the first day of the month, the waters were dried from off the earth; and Noah removed the covering of the ark, and looked, and behold, the face of the ground was dry. [14] In the second month, on the twenty-seventh day of the month, the earth was dry. [15] Then God said to Noah, [16] "Go forth from the ark, you and your wife, and your sons and your sons' wives with you. [17] Bring forth with you every living thing that is with you of all flesh—birds and animals and every creeping thing that creeps on the earth—that they

7.21
Gen 6.13,17
7.22
Gen 2.7
7.23
1 Pet 3.20;
2 Pet 2.5
7.24
Gen 8.3

8.1
Gen 19.29;
Ex 2.24;
1 Sam 1.19;
Ex 14.21;
Job 12.15;
Ps 29.10;
Isa 44.27;
Nah 1.4
8.2
Gen 7.11;
Job 38.37
8.3
Gen 7.24
*8.4
Jer 51.27
8.6
2 Pet 2.5
8.7
1 Ki 17.4,6
8.11
Mt 10.16
8.13
2 Pet 3.5,6
8.16
Gen 7.13
8.17
Gen 1.22

8.4 The *mountains of Ararat* constituted a range of mountains, the highest peak of which rose almost 17,000 feet above sea level. The ark hardly could have come to rest on the highest peak. Probably it rested on one of the smaller ones far closer to sea level. The Babylonian flood epic has the ark coming to rest on Mt. Nisir, east of the Tigris.

may breed abundantly on the earth, and be fruitful and multiply upon the earth." 18 So Noah went forth, and his sons and his wife and his sons' wives with him. 19And every beast, every creeping thing, and every bird, everything that moves upon the earth, went forth by families out of the ark.

F. The altar of sacrifice:
God will never curse the earth again

20 Then Noah built an altar to the LORD, and took of every clean animal and of every clean bird, and offered burnt offerings on the altar. 21And when the LORD smelled the pleasing odor, the LORD said in his heart, "I will never again curse the ground because of man, for the imagination of man's heart is evil from his youth; neither will I ever again destroy every living creature as I have done. 22 While the earth remains, seedtime and harvest, cold and heat, summer and winter, day and night, shall not cease."

G. God allows meat but forbids blood

9 And God blessed Noah and his sons, and said to them, "Be fruitful and multiply, and fill the earth. 2 The fear of you and the dread of you shall be upon every beast of the earth, and upon every bird of the air, upon everything that creeps on the ground and all the fish of the sea; into your hand they are delivered. 3 Every moving thing that lives shall be food for you; and as I gave you the green plants, I give you everything. 4 Only you shall not eat flesh with its life, that is, its blood. 5 For your lifeblood I will surely require a reckoning; of every beast I will require it and of man; of every man's brother I will require the life of man. 6 Whoever sheds the blood of man, by man shall his blood be shed; for God made man in his own image. 7And you, be fruitful and multiply, bring forth abundantly on the earth and multiply in it."

H. The Noahic covenant: the rainbow

8 Then God said to Noah and to his sons with him, 9 "Behold, I establish my covenant with you and your descendants after you, 10 and with every living creature that is with you, the birds, the cattle, and every beast of the earth with you, as many as came out of the ark.ⁱ 11 I establish my covenant with you, that never again shall all flesh be cut off by the waters of a flood, and never again shall there be a flood to destroy the earth." 12And God said, "This is the sign of the covenant which I make between me and you and every living creature that is with you, for all future generations: 13 I set my bow in the cloud, and it shall be a sign of the covenant between me and the earth. 14 When I bring clouds over the earth

ⁱ Gk: Heb repeats *every beast of the earth*

8.20
Gen 12.7,8;
13.18;22.9;
7.2; 22.2;
Ex 10.25
★8.21
Lev 1.9;
2 Cor 2.15;
Gen 3.17;
6.17;
9.11,15
8.22
Isa 54.9;
Jer 33.20,25

★9.1
ver 7;
Gen 1.28
9.3
Deut 12.15;
Gen 1.29
9.4
Lev 17.10–16;
Deut 12.23;
1 Sam 14.33
9.5
Ex 21.28;
Gen 4.9,10
9.6
Ex 21.12,14;
Lev 24.17;
Mt 26.52;
Gen 1.27
9.7
ver 1,19

9.9
Gen 6.18;
Isa 54.9
9.10
Ps 149.9
9.11
Isa 54.9
9.12
Gen 17.11

9.13
Ezek 1.28;
Rev 4.3

8.21 A change of heart (see 3.17).

9.1 After the flood, God made a covenant with Noah. It embraced the following elements: (1) the orderliness and regularity of the seasons and of nature generally were confirmed (8.22); (2) Noah's seed was to be fruitful and replenish the earth (9.1); (3) a system of law and government was begun, together with penalties for crime (9.1–6); (4) the fruit of the earth was given to man for food, and all meat, except for the blood (9.3, 4); (5) the seal of the covenant was the rainbow (9.16, 17); (6) the promise of the covenant was that the earth should never again be destroyed by a universal flood such as this. (9.15).

9.15
Lev 26.42,
45;
Deut 7.9

9.16
Gen 17.13,
19

*9.17

and the bow is seen in the clouds, 15 I will remember my covenant which is between me and you and every living creature of all flesh; and the waters shall never again become a flood to destroy all flesh. 16 When the bow is in the clouds, I will look upon it and remember the everlasting covenant between God and every living creature of all flesh that is upon the earth." 17 God said to Noah, "This is the sign of the covenant which I have established between me and all flesh that is upon the earth."

9.18
Gen 10.6
9.19
Gen 5.32

18 The sons of Noah who went forth from the ark were Shĕm, Ham, and Jāphĕth. Ham was the father of Cānaán. 19 These three were the sons of Noah; and from these the whole earth was peopled.

I. Canaan cursed; Shem blessed

*9.21

20 Noah was the first tiller of the soil. He planted a vineyard; 21 and he drank of the wine, and became drunk, and lay uncovered in his tent. 22And Ham, the father of Cānaán, saw the nakedness of

9.23
Ex 20.12

his father, and told his two brothers outside. 23 Then Shĕm and Jāphĕth took a garment, laid it upon both their shoulders, and walked backward and covered the nakedness of their father; their faces were turned away, and they did not see their father's nakedness. 24 When Noah awoke from his wine and knew what his

*9.25
Deut 27.16

youngest son had done to him, 25 he said,

"Cursed be Cānaán;
a slave of slaves shall he be to his brothers."

9.26
Ps 144.15

26 He also said,

"Blessed by the LORD my God be Shĕm;*m*
and let Cānaán be his slave.

9.27
Eph 2.13,
14; 3.6

27 God enlarge Jāphĕth,
and let him dwell in the tents of Shĕm;
and let Cānaán be his slave."

28 After the flood Noah lived three hundred and fifty years. 29All the days of Noah were nine hundred and fifty years; and he died.

m Or *Blessed be the* LORD, *the God of Shem*

9.17 When God made a covenant between himself and man he was bound by his own agreement. Seals or signs were given by God as evidence that a covenant had been made. The seal of the Abrahamic covenant was circumcision (see note to 17.9, 10). Here (9.17) God covenanted never to destroy life again by a flood. The sign or seal of this covenant was the rainbow across the sky. This was God's guarantee against a similar visitation. Scripture does forecast that the next cataclysmic judgment will take place by means of fire (2 Pet 3.10, 11).

9.21 Noah was never reproved by God for his drunkenness. Fermentation, which turned the juice of the grape into wine, may have become common subsequent to the flood. Scripture affords no evidence of drunkenness prior to this incident.

9.25 Canaan was the son of Ham (10.6) and it is against Canaan that the curse of Noah is directed. The idea that Ham was a Negro and that slavery and other restrictions against Negroes are of divine origin is com-

pletely untenable. The statement of Noah was prophetically fulfilled when the Canaanites were conquered by the descendants of Shem and later by the Persians, Greeks, and Romans. Ham's descendants, the Canaanites, developed into seven great nations of people in Canaan (Deut 7.1) but they were idolatrous (Deut 29.17) and superstitious (Deut 18.9–11) as well as abominably wicked (Lev 18.27). Abraham dwelt among them (12.5, 6) and the land they occupied was promised to him by God (12.7). Centuries went by before Abraham's posterity entered the land to occupy it and when they did, God commanded them: (1) to make no covenant with the Canaanites and show no mercy to them (Deut 7.2); (2) not to follow, but to destroy their idols (Ex 23.24; Deut 7.5, 25); (3) not to follow their customs (Lev 18.26, 27); (4) not to be afraid of them (Deut 7.17,18; 31.7). Because of Israel's transgression, God permitted a remnant of the Canaanites to remain in the land and to try and to chastise Israel (Judg 2.21, 22; 3.1–4; Num 33.55; Judg 2.3; 4.2).

IV. The generations of the sons of Noah 10.1–11.9

A. The sons of Japheth

10 These are the generations of the sons of Noah, Shĕm, Ham, and Jāphĕth; sons were born to them after the flood. 2 The sons of Jāphĕth: Gōmĕr, Māgŏg, Mādaī, Jāvăn, Tŭbăl, Mĕshĕçh, and Tīrăs. 3 The sons of Gōmĕr: Ăsh'kĕnăz, Rĭphăth, and Tŏgar'măh. 4 The sons of Jāvăn: Ĕlĭ'shăh, Tarshĭsh, Kĭttĭm, and Dō'dănĭm. 5 From these the coastland peoples spread. These are the sons of Jāphĕth[n] in their lands, each with his own language, by their families, in their nations.

*10.1ff

10.2
1 Chr 1.5–7

10.5
Gen 5.32

B. The sons of Ham

6 The sons of Ham: Cŭsh, Egypt, Put, and Cānaăn. 7 The sons of Cŭsh: Sēbă, Hăv'ĭlăh, Săbtăh, Ră'amăh, and Săb'tĕcă. The sons of Raamah: Shēb'á and Dēdăn. 8 Cŭsh became the father of Nĭm-rŏd; he was the first on earth to be a mighty man. 9 He was a mighty hunter before the LORD; therefore it is said, "Like Nĭm-rŏd a mighty hunter before the LORD." 10 The beginning of his kingdom was Bābĕl, Ĕrĕçh, and Ăccăd, all of them in the land of Shīnar. 11From that land he went into Assyria, and built Nĭn'-ĕvĕh, Rēhō'bŏth-Ĭr', Cālăh, and 12 Rĕṣĕn between Nĭn'ĕvĕh and Cālăh; that is the great city. 13 Egypt became the father of Lŭdĭm, Ăn'amĭm, Lĕhā'bĭm, Năph-tu'hĭm, 14 Păthru'sĭm, Căslu'hĭm (whence came the Philĭs'tīneṣ), and Căph'tŏrĭm.

15 Cānaăn became the father of Sīdŏn his first-born, and Hĕth, 16 and the Jĕb'ūsītes, the Ăm'ŏrītes, the Gĭr'găshītes, 17 the Hīvītes, the Arkītes, the Sīnītes, 18 the Ar'vădītes, the Zĕm'arītes, and the Hā'măthītes. Afterward the families of the Cā'naănītes spread abroad. 19And the territory of the Cā'naănītes extended from Sīdŏn, in the direction of Gērar, as far as Gază, and in the direction of Sŏdŏm, Gŏmor'răh, Ădmăh, and Zĕboi'ĭm, as far as Lāshă. 20 These are the sons of Ham, by their families, their languages, their lands, and their nations.

10.6
1 Chr 1.8–10

10.9
Mic 5.6

10.10
Mic 5.6

10.13
1 Chr 1.8,11

10.15
1 Chr 1.13

10.18
1 Chr 1.16;
18.3
10.19
Num 34.2–12

C. The sons of Shem

21 To Shĕm also, the father of all the children of Ē'bĕr, the elder brother of Jāphĕth, children were born. 22 The sons of Shĕm: Ēlăm, Ăsshŭr, Arpăçh'shăd, Lŭd, and Ărăm. 23 The sons

10.22
1 Chr 1.17;
Gen 14.1,9;
2 Ki 15.29;
Gen 11.10;
Isa 66.19
10.23
Job 1.1

---

[n] Compare verses 20, 31. Heb lacks *These are the sons of Japheth*

10.1–32 In this unique genealogy (nothing like it has been found among the non-biblical sources of the ancient world) the biblical writer classifies the peoples known to him under the three sons of Noah. In places, however, the alignment is to be understood politically, not racially. For example, the Canaanites, who were Semites (sons of Shem), are listed as sons of Ham (10.6) because for many centuries prior to the invasion by the Israelites the land of Canaan was under the control of the Hamites, the peoples of north-east Africa. If Lud is a reference to the Lydians of Asia Minor, then racially it belongs under Japheth, not Shem (10.22). Many of the names have been found on ancient inscriptions and positive or very probable identification can be made in a number of cases: for example, *Madai* (10.2) = the Medes, *Javan* = the Ionians (Greeks), *Ashkenaz* (10.3) is probably the Scythians, *Elishah* (10.4) is most likely Alashiya, an ancient designation for the island of Cyprus, *Tarshish* (10–4) is probably southern Spain or Sardinia, *Kittim* (10–4) = people of Cyprus, *Put* (10.6) = Cyrenaica of N. Africa, *Shinar* (10.10) is an ancient name for Babylonia, *Caphtorim* (10.14) = people of Crete, *Heth* (10.15) = the Hittites, and *Sheba* (10.28) the country in southwest Arabia (approximately present-day Yemen) whose queen visited Solomon.

of Áràm: Ŭz, Hŭl, Gĕthér, and Măsh. ²⁴Arpăch'shăd became the
father of Shĕláh; and Shelah became the father of Ē'bĕr. ²⁵ To
Ē'bĕr were born two sons: the name of the one was Pĕlĕg,ᵒ for
in his days the earth was divided, and his brother's name
was Jŏktán. ²⁶ Jŏktán became the father of Ălmō'dăd, Shĕlĕph,
Hă'zarmă'vĕth, Jĕráh, ²⁷ Hádor'ám, Ūzál, Dĭkláh, ²⁸ Ōbál,
Ăbĭm'ä-él, Shĕbá, ²⁹ Ōphĭr, Hăv'ĭláh, and Jŏbăb; all these were
the sons of Jŏktán. ³⁰ The territory in which they lived extended
from Mĕshá in the direction of Sĕphar to the hill country of the
east. ³¹ These are the sons of Shĕm, by their families, their languages, their lands, and their nations.

32 These are the families of the sons of Noah, according to their
genealogies, in their nations; and from these the nations spread
abroad on the earth after the flood.

D. *The tower of Babel: the confusion of tongues*

11 Now the whole earth had one language and few words.
²And as men migrated from the east, they found a plain
in the land of Shīnar and settled there. ³And they said to one
another, "Come, let us make bricks, and burn them thoroughly."
And they had brick for stone, and bitumen for mortar. ⁴ Then
they said, "Come, let us build ourselves a city, and a tower with
its top in the heavens, and let us make a name for ourselves, lest
we be scattered abroad upon the face of the whole earth." ⁵And
the LORD came down to see the city and the tower, which the sons
of men had built. ⁶And the LORD said, "Behold, they are one
people, and they have all one language; and this is only the beginning of what they will do; and nothing that they propose to do
will now be impossible for them. ⁷ Come, let us go down, and
there confuse their language, that they may not understand one
another's speech." ⁸ So the LORD scattered them abroad from
there over the face of all the earth, and they left off building the
city. ⁹ Therefore its name was called Bábĕl, because there the
LORD confusedᵖ the language of all the earth; and from there the
LORD scattered them abroad over the face of all the earth.

V. *The generations of Shem 11.10–26*

10 These are the descendants of Shĕm. When Shem was a hun-

ᵒ That is *Division* ᵖ Compare Heb *balal*, confuse

11.1 The languages of men differed at the time of the flood. After the flood, in the area covered there was now a single language— that which was spoken by Noah and his family. It is true that 10.5, 20, 31 speaks of various languages but these verses look for- ward to the history of the Noahic descendants after the incident of the tower of Babel. Subsequent to the flood, the sons of Noah were directed to replenish the earth. This meant geographical dispersion as well as numerical increase. Sin, which was expressed by the building of the tower of Babel, was judged by the confusion of tongues which shall continue until the end of the age.

11.3 Since stone was very scarce in Baby- lonia (Shinar), it was the custom to build with fired bricks and bitumen mortar.

11.4-9 The Assyrian *Bab-ili* is the native name for the Greek Babylon. It means *Gate of God*. There is no connection between this word and the Hebrew word *balal* which means "to confound." The story of the tower of Babel has other counterparts such as the Greek myth of the Titans who tried to climb to heaven. The biblical account is far older and from it many of the later tales may have been taken. Various suggestions have been made as to the location of the tower of Babel, e.g. Birs Nimrud which is seven miles from Babylon, and Amran which is within the city. In later history Nebuchadnezzar speaks of the Ziggurat Babili (Tower of Babylon) which had been commenced by a previous king but which had fallen into a ruinous state until Nebuchadnezzar restored and completed it.

Marginal references:
10.24
Gen 11.12;
Lk 3.35
10.25
1 Chr 1.19
10.26-29
1 Chr 1.20-23
10.32
ver 1
*11.1
11.2
Ex 1.11,14;
5.7–19
*11.3
*11.4ff
Deut 1.28
11.5
Gen 18.21
11.6
Acts 17.26;
Gen 9.19
11.7
Gen 1.26;
42.23;
Ex 4.11;
1 Cor 14.2,
11
11.8
Lk 1.51;
Gen 10.25,
32
11.9
Gen 10.10
11.10
Gen 10.22;
1 Chr 1.17

dred years old, he became the father of Arpăçh'shăd two years
after the flood; 11 and Shĕm lived after the birth of Arpăçh'shăd
five hundred years, and had other sons and daughters.

12 When Arpăçh'shăd had lived thirty-five years, he became
the father of Shēláh; 13 and Arpăçh'shăd lived after the birth of
Shēláh four hundred and three years, and had other sons and
daughters.

11.12
Lk 3.36

14 When Shēláh had lived thirty years, he became the father of
Ē'bėr; 15 and Shēláh lived after the birth of Ē'bėr four hundred
and three years, and had other sons and daughters.

16 When Ē'bėr had lived thirty-four years, he became the father
of Pĕlĕg; 17 and Ē'bėr lived after the birth of Pĕlĕg four hundred
and thirty years, and had other sons and daughters.

11.16
1 Chr 1.19

18 When Pĕlĕg had lived thirty years, he became the father of
Rē'ū; 19 and Pĕlĕg lived after the birth of Rē'ū two hundred and
nine years, and had other sons and daughters.

20 When Rē'ū had lived thirty-two years, he became the father
of Sērùg; 21 and Rē'ū lived after the birth of Sērùg two hundred
and seven years, and had other sons and daughters.

11.20
Lk 3.35

22 When Sērùg had lived thirty years, he became the father of
Nāhor; 23 and Sērùg lived after the birth of Nāhor two hundred
years, and had other sons and daughters.

24 When Nāhor had lived twenty-nine years, he became the
father of Tēráh; 25 and Nāhor lived after the birth of Tēráh a
hundred and nineteen years, and had other sons and daughters.

11.24
Lk 3.34

26 When Tēráh had lived seventy years, he became the father
of Abram, Nāhor, and Hārán.

11.26
Josh 24.2

VI. *The generations of Terah 11.27–25.11*

A. *The genealogy of Abraham*

27 Now these are the descendants of Tēráh. Terah was the
father of Abram, Nāhor, and Hārán; and Haran was the father of
Lot. 28 Hārán died before his father Tēráh in the land of his birth,
in Ŭr of the Çhăldē'áns̩. 29And Abram and Nāhor took wives; the
name of Abram's wife was Saraī, and the name of Nāhor's̩ wife,
Mĭlcáh, the daughter of Hārán the father of Milcah and Ĭscáh.
30 Now Saraī was barren; she had no child.

*11.27f

11.29
Gen 24.10;
17.15;
20.12;
22.20

11.30
Gen 16.1

31 Tēráh took Abram his son and Lot the son of Hārán, his
grandson, and Saraī his daughter-in-law, his son Abram's wife,
and they went forth together from Ŭr of the Çhăldē'áns to go into
the land of Cānaán; but when they came to Haran, they settled
there. 32 The days of Tēráh were two hundred and five years;
and Terah died in Hārán.

*11.31
Gen 15.7;
Neh 9.7;
Acts 7.4

11.27, 28 Abraham has often been conceived of as an ignorant nomad, an illiterate
and uneducated ancient. This is not so.
Archaeological discoveries have shown that
Ur of the Chaldees was a center of advanced
culture. There were libraries in the schools
and temples. The people used grammars,
dictionaries, encyclopedias, and reference
works along with textbooks on mathematics,
religion, and politics. What was true for

Babylonia was also true for Egypt where more
than a thousand years before Abraham's time,
writing was well established. It is quite
possible, therefore, that Abraham left written
records which were incorporated in the
Pentateuch.

11.31 Abraham's ancestors stemmed from
this area because near Haran were towns
called Peleg, Serug, Nahor, and Terah, all
names of Abraham's ancestors.

B. The call of Abraham

1. *The promise to make him a blessing*

12 Now the LORD said to Abram, "Go from your country and your kindred and your father's house to the land that I will show you. ²And I will make of you a great nation, and I will bless you, and make your name great, so that you will be a blessing. ³ I will bless those who bless you, and him who curses you I will curse; and by you all the families of the earth shall bless themselves."*q*

2. *The promise of Canaanland*

4 So Abram went, as the LORD had told him; and Lot went with him. Abram was seventy-five years old when he departed from Hārán. ⁵And Abram took Saraī his wife, and Lot his brother's son, and all their possessions which they had gathered, and the persons that they had gotten in Hārán; and they set forth to go to the land of Cānaán. When they had come to the land of Canaan, ⁶Abram passed through the land to the place at Shĕchĕm, to the oak*r* of Moreh. At that time the Cā'naánītes were in the land. ⁷ Then the LORD appeared to Abram, and said, "To your descendants I will give this land." So he built there an altar to the LORD, who had appeared to him. ⁸ Thence he removed to the mountain on the east of Bĕthĕl, and pitched his tent, with Bethel on the west and Āī on the east; and there he built an altar to the LORD and called on the name of the LORD. ⁹And Abram journeyed on, still going toward the Nĕgĕb.

3. *The sojourn in Egypt*

10 Now there was a famine in the land. So Abram went down to Egypt to sojourn there, for the famine was severe in the land. ¹¹ When he was about to enter Egypt, he said to Saraī his wife, "I know that you are a woman beautiful to behold; ¹² and when the Egyptians see you, they will say, 'This is his wife'; then they will kill me, but they will let you live. ¹³ Say you are my sister, that it may go well with me because of you, and that my life may be spared on your account." ¹⁴ When Abram entered Egypt the Egyptians saw that the woman was very beautiful. ¹⁵And when

q Or in you all the families of the earth shall be blessed r Or terebinth

12.2 The Abrahamic covenant is mentioned several times in Genesis (12.2, 3, 7; 13.14–17; ch 15; 17; 18; 21.12; 22.16–18). The covenant was essentially one of promise, the only requirement being Abraham's response in trust and faith to the new God calling him from his family and land. The covenant takes many variations in Genesis, but the two basic features of it are "land" and "descendants." The progeny of Abraham were to be a blessing to all and Abraham was guaranteed a son through whom his line would be perpetuated.

12.7 Abraham's altar at Shechem implies animal sacrifice which was common to all Semites.

12.9 The reference to the Negeb here and elsewhere in Genesis takes on further significance since Nelson Glueck's findings which show that the Negeb was occupied from 2100–

1800 B.C., the period of Abraham. Thus, when he made his round trip to Egypt he followed a series of water stations from Mamre (Hebron) southwest to Kadesh. (Later called Kadesh-barnea.) Jacob and Moses knew of this route also.

12.10 In times of famine it was customary, according to Egyptian records, for peoples of Palestine and Syria to seek refuge in Egypt.

12.13 God's will, done God's way, never lacks for God's blessing. *Say you are my sister.* Here Abraham did not tell the truth. Selfishness overtook this man of faith. Fear for his own life made him forget what consequences his deceit would bring for Sarah and others. Although Abraham was a man of faith he was not a perfect man. This incident serves to illustrate the fact that the end does not justify the means. The means and the end must both be right.

the princes of Phạraōh saw her, they praised her to Pharaoh. And the woman was taken into Phạraōh's house. ¹⁶And for her sake he dealt well with Abram; and he had sheep, oxen, he-asses, menservants, maidservants, she-asses, and camels.

17 But the LORD afflicted Phạraōh and his house with great plagues because of Sạraī, Abram's wife. ¹⁸ So Phạraōh called Abram, and said, "What is this you have done to me? Why did you not tell me that she was your wife? ¹⁹ Why did you say, 'She is my sister,' so that I took her for my wife? Now then, here is your wife, take her, and be gone." ²⁰And Phạraōh gave men orders concerning him; and they set him on the way, with his wife and all that he had.

13 So Abram went up from Egypt, he and his wife, and all that he had, and Lot with him, into the Nĕgĕb.

C. The separation of Abraham and Lot

1. The strife between the herdsmen of Lot and Abraham

2 Now Abram was very rich in cattle, in silver, and in gold. ³And he journeyed on from the Nĕgĕb as far as Bĕthĕl, to the place where his tent had been at the beginning, between Bethel and Āī, ⁴ to the place where he had made an altar at the first; and there Abram called on the name of the LORD. ⁵And Lot, who went with Abram, also had flocks and herds and tents, ⁶ so that the land could not support both of them dwelling together; for their possessions were so great that they could not dwell together, ⁷ and there was strife between the herdsmen of Abram's cattle and the herdsmen of Lot's cattle. At that time the Cā'naȧnītes and the Pĕr'ịzzītes dwelt in the land.

2. Lot chooses Sodom

8 Then Abram said to Lot, "Let there be no strife between you and me, and between your herdsmen and my herdsmen; for we are kinsmen. ⁹ Is not the whole land before you? Separate yourself from me. If you take the left hand, then I will go to the right; or if you take the right hand, then I will go to the left." ¹⁰And Lot lifted up his eyes, and saw that the Jordan valley was well watered everywhere like the garden of the LORD, like the land of Egypt, in the direction of Zō'ar; this was before the LORD destroyed Sŏdŏm and Gŏmor'rȧh. ¹¹ So Lot chose for himself all the Jordan valley, and Lot journeyed east; thus they separated from each other. ¹²Abram dwelt in the land of Cānaȧn, while Lot dwelt among the cities of the valley and moved his tent as far as Sŏdŏm. ¹³ Now the men of Sŏdŏm were wicked, great sinners against the LORD.

3. Abraham chooses Hebron

14 The LORD said to Abram, after Lot had separated from him, "Lift up your eyes, and look from the place where you are, northward and southward and eastward and westward; ¹⁵ for all the land which you see I will give to you and to your descendants for ever. ¹⁶ I will make your descendants as the dust of the earth;

12.16	Gen 20.14
12.17	Gen 20.18; 1 Chr 16.21; Ps 105.14
12.18	Gen 20.9,10
12.20	Prov 21.1
13.1	Gen 12.9
13.3	Gen 12.8,9
13.4	Gen 12.7,8
★13.7	Gen 26.20
13.8	Prov 15.18; 20.3
13.10	Gen 19.17–29; Deut 34.3; Gen 2.8; 47.6;14.8
13.12	Gen 19.29
13.13	Gen 18.20; 2 Pet 2.7,8
13.14	Gen 28.14; Deut 3.27
13.15	Gen 12.7; 17.8; Deut 34.3; Acts 7.5; 2 Chr 20.7
13.16	Gen 16.10; 28.14

13.7 The strife between the herdsmen of Abraham and Lot represents the first threat to the promise of God that Abraham would possess the land. Abraham lived above this threat in faith and his gracious attitude toward Lot was rewarded by another confirmation of the promise by God. (Read verses 14–17 and chapter 15.)

13.17
Num 13.17–
24
13.18
Gen 14.13;
35.27

14.1
Isa 11.11;
Dan 8.2
14.2
Gen 10.19;
Deut 29.23;
Gen 13.10
14.3
Num 34.12;
Deut 3.17;
Josh 3.16
14.5
Gen 15.20;
Deut 2.20
14.6
Deut 2.12,
22
*14.7
2 Chr 20.2

14.11
ver 16,21
*14.12
Gen 12.5;
13.12

14.13
Gen 13.18;
ver 24
*14.14
Gen 13.8;
15.3

so that if one can count the dust of the earth, your descendants also can be counted. ¹⁷Arise, walk through the length and the breadth of the land, for I will give it to you." ¹⁸ So Abram moved his tent, and came and dwelt by the oaks^s of Mămrĕ, which are at Hēbrón; and there he built an altar to the LORD.

D. Abraham delivers Lot

1. *The war of the kings*

14 In the days of Ăm'răphĕl king of Shīnar, Ạr'ĭŏçh king of Ĕllā'sẳr, Çhĕd'-ôr-läō'mĕr king of Ēlăm, and Tīdăl king of Goi'ĭm, ² these kings made war with Bērạ king of Sŏdồm, Bĭrshạ king of Gŏmor'răh, Shīnăb king of Ădmáh, Shĕmĕ'bér king of Zĕboi'ĭm, and the king of Bĕlả (that is, Zō'ar). ³And all these joined forces in the Valley of Sĭddĭm (that is, the Salt Sea). ⁴ Twelve years they had served Çhĕd'-ôr-läō'mĕr, but in the thirteenth year they rebelled. ⁵ In the fourteenth year Çhĕd'-ôr-läō'mĕr and the kings who were with him came and subdued the Rĕph'äĭm in Ăsh'tĕrŏth-karnä'ĭm, the Zuzĭm in Ham, the Ēmĭm in Shā'vĕh-kĭriăthā'ĭm, ⁶ and the Horĭtes in their Mount Sēịr as far as Ĕl-pā'rán on the border of the wilderness; ⁷ then they turned back and came to Ĕnmĭsh'pát (that is, Kādĕsh), and subdued all the country of the Ămăl'ĕkītes, and also the Ăm'órĭtes who dwelt in Hăz'ăzòn-tā'mȧr. ⁸ Then the king of Sŏdồm, the king of Gồmor'răh, the king of Ădmáh, the king of Zĕboi'ĭm, and the king of Bĕlả (that is, Zō'ar) went out, and they joined battle in the Valley of Sĭddĭm ⁹ with Çhĕd'-ôr-läō'mĕr king of Ēlăm, Tīdăl king of Goi'ĭm, Ăm'răphĕl king of Shīnar, and Ạr'ĭŏçh king of Ĕllā'sẳr, four kings against five. ¹⁰ Now the Valley of Sĭddĭm was full of bitumen pits; and as the kings of Sŏdồm and Gồmor'răh fled, some fell into them, and the rest fled to the mountain. ¹¹ So the enemy took all the goods of Sŏdồm and Gồmor'răh, and all their provisions, and went their way; ¹² they also took Lot, the son of Abram's brother, who dwelt in Sŏdồm, and his goods, and departed.

13 Then one who had escaped came, and told Abram the Hebrew, who was living by the oaks^s of Mămrĕ the Ăm'órĭte, brother of Ēshcòl and of Ānér; these were allies of Abram. ¹⁴ When Abram heard that his kinsman had been taken captive, he led forth his trained men, born in his house, three hundred and eighteen of them, and went in pursuit as far as Dan. ¹⁵And he divided his forces against them by night, he and his servants, and routed them and pursued them to Hōbáh, north of Damascus.

^s Or *terebinths*

14.7 The fact that the four eastern kings devastated the area from Transjordan down to Kadesh-barnea is borne out by Glueck's findings that sedentary culture in Transjordania ceased about the 20th century B.C.
14.12 Lot's initial choice of Sodom and Gomorrah was wrong. 2 Pet 2.8 states that Lot *was vexed . . . with their lawless deeds*. But nowhere are we told that Lot needed to remain in this environment. So he was taken prisoner in the raid of the four kings, only to be delivered by Abraham; returning again, he

remained until the destruction of Sodom and Gomorrah, when he was delivered by God. The mercy and goodness of God toward a backslidden yet truly converted believer is a revelation of God's grace.
14.14 Before its capture by the Danites, Dan was known as Laish (Judg 18.29). The name was modernized in Genesis so that the reader could readily identify the familiar Danite city. Abraham had three hundred and eighteen trained men born in his house even before he had a son of his own.

16 Then he brought back all the goods, and also brought back his kinsman Lot with his goods, and the women and the people.

2. Melchizedek and Abraham's tithe

17 After his return from the defeat of Chĕd´-ŏr-läō´mĕr and the kings who were with him, the king of Sŏdŏm went out to meet him at the Valley of Shāvĕh (that is, the King's Valley). 18And Mĕl-chĭz´ĕdĕk king of Sālĕm brought out bread and wine; he was priest of God Most High. 19And he blessed him and said,
"Blessed be Abram by God Most High,
    maker of heaven and earth;
20 and blessed be God Most High,
    who has delivered your enemies into your hand!"

3. Abraham's refusal to take spoil

And Abram gave him a tenth of everything. 21And the king of Sŏdŏm said to Abram, "Give me the persons, but take the goods for yourself." 22 But Abram said to the king of Sŏdŏm, "I have sworn to the LORD God Most High, maker of heaven and earth, 23 that I would not take a thread or a sandal-thong or anything that is yours, lest you should say, 'I have made Abram rich.' 24 I will take nothing but what the young men have eaten, and the share of the men who went with me; let Ānĕr, Ĕshcŏl, and Mămrĕ take their share."

E. The Abrahamic covenant

1. The promise of an heir

15 After these things the word of the LORD came to Abram in a vision, "Fear not, Abram, I am your shield; your reward shall be very great." 2 But Abram said, "O Lord GOD, what wilt thou give me, for I continue childless, and the heir of my house is Ĕlĭē´zĕr of Damascus?" 3And Abram said, "Behold, thou hast given me no offspring; and a slave born in my house will be my heir." 4And behold, the word of the LORD came to him, "This man shall not be your heir; your own son shall be your heir." 5And he brought him outside and said, "Look toward heaven, and number the stars, if you are able to number them." Then he said to him,

Cross-references

14.16 ver 11,12

14.17 2 Sam 18.6, 18

*14.18 Heb 7.1; Ps 110.4; Heb 5.6,10

14.19 ver 22; Mt 11.25

14.20 Gen 24.27; Heb 7.4

*14.22 Dan 12.7; ver 19

14.23 2 Ki 5.16

15.1 Dan 10.1; Gen 21.17; 26.24; Deut 33.29; Prov 11.8

*15.2f Acts 7.5

15.3 Gen 14.14

15.4 Gal 4.28

15.5 Ps 147.4; Jer 33.22; Gen 22.17; Rom 4.18; Heb 11.12

14.18 *Melchizedek* (king of righteousness) was both priest and king of Salem (*peace*, probably the old name for Jerusalem). In the book of Hebrews the priestly function is stressed when Melchizedek is presented as a type of Christ. This emphasis rests on Ps 110.4 where the LORD says through David, "*You are a priest for ever after the order of Melchizedek.*" In Hebrews (7.1–17) the eternal priesthood of Melchizedek is shown to be superior to the Aaronic priesthood, which was transitory and imperfect.

14.22 Oaths have been employed from the earliest times, as evidenced by this one of Abraham. The purpose of an oath is explained in Heb 6.16. In the Old Testament they were employed for: (1) confirming covenants (26.28; 31.44, 53); (2) resolving controversies in courts of law (Ex 22.11; Num 5.19); (3)

guaranteeing the fulfilment of promised acts or sacred duties (24.3, 4; 50.25; Num 30.2; 2 Chr 15.14, 15). Believers have always been forbidden to take oaths in the name of idols or created things (Josh 23.7; Mt 5.34–36; Jas 5.12). God himself used an oath to show His immutability (22.16; Num 14.28; Heb 6.17). But the Lord Jesus admonished believers to fulfil their promises without the need of resorting to any oaths, so their word would be as good as their bond (Mt 5.34–37).

15.2, 3 The concern of Abraham here is made intelligible by the Nuzu tablets. From these tablets we learn that childless couples used to adopt a slave on condition that he would care for them and give them a proper burial. If a natural son should be born later the slave heir was disinherited to a great extent.

*15.6

"So shall your descendants be." 6And he believed the LORD; and he reckoned it to him as righteousness.

2. The sacrifice offered

15.7
Gen 11.31;
13.15,17

15.8
Lk 1.18

7 And he said to him, "I am the LORD who brought you from Úr of the Chăldē'ăns, to give you this land to possess." 8 But he said, "O Lord GOD, how am I to know that I shall possess it?" 9 He said to him, "Bring me a heifer three years old, a she-goat three years old, a ram three years old, a turtledove, and a young pigeon." 10And he brought him all these, cut them in two, and laid each half over against the other; but he did not cut the birds in two. 11And when birds of prey came down upon the carcasses, Abram drove them away.

*15.10
Jer 34.18;
Lev 1.17

15.12
Gen 2.21
*15.13
Acts 7.6;
Ex 12.40

12 As the sun was going down, a deep sleep fell on Abram; and lo, a dread and great darkness fell upon him. 13 Then the LORD said to Abram, "Know of a surety that your descendants will be sojourners in a land that is not theirs, and will be slaves there, and they will be oppressed for four hundred years; 14 but I will bring judgment on the nation which they serve, and afterward they shall come out with great possessions. 15As for yourself, you shall go to your fathers in peace; you shall be buried in a good old age. 16And they shall come back here in the fourth generation; for the iniquity of the Ăm'ŏrītes is not yet complete."

15.14
Ex 12.36

15.15
Gen 25.8

15.16
1 Ki 21.26

3. The promise of a land

15.17
Jer 34.18,19

15.18
Gen 24.7;
12.7;
Ex 23.31;
Num 34.3;
Deut 11.24;
Josh 1.4

17 When the sun had gone down and it was dark, behold, a smoking fire pot and a flaming torch passed between these pieces. 18 On that day the LORD made a covenant with Abram, saying, "To your descendants I give this land, from the river of Egypt to the great river, the river Eūphrā'tēs, 19 the land of the Kēnītes, the Kĕn'ĭzzītes, the Kăd'mŏnītes, 20 the Hĭttītes, the Pĕr'ĭzzītes, the Rĕph'āīm, 21 the Ăm'ŏrītes, the Cā'naănītes, the Gĭr'găshītes and the Jĕb'ūsītes."

F. The birth of Ishmael

1. Sarai gives Hagar to Abraham

16.1
Gen 11.30;
21.9;
Gal 4.24

16.2
Gen 30.3,4,
9,10

16 Now Sạraī, Abram's wife, bore him no children. She had an Egyptian maid whose name was Hāgar; 2 and Sạraī said to Abram, "Behold now, the LORD has prevented me from bearing children; go in to my maid; it may be that I shall obtain children by her." And Abram hearkened to the voice of Sarai.

15.6 *reckoned it to him as righteousness.* Under the old covenant salvation was the gift of the grace of God through faith just as it is under the new covenant. In Romans (ch 4) the Apostle Paul uses Abraham as an example of one whose faith, and not his works, justified him. Indeed he argues that Abraham was justified *before* he was circumcised, a seal that follows faith, not precedes it.

15.10 Cutting the animals in halves may have been part of the normal custom or ritual at a covenant sealing. The Hebrew of 15.18 reads that God "cut a covenant" with Abraham. For a long time Old Testament scholars doubted the accuracy of this ex-

pression, but texts have been uncovered in Qatna and Mari informing us that covenants were sealed by some ritual involving the cutting up of asses.

15.13 God here revealed to Abraham future history and events in the life of the promised seed. The bondage in Egypt is foretold and its length marked as four hundred years or four generations. The Egyptian bondage, then, was part of the plan of God for the cradling of the Hebrew race. But it also reveals the mercy and kindness of God toward the Amorites to whom He extended time for repentance before judgment should befall them. (See also note to 12.10.)

3 So, after Abram had dwelt ten years in the land of Cānaàn, Saraī, Abram's wife, took Hāgar the Egyptian, her maid, and gave her to Abram her husband as a wife. 4And he went in to Hāgar, and she conceived; and when she saw that she had conceived, she looked with contempt on her mistress. 5And Saraī said to Abram, "May the wrong done to me be on you! I gave my maid to your embrace, and when she saw that she had conceived, she looked on me with contempt. May the LORD judge between you and me!" 6 But Abram said to Saraī, "Behold, your maid is in your power; do to her as you please." Then Sarai dealt harshly with her, and she fled from her.

2. God's promise to Hagar

7 The angel of the LORD found her by a spring of water in the wilderness, the spring on the way to Shŭr. 8And he said, "Hāgar, maid of Saraī, where have you come from and where are you going?" She said, "I am fleeing from my mistress Sarai." 9 The angel of the LORD said to her, "Return to your mistress, and submit to her." 10 The angel of the LORD also said to her, "I will so greatly multiply your descendants that they cannot be numbered for multitude." 11And the angel of the LORD said to her, "Behold, you are with child, and shall bear a son; you shall call his name Īsh'mäël;ᵗ because the LORD has given heed to your affliction. 12 He shall be a wild ass of a man, his hand against every man and every man's hand against him; and he shall dwell over against all his kinsmen." 13 So she called the name of the LORD who spoke to her, "Thou art a God of seeing"; for she said, "Have I really seen God and remained alive after seeing him?"ᵘ 14 Therefore the well was called Beër-làhaï'-roi;ᵛ it lies between Kādĕsh and Bĕrĕd.

3. The birth of the baby

15 And Hāgar bore Abram a son; and Abram called the name of his son, whom Hagar bore, Īsh'mäël. 16Abram was eighty-six years old when Hāgar bore Īsh'mäël to Abram.

ᵗ That is God hears ᵘ Cn: Heb have I even here seen after him who sees me?
ᵛ That is the well of one who sees and lives

*16.3	Gen 12.5
16.5	Gen 31.53
16.7	Gen 21.17, 18; 22.11, 15; 31.11; 20.1
16.10	Gen 17.20
16.11	Ex 3.7,9
16.12	Gen 25.18
16.13	Gen 32.30
*16.14	
16.15	Gal 4.22

16.3 The story of Hagar and Ishmael has real spiritual value and instruction for the believer. Abraham was seventy-five years old when he left Haran and received God's covenantal promise (12.4). Inherent in the covenant was the promise of seed. Now at eighty-five years it appeared quite impossible of fulfilment. *Sarai, Abram's wife, took Hagar . . . and gave her to Abram her husband as a wife.* Archeological evidence of Nuzu customs indicates that in some marriage contracts a childless wife was required to furnish a substitute for her husband. In oriental eyes, childlessness was the greatest of tragedies. Nuzu custom stipulated further that the slave wife and her children could not be sent away. Thus the action of Sarah and Abraham was undoubtedly consonant with the customs of that day. When Abraham was eighty-six years of age Hagar gave birth to Ishmael (16.16). This incident reveals how two genuine believers may seek to fulfil God's will by normally acceptable methods but spiritually carnal ones. The promise of God was not to Hagar but to Sarah. Sarah suggested the use of Hagar, and Abraham consented to the arrangement. Both were guilty. The birth of Ishmael introduced a people (the nucleus of the later Mohammedans) which has been a challenge both to the Jews and the Christian Church. It was not until Abraham was a hundred years old that Isaac was born (21.5). From the length of time between the promise and the fulfilment we can draw the lessons that God's ways are not our ways and His thoughts are higher than our thoughts (Isa 55.8, 9). Patient waiting would have produced the desired results without the additional problems created by impatience and lack of faith. God always rewards those who have faith to believe his promises.

16.14 The well Beer-lahairoi, near Kadesh (called Kadesh-barnea in 32.8; 34.4; and in Deuteronomy and Joshua), indicates that Hagar wandered quite a way in the wilderness. 24.62; 25.11 claim that Isaac dwelt in this region.

G. The circumcision of Abraham

1. The covenant restated

★17.1
Gen 28.3;
Ex 6.3;
Deut 18.13
17.2
Gen 15.18
17.4
Gen 35.11;
48.19
17.5
Neh 9.7;
Rom 4.17
17.6
Gen 35.11;
Mt 1.6
17.7
Gal 3.17;
Gen 26.24;
28.13;
Rom 9.8
17.8
Gen 12.7;
Ps 105.9,11;
Gen 23.4;
28.4;
Ex 6.7;
Lev 26.12

17 When Abram was ninety-nine years old the LORD appeared to Abram, and said to him, "I am God Almighty;*w* walk before me, and be blameless. ²And I will make my covenant between me and you, and will multiply you exceedingly." ³ Then Abram fell on his face; and God said to him, ⁴ "Behold, my covenant is with you, and you shall be the father of a multitude of nations. ⁵ No longer shall your name be Abram,*x* but your name shall be Abraham;*y* for I have made you the father of a multitude of nations. ⁶ I will make you exceedingly fruitful; and I will make nations of you, and kings shall come forth from you. ⁷And I will establish my covenant between me and you and your descendants after you throughout their generations for an everlasting covenant, to be God to you and to your descendants after you. ⁸And I will give to you, and to your descendants after you, the land of your sojournings, all the land of Cānaàn, for an everlasting possession; and I will be their God."

2. The sign of the covenant

★17.9f
17.10
Acts 7.8
17.11
Ex 12.48;
Deut 10.16;
Rom 4.11
17.12
Lev 12.3;
Lk 2.21
17.14
Ex 4.24

9 And God said to Abraham, "As for you, you shall keep my covenant, you and your descendants after you throughout their generations. 10 This is my covenant, which you shall keep, between me and you and your descendants after you: Every male among you shall be circumcised. 11 You shall be circumcised in the flesh of your foreskins, and it shall be a sign of the covenant between me and you. 12 He that is eight days old among you shall be circumcised; every male throughout your generations, whether born in your house, or bought with your money from any foreigner who is not of your offspring, 13 both he that is born in your house and he that is bought with your money, shall be circumcised. So shall my covenant be in your flesh an everlasting covenant. 14Any uncircumcised male who is not circumcised in the flesh of his foreskin shall be cut off from his people; he has broken my covenant."

3. The promise of Isaac

17.16
Gen 18.10;
35.11;
Gal 4.31

15 And God said to Abraham, "As for Saraī your wife, you shall not call her name Sarai, but Sarah shall be her name. 16 I will bless her, and moreover I will give you a son by her; I will bless her, and she shall be a mother of nations; kings of peoples shall come from

---

w Heb *Ĕl Shăd'dāï*   *x* That is *exalted father*   *y* Here taken to mean *father of a multitude*

17.1 *El Shaddai* (Hebrew), meaning *God Almighty*, from the root *shadad* (be violent, irresistibly strong). Some accept another interpretation, "God of the mountain," which is not to be taken as worship of nature (animism) but that God appeared to Abraham on the mountain. El Shaddai appears to Abraham when he is ninety-nine years of age, and when the birth of an heir seems literally impossible. The mighty God steps in and does the impossible. God changes Abram's name to Abraham, *father of a multitude* (17.5), and the following year Isaac is born as the seed of promise. See also note to 2.4 on the names of God.

17.9, 10 Circumcision was convenantal in nature, being the outward sign or seal of the Abrahamic agreement which God made (17.11). The failure to be circumcised separated one from the people of Israel. The command was perpetuated in the Law of Moses (Lev 12.3; Jn 7.22,23). In the gospel dispensation, circumcision was abolished (Eph 2.11–15; Col 3.11) and to require it now is to revert to legalism. Circumcision in this age is of the heart and not of the flesh, but even when it was binding it had no value unless accompanied by faith and obedience (Rom 3.30; Gal 5.6; Rom 2.25; 1 Cor 7.19).

her." 17 Then Abraham fell on his face and laughed, and said to himself, "Shall a child be born to a man who is a hundred years old? Shall Sarah, who is ninety years old, bear a child?" 18And Abraham said to God, "O that Ĭsh′mäël might live in thy sight!" 19 God said, "No, but Sarah your wife shall bear you a son, and you shall call his name Isaac.ᶻ I will establish my covenant with him as an everlasting covenant for his descendants after him. 20As for Ĭsh′mäël, I have heard you; behold, I will bless him and make him fruitful and multiply him exceedingly; he shall be the father of twelve princes, and I will make him a great nation. 21 But I will establish my covenant with Isaac, whom Sarah shall bear to you at this season next year."

4. The circumcisions performed

22 When he had finished talking with him, God went up from Abraham. 23 Then Abraham took Ĭsh′mäël his son and all the slaves born in his house or bought with his money, every male among the men of Abraham's house, and he circumcised the flesh of their foreskins that very day, as God had said to him. 24Abraham was ninety-nine years old when he was circumcised in the flesh of his foreskin. 25And Ĭsh′mäël his son was thirteen years old when he was circumcised in the flesh of his foreskin. 26 That very day Abraham and his son Ĭsh′mäël were circumcised; 27 and all the men of his house, those born in the house and those bought with money from a foreigner, were circumcised with him.

H. Sodom and Gomorrah destroyed

1. Abraham entertains heavenly visitors

18 And the LORD appeared to him by the oaksᵃ of Mămrë, as he sat at the door of his tent in the heat of the day. 2 He lifted up his eyes and looked, and behold, three men stood in front of him. When he saw them, he ran from the tent door to meet them, and bowed himself to the earth, 3 and said, "My lord, if I have found favor in your sight, do not pass by your servant. 4 Let a little water be brought, and wash your feet, and rest yourselves under the tree, 5 while I fetch a morsel of bread, that you may refresh yourselves, and after that you may pass on—since you have come to your servant." So they said, "Do as you have said." 6And Abraham hastened into the tent to Sarah, and said, "Make ready quickly three measuresᵇ of fine meal, knead it, and make cakes." 7And Abraham ran to the herd, and took a calf, tender and good, and gave it to the servant, who hastened to prepare it. 8 Then he took curds, and milk, and the calf which he had prepared, and set it before them; and he stood by them under the tree while they ate.

ᶻ That is he laughs   ᵃ Or terebinths   ᵇ Heb seahs

Side references:

★17.17 Gen 18.12; 21.6
★17.18
17.19 Gen 18.10; 21.2; 26.2–5
17.20 Gen 16.10; 25.12,16
★17.22ff
17.23 Gen 14.14
17.24 Rom 4.11
18.1 Gen 13.18; 14.13
18.2 ver 16,22; Gen 32.24; Josh 5.13; Judg 13.6–11
18.4 Gen 19.2; 43.24
18.5 Judg 6.18, 19;13.15,16
18.8 Gen 19.3

17.17 After twenty-four years of impatient waiting, the words of God seem an idle fancy to Abraham. All of the outward circumstances were against him. The biological facts of life stood over against the promise of God. Sight and sense told him the promise was impossible of fulfilment. Yet Abraham was a man of faith who had moments of doubt. How much we can learn from his laugh of disbelief here!

17.18 Abraham still hoped that Ishmael would be recognized but this plea and God's answer in verse 19 show that man's answers and ways can never be substituted for God's.

17.22-27 Abraham's faith triumphed over his doubts. He responded to the covenant by circumcising himself and all his males. Thus he passed another crucial stage in his walk and experience with the covenant-keeping God.

2. Sarah laughs

9 They said to him, "Where is Sarah your wife?" And he said, "She is in the tent." 10 The LORD said, "I will surely return to you in the spring, and Sarah your wife shall have a son." And Sarah was listening at the tent door behind him. 11 Now Abraham and Sarah were old, advanced in age; it had ceased to be with Sarah after the manner of women. 12 So Sarah laughed to herself, saying, "After I have grown old, and my husband is old, shall I have pleasure?" 13 The LORD said to Abraham, "Why did Sarah laugh, and say, 'Shall I indeed bear a child, now that I am old?' 14 Is anything too hard^c for the LORD? At the appointed time I will return to you, in the spring, and Sarah shall have a son." 15 But Sarah denied, saying, "I did not laugh"; for she was afraid. He said, "No, but you did laugh."

3. God informs Abraham of the end of Sodom and Gomorrah

16 Then the men set out from there, and they looked toward Sŏdŏm; and Abraham went with them to set them on their way. 17 The LORD said, "Shall I hide from Abraham what I am about to do, 18 seeing that Abraham shall become a great and mighty nation, and all the nations of the earth shall bless themselves by him?^{d} 19 No, for I have chosen^e him, that he may charge his children and his household after him to keep the way of the LORD by doing righteousness and justice; so that the LORD may bring to Abraham what he has promised him." 20 Then the LORD said, "Because the outcry against Sŏdŏm and Gŏmor'răh is great and their sin is very grave, 21 I will go down to see whether they have done altogether according to the outcry which has come to me; and if not, I will know."

4. Abraham intercedes for Sodom

22 So the men turned from there, and went toward Sŏdŏm; but Abraham still stood before the LORD. 23 Then Abraham drew near, and said, "Wilt thou indeed destroy the righteous with the wicked? 24 Suppose there are fifty righteous within the city; wilt thou then destroy the place and not spare it for the fifty righteous who are in it? 25 Far be it from thee to do such a thing, to slay the righteous with the wicked, so that the righteous fare as the wicked! Far be that from thee! Shall not the Judge of all the earth do right?" 26 And the LORD said, "If I find at Sŏdŏm fifty righteous in the city, I will spare the whole place for their sake." 27 Abraham answered, "Behold, I have taken upon myself to speak to the Lord, I who am but dust and ashes. 28 Suppose five of the fifty

---

Marginal references:

18.10 Rom 9.9
18.11 Gen 17.17; Rom 4.19
*18.12ff 1 Pet 3.6
18.14 Jer 32.17, 27; Zech 8.6; Mt 3.9; Lk 1.37
18.18 Gal 3.8
18.19 Deut 4.9, 10; 6.7; Josh 24.15; Eph 6.4
18.20 Gen 19.13; Ezek 16.49, 50
18.21 Gen 11.5
18.22 Gen 19.1
18.23 Heb 10.22; Num 16.22
18.24 Jer 5.1
*18.25 Job 8.20; Isa 3.10,11; Rom 3.6
18.27 Gen 3.19; Job 4.19; 30.19; 42.6; 2 Cor 5.1

---

c Or *wonderful*   *d* Or *in him all the nations of the earth shall be blessed*   *e* Heb *known*

18.12-15 Sarah, like Abraham, passed through periods of doubt and disbelief. It was the laughter of doubt in her heart which caused God to pose the question, *Is anything too hard for the LORD?* (ver 14). God who changes not continues faithful despite the sin of unbelief in His people. In 17.15 the name Sarai, meaning "contentious" or "princely," was changed to Sarah which means "princess."

18.25 God is love (1 Jn 4.8), but because He loves holiness and truth, He is also just (Ps 89.14; 145.17). His judgments are: (1)

according to truth (Rev 19.2); (2) universal and certain (Rom 2.6); (3) impersonal and impartial (Rom 2.11); (4) concerned with motive as well as outward conduct (Rom 2.16; Lk 12.2, 3). Three major judgments are mentioned in Scripture: (1) the judgment of believers' sins, which is past, having been inflicted on the Christ at Calvary (Jn 5.24; Rom 8.1); (2) the believers' judgment for rewards (2 Cor 5.10; Rom 14.10; 1 Cor 3.10–15); (3) the judgment of unbelievers (Rev 20.11–15).

righteous are lacking? Wilt thou destroy the whole city for lack of
five?" And he said, "I will not destroy it if I find forty-five there."
29Again he spoke to him, and said, "Suppose forty are found
there." He answered, "For the sake of forty I will not do it."
30 Then he said, "Oh let not the Lord be angry, and I will speak.
Suppose thirty are found there." He answered, "I will not do it,
if I find thirty there." 31 He said, "Behold, I have taken upon
myself to speak to the Lord. Suppose twenty are found there."
He answered, "For the sake of twenty I will not destroy it."
32 Then he said, "Oh let not the Lord be angry, and I will speak
again but this once. Suppose ten are found there." He answered,
"For the sake of ten I will not destroy it." 33And the LORD went
his way, when he had finished speaking to Abraham; and Abraham
returned to his place.

*18.32
Judg 6.39;
Jas 5.16

5. Lot entertains two angels

19 The two angels came to Sŏdŏm in the evening; and Lot
was sitting in the gate of Sodom. When Lot saw them, he
rose to meet them, and bowed himself with his face to the earth,
2 and said, "My lords, turn aside, I pray you, to your servant's
house and spend the night, and wash your feet; then you may rise
up early and go on your way." They said, "No; we will spend the
night in the street." 3 But he urged them strongly; so they turned
aside to him and entered his house; and he made them a feast, and
baked unleavened bread, and they ate. 4 But before they lay down,
the men of the city, the men of Sŏdŏm, both young and old, all the
people to the last man, surrounded the house; 5 and they called
to Lot, "Where are the men who came to you tonight? Bring them
out to us, that we may know them." 6 Lot went out of the door to
the men, shut the door after him, 7 and said, "I beg you, my brothers, do not act so wickedly. 8 Behold, I have two daughters who
have not known man; let me bring them out to you, and do to them
as you please; only do nothing to these men, for they have come
under the shelter of my roof." 9 But they said, "Stand back!" And
they said, "This fellow came to sojourn, and he would play the
judge! Now we will deal worse with you than with them." Then
they pressed hard against the man Lot, and drew near to break the
door. 10 But the men put forth their hands and brought Lot into
the house to them, and shut the door. 11And they struck with
blindness the men who were at the door of the house, both small
and great, so that they wearied themselves groping for the door.

*19.1
Gen 18.22;
18.1ff

19.2
Heb 13.2;
Gen 18.4

19.3
Gen 18.8

19.5
Isa 3.9;
Judg 19.22;
Rom 1.24
19.6
Judg 19.23
19.8
see Judg
19.24
19.9
2 Pet 2.7,8;
Ex 2.14

19.11
see 2 Ki
6.18;
Acts 13.11

6. Lot informed of the imminent destruction

12 Then the men said to Lot, "Have you any one else here?
Sons-in-law, sons, daughters, or any one you have in the city,
bring them out of the place; 13 for we are about to destroy this
place, because the outcry against its people has become great

19.12
Gen 7.1;
2 Pet 2.7,9
19.13
Gen 18.20;
1 Chr 21.15

18.32 Six times Abraham beseeches God
to spare Sodom. Each time God grants his
petition. This incident should encourage
believers to intercede effectively and to expect
responses to prayer. It is a solemn commentary on the awful condition of Sodom that
there were not even ten righteous people to
be found within its gates.
19.1 Lot and Abraham both were righteous

men (15.6; 2 Pet 2.7, 8), and both enjoyed
similar backgrounds and advantages. Abraham, however, *looked forward to the city
which has foundations, whose builder and maker
is God* (Heb 11.10). Lot, on the contrary,
looked toward the city without heavenly foundations, choosing for the present time without
concern for eternity (13.5-18). Lot's misfortune should be a warning for all.

19.14
Num 16.21;
Ex 9.21;
Lk 17.28

before the LORD, and the LORD has sent us to destroy it." 14 So Lot went out and said to his sons-in-law, who were to marry his daughters, "Up, get out of this place; for the LORD is about to destroy the city." But he seemed to his sons-in-law to be jesting.

7. The departure of the family of Lot

19.15
Num 16.24,
26;
Rev 18.4
19.16
Lk 18.13;
Ps 34.22
19.17
1 Ki 19.3;
Jer 48.6;
ver 26

15 When morning dawned, the angels urged Lot, saying, "Arise, take your wife and your two daughters who are here, lest you be consumed in the punishment of the city." 16 But he lingered; so the men seized him and his wife and his two daughters by the hand, the LORD being merciful to him, and they brought him forth and set him outside the city. 17And when they had brought them forth, they^f said, "Flee for your life; do not look back or stop anywhere in the valley; flee to the hills, lest you be consumed." 18And Lot said to them, "Oh, no, my lords; 19 behold, your servant has found favor in your sight, and you have shown me great kindness in saving my life; but I cannot flee to the hills, lest the disaster overtake me, and I die. 20 Behold, yonder city is near enough to flee to, and it is a little one. Let me escape there—is it not a little one?—and my life will be saved!" 21 He said to him, "Behold, I grant you this favor also, that I will not overthrow the city of which you have spoken. 22 Make haste, escape there; for I can do nothing till you arrive there." Therefore the name of the city was called Zō'ar.^g 23 The sun had risen on the earth when Lot came to Zō'ar.

19.21
Job 42.8,9;
Ps 145.9

8. Sodom and Gomorrah destroyed

*19.24
Deut 29.23;
Isa 13.19;
Lk 17.29;
Jude 7
19.25
Ps 107.34
19.26
Lk 17.32
19.27
Gen 18.22
19.28
Rev 9.2;
18.9
19.29
2 Pet 2.7

24 Then the LORD rained on Sŏdŏm and Gŏmor'rȧh brimstone and fire from the LORD out of heaven; 25 and he overthrew those cities, and all the valley, and all the inhabitants of the cities, and what grew on the ground. 26 But Lot's wife behind him looked back, and she became a pillar of salt. 27And Abraham went early in the morning to the place where he had stood before the LORD; 28 and he looked down toward Sŏdŏm and Gŏmor'rȧh and toward all the land of the valley, and beheld, and lo, the smoke of the land went up like the smoke of a furnace.

29 So it was that, when God destroyed the cities of the valley, God remembered Abraham, and sent Lot out of the midst of the overthrow, when he overthrew the cities in which Lot dwelt.

9. The sin of Lot's daughters: the origins of the Moabites and Ammonites

30 Now Lot went up out of Zō'ar, and dwelt in the hills with his two daughters, for he was afraid to dwell in Zoar; so he dwelt in a cave with his two daughters. 31And the first-born said to the younger, "Our father is old, and there is not a man on earth to come in to us after the manner of all the earth. 32 Come, let us make our father drink wine, and we will lie with him, that we may preserve offspring through our father." 33 So they made their father drink wine that night; and the first-born went in, and lay with her father; he did not know when she lay down or when she

19.31
Gen 38.8,9;
Deut 25.5
19.32
Mk 12.19

---

^f Gk Syr Vg: Heb he   ^g That is Little

19.24 Sodom and Gomorrah, in the Valley of Siddim (Dead Sea) filled with *bitumen* pits (14.3, 10), were probably destroyed by lightning and possibly an earthquake (ver 25).

arose. 34And on the next day, the first-born said to the younger, "Behold, I lay last night with my father; let us make him drink wine tonight also; then you go in and lie with him, that we may preserve offspring through our father." 35 So they made their father drink wine that night also; and the younger arose, and lay with him; and he did not know when she lay down or when she arose. 36 Thus both the daughters of Lot were with child by their father. 37 The first-born bore a son, and called his name Mōăb; he is the father of the Mōʼăbĭtes to this day. 38 The younger also bore a son, and called his name Bĕn-ămʼmĭ; he is the father of the Ămʼmŏnĭtes to this day.

19.37
Deut 2.9
19.38
Deut 2.19

I. Abraham and Abimelech

1. Abimelech's sin of ignorance

20 From there Abraham journeyed toward the territory of the Nĕgĕb, and dwelt between Kādĕsh and Shŭr; and he sojourned in Gērar. 2And Abraham said of Sarah his wife, "She is my sister." And Ăbĭmʼĕlĕch king of Gērar sent and took Sarah. 3 But God came to Ăbĭmʼĕlĕch in a dream by night, and said to him, "Behold, you are a dead man, because of the woman whom you have taken; for she is a man's wife." 4 Now Ăbĭmʼĕlĕch had not approached her; so he said, "Lord, wilt thou slay an innocent people? 5 Did he not himself say to me, 'She is my sister'? And she herself said, 'He is my brother.' In the integrity of my heart and the innocence of my hands I have done this." 6 Then God said to him in the dream, "Yes, I know that you have done this in the integrity of your heart, and it was I who kept you from sinning against me; therefore I did not let you touch her. 7 Now then restore the man's wife; for he is a prophet, and he will pray for you, and you shall live. But if you do not restore her, know that you shall surely die, you, and all that are yours."

20.1
Gen 18.1;
16.7,14;
26.6
20.2
ver 12;
Gen 12.13,
15
20.3
Ps 105.14;
Job 33.15;
Gen 26.11
20.5
1 Ki 9.4;
2 Ki 20.3

20.7
1 Sam 7.5;
Job 42.8

2. Abraham's prayer for Abimelech

8 So Ăbĭmʼĕlĕch rose early in the morning, and called all his servants, and told them all these things; and the men were very much afraid. 9 Then Abĭmʼĕlĕch called Abraham, and said to him, "What have you done to us? And how have I sinned against you, that you have brought on me and my kingdom a great sin? You have done to me things that ought not to be done." 10And Abĭmʼĕlĕch said to Abraham, "What were you thinking of, that you did this thing?" 11Abraham said, "I did it because I thought, There is no fear of God at all in this place, and they will kill me because of my wife. 12 Besides she is indeed my sister, the daughter of my father but not the daughter of my mother; and she became my wife. 13And when God caused me to wander from my father's house, I said to her, 'This is the kindness you must do me: at every place to which we come, say of me, He is my brother.'" 14 Then Abĭmʼĕlĕch took sheep and oxen, and male and female slaves, and gave them to Abraham, and restored Sarah his wife to him. 15And Abĭmʼĕlĕch said, "Behold, my land is before you; dwell where it pleases you." 16 To Sarah he said, "Behold, I have given your brother a thousand pieces of silver; it is your vindication in the eyes of all who are with you; and before every one you are righted." 17 Then Abraham prayed to God; and God healed

20.9
Gen 26.10;
Ex 32.21;
Josh 7.25;
Gen 34.7

20.11
Ps 36.1;
Gen 12.12;
26.7

20.13
ver 5

20.14
Gen 12.16

20.15
Gen 13.9

20.17
Num 12.13;
Job 42.9

Åbĭm′ĕlĕçh, and also healed his wife and female slaves so that they bore children. [18] For the LORD had closed all the wombs of the house of Åbĭm′ĕlĕçh because of Sarah, Abraham's wife.

20.18
Gen 12.17

J. The birth of Isaac

1. Birth and circumcision

21 The LORD visited Sarah as he had said, and the LORD did to Sarah as he had promised. [2]And Sarah conceived, and bore Abraham a son in his old age at the time of which God had spoken to him. [3]Abraham called the name of his son who was born to him, whom Sarah bore him, Isaac. [4]And Abraham circumcised his son Isaac when he was eight days old, as God had commanded him. [5]Abraham was a hundred years old when his son Isaac was born to him. [6]And Sarah said, "God has made laughter for me; every one who hears will laugh over me." [7]And she said, "Who would have said to Abraham that Sarah would suckle children? Yet I have borne him a son in his old age."

21.1
1 Sam 2.21;
Gen 17.16,
21;
Gal 4.23
21.2
Acts 7.8;
Gal 4.22;
Heb 11.11;
Gen 17.21
21.3
Gen 17.19
21.4
Gen 17.12;
Acts 7.8
21.5
Gen 17.17
21.6
Ps 126.2;
Isa 54.1
21.7
Gen 18.13

2. The expulsion of Ishmael

8 And the child grew, and was weaned; and Abraham made a great feast on the day that Isaac was weaned. 9 But Sarah saw the son of Hāgar the Egyptian, whom she had borne to Abraham, playing with her son Isaac.[h] 10 So she said to Abraham, "Cast out this slave woman with her son; for the son of this slave woman shall not be heir with my son Isaac." [11]And the thing was very displeasing to Abraham on account of his son. 12 But God said to Abraham, "Be not displeased because of the lad and because of your slave woman; whatever Sarah says to you, do as she tells you, for through Isaac shall your descendants be named. [13]And I will make a nation of the son of the slave woman also, because he is your offspring." 14 So Abraham rose early in the morning, and took bread and a skin of water, and gave it to Hāgar, putting it on her shoulder, along with the child, and sent her away. And she departed, and wandered in the wilderness of Beër-shē′bà.

21.9
Gen 16.15;
Gal 4.29
21.10
Gal 4.30
*21.11
Gen 17.18
21.12
Rom 9.7;
Heb 11.18
21.13
ver 18;
Gen 16.10;
17.20

3. The deliverance of Hagar and Ishmael

15 When the water in the skin was gone, she cast the child under one of the bushes. 16 Then she went, and sat down over against him a good way off, about the distance of a bowshot; for she said, "Let me not look upon the death of the child." And as she sat over against him, the child lifted up his voice[i] and wept. [17]And God heard the voice of the lad; and the angel of God called to Hāgar from heaven, and said to her, "What troubles you, Hāgar? Fear not; for God has heard the voice of the lad where he is. [18]Arise, lift up the lad, and hold him fast with your hand; for I will make him a great nation." 19 Then God opened her eyes, and she saw a well of water; and she went, and filled the skin with water, and gave the lad a drink. [20]And God was with the lad, and he grew up; he lived in the wilderness, and became an expert with the

21.17
Ex 3.7

21.18
ver 13

21.19
Num 22.31

21.20
Gen 28.15;
39.2,3,21

h Gk Vg: Heb lacks *with her son Isaac*   i Gk: Heb *she lifted up her voice*

21.11 Abraham's displeasure may well have been a reflection of the fact that custom-ary law of his day forbade the expulsion of a slave wife and her children.

bow. 21 He lived in the wilderness of Pārȧn; and his mother took a wife for him from the land of Egypt.

21.21
Gen 24.4

4. *The discord between Abraham and Abimelech*

22 At that time Abïm′ělěçh and Phïcòl the commander of his army said to Abraham, "God is with you in all that you do; 23 now therefore swear to me here by God that you will not deal falsely with me or with my offspring or with my posterity, but as I have dealt loyally with you, you will deal with me and with the land where you have sojourned." 24And Abraham said, "I will swear."

21.22
Gen 20.2;
26.26,28

25 When Abraham complained to Abïm′ělěçh about a well of water which Abïm′ělěçh's servants had seized, 26Abïm′ělěçh said, "I do not know who has done this thing; you did not tell me, and I have not heard of it until today." 27 So Abraham took sheep and oxen and gave them to Abïm′ělěçh, and the two men made a covenant. 28Abraham set seven ewe lambs of the flock apart. 29And Abïm′ělěçh said to Abraham, "What is the meaning of these seven ewe lambs which you have set apart?" 30 He said, "These seven ewe lambs you will take from my hand, that you may be a witness for me that I dug this well." 31 Therefore that place was called Beër-shē′bȧ;ʲ because there both of them swore an oath. 32 So they made a covenant at Beër-shē′bȧ. Then Abïm′-ělěçh and Phïcòl the commander of his army rose up and returned to the land of the Philis′tïneş. 33Abraham planted a tamarisk tree in Beër-shē′bȧ, and called there on the name of the LORD, the Everlasting God. 34And Abraham sojourned many days in the land of the Philis′tïneş.

21.25
Gen 26.15,
18,20—22

21.27
Gen 26.31

21.30
Gen 31.48,
52
21.31
Gen 26.33

*21.32

21.33
Gen 4.26;
Deut 33.27

K. Abraham's sacrifice of Isaac
1. *God tests Abraham*

22 After these things God tested Abraham, and said to him, "Abraham!" And he said, "Here am I." 2 He said, "Take your son, your only son Isaac, whom you love, and go to the land of Mòrï′äh, and offer him there as a burnt offering upon one of the mountains of which I shall tell you." 3 So Abraham rose early in the morning, saddled his ass, and took two of his young men with him, and his son Isaac; and he cut the wood for the burnt offering, and arose and went to the place of which God had told him. 4 On the third day Abraham lifted up his eyes and saw the place afar off. 5 Then Abraham said to his young men, "Stay here with the ass; I and the lad will go yonder and worship, and come again to you." 6And Abraham took the wood of the burnt

*22.2
Heb 11.17;
2 Chr 3.1

22.6
Jn 19.17

ʲ That is *Well of seven* or *Well of the oath*

21.32 *land of the Philistines.* This designation for Canaan could be ascribed to a late editor, for the Philistines probably entered the land long after the time of Abraham.

22.2 On the basis of 2 Chr 3.1 Christian tradition has assumed that Jerusalem was the place where Abraham offered up Isaac. Glueck has called attention to the fact that it would have been odd for Abraham to have carried wood for the offering from Beersheba to the wooded country around Jerusalem where he could easily have secured all the wood he needed. Probably the *land of* Moriah of this text was in the treeless ranges of Sinai down near Kadesh. Abraham knew this country well. Moreover, Isaac here may be understood to be a type of Christ. He was an only son. He was offered up as a sacrifice. It was through Isaac that the descendants of Abraham should be named. And Abraham believed that God was able to raise Isaac from the dead, and, in a manner of speaking, did receive him back from the dead (Heb 11.17–19). Christ, from whom the type is taken, was an only son; He was offered up as a sacrifice; He was raised from the dead.

offering, and laid it on Isaac his son; and he took in his hand the fire and the knife. So they went both of them together. 7And Isaac said to his father Abraham, "My father!" And he said, "Here am I, my son." He said, "Behold, the fire and the wood; but where is the lamb for a burnt offering?" 8Abraham said, "God will provide himself the lamb for a burnt offering, my son." So they went both of them together.

*22.7
Jn 1.29,36;
Rev 13.8

2. God stops obedient Abraham

22.9
Heb 11.17–19

9 When they came to the place of which God had told him, Abraham built an altar there, and laid the wood in order, and bound Isaac his son, and laid him on the altar, upon the wood. 10 Then Abraham put forth his hand, and took the knife to slay his son. 11 But the angel of the LORD called to him from heaven, and said, "Abraham, Abraham!" And he said, "Here am I." 12 He said, "Do not lay your hand on the lad or do anything to him; for now I know that you fear God, seeing you have not withheld your son, your only son, from me." 13And Abraham lifted up his eyes and looked, and behold, behind him was a ram, caught in a thicket by his horns; and Abraham went and took the ram, and offered it up as a burnt offering instead of his son. 14 So Abraham called the name of that place The LORD will provide;k as it is said to this day, "On the mount of the LORD it shall be provided."l

*22.11
22.12
Gen 26.5;
1 Sam 15.22
*22.13

3. God's blessing repeated

22.16
Heb 6.13,14
22.17
Gen 15.5;
26.4;
32.12;
24.60
22.18
Gal 3.8,16;
Acts 3.25;
Gen 18.19

15 And the angel of the LORD called to Abraham a second time from heaven, 16 and said, "By myself I have sworn, says the LORD, because you have done this, and have not withheld your son, your only son, 17 I will indeed bless you, and I will multiply your descendants as the stars of heaven and as the sand which is on the seashore. And your descendants shall possess the gate of their enemies, 18 and by your descendants shall all the nations of the earth bless themselves, because you have obeyed my voice." 19 So Abraham returned to his young men, and they arose and went together to Beër-shē'ba; and Abraham dwelt at Beer-sheba.

20 Now after these things it was told Abraham, "Behold, Mīl-cåh also has borne children to your brother Nāhor: 21 Ūz the first-born, Būz his brother, Kĕm'ūėl the father of Aram, 22 Chĕsĕd, Hāzō, Pīldäsh, Jīdlăph, and Bēthu'ėl." 23 Bēthu'ėl became the father of Rēbĕk'åh. These eight Mīlcåh bore to Nāhor, Abraham's brother. 24 Moreover, his concubine, whose name was Reumåh, bore Tēbåh, Gāhåm, Tāhăsh, and Mā'åcåh.

22.23
Gen 24.15

k Or see   l Or he will be seen

22.7 How stunned Abraham must have been when Isaac, carrying the wood, inquires about the missing lamb! Would God require Abraham to carry through with the command of killing his son! Yet with unflinching faith in God he prepared to sacrifice Isaac.
22.11 Here am I. Abraham heard God call him; he was quick to respond. Had he not been listening he could not have responded. Had he been disobedient he would not have answered yes.
22.13 The ram caught in the thicket was a revelatory event of God to Abraham. When Abraham prepared to offer his only son Isaac

in obedience to God's command, his dilemma was this; how could he reconcile the command of God to slay his son with God's previous promise that through this son should come a great posterity? He did not solve the problem by deciding to disobey God's command to offer up Isaac. Rather by faith he concluded that God himself could raise Isaac from the dead after he had been offered. Spiritually there is a deeper lesson. God, like Abraham, did not spare His own Son (Rom 8.32). And, as Abraham received back Isaac as though he had been raised from the dead, so Christ has been raised by the Father from the dead.

L. *The death and burial of Sarah*

23 Sarah lived a hundred and twenty-seven years; these were the years of the life of Sarah. ²And Sarah died at Kĭr'ĭăth-ar'bá (that is, Hēbrŏn) in the land of Cānaăn; and Abraham went in to mourn for Sarah and to weep for her. ³And Abraham rose up from before his dead, and said to the Hĭttītes, ⁴ "I am a stranger and a sojourner among you; give me property among you for a burying place, that I may bury my dead out of my sight." ⁵ The Hĭttītes answered Abraham, ⁶ "Hear us, my lord; you are a mighty prince among us. Bury your dead in the choicest of our sepulchres; none of us will withhold from you his sepulchre, or hinder you from burying your dead." ⁷Abraham rose and bowed to the Hĭttītes, the people of the land. ⁸And he said to them, "If you are willing that I should bury my dead out of my sight, hear me, and entreat for me Ēphrŏn the son of Zōhar, ⁹ that he may give me the cave of Măch-pē'láh, which he owns; it is at the end of his field. For the full price let him give it to me in your presence as a possession for a burying place." ¹⁰ Now Ēphrŏn was sitting among the Hĭttītes; and Ephron the Hĭttīte answered Abraham in the hearing of the Hittites, of all who went in at the gate of his city, ¹¹ "No, my lord, hear me; I give you the field, and I give you the cave that is in it; in the presence of the sons of my people I give it to you; bury your dead." ¹² Then Abraham bowed down before the people of the land. ¹³And he said to Ēphrŏn in the hearing of the people of the land, "But if you will, hear me; I will give the price of the field; accept it from me, that I may bury my dead there." ¹⁴ Ēphrŏn answered Abraham, ¹⁵ "My lord, listen to me; a piece of land worth four hundred shekels of silver, what is that between you and me? Bury your dead." ¹⁶Abraham agreed with Ēphrŏn; and Abraham weighed out for Ephron the silver which he had named in the hearing of the Hĭttītes, four hundred shekels of silver, according to the weights current among the merchants.

17 So the field of Ēphrŏn in Măch-pē'láh, which was to the east of Mămrë, the field with the cave which was in it and all the trees that were in the field, throughout its whole area, was made over ¹⁸ to Abraham as a possession in the presence of the Hĭttītes, before all who went in at the gate of his city. ¹⁹After this, Abraham buried Sarah his wife in the cave of the field of Măch-pē'láh east of Mămrë (that is, Hēbrŏn) in the land of Cānaăn. ²⁰ The field and the cave that is in it were made over to Abraham as a possession for a burying place by the Hĭttītes.

M. *The marriage of Isaac*

1. *Abraham's instructions to his servant*

24 Now Abraham was old, well advanced in years; and the LORD had blessed Abraham in all things. ²And Abraham said to his servant, the oldest of his house, who had charge of all that he had, "Put your hand under my thigh, ³ and I will make you swear by the LORD, the God of heaven and of the earth, that you will not take a wife for my son from the daughters of the

Marginal references

23.2 Josh 14.15; ver 19; Gen 13.18

23.4 1 Chr 29.15; Ps 105.12; Heb 11.9,13

23.6 Gen 14.14; 24.35

23.8 Gen 25.9

23.10 Gen 24.20, 24; Ruth 4.4

23.11 see 2 Sam 24.21–24

23.15 Ex 30.13; Ezek 45.12

23.16 Jer 32.9; Zech 11.12

★23.17 Gen 25.9; 49.30–32; 50.13; Acts 7.16

24.1 ver 35; Gen 13.2

★24.2 Gen 47.29

24.3 Gen 14.22; 10.18,19; 26.34,35; 28.1,2,8

23.17 Hittite real estate transactions made specific reference to the trees on the property.

24.2 *hand under my thigh*, an ancient custom for confirming a solemn oath.

24.4
Gen 28.2;
12.1

24.7
Gen 12.7;
13.15;
15.18;
Ex 23.20,23

24.9
ver 2

*24.10
Gen 11.31,
32; 27.43
24.11
1 Sam 9.11

24.12
ver 27;
Gen 26.24;
Ex 3.6
24.13
ver 43
24.14
see Judg
6.17,37;
1 Sam 6.7

24.15
ver 45;
Gen 22.20,
23
24.16
Gen 26.7

24.18
ver 14,16
24.19
ver 14

24.21
ver 12–14;
56

24.22
ver 47

24.24
ver 15

Cā'naànītes, among whom I dwell, 4 but will go to my country and to my kindred, and take a wife for my son Isaac." 5 The servant said to him, "Perhaps the woman may not be willing to follow me to this land; must I then take your son back to the land from which you came?" 6Abraham said to him, "See to it that you do not take my son back there. 7 The LORD, the God of heaven, who took me from my father's house and from the land of my birth, and who spoke to me and swore to me, 'To your descendants I will give this land,' he will send his angel before you, and you shall take a wife for my son from there. 8 But if the woman is not willing to follow you, then you will be free from this oath of mine; only you must not take my son back there." 9 So the servant put his hand under the thigh of Abraham his master, and swore to him concerning this matter.

2. *The servant's prayer for guidance*

10 Then the servant took ten of his master's camels and departed, taking all sorts of choice gifts from his master; and he arose, and went to Mĕsôpôtā'mĭă, to the city of Nāhor. 11And he made the camels kneel down outside the city by the well of water at the time of evening, the time when women go out to draw water. 12And he said, "O LORD, God of my master Abraham, grant me success today, I pray thee, and show steadfast love to my master Abraham. 13 Behold, I am standing by the spring of water, and the daughters of the men of the city are coming out to draw water. 14 Let the maiden to whom I shall say, 'Pray let down your jar that I may drink,' and who shall say, 'Drink, and I will water your camels'—let her be the one whom thou hast appointed for thy servant Isaac. By this I shall know that thou hast shown steadfast love to my master."

3. *The servant's meeting with Rebekah*

15 Before he had done speaking, behold, Rĕbĕk'áh, who was born to Bĕthu'ĕl the son of Mĭlcáh, the wife of Nāhor, Abraham's brother, came out with her water jar upon her shoulder. 16 The maiden was very fair to look upon, a virgin, whom no man had known. She went down to the spring, and filled her jar, and came up. 17 Then the servant ran to meet her, and said, "Pray give me a little water to drink from your jar." 18 She said, "Drink, my lord"; and she quickly let down her jar upon her hand, and gave him a drink. 19 When she had finished giving him a drink, she said, "I will draw for your camels also, until they have done drinking." 20 So she quickly emptied her jar into the trough and ran again to the well to draw, and she drew for all his camels. 21 The man gazed at her in silence to learn whether the LORD had prospered his journey or not.

22 When the camels had done drinking, the man took a gold ring weighing a half shekel, and two bracelets for her arms weighing ten gold shekels, 23 and said, "Tell me whose daughter you are. Is there room in your father's house for us to lodge in?" 24 She said to him, "I am the daughter of Bĕthu'ĕl the son of Mĭlcáh, whom she bore to Nāhor." 25 She added, "We have both straw and

---

24.10 *Mesopotamia*, Hebrew *Aram-naha-raim* (Aram of the Two Rivers), the region also called *Paddan-aram* (25.20; 28.2). *city of* *Nahor*, a town near Haran, with slightly different spelling in Hebrew from Nahor, Abraham's brother (ver 15).

provender enough, and room to lodge in." 26 The man bowed his
head and worshiped the LORD, 27 and said, "Blessed be the LORD,
the God of my master Abraham, who has not forsaken his steadfast love and his faithfulness toward my master. As for me, the
LORD has led me in the way to the house of my master's kinsmen."
28 Then the maiden ran and told her mother's household about
these things. 29 Rĕbĕk'äh had a brother whose name was Lābán;
and Laban ran out to the man, to the spring. 30 When he saw the
ring, and the bracelets on his sister's arms, and when he heard the
words of Rĕbĕk'äh his sister, "Thus the man spoke to me," he
went to the man; and behold, he was standing by the camels at the
spring. 31 He said, "Come in, O blessed of the LORD; why do you
stand outside? For I have prepared the house and a place for the
camels." 32 So the man came into the house; and Lābán ungirded
the camels, and gave him straw and provender for the camels,
and water to wash his feet and the feet of the men who were with
him. 33 Then food was set before him to eat; but he said, "I will
not eat until I have told my errand." He said, "Speak on."

4. The servant's request for the hand of Rebekah for Isaac

34 So he said, "I am Abraham's servant. 35 The LORD has
greatly blessed my master, and he has become great; he has given
him flocks and herds, silver and gold, menservants and maidservants, camels and asses. 36And Sarah my master's wife bore a son
to my master when she was old; and to him he has given all that
he has. 37 My master made me swear, saying, 'You shall not take a
wife for my son from the daughters of the Cā'naánītes, in whose
land I dwell; 38 but you shall go to my father's house and to my
kindred, and take a wife for my son.' 39 I said to my master, 'Perhaps the woman will not follow me.' 40 But he said to me, 'The
LORD, before whom I walk, will send his angel with you and
prosper your way; and you shall take a wife for my son from my
kindred and from my father's house; 41 then you will be free from
my oath, when you come to my kindred; and if they will not give
her to you, you will be free from my oath.'
42 "I came today to the spring, and said, 'O LORD, the God of
my master Abraham, if now thou wilt prosper the way which I go,
43 behold, I am standing by the spring of water; let the young
woman who comes out to draw, to whom I shall say, "Pray give
me a little water from your jar to drink," 44 and who will say to
me, "Drink, and I will draw for your camels also," let her be the
woman whom the LORD has appointed for my master's son.'
45 "Before I had done speaking in my heart, behold, Rĕbĕk'äh
came out with her water jar on her shoulder; and she went down
to the spring, and drew. I said to her, 'Pray let me drink.' 46 She
quickly let down her jar from her shoulder, and said, 'Drink, and I
will give your camels drink also.' So I drank, and she gave the
camels drink also. 47 Then I asked her, 'Whose daughter are you?'
She said, 'The daughter of Bĕthu'ĕl, Nāhor's son, whom Mĭlcáh
bore to him.' So I put the ring on her nose, and the bracelets on
her arms. 48 Then I bowed my head and worshiped the LORD, and
blessed the LORD, the God of my master Abraham, who had led
me by the right way to take the daughter of my master's kinsman
for his son. 49 Now then, if you will deal loyally and truly with my

24.26
ver 48,52
24.27
ver 42,48,21

24.29
Gen 29.5,13

24.31
Gen 26.29
24.32
Gen 43,24;
Judg 19.21

24.35
ver 1;
Gen 13.2

24.36
Gen 21.2,
10; 25.5
24.37
ver 2–4
24.38
ver 4
24.39
ver 5
24.40
ver 7
24.41
ver 8

24.42
ver 11,12

24.43
ver 13,14

24.45
ver 15,17;
1 Sam 1.13
24.46
ver 18

24.47
ver 23,24

24.48
ver 26,27

24.49
Gen 47.29;
Josh 2.14

master, tell me; and if not, tell me; that I may turn to the right hand or to the left."

5. Rebekah goes with Abraham's servant

50 Then Lában and Bēthu'ēl answered, "The thing comes from the LORD; we cannot speak to you bad or good. 51 Behold, Rĕbĕk'-áh is before you, take her and go, and let her be the wife of your master's son, as the LORD has spoken."

52 When Abraham's servant heard their words, he bowed himself to the earth before the LORD. 53And the servant brought forth jewelry of silver and of gold, and raiment, and gave them to Rĕbĕk'áh; he also gave to her brother and to her mother costly ornaments. 54And he and the men who were with him ate and drank, and they spent the night there. When they arose in the morning, he said, "Send me back to my master." 55 Her brother and her mother said, "Let the maiden remain with us a while, at least ten days; after that she may go." 56 But he said to them, "Do not delay me, since the LORD has prospered my way; let me go that I may go to my master." 57 They said, "We will call the maiden, and ask her." 58And they called Rĕbĕk'áh, and said to her, "Will you go with this man?" She said, "I will go." 59 So they sent away Rĕbĕk'áh their sister and her nurse, and Abraham's servant and his men. 60And they blessed Rĕbĕk'áh, and said to her, "Our sister, be the mother of thousands of ten thousands; and may your descendants possess the gate of those who hate them!" 61 Then Rĕbĕk'áh and her maids arose, and rode upon the camels and followed the man; thus the servant took Rebekah, and went his way.

6. Isaac and Rebekah marry

62 Now Isaac had come from[n] Beër-láhaï'-roi, and was dwelling in the Nĕgĕb. 63And Isaac went out to meditate in the field in the evening; and he lifted up his eyes and looked, and behold, there were camels coming. 64And Rĕbĕk'áh lifted up her eyes, and when she saw Isaac, she alighted from the camel, 65 and said to the servant, "Who is the man yonder, walking in the field to meet us?" The servant said, "It is my master." So she took her veil and covered herself. 66And the servant told Isaac all the things that he had done. 67 Then Isaac brought her into the tent,[o] and took Rĕbĕk'áh, and she became his wife; and he loved her. So Isaac was comforted after his mother's death.

N. Abraham's seed by Keturah

25 Abraham took another wife, whose name was Kĕtu'ráh. 2 She bore him Zĭmrán, Jŏkshán, Mēdán, Mĭd'ĭán, Ĭshbăk, and Shuáh. 3 Jŏkshán was the father of Shēbá and Dēdán. The sons of Dedan were Ăssh'urĭm, Lĕtu'shĭm, and Lĕ-ŭm'mĭm. 4 The sons of Mĭd'ĭán were Ēpháh, Ēphĕr, Hānoch, Ăbī'dá, and Ĕldā'áh. All these were the children of Kĕtu'ráh. 5Abraham gave all he had to Isaac. 6 But to the sons of his concubines Abraham gave gifts, and while he was still living he sent them away from his son Isaac, eastward to the east country.

Marginal references:
24.50 Ps 118.23; Gen 31.24
24.52 ver 26
24.53 ver 10,22
24.54 ver 56,59
24.59 Gen 35.8
24.60 Gen 17.16; 22.17
24.62 Gen 16.14; 25.11;20.1
24.63 Ps 1.2; 77.12; 119.15; 143.5; 145.5
24.67 Gen 29.18; 23.1,2; 25.20
25.2 1 Chr 1,32,33
25.5 Gen 24.35,36

[n] Syr Tg: Heb from coming to
[o] Heb adds Sarah his mother

O. *The death of Abraham*

7 These are the days of the years of Abraham's life, a hundred
and seventy-five years. ⁸Abraham breathed his last and died in a
good old age, an old man and full of years, and was gathered to
his people. ⁹ Isaac and Ĭsh'mäël his sons buried him in the cave of
Măch-pē'läh, in the field of Ēphrŏn the son of Zōhar the Hĭttīte,
east of Mămrë, ¹⁰ the field which Abraham purchased from the
Hĭttītes. There Abraham was buried, with Sarah his wife. ¹¹After
the death of Abraham God blessed Isaac his son. And Isaac dwelt
at Beër-lähaī'-roi.

25.8
Gen 15.15;
35.29;
49.29,33
*25.9
25.10
Gen 23.16
25.11
Gen 24.62

VII. *The generations of Ishmael 25.12–18*

12 These are the descendants of Ĭsh'mäël, Abraham's son,
whom Hāgar the Egyptian, Sarah's maid, bore to Abraham.
¹³ These are the names of the sons of Ĭsh'mäël, named in the order
of their birth: Nēbāi'ŏth, the first-born of Ishmael; and Kēdar,
Ădbeēl, Mĭbsäm, ¹⁴ Mĭshmä, Dumäh, Mässä, ¹⁵ Hādäd, Tēmä, Jē-
túr, Nāphĭsh, and Kĕd'ëmäh. ¹⁶ These are the sons of Ĭsh'mäël
and these are their names, by their villages and by their encampments, twelve princes according to their tribes. ¹⁷ (These are the
years of the life of Ĭsh'mäël, a hundred and thirty-seven years;
he breathed his last and died, and was gathered to his kindred.)
¹⁸ They dwelt from Hăv'ĭläh to Shŭr, which is opposite Egypt
in the direction of Assyria; he settledᵖ over against all his people.

25.12
Gen 16.15
25.13
1 Chr 1.29–
31

25.16
Gen 17.20
25.17
ver 8

25.18
Gen 16.12

VIII. *The generations of Isaac 25.19–35.29*

A. *The birth of Jacob and Esau*

1. *The elder shall serve the younger*

19 These are the descendants of Isaac, Abraham's son: Abraham was the father of Isaac, ²⁰ and Isaac was forty years old when
he took to wife Rĕbĕk'äh, the daughter of Bĕthu'ĕl the Ărämē'än of
Păd'dän-ąr'äm, the sister of Lābän the Aramean. ²¹And Isaac
prayed to the LORD for his wife, because she was barren; and the
LORD granted his prayer, and Rĕbĕk'äh his wife conceived. ²² The
children struggled together within her; and she said, "If it is thus,
why do I live?"�q So she went to inquire of the LORD. ²³And the
LORD said to her,
"Two nations are in your womb,
    and two peoples, born of you, shall be divided;
the one shall be stronger than the other,
    the elder shall serve the younger."
²⁴ When her days to be delivered were fulfilled, behold, there were

25.20
Gen 24.15,
19
25.21
1 Sam 1.17;
Ps 127.3

25.23
Gen 17.16;
Num 20.14;
Gen 27.29;
Mal 1.3;
Rom 9.12

ᵖ Heb *fell*   �q Syr: Heb obscure

25.9 *Isaac and Ishmael his sons buried him.*
Abraham was one hundred years old when
Isaac was born. Thus Isaac was seventy-five
years old when his father died. Ishmael
was fourteen years older than Isaac. Evidently whatever friction existed between Isaac
and Ishmael they must have been in close
contact with each other. Here we find them,
at the death of their father Abraham, burying him next to Isaac's mother, Sarah, in
the cave of Machpelah. The descendants
of Ishmael and Isaac have had almost
nothing in common with each other for
many centuries despite the fact that both
sprang from the loins of a common father,
Abraham.

*25.25
Gen 27.11
25.26
Hos 12.3;
Gen 27.36

twins in her womb. 25 The first came forth red, all his body like a hairy mantle; so they called his name Ēsau. 26Afterward his brother came forth, and his hand had taken hold of Esau's heel; so his name was called Jacob.ʳ Isaac was sixty years old when she bore them.

2. Esau sells his birthright to Jacob

25.27
Gen 27.3,5

27 When the boys grew up, Ēsau wás a skilful hunter, a man of the field, while Jacob was a quiet man, dwelling in tents. 28 Isaac loved Ēsau, because he ate of his game; but Rëbĕk´áh loved Jacob.

29 Once when Jacob was boiling pottage, Ēsau came in from the field, and he was famished. 30And Ēsau said to Jacob, "Let me eat some of that red pottage, for I am famished!" (Therefore

*25.31

his name was called Ēdŏm.ˢ) 31 Jacob said, "First sell me your birthright." 32 Ēsau said, "I am about to die; of what use is a

25.33
Heb 12.16

birthright to me?" 33 Jacob said, "Swear to me first."ᵗ So he swore to him, and sold his birthright to Jacob. 34 Then Jacob gave Ēsau bread and pottage of lentils, and he ate and drank, and rose and went his way. Thus Ēsau despised his birthright

B. Isaac and Abimelech

1. The covenant confirmed to Isaac

26.1
Gen 12.10;
20.1,2
26.2
Gen 12.7;
17.1;18.1;
12.1
26.3
Gen 20.1;
12.2,7;
13.15;
15.18;
22.16–18
26.4
Gen 15.5;
22.17;
Ex 32.15;
Gen 12.3;
22.18;
Gal 3.8

26 Now there was a famine in the land, besides the former famine that was in the days of Abraham. And Isaac went to Gērar, to Ábĭm´ĕlĕçh king of the Phĭlĭs´tĭnĕs. 2And the LORD appeared to him, and said, "Do not go down to Egypt; dwell in the land of which I shall tell you. 3 Sojourn in this land, and I will be with you, and will bless you; for to you and to your descendants I will give all these lands, and I will fulfil the oath which I swore to Abraham your father. 4 I will multiply your descendants as the stars of heaven, and will give to your descendants all these lands; and by your descendants all the nations of the earth shall bless themselves: 5 because Abraham obeyed my voice and kept my charge, my commandments, my statutes, and my laws."

ʳ That is He takes by the heel or He supplants   ˢ That is Red   ᵗ Heb today

25.25
Esau was the twin brother of Jacob and the elder one with a natal claim to all the rights and privileges of the first-born, including the domestic priesthood, probably a double portion of the inheritance, and the precedence and authority after his father's death. The name Esau means "hairy." The name Edom which was given to Esau and which became the name of his descendants the Edomites, means "red." The story of Esau's life may be written in four parts: (1) the sale of his birthright to Jacob for the mess of pottage (25.27–34) which indicated that he despised his birthright and was willing to barter it away for a small consideration; (2) the marriages of Esau which were consummated with women who were not related to his father's family except for Mahalath who was his third wife and whom he married to placate his parents; (3) his failure to secure the patriarchal blessing just prior to the death of his father Isaac; (4) the re-establishment of brotherly relations with Jacob, and his departure from Canaan

for Seir. Esau was careless, motivated by animal appetites, and revengeful after the blessing was stolen from him by Jacob.

25.31 The birthright was of little practical importance when there was an only son. Isaac was Abraham's only true heir, Ishmael not being of the seed of promise. Thus Isaac was the only one in the line of promise and the natural heir of his father's possessions. But Isaac's wife bore him two sons, Esau and Jacob. Now the birthright assumed greater significance. Esau, as the first-born, should have been the one through whom the people of God descended. But he foolishly sold that birthright for carnal considerations and lost it to Jacob. Jacob claimed the privileges of the birthright and from him came the twelve tribes of Israel. The first-born received a double portion of the inheritance (cf. Deut 21.16–17) and, at least before the establishment of the Aaronic priesthood, the first-born in each family exercised the priestly prerogatives in the home after his father's death.

2. Isaac deceives Abimelech about Rebekah

6 So Isaac dwelt in Gērar. 7 When the men of the place asked him about his wife, he said, "She is my sister"; for he feared to say, "My wife," thinking, "lest the men of the place should kill me for the sake of Rĕbĕk′áh"; because she was fair to look upon. 8 When he had been there a long time, Ăbĭm′ĕlĕçh king of the Phĭlĭs′tĭneṣ looked out of a window and saw Isaac fondling Rĕbĕk′áh his wife. 9 So Ăbĭm′ĕlĕçh called Isaac, and said, "Behold, she is your wife; how then could you say, 'She is my sister'?" Isaac said to him, "Because I thought, 'Lest I die because of her.'" 10 Ăbĭm′ĕlĕçh said, "What is this you have done to us? One of the people might easily have lain with your wife, and you would have brought guilt upon us." 11 So Ăbĭm′ĕlĕçh warned all the people, saying, "Whoever touches this man or his wife shall be put to death."

26.7
Gen 12.13;
20.2,12,13

26.10
Gen 20.9

3. Isaac's riches

12 And Isaac sowed in that land, and reaped in the same year a hundredfold. The LORD blessed him, 13 and the man became rich, and gained more and more until he became very wealthy. 14 He had possessions of flocks and herds, and a great household, so that the Phĭlĭs′tĭneṣ envied him. 15 (Now the Phĭlĭs′tĭneṣ had stopped and filled with earth all the wells which his father's servants had dug in the days of Abraham his father.) 16 And Ăbĭm′ĕlĕçh said to Isaac, "Go away from us; for you are much mightier than we."

26.12
ver 3

26.14
Gen 24.35;
37.11
26.15
Gen 21.25,
30

4. Isaac's trouble with Abimelech over the wells: their covenant

17 So Isaac departed from there, and encamped in the valley of Gērar and dwelt there. 18 And Isaac dug again the wells of water which had been dug in the days of Abraham his father; for the Phĭlĭs′tĭneṣ had stopped them after the death of Abraham; and he gave them the names which his father had given them. 19 But when Isaac's servants dug in the valley and found there a well of springing water, 20 the herdsmen of Gērar quarreled with Isaac's herdsmen, saying, "The water is ours." So he called the name of the well Ēsĕk,ᵘ because they contended with him. 21 Then they dug another well, and they quarreled over that also; so he called its name Sĭtnáh.ᵛ 22 And he moved from there and dug another well, and over that they did not quarrel; so he called its name Rĕhō′bŏth,ʷ saying, "For now the LORD has made room for us, and we shall be fruitful in the land."

26.18
Gen 21.31

26.22
Gen 17.6

23 From there he went up to Beër-shē′bà. 24 And the LORD appeared to him the same night and said, "I am the God of Abraham your father; fear not, for I am with you and will bless you and multiply your descendants for my servant Abraham's sake." 25 So he built an altar there and called upon the name of the LORD, and pitched his tent there. And there Isaac's servants dug a well.

26.24
Gen 17.7;
24.12;
Ex 3.6

26.25
Gen 12.7,8;
13.4,18;
Ps 116.17

26 Then Ăbĭm′ĕlĕçh went to him from Gērar with Ăhŭz′zăth his adviser and Phīcŏl the commander of his army. 27 Isaac said to them, "Why have you come to me, seeing that you hate me

26.26
Gen 21.22

26.27
ver 16

ᵘ That is Contention   ᵛ That is Enmity   ʷ That is Broad places or Room

26.28
Gen 21.22,
23

and have sent me away from you?" 28 They said, "We see plainly that the LORD is with you; so we say, let there be an oath between you and us, and let us make a covenant with you, 29 that you will do us no harm, just as we have not touched you and have done to you nothing but good and have sent you away in peace. You are now the blessed of the LORD." 30 So he made them a feast,

26.31
Gen 21.31

and they ate and drank. 31 In the morning they rose early and took oath with one another; and Isaac set them on their way, and they departed from him in peace. 32 That same day Isaac's servants came and told him about the well which they had dug, and said to

26.33
Gen 21.31

him, "We have found water." 33 He called it Shībah; therefore the name of the city is Beër-shē'ba to this day.

C. Esau's marriages: Isaac's sorrow

26.34
Gen 28.8;
36.2
26.35
Gen 27.46

34 When Ēsau was forty years old, he took to wife Judïth the daughter of Be-ër'ï the Hïttïte, and Băs'ēmăth the daughter of Ēlŏn the Hittite; 35 and they made life bitter for Isaac and Rē-bĕk'ăh.

D. The stolen blessing

1. Esau hunts for game

27.1
Gen 48.10;
1 Sam 3.2
27.2
Gen 47.29
27.3
Gen 25.27,
28
27.4
ver 27;
Gen 48.9,
15;49.28

27 When Isaac was old and his eyes were dim so that he could not see, he called Ēsau his older son, and said to him, "My son"; and he answered, "Here I am." 2 He said, "Behold, I am old; I do not know the day of my death. 3 Now then, take your weapons, your quiver and your bow, and go out to the field, and hunt game for me, 4 and prepare for me savory food, such as I love, and bring it to me that I may eat; that I may bless you before I die."

2. Rebekah schemes with Jacob

27.8
ver 13

5 Now Rēbĕk'ăh was listening when Isaac spoke to his son Ēsau. So when Ēsau went to the field to hunt for game and bring it, 6 Rēbĕk'ăh said to her son Jacob, "I heard your father speak to your brother Ēsau, 7 'Bring me game, and prepare for me savory food, that I may eat it, and bless you before the LORD before I die.' 8 Now therefore, my son, obey my word as I command you. 9 Go to the flock, and fetch me two good kids, that I may prepare from them savory food for your father, such as he loves; 10 and you shall bring it to your father to eat, so that he may bless you before he

27.11
Gen 25.25
27.12
ver 21,22
27.13
ver 8;
Mt 27.25

dies." 11 But Jacob said to Rēbĕk'ăh his mother, "Behold, my brother Ēsau is a hairy man, and I am a smooth man. 12 Perhaps my father will feel me, and I shall seem to be mocking him, and bring a curse upon myself and not a blessing." 13 His mother said to him, "Upon me be your curse, my son; only obey my word, and go, fetch them to me." 14 So he went and took them and brought them to his mother; and his mother prepared savory food, such

27.15
ver 27

as his father loved. 15 Then Rēbĕk'ăh took the best garments of Ēsau her older son, which were with her in the house, and put them on Jacob her younger son; 16 and the skins of the kids she put upon his hands and upon the smooth part of his neck; 17 and she gave the savory food and the bread, which she had prepared, into the hand of her son Jacob.

3. *Jacob pretends to be Esau: he obtains the blessing*

18 So he went in to his father, and said, "My father"; and he said, "Here I am; who are you, my son?" 19 Jacob said to his father, "I am Ēsau your first-born. I have done as you told me; now sit up and eat of my game, that you may bless me." 20 But Isaac said to his son, "How is it that you have found it so quickly, my son?" He answered, "Because the LORD your God granted me success." 21 Then Isaac said to Jacob, "Come near, that I may feel you, my son, to know whether you are really my son Ēsau or not." 22 So Jacob went near to Isaac his father, who felt him and said, "The voice is Jacob's voice, but the hands are the hands of Ēsau." 23And he did not recognize him, because his hands were hairy like his brother Ēsau's hands; so he blessed him. 24 He said, "Are you really my son Ēsau?" He answered, "I am." 25 Then he said, "Bring it to me, that I may eat of my son's game and bless you." So he brought it to him, and he ate; and he brought him wine, and he drank. 26 Then his father Isaac said to him, "Come near and kiss me, my son." 27 So he came near and kissed him; and he smelled the smell of his garments, and blessed him, and said,

"See, the smell of my son
    is as the smell of a field which the LORD has blessed!
28 May God give you of the dew of heaven,
    and of the fatness of the earth,
    and plenty of grain and wine.
29 Let peoples serve you,
    and nations bow down to you.
Be lord over your brothers,
    and may your mother's sons bow down to you.
Cursed be every one who curses you,
    and blessed be every one who blesses you!"

4. *Esau learns of the deception*

30 As soon as Isaac had finished blessing Jacob, when Jacob had scarcely gone out from the presence of Isaac his father, Ēsau his brother came in from his hunting. 31 He also prepared savory food, and brought it to his father. And he said to his father, "Let my father arise, and eat of his son's game, that you may bless me." 32 His father Isaac said to him, "Who are you?" He answered, "I am your son, your first-born, Ēsau." 33 Then Isaac trembled violently, and said, "Who was it then that hunted game and brought it to me, and I ate it all[x] before you came, and I have blessed him?—yes, and he shall be blessed." 34 When Ēsau heard the words of his father, he cried out with an exceedingly great and bitter cry, and said to his father, "Bless me, even me also, O my father!" 35 But he said, "Your brother came with guile, and he has taken away your blessing." 36 Ēsau said, "Is he not rightly named Jacob? For he has supplanted me these two times. He

x Cn: Heb *of all*

27.19
ver 4

27.21
ver 12

27.23
ver 16

27.25
ver 4,10,19,
31

27.27
Heb 11.20;
Sol 4.11

27.28
Deut 33.13,
28;
Gen 45.18

27.29
Gen 9.25;
25.23;
49.8;12.3;
Num 24.9;
Zeph 2.8

27.31
ver 4

27.32
ver 18
27.33
Gen 28.3,4;
Rom 11.29

27.34
Heb 12.17

27.36
Gen 25.26,
32–34

27.19 Rebekah and Jacob deceived Isaac in order to obtain the blessing. Esau, long before this, had sold the birthright (25.27–34) to his brother. God would undoubtedly have worked out His will for Jacob to obtain the blessing in the end without resort to fraud. This incident is a sad illustration of what happens when believers seek to promote the will of God by dishonest means. Jacob had to pay the price in long years of exile.

took away my birthright; and behold, now he has taken away my blessing." Then he said, "Have you not reserved a blessing for

27.37
ver 28,29

me?" 37 Isaac answered Ēsau, "Behold, I have made him your lord, and all his brothers I have given to him for servants, and with grain and wine I have sustained him. What then can I do

27.38
Heb 12.17

for you, my son?" 38 Ēsau said to his father, "Have you but one blessing, my father? Bless me, even me also, O my father." And Esau lifted up his voice and wept.

27.39
ver 28

39 Then Isaac his father answered him:
"Behold, away from^y the fatness of the earth shall your dwelling
     be,
     and away from^y the dew of heaven on high.

27.40
Gen 25.23;
2 Ki 8.20–
22

40 By your sword you shall live,
     and you shall serve your brother;
but when you break loose
     you shall break his yoke from your neck."

5. *Rebekah schemes for Jacob to visit Laban*

27.41
Gen 32.3–
11

41 Now Ēsau hated Jacob because of the blessing with which his father had blessed him, and Esau said to himself, "The days of mourning for my father are approaching; then I will kill my brother Jacob." 42 But the words of Ēsau her older son were told to Rēbĕk'áh; so she sent and called Jacob her younger son, and said to him, "Behold, your brother Esau comforts himself by plan-

27.43
ver 8,13;
Gen 24.29

ning to kill you. 43 Now therefore, my son, obey my voice; arise, flee to Lābán my brother in Hārán, 44 and stay with him a while, until your brother's fury turns away; 45 until your brother's anger turns away, and he forgets what you have done to him; then I will send, and fetch you from there. Why should I be bereft of you both in one day?"

27.46
Gen 26.34,
35

46 Then Rēbĕk'áh said to Isaac, "I am weary of my life because of the Hĭttīte women. If Jacob marries one of the Hittite women such as these, one of the women of the land, what good will my

6. *Isaac sends Jacob to Laban*

28.1
Gen 24.3,4

28 life be to me?" 1 Then Isaac called Jacob and blessed him, and charged him, "You shall not marry one of the Cā'-

28.2
Gen 25.20

naánīte women. 2Arise, go to Păd'dăn-ạr'ám to the house of Bĕthu'ĕl your mother's father; and take as wife from there one of

28.3
Gen 17.1,6

the daughters of Lābán your mother's brother. 3 God Almighty^z bless you and make you fruitful and multiply you, that you may

28.4
Gen 12.2;
17.8

become a company of peoples. 4 May he give the blessing of Abraham to you and to your descendants with you, that you may take possession of the land of your sojournings which God gave to Abraham!" 5 Thus Isaac sent Jacob away; and he went to Păd'-dăn-ạr'ám to Lābán, the son of Bĕthu'ĕl the Ạrámē'án, the brother of Rēbĕk'áh, Jacob's and Ēsau's mother.

E. *Esau's third wife*

28.6
ver 1

6 Now Ēsau saw that Isaac had blessed Jacob and sent him away to Păd'dăn-ạr'ám to take a wife from there, and that as he blessed him he charged him, "You shall not marry one of the Cā'naánīte women," 7 and that Jacob had obeyed his father and his mother

---

^{y} Or *of* ^{z} Heb *Ĕl Shăd'dāī*

and gone to Păd′dăn-ặr′ám. 8 So when Ēsau saw that the Cā′-naănīte women did not please Isaac his father, 9 Ēsau went to Ĭsh′măël and took to wife, besides the wives he had, Mā′hăläth the daughter of Ishmael Abraham's son, the sister of Nĕbāi′óth.

F. Jacob's dream at Bethel

10 Jacob left Beër-shē′bả, and went toward Hărản. 11And he came to a certain place, and stayed there that night, because the sun had set. Taking one of the stones of the place, he put it under his head and lay down in that place to sleep. 12And he dreamed that there was a ladder set up on the earth, and the top of it reached to heaven; and behold, the angels of God were ascending and descending on it! 13And behold, the LORD stood above it*a* and said, "I am the LORD, the God of Abraham your father and the God of Isaac; the land on which you lie I will give to you and to your descendants; 14 and your descendants shall be like the dust of the earth, and you shall spread abroad to the west and to the east and to the north and to the south; and by you and your descendants shall all the families of the earth bless themselves.*b* 15 Behold, I am with you and will keep you wherever you go, and will bring you back to this land; for I will not leave you until I have done that of which I have spoken to you." 16 Then Jacob awoke from his sleep and said, "Surely the LORD is in this place; and I did not know it." 17And he was afraid, and said, "How awesome is this place! This is none other than the house of God, and this is the gate of heaven."

18 So Jacob rose early in the morning, and he took the stone which he had put under his head and set it up for a pillar and poured oil on the top of it. 19 He called the name of that place Bĕthĕl;*c* but the name of the city was Lùz at the first. 20 Then Jacob made a vow, saying, "If God will be with me, and will keep me in this way that I go, and will give me bread to eat and clothing to wear, 21 so that I come again to my father's house in peace, then the LORD shall be my God, 22 and this stone, which I have set up for a pillar, shall be God's house; and of all that thou givest me I will give the tenth to thee."

G. Jacob and Laban

1. Jacob meets Rachel

29 Then Jacob went on his journey, and came to the land of the people of the east. 2As he looked, he saw a well in the

a Or beside him   *b* Or be blessed   *c* That is The house of God

---

28.8
Gen 24.3;
26.35
28.9
Gen 36.3

28.12
Jn 1.51
28.13
Gen 35.1;
48.3;
26.24;
13.15;
35.12
28.14
Gen 13.14–
16; 22.17;
12.3;
18.18;
22.18; 26.4
28.15
Gen 26.3;
Num 6.24;
Ps 121.7,8;
Gen 48.21;
Deut 31.6,8
28.16
Ex 3.5;
Josh 5.15
★28.18
Gen 35.14;
Lev 8.10–12
★28.19
Judg 1.23,
26;
Hos 4.15
★28.20ff
Gen 31.13;
ver 15;
1 Tim 6.8
28.21
Judg 11.31;
2 Sam
19.24, 30;
Deut 26.17;
2 Sam 15.8
28.22
Gen 35.7,
14;
Lev 27.30

29.1
Judg 6.3,33

28.18 *pillar*, a memorial stone; *oil*, consecrating the holy place as an altar to God.

28.19 *Luz*, probably meaning "almond-tree," was renamed by Jacob *Bethel*, meaning "house of God," and became a holy place to the children of Israel. It was located on land which later was granted to the tribe of Benjamin and was about twelve miles north of Jerusalem. This sacred place was defiled when Jeroboam erected a golden calf (1 Ki 12.28–33), therefore God decreed the destruction of the altar (1 Ki 13.1–5; 2 Ki 23.15–17; Amos 3.14, 15).

28.20-22 Jacob here was not expressing doubt as to whether God would keep His promise of verses 13–15; he used the particle *if* in the sense of "on the basis of the fact that" (cf. Rom 8.31: *If God is for us*). Nor was he necessarily making a bargain with God, as if he would bribe Him to keep His word. He was simply specifying in the form of a vow the particular expression he would give to his gratitude for God's surprising and wholly undeserved favor. This became a customary type of thanksgiving in Israelite practice and was often solemnized by a votive offering.

field, and lo, three flocks of sheep lying beside it; for out of that well the flocks were watered. The stone on the well's mouth was large, 3 and when all the flocks were gathered there, the shepherds would roll the stone from the mouth of the well, and water the sheep, and put the stone back in its place upon the mouth of the well.

29.4
Gen 28.10
29.5
Gen 24.24,
29
29.6
Gen 43.27

4 Jacob said to them, "My brothers, where do you come from?" They said, "We are from Hārán." 5 He said to them, "Do you know Lábán the son of Nāhor?" They said, "We know him." 6 He said to them, "Is it well with him?" They said, "It is well; and see, Rachel his daughter is coming with the sheep!" 7 He said, "Behold, it is still high day, it is not time for the animals to be gathered together; water the sheep, and go, pasture them." 8 But they said, "We cannot until all the flocks are gathered together, and the stone is rolled from the mouth of the well; then we water the sheep."

29.9
Ex 2.16
29.10
Ex 2.17

9 While he was still speaking with them, Rachel came with her father's sheep; for she kept them. 10 Now when Jacob saw Rachel the daughter of Lábán his mother's brother, and the sheep of Laban his mother's brother, Jacob went up and rolled the stone from the well's mouth, and watered the flock of Laban his mother's

29.12
Gen 13.8;
14.14,16;
24.28

brother. 11 Then Jacob kissed Rachel, and wept aloud. 12And Jacob told Rachel that he was her father's kinsman, and that he was Rëbëk'áh's son; and she ran and told her father.

29.13
Gen 24.29,
31;33.4
29.14
Judg 9.2

13 When Lábán heard the tidings of Jacob his sister's son, he ran to meet him, and embraced him and kissed him, and brought him to his house. Jacob told Laban all these things, 14 and Lábán said to him, "Surely you are my bone and my flesh!" And he stayed with him a month.

2. Jacob's marriages to Leah and Rachel

15 Then Lábán said to Jacob, "Because you are my kinsman, should you therefore serve me for nothing? Tell me, what shall your wages be?" 16 Now Lábán had two daughters; the name of the older was Lēáh, and the name of the younger was Rachel.

29.18
Hos 12.12

17 Lēáh's eyes were weak, but Rachel was beautiful and lovely. 18 Jacob loved Rachel; and he said, "I will serve you seven years for your younger daughter Rachel." 19 Lábán said, "It is better

29.21
Judg 15.1
29.22
Judg 14.10;
Jn 2.1,2

that I give her to you than that I should give her to any other man; stay with me." 20 So Jacob served seven years for Rachel, and they seemed to him but a few days because of the love he had for her.

21 Then Jacob said to Lábán, "Give me my wife that I may go in to her, for my time is completed." 22 So Lábán gathered together all the men of the place, and made a feast. 23 But in the evening he took his daughter Lēáh and brought her to Jacob; and he went in to her. 24 (Lábán gave his maid Zílpáh to his daughter

*29.25

Lēáh to be her maid.) 25And in the morning, behold, it was Lēáh; and Jacob said to Lábán, "What is this you have done to me? Did I not serve with you for Rachel? Why then have you de-

---

29.25 We have here an illustration of how a man must reap as he has sown. The deceit which Jacob practiced on Esau was returned to him by Laban, who practiced the same kind of deceit. For all of that, however, Jacob was under the covenant care of God and did not come out a loser in the end. Yet in later years Jacob's own sons practiced on him a similar form of deceit in connection with Joseph's abduction (37.32-36).

ceived me?" 26 Lābán said, "It is not so done in our country, to give the younger before the first-born. 27 Complete the week of this one, and we will give you the other also in return for serving me another seven years." 28 Jacob did so, and completed her week; then Lābán gave him his daughter Rachel to wife. 29 (Lābán gave his maid Bïlháh to his daughter Rachel to be her maid.) 30 So Jacob went in to Rachel also, and he loved Rachel more than Lēáh, and served Lābán for another seven years.

3. Jacob's children
a. Leah's four sons

31 When the LORD saw that Lēáh was hated, he opened her womb; but Rachel was barren. 32 And Lēáh conceived and bore a son, and she called his name Reubën;*d* for she said, "Because the LORD has looked upon my affliction; surely now my husband will love me." 33 She conceived again and bore a son, and said, "Because the LORD has heard*e* that I am hated, he has given me this son also"; and she called his name Sïm'ëón. 34 Again she conceived and bore a son, and said, "Now this time my husband will be joined*f* to me, because I have borne him three sons"; therefore his name was called Lēvï. 35 And she conceived again and bore a son, and said, "This time I will praise*g* the LORD"; therefore she called his name Judah; then she ceased bearing.

b. Bilhah's two sons

30 When Rachel saw that she bore Jacob no children, she envied her sister; and she said to Jacob, "Give me children, or I shall die!" 2 Jacob's anger was kindled against Rachel, and he said, "Am I in the place of God, who has withheld from you the fruit of the womb?" 3 Then she said, "Here is my maid Bïlháh; go in to her, that she may bear upon my knees, and even I may have children through her." 4 So she gave him her maid Bïlháh as a wife; and Jacob went in to her. 5 And Bïlháh conceived and bore Jacob a son. 6 Then Rachel said, "God has judged me, and has also heard my voice and given me a son"; therefore she called his name Dan.*h* 7 Rachel's maid Bïlháh conceived again and bore Jacob a second son. 8 Then Rachel said, "With mighty wrestlings I have wrestled*i* with my sister, and have prevailed"; so she called his name Năph'tālï.

c. Zilpah's two sons

9 When Lēáh saw that she had ceased bearing children, she took her maid Zïlpáh and gave her to Jacob as a wife. 10 Then Lēáh's maid Zïlpáh bore Jacob a son. 11 And Lēáh said, "Good fortune!" so she called his name Găd.*j* 12 Lēáh's maid Zïlpáh bore Jacob a second son. 13 And Lēáh said, "Happy am I! For the women will call me happy"; so she called his name Ásher.*k*

d. Leah's last two sons: Rachel's first one

14 In the days of wheat harvest Reubën went and found mandrakes in the field, and brought them to his mother Lēáh. Then Rachel said to Leah, "Give me, I pray, some of your son's mandrakes." 15 But she said to her, "Is it a small matter that you have taken away my husband? Would you take away my son's

d That is See, a son   *e* Heb shama   *f* Heb lawah   *g* Heb hodah   *h* That is He judged
i Heb niphtal   *j* That is Fortune   *k* That is Happy

29.27
Judg 14.12

29.30
ver 17 18

29.31
Ps 127.3;
Gen 30.1
29.32
Gen 16.11;
31.42

29.34
Gen 49.5

29.35
Gen 49.8;
Mt 1.2

30.1
1 Sam 1.5,6
30.2
Gen 20.18;
29.31
30.3
Gen 16.2
30.4
Gen 16.3,4
30.6
Lam 3.59

30.8
Mt 4.13

30.9
ver 4

30.13
Prov 31.28

30.14
Gen 25.30
30.15
Num 16.9
13

mandrakes also?" Rachel said, "Then he may lie with you tonight for your son's mandrakes." 16 When Jacob came from the field in the evening, Lēáh went out to meet him, and said, "You must come in to me; for I have hired you with my son's mandrakes." So he lay with her that night. 17And God hearkened to Lēáh, and she conceived and bore Jacob a fifth son. 18 Lēáh said, "God has given me my hire*l* because I gave my maid to my husband"; so she called his name Ĭs'sáçhar. 19And Lēáh conceived again, and she bore Jacob a sixth son. 20 Then Lēáh said, "God has endowed me with a good dowry; now my husband will honor*m* me, because I have borne him six sons"; so she called his name Zĕb'ŭlŭn. 21Afterwards she bore a daughter, and called her name Dinah. 22 Then God remembered Rachel, and God hearkened to her and opened her womb. 23 She conceived and bore a son, and said, "God has taken away my reproach"; 24 and she called his name Joseph,*n* saying, "May the LORD add to me another son!"

4. Jacob's bargain with Laban

25 When Rachel had borne Joseph, Jacob said to Lābán, "Send me away, that I may go to my own home and country. 26 Give me my wives and my children for whom I have served you, and let me go; for you know the service which I have given you." 27 But Lābán said to him, "If you will allow me to say so, I have learned by divination that the LORD has blessed me because of you; 28 name your wages, and I will give it." 29 Jacob said to him, "You yourself know how I have served you, and how your cattle have fared with me. 30 For you had little before I came, and it has increased abundantly; and the LORD has blessed you wherever I turned. But now when shall I provide for my own household also?" 31 He said, "What shall I give you?" Jacob said, "You shall not give me anything; if you will do this for me, I will again feed your flock and keep it: 32 let me pass through all your flock today, removing from it every speckled and spotted sheep and every black lamb, and the spotted and speckled among the goats; and such shall be my wages. 33 So my honesty will answer for me later, when you come to look into my wages with you. Every one that is not speckled and spotted among the goats and black among the lambs, if found with me, shall be counted stolen." 34 Lābán said, "Good! Let it be as you have said." 35 But that day Lābán removed the he-goats that were striped and spotted, and all the she-goats that were speckled and spotted, every one that had white on it, and every lamb that was black, and put them in charge of his sons; 36 and he set a distance of three days' journey between himself and Jacob; and Jacob fed the rest of Lābán's flock.

37 Then Jacob took fresh rods of poplar and almond and plane, and peeled white streaks in them, exposing the white of the rods. 38 He set the rods which he had peeled in front of the flocks in the runnels, that is, the watering troughs, where the flocks came to drink. And since they bred when they came to drink, 39 the flocks bred in front of the rods and so the flocks brought forth striped, speckled, and spotted. 40And Jacob separated the lambs, and set the faces of the flocks toward the striped and all the black in the flock of Lābán; and he put his own droves apart, and did not put them with Lābán's flock. 41 Whenever the stronger of the flock

Marginal references (left column):

30.20
Mt 4.13

30.22
1 Sam
1.19,20;
Gen 29.31

30.23
Isa 4.1;
Lk 1.25

30.24
Gen 35.17

30.25
Gen 24.54,
56

30.26
Gen 29.20,
30;
Hos 12.12

30.27
Gen 39.3,5

30.28
Gen 29.15

30.29
Gen 31.38–
40

30.30
1 Tim 5.8

30.32
Gen 31.8

30.33
Ps 37.6

30.37
Gen 31.9–
12

l Heb *sakar* *m* Heb *zabal* *n* That is *He adds*

were breeding Jacob laid the rods in the runnels before the eyes
of the flock, that they might breed among the rods, 42 but for the
feebler of the flock he did not lay them there; so the feebler were
Lābàn's, and the stronger Jacob's. 43 Thus the man grew exceedingly rich, and had large flocks, maidservants and menservants, and camels and asses.

30.43
Gen 12.16;
13.2;24.35;
26.13,14

5. *Jacob plans to return home*

31 Now Jacob heard that the sons of Lābàn were saying,
"Jacob has taken all that was our father's; and from what
was our father's he has gained all this wealth." 2And Jacob saw
that Lābàn did not regard him with favor as before. 3 Then the
LORD said to Jacob, "Return to the land of your fathers and to
your kindred, and I will be with you." 4 So Jacob sent and called
Rachel and Lèàh into the field where his flock was, 5 and said to
them, "I see that your father does not regard me with favor as
he did before. But the God of my father has been with me. 6 You
know that I have served your father with all my strength; 7 yet
your father has cheated me and changed my wages ten times, but
God did not permit him to harm me. 8 If he said, 'The spotted
shall be your wages,' then all the flock bore spotted; and if he said,
'The striped shall be your wages,' then all the flock bore striped.
9 Thus God has taken away the cattle of your father, and given
them to me. 10 In the mating season of the flock I lifted up my
eyes, and saw in a dream that the he-goats which leaped upon
the flock were striped, spotted, and mottled. 11 Then the angel of
God said to me in the dream, 'Jacob,' and I said, 'Here I am!'
12And he said, 'Lift up your eyes and see, all the goats that leap
upon the flock are striped, spotted, and mottled; for I have seen all
that Lābàn is doing to you. 13 I am the God of Bĕthèl, where you
anointed a pillar and made a vow to me. Now arise, go forth from
this land, and return to the land of your birth.' " 14 Then Rachel
and Lèàh answered him, "Is there any portion or inheritance left
to us in our father's house? 15Are we not regarded by him as
foreigners? For he has sold us, and he has been using up the
money given for us. 16All the property which God has taken away
from our father belongs to us and to our children; now then,
whatever God has said to you, do."

*31.1

31.3
Gen 28.15,
20,21; 32.9

31.5
ver 3,42;
Gen 48.15

31.7
ver 41;
Job 19.3;
Ps 37.28;
105.14
31.8
Gen 30.32

31.11
Gen 48.16

31.13
Gen 28.13,
18,20
31.14
Gen 29,15,
27

6. *Jacob's flight from Laban*
a. *Jacob steals away*

17 So Jacob arose, and set his sons and his wives on camels;
18 and he drove away all his cattle, all his livestock which he had
gained, the cattle in his possession which he had acquired in Pād'-
dàn-ar'àm, to go to the land of Cānaàn to his father Isaac. 19 Lābàn had gone to shear his sheep, and Rachel stole her father's
household gods. 20And Jacob outwitted Lābàn the Arāmè'àn, in
that he did not tell him that he intended to flee. 21 He fled with all
that he had, and arose and crossed the Eūphrā'tēs, and set his
face toward the hill country of Gĭl'ĕàd.

*31.19
ver 30,34;
Judg 17.5;
1 Sam 19.
13;
Hos 3.4
31.21
Gen 37.25

b. *Laban overtakes Jacob*

22 When it was told Lābàn on the third day that Jacob had
fled, 23 he took his kinsmen with him and pursued him for seven

31.23
Gen 13.8

31.1 *Laban*, see note to Gen 29.25.   **31.19** *household gods*, idols of clay or metal.

days and followed close after him into the hill country of Gĭl'ëåd.
²⁴ But God came to Lābån the Ạrámē'án in a dream by night, and
said to him, "Take heed that you say not a word to Jacob, either
good or bad."

25 And Lābån overtook Jacob. Now Jacob had pitched his tent
in the hill country, and Laban with his kinsmen encamped in
the hill country of Gĭl'ëåd. ²⁶And Lābån said to Jacob, "What
have you done, that you have cheated me, and carried away my
daughters like captives of the sword? ²⁷ Why did you flee secretly,
and cheat me, and did not tell me, so that I might have sent you
away with mirth and songs, with tambourine and lyre? ²⁸And why
did you not permit me to kiss my sons and my daughters farewell?
Now you have done foolishly. ²⁹ It is in my power to do you
harm; but the God of your father spoke to me last night, saying,
'Take heed that you speak to Jacob neither good nor bad.' ³⁰And
now you have gone away because you longed greatly for your
father's house, but why did you steal my gods?" ³¹ Jacob answered
Lābån, "Because I was afraid, for I thought that you would take
your daughters from me by force. ³²Any one with whom you find
your gods shall not live. In the presence of our kinsmen point
out what I have that is yours, and take it." Now Jacob did not
know that Rachel had stolen them.

c. Rachel and Laban's idols

33 So Lābån went into Jacob's tent, and into Lēåh'ş tent, and
into the tent of the two maidservants, but he did not find them.
And he went out of Leah's tent, and entered Rachel's. ³⁴ Now
Rachel had taken the household gods and put them in the camel's
saddle, and sat upon them. Lābån felt all about the tent, but did
not find them. ³⁵And she said to her father, "Let not my lord be
angry that I cannot rise before you, for the way of women is upon
me." So he searched, but did not find the household gods.

36 Then Jacob became angry, and upbraided Lābån; Jacob
said to Laban, "What is my offense? What is my sin, that you have
hotly pursued me? ³⁷Although you have felt through all my goods,
what have you found of all your household goods? Set it here
before my kinsmen and your kinsmen, that they may decide
between us two. ³⁸ These twenty years I have been with you; your
ewes and your she-goats have not miscarried, and I have not eaten
the rams of your flocks. ³⁹ That which was torn by wild beasts I
did not bring to you; I bore the loss of it myself; of my hand you
required it, whether stolen by day or stolen by night. ⁴⁰ Thus I
was; by day the heat consumed me, and the cold by night, and
my sleep fled from my eyes. ⁴¹ These twenty years I have been
in your house; I served you fourteen years for your two daughters,
and six years for your flock, and you have changed my wages ten
times. ⁴² If the God of my father, the God of Abraham and the
Fear of Isaac, had not been on my side, surely now you would
have sent me away empty-handed. God saw my affliction and the
labor of my hands, and rebuked you last night."

d. The covenant between Jacob and Laban: Mizpah

43 Then Lābån answered and said to Jacob, "The daughters

31.24
Gen 20.3;
Job 33.15;
Gen 24.50

31.26
1 Sam 30.2

31.27
ver 55;
Ruth 1.9,
14;
Acts 20.37

31.29
ver 53,24

31.30
ver 19

31.32
Gen 44.9

*31.35
Ex 20.12;
Lev 19.32

31.39
Ex 22.10–13

31.41
Gen 29.27,
30;
ver 7

*31.42
Ps 124.1,2;
ver 53;
Isa 8.13;
Gen 29.32;
1 Chr 12.17

31.35 Rachel deceived her father by pretending to be "unclean."

31.42 *Fear of Isaac* (a term used for Israel's God), object of Isaac's reverence.

are my daughters, the children are my children, the flocks are my
flocks, and all that you see is mine. But what can I do this day
to these my daughters, or to their children whom they have
borne? 44 Come now, let us make a covenant, you and I; and let
it be a witness between you and me." 45 So Jacob took a stone, and
set it up as a pillar. 46 And Jacob said to his kinsmen, "Gather
stones," and they took stones, and made a heap; and they ate there
by the heap. 47 Lābȧn called it Jē'gar-sāhȧdu'thȧ:[o] but Jacob
called it Gălеēd.[p] 48 Lābȧn said, "This heap is a witness between
you and me today." Therefore he named it Gălеēd, 49 and the
pillar[q] Mĭzpȧh,[r] for he said, "The LORD watch between you and
me, when we are absent one from the other. 50 If you ill-treat my
daughters, or if you take wives besides my daughters, although no
man is with us, remember, God is witness between you and me."
51 Then Lābȧn said to Jacob, "See this heap and the pillar,
which I have set between you and me. 52 This heap is a witness,
and the pillar is a witness, that I will not pass over this heap to
you, and you will not pass over this heap and this pillar to me,
for harm. 53 The God of Abraham and the God of Nāhor, the God
of their father, judge between us." So Jacob swore by the Fear of
his father Isaac, 54 and Jacob offered a sacrifice on the mountain
and called his kinsmen to eat bread; and they ate bread and tarried
all night on the mountain.
55[s] Early in the morning Lābȧn arose, and kissed his grandchildren and his daughters and blessed them; then he departed
and returned home.

H. *Jacob's meeting with Esau*

1. *The preparations*

32 Jacob went on his way and the angels of God met him;
2 and when Jacob saw them he said, "This is God's army!"
So he called the name of that place Māhȧnā'ĭm.[t]
3 And Jacob sent messengers before him to Ēsau his brother in
the land of Sēịr, the country of Ēdȯm, 4 instructing them, "Thus
you shall say to my lord Ēsau: Thus says your servant Jacob, 'I
have sojourned with Lābȧn, and stayed until now; 5 and I have
oxen, asses, flocks, menservants, and maidservants; and I have
sent to tell my lord, in order that I may find favor in your sight.' "
6 And the messengers returned to Jacob, saying, "We came to
your brother Ēsau, and he is coming to meet you, and four hundred men with him." 7 Then Jacob was greatly afraid and distressed; and he divided the people that were with him, and the
flocks and herds and camels, into two companies, 8 thinking, "If
Ēsau comes to the one company and destroys it, then the company
which is left will escape."
9 And Jacob said, "O God of my father Abraham and God of

31.44 Gen 21.27, 32; 26.28; Josh 24.27
31.45 Gen 28.18
31.48 Josh 24.27
★31.49 Judg 11.29; 1 Sam 7.5
31.53 Gen 16.5; 21.23; 28.13; ver 42
31.55 Gen 18.33; 30.25
32.1 Ps 34.7; 91.11; Heb 1.14
32.2 Ps 103.21
32.3 Gen 33.14, 16; 25.30; 36.8,9
32.4 Prov 15.1
32.5 Gen 30.43; 33.8,15
32.6 Gen 33.1
32.7 ver 11
★32.9 Gen 31.42; 28.15; 31.13

[o] In Aramaic *The heap of witness* [p] In Hebrew *The heap of witness*
[q] Compare Sam: Heb lacks *the pillar*
[r] That is *Watchpost* [s] Ch 32.1 in Heb [t] Here taken to mean *Two armies*

31.49 God is called as a witness so that if either Jacob or Laban breaks the agreement the LORD will enforce the covenant.

32.9 Jacob's prayer for deliverance was graciously answered. God granted His favor to an undeserving sinner who cast himself wholly upon His mercy. Notice, however, that Jacob acted in accord with the proposition that often we should work as though we had never prayed.

my father Isaac, O LORD who didst say to me, 'Return to your country and to your kindred, and I will do you good,' 10 I am not worthy of the least of all the steadfast love and all the faithfulness which thou hast shown to thy servant, for with only my staff I crossed this Jordan; and now I have become two companies. 11 Deliver me, I pray thee, from the hand of my brother, from the hand of Ēsau, for I fear him, lest he come and slay us all, the mothers with the children. 12 But thou didst say, 'I will do you good, and make your descendants as the sand of the sea, which cannot be numbered for multitude.' "

13 So he lodged there that night, and took from what he had with him a present for his brother Ēsau, 14 two hundred she-goats and twenty he-goats, two hundred ewes and twenty rams, 15 thirty milch camels and their colts, forty cows and ten bulls, twenty she-asses and ten he-asses. 16 These he delivered into the hand of his servants, every drove by itself, and said to his servants, "Pass on before me, and put a space between drove and drove." 17 He instructed the foremost, "When Ēsau my brother meets you, and asks you, 'To whom do you belong? Where are you going? And whose are these before you?' 18 then you shall say, 'They belong to your servant Jacob; they are a present sent to my lord Ēsau; and moreover he is behind us.' " 19 He likewise instructed the second and the third and all who followed the droves, "You shall say the same thing to Ēsau when you meet him, 20 and you shall say, 'Moreover your servant Jacob is behind us.' " For he thought, "I may appease him with the present that goes before me, and afterwards I shall see his face; perhaps he will accept me." 21 So the present passed on before him; and he himself lodged that night in the camp.

2. Jacob becomes Israel: wrestling at the Jabbok

22 The same night he arose and took his two wives, his two maids, and his eleven children, and crossed the ford of the Jăbbŏk. 23 He took them and sent them across the stream, and likewise everything that he had. 24 And Jacob was left alone; and a man wrestled with him until the breaking of the day. 25 When the man saw that he did not prevail against Jacob, he touched the hollow of his thigh; and Jacob's thigh was put out of joint as he wrestled with him. 26 Then he said, "Let me go, for the day is breaking." But Jacob said, "I will not let you go, unless you bless me." 27 And he said to him, "What is your name?" And he said, "Jacob." 28 Then he said, "Your name shall no more be called Jacob, but Israel,ᵘ for you have striven with God and with men, and have prevailed." 29 Then Jacob asked him, "Tell me, I pray, your name?" But he said, "Why is it that you ask my name?" And there he blessed him. 30 So Jacob called the name of the place Pĕnī'ĕl,ᵛ saying, "For I have seen God face to face, and yet my life is preserved." 31 The sun rose upon him as he passed Pĕnü'ĕl, limping because of his thigh. 32 Therefore to this day the Israelites

32.10
Gen 24.27;
Job 8.7

32.11
Gen 27.41,
42; 33.4

32.12
Gen 28.13–
15

32.13
Gen 43.11;
Prov 18.16

32.20
Prov 21.14

32.22
Deut 3.16;
Josh 12.2

32.24
Hos 12.3,4

32.26
Hos 12.4

★32.28
Gen 35.10;
1 Ki 18.31

32.29
Judg 13.17,
18

32.30
Gen 16.13;
Ex 24.11;
Num 12.8;
Judg 6.22;
13.22

★32.31

ᵘ That is *He who strives with God* or *God strives*   ᵛ That is *The face of God*

32.28 Just as God changed Abram's name to Abraham, he now changes Jacob's name to Israel, by which the Hebrews are henceforth to be known. It is a name for the people and for an individual. The normative use of *Israel* in the Bible denotes the people just as *American* denotes a citizen of the United States.
32.31 *Penuel*, Peniel (ver 30).

do not eat the sinew of the hip which is upon the hollow of the thigh, because he touched the hollow of Jacob's thigh on the sinew of the hip.

3. Jacob and Esau meet

33 And Jacob lifted up his eyes and looked, and behold, Ēsau was coming, and four hundred men with him. So he divided the children among Lēah and Rachel and the two maids. ²And he put the maids with their children in front, then Lēah with her children, and Rachel and Joseph last of all. ³ He himself went on before them, bowing himself to the ground seven times, until he came near to his brother.

4 But Ēsau ran to meet him, and embraced him, and fell on his neck and kissed him, and they wept. ⁵And when Ēsau raised his eyes and saw the women and children, he said, "Who are these with you?" Jacob said, "The children whom God has graciously given your servant." 6 Then the maids drew near, they and their children, and bowed down; 7 Lēah likewise and her children drew near and bowed down; and last Joseph and Rachel drew near, and they bowed down. 8 Ēsau said, "What do you mean by all this company which I met?" Jacob answered, "To find favor in the sight of my lord." 9 But Ēsau said, "I have enough, my brother; keep what you have for yourself." 10 Jacob said, "No, I pray you, if I have found favor in your sight, then accept my present from my hand; for truly to see your face is like seeing the face of God, with such favor have you received me. ¹¹Accept, I pray you, my gift that is brought to you, because God has dealt graciously with me, and because I have enough." Thus he urged him, and he took it.

12 Then Ēsau said, "Let us journey on our way, and I will go before you." 13 But Jacob said to him, "My lord knows that the children are frail, and that the flocks and herds giving suck are a care to me; and if they are overdriven for one day, all the flocks will die. ¹⁴ Let my lord pass on before his servant, and I will lead on slowly, according to the pace of the cattle which are before me and according to the pace of the children, until I come to my lord in Sēir."

4. Jacob journeys to Shechem

15 So Ēsau said, "Let me leave with you some of the men who are with me." But he said, "What need is there? Let me find favor in the sight of my lord." 16 So Ēsau returned that day on his way to Sēir. 17 But Jacob journeyed to Súccóth,ʷ and built himself a house, and made booths for his cattle; therefore the name of the place is called Succoth.

18 And Jacob came safely to the city of Shĕchĕm, which is in the land of Cānaàn, on his way from Pãd'dăn-ạr'ảm; and he camped before the city. ¹⁹And from the sons of Hãmor, Shĕchĕm's father, he bought for a hundred pieces of moneyˣ the piece of land on which he had pitched his tent. 20 There he erected an altar and called it Ēl-Ēl'ōhĕ-Ĭṣ'räël.ʸ

ʷ That is *Booths*   ˣ Heb *a hundred qesitah*   ʸ That is *God, the God of Israel*

Side references: 33.1 Gen 32.6; 33.3 Gen 18.2; 42.6; ★33.4 Gen 45.14,15; 33.5 Gen 48.9; Ps 127.3; Isa 8.18; 33.8 Gen 32.14–16; 33.10 Gen 43.3; 2 Sam 3.13; 33.11 1 Sam 25.27; 33.14 Gen 32.3; 33.15 Gen 34.11; 47.25; Ruth 2.13; ★33.16; 33.17 Judg 8.5,14; Ps 60.6; 33.18 Josh 24.1; Judg 9.1; Gen 25.20; 28.2; 33.19 Josh 24.32; Jn 4.5

33.4 Only God working in the heart of Esau explains the change in him as he greets Jacob in a friendly, not in a hostile, manner. **33.16** *Seir,* Edom.

I. Jacob's later life

1. *The humbling of Dinah*

34.1
Gen 30.21

34 Now Dinah the daughter of Lĕah, whom she had borne to Jacob, went out to visit the women of the land; 2 and when Shĕçhĕm the son of Hāmor the Hĭvīte, the prince of the land, saw her, he seized her and lay with her and humbled her. 3And his soul was drawn to Dinah the daughter of Jacob; he loved the maiden and spoke tenderly to her. 4 So Shĕçhĕm spoke to his father Hāmor, saying, "Get me this maiden for my wife." 5 Now Jacob heard that he had defiled his daughter Dinah; but his sons were with his cattle in the field, so Jacob held his peace until they came. 6And Hāmor the father of Shĕçhĕm went out to Jacob to speak with him. 7 The sons of Jacob came in from the field when they heard of it; and the men were indignant and very angry, because he had wrought folly in Israel by lying with Jacob's daughter, for such a thing ought not to be done.

34.4
Judg 14.2

34.7
Deut 22.21;
Josh 7.15;
Judg 20.6;
2 Sam 13.12

8 But Hāmor spoke with them, saying, "The soul of my son Shĕçhĕm longs for your daughter; I pray you, give her to him in marriage. 9 Make marriages with us; give your daughters to us, and take our daughters for yourselves. 10 You shall dwell with us; and the land shall be open to you; dwell and trade in it, and get property in it." 11 Shĕçhĕm also said to her father and to her brothers, "Let me find favor in your eyes, and whatever you say to me I will give. 12Ask of me ever so much as marriage present and gift, and I will give according as you say to me; only give me the maiden to be my wife."

34.10
Gen 13.9;
20.15

34.12
Ex 22.16;
Deut 22.29;
1 Sam 18.25

13 The sons of Jacob answered Shĕçhĕm and his father Hāmor deceitfully, because he had defiled their sister Dinah. 14 They said to them, "We cannot do this thing, to give our sister to one who is uncircumcised, for that would be a disgrace to us. 15 Only on this condition will we consent to you: that you will become as we are and every male of you be circumcised. 16 Then we will give our daughters to you, and we will take your daughters to ourselves, and we will dwell with you and become one people. 17 But if you will not listen to us and be circumcised, then we will take our daughter, and we will be gone."

34.14
Gen 17.14

2. *The revenge for the humbling of Dinah*

18 Their words pleased Hāmor and Hāmor's son Shĕçhĕm. 19And the young man did not delay to do the thing, because he had delight in Jacob's daughter. Now he was the most honored of all his family. 20 So Hāmor and his son Shĕçhĕm came to the gate of their city and spoke to the men of their city, saying, 21 "These men are friendly with us; let them dwell in the land and trade in it, for behold, the land is large enough for them; let us take their daughters in marriage, and let us give them our daughters. 22 Only on this condition will the men agree to dwell with us, to become one people: that every male among us be circumcised as they are circumcised. 23 Will not their cattle, their property and all their beasts be ours? Only let us agree with them, and they will dwell with us." 24And all who went out of the gate of his city hearkened to Hāmor and his son Shĕçhĕm; and every male was circumcised, all who went out of the gate of his city.

34.19
1 Chr 4.9

34.24
Gen 23.10

34.25
Gen 49.5–7

25 On the third day, when they were sore, two of the sons of

Jacob, Sïm'ëön and Lēvī, Dinah's brothers, took their swords and came upon the city unawares, and killed all the males. 26 They slew Hāmor and his son Shĕçhĕm with the sword, and took Dinah out of Shĕçhĕm's house, and went away. 27And the sons of Jacob came upon the slain, and plundered the city, because their sister had been defiled; 28 they took their flocks and their herds, their asses, and whatever was in the city and in the field; 29 all their wealth, all their little ones and their wives, all that was in the houses, they captured and made their prey. 30 Then Jacob said to Sïm'ëön and Lēvī, "You have brought trouble on me by making me odious to the inhabitants of the land, the Cā'naänītes and the Pĕr'ịzzītes; my numbers are few, and if they gather themselves against me and attack me, I shall be destroyed, both I and my household." 31 But they said, "Should he treat our sister as a harlot?"

3. Jacob returns to Bethel: God renews the covenant promises

35 God said to Jacob, "Arise, go up to Bĕthĕl, and dwell there; and make there an altar to the God who appeared to you when you fled from your brother Ēsau." 2 So Jacob said to his household and to all who were with him, "Put away the foreign gods that are among you, and purify yourselves, and change your garments; 3 then let us arise and go up to Bĕthĕl, that I may make there an altar to the God who answered me in the day of my distress and has been with me wherever I have gone." 4 So they gave to Jacob all the foreign gods that they had, and the rings that were in their ears; and Jacob hid them under the oak which was near Shĕçhĕm.

5 And as they journeyed, a terror from God fell upon the cities that were round about them, so that they did not pursue the sons of Jacob. 6And Jacob came to Lùz (that is, Bĕthĕl), which is in the land of Cānaän, he and all the people who were with him, 7 and there he built an altar, and called the place Ĕl-bĕth'ĕl,z because there God had revealed himself to him when he fled from his brother. 8And Deborah, Rĕbĕk'áh's nurse, died, and she was buried under an oak below Bĕthĕl; so the name of it was called Ăllón-băc'úth.a

9 God appeared to Jacob again, when he came from Păd́dăn-ạr'ám, and blessed him. 10And God said to him, "Your name is Jacob; no longer shall your name be called Jacob, but Israel shall be your name." So his name was called Israel. 11And God said to him, "I am God Almighty:b be fruitful and multiply; a nation and a company of nations shall come from you, and kings shall spring from you. 12 The land which I gave to Abraham and Isaac I will give to you, and I will give the land to your descendants after you." 13 Then God went up from him in the place where he had spoken with him. 14And Jacob set up a pillar in the place where he

z That is God of Bĕthĕl   a That is Oak of weeping   b Heb Ĕl Shăd'dăï

34.30
Gen 49.6;
Ex 5.21;
Gen 36.26,
27

35.1
Gen 28.19,
13; 27.43
35.2
Gen 31.19,
30,34;
Ex 19.10,14
35.3
Gen 32.7,
24;
28.20–22;
28.15
35.4
Hos 2.13;
Josh 24.26

35.6
Gen 28.19;
48.3
35.7
Gen 28.13
35.8
Gen 24.59
35.9
Hos 12.4;
Gen 32.29
35.10
Gen 32.28
35.11
Gen 17.1;
28.3; 48.4;
17.6,16;
36.31
35.12
Gen 13.15;
26.3; 28.13
35.13
Gen 17.22
*35.14
Gen 28.18

35.14 This is the first mention of the drink offering in the Old Testament. Mosaic sacrifices were often accompanied by drink offerings (Ex 29.40; Lev 23.13). In Num 15.3–10 the quantity is prescribed according to the type of blood sacrifice to be presented. Its use was perverted by the Jews who offered it along with their sacrificial cakes to Ash-toreth, the queen of heaven (Jer 44.17–19). God reproved Israel for offering it to idols (Isa 57.5, 6 and 65.11; Jer 19.13; Ezek 20.28). The drink offering is symbolic of the outpoured blood of Christ on Calvary (Isa 53.12; Mt 26.28; Heb 9.11–14) and of the outpouring of the Holy Spirit upon His Church (Joel 2.28; Acts 2.17, 18; 10.45).

had spoken with him, a pillar of stone; and he poured out a drink
offering on it, and poured oil on it. 15 So Jacob called the name of
the place where God had spoken with him, Bĕthĕl.

*35.15
Gen 28.19

35.17
Gen 30.24
*35.18
35.19
Gen 48.7;
Ruth 1.2;
Mic 5.2;
Mt 2.6
35.20
1 Sam 10.2
35.5
Ex 15.16;
Deut 2.25;
11.25
35.22
Gen 49.2;
1 Chr 5.1;
1 Cor 5.1

4. Benjamin's birth: Rachel's death

16 Then they journeyed from Bĕthĕl; and when they were still
some distance from Ēphrăth, Rachel travailed, and she had hard
labor. 17And when she was in her hard labor, the midwife said to
her, "Fear not; for now you will have another son." 18And as her
soul was departing (for she died), she called his name Bĕn-ō'nī;c
but his father called his name Benjamin.d 19 So Rachel died, and
she was buried on the way to Ēphrăth (that is, Bĕth'lĕhĕm), 20 and
Jacob set up a pillar upon her grave; it is the pillar of Rachel's
tomb, which is there to this day. 21 Israel journeyed on, and
pitched his tent beyond the tower of Ēdĕr.

5. The sin of Reuben

22 While Israel dwelt in that land Reubĕn went and lay with
Bĭlhăh his father's concubine; and Israel heard of it.

6. The sons of Jacob

Now the sons of Jacob were twelve. 23 The sons of Lēăh: Reubĕn (Jacob's first-born), Sĭm'ĕŏn, Lēvī, Judah, Ĭs'săchar, and
Zĕb'ŭlŭn. 24 The sons of Rachel: Joseph and Benjamin. 25 The
sons of Bĭlhăh, Rachel's maid: Dan and Năph'tălī. 26 The sons of
Zĭlpăh, Lēăh's maid: Găd and Āshĕr. These were the sons of Jacob
who were born to him in Păd'dăn-ar'ăm.

7. The death of Isaac

35.27
Gen 18.1;
23.9
35.29
Gen 25.8;
15.15

27 And Jacob came to his father Isaac at Mămrĕ, or Kĭr'iăth-
ar'bă (that is, Hēbrŏn), where Abraham and Isaac had sojourned.
28 Now the days of Isaac were a hundred and eighty years. 29And
Isaac breathed his last; and he died and was gathered to his people, old and full of days; and his sons Ēsau and Jacob buried him.

IX. The generations of Esau 36.1–43

36.1
Gen 25.30
36.2
Gen 26.34;
28.9

36 These are the descendants of Ēsau (that is, Ēdŏm). 2 Ēsau
took his wives from the Cā'naănītes: Ādăh the daughter of
Ēlŏn the Hĭttīte, Ōhōlĭbă'măh the daughter of Ānăh the sone of
Zĭbĕŏn the Hīvīte, 3 and Băs'ĕmăth, Ĭsh'măĕl's daughter, the
sister of Nĕbāi'ŏth. 4And Ādăh bore to Ēsau, Ĕl'īphăz; Băs'ĕmăth
bore Reu'ĕl; 5 and Ōhōlĭbă'măh bore Jĕ'ŭsh, Jālăm, and Kōrăh.
These are the sons of Ēsau who were born to him in the land of
Cānaăn.

c That is Son of my sorrow
d That is Son of the right hand or Son of the South   e Sam Gk Syr: Heb daughter

---

35.15 See here note to 28.19.
35.18 Benjamin was the twelfth and last
son of Jacob. He was full brother to Joseph,
being born of Rachel, the favorite wife of
Jacob. Benjamin alone was born in Canaan
rather than Paddan-aram, and his mother was
buried on the way to Bethlehem in the region
later assigned to Benjamin. He and Joseph
were special objects of the affection of Jacob

because their mother was Rachel. In her dying
agonies Rachel gave him the name of Benoni,
"son of my sorrow," but Jacob named him
Benjamin, "son of the right hand." The
peculiar concern of Joseph for Benjamin during the Egyptian episode may be understood
by the fact that they were full brothers, whose
half brothers looked upon them with envy
because of Jacob's special love for them.

6 Then Ēsau took his wives, his sons, his daughters, and all the members of his household, his cattle, all his beasts, and all his property which he had acquired in the land of Cānaàn; and he went into a land away from his brother Jacob. 7 For their possessions were too great for them to dwell together; the land of their sojournings could not support them because of their cattle. 8 So Ēsau dwelt in the hill country of Sēir; Esau is Ēdóm.

9 These are the descendants of Ēsau the father of the Ē'dòmītes in the hill country of Sēir. 10 These are the names of Ēsau's sons: Ēl'iphăz the son of Ādáh the wife of Ēsau, Reu'ēl the son of Băs'ēmăth the wife of Esau. 11 The sons of Ēl'iphăz were Tēmàn, Ōmar, Zēphō, Gātám, and Kēnăz. 12 (Tīmnà was a concubine of Ēl'iphăz, Ēsau's son; she bore Ăm'álĕk to Eliphaz.) These are the sons of Adáh, Esau's wife. 13 These are the sons of Reu'ēl: Nāhǎth, Zērǎh, Shǎmmáh, and Mǐzzàh. These are the sons of Băs'ēmăth, Ēsau's wife. 14 These are the sons of Ōhōlibā'máh the daughter of Ānáh the sonᶠ of Zīb'ëön, Ēsau's wife: she bore to Ēsau Jē'üsh, Jālàm, and Kōráh.

15 These are the chiefs of the sons of Ēsau. The sons of Ēl'iphăz the first-born of Esau: the chiefs Tēmán, Ōmar, Zēphō, Kēnăz, 16 Kōráh, Gátám, and Ăm'álĕk; these are the chiefs of Ēl'iphăz in the land of Ēdóm; they are the sons of Ādáh. 17 These are the sons of Reu'ēl, Ēsau's son: the chiefs Nāháth, Zēráh, Shǎmmáh, and Mǐzzàh; these are the chiefs of Reuel in the land of Ēdóm; they are the sons of Băs'ēmăth, Esau's wife. 18 These are the sons of Ōhōlibā'máh, Ēsau's wife: the chiefs Jē'üsh, Jālàm, and Kōráh; these are the chiefs born of Oholibamah the daughter of Ānáh, Esau's wife. 19 These are the sons of Ēsau (that is, Ēdòm), and these are their chiefs.

20 These are the sons of Sēir the Horīte, the inhabitants of the land: Lōtán, Shōbǎl, Zǐb'ëön, Ānáh, 21 Dīshòn, Ēzér, and Dīshǎn; these are the chiefs of the Horītes, the sons of Sēir in the land of Ēdóm. 22 The sons of Lōtàn were Hōrī and Hēmàn; and Lōtàn's sister was Tīmnà. 23 These are the sons of Shōbǎl: Ālvan, Manā'hàth, Ēbál, Shēphō, and Ōnàm. 24 These are the sons of Zīb'ëön: Ā'iah and Ānáh; he is the Anah who found the hot springs in the wilderness, as he pastured the asses of Zǐb'eon his father. 25 These are the children of Ānáh: Dīshòn and Ōhōlibā'máh the daughter of Anah. 26 These are the sons of Dīshòn: Hěmdăn, Ēshbàn, Ĭthrǎn, and Chērán. 27 These are the sons of Ēzér: Bīlhàn, Zā'ávàn, and Ākán. 28 These are the sons of Dīshǎn: Úz and Āràn. 29 These are the chiefs of the Horītes: the chiefs Lōtàn, Shōbǎl, Zǐb'ëön, Ānáh, 30 Dīshòn, Ēzér, and Dīshǎn; these are the chiefs of the Horītes, according to their clans in the land of Sēir.

31 These are the kings who reigned in the land of Ēdóm, before any king reigned over the Israelites. 32 Bēlà the son of Bēor

36.6 Gen 12.5
36.7 Gen 13.6, 11; 17.8; 28.4
36.8 Gen 32.3 *36.9
36.10 1 Chr 1.35
36.12 Ex 17.8,14
36.15 1 Chr 1.34
36.17 1 Chr 1.35, 37
36.18 ver 25; 1 Chr 1.52
36.20 Gen 14.6; Deut 2.12, 22; 1 Chr 1.38
36.25 ver 18; 1 Chr 1.52
36.27 1 Chr 1.42
*36.31 1 Chr 1.43

ᶠ Gk Syr: Heb daughter

36.9 The Edomites sprang from Esau and dwelt in the hill country of Seir. They were inveterate enemies of Israel (Ezek 35.5) although God forbade His people to hate or to despoil them (Deut 23.7; 2.4–6; 2 Chr 20.10). Edom became a symbol of the hardened unbelief and hostility of the world to the people of God and as such was declared by the prophets to be the object of God's wrath and conquering power in the Last Days (Isa 11.14; 34.5–6; Obad 1.1–4; Amos 9.12). 36.31 before any king reigned may be regarded as an indication that this phrase or perhaps the whole list was incorporated after the Israelite monarchy began; or as a prophetic revelation of the kingdoms of Saul and David.

reigned in Ēdŏm, the name of his city being Dĭnhā'bāh. ³³ Bēlá
died, and Jōbăb the son of Zĕráh of Bŏzráh reigned in his stead.
³⁴ Jōbăb died, and Hūshám of the land of the Tē'mánītes reigned
in his stead. ³⁵ Hūshám died, and Hădăd the son of Bĕdăd, who
defeated Mĭd'ĭán in the country of Mōăb, reigned in his stead,
the name of his city being Āvĭth. ³⁶ Hădăd died, and Sămláh
of Măsrē'kăh reigned in his stead. ³⁷ Sămláh died, and Shaul of
Rēhō'bŏth on the Eūphrā'tĕş reigned in his stead. ³⁸ Shaul died,

36.39
1 Chr 1.50

and Bā'ăl-hā'năn the son of Ăchbor reigned in his stead. ³⁹ Bā'ăl-
hā'năn the son of Ăchbor died, and Hādar reigned in his stead,
the name of his city being Pā'ū; his wife's name was Mĕhĕt'ăbĕl,
the daughter of Mătrĕd, daughter of Mĕ'záhăb.

36.40
1 Chr 1.51

40 These are the names of the chiefs of Ēsau, according to their
families and their dwelling places, by their names: the chiefs
Tĭmná, Ălvăh, Jēthĕth, ⁴¹ Ōhōlibā'máh, Ēláh, Pīnŏn, ⁴² Kēnăz,
Tēmán, Mĭbzar, ⁴³ Măg'dĭĕl, and Īrăm; these are the chiefs of
Ēdŏm (that is, Ēsau, the father of Edom), according to their
dwelling places in the land of their possession.

X. The generations of Jacob 37.1–50.26

A. Joseph sold into slavery

1. Joseph's dream: his brothers' hatred

37.1
Gen 17.8;
28.4

37 Jacob dwelt in the land of his father's sojournings, in
the land of Cānaán. ² This is the history of the family of
Jacob.

Joseph, being seventeen years old, was shepherding the flock
with his brothers; he was a lad with the sons of Bĭlháh and Zĭlpáh,
his father's wives; and Joseph brought an ill report of them to their

37.3
Gen 44.20

father. ³ Now Israel loved Joseph more than any other of his children, because he was the son of his old age; and he made him a

37.4
Gen 27.41;
49.22,23

long robe with sleeves. ⁴ But when his brothers saw that their
father loved him more than all his brothers, they hated him, and
could not speak peaceably to him.

5 Now Joseph had a dream, and when he told it to his brothers
they only hated him the more. ⁶ He said to them, "Hear this

37.7
Gen 42.6,9;
43.26;
44.14

dream which I have dreamed: ⁷ behold, we were binding sheaves
in the field, and lo, my sheaf arose and stood upright; and behold,
your sheaves gathered round it, and bowed down to my sheaf."

37.8
Gen 49.26

⁸ His brothers said to him, "Are you indeed to reign over us? Or
are you indeed to have dominion over us?" So they hated him yet
more for his dreams and for his words. ⁹ Then he dreamed another
dream, and told it to his brothers, and said, "Behold, I have
dreamed another dream; and behold, the sun, the moon, and

37.10
Gen 27.29

eleven stars were bowing down to me." ¹⁰ But when he told it
to his father and to his brothers, his father rebuked him, and said
to him, "What is this dream that you have dreamed? Shall I and
your mother and your brothers indeed come to bow ourselves to

37.11
Acts 7.9

the ground before you?" ¹¹And his brothers were jealous of him,
but his father kept the saying in mind.

2. The conspiracy to kill Joseph

12 Now his brothers went to pasture their father's flock near

Shĕçhĕm. 13And Israel said to Joseph, "Are not your brothers
pasturing the flock at Shĕçhĕm? Come, I will send you to them."
And he said to him, "Here I am." 14 So he said to him, "Go now,
see if it is well with your brothers, and with the flock; and bring
me word again." So he sent him from the valley of Hēbrŏn, and
he came to Shĕçhĕm. 15And a man found him wandering in the
fields; and the man asked him, "What are you seeking?" 16 "I am
seeking my brothers," he said, "tell me, I pray you, where they are
pasturing the flock." 17And the man said, "They have gone away,
for I heard them say, 'Let us go to Dōthăn.' " So Joseph went
after his brothers, and found them at Dothan. 18 They saw him
afar off, and before he came near to them they conspired against
him to kill him. 19 They said to one another, "Here comes this
dreamer. 20 Come now, let us kill him and throw him into one of
the pits; then we shall say that a wild beast has devoured him, and
we shall see what will become of his dreams." 21 But when
Reubĕn heard it, he delivered him out of their hands, saying, "Let
us not take his life." 22And Reubĕn said to them, "Shed no blood;
cast him into this pit here in the wilderness, but lay no hand upon
him"—that he might rescue him out of their hand, to restore him
to his father. 23 So when Joseph came to his brothers, they stripped
him of his robe, the long robe with sleeves that he wore; 24 and
they took him and cast him into a pit. The pit was empty, there
was no water in it.

3. Joseph sold to traders

25 Then they sat down to eat; and looking up they saw a caravan
of Ĭsh'mäĕlītes coming from Gĭl'ĕăd, with their camels bearing
gum, balm, and myrrh, on their way to carry it down to Egypt.
26 Then Judah said to his brothers, "What profit is it if we slay our
brother and conceal his blood? 27 Come, let us sell him to the
Ĭsh'mäĕlītes, and let not our hand be upon him, for he is our
brother, our own flesh." And his brothers heeded him. 28 Then
Mĭd'ĭănīte traders passed by; and they drew Joseph up and lifted
him out of the pit, and sold him to the Ĭsh'mäĕlītes for twenty
shekels of silver; and they took Joseph to Egypt.

4. Reuben's distress and Jacob's grief

29 When Reubĕn returned to the pit and saw that Joseph was
not in the pit, he rent his clothes 30 and returned to his brothers,
and said, "The lad is gone; and I, where shall I go?" 31 Then they
took Joseph's robe, and killed a goat, and dipped the robe in the
blood; 32 and they sent the long robe with sleeves and brought it
to their father, and said, "This we have found; see now whether it
is your son's robe or not." 33And he recognized it, and said, "It is
my son's robe; a wild beast has devoured him; Joseph is without
doubt torn to pieces." 34 Then Jacob rent his garments, and put
sackcloth upon his loins, and mourned for his son many days.

37.14
Gen 35.27

37.17
2 Ki 6.13

37.18
1 Sam 19.1;
Mt 27.1;
Acts 23.12

37.21
Gen 42.22

37.25
ver 28,36;
Gen 43.11;
Jer 8.22

37.26
ver 20;
Gen 4.10;
Job 16.18

37.27
Gen 42.21

★37.28
Judg 6.3;
Gen 45.4,5;
Acts 7.9;
Gen 39.1

37.29
Gen 44.13

37.30
Gen 42.13,
36

37.31
ver 3,23

37.33
ver 20;
Gen 44.28

★37.34
ver 29;
2 Sam 3.31

37.28 *Midianite traders.* It is not clear how
these descendants of Abraham and Keturah
(25.2) were involved in the sale of Joseph to
the Ishmaelites, descendants of Abraham and
Hagar (16.15). See also 37.36 and 39.2.
37.34 Jacob's experience reflects some
fulfilment of the dictum that "as a man sows

so shall he also reap." Himself a deceiver who
stole Esau's blessing and bought his birthright, he is now cruelly deceived by his own
sons. Twenty years later the deceiving sons
are to experience the anguish of guilty consciences as they see themselves threatened
with retribution (see 42.21).

37.35
2 Sam
12.17;
Gen 42.38;
44.29,31
37.36
Gen 39.1

35All his sons and all his daughters rose up to comfort him; but he refused to be comforted, and said, "No, I shall go down to Shēōl to my son, mourning." Thus his father wept for him. 36 Meanwhile the Mĭd′iănītes had sold him in Egypt to Pŏt′ĭ-phăr, an officer of Phăraōh, the captain of the guard.

B. Judah's adultery

1. The birth of Er and his marriage to Tamar

38 It happened at that time that Judah went down from his brothers, and turned in to a certain Ădŭl′lămīte, whose name was Hīrăh. 2 There Judah saw the daughter of a certain Cā′naănīte whose name was Shuă; he married her and went in to her, 3 and she conceived and bore a son, and he called his name Ĕr. 4Again she conceived and bore a son, and she called his name Ōnăn. 5 Yet again she bore a son, and she called his name Shēlăh. Sheg was in Chĕzĭb when she bore him. 6And Judah took a wife for Ĕr his first-born, and her name was Tāmar. 7 But Ĕr, Judah's first-born, was wicked in the sight of the LORD; and the LORD slew him. 8 Then Judah said to Ōnăn, "Go in to your brother's wife, and perform the duty of a brother-in-law to her, and raise up offspring for your brother." 9 But Ōnăn knew that the offspring would not be his; so when he went in to his brother's wife he spilled the semen on the ground, lest he should give offspring to his brother. 10And what he did was displeasing in the sight of the LORD, and he slew him also. 11 Then Judah said to Tāmar his daughter-in-law, "Remain a widow in your father's house, till Shēlăh my son grows up"—for he feared that he would die, like his brothers. So Tamar went and dwelt in her father's house.

38.3
Gen 46.12;
Num 26.19

38.7
1 Chr 2.3

*38.8
Deut 25.5;
Mt 22.24

38.9
Deut 25.6

38.11
Ruth 1.12,
13

2. Judah goes in to Tamar

12 In course of time the wife of Judah, Shuă′ṣ daughter, died; and when Judah was comforted, he went up to Tĭmnăh to his sheepshearers, he and his friend Hīrăh the Ădŭl′lămīte. 13And when Tāmar was told, "Your father-in-law is going up to Tĭmnăh to shear his sheep," 14 she put off her widow's garments, and put on a veil, wrapping herself up, and sat at the entrance to Ēnā′ĭm, which is on the road to Tĭmnăh; for she saw that Shēlăh was grown up, and she had not been given to him in marriage. 15 When Judah saw her, he thought her to be a harlot, for she had covered her face. 16 He went over to her at the road side, and said, "Come, let me come in to you," for he did not know that she was his daughter-in-law. She said, "What will you give me, that you may come in to me?" 17 He answered, "I will send you a kid from the flock." And she said, "Will you give me a pledge, till you send it?" 18 He said, "What pledge shall I give you?" She replied, "Your signet and your cord, and your staff that is in your hand." So he gave them to her, and went in to her, and she conceived by him. 19 Then she arose and went away, and taking off her veil she put on the garments of her widowhood.

20 When Judah sent the kid by his friend the Ădŭl′lămīte, to receive the pledge from the woman's hand, he could not find her.

38.12
Josh 15.10,
57

*38.15

38.17
Ezek 16.33;
ver 20
38.18
ver 25

38.19
ver 14

g Gk: Heb He

38.8 See note to Deut 25.5–10.   38.15 thought . . . harlot. See Prov 7.10.

21And he asked the men of the place, "Where is the harlot[h] who was at Ēnā'im by the wayside?" And they said, "No harlot[h] has been here." 22 So he returned to Judah, and said, "I have not found her; and also the men of the place said, 'No harlot[h] has been here.' " 23And Judah replied, "Let her keep the things as her own, lest we be laughed at; you see, I sent this kid, and you could not find her."

3. Tamar justified: Perez and Zerah born

24 About three months later Judah was told, "Tāmar your daughter-in-law has played the harlot; and moreover she is with child by harlotry." And Judah said, "Bring her out, and let her be burned." 25As she was being brought out, she sent word to her father-in-law, "By the man to whom these belong, I am with child." And she said, "Mark, I pray you, whose these are, the signet and the cord and the staff." 26 Then Judah acknowledged them and said, "She is more righteous than I, inasmuch as I did not give her to my son Shēláh." And he did not lie with her again.

27 When the time of her delivery came, there were twins in her womb. 28And when she was in labor, one put out a hand; and the midwife took and bound on his hand a scarlet thread, saying, "This came out first." 29 But as he drew back his hand, behold, his brother came out; and she said, "What a breach you have made for yourself!" Therefore his name was called Pērĕz.[i] 30Afterward his brother came out with the scarlet thread upon his hand; and his name was called Zēráh.

C. Joseph, man of integrity

1. His prosperity

39 Now Joseph was taken down to Egypt, and Pŏt'ĭ-phảr, an officer of Phạraōh, the captain of the guard, an Egyptian, bought him from the Ísh'mäĕlītes who had brought him down there. 2 The LORD was with Joseph, and he became a successful man; and he was in the house of his master the Egyptian, 3 and his master saw that the LORD was with him, and that the LORD caused all that he did to prosper in his hands. 4 So Joseph found favor in his sight and attended him, and he made him overseer of his house and put him in charge of all that he had. 5 From the time that he made him overseer in his house and over all that he had the LORD blessed the Egyptian's house for Joseph's sake; the blessing of the LORD was upon all that he had, in house and field. 6 So he left all that he had in Joseph's charge; and having him he had no concern for anything but the food which he ate.

h Or *cult prostitute* *i* That is *A breach*

	38.24 Lev 21.9; Deut 22.21
	38.25 ver 18
	38.26 1 Sam 24.17; ver 14
	38.29 Gen 46.12; Num 26.20; Mt 1.3
	39.1 Gen 37.28, 36; Ps 105.17
	★39.2 ver 3,21,23
	39.3 Gen 21.22; 26.28; Acts 7.9
	39.4 ver 8,22
	39.5 Gen 30.27

39.2 When Joseph was sold as a slave he could hardly have known that God was arranging circumstances which would make possible the fulfilment of his dreams (37.5–10). Nor could he have suspected the long years needed before the fulfilment. But of one truth he early became aware—that God was with him, for no adversity could make him bitter or distrustful of God. Twice we are told *the* LORD *was with Joseph* (39.2, 21). Joseph's rich spiritual insight was plainly evidenced when he attributed to God his imprisonment and slavery as well as his rise to power (45.7, 8). His brothers sinned as they wrought their own wilful wickedness, but God used it for the accomplishment of the divine purpose (45.7; 50.20; Ps 76.10).

2. The solicitation to sin

39.7
2 Sam
13.11;
Prov 7.15–
20

★39.9
Gen 20.6;
42.18;
2 Sam 12.13

39.12
Prov 7.13–
25

39.17
Ex 23.1;
Ps 120.3

Now Joseph was handsome and good-looking. 7And after a time his master's wife cast her eyes upon Joseph, and said, "Lie with me." 8 But he refused and said to his master's wife, "Lo, having me my master has no concern about anything in the house, and he has put everything that he has in my hand; 9 he is not greater in this house than I am; nor has he kept back anything from me except yourself, because you are his wife; how then can I do this great wickedness, and sin against God?" 10And although she spoke to Joseph day after day, he would not listen to her, to lie with her or to be with her. 11 But one day, when he went into the house to do his work and none of the men of the house was there in the house, 12 she caught him by his garment, saying, "Lie with me." But he left his garment in her hand, and fled and got out of the house. 13And when she saw that he had left his garment in her hand, and had fled out of the house, 14 she called to the men of her household and said to them, "See, he has brought among us a Hebrew to insult us; he came in to me to lie with me, and I cried out with a loud voice; 15 and when he heard that I lifted up my voice and cried, he left his garment with me, and fled and got out of the house." 16 Then she laid up his garment by her until his master came home, 17 and she told him the same story, saying, "The Hebrew servant, whom you have brought among us, came in to me to insult me; 18 but as soon as I lifted up my voice and cried, he left his garment with me, and fled out of the house."

3. Joseph wrongly cast into prison

39.19
Prov 6.34,
35

39.20
Ps 105.18

39.21
ver 21;
Ps 105.19;
Ex 3.21;
Dan 1.9

39.22
ver 4

39.23
ver 2,3,8

19 When his master heard the words which his wife spoke to him, "This is the way your servant treated me," his anger was kindled. 20And Joseph's master took him and put him into the prison, the place where the king's prisoners were confined, and he was there in prison. 21 But the LORD was with Joseph and showed him steadfast love, and gave him favor in the sight of the keeper of the prison. 22And the keeper of the prison committed to Joseph's care all the prisoners who were in the prison; and whatever was done there, he was the doer of it; 23 the keeper of the prison paid no heed to anything that was in Joseph's care, because the LORD was with him; and whatever he did, the LORD made it prosper.

D. Joseph, interpreter of dreams

1. The butler and the baker

40.1
ver 11,13

40.3
Gen 39.20,
23

40 Some time after this, the butler of the king of Egypt and his baker offended their lord the king of Egypt. 2And Pharaōh was angry with his two officers, the chief butler and the chief baker, 3 and he put them in custody in the house of the captain of the guard, in the prison where Joseph was confined. 4 The captain of the guard charged Joseph with them, and he waited on them; and they continued for some time in custody. 5And one night they both dreamed—the butler and the baker of

---

39.9 Joseph had to choose between his position and his purity. He chose the latter only to suffer unjust accusation and punishment for a crime he did not commit. Yet his noble stand was not in vain, for it resulted in his meeting with the king's butler and baker, and this contact in turn made possible his becoming premier of Egypt under the Pharaoh.

the king of Egypt, who were confined in the prison—each his own
dream, and each dream with its own meaning. 6 When Joseph
came to them in the morning and saw them, they were troubled.
7 So he asked Pharaōh's officers who were with him in custody in
his master's house, "Why are your faces downcast today?" 8 They
said to him, "We have had dreams, and there is no one to interpret
them." And Joseph said to them, "Do not interpretations belong
to God? Tell them to me, I pray you."

40.8
Gen 41.16;
Dan 2.27,28

2. The butler's dream and interpretation

9 So the chief butler told his dream to Joseph, and said to him,
"In my dream there was a vine before me, 10 and on the vine there
were three branches; as soon as it budded, its blossoms shot forth,
and the clusters ripened into grapes. 11 Pharaōh's cup was in my
hand; and I took the grapes and pressed them into Pharaoh's cup,
and placed the cup in Pharaoh's hand." 12 Then Joseph said to
him, "This is its interpretation: the three branches are three days;
13 within three days Pharaōh will lift up your head and restore you
to your office; and you shall place Pharaōh's cup in his hand as
formerly, when you were his butler. 14 But remember me, when
it is well with you, and do me the kindness, I pray you, to make
mention of me to Pharaōh, and so get me out of this house. 15 For
I was indeed stolen out of the land of the Hebrews; and here also I
have done nothing that they should put me into the dungeon."

40.12
Gen 41.12,
25;
Dan 2.36;
4.19

40.14
Lk 23.42;
Josh 2.12

40.15
Gen 37.26–
28

3. The baker's dream and interpretation

16 When the chief baker saw that the interpretation was favorable, he said to Joseph, "I also had a dream: there were three
cake baskets on my head, 17 and in the uppermost basket there
were all sorts of baked food for Pharaōh, but the birds were eating
it out of the basket on my head." 18 And Joseph answered, "This
is its interpretation: the three baskets are three days; 19 within
three days Pharaōh will lift up your head—from you!—and hang
you on a tree; and the birds will eat the flesh from you."

40.18
ver 12

40.19
ver 13

4. The fulfilment of the interpretations

20 On the third day, which was Pharaōh's birthday, he made a
feast for all his servants, and lifted up the head of the chief butler
and the head of the chief baker among his servants. 21 He restored
the chief butler to his butlership, and he placed the cup in
Pharaōh's hand; 22 but he hanged the chief baker, as Joseph had
interpreted to them. 23 Yet the chief butler did not remember
Joseph, but forgot him.

40.20
ver 13,19

40.21
ver 13

40.22
ver.19

E. Joseph and Pharaoh

1. Pharaoh's dream

41 After two whole years, Pharaōh dreamed that he was
standing by the Nile, 2 and behold, there came up out of
the Nile seven cows sleek and fat, and they fed in the reed grass.
3 And behold, seven other cows, gaunt and thin, came up out of
the Nile after them, and stood by the other cows on the bank of
the Nile. 4 And the gaunt and thin cows ate up the seven sleek and
fat cows. And Pharaōh awoke. 5 And he fell asleep and dreamed a
second time; and behold, seven ears of grain, plump and good,

*41.6

*41.8
Dan 2.1,3;
4.5,19;
Ex 7.11,22;
Dan 2.27;
4.7

41.10
Gen 40.2,3

41.11
Gen 40.5

41.12
Gen 40.12ff

41.13
Gen 40.21,
22

41.14
Ps 105.20;
Dan 2.25;
Ps 113.7,8

41.15
ver 12

41.16
Dan 2.30;
Acts 3.12;
2 Cor 3.5;
Gen 40.8

41.24
ver 8

41.25
ver 28,32

41.27
2 Ki 8.1

41.28
ver 25,32

41.29
ver 47

41.30
ver 54,56;
Gen 47.13

were growing on one stalk. 6And behold, after them sprouted seven ears, thin and blighted by the east wind. 7And the thin ears swallowed up the seven plump and full ears. And Pharaōh awoke, and behold, it was a dream. 8 So in the morning his spirit was troubled; and he sent and called for all the magicians of Egypt and all its wise men; and Pharaōh told them his dream, but there was none who could interpret it*j* to Pharaoh.

2. *The butler remembers Joseph*

9 Then the chief butler said to Pharaōh, "I remember my faults today. 10 When Pharaōh was angry with his servants, and put me and the chief baker in custody in the house of the captain of the guard, 11 we dreamed on the same night, he and I, each having a dream with its own meaning. 12A young Hebrew was there with us, a servant of the captain of the guard; and when we told him, he interpreted our dreams to us, giving an interpretation to each man according to his dream. 13And as he interpreted to us, so it came to pass; I was restored to my office, and the baker was hanged.

3. *Pharaoh tells his dream to Joseph*

14 Then Pharaōh sent and called Joseph, and they brought him hastily out of the dungeon; and when he had shaved himself and changed his clothes, he came in before Pharaoh. 15And Pharaōh said to Joseph, "I have had a dream, and there is no one who can interpret it; and I have heard it said of you that when you hear a dream you can interpret it." 16 Joseph answered Pharaōh, "It is not in me; God will give Pharaoh a favorable answer." 17 Then Pharaōh said to Joseph, "Behold, in my dream I was standing on the banks of the Nile; 18 and seven cows, fat and sleek, came up out of the Nile and fed in the reed grass; 19 and seven other cows came up after them, poor and very gaunt and thin, such as I had never seen in all the land of Egypt. 20And the thin and gaunt cows ate up the first seven fat cows, 21 but when they had eaten them no one would have known that they had eaten them, for they were still as gaunt as at the beginning. Then I awoke. 22 I also saw in my dream seven ears growing on one stalk, full and good; 23 and seven ears, withered, thin, and blighted by the east wind, sprouted after them, 24 and the thin ears swallowed up the seven good ears. And I told it to the magicians, but there was no one who could explain it to me."

4. *Joseph interprets Pharaoh's dream:*
he proposes a solution

25 Then Joseph said to Pharaōh, "The dream of Pharaoh is one; God has revealed to Pharaoh what he is about to do. 26 The seven good cows are seven years, and the seven good ears are seven years; the dream is one. 27 The seven lean and gaunt cows that came up after them are seven years, and the seven empty ears blighted by the east wind are also seven years of famine. 28 It is as I told Pharaōh, God has shown to Pharaoh what he is about to do. 29 There will come seven years of great plenty throughout all the land of Egypt, 30 but after them there will arise seven years of

j Gk: Heb *them*

41.6 *east wind*, the sirocco, a hot wind.   **41.8** Shows the futility of pagan practice.

famine, and all the plenty will be forgotten in the land of Egypt; the famine will consume the land, 31 and the plenty will be unknown in the land by reason of that famine which will follow, for it will be very grievous. 32And the doubling of Pharaōh's dream means that the thing is fixed by God, and God will shortly bring it to pass. 33 Now therefore let Pharaōh select a man discreet and wise, and set him over the land of Egypt. 34 Let Pharaōh proceed to appoint overseers over the land, and take the fifth part of the produce of the land of Egypt during the seven plenteous years. 35And let them gather all the food of these good years that are coming, and lay up grain under the authority of Pharaōh for food in the cities, and let them keep it. 36 That food shall be a reserve for the land against the seven years of famine which are to befall the land of Egypt, so that the land may not perish through the famine."

41.32
Num 23.19;
Isa 46.10,11

41.35
ver 48

5. *Pharaoh makes Joseph a ruler*

37 This proposal seemed good to Pharaōh and to all his servants. 38And Pharaōh said to his servants, "Can we find such a man as this, in whom is the Spirit of God?" 39 So Pharaōh said to Joseph, "Since God has shown you all this, there is none so discreet and wise as you are; 40 you shall be over my house, and all my people shall order themselves as you command; only as regards the throne will I be greater than you." 41And Pharaōh said to Joseph, "Behold, I have set you over all the land of Egypt." 42 Then Pharaōh took his signet ring from his hand and put it on Joseph's hand, and arrayed him in garments of fine linen, and put a gold chain about his neck; 43 and he made him to ride in his second chariot; and they cried before him, "Bow the knee!"*k* Thus he set him over all the land of Egypt. 44 Moreover Pharaōh said to Joseph, "I am Pharaoh, and without your consent no man shall lift up hand or foot in all the land of Egypt." 45And Pharaōh called Joseph's name Zăph'ĕnăth-păne'ah; and he gave him in marriage Ăs'ĕnăth, the daughter of Pŏt'ĭphĕr'ă priest of On. So Joseph went out over the land of Egypt.

41.38
Num 27.18;
Dan 4.8,18

★41.40
Ps 105.21,
22;
Acts 7.10

41.41
Gen 42.6

41.42
Est 3.10;
Dan 5.7,16,
29

41.43
Est 6.9

41.44
Ps 105.22

★41.45

6. *The fulfilment of the dream*

46 Joseph was thirty years old when he entered the service of Pharaōh king of Egypt. And Joseph went out from the presence of Pharaoh, and went through all the land of Egypt. 47 During the seven plenteous years the earth brought forth abundantly, 48 and he gathered up all the food of the seven years when there was plenty*l* in the land of Egypt, and stored up food in the cities; he stored up in every city the food from the fields around it. 49And

★41.46
Gen 37.2

k Abrek, probably an Egyptian word similar in sound to the Hebrew word meaning *to kneel*
l Sam Gk: Heb *which were*

41.40 *over my house*, meaning the office of prime minister or vizier.
41.45 *On* was a city in Lower (northern) Egypt noted for its chief temple of the sun god Re. It was known to the Greeks as Heliopolis, meaning "city of the sun." References are made to it in Isa 19.18 and in Jer 43.13 (where the RSV translators call it *Heliopolis*). *On* was also the most important seat of learning in the country.

41.46 At least twenty years passed before Joseph's boyhood dreams were fulfilled. He first dreamed when seventeen years of age (37.2). He appeared before Pharaoh thirteen years later (41.46). The seven years of plenty followed. Then came the years of famine. This meant that his brothers had not seen him for at least twenty years. He knew them, but they were unable to recognize him in his new role of splendor and authority.

Joseph stored up grain in great abundance, like the sand of the sea, until he ceased to measure it, for it could not be measured.

41.50
Gen 46.20
50 Before the year of famine came, Joseph had two sons, whom Ăs'ĕnäth, the daughter of Pŏt'įphĕr'á priest of On, bore to him. 51 Joseph called the name of the first-born Mănăs'sĕh,*m* "For," he said, "God has made me forget all my hardship and all my father's house." 52 The name of the second he called Ē'phrăįm,*n* "For God has made me fruitful in the land of my affliction."

41.52
Gen 17.6;
28.3; 49.22
53 The seven years of plenty that prevailed in the land of Egypt came to an end; 54 and the seven years of famine began to come, as Joseph had said. There was famine in all lands; but in all the land of Egypt there was bread. 55 When all the land of Egypt was famished, the people cried to Pharaōh for bread; and Pharaoh said to all the Egyptians, "Go to Joseph; what he says to you, do." 56 So when the famine had spread over all the land, Joseph opened all the storehouses,*o* and sold to the Egyptians, for the famine was severe in the land of Egypt. 57 Moreover, all the earth came to Egypt to Joseph to buy grain, because the famine was severe over all the earth.

41.54
ver 30;
Ps 105.16;
Acts 7.11

41.56
Gen 42.6

F. Joseph's brothers in Egypt

1. Jacob sends ten sons

42 When Jacob learned that there was grain in Egypt, he said to his sons, "Why do you look at one another?" 2 And he said, "Behold, I have heard that there is grain in Egypt; go down and buy grain for us there, that we may live, and not die." 3 So ten of Joseph's brothers went down to buy grain in Egypt. 4 But Jacob did not send Benjamin, Joseph's brother, with his brothers, for he feared that harm might befall him. 5 Thus the sons of Israel came to buy among the others who came, for the famine was in the land of Cānaàn.

42.1
Acts 7.12
42.2
Gen 43.8

42.4
Gen 35.24

42.5
Gen 41.57;
Acts 7.11

2. Joseph encounters his brothers

6 Now Joseph was governor over the land; he it was who sold to all the people of the land. And Joseph's brothers came, and bowed themselves before him with their faces to the ground. 7 Joseph saw his brothers, and knew them, but he treated them like strangers and spoke roughly to them. "Where do you come from?" he said. They said, "From the land of Cānaàn, to buy food." 8 Thus Joseph knew his brothers, but they did not know him. 9 And Joseph remembered the dreams which he had dreamed of them; and he said to them, "You are spies, you have come to see the weakness of the land." 10 They said to him, "No, my lord, but to buy food have your servants come. 11 We are all sons of one man, we are honest men, your servants are not spies." 12 He said to them, "No, it is the weakness of the land that you have come to see." 13 And they said, "We, your servants, are twelve brothers, the sons of one man in the land of Cānaàn; and behold, the youngest is this day with our father, and one is no more." 14 But Joseph said to them, "It is as I said to you, you are spies. 15 By this you shall be tested: by the life of Pharaōh, you shall not go from this place unless your youngest brother comes here. 16 Send one of you, and

42.6
Gen 41.41,
55;
37.7
42.7
ver 30

42.9
Gen 37.6–9

42.13
Gen 43.7;
37.30

m That is *Making to forget*   *n* From a Hebrew word meaning *to be fruitful*
o Gk Vg Compare Syr: Heb *all that was in them*

let him bring your brother, while you remain in prison, that your words may be tested, whether there is truth in you; or else, by the life of Phạraōh, surely you are spies." 17And he put them all together in prison for three days.

3. *Joseph gives them grain*

18 On the third day Joseph said to them, "Do this and you will live, for I fear God: 19 if you are honest men, let one of your brothers remain confined in your prison, and let the rest go and carry grain for the famine of your households, 20 and bring your youngest brother to me; so your words will be verified, and you shall not die." And they did so. 21 Then they said to one another, "In truth we are guilty concerning our brother, in that we saw the distress of his soul, when he besought us and we would not listen; therefore is this distress come upon us." 22And Reubën answered them, "Did I not tell you not to sin against the lad? But you would not listen. So now there comes a reckoning for his blood." 23 They did not know that Joseph understood them, for there was an interpreter between them. 24 Then he turned away from them and wept; and he returned to them and spoke to them. And he took Sïm′ëön from them and bound him before their eyes. 25And Joseph gave orders to fill their bags with grain, and to replace every man's money in his sack, and to give them provisions for the journey. This was done for them.

26 Then they loaded their asses with their grain, and departed. 27And as one of them opened his sack to give his ass provender at the lodging place, he saw his money in the mouth of his sack; 28 and he said to his brothers, "My money has been put back; here it is in the mouth of my sack!" At this their hearts failed them, and they turned trembling to one another, saying, "What is this that God has done to us?"

4. *The ten sons report to Jacob*

29 When they came to Jacob their father in the land of Cānaán, they told him all that had befallen them, saying, 30 "The man, the lord of the land, spoke roughly to us, and took us to be spies of the land. 31 But we said to him, 'We are honest men, we are not spies; 32 we are twelve brothers, sons of our father; one is no more, and the youngest is this day with our father in the land of Cānaán.' 33 Then the man, the lord of the land, said to us, 'By this I shall know that you are honest men: leave one of your brothers with me, and take grain for the famine of your households, and go your way. 34 Bring your youngest brother to me; then I shall know that you are not spies but honest men, and I will deliver to you your brother, and you shall trade in the land.' "

35 As they emptied their sacks, behold, every man's bundle of money was in his sack; and when they and their father saw their bundles of money, they were dismayed. 36And Jacob their father said to them, "You have bereaved me of my children: Joseph is no more, and Sïm′ëön is no more, and now you would take Benjamin; all this has come upon me." 37 Then Reubën said to his father, "Slay my two sons if I do not bring him back to you; put him in my hands, and I will bring him back to you." 38 But he said, "My son shall not go down with you, for his brother is dead, and he only is left. If harm should befall him on the journey that

---

42.18
Lev 25.43

42.20
ver 34

42.21
Hos 5.15;
Prov 21.13

42.22
Gen 37.22;
9.5,6

42.24
Gen 43.30;
45.14,15;
43.14,23

42.25
Gen 44.1;
Rom 12.17,
20,21

42.26
Gen 37.31–
35

42.30
ver 7

42.31
ver 11

42.33
Gen 15.19,
20

42.35
Gen 43.12,
15

42.36
Gen 43.14

42.38
Gen 37.33,
35;
44.31

you are to make, you would bring down my gray hairs with sorrow
to Shēōl."

G. The second trip to Egypt with Benjamin

1. Jacob unwillingly sends Benjamin

43 Now the famine was severe in the land. ²And when they
had eaten the grain which they had brought from Egypt,
their father said to them, "Go again, buy us a little food." ³ But
Judah said to him, "The man solemnly warned us, saying, 'You
shall not see my face, unless your brother is with you.' ⁴ If you will
send our brother with us, we will go down and buy you food; ⁵ but
if you will not send him, we will not go down, for the man said to
us, 'You shall not see my face, unless your brother is with you.' "
⁶ Israel said, "Why did you treat me so ill as to tell the man that
you had another brother?" ⁷ They replied, "The man questioned
us carefully about ourselves and our kindred, saying, 'Is your
father still alive? Have you another brother?' What we told him
was in answer to these questions; could we in any way know that
he would say, 'Bring your brother down'?" ⁸And Judah said to
Israel his father, "Send the lad with me, and we will arise and go,
that we may live and not die, both we and you and also our little
ones. ⁹ I will be surety for him; of my hand you shall require
him. If I do not bring him back to you and set him before you,
then let me bear the blame for ever; ¹⁰ for if we had not delayed,
we would now have returned twice."

¹¹ Then their father Israel said to them, "If it must be so, then
do this: take some of the choice fruits of the land in your bags, and
carry down to the man a present, a little balm and a little honey,
gum, myrrh, pistachio nuts, and almonds. ¹² Take double the
money with you; carry back with you the money that was returned
in the mouth of your sacks; perhaps it was an oversight. ¹³ Take
also your brother, and arise, go again to the man; ¹⁴ may God
Almighty^p grant you mercy before the man, that he may send
back your other brother and Benjamin. If I am bereaved of my
children, I am bereaved." ¹⁵ So the men took the present, and they
took double the money with them, and Benjamin; and they arose
and went down to Egypt, and stood before Joseph.

2. Joseph dines with his brothers

¹⁶ When Joseph saw Benjamin with them, he said to the
steward of his house, "Bring the men into the house, and slaughter
an animal and make ready, for the men are to dine with me at
noon." ¹⁷ The man did as Joseph bade him, and brought the men
to Joseph's house. ¹⁸And the men were afraid because they were
brought to Joseph's house, and they said, "It is because of the
money, which was replaced in our sacks the first time, that we are
brought in, so that he may seek occasion against us and fall upon
us, to make slaves of us and seize our asses." ¹⁹ So they went up
to the steward of Joseph's house, and spoke with him at the door
of the house, ²⁰ and said, "Oh, my lord, we came down the first
time to buy food; ²¹ and when we came to the lodging place we
opened our sacks, and there was every man's money in the mouth
of his sack, our money in full weight; so we have brought it again

^{p} Heb *Ēl Shăd'dāï*

with us, 22 and we have brought other money down in our hand to buy food. We do not know who put our money in our sacks." 23 He replied, "Rest assured, do not be afraid; your God and the God of your father must have put treasure in your sacks for you; I received your money." Then he brought Sïm'ëón out to them. 24And when the man had brought the men into Joseph's house, and given them water, and they had washed their feet, and when he had given their asses provender, 25 they made ready the present for Joseph's coming at noon, for they heard that they should eat bread there.

26 When Joseph came home, they brought into the house to him the present which they had with them, and bowed down to him to the ground. 27And he inquired about their welfare, and said, "Is your father well, the old man of whom you spoke? Is he still alive?" 28 They said, "Your servant our father is well, he is still alive." And they bowed their heads and made obeisance. 29And he lifted up his eyes, and saw his brother Benjamin, his mother's son, and said, "Is this your youngest brother, of whom you spoke to me? God be gracious to you, my son!" 30 Then Joseph made haste, for his heart yearned for his brother, and he sought a place to weep. And he entered his chamber and wept there. 31 Then he washed his face and came out; and controlling himself he said, "Let food be served." 32 They served him by himself, and them by themselves, and the Egyptians who ate with him by themselves, because the Egyptians might not eat bread with the Hebrews, for that is an abomination to the Egyptians. 33And they sat before him, the first-born according to his birthright and the youngest according to his youth; and the men looked at one another in amazement. 34 Portions were taken to them from Joseph's table, but Benjamin's portion was five times as much as any of theirs. So they drank and were merry with him.

3. The seizure of Benjamin

44 Then he commanded the steward of his house, "Fill the men's sacks with food, as much as they can carry, and put each man's money in the mouth of his sack, 2 and put my cup, the silver cup, in the mouth of the sack of the youngest, with his money for the grain." And he did as Joseph told him. 3As soon as the morning was light, the men were sent away with their asses. 4 When they had gone but a short distance from the city, Joseph said to his steward, "Up, follow after the men; and when you overtake them, say to them, 'Why have you returned evil for good? Why have you stolen my silver cup?q 5 Is it not from this that my lord drinks, and by this that he divines? You have done wrong in so doing.' "

6 When he overtook them, he spoke to them these words. 7 They said to him, "Why does my lord speak such words as these? Far be it from your servants that they should do such a thing! 8 Behold, the money which we found in the mouth of our sacks, we brought back to you from the land of Cānaản; how then should we steal silver or gold from your lord's house? 9 With whomever of your servants it be found, let him die, and we also will be my lord's slaves." 10 He said, "Let it be as you say: he with whom it is found shall be my slave, and the rest of you shall be

---

q Gk Compare Vg: Heb lacks *Why have you stolen my silver cup?*

43.23
Gen 42.24

43.24
Gen 18.4;
19.2; 24.32

43.26
Gen 37.7,10
43.27
ver 7;
Gen 45.3
43.28
Gen 37..7,10
43.29
Gen 35.17,
18; 42.13;
Num 6.25;
Ps 67.1
43.30
Gen 42.24;
45.2,14,15;
46.29
43.31
Gen 45.1
43.32
Gen 46.34

43.34
Gen 45.22

44.1
Gen 42.25

44.5
ver 15;
Lev 19.26;
Deut 18.10–
14

44.8
Gen 43.21

44.9
Gen 31.32

blameless." 11 Then every man quickly lowered his sack to the ground, and every man opened his sack. 12And he searched, beginning with the eldest and ending with the youngest; and the cup was found in Benjamin's sack. 13 Then they rent their clothes, and every man loaded his ass, and they returned to the city.

4. His brothers bow before Joseph

14 When Judah and his brothers came to Joseph's house, he was still there; and they fell before him to the ground. 15 Joseph said to them, "What deed is this that you have done? Do you not know that such a man as I can indeed divine?" 16And Judah said, "What shall we say to my lord? What shall we speak? Or how can we clear ourselves? God has found out the guilt of your servants; behold, we are my lord's slaves, both we and he also in whose hand the cup has been found." 17 But he said, "Far be it from me that I should do so! Only the man in whose hand the cup was found shall be my slave; but as for you, go up in peace to your father."

18 Then Judah went up to him and said, "O my lord, let your servant, I pray you, speak a word in my lord's ears, and let not your anger burn against your servant; for you are like Phạraōh himself. 19 My lord asked his servants, saying, 'Have you a father, or a brother?' 20And we said to my lord, 'We have a father, an old man, and a young brother, the child of his old age; and his brother is dead, and he alone is left of his mother's children; and his father loves him.' 21 Then you said to your servants, 'Bring him down to me, that I may set my eyes upon him.' 22 We said to my lord, 'The lad cannot leave his father, for if he should leave his father, his father would die.' 23 Then you said to your servants, 'Unless your youngest brother comes down with you, you shall see my face no more.' 24 When we went back to your servant my father we told him the words of my lord. 25And when our father said, 'Go again, buy us a little food,' 26 we said, 'We cannot go down. If our youngest brother goes with us, then we will go down; for we cannot see the man's face unless our youngest brother is with us.' 27 Then your servant my father said to us, 'You know that my wife bore me two sons; 28 one left me, and I said, Surely he has been torn to pieces; and I have never seen him since. 29 If you take this one also from me, and harm befalls him, you will bring down my gray hairs in sorrow to Shēōl.' 30 Now therefore, when I come to your servant my father, and the lad is not with us, then, as his life is bound up in the lad's life, 31 when he sees that the lad is not with us, he will die; and your servants will bring down the gray hairs of your servant our father with sorrow to Shēōl. 32 For your servant became surety for the lad to my father, saying, 'If I do not bring him back to you, then I shall bear the blame in the sight of my father all my life.' 33 Now therefore, let your servant, I pray you, remain instead of the lad as a slave to my lord; and let the lad go back with his brothers. 34 For how can I go back to my father if the lad is not with me? I fear to see the evil that would come upon my father."

5. Joseph discloses his identity

45 Then Joseph could not control himself before all those who stood by him; and he cried, "Make every one go out from me." So no one stayed with him when Joseph made himself

known to his brothers. ²And he wept aloud, so that the Egyptians heard it, and the household of Phạraōh heard it. ³And Joseph said to his brothers, "I am Joseph; is my father still alive?" But his brothers could not answer him, for they were dismayed at his presence.

4 So Joseph said to his brothers, "Come near to me, I pray you." And they came near. And he said, "I am your brother, Joseph, whom you sold into Egypt. ⁵And now do not be distressed, or angry with yourselves, because you sold me here; for God sent me before you to preserve life. ⁶ For the famine has been in the land these two years; and there are yet five years in which there will be neither plowing nor harvest. ⁷And God sent me before you to preserve for you a remnant on earth, and to keep alive for you many survivors. ⁸ So it was not you who sent me here, but God; and he has made me a father to Phạraōh, and lord of all his house and ruler over all the land of Egypt. ⁹ Make haste and go up to my father and say to him, 'Thus says your son Joseph, God has made me lord of all Egypt; come down to me, do not tarry; ¹⁰ you shall dwell in the land of Gōshèn, and you shall be near me, you and your children and your children's children, and your flocks, your herds, and all that you have; ¹¹ and there I will provide for you, for there are yet five years of famine to come; lest you and your household, and all that you have, come to poverty.' ¹²And now your eyes see, and the eyes of my brother Benjamin see, that it is my mouth that speaks to you. ¹³ You must tell my father of all my splendor in Egypt, and of all that you have seen. Make haste and bring my father down here." ¹⁴ Then he fell upon his brother Benjamin's neck and wept; and Benjamin wept upon his neck. ¹⁵And he kissed all his brothers and wept upon them; and after that his brothers talked with him.

6. Pharaoh invites Joseph's kin to Egypt

16 When the report was heard in Phạraōh's house, "Joseph's brothers have come," it pleased Phạraōh and his servants well. ¹⁷And Phạraōh said to Joseph, "Say to your brothers, 'Do this: load your beasts and go back to the land of Cānaàn; ¹⁸ and take your father and your households, and come to me, and I will give you the best of the land of Egypt, and you shall eat the fat of the land.' ¹⁹ Command them‍ʳ also, 'Do this: take wagons from the land of Egypt for your little ones and for your wives, and bring your father, and come. ²⁰ Give no thought to your goods, for the best of all the land of Egypt is yours.' "

21 The sons of Israel did so; and Joseph gave them wagons, according to the command of Phạraōh, and gave them provisions for the journey. ²² To each and all of them he gave festal garments; but to Benjamin he gave three hundred shekels of silver and five festal garments. ²³ To his father he sent as follows: ten asses loaded with the good things of Egypt, and ten she-asses loaded with grain, bread, and provision for his father on the journey. ²⁴ Then he sent his brothers away, and as they departed, he said to them, "Do not quarrel on the way." ²⁵ So they went up out of

---

ʳ Compare Gk Vg: Heb you are commanded

45.10 Goshen, fertile grazing land in the eastern section of the Nile Delta. This verse agrees with 47.6 where Pharaoh tells Joseph to settle his family in Goshen.

Marginal references

45.2
ver 14,15;
Gen 46.29
45.3
Gen 43.27

45.4
Gen 37.28

45.5
Isa 40.2;
Gen 37.28;
44.20;
50.20

45.8
Gen 41.43

★45.10
Gen 46.28,
34; 47.1

45.13
Acts 7.14

45.18
Gen 27.28;
Num 18.12,
29

45.22
Gen 43.34

Egypt, and came to the land of Cānaán to their father Jacob. 26And they told him, "Joseph is still alive, and he is ruler over all the land of Egypt." And his heart fainted, for he did not believe them. 27 But when they told him all the words of Joseph, which he had said to them, and when he saw the wagons which Joseph had sent to carry him, the spirit of their father Jacob revived; 28 and Israel said, "It is enough; Joseph my son is still alive; I will go and see him before I die."

H. Jacob goes to Egypt

46 So Israel took his journey with all that he had, and came to Beër-shē'bá, and offered sacrifices to the God of his father Isaac. 2And God spoke to Israel in visions of the night, and said, "Jacob, Jacob." And he said, "Here am I." 3 Then he said, "I am God, the God of your father; do not be afraid to go down to Egypt; for I will there make of you a great nation. 4 I will go down with you to Egypt, and I will also bring you up again; and Joseph's hand shall close your eyes." 5 Then Jacob set out from Beër-shē'-bá; and the sons of Israel carried Jacob their father, their little ones, and their wives, in the wagons which Phạraōh had sent to carry him. 6 They also took their cattle and their goods, which they had gained in the land of Cānaán, and came into Egypt, Jacob and all his offspring with him, 7 his sons, and his sons' sons with him, his daughters, and his sons' daughters; all his offspring he brought with him into Egypt.

I. The descendants of Jacob

8 Now these are the name of the descendants of Israel, who came into Egypt, Jacob and his sons. Reubën, Jacob's first-born, 9 and the sons of Reubën: Hānoçh, Pǎllu, Hězrȯn, and Carmī. 10 The sons of Sǐm'ëön: Jěm'üël, Jāmǐn, Ōhǎd, Jāçhǐn, Zōhar, and Shaul, the son of a Cā'naánī'tǐsh woman. 11 The sons of Lēvī: Gěrshȯn, Kōhǎth, and Měrar'ȉ. 12 The sons of Judah: Ėr, Onȧn, Shēláh, Pěrěz, and Zērȧh (but Er and Onan died in the land of Cānaán); and the sons of Perez were Hězrȯn and Hāmùl. 13 The sons of Ȉs'sáçhar: Tōlȧ, Pūvȧh, Ị̌ōb, and Shǐmrȯn. 14 The sons of Zěb'ụlùn: Sěrěd, Ēlȯn, and Jah'leël 15 (these are the sons of Lēȧh, whom she bore to Jacob in Pǎd'dȧn-ar'ȧm, together with his daughter Dinah; altogether his sons and his daughters numbered thirty-three). 16 The sons of Gǎd: Zǐph'ȉȯn, Hǎggī, Shunī, Ěz-bȯn, Ērī, Ạr'ȯdī, and Ạrē'lī. 17 The sons of Āsher: Ȉmnȧh, Ȉsh-vȧh, Ȉshvī, Běrī'ȧh, with Sěrȧh their sister. And the sons of Beri'ah: Hēběr and Mǎl'çhȉël 18 (these are the sons of Zȋlpȧh, whom Lābȧn gave to Lēȧh his daughter; and these she bore to Jacob—sixteen persons). 19 The sons of Rachel, Jacob's wife: Joseph and Benja-min. 20And to Joseph in the land of Egypt were born Mȧnǎs'sěh

46.1
Gen 28.10;
  26.24;
  28.13
46.2
Job 33.14,
  15;
Gen 22.11;
  31.11
*46.3
Gen 28.13;
  12.2
46.4
Gen 28.15;
  50.13,24,
  25; Ex 3.8;
Gen 50.1
46.5
Gen 45.19,
  21
46.6
Acts 7.15;
Deut 26.5;
Josh 24.4;
Ps 105.23;
Isa 52.4

46.8
Ex 1.1

46.10
Ex 6.15
46.11
1 Chr 6.1,16
*46.12
1 Chr 2.3;
4.21; 38.3,
  7,10,29

46.17
1 Chr 7.30
46.18
Gen 30.10;
  29.24
46.19
Gen 44.27
46.20
Gen 41.50

46.3 It has been imagined by some that Jacob was denying the directive will of God when he went down into Egypt and that he was only in the permissive will of God. But this erroneous interpretation is based upon the notion that Egypt always symbolizes sin and compromise. It was really God who told Jacob to go to Egypt, for it was in Egypt that God purposed to develop His family into a great nation strong enough to conquer Canaan.

46.12 Hezron and Hamul, these grandsons of Judah were most likely born in Egypt but included to take the places of Er and Onan who died in Canaan. This is similar to including Manasseh and Ephraim, born in Egypt (ver 20), with those who "came into Egypt."

and Ē'phrāịm, whom Ăs'ĕnăth, the daughter of Pŏt'ĭphĕr'ȧ the
priest of On, bore to him. 21And the sons of Benjamin: Bēlȧ,
Bēçhĕr, Ăshbél, Gērȧ, Nā'ȧmȧn, Ēhī, Rōsh, Mŭppĭm, Hŭppĭm,
and Ard 22 (these are the sons of Rachel, who were born to Jacob—
fourteen persons in all). 23 The sons of Dan: Hūshĭm. 24 The sons
of Năph'tȧlī: Jahzeēl, Gunī, Jēzĕr, and Shĭllĕm 25 (these are the
sons of Bĭlhȧh, whom Lābȧn gave to Rachel his daughter, and
these she bore to Jacob—seven persons in all). 26All the persons
belonging to Jacob who came into Egypt, who were his own offspring, not including Jacob's sons' wives, were sixty-six persons
in all; 27 and the sons of Joseph, who were born to him in Egypt,
were two; all the persons of the house of Jacob, that came into
Egypt, were seventy.

J. The settlement in Egypt

28 He sent Judah before him to Joseph, to appearˢ before him
in Gōshĕn; and they came into the land of Goshen. 29 Then Joseph
made ready his chariot and went up to meet Israel his father in
Gōshĕn; and he presented himself to him, and fell on his neck,
and wept on his neck a good while. 30 Israel said to Joseph, "Now
let me die, since I have seen your face and know that you are still
alive." 31 Joseph said to his brothers and to his father's household,
"I will go up and tell Phạraōh, and will say to him, 'My brothers
and my father's household, who were in the land of Cānaȧn, have
come to me; 32 and the men are shepherds, for they have been
keepers of cattle; and they have brought their flocks, and their
herds, and all that they have.' 33 When Phạraōh calls you, and
says, 'What is your occupation?' 34 you shall say, 'Your servants
have been keepers of cattle from our youth even until now, both
we and our fathers,' in order that you may dwell in the land of
Gōshĕn; for every shepherd is an abomination to the Egyptians."

47 So Joseph went in and told Phạraōh, "My father and my
brothers, with their flocks and herds and all that they
possess, have come from the land of Cānaȧn; they are now in the
land of Gōshĕn." 2And from among his brothers he took five men
and presented them to Phạraōh. 3 Phạraōh said to his brothers,
"What is your occupation?" And they said to Pharaoh, "Your
servants are shepherds, as our fathers were." 4 They said to Phạraōh, "We have come to sojourn in the land; for there is no pasture
for your servants' flocks, for the famine is severe in the land of
Cānaȧn; and now, we pray you, let your servants dwell in the land
of Gōshĕn." 5 Then Phạraōh said to Joseph, "Your father and
your brothers have come to you. 6 The land of Egypt is before
you; settle your father and your brothers in the best of the land;
let them dwell in the land of Gōshĕn; and if you know any able
men among them, put them in charge of my cattle."
7 Then Joseph brought in Jacob his father, and set him before
Phạraōh, and Jacob blessed Pharaoh. 8And Phạraōh said to Jacob,

ˢ Sam Syr Compare Gk Vg: Heb to show the way

46.21
1 Chr 7.6;
8.1
46.23
1 Chr 7.12
46.24
1 Chr 7.13
46.25
Gen 30.5,7;
29.29
46.26
Ex 1.5
★46.27
Deut 10.22;
Acts 7.14

46.28
Gen 47.1
★46.29
Gen 45.14,
15

46.31
Gen 47.1

46.33
Gen 47.2,3
46.34
Gen 13.7,8;
26.20;
37.2;
45.10,18;
Ex 8.26
47.1
Gen 46.31

47.3
Gen 46.33,
34
47.4
Gen 15.13;
Deut 26.5;
Gen 43.1;
46.34
47.6
ver 11;
Gen 45.10,
18
47.8
Ps 39.12;
Heb 11.9,
13;
Job 14.1;
Gen 25.7;
35.28

46.27 Compare this with Acts 7.14 where
the number *seventy-five* is likely derived
from the LXX (Septuagint—Greek translation of the Old Testament Scriptures), which
includes two descendants of Manasseh and

three descendants of Ephraim in verse 20,
making a total of five more than the *seventy*
noted in 46.27 of the Masoretic Text (standard Hebrew text of the Old Testament).
46.29 *Israel.* Another name for Jacob.

*47.9

"How many are the days of the years of your life?" 9And Jacob said to Pharaōh, "The days of the years of my sojourning are a hundred and thirty years; few and evil have been the days of the years of my life, and they have not attained to the days of the years of the life of my fathers in the days of their sojourning." 10And Jacob blessed Pharaōh, and went out from the presence of Pharaoh. 11 Then Joseph settled his father and his brothers, and gave them a possession in the land of Egypt, in the best of the land, in the land of Răm′ēsēs, as Pharaōh had commanded. 12And Joseph provided his father, his brothers, and all his father's household with food, according to the number of their dependents.

47.10
ver 7
*47.11
Ex 1.11;
12.37;
ver 6.27

K. The land policies of Joseph

47.13
Gen 41.30;
Acts 7.11
47.14
Gen 41.56
47.15
ver 19

13 Now there was no food in all the land; for the famine was very severe, so that the land of Egypt and the land of Cānaán languished by reason of the famine. 14And Joseph gathered up all the money that was found in the land of Egypt and in the land of Cānaán, for the grain which they bought; and Joseph brought the money into Pharaōh's house. 15And when the money was all spent in the land of Egypt and in the land of Cānaán, all the Egyptians came to Joseph, and said, "Give us food; why should we die before your eyes? For our money is gone." 16And Joseph answered, "Give your cattle, and I will give you food in exchange for your cattle, if your money is gone." 17 So they brought their cattle to Joseph; and Joseph gave them food in exchange for the horses, the flocks, the herds, and the asses: and he supplied them with food in exchange for all their cattle that year. 18And when that year was ended, they came to him the following year, and said to him, "We will not hide from my lord that our money is all spent; and the herds of cattle are my lord's; there is nothing left in the sight of my lord but our bodies and our lands. 19 Why should we die before your eyes, both we and our land? Buy us and our land for food, and we with our land will be slaves to Pharaōh; and give us seed, that we may live, and not die, and that the land may not be desolate."

20 So Joseph bought all the land of Egypt for Pharaōh; for all the Egyptians sold their fields, because the famine was severe upon them. The land became Pharaōh's; 21 and as for the people, he made slaves of them[f] from one end of Egypt to the other. 22 Only the land of the priests he did not buy; for the priests had a fixed allowance from Pharaōh, and lived on the allowance which Pharaoh gave them; therefore they did not sell their land. 23 Then Joseph said to the people, "Behold, I have this day bought you and your land for Pharaōh. Now here is seed for you, and you shall sow the land. 24And at the harvests you shall give a fifth to Pharaōh, and four fifths shall be your own, as seed for the field and

47.22
Ezra 7.24
47.24
Gen 41.34

---

f Sam Gk Compare Vg: Heb he removed them to the cities

47.9 Scripture describes believers of every age as *strangers, pilgrims, sojourners,* and *exiles.* Believers are not of this world (Jn 17.16). Rather they: (1) look for the city whose maker is God (Heb 11.16); (2) live in the fear of God during the days of their temporary sojourn (1 Pet 1.17); (3) constitute a heavenly commonwealth (Phil 3.20). Exposed to persecution by the world (Jn 17.14), they are not to be anxious about earthly concerns (Mt 6.25). They are to lay up their spiritual treasures in heaven (Mt 6.19), abstaining from the passions of the flesh (1 Pet 2.11) and shining as lights in the world (Phil 2.15).

47.11 *land of Rameses,* later called Goshen.

as food for yourselves and your households, and as food for your little ones." 25And they said, "You have saved our lives; may it please my lord, we will be slaves to Pharaōh." 26 So Joseph made it a statute concerning the land of Egypt, and it stands to this day, that Pharaōh should have the fifth; the land of the priests alone did not become Pharaōh's.

L. Joseph's promise to Jacob

27 Thus Israel dwelt in the land of Egypt, in the land of Gōshĕn; and they gained possessions in it, and were fruitful and multiplied exceedingly. 28And Jacob lived in the land of Egypt seventeen years; so the days of Jacob, the years of his life, were a hundred and forty-seven years.

29 And when the time drew near that Israel must die, he called his son Joseph and said to him, "If now I have found favor in your sight, put your hand under my thigh, and promise to deal loyally and truly with me. Do not bury me in Egypt, 30 but let me lie with my fathers; carry me out of Egypt and bury me in their burying place." He answered, "I will do as you have said." 31And he said, "Swear to me"; and he swore to him. Then Israel bowed himself upon the head of his bed.

M. Jacob's last days

1. *Jacob blesses Joseph's sons:*
Ephraim preferred over Manasseh

48 After this Joseph was told, "Behold, your father is ill"; so he took with him his two sons, Mănăs'sĕh and Ē'phrăịm. 2And it was told to Jacob, "Your son Joseph has come to you"; then Israel summoned his strength, and sat up in bed. 3And Jacob said to Joseph, "God Almighty[u] appeared to me at Lūz in the land of Cānaán and blessed me, 4 and said to me, 'Behold, I will make you fruitful, and multiply you, and I will make of you a company of peoples, and will give this land to your descendants after you for an everlasting possession.' 5And now your two sons, who were born to you in the land of Egypt before I came to you in Egypt, are mine; Ē'phrăịm and Mănăs'sĕh shall be mine, as Reu-bĕn and Sĭm'ĕŏn are. 6And the offspring born to you after them shall be yours; they shall be called by the name of their brothers in their inheritance. 7 For when I came from Păddăn, Rachel to my sorrow died in the land of Cānaán on the way, when there was still some distance to go to Ēphrăth; and I buried her there on the way to Ephrath (that is, Bĕth'lĕhĕm)."

8 When Israel saw Joseph's sons, he said, "Who are these?" 9 Joseph said to his father, "They are my sons, whom God has given me here." And he said, "Bring them to me, I pray you, that I may bless them." 10 Now the eyes of Israel were dim with age, so that he could not see. So Joseph brought them near him; and he kissed them and embraced them. 11And Israel said to Joseph, "I had not thought to see your face; and lo, God has let me see your

[u] Heb *Ēl Shăd'dăi*

47.25
Gen 33.15
47.26
ver 22

47.27
ver 11;
Gen 46.3;
Ex 1.7

*47.29
Deut 31.14;
Gen 24.2,49

47.30
Gen 49.29;
50.5,13
47.31
Gen 21.23,
24; 24.3;
31.53;
50.25

48.3
Gen 35.9–
12; 28.19;
35.6
48.4
Gen 18.8

*48.5
Gen 46.20;
Josh 13.7;
14.4

48.7
Gen 33.18;
35.19,20

48.9
Gen 33.5

48.10
Gen 27.1,27

48.11
Gen 45.26

47.29 *thigh*, see note to 24.2.
48.5 *are mine*, meaning that Jacob adopted his grandsons and gave them the same rank as his own sons. Thus when Levi was made the priestly tribe and given no inheritance there were still twelve tribes.

children also." 12 Then Joseph removed them from his knees, and
he bowed himself with his face to the earth. 13And Joseph took
them both, Ē'phraïm in his right hand toward Israel's left hand,
and Mánăs'sĕh in his left hand toward Israel's right hand, and

48.14
ver 19

brought them near him. 14And Israel stretched out his right hand
and laid it upon the head of Ē'phraïm, who was the younger, and
his left hand upon the head of Mánăs'seh, crossing his hands, for

48.15
Gen 17.1;
Heb 11.21

Manas'seh was the first-born. 15And he blessed Joseph, and said,
   "The God before whom my fathers Abraham and Isaac walked,
      the God who has led me all my life long to this day,

48.16
Gen 28.15;
31.11,13,
24; 28.14;
46.3

16 the angel who has redeemed me from all evil, bless the lads;
      and in them let my name be perpetuated, and the name of my
            fathers Abraham and Isaac;
      and let them grow into a multitude in the midst of the earth."

48.17
ver 14

17 When Joseph saw that his father laid his right hand upon
the head of Ē'phraïm, it displeased him; and he took his father's
hand, to remove it from Ē'phraïm's head to Mánăs'sĕh's head.
18And Joseph said to his father, "Not so, my father; for this one

48.19
ver 14;
Num 1.33,
35

is the first-born; put your right hand upon his head." 19 But his
father refused, and said, "I know, my son, I know; he also shall
become a people, and he also shall be great; nevertheless his
younger brother shall be greater than he, and his descendants shall
become a multitude of nations." 20 So he blessed them that day,
saying,
   "By you Israel will pronounce blessings, saying,
      'God make you as Ē'phraïm and as Mánăs'sĕh' ";

48.21
Gen 26.3;
28.15;
46.4; 50.24
*48.22
Josh 24.32;
Jn 4.5

and thus he put Ephraim before Manasseh. 21 Then Israel said to
Joseph, "Behold, I am about to die, but God will be with you, and
will bring you again to the land of your fathers. 22 Moreover I have
given to you rather than to your brothers one mountain slope^v
which I took from the hand of the Ăm'ŏrītes with my sword and
with my bow."

2. Jacob blesses his sons

49.1
Num 24.14

49 Then Jacob called his sons, and said, "Gather yourselves
   together, that I may tell you what shall befall you in days
to come.
2 Assemble and hear, O sons of Jacob,
      and hearken to Israel your father.

49.3
Gen 29.32;
Deut 21.17

3 Reubën, you are my first-born,
      my might, and the first fruits of my strength,
      pre-eminent in pride and pre-eminent in power.

*49.4
Gen 35.22;
Deut 27.20

4 Unstable as water, you shall not have pre-eminence
      because you went up to your father's bed;
      then you defiled it—you^w went up to my couch!

49.5
Gen 34.25-
30

5 Sĭm'ĕŏn and Lēvī are brothers;
      weapons of violence are their swords.

49.6
Prov 1.15;
Eph 5.11;
Gen 34.26

6 O my soul, come not into their council;

^v Heb shekem, shoulder   ^w Gk Syr Tg: Heb he

48.22 one mountain slope, probably a reference to the town of Shechem at the foot of
Mount Gerizim.
49.4 you shall not have pre-eminence. As

the first-born Reuben would normally have
had pre-eminence. This prediction reversed
it. The tribe early lost its territory to the
Moabites.

O my spirit,[x] be not joined to their company;
for in their anger they slay men,
   and in their wantonness they hamstring oxen.
7 Cursed be their anger, for it is fierce;
   and their wrath, for it is cruel!
I will divide them in Jacob
   and scatter them in Israel.

8 Judah, your brothers shall praise you;
   your hand shall be on the neck of your enemies;
   your father's sons shall bow down before you.
9 Judah is a lion's whelp;
   from the prey, my son, you have gone up.
He stooped down, he couched as a lion,
   and as a lioness; who dares rouse him up?
10 The scepter shall not depart from Judah,
   nor the ruler's staff from between his feet,
until he comes to whom it belongs;[y]
   and to him shall be the obedience of the peoples.
11 Binding his foal to the vine
   and his ass's colt to the choice vine,
he washes his garments in wine
   and his vesture in the blood of grapes;
12 his eyes shall be red with wine,
   and his teeth white with milk.

13 Zĕb'ŭlŭn shall dwell at the shore of the sea;
   he shall become a haven for ships,
   and his border shall be at Sīdŏn.

14 Ĭs'sȧchar is a strong ass,
   crouching between the sheepfolds;
15 he saw that a resting place was good,
   and that the land was pleasant;
so he bowed his shoulder to bear,
   and became a slave at forced labor.

16 Dan shall judge his people
   as one of the tribes of Israel.
17 Dan shall be a serpent in the way,
   a viper by the path,
that bites the horse's heels
   so that his rider falls backward.
18 I wait for thy salvation, O Lord.

19 Raiders[z] shall raid Găd,
   but he shall raid at their heels.

20 Ăshĕr's food shall be rich,
   and he shall yield royal dainties.

*49.7
Josh 19.1,9;
21.1–42

49.8
Deut 33.7;
1 Chr 5.2

49.9
Ezek 19.5–
7;
Mic 5.8

*49.10
Num 24.17;
Ps 60.7;
Lk 1.32;
Isa 2.2;
11.1

49.13
Deut 33.18,
19;
Josh 19.10,
11

49.16
Deut 33.22;
Judg 18.1,2
49.17
Judg 18.26,
27
49.18
Ex 15.2;
Ps 25.5;
119.166,
174;
Isa 25.9;
Mic 7.7
49.19
Deut 33.20;
1 Chr 5.18
49.20
Deut 33.24,
25;
Josh 19.24

x Or glory   y Syr Compare Tg: Heb until Shĭlōh comes or until he comes to Shiloh
z Heb gedud, a raiding troop

49.7 scatter them in Israel. Levi received
no assigned territory, and Simeon, assigned
portions within Judah's territory, was soon
absorbed.

49.10 he comes . . . belongs, is a variant for the
Hebrew Shĭlōh comes, meaning either the Davidic period or the Messiah, or it may refer to
both David and to the Davidic Messiah.

49.21
Deut 33.23

49.22
Deut 33.13–
17

49.23
Gen 37.4,
24,28

49.24
Ps 18.34;
Isa 41.10;
Ps 132.2,5;
Isa 1.24;
Ps 23.1;
Isa 28.16;
1 Pet 2.6–8

★49.25
Gen 28.3,
13;
32.9; 48.3;
27.28

49.26
Deut 33.15,
16

49.28
Gen 23.16–
20

49.29
Gen 25.8;
47.30

49.30
Gen 23.16

49.31
Gen 23.19;
25.9; 35.29

49.33
Gen 25.8;
Acts 7.15;
ver 29

50.1
Gen 46.4

★50.2
ver 26

50.3
ver 10;
Num 20.29;
Deut 34.8

21 Năph'tālī is a hind let loose,
that bears comely fawns.[a]

22 Joseph is a fruitful bough,
a fruitful bough by a spring;
his branches run over the wall.

23 The archers fiercely attacked him,
shot at him, and harassed him sorely;

24 yet his bow remained unmoved,
his arms[b] were made agile
by the hands of the Mighty One of Jacob
(by the name of the Shepherd, the Rock of Israel),

25 by the God of your father who will help you,
by God Almighty[u] who will bless you
with blessings of heaven above,
blessings of the deep that couches beneath,
blessings of the breasts and of the womb.

26 The blessings of your father
are mighty beyond the blessings of the eternal mountains,[c]
the bounties of the everlasting hills;
may they be on the head of Joseph,
and on the brow of him who was separate from his brothers.

27 Benjamin is a ravenous wolf,
in the morning devouring the prey,
and at even dividing the spoil."

3. *The death and burial of Jacob*

28 All these are the twelve tribes of Israel; and this is what their
father said to them as he blessed them, blessing each with the
blessing suitable to him. 29 Then he charged them, and said to
them, "I am to be gathered to my people; bury me with my fathers
in the cave that is in the field of Ēphrŏn the Hĭttīte, 30 in the cave
that is in the field at Măch-pē'lăh, to the east of Mămrë, in the
land of Cānaán, which Abraham bought with the field from
Ēphrŏn the Hĭttīte to possess as a burying place. 31 There they
buried Abraham and Sarah his wife; there they buried Isaac and
Rēbĕk'áh his wife; and there I buried Lēăh—32 the field and the
cave that is in it were purchased from the Hĭttītes." 33 When Jacob
finished charging his sons, he drew up his feet into the bed, and
breathed his last, and was gathered to his people.

50 Then Joseph fell on his father's face, and wept over him,
and kissed him. 2 And Joseph commanded his servants the
physicians to embalm his father. So the physicians embalmed
Israel; 3 forty days were required for it, for so many are required
for embalming. And the Egyptians wept for him seventy days.

4 And when the days of weeping for him were past, Joseph
spoke to the household of Phạraŏh, saying, "If now I have found
favor in your eyes, speak, I pray you, in the ears of Pharaoh, say-

a Or *who gives beautiful words*   *b* Heb *the arms of his hands*
u Heb *Ĕl Shăd'däi*   *c* Compare Gk: Heb *of my progenitors to*

49.25 *blessings of heaven*, rain and sunshine;
blessings of the deep, rivers and springs.

50.2 *embalm*, Egyptian practice of preparing noted persons for burial.

ing, 5 My father made me swear, saying, 'I am about to die: in my tomb which I hewed out for myself in the land of Cānaản, there shall you bury me.' Now therefore let me go up, I pray you, and bury my father; then I will return." 6And Phạraỏh answered, "Go up, and bury your father, as he made you swear." 7 So Joseph went up to bury his father; and with him went up all the servants of Phạraỏh, the elders of his household, and all the elders of the land of Egypt, 8 as well as all the household of Joseph, his brothers, and his father's household; only their children, their flocks, and their herds were left in the land of Gōshèn. 9And there went up with him both chariots and horsemen; it was a very great company. 10 When they came to the threshing floor of Ātăd, which is beyond the Jordan, they lamented there with a very great and sorrowful lamentation; and he made a mourning for his father seven days. 11 When the inhabitants of the land, the Cā'naảnĩtes, saw the mourning on the threshing floor of Ātăd, they said, "This is a grievous mourning to the Egyptians." Therefore the place was named Ā'bèl-mĩzrā'ĩm;*d* it is beyond the Jordan. 12 Thus his sons did for him as he had commanded them; 13 for his sons carried him to the land of Cānaản, and buried him in the cave of the field at Măch-pē'lảh, to the east of Mămrë, which Abraham bought with the field from Ēphrỏn the Hĩttĩte, to possess as a burying place. 14After he had buried his father, Joseph returned to Egypt with his brothers and all who had gone up with him to bury his father.

N. Joseph's kindness to his brethren

15 When Joseph's brothers saw that their father was dead, they said, "It may be that Joseph will hate us and pay us back for all the evil which we did to him." 16 So they sent a message to Joseph, saying, "Your father gave this command before he died, 17 'Say to Joseph, Forgive, I pray you, the transgression of your brothers and their sin, because they did evil to you.' And now, we pray you, forgive the transgression of the servants of the God of your father." Joseph wept when they spoke to him. 18 His brothers also came and fell down before him, and said, "Behold, we are your servants." 19 But Joseph said to them, "Fear not, for am I in the place of God? 20As for you, you meant evil against me; but God meant it for good, to bring it about that many people should be kept alive, as they are today. 21 So do not fear; I will provide for you and your little ones." Thus he reassured them and comforted them.

O. The death and embalming of Joseph

22 So Joseph dwelt in Egypt, he and his father's house; and Joseph lived a hundred and ten years. 23And Joseph saw Ē'phrặỉm's children of the third generation; the children also of Mảchĩr the son of Mảnăs'sèh were born upon Joseph's knees. 24And Joseph said to his brothers, "I am about to die; but God will visit you, and bring you up out of this land to the land which he swore to Abraham, to Isaac, and to Jacob." 25 Then Joseph took an oath of the sons of Israel, saying, "God will visit you, and you shall carry up my bones from here." 26 So Joseph died, being a hundred and ten years old; and they embalmed him, and he was put in a coffin in Egypt.

d That is meadow (or mourning) of Egypt

50.5
Gen
47.29–31

50.8
Ex 8.22

50.10
2 Sam 1.17;
1 Sam
31.13;
Job 2.13

50.13
Gen 49.29,
30; 23.16

50.15
Gen 37.28;
42.21,22

50.18
Gen 37.7,
10;41.43

50.19
Gen 45.5;
Deut 32.35;
Rom 12.19;
Heb 10.30

50.20
Gen 37.26,
27; 45.5,7

50.21
Gen 45.11;
47.12

50.24
Gen 48.21;
Heb 11.22;
Gen 13.15,
17; 15.7,8;
26.3;
28.13;
35.12

INTRODUCTION TO

THE SECOND BOOK OF MOSES

COMMONLY CALLED

EXODUS

Authorship and Background: Exodus is the second of the five books of the Pentateuch ascribed to Moses. The name Exodus, meaning "going out," "departure," is the Greek title given to the book by the Septuagint translators. The Hebrew title, according to the ancient custom, consists in the opening words of the Hebrew text, "And these are the names."

Although the RSV starts the book with the word "These," "And" in the Hebrew suggests that it is a continuation of the story begun in Genesis. Without that background the account in Exodus would be puzzling indeed. Moses is the central figure in the book; no other Old Testament character towers as high as he does. He was a military leader, lawgiver, and key figure in the founding of Israel's religion. The chief event of the book is the crossing of the Red (or Reed) Sea. The prophets and psalmists continually refer back to this mighty act of deliverance. The date of the Exodus is still debated. Some scholars hold to a date around 1440 B.C.; most in recent years have supported a date around 1290 B.C.

Characteristics: Exodus is essentially the history of the origin and early years of Israel as God's chosen people of the covenant. The fortunes of this people are traced from Egypt to the wilderness under the leadership of Moses. The rise of the nation Israel as a theocracy, a form of government in which God is king, is unfolded in its pages. Guiding spiritual and moral principles characteristic of the Christian faith for centuries have their foundation in Exodus. There is considerable drama in the events as they unfold, and the effects are heightened by the manner in which they are recounted. The contests of Moses with Pharaoh, the crossing of the Red Sea, the provision of manna, the giving of the Law, and the account of Aaron and the golden calf are samples of events marked by emotion, anger, suspense, and retribution. In it all, however, may be seen the mighty power of the LORD God.

Contents:

I.   The deliverance from Egypt. 1.1—15.21: Israel is oppressed in Egypt. Moses' birth and education; his flight from Egypt. God calls him to be deliverer of Israel. Moses engages Pharaoh in successive tests marked by miraculous events. Directions for celebrating the Passover. Israel leaves Egypt. The first-born are sanctified, the Red Sea crossed, and the Egyptians drowned. The Song of Moses.

II.   The journey to Sinai. 15.22—18.27: The bitter waters of Marah made sweet. The people murmur and God provides manna for food. Sabbath instruction. Moses strikes the rock at Horeb to secure water. The battle against Amalek. Jethro becomes advisor to Moses, his son-in-law.

III.   The covenant and the Law. 19.1—24.18: Israel prepares to receive the covenant. The Ten Commandments given. Various judgments and moral statutes prescribed and the rewards of obedience stated. The people ratify the covenant. Moses returns to Sinai.

IV.   The tabernacle in the wilderness. 25.1—40.38: The divine plan for the tabernacle including the furniture, altar, court, priestly garments and their consecration. God promises His presence, adds directions for the tabernacle. The Sabbath, and the tables of testimony. The making of the golden calf, Moses' intercession on behalf of Israel, the punishment. Moses' further intercession and his vision of the glory of God. The covenant is renewed. The tabernacle is constructed, set up, and the glory of God fills it.

THE SECOND BOOK OF MOSES

COMMONLY CALLED

EXODUS

I. The deliverance from Egypt 1.1–15.21

A. Introduction

1. *The numerical growth of Israel*

Gen 46.8–
27
1.5
Gen 46.27
1.6
Gen 50.26
★1.7
Gen 46.3;
47.27;
Acts 7.17

1.1

1 These are the names of the sons of Israel who came to Egypt with Jacob, each with his household: 2 Reubën, Sĭm′ëŏn, Lēvī, and Judah, 3 Ĭs′sȧçhar, Zĕb′ŭlŭn, and Benjamin, 4 Dan and Năph′tȧlī, Găd and Ăshĕr. 5All the offspring of Jacob were seventy persons; Joseph was already in Egypt. 6 Then Joseph died, and all his brothers, and all that generation. 7 But the descendants of Israel were fruitful and increased greatly; they multiplied and grew exceedingly strong; so that the land was filled with them.

2. *Israel in bondage*

1.8
Acts 7.18,
19
1.9
Ps 105.24,
25
★1.11
Ex 3.7; 5.6

8 Now there arose a new king over Egypt, who did not know Joseph. 9And he said to his people, "Behold, the people of Israel are too many and too mighty for us. 10 Come, let us deal shrewdly with them, lest they multiply, and, if war befall us, they join our enemies and fight against us and escape from the land." 11 Therefore they set taskmasters over them to afflict them with heavy burdens; and they built for Phȧraōh store-cities, Pĭthŏm and Rā-ăm′sēṣ. 12 But the more thev were oppressed, the more they multiplied and the more they spread abroad. And the Egyptians were in dread of the people of Israel. 13 So they made the people of Israel serve with rigor, 14 and made their lives bitter with hard service, in mortar and brick, and in all kinds of work in the field; in all their work they made them serve with rigor.

1.14
Ps 81.6

3. *The background for Moses*

1.16
Acts 7.19

1.17
ver 21

1.20
ver 12;
Isa 3.10
1.21
1 Sam 2.35
1.22
Acts 7.19

15 Then the king of Egypt said to the Hebrew midwives, one of whom was named Shĭph′rȧh and the other Pŭȧh, 16 "When you serve as midwife to the Hebrew women, and see them upon the birthstool, if it is a son, you shall kill him; but if it is a daughter, she shall live." 17 But the midwives feared God, and did not do as the king of Egypt commanded them, but let the male children live. 18 So the king of Egypt called the midwives, and said to them, "Why have you done this, and let the male children live?" 19 The midwives said to Phȧraōh, "Because the Hebrew women are not like the Egyptian women; for they are vigorous and are delivered before the midwife comes to them." 20 So God dealt well with the midwives; and the people multiplied and grew very strong. 21And because the midwives feared God he gave them families. 22 Then Phȧraōh commanded all his people, "Every son that is born to the Hebrews*a* you shall cast into the Nile, but you shall let every daughter live."

a Sam Gk Tg: Heb lacks *to the Hebrews*

1.7 *land*, the land of Goshen or Rameses.
1.11 *Pithom and Raamses*, cities in the Nile Delta. If this is a reference to the building operations of the 19th Dynasty kings of Egypt, then the exodus took place shortly after 1300 B.C.

84

B. God's servant Moses

1. Moses' birth

2 Now a man from the house of Lēvī went and took to wife a daughter of Levi. 2 The woman conceived and bore a son; and when she saw that he was a goodly child, she hid him three months. 3And when she could hide him no longer she took for him a basket made of bulrushes, and daubed it with bitumen and pitch; and she put the child in it and placed it among the reeds at the river's brink. 4And his sister stood at a distance, to know what would be done to him. 5 Now the daughter of Pharaōh came down to bathe at the river, and her maidens walked beside the river; she saw the basket among the reeds and sent her maid to fetch it. 6 When she opened it she saw the child; and lo, the babe was crying. She took pity on him and said, "This is one of the Hebrews' children." 7 Then his sister said to Pharaōh's daughter, "Shall I go and call you a nurse from the Hebrew women to nurse the child for you?" 8And Pharaōh's daughter said to her, "Go." So the girl went and called the child's mother. 9And Pharaōh's daughter said to her, "Take this child away, and nurse him for me, and I will give you your wages." So the woman took the child and nursed him. 10And the child grew, and she brought him to Pharaōh's daughter, and he became her son; and she named him Moses,[b] for she said, "Because I drew him out[c] of the water."

2. Moses' crime and flight

11 One day, when Moses had grown up, he went out to his people and looked on their burdens; and he saw an Egyptian beating a Hebrew, one of his people. 12 He looked this way and that, and seeing no one he killed the Egyptian and hid him in the sand. 13 When he went out the next day, behold, two Hebrews were struggling together; and he said to the man that did the wrong, "Why do you strike your fellow?" 14 He answered, "Who made you a prince and a judge over us? Do you mean to kill me as you killed the Egyptian?" Then Moses was afraid, and thought, "Surely the thing is known." 15 When Pharaōh heard of it, he sought to kill Moses.

But Moses fled from Pharaoh, and stayed in the land of Mid'ian; and he sat down by a well. 16 Now the priest of Mid'ian had seven daughters; and they came and drew water, and filled the troughs to water their father's flock. 17 The shepherds came and drove them away; but Moses stood up and helped them, and

b Heb *Mosheh*   c Heb *mashah*

Marginal references:
2.1 Ex 6.19,20
2.2 Acts 7.20; Heb 11.23
*2.3
2.4 Ex 15.20; Num 26.59
*2.10 Acts 7.21
2.11 Acts 7.23; Heb 11.24–26
2.12 Acts 7.24
2.13 Acts 7.26–28
2.14 Gen 19.9; Acts 7.27
*2.15 Acts 7.29; Gen 24.11; 29.2
2.16 Ex 3.1; 18.12; Gen 24.13,19
2.17 Gen 29.3,10

2.3 *bulrushes*, papyrus reeds; *bitumen*, or asphalt, making the basket watertight.

2.10 Moses was one of the two greatest Old Testament characters—the other being Abraham— and he certainly ranks among the greatest men of all time. He was well educated in Egypt where his training doubtless included athletics, art, writing, music, geometry, literature, law, astronomy, medicine, and philosophy. Apparently he could have chosen an official life, a literary life, or the life of a soldier. As the leader of Israel he occupied a unique position. He was deliverer, lawgiver, builder, commander-in-chief, judge, author, and intermediary between God and Israel. At forty (according to 2.15; Acts 7.23–29) he fled for his life from Egypt. At eighty he delivered Israel from Egypt. At one hundred and twenty his ministry was completed. As a member of the tribe of Levi, he consecrated his brother Aaron to the high priesthood and thus, under God, made him the forefather of the priestly line. Faithful and unselfish, Moses was meek before the Lord and courageous before men.

2.15 *land of Midian*, properly speaking, in Arabia, but broadened here to include the Mt. Sinai region.

*2.18
Ex 3.1;
Num 10.29
2.20
Gen 31.54
2.21
Acts 7.29;
Gen 4.25;
18.2
2.22
Ex 18.3;
Heb 11.13,
14

2.23
Acts 7.30;
Deut 26.7;
Ex 3.9;
Jas 5.4
2.24
Ex 6.5;
Ps 105.8,42;
Gen 22.16-
18
2.25
Ex 4.31;
3.7;
4.27;18.5
3.1
Ex 2.18
*3.2
Deut 33.16;
Mk 12.26
3.3
Acts 7.31

3.5
Josh 5.15;
Acts 7.33
3.6
Mt 22.31,
32;
Mk 12.26;
Lk 20.37;
Acts 7.32
3.7
Ex 2.25;
Neh 9.9;
Acts 7.34
3.8
Gen 50.24,
25;
ver 17;
Josh 24.11
3.9
Ex 2.23;
1.13,14
3.10
Mic 6.4

3.12
Gen 31.3;
Josh 1.5

watered their flock. 18 When they came to their father Reu'el, he said, "How is it that you have come so soon today?" 19 They said, "An Egyptian delivered us out of the hand of the shepherds, and even drew water for us and watered the flock." 20 He said to his daughters, "And where is he? Why have you left the man? Call him, that he may eat bread." 21And Moses was content to dwell with the man, and he gave Moses his daughter Zippō'rah. 22 She bore a son, and he called his name Gērshŏm; for he said, "I have been a sojourner[d] in a foreign land."

3. The call of Moses at the burning bush
a. Moses' conversations with God

23 In the course of those many days the king of Egypt died. And the people of Israel groaned under their bondage, and cried out for help, and their cry under bondage came up to God. 24And God heard their groaning, and God remembered his covenant with Abraham, with Isaac, and with Jacob. 25And God saw the people of Israel, and God knew their condition.

3 Now Moses was keeping the flock of his father-in-law, Jĕthrō, the priest of Mĭd'iăn; and he led his flock to the west side of the wilderness, and came to Horĕb, the mountain of God. 2And the angel of the LORD appeared to him in a flame of fire out of the midst of a bush; and he looked, and lo, the bush was burning, yet it was not consumed. 3And Moses said, "I will turn aside and see this great sight, why the bush is not burnt." 4 When the LORD saw that he turned aside to see, God called to him out of the bush, "Moses, Moses!" And he said, "Here am I." 5 Then he said, "Do not come near; put off your shoes from your feet, for the place on which you are standing is holy ground." 6And he said, "I am the God of your father, the God of Abraham, the God of Isaac, and the God of Jacob." And Moses hid his face, for he was afraid to look at God.

7 Then the LORD said, "I have seen the affliction of my people who are in Egypt, and have heard their cry because of their taskmasters; I know their sufferings, 8 and I have come down to deliver them out of the hand of the Egyptians, and to bring them up out of that land to a good and broad land, a land flowing with milk and honey, to the place of the Cā'naănĭtes, the Hĭttītes, the Ăm'ŏrĭtes, the Pĕr'ĭzzītes, the Hĭvītes, and the Jĕb'ūsītes. 9And now, behold, the cry of the people of Israel has come to me, and I have seen the oppression with which the Egyptians oppress them. 10 Come, I will send you to Phăraōh that you may bring forth my people, the sons of Israel, out of Egypt." 11 But Moses said to God, "Who am I that I should go to Phăraōh, and bring the sons of Israel out of Egypt?" 12 He said, "But I will be with you; and this shall be the sign for you, that I have sent you: when you have brought forth the people out of Egypt, you shall serve God upon this mountain."

[d] Heb ger

2.18 *Reuel*, Moses' father-in-law to be, is called Jethro (3.1) and Hobab (Judg 4.11), although in Num 10.29 Hobab is called the son of Reuel.
3.2 The phrase *angel of the* LORD may indicate an appearance of the pre-incarnate Christ in the Old Testament, as, for example, in Judg 2.1; 6.12-16; 13.3-22, where the texts clearly show that the angel was God Himself.

13 Then Moses said to God, "If I come to the people of Israel and say to them, 'The God of your fathers has sent me to you,' and they ask me, 'What is his name?' what shall I say to them?" 14 God said to Moses, "I AM WHO I AM."[e] And he said, "Say this to the people of Israel, 'I AM has sent me to you.'" 15 God also said to Moses, "Say this to the people of Israel, 'The LORD,[f] the God of your fathers, the God of Abraham, the God of Isaac, and the God of Jacob, has sent me to you': this is my name for ever, and thus I am to be remembered throughout all generations. 16 Go and gather the elders of Israel together, and say to them, 'The LORD, the God of your fathers, the God of Abraham, of Isaac, and of Jacob, has appeared to me, saying, "I have observed you and what has been done to you in Egypt; 17 and I promise that I will bring you up out of the affliction of Egypt, to the land of the Cānaánites, the Hĭttītes, the Ăm'órites, the Pĕr'ĭzzītes, the Hĭvītes, and the Jĕb'ūsītes, a land flowing with milk and honey."' 18And they will hearken to your voice; and you and the elders of Israel shall go to the king of Egypt and say to him, 'The LORD, the God of the Hebrews, has met with us; and now, we pray you, let us go a three days' journey into the wilderness, that we may sacrifice to the LORD our God.' 19 I know that the king of Egypt will not let you go unless compelled by a mighty hand.[g] 20 So I will stretch out my hand and smite Egypt with all the wonders which I will do in it; after that he will let you go. 21And I will give this people favor in the sight of the Egyptians; and when you go, you shall not go empty, 22 but each woman shall ask of her neighbor, and of her who sojourns in her house, jewelry of silver and of gold, and clothing, and you shall put them on your sons and on your daughters; thus you shall despoil the Egyptians."

3.14
Ex 6.3;
Jn 8.58;
Heb 13.8
3.15
Ps 135.13;
Hos 12.5

3.17
Gen 15.14,
16;
Josh 24.11
3.18
Ex 4.31;
5.1,3

3.19
Ex 5.2; 6.1
3.20
Ex 6.6;
9.15;
Deut 6.22;
Neh 9.10;
Ex 12.31
3.21
Ex 11.3;
12.36
3.22
Ex 11.2,3;
12.35,36

b. *God equips Moses*

4 Then Moses answered, "But behold, they will not believe me or listen to my voice, for they will say, 'The LORD did not appear to you.'" 2 The LORD said to him, "What is that in your hand?" He said, "A rod." 3And he said, "Cast it on the ground." So he cast it on the ground, and it became a serpent; and Moses fled from it. 4 But the LORD said to Moses, "Put out your hand, and take it by the tail"—so he put out his hand and caught it, and it became a rod in his hand— 5"that they may believe that the LORD, the God of their fathers, the God of Abraham, the God of Isaac, and the God of Jacob, has appeared to you."

4.1
Ex 3.18;
6.30
*4.2
ver 17,20

[e] Or I AM WHAT I AM or I WILL BE WHAT I WILL BE
[f] The word LORD when spelled with capital letters, stands for the divine name, YHWH, which is here connected with the verb *hayah*, to be
[g] Gk Vg: Heb *no, not by a mighty hand*

4.2 Moses asked God for some sign by which he might impress Pharaoh that he had come from God. He was given the rod-serpent and the leprous hand (ver 6); however, his credentials served only to prove that unbelief will not be moved by mere signs and wonders. As it turned out, neither sign induced Pharaoh to let Israel go. Another aspect of this incident concerns believers in their walk with God: all God needed was what Moses had in his hand—a rod. When yielded to the Lord in complete surrender and trust, it became a miracle-working instru-ment. Pebbles and a sling were all David had to oppose Goliath, but God made them enough. So it has always been. Even the smallest and most insignificant object which is wholly dedicated to God in the hands of a willing believer may be used for God's glory and the accomplishment of His will. In this experience of Moses one fact should be care-fully noted. Though the signs may not have convinced Pharaoh, they did serve to con-vince the children of Israel that Moses was truly God's messenger of deliverance (ver 29–31).

4.6
Num 12.10;
2 Ki 5.27
4.7
Num 12.13,
14;
Deut 32.39;
2 Ki 5.14;
Mt 8.3

4.9
Ex 7.19

⁶Again, the LORD said to him, "Put your hand into your bosom." And he put his hand into his bosom; and when he took it out, behold, his hand was leprous, as white as snow. ⁷ Then God said, "Put your hand back into your bosom." So he put his hand back into his bosom; and when he took it out, behold, it was restored like the rest of his flesh. ⁸ "If they will not believe you," God said, "or heed the first sign, they may believe the latter sign. ⁹ If they will not believe even these two signs or heed your voice, you shall take some water from the Nile and pour it upon the dry ground; and the water which you shall take from the Nile will become blood upon the dry ground."

c. God provides Aaron to speak

4.10
Ex 6.12;
Jer 1.6
4.11
Ps 94.9;
Mt 11.5
4.12
Isa 50.4;
Jer 1.9;
Mt 10.19;
Mk 13.11;
Lk 12.11;
12;21.14,15
4.14
ver 27
4.15
Ex 7.1,2;
Num 23.5,
12,16;
Deut 5.31
4.17
ver 2;
Ex 7.9–20
4.19
Ex 2.15,23

10 But Moses said to the LORD, "Oh, my Lord, I am not eloquent, either heretofore or since thou hast spoken to thy servant; but I am slow of speech and of tongue." ¹¹ Then the LORD said to him, "Who has made man's mouth? Who makes him dumb, or deaf, or seeing, or blind? Is it not I, the LORD? ¹² Now therefore go, and I will be with your mouth and teach you what you shall speak." ¹³ But he said, "Oh, my Lord, send, I pray, some other person." ¹⁴ Then the anger of the LORD was kindled against Moses and he said, "Is there not Aaron, your brother, the Levite? I know that he can speak well; and behold, he is coming out to meet you, and when he sees you he will be glad in his heart. ¹⁵And you shall speak to him and put the words in his mouth; and I will be with your mouth and with his mouth, and will teach you what you shall do. ¹⁶ He shall speak for you to the people; and he shall be a mouth for you, and you shall be to him as God. ¹⁷And you shall take in your hand this rod, with which you shall do the signs."

d. Moses starts for Egypt

4.20
Ex 17.9;
Num 20.8
*4.21
Ex 7.3,13;
9.12,35;
10.1;14.8;
Deut 2.30;
Jn 12.40;
Rom 19.18
4.22
Isa 63.16;
64.8;
Hos 11.1;
Rom 9.4;
Jer 31.9
4.23
Ex 5.1;
6.11; 7.16;
12.29
*4.24ff
Num 22.22;
Gen 17.14
4.25
Josh 5.2,3

18 Moses went back to Jethro his father-in-law and said to him, "Let me go back, I pray, to my kinsmen in Egypt and see whether they are still alive." And Jethro said to Moses, "Go in peace." ¹⁹And the LORD said to Moses in Mid'ian, "Go back to Egypt; for all the men who were seeking your life are dead." ²⁰ So Moses took his wife and his sons and set them on an ass, and went back to the land of Egypt; and in his hand Moses took the rod of God.

21 And the LORD said to Moses, "When you go back to Egypt, see that you do before Pharaoh all the miracles which I have put in your power; but I will harden his heart, so that he will not let the people go. ²²And you shall say to Pharaoh, 'Thus says the LORD, Israel is my first-born son, ²³ and I say to you, "Let my son go that he may serve me"; if you refuse to let him go, behold, I will slay your first-born son.' "

24 At a lodging place on the way the LORD met him and sought to kill him. ²⁵ Then Zippo'rah took a flint and cut off her son's

---

4.21 Moses records not only that God hardened Pharaoh's heart (e.g., 9.12; 10.1), but also that Pharaoh hardened his own heart (e.g., 8.15, 32; 9.34). Nowhere are we told that God forced Pharaoh contrary to his own voluntary choice. Rather it seems that God sent circumstances into Pharaoh's life which hardened his own heart and caused him to reject the claims of God. Resisting God must always result in a hardened heart.

4.24-26 The reason that Moses had not circumcised his son is not made clear in the narrative. It may have been that, to please his wife, he had neglected this seal of the Abrahamic covenant. But God made it perfectly evident that he could not effectively serve as God's deliverer until he had fulfilled the covenant condition. Because of Moses' grave illness at the inn, Zipporah, much against her will, had to perform the circum-

foreskin, and touched Moses' feet with it, and said, "Surely you are a bridegroom of blood to me!" 26 So he let him alone. Then it was that she said, "You are a bridegroom of blood," because of the circumcision.

27 The LORD said to Aaron, "Go into the wilderness to meet Moses." So he went, and met him at the mountain of God and kissed him. 28And Moses told Aaron all the words of the LORD with which he had sent him, and all the signs which he had charged him to do. 29 Then Moses and Aaron went and gathered together all the elders of the people of Israel. 30And Aaron spoke all the words which the LORD had spoken to Moses, and did the signs in the sight of the people. 31And the people believed; and when they heard that the LORD had visited the people of Israel and that he had seen their affliction, they bowed their heads and worshiped.

4.27
ver 14;
Ex 3.1
4.28
ver 15,16;
8.9
4.29
Ex 3.16
4.30
ver 16
4.31
ver 8,9;
Ex 3.18;
2.25; 3.7;
12.27

C. God's method of deliverance

1. Moses and Aaron meet with Pharaoh

a. Pharaoh refuses to let Israel go

5 Afterward Moses and Aaron went to Pharaōh and said, "Thus says the LORD, the God of Israel, 'Let my people go, that they may hold a feast to me in the wilderness.' " 2 But Pharaōh said, "Who is the LORD, that I should heed his voice and let Israel go? I do not know the LORD, and moreover I will not let Israel go." 3 Then they said, "The God of the Hebrews has met with us; let us go, we pray, a three days' journey into the wilderness, and sacrifice to the LORD our God, lest he fall upon us with pestilence or with the sword." 4 But the king of Egypt said to them, "Moses and Aaron, why do you take the people away from their work? Get to your burdens." 5And Pharaōh said, "Behold, the people of the land are now many and you make them rest from their burdens!" 6 The same day Pharaōh commanded the taskmasters of the people and their foremen, 7 "You shall no longer give the people straw to make bricks, as heretofore; let them go and gather straw for themselves. 8 But the number of bricks which they made heretofore you shall lay upon them, you shall by no means lessen it; for they are idle; therefore they cry, 'Let us go and offer sacrifice to our God.' 9 Let heavier work be laid upon the men that they may labor at it and pay no regard to lying words."

5.1
Ex 3.18;
4.23; 10.9
5.2
Job 21.15;
Ex 3.19
5.3
Ex 3.18
5.4
Ex 1.11;
2.11; 6.6,7
5.5
Ex 1.7,9
5.6
Ex 1.11;
3.7
5.8
ver 17

b. Israel's task made heavier

10 So the taskmasters and the foremen of the people went out and said to the people, "Thus says Pharaōh, 'I will not give you straw. 11 Go yourselves, get your straw wherever you can find it; but your work will not be lessened in the least.' " 12 So the people were scattered abroad throughout all the land of Egypt, to gather stubble for straw. 13 The taskmasters were urgent, saying, "Complete your work, your daily task, as when there was straw." 14And the foremen of the people of Israel, whom Pharaōh's taskmasters

5.10
ver 6

5.14
ver 6;
Isa 10.24

cision. Not to circumcise was tantamount to abrogating the covenant (Gen 17.14) and meant that the uncircumcised was cut off from inclusion in the covenant people. Since the advent of Christ, real circumcision has been of the heart and not of the flesh (Rom 2.29).

had set over them, were beaten, and were asked, "Why have you not done all your task of making bricks today, as hitherto?"

15 Then the foremen of the people of Israel came and cried to Pharaōh, "Why do you deal thus with your servants? 16 No straw is given to your servants, yet they say to us, 'Make bricks!' And behold, your servants are beaten; but the fault is in your own people." 17 But he said, "You are idle, you are idle; therefore you say, 'Let us go and sacrifice to the LORD.' 18 Go now, and work; for no straw shall be given you, yet you shall deliver the same number of bricks." 19 The foremen of the people of Israel saw that they were in evil plight, when they said, "You shall by no means lessen your daily number of bricks." 20 They met Moses and Aaron, who were waiting for them, as they came forth from Pharaōh; 21 and they said to them, "The LORD look upon you and judge, because you have made us offensive in the sight of Pharaōh and his servants, and have put a sword in their hand to kill us."

c. God's promise of deliverance to Moses

22 Then Moses turned again to the LORD and said, "O LORD, why hast thou done evil to this people? Why didst thou ever send me? 23 For since I came to Pharaōh to speak in thy name, he has done evil to this people, and thou hast not delivered thy people at all." 1 But the LORD said to Moses, "Now you shall see what I will do to Pharaōh; for with a strong hand he will send them out, yea, with a strong hand he will drive them out of his land."

2 And God said to Moses, "I am the LORD. 3 I appeared to Abraham, to Isaac, and to Jacob, as God Almighty,ʰ but by my name the LORD I did not make myself known to them. 4 I also established my covenant with them, to give them the land of Cānaán, the land in which they dwelt as sojourners. 5 Moreover I have heard the groaning of the people of Israel whom the Egyptians hold in bondage and I have remembered my covenant. 6 Say therefore to the people of Israel, 'I am the LORD, and I will bring you out from under the burdens of the Egyptians, and I will deliver you from their bondage, and I will redeem you with an outstretched arm and with great acts of judgment, 7 and I will take you for my people, and I will be your God; and you shall know that I am the LORD your God, who has brought you out from under the burdens of the Egyptians. 8And I will bring you into the land which I swore to give to Abraham, to Isaac, and to Jacob; I will give it to you for a possession. I am the LORD.' " 9 Moses

ʰ Heb Ĕl Shăd'dăi

5.22 The perplexity of Moses is easy to understand. God had guaranteed to deliver Israel, but their situation seemed to be worsening. Moses did not understand that God's special deliverance is often preceded by great difficulties and apparently unfavorable conditions. Since a believer is to walk by faith and not by sight, he is not to be subject to mere external appearances but to trust God's faithfulness whatever happens. Before Joseph became premier of Egypt he first had become a slave and then was imprisoned for a crime he never committed. Strong faith is challenged, not defeated, by adverse circumstances.

6.3 This verse poses some difficulties because in Gen 12.8 it states that when Abraham came to the Bethel area *he built an altar . . . of the* LORD. The name "LORD" (with small capital letters) is the common designation in the KJV and RSV for *Yahweh*, the personal name for the God of Israel. If the name *Yahweh* was used as early as Gen 12.8, then 6.3 means that *Yahweh* took on new meaning after God's revelation to Moses. However, if 6.3 is to be interpreted as the origin of the name *Yahweh*, then earlier uses represent a reading back of the name of the God of Israel into earlier patriarchal records.

Margin refs: 5.17 ver 8; 5.21 Ex 14.11; 15.24; Gen 16.5; 34.30; *5.22 Num 11.11; Jer 4.10; 5.23 Ex 3.8; 6.1 Ex 3.19,20; 7.4,5; 12.31,33,39; *6.3 Ps 68.4; 83.18; Isa 52.6; Jer 16.21; Ezek 37.6,13; 6.4 Gen 15.18; 28.4; 6.5 Ex 2.24; 6.6 Deut 26.8; 6.7 Deut 4.20; 26.8; Ps 81.6; Ex 16.12; Isa 41.20; 6.8 Gen 15.18

spoke thus to the people of Israel; but they did not listen to Moses,
because of their broken spirit and their cruel bondage.

10 And the LORD said to Moses, 11 "Go in, tell Phạraōh king of
Egypt to let the people of Israel go out of his land." 12 But Moses
said to the LORD, "Behold, the people of Israel have not listened
to me; how then shall Phạraōh listen to me, who am a man of
uncircumcised lips?" 13 But the LORD spoke to Moses and Aaron,
and gave them a charge to the people of Israel and to Phạraōh king
of Egypt to bring the people of Israel out of the land of Egypt.

d. The genealogy of Israel

14 These are the heads of their fathers' houses: the sons of
Reubën, the first-born of Israel: Hānoch, Păllu, Hĕzrón, and
Carmī; these are the families of Reuben. 15 The sons of Sĭm'ëön:
Jĕm'ūĕl, Jāmĭn, Ōhăd, Jāchĭn, Zōhar, and Shaul, the son of a
Cā'naánīte woman; these are the families of Simeon. 16 These are
the names of the sons of Lēvī according to their generations:
Gèrshòn, Kōhăth, and Mèrar'ĭ, the years of the life of Levi being
a hundred and thirty-seven years. 17 The sons of Gèrshòn: Lĭbnī
and Shĭm'ë-ī, by their families. 18 The sons of Kōhăth: Ȧmrăm,
Ĭzhar, Hēbrón, and Ŭzzĭ'ĕl, the years of the life of Kohath being a
hundred and thirty-three years. 19 The sons of Mèrar'ĭ: Mahlī
and Mushī. These are the families of the Lēvītes according to their
generations. 20Ȧmrăm took to wife Jŏch'ĕbĕd his father's sister
and she bore him Aaron and Moses, the years of the life of Ȧmrăm
being one hundred and thirty-seven years. 21 The sons of Ĭzhar:
Kōrăh, Nĕphĕg, and Zĭchrī. 22And the sons of Ŭzzĭ'ĕl: Mĭsh'ä-ĕl,
Ĕlzā'phản, and Sĭthrī. 23Aaron took to wife Ĕlĭ'shĕbȧ, the daughter
of Ȧmmĭn'ȧdȧb and the sister of Nahshòn; and she bore him
Nādăb, Ȧbĭ'hū, Ĕlëä'zȧr, and Ĭth'ȧmar. 24 The sons of Kōrăh:
Ȧssir, Ĕlkā'năh, and Ȧbĭ'ȧsăph; these are the families of the
Kō'răhītes. 25 Ĕlëä'zȧr, Aaron's son, took to wife one of the
daughters of Pū'tĭ-ĕl; and she bore him Phĭn'ëhȧs. These are the
heads of the fathers' houses of the Lēvītes by their families.

26 These are the Aaron and Moses to whom the LORD said:
"Bring out the people of Israel from the land of Egypt by their
hosts." 27 It was they who spoke to Phạraōh king of Egypt about
bringing out the people of Israel from Egypt, this Moses and this
Aaron.

e. Moses commanded to speak to Pharaoh again

28 On the day when the LORD spoke to Moses in the land of
Egypt, 29 the LORD said to Moses, "I am the LORD; tell Phạraōh
king of Egypt all that I say to you." 30 But Moses said to the LORD,
"Behold, I am of uncircumcised lips; how then shall Phạraōh listen
7 to me?" 1And the LORD said to Moses, "See, I make you as
God to Phạraōh; and Aaron your brother shall be your prophet. 2 You shall speak all that I command you; and Aaron your
brother shall tell Phạraōh to let the people of Israel go out of his
land. 3 But I will harden Phạraōh's heart, and though I multiply
my signs and wonders in the land of Egypt, 4 Phạraōh will not
listen to you; then I will lay my hand upon Egypt and bring forth
my hosts, my people the sons of Israel, out of the land of Egypt
by great acts of judgment. 5And the Egyptians shall know that I

6.14
Gen 46.9;
Num 26.5–
11
6.15
Gen 46.10;
1 Chr 4.24
6.16
Gen 46.11;
Num 3.17
6.17
1 Chr 6.17
6.18
1 Chr 6.2,18
6.19
1 Chr 6.19
6.20
Ex 2.1,2;
Num 26.59
6.21
Num 16.1;
1 Chr 6.37,
38
6.22
Lev 10.4;
Num 3.30
6.24
Num 26.11
6.25
Josh 24.33;
Num 25.7–
11;
Ps 106.30

6.29
ver 11;
Ex 7.2
*6.30
ver 12;
Ex 4.10
7.1
Ex 4.16
7.2
Ex 4.15
*7.3
Ex 4.21;
11.9
7.4
Ex 3.19,20;
10.1; 11.9;
12.51;
13.3,9; 6.6
7.5
ver 17;
Ex 8.19;
3.20

6.30 uncircumcised lips, stammering lips.   **7.3** will harden, see note to 4.21.

am the LORD, when I stretch forth my hand upon Egypt and bring

7.6
ver 2

out the people of Israel from among them." 6And Moses and

7.7
Deut 34.7;
Acts 7.23,
30

Aaron did so; they did as the LORD commanded them. 7 Now Moses was eighty years old, and Aaron eighty-three years old, when they spoke to Pharaōh.

2. The miracles of Moses
a. The rod becomes a serpent

7.9
Isa 7.11;
Jn 2.18;
Ex 4.2,17

8 And the LORD said to Moses and Aaron, 9 "When Pharaōh says to you, 'Prove yourselves by working a miracle,' then you shall say to Aaron, 'Take your rod and cast it down before Phar-

7.10
ver 9;
Ex 4.3

aoh, that it may become a serpent.' " 10 So Moses and Aaron went to Pharaōh and did as the LORD commanded; Aaron cast down his rod before Pharaoh and his servants, and it became a

7.11
Gen 41.8;
ver 22;
Ex 8.7,18

serpent. 11 Then Pharaōh summoned the wise men and the sorcerers; and they also, the magicians of Egypt, did the same by their secret arts. 12 For every man cast down his rod, and they became

*7.12
7.13
ver 4;
Ex 4.21

serpents. But Aaron's rod swallowed up their rods. 13 Still Pharaōh's heart was hardened, and he would not listen to them; as the LORD had said.

b. The water turned into blood

7.14
Ex 8.15;
10.1,20,27

14 Then the LORD said to Moses, "Pharaōh's heart is hardened, he refuses to let the people go. 15 Go to Pharaōh in the morning, as

7.15
ver 10;
Ex 4.2,3

he is going out to the water; wait for him by the river's brink, and take in your hand the rod which was turned into a serpent. 16And

7.16
Ex 3.12,18;
5.1,3

you shall say to him, 'The LORD, the God of the Hebrews, sent me to you, saying, "Let my people go, that they may serve me in the wilderness; and behold, you have not yet obeyed." 17 Thus

7.17
ver 5;
Ex 5.2;4.9;
Rev 11.6;
16.4,6

says the LORD, "By this you shall know that I am the LORD: behold, I will strike the water that is in the Nile with the rod that is in my hand, and it shall be turned to blood, 18 and the fish in the

7.18
ver 21,24

Nile shall die, and the Nile shall become foul, and the Egyptians

7.19
Ex 8.5,6,16;
9.22;
10.12,21;
14.21,26

will loathe to drink water from the Nile." ' " 19And the LORD said to Moses, "Say to Aaron, 'Take your rod and stretch out your hand over the waters of Egypt, over their rivers, their canals, and their ponds, and all their pools of water, that they may become blood; and there shall be blood throughout all the land of Egypt, both in vessels of wood and in vessels of stone.' "

7.20
Ps 78.44;
105.29

20 Moses and Aaron did as the LORD commanded; in the sight of Pharaōh and in the sight of his servants, he lifted up the rod and struck the water that was in the Nile, and all the water that was in

7.21
ver 18

the Nile turned to blood. 21And the fish in the Nile died; and the Nile became foul, so that the Egyptians could not drink water from the Nile; and there was blood throughout all the land of Egypt.

7.22
ver 11;
Ex 8.7

22 But the magicians of Egypt did the same by their secret arts; so Pharaōh's heart remained hardened, and he would not listen to them; as the LORD had said. 23 Pharaōh turned and went into his house, and he did not lay even this to heart. 24And all the Egyptians dug round about the Nile for water to drink, for they could not drink the water of the Nile.

7.12 Two miracles are here recorded. The first occurred when Aaron's rod became a serpent, only to be challenged by a counter-miracle when the rods of the Egyptians also became serpents. But the supreme power of God was demonstrated when (second miracle) Aaron's serpent swallowed the serpents of the Egyptians.

c. *The plague of frogs*

25 Seven days passed after the LORD had struck the Nile.
8 ⁱ 1 Then the LORD said to Moses, "Go in to Pharaōh and say to
him, 'Thus says the LORD, "Let my people go, that they may
serve me. 2 But if you refuse to let them go, behold, I will plague
all your country with frogs; 3 the Nile shall swarm with frogs
which shall come up into your house, and into your bedchamber
and on your bed, and into the houses of your servants and of your
people,^j and into your ovens and your kneading bowls; 4 the frogs
shall come up on you and on your people and on all your servants." ' " 5k And the LORD said to Aaron, "Stretch
out your hand with your rod over the rivers, over the canals, and
over the pools, and cause frogs to come upon the land of Egypt!' "
6 So Aaron stretched out his hand over the waters of Egypt; and
the frogs came up and covered the land of Egypt. 7 But the magicians did the same by their secret arts, and brought frogs upon
the land of Egypt.

8 Then Pharaōh called Moses and Aaron, and said, "Entreat
the LORD to take away the frogs from me and from my people; and
I will let the people go to sacrifice to the LORD." 9 Moses said to
Pharaōh, "Be pleased to command me when I am to entreat, for
you and for your servants and for your people, that the frogs be
destroyed from you and your houses and be left only in the Nile."
10And he said, "Tomorrow." Moses said, "Be it as you say, that
you may know that there is no one like the LORD our God. 11 The
frogs shall depart from you and your houses and your servants and
your people; they shall be left only in the Nile." 12 So Moses
and Aaron went out from Pharaōh; and Moses cried to the LORD
concerning the frogs, as he had agreed with Pharaoh.^l 13And the
LORD did according to the word of Moses; the frogs died out of
the houses and courtyards and out of the fields. 14And they gathered them together in heaps, and the land stank. 15 But when
Pharaōh saw that there was a respite, he hardened his heart, and
would not listen to them; as the LORD had said.

d. *The plague of gnats*

16 Then the LORD said to Moses, "Say to Aaron, 'Stretch out
your rod and strike the dust of the earth, that it may become gnats
throughout all the land of Egypt.' " 17And they did so; Aáron
stretched out his hand with his rod, and struck the dust of the
earth, and there came gnats on man and beast; all the dust of the
earth became gnats throughout all the land of Egypt. 18 The
magicians tried by their secret arts to bring forth gnats, but they
could not. So there were gnats on man and beast. 19And the
magicians said to Pharaōh, "This is the finger of God." But
Pharaōh's heart was hardened, and he would not listen to them;
as the LORD had said.

i Ch 7.26 in Heb *j* Gk: Heb *upon your people*
k Ch 8.1 in Heb *l* Or *which he had brought upon Pharaoh*

Side references:
8.1 Ex 3.12,18
8.3 Ps 105.30
8.5 Ex 7.19
8.6 Ps 78.45; 105.30
8.7 Ex 7.11
8.8 ver 25,28; Ex 9.27,28; 10.17
8.10 Ex 9.14; Deut 33.26; Ps 86.8; Isa 46.9; Jer 10.6,7
8.12 ver 30; Ex 9.33; 10.18
8.15 Ex 7.4
8.17 Ps 105.31
8.18 Ex 7.11
*8.19 Ex 7.5; 10.7

8.19 The magicians of Pharaoh were at
last convinced that Moses and Aaron were
truly from God, because they themselves
could no longer reproduce the miracles of
Moses and Aaron. Yet the heart of Pharaoh
remained as stone, demonstrating the obsti-
nacy of the rebellious human heart which
remains unconvinced of the truth of God's
Word, even in the face of overwhelming
evidence.

e. The swarms of flies

8.20
Ex 9.13;
7.15; ver 1

20 Then the LORD said to Moses, "Rise up early in the morning and wait for Phạraōh, as he goes out to the water, and say to him, 'Thus says the LORD, "Let my people go, that they may serve me. 21 Else, if you will not let my people go, behold, I will send swarms of flies on you and your servants and your people, and into your houses; and the houses of the Egyptians shall be filled with swarms of flies, and also the ground on which they stand.

8.22
Ex 9.4,6,26;
10.23;
11.6,7

22 But on that day I will set apart the land of Gōshèn, where my people dwell, so that no swarms of flies shall be there; that you may know that I am the LORD in the midst of the earth. 23 Thus I will put a division^m between my people and your people. By tomorrow shall this sign be." ' " 24And the LORD did so; there came great swarms of flies into the house of Phạraōh and into his servants' houses, and in all the land of Egypt the land was ruined by reason of the flies.

8.24
Ps 78.45;
105.31

25 Then Phạraōh called Moses and Aaron, and said, "Go, sacrifice to your God within the land." 26 But Moses said, "It would not be right to do so; for we shall sacrifice to the LORD our God offerings abominable to the Egyptians. If we sacrifice offerings abominable to the Egyptians before their eyes, will they not stone us? 27 We must go three days' journey into the wilderness and sacrifice to the LORD our God as he will command us." 28 So Phạraōh said, "I will let you go, to sacrifice to the LORD your God in the wilderness; only you shall not go very far away. Make entreaty for me." 29 Then Moses said, "Behold, I am going out from you and I will pray to the LORD that the swarms of flies may depart from Phạraōh, from his servants, and from his people, tomorrow; only let not Pharaoh deal falsely again by not letting the people go to sacrifice to the LORD." 30 So Moses went out from Phạraōh and prayed to the LORD. 31And the LORD did as Moses asked, and removed the swarms of flies from Phạraōh, from his servants, and from his people; not one remained. 32 But Phạraōh hardened his heart this time also, and did not let the people go.

8.27
Ex 3.18;
5.3
8.28
ver 8,15,29,
32
8.29
ver 8,15

8.32
ver 8,15;
Ex 4.21

f. The death of the Egyptian cattle

9.1
Ex 8.1

9 Then the LORD said to Moses, "Go in to Phạraōh, and say to him, 'Thus says the LORD, the God of the Hebrews, "Let my people go, that they may serve me. 2 For if you refuse to let them go and still hold them, 3 behold, the hand of the LORD will fall with a very severe plague upon your cattle which are in the field, the horses, the asses, the camels, the herds, and the flocks. 4 But the LORD will make a distinction between the cattle of Israel and the cattle of Egypt, so that nothing shall die of all that belongs to the people of Israel." ' " 5And the LORD set a time, saying, "Tomorrow the LORD will do this thing in the land." 6And on the morrow the LORD did this thing; all the cattle of the Eygptians died, but of the cattle of the people of Israel not one died. 7And Phạraōh sent, and behold, not one of the cattle of the Israelites was dead. But the heart of Pharaoh was hardened, and he did not let the people go.

9.2
Ex 8.2

9.4
Ex 8.22

9.6
Ex 11.5;
ver 4
9.7
Ex 7.14;
8.32

g. The boils and sores

8 And the LORD said to Moses and Aaron, "Take handfuls of

---

m Gk Vg: Heb set redemption

ashes from the kiln, and let Moses throw them toward heaven in the sight of Pharaōh. 9And it shall become fine dust over all the land of Egypt, and become boils breaking out in sores on man and beast throughout all the land of Egypt." 10 So they took ashes from the kiln, and stood before Pharaōh, and Moses threw them toward heaven, and it became boils breaking out in sores on man and beast. 11And the magicians could not stand before Moses because of the boils, for the boils were upon the magicians and upon all the Egyptians. 12 But the LORD hardened the heart of Pharaōh, and he did not listen to them; as the LORD had spoken to Moses.

h. *The hail and fire*

13 Then the LORD said to Moses, "Rise up early in the morning and stand before Pharaōh, and say to him, 'Thus says the LORD, the God of the Hebrews, "Let my people go, that they may serve me. 14 For this time I will send all my plagues upon your heart, and upon your servants and your people, that you may know that there is none like me in all the earth. 15 For by now I could have put forth my hand and struck you and your people with pestilence, and you would have been cut off from the earth; 16 but for this purpose have I let you live, to show you my power, so that my name may be declared throughout all the earth. 17 You are still exalting yourself against my people, and will not let them go. 18 Behold, tomorrow about this time I will cause very heavy hail to fall, such as never has been in Egypt from the day it was founded until now. 19 Now therefore send, get your cattle and all that you have in the field into safe shelter; for the hail shall come down upon every man and beast that is in the field and is not brought home, and they shall die." ' " 20 Then he who feared the word of the LORD among the servants of Pharaōh made his slaves and his cattle flee into the houses; 21 but he who did not regard the word of the LORD left his slaves and his cattle in the field.

22 And the LORD said to Moses, "Stretch forth your hand toward heaven, that there may be hail in all the land of Egypt, upon man and beast and every plant of the field, throughout the land of Egypt." 23 Then Moses stretched forth his rod toward heaven; and the LORD sent thunder and hail, and fire ran down to the earth. And the LORD rained hail upon the land of Egypt; 24 there was hail, and fire flashing continually in the midst of the hail, very heavy hail, such as had never been in all the land of Egypt since it became a nation. 25 The hail struck down everything that was in the field throughout all the land of Egypt, both man and beast; and the hail struck down every plant of the field, and shattered every tree of the field. 26 Only in the land of Gōshen, where the people of Israel were, there was no hail.

27 Then Pharaōh sent, and called Moses and Aaron, and said to them, "I have sinned this time; the LORD is in the right, and I and my people are in the wrong. 28 Entreat the LORD; for there has been enough of this thunder and hail; I will let you go, and you shall stay no longer." 29 Moses said to him, "As soon as I have gone out of the city, I will stretch out my hands to the LORD; the thunder will cease, and there will be no more hail, that you may know that the earth is the LORD's. 30 But as for you and your servants, I know that you do not yet fear the LORD God." 31 (The flax and the barley were ruined, for the barley was in the ear and the

9.9
Rev 16.2

9.12
Ex 4.21

9.13
Ex 8.20

9.14
Ex 8.10

9.15
Ex 3.20

9.16
Rom 9.17

9.18
ver 23,24

9.20
Prov 13.13

9.22
Rev 16.21

9.23
Gen 19.24;
Josh 10.11;
Ps 78.47;
Isa 30.30;
Ezek 38.22;
Rev 8.7

9.25
ver 19;
Ps 78.47;
105.32,33

9.26
Ex 8.22;
9.4,6;
10.23;
11.7; 12.13

9.27
Ex 8.8;
10.16,17;
2 Chr 12.6;
Ps 129.4

9.28
Ex 8.8;
10.17

9.29
1 Ki 8.22;
Ps 143.6;
Ex 8.22;
19.5;
20.11;
Ps 24.1

flax was in bud. 32 But the wheat and the spelt were not ruined, for
they are late in coming up.) 33 So Moses went out of the city from
Pharaōh, and stretched out his hands to the LORD; and the thunder
and the hail ceased, and the rain no longer poured upon the earth.
34 But when Pharaōh saw that the rain and the hail and the thunder
had ceased, he sinned yet again, and hardened his heart, he and

9.35
Ex 4.21

his servants. 35 So the heart of Pharaōh was hardened, and he did
not let the people of Israel go; as the LORD had spoken through
Moses.

i. *The plague of locusts*

10.1
Ex 4.21;
7.14

10 Then the LORD said to Moses, "Go in to Pharaōh; for I
have hardened his heart and the heart of his servants, that
I may show these signs of mine among them, 2 and that you may

10.2
Ex 12.26,
27;
13.8,14,15;
Deut 4.9;
Ps 44.1;
Ex 7.5,15

tell in the hearing of your son and of your son's son how I have
made sport of the Egyptians and what signs I have done among
them; that you may know that I am the LORD."

10.3
Jas 4.10;
1 Pet 5.6;
Ex 4.23

3 So Moses and Aaron went in to Pharaōh, and said to him,
"Thus says the LORD, the God of the Hebrews, 'How long will
you refuse to humble yourself before me? Let my people go, that

10.4
Rev 9.3

they may serve me. 4 For if you refuse to let my people go, behold,
tomorrow I will bring locusts into your country, 5 and they shall

10.5
Ex 9.32;
Joel 1.4;
2.25

cover the face of the land, so that no one can see the land; and they
shall eat what is left to you after the hail, and they shall eat every
tree of yours which grows in the field, 6 and they shall fill your

10.6
Ex 8.3,21

houses, and the houses of all your servants and of all the Egyptians;
as neither your fathers nor your grandfathers have seen, from the
day they came on earth to this day.' " Then he turned and went
out from Pharaōh.

10.7
Ex 7.5;
8.19;
12.33

7 And Pharaōh's servants said to him, "How long shall this
man be a snare to us? Let the men go, that they may serve the
LORD their God; do you not yet understand that Egypt is ruined?"

10.8
Ex 8.8,25

8 So Moses and Aaron were brought back to Pharaōh; and he said

10.9
Ex 12.37,
38;
ver 26;
Ex 5.1

to them, "Go, serve the LORD your God; but who are to go?" 9And
Moses said, "We will go with our young and our old; we will go
with our sons and daughters and with our flocks and herds, for we
must hold a feast to the LORD." 10And he said to them, "The LORD

10.11
ver 28

be with you, if ever I let you and your little ones go! Look, you
have some evil purpose in mind.[n] 11 No! Go, the men among you,
and serve the LORD, for that is what you desire." And they were
driven out from Pharaōh's presence.

10.12
Ex 7.19;
ver 4,5

12 Then the LORD said to Moses, "Stretch out your hand over
the land of Egypt for the locusts, that they may come upon the
land of Egypt, and eat every plant in the land, all that the hail has
left." 13 So Moses stretched forth his rod over the land of Egypt,
and the LORD brought an east wind upon the land all that day
and all that night; and when it was morning the east wind had

10.14
Ps 78.46;
105.34;
Joel 2.1–11

brought the locusts. 14And the locusts came up over all the land
of Egypt, and settled on the whole country of Egypt, such a dense
swarm of locusts as had never been before, nor ever shall be again.

10.15
ver 5;
Ps 105.35

15 For they covered the face of the whole land, so that the land was
darkened, and they ate all the plants in the land and all the fruit
of the trees which the hail had left; not a green thing remained,
neither tree nor plant of the field, through all the land of Egypt.

n Heb *before your face*

16 Then Pharaōh called Moses and Aaron in haste, and said, "I
have sinned against the LORD your God, and against you. 17 Now
therefore, forgive my sin, I pray you, only this once, and entreat
the LORD your God only to remove this death from me." 18 So he
went out from Pharaōh, and entreated the LORD. 19And the LORD
turned a very strong west wind, which lifted the locusts and drove
them into the Red Sea; not a single locust was left in all the country
of Egypt. 20 But the LORD hardened Pharaōh's heart, and he did
not let the children of Israel go.

j. The three days' darkness

21 Then the LORD said to Moses, "Stretch out your hand toward heaven that there may be darkness over the land of Egypt,
a darkness to be felt." 22 So Moses stretched out his hand toward
heaven, and there was thick darkness in all the land of Egypt three
days; 23 they did not see one another, nor did any rise from his
place for three days; but all the people of Israel had light where
they dwelt. 24 Then Pharaōh called Moses, and said, "Go, serve the
LORD; your children also may go with you; only let your flocks and
your herds remain behind." 25 But Moses said, "You must also
let us have sacrifices and burnt offerings, that we may sacrifice to
the LORD our God. 26 Our cattle also must go with us; not a hoof
shall be left behind, for we must take of them to serve the LORD
our God, and we do not know with what we must serve the LORD
until we arrive there." 27 But the LORD hardened Pharaōh's heart,
and he would not let them go. 28 Then Pharaōh said to him, "Get
away from me; take heed to yourself; never see my face again; for
in the day you see my face you shall die." 29 Moses said, "As you
say! I will not see your face again."

k. The death of the first-born
(1) THE ANNOUNCEMENT BY GOD

11 The LORD said to Moses, "Yet one plague more I will
bring upon Pharaōh and upon Egypt; afterwards he will let
you go hence; when he lets you go, he will drive you away completely. 2 Speak now in the hearing of the people, that they ask,
every man of his neighbor and every woman of her neighbor,
jewelry of silver and of gold." 3And the LORD gave the people
favor in the sight of the Egyptians. Moreover, the man Moses
was very great in the land of Egypt, in the sight of Pharaōh's
servants and in the sight of the people.
4 And Moses said, "Thus says the LORD: About midnight I
will go forth in the midst of Egypt; 5 and all the first-born in the
land of Egypt shall die, from the first-born of Pharaōh who sits
upon his throne, even to the first-born of the maidservant who is
behind the mill; and all the first-born of the cattle. 6And there
shall be a great cry throughout all the land of Egypt, such as there
has never been, nor ever shall be again. 7 But against any of the
people of Israel, either man or beast, not a dog shall growl; that
you may know that the LORD makes a distinction between the
Egyptians and Israel. 8And all these your servants shall come down
to me, and bow down to me, saying, 'Get you out, and all the
people who follow you.' And after that I will go out." And he
went out from Pharaōh in hot anger. 9 Then the LORD said to
Moses, "Pharaōh will not listen to you; that my wonders may
be multiplied in the land of Egypt."

10.16 Ex 9.27
10.17 Ex 8.8,29
10.20 Ex 4.21; 11.10
10.21 Deut 28.29
10.22 Ps 105.28
10.24 ver 8,10
10.26 ver 9
10.27 ver 20
10.28 ver 11
10.29 Heb 11.27
11.1 Ex 12.31,33,39
11.2 Ex 3.22; 12.35,36
11.3 Ex 3.21; 12.36; Deut 34.10-12
11.4 Ex 12.29
11.5 Ex 12.12,29; Ps 78.51; 105.36; 135.8; 136.10
11.6 Ex 12.30
11.7 Ex 8.22
11.8 Ex 12.31-33
11.9 Ex 7.3,4

11.10 Ex 4.21; 10.20,27	10 Moses and Aaron did all these wonders before Phạraōh; and the LORD hardened Phạraōh'ş heart, and he did not let the people of Israel go out of his land.

(2) THE INSTITUTION OF THE PASSOVER

★12.2
Ex 13.4;
Deut 16.1
★12.3

12 The LORD said to Moses and Aaron in the land of Egypt, 2 "This month shall be for you the beginning of months; it shall be the first month of the year for you. 3 Tell all the congregation of Israel that on the tenth day of this month they shall take every man a lamb according to their fathers' houses, a lamb for a household; 4 and if the household is too small for a lamb, then a man and his neighbor next to his house shall take according to the number of persons; according to what each can eat you shall make

12.5
Lev 22.18–
20
12.6
Lev 23.5;
Num 9.3;
Deut 16.1,6

your count for the lamb. 5 Your lamb shall be without blemish, a male a year old; you shall take it from the sheep or from the goats; 6 and you shall keep it until the fourteenth day of this month, when the whole assembly of the congregation of Israel shall kill their lambs in the evening.ᵒ 7 Then they shall take some of the blood, and put it on the two doorposts and the lintel of the houses in which they eat them. 8 They shall eat the flesh that night,

12.8
Ex 34.25;
Num 9.11,
12;
Deut 16.7
12.10
Ex 23.18;
34.25
★12.11
ver 27

roasted; with unleavened bread and bitter herbs they shall eat it. 9 Do not eat any of it raw or boiled with water, but roasted, its head with its legs and its inner parts. 10 And you shall let none of it remain until the morning, anything that remains until the morning you shall burn. 11 In this manner you shall eat it: your loins girded, your sandals on your feet, and your staff in your hand; and you shall eat it in haste. It is the LORD'S passover. 12 For I

12.12
Ex 11.4,5;
Num 33.4

will pass through the land of Egypt that night, and I will smite all the first-born in the land of Egypt, both man and beast; and on all the gods of Egypt I will execute judgments: I am the LORD. 13 The blood shall be a sign for you, upon the houses where you are; and when I see the blood, I will pass over you, and no plague shall fall upon you to destroy you, when I smite the land of Egypt.

12.14
ver 6;
Ex 13.9;
ver 17;
Ex 13.10
12.15
Ex 23.15;
34.18;
Lev 23.5,6;
Deut 16.3;
ver 19;
Num 9.13
12.16
Lev 23.7,8
12.17
ver 41;
Ex 13.3

14 "This day shall be for you a memorial day, and you shall keep it as a feast to the LORD; throughout your generations you shall observe it as an ordinance for ever. 15 Seven days you shall eat unleavened bread; on the first day you shall put away leaven out of your houses, for if any one eats what is leavened, from the first day until the seventh day, that person shall be cut off from Israel. 16 On the first day you shall hold a holy assembly, and on the seventh day a holy assembly; no work shall be done on those days; but what every one must eat, that only may be prepared by you. 17 And you shall observe the feast of unleavened bread, for on this very day I brought your hosts out of the land of Egypt: therefore you shall observe this day, throughout your generations, as an

ᵒ Heb between the two evenings

12.2 *first month of the year*, Nisan, the latter part of March and the first of April.
12.3 The lamb had to be without blemish. It was to be slain and its blood applied. It was offered as a substitute. Christ met all of these requirements; he was the perfect Lamb of God (Jn 1.29), who delivered his people from the tyranny of sin, a greater oppressor than Pharaoh.
12.11 On that Passover night the angel of

death had respect only for those households over whose doors the blood had been sprinkled (12.13). The works and characters of the individual believers had nothing to do with its saving benefit. It was the blood alone which authorized the death angel to pass over. So Christ is the perfect sacrifice, slain and offered. When His blood is personally applied by faith, the sinner is declared righteous and his sins are forgiven (Rom 3.22; 1 Pet 1.18,19).

ordinance for ever. 18 In the first month, on the fourteenth day of the month at evening, you shall eat unleavened bread, and so until the twenty-first day of the month at evening. 19 For seven days no leaven shall be found in your houses; for if any one eats what is leavened, that person shall be cut off from the congregation of Israel, whether he is a sojourner or a native of the land. 20 You shall eat nothing leavened; in all your dwellings you shall eat unleavened bread."

21 Then Moses called all the elders of Israel, and said to them, "Select lambs for yourselves according to your families, and kill the passover lamb. 22 Take a bunch of hyssop and dip it in the blood which is in the basin, and touch the lintel and the two doorposts with the blood which is in the basin; and none of you shall go out of the door of his house until the morning. 23 For the LORD will pass through to slay the Egyptians; and when he sees the blood on the lintel and on the two doorposts, the LORD will pass over the door, and will not allow the destroyer to enter your houses to slay you. 24 You shall observe this rite as an ordinance for you and for your sons for ever. 25And when you come to the land which the LORD will give you, as he has promised, you shall keep this service. 26And when your children say to you, 'What do you mean by this service?' 27 you shall say, 'It is the sacrifice of the LORD's passover, for he passed over the houses of the people of Israel in Egypt, when he slew the Egyptians but spared our houses.' " And the people bowed their heads and worshiped.

28 Then the people of Israel went and did so; as the LORD had commanded Moses and Aaron, so they did.

(3) THE FIRST-BORN KILLED

29 At midnight the LORD smote all the first-born in the land of Egypt, from the first-born of Phạraōh who sat on his throne to the first-born of the captive who was in the dungeon, and all the first-born of the cattle. 30And Phạraōh rose up in the night, he, and all his servants, and all the Egyptians; and there was a great cry in Egypt, for there was not a house where one was not dead. 31And he summoned Moses and Aaron by night, and said, "Rise up, go forth from among my people, both you and the people of Israel; and go, serve the LORD, as you have said. 32 Take your flocks and your herds, as you have said, and be gone; and bless me also!"

33 And the Egyptians were urgent with the people, to send them out of the land in haste; for they said, "We are all dead men." 34 So the people took their dough before it was leavened, their kneading bowls being bound up in their mantles on their shoulders. 35 The people of Israel had also done as Moses told them, for they had asked of the Egyptians jewelry of silver and of gold, and clothing; 36 and the LORD had given the people favor in the sight of the Egyptians, so that they let them have what they asked. Thus they despoiled the Egyptians.

D. The exodus begun

1. The unleavened bread

37 And the people of Israel journeyed from Răm'ĕsĕṣ to Sŭc'-cŏth, about six hundred thousand men on foot, besides women

---

12.18
ver 2;
Lev 23.5–8;
Num
28.16–25
12.19
ver 15

12.21
Heb 11.28;
ver 11;
Num 9.4
12.22
ver 7
12.23
ver 12,13

12.24
Ex 13.5,10

12.26
Ex 13.14,
15;
Josh 4.6
12.27
ver 11;
Ex 4.31

12.29
Ex 11.4;
4.23; 9.6;
Ps 78.51;
105.36
12.30
Ex 11.6
12.31
Ex 8.8,25

12.32
Ex 10.9,26

12.33
ver 39;
Ex 10.7;
11.1;
Ps 105.38

12.35
Ex 3.21,22;
11.2,3
12.36
Ex 3.22

12.37
Num 33.3,
4;
Ex 38.26;
Num 1.46;
11.21

12.38
Num 11.4;
Ex 17.3
12.39
ver 31–33;
Ex 11.1

12.40
Gen 15.13;
Acts 7.6;
Gal 3.17
12.41
ver 17;
Ex 3.8,10;
6.6
12.42
Ex 13.10;
Deut 16.1

12.43
ver 11,48
12.44
Gen 17.12,
13;
Lev 22.11
12.46
Num 9.12;
Jn 19.33,36
12.47
Num 9.13,
14

12.49
Num 15.15,
16;
Gal 3.28
12.51
ver 41
13.2
ver 12,13,
15;
Ex 22.29;
Lk 2.23

13.3
Ex 3.20;
6.1; 12.19

13.5
Ex 3.8;
12.25,26

13.6
Ex 12.15–20

13.8
ver 14;
Ex 10.2
13.9
ver 16;
Ex 12.14;
Deut 6.8;
11.18
13.10
Ex 12.24,25

and children. 38A mixed multitude also went up with them, and very many cattle, both flocks and herds. 39And they baked unleavened cakes of the dough which they had brought out of Egypt, for it was not leavened, because they were thrust out of Egypt and could not tarry, neither had they prepared for themselves any provisions.

40 The time that the people of Israel dwelt in Egypt was four hundred and thirty years. 41And at the end of four hundred and thirty years, on that very day, all the hosts of the LORD went out from the land of Egypt. 42 It was a night of watching by the LORD, to bring them out of the land of Egypt; so this same night is a night of watching kept to the LORD by all the people of Israel throughout their generations.

2. The law of the Passover

43 And the LORD said to Moses and Aaron, "This is the ordinance of the passover: no foreigner shall eat of it; 44 but every slave that is bought for money may eat of it after you have circumcised him. 45 No sojourner or hired servant may eat of it. 46 In one house shall it be eaten; you shall not carry forth any of the flesh outside the house; and you shall not break a bone of it. 47All the congregation of Israel shall keep it. 48And when a stranger shall sojourn with you and would keep the passover to the LORD, let all his males be circumcised, then he may come near and keep it; he shall be as a native of the land. But no uncircumcised person shall eat of it. 49 There shall be one law for the native and for the stranger who sojourns among you."

50 Thus did all the people of Israel; as the LORD commanded Moses and Aaron, so they did. 51And on that very day the LORD brought the people of Israel out of the land of Egypt by their hosts.

13 The LORD said to Moses, 2 "Consecrate to me all the first-born; whatever is the first to open the womb among the people of Israel, both of man and of beast, is mine."

3. The speech of Moses

3 And Moses said to the people, "Remember this day, in which you came out from Egypt, out of the house of bondage, for by strength of hand the LORD brought you out from this place; no leavened bread shall be eaten. 4 This day you are to go forth, in the month of Ābīb. 5And when the LORD brings you into the land of the Cā'naánites, the Hĭttītes, the Ăm'órītes, the Hĭvītes, and the Jĕb'ūsītes, which he swore to your fathers to give you, a land flowing with milk and honey, you shall keep this service in this month. 6 Seven days you shall eat unleavened bread, and on the seventh day there shall be a feast to the LORD. 7 Unleavened bread shall be eaten for seven days; no leavened bread shall be seen with you, and no leaven shall be seen with you in all your territory. 8And you shall tell your son on that day, 'It is because of what the LORD did for me when I came out of Egypt.' 9And it shall be to you as a sign on your hand and as a memorial between your eyes, that the law of the LORD may be in your mouth; for with a strong hand the LORD has brought you out of Egypt. 10 You shall therefore keep this ordinance at its appointed time from year to year.

11 "And when the LORD brings you into the land of the Cā'-naänītes, as he swore to you and your fathers, and shall give it to you, 12 you shall set apart to the LORD all that first opens the womb. All the firstlings of your cattle that are males shall be the LORD's. 13 Every firstling of an ass you shall redeem with a lamb, or if you will not redeem it you shall break its neck. Every first-born of man among your sons you shall redeem. 14And when in time to come your son asks you, 'What does this mean?' you shall say to him, 'By strength of hand the LORD brought us out of Egypt, from the house of bondage. 15 For when Pharaōh stubbornly refused to let us go, the LORD slew all the first-born in the land of Egypt, both the first-born of man and the first-born of cattle. Therefore I sacrifice to the LORD all the males that first open the womb; but all the first-born of my sons I redeem.' 16 It shall be as a mark on your hand or frontlets between your eyes; for by a strong hand the LORD brought us out of Egypt."

4. *The pillar of cloud and of fire*

17 When Pharaōh let the people go, God did not lead them by way of the land of the Philis'tines, although that was near; for God said, "Lest the people repent when they see war, and return to Egypt." 18 But God led the people round by the way of the wilderness toward the Red Sea. And the people of Israel went up out of the land of Egypt equipped for battle. 19And Moses took the bones of Joseph with him; for Joseph had solemnly sworn the people of Israel, saying, "God will visit you; then you must carry my bones with you from here." 20And they moved on from Succoth, and encamped at Ētham, on the edge of the wilderness. 21And the LORD went before them by day in a pillar of cloud to lead them along the way, and by night in a pillar of fire to give them light, that they might travel by day and by night; 22 the pillar of cloud by day and the pillar of fire by night did not depart from before the people.

5. *Crossing the Red Sea*

14 Then the LORD said to Moses, 2 "Tell the people of Israel to turn back and encamp in front of Pī'hà-hī'ròth, between Migdōl and the sea, in front of Bā'àl-zēphōn; you shall encamp over against it, by the sea. 3 For Pharaōh will say of the people of Israel, 'They are entangled in the land; the wilderness has shut them in.' 4And I will harden Pharaōh's heart, and he will pursue them and I will get glory over Pharaōh and all his host; and the Egyptians shall know that I am the LORD." And they did so.

5 When the king of Egypt was told that the people had fled, the mind of Pharaōh and his servants was changed toward the people, and they said, "What is this we have done, that we have let Israel

---

13.12
ver 2;
Ex 22.29;
34.19
13.13
Ex 34.20;
Num 18.15,
16
13.14
Ex 12.26,
27;
Deut 6.20;
ver 3,9
13.15
Ex 12.29

13.16
ver 9

13.17
Ex 14.11,
12;
Num 14.1–
4;
Deut 17.16
13.19
Gen 50.25,
26;
Josh 24.32;
Acts 7.16
13.20
Num 33.6–
8
★**13.21f**
Ex 14.19,
24;
33.9,10;
Ps 78.14;
105.39;
1 Cor 10.1

14.2
Num 33.7,8

14.4
ver 17;
Ex 4.21;
7.5

★**14.5**

13.21, 22 The cloud of glory, which later became known as the *Shekinah* ("abiding," or "dwelling") was called by various names in the Old Testament: *my glory* (*kabod*) (29.43); *the cloud* (34.5); *the pillar of cloud* (33.9, 10); *the cloud of fire* (Num 10.34); *my presence* (33.14, 15). The purposes of the *Shekinah* were various: (1) to guide Israel (13.21; Neh 9.19); (2) to control the movements of Israel in the wilderness until they were settled in the land (40.36, 37; Num 9.17–25); (3) to defend Israel (14.19; Ps 105.39). The cloud of glory appeared at other times both in the Old and New Testaments. Of particular significance is its appearance at the Transfiguration (Mt 17.5) and the Ascension (Acts 1.9). At His Second Advent Christ will come *in a cloud with power and great glory* (Lk 21.27; cf. Acts 1.11).
14.5 *had fled*, i.e., permitted to leave.

go from serving us?" 6 So he made ready his chariot and took his army with him, 7 and took six hundred picked chariots and all the other chariots of Egypt with officers over all of them. 8And the LORD hardened the heart of Phạraōh king of Egypt and he pursued the people of Israel as they went forth defiantly. 9 The Egyptians pursued them, all Phạraōh'ş horses and chariots and his horsemen and his army, and overtook them encamped at the sea, by Pī'hȧ-hī'rŏth, in front of Bā'ȧl-zëphŏn.

10 When Phạraōh drew near, the people of Israel lifted up their eyes, and behold, the Egyptians were marching after them; and they were in great fear. And the people of Israel cried out to the LORD; 11 and they said to Moses, "Is it because there are no graves in Egypt that you have taken us away to die in the wilderness? What have you done to us, in bringing us out of Egypt? 12 Is not this what we said to you in Egypt, 'Let us alone and let us serve the Egyptians'? For it would have been better for us to serve the Egyptians than to die in the wilderness." 13And Moses said to the people, "Fear not, stand firm, and see the salvation of the LORD, which he will work for you today; for the Egyptians whom you see today, you shall never see again. 14 The LORD will fight for you, and you have only to be still." 15 The LORD said to Moses, "Why do you cry to me? Tell the people of Israel to go forward. 16 Lift up your rod, and stretch out your hand over the sea and divide it, that the people of Israel may go on dry ground through the sea. 17And I will harden the hearts of the Egyptians so that they shall go in after them, and I will get glory over Phạraōh and all his host, his chariots, and his horsemen. 18And the Egyptians shall know that I am the LORD, when I have gotten glory over Phạraōh, his chariots, and his horsemen."

19 Then the angel of God who went before the host of Israel moved and went behind them; and the pillar of cloud moved from before them and stood behind them, 20 coming between the host of Egypt and the host of Israel. And there was the cloud and the darkness; and the night passed[p] without one coming near the other all night.

21 Then Moses stretched out his hand over the sea; and the LORD drove the sea back by a strong east wind all night, and made the sea dry land, and the waters were divided. 22And the people of Israel went into the midst of the sea on dry ground, the waters being a wall to them on their right hand and on their left. 23 The Egyptians pursued, and went in after them into the midst of the sea, all Phạraōh'ş horses, his chariots, and his horsemen. 24And in the morning watch the LORD in the pillar of fire and of cloud

p Gk: Heb and it lit up the night

Cross-references (left margin):

14.8 ver 4; Num 33.3; Acts 13.17

*14.9 Ex 15.9

14.10 Neh 9.9

14.11 Ps 106.7,8

*14.13 Gen 15.1; ver 30; Ex 15.2

14.14 Ex 15.3; Deut 1.30; 3.22; Isa 30.15

14.16 Ex 4.17; Num 20.8, 9,11; Isa 10.26

14.17 ver 4

14.18 ver 25

14.19 Ex 13.21,22

14.21 ver 16; Ps 106.9; 114.3,5; Isa 63.12,13

14.22 Ex 15.19; Neh 9.11; Heb 11.29

14.24 Ex 13.21

14.9 *sea.* The fortress towns named indicate that the "Red Sea" which the Israelites crossed was to the north of the Red Sea proper. The name would be more accurately translated "Reed Sea."

14.13 Almost from the beginning of the exodus, the children of Israel manifested a complaining spirit. They allowed circumstances to move them. It is true that the Red Sea was before them and the Pharaoh and his soldiers behind them, but they forgot God who was above them. Moses displayed his great faith in the delivering power of God, but even he failed to see how that power would operate. He told Israel to stand still and watch God intervene on their behalf. But then God told them to move forward in faith and against the waters of the sea. Moses used his rod; God parted the waters *by a strong east wind all night* (ver 21); and the children of Israel moved forward dry-shod. God does lead his children forward against apparently impassable barriers, opening doors previously shut fast.

looked down upon the host of the Egyptians, and discomfited the host of the Egyptians, 25 clogging[q] their chariot wheels so that they drove heavily; and the Egyptians said, "Let us flee from before Israel; for the LORD fights for them against the Egyptians."

26 Then the LORD said to Moses, "Stretch out your hand over the sea, that the water may come back upon the Egyptians, upon their chariots, and upon their horsemen." 27 So Moses stretched forth his hand over the sea, and the sea returned to its wonted flow when the morning appeared; and the Egyptians fled into it, and the LORD routed[r] the Egyptians in the midst of the sea. 28 The waters returned and covered the chariots and the horsemen and all the host[s] of Pharaōh that had followed them into the sea; not so much as one of them remained. 29 But the people of Israel walked on dry ground through the sea, the waters being a wall to them on their right hand and on their left.

30 Thus the LORD saved Israel that day from the hand of the Egyptians; and Israel saw the Egyptians dead upon the seashore. 31And Israel saw the great work which the LORD did against the Egyptians, and the people feared the LORD; and they believed in the LORD and in his servant Moses.

6. *The song of Moses*

15 Then Moses and the people of Israel sang this song to the LORD, saying,

"I will sing to the LORD, for he has triumphed gloriously;
the horse and his rider[t] he has thrown into the sea.

2 The LORD is my strength and my song,
and he has become my salvation;
this is my God, and I will praise him,
my father's God, and I will exalt him.

3 The LORD is a man of war;
the LORD is his name.

4 "Pharaōh's chariots and his host he cast into the sea;
and his picked officers are sunk in the Red Sea.

5 The floods cover them;
they went down into the depths like a stone.

6 Thy right hand, O LORD, glorious in power,
thy right hand, O LORD, shatters the enemy.

7 In the greatness of thy majesty thou overthrowest thy adversaries;
thou sendest forth thy fury, it consumes them like stubble.

8 At the blast of thy nostrils the waters piled up,
the floods stood up in a heap;
the deeps congealed in the heart of the sea.

9 The enemy said, 'I will pursue, I will overtake,
I will divide the spoil, my desire shall have its fill of them.
I will draw my sword, my hand shall destroy them.'

10 Thou didst blow with thy wind, the sea covered them;
they sank as lead in the mighty waters.

Cross-references (margin):

14.25 ver 4,18
14.27 Ex 15.1,7
14.28 Ps 78.53; 106.11
14.29 Ex 15.19; Neh 9.11; Heb 11.29
14.30 Ps 106.8
14.31 Ps 106.12
*15.1 Ps 106.12; Rev 15.3
15.2 Ps 59.17; Ex 3.15,16
15.3 Ps 24.8; 83.18
15.4 Ex 14.6,7, 17,28
15.5 ver 10; Neh 9.11
15.6 Ps 118.15
15.7 Ex 14.27; Ps 78.49,50
15.8 Ex 14.22, 29; Ps 78.13
15.9 Ex 14.5
15.10 Ex 14.28

---

[q] Or *binding*. Sam Gk Syr: Heb *removing*   [r] Heb *shook off*
[s] Gk Syr: Heb *to all the host*   [t] Or *its chariot*

15.1 Singing is an expression of love and thanksgiving, encouraged in Scripture with such phrases as *spiritual songs, singing ... melody* (Eph 5.19) and *song of the Lamb* (Rev 15.3).

*15.11
Ex 8.10;
Deut 3.24;
Isa 6.3;
Rev 4.8;
Ps 22.23;
72.18

11 "Who is like thee, O LORD, among the gods?
    Who is like thee, majestic in holiness,
    terrible in glorious deeds, doing wonders?
12 Thou didst stretch out thy right hand,
    the earth swallowed them.

15.13
Neh 9.12;
Ps 77.15;
78.54

13 "Thou hast led in thy steadfast love the people whom thou hast
    redeemed,
    thou hast guided them by thy strength to thy holy abode.

15.14
Deut 2.25;
Hab 3.7

14 The peoples have heard, they tremble;
    pangs have seized on the inhabitants of Phĭlĭs'tĭä.

15.15
Gen 36.15;
Num 22.3;
Josh 5.1

15 Now are the chiefs of Ēdŏm dismayed;
    the leaders of Mŏăb, trembling seizes them;
    all the inhabitants of Cānaăn have melted away.

15.16
Ex 23.27;
1 Sam 25.
37;
Ps 74.2

16 Terror and dread fall upon them;
    because of the greatness of thy arm, they are as still as a stone,
    till thy people, O LORD, pass by,
    till the people pass by whom thou hast purchased.

15.17
Ps 44.2;
78.54

17 Thou wilt bring them in, and plant them on thy own mountain,
    the place, O LORD, which thou hast made for thy abode,
    the sanctuary, O LORD, which thy hands have established.

15.18
Ps 10.16

18 The LORD will reign for ever and ever."

7. The song of Miriam

15.19
Ex 14.23,28

19 For when the horses of Phặraōh with his chariots and his
horsemen went into the sea, the LORD brought back the waters of
the sea upon them; but the people of Israel walked on dry ground
in the midst of the sea. 20 Then Miriam, the prophetess, the sister
of Aaron, took a timbrel in her hand; and all the women went out
after her with timbrels and dancing. 21And Miriam sang to them:
"Sing to the LORD, for he has triumphed gloriously;
    the horse and his rider he has thrown into the sea."

15.20
Judg 4.4;
Num 26.59;
1 Sam 18.6;
Ps 30.11;
150.4

15.21
ver 1

II. The journey to Sinai 15.22–18.27

A. The bitter waters of Marah made sweet

*15.22
Ps 77.20;
Num 33.8

*15.23
Num 33.8

15.24
Ex 14.11;
Ps 106.13

15.25
Ex 14.10;
Ps 50.15

22 Then Moses led Israel onward from the Red Sea, and they
went into the wilderness of Shŭr; they went three days in the
wilderness and found no water. 23 When they came to Marăh,
they could not drink the water of Marah because it was bitter;
therefore it was named Marah.ᵘ 24And the people murmured
against Moses, saying, "What shall we drink?" 25And he cried
to the LORD; and the LORD showed him a tree, and he threw it
into the water, and the water became sweet.

ᵘ That is Bitterness

15.11 One of the chief attributes of God is
His holiness, that is, His complete separation
from the finite, from frailty, and from all that
is sinful or impure. This holiness of the LORD
is incomparable (1 Sam 2.2). It may be seen
in His character (Ps 22.3), in His Name (Isa
57.15), and in His words (Jer 23.9). We are
to praise Him for His holiness (Ps 30.4) and
imitate it (Lev 11.44; 1 Pet 1.15, 16).
15.22 This was the end of the exodus.

15.23 The bitter waters of Marah provide
a spiritual lesson for believers. The pathway
of obedience may lead to adversity and
trouble which are not of the believer's
devising nor a consequence of his disobedience or sin. This was the case at Marah.
But here God had an opportunity to show
His mighty power to deliver, and to put His
children's faith to the test that it might be
strengthened by this experience.

There the LORD[v] made for them a statute and an ordinance and there he proved them, 26 saying, "If you will diligently hearken to the voice of the LORD your God, and do that which is right in his eyes, and give heed to his commandments and keep all his statutes, I will put none of the diseases upon you which I put upon the Egyptians; for I am the LORD, your healer."

15.26
Deut 7.12;
28.27

27 Then they came to Elim, where there were twelve springs of water and seventy palm trees; and they encamped there by the water.

15.27
Num 33.9,
10

B. The manna and the quail

1. The murmuring of the Israelites

16 They set out from Elim, and all the congregation of the people of Israel came to the wilderness of Sin, which is between Elim and Si'nai, on the fifteenth day of the second month after they had departed from the land of Egypt. 2And the whole congregation of the people of Israel murmured against Moses and Aaron in the wilderness, 3 and said to them, "Would that we had died by the hand of the LORD in the land of Egypt, when we sat by the fleshpots and ate bread to the full; for you have brought us out into this wilderness to kill this whole assembly with hunger."

16.1
Num 33.11,
12

*16.2
Ex 14.11;
1 Cor 10.10

16.3
Ex 17.3;
Num 11.4,5

2. God promises bread and meat

4 Then the LORD said to Moses, "Behold, I will rain bread from heaven for you; and the people shall go out and gather a day's portion every day, that I may prove them, whether they will walk in my law or not. 5 On the sixth day, when they prepare what they bring in, it will be twice as much as they gather daily." 6 So Moses and Aaron said to all the people of Israel, "At evening you shall know that it was the LORD who brought you out of the land of Egypt, 7 and in the morning you shall see the glory of the LORD, because he has heard your murmurings against the LORD. For what are we, that you murmur against us?" 8And Moses said, "When the LORD gives you in the evening flesh to eat and in the morning bread to the full, because the LORD has heard your murmurings which you murmur against him—what are we? Your murmurings are not against us but against the LORD."

16.4
Jn 6.31;
1 Cor 10.3;
Deut 8.2,16

16.5
ver 22

16.7
ver 12;
Num 14.27;
16.11

9 And Moses said to Aaron, "Say to the whole congregation of the people of Israel, 'Come near before the LORD, for he has heard your murmurings.' " 10And as Aaron spoke to the whole congregation of the people of Israel, they looked toward the wilderness, and behold, the glory of the LORD appeared in the cloud. 11And the LORD said to Moses, 12 "I have heard the murmurings of the people of Israel; say to them, 'At twilight you shall eat flesh, and in the morning you shall be filled with bread; then you shall know that I am the LORD your God.' "

16.9
Num 16.16

16.10
ver 7;
Num 16.19

3. God sends quail and gives bread

13 In the evening quails came up and covered the camp; and in the morning dew lay round about the camp. 14And when the dew had gone up, there was on the face of the wilderness a fine, flake-

16.13
Num 11.31;
Ps 78.27,
28; 105.40

16.14
Num 11.7-
9;
ver 31

[v] Heb he

16.2 *congregation . . . murmured.* This was the recurring sin of the Israelites—complain- | ing against God. It sprang from unbelief, from distrust of God.

16.15
ver 4

16.18
2 Cor 8.15

16.19
ver 23;
Ex 12.10;
23.18

16.22
ver 5;
Ex 34.31

16.23ff
Ex 20.8;
23.12

16.24
ver 20

16.28
Ps 78.10

16.31
Num
11.6–9

16.33
Heb 9.4

16.34
Ex 25.16,21

16.35
Josh 5.12;
Neh 9.20,21

like thing, fine as hoarfrost on the ground. 15 When the people of Israel saw it, they said to one another, "What is it?"ʷ For they did not know what it was. And Moses said to them, "It is the bread which the LORD has given you to eat. 16 This is what the LORD has commanded: 'Gather of it, every man of you, as much as he can eat; you shall take an omer apiece, according to the number of the persons whom each of you has in his tent.' " 17And the people of Israel did so; they gathered, some more, some less. 18 But when they measured it with an omer, he that gathered much had nothing over, and he that gathered little had no lack; each gathered according to what he could eat. 19And Moses said to them, "Let no man leave any of it till the morning." 20 But they did not listen to Moses; some left part of it till the morning, and it bred worms and became foul; and Moses was angry with them. 21 Morning by morning they gathered it, each as much as he could eat; but when the sun grew hot, it melted.

4. The Sabbath commandment

22 On the sixth day they gathered twice as much bread, two omers apiece; and when all the leaders of the congregation came and told Moses, 23 he said to them, "This is what the LORD has commanded: 'Tomorrow is a day of solemn rest, a holy sabbath to the LORD; bake what you will bake and boil what you will boil, and all that is left over lay by to be kept till the morning.' " 24 So they laid it by till the morning, as Moses bade them; and it did not become foul, and there were no worms in it. 25 Moses said, "Eat it today, for today is a sabbath to the LORD; today you will not find it in the field. 26 Six days you shall gather it; but on the seventh day, which is a sabbath, there will be none." 27 On the seventh day some of the people went out to gather, and they found none. 28And the LORD said to Moses, "How long do you refuse to keep my commandments and my laws? 29 See! The LORD has given you the sabbath, therefore on the sixth day he gives you bread for two days; remain every man of you in his place, let no man go out of his place on the seventh day." 30 So the people rested on the seventh day.

5. An omer of manna kept for a memorial

31 Now the house of Israel called its name manna; it was like coriander seed, white, and the taste of it was like wafers made with honey. 32And Moses said, "This is what the LORD has commanded: 'Let an omer of it be kept throughout your generations, that they may see the bread with which I fed you in the wilderness, when I brought you out of the land of Egypt.' " 33And Moses said to Aaron, "Take a jar, and put an omer of manna in it, and place it before the LORD, to be kept throughout your generations." 34As the LORD commanded Moses, so Aaron placed it before the testimony, to be kept. 35And the people of Israel ate the

ʷ Or "It is manna." Heb man hu

16.15 The bread was a free gift from above; it came daily in sufficient quantity for the needs of each day; it was life-giving and sustained the eater; and there was enough of it for all who wished to partake of it by appropriation. Christ (the bread which came down from heaven) is the one from whom the type is taken. The fulfilment far exceeds the type itself. (See Jn 6.30–41.)

16.23-26 These verses indicate that the idea of the Sabbath existed before the commandment of 20.8–11 and the Sabbath itself was observed before it, too.

16.34 the testimony, a name for the ark.

manna forty years, till they came to a habitable land; they ate the manna, till they came to the border of the land of Cānaàn. 36 (An omer is the tenth part of an ephah.)

C. Water from the smitten rock at Rephidim

17 All the congregation of the people of Israel moved on from the wilderness of Sin by stages, according to the commandment of the LORD, and camped at Rĕph'ĭdĭm; but there was no water for the people to drink. 2 Therefore the people found fault with Moses, and said, "Give us water to drink." And Moses said to them, "Why do you find fault with me? Why do you put the LORD to the proof?" 3 But the people thirsted there for water, and the people murmured against Moses, and said, "Why did you bring us up out of Egypt, to kill us and our children and our cattle with thirst?" 4 So Moses cried to the LORD, "What shall I do with this people? They are almost ready to stone me." 5And the LORD said to Moses, "Pass on before the people, taking with you some of the elders of Israel; and take in your hand the rod with which you struck the Nile, and go. 6 Behold, I will stand before you there on the rock at Horĕb; and you shall strike the rock, and water shall come out of it, that the people may drink." And Moses did so, in the sight of the elders of Israel. 7And he called the name of the place Mãssãh˟ and Mĕr'ĭbah,ʸ because of the faultfinding of the children of Israel, and because they put the LORD to the proof by saying, "Is the LORD among us or not?"

D. The defeat of the Amalekites

8 Then came Ăm'ălĕk and fought with Israel at Rĕph'ĭdĭm. 9And Moses said to Joshua, "Choose for us men, and go out, fight with Ăm'ălĕk; tomorrow I will stand on the top of the hill with the rod of God in my hand." 10 So Joshua did as Moses told him, and fought with Ăm'ălĕk; and Moses, Aaron, and Húr went up to the top of the hill. 11 Whenever Moses held up his hand, Israel prevailed; and whenever he lowered his hand, Ăm'ălĕk prevailed. 12 But Moses' hands grew weary; so they took a stone and put it under him, and he sat upon it, and Aaron and Húr held up his hands, one on one side, and the other on the other side; so his hands were steady until the going down of the sun. 13And Joshua mowed down Ăm'ălĕk and his people with the edge of the sword.

14 And the LORD said to Moses, "Write this as a memorial in a book and recite it in the ears of Joshua, that I will utterly blot out the remembrance of Ăm'ălĕk from under heaven." 15And Moses built an altar and called the name of it, The LORD is my banner, 16 saying, "A hand upon the banner of the LORD!ᶻ The LORD will have war with Ăm'ălĕk from generation to generation."

˟ That is *Proof* ʸ That is *Contention* ᶻ Cn: Heb obscure

17.6 The rock spoken of here is a type of Christ (1 Cor 10.4). Just as the life-giving water flowed from the rock, so does eternal life flow from the Rock Christ Jesus. And as the water was there for all who appropriated it, so is salvation available for all who lay hold of it by faith (Jn 1.12). As thirst is quenched by water, so spiritual thirst is satisfied forever by faith in Christ (Jn 4.14). (See Num 20.8.)
17.8 *Amalek*, a nomadic tribe of the Sinai Peninsula and the Negeb which resisted the Israelites as intruders.
17.9 *Joshua*, first mentioned here, was probably chosen to assist Moses soon after leaving Egypt.

17.1 Ex 16.1
17.2 Num 20.3; Deut 6.16; 1 Cor 10.9
17.3 Ex 16.2,3
17.4 Ex 14.15; Num 14.10; 1 Sam 30.6
17.5 Ex 3.16,18; 7.20
★17.6 Num 20.10; Ps 114.8; 1 Cor 10.4
17.7 Ps 81.7
★17.8 Num 24.20; Deut 25.17–19
★17.9 Ex 4.20
17.14 Ex 34.27; Num 24.20; Deut 29.19

E. The visit of Jethro, Moses' father-in-law

1. Jethro's advent: the burnt offering and breaking of bread

18 Jĕthrō, the priest of Mĭd'ĭăn, Moses' father-in-law, heard of all that God had done for Moses and for Israel his people, how the LORD had brought Israel out of Egypt. 2 Now Jĕthrō, Moses' father-in-law, had taken Zĭppō'răh, Moses' wife, after he had sent her away, 3 and her two sons, of whom the name of the one was Gėrshŏm (for he said, "I have been a sojourner[a] in a foreign land"), 4 and the name of the other, Ėlĭĕ'zĕr[b] (for he said, "The God of my father was my help, and delivered me from the sword of Phạraōh"). 5 And Jĕthrō, Moses' father-in-law, came with his sons and his wife to Moses in the wilderness where he was encamped at the mountain of God. 6 And when one told Moses, "Lo,[c] your father-in-law Jĕthrō is coming to you with your wife and her two sons with her," 7 Moses went out to meet his father-in-law, and did obeisance and kissed him; and they asked each other of their welfare, and went into the tent. 8 Then Moses told his father-in-law all that the LORD had done to Phạraōh and to the Egyptians for Israel's sake, all the hardship that had come upon them in the way, and how the LORD had delivered them. 9 And Jĕthrō rejoiced for all the good which the LORD had done to Israel, in that he had delivered them out of the hand of the Egyptians.

10 And Jĕthrō said, "Blessed be the LORD, who has delivered you out of the hand of the Egyptians and out of the hand of Phạraōh. 11 Now I know that the LORD is greater than all gods, because he delivered the people from under the hand of the Egyptians,[d] when they dealt arrogantly with them." 12 And Jĕthrō, Moses' father-in-law, offered[e] a burnt offering and sacrifices to God; and Aaron came with all the elders of Israel to eat bread with Moses' father-in-law before God.

2. The selection of judges: the departure of Jethro

13 On the morrow Moses sat to judge the people, and the people stood about Moses from morning till evening. 14 When Moses' father-in-law saw all that he was doing for the people, he said, "What is this that you are doing for the people? Why do you sit alone, and all the people stand about you from morning till evening?" 15 And Moses said to his father-in-law, "Because the people come to me to inquire of God; 16 when they have a dispute, they come to me and I decide between a man and his neighbor, and I make them know the statutes of God and his decisions." 17 Moses' father-in-law said to him, "What you are doing is not good. 18 You and the people with you will wear yourselves out, for the thing is too heavy for you; you are not able to perform it alone. 19 Listen now to my voice; I will give you counsel, and God be with you! You shall represent the people before God, and bring their cases to God; 20 and you shall teach them the statutes and the decisions, and make them know the way in which they must

Margin references: *18.1 Ex 2.16; 3.1 · 18.2 Ex 4.25 · 18.3 Acts 7.29; Ex 2.22 · 18.5 Ex 3.1,12 · 18.7 Gen 43.26–28; Ex 4.27 · 18.8 Ps 81.7 · 18.10 Ps 68.19,20 · 18.11 Ex 12.12; 15.11; 1 Sam 2.3 · 18.15 Num 9.8; Deut 17.8–13 · 18.18 Num 11.14,17 · 18.19 Ex 3.12; Num 27.5 · 18.20 Deut 1.18

a Heb ger   *b* Heb Eli, my God, ezer, help   *c* Sam Gk Syr: Heb I
d Transposing the last clause of v. 10 to v. 11   *e* Syr Tg Vg: Heb took

18.1 Jethro, Moses' father-in-law, is called *the priest of Midian*. In verse 10 he blessed the LORD, in 12 he offered *a burnt offering and sacrifices* and in 17ff he advised Moses.

walk and what they must do. 21 Moreover choose able men from all the people, such as fear God, men who are trustworthy and who hate a bribe; and place such men over the people as rulers of thousands, of hundreds, of fifties, and of tens. 22And let them judge the people at all times; every great matter they shall bring to you, but any small matter they shall decide themselves; so it will be easier for you, and they will bear the burden with you. 23 If you do this, and God so commands you, then you will be able to endure, and all this people also will go to their place in peace."

24 So Moses gave heed to the voice of his father-in-law and did all that he had said. 25 Moses chose able men out of all Israel, and made them heads over the people, rulers of thousands, of hundreds, of fifties, and of tens. 26And they judged the people at all times; hard cases they brought to Moses, but any small matter they decided themselves. 27 Then Moses let his father-in-law depart, and he went his way to his own country.

III. *The covenant and the Law 19.1—24.18*

A. *The covenant made*

1. *The people at Sinai*

19 On the third new moon after the people of Israel had gone forth out of the land of Egypt, on that day they came into the wilderness of Sī'näï. 2And when they set out from Rĕph'ĭdĭm and came into the wilderness of Sī'näï, they encamped in the wilderness; and there Israel encamped before the mountain. 3And Moses went up to God, and the LORD called to him out of the mountain, saying, "Thus you shall say to the house of Jacob, and tell the people of Israel: 4 You have seen what I did to the Egyptians, and how I bore you on eagles' wings and brought you to myself. 5 Now therefore, if you will obey my voice and keep my covenant, you shall be my own possession among all peoples; for all the earth is mine, 6 and you shall be to me a kingdom of priests and a holy nation. These are the words which you shall speak to the children of Israel."

7 So Moses came and called the elders of the people, and set before them all these words which the LORD had commanded him. 8And all the people answered together and said, "All that

Marginal references:

★18.21ff
ver 25;
Deut 1.13,
15

★18.22
Deut 1.17,
18;
Num 11.17

18.25
Deut 1.15

18.26
ver 22

18.27
Num 10.29,
30

19.2
Ex 17.1;
18.5

19.3
Ex 20.21;
Acts 7.38

★19.4
Deut 29.2;
Isa 63.9

★19.5ff
Deut 5.2;
7.6; 10.14

★19.6
1 Pet 2.5;
Rev 1.6;
5.10;
Deut 14.21;
26.19

★19.8
Ex 24.3,7

18.21ff Jethro's sound counsel to Moses was blessed of God. Num 11.14–17 makes this evident. God summoned the seventy elders whom Moses had chosen, that they might appear before Him and that He might make His presence known to them (see also 24.9). In imitation of these seventy elders, the number of the New Testament Sanhedrin was fixed at seventy. The same problem of overwork which vexed Moses led the early church to establish the office of deacon in order to free the Apostles for their spiritual duties.

19.4 Israel was governed as a theocracy (immediate government by God). Israel's movements were directed by God (40.36, 37), war was proclaimed by God (Num 31.1, 2), leaders were appointed by Him (Num 27.18,

20), and land in Canaan was distributed by Him (Jos 13.1–7). God used Moses, Joshua, and later the prophets (e.g., Samuel) as the intermediaries through whom He governed. Saul proved unworthy to continue as God's representative, and so David was chosen by the LORD to serve as His theocratic king—an authority conditioned upon covenant-obedience, but vouchsafed to David's posterity forever (2 Sam 7.12–16).

19.5-8 Israel here accepts the covenant proposed by God. Oftentimes this relationship has been denominated as God's theocratic rule over Israel. Two things are quite clear: (1) this covenant may be regarded as a fulfilment of the promise made to Abraham; and (2) this covenant was similar in form to a suzerainty treaty in which fealty is acknowl-

*19.9
ver 16;
Ex 24.15

*19.10
Lev 11.44,
45;
Heb 10.22;
Gen 35.2;
Num 8.7;
19.19

19.11
ver 16

19.12
Heb 12.20

19.13
ver 17

the LORD has spoken we will do." And Moses reported the words of the people to the LORD. 9And the LORD said to Moses, "Lo, I am coming to you in a thick cloud, that the people may hear when I speak with you, and may also believe you for ever."

2. The consecration of the people

Then Moses told the words of the people to the LORD. 10And the LORD said to Moses, "Go to the people and consecrate them today and tomorrow, and let them wash their garments, 11 and be ready by the third day; for on the third day the LORD will come down upon Mount Si'naï in the sight of all the people. 12And you shall set bounds for the people round about, saying, 'Take heed that you do not go up into the mountain or touch the border of it; whoever touches the mountain shall be put to death; 13 no hand shall touch him, but he shall be stoned or shot; whether beast or man, he shall not live.' When the trumpet sounds a long blast, they shall come up to the mountain." 14 So Moses went down from the mountain to the people, and consecrated the people; and they washed their garments. 15And he said to the people, "Be ready by the third day; do not go near a woman."

3. Moses meets God on Mount Sinai

19.16
Heb 12.18,
19;
Ex 40.34

*19.18
Ps 104.32;
Heb 12.18;
Gen 19.28;
Ps 68.7,8

19.19
Heb 12.21;
Ps 81.7

19.21
Ex 3.5

19.22
Lev 10.3;
2 Sam 6.7

19.23
ver 12

16 On the morning of the third day there were thunders and lightnings, and a thick cloud upon the mountain, and a very loud trumpet blast, so that all the people who were in the camp trembled. 17 Then Moses brought the people out of the camp to meet God; and they took their stand at the foot of the mountain. 18And Mount Si'naï was wrapped in smoke, because the LORD descended upon it in fire; and the smoke of it went up like the smoke of a kiln, and the whole mountain quaked greatly. 19And as the sound of the trumpet grew louder and louder, Moses spoke, and God answered him in thunder. 20And the LORD came down upon Mount Si'naï, to the top of the mountain; and the LORD called Moses to the top of the mountain, and Moses went up. 21And the LORD said to Moses, "Go down and warn the people, lest they break through to the LORD to gaze and many of them perish. 22And also let the priests who come near to the LORD consecrate themselves, lest the LORD break out upon them." 23And Moses said to the LORD, "The people cannot come up to Mount Si'naï; for thou thyself didst charge us, saying, 'Set bounds about the mountain, and consecrate it.' " 24And the LORD said to him, "Go down, and come up bringing Aaron with you; but do not let the priests and the people break through to come up to the LORD, lest he break out against them." 25 So Moses went down to the people and told them.

---

edged to a superior lord. The covenant was conditioned upon two things: (1) faith, and (2) obedience. The terms clearly stated that unbelief and disobedience would break the covenant, and as a result, the promised blessings flowing from faith and obedience would be withdrawn.

The melancholy history of Israel is a clear example of failure to believe God and to obey Him. Judgment, dispersion among the nations, and the withdrawal of the blessing of God inevitably followed.

19.9 *believe you for ever.* One of the re-

curring sins of Israel was to doubt and disbelieve Moses despite the fact that God gave Israel evident tokens that he was God's representative who enjoyed divine approval.

19.10 Moses was commanded to *consecrate* (separate or set apart) the people and to have them wash their clothes. Since they were to come into the presence of a holy God these preparatory measures were essential.

19.18 *the LORD descended . . . in fire.* As a symbol of holiness, fire is mentioned often in Scripture. Examples may be found in 3.2; 2 Ki 2.11; 2 Thess 1.8.

B. *The Law given*

20 And God spoke all these words, saying,
2 "I am the LORD your God, who brought you out of the land of Egypt, out of the house of bondage.

3 "You shall have no other gods before*ᶠ* me.

4 "You shall not make for yourself a graven image, or any likeness of anything that is in heaven above, or that is in the earth beneath, or that is in the water under the earth; 5 you shall not bow down to them or serve them; for I the LORD your God am a jealous God, visiting the iniquity of the fathers upon the children to the third and the fourth generation of those who hate me, 6 but showing steadfast love to thousands of those who love me and keep my commandments.

7 "You shall not take the name of the LORD your God in vain; for the LORD will not hold him guiltless who takes his name in vain.

8 "Remember the sabbath day, to keep it holy. 9 Six days you shall labor, and do all your work; 10 but the seventh day is a sabbath to the LORD your God; in it you shall not do any work, you, or your son, or your daughter, your manservant, or your maidservant, or your cattle, or the sojourner who is within your gates; 11 for in six days the LORD made heaven and earth, the sea, and all that is in them, and rested the seventh day; therefore the LORD blessed the sabbath day and hallowed it.

12 "Honor your father and your mother, that your days may be long in the land which the LORD your God gives you.

13 "You shall not kill.

14 "You shall not commit adultery.

15 "You shall not steal.

ᶠ Or besides

★20.1	Deut 5.22
20.2	Deut 5.6; 7.8
★20.3	Jer 35.15
20.4	Lev 26.1; Deut 4.15–19; Ps 97.7
20.5	Isa 44.15, 19; Deut 4.24; Jer 32.18
20.6	Deut 7.9
20.7	Lev 19.12; Mt 5.33
20.8	Ex 23.12; 31.15
20.9	Ex 34.21; Lk 13.14
★20.11	Gen 2.2,3
20.12	Lev 19.3; Mt 15.4; Mk 7.10; Eph 6.2
20.13	Rom 13.9
20.14	Mt 19.18
20.15	Mt 19.18

20.1 The Ten Commandments of chapter 20 follow Israel's acceptance of God's theocratic rule over them. The commandments are an expression of the eternal moral nature of God. They embody the basic principles which govern a life of faith, that is, loyalty and reverence toward God and moral responsibility toward man. They were never intended to serve as a basis for man's self-justification (as the legalists of Christ's day supposed), but only as a guide for the already-saved who love God and seek to please their divine Redeemer and carry out His will. Scripture states that these commandments were spoken by God (Deut 5.4, 22), and were written by Him (32.16; Deut 4.13; 10.4). Christ summed up the two tables of the Law by asserting that men are to love the Lord their God with all their hearts, and souls, and minds, and their neighbors as themselves (Mt 22.35–40). The commandments contain an indictment against all human righteousness and convey the sentence of death upon all who would misuse them for purposes of merit-earning or self-justification. But the same God who promulgated the Ten Commandments also made ample provision for the cleansing of sinners who transgressed these commandments and who in repentance cast themselves upon His grace. This forgiveness was symbolized through the shedding of the blood of the innocent victim at the altar of sacrifice. Contrary to what most people think, the Law means more than external conformity to rules; it is spiritual, for Christ states that the true locus of sin is in the heart (Mt 5.28; 12.34; Lk 12.34). The tenth commandment, against coveting, refers explicitly to the motives of man and shows the spiritual nature of the Law. Thus the overt act is only a revelation of what is in the heart; even if the overt act is not performed, a person is already guilty of having broken the Law by the inward condition of the heart (Mt 5.28; Rom 7.14).

20.3 Idolatry is strictly and sternly forbidden in Scripture. Everywhere it is regarded as an abomination. The objects of idol worship are called "foreign gods," "gods of wood and stone," "wooden idols." Idolatry consists in: (1) worshiping or bowing down to images whether of God or of man (20.5; Isa 44.17; Dan 3.5, 10, 15); (2) sacrificing to other gods or images (22.20; Ps 106.38; Acts 7.41); (3) worshiping of angels (Col 2.18); (4) covetousness (Eph 5.5); (5) sensuality (Phil 3.19). (Compare the note at 32.1.) In a general fashion it may be said that idolatry occurs when we place anything before God as the first object of our affection and obedience.

20.11 See here Deut 5.15 where another reason for keeping the Sabbath is given.

20.16
Ex 23.1;
Mt 19.18
20.17
Rom 7.7;
13.9

16 "You shall not bear false witness against your neighbor.

17 "You shall not covet your neighbor's house; you shall not covet your neighbor's wife, or his manservant, or his maidservant, or his ox, or his ass, or anything that is your neighbor's."

C. The people afraid

20.18
Heb 12.18;
Ex 19.18
20.19
Deut 5.23–
27
20.20
Ex 14.13;
15.25;
Deut 4.10

18 Now when all the people perceived the thunderings and the lightnings and the sound of the trumpet and the mountain smoking, the people were afraid and trembled; and they stood afar off, 19 and said to Moses, "You speak to us, and we will hear; but let not God speak to us, lest we die." 20And Moses said to the people, "Do not fear; for God has come to prove you, and that the fear of him may be before your eyes, that you may not sin."

D. The laws of the covenant

1. *The law of the altar*

20.21
Deut 5.22
20.22
Neh 9.13
20.23
ver 3;
Ex 32.1,2,4
20.24
Lev 1.2;
Deut 12.5;
Gen 12.2
20.25
Deut 27.5,6

*20.26

21 And the people stood afar off, while Moses drew near to the thick darkness where God was. 22And the LORD said to Moses, "Thus you shall say to the people of Israel: 'You have seen for yourselves that I have talked with you from heaven. 23 You shall not make gods of silver to be with me, nor shall you make for yourselves gods of gold. 24An altar of earth you shall make for me and sacrifice on it your burnt offerings and your peace offerings, your sheep and your oxen; in every place where I cause my name to be remembered I will come to you and bless you. 25And if you make me an altar of stone, you shall not build it of hewn stones; for if you wield your tool upon it you profane it. 26And you shall not go up by steps to my altar, that your nakedness be not exposed on it.'

2. *Laws concerning slaves*

*21.1
Deut 4.14
21.2
Lev 25.39–
41;
Deut 15.12–
18

21 "Now these are the ordinances which you shall set before them. 2 When you buy a Hebrew slave, he shall serve six years, and in the seventh he shall go out free, for nothing. 3 If he comes in single, he shall go out single; if he comes in married, then his wife shall go out with him. 4 If his master gives him a wife and she bears him sons or daughters, the wife and her children shall be her master's and he shall go out alone. 5 But if the slave plainly says, 'I love my master, my wife, and my children; I will not go out free,' 6 then his master shall bring him to God, and he shall bring him to the door or the doorpost; and his master shall bore his ear through with an awl; and he shall serve him for life.

21.6
Ex 22.8,9,
28

21.7
Neh 5.5;
ver 2,3

7 "When a man sells his daughter as a slave, she shall not go out as the male slaves do. 8 If she does not please her master, who has

---

20.26 See here Ezek 43.17 where the altar has steps.

21.1 Under the theocracy (see note to 19.4) God legislated civil statutes or laws which were to govern such a society under the cultural conditions that prevailed in that day. The unit of ordinances found in 21.1–23.33 apparently called *the book of the covenant* in 24.7, is characterized by case law, "if . . . , then . . . ." A number of laws have parallels or similar features to the law codes of Sumer and Babylonia which date some centuries before Moses. But the apodictic form of the Ten Commandments, "Thou shalt not . . . ," is unique to Israel. In the era of the Christian church many of the Pentateuchal regulations are inapplicable. Yet the underlying principles of justice and fairness and equality remain ever valid and foundational for sound jurisprudence.

designated her[g] for himself, then he shall let her be redeemed; he shall have no right to sell her to a foreign people, since he has dealt faithlessly with her. 9 If he designates her for his son, he shall deal with her as with a daughter. 10 If he takes another wife to himself, he shall not diminish her food, her clothing, or her marital rights. 11And if he does not do these three things for her, she shall go out for nothing, without payment of money.

3. *Laws relating to murder*

12 "Whoever strikes a man so that he dies shall be put to death. 13 But if he did not lie in wait for him, but God let him fall into his hand, then I will appoint for you a place to which he may flee. 14 But if a man willfully attacks another to kill him treacherously, you shall take him from my altar, that he may die.

15 "Whoever strikes his father or his mother shall be put to death.

16 "Whoever steals a man, whether he sells him or is found in possession of him, shall be put to death.

17 "Whoever curses his father or his mother shall be put to death.

4. *Laws relating to non-capital offenses*

18 "When men quarrel and one strikes the other with a stone or with his fist and the man does not die but keeps his bed, 19 then if the man rises again and walks abroad with his staff, he that struck him shall be clear; only he shall pay for the loss of his time, and shall have him thoroughly healed.

20 "When a man strikes his slave, male or female, with a rod and the slave dies under his hand, he shall be punished. 21 But if the slave survives a day or two, he is not to be punished; for the slave is his money.

22 "When men strive together, and hurt a woman with child, so that there is a miscarriage, and yet no harm follows, the one who hurt her shall[h] be fined, according as the woman's husband shall lay upon him; and he shall pay as the judges determine. 23 If any harm follows, then you shall give life for life, 24 eye for eye, tooth for tooth, hand for hand, foot for foot, 25 burn for burn, wound for wound, stripe for stripe.

26 "When a man strikes the eye of his slave, male or female, and destroys it, he shall let the slave go free for the eye's sake. 27 If he knocks out the tooth of his slave, male or female, he shall let the slave go free for the tooth's sake.

28 "When an ox gores a man or a woman to death, the ox shall be stoned, and its flesh shall not be eaten; but the owner of the ox shall be clear. 29 But if the ox has been accustomed to gore in the past, and its owner has been warned but has not kept it in, and it kills a man or a woman, the ox shall be stoned, and its owner also shall be put to death. 30 If a ransom is laid on him, then he shall give for the redemption of his life whatever is laid upon him. 31 If it gores a man's son or daughter, he shall be dealt with according

21.10
1 Cor 7.3,5

21.12
Gen 9.6;
Lev 24.17

21.13
Num 35.22;
Deut 19.4,5

21.14
Deut 19.11,
12;
Heb 10.26;
1 Ki 2.28–
34

21.16
Deut 24.7

21.17
Lev 20.9;
Mt 15.4;
Mk 7.10

21.21
Lev 25.45,
46

*21.23ff
Lev 24.19
*21.24
Mt 5.38

21.28
Gen 9.5

21.30
ver 22

[g] Another reading is *so that he has not designated her*   [h] Heb *he shall*

21.23-25 The concept of punishment equal to the crime was a tremendous advance over the law of revenge illustrated by Gen 4.24: *If Cain is avenged sevenfold, truly Lamech seventy-sevenfold*. The New Testament principle of forgiveness until "seventy times seven times" makes very clear what the attitude of the individual to his fellowman must be.

21.32
see Zech
11.12,13;
Mt 26.15

to this same rule. 32 If the ox gores a slave, male or female, the owner shall give to their master thirty shekels of silver, and the ox shall be stoned.

5. *Laws relating to property rights*

21.33
Lk 14.5

33 "When a man leaves a pit open, or when a man digs a pit and does not cover it, and an ox or an ass falls into it, 34 the owner of the pit shall make it good; he shall give money to its owner, and the dead beast shall be his.

35 "When one man's ox hurts another's, so that it dies, then they shall sell the live ox and divide the price of it; and the dead beast also they shall divide. 36 Or if it is known that the ox has been accustomed to gore in the past, and its owner has not kept it in, he shall pay ox for ox, and the dead beast shall be his.

22.1
2 Sam 12.6

22 *i* "If a man steals an ox or a sheep, and kills it or sells it, he shall pay five oxen for an ox, and four sheep for a sheep. *j*He shall make restitution; if he has nothing, then he shall be sold for his theft. 4 If the stolen beast is found alive in his possession, whether it is an ox or an ass or a sheep, he shall pay double.

22.2
Mt 24.43;
Num 35.27
22.3
Ex 21.2

2*k* "If a thief is found breaking in, and is struck so that he dies, there shall be no bloodguilt for him; 3 but if the sun has risen upon him, there shall be bloodguilt for him.

5 "When a man causes a field or vineyard to be grazed over, or lets his beast loose and it feeds in another man's field, he shall make restitution from the best in his own field and in his own vineyard.

6 "When fire breaks out and catches in thorns so that the stacked grain or the standing grain or the field is consumed, he that kindled the fire shall make full restitution.

22.7
ver 4

7 "If a man delivers to his neighbor money or goods to keep, and it is stolen out of the man's house, then, if the thief is found, he shall pay double. 8 If the thief is not found, the owner of the house shall come near to God, to show whether or not he has put his hand to his neighbor's goods.

22.8
ver 28;
Ex 21.6;
Deut 17.8,
9;19.17
22.9
ver 8,28

9 "For every breach of trust, whether it is for ox, for ass, for sheep, for clothing, or for any kind of lost thing, of which one says, 'This is it,' the case of both parties shall come before God; he whom God shall condemn shall pay double to his neighbor.

10 "If a man delivers to his neighbor an ass or an ox or a sheep or any beast to keep, and it dies or is hurt or is driven away, without any one seeing it, 11 an oath by the LORD shall be between them both to see whether he has not put his hand to his neighbor's property; and the owner shall accept the oath, and he shall not make restitution. 12 But if it is stolen from him, he shall make restitution to its owner. 13 If it is torn by beasts, let him bring it as evidence; he shall not make restitution for what has been torn.

22.11
Heb 6.16

22.12
Gen 31.39

14 "If a man borrows anything of his neighbor, and it is hurt or dies, the owner not being with it, he shall make full restitution. 15 If the owner was with it, he shall not make restitution; if it was hired, it came for its hire.*l*

22.16
Deut
22.28,29

16 "If a man seduces a virgin who is not betrothed, and lies with her, he shall give the marriage present for her, and make her

i Ch 21.37 in Heb
j Restoring the second half of verse 3 with 4 to their place immediately following verse 1
k Ch 22.1 in Heb   *l* Or *it is reckoned in* (Heb *comes into*) *its hire*

his wife. 17 If her father utterly refuses to give her to him, he shall pay money equivalent to the marriage present for virgins.

6. *Other laws*
a. *Crimes punishable by death*

18 "You shall not permit a sorceress to live.

19 "Whoever lies with a beast shall be put to death.

20 "Whoever sacrifices to any god, save to the LORD only, shall be utterly destroyed.

b. *Sundry duties*

21 "You shall not wrong a stranger or oppress him, for you were strangers in the land of Egypt. 22 You shall not afflict any widow or orphan. 23 If you do afflict them, and they cry out to me, I will surely hear their cry; 24 and my wrath will burn, and I will kill you with the sword, and your wives shall become widows and your children fatherless.

25 "If you lend money to any of my people with you who is poor, you shall not be to him as a creditor, and you shall not exact interest from him. 26 If ever you take your neighbor's garment in pledge, you shall restore it to him before the sun goes down; 27 for that is his only covering, it is his mantle for his body; in what else shall he sleep? And if he cries to me, I will hear, for I am compassionate.

28 "You shall not revile God, nor curse a ruler of your people.

29 "You shall not delay to offer from the fulness of your harvest and from the outflow of your presses.

"The first-born of your sons you shall give to me. 30 You shall do likewise with your oxen and with your sheep: seven days it shall be with its dam; on the eighth day you shall give it to me.

31 "You shall be men consecrated to me; therefore you shall not eat any flesh that is torn by beasts in the field; you shall cast it to the dogs.

c. *Ethical instructions*

23 "You shall not utter a false report. You shall not join hands with a wicked man, to be a malicious witness. 2 You shall not follow a multitude to do evil; nor shall you bear witness in a suit, turning aside after a multitude, so as to pervert justice; 3 nor shall you be partial to a poor man in his suit.

4 "If you meet your enemy's ox or his ass going astray, you shall bring it back to him. 5 If you see the ass of one who hates you lying under its burden, you shall refrain from leaving him with it, you shall help him to lift it up.*m*

6 "You shall not pervert the justice due to your poor in his suit. 7 Keep far from a false charge, and do not slay the innocent and righteous, for I will not acquit the wicked. 8 And you shall take no bribe, for a bribe blinds the officials, and subverts the cause of those who are in the right.

m Gk: Heb obscure

23.1 Slander is a gross sin which is strictly forbidden by God (Prov 6.16, 19; Eph 4.31; Jas 4.11). Included within this general category are such sins as: (1) gossip (Rom 1.29; 2 Cor 12.20); (2) tattling (1 Tim 5.13); (3) defaming (Jer 20.10); (4) base suspicion (1 Tim 6.4). Life in the Spirit enables believers to gain even more victories over this sin; by God's grace they are led to love their neighbors (even the less lovable ones) as themselves.

23.9
Ex 22.21

9 "You shall not oppress a stranger; you know the heart of a stranger, for you were strangers in the land of Egypt.

7. *Laws of festivals and holidays*

23.10
Lev 25.3
*23.11

10 "For six years you shall sow your land and gather in its yield; 11 but the seventh year you shall let it rest and lie fallow, that the poor of your people may eat; and what they leave the wild beasts may eat. You shall do likewise with your vineyard, and with your olive orchard.

23.12
Ex 20.8–11

12 "Six days you shall do your work, but on the seventh day you shall rest; that your ox and your ass may have rest, and the son of your bondmaid, and the alien, may be refreshed. 13 Take heed to all that I have said to you; and make no mention of the names of other gods, nor let such be heard out of your mouth.

23.13
Ps 39.1;
Eph 5.15

*23.14
Ex 34.23
23.15
Ex 12.15;
34.20

14 "Three times in the year you shall keep a feast to me. 15 You shall keep the feast of unleavened bread; as I commanded you, you shall eat unleavened bread for seven days at the appointed time in the month of Ābīb, for in it you came out of Egypt. None shall appear before me empty-handed. 16 You shall keep the feast of harvest, of the first fruits of your labor, of what you sow in the field. You shall keep the feast of ingathering at the end of the year, when you gather in from the field the fruit of your labor. 17 Three times in the year shall all your males appear before the Lord GOD.

*23.16
Ex 34.22;
Deut 16.13

23.17
Deut 16.16

23.18
Ex 34.25

18 "You shall not offer the blood of my sacrifice with leavened bread, or let the fat of my feast remain until the morning.

23.19
Ex 22.29;
Deut 14.21

19 "The first of the first fruits of your ground you shall bring into the house of the LORD your God.

"You shall not boil a kid in its mother's milk.

8. *God's final injunctions*

23.20
Ex 32.34;
15.16,17
23.21
Num 14.11;
Ps 78.40,56;
Num 14.35

20 "Behold, I send an angel before you, to guard you on the way and to bring you to the place which I have prepared. 21 Give heed to him and hearken to his voice, do not rebel against him, for he will not pardon your transgression; for my name is in him.

23.22
Gen 12.2

22 "But if you hearken attentively to his voice and do all that

---

23.11 The Feast of the Sabbatical Year was kept every seventh year. Its purpose was to provide a Sabbath or fallow year for the land (Lev 25.2). The people were to live on the fruits of their labor for the sixth year (Lev 25.20–22). Special commandments governed this year. Field labor was to cease, the fruits of the earth were to be common property, debts were to be remitted, Hebrew servants manumitted, and the Law was to be publicly read (see Lev 25.4ff; Deut 15.1–3; Neh 10.31; Deut 15.12; 31.10–13). Strangers or non-Israelites were not necessarily to be freed from debts in the sabbatic year (Deut 15.3). The Babylonian captivity centuries later was partly a consequence of failure to observe these sabbatical years (2 Chr 36.20, 21).

23.14 Three times a year all of the male Israelites were to appear before God at the tabernacle: *the feast of unleavened bread* (ver 15), *the feast of harvest* (ver 16), and *the feast of ingathering* (ver 16). Elsewhere they were spoken of as the feasts of Passover, Pentecost and Tabernacles. (See notes to 12.11; Lev

23.15; Ex 23.16; Mk 14.1).

23.16 The Feast of Tabernacles was one of the three national feasts of the Jews (the other two being Passover and Pentecost). It was also called the *feast of ingathering* (34.22) and was begun on the fifteenth day of Tishri, the seventh month (Lev 23.34, 39). It was celebrated after the harvest and vintage had been gathered in (Deut 16.13) and lasted for seven days (Lev 23.34, 41; Deut 16.13, 15). All males were obligated to attend the feast (23.16, 17), the first and last days of which were to be celebrated by holy convocations (Lev 23.35, 39; Num 29.12, 35). During the period of the observance the people camped out in booths, family by family (Lev 23.42). This feast was to be observed perpetually and with thanksgiving (Lev 23.41; Deut 16.14, 15). It was also called the *feast of booths*, and it memorialized the redemption of Israel out of Egypt (Lev 23.34–44). Zechariah prophetically declares that this feast will ultimately become a memorial feast for all nations (Zech 14.16–21).

I say, then I will be an enemy to your enemies and an adversary
to your adversaries.
23 "When my angel goes before you, and brings you in to the
Ăm'ŏrītes, and the Hĭttītes, and the Pĕr'ĭzzītes, and the Cā'-
naănītes, the Hĭvītes, and the Jĕb'ūsītes, and I blot them out,
24 you shall not bow down to their gods, nor serve them, nor do
according to their works, but you shall utterly overthrow them
and break their pillars in pieces. 25 You shall serve the LORD your
God, and I[n] will bless your bread and your water; and I will take
sickness away from the midst of you. 26 None shall cast her young
or be barren in your land; I will fulfil the number of your days.
27 I will send my terror before you, and will throw into confusion
all the people against whom you shall come, and I will make all
your enemies turn their backs to you. 28And I will send hornets
before you, which shall drive out Hĭvīte, Cā'naănīte, and Hĭttīte
from before you. 29 I will not drive them out from before you in
one year, lest the land become desolate and the wild beasts multiply against you. 30 Little by little I will drive them out from
before you, until you are increased and possess the land. 31And I
will set your bounds from the Red Sea to the sea of the Phĭlĭs'-
tĭnĕs, and from the wilderness to the Eūphrā'tĕs; for I will deliver
the inhabitants of the land into your hand, and you shall drive
them out before you. 32 You shall make no covenant with them or
with their gods. 33 They shall not dwell in your land, lest they
make you sin against me; for if you serve their gods, it will surely
be a snare to you."

9. Israel's acceptance of the covenant
a. The covenant sealed by blood

24 And he said to Moses, "Come up to the LORD, you and
Aaron, Nādăb, and Ábī'hū, and seventy of the elders of
Israel, and worship afar off. 2 Moses alone shall come near to the
LORD; but the others shall not come near, and the people shall
not come up with him."
3 Moses came and told the people all the words of the LORD
and all the ordinances; and all the people answered with one voice,
and said, "All the words which the LORD has spoken we will do."
4And Moses wrote all the words of the LORD. And he rose early
in the morning, and built an altar at the foot of the mountain, and
twelve pillars, according to the twelve tribes of Israel. 5And he
sent young men of the people of Israel, who offered burnt offerings and sacrificed peace offerings of oxen to the LORD. 6And
Moses took half of the blood and put it in basins, and half of the
blood he threw against the altar. 7 Then he took the book of the
covenant, and read it in the hearing of the people; and they said,
"All that the LORD has spoken we will do, and we will be obedient." 8And Moses took the blood and threw it upon the people,
and said, "Behold the blood of the covenant which the LORD has
made with you in accordance with all these words."
9 Then Moses and Aaron, Nādăb, and Ábī'hū, and seventy of

[n] Gk Vg: Heb he

23.23	Josh 24.8, 11
23.24	Ex 20.5; Lev 18.3; Ex 34.13
23.25	Deut 6.13; Mt 4.10; Deut 28.5; Ex 15.26
23.26	Deut 7.14; Mal 3.11; Job 5.26
23.27	Ex 15.14, 16; Deut 7.23
23.28	Deut 7.20; Josh 24.12
23.29	Deut 7.22
★23.30	
23.31	Gen 15.18; Josh 21.44; 24.12,18
23.32	Deut 7.2; ver 13,24
23.33	Deut 7.1–5, 16
24.1	Lev 10.1,2; Num 11.16
24.3	ver 7; Ex 19.8
24.4	Deut 31.9; Gen 28.18
24.6	Heb 9.18
24.7	Heb 9.19; ver 3
24.8	Heb 9.20; 1 Pet 1.2
24.9	ver 1

23.30 It was not the intention of God for Israel to subjugate Palestine quickly. The conquest was to be accomplished over a period of time. God commanded Israel to drive out the inhabitants as they went. It was the failure to do this which became a stumbling block to Israel.

*24.10
Ezek 1.26;
Rev 4.3;
Mt 17.2
24.11
Ex 19.21;
Gen 32.30;
31.54

the elders of Israel went up, 10 and they saw the God of Israel; and there was under his feet as it were a pavement of sapphire stone, like the very heaven for clearness. 11And he did not lay his hand on the chief men of the people of Israel; they beheld God, and ate and drank.

b. Moses on the mount for forty days

24.12
ver 2,15;
Ex 32.15,16
24.13
Ex 17.9-14;
3.1

12 The LORD said to Moses, "Come up to me on the mountain, and wait there; and I will give you the tables of stone, with the law and the commandment, which I have written for their instruction." 13 So Moses rose with his servant Joshua, and Moses went up into the mountain of God. 14And he said to the elders, "Tarry here for us, until we come to you again; and, behold, Aaron and Hùr are with you; whoever has a cause, let him go to them."

24.15
Ex 19.9
24.16
Ex 16.10
24.17
Ex 3.2;
Deut 4.36;
Heb 12.18,
29
24.18
Ex 34.28;
Deut 9.9

15 Then Moses went up on the mountain, and the cloud covered the mountain. 16 The glory of the LORD settled on Mount Si'näi, and the cloud covered it six days; and on the seventh day he called to Moses out of the midst of the cloud. 17 Now the appearance of the glory of the LORD was like a devouring fire on the top of the mountain in the sight of the people of Israel. 18And Moses entered the cloud, and went up on the mountain. And Moses was on the mountain forty days and forty nights.

IV. The tabernacle in the wilderness 25.1–40.38

A. The offering for the tabernacle

25.2
Ex 35.5,21;
2 Cor 8.12;
9.7
25.6
Ex 27.20;
30.23,34
25.7
Ex 28.4,6,
15
25.8
Ex 36.1,3,4;
Heb 9.1,2;
Ex 29.45;
Rev 21.3
*25.9
ver 40;
Acts 7.44;
Heb 8.2,5

25 The LORD said to Moses, 2 "Speak to the people of Israel, that they take for me an offering; from every man whose heart makes him willing you shall receive the offering for me. 3And this is the offering which you shall receive from them: gold, silver, and bronze, 4 blue and purple and scarlet stuff and fine twined linen, goats' hair, 5 tanned rams' skins, goatskins, acacia wood, 6 oil for the lamps, spices for the anointing oil and for the fragrant incense, 7 onyx stones, and stones for setting, for the ephod and for the breastpiece. 8And let them make me a sanctuary, that I may dwell in their midst. 9According to all that I show you concerning the pattern of the tabernacle, and of all its furniture, so you shall make it.

24.10 A theophany is a visible appearance of God to men. This appearance might take place in different ways and under different circumstances. Among the appearances recorded in Scripture the following may be cited: (1) Here in 24.10 where Moses, Aaron, Nadab, Abihu, and the seventy elders saw a manifestation of the glory and person of God without any suggestion that it was by other than ordinary vision; (2) in 33.11 where God spoke to Moses *face to face* which must be understood in the context of verses 17–23; (3) in Isa 6, Ezek 1 and Dan 7.9 where God was seen in a vision or a dream; (4) in Gen 16.7 where the angel of the LORD appeared to Hagar (although the angel of the LORD does not always mean the appearance of God or Christ); (5) in 14.19 where God appeared in the pillar of cloud; (6) in Deut 5.24 and

elsewhere where Scripture speaks of men beholding the LORD's glory and greatness. The supreme revelation of God to man is found in the incarnation of Jesus Christ who *became flesh and dwelt among us* (Jn 1.14).

25.9 God commanded Moses to make the tabernacle. It was a movable tent appropriate to the unsettled life of the people (2 Sam 7.6, 7). The Levites were appointed to have charge over it (Num 1.50; Num 18.2–4). God's presence or cloud of glory filled the holy place and remained over the ark of the covenant (25.22; Lev 16.2; Num 7.89). During the wilderness wanderings of Israel the cloud of glory rested over the tabernacle both day and night, and the movements of the people were guided by the movement of the cloud (40.36–38; Num 9.15, 16).

B. *The ark*

10 "They shall make an ark of acacia wood; two cubits and a half shall be its length, a cubit and a half its breadth, and a cubit and a half its height. ¹¹And you shall overlay it with pure gold, within and without shall you overlay it, and you shall make upon it a molding of gold round about. ¹²And you shall cast four rings of gold for it and put them on its four feet, two rings on the one side of it, and two rings on the other side of it. ¹³ You shall make poles of acacia wood, and overlay them with gold. ¹⁴And you shall put the poles into the rings on the sides of the ark, to carry the ark by them. ¹⁵ The poles shall remain in the rings of the ark; they shall not be taken from it. ¹⁶And you shall put into the ark the testimony which I shall give you. ¹⁷ Then you shall make a mercy seat° of pure gold; two cubits and a half shall be its length, and a cubit and a half its breadth. ¹⁸And you shall make two cherubim of gold; of hammered work shall you make them, on the two ends of the mercy seat. ¹⁹ Make one cherub on the one end, and one cherub on the other end; of one piece with the mercy seat shall you make the cherubim on its two ends. ²⁰ The cherubim shall spread out their wings above, overshadowing the mercy seat with their wings, their faces one to another; toward the mercy seat shall the faces of the cherubim be. ²¹And you shall put the mercy seat on the top of the ark; and in the ark you shall put the testimony that I shall give you. ²² There I will meet with you, and from above the mercy seat, from between the two cherubim that are upon the ark of the testimony, I will speak with you of all that I will give you in commandment for the people of Israel.

C. *The table*

23 "And you shall make a table of acacia wood; two cubits shall be its length, a cubit its breadth, and a cubit and a half its height. ²⁴ You shall overlay it with pure gold, and make a molding of gold around it. ²⁵And you shall make around it a frame a handbreadth wide, and a molding of gold around the frame. ²⁶And you shall make for it four rings of gold, and fasten the rings to the four corners at its four legs. ²⁷ Close to the frame the rings shall lie, as holders for the poles to carry the table. ²⁸ You shall make the poles of acacia wood, and overlay them with gold, and the table

*25.10
Ex 37.1–9

25.16
Deut 31.26;
Heb 9.4
*25.17
Ex 37.6;
Rom 3.25;
Heb 9.5

25.20
1 Ki 8.7;
Heb 9.5

25.21
Ex 26.34;
ver 16
*25.22
Ex 29.42,
43; 30.6,36;
Num 7.89;
Ps 80.1

25.23
Ex 37.10–
16;
Heb 9.2

o Or *cover*

25.10 The ark was a chest made of acacia wood overlaid with gold. Reckoning the cubit at 18 inches, this chest was 3.75 feet long, 2.25 feet wide, and 2.25 feet deep. See also notes to 25.17; 26.33.
25.17 The *mercy seat* was the lid of the ark; the Hebrew term means "propitiatory" and comes from the verb *kippĕr*, "to atone." It was made of solid gold, beaten out into the form of two cherubs (winged lions with human heads) which faced each other at either end. Their wings were outspread in front of them as they looked down at the mercy seat. Within the ark itself (or in front of it) were Aaron's rod, a pot of manna, and the two tables of the Law. The symbolism of the mercy seat surmounting the tables of the

Law is representative of the covering of law by mercy. Thus it speaks of Christ and His perfect atonement which met the demands of the Law, making possible divine mercy. The mercy seat is a type of Christ. Once a year the high priest came with blood to make atonement for his sins and the sins of the people (Lev 16.29–34; Heb 9.5–7). At the mercy seat God met and communed with those who came through blood (25.22). All believers now have access to the mercy seat through Christ, their High Priest (Rom 3.25; Heb 4.14–16).
25.22 *the two cherubim.* The concept that the LORD of hosts was enthroned on the cherubim is noted explicitly in 1 Sam 4.4; 2 Sam 6.2; 2 Ki 19.15; Isa 37.16; 1 Chr 13.6.

25.29
Ex 37.16;
Num 4.7
25.30
Lev 24.5-9

shall be carried with these. 29And you shall make its plates and dishes for incense, and its flagons and bowls with which to pour libations; of pure gold you shall make them. 30And you shall set the bread of the Presence on the table before me always.

D. *The lampstand*

25.31
Ex 37.17;
Heb 9.2;
Rev 1.12
25.32
Ex 38.18

31 "And you shall make a lampstand of pure gold. The base and the shaft of the lampstand shall be made of hammered work; its cups, its capitals, and its flowers shall be of one piece with it; 32 and there shall be six branches going out of its sides, three branches of the lampstand out of one side of it and three branches of the lampstand out of the other side of it; 33 three cups made like almonds, each with capital and flower, on one branch, and three cups made like almonds, each with capital and flower, on the other branch—so for the six branches going out of the lamp-

25.34
Ex 37.20

stand; 34 and on the lampstand itself four cups made like almonds, with their capitals and flowers, 35 and a capital of one piece with it under each pair of the six branches going out from the lamp-stand. 36 Their capitals and their branches shall be of one piece with it, the whole of it one piece of hammered work of pure gold.

25.37
Ex 27.21;
Lev 24.3,4

37And you shall make the seven lamps for it; and the lamps shall be set up so as to give light upon the space in front of it. 38 Its snuffers and their trays shall be of pure gold. 39 Of a talent of pure gold shall it be made, with all these utensils. 40And see that you

25.40
Ex 26.30;
Acts 7.44;
Heb 8.5

make them after the pattern for them, which is being shown you on the mountain.

E. *The tabernacle*

26.1
Ex 36.8

26 "Moreover you shall make the tabernacle with ten cur-tains of fine twined linen and blue and purple and scarlet stuff; with cherubim skilfully worked shall you make them. 2 The length of each curtain shall be twenty-eight cubits, and the breadth of each curtain four cubits; all the curtains shall have one measure.

26.3
Ex 36.10

3 Five curtains shall be coupled to one another; and the other five curtains shall be coupled to one another. 4And you shall make loops of blue on the edge of the outmost curtain in the first set; and likewise you shall make loops on the edge of the outmost cur-tain in the second set. 5 Fifty loops you shall make on the one

26.5
Ex 36.12

curtain, and fifty loops you shall make on the edge of the curtain that is in the second set; the loops shall be opposite one another. 6And you shall make fifty clasps of gold, and couple the curtains one to the other with the clasps, that the tabernacle may be one whole.

26.7
Ex 36.14

7 "You shall also make curtains of goats' hair for a tent over the tabernacle; eleven curtains shall you make. 8 The length of each curtain shall be thirty cubits, and the breadth of each curtain four cubits; the eleven curtains shall have the same measure. 9And you shall couple five curtains by themselves, and six curtains by themselves, and the sixth curtain you shall double over at the front of the tent. 10And you shall make fifty loops on the edge of the curtain that is outmost in one set, and fifty loops on the edge of the curtain which is outmost in the second set.

26.11
Ex 36.18

11 "And you shall make fifty clasps of bronze, and put the

clasps into the loops, and couple the tent together that it may be one whole. 12And the part that remains of the curtains of the tent, the half curtain that remains, shall hang over the back of the tabernacle. 13And the cubit on the one side, and the cubit on the other side, of what remains in the length of the curtains of the tent shall hang over the sides of the tabernacle, on this side and that side, to cover it. 14And you shall make for the tent a covering of tanned rams' skins and goatskins.

26.14
Ex 36.19

15 "And you shall make upright frames for the tabernacle of acacia wood. 16 Ten cubits shall be the length of a frame, and a cubit and a half the breadth of each frame. 17 There shall be two tenons in each frame, for fitting together; so shall you do for all the frames of the tabernacle. 18 You shall make the frames for the tabernacle: twenty frames for the south side; 19 and forty bases of silver you shall make under the twenty frames, two bases under one frame for its two tenons, and two bases under another frame for its two tenons; 20 and for the second side of the tabernacle, on the north side twenty frames, 21 and their forty bases of silver, two bases under one frame, and two bases under another frame; 22 and for the rear of the tabernacle westward you shall make six frames. 23And you shall make two frames for corners of the tabernacle in the rear; 24 they shall be separate beneath, but joined at the top, at the first ring; thus shall it be with both of them; they shall form the two corners. 25And there shall be eight frames, with their bases of silver, sixteen bases; two bases under one frame, and two bases under another frame.

26.15
Ex 36.20

26.20
Ex 36.23

26.25
Ex 36.30

26 "And you shall make bars of acacia wood, five for the frames of the one side of the tabernacle, 27 and five bars for the frames of the other side of the tabernacle, and five bars for the frames of the side of the tabernacle at the rear westward. 28 The middle bar, halfway up the frames, shall pass through from end to end. 29 You shall overlay the frames with gold, and shall make their rings of gold for holders for the bars; and you shall overlay the bars with gold. 30And you shall erect the tabernacle according to the plan for it which has been shown you on the mountain.

26.30
Ex 25.9,40;
27.8;
Acts 7.44;
Heb 8.5

F. The veil

31 "And you shall make a veil of blue and purple and scarlet stuff and fine twined linen; in skilled work shall it be made, with cherubim; 32 and you shall hang it upon four pillars of acacia overlaid with gold, with hooks of gold, upon four bases of silver. 33And you shall hang the veil from the clasps, and bring the ark of the

★26.31
Ex 36.35;
Mt 27.51;
Heb 9.3
★26.33
Ex 25.16;
40.21;
Lev 16.2;
Heb 9.2,3

26.31 The veil in the tabernacle separated the Holy of Holies from all men, even the priests. It was entered but once a year by the high priest and then only with an offering of blood both for his own sins and for the sins of the people. The figure is plain: man was separated from God by his sin and an approach could be made only by blood and through the priesthood. (See note to Mt 27.51.)

26.33 The veil here described shut off the Holy of Holies from the outer holy place of the tabernacle. This innermost chamber, called the Holy of Holies, was variously denominated as *the sanctuary* (Lev 4.6); *the holy place*

(Lev 16.2), which is literally in Hebrew "Holy of Holies"; *most holy* in this verse. In this innermost sanctum was the ark of the covenant. The mercy seat was the lid, made of solid gold. The cherubim were on top of the lid and were of one piece with it. Inside the ark were the golden urn holding manna from the wilderness (16.33), Aaron's rod (Num 17.10), and a copy of the Law (Deut 31.26; 2 Ki 22.8). Because the golden altar of incense was placed right in front of the inner veil (which curtained off the innermost sanctum from the holy place), and because the smoke of its incense wafted through

testimony in thither within the veil; and the veil shall separate for you the holy place from the most holy. 34 You shall put the mercy seat upon the ark of the testimony in the most holy place. 35And you shall set the table outside the veil, and the lampstand on the south side of the tabernacle opposite the table; and you shall put the table on the north side.

36 "And you shall make a screen for the door of the tent, of blue and purple and scarlet stuff and fine twined linen, embroidered with needlework. 37And you shall make for the screen five pillars of acacia, and overlay them with gold; their hooks shall be of gold, and you shall cast five bases of bronze for them.

G. The altar

27 "You shall make the altar of acacia wood, five cubits long and five cubits broad; the altar shall be square, and its height shall be three cubits. 2And you shall make horns for it on its four corners; its horns shall be of one piece with it, and you shall overlay it with bronze. 3 You shall make pots for it to receive its ashes, and shovels and basins and forks and firepans; all its utensils you shall make of bronze. 4 You shall also make for it a grating, a network of bronze; and upon the net you shall make four bronze rings at its four corners. 5And you shall set it under the ledge of the altar so that the net shall extend halfway down the altar. 6And you shall make poles for the altar, poles of acacia wood, and overlay them with bronze; 7 and the poles shall be put through the rings, so that the poles shall be upon the two sides of the altar, when it is carried. 8 You shall make it hollow, with boards; as it has been shown you on the mountain, so shall it be made.

H. The court of the tabernacle

9 "You shall make the court of the tabernacle. On the south side the court shall have hangings of fine twined linen a hundred cubits long for one side; 10 their pillars shall be twenty and their bases twenty, of bronze, but the hooks of the pillars and their fillets shall be of silver. 11And likewise for its length on the north side there shall be hangings a hundred cubits long, their pillars twenty and their bases twenty, of bronze, but the hooks of the pillars and their fillets shall be of silver. 12And for the breadth of the court on the west side there shall be hangings for fifty cubits, with ten pillars and ten bases. 13 The breadth of the court on the front to the east shall be fifty cubits. 14 The hangings for the one side of the gate shall be fifteen cubits, with three pillars and three bases. 15 On the other side the hangings shall be fifteen cubits, with three pillars and three bases. 16 For the gate of the court there shall be a screen twenty cubits long, of blue and purple and scarlet stuff and fine twined linen, embroidered with needlework; it shall have four pillars and with them four bases. 17All the pillars around the court shall be filleted with silver; their hooks shall be of silver, and their bases of bronze. 18 The length of the court shall be a

Marginal references:
26.34 Ex 25.21; 40.20; Heb 9.5
26.35 Ex 40.22, 24; Heb 9.2
26.36 Ex 36.37
26.37 Ex 36.38
27.1 Ex 38.1; Ezek 43.13
27.3 Num 4.14
27.8 Ex 25.40; 26.30
27.9 Ex 38.9
27.10 Ex 38.17
27.14 Ex 38.15
27.16 Ex 36.37

hundred cubits, the breadth fifty, and the height five cubits, with hangings of fine twined linen and bases of bronze. 19All the utensils of the tabernacle for every use, and all its pegs and all the pegs of the court, shall be of bronze.

I. The service and ritual

1. Oil for the lamp

20 "And you shall command the people of Israel that they bring to you pure beaten olive oil for the light, that a lamp may be set up to burn continually. 21 In the tent of meeting, outside the veil which is before the testimony, Aaron and his sons shall tend it from evening to morning before the LORD. It shall be a statute for ever to be observed throughout their generations by the people of Israel.

2. The garments for the priesthood

28 "Then bring near to you Aaron your brother, and his sons with him, from among the people of Israel, to serve me as priests—Aaron and Aaron's sons, Nādăb and Ăbi'hū, Ĕlëä'zăr and Ĭth'ámar. 2And you shall make holy garments for Aaron your brother, for glory and for beauty. 3And you shall speak to all who have ability, whom I have endowed with an able mind, that they make Aaron's garments to consecrate him for my priesthood. 4 These are the garments which they shall make: a breastpiece, an ephod, a robe, a coat of checker work, a turban, and a girdle; they shall make holy garments for Aaron your brother and his sons to serve me as priests.

5 "They shall receive gold, blue and purple and scarlet stuff, and fine twined linen. 6And they shall make the ephod of gold, of blue and purple and scarlet stuff, and of fine twined linen, skilfully worked. 7 It shall have two shoulder-pieces attached to its two edges, that it may be joined together. 8And the skilfully woven band upon it, to gird it on, shall be of the same workmanship and materials, of gold, blue and purple and scarlet stuff, and fine twined linen. 9And you shall take two onyx stones, and engrave on them the names of the sons of Israel, 10 six of their names on the one stone, and the names of the remaining six on the other stone, in the order of their birth. 11As a jeweler engraves signets, so shall you engrave the two stones with the names of the sons of Israel; you shall enclose them in settings of gold filigree. 12And you shall set the two stones upon the shoulder-pieces of the ephod, as stones of remembrance for the sons of Israel; and Aaron shall bear their names before the LORD upon his two shoulders for remembrance. 13And you shall make settings of gold filigree, 14 and two chains of pure gold, twisted like cords; and you shall attach the corded chains to the settings.

15 "And you shall make a breastpiece of judgment, in skilled work; like the work of the ephod you shall make it; of gold, blue and purple and scarlet stuff, and fine twined linen shall you make

Marginal references

27.20
Lev 24.2

*27.21
Ex 26.31,
33; 30.8;
28.43;
Lev 3.17;
16.34

*28.1
Num 18.7;
Heb 5.1,4

28.2
Ex 29.5,29;
31.10

28.3
Ex 31.3,6

28.4
see ver 6,15,
31,39

28.6
Ex 39.2

28.9
1 Chr 9.2 2

28.12
ver 29;
Ex 39.7

28.15
Ex 39.8

27.21 *tent of meeting*, clearly another designation for the tabernacle which was the meeting place between God and His people.
28.1 *Aaron*, the high priest, represents Christ, our High Priest. In Heb 5.6ff the priesthood of Christ (*after the order of Melchizedek*) is contrasted with that of Aaron and is shown to surpass it in efficacy.

it. 16 It shall be square and double, a span its length and a span
its breadth. 17And you shall set in it four rows of stones. A row of
sardius, topaz, and carbuncle shall be the first row; 18 and the
second row an emerald, a sapphire, and a diamond; 19 and the
third row a jacinth, an agate, and an amethyst; 20 and the fourth
row a beryl, an onyx, and a jasper; they shall be set in gold filigree.
21 There shall be twelve stones with their names according to the
names of the sons of Israel; they shall be like signets, each engraved
with its name, for the twelve tribes. 22And you shall make for the
breastpiece twisted chains like cords, of pure gold; 23 and you shall
make for the breastpiece two rings of gold, and put the two rings
on the two edges of the breastpiece. 24And you shall put the two
cords of gold in the two rings at the edges of the breastpiece;
25 the two ends of the two cords you shall attach to the two settings
of filigree, and so attach it in front to the shoulder-pieces of the
ephod. 26And you shall make two rings of gold, and put them at
the two ends of the breastpiece, on its inside edge next to the
ephod. 27And you shall make two rings of gold, and attach them
in front to the lower part of the two shoulder-pieces of the ephod,
at its joining above the skilfully woven band of the ephod. 28And
they shall bind the breastpiece by its rings to the rings of the
ephod with a lace of blue, that it may lie upon the skilfully woven
band of the ephod, and that the breastpiece shall not come loose
from the ephod. 29 So Aaron shall bear the names of the sons of
Israel in the breastpiece of judgment upon his heart, when he goes
into the holy place, to bring them to continual remembrance before the LORD. 30And in the breastpiece of judgment you shall put
the Urim and the Thummim, and they shall be upon Aaron's
heart, when he goes in before the LORD; thus Aaron shall bear the
judgment of the people of Israel upon his heart before the LORD
continually.

31 "And you shall make the robe of the ephod all of blue. 32 It
shall have in it an opening for the head, with a woven binding
around the opening, like the opening in a garment,ᵖ that it may
not be torn. 33 On its skirts you shall make pomegranates of blue
and purple and scarlet stuff, around its skirts, with bells of gold
between them, 34 a golden bell and a pomegranate, a golden bell
and a pomegranate, round about on the skirts of the robe. 35And
it shall be upon Aaron when he ministers, and its sound shall be
heard when he goes into the holy place before the LORD, and
when he comes out, lest he die.

36 "And you shall make a plate of pure gold, and engrave on it,
like the engraving of a signet, 'Holy to the LORD.' 37And you shall
fasten it on the turban by a lace of blue; it shall be on the front of

28.17 Ex 39.10ff
28.21 Ex 39.14
28.24 Ex 39.17
28.26 Ex 39.17
28.29 ver 12
*28.30 Lev 8.8; Num 27.21
28.31 Ex 39.22
28.36 Ex 39.30,31

ᵖ The Hebrew word is of uncertain meaning

28.30 Urim and Thummim signify literally "lights" and "perfections." The precise
nature of these is still unclear. They were
perhaps two gem-stones which were laid in a
receptacle in the breastplate of the high
priest. Num 27.21, 1 Sam 14.37–42, and
28.6 are passages construed by some to show
that these two stones could be cast as lots in
determining God's reply to questions of
national interest to Israel. There are difficulties with this view; but no other seems to
be better. Whatever the correct explanation,
Scripture does indicate that the use of them
was a medium whereby guilt or innocence of
suspected persons might be ascertained and
the will of God discovered (1 Sam 14). The
use of the Urim and Thummim is not
mentioned after the reign of David. Ezra
2.63 and Neh 7.65 note that after the
Babylonian exile Israel had no priest with
Urim and Thummim. There is no biblical
reference to them thereafter.

the turban. 38 It shall be upon Aaron's forehead, and Aaron shall take upon himself any guilt incurred in the holy offering which the people of Israel hallow as their holy gifts; it shall always be upon his forehead, that they may be accepted before the LORD.

39 "And you shall weave the coat in checker work of fine linen, and you shall make a turban of fine linen, and you shall make a girdle embroidered with needlework.

40 "And for Aaron's sons you shall make coats and girdles and caps; you shall make them for glory and beauty. 41And you shall put them upon Aaron your brother, and upon his sons with him, and shall anoint them and ordain them and consecrate them, that they may serve me as priests. 42And you shall make for them linen breeches to cover their naked flesh; from the loins to the thighs they shall reach; 43 and they shall be upon Aaron, and upon his sons, when they go into the tent of meeting, or when they come near the altar to minister in the holy place; lest they bring guilt upon themselves and die. This shall be a perpetual statute for him and for his descendants after him.

3. The ordination of the priests
a. The ordination ritual

29 "Now this is what you shall do to them to consecrate them, that they may serve me as priests. Take one young bull and two rams without blemish, 2 and unleavened bread, unleavened cakes mixed with oil, and unleavened wafers spread with oil. You shall make them of fine wheat flour. 3And you shall put them in one basket and bring them in the basket, and bring the bull and the two rams. 4 You shall bring Aaron and his sons to the door of the tent of meeting, and wash them with water. 5And you shall take the garments, and put on Aaron the coat and the robe of the ephod, and the ephod, and the breastpiece, and gird him with the skilfully woven band of the ephod; 6 and you shall set the turban on his head, and put the holy crown upon the turban. 7And you shall take the anointing oil, and pour it on his head and anoint him. 8 Then you shall bring his sons, and put coats on them, 9 and you shall gird them with girdles^q and bind caps on them; and the priesthood shall be theirs by a perpetual statute. Thus you shall ordain Aaron and his sons.

b. The sin offering

10 "Then you shall bring the bull before the tent of meeting. Aaron and his sons shall lay their hands upon the head of the bull, 11 and you shall kill the bull before the LORD, at the door of the tent of meeting, 12 and shall take part of the blood of the bull and put it upon the horns of the altar with your finger, and the rest of^r the blood you shall pour out at the base of the altar. 13And you shall take all the fat that covers the entrails, and the appendage of the liver, and the two kidneys with the fat that is on them, and burn them upon the altar. 14 But the flesh of the bull, and its skin, and its dung, you shall burn with fire outside the camp; it is a sin offering.

c. The burnt offering

15 "Then you shall take one of the rams, and Aaron and his

q Gk: Heb girdles, Aaron and his sons   r Heb all

28.38 ver 43; Lev 10.17; Num 18.1; Heb 9.28; 1 Pet 2.24

28.40 ver 4; Ex 39.27-29
28.41 Ex 29.7-9; 30.30; Lev ch 8; Heb 7.28
28.42 Ex 39.28
28.43 Ex 20.26; Lev 20.19, 20; Ex 27.21; Lev 17.7

29.1 Lev 8.2
29.2 Lev 6.19-23
29.4 Ex 40.12; Heb 10.22
29.5 Ex 28.2,8
29.6 Lev 8.9
29.7 Lev 8.12
29.8 Lev 8.13
29.9 Num 18.7; Ex 28.41

29.10 Lev 1.4; 8.14
29.12 Lev 8.15; Ex 27.2
29.13 Lev 3.3
29.14 Lev 4.11, 12,21

sons shall lay their hands upon the head of the ram, 16 and you
shall slaughter the ram, and shall take its blood and throw it
against the altar round about. 17 Then you shall cut the ram into
pieces, and wash its entrails and its legs, and put them with its

29.18
Gen 8.21

pieces and its head, 18 and burn the whole ram upon the altar;
it is a burnt offering to the LORD; it is a pleasing odor, an offering by fire to the LORD.

d. *The sacrifice on ordination*

19 "You shall take the other ram; and Aaron and his sons shall
lay their hands upon the head of the ram, 20 and you shall kill
the ram, and take part of its blood and put it upon the tip of the
right ear of Aaron and upon the tips of the right ears of his sons,
and upon the thumbs of their right hands, and upon the great
toes of their right feet, and throw the rest of the blood against the

29.21
Ex 30.25,
31;
ver 1;
Heb 9.22

altar round about. 21 Then you shall take part of the blood that is
on the altar, and of the anointing oil, and sprinkle it upon Aaron
and his garments, and upon his sons and his sons' garments with
him; and he and his garments shall be holy, and his sons and his
sons' garments with him.

22 "You shall also take the fat of the ram, and the fat tail, and
the fat that covers the entrails, and the appendage of the liver, and
the two kidneys with the fat that is on them, and the right thigh

29.23
Lev 8.26

(for it is a ram of ordination), 23 and one loaf of bread, and one
cake of bread with oil, and one wafer, out of the basket of un-

29.24
Lev 7.30

leavened bread that is before the LORD; 24 and you shall put all
these in the hands of Aaron and in the hands of his sons, and

29.25
Lev 8.28

wave them for a wave offering before the LORD. 25Then you
shall take them from their hands, and burn them on the altar
in addition to the burnt offering, as a pleasing odor before the
LORD; it is an offering by fire to the LORD.

29.26
Lev 8.29

26 "And you shall take the breast of the ram of Aaron's ordination and wave it for a wave offering before the LORD; and it shall be

29.27
Lev 7.31,
34;
Deut 18.3

your portion. 27And you shall consecrate the breast of the wave
offering, and the thigh of the priests' portion, which is waved, and
which is offered from the ram of ordination, since it is for Aaron
and for his sons. 28 It shall be for Aaron and his sons as a per-

29.28
Lev 10.15

petual due from the people of Israel, for it is the priests' portion
to be offered by the people of Israel from their peace offerings;
it is their offering to the LORD.

29.29
Num 20.26,
28; 18.8

29 "The holy garments of Aaron shall be for his sons after him,
to be anointed in them and ordained in them. 30 The son who is

29.30
Num 20.28;
Lev 8.35;
9.1,8

priest in his place shall wear them seven days, when he comes into
the tent of meeting to minister in the holy place.

29.31
Lev 8.31

31 "You shall take the ram of ordination, and boil its flesh in a
holy place; 32 and Aaron and his sons shall eat the flesh of the ram

29.32
Mt 12.4

and the bread that is in the basket, at the door of the tent of meeting. 33 They shall eat those things with which atonement was

29.33
Lev 10.14,
15,17;
22.10

made, to ordain and consecrate them, but an outsider shall not
eat of them, because they are holy. 34And if any of the flesh for the
ordination, or of the bread, remain until the morning, then you

29.34
Lev 8.32

shall burn the remainder with fire; it shall not be eaten, because
it is holy.

29.35
Lev 8.33

35 "Thus you shall do to Aaron and to his sons, according to
all that I have commanded you; through seven days shall you or-

dain them, 36 and every day you shall offer a bull as a sin offering for atonement. Also you shall offer a sin offering for the altar, when you make atonement for it, and shall anoint it, to consecrate it. 37 Seven days you shall make atonement for the altar, and consecrate it, and the altar shall be most holy; whatever touches the altar shall become holy.

e. The altar of burnt offering

38 "Now this is what you shall offer upon the altar: two lambs a year old day by day continually. 39 One lamb you shall offer in the morning, and the other lamb you shall offer in the evening; 40 and with the first lamb a tenth measure of fine flour mingled with a fourth of a hin of beaten oil, and a fourth of a hin of wine for a libation. 41 And the other lamb you shall offer in the evening, and shall offer with it a cereal offering and its libation, as in the morning, for a pleasing odor, an offering by fire to the LORD. 42 It shall be a continual burnt offering throughout your generations at the door of the tent of meeting before the LORD, where I will meet with you, to speak there to you. 43 There I will meet with the people of Israel, and it shall be sanctified by my glory; 44 I will consecrate the tent of meeting and the altar; Aaron also and his sons I will consecrate, to serve me as priests. 45 And I will dwell among the people of Israel, and will be their God. 46 And they shall know that I am the LORD their God, who brought them forth out of the land of Egypt that I might dwell among them; I am the LORD their God.

4. The altar of incense

30 "You shall make an altar to burn incense upon; of acacia wood shall you make it. 2 A cubit shall be its length, and a cubit its breadth; it shall be square, and two cubits shall be its height; its horns shall be of one piece with it. 3 And you shall overlay it with pure gold, its top and its sides round about and its horns; and you shall make for it a molding of gold round about. 4 And two golden rings shall you make for it; under its molding on two opposite sides of it shall you make them, and they shall be holders for poles with which to carry it. 5 You shall make the poles of acacia wood, and overlay them with gold. 6 And you shall put it before the veil that is by the ark of the testimony, before the mercy seat that is over the testimony, where I will meet with you. 7 And Aaron shall burn fragrant incense on it; every morning when he dresses the lamps he shall burn it, 8 and when Aaron sets up the lamps in the evening, he shall burn it, a perpetual incense before the LORD throughout your generations. 9 You shall offer no unholy incense thereon, nor burnt offering, nor cereal offering; and you shall pour no libation thereon. 10 Aaron shall make atonement upon its horns once a year; with the blood of the sin offering of atonement he shall make atonement for it once in the year throughout your generations; it is most holy to the LORD."

5. The offerings for the tabernacle

11 The LORD said to Moses, 12 "When you take the census of

29.36
Heb 10.11;
Ex 40.10

29.37
Ex 40.10;
Mt 23.19

29.38
Num 28.3

29.42
Ex 30.8
29.43
1 Ki 8.11
29.44
Lev 21.15
29.45
Ex 25.8;
Lev 26.12;
Rev 21.3
29.46
Ex 20.2

30.1
Ex 37.25

30.6
Ex 25.21,22

30.7
ver 34,35;
Ex 27.21

30.9
Lev 10.1

*30.10
Lev 16.18

*30.12
Num 1.2,5;
31.50;
Mt 20.28;
2 Sam 24.15

30.10 *once a year* is a reference to the Day of Atonement. (See note to Lev 16.6.)
30.12 *a ransom for himself* was the half-shekel sanctuary (later, temple) tax which was to stay the plague the ancients associated with a census.

the people of Israel, then each shall give a ransom for himself to the LORD when you number them, that there be no plague among them when you number them. 13 Each who is numbered in the census shall give this: half a shekel according to the shekel of the sanctuary (the shekel is twenty gerahs), half a shekel as an offering to the LORD. 14 Every one who is numbered in the census, from twenty years old and upward, shall give the LORD's offering. 15 The rich shall not give more, and the poor shall not give less, than the half shekel, when you give the LORD's offering to make atonement for yourselves. 16And you shall take the atonement money from the people of Israel, and shall appoint it for the service of the tent of meeting; that it may bring the people of Israel to remembrance before the LORD, so as to make atonement for yourselves."

6. The bronze laver

17 The LORD said to Moses, 18 "You shall also make a laver of bronze, with its base of bronze, for washing. And you shall put it between the tent of meeting and the altar, and you shall put water in it, 19 with which Aaron and his sons shall wash their hands and their feet. 20 When they go into the tent of meeting, or when they come near the altar to minister, to burn an offering by fire to the LORD, they shall wash with water, lest they die. 21 They shall wash their hands and their feet, lest they die: it shall be a statute for ever to them, even to him and to his descendants throughout their generations."

7. The anointing oil

22 Moreover, the LORD said to Moses, 23 "Take the finest spices: of liquid myrrh five hundred shekels, and of sweet-smelling cinnamon half as much, that is, two hundred and fifty, and of aromatic cane two hundred and fifty, 24 and of cassia five hundred, according to the shekel of the sanctuary, and of olive oil a hin; 25 and you shall make of these a sacred anointing oil blended as by the perfumer; a holy anointing oil it shall be. 26And you shall anoint with it the tent of meeting and the ark of the testimony, 27 and the table and all its utensils, and the lampstand and its utensils, and the altar of incense, 28 and the altar of burnt offering with all its utensils and the laver and its base; 29 you shall consecrate them, that they may be most holy; whatever touches them will become holy. 30And you shall anoint Aaron and his sons, and consecrate them, that they may serve me as priests. 31And you shall say to the people of Israel, 'This shall be my holy anointing oil throughout your generations. 32 It shall not be poured upon the bodies of ordinary men, and you shall make no other like it in composition; it is holy, and it shall be holy to you. 33 Whoever compounds any like it or whoever puts any of it on an outsider shall be cut off from his people.' "

8. The incense

34 And the LORD said to Moses, "Take sweet spices, stacte, and onycha, and galbanum, sweet spices with pure frankincense (of each shall there be an equal part), 35 and make an incense blended as by the perfumer, seasoned with salt, pure and holy; 36 and you shall beat some of it very small, and put part of it before the testimony in the tent of meeting where I shall meet with you; it

30.13
Mt 17.24

30.15
Prov 22.2

30.16
Ex 38.25;
Num 16.40

30.18
Ex 38.8;
40.7,30

30.19
Ex 40.31,32

30.21
Ex 28.43

30.25
Ex 37.29;
40.9

30.26
Lev 8.10

30.29
Ex 29.37

30.30
Lev 8.12,30

30.32
ver 25,37

30.33
ver 38;
Ex 12.15

30.35
ver 25

30.36
Ex 29.42;
Lev 16.2;
ver 32;
Ex 29.37;
Lev 2.3

shall be for you most holy. 37And the incense which you shall make according to its composition, you shall not make for yourselves; it shall be for you holy to the LORD. 38 Whoever makes any like it to use as perfume shall be cut off from his people."

J. The appointment of the workmen

31 The LORD said to Moses, 2 "See, I have called by name Bĕz'álĕl the son of Ū́rī, son of Hŭr, of the tribe of Judah: 3 and I have filled him with the Spirit of God, with ability and intelligence, with knowledge and all craftsmanship, 4 to devise artistic designs, to work in gold, silver, and bronze, 5 in cutting stones for setting, and in carving wood, for work in every craft. 6And behold, I have appointed with him Ŏhŏ'liăb, the son of Áhĭs'ámăch, of the tribe of Dan; and I have given to all able men ability, that they may make all that I have commanded you: 7 the tent of meeting, and the ark of the testimony, and the mercy seat that is thereon, and all the furnishings of the tent, 8 the table and its utensils, and the pure lampstand with all its utensils, and the altar of incense, 9 and the altar of burnt offering with all its utensils, and the laver and its base, 10 and the finely worked garments, the holy garments for Aaron the priest and the garments of his sons, for their service as priests, 11 and the anointing oil and the fragrant incense for the holy place. According to all that I have commanded you they shall do."

K. The observance of the Sabbath

12 And the LORD said to Moses, 13 "Say to the people of Israel, 'You shall keep my sabbaths, for this is a sign between me and you throughout your generations, that you may know that I, the LORD, sanctify you. 14 You shall keep the sabbath, because it is holy for you; every one who profanes it shall be put to death; whoever does any work on it, that soul shall be cut off from among his people. 15 Six days shall work be done, but the seventh day is a sabbath of solemn rest, holy to the LORD; whoever does any work on the sabbath day shall be put to death. 16 Therefore the people of Israel shall keep the sabbath, observing the sabbath throughout their generations, as a perpetual covenant. 17 It is a sign for ever between me and the people of Israel that in six days the LORD made heaven and earth, and on the seventh day he rested, and was refreshed.' "

18 And he gave to Moses, when he had made an end of speaking with him upon Mount Sī́nāï, the two tables of the testimony, tables of stone, written with the finger of God.

L. Israel breaks the covenant by idolatry

1. Aaron makes a golden calf

32 When the people saw that Moses delayed to come down from the mountain, the people gathered themselves together to Aaron, and said to him, "Up, make us gods, who shall go before us; as for this Moses, the man who brought us up out of

31.2
Ex 35.30–
36.1

31.6
Ex 35.34

31.7
Ex 36.8;
37.1,6
31.8
Ex 37.10,17

31.11
Ex 30.25,
31; 37.29;
30.34

31.13
Lev 19.3,
30;
Ezek 20.12,
20
31.14
Ex 35.2;
Num 15.32,
35
31.15
Ex 16.23;
20.9,10

31.17
ver 13;
Gen 2.2,3

31.18
Ex 24.12;
32.15,16;
34.1,28

★32.1
Ex 24.18;
Deut 9.9;
Acts 7.40;
Ex 13.21

32.1 The making of the golden calf with Aaron's consent was flagrant idolatry. God had delivered His people from Egypt and had worked miracles. They were fed with manna and enjoyed the fire and the cloud for guidance. Yet they turned away from God. This

the land of Egypt, we do not know what has become of him."
2And Aaron said to them, "Take off the rings of gold which are in the ears of your wives, your sons, and your daughters, and bring them to me." 3 So all the people took off the rings of gold which were in their ears, and brought them to Aaron. 4And he received the gold at their hand, and fashioned it with a graving tool, and made a molten calf; and they said, "These are your gods, O Israel, who brought you up out of the land of Egypt!" 5 When Aaron saw this, he built an altar before it; and Aaron made proclamation and said, "Tomorrow shall be a feast to the LORD." 6And they rose up early on the morrow, and offered burnt offerings and brought peace offerings; and the people sat down to eat and drink, and rose up to play.

2. Moses intercedes for sinful Israel

7 And the LORD said to Moses, "Go down; for your people, whom you brought up out of the land of Egypt, have corrupted themselves; 8 they have turned aside quickly out of the way which I commanded them; they have made for themselves a molten calf, and have worshiped it and sacrificed to it, and said, 'These are your gods, O Israel, who brought you up out of the land of Egypt!' " 9And the LORD said to Moses, "I have seen this people, and behold, it is a stiff-necked people; 10 now therefore let me alone, that my wrath may burn hot against them and I may consume them; but of you I will make a great nation."

11 But Moses besought the LORD his God, and said, "O LORD, why does thy wrath burn hot against thy people, whom thou hast brought forth out of the land of Egypt with great power and with a mighty hand? 12 Why should the Egyptians say, 'With evil intent did he bring them forth, to slay them in the mountains, and to consume them from the face of the earth'? Turn from thy fierce wrath, and repent of this evil against thy people. 13 Remember Abraham, Isaac, and Israel, thy servants, to whom thou didst swear by thine own self, and didst say to them, 'I will multiply your descendants as the stars of heaven, and all this land that I have promised I will give to your descendants, and they shall inherit it for ever.' " 14And the LORD repented of the evil which he thought to do to his people.

3. Moses destroys the calf and breaks the tables of the law

15 And Moses turned, and went down from the mountain with the two tables of the testimony in his hands, tables that were written on both sides; on the one side and on the other were they written. 16And the tables were the work of God, and the writing was the writing of God, graven upon the tables. 17 When Joshua

32.2
Ex 35.22

32.4
Deut 9.16;
Acts 7.41

32.6
1 Cor 10.7

32.7
Deut 9.12;
Dan 9.24;
Gen 6.11,12
32.8
Ex 20.3,4,
23;
1 Ki 12.28
32.9
Num
14.11–20;
Ex 33.3,5;
34.9;
Acts 7.31
32.10
Deut 9.14;
Num 14.12
32.11
Deut 9.18
32.12
Num 14.13;
Deut 9.28;
ver 14
32.13
Gen 22.16;
Heb 6.13;
Gen 12.7;
13.15;
Ex 13.5
32.14
Ps 106.45

32.15
Deut 9.15

32.16
Ex 31.18

act is called: (1) great sin (32.21, 30, 31); (2) disobedience (Deut 9.12, 16); (3) a forgetting of God (Ps 106.21). Paul warns against this kind of wickedness (1 Cor 10.5–7). It is important to observe that the golden calf in this case was intended as a representation of the LORD Himself (or at least of the pedestal upon which He invisibly stood). Aaron inaugurated its worship by proclaiming a feast to the LORD (ver 5). Thus God's hot anger was directed against a worship of Himself which was accompanied by the use of images contrary to His command. Certainly any pictorial representation of God is included in the prohibition of the second commandment: "You shall not make for yourself a graven image, or any likeness of anything that is in heaven above. . . ." By the same token this would forbid the bowing before any image of angel or saint dwelling in heaven above. Israel should have known this and was sternly punished for violating God's command.

heard the noise of the people as they shouted, he said to Moses, "There is a noise of war in the camp." [18] But he said, "It is not the sound of shouting for victory, or the sound of the cry of defeat, but the sound of singing that I hear." [19]And as soon as he came near the camp and saw the calf and the dancing, Moses' anger burned hot, and he threw the tables out of his hands and broke them at the foot of the mountain. [20]And he took the calf which they had made, and burnt it with fire, and ground it to powder, and scattered it upon the water, and made the people of Israel drink it.

32.19
Deut 9.16, 17

32.20
Deut 9.21

21 And Moses said to Aaron, "What did this people do to you that you have brought a great sin upon them?" [22]And Aaron said, "Let not the anger of my lord burn hot; you know the people, that they are set on evil. 23 For they said to me, 'Make us gods, who shall go before us; as for this Moses, the man who brought us up out of the land of Egypt, we do not know what has become of him.' [24]And I said to them, 'Let any who have gold take it off'; so they gave it to me, and I threw it into the fire, and there came out this calf."

32.21
Gen 26.10
32.22
Deut 9.24
32.23
ver 1

32.24
ver 4

4. The slaughter by the Levites

25 And when Moses saw that the people had broken loose (for Aaron had let them break loose, to their shame among their enemies), 26 then Moses stood in the gate of the camp, and said, "Who is on the LORD's side? Come to me." And all the sons of Lēvī gathered themselves together to him. [27]And he said to them, "Thus says the LORD God of Israel, 'Put every man his sword on his side, and go to and fro from gate to gate throughout the camp, and slay every man his brother, and every man his companion, and every man his neighbor.' " [28]And the sons of Lēvī did according to the word of Moses; and there fell of the people that day about three thousand men. [29]And Moses said, "Today you have ordained yourselvesˢ for the service of the LORD, each one at the cost of his son and of his brother, that he may bestow a blessing upon you this day."

32.27
Num 25.7-13;
Deut 33.9

32.30
1 Sam 12.20,23;
2 Sam 16.12;
Num 25.13

*32.31
Deut 9.18;
Ex 20.23

5. The second intercession of Moses

30 On the morrow Moses said to the people, "You have sinned a great sin. And now I will go up to the LORD; perhaps I can make atonement for your sin." 31 So Moses returned to the LORD and said, "Alas, this people have sinned a great sin; they have made for themselves gods of gold. 32 But now, if thou wilt forgive their sin—and if not, blot me, I pray thee, out of thy book which thou hast written." 33 But the LORD said to Moses, "Whoever has sinned against me, him will I blot out of my book. 34 But now go, lead the people to the place of which I have spoken to you; behold,

32.32
Ps 69.28;
Rom 9.3;
Dan 12.1;
Rev 3.5;
13.8; 17.8;
21.27

32.33
Deut 29.20;
Ps 9.5

32.34
Ex 3.17;
23.20;
Ps 99.8

ˢ Gk Vg See Tg: Heb ordain yourselves

32.31 Moses confessed to God the sin of Israel in the making of the golden calf. He prayed for forgiveness as an intercessor for the people. God did freely forgive them, but there were consequences of the sin which were unavoidable (see ver 35). The biblical principle established here is that guilt and penalty may be set aside in response to repentance and confession, but the temporal consequences of the sin may continue all the days of this life. An example of this is Moses arrogantly striking the rock to which he was only supposed to speak (Num 20.12). His sin was forgiven and the guilt and penalty removed, but the temporal consequence endured —he could not enter the promised land.

my angel shall go before you. Nevertheless, in the day when I visit, I will visit their sin upon them."

32.35
ver 4,24,28

35 And the LORD sent a plague upon the people, because they made the calf which Aaron made.

6. *The renewal of the covenant*
a. *God's command to depart*

33.1
Ex 32.7,13;
Gen 12.7

33 The LORD said to Moses, "Depart, go up hence, you and the people whom you have brought up out of the land of Egypt, to the land of which I swore to Abraham, Isaac, and Jacob, saying, 'To your descendants I will give it.' 2And I will

33.2
Ex 32.34;
23,27-31

send an angel before you, and I will drive out the Cā'naànītes, the Ăm'órītes, the Hĭttītes, the Pĕr'ĭzzītes, the Hĭvītes, and the Jĕb'ūsītes. 3 Go up to a land flowing with milk and honey; but

33.3
Ex 3.8,17;
32.9,10

I will not go up among you, lest I consume you in the way, for you are a stiff-necked people."

33.4
Num 14.1,
39

4 When the people heard these evil tidings, they mourned; and no man put on his ornaments. 5 For the LORD had said to Moses,

33.5
ver 3

"Say to the people of Israel, 'You are a stiff-necked people; if for a single moment I should go up among you, I would consume you. So now put off your ornaments from you, that I may know what to do with you.' " 6 Therefore the people of Israel stripped themselves of their ornaments, from Mount Horĕb onward.

b. *The tent of meeting*

33.7
Ex 29.42,
43;
Deut 4.29

7 Now Moses used to take the tent and pitch it outside the camp, far off from the camp; and he called it the tent of meeting. And every one who sought the LORD would go out to the tent of

33.8
Num 16.27

meeting, which was outside the camp. 8 Whenever Moses went out to the tent, all the people rose up, and every man stood at his tent door, and looked after Moses, until he had gone into the tent.

33.9
Ex 25.22;
31.18;
Ps 99.7

9 When Moses entered the tent, the pillar of cloud would descend and stand at the door of the tent, and the LORD would speak with Moses. 10And when all the people saw the pillar of cloud standing at the door of the tent, all the people would rise up and worship,

33.11
Num 12.8;
Deut 34.10;
Ex 24.13

every man at his tent door. 11 Thus the LORD used to speak to Moses face to face, as a man speaks to his friend. When Moses turned again into the camp, his servant Joshua the son of Nùn, a young man, did not depart from the tent.

c. *The promise of God's presence*

33.12
Ex 32.34;
ver 17;
Jer 1.5;
Jn 10.14,15;
2 Tim 2.19

12 Moses said to the LORD, "See, thou sayest to me, 'Bring up this people'; but thou hast not let me know whom thou wilt send with me. Yet thou hast said, 'I know you by name, and you have also found favor in my sight.' 13 Now therefore, I pray thee, if I

33.13
Ex 34.9;
Ps 25.4;
Deut 9.26,
29

have found favor in thy sight, show me now thy ways, that I may know thee and find favor in thy sight. Consider too that this nation is thy people." 14And he said, "My presence will go with you, and I will give you rest." 15And he said to him, "If thy presence will

33.14
Isa 63.9;
Josh 22.4

not go with me, do not carry us up from here. 16 For how shall it

33.16
Num 14.14;
Ex 34.10

be known that I have found favor in thy sight, I and thy people? Is it not in thy going with us, so that we are distinct, I and thy people, from all other people that are upon the face of the earth?"

d. *Moses beholds God's glory*

33.17
ver 12

17 And the LORD said to Moses, "This very thing that you have

spoken I will do; for you have found favor in my sight, and I know you by name." ¹⁸ Moses said, "I pray thee, show me thy glory." ¹⁹And he said, "I will make all my goodness pass before you, and will proclaim before you my name 'The LORD'; and I will be gracious to whom I will be gracious, and will show mercy on whom I will show mercy. ²⁰ But," he said, "you cannot see my face; for man shall not see me and live." ²¹And the LORD said, "Behold, there is a place by me where you shall stand upon the rock; ²² and while my glory passes by I will put you in a cleft of the rock, and I will cover you with my hand until I have passed by; ²³ then I will take away my hand, and you shall see my back; but my face shall not be seen."

e. The second tables of stone: the covenant promise repeated

34 The LORD said to Moses, "Cut two tables of stone like the first; and I will write upon the tables the words that were on the first tables, which you broke. ² Be ready in the morning, and come up in the morning to Mount Sī'naï, and present yourself there to me on the top of the mountain. ³ No man shall come up with you, and let no man be seen throughout all the mountain; let no flocks or herds feed before that mountain." ⁴ So Moses cut two tables of stone like the first; and he rose early in the morning and went up on Mount Sī'naï, as the LORD had commanded him, and took in his hand two tables of stone. ⁵And the LORD descended in the cloud and stood with him there, and proclaimed the name of the LORD. ⁶ The LORD passed before him, and proclaimed, "The LORD, the LORD, a God merciful and gracious, slow to anger, and abounding in steadfast love and faithfulness, ⁷ keeping steadfast love for thousands, forgiving iniquity and transgression and sin, but who will by no means clear the guilty, visiting the iniquity of the fathers upon the children and the children's children, to the third and the fourth generation." ⁸And Moses made haste to bow his head toward the earth, and worshiped. ⁹And he said, "If now I have found favor in thy sight, O Lord, let the Lord, I pray thee, go in the midst of us, although it is a stiff-necked people; and pardon our iniquity and our sin, and take us for thy inheritance."

10 And he said, "Behold, I make a covenant. Before all your people I will do marvels, such as have not been wrought in all the earth or in any nation; and all the people among whom you are shall see the work of the LORD; for it is a terrible thing that I will do with you.

f. Warning against heathen idolatry

11 "Observe what I command you this day. Behold, I will drive out before you the Am'orites, the Cā'naänites, the Hittītes, the Pěr'izzītes, the Hivītes, and the Jěb'ūsītes. ¹² Take heed to yourself, lest you make a covenant with the inhabitants of the land whither you go, lest it become a snare in the midst of you. ¹³ You

Marginal references:
33.18 ver 20,23
33.19 Rom 9.15, 16,18
33.20 Gen 32.20; Isa 6.5
33.23 Jn 1.18
34.1 Ex 32.16, 19; ver 28
34.2 Ex 19.20
34.3 Ex 19.12, 13,21
34.5 Ex 33.19
34.6 Num 14.18; Neh 9.17; Ps 86.15; 103.8
34.7 Ex 20.6,7; Ps 103.3; Dan 9.9; Eph 4.32
34.8 Ex 4.31
34.9 Ex 33.3, 15,16
34.10 Deut 5.2; 4.32
34.11 Deut 6.3; Ex 33.2
34.12 Ex 23.32,33
*34.13 Ex 23.24; 2 Ki 18.4

34.13 *Asherim*, symbols of Asherah, the Canaanite mother-goddess, who figured prominently in the fertility cult of the Canaanites. These objects were certainly of wood because they are referred to as a tree, or a pole, and they could be cut down, burned, plucked up, or broken in pieces (34.13; Deut 16.21; Mic 5.14; 2 Chr 34.4). Some scholars suggest that all the Asherim were images of the goddess. In any case, they were associated with an idolatry of the most immoral character, and they became a snare to Israel who disobeyed the second commandment (20.3–5; Deut 5.8, 9).

★34.14 Ex 20.3,5; Deut 4.24
34.15 Judg 2.17; Num 25.2; 1 Cor 8.4, 7,10
34.16 Deut 7.3; Num 25.1

shall tear down their altars, and break their pillars, and cut down their Āshē′rīm 14 (for you shall worship no other god, for the LORD, whose name is Jealous, is a jealous God), 15 lest you make a covenant with the inhabitants of the land, and when they play the harlot after their gods and sacrifice to their gods and one invites you, you eat of his sacrifice, 16 and you take of their daughters for your sons, and their daughters play the harlot after their gods and make your sons play the harlot after their gods.

g. Diverse commands

34.17 Ex 32.8

17 "You shall make for yourself no molten gods.

34.18 Ex 12.2,15–17; 13.4

18 "The feast of unleavened bread you shall keep. Seven days you shall eat unleavened bread, as I commanded you, at the time appointed in the month Ābīb; for in the month Ābīb you came out from Egypt.

34.19 Ex 13.2; 22.29

19All that opens the womb is mine, all your male^x cattle, the firstlings of cow and sheep.

34.20 Ex 13.13; 23.15

20 The firstling of an ass you shall redeem with a lamb, or if you will not redeem it you shall break its neck. All the first-born of your sons you shall redeem. And none shall appear before me empty.

34.21 Ex 20.9; Lk 13.14

21 "Six days you shall work, but on the seventh day you shall rest; in plowing time and in harvest you shall rest.

34.22 Ex 23.16

22And you shall observe the feast of weeks, the first fruits of wheat harvest, and the feast of ingathering at the year's end.

34.23 Ex 23.14–17

23 Three times in the year shall all your males appear before the LORD God, the God of Israel. 24 For I will cast out nations before you, and enlarge your borders; neither shall any man desire your land, when you go up to appear before the LORD your God three times in the year.

34.25 Ex 23.18; 12.10

25 "You shall not offer the blood of my sacrifice with leaven; neither shall the sacrifice of the feast of the passover be left until the morning.

34.26 Ex 23.19

26 The first of the first fruits of your ground you shall bring to the house of the LORD your God. You shall not boil a kid in its mother's milk."

34.27 Ex 17.14; 24.4

27 And the LORD said to Moses, "Write these words; in accordance with these words I have made a covenant with you and with Israel."

34.28 Ex 24.18; 31.18; 34.1; Deut 4.13; 10.4

28And he was there with the LORD forty days and forty nights; he neither ate bread nor drank water. And he wrote upon the tables the words of the covenant, the ten commandments.^t

h. Moses' shining face: the veil

34.29 Ex 32.15; Mt 17.2; 2 Cor 3.7,13

29 When Moses came down from Mount Sī′naï, with the two tables of the testimony in his hand as he came down from the mountain, Moses did not know that the skin of his face shone because he had been talking with God. 30And when Aaron and all the people of Israel saw Moses, behold, the skin of his face shone, and they were afraid to come near him. 31 But Moses called to them; and Aaron and all the leaders of the congregation returned

34.32 Ex 24.3

to him, and Moses talked with them. 32And afterward all the people of Israel came near, and he gave them in commandment all that the LORD had spoken with him in Mount Sī′naï.

34.33 2 Cor 3.13

33And when Moses had finished speaking with them, he put a veil on his

---

^x Gk Theodotion Vg Tg: Heb uncertain   ^t Heb *words*

34.14 *Jealous . . . God* is a very appropriate way to describe God. When God's just and righteous claim on His creatures is rejected He is warranted in being angry. In fact, His anger springs from man's refusal to respond to His love and is in full accord with His justice.

face; 34 but whenever Moses went in before the LORD to speak with him, he took the veil off, until he came out; and when he came out, and told the people of Israel what he was commanded, 35 the people of Israel saw the face of Moses, that the skin of Moses' face shone; and Moses would put the veil upon his face again, until he went in to speak with him.

M. *The building of the tabernacle*

1. *The gathering of the materials*

35 Moses assembled all the congregation of the people of Israel, and said to them, "These are the things which the LORD has commanded you to do. 2 Six days shall work be done, but on the seventh day you shall have a holy sabbath of solemn rest to the LORD; whoever does any work on it shall be put to death; 3 you shall kindle no fire in all your habitations on the sabbath day."

4 Moses said to all the congregation of the people of Israel, "This is the thing which the LORD has commanded. 5 Take from among you an offering to the LORD; whoever is of a generous heart, let him bring the LORD's offering: gold, silver, and bronze; 6 blue and purple and scarlet stuff and fine twined linen; goats' hair, 7 tanned rams' skins, and goatskins; acacia wood, 8 oil for the light, spices for the anointing oil and for the fragrant incense, 9 and onyx stones and stones for setting, for the ephod and for the breastpiece.

10 "And let every able man among you come and make all that the LORD has commanded: the tabernacle, 11 its tent and its covering, its hooks and its frames, its bars, its pillars, and its bases; 12 the ark with its poles, the mercy seat, and the veil of the screen; 13 the table with its poles and all its utensils, and the bread of the Presence; 14 the lampstand also for the light, with its utensils and its lamps, and the oil for the light; 15 and the altar of incense, with its poles, and the anointing oil and the fragrant incense, and the screen for the door, at the door of the tabernacle; 16 the altar of burnt offering, with its grating of bronze, its poles, and all its utensils, the laver and its base; 17 the hangings of the court, its pillars and its bases, and the screen for the gate of the court; 18 the pegs of the tabernacle and the pegs of the court, and their cords; 19 the finely wrought garments for ministering in the holy place, the holy garments for Aaron the priest, and the garments of his sons, for their service as priests."

20 Then all the congregation of the people of Israel departed from the presence of Moses. 21And they came, every one whose heart stirred him, and every one whose spirit moved him, and brought the LORD's offering to be used for the tent of meeting, and for all its service, and for the holy garments. 22 So they came, both men and women; all who were of a willing heart brought brooches and earrings and signet rings and armlets, all sorts of gold objects, every man dedicating an offering of gold to the LORD. 23And every man with whom was found blue or purple or scarlet stuff or fine linen or goats' hair or tanned rams' skins or goatskins, brought them. 24 Every one who could make an offering of silver or bronze brought it as the LORD's offering; and every man with whom was found acacia wood of any use in the work, brought it. 25And all women who had ability spun with their hands, and

34.34
2 Cor 3.16

35.1
Ex 34.32
35.2
Ex 31.15
35.3
Ex 16.23
35.4
Ex 25.1–9

35.10
Ex 31.6
35.11
Ex 26.1ff

35.13
Ex 25.23,
30;
Lev 24.5,6
35.15
Ex 30.1

35.19
Ex 31.10

35.21
Ex 25.2

35.23
1 Chr 29.8

35.25
Ex 28.3

brought what they had spun in blue and purple and scarlet stuff and fine twined linen; 26 all the women whose hearts were moved with ability spun the goats' hair. 27And the leaders brought onyx stones and stones to be set, for the ephod and for the breastpiece, 28 and spices and oil for the light, and for the anointing oil, and for the fragrant incense. 29All the men and women, the people of Israel, whose heart moved them to bring anything for the work which the LORD had commanded by Moses to be done, brought it as their freewill offering to the LORD.

2. The workmen gathered

30 And Moses said to the people of Israel, "See, the LORD has called by name Bĕz'ălĕl the son of Ūrī, son of Hŭr, of the tribe of Judah; 31 and he has filled him with the Spirit of God, with ability, with intelligence, with knowledge, and with all craftsmanship, 32 to devise artistic designs, to work in gold and silver and bronze, 33 in cutting stones for setting, and in carving wood, for work in every skilled craft. 34And he has inspired him to teach, both him and Ŏhō'lĭăb the son of Ăhĭs'ămăch of the tribe of Dan. 35 He has filled them with ability to do every sort of work done by a craftsman or by a designer or by an embroiderer in blue and purple and scarlet stuff and fine twined linen, or by a weaver—by any sort of workman or skilled designer. 36 1 Bĕz'ălĕl and Ŏhō'lĭăb and every able man in whom the LORD has put ability and intelligence to know how to do any work in the construction of the sanctuary shall work in accordance with all that the LORD has commanded."

2 And Moses called Bĕz'ălĕl and Ŏhō'lĭăb and every able man in whose mind the LORD had put ability, every one whose heart stirred him up to come to do the work; 3 and they received from Moses all the freewill offering which the people of Israel had brought for doing the work on the sanctuary. They still kept bringing him freewill offerings every morning, 4 so that all the able men who were doing every sort of task on the sanctuary came, each from the task that he was doing, 5 and said to Moses, "The people bring much more than enough for doing the work which the LORD has commanded us to do." 6 So Moses gave command, and word was proclaimed throughout the camp, "Let neither man nor woman do anything more for the offering for the sanctuary." So the people were restrained from bringing; 7 for the stuff they had was sufficient to do all the work, and more.

3. The curtain and coverings made

8 And all the able men among the workmen made the tabernacle with ten curtains; they were made of fine twined linen and blue and purple and scarlet stuff, with cherubim skilfully worked. 9 The length of each curtain was twenty-eight cubits, and the breadth of each curtain four cubits; all the curtains had the same measure.

10 And he coupled five curtains to one another, and the other five curtains he coupled to one another. 11And he made loops of blue on the edge of the outmost curtain of the first set; likewise he made them on the edge of the outmost curtain of the second set; 12 he made fifty loops on the one curtain, and he made fifty loops on the edge of the curtain that was in the second set; the

35.27 1 Chr 29.6; Ezra 2.68
35.28 Ex 30.23
35.29 ver 21
35.30 Ex 31.1–6
35.35 ver 31
36.1 Ex 25.8
36.2 Ex 35.21, 26; 1 Chr 29.5
36.3 Ex 35.27
36.5 2 Chr 24.14; 31.6–10; 2 Cor 8.23
36.8 Ex 26.1–14
36.12 Ex 26.5

loops were opposite one another. 13And he made fifty clasps of gold, and coupled the curtains one to the other with clasps; so the tabernacle was one whole.

14 He also made curtains of goats' hair for a tent over the tabernacle; he made eleven curtains. 15 The length of each curtain was thirty cubits, and the breadth of each curtain four cubits; the eleven curtains had the same measure. 16 He coupled five curtains by themselves, and six curtains by themselves. 17And he made fifty loops on the edge of the outmost curtain of the one set, and fifty loops on the edge of the other connecting curtain. 18And he made fifty clasps of bronze to couple the tent together that it might be one whole. 19And he made for the tent a covering of tanned rams' skins and goatskins.

4. *The framework of the tabernacle constructed*

20 Then he made the upright frames for the tabernacle of acacia wood. 21 Ten cubits was the length of a frame, and a cubit and a half the breadth of each frame. 22 Each frame had two tenons, for fitting together; he did this for all the frames of the tabernacle. 23 The frames for the tabernacle he made thus: twenty frames for the south side; 24 and he made forty bases of silver under the twenty frames, two bases under one frame for its two tenons, and two bases under another frame for its two tenons. 25And for the second side of the tabernacle, on the north side, he made twenty frames 26 and their forty bases of silver, two bases under one frame and two bases under another frame. 27And for the rear of the tabernacle westward he made six frames. 28And he made two frames for corners of the tabernacle in the rear. 29And they were separate beneath, but joined at the top, at the first ring; he made two of them thus, for the two corners. 30 There were eight frames with their bases of silver: sixteen bases, under every frame two bases.

31 And he made bars of acacia wood, five for the frames of the one side of the tabernacle, 32 and five bars for the frames of the other side of the tabernacle, and five bars for the frames of the tabernacle at the rear westward. 33And he made the middle bar to pass through from end to end halfway up the frames. 34And he overlaid the frames with gold, and made their rings of gold for holders for the bars, and overlaid the bars with gold.

5. *The making of the veil*

35 And he made the veil of blue and purple and scarlet stuff and fine twined linen; with cherubim skilfully worked he made it. 36And for it he made four pillars of acacia, and overlaid them with gold; their hooks were of gold, and he cast for them four bases of silver. 37 He also made a screen for the door of the tent, of blue and purple and scarlet stuff and fine twined linen, embroidered with needlework; 38 and its five pillars with their hooks. He overlaid their capitals, and their fillets were of gold, but their five bases were of bronze.

6. *The construction of the ark*

37 Bĕz'álĕl made the ark of acacia wood; two cubits and a half was its length, a cubit and a half its breadth, and a cubit and a half its height. 2And he overlaid it with pure gold within and

36.14 Ex 26.7
36.19 Ex 26.14
36.20 Ex 26.15–29
36.24 Ex 26.21
36.27 Ex 26.22
36.31 Ex 26.26
36.35 Ex 26.31–37
37.1 Ex 25.10–20

without, and made a molding of gold around it. 3And he cast for it four rings of gold for its four corners, two rings on its one side and two rings on its other side. 4And he made poles of acacia wood, and overlaid them with gold, 5 and put the poles into the rings on the sides of the ark, to carry the ark. 6And he made a mercy seat of pure gold; two cubits and a half was its length, and a cubit and a half its breadth. 7And he made two cherubim of hammered gold; on the two ends of the mercy seat he made them, 8 one cherub on the one end, and one cherub on the other end; of one piece with the mercy seat he made the cherubim on its two ends. 9 The cherubim spread out their wings above, overshadowing the mercy seat with their wings, with their faces one to another; toward the mercy seat were the faces of the cherubim.

7. *The building of the table*

10 He also made the table of acacia wood; two cubits was its length, a cubit its breadth, and a cubit and a half its height; 11 and he overlaid it with pure gold, and made a molding of gold around it. 12And he made around it a frame a handbreadth wide, and made a molding of gold around the frame. 13 He cast for it four rings of gold, and fastened the rings to the four corners at its four legs. 14 Close to the frame were the rings, as holders for the poles to carry the table. 15 He made the poles of acacia wood to carry the table, and overlaid them with gold. 16And he made the vessels of pure gold which were to be upon the table, its plates and dishes for incense, and its bowls and flagons with which to pour libations.

8. *The making of the lampstand*

17 He also made the lampstand of pure gold. The base and the shaft of the lampstand were made of hammered work; its cups, its capitals, and its flowers were of one piece with it. 18And there were six branches going out of its sides, three branches of the lampstand out of one side of it and three branches of the lampstand out of the other side of it; 19 three cups made like almonds, each with capital and flower, on one branch, and three cups made like almonds, each with capital and flower, on the other branch—so for the six branches going out of the lampstand. 20And on the lampstand itself were four cups made like almonds, with their capitals and flowers, 21 and a capital of one piece with it under each pair of the six branches going out of it. 22 Their capitals and their branches were of one piece with it; the whole of it was one piece of hammered work of pure gold. 23And he made its seven lamps and its snuffers and its trays of pure gold. 24 He made it and all its utensils of a talent of pure gold.

9. *The construction of the altar of incense*

25 He made the altar of incense of acacia wood; its length was a cubit, and its breadth was a cubit; it was square, and two cubits was its height; its horns were of one piece with it. 26 He overlaid it with pure gold, its top, and its sides round about, and its horns; and he made a molding of gold round about it, 27 and made two rings of gold on it under its molding, on two opposite sides of it, as holders for the poles with which to carry it. 28And he made the poles of acacia wood, and overlaid them with gold.

37.3
Ex 25.12

37.6
Ex 25.17

37.16
Ex 25.29

37.17
Ex 25.31–39

37.19
Ex 25.33

37.21
Ex 25.35

37.25
Ex 30.1–5

10. *The oil and incense*

29 He made the holy anointing oil also, and the pure fragrant incense, blended as by the perfumer.

37.29
Ex 30.23,34

11. *The making of the altar of burnt offering*

38 He made the altar of burnt offering also of acacia wood; five cubits was its length, and five cubits its breadth; it was square, and three cubits was its height. 2 He made horns for it on its four corners; its horns were of one piece with it, and he overlaid it with bronze. 3And he made all the utensils of the altar, the pots, the shovels, the basins, the forks, and the firepans: all its utensils he made of bronze. 4And he made for the altar a grating, a network of bronze, under its ledge, extending halfway down. 5 He cast four rings on the four corners of the bronze grating as holders for the poles; 6 he made the poles of acacia wood, and overlaid them with bronze. 7And he put the poles through the rings on the sides of the altar, to carry it with them; he made it hollow, with boards.

38.1
Ex 27.1–8

8 And he made the laver of bronze and its base of bronze, from the mirrors of the ministering women who ministered at the door of the tent of meeting.

38.8
Ex 30.18

12. *The construction of the court*

9 And he made the court; for the south side the hangings of the court were of fine twined linen, a hundred cubits; 10 their pillars were twenty and their bases twenty, of bronze, but the hooks of the pillars and their fillets were of silver. 11And for the north side a hundred cubits, their pillars twenty, their bases twenty, of bronze, but the hooks of the pillars and their fillets were of silver. 12And for the west side were hangings of fifty cubits, their pillars ten, and their sockets ten; the hooks of the pillars and their fillets were of silver. 13And for the front to the east, fifty cubits. 14 The hangings for one side of the gate were fifteen cubits, with three pillars and three bases. 15And so for the other side; on this hand and that hand by the gate of the court were hangings of fifteen cubits, with three pillars and three bases. 16All the hangings round about the court were of fine twined linen. 17And the bases for the pillars were of bronze, but the hooks of the pillars and their fillets were of silver; the overlaying of their capitals was also of silver, and all the pillars of the court were filleted with silver. 18And the screen for the gate of the court was embroidered with needlework in blue and purple and scarlet stuff and fine twined linen; it was twenty cubits long and five cubits high in its breadth, corresponding to the hangings of the court. 19And their pillars were four; their four bases were of bronze, their hooks of silver, and the overlaying of their capitals and their fillets of silver. 20And all the pegs for the tabernacle and for the court round about were of bronze.

38.9
Ex 27.9–19

38.11
Ex 27.11

38.14
Ex 27.14

38.18
Ex 27.16

13. *The sum of the metals used*

21 This is the sum of the things for the tabernacle, the tabernacle of the testimony, as they were counted at the commandment of Moses, for the work of the Lēvītes under the direction of Ĭth'-ămar the son of Aaron the priest. 22 Bĕz'ălĕl the son of Ūrī, son of Hûr, of the tribe of Judah, made all that the LORD commanded

38.21
Num 4.28, 33

38.22
Ex 31.2,6

Moses; 23 and with him was Ŏhŏ′liäb the son of Ȧhĭs′ȧmăch, of
the tribe of Dan, a craftsman and designer and embroiderer in
blue and purple and scarlet stuff and fine twined linen.

38.24
Ex 30.13

24 All the gold that was used for the work, in all the construction of the sanctuary, the gold from the offering, was twenty-nine
talents and seven hundred and thirty shekels, by the shekel of the

38.25
Ex 30.11–16

sanctuary. 25And the silver from those of the congregation who
were numbered was a hundred talents and a thousand seven hundred and seventy-five shekels, by the shekel of the sanctuary: 26 a

38.26
Ex 30.13,
15;
Num 1.46

bēká a head (that is, half a shekel, by the shekel of the sanctuary),
for every one who was numbered in the census, from twenty years
old and upward, for six hundred and three thousand, five hundred

38.27
Ex 26.19,
21,25,32

and fifty men. 27 The hundred talents of silver were for casting the
bases of the sanctuary, and the bases of the veil; a hundred bases
for the hundred talents, a talent for a base. 28And of the thousand
seven hundred and seventy-five shekels he made hooks for the
pillars, and overlaid their capitals and made fillets for them. 29And
the bronze that was contributed was seventy talents, and two
thousand and four hundred shekels; 30 with it he made the bases
for the door of the tent of meeting, the bronze altar and the
bronze grating for it and all the utensils of the altar, 31 the bases
round about the court, and the bases of the gate of the court, all
the pegs of the tabernacle, and all the pegs round about the court.

14. *The making of the dress of the priesthood*
a. *The materials*

39.1
Ex 35.23;
28.4

39 And of the blue and purple and scarlet stuff they made
finely wrought garments, for ministering in the holy place;
they made the holy garments for Aaron; as the LORD had commanded Moses.

b. *The making of the ephod*

39.2
Ex 28.6–12

2 And he made the ephod of gold, blue and purple and scarlet
stuff, and fine twined linen. 3And gold leaf was hammered out and
cut into threads to work into the blue and purple and the scarlet
stuff, and into the fine twined linen, in skilled design. 4 They made
for the ephod shoulder-pieces, joined to it at its two edges.
5And the skilfully woven band upon it, to gird it on, was of the
same materials and workmanship, of gold, blue and purple and
scarlet stuff, and fine twined linen; as the LORD had commanded
Moses.

39.6
Ex 28.9
39.7
Ex 28.12

6 The onyx stones were prepared, enclosed in settings of gold
filigree and engraved like the engravings of a signet, according to
the names of the sons of Israel. 7And he set them on the shoulder-
pieces of the ephod, to be stones of remembrance for the sons of
Israel; as the LORD had commanded Moses.

c. *The making of the breastpiece*

39.8
Ex 28.15–28

8 He made the breastpiece, in skilled work, like the work of the
ephod, of gold, blue and purple and scarlet stuff, and fine twined
linen. 9 It was square; the breastpiece was made double, a span
its length and a span its breadth when doubled. 10And they set
in it four rows of stones. A row of sardius, topaz, and carbuncle

39.11
Ex 28.18

was the first row; 11 and the second row, an emerald, a sapphire,
and a diamond; 12 and the third row, a jacinth, an agate, and an

amethyst; 13 and the fourth row, a beryl, an onyx, and a jasper; they were enclosed in settings of gold filigree. 14 There were twelve stones with their names according to the names of the sons of Israel; they were like signets, each engraved with its name, for the twelve tribes. 15And they made on the breastpiece twisted chains like cords, of pure gold; 16 and they made two settings of gold filigree and two gold rings, and put the two rings on the two edges of the breastpiece; 17 and they put the two cords of gold in the two rings at the edges of the breastpiece. 18 Two ends of the two cords they had attached to the two settings of filigree; thus they attached it in front to the shoulder-pieces of the ephod. 19 Then they made two rings of gold, and put them at the two ends of the breastpiece, on its inside edge next to the ephod. 20And they made two rings of gold, and attached them in front to the lower part of the two shoulder-pieces of the ephod, at its joining above the skilfully woven band of the ephod. 21And they bound the breastpiece by its rings to the rings of the ephod with a lace of blue, so that it should lie upon the skilfully woven band of the ephod, and that the breastpiece should not come loose from the ephod; as the LORD had commanded Moses.

d. *The robe of the ephod*

22 He also made the robe of the ephod woven all of blue; 23 and the opening of the robe in it was like the opening in a garment, with a binding around the opening, that it might not be torn. 24 On the skirts of the robe they made pomegranates of blue and purple and scarlet stuff and fine twined linen. 25 They also made bells of pure gold, and put the bells between the pomegranates upon the skirts of the robe round about, between the pomegranates; 26 a bell and a pomegranate, a bell and a pomegranate round about upon the skirts of the robe for ministering; as the LORD had commanded Moses.

e. *The remainder of the garments*

27 They also made the coats, woven of fine linen, for Aaron and his sons, 28 and the turban of fine linen, and the caps of fine linen, and the linen breeches of fine twined linen, 29 and the girdle of fine twined linen and of blue and purple and scarlet stuff, embroidered with needlework; as the LORD had commanded Moses.

30 And they made the plate of the holy crown of pure gold, and wrote upon it an inscription, like the engraving of a signet, "Holy to the LORD." 31And they tied to it a lace of blue, to fasten it on the turban above; as the LORD had commanded Moses.

15. *Moses inspects and blesses the completed work*

32 Thus all the work of the tabernacle of the tent of meeting was finished; and the people of Israel had done according to all that the LORD had commanded Moses; so had they done. 33And they brought the tabernacle to Moses, the tent and all its utensils, its hooks, its frames, its bars, its pillars, and its bases; 34 the covering of tanned rams' skins and goatskins, and the veil of the screen; 35 the ark of the testimony with its poles and the mercy seat; 36 the table with all its utensils, and the bread of the Presence; 37 the lampstand of pure gold and its lamps with the lamps set and all its utensils, and the oil for the light; 38 the golden altar, the

39.14
Ex 28.21

39.16
Ex 28.24

39.19
Ex 28.26

39.22
Ex 28.31–34

39.27
Ex 28.39,
40,42

39.30
Ex 28.36,37

39.32
ver 42,43;
Ex 25.40

39.35
Ex 25.16;
30.6

anointing oil and the fragrant incense, and the screen for the door of the tent; 39 the bronze altar, and its grating of bronze, its poles, and all its utensils; the laver and its base; 40 the hangings of the court, its pillars, and its bases, and the screen for the gate of the court, its cords, and its pegs; and all the utensils for the service of the tabernacle, for the tent of meeting; 41 the finely worked garments for ministering in the holy place, the holy garments for Aaron the priest, and the garments of his sons to serve as priests. 42According to all that the LORD had commanded Moses, so the people of Israel had done all the work. 43And Moses saw all the work, and behold, they had done it; as the LORD had commanded, so had they done it. And Moses blessed them.

16. *The assembling and dedication of the tabernacle*

a. *The command of God to assemble the tabernacle*

40 The LORD said to Moses, 2 "On the first day of the first month you shall erect the tabernacle of the tent of meeting. 3And you shall put in it the ark of the testimony, and you shall screen the ark with the veil. 4And you shall bring in the table, and set its arrangements in order; and you shall bring in the lampstand, and set up its lamps. 5And you shall put the golden altar for incense before the ark of the testimony, and set up the screen for the door of the tabernacle. 6 You shall set the altar of burnt offering before the door of the tabernacle of the tent of meeting, 7 and place the laver between the tent of meeting and the altar, and put water in it. 8And you shall set up the court round about, and hang up the screen for the gate of the court. 9 Then you shall take the anointing oil, and anoint the tabernacle and all that is in it, and consecrate it and all its furniture; and it shall become holy. 10 You shall also anoint the altar of burnt offering and all its utensils, and consecrate the altar; and the altar shall be most holy. 11 You shall also anoint the laver and its base, and consecrate it. 12 Then you shall bring Aaron and his sons to the door of the tent of meeting, and shall wash them with water, 13 and put upon Aaron the holy garments, and you shall anoint him and consecrate him, that he may serve me as priest. 14 You shall bring his sons also and put coats on them, 15 and anoint them, as you anointed their father, that they may serve me as priests: and their anointing shall admit them to a perpetual priesthood throughout their generations."

b. *The obedience of Moses*

16 Thus did Moses; according to all that the LORD commanded him, so he did. 17And in the first month in the second year, on the first day of the month, the tabernacle was erected. 18 Moses erected the tabernacle; he laid its bases, and set up its frames, and put in its poles, and raised up its pillars; 19 and he spread the tent over the tabernacle, and put the covering of the tent over it, as the LORD had commanded Moses. 20And he took the testimony and put it into the ark, and put the poles on the ark, and set the mercy seat above on the ark; 21 and he brought the ark into the tabernacle, and set up the veil of the screen, and screened the ark of the testimony; as the LORD had commanded Moses. 22And he put the table in the tent of meeting, on the north side of the tabernacle, outside the veil, 23 and set the bread in order on it

---

Marginal references (left column):

39.41
Ex 26.33

39.43
Lev 9.22,23

40.2
Ex 12.2;
13.4;
ver 17
40.3
ver 21–30

40.9
Ex 30.26

40.10
Ex 29.36,37

40.12
Lev 8.1–13
40.13
Ex 28.41

40.15
Num 25.13

40.20
Ex 25.16

40.21
Ex 26.33;
35.12
40.22
Ex 26.35
40.23
ver 4

before the LORD; as the LORD had commanded Moses. 24And he put the lampstand in the tent of meeting, opposite the table on the south side of the tabernacle, 25 and set up the lamps before the LORD; as the LORD had commanded Moses. 26And he put the golden altar in the tent of meeting before the veil, 27 and burnt fragrant incense upon it; as the LORD had commanded Moses. 28And he put in place the screen for the door of the tabernacle. 29And he set the altar of burnt offering at the door of the tabernacle of the tent of meeting, and offered upon it the burnt offering and the cereal offering; as the LORD had commanded Moses. 30And he set the laver between the tent of meeting and the altar, and put water in it for washing, 31 with which Moses and Aaron and his sons washed their hands and their feet; 32 when they went into the tent of meeting, and when they approached the altar, they washed; as the LORD commanded Moses. 33And he erected the court round the tabernacle and the altar, and set up the screen of the gate of the court. So Moses finished the work.

40.25
Ex 25.37
40.26
ver 5

40.28
Ex 26.36

40.30
ver 7

40.32
Ex 30.19, 20

c. *The glory of the* LORD *fills the tabernacle*

34 Then the cloud covered the tent of meeting, and the glory of the LORD filled the tabernacle. 35And Moses was not able to enter the tent of meeting, because the cloud abode upon it, and the glory of the LORD filled the tabernacle. 36 Throughout all their journeys, whenever the cloud was taken up from over the tabernacle, the people of Israel would go onward; 37 but if the cloud was not taken up, then they did not go onward till the day that it was taken up. 38 For throughout all their journeys the cloud of the LORD was upon the tabernacle by day, and fire was in it by night, in the sight of all the house of Israel.

*40.34
Num 9.15–
23

40.36
Num 9.17;
10.11;
Neh 9.19

40.38
Ex 13.21;
Num 9.15

40.34 See also note to 13.21. *The glory of the* LORD *filled the tabernacle* as it later filled the Solomonic Temple (2 Chr 5.13, 14). But at the apostasy of Zedekiah's reign that glory departed (cf. Ezek 43.1–4) and never returned in visible splendor when the Temple was rebuilt in 516 B.C. Nevertheless the LORD promised the builders of the second Temple that the splendor (KJV "glory") of that latter sanctuary would some day surpass that of the former (Hag 2.9). This came to pass when our Savior came to cleanse the Temple and to teach in it five centuries later. When He was afterwards rejected and crucified, the spiritual glory departed from the Temple forever, and God decreed its destruction within forty years thereafter (A.D. 70). He no longer had any use for it, for now His Temple consisted of the New Testament church, the mystical body of Christ.

INTRODUCTION TO
THE THIRD BOOK OF MOSES
COMMONLY CALLED
LEVITICUS

Authorship and Background: The name Leviticus, meaning "pertaining to the Levites," is the Septuagint title of the book. The Israelite priesthood was drawn from the tribe of Levi, and the title Leviticus suggests that the book discusses the ministry of the Levitical priesthood. The Hebrew title is the first phrase of the Hebrew text, "And he called." The key idea of the book is embodied in the command, ". . . you shall therefore be holy, for I am holy" (11.45). In Exodus the people covenanted to be the LORD's holy nation. It was fitting, therefore, that specific ways by which priest and people alike might manifest holiness should be set forth in Leviticus. It is reiterated again and again that these laws were given through Moses, who evidently either wrote them down himself, or had them written under his direction and supervision (4.1; 6.1; 8.1; 11.1; 12.1; 13.1, etc.). Leviticus is the third of the five books known as the "Law" of Moses.

Characteristics: In Leviticus there is a blending together of two apparently incompatible concepts, i.e., of law and grace. The book is probably the most legalistic of all the Old Testament scriptures, demanding of men that they render perfect obedience to all the moral laws of God. At the same time, it makes clear that such obedience is required as the response of the people to the grace and mercy of God who makes communion with Himself possible by forgiving the sins of the penitent believer. Thus the New Testament gospel is found at the heart of the ritual of sacrifice, and particularly in the rites of the Day of Atonement. The laws laid down are both general and specific; they are moral and ceremonial. Some are forever binding while others are of value only for the Mosaic dispensation. There is a striking progression of revealed truth which, commencing in Genesis, the book of beginnings, and continuing in Exodus, the book of redemption, culminates in Leviticus which may be termed the book of communion and religious worship.

Contents:

I.   The way of approach to a holy God. 1.1—16.34: The law of sacrifice enunciated with particular reference to the burnt offerings, the meal offering, the peace offering, the sin offering, the guilt offering, and various sacrifices. The law of the consecration of the priests, including washing and anointing, and the ceremony of sacrifice and induction into the office. Aaron and his sons are consecrated. Nadab and Abihu offer strange fire and judgment falls upon them. Instructions given to

the priests concerning abstinence from wine and the eating of holy things. Clean and unclean animals. The laws governing purification of women after childbirth. The laws of leprosy relating to persons, clothing, houses, and purifications. Rules given for diseases which have secretions. The rites for the day of atonement in which expiation is made by the high priest for his own sins and the sins of the people.

II.   The maintaining of fellowship with a holy God. 17.1—27.34: The place of sacrifice and the sanctity of blood as the sacrificial element. Religious and ethical laws which involve incest and sexual sins; sundry warnings. Laws of conduct toward a neighbor and punishments for violations of the statutes. The priests, who are holy, forbidden to defile themselves by contact with the dead. Marriage of the priesthood and physical impediments; also sacred oblations. The laws of holy convocations, including the Sabbath, the annual feasts, first fruits, harvest, pentecost, the Day of Atonement, and the Feast of Tabernacles. The oil and the bread. The penalty for blasphemy. The laws of the sabbatic and jubilee years, together with laws regarding property and personal freedom for servants. God commands obedience and promises blessings upon the obedient, and cursings with strong warnings of the consequences of disobedience. The dispersion predicted. The laws concerning vows relative to persons, animals, houses, land, firstlings, devoted things, and the tithe of the land.

THE THIRD BOOK OF MOSES

COMMONLY CALLED

LEVITICUS

I. *The way of approach to a holy God 1.1–16.34*

A. *The laws and rituals of worship*

1. *The law of burnt offering*

1.1
Num 7.89
*1.2f
Lev 22.18,
19
1.3
Deut 15.21;
Heb 9.14;
1 Pet 1.19
*1.4f
Ex 29.10;
Lev 9.7;
Num 15.25
1.5
Ex 29.11;
Heb 10.11;
12.24;
1 Pet 1.2
1.7
Lev 6.8–13

1.9
Num 15.8–
10;
Eph 5.2

1.11
ver 5

1.14
Lev 5.7

The LORD called Moses, and spoke to him from the tent of meeting, saying, 2 "Speak to the people of Israel, and say to them, When any man of you brings an offering to the LORD, you shall bring your offering of cattle from the herd or from the flock.

3 "If his offering is a burnt offering from the herd, he shall offer a male without blemish; he shall offer it at the door of the tent of meeting, that he may be accepted before the LORD; 4 he shall lay his hand upon the head of the burnt offering, and it shall be accepted for him to make atonement for him. 5 Then he shall kill the bull before the LORD; and Aaron's sons the priests shall present the blood, and throw the blood round about against the altar that is at the door of the tent of meeting. 6 And he shall flay the burnt offering and cut it into pieces; 7 and the sons of Aaron the priest shall put fire on the altar, and lay wood in order upon the fire; 8 and Aaron's sons the priests shall lay the pieces, the head, and the fat, in order upon the wood that is on the fire upon the altar; 9 but its entrails and its legs he shall wash with water. And the priest shall burn the whole on the altar, as a burnt offering, an offering by fire, a pleasing odor to the LORD.

10 "If his gift for a burnt offering is from the flock, from the sheep or goats, he shall offer a male without blemish; 11 and he shall kill it on the north side of the altar before the LORD, and Aaron's sons the priests shall throw its blood against the altar round about. 12 And he shall cut it into pieces, with its head and its fat, and the priest shall lay them in order upon the wood that is on the fire upon the altar; 13 but the entrails and the legs he shall wash with water. And the priest shall offer the whole, and burn it on the altar; it is a burnt offering, an offering by fire, a pleasing odor to the LORD.

14 "If his offering to the LORD is a burnt offering of birds, then

---

1.2, 3 The burnt offering is a type of Christ as the One who offered Himself in atonement for sin (Heb 10.10). This offering was intended as a substitute for the sinner himself. By laying his hand upon the animal's head, the offerer symbolically identified himself with it (ver 4). This act of faith, of which the outward evidence was the laying of the hand on the animal, had validity in view of the sacrifice of Christ. It was then that the animal was to be slain and its blood sprinkled upon the altar. So also Christ atoned for our sin and Himself stood in the sinner's place as his representative (1 Pet 1.18–20). Different animals could be offered, depending upon the financial resources of the one who brought the sacrifice. Acceptable sacrifices included an unblemished bull, a sheep, a goat, a turtledove, or pigeon. As distinct from

all other sacrifices, the burnt offering was to be wholly consumed by fire on the altar; no part could be eaten by priest or worshiper. It pointed forward to the efficacy of the Cross in providing atonement for the totality of sin of fallen man.

1.4, 5 In the Old Testament the principle of life is declared to be in the blood (Gen 9.4). As a basic principle, Scripture also insists that no atonement for sin is possible without the sacrifice of life, the visible representation being the blood (17.11). When the blood was presented it was evidence in God's sight that life had been given. While Jesus Christ did not die from the loss of blood (for he voluntarily yielded up his spirit, Mt 27.50), the blood from his crown, nail wounds, and pierced side attested to the sacrifice of his life, the condition for the atonement for our sins.

he shall bring his offering of turtledoves or of young pigeons. 15And the priest shall bring it to the altar and wring off its head, and burn it on the altar; and its blood shall be drained out on the side of the altar; 16 and he shall take away its crop with the feathers, and cast it beside the altar on the east side, in the place for ashes; 17 he shall tear it by its wings, but shall not divide it asunder. And the priest shall burn it on the altar, upon the wood that is on the fire; it is a burnt offering, an offering by fire, a pleasing odor to the LORD.

2. The law of the cereal (meal) offerings
a. Flour, oil, and frankincense

2 "When any one brings a cereal offering as an offering to the LORD, his offering shall be of fine flour; he shall pour oil upon it, and put frankincense on it, 2 and bring it to Aaron's sons the priests. And he shall take from it a handful of the fine flour and oil, with all of its frankincense; and the priest shall burn this as its memorial portion upon the altar, an offering by fire, a pleasing odor to the LORD. 3And what is left of the cereal offering shall be for Aaron and his sons; it is a most holy part of the offerings by fire to the LORD.

4 "When you bring a cereal offering baked in the oven as an offering, it shall be unleavened cakes of fine flour mixed with oil, or unleavened wafers spread with oil. 5And if your offering is a cereal offering baked on a griddle, it shall be of fine flour unleavened, mixed with oil; 6 you shall break it in pieces, and pour oil on it; it is a cereal offering. 7And if your offering is a cereal offering cooked in a pan, it shall be made of fine flour with oil. 8And you shall bring the cereal offering that is made of these things to the LORD; and when it is presented to the priest, he shall bring it to the altar. 9And the priest shall take from the cereal offering its memorial portion, and burn this on the altar, an offering by fire, a pleasing odor to the LORD. 10And what is left of the cereal offering shall be for Aaron and his sons; it is a most holy part of the offerings by fire to the LORD.

b. Leaven and salt

11 "No cereal offering which you bring to the LORD shall be made with leaven; for you shall burn no leaven nor any honey as an offering by fire to the LORD. 12As an offering of first fruits you may bring them to the LORD, but they shall not be offered on the altar for a pleasing odor. 13 You shall season all your cereal offerings with salt; you shall not let the salt of the covenant with your God be lacking from your cereal offering; with all your offerings you shall offer salt.

14 "If you offer a cereal offering of first fruits to the LORD, you shall offer for the cereal offering of your first fruits crushed new grain from fresh ears, parched with fire. 15And you shall put oil

1.15 Lev 5.9
1.16 Lev 6.10
1.17 Lev 5.8; Gen 15.10
*2.1 Lev 6.14
2.2 ver 9,16; Lev 5.12; 6.15; Acts 10.4
2.3 Lev 6.16; 10.12,13
2.9 ver 2; Ex 29.18
2.10 ver 3
2.11 Lev 6.16, 17; Ex 23.18; 34.25
2.12 Lev 7.13; 23.10,11
*2.13 Mk 9.49; Num 18.19
2.14 Lev 23.10, 14

2.1 The *cereal* (or meal) *offering* ("meat" in KJV) was made of fine flour, unleavened, seasoned with salt, and presented with oil and incense (2.1, 4, 5, 7, 13–15). This sacrifice was not to be offered on the altar of incense (Ex 30.9) but only on the altar of burnt offering (Ex 40.29). When offered by a priest it was to be wholly consumed by fire (6.23). When offered by others the priesthood kept the remainder of it for their own food, after the memorial handful had been consigned to the altar flames (6.15, 17).

2.13 *salt of the covenant* represents the fact that ancient covenants were ratified by meals of food seasoned with salt. Apparently salt became a symbol for the covenant between God and Israel (see Num 18.19; 2 Chr 13.5).

2.16 ver 2	upon it, and lay frankincense on it; it is a cereal offering. ¹⁶And the priest shall burn as its memorial portion part of the crushed grain and of the oil with all of its frankincense; it is an offering by fire to the LORD.

3. The law of the peace offerings

3.1
Lev 7.11,
19; 22.21

3 "If a man's offering is a sacrifice of peace offering, if he offers an animal from the herd, male or female, he shall offer it without blemish before the LORD.

3.2
Lev 1.4;
Ex 29.11,
16,20

²And he shall lay his hand upon the head of his offering and kill it at the door of the tent of meeting; and Aaron's sons the priests shall throw the blood against the altar round about.

3.3
Ex 29.13,22

³And from the sacrifice of the peace offering, as an offering by fire to the LORD, he shall offer the fat covering the entrails and all the fat that is on the entrails, ⁴ and the two kidneys with the fat that is on them at the loins, and the appendage of the liver which he shall take away with the kidneys.

3.5
Lev
7.28–34;
Ex 29.13

⁵ Then Aaron's sons shall burn it on the altar upon the burnt offering, which is upon the wood on the fire; it is an offering by fire, a pleasing odor to the LORD.

3.6
ver 1

6 "If his offering for a sacrifice of peace offering to the LORD is an animal from the flock, male or female, he shall offer it without blemish.

3.7
Lev 17.8,9

⁷ If he offers a lamb for his offering, then he shall offer it before the LORD,

3.8
Lev 1.4,5;
ver 2

⁸ laying his hand upon the head of his offering and killing it before the tent of meeting; and Aaron's sons shall throw its blood against the altar round about. ⁹ Then from the sacrifice of the peace offering as an offering by fire to the LORD he shall offer its fat, the fat tail entire, taking it away close by the backbone, and the fat that covers the entrails, and all the fat that is

3.10
ver 4

on the entrails, ¹⁰ and the two kidneys with the fat that is on them at the loins, and the appendage of the liver which he shall take away with the kidneys.

3.11
ver 5,16;
Lev 21.6,
8,17

¹¹And the priest shall burn it on the altar as food offered by fire to the LORD.

12 "If his offering is a goat, then he shall offer it before the LORD, ¹³ and lay his hand upon its head, and kill it before the tent of meeting; and the sons of Aaron shall throw its blood against the altar round about. ¹⁴ Then he shall offer from it, as his offering for an offering by fire to the LORD, the fat covering the entrails, and all the fat that is on the entrails, ¹⁵ and the two kidneys with the fat that is on them at the loins, and the appendage of the liver which

3.16
Lev 7.23–25

he shall take away with the kidneys. ¹⁶And the priest shall burn them on the altar as food offered by fire for a pleasing odor. All fat

3.17
Gen 9.4;
Lev 17.10,
14;
Deut 12.16

is the LORD's. ¹⁷ It shall be a perpetual statute throughout your generations, in all your dwelling places, that you eat neither fat nor blood."

4. The law of sin offerings
a. The offering for the priest

4.2
Lev 5.15–
18;
Ps 19.12

4 And the LORD said to Moses, 2 "Say to the people of Israel, If any one sins unwittingly in any of the things which the

---

3.1 The *peace offering*, with the exception of the fat and kidneys, was eaten by the priests and worshipers. As such it was a fellowship meal signifying the peace which existed in the covenant relation between God and man and also between men.

4.2 Sins of ignorance were sins wrongfully committed by an Israelite out of weakness or waywardness without any intent to renounce the sovereignty of God. Sins committed with the intention of rejecting God's sovereignty were to be punished by cutting off

LORD has commanded not to be done, and does any one of them,
3 if it is the anointed priest who sins, thus bringing guilt on the
people, then let him offer for the sin which he has committed a
young bull without blemish to the LORD for a sin offering. 4 He
shall bring the bull to the door of the tent of meeting before the
LORD, and lay his hand on the head of the bull, and kill the bull
before the LORD. 5And the anointed priest shall take some of the
blood of the bull and bring it to the tent of meeting; 6 and the
priest shall dip his finger in the blood and sprinkle part of the
blood seven times before the LORD in front of the veil of the
sanctuary. 7And the priest shall put some of the blood on the
horns of the altar of fragrant incense before the LORD which is in
the tent of meeting, and the rest of the blood of the bull he shall
pour out at the base of the altar of burnt offering which is at the
door of the tent of meeting. 8And all the fat of the bull of the sin
offering he shall take from it, the fat that covers the entrails and
all the fat that is on the entrails, 9 and the two kidneys with the
fat that is on them at the loins, and the appendage of the liver
which he shall take away with the kidneys 10 (just as these are
taken from the ox of the sacrifice of the peace offerings), and the
priest shall burn them upon the altar of burnt offering. 11 But the
skin of the bull and all its flesh, with its head, its legs, its entrails,
and its dung, 12 the whole bull he shall carry forth outside the
camp to a clean place, where the ashes are poured out, and shall
burn it on a fire of wood; where the ashes are poured out it shall
be burned.

b. The offering for the whole congregation

13 "If the whole congregation of Israel commits a sin unwittingly and the thing is hidden from the eyes of the assembly,
and they do any one of the things which the LORD has commanded
not to be done and are guilty; 14 when the sin which they have
committed becomes known, the assembly shall offer a young bull
for a sin offering and bring it before the tent of meeting; 15 and
the elders of the congregation shall lay their hands upon the head
of the bull before the LORD, and the bull shall be killed before the
LORD. 16 Then the anointed priest shall bring some of the blood
of the bull to the tent of meeting, 17 and the priest shall dip his
finger in the blood and sprinkle it seven times before the LORD
in front of the veil. 18And he shall put some of the blood on the
horns of the altar which is in the tent of meeting before the LORD;
and the rest of the blood he shall pour out at the base of the altar of

Marginal references: *4.3ff ver 14,23,28; 4.4 Lev 1.4; 4.5 Lev 16.14; 4.7 Lev 8.15; 9.9; Lev 5.9; 4.8 Lev 3.3–5; 4.12 Lev 6.11; Heb 13.11; 4.13 Num 15.24–26; Lev 5.2–4, 17; 4.14 ver 3,23,28; 4.15 Lev 1.4; 4.17 ver 6

their perpetrators from among the people (Num 15.30–31). That atonement should be required for sins of ignorance demonstrates that ignorance is no adequate excuse for failure to keep the Laws of God. Believers are enjoined to study the Scriptures (2 Tim 2.15) and failure to acquaint themselves with the commandments of God affords no excuse. This kind of sin must also be confessed and forgiven (1 Jn 1.9). Even in the case of unbelievers, ignorance is basically wilful, according to Rom 1.21, 28.

4.3ff What was prefigured in the Old Testament sacrifices was fulfilled by Christ at Calvary. The sin offering: (1) met the demands of the Law (justice was satisfied and vindicated—Heb 10.10–12); (2) was to be perfect (Christ was the sinless servant—Heb 4.15); (3) was a substitute offered in the stead of the offerer (Christ was the substitute who bore our sins—1 Pet 2.24; 2 Cor 5.21); (4) removed the guilt and the penalty of the sin. In contradistinction to the burnt offering (which was not related to particular transgressions but which symbolized an approach to a holy God and gave standing in His sight), the sin offering made an atonement for specific sins for which the offering provided a "covering," and the sin was forgiven.

burnt offering which is at the door of the tent of meeting. ¹⁹And
all its fat he shall take from it and burn upon the altar. ²⁰ Thus
shall he do with the bull; as he did with the bull of the sin offering,
so shall he do with this; and the priest shall make atonement for
them, and they shall be forgiven. ²¹And he shall carry forth the bull
outside the camp, and burn it as he burned the first bull; it is the
sin offering for the assembly.

c. *The offering for a ruler*

22 "When a ruler sins, doing unwittingly any one of all the
things which the LORD his God has commanded not to be done,
and is guilty, 23 if the sin which he has committed is made known
to him, he shall bring as his offering a goat, a male without blemish, 24 and shall lay his hand upon the head of the goat, and kill it
in the place where they kill the burnt offering before the LORD;
it is a sin offering. 25 Then the priest shall take some of the blood
of the sin offering with his finger and put it on the horns of the
altar of burnt offering, and pour out the rest of its blood at the
base of the altar of burnt offering. ²⁶And all its fat he shall burn
on the altar, like the fat of the sacrifice of peace offerings; so the
priest shall make atonement for him for his sin, and he shall be
forgiven.

d. *The offering for the common man*

27 "If any one of the common people sins unwittingly in doing
any one of the things which the LORD has commanded not to be
done, and is guilty, 28 when the sin which he has committed is
made known to him he shall bring for his offering a goat, a female
without blemish, for his sin which he has committed. ²⁹And he
shall lay his hand on the head of the sin offering, and kill the sin
offering in the place of burnt offering. ³⁰And the priest shall take
some of its blood with his finger and put it on the horns of the
altar of burnt offering, and pour out the rest of its blood at the
base of the altar. ³¹And all its fat he shall remove, as the fat is
removed from the peace offerings, and the priest shall burn it upon
the altar for a pleasing odor to the LORD; and the priest shall make
atonement for him, and he shall be forgiven.

32 "If he brings a lamb as his offering for a sin offering, he shall
bring a female without blemish, 33 and lay his hand upon the head
of the sin offering, and kill it for a sin offering in the place where
they kill the burnt offering. 34 Then the priest shall take some of
the blood of the sin offering with his finger and put it on the horns
of the altar of burnt offering, and pour out the rest of its blood at
the base of the altar. ³⁵And all its fat he shall remove as the fat of
the lamb is removed from the sacrifice of peace offerings, and the
priest shall burn it on the altar, upon the offerings by fire to the
LORD; and the priest shall make atonement for him for the sin
which he has committed, and he shall be forgiven.

e. *Acts requiring a sin offering*

5 "If any one sins in that he hears a public adjuration to testify
and though he is a witness, whether he has seen or come to
know the matter, yet does not speak, he shall bear his iniquity.
2 Or if any one touches an unclean thing, whether the carcass of an
unclean beast or a carcass of unclean cattle or a carcass of unclean

swarming things, and it is hidden from him, and he has become unclean, he shall be guilty. 3 Or if he touches human uncleanness, of whatever sort the uncleanness may be with which one becomes unclean, and it is hidden from him, when he comes to know it he shall be guilty. 4 Or if any one utters with his lips a rash oath to do evil or to do good, any sort of rash oath that men swear, and it is hidden from him, when he comes to know it he shall in any of these be guilty. 5 When a man is guilty in any of these, he shall confess the sin he has committed, 6 and he shall bring his guilt offering to the LORD for the sin which he has committed, a female from the flock, a lamb or a goat, for a sin offering; and the priest shall make atonement for him for his sin.

*5.5
Lev 16.21;
26.40;
Num 5.7;
Prov 28.13

f. Different sin offerings allowed for the poor

7 "But if he cannot afford a lamb, then he shall bring, as his guilt offering to the LORD for the sin which he has committed, two turtledoves or two young pigeons, one for a sin offering and the other for a burnt offering. 8 He shall bring them to the priest, who shall offer first the one for the sin offering; he shall wring its head from its neck, but shall not sever it, 9 and he shall sprinkle some of the blood of the sin offering on the side of the altar, while the rest of the blood shall be drained out at the base of the altar; it is a sin offering. 10 Then he shall offer the second for a burnt offering according to the ordinance; and the priest shall make atonement for him for the sin which he has committed, and he shall be forgiven.

5.7
Lev 12.8;
14.21

5.8
Lev 1.15,17

5.9
Lev 4.7,18,
30,34

5.10
Lev 1.14–17

11 "But if he cannot afford two turtledoves or two young pigeons, then he shall bring, as his offering for the sin which he has committed, a tenth of an ephah of fine flour for a sin offering; he shall put no oil upon it, and shall put no frankincense on it, for it is a sin offering. 12 And he shall bring it to the priest, and the priest shall take a handful of it as its memorial portion and burn this on the altar, upon the offerings by fire to the LORD; it is a sin offering. 13 Thus the priest shall make atonement for him for the sin which he has committed in any one of these things, and he shall be forgiven. And the remainder shall be for the priest, as in the cereal offering."

5.11
Lev 2.1,2

5.13
Lev 4.26;
2.3

5. The law of the guilt offering

14 The LORD said to Moses, 15 "If any one commits a breach of faith and sins unwittingly in any of the holy things of the LORD, he shall bring, as his guilt offering to the LORD, a ram without blemish out of the flock, valued by you in shekels of silver, according to the shekel of the sanctuary; it is a guilt offering. 16 He shall also make restitution for what he has done amiss in the holy thing,

5.14
Lev 22.14;
7.1–10;
Ex 30.13
*5.16
Lev 6.5;
22.14;
Num 5.7,8;
Lev 4.26

5.5 Confession of sin is essential to a godly walk and life. It is required by God of those who have sinned (5.5; Hos 5.15); for without repentance and confession it is vain to appeal to the blood-sacrifice. The New Testament also bids men to confess their sins (Jas 5.16) with the assurance that there is pardon and cleansing (1 Jn 1.9; cf. Ps 32.5). True confession includes: (1) godly sorrow for sin (Ps 38.18); (2) self-abasement (Jer 3.25); (3) a prayer for forgiveness (Ps 51.1); (4) a willingness to make restitution (Num 5.6, 7); (5) a humble acceptance of the cor-

recting hand of God in punishment (Ezra 9.13; Neh 9.33); (6) a turning away from that sin (Prov 28.13). Two of the finest examples of people who confessed their sins are the prodigal son and the tax collector.

5.16 The *guilt offering* (or, trespass-offering) provided for overt sins or offenses which could be assessed as to the amount of damages; otherwise it resembled the sin offering in all of its requirements. Explicit in the guilt offering are: (1) the principle of the shed blood which provides atonement (6.7); (2) the principle of restitution over and above

and shall add a fifth to it and give it to the priest; and the priest shall make atonement for him with the ram of the guilt offering, and he shall be forgiven.

5.17
ver 15;
4.2,13,
22,27
5.18
ver 15–17

6.2
Num 5.6;
Acts 5.4;
Col 3.9;
Ex 22.7,10;
Prov 24.28
6.3
Deut 22.1–3

6.5
Lev 5.16;
Num 5.7,8
6.6
Lev 5.15

6.7
Lev 4.26

6.10
Ex 28.39–
41,43;
39.27,28

*6.13

17 "If any one sins, doing any of the things which the LORD has commanded not to be done, though he does not know it, yet he is guilty and shall bear his iniquity. 18 He shall bring to the priest a ram without blemish out of the flock, valued by you at the price for a guilt offering, and the priest shall make atonement for him for the error which he committed unwittingly, and he shall be forgiven. 19 It is a guilt offering; he is guilty before the LORD."

6^a The LORD said to Moses, 2 "If any one sins and commits a breach of faith against the LORD by deceiving his neighbor in a matter of deposit or security, or through robbery, or if he has oppressed his neighbor 3 or has found what was lost and lied about it, swearing falsely—in any of all the things which men do and sin therein, 4 when one has sinned and become guilty, he shall restore what he took by robbery, or what he got by oppression, or the deposit which was committed to him, or the lost thing which he found, 5 or anything about which he has sworn falsely; he shall restore it in full, and shall add a fifth to it, and give it to him to whom it belongs, on the day of his guilt offering. 6 And he shall bring to the priest his guilt offering to the LORD, a ram without blemish out of the flock, valued by you at the price for a guilt offering; 7 and the priest shall make atonement for him before the LORD, and he shall be forgiven for any of the things which one may do and thereby become guilty."

6. Instructions for the priests
a. On burnt offerings

8^b The LORD said to Moses, 9 "Command Aaron and his sons, saying, This is the law of the burnt offering. The burnt offering shall be on the hearth upon the altar all night until the morning, and the fire of the altar shall be kept burning on it. 10 And the priest shall put on his linen garment, and put his linen breeches upon his body, and he shall take up the ashes to which the fire has consumed the burnt offering on the altar, and put them beside the altar. 11 Then he shall put off his garments, and put on other garments, and carry forth the ashes outside the camp to a clean place. 12 The fire on the altar shall be kept burning on it, it shall not go out; the priest shall burn wood on it every morning, and he shall lay the burnt offering in order upon it, and shall burn on it the fat of the peace offerings. 13 Fire shall be kept burning upon the altar continually; it shall not go out.

^a Ch 5.20 in Heb   ^b Ch 6.1 in Heb

the damage inflicted (six-fifths compensation) to the brother who has suffered loss (6.5); (3) the principle of confession of sin, of which the very act of bringing the offering is outward proof (6.6); (4) the principle of faith, evidenced by the erring believer's acceptance of God's atoning provision for his trespass (6.6); (5) the principle of forgiveness by which the sinner, having met the divine conditions, can be assured that his sin is cared for (6.7). In Isa 53.10 the word translated *an offering for sin* is really this term: *guilt offering (asham).*

6.13 The first fire which enkindled the wood of the sacrifice after the formal consecration of Aaron was kindled by God (9.24). This supernatural origin of the altar fire indicated that only by God's grace could man's sacrifice be acceptable for purposes of atonement. No man-made fire could be used on the altar of the LORD and it was most important that once the fire was kindled the priests keep it burning. It was the sin of bringing *unholy fire* (i.e., fire which they had enkindled themselves) that resulted in the death of Nadab and Abihu (10.1, 2).

b. On cereal offerings

14 "And this is the law of the cereal offering. The sons of Aaron shall offer it before the LORD, in front of the altar. ¹⁵And one shall take from it a handful of the fine flour of the cereal offering with its oil and all the frankincense which is on the cereal offering, and burn this as its memorial portion on the altar, a pleasing odor to the LORD. ¹⁶And the rest of it Aaron and his sons shall eat; it shall be eaten unleavened in a holy place; in the court of the tent of meeting they shall eat it. ¹⁷ It shall not be baked with leaven. I have given it as their portion of my offerings by fire; it is a thing most holy, like the sin offering and the guilt offering. ¹⁸ Every male among the children of Aaron may eat of it, as decreed for ever throughout your generations, from the LORD's offerings by fire; whoever touches them shall become holy."

19 The LORD said to Moses, ²⁰ "This is the offering which Aaron and his sons shall offer to the LORD on the day when he is anointed: a tenth of an ephah of fine flour as a regular cereal offering, half of it in the morning and half in the evening. ²¹ It shall be made with oil on a griddle; you shall bring it well mixed, in baked^c pieces like a cereal offering, and offer it for a pleasing odor to the LORD. ²² The priest from among Aaron's sons, who is anointed to succeed him, shall offer it to the LORD as decreed for ever; the whole of it shall be burned. ²³ Every cereal offering of a priest shall be wholly burned; it shall not be eaten."

c. On sin offerings

24 The LORD said to Moses, ²⁵ "Say to Aaron and his sons, This is the law of the sin offering. In the place where the burnt offering is killed shall the sin offering be killed before the LORD; it is most holy. ²⁶ The priest who offers it for sin shall eat it; in a holy place it shall be eaten, in the court of the tent of meeting. ²⁷ Whatever^d touches its flesh shall be holy; and when any of its blood is sprinkled on a garment, you shall wash that on which it was sprinkled in a holy place. ²⁸And the earthen vessel in which it is boiled shall be broken; but if it is boiled in a bronze vessel, that shall be scoured, and rinsed in water. ²⁹ Every male among the priests may eat of it; it is most holy. ³⁰ But no sin offering shall be eaten from which any blood is brought into the tent of meeting to make atonement in the holy place; it shall be burned with fire.

d. On guilt offerings

7 "This is the law of the guilt offering. It is most holy; ² in the place where they kill the burnt offering they shall kill the guilt offering, and its blood shall be thrown on the altar round about. ³And all its fat shall be offered, the fat tail, the fat that covers the entrails, ⁴ the two kidneys with the fat that is on them at the loins, and the appendage of the liver which he shall take away with the kidneys; ⁵ the priest shall burn them on the altar as an offering by fire to the LORD; it is a guilt offering. ⁶ Every male among the priests may eat of it; it shall be eaten in a holy place; it is most holy. ⁷ The guilt offering is like the sin offering, there is one law for them; the priest who makes atonement with it shall have it. ⁸And the priest who offers any man's burnt offering shall have for himself the skin of the burnt offering which he has offered.

c Meaning of Heb is uncertain   d Or Whoever

6.14
Lev 2.1,2

6.16
Lev 2.3

6.17
Lev 2.11;
ver 26,29,30
6.18
ver 29;
Num 18.10;
ver 27

6.20
Ex 29.1,2

6.21
Lev 2.5

6.25
Lev 4.2,24,
29,33;
1.3,5,11
6.26
Lev 10.17,
18;
ver 16
6.27
Ex 29.37
6.28
Ex 11.33;
15.12
6.29
ver 18,25
6.30
Lev 4.1,7,
11,12,18,21

7.1
Lev 5.14—
6.7
7.2
Lev 1.11

7.4
Lev 3.4

7.6
Lev 6.16—
18; 2.3
7.7
Lev 6.25,26

7.9
Lev 2.3,10
9And every cereal offering baked in the oven and all that is prepared on a pan or a griddle shall belong to the priest who offers it. 10And every cereal offering, mixed with oil or dry, shall be for all the sons of Aaron, one as well as another.

e. On peace offerings

11 "And this is the law of the sacrifice of peace offerings which one may offer to the LORD. 12 If he offers it for a thanksgiving, then he shall offer with the thank offering unleavened cakes mixed with oil, unleavened wafers spread with oil, and cakes of fine flour well mixed with oil. 13 With the sacrifice of his peace offerings for thanksgiving he shall bring his offering with cakes of leavened

7.14
Num 18.8,
11,19
bread. 14And of such he shall offer one cake from each offering, as an offering to the LORD; it shall belong to the priest who throws the
7.15
Lev 22.30
blood of the peace offerings. 15And the flesh of the sacrifice of his peace offerings for thanksgiving shall be eaten on the day of his
7.16
Lev 19.6–8
offering; he shall not leave any of it until the morning. 16 But if the sacrifice of his offering is a votive offering or a freewill offering, it shall be eaten on the day that he offers his sacrifice, and on the morrow what remains of it shall be eaten, 17 but what remains of the flesh of the sacrifice on the third day shall be burned with
7.18
Lev 19.7;
Num 18.27
fire. 18 If any of the flesh of the sacrifice of his peace offering is eaten on the third day, he who offers it shall not be accepted, neither shall it be credited to him; it shall be an abomination, and he who eats of it shall bear his iniquity.

19 "Flesh that touches any unclean thing shall not be eaten; it
7.20
Lev 22.3
shall be burned with fire. All who are clean may eat flesh, 20 but the person who eats of the flesh of the sacrifice of the LORD's peace offerings while an uncleanness is on him, that person shall be cut
7.21
Lev
11.24,28
off from his people. 21And if any one touches an unclean thing, whether the uncleanness of man or an unclean beast or any unclean abomination, and then eats of the flesh of the sacrifice of the LORD's peace offerings, that person shall be cut off from his people."

f. Forbidden portions

7.23
Lev 3.17
22 The LORD said to Moses, 23 "Say to the people of Israel, You shall eat no fat, of ox, or sheep, or goat. 24 The fat of an animal that dies of itself, and the fat of one that is torn by beasts, may be put to any other use, but on no account shall you eat it. 25 For every person who eats of the fat of an animal of which an offering by fire is made to the LORD shall be cut off from his people.
*7.26
Lev
17.10–14
26 Moreover you shall eat no blood whatever, whether of fowl or of animal, in any of your dwellings. 27 Whoever eats any blood, that person shall be cut off from his people."

g. The portion for the priesthood

7.29
Lev 3.1
28 The LORD said to Moses, 29 "Say to the people of Israel, He that offers the sacrifice of his peace offerings to the LORD shall bring his offering to the LORD; from the sacrifice of his peace offerings 30 he shall bring with his own hands the offerings by fire to the

---

7.26 *eat no blood whatever.* Since shed blood represented the loss of life (Gen 9.4) and was to be used solely for atonement, it was never to be eaten or drunk. This prohibition refers to the eating or drinking of blood as an item of food; it has nothing to do with the medical use of blood-transfusion, as some cultists have claimed. If anything, blood-transfusion, serves as a beautiful illustration of the life-giving efficacy of Christ's atoning blood for us.

LORD; he shall bring the fat with the breast, that the breast may be
waved as a wave offering before the LORD. 31 The priest shall burn
the fat on the altar, but the breast shall be for Aaron and his sons.
32And the right thigh you shall give to the priest as an offering
from the sacrifice of your peace offerings; 33 he among the sons of
Aaron who offers the blood of the peace offerings and the fat shall
have the right thigh for a portion. 34 For the breast that is waved
and the thigh that is offered I have taken from the people of Israel,
out of the sacrifices of their peace offerings, and have given them
to Aaron the priest and to his sons, as a perpetual due from the
people of Israel. 35 This is the portion of Aaron and of his sons
from the offerings made by fire to the LORD, consecrated to them
on the day they were presented to serve as priests of the LORD;
36 the LORD commanded this to be given them by the people of
Israel, on the day that they were anointed; it is a perpetual due
throughout their generations."

h. *Summary*

37 This is the law of the burnt offering, of the cereal offering,
of the sin offering, of the guilt offering, of the consecration, and of
the peace offerings, 38 which the LORD commanded Moses on
Mount Sī′näï, on the day that he commanded the people of Israel
to bring their offerings to the LORD, in the wilderness of Sinai.

B. *The priestly regulations*

1. *The consecration of the priesthood*
a. *Their anointing*

8 The LORD said to Moses, 2 "Take Aaron and his sons with
him, and the garments, and the anointing oil, and the bull of
the sin offering, and the two rams, and the basket of unleavened
bread; 3 and assemble all the congregation at the door of the tent
of meeting." 4And Moses did as the LORD commanded him; and
the congregation was assembled at the door of the tent of meeting.

5 And Moses said to the congregation, "This is the thing which
the LORD has commanded to be done." 6And Moses brought
Aaron and his sons, and washed them with water. 7And he put
on him the coat, and girded him with the girdle, and clothed him
with the robe, and put the ephod upon him, and girded him with
the skilfully woven band of the ephod, binding it to him therewith.
8And he placed the breastpiece on him; and in the breastpiece he
put the Ūrĭm and the Thŭmmĭm. 9And he set the turban upon
his head, and on the turban, in front, he set the golden plate, the
holy crown, as the LORD commanded Moses.

10 Then Moses took the anointing oil, and anointed the tabernacle and all that was in it, and consecrated them. 11And he
sprinkled some of it on the altar seven times, and anointed the
altar and all its utensils, and the laver and its base, to consecrate
them. 12And he poured some of the anointing oil on Aaron's
head, and anointed him, to consecrate him. 13And Moses brought
Aaron's sons, and clothed them with coats, and girded them with
girdles, and bound caps on them, as the LORD commanded Moses.

7.31
ver 34

7.34
Num 18.18,
19

7.37
Lev 6.9,14,
20,25;
ver 1,11
7.38
Lev 1.1,2

*8.2
Ex 29.1–3;
28.2,4;
30.24,25

8.6
Ex 29.4–6

*8.8
Ex 28.30
8.9
Ex 28.36,37

8.10
ver 2

8.12
Ex 30.30;
Ps 133.2
8.13
Ex 29.8,9

8.2 *Aaron and his sons*, set aside as priests
of God, had duties distinct from those religious services which were performed by the
Levites as a whole.
8.8 *Urim and the Thummim*, see note to
Ex 28.30 for explanation.

b. *The sin offering*

8.14
Ex 29.10;
Lev 4.4

8.15
Lev 4.7;
Heb 9.22

8.16
Lev 4.8

8.17
Lev 4.11,12

14 Then he brought the bull of the sin offering; and Aaron and his sons laid their hands upon the head of the bull of the sin offering. ¹⁵And Moses killed it, and took the blood, and with his finger put it on the horns of the altar round about, and purified the altar, and poured out the blood at the base of the altar, and consecrated it, to make atonement for it. ¹⁶And he took all the fat that was on the entrails, and the appendage of the liver, and the two kidneys with their fat, and Moses burned them on the altar. ¹⁷ But the bull, and its skin, and its flesh, and its dung, he burned with fire outside the camp, as the LORD commanded Moses.

c. *The burnt offering*

8.18
Ex 29.15

8.21
Ex 29.18

18 Then he presented the ram of the burnt offering; and Aaron and his sons laid their hands on the head of the ram. ¹⁹And Moses killed it, and threw the blood upon the altar round about. ²⁰And when the ram was cut into pieces, Moses burned the head and the pieces and the fat. ²¹And when the entrails and the legs were washed with water, Moses burned the whole ram on the altar, as a burnt offering, a pleasing odor, an offering by fire to the LORD, as the LORD commanded Moses.

d. *The ram of ordination*

8.22
Ex 29.19,31

8.25
Ex 29.22

8.26
Ex 29.23

8.28
Ex 29.25

8.29
Ex 29.26

22 Then he presented the other ram, the ram of ordination; and Aaron and his sons laid their hands on the head of the ram. ²³And Moses killed it, and took some of its blood and put it on the tip of Aaron's right ear and on the thumb of his right hand and on the great toe of his right foot. ²⁴And Aaron's sons were brought, and Moses put some of the blood on the tips of their right ears and on the thumbs of their right hands and on the great toes of their right feet; and Moses threw the blood upon the altar round about. ²⁵ Then he took the fat, and the fat tail, and all the fat that was on the entrails, and the appendage of the liver, and the two kidneys with their fat, and the right thigh; ²⁶ and out of the basket of unleavened bread which was before the LORD he took one unleavened cake, and one cake of bread with oil, and one wafer, and placed them on the fat and on the right thigh; ²⁷ and he put all these in the hands of Aaron and in the hands of his sons, and waved them as a wave offering before the LORD. ²⁸ Then Moses took them from their hands, and burned them on the altar with the burnt offering, as an ordination offering, a pleasing odor, an offering by fire to the LORD. ²⁹And Moses took the breast, and waved it for a wave offering before the LORD; it was Moses' portion of the ram of ordination, as the LORD commanded Moses.

8.30
Ex 30.30;
Num 3.3

30 Then Moses took some of the anointing oil and of the blood which was on the altar, and sprinkled it upon Aaron and his garments, and also upon his sons and his sons' garments; so he consecrated Aaron and his garments, and his sons and his sons' garments with him.

e. *The seven days of the ordination*

8.31
Ex 29.31,32

31 And Moses said to Aaron and his sons, "Boil the flesh at the door of the tent of meeting, and there eat it and the bread that is in the basket of ordination offerings, as I commanded, saying,

'Aaron and his sons shall eat it'; 32 and what remains of the flesh and the bread you shall burn with fire. 33And you shall not go out from the door of the tent of meeting for seven days, until the days of your ordination are completed, for it will take seven days to ordain you. 34As has been done today, the LORD has commanded to be done to make atonement for you. 35At the door of the tent of meeting you shall remain day and night for seven days, performing what the LORD has charged, lest you die; for so I am commanded." 36And Aaron and his sons did all the things which the LORD commanded by Moses.

2. *The sacrifices*
a. *The offering for the priesthood*

9 On the eighth day Moses called Aaron and his sons and the elders of Israel; 2 and he said to Aaron, "Take a bull calf for a sin offering, and a ram for a burnt offering, both without blemish, and offer them before the LORD. 3And say to the people of Israel, 'Take a male goat for a sin offering, and a calf and a lamb, both a year old without blemish, for a burnt offering, 4 and an ox and a ram for peace offerings, to sacrifice before the LORD, and a cereal offering mixed with oil; for today the LORD will appear to you.' " 5And they brought what Moses commanded before the tent of meeting; and all the congregation drew near and stood before the LORD. 6And Moses said, "This is the thing which the LORD commanded you to do; and the glory of the LORD will appear to you." 7 Then Moses said to Aaron, "Draw near to the altar, and offer your sin offering and your burnt offering, and make atonement for yourself and for the people; and bring the offering of the people, and make atonement for them; as the LORD has commanded."

8 So Aaron drew near to the altar, and killed the calf of the sin offering, which was for himself. 9And the sons of Aaron presented the blood to him, and he dipped his finger in the blood and put it on the horns of the altar, and poured out the blood at the base of the altar; 10 but the fat and the kidneys and the appendage of the liver from the sin offering he burned upon the altar, as the LORD commanded Moses. 11 The flesh and the skin he burned with fire outside the camp.

12 And he killed the burnt offering; and Aaron's sons delivered to him the blood, and he threw it on the altar round about. 13And they delivered the burnt offering to him, piece by piece, and the head; and he burned them upon the altar. 14And he washed the entrails and the legs, and burned them with the burnt offering on the altar.

b. *The offering for the people*

15 Then he presented the people's offering, and took the goat of the sin offering which was for the people, and killed it, and offered it for sin, like the first sin offering. 16And he presented the burnt offering, and offered it according to the ordinance. 17And he presented the cereal offering, and filled his hand from it, and burned it upon the altar, besides the burnt offering of the morning.

18 He killed the ox also and the ram, the sacrifice of peace offerings for the people; and Aaron's sons delivered to him the blood, which he threw upon the altar round about, 19 and the fat of the ox and of the ram, the fat tail, and that which covers the entrails,

8.32
Ex 29.34
8.33
Ex 29.30,35

8.34
Heb 7.16

9.2
Lev 8.18;
Ex 29.1
9.3
Lev 4.23

9.6
ver 23
9.7
Heb 5.1,3

9.8
Lev 4.1–12
9.9
ver 12,18

9.11
Lev 4.11;
8.17

9.15
Lev 4.27–31
9.16
Lev 1.3,10
9.17
Lev 2.1,2;
3.5

9.18
Lev 3.1–11

and the kidneys, and the appendage of the liver; 20 and they put the fat upon the breasts, and he burned the fat upon the altar, 21 but the breasts and the right thigh Aaron waved for a wave offering before the LORD; as Moses commanded.

22 Then Aaron lifted up his hands toward the people and blessed them; and he came down from offering the sin offering and the burnt offering and the peace offerings. 23And Moses and Aaron went into the tent of meeting; and when they came out they blessed the people, and the glory of the LORD appeared to all the people. 24And fire came forth from before the LORD and consumed the burnt offering and the fat upon the altar; and when all the people saw it, they shouted, and fell on their faces.

3. The death of Nadab and Abihu: their strange fire

10 Now Nādăb and Ăbī′hū, the sons of Aaron, each took his censer, and put fire in it, and laid incense on it, and offered unholy fire before the LORD, such as he had not commanded them. 2And fire came forth from the presence of the LORD and devoured them, and they died before the LORD. 3 Then Moses said to Aaron, "This is what the LORD has said, 'I will show myself holy among those who are near me, and before all the people I will be glorified.' " And Aaron held his peace.

4 And Moses called Mĭsh′ä-ĕl and Ĕlzā′phăn, the sons of Ŭzzī′ĕl the uncle of Aaron, and said to them, "Draw near, carry your brethren from before the sanctuary out of the camp." 5 So they drew near, and carried them in their coats out of the camp, as Moses had said. 6And Moses said to Aaron and to Ĕlĕä′zăr and Ĭth′ămar, his sons, "Do not let the hair of your heads hang loose, and do not rend your clothes, lest you die, and lest wrath come upon all the congregation; but your brethren, the whole house of Israel, may bewail the burning which the LORD has kindled. 7And do not go out from the door of the tent of meeting, lest you die; for the anointing oil of the LORD is upon you." And they did according to the word of Moses.

4. The command against wine for the performing priesthood

8 And the LORD spoke to Aaron, saying, 9 "Drink no wine nor strong drink, you nor your sons with you, when you go into the tent of meeting, lest you die; it shall be a statute for ever throughout your generations. 10 You are to distinguish between the holy

Margin references:
9.21
Lev 7.30–34

9.23
ver 6;
Num 14.10

*9.24
1 Ki 18.38, 39

*10.1
Num 3.3,4;
Lev 16.12;
Ex 30.9

10.2
Num 3.4;
26.61

10.3
Ex 19.22;
30.30;
Lev 21.6

10.4
Ex 6.18,22;
Acts 5.6,9, 10

10.6
Lev 21.1,10;
Num 16.22, 46;
Josh 7.1;
22.18–20

10.7
Lev 21.12

*10.9
Ezek 44.21

*10.10
Lev 11.47;
20.25;
Ezek 22.26

9.24 Fire has been regarded as a sacred symbol by almost all peoples and in almost all religions. As a symbol it illustrates many biblical truths. Fire was employed to provide God's protection (Num 9.16); as a weapon of divine vengeance (Deut 4.24; Heb 12.29); and as a symbol of the Holy Spirit (Isa 4.4; Acts 2.3). In this verse fire came down from God to enkindle the sacrifice upon His altar. All burnt offerings were to be consumed by fire (6.9, 12). As a symbol it was used supernaturally in Scripture in many instances: the burning bush (Ex 3.2); at the giving of the Law on Mt. Sinai (Deut 4.11, 36); and again on Mt. Carmel when Elijah overcame the prophets of Baal (1 Ki 18.38). On some occasions God Himself appeared in fire (Ex 3.2 and 19.18). At the end of the age we are told that Christ will return to earth in flaming fire (2 Thess 1.7). It may be thought of as a consuming, purifying, and melting agency, and it certainly connotes the holiness of God (our God is a consuming fire, Heb 12.29; cf. Deut 9.3).

10.1 See note to 6.13. It has been inferred from verse 9 of this chapter that Nadab and Abihu had committed their fatal offense while under the influence of intoxicating drink. Hence the appropriateness of the regulation forbidding descendants of Aaron ever to touch fermented drinks before entering upon their sacred duties.

10.9 strong drink was probably beer, for the ancients did not have distilled liquors.

10.10 unclean does not mean dirty, but ceremonially unclean.

and the common, and between the unclean and the clean; 11 and
you are to teach the people of Israel all the statutes which the
LORD has spoken to them by Moses."

10.11
Deut 24.8;
Mal 2.7

5. *The law of the eating of holy things*

12 And Moses said to Aaron and to Ĕlĕā′zăr and Ĭth′ămar, his
sons who were left, "Take the cereal offering that remains of the
offerings by fire to the LORD, and eat it unleavened beside the
altar, for it is most holy; 13 you shall eat it in a holy place, because
it is your due and your sons' due, from the offerings by fire to the
LORD; for so I am commanded. 14 But the breast that is waved
and the thigh that is offered you shall eat in any clean place, you
and your sons and your daughters with you; for they are given as
your due and your sons' due, from the sacrifices of the peace offerings of the people of Israel. 15 The thigh that is offered and the
breast that is waved they shall bring with the offerings by fire of
the fat, to wave for a wave offering before the LORD, and it shall be
yours, and your sons' with you, as a due for ever; as the LORD
has commanded."

10.12
Lev 6.14–
18; 21.22

10.14
Ex 29.24,
26,27

10.15
Lev 7.29,
30,34

16 Now Moses diligently inquired about the goat of the sin
offering, and behold, it was burned! And he was angry with
Ĕlĕā′zăr and Ĭth′ămar, the sons of Aaron who were left, saying,
17 "Why have you not eaten the sin offering in the place of the
sanctuary, since it is a thing most holy and has been given to you
that you may bear the iniquity of the congregation, to make atonement for them before the LORD? 18 Behold, its blood was not
brought into the inner part of the sanctuary. You certainly ought
to have eaten it in the sanctuary, as I commanded." 19And Aaron
said to Moses, "Behold, today they have offered their sin offering
and their burnt offering before the LORD; and yet such things as
these have befallen me! If I had eaten the sin offering today,
would it have been acceptable in the sight of the LORD?" 20And
when Moses heard that, he was content.

10.17
Lev 6.24–30

★10.19
Lev 9.8,12

C. *The laws of purification*

1. *Clean and unclean animals*

11 And the LORD said to Moses and Aaron, 2 "Say to the
people of Israel, These are the living things which you may
eat among all the beasts that are on the earth. 3 Whatever parts
the hoof and is cloven-footed and chews the cud, among the
animals, you may eat. 4 Nevertheless among those that chew the
cud or part the hoof, you shall not eat these: The camel, because
it chews the cud but does not part the hoof, is unclean to you.
5And the rock badger, because it chews the cud but does not part

★11.2
Deut 14.3–
21

10.19 *such things*, the death of Nadab and
Abihu.

11.2 The dietary restrictions under the
Hebrew theocracy have been rendered obsolete by the atoning work of Christ who
fulfilled all the symbolism of the ceremonial
law (cf. Acts 10.14, 15; Col 2.16; 1 Tim 4.3,
4). The distinction between clean and unclean foods seems to have been based on the
following considerations: (1) the flesh of
unclean animals or birds was unwholesome
or unsuitable for sanitary reasons, usually be-

cause they fed upon carrion or that which had
putrified; (2) the animal in question was
especially associated with depraved heathen
worship (such as the pig, which was offered
to the gods of the nether world); (3) their
habits of life or behavior had an objectionable
association, such as "creeping things" which
were serpent-like in their movements, or bats,
which were at home in dark, dank caves and
hated the light. The New Testament teaches
that these pre-Christian regulations are not
binding upon believers today.

11.7
Isa 65.4;
66.3,17
11.8
Isa 52.11;
Heb 9.10
11.9
Deut 14.9
11.10
Lev 7.18;
Deut 14.3

11.13
Deut 14.12

11.22
Mt 3.4;
Mk 1.6

11.25
ver 40

11.29
Isa 66.17

11.32
Lev 15.12

11.33
Lev 6.28;
15.12

the hoof, is unclean to you. 6And the hare, because it chews the cud but does not part the hoof, is unclean to you. 7And the swine, because it parts the hoof and is cloven-footed but does not chew the cud, is unclean to you. 8 Of their flesh you shall not eat, and their carcasses you shall not touch; they are unclean to you.

9 "These you may eat, of all that are in the waters. Everything in the waters that has fins and scales, whether in the seas or in the rivers, you may eat. 10 But anything in the seas or the rivers that has not fins and scales, of the swarming creatures in the waters and of the living creatures that are in the waters, is an abomination to you. 11 They shall remain an abomination to you; of their flesh you shall not eat, and their carcasses you shall have in abomination. 12 Everything in the waters that has not fins and scales is an abomination to you.

13 "And these you shall have in abomination among the birds, they shall not be eaten, they are an abomination: the eagle, the vulture, the osprey, 14 the kite, the falcon according to its kind, 15 every raven according to its kind, 16 the ostrich, the nighthawk, the sea gull, the hawk according to its kind, 17 the owl, the cormorant, the ibis, 18 the water hen, the pelican, the carrion vulture, 19 the stork, the heron according to its kind, the hoopoe, and the bat.

20 "All winged insects that go upon all fours are an abomination to you. 21 Yet among the winged insects that go on all fours you may eat those which have legs above their feet, with which to leap on the earth. 22 Of them you may eat: the locust according to its kind, the bald locust according to its kind, the cricket according to its kind, and the grasshopper according to its kind. 23 But all other winged insects which have four feet are an abomination to you.

24 "And by these you shall become unclean; whoever touches their carcass shall be unclean until the evening, 25 and whoever carries any part of their carcass shall wash his clothes and be unclean until the evening. 26 Every animal which parts the hoof but is not cloven-footed or does not chew the cud is unclean to you; every one who touches them shall be unclean. 27And all that go on their paws, among the animals that go on all fours, are unclean to you; whoever touches their carcass shall be unclean until the evening, 28 and he who carries their carcass shall wash his clothes and be unclean until the evening; they are unclean to you.

29 "And these are unclean to you among the swarming things that swarm upon the earth: the weasel, the mouse, the great lizard according to its kind, 30 the gecko, the land crocodile, the lizard, the sand lizard, and the chameleon. 31 These are unclean to you among all that swarm; whoever touches them when they are dead shall be unclean until the evening. 32And anything upon which any of them falls when they are dead shall be unclean, whether it is an article of wood or a garment or a skin or a sack, any vessel that is used for any purpose; it must be put into water, and it shall be unclean until the evening; then it shall be clean. 33And if any of them falls into any earthen vessel, all that is in it shall be unclean, and you shall break it. 34Any food in it which may be eaten, upon which water may come, shall be unclean; and all drink which may be drunk from every such vessel shall be unclean. 35And everything upon which any part of their carcass falls shall be un-

clean; whether oven or stove, it shall be broken in pieces; they are unclean, and shall be unclean to you. 36 Nevertheless a spring or a cistern holding water shall be clean; but whatever touches their carcass shall be unclean. 37And if any part of their carcass falls upon any seed for sowing that is to be sown, it is clean; 38 but if water is put on the seed and any part of their carcass falls on it, it is unclean to you.

39 "And if any animal of which you may eat dies, he who touches its carcass shall be unclean until the evening, 40 and he who eats of its carcass shall wash his clothes and be unclean until the evening; he also who carries the carcass shall wash his clothes and be unclean until the evening.

41 "Every swarming thing that swarms upon the earth is an abomination; it shall not be eaten. 42 Whatever goes on its belly, and whatever goes on all fours, or whatever has many feet, all the swarming things that swarm upon the earth, you shall not eat; for they are an abomination. 43 You shall not make yourselves abominable with any swarming thing that swarms; and you shall not defile yourselves with them, lest you become unclean. 44 For I am the LORD your God; consecrate yourselves therefore, and be holy, for I am holy. You shall not defile yourselves with any swarming thing that crawls upon the earth. 45 For I am the LORD who brought you up out of the land of Egypt, to be your God; you shall therefore be holy, for I am holy."

46 This is the law pertaining to beast and bird and every living creature that moves through the waters and every creature that swarms upon the earth, 47 to make a distinction between the unclean and the clean and between the living creature that may be eaten and the living creature that may not be eaten.

2. Purification of a woman after childbirth

12 The LORD said to Moses, 2 "Say to the people of Israel, If a woman conceives, and bears a male child, then she shall be unclean seven days; as at the time of her menstruation, she shall be unclean. 3And on the eighth day the flesh of his foreskin shall be circumcised. 4 Then she shall continue for thirty-three days in the blood of her purifying; she shall not touch any hallowed thing, nor come into the sanctuary, until the days of her purifying are completed. 5 But if she bears a female child, then she shall be unclean two weeks, as in her menstruation; and she shall continue in the blood of her purifying for sixty-six days.

6 "And when the days of her purifying are completed, whether for a son or for a daughter, she shall bring to the priest at the door of the tent of meeting a lamb a year old for a burnt offering, and a young pigeon or a turtledove for a sin offering, 7 and he shall offer it before the LORD, and make atonement for her; then she shall be clean from the flow of her blood. This is the law for her who bears a child, either male or female. 8And if she cannot afford a lamb, then she shall take two turtledoves or two young pigeons, one for a burnt offering and the other for a sin offering; and the priest shall make atonement for her, and she shall be clean."

Marginal references

11.40 Lev 17.15; 22.8

*11.41 ver 29

11.43 Lev 20.25

11.44 Ex 6.7; 19.6; Lev 19.2; 1 Pet 1.15, 16

11.45 Ex 6.7

11.47 Lev 10.10

12.2 Lev 15.19; 18.19

12.3 Gen 17.12

12.6 Lk 2.22

12.8 Lk 2.22–24; Lev 5.7; 4.26

11.41 abomination, "whatever is offensive to God and His plan for man's righteous way of life, whether 'unclean' items of tabooed food, worship of idols, harlotry, or dishonesty." (HARPER'S BIBLE DICTIONARY, p.3.) (See also note to Dan 9.27 on abomination of desolation.)

3. *The laws of leprosy*
a. *Diagnosis and treatment of leprosy in man*

*13.2
Deut 24.8

13 The Lord said to Moses and Aaron, 2 "When a man has on the skin of his body a swelling or an eruption or a spot, and it turns into a leprous disease on the skin of his body, then he shall be brought to Aaron the priest or to one of his sons the priests, 3 and the priest shall examine the diseased spot on the skin of his body; and if the hair in the diseased spot has turned white and the disease appears to be deeper than the skin of his body, it is a leprous disease; when the priest has examined him he shall

13.4
ver 21

pronounce him unclean. 4 But if the spot is white in the skin of his body, and appears no deeper than the skin, and the hair in it has not turned white, the priest shall shut up the diseased person for seven days; 5 and the priest shall examine him on the seventh day, and if in his eyes the disease is checked and the disease has not spread in the skin, then the priest shall shut him up seven days

13.6
Lev 11.25;
14.8

more; 6 and the priest shall examine him again on the seventh day, and if the diseased spot is dim and the disease has not spread in the skin, then the priest shall pronounce him clean; it is only

13.7
Lk 5.14

an eruption; and he shall wash his clothes, and be clean. 7 But if the eruption spreads in the skin, after he has shown himself to the priest for his cleansing, he shall appear again before the priest; 8 and the priest shall make an examination, and if the eruption has spread in the skin, then the priest shall pronounce him unclean; it is leprosy.

9 "When a man is afflicted with leprosy, he shall be brought to

13.10
Num 12.10;
2 Ki 5.27;
2 Chr 26.20

the priest; 10 and the priest shall make an examination, and if there is a white swelling in the skin, which has turned the hair white, and there is quick raw flesh in the swelling, 11 it is a chronic leprosy in the skin of his body, and the priest shall pronounce him

13.12
Lk 5.12

unclean; he shall not shut him up, for he is unclean. 12 And if the leprosy breaks out in the skin, so that the leprosy covers all the skin of the diseased person from head to foot, so far as the priest can see, 13 then the priest shall make an examination, and if the leprosy has covered all his body, he shall pronounce him clean of the disease; it has all turned white, and he is clean. 14 But when

13.15
Mt 8.3

raw flesh appears on him, he shall be unclean. 15 And the priest shall examine the raw flesh, and pronounce him unclean; raw flesh is unclean, for it is leprosy. 16 But if the raw flesh turns again and is changed to white, then he shall come to the priest, 17 and the priest shall examine him, and if the disease has turned white, then the priest shall pronounce the diseased person clean; he is clean.

13.18
Ex 9.9
13.19
ver 43

18 "And when there is in the skin of one's body a boil that has healed, 19 and in the place of the boil there comes a white swelling or a reddish-white spot, then it shall be shown to the priest; 20 and the priest shall make an examination, and if it appears deeper than the skin and its hair has turned white, then the priest shall pronounce him unclean; it is the disease of leprosy, it has broken out

13.21
Num 12.14,
15

in the boil. 21 But if the priest examines it, and the hair on it is not white and it is not deeper than the skin, but is dim, then the

---

13.2 *leprous disease*, a term which was used to cover a variety of skin diseases. It was extended to include molds or defects in gar-ments (13.47–59) and in houses (14.34–53). Sometimes tetter (see 13.39), a cutaneous disease, was mistaken for leprosy.

priest shall shut him up seven days; 22 and if it spreads in the skin, then the priest shall pronounce him unclean; it is diseased. 23 But if the spot remains in one place and does not spread, it is the scar of the boil; and the priest shall pronounce him clean.

24 "Or, when the body has a burn on its skin and the raw flesh of the burn becomes a spot, reddish-white or white, 25 the priest shall examine it, and if the hair in the spot has turned white and it appears deeper than the skin, then it is leprosy; it has broken out in the burn, and the priest shall pronounce him unclean; it is a leprous disease. 26 But if the priest examines it, and the hair in the spot is not white and it is no deeper than the skin, but is dim, the priest shall shut him up seven days, 27 and the priest shall examine him the seventh day; if it is spreading in the skin, then the priest shall pronounce him unclean; it is a leprous disease. 28 But if the spot remains in one place and does not spread in the skin, but is dim, it is a swelling from the burn, and the priest shall pronounce him clean; for it is the scar of the burn.

29 "When a man or woman has a disease on the head or the beard, 30 the priest shall examine the disease; and if it appears deeper than the skin, and the hair in it is yellow and thin, then the priest shall pronounce him unclean; it is an itch, a leprosy of the head or the beard. 31And if the priest examines the itching disease, and it appears no deeper than the skin and there is no black hair in it, then the priest shall shut up the person with the itching disease for seven days, 32 and on the seventh day the priest shall examine the disease; and if the itch has not spread, and there is in it no yellow hair, and the itch appears to be no deeper than the skin, 33 then he shall shave himself, but the itch he shall not shave; and the priest shall shut up the person with the itching disease for seven days more; 34 and on the seventh day the priest shall examine the itch, and if the itch has not spread in the skin and it appears to be no deeper than the skin, then the priest shall pronounce him clean; and he shall wash his clothes, and be clean. 35 But if the itch spreads in the skin after his cleansing, 36 then the priest shall examine him, and if the itch has spread in the skin, the priest need not seek for the yellow hair; he is unclean. 37 But if in his eyes the itch is checked, and black hair has grown in it, the itch is healed, he is clean; and the priest shall pronounce him clean.

38 "When a man or a woman has spots on the skin of the body, white spots, 39 the priest shall make an examination, and if the spots on the skin of the body are of a dull white, it is tetter that has broken out in the skin; he is clean.

40 "If a man's hair has fallen from his head, he is bald but he is clean. 41And if a man's hair has fallen from his forehead and temples, he has baldness of the forehead but he is clean. 42 But if there is on the bald head or the bald forehead a reddish-white diseased spot, it is leprosy breaking out on his bald head or his bald forehead. 43 Then the priest shall examine him, and if the diseased swelling is reddish-white on his bald head or on his bald forehead, like the appearance of leprosy in the skin of the body, 44 he is a leprous man, he is unclean; the priest must pronounce him unclean; his disease is on his head.

45 "The leper who has the disease shall wear torn clothes and let the hair of his head hang loose, and he shall cover his upper lip and cry, 'Unclean, unclean.' 46 He shall remain unclean as long

13.25
ver 15

13.27
ver 5

13.29
ver 44

13.32
ver 5

13.34
Lev 14.8

13.36
ver 30

13.40
Ezek 29.18

13.44
ver 29
13.45
Ezek 24.17, 22;
Mic 3.7;
Lam 4.15
13.46
Num 5.2;
12.14;
2 Ki 7.3;
15.5;
Lk 17.12

as he has the disease; he is unclean; he shall dwell alone in a habitation outside the camp.

b. *Diagnosis and treatment of leprosy in garments*

47 "When there is a leprous disease in a garment, whether a woolen or a linen garment, 48 in warp or woof of linen or wool, or in a skin or in anything made of skin, 49 if the disease shows greenish or reddish in the garment, whether in warp or woof or in skin or in anything made of skin, it is a leprous disease and shall be shown to the priest. 50And the priest shall examine the disease, and shut up that which has the disease for seven days; 51 then he shall examine the disease on the seventh day. If the disease has spread in the garment, in warp or woof, or in the skin, whatever be the use of the skin, the disease is a malignant leprosy; it is unclean. 52And he shall burn the garment, whether diseased in warp or woof, woolen or linen, or anything of skin, for it is a malignant leprosy; it shall be burned in the fire.

53 "And if the priest examines, and the disease has not spread in the garment in warp or woof or in anything of skin, 54 then the priest shall command that they wash the thing in which is the disease, and he shall shut it up seven days more; 55 and the priest shall examine the diseased thing after it has been washed. And if the diseased spot has not changed color, though the disease has not spread, it is unclean; you shall burn it in the fire, whether the leprous spot is on the back or on the front.

56 "But if the priest examines, and the disease is dim after it is washed, he shall tear the spot out of the garment or the skin or the warp or woof; 57 then if it appears again in the garment, in warp or woof, or in anything of skin, it is spreading; you shall burn with fire that in which is the disease. 58 But the garment, warp or woof, or anything of skin from which the disease departs when you have washed it, shall then be washed a second time, and be clean."

59 This is the law for a leprous disease in a garment of wool or linen, either in warp or woof, or in anything of skin, to decide whether it is clean or unclean.

c. *The laws of purification for leprosy*

14 The LORD said to Moses, 2 "This shall be the law of the leper for the day of his cleansing. He shall be brought to the priest; 3 and the priest shall go out of the camp, and the priest shall make an examination. Then, if the leprous disease is healed in the leper, 4 the priest shall command them to take for him who is to be cleansed two living clean birds and cedarwood and scarlet stuff and hyssop; 5 and the priest shall command them to kill one of the birds in an earthen vessel over running water. 6 He shall take the living bird with the cedarwood and the scarlet stuff and the hyssop, and dip them and the living bird in the blood of the bird that was killed over the running water; 7 and he shall sprinkle it seven times upon him who is to be cleansed of leprosy; then he shall pronounce him clean, and shall let the living bird go into the open field. 8And he who is to be cleansed shall wash his clothes, and shave off all his hair, and bathe himself in water, and he shall be clean; and after that he shall come into the camp, but shall dwell outside his tent seven days. 9And on the seventh day he

13.51
Lev 14.44

13.52
Lev 14.44

13.54
ver 4

13.56
Lev 14.8

14.2
Mt 8.2,4;
Mk 1.40,44;
Lk 5.12,14;
17.14

14.4
ver 6,49,
51,52;
Num 19.6

14.7
2 Ki 5.10,14

14.8
Lev 13.6;
Num 8.7

shall shave all his hair off his head; he shall shave off his beard and his eyebrows, all his hair. Then he shall wash his clothes, and bathe his body in water, and he shall be clean.

10 "And on the eighth day he shall take two male lambs without blemish, and one ewe lamb a year old without blemish, and a cereal offering of three tenths of an ephah of fine flour mixed with oil, and one log of oil. 11And the priest who cleanses him shall set the man who is to be cleansed and these things before the LORD, at the door of the tent of meeting. 12And the priest shall take one of the male lambs, and offer it for a guilt offering, along with the log of oil, and wave them for a wave offering before the LORD; 13 and he shall kill the lamb in the place where they kill the sin offering and the burnt offering, in the holy place; for the guilt offering, like the sin offering, belongs to the priest; it is most holy. 14 The priest shall take some of the blood of the guilt offering, and the priest shall put it on the tip of the right ear of him who is to be cleansed, and on the thumb of his right hand, and on the great toe of his right foot. 15 Then the priest shall take some of the log of oil, and pour it into the palm of his own left hand, 16 and dip his right finger in the oil that is in his left hand, and sprinkle some oil with his finger seven times before the LORD. 17And some of the oil that remains in his hand the priest shall put on the tip of the right ear of him who is to be cleansed, and on the thumb of his right hand, and on the great toe of his right foot, upon the blood of the guilt offering; 18 and the rest of the oil that is in the priest's hand he shall put on the head of him who is to be cleansed. Then the priest shall make atonement for him before the LORD. 19 The priest shall offer the sin offering, to make atonement for him who is to be cleansed from his uncleanness. And afterward he shall kill the burnt offering; 20 and the priest shall offer the burnt offering and the cereal offering on the altar. Thus the priest shall make atonement for him, and he shall be clean.

21 "But if he is poor and cannot afford so much, then he shall take one male lamb for a guilt offering to be waved, to make atonement for him, and a tenth of an ephah of fine flour mixed with oil for a cereal offering, and a log of oil; 22 also two turtledoves or two young pigeons, such as he can afford; the one shall be a sin offering and the other a burnt offering. 23And on the eighth day he shall bring them for his cleansing to the priest, to the door of the tent of meeting, before the LORD; 24 and the priest shall take the lamb of the guilt offering, and the log of oil, and the priest shall wave them for a wave offering before the LORD. 25And he shall kill the lamb of the guilt offering; and the priest shall take some of the blood of the guilt offering, and put it on the tip of the right ear of him who is to be cleansed, and on the thumb of his right hand, and on the great toe of his right foot. 26And the priest shall pour some of the oil into the palm of his own left hand; 27 and shall sprinkle with his right finger some of the oil that is in his left hand seven times before the LORD; 28 and the priest shall put some of the oil that is in his hand on the tip of the right ear of him who is to be cleansed, and on the thumb of his right hand, and the great toe of his right foot, in the place where the blood of the guilt offering was put; 29 and the rest of the oil that is in the priest's hand he shall put on the head of him who is to be cleansed, to make atonement for him before the LORD. 30And he shall offer, of the turtledoves

14.10
Mt 8.4;
Mk 1.44;
Lk 5.14

14.12
Lev 5.2,8;
6.6,7;
Ex 29.24
14.13
Lev 1.5,11;
6.24–30;
2.3; 7.6
14.14
Lev 8.23

14.18
Lev 4.26
14.19
ver 12

14.21
Lev 5.7,11;
12.8;
ver 22
14.22
Lev 12.8;
15.14,15
14.23
ver 10,11
14.24
ver 12
14.25
ver 14

14.28
Lev 5.6

14.30
ver 22;
Lev 15.15

14.31
Lev 5.7
or young pigeons such as he can afford, 31 one[x] for a sin offering and the other for a burnt offering, along with a cereal offering; and the priest shall make atonement before the LORD for him who is being cleansed. 32 This is the law for him in whom is a leprous disease, who cannot afford the offerings for his cleansing."

d. *Diagnosis and treatment of leprosy in houses*

14.34
Gen 17.8;
Num 32.22;
Deut 7.1
14.35
Ps 91.10;
Prov 3.33
33 The LORD said to Moses and Aaron, 34 "When you come into the land of Cānaàn, which I give you for a possession, and I put a leprous disease in a house in the land of your possession, 35 then he who owns the house shall come and tell the priest, 'There seems to me to be some sort of disease in my house.' 36 Then the priest shall command that they empty the house before the priest goes to examine the disease, lest all that is in the house be declared unclean; and afterward the priest shall go in to see the house. 37And he shall examine the disease; and if the disease is in the walls of the house with greenish or reddish spots, and if it appears to be deeper than the surface, 38 then the priest shall go out of the house

14.38
Num 12.15
to the door of the house, and shut up the house seven days. 39And the priest shall come again on the seventh day, and look; and if the disease has spread in the walls of the house, 40 then the priest shall

14.40
ver 45
command that they take out the stones in which is the disease and throw them into an unclean place outside the city; 41 and he shall cause the inside of the house to be scraped round about, and the plaster that they scrape off they shall pour into an unclean place outside the city; 42 then they shall take other stones and put them in the place of those stones, and he shall take other plaster and plaster the house.

43 "If the disease breaks out again in the house, after he has taken out the stones and scraped the house and plastered it,

14.44
Lev 13.51
44 then the priest shall go and look; and if the disease has spread in the house, it is a malignant leprosy in the house; it is unclean. 45And he shall break down the house, its stones and timber and all the plaster of the house; and he shall carry them forth out of the city to an unclean place. 46 Moreover he who enters the house while it is shut up shall be unclean until the evening; 47 and he who lies down in the house shall wash his clothes; and he who eats in the house shall wash his clothes.

48 "But if the priest comes and makes an examination, and the disease has not spread in the house after the house was plastered, then the priest shall pronounce the house clean, for the disease is healed. 49And for the cleansing of the house he shall take two small

14.49
ver 4
birds, with cedarwood and scarlet stuff and hyssop, 50 and shall

14.51
Ps 51.7
kill one of the birds in an earthen vessel over running water, 51 and shall take the cedarwood and the hyssop and the scarlet stuff, along with the living bird, and dip them in the blood of the bird that was killed and in the running water, and sprinkle the house seven times. 52 Thus he shall cleanse the house with the blood of the bird, and with the running water, and with the living bird, and with the cedarwood and hyssop and scarlet stuff; 53 and he

14.53
ver 20
shall let the living bird go out of the city into the open field; so he

14.54
Lev 13.30
14.56
Lev 13.2
shall make atonement for the house, and it shall be clean."

54 This is the law for any leprous disease: for an itch, 55 for leprosy in a garment or in a house, 56 and for a swelling or an erup-

---

[x] Gk Syr: Heb *afford*, 31*such as he can afford, one*

tion or a spot, [57] to show when it is unclean and when it is clean. This is the law for leprosy.

4. *Unclean secretions and cleansing*
a. *Uncleanness in man: purification*

15 The LORD said to Moses and Aaron, [2] "Say to the people of Israel, When any man has a discharge from his body, his discharge is unclean. [3] And this is the law of his uncleanness for a discharge: whether his body runs with his discharge, or his body is stopped from discharge, it is uncleanness in him. [4] Every bed on which he who has the discharge lies shall be unclean; and everything on which he sits shall be unclean. [5] And any one who touches his bed shall wash his clothes, and bathe himself in water, and be unclean until the evening. [6] And whoever sits on anything on which he who has the discharge has sat shall wash his clothes, and bathe himself in water, and be unclean until the evening. [7] And whoever touches the body of him who has the discharge shall wash his clothes, and bathe himself in water, and be unclean until the evening. [8] And if he who has the discharge spits on one who is clean, then he shall wash his clothes, and bathe himself in water, and be unclean until the evening. [9] And any saddle on which he who has the discharge rides shall be unclean. [10] And whoever touches anything that was under him shall be unclean until the evening; and he who carries such a thing shall wash his clothes, and bathe himself in water, and be unclean until the evening. [11] Any one whom he that has the discharge touches without having rinsed his hands in water shall wash his clothes, and bathe himself in water, and be unclean until the evening. [12] And the earthen vessel which he who has the discharge touches shall be broken; and every vessel of wood shall be rinsed in water.

[13] "And when he who has a discharge is cleansed of his discharge, then he shall count for himself seven days for his cleansing, and wash his clothes; and he shall bathe his body in running water, and shall be clean. [14] And on the eighth day he shall take two turtledoves or two young pigeons, and come before the LORD to the door of the tent of meeting, and give them to the priest; [15] and the priest shall offer them, one for a sin offering and the other for a burnt offering; and the priest shall make atonement for him before the LORD for his discharge.

[16] "And if a man has an emission of semen, he shall bathe his whole body in water, and be unclean until the evening. [17] And every garment and every skin on which the semen comes shall be washed with water, and be unclean until the evening. [18] If a man lies with a woman and has an emission of semen, both of them shall bathe themselves in water, and be unclean until the evening.

b. *Uncleanness in woman: purification*

[19] "When a woman has a discharge of blood which is her regular discharge from her body, she shall be in her impurity for seven days, and whoever touches her shall be unclean until the evening. [20] And everything upon which she lies during her impurity shall be unclean; everything also upon which she sits shall be unclean. [21] And whoever touches her bed shall wash his clothes, and bathe himself in water, and be unclean until the evening. [22] And whoever touches anything upon which she sits shall wash

15.2
Lev 22.4;
Num 5.2;
2 Sam 3.29;
Mt 9.20

15.7
Num 19.19

15.10
Num 19.10

15.12
Lev 6.28;
11.32,33

15.13
ver 28

15.14
Lev 14.22,
23
15.15
Lev 14.30,
31

15.16
Lev 22.4;
Deut 23.10

15.18
1 Sam 21.4

15.19
Lev 12.2

15.21
ver 27

his clothes, and bathe himself in water, and be unclean until the evening; 23 whether it is the bed or anything upon which she sits, when he touches it he shall be unclean until the evening. 24And if any man lies with her, and her impurity is on him, he shall be unclean seven days; and every bed on which he lies shall be unclean.

25 "If a woman has a discharge of blood for many days, not at the time of her impurity, or if she has a discharge beyond the time of her impurity, all the days of the discharge she shall continue in uncleanness; as in the days of her impurity, she shall be unclean. 26 Every bed on which she lies, all the days of her discharge, shall be to her as the bed of her impurity; and everything on which she sits shall be unclean, as in the uncleanness of her impurity. 27And whoever touches these things shall be unclean, and shall wash his clothes, and bathe himself in water, and be unclean until the evening. 28 But if she is cleansed of her discharge, she shall count for herself seven days, and after that she shall be clean. 29And on the eighth day she shall take two turtledoves or two young pigeons, and bring them to the priest, to the door of the tent of meeting. 30And the priest shall offer one for a sin offering and the other for a burnt offering; and the priest shall make atonement for her before the LORD for her unclean discharge.

31 "Thus you shall keep the people of Israel separate from their uncleanness, lest they die in their uncleanness by defiling my tabernacle that is in their midst."

32 This is the law for him who has a discharge and for him who has an emission of semen, becoming unclean thereby; 33 also for her who is sick with her impurity; that is, for any one, male or female, who has a discharge, and for the man who lies with a woman who is unclean.

D. The Day of Atonement

1. The institution of the ceremony

16 The LORD spoke to Moses, after the death of the two sons of Aaron, when they drew near before the LORD and died; 2 and the LORD said to Moses, "Tell Aaron your brother not to come at all times into the holy place within the veil, before the mercy seat which is upon the ark, lest he die; for I will appear in the cloud upon the mercy seat. 3 But thus shall Aaron come into the holy place: with a young bull for a sin offering and a ram for a burnt offering. 4 He shall put on the holy linen coat, and shall have the linen breeches on his body, be girded with the linen girdle, and wear the linen turban; these are the holy garments. He shall bathe his body in water, and then put them on. 5And he shall take from the congregation of the people of Israel two male goats for a sin offering, and one ram for a burnt offering.

6 "And Aaron shall offer the bull as a sin offering for himself,

---

Marginal references (left column):

15.24
Lev 20.18

15.25
Mt 9.20;
Mk 5.25;
Lk 8.43

15.27
ver 21

15.29
Gen 15.9

15.31
Ezek 44.23;
Num 5.3;
19.13,20;
Ezek 5.11;
23.38
15.32
ver 2,16
15.33
ver 19,24,25

16.1
Lev 10.1,2
16.2
Ex 30.10;
Heb 9.7;
10.19;
Ex 25.21,22
16.3
Heb 9.7,
12,24,25;
Lev 4.3
16.4
Ex 28.39,
42,43;
ver 24
16.5
Lev 4.13–21
★16.6
Lev 9.7;
Heb 5.2;
7.27,28;
9.7

16.6a The nature of Christ's offering of Himself on the cross is comprehended under the word atonement (kippūr). This word (derived from the Hebrew kippēr, "to atone") means to cover over by an expiatory sacrifice. It includes Christ's payment of the penalty for sin and His rendering to God a life of perfect obedience. He suffered vicariously, i.e., as a substitute, the just for the unjust, dying in our place and stead (2 Cor 5.21; 1 Pet 2.24). In the New Testament the word reconciliation is used (from the Greek katallage), which means to effect reparation legally and morally for injury done (Rom 5.11) and thus to bring about a restored relationship between those who were at

and shall make atonement for himself and for his house. 7 Then
he shall take the two goats, and set them before the LORD at the
door of the tent of meeting; 8 and Aaron shall cast lots upon the
two goats, one lot for the LORD and the other lot for Azā'zel. 9And
Aaron shall present the goat on which the lot fell for the LORD, and
offer it as a sin offering; 10 but the goat on which the lot fell for
Azā'zel shall be presented alive before the LORD to make atonement over it, that it may be sent away into the wilderness to Azazel.

2. The sin offering for the high priest

11 "Aaron shall present the bull as a sin offering for himself, and
shall make atonement for himself and for his house; he shall kill
the bull as a sin offering for himself. 12And he shall take a censer
full of coals of fire from the altar before the LORD, and two handfuls of sweet incense beaten small; and he shall bring it within the
veil 13 and put the incense on the fire before the LORD, that the
cloud of the incense may cover the mercy seat which is upon the
testimony, lest he die; 14 and he shall take some of the blood of the
bull, and sprinkle it with his finger on the front of the mercy seat,
and before the mercy seat he shall sprinkle the blood with his
finger seven times.

3. The sin offering for the people

15 "Then he shall kill the goat of the sin offering which is for
the people, and bring its blood within the veil, and do with its
blood as he did with the blood of the bull, sprinkling it upon the
mercy seat and before the mercy seat; 16 thus he shall make atonement for the holy place, because of the uncleannesses of the people
of Israel, and because of their transgressions, all their sins; and
so he shall do for the tent of meeting, which abides with them in
the midst of their uncleannesses. 17 There shall be no man in the
tent of meeting when he enters to make atonement in the holy

Margin references:

*16.8

16.11
Heb 7.27;
9.7
16.12
Lev 10.1;
Ex 30.34
16.13
Lev 22.9
16.14
Heb 9.13,
25;
Lev 4.6,17

16.15
Heb 9.3,7,
12

16.16
Ex 29.36;
Heb 2.17

---

enmity with each other. Man had broken the
law and God's justice required the penalty of
death from the sinner. This penalty Christ
paid in the atonement. The effect of the
atonement is to provide righteousness and
eternal life for those who accept it by faith in
Christ (Eph 2.8–10).

16.6b Day of Atonement. The sacrifice of
bulls and goats did not remove sin (Heb 10.4),
for only the death of Christ on Calvary could
do that. But redemption before Calvary was
possible. The Old Testament sacrificial system enabled men to manifest their faith so that
their sins were "covered," looking forward to
the death of Christ. Thus, in a sense, each sacrifice was like a check drawn against a bank
deposit; in and of itself a check is but a scrap
of paper, but it effects true payment nevertheless, because eventually the money itself is
transmitted to honor the check. Every faith-
supported sacrifice of pre-Christian times
was drawn against the account of Christ's
atoning merit on Calvary. In the Old Testament era the sacrifice of the Day of Atonement
was repeated annually when the high priest
entered the holy of holies (and not without
blood) to atone for himself and for his people
(Heb 9.7). Since the sacrifices were a type of
Christ's perfect and final sacrifice, the old
dispensation ended with Christ's death and

there was and is no further need for animal
sacrifices (Heb 9.12–28).

16.8 Azazel, "the scapegoat" in the KJV.
The Scripture does not throw much light on
Azazel or even make it clear that it is a name.
The word appears in the non-canonical Book
of Enoch as a name applied to a certain fallen
angel who misled mankind. Outside of the
few biblical references, and that in Enoch,
there is nothing further mentioned. We do
know that the ceremony spoken of in chapter
16 symbolized the fact that guilt had been
removed both from land and people. In some
sense it is typical of Christ (Isa 53.6, 11, 12).
(The theory that Azazel is a name for Satan
is as old as the third century A.D. but has
little to commend it; the notion of a sacrifice
to Satan is altogether pagan and contrary to
Scripture.) Some understand the Hebrew
word as a reduplicated root from *azal* ("depart" or "remove") signifying "removal" or
"that which is removed." Others, like the
early translators Aquila and Jerome, construe
it as a compound word: "goat of departure or
removal." This seems to have been the basis
of the rendering "scapegoat," (i.e., escape-
goat) in the KJV. Still others consider
Azazel as the first two words (meaning
"strength has passed away") of the ritual
recited when the goat was sent away.

16.18
Lev 4.25;
Ezek 43.20,
22

16.19
ver 14

16.21
Isa 53.6

16.22
Isa 53.11,12

16.23
ver 4;
Ezek 42.14;
44.19
16.24
ver 3–5

16.27
Lev 4.12,
21; 6.30;
Heb 13.11

*16.29
Lev 23.27;
Num 29.7

16.31
Lev 23.32;
Isa 58.3,5
16.32
ver 4;
Num 20.26,
28
16.33
ver 6,16–18,
24

place until he comes out and has made atonement for himself and for his house and for all the assembly of Israel. 18 Then he shall go out to the altar which is before the LORD and make atonement for it, and shall take some of the blood of the bull and of the blood of the goat, and put it on the horns of the altar round about. 19And he shall sprinkle some of the blood upon it with his finger seven times, and cleanse it and hallow it from the uncleannesses of the people of Israel.

4. The scapegoat

20 "And when he has made an end of atoning for the holy place and the tent of meeting and the altar, he shall present the live goat; 21 and Aaron shall lay both his hands upon the head of the live goat, and confess over him all the iniquities of the people of Israel, and all their transgressions, all their sins; and he shall put them upon the head of the goat, and send him away into the wilderness by the hand of a man who is in readiness. 22 The goat shall bear all their iniquities upon him to a solitary land; and he shall let the goat go in the wilderness.

23 "Then Aaron shall come into the tent of meeting, and shall put off the linen garments which he put on when he went into the holy place, and shall leave them there; 24 and he shall bathe his body in water in a holy place, and put on his garments, and come forth, and offer his burnt offering and the burnt offering of the people, and make atonement for himself and for the people. 25And the fat of the sin offering he shall burn upon the altar. 26And he who lets the goat go to Azā′zĕl shall wash his clothes and bathe his body in water, and afterward he may come into the camp. 27And the bull for the sin offering and the goat for the sin offering, whose blood was brought in to make atonement in the holy place, shall be carried forth outside the camp; their skin and their flesh and their dung shall be burned with fire. 28And he who burns them shall wash his clothes and bathe his body in water, and afterward he may come into the camp.

5. The Day of Atonement a perpetual statute

29 "And it shall be a statute to you for ever that in the seventh month, on the tenth day of the month, you shall afflict yourselves, and shall do no work, either the native or the stranger who sojourns among you; 30 for on this day shall atonement be made for you, to cleanse you; from all your sins you shall be clean before the LORD. 31 It is a sabbath of solemn rest to you, and you shall afflict yourselves; it is a statute for ever. 32And the priest who is anointed and consecrated as priest in his father's place shall make atonement, wearing the holy linen garments; 33 he shall make atonement for the sanctuary, and he shall make atonement for the tent of meeting and for the altar, and he shall make atonement for

---

16.29 Fasting, which is here referred to by the verb *afflict yourselves*, was a practice common to both the Old and New Testaments. It involved not only abstinence from food but also self-abasement and mourning (Deut 9.18; Neh 9.1; Joel 2.12); confession of sin (1 Sam 7.6; Neh 9.1, 2); and supplicatory prayer (Ezra 8.23; Dan 9.3). Fasting was intended to provide self-chastening and humility of which the fasting was an outward sign (Ps 35.13; 69.10). It was resorted to in the face of calamities, afflictions, misfortune, and approaching danger. Individuals and nations employed it. Hypocrites used it to gain a reputation for godliness before men, even though they could not impose upon a God who knew how to read the heart. Noteworthy examples of those who fasted are David (2 Sam 12.16); Daniel (Dan 9.3); Cornelius (Acts 10.30); Paul (2 Cor 11:27).

the priests and for all the people of the assembly. 34And this shall be an everlasting statute for you, that atonement may be made for the people of Israel once in the year because of all their sins." And Moses did as the LORD commanded him.

16.34
Heb 9.7,25

II. *The maintaining of fellowship with a holy God*
17.1–27.34

A. *Rules for killing of animals*

17 And the LORD said to Moses, 2 "Say to Aaron and his sons, and to all the people of Israel, This is the thing which the LORD has commanded. 3 If any man of the house of Israel kills an ox or a lamb or a goat in the camp, or kills it outside the camp, 4 and does not bring it to the door of the tent of meeting, to offer it as a gift to the LORD before the tabernacle of the LORD, bloodguilt shall be imputed to that man; he has shed blood; and that man shall be cut off from among his people. 5 This is to the end that the people of Israel may bring their sacrifices which they slay in the open field, that they may bring them to the LORD, to the priest at the door of the tent of meeting, and slay them as sacrifices of peace offerings to the LORD; 6 and the priest shall sprinkle the blood on the altar of the LORD at the door of the tent of meeting, and burn the fat for a pleasing odor to the LORD. 7 So they shall no more slay their sacrifices for satyrs, after whom they play the harlot. This shall be a statute for ever to them throughout their generations.

8 "And you shall say to them, Any man of the house of Israel, or of the strangers that sojourn among them, who offers a burnt offering or sacrifice, 9 and does not bring it to the door of the tent of meeting, to sacrifice it to the LORD; that man shall be cut off from his people.

*17.1ff

*17.4
Deut 12.5–21;
Rom 5.13

17.6
Lev 3.2;
Num 18.17
17.7
Ex 22.20;
32.8;
34.15;
Deut 32.17;
2 Chr 11.15

17.9
ver 4

B. *The eating of blood prohibited*

10 "If any man of the house of Israel or of the strangers that sojourn among them eats any blood, I will set my face against that person who eats blood, and will cut him off from among his people. 11 For the life of the flesh is in the blood; and I have given it for you upon the altar to make atonement for your souls; for it is the blood that makes atonement, by reason of the life. 12 Therefore I have said to the people of Israel, No person among you shall eat blood, neither shall any stranger who sojourns among you eat blood. 13Any man also of the people of Israel, or of the strangers that sojourn among them, who takes in hunting any beast or bird that may be eaten shall pour out its blood and cover it with dust.

14 "For the life of every creature is the blood of it;*e* therefore

17.10
Lev 3.17;
Deut 12.16,
23
*17.11
ver 14;
Gen 9.4;
Heb 9.22

17.13
Lev 7.26;
Deut 12.16
17.14
ver 11

e Gk Syr Compare Vg: Heb *for the life of all flesh, its blood is in its life*

17.1ff The section of laws (17.1–26.45), given by Moses at Sinai (26.46), is commonly called "The Holiness Code" because it sets forth the conditions required of Israel if they were to be a holy people.
17.4 God commanded that all blood sacri-

fices be made at the tabernacle rather than at shrines of man's own choosing. Otherwise bloodguilt, not forgiveness, would be the result. The right sacrifice made in the wrong way or place availed nothing.
17.11 See note 1.4, 5 on atonement.

I have said to the people of Israel, You shall not eat the blood of any creature, for the life of every creature is its blood; whoever eats it shall be cut off. 15And every person that eats what dies of itself or what is torn by beasts, whether he is a native or a sojourner, shall wash his clothes, and bathe himself in water, and be unclean until the evening; then he shall be clean. 16 But if he does not wash them or bathe his flesh, he shall bear his iniquity."

17.15
Ex 22.31;
Deut 14.21

C. Laws on sexual relations

1. Introduction

18.2
Ex 6.7;
Lev 11.44
18.3
Ezek
20.7,8;
Ex 23.24;
Lev 20.23
18.5
Ezek 20.11;
Lk 10.28;
Rom 10.5;
Gal 3.12

18 And the LORD said to Moses, 2 "Say to the people of Israel, I am the LORD your God. 3 You shall not do as they do in the land of Egypt, where you dwelt, and you shall not do as they do in the land of Cānaän, to which I am bringing you. You shall not walk in their statutes. 4 You shall do my ordinances and keep my statutes and walk in them. I am the LORD your God. 5 You shall therefore keep my statutes and my ordinances, by doing which a man shall live: I am the LORD.

2. Incest forbidden

*18.6
18.7
Lev 20.11

6 "None of you shall approach any one near of kin to him to uncover nakedness. I am the LORD. 7 You shall not uncover the nakedness of your father, which is the nakedness of your mother; she is your mother, you shall not uncover her nakedness. 8 You shall not uncover the nakedness of your father's wife; it is your father's nakedness. 9 You shall not uncover the nakedness of your sister, the daughter of your father or the daughter of your mother, whether born at home or born abroad. 10 You shall not uncover the nakedness of your son's daughter or of your daughter's daughter, for their nakedness is your own nakedness. 11 You shall not uncover the nakedness of your father's wife's daughter, begotten by your father, since she is your sister. 12 You shall not uncover the nakedness of your father's sister; she is your father's near kinswoman. 13 You shall not uncover the nakedness of your mother's sister, for she is your mother's near kinswoman. 14 You shall not uncover the nakedness of your father's brother, that is, you shall not approach his wife; she is your aunt. 15 You shall not uncover the nakedness of your daughter-in-law; she is your son's wife, you shall not uncover her nakedness. 16 You shall not uncover the nakedness of your brother's wife; she is your brother's nakedness. 17 You shall not uncover the nakedness of a woman and of her daughter, and you shall not take her son's daughter or her daughter's daughter to uncover her nakedness; they are your f near kinswomen; it is wickedness. 18And you shall not take a woman as a rival wife to her sister, uncovering her nakedness while her sister is yet alive.

18.9
Lev 20.17

18.12
Lev 20.19

18.14
Lev 20.20

18.15
Lev 20.12

18.16
Lev 20.21

18.17
Lev 20.14

f Gk: Heb lacks your

18.6 God laid down laws relative to marriage. It is true that in the first days of the human race brother married sister since there was no one else to marry. With the firm establishment of the race God forbade marriages between people who were closely related by blood. For example, under the Law of Moses a man could not marry his sister or his mother's sister or his daughter-in-law. These same prohibitions for the most part prevail in our modern world even in non-Christian societies.

3. *Other sins of the flesh forbidden*

19 "You shall not approach a woman to uncover her nakedness while she is in her menstrual uncleanness. 20And you shall not lie carnally with your neighbor's wife, and defile yourself with her. 21 You shall not give any of your children to devote them by fire to Mōlĕch, and so profane the name of your God: I am the LORD. 22 You shall not lie with a male as with a woman; it is an abomination. 23And you shall not lie with any beast and defile yourself with it, neither shall any woman give herself to a beast to lie with it: it is perversion.

4. *Warnings*

24 "Do not defile yourselves by any of these things, for by all these the nations I am casting out before you defiled themselves; 25 and the land became defiled, so that I punished its iniquity, and the land vomited out its inhabitants. 26 But you shall keep my statutes and my ordinances and do none of these abominations, either the native or the stranger who sojourns among you 27 (for all of these abominations the men of the land did, who were before you, so that the land became defiled); 28 lest the land vomit you out, when you defile it, as it vomited out the nation that was before you. 29 For whoever shall do any of these abominations, the persons that do them shall be cut off from among their people. 30 So keep my charge never to practice any of these abominable customs which were practiced before you, and never to defile yourselves by them: I am the LORD your God."

D. Holiness and personal conduct: the law of love

19 And the LORD said to Moses, 2 "Say to all the congregation of the people of Israel, You shall be holy; for I the LORD your God am holy. 3 Every one of you shall revere his mother and his father, and you shall keep my sabbaths: I am the LORD your God. 4 Do not turn to idols or make for yourselves molten gods: I am the LORD your God.

5 "When you offer a sacrifice of peace offerings to the LORD, you shall offer it so that you may be accepted. 6 It shall be eaten the same day you offer it, or on the morrow; and anything left over until the third day shall be burned with fire. 7 If it is eaten at all on the third day, it is an abomination; it will not be accepted, 8 and every one who eats it shall bear his iniquity, because he has profaned a holy thing of the LORD; and that person shall be cut off from his people.

9 "When you reap the harvest of your land, you shall not reap your field to its very border, neither shall you gather the gleanings after your harvest. 10And you shall not strip your vineyard bare, neither shall you gather the fallen grapes of your vineyard; you shall leave them for the poor and for the sojourner: I am the LORD your God.

11 "You shall not steal, nor deal falsely, nor lie to one another. 12And you shall not swear by my name falsely, and so profane the name of your God: I am the LORD.

18.21 See note to Zeph 1.5 for *Molech*, or *Milcom*.

19.9 See the Book of Ruth for a beautiful fulfilment of this law.

18.19 Lev 15.24; 20.18
18.20 Lev 20.10; Ex 20.14; Prov 6.32; Mt 5.27
*18.21 Lev 20.2–5; 19.12; 21.6
18.22 Lev 20.13; Rom 1.27
18.23 Ex 22.19; Lev 20.15; Deut 27.21
18.24 ver 3; Lev 20.23
18.25 Lev 20.23; Deut 9.5; 18.12; ver 28
18.30 Lev 22.9; Deut 11.1; ver 2
19.2 1 Pet 1.16
19.3 Ex 20.8,12; Lev 11.44
19.4 Lev 26.1; Ps 96.5; Ex 20.23; 34.17
*19.9 Lev 23.22; Deut 24.20–22
19.11 Ex 20.15; Lev 6.2; Eph 4.25; Col 3.9
19.12 Ex 20.7; Lev 18.21

19.13
Ex 22.7–15;
21–27;
Deut 24.15;
Jas 5.4

19.14
Deut 27.18

19.15
Ex 23.6;
Deut 1.17

19.16
Ps 15.3;
Ezek 22.9;
Ex 23.7

19.17
1 Jn 2.9,11;
3.15;
Lk 17.3;
Gal 6.1

*19.18
Rom 12.19;
Ps 103.9;
Mt 19.19;
Mk 12.31;
Rom 13.9

19.19
Deut 22.9,
11

19.21
Lev 5.15

19.24
Deut 12.17,
18;
Prov 3.9

19.26
Lev 17.10;
Deut 18.10

19.27
Lev 21.5

19.28
Lev 21.5

19.29
Deut 23.17

19.30
ver 3;
Lev 26.2

19.31
Lev 20.6,
27;
Deut 18.10,
11

19.33
Ex 22.21

19.34
Ex 12.48,
49;
Deut 10.19

13 "You shall not oppress your neighbor or rob him. The wages of a hired servant shall not remain with you all night until the morning. 14 You shall not curse the deaf or put a stumbling block before the blind, but you shall fear your God: I am the LORD.

15 "You shall do no injustice in judgment; you shall not be partial to the poor or defer to the great, but in righteousness shall you judge your neighbor. 16 You shall not go up and down as a slanderer among your people, and you shall not stand forth against the life^g of your neighbor: I am the LORD.

17 "You shall not hate your brother in your heart, but you shall reason with your neighbor, lest you bear sin because of him. 18 You shall not take vengeance or bear any grudge against the sons of your own people, but you shall love your neighbor as yourself: I am the LORD.

19 "You shall keep my statutes. You shall not let your cattle breed with a different kind; you shall not sow your field with two kinds of seed; nor shall there come upon you a garment of cloth made of two kinds of stuff.

20 "If a man lies carnally with a woman who is a slave, betrothed to another man and not yet ransomed or given her freedom, an inquiry shall be held. They shall not be put to death, because she was not free; 21 but he shall bring a guilt offering for himself to the LORD, to the door of the tent of meeting, a ram for a guilt offering. 22 And the priest shall make atonement for him with the ram of the guilt offering before the LORD for his sin which he has committed; and the sin which he has committed shall be forgiven him.

23 "When you come into the land and plant all kinds of trees for food, then you shall count their fruit as forbidden;^{h} three years it shall be forbidden to you, it must not be eaten. 24 And in the fourth year all their fruit shall be holy, an offering of praise to the LORD. 25 But in the fifth year you may eat of their fruit, that they may yield more richly for you: I am the LORD your God.

26 "You shall not eat any flesh with the blood in it. You shall not practice augury or witchcraft. 27 You shall not round off the hair on your temples or mar the edges of your beard. 28 You shall not make any cuttings in your flesh on account of the dead or tattoo any marks upon you: I am the LORD.

29 "Do not profane your daughter by making her a harlot, lest the land fall into harlotry and the land become full of wickedness. 30 You shall keep my sabbaths and reverence my sanctuary: I am the LORD.

31 "Do not turn to mediums or wizards; do not seek them out, to be defiled by them: I am the LORD your God.

32 "You shall rise up before the hoary head, and honor the face of an old man, and you shall fear your God: I am the LORD.

33 "When a stranger sojourns with you in your land, you shall not do him wrong. 34 The stranger who sojourns with you shall be to you as the native among you, and you shall love him as yourself; for you were strangers in the land of Egypt: I am the LORD your God.

g Heb blood h Heb their uncircumcision

19.18 love your neighbor indicates that the moral aspect is not neglected even in laws chiefly concerned with priests and ritual. Jesus considered this law and Deut 6.4 as the essence of the moral law. (See, for example, Mt 19.19 and Lk 10.27.)

35 "You shall do no wrong in judgment, in measures of length
or weight or quantity. 36 You shall have just balances, just weights,
a just ephah, and a just hin: I am the LORD your God, who brought
you out of the land of Egypt. 37And you shall observe all my
statutes and all my ordinances, and do them: I am the LORD."

E. Punishments for sin

1. Giving children to Molech

20 The LORD said to Moses, 2 "Say to the people of Israel,
Any man of the people of Israel, or of the strangers that
sojourn in Israel, who gives any of his children to Mōlĕch shall be
put to death; the people of the land shall stone him with stones.
3 I myself will set my face against that man, and will cut him off
from among his people, because he has given one of his children
to Mōlĕch, defiling my sanctuary and profaning my holy name.
4And if the people of the land do at all hide their eyes from that
man, when he gives one of his children to Mōlĕch, and do not
put him to death, 5 then I will set my face against that man and
against his family, and will cut them off from among their people,
him and all who follow him in playing the harlot after Mōlĕch.

2. Consulting mediums and wizards

6 "If a person turns to mediums and wizards, playing the harlot
after them, I will set my face against that person, and will cut him
off from among his people. 7 Consecrate yourselves therefore, and
be holy; for I am the LORD your God. 8 Keep my statutes, and do
them; I am the LORD who sanctify you. 9 For every one who curses
his father or his mother shall be put to death; he has cursed his
his father or his mother, his blood is upon him.

3. Adultery

10 "If a man commits adultery with the wife of[i] his neighbor,
both the adulterer and the adulteress shall be put to death. 11 The
man who lies with his father's wife has uncovered his father's nakedness; both of them shall be put to death, their blood is upon them.
12 If a man lies with his daughter-in-law, both of them shall be put
to death; they have committed incest, their blood is upon them.
13 If a man lies with a male as with a woman, both of them have
committed an abomination; they shall be put to death, their blood
is upon them. 14 If a man takes a wife and her mother also, it is
wickedness; they shall be burned with fire, both he and they, that
there may be no wickedness among you. 15 If a man lies with a
beast, he shall be put to death; and you shall kill the beast. 16 If a
woman approaches any beast and lies with it, you shall kill the
woman and the beast; they shall be put to death, their blood is
upon them.

4. Other sins of the flesh

17 "If a man takes his sister, a daughter of his father or a daughter of his mother, and sees her nakedness, and she sees his nakedness, it is a shameful thing, and they shall be cut off in the sight of
the children of their people; he has uncovered his sister's nakedness, he shall bear his iniquity. 18 If a man lies with a woman hav-

i Heb repeats if a man commits adultery with the wife of

20.2
Lev 18.21

20.3
Lev 15.31;
18.21

20.4
Deut 17.2,
3,5

20.6
Lev 19.31
20.7
1 Pet 1.16
20.8
Lev 19.37;
Ex 31.13
20.9
Ex 21.17;
Deut 27.16

20.10
Lev 18.20;
Deut 22.22
20.11
Lev 18.7,8
20.12
Lev 18.15
20.13
Lev 18.22
20.14
Deut 27.23
20.15
Lev 18.23

20.17
Lev 18.9

20.18
Lev 18.19

ing her sickness, and uncovers her nakedness, he has made naked her fountain, and she has uncovered the fountain of her blood; both of them shall be cut off from among their people. 19 You shall not uncover the nakedness of your mother's sister or of your father's sister, for that is to make naked one's near kin; they shall bear their iniquity. 20 If a man lies with his uncle's wife, he has uncovered his uncle's nakedness; they shall bear their sin, they shall die childless. 21 If a man takes his brother's wife, it is impurity; he has uncovered his brother's nakedness, they shall be childless.

5. *Command to be holy*

22 "You shall therefore keep all my statutes and all my ordinances, and do them; that the land where I am bringing you to dwell may not vomit you out. 23 And you shall not walk in the customs of the nation which I am casting out before you; for they did all these things, and therefore I abhorred them. 24 But I have said to you, 'You shall inherit their land, and I will give it to you to possess, a land flowing with milk and honey.' I am the LORD your God, who have separated you from the peoples. 25 You shall therefore make a distinction between the clean beast and the unclean, and between the unclean bird and the clean; you shall not make yourselves abominable by beast or by bird or by anything with which the ground teems, which I have set apart for you to hold unclean. 26 You shall be holy to me; for I the LORD am holy, and have separated you from the peoples, that you should be mine.

6. *Penalty for being a medium or wizard*

27 "A man or a woman who is a medium or a wizard shall be put to death; they shall be stoned with stones, their blood shall be upon them."

F. Rules for the priesthood

1. *The sanctity of the priesthood*

21 And the LORD said to Moses, "Speak to the priests, the sons of Aaron, and say to them that none of them shall defile himself for the dead among his people, 2 except for his nearest of kin, his mother, his father, his son, his daughter, his brother, 3 or his virgin sister (who is near to him because she has had no husband; for her he may defile himself). 4 He shall not defile himself as a husband among his people and so profane himself. 5 They shall not make tonsures upon their heads, nor shave off the edges of their beards, nor make any cuttings in their flesh. 6 They shall be holy to their God, and not profane the name of their God; for they offer the offerings by fire to the LORD, the bread of their God; therefore they shall be holy. 7 They shall not marry a harlot or a woman who has been defiled; neither shall they marry a woman divorced from her husband; for the priest is holy to his God. 8 You shall consecrate him, for he offers the bread of your God; he shall be holy to you; for I the LORD, who sanctify you, am holy. 9 And the daughter of any priest, if she profanes herself by playing the harlot, profanes her father; she shall be burned with fire.

10 "The priest who is chief among his brethren, upon whose head the anointing oil is poured, and who has been consecrated to wear the garments, shall not let the hair of his head hang loose, nor rend his clothes; 11 he shall not go in to any dead body, nor defile

20.19
Lev 18.12,
13

20.20
Lev 18.14

20.21
Lev 18.16

20.22
Lev 18.25,
26,28

20.23
Lev 18.3,
24,27,30

20.24
Ex 13.5;
33.3,16;
ver 26

20.25
Lev 11.1–
47;
Deut 14.3–
21

20.26
ver 24

20.27
Lev 19.31

21.1
Lev 19.28;
Ezek 44.25

21.5
Deut 14.1;
Ezek 44.20;
Lev 19.27

21.6
Lev 18.21;
3.11

21.7
ver 13,14

21.10
Lev 16.32;
10.6,7

21.11
Lev 19.28

himself, even for his father or for his mother; 12 neither shall he go out of the sanctuary, nor profane the sanctuary of his God; for the consecration of the anointing oil of his God is upon him: I am the LORD. 13And he shall take a wife in her virginity. 14A widow, or one divorced, or a woman who has been defiled, or a harlot, these he shall not marry; but he shall take to wife a virgin of his own people, 15 that he may not profane his children among his people; for I am the LORD who sanctify him."

16 And the LORD said to Moses, 17 "Say to Aaron, None of your descendants throughout their generations who has a blemish may approach to offer the bread of his God. 18 For no one who has a blemish shall draw near, a man blind or lame, or one who has a mutilated face or a limb too long, 19 or a man who has an injured foot or an injured hand, 20 or a hunchback, or a dwarf, or a man with a defect in his sight or an itching disease or scabs or crushed testicles; 21 no man of the descendants of Aaron the priest who has a blemish shall come near to offer the LORD'S offerings by fire; since he has a blemish, he shall not come near to offer the bread of his God. 22 He may eat the bread of his God, both of the most holy and of the holy things, 23 but he shall not come near the veil or approach the altar, because he has a blemish, that he may not profane my sanctuaries; for I am the LORD who sanctify them." 24 So Moses spoke to Aaron and to his sons and to all the people of Israel.

22 And the LORD said to Moses, 2 "Tell Aaron and his sons to keep away from the holy things of the people of Israel, which they dedicate to me, so that they may not profane my holy name: I am the LORD. 3 Say to them, 'If any one of all your descendants throughout your generations approaches the holy things, which the people of Israel dedicate to the LORD, while he has an uncleanness, that person shall be cut off from my presence: I am the LORD. 4 None of the line of Aaron who is a leper or suffers a discharge may eat of the holy things until he is clean. Whoever touches anything that is unclean through contact with the dead or a man who has had an emission of semen, 5 and whoever touches a creeping thing by which he may be made unclean or a man from whom he may take uncleanness, whatever his uncleanness may be— 6 the person who touches any such shall be unclean until the evening and shall not eat of the holy things unless he has bathed his body in water. 7 When the sun is down he shall be clean; and afterward he may eat of the holy things, because such are his food. 8 That which dies of itself or is torn by beasts he shall not eat, defiling himself by it: I am the LORD.' 9 They shall therefore keep my charge, lest they bear sin for it and die thereby when they profane it: I am the LORD who sanctify them.

21.12 Lev 10.7; Ex 29.6,7
21.13 ver 7; Ezek 44.22
*21.17ff ver 6
21.18 Lev 22.23
21.20 Deut 23.1
21.21 ver 6
21.23 ver 12
*22.3 Lev 7.20
22.4 Lev 14.1–32; Num 19.11,12; 15.16,17
22.5 Lev 11.24,43,44; 15.7,19
22.8 Ex 22.31; Lev 17.15
22.9 Lev 18.30; ver 16

21.17ff Scripture distinguishes between a man's person and the office he occupies. Thus no one of the seed of Aaron could occupy the office of the priesthood if he suffered from certain physical imperfections and disabilities (ver 18–20). While a descendant of Aaron might be physically disqualified from exercising the priestly function, he was not debarred from receiving his share of the offerings for his personal support (ver 22). (So in the ministry of the church there may be things which would disqualify a man from holding its various offices but which would not bar him from its worship and fellowship.) Thus both the priest and the sacrificial animal itself had to be without blemish in order to be satisfactory. Christ met both of these demands. He was without blemish in Himself and His sacrifice of His own body was a perfect one (2 Cor 5.21; 1 Pet 1.19).

22.3 holy things were the portions of the sacrifice given to the priest.

22.10
ver 13

10 "An outsider shall not eat of a holy thing. A sojourner of the priest's or a hired servant shall not eat of a holy thing; 11 but if a priest buys a slave as his property for money, the slave may eat of it; and those that are born in his house may eat of his food. 12 If a priest's daughter is married to an outsider she shall not eat of the offering of the holy things. 13 But if a priest's daughter is a widow or divorced, and has no child, and returns to her father's house, as in her youth, she may eat of her father's food; yet no outsider shall eat of it. 14And if a man eats of a holy thing unwittingly, he shall add the fifth of its value to it, and give the holy thing to the priest. 15 The priests shall not profane the holy things of the people of Israel, which they offer to the LORD, 16 and so cause them to bear iniquity and guilt, by eating their holy things: for I am the LORD who sanctify them.''

22.13
ver 10

22.14
Lev 5.15,16

22.16
ver 9

2. Acceptable and unacceptable offerings

17 And the LORD said to Moses, 18 "Say to Aaron and his sons and all the people of Israel, When any one of the house of Israel or of the sojourners in Israel presents his offering, whether in payment of a vow or as a freewill offering which is offered to the LORD as a burnt offering, 19 to be accepted you shall offer a male without blemish, of the bulls or the sheep or the goats. 20 You shall not offer anything that has a blemish, for it will not be acceptable for you. 21And when any one offers a sacrifice of peace offerings to the LORD, to fulfil a vow or as a freewill offering, from the herd or from the flock, to be accepted it must be perfect; there shall be no blemish in it. 22Animals blind or disabled or mutilated or having a discharge or an itch or scabs, you shall not offer to the LORD or make of them an offering by fire upon the altar to the LORD. 23A bull or a lamb which has a part too long or too short you may present for a freewill offering; but for a votive offering it cannot be accepted. 24Any animal which has its testicles bruised or crushed or torn or cut, you shall not offer to the LORD or sacrifice within your land; 25 neither shall you offer as the bread of your God any such animals gotten from a foreigner. Since there is a blemish in them, because of their mutilation, they will not be accepted for you.''

22.19
Lev 1.3
22.20
Deut 15.21;
17.1;
Heb 9.14;
1 Pet 1.19
22.21
Lev 3.1,6

22.25
Lev 21.6,17

22.27
Ex 22.30

26 And the LORD said to Moses, 27 "When a bull or sheep or goat is born, it shall remain seven days with its mother; and from the eighth day on it shall be acceptable as an offering by fire to the LORD. 28And whether the mother is a cow or a ewe, you shall not kill both her and her young in one day. 29And when you sacrifice a sacrifice of thanksgiving to the LORD, you shall sacrifice it so that you may be accepted. 30 It shall be eaten on the same day, you shall leave none of it until morning: I am the LORD.

22.28
Deut 22.6,7
22.29
Lev 7.12
22.30
Lev 7.15
22.31
Lev 19.37
22.32
Lev 18.21;
10.3
22.33
Ex 6.7;
Lev 11.45

31 "So you shall keep my commandments and do them: I am the LORD. 32And you shall not profane my holy name, but I will be hallowed among the people of Israel; I am the LORD who sanctify you, 33 who brought you out of the land of Egypt to be your God: I am the LORD.''

G. Laws concerning festivals
1. The Sabbath

23.2
ver 4,37,44;
Num 29.39

23 The LORD said to Moses, 2 "Say to the people of Israel, The appointed feasts of the LORD which you shall pro-

claim as holy convocations, my appointed feasts, are these. 3 Six days shall work be done; but on the seventh day is a sabbath of solemn rest, a holy convocation; you shall do no work; it is a sabbath to the LORD in all your dwellings.

2. The Passover and Unleavened Bread

4 "These are the appointed feasts of the LORD, the holy convocations, which you shall proclaim at the time appointed for them. 5 In the first month, on the fourteenth day of the month in the evening,*j* is the LORD'S passover. 6And on the fifteenth day of the same month is the feast of unleavened bread to the LORD; seven days you shall eat unleavened bread. 7 On the first day you shall have a holy convocation; you shall do no laborious work. 8 But you shall present an offering by fire to the LORD seven days; on the seventh day is a holy convocation; you shall do no laborious work."

3. The Feast of First Fruits

9 And the LORD said to Moses, 10 "Say to the people of Israel, When you come into the land which I give you and reap its harvest, you shall bring the sheaf of the first fruits of your harvest to the priest; 11 and he shall wave the sheaf before the LORD, that you may find acceptance; on the morrow after the sabbath the priest shall wave it. 12And on the day when you wave the sheaf, you shall offer a male lamb a year old without blemish as a burnt offering to the LORD. 13And the cereal offering with it shall be two tenths of an ephah of fine flour mixed with oil, to be offered by fire to the LORD, a pleasing odor; and the drink offering with it shall be of wine, a fourth of a hin. 14And you shall eat neither bread nor grain parched or fresh until this same day, until you have brought the offering of your God: it is a statute for ever throughout your generations in all your dwellings.

4. Pentecost

15 "And you shall count from the morrow after the sabbath, from the day that you brought the sheaf of the wave offering; seven full weeks shall they be, 16 counting fifty days to the morrow after the seventh sabbath; then you shall present a cereal offering of new grain to the LORD. 17 You shall bring from your dwellings

*j*Heb between the two evenings

23.3 Lev 19.3; Ex 31.13-17; Deut 5.13
23.4 ver 2
*23.5** Ex 12.18, 19; Num 28.16, 17
*23.6**
23.8 ver 8,21, 25,35,36
23.10 Ex 23.16,19; 34.22,26
23.13 Lev 2.14-16
*23.15** Deut 16.9
23.16 Num 28.26
23.17 Lev 2.12; 7.13

23.5 *passover*, see notes to Ex 12.11; Mk 14.1.

23.6 *the feast of unleavened bread* is to be kept distinct from the Passover, although they have a close connection with each other. The Passover was celebrated on the fourteenth day (ver 5) whereas the Feast of Unleavened Bread began on the fifteenth day and continued for seven days. Together they formed a double festival just as the Feast of Tabernacles and the Day of Atonement formed a double celebration. In Mk 14.1, 12 and Lk 22.1 the two feasts (Passover and Unleavened Bread) are spoken of as virtually one. This was due, no doubt, to the fact that they were not separated by any interval of time. The regulations for the Feast of Unleavened Bread are detailed in verses 6-8.

23.15 In Old Testament times this event was known as the *Feast of Weeks* or the *Feast of Harvest*. Its New Testament name derives from the Greek word "fiftieth" which, in turn, derives from the fact that the feast took place on the fiftieth day after the feast of Unleavened Bread had been celebrated. (According to our reckoning it would be forty-nine days.) The feast was a prophetic type pointing forward to the descent of the Holy Spirit, who came upon the apostolic church with power on the fiftieth day after the Resurrection of Christ from the dead (Acts 2.1ff). In Old Testament times this feast celebrated the harvest of fruits of the earth; in New Testament times the 120 in the apostolic band constituted the first-fruits of Christ's harvest, even as the gift of the Holy Spirit is the first-fruit of the believer's heavenly inheritance (see Rom 8.23; 11.16; Jas 1.18).

two loaves of bread to be waved, made of two tenths of an ephah; they shall be of fine flour, they shall be baked with leaven, as first fruits to the LORD. 18And you shall present with the bread seven lambs a year old without blemish, and one young bull, and two rams; they shall be a burnt offering to the LORD, with their cereal offering and their drink offerings, an offering by fire, a pleasing odor to the LORD. 19And you shall offer one male goat for a sin offering, and two male lambs a year old as a sacrifice of peace offerings. 20And the priest shall wave them with the bread of the first fruits as a wave offering before the LORD, with the two lambs; they shall be holy to the LORD for the priest. 21And you shall make proclamation on the same day; you shall hold a holy convocation; you shall do no laborious work: it is a statute for ever in all your dwellings throughout your generations.

22 "And when you reap the harvest of your land, you shall not reap your field to its very border, nor shall you gather the gleanings after your harvest; you shall leave them for the poor and for the stranger: I am the LORD your God."

5. *The Feast of Trumpets*

23 And the LORD said to Moses, 24 "Say to the people of Israel, In the seventh month, on the first day of the month, you shall observe a day of solemn rest, a memorial proclaimed with blasts of trumpets, a holy convocation. 25 You shall do no laborious work; and you shall present an offering by fire to the LORD."

6. *The Day of Atonement*

26 And the LORD said to Moses, 27 "On the tenth day of this seventh month is the day of atonement; it shall be for you a time of holy convocation, and you shall afflict yourselves and present an offering by fire to the LORD. 28And you shall do no work on this same day; for it is a day of atonement, to make atonement for you before the LORD your God. 29 For whoever is not afflicted on this same day shall be cut off from his people. 30And whoever does any work on this same day, that person I will destroy from among his people. 31 You shall do no work: it is a statute for ever throughout your generations in all your dwellings. 32 It shall be to you a sabbath of solemn rest, and you shall afflict yourselves; on the ninth day of the month beginning at evening, from evening to evening shall you keep your sabbath."

7. *The Feast of Tabernacles*

33 And the LORD said to Moses, 34 "Say to the people of Israel, On the fifteenth day of this seventh month and for seven days is the feast of booths*k* to the LORD. 35 On the first day shall be a holy convocation; you shall do no laborious work. 36 Seven days you

k Or *tabernacles*

Side references:

23.19
Num 28.30;
Lev 3.1

23.21
ver 7

23.22
Lev 19.9

★23.24
Num 29.1;
Lev 25.9

★23.27
Lev 16.29,
30

23.29
Gen 17.14
23.30
Lev 20.3,5,
6

★23.34
Ex 23.16;
Num 29.12;
ver 42,43
23.36
Num 29.12–
38

23.24 "The Feast of Trumpets" was celebrated the first day of Tishri, the seventh month. Trumpets were blown and sacrifices offered (Num 29.1–6). It was a day of holy convocation and rest (23.24, 25). Since it inaugurated the seventh month of the religious calendar, the feast was connected with the institution of the Sabbath and is mentioned again in Neh 8.9, 10. It constituted the New Year's Day of the civil calendar, and as such is celebrated to this day by the Jews as Rosh Hashanah.

23.27 *day of atonement*, see note to 16.6.

23.34 *feast of booths* (also known as the "feast of tabernacles" and "feast of ingathering"), see note to Ex 23.16.

shall present offerings by fire to the LORD; on the eighth day you
shall hold a holy convocation and present an offering by fire to the
LORD; it is a solemn assembly; you shall do no laborious work.

37 "These are the appointed feasts of the LORD, which you shall
proclaim as times of holy convocation, for presenting to the LORD
offerings by fire, burnt offerings and cereal offerings, sacrifices and
drink offerings, each on its proper day; 38 besides the sabbaths of
the LORD, and besides your gifts, and besides all your votive offerings, and besides all your freewill offerings, which you give to the
LORD.

23.37
ver 2,4

39 "On the fifteenth day of the seventh month, when you have
gathered in the produce of the land, you shall keep the feast of the
LORD seven days; on the first day shall be a solemn rest, and on
the eighth day shall be a solemn rest. 40And you shall take on the
first day the fruit of goodly trees, branches of palm trees, and
boughs of leafy trees, and willows of the brook; and you shall
rejoice before the LORD your God seven days. 41 You shall keep
it as a feast to the LORD seven days in the year; it is a statute for
ever throughout your generations; you shall keep it in the seventh
month. 42 You shall dwell in booths for seven days; all that are
native in Israel shall dwell in booths, 43 that your generations may
know that I made the people of Israel dwell in booths when I
brought them out of the land of Egypt: I am the LORD your God."

23.39
Ex 23.16;
Deut 16.13

23.40
Neh 8.15;
Deut 16.14,
15

23.42
Neh
8.14–16

44 Thus Moses declared to the people of Israel the appointed
feasts of the LORD.

23.44
ver 2,37

H. Laws of ritual and ethics

1. The oil and the showbread

24 The LORD said to Moses, 2 "Command the people of
Israel to bring you pure oil from beaten olives for the lamp,
that a light may be kept burning continually. 3 Outside the veil of
the testimony, in the tent of meeting, Aaron shall keep it in order
from evening to morning before the LORD continually; it shall be
a statute for ever throughout your generations. 4 He shall keep
the lamps in order upon the lampstand of pure gold before the
LORD continually.

24.2
Ex 27.20,21

24.4
Ex 31.8;
39.37

5 "And you shall take fine flour, and bake twelve cakes of it;
two tenths of an ephah shall be in each cake. 6And you shall set
them in two rows, six in a row, upon the table of pure gold. 7And
you shall put pure frankincense with each row, that it may go with
the bread as a memorial portion to be offered by fire to the LORD.
8 Every sabbath day Aaron shall set it in order before the LORD
continually on behalf of the people of Israel as a covenant for ever.
9And it shall be for Aaron and his sons, and they shall eat it in a
holy place, since it is for him a most holy portion out of the offerings by fire to the LORD, a perpetual due."

24.5
Ex 25.30
24.6
Ex 25.24;
1 Ki 7.48

24.8
Num 4.7;
1 Chr 9.32;
2 Chr 2.4
24.9
Mt 12.4;
Mk 2.26;
Lk 6.4;
Lev 8.31

2. Death for blasphemy

10 Now an Israelite woman's son, whose father was an Egyptian, went out among the people of Israel; and the Israelite woman's son and a man of Israel quarreled in the camp, 11 and the
Israelite woman's son blasphemed the Name, and cursed. And
they brought him to Moses. His mother's name was Shĕlō'mĭth,
the daughter of Dĭbrī, of the tribe of Dan. 12And they put him in

24.11
ver 16
24.12
Num 15.34;
Ex 18.15,16

24.14
Deut 13.9;
17.7;
Lev 20.2,
27;
Deut 21.21
★24.16
1 Ki 21.10,
13;
Mt 12.31;
Mk 3.28
24.17
Ex 21.12;
Num 35.30,
31;
Deut 19.11,
12
24.18
ver 21
24.20
Ex 21.23,
24;
Deut 19.21;
Mt 5.38
24.21
ver 17,18
24.22
Ex 12.49;
Num 15.16

custody, till the will of the LORD should be declared to them. 13 And the LORD said to Moses, 14 "Bring out of the camp him who cursed; and let all who heard him lay their hands upon his head, and let all the congregation stone him. 15And say to the people of Israel, Whoever curses his God shall bear his sin. 16 He who blasphemes the name of the LORD shall be put to death; all the congregation shall stone him; the sojourner as well as the native, when he blasphemes the Name, shall be put to death. 17 He who kills a man shall be put to death. 18 He who kills a beast shall make it good, life for life. 19 When a man causes a disfigurement in his neighbor, as he has done it shall be done to him, 20 fracture for fracture, eye for eye, tooth for tooth; as he has disfigured a man, he shall be disfigured. 21 He who kills a beast shall make it good; and he who kills a man shall be put to death. 22 You shall have one law for the sojourner and for the native; for I am the LORD your God." 23 So Moses spoke to the people of Israel; and they brought him who had cursed out of the camp, and stoned him with stones. Thus the people of Israel did as the LORD commanded Moses.

I. Laws for the sabbatical and jubilee years

1. The sabbatical year

25.2
Ex 23.10,11

25 The LORD said to Moses on Mount Sī'näï, 2 "Say to the people of Israel, When you come into the land which I give you, the land shall keep a sabbath to the LORD. 3 Six years you shall sow your field, and six years you shall prune your vineyard, and gather in its fruits; 4 but in the seventh year there shall be a sabbath of solemn rest for the land, a sabbath to the LORD; you shall not sow your field or prune your vineyard. 5 What grows of itself in your harvest you shall not reap, and the grapes of your undressed vine you shall not gather; it shall be a year of solemn rest for the land. 6 The sabbath of the land shall provide food for you, for yourself and for your male and female slaves and for your hired servant and the sojourner who lives with you; 7 for your cattle also and for the beasts that are in your land all its yield shall be for food.

25.6
ver 20,21

2. The year of Jubilee

★25.8ff

8 "And you shall count seven weeks[l] of years, seven times seven years, so that the time of the seven weeks of years shall be to you forty-nine years. 9 Then you shall send abroad the loud trumpet on the tenth day of the seventh month; on the day of atonement you shall send abroad the trumpet throughout all your land.

25.9
Lev
23.24,27

[l] Or sabbaths

24.16 To blaspheme is to scoff at or revile the name of God, and the Old Testament penalty was death. Ungodly men are peculiarly addicted to blasphemy (Ps 74.18; Isa 52.5). Idolatry in the Old Testament was also regarded as blasphemy (Isa 65.7) because it implied a contempt for His name as the one true God. Examples of blasphemers include the profane Danite of this chapter (ver 11); King Sennacherib of Assyria (2 Ki 19.4, 10, 22); and Hymenaeus, a heretic of the early Church (1 Tim 1.20). Unbelievers take delight in accusing the saints of the very sin of which they themselves are guilty. Christ was accused of this crime on the ground that He, being a man, made Himself out to be God (Mt 26.65; Lk 22.66–71). Members of the early church were also charged with the offense because they affirmed His deity (Acts 6.11–14).

25.8-10 The observance of the Jubilee was held every fiftieth year. It commenced on the Day of Atonement. It was called by various names, such as the year of liberty (Ezek 46.17), the year of redemption (Isa 63.4), and even in

10And you shall hallow the fiftieth year, and proclaim liberty throughout the land to all its inhabitants; it shall be a jubilee for you, when each of you shall return to his property and each of you shall return to his family. 11A jubilee shall that fiftieth year be to you; in it you shall neither sow, nor reap what grows of itself, nor gather the grapes from the undressed vines. 12 For it is a jubilee; it shall be holy to you; you shall eat what it yields out of the field.

13 "In this year of jubilee each of you shall return to his property. 14And if you sell to your neighbor or buy from your neighbor, you shall not wrong one another. 15According to the number of years after the jubilee, you shall buy from your neighbor, and according to the number of years for crops he shall sell to you. 16 If the years are many you shall increase the price, and if the years are few you shall diminish the price, for it is the number of the crops that he is selling to you. 17 You shall not wrong one another, but you shall fear your God; for I am the LORD your God.

18 "Therefore you shall do my statutes, and keep my ordinances and perform them; so you will dwell in the land securely. 19 The land will yield its fruit, and you will eat your fill, and dwell in it securely. 20And if you say, 'What shall we eat in the seventh year, if we may not sow or gather in our crop?' 21 I will command my blessing upon you in the sixth year, so that it will bring forth fruit for three years. 22 When you sow in the eighth year, you will be eating old produce; until the ninth year, when its produce comes in, you shall eat the old. 23 The land shall not be sold in perpetuity, for the land is mine; for you are strangers and sojourners with me. 24And in all the country you possess, you shall grant a redemption of the land.

3. Redemption of property

25 "If your brother becomes poor, and sells part of his property, then his next of kin shall come and redeem what his brother has sold. 26 If a man has no one to redeem it, and then himself becomes prosperous and finds sufficient means to redeem it, 27 let him reckon the years since he sold it and pay back the overpayment to the man to whom he sold it; and he shall return to his property. 28 But if he has not sufficient means to get it back for himself, then what he sold shall remain in the hand of him who bought it until the year of jubilee; in the jubilee it shall be released, and he shall return to his property.

29 "If a man sells a dwelling house in a walled city, he may redeem it within a whole year after its sale; for a full year he shall have the right of redemption. 30 If it is not redeemed within a full year, then the house that is in the walled city shall be made sure in perpetuity to him who bought it, throughout his generations; it shall not be released in the jubilee. 31 But the houses of the villages which have no wall around them shall be reckoned with the fields

*25.10 ver 13,28,54
25.13 ver 10
25.14 Lev 19.13; 1 Sam 12.3, 4; 1 Cor 6.8
25.15 Lev 27.18, 23
25.17 ver 14; Lev 19.14, 32
25.18 Lev 19.37; 26.4,5
25.20 ver 4,5
25.22 Lev 26.10
25.23 Ex 19.5; Gen 23.4; 1 Chr 29.15; Ps 39.12
25.25 Ruth 2.20; 4.4,6
25.27 ver 50–52
25.28 ver 13

the expression *year of the* LORD's *favor* (Isa 61.2) there are Jubilee overtones. It was a holy year (ver 12) and was ushered in by the solemn blowing of trumpets (ver 9; Ps 89.15). During this fiftieth year all field labor was to cease, and the people were to eat of what they had stored up from the previous year. Non-urban property that had been sold could be redeemed, inheritances restored, and slaves set free from their servitude. The Year of Jubilee is spoken of as fulfilled in the Gospel (Lk 4.18, 19), which sets men free from their bondage and brings them into the glorious liberty of the sons of God.

of the country; they may be redeemed, and they shall be released in the jubilee. 32 Nevertheless the cities of the Lēvītes, the houses in the cities of their possession, the Levites may redeem at any time. 33And if one of the Lēvītes does not exercise*m* his right of redemption, then the house that was sold in a city of their possession shall be released in the jubilee; for the houses in the cities of the Levites are their possession among the people of Israel. 34 But the fields of common land belonging to their cities may not be sold; for that is their perpetual possession.

4. The law of usury

35 "And if your brother becomes poor, and cannot maintain himself with you, you shall maintain him; as a stranger and a sojourner he shall live with you. 36 Take no interest from him or increase, but fear your God; that your brother may live beside you. 37 You shall not lend him your money at interest, nor give him your food for profit. 38 I am the LORD your God, who brought you forth out of the land of Egypt to give you the land of Cānaān, and to be your God.

5. The redemption of servants

39 "And if your brother becomes poor beside you, and sells himself to you, you shall not make him serve as a slave: 40 he shall be with you as a hired servant and as a sojourner. He shall serve with you until the year of the jubilee; 41 then he shall go out from you, he and his children with him, and go back to his own family, and return to the possession of his fathers. 42 For they are my servants, whom I brought forth out of the land of Egypt; they shall not be sold as slaves. 43 You shall not rule over him with harshness, but shall fear your God. 44As for your male and female slaves whom you may have: you may buy male and female slaves from among the nations that are round about you. 45 You may also buy from among the strangers who sojourn with you and their families that are with you, who have been born in your land; and they may be your property. 46 You may bequeath them to your sons after you, to inherit as a possession for ever; you may make slaves of them, but over your brethren the people of Israel you shall not rule, one over another, with harshness.

47 "If a stranger or sojourner with you becomes rich, and your brother beside him becomes poor and sells himself to the stranger or sojourner with you, or to a member of the stranger's family, 48 then after he is sold he may be redeemed; one of his brothers may redeem him, 49 or his uncle, or his cousin may redeem him, or a near kinsman belonging to his family may redeem him; or if he grows rich he may redeem himself. 50 He shall reckon with him who bought him from the year when he sold himself to him until the year of jubilee, and the price of his release shall be according to the number of years; the time he was with his owner shall be rated as the time of a hired servant. 51 If there are still many years, according to them he shall refund out of the price paid for him the price for his redemption. 52 If there remain but a few years until the year of jubilee, he shall make a reckoning with him; according to the years of service due from him he shall refund the money for his redemption. 53As a servant hired year by year shall

Cross-references (margin)

25.32 Num 35.1–8

25.35 Deut 15.7–11; Ps 37.26; Lk 6.35

25.36 Ex 22.25; Deut 23.19,20

25.38 Lev 11.45

25.39 Ex 21.2; Deut 15.12; 1 Ki 9.22

25.41 Ex 21.3; ver 28

25.43 ver 46,53; Ex 1.13,14

25.45 Isa 56.3,6

25.46 ver 43

25.48 Neh 5.5

25.49 ver 26

25.50 Job 7.1; Isa 16.14; 21.16

25.51 Jer 32.7

---

m Compare Vg: Heb *exercises*

he be with him; he shall not rule with harshness over him in your sight. ⁵⁴And if he is not redeemed by these means, then he shall be released in the year of jubilee, he and his children with him. ⁵⁵ For to me the people of Israel are servants, they are my servants whom I brought forth out of the land of Egypt: I am the Lord your God.

J. Promises and warnings

1. The blessings for obedience

26 "You shall make for yourselves no idols and erect no graven image or pillar, and you shall not set up a figured stone in your land, to bow down to them; for I am the Lord your God. ² You shall keep my sabbaths and reverence my sanctuary: I am the Lord.

3 "If you walk in my statutes and observe my commandments and do them, ⁴ then I will give you your rains in their season, and the land shall yield its increase, and the trees of the field shall yield their fruit. ⁵And your threshing shall last to the time of vintage, and the vintage shall last to the time for sowing; and you shall eat your bread to the full, and dwell in your land securely. ⁶And I will give peace in the land, and you shall lie down, and none shall make you afraid; and I will remove evil beasts from the land, and the sword shall not go through your land. ⁷And you shall chase your enemies, and they shall fall before you by the sword. ⁸ Five of you shall chase a hundred, and a hundred of you shall chase ten thousand; and your enemies shall fall before you by the sword. ⁹And I will have regard for you and make you fruitful and multiply you, and will confirm my covenant with you. ¹⁰And you shall eat old store long kept, and you shall clear out the old to make way for the new. ¹¹And I will make my abode among you, and my soul shall not abhor you. ¹²And I will walk among you, and will be your God, and you shall be my people. ¹³ I am the Lord your God, who brought you forth out of the land of Egypt, that you should not be their slaves; and I have broken the bars of your yoke and made you walk erect.

2. The punishments for disobedience

14 "But if you will not hearken to me, and will not do all these commandments, ¹⁵ if you spurn my statutes, and if your soul abhors my ordinances, so that you will not do all my commandments, but break my covenant, ¹⁶ I will do this to you: I will appoint over you sudden terror, consumption, and fever that waste the eyes and cause life to pine away. And you shall sow your seed in vain, for your enemies shall eat it; ¹⁷ I will set my face against you, and you shall be smitten before your enemies; those who hate you shall rule over you, and you shall flee when none pursues you. ¹⁸And if in spite of this you will not hearken to me, then I will chastise you again sevenfold for your sins, ¹⁹ and I will break the pride of your power, and I will make your heavens like

25.54 ver 10,13,28

26.1 Ex 20.4,5; Lev 19.4; Deut 5.8

26.2 Lev 19.30

26.3 Deut 28.1

26.5 Amos 9.13; Lev 25.18, 19

26.6 Ps 29.11; 147.14; Zeph 3.13; ver 22,25

*26.8 Deut 32.30; Josh 23.10

26.9 Gen 17.6,7; 22.17; Neh 9.23

26.10 Lev 25.22

26.11 Ex 25.8; Ps 76.2

26.12 2 Cor 6.16

26.14 Deut 28.15; Mal 2.2

26.16 Deut 28.22; 1 Sam 2.33; Deut 28.35, 51

26.17 Lev 17.10; Deut 28.25; Ps 106.41; 53.5; ver 36,37

26.18 ver 21,24,28

26.19 Isa 25.11; Deut 28.23

26.8 In spiritual things the law which governs is not that of arithmetic progression but of an accumulative effect as the numbers rise. Symbolically, five will chase one hundred but one hundred will chase ten thousand. Especially in prayer may it be said that the power generated will be proportionately greater as more people pray. Thus the more of God's people who work and pray together the more significant will be the results.

26.20
Isa 17.10,
11;
Deut 11.17

26.21
ver 18,24,
27,40
26.22
Deut 32.24

26.23
Jer 2.30;
5.3
26.24
ver 21,28,41
26.25
Ezek 5.17;
Num 14.12
*26.26
Ps 105.16;
Isa 3.1;
Mic 6.14

26.28
ver 24,41
26.29
Deut 28.53
26.30
2 Chr 34.3;
Ezek 6.3–6,
13
26.31
Ps 74.7;
Isa 63.18
*26.32
Jer 9.11;
19.18
26.33
Deut 4.27;
Ezek 12.15
26.34
ver 43;
2 Chr 36.21

26.36
Ezek 21.7

26.37
Josh 7.12,
13
26.38
Deut 4.26
26.39
Deut 4.27;
Ezek 4.17
*26.40ff
Jer 3.12–15;
Lk 15.18;
1 Jn 1.9

iron and your earth like brass; 20 and your strength shall be spent in vain, for your land shall not yield its increase, and the trees of the land shall not yield their fruit.

21 "Then if you walk contrary to me, and will not hearken to me, I will bring more plagues upon you, sevenfold as many as your sins. 22And I will let loose the wild beasts among you, which shall rob you of your children, and destroy your cattle, and make you few in number, so that your ways shall become desolate.

23 "And if by this discipline you are not turned to me, but walk contrary to me, 24 then I also will walk contrary to you, and I myself will smite you sevenfold for your sins. 25And I will bring a sword upon you, that shall execute vengeance for the covenant; and if you gather within your cities I will send pestilence among you, and you shall be delivered into the hand of the enemy. 26 When I break your staff of bread, ten women shall bake your bread in one oven, and shall deliver your bread again by weight; and you shall eat, and not be satisfied.

27 "And if in spite of this you will not hearken to me, but walk contrary to me, 28 then I will walk contrary to you in fury, and chastise you myself sevenfold for your sins. 29 You shall eat the flesh of your sons, and you shall eat the flesh of your daughters. 30And I will destroy your high places, and cut down your incense altars, and cast your dead bodies upon the dead bodies of your idols; and my soul will abhor you. 31And I will lay your cities waste, and will make your sanctuaries desolate, and I will not smell your pleasing odors. 32And I will devastate the land, so that your enemies who settle in it shall be astonished at it. 33And I will scatter you among the nations, and I will unsheathe the sword after you; and your land shall be a desolation, and your cities shall be a waste.

34 "Then the land shall enjoy[n] its sabbaths as long as it lies desolate, while you are in your enemies' land; then the land shall rest, and enjoy[n] its sabbaths. 35As long as it lies desolate it shall have rest, the rest which it had not in your sabbaths when you dwelt upon it. 36And as for those of you that are left, I will send faintness into their hearts in the lands of their enemies; the sound of a driven leaf shall put them to flight, and they shall flee as one flees from the sword, and they shall fall when none pursues. 37 They shall stumble over one another, as if to escape a sword, though none pursues; and you shall have no power to stand before your enemies. 38And you shall perish among the nations, and the land of your enemies shall eat you up. 39And those of you that are left shall pine away in your enemies' lands because of their iniquity; and also because of the iniquities of their fathers they shall pine away like them.

40 "But if they confess their iniquity and the iniquity of their

---

[n] Or *pay for*

26.26 *staff* in this sense, "sustenance."
26.32 God here lays down the punishment which will be meted out to His people for persistent disobedience and disregard of the covenant. The warning is amplified in Deut 28.58–67. The punishment was meted out in the Babylonian captivity of 587 B.C.
26.40ff The Abrahamic covenant was not to be abrogated by Israel's future disobedience. It would continue in accord with the conditions which governed it. When and if Israel repented of her sins and turned to God, the land would be returned to Israel. This was fulfilled after the fall of Babylon in 539 B.C. and a remnant returned to Palestine under Zerubbabel.

fathers in their treachery which they committed against me, and also in walking contrary to me, 41 so that I walked contrary to them and brought them into the land of their enemies; if then their uncircumcised heart is humbled and they make amends for their iniquity; 42 then I will remember my covenant with Jacob, and I will remember my covenant with Isaac and my covenant with Abraham, and I will remember the land. 43 But the land shall be left by them, and enjoy*n* its sabbaths while it lies desolate without them; and they shall make amends for their iniquity, because they spurned my ordinances, and their soul abhorred my statutes. 44 Yet for all that, when they are in the land of their enemies, I will not spurn them, neither will I abhor them so as to destroy them utterly and break my covenant with them; for I am the LORD their God; 45 but I will for their sake remember the covenant with their forefathers, whom I brought forth out of the land of Egypt in the sight of the nations, that I might be their God: I am the LORD."

46 These are the statutes and ordinances and laws which the LORD made between him and the people of Israel on Mount Si'näi by Moses.

26.41
Ezek 44.9;
2 Chr 12.6,7

26.42
Gen 28.13–
15; 26.2–5;
22.15–18

26.43
ver 34,35,15

26.44
Deut 4.31;
Rom 11.2

26.45
Ex 6.6–8;
Lev 25.38;
Gen 17.7

★26.46
Lev 7.38;
27.34; 25.1

K. Appendix: the making of vows

1. Vows involving persons

27 The LORD said to Moses, 2 "Say to the people of Israel, When a man makes a special vow of persons to the LORD at your valuation, 3 then your valuation of a male from twenty years old up to sixty years old shall be fifty shekels of silver, according to the shekel of the sanctuary. 4 If the person is a female, your valuation shall be thirty shekels. 5 If the person is from five years old up to twenty years old, your valuation shall be for a male twenty shekels, and for a female ten shekels. 6 If the person is from a month old up to five years old, your valuation shall be for a male five shekels of silver, and for a female your valuation shall be three shekels of silver. 7And if the person is sixty years old and upward, then your valuation for a male shall be fifteen shekels, and for a female ten shekels. 8And if a man is too poor to pay your valuation, then he shall bring the person before the priest, and the priest shall value him; according to the ability of him who vowed the priest shall value him.

27.3
Ex 30.13

27.6
Num 18.16

27.8
ver 12

2. Vows involving animals

9 "If it is an animal such as men offer as an offering to the LORD,

n Or *pay for*

26.46 The Law of Moses is used to describe the Old Testament economy under which the people of Israel lived in relation to God. The Law can be divided into three categories: (1) the moral law or the Ten Commandments (Deut 5.22; 10.4); (2) the ceremonial law setting forth the proper approach to God in worship (7.37, 38); (3) the civil law under which the people were to live and be governed (Deut 17.9–11). The ceremonial law has been completely fulfilled by the Lord Jesus Christ and is hence not binding upon New Testament believers. The civil law was designed especially for the pre-Christian Jewish theocracy, and other nations living under different cultural conditions need not be subject to it. But the basic moral law applies to all people of all ages and serves to: (1) demonstrate to all men that they are sinners in need of a Savior; (2) reveal what is the rule of godly conduct by which believers who love the Lord may know how they can please Him; (3) exercise a certain restraining influence upon mankind as a whole so that a law-governed society is rendered possible. Technically (1) is known as the pedagogic use of the Law; (2) is the normative use; (3) is the political use.

all of such that any man gives to the LORD is holy. 10 He shall not substitute anything for it or exchange it, a good for a bad, or a bad for a good; and if he makes any exchange of beast for beast, then both it and that for which it is exchanged shall be holy. 11And if it is an unclean animal such as is not offered as an offering to the LORD, then the man shall bring the animal before the priest, 12 and the priest shall value it as either good or bad; as you, the priest, value it, so it shall be. 13 But if he wishes to redeem it, he shall add a fifth to the valuation.

3. *Vows involving a house*

14 "When a man dedicates his house to be holy to the LORD, the priest shall value it as either good or bad; as the priest values it, so it shall stand. 15And if he who dedicates it wishes to redeem his house, he shall add a fifth of the valuation in money to it, and it shall be his.

4. *Vows involving land*

16 "If a man dedicates to the LORD part of the land which is his by inheritance, then your valuation shall be according to the seed for it; a sowing of a homer of barley shall be valued at fifty shekels of silver. 17 If he dedicates his field from the year of jubilee, it shall stand at your full valuation; 18 but if he dedicates his field after the jubilee, then the priest shall compute the money-value for it according to the years that remain until the year of jubilee, and a deduction shall be made from your valuation. 19And if he who dedicates the field wishes to redeem it, then he shall add a fifth of the valuation in money to it, and it shall remain his. 20 But if he does not wish to redeem the field, or if he has sold the field to another man, it shall not be redeemed any more; 21 but the field, when it is released in the jubilee, shall be holy to the LORD, as a field that has been devoted; the priest shall be in possession of it. 22 If he dedicates to the LORD a field which he has bought, which is not a part of his possession by inheritance, 23 then the priest shall compute the valuation for it up to the year of jubilee, and the man shall give the amount of the valuation on that day as a holy thing to the LORD. 24 In the year of jubilee the field shall return to him from whom it was bought, to whom the land belongs as a possession by inheritance. 25 Every valuation shall be according to the shekel of the sanctuary: twenty gerahs shall make a shekel.

5. *Vows involving firstlings*

26 "But a firstling of animals, which as a firstling belongs to the LORD, no man may dedicate; whether ox or sheep, it is the LORD's. 27And if it is an unclean animal, then he shall buy it back at your valuation, and add a fifth to it; or, if it is not redeemed, it shall be sold at your valuation.

6. *Vows involving devoted things*

28 "But no devoted thing that a man devotes to the LORD, of anything that he has, whether of man or beast, or of his inherited field, shall be sold or redeemed; every devoted thing is most holy to the LORD. 29 No one devoted, who is to be utterly destroyed from among men, shall be ransomed; he shall be put to death.

27.12 ver 8
27.13 ver 15,19
27.15 ver 20
27.18 Lev 25.15,16
27.21 Lev 25.10,28,31; Num 18.14
27.23 ver 18
27.24 Lev 25.28
27.25 Ex 30.13
27.26 Ex 13.2,12
27.27 ver 11,12
27.28 Josh 6.17–19

7. *Redeeming the tithe*

30 "All the tithe of the land, whether of the seed of the land or of the fruit of the trees, is the LORD's; it is holy to the LORD. 31 If a man wishes to redeem any of his tithe, he shall add a fifth to it. 32And all the tithe of herds and flocks, every tenth animal of all that pass under the herdsman's staff, shall be holy to the LORD. 33A man shall not inquire whether it is good or bad, neither shall he exchange it; and if he exchanges it, then both it and that for which it is exchanged shall be holy; it shall not be redeemed."

34 These are the commandments which the LORD commanded Moses for the people of Israel on Mount Si'näi.

27.30
Gen 28.22;
Mal 3.8,10
27.31
ver 13

27.33
ver 10

27.34
Lev 26.46;
Deut 4.5

INTRODUCTION TO
THE FOURTH BOOK OF MOSES

COMMONLY CALLED

NUMBERS

Authorship and Background: The fourth book of the Pentateuch is called Numbers in the Septuagint because of the numberings described in chapters 1 and 26. Far more appropriate is the Hebrew title "in the wilderness," the fifth word in the first line of the Hebrew text. The story traces the journey of the Israelites from Sinai to the plains of Moab. Moses is the key figure; the text of 33.2 notes that he kept a log of the journey "stage by stage."

In Exodus the covenant is made, the Law given, and the tabernacle completed. In Leviticus the priests and people alike receive religious instruction, and then in Numbers the Israelites are prepared for their ultimate goal—the entrance into, and the conquest of, Canaan. Most of the events in Numbers occur in the second and fortieth years of the forty-year period between the exodus and the entering of Canaan. Aside from two events, the thirty-eight weary years in the wilderness are passed over in silence.

Characteristics: There is more to the Book of Numbers than the history of the wilderness wanderings. The account manifests the guiding, delivering, sustaining, and protecting hand of God among His people. Disobedience receives its due reward. Repentance results in pardon and restoration. By type and figure the principles underlying this relationship between God and His people may be carried over into the New Testament and even applied to the church today. God indeed is with His people and these things "were written down for our instruction" (1 Cor 10.11). Rich spiritual lessons may be learned from a study of this book. The narrative sections of Numbers are made more difficult to read by the statistical and geographical summaries (ch 1, 33, etc.). Some segments of the book appear in poetic form.

Contents:

I. The preparations for leaving Sinai. 1.1—10.10: The tribes are numbered and their positions assigned. The Levites are numbered and their duties outlined. Miscellaneous laws and regulations for the removal of uncleanness and defilement; ordeal of jealousy. Nazirite regulations. The arrangements for the religious life of the camp given: the golden lampstand, rules for the Levites, the Passover, the fiery cloud, and the silver trumpets.

II. The journey from Sinai to Moab. 10.11—21.35: The departure from Sinai. The people's complaint about the manna and the demand for flesh. Miriam and Aaron complain against Moses; God vindicates him;

Moses intercedes for leprosy-stricken Miriam. Israel sojourns in Paran; spies are sent out. Their reports are received and Israel accepts the report of the ten spies and rejects the counsel of Joshua and Caleb. Judgment is about to fall and Moses intercedes with God for the people. Miscellaneous legislation enacted. Korah, Dathan, and Abiram rebel and are punished. Aaron's rod sprouts. The duties and dues of the Levites. Israel marches from Kadesh to Moab. Miriam dies. The miracle of Meribah. Israel clashes with Edom. Aaron dies. Israel wars with the Amorites and Og who are defeated. The bronze serpent.

III.   Events in Moab. 22.1—36.13: The story of Balaam: Balak, Moab, the ass, and Balaam's oracles. Various laws and incidents: marriage with women of Moab and Midian, the second census, the laws of female inheritance, the appointment of Joshua, the laws of worship relating to daily sacrifices, Sabbath, new moon, unleavened bread, feast of weeks and trumpets, Day of Atonement and the feast of booths. Vows made by women. Israel destroys the Midianites and begins settlements in Trans-Jordan. Gad and Reuben build cities and Manasseh makes settlements in Gilead. The journey from Egypt to Moab summarized and plans formulated for the division of Canaan. The Levitical cities and the laws for murder. Laws concerning the marriage of heiresses.

THE FOURTH BOOK OF MOSES

COMMONLY CALLED

NUMBERS

I. Preparations for the march from Sinai 1.1–10.10

A. The census

1. Selection of the census takers

★1.1
Ex 19.1;
40.2,17

1 The LORD spoke to Moses in the wilderness of Sī′näï, in the tent of meeting, on the first day of the second month, in the second year after they had come out of the land of Egypt, saying,

1.2
Ex 38.26;
Num 26.2

2 "Take a census of all the congregation of the people of Israel, by families, by fathers' houses, according to the number of names, every male, head by head; 3 from twenty years old and upward, all in Israel who are able to go forth to war, you and Aaron shall number them, company by company.

1.4
ver 16

4And there shall be with you a man from each tribe, each man being the head of the house of his fathers. 5And these are the names of the men who shall attend you. From Reubën, Ēlī′zúr the son of Shėdē′úr; 6 from Sĭm′ëŏn, Shėlu′mĭ-ėl the son of Zurĭshăd′däï; 7 from Judah, Nahshòn the son of Ǎmmĭn′ǎdàb; 8 from Ĭs′sȧchar, Nēthăn′ėl the son of Zu′ar; 9 from Zĕb′ụlún, Ēlī′ab the son of Hēlòn; 10 from the sons of Joseph, from Ē′phräïm, Ēlī′shȧmȧ the son of Ǎmmī′hŭd, and from Mȧnȧs′sėh, Gȧmā′lĭėl the son of Pėdah′zúr; 11 from Benjamin, Ǎb′ĭdăn the son of Gĭdëŏ′nī; 12 from Dan, Āhī-ē′zėr the son of Ǎmmĭshăd′däï; 13 from Ǎshėr, Pā′ġïėl the son of Ŏchrȧn;

1.14
Num 2.14,
Reuel

14 from Găd, Ēlī′ȧsȧph the son of Deu′ėl; 15 from Năph′tȧlī, Ǎhī′rȧ the son of Ēnȧn."

1.16
Num 16.2;
26.9

16 These were the ones chosen from the congregation, the leaders of their ancestral tribes, the heads of the clans of Israel.

2. The numbering of Israel

17 Moses and Aaron took these men who have been named, 18 and on the first day of the second month, they assembled the whole congregation together, who registered themselves by families, by fathers' houses, according to the number of names from twenty years old and upward, head by head, 19 as the LORD commanded Moses. So he numbered them in the wilderness of Sī′näï.

1.20
Num
26.5–11

20 The people of Reubën, Israel's first-born, their generations, by their families, by their fathers' houses, according to the number of names, head by head, every male from twenty years old and upward, all who were able to go forth to war: 21 the number of the tribe of Reubën was forty-six thousand five hundred.

1.22
Num
26.12–14

22 Of the people of Sĭm′ëŏn, their generations, by their families, by their fathers' houses, those of them that were numbered, according to the number of names, head by head, every male from twenty years old and upward, all who were able to go forth to war: 23 the number of the tribe of Sĭm′ëŏn was fifty-nine thousand three hundred.

1.24
Num
26.15–18

24 Of the people of Găd, their generations, by their families, by their fathers' houses, according to the number of the names, from

---

1.1 *second month,* just a month after the erection of the tabernacle (Ex 40.17). The events described in 1.1—10.10 occurred in just nineteen days (10.11).

twenty years old and upward, all who were able to go forth to war:
25 the number of the tribe of Găd was forty-five thousand six hundred and fifty.

26 Of the people of Judah, their generations, by their families, by their fathers' houses, according to the number of names, from twenty years old and upward, every man able to go forth to war: 27 the number of the tribe of Judah was seventy-four thousand six hundred.

28 Of the people of Ĭs'sáchar, their generations, by their families, by their fathers' houses, according to the number of names, from twenty years old and upward, every man able to go forth to war: 29 the number of the tribe of Ĭs'sàchar was fifty-four thousand four hundred.

30 Of the people of Zĕb'ụlủn, their generations, by their families, by their fathers' houses, according to the number of names, from twenty years old and upward, every man able to go forth to war: 31 the number of the tribe of Zĕb'ụlùn was fifty-seven thousand four hundred.

32 Of the people of Joseph, namely, of the people of Ē'phräịm, their generations, by their families, by their fathers' houses, according to the number of names, from twenty years old and upward, every man able to go forth to war: 33 the number of the tribe of Ē'phräịm was forty thousand five hundred.

34 Of the people of Mảnăs'sẻh, their generations, by their families, by their fathers' houses, according to the number of names, from twenty years old and upward, every man able to go forth to war: 35 the number of the tribe of Mảnăs'sẻh was thirty-two thousand two hundred.

36 Of the people of Benjamin, their generations, by their families, by their fathers' houses, according to the number of names, from twenty years old and upward, every man able to go forth to war: 37 the number of the tribe of Benjamin was thirty-five thousand four hundred.

38 Of the people of Dan, their generations, by their families, by their fathers' houses, according to the number of names, from twenty years old and upward, every man able to go forth to war: 39 the number of the tribe of Dan was sixty-two thousand seven hundred.

40 Of the people of Ăshẻr, their generations, by their families, by their fathers' houses, according to the number of names, from twenty years old and upward, every man able to go forth to war: 41 the number of the tribe of Ăshẻr was forty-one thousand five hundred.

42 Of the people of Năph'tảlī, their generations, by their families, by their fathers' houses, according to the number of names, from twenty years old and upward, every man able to go forth to war: 43 the number of the tribe of Năph'tảlī was fifty-three thousand four hundred.

44 These are those who were numbered, whom Moses and Aaron numbered with the help of the leaders of Israel, twelve men, each representing his fathers' house. 45 So the whole number of the people of Israel, by their fathers' houses, from twenty years old and upward, every man able to go forth to war in Israel— 46 their whole number was six hundred and three thousand five hundred and fifty.

1.26
Num 26.19–22

1.28
Num 26.23–25

1.30
Num 26.26, 27

1.32
Num 26.35–37

1.34
Num 26.28–34

1.36
Num 26.38–41

1.38
Num 26.42, 43

1.40
Num 26.44–47

1.42
Num 26.48–50

1.44
Num 26.64

1.46
Num 2.32; 26.51; Ex 12.37; 38.26

3. *The Levites not numbered: their duties*

1.47
Num 2.33;
ch 3,4;
26.57
*1.49
1.50
Num 3.25–
37
1.51
Num 4.1–
33
1.52
Num 2.2
1.53
ver 50

47 But the Lēvītes were not numbered by their ancestral tribe along with them. 48 For the LORD said to Moses, 49 "Only the tribe of Lēvī you shall not number, and you shall not take a census of them among the people of Israel; 50 but appoint the Lēvītes over the tabernacle of the testimony, and over all its furnishings, and over all that belongs to it; they are to carry the tabernacle and all its furnishings, and they shall tend it, and shall encamp around the tabernacle. 51 When the tabernacle is to set out, the Lēvītes shall take it down; and when the tabernacle is to be pitched, the Levites shall set it up. And if any one else comes near, he shall be put to death. 52 The people of Israel shall pitch their tents by their companies, every man by his own camp and every man by his own standard; 53 but the Lēvītes shall encamp around the tabernacle of the testimony, that there may be no wrath upon the congregation of the people of Israel; and the Levites shall keep charge of the tabernacle of the testimony." 54 Thus did the people of Israel; they did according to all that the LORD commanded Moses.

B. *The camps and leaders of the tribes*

2.2
Num 1.52

2.3
Num 10.14

2.5
Num 1.8

2.9
Num 10.14

2.10
Num 1.5

2.12
Num 1.6

2.14
Num 1.14,
Deuel

2.17
Num 1.53

2 The LORD said to Moses and Aaron, 2 "The people of Israel shall encamp each by his own standard, with the ensigns of their fathers' houses; they shall encamp facing the tent of meeting on every side. 3 Those to encamp on the east side toward the sunrise shall be of the standard of the camp of Judah by their companies, the leader of the people of Judah being Nahshŏn the son of Ămmĭn′ădăb, 4 his host as numbered being seventy-four thousand six hundred. 5 Those to encamp next to him shall be the tribe of Is′sȧchar, the leader of the people of Issachar being Néthăn′ĕl the son of Zu′ar, 6 his host as numbered being fifty-four thousand four hundred. 7 Then the tribe of Zĕb′ulŭn, the leader of the people of Zebulun being Ēlī′áb the son of Hēlŏn, 8 his host as numbered being fifty-seven thousand four hundred. 9 The whole number of the camp of Judah, by their companies, is a hundred and eighty-six thousand four hundred. They shall set out first on the march.

10 "On the south side shall be the standard of the camp of Reubën by their companies, the leader of the people of Reuben being Ēlī′zŭr the son of Shédē′ŭr, 11 his host as numbered being forty-six thousand five hundred. 12 And those to encamp next to him shall be the tribe of Sĭm′ëŏn, the leader of the people of Simeon being Shĕlu′mĭ-ĕl the son of Zurĭshăd′däï, 13 his host as numbered being fifty-nine thousand three hundred. 14 Then the tribe of Găd, the leader of the people of Gad being Ēlī′ȧsăph the son of Reu′ĕl, 15 his host as numbered being forty-five thousand six hundred and fifty. 16 The whole number of the camp of Reubën, by their companies, is a hundred and fifty-one thousand four hundred and fifty. They shall set out second.

17 "Then the tent of meeting shall set out, with the camp of the Lēvītes in the midst of the camps; as they encamp, so shall they set out, each in position, standard by standard.

1.49 *you shall not number* simply means that the Levites were not to be numbered along with the twelve tribes. They were numbered separately later (3.15).

18 "On the west side shall be the standard of the camp of
Ē'phräim by their companies, the leader of the people of Ephraim
being Ēlī'shämä the son of Ammī'hŭd, 19 his host as numbered
being forty thousand five hundred. 20And next to him shall be
the tribe of Mänäs'sĕh, the leader of the people of Manasseh being
Gämä'lĭĕl the son of Pĕdah'zŭr, 21 his host as numbered being
thirty-two thousand two hundred. 22 Then the tribe of Benjamin,
the leader of the people of Benjamin being Ăb'ĭdän the son of
Gĭdĕō'nī, 23 his host as numbered being thirty-five thousand four
hundred. 24 The whole number of the camp of Ē'phräjm, by their
companies, is a hundred and eight thousand one hundred. They
shall set out third on the march.

25 "On the north side shall be the standard of the camp of Dan
by their companies, the leader of the people of Dan being Āhī-
ē'zĕr the son of Ammĭshäd'däī, 26 his host as numbered being
sixty-two thousand seven hundred. 27And those to encamp next
to him shall be the tribe of Āshĕr, the leader of the people of
Asher being Pä'ğĭĕl the son of Ōçhrán, 28 his host as numbered
being forty-one thousand five hundred. 29 Then the tribe of
Năph'tälī, the leader of the people of Naphtali being Ahī'rä the
son of Ēnän, 30 his host as numbered being fifty-three thousand
four hundred. 31 The whole number of the camp of Dan is a hundred and fifty-seven thousand six hundred. They shall set out last,
standard by standard."

32 These are the people of Israel as numbered by their fathers'
houses; all in the camps who were numbered by their companies
were six hundred and three thousand five hundred and fifty. 33 But
the Lēvītes were not numbered among the people of Israel, as the
LORD commanded Moses.

34 Thus did the people of Israel. According to all that the LORD
commanded Moses, so they encamped by their standards, and so
they set out, every one in his family, according to his fathers'
house.

C. The Levites

1. The sons of Aaron

3 These are the generations of Aaron and Moses at the time
when the LORD spoke with Moses on Mount Sī'näī. 2 These
are the names of the sons of Aaron: Nädäb the first-born, and
Abī'hū, Ēlĕä'zär, and Ĭth'ämar; 3 these are the names of the sons
of Aaron, the anointed priests, whom he ordained to minister
in the priest's office. 4 But Nädäb and Abī'hū died before the
LORD when they offered unholy fire before the LORD in the wilderness of Sī'näī; and they had no children. So Ēlĕä'zär and
Ĭth'ämar served as priests in the lifetime of Aaron their father.

2. The responsibilities of the Levites

5 And the LORD said to Moses, 6 "Bring the tribe of Lēvī near,
and set them before Aaron the priest, that they may minister to
him. 7 They shall perform duties for him and for the whole
congregation before the tent of meeting, as they minister at the
tabernacle; 8 they shall have charge of all the furnishings of the
tent of meeting, and attend to the duties for the people of Israel
as they minister at the tabernacle. 9And you shall give the Lēvītes

2.20
Num 1.10

2.24
Num 10.22

2.25
Num 1.12

2.27
Num 1.13

2.31
Num 10.25

2.32
Num 1.46;
Ex 38.26
2.33
Num 1.47

3.2
Num 26.60

3.4
Num 26.61

3.6
Num 8.6–
22; 18.1-7

3.9
Num 18.6

3.10
Ex 29.9;
Num 1.51

to Aaron and his sons; they are wholly given to him from among the people of Israel. 10And you shall appoint Aaron and his sons, and they shall attend to their priesthood; but if any one else comes near, he shall be put to death."

3. God chooses the Levites instead of every first-born

3.12
ver 41;
Num 8.16;
18.6

3.13
Ex 13.2,
12,15;
Num 8.17

11 And the LORD said to Moses, 12 "Behold, I have taken the Lēvītes from among the people of Israel instead of every first-born that opens the womb among the people of Israel. The Levites shall be mine, 13 for all the first-born are mine; on the day that I slew all the first-born in the land of Egypt, I consecrated for my own all the first-born in Israel, both of man and of beast; they shall be mine: I am the LORD."

4. The Levites numbered: duties assigned

3.15
ver 39

3.17
Ex 6.16–22

3.20
Gen 46.11

14 And the LORD said to Moses in the wilderness of Sī′näi, 15 "Number the sons of Lēvī, by fathers' houses and by families; every male from a month old and upward you shall number." 16 So Moses numbered them according to the word of the LORD, as he was commanded. 17And these were the sons of Lēvī by their names: Gērshŏn and Kōhăth and Mĕrar′ī. 18And these are the names of the sons of Gērshŏn by their families: Lĭbnī and Shĭm′-ĕ-ī. 19And the sons of Kōhăth by their families: Ămrăm, Ĭzhar, Hēbrŏn, and Ŭzzī′ĕl. 20And the sons of Mĕrar′ī by their families: Mahlī and Mushī. These are the families of the Lēvītes, by their fathers' houses.

3.21
Ex 6.17

3.25
Num 4.24–
26; Ex 25.9

21 Of Gērshŏn were the family of the Lĭbnītes and the family of the Shĭm′ĕ-ītes; these were the families of the Gēr′shŏnītes. 22 Their number according to the number of all the males from a month old and upward was[a] seven thousand five hundred. 23 The families of the Gēr′shŏnītes were to encamp behind the tabernacle on the west, 24 with Ēlī′ăsăph, the son of Lāĕl as head of the fathers' house of the Gēr′shŏnītes. 25And the charge of the sons of Gērshŏn in the tent of meeting was to be the tabernacle, the tent with its covering, the screen for the door of the tent of meeting, 26 the hangings of the court, the screen for the door of the court which is around the tabernacle and the altar, and its cords; all the service pertaining to these.

3.27
1 Chr 26.23

3.29
Ex 6.18

27 Of Kōhăth were the family of the Ăm′rămites, and the family of the Ĭz′harītes, and the family of the Hē′brŏnītes, and the family of the Ŭzzī′ĕlītes; these are the families of the Kō′hăthītes. 28According to the number of all the males, from a month old and upward, there were eight thousand six hundred, attending to the duties of the sanctuary. 29 The families of the sons of Kōhăth were to encamp on the south side of the tabernacle, 30 with Ēlīz′ăphăn the son of Ŭzzī′ĕl as head of the fathers' house of the families of the Kō′hăthītes. 31And their charge was to be the ark, the table, the lampstand, the altars, the vessels of the sanctuary with which the priests minister, and the screen; all the service pertaining to these. 32And Ēlëă′zăr the son of Aaron the priest was to be chief over the leaders of the Lēvītes, and to have oversight of those who had charge of the sanctuary.

3.33
Ex 6.19

33 Of Mĕrar′ī were the family of the Mahlītes and the family of the Mushītes: these are the families of Merari. 34 Their number

a Heb *their number was*

according to the number of all the males from a month old and
upward was six thousand two hundred. 35And the head of the
fathers' house of the families of Mèrar'ĭ was Zu'rĭĕl the son of
Ăb'ĭhāil; they were to encamp on the north side of the tabernacle.
36And the appointed charge of the sons of Mèrar'ĭ was to be the
frames of the tabernacle, the bars, the pillars, the bases, and all
their accessories; all the service pertaining to these; 37 also the
pillars of the court round about, with their bases and pegs and
cords.

3.36
Num 4.29–
32

38 And those to encamp before the tabernacle on the east, before the tent of meeting toward the sunrise, were Moses and Aaron
and his sons, having charge of the rites within the sanctuary, whatever had to be done for the people of Israel; and any one else who
came near was to be put to death. 39All who were numbered of
the Lĕvītes, whom Moses and Aaron numbered at the commandment of the LORD, by families, all the males from a month old
and upward, were twenty-two thousand.

3.38
Num 18.5;
ver 7,8,10

★3.39
Num 26.62

5. The numbering of first-born males

40 And the LORD said to Moses, "Number all the first-born
males of the people of Israel, from a month old and upward, taking
their number by names. 41And you shall take the Lĕvītes for me—I
am the LORD—instead of all the first-born among the people of
Israel, and the cattle of the Levites instead of all the firstlings
among the cattle of the people of Israel." 42 So Moses numbered
all the first-born among the people of Israel, as the LORD commanded him. 43And all the first-born males, according to the
number of names, from a month old and upward as numbered
were twenty-two thousand two hundred and seventy-three.

3.41
ver 12,45

3.43
ver 39

44 And the LORD said to Moses, 45 "Take the Lĕvītes instead of
all the first-born among the people of Israel, and the cattle of the
Levites instead of their cattle; and the Levites shall be mine: I am
the LORD. 46And for the redemption of the two hundred and
seventy-three of the first-born of the people of Israel, over and
above the number of the male Lĕvītes, 47 you shall take five shekels
apiece; reckoning by the shekel of the sanctuary, the shekel of
twenty gerahs, you shall take them, 48 and give the money by
which the excess number of them is redeemed to Aaron and his
sons." 49 So Moses took the redemption money from those who
were over and above those redeemed by the Lĕvītes; 50 from the
first-born of the people of Israel he took the money, one thousand
three hundred and sixty-five shekels, reckoned by the shekel of the
sanctuary; 51 and Moses gave the redemption money to Aaron and
his sons, according to the word of the LORD, as the LORD commanded Moses.

3.45
ver 12,41

3.46
Ex 13.13;
Num 18.15
3.47
Ex 30.13

3.50
ver 46–48

6. Numbering and service of the Levites
a. The sons of Kohath

4 The LORD said to Moses and Aaron, 2 "Take a census of the
sons of Kōhăth from among the sons of Lĕvi, by their families
and their fathers' houses, 3 from thirty years old up to fifty years

4.3
Num 8.24;
ver 23,30,
35

3.39 Compare this with 26.62. In the
latter account there are one thousand more.
Evidently between the time of the first
and the second mention the number of

Levites from one month of age and over had
increased by this number. Round figures are
used, a common practice in history at all
times.

old, all who can enter the service, to do the work in the tent of meeting. 4 This is the service of the sons of Kōhăth in the tent of meeting: the most holy things. 5 When the camp is to set out, Aaron and his sons shall go in and take down the veil of the screen, and cover the ark of the testimony with it; 6 then they shall put on it a covering of goatskin, and spread over that a cloth all of blue, and shall put in its poles. 7And over the table of the bread of the Presence they shall spread a cloth of blue, and put upon it the plates, the dishes for incense, the bowls, and the flagons for the drink offering; the continual bread also shall be on it; 8 then they shall spread over them a cloth of scarlet, and cover the same with a covering of goatskin, and shall put in its poles. 9And they shall take a cloth of blue, and cover the lampstand for the light, with its lamps, its snuffers, its trays, and all the vessels for oil with which it is supplied: 10 and they shall put it with all its utensils in a covering of goatskin and put it upon the carrying frame. 11And over the golden altar they shall spread a cloth of blue, and cover it with a covering of goatskin, and shall put in its poles; 12 and they shall take all the vessels of the service which are used in the sanctuary, and put them in a cloth of blue, and cover them with a covering of goatskin, and put them on the carrying frame. 13And they shall take away the ashes from the altar, and spread a purple cloth over it; 14 and they shall put on it all the utensils of the altar, which are used for the service there, the firepans, the forks, the shovels, and the basins, all the utensils of the altar; and they shall spread upon it a covering of goatskin, and shall put in its poles. 15And when Aaron and his sons have finished covering the sanctuary and all the furnishings of the sanctuary, as the camp sets out, after that the sons of Kōhăth shall come to carry these, but they must not touch the holy things, lest they die. These are the things of the tent of meeting which the sons of Kohath are to carry.

16 "And Ēlëä´zăr the son of Aaron the priest shall have charge of the oil for the light, the fragrant incense, the continual cereal offering, and the anointing oil, with the oversight of all the tabernacle and all that is in it, of the sanctuary and its vessels."

17 The LORD said to Moses and Aaron, 18 "Let not the tribe of the families of the Kō´hăthītes be destroyed from among the Lēvītes; 19 but deal thus with them, that they may live and not die when they come near to the most holy things: Aaron and his sons shall go in and appoint them each to his task and to his burden, 20 but they shall not go in to look upon the holy things even for a moment, lest they die."

b. The sons of Gershon

21 The LORD said to Moses, 22 "Take a census of the sons of Gėrshón also, by their families and their fathers' houses; 23 from thirty years old up to fifty years old, you shall number them, all who can enter for service, to do the work in the tent of meeting. 24 This is the service of the families of the Gėr´shónītes, in serving and bearing burdens: 25 they shall carry the curtains of the tabernacle, and the tent of meeting with its covering, and the covering of goatskin that is on top of it, and the screen for the door of the tent of meeting, 26 and the hangings of the court, and the screen for the entrance of the gate of the court which is around the tabernacle and the altar, and their cords, and all the equipment for

their service; and they shall do all that needs to be done with regard to them. 27All the service of the sons of the Gėr′shŏnītes shall be at the command of Aaron and his sons, in all that they are to carry, and in all that they have to do; and you shall assign to their charge all that they are to carry. 28 This is the service of the families of the sons of the Gėr′shŏnītes in the tent of meeting, and their work is to be under the oversight of Ĭth′ámar the son of Aaron the priest.

c. *The sons of Merari*

29 "As for the sons of Mėrar′ī, you shall number them by their families and their fathers' houses; 30 from thirty years old up to fifty years old, you shall number them, every one that can enter the service, to do the work of the tent of meeting. 31And this is what they are charged to carry, as the whole of their service in the tent of meeting: the frames of the tabernacle, with its bars, pillars, and bases, 32 and the pillars of the court round about with their bases, pegs, and cords, with all their equipment and all their accessories; and you shall assign by name the objects which they are required to carry. 33 This is the service of the families of the sons of Mėrar′ī, the whole of their service in the tent of meeting, under the hand of Ĭth′ámar the son of Aaron the priest."

d. *The results of the census*

34 And Moses and Aaron and the leaders of the congregation numbered the sons of the Kō′háthītes, by their families and their fathers' houses, 35 from thirty years old up to fifty years old, every one that could enter the service, for work in the tent of meeting; 36 and their number by families was two thousand seven hundred and fifty. 37 This was the number of the families of the Kō′háthītes, all who served in the tent of meeting, whom Moses and Aaron numbered according to the commandment of the LORD by Moses.

38 The number of the sons of Gėrshŏn, by their families and their fathers' houses, 39 from thirty years old up to fifty years old, every one that could enter the service for work in the tent of meeting—40 their number by their families and their fathers' houses was two thousand six hundred and thirty. 41 This was the number of the families of the sons of Gėrshŏn, all who served in the tent of meeting, whom Moses and Aaron numbered according to the commandment of the LORD.

42 The number of the families of the sons of Mėrar′ī, by their families and their fathers' houses, 43 from thirty years old up to fifty years old, every one that could enter the service, for work in the tent of meeting—44 their number by families was three thousand two hundred. 45 These are those who were numbered of the families of the sons of Mėrar′ī, whom Moses and Aaron numbered according to the commandment of the LORD by Moses.

46 All those who were numbered of the Lēvītes, whom Moses and Aaron and the leaders of Israel numbered, by their families and their fathers' houses, 47 from thirty years old up to fifty years old, every one that could enter to do the work of service and the work of bearing burdens in the tent of meeting, 48 those who were numbered of them were eight thousand five hundred and eighty. 49According to the commandment of the LORD through Moses

4.27
Num 3.21

4.30
ver 3

4.31
Num 3.36,
37

4.33
ver 28

4.34
ver 2

4.37
Num 3.27

4.38
Gen 46.11

4.41
ver 22

4.45
ver 29

4.47
ver 3,23,30

they were appointed, each to his task of serving or carrying; thus they were numbered by him, as the LORD commanded Moses.

D. Camp laws and regulations

1. *The unclean to be put out of the camp*

*5.2ff
Lev 13.3,
46; 15.2;
19.11

5.3
Lev 26.11,
12; 2 Cor
6.16

5 The LORD said to Moses, 2 "Command the people of Israel that they put out of the camp every leper, and every one having a discharge, and every one that is unclean through contact with the dead; 3 you shall put out both male and female, putting them outside the camp, that they may not defile their camp, in the midst of which I dwell." 4And the people of Israel did so, and drove them outside the camp; as the LORD said to Moses, so the people of Israel did.

2. *The law of restitution*

5.6
Lev 6.2,3

5.7
Lev 5.5;
26.40; 6.5

5.8
Lev 6.6,7;
7.7

5.9
Lev 6.17,
18,26; 7.6–
14
5.10
Lev 10.13

5 And the LORD said to Moses, 6 "Say to the people of Israel, When a man or woman commits any of the sins that men commit by breaking faith with the LORD, and that person is guilty, 7 he shall confess his sin which he has committed; and he shall make full restitution for his wrong, adding a fifth to it, and giving it to him to whom he did the wrong. 8 But if the man has no kinsman to whom restitution may be made for the wrong, the restitution for wrong shall go to the LORD for the priest, in addition to the ram of atonement with which atonement is made for him. 9And every offering, all the holy things of the people of Israel, which they bring to the priest, shall be his; 10 and every man's holy things shall be his; whatever any man gives to the priest shall be his."

3. *The law concerning jealousy*

*5.11ff
5.12
Ex 20.14
5.13
Lev 18.20

5.15
Ezek 29.16

5.18
1 Cor 11.6

11 And the LORD said to Moses, 12 "Say to the people of Israel, If any man's wife goes astray and acts unfaithfully against him, 13 if a man lies with her carnally, and it is hidden from the eyes of her husband, and she is undetected though she has defiled herself, and there is no witness against her, since she was not taken in the act; 14 and if the spirit of jealousy comes upon him, and he is jealous of his wife who has defiled herself; or if the spirit of jealousy comes upon him, and he is jealous of his wife, though she has not defiled herself; 15 then the man shall bring his wife to the priest, and bring the offering required of her, a tenth of an ephah of barley meal; he shall pour no oil upon it and put no frankincense on it, for it is a cereal offering of jealousy, a cereal offering of remembrance, bringing iniquity to remembrance.

16 "And the priest shall bring her near, and set her before the LORD; 17 and the priest shall take holy water in an earthen vessel, and take some of the dust that is on the floor of the tabernacle and put it into the water. 18And the priest shall set the woman before the LORD, and unbind the hair of the woman's head, and place in her hands the cereal offering of remembrance, which is the cereal offering of jealousy. And in his hand the priest shall have the

5.2ff Addenda to the laws in Leviticus.
5.11ff Moses outlines here (ver 11–31) the law of jealousy by which suspicion of marital unfaithfulness could be cleared or confirmed. The rite prescribed was, in effect, an appeal to God to determine the guilt or innocence of the suspected party. Specific examples of the use of this rite do not exist in Scripture. The custom was not practiced in post-biblical times, although during the history of the church ordeals were resorted to which bore some affinities to the law of jealousy.

water of bitterness that brings the curse. 19 Then the priest shall make her take an oath, saying, 'If no man has lain with you, and if you have not turned aside to uncleanness, while you were under your husband's authority, be free from this water of bitterness that brings the curse. 20 But if you have gone astray, though you are under your husband's authority, and if you have defiled yourself, and some man other than your husband has lain with you, 21 then' (let the priest make the woman take the oath of the curse, and say to the woman) 'the LORD make you an execration and an oath among your people, when the LORD makes your thigh fall away and your body swell; 22 may this water that brings the curse pass into your bowels and make your body swell and your thigh fall away.' And the woman shall say, 'Amen, Amen.'

23 "Then the priest shall write these curses in a book, and wash them off into the water of bitterness; 24 and he shall make the woman drink the water of bitterness that brings the curse, and the water that brings the curse shall enter into her and cause bitter pain. 25And the priest shall take the cereal offering of jealousy out of the woman's hand, and shall wave the cereal offering before the LORD and bring it to the altar; 26 and the priest shall take a handful of the cereal offering, as its memorial portion, and burn it upon the altar, and afterward shall make the woman drink the water. 27And when he has made her drink the water, then, if she has defiled herself and has acted unfaithfully against her husband, the water that brings the curse shall enter into her and cause bitter pain, and her body shall swell, and her thigh shall fall away, and the woman shall become an execration among her people. 28 But if the woman has not defiled herself and is clean, then she shall be free and shall conceive children.

29 "This is the law in cases of jealousy, when a wife, though under her husband's authority, goes astray and defiles herself, 30 or when the spirit of jealousy comes upon a man and he is jealous of his wife; then he shall set the woman before the LORD, and the priest shall execute upon her all this law. 31 The man shall be free from iniquity, but the woman shall bear her iniquity."

4. The law for a Nazirite

6 And the LORD said to Moses, 2 "Say to the people of Israel, When either a man or a woman makes a special vow, the vow of a Năz'irīte,[b] to separate himself to the LORD, 3 he shall separate himself from wine and strong drink; he shall drink no vinegar made from wine or strong drink, and shall not drink any juice of grapes or eat grapes, fresh or dried. 4All the days of his separation[c] he shall eat nothing that is produced by the grapevine, not even the seeds or the skins.

---

[b] That is one separated or one consecrated   [c] Or Năz'irīte'ship

---

Marginal references:

5.21
Josh 6.26;
1 Sam
14.24;
Neh 10.29
5.22
Deut 27.15;
Ps 109.18

5.25
Lev 8.27

5.27
Jer 29.18;
42.18;
Zech 8.13

5.29
ver 12,19

*6.2
Judg 13.5;
16.17;
Amos 2.11,
12

6.2 Scripture warns against making vows lightly (Prov 20.25), but once made they are regarded as binding. Indeed Scripture insists upon performance even though the vower may have changed his preference (30.2) and urges prompt discharge of his vows (Deut 23.21, 23). There is nothing in Scripture which would require one to fulfil a vow made in good faith but which later is discovered to be wrong or sinful. To refrain from making a vow is not sinful (Deut 23.22). Certain restrictions were laid down to prevent misuse of the vow: (1) vows of children required the consent of their parents (30.3–5); (2) vows of wives required the consent of their husbands (30.6–8, 10–13); (3) but vows of widows and divorced women were binding upon them (30.9). Illustrations of those who made vows include: (1) Jephthah (Judg 11.30, 31); (2) Hannah (1 Sam 1.11); (3) David (Ps 132.2–5); (4) Paul (Acts 18.18); (5) the Jews whom Paul sponsored (Acts 21.23, 24, 26).

6.5
Sam 1.11

5 "All the days of his vow of separation no razor shall come upon his head; until the time is completed for which he separates himself to the LORD, he shall be holy; he shall let the locks of hair of his head grow long.

6.6
Lev 19.11–
22; 21.1–3

6 "All the days that he separates himself to the LORD he shall not go near a dead body. 7 Neither for his father nor for his mother, nor for brother or sister, if they die, shall he make himself unclean; because his separation to God is upon his head. 8 All the days of his separation he is holy to the LORD.

9 "And if any man dies very suddenly beside him, and he defiles his consecrated head, then he shall shave his head on the day of

6.10
Lev 5.7

his cleansing; on the seventh day he shall shave it. 10 On the eighth day he shall bring two turtledoves or two young pigeons to the priest to the door of the tent of meeting, 11 and the priest shall offer one for a sin offering and the other for a burnt offering, and make atonement for him, because he sinned by reason of the dead body.

6.12
Lev 5.6

And he shall consecrate his head that same day, 12 and separate himself to the LORD for the days of his separation, and bring a male lamb a year old for a guilt offering; but the former time shall be void, because his separation was defiled.

6.13
Acts 21.26

13 "And this is the law for the Năz′irīte, when the time of his separation has been completed: he shall be brought to the door of

6.14
Num 15.27;
Lev 14.10

the tent of meeting, 14 and he shall offer his gift to the LORD, one male lamb a year old without blemish for a burnt offering, and one ewe lamb a year old without blemish as a sin offering, and one

6.15
Num 15.1–
7

ram without blemish as a peace offering, 15 and a basket of unleavened bread, cakes of fine flour mixed with oil, and unleavened wafers spread with oil, and their cereal offering and their drink offerings. 16 And the priest shall present them before the LORD and offer his sin offering and his burnt offering, 17 and he shall offer the ram as a sacrifice of peace offering to the LORD, with the basket of unleavened bread; the priest shall offer also its cereal offering

6.18
ver 9;
Acts 21.24

and its drink offering. 18 And the Năz′irīte shall shave his consecrated head at the door of the tent of meeting, and shall take the hair from his consecrated head and put it on the fire which is under the sacrifice of the peace offering. 19 And the priest shall take the shoulder of the ram, when it is boiled, and one unleavened cake out of the basket, and one unleavened wafer, and shall put them upon the hands of the Năz′irīte, after he has shaven the hair of his consecration, 20 and the priest shall wave them for a wave offering before the LORD; they are a holy portion for the priest, together with the breast that is waved and the thigh that is offered; and after that the Năz′irīte may drink wine.

21 "This is the law for the Năz′irīte who takes a vow. His offering to the LORD shall be according to his vow as a Nazirite, apart from what else he can afford; in accordance with the vow which he takes, so shall he do according to the law for his separation as a Nazirite."

5. *The Aaronic benediction*

6.23
1 Chr 23.13

22 The LORD said to Moses, 23 "Say to Aaron and his sons, Thus you shall bless the people of Israel: you shall say to them,

6.24
Deut 28.3–6

24 The LORD bless you and keep you:

6.25
Ps 80.3,7,
19;
119.135;
Gen 43.29

25 The LORD make his face to shine upon you, and be gracious to you:

26 The LORD lift up his countenance upon you, and give you peace.

27 "So shall they put my name upon the people of Israel, and I will bless them."

6.26
Ps 4.6;
44.3; Jn
14.27
6.27
Deut 28.10;
2 Chr 7.14

E. The offerings for the tabernacle

1. The dedication of the altar

7 On the day when Moses had finished setting up the tabernacle, and had anointed and consecrated it with all its furnishings, and had anointed and consecrated the altar with all its utensils, 2 the leaders of Israel, heads of their fathers' houses, the leaders of the tribes, who were over those who were numbered, 3 offered and brought their offerings before the LORD, six covered wagons and twelve oxen, a wagon for every two of the leaders, and for each one an ox; they offered them before the tabernacle. 4 Then the LORD said to Moses, 5 "Accept these from them, that they may be used in doing the service of the tent of meeting, and give them to the Lēvītes, to each man according to his service." 6 So Moses took the wagons and the oxen, and gave them to the Lēvītes. 7 Two wagons and four oxen he gave to the sons of Gērshŏn, according to their service; 8 and four wagons and eight oxen he gave to the sons of Mērar'ï, according to their service, under the direction of Ith'āmar the son of Aaron the priest. 9 But to the sons of Kōhăth he gave none, because they were charged with the care of the holy things which had to be carried on the shoulder. 10And the leaders offered offerings for the dedication of the altar on the day it was anointed; and the leaders offered their offering before the altar. 11And the LORD said to Moses, "They shall offer their offerings, one leader each day, for the dedication of the altar."

7.1
Ex 40.18

7.2
Num 1.5–
16

7.7
Num 4.25
7.8
Num 4.28,
31,33
7.9
Num 4.5–
15
7.10
2 Chr 7.9

2. Nahshon of Judah

12 He who offered his offering the first day was Nahshŏn the son of Ămmĭn'ădăb, of the tribe of Judah; 13 and his offering was one silver plate whose weight was a hundred and thirty shekels, one silver basin of seventy shekels, according to the shekel of the sanctuary, both of them full of fine flour mixed with oil for a cereal offering; 14 one golden dish of ten shekels, full of incense; 15 one young bull, one ram, one male lamb a year old, for a burnt offering; 16 one male goat for a sin offering; 17 and for the sacrifice of peace offerings, two oxen, five rams, five male goats, and five male lambs a year old. This was the offering of Nahshŏn the son of Ămmĭn'ădăb.

7.13
Num 3.47

7.14
Ex 30.34

7.17
Lev 3.1

3. Nethanel of Issachar

18 On the second day Nĕthăn'ĕl the son of Zu'ar, the leader of Ĭs'săchar, made an offering; 19 he offered for his offering one silver plate, whose weight was a hundred and thirty shekels, one silver basin of seventy shekels, according to the shekel of the sanctuary, both of them full of fine flour mixed with oil for a cereal offering; 20 one golden dish of ten shekels, full of incense; 21 one young bull, one ram, one male lamb a year old, for a burnt offering; 22 one male goat for a sin offering; 23 and for the sacrifice of peace offerings, two oxen, five rams, five male goats, and five male lambs a

7.18
Num 1.8

7.23
ver 18

year old. This was the offering of Néthăn'ĕl the son of Zu'ar.

4. Eliab of Zebulun

7.24
Num 1.9

24 On the third day Ēlī'áb the son of Hēlón, the leader of the men of Zĕb'ŭlún: 25 his offering was one silver plate, whose weight was a hundred and thirty shekels, one silver basin of seventy shekels, according to the shekel of the sanctuary, both of them full of fine flour mixed with oil for a cereal offering; 26 one golden dish of ten shekels, full of incense; 27 one young bull, one ram, one male lamb a year old, for a burnt offering; 28 one male goat for a sin offering; 29 and for the sacrifice of peace offerings, two oxen, five rams, five male goats, and five male lambs a year old. This was the offering of Ēlī'áb the son of Hēlón.

7.29
Lev 7.32

5. Elizur of Reuben

7.30
Num 1.5

30 On the fourth day Ēlī'zùr the son of Shĕdē'ùr, the leader of the men of Reubën: 31 his offering was one silver plate whose weight was a hundred and thirty shekels, one silver basin of seventy shekels, according to the shekel of the sanctuary, both of them full of fine flour mixed with oil for a cereal offering; 32 one golden dish of ten shekels, full of incense; 33 one young bull, one ram, one male lamb a year old, for a burnt offering; 34 one male goat for a sin offering; 35 and for the sacrifice of peace offerings, two oxen, five rams, five male goats, and five male lambs a year old. This was the offering of Ēlī'zùr the son of Shĕdē'ùr.

7.34
Heb 10.4

6. Shelumiel of Simeon

7.36
Num 1.6

36 On the fifth day Shēlù'mĭ-ĕl the son of Zurïshăd'däi, the leader of the men of Sïm'ĕŏn: 37 his offering was one silver plate, whose weight was a hundred and thirty shekels, one silver basin of seventy shekels, according to the shekel of the sanctuary, both of them full of fine flour mixed with oil for a cereal offering; 38 one golden dish of ten shekels, full of incense; 39 one young bull, one ram, one male lamb a year old, for a burnt offering; 40 one male goat for a sin offering; 41 and for the sacrifice of peace offerings, two oxen, five rams, five male goats, and five male lambs a year old. This was the offering of Shēlù'mĭ-ĕl the son of Zurïshăd'däi.

7.40
ver 34

7. Eliasaph of Gad

7.42
Num 1.14
Reuel

42 On the sixth day Ēlī'ásăph the son of Deu'ĕl, the leader of the men of Găd: 43 his offering was one silver plate, whose weight was a hundred and thirty shekels, one silver basin of seventy shekels, according to the shekel of the sanctuary, both of them full of fine flour mixed with oil for a cereal offering; 44 one golden dish of ten shekels, full of incense; 45 one young bull, one ram, one male lamb a year old, for a burnt offering; 46 one male goat for a sin offering; 47 and for the sacrifice of peace offerings, two oxen, five rams, five male goats, and five male lambs a year old. This was the offering of Ēlī'ásăph the son of Deu'ĕl.

7.46
ver 34

8. Elishama of Ephraim

7.48
Num 1.10

48 On the seventh day Ēlī'shămá the son of Ămmī'hŭd, the leader of the men of Ē'phräïm: 49 his offering was one silver plate, whose weight was a hundred and thirty shekels, one silver basin of seventy shekels, according to the shekel of the sanctuary, both

of them full of fine flour mixed with oil for a cereal offering; 50 one
golden dish of ten shekels, full of incense; 51 one young bull, one
ram, one male lamb a year old, for a burnt offering; 52 one male
goat for a sin offering; 53 and for the sacrifice of peace offerings,
two oxen, five rams, five male goats, and five male lambs a year
old. This was the offering of Ĕlī'shämä the son of Ammī'hŭd.

9. *Gamaliel of Manasseh*

54 On the eighth day Gämä'lĭĕl the son of Pĕdah'zŭr, the leader
of the men of Mänăs'sĕh: 55 his offering was one silver plate,
whose weight was a hundred and thirty shekels, one silver basin
of seventy shekels, according to the shekel of the sanctuary, both
of them full of fine flour mixed with oil for a cereal offering;
56 one golden dish of ten shekels, full of incense; 57 one young
bull, one ram, one male lamb a year old, for a burnt offering;
58 one male goat for a sin offering; 59 and for the sacrifice of peace
offerings, two oxen, five rams, five male goats, and five male lambs
a year old. This was the offering of Gämä'lĭĕl the son of Pĕdah'zŭr.

10. *Abidan of Benjamin*

60 On the ninth day Ăb'ĭdän the son of Gĭdëö'nī, the leader of
the men of Benjamin: 61 his offering was one silver plate, whose
weight was a hundred and thirty shekels, one silver basin of seventy shekels, according to the shekel of the sanctuary, both of them
full of fine flour mixed with oil for a cereal offering; 62 one golden
dish of ten shekels, full of incense; 63 one young bull, one ram, one
male lamb a year old, for a burnt offering; 64 one male goat for a
sin offering; 65 and for the sacrifice of peace offerings, two oxen,
five rams, five male goats, and five male lambs a year old. This was
the offering of Ăb'ĭdän the son of Gĭdëö'nī.

11. *Ahiezer of Dan*

66 On the tenth day Āhī-ē'zĕr the son of Ămmĭshăd'däī, the
leader of the men of Dan: 67 his offering was one silver plate,
whose weight was a hundred and thirty shekels, one silver basin
of seventy shekels, according to the shekel of the sanctuary, both of
them full of fine flour mixed with oil for a cereal offering; 68 one
golden dish of ten shekels, full of incense; 69 one young bull, one
ram, one male lamb a year old, for a burnt offering; 70 one male
goat for a sin offering; 71 and for the sacrifice of peace offerings,
two oxen, five rams, five male goats, and five male lambs a year
old. This was the offering of Āhī-ē'zĕr the son of Ămmĭshăd'däī.

12. *Pagiel of Asher*

72 On the eleventh day Pä'gĭĕl the son of Ŏçhrän, the leader of
the men of Ăshĕr: 73 his offering was one silver plate, whose weight
was a hundred and thirty shekels, one silver basin of seventy
shekels, according to the shekel of the sanctuary, both of them
full of fine flour mixed with oil for a cereal offering; 74 one golden
dish of ten shekels, full of incense; 75 one young bull, one ram, one
male lamb a year old, for a burnt offering; 76 one male goat for a
sin offering; 77 and for the sacrifice of peace offerings, two oxen,
five rams, five male goats, and five male lambs a year old. This was
the offering of Pä'gĭĕl the son of Ŏçhrän.

7.52
Heb 10.4

7.54
Num 1.10

7.58
ver 52

7.60
Num 1.11

7.64
ver 52

7.66
Num 1.12

7.70
Heb 10.4

7.72
Num 1.13

7.76
ver 70

13. *Ahira of Naphtali*

7.78
Num 1.15

78 On the twelfth day Ăhī′rà the son of Ēnán, the leader of the men of Năph′tàlī: 79 his offering was one silver plate, whose weight was a hundred and thirty shekels, one silver basin of seventy shekels, according to the shekel of the sanctuary, both of them full of fine flour mixed with oil for a cereal offering; 80 one golden dish of ten shekels, full of incense; 81 one young bull, one ram, one male lamb a year old, for a burnt offering; 82 one male goat for a sin offering; 83 and for the sacrifice of peace offerings, two oxen, five rams, five male goats, and five male lambs a year old. This was the offering of Ăhī′rà the son of Enán.

7.82
ver 70

7.84
ver 1,10

84 This was the dedication offering for the altar, on the day when it was anointed, from the leaders of Israel: twelve silver plates, twelve silver basins, twelve golden dishes, 85 each silver plate weighing a hundred and thirty shekels and each basin seventy, all the silver of the vessels two thousand four hundred shekels according to the shekel of the sanctuary, 86 the twelve golden dishes, full of incense, weighing ten shekels apiece according to the shekel of the sanctuary, all the gold of the dishes being a hundred and twenty shekels; 87 all the cattle for the burnt offering twelve bulls, twelve rams, twelve male lambs a year old, with their cereal offering; and twelve male goats for a sin offering; 88 and all the cattle for the sacrifice of peace offerings twenty-four bulls, the rams sixty, the male goats sixty, the male lambs a year old sixty. This was the dedication offering for the altar, after it was anointed.

7.87
Gen 8.20

14. *The voice from above the mercy seat*

*7.89
Ex 33.9,11;
25.21,22

89 And when Moses went into the tent of meeting to speak with the LORD, he heard the voice speaking to him from above the mercy seat that was upon the ark of the testimony, from between the two cherubim; and it spoke to him.

F. *Final details before the march*

1. *The lampstand*

8.2
Ex 25.37;
Lev 24.2,4

8 Now the LORD said to Moses, 2 "Say to Aaron, When you set up the lamps, the seven lamps shall give light in front of the lampstand." 3And Aaron did so; he set up its lamps to give light in front of the lampstand, as the LORD commanded Moses. 4And this was the workmanship of the lampstand, hammered work of gold; from its base to its flowers, it was hammered work; according to the pattern which the LORD had shown Moses, so he made the lampstand.

8.4
Ex 25.31–
40; 25.18

2. *Purification of the Levites*

8.7
Num 19.9,
17,18; Lev
14.8,9; ver
21

5 And the LORD said to Moses, 6 "Take the Lēvītes from among the people of Israel, and cleanse them. 7And thus you shall do to them, to cleanse them: sprinkle the water of expiation upon them, and let them go with a razor over all their body, and wash their clothes and cleanse themselves. 8 Then let them take a young bull and its cereal offering of fine flour mixed with oil, and you shall take another young bull for a sin offering. 9And you shall present

8.8
Lev 2.1
*8.9
Lev 8.3

---

the Lĕvītes before the tent of meeting, and assemble the whole
congregation of the people of Israel. 10 When you present the
Lĕvītes before the LORD, the people of Israel shall lay their hands
upon the Levites, 11 and Aaron shall offer the Lĕvītes before the
LORD as a wave offering from the people of Israel, that it may be
theirs to do the service of the LORD. 12 Then the Lĕvītes shall lay
their hands upon the heads of the bulls; and you shall offer the
one for a sin offering and the other for a burnt offering to the
LORD, to make atonement for the Levites. 13And you shall cause
the Lĕvītes to attend Aaron and his sons, and shall offer them as a
wave offering to the LORD.

14 "Thus you shall separate the Lĕvītes from among the people
of Israel, and the Levites shall be mine. 15And after that the Lĕvītes shall go in to do service at the tent of meeting, when you have
cleansed them and offered them as a wave offering. 16 For they are
wholly given to me from among the people of Israel; instead of
all that open the womb, the first-born of all the people of Israel, I
have taken them for myself. 17 For all the first-born among the
people of Israel are mine, both of man and of beast; on the day
that I slew all the first-born in the land of Egypt I consecrated
them for myself, 18 and I have taken the Lĕvītes instead of all the
first-born among the people of Israel. 19And I have given the Lĕvītes as a gift to Aaron and his sons from among the people of Israel, to do the service for the people of Israel at the tent of meeting,
and to make atonement for the people of Israel, that there may be
no plague among the people of Israel in case the people of Israel
should come near the sanctuary."

20 Thus did Moses and Aaron and all the congregation of the
people of Israel to the Lĕvītes; according to all that the LORD commanded Moses concerning the Levites, the people of Israel did to
them. 21And the Lĕvītes purified themselves from sin, and washed
their clothes; and Aaron offered them as a wave offering before
the LORD, and Aaron made atonement for them to cleanse them.
22And after that the Lĕvītes went in to do their service in the tent
of meeting in attendance upon Aaron and his sons; as the LORD
had commanded Moses concerning the Levites, so they did to
them.

3. *Age of service for the Levites*

23 And the LORD said to Moses, 24 "This is what pertains to the
Lĕvītes: from twenty-five years old and upward they shall go in to
perform the work in the service of the tent of meeting; 25 and from
the age of fifty years they shall withdraw from the work of the
service and serve no more, 26 but minister to their brethren in the
tent of meeting, to keep the charge, and they shall do no service.
Thus shall you do to the Lĕvītes in assigning their duties."

4. *The Passover command*

9 And the LORD spoke to Moses in the wilderness of Sī′naï, in
the first month of the second year after they had come out of
the land of Egypt, saying, 2 "Let the people of Israel keep the passover at its appointed time. 3 On the fourteenth day of this month,
in the evening, you shall keep it at its appointed time; according to
all its statutes and all its ordinances you shall keep it." 4 So Moses
told the people of Israel that they should keep the passover. 5And

8.12
Ex 29.10

8.14
Num 3.12,
45

8.15
ver 11,13

8.16
Num 3.12,
45

8.19
Num 1.53

8.21
ver 7,11,12

8.24
Num 4.3

9.1
Num 1.1

9.2
Ex 12.6

9.5
Josh 5.10

they kept the passover in the first month, on the fourteenth day of the month, in the evening, in the wilderness of Sī'näi; according to all that the LORD commanded Moses, so the people of Israel did. 6And there were certain men who were unclean through touching the dead body of a man, so that they could not keep the passover on that day; and they came before Moses and Aaron on that day; 7 and those men said to him, "We are unclean through touching the dead body of a man; why are we kept from offering the LORD's offering at its appointed time among the people of Israel?" 8And Moses said to them, "Wait, that I may hear what the LORD will command concerning you."

9 The LORD said to Moses, 10 "Say to the people of Israel, If any man of you or of your descendants is unclean through touching a dead body, or is afar off on a journey, he shall still keep the passover to the LORD. 11 In the second month on the fourteenth day in the evening they shall keep it; they shall eat it with unleavened bread and bitter herbs. 12 They shall leave none of it until the morning, nor break a bone of it; according to all the statute for the passover they shall keep it. 13 But the man who is clean and is not on a journey, yet refrains from keeping the passover, that person shall be cut off from his people, because he did not offer the LORD's offering at its appointed time; that man shall bear his sin. 14And if a stranger sojourns among you, and will keep the passover to the LORD, according to the statute of the passover and according to its ordinance, so shall he do; you shall have one statute, both for the sojourner and for the native."

5. The cloud of guidance

15 On the day that the tabernacle was set up, the cloud covered the tabernacle, the tent of the testimony; and at evening it was over the tabernacle like the appearance of fire until morning. 16 So it was continually; the cloud covered it by day,*d* and the appearance of fire by night. 17And whenever the cloud was taken up from over the tent, after that the people of Israel set out; and in the place where the cloud settled down, there the people of Israel encamped. 18At the command of the LORD the people of Israel set out, and at the command of the LORD they encamped; as long as the cloud rested over the tabernacle, they remained in camp. 19 Even when the cloud continued over the tabernacle many days, the people of Israel kept the charge of the LORD, and did not set out. 20 Sometimes the cloud was a few days over the tabernacle, and according to the command of the LORD they remained in camp; then according to the command of the LORD they set out. 21And sometimes the cloud remained from evening until morning; and when the cloud was taken up in the morning, they set out, or if it continued for a day and a night, when the cloud was taken up they set out. 22 Whether it was two days, or a month, or a longer time, that the cloud continued over the tabernacle, abiding there, the people of Israel remained in camp and did not set out; but when it was taken up they set out. 23At the command of the LORD they encamped,

d Gk Syr Vg: Heb lacks *by day*

Cross-references (margin)

- 9.6 Num 19.11–22
- 9.8 Ex 18.15; Num 27.5
- *9.10f
- 9.11 Ex 12.8
- 9.12 Ex 12.10, 43,46; Jn 19.36
- 9.13 ver 7; Ex 12.15
- 9.14 Ex 12.48,49
- 9.15 Ex 40.34; Neh 9.12, 19; Ps 78.4; Ex 13.21; 40.38
- 9.17 Num 10.11, 12; Ex 40.36–38
- 9.18 1 Cor 10.1
- 9.19 Num 1.53; 3.8
- 9.22 Ex 40.36,37

9.10, 11 Special provision was made for those who, for some reason, did not observe the regular Passover so that they could keep it a month later.

and at the command of the LORD they set out; they kept the charge of the LORD, at the command of the LORD by Moses.

6. *The two silver trumpets*

10 The LORD said to Moses, 2 "Make two silver trumpets; of hammered work you shall make them; and you shall use them for summoning the congregation, and for breaking camp. 3And when both are blown, all the congregation shall gather themselves to you at the entrance of the tent of meeting. 4 But if they blow only one, then the leaders, the heads of the tribes of Israel, shall gather themselves to you. 5 When you blow an alarm, the camps that are on the east side shall set out. 6And when you blow an alarm the second time, the camps that are on the south side shall set out. An alarm is to be blown whenever they are to set out. 7 But when the assembly is to be gathered together, you shall blow, but you shall not sound an alarm. 8And the sons of Aaron, the priests, shall blow the trumpets. The trumpets shall be to you for a perpetual statute throughout your generations. 9And when you go to war in your land against the adversary who oppresses you, then you shall sound an alarm with the trumpets, that you may be remembered before the LORD your God, and you shall be saved from your enemies. 10 On the day of your gladness also, and at your appointed feasts, and at the beginnings of your months, you shall blow the trumpets over your burnt offerings and over the sacrifices of your peace offerings; they shall serve you for remembrance before your God: I am the LORD your God."

II. *The journey from Sinai to Moab 10.11–21.35*

A. *The departure*

1. *The order of march*

11 In the second year, in the second month, on the twentieth day of the month, the cloud was taken up from over the tabernacle of the testimony, 12 and the people of Israel set out by stages from the wilderness of Sī'näï; and the cloud settled down in the wilderness of Pärän. 13 They set out for the first time at the command of the LORD by Moses. 14 The standard of the camp of the men of Judah set out first by their companies; and over their host was Nahshón the son of Ammïn'ádǎb. 15And over the host of the tribe of the men of Ĭs'sáchar was Néthän'él the son of Zu'ar. 16And over the host of the tribe of the men of Zĕb'ŭlŭn was Ĕlī'áb the son of Hēlón.

17 And when the tabernacle was taken down, the sons of Gérshón and the sons of Mérar'ĭ, who carried the tabernacle, set out. 18And the standard of the camp of Reubën set out by their companies; and over their host was Ĕlī'zŭr the son of Shĕdē'ŭr. 19And over the host of the tribe of the men of Sĭm'ëón was Shĕlu'mĭ-él the son of Zurĭshǎd'däï. 20And over the host of the tribe of the men of Gǎd was Ĕlī'ásǎph the son of Deu'él.

Margin references

10.3 Jer 4.5
10.5 ver 14
10.6 ver 18
10.8 Num 31.6
10.9 Num 31.6; Judg 2.18; Ps 106.4
*10.10 Num 29.1; Lev 23.24; Ps 81.3–5
10.11 Num 9.17
10.13 Deut 1.6
10.14 Num 2.3–9
10.17 Num 4.21–32
10.18 Num 2.10–16

10.10 The Feast of the New Moon was held on the first day of the month. In celebration of it, sacrifices were to be offered (28.11–15), and the priestly trumpets were to be blown (10.10; Ps 81.3, 4). God condemned the keeping of this feast (as well as all the others) when it was simply an insincere, formal observance (Isa 1.13, 14). The feast required a cessation from all business and work, which made it irksome to the ungodly (Amos 8.5). New Testament believers, of course, are not expected to keep feasts which have been abolished by the perfect sacrifice of Christ (Col 2.16; Gal 4.10, 11).

10.21
Num 4.4–
20
10.22
Num 2.18–
24

10.25
Num 2.25–
31;
Josh 6.9,13

10.29
Judg 4.11;
Ex 2.18;
Gen 12.7;
32.12;
Ex 3.8

★10.31

10.32
Ps 22.27–
31; Lev
19.34

10.33
ver 11;
Deut 1.33;
Isa 11.10
10.34
Num 9.15–
23
10.35
Ps 68.1,2;
Deut 7.10;
32.41

11.1
Num 14.2;
16.11;
17.5;
16.35;
Lev 10.2
11.2
Num 21.7

★11.4
Ex 12.38;
Ps 78.18;
1 Cor 10.6

21 Then the Kō'hăthītes set out, carrying the holy things, and the tabernacle was set up before their arrival. 22And the standard of the camp of the men of Ē'phrăim set out by their companies; and over their host was Ĕlī'shămă the son of Ammī'hŭd. 23And over the host of the tribe of the men of Mănăs'sĕh was Găma'lĭĕl the son of Pĕdah'zŭr. 24And over the host of the tribe of the men of Benjamin was Ăb'ĭdăn the son of Gĭdĕō'nĭ.

25 Then the standard of the camp of the men of Dan, acting as the rear guard of all the camps, set out by their companies; and over their host was Āhī-ē'zĕr the son of Ămmĭshăd'dāi. 26And over the host of the tribe of the men of Ăshĕr was Pā'ġĭĕl the son of Ŏçhrăn. 27And over the host of the tribe of the men of Năph'tălī was Ahī'ră the son of Ēnăn. 28 This was the order of march of the people of Israel according to their hosts, when they set out.

2. *The appeal to Hobab*

29 And Moses said to Hōbăb the son of Reu'ĕl the Mĭd'ĭănīte, Moses' father-in-law, "We are setting out for the place of which the LORD said, 'I will give it to you'; come with us, and we will do you good; for the LORD has promised good to Israel." 30 But he said to him, "I will not go; I will depart to my own land and to my kindred." 31And he said, "Do not leave us, I pray you, for you know how we are to encamp in the wilderness, and you will serve as eyes for us. 32And if you go with us, whatever good the LORD will do to us, the same will we do to you."

3. *The ark and the cloud of guidance*

33 So they set out from the mount of the LORD three days' journey; and the ark of the covenant of the LORD went before them three days' journey, to seek out a resting place for them. 34And the cloud of the LORD was over them by day, whenever they set out from the camp.

35 And whenever the ark set out, Moses said, "Arise, O LORD, and let thy enemies be scattered; and let them that hate thee flee before thee." 36And when it rested, he said, "Return, O LORD, to the ten thousand thousands of Israel."

B. The sins of Israel

1. *Complaining at Taberah*

11 And the people complained in the hearing of the LORD about their misfortunes; and when the LORD heard it, his anger was kindled, and the fire of the LORD burned among them, and consumed some outlying parts of the camp. 2 Then the people cried to Moses; and Moses prayed to the LORD, and the fire abated. 3 So the name of that place was called Tăb'ĕráh,*e* because the fire of the LORD burned among them.

2. *The cry for meat*

4 Now the rabble that was among them had a strong craving;

e That is *Burning*

10.31 *serve as eyes for us.* Hobab, Moses' brother-in-law, knew the region well and could serve as guide.

11.4 *rabble,* probably the non-Israelites referred to in Ex 12.38 as the *mixed multitude.*

and the people of Israel also wept again, and said, "O that we had meat to eat! 5 We remember the fish we ate in Egypt for nothing, the cucumbers, the melons, the leeks, the onions, and the garlic; 6 but now our strength is dried up, and there is nothing at all but this manna to look at."

7 Now the manna was like coriander seed, and its appearance like that of bdellium. 8 The people went about and gathered it, and ground it in mills or beat it in mortars, and boiled it in pots, and made cakes of it; and the taste of it was like the taste of cakes baked with oil. 9 When the dew fell upon the camp in the night, the manna fell with it.

3. Moses' prayer for help

10 Moses heard the people weeping throughout their families, every man at the door of his tent; and the anger of the LORD blazed hotly, and Moses was displeased. 11 Moses said to the LORD, "Why hast thou dealt ill with thy servant? And why have I not found favor in thy sight, that thou dost lay the burden of all this people upon me? 12 Did I conceive all this people? Did I bring them forth, that thou shouldst say to me, 'Carry them in your bosom, as a nurse carries the sucking child, to the land which thou didst swear to give their fathers?' 13 Where am I to get meat to give to all this people? For they weep before me and say, 'Give us meat, that we may eat.' 14 I am not able to carry all this people alone, the burden is too heavy for me. 15 If thou wilt deal thus with me, kill me at once, if I find favor in thy sight, that I may not see my wretchedness."

4. God's reply to Moses:
the appointment of the seventy elders

16 And the LORD said to Moses, "Gather for me seventy men of the elders of Israel, whom you know to be the elders of the people and officers over them; and bring them to the tent of meeting, and let them take their stand there with you. 17And I will come down and talk with you there; and I will take some of the spirit which is upon you and put it upon them; and they shall bear the burden of the people with you, that you may not bear it yourself alone. 18And say to the people, 'Consecrate yourselves for tomorrow, and you shall eat meat; for you have wept in the hearing of the LORD, saying, "Who will give us meat to eat? For it was well with us in Egypt." Therefore the LORD will give you meat, and you shall eat. 19 You shall not eat one day, or two days, or five days, or ten days, or twenty days, 20 but a whole month, until it comes out at your nostrils and becomes loathsome to you, because you have rejected the LORD who is among you, and have wept before him, saying, "Why did we come forth out of Egypt?"' " 21 But Moses said, "The people among whom I am number six hundred thousand on foot; and thou hast said, 'I will give them meat, that they may eat a whole month!' 22 Shall flocks and herds be slaughtered for them, to suffice them? Or shall all the fish of the sea be gathered together for them, to suffice them?" 23And the LORD said to Moses, "Is the LORD's hand shortened? Now you shall see whether my word will come true for you or not."

24 So Moses went out and told the people the words of the LORD; and he gathered seventy men of the elders of the people, and

11.5
Ex 16.3

11.6
Lev 21.5

11.7
Ex 16.14,31

11.9
Ex 16.13,14

11.10
Ps 78.21

11.12
Isa 40.11;
49.23;
Gen 26.3;
Ex 13.5

11.13
ver 21,22;
Jn 6.5–9

11.14
Ex 18.18

11.15
1 Ki 19.4;
Jon 4.3

11.16
Ex 24.1,9;
Deut 16.18

11.17
ver 25;
Ex 19.20;
1 Sam 10.6;
2 Ki 2.15

11.18
Ex 19.10;
16.7; ver 5;
Acts 7.39

11.19
Ps 78.29;
106.15;
Num 21.5

11.22
Mt 15.33

11.23
Isa 50.2;
59.1;
Num 23.19

11.24
ver 16

Numbers 11.25—12.5

placed them round about the tent. ²⁵ Then the LORD came down in the cloud and spoke to him, and took some of the spirit that was upon him and put it upon the seventy elders; and when the spirit rested upon them, they prophesied. But they did so no more.

26 Now two men remained in the camp, one named Ĕldăd, and the other named Mĕdăd, and the spirit rested upon them; they were among those registered, but they had not gone out to the tent, and so they prophesied in the camp. ²⁷And a young man ran and told Moses, "Ĕldăd and Mĕdăd are prophesying in the camp." ²⁸And Joshua the son of Nûn, the minister of Moses, one of his chosen men, said, "My lord Moses, forbid them." ²⁹ But Moses said to him, "Are you jealous for my sake? Would that all the LORD's people were prophets, that the LORD would put his spirit upon them!" ³⁰And Moses and the elders of Israel returned to the camp.

5. God sends quail for meat

31 And there went forth a wind from the LORD, and it brought quails from the sea, and let them fall beside the camp, about a day's journey on this side and a day's journey on the other side, round about the camp, and about two cubits above the face of the earth. ³²And the people rose all that day, and all night, and all the next day, and gathered the quails; he who gathered least gathered ten homers; and they spread them out for themselves all around the camp. ³³ While the meat was yet between their teeth, before it was consumed, the anger of the LORD was kindled against the people, and the LORD smote the people with a very great plague. ³⁴ Therefore the name of that place was called Kĭb′rŏth-hăttā′ăvăh,ᶠ because there they buried the people who had the craving. ³⁵ From Kĭb′rŏth-hăttā′ăvăh the people journeyed to Hăzē′rŏth; and they remained at Hazeroth.

C. Miriam and Aaron oppose Moses

1. God vindicates Moses

12 Miriam and Aaron spoke against Moses because of the Cŭshĭte woman whom he had married, for he had married a Cushite woman; 2 and they said, "Has the LORD indeed spoken only through Moses? Has he not spoken through us also?" And the LORD heard it. 3 Now the man Moses was very meek, more than all men that were on the face of the earth. ⁴And suddenly the LORD said to Moses and to Aaron and Miriam, "Come out, you three, to the tent of meeting." And the three of them came out. ⁵And the LORD came down in a pillar of cloud, and stood at the

ᶠ That is Graves of craving

11.25 ver 17; Num 12.5; 1 Sam 10.5, 6,10; Acts 2.17,18
*11.26 1 Sam 10.6; 20.26
11.28 Mk 9.38-40
11.29 1 Cor 14.5
11.31 Ex 16.13; Ps 78.26-28; 105.40
11.33 Ps 78.30, 31; 106.15
11.34 Deut 9.22
11.35 Num 33.17
*12.1 Ex 2.21
12.2 Num 16.3
*12.3 Mt 11.29
12.5 Num 11.25; 16.19

11.26 This display of sectarian spirit (for one Israelite conveyed to Moses the news that others were prophesying when he thought only Moses should do so) is suggestive of the incident recorded in Mk 9.38-41. There the disciples requested Jesus to forbid anyone to cast out demons in His name unless he belonged to the same group as the disciples. Sectarianism was an attitude condemned both by Moses and Jesus, and this condemnation should serve as a warning to believers today.
12.1 Cushite woman, generally considered to be an Ethiopian. Whether she was a Negress is debatable. In any case, it was the authority of Moses, not his wife, which was at stake in this incident.
12.3 Some believe that this verse was the work of a later editor.

door of the tent, and called Aaron and Miriam; and they both
came forward. 6 And he said, "Hear my words: If there is a prophet
among you, I the LORD make myself known to him in a vision, I
speak with him in a dream. 7 Not so with my servant Moses; he is
entrusted with all my house. 8 With him I speak mouth to mouth,
clearly, and not in dark speech; and he beholds the form of the
LORD. Why then were you not afraid to speak against my servant
Moses?"

12.6 Gen 46.2; 31.10,11; 1 Ki 3.5
***12.7** Ps 105.26; Heb 3.2,5
12.8 Ex 33.11; Deut 34.10; Ex 33.19

2. *Miriam becomes a leper; Moses prays for her healing*

9 And the anger of the LORD was kindled against them, and he
departed; 10 and when the cloud removed from over the tent, behold, Miriam was leprous, as white as snow. And Aaron turned
towards Miriam, and behold, she was leprous. 11 And Aaron said
to Moses, "Oh, my lord, do not[g] punish us because we have done
foolishly and have sinned. 12 Let her not be as one dead, of whom
the flesh is half consumed when he comes out of his mother's
womb." 13 And Moses cried to the LORD, "Heal her, O God, I beseech thee." 14 But the LORD said to Moses, "If her father had but
spit in her face, should she not be shamed seven days? Let her be
shut up outside the camp seven days, and after that she may be
brought in again." 15 So Miriam was shut up outside the camp
seven days; and the people did not set out on the march till Miriam
was brought in again. 16 After that the people set out from Hȧzē'-
rȯth, and encamped in the wilderness of Pārȧn.

12.10 Deut 24.9; 2 Ki 5.27; 15.5
12.11 2 Sam 19.19; 24.10
12.14 Lev 13.46; Num 5.2,3

D. *The twelve spies*

1. *The spies chosen*

13 The LORD said to Moses, 2 "Send men to spy out the land
of Cānaȧn, which I give to the people of Israel; from each
tribe of their fathers shall you send a man, every one a leader
among them." 3 So Moses sent them from the wilderness of
Pārȧn, according to the command of the LORD, all of them men
who were heads of the people of Israel. 4 And these were their
names: From the tribe of Reubĕn, Shăm'mū-ȧ the son of Zăccŭr;
5 from the tribe of Sĭm'ēȯn, Shāphăt the son of Hōrī; 6 from the
tribe of Judah, Cālėb the son of Jėphŭn'nėh; 7 from the tribe of
Ĭs'sạchar, Īgăl the son of Joseph; 8 from the tribe of Ē'phrạịm,
Hōshe'ȧ the son of Nŭn; 9 from the tribe of Benjamin, Păltī the
son of Rāphū; 10 from the tribe of Zĕb'ụlŭn, Găd'dĭėl the son of
Sōdī; 11 from the tribe of Joseph (that is from the tribe of Mȧnăs'-
sėh), Găddī the son of Suṣī; 12 from the tribe of Dan, Ăm'mĭėl the
son of Gėmăl'lī; 13 from the tribe of Ăshėr, Sēthŭr the son of
Michael; 14 from the tribe of Năph'tȧlī, Nahbī the son of Vŏphsī;
15 from the tribe of Găd, Gėū'ėl the son of Māc̣hī. 16 These were
the names of the men whom Moses sent to spy out the land. And
Moses called Hōshe'ȧ the son of Nŭn Joshua.

***13.2** Deut 1.22
13.8 ver 16
13.16 ver 8

g Heb *lay not sin upon us*

12.7 Moses was in many respects a type of Christ. (1) He was God's chosen deliverer (Ex 3.1–10; Acts 7.25); (2) he was a prophet (Deut 18.15; Acts 3.20–22); (3) he was a faithful servant in His spiritual house (12.7; Heb 3.2–6), although Christ had status as the divine Son, whereas Moses was but a human servant; (4) Moses was an earnest advocate and intercessor for Israel even as Christ is for His church (Ex 32.30–35; 1 Jn 2.1, 2; Ex 17.1–7; Heb 7.25).

13.2 *men.* These were the "secret scouts."

2. The spies sent out

*13.17
ver 21

13.20
Deut 1.24,
25; 31.6,
23

*13.22
Josh 15.13,
14;
ver 28,33;
Ps 78.12

*13.26
ver 3;
Num 20.1,
16; 32.8

13.27
Ex 3.8;
Deut 1.25
*13.28
Deut 1.28

13.29
Num 14.43

13.30
Num 14.6,
24

17 Moses sent them to spy out the land of Cānaán, and said to them, "Go up into the Něgěb yonder, and go up into the hill country, 18 and see what the land is, and whether the people who dwell in it are strong or weak, whether they are few or many, 19 and whether the land that they dwell in is good or bad, and whether the cities that they dwell in are camps or strongholds, 20 and whether the land is rich or poor, and whether there is wood in it or not. Be of good courage, and bring some of the fruit of the land." Now the time was the season of the first ripe grapes.

21 So they went up and spied out the land from the wilderness of Zĭn to Rĕhŏb, near the entrance of Hāmáth. 22 They went up into the Něgěb, and came to Hēbrón; and Ăhĭ'mán, Shĕshaī, and Tălmaī, the descendants of Ānăk, were there. (Hebron was built seven years before Zōăn in Egypt.) 23And they came to the Valley of Ĕshcól, and cut down from there a branch with a single cluster of grapes, and they carried it on a pole between two of them; they brought also some pomegranates and figs. 24 That place was called the Valley of Ĕshcól,ʰ because of the cluster which the men of Israel cut down from there.

3. The adverse report of the majority

25 At the end of forty days they returned from spying out the land. 26And they came to Moses and Aaron and to all the congregation of the people of Israel in the wilderness of Pārán, at Kādĕsh; they brought back word to them and to all the congregation, and showed them the fruit of the land. 27And they told him, "We came to the land to which you sent us; it flows with milk and honey, and this is its fruit. 28 Yet the people who dwell in the land are strong, and the cities are fortified and very large; and besides, we saw the descendants of Ānăk there. 29 The Ămăl'ĕkītes dwell in the land of the Něgěb; the Hĭttītes, the Jĕb'ūsītes, and the Ăm'órītes dwell in the hill country; and the Cā'naánītes dwell by the sea, and along the Jordan."

30 But Cālĕb quieted the people before Moses, and said, "Let

ʰ That is Cluster

13.17 Negeb ... hill country. The direct route to Canaan led northeast from Kadesh along some water stations in the Negeb (meaning "parched") up to Hebron in the hill country. Abraham and Jacob probably used this route going down to Egypt.

13.22 Zoan, also known as "Avaris" or "Tanis," was built about 1700 B.C. in the Nile delta by the Hyksos. Just seven years previously, Hebron was built at the place known to Abraham as Kiriath-arba or Mamre (Gen 23.2, 19). The fields of Zoan (Ps 78.12, 43) refers to Goshen where the Israelites dwelt.

13.26 All during the exodus journey Israel constantly fell into discontent, rebellion, and unbelief. Here at Kadesh this rebelliousness came to a head. God had miraculously delivered them from Egypt, preserved them from the attack of the Pharaoh, opened the passage across the sea, fed them with manna, and protected them against their foes. And now, after all these demonstrations of God's faithfulness, Israel proved ready to lend

credence to the adverse report of the ten spies more than to the God-honoring testimony of Joshua and Caleb. They walked by sight rather than by faith. Hence the report which magnified the difficulties in the way of conquest plunged them into despair and disbelief in the promises of God. Outward circumstances rather than a trust in God's faithfulness resulted in their shameful failure to enter the land by faith. Such unbelief could only be dealt with by discipline, if the nation was ever to be educated for its task of conquest and of possessing the Promised Land in the name of the LORD. The forty years of wandering in the wilderness would give time for the old, craven-hearted generation to die off and for a new generation, reared in freedom rather than slavery, to fulfil Israel's destiny. Only Caleb and Joshua would remain to lead them in and to serve as a testimony of God's faithfulness to those who sincerely trust Him.

13.28 fortified. Some Canaanite cities had walls 12 to 15 feet thick and 30 to 50 feet high.

us go up at once, and occupy it; for we are well able to overcome it." 31 Then the men who had gone up with him said, "We are not able to go up against the people; for they are stronger than we." 32 So they brought to the people of Israel an evil report of the land which they had spied out, saying, "The land, through which we have gone, to spy it out, is a land that devours its inhabitants; and all the people that we saw in it are men of great stature. 33And there we saw the Nĕph′ilim (the sons of Ānăk, who come from the Nephilim); and we seemed to ourselves like grasshoppers, and so we seemed to them."

4. *The rebellion of Israel*
a. *Their murmuring*

14 Then all the congregation raised a loud cry; and the people wept that night. 2And all the people of Israel murmured against Moses and Aaron; the whole congregation said to them, "Would that we had died in the land of Egypt! Or would that we had died in this wilderness! 3 Why does the LORD bring us into this land, to fall by the sword? Our wives and our little ones will become a prey; would it not be better for us to go back to Egypt?"

b. *The plea of Joshua and Caleb*

4 And they said to one another, "Let us choose a captain, and go back to Egypt." 5 Then Moses and Aaron fell on their faces before all the assembly of the congregation of the people of Israel. 6And Joshua the son of Nŭn and Cālĕb the son of Jĕphŭn′nĕh, who were among those who had spied out the land, rent their clothes, 7 and said to all the congregation of the people of Israel, "The land, which we passed through to spy it out, is an exceedingly good land. 8 If the LORD delights in us, he will bring us into this land and give it to us, a land which flows with milk and honey. 9 Only, do not rebel against the LORD; and do not fear the people of the land, for they are bread for us; their protection is removed from them, and the LORD is with us; do not fear them." 10 But all the congregation said to stone them with stones.

c. *The anger of God*

Then the glory of the LORD appeared at the tent of meeting to all the people of Israel. 11And the LORD said to Moses, "How long will this people despise me? And how long will they not believe in me, in spite of all the signs which I have wrought among them? 12 I will strike them with the pestilence and disinherit them, and I will make of you a nation greater and mightier than they."

d. *Moses intercedes for the people*

13 But Moses said to the LORD, "Then the Egyptians will hear of it, for thou didst bring up this people in thy might from among them, 14 and they will tell the inhabitants of this land. They have heard that thou, O LORD, art in the midst of this people; for thou, O LORD, art seen face to face, and thy cloud stands over them and thou goest before them, in a pillar of cloud by day and in a pillar of fire by night. 15 Now if thou dost kill this people as one man, then the nations who have heard thy fame will say, 16 'Because the LORD was not able to bring this people into the land which he swore to give to them, therefore he has slain them in the wilderness.' 17And now, I pray thee, let the power of the LORD be

---

13.31
Deut 1.28

13.32
Num 14.36;
Ps 106.24;
Amos 2.9

13.33
Deut 1.28;
9.2

14.2
Num 11.1,
5

14.5
Num 16.4,
22

14.7
Num 13.27;
Deut 1.25

14.8
Deut 10.15;
Num 13.27

14.9
Deut 9.7,
23, 24;
7.18; 20.1,
3,4

14.10
Ex 17.4;
16.10;
Lev 9.23

14.11
Deut 9.7,8;
Ps 78.22;
106.24

14.12
Ex 32.10

14.13
Ps 106.23

14.14
Ex 15.14;
Josh 2.9,
10;
Ex 13.21

14.16
Deut 9.28

14.18
Ex 34.6,7;
Ps 103.8;
Ex 20.5

great as thou hast promised, saying, 18 'The Lord is slow to anger, and abounding in steadfast love, forgiving iniquity and transgression, but he will by no means clear the guilty, visiting the iniquity of fathers upon children, upon the third and upon the fourth generation.' 19 Pardon the iniquity of this people, I pray thee, according to the greatness of thy steadfast love, and according as thou hast forgiven this people, from Egypt even until now."

14.19
Ex 34.9;
Ps 106.45;
78.38

e. God pronounces judgment on Israel for unbelief

14.20
Ps 106.23
14.21
Ps 72.19

20 Then the Lord said, "I have pardoned, according to your word; 21 but truly, as I live, and as all the earth shall be filled with the glory of the Lord, 22 none of the men who have seen my glory and my signs which I wrought in Egypt and in the wilderness, and yet have put me to the proof these ten times and have not hearkened to my voice, 23 shall see the land which I swore to give to their fathers; and none of those who despised me shall see it.

14.24
ver 7–9;
Num 32.12;
Josh 14.6–
15
14.25
Deut 1.40

24 But my servant Cāléb, because he has a different spirit and has followed me fully, I will bring into the land into which he went, and his descendants shall possess it. 25 Now, since the Ămăl'-ékītes and the Cā'naánītes dwell in the valleys, turn tomorrow and set out for the wilderness by the way to the Red Sea."

14.27
Num 11.1;
Ex 16.12

26 And the Lord said to Moses and to Aaron, 27 "How long shall this wicked congregation murmur against me? I have heard the murmurings of the people of Israel, which they murmur against me. 28 Say to them, 'As I live,' says the Lord, 'what you have said in my hearing I will do to you: 29 your dead bodies shall fall in this wilderness; and of all your number, numbered from twenty years old and upward, who have murmured against me, 30 not one shall come into the land where I swore that I would make you dwell, except Cāléb the son of Jéphŭn'néh and Joshua the son of Nŭn. 31 But your little ones, who you said would become a prey, I will bring in, and they shall know the land which you have despised. 32 But as for you, your dead bodies shall fall in this wilderness. 33 And your children shall be shepherds in the wilderness forty years, and shall suffer for your faithlessness, until the last of your dead bodies lies in the wilderness. 34 According to the number of the days in which you spied out the land, forty days, for every day a year, you shall bear your iniquity, forty years, and you shall know my displeasure.' 35 I, the Lord, have spoken; surely this will I do to all this wicked congregation that are gathered together against me: in this wilderness they shall come to a full end, and there they shall die."

14.28
ver 21;
Deut 1.35;
see ver 2
14.29
Num 1.45;
26.64
14.30
ver 24;
Deut 1.36
14.31
Deut 1.39;
Ps 106.24
14.32
1 Cor 10.5
14.33
Num 32.13;
Ps 107.40
14.34
Num 13.25;
Ps 95.10
14.35
Num 23.19;
26.65

14.36
Num 13.4–
16,32

36 And the men whom Moses sent to spy out the land, and who returned and made all the congregation to murmur against him by bringing up an evil report against the land, 37 the men who brought up an evil report of the land, died by plague before the Lord. 38 But Joshua the son of Nŭn and Cāléb the son of Jéphŭn'néh remained alive, of those men who went to spy out the land.

14.38
Josh 14.6

f. Israel's defeat by the Amalekites and Canaanites

14.39
Ex 33.4
14.40
Deut 1.41

39 And Moses told these words to all the people of Israel, and the people mourned greatly. 40 And they rose early in the morning, and went up to the heights of the hill country, saying, "See, we are here, we will go up to the place which the Lord has promised; for we have sinned." 41 But Moses said, "Why now are you trans-

gressing the command of the LORD, for that will not succeed? **14.42**
42 Do not go up lest you be struck down before your enemies, for   **Deut 1.42**
the LORD is not among you. 43 For there the Ămăl'ĕkītes and the
Cā'naănītes are before you, and you shall fall by the sword; because you have turned back from following the LORD, the LORD   **14.44**
will not be with you." 44 But they presumed to go up to the   **Deut 1.43**
heights of the hill country, although neither the ark of the covenant of the LORD, nor Moses, departed out of the camp. 45 Then   **14.45**
the Ămăl'ĕkītes and the Cā'naănītes who dwelt in that hill country **Deut 1.44;**
came down, and defeated them and pursued them, even to   **Num 21.3**
Hormăh.

E. Additional laws and regulations

1. Cereal offerings

15 The LORD said to Moses, 2 "Say to the people of Israel,   ***15.2**
When you come into the land you are to inhabit, which I   **ver 18**
give you, 3 and you offer to the LORD from the herd or from the   **15.3**
flock an offering by fire or a burnt offering or a sacrifice, to fulfil **Lev 23.1–44**
a vow or as a freewill offering or at your appointed feasts, to make
a pleasing odor to the LORD, 4 then he who brings his offering shall **15.4**
offer to the LORD a cereal offering of a tenth of an ephah of fine **Lev 2.1;**
flour, mixed with a fourth of a hin of oil; 5 and wine for the drink **6.14;**
offering, a fourth of a hin, you shall prepare with the burnt offer- **Ex 29.40;**
ing, or for the sacrifice, for each lamb. 6 Or for a ram, you shall **Lev 23.13;**
prepare for a cereal offering two tenths of an ephah of fine flour   **14.10;**
mixed with a third of a hin of oil; 7 and for the drink offering you **Num 28.5**
shall offer a third of a hin of wine, a pleasing odor to the LORD. **15.5**
8And when you prepare a bull for a burnt offering, or for a sac-   **Num 28.7,**
rifice, to fulfil a vow, or for peace offerings to the LORD, 9 then one **14**
shall offer with the bull a cereal offering of three tenths of an   **15.6**
ephah of fine flour, mixed with half a hin of oil, 10 and you shall **Num 28.12,**
offer for the drink offering half a hin of wine, as an offering by fire, **14**
a pleasing odor to the LORD.   **15.8**
                                                                    Lev 7.11
11 "Thus it shall be done for each bull or ram, or for each of   **15.9**
the male lambs or the kids. 12According to the number that you   **Num 28.12,**
prepare, so shall you do with every one according to their number. **14**
13All who are native shall do these things in this way, in offering
an offering by fire, a pleasing odor to the LORD. 14And if a stranger
is sojourning with you, or any one is among you throughout your
generations, and he wishes to offer an offering by fire, a pleasing
odor to the LORD, he shall do as you do. 15 For the assembly, there **15.15**
shall be one statute for you and for the stranger who sojourns with **ver 29;**
you, a perpetual statute throughout your generations; as you are, **Num 9.14**
so shall the sojourner be before the LORD. 16 One law and one
ordinance shall be for you and for the stranger who sojourns with
you."

2. The coarse meal offering

17 The LORD said to Moses, 18 "Say to the people of Israel,   **15.18**
                                                                   ver 2

15.2 Unbelief at Kadesh did not result in   would enter the land despite the punishment
a permanent denial of entrance into the   for their disobedience. For the believer, this
Promised Land but only a delay. The instruc-   incident is illustrative of the truth that sin
tions given by God for offerings in the land   breaks fellowship and results in chastening,
were intended to reassure Israel that they   but God stands ready to forgive.

15.19
Josh 5.11,12
15.20
Deut 26.2,
10;
Lev 2.14

When you come into the land to which I bring you 19 and when you eat of the food of the land, you shall present an offering to the LORD. 20 Of the first of your coarse meal you shall present a cake as an offering; as an offering from the threshing floor, so shall you present it. 21 Of the first of your coarse meal you shall give to the LORD an offering throughout your generations.

3. Offering for sins done ignorantly

15.22
Lev 4.2

22 "But if you err, and do not observe all these commandments which the LORD has spoken to Moses, 23 all that the LORD has commanded you by Moses, from the day that the LORD gave commandment, and onward throughout your generations, 24 then if it was done unwittingly without the knowledge of the congregation, all the congregation shall offer one young bull for a burnt offering, a pleasing odor to the LORD, with its cereal offering and its drink offering, according to the ordinance, and one male goat for a sin offering. 25And the priest shall make atonement for all the congregation of the people of Israel, and they shall be forgiven; because it was an error, and they have brought their offering, an offering by fire to the LORD, and their sin offering before the LORD, for their error. 26And all the congregation of the people of Israel shall be forgiven, and the stranger who sojourns among them, because the whole population was involved in the error.

15.24
Lev 4.13;
ver 8–10

15.25
Lev 4.20

15.27
Lev 4.27,
28
15.28
Lev 4.35

27 "If one person sins unwittingly, he shall offer a female goat a year old for a sin offering. 28And the priest shall make atonement before the LORD for the person who commits an error, when he sins unwittingly, to make atonement for him; and he shall be forgiven. 29 You shall have one law for him who does anything unwittingly, for him who is native among the people of Israel, and for the stranger who sojourns among them. 30 But the person who does anything with a high hand, whether he is native or a sojourner, reviles the LORD, and that person shall be cut off from among his people. 31 Because he has despised the word of the LORD, and has broken his commandment, that person shall be utterly cut off; his iniquity shall be upon him."

15.29
ver 15
*15.30

15.31
2 Sam 12.9;
Lev 5.1;
Ezek 18.20

4. Stoning of Sabbath breakers

15.32
Ex 31.14,
15; 35.2,3

32 While the people of Israel were in the wilderness, they found a man gathering sticks on the sabbath day. 33And those who found him gathering sticks brought him to Moses and Aaron, and to all the congregation. 34 They put him in custody, because it had not been made plain what should be done to him. 35And the LORD said to Moses, "The man shall be put to death; all the congregation shall stone him with stones outside the camp." 36And all the congregation brought him outside the camp, and stoned him to death with stones, as the LORD commanded Moses.

15.34
Lev 24.12
15.35
Ex 31.14,
15;
Lev 24.14;
Acts 7.58

5. The tassels of remembrance

*15.38
Deut 22.12;
Mt 23.5

37 The LORD said to Moses, 38 "Speak to the people of Israel, and bid them to make tassels on the corners of their garments throughout their generations, and to put upon the tassel of each corner a cord of blue; 39 and it shall be to you a tassel to look upon and remember all the commandments of the LORD, to do them,

15.39
Deut 4.23;
Ps 73.27

15.30 *high hand*, see note to Lev 4.2.   15.38 *tassels*, part of the praying mantle.

not to follow after your own heart and your own eyes, which you are inclined to go after wantonly. 40 So you shall remember and do all my commandments, and be holy to your God. 41 I am the LORD your God, who brought you out of the land of Egypt, to be your God; I am the LORD your God."

15.40
Lev 11.44;
Rom 12.1;
Col 1.22;
1 Pet 1.15,
16

F. The rebellion and death of Korah, Dathan, and Abiram

1. Korah's revolt

16 Now Kōráh the son of Ĭzhar, son of Kōhắth, son of Lēvī, and Dāthắn and Ábĭ'rắm the sons of Ĕlī'áb, and On the son of Pĕlĕth, sons of Reubĕn, 2 took men; and they rose up before Moses, with a number of the people of Israel, two hundred and fifty leaders of the congregation, chosen from the assembly, well-known men; 3 and they assembled themselves together against Moses and against Aaron, and said to them, "You have gone too far! For all the congregation are holy, every one of them, and the LORD is among them; why then do you exalt yourselves above the assembly of the LORD?" 4 When Moses heard it, he fell on his face; 5 and he said to Kōráh and all his company, "In the morning the LORD will show who is his, and who is holy, and will cause him to come near to him; him whom he will choose he will cause to come near to him. 6 Do this: take censers, Kōráh and all his company; 7 put fire in them and put incense upon them before the LORD tomorrow, and the man whom the LORD chooses shall be the holy one. You have gone too far, sons of Lēvī!" 8And Moses said to Kōráh, "Hear now, you sons of Lēvī: 9 is it too small a thing for you that the God of Israel has separated you from the congregation of Israel, to bring you near to himself, to do service in the tabernacle of the LORD, and to stand before the congregation to minister to them; 10 and that he has brought you near him, and all your brethren the sons of Lēvī with you? And would you seek the priesthood also? 11 Therefore it is against the LORD that you and all your company have gathered together; what is Aaron that you murmur against him?"

*16.1
Ex 6.21;
Jude 11
16.2
Num 26.9

16.3
Ps 106.16;
Ex 19.6;
Num 14.14

16.4
Num 14.5
16.5
Lev 10.3;
Ps 65.4;
Num 17.5,8

16.9
Num 3.6,9;
8.14;
Deut 10.8

16.11
Ex 16.7,8;
1 Cor 10.10

2. The rebellion of Dathan and Abiram

12 And Moses sent to call Dāthắn and Ábĭ'rắm the sons of Ĕlī'áb; and they said, "We will not come up. 13 Is it a small thing that you have brought us up out of a land flowing with milk and honey, to kill us in the wilderness, that you must also make yourself a prince over us? 14 Moreover you have not brought us into a land flowing with milk and honey, nor given us inheritance of fields and vineyards. Will you put out the eyes of these men? We will not come up."

16.13
Num 11.4–
6; Ex 2.14;
Acts 7.27,
35
16.14
Lev 20.24

3. The punishment of the rebels

15 And Moses was very angry, and said to the LORD, "Do not

16.15
Gen 4.4,5;
1 Sam 12.3

16.1 Korah's sin consisted in rebellion against God's authority to appoint as leaders men of His own choosing. It was a sizable revolt both in numbers and in the position of those who joined him. Specifically named with Korah are Dathan and Abiram, who were descendants of Reuben. Thus it involved an intrusion by non-Levites into the office reserved for the Levites alone, although Korah himself was of the priestly tribe. God destroyed the guilty men and their families (except for the descendants of Korah—cf. 26.11), but the congregation of Israel accused Moses and Aaron of having killed the people of the LORD (ver 41). As a consequence God slew 14,700 more by a sudden plague (ver 49).

respect their offering. I have not taken one ass from them, and I have not harmed one of them." 16And Moses said to Kōrah, "Be present, you and all your company, before the LORD, you and they, and Aaron, tomorrow; 17 and let every one of you take his censer, and put incense upon it, and every one of you bring before the LORD his censer, two hundred and fifty censers; you also, and Aaron, each his censer." 18 So every man took his censer, and they put fire in them and laid incense upon them, and they stood at the entrance of the tent of meeting with Moses and Aaron. 19 Then Kōrah assembled all the congregation against them at the entrance of the tent of meeting. And the glory of the LORD appeared to all the congregation.

20 And the LORD said to Moses and to Aaron, 21 "Separate yourselves from among this congregation, that I may consume them in a moment." 22And they fell on their faces, and said, "O God, the God of the spirits of all flesh, shall one man sin, and wilt thou be angry with all the congregation?" 23And the LORD said to Moses, 24 "Say to the congregation, Get away from about the dwelling of Kōrah, Dāthan, and Abī'ram."

25 Then Moses rose and went to Dāthan and Abī'ram; and the elders of Israel followed him. 26And he said to the congregation, "Depart, I pray you, from the tents of these wicked men, and touch nothing of theirs, lest you be swept away with all their sins." 27 So they got away from about the dwelling of Kōrah, Dāthan, and Abī'ram; and Dathan and Abiram came out and stood at the door of their tents, together with their wives, their sons, and their little ones. 28And Moses said, "Hereby you shall know that the LORD has sent me to do all these works, and that it has not been of my own accord. 29 If these men die the common death of all men, or if they are visited by the fate of all men, then the LORD has not sent me. 30 But if the LORD creates something new, and the ground opens its mouth, and swallows them up, with all that belongs to them, and they go down alive into Shēōl, then you shall know that these men have despised the LORD."

31 And as he finished speaking all these words, the ground under them split asunder; 32 and the earth opened its mouth and swallowed them up, with their households and all the men that belonged to Kōrah and all their goods. 33 So they and all that belonged to them went down alive into Shēōl; and the earth closed over them, and they perished from the midst of the assembly. 34And all Israel that were round about them fled at their cry; for they said, "Lest the earth swallow us up!" 35And fire came forth from the LORD, and consumed the two hundred and fifty men offering the incense.

36i Then the LORD said to Moses, 37 "Tell Ēlëä'zar the son of Aaron the priest to take up the censers out of the blaze; then scatter the fire far and wide. For they are holy, 38 the censers of these men who have sinned at the cost of their lives; so let them be made into hammered plates as a covering for the altar, for they offered them before the LORD; therefore they are holy. Thus they shall be a sign to the people of Israel." 39 So Ēlëä'zar the priest took the bronze censers, which those who were burned had offered; and they were hammered out as a covering for the altar, 40 to be a reminder to the people of Israel, so that no one who is not a priest, who is not

16.16 ver 6,7
16.19 ver 42; Num 14.10; Ex 16.7,10; Lev 9.6,23
16.21 ver 45; Ex 32.10,12
16.22 ver 45; Num 14.5
16.26 Gen 19.12,14
16.28 Ex 3.12; Jn 5.36; Num 24.13; Jn 6.38
16.30 ver 33; Ps 55.15
16.31 Num 26.10
16.32 Num 26.11
16.35 Num 11.1–3; 26.10
16.38 Prov 20.2; Num 26.10
16.40 Num 3.10; 2 Chr 26.18

of the descendants of Aaron, should draw near to burn incense before the LORD, lest he become as Kōrȧh and as his company—as the LORD said to Ĕlë'zȧr through Moses.

4. *The murmuring of the people: the plague*

41 But on the morrow all the congregation of the people of Israel murmured against Moses and against Aaron, saying, "You have killed the people of the LORD." 42And when the congregation had assembled against Moses and against Aaron, they turned toward the tent of meeting; and behold, the cloud covered it, and the glory of the LORD appeared. 43And Moses and Aaron came to the front of the tent of meeting, 44 and the LORD said to Moses, 45 "Get away from the midst of this congregation, that I may consume them in a moment." And they fell on their faces. 46And Moses said to Aaron, "Take your censer, and put fire therein from off the altar, and lay incense on it, and carry it quickly to the congregation, and make atonement for them; for wrath has gone forth from the LORD, the plague has begun." 47 So Aaron took it as Moses said, and ran into the midst of the assembly; and behold, the plague had already begun among the people; and he put on the incense, and made atonement for the people. 48And he stood between the dead and the living; and the plague was stopped. 49 Now those who died by the plague were fourteen thousand seven hundred, besides those who died in the affair of Kōrȧh. 50And Aaron returned to Moses at the entrance of the tent of meeting, when the plague was stopped.

16.41
ver 3

16.42
Ex 40.34;
ver 19;
Num 20.6

16.45
ver 21, 24

16.46
Num 8.19;
Ps 106.29

16.47
Num 25.7,
8,13

16.48
Ps 106.30
16.49
ver 32,35

5. *The budding of Aaron's rod*

17[j] The LORD said to Moses, 2 "Speak to the people of Israel, and get from them rods, one for each fathers' house, from all their leaders according to their fathers' houses, twelve rods. Write each man's name upon his rod, 3 and write Aaron's name upon the rod of Lēvī. For there shall be one rod for the head of each fathers' house. 4 Then you shall deposit them in the tent of meeting before the testimony, where I meet with you. 5And the rod of the man whom I choose shall sprout; thus I will make to cease from me the murmurings of the people of Israel, which they murmur against you." 6 Moses spoke to the people of Israel; and all their leaders gave him rods, one for each leader, according to their fathers' houses, twelve rods; and the rod of Aaron was among their rods. 7And Moses deposited the rods before the LORD in the tent of the testimony.

8 And on the morrow Moses went into the tent of the testimony; and behold, the rod of Aaron for the house of Lēvī had sprouted and put forth buds, and produced blossoms, and it bore ripe almonds. 9 Then Moses brought out all the rods from before the LORD to all the people of Israel; and they looked, and each man took his rod. 10And the LORD said to Moses, "Put back the rod of

17.4
Ex 25.22;
29.42,43
17.5
Num 16.5,
11

17.7
Num 18.2;
Acts 7.44
*17.8

17.10
Heb 9.4;
ver 5

[j] Ch 17.16 in Heb

17.8 Both Moses and Aaron had rods. In Ex 7.12 Aaron's rod, in the form of a serpent, swallowed the rods of the Egyptians. Since Aaron's unique authority as high priest was challenged by the other Israelites, an appeal was made to God directly by placing a staff for each tribe before the ark to see which one would be accepted by Him. Only Aaron's rod put forth blossoms. This miracle of God revealed that Aaron and his house should be the sole possessors of the priestly prerogatives. The rod itself was placed in front of the ark (the testimony) and later, apparently, within the ark (Heb 9.4).

Aaron before the testimony, to be kept as a sign for the rebels, that you may make an end of their murmurings against me, lest they die." 11 Thus did Moses; as the LORD commanded him, so he did.

12 And the people of Israel said to Moses, "Behold, we perish, we are undone, we are all undone. 13 Every one who comes near, who comes near to the tabernacle of the LORD, shall die. Are we all to perish?"

G. The laws of the priests and Levites

1. *The duties of the Levites*

18 So the LORD said to Aaron, "You and your sons and your fathers' house with you shall bear iniquity in connection with the sanctuary; and you and your sons with you shall bear iniquity in connection with your priesthood. 2And with you bring your brethren also, the tribe of Lēvī, the tribe of your father, that they may join you, and minister to you while you and your sons with you are before the tent of the testimony. 3 They shall attend you and attend to all duties of the tent; but shall not come near to the vessels of the sanctuary or to the altar, lest they, and you, die. 4 They shall join you, and attend to the tent of meeting, for all the service of the tent; and no one else shall come near you. 5And you shall attend to the duties of the sanctuary and the duties of the altar, that there be wrath no more upon the people of Israel. 6And behold, I have taken your brethren the Lēvītes from among the people of Israel; they are a gift to you, given to the LORD, to do the service of the tent of meeting. 7And you and your sons with you shall attend to your priesthood for all that concerns the altar and that is within the veil; and you shall serve. I give your priesthood as a gift,*k* and any one else who comes near shall be put to death."

2. *The offerings which belong to the priests*

8 Then the LORD said to Aaron, "And behold, I have given you whatever is kept of the offerings made to me, all the consecrated things of the people of Israel; I have given them to you as a portion, and to your sons as a perpetual due. 9 This shall be yours of the most holy things, reserved from the fire; every offering of theirs, every cereal offering of theirs and every sin offering of theirs and every guilt offering of theirs, which they render to me, shall be most holy to you and to your sons. 10 In a most holy place shall you eat of it; every male may eat of it; it is holy to you. 11 This also is yours, the offering of their gift, all the wave offerings of the people of Israel; I have given them to you, and to your sons and daughters with you, as a perpetual due; every one who is clean in your house may eat of it. 12All the best of the oil, and all the best of the wine and of the grain, the first fruits of what they give to the LORD, I give to you. 13 The first ripe fruits of all that is in their land, which they bring to the LORD, shall be yours; every one who is clean in your house may eat of it. 14 Every devoted thing in Israel shall be yours. 15 Everything that opens the womb of all flesh, whether man or beast, which they offer to the LORD, shall be yours; nevertheless the first-born of man you shall redeem, and the firstling of unclean beasts you shall redeem. 16And their redemption price

Marginal references

17.13
Num 1.51,
53

18.1
Ex 28.38

18.2
Num 3.5–
10

18.3
Num 3.25,
31,36; 4.15

18.4
Num 3.10

18.5
Num 16.46

18.6
Num 3.9,
12,45

18.7
Num 3.10;
Heb 9.3, 6

18.8
Lev 6.16,
18; 7.6,32;
Ex 29.29;
40.13,15

18.9
Lev 2.2,3;
10.12,13;
6.25,26;
7.7

18.10
Lev 6.16,26

18.11
Ex 29.27,
28;
Lev 22.1–16

18.12
Ex 23.19;
Deut 18.4;
Neh 10.35;
Ex 22.29

18.13
Ex 22.29;
23.19;
34.26

18.14
Lev 27.28

18.15
Ex 13.2;
Lev 27.26;
Ex 13.13

18.16
Lev 27.6

k Heb *service of gift*

(at a month old you shall redeem them) you shall fix at five shekels in silver, according to the shekel of the sanctuary, which is twenty gerahs. 17 But the firstling of a cow, or the firstling of a sheep, or the firstling of a goat, you shall not redeem; they are holy. You shall sprinkle their blood upon the altar, and shall burn their fat as an offering by fire, a pleasing odor to the LORD; 18 but their flesh shall be yours, as the breast that is waved and as the right thigh are yours. 19All the holy offerings which the people of Israel present to the LORD I give to you, and to your sons and daughters with you, as a perpetual due; it is a covenant of salt for ever before the LORD for you and for your offspring with you." 20And the LORD said to Aaron, "You shall have no inheritance in their land, neither shall you have any portion among them; I am your portion and your inheritance among the people of Israel.

18.17
Lev 3.2,5

18.19
ver 11;
2 Chr 13.5

18.20
Deut 10.9;
12.12;
14.27, 29;
18.1,2;
Josh 13.33;
Ezek 44.28

3. The tithe for the Levites

21 "To the Lēvītes I have given every tithe in Israel for an inheritance, in return for their service which they serve, their service in the tent of meeting. 22And henceforth the people of Israel shall not come near the tent of meeting, lest they bear sin and die. 23 But the Lēvītes shall do the service of the tent of meeting, and they shall bear their iniquity; it shall be a perpetual statute throughout your generations; and among the people of Israel they shall have no inheritance. 24 For the tithe of the people of Israel, which they present as an offering to the LORD, I have given to the Lēvītes for an inheritance; therefore I have said of them that they shall have no inheritance among the people of Israel."

18.21
Lev 27.30–
33
18.22
Num 1.51
18.23
Num 3.7;
ver 1,20

4. The Levites' tithe of the tithe

25 And the LORD said to Moses, 26 "Moreover you shall say to the Lēvītes, 'When you take from the people of Israel the tithe which I have given you from them for your inheritance, then you shall present an offering from it to the LORD, a tithe of the tithe. 27And your offering shall be reckoned to you as though it were the grain of the threshing floor, and as the fulness of the wine press. 28 So shall you also present an offering to the LORD from all your tithes, which you receive from the people of Israel; and from it you shall give the LORD's offering to Aaron the priest. 29 Out of all the gifts to you, you shall present every offering due to the LORD, from all the best of them, giving the hallowed part from them.' 30 Therefore you shall say to them, 'When you have offered from it the best of it, then the rest shall be reckoned to the Lēvītes as produce of the threshing floor, and as produce of the wine press; 31 and you may eat it in any place, you and your households; for it is your reward in return for your service in the tent of meeting. 32And you shall bear no sin by reason of it, when you have offered the best of it. And you shall not profane the holy things of the people of Israel, lest you die.' "

18.26
Neh 10.38

18.28
Ex 29.27

18.32
Lev 19.8;
22.2,15,16

H. Purification of the unclean

1. The red heifer

19 Now the LORD said to Moses and to Aaron, 2 "This is the statute of the law which the LORD has commanded: Tell the people of Israel to bring you a red heifer without defect, in which

19.2
Deut 21.3

there is no blemish, and upon which a yoke has never come. ³And you shall give her to Ĕlĕä′zär the priest, and she shall be taken outside the camp and slaughtered before him; ⁴ and Ĕlĕä′zär the priest shall take some of her blood with his finger, and sprinkle some of her blood toward the front of the tent of meeting seven times. ⁵And the heifer shall be burned in his sight; her skin, her flesh, and her blood, with her dung, shall be burned; ⁶ and the priest shall take cedarwood and hyssop and scarlet stuff, and cast them into the midst of the burning of the heifer. ⁷ Then the priest shall wash his clothes and bathe his body in water, and afterwards he shall come into the camp; and the priest shall be unclean until evening. ⁸ He who burns the heifer shall wash his clothes in water and bathe his body in water, and shall be unclean until evening. ⁹And a man who is clean shall gather up the ashes of the heifer, and deposit them outside the camp in a clean place; and they shall be kept for the congregation of the people of Israel for the water for impurity, for the removal of sin. ¹⁰And he who gathers the ashes of the heifer shall wash his clothes, and be unclean until evening. And this shall be to the people of Israel, and to the stranger who sojourns among them, a perpetual statute.

2. Purification of uncleanness with water

11 "He who touches the dead body of any person shall be unclean seven days; ¹² he shall cleanse himself with the water on the third day and on the seventh day, and so be clean; but if he does not cleanse himself on the third day and on the seventh day, he will not become clean. ¹³ Whoever touches a dead person, the body of any man who has died, and does not cleanse himself, defiles the tabernacle of the LORD, and that person shall be cut off from Israel; because the water for impurity was not thrown upon him, he shall be unclean; his uncleanness is still on him.

14 "This is the law when a man dies in a tent: every one who comes into the tent, and every one who is in the tent, shall be unclean seven days. ¹⁵And every open vessel, which has no cover fastened upon it, is unclean. ¹⁶ Whoever in the open field touches one who is slain with a sword, or a dead body, or a bone of a man, or a grave, shall be unclean seven days. ¹⁷ For the unclean they shall take some ashes of the burnt sin offering, and running water shall be added in a vessel; ¹⁸ then a clean person shall take hyssop, and dip it in the water, and sprinkle it upon the tent, and upon all the furnishings, and upon the persons who were there, and upon him who touched the bone, or the slain, or the dead, or the grave; ¹⁹ and the clean person shall sprinkle upon the unclean on the third day and on the seventh day; thus on the seventh day he shall cleanse him, and he shall wash his clothes and bathe himself in water, and at evening he shall be clean.

20 "But the man who is unclean and does not cleanse himself, that person shall be cut off from the midst of the assembly, since he has defiled the sanctuary of the LORD; because the water for impurity has not been thrown upon him, he is unclean. ²¹And it shall be a perpetual statute for them. He who sprinkles the water for impurity shall wash his clothes; and he who touches the water for impurity shall be unclean until evening. ²²And whatever the unclean person touches shall be unclean; and any one who touches it shall be unclean until evening."

I. Incidents at Kadesh

1. The death of Miriam

20 And the people of Israel, the whole congregation, came into the wilderness of Zĭn in the first month, and the people stayed in Kādĕsh; and Miriam died there, and was buried there.

*20.1
Num 33.36

2. Water from the rock (Meribah)

2 Now there was no water for the congregation; and they assembled themselves together against Moses and against Aaron. ³And the people contended with Moses, and said, "Would that we had died when our brethren died before the LORD! ⁴ Why have you brought the assembly of the LORD into this wilderness, that we should die here, both we and our cattle? ⁵And why have you made us come up out of Egypt, to bring us to this evil place? It is no place for grain, or figs, or vines, or pomegranates; and there is no water to drink." ⁶ Then Moses and Aaron went from the presence of the assembly to the door of the tent of meeting, and fell on their faces. And the glory of the LORD appeared to them, ⁷ and the LORD said to Moses, ⁸ "Take the rod, and assemble the congregation, you and Aaron your brother, and tell the rock before their eyes to yield its water; so you shall bring water out of the rock for them; so you shall give drink to the congregation and their cattle." ⁹And Moses took the rod from before the LORD, as he commanded him.

20.2
Ex 17.1

20.3
Ex 17.2;
Num 14.2,
3; 16.31–35

20.4
Ex 17.3

20.6
Num 14.5,
10

*20.8
Ex 17.5;
Neh 9.15;
Isa 43.20;
48.21

3. The sin of Moses: his exclusion from Canaan

10 And Moses and Aaron gathered the assembly together before the rock, and he said to them, "Hear now, you rebels; shall we bring forth water for you out of this rock?" ¹¹And Moses lifted up his hand and struck the rock with his rod twice; and water came forth abundantly, and the congregation drank, and their cattle. ¹²And the LORD said to Moses and Aaron, "Because you did not believe in me, to sanctify me in the eyes of the people of Israel, therefore you shall not bring this assembly into the land which I have given them." ¹³ These are the waters of Mĕr′ĭbah,[l] where the people of Israel contended with the LORD, and he showed himself holy among them.

20.10
Ps 106.32,
33

20.11
Ps 78.16;
Isa 48.21;
1 Cor 10.14

20.12
Num 27.14;
Deut 1.37;
3.26, 27;
Lev 10.3

20.13
Deut 33.8;
Ps 95.8

4. Israel refused passage through Edom

14 Moses sent messengers from Kādĕsh to the king of Ēdŏm, "Thus says your brother Israel: You know all the adversity that has befallen us: ¹⁵ how our fathers went down to Egypt, and we dwelt in Egypt a long time; and the Egyptians dealt harshly with us and our fathers; ¹⁶ and when we cried to the LORD, he heard our voice, and sent an angel and brought us forth out of Egypt; and

20.14
Deut 2.4

20.15
Gen 46.6;
Acts 7.15,
19;
Ex 12.40;
Deut 26.6

20.16
Ex 2.23;
14.19

[l] That is Contention

20.1 first month, apparently in a year near the end of the wilderness sojourn. Thus this summary verse covers a period of about 37 years, the Israelites having arrived at Kadesh (13.26) not long after leaving Sinai. See Deut 2.14.

20.8 Moses was commanded to smite a rock at Horeb in Ex 17.6. Here he is com-

manded to speak to the rock at Kadesh (later known as Kadesh-barnea), but angrily he struck it twice. There was a note of carnal self-importance and pride in his query, "Hear now, you rebels; shall we bring forth water for you out of this rock?" (20.10). He was punished for his unbelief and disobedience.

*20.17

20.19
Deut 2.6,
28

20.21
Judg 11.17;
Deut 2.8

20.22
Num 33.37;
21.4

20.24
Gen 25.8;
ver 12

20.25
Num 33.38;
Deut 32.50

20.28
Num 33.38;
Deut 10.6

21.1
Num 33.40;
Judg 1.16;
Num 13.21

21.4
Num 20.22
21.5
Ps 78.19;
Ex 16.3;
17.3;
Num 11.6
21.6
Deut 8.15;
1 Cor 10.9

here we are in Kādësh, a city on the edge of your territory. 17 Now let us pass through your land. We will not pass through field or vineyard, neither will we drink water from a well; we will go along the King's Highway, we will not turn aside to the right hand or to the left, until we have passed through your territory." 18 But Ēdòm said to him, "You shall not pass through, lest I come out with the sword against you." 19And the people of Israel said to him, "We will go up by the highway; and if we drink of your water, I and my cattle, then I will pay for it; let me only pass through on foot, nothing more." 20 But he said, "You shall not pass through." And Ēdòm came out against them with many men, and with a strong force. 21 Thus Ēdòm refused to give Israel passage through his territory; so Israel turned away from him.

J. Events from Kadesh to Moab

1. The death of Aaron

22 And they journeyed from Kādësh, and the people of Israel, the whole congregation, came to Mount Hor. 23And the LORD said to Moses and Aaron at Mount Hor, on the border of the land of Ēdòm, 24 "Aaron shall be gathered to his people; for he shall not enter the land which I have given to the people of Israel, because you rebelled against my command at the waters of Mĕr′ĭbah. 25 Take Aaron and Ēlëä′zär his son, and bring them up to Mount Hor; 26 and strip Aaron of his garments, and put them upon Ēlëä′zär his son; and Aaron shall be gathered to his people, and shall die there." 27 Moses did as the LORD commanded; and they went up Mount Hor in the sight of all the congregation. 28And Moses stripped Aaron of his garments, and put them upon Ēlëä′zär his son; and Aaron died there on the top of the mountain. Then Moses and Eleazar came down from the mountain. 29And when all the congregation saw that Aaron was dead, all the house of Israel wept for Aaron thirty days.

2. The victory over Arad at Hormah

21 When the Cā′naànīte, the king of Ạrạd, who dwelt in the Nĕgĕb, heard that Israel was coming by the way of Ăth′ärĭm, he fought against Israel, and took some of them captive. 2And Israel vowed a vow to the LORD, and said, "If thou wilt indeed give this people into my hand, then I will utterly destroy their cities." 3And the LORD hearkened to the voice of Israel, and gave over the Cā′naànītes; and they utterly destroyed them and their cities; so the name of the place was called Hormāh.ᵐ

3. The fiery serpents: the murmuring of Israel

4 From Mount Hor they set out by the way to the Red Sea, to go around the land of Ēdòm; and the people became impatient on the way. 5And the people spoke against God and against Moses, "Why have you brought us up out of Egypt to die in the wilderness? For there is no food and no water, and we loathe this worthless food." 6 Then the LORD sent fiery serpents among the people,

m Heb *Destruction*

20.17 *King's Highway*, meaning the ancient route through Trans-Jordan. Note that passage was refused. (Incidentally, today the route is a paved thoroughfare.)

and they bit the people, so that many people of Israel died. 7And the people came to Moses, and said, "We have sinned, for we have spoken against the LORD and against you; pray to the LORD, that he take away the serpents from us." So Moses prayed for the people. 8And the LORD said to Moses, "Make a fiery serpent, and set it on a pole; and every one who is bitten, when he sees it, shall live." 9 So Moses made a bronze serpent, and set it on a pole; and if a serpent bit any man, he would look at the bronze serpent and live.

4. Israel on the march

10 And the people of Israel set out, and encamped in Ōbŏth. 11And they set out from Ōbŏth, and encamped at Ī′yĕ-ăb′ărĭm, in the wilderness which is opposite Mŏăb, toward the sunrise. 12 From there they set out, and encamped in the Valley of Zĕrĕd. 13 From there they set out, and encamped on the other side of the Arnŏn, which is in the wilderness, that extends from the boundary of the Ăm′ŏrĭtes; for the Arnon is the boundary of Mŏăb, between Moab and the Amorites. 14 Wherefore it is said in the Book of the Wars of the LORD,

"Wahĕb in Suphăh,
    and the valleys of the Arnŏn,
15 and the slope of the valleys
    that extends to the seat of Ar,
    and leans to the border of Mŏăb."

16 And from there they continued to Beër;[n] that is the well of which the LORD said to Moses, "Gather the people together, and I will give them water." 17 Then Israel sang this song:
"Spring up, O well!—Sing to it!—
18 the well which the princes dug,
    which the nobles of the people delved,
    with the scepter and with their staves."
And from the wilderness they went on to Măt′tănăh, 19 and from Măt′tănăh to Năhā′lĭĕl, and from Nahaliel to Bāmŏth, 20 and from Bāmŏth to the valley lying in the region of Mŏăb by the top of Pĭṣ′găh which looks down upon the desert.[o]

5. Defeat of Sihon, king of the Amorites

21 Then Israel sent messengers to Sīhŏn king of the Ăm′ŏrĭtes, saying, 22 "Let me pass through your land; we will not turn aside into field or vineyard; we will not drink the water of a well; we will go by the King's Highway, until we have passed through your territory." 23 But Sīhŏn would not allow Israel to pass through his territory. He gathered all his men together, and went out against Israel to the wilderness, and came to Jāhăz, and fought against Israel. 24And Israel slew him with the edge of the sword, and took possession of his land from the Arnŏn to the Jăbbŏk, as far as to

n That is Well o Or Jĕsh′ĭmŏn

21.7	Ps 78.34
*21.9	2 Ki 18.4; Jn 3.14,15
21.10	Num 33.43
21.11	Num 33.44
21.12	Deut 2.13
21.15	ver 28; Deut 2.18, 29
21.21	Deut 2.26, 27
21.22	Num 20.16, 17
21.23	Num 20.21; Deut 2.32
21.24	Deut 2.33; Josh 12.1, 2; Ps 135.10, 11

21.9 The bronze serpent was a type of Christ (Jn 3.14, 15). As men bitten by the fiery serpents died, so men bitten by the Satanic serpent of sin must suffer spiritual death. As the bronze serpent was lifted up in the wilderness, so Christ was lifted up to bear the sins of many (Jn 12.32). Men who had been bitten needed only to look at the bronze serpent which Moses had erected, and they were instantly healed. So, in type, sinners need only look to Him who has been lifted up on the Cross and they will be saved from the guilt, the penalty, and the power of sin (Jn 1.12; 3.16).

the Ăm′mȯnītes; for Jāzėr was the boundary of the Ammonites.[p]
25 And Israel took all these cities, and Israel settled in all the cities
of the Am′ȯrītes, in Hĕshbȯn, and in all its villages. 26 For Hĕshbȯn was the city of Sīhȯn the king of the Ăm′ȯrītes, who had
fought against the former king of Mōăb and taken all his land out
of his hand, as far as the Arnȯn. 27 Therefore the ballad singers
say,

"Come to Hĕshbȯn, let it be built,
 let the city of Sīhȯn be established.

21.28 Jer 48.45, 46; Deut 2.9, 18; Isa 15.1

28 For fire went forth from Hĕshbȯn,
 flame from the city of Sīhȯn.
It devoured Ar of Mōăb,
 the lords of the heights of the Arnȯn.

21.29 Judg 11.24; 1 Ki 11.7, 33; 2 Ki 23.13; Jer 48.7,13

29 Woe to you, O Mōăb!
 You are undone, O people of C̣hēmŏsh!
He has made his sons fugitives,
 and his daughters captives,
 to an Ăm′ȯrīte king, Sīhȯn.

21.30 Num 32.3, 34; Jer 48.18, 22

30 So their posterity perished from Hĕshbȯn,[q] as far as Dībȯn,
 and we laid waste until fire spread to Mĕd′ėbȧ."[r]

6. *Defeat of Og, king of Bashan*

21.32 Num 32.1; Jer 48.32
21.33 Deut 3.1–7; Josh 13.12
21.34 Deut 3.2; ver 24

31 Thus Israel dwelt in the land of the Ăm′ȯrītes. 32 And Moses
sent to spy out Jāzėr; and they took its villages, and dispossessed
the Ăm′ȯrītes that were there. 33 Then they turned and went up
by the way to Bāshȧn; and Ŏg the king of Bashan came out against
them, he and all his people, to battle at Ĕd′rĕ-ī. 34 But the LORD
said to Moses, "Do not fear him; for I have given him into your
hand, and all his people, and his land; and you shall do to him as
you did to Sīhȯn king of the Ăm′ȯrītes, who dwelt at Hĕshbȯn."
35 So they slew him, and his sons, and all his people, until there
was not one survivor left to him; and they possessed his land.

III. *Events in Moab 22.1–36.13*

A. *Balak and Balaam*

1. *Balak sends for Balaam*

★22.1 Num 33.48
22.3 Ex 15.15
22.4 Num 31.1–3,8
★22.5 Num 23.7; Josh 24.9; Deut 23.4

22 Then the people of Israel set out, and encamped in the
plains of Mōăb beyond the Jordan at Jĕr′ĭc̣hō. 2 And Bālȧk
the son of Zĭppor saw all that Israel had done to the Ăm′ȯrītes.
3 And Mōăb was in great dread of the people, because they were
many; Moab was overcome with fear of the people of Israel. 4 And
Mōăb said to the elders of Mĭd′ĭȧn, "This horde will now lick
up all that is round about us, as the ox licks up the grass of the
field." So Bālȧk the son of Zĭppor, who was king of Moab at that
time, 5 sent messengers to Bālaȧm the son of Bēor at Pēthor, which
is near the River, in the land of Ămaw to call him, saying, "Behold, a people has come out of Egypt; they cover the face of the

[p] Gk: Heb *the boundary of the Ammonites was strong*
[q] Gk: Heb *we have shot at them. Heshbon has perished*
[r] Compare Sam and Gk: Heb *we have laid waste to Nophah which to Medeba*

22.1 *beyond the Jordan*, see note to Deut 1.1 for clarification.

22.5*a* The importance of this incident involving Balaam may be seen from the fact

earth, and they are dwelling opposite me. 6 Come now, curse this people for me, since they are too mighty for me; perhaps I shall be able to defeat them and drive them from the land; for I know that he whom you bless is blessed, and he whom you curse is cursed."

2. God forbids Balaam to go to Balak

7 So the elders of Mōăb and the elders of Mĭd′ĭăn departed with the fees for divination in their hand; and they came to Bālaăm, and gave him Bālăk's message. 8And he said to them, "Lodge here this night, and I will bring back word to you, as the LORD speaks to me"; so the princes of Mōăb stayed with Bālaăm. 9And God came to Bālaăm and said, "Who are these men with you?" 10And Bālaăm said to God, "Bālăk the son of Zĭppor, king of Mōăb, has sent to me, saying, 11 'Behold, a people has come out of Egypt, and it covers the face of the earth; now come, curse them for me; perhaps I shall be able to fight against them and drive them out.' " 12 God said to Bālaăm, "You shall not go with them; you shall not curse the people, for they are blessed." 13 So Bālaăm rose in the morning, and said to the princes of Bālăk, "Go to your own land; for the LORD has refused to let me go with you." 14 So the princes of Mōăb rose and went to Bālăk, and said, "Bālaăm refuses to come with us."

3. God lets Balaam go

15 Once again Bālăk sent princes, more in number and more honorable than they. 16And they came to Bālaăm and said to him, "Thus says Bālăk the son of Zĭppor: 'Let nothing hinder you from coming to me; 17 for I will surely do you great honor, and whatever you say to me I will do; come, curse this people for me.' " 18 But Bālaăm answered and said to the servants of Bālăk, "Though Balak were to give me his house full of silver and gold, I could not go beyond the command of the LORD my God, to do less or more. 19 Pray, now, tarry here this night also, that I may know what more the LORD will say to me." 20And God came to Bālaăm at night and said to him, "If the men have come to call you, rise, go with them; but only what I bid you, that shall you do."

4. Balaam's ass: God's anger at Balaam's disobedience

21 So Bālaăm rose in the morning, and saddled his ass, and went with the princes of Mōăb. 22 But God's anger was kindled because he went; and the angel of the LORD took his stand in the way as his

22.6
ver 17;
Num 23.7

22.7
Num 23.23;
24.1

22.8
ver 19

22.12
Num 23.20

22.17
ver 6

22.18
Num 24.13;
1 Ki 22.14;
2 Chr 18.13

*22.19

22.20
ver 35;
Num 23.12,
26; 24.13

22.21
2 Pet 2.15

*22.22

---

that it is referred to by three different New Testament writers (see 2 Pet 2.15; Jude 11; Rev 2.14). Balaam began as a conscientious prophet of the LORD, but through love of money he became a hireling. In each instance God thwarted the purpose of Balak to harm Israel, for Balaam never did curse the people of God as Balak desired him to do. But Balak did succeed by another device—craftily suggested to him by Balaam—for he corrupted Israel by the allurement of sexual license. This is what might be termed the teaching of Balaam (25.1ff; Rev 2.14).

22.5b land of Amaw, along the upper Euphrates near Carchemish. This area was noted for its diviners.

22.19 This is one of the clearest biblical

instances of the permissive will of God. Balaam knew perfectly well that it was not the will of God for him to go at the bidding of Balak. He needed no further instruction about God's will. He merely needed to obey it. Instead he trifled with the known will of God and then it was that God's permissive will came into action. God let him go with the stipulation that the outcome of his disobedience would do no harm to the people of God.

22.22 adversary, in Hebrew satan. In The Book of Job "the satan" or "adversary" accuses Job of serving God for material considerations. After the exile, the term, as the name Satan, was applied to the arch enemy of God. See Zech 3.1 where the angel of the LORD and Satan are clearly distinguished.

adversary. Now he was riding on the ass, and his two servants were with him. 23And the ass saw the angel of the LORD standing in the road, with a drawn sword in his hand; and the ass turned aside out of the road, and went into the field; and Bālaàm struck the ass, to turn her into the road. 24 Then the angel of the LORD stood in a narrow path between the vineyards, with a wall on either side. 25And when the ass saw the angel of the LORD, she pushed against the wall, and pressed Bālaàm's foot against the wall; so he struck her again. 26 Then the angel of the LORD went ahead, and stood in a narrow place, where there was no way to turn either to the right or to the left. 27 When the ass saw the angel of the LORD, she lay down under Bālaàm; and Bālaàm's anger was kindled, and he struck the ass with his staff. 28 Then the LORD opened the mouth of the ass, and she said to Bālaàm, "What have I done to you, that you have struck me these three times?" 29And Bālaàm said to the ass, "Because you have made sport of me. I wish I had a sword in my hand, for then I would kill you." 30And the ass said to Bālaàm, "Am I not your ass, upon which you have ridden all your life long to this day? Was I ever accustomed to do so to you?" And he said, "No."

31 Then the LORD opened the eyes of Bālaàm, and he saw the angel of the LORD standing in the way, with his drawn sword in his hand; and he bowed his head, and fell on his face. 32And the angel of the LORD said to him, "Why have you struck your ass these three times? Behold, I have come forth to withstand you, because your way is perverse before me; 33 and the ass saw me, and turned aside before me these three times. If she had not turned aside from me, surely just now I would have slain you and let her live." 34 Then Bālaàm said to the angel of the LORD, "I have sinned, for I did not know that thou didst stand in the road against me. Now therefore, if it is evil in thy sight, I will go back again." 35And the angel of the LORD said to Bālaàm, "Go with the men; but only the word which I bid you, that shall you speak." So Bālaàm went on with the princes of Bālak.

5. Balaam visits Balak

36 When Bālak heard that Bālaàm had come, he went out to meet him at the city of Mōäb, on the boundary formed by the Arnòn, at the extremity of the boundary. 37And Bālak said to Bālaàm, "Did I not send to you to call you? Why did you not come to me? Am I not able to honor you?" 38 Bālaàm said to Bālak, "Lo, I have come to you! Have I now any power at all to speak anything? The word that God puts in my mouth, that must I speak." 39 Then Bālaàm went with Bālak, and they came to Kǐr'ǐăth-hū'-zóth. 40And Bālak sacrificed oxen and sheep, and sent to Bālaàm and to the princes who were with him.

6. Balaam's first blessing

41 And on the morrow Bālak took Bālaàm and brought him up to Bā'môth-bā'ál; and from there he saw the nearest of the people.

23 1And Bālaàm said to Bālak, "Build for me here seven altars, and provide for me here seven bulls and seven rams." 2 Bālak did as Bālaàm had said; and Balak and Balaam offered on each altar a bull and a ram. 3And Bālaàm said to Bālak, "Stand beside your burnt offering, and I will go; perhaps the LORD will

22.23
2 Pet 2.16

22.24
Judg 6.12

22.28
2 Pet 2.16

22.29
Prov 12.10

22.30
2 Pet 2.16

22.31
Josh 5.13-
15

22.34
Num 14.40;
1 Sam
15.24,30;
2 Sam 12.13
22.35
ver 20

22.37
ver 17;
Num 24.11
22.38
ver 18;
Num 23.26;
24.13

22.41
Deut 12.2

23.1
ver 29

23.2
ver 14,30
23.3
ver 15

come to meet me; and whatever he shows me I will tell you." And
he went to a bare height. ⁴And God met Bālaám; and Balaam said
to him, "I have prepared the seven altars, and I have offered upon
each altar a bull and a ram." ⁵And the LORD put a word in
Bālaám's mouth, and said, "Return to Bālak, and thus you shall
speak." ⁶And he returned to him, and lo, he and all the princes of
Mōáb were standing beside his burnt offering. ⁷And Bālaám took
up his discourse, and said,

"From Arám Bālák has brought me,
　　the king of Mōáb from the eastern mountains:
'Come, curse Jacob for me,
　　and come, denounce Israel!'
⁸ How can I curse whom God has not cursed?
　　How can I denounce whom the LORD has not denounced?
⁹ For from the top of the mountains I see him,
　　from the hills I behold him;
lo, a people dwelling alone,
　　and not reckoning itself among the nations!
¹⁰ Who can count the dust of Jacob,
　　or number the fourth part$ of Israel?
Let me die the death of the righteous,
　　and let my end be like his!"

11 And Bālák said to Bālaám, "What have you done to me? I
took you to curse my enemies, and behold, you have done nothing
but bless them." ¹²And he answered, "Must I not take heed to
speak what the LORD puts in my mouth?"

7. Balaam's second blessing

13 And Bālák said to him, "Come with me to another place,
from which you may see them; you shall see only the nearest of
them, and shall not see them all; then curse them for me from
there." ¹⁴And he took him to the field of Zōphĭm, to the top of
Pĭsgáh, and built seven altars, and offered a bull and a ram on each
altar. 15 Bālaám said to Bālák, "Stand here beside your burnt offering, while I meet the LORD yonder." ¹⁶And the LORD met Bālaám,
and put a word in his mouth, and said, "Return to Bālák, and thus
shall you speak." ¹⁷And he came to him, and, lo, he was standing
beside his burnt offering, and the princes of Mōáb with him. And
Bālák said to him, "What has the LORD spoken?" ¹⁸And Bālaám
took up his discourse, and said,

"Rise, Bālák, and hear;
　　hearken to me, O son of Zĭppor:
¹⁹ God is not man, that he should lie,
　　or a son of man, that he should repent.
Has he said, and will he not do it?
　　Or has he spoken, and will he not fulfil it?
²⁰ Behold, I received a command to bless:
　　he has blessed, and I cannot revoke it.
²¹ He has not beheld misfortune in Jacob;
　　nor has he seen trouble in Israel.

$ Or dust clouds

23.4 These rites were used by Babylonian
diviners. (See also ver 2, 30.) Note that these
were the pagan offerings of Balak and as such
could not commend him toward God.

23.4
ver 16

23.5
ver 16;
Num 22.35;
Deut 18.18;
Jer 1.9

23.7
ver 18;
Num 24.3,
15,23;
Job 27.1;
29.1;
Ps 78.2;
Num 22.6

23.8
Num 22.12

23.9
Ex 33.16;
Deut 32.8;
33.28

23.10
Gen 13.16;
Ps 116.15

23.11
Num 24.10

23.12
Num 22.20,
38

*23.14
ver 1,2

23.16
Num 22.20

23.19
1 Sam
15.29;
Mal 3.6;
Rom 11.29;
Tit 1.2;
Jas 1.17

23.20
Isa 43.13

23.21
Ps 32.2,5;
Rom 4.7,8;
Isa 40.2;
Ex 29.45,
46; Ps 89.15

The LORD their God is with them,
  and the shout of a king is among them.

23.22
Num 24.8
22 God brings them out of Egypt;
  they have as it were the horns of the wild ox.
23 For there is no enchantment against Jacob,
  no divination against Israel;
now it shall be said of Jacob and Israel,
  'What has God wrought!'

23.24
Gen 49.9,
27
24 Behold, a people! As a lioness it rises up
  and as a lion it lifts itself;
it does not lie down till it devours the prey,
  and drinks the blood of the slain."

8. *Balaam's third blessing*

23.26
ver 12;
Num 22.38
23.27
ver 13
25 And Bālák said to Balaám, "Neither curse them at all, nor bless them at all." 26 But Balaám answered Bālák, "Did I not tell you, 'All that the LORD says, that I must do'?" 27And Bālák said to Balaám, "Come now, I will take you to another place; perhaps it will please God that you may curse them for me from there." 28 So Bālák took Balaám to the top of Pēʹor, that overlooks the desert.*t*

23.29
ver 1
29And Balaám said to Bālák, "Build for me here seven altars, and provide for me here seven bulls and seven rams." 30And Bālák did as Balaám had said, and offered a bull and a ram on each altar.

24.1
Num 23.3,
15
24.2
Num 11.25,
26;
1 Sam
10.10;
2 Chr 15.1
24 When Balaám saw that it pleased the LORD to bless Israel, he did not go, as at other times, to look for omens, but set his face toward the wilderness. 2And Balaám lifted up his eyes, and saw Israel encamping tribe by tribe. And the Spirit of God came upon him, 3 and he took up his discourse, and said,

"The oracle of Balaám the son of Bēor,
  the oracle of the man whose eye is opened,*u*

24.3
Num 23.7,
18
24.4
Num 22.20;
12.6
4 the oracle of him who hears the words of God,
  who sees the vision of the Almighty,
  falling down, but having his eyes uncovered:
5 how fair are your tents, O Jacob,
  your encampments, O Israel!

24.6
Ps 1.3;
104.16
6 Like valleys that stretch afar,
  like gardens beside a river,
like aloes that the LORD has planted,
  like cedar trees beside the waters.

24.7
ver 20;
1 Sam
15.8,9;
2 Sam 5.12;
1 Chr 14.2
7 Water shall flow from his buckets,
  and his seed shall be in many waters,
his king shall be higher than Āgăg,
  and his kingdom shall be exalted.

24.8
Num 23.22,
24;
Ps 2.9;
45.5;
Jer 50.9,17
8 God brings him out of Egypt;
  he has as it were the horns of the wild ox,
he shall eat up the nations his adversaries,
  and shall break their bones in pieces,
  and pierce them through with his arrows.

24.9
Gen 49.9;
12.3;
27.29
9 He couched, he lay down like a lion,
  and like a lioness; who will rouse him up?
Blessed be every one who blesses you,
  and cursed be every one who curses you."

---

t Or *Jĕshʹimŏn* *u* Or *closed* or *perfect*

9. Balaam's fourth blessing and prophecy

10 And Bālák's anger was kindled against Balaám, and he struck his hands together; and Balak said to Balaam, "I called you to curse my enemies, and behold, you have blessed them these three times. 11 Therefore now flee to your place; I said, 'I will certainly honor you,' but the LORD has held you back from honor." 12And Bālaám said to Bālák, "Did I not tell your messengers whom you sent to me, 13 'If Bālák should give me his house full of silver and gold, I would not be able to go beyond the word of the LORD, to do either good or bad of my own will; what the LORD speaks, that will I speak'? 14And now, behold, I am going to my people; come, I will let you know what this people will do to your people in the latter days." 15And he took up his discourse, and said,

"The oracle of Balaám the son of Bēor,
    the oracle of the man whose eye is opened,[v]
16 the oracle of him who hears the words of God,
    and knows the knowledge of the Most High,
who sees the vision of the Almighty,
    falling down, but having his eyes uncovered:
17 I see him, but not now;
    I behold him, but not nigh:
a star shall come forth out of Jacob,
    and a scepter shall rise out of Israel;
it shall crush the forehead[w] of Mōáb,
    and break down all the sons of Shēth.
18 Ēdóm shall be dispossessed,
    Sēir also, his enemies, shall be dispossessed,
    while Israel does valiantly.
19 By Jacob shall dominion be exercised,
    and the survivors of cities be destroyed!"
20 Then he looked on Ăm′álěk, and took up his discourse, and said,
"Amalek was the first of the nations,
    but in the end he shall come to destruction."
21 And he looked on the Kēnīte, and took up his discourse, and said,
"Enduring is your dwelling place,
    and your nest is set in the rock;
22 nevertheless Kāin shall be wasted.
    How long shall Ăsshúr take you away captive?"
23 And he took up his discourse, and said,
"Alas, who shall live when God does this?
24   But ships shall come from Kĭttĭm
    and shall afflict Ăsshúr and Ē′bèr;
    and he also shall come to destruction."

Cross references (right margin):
24.11 Num 22.17, 37
24.13 Num 22.18, 20
24.14 Gen 49.1; Dan 2.28; Mic 6.5
*24.17 Rev 1.7; Mt 2.2; Gen 49.10
24.18 2 Sam 8.14
24.19 Gen 49.10; Mic 5.2
24.20 Ex 17.8, 14,16
*24.21
24.24 Gen 10.4, 21; ver 20

[v] Or closed or perfect   [w] Heb corners (of the head)

24.17 This prophecy of Israel's supremacy over Moab and Edom came true in David's reign, but it extends beyond that to David's greater son. Balaam did not understand the implications of his prophetic words, for ultimately Jesus Christ is the star . . . out of Jacob and in His hands is the scepter of kingship. As the Messianic descendant of Jacob He shall exercise dominion over all the earth. Christ's kingdom has been estab-

lished as a spiritual reign. Some Christians look forward to a literal and earthly manifestation when, during the millennial age, He will rule over the nations with a rod of iron (Rev 19.15).
Sheth, an ancient name for Moab which has been found in nonbiblical texts.
24.21 Kenite, meaning a smith, is probably a reference to those who mined and smelted copper from Edomite mines.

24.25
Num 31.8

25 Then Bālaăm rose, and went back to his place; and Bālăk also went his way.

B. Israel's idolatry in Shittim

1. Israelites yoked to Baal of Peor

25.1
Mic 6.5;
Num 31.16;
1 Cor 10.8;
Rev 2.14

25 While Israel dwelt in Shĭttĭm the people began to play the harlot with the daughters of Mŏăb. 2 These invited the people to the sacrifices of their gods, and the people ate, and bowed down to their gods. 3 So Israel yoked himself to Bāăl of Pē′or. And the anger of the LORD was kindled against Israel; 4 and the LORD said to Moses, "Take all the chiefs of the people, and hang them in the sun before the LORD, that the fierce anger of the LORD may turn away from Israel." 5And Moses said to the judges of Israel, "Every one of you slay his men who have yoked themselves to Bāăl of Pē′or."

25.2
Ex 34.15;
20.5;
1 Cor 10.20

25.3
Ps 106.28,
29;
Hos 9.10

25.4
Deut 4.3

2. Phinehas slays the Midianite woman

6 And behold, one of the people of Israel came and brought a Mĭd′ĭănīte woman to his family, in the sight of Moses and in the sight of the whole congregation of the people of Israel, while they were weeping at the door of the tent of meeting. 7 When Phĭn′ĕhăs the son of Ĕlĕā′zăr, son of Aaron the priest, saw it, he rose and left the congregation, and took a spear in his hand 8 and went after the man of Israel into the inner room, and pierced both of them, the man of Israel and the woman, through her body. Thus the plague was stayed from the people of Israel. 9 Nevertheless those that died by the plague were twenty-four thousand.

25.7
Ps 106.30

25.9
Deut 4.3;
1 Cor 10.8

10 And the LORD said to Moses, 11 "Phĭn′ĕhăs the son of Ĕlĕā′-zăr, son of Aaron the priest, has turned back my wrath from the people of Israel, in that he was jealous with my jealousy among them, so that I did not consume the people of Israel in my jealousy. 12 Therefore say, 'Behold, I give to him my covenant of peace; 13 and it shall be to him, and to his descendants after him, the covenant of a perpetual priesthood, because he was jealous for his God, and made atonement for the people of Israel.' "

25.11
Ps 106.30;
Ex 20.5;
Deut 32.16,
21

25.12
Isa 54.10;
Mal 2.4,5

25.13
Ex 40.15;
Num 16.46;
Heb 2.17

14 The name of the slain man of Israel, who was slain with the Mĭd′ĭănīte woman, was Zĭmrī the son of Sālū, head of a fathers' house belonging to the Sĭm′ĕŏnītes. 15And the name of the Mĭd′-ĭănīte woman who was slain was Cŏzbī the daughter of Zŭr, who was the head of the people of a fathers' house in Mĭd′ĭăn.

25.15
Num 31.8

16 And the LORD said to Moses, 17 "Harass the Mĭd′ĭănītes, and smite them; 18 for they have harassed you with their wiles, with which they beguiled you in the matter of Pē′or, and in the matter of Cŏzbī, the daughter of the prince of Mĭd′ĭăn, their sister, who was slain on the day of the plague on account of Peor."

25.17
Num 31.2

25.18
Num 31.16

C. Israel's second census

1. The command to take the census

26.2
Ex 30.12;
38.25,26;
Num 1.2

26 After the plague the LORD said to Moses and to Ĕlĕā′zăr the son of Aaron, the priest, 2 "Take a census of all the congregation of the people of Israel, from twenty years old and upward, by their fathers' houses, all in Israel who are able to go

forth to war." ³And Moses and Ĕlëä′zăr the priest spoke with them in the plains of Mŏăb by the Jordan at Jĕr′ĭchō, saying, ⁴ "Take a census of the people,ˣ from twenty years old and upward," as the LORD commanded Moses. The people of Israel, who came forth out of the land of Egypt, were:

2. The numbering of the tribes

5 Reubën, the first-born of Israel; the sons of Reuben: of Hānŏch, the family of the Hā′nŏchītes; of Păllu, the family of the Păl′luītes; ⁶ of Hĕzrŏn, the family of the Hĕz′rŏnītes; of Carmī, the family of the Carmītes. ⁷ These are the families of the Reubënītes; and their number was forty-three thousand seven hundred and thirty. ⁸And the sons of Păllu: Ĕlī′ăb. ⁹ The sons of Ĕlī′ăb: Nĕm′ū-ĕl, Dāthăn, and Ăbī′răm. These are the Dathan and Abiram, chosen from the congregation, who contended against Moses and Aaron in the company of Kŏrăh, when they contended against the LORD, ¹⁰ and the earth opened its mouth and swallowed them up together with Kŏrăh, when that company died, when the fire devoured two hundred and fifty men; and they became a warning. ¹¹ Notwithstanding, the sons of Kŏrăh did not die.

12 The sons of Sĭm′ëŏn according to their families: of Nĕm′-ū-ĕl, the family of the Nĕm′üĕlītes; of Jāmĭn, the family of the Jā′mĭnītes; of Jāchĭn, the family of the Jā′chĭnītes; ¹³ of Zĕrăh, the family of the Zĕr′ăhītes; of Shaul, the family of the Shaulītes. ¹⁴ These are the families of the Sĭm′ëŏnītes, twenty-two thousand two hundred.

15 The sons of Găd according to their families: of Zēphŏn, the family of the Zē′phŏnītes; of Hăggī, the family of the Hăggītes; of Shunī, the family of the Shunītes; ¹⁶ of Ŏznī, the family of the Ŏznītes; of Ērī, the family of the Ērītes; ¹⁷ of Ărŏd, the family of the Ăr′ŏdītes; of Ărē′lī, the family of the Ărē′lītes. ¹⁸ These are the families of the sons of Găd according to their number, forty thousand five hundred.

19 The sons of Judah were Ĕr and Ōnăn; and Er and Onan died in the land of Cānaăn. ²⁰And the sons of Judah according to their families were: of Shēlăh, the family of the Shē′lănītes; of Pĕrĕz, the family of the Pĕr′ĕzītes; of Zērăh, the family of the Zĕr′ăhītes. ²¹And the sons of Pĕrĕz were: of Hĕzrŏn, the family of the Hĕz′-rŏnītes; of Hāmŭl, the family of the Hā′mŭlītes. ²² These are the families of Judah according to their number, seventy-six thousand five hundred.

23 The sons of Ĭs′săchar according to their families: of Tŏlă, the family of the Tŏ′lăītes; of Pūvăh, the family of the Pūnītes; ²⁴ of Jāshŭb, the family of the Jā′shŭbītes; of Shĭmrŏn, the family of the Shĭm′rŏnītes. ²⁵ These are the families of Ĭs′săchar according to their number, sixty-four thousand three hundred.

26 The sons of Zĕb′ŭlŭn, according to their families: of Sērĕd, the family of the Sĕr′ĕdītes; of Ēlŏn, the family of the Ē′lŏnītes; of Jahleĕl, the family of the Jah′leĕlītes. ²⁷ These are the families of the Zĕb′ŭlŭnītes according to their number, sixty thousand five hundred.

28 The sons of Joseph according to their families: Mănăs′sĕh and Ē′phrăĭm. ²⁹ The sons of Mănăs′sĕh: of Māchĭr, the family of the Mā′chĭrītes; and Machir was the father of Gĭl′ëăd; of Gilead,

26.5
Ex 6.14

26.9
Num 16.1,2

26.10
Num 16.32,
35,38

26.11
Deut 24.16
26.12
Ex 6.15
Jemuel;
1 Chr 4.24
Jarib
26.13
Gen 46.10
Zohar

26.15
Gen 46.16
Ziphion
26.16
Gen 46.16
Ezbon
26.17
Gen 46.16
Arodi
26.18
Num 1.25

26.22
Num 1.27

26.24
Gen 46.13
Job
26.25
Num 1.29

26.27
Num 1.31

ˣ Supplying *take a census of the people* Compare verse 2

26.30
see Josh
17.2
Abiezer

the family of the Gĭl′ĕădītes. 30 These are the sons of Gĭl′ĕăd: of Ĭĕ′zĕr, the family of the Ĭĕz′ĕrītes; of Hēlĕk, the family of the Hē′lĕkītes; 31 and of Ăs′rĭĕl, the family of the Ăs′rĭĕlītes; and of Shĕçhĕm, the family of the Shĕçh′ĕmītes; 32 and of Shĕmī′dă, the family of the Shĕmī′dāites; and of Hēphĕr, the family of the Hē′phĕrītes. 33 Now Zĕlō′phĕhăd the son of Hēphĕr had no sons, but daughters: and the names of the daughters of Zelophehad were Mahlăh, Noah, Hŏglăh, Mĭlcăh, and Tĭrzăh. 34 These are the families of Mănăs′sĕh; and their number was fifty-two thousand seven hundred.

26.35
1 Chr 7.20
Bered

35 These are the sons of Ē′phrăĭm according to their families: of Shŭthē′lăh, the family of the Shŭthē′lăhītes; of Bĕçhĕr, the family of the Bē′çhĕrītes; of Tāhăn, the family of the Tā′hănītes. 36 And these are the sons of Shŭthē′lăh: of Ērăn, the family of the Ē′rănītes.

26.37
Num 1.33

37 These are the families of the sons of Ē′phrăĭm according to their number, thirty-two thousand five hundred. These are the sons of Joseph according to their families.

26.38
Gen 46.21
Ehi
26.39
Gen 46.21
Muppim
Huppim
26.40
1 Chr 8.3
Addar
26.41
Num 1.37

38 The sons of Benjamin according to their families: of Bēlă, the family of the Bē′lă-ītes; of Ăshbĕl, the family of the Ăsh′bĕlītes; of Ăhī′răm, the family of the Ăhī′rămītes; 39 of Shĕphu′phăm, the family of the Shu′phămītes; of Hūphăm, the family of the Hū′phămītes. 40 And the sons of Bēlă were Ard and Nā′ămăn: of Ard, the family of the Ard′ītes; of Naaman, the family of the Nā′ămītes. 41 These are the sons of Benjamin according to their families; and their number was forty-five thousand six hundred.

26.42
Gen 46.23
Hushim
26.43
Num 1.39

42 These are the sons of Dan according to their families: of Shuhăm, the family of the Shu′hămītes. These are the families of Dan according to their families. 43 All the families of the Shu′hămītes, according to their number, were sixty-four thousand four hundred.

44 The sons of Ăshĕr according to their families: of Ĭmnăh, the family of the Ĭmnītes; of Ĭshvī, the family of the Ĭshvītes; of Bĕrī′ăh, the family of the Bĕrī′ītes. 45 Of the sons of Bĕrī′ăh: of Hēbĕr, the family of the Hē′bĕrītes; of Măl′çhĭ-ĕl, the family of the Măl′çhĭ-ĕlītes. 46 And the name of the daughter of Ăshĕr was Sērăh.

26.47
Num 1.41

47 These are the families of the sons of Ăshĕr according to their number, fifty-three thousand four hundred.

48 The sons of Năph′tălī according to their families: of Jahzēĕl, the family of the Jah′zeēlītes; of Gunī, the family of the Gunītes; 49 of Jēzĕr, the family of the Jĕz′ĕrītes; of Shĭllĕm, the family of the Shĭl′lĕmītes.

26.50
Num 1.43

50 These are the families of Năph′tălī according to their families; and their number was forty-five thousand four hundred.

51 This was the number of the people of Israel, six hundred and one thousand seven hundred and thirty.

3. The division of the land

26.53
Josh 11.23;
14.1
26.54
Num 33.54
26.55
Num 33.54;
34.13

52 The LORD said to Moses: 53 "To these the land shall be divided for inheritance according to the number of names. 54 To a large tribe you shall give a large inheritance, and to a small tribe you shall give a small inheritance; every tribe shall be given its inheritance according to its numbers. 55 But the land shall be divided by lot; according to the names of the tribes of their fathers they shall inherit. 56 Their inheritance shall be divided according to lot between the larger and the smaller."

4. *The numbering of the Levites*

57 These are the Lēvītes as numbered according to their families: of Gērshón, the family of the Gēr′shónītes; of Kōhăth, the family of the Kō′hăthītes; of Mērar′ĭ, the family of the Mērar′- ītes. 58 These are the families of Lēvī: the family of the Lībnītes, the family of the Hē′brónītes, the family of the Mahlītes, the family of the Mushītes, the family of the Kō′rāhītes. And Kōhăth was the father of Ămrăm. 59 The name of Ămrăm's wife was Jŏch′ĕbĕd the daughter of Lēvī, who was born to Levi in Egypt; and she bore to Ămrăm Aaron and Moses and Miriam their sister. 60And to Aaron were born Nādăb, Abī′hū, Ēlëä′zăr and Ith′ámar. 61 But Nādăb and Åbī′hū died when they offered unholy fire before the LORD. 62And those numbered of them were twenty-three thousand, every male from a month old and upward; for they were not numbered among the people of Israel, because there was no inheritance given to them among the people of Israel.

26.59
Ex 6.20

26.60
Num 3.2
26.61
Lev 10.1,2;
Num 3.4
26.62
Num 1.47;
18.20,23,
24

5. *Summary*

63 These were those numbered by Moses and Ēlëä′zăr the priest, who numbered the people of Israel in the plains of Mōăb by the Jordan at Jĕr′ĭchō. 64 But among these there was not a man of those numbered by Moses and Aaron the priest, who had numbered the people of Israel in the wilderness of Sī′näī. 65 For the LORD had said of them, "They shall die in the wilderness." There was not left a man of them, except Cālĕb the son of Jĕphŭn′- nĕh and Joshua the son of Nún.

26.64
Deut 2.14,
15

26.65
Num 14.28,
29;
1 Cor 10.5,
6;
Num 14.30

D. *The case of Zelophehad's daughters*

1. *Zelophehad's death without male issue*

27 Then drew near the daughters of Zēlō′phēhăd the son of Hēphĕr, son of Gĭl′ëăd, son of Māchĭr, son of Mănăs′sĕh, from the families of Manasseh the son of Joseph. The names of his daughters were: Mahlăh, Noah, Hŏglăh, Mĭlcăh, and Tĭrzăh. 2And they stood before Moses, and before Ēlëä′zăr the priest, and before the leaders and all the congregation, at the door of the tent of meeting, saying, 3 "Our father died in the wilderness; he was not among the company of those who gathered themselves together against the LORD in the company of Kōrăh, but died for his own sin; and he had no sons. 4 Why should the name of our father be taken away from his family, because he had no son? Give to us a possession among our father's brethren."

*27.1ff
Num 26.33;
36.1

27.3
Num 26.64,
65; 26.33;
16.1,2

27.4
Josh 17.4

2. *The inheritance to pass through the daughters*

5 Moses brought their case before the LORD. 6And the LORD said to Moses, 7 "The daughters of Zēlō′phēhăd are right; you shall give them possession of an inheritance among their father's brethren and cause the inheritance of their father to pass to them. 8And you shall say to the people of Israel, 'If a man dies, and has no son, then you shall cause his inheritance to pass to his daughter. 9And if he has no daughter, then you shall give his inheritance to his brothers. 10And if he has no brothers, then you shall give his

27.5
Num 9.8
27.6
Num 36.2

27.1-10 Provision for inheritance by daughters and others was necessary, otherwise the lack of a son would mean the loss of inheritance of the land allotted. See 36.6, 7.

*27.11	inheritance to his father's brothers. 11And if his father has no brothers, then you shall give his inheritance to his kinsman that is next to him of his family, and he shall possess it. And it shall be to the people of Israel a statute and ordinance, as the LORD commanded Moses.' "

E. The selection of Joshua to succeed Moses

*27.12
Num 33.47;
Deut 32.49
27.13
Num 31.2
27.14
Num 20.12:
Ex 17.7

12 The LORD said to Moses, "Go up into this mountain of Ăb'árĭm, and see the land which I have given to the people of Israel. 13And when you have seen it, you also shall be gathered to your people, as your brother Aaron was gathered, 14 because you rebelled against my word in the wilderness of Zĭn during the strife of the congregation, to sanctify me at the waters before their eyes." (These are the waters of Mĕr'ĭbah of Kādĕsh in the wilderness of Zĭn.) 15 Moses said to the LORD, 16 "Let the LORD, the God of the spirits of all flesh, appoint a man over the congregation, 17 who shall go out before them and come in before them, who shall lead them out and bring them in; that the congregation of the LORD may not be as sheep which have no shepherd." 18And the LORD said to Moses, "Take Joshua the son of Nŭn, a man in whom is the spirit, and lay your hand upon him; 19 cause him to stand before Elĕā'zăr the priest and all the congregation, and you shall commission him in their sight. 20 You shall invest him with some of your authority, that all the congregation of the people of Israel may obey. 21And he shall stand before Elĕā'zăr the priest, who shall inquire for him by the judgment of the Urĭm before the LORD; at his word they shall go out, and at his word they shall come in, both he and all the people of Israel with him, the whole congregation." 22And Moses did as the LORD commanded him; he took Joshua and caused him to stand before Elĕā'zăr the priest and the whole congregation, 23 and he laid his hands upon him, and commissioned him as the LORD directed through Moses.

*27.15
27.16
Num 16.22
27.17
Deut 31.2;
Mt 9.36;
Mk 6.34
27.18
Num 11.25–
29;
Deut 34.9
27.19
Deut 31.3,
7,8,23
27.20
Josh 1.16,
17
27.21
Ex 28.30

F. The laws of offerings repeated and explained

1. The daily burnt offering

28.2
Lev 3.11

28.3
Ex 29.38

28.7
Ex 29.42

28 The LORD said to Moses, 2 "Command the people of Israel, and say to them, 'My offering, my food for my offerings by fire, my pleasing odor, you shall take heed to offer to me in its due season.' 3And you shall say to them, This is the offering by fire which you shall offer to the LORD: two male lambs a year old without blemish, day by day, as a continual offering. 4 The one lamb you shall offer in the morning, and the other lamb you shall offer in the evening; 5 also a tenth of an ephah of fine flour for a cereal offering, mixed with a fourth of a hin of beaten oil. 6 It is a continual burnt offering, which was ordained at Mount Sĭ'nāï for a pleasing odor, an offering by fire to the LORD. 7 Its drink offering shall be a fourth of a hin for each lamb; in the holy place you shall pour out a drink offering of strong drink to the LORD. 8 The other lamb you shall offer in the evening; like the

---

27.11 See note to Num 27.1–10
27.12 *mountain of Abarim*, probably another designation for the hill country of Mt. Nebo.

27.15 In answer to Moses' request for a new leader over the people the LORD tells him to take Joshua (ver 18).

cereal offering of the morning, and like its drink offering, you shall offer it as an offering by fire, a pleasing odor to the LORD.

2. *The offering on the Sabbath*

9 "On the sabbath day two male lambs a year old without blemish, and two tenths of an ephah of fine flour for a cereal offering, mixed with oil, and its drink offering: 10 this is the burnt offering of every sabbath, besides the continual burnt offering and its drink offering.

28.10
ver 3

3. *The offering on the new moon*

11 "At the beginnings of your months you shall offer a burnt offering to the LORD: two young bulls, one ram, seven male lambs a year old without blemish; 12 also three tenths of an ephah of fine flour for a cereal offering, mixed with oil, for each bull; and two tenths of fine flour for a cereal offering, mixed with oil, for the one ram; 13 and a tenth of fine flour mixed with oil as a cereal offering for every lamb; for a burnt offering of pleasing odor, an offering by fire to the LORD. 14 Their drink offerings shall be half a hin of wine for a bull, a third of a hin for a ram, and a fourth of a hin for a lamb; this is the burnt offering of each month throughout the months of the year. 15Also one male goat for a sin offering to the LORD; it shall be offered besides the continual burnt offering and its drink offering.

28.11
Num 10.10;
Ezek 45.17;
46.6
28.12
Num 15.4–
12

28.15
ver 3

4. *The offerings on the Feast of Unleavened Bread*

16 "On the fourteenth day of the first month is the LORD's passover. 17And on the fifteenth day of this month is a feast; seven days shall unleavened bread be eaten. 18 On the first day there shall be a holy convocation: you shall do no laborious work, 19 but offer an offering by fire, a burnt offering to the LORD: two young bulls, one ram, and seven male lambs a year old; see that they are without blemish; 20 also their cereal offering of fine flour mixed with oil; three tenths of an ephah shall you offer for a bull, and two tenths for a ram; 21 a tenth shall you offer for each of the seven lambs; 22 also one male goat for a sin offering, to make atonement for you. 23 You shall offer these besides the burnt offering of the morning, which is for a continual burnt offering. 24 In the same way you shall offer daily, for seven days, the food of an offering by fire, a pleasing odor to the LORD; it shall be offered besides the continual burnt offering and its drink offering. 25And on the seventh day you shall have a holy convocation; you shall do no laborious work.

28.16
Ex 12.6,18;
Lev 23.5;
Deut 16.1
28.17
Lev 23.6
28.18
Ex 12.16;
Lev 23.7

28.23
ver 3

28.25
Ex 12.16

5. *First fruits (Pentecost) offerings*

26 "On the day of the first fruits, when you offer a cereal offering of new grain to the LORD at your feast of weeks, you shall have a holy convocation; you shall do no laborious work, 27 but offer a burnt offering, a pleasing odor to the LORD: two young bulls, one ram, seven male lambs a year old; 28 also their cereal offering of fine flour mixed with oil, three tenths of an ephah for each bull, two tenths for one ram, 29 a tenth for each of the seven lambs; 30 with one male goat, to make atonement for you. 31 Besides the continual burnt offering and its cereal offering, you shall offer them and their drink offering. See that they are without blemish.

28.26
Ex 23.16;
34.22;
Lev 23.10,
15;
Deut 16.10

28.31
ver 3,19

6. *Feast of Trumpets*

29.1
Ex 23.16;
34.22;
Lev 23.24

29 "On the first day of the seventh month you shall have a holy convocation; you shall do no laborious work. It is a day for you to blow the trumpets, 2 and you shall offer a burnt offering, a pleasing odor to the LORD: one young bull, one ram, seven male lambs a year old without blemish; 3 also their cereal offering of fine flour mixed with oil, three tenths of an ephah for the bull, two tenths for the ram, 4 and one tenth for each of the seven lambs; 5 with one male goat for a sin offering, to make atone-

29.6
Num 28.3,
11

ment for you; 6 besides the burnt offering of the new moon, and its cereal offering, and the continual burnt offering and its cereal offering, and their drink offering, according to the ordinance for them, a pleasing odor, an offering by fire to the LORD.

7. *The offering on the Day of Atonement*

29.7
Lev 16.29–
34;
23.26–32

7 "On the tenth day of this seventh month you shall have a holy convocation, and afflict yourselves; you shall do no work, 8 but you shall offer a burnt offering to the LORD, a pleasing odor: one young bull, one ram, seven male lambs a year old; they shall be to you without blemish; 9 and their cereal offering of fine flour mixed with oil, three tenths of an ephah for the bull, two tenths for the

29.11
Lev 16.3,5;
Num 28.3

one ram, 10 a tenth for each of the seven lambs: 11 also one male goat for a sin offering, besides the sin offering of atonement, and the continual burnt offering and its cereal offering, and their drink offerings.

8. *Offerings at the Feast of Tabernacles*

29.12
Lev 23.33–
35

12 "On the fifteenth day of the seventh month you shall have a holy convocation; you shall do no laborious work, and you shall keep a feast to the LORD seven days; 13 and you shall offer a burnt offering, an offering by fire, a pleasing odor to the LORD, thirteen young bulls, two rams, fourteen male lambs a year old; they shall be without blemish; 14 and their cereal offering of fine flour mixed with oil, three tenths of an ephah for each of the thirteen bulls, two tenths for each of the two rams, 15 and a tenth for each of the

29.16
ver 11

fourteen lambs; 16 also one male goat for a sin offering, besides the continual burnt offering, its cereal offering and its drink offering.

29.18
ver 3,4,9,
10;
Num 15.12;
28.7,14

17 "On the second day twelve young bulls, two rams, fourteen male lambs a year old without blemish, 18 with the cereal offering and the drink offerings for the bulls, for the rams, and for the lambs, by number, according to the ordinance; 19 also one male goat for a sin offering, besides the continual burnt offering and its cereal offering, and their drink offerings.

20 "On the third day eleven bulls, two rams, fourteen male lambs a year old without blemish, 21 with the cereal offering and the drink offerings for the bulls, for the rams, and for the lambs, by number, according to the ordinance; 22 also one male goat for a

29.22
Num 28.15

sin offering, besides the continual burnt offering and its cereal offering and its drink offering.

23 "On the fourth day ten bulls, two rams, fourteen male lambs a year old without blemish, 24 with the cereal offering and the drink offerings for the bulls, for the rams, and for the lambs, by number, according to the ordinance; 25 also one male goat for a sin offering, besides the continual burnt offering, its cereal offering and its drink offering.

26 "On the fifth day nine bulls, two rams, fourteen male lambs a year old without blemish, 27 with the cereal offering and the drink offerings for the bulls, for the rams, and for the lambs, by number, according to the ordinance; 28 also one male goat for a sin offering; besides the continual burnt offering and its cereal offering and its drink offering.

29 "On the sixth day eight bulls, two rams, fourteen male lambs a year old without blemish, 30 with the cereal offering and the drink offerings for the bulls, for the rams, and for the lambs, by number, according to the ordinance; 31 also one male goat for a sin offering; besides the continual burnt offering, its cereal offering, and its drink offerings.

32 "On the seventh day seven bulls, two rams, fourteen male lambs a year old without blemish, 33 with the cereal offering and the drink offerings for the bulls, for the rams, and for the lambs, by number, according to the ordinance; 34 also one male goat for a sin offering; besides the continual burnt offering, its cereal offering, and its drink offering.

35 "On the eighth day you shall have a solemn assembly: you shall do no laborious work, 36 but you shall offer a burnt offering, an offering by fire, a pleasing odor to the LORD: one bull, one ram, seven male lambs a year old without blemish, 37 and the cereal offering and the drink offerings for the bull, for the ram, and for the lambs, by number, according to the ordinance; 38 also one male goat for a sin offering; besides the continual burnt offering and its cereal offering and its drink offering.

39 "These you shall offer to the LORD at your appointed feasts, in addition to your votive offerings and your freewill offerings, for your burnt offerings, and for your cereal offerings, and for your drink offerings, and for your peace offerings."

40ʸ And Moses told the people of Israel everything just as the LORD had commanded Moses.

G. The laws of vows

30 Moses said to the heads of the tribes of the people of Israel, "This is what the LORD has commanded. 2 When a man vows a vow to the LORD, or swears an oath to bind himself by a pledge, he shall not break his word; he shall do according to all that proceeds out of his mouth. 3 Or when a woman vows a vow to the LORD, and binds herself by a pledge, while within her father's house, in her youth, 4 and her father hears of her vow and of her pledge by which she has bound herself, and says nothing to her; then all her vows shall stand, and every pledge by which she has bound herself shall stand. 5 But if her father expresses disapproval to her on the day that he hears of it, no vow of hers, no pledge by which she has bound herself, shall stand; and the LORD will forgive her, because her father opposed her. 6And if she is married to a husband, while under her vows or any thoughtless utterance of her lips by which she has bound herself, 7 and her husband hears of it, and says nothing to her on the day that he hears; then her vows shall stand, and her pledges by which she

ʸ Ch 30.1 in Heb

30.2 See note to Num 6.2 for a detailed explanation on the meaning of vows. It is also interesting to compare Mt 5.33–37 where Jesus says, "You shall not swear falsely. . . ."

30.8
Gen 3.16

has bound herself shall stand. 8 But if, on the day that her husband comes to hear of it, he expresses disapproval, then he shall make void her vow which was on her, and the thoughtless utterance of her lips, by which she bound herself; and the LORD will forgive her. 9 But any vow of a widow or of a divorced woman, anything by which she has bound herself, shall stand against her. 10And if she vowed in her husband's house, or bound herself by a pledge with an oath, 11 and her husband heard of it, and said nothing to her, and did not oppose her; then all her vows shall stand, and every pledge by which she bound herself shall stand.

30.12
Eph 5.22

12 But if her husband makes them null and void on the day that he hears them, then whatever proceeds out of her lips concerning her vows, or concerning her pledge of herself, shall not stand: her husband has made them void, and the LORD will forgive her. 13Any vow and any binding oath to afflict herself, her husband may establish, or her husband may make void. 14 But if her husband says nothing to her from day to day, then he establishes all her vows, or all her pledges, that are upon her; he has established them, because he said nothing to her on the day that he heard of them.

30.15
Col 3.18

15 But if he makes them null and void after he has heard of them, then he shall bear her iniquity."

30.16
Ex 15.26

16 These are the statutes which the LORD commanded Moses, as between a man and his wife, and between a father and his daughter, while in her youth, within her father's house.

H. *The destruction of the Midianites*

1. *The slaying of the Midianites*

31.2
Num 25.1,
16,17;
27.13

31 The LORD said to Moses, 2 "Avenge the people of Israel on the Mĭd'ĭănītes; afterward you shall be gathered to your people." 3And Moses said to the people, "Arm men from among you for the war, that they may go against Mĭd'ĭăn, to execute the LORD's vengeance on Midian. 4 You shall send a thousand from each of the tribes of Israel to the war." 5 So there were provided, out of the thousands of Israel, a thousand from each tribe, twelve thousand armed for war.

31.6
Num 10.9

6And Moses sent them to the war, a thousand from each tribe, together with Phĭn'ĕhăs the son of Elĕā'zăr the priest, with the vessels of the sanctuary and the trumpets for the alarm in his hand. 7 They warred against Mĭd'ĭăn, as the LORD commanded Moses, and slew every male. 8 They slew

31.8
Josh 13.21,
22;
ver 16

the kings of Mĭd'ĭăn with the rest of their slain, Ēvī, Rĕkĕm, Zúr, Húr, and Rēbá, the five kings of Midian; and they also slew Bālaăm the son of Bēor with the sword. 9And the people of Israel took captive the women of Mĭd'ĭăn and their little ones; and they took as booty all their cattle, their flocks, and all their goods. 10All their cities in the places where they dwelt, and all their encampments, they burned with fire, 11 and took all the spoil and all the

31.11
Deut 20.14

booty, both of man and of beast. 12 Then they brought the captives and the booty and the spoil to Moses, and to Elĕā'zăr the priest, and to the congregation of the people of Israel, at the camp on the plains of Mōăb by the Jordan at Jĕr'ĭchō.

2. *The command to exterminate: rite of purification*

13 Moses, and Elĕā'zăr the priest, and all the leaders of the congregation, went forth to meet them outside the camp. 14And

Moses was angry with the officers of the army, the commanders of thousands and the commanders of hundreds, who had come from service in the war. 15 Moses said to them, "Have you let all the women live? 16 Behold, these caused the people of Israel, by the counsel of Bālaàm, to act treacherously against the LORD in the matter of Pē′or, and so the plague came among the congregation of the LORD. 17 Now therefore, kill every male among the little ones, and kill every woman who has known man by lying with him. 18 But all the young girls who have not known man by lying with him, keep alive for yourselves. 19 Encamp outside the camp seven days; whoever of you has killed any person, and whoever has touched any slain, purify yourselves and your captives on the third day and on the seventh day. 20 You shall purify every garment, every article of skin, all work of goats' hair, and every article of wood."

21 And Ēlēä′zàr the priest said to the men of war who had gone to battle: "This is the statute of the law which the LORD has commanded Moses: 22 only the gold, the silver, the bronze, the iron, the tin, and the lead, 23 everything that can stand the fire, you shall pass through the fire, and it shall be clean. Nevertheless it shall also be purified with the water of impurity; and whatever cannot stand the fire, you shall pass through the water. 24 You must wash your clothes on the seventh day, and you shall be clean; and afterward you shall come into the camp."

3. The division of the booty

25 The LORD said to Moses, 26 "Take the count of the booty that was taken, both of man and of beast, you and Ēlēä′zàr the priest and the heads of the fathers' houses of the congregation; 27 and divide the booty into two parts, between the warriors who went out to battle and all the congregation. 28 And levy for the LORD a tribute from the men of war who went out to battle, one out of five hundred, of the persons and of the oxen and of the asses and of the flocks; 29 take it from their half, and give it to Ēlēä′zàr the priest as an offering to the LORD. 30 And from the people of Israel's half you shall take one drawn out of every fifty, of the persons, of the oxen, of the asses, and of the flocks, of all the cattle, and give them to the Lēvītes who have charge of the tabernacle of the LORD." 31 And Moses and Ēlēä′zàr the priest did as the LORD commanded Moses.

32 Now the booty remaining of the spoil that the men of war took was: six hundred and seventy-five thousand sheep, 33 seventy-two thousand cattle, 34 sixty-one thousand asses, 35 and thirty-two thousand persons in all, women who had not known man by lying with him. 36 And the half, the portion of those who had gone out to war, was in number three hundred and thirty-seven thousand five hundred sheep, 37 and the LORD's tribute of sheep was six hundred and seventy-five. 38 The cattle were thirty-six thousand, of which the LORD's tribute was seventy-two. 39 The asses were thirty thousand five hundred, of which the LORD's tribute was sixty-one. 40 The persons were sixteen thousand, of which the LORD's tribute was thirty-two persons. 41 And Moses gave the

Cross-references (margin)

31.16 Num 25.1–9; 24.14; 2 Pet 2.15; Rev 2.14
*31.17 Judg 21.11
31.19 Num 19.11–22
31.23 Num 19.9, 17
31.24 Lev 11.25
*31.26ff
31.28 Num 18.21–30
31.30 Num 3.7,8, 25; 18.3,4
31.32 Gen 49.27; Ex 15.9
31.37 ver 38,41
31.41 see Num 18.8,9

31.17 However, the Midianites were not exterminated for they oppressed the Israelites later on in Canaan. See Judg 6.1, 2.

31.26ff The *booty* (all that had been seized) was counted and equally divided among everyone, whether soldier or civilian.

tribute, which was the offering for the LORD, to Ĕlëä′zăr the priest, as the LORD commanded Moses.

42 From the people of Israel's half, which Moses separated from that of the men who had gone to war— 43 now the congregation's half was three hundred and thirty-seven thousand five hundred sheep, 44 thirty-six thousand cattle, 45 and thirty thousand five hundred asses, 46 and sixteen thousand persons— 47 from the people of Israel's half Moses took one of every fifty, both of persons and of beasts, and gave them to the Lēvītes who had charge of the tabernacle of the LORD; as the LORD commanded Moses.

31.47
ver 30

4. The offerings of the officers and captains

48 Then the officers who were over the thousands of the army, the captains of thousands and the captains of hundreds, came near to Moses, 49 and said to Moses, "Your servants have counted the men of war who are under our command, and there is not a man missing from us. 50And we have brought the LORD's offering, what each man found, articles of gold, armlets and bracelets, signet rings, earrings, and beads, to make atonement for ourselves before the LORD." 51And Moses and Ĕlëä′zăr the priest received from them the gold, all wrought articles. 52And all the gold of the offering that they offered to the LORD, from the commanders of thousands and the commanders of hundreds, was sixteen thousand seven hundred and fifty shekels. 53 (The men of war had taken booty, every man for himself.) 54And Moses and Ĕlëä′zăr the priest received the gold from the commanders of thousands and of hundreds, and brought it into the tent of meeting, as a memorial for the people of Israel before the LORD.

31.50
Ex 30.12,
16

31.53
ver 32;
Deut 20.14
31.54
Ex 30.16

l. The beginning of the settlements: Reuben and Gad in Gilead

1. Their desire to settle east of Jordan

32 Now the sons of Reubën and the sons of Găd had a very great multitude of cattle; and they saw the land of Jāzĕr and the land of Gĭl′ëăd, and behold, the place was a place for cattle. 2 So the sons of Găd and the sons of Reubën came and said to Moses and to Ĕlëä′zăr the priest and to the leaders of the congregation, 3 "Ăt′ărŏth, Dībŏn, Jāzĕr, Nĭmrăh, Hĕshbŏn, Ĕlëä′lĕh, Sēbăm, Nēbō, and Bēŏn, 4 the land which the LORD smote before the congregation of Israel, is a land for cattle; and your servants have cattle." 5And they said, "If we have found favor in your sight, let this land be given to your servants for a possession; do not take us across the Jordan."

32.1
Ex 12.38;
Num 21.32

32.3
ver 36
Beth-
nimrah;
ver 38
Sibmah;
ver 38
Baal-meon

6 But Moses said to the sons of Găd and to the sons of Reubën, "Shall your brethren go to the war while you sit here? 7 Why will you discourage the heart of the people of Israel from going over into the land which the LORD has given them? 8 Thus did your fathers, when I sent them from Kā′dĕsh-barnē′ă to see the land. 9 For when they went up to the Valley of Ĕshcŏl, and saw the land, they discouraged the heart of the people of Israel from going into the land which the LORD had given them. 10And the LORD's anger was kindled on that day, and he swore, saying, 11 'Surely none of the men who came up out of Egypt, from twenty years old and upward, shall see the land which I swore to give to Abraham, to Isaac, and to Jacob, because they have not wholly followed me;

32.7
Num 13.27–
14.4
32.8
Num 13.3,
26

32.10
Num 14.11,
21;
Deut 1.34
32.11
Num 14.28–
30;
Deut 1.35

12 none except Cālĕb the son of Jĕphŭn′nĕh the Kĕn′ĭzzīte and Joshua the son of Nŭn, for they have wholly followed the LORD.' 13And the LORD's anger was kindled against Israel, and he made them wander in the wilderness forty years, until all the generation that had done evil in the sight of the LORD was consumed. 14And behold, you have risen in your fathers' stead, a brood of sinful men, to increase still more the fierce anger of the LORD against Israel! 15 For if you turn away from following him, he will again abandon them in the wilderness; and you will destroy all this people."

2. The agreement to help the others settle west of Jordan

16 Then they came near to him, and said, "We will build sheepfolds here for our flocks, and cities for our little ones, 17 but we will take up arms, ready to go before the people of Israel, until we have brought them to their place; and our little ones shall live in the fortified cities because of the inhabitants of the land. 18 We will not return to our homes until the people of Israel have inherited each his inheritance. 19 For we will not inherit with them on the other side of the Jordan and beyond; because our inheritance has come to us on this side of the Jordan to the east." 20 So Moses said to them, "If you will do this, if you will take up arms to go before the LORD for the war, 21 and every armed man of you will pass over the Jordan before the LORD, until he has driven out his enemies from before him 22 and the land is subdued before the LORD; then after that you shall return and be free of obligation to the LORD and to Israel; and this land shall be your possession before the LORD. 23 But if you will not do so, behold, you have sinned against the LORD; and be sure your sin will find you out. 24 Build cities for your little ones, and folds for your sheep; and do what you have promised." 25And the sons of Găd and the sons of Reubĕn said to Moses, "Your servants will do as my lord commands. 26 Our little ones, our wives, our flocks, and all our cattle, shall remain there in the cities of Gĭl′ĕăd; 27 but your servants will pass over, every man who is armed for war, before the LORD to battle, as my lord orders."

3. Moses' decision

28 So Moses gave command concerning them to Ĕleā′zăr the priest, and to Joshua the son of Nŭn, and to the heads of the fathers' houses of the tribes of the people of Israel. 29And Moses said to them, "If the sons of Găd and the sons of Reubĕn, every man who is armed to battle before the LORD, will pass with you over the Jordan and the land shall be subdued before you, then you shall give them the land of Gĭl′ĕăd for a possession; 30 but if they will not pass over with you armed, they shall have possessions among you in the land of Cānaàn." 31And the sons of Găd and the sons of Reubĕn answered, "As the LORD has said to your servants, so we will do. 32 We will pass over armed before the LORD into the land of Cānaàn, and the possession of our inheritance shall remain with us beyond the Jordan."

4. The half-tribe of Manasseh settles in Gilead

33 And Moses gave to them, to the sons of Găd and to the sons of Reubĕn and to the half-tribe of Mănăs′sĕh the son of Joseph,

32.12
Num 14.24;
Deut 1.36

32.13
Num 14.33–35;
26.64,65

32.15
Deut 30.17, 18

32.17
Josh 4.12, 13

32.18
Josh 22.1–4

32.19
ver 33

32.20
Deut 3.18

32.22
Deut 3.12–20

32.24
ver 16,34

32.26
Josh 1.14
32.27
Josh 4.12

32.28
Josh 1.13

32.29
ver 1

32.33
Deut 3.12–17;
Josh 12.1–6;
Num 21.24, 33,35

the kingdom of Sĭhón king of the Ăm'órītes and the kingdom of Og king of Báshán, the land and its cities with their territories, the cities of the land throughout the country. 34And the sons of Găd built Dībón, At'áróth, Arō'ér, 35At'róth-shō'phăn, Jāzér, Jŏg'bëháh, 36 Běth-nĭm'ráh and Běth-hā'rán, fortified cities, and folds for sheep. 37And the sons of Reubën built Hěshbón, Ëlëä'lëh, Kĭr'ĭáthā'ĭm, 38 Nēbō, and Bā'ál-mē'ón (their names to be changed), and Sĭbmáh; and they gave other names to the cities which they built. 39And the sons of Măçhĭr the son of Mánăs'sĕh went to Gĭl'ëäd and took it, and dispossessed the Ăm'órītes who were in it. 40And Moses gave Gĭl'ëäd to Măçhĭr the son of Mánăs'-

32.41
Judg 10.4

sĕh, and he settled in it. 41And Jāĭr the son of Mánăs'sĕh went and took their villages, and called them Hăvvóth-jā'ĭr.z 42And Nōbáh went and took Kēnáth and its villages, and called it Nobah, after his own name.

J. The stages of Israel's journey from Egypt to Canaan

33.1
Ps 77.20;
Mic 6.4

33 These are the stages of the people of Israel, when they went forth out of the land of Egypt by their hosts under the leadership of Moses and Aaron. 2 Moses wrote down their starting places, stage by stage, by command of the LORD; and these are their stages according to their starting places. 3 They set

33.3
Ex 12.37;
14.8

out from Răm'ĕsḝs in the first month, on the fifteenth day of the first month; on the day after the passover the people of Israel

33.4
Ex 12.12

went out triumphantly in the sight of all the Egyptians, 4 while the Egyptians were burying all their first-born, whom the LORD had struck down among them; upon their gods also the LORD executed judgments.

5 So the people of Israel set out from Răm'ĕsḝs, and encamped

33.6
Ex 13.20
33.7
Ex 14.2,9
33.8
Ex 14.22

at Sŭccóth. 6 And they set out from Sŭccóth, and encamped at Ēthám, which is on the edge of the wilderness. 7And they set out from Ēthám, and turned back to Pī'-háhī'róth, which is east of Bā'ál-zĕphŏn; and they encamped before Mĭgdŏl. 8And they set out from before Háhī'róth, and passed through the midst of the sea into the wilderness, and they went a three days' journey in the

33.9
Ex 15.27

wilderness of Ēthám, and encamped at Maráh. 9And they set out from Maráh, and came to Ēlĭm; at Elim there were twelve springs of water and seventy palm trees, and they encamped there.

33.11
Ex 16.1

10And they set out from Ēlĭm, and encamped by the Red Sea. 11And they set out from the Red Sea, and encamped in the wilderness of Sin. 12And they set out from the wilderness of Sin, and encamped at Dŏphkáh. 13And they set out from Dŏphkáh, and

33.14
Ex 17.1

encamped at Ālúsh. 14And they set out from Ālúsh, and encamped at Rěph'ĭdĭm, where there was no water for the people to drink.

33.15
Ex 19.1
33.16
Num 11.34
33.17
Num 11.35

15And they set out from Rěph'ĭdĭm, and encamped in the wilderness of Sī'näï. 16And they set out from the wilderness of Sī'näï, and encamped at Kĭb'róth-hăttā'áváh. 17And they set out from Kĭb'róth-hăttā'áváh, and encamped at Házē'róth. 18And they set out from Házē'róth, and encamped at Rĭthmáh. 19And they set out

33.20
see Josh
10.29

from Rĭthmáh, and encamped at Rĭm'mòn-pē'rĕz. 20And they set out from Rĭm'mòn-pē'rĕz, and encamped at Lĭbnáh. 21And they set out from Lĭbnáh, and encamped at Rĭssáh. 22And they set out from Rĭssáh, and encamped at Kēhēlā'tháh. 23And they set

z That is the villages of Jair

out from Kēhėlā'tháh, and encamped at Mount Shēphėr. 24And
they set out from Mount Shēphėr, and encamped at Hárā'dáh.
25And they set out from Hárā'dáh, and encamped at Măkhē'lŏth.
26And they set out from Măkhē'lŏth, and encamped at Tāhăth.
27And they set out from Tāhăth, and encamped at Tērāh. 28And
they set out from Tērāh, and encamped at Mīthkáh. 29 And they
set out from Mīthkáh, and encamped at Hăshmō'náh. 30And they
set out from Hăshmō'náh, and encamped at Mȯṣē'rŏth. 31And
they set out from Mȯṣē'rŏth, and encamped at Běnė-jā'ákán. 32And
they set out from Běnė-jā'ákán, and encamped at Hor'-hăggĭd'găd.
33And they set out from Hor'-hăggĭd'găd, and encamped at
Jŏt'bátháh. 34And they set out from Jŏt'bátháh, and encamped at
Ăbrō'náh. 35And they set out from Ăbrō'náh, and encamped at
Ēz'ĭŏn-gē'bėr. 36And they set out from Ēz'ĭŏn-gē'bėr, and encamped in the wilderness of Zĭn (that is, Kādësh). 37And they set
out from Kādësh, and encamped at Mount Hor, on the edge of
the land of Ēdȯm.

38 And Aaron the priest went up Mount Hor at the command
of the LORD, and died there, in the fortieth year after the people of
Israel had come out of the land of Egypt, on the first day of the
fifth month. 39And Aaron was a hundred and twenty-three years
old when he died on Mount Hor.

40 And the Cā'naánīte, the king of Ąrȧd, who dwelt in the
Nĕgĕb in the land of Cānaán, heard of the coming of the people
of Israel.

41 And they set out from Mount Hor, and encamped at Zălmō'-
náh. 42And they set out from Zălmō'náh, and encamped at Pūnȯn.
43And they set out from Pūnȯn, and encamped at Ōbŏth. 44And
they set out from Ōbŏth, and encamped at Ī'yė-ăb'árĭm, in the
territory of Mōáb. 45And they set out from Ĭyĭm, and encamped at
Dĭ'bȯn-găd. 46And they set out from Dĭ'bȯn-găd, and encamped
at Ăl'mȯn-dĭblȧthā'ĭm. 47And they set out from Ăl'mȯn-dĭblȧthā'-
ĭm, and encamped in the mountains of Ăb'árĭm, before Nēbō.
48And they set out from the mountains of Ăb'árĭm, and encamped
in the plains of Mōáb by the Jordan at Jĕr'ĭçhō; 49 they encamped
by the Jordan from Bĕth-jĕsh'ĭmȯth as far as Ā'bėl-shĭt'tĭm in the
plains of Mōáb.

K. God's commands concerning Canaan

1. The command to drive out the inhabitants

50 And the LORD said to Moses in the plains of Mōáb by the
Jordan at Jĕr'ĭçhō, 51 "Say to the people of Israel, When you pass
over the Jordan into the land of Cānaán, 52 then you shall drive
out all the inhabitants of the land from before you, and destroy
all their figured stones, and destroy all their molten images, and
demolish all their high places; 53 and you shall take possession of
the land and settle in it, for I have given the land to you to possess
it. 54 You shall inherit the land by lot according to your families;
to a large tribe you shall give a large inheritance, and to a small
tribe you shall give a small inheritance; wherever the lot falls to any
man, that shall be his; according to the tribes of your fathers you

Marginal references (right column):

33.30
Deut 10.6

33.33
Deut 10.7

33.35
Deut 2.8
*33.36
Num 20.1

33.37
Num 20.16,
22; 21.4

33.38
Num 20.25,
28;
Deut 10.6

33.40
Num 21.1

*33.41

33.43
Num 21.10
33.44
Num 21.11

33.47
Num 27.12

33.48
Num 22.1
33.49
Num 25.1

33.52
Ex 23.24,
33; 34.13;
Deut 7.2,5;
12.3;
Josh 11.12

33.54
Num 26.53-
55

33.36 Ezion-geber, see note to 1 Ki 9.26.
33.41 Zalmonah. The exact location is not
known, however, the camp site is obviously
en route to Canaan from Egypt.

*33.55
Josh 23.13;
Ps 106.34,
36

shall inherit. 55 But if you do not drive out the inhabitants of the land from before you, then those of them whom you let remain shall be as pricks in your eyes and thorns in your sides, and they shall trouble you in the land where you dwell. 56And I will do to you as I thought to do to them."

2. *The boundaries of the land*

34.2
Gen 17.8;
Deut 1.7;
Ps 78.55;
Ezek 47.15
34.3
Josh 15.1–3

34 The LORD said to Moses, 2 "Command the people of Israel, and say to them, When you enter the land of Cānaån (this is the land that shall fall to you for an inheritance, the land of Canaan in its full extent), 3 your south side shall be from the wilderness of Zĭn along the side of Ēdŏm, and your southern boundary shall be from the end of the Salt Sea on the east; 4 and your boundary shall turn south of the ascent of Ăkrăb′bĭm, and cross to Zĭn, and its end shall be south of Kā′dĕsh-barnē′å; then it shall

34.5
Gen 15.18;
Josh 15.4,
47

go on to Hā′zar-ăd′dar, and pass along to Ăzmŏn; 5 and the boundary shall turn from Ăzmŏn to the Brook of Egypt, and its termination shall be at the sea.

6 "For the western boundary, you shall have the Great Sea and its*a* coast; this shall be your western boundary.

34.7
Ezek 47.15–
17
*34.8
Num 13.21

7 "This shall be your northern boundary: from the Great Sea you shall mark out your line to Mount Hor; 8 from Mount Hor you shall mark it out to the entrance of Hāmăth, and the end of the boundary shall be at Zēdăd; 9 then the boundary shall extend to Zĭphrŏn, and its end shall be at Hā′zar-ē′năn; this shall be your northern boundary.

34.11
2 Ki 23.33;
Deut 3.17;
Josh 11.2

10 "You shall mark out your eastern boundary from Hā′zar-ē′năn to Shĕphăm; 11 and the boundary shall go down from Shĕphăm to Rĭblăh on the east side of Ă′ĭn; and the boundary shall go down, and reach to the shoulder of the sea of Chĭn′nĕrĕth on the east; 12 and the boundary shall go down to the Jordan, and its end shall be at the Salt Sea. This shall be your land with its boundaries all round."

34.13
Josh 14.1,2

13 Moses commanded the people of Israel, saying, "This is the land which you shall inherit by lot, which the LORD has commanded to give to the nine tribes and to the half-tribe; 14 for the

34.14
Num 32.33;
Josh 14.2,3

tribe of the sons of Reubĕn by fathers' houses and the tribe of the sons of Găd by their fathers' houses have received their inheritance, and also the half-tribe of Mănăs′sĕh; 15 the two tribes and the half-tribe have received their inheritance beyond the Jordan at Jĕr′ĭchō eastward, toward the sunrise."

3. *The men chosen to divide the land*

34.17
Josh 14.1

16 The LORD said to Moses, 17 "These are the names of the men who shall divide the land to you for inheritance: Ēlĕ-ā′zăr the priest and Joshua the son of Nŭn. 18 You shall take one leader of

34.18
Num 1.4,16

every tribe, to divide the land for inheritance. 19 These are the

a Syr: Heb lacks *its*

33.55 Incomplete obedience invites evil consequences. God's charge to Israel to drive all the heathen inhabitants from Canaan was never completely obeyed and the malign influence of these depraved people contaminated Israel. It hastened their religious apostasy and led to the Babylonian captivity.

34.8 *to the entrance of Hamath*, that is, near Riblah. The boundary did not reach this far north until the reign of David.

names of the men: Of the tribe of Judah, Cālĕb the son of Jĕphŭn'-nĕh. 20 Of the tribe of the sons of Sĭm'ëon, Shĕm'ŭĕl the son of Ămmĭ'hŭd. 21 Of the tribe of Benjamin, Ĕlĭ'dăd the son of Chĭslón. 22 Of the tribe of the sons of Dan a leader, Bŭkkī the son of Jŏglī. 23 Of the sons of Joseph: of the tribe of the sons of Mănăs'sĕh a leader, Hăn'nĭĕl the son of Ē'phŏd. 24And of the tribe of the sons of Ē'phrăĭm a leader, Kĕm'ŭĕl the son of Shĭphtán. 25 Of the tribe of the sons of Zĕb'ŭlún a leader, Ĕlĭz'áphán the son of Parnăch. 26 Of the tribe of the sons of Ĭs'sáchar a leader, Păl'tĭĕl the son of Ăzzăn. 27And of the tribe of the sons of Ăshĕr a leader, Ăhĭ'hŭd the son of Shĕlŏ'mī. 28 Of the tribe of the sons of Năph'tálī a leader, Pĕd'áhĕl the son of Ămmĭ'hŭd. 29 These are the men whom the LORD commanded to divide the inheritance for the people of Israel in the land of Cănaán."

4. The Levitical cities
a. The forty-eight cities and pasture land

35 The LORD said to Moses in the plains of Mōăb by the Jordan at Jĕr'ĭchō, 2 "Command the people of Israel, that they give to the Lēvītes, from the inheritance of their possession, cities to dwell in; and you shall give to the Levites pasture lands round about the cities. 3 The cities shall be theirs to dwell in, and their pasture lands shall be for their cattle and for their livestock and for all their beasts. 4 The pasture lands of the cities, which you shall give to the Lēvītes, shall reach from the wall of the city outward a thousand cubits all round. 5And you shall measure, outside the city, for the east side two thousand cubits, and for the south side two thousand cubits, and for the west side two thousand cubits, and for the north side two thousand cubits, the city being in the middle; this shall belong to them as pasture land for their cities. 6 The cities which you give to the Lēvītes shall be the six cities of refuge, where you shall permit the manslayer to flee, and in addition to them you shall give forty-two cities. 7All the cities which you give to the Lēvītes shall be forty-eight, with their pasture lands. 8And as for the cities which you shall give from the possession of the people of Israel, from the larger tribes you shall take many, and from the smaller tribes you shall take few; each, in proportion to the inheritance which it inherits, shall give of its cities to the Lēvītes."

b. The cities of refuge

9 And the LORD said to Moses, 10 "Say to the people of Israel, When you cross the Jordan into the land of Cănaán, 11 then you shall select cities to be cities of refuge for you, that the manslayer who kills any person without intent may flee there. 12 The cities shall be for you a refuge from the avenger, that the manslayer may not die until he stands before the congregation for judgment. 13And the cities which you give shall be your six cities of refuge. 14 You shall give three cities beyond the Jordan, and three cities in the land of Cănaán, to be cities of refuge. 15 These six cities shall be for refuge for the people of Israel, and for the stranger and for

35.2
Lev 25.32–34;
Josh 14.3,4

35.6
Josh 20.7–9; 21.3,13,21,27,32,36,38

35.8
Num 26.54;
Lev 25.32–34;
Josh 21.1–42

35.11
Deut 19.1–13;
Ex 21.13
*35.12
Josh 20.2–6

35.15
ver 11

35.12 *from the avenger.* The cities of refuge implemented the new law, "an eye for an eye," by protecting the manslayer from the kinsman who, under the ancient custom of vendetta, was to avenge the death of the deceased.

the sojourner among them, that any one who kills any person without intent may flee there.

35.16
Ex 21.12,
14;
Lev 24.17

16 "But if he struck him down with an instrument of iron, so that he died, he is a murderer; the murderer shall be put to death. 17And if he struck him down with a stone in the hand, by which a man may die, and he died, he is a murderer; the murderer shall be put to death. 18 Or if he struck him down with a weapon of wood in the hand, by which a man may die, and he died, he is a mur-derer; the murderer shall be put to death. 19 The avenger of blood

35.19
ver 21,24,
27

shall himself put the murderer to death; when he meets him, he shall put him to death. 20And if he stabbed him from hatred, or hurled at him, lying in wait, so that he died, 21 or in enmity struck him down with his hand, so that he died, then he who struck the blow shall be put to death; he is a murderer; the avenger of blood shall put the murderer to death, when he meets him.

35.22
ver 11;
Ex 21.13

22 "But if he stabbed him suddenly without enmity, or hurled anything on him without lying in wait, 23 or used a stone, by which a man may die, and without seeing him cast it upon him, so that he died, though he was not his enemy, and did not seek his

35.24
ver 12

harm; 24 then the congregation shall judge between the manslayer and the avenger of blood, in accordance with these ordinances; 25 and the congregation shall rescue the manslayer from the hand of the avenger of blood, and the congregation shall restore him to his city of refuge, to which he had fled, and he shall live in it until the death of the high priest who was anointed with the holy oil. 26 But if the manslayer shall at any time go beyond the bounds of his city of refuge to which he fled, 27 and the avenger of blood finds him outside the bounds of his city of refuge, and the avenger of blood slays the manslayer, he shall not be guilty of blood. 28 For the man must remain in his city of refuge until the death of the high priest; but after the death of the high priest the manslayer may return to the land of his possession.

29 "And these things shall be for a statute and ordinance to you

35.30
ver 16;
Deut 17.6;
19.15;
Mt 18.16;
2 Cor 13.1;
Heb 10.28

throughout your generations in all your dwellings. 30 If any one kills a person, the murderer shall be put to death on the evidence of witnesses; but no person shall be put to death on the testimony of one witness. 31 Moreover you shall accept no ransom for the life of a murderer, who is guilty of death; but he shall be put to death. 32And you shall accept no ransom for him who has fled to his city of refuge, that he may return to dwell in the land before the death of the high priest. 33 You shall not thus pollute the land in which

35.33
Ps 106.38;
Gen 9.6

you live; for blood pollutes the land, and no expiation can be made for the land, for the blood that is shed in it, except by the blood

35.34
Lev 18.25;
Ex 29.45,
46

of him who shed it. 34 You shall not defile the land in which you live, in the midst of which I dwell; for I the LORD dwell in the midst of the people of Israel."

5. Laws concerning the marriage of heiresses

36.1
Num 26.29;
27.1

36 The heads of the fathers' houses of the families of the sons of Gĭl'ĕăd the son of Māchĭr, son of Mănăs'sĕh, of the fathers' houses of the sons of Joseph, came near and spoke before Moses and before the leaders, the heads of the fathers' houses of the people of Israel; 2 they said, "The LORD commanded my lord

36.2
Num 26.55;
33.54;
27.1,7

to give the land for inheritance by lot to the people of Israel; and my lord was commanded by the LORD to give the inheritance of

Zĕlō'phëhăd our brother to his daughters. 3 But if they are married
to any of the sons of the other tribes of the people of Israel then
their inheritance will be taken from the inheritance of our fathers,
and added to the inheritance of the tribe to which they belong; so it
will be taken away from the lot of our inheritance. 4And when the
jubilee of the people of Israel comes, then their inheritance will be
added to the inheritance of the tribe to which they belong; and
their inheritance will be taken from the inheritance of the tribe
of our fathers."

5 And Moses commanded the people of Israel according to the
word of the LORD, saying, "The tribe of the sons of Joseph is right.
6 This is what the LORD commands concerning the daughters of
Zĕlō'phëhăd, 'Let them marry whom they think best; only, they
shall marry within the family of the tribe of their father. 7 The
inheritance of the people of Israel shall not be transferred from
one tribe to another; for every one of the people of Israel shall
cleave to the inheritance of the tribe of his fathers. 8And every
daughter who possesses an inheritance in any tribe of the people
of Israel shall be wife to one of the family of the tribe of her father,
so that every one of the people of Israel may possess the inheritance
of his fathers. 9 So no inheritance shall be transferred from one
tribe to another; for each of the tribes of the people of Israel shall
cleave to its own inheritance.' "

10 The daughters of Zĕlō'phëhăd did as the LORD commanded
Moses; 11 for Mahlăh, Tĭrzăh, Hŏglăh, Mĭlcăh, and Noah, the
daughters of Zĕlō'phëhăd, were married to sons of their father's
brothers. 12 They were married into the families of the sons of
Mănăs'sĕh the son of Joseph, and their inheritance remained in
the tribe of the family of their father.

13 These are the commandments and the ordinances which the
LORD commanded by Moses to the people of Israel in the plains
of Mōăb by the Jordan at Jĕr'ĭchō.

36.4
Lev 25.10

36.6
ver 12

36.8
1 Chr 23.22

36.11
Num 27.1

36.13
Num 22.1;
Lev 26.46;
27.34

INTRODUCTION TO

THE FIFTH BOOK OF MOSES

COMMONLY CALLED

DEUTERONOMY

Authorship and Background: The title of this book is the English form of the Greek word *deuteronomion*, "second law," or "repetition of the law," which is the Septuagint title for the fifth book of the Pentateuch. The Hebrew title, "These are the words," is simply the first two Hebrew words in the text. Jewish and Samaritan traditions represent Moses as the author. In modern times Mosaic authorship has been disputed by some critical scholars. Many acknowledge, however, that the contents of the book are generally of Mosaic origin. The death of Moses is clearly an addition after his time. The book itself claims Mosaic authority, asserting that "Moses undertook to explain this law, saying" (1.5) and "Moses wrote this law" (31.9) and commanded the Levites, "Take this book of the law, and put it by the side of the ark of the covenant" (31.26).

Deuteronomy presupposes what is found in Exodus and Leviticus. Israel had wandered in the wilderness for almost two decades and now camped outside the Promised Land, ready to go in. But Moses, because of his sin, had been refused permission to enter Canaan. He was to be replaced by Joshua. Before taking his departure from the people, Moses oriented the new generation to the covenantal relationship which they bore to God and explained the terms of that covenant and its indispensable condition of obedience.

Characteristics: Deuteronomy is hortatory in the sense that Moses warns the people of the consequences of disobedience, and urges upon them the necessity of walking according to the will of God. In some measure the book is an inspired account of reminiscences of the prayers, inner life, and thoughts of Moses. Written in prose and poetry, the material is imaginative yet didactic. Moses evidences outbursts of human passion in indignation and personal appeal (9.13–21; 10.10–21). He addresses all of the people in language easily comprehended, specifying what God requires of them. The substance of his discourses is summed up in the words, "What does the LORD your God require of you, but to fear the LORD your God, to walk in all his ways, to love him, to serve the LORD your God with all your heart and with all your soul" (10.12).

Contents:

I.   Moses' first discourse. 1.1—4.43: Moses recounts in retrospect what God has done for Israel: the journey, the successes, and God's gift of the land to the people. How Moses bore with the sins of the people. God having acted, Israel must listen and obey. Idolatry is a peril. The LORD is God. The three cities of refuge designated.

II.   Moses' second address. 4.44—26.19: An extended review of the Ten
         Commandments. God on the mountain; the purpose of the Law; the
         greatest commandment; what children are to be taught. The command
         to wipe out idolatry by exterminating the Canaanites. Illustrations of
         past discipline because of sins like the golden calf. An exhortation to
         obedience with blessing. Moses' exposition of principal laws. The one
         central place of worship. Idolatry to be punished. The law of unclean
         food and the tithe of fruit. Directions about slaves and the poor;
         manumission. The feasts of the Passover, harvest, and tabernacles.
         The duties of officials in the administration of justice: courts, the king,
         priests, and the prophet. Moses' word on criminal law: homicide, theft,
         and perjury. The laws concerning wars in the future. Sundry laws:
         unsolved murder, women taken in war, inheritance, wicked sons, sex,
         divorce, corporal punishment. Thanksgiving.

III.   The covenant renewed. 27.1—30.20: Stones to be erected when the
         Jordan is crossed. The Law to be ratified. Blessings for obedience and
         cursing for disobedience. The covenant renewed; the choice of life
         and death set before the people.

IV.   Moses' final words and death. 31.1—34.12: Moses' last words: Joshua
         appointed and commissioned; the Law to be placed in the ark. The son
         of Moses. The blessing of Moses. The command to prepare for death.
         The death and burial of Moses.

THE FIFTH BOOK OF MOSES

COMMONLY CALLED

DEUTERONOMY

I. Moses' first address 1.1–4.43

A. The introduction

★1.1

1 These are the words that Moses spoke to all Israel beyond the Jordan in the wilderness, in the Ạr'ȧbȧh over against Suph, between Pāràn and Tōphėl, Lābȧn, Hȧzē'rȯth, and Dī'-zȧhȧb.

★1.2
★1.3
Num 33.38

2 It is eleven days' journey from Horĕb by the way of Mount Sēir to Kā'dĕsh-barnē'ȧ. ³And in the fortieth year, on the first day of the eleventh month, Moses spoke to the people of Israel according to all that the LORD had given him in commandment to them,

1.4
Num 21.24,
33
★1.5

⁴ after he had defeated Sīhȯn the king of the Ȧm'ȯrītes, who lived in Hĕshbȯn, and Ŏg the king of Bāshȧn, who lived in Ȧsh'tȧrŏth and in Ĕd'rë-ī. ⁵ Beyond the Jordan, in the land of Mȯȧb, Moses

B. The guidance of God from Horeb to Kadesh

1. The command to enter the land

1.6
Ex 3.1;
Num 10.11–
13

undertook to explain this law, saying, 6 "The LORD our God said to us in Horĕb, 'You have stayed long enough at this mountain; ⁷ turn and take your journey, and go to the hill country of the Ȧm'ȯrītes, and to all their neighbors in the Ạr'ȧbȧh, in the hill country and in the lowland, and in the Nĕgĕb, and by the seacoast, the land of the Cā'naȧnītes, and Lebanon, as far as the great river,

1.8
Gen 12.7;
15.18;
17.7,8;
26.4; 28.13

the river Eūphrā'tēṣ. 8 Behold, I have set the land before you; go in and take possession of the land which the LORD swore to your fathers, to Abraham, to Isaac, and to Jacob, to give to them and to their descendants after them.'

2. The choice of leaders

1.9
Ex 18.18
1.10
Gen 15.5;
Deut 10.22
1.11
Gen 22.17;
Ex 32.13
1.13
Ex 18.21

9 "At that time I said to you, 'I am not able alone to bear you; ¹⁰ the LORD your God has multiplied you, and behold, you are this day as the stars of heaven for multitude. ¹¹ May the LORD, the God of your fathers, make you a thousand times as many as you are, and bless you, as he has promised you! ¹² How can I bear alone the weight and burden of you and your strife? ¹³ Choose wise, understanding, and experienced men, according to your tribes,

---

1.1 *beyond the Jordan.* This expression has been interpreted by many to be equivalent to our name "Trans-Jordan," but in 3.20, 25; 11.30 it is not used in this technical sense and clearly means "Canaan." Some believe that the expression in Deuteronomy is used relative to the speaker or writer. Since Moses never got beyond Moab, *beyond the Jordan* in verses 1 and 5 implies that the writer of the introduction was in Canaan.

1.2 *eleven days' journey.* This interesting note, confirmed by modern travelers, highlights the thirty-eight lost years resulting from Israel's disobedience at Kadesh-barnea.

Horeb, an alternate designation for Sinai.

The name occurs only twelve times in the Pentateuch, and nine of these are in Deuteronomy. The name Sinai occurs thirty-one times in the Pentateuch, but it appears only once in Deuteronomy (33.2).

1.3 *fortieth year,* after the exodus from Egypt. The Israelites crossed the Jordan in the first month of the next year (Josh 4.19), and of this period of about 40 days, 30 were spent in mourning for Moses (34.8). Therefore, the events in this book took place within a week or so.

1.5 *undertook to explain* clearly indicates that Deuteronomy is an interpretation, not a mere repetition of the law.

and I will appoint them as your heads.' ¹⁴And you answered me, 'The thing that you have spoken is good for us to do.' ¹⁵ So I took the heads of your tribes, wise and experienced men, and set them as heads over you, commanders of thousands, commanders of hundreds, commanders of fifties, commanders of tens, and officers, throughout your tribes. ¹⁶And I charged your judges at that time, 'Hear the cases between your brethren, and judge righteously between a man and his brother or the alien that is with him. ¹⁷ You shall not be partial in judgment; you shall hear the small and the great alike; you shall not be afraid of the face of man, for the judgment is God's; and the case that is too hard for you, you shall bring to me, and I will hear it.' ¹⁸And I commanded you at that time all the things that you should do.

3. *The episode at Kadesh-barnea: the report of the spies*

¹⁹ "And we set out from Horĕb, and went through all that great and terrible wilderness which you saw, on the way to the hill country of the Ăm'ŏrītes, as the LORD our God commanded us; and we came to Kā'dĕsh-barnē'ă. ²⁰And I said to you, 'You have come to the hill country of the Ăm'ŏrītes, which the LORD our God gives us. ²¹ Behold, the LORD your God has set the land before you; go up, take possession, as the LORD, the God of your fathers, has told you; do not fear or be dismayed.' ²² Then all of you came near me, and said, 'Let us send men before us, that they may explore the land for us, and bring us word again of the way by which we must go up and the cities into which we shall come.' ²³ The thing seemed good to me, and I took twelve men of you, one man for each tribe; ²⁴ and they turned and went up into the hill country, and came to the Valley of Ĕshcŏl and spied it out. ²⁵And they took in their hands some of the fruit of the land and brought it down to us, and brought us word again, and said, 'It is a good land which the LORD our God gives us.'

²⁶ "Yet you would not go up, but rebelled against the command of the LORD your God; ²⁷ and you murmured in your tents, and said, 'Because the LORD hated us he has brought us forth out of the land of Egypt, to give us into the hand of the Ăm'ŏrītes, to destroy us. ²⁸ Whither are we going up? Our brethren have made our hearts melt, saying, "The people are greater and taller than we; the cities are great and fortified up to heaven; and moreover we have seen the sons of the Ăn'ăkĭm there."' ²⁹ Then I said to you, 'Do not be in dread or afraid of them. ³⁰ The LORD your God who goes before you will himself fight for you, just as he did for you in Egypt before your eyes, ³¹ and in the wilderness, where you have seen how the LORD your God bore you, as a man bears his son, in all the way that you went until you came to this place.' ³² Yet in spite of this word you did not believe the LORD your God, ³³ who went before you in the way to seek you out a place to pitch your tents, in fire by night, to show you by what way you should go, and in the cloud by day.

³⁴ "And the LORD heard your words, and was angered, and he swore, ³⁵ 'Not one of these men of this evil generation shall see the good land which I swore to give to your fathers, ³⁶ except

1.15 Ex 18.25
1.16 Deut 16.18; Lev 24.22
1.17 Lev 19.15; Jas 2.1; Ex 18.19–26
1.19 ver 2; Deut 8.15; Num 13.26
1.21 Josh 1.9
1.23 Num 13.1–3
1.24 Num 13.22–24
1.25 Num 13.27
1.26 Num 14.1–4
1.27 Deut 9.28; Ps 106.25
*1.28 Num 13.28, 31–33; Deut 9.1,2
1.30 Ex 14.14; Deut 3.22
1.31 Deut 32.11, 12; Acts 13.18
1.32 Ps 106.24
1.33 Ex 13.21; Num 10.33
1.34 Num 14.22–30
*1.36

1.28 *fortified up to heaven.* The walls of the large Canaanite cities ranged from 30 to 50 feet high.

1.36 Caleb and Joshua both are commended as men who *wholly followed the* LORD (see Num 32.12; Josh 14.8, 9,14). They

Cāleb the son of Jĕphŭn'nĕh; he shall see it, and to him and to his children I will give the land upon which he has trodden, because he has wholly followed the LORD!' 37 The LORD was angry with me also on your account, and said, 'You also shall not go in there; 38 Joshua the son of Nŭn, who stands before you, he shall enter; encourage him, for he shall cause Israel to inherit it. 39 Moreover your little ones, who you said would become a prey, and your children, who this day have no knowledge of good or evil, shall go in there, and to them I will give it, and they shall possess it. 40 But as for you, turn, and journey into the wilderness in the direction of the Red Sea.'

41 Then you answered me, 'We have sinned against the LORD; we will go up and fight, just as the LORD our God commanded us.' And every man of you girded on his weapons of war, and thought it easy to go up into the hill country. 42And the LORD said to me, 'Say to them, Do not go up or fight, for I am not in the midst of you; lest you be defeated before your enemies.' 43 So I spoke to you, and you would not hearken; but you rebelled against the command of the LORD, and were presumptuous and went up into the hill country. 44 Then the Ăm'ŏrītes who lived in that hill country came out against you and chased you as bees do and beat you down in Sĕir as far as Hormȧh. 45And you returned and wept before the LORD; but the LORD did not hearken to your voice or give ear to you. 46 So you remained at Kādĕsh many days, the days that you remained there.

C. The years in the wilderness

1. The command to leave the Edomites alone

2 "Then we turned, and journeyed into the wilderness in the direction of the Red Sea, as the LORD told me; and for many days we went about Mount Sĕir. 2 Then the LORD said to me, 3 'You have been going about this mountain country long enough; turn northward. 4And command the people, You are about to pass through the territory of your brethren the sons of Ēsau, who live in Sĕir; and they will be afraid of you. So take good heed; 5 do not contend with them; for I will not give you any of their land, no, not so much as for the sole of the foot to tread on, because I have given Mount Sĕir to Ēsau as a possession. 6 You shall purchase food from them for money, that you may eat; and you shall also buy water of them for money, that you may drink. 7 For the LORD your God has blessed you in all the work of your hands; he knows your going through this great wilderness; these forty years the LORD your God has been with you; you have lacked nothing.' 8 So we went on, away from our brethren the sons of Ēsau who live in Sĕir, away from the Ăr'abȧh road from Ēlăth and Ēz'ĭ-ŏn-gē'bĕr.

2. The command to leave the Moabites alone

"And we turned and went in the direction of the wilderness of Mōȧb. 9And the LORD said to me, 'Do not harass Mōȧb or contend with them in battle, for I will not give you any of their land for a

1.37
Num 20.12;
Deut 3.26;
Ps 106.32
1.38
Num 14.30;
Deut 3.28;
31.7
1.39
Num 14.3,
31
1.40
Num 14.25
1.41
Num 14.40

1.42
Num 14.42

1.43
Num 14.44,
45

1.44
Ps 118.12

2.1
Num 21.4

2.4
Num 20.14

2.5
Josh 24.4

2.7
Deut 8.2–4

2.8
Judg 11.18

2.9
ver 18;
Num 21.28;
Gen 19.36,
37

were not perfect in the sense that they were sinless. Rather they were blameless in that they walked in obedience to what God commanded them with respect to entering the Promised Land. No higher commendation can be given a man.

possession, because I have given Ar to the sons of Lot for a possession.' 10 (The Ēmĭm formerly lived there, a people great and many, and tall as the Ăn'ākĭm; 11 like the Ăn'ākĭm they are also known as Rĕph'āĭm, but the Mō'ābĭtes call them Ēmĭm. 12 The Horītes also lived in Sēĭr formerly, but the sons of Ēsau dispossessed them, and destroyed them from before them, and settled in their stead; as Israel did to the land of their possession, which the LORD gave to them.) 13 'Now rise up, and go over the brook Zĕrĕd.' So we went over the brook Zered. 14And the time from our leaving Kā'dĕsh-barnē'ă until we crossed the brook Zĕrĕd was thirty-eight years, until the entire generation, that is, the men of war, had perished from the camp, as the LORD had sworn to them. 15 For indeed the hand of the LORD was against them, to destroy them from the camp, until they had perished.

*2.10ff
Gen 14.5;
Num 13.22, 33

2.12
ver 22

2.14
Num 13.26;
14.29–35;
26.64;
Deut 1.34, 35

2.15
Ps 106.26

3. The command to leave the Ammonites alone

16 "So when all the men of war had perished and were dead from among the people, 17 the LORD said to me, 18 'This day you are to pass over the boundary of Mōăb at Ar; 19 and when you approach the frontier of the sons of Ămmŏn, do not harass them or contend with them, for I will not give you any of the land of the sons of Ammon as a possession, because I have given it to the sons of Lot for a possession.' 20 (That also is known as a land of Rĕph'āĭm; Rephaim formerly lived there, but the Ăm'mŏnītes call them Zămzŭm'mĭm, 21 a people great and many, and tall as the Ăn'ākĭm; but the LORD destroyed them before them; and they dispossessed them, and settled in their stead; 22 as he did for the sons of Ēsau, who live in Sēĭr, when he destroyed the Horītes before them, and they dispossessed them, and settled in their stead even to this day. 23As for the Ăvvĭm, who lived in villages as far as Gază, the Căph'tŏrĭm, who came from Căphtor, destroyed them and settled in their stead.) 24 'Rise up, take your journey, and go over the valley of the Arnŏn; behold, I have given into your hand Sīhŏn the Ăm'ŏrīte, king of Hĕshbŏn, and his land; begin to take possession, and contend with him in battle. 25 This day I will begin to put the dread and fear of you upon the peoples that are under the whole heaven, who shall hear the report of you and shall tremble and be in anguish because of you.'

2.19
ver 9

2.21
See ver 10

*2.22
Gen 36.8;
ver 12

*2.23
Josh 13.3;
Gen 10.14;
Amos 9.7

2.24
Judg 11.18

2.25
Ex 15.14, 15;
Deut 11.25;
Josh 2.9,10

D. The victories over the Amorites

1. Over Sihon, king of Heshbon

26 "So I sent messengers from the wilderness of Kĕd'ĕmŏth to Sīhŏn the king of Hĕshbŏn, with words of peace, saying, 27 'Let me pass through your land; I will go only by the road, I will turn aside neither to the right nor to the left. 28 You shall sell me food for money, that I may eat, and give me water for money, that I may drink; only let me pass through on foot, 29 as the sons of Ēsau who live in Sēĭr and the Mō'ābĭtes who live in Ar did for me, until I go over the Jordan into the land which the LORD our God

2.26
Deut 20.10

2.27
Num 21.21, 22

2.28
Num 20.19

2.10-12 Some regard these verses as a scribal insertion; similarly 2.20–23; 3.9, 11, 13, 14.

2.22 to this day, that is, the time of the writing of the note. This is a very common expression in the historical books. See especially Gen 22.14; 32.32; 35.20; Deut 3.14; 34.6; Josh 4.9; 7.26; Judg 1.21; 10.4; 1 Sam 6.18; 2 Sam 4.3; 1 Ki 9.13; 2 Ki 8.22.

2.23 Caphtor, the island of Crete.

*2.30
Num 21.23

2.31
Deut 1.8

2.32
Num 21.23,
24;
Deut 7.2;
20.16
*2.34
Deut 3.6

2.36
Deut 3.12;
4.48;
Ps 44.3

2.37
Num 21.24

3.1
Num
21.33-35
3.2
Num 21.34

3.3
Num 21.35

3.4
1 Ki 4.13

3.6
Deut 2.24,
34

3.9
Ps 29.6

3.11
Amos 2.9;
Gen 14.5;
2 Sam
12.26;
Jer 49.2

3.12
Deut 2.36;
Num 32.32-
38;
Josh 13.8-
13

gives to us.' 30 But Sīhŏn the king of Hĕshbŏn would not let us pass by him; for the LORD your God hardened his spirit and made his heart obstinate, that he might give him into your hand, as at this day. 31And the LORD said to me, 'Behold, I have begun to give Sīhŏn and his land over to you; begin to take possession, that you may occupy his land.' 32 Then Sīhŏn came out against us, he and all his people, to battle at Jāhăz. 33And the LORD our God gave him over to us; and we defeated him and his sons and all his people. 34And we captured all his cities at that time and utterly destroyed every city, men, women, and children; we left none remaining; 35 only the cattle we took as spoil for ourselves, with the booty of the cities which we captured. 36 From Ărŏ'ĕr, which is on the edge of the valley of the Arnŏn, and from the city that is in the valley, as far as Gĭl'ĕăd, there was not a city too high for us; the LORD our God gave all into our hands. 37 Only to the land of the sons of Ămmŏn you did not draw near, that is, to all the banks of the river Jăbbŏk and the cities of the hill country, and wherever the LORD our God forbade us.

2. Over Og, king of Bashan

3 "Then we turned and went up the way to Bāshăn; and Ŏg the king of Bashan came out against us, he and all his people, to battle at Ĕd'rĕ-ī. 2 But the LORD said to me, 'Do not fear him; for I have given him and all his people and his land into your hand; and you shall do to him as you did to Sīhŏn the king of the Ăm'- ŏrītes, who dwelt at Hĕshbŏn.' 3 So the LORD our God gave into our hand Ŏg also, the king of Bāshăn, and all his people; and we smote him until no survivor was left to him. 4And we took all his cities at that time—there was not a city which we did not take from them—sixty cities, the whole region of Argŏb, the kingdom of Ŏg in Bāshăn. 5All these were cities fortified with high walls, gates, and bars, besides very many unwalled villages. 6And we utterly destroyed them, as we did to Sīhŏn the king of Hĕshbŏn, destroying every city, men, women, and children. 7 But all the cattle and the spoil of the cities we took as our booty. 8 So we took the land at that time out of the hand of the two kings of the Ăm'- ŏrītes who were beyond the Jordan, from the valley of the Arnŏn to Mount Hĕrmŏn 9 (the Sīdŏ'nĭănş call Hĕrmŏn Sĭr'ĭŏn, while the Ăm'ŏrītes call it Sĕnĭr), 10 all the cities of the tableland and all Gĭl'ĕăd and all Bāshăn, as far as Săl'ĕcăh and Ĕd'rĕ-ī, cities of the kingdom of Ŏg in Bashan. 11 (For only Ŏg the king of Bāshăn was left of the remnant of the Rĕph'ăïm; behold, his bedstead was a bedstead of iron; is it not in Răbbăh of the Ăm'mŏnītes? Nine cubits was its length, and four cubits its breadth, according to the common cubit.ᵃ)

3. The distribution of the land

12 "When we took possession of this land at that time, I gave to the Reu'bĕnītes and the Gădītes the territory beginning at Ărŏ'ĕr, which is on the edge of the valley of the Arnŏn, and half

ᵃ Heb cubit of a man

2.30 *hardened his spirit.* See note to Ex 4.21.
2.34 *left . . . remaining.* This ancient practice was called *herem*, "devotion to destruction." The enemy and its possessions were de- voted to Yahweh. Thus, in this holy war the males, and in some cases women and children (20.16), were slain and the cities destroyed. The booty was divided among the victors.

the hill country of Gĭl'ëăd with its cities; 13 the rest of Gĭl'ëăd, and all Bāshán, the kingdom of Ŏg, that is, all the region of Argób, I gave to the half-tribe of Mánăs'seh. (The whole of that Bashan is called the land of Rĕph'aïm. 14 Jāĭr the Mánăs'sĭte took all the region of Argób, that is, Bāshán, as far as the border of the Gĕsh'-úrītes and the Mā-ăc'áthītes, and called the villages after his own name, Hăvvôth-jā'ĭr, as it is to this day.) 15 To Māchĭr I gave Gĭl'ëăd, 16 and to the Reu'bënītes and the Gădītes I gave the territory from Gĭlëăd as far as the valley of the Arnôn, with the middle of the valley as a boundary, as far over as the river Jăbbók, the boundary of the Ăm'mónītes; 17 the Ạr'ábăh also, with the Jordan as the boundary, from Chĭn'nerĕth as far as the sea of the Arabah, the Salt Sea, under the slopes of Pĭṣgáh on the east.

18 "And I commanded you at that time, saying, 'The LORD your God has given you this land to possess; all your men of valor shall pass over armed before your brethren the people of Israel. 19 But your wives, your little ones, and your cattle (I know that you have many cattle) shall remain in the cities which I have given you, 20 until the LORD gives rest to your brethren, as to you, and they also occupy the land which the LORD your God gives them beyond the Jordan; then you shall return every man to his possession which I have given you.' 21And I commanded Joshua at that time, 'Your eyes have seen all that the LORD your God has done to these two kings; so will the LORD do to all the kingdoms into which you are going over. 22 You shall not fear them; for it is the LORD your God who fights for you.'

4. Moses forbidden to cross the Jordan

23 "And I besought the LORD at that time, saying, 24 'O Lord GOD, thou hast only begun to show thy servant thy greatness and thy mighty hand; for what god is there in heaven or on earth who can do such works and mighty acts as thine? 25 Let me go over, I pray, and see the good land beyond the Jordan, that goodly hill country, and Lebanon.' 26 But the LORD was angry with me on your account, and would not hearken to me; and the LORD said to me, 'Let it suffice you; speak no more to me of this matter. 27 Go up to the top of Pĭṣgáh, and lift up your eyes westward and northward and southward and eastward, and behold it with your eyes; for you shall not go over this Jordan. 28 But charge Joshua, and encourage and strengthen him; for he shall go over at the head of this people, and he shall put them in possession of the land which you shall see.' 29 So we remained in the valley opposite Bĕth'-pëor.

E. The exhortation of Moses

1. The command to obedience

4 "And now, O Israel, give heed to the statutes and the ordinances which I teach you, and do them; that you may live, and go in and take possession of the land which the LORD, the God of your fathers, gives you. 2 You shall not add to the word which I command you, nor take from it; that you may keep the commandments of the LORD your God which I command you. 3 Your

Marginal references:
3.14 Num 32.41; 1 Chr 2.22
3.15 Num 32.39, 40
*3.17 Num 34.11; Josh 13.27
3.18 Num 32.20
3.20 Josh 22.4
3.22 Deut 1.30
3.24 Ex 15.11; Ps 86.8
3.26 Deut 1.37; 31.2
3.27 Num 27.12
3.28 Num 27.18, 23; Deut 31.3,7
*3.29 Deut 4.46; 34.6
4.1 Deut 5.33; 8.1; 16.20; 30.16,19
4.2 Deut 12.32; Josh 1.7; Rev 22.18, 19
4.3 Num 25.4; Ps 106.28, 29

3.17 *Chinnereth*, Lake Gennesaret, or Sea of Galilee.

3.29 *Beth-peor*, an elevated area close to the burial place of Moses.

eyes have seen what the LORD did at Bā′ăl-pëor; for the LORD your God destroyed from among you all the men who followed the Bāăl of Pē′or; 4 but you who held fast to the LORD your God are all alive this day. 5 Behold, I have taught you statutes and ordinances, as the LORD my God commanded me, that you should do them in the land which you are entering to take possession of it. 6 Keep them and do them; for that will be your wisdom and your understanding in the sight of the peoples, who, when they hear all these statutes, will say, 'Surely this great nation is a wise and understanding people.' 7 For what great nation is there that has a god so near to it as the LORD our God is to us, whenever we call upon him? 8And what great nation is there, that has statutes and ordinances so righteous as all this law which I set before you this day?

9 "Only take heed, and keep your soul diligently, lest you forget the things which your eyes have seen, and lest they depart from your heart all the days of your life; make them known to your children and your children's children—10 how on the day that you stood before the LORD your God at Horeb, the LORD said to me, 'Gather the people to me, that I may let them hear my words, so that they may learn to fear me all the days that they live upon the earth, and that they may teach their children so.' 11And you came near and stood at the foot of the mountain, while the mountain burned with fire to the heart of heaven, wrapped in darkness, cloud, and gloom. 12 Then the LORD spoke to you out of the midst of the fire; you heard the sound of words, but saw no form; there was only a voice. 13And he declared to you his covenant, which he commanded you to perform, that is, the ten commandments;*b* and he wrote them upon two tables of stone. 14And the LORD commanded me at that time to teach you statutes and ordinances, that you might do them in the land which you are going over to possess.

2. Idolatry forbidden

15 "Therefore take good heed to yourselves. Since you saw no form on the day that the LORD spoke to you at Horeb out of the midst of the fire, 16 beware lest you act corruptly by making a graven image for yourselves, in the form of any figure, the likeness of male or female, 17 the likeness of any beast that is on the earth, the likeness of any winged bird that flies in the air, 18 the likeness of anything that creeps on the ground, the likeness of any fish that is in the water under the earth. 19And beware lest you lift up your eyes to heaven, and when you see the sun and the moon and the stars, all the host of heaven, you be drawn away and worship them and serve them, things which the LORD your God has allotted to all the peoples under the whole heaven. 20 But the LORD has taken you, and brought you forth out of the iron furnace, out of Egypt, to be a people of his own possession, as at this day. 21 Furthermore the LORD was angry with me on your account, and he swore that I should not cross the Jordan, and that I should not enter the good land which the LORD your God gives you for an inheritance. 22 For I must die in this land, I must not go over the

b Heb words

4.15 *saw no form.* God is a spirit and thus is nonmaterial.   **4.20** *iron furnace.* This designation for Egypt also occurs in Jer 11.4.

Jordan; but you shall go over and take possession of that good land. 23 Take heed to yourselves, lest you forget the covenant of the LORD your God, which he made with you, and make a graven image in the form of anything which the LORD your God has forbidden you. 24 For the LORD your God is a devouring fire, a jealous God.

25 "When you beget children and children's children, and have grown old in the land, if you act corruptly by making a graven image in the form of anything, and by doing what is evil in the sight of the LORD your God, so as to provoke him to anger, 26 I call heaven and earth to witness against you this day, that you will soon utterly perish from the land which you are going over the Jordan to possess; you will not live long upon it, but will be utterly destroyed. 27And the LORD will scatter you among the peoples, and you will be left few in number among the nations where the LORD will drive you. 28And there you will serve gods of wood and stone, the work of men's hands, that neither see, nor hear, nor eat, nor smell. 29 But from there you will seek the LORD your God, and you will find him, if you search after him with all your heart and with all your soul. 30 When you are in tribulation, and all these things come upon you in the latter days, you will return to the LORD your God and obey his voice, 31 for the LORD your God is a merciful God; he will not fail you or destroy you or forget the covenant with your fathers which he swore to them.

3. The peculiar relation of Israel as a chosen nation

32 "For ask now of the days that are past, which were before you, since the day that God created man upon the earth, and ask from one end of heaven to the other, whether such a great thing as this has ever happened or was ever heard of. 33 Did any people ever hear the voice of a god speaking out of the midst of the fire, as you have heard, and still live? 34 Or has any god ever attempted to go and take a nation for himself from the midst of another nation, by trials, by signs, by wonders, and by war, by a mighty hand and an outstretched arm, and by great terrors, according to all that the LORD your God did for you in Egypt before your eyes? 35 To you it was shown, that you might know that the LORD is God; there is no other besides him. 36 Out of heaven he let you hear his voice, that he might discipline you; and on earth he let you see his great fire, and you heard his words out of the midst of the fire. 37And because he loved your fathers and chose their descendants after them, and brought you out of Egypt with his own presence, by his great power, 38 driving out before you nations greater and mightier than yourselves, to bring you in, to give you their land for an inheritance, as at this day; 39 know therefore this day, and lay it to your heart, that the LORD is God in heaven above and on the earth beneath; there is no other. 40 Therefore you shall keep his statutes and his commandments, which I command you this day, that it may go well with you, and with your children after you, and that you may prolong your days in the land which the LORD your God gives you for ever."

F. The cities of refuge

41 Then Moses set apart three cities in the east beyond the

Cross references (right margin):

4.23
ver 9,16;
Ex 20.4,5

4.24
Ex 24.17;
Deut 9.3;
Heb 12.29;
Deut 6.15

4.25
ver 16,23;
2 Ki 17.17

4.26
Deut 30.18,
19

4.27
Deut 28.62,
64

4.28
Deut 28.64;
1 Sam
26.19;
Ps 115.4,5

4.29
Deut 30.1–
3;
2 Chr 15.4;
Isa 55.6,7;
Jer 29.12–
14

4.31
2 Chr 30.9;
Ps 116.5

4.32
Deut 32.7;
Gen 1.27;
Deut 28.64

4.33
Ex 20.22;
Deut 5.24,
26

4.34
Deut 7.19;
Ex 7.3;
13.3; 6.6;
Deut 26.8;
34.12

4.35
Deut 32.39;
1 Sam 2.2;
Isa 45.5,18;
Mk 12.29

4.36
Ex 19.9,19;
Heb 12.18

4.37
Deut 10.15;
Ex 13.3,9,
14

4.38
Deut 7.1;
9.1,4,5

4.39
ver 35;
Josh 2.11

4.40
Lev 22.31;
Deut 5.16,
29,33;
Eph 6.2, 3

4.41
Num 35.6

Jordan, 42 that the manslayer might flee there, who kills his neighbor unintentionally, without being at enmity with him in time past, and that by fleeing to one of these cities he might save his life: 43 Bēzĕr in the wilderness on the tableland for the Reu'bēnītes, and Rāmŏth in Gĭl'ĕăd for the Gădītes, and Gōlăn in Bāshán for the Mănăs'sītes.

II. Moses' second address 4.44–26.19

A. Introduction

44 This is the law which Moses set before the children of Israel; 45 these are the testimonies, the statutes, and the ordinances, which Moses spoke to the children of Israel when they came out of Egypt, 46 beyond the Jordan in the valley opposite Bĕth'-pĕor, in the land of Sīhŏn the king of the Ăm'ŏrītes, who lived at Hĕshbŏn, whom Moses and the children of Israel defeated when they came out of Egypt. 47And they took possession of his land and the land of Ŏg the king of Bāshăn, the two kings of the Ăm'ŏrītes, who lived to the east beyond the Jordan; 48 from Arŏ'ĕr, which is on the edge of the valley of the Arnŏn, as far as Mount Sĭr'ĭŏn^c (that is, Hĕrmŏn), 49 together with all the Ar'ăbăh on the east side of the Jordan as far as the Sea of the Arabah, under the slopes of Pĭşgăh.

B. The covenant: the Ten Commandments

1. The Commandments stated

5 And Moses summoned all Israel, and said to them, "Hear, O Israel, the statutes and the ordinances which I speak in your hearing this day, and you shall learn them and be careful to do them. 2 The LORD our God made a covenant with us in Horĕb. 3 Not with our fathers did the LORD make this covenant, but with us, who are all of us here alive this day. 4 The LORD spoke with you face to face at the mountain, out of the midst of the fire, 5 while I stood between the LORD and you at that time, to declare to you the word of the LORD; for you were afraid because of the fire, and you did not go up into the mountain. He said:

6 " 'I am the LORD your God, who brought you out of the land of Egypt, out of the house of bondage.

7 " 'You shall have no other gods before^d me.

8 " 'You shall not make for yourself a graven image, or any likeness of anything that is in heaven above, or that is on the earth beneath, or that is in the water under the earth; 9 you shall not bow down to them or serve them; for I the LORD your God am a jealous God, visiting the iniquity of the fathers upon the children to the third and fourth generation of those who hate me, 10 but showing steadfast love to thousands of those who love me and keep my commandments.

11 " 'You shall not take the name of the LORD your God in vain: for the LORD will not hold him guiltless who takes his name in vain.

12 " 'Observe the sabbath day, to keep it holy, as the LORD your

c Syr: Heb Sĭŏn   d Or besides

5.9 *jealous God*, see note to Ex 34.14.   5.12 *Observe*. Ex 20.8 has *remember*.

4.46
Deut 3.29;
Num 21.21–
25

4.48
Deut 2.36;
3.12

5.2
Ex 19.5

5.4
Ex 19.9,
19;
Deut 4.33,
36
5.5
Ex 20.18,
21
5.6
Ex 20.2–17

*5.9
Ex 34.7

5.10
Jer 32.18

*5.12

God commanded you. 13 Six days you shall labor, and do all your work; 14 but the seventh day is a sabbath to the LORD your God; in it you shall not do any work, you, or your son, or your daughter, or your manservant, or your maidservant, or your ox, or your ass, or any of your cattle, or the sojourner who is within your gates, that your manservant and your maidservant may rest as well as you. 15 You shall remember that you were a servant in the land of Egypt, and the LORD your God brought you out thence with a mighty hand and an outstretched arm; therefore the LORD your God commanded you to keep the sabbath day.

16 " 'Honor your father and your mother, as the LORD your God commanded you; that your days may be prolonged, and that it may go well with you, in the land which the LORD your God gives you.

17 " 'You shall not kill.

18 " 'Neither shall you commit adultery.

19 " 'Neither shall you steal.

20 " 'Neither shall you bear false witness against your neighbor.

21 " 'Neither shall you covet your neighbor's wife; and you shall not desire your neighbor's house, his field, or his manservant, or his maidservant, his ox, or his ass, or anything that is your neighbor's.'

2. *God and Moses at Sinai*

22 "These words the LORD spoke to all your assembly at the mountain out of the midst of the fire, the cloud, and the thick darkness, with a loud voice; and he added no more. And he wrote them upon two tables of stone, and gave them to me. 23And when you heard the voice out of the midst of the darkness, while the mountain was burning with fire, you came near to me, all the heads of your tribes, and your elders; 24 and you said, 'Behold, the LORD our God has shown us his glory and greatness, and we have heard his voice out of the midst of the fire; we have this day seen God speak with man and man still live. 25 Now therefore why should we die? For this great fire will consume us; if we hear the voice of the LORD our God any more, we shall die. 26 For who is there of all flesh, that has heard the voice of the living God speaking out of the midst of fire, as we have, and has still lived? 27 Go near, and hear all that the LORD our God will say; and speak to us all that the LORD our God will speak to you; and we will hear and do it.'

28 "And the LORD heard your words, when you spoke to me; and the LORD said to me, 'I have heard the words of this people, which they have spoken to you; they have rightly said all that they have spoken. 29 Oh that they had such a mind as this always, to fear me and to keep all my commandments, that it might go well with them and with their children for ever! 30 Go and say to them, "Return to your tents." 31 But you, stand here by me, and I will tell you all the commandment and the statutes and the ordinances which you shall teach them, that they may do them in the land which I give them to possess.' 32 You shall be careful to do there-

Marginal references
5.14 Gen 2.2; Ex 16.29,30
*5.15 Deut 15.16; 4.34,37
*5.16
5.21 Rom 7.7; 13.9
5.22 Ex 31.18; Deut 4.13
5.24 Ex 19.19
5.25 Deut 18.16
5.26 Deut 4.33
5.28 Deut 18.17
5.29 Ps 81.13; Isa 48.18; Deut 4.40
5.31 Ex 24.12
5.32 Deut 17.20; 28.14; Josh 1.7; 23.6

5.15 See Ex 20.11 where another reason is given for keeping the Sabbath.
5.16 *as the LORD your God commanded you.*

This expression also occurs in verse 12 and, with slight variations, is used throughout Deuteronomy.

fore as the LORD your God has commanded you; you shall not turn aside to the right hand or to the left. 33 You shall walk in all the way which the LORD your God has commanded you, that you may live, and that it may go well with you, and that you may live long in the land which you shall possess.

5.33
Deut 4.40

3. The purpose of the Law

6 "Now this is the commandment, the statutes and the ordinances which the LORD your God commanded me to teach you, that you may do them in the land to which you are going over, to possess it; 2 that you may fear the LORD your God, you and your son and your son's son, by keeping all his statutes and his commandments, which I command you, all the days of your life; and that your days may be prolonged. 3 Hear therefore, O Israel, and be careful to do them; that it may go well with you, and that you may multiply greatly, as the LORD, the God of your fathers, has promised you, in a land flowing with milk and honey.

6.2
Ex 20.20;
Deut 10.12,
13

6.3
Deut 5.33;
Gen 15.5;
Ex 3.8

4. The law of love

4 "Hear, O Israel: The LORD our God is one LORD;[e] 5 and you shall love the LORD your God with all your heart, and with all your soul, and with all your might. 6And these words which I command you this day shall be upon your heart; 7 and you shall teach them diligently to your children, and shall talk of them when you sit in your house, and when you walk by the way, and when you lie down, and when you rise. 8And you shall bind them as a sign upon your hand, and they shall be as frontlets between your eyes. 9And you shall write them on the doorposts of your house and on your gates.

*6.4ff
Mk 12.29,
32;
Jn 17.3;
1 Cor 8.4,6
*6.5
Deut 10.12;
Mt 22.37;
Lk 10.27
6.7
Deut 4.9;
Eph 6.4
6.8
Ex 13.9,
16;
Deut 11.18
6.9
Deut 11.20

10 "And when the LORD your God brings you into the land which he swore to your fathers, to Abraham, to Isaac, and to Jacob, to give you, with great and goodly cities, which you did not build, 11 and houses full of all good things, which you did not fill, and cisterns hewn out, which you did not hew, and vineyards and olive trees, which you did not plant, and when you eat and are full, 12 then take heed lest you forget the LORD, who brought you out of the land of Egypt, out of the house of bondage. 13 You shall fear the LORD your God; you shall serve him, and swear by his name. 14 You shall not go after other gods, of the gods of the peoples who are round about you; 15 for the LORD your God in the midst of you is a jealous God; lest the anger of the LORD your God be kindled against you, and he destroy you from off the face of the earth.

6.10
Deut 9.1;
Josh 24.13
6.11
Deut 8.10

*6.13
Deut 10.20

6.15
Deut 4.24

e Or the LORD our God, the LORD is one
  Or the LORD is our God, the LORD is one
  Or the LORD is our God, the LORD alone

6.4-9 Later in Israel there arose the practice of reciting these basic verses, called the *Shema* ("Hear"), twice daily.

The great teaching of the Scripture about God is that there is a unity in a trinity—three Persons make up the Godhead, yet they constitute but one essence. It is, therefore, a tri-unity, for God is one yet three. This is a great mystery but it is the only way of recon-ciling all that the Bible says about God. (See also note to Mt 28.19 on the Trinity.)

6.5 This verse, according to Jesus, is the first and great commandment. Since *heart* in Hebrew thought was also considered the seat of intelligence, Jesus was warranted in adding a fourth item, *mind* (Mk 12.30; Lk 10.27).

6.13 *fear*, that is, reverence, obedience, submissiveness.

16 "You shall not put the LORD your God to the test, as you tested him at Mǎssàh. 17 You shall diligently keep the commandments of the LORD your God, and his testimonies, and his statutes, which he has commanded you. 18And you shall do what is right and good in the sight of the LORD, that it may go well with you, and that you may go in and take possession of the good land which the LORD swore to give to your fathers 19 by thrusting out all your enemies from before you, as the LORD has promised.

5. Explaining the Law to their children

20 "When your son asks you in time to come, 'What is the meaning of the testimonies and the statutes and the ordinances which the LORD our God has commanded you?' 21 then you shall say to your son, 'We were Phạraōh's slaves in Egypt; and the LORD brought us out of Egypt with a mighty hand; 22 and the LORD showed signs and wonders, great and grievous, against Egypt and against Phạraōh and all his household, before our eyes; 23 and he brought us out from there, that he might bring us in and give us the land which he swore to give to our fathers. 24And the LORD commanded us to do all these statutes, to fear the LORD our God, for our good always, that he might preserve us alive, as at this day. 25And it will be righteousness for us, if we are careful to do all this commandment before the LORD our God, as he has commanded us.'

6. Extermination of the Canaanites
a. The evils of idolatry

7 "When the LORD your God brings you into the land which you are entering to take possession of it, and clears away many nations before you, the Hittītes, the Gịr'gáshītes, the Ăm'órītes, the Cā'naànītes, the Pěr'ịzzītes, the Hivītes, and the Jĕb'ūsītes, seven nations greater and mightier than yourselves, 2 and when the LORD your God gives them over to you, and you defeat them; then you must utterly destroy them; you shall make no covenant with them, and show no mercy to them. 3 You shall not make marriages with them, giving your daughters to their sons or taking their daughters for your sons. 4 For they would turn away your sons from following me, to serve other gods; then the anger of the LORD would be kindled against you, and he would destroy you quickly. 5 But thus shall you deal with them: you shall break down

Marginal references:
6.16 Mt 4.7; Ex 17.2,7
6.17 Deut 11.22
6.18 Deut 4.40
6.20 Ex 13.14
6.24 Deut 10.12
6.25 Deut 24.13
7.1 Deut 31.3; Acts 13.19
*7.2 Ex 23.32; Deut 13.8
7.3 Ex 34.15, 16
7.4 Deut 6.15
7.5 Ex 23.24

7.2 God at times commanded Israel to annihilate certain peoples. This aspect of God's character has occasioned difficult questions concerning His love, righteousness, and mercy. Because of these problems, some scholars have attempted to distinguish between the God of wrath of the Old Testament and the God of love of the New Testament. This distinction is false. God is the one and same God, both in the Old Testament and the New Testament. That He did execute wrath against certain nations admits of no doubt; that He promises to do so again in the end time is clear from the Revelation to John. God's love is a holy and righteous love; He will not show an unfeeling disregard toward the victims of crime by sparing the unrepentant criminal who has injured them. In decreeing their punishment, God shows love towards His moral order and those principles of justice and retribution without which life makes no sense. (Justice and retribution were at work even when Christ, God's love-gift for sinners, bore the sinners' guilt and paid their penalty for them.) The proposition that God is love cannot mean that God loves evil or protects wickedness. Even so, in these ancient times the wickedness of the people to be destroyed was so great, the patience of God toward them so long-suffering, and the opportunities for repentance so many, that when judgment did fall it came as a just recompense for awful sinfulness. It might be added that judgment in time is no worse than judgment in eternity, and to deny one is just as fallacious as to deny the other.

their altars, and dash in pieces their pillars, and hew down their
Åshē'rǐm, and burn their graven images with fire.

b. *The peculiar status of Israel*

6 "For you are a people holy to the LORD your God; the LORD
your God has chosen you to be a people for his own possession,
out of all the peoples that are on the face of the earth. 7 It was not
because you were more in number than any other people that the
LORD set his love upon you and chose you, for you were the fewest
of all peoples; 8 but it is because the LORD loves you, and is keeping the oath which he swore to your fathers, that the LORD has
brought you out with a mighty hand, and redeemed you from the
house of bondage, from the hand of Pharaōh king of Egypt.
9 Know therefore that the LORD your God is God, the faithful God
who keeps covenant and steadfast love with those who love him
and keep his commandments, to a thousand generations, 10 and requites to their face those who hate him, by destroying them; he will
not be slack with him who hates him, he will requite him to his
face. 11 You shall therefore be careful to do the commandment,
and the statutes, and the ordinances, which I command you
this day.

12 "And because you hearken to these ordinances, and keep and
do them, the LORD your God will keep with you the covenant and
the steadfast love which he swore to your fathers to keep; 13 he will
love you, bless you, and multiply you; he will also bless the fruit
of your body and the fruit of your ground, your grain and your
wine and your oil, the increase of your cattle and the young of
your flock, in the land which he swore to your fathers to give you.
14 You shall be blessed above all peoples; there shall not be male
or female barren among you, or among your cattle. 15 And the LORD
will take away from you all sickness; and none of the evil diseases
of Egypt, which you knew, will he inflict upon you, but he will lay
them upon all who hate you. 16 And you shall destroy all the peoples that the LORD your God will give over to you, your eye shall
not pity them; neither shall you serve their gods, for that would
be a snare to you.

c. *God is greater than the Canaanites: Israel need not fear*

17 "If you say in your heart, 'These nations are greater than I;
how can I dispossess them?' 18 you shall not be afraid of them, but
you shall remember what the LORD your God did to Pharaōh and
to all Egypt, 19 the great trials which your eyes saw, the signs, the
wonders, the mighty hand, and the outstretched arm, by which the
LORD your God brought you out; so will the LORD your God do to
all the peoples of whom you are afraid. 20 Moreover the LORD your
God will send hornets among them, until those who are left and
hide themselves from you are destroyed. 21 You shall not be in
dread of them; for the LORD your God is in the midst of you, a
great and terrible God. 22 The LORD your God will clear away
these nations before you little by little; you may not make an end
of them at once,ᶠ lest the wild beasts grow too numerous for you.

ᶠ Or *quickly*

7.6 *a people holy to the* LORD. Because the
people of Israel were God's *own possession,*
they were to *utterly destroy* (ver 2) the
peoples in Canaan.

(marginal references)

*7.6
Ex 19.5,6;
Deut 14.2
7.7
Deut 10.22

7.8
Deut 10.15;
Ex 32.13;
13.3,14

7.9
Deut 4.35,
39;
Neh 1.5

7.12
Lev 26.3;
Deut 28.1;
Ps 105.8,9
7.13
Deut 28.4

7.14
Ex 23.26
7.15
Ex 15.26

7.16
ver 2;
Ex 23.33

7.18
Deut 31.6

7.19
Deut 4.34

7.20
Ex 23.28;
Josh 24.12
7.21
Deut 10.17

7.22
Ex 23.29,
30*

23 But the LORD your God will give them over to you, and throw them into great confusion, until they are destroyed. 24And he will give their kings into your hand, and you shall make their name perish from under heaven; not a man shall be able to stand against you, until you have destroyed them. 25 The graven images of their gods you shall burn with fire; you shall not covet the silver or the gold that is on them, or take it for yourselves, lest you be ensnared by it; for it is an abomination to the LORD your God. 26And you shall not bring an abominable thing into your house, and become accursed like it; you shall utterly detest and abhor it; for it is an accursed thing.

7. Moses' reminder of God's past mercies
a. Wilderness mercies

8 "All the commandment which I command you this day you shall be careful to do, that you may live and multiply, and go in and possess the land which the LORD swore to give to your fathers. 2And you shall remember all the way which the LORD your God has led you these forty years in the wilderness, that he might humble you, testing you to know what was in your heart, whether you would keep his commandments, or not. 3And he humbled you and let you hunger and fed you with manna, which you did not know, nor did your fathers know; that he might make you know that man does not live by bread alone, but that man lives by everything that proceeds out of the mouth of the LORD. 4 Your clothing did not wear out upon you, and your foot did not swell, these forty years. 5 Know then in your heart that, as a man disciplines his son, the LORD your God disciplines you. 6 So you shall keep the commandments of the LORD your God, by walking in his ways and by fearing him. 7 For the LORD your God is bringing you into a good land, a land of brooks of water, of fountains and springs, flowing forth in valleys and hills, 8 a land of wheat and barley, of vines and fig trees and pomegranates, a land of olive trees and honey, 9 a land in which you will eat bread without scarcity, in which you will lack nothing, a land whose stones are iron, and out of whose hills you can dig copper. 10And you shall eat and be full, and you shall bless the LORD your God for the good land he has given you.

b. Admonition against pride

11 "Take heed lest you forget the LORD your God, by not keeping his commandments and his ordinances and his statutes, which I command you this day: 12 lest, when you have eaten and are full, and have built goodly houses and live in them, 13 and when your herds and flocks multiply, and your silver and gold is multiplied, and all that you have is multiplied, 14 then your heart be lifted up, and you forget the LORD your God, who brought you out of the land of Egypt, out of the house of bondage, 15 who led you through the great and terrible wilderness, with its fiery serpents and scorpions and thirsty ground where there was no water, who brought you water out of the flinty rock, 16 who fed you in the wilderness with manna which your fathers did not know, that he might humble you and test you, to do you good in the end. 17 Beware lest you say in your heart, 'My power and the might of my hand have

Marginal references:
7.24 ver 16
7.25 1 Chr 14.12; Josh 7.1, 21; Judg 8.27
8.1 Deut 4.1
8.2 Deut 29.5; 13.3
8.3 Ex 16.2,3, 12, 14,35; Mt 4.4; Lk 4.7
8.4 Deut 29.5
8.5 Prov 3.12; Heb 12.5,6
8.6 Deut 5.33
8.7 Deut 11.10–12
*8.9
8.10 Deut 6.11, 12
8.14 Ps 106.21
8.15 Num 21.6; 20.11; Ps 78.15; 114.8
8.16 ver 2,3; Ex 16.15

8.9 *a land whose stones are iron, and out of whose hills you can dig copper.* Modern explorations have confirmed this to be true in the great rift of the Arabah south of the Dead Sea.

8.18
Prov 10.22;
Hos 2.8

8.19
Deut 4.26;
30.18

9.1
Deut 11.31

9.2
Num 13.22,
28,32,33

9.3
Deut 31.3;
4.24; 7.23,
24

9.4
Deut 8.17;
18.12;
Lev 18.24,
25

9.5
Gen 12.7

9.6
ver 13;
Ex 32.9;
Deut 31.27

9.8
Ex 32.7–10

9.9
Ex 24.12,
15,18

9.10
Ex 31.18;
Deut 4.13

9.12
Ex 32.7,8;
Deut 31.29

9.13
Ex 32.9;
ver 6

9.14
Ex 32.10;
Deut 29.20;
Num 14.12

gotten me this wealth.' 18 You shall remember the LORD your God, for it is he who gives you power to get wealth; that he may confirm his covenant which he swore to your fathers, as at this day. 19And if you forget the LORD your God and go after other gods and serve them and worship them, I solemnly warn you this day that you shall surely perish. 20 Like the nations that the LORD makes to perish before you, so shall you perish, because you would not obey the voice of the LORD your God.

c. God will give Israel the land:
not because of their righteousness

9 "Hear, O Israel; you are to pass over the Jordan this day, to go in to dispossess nations greater and mightier than yourselves, cities great and fortified up to heaven, 2 a people great and tall, the sons of the Ăn'ákĭm, whom you know, and of whom you have heard it said, 'Who can stand before the sons of Ānăk?' 3 Know therefore this day that he who goes over before you as a devouring fire is the LORD your God; he will destroy them and subdue them before you; so you shall drive them out, and make them perish quickly, as the LORD has promised you.

4 "Do not say in your heart, after the LORD your God has thrust them out before you, 'It is because of my righteousness that the LORD has brought me in to possess this land'; whereas it is because of the wickedness of these nations that the LORD is driving them out before you. 5 Not because of your righteousness or the uprightness of your heart are you going in to possess their land; but because of the wickedness of these nations the LORD your God is driving them out from before you, and that he may confirm the word which the LORD swore to your fathers, to Abraham, to Isaac, and to Jacob.

d. Israel's own sin: the golden calf

6 "Know therefore, that the LORD your God is not giving you this good land to possess because of your righteousness; for you are a stubborn people. 7 Remember and do not forget how you provoked the LORD your God to wrath in the wilderness; from the day you came out of the land of Egypt, until you came to this place, you have been rebellious against the LORD. 8 Even at Horĕb you provoked the LORD to wrath, and the LORD was so angry with you that he was ready to destroy you. 9 When I went up the mountain to receive the tables of stone, the tables of the covenant which the LORD made with you, I remained on the mountain forty days and forty nights; I neither ate bread nor drank water. 10And the LORD gave me the two tables of stone written with the finger of God; and on them were all the words which the LORD had spoken with you on the mountain out of the midst of the fire on the day of the assembly. 11And at the end of forty days and forty nights the LORD gave me the two tables of stone, the tables of the covenant. 12 Then the LORD said to me, 'Arise, go down quickly from here; for your people whom you have brought from Egypt have acted corruptly; they have turned aside quickly out of the way which I commanded them; they have made themselves a molten image.'

13 "Furthermore the LORD said to me, 'I have seen this people, and behold, it is a stubborn people; 14 let me alone, that I may destroy them and blot out their name from under heaven; and I

will make of you a nation mightier and greater than they.' ¹⁵ So I turned and came down from the mountain, and the mountain was burning with fire; and the two tables of the covenant were in my two hands. ¹⁶And I looked, and behold, you had sinned against the LORD your God; you had made yourselves a molten calf; you had turned aside quickly from the way which the LORD had commanded you. ¹⁷ So I took hold of the two tables, and cast them out of my two hands, and broke them before your eyes. ¹⁸ Then I lay prostrate before the LORD as before, forty days and forty nights; I neither ate bread nor drank water, because of all the sin which you had committed, in doing what was evil in the sight of the LORD, to provoke him to anger. ¹⁹ For I was afraid of the anger and hot displeasure which the LORD bore against you, so that he was ready to destroy you. But the LORD hearkened to me that time also. ²⁰And the LORD was so angry with Aaron that he was ready to destroy him; and I prayed for Aaron also at the same time. ²¹ Then I took the sinful thing, the calf which you had made, and burned it with fire and crushed it, grinding it very small, until it was as fine as dust; and I threw the dust of it into the brook that descended out of the mountain.

e. *Israel's other sins*

²² "At Tăb'ĕràh also, and at Măssáh, and at Kĭb'rŏth-hăttä'-àváh, you provoked the LORD to wrath. ²³And when the LORD sent you from Kā'dĕsh-barnē'á, saying, 'Go up and take possession of the land which I have given you,' then you rebelled against the commandment of the LORD your God, and did not believe him or obey his voice. ²⁴ You have been rebellious against the LORD from the day that I knew you.

f. *Moses intercedes for Israel*

²⁵ "So I lay prostrate before the LORD for these forty days and forty nights, because the LORD had said he would destroy you. ²⁶And I prayed to the LORD, 'O Lord GOD, destroy not thy people and thy heritage, whom thou hast redeemed through thy greatness, whom thou hast brought out of Egypt with a mighty hand. ²⁷ Remember thy servants, Abraham, Isaac, and Jacob; do not regard the stubbornness of this people, or their wickedness, or their sin, ²⁸ lest the land from which thou didst bring us say, "Because the LORD was not able to bring them into the land which he promised them, and because he hated them, he has brought them out to slay them in the wilderness." ²⁹ For they are thy people and thy heritage, whom thou didst bring out by thy great power and by thy outstretched arm.'

g. *The two tables of stone*

10 "At that time the LORD said to me, 'Hew two tables of stone like the first, and come up to me on the mountain, and make an ark of wood. ²And I will write on the tables the words that were on the first tables which you broke, and you shall put them in the ark.' ³ So I made an ark of acacia wood, and hewed two tables of stone like the first, and went up the mountain with the two tables in my hand. ⁴And he wrote on the tables, as at the first writing, the ten commandments^g which the LORD had spoken

g Heb *words*

9.15 Ex 32.15–19; 19.18
9.16 Ex 32.19
9.18 Ex 34.28
9.19 Ex 32.10–14
9.21 Ex 32.20
9.22 Num 11.3, 34; Ex 17.7
9.24 ver 7; Deut 31.27
9.25 ver 18
9.26 Ex 32.11–13
9.29 Deut 4.20, 34
10.1 Ex 34.1,2; 25.10
10.2 Deut 4.13; Ex 25.16,21
10.3 Ex 37.1; 34.4
10.4 Ex 20.1

to you on the mountain out of the midst of the fire on the day of
the assembly; and the LORD gave them to me. 5 Then I turned and
came down from the mountain, and put the tables in the ark which
I had made; and there they are, as the LORD commanded me.

6 (The people of Israel journeyed from Be-ër′ŏth Bĕnĕ-jā′á-
kăn[h] to Mŏṣē′răh. There Aaron died, and there he was buried;
and his son Ĕlëä′zăr ministered as priest in his stead. 7 From there
they journeyed to Gŭdgŏ′dăh, and from Gudgodah to Jŏt′băthăh,
a land with brooks of water. 8At that time the LORD set apart the
tribe of Lēvī to carry the ark of the covenant of the LORD, to stand
before the LORD to minister to him and to bless in his name, to this
day. 9 Therefore Lēvī has no portion or inheritance with his
brothers; the LORD is his inheritance, as the LORD your God said
to him.)

10 "I stayed on the mountain, as at the first time, forty days and
forty nights, and the LORD hearkened to me that time also; the
LORD was unwilling to destroy you. 11And the LORD said to me,
'Arise, go on your journey at the head of the people, that they may
go in and possess the land, which I swore to their fathers to
give them.'

8. God's great requirement

12 "And now, Israel, what does the LORD your God require of
you, but to fear the LORD your God, to walk in all his ways, to love
him, to serve the LORD your God with all your heart and with all
your soul, 13 and to keep the commandments and statutes of the
LORD, which I command you this day for your good? 14 Behold,
to the LORD your God belong heaven and the heaven of heavens,
the earth with all that is in it; 15 yet the LORD set his heart in love
upon your fathers and chose their descendants after them, you
above all peoples, as at this day. 16 Circumcise therefore the foreskin of your heart, and be no longer stubborn. 17 For the LORD
your God is God of gods and Lord of lords, the great, the mighty,
and the terrible God, who is not partial and takes no bribe. 18 He
executes justice for the fatherless and the widow, and loves the
sojourner, giving him food and clothing. 19 Love the sojourner
therefore; for you were sojourners in the land of Egypt. 20 You
shall fear the LORD your God; you shall serve him and cleave to
him, and by his name you shall swear. 21 He is your praise; he is
your God, who has done for you these great and terrible things
which your eyes have seen. 22 Your fathers went down to Egypt
seventy persons; and now the LORD your God has made you as
the stars of heaven for multitude.

9. Moses' concluding exhortation
a. The command to love God

11 "You shall therefore love the LORD your God, and keep
his charge, his statutes, his ordinances, and his commandments always. 2And consider this day (since I am not speaking to
your children who have not known or seen it), consider the discipline[i] of the LORD your God, his greatness, his mighty hand and
his outstretched arm, 3 his signs and his deeds which he did in

---

h Or the wells of the Bene-jaakan   i Or instruction

10.5 Compare this to 1 Ki 8.9.   **10.8** *to bless,* as in Num 6.24–26.

Margin references

*10.5
Ex 40.20

10.6
Num 33.30,
31,38
10.7
Num
33.32-34
*10.8
Num 3.6;
4.15;
Deut 18.5;
21.5
10.9
Num 18.20,
24

10.10
Deut 9.18,
25;
Ex 33.17

10.12
Mic 6.8;
Deut 6.13;
5.33; 6.5
10.14
1 Ki 8.27;
Ex 19.5
10.15
Deut 4.37
10.16
Jer 4.4;
Deut 9.6
10.17
Josh 22.22;
Rev 19.16;
Acts 10.34
10.18
Ps 68.5
10.19
Lev 19.34
10.20
Mt 4.10;
Deut 11.22;
Ps 63.11
10.21
Ex 15.2;
Ps 106.21,
22
10.22
Gen 46.27;
Deut 1.10

11.1
Deut 10.12;
Zech 3.7
11.2
Deut 8.5;
5.24

Egypt to Pharaōh the king of Egypt and to all his land; 4 and what
he did to the army of Egypt, to their horses and to their chariots;
how he made the water of the Red Sea overflow them as they pursued after you, and how the LORD has destroyed them to this day;
5 and what he did to you in the wilderness, until you came to this
place; 6 and what he did to Dāthàn and Àbī′ràm the sons of
Ēlī′àb, son of Reubën; how the earth opened its mouth and swallowed them up, with their households, their tents, and every living
thing that followed them, in the midst of all Israel; 7 for your eyes
have seen all the great work of the LORD which he did.

b. *The order to keep God's commandments*

8 "You shall therefore keep all the commandment which I command you this day, that you may be strong, and go in and take
possession of the land which you are going over to possess, 9 and
that you may live long in the land which the LORD swore to your
fathers to give to them and to their descendants, a land flowing
with milk and honey. 10 For the land which you are entering to
take possession of it is not like the land of Egypt, from which you
have come, where you sowed your seed and watered it with your
feet, like a garden of vegetables; 11 but the land which you are
going over to possess is a land of hills and valleys, which drinks
water by the rain from heaven, 12 a land which the LORD your
God cares for; the eyes of the LORD your God are always upon it,
from the beginning of the year to the end of the year.

c. *The consequences of obedience and disobedience*

13 "And if you will obey my commandments which I command
you this day, to love the LORD your God, and to serve him with all
your heart and with all your soul, 14 he*j* will give the rain for your
land in its season, the early rain and the later rain, that you may
gather in your grain and your wine and your oil. 15And he*j* will
give grass in your fields for your cattle, and you shall eat and be
full. 16 Take heed lest your heart be deceived, and you turn aside
and serve other gods and worship them, 17 and the anger of the
LORD be kindled against you, and he shut up the heavens, so that
there be no rain, and the land yield no fruit, and you perish
quickly off the good land which the LORD gives you.

d. *The command to lay up God's Law*
and to teach it to children

18 "You shall therefore lay up these words of mine in your
heart and in your soul; and you shall bind them as a sign upon
your hand, and they shall be as frontlets between your eyes. 19And
you shall teach them to your children, talking of them when you
are sitting in your house, and when you are walking by the way,
and when you lie down, and when you rise. 20And you shall write
them upon the doorposts of your house and upon your gates,
21 that your days and the days of your children may be multiplied
in the land which the LORD swore to your fathers to give them, as
long as the heavens are above the earth. 22 For if you will be careful to do all this commandment which I command you to do,
loving the LORD your God, walking in all his ways, and cleaving
to him, 23 then the LORD will drive out all these nations before you,

*j*Sam Gk Vg: Heb *I*

11.4
Ex 14.27,28

11.6
Num
16.31–33

11.8
Josh 1.6,7

11.9
Deut 4.40;
9.5; Ex 3.8

11.11
Deut 8.7

11.13
ver 22;
Deut 6.17;
10.12
11.14
Deut 28.12;
Joel 2.23
11.15
Deut 6.11
11.16
Deut 29.18;
8.19
11.17
Deut 6.15;
1 Ki 8.35;
Deut 4.26

11.18
Deut 6.6,8
11.19
Deut 4.9,
10; 6.7
11.20
Deut 6.9

11.22
Deut 6.17;
10.20
11.23
Deut 9.1,5

and you will dispossess nations greater and mightier than yourselves. 24 Every place on which the sole of your foot treads shall be yours; your territory shall be from the wilderness and Lebanon and from the River, the river Eūphrā'tēṣ, to the western sea. 25 No man shall be able to stand against you; the LORD your God will lay the fear of you and the dread of you upon all the land that you shall tread, as he promised you.

e. A blessing and a curse: Israel must choose for herself

26 "Behold, I set before you this day a blessing and a curse: 27 the blessing, if you obey the commandments of the LORD your God, which I command you this day, 28 and the curse, if you do not obey the commandments of the LORD your God, but turn aside from the way which I command you this day, to go after other gods which you have not known. 29And when the LORD your God brings you into the land which you are entering to take possession of it, you shall set the blessing on Mount Gĕr'izĭm and the curse on Mount Ēbál. 30Are they not beyond the Jordan, west of the road, toward the going down of the sun, in the land of the Cā'naaănītes who live in the Ạr'ábáh, over against Gĭlgăl, beside the oak[k] of Morĕh? 31 For you are to pass over the Jordan to go in to take possession of the land which the LORD your God gives you; and when you possess it and live in it, 32 you shall be careful to do all the statutes and the ordinances which I set before you this day.

C. Moses' exposition of the principal Laws

1. Israel shall erect an altar: the place which the LORD will choose

12 "These are the statutes and ordinances which you shall be careful to do in the land which the LORD, the God of your fathers, has given you to possess, all the days that you live upon the earth. 2 You shall surely destroy all the places where the nations whom you shall dispossess served their gods, upon the high mountains and upon the hills and under every green tree; 3 you shall tear down their altars, and dash in pieces their pillars, and burn their Ashĕ'rĭm with fire; you shall hew down the graven images of their gods, and destroy their name out of that place. 4 You shall not do so to the LORD your God. 5 But you shall seek the place which the LORD your God will choose out of all your tribes to put his name and make his habitation there; thither you shall go, 6 and thither you shall bring your burnt offerings and your sacrifices, your tithes and the offering that you present, your votive offerings, your freewill offerings, and the firstlings of your herd and of your flock; 7 and there you shall eat before the LORD your God, and you shall rejoice, you and your households, in all that you undertake, in which the LORD your God has blessed you. 8 You shall not do according to all that we are doing here this day,

---

k Gk Syr: See Gen 12.6. Heb oaks or terebinths

11.24 Josh 1.3; Gen 15.18; Ex 23.31
11.25 Deut 7.24; Ex 23.27
11.26 Deut 30.1, 19
11.27 Deut 28.2
11.28 Deut 28.15
11.29 Deut 27.12; Josh 8.33
11.30 Josh 4.19; Gen 12.6
11.31 Deut 9.1; Josh 1.11
12.1 Deut 4.9, 10
*12.3 Deut 7.5
*12.5 ver 11
12.7 Deut 14.26; ver 12,18

12.3 *pillars*, large upright stones at Canaanite sanctuaries. Some suggest that they may have been symbols of Baal, the Canaanite fertility god. *Asherim*, see note to Ex 34.13.

12.5 *the place*. As a safeguard against idolatry Israel was to have only one legitimate sanctuary. It was originally at Shiloh, but David moved the sanctuary to Jerusalem.

every man doing whatever is right in his own eyes; 9 for you have not as yet come to the rest and to the inheritance which the LORD your God gives you. 10 But when you go over the Jordan, and live in the land which the LORD your God gives you to inherit, and when he gives you rest from all your enemies round about, so that you live in safety, 11 then to the place which the LORD your God will choose, to make his name dwell there, thither you shall bring all that I command you: your burnt offerings and your sacrifices, your tithes and the offering that you present, and all your votive offerings which you vow to the LORD. 12And you shall rejoice before the LORD your God, you and your sons and your daughters, your menservants and your maidservants, and the Lēvīte that is within your towns, since he has no portion or inheritance with you. 13 Take heed that you do not offer your burnt offerings at every place that you see; 14 but at the place which the LORD will choose in one of your tribes, there you shall offer your burnt offerings, and there you shall do all that I am commanding you.

15 "However, you may slaughter and eat flesh within any of your towns, as much as you desire, according to the blessing of the LORD your God which he has given you; the unclean and the clean may eat of it, as of the gazelle and as of the hart. 16 Only you shall not eat the blood; you shall pour it out upon the earth like water. 17 You may not eat within your towns the tithe of your grain or of your wine or of your oil, or the firstlings of your herd or of your flock, or any of your votive offerings which you vow, or your free-will offerings, or the offering that you present; 18 but you shall eat them before the LORD your God in the place which the LORD your God will choose, you and your son and your daughter, your manservant and your maidservant, and the Lēvīte who is within your towns; and you shall rejoice before the LORD your God in all that you undertake. 19 Take heed that you do not forsake the Lēvīte as long as you live in your land.

20 "When the LORD your God enlarges your territory, as he has promised you, and you say, 'I will eat flesh,' because you crave flesh, you may eat as much flesh as you desire. 21 If the place which the LORD your God will choose to put his name there is too far from you, then you may kill any of your herd or your flock, which the LORD has given you, as I have commanded you; and you may eat within your towns as much as you desire. 22 Just as the gazelle or the hart is eaten, so you may eat of it; the unclean and the clean alike may eat of it. 23 Only be sure that you do not eat the blood; for the blood is the life, and you shall not eat the life with the flesh. 24 You shall not eat it; you shall pour it out upon the earth like water. 25 You shall not eat it; that all may go well with you and with your children after you, when you do what is right in the sight of the LORD. 26 But the holy things which are due from you, and your votive offerings, you shall take, and you shall go to the place which the LORD will choose, 27 and offer your burnt offerings, the flesh and the blood, on the altar of the LORD your God; the blood of your sacrifices shall be poured out on the altar of the LORD your God, but the flesh you may eat. 28 Be careful to heed all these words which I command you, that it may go well with you and with your children after you for ever, when you do what is good and right in the sight of the LORD your God.

29 "When the LORD your God cuts off before you the nations

12.10
Deut 11.31

12.11
ver 5

12.12
ver 7;
Deut 10.9

12.14
ver 11

12.15
ver 20–23;
Deut 14.5

12.16
Lev 17.10–12

12.18
ver 5,7,12

12.19
Deut 14.27

12.20
Gen 15.18

12.22
ver 15

12.23
ver 16;
Lev 17.11,14

12.25
Deut 4.40;
13.18

12.26
ver 17

12.28
ver 25;
Deut 4.40

whom you go in to dispossess, and you dispossess them and dwell in their land, 30 take heed that you be not ensnared to follow them, after they have been destroyed before you, and that you do not inquire about their gods, saying, 'How did these nations serve their gods?—that I also may do likewise.' 31 You shall not do so to the LORD your God; for every abominable thing which the LORD hates they have done for their gods; for they even burn their sons and their daughters in the fire to their gods.

12.31
*Deut 9.5;
18.10*

32[1] "Everything that I command you you shall be careful to do; you shall not add to it or take from it.

12.32
Deut 4.2

2. The second commandment
a. False prophets to die

13 "If a prophet arises among you, or a dreamer of dreams, and gives you a sign or a wonder, 2 and the sign or wonder which he tells you comes to pass, and if he says, 'Let us go after other gods,' which you have not known, 'and let us serve them,' 3 you shall not listen to the words of that prophet or to that dreamer of dreams; for the LORD your God is testing you, to know whether you love the LORD your God with all your heart and with all your soul. 4 You shall walk after the LORD your God and fear him, and keep his commandments and obey his voice, and you shall serve him and cleave to him. 5 But that prophet or that dreamer of dreams shall be put to death, because he has taught rebellion against the LORD your God, who brought you out of the land of Egypt and redeemed you out of the house of bondage, to make you leave the way in which the LORD your God commanded you to walk. So you shall purge the evil from the midst of you.

*13.1
Mt 24.24;
Mk 13.22*

*13.2
ver 6,13*

*13.3
Deut 8.2,
16*

*★13.4
2 Ki 23.3;
Deut 10.20*

*13.5
Deut 18.20;
17.7*

b. Secret idolaters to be cut off

6 "If your brother, the son of your mother, or your son, or your daughter, or the wife of your bosom, or your friend who is as your own soul, entices you secretly, saying, 'Let us go and serve other gods,' which neither you nor your fathers have known, 7 some of the gods of the peoples that are round about you, whether near you or far off from you, from the one end of the earth to the other, 8 you shall not yield to him or listen to him, nor shall your eye pity him, nor shall you spare him, nor shall you conceal him; 9 but you shall kill him; your hand shall be first against him to put him to death, and afterwards the hand of all the people. 10 You shall stone him to death with stones, because he sought to draw you away from the LORD your God, who brought you out of the land of Egypt, out of the house of bondage. 11And all Israel shall hear, and fear, and never again do any such wickedness as this among you.

*13.6
Deut 17.2–
7; 29.18*

*13.9
Deut 17.5,7*

*13.11
Deut 19.20*

[1] Ch 13.1 in Heb

13.4 In all ages the indispensable test of one's faith toward God has been grounded in obedience. Obedience must spring from the heart (Rom 6.17); it must be willing and without reservation (Isa 1.19; Josh 22.2, 3); it must be constant in its intention (Phil 2.12). It springs from faith (Heb 11.6) and consists of the following: (1) obedience to the law of God (11.27; Isa 42.24); (2) obedience to the voice of God (Ex 19.5; Jer 7.23); (3) obedience to Christ (2 Cor 10.5); (4) obedience to the gospel (Rom 1.5; 6.17; 10.16, 17); (5) obedience to governing authorities (Rom 13.1). Punishments are threatened for those who disobey, just as blessings are promised those who obey. Scripture abounds with illustrations of individuals who were obedient and followed God.

c. Idolatrous cities to be destroyed

12 "If you hear in one of your cities, which the LORD your God gives you to dwell there, 13 that certain base fellows have gone out among you and have drawn away the inhabitants of the city, saying, 'Let us go and serve other gods,' which you have not known, 14 then you shall inquire and make search and ask diligently; and behold, if it be true and certain that such an abominable thing has been done among you, 15 you shall surely put the inhabitants of that city to the sword, destroying it utterly, all who are in it and its cattle, with the edge of the sword. 16 You shall gather all its spoil into the midst of its open square, and burn the city and all its spoil with fire, as a whole burnt offering to the LORD your God; it shall be a heap for ever, it shall not be built again. 17 None of the devoted things shall cleave to your hand; that the LORD may turn from the fierceness of his anger, and show you mercy, and have compassion on you, and multiply you, as he swore to your fathers, 18 if you obey the voice of the LORD your God, keeping all his commandments which I command you this day, and doing what is right in the sight of the LORD your God.

3. Clean and unclean animals

14 "You are the sons of the LORD your God; you shall not cut yourselves or make any baldness on your foreheads for the dead. 2 For you are a people holy to the LORD your God, and the LORD has chosen you to be a people for his own possession, out of all the peoples that are on the face of the earth.

3 "You shall not eat any abominable thing. 4 These are the animals you may eat: the ox, the sheep, the goat, 5 the hart, the gazelle, the roebuck, the wild goat, the ibex, the antelope, and the mountain-sheep. 6 Every animal that parts the hoof and has the hoof cloven in two, and chews the cud, among the animals, you may eat. 7 Yet of those that chew the cud or have the hoof cloven you shall not eat these: the camel, the hare, and the rock badger, because they chew the cud but do not part the hoof, are unclean for you. 8 And the swine, because it parts the hoof but does not chew the cud, is unclean for you. Their flesh you shall not eat, and their carcasses you shall not touch.

9 "Of all that are in the waters you may eat these: whatever has fins and scales you may eat. 10 And whatever does not have fins and scales you shall not eat; it is unclean for you.

11 "You may eat all clean birds. 12 But these are the ones which you shall not eat: the eagle, the vulture, the osprey, 13 the buzzard, the kite, after their kinds; 14 every raven after its kind; 15 the ostrich, the nighthawk, the sea gull, the hawk, after their kinds; 16 the little owl and the great owl, the water hen 17 and the pelican, the carrion vulture and the cormorant, 18 the stork, the heron, after their kinds; the hoopoe and the bat. 19 And all winged insects are unclean for you; they shall not be eaten. 20 All clean winged things you may eat.

21 "You shall not eat anything that dies of itself; you may give it to the alien who is within your towns, that he may eat it, or you may sell it to a foreigner; for you are a people holy to the LORD your God.

"You shall not boil a kid in its mother's milk.

13.13
ver 2,6;
see 1 Jn 2.19

13.15
Ex 22.20

13.16
Josh 6.24;
8.28

13.17
Num 25.4;
Deut 30.3;
7.13

13.18
Deut 12.28

14.1
Rom 8.16;
Lev 21.5

14.2
Deut 7.6

14.4
Lev 11.2–
45;
Acts 10.14

14.8
Lev 11.26,
27

14.9
Lev 11.9

14.12
Lev 11.3

14.19
Lev 11.20

14.21
Lev 17.15;
ver 2;
Ex 29.19;
34.26

4. *The tithe of fruits*

*14.22ff
Lev 27.30
14.23
Deut 12.5–
7; 4.10

22 "You shall tithe all the yield of your seed, which comes forth from the field year by year. 23And before the LORD your God, in the place which he will choose, to make his name dwell there, you shall eat the tithe of your grain, of your wine, and of your oil, and the firstlings of your herd and flock; that you may learn to fear the LORD your God always. 24And if the way is too long for you, so

14.24
Deut 12.5,
21

that you are not able to bring the tithe, when the LORD your God blesses you, because the place is too far from you, which the LORD your God chooses, to set his name there, 25 then you shall turn it into money, and bind up the money in your hand, and go to the

*14.26
Deut 12.7,
18

place which the LORD your God chooses, 26 and spend the money for whatever you desire, oxen, or sheep, or wine or strong drink, whatever your appetite craves; and you shall eat there before the LORD your God and rejoice, you and your household. 27And you

14.27
Deut 12.12;
Num 18.20

shall not forsake the Lēvīte who is within your towns, for he has no portion or inheritance with you.

14.28
Deut 26.12

28 "At the end of every three years you shall bring forth all the tithe of your produce in the same year, and lay it up within your towns; 29 and the Lēvīte, because he has no portion or inheritance

14.29
Deut 26.12;
ver 27;
Deut 15.10

with you, and the sojourner, the fatherless, and the widow, who are within your towns, shall come and eat and be filled; that the LORD your God may bless you in all the work of your hands that you do.

5. *Laws relating to slaves and the poor*
a. *The year of release*

15.1
Deut 31.10

15 "At the end of every seven years you shall grant a release. 2And this is the manner of the release: every creditor shall release what he has lent to his neighbor; he shall not exact it of his neighbor, his brother, because the LORD's release has been proclaimed. 3 Of a foreigner you may exact it; but whatever of yours is with your brother your hand shall release. 4 But there will be no poor among you (for the LORD will bless you in the land which the LORD your God gives you for an inheritance to possess), 5 if

15.5
Deut 28.1

only you will obey the voice of the LORD your God, being careful to do all this commandment which I command you this day. 6 For

15.6
Deut 28.12,
13

the LORD your God will bless you, as he promised you, and you shall lend to many nations, but you shall not borrow; and you shall rule over many nations, but they shall not rule over you.

15.7
1 Jn 3.17

7 "If there is among you a poor man, one of your brethren, in any of your towns within your land which the LORD your God gives you, you shall not harden your heart or shut your hand against your poor brother, 8 but you shall open your hand to him,

15.8
Lev 25.35
15.9
ver 1;
Deut 24.15

and lend him sufficient for his need, whatever it may be. 9 Take heed lest there be a base thought in your heart, and you say, 'The seventh year, the year of release is near,' and your eye be hostile to your poor brother, and you give him nothing, and he cry to the

15.10
2 Cor 9.5,
7;
Deut 24.19

LORD against you, and it be sin in you. 10 You shall give to him freely, and your heart shall not be grudging when you give to him; because for this the LORD your God will bless you in all your work

---

14.22-27 This law of the tithe is different from the law of the tithe found in Num 18.21–24. The one apparently superseded the other.
14.26 *wine*, Hebrew *yayin*, fermented grape juice. *strong drink*, Hebrew *shekar*, probably beer, since the Israelites did not have distilled liquors. The Hebrew word for *strong drink* comes from the verb meaning "to be drunk."

and in all that you undertake. 11 For the poor will never cease out of the land; therefore I command you, You shall open wide your hand to your brother, to the needy and to the poor, in the land.

b. *Manumission of slaves*

12 "If your brother, a Hebrew man, or a Hebrew woman, is sold to you, he shall serve you six years, and in the seventh year you shall let him go free from you. 13And when you let him go free from you, you shall not let him go empty-handed; 14 you shall furnish him liberally out of your flock, out of your threshing floor, and out of your wine press; as the LORD your God has blessed you, you shall give to him. 15 You shall remember that you were a slave in the land of Egypt, and the LORD your God redeemed you; therefore I command you this today. 16 But if he says to you, 'I will not go out from you,' because he loves you and your household, since he fares well with you, 17 then you shall take an awl, and thrust it through his ear into the door, and he shall be your bondman for ever. And to your bondwoman you shall do likewise. 18 It shall not seem hard to you, when you let him go free from you; for at half the cost of a hired servant he has served you six years. So the LORD your God will bless you in all that you do.

c. *Sacrifice of firstling males*

19 "All the firstling males that are born of your herd and flock you shall consecrate to the LORD your God; you shall do no work with the firstling of your herd, nor shear the firstling of your flock. 20 You shall eat it, you and your household, before the LORD your God year by year at the place which the LORD will choose. 21 But if it has any blemish, if it is lame or blind, or has any serious blemish whatever, you shall not sacrifice it to the LORD your God. 22 You shall eat it within your towns; the unclean and the clean alike may eat it, as though it were a gazelle or a hart. 23 Only you shall not eat its blood; you shall pour it out on the ground like water.

6. *The Passover*

16 "Observe the month of Ābïb, and keep the passover to the LORD your God; for in the month of Abib the LORD your God brought you out of Egypt by night. 2And you shall offer the passover sacrifice to the LORD your God, from the flock or the herd, at the place which the LORD will choose, to make his name dwell there. 3 You shall eat no leavened bread with it; seven days you shall eat it with unleavened bread, the bread of affliction—for you came out of the land of Egypt in hurried flight—that all the days of your life you may remember the day when you came out of the land of Egypt. 4 No leaven shall be seen with you in all your territory for seven days; nor shall any of the flesh which you sacrifice on the evening of the first day remain all night until morning. 5 You may not offer the passover sacrifice within any of your towns which the LORD your God gives you; 6 but at the place which the LORD your God will choose, to make his name dwell in it, there

15.11 Mt 26.11; Mk 14.7; Jn 12.8

15.12 Ex 21.2; Lev 25.39

15.15 Deut 5.15; 16.12 *15.16 Ex 21.5,6

15.19 Ex 13.2

15.20 Deut 12.5–7,17

15.21 Lev 22.19–25

15.22 Deut 12.15, 22

15.23 Deut 12.16, 23

16.1 Ex 12.2,29, 42; 13.4

16.2 Deut 12.5, 26

16.3 Ex 12.8,15

16.4 Ex 13.7; 12.10

16.6 Deut 12.5; Ex 12.6

15.16 God had redeemed Israel from slavery in Egypt, therefore no Israelite could be held in slavery perpetually without the consent of the person. In some cases slavery offered more security and better conditions than individual freedom could give.

you shall offer the passover sacrifice, in the evening at the going
down of the sun, at the time you came out of Egypt. 7And you shall
boil it and eat it at the place which the LORD your God will choose;
and in the morning you shall turn and go to your tents. 8 For six
days you shall eat unleavened bread; and on the seventh day there
shall be a solemn assembly to the LORD your God; you shall do
no work on it.

7. The Feast of Weeks

9 "You shall count seven weeks; begin to count the seven weeks
from the time you first put the sickle to the standing grain. 10 Then
you shall keep the feast of weeks to the LORD your God with the
tribute of a freewill offering from your hand, which you shall give
as the LORD your God blesses you; 11 and you shall rejoice before
the LORD your God, you and your son and your daughter, your
manservant and your maidservant, the Lēvīte who is within your
towns, the sojourner, the fatherless, and the widow who are
among you, at the place which the LORD your God will choose, to
make his name dwell there. 12 You shall remember that you were a
slave in Egypt; and you shall be careful to observe these statutes.

8. The Feast of Tabernacles

13 "You shall keep the feast of booths seven days, when you
make your ingathering from your threshing floor and your wine
press; 14 you shall rejoice in your feast, you and your son and your
daughter, your manservant and your maidservant, the Lēvīte, the
sojourner, the fatherless, and the widow who are within your
towns. 15 For seven days you shall keep the feast to the LORD your
God at the place which the LORD will choose; because the LORD
your God will bless you in all your produce and in all the work of
your hands, so that you will be altogether joyful.

16 "Three times a year all your males shall appear before the
LORD your God at the place which he will choose: at the feast of
unleavened bread, at the feast of weeks, and at the feast of booths.
They shall not appear before the LORD empty-handed; 17 every
man shall give as he is able, according to the blessing of the LORD
your God which he has given you.

9. The administration of justice
a. Judges

18 "You shall appoint judges and officers in all your towns
which the LORD your God gives you, according to your tribes; and
they shall judge the people with righteous judgment. 19 You shall
not pervert justice; you shall not show partiality; and you shall not
take a bribe, for a bribe blinds the eyes of the wise and subverts
the cause of the righteous. 20 Justice, and only justice, you shall
follow, that you may live and inherit the land which the LORD
your God gives you.

b. Prohibitions: idolatry and blemished sacrifices

21 "You shall not plant any tree as an Ashē'ráh beside the altar
of the LORD your God which you shall make. 22And you shall not
set up a pillar, which the LORD your God hates.

17 "You shall not sacrifice to the LORD your God an ox or a
sheep in which is a blemish, any defect whatever; for that
is an abomination to the LORD your God.

16.7
Ex 12.8,9

16.8
Ex 12.16

16.9
Ex 23.16;
34.22;
Lev 23.15;
Num 28.26

16.11
Deut 12.7,
12

16.12
Deut 15.15

16.13
Ex 23.16;
Lev 23.34
16.14
ver 11

16.15
Lev 23.39

16.16
Ex 23.14–
17; 34.20,
23

16.18
Deut 1.16

16.19
Deut 1.17;
Ex 23.8

16.21
Ex 34.13;
Deut 7.5

17.1
Deut 15.21;
Mal 1.8,13

2 "If there is found among you, within any of your towns which the LORD your God gives you, a man or woman who does what is evil in the sight of the LORD your God, in transgressing his covenant, 3 and has gone and served other gods and worshiped them, or the sun or the moon or any of the host of heaven, which I have forbidden, 4 and it is told you and you hear of it; then you shall inquire diligently, and if it is true and certain that such an abominable thing has been done in Israel, 5 then you shall bring forth to your gates that man or woman who has done this evil thing, and you shall stone that man or woman to death with stones. 6 On the evidence of two witnesses or of three witnesses he that is to die shall be put to death; a person shall not be put to death on the evidence of one witness. 7 The hand of the witnesses shall be first against him to put him to death, and afterward the hand of all the people. So you shall purge the evil from the midst of you.

c. *The court of appeal*

8 "If any case arises requiring decision between one kind of homicide and another, one kind of legal right and another, or one kind of assault and another, any case within your towns which is too difficult for you, then you shall arise and go up to the place which the LORD your God will choose, 9 and coming to the Lévĭt́-ĭcăl priests, and to the judge who is in office in those days, you shall consult them, and they shall declare to you the decision. 10 Then you shall do according to what they declare to you from that place which the LORD will choose; and you shall be careful to do according to all that they direct you; 11 according to the instructions which they give you, and according to the decision which they pronounce to you, you shall do; you shall not turn aside from the verdict which they declare to you, either to the right hand or to the left. 12 The man who acts presumptuously, by not obeying the priest who stands to minister there before the LORD your God, or the judge, that man shall die; so you shall purge the evil from Israel. 13 And all the people shall hear, and fear, and not act presumptuously again.

10. *The choice of a king*

14 "When you come to the land which the LORD your God gives you, and you possess it and dwell in it, and then say, 'I will set a king over me, like all the nations that are round about me'; 15 you may indeed set as king over you him whom the LORD your God will choose. One from among your brethren you shall set as king over you; you may not put a foreigner over you, who is not your brother. 16 Only he must not multiply horses for himself, or cause the people to return to Egypt in order to multiply horses, since the LORD has said to you, 'You shall never return that way again.' 17 And he shall not multiply wives for himself, lest his heart turn away; nor shall he greatly multiply for himself silver and gold.

17.2 Deut 13.6
17.4 Deut 13.12, 14
17.6 Num 35.30; Deut 19.15; Mt 18.16
17.7 Deut 13.5,9
17.8 Deut 12.5
17.9 Deut 19.17; Ezek 44.24
17.11 Deut 25.1
17.13 Deut 13.11; 19.20
★**17.14** Deut 11.31; 1 Sam 8.5, 19,20
17.15 Jer 30.21
★**17.16ff** 1 Ki 4.26; 10.26,28; Isa 31.1; Ezek 17.15
17.17 cf. 1 Ki 11.3,4

17.14 Moses predicted that Israel would ask for a king. Although the people's motive would be offensive to God, He had included all this in His plan and had decreed the eventual establishment of the Davidic throne in anticipation of the reign of Christ.

17.16-20 In the historical books we frequently read of otherwise godly people multiplying horses, wives, silver, and gold contrary to these regulations. David and Solomon had God's blessing in spite of their violating these precepts.

18.10 | Deut 31.24–26
17.18
17.19 | Josh 1.8
17.20 | Deut 5.32

18 "And when he sits on the throne of his kingdom, he shall write for himself in a book a copy of this law, from that which is in charge of the Levit'ical priests; 19 and it shall be with him, and he shall read in it all the days of his life, that he may learn to fear the LORD his God, by keeping all the words of this law and these statutes, and doing them; 20 that his heart may not be lifted up above his brethren, and that he may not turn aside from the commandment, either to the right hand or to the left; so that he may continue long in his kingdom, he and his children, in Israel.

11. The portion of the priests and Levites

18.1 | Deut 10.9; 1 Cor 9.13

18 "The Levit'ical priests, that is, all the tribe of Levi, shall have no portion or inheritance with Israel; they shall eat the offerings by fire to the LORD, and his rightful dues. 2 They shall have no inheritance among their brethren; the LORD is their inheritance, as he promised them. 3 And this shall be the priests' due from the people, from those offering a sacrifice, whether it be ox or sheep: they shall give to the priest the shoulder and the two cheeks and the stomach. 4 The first fruits of your grain, of your wine and of your oil, and the first of the fleece of your sheep, you shall give him. 5 For the LORD your God has chosen him out of all your tribes, to stand and minister in the name of the LORD, him and his sons for ever.

18.3 | Lev 7.30–34
18.4 | Ex 22.29; Num 18.12
18.5 | Ex 28.1; Deut 10.8

6 "And if a Levite comes from any of your towns out of all Israel, where he lives—and he may come when he desires—to the place which the LORD will choose, 7 then he may minister in the name of the LORD his God, like all his fellow-Levites who stand to minister there before the LORD. 8 They shall have equal portions to eat, besides what he receives from the sale of his patrimony.m

18.8 | Neh 12.44, 47

12. The law of the prophet
a. Canaanitish abominations forbidden

18.9 | Deut 12.29–31
*18.10 | Deut 12.31; Lev 19.26, 31
18.12 | Deut 9.4

9 "When you come into the land which the LORD your God gives you, you shall not learn to follow the abominable practices of those nations. 10 There shall not be found among you any one who burns his son or his daughter as an offering,n any one who practices divination, a soothsayer, or an augur, or a sorcerer, 11 or a charmer, or a medium, or a wizard, or a necromancer. 12 For whoever does these things is an abomination to the LORD; and because of these abominable practices the LORD your God is driving them out before you. 13 You shall be blameless before the LORD your God. 14 For these nations, which you are about to dispossess, give heed to soothsayers and to diviners; but as for you, the LORD your God has not allowed you so to do.

m Heb obscure n Heb makes his son or his daughter pass through the fire

18.10 Divination as practiced by the heathen is sternly forbidden by Scripture. The following classes or categories of diviners are included: diviner, soothsayer, augur, sorcerer, charmer, medium, necromancer (18.10, 11), magician (Gen 41.8; Dan 4.7), astrologer (Isa 47.13; Dan 4.7). According to the Mari tablets, divination flourished in upper Mesopotamia and Syria. One of its chief functions was to determine the proper move. Every army had a diviner whose task it was to decide, for example, which route to take at the fork of the road. Israel had Yahweh to lead it, therefore such heathen practices were inconsistent with true faith. In the Old Testament, those who practiced these forbidden arts were subject to the death penalty (Ex 22.18; Lev 20.27). In the New Testament, it is stated that sorcerers shall not inherit the kingdom of God (Gal 5.20; Rev 22.15), although there is no injunction that such profane people should be killed today.

b. The predicted coming of the prophet Messiah:
the test of a false prophet

15 "The LORD your God will raise up for you a prophet like me from among you, from your brethren—him you shall heed— 16 just as you desired of the LORD your God at Horĕb on the day of the assembly, when you said, 'Let me not hear again the voice of the LORD my God, or see this great fire any more, lest I die.' 17And the LORD said to me, 'They have rightly said all that they have spoken. 18 I will raise up for them a prophet like you from among their brethren; and I will put my words in his mouth, and he shall speak to them all that I command him. 19And whoever will not give heed to my words which he shall speak in my name, I myself will require it of him. 20 But the prophet who presumes to speak a word in my name which I have not commanded him to speak, or who speaks in the name of other gods, that same prophet shall die.' 21And if you say in your heart, 'How may we know the word which the LORD has not spoken?'—22 when a prophet speaks in the name of the LORD, if the word does not come to pass or come true, that is a word which the LORD has not spoken; the prophet has spoken it presumptuously, you need not be afraid of him.

13. Criminal laws
a. Cities of refuge for accidental manslaughter

19 "When the LORD your God cuts off the nations whose land the LORD your God gives you, and you dispossess them and dwell in their cities and in their houses, 2 you shall set apart three cities for you in the land which the LORD your God gives you to possess. 3 You shall prepare the roads, and divide into three parts the area of the land which the LORD your God gives you as a possession, so that any manslayer can flee to them.

4 "This is the provision for the manslayer, who by fleeing there may save his life. If any one kills his neighbor unintentionally without having been at enmity with him in time past—5 as when a man goes into the forest with his neighbor to cut wood, and his hand swings the axe to cut down a tree, and the head slips from the handle and strikes his neighbor so that he dies—he may flee to one of these cities and save his life; 6 lest the avenger of blood in hot anger pursue the manslayer and overtake him, because the way is long, and wound him mortally, though the man did not deserve to die, since he was not at enmity with his neighbor in time past. 7 Therefore I command you, You shall set apart three cities. 8And if the LORD your God enlarges your border, as he has sworn to your fathers, and gives you all the land which he promised to give to your fathers—9 provided you are careful to keep all this commandment, which I command you this day, by loving the LORD your God and by walking ever in his ways—then you shall add three other cities to these three, 10 lest innocent blood be shed in your land which the LORD your God gives you for an inheritance, and so the guilt of bloodshed be upon you.

*18.15ff Jn 1.21; Acts 3.22; 7.37
18.16 Deut 5.23-27; Ex 20.19
18.17 Deut 5.28
18.18 ver 15; Isa 51.16; Jn 4.25,26
18.19 Acts 3.23
18.20 Deut 13.1,2,5
18.22 Jer 28.9; ver 20
19.1 Deut 12.29
19.2 Num 35.10,14
19.4 Num 35.15
19.6 Num 35.12
19.9 Josh 20.7,8
19.10 Deut 21.1-9; Num 35.33

18.15-22 Since divination of all sorts is outlawed, God promises to raise up a prophet like Moses in succeeding generations. Each of these prophets will speak God's words, and instruct the people in the way they should go. The false prophet will be proven wrong and he will die for his presumption. The ultimate prophet like Moses was to be Jesus Christ. To see and hear him was to see and hear God.

b. *Punishment for murderers*

11 "But if any man hates his neighbor, and lies in wait for him, and attacks him, and wounds him mortally so that he dies, and the man flees into one of these cities, 12 then the elders of his city shall send and fetch him from there, and hand him over to the avenger of blood, so that he may die. 13 Your eye shall not pity him, but you shall purge the guilt of innocent blood*o* from Israel, so that it may be well with you.

c. *Removing landmarks*

14 "In the inheritance which you will hold in the land that the LORD your God gives you to possess, you shall not remove your neighbor's landmark, which the men of old have set.

d. *The law of witnesses*

15 "A single witness shall not prevail against a man for any crime or for any wrong in connection with any offense that he has committed; only on the evidence of two witnesses, or of three witnesses, shall a charge be sustained. 16 If a malicious witness rises against any man to accuse him of wrongdoing, 17 then both parties to the dispute shall appear before the LORD, before the priests and the judges who are in office in those days; 18 the judges shall inquire diligently, and if the witness is a false witness and has accused his brother falsely, 19 then you shall do to him as he had meant to do to his brother; so you shall purge the evil from the midst of you. 20 And the rest shall hear, and fear, and shall never again commit any such evil among you. 21 Your eye shall not pity; it shall be life for life, eye for eye, tooth for tooth, hand for hand, foot for foot.

14. *Laws of war*
a. *Military service*

20 "When you go forth to war against your enemies, and see horses and chariots and an army larger than your own, you shall not be afraid of them; for the LORD your God is with you, who brought you up out of the land of Egypt. 2 And when you draw near to the battle, the priest shall come forward and speak to the people, 3 and shall say to them, 'Hear, O Israel, you draw near this day to battle against your enemies: let not your heart faint; do not fear, or tremble, or be in dread of them; 4 for the LORD your God is he that goes with you, to fight for you against your enemies, to give you the victory.' 5 Then the officers shall speak to the people, saying, 'What man is there that has built a new house and has not dedicated it? Let him go back to his house, lest he die in the battle and another man dedicate it. 6 And what man is there that has planted a vineyard and has not enjoyed its fruit? Let him go back to his house, lest he die in the battle and another man enjoy its fruit. 7 And what man is there that has betrothed a wife and has not taken her? Let him go back to his house, lest he die in the battle and another man take her.' 8 And the officers shall speak further to the people, and say, 'What man is there that is

o Or *the blood of the innocent*

19.14 *landmark*. Evidently it was a common practice to move the boundary stones, thereby encroaching and eventually robbing the poor neighbor of some property.

Margin references:
19.13 Deut 7.2
*19.14 Deut 27.17
19.15 Num 35.30; Deut 17.6; Mt 18.16; 2 Cor 13.1
19.16 Ex 23.1; Ps 27.12
19.17 Deut 17.9
19.19 Prov 19.5,9
19.21 ver 13; Ex 21.23; Lev 24.20; Mt 5.38
20.1 Deut 31.6, 8
20.3 ver 1; Josh 23.10
20.4 Deut 1.30
20.6 1 Cor 9.7
20.7 Deut 24.5
20.8 Judg 7.3

fearful and fainthearted? Let him go back to his house, lest the heart of his fellows melt as his heart.' 9And when the officers have made an end of speaking to the people, then commanders shall be appointed at the head of the people.

b. *Sieges*

10 "When you draw near to a city to fight against it, offer terms of peace to it. 11And if its answer to you is peace and it opens to you, then all the people who are found in it shall do forced labor for you and shall serve you. 12 But if it makes no peace with you, but makes war against you, then you shall besiege it; 13 and when the LORD your God gives it into your hand you shall put all its males to the sword, 14 but the women and the little ones, the cattle, and everything else in the city, all its spoil, you shall take as booty for yourselves; and you shall enjoy the spoil of your enemies, which the LORD your God has given you. 15 Thus you shall do to all the cities which are very far from you, which are not cities of the nations here. 16 But in the cities of these peoples that the LORD your God gives you for an inheritance, you shall save alive nothing that breathes, 17 but you shall utterly destroy them, the Hĭttĭtes and the Ăm'ŏrĭtes, the Cā'naánĭtes and the Pĕr'ĭzzĭtes, the Hĭvĭtes and the Jĕb'ūsĭtes, as the LORD your God has commanded; 18 that they may not teach you to do according to all their abominable practices which they have done in the service of their gods, and so to sin against the LORD your God.

19 "When you besiege a city for a long time, making war against it in order to take it, you shall not destroy its trees by wielding an axe against them; for you may eat of them, but you shall not cut them down. Are the trees in the field men that they should be besieged by you? 20 Only the trees which you know are not trees for food you may destroy and cut down that you may build siegeworks against the city that makes war with you, until it falls.

15. *Sundry laws*
a. *Sacrifice for unknown murderer's crime*

21 "If in the land which the LORD your God gives you to possess, any one is found slain, lying in the open country, and it is not known who killed him, 2 then your elders and your judges shall come forth, and they shall measure the distance to the cities which are around him that is slain; 3 and the elders of the city which is nearest to the slain man shall take a heifer which has never been worked and which has not pulled in the yoke. 4And the elders of that city shall bring the heifer down to a valley with running water, which is neither plowed nor sown, and shall break the heifer's neck there in the valley. 5And the priests the sons of Lēvī shall come forward, for the LORD your God has chosen them to minister to him and to bless in the name of the LORD, and by their word every dispute and every assault shall be settled. 6And all the elders of that city nearest to the slain man shall wash their hands over the heifer whose neck was broken in the valley; 7 and they shall testify, 'Our hands did not shed this blood, neither did

*20.10ff
Lk 14.31

20.14
Josh 8.2;
22.8

20.16
Deut 7.1,2;
Josh 11.14

20.18
Ex 23.33

21.1
Josh 1.6

21.5
Deut 17.8–
11

*21.7

20.10-18 See note to 2.34.
21.7 This verse shows that crime and sin have corporate, as well as individual, implications. (See also ver 9.)

21.8
Jon 1.8
our eyes see it shed. 8 Forgive, O LORD, thy people Israel, whom thou hast redeemed, and set not the guilt of innocent blood in the midst of thy people Israel; but let the guilt of blood be forgiven them.' 9 So you shall purge the guilt of innocent blood from your midst, when you do what is right in the sight of the LORD.

21.9
Deut 19.13

b. *Marrying a captive woman*

21.12
Lev 14.8,9;
Num 6.9
10 "When you go forth to war against your enemies, and the LORD your God gives them into your hands, and you take them captive, 11 and see among the captives a beautiful woman, and you have desire for her and would take her for yourself as wife, 12 then you shall bring her home to your house, and she shall shave her head and pare her nails. 13And she shall put off her captive's garb, and shall remain in your house and bewail her father and her mother a full month; after that you may go in to her, and be her husband, and she shall be your wife. 14 Then, if you have no delight in her, you shall let her go where she will; but you shall not sell her for money, you shall not treat her as a slave, since you have humiliated her.

c. *The law of the first-born*

21.16
1 Chr 26.10
15 "If a man has two wives, the one loved and the other disliked, and they have borne him children, both the loved and the disliked, and if the first-born son is hers that is disliked, 16 then on the day when he assigns his possessions as an inheritance to his sons, he may not treat the son of the loved as the first-born in preference to the son of the disliked, who is the first-born, 17 but he shall acknowledge the first-born, the son of the disliked, by giving him a double portion of all that he has, for he is the first issue of his strength; the right of the first-born is his.

21.17
Gen 49.3

d. *Stoning of a rebellious son*

21.18
Isa 30.1
18 "If a man has a stubborn and rebellious son, who will not obey the voice of his father or the voice of his mother, and, though they chastise him, will not give heed to them, 19 then his father and his mother shall take hold of him and bring him out to the elders of his city at the gate of the place where he lives, 20 and they shall say to the elders of his city, 'This our son is stubborn and rebellious, he will not obey our voice; he is a glutton and a drunkard.' 21 Then all the men of the city shall stone him to death with stones; so you shall purge the evil from your midst; and all Israel shall hear, and fear.

21.21
Deut 13.5,
11

e. *Burying a hanged criminal*

21.23
Josh 8.29;
10.26,27;
Jn 19.31;
Gal 3.13
22 "And if a man has committed a crime punishable by death and he is put to death, and you hang him on a tree, 23 his body shall not remain all night upon the tree, but you shall bury him the same day, for a hanged man is accursed by God; you shall not defile your land which the LORD your God gives you for an inheritance.

f. *The law of neighborliness*

22.1
Ex 23.4
22 "You shall not see your brother's ox or his sheep go astray, and withhold your help*p* from them; you shall take them back to your brother. 2And if he is not near you, or if you do not know him, you shall bring it home to your house, and it shall be

p Heb *hide yourself*

with you until your brother seeks it; then you shall restore it to him. ³And so you shall do with his ass; so you shall do with his garment; so you shall do with any lost thing of your brother's, which he loses and you find; you may not withhold your help. ⁴ You shall not see your brother's ass or his ox fallen down by the way, and withhold your help*p* from them; you shall help him to lift them up again.

g. *Incidental laws*

5 "A woman shall not wear anything that pertains to a man, nor shall a man put on a woman's garment; for whoever does these things is an abomination to the LORD your God.

6 "If you chance to come upon a bird's nest, in any tree or on the ground, with young ones or eggs and the mother sitting upon the young or upon the eggs, you shall not take the mother with the young; ⁷ you shall let the mother go, but the young you may take to yourself; that it may go well with you, and that you may live long.

8 "When you build a new house, you shall make a parapet for your roof, that you may not bring the guilt of blood upon your house, if any one fall from it.

9 "You shall not sow your vineyard with two kinds of seed, lest the whole yield be forfeited to the sanctuary,*q* the crop which you have sown and the yield of the vineyard. ¹⁰ You shall not plow with an ox and an ass together. ¹¹ You shall not wear a mingled stuff, wool and linen together.

12 "You shall make yourself tassels on the four corners of your cloak with which you cover yourself.

h. *The laws of sexual relationships*

13 "If any man takes a wife, and goes in to her, and then spurns her, ¹⁴ and charges her with shameful conduct, and brings an evil name upon her, saying, 'I took this woman, and when I came near her, I did not find in her the tokens of virginity,' ¹⁵ then the father of the young woman and her mother shall take and bring out the tokens of her virginity to the elders of the city in the gate; ¹⁶ and the father of the young woman shall say to the elders, 'I gave my daughter to this man to wife, and he spurns her; ¹⁷ and lo, he has made shameful charges against her, saying, "I did not find in your daughter the tokens of virginity." And yet these are the tokens of my daughter's virginity.' And they shall spread the garment before the elders of the city. ¹⁸ Then the elders of that city shall take the man and whip him; ¹⁹ and they shall fine him a hundred shekels of silver, and give them to the father of the young woman, because he has brought an evil name upon a virgin of Israel; and she shall be his wife; he may not put her away all his days. ²⁰ But if the thing is true, that the tokens of virginity were not found in the young woman, ²¹ then they shall bring out the young woman to the door of her father's house, and the men of her city shall stone her to death with stones, because she has wrought folly in Israel by playing the harlot in her father's house; so you shall purge the evil from the midst of you.

22 "If a man is found lying with the wife of another man, both of them shall die, the man who lay with the woman, and the woman; so you shall purge the evil from Israel.

---

p Heb *hide yourself*   *q* Heb *become holy*

22.4
Ex 23.5

22.6
Lev 22.28

22.7
Deut 4.40

22.9
Lev 19.19

22.11
Lev 19.19
22.12
Num
15.37–41;
Mt 23.5

22.13
Deut 24.1

22.15
ver 23ff

22.21
Deut 23.17,
18; 13.5

22.22
Lev 20.10;
Jn 8.5

23 "If there is a betrothed virgin, and a man meets her in the
22.24
ver 21,22
city and lies with her, 24 then you shall bring them both out to the
gate of that city, and you shall stone them to death with stones, the
young woman because she did not cry for help though she was in
the city, and the man because he violated his neighbor's wife; so
you shall purge the evil from the midst of you.

22.25
Jn 8.1–11
25 "But if in the open country a man meets a young woman who
is betrothed, and the man seizes her and lies with her, then only
the man who lay with her shall die. 26 But to the young woman
you shall do nothing; in the young woman there is no offense punishable by death, for this case is like that of a man attacking and
murdering his neighbor; 27 because he came upon her in the open
country, and though the betrothed young woman cried for help
there was no one to rescue her.

22.28
Ex 22.16,17
28 "If a man meets a virgin who is not betrothed, and seizes her
and lies with her, and they are found, 29 then the man who lay
with her shall give to the father of the young woman fifty shekels
of silver, and she shall be his wife, because he has violated her;
he may not put her away all his days.

22.30
Deut 27.20
30ʳ "A man shall not take his father's wife, nor shall he uncover
her who is his father's.ˢ

i. *Those excluded from the congregation of Israel*

23 "He whose testicles are crushed or whose male member is
cut off shall not enter the assembly of the LORD.
2 "No bastard shall enter the assembly of the LORD; even to the
tenth generation none of his descendants shall enter the assembly
of the LORD.

23.3
Neh 13.1,2
3 "No Am'monīte or Mō'ābīte shall enter the assembly of the
LORD; even to the tenth generation none belonging to them shall
23.4
Num 22.5,6
enter the assembly of the LORD for ever; 4 because they did not
meet you with bread and with water on the way, when you came
forth out of Egypt, and because they hired against you Bālaàm the
son of Bēor from Pēthor of Mĕsŏpŏtā'miă, to curse you. 5 Nevertheless the LORD your God would not hearken to Bālaàm; but the
LORD your God turned the curse into a blessing for you, because
the LORD your God loved you. 6 You shall not seek their peace or
their prosperity all your days for ever.

23.7
Gen 25.24–
26
7 "You shall not abhor an Ē'dŏmīte, for he is your brother; you
shall not abhor an Egyptian, because you were a sojourner in his
land. 8 The children of the third generation that are born to them
may enter the assembly of the LORD.
9 "When you go forth against your enemies and are in camp,
then you shall keep yourself from every evil thing.

j. *Camp sanitation in wartime*

23.10
Lev 15.16
10 "If there is among you any man who is not clean by reason of
what chances to him by night, then he shall go outside the camp,
he shall not come within the camp; 11 but when evening comes on,
he shall bathe himself in water, and when the sun is down, he may
come within the camp.
12 "You shall have a place outside the camp and you shall go
out to it; 13 and you shall have a stick with your weapons; and
when you sit down outside, you shall dig a hole with it, and turn

ʳ Ch 23.1 in Heb   ˢ Heb *uncover his father's skirt*

back and cover up your excrement. 14 Because the LORD your
God walks in the midst of your camp, to save you and to give up
your enemies before you, therefore your camp must be holy, that
he may not see anything indecent among you, and turn away
from you.

k. Incidental laws

15 "You shall not give up to his master a slave who has escaped
from his master to you; 16 he shall dwell with you, in your midst,
in the place which he shall choose within one of your towns, where
it pleases him best; you shall not oppress him.

17 "There shall be no cult prostitute of the daughters of Israel,
neither shall there be a cult prostitute of the sons of Israel. 18 You
shall not bring the hire of a harlot, or the wages of a dog,ᵗ into
the house of the LORD your God in payment for any vow; for both
of these are an abomination to the LORD your God.

19 "You shall not lend upon interest to your brother, interest on
money, interest on victuals, interest on anything that is lent for
interest. 20 To a foreigner you may lend upon interest, but to
your brother you shall not lend upon interest; that the LORD your
God may bless you in all that you undertake in the land which you
are entering to take possession of it.

21 "When you make a vow to the LORD your God, you shall not
be slack to pay it; for the LORD your God will surely require it of
you, and it would be sin in you. 22 But if you refrain from vowing,
it shall be no sin in you. 23 You shall be careful to perform what
has passed your lips, for you have voluntarily vowed to the LORD
your God what you have promised with your mouth.

24 "When you go into your neighbor's vineyard, you may eat
your fill of grapes, as many as you wish, but you shall not put any
in your vessel. 25 When you go into your neighbor's standing grain,
you may pluck the ears with your hand, but you shall not put a
sickle to your neighbor's standing grain.

1. Additional incidental laws

24 "When a man takes a wife and marries her, if then she
finds no favor in his eyes because he has found some indecency
in her, and he writes her a bill of divorce and puts it in her hand
and sends her out of his house, and she departs out of his house,
2 and if she goes and becomes another man's wife, 3 and the latter

Reference column:
23.14 Lev 26.12
*23.17 Deut 22.21
23.19 Ex 22.25; Lev 25.36, 37
23.20 Deut 28.12
23.21 Num 30.2; Mt 5.33
23.25 Mt 12.1; Mk 2.23; Lk 6.1
*24.1 Deut 22.13-21; Mt 5.31; 19.7; Mk 10.4

ᵗ Or sodomite

23.17 Sacred prostitution, both male and female, was part of the idolatrous Canaanite worship. In fact, the designations for these prostitutes derives from the word meaning "to be holy."

24.1 This provision was designed to protect the property rights of a divorced woman; this "bill of divorcement" compelled the husband to surrender his claim on her dowry. Christ made it clear that divorce was permitted in Old Testament times because of hardness of heart (Mt 19.8); it did not imply divine endorsement of divorce, for God's purpose in the institution of marriage was set forth clearly in Gen 2.24. But for Christians, as citizens of the kingdom of heaven, Christ forbade divorce except on the grounds of adultery (Mt 5.32 and 19.9). Since the adulterous act, like death, breaks the marriage bond, most Christians feel that Jesus implied the right of the innocent party to remarry. Some have suggested that wilful desertion is also grounds for divorce and remarriage although there is no clear Scripture to support this. Beyond these two reasons there seem to be no others which are acceptable grounds for breaking the marriage relationship. A Christian who marries the innocent party to a divorce is not guilty of sin; but for a Christian to marry a divorced person who was the guilty partner or who was divorced for no biblical reason is to commit adultery in the eyes of heaven. Some argue that marriage may be dissolved only by death.

husband dislikes her and writes her a bill of divorce and puts it in her hand and sends her out of his house, or if the latter husband dies, who took her to be his wife, 4 then her former husband, who sent her away, may not take her again to be his wife, after she has been defiled; for that is an abomination before the LORD, and you shall not bring guilt upon the land which the LORD your God gives you for an inheritance.

5 "When a man is newly married, he shall not go out with the army or be charged with any business; he shall be free at home one year, to be happy with his wife whom he has taken.

6 "No man shall take a mill or an upper millstone in pledge; for he would be taking a life in pledge.

7 "If a man is found stealing one of his brethren, the people of Israel, and if he treats him as a slave or sells him, then that thief shall die; so you shall purge the evil from the midst of you.

8 "Take heed, in an attack of leprosy, to be very careful to do according to all that the Levit'ical priests shall direct you; as I commanded them, so you shall be careful to do. 9 Remember what the LORD your God did to Miriam on the way as you came forth out of Egypt.

10 "When you make your neighbor a loan of any sort, you shall not go into his house to fetch his pledge. 11 You shall stand outside, and the man to whom you make the loan shall bring the pledge out to you. 12And if he is a poor man, you shall not sleep in his pledge; 13 when the sun goes down, you shall restore to him the pledge that he may sleep in his cloak and bless you; and it shall be righteousness to you before the LORD your God.

14 "You shall not oppress a hired servant who is poor and needy, whether he is one of your brethren or one of the sojourners who are in your land within your towns; 15 you shall give him his hire on the day he earns it, before the sun goes down (for he is poor, and sets his heart upon it); lest he cry against you to the LORD, and it be sin in you.

16 "The fathers shall not be put to death for the children, nor shall the children be put to death for the fathers; every man shall be put to death for his own sin.

17 "You shall not pervert the justice due to the sojourner or to the fatherless, or take a widow's garment in pledge; 18 but you shall remember that you were a slave in Egypt and the LORD your God redeemed you from there; therefore I command you to do this.

19 "When you reap your harvest in your field, and have forgotten a sheaf in the field, you shall not go back to get it; it shall be for the sojourner, the fatherless, and the widow; that the LORD your God may bless you in all the work of your hands. 20 When you beat your olive trees, you shall not go over the boughs again; it shall be for the sojourner, the fatherless, and the widow. 21 When you gather the grapes of your vineyard, you shall not glean it afterward; it shall be for the sojourner, the fatherless, and the widow. 22 You shall remember that you were a slave in the land of Egypt; therefore I command you to do this.

25 "If there is a dispute between men, and they come into court, and the judges decide between them, acquitting the innocent and condemning the guilty, 2 then if the guilty man deserves to be beaten, the judge shall cause him to lie down and be

24.4
Jer 3.1

24.5
Deut 20.7

24.7
Ex 21.16

24.8
Lev 13.2;
14.2
24.9
Num 12.10

24.13
Ex 22.26;
Deut 6.25

24.14
Lev 25.35-
43;
Deut 15.7-
18
24.15
Lev 19.13;
Jas 5.4;
Deut 15.9
24.16
2 Ki 14.6;
2 Chr 25.4;
Jer 31.29,
30;
Ezek 18.20
24.17
Deut 1.17;
10.17;
16.19
24.18
Deut 16.12
24.19
Lev 19.9,
10; 23.22
24.20
Lev 19.10

24.22
ver 18

25.1
Deut 19.17;
1.16,17

beaten in his presence with a number of stripes in proportion to his offense. ³ Forty stripes may be given him, but not more; lest, if one should go on to beat him with more stripes than these, your brother be degraded in your sight.

25.3
2 Cor 11.24

4 "You shall not muzzle an ox when it treads out the grain.

25.4
1 Cor 9.9;
1 Tim 5.18

5 "If brothers dwell together, and one of them dies and has no son, the wife of the dead shall not be married outside the family to a stranger; her husband's brother shall go in to her, and take her as his wife, and perform the duty of a husband's brother to her. ⁶And the first son whom she bears shall succeed to the name of his brother who is dead, that his name may not be blotted out of Israel. ⁷And if the man does not wish to take his brother's wife, then his brother's wife shall go up to the gate to the elders, and say, 'My husband's brother refuses to perpetuate his brother's name in Israel; he will not perform the duty of a husband's brother to me.' ⁸ Then the elders of his city shall call him, and speak to him: and if he persists, saying, 'I do not wish to take her,' ⁹ then his brother's wife shall go up to him in the presence of the elders, and pull his sandal off his foot, and spit in his face; and she shall answer and say, 'So shall it be done to the man who does not build up his brother's house.' ¹⁰And the name of his house^u shall be called in Israel, The house of him that had his sandal pulled off.

★25.5ff
Mt 22.24;
Mk 12.19;
Lk 20.28

25.6
Gen 38.9;
Ruth 4.10

25.7
Ruth 4.1,2

25.8
Ruth 4.6
★25.9f
Ruth 4.7,11

11 "When men fight with one another, and the wife of the one draws near to rescue her husband from the hand of him who is beating him, and puts out her hand and seizes him by the private parts, ¹² then you shall cut off her hand; your eye shall have no pity.

13 "You shall not have in your bag two kinds of weights, a large and a small. ¹⁴ You shall not have in your house two kinds of measures, a large and a small. ¹⁵A full and just weight you shall have, a full and just measure you shall have; that your days may be prolonged in the land which the LORD your God gives you. ¹⁶ For all who do such things, all who act dishonestly, are an abomination to the LORD your God.

25.13
Lev 19.35–
37

25.16
Prov 11.1

17 "Remember what Ăm'ălĕk did to you on the way as you came out of Egypt, ¹⁸ how he attacked you on the way, when you were faint and weary, and cut off at your rear all who lagged behind you; and he did not fear God. ¹⁹ Therefore when the LORD your God has given you rest from all your enemies round about, in the land which the LORD your God gives you for an inheritance to possess, you shall blot out the remembrance of Ăm'ălĕk from under heaven; you shall not forget.

★25.17
Ex 17.8

25.19
1 Sam 15.2,
3

^u Heb *its name*

25.5-10 The Deuteronomic code provided that when a man died childless his brother, if unmarried, was supposed to raise up seed by the widow. This is known as levirate (Latin *levir*, husband's brother) marriage. The reason for this command is not explicitly stated, but it has been supposed that it was enjoined to protect the land rights of the dead man through the continuation of his seed. The first son of a levirate marriage enjoyed the same rights as though begotten by his mother's dead husband. All children after that were regarded as legal heirs of the father and not

of the dead man. The custom is pre-Mosaic, being mentioned in the Nuzi Tablets (14th century B.C.). Tamar, in Gen 38, insisted upon this right against her father-in-law, Judah, and maneuvered him into compliance before the custom was written into the Mosaic Law. This regulation furnished the basis of a Sadducean argument against bodily resurrection in Mt 22.23-33.

25.9, 10 Compare the custom described in Ruth 4.7, 8.

25.17 *Remember what Amalek did.* The Amalekites were inveterate enemies of early Israel.

m. Offerings and thanksgiving

26 "When you come into the land which the LORD your God gives you for an inheritance, and have taken possession of it, and live in it, 2 you shall take some of the first of all the fruit of the ground, which you harvest from your land that the LORD your God gives you, and you shall put it in a basket, and you shall go to the place which the LORD your God will choose, to make his name to dwell there. 3And you shall go to the priest who is in office at that time, and say to him, 'I declare this day to the LORD your God that I have come into the land which the LORD swore to our fathers to give us.' 4 Then the priest shall take the basket from your hand, and set it down before the altar of the LORD your God.

5 "And you shall make response before the LORD your God, 'A wandering Árámē'án was my father; and he went down into Egypt and sojourned there, few in number; and there he became a nation, great, mighty, and populous. 6And the Egyptians treated us harshly, and afflicted us, and laid upon us hard bondage. 7 Then we cried to the LORD the God of our fathers, and the LORD heard our voice, and saw our affliction, our toil, and our oppression; 8 and the LORD brought us out of Egypt with a mighty hand and an outstretched arm, with great terror, with signs and wonders; 9 and he brought us into this place and gave us this land, a land flowing with milk and honey. 10And behold, now I bring the first of the fruit of the ground, which thou, O LORD, hast given me.' And you shall set it down before the LORD your God, and worship before the LORD your God; 11 and you shall rejoice in all the good which the LORD your God has given to you and to your house, you, and the Lēvīte, and the sojourner who is among you.

12 "When you have finished paying all the tithe of your produce in the third year, which is the year of tithing, giving it to the Lēvīte, the sojourner, the fatherless, and the widow, that they may eat within your towns and be filled, 13 then you shall say before the LORD your God, 'I have removed the sacred portion out of my house, and moreover I have given it to the Lēvīte, the sojourner, the fatherless, and the widow, according to all thy commandment which thou hast commanded me; I have not transgressed any of thy commandments, neither have I forgotten them; 14 I have not eaten of the tithe while I was mourning, or removed any of it while I was unclean, or offered any of it to the dead; I have obeyed the voice of the LORD my God, I have done according to all that thou hast commanded me. 15 Look down from thy holy habitation, from heaven, and bless thy people Israel and the ground which thou hast given us, as thou didst swear to our fathers, a land flowing with milk and honey.'

16. Moses' command to obey God

16 "This day the LORD your God commands you to do these statutes and ordinances; you shall therefore be careful to do them with all your heart and with all your soul. 17 You have declared

---

26.2
Ex 22.29;
23.16,19;
Num 18.13

*26.5
Hos 12.12;
Gen 43.1,
2; 45.7,11;
46.27;
Deut 10.22
26.6
Ex 1.11,14
26.7
Ex 2.23–25
26.8
Deut 4.34
26.9
Ex 3.8

26.11
Deut 12.7

26.12
Deut 14.28,
29;
Heb 7.5,
9,10
26.13
Ps 119.141,
153,176

*26.14
Lev 7.20;
Hos 9.4

26.16
Deut 4.29

26.5 *wandering Aramean* is a reference to Jacob. This accords with his close ties to Paddan-aram or Aram-naharaim.
26.14 *offered any of it to the dead* refers to the use of some of the tithe as an offering placed in or near the tomb. There is no indication that the Israelites sacrificed to the spirits of the dead.

this day concerning the Lord that he is your God, and that you will walk in his ways, and keep his statutes and his commandments and his ordinances, and will obey his voice; 18 and the Lord has declared this day concerning you that you are a people for his own possession, as he has promised you, and that you are to keep all his commandments, 19 that he will set you high above all nations that he has made, in praise and in fame and in honor, and that you shall be a people holy to the Lord your God, as he has spoken."

26.18
Deut 7.6

26.19
Deut 28.1;
Ps 148.14;
Deut 7.6

III. The covenant renewed 27.1–30.20

A. The altar at Mount Ebal

27 Now Moses and the elders of Israel commanded the people, saying, "Keep all the commandment which I command you this day. 2And on the day you pass over the Jordan to the land which the Lord your God gives you, you shall set up large stones, and plaster them with plaster; 3 and you shall write upon them all the words of this law, when you pass over to enter the land which the Lord your God gives you, a land flowing with milk and honey, as the Lord, the God of your fathers, has promised you. 4And when you have passed over the Jordan, you shall set up these stones, concerning which I command you this day, on Mount Ēbàl, and you shall plaster them with plaster. 5And there you shall build an altar to the Lord your God, an altar of stones; you shall lift up no iron tool upon them. 6 You shall build an altar to the Lord your God of unhewn[v] stones; and you shall offer burnt offerings on it to the Lord your God; 7 and you shall sacrifice peace offerings, and shall eat there; and you shall rejoice before the Lord your God. 8And you shall write upon the stones all the words of this law very plainly."

*27.1

27.2
Josh 8.30–32
27.3
Deut 26.9

27.5
Ex 20.25;
Josh 8.31

9 And Moses and the Lèvìt'ĭcăl priests said to all Israel, "Keep silence and hear, O Israel: this day you have become the people of the Lord your God. 10 You shall therefore obey the voice of the Lord your God, keeping his commandments and his statutes, which I command you this day."

27.9
Deut 26.18

11 And Moses charged the people the same day, saying, 12 "When you have passed over the Jordan, these shall stand upon Mount Gĕr'ĭzĭm to bless the people: Sĭm'ëŏn, Lēvī, Judah, Ĭs'-sáchar, Joseph, and Benjamin. 13And these shall stand upon Mount Ēbàl for the curse: Reubën, Găd, Ăshèr, Zĕb'ūlún, Dan, and Năph'tàlī. 14And the Lēvītes shall declare to all the men of Israel with a loud voice:

27.12
Josh 8.33–35

B. The twelve curses at Mount Ebal

15 " 'Cursed be the man who makes a graven or molten image, an abomination to the Lord, a thing made by the hands of a craftsman, and sets it up in secret.' And all the people shall answer and say, 'Amen.'

27.15
Ex 20.4,23;
34.17

[v] Heb whole

27.1 Chapter 27, which speaks of Moses in the third person, is thought by some to be out of place here because it interrupts the smooth flow of Moses' address. This would be remedied if 28.1 were connected directly to 26.19, without the interference of chapter 27.

27.16
Ex 21.17;
Lev 20.9
27.17
Lev 19.14
27.18
Lev 19.14
27.19
Deut 10.18;
24.17
27.20
Lev 18.8;
Deut 22.30
27.21
Lev 18.23
27.22
Lev 18.9;
20.17
27.23
Lev 20.14
27.24
Lev 24.17;
Num 35.31
27.25
Ex 23.7,8
27.26
Deut 28.15;
Gal 3.10

16 " 'Cursed be he who dishonors his father or his mother.' And all the people shall say, 'Amen.'

17 " 'Cursed be he who removes his neighbor's landmark.' And all the people shall say, 'Amen.'

18 " 'Cursed be he who misleads a blind man on the road.' And all the people shall say, 'Amen.'

19 " 'Cursed be he who perverts the justice due to the sojourner, the fatherless, and the widow.' And all the people shall say, 'Amen.'

20 " 'Cursed be he who lies with his father's wife, because he has uncovered her who is his father's.'ʷ And all the people shall say, 'Amen.'

21 " 'Cursed be he who lies with any kind of beast.' And all the people shall say, 'Amen.'

22 " 'Cursed be he who lies with his sister, whether the daughter of his father or the daughter of his mother.' And all the people shall say, 'Amen.'

23 " 'Cursed be he who lies with his mother-in-law.' And all the people shall say, 'Amen.'

24 " 'Cursed be he who slays his neighbor in secret.' And all the people shall say, 'Amen.'

25 " 'Cursed be he who takes a bribe to slay an innocent person.' And all the people shall say, 'Amen.'

26 " 'Cursed be he who does not confirm the words of this law by doing them.' And all the people shall say, 'Amen.'

C. The blessings of obedience

28.1
Deut 7.12–
26; 26.19

28 "And if you obey the voice of the LORD your God, being careful to do all his commandments which I command you this day, the LORD your God will set you high above all the nations of the earth. 2And all these blessings shall come upon you and overtake you, if you obey the voice of the LORD your God.

28.3
Gen 39.5;
Ps 128.14
28.4
Gen 49.25;
Ps 107.38;
Prov 10.22

3 Blessed shall you be in the city, and blessed shall you be in the field. 4 Blessed shall be the fruit of your body, and the fruit of your ground, and the fruit of your beasts, the increase of your cattle, and the young of your flock. 5 Blessed shall be your basket and your kneading-trough. 6 Blessed shall you be when you come in, and blessed shall you be when you go out.

28.7
Lev 26.7,8

7 "The LORD will cause your enemies who rise against you to be defeated before you; they shall come out against you one way, and flee before you seven ways. 8 The LORD will command the blessing upon you in your barns, and in all that you undertake; and he will bless you in the land which the LORD your God gives you.

28.9
Deut 7.6

9 The LORD will establish you as a people holy to himself, as he has sworn to you, if you keep the commandments of the LORD your God, and walk in his ways.

28.10
2 Chr 7.14

10And all the peoples of the earth shall see that you are called by the name of the LORD; and they shall be afraid of you.

28.11
Deut 30.9

11And the LORD will make you abound in prosperity, in the fruit of your body, and in the fruit of your cattle, and in the fruit of your ground, within the land which the LORD swore to your fathers to give you.

28.12
Lev 26.4;
Deut 15.6

12 The LORD will open to you his good treasury the heavens, to give the rain of your land in its season and to bless all the work of your hands; and you shall lend to many

w Heb uncovered his father's skirt

nations, but you shall not borrow. 13And the LORD will make you the head, and not the tail; and you shall tend upward only, and not downward; if you obey the commandments of the LORD your God, which I command you this day, being careful to do them, 14 and if you do not turn aside from any of the words which I command you this day, to the right hand or to the left, to go after other gods to serve them.

28.14
Deut 5.32

D. The curses of disobedience

15 "But if you will not obey the voice of the LORD your God or be careful to do all his commandments and his statutes which I command you this day, then all these curses shall come upon you and overtake you. 16 Cursed shall you be in the city, and cursed shall you be in the field. 17 Cursed shall be your basket and your kneading-trough. 18 Cursed shall be the fruit of your body, and the fruit of your ground, the increase of your cattle, and the young of your flock. 19 Cursed shall you be when you come in, and cursed shall you be when you go out.

28.15
Lev 26.14;
Josh 23.15;
Mal 2.2

20 "The LORD will send upon you curses, confusion, and frustration, in all that you undertake to do, until you are destroyed and perish quickly, on account of the evil of your doings, because you have forsaken me. 21 The LORD will make the pestilence cleave to you until he has consumed you off the land which you are entering to take possession of it. 22 The LORD will smite you with consumption, and with fever, inflammation, and fiery heat, and with drought,ˣ and with blasting, and with mildew; they shall pursue you until you perish. 23And the heavens over your head shall be brass, and the earth under you shall be iron. 24 The LORD will make the rain of your land powder and dust; from heaven it shall come down upon you until you are destroyed.

28.20
Deut 4.26

28.21
Lev 26.25;
Jer 24.10
28.22
Lev 26.16;
Amos 4.9

28.23
Lev 26.19

25 "The LORD will cause you to be defeated before your enemies; you shall go out one way against them, and flee seven ways before them; and you shall be a horror to all the kingdoms of the earth. 26And your dead body shall be food for all birds of the air, and for the beasts of the earth; and there shall be no one to frighten them away. 27 The LORD will smite you with the boils of Egypt, and with the ulcers and the scurvy and the itch, of which you cannot be healed. 28 The LORD will smite you with madness and blindness and confusion of mind; 29 and you shall grope at noonday, as the blind grope in darkness, and you shall not prosper in your ways; and you shall be only oppressed and robbed continually, and there shall be no one to help you. 30 You shall betroth a wife, and another man shall lie with her; you shall build a house, and you shall not dwell in it; you shall plant a vineyard, and you shall not use the fruit of it. 31 Your ox shall be slain before your eyes, and you shall not eat of it; your ass shall be violently taken away before your face, and shall not be restored to you; your sheep shall be given to your enemies, and there shall be no one to help you. 32 Your sons and your daughters shall be given to another people, while your eyes look on and fail with longing for them all the day; and it shall not be in the power of your hand to prevent it. 33 A nation which you have not known shall eat up the fruit of your ground and of all your

28.25
Lev 26.17,
37;
Jer 15.4

28.26
Jer 7.33;
16.4; 34.20
28.27
ver 60,61

28.29
Job 5.14;
Isa 59.10

28.30
Jer 8.10;
12.13;
Amos 5.11

28.32
ver 41

28.33
Jer 5.17

ˣ Another reading is *sword*

labors; and you shall be only oppressed and crushed continually; 34 so that you shall be driven mad by the sight which your eyes shall see. 35 The LORD will smite you on the knees and on the legs with grievous boils of which you cannot be healed, from the sole of your foot to the crown of your head.

36 "The LORD will bring you, and your king whom you set over you, to a nation that neither you nor your fathers have known; and there you shall serve other gods, of wood and stone. 37And you shall become a horror, a proverb, and a byword, among all the peoples where the LORD will lead you away. 38 You shall carry much seed into the field, and shall gather little in; for the locust shall consume it. 39 You shall plant vineyards and dress them, but you shall neither drink of the wine nor gather the grapes; for the worm shall eat them. 40 You shall have olive trees throughout all your territory, but you shall not anoint yourself with the oil; for your olives shall drop off. 41 You shall beget sons and daughters, but they shall not be yours; for they shall go into captivity. 42All your trees and the fruit of your ground the locust shall possess. 43 The sojourner who is among you shall mount above you higher and higher; and you shall come down lower and lower. 44 He shall lend to you, and you shall not lend to him; he shall be the head, and you shall be the tail. 45All these curses shall come upon you and pursue you and overtake you, till you are destroyed, because you did not obey the voice of the LORD your God, to keep his commandments and his statutes which he commanded you. 46 They shall be upon you as a sign and a wonder, and upon your descendants for ever.

47 "Because you did not serve the LORD your God with joyfulness and gladness of heart, by reason of the abundance of all things, 48 therefore you shall serve your enemies whom the LORD will send against you, in hunger and thirst, in nakedness, and in want of all things; and he will put a yoke of iron upon your neck, until he has destroyed you. 49 The LORD will bring a nation against you from afar, from the end of the earth, as swift as the eagle flies, a nation whose language you do not understand, 50 a nation of stern countenance, who shall not regard the person of the old or show favor to the young, 51 and shall eat the offspring of your cattle and the fruit of your ground, until you are destroyed; who also shall not leave you grain, wine, or oil, the increase of your cattle or the young of your flock, until they have caused you to perish. 52 They shall besiege you in all your towns, until your high and fortified walls, in which you trusted, come down throughout all your land; and they shall besiege you in all your towns throughout all your land, which the LORD your God has given you. 53And you shall eat the offspring of your own body, the flesh of your sons and daughters, whom the LORD your God has given you, in the siege and in the distress with which your enemies shall distress you. 54 The man who is the most tender and delicately bred among you will grudge food to his brother, to the wife of his bosom, and to the last of the children who remain to him; 55 so that he will not give to any of them any of the flesh of his children whom he is eating, because he has nothing left him, in the siege and in the distress with which your enemy shall distress you in all your towns. 56 The most tender and delicately bred woman among you, who would not venture to set the sole of her foot upon the ground be-

28.35
ver 27

28.36
2 Ki 17.4,
6; 24.12,
14; 25.7,11;
Deut 4.28
28.37
Jer 24.9;
Ps 44.14
28.38
Mic 6.15;

28.41
ver 32
28.42
ver 38
28.43
ver 13
28.44
ver 12,13
28.45
ver 15

28.47
Deut 32.15

28.48
Jer 28.13,
14

28.49
Jer 5.15

28.51
ver 33

28.52
Jer 10.17,
18;
Zeph 1.15,
16; Josh 1.4
28.53
Lev 26.29;
Jer 19.9;
Lam 2.20

28.56
ver 54

cause she is so delicate and tender, will grudge to the husband of her bosom, to her son and to her daughter, 57 her afterbirth that comes out from between her feet and her children whom she bears, because she will eat them secretly, for want of all things, in the siege and in the distress with which your enemy shall distress you in your towns.

58 "If you are not careful to do all the words of this law which are written in this book, that you may fear this glorious and awful name, the LORD your God, 59 then the LORD will bring on you and your offspring extraordinary afflictions, afflictions severe and lasting, and sicknesses grievous and lasting. 60And he will bring upon you again all the diseases of Egypt, which you were afraid of; and they shall cleave to you. 61 Every sickness also, and every affliction which is not recorded in the book of this law, the LORD will bring upon you, until you are destroyed. 62 Whereas you were as the stars of heaven for multitude, you shall be left few in number; because you did not obey the voice of the LORD your God. 63And as the LORD took delight in doing you good and multiplying you, so the LORD will take delight in bringing ruin upon you and destroying you; and you shall be plucked off the land which you are entering to take possession of it. 64And the LORD will scatter you among all peoples, from one end of the earth to the other; and there you shall serve other gods, of wood and stone, which neither you nor your fathers have known. 65And among these nations you shall find no ease, and there shall be no rest for the sole of your foot; but the LORD will give you there a trembling heart, and failing eyes, and a languishing soul; 66 your life shall hang in doubt before you; night and day you shall be in dread, and have no assurance of your life. 67 In the morning you shall say, 'Would it were evening!' and at evening you shall say, 'Would it were morning!' because of the dread which your heart shall fear, and the sights which your eyes shall see. 68And the LORD will bring you back in ships to Egypt, a journey which I promised that you should never make again; and there you shall offer yourselves for sale to your enemies as male and female slaves, but no man will buy you."

E. The exhortation to keep the covenant

29[y] These are the words of the covenant which the LORD commanded Moses to make with the people of Israel in the land of Mōăb, besides the covenant which he had made with them at Horĕb.

2[z] And Moses summoned all Israel and said to them: "You

[y] Ch 28.69 in Heb   [z] Ch 29.1 in Heb

Marginal references:

28.58 Ex 6.3

28.60 ver 27

28.61 Deut 4.25, 26

28.62 Deut 4.27; 10.22

*28.63 Jer 12.14; 45.4

28.64 Deut 4.27, 28

28.65 Lev 26.16, 36

28.67 ver 34

*29.1 Deut 5.2,3

29.2 Ex 19.4

28.63 This prophetic Scripture was literally fulfilled in the Babylonian captivity and in the dispersion of the Jews by the Roman government and also by the indignities and hardships suffered by them over many centuries. The present persecutions are part of this prophecy (ver 63–68) and they will continue until the Jews turn to God in repentance and faith. Yet, Gen 12.3 makes clear God's displeasure with those who unjustly oppress these people, and His blessing upon those who grant them toleration and kindness.

29.1 This covenant (actually only a phase of the Abrahamic covenant) made in Moab governed the entrance of Israel into the land of promise. The conditions were as follows: (1) obedience to God's commands as the indispensable condition of blessing (28.1ff); (2) chastisement promised for disobedience (28.15ff); (3) dispersion promised as a judgment upon apostasy (28.63ff); (4) regathering of Israel promised when they repent (30.1ff); (5) repossession of the land promised (30.5); (6) judgment of Israel's enemies (30.7); (7) future prosperity assured (30.9).

have seen all that the LORD did before your eyes in the land of Egypt, to Pharaōh and to all his servants and to all his land, 3 the great trials which your eyes saw, the signs, and those great wonders; 4 but to this day the LORD has not given you a mind to understand, or eyes to see, or ears to hear. 5 I have led you forty years in the wilderness; your clothes have not worn out upon you, and your sandals have not worn off your feet; 6 you have not eaten bread, and you have not drunk wine or strong drink; that you may know that I am the LORD your God. 7And when you came to this place, Sīhōn the king of Hĕshbŏn and Ŏg the king of Bāshán came out against us to battle, but we defeated them; 8 we took their land, and gave it for an inheritance to the Reu′bĕnītes, the Gădītes, and the half-tribe of the Mănăs′sītes. 9 Therefore be careful to do the words of this covenant, that you may prosper*a* in all that you do.

10 "You stand this day all of you before the LORD your God; the heads of your tribes,*b* your elders, and your officers, all the men of Israel, 11 your little ones, your wives, and the sojourner who is in your camp, both he who hews your wood and he who draws your water, 12 that you may enter into the sworn covenant of the LORD your God, which the LORD your God makes with you this day; 13 that he may establish you this day as his people, and that he may be your God, as he promised you, and as he swore to your fathers, to Abraham, to Isaac, and to Jacob. 14 Nor is it with you only that I make this sworn covenant, 15 but with him who is not here with us this day as well as with him who stands here with us this day before the LORD our God.

F. The punishment for forsaking the covenant

16 "You know how we dwelt in the land of Egypt, and how we came through the midst of the nations through which you passed; 17 and you have seen their detestable things, their idols of wood and stone, of silver and gold, which were among them. 18 Beware lest there be among you a man or woman or family or tribe, whose heart turns away this day from the LORD our God to go and serve the gods of those nations; lest there be among you a root bearing poisonous and bitter fruit, 19 one who, when he hears the words of this sworn covenant, blesses himself in his heart, saying, 'I shall be safe, though I walk in the stubbornness of my heart.' This would lead to the sweeping away of moist and dry alike. 20 The LORD would not pardon him, but rather the anger of the LORD and his jealousy would smoke against that man, and the curses written in this book would settle upon him, and the LORD would blot out his name from under heaven. 21And the LORD would single him out from all the tribes of Israel for calamity, in accordance with all the curses of the covenant written in this book of the law. 22And the generation to come, your children who rise up after you, and the foreigner who comes from a far land, would say, when they see the afflictions of that land and the sicknesses with which the LORD has made it sick— 23 the whole land brimstone and salt, and a burnt-out waste, unsown, and growing nothing, where no grass can sprout, an overthrow like that of Sŏdŏm and Gŏmor′ráh, Ădmáh and Zĕboi′ĭm, which the LORD overthrew in his anger and

a Or deal wisely   b Gk Syr: Heb your heads, your tribes

29.4
Isa 6.9,10;
Acts 28.26,
27;
Eph 4.18
29.5
Deut 8.4
29.6
Deut 8.3
29.7
Num
21.21–24,
33–35;
Deut 2.32;
3.1
29.8
Num 32.33;
Deut 3.12,
13
29.9
Deut 4.6;
Josh 1.7
29.11
Josh 9.21,
23,27

29.13
Deut 28.9;
Ex 6.7;
Gen 17.7

29.17
Deut 28.26
29.18
Deut 11.16;
Heb 12.15

29.20
Ps 74.1;
79.5;
Deut 9.14;
Ex 32.33

29.21
Mt 24.51

29.22
Jer 19.8

29.23
Gen 19.24;
Isa 34.9;
Jer 20.16

wrath— 24 yea, all the nations would say, 'Why has the LORD done thus to this land? What means the heat of this great anger?' 25 Then men would say, 'It is because they forsook the covenant of the LORD, the God of their fathers, which he made with them when he brought them out of the land of Egypt, 26 and went and served other gods and worshiped them, gods whom they had not known and whom he had not allotted to them; 27 therefore the anger of the LORD was kindled against this land, bringing upon it all the curses written in this book; 28 and the LORD uprooted them from their land in anger and fury and great wrath, and cast them into another land, as at this day.'

29 "The secret things belong to the LORD our God; but the things that are revealed belong to us and to our children for ever, that we may do all the words of this law.

G. Repentance to be followed by forgiveness and blessing

30 "And when all these things come upon you, the blessing and the curse, which I have set before you, and you call them to mind among all the nations where the LORD your God has driven you, 2 and return to the LORD your God, you and your children, and obey his voice in all that I command you this day, with all your heart and with all your soul; 3 then the LORD your God will restore your fortunes, and have compassion upon you, and he will gather you again from all the peoples where the LORD your God has scattered you. 4 If your outcasts are in the uttermost parts of heaven, from there the LORD your God will gather you, and from there he will fetch you; 5 and the LORD your God will bring you into the land which your fathers possessed, that you may possess it; and he will make you more prosperous and numerous than your fathers. 6And the LORD your God will circumcise your heart and the heart of your offspring, so that you will love the LORD your God with all your heart and with all your soul, that you may live. 7And the LORD your God will put all these curses upon your foes and enemies who persecuted you. 8And you shall again obey the voice of the LORD, and keep all his commandments which I command you this day. 9 The LORD your God will make you abundantly prosperous in all the work of your hand, in the fruit of your body, and in the fruit of your cattle, and in the fruit of your ground; for the LORD will again take delight in prospering you, as he took delight in your fathers, 10 if you obey the voice of the LORD your God, to keep his commandments and his statutes which are written in this book of the law, if you turn to the LORD your God with all your heart and with all your soul.

H. Closing admonition

1. The nearness of God's word

11 "For this commandment which I command you this day is not too hard for you, neither is it far off. 12 It is not in heaven, that you should say, 'Who will go up for us to heaven, and bring it to

Margin references:
29.24 Jer 22.8,9
29.28 1 Ki 14.15; 2 Chr 7.20
*29.29
30.1 ver 15,19; Deut 11.26; 28.64; 29.28
30.2 Deut 4.29, 30
30.3 Jer 29.14; 32.37
30.4 Neh 1.9; Isa 43.6
30.6 Jer 32.39
30.9 Deut 28.11; Jer 32.41
30.11 Isa 45.19
30.12 Rom 10.6-8

29.29 This exceptional verse foresees what 30.11–14 unequivocally tells: the clarity and feasibility of God's revelation. Generally speaking, therefore, disobedience indicates a lack of will or proper motivation, not knowledge.

us, that we may hear it and do it?' 13 Neither is it beyond the sea, that you should say, 'Who will go over the sea for us, and bring it to us, that we may hear it and do it?' 14 But the word is very near you; it is in your mouth and in your heart, so that you can do it.

2. The choice of life versus death

15 "See, I have set before you this day life and good, death and evil. 16 If you obey the commandments of the LORD your God[c] which I command you this day, by loving the LORD your God, by walking in his ways, and by keeping his commandments and his statutes and his ordinances, then you shall live and multiply, and the LORD your God will bless you in the land which you are entering to take possession of it. 17 But if your heart turns away, and you will not hear, but are drawn away to worship other gods and serve them, 18 I declare to you this day, that you shall perish; you shall not live long in the land which you are going over the Jordan to enter and possess. 19 I call heaven and earth to witness against you this day, that I have set before you life and death, blessing and curse; therefore choose life, that you and your descendants may live, 20 loving the LORD your God, obeying his voice, and cleaving to him; for that means life to you and length of days, that you may dwell in the land which the LORD swore to your fathers, to Abraham, to Isaac, and to Jacob, to give them."

IV. Moses' final words and death 31.1–34.12

A. Moses' final arrangements

1. The appointment of Joshua

31 So Moses continued to speak these words to all Israel. 2And he said to them, "I am a hundred and twenty years old this day; I am no longer able to go out and come in. The LORD has said to me, 'You shall not go over this Jordan.' 3 The LORD your God himself will go over before you; he will destroy these nations before you, so that you shall dispossess them; and Joshua will go over at your head, as the LORD has spoken. 4And the LORD will do to them as he did to Sîhòn and Ŏg, the kings of the Ăm'-òrĭtes, and to their land, when he destroyed them. 5And the LORD will give them over to you, and you shall do to them according to all the commandment which I have commanded you. 6 Be strong and of good courage, do not fear or be in dread of them: for it is the LORD your God who goes with you; he will not fail you or forsake you."

7 Then Moses summoned Joshua, and said to him in the sight of all Israel, "Be strong and of good courage; for you shall go with this people into the land which the LORD has sworn to their fathers to give them; and you shall put them in possession of it. 8 It is the LORD who goes before you; he will be with you, he will not fail you or forsake you; do not fear or be dismayed."

2. The teaching of the Law

9 And Moses wrote this law, and gave it to the priests the sons of Lēvī, who carried the ark of the covenant of the LORD, and to

---

c Gk: Heb lacks If you obey the commandments of the LORD your God

Marginal references

30.15 ver 1,19

30.18 Deut 4.26

30.19 Deut 4.26; ver 1

30.20 Deut 6.5; 10.20; Ps 27.1; Jn 11.25

31.2 Deut 34.7; 3.27

31.3 Deut 9.3; 3.28

31.5 Deut 7.2

31.6 Josh 10.25; Deut 1.29; 20.4; Heb 13.5

31.7 Deut 1.38; 3.28

31.8 ver 6

31.9 ver 25; Num 4.15

all the elders of Israel. [10]And Moses commanded them, "At the end of every seven years, at the set time of the year of release, at the feast of booths, [11] when all Israel comes to appear before the LORD your God at the place which he will choose, you shall read this law before all Israel in their hearing. [12]Assemble the people, men, women, and little ones, and the sojourner within your towns, that they may hear and learn to fear the LORD your God, and be careful to do all the words of this law, [13] and that their children, who have not known it, may hear and learn to fear the LORD your God, as long as you live in the land which you are going over the Jordan to possess."

3. God appears to Moses and Joshua

14 And the LORD said to Moses, "Behold, the days approach when you must die; call Joshua, and present yourselves in the tent of meeting, that I may commission him." And Moses and Joshua went and presented themselves in the tent of meeting. [15]And the LORD appeared in the tent in a pillar of cloud; and the pillar of cloud stood by the door of the tent.

16 And the LORD said to Moses, "Behold, you are about to sleep with your fathers; then this people will rise and play the harlot after the strange gods of the land, where they go to be among them, and they will forsake me and break my covenant which I have made with them. [17] Then my anger will be kindled against them in that day, and I will forsake them and hide my face from them, and they will be devoured; and many evils and troubles will come upon them, so that they will say in that day, 'Have not these evils come upon us because our God is not among us?' [18]And I will surely hide my face in that day on account of all the evil which they have done, because they have turned to other gods. [19] Now therefore write this song, and teach it to the people of Israel; put it in their mouths, that this song may be a witness for me against the people of Israel. [20] For when I have brought them into the land flowing with milk and honey, which I swore to give to their fathers, and they have eaten and are full and grown fat, they will turn to other gods and serve them, and despise me and break my covenant. [21]And when many evils and troubles have come upon them, this song shall confront them as a witness (for it will live unforgotten in the mouths of their descendants); for I know the purposes which they are already forming, before I have brought them into the land that I swore to give." [22] So Moses wrote this song the same day, and taught it to the people of Israel.

23 And the LORD commissioned Joshua the son of Nún and said, "Be strong and of good courage; for you shall bring the children of Israel into the land which I swore to give them: I will be with you."

4. Moses' counsel to the Levites

24 When Moses had finished writing the words of this law in a book, to the very end, [25] Moses commanded the Lēvītes who carried the ark of the covenant of the LORD, [26] "Take this book of

31.10	Deut 15.1; Lev 23.34
31.11	Deut 16.16; Josh 8.34, 35
31.12	Deut 4.10
31.13	Deut 11.2; Ps 78.6,7
31.14	Deut 32.49, 50; ver 23
31.15	Ex 33.9
31.16	Judg 2.11, 12; 10.6,13
31.17	Judg 2.14; 6.13; Deut 32.20; Num 14.42
31.20	Deut 6.10–12; 32.15–17; ver 16
31.21	ver 17; Hos 5.3
★31.22	ver 19
31.23	ver 7; Josh 1.6
★31.24 **31.25**	ver 9
31.26	ver 19

31.22 *this song*, that is, the song recorded in 32.1–43.   **31.24** *this law* (also in ver 9) refers explicitly to the Deuteronomic Law.

the law, and put it by the side of the ark of the covenant of the LORD your God, that it may be there for a witness against you.

31.27
Deut 9.6, 24
27 For I know how rebellious and stubborn you are; behold, while I am yet alive with you, today you have been rebellious against the LORD; how much more after my death!

31.28
Deut 4.26
28Assemble to me all the elders of your tribes, and your officers, that I may speak these words in their ears and call heaven and earth to witness against them.

31.29
Deut 32.5; 28.15
29 For I know that after my death you will surely act corruptly, and turn aside from the way which I have commanded you; and in the days to come evil will befall you, because you will do what is evil in the sight of the LORD, provoking him to anger through the work of your hands."

B. *The song of Moses*

1. *Introduction*

30 Then Moses spoke the words of this song until they were finished, in the ears of all the assembly of Israel:

32.1
Isa 1.2
32 "Give ear, O heavens, and I will speak;
and let the earth hear the words of my mouth.

32.2
Isa 55.10, 11
2 May my teaching drop as the rain,
   my speech distil as the dew,
as the gentle rain upon the tender grass,
   and as the showers upon the herb.

32.3
Ex 33.19;
Deut 3.24
3 For I will proclaim the name of the LORD.
   Ascribe greatness to our God!

2. *Faithfulness of God contrasted with the faithlessness of Israel*

32.4
ver 15,18, 30;
Deut 7.9;
Ps 92.15
4 "The Rock, his work is perfect;
   for all his ways are justice.
A God of faithfulness and without iniquity,
   just and right is he.

32.5
Deut 31.29;
Lk 9.41
5 They have dealt corruptly with him,
   they are no longer his children because of their blemish;
   they are a perverse and crooked generation.

32.6
Deut 1.31
6 Do you thus requite the LORD,
   you foolish and senseless people?
Is not he your father, who created you,
   who made you and established you?

32.7
Ex 13.14
7 Remember the days of old,
   consider the years of many generations;
ask your father, and he will show you;
   your elders, and they will tell you.

32.8
Gen 11.8;
Acts 17.26
8 When the Most High gave to the nations their inheritance,
   when he separated the sons of men,
he fixed the bounds of the peoples
   according to the number of the sons of God.*d*

32.9
1 Ki 8.51, 53;
Jer 10.16
9 For the LORD's portion is his people,
   Jacob his allotted heritage.

32.10
Jer 2.6;
Zech 2.8
10 "He found him in a desert land,
   and in the howling waste of the wilderness;

---

d Compare Gk: Heb *Israel*

he encircled him, he cared for him,
   he kept him as the apple of his eye.

11 Like an eagle that stirs up its nest,
   that flutters over its young,
spreading out its wings, catching them,
   bearing them on its pinions,

32.11
Ex 19.4;
Isa 31.5

12 the LORD alone did lead him,
   and there was no foreign god with him.

32.12
ver 39

13 He made him ride on the high places of the earth,
   and he ate the produce of the field;
and he made him suck honey out of the rock,
   and oil out of the flinty rock.

32.13
Isa 58.14;
Job 29.6

14 Curds from the herd, and milk from the flock,
   with fat of lambs and rams,
   herds of Bāshán and goats,
with the finest of the wheat—
   and of the blood of the grape you drank wine.

32.14
Ps 147.14

15 "But Jĕsh'úrún waxed fat, and kicked;
   you waxed fat, you grew thick, you became sleek;
then he forsook God who made him,
   and scoffed at the Rock of his salvation.

*32.15
Deut 33.5,
26; Isa 1.4;
ver 6,4

16 They stirred him to jealousy with strange gods;
   with abominable practices they provoked him to anger.

32.16
Ps 78.58;
1 Cor 10.22

17 They sacrificed to demons which were no gods,
   to gods they had never known,
to new gods that had come in of late,
   whom your fathers had never dreaded.

32.17
Ps 106.37;
Deut 28.64;
Judg 5.8

18 You were unmindful of the Rock that begot[e] you,
   and you forgot the God who gave you birth.

32.18
Isa 17.10;
Ps 106.21

3. Why God punished Israel

19 "The LORD saw it, and spurned them,
   because of the provocation of his sons and his daughters.

32.19
Ps 106.40;
Jer 44.21–
23

20 And he said, 'I will hide my face from them,
   I will see what their end will be,
for they are a perverse generation,
   children in whom is no faithfulness.

32.20
Deut 31.17,
29; ver 5

21 They have stirred me to jealousy with what is no god;
   they have provoked me with their idols.
So I will stir them to jealousy with those who are no people;
   I will provoke them with a foolish nation.

32.21
ver 16;
Rom 10.19

22 For a fire is kindled by my anger,
   and it burns to the depths of Shēōl,
devours the earth and its increase,
   and sets on fire the foundations of the mountains.

*32.22
Jer 15.14

e Or bore

32.15 *Jeshurun*, meaning "Upright One," may be an ironical title for Israel. See 33.5.
32.22 *Sheol*, translated *hades* in the Septuagint, was the underworld abode of the departed spirits of the dead, both righteous and evil. God's spirit was there (Ps 139.8), his anger extended there (32.22), it was a gloomy place with worms (Job 17.13–15), a pit where God could not be praised (Ps 6.5; Isa 38.18). This concept was carried over into the New Testament as *hades*, the abode of the wicked (see note to Lk 10.15), and associated with the concept of Gehenna. The whole idea of *sheol* was very complex in the Old Testament. The basic idea was delimited in some cases to the wicked (Ps 9.17) but this emphasis was a clear development in the Intertestamental period.

<table>
<tr><td>

32.23
Deut 29.21;
Ezek 5.16
32.24
Deut 28.22;
Lev 26.22;
ver 33

32.25
Ezek 7.15;
2 Chr 36.17

32.26
Deut 4.27;
Ps 34.16

32.27
Deut 9.26–
28;
Isa 10.13

32.29
Ps 81.13
32.30
Lev 26.7,8;
ver 4

32.31
1 Sam 2.2;
4.8

32.33
Ps 58.4

32.34
Hos 13.12

32.35
Rom 12.19;
Heb 10.30

32.36
Ps 135.14;
106.45;
Judg 2.18;
Joel 2.14

32.37
Jer 2.28

</td><td>

23 " 'And I will heap evils upon them;
    I will spend my arrows upon them;
24 they shall be wasted with hunger,
    and devoured with burning heat
    and poisonous pestilence;
and I will send the teeth of beasts against them,
    with venom of crawling things of the dust.
25 In the open the sword shall bereave,
    and in the chambers shall be terror,
destroying both young man and virgin,
    the sucking child with the man of gray hairs.
26 I would have said, "I will scatter them afar,
    I will make the remembrance of them cease from among
    men,"
27 had I not feared provocation by the enemy,
    lest their adversaries should judge amiss,
    lest they should say, "Our hand is triumphant,
    the LORD has not wrought all this." '

28 "For they are a nation void of counsel,
    and there is no understanding in them.
29 If they were wise, they would understand this,
    they would discern their latter end!
30 How should one chase a thousand,
    and two put ten thousand to flight,
unless their Rock had sold them,
    and the LORD had given them up?
31 For their rock is not as our Rock,
    even our enemies themselves being judges.
32 For their vine comes from the vine of Sŏdŏm,
    and from the fields of Gŏmor′rȧh;
    their grapes are grapes of poison,
    their clusters are bitter;
33 their wine is the poison of serpents,
    and the cruel venom of asps.

4. God will show mercy to Israel
and vengeance to her enemies

34 "Is not this laid up in store with me,
    sealed up in my treasuries?
35 Vengeance is mine, and recompense,
    for the time when their foot shall slip;
for the day of their calamity is at hand,
    and their doom comes swiftly.
36 For the LORD will vindicate his people
    and have compassion on his servants,
when he sees that their power is gone,
    and there is none remaining, bond or free.
37 Then he will say, 'Where are their gods,
    the rock in which they took refuge,
38 who ate the fat of their sacrifices,
    and drank the wine of their drink offering?
Let them rise up and help you,
    let them be your protection!

</td></tr>
</table>

39 " 'See now that I, even I, am he,
   and there is no god beside me;
I kill and I make alive;
   I wound and I heal;
   and there is none that can deliver out of my hand.
40 For I lift up my hand to heaven,
   and swear, As I live for ever,
41 if I whet my glittering sword,*f*
   and my hand takes hold on judgment,
I will take vengeance on my adversaries,
   and will requite those who hate me.
42 I will make my arrows drunk with blood,
   and my sword shall devour flesh—
with the blood of the slain and the captives,
   from the long-haired heads of the enemy.'

43 "Praise his people, O you nations;
   for he avenges the blood of his servants,
and takes vengeance on his adversaries,
   and makes expiation for the land of his people."*g*

44 Moses came and recited all the words of this song in the
hearing of the people, he and Joshua*h* the son of Nùn. 45And when
Moses had finished speaking all these words to all Israel, 46 he
said to them, "Lay to heart all the words which I enjoin upon you
this day, that you may command them to your children, that they
may be careful to do all the words of this law. 47 For it is no trifle
for you, but it is your life, and thereby you shall live long in the
land which you are going over the Jordan to possess."

C. God summons Moses to die

48 And the LORD said to Moses that very day, 49 "Ascend this
mountain of the Ăb'ărim, Mount Nēbō, which is in the land of
Mŏăb, opposite Jĕr'ĭchō; and view the land of Cānaăn, which I
give to the people of Israel for a possession; 50 and die on the
mountain which you ascend, and be gathered to your people, as
Aaron your brother died in Mount Hor and was gathered to his
people; 51 because you broke faith with me in the midst of the
people of Israel at the waters of Mĕr'ĭ-băth-kā'dĕsh, in the wilderness of Zĭn; because you did not revere me as holy in the midst of
the people of Israel. 52 For you shall see the land before you; but
you shall not go there, into the land which I give to the people
of Israel."

D. Moses blesses the people of Israel

33 This is the blessing with which Moses the man of God
   blessed the children of Israel before his death. 2 He said,
"The LORD came from Sĭ'nāï,
   and dawned from Sēïr upon us;*i*
he shone forth from Mount Pārăn,
he came from the ten thousands of holy ones,
   with flaming fire*j* at his right hand.

Reference column:

32.39 Isa 41.4; Ps 50.22

32.41 Ezek 21.9, 10

32.42 Jer 46.10

32.43 Rom 15.10; Rev 19.2; Ps 85.1

32.46 Deut 6.6; Ezek 40.4

32.47 Deut 30.20

32.49 Num 27.12–14

32.51 Num 20.11–13; 27.14

32.52 Deut 34.1–3; 1.37

33.1 Josh 14.6

33.2 Hab 3.3; Dan 7.10; Acts 7.53; Gal 3.19; Rev 5.11

---

f Heb *the lightning of my sword* *g* Gk Vg: Heb *his land his people* *h* Gk Syr Vg: Heb *Hōshe'ă*
i Gk Syr Vg: Heb *them* *j* The meaning of the Hebrew word is uncertain

33.3
Hos 11.1;
Deut 14.2
3 Yea, he loved his people;*k*
  all those consecrated to him were in his*x* hand;
so they followed*j* in thy steps,
  receiving direction from thee,

33.4
Jn 1.17;
Ps 119.111
4 when Moses commanded us a law,
  as a possession for the assembly of Jacob.
5 Thus the LORD became king in Jĕsh′ŭrŭn,
  when the heads of the people were gathered,
  all the tribes of Israel together.

6 "Let Reubĕn live, and not die,
  nor let his men be few."

*33.7
Gen 49.8–
12
7 And this he said of Judah:
"Hear, O LORD, the voice of Judah,
  and bring him in to his people.
With thy hands contend*l* for him,
  and be a help against his adversaries."

33.8
Ex 28.30;
17.7
8 And of Lēvī he said,
"Give to Levi*m* thy Thŭmmĭm,
  and thy Ūrĭm to thy godly one,
whom thou didst test at Măssăh,
  with whom thou didst strive at the waters of Mĕr′ĭbah;

33.9
Ex 32.26–29
9 who said of his father and mother,
  'I regard them not';
he disowned his brothers,
  and ignored his children.
For they observed thy word,
  and kept thy covenant.

33.10
Deut 31.9–
13;
Ex 30.7,8;
Ps 51.19
10 They shall teach Jacob thy ordinances,
  and Israel thy law;
they shall put incense before thee,
  and whole burnt offering upon thy altar.

33.11
2 Sam
24.23;
Ps 20.3
11 Bless, O LORD, his substance,
  and accept the work of his hands;
crush the loins of his adversaries,
  of those that hate him, that they rise not again."

12 Of Benjamin he said,
"The beloved of the LORD,
  he dwells in safety by him;
he encompasses him all the day long,
  and makes his dwelling between his shoulders."

33.13
Gen 49.25;
27.28
13 And of Joseph he said,
"Blessed by the LORD be his land,
  with the choicest gifts of heaven above,*n*
  and of the deep that couches beneath,
14 with the choicest fruits of the sun,

k Gk: Heb *peoples* *x* Heb *thy* *l* The meaning of the Hebrew word is uncertain
l Cn: Heb *with his hands he contended* *m* Gk: Heb lacks *Give to Levi*
n Two Heb Mss and Tg: Heb *with the dew*

33.7 The tribe of Simeon, missing from the blessing, may have been implicitly asso-ciated with Judah within whose borders it dwelt.

and the rich yield of the months,
15 with the finest produce of the ancient mountains,
    and the abundance of the everlasting hills,

33.15
Gen 49.26

16 with the best gifts of the earth and its fulness,
    and the favor of him that dwelt in the bush.
Let these come upon the head of Joseph,
    and upon the crown of the head of him that is prince among
      his brothers.

33.16
Ex 3.2,4;
Acts 7.30,
35

17 His firstling bull has majesty,
    and his horns are the horns of a wild ox;
with them he shall push the peoples,
    all of them, to the ends of the earth;
such are the ten thousands of Ē′phräïm,
    and such are the thousands of Mănăs′sĕh."

33.17
Num 23.22;
Ps 44.5

18 And of Zĕb′ŭlŭn he said,
"Rejoice, Zebulun, in your going out;
    and Is′săchar, in your tents.
19 They shall call peoples to their mountain;
    there they offer right sacrifices;
for they suck the affluence of the seas
    and the hidden treasures of the sand."

33.18
Gen 49.13–
15

33.19
Isa 2.3;
Ps 4.5

20 And of Găd he said,
"Blessed be he who enlarges Gad!
Gad couches like a lion,
    he tears the arm, and the crown of the head.
21 He chose the best of the land for himself,
    for there a commander's portion was reserved;
and he came to the heads of the people,
    with Israel he executed the commands
    and just decrees of the LORD."

33.20
Gen 49.19

33.21
Num 32.1–
5,31,32;
Josh 4.12;
22.1–3

22 And of Dan he said,
"Dan is a lion's whelp,
    that leaps forth from Bāshăn."

33.22
Gen 49.16

23 And of Năph′tălī he said,
"O Naphtali, satisfied with favor,
    and full of the blessing of the LORD,
    possess the lake and the south."

33.23
Gen 49.21

24 And of Ăshĕr he said,
"Blessed above sons be Asher;
    let him be the favorite of his brothers,
    and let him dip his foot in oil.
25 Your bars shall be iron and bronze;
    and as your days, so shall your strength be.

33.24
Gen 49.20;
Job 29.6

33.25
Deut 4.40;
32.49

26 "There is none like God, O Jĕsh′ŭrŭn,
    who rides through the heavens to your help,
    and in his majesty through the skies.
27 The eternal God is your dwelling place,
    and underneath are the everlasting arms.
And he thrust out the enemy before you,
    and said, Destroy.

33.26
Ex 15.11;
Ps 68.33,34

33.27
Ps 90.1,2;
Josh 24.18

33.28
Num 23.9;
Gen 27.28

28 So Israel dwelt in safety,
   the fountain of Jacob alone,
in a land of grain and wine;
   yea, his heavens drop down dew.

33.29
Ps 144.15;
2 Sam 7.23;
Ps 18.14;
Deut 32.13

29 Happy are you, O Israel! Who is like you,
   a people saved by the LORD,
the shield of your help,
   and the sword of your triumph!
Your enemies shall come fawning to you;
   and you shall tread upon their high places."

E. The death and burial of Moses

34.1
Deut 32.49,
52

34 And Moses went up from the plains of Mŏăb to Mount Nēbō, to the top of Pĭṣgăh, which is opposite Jĕr'ĭchō. And the LORD showed him all the land, Gĭl'ĕăd as far as Dan, 2 all Năph'tălī, the land of Ē'phrăĭm and Mănăs'sĕh, all the land of Judah as far as the Western Sea, 3 the Nĕgĕb, and the Plain, that

34.4
Gen 12.7;
28.13

is, the valley of Jĕr'ĭchō the city of palm trees, as far as Zŏ'ar. 4And the LORD said to him, "This is the land of which I swore to Abraham, to Isaac, and to Jacob, 'I will give it to your descendants.' I have let you see it with your eyes, but you shall not go over

34.5
Deut 32.50;
Josh 1.1,2

there." 5 So Moses the servant of the LORD died there in the land of Mŏăb, according to the word of the LORD, 6 and he buried him in the valley in the land of Mŏăb opposite Bĕth'-pĕor; but no man

34.7
Deut 31.2

knows the place of his burial to this day. 7 Moses was a hundred and twenty years old when he died; his eye was not dim, nor his natural force abated. 8And the people of Israel wept for Moses in the plains of Mŏăb thirty days; then the days of weeping and mourning for Moses were ended.

34.9
Isa 11.2;
Num 27.18,
23
34.10
Num 12.6,8
34.11
Deut 4.34

9 And Joshua the son of Nŭn was full of the spirit of wisdom, for Moses had laid his hands upon him; so the people of Israel obeyed him, and did as the LORD had commanded Moses. 10And there has not arisen a prophet since in Israel like Moses, whom the LORD knew face to face, 11 none like him for all the signs and the wonders which the LORD sent him to do in the land of Egypt, to Phạraōh and to all his servants and to all his land, 12 and for all the mighty power and all the great and terrible deeds which Moses wrought in the sight of all Israel.

INTRODUCTION TO
THE BOOK OF
JOSHUA

Authorship and Background: This book is named after its chief character, Joshua, of the tribe of Ephraim. His name was originally Hoshea, "salvation" (Num 13.8), but Moses changed it to Joshua (Jehoshua), "Yahweh is salvation" (Num 13.16). Jesus, the Septuagint spelling of Joshua, was the name given the Christ at his birth. The authorship of the book cannot be determined definitely. Jewish tradition attributed it to Joshua, but also held that Eleazar appended the account of Joshua's death, after which Phinehas noted the death of Eleazar. The recurring expression "to this day" implies that the unknown author compiled the book some time after the events occurred, although the sources from which the book is derived were contemporary with the historical incidents. In the Hebrew Bible the historical books of Joshua through 2 Kings (with the exception of Ruth) are listed as "The Former Prophets" because ancient Jewish rabbis considered the traditional authors (Joshua, Samuel, Nathan, Gad, and others) as prophets.

Characteristics: The Book of Joshua is both history and biography, for the story of Joshua's life is intermingled with the history of Israel during the time of the conquest of Canaan. The book commences with the call and commission of Joshua; it ends with his death. Joshua is pictured as a man of courage and faith. He is a consecrated leader, a military strategist, and a wise governor of men. Together with Caleb he had earlier submitted a minority report contrary to the discouraging account of the other ten spies. The Book of Joshua recounts the success of Israel in the conquest of Canaan. This success is a token of God's faithfulness in the fulfilment of the divine promise made years before. The destruction of the Amorites is an example of divine judgment against national iniquity. Joshua has often been pictured as a type of Christ, the leader of his people. The style of the work is similar to that of the other historical writings.

Contents:

I.   The conquest of Canaan. 1.1—12.24: Joshua commissioned; the army mobilized; the spies sent. The Jordan crossed; the twelve stones of memorial erected. Israel circumcised; the Passover celebrated; the unseen Captain present. Jericho captured. The fall of Ai. The monument erected on Mt. Ebal. The deception of the Gibeonites. Victory over the five kings. Conquest of southern and northern Canaan; summary of conquests. List of the conquered kings.

II.   The partition of the Promised Land. 13.1—21.45: The command to divide the land. East Canaan given to Reuben, Gad, and the half-tribe of Manasseh. West Canaan partitioned: Caleb's portion; Judah's

portion; Ephraim's and Manasseh's portions. The erection of the
tabernacle at Shiloh. The division of the remaining land among the
tribes of Benjamin, Simeon, Zebulun, Issachar, Asher, Naphtali, and
Dan. The six cities of refuge; the forty-eight cities apportioned to the
priests and Levites.

III. The farewell addresses of Joshua. 22.1—24.33: His last words to the
two and a half tribes of east Canaan. Their altar at the Jordan; the
protest by the other tribes; the apology of the two and a half tribes for
erecting the altar. Joshua's last words to the tribes of west Canaan; a
rehearsal of the benefits, the promised blessings, and warnings.
Joshua's message to the twelve tribes: his own covenant, ". . . for me
and my house, we will serve the LORD" (24.15). The death and burial
of Joshua; the burial of Joseph's bones; the death and burial of Eleazar.

THE BOOK OF
JOSHUA

I. The conquest of Canaan 1.1–12.24

A. Introduction: God's instructions to Joshua

1 After the death of Moses the servant of the LORD, the LORD said to Joshua the son of Nún, Moses' minister, 2 "Moses my servant is dead; now therefore arise, go over this Jordan, you and all this people, into the land which I am giving to them, to the people of Israel. 3 Every place that the sole of your foot will tread upon I have given to you, as I promised to Moses. 4 From the wilderness and this Lebanon as far as the great river, the river Eūphrā'tēṣ, all the land of the Hĭttĭtes to the Great Sea toward the going down of the sun shall be your territory. 5 No man shall be able to stand before you all the days of your life; as I was with Moses, so I will be with you; I will not fail you or forsake you. 6 Be strong and of good courage; for you shall cause this people to inherit the land which I swore to their fathers to give them. 7 Only be strong and very courageous, being careful to do according to all the law which Moses my servant commanded you; turn not from it to the right hand or to the left, that you may have good success wherever you go. 8 This book of the law shall not depart out of your mouth, but you shall meditate on it day and night, that you may be careful to do according to all that is written in it; for then you shall make your way prosperous, and then you shall have good success. 9 Have I not commanded you? Be strong and of good courage; be not frightened, neither be dismayed; for the LORD your God is with you wherever you go."

B. Preparations for crossing the Jordan

1. The order issued

10 Then Joshua commanded the officers of the people, 11 "Pass through the camp, and command the people, 'Prepare your provisions; for within three days you are to pass over this Jordan, to go in to take possession of the land which the LORD your God gives you to possess.' "

2. The reminder to Reubenites, Gadites, and half-tribe of Manasseh

12 And to the Reu'bēnĭtes, the Gădĭtes, and the half-tribe of Mănăs'sĕh Joshua said, 13 "Remember the word which Moses the servant of the LORD commanded you, saying, 'The LORD your God is providing you a place of rest, and will give you this land.' 14 Your wives, your little ones, and your cattle shall remain in the land which Moses gave you beyond the Jordan; but all the men of

1.2
Num 12.7;
Deut 34.5;
ver 11

1.3
Deut 11.24
*1.4
Gen 15.18

*1.5
Deut 7.24;
31.6–8

1.7
Deut 5.32;
28.14

1.8
Deut 17.8,
9; Ps 1.1–3

1.9
Deut 31.7,
8,23;
Jer 1.8

1.11
Joel 3.2

1.12
Num 32.20–
22
1.13
Deut 3.18–
20

1.4 *Great Sea*, the Mediterranean.
1.5 Joshua (shortened from Jehoshua, "Yahweh is salvation") was a type of Christ. In fact, his name becomes "Jesus" in Greek. He led the people of God into the Promised Land. He interceded for them when they went astray. He led them to victory over the forces of evil. Likewise Jesus is the captain of our salvation who intercedes for His people, brings them into the promised rest, gives them an inheritance, and makes victory over sin possible. (See Heb 4.8, 9; Acts 20.32; Heb 2.10, 11; Rom 8.37; 2 Cor 1.10; 2.14; Josh 7.5–9; 1 Jn 2.1.)

valor among you shall pass over armed before your brethren and
shall help them, 15 until the LORD gives rest to your brethren as
well as to you, and they also take possession of the land which the
LORD your God is giving them; then you shall return to the land
of your possession, and shall possess it, the land which Moses the
servant of the LORD gave you beyond the Jordan toward the sunrise." 16And they answered Joshua, "All that you have commanded
us we will do, and wherever you send us we will go. 17 Just as we
obeyed Moses in all things, so we will obey you; only may the
LORD your God be with you, as he was with Moses! 18 Whoever
rebels against your commandment and disobeys your words,
whatever you command him, shall be put to death. Only be strong
and of good courage."

3. *Two spies sent to Jericho*
a. *Rahab hides the spies*

2 And Joshua the son of Nún sent two men secretly from Shït-
tìm as spies, saying, "Go, view the land, especially Jĕr′ĭchō."
And they went, and came into the house of a harlot whose name
was Rāhăb, and lodged there. 2And it was told the king of Jĕr′ĭchō,
"Behold, certain men of Israel have come here tonight to search
out the land." 3 Then the king of Jĕr′ĭchō sent to Rāhăb, saying,
"Bring forth the men that have come to you, who entered your
house; for they have come to search out all the land." 4 But the
woman had taken the two men and hidden them; and she said,
"True, men came to me, but I did not know where they came
from; 5 and when the gate was to be closed, at dark, the men went
out; where the men went I do not know; pursue them quickly, for
you will overtake them." 6 But she had brought them up to the
roof, and hid them with the stalks of flax which she had laid in
order on the roof. 7 So the men pursued after them on the way to
the Jordan as far as the fords; and as soon as the pursuers had gone
out, the gate was shut.

b. *Rahab secures a promise of safety from the spies*

8 Before they lay down, she came up to them on the roof, 9 and
said to the men, "I know that the LORD has given you the land,
and that the fear of you has fallen upon us, and that all the inhabitants of the land melt away before you. 10 For we have heard
how the LORD dried up the water of the Red Sea before you when
you came out of Egypt, and what you did to the two kings of
the Ăm′ŏrītes that were beyond the Jordan, to Sīhŏn and Ŏg, whom
you utterly destroyed. 11And as soon as we heard it, our hearts
melted, and there was no courage left in any man, because of you;
for the LORD your God is he who is God in heaven above and on
earth beneath. 12 Now then, swear to me by the LORD that as I
have dealt kindly with you, you also will deal kindly with my
father's house, and give me a sure sign, 13 and save alive my father

Margin references:
1.15
Josh 22.1–4

1.17
ver 5,9

2.1
Num 25.1;
Heb 11.31;
Jas 2.25

*2.4

2.6
Jas 2.25

2.9
Ex 23.27;
Deut 2.25

2.10
Ex 14.21;
Num 21.24,
34,35

2.11
Ex 15.14,
15;
Josh 5.1;
Deut 4.39

2.12
ver 18

2.4 Rahab deliberately told a falsehood to protect the Hebrew spies. Some have argued that her act makes it permissible to lie on certain occasions. Calvin said, "As to the falsehood, we must admit that though it was done for a good purpose, it was not free from fault." In the New Testament Rahab is commended for her faith in God (for she risked her life to save the two spies from death), but nothing is said to suggest that her lie was commended (Heb 11.31; Jas 2.25). God would have been able to save the spies from death without the aid of man's (or woman's) sin. Scripture nowhere supports the position that it is justifiable to lie (Ex 20.16; Deut 5.20; Mt 19.19).

and mother, my brothers and sisters, and all who belong to them, and deliver our lives from death." ¹⁴And the men said to her, "Our life for yours! If you do not tell this business of ours, then we will deal kindly and faithfully with you when the LORD gives us the land."

2.14
Judg 1.24

c. The promise of the scarlet cord

15 Then she let them down by a rope through the window, for her house was built into the city wall, so that she dwelt in the wall. ¹⁶And she said to them, "Go into the hills, lest the pursuers meet you; and hide yourselves there three days, until the pursuers have returned; then afterward you may go your way." ¹⁷ The men said to her, "We will be guiltless with respect to this oath of yours which you have made us swear. ¹⁸ Behold, when we come into the land, you shall bind this scarlet cord in the window through which you let us down; and you shall gather into your house your father and mother, your brothers, and all your father's household. ¹⁹ If any one goes out of the doors of your house into the street, his blood shall be upon his head, and we shall be guiltless; but if a hand is laid upon any one who is with you in the house, his blood shall be on our head. ²⁰ But if you tell this business of ours, then we shall be guiltless with respect to your oath which you have made us swear." ²¹And she said, "According to your words, so be it." Then she sent them away, and they departed; and she bound the scarlet cord in the window.

*2.15

2.16
Jas 2.25

2.17
Gen 24.8

2.18
ver 12;
Josh 6.23

2.19
Ezek 33.4

d. The return of the spies

22 They departed, and went into the hills, and remained there three days, until the pursuers returned; for the pursuers had made search all along the way and found nothing. ²³ Then the two men came down again from the hills, and passed over and came to Joshua the son of Nún; and they told him all that had befallen them. ²⁴And they said to Joshua, "Truly the LORD has given all the land into our hands; and moreover all the inhabitants of the land are fainthearted because of us."

2.24
ver 9;
Josh 6.2

C. Israel crossing the Jordan

1. The final preparations

3 Early in the morning Joshua rose and set out from Shǐttĭm, with all the people of Israel; and they came to the Jordan, and lodged there before they passed over. ²At the end of three days the officers went through the camp ³ and commanded the people, "When you see the ark of the covenant of the LORD your God being carried by the Lėvĭt′ĭcȧl priests, then you shall set out from your place and follow it, ⁴ that you may know the way you shall go, for you have not passed this way before. Yet there shall be a space between you and it, a distance of about two thousand cubits; do not come near it." ⁵And Joshua said to the people, "Sanctify yourselves; for tomorrow the LORD will do wonders among you." ⁶And Joshua said to the priests, "Take up the ark of the covenant,

3.1
Josh 2.1

3.2
Josh 1.11
3.3
Deut 31.9

3.5
Ex 19.10,
14;
Josh 7.13

2.15 *built into the city wall*, literally means "in the wall of the wall." Jericho, like other Canaanite cities, had two walls about 12 to 15 feet apart. Crowded conditions resulted in houses (such as Rahab's) being built on timbers extended across the walls. Escape was facilitated because the window was over the outer wall.

and pass on before the people." And they took up the ark of the covenant, and went before the people.

2. *The promise of God*

3.7
Josh 4.7;
1.5
3.8
ver 3,17

7 And the LORD said to Joshua, "This day I will begin to exalt you in the sight of all Israel, that they may know that, as I was with Moses, so I will be with you. 8And you shall command the priests who bear the ark of the covenant, 'When you come to the brink of the waters of the Jordan, you shall stand still in the Jordan.'"

3.10
Deut 7.1

9And Joshua said to the people of Israel, "Come hither, and hear the words of the LORD your God." 10And Joshua said, "Hereby you shall know that the living God is among you, and that he will without fail drive out from before you the Cā´naánītes, the Hĭt-tītes, the Hīvītes, the Pĕr´ĭzzītes, the Gĭr´gàshītes, the Ăm´órītes, and the Jĕb´ūsītes. 11 Behold, the ark of the covenant of the Lord

3.12
Josh 4.2

of all the earth is to pass over before you into the Jordan. 12 Now therefore take twelve men from the tribes of Israel, from each tribe a man. 13And when the soles of the feet of the priests who

3.13
Ex 15.8;
Ps 78.13

bear the ark of the LORD, the Lord of all the earth, shall rest in the waters of the Jordan, the waters of the Jordan shall be stopped from flowing, and the waters coming down from above shall stand in one heap.''

3. *The crossing commenced; the Jordan parted*

14 So, when the people set out from their tents, to pass over the Jordan with the priests bearing the ark of the covenant before the

3.15
Josh 4.18

people, 15 and when those who bore the ark had come to the Jordan, and the feet of the priests bearing the ark were dipped in the brink of the water (the Jordan overflows all its banks throughout the time of harvest), 16 the waters coming down from above stood

*3.16
Ps 66.6;
74.15;
ver 13

and rose up in a heap far off, at Adam, the city that is beside Zar´ĕthàn, and those flowing down toward the sea of the Ar´ábáh, the Salt Sea, were wholly cut off; and the people passed over opposite Jĕr´ĭchō. 17And while all Israel were passing over on dry

3.17
Ex 14.29

ground, the priests who bore the ark of the covenant of the LORD stood on dry ground in the midst of the Jordan, until all the nation finished passing over the Jordan.

4. *The twelve stones of memorial*

4.2
Josh 3.12
4.3
ver 19,20

4 When all the nation had finished passing over the Jordan, the LORD said to Joshua, 2 "Take twelve men from the people, from each tribe a man, 3 and command them, 'Take twelve stones from here out of the midst of the Jordan, from the very place where the priests' feet stood, and cárry them over with you, and lay them down in the place where you lodge tonight.'" 4 Then Joshua called the twelve men from the people of Israel, whom he had appointed, a man from each tribe; 5 and Joshua said to them,

4.6
ver 21;
Ex 12.26;
13.14

"Pass on before the ark of the LORD your God into the midst of the Jordan, and take up each of you a stone upon his shoulder, according to the number of the tribes of the people of Israel, 6 that this may be a sign among you, when your children ask in time to

---

3.16 This miracle (or special providential act) may have been one of timing in which an earthquake blocked the river. As recently as 1927 a tremor dislodged some of the cliffs overlooking the river, completely blocking the Jordan for over 21 hours.

come, 'What do those stones mean to you?' 7 Then you shall tell
them that the waters of the Jordan were cut off before the ark of
the covenant of the LORD; when it passed over the Jordan, the
waters of the Jordan were cut off. So these stones shall be to the
people of Israel a memorial for ever."

8 And the men of Israel did as Joshua commanded, and took up
twelve stones out of the midst of the Jordan, according to the
number of the tribes of the people of Israel, as the LORD told
Joshua; and they carried them over with them to the place where
they lodged, and laid them down there. 9And Joshua set up twelve
stones in the midst of the Jordan, in the place where the feet of
the priests bearing the ark of the covenant had stood; and they
are there to this day. 10 For the priests who bore the ark stood in
the midst of the Jordan, until everything was finished that the
LORD commanded Joshua to tell the people, according to all that
Moses had commanded Joshua.

The people passed over in haste; 11 and when all the people had
finished passing over, the ark of the LORD and the priests passed
over before the people. 12 The sons of Reubën and the sons of Găd
and the half-tribe of Mănăs′sëh passed over armed before the
people of Israel, as Moses had bidden them; 13 about forty thousand ready armed for war passed over before the LORD for battle,
to the plains of Jĕr′ĭchō. 14 On that day the LORD exalted Joshua
in the sight of all Israel; and they stood in awe of him, as they had
stood in awe of Moses, all the days of his life.

5. The crossing completed: the Jordan flows

15 And the LORD said to Joshua, 16 "Command the priests who
bear the ark of the testimony to come up out of the Jordan."
17 Joshua therefore commanded the priests, "Come up out of the
Jordan." 18And when the priests bearing the ark of the covenant
of the LORD came up from the midst of the Jordan, and the soles
of the priests' feet were lifted up on dry ground, the waters of the
Jordan returned to their place and overflowed all its banks, as
before.

6. The meaning of the stones

19 The people came up out of the Jordan on the tenth day of
the first month, and they encamped in Gĭlgăl on the east border of
Jĕr′ĭchō. 20And those twelve stones, which they took out of the
Jordan, Joshua set up in Gĭlgăl. 21And he said to the people of
Israel, "When your children ask their fathers in time to come,
'What do these stones mean?' 22 then you shall let your children
know, 'Israel passed over this Jordan on dry ground.' 23 For the
LORD your God dried up the waters of the Jordan for you until you
passed over, as the LORD your God did to the Red Sea, which he
dried up for us until we passed over, 24so that all the peoples of the

*4.7 Josh 3.13 · 4.8 ver 19,20 · *4.9 Ex 28.21 · 4.12 Num 32.17 · 4.14 Josh 3.7 · 4.18 Josh 3.15 · 4.19 Josh 5.9 · 4.20 ver 3,8 · 4.21 ver 6 · 4.22 Josh 3.17 · 4.23 Ex 14.21 · 4.24 1 Ki 8.42, 43; Ps 89.13; Ex 14.31

4.7 The stones of memorial were to be set up not simply to commemorate the crossing of the Jordan, but as a testimony to the people of God concerning His miraculous and delivering power. The stones would recall what God had done in the past, so that in future difficulties Israel could look to the God who had formerly delivered them. Today the believer should erect some stones of remembrance in his own experience which will stand him in good stead when facing great difficulties. Then he will be able to say, "Hitherto the Lord has led."
4.9 *there to this day*. Apparently the heap of stones could be seen when the river level was low.

earth may know that the hand of the LORD is mighty; that you may fear the LORD your God for ever."

5.1
Num 13.29;
Josh 2.9–11

5 When all the kings of the Ăm′ŏrītes that were beyond the Jordan to the west, and all the kings of the Cā′naánītes that were by the sea, heard that the LORD had dried up the waters of the Jordan for the people of Israel until they had crossed over, their heart melted, and there was no longer any spirit in them, because of the people of Israel.

D. The encampment at Gilgal

1. The covenant of circumcision fulfilled

*5.2
Ex 4.25

2 At that time the LORD said to Joshua, "Make flint knives and circumcise the people of Israel again the second time." 3 So Joshua made flint knives, and circumcised the people of Israel at Gĭb′-

5.4
Deut 2.16

ëăth-hăar′ălōth.ᵃ 4And this is the reason why Joshua circumcised them: all the males of the people who came out of Egypt, all the men of war, had died on the way in the wilderness after they had come out of Egypt. 5 Though all the people who came out had been circumcised, yet all the people that were born on the way in the wilderness after they had come out of Egypt had not been circumcised.

5.6
Deut 2.7,
14;
Num 14.23

6 For the people of Israel walked forty years in the wilderness, till all the nation, the men of war that came forth out of Egypt, perished, because they did not hearken to the voice of the LORD; to them the LORD swore that he would not let them see the land which the LORD had sworn to their fathers to give us, a land flowing with milk and honey. 7 So it was their children, whom he

*5.7

raised up in their stead, that Joshua circumcised; for they were uncircumcised, because they had not been circumcised on the way.

8 When the circumcising of all the nation was done, they remained in their places in the camp till they were healed. 9 And the LORD said to Joshua, "This day I have rolled away the reproach of Egypt from you." And so the name of that place is called Gĭlgălᵇ to this day.

2. The Passover kept

5.10
Ex 12.6,8

10 While the people of Israel were encamped in Gĭlgăl they kept the passover on the fourteenth day of the month at evening in the plains of Jĕr′ĭchō. 11And on the morrow after the passover, on that very day, they ate of the produce of the land, unleavened

5.12
Ex 16.35

cakes and parched grain. 12And the manna ceased on the morrow, when they ate of the produce of the land; and the people of Israel had manna no more, but ate of the fruit of the land of Cānaán that year.

ᵃ That is the hill of the foreskins   ᵇ From Heb galal to roll

---

5.2 Circumcision was the seal attached to the Abrahamic covenant (see Gen 17.9, 10). It had no saving value in itself unless it was accompanied by faith. But the rite was neglected during the years of wandering. While KJV, RSV, and MT (Masoretic Text) indicate otherwise, the LXX (Septuagint) says some in Egypt were not circumcised. Now, as they were about to enter the land, God told Joshua to circumcise all the males upon which the LORD rolled away the re-

proach of Egypt (ver 9). Early in the history of the church baptism replaced circumcision as the outward rite or means of admission to the fellowship.
5.7 No explicit reason is given for the failure to circumcise each male when he was eight days old. The ritual was instituted by Abraham (Gen 17.12) as a sign of the covenant, Moses realized its importance (Ex 4.24–26), and the LORD instructed Moses to incorporate it in the Sinaitic code (Lev 12.3).

3. The angel of the LORD

13 When Joshua was by Jĕr'ĭchō, he lifted up his eyes and looked, and behold, a man stood before him with his drawn sword in his hand; and Joshua went to him and said to him, "Are you for us, or for our adversaries?" 14And he said, "No; but as commander of the army of the LORD I have now come." And Joshua fell on his face to the earth, and worshiped, and said to him, "What does my lord bid his servant?" 15And the commander of the LORD's army said to Joshua, "Put off your shoes from your feet; for the place where you stand is holy." And Joshua did so.

E. The conquest of Jericho

1. The six-day march around Jericho

6 Now Jĕr'ĭchō was shut up from within and from without because of the people of Israel; none went out, and none came in. 2And the LORD said to Joshua, "See, I have given into your hand Jĕr'ĭchō, with its king and mighty men of valor. 3 You shall march around the city, all the men of war going around the city once. Thus shall you do for six days. 4And seven priests shall bear seven trumpets of rams' horns before the ark; and on the seventh day you shall march around the city seven times, the priests blowing the trumpets. 5And when they make a long blast with the ram's horn, as soon as you hear the sound of the trumpet, then all the people shall shout with a great shout; and the wall of the city will fall down flat, and the people shall go up every man straight before him." 6 So Joshua the son of Nûn called the priests and said to them, "Take up the ark of the covenant, and let seven priests bear seven trumpets of rams' horns before the ark of the LORD." 7And he said to the people, "Go forward; march around the city, and let the armed men pass on before the ark of the LORD."

8 And as Joshua had commanded the people, the seven priests bearing the seven trumpets of rams' horns before the LORD went forward, blowing the trumpets, with the ark of the covenant of the LORD following them. 9And the armed men went before the priests who blew the trumpets, and the rear guard came after the ark, while the trumpets blew continually. 10 But Joshua commanded the people, "You shall not shout or let your voice be heard, neither shall any word go out of your mouth, until the day I bid you shout; then you shall shout." 11 So he caused the ark of the LORD to compass the city, going about it once; and they came into the camp, and spent the night in the camp.

12 Then Joshua rose early in the morning, and the priests took up the ark of the LORD. 13And the seven priests bearing the seven trumpets of rams' horns before the ark of the LORD passed on, blowing the trumpets continually; and the armed men went before them, and the rear guard came after the ark of the LORD, while the

5.13 Gen 18.2; 32.24; Num 22.31

5.14 Gen 17.3

5.15 Ex 3.5

*6.1

6.2 Josh 2.9, 24; Deut 7.24

6.4 Num 10.8

6.5 Lev 25.9

6.7 Ex 14.15

6.9 ver 13; Isa 52.12

6.13 ver 4,9

6.1 Jericho was conquered by spiritual rather than carnal means. Once again God illustrates how He uses foolish things to confound the wise, viz., the wooden rod of Moses, the crude slingshot of David, and the ram's-horn trumpets of Joshua. Whether the falling of the walls occurred because of an earthquake or because God performed a special miracle at that moment is immaterial. He chooses his own means to accomplish the divine will. The unchanging fact remains that the walls fell at the moment they were supposed to, and the means by which God caused it are secondary.

trumpets blew continually. 14And the second day they marched around the city once, and returned into the camp. So they did for six days.

2. The fall of the city

15 On the seventh day they rose early at the dawn of day, and marched around the city in the same manner seven times: it was only on that day that they marched around the city seven times. 16And at the seventh time, when the priests had blown the trumpets, Joshua said to the people, "Shout; for the LORD has given you the city. 17And the city and all that is within it shall be devoted to the LORD for destruction; only Rāhǎb the harlot and all who are with her in her house shall live, because she hid the messengers that we sent. 18But you, keep yourselves from the things devoted to destruction, lest when you have devoted them you take any of the devoted things and make the camp of Israel a thing for destruction, and bring trouble upon it. 19 But all silver and gold, and vessels of bronze and iron, are sacred to the LORD; they shall go into the treasury of the LORD." 20 So the people shouted, and the trumpets were blown. As soon as the people heard the sound of the trumpet, the people raised a great shout, and the wall fell down flat, so that the people went up into the city, every man straight before him, and they took the city. 21 Then they utterly destroyed all in the city, both men and women, young and old, oxen, sheep, and asses, with the edge of the sword.

3. The rescue of Rahab

22 And Joshua said to the two men who had spied out the land, "Go into the harlot's house, and bring out from it the woman, and all who belong to her, as you swore to her." 23 So the young men who had been spies went in, and brought out Rāhǎb, and her father and mother and brothers and all who belonged to her; and they brought all her kindred, and set them outside the camp of Israel. 24And they burned the city with fire, and all within it; only the silver and gold, and the vessels of bronze and of iron, they put into the treasury of the house of the LORD. 25 But Rāhǎb the harlot, and her father's household, and all who belonged to her, Joshua saved alive; and she dwelt in Israel to this day, because she hid the messengers whom Joshua sent to spy out Jěr'íchō.

4. The curse on Jericho

26 Joshua laid an oath upon them at that time, saying, "Cursed before the LORD be the man that rises up and rebuilds this city, Jěr'íchō.

At the cost of his first-born shall he lay its foundation,
and at the cost of his youngest son shall he set up its gates."

27 So the LORD was with Joshua; and his fame was in all the land.

6.17
Lev 27.28;
Josh 2.4

6.18
Josh 7.1,25

*6.20
ver 5;
Heb 11.30

6.21
Deut 7.2;
20.16

6.22
Josh 2.14;
Heb 11.31

6.23
Josh 2.13

6.24
ver 19

*6.25
Heb 11.31

6.26
1 Ki 16.34

6.27
Josh 1.5;
9.1,3

6.17a *devoted to the* LORD, see note to Deut 2.34 for an explanation.
6.17b *harlot.* Some, like Josephus, have tried to soften this to "innkeeper," but the Hebrew word and the Septuagint translation make this impossible to do.
6.20 *the wall fell down flat.* For six days the soldiers marched around the city once a day.

On the seventh day they went around seven times. Whether the collapse was a result of this, or a providential coincidence, or a miracle, the text does not say.
6.25 *But Rahab . . . and all who belonged to her.* Because of her coalition with Joshua he saw to it that Rahab and her entire family escaped when Jericho was destroyed.

F. The conquest of Ai

1. Israel flees from Ai

7 But the people of Israel broke faith in regard to the devoted things; for Āchản the son of Carmī, son of Zăbdī, son of Zērảh, of the tribe of Judah, took some of the devoted things; and the anger of the LORD burned against the people of Israel.

2 Joshua sent men from Jĕr′içhō to Āī, which is near Bĕth-ăvĕn, east of Bĕthĕl, and said to them, "Go up and spy out the land." And the men went up and spied out Ai. 3 And they returned to Joshua, and said to him, "Let not all the people go up, but let about two or three thousand men go up and attack Āī; do not make the whole people toil up there, for they are but few." 4 So about three thousand went up there from the people; and they fled before the men of Āī, 5 and the men of Āī killed about thirty-six men of them, and chased them before the gate as far as Shĕb′-ảrĭm, and slew them at the descent. And the hearts of the people melted, and became as water.

2. Joshua's grief

6 Then Joshua rent his clothes, and fell to the earth upon his face before the ark of the LORD until the evening, he and the elders of Israel; and they put dust upon their heads. 7 And Joshua said, "Alas, O Lord GOD, why hast thou brought this people over the Jordan at all, to give us into the hands of the Ăm′ŏrītes, to destroy us? Would that we had been content to dwell beyond the Jordan! 8 O Lord, what can I say, when Israel has turned their backs before their enemies! 9 For the Că′naănītes and all the inhabitants of the land will hear of it, and will surround us, and cut off our name from the earth; and what wilt thou do for thy great name?"

3. God's way of uncovering sin

10 The LORD said to Joshua, "Arise, why have you thus fallen upon your face? 11 Israel has sinned; they have transgressed my covenant which I commanded them; they have taken some of the devoted things; they have stolen, and lied, and put them among their own stuff. 12 Therefore the people of Israel cannot stand before their enemies; they turn their backs before their enemies, because they have become a thing for destruction. I will be with you no more, unless you destroy the devoted things from among you. 13 Up, sanctify the people, and say, 'Sanctify yourselves for tomorrow; for thus says the LORD, God of Israel, "There are devoted things in the midst of you, O Israel; you cannot stand before your enemies, until you take away the devoted things from among you." 14 In the morning therefore you shall be brought near by your tribes; and the tribe which the LORD takes shall come near by families; and the family which the LORD takes shall come near by

*7.1
Josh 6.17-19

7.4
Lev 26.17;
28.25

7.6
Job 2.12;
Rev 18.19
7.7
Ex 5.22

7.9
Ex 32.12;
Deut 9.28

7.11
ver 1;
Josh 6.18,
19;
See Acts
5.1,2

7.13
Josh 3.5;
6.18

7.1 Valuable lessons may be learned from the sin of Achan. God looked upon Israel as an entity, so that the sin of one brought punishment upon all. The essential unity of the people of God is thus evident. Since man neither lives nor dies for himself, his activities inevitably affect the lives of many people. Israel's first attack on Ai, which was repulsed, shows this to be true. Achan's sin did not consist in the seizure of the enemy's goods, nor was covetousness the worst of his offenses. His chief sin was flagrant disobedience of God's express command. Israel was released from her own involvement in guilt only after Achan and his family had been dealt with. The terrible punishment meted out to him was a warning to all never to allow greed to lure them into disregard of God's will.

households; and the household which the LORD takes shall come near man by man. 15And he who is taken with the devoted things shall be burned with fire, he and all that he has, because he has transgressed the covenant of the LORD, and because he has done a shameful thing in Israel.' "

4. The sin of Achan uncovered

16 So Joshua rose early in the morning, and brought Israel near tribe by tribe, and the tribe of Judah was taken; 17 and he brought near the families of Judah, and the family of the Zĕr′ăhītes was taken; and he brought near the family of the Zerahites man by man, and Zăbdī was taken; 18 and he brought near his household man by man, and Ăchăn the son of Carmī, son of Zăbdī, son of Zĕrăh, of the tribe of Judah, was taken. 19 Then Joshua said to Ăchăn, "My son, give glory to the LORD God of Israel, and render praise to him; and tell me now what you have done; do not hide it from me." 20And Ăchăn answered Joshua, "Of a truth I have sinned against the LORD God of Israel, and this is what I did: 21 when I saw among the spoil a beautiful mantle from Shīnar, and two hundred shekels of silver, and a bar of gold weighing fifty shekels, then I coveted them, and took them; and behold, they are hidden in the earth inside my tent, with the silver underneath."

5. The stoning of Achan and his family

22 So Joshua sent messengers, and they ran to the tent; and behold, it was hidden in his tent with the silver underneath. 23And they took them out of the tent and brought them to Joshua and all the people of Israel; and they laid them down before the LORD. 24And Joshua and all Israel with him took Ăchăn the son of Zĕrăh, and the silver and the mantle and the bar of gold, and his sons and daughters, and his oxen and asses and sheep, and his tent, and all that he had; and they brought them up to the Valley of Ăchŏr. 25And Joshua said, "Why did you bring trouble on us? The LORD brings trouble on you today." And all Israel stoned him with stones; they burned them with fire, and stoned them with stones. 26And they raised over him a great heap of stones that remains to this day; then the LORD turned from his burning anger. Therefore to this day the name of that place is called the Valley of Ăchŏr.c

6. The battle for Ai
a. The plan of battle

8 And the LORD said to Joshua, "Do not fear or be dismayed; take all the fighting men with you, and arise, go up to Āī; see, I have given into your hand the king of Ai, and his people, his city, and his land; 2 and you shall do to Āī and its king as you did to Jĕr′ĭchŏ and its king; only its spoil and its cattle you shall take as booty for yourselves; lay an ambush against the city, behind it."

3 So Joshua arose, and all the fighting men, to go up to Āī; and Joshua chose thirty thousand mighty men of valor, and sent them forth by night. 4And he commanded them, "Behold, you shall lie in ambush against the city, behind it; do not go very far from the city, but hold yourselves all in readiness; 5 and I, and all the people who are with me, will approach the city. And when they come

---

c That is Trouble

7.15
ver 11

7.17
Num 26.20

7.19
Jer 13.16;
Jn 9.24;
Num 5.6,7;
1 Sam 14.43
7.20
Josh 22.20;
1 Chr 2.7

7.24
Josh 15.7

7.25
Josh 6.18;
Deut 17.5

7.26
Deut 13.17;
Isa 65.10;
Hos 2.15

8.1
Deut 1.21;
7.18;
Josh 1.9;
6.2
8.2
ver 27;
Deut 20.14

8.4
see Judg
20.29–32

out against us, as before, we shall flee before them; 6 and they will
come out after us, till we have drawn them away from the city; for
they will say, 'They are fleeing from us, as before.' So we will flee
from them; 7 then you shall rise up from the ambush, and seize the
city; for the LORD your God will give it into your hand. 8And when
you have taken the city, you shall set the city on fire, doing as the
LORD has bidden; see, I have commanded you." 9 So Joshua sent
them forth; and they went to the place of ambush, and lay between
Běthěl and Āī, to the west of Ai; but Joshua spent that night
among the people.

b. *The seizure of the city*

10 And Joshua arose early in the morning and mustered the
people, and went up, with the elders of Israel, before the people to
Āī. 11And all the fighting men who were with him went up, and
drew near before the city, and encamped on the north side of Āī,
with a ravine between them and Ai. 12And he took about five
thousand men, and set them in ambush between Běthěl and Āī, to
the west of the city. 13 So they stationed the forces, the main encampment which was north of the city and its rear guard west
of the city. But Joshua spent that night in the valley. 14And when
the king of Āī saw this he and all his people, the men of the city,
made haste and went out early to the descent*d* toward the Ar′ábáh
to meet Israel in battle; but he did not know that there was an
ambush against him behind the city. 15And Joshua and all Israel
made a pretense of being beaten before them, and fled in the direction of the wilderness. 16 So all the people who were in the city
were called together to pursue them, and as they pursued Joshua
they were drawn away from the city. 17 There was not a man left
in Āī or Běthěl, who did not go out after Israel; they left the city
open, and pursued Israel.

18 Then the LORD said to Joshua, "Stretch out the javelin that
is in your hand toward Āī; for I will give it into your hand."
And Joshua stretched out the javelin that was in his hand toward
the city. 19And the ambush rose quickly out of their place, and as
soon as he had stretched out his hand, they ran and entered the
city and took it; and they made haste to set the city on fire. 20 So
when the men of Āī looked back, behold, the smoke of the city
went up to heaven; and they had no power to flee this way or
that, for the people that fled to the wilderness turned back upon
the pursuers. 21And when Joshua and all Israel saw that the ambush had taken the city, and that the smoke of the city went up,
then they turned back and smote the men of Āī. 22And the others
came forth from the city against them; so they were in the midst
of Israel, some on this side, and some on that side; and Israel
smote them, until there was left none that survived or escaped.
23 But the king of Āī they took alive, and brought him to Joshua.

c. *The slaughter of the inhabitants*

24 When Israel had finished slaughtering all the inhabitants of
Āī in the open wilderness where they pursued them and all of them
to the very last had fallen by the edge of the sword, all Israel returned to Ai, and smote it with the edge of the sword. 25And all
who fell that day, both men and women, were twelve thousand,

d Cn: Heb *appointed time*

8.8
ver 2

8.10
ver 33

8.14
Josh 3.16;
Judg 20.34

8.18
ver 26;
Ex 14.16;
17.9–13
8.19
ver 8

8.22
Deut 7.2

8.25
Deut 20.16–
18

8.26
Ex 17.11,12

8.27
ver 2;
Num 31.22

*8.28
Deut 13.16

8.29
Deut 21.22,
23

all the people of Āi. 26 For Joshua did not draw back his hand, with which he stretched out the javelin, until he had utterly destroyed all the inhabitants of Āi. 27 Only the cattle and the spoil of that city Israel took as their booty, according to the word of the LORD which he commanded Joshua. 28 So Joshua burned Āi, and made it for ever a heap of ruins, as it is to this day. 29And he hanged the king of Āi on a tree until evening; and at the going down of the sun Joshua commanded, and they took his body down from the tree, and cast it at the entrance of the gate of the city, and raised over it a great heap of stones, which stands there to this day.

7. An altar erected in Mount Ebal

8.30
Deut 27.2–8

8.31
Ex 20.24,
25; Deut
27.5,6

*8.32
Deut 27.2,
8

8.33
Deut 31.9,
12;
27.11–14

*8.34f
Deut 31.11;
Josh 1.8

8.35
Deut 31.12

30 Then Joshua built an altar in Mount Ēbál to the LORD, the God of Israel, 31 as Moses the servant of the LORD had commanded the people of Israel, as it is written in the book of the law of Moses, "an altar of unhewn stones, upon which no man has lifted an iron tool"; and they offered on it burnt offerings to the LORD, and sacrificed peace offerings. 32And there, in the presence of the people of Israel, he wrote upon the stones a copy of the law of Moses, which he had written. 33And all Israel, sojourner as well as homeborn, with their elders and officers and their judges, stood on opposite sides of the ark before the Lévit'ĭcăl priests who carried the ark of the covenant of the LORD, half of them in front of Mount Gĕr'ĭzĭm and half of them in front of Mount Ēbál, as Moses the servant of the LORD had commanded at the first, that they should bless the people of Israel. 34And afterward he read all the words of the law, the blessing and the curse, according to all that is written in the book of the law. 35 There was not a word of all that Moses commanded which Joshua did not read before all the assembly of Israel, and the women, and the little ones, and the sojourners who lived among them.

G. The stratagem of Gibeon

1. The coalition of kings

9.1
Josh 3.10

9 When all the kings who were beyond the Jordan in the hill country and in the lowland all along the coast of the Great Sea toward Lebanon, the Hĭttītes, the Ăm'ŏrītes, the Cā'naănītes, the Pĕr'ĭzzītes, the Hīvītes, and the Jĕb'ūsītes, heard of this, 2 they gathered together with one accord to fight Joshua and Israel.

2. The treaty with Gibeon

9.3
Josh 10.2;
6.27

9.6
Josh 5.10

3 But when the inhabitants of Gĭb'ĕŏn heard what Joshua had done to Jĕr'ĭchō and to Āi, 4 they on their part acted with cunning, and went and made ready provisions, and took worn-out sacks upon their asses, and wineskins, worn-out and torn and mended, 5 with worn-out, patched sandals on their feet, and worn-out clothes; and all their provisions were dry and moldy. 6And they

---

8.28 *Ai*, meaning "ruins," was destroyed about 2200 B.C. and not occupied at all during the Israelite conquest. A probable explanation is that Joshua took Bethel, which was a mile from Ai (see Judg 1.22–26). Ai may have been a military outpost of Bethel.
8.32, 34, 35 Besides the "blessing" and the "curse" (see Deut 27.3, 8, 12–26), it is im-

possible to determine how much of the Law of Moses was inscribed on the stones and read to the people. At the covenant ceremony at Sinai, Moses read *the book of the covenant*, probably Ex 21–23 (see Ex 24.7). The limitations of space and time indicate that the reading of the law at Ebal and Gerizim was not much, if any, longer.

went to Joshua in the camp at Gilgal, and said to him and to the men of Israel, "We have come from a far country; so now make a covenant with us." 7 But the men of Israel said to the Hivites, "Perhaps you live among us; then how can we make a covenant with you?" 8 They said to Joshua, "We are your servants." And Joshua said to them, "Who are you? And where do you come from?" 9 They said to him, "From a very far country your servants have come, because of the name of the LORD your God; for we have heard a report of him, and all that he did in Egypt, 10 and all that he did to the two kings of the Am'orites who were beyond the Jordan, Sihon the king of Heshbon, and Og king of Bashan, who dwelt in Ash'taroth. 11And our elders and all the inhabitants of our country said to us, 'Take provisions in your hand for the journey, and go to meet them, and say to them, "We are your servants; come now, make a covenant with us." ' 12 Here is our bread; it was still warm when we took it from our houses as our food for the journey, on the day we set forth to come to you, but now, behold, it is dry and moldy; 13 these wineskins were new when we filled them, and behold, they are burst; and these garments and shoes of ours are worn out from the very long journey." 14 So the men partook of their provisions, and did not ask direction from the LORD. 15And Joshua made peace with them, and made a covenant with them, to let them live; and the leaders of the congregation swore to them.

3. The punishment of the Gibeonites for their deceit

16 At the end of three days after they had made a covenant with them, they heard that they were their neighbors, and that they dwelt among them. 17And the people of Israel set out and reached their cities on the third day. Now their cities were Gib'eon, Chephi'rah, Be-er'oth, and Kir'iath-je'arim. 18 But the people of Israel did not kill them, because the leaders of the congregation had sworn to them by the LORD, the God of Israel. Then all the congregation murmured against the leaders. 19 But all the leaders said to all the congregation, "We have sworn to them by the LORD, the God of Israel, and now we may not touch them. 20 This we will do to them, and let them live, lest wrath be upon us, because of the oath which we swore to them." 21And the leaders said to them, "Let them live." So they became hewers of wood and drawers of water for all the congregation, as the leaders had said of them.

22 Joshua summoned them, and he said to them, "Why did you deceive us, saying, 'We are very far from you,' when you dwell among us? 23 Now therefore you are cursed, and some of you shall always be slaves, hewers of wood and drawers of water for the house of my God." 24 They answered Joshua, "Because it was told to your servants for a certainty that the LORD your God had commanded his servant Moses to give you all the land, and to destroy all the inhabitants of the land from before you; so we feared

Marginal references:

9.7; ver 2; Josh 11.19; Ex 23.32

9.8 Deut 20.11

9.9 Deut 20.15; ver 16,17, 24;
Josh 2.9,10

9.10 Num 21.24, 33

*9.14 Num 27.21

9.15 Ex 23.32

9.17 Josh 18.25–28; Ezra 2.25

9.18 Ps 15.4; Ecc 5.2

9.21 ver 15

9.22 ver 6.9,16, 17

9.23 Gen 9.25; ver 21,27

9.24 Deut 7.1,2

9.14 The Gibeonites obtained a treaty of friendship by deception. Yet Israel was not without guilt, nor was it necessary for them to be deceived. They *did not ask direction from the* LORD. Had they done so they would have been delivered from this error in judg-ment. No matter how favorable the external appearances, we must never rely upon our own good judgment or common sense when making a covenantal commitment; we must wait upon God and ascertain His will in the matter.

greatly for our lives because of you, and did this thing. 25And now, behold, we are in your hand: do as it seems good and right in your sight to do to us." 26 So he did to them, and delivered them out of the hand of the people of Israel; and they did not kill them. 27 But Joshua made them that day hewers of wood and drawers of water for the congregation and for the altar of the LORD, to continue to this day, in the place which he should choose.

H. The conquest of southern Canaan

1. The victory over the Amorites

a. The confederation

10 When Ădŏn'ĭ-zē'dĕk king of Jerusalem heard how Joshua had taken Āī, and had utterly destroyed it, doing to Ai and its king as he had done to Jĕr'ĭçhō and its king, and how the inhabitants of Gĭb'ëŏn had made peace with Israel and were among them, 2 hex feared greatly, because Gĭb'ëŏn was a great city, like one of the royal cities, and because it was greater than Āī, and all its men were mighty. 3 So Ădŏn'ĭ-zē'dĕk king of Jerusalem sent to Hōhăm king of Hēbrŏn, to Pīrăm king of Jarmŭth, to Jăphī'ă king of Lāchĭsh, and to Dēbir king of Ĕglŏn, saying, 4 "Come up to me, and help me, and let us smite Gĭb'ëŏn; for it has made peace with Joshua and with the people of Israel." 5 Then the five kings of the Ăm'ŏrītes, the king of Jerusalem, the king of Hēbrŏn, the king of Jarmŭth, the king of Lāchĭsh, and the king of Ĕglŏn, gathered their forces, and went up with all their armies and encamped against Gĭb'ëŏn, and made war against it.

b. The battle: God sends hailstones

6 And the men of Gĭb'ëŏn sent to Joshua at the camp in Gĭlgăl, saying, "Do not relax your hand from your servants; come up to us quickly, and save us, and help us; for all the kings of the Ăm'-ŏrītes that dwell in the hill country are gathered against us." 7 So Joshua went up from Gĭlgăl, he and all the people of war with him, and all the mighty men of valor. 8And the LORD said to Joshua, "Do not fear them, for I have given them into your hands; there shall not a man of them stand before you." 9 So Joshua came upon them suddenly, having marched up all night from Gĭlgăl. 10And the LORD threw them into a panic before Israel, who slew them with a great slaughter at Gĭb'ëŏn, and chased them by the way of the ascent of Bĕth-hor'ŏn, and smote them as far as Ăzē'kăh and Măkkē'dăh. 11And as they fled before Israel, while they were going down the ascent of Bĕth-hor'ŏn, the LORD threw down great stones from heaven upon them as far as Ăzē'kăh, and they died; there were more who died because of the hailstones than the men of Israel killed with the sword.

c. The sun stands still

12 Then spoke Joshua to the LORD in the day when the LORD gave the Ăm'ŏrītes over to the men of Israel; and he said in the sight of Israel,
"Sun, stand thou still at Gĭb'ëŏn,
and thou Moon in the valley of Āī'jălŏn."

x Heb they

Marginal references:

9.25 Gen 16.6

9.27 ver 21,23; Deut 12.5

10.1 Josh 6.21; 8.22,26,28; 9.15

10.4 ver 1

10.5 Josh 9.2

10.8 Josh 1.5,9; 11.6

10.10 Deut 7.23

10.11 Ps 18.13, 14; Isa 30.30

10.12 Hab 3.11

13 And the sun stood still, and the moon stayed,
   until the nation took vengeance on their enemies.
Is this not written in the Book of Jăshár? The sun stayed in the
midst of heaven, and did not hasten to go down for about a whole
day. 14 There has been no day like it before or since, when the
LORD hearkened to the voice of a man; for the LORD fought for
Israel.

15 Then Joshua returned, and all Israel with him, to the camp
at Gĭlgăl.

d. The slaughter of the five kings

16 These five kings fled, and hid themselves in the cave at
Măkkē′dăh. 17And it was told Joshua, "The five kings have been
found, hidden in the cave at Măkkē′dăh." 18And Joshua said,
"Roll great stones against the mouth of the cave, and set men by it
to guard them; 19 but do not stay there yourselves, pursue your
enemies, fall upon their rear, do not let them enter their cities;
for the LORD your God has given them into your hand." 20 When
Joshua and the men of Israel had finished slaying them with a very
great slaughter, until they were wiped out, and when the remnant
which remained of them had entered into the fortified cities, 21 all
the people returned safe to Joshua in the camp at Măkkē′dăh;
not a man moved his tongue against any of the people of Israel.
22 Then Joshua said, "Open the mouth of the cave, and bring
those five kings out to me from the cave." 23And they did so, and
brought those five kings out to him from the cave, the king of
Jerusalem, the king of Hēbrŏn, the king of Jarmŭth, the king of
Lăchĭsh, and the king of Ĕglŏn. 24And when they brought those
kings out to Joshua, Joshua summoned all the men of Israel, and
said to the chiefs of the men of war who had gone with him,
"Come near, put your feet upon the necks of these kings." Then
they came near, and put their feet on their necks. 25And Joshua
said to them, "Do not be afraid or dismayed; be strong and of good
courage; for thus the LORD will do to all your enemies against
whom you fight." 26And afterward Joshua smote them and put
them to death, and he hung them on five trees. And they hung
upon the trees until evening; 27 but at the time of the going down
of the sun, Joshua commanded, and they took them down from
the trees, and threw them into the cave where they had hidden
themselves, and they set great stones against the mouth of the
cave, which remain to this very day.

2. The conquest completed

28 And Joshua took Măkkē′dăh on that day, and smote it and
its king with the edge of the sword; he utterly destroyed every
person in it, he left none remaining; and he did to the king of
Makkedah as he had done to the king of Jĕr′ĭchō.

★10.13
2 Sam 1.18;
Isa 38.8

10.14
ver 42

★10.15
ver 43

10.16
ver 5

10.20
Deut 20.16

10.21
Ex 11.7

10.22
Deut 7.24

★10.24
Ps 110.5;
Isa 26.5,6;
Mal 4.3

10.25
ver 8

10.26
Josh 8.29

10.27
Deut 21.23;
Josh 8.9

10.28
Deut 20.16;
Josh 6.21

10.13 *the sun stood still*, has been understood by some to be a figure of speech; by
others as evidence of a miracle. It is not a case
of whether God could have performed a miracle, but rather whether Scripture teaches that
He did so on this occasion. Some hold that
verses 7–18 give the historical happenings, and
verses 12–14 the poetic interpretation from the
Book of Jasher. Others hold that verses 12–14

must be taken literally.
10.15 This verse, identical with 10.43, is
out of place here. Return to Gilgal is incon-
gruous because verse 16 continues the story
about the five kings. Had Joshua returned,
the kings would not have had to hide in a cave.
10.24 *feet upon the necks*. This action,
symbolic of victory, is found many times in
Egyptian and Assyrian sculptures.

10.29
1 Chr 6.57

29 Then Joshua passed on from Măkkē'dȧh, and all Israel with him, to Lĭbnȧh, and fought against Libnah; 30 and the LORD gave it also and its king into the hand of Israel; and he smote it with the edge of the sword, and every person in it; he left none remaining in it; and he did to its king as he had done to the king of Jĕr'ĭc̨hō.

10.31
2 Ki 14.19

31 And Joshua passed on from Lĭbnȧh, and all Israel with him, to Lāc̨hĭsh, and laid siege to it, and assaulted it: 32 and the LORD gave Lāc̨hĭsh into the hand of Israel, and he took it on the second day, and smote it with the edge of the sword, and every person in it, as he had done to Lĭbnȧh.

33 Then Horȧm king of Gēzėr came up to help Lāc̨hĭsh; and Joshua smote him and his people, until he left none remaining.

34 And Joshua passed on with all Israel from Lāc̨hĭsh to Ĕglŏn; and they laid siege to it, and assaulted it; 35 and they took it on that day, and smote it with the edge of the sword; and every person in it he utterly destroyed that day, as he had done to Lāc̨hĭsh.

10.36
Josh 14.13;
15.13;
Judg 1.10
★**10.37**

36 Then Joshua went up with all Israel from Ĕglŏn to Hēbrŏn; and they assaulted it, 37 and took it, and smote it with the edge of the sword, and its king and its towns, and every person in it; he left none remaining, as he had done to Ĕglŏn, and utterly destroyed it with every person in it.

10.38
Josh 15.15;
Judg 1.11

38 Then Joshua, with all Israel, turned back to Dēbĭr and assaulted it, 39 and he took it with its king and all its towns; and they smote them with the edge of the sword, and utterly destroyed every person in it; he left none remaining; as he had done to Hēbrŏn and to Lĭbnȧh and its king, so he did to Dēbĭr and to its king.

★**10.40**
Deut 1.7;
7.24;
20.16,17

40 So Joshua defeated the whole land, the hill country and the Nĕgĕb and the lowland and the slopes, and all their kings; he left none remaining, but utterly destroyed all that breathed, as the LORD God of Israel commanded. 41And Joshua defeated them from Kā'dĕsh-barnē'ȧ to Gaza, and all the country of Gōshėn, as far as Gĭb'ëön. 42And Joshua took all these kings and their land at one time, because the LORD God of Israel fought for Israel. 43 Then Joshua returned, and all Israel with him, to the camp at Gĭlgȧl.

★**10.41**
Josh 11.16;
15.51
10.42
ver 14

I. The conquest of northern Canaan

11.1
ver 10

11.2
Josh 12.3ff

11 When Jābĭn king of Hāzor heard of this, he sent to Jōbăb king of Mādŏn, and to the king of Shĭmrŏn, and to the king of Ȧc̨h'shȧph, 2 and to the kings who were in the northern hill country, and in the Ȧr'ābȧh south of C̨hĭn'nėrŏth, and in the lowland, and in Nā'phŏth-dor' on the west, 3 to the Cā'naȧnītes in the east and the west, the Ăm'ŏrītes, the Hĭttītes, the Pĕr'-ĭzzītes, and the Jĕb'ūsītes in the hill country, and the Hĭvītes under

---

10.37 *its king*, the king of Hebron. He must have been a recent claimant or successor to the throne because the king of Hebron was one of the five kings slain by Joshua (10.26).
10.40 This all-inclusive statement, like those in 11.16–19; 21.44–45, applies only to the enemies which Joshua defeated in certain areas. Judg 1.27–33 states that there were a

number of Canaanite cities which the Israelites did not capture and destroy. In fact, some did not fall until the time of David and Solomon. These statements must be understood in terms of extent. Joshua had general control over the whole land, even though there were islands of resistance.
10.41 *Goshen*, not the Goshen in Egypt.

Hèrmòn in the land of Mĭzpàh. [4]And they came out, with all their troops, a great host, in number like the sand that is upon the sea-shore, with very many horses and chariots. [5]And all these kings joined their forces, and came and encamped together at the waters of Mèròm, to fight with Israel.

6 And the LORD said to Joshua, "Do not be afraid of them, for tomorrow at this time I will give over all of them, slain, to Israel; you shall hamstring their horses, and burn their chariots with fire." [7] So Joshua came suddenly upon them with all his people of war, by the waters of Mèròm, and fell upon them. [8]And the LORD gave them into the hand of Israel, who smote them and chased them as far as Great Sĭdòn and Mĭs'rèphòth-mā'ĭm, and eastward as far as the valley of Mĭzpèh; and they smote them, until they left none remaining. [9]And Joshua did to them as the LORD bade him; he hamstrung their horses, and burned their chariots with fire.

10 And Joshua turned back at that time, and took Hāzor, and smote its king with the sword; for Hazor formerly was the head of all those kingdoms. [11]And they put to the sword all who were in it, utterly destroying them; there was none left that breathed, and he burned Hāzor with fire. [12]And all the cities of those kings, and all their kings, Joshua took, and smote them with the edge of the sword, utterly destroying them, as Moses the servant of the LORD had commanded. [13] But none of the cities that stood on mounds did Israel burn, except Hāzor only; that Joshua burned. [14]And all the spoil of these cities and the cattle, the people of Israel took for their booty; but every man they smote with the edge of the sword, until they had destroyed them, and they did not leave any that breathed. [15]As the LORD had commanded Moses his servant, so Moses commanded Joshua, and so Joshua did; he left nothing undone of all that the LORD had commanded Moses.

J. Summary of the conquests

16 So Joshua took all that land, the hill country and all the Nĕgĕb and all the land of Gòshèn and the lowland and the Ar'àbàh and the hill country of Israel and its lowland [17]from Mount Hālăk, that rises toward Sèir, as far as Bā'àl-găd in the valley of Lebanon below Mount Hèrmòn. And he took all their kings, and smote them, and put them to death. [18] Joshua made war a long time with all those kings. [19] There was not a city that made peace with the people of Israel, except the Hĭvītes, the inhabitants of Gĭbëòn; they took all in battle. [20] For it was the LORD's doing to harden their hearts that they should come against Israel in battle, in order that they should be utterly destroyed, and should receive no mercy but be exterminated, as the LORD commanded Moses.

21 And Joshua came at that time, and wiped out the Ăn'ákĭm from the hill country, from Hèbròn, from Dèbĭr, from Ănăb, and from all the hill country of Judah, and from all the hill country of Israel; Joshua utterly destroyed them with their cities. [22] There was none of the Ăn'ákĭm left in the land of the people of Israel; only in Gazà, in Găth, and in Ăshdŏd, did some remain. [23] So Joshua took the whole land, according to all that the LORD had spoken to Moses; and Joshua gave it for an inheritance to Israel according to their tribal allotments. And the land had rest from war.

11.4
Judg 7.12

11.6
Josh 10.8;
2 Sam 8.4

11.8
Josh 13.6

11.9
ver 6

11.11
Deut 20.16, 17

11.14
Num 31.11, 12

11.15
Ex 34.11, 12;
Deut 7.2;
Josh 1.7

11.16
Josh 10.40, 41; ver 2
11.17
Josh 12.7;
Deut 7.24

11.19
Josh 9.3,7

11.20
Deut 2.30;
Rom 9.18;
Deut 20.16, 17

11.21
Num 13.33;
Deut 9.2

11.23
Num 34.2ff

K. The list of conquered kings

1. The kings of east Canaan

12 Now these are the kings of the land, whom the people of Israel defeated, and took possession of their land beyond the Jordan toward the sunrising, from the valley of the Arnòn to Mount Hèrmòn, with all the Ạr'ạbạh eastward: 2 Sìhòn king of the Ạm'òrites who dwelt at Hèshbòn, and ruled from Ạrõ'èr, which is on the edge of the valley of the Arnòn, and from the middle of the valley as far as the river Jäbbòk, the boundary of the Ạm'mònites, that is, half of Gìl'ëäd, 3 and the Ạr'ạbạh to the Sea of Chìn'nèròth eastward, and in the direction of Bèth-jèsh'ìmòth, to the sea of the Arabah, the Salt Sea, southward to the foot of the slopes of Pìsgäh; 4 and Õgᵉ king of Bäshàn, one of the remnant of the Rèph'äim, who dwelt at Ạsh'tàròth and at Ĕd'rë-ì 5 and ruled over Mount Hèrmòn and Sạl'ècàh and all Bäshàn to the boundary of the Gèsh'ùrites and the Mä-äc'äthìtes, and over half of Gìl'ëäd to the boundary of Sìhòn king of Hèshbòn. 6 Moses, the servant of the LORD, and the people of Israel defeated them; and Moses the servant of the LORD gave their land for a possession to the Reu'bènites and the Gạdìtes and the half-tribe of Mạnạs'sèh.

2. The kings of west Canaan

7 And these are the kings of the land whom Joshua and the people of Israel defeated on the west side of the Jordan, from Bä'äl-gäd in the valley of Lebanon to Mount Häläk, that rises toward Seir (and Joshua gave their land to the tribes of Israel as a possession according to their allotments, 8 in the hill country, in the lowland, in the Ạr'ạbạh, in the slopes, in the wilderness, and in the Nègĕb, the land of the Hìttìtes, the Ạm'òrites, the Cä'naànìtes, the Pĕr'ìzzìtes, the Hìvìtes, and the Jèb'ùsìtes): 9 the king of Jèr'ìchò, one; the king of Ạì, which is beside Bèthèl, one; 10 the king of Jerusalem, one; the king of Hèbròn, one; 11 the king of Jarmùth, one; the king of Lächìsh, one; 12 the king of Ĕglòn, one; the king of Gèzèr, one; 13 the king of Dèbìr, one; the king of Gèdèr, one; 14 the king of Hormàh, one; the king of Ạràd, one; 15 the king of Lìbnàh, one; the king of Ạdùl'làm, one; 16 the king of Mạkkè'dàh, one; the king of Bèthèl, one; 17 the king of Tàppū'äh, one; the king of Hèphèr, one; 18 the king of Ạphĕk, one; the king of Lä-shạr'òn, one; 19 the king of Mädòn, one; the king of Hāzor, one; 20 the king of Shìm'ròn-mèr'òn, one; the king of Ạch'shàph, one; 21 the king of Tä'änàch, one; the king of Mègìd'dò, one; 22 the king of Kĕdësh, one; the king of Jŏk'nè-àm in Carmèl, one; 23 the king of Dor in Nä'phäth-dor', one; the king of Goi'ìm in Gạl'ilëē, ᶠ one; 24 the king of Tìrzàh, one: in all, thirty-one kings.

II. The partition of the Promised Land 13.1–21.45

A. The command to divide the land

13 Now Joshua was old and advanced in years; and the LORD said to him, "You are old and advanced in years, and there

ᵉ Gk: Heb *the boundary of Og*   ᶠ Gk: Heb *Gilgäl*

12.9-24 Compare this with Judg 1.27–29.   **13.1** Beginning the second half of Joshua.

12.1
Deut 3.8,9

12.2
Deut 2.33,
36

12.3
Josh 11.2;
13.20

12.4
Deut 3.11
12.5
Deut 3.8ff

12.6
Num 21.24,
33; 32.29,
33

12.7
Josh 11.17,
23

12.8
Josh 11.16

*12.9ff
Josh 6.2;
8.29

12.12
Josh 10.33
12.13
Josh 10.38

12.24
Deut 7.24

*13.1
Josh 14.10

remains yet very much land to be possessed. 2 This is the land
that yet remains: all the regions of the Phĭlĭs′tĭneṣ, and all those
of the Gĕsh′ŭrītes 3 (from the Shīhor, which is east of Egypt,
northward to the boundary of Ĕkrŏn, it is reckoned as Cā′naănīte;
there are five rulers of the Phĭlĭs′tĭneṣ, those of Gazȧ, Ăshdŏd,
Ăsh′kĕlŏn, Găth, and Ekron), and those of the Ăvvĭm, 4 in the
south, all the land of the Cā′naănītes, and Mê-ă′rȧh which belongs
to the Sīdō′nĭăṇṣ, to Āphĕk, to the boundary of the Ăm′ŏrītes,
5 and the land of the Gĕ′bȧlītes, and all Lebanon, toward the sunrising, from Bā′ăl-găd below Mount Hermŏn to the entrance of
Hāmȧth, 6 all the inhabitants of the hill country from Lebanon to
Mĭs′rĕphŏth-mā′ĭm, even all the Sīdō′nĭăṇṣ. I will myself drive
them out from before the people of Israel; only allot the land to
Israel for an inheritance, as I have commanded you. 7 Now therefore divide this land for an inheritance to the nine tribes and half
the tribe of Mȧnăs′sĕh.''

B. The division of east Canaan

1. *The boundaries*

8 With the other half of the tribe of Mȧnăs′sĕh g the Reu′bĕnītes
and the Gădītes received their inheritance, which Moses gave
them, beyond the Jordan eastward, as Moses the servant of the
LORD gave them: 9 from Ȧrō′ĕr, which is on the edge of the valley
of the Arnŏn, and the city that is in the middle of the valley, and all
the tableland of Mĕd′ĕbȧ as far as Dībŏn; 10 and all the cities of
Sīhŏn king of the Ăm′ŏrītes, who reigned in Hĕshbŏn, as far as
the boundary of the Ăm′mŏnītes; 11 and Gĭl′ĕăd, and the region of
the Gĕsh′ŭrītes and Mā-ăc′ăthītes, and all Mount Hermŏn, and
all Bāshȧn ṭo Săl′ĕcȧh; 12 all the kingdom of Ŏg in Bāshȧn, who
reigned in Ăsh′tȧrŏth and in Ĕd′rë-ī (he alone was left of the remnant of the Rĕph′ăim); these Moses had defeated and driven out.
13 Yet the people of Israel did not drive out the Gĕsh′ŭrītes or
the Mā-ăc′ăthītes; but Gĕshȯr and Mā′ăcăth dwell in the midst of
Israel to this day.

14 To the tribe of Lĕvī alone Moses gave no inheritance; the
offerings by fire to the LORD God of Israel are their inheritance,
as he said to him.

2. *Inheritance of the Reubenites*

15 And Moses gave an inheritance to the tribe of the Reu′bĕnītes
according to their families. 16 So their territory was from Ȧrō′ĕr,
which is on the edge of the valley of the Arnŏn, and the city that
is in the middle of the valley, and all the tableland by Mĕd′ĕbȧ;
17 with Hĕshbŏn, and all its cities that are in the tableland; Dībŏn,
and Bā′mŏth-bā′ăl, and Bĕth-bā′ăl-mëŏn, 18 and Jăhăz, and Kĕd′-
ĕmŏth, and Mĕphā′-ăth, 19 and Kĭr′iăthā′ĭm, and Sĭbmȧh, and
Zĕr′ĕth-shā′har on the hill of the valley, 20 and Bĕth′-pëor, and
the slopes of Pĭṣgȧh, and Bĕth-jĕsh′ĭmŏth, 21 that is, all the cities of
the tableland, and all the kingdom of Sīhŏn king of the Ăm′ŏrītes,
who reigned in Hĕshbŏn, whom Moses defeated with the leaders
of Mĭd′iăn, Ēvī and Rĕkĕm and Zŭr and Hŭr and Rēbȧ, the
princes of Sihon, who dwelt in the land. 22 Bālaăm also, the son of
Bēor, the soothsayer, the people of Israel killed with the sword

g Cn: Heb *With it*

13.3
Judg 3.3;
Deut 2.23

13.6
Josh 11.8

13.8
Josh 12.1–6

13.9
ver 16

13.10
Num 21.24,
25

13.12
Deut 3.11;
Num 21.24,
35

13.14
Deut 18.1,2

13.16
Josh 12.2

13.21
Num 31.8

13.22
Num 31.8

among the rest of their slain. 23And the border of the people of
Reuben was the Jordan as a boundary. This was the inheritance
of the Reu'bënītes, according to their families with their cities and
villages.

3. *Inheritance of the Gadites*

24 And Moses gave an inheritance also to the tribe of the
Gădītes, according to their families. 25 Their territory was Jāzėr,
and all the cities of Gĭl'ėăd, and half the land of the Ăm'mŏnītes,
to Arŏ'ėr, which is east of Răbbăh, 26 and from Hĕshbŏn to Rā'-
măth-mĭz'pėh and Bĕt'ŏnĭm, and from Māhănā'ĭm to the territory of Dėbĭr,ʰ 27 and in the valley Bĕth-hā'răm, Bĕth-nĭm'răh,
Sŭccŏth, and Zāphŏn, the rest of the kingdom of Sīhŏn king of
Hĕshbŏn, having the Jordan as a boundary, to the lower end of the
Sea of Chĭn'nĕrĕth, eastward beyond the Jordan. 28 This is the
inheritance of the Gădītes according to their families, with their
cities and villages.

4. *Inheritance of the half-tribe of Manasseh*

29 And Moses gave an inheritance to the half-tribe of Mănăs'-
sėh; it was allotted to the half-tribe of the Mănăs'sītes according
to their families. 30 Their region extended from Māhănā'ĭm,
through all Bāshăn, the whole kingdom of Ŏg king of Bashan, and
all the towns of Jāĭr, which are in Bashan, sixty cities, 31 and half
Gĭl'ėăd, and Ăsh'tărŏth, and Ĕd'rë-ī, the cities of the kingdom of
Ŏg in Bāshăn; these were allotted to the people of Māchĭr the son
of Mănăs'sėh for the half of the Mā'chĭrītes according to their
families.

32 These are the inheritances which Moses distributed in the
plains of Mōăb, beyond the Jordan east of Jĕr'ĭchŏ. 33 But to the
tribe of Lēvī Moses gave no inheritance; the LORD God of Israel
is their inheritance, as he said to them.

C. *The division of west Canaan*

1. *Introduction*

14 And these are the inheritances which the people of Israel
received in the land of Cānaăn, which Ēlëā'zăr the priest,
and Joshua the son of Nŭn, and the heads of the fathers' houses
of the tribes of the people of Israel distributed to them. 2 Their
inheritance was by lot, as the LORD had commanded Moses for the
nine and one-half tribes. 3 For Moses had given an inheritance
to the two and one-half tribes beyond the Jordan; but to the
Lēvītes he gave no inheritance among them. 4 For the people of
Joseph were two tribes, Mănăs'sėh and Ē'phraĭm; and no portion
was given to the Lēvītes in the land, but only cities to dwell in,
with their pasture lands for their cattle and their substance. 5 The
people of Israel did as the LORD commanded Moses; they allotted
the land.

2. *Caleb receives Hebron*

6 Then the people of Judah came to Joshua at Gĭlgăl; and Cālėb

---

Margin references (left column):

13.25
Num 21.32

13.27
Num 34.11

13.30
Num 32.41

13.33
ver 14;
Num 18.20;
Deut 10.9;
18.1,2

14.1
Num 34.17,
18

14.2
Num 26.55

14.3
Num 32.33;
Josh 13.14

14.4
Gen 48.5

14.6
Num 13.6,
26, 30;
14.6, 24, 30

ʰ Gk Syr Vg: Heb Lĭdĕb'ir

the son of Jĕphŭn'nĕh the Kĕn'ĭzzīte said to him, "You know what
the LORD said to Moses the man of God in Kā'dĕsh-barnē'á concerning you and me. 7 I was forty years old when Moses the servant of the LORD sent me from Kā'dĕsh-barnē'á to spy out the land;
and I brought him word again as it was in my heart. 8 But my brethren who went up with me made the heart of the people melt; yet I
wholly followed the LORD my God. 9And Moses swore on that
day, saying, 'Surely the land on which your foot has trodden shall
be an inheritance for you and your children for ever, because you
have wholly followed the LORD my God.' 10And now, behold, the
LORD has kept me alive, as he said, these forty-five years since the
time that the LORD spoke this word to Moses, while Israel walked
in the wilderness; and now, lo, I am this day eighty-five years old.
11 I am still as strong to this day as I was in the day that Moses
sent me; my strength now is as my strength was then, for war, and
for going and coming. 12 So now give me this hill country of which
the LORD spoke on that day; for you heard on that day how the
Ăn'ákĭm were there, with great fortified cities: it may be that the
LORD will be with me, and I shall drive them out as the LORD
said."

13 Then Joshua blessed him; and he gave Hēbrŏn to Cālĕb the
son of Jĕphŭn'nĕh for an inheritance. 14 So Hēbrŏn became the
inheritance of Cālĕb the son of Jĕphŭn'nĕh the Kĕn'ĭzzīte to this
day, because he wholly followed the LORD, the God of Israel.
15 Now the name of Hēbrŏn formerly was Kĭr'ĭăth-ar'bá;[i] this
Arbá was the greatest man among the Ăn'ákĭm. And the land had
rest from war.

3. The inheritance of Judah
a. The boundaries of Judah

15 The lot for the tribe of the people of Judah according to
their families reached southward to the boundary of Ēdŏm,
to the wilderness of Zĭn at the farthest south. 2And their south
boundary ran from the end of the Salt Sea, from the bay that
faces southward; 3 it goes out southward of the ascent of Ăkrăb'bĭm,
passes along to Zĭn, and goes up south of Kā'dĕsh-barnē'á, along
by Hĕzrŏn, up to Ăddar, turns about to Karkà, 4 passes along to
Ăzmŏn, goes out by the Brook of Egypt, and comes to its end at
the sea. This shall be your south boundary. 5And the east boundary is the Salt Sea, to the mouth of the Jordan. And the boundary
on the north side runs from the bay of the sea at the mouth of the
Jordan; 6 and the boundary goes up to Bĕth-hŏg'láh, and passes
along north of Bĕth-ar'ábáh; and the boundary goes up to the
stone of Bōhăn the son of Reubĕn; 7 and the boundary goes up to
Dēbĭr from the Valley of Ăçhor, and so northward, turning toward
Gĭlgăl, which is opposite the ascent of Ădŭm'mĭm, which is on
the south side of the valley; and the boundary passes along to the
waters of Ĕn-shĕm'ĕsh, and ends at Ĕn-rō'gĕl; 8 then the boundary
goes up by the valley of the son of Hĭnnŏm at the southern shoulder of the Jĕb'ūsīte (that is, Jerusalem); and the boundary goes up
to the top of the mountain that lies over against the valley of Hinnom, on the west, at the northern end of the valley of Rĕph'áĭm;
9 then the boundary extends from the top of the mountain to the
spring of the Waters of Nĕphtō'áh, and from there to the cities

Margin references:
14.7 Num 13.6; 14.6
14.8 Num 13.31, 32; 14.24
14.9 Deut 1.36
14.10 Num 14.30
14.12 Num 13.33
14.14 Josh 22.6; ver 8,9
14.15 Josh 11.23
15.1 Num 34.3, 4; 33.36
15.3 Num 34.4
15.4 Num 34.5
15.6 Josh 18.17, 19
15.7 Josh 7.24
15.8 ver 63
15.9 Josh 18.15

---

i That is The city of Arba

15.10
Judg 14.1

15.12
ver 47

15.13
Jn 14.13–
15

15.14
Josh 11.21,
22;
Num 13.22

15.15
Josh 10.38
15.16
Judg 1.12,
13; 3.9

15.18
Judg 1.14

15.28
Gen 21.31
15.31
1 Sam 27.6
★15.32

15.33
Judg 13.25;
16.31
15.35
1 Sam 22.1

15.38
2 Ki 14.7
15.39
Josh 10.3;
2 Ki 14.19

of Mount Ēphròn; then the boundary bends round to Bā'àlàh
(that is, Kīr'iàth-jē'àrìm); 10 and the boundary circles west of
Bā'àlàh to Mount Sēir, passes along to the northern shoulder of
Mount Jē'àrìm (that is, Chĕs'àlòn), and goes down to Bĕth-shĕ'-
mĕsh, and passes along by Tìmnàh; 11 the boundary goes out to
the shoulder of the hill north of Ēkròn, then the boundary bends
round to Shĭk'kĕròn, and passes along to Mount Bā'àlàh, and goes
out to Jàbneēl; then the boundary comes to an end at the sea.
12And the west boundary was the Great Sea with its coast-line.
This is the boundary round about the people of Judah according
to their families.

b. *Caleb's inheritance*

13 According to the commandment of the LORD to Joshua, he
gave to Cālèb the son of Jéphùn'nèh a portion among the people
of Judah, Kīr'iàth-ar'bà, that is, Hēbròn (Arbà was the father of
Ānàk). 14And Cālèb drove out from there the three sons of Ānàk,
Shēshaī and Àhì'màn and Tàlmaī, the descendants of Anak.
15And he went up from there against the inhabitants of Dēbìr;
now the name of Debir formerly was Kīr'iàth-sē'phèr. 16And
Cālèb said, "Whoever smites Kīr'iàth-sē'phèr, and takes it, to him
will I give Àchsàh my daughter as wife." 17And Ōth'nĭ-èl the son
of Kēnàz, the brother of Cālèb, took it; and he gave him Àchsàh
his daughter as wife. 18 When she came to him, she urged him to
ask her father for a field; and she alighted from her ass, and Cālèb
said to her, "What do you wish?" 19 She said to him, "Give me a
present; since you have set me in the land of the Nĕgĕb, give me
also springs of water." And Cālèb gave her the upper springs and
the lower springs.

c. *The cities of Judah*

20 This is the inheritance of the tribe of the people of Judah
according to their families. 21 The cities belonging to the tribe
of the people of Judah in the extreme South, toward the boundary
of Ēdòm, were Kàbzeēl, Ēdèr, Jàgùr, 22 Kīnàh, Dīmō'nàh, Àda'-
dàh, 23 Kĕdĕsh, Hāzor, Ĭthnăn, 24 Zìph, Tĕlĕm, Bē'-àlŏth, 25 Hā'-
zor-hàdăt'tàh, Kĕr'ĭ-òth-hĕz'ròn (that is, Hāzor), 26 Āmàm,
Shēmà, Mōlà'dàh, 27 Hā'zar-gàd'dàh, Hĕshmòn, Bĕth-pĕl'èt,
28 Hā'zar-shu'àl, Beēr-shē'bà, Bìzìothì'àh, 29 Bā'àlàh, Ī'ìm, Ēzèm,
30 Ēltō'làd, Chĕsìl, Hormàh, 31 Zìklăg, Màdmăn'nàh, Sănsăn'nàh,
32 Lèbà'òth, Shìlhìm, Ā'ìn, and Rìmmòn: in all, twenty-nine cities,
with their villages.

33 And in the lowland, Ĕsh'tàòl, Zoràh, Àshnàh, 34 Zànō'àh,
Ēn-gàn'nìm, Tàppū'àh, Ēnàm, 35 Jarmŭth, Àdŭl'làm, Sōcōh,
Àzē'kàh, 36 Shà-àrā'ìm, Àdīthā'ìm, Gèdē'ràh, Gĕd'èròthā'ìm:
fourteen cities with their villages.

37 Zēnàn, Hàdàsh'àh, Mĭg'dàl-gàd, 38 Dì'lèàn, Mìzpèh, Jŏk-
theēl, 39 Lāchìsh, Bŏzkàth, Ēglòn, 40 Càbbòn, Lahmăm, Chìtlìsh,
41 Gĕd'èròth, Bĕth-dā'gòn, Nā'àmàh, and Màkkē'dàh: sixteen
cities with their villages.

42 Lìbnàh, Ēthèr, Āshàn, 43 Ĭphtàh, Àshnàh, Nēzìb, 44 Keīlàh,
Àchzìb, and Màrē'shàh: nine cities with their villages.

15.32 *twenty-nine cities, with their villages.*
Thirty-six are listed in verses 21–32. Presum-
ably, names were added sometime in the proc- | ess of transmission. Similarly, verse 36 says
fourteen cities with their villages, whereas
fifteen are recorded in verses 33–36.

45 Ĕkrŏn, with its towns and its villages; 46 from Ĕkrŏn to the sea, all that were by the side of Ăshdŏd, with their villages.

47 Ăshdŏd, its towns and its villages; Gază, its towns and its villages; to the Brook of Egypt, and the Great Sea with its coastline.

15.47
ver 4;
Num 34.6

48 And in the hill country, Shāmĭr, Jăttĭr, Sŏcōh, 49 Dănnáh, Kĭr'iăth-săn'nàh (that is, Dēbĭr), 50 Ănăb, Ĕsh'tĕmōh, Ănĭm, 51 Gōshĕn, Hōlŏn, and Gĭlōh: eleven cities with their villages.

15.51
Josh 10.41;
11.16

52 Arab, Dumáh, Ēshàn, 53 Jānĭm, Bĕth-tăppū'áh, Aphē'kàh, 54 Hŭmtàh, Kĭr'iăth-ar'bà (that is, Hēbròn), and Zĭ'or: nine cities with their villages.

55 Mă'ŏn, Carmĕl, Zĭph, Jŭttàh, 56 Jĕzreĕl, Jŏk'dĕ-àm, Zănō'-àh, 57 Kāin, Gĭb'ĕ-àh, and Tĭmnàh: ten cities with their villages.

58 Hălhŭl, Beth-zŭr, Gĕdor, 59 Mă'àrăth, Bĕth-ā'nŏth, and Ĕltĕ'kŏn: six cities with their villages.

60 Kĭr'iăth-bā'ál (that is, Kĭr'iăth-jĕ'árĭm), and Răbbàh: two cities with their villages.

15.60
Josh 18.14

61 In the wilderness, Bĕth-ar'ábàh, Mĭddĭn, Sĕcā'càh, 62 Nĭbshăn, the City of Salt, and Ĕn-gĕ'dī: six cities with their villages.

*15.62

63 But the Jĕb'ūsītes, the inhabitants of Jerusalem, the people of Judah could not drive out; so the Jebusites dwell with the people of Judah at Jerusalem to this day.

15.63
Judg 1.21;
2 Sam 5.6

4. The inheritance of Joseph
a. The general boundaries

16 The allotment of the descendants of Joseph went from the Jordan by Jĕr'ĭchō, east of the waters of Jericho, into the wilderness, going up from Jericho into the hill country to Bĕthĕl; 2 then going from Bĕthĕl to Lŭz, it passes along to Ăt'árŏth, the territory of the Archĭtes; 3 then it goes down westward to the territory of the Jăph'lĕtītes, as far as the territory of Lower Bĕth-hor'ŏn, then to Gĕzĕr, and it ends at the sea.

16.1
Josh 18.12

16.2
Josh 18.13
16.3
Josh 18.13;
2 Chr 8.5

4 The people of Joseph, Mănăs'sĕh and Ē'phrăĭm, received their inheritance.

b. The territory of the Ephraimites

5 The territory of the Ē'phräĭmītes by their families was as follows: the boundary of their inheritance on the east was Ăt'-árŏth-ăd'dar as far as Upper Bĕth-hor'ŏn, 6 and the boundary goes thence to the sea; on the north is Mĭchmĕ'thăth; then on the east the boundary turns round toward Tā'ánăth-shī'lōh, and passes along beyond it on the east to Jănō'áh, 7 then it goes down from Jănō'áh to Ăt'árŏth and to Nă'áràh, and touches Jĕr'ĭchō, ending at the Jordan. 8 From Tăppū'áh the boundary goes westward to the brook Kānàh, and ends at the sea. Such is the inheritance of the tribe of the Ē'phräĭmītes by their families, 9 together with the towns which were set apart for the Ē'phräĭmītes within the inheritance of the Mănăs'sītes, all those towns with their villages. 10 However they did not drive out the Că'naànītes that dwelt in Gĕzĕr: so the Canaanites have dwelt in the midst of Ē'phrăĭm to this day but have become slaves to do forced labor.

16.5
Josh 18.13

16.6
Josh 17.7

16.7
1 Chr 7.28

16.8
Josh 17.8,9

16.10
Judg 1.29;
1 Ki 9.16;
Josh 17.12,
13

15.62 *City of Salt*, probably the ancient name for Qumran, where the Dead Sea Scrolls were found. These scrolls are also known as the Qumran manuscripts.

c. The allotment to the half-tribe of Manasseh

17.1
Gen 41.41;
50.23;
Deut 3.15

17.2
Num
26.29–32

17 Then allotment was made to the tribe of Mănăs'seh, for he was the first-born of Joseph. To Măchĭr the first-born of Manasseh, the father of Gĭl'eăd, were allotted Gilead and Băshăn, because he was a man of war. ²And allotments were made to the rest of the tribe of Mănăs'seh, by their families, Ăbĭe'zĕr, Hēlĕk, Ăs'rĭ-ĕl, Shĕchĕm, Hĕphĕr, and Shĕmĭ'dă; these were the male descendants of Manasseh the son of Joseph, by their families.

17.3
Num 26.33;
27.1–7

17.4
Num
27.5–7

3 Now Zĕlō'phĕhăd the son of Hĕphĕr, son of Gĭl'eăd, son of Măchĭr, son of Mănăs'seh, had no sons, but only daughters; and these are the names of his daughters: Mahlăh, Noah, Hŏglăh, Mĭlcăh, and Tĭrzăh. ⁴ They came before Ēlĕă'zăr the priest and Joshua the son of Nŭn and the leaders, and said, "The Lord commanded Moses to give us an inheritance along with our brethren." So according to the commandment of the Lord he gave them an inheritance among the brethren of their father. ⁵ Thus there fell to Mănăs'seh ten portions, besides the land of Gĭl'eăd

17.6
Josh 13.30,
31

and Băshăn, which is on the other side of the Jordan; ⁶ because the daughters of Mănăs'seh received an inheritance along with his sons. The land of Gĭl'eăd was allotted to the rest of the Mănăs'sites.

17.7
Josh 16.6

17.8
Josh 16.8

17.9
Josh 16.8,9

7 The territory of Mănăs'seh reached from Ăshĕr to Mĭchmĕ'-thăth, which is east of Shĕchĕm; then the boundary goes along southward to the inhabitants of Ĕn-tăppū'ăh. ⁸ The land of Tăp-pū'ăh belonged to Mănăs'seh, but the town of Tappuah on the boundary of Manasseh belonged to the sons of Ē'phrăĭm. ⁹ Then the boundary went down to the brook Kănăh. The cities here, to the south of the brook, among the cities of Mănăs'seh, belong to Ē'phrăĭm. Then the boundary of Manasseh goes on the north side of the brook and ends at the sea; ¹⁰ the land to the south being Ē'phrăĭm's and that to the north being Mănăs'seh's, with the sea forming its boundary; on the north Ăshĕr is reached, and on the east Ĭs'săchar.

17.11
1 Chr 7.29

¹¹Also in Ĭs'săchar and in Ăshĕr Mănăs'seh had Bĕth-shĕ'ăn and its villages, and Ĭb'lĕ-ăm and its villages, and the inhabitants of Dor and its villages, and the inhabitants of Ĕn-dor and its villages, and the inhabitants of Tā'ănăch and its villages, and the inhabitants of Mĕgĭd'dō and its villages; the third is

17.12
Judg 1.27,
28

17.13
Josh 16.10

Năphăth.ʲ ¹² Yet the sons of Mănăs'seh could not take possession of those cities; but the Cā'naănītes persisted in dwelling in that land. ¹³ But when the people of Israel grew strong, they put the Cā'naănītes to forced labor, and did not utterly drive them out.

d. The complaint of the tribe of Joseph

17.14
Num 26.34,
37

14 And the tribe of Joseph spoke to Joshua, saying, "Why have you given me but one lot and one portion as an inheritance, although I am a numerous people, since hitherto the Lord has blessed me?" ¹⁵And Joshua said to them, "If you are a numerous people, go up to the forest, and there clear ground for yourselves in the land of the Pĕr'izzītes and the Rĕph'ăĭm, since the hill country of Ē'phrăĭm is too narrow for you." ¹⁶ The tribe of Joseph

17.16
Judg 1.19;
4.3

said, "The hill country is not enough for us; yet all the Cā'-naănītes who dwell in the plain have chariots of iron, both those in Bĕth-shĕ'ăn and its villages and those in the Valley of Jĕzreĕl." ¹⁷ Then Joshua said to the house of Joseph, to Ē'phrăĭm and

ʲ Heb obscure

Mánăs′sĕh, "You are a numerous people, and have great power; you shall not have one lot only, 18 but the hill country shall be yours, for though it is a forest, you shall clear it and possess it to its farthest borders; for you shall drive out the Cā′naánītes, though they have chariots of iron, and though they are strong."

5. The division of the remaining land
a. The land survey: casting the lot

18 Then the whole congregation of the people of Israel assembled at Shīlōh, and set up the tent of meeting there; the land lay subdued before them.

2 There remained among the people of Israel seven tribes whose inheritance had not yet been apportioned. 3 So Joshua said to the people of Israel, "How long will you be slack to go in and take possession of the land, which the LORD, the God of your fathers, has given you? 4 Provide three men from each tribe, and I will send them out that they may set out and go up and down the land, writing a description of it with a view to their inheritances, and then come to me. 5 They shall divide it into seven portions, Judah continuing in his territory on the south, and the house of Joseph in their territory on the north. 6 And you shall describe the land in seven divisions and bring the description here to me; and I will cast lots for you here before the LORD our God. 7 The Lēvītes have no portion among you, for the priesthood of the LORD is their heritage; and Găd and Reubën and half the tribe of Mánăs′sĕh have received their inheritance beyond the Jordan eastward, which Moses the servant of the LORD gave them."

8 So the men started on their way; and Joshua charged those who went to write the description of the land, saying, "Go up and down and write a description of the land, and come again to me; and I will cast lots for you here before the LORD in Shīlōh." 9 So the men went and passed up and down in the land and set down in a book a description of it by towns in seven divisions; then they came to Joshua in the camp at Shīlōh, 10 and Joshua cast lots for them in Shīlōh before the LORD; and there Joshua apportioned the land to the people of Israel, to each his portion.

b. The inheritance of Benjamin

11 The lot of the tribe of Benjamin according to its families came up, and the territory allotted to it fell between the tribe of Judah and the tribe of Joseph. 12 On the north side their boundary began at the Jordan; then the boundary goes up to the shoulder north of Jĕr′ĭchō, then up through the hill country westward; and it ends at the wilderness of Bĕth-ā′vĕn. 13 From there the boundary passes along southward in the direction of Lùz, to the shoulder of Luz (the same is Bĕthĕl), then the boundary goes down to Ăt′-ărŏth-ăd′dar, upon the mountain that lies south of Lower Bĕth-hor′ón. 14 Then the boundary goes in another direction, turning on the western side southward from the mountain that lies to the south, opposite Bĕth-hor′ón, and it ends at Kĭr′ĭăth-bā′ál (that is, Kĭr′ĭăth-jē′ărĭm), a city belonging to the tribe of Judah. This

*18.1
Josh 19.51;
Jer 7.12;
Judg 18.31

18.3
Judg 18.9

18.5
Josh 15.1;
16.1,4

18.7
Josh 13.33;
13.8

18.8
ver 1;
Judg 18.31

18.10
Josh 19.51

18.13
Gen 28.19;
Josh 16.3

18.14
Josh 15.9

18.1 The allotment of Canaan, begun in Gilgal, is continued at Shiloh. It is not apparent why Judah, Ephraim, and half of Manasseh should get such a large portion of the land before the remaining seven tribes were given their share.

forms the western side. [15]And the southern side begins at the outskirts of Kĭr'ĭăth-jē'ărĭm; and the boundary goes from there to Ēphrŏn,[k] to the spring of the Waters of Nĕphtō'áh; [16] then the boundary goes down to the border of the mountain that overlooks the valley of the son of Hĭnnŏm, which is at the north end of the valley of Rĕph'áĭm; and it then goes down the valley of Hinnom, south of the shoulder of the Jĕb'ūsītes, and downward to Ĕn-rō'gĕl; [17] then it bends in a northerly direction going on to Ĕn-shĕm'ĕsh, and thence goes to Gĕlī'lŏth, which is opposite the ascent of Ădŭm'mĭm; then it goes down to the Stone of Bōhăn the son of Reubĕn; [18] and passing on to the north of the shoulder of Bĕth-ar'ábáh[l] it goes down to the Ar'ábáh; [19] then the boundary passes on to the north of the shoulder of Bĕth-hŏg'láh; and the boundary ends at the northern bay of the Salt Sea, at the south end of the Jordan: this is the southern border. [20] The Jordan forms its boundary on the eastern side. This is the inheritance of the tribe of Benjamin, according to its families, boundary by boundary round about.

21 Now the cities of the tribe of Benjamin according to their families were Jĕr'ĭchō, Bĕth-hŏg'láh, Ē'mĕk-kĕzĭz', [22] Bĕthar'ábáh, Zĕmārā'ĭm, Bĕthĕl, [23] Ăvvĭm, Pāráh, Ōphráh, [24] Chĕ'phar-ăm'mŏnī, Ōphnī, Gĕbá—twelve cities with their villages: [25] Gĭb'ĕŏn, Rāmáh, Bĕ-ēr'ŏth, [26] Mĭzpĕh, Chĕphī'ráh, Mōzáh, [27] Rĕkĕm, Ĭrpĕ'ĕl, Tar'áláh, [28] Zĕlá, Hă-ĕl'ĕph, Jĕbŭs[m] (that is, Jerusalem), Gĭb'ĕ-áh[n] and Kĭr'ĭăth-jē'ărĭm[o]—fourteen cities with their villages. This is the inheritance of the tribe of Benjamin according to its families.

c. The inheritance of Simeon

19 The second lot came out for Sĭm'ĕŏn, for the tribe of Simeon, according to its families; and its inheritance was in the midst of the inheritance of the tribe of Judah. [2] And it had for its inheritance Beĕr-shē'bá, Shĕbá, Mōlá'dáh, [3] Hā'zar-shu'ăl, Bāláh, Ēzĕm, [4] Ĕltō'lád, Bĕthŭl, Hormáh, [5] Zĭklăg, Bĕth-mar'cábŏth, Hā'zar-su'sáh, [6] Bĕth-lĕbá'ŏth, and Sháru'hĕn—thirteen cities with their villages; [7] Ĕn-rĭm'mŏn, Ēthĕr, and Ăshán—four cities with their villages; [8] together with all the villages round about these cities as far as Bā'áláth-beĕr, Rāmáh of the Nĕgĕb. This was the inheritance of the tribe of Sĭm'ĕŏn according to its families. [9] The inheritance of the tribe of Sĭm'ĕŏn formed part of the territory of Judah; because the portion of the tribe of Judah was too large for them, the tribe of Simeon obtained an inheritance in the midst of their inheritance.

d. The inheritance of Zebulun

10 The third lot came up for the tribe of Zĕb'ŭlŭn, according to its families. And the territory of its inheritance reached as far as Sārĭd; [11] then its boundary goes up westward, and on to Mar'ĕál, and touches Dăb'bĕshĕth, then the brook which is east of Jŏk'nĕ-ám; [12] from Sārĭd it goes in the other direction eastward

---

[k] Cn See 15.9. Heb westward [l] Gk: Heb to the shoulder over against the Arabah
[m] Gk Syr Vg: Heb the Jĕb'ŭsite [n] Heb Gĭb'ĕáth [o] Gk: Heb Kĭr'ĭáth

---

19.6 The total is fourteen. (In ver 7, three.)   into Judah and seldom mentioned thereafter.
19.9 The tribe of Simeon was absorbed   See note to Deut 33.7.

18.15
Josh 15.5–9

18.16
2 Ki 23.10

18.20
Josh 21.4,
17

18.28
Josh 15.8

19.1
ver 9

19.5
1 Sam 30.1
*19.6

*19.9
ver 1

19.11
Josh 21.34

toward the sunrise to the boundary of Chĭs'lŏth-tā'bŏr; thence it goes to Dăb'ĕrăth, then up to Jáphī'á; 13 from there it passes along on the east toward the sunrise to Găth-hē'phĕr, to Ĕth-kāzĭn, and going on to Rĭmmŏn it bends toward Nē'áh; 14 then on the north the boundary turns about to Hăn'náthŏn, and it ends at the valley of Ĭph'tăhĕl; 15 and Kăttáth, Nā'hálăl, Shĭmrŏn, Ĭd'álàh, and Bĕth'lĕhĕm—twelve cities with their villages. 16 This is the inheritance of the tribe of Zĕb'ųlŭn, according to its families—these cities with their villages.

19.15
Mic 5.2

e. *The inheritance of Issachar*

17 The fourth lot came out for Ĭs'sáchar, for the tribe of Issachar, according to its families. 18 Its territory included Jĕzreēl', Chĕsŭl'lŏth, Shunĕm, 19 Hăph'árā'-ĭm, Shĭŏn, Ànā'hárăth, 20 Răbbĭth, Kĭsh'ĭŏn, Ēbĕz, 21 Rĕmĕth, Ĕn-găn'nĭm, Ĕn-hăd'dáh, Bĕthpăz'zĕz; 22 the boundary also touches Tābŏr, Shāhăzu'máh, and Bĕth-shĕ'mĕsh, and its boundary ends at the Jordan—sixteen cities with their villages. 23 This is the inheritance of the tribe of Ĭs'sąchar, according to its families—the cities with their villages.

19.17
2 Sam 2.9

f. *The inheritance of Asher*

24 The fifth lot came out for the tribe of Ăshĕr according to its families. 25 Its territory included Hĕlkăth, Hālī, Bĕtĕn, Ăchsháph, 26Ăllăm'mĕlĕch, Āmăd, and Mīshál; on the west it touches Carmĕl and Shī'horlĭb'năth, 27 then it turns eastward, it goes to Bĕthdā'gŏn, and touches Zĕb'ųlŭn and the valley of Ĭph'tăhĕl northward to Bĕth-ē'mĕk and Neĭ'ĕl; then it continues in the north to Cābŭl, 28 Ēbrŏn, Rĕhŏb, Hămmŏn, Kānăh, as far as Sīdŏn the Great; 29 then the boundary turns to Rāmáh, reaching to the fortified city of Tȳre; then the boundary turns to Hōṣáh, and it ends at the sea; Mā'hálăb,ᵖ Ăchzĭb, 30 Ŭmmáh, Āphĕk and Rĕhŏb—twenty-two cities with their villages. 31 This is the inheritance of the tribe of Ăshĕr according to its families—these cities with their villages.

19.28
Josh 11.8

19.30
Josh 21.31

g. *The inheritance of Naphtali*

32 The sixth lot came out for the tribe of Năph'tálī, for the tribe of Naphtali, according to its families. 33And its boundary ran from Hēlĕph, from the oak in Zā-ánăn'nĭm, and Ăd'ámī-nē'kĕb, and Jăbneēl, as far as Lăkkùm; and it ended at the Jordan; 34 then the boundary turns westward to Ăz'nŏth-tā'bor, and goes from there to Hŭkkŏk, touching Zĕb'ųlŭn at the south, and Ăshĕr on the west, and Judah on the east at the Jordan. 35 The fortified cities are Zĭddĭm, Zĕr, Hămmáth, Răkkáth, Chĭn'nĕrĕth, 36Ăd'ámăh, Rāmáh, Hāzor, 37 Kĕdĕsh, Ĕd'rĕ-ī, Ĕn-hā'zŏr, 38 Yĭrŏn, Mĭg'dàl-ĕl, Horĕm, Bĕth-ā'năth, and Bĕth-shĕ'mĕsh—nineteen cities with their villages. 39 This is the inheritance of the tribe of Năph'tálī according to its families—the cities with their villages.

19.34
Deut 33.23

h. *The inheritance of Dan*

40 The seventh lot came out for the tribe of Dan, according to its families. 41And the territory of its inheritance included Zoráh, Ĕsh'tä-ŏl, Ĭrshĕm'ĕsh, 42 Shā-álăb'bĭn, Ăi'jálŏn, Ĭthláh, 43 Ēlŏn, Tĭmnáh, Ĕkrŏn, 44 Ĕltĕ'kĕh, Gĭb'bĕthŏn, Bā'áláth, 45 Jĕhŭd,

19.42
Judg 1.35

ᵖ Cn Compare Gk: Heb *Mēhē'bĕl*

Bĕnĕ-bĕ′råk, Găth-rĭm′mȯn, 46 and Mė-jar′kȯn and Răkkȯn with
the territory over against Jȯppá. 47 When the territory of the
Dănĭtes was lost to them, the Danites went up and fought against
Lĕshĕm, and after capturing it and putting it to the sword they
took possession of it and settled in it, calling Leshem, Dan, after
the name of Dan their ancestor. 48 This is the inheritance of the
tribe of Dan, according to their families—these cities with their
villages.

i. *Summary*

49 When they had finished distributing the several territories
of the land as inheritances, the people of Israel gave an inheritance
among them to Joshua the son of Nŭn. 50 By command of the
LORD they gave him the city which he asked, Tĭm′năth-sĕ′råh in
the hill country of Ē′phrȧĭm; and he rebuilt the city, and settled
in it.

51 These are the inheritances which Ĕlëä′zȧr the priest and
Joshua the son of Nŭn and the heads of the fathers' houses of the
tribes of the people of Israel distributed by lot at Shĭlōh before
the LORD, at the door of the tent of meeting. So they finished
dividing the land.

6. *The six cities of refuge*

20 Then the LORD said to Joshua, 2 "Say to the people of
Israel, 'Appoint the cities of refuge, of which I spoke to you
through Moses, 3 that the manslayer who kills any person without
intent or unwittingly may flee there; they shall be for you a refuge
from the avenger of blood. 4 He shall flee to one of these cities and
shall stand at the entrance of the gate of the city, and explain his
case to the elders of that city; then they shall take him into the
city, and give him a place, and he shall remain with them. 5And
if the avenger of blood pursues him, they shall not give up the
slayer into his hand; because he killed his neighbor unwittingly,
having had no enmity against him in times past. 6And he shall
remain in that city until he has stood before the congregation for
judgment, until the death of him who is high priest at the time:
then the slayer may go again to his own town and his own home,
to the town from which he fled.' "

7 So they set apart Kĕdĕsh in Găl′ĭlëē in the hill country of
Năph′tålī, and Shĕchĕm in the hill country of Ē′phrȧĭm, and
Kĭr′ĭăth-ar′bȧ (that is, Hēbrȯn) in the hill country of Judah. 8And
beyond the Jordan east of Jĕr′ĭçhō, they appointed Bĕzĕr in the
wilderness on the tableland, from the tribe of Reubĕn, and Rāmȯth
in Gĭl′ëäd, from the tribe of Găd, and Gōlȧn in Bāshȧn, from the
tribe of Mănăs′sĕh. 9 These were the cities designated for all the
people of Israel, and for the stranger sojourning among them, that
any one who killed a person without intent could flee there, so that
he might not die by the hand of the avenger of blood, till he stood
before the congregation.

7. *The Levitical cities*
a. *The method of distribution*

21 Then the heads of the fathers' houses of the Lēvĭtes came
to Ĕlëä′zar the priest and to Joshua the son of Nŭn and to
the heads of the fathers' houses of the tribes of the people of Israel;

Margin references (left column):

19.47
Judg 18.27–31

19.50
Josh 24.30

19.51
Josh 14.1;
18.1,10

20.2
Num 35.6–34;
Deut 4.41;
19.2

20.4
Ruth 4.1,2

20.5
Num 35.12

20.6
Num 35.25

20.7
Josh 21.32;
1 Chr 6.76;
Josh 21.11;
Lk 1.39
20.8
Josh 21.27,
36,38

20.9
Num 35.15;
ver 6

21.1
Num 35.1–8

2 and they said to them at Shīlōh in the land of Cānaàn, "The LORD commanded through Moses that we be given cities to dwell in, along with their pasture lands for our cattle." 3 So by command of the LORD the people of Israel gave to the Lēvītes the following cities and pasture lands out of their inheritance.

4 The lot came out for the families of the Kō'hàthītes. So those Lēvītes who were descendants of Aaron the priest received by lot from the tribes of Judah, Sĭm'ëŏn, and Benjamin, thirteen cities.

5 And the rest of the Kō'hàthītes received by lot from the families of the tribe of Ē'phrāïm, from the tribe of Dan and the half-tribe of Mànăs'sèh, ten cities.

6 The Gēr'shŏnītes received by lot from the families of the tribe of Ĭs'sàchar, from the tribe of Āshèr, from the tribe of Năph'-tālī, and from the half-tribe of Mànăs'sèh in Bāshàn, thirteen cities.

7 The Mèrar'ītes according to their families received from the tribe of Reubën, the tribe of Găd, and the tribe of Zĕb'ŭlún, twelve cities.

b. The assignment of the cities

8 These cities and their pasture lands the people of Israel gave by lot to the Lēvītes, as the LORD had commanded through Moses.

9 Out of the tribe of Judah and the tribe of Sĭm'ëŏn they gave the following cities mentioned by name, 10 which went to the descendants of Aaron, one of the families of the Kō'hàthītes who belonged to the Lēvītes; since the lot fell to them first. 11 They gave them Kĭr'ĭăth-ar'bà (Arbà being the father of Ānăk), that is Hēbrŏn, in the hill country of Judah, along with the pasture lands round about it. 12 But the fields of the city and its villages had been given to Cālĕb the son of Jĕphŭn'nèh as his possession.

13 And to the descendants of Aaron the priest they gave Hēbrŏn, the city of refuge for the slayer, with its pasture lands, Lĭbnàh with its pasture lands, 14 Jăttĭr with its pasture lands, Ĕshtĕmō'à with its pasture lands, 15 Hōlŏn with its pasture lands, Dēbĭr with its pasture lands, 16 Ā'ĭn with its pasture lands, Jŭttàh with its pasture lands, Bĕth-shĕ'mĕsh with its pasture lands—nine cities out of these two tribes; 17 then out of the tribe of Benjamin, Gĭb'ëŏn with its pasture lands, Gēbà with its pasture lands, 18 Ăn'-àthŏth with its pasture lands, and Ălmŏn with its pasture lands—four cities. 19 The cities of the descendants of Aaron, the priests, were in all thirteen cities with their pasture lands.

20 As to the rest of the Kō'hàthītes belonging to the Kō'hàthīte families of the Lēvītes, the cities allotted to them were out of the tribe of Ē'phrāïm. 21 To them were given Shĕchĕm, the city of refuge for the slayer, with its pasture lands in the hill country of Ē'phrāïm, Gēzĕr with its pasture lands, 22 Kĭbzā'-ĭm with its pasture lands, Bĕth-hor'ŏn with its pasture lands—four cities; 23 and out of the tribe of Dan, Ĕltē'kĕ with its pasture lands, Gĭb'bĕthŏn with its pasture lands, 24 Ăi'jàlŏn with its pasture lands, Găth-rĭm'mŏn with its pasture lands—four cities; 25 and out of the half-tribe of Mànăs'sèh, Tā'ànăch with its pasture lands, and Găth-rĭm'mŏn with its pasture lands—two cities. 26 The cities of the families of the rest of the Kō'hàthītes were ten in all with their pasture lands.

27 And to the Gēr'shŏnītes, one of the families of the Lēvītes,

21.2	Num 35.2
21.4	ver 8,19
21.5	ver 20ff
21.6	ver 27ff
21.7	ver 34ff
21.8	ver 3
21.11	Josh 15.13, 14; 1 Chr 6.55
21.13	Josh 15.42, 54; 20.7; 1 Chr 6.57
21.15	Josh 15.49, 51; 1 Chr 6.58
21.16	Josh 15.10, 15; 1 Chr 6.59
21.18	1 Chr 6.60
21.21	Josh 20.7
21.27	ver 6

were given out of the half-tribe of Mànăs'sĕh, Gōlán in Bāshán with its pasture lands, the city of refuge for the slayer, and Bĕ-ĕsh'tĕrăh with its pasture lands—two cities; 28 and out of the tribe of Ĭs'sáchar, Kish'ĭŏn with its pasture lands, Dăb'ĕrăth with its pasture lands, 29 Jarmŭth with its pasture lands, Ĕn-găn'nĭm with its pasture lands—four cities; 30 and out of the tribe of Ăshér, Mĭshál with its pasture lands, Ābdŏn with its pasture lands, 31 Hĕlkăth with its pasture lands, and Rĕhŏb with its pasture lands—four cities; 32 and out of the tribe of Năph'tālī, Kĕdĕsh in Găl'ĭleē with its pasture lands, the city of refuge for the slayer, Hămmoth-dor' with its pasture lands, and Kartán with its pasture lands—three cities. 33 The cities of the several families of the Gĕr'shŏnītes were in all thirteen cities with their pasture lands.

34 And to the rest of the Lēvītes, the Mĕrar'īte families, were given out of the tribe of Zĕb'ŭlŭn, Jŏk'nĕ-ám with its pasture lands, Kartáh with its pasture lands, 35 Dĭmnáh with its pasture lands, Nā'hálăl with its pasture lands—four cities; 36 and out of the tribe of Reubĕn, Bēzĕr with its pasture lands, Jāhăz with its pasture lands, 37 Kĕd'ĕmŏth with its pasture lands, and Mĕphā'áth with its pasture lands—four cities; 38 and out of the tribe of Găd, Rāmŏth in Gĭl'ĕăd with its pasture lands, the city of refuge for the slayer, Māhánā'ĭm with its pasture lands, 39 Hĕshbŏn with its pasture lands, Jāzĕr with its pasture lands—four cities in all. 40As for the cities of the several Mĕrar'īte families, that is, the remainder of the families of the Lēvītes, those allotted to them were in all twelve cities.

41 The cities of the Lēvītes in the midst of the possession of the people of Israel were in all forty-eight cities with their pasture lands. 42 These cities had each its pasture lands round about it; so it was with all these cities.

8. The fulfilment of the divine promise

43 Thus the LORD gave to Israel all the land which he swore to give to their fathers; and having taken possession of it, they settled there. 44And the LORD gave them rest on every side just as he had sworn to their fathers; not one of all their enemies had withstood them, for the LORD had given all their enemies into their hands. 45 Not one of all the good promises which the LORD had made to the house of Israel had failed; all came to pass.

III. The farewell addresses of Joshua 22.1–24.33

A. The message to the two-and-a-half tribes

1. Joshua's blessing

22 Then Joshua summoned the Reu'bĕnītes, and the Gădītes, and the half-tribe of Mànăs'sĕh, 2 and said to them, "You have kept all that Moses the servant of the LORD commanded you, and have obeyed my voice in all that I have commanded you;

Marginal references (left column):

21.32
Josh 20.7

21.34
ver 7

21.36
Josh 20.8

*21.39

21.41
Num 35.7

*21.43ff
Gen 13.15;
Deut 11.31

21.44
Josh 1.13;
11.23;
Deut 7.24

21.45
Josh 23.14

22.2
Num 32.20

21.39 Heshbon, originally assigned to Reuben (13.17), is included here under Gad. This is an indication that the Reubenites, like Simeon, gradually were absorbed and lost their identity. The allotment was made, although territories remained to be possessed by individual tribes.

21.43-45 The intent of this sweeping statement is to show how the promise of 1.5 was essentially fulfilled.

3 you have not forsaken your brethren these many days, down to this day, but have been careful to keep the charge of the LORD your God. 4And now the LORD your God has given rest to your brethren, as he promised them; therefore turn and go to your home in the land where your possession lies, which Moses the servant of the LORD gave you on the other side of the Jordan. 5 Take good care to observe the commandment and the law which Moses the servant of the LORD commanded you, to love the LORD your God, and to walk in all his ways, and to keep his commandments, and to cleave to him, and to serve him with all your heart and with all your soul." 6 So Joshua blessed them, and sent them away; and they went to their homes.

7 Now to the one half of the tribe of Mánás'seh Moses had given a possession in Báshán; but to the other half Joshua had given a possession beside their brethren in the land west of the Jordan. And when Joshua sent them away to their homes and blessed them, 8 he said to them, "Go back to your homes with much wealth, and with very many cattle, with silver, gold, bronze, and iron, and with much clothing; divide the spoil of your enemies with your brethren." 9 So the Reu'bënïtes and the Gädïtes and the half-tribe of Mánás'seh returned home, parting from the people of Israel at Shïlöh, which is in the land of Cänaán, to go to the land of Gïl'ëäd, their own land of which they had possessed themselves by command of the LORD through Moses.

2. The altar by the Jordan

10 And when they came to the region about the Jordan, that lies in the land of Cänaán, the Reu'bënïtes and the Gädïtes and the half-tribe of Mánás'seh built there an altar by the Jordan, an altar of great size. 11And the people of Israel heard say, "Behold, the Reu'bënïtes and the Gädïtes and the half-tribe of Mánás'seh have built an altar at the frontier of the land of Cänaán, in the region about the Jordan, on the side that belongs to the people of Israel." 12And when the people of Israel heard of it, the whole assembly of the people of Israel gathered at Shïlöh, to make war against them.

13 Then the people of Israel sent to the Reu'bënïtes and the Gädïtes and the half-tribe of Mánás'seh, in the land of Gïl'ëäd, Phín'ëhás the son of Ëlëä'zär the priest, 14 and with him ten chiefs, one from each of the tribal families of Israel, every one of them the head of a family among the clans of Israel. 15And they came to the Reu'bënïtes, the Gädïtes, and the half-tribe of Mánás'seh, in the land of Gïl'ëäd, and they said to them, 16 "Thus says the whole congregation of the LORD, 'What is this treachery which you have committed against the God of Israel in turning away this day from following the LORD, by building yourselves an altar this day in rebellion against the LORD? 17 Have we not had enough of the sin at Pë'or from which even yet we have not cleansed ourselves, and for which there came a plague upon the congregation of the LORD, 18 that you must turn away this day from following the LORD? And if you rebel against the LORD today he will be angry with the whole congregation of Israel tomorrow. 19 But now, if your land is unclean, pass over into the LORD's land where the LORD's tabernacle stands, and take for yourselves a possession among us; only do not rebel against the LORD, or make us as rebels by building yourselves

22.4 Num 32.18; Deut 3.20

22.5 Deut 6.6, 17; 10.12

22.7 Num 32.33; Josh 17.5

22.9 Num 32.1, 26,29

22.11 ver 19

22.12 Josh 18.1

22.13 Deut 13.14; Num 25.7

22.16 ver 11; Deut 12.13, 14

22.17 Num 25.1-9

22.19 ver 11

22.20
Josh 7.1–26

22.22
Deut 10.17;
1 Ki 8.39
22.23
Deut 18.19;
1 Sam 20.16

22.27
Josh 24.27

22.29
Deut 12.13,
14

22.31
Lev 26.11,
12;
2 Chr 15.2

22.33
1 Chr 29.20

22.34
Josh 24.27

23.1
Josh 21.44;
13.1
23.2
Josh 24.1

an altar other than the altar of the LORD our God. 20 Did not
Āchán the son of Zērāh break faith in the matter of the devoted
things, and wrath fell upon all the congregation of Israel? And
he did not perish alone for his iniquity.' "

21 Then the Reu'bēnītes, the Gădītes, and the half-tribe of
Mánăs'sĕh said in answer to the heads of the families of Israel,
22 "The Mighty One, God, the LORD! The Mighty One, God,
the LORD! He knows; and let Israel itself know! If it was in rebellion or in breach of faith toward the LORD, spare us not today 23 for
building an altar to turn away from following the LORD; or if we
did so to offer burnt offerings or cereal offerings or peace offerings on it, may the LORD himself take vengeance. 24 Nay, but we
did it from fear that in time to come your children might say to
our children, 'What have you to do with the LORD, the God of
Israel? 25 For the LORD has made the Jordan a boundary between
us and you, you Reu'bēnītes and Gădītes; you have no portion in
the LORD.' So your children might make our children cease to
worship the LORD. 26 Therefore we said, 'Let us now build an
altar, not for burnt offering, nor for sacrifice, 27 but to be a witness
between us and you, and between the generations after us, that we
do perform the service of the LORD in his presence with our burnt
offerings and sacrifices and peace offerings; lest your children say
to our children in time to come, "You have no portion in the
LORD." ' 28 And we thought, If this should be said to us or to our
descendants in time to come, we should say, 'Behold the copy of
the altar òf the LORD, which our fathers made, not for burnt
offerings, nor for sacrifice, but to be a witness between us and
you.' 29 Far be it from us that we should rebel against the LORD,
and turn away this day from following the LORD by building an
altar for burnt offering, cereal offering, or sacrifice, other than the
altar of the LORD our God that stands before his tabernacle!"

30 When Phĭn'ĕhăs the priest and the chiefs of the congregation, the heads of the families of Israel who were with him, heard
the words that the Reu'bēnītes and the Gădītes and the Mánăs'-
sītes spoke, it pleased them well. 31 And Phĭn'ĕhăs the son of
Ēlĕä'zăr the priest said to the Reu'bēnītes and the Gădītes and the
Mánăs'sītes, "Today we know that the LORD is in the midst of us,
because you have not committed this treachery against the LORD;
now you have saved the people of Israel from the hand of the
LORD."

32 Then Phĭn'ĕhăs the son of Ēlĕä'zăr the priest, and the chiefs,
returned from the Reu'bēnītes and the Gădītes in the land of
Gĭl'ĕăd to the land of Cānăàn, to the people of Israel, and brought
back word to them. 33 And the report pleased the people of Israel;
and the people of Israel blessed God and spoke no more of making
war against them, to destroy the land where the Reu'bēnītes and
the Gădītes were settled. 34 The Reu'bēnītes and the Gădītes
called the altar Witness; "For," said they, "it is a witness between
us that the LORD is God."

B. *Joshua's address to the nine-and-a-half tribes*

23 A long time afterward, when the LORD had given rest to
Israel from all their enemies round about, and Joshua was
old and well advanced in years, 2 Joshua summoned all Israel,

their elders and heads, their judges and officers, and said to them, "I am now old and well advanced in years; 3 and you have seen all that the LORD your God has done to all these nations for your sake, for it is the LORD your God who has fought for you. 4 Behold, I have allotted to you as an inheritance for your tribes those nations that remain, along with all the nations that I have already cut off, from the Jordan to the Great Sea in the west. 5 The LORD your God will push them back before you, and drive them out of your sight; and you shall possess their land, as the LORD your God promised you. 6 Therefore be very steadfast to keep and do all that is written in the book of the law of Moses, turning aside from it neither to the right hand nor to the left, 7 that you may not be mixed with these nations left here among you, or make mention of the names of their gods, or swear by them, or serve them, or bow down yourselves to them, 8 but cleave to the LORD your God as you have done to this day. 9 For the LORD has driven out before you great and strong nations; and as for you, no man has been able to withstand you to this day. 10 One man of you puts to flight a thousand, since it is the LORD your God who fights for you, as he promised you. 11 Take good heed to yourselves, therefore, to love the LORD your God. 12 For if you turn back, and join the remnant of these nations left here among you, and make marriages with them, so that you marry their women and they yours, 13 know assuredly that the LORD your God will not continue to drive out these nations before you; but they shall be a snare and a trap for you, a scourge on your sides, and thorns in your eyes, till you perish from off this good land which the LORD your God has given you.

14 "And now I am about to go the way of all the earth, and you know in your hearts and souls, all of you, that not one thing has failed of all the good things which the LORD your God promised concerning you; all have come to pass for you, not one of them has failed. 15 But just as all the good things which the LORD your God promised concerning you have been fulfilled for you, so the LORD will bring upon you all the evil things, until he have destroyed you from off this good land which the LORD your God has given you, 16 if you transgress the covenant of the LORD your God, which he commanded you, and go and serve other gods and bow down to them. Then the anger of the LORD will be kindled against you, and you shall perish quickly from off the good land which he has given to you."

C. Joshua's last message

1. Review of God's past dealings with Israel

24 Then Joshua gathered all the tribes of Israel to Shĕchĕm, and summoned the elders, the heads, the judges, and the officers of Israel; and they presented themselves before God. 2And Joshua said to all the people, "Thus says the LORD, the God of Israel, 'Your fathers lived of old beyond the Eūphrā′tĕs, Tĕráh,

Cross references

23.3 Josh 10.14, 42
23.5 Num 33.53
23.6 Deut 5.32; Josh 1.7
23.7 Ex 23.33; Deut 7.2,3; Ex 23.13; Ps 16.4
23.8 Deut 10.20
23.9 Deut 11.23; Josh 1.5
★23.10 Lev 26.8; ver 3; Deut 3.22
23.12 Ex 34.15, 16; Deut 7.3
23.13 Judg 2.3; Ex 23.33; Num 33.55
23.14 1 Ki 2.2; Josh 21.45
23.15 Lev 26.16; Deut 28.15
24.1 Josh 23.2
24.2 Gen 11.27–32

23.10 This verse seems to employ a rather startling hyperbole, promising that a single Hebrew warrior shall chase a thousand of his foes. But the point here and elsewhere in Scripture is that one man plus God is a majority. The Bible everywhere (Ex 14.14, 25; Deut 1.30; 3.22ff, etc.) affirms that God may see fit to intervene in the affairs of men and His intervention does make the difference between victory and defeat.

the father of Abraham and of Nāhŏr; and they served other gods.
³ Then I took your father Abraham from beyond the River and
led him through all the land of Cānaän, and made his offspring
many. I gave him Isaac; ⁴ and to Isaac I gave Jacob and Ēsau. And
I gave Esau the hill country of Sēïr to possess, but Jacob and his
children went down to Egypt. ⁵And I sent Moses and Aaron, and
I plagued Egypt with what I did in the midst of it; and afterwards
I brought you out. ⁶ Then I brought your fathers out of Egypt,
and you came to the sea; and the Egyptians pursued your fathers
with chariots and horsemen to the Red Sea. ⁷And when they cried
to the LORD, he put darkness between you and the Egyptians, and
made the sea come upon them and cover them; and your eyes saw
what I did to Egypt; and you lived in the wilderness a long time.
⁸ Then I brought you to the land of the Ăm'ŏrītes, who lived on
the other side of the Jordan; they fought with you, and I gave them
into your hand, and you took possession of their land, and I destroyed them before you. ⁹ Then Bālăk the son of Zĭppor, king of
Mōăb, arose and fought against Israel; and he sent and invited
Bālaăm the son of Bēor to curse you, ¹⁰ but I would not listen to
Bālaăm; therefore he blessed you; so I delivered you out of his
hand. ¹¹And you went over the Jordan and came to Jĕr'ĭchō, and
the men of Jericho fought against you, and also the Ăm'ŏrītes, the
Pĕr'ĭzzītes, the Cā'naänītes, the Hĭttītes, the Gĭr'gåshītes, the
Hĭvītes, and the Jĕb'ūsītes; and I gave them into your hand. ¹²And
I sent the hornet before you, which drove them out before you,
the two kings of the Ăm'ŏrītes; it was not by your sword or by
your bow. ¹³ I gave you a land on which you had not labored, and
cities which you had not built, and you dwell therein; you eat the
fruit of vineyards and oliveyards which you did not plant.'

2. Joshua's challenge to serve the LORD

14 "Now therefore fear the LORD, and serve him in sincerity
and in faithfulness; put away the gods which your fathers served
beyond the River, and in Egypt, and serve the LORD. ¹⁵And if you
be unwilling to serve the LORD, choose this day whom you will
serve, whether the gods your fathers served in the region beyond
the River, or the gods of the Ăm'ŏrītes in whose land you dwell;
but as for me and my house, we will serve the LORD."

3. Israel chooses the LORD

16 Then the people answered, "Far be it from us that we should
forsake the LORD, to serve other gods; ¹⁷ for it is the LORD our God
who brought us and our fathers up from the land of Egypt, out of
the house of bondage, and who did those great signs in our sight,
and preserved us in all the way that we went, and among all the
peoples through whom we passed; ¹⁸ and the LORD drove out
before us all the peoples, the Ăm'ŏrītes who lived in the land;
therefore we also will serve the LORD, for he is our God."

19 But Joshua said to the people, "You cannot serve the LORD;
for he is a holy God; he is a jealous God; he will not forgive your
transgressions or your sins. ²⁰ If you forsake the LORD and serve
foreign gods, then he will turn and do you harm, and consume
you, after having done you good." ²¹And the people said to Joshua,
"Nay; but we will serve the LORD." ²² Then Joshua said to the
people, "You are witnesses against yourselves that you have chosen

Marginal references

24.3 Gen 12.1; 15.5; 21.3
24.4 Gen 25.25, 26; Deut 2.5; Gen 46.6,7
24.5 Ex 3.10
24.6 Ex 12.51; 14.2–31
24.8 Num 21.21–35
24.9 Num 22.2,5
24.11 Josh 3.16, 17; 6.1
24.12 Ex 23.28; Deut 7.20; Ps 44.3,6
24.13 Deut 6.10, 11
24.14 Deut 10.12; 18.13; 2 Cor 1.12
24.15 Ruth 1.15; 1 Ki 18.21; Ezek 20.39
24.19 Lev 19.2; Ex 20.5; 23.21
24.20 1 Chr 28.9; Josh 23.15

the LORD, to serve him." And they said, "We are witnesses."
23 He said, "Then put away the foreign gods which are among you,
and incline your heart to the LORD, the God of Israel." 24And the
people said to Joshua, "The LORD our God we will serve, and his
voice we will obey." 25 So Joshua made a covenant with the people
that day, and made statutes and ordinances for them at Shĕçhĕm.
26And Joshua wrote these words in the book of the law of God; and
he took a great stone, and set it up there under the oak in the
sanctuary of the LORD. 27And Joshua said to all the people, "Behold, this stone shall be a witness against us; for it has heard all
the words of the LORD which he spoke to us; therefore it shall be
a witness against you, lest you deal falsely with your God." 28 So
Joshua sent the people away, every man to his inheritance.

D. The death and burial of Joshua

29 After these things Joshua the son of Nùn, the servant of the
LORD, died, being a hundred and ten years old. 30And they buried
him in his own inheritance at Tìm'nǎth-sē'rǎh, which is in the hill
country of Ē'phrǎįm, north of the mountain of Gǎǎsh.

31 And Israel served the LORD all the days of Joshua, and all
the days of the elders who outlived Joshua and had known all the
work which the LORD did for Israel.

E. The burial of Joseph

32 The bones of Joseph which the people of Israel brought up
from Egypt were buried at Shĕçhĕm, in the portion of ground
which Jacob bought from the sons of Hāmor the father of Shechem
for a hundred pieces of money;q it became an inheritance of the
descendants of Joseph.

F. The death and burial of Eleazar

33 And Ēlĕā'zàr the son of Aaron died; and they buried him at
Gĭb'ĕ-ǎh, the town of Phĭn'ĕhàs his son, which had been given
him in the hill country of Ē'phrǎįm.

q Heb qesitah

24.23
Judg 10.16
24.24
Ex 19.8;
24.3,7;
Deut 5.27
24.25
Ex 24.8

24.27
Josh 22.27

24.29
Judg 2.8
24.30
Josh 19.50

24.31
Judg 2.7

24.32
Gen 50.24,
25;
Ex 13.19;
Gen 33.19

24.33
Josh 22.13

INTRODUCTION TO
THE BOOK OF
JUDGES

Authorship and Background: The title of the book in Hebrew, the Septuagint, and English derives from the Hebrew word *shophetim*, "judges," which designated the rulers who figured prominently in this period. Rabbinic tradition assigned the authorship of the book to Samuel, but there are internal indications of a later date. In any event, the author obtained his material from diverse sources, oral and written. Some of the material is ancient, such as the Song of Deborah (5.1–31), which may be dated around 1125 B.C. The statement "as long as the house of God was at Shiloh" (18.31) implies a date after the destruction of Shiloh by the Philistines (1 Sam 4.10–12; Jer 7.12). A later date, somewhere during the time of the monarchy, is indicated by the notice "In those days there was no king in Israel" (17.6; 18.1; 19.1; 21.25).

The period of Judges lasted for several centuries. The chronology is related to the date chosen for the Exodus. It is clear that although the various judges are discussed consecutively, few of them were supported by more than half of the tribes. In all likelihood, therefore, some of the judges ruled concurrently in different geographical areas.

Characteristics: The author of Judges reflects a philosophy of history often identified as the Deuteronomic philosophy of history, for in that book it finds its finest expression. Prosperity is due to obedience to the will of God; adversity is due to disobedience and rebellion against God. The history of Israel during the period of the Judges bears this out. When the twelve tribes are obedient to God and the covenant requirements, they have a strength and a unity which protects them from their enemies. When their loyalty to the central sanctuary at Shechem or Shiloh is dissipated by Baal worship the tribes become isolated, disorganized units which fall easy prey to their alert foes. The book is cyclical. Apostasy leads to oppression by Israel's enemies. The oppression leads to renewal and repentance, followed by deliverance through some judge. Then apostasy sets in, followed by oppression, repentance, and again deliverance by some judge.

Contents:

I.   Introduction. 1.1—2.5: Efforts to finish the conquest of Canaan by Judah and Simeon. The efforts by the tribes of Benjamin and Joseph. The failure to complete the conquest in Ephraim, Zebulun, Asher, Naphtali, and Dan. A review of Israel's blessings, apostasies, disasters, and deliverances.

II.   The judges of Israel. 2.6—16.31: The first apostasy: servitude under Cushan-rishathaim of Mesopotamia; deliverance by Othniel of Judah. The second apostasy: servitude under Eglon of Moab; deliverance by

Ehud; Shamgar. The third apostasy: servitude under Jabin the Canaanite; deliverance by Deborah and Barak. The fourth apostasy: servitude under the Midianites; deliverance by Gideon of Manasseh to whom God grants miraculous signs and who refuses to be made king. The fifth apostasy: servitude under Abimelech who is made king over Shechem; deliverance by Tola of Issachar and Jair of Gilead. The sixth apostasy: servitude under the Philistines; deliverance by Jephthah; Ibzan, Elon, and Abdon. The seventh apostasy: servitude under the Philistines; deliverance by Samson, a Nazirite who marries a Philistine, sins at Gaza, and reveals his strength to Delilah.

III.   The appendices. 17.1—21.25: Micah sets up his own sanctuary; he secures his own priest. Some Danites remove his priest and rob his sanctuary. The expedition against Laish which is captured and renamed Dan. Micah's idols and priests. The Levite seeks his concubine. The men of Gibeah abuse the concubine. The Levite calls for help to all Israel. Israel defeats her own tribe of Benjamin which is nearly extinguished. The remnant of Benjamin preserved from extinction by taking wives from among the virgins of Jabesh-gilead and from maidens at one of the feasts at Shiloh.

THE BOOK OF
JUDGES

I. Introduction 1.1–2.5

A. Conquests by the men of Judah and Simeon

*1.1
Num 27.21

1 After the death of Joshua the people of Israel inquired of the LORD, "Who shall go up first for us against the Cā'naánites, to fight against them?" 2 The LORD said, "Judah shall go up; behold, I have given the land into his hand." 3And Judah said to Sĭm'ëŏn his brother, "Come up with me into the territory allotted to me, that we may fight against the Cā'naánites; and I likewise will go with you into the territory allotted to you." So Simeon went with him. 4 Then Judah went up and the LORD gave the Cā'naánites and the Pĕr'ĭzzītes into their hand; and they defeated ten thousand of them at Bēzĕk. 5 They came upon Àdŏn'ĭ-bĕ'zĕk at Bēzĕk, and fought against him, and defeated the Cā'-naánites and the Pĕr'ĭzzītes. 6Àdŏn'ĭ-bĕ'zĕk fled; but they pursued him, and caught him, and cut off his thumbs and his great toes. 7And Àdŏn'ĭ-bĕ'zĕk said, "Seventy kings with their thumbs and their great toes cut off used to pick up scraps under my table; as I have done, so God has requited me." And they brought him to Jerusalem, and he died there.

1.3
ver 17

1.4
Gen 13.7

8 And the men of Judah fought against Jerusalem, and took it, and smote it with the edge of the sword, and set the city on fire. 9And afterward the men of Judah went down to fight against the Cā'naánites who dwelt in the hill country, in the Nĕgĕb, and in the lowland. 10And Judah went against the Cā'naánites who dwelt in Hēbrŏn (now the name of Hebron was formerly Kĭr'ĭath-ar'bà); and they defeated Shēshaī and Àhī'mán and Tălmaī.

1.8
ver 21;
Josh 15.63

1.10
Josh 15.13–19

11 From there they went against the inhabitants of Dēbĭr. The name of Debir was formerly Kĭr'ĭath-sē'phĕr. 12And Cālĕb said, "He who attacks Kĭr'ĭath-sē'phĕr and takes it, I will give him Àchsáh my daughter as wife." 13And Ŏth'nĭ-ĕl the son of Kēnăz, Cālĕb's younger brother, took it; and he gave him Àchsáh his daughter as wife. 14 When she came to him, she urged him to ask her father for a field; and she alighted from her ass, and Cālĕb said to her, "What do you wish?" 15 She said to him, "Give me a present; since you have set me in the land of the Nĕgĕb, give me also springs of water." And Cālĕb gave her the upper springs and the lower springs.

1.13
Judg 3.9

1.14
Josh 15.18, 19

16 And the descendants of the Kēnīte, Moses' father-in-law, went up with the people of Judah from the city of palms into the wilderness of Judah, which lies in the Nĕgĕb near Àràd; and they went and settled with the people. 17And Judah went with Sĭm'ëŏn his brother, and they defeated the Cā'naánites who inhabited

1.16
Judg 4.11,
17;
Deut 34.3;
Judg 3.13

1.17
ver 3;
Num 21.3

1.1 *After the death of Joshua.* Some have felt that the accounts of the conquest of Canaan as given in Joshua and Judges are at variance since Joshua implies that Israel has achieved full possession of the Promised Land, while Judges describes the process as gradual and lengthy. The two accounts are supplementary rather than contradictory. Joshua did defeat strong Canaanite forces, but he did not *occupy* all of Palestine. The Book of Judges fills in the picture painted in Joshua, but both books depict the conquest of Canaan as incomplete. It was left to each tribe to occupy the territories allocated to it.

Zĕphăth, and utterly destroyed it. So the name of the city was
called Hormăh. ¹⁸ Judah also took Gază with its territory, and
Ăsh′kĕlŏn with its territory, and Ĕkrŏn with its territory. ¹⁹And
the LORD was with Judah, and he took possession of the hill country, but he could not drive out the inhabitants of the plain, because
they had chariots of iron. ²⁰And Hĕbrŏn was given to Cālĕb, as
Moses had said; and he drove out from it the three sons of Ānăk.
²¹ But the people of Benjamin did not drive out the Jĕb′ūsītes who
dwelt in Jerusalem; so the Jebusites have dwelt with the people
of Benjamin in Jerusalem to this day.

*1.19
ver 2;
Josh 17.16,
18
1.20
Josh 14.9;
15.13,14;
ver 10
1.21
Josh 15.63

B. The incomplete conquests of Israel

22 The house of Joseph also went up against Bĕthĕl; and the
LORD was with them. ²³And the house of Joseph sent to spy out
Bĕthĕl. (Now the name of the city was formerly Lŭz.) ²⁴And the
spies saw a man coming out of the city, and they said to him,
"Pray, show us the way into the city, and we will deal kindly with
you." ²⁵And he showed them the way into the city; and they smote
the city with the edge of the sword, but they let the man and all his
family go. ²⁶And the man went to the land of the Hĭttītes and built
a city, and called its name Lŭz; that is its name to this day.

1.23
Gen 28.19

1.25
Josh 6.25

27 Mănăs′sĕh did not drive out the inhabitants of Bĕth-shĕ′ăn
and its villages, or Tā′ănăch and its villages, or the inhabitants of
Dor and its villages, or the inhabitants of Ĭb′lĕ-ăm and its villages,
or the inhabitants of Mĕgĭd′dō and its villages; but the Cā′naănītes
persisted in dwelling in that land. ²⁸ When Israel grew strong, they
put the Cā′naănītes to forced labor, but did not utterly drive
them out.

*1.27
Josh 17.11–
13

29 And Ē′phrăĭm did not drive out the Cā′naănītes who dwelt
in Gĕzĕr; but the Canaanites dwelt in Gezer among them.

1.29
Josh 16.10

30 Zĕb′ŭlŭn did not drive out the inhabitants of Kĭtrŏn, or the
inhabitants of Nā′hălŏl; but the Cā′naănītes dwelt among them,
and became subject to forced labor.

31 Ăshĕr did not drive out the inhabitants of Ăccō, or the inhabitants of Sīdŏn, or of Ahlăb, or of Ăchzĭb, or of Hĕlbăh, or of
Āphĭk, or of Rĕhŏb; ³² but the Ăsh′ĕrītes dwelt among the Cā′-
naănītes, the inhabitants of the land; for they did not drive them
out.

1.31
Judg 10.6

33 Năph′tălī did not drive out the inhabitants of Bĕth-shĕ′-
mĕsh, or the inhabitants of Bĕth-ā′năth, but dwelt among the
Cā′naănītes, the inhabitants of the land; nevertheless the inhabitants of Beth-shemesh and of Beth-anath became subject to
forced labor for them.

34 The Ăm′ŏrītes pressed the Dănītes back into the hill coun-
try, for they did not allow them to come down to the plain; ³⁵ the
Ăm′ŏrītes persisted in dwelling in Har-hĕ′rĕs, in Āi′jălŏn, and in
Shă-ăl′bĭm, but the hand of the house of Joseph rested heavily

1.34
Ex 3.17

1.19 The Israelites, good hand-to-hand
fighters, were successful against their enemies
in the hill country, but they were no match
for the chariots of iron in the plains, even
though the LORD was with them (see 1 Ki
20.23). Scripture sometimes describes history
in terms of God's power and sometimes in

terms of man's power, but God is always
behind history. God is always the ultimate
source of power, man is the proximate, or
secondary source. In this particular case the
superior military power of the enemy prevailed.
1.27 See notes to Josh 10.40; 12.9–24.

1.36
Josh 15.3

upon them, and they became subject to forced labor. 36And the border of the Ăm'órītes ran from the ascent of Ăkrăb'bǐm, from Sēlă and upward.

C. The failure of Israel to keep the covenant

*2.1
ver 5;
Judg 6.11;
Ex 20.2;
Gen 17.7;
Deut 7.9
2.2
Ex 23.32;
34.12,13
2.3
Josh 23.13;
Judg 3.6;
Deut 7.16;
Ps 106.36

2 Now the angel of the LORD went up from Gĭlgăl to Bōçhĭm. And he said, "I brought you up from Egypt, and brought you into the land which I swore to give to your fathers. I said, 'I will never break my covenant with you, 2 and you shall make no covenant with the inhabitants of this land; you shall break down their altars.' But you have not obeyed my command. What is this you have done? 3 So now I say, I will not drive them out before you; but they shall become adversaries*a* to you, and their gods shall be a snare to you." 4 When the angel of the LORD spoke these words to all the people of Israel, the people lifted up their voices and wept. 5And they called the name of that place Bōçhĭm;*b* and they sacrificed there to the LORD.

II. The judges of Israel 2.6–16.31

A. The death and burial of Joshua

2.6
Josh 24.28–31

6 When Joshua dismissed the people, the people of Israel went each to his inheritance to take possession of the land. 7And the people served the LORD all the days of Joshua, and all the days of the elders who outlived Joshua, who had seen all the great work which the LORD had done for Israel. 8And Joshua the son of Nŭn, the servant of the LORD, died at the age of one hundred and ten years. 9And they buried him within the bounds of his inheritance in Tĭm'năth-hē'rĕs, in the hill country of Ē'phrăĭm, north of the mountain of Gāăsh. 10And all that generation also were gathered to their fathers; and there arose another generation after them, who did not know the LORD or the work which he had done for Israel.

2.10
1 Sam 2.12;
1 Chr 28.9;
Gal 4.8

B. The apostasy of Israel

2.11
Judg 3.7,
12; 4.1;
6.1,25;
8.33; 10.6
2.12
Deut 31.16
*2.13
Judg 10.6
2.14
Judg 3.8;
Ps 106.40–42;
Deut 28.25

11 And the people of Israel did what was evil in the sight of the LORD and served the Bāăls; 12 and they forsook the LORD, the God of their fathers, who had brought them out of the land of Egypt; they went after other gods, from among the gods of the peoples who were round about them, and bowed down to them; and they provoked the LORD to anger. 13 They forsook the LORD, and served the Bāăls and the Ăsh'tărŏth. 14 So the anger of the LORD was kindled against Israel, and he gave them over to plunderers, who plundered them; and he sold them into the power of their enemies round about, so that they could no longer withstand their

a Vg Old Latin Compare Gk: Heb *sides*   *b* That is *Weepers*

2.1 This is obviously the Abrahamic covenant as renewed in Ex 34.10ff. It was not completely unconditional but was dependent upon personal obedience to the voice of God. The failure of Israel to drive all of the inhabitants out of the land led to disaster (ver 2, 3).

2.13 *Baals*, local representations of Baal, the lord of the Canaanite pantheon. *Ashtaroth* is the plural of Astarte, the Canaanite goddess of fertility and war.

enemies. 15 Whenever they marched out, the hand of the LORD was against them for evil, as the LORD had warned, and as the LORD had sworn to them; and they were in sore straits.

C. Deliverance through judges and repeated apostasy

16 Then the LORD raised up judges, who saved them out of the power of those who plundered them. 17And yet they did not listen to their judges; for they played the harlot after other gods and bowed down to them; they soon turned aside from the way in which their fathers had walked, who had obeyed the commandments of the LORD, and they did not do so. 18 Whenever the LORD raised up judges for them, the LORD was with the judge, and he saved them from the hand of their enemies all the days of the judge; for the LORD was moved to pity by their groaning because of those who afflicted and oppressed them. 19 But whenever the judge died, they turned back and behaved worse than their fathers, going after other gods, serving them and bowing down to them; they did not drop any of their practices or their stubborn ways. 20 So the anger of the LORD was kindled against Israel; and he said, "Because this people have transgressed my covenant which I commanded their fathers, and have not obeyed my voice, 21 I will not henceforth drive out before them any of the nations that Joshua left when he died, 22 that by them I may test Israel, whether they will take care to walk in the way of the LORD as their fathers did, or not." 23 So the LORD left those nations, not driving them out at once, and he did not give them into the power of Joshua.

D. The nations left to test Israel

3 Now these are the nations which the LORD left, to test Israel by them, that is, all in Israel who had no experience of any war in Cānaàn; 2 it was only that the generations of the people of Israel might know war, that he might teach war to such at least as had not known it before. 3 These are the nations: the five lords of the Philĭs'tĭnes, and all the Cā'naànītes, and the Sīdŏ'nĭàns, and the Hīvītes who dwelt on Mount Lebanon, from Mount Bā'àl-hèr'mòn as far as the entrance of Hāmàth. 4 They were for the testing of Israel, to know whether Israel would obey the commandments of the LORD, which he commanded their fathers by Moses. 5 So the people of Israel dwelt among the Cā'naànītes, the Hĭttītes, the Ăm'órītes, the Pĕr'ĭzzītes, the Hīvītes, and the Jĕb'ūsītes; 6 and they took their daughters to themselves for wives, and their own daughters they gave to their sons; and they served their gods.

*2.16
Ps 106.43–45;
Acts 13.20
2.17
ver 7

2.19
Judg 3.12;
4.1; 8.33

2.20
ver 14;
Josh 23.16

2.21
Josh 23.13
2.22
Judg 3.1,4
*2.23

3.1
Judg 2.21, 22

3.3
Josh 13.3

3.4
Deut 8.2;
Judg 2.22

3.6
Ex 34.16;
Deut 7.3,4

2.16 After the death of Joshua the power of Israel began to decline due to religious apostasy. The history of God's people was from that time on characterized by recurring eras of subjugation by, and deliverance from, the peoples of the land. In this period before the appointment of the prophets, when Israel went from apostasy to repentance and back to apostasy, God provided deliverers such as Othniel, Ehud, Deborah, and Samson. These leaders were called "judges" (a term which in Hebrew implied leadership in government and war as well as in legal cases), and were raised up by God under His theocratic government. None of these judges was of a stature comparable to Moses or Joshua before them, or Samuel and David after them, and none of them had the unified support of all twelve tribes. It was a time of confusion. The description *every man did what was right in his own eyes* (17.6; 21.25) was all too true.

2.23 *Joshua* is apparently a reference to Israel, the people led into Canaan by Joshua.

E. *The judgeship of Othniel*

| ★3.7
Judg 2.11,
13;
Deut 4.9 |
| ★3.8 |

7 And the people of Israel did what was evil in the sight of the LORD, forgetting the LORD their God, and serving the Bāáls and the Ashē′róth. 8 Therefore the anger of the LORD was kindled against Israel, and he sold them into the hand of Cŭ′shăn-rĭsh-áthā′ĭm king of Mĕsôpôtá′mĭá; and the people of Israel served Cushan-rishathaim eight years. 9 But when the people of Israel cried to the LORD, the LORD raised up a deliverer for the people of Israel, who delivered them, Ŏth′nĭ-ĕl the son of Kēnăz, Cālĕb's younger brother. 10 The Spirit of the LORD came upon him, and he judged Israel; he went out to war, and the LORD gave Cŭ′shăn-rĭsháthā′ĭm king of Mĕsôpôtá′mĭá into his hand; and his hand prevailed over Cushan-rishathaim. 11 So the land had rest forty years. Then Ŏth′nĭ-ĕl the son of Kēnáz died.

F. *The judgeship of Ehud*

1. *The sin of Israel: oppression by Moab*

12 And the people of Israel again did what was evil in the sight of the LORD; and the LORD strengthened Ĕglŏn the king of Mŏăb against Israel, because they had done what was evil in the sight of the LORD. 13 He gathered to himself the Ăm′mŏnītes and the Ămăl′ĕkītes, and went and defeated Israel; and they took possession of the city of palms. 14And the people of Israel served Ĕglŏn the king of Mŏăb eighteen years.

2. *Ehud assassinates Eglon*

15 But when the people of Israel cried to the LORD, the LORD raised up for them a deliverer, Ēhŭd, the son of Gērá, the Benjaminite, a left-handed man. The people of Israel sent tribute by him to Ĕglŏn the king of Mŏăb. 16And Ēhŭd made for himself a sword with two edges, a cubit in length; and he girded it on his right thigh under his clothes. 17And he presented the tribute to Ĕglŏn king of Mŏăb. Now Eglon was a very fat man. 18And when Ēhŭd had finished presenting the tribute, he sent away the people that carried the tribute. 19 But he himself turned back at the sculptured stones near Gĭlgăl, and said, "I have a secret message for you, O king." And he commanded, "Silence." And all his attendants went out from his presence. 20And Ēhŭd came to him, as he was sitting alone in his cool roof chamber. And Ehud said, "I have a message from God for you." And he arose from his seat. 21And Ēhŭd reached with his left hand, took the sword from his right thigh, and thrust it into his belly; 22 and the hilt also went in after the blade, and the fat closed over the blade, for he did not draw the sword out of his belly; and the dirt came out. 23 Then Ēhŭd went out into the vestibule,c and closed the doors of the roof chamber upon him, and locked them.

c The meaning of the Hebrew word is unknown

3.7 *Asheroth*, the plural of Asherah, the Canaanite mother-goddess who, like Ashtaroth in 2.13, was prominent in the fertility rites of the Canaanites.
3.8 *Mesopotamia*, Hebrew *Aram-naharaim*, the region around Haran. Evidently Cushan-rishathaim was an Aramean prince.
3.12 After the death of Othniel, Israel reverted to apostasy. It was only after eighteen years of oppression by Eglon that Israel came to her senses and sought the help of the LORD. Then the LORD heard and delivered Israel.

Cross-references: 3.9 ver 15; Judg 1.13 · 3.10 Num 11.25, 29; 24.2; Judg 6.34 · ★3.12 Judg 2.11, 14 · 3.13 Judg 1.16 · 3.15 Ps 107.13 · 3.17 ver 12

3. The discovery of the assassination

24 When he had gone, the servants came; and when they saw that the doors of the roof chamber were locked, they thought, "He is only relieving himself in the closet of the cool chamber." 25And they waited till they were utterly at a loss; but when he still did not open the doors of the roof chamber, they took the key and opened them; and there lay their lord dead on the floor.

3.24
1 Sam 24.3

3.25
2 Ki 2.17;
8.11

4. The defeat of the Moabites

26 Ēhŭd escaped while they delayed, and passed beyond the sculptured stones, and escaped to Sē-ī'răh. 27 When he arrived, he sounded the trumpet in the hill country of Ē'phrăim; and the people of Israel went down with him from the hill country, having him at their head. 28And he said to them, "Follow after me; for the LORD has given your enemies the Mōábītes into your hand." So they went down after him, and seized the fords of the Jordan against the Moabites, and allowed not a man to pass over. 29And they killed at that time about ten thousand of the Mōábītes, all strong, able-bodied men; not a man escaped. 30 So Mōáb was subdued that day under the hand of Israel. And the land had rest for eighty years.

3.28
Judg 7.9,
15,24; 12.5

3.30
ver 11

G. Delivery by Shamgar

31 After him was Shămgar the son of Ānăth, who killed six hundred of the Phĭlĭs'tĭnes with an oxgoad; and he too delivered Israel.

3.31
Judg 5.6

H. The judgeships of Deborah and Barak

1. The oppression by the Canaanites

4 And the people of Israel again did what was evil in the sight of the LORD, after Ēhŭd died. 2And the LORD sold them into the hand of Jābĭn king of Cānaán, who reigned in Hāzor; the commander of his army was Sĭs'ĕrå, who dwelt in Hăró'shĕth-há-goi'ĭm. 3 Then the people of Israel cried to the LORD for help; for he had nine hundred chariots of iron, and oppressed the people of Israel cruelly for twenty years.

4.1
Judg 2.19
4.2
Josh 11.1,
10;
ver 13,16;
Ps 83.9
4.3
Judg 1.19

2. Deborah summons Barak

4 Now Deborah, a prophetess, the wife of Lăp'pĭdŏth, was judging Israel at that time. 5 She used to sit under the palm of Deborah between Rāmáh and Bĕthĕl in the hill country of Ē'-phrăim; and the people of Israel came up to her for judgment. 6 She sent and summoned Băråk the son of Ȧbĭn'ō-ăm from Kĕdĕsh in Năph'tálī, and said to him, "The LORD, the God of Israel, commands you, 'Go, gather your men at Mount Tābŏr, taking ten thousand from the tribe of Naphtali and the tribe of Zĕb'ŭlŭn. 7And I will draw out Sĭs'ĕrå, the general of Jābĭn's army, to meet you by the river Kĭshŏn with his chariots and his troops; and I will give him into your hand.' " 8 Băråk said to her, "If you will go with me, I will go; but if you will not go with me, I will not go." 9And she said, "I will surely go with you; nevertheless, the road on which you are going will not lead to your glory,

4.6
Heb 11.32

4.7
Ps 83.9

4.9
ver 21

for the LORD will sell Sĭs′ĕrà into the hand of a woman." Then Deborah arose, and went with Bàràk to Kĕdĕsh. ¹⁰And Bàràk summoned Zĕb′ūlùn and Năph′tàlī to Kĕdĕsh; and ten thousand men went up at his heels; and Deborah went up with him.

4.10
Judg 5.18;
ver 14;
Judg 5.15

3. The victory over the Canaanites

*4.11
Judg 1.16;
ver 6

11 Now Hēbèr the Kēnīte had separated from the Kēnītes, the descendants of Hōbăb the father-in-law of Moses, and had pitched his tent as far away as the oak in Zā-ànăn′nĭm, which is near Kĕdĕsh.

4.13
ver 3
4.14
Deut 9.3

12 When Sĭs′ĕrà was told that Bàràk the son of Àbĭn′ō-àm had gone up to Mount Tābòr, ¹³Sĭs′ĕrà called out all his chariots, nine hundred chariots of iron, and all the men who were with him, from Hàrō′shĕth-hà-goi′ĭm to the river Kĭshón. ¹⁴And Deborah said to Bàràk, "Up! For this is the day in which the LORD has given Sĭs′ĕrà into your hand. Does not the LORD go out before you?" So Barak went down from Mount Tābòr with ten thousand men

4.15
Josh 10.10
4.16
Ps 83.9

following him. ¹⁵And the LORD routed Sĭs′ĕrà and all his chariots and all his army before Bàràk at the edge of the sword; and Sisera alighted from his chariot and fled away on foot. ¹⁶And Bàràk pursued the chariots and the army to Hàrō′shĕth-hà-goi′ĭm, and all the army of Sĭs′ĕrà fell by the edge of the sword; not a man was left.

4. Jael slays Sisera

4.19
Judg 5.25

17 But Sĭs′ĕrà fled away on foot to the tent of Jàèl, the wife of Hēbèr the Kēnīte; for there was peace between Jābĭn the king of Hāzor and the house of Heber the Kenite. ¹⁸And Jàèl came out to meet Sĭs′ĕrà, and said to him, "Turn aside, my lord, turn aside to me; have no fear." So he turned aside to her into the tent, and she covered him with a rug. ¹⁹And he said to her, "Pray, give me a little water to drink; for I am thirsty." So she opened a skin of milk and gave him a drink and covered him. ²⁰And he said to her, "Stand at the door of the tent, and if any man comes and asks you, 'Is any one here?' say, No." ²¹ But Jàèl the wife of Hēbèr took a

4.21
Judg 5.26

tent peg, and took a hammer in her hand, and went softly to him and drove the peg into his temple, till it went down into the ground, as he was lying fast asleep from weariness. So he died. ²²And behold, as Bàràk pursued Sĭs′ĕrà, Jàèl went out to meet him, and said to him, "Come, and I will show you the man whom you are seeking." So he went in to her tent; and there lay Sisera dead, with the tent peg in his temple.

5. Jabin destroyed

23 So on that day God subdued Jābĭn the king of Cānaàn before the people of Israel. ²⁴And the hand of the people of Israel bore harder and harder on Jābĭn the king of Cānaàn, until they destroyed Jabin king of Canaan.

6. The song of Deborah

*5.1
Ex 15.1
5.2
Deut 32.41

5 Then sang Deborah and Bàràk the son of Àbĭn′ō-àm on that day:
2 "That the leaders took the lead in Israel,

4.11 *Hobab.* See note to Ex 2.18.   **5.1** The war song in poetic form.

that the people offered themselves willingly,
bless[d] the Lord!

3 "Hear, O kings; give ear, O princes;
to the Lord I will sing,
I will make melody to the Lord, the God of Israel.

5.3
Ps 27.6

4 "Lord, when thou didst go forth from Sḕir,
when thou didst march from the region of Ēdȯm,
the earth trembled,
and the heavens dropped,
yea, the clouds dropped water.

5.4
Deut 33.2;
Ps 68.7–9

5 The mountains quaked before the Lord,
yon Sī′näï before the Lord, the God of Israel.

5.5
Ps 97.5;
Isa 64.1,3;
Ps 68.8

6 "In the days of Shămgar, son of Ānăth,
in the days of Jāêl, caravans ceased
and travelers kept to the byways.

5.6
Judg 3.31;
4.17

7 The peasantry ceased in Israel, they ceased
until you arose, Deborah,
arose as a mother in Israel.

8 When new gods were chosen,
then war was in the gates.
Was shield or spear to be seen
among forty thousand in Israel?

5.8
Deut 32.17

9 My heart goes out to the commanders of Israel
who offered themselves willingly among the people.
Bless the Lord.

10 "Tell of it, you who ride on tawny asses,
you who sit on rich carpets[e]
and you who walk by the way.

11 To the sound of musicians[e] at the watering places,
there they repeat the triumphs of the Lord,
the triumphs of his peasantry in Israel.

5.11
1 Sam 12.7;
Mic 6.5

"Then down to the gates marched the people of the Lord.

12 "Awake, awake, Deborah!
Awake, awake, utter a song!
Arise, Bạrák, lead away your captives,
O son of Ăbĭn′ō-ám.

5.12
Ps 57.8;
68.18

13 Then down marched the remnant of the noble;
the people of the Lord marched down for him[f] against the
mighty.

14 From Ē′phrăĭm they set out thither[x] into the valley,[g]
following you, Benjamin, with your kinsmen;
from Măchir marched down the commanders,
and from Zĕb′ŭlŭn those who bear the marshal's staff;

5.14
Judg 3.13,
27;
Num 32.39

15 the princes of Ĭs′săchar came with Deborah,
and Issachar faithful to Bạrák;
into the valley they rushed forth at his heels.

5.15
Judg 4.10

---

d Or *You who offered yourselves willingly among the people, bless*
e The meaning of the Hebrew word is uncertain   f Gk: Heb *me*
x Cn: Heb *From Ephraim their root*   g Gk: Heb in *Am′ălĕk*

Among the clans of Reubën
there were great searchings of heart.

5.16
Num 32.1

16 Why did you tarry among the sheepfolds,
to hear the piping for the flocks?
Among the clans of Reubën
there were great searchings of heart.

5.17
Josh 13.24–
28; 19.29,
46

17 Gĭl'ëäd stayed beyond the Jordan;
and Dan, why did he abide with the ships?
Ăshër sat still at the coast of the sea,
settling down by his landings.

5.18
Judg 4.6,10

18 Zĕb'ŭlŭn is a people that jeoparded their lives to the death;
Năph'tălī too, on the heights of the field.

*5.19ff
Josh 11.1,
2;
Judg 1.27

19 "The kings came, they fought;
then fought the kings of Cānaăn,
at Tā'ănăch, by the waters of Mĕgĭd'dō;
they got no spoils of silver.

5.20
Josh 10.11–
14

20 From heaven fought the stars,
from their courses they fought against Sĭs'erä.

5.21
Judg 4.7

21 The torrent Kĭshŏn swept them away,
the onrushing torrent, the torrent Kishon.
March on, my soul, with might!

22 "Then loud beat the horses' hoofs
with the galloping, galloping of his steeds.

23 "Curse Mērŏz, says the angel of the Lord,
curse bitterly its inhabitants,
because they came not to the help of the Lord,
to the help of the Lord against the mighty.

5.24
Judg 4.17,
19–21

24 "Most blessed of women be Jäĕl,
the wife of Hēbĕr the Kēnīte,
of tent-dwelling women most blessed.

5.25
Judg 4.19

25 He asked water and she gave him milk,
she brought him curds in a lordly bowl.

5.26
Judg 4.21

26 She put her hand to the tent peg
and her right hand to the workmen's mallet;
she struck Sĭs'erä a blow,
she crushed his head,
she shattered and pierced his temple.

*5.27

27 He sank, he fell,
he lay still at her feet;
at her feet he sank, he fell;
where he sank, there he fell dead.

5.28
Prov 7.6

28 "Out of the window she peered,
the mother of Sĭs'erä gazed[h] through the lattice:
'Why is his chariot so long in coming?
Why tarry the hoofbeats of his chariots?'
29 Her wisest ladies make answer,

---

[h] Gk Compare Tg: Heb *exclaimed*

5.19–22 A dramatic account of the raging battle at Taanach.

5.27 This verse is apparently a poetic description of the incident in 4.21.

nay, she gives answer to herself,
30 'Are they not finding and dividing the spoil?—
    A maiden or two for every man;
  spoil of dyed stuffs for Sĭs′ĕrȧ,
    spoil of dyed stuffs embroidered,
    two pieces of dyed work embroidered for my neck as spoil?'

31 "So perish all thine enemies, O LORD!
  But thy friends be like the sun as he rises in his might."

And the land had rest for forty years.

I. The judgeship of Gideon

1. Apostasy and servitude

6 The people of Israel did what was evil in the sight of the LORD; and the LORD gave them into the hand of Mĭd′ĭȧn seven years. 2And the hand of Mĭd′ĭȧn prevailed over Israel; and because of Midian the people of Israel made for themselves the dens which are in the mountains, and the caves and the strongholds. 3 For whenever the Israelites put in seed the Mĭd′ĭȧnītes and the Ȧmȧl′ĕkītes and the people of the East would come up and attack them; 4 they would encamp against them and destroy the produce of the land, as far as the neighborhood of Gazȧ, and leave no sustenance in Israel, and no sheep or ox or ass. 5 For they would come up with their cattle and their tents, coming like locusts for number; both they and their camels could not be counted; so that they wasted the land as they came in. 6And Israel was brought very low because of Mĭd′ĭȧn; and the people of Israel cried for help to the LORD.

2. The advent of a prophet

7 When the people of Israel cried to the LORD on account of the Mĭd′ĭȧnītes, 8 the LORD sent a prophet to the people of Israel; and he said to them, "Thus says the LORD, the God of Israel: I led you up from Egypt, and brought you out of the house of bondage; 9 and I delivered you from the hand of the Egyptians, and from the hand of all who oppressed you, and drove them out before you, and gave you their land; 10 and I said to you, 'I am the LORD your God; you shall not pay reverence to the gods of the Ăm′ôrītes, in whose land you dwell.' But you have not given heed to my voice."

3. Gideon called of the LORD

11 Now the angel of the LORD came and sat under the oak at Ŏph′rȧh, which belonged to Jō′ȧsh the Ăbĭĕz′rīte, as his son Gideon was beating out wheat in the wine press, to hide it from the Mĭd′-ĭȧnītes. 12And the angel of the LORD appeared to him and said to him, "The LORD is with you, you mighty man of valor." 13And Gideon said to him, "Pray, sir, if the LORD is with us, why then has all this befallen us? And where are all his wonderful deeds which our fathers recounted to us, saying, 'Did not the LORD bring us up from Egypt?' But now the LORD has cast us off, and

Margin references:
5.30 Ex 15.9
5.31 Ps 68.2; 92.9; 19.4,5; Judg 3.11
*6.1 Judg 2.11, 19; Num 25.15-18; 31.1-3
6.3 Judg 3.13
6.4 Lev 26.16; Deut 28.30, 33,51
*6.5 Judg 7.12
6.6 Judg 3.15
6.8 Judg 2.1,2
6.9 Ps 44.2,3
6.11 Josh 17.2
6.12 Josh 1.5
6.13 Ps 44.1; 2 Chr 15.2

6.1 Cf. with 3.14 where it took eighteen years for Israel to come to her senses.   6.5 *camels.* This is the first known use of domesticated camels in warfare.

6.14
Heb 11.32,
34;
Judg 4.6
6.15
Ex 3.11;
1 Sam 9.21
6.16
Ex 3.12;
Josh 1.5
6.17
ver 36,37;
Isa 38.7,8

6.19
Gen 18.6–8

6.20
Judg 13.19
6.21
Lev 9.24

6.22
Judg 13.21

6.25
Ex 34.13;
Deut 7.5

6.28
1 Ki 16.32

6.32
Judg 7.1;
1 Sam 12.11
6.33
ver 3;
Josh 17.16

given us into the hand of Mĭd'ĭán." 14And the LORD turned to him and said, "Go in this might of yours and deliver Israel from the hand of Mĭd'ĭán; do not I send you?" 15And he said to him, "Pray, Lord, how can I deliver Israel? Behold, my clan is the weakest in Mánăs'sĕh, and I am the least in my family." 16And the LORD said to him, "But I will be with you, and you shall smite the Mĭd'ĭănītes as one man." 17And he said to him, "If now I have found favor with thee, then show me a sign that it is thou who speakest with me. 18 Do not depart from here, I pray thee, until I come to thee, and bring out my present, and set it before thee." And he said, "I will stay till you return."

19 So Gideon went into his house and prepared a kid, and unleavened cakes from an ephah of flour; the meat he put in a basket, and the broth he put in a pot, and brought them to him under the oak and presented them. 20And the angel of God said to him, "Take the meat and the unleavened cakes, and put them on this rock, and pour the broth over them." And he did so. 21 Then the angel of the LORD reached out the tip of the staff that was in his hand, and touched the meat and the unleavened cakes; and there sprang up fire from the rock and consumed the flesh and the unleavened cakes; and the angel of the LORD vanished from his sight. 22 Then Gideon perceived that he was the angel of the LORD; and Gideon said, "Alas, O Lord GOD! For now I have seen the angel of the LORD face to face." 23 But the LORD said to him, "Peace be to you; do not fear, you shall not die." 24 Then Gideon built an altar there to the LORD, and called it, The LORD is peace. To this day it still stands at Ŏph'răh, which belongs to the Ăbĭĕz'rītes.

4. Gideon destroys the altar to Baal

25 That night the LORD said to him, "Take your father's bull, the second bull seven years old, and pull down the altar of Bāăl which your father has, and cut down the Ăshē'răh that is beside it; 26 and build an altar to the LORD your God on the top of the stronghold here, with stones laid in due order; then take the second bull, and offer it as a burnt offering with the wood of the Ăshē'răh which you shall cut down." 27 So Gideon took ten men of his servants, and did as the LORD had told him; but because he was too afraid of his family and the men of the town to do it by day, he did it by night.

28 When the men of the town rose early in the morning, behold, the altar of Bāăl was broken down, and the Ăshē'răh beside it was cut down, and the second bull was offered upon the altar which had been built. 29And they said to one another, "Who has done this thing?" And after they had made search and inquired, they said, "Gideon the son of Jō'ăsh has done this thing." 30 Then the men of the town said to Jō'ăsh, "Bring out your son, that he may die, for he has pulled down the altar of Bāăl and cut down the Ăshē'răh beside it." 31 But Jō'ăsh said to all who were arrayed against him, "Will you contend for Bāăl? Or will you defend his cause? Whoever contends for him shall be put to death by morning. If he is a god, let him contend for himself, because his altar has been pulled down." 32 Therefore on that day he was called Jĕrŭbbā'ăl, that is to say, "Let Bāăl contend against him," because he pulled down his altar.

33 Then all the Mĭd'ĭănītes and the Ămăl'ĕkītes and the people

of the East came together, and crossing the Jordan they encamped in the Valley of Jĕzreĕl'. 34 But the Spirit of the LORD took possession of Gideon; and he sounded the trumpet, and the Ăbĭĕz'-rītes were called out to follow him. 35And he sent messengers throughout all Mănăs'sĕh; and they too were called out to follow him. And he sent messengers to Ăshĕr, Zĕb'ūlŭn, and Năph'tālī; and they went up to meet them.

5. Gideon puts out the fleece

36 Then Gideon said to God, "If thou wilt deliver Israel by my hand, as thou hast said, 37 behold, I am laying a fleece of wool on the threshing floor; if there is dew on the fleece alone, and it is dry on all the ground, then I shall know that thou wilt deliver Israel by my hand, as thou hast said." 38And it was so. When he rose early next morning and squeezed the fleece, he wrung enough dew from the fleece to fill a bowl with water. 39 Then Gideon said to God, "Let not thy anger burn against me, let me speak but this once; pray, let me make trial only this once with the fleece; pray, let it be dry only on the fleece, and on all the ground let there be dew." 40And God did so that night; for it was dry on the fleece only, and on all the ground there was dew.

6. The defeat of the Midianites
a. The selection of the three hundred

7 Then Jĕrŭbbā'ăl (that is, Gideon) and all the people who were with him rose early and encamped beside the spring of Hārŏd; and the camp of Mĭd'iăn was north of them, by the hill of Morĕh, in the valley.

2 The LORD said to Gideon, "The people with you are too many for me to give the Mĭd'iănītes into their hand, lest Israel vaunt themselves against me, saying, 'My own hand has delivered me.' 3 Now therefore proclaim in the ears of the people, saying, 'Whoever is fearful and trembling, let him return home.' " And Gideon tested them;[i] twenty-two thousand returned, and ten thousand remained.

4 And the LORD said to Gideon, "The people are still too many; take them down to the water and I will test them for you there; and he of whom I say to you, 'This man shall go with you,' shall go with you; and any of whom I say to you, 'This man shall not go with you,' shall not go." 5 So he brought the people down to the water; and the LORD said to Gideon, "Every one that laps the water with his tongue, as a dog laps, you shall set by himself; likewise every one that kneels down to drink." 6And the number of those that lapped, putting their hands to their mouths, was three hundred men; but all the rest of the people knelt down to drink water. 7And the LORD said to Gideon, "With the three hundred men that lapped I will deliver you, and give the Mĭd'iănītes into your hand; and let all the others go every man to his home." 8 So he took the jars of the people from their

i Cn: Heb and depart from Mount Gil'ĕăd

6.34 Judg 3.10, 27; 1 Chr 12.18; 2 Chr 24.20

*6.37 see Ex 4.3–7

6.39 Gen 18.32

7.1 Judg 6.32

7.2 Deut 8.17; Isa 10.13; 2 Cor 4.7

7.3 Deut 20.8

7.4 1 Sam 14.6

7.7 1 Sam 14.6

6.37 Gideon and the fleece illustrate one method by which God may guide His children in the decisions of life (ver 37–40). However illusory the test of Gideon might appear to modern thinking, the results of the putting out of the fleece confirmed to him the will of God and led him to very definite victory over the Midianites.

hands,[j] and their trumpets; and he sent all the rest of Israel every man to his tent, but retained the three hundred men; and the camp of Mĭd′ĭăn was below him in the valley.

b. *The prophecy against Midian*

7.9
Josh 2.24;
10.8; 11.6

7.11
ver 13–15

7.12
Judg 6.5;
8.10;
Josh 11.4

7.14
ver 20

9 That same night the LORD said to him, "Arise, go down against the camp; for I have given it into your hand. 10 But if you fear to go down, go down to the camp with Pū′răh your servant; 11 and you shall hear what they say, and afterward your hands shall be strengthened to go down against the camp." Then he went down with Pū′răh his servant to the outposts of the armed men that were in the camp. 12 And the Mĭd′ĭănītes and the Ȧmăl′ĕkītes and all the people of the East lay along the valley like locusts for multitude; and their camels were without number, as the sand which is upon the seashore for multitude. 13 When Gideon came, behold, a man was telling a dream to his comrade; and he said, "Behold, I dreamed a dream; and lo, a cake of barley bread tumbled into the camp of Mĭd′ĭăn, and came to the tent, and struck it so that it fell, and turned it upside down, so that the tent lay flat." 14 And his comrade answered, "This is no other than the sword of Gideon the son of Jō′ăsh, a man of Israel; into his hand God has given Mĭd′ĭăn and all the host."

c. *Battle orders*

7.15
1 Sam 15.31

7.18
ver 14,20

15 When Gideon heard the telling of the dream and its interpretation, he worshiped; and he returned to the camp of Israel, and said, "Arise; for the LORD has given the host of Mĭd′ĭăn into your hand." 16 And he divided the three hundred men into three companies, and put trumpets into the hands of all of them and empty jars, with torches inside the jars. 17 And he said to them, "Look at me, and do likewise; when I come to the outskirts of the camp, do as I do. 18 When I blow the trumpet, I and all who are with me, then blow the trumpets also on every side of all the camp, and shout, 'For the LORD and for Gideon.' "

d. *The flight of the Midianites*

7.20
ver 14

7.21
2 Ki 7.7

7.22
Josh 6.4;
16.20;
1 Sam 14.20

7.23
Judg 6.35

7.24
Judg 3.27,
28

19 So Gideon and the hundred men who were with him came to the outskirts of the camp at the beginning of the middle watch, when they had just set the watch; and they blew the trumpets and smashed the jars that were in their hands. 20 And the three companies blew the trumpets and broke the jars, holding in their left hands the torches, and in their right hands the trumpets to blow; and they cried, "A sword for the LORD and for Gideon!" 21 They stood every man in his place round about the camp, and all the army ran; they cried out and fled. 22 When they blew the three hundred trumpets, the LORD set every man's sword against his fellow and against all the army; and the army fled as far as Bĕth-shĭt′tăh toward Zĕr′erăh,[k] as far as the border of Ȧ′bĕl-mĕhō′lăh, by Tăbbăth. 23 And the men of Israel were called out from Năph′-tălī and from Ăshĕr and from all Mănăs′sĕh, and they pursued after Mĭd′ĭăn.

24 And Gideon sent messengers throughout all the hill country of Ē′phrāĭm, saying, "Come down against the Mĭd′ĭănītes and seize the waters against them, as far as Bĕth-bar′ăh, and also the

---

j Cn: Heb *the people took provisions in their hands*   *k* Another reading is *Zĕr′ēdăh*

Jordan." So all the men of Ephraim were called out, and they seized the waters as far as Beth-barah, and also the Jordan. 25And they took the two princes of Mĭd'ĭăn, Ōrĕb and Zeēb; they killed Oreb at the rock of Oreb, and Zeeb they killed at the wine press of Zeeb, as they pursued Midian; and they brought the heads of Oreb and Zeeb to Gideon beyond the Jordan.

7.25
Judg 8.3,4;
Ps 83.11;
Isa 10.26

e. *Gideon's trouble with Ephraim*

8 And the men of Ē'phrăĭm said to him, "What is this that you have done to us, not to call us when you went to fight with Mĭd'ĭăn?" And they upbraided him violently. 2And he said to them, "What have I done now in comparison with you? Is not the gleaning of the grapes of Ē'phrăĭm better than the vintage of Ăbĭē'zĕr? 3 God has given into your hands the princes of Mĭd'ĭăn, Ōrĕb and Zeēb; what have I been able to do in comparison with you?" Then their anger against him was abated, when he had said this.

8.1
Judg 12.1

8.3
Judg 7.24,
25

f. *Succoth and Penuel refuse Gideon supplies*

4 And Gideon came to the Jordan and passed over, he and the three hundred men who were with him, faint yet pursuing. 5 So he said to the men of Sŭccŏth, "Pray, give loaves of bread to the people who follow me; for they are faint, and I am pursuing after Zēbáh and Zălmŭn'nă, the kings of Mĭd'ĭăn." 6And the officials of Sŭccŏth said, "Are Zēbáh and Zălmŭn'nă already in your hand, that we should give bread to your army?" 7And Gideon said, "Well then, when the LORD has given Zēbáh and Zălmŭn'nă into my hand, I will flail your flesh with the thorns of the wilderness and with briers." 8And from there he went up to Pĕnū'ĕl, and spoke to them in the same way; and the men of Penuel answered him as the men of Sŭccŏth had answered. 9And he said to the men of Pĕnū'ĕl, "When I come again in peace, I will break down this tower."

8.5
Gen 33.17

8.6
ver 15

8.7
Judg 7.15

8.8
Gen 32.30,
31
8.9
ver 18

g. *The capture of Zebah and Zalmunna*

10 Now Zēbáh and Zălmŭn'nă were in Karkor with their army, about fifteen thousand men, all who were left of all the army of the people of the East; for there had fallen a hundred and twenty thousand men who drew the sword. 11And Gideon went up by the caravan route east of Nōbáh and Jŏg'bĕháh, and attacked the army; for the army was off its guard. 12And Zēbáh and Zălmŭn'nă fled; and he pursued them and took the two kings of Mĭd'ĭăn, Zebah and Zalmunna, and he threw all the army into a panic.

8.12
Ps 83.11

h. *The punishment of Succoth and Penuel*

13 Then Gideon the son of Jō'ăsh returned from the battle by the ascent of Hērĕş. 14And he caught a young man of Sŭccŏth, and questioned him; and he wrote down for him the officials and elders of Succoth, seventy-seven men. 15And he came to the men of Sŭccŏth, and said, "Behold Zēbáh and Zălmŭn'nă, about whom you taunted me, saying, 'Are Zebah and Zalmunna already in your hand, that we should give bread to your men who are faint?'" 16And he took the elders of the city and he took thorns of the wilderness and briers and with them taught the men of Sŭccŏth. 17And he broke down the tower of Pĕnū'ĕl, and slew the men of the city.

8.15
ver 6

8.16
ver 7

8.17
ver 9

i. *The death of Zebah and Zalmunna*

8.18
Judg 4.6

18 Then he said to Zēbáh and Zälmùn′ná, "Where are the men whom you slew at Tābòr?" They answered, "As you are, so were they, every one of them; they resembled the sons of a king." ¹⁹And he said, "They were my brothers, the sons of my mother; as the LORD lives, if you had saved them alive, I would not slay you." ²⁰And he said to Jēthèr his first-born, "Rise, and slay them." But the youth did not draw his sword; for he was afraid, because

8.21
Ps 83.11;
ver 26

he was still a youth. 21 Then Zēbáh and Zälmùn′ná said, "Rise yourself, and fall upon us; for as the man is, so is his strength." And Gideon arose and slew Zebah and Zalmunna; and he took the crescents that were on the necks of their camels.

7. *Gideon refuses the kingship and makes an ephod*

8.23
1 Sam 8.7;
10.19;
12.12

22 Then the men of Israel said to Gideon, "Rule over us, you and your son and your grandson also; for you have delivered us out of the hand of Mĭd′ĭán." 23 Gideon said to them, "I will not rule over you, and my son will not rule over you; the LORD will rule over you." ²⁴And Gideon said to them, "Let me make a request of you; give me every man of you the earrings of his spoil." (For they had golden earrings, because they were Ish′mäèlītes.) ²⁵And they answered, "We will willingly give them." And they spread a garment, and every man cast in it the earrings of his spoil. ²⁶And the weight of the golden earrings that he requested was one thousand seven hundred shekels of gold; besides the crescents and the pendants and the purple garments worn by the kings of Mĭd′ĭán, and besides the collars that were about the necks of their camels.

*8.27
Judg 17.5;
Ps 106.39;
Deut 7.16
8.28
Judg 5.31

²⁷And Gideon made an ephod of it and put it in his city, in Ōphráh; and all Israel played the harlot after it there, and it became a snare to Gideon and to his family. 28 So Mĭd′ĭán was subdued before the people of Israel, and they lifted up their heads no more. And the land had rest forty years in the days of Gideon.

8. *Gideon's death*

8.29
Judg 7.1
8.30
Judg 9.2,5
8.31
Judg 9.1

29 Jĕrúbbā′ál the son of Jō′ásh went and dwelt in his own house. ³⁰ Now Gideon had seventy sons, his own offspring, for he had many wives. ³¹And his concubine who was in Shĕçhèm also bore him a son, and he called his name Åbĭm′èlèçh. ³²And Gideon the son of Jō′ásh died in a good old age, and was buried in the tomb of Joash his father, at Ōphráh of the Åbĭĕz′rītes.

9. *Israel's apostasy after Gideon's death*

*8.33
Judg 2.17,
19; 9.4,46
8.34
Judg 3.7;
Deut 4.9

33 As soon as Gideon died, the people of Israel turned again and played the harlot after the Bääls, and made Bā′ál-bē′rīth their god. ³⁴And the people of Israel did not remember the LORD their God, who had rescued them from the hand of all their enemies on every side; 35 and they did not show kindness to the family of Jĕrúbbā′ál (that is, Gideon) in return for all the good that he had done to Israel.

8.27 *ephod* here does not seem to be the usual priestly garment of white linen, but rather some kind of image or idol made out of the spoil of battle. This ephod was "set up" in the city and became a center of idolatrous worship. It became *a snare to Gideon and to his family*.

8.33 *Baal-berith,* "Baal (Lord) of the Covenant," was the god worshiped by the Canaanites at Shechem and elsewhere. In 9.46 he is called *El-berith,* "God of the Covenant." Excavators have found ruins of a temple to this god (see 9.4).

J. Abimelech the son of Gideon

1. *He murders seventy of his brothers and becomes king of Shechem*

9 Now Åbǐm'ẹ̆lẹ̆ch the son of Jĕrǔbbā'ȧl went to Shẹ̆chẹ̆m to his mother's kinsmen and said to them and to the whole clan of his mother's family, ² "Say in the ears of all the citizens of Shẹ̆chẹ̆m, 'Which is better for you, that all seventy of the sons of Jĕrǔbbā'ȧl rule over you, or that one rule over you?' Remember also that I am your bone and your flesh." ³And his mother's kinsmen spoke all these words on his behalf in the ears of all the men of Shẹ̆chẹ̆m; and their hearts inclined to follow Åbǐm'ẹ̆lẹ̆ch, for they said, "He is our brother." ⁴And they gave him seventy pieces of silver out of the house of Bā'ȧl-bē'rǐth with which Åbǐm'ẹ̆lẹ̆ch hired worthless and reckless fellows, who followed him. ⁵And he went to his father's house at Ōphrȧh, and slew his brothers the sons of Jĕrǔbbā'ȧl, seventy men, upon one stone; but Jōthȧm the youngest son of Jerubbaal was left, for he hid himself. ⁶And all the citizens of Shẹ̆chẹ̆m came together, and all Bĕth-mǐl'lō, and they went and made Åbǐm'ẹ̆lẹ̆ch king, by the oak of the pillar at Shechem.

2. *Jotham's parable of the bramble*

7 When it was told to Jōthȧm, he went and stood on the top of Mount Gĕr'ĭzǐm, and cried aloud and said to them, "Listen to me, you men of Shẹ̆chẹ̆m, that God may listen to you. ⁸ The trees once went forth to anoint a king over them; and they said to the olive tree, 'Reign over us.' ⁹ But the olive tree said to them, 'Shall I leave my fatness, by which gods and men are honored, and go to sway over the trees?' ¹⁰And the trees said to the fig tree, 'Come you, and reign over us.' ¹¹ But the fig tree said to them, 'Shall I leave my sweetness and my good fruit, and go to sway over the trees?' ¹²And the trees said to the vine, 'Come you, and reign over us.' ¹³ But the vine said to them, 'Shall I leave my wine which cheers gods and men, and go to sway over the trees?' ¹⁴ Then all the trees said to the bramble, 'Come you, and reign over us.' ¹⁵And the bramble said to the trees, 'If in good faith you are anointing me king over you, then come and take refuge in my shade; but if not, let fire come out of the bramble and devour the cedars of Lebanon.'

3. *The application of the parable*

16 "Now therefore, if you acted in good faith and honor when you made Åbǐm'ẹ̆lẹ̆ch king, and if you have dealt well with Jĕrǔbbā'ȧl and his house, and have done to him as his deeds deserved — ¹⁷ for my father fought for you, and risked his life, and rescued you from the hand of Mǐd'ĭȧn; ¹⁸ and you have risen up against my father's house this day, and have slain his sons, seventy men on one stone, and have made Åbǐm'ẹ̆lẹ̆ch, the son of his maidservant, king over the citizens of Shẹ̆chẹ̆m, because he is your kinsman— ¹⁹ if you then have acted in good faith and honor with Jĕrǔbbā'ȧl and with his house this day, then rejoice in Åbǐm'ẹ̆lẹ̆ch, and let him also rejoice in you; ²⁰ but if not, let fire come out from Åbǐm'-ẹ̆lẹ̆ch, and devour the citizens of Shẹ̆chẹ̆m, and Bĕth-mǐl'lō; and let fire come out from the citizens of Shechem, and from Beth-

9.1
Judg 8.31

9.2
Judg 8.30;
Gen 29.14

9.4
Judg 8.33

9.5
ver 2

9.7
Deut 11.29;
27.12;
Jn 4.20

9.15
Isa 30.2;
ver 20

9.16
Judg 8.35

9.18
ver 5,6;
Judg 8.31

9.19
Judg 8.35

millo, and devour Abimelech." ²¹And Jōthȧm ran away and fled,
and went to Beër and dwelt there, for fear of Àbĭm'ĕlĕçh his
brother.

4. *Discord between Abimelech and Shechem*

9.23
1 Sam
16.14;
18.9,10
9.24
ver 56,57;
Deut 27.25;
Num 35.33

22 Àbĭm'ĕlĕçh ruled over Israel three years. ²³And God sent an
evil spirit between Àbĭm'ĕlĕçh and the men of Shĕçhĕm; and the
men of Shechem dealt treacherously with Abimelech; ²⁴ that the
violence done to the seventy sons of Jĕrŭbbā'ȧl might come and
their blood be laid upon Àbĭm'ĕlĕçh their brother, who slew them,
and upon the men of Shĕçhĕm, who strengthened his hands to
slay his brothers. ²⁵And the men of Shĕçhĕm put men in ambush
against him on the mountain tops, and they robbed all who passed
by them along that way; and it was told Àbĭm'ĕlĕçh.

5. *The revolt of Gaal*

9.27
Judg 8.33

26 And Gāȧl the son of Ēbĕd moved into Shĕçhĕm with his
kinsmen; and the men of Shechem put confidence in him. ²⁷And
they went out into the field, and gathered the grapes from their
vineyards and trod them, and held festival, and went into the house
of their god, and ate and drank and reviled Abĭm'ĕlĕçh. ²⁸And

9.28
Gen 34.2,6

Gāȧl the son of Ēbĕd said, "Who is Àbĭm'ĕlĕçh, and who are we
of Shĕçhĕm, that we should serve him? Did not the son of Jĕrŭbbā'ȧl and Zēbŭl his officer serve the men of Hāmor the father of
Shechem? Why then should we serve him? ²⁹ Would that this

9.29
2 Sam 15.4

people were under my hand! then I would remove Àbĭm'ĕlĕçh.
I would say*l* to Abimelech, 'Increase your army, and come out.' "

6. *Abimelech informed of Gaal's treachery*

30 When Zēbŭl the ruler of the city heard the words of Gāȧl the
son of Ēbĕd, his anger was kindled. ³¹And he sent messengers to
Àbĭm'ĕlĕçh at Àru'mȧh,*m* saying, "Behold, Gāȧl the son of Ēbĕd
and his kinsmen have come to Shĕçhĕm, and they are stirring
up*n* the city against you. ³² Now therefore, go by night, you and
the men that are with you, and lie in wait in the fields. ³³ Then in

9.33
1 Sam 10.7

the morning, as soon as the sun is up, rise early and rush upon the
city; and when he and the men that are with him come out against
you, you may do to them as occasion offers."

7. *Abimelech quells Gaal's revolt*

34 And Àbĭm'ĕlĕçh and all the men that were with him rose up
by night, and laid wait against Shĕçhĕm in four companies. ³⁵And
Gāȧl the son of Ēbĕd went out and stood in the entrance of the
gate of the city; and Àbĭm'ĕlĕçh and the men that were with him
rose from the ambush. ³⁶And when Gāȧl saw the men, he said to
Zēbŭl, "Look, men are coming down from the mountain tops!"
And Zebul said to him, "You see the shadow of the mountains as

9.37
Ezek 38.12

if they were men." ³⁷ Gāȧl spoke again and said, "Look, men are
coming down from the center of the land, and one company is
coming from the direction of the Diviners' Oak." ³⁸ Then Zēbŭl

9.38
ver 28,29

said to him, "Where is your mouth now, you who said, 'Who is
Àbĭm'ĕlĕçh, that we should serve him?' Are not these the men
whom you despised? Go out now and fight with them." ³⁹And

9.39
Gen 35.4

Gāȧl went out at the head of the men of Shĕçhĕm, and fought with

l Gk: Heb *and he said*   *m* Cn See 9.41. Heb *Tormah*   *n* Cn: Heb *besieging*

Åbĭm′ĕlĕçh. 40And Åbĭm′ĕlĕçh chased him, and he fled before
him; and many fell wounded, up to the entrance of the gate. 41And
Åbĭm′ĕlĕçh dwelt at Åru′mäh; and Zēbŭl drove out Gāäl and his
kinsmen, so that they could not live on at Shĕçhĕm.

8. *Abimelech razes Shechem*

42 On the following day the men went out into the fields. And
Åbĭm′ĕlĕçh was told. 43 He took his men and divided them into
three companies, and laid wait in the fields; and he looked and
saw the men coming out of the city, and he rose against them and
slew them. 44Åbĭm′ĕlĕçh and the company° that was with him
rushed forward and stood at the entrance of the gate of the city,
while the two companies rushed upon all who were in the fields
and slew them. 45And Åbĭm′ĕlĕçh fought against the city all that
day; he took the city, and killed the people that were in it; and
he razed the city and sowed it with salt.

9.45
ver 20;
Deut 29.23

9. *The Tower of Shechem burned*

46 When all the people of the Tower of Shĕçhĕm heard of it,
they entered the stronghold of the house of Ĕl-bē′rĭth. 47Åbĭm′-
ĕlĕçh was told that all the people of the Tower of Shĕçhĕm were
gathered together. 48And Åbĭm′ĕlĕçh went up to Mount Zălmŏn,
he and all the men that were with him; and Abimelech took an axe
in his hand, and cut down a bundle of brushwood, and took it up
and laid it on his shoulder. And he said to the men that were with
him, "What you have seen me do, make haste to do, as I have
done." 49 So every one of the people cut down his bundle and
following Åbĭm′ĕlĕçh put it against the stronghold, and they set
the stronghold on fire over them, so that all the people of the
Tower of Shĕçhĕm also died, about a thousand men and women.

9.46
Judg 8.33

9.48
Ps 68.14

10. *Abimelech's death*

50 Then Åbĭm′ĕlĕçh went to Thĕbĕz, and encamped against
Thebez, and took it. 51 But there was a strong tower within the
city, and all the people of the city fled to it, all the men and women,
and shut themselves in; and they went to the roof of the tower.
52And Åbĭm′ĕlĕçh came to the tower, and fought against it, and
drew near to the door of the tower to burn it with fire. 53And a
certain woman threw an upper millstone upon Åbĭm′ĕlĕçh's head,
and crushed his skull. 54 Then he called hastily to the young man
his armor-bearer, and said to him, "Draw your sword and kill me,
lest men say of me, 'A woman killed him.'" And his young man
thrust him through, and he died. 55And when the men of Israel
saw that Åbĭm′ĕlĕçh was dead, they departed every man to his
home. 56 Thus God requited the crime of Åbĭm′ĕlĕçh, which he
committed against his father in killing his seventy brothers; 57 and
God also made all the wickedness of the men of Shĕçhĕm fall back
upon their heads, and upon them came the curse of Jŏthăm the son
of Jĕrŭbbā′ăl.

9.50
2 Sam 11.21

9.53
ver 50

9.56
ver 24;
Ps 94.23
9.57
ver 20

K. *The judgeship of Tola*

10 After Åbĭm′ĕlĕçh there arose to deliver Israel Tōlä the
son of Pūäh, son of Dōdō, a man of Ĭs′säçhar; and he lived

10.1
Judg 2.16

° Vg and some Mss of Gk: Heb *companies*

at Shāmĭr in the hill country of Ē'phräĭm. 2And he judged Israel twenty-three years. Then he died, and was buried at Shāmĭr.

L. The judgeship of Jair

3 After him arose Jāĭr the Gĭl'ëädīte, who judged Israel twenty-two years. 4And he had thirty sons who rode on thirty asses; and they had thirty cities, called Hăvvŏth-jā'ĭr to this day, which are in the land of Gĭl'ëäd. 5And Jāĭr died, and was buried in Kāmŏn.

M. The judgeship of Jephthah

1. The apostasy and oppression

6 And the people of Israel again did what was evil in the sight of the LORD, and served the Bāălṣ and the Ăsh'tărŏth, the gods of Syria, the gods of Sīdŏn, the gods of Mōăb, the gods of the Ăm'-mŏnītes, and the gods of the Phĭlĭs'tĭneṣ; and they forsook the LORD, and did not serve him. 7And the anger of the LORD was kindled against Israel, and he sold them into the hand of the Phĭlĭs'tĭneṣ and into the hand of the Ăm'mŏnītes, 8 and they crushed and oppressed the children of Israel that year. For eighteen years they oppressed all the people of Israel that were beyond the Jordan in the land of the Ăm'ŏrītes, which is in Gĭl'ëäd. 9And the Ăm'mŏnītes crossed the Jordan to fight also against Judah and against Benjamin and against the house of Ē'phräĭm; so that Israel was sorely distressed.

2. Israel cries to the LORD for deliverance

10 And the people of Israel cried to the LORD, saying, "We have sinned against thee, because we have forsaken our God and have served the Bāălṣ." 11And the LORD said to the people of Israel, "Did I not deliver you from the Egyptians and from the Ăm'ŏrītes, from the Ăm'mŏnītes and from the Phĭlĭs'tĭneṣ? 12 The Sīdŏ'nĭänṣ also, and the Amăl'ékītes, and the Mā'ŏnītes, oppressed you; and you cried to me, and I delivered you out of their hand. 13 Yet you have forsaken me and served other gods; therefore I will deliver you no more. 14 Go and cry to the gods whom you have chosen; let them deliver you in the time of your distress." 15And the people of Israel said to the LORD, "We have sinned; do to us whatever seems good to thee; only deliver us, we pray thee, this day." 16 So they put away the foreign gods from among them and served the LORD; and he became indignant over the misery of Israel.

17 Then the Am'mŏnītes were called to arms, and they encamped in Gĭl'ëäd; and the people of Israel came together, and they encamped at Mĭzpäh. 18And the people, the leaders of Gĭl'-ëäd, said one to another, "Who is the man that will begin to fight against the Ăm'mŏnītes? He shall be head over all the inhabitants of Gilead."

3. Jephthah's background

11 Now Jĕphthăh the Gĭl'ëädīte was a mighty warrior, but he was the son of a harlot. Gĭl'ëäd was the father of Jephthah. 2And Gĭl'ëäd'ṣ wife also bore him sons; and when his wife's sons grew up, they thrust Jĕphthăh out, and said to him, "You shall not inherit in our father's house; for you are the son of

---

Marginal references (left column):

10.4
Num 32.41

10.6
Judg 2.11–13;
Deut 31.16,
17; 32.15

10.7
Judg 2.14

10.10
1 Sam 12.10

10.11
Ex 14.30;
Num 21.21;
24.25;
Judg 3.12,
13,31

10.12
Judg 5.19;
Ps 106.42,
43

10.14
Deut 32.37

10.15
1 Sam 3.18

10.16
Josh 24.23;
Jer 18.7,8;
Deut 32.36;
Ps 106.44,
45

10.17
Judg 11.29

10.18
Judg 11.8,
11

11.1
Heb 11.32

another woman." ³ Then Jĕphtháh fled from his brothers, and
dwelt in the land of Tŏb; and worthless fellows collected round
Jephthah, and went raiding with him.

11.3
2 Sam 10.6,
8

4. Israel appeals to Jephthah for deliverance

4 After a time the Ăm′mŏnītes made war against Israel. ⁵And
when the Ăm′mŏnītes made war against Israel, the elders of
Gĭl′ëád went to bring Jĕphtháh from the land of Tŏb; ⁶ and they
said to Jĕphtháh, "Come and be our leader, that we may fight
with the Ăm′mŏnītes." ⁷ But Jĕphtháh said to the elders of Gĭl′-
ëád, "Did you not hate me, and drive me out of my father's house?
Why have you come to me now when you are in trouble?" ⁸And
the elders of Gĭl′ëád said to Jĕphtháh, "That is why we have
turned to you now, that you may go with us and fight with the
Ăm′mŏnītes, and be our head over all the inhabitants of Gilead."
⁹ Jĕphtháh said to the elders of Gĭl′ëád, "If you bring me home
again to fight with the Ăm′mŏnītes, and the LORD gives them over
to me, I will be your head." ¹⁰And the elders of Gĭl′ëád said to
Jĕphtháh, "The LORD will be witness between us; we will surely
do as you say." ¹¹ So Jĕphtháh went with the elders of Gĭl′ëád,
and the people made him head and leader over them; and Jephthah spoke all his words before the LORD at Mĭzpáh.

11.4
Judg 10.9,
17

11.8
Judg 10.18

11.10
Jer 42.5

11.11
ver 8;
Judg 10.17

5. The Ammonites want East Canaan

12 Then Jĕphtháh sent messengers to the king of the Ăm′-
mŏnītes and said, "What have you against me, that you have come
to me to fight against my land?" ¹³And the king of the Ăm′mŏnītes
answered the messengers of Jĕphtháh, "Because Israel on coming
from Egypt took away my land, from the Arnón to the Jăbbók and
to the Jordan; now therefore restore it peaceably." ¹⁴And Jĕphtháh
sent messengers again to the king of the Ăm′mŏnītes ¹⁵ and said
to him, "Thus says Jĕphtháh: Israel did not take away the land of
Mŏăb or the land of the Ăm′mŏnītes, ¹⁶ but when they came up
from Egypt, Israel went through the wilderness to the Red Sea
and came to Kādĕsh. ¹⁷ Israel then sent messengers to the king
of Ēdóm, saying, 'Let us pass, we pray, through your land'; but
the king of Edom would not listen. And they sent also to the king
of Mŏăb, but he would not consent. So Israel remained at Kādĕsh.
¹⁸ Then they journeyed through the wilderness, and went around
the land of Ēdóm and the land of Mŏăb, and arrived on the east
side of the land of Moab, and camped on the other side of the
Arnón; but they did not enter the territory of Moab, for the Arnon
was the boundary of Moab. ¹⁹ Israel then sent messengers to
Sĭhón king of the Ăm′orītes, king of Hĕshbón; and Israel said to
him, 'Let us pass, we pray, through your land to our country.'
20 But Sĭhón did not trust Israel to pass through his territory; so
Sihon gathered all his people together, and encamped at Jāhăz,
and fought with Israel. ²¹And the LORD, the God of Israel, gave
Sĭhón and all his people into the hand of Israel, and they defeated
them; so Israel took possession of all the land of the Ăm′orītes,
who inhabited that country. ²²And they took possession of all the
territory of the Ăm′orītes from the Arnón to the Jăbbók and from
the wilderness to the Jordan. ²³ So then the LORD, the God of
Israel, dispossessed the Ăm′orītes from before his people Israel;
and are you to take possession of them? ²⁴ Will you not possess

11.13
Num
21.24–26

11.15
Deut 2.9,19

11.16
Num 14.25;
20.1,14–21

11.18
Num 21.4;
Deut 2.1–9,
18,19

11.19
Num 21.21,
22;
Deut 2.26,
27
11.20
Num 21.23;
Deut 2.32
11.21
Num 21.24,
25;
Deut 2.33,
34
11.22
Deut 2.36
11.24
Num 21.29;
1 Ki 11.7;
Josh 3.10

what Chĕmŏsh your god gives you to possess? And all that the LORD our God has dispossessed before us, we will possess. 25 Now are you any better than Bālăk the son of Zĭppor, king of Mōăb? Did he ever strive against Israel, or did he ever go to war with them? 26 While Israel dwelt in Hĕshbŏn and its villages, and in Arŏ′ĕr and its villages, and in all the cities that are on the banks of the Arnŏn, three hundred years, why did you not recover them within that time? 27 I therefore have not sinned against you, and you do me wrong by making war on me; the LORD, the Judge, decide this day between the people of Israel and the people of Ămmŏn." 28 But the king of the Ăm′mŏnītes did not heed the message of Jĕphthăh which he sent to him.

6. *Jephthah's vow: defeat of the Ammonites*

29 Then the Spirit of the LORD came upon Jĕphthăh, and he passed through Gĭl′ĕăd and Mănăs′sĕh, and passed on to Mĭzpăh of Gilead, and from Mizpah of Gilead he passed on to the Ăm′-mŏnītes. 30And Jĕphthăh made a vow to the LORD, and said, "If thou wilt give the Ăm′mŏnītes into my hand, 31 then whoever comes forth from the doors of my house to meet me, when I return victorious from the Ăm′mŏnītes, shall be the LORD'S, and I will offer him up for a burnt offering." 32 So Jĕphthăh crossed over to the Ăm′mŏnītes to fight against them; and the LORD gave them into his hand. 33And he smote them from Arŏ′ĕr to the neighborhood of Mĭnnĭth, twenty cities, and as far as Ā′bĕl-kĕr′ămĭm, with a very great slaughter. So the Ăm′mŏnītes were subdued before the people of Israel.

7. *Jephthah fulfils his vow*

34 Then Jĕphthăh came to his home at Mĭzpăh; and behold, his daughter came out to meet him with timbrels and with dances; she was his only child; beside her he had neither son nor daughter. 35And when he saw her, he rent his clothes, and said, "Alas, my daughter! you have brought me very low, and you have become the cause of great trouble to me; for I have opened my mouth to the LORD, and I cannot take back my vow." 36And she said to him, "My father, if you have opened your mouth to the LORD, do to me according to what has gone forth from your mouth, now that the LORD has avenged you on your enemies, on the Ăm′-mŏnītes." 37And she said to her father, "Let this thing be done for me; let me alone two months, that I may go and wander*p* on the mountains, and bewail my virginity, I and my companions." 38And he said, "Go." And he sent her away for two months; and she departed, she and her companions, and bewailed her virginity

p Cn: Heb *go down*

Marginal references:

11.25 Num 22.2; Josh 24.9

*11.26 Num 21.25; Deut 2.36

11.27 Gen 16.5; 18.25; 31.53; 1 Sam 24.12,15

11.29 Judg 3.10

*11.30f

11.33 Ezek 27.17

11.34 Judg 10.17; Ex 15.20; 1 Sam 18.6; Jer 31.4

11.35 Num 30.2; Ecc 5.2,4,5

11.36 Num 30.2; 2 Sam 18.19,31; Lk 1.38

11.26 *three hundred years.* Probably a round number for the 319 years noted thus far in the period of the judges. However, it may be that some of these judges were ruling concurrently.

11.30, 31 Jephthah vowed that if God delivered the children of Ammon into his hands he would offer up a sacrifice. Whether he meant by this a human sacrifice or a living and unbloody sacrifice has been the subject of much discussion. The term '*olah* used here means "whole burnt offering." Unless the meaning of the word is changed, Jephthah very likely offered his daughter as a human sacrifice. If this is true, it does not mean that it was right for him to do so, but Jephthah's rough background may account for his lack of spiritual discernment (cf. 11.1-3).

upon the mountains. 39And at the end of two months, she returned
to her father, who did with her according to his vow which he had
made. She had never known a man. And it became a custom in
Israel 40 that the daughters of Israel went year by year to lament
the daughter of Jĕphthăh the Gĭl′ĕădīte four days in the year.

*11.39

8. *Jephthah's quarrel with Ephraim: Shibboleth or Sibboleth*

12 The men of Ē′phrăịm were called to arms, and they
crossed to Zāphòn and said to Jĕphthăh, "Why did you
cross over to fight against the Ăm′mŏnītes, and did not call us to
go with you? We will burn your house over you with fire." 2And
Jĕphthăh said to them, "I and my people had a great feud with
the Ăm′mŏnītes; and when I called you, you did not deliver me
from their hand. 3And when I saw that you would not deliver me,
I took my life in my hand, and crossed over against the Ăm′-
mŏnītes, and the LORD gave them into my hand; why then have
you come up to me this day, to fight against me?" 4 Then Jĕphthăh
gathered all the men of Gĭl′ĕăd and fought with Ē′phrăịm; and
the men of Gilead smote Ēphraịm, because they said, "You are
fugitives of Ephraim, you Gĭl′ĕădītes, in the midst of Ephraim and
Mănăs′sĕh." 5And the Gĭl′ĕădītes took the fords of the Jordan
against the Ē′phrăịmītes. And when any of the fugitives of Ē′-
phrăịm said, "Let me go over," the men of Gĭl′ĕăd said to him,
"Are you an Ē′phrăịmīte?" When he said, "No," 6 they said to
him, "Then say Shĭb′bŏlĕth," and he said, "Sĭb′bŏlĕth," for he
could not pronounce it right; then they seized him and slew him at
the fords of the Jordan. And there fell at that time forty-two
thousand of the Ē′phrăịmītes.

12.1
Judg 8.1

12.3
1 Sam 19.5;
28.21;
Job 13.14

12.4
Judg 3.28;
7.24

12.5
Judg 3.28;
7.24;
Josh 22.11

7 Jĕphthăh judged Israel six years. Then Jephthah the Gĭl′-
ĕădīte died, and was buried in his city in Gĭl′ĕăd.q

12.7
Heb 11.32

N. *The judgeship of Ibzan*

8 After him Ĭbzăn of Bĕth′lĕhĕm judged Israel. 9 He had thirty
sons; and thirty daughters he gave in marriage outside his clan,
and thirty daughters he brought in from outside for his sons. And
he judged Israel seven years. 10 Then Ĭbzăn died, and was buried
at Bĕth′lĕhĕm.

O. *The judgeship of Elon*

11 After him Ēlòn the Zĕb′ụlùnīte judged Israel; and he judged
Israel ten years. 12 Then Ēlòn the Zĕb′ụlùnīte died, and was buried
at Āī′jàlòn in the land of Zĕb′ụlùn.

P. *The judgeship of Abdon*

13 After him Ăbdòn the son of Hĭllĕl the Pĭrā′thŏnīte judged
Israel. 14 He had forty sons and thirty grandsons, who rode on
seventy asses; and he judged Israel eight years. 15 Then Ăbdòn the
son of Hĭllĕl the Pĭrā′thŏnīte died, and was buried at Pĭr′àthòn in
the land of Ē′phrăịm, in the hill country of the Ămăl′ĕkītes.

12.14
Judg 5.10;
10.4

q Gk: Heb *in the cities of Gilead*

11.39 *custom in Israel.* This annual four-
day feast of lamentation is never mentioned
again in Scripture. Apparently it was observed
only in Gilead.

Q. The judgeship of Samson

1. Israel's apostasy and servitude

*13.1
Judg 2.11;
1 Sam 12.9

13 And the people of Israel again did what was evil in the sight of the LORD; and the LORD gave them into the hand of the Philis'tines for forty years.

2. The backgrounds of Samson
a. The promise to Manoah and his wife

13.2
Josh 19.41

13.3
ver 6,8,10;
Judg 6.12
13.4
ver 14;
Num 6.2,3
*13.5
Lk 1.15;
Num 6.2,5

*13.6
1 Sam 2.27;
Mt 28.3;
ver 17,18

2 And there was a certain man of Zorah, of the tribe of the Danites, whose name was Mano'ah; and his wife was barren and had no children. 3And the angel of the LORD appeared to the woman and said to her, "Behold, you are barren and have no children; but you shall conceive and bear a son. 4 Therefore beware, and drink no wine or strong drink, and eat nothing unclean, 5 for lo, you shall conceive and bear a son. No razor shall come upon his head, for the boy shall be a Naz'irite to God from birth; and he shall begin to deliver Israel from the hand of the Philis'tines." 6 Then the woman came and told her husband, "A man of God came to me, and his countenance was like the countenance of the angel of God, very terrible; I did not ask him whence he was, and he did not tell me his name; 7 but he said to me, 'Behold, you shall conceive and bear a son; so then drink no wine or strong drink, and eat nothing unclean, for the boy shall be a Naz'irite to God from birth to the day of his death.'"

b. Manoah and the angel of the LORD

13.8
ver 3,7

8 Then Mano'ah entreated the LORD, and said, "O LORD, I pray thee, let the man of God whom thou didst send come again to us, and teach us what we are to do with the boy that will be born." 9And God listened to the voice of Mano'ah, and the angel of God came again to the woman as she sat in the field; but Manoah her husband was not with her. 10And the woman ran in haste and told her husband, "Behold, the man who came to me the other day has appeared to me." 11And Mano'ah arose and went after his wife, and came to the man and said to him, "Are you the man who spoke to this woman?" And he said, "I am." 12And Mano'ah said, "Now when your words come true, what is to be the boy's manner of life, and what is he to do?" 13And the angel of the LORD said to Mano'ah, "Of all that I said to the woman let her beware. 14 She may not eat of anything that comes from the vine, neither let her

13.13
ver 4,11
13.14
Num 6.4

13.1 *Philistines.* According to Deut 2.23, Amos 9.7, and Jer 47.4, the Philistines came from Caphtor, the island of Crete. They were part of the sea peoples who, having been repulsed by Egypt, settled along the coast of Canaan about 1200 B.C. At that time they began to infiltrate the foothills of Dan and Judah. Deliverance under Samson was far from permanent, because the Philistines plagued the Israelites until David's time. (See also note to 14.4 describing Israel's deliverance under Samson.)

13.5 A Nazirite was a person consecrated to God by a special vow and could be either male or female (Num 6.2). In the cases of Samson and John the Baptist they were Nazirites from the womb or before birth

(13.5; Lk 1.15). Certain prohibitions governed those who were Nazirites and among them were: (1) avoidance of wine or strong drink (Num 6.3; Lk 1.15); (2) avoidance of contact with the dead (Num 6.6, 7); (3) no shaving of the head (Num 6.5; Judg 13.5; 16.17); (4) no contact with grapes or any product of the vine (Num 6.3, 4; Judg 13.14). These prohibitions lasted as long as the vow was in force. When the term of the vow ended, the individual was brought to the tabernacle door, his head was shaved, sacrifices were offered, and the left shoulder of a ram was presented by the priest as a wave-offering (Num 6.13–20; Acts 18.18; 21.24; Lev 7.32).

13.6 *terrible*, that is, inspiring awe and reverence.

drink wine or strong drink, or eat any unclean thing; all that I commanded her let her observe."

15 Mánō'áh said to the angel of the LORD, "Pray, let us detain you, and prepare a kid for you." ¹⁶And the angel of the LORD said to Mánō'áh, "If you detain me, I will not eat of your food; but if you make ready a burnt offering, then offer it to the LORD." (For Manaoh did not know that he was the angel of the LORD.) ¹⁷And Mánō'áh said to the angel of the LORD, "What is your name, so that, when your words come true, we may honor you?" ¹⁸And the angel of the LORD said to him, "Why do you ask my name, seeing it is wonderful?" ¹⁹ So Mánō'áh took the kid with the cereal offering, and offered it upon the rock to the LORD, to him who works⁷ wonders.⁵ ²⁰And when the flame went up toward heaven from the altar, the angel of the LORD ascended in the flame of the altar while Mánō'áh and his wife looked on; and they fell on their faces to the ground.

c. The birth of Samson

21 The angel of the LORD appeared no more to Mánō'áh and to his wife. Then Manoah knew that he was the angel of the LORD. ²²And Mánō'áh said to his wife, "We shall surely die, for we have seen God." ²³ But his wife said to him, "If the LORD had meant to kill us, he would not have accepted a burnt offering and a cereal offering at our hands, or shown us all these things, or now announced to us such things as these." ²⁴And the woman bore a son, and called his name Sămsón; and the boy grew, and the LORD blessed him. ²⁵And the Spirit of the LORD began to stir him in Mā'hánĕh-dăn', between Zoráh and Ésh'tä-ól.

3. Samson's marriage to the woman of Timnah
a. Samson falls in love

14 Sămsón went down to Tìmnáh, and at Timnah he saw one of the daughters of the Philis'tines. ² Then he came up, and told his father and mother, "I saw one of the daughters of the Philis'tines at Timnàh; now get her for me as my wife." ³ But his father and mother said to him, "Is there not a woman among the daughters of your kinsmen, or among all our people, that you must go to take a wife from the uncircumcised Philis'tines?" But Sămsón said to his father, "Get her for me; for she pleases me well."

4 His father and mother did not know that it was from the LORD;

Side references:
13.15 ver 3
13.16 Judg 6.20
13.17 Gen 32.29
*13.18 Isa 9.6
13.19 Judg 6.20, 21
13.20 Lev 9.24
13.21 ver 16
13.22 Judg 6.22; Deut 5.26
*13.24 Heb 11.32; 1 Sam 3.19
13.25 Judg 3.10; 18.11
14.2 Gen 21.21; 34.4
*14.4 Josh 11.20; Judg 13.1

⁷ Gk Vg: Heb *and working* ⁵ Heb *wonders, while Manoah and his wife looked on*

13.18 *wonderful*, that is, beyond knowledge, ineffable (see Ps 139.6).
13.24 Samson succumbed to various carnal desires. Beginning with everything in his favor (he was a Nazirite, his birth was foretold by an angel, and he was separated from sin), he backslid until he was captured and rendered sightless. His life illustrates the truth that small sins lead to big ones and that a stubborn insistence upon one's own will (cf. 14.3) leads ultimately to a ruined life. One of the most pathetic verses of Scripture is Judg 16.20. However, Samson repented before he died (16.28), and his name is mentioned in Hebrews 11.32 as one who gave his life to vindicate God before the blasphemous heathen. Despite his carnal life he had great faith in God and this faith justified him.

14.4 Scripture here illustrates the truth that even the mistaken decisions of those who profess God may be used to accomplish the purposes of God. Samson was out of the will of God when he insisted that his parents arrange for his marriage to the Philistine woman from Timnah. It was altogether Samson's own choice. But God used it indirectly to deliver Israel from the Philistines. In no sense, however, did this excuse Samson from his responsibility for his decision.

for he was seeking an occasion against the Phĭlĭs′tĭneș. At that time the Philistines had dominion over Israel.

b. *The slaying of the lion*

5 Then Sămsŏn went down with his father and mother to Tĭm-năh, and he came to the vineyards of Timnah. And behold, a young lion roared against him; 6 and the Spirit of the LORD came mightily upon him, and he tore the lion asunder as one tears a kid; and he had nothing in his hand. But he did not tell his father or his mother what he had done. 7 Then he went down and talked with the woman; and she pleased Sămsŏn well. 8And after a while he returned to take her; and he turned aside to see the carcass of the lion, and behold, there was a swarm of bees in the body of the lion, and honey. 9 He scraped it out into his hands, and went on, eating as he went; and he came to his father and mother, and gave some to them, and they ate. But he did not tell them that he had taken the honey from the carcass of the lion.

c. *Samson's riddle at the wedding feast*

10 And his father went down to the woman, and Sămsŏn made a feast there; for so the young men used to do. 11And when the people saw him, they brought thirty companions to be with him. 12And Sămsŏn said to them, "Let me now put a riddle to you; if you can tell me what it is, within the seven days of the feast, and find it out, then I will give you thirty linen garments and thirty festal garments; 13 but if you cannot tell me what it is, then you shall give me thirty linen garments and thirty festal garments." And they said to him, "Put your riddle, that we may hear it." 14And he said to them,

"Out of the eater came something to eat.
Out of the strong came something sweet."

And they could not in three days tell what the riddle was.

d. *The solution of the riddle: the treachery of Samson's wife*

15 On the fourth*ᵗ* day they said to Sămsŏn′ș wife, "Entice your husband to tell us what the riddle is, lest we burn you and your father's house with fire. Have you invited us here to impoverish us?" 16And Sămsŏn′ș wife wept before him, and said, "You only hate me, you do not love me; you have put a riddle to my country-men, and you have not told me what it is." And he said to her, "Behold, I have not told my father nor my mother, and shall I tell you?" 17 She wept before him the seven days that their feast lasted; and on the seventh day he told her, because she pressed him hard. Then she told the riddle to her countrymen. 18And the men of the city said to him on the seventh day before the sun went down,

"What is sweeter than honey?
What is stronger than a lion?"

And he said to them,

"If you had not plowed with my heifer,
you would not have found out my riddle."

19And the Spirit of the LORD came mightily upon him, and he went down to Ăsh′kĕlŏn and killed thirty men of the town, and took their spoil and gave the festal garments to those who had

---

ᵗ Gk Syr: Heb *seventh*

14.6
Judg 3.10;
13.25

14.7
ver 3

14.12
1 Ki 10.2;
Ezek 17.2;
Gen 29.27

14.15
Judg 16.5;
15.6

14.18
ver 14

14.19
Judg 3.10

told the riddle. In hot anger he went back to his father's house.
²⁰And Sämsŏn'ṣ wife was given to his companion, who had been
his best man.

4. The Philistines slay Samson's wife and father-in-law

15 After a while, at the time of wheat harvest, Sämsŏn went
to visit his wife with a kid; and he said, "I will go in to my
wife in the chamber." But her father would not allow him to go
in. ²And her father said, "I really thought that you utterly hated
her; so I gave her to your companion. Is not her younger sister
fairer than she? Pray take her instead." ³And Sämsŏn said to them,
"This time I shall be blameless in regard to the Philĭs'tĭneṣ, when
I do them mischief." ⁴ So Sämsŏn went and caught three hundred
foxes, and took torches; and he turned them tail to tail, and put a
torch between each pair of tails. ⁵And when he had set fire to the
torches, he let the foxes go into the standing grain of the Philĭs'-
tĭneṣ, and burned up the shocks and the standing grain, as well
as the olive orchards. ⁶ Then the Philĭs'tĭneṣ said, "Who has done
this?" And they said, "Sämsŏn, the son-in-law of the Tĭmnĭte,
because he has taken his wife and given her to his companion."
And the Philistines came up, and burned her and her father with
fire. ⁷And Sämsŏn said to them, "If this is what you do, I swear I
will be avenged upon you, and after that I will quit." ⁸And he
smote them hip and thigh with great slaughter; and he went down
and stayed in the cleft of the rock of Ētăm.

5. Samson in the hands of the Philistines
a. Judah delivers him

9 Then the Philĭs'tĭneṣ came up and encamped in Judah, and
made a raid on Lēhī. ¹⁰And the men of Judah said, "Why have
you come up against us?" They said, "We have come up to bind
Sämsŏn, to do to him as he did to us." ¹¹ Then three thousand men
of Judah went down to the cleft of the rock of Ētăm, and said to
Sämsŏn, "Do you not know that the Philĭs'tĭneṣ are rulers over
us? What then is this that you have done to us?" And he said to
them, "As they did to me, so have I done to them." ¹²And they
said to him, "We have come down to bind you, that we may give
you into the hands of the Philĭs'tĭneṣ." And Sämsŏn said to them,
"Swear to me that you will not fall upon me yourselves." ¹³ They
said to him, "No; we will only bind you and give you into their
hands; we will not kill you." So they bound him with two new
ropes, and brought him up from the rock.

b. Samson's vengeance on the Philistines

14 When he came to Lēhī, the Philĭs'tĭneṣ came shouting to
meet him; and the Spirit of the LORD came mightily upon him,
and the ropes which were on his arms became as flax that has
caught fire, and his bonds melted off his hands. ¹⁵And he found
a fresh jawbone of an ass, and put out his hand and seized it, and
with it he slew a thousand men. ¹⁶And Sämsŏn said,

14.20 Judg 15.2; Jn 3.29

15.2 Judg 14.20

15.6 Judg 14.15

15.9 ver 19

15.11 Judg 13.1; 14.4

15.14 Judg 14.19; 1 Sam 11.6

*15.15 Lev 26.8; Josh 23.10; Judg 3.31

15.15 The secret of Samson's strength did not lie in his pledge to refrain from touching strong drink and cutting his hair. Rather it lay in his inner relationship to God, the outward symbols of which were the vows of abstinence to which he solemnly adhered until Delilah tricked him. Samson himself realized that God was the source of his superior strength (ver 18).

"With the jawbone of an ass,
　heaps upon heaps,
　with the jawbone of an ass
　　have I slain a thousand men."

17 When he had finished speaking, he threw away the jawbone out of his hand; and that place was called Rā'māth-lē'hī.[u]

18 And he was very thirsty, and he called on the LORD and said, "Thou hast granted this great deliverance by the hand of thy servant; and shall I now die of thirst, and fall into the hands of the uncircumcised?" 19And God split open the hollow place that is at Lēhī, and there came water from it; and when he drank, his spirit returned, and he revived. Therefore the name of it was called Ĕn-hăk'kŏrē;[v] it is at Lehi to this day. 20And he judged Israel in the days of the Phịlĭs'tĭneṣ twenty years.

6. *Samson and the harlot at Gaza*

16 Sămsȯn went to Gazȧ, and there he saw a harlot, and he went in to her. 2 The Gāzītes were told, "Sămsȯn has come here," and they surrounded the place and lay in wait for him all night at the gate of the city. They kept quiet all night, saying, "Let us wait till the light of the morning; then we will kill him." 3 But Sămsȯn lay till midnight, and at midnight he arose and took hold of the doors of the gate of the city and the two posts, and pulled them up, bar and all, and put them on his shoulders and carried them to the top of the hill that is before Hēbrȯn.

7. *Samson and Delilah*
a. *Delilah seeks the source of Samson's strength*

4 After this he loved a woman in the valley of Sorĕk, whose name was Dĕlī'läh. 5And the lords of the Phịlĭs'tĭneṣ came to her and said to her, "Entice him, and see wherein his great strength lies, and by what means we may overpower him, that we may bind him to subdue him; and we will each give you eleven hundred pieces of silver." 6And Dĕlī'läh said to Sămsȯn, "Please tell me wherein your great strength lies, and how you might be bound, that one could subdue you." 7And Samson said to her, "If they bind me with seven fresh bowstrings which have not been dried, then I shall become weak, and be like any other man." 8 Then the lords of the Phịlĭs'tĭneṣ brought her seven fresh bowstrings which had not been dried, and she bound him with them. 9 Now she had men lying in wait in an inner chamber. And she said to him, "The Phịlĭs'tĭneṣ are upon you, Sămsȯn!" But he snapped the bowstrings, as a string of tow snaps when it touches the fire. So the secret of his strength was not known.

b. *Delilah's second attempt*

10 And Dĕlī'läh said to Sămsȯn, "Behold, you have mocked me, and told me lies; please tell me how you might be bound." 11And he said to her, "If they bind me with new ropes that have not been used, then I shall become weak, and be like any other man." 12 So Dĕlī'läh took new ropes and bound him with them, and said to him, "The Phịlĭs'tĭneṣ are upon you, Sămsȯn!" And the men lying in wait were in an inner chamber. But he snapped the ropes off his arms like a thread.

15.18
Judg 16.28

15.19
Gen 45.27;
Isa 40.29
15.20
Heb 11.32;
Judg 13.1;
16.31

16.2
Ps 118.10–
12

16.5
Judg 14.15

16.10
ver 13,15

---

[u] That is *The hill of the jawbone*　[v] That is *The spring of him who called*

c. *Delilah's third attempt*

13 And Dĕlī'läh said to Sămsŏn, "Until now you have mocked me, and told me lies; tell me how you might be bound." And he said to her, "If you weave the seven locks of my head with the web and make it tight with the pin, then I shall become weak, and be like any other man." 14 So while he slept, Dĕlī'läh took the seven locks of his head and wove them into the web. [w] And she made them tight with the pin, and said to him, "The Phĭlĭs'tĭneṣ are upon you, Sămsŏn!" But he awoke from his sleep, and pulled away the pin, the loom, and the web.

d. *Samson succumbs to Delilah's wiles*

15 And she said to him, "How can you say, 'I love you,' when your heart is not with me? You have mocked me these three times, and you have not told me wherein your great strength lies." 16And when she pressed him hard with her words day after day, and urged him, his soul was vexed to death. 17And he told her all his mind, and said to her, "A razor has never come upon my head; for I have been a Năz'ĭrīte to God from my mother's womb. If I be shaved, then my strength will leave me, and I shall become weak, and be like any other man."

e. *The Philistines seize Samson*

18 When Dĕlī'läh saw that he had told her all his mind, she sent and called the lords of the Phĭlĭs'tĭneṣ, saying, "Come up this once, for he has told me all his mind." Then the lords of the Philistines came up to her, and brought the money in their hands. 19 She made him sleep upon her knees; and she called a man, and had him shave off the seven locks of his head. Then she began to torment him, and his strength left him. 20And she said, "The Phĭlĭs'tĭneṣ are upon you, Sămsŏn!" And he awoke from his sleep, and said, "I will go out as at other times, and shake myself free." And he did not know that the LORD had left him. 21And the Phĭlĭs'tĭneṣ seized him and gouged out his eyes, and brought him down to Gazä, and bound him with bronze fetters; and he ground at the mill in the prison. 22 But the hair of his head began to grow again after it had been shaved.

f. *Samson's final revenge and death*

23 Now the lords of the Phĭlĭs'tĭneṣ gathered to offer a great sacrifice to Dāgŏn their god, and to rejoice; for they said, "Our god has given Sămsŏn our enemy into our hand." 24And when the people saw him, they praised their god; for they said, "Our god has given our enemy into our hand, the ravager of our country, who has slain many of us." 25And when their hearts were merry, they said, "Call Sămsŏn, that he may make sport for us." So they called Samson out of the prison, and he made sport before them. They made him stand between the pillars; 26and Sămsŏn said to the lad who held him by the hand, "Let me feel the pillars on which the house rests, that I may lean against them." 27 Now the house was full of men and women; all the lords of the Phĭlĭs'tĭneṣ were there, and on the roof there were about three thousand men and women, who looked on while Sămsŏn made sport.

28 Then Sămsŏn called to the LORD and said, "O Lord GOD,

w Compare Gk: Heb lacks *and make it tight . . . into the web*

16.13
ver 10,15

16.15
Judg 14.16

16.17
Mic 7.5;
Num 6.5;
Judg 13.5

16.19
Prov 7.26,
27
16.20
Josh 7.12;
1 Sam
16.14;
18.12

16.23
1 Sam 5.2

16.24
Dan 5.4

16.25
Judg 9.27

16.27
Deut 22.8

16.28
Judg 15.18;
Jer 15.15

remember me, I pray thee, and strengthen me, I pray thee, only this once, O God, that I may be avenged upon the Philis'tines for one of my two eyes." 29And Sămsòn grasped the two middle pillars upon which the house rested, and he leaned his weight upon them, his right hand on the one and his left hand on the other. 30And Sămsòn said, "Let me die with the Philis'tines." Then he bowed with all his might; and the house fell upon the lords and upon all the people that were in it. So the dead whom he slew at his death were more than those whom he had slain during his life. 31 Then his brothers and all his family came down and took him and brought him up and buried him between Zorăh and Esh'tä-ól in the tomb of Mảnō'åh his father. He had judged Israel twenty years.

<small>16.31
Judg 15.20</small>

III. The appendices 17.1–21.25

A. Micah the Ephraimite and his priest

1. Micah makes his own idols

17 There was a man of the hill country of Ē'phrȧim, whose name was Mĭcȧh. 2And he said to his mother, "The eleven hundred pieces of silver which were taken from you, about which you uttered a curse, and also spoke it in my ears, behold, the silver is with me; I took it." And his mother said, "Blessed be my son by the LORD." 3And he restored the eleven hundred pieces of silver to his mother; and his mother said, "I consecrate the silver to the LORD from my hand for my son, to make a graven image and a molten image; now therefore I will restore it to you." 4 So when he restored the money to his mother, his mother took two hundred pieces of silver, and gave it to the silversmith, who made it into a graven image and a molten image; and it was in the house of Mĭcȧh. 5And the man Mĭcȧh had a shrine, and he made an ephod and teraphim, and installed one of his sons, who became his priest. 6 In those days there was no king in Israel; every man did what was right in his own eyes.

<small>17.3
Ex 20.4,23;
34.17;
Lev 19.4</small>

<small>17.5
Judg 18.24;
8.27;
18.14;
Gen 31.19</small>

<small>*17.6
Judg 18.1;
19.1;
Deut 12.8</small>

2. Micah hires a Levite as priest

7 Now there was a young man of Bĕth'lĕhĕm in Judah, of the family of Judah, who was a Lēvīte; and he sojourned there. 8And the man departed from the town of Bĕth'lĕhĕm in Judah, to live where he could find a place; and as he journeyed, he came to the hill country of Ē'phrȧim to the house of Mĭcȧh. 9And Mĭcȧh said to him, "From where do you come?" And he said to him, "I am a Lēvīte of Bĕth'lĕhĕm in Judah, and I am going to sojourn where I may find a place." 10And Mĭcȧh said to him, "Stay with me, and be to me a father and a priest, and I will give you ten pieces of silver a year, and a suit of apparel, and your living."w 11And the Lēvīte was content to dwell with the man; and the young man became to him like one of his sons. 12And Mĭcȧh installed the Lēvīte, and the young man became his priest, and was in the house of Micah. 13 Then Mĭcȧh said, "Now I know that the LORD will prosper me, because I have a Lēvīte as priest."

<small>17.7
Judg 19.1;
Ruth 1.1,2;
Mic 5.2;
Mt 2.1</small>

<small>17.10
Judg 18.19</small>

<small>17.12
ver 5;
Judg 13.25</small>

w Heb living, and the Lēvīte went

17.6 no king in Israel. This statement (repeated in 18.1; 19.1; 21.25) is clear indication that The Book of Judges was put in its present form sometime during the monarchy.

3. *The Danite spies: their report*

18 In those days there was no king in Israel. And in those days the tribe of the Dănītes was seeking for itself an inheritance to dwell in; for until then no inheritance among the tribes of Israel had fallen to them. 2 So the Dănītes sent five able men from the whole number of their tribe, from Zoràh and from Ēsh′tä-òl, to spy out the land and to explore it; and they said to them, "Go and explore the land." And they came to the hill country of Ē′phräịm, to the house of Mīcàh, and lodged there. 3 When they were by the house of Mīcàh, they recognized the voice of the young Lēvīte; and they turned aside and said to him, "Who brought you here? What are you doing in this place? What is your business here?" 4And he said to them, "Thus and thus has Mīcàh dealt with me: he has hired me, and I have become his priest." 5And they said to him, "Inquire of God, we pray thee, that we may know whether the journey on which we are setting out will succeed." 6And the priest said to them, "Go in peace. The journey on which you go is under the eye of the Lord."

7 Then the five men departed, and came to Lā′ïsh, and saw the people who were there, how they dwelt in security, after the manner of the Sīdō′nïäns, quiet and unsuspecting, lacking^x nothing that is in the earth, and possessing wealth, and how they were far from the Sidonians and had no dealings with any one. 8And when they came to their brethren at Zoràh and Ēsh′tä-òl, their brethren said to them, "What do you report?" 9 They said, "Arise, and let us go up against them; for we have seen the land, and behold, it is very fertile. And will you do nothing? Do not be slow to go, and enter in and possess the land. 10 When you go, you will come to an unsuspecting people. The land is broad; yea, God has given it into your hands, a place where there is no lack of anything that is in the earth."

11 And six hundred men of the tribe of Dan, armed with weapons of war, set forth from Zoràh and Ēsh′tä-òl, 12 and went up and encamped at Kĭr′ĭäth-jē′àrĭm in Judah. On this account that place is called Mā′hànĕh-dăn′^y to this day; behold, it is west of Kiriath-jearim. 13And they passed on from there to the hill country of Ē′phräịm, and came to the house of Mīcàh.

4. *The Danites take Micah's idols and priest*

14 Then the five men who had gone to spy out the country of Lā′ïsh said to their brethren, "Do you know that in these houses there are an ephod, teraphim, a graven image, and a molten image? Now therefore consider what you will do." 15And they turned aside thither, and came to the house of the young Lēvīte, at the home of Mīcàh, and asked him of his welfare. 16 Now the six hundred men of the Dănītes, armed with their weapons of war, stood by the entrance of the gate; 17 and the five men who had gone to spy out the land went up, and entered and took the graven image, the ephod, the teraphim, and the molten image, while the

^x Cn Compare 18.10. The Hebrew text is uncertain　　^y That is *Camp of Dan*

18.1 no inheritance . . . had fallen to them, that is, they had not been able to conquer the territory assigned (see Josh 19.47 for the Danites capture of Lesham). In the lowlands assigned to Dan were fertile plains occupied by the Amorites who had iron chariots. The tribe of Dan was wanting an all-conquering faith in God. Even if they had had such faith in *any* measure it would have enabled them to overcome their enemies.

Marginal references:
18.1 Judg 17.6; 19.1; Josh 19.47
18.2 Judg 13.25; Josh 2.1; Judg 17.1
18.4 Judg 17.10, 12
18.5 1 Ki 22.5
18.6 1 Ki 22.6
18.7 ver 27,28; Josh 19.47
18.8 ver 2
18.9 Num 13.30; 1 Ki 22.3
18.10 ver 7,27; Deut 8.9
18.12 Judg 13.25
18.13 ver 2
18.14 Judg 17.5
18.16 ver 11
18.17 ver 2,14

priest stood by the entrance of the gate with the six hundred men armed with weapons of war. 18And when these went into Mĭcăh's house and took the graven image, the ephod, the teraphim, and the molten image, the priest said to them, "What are you doing?" 19And they said to him, "Keep quiet, put your hand upon your mouth, and come with us, and be to us a father and a priest. Is it better for you to be priest to the house of one man, or to be priest to a tribe and family in Israel?" 20And the priest's heart was glad; he took the ephod, and the teraphim, and the graven image, and went in the midst of the people.

5. *Micah's failure to recover his idols*

21 So they turned and departed, putting the little ones and the cattle and the goods in front of them. 22 When they were a good way from the home of Mĭcăh, the men who were in the houses near Mĭcăh's house were called out, and they overtook the Dănĭtes. 23And they shouted to the Dănĭtes, who turned round and said to Mĭcăh, "What ails you that you come with such a company?" 24And he said, "You take my gods which I made, and the priest, and go away, and what have I left? How then do you ask me, 'What ails you?'" 25And the Dănĭtes said to him, "Do not let your voice be heard among us, lest angry fellows fall upon you, and you lose your life with the lives of your household." 26 Then the Dănĭtes went their way; and when Mĭcăh saw that they were too strong for him, he turned and went back to his home.

6. *The Danites burn Laish and rebuild it*

27 And taking what Mĭcăh had made, and the priest who belonged to him, the Dănĭtes came to Lā'ĭsh, to a people quiet and unsuspecting, and smote them with the edge of the sword, and burned the city with fire. 28And there was no deliverer because it was far from Sĭdŏn, and they had no dealings with any one. It was in the valley which belongs to Bĕth-rē'hŏb. And they rebuilt the city, and dwelt in it. 29And they named the city Dan, after the name of Dan their ancestor, who was born to Israel; but the name of the city was Lā'ĭsh at the first. 30And the Dănĭtes set up the graven image for themselves; and Jonathan the son of Gĕrshŏm, son of Moses,z and his sons were priests to the tribe of the Danites until the day of the captivity of the land. 31 So they set up Mĭcăh's graven image which he made, as long as the house of God was at Shĭlōh.

B. The Levite and his concubine

1. *The Levite recovers his concubine*

19 In those days, when there was no king in Israel, a certain Lĕvĭte was sojourning in the remote parts of the hill country of Ē'phrăĭm, who took to himself a concubine from Bĕth-

z Another reading is *Mănăs'sĕh*

18.29 Laish. *Leshem* in Josh 19.47.
18.30 *captivity of the land* refers to the captivity of northern Palestine by the Assyrian king Tiglath-pileser III. Reference to this event, which took place about 732 B.C., indicates that the compilation of the book was quite late in the monarchy. Others believe that it refers to the captivity of the ark under Eli.
18.31 The Philistines captured the ark and destroyed Shiloh about 1050 B.C.

Margin references:
18.19 Job 21.5; Judg 17.10
18.24 Judg 17.5
18.27 ver 7,10; Josh 19.47
18.28 ver 7; 2 Sam 10.6
*18.29 Josh 19.47
*18.30 Judg 17.3, 5; Ex 2.22
*18.31 Josh 18.1
19.1 Judg 18.1

lēhĕm in Judah. [2]And his concubine became angry with[a] him, and she went away from him to her father's house at Bĕth'lĕhĕm in Judah, and was there some four months. [3] Then her husband arose and went after her, to speak kindly to her and bring her back. He had with him his servant and a couple of asses. And he came[b] to her father's house; and when the girl's father saw him, he came with joy to meet him. [4]And his father-in-law, the girl's father, made him stay, and he remained with him three days; so they ate and drank, and lodged there. [5]And on the fourth day they arose early in the morning, and he prepared to go; but the girl's father said to his son-in-law, "Strengthen your heart with a morsel of bread, and after that you may go." [6] So the two men sat and ate and drank together; and the girl's father said to the man, "Be pleased to spend the night, and let your heart be merry." [7]And when the man rose up to go, his father-in-law urged him, till he lodged there again. [8]And on the fifth day he arose early in the morning to depart; and the girl's father said, "Strengthen your heart, and tarry until the day declines." So they ate, both of them. [9]And when the man and his concubine and his servant rose up to depart, his father-in-law, the girl's father, said to him, "Behold, now the day has waned toward evening; pray tarry all night. Behold, the day draws to its close; lodge here and let your heart be merry; and tomorrow you shall arise early in the morning for your journey, and go home."

2. They spend the night at Gibeah

10 But the man would not spend the night; he rose up and departed, and arrived opposite Jēbŭs (that is, Jerusalem). He had with him a couple of saddled asses, and his concubine was with him. [11] When they were near Jēbŭs, the day was far spent, and the servant said to his master, "Come now, let us turn aside to this city of the Jĕb'ŭsītes, and spend the night in it." [12]And his master said to him, "We will not turn aside into the city of foreigners, who do not belong to the people of Israel; but we will pass on to Gĭb'ë-äh." [13]And he said to his servant, "Come and let us draw near to one of these places, and spend the night at Gĭb'ë-äh or at Rā-mäh." [14] So they passed on and went their way; and the sun went down on them near Gĭb'ë-äh, which belongs to Benjamin, [15] and they turned aside there, to go in and spend the night at Gĭb'ë-äh. And he went in and sat down in the open square of the city; for no man took them into his house to spend the night.

3. The Ephraimite's hospitality

16 And behold, an old man was coming from his work in the field at evening; the man was from the hill country of Ē'phräim, and he was sojourning in Gĭb'ë-äh; the men of the place were Benjaminites. [17]And he lifted up his eyes, and saw the wayfarer in the open square of the city; and the old man said, "Where are you going? and whence do you come?" [18]And he said to him, "We are passing from Bĕth'lĕhĕm in Judah to the remote parts of the hill country of Ē'phräim, from which I come. I went to Bethlehem in Judah, and I am going to my home;[c] and nobody takes me into his house. [19] We have straw and provender for our asses, with

a Gk Old Latin: Heb *played the harlot against*
b Gk: Heb *she brought him*   *c* Gk Compare 19.29. Heb *to the house of the* LORD

Margin references:

19.3
Gen 34.3;
50.21

19.5
ver 8;
Gen 18.5

19.6
ver 9,22

19.10
1 Chr 11.4,5

19.11
Judg 1.21

19.12
Heb 11.13

19.15
Heb 13.2

19.16
Ps 104.23;
ver 14

19.18
Judg 18.31;
20.18

bread and wine for me and your maidservant and the young man with your servants; there is no lack of anything." 20And the old man said, "Peace be to you; I will care for all your wants; only, do not spend the night in the square." 21 So he brought him into his house, and gave the asses provender; and they washed their feet, and ate and drank.

19.21
Gen 24.32,
33

4. *The abuse of the concubine*

22 As they were making their hearts merry, behold, the men of the city, base fellows, beset the house round about, beating on the door; and they said to the old man, the master of the house, "Bring out the man who came into your house, that we may know him." 23And the man, the master of the house, went out to them and said to them, "No, my brethren, do not act so wickedly; seeing that this man has come into my house, do not do this vile thing. 24 Behold, here are my virgin daughter and his concubine; let me bring them out now. Ravish them and do with them what seems good to you; but against this man do not do so vile a thing." 25 But the men would not listen to him. So the man seized his concubine, and put her out to them; and they knew her, and abused her all night until the morning. And as the dawn began to break, they let her go. 26And as morning appeared, the woman came and fell down at the door of the man's house where her master was, till it was light.

19.22
Gen 19.4;
Deut 13.13;
Rom 1.26,
27
19.23
Gen 34.7;
Deut 22.21;
2 Sam 13.12
19.24
Gen 19.8;
Deut 21.14

5. *The Levite's anger*

27 And her master rose up in the morning, and when he opened the doors of the house and went out to go on his way, behold, there was his concubine lying at the door of the house, with her hands on the threshold. 28 He said to her, "Get up, let us be going." But there was no answer. Then he put her upon the ass; and the man rose up and went away to his home. 29And when he entered his house, he took a knife, and laying hold of his concubine he divided her, limb by limb, into twelve pieces, and sent her throughout all the territory of Israel. 30And all who saw it said, "Such a thing has never happened or been seen from the day that the people of Israel came up out of the land of Egypt until this day; consider it, take counsel, and speak."

19.28
Judg 20.5
19.29
1 Sam 11.7
19.30
Judg 20.7

6. *War between Israel and Benjamin*
a. *Israel gathers at Mizpah: the Levite tells his tale*

20 Then all the people of Israel came out, from Dan to Beër-shē'bà, including the land of Gĭl'ëäd, and the congregation assembled as one man to the LORD at Mĭzpáh. 2And the chiefs of all the people, of all the tribes of Israel, presented themselves in the assembly of the people of God, four hundred thousand men on foot that drew the sword. 3 (Now the Benjaminites heard that the people of Israel had gone up to Mĭzpáh.) And the people of Israel said, "Tell us, how was this wickedness brought to pass?" 4And the Lēvīte, the husband of the woman who was murdered, answered and said, "I came to Gĭb'ë-äh that belongs to Benjamin, I and my concubine, to spend the night. 5And the men of Gĭb'ë-äh rose against me, and beset the house round about me by night; they meant to kill me, and they ravished my concubine, and she is dead. 6And I took my concubine and cut her in pieces, and sent her throughout all the country of the inheritance of Israel; for they have

20.1
Judg 21.5;
1 Sam 7.5
20.4
Judg 19.15
20.5
Judg 19.22,
25,26
20.6
Judg 19.29;
Josh 7.15

committed abomination and wantonness in Israel. 7 Behold, you people of Israel, all of you, give your advice and counsel here." | 20.7
Judg 19.30

8 And all the people arose as one man, saying, "We will not any of us go to his tent, and none of us will return to his house. 9 But now this is what we will do to Gĭb′ĕ-ăh: we will go up against it by lot, 10 and we will take ten men of a hundred throughout all the tribes of Israel, and a hundred of a thousand, and a thousand of ten thousand, to bring provisions for the people, that when they come they may requite Gĭb′ĕ-ăh of Benjamin, for all the wanton crime which they have committed in Israel." 11 So all the men of Israel gathered against the city, united as one man.

b. *The Benjaminites refuse to repent*

12 And the tribes of Israel sent men through all the tribe of Benjamin, saying, "What wickedness is this that has taken place among you? 13 Now therefore give up the men, the base fellows in Gĭb′ĕ-ăh, that we may put them to death, and put away evil from Israel." But the Benjaminites would not listen to the voice of their brethren, the people of Israel. 14And the Benjaminites came together out of the cities to Gĭb′ĕ-ăh, to go out to battle against the people of Israel. 15And the Benjaminites mustered out of their cities on that day twenty-six thousand men that drew the sword, besides the inhabitants of Gĭb′ĕ-ăh, who mustered seven hundred picked men. 16Among all these were seven hundred picked men who were left-handed; every one could sling a stone at a hair, and not miss. 17And the men of Israel, apart from Benjamin, mustered four hundred thousand men that drew sword; all these were men of war. | 20.12
Deut 13.14, 15
20.13
Judg 19.22
20.16
Judg 3.15; 1 Chr 12.2

c. *Israel seeks the will of God*

18 The people of Israel arose and went up to Bĕth′ĕl, and inquired of God, "Which of us shall go up first to battle against the Benjaminites?" And the LORD said, "Judah shall go up first." | 20.18
ver 23,26, 27;
Num 27.21

d. *The initial victory of Benjamin*

19 Then the people of Israel rose in the morning, and encamped against Gĭb′ĕ-ăh. 20And the men of Israel went out to battle against Benjamin; and the men of Israel drew up the battle line against them at Gĭb′ĕ-ăh. 21 The Benjaminites came out of Gĭb′ĕ-ăh, and felled to the ground on that day twenty-two thousand men of the Israelites. 22 But the people, the men of Israel, took courage, and again formed the battle line in the same place where they had formed it on the first day. 23And the people of Israel went up and wept before the LORD until the evening; and they inquired of the LORD, "Shall we again draw near to battle against our brethren the Benjaminites?" And the LORD said, "Go up against them." | 20.21
ver 25
20.23
ver 18

e. *Benjamin's second victory*

24 So the people of Israel came near against the Benjaminites the second day. 25And Benjamin went against them out of Gĭb′ĕ-ăh the second day, and felled to the ground eighteen thousand men of the people of Israel; all these were men who drew the sword. 26 Then all the people of Israel, the whole army, went up and came to Bĕth′ĕl and wept; they sat there before the LORD, and fasted | 20.25
ver 21
20.26
ver 23;
Judg 21.2

that day until evening, and offered burnt offerings and peace
offerings before the LORD. [27]And the people of Israel inquired of
the LORD (for the ark of the covenant of God was there in those
days, [28] and Phin′ehas the son of Ēleā′zàr, son of Aaron, ministered before it in those days), saying, "Shall we yet again go
out to battle against our brethren the Benjaminites, or shall we
cease?" And the LORD said, "Go up; for tomorrow I will give
them into your hand."

f. *The rout of Benjamin*

[29] So Israel set men in ambush round about Gĭb′ë-åh. [30]And
the people of Israel went up against the Benjaminites on the third
day, and set themselves in array against Gĭb′ë-åh, as at other times.
[31]And the Benjaminites went out against the people, and were
drawn away from the city; and as at other times they began to
smite and kill some of the people, in the highways, one of which
goes up to Bĕthĕl and the other to Gĭb′ë-åh, and in the open country, about thirty men of Israel. [32]And the Benjaminites said,
"They are routed before us, as at the first." But the men of Israel
said, "Let us flee, and draw them away from the city to the highways." [33]And all the men of Israel rose up out of their place, and
set themselves in array at Bā′al-tā′mar; and the men of Israel who
were in ambush rushed out of their place west[d] of Gēbà. [34]And
there came against Gĭb′ë-åh ten thousand picked men out of all
Israel, and the battle was hard; but the Benjaminites did not know
that disaster was close upon them. [35]And the LORD defeated Benjamin before Israel; and the men of Israel destroyed twenty-five
thousand one hundred men of Benjamin that day; all these were
men who drew the sword. [36] So the Benjaminites saw that they
were defeated.

The men of Israel gave ground to Benjamin, because they
trusted to the men in ambush whom they had set against Gĭb′ë-åh.
[37]And the men in ambush made haste and rushed upon Gĭb′ë-åh;
the men in ambush moved out and smote all the city with the edge
of the sword. [38] Now the appointed signal between the men of
Israel and the men in ambush was that when they made a great
cloud of smoke rise up out of the city [39]the men of Israel should
turn in battle. Now Benjamin had begun to smite and kill about
thirty men of Israel; they said, "Surely they are smitten down
before us, as in the first battle." [40] But when the signal began to
rise out of the city in a column of smoke, the Benjaminites looked
behind them; and behold, the whole of the city went up in smoke
to heaven. [41] Then the men of Israel turned, and the men of Benjamin were dismayed, for they saw that disaster was close upon
them. [42] Therefore they turned their backs before the men of Israel in the direction of the wilderness; but the battle overtook
them, and those who came out of the cities destroyed them in the
midst of them. [43] Cutting down[e] the Benjaminites, they pursued
them and trod them down from Nōhàh[f] as far as opposite Gĭb′ë-åh
on the east. [44] Eighteen thousand men of Benjamin fell, all of them
men of valor. [45]And they turned and fled toward the wilderness

20.27
Josh 18.1

★20.28
Josh 24.33;
Deut 18.5;
Judg 7.9

20.29
Josh 8.4

20.31
Josh 8.16

20.33
Josh 8.19

20.34
Josh 8.14

20.36
Josh 8.15

★20.37
Josh 8.19

20.38
Josh 8.20

20.39
ver 32

★20.40
Josh 8.20

20.45
Judg 21.13

d Gk Vg: Heb *in the plain*   *e* Gk: Heb *surrounding*   *f* Gk: Heb *(at their) resting place*

20.28 Initial defeat did not mean ultimate
defeat. Victory came after the first disaster.

20.37, 40 Evidences of this destruction
have been found by excavators at Gibeah.

to the rock of Rĭmmŏn; five thousand men of them were cut down
in the highways, and they were pursued hard to Gĭdŏm, and two
thousand men of them were slain. 46 So all who fell that day of
Benjamin were twenty-five thousand men that drew the sword,
all of them men of valor. 47 But six hundred men turned and fled
toward the wilderness to the rock of Rĭmmŏn, and abode at the
rock of Rimmon four months. 48And the men of Israel turned back
against the Benjaminites, and smote them with the edge of the
sword, men and beasts and all that they found. And all the towns
which they found they set on fire.

20.47
Judg 21.13

7. The preservation of the tribe of Benjamin
a. Israel weeps for Benjamin

21 Now the men of Israel had sworn at Mĭzpáh, "No one of
us shall give his daughter in marriage to Benjamin." 2And
the people came to Bĕthĕl, and sat there till evening before God,
and they lifted up their voices and wept bitterly. 3And they said,
"O LORD, the God of Israel, why has this come to pass in Israel,
that there should be today one tribe lacking in Israel?" 4And on
the morrow the people rose early, and built there an altar, and
offered burnt offerings and peace offerings. 5And the people of
Israel said, "Which of all the tribes of Israel did not come up in
the assembly to the LORD?" For they had taken a great oath concerning him who did not come up to the LORD to Mĭzpáh, saying,
"He shall be put to death." 6And the people of Israel had compassion for Benjamin their brother, and said, "One tribe is cut off
from Israel this day. 7 What shall we do for wives for those who
are left, since we have sworn by the LORD that we will not give
them any of our daughters for wives?"

21.1
ver 7,18
21.2
Judg 20.18,
26

21.4
2 Sam 24.25

21.7
ver 1

b. Wives for the Benjaminites
(1) THE VIRGINS OF JABESH-GILEAD

8 And they said, "What one is there of the tribes of Israel that
did not come up to the LORD to Mĭzpáh?" And behold, no one
had come to the camp from Jā′bĕsh-gĭl′ĕăd, to the assembly. 9 For
when the people were mustered, behold, not one of the inhabitants
of Jā′bĕsh-gĭl′ĕăd was there. 10 So the congregation sent thither
twelve thousand of their bravest men, and commanded them, "Go
and smite the inhabitants of Jā′bĕsh-gĭl′ĕăd with the edge of the
sword; also the women and the little ones. 11 This is what you shall
do; every male and every woman that has lain with a male you
shall utterly destroy." 12And they found among the inhabitants of
Jā′bĕsh-gĭl′ĕăd four hundred young virgins who had not known
man by lying with him; and they brought them to the camp at
Shĭlōh, which is in the land of Cānaăn.

13 Then the whole congregation sent word to the Benjaminites
who were at the rock of Rĭmmŏn, and proclaimed peace to them.
14And Benjamin returned at that time; and they gave them the
women whom they had saved alive of the women of Jā′bĕsh-
gĭl′ĕăd; but they did not suffice for them. 15And the people had
compassion on Benjamin because the LORD had made a breach
in the tribes of Israel.

★21.8

21.11
Num 31.17

21.13
Judg 20.47;
Deut 20.10

21.15
ver 6

21.8 Apparently the old marriage ties between the Benjaminites and Machir (Gilead)
(see 1 Chr 7.12, 15) explain why no inhabitants
of Jabesh-gilead came up to fight Benjamin.

(2) THE DAUGHTERS OF SHILOH

16 Then the elders of the congregation said, "What shall we do for wives for those who are left, since the women are destroyed out of Benjamin?" 17And they said, "There must be an inheritance for the survivors of Benjamin, that a tribe be not blotted out from Israel. 18 Yet we cannot give them wives of our daughters." For the people of Israel had sworn, "Cursed be he who gives a wife to Benjamin." 19 So they said, "Behold, there is the yearly feast of the LORD at Shīlōh, which is north of Bĕthĕl, on the east of the highway that goes up from Bethel to Shĕçhĕm, and south of Lĕbō′nàh." 20And they commanded the Benjaminites, saying, "Go and lie in wait in the vineyards, 21 and watch; if the daughters of Shīlōh come out to dance in the dances, then come out of the vineyards and seize each man his wife from the daughters of Shiloh, and go to the land of Benjamin. 22And when their fathers or their brothers come to complain to us, we will say to them, 'Grant them graciously to us; because we did not take for each man of them his wife in battle, neither did you give them to them, else you would now be guilty.' " 23And the Benjaminites did so, and took their wives, according to their number, from the dancers whom they carried off; then they went and returned to their inheritance, and rebuilt the towns, and dwelt in them. 24And the people of Israel departed from there at that time, every man to his tribe and family, and they went out from there every man to his inheritance.

8. Summary of the age of the judges

25 In those days there was no king in Israel; every man did what was right in his own eyes.

Marginal references (left column):

21.18
ver 18

21.19
Judg 18.31;
1 Sam 1.3

21.21
Ex 15.20;
Judg 11.34

*21.22
ver 1,18

21.23
Judg 20.48

21.25
Judg 17.6;
18.1; 19.1

21.22 *neither did you give them.* Israel circumvented its vow, and any guilt from breaking it, by allowing Benjamin to *take* wives from the girls who danced during the feast at Shiloh. This prosperous town had become Israel's headquarters.

INTRODUCTION TO

THE BOOK OF

RUTH

Authorship and Background: Jewish tradition attributed this book to Samuel, but the reference to David (4. 17, 21) suggests a later period. The story was most likely transmitted orally around Bethlehem until the reign of David when it came into prominence. The book names Boaz as the great-grandfather of David which would place the time of the story around 1100 B.C. This beautiful story, sometimes referred to as the second appendix to The Book of Judges, shines brilliantly against the dark background of the anarchy pictured in Judges 17–21. In the Hebrew Bible, however, The Book of Ruth is placed in the third, and last, division (*kethubim*, "writings") following Psalms, Job, and Proverbs, and is established as part of the Rolls along with The Song of Solomon, Ecclesiastes, Lamentations, and Esther. The order in the English Bible stems from the Septuagint. Ruth was a Moabitess, and apparently in her day marriages among the people of Moab and Israel were contracted (see Deut 23. 3–6). Ruth, a non-Israelite, became an ancestress of Jesus, the greater David, who came to break down the dividing wall of hostility between Jews and Gentiles. The author of Ruth is unknown and the date it was written cannot be determined conclusively.

Relating a story from the period of Judges which was characterized by savagery, lust, strife, and lawlessness, The Book of Ruth presents a strange contrast. Instead of war, bloodshed, cruelty, politics, and intrigue, there is love and marriage, simple faith, and the tilling of the land; the common customs of ordinary people as they lived and died amid the turbulence of their age.

Characteristics: Ruth is the record of tragedy and love in the lives of average people. In it we see the fortunes of Elimelech of Bethlehem, who, with his wife Naomi and his two sons, goes to Moab in time of famine. He and his sons die there. Naomi yearns for her homeland and brings back Ruth, a young Moabitess who had been married to her deceased son. The story is told in simple language; the customs of the people are unfolded. The attractiveness of the story derives from the suspense factor as faithful Ruth, still young and marriageable, is rewarded for her faithfulness when she meets and marries Boaz, a near kinsman. Boaz's preliminary reaction to his kinsman's role, and the refusal of a nearer kinsman to marry Ruth add further suspense to the story. The happy ending and the sequel which marks David as a descendant of Ruth and Boaz add luster to the narrative.

Contents:

I.   Ruth returns with Naomi. 1.1–22: The famine in Bethlehem. Elimelech migrates. He and his sons die. Naomi and Ruth decide to return to Judah. Orpah turns back to Moab. Ruth goes with Naomi.

Introduction to Ruth

II.   Ruth meets Boaz. 2.1–23: Ruth gleans in the field of a near kinsman,
      Boaz, who is kind to her. She confides in Naomi. Ruth stays close to
      Boaz's maidens through the barley and wheat harvests.

III. Boaz decides. 3.1–18: Naomi tells Ruth to approach Boaz as a kins-
      man. Boaz refuses because there is a closer kinsman. Ruth returns to
      Naomi with Boaz's gift of six measures of barley. Naomi advises Ruth
      to wait for Boaz to settle the issue.

IV.   Boaz and Ruth marry. 4.1–22: The nearest kinsman refuses to marry
      Ruth lest he impair his own inheritance. The transaction is com-
      pleted with witnesses. Ruth becomes the wife of Boaz. Obed is born
      and Naomi cares for the child. Obed becomes the father of Jesse who
      becomes the father of David.

THE BOOK OF

RUTH

I. Ruth returns with Naomi 1.1–22

A. Naomi's afflictions

1 In the days when the judges ruled there was a famine in the land, and a certain man of Bĕth'lĕhĕm in Judah went to sojourn in the country of Mōăb, he and his wife and his two sons. ² The name of the man was Ēlĭm'ĕlĕch and the name of his wife Nāō'mĭ, and the names of his two sons were Mahlŏn and Chĭl'ĭŏn; they were Ēph'răthītes from Bĕth'lĕhĕm in Judah. They went into the country of Mōăb and remained there. ³ But Ēlĭm'ĕlĕch, the husband of Nāō'mĭ, died, and she was left with her two sons. ⁴ These took Mō'ăbīte wives; the name of the one was Orpăh and the name of the other Ruth. They lived there about ten years; ⁵ and both Mahlŏn and Chĭl'ĭŏn died, so that the woman was bereft of her two sons and her husband.

B. Naomi decides to return to Bethlehem

6 Then she started with her daughters-in-law to return from the country of Mōăb, for she had heard in the country of Moab that the LORD had visited his people and given them food. ⁷ So she set out from the place where she was, with her two daughters-in-law, and they went on the way to return to the land of Judah. ⁸ But Nāō'mĭ said to her two daughters-in-law, "Go, return each of you to her mother's house. May the LORD deal kindly with you, as you have dealt with the dead and with me. ⁹ The LORD grant that you may find a home, each of you in the house of her husband!" Then she kissed them, and they lifted up their voices and wept. ¹⁰And they said to her, "No, we will return with you to your people." ¹¹ But Nāō'mĭ said, "Turn back, my daughters, why will you go with me? Have I yet sons in my womb that they may become your husbands? ¹² Turn back, my daughters, go your way, for I am too old to have a husband. If I should say I have hope, even if I should have a husband this night and should bear sons, ¹³ would you therefore wait till they were grown? Would you therefore refrain from marrying? No, my daughters, for it is exceedingly bitter to me for your sake that the hand of the LORD has gone forth against me." ¹⁴ Then they lifted up their voices and wept again; and Orpăh kissed her mother-in-law, but Ruth clung to her.

*1.1
Judg 2.16

1.2
Gen 35.19;
Judg 3.30

*1.4

1.6
Ex 4.31

1.8
ver 5;
Ruth 2.20
1.9
Ruth 3.1

*1.11
Deut 25.5

1.13
Judg 2.15;
Ps 32.4

1.1 *when the judges ruled.* The order, peace, and love of the God-honoring society described in this beautiful story are in marked contrast to the dark, chaotic days which characterized Canaan when "there was no king in Israel" and it was every man for himself.
1.4 Ruth was a Moabitess. The Moabites descended from Moab, who was the son of Lot and his daughter (Gen 19.36, 37). Eventually Ruth the Moabitess, as the wife

of Boaz, became an ancestress of Jesus Christ. Matthew lists the names of four women in the Messianic line and three of them were Gentiles after the flesh: *Rahab, Ruth,* and *the wife of Uriah,* or "Bath-sheba" (Mt 1.5, 6).
1.11 Back of Naomi's questions is the concept of levirate marriage, Deut 25.5, 6, whereby the brother of a deceased husband marries the widow. This is specifically stated in Deut 25.5, 6. (Also see note to Deut 25.5–10 for a complete survey of this custom.)

C. Ruth refuses to leave Naomi

*1.16
2 Ki 2.2,
4,6;
Ruth 2.11,
12

15 And she said, "See, your sister-in-law has gone back to her people and to her gods; return after your sister-in-law." 16 But Ruth said, "Entreat me not to leave you or to return from following you; for where you go I will go, and where you lodge I will lodge; your people shall be my people, and your God my God; 17 where you die I will die, and there will I be buried. May the LORD do so to me and more also if even death parts me from you."

1.18
Acts 21.14

18And when Nāō'mĭ saw that she was determined to go with her, she said no more.

D. Ruth and Naomi return together

1.20
Ex 6.3;
Job 6.4
1.21
Job 1.21

19 So the two of them went on until they came to Bĕth'lĕhĕm. And when they came to Bethlehem, the whole town was stirred because of them; and the women said, "Is this Nāō'mĭ?" 20 She said to them, "Do not call me Nāō'mĭ,ᵃ call me Mara,ᵇ for the Almighty has dealt very bitterly with me. 21 I went away full, and the LORD has brought me back empty. Why call me Nāō'mĭ, when the LORD has afflictedᶜ me and the Almighty has brought calamity upon me?"

1.22
Ex 9.31,32;
Ruth 2.23

22 So Nāō'mĭ returned, and Ruth the Mōȧbīt'ĕss her daughter-in-law with her, who returned from the country of Mōȧb. And they came to Bĕth'lĕhĕm at the beginning of barley harvest.

II. Ruth meets Boaz 2.1–23

A. Ruth gleans in Boaz's field

2.1
Ruth 1.2;
3.2,12
*2.2
ver 7;
Lev 19.9;
Deut 24.19

2 Now Nāō'mĭ had a kinsman of her husband's, a man of wealth, of the family of Ĕlĭm'ĕlĕch, whose name was Bōȧz. 2And Ruth the Mōȧbīt'ĕss said to Nāō'mĭ, "Let me go to the field, and glean among the ears of grain after him in whose sight I shall find favor." And she said to her, "Go, my daughter." 3 So she set forth and went and gleaned in the field after the reapers; and she happened to come to the part of the field belonging to Bōȧz, who was of the family of Ĕlĭm'ĕlĕch. 4And behold, Bōȧz came from Bĕth'lĕhĕm; and he said to the reapers, "The LORD be with you!" And they answered, "The LORD bless you." 5 Then Bōȧz said to his servant who was in charge of the reapers, "Whose maiden is this?" 6And the servant who was in charge of the reapers answered, "It is the Mō'ȧbīte maiden, who came back with Nāō'mĭ from the country of Mōȧb. 7 She said, 'Pray, let me glean and gather among the sheaves after the reapers.' So she came, and she has continued from early morning until now, without resting even for a moment."ᵈ

2.4
Ps 129.7,8;
Lk 1.28

2.6
Ruth 1.22

ᵃ That is *Pleasant* ᵇ That is *Bitter* ᶜ Gk Syr Vg: Heb *testified against*
ᵈ Compare Gk Vg: the meaning of the Hebrew text is uncertain

1.16 This beautiful passage has been widely acclaimed and many brides have used it as part of the wedding ceremony. No woman should make the God of her husband her God unless: (1) her husband's God is the true God and not a false one; (2) her choice is rooted in her own faith in God for, however good her intention, her choice has no validity if it is not accompanied by saving faith.
2.2 This custom is in accord with Deut 24.19.

B. *Boaz commends faithful Ruth*

8 Then Bōăz said to Ruth, "Now, listen, my daughter, do not go to glean in another field or leave this one, but keep close to my maidens. 9 Let your eyes be upon the field which they are reaping, and go after them. Have I not charged the young men not to molest you? And when you are thirsty, go to the vessels and drink what the young men have drawn." 10 Then she fell on her face, bowing to the ground, and said to him, "Why have I found favor in your eyes, that you should take notice of me, when I am a foreigner?" 11 But Bōăz answered her, "All that you have done for your mother-in-law since the death of your husband has been fully told me, and how you left your father and mother and your native land and came to a people that you did not know before. 12 The LORD recompense you for what you have done, and a full reward be given you by the LORD, the God of Israel, under whose wings you have come to take refuge!" 13 Then she said, "You are most gracious to me, my lord, for you have comforted me and spoken kindly to your maidservant, though I am not one of your maid-servants."

14 And at mealtime Bōăz said to her, "Come here, and eat some bread, and dip your morsel in the wine." So she sat beside the reapers, and he passed to her parched grain; and she ate until she was satisfied, and she had some left over. 15 When she rose to glean, Bōăz instructed his young men, saying, "Let her glean even among the sheaves, and do not reproach her. 16And also pull out some from the bundles for her, and leave it for her to glean, and do not rebuke her."

C. *Ruth confides in Naomi*

17 So she gleaned in the field until evening; then she beat out what she had gleaned, and it was about an ephah of barley. 18And she took it up and went into the city; she showed her mother-in-law what she had gleaned, and she also brought out and gave her what food she had left over after being satisfied. 19And her mother-in-law said to her, "Where did you glean today? And where have you worked? Blessed be the man who took notice of you." So she told her mother-in-law with whom she had worked, and said, "The man's name with whom I worked today is Bōăz." 20And Nāō′mĭ said to her daughter-in-law, "Blessed be he by the LORD, whose kindness has not forsaken the living or the dead!" Naomi also said to her, "The man is a relative of ours, one of our nearest kin." 21And Ruth the Mōăbīt′ĕss said, "Besides, he said to me, 'You shall keep close by my servants, till they have finished all my harvest.'" 22And Nāō′mĭ said to Ruth, her daughter-in-law, "It is well, my daughter, that you go out with his maidens, lest in another field you be molested." 23 So she kept close to the maidens of Bōăz, gleaning until the end of the barley and wheat harvests; and she lived with her mother-in-law.

Margin references:

2.10 1 Sam 25.23

★2.11 Ruth 1.14; 16,17

2.12 1 Sam 24.19; Ps 17.8; Ruth 1.16

2.14 ver 18

2.18 ver 14

2.19 ver 10

2.20 Ruth 3.10; Prov 17.17; Ruth 3.9; 4.6

★2.23 Deut 16.9

2.11 Refer back to verse 5 where it is evident that Boaz does not know who Ruth is, but evidently he is fully aware of Ruth's good reputation and character without any knowledge of her identity.

2.23 This verse further illustrates Ruth's compliance, obedience, and moral goodness—qualities that attracted Boaz to her.

III. Boaz decides 3.1–18

A. Naomi counsels Ruth

3 Then Nāŏ′mĭ her mother-in-law said to her, "My daughter, should I not seek a home for you, that it may be well with you? ²Now is not Bŏ̆ăz our kinsman, with whose maidens you were? See, he is winnowing barley tonight at the threshing floor. ³Wash therefore and anoint yourself, and put on your best clothes and go down to the threshing floor; but do not make yourself known to the man until he has finished eating and drinking. ⁴But when he lies down, observe the place where he lies; then, go and uncover his feet and lie down; and he will tell you what to do." ⁵And she replied, "All that you say I will do."

B. Ruth follows Naomi's counsel: Boaz determines to act

6 So she went down to the threshing floor and did just as her mother-in-law had told her. ⁷And when Bŏ̆ăz had eaten and drunk, and his heart was merry, he went to lie down at the end of the heap of grain. Then she came softly, and uncovered his feet, and lay down. ⁸At midnight the man was startled, and turned over, and behold, a woman lay at his feet! ⁹He said, "Who are you?" And she answered, "I am Ruth, your maidservant; spread your skirt over your maidservant, for you are next of kin." ¹⁰And he said, "May you be blessed by the LORD, my daughter; you have made this last kindness greater than the first, in that you have not gone after young men, whether poor or rich. ¹¹And now, my daughter, do not fear, I will do for you all that you ask, for all my fellow townsmen know that you are a woman of worth. ¹²And now it is true that I am a near kinsman, yet there is a kinsman nearer than I. ¹³Remain this night, and in the morning, if he will do the part of the next of kin for you, well; let him do it; but if he is not willing to do the part of the next of kin for you, then, as the LORD lives, I will do the part of the next of kin for you. Lie down until the morning."

C. Ruth returns to Naomi

14 So she lay at his feet until the morning, but arose before one could recognize another; and he said, "Let it not be known that the woman came to the threshing floor." ¹⁵And he said, "Bring the mantle you are wearing and hold it out." So she held it, and he measured out six measures of barley, and laid it upon her; then she went into the city. ¹⁶And when she came to her mother-in-law, she said, "How did you fare, my daughter?" Then she told her all that the man had done for her, ¹⁷saying, "These six measures of barley he gave to me, for he said, 'You must not go back

Margin refs: *3.1 Ruth 1.9; 3.2 Deut 25.5–10; Ruth 2.8; 3.3 2 Sam 14.2; 3.7 Judg 19.6, 9.22; 2 Sam 13.28; *3.9 ver 12; Ruth 2.20; 3.11 Prov 12.4; *3.12 ver 9; Ruth 4.1; 3.13 Ruth 4.5

3.1 Naomi suggests a course of action consonant with the intention of Israel's levirate custom (see note to 1.11). When this custom was followed, the first-born was thought of as the son of the woman's deceased husband but all subsequent children were recognized as those of her second one. By such action the family ownership of land could be perpetuated.

3.9 Ruth's action invited Boaz to perform the function of nearest kinsman and as such was both proper and devoid of any immorality. The custom was common to Israelitish society, however, no biblical sanction exists for its use today.
3.12 The propriety of Boaz's conduct bespeaks the worth of his character and life.

empty-handed to your mother-in-law.' " 18 She replied, "Wait, my daughter, until you learn how the matter turns out, for the man will not rest, but will settle the matter today."

3.18
Ps 37.3-5

IV. Boaz and Ruth marry 4.1–22

A. Boaz seeks out the nearest kinsman: the kinsman declines

4 And Bōăz went up to the gate and sat down there; and behold, the next of kin, of whom Boaz had spoken, came by. So Boaz said, "Turn aside, friend; sit down here"; and he turned aside and sat down. 2And he took ten men of the elders of the city, and said, "Sit down here"; so they sat down. 3 Then he said to the next of kin, "Nāō'mĭ, who has come back from the country of Mōăb, is selling the parcel of land which belonged to our kinsman Ëlĭm'ĕlĕch. 4 So I thought I would tell you of it, and say, Buy it in the presence of those sitting here, and in the presence of the elders of my people. If you will redeem it, redeem it; but if you will not, tell me, that I may know, for there is no one besides you to redeem it, and I come after you." And he said, "I will redeem it." 5 Then Bōăz said, "The day you buy the field from the hand of Nāō'mĭ, you are also buying Ruth[e] the Mōăbīt'ĕss, the widow of the dead, in order to restore the name of the dead to his inheritance." 6 Then the next of kin said, "I cannot redeem it for myself, lest I impair my own inheritance. Take my right of redemption yourself, for I cannot redeem it."

4.1
Ruth 3.12

4.3
Lev 25.25

4.4
Jer 32.7,8;
Lev 25.25

★4.5ff
Deut 25.5,6

4.6
Ruth 3.12,
13

B. Boaz fulfils the legal requirements

7 Now this was the custom in former times in Israel concerning redeeming and exchanging: to confirm a transaction, the one drew off his sandal and gave it to the other, and this was the manner of attesting in Israel. 8 So when the next of kin said to Bōăz, "Buy it for yourself," he drew off his sandal. 9 Then Bōăz said to the elders and all the people, "You are witnesses this day that I have bought from the hand of Nāō'mĭ all that belonged to Ëlĭm'ĕlĕch and all that belonged to Chĭl'ĭŏn and to Mahlŏn. 10Also Ruth the Mōăbīt'ĕss, the widow of Mahlŏn, I have bought to be my wife, to perpetuate the name of the dead in his inheritance, that the name of the dead may not be cut off from among his brethren and from the gate of his native place; you are witnesses this day." 11 Then all the people who were at the gate, and the elders, said, "We are witnesses. May the LORD make the woman, who is coming into your house, like Rachel and Lēah, who together built up the house of Israel. May you prosper in Ëph'răthăh and be renowned in

4.7
Deut 25.7,9

4.10
Deut 25.6

4.11
Ps 127.3

e Old Latin Vg: Heb of Naomi and from Ruth

4.5a Boaz carefully ties the purchase of the land to the marriage of Ruth and evidently was aware of the fact that the nearer kinsman would decline to buy the land if he had to take Ruth with it. (Read Deut 25.5, 6 in this connection.)

4.5b-10 The right of redemption exercised by Boaz involved property (Lev 25.25) and marriage (Deut 25.5-10), but the precise details are not exactly in accord with the regulations; for example, while Boaz was a near kinsman, he was not the brother of Mahlon.

*4.12
ver 18;
Gen 38.29

Běth'lěhěm; 12 and may your house be like the house of Pěrěz, whom Tāmar bore to Judah, because of the children that the LORD will give you by this young woman."

C. Boaz and Ruth marry: Obed is born

4.13
Ruth 3.11;
Gen 29.31;
33.5
4.14
Lk 1.58
4.15
Ruth 1.16,
17; 2.11,12

13 So Bōăz took Ruth and she became his wife; and he went in to her, and the LORD gave her conception, and she bore a son. 14 Then the women said to Nāō'mĭ, "Blessed be the LORD, who has not left you this day without next of kin; and may his name be renowned in Israel! 15 He shall be to you a restorer of life and a nourisher of your old age; for your daughter-in-law who loves you, who is more to you than seven sons, has borne him." 16 Then Nāō'mĭ took the child and laid him in her bosom, and became his nurse. 17And the women of the neighborhood gave him a name, saying, "A son has been born to Nāō'mĭ." They named him Ōběd; he was the father of Jěssě, the father of David.

D. Ruth enters the Davidic line

*4.18
Mt 1.3-6

18 Now these are the descendants of Pěrěz: Perez was the father of Hězrŏn, 19 Hězrŏn of Ram, Ram of Ămmĭn'ădăb, 20Ămmĭn'-ădăb of Nahshŏn, Nahshon of Sălmŏn, 21 Sălmŏn of Bōăz, Boaz of Ōběd, 22 Ōběd of Jěssě, and Jesse of David.

4.12 Tamar determined to play the role of a harlot in order to force Judah to perform the part of the near kinsman since Judah had refused to allow Tamar's brother-in-law to perform this function. However, Tamar protected her purity and any odium belonged to Judah alone in this instance.

4.18 The genealogy is traced from Perez who was born to Tamar in contrast to the birth of Obed which, compared to the birth of Perez, is a beautiful and moving, as well as a pure and rightly motivated incident.

INTRODUCTION TO
THE FIRST BOOK OF
SAMUEL

Authorship and Background: 1 and 2 Samuel, like the two books of Kings, were originally a single book. The Septuagint translators considered these two larger books a complete history of the kingdoms of Israel and Judah, and, after dividing them into four books, they named them "Books of Kingdoms" instead of the Hebrew titles "Samuel" and "Kings." Jerome followed the same division in his Latin Vulgate, but he changed the title to "Books of Kings." The various English Bibles have retained the Hebrew titles while following the Septuagint-Vulgate divisions. In some instances the four books are subtitled "The First, Second, Third, and Fourth Book of the Kings" as in the Vulgate.

A late Jewish tradition attributed the two books of Samuel to the prophet Samuel, but internal evidence shows that the writer lived later than the events which he recorded and he made use of early source materials such as the Chronicles of Samuel, Nathan, and Gad referred to in 1 Chr 29.29. For example, 2 Sam 9–20 may well be based on an old historical record from the royal court of David. The fact that the books were named for Samuel indicates the high regard in which he was held. He was ordained of God to deliver Israel when its national situation appeared hopeless. Probably he was the founder of the schools of the prophets. He lived and ministered during the changeover from the judges to the monarchy, and was privileged to train David who became Israel's great shepherd-king.

Characteristics: The books of Samuel cover the history of Israel from the period of Judges to the close of the reign of David. There are three main characters: Samuel, Saul, and David. Samuel the prophet was, like Moses, a man of destiny. As the last of the judges he anointed both Saul and David kings. Thus he was a crucial link in the transition from the dark and forbidding days of the judges to the establishment of the Davidic monarchy. The books of Samuel are both history and biography. No effort is made to gloss over the defects and sins of the chief characters; indeed the weight is on the side of holiness. The stories of their lives reveal them to have been both good and bad, having high ideals at times and falling into disobedience and sin at others. In devotion and obedience to God, Samuel stands out as one of the great Old Testament characters. Yet his sons, like those of Eli, wrought wickedness.

Contents:

I.   The judgeship of Samuel. 1.1—7.17: Samuel's birth and consecration. His ministry before God in the house of Eli. His prophecy concerning the sons of Eli and of God's new and faithful priest. Eli's house judged. Israel overcome by the Philistines; the Ark seized. The

Introduction to 1 Samuel

death of Eli and the birth of Ichabod. God punishes the Philistines for
taking the Ark. It is sent to Kiriath-jearim. Israel repents and is victorious at Mizpah; the Ebenezer stone. Samuel is circuit judge at
Bethel, Gilgal, Mizpah, and Ramah.

II. The reign of Saul. 8.1—31.13: The evil of Samuel's sons. Israel asks
for a king. God's description of what the king will be like. God as-
sents to a king and Saul of Benjamin is selected. Saul is secretly
anointed and later crowned publicly. Saul wars against Ammon victoriously. Samuel defends his record, and reproves Israel; the people
confess their sins. Samuel exhorts to obedience and offers hope to the
repentant, and wrath against the disobedient. Saul wars against the
Philistines. Geba attacked by Jonathan. Saul offers sacrifice; Samuel
reproves him. Saul's army unprepared. Jonathan's victory at Michmash. Saul orders the army not to eat. Jonathan transgresses the order,
is found guilty, and rescued by the people. Saul wars against the
Amalekites. He spares Agag and keeps some of the spoil. God rejects
Saul. Samuel laments. David is anointed king. Saul's mind is darkened. David comes to Saul's court. David wins a victory over Goliath.
Jonathan loves David; Saul hates him. Saul secretly persecutes David,
then openly. David's first escape and flight; his second escape and
flight. Jonathan tries to reconcile Saul and David; David goes to Nob,
then Gath, then Adullam, then Mizpeh. Saul murders the priests
at Nob. David flees the third time: he goes to Keilah. His fourth flight
takes him to Ziph. The fifth time he flees to Maon. In his sixth flight
David goes to En-gedi. He cuts off Saul's skirt. Samuel dies and David
flees the seventh time: the affair with Nabal; David's wives; the
seizure of Saul's spear and water jug. Saul confesses his wickedness.
David goes to the Philistines. Saul consults the medium at Endor. The
Philistines send David away. He destroys Amalek. Saul dies in battle
against the Philistines; his corpse is mutilated and his remains buried.

THE FIRST BOOK OF
SAMUEL

I. The judgeship of Samuel 1.1–7.17

A. Samuel's birth, growth, and background

1. Samuel born in answer to prayer

1 There was a certain man of Rā'màthā'ïm-zō'phïm of the hill country of Ē'phräïm, whose name was Ĕlkā'näh the son of Jĕrō'hàm, son of Ēlī'hū, son of Tōhū, son of Zúph, an Ē'phräïmïte. ² He had two wives; the name of the one was Hannah, and the name of the other Pĕnïn'näh. And Peninnah had children, but Hannah had no children.

3 Now this man used to go up year by year from his city to worship and to sacrifice to the LORD of hosts at Shīlōh, where the two sons of Ēlī, Hŏphnī and Phïn'ëhàs, were priests of the LORD. ⁴ On the day when Ĕlkā'näh sacrificed, he would give portions to Pĕnïn'näh his wife and to all her sons and daughters; ⁵ and, although*a* he loved Hannah, he would give Hannah only one portion, because the LORD had closed her womb. ⁶And her rival used to provoke her sorely, to irritate her, because the LORD had closed her womb. ⁷ So it went on year by year; as often as she went up to the house of the LORD, she used to provoke her. Therefore Hannah wept and would not eat. ⁸And Ĕlkā'näh, her husband, said to her, "Hannah, why do you weep? And why do you not eat? And why is your heart sad? Am I not more to you than ten sons?"

9 After they had eaten and drunk in Shīlōh, Hannah rose. Now Ēlī the priest was sitting on the seat beside the doorpost of the temple of the LORD. ¹⁰ She was deeply distressed and prayed to the LORD, and wept bitterly. ¹¹And she vowed a vow and said, "O LORD of hosts, if thou wilt indeed look on the affliction of thy maidservant, and remember me, and not forget thy maidservant, but wilt give to thy maidservant a son, then I will give him to the LORD all the days of his life, and no razor shall touch his head."

12 As she continued praying before the LORD, Ēlī observed her mouth. ¹³ Hannah was speaking in her heart; only her lips moved, and her voice was not heard; therefore Ēlī took her to be a drunken woman. ¹⁴And Ēlī said to her, "How long will you be drunken? Put away your wine from you." ¹⁵ But Hannah answered, "No, my lord, I am a woman sorely troubled; I have drunk neither wine nor strong drink, but I have been pouring out my soul before the LORD. ¹⁶ Do not regard your maidservant as a base woman, for all along I have been speaking out of my great anxiety and vexation." ¹⁷ Then Ēlī answered, "Go in peace, and the God of Israel grant your petition which you have made to him." ¹⁸And she said, "Let your maidservant find favor in your eyes." Then the woman

a Gk: Heb obscure

1.1
Josh 17.17, 18;
1 Chr 6.27
1.2
Deut 21.15–17;
Lk 2.36
1.3
Ex 34.23;
Deut 12.5;
Josh 18.1
1.4
Deut 12.17
1.5
Gen 16.1;
30.2
1.6
Job 24.21
1.8
Ruth 4.15
1.9
1 Sam 3.3
*1.10
1.11
Gen 28.20;
29.32;
Num 6.5;
Judg 13.5
1.13
Gen 24.42–45
1.14
Acts 2.4,13
1.15
Ps 62.8
1.17
Judg 18.6;
1 Sam 25.35;
Mk 5.34
1.18
Ruth 2.13;
Ecc 9.7

1.10 The principles which govern effective prayer are beautifully illustrated in the experience of Hannah (ver 10–20): (1) She was rightly related to God as a believer. (2) She had intensity of desire. (3) She petitioned for what she wanted. (4) She had faith to believe. (5) She received the promise by faith before it actually came in experience. And when her prayer had been answered she acknowledged it by naming her son *Samuel,* which means *His name is God* (or possibly, *Heard of God*).

went her way and ate, and her countenance was no longer sad.

1.19
Gen 4.1;
30.22
1.20
Gen 41.51,
52;
Ex 2.10,22

19 They rose early in the morning and worshiped before the LORD; then they went back to their house at Rāmáh. And Ĕlkā'náh knew Hannah his wife, and the LORD remembered her; 20 and in due time Hannah conceived and bore a son, and she called his name Samuel, for she said, "I have asked him of the LORD."

2. *Samuel dedicated*

1.21
ver 3
1.22
Lk 2.22;
1 Sam 2.11,
18
1.23
Num 30.7;
ver 17

21 And the man Ĕlkā'náh and all his house went up to offer to the LORD the yearly sacrifice, and to pay his vow. 22 But Hannah did not go up, for she said to her husband, "As soon as the child is weaned, I will bring him, that he may appear in the presence of the LORD, and abide there for ever." 23 Ĕlkā'náh her husband said to her, "Do what seems best to you, wait until you have weaned him; only, may the LORD establish his word." So the woman remained and nursed her son, until she weaned him.

1.24
Deut 12.5;
Josh 18.1

24And when she had weaned him, she took him up with her, along with a three-year-old bull,[b] an ephah of flour, and a skin of wine; and she brought him to the house of the LORD at Shīlōh; and the child was young. 25 Then they slew the bull, and they brought the child to Ēlī. 26And she said, "Oh, my lord! As you live, my lord, I am the woman who was standing here in your presence, praying to the LORD. 27 For this child I prayed; and the LORD has granted me my petition which I made to him. 28 Therefore I have lent him to the LORD; as long as he lives, he is lent to the LORD."

*1.25
Lev 1.5;
Lk 2.22
1.26
2 Ki 2.2
1.27
ver 11–13
1.28
ver 11,22

And they[x] worshiped the LORD there.

3. *Hannah's song of praise*

2.1
Lk 1.46–55;
Ps 89.17;
Isa 12.2,3

2 Hannah also prayed and said,
"My heart exults in the LORD;
   my strength is exalted in the LORD.
My mouth derides my enemies,
   because I rejoice in thy salvation.

2.2
Lev 19.2;
2 Sam
22.32;
Deut 32.30,
31

2 "There is none holy like the LORD,
   there is none besides thee;
   there is no rock like our God.

2.3
Prov 8.13;
1 Sam 16.7;
1 Ki 8.39;
Prov 16.2;
24.12

3 Talk no more so very proudly,
   let not arrogance come from your mouth;
for the LORD is a God of knowledge,
   and by him actions are weighed.

2.4
Ps 76.3

4 The bows of the mighty are broken,
   but the feeble gird on strength.

2.5
Ps 113.9;
Jer 15.9

5 Those who were full have hired themselves out for bread,
   but those who were hungry have ceased to hunger.
The barren has borne seven,
   but she who has many children is forlorn.

2.6
Deut 32.39;
Isa 26.19

6 The LORD kills and brings to life;
   he brings down to Shēōl and raises up.

2.7
Deut 8.17,
18;
Job 5.11;
Ps 75.6,7

7 The LORD makes poor and makes rich;
   he brings low, he also exalts.

b Gk Syr: Heb *three bulls*   *x* Heb *he*

1.25 *they slew.* Evidently Elkanah was with Hannah. A text of Samuel found at Qumran indicates this. Moreover, Elkanah returns home after Hannah's prayer at Shiloh (2.11).

8 He raises up the poor from the dust;
  he lifts the needy from the ash heap,
to make them sit with princes
  and inherit a seat of honor.
For the pillars of the earth are the LORD's,
  and on them he has set the world.

9 "He will guard the feet of his faithful ones;
  but the wicked shall be cut off in darkness;
  for not by might shall a man prevail.
10 The adversaries of the LORD shall be broken to pieces;
  against them he will thunder in heaven.
The LORD will judge the ends of the earth;
  he will give strength to his king,
  and exalt the power of his anointed."

4. Samuel ministers before the LORD

11 Then Ĕlkā′nåh went home to Rāmáh. And the boy ministered to the LORD, in the presence of Ēlī the priest.

12 Now the sons of Ēlī were worthless men; they had no regard for the LORD. 13 The custom of the priests with the people was that when any man offered sacrifice, the priest's servant would come, while the meat was boiling, with a three-pronged fork in his hand, 14 and he would thrust it into the pan, or kettle, or caldron, or pot; all that the fork brought up the priest would take for himself.ᶜ So they did at Shīlōh to all the Israelites who came there. 15 Moreover, before the fat was burned, the priest's servant would come and say to the man who was sacrificing, "Give meat for the priest to roast; for he will not accept boiled meat from you, but raw." 16And if the man said to him, "Let them burn the fat first, and then take as much as you wish," he would say, "No, you must give it now; and if not, I will take it by force." 17 Thus the sin of the young men was very great in the sight of the LORD; for the men treated the offering of the LORD with contempt.

18 Samuel was ministering before the LORD, a boy girded with a linen ephod. 19And his mother used to make for him a little robe and take it to him each year, when she went up with her husband to offer the yearly sacrifice. 20 Then Ēlī would bless Ĕlkā′nåh and his wife, and say, "The LORD give you children by this woman for the loan which she lent toᵈ the LORD"; so then they would return to their home.

21 And the LORD visited Hannah, and she conceived and bore three sons and two daughters. And the boy Samuel grew in the presence of the LORD.

22 Now Ēlī was very old, and he heard all that his sons were doing to all Israel, and how they lay with the women who served at the entrance to the tent of meeting. 23And he said to them, "Why do you do such things? For I hear of your evil dealings from all the people. 24 No, my sons; it is no good report that I hear the people of the LORD spreading abroad. 25 If a man sins against a man, God will mediate for him; but if a man sins against the LORD, who can intercede for him?" But they would not listen to the voice of their father; for it was the will of the LORD to slay them.

2.8
Ps 113.7,8;
Job 36.7;
38.4,5

2.9
Ps 91.11,12;
Mt 8.12;
Ps 33.16,17

2.10
Ps 2.9;
18.13;
96.13;
21.1,7;
89.24

2.11
1 Sam 3.1

2.12
Jer 2.8;
9.3,6
2.13
Lev 7.29–34

2.15
Lev 3.3,4

2.17
Mal 2.7–9

2.18
ver 11,28;
1 Sam 3.1
2.19
1 Sam 1.3
2.20
Lk 2.34;
1 Sam 1.11,
27,28

2.21
Gen 21.1;
ver 26;
1 Sam 3.19;
Lk 2.40
2.22
Ex 38.8

2.24
1 Ki 15.26
2.25
Deut 1.17;
Num 15.30;
Josh 11.20

ᶜ Gk Syr Vg: Heb with it   ᵈ Or for the petition which she asked of

2.26
ver 21;
Lk 2.52

26 Now the boy Samuel continued to grow both in stature and in favor with the LORD and with men.

5. *The prophet announces the doom of Eli's house*

2.27
1 Ki 13.1;
Ex 4.14–16
2.28
Ex 28.1–4;
Lev 8.7,8

27 And there came a man of God to Ēlī, and said to him, "Thus the LORD has said, 'I revealed[e] myself to the house of your father when they were in Egypt subject to the house of Phạraōh. 28 And I chose him out of all the tribes of Israel to be my priest, to go up to my altar, to burn incense, to wear an ephod before me; and I gave to the house of your father all my offerings by fire from the people of Israel.

2.29
ver 13–17;
Deut 12.5;
Mt 10.37

29 Why then look with greedy eye at[f] my sacrifices and my offerings which I commanded, and honor your sons above me by fattening yourselves upon the choicest parts of every offering of my people Israel?'

2.30
Ex 29.9;
Ps 91.14;
Mal 2.9

30 Therefore the LORD the God of Israel declares: 'I promised that your house and the house of your father should go in and out before me for ever'; but now the LORD declares: 'Far be it from me; for those who honor me I will honor, and those who despise me shall be lightly esteemed.

2.31
1 Sam 4.11–18;
22.17–20

31 Behold, the days are coming, when I will cut off your strength and the strength of your father's house, so that there will not be an old man in your house.

2.32
1 Ki 2.26,27;
Zech 8.4

32 Then in distress you will look with envious eye on all the prosperity which shall be bestowed upon Israel; and there shall not be an old man in your house for ever. 33 The man of you whom I shall not cut off from my altar shall be spared to weep out his[g] eyes and grieve his[g] heart; and all the increase of your house shall die by the sword of men.[h]

2.34
1 Ki 13.3;
1 Sam 4.11
★2.35
1 Ki 2.35;
2 Sam 7.11,27;
1 Ki 11.38;
1 Sam 12.3;
16.13

34 And this which shall befall your two sons, Hŏphnī and Phīn′ëhȧs, shall be the sign to you: both of them shall die on the same day. 35 And I will raise up for myself a faithful priest, who shall do according to what is in my heart and in my mind; and I will build him a sure house, and he shall go in and out before my anointed for ever.

2.36
1 Ki 2.27

36 And every one who is left in your house shall come to implore him for a piece of silver or a loaf of bread, and shall say, "Put me, I pray you, in one of the priest's places, that I may eat a morsel of bread."'"

6. *Samuel announces the doom of Eli's house*
a. *Samuel before the LORD*

3.1
1 Sam 2.11,18;
Ps 74.9;
Amos 8.11

3 Now the boy Samuel was ministering to the LORD under Ēlī. And the word of the LORD was rare in those days; there was no frequent vision.

b. *The call of God to Samuel*

3.2
1 Sam 4.15
3.3
Lev 24.2–4
3.4
Isa 6.8

2 At that time Ēlī, whose eyesight had begun to grow dim, so that he could not see, was lying down in his own place; 3 the lamp of God had not yet gone out, and Samuel was lying down within the temple of the LORD, where the ark of God was. 4 Then the LORD called, "Samuel! Samuel!"[i] and he said, "Here I am!" 5 and ran to Ēlī, and said, "Here I am, for you called me." But he said, "I did not call; lie down again." So he went and lay down. 6 And the LORD called again, "Samuel!" And Samuel arose and went

---

e Gk Tg: Heb *Did I reveal*   *f* Or *treat with scorn* Gk: Heb *kick at*
g Gk: Heb *your*   *h* Gk: Heb *die as men*   *i* Gk See 3.10: Heb *the* LORD *called Samuel*

2.35 *a faithful priest.* According to 1 Ki 2.27, 35 this verse was a prediction of Zadok, the priest appointed by Solomon in place of Abiathar, Eli's great-grandson.

to Ēlī, and said, "Here I am, for you called me." But he said, "I did not call, my son; lie down again." 7 Now Samuel did not yet know the LORD, and the word of the LORD had not yet been revealed to him. 8And the LORD called Samuel again the third time. And he arose and went to Ēlī, and said, "Here I am, for you called me." Then Eli perceived that the LORD was calling the boy. 9 Therefore Ēlī said to Samuel, "Go, lie down; and if he calls you, you shall say, 'Speak, LORD, for thy servant hears.' " So Samuel went and lay down in his place.

c. God pronounces judgment on Eli's house

10 And the LORD came and stood forth, calling as at other times, "Samuel! Samuel!" And Samuel said, "Speak, for thy servant hears." 11 Then the LORD said to Samuel, "Behold, I am about to do a thing in Israel, at which the two ears of every one that hears it will tingle. 12 On that day I will fulfil against Ēlī all that I have spoken concerning his house, from beginning to end. 13And I tell him that I am about to punish his house for ever, for the iniquity which he knew, because his sons were blaspheming God,ʲ and he did not restrain them. 14 Therefore I swear to the house of Ēlī that the iniquity of Ēlī's house shall not be expiated by sacrifice or offering for ever."

d. Samuel tells Eli of the judgment of God

15 Samuel lay until morning; then he opened the doors of the house of the LORD. And Samuel was afraid to tell the vision to Ēlī. 16 But Ēlī called Samuel and said, "Samuel, my son." And he said, "Here I am." 17And Ēlī said, "What was it that he told you? Do not hide it from me. May God do so to you and more also, if you hide anything from me of all that he told you." 18 So Samuel told him everything and hid nothing from him. And he said, "It is the LORD; let him do what seems good to him."

e. Samuel established as a prophet

19 And Samuel grew, and the LORD was with him and let none of his words fall to the ground. 20And all Israel from Dan to Beër-shē′bà knew that Samuel was established as a prophet of the LORD. 21And the LORD appeared again at Shīlōh, for the LORD revealed
4 himself to Samuel at Shiloh by the word of the LORD. 1And the word of Samuel came to all Israel.

B. Samuel welds the theocracy together

1. The defeat of Israel; the capture of the ark

Now Israel went out to battle against the Phĭlĭs′tĭneṣ; they encamped at Ēbĕnē′zĕr, and the Philistines encamped at Aphĕk. 2 The Phĭlĭs′tĭneṣ drew up in line against Israel, and when the battle spread, Israel was defeated by the Philistines, who slew about four thousand men on the field of battle. 3And when the troops came to the camp, the elders of Israel said, "Why has the LORD put us to rout today before the Phĭlĭs′tĭneṣ? Let us bring

ʲ Another reading is for themselves

Marginal references

3.7
Acts 19.2

3.11
2 Ki 21.12;
Jer 19.3
3.12
1 Sam 2.30–36
3.13
1 Sam 2.12,
17,22,
29–31
3.14
Lev 15.30,
31;
Isa 22.14

3.17
Ruth 1.17;
2 Sam 3.35
3.18
Job 2.10;
Isa 39.8

★3.19
1 Sam 2.21;
Gen 21.22;
39.2;
1 Sam 9.6
3.20
Judg 20.1
3.21
ver 10
★4.1
1 Sam 7.12

4.3
Josh 7.7,8;
Num 10.35

3.19 This verse confirms Samuel's prophetic powers.

4.1 *Philistines*, see note to Judg 13.1 for background.

the ark of the covenant of the LORD here from Shīlōh, that he may come among us and save us from the power of our enemies." ⁴ So the people sent to Shīlōh, and brought from there the ark of the covenant of the LORD of hosts, who is enthroned on the cherubim; and the two sons of Ēlī, Hŏphnī and Phǐn'ēhás, were there with the ark of the covenant of God.

*4.4
2 Sam 6.2;
Ex 25.18.22

4.5
Josh 6.5,20
4.6
Ex 15.14

5 When the ark of the covenant of the LORD came into the camp, all Israel gave a mighty shout, so that the earth resounded. ⁶And when the Phǐlǐs'tīneṣ heard the noise of the shouting, they said, "What does this great shouting in the camp of the Hebrews mean?" And when they learned that the ark of the LORD had come to the camp, ⁷ the Phǐlǐs'tīneṣ were afraid; for they said, "A god has come into the camp." And they said, "Woe to us! For nothing like this has happened before. ⁸ Woe to us! Who can deliver us from the power of these mighty gods? These are the gods who smote the Egyptians with every sort of plague in the wilderness. ⁹ Take courage, and acquit yourselves like men, O Phǐlǐs'tīneṣ, lest you become slaves to the Hebrews as they have been to you; acquit yourselves like men and fight."

4.9
1 Cor 16.13;
Judg 13.1
4.10
ver 2;
Deut 28.25;
2 Sam
18.17;
2 Ki 14.12
4.11
1 Sam 2.34;
Ps 78.56–64

10 So the Phǐlǐs'tīneṣ fought, and Israel was defeated, and they fled, every man to his home; and there was a very great slaughter, for there fell of Israel thirty thousand foot soldiers. ¹¹And the ark of God was captured; and the two sons of Ēlī, Hŏphnī and Phǐn'ēhás, were slain.

2. The death of Eli
a. His accident

*4.12
Josh 7.6;
2 Sam 1.2;
Neh 9.1
4.13
ver 18;
1 Sam 1.9

12 A man of Benjamin ran from the battle line, and came to Shīlōh the same day, with his clothes rent and with earth upon his head. ¹³ When he arrived, Ēlī was sitting upon his seat by the road watching, for his heart trembled for the ark of God. And when the man came into the city and told the news, all the city cried out. ¹⁴ When Ēlī heard the sound of the outcry, he said, "What is this uproar?" Then the man hastened and came and told Eli. ¹⁵ Now Ēlī was ninety-eight years old and his eyes were set, so that he could not see. ¹⁶And the man said to Ēlī, "I am he who has come from the battle; I fled from the battle today." And he said, "How did it go, my son?" ¹⁷ He who brought the tidings answered and said, "Israel has fled before the Phǐlǐs'tīneṣ, and there has also been a great slaughter among the people; your two sons also, Hŏphnī and Phǐn'ēhás, are dead, and the ark of God has been captured." ¹⁸ When he mentioned the ark of God, Ēlī fell over backward from his seat by the side of the gate; and his neck was broken and he died, for he was an old man, and heavy. He had judged Israel forty years.

4.15
1 Sam 3.2
4.16
2 Sam 1.4
4.18
ver 13

b. The birth of Ichabod

19 Now his daughter-in-law, the wife of Phǐn'ēhás, was with child, about to give birth. And when she heard the tidings that the ark of God was captured, and that her father-in-law and her husband were dead, she bowed and gave birth; for her pains came

---

4.4 enthroned on the cherubim, see note to Ex 25.22.
4.12 Shiloh. The story does not tell of the destruction of Shiloh, but archaeological evidence confirms the fact reported in Jer 7.12; 26.6.

upon her. ²⁰And about the time of her death the women attending her said to her, "Fear not, for you have borne a son." But she did not answer or give heed. ²¹And she named the child Ĭch'ábŏd, saying, "The glory has departed from Israel!" because the ark of God had been captured and because of her father-in-law and her husband. ²²And she said, "The glory has departed from Israel, for the ark of God has been captured."

3. The ark in the hands of the Philistines
a. The ark at Ashdod in the house of Dagon

5 When the Phĭlĭs'tĭneṣ captured the ark of God, they carried it from Ĕbĕnĕ'zĕr to Ăshdŏd; ² then the Phĭlĭs'tĭneṣ took the ark of God and brought it into the house of Dāgŏn and set it up beside Dagon. ³And when the people of Ăshdŏd rose early the next day, behold, Dāgŏn had fallen face downward on the ground before the ark of the Lᴏʀᴅ. So they took Dagon and put him back in his place. ⁴ But when they rose early on the next morning, behold, Dāgŏn had fallen face downward on the ground before the ark of the Lᴏʀᴅ, and the head of Dagon and both his hands were lying cut off upon the threshold; only the trunk of Dagon was left to him. ⁵ This is why the priests of Dāgŏn and all who enter the house of Dagon do not tread on the threshold of Dagon in Ăshdŏd to this day.

b. The ark at Gath and Ekron

6 The hand of the Lᴏʀᴅ was heavy upon the people of Ăshdŏd, and he terrified and afflicted them with tumors, both Ashdod and its territory. ⁷And when the men of Ăshdŏd saw how things were, they said, "The ark of the God of Israel must not remain with us; for his hand is heavy upon us and upon Dāgŏn our god." ⁸ So they sent and gathered together all the lords of the Phĭlĭs'tĭneṣ, and said, "What shall we do with the ark of the God of Israel?" They answered, "Let the ark of the God of Israel be brought around to Găth." So they brought the ark of the God of Israel there. ⁹ But after they had brought it around, the hand of the Lᴏʀᴅ was against the city, causing a very great panic, and he afflicted the men of the city, both young and old, so that tumors broke out upon them. ¹⁰ So they sent the ark of God to Ĕkrŏn. But when the ark of God came to Ekron, the people of Ekron cried out, "They have brought around to us the ark of the God of Israel to slay us and our people." ¹¹ They sent therefore and gathered together all the lords of the Phĭlĭs'tĭneṣ, and said, "Send away the ark of the God of Israel, and let it return to its own place, that it may not slay us and our people." For there was a deathly panic throughout the whole city. The hand of God was very heavy there; ¹² the men who did not die were stricken with tumors, and the cry of the city went up to heaven.

4. The return of the ark
a. The ark sent away with sacrifices

6 The ark of the Lᴏʀᴅ was in the country of the Phĭlĭs'tĭneṣ seven months. ²And the Phĭlĭs'tĭneṣ called for the priests and

---

Marginal references:

4.20 Gen 35.16-19
*4.21
4.22 Jer 2.11; ver 11
5.1 1 Sam 4.1; 7.12
*5.2 Judg 16.23
5.3 Isa 19.1; 46.1,2,7
5.4 Ezek 6.4,6
5.6 ver 7,11; Ex 9.3; 1 Sam 6.5; Deut 28.27; Ps 78.66
5.8 ver 11
5.9 ver 6,11; 1 Sam 7.13; Ps 78.66
5.11 ver 6,8,9
6.2 Gen 41.8; Ex 7.11; Isa 2.6

4.21 *Ichabod*, that is, "without glory." So named because of his ill-timed birth.   **5.2** *house of Dagon*, the temple containing the image of Dagon (the grain-god).

the diviners and said, "What shall we do with the ark of the LORD? Tell us with what we shall send it to its place." 3 They said, "If you send away the ark of the God of Israel, do not send it empty, but by all means return him a guilt offering. Then you will be healed, and it will be known to you why his hand does not turn away from you." 4And they said, "What is the guilt offering that we shall return to him?" They answered, "Five golden tumors and five golden mice, according to the number of the lords of the Philis'tines; for the same plague was upon all of you and upon your lords. 5 So you must make images of your tumors and images of your mice that ravage the land, and give glory to the God of Israel; perhaps he will lighten his hand from off you and your gods and your land. 6 Why should you harden your hearts as the Egyptians and Pharaōh hardened their hearts? After he had made sport of them, did not they let the people go, and they departed? 7 Now then, take and prepare a new cart and two milch cows upon which there has never come a yoke, and yoke the cows to the cart, but take their calves home, away from them. 8And take the ark of the LORD and place it on the cart, and put in a box at its side the figures of gold, which you are returning to him as a guilt offering. Then send it off, and let it go its way. 9And watch; if it goes up on the way to its own land, to Bĕth-shĕ'mĕsh, then it is he who has done us this great harm; but if not, then we shall know that it is not his hand that struck us, it happened to us by chance."

10 The men did so, and took two milch cows and yoked them to the cart, and shut up their calves at home. 11And they put the ark of the LORD on the cart, and the box with the golden mice and the images of their tumors. 12And the cows went straight in the direction of Bĕth-shĕ'mĕsh along one highway, lowing as they went; they turned neither to the right nor to the left, and the lords of the Philis'tines went after them as far as the border of Beth-shemesh. 13 Now the people of Bĕth-shĕ'mĕsh were reaping their wheat harvest in the valley; and when they lifted up their eyes and saw the ark, they rejoiced to see it. 14 The cart came into the field of Joshua of Bĕth-shĕ'mĕsh, and stopped there. A great stone was there; and they split up the wood of the cart and offered the cows as a burnt offering to the LORD. 15And the Lēvītes took down the ark of the LORD and the box that was beside it, in which were the golden figures, and set them upon the great stone; and the men of Bĕth-shĕ'mĕsh offered burnt offerings and sacrificed sacrifices on that day to the LORD. 16And when the five lords of the Philis'tines saw it, they returned that day to Ēkrŏn.

b. The ark sent from Beth-shemesh to Kiriath-jearim

17 These are the golden tumors, which the Philis'tines returned as a guilt offering to the LORD: one for Ăshdŏd, one for Gazà, one for Ăsh'kĕlŏn, one for Găth, one for Ēkrŏn; 18 also the golden mice, according to the number of all the cities of the Philis'tines belonging to the five lords, both fortified cities and unwalled villages. The great stone, beside which they set down the ark of the LORD, is a witness to this day in the field of Joshua of Bĕth-shĕ'mĕsh.

19 And he slew some of the men of Bĕth-shĕ'mĕsh, because they looked into the ark of the LORD; he slew seventy men of them,[k] and the people mourned because the LORD had made a great

k Cn: Heb of the people seventy men, fifty thousand men

slaughter among the people. 20 Then the men of Bĕth-shĕ'mĕsh said, "Who is able to stand before the LORD, this holy God? And to whom shall he go up away from us?" 21 So they sent messengers to the inhabitants of Kĭr'ĭăth-jē'ărĭm, saying, "The Phĭlĭs'tĭneş have returned the ark of the LORD. Come down and take it up to you." 1 And the men of Kĭr'ĭăth-jē'ărĭm came and took up the ark of the LORD, and brought it to the house of Ábĭn'ádăb on the hill; and they consecrated his son, Ēlëä'zăr, to have charge of the ark of the LORD. 2 From the day that the ark was lodged at Kĭr'ĭăth-jē'ărĭm, a long time passed, some twenty years, and all the house of Israel lamented after the LORD.

5. *Samuel overcomes the Philistines*
a. *The call to repentance*

3 Then Samuel said to all the house of Israel, "If you are returning to the LORD with all your heart, then put away the foreign gods and the Ăsh'tărŏth from among you, and direct your heart to the LORD, and serve him only, and he will deliver you out of the hand of the Phĭlĭs'tĭneş." 4 So Israel put away the Bāálş and the Ăsh'tărŏth, and they served the LORD only.

b. *The defeat of the Philistines*

5 Then Samuel said, "Gather all Israel at Mĭzpăh, and I will pray to the LORD for you." 6 So they gathered at Mĭzpăh, and drew water and poured it out before the LORD, and fasted on that day, and said there, "We have sinned against the LORD." And Samuel judged the people of Israel at Mizpah. 7 Now when the Phĭlĭs'tĭneş heard that the people of Israel had gathered at Mĭzpăh, the lords of the Philistines went up against Israel. And when the people of Israel heard of it they were afraid of the Phĭlistines. 8 And the people of Israel said to Samuel, "Do not cease to cry to the LORD our God for us, that he may save us from the hand of the Phĭlĭs'-tĭneş." 9 So Samuel took a sucking lamb and offered it as a whole burnt offering to the LORD; and Samuel cried to the LORD for Israel, and the LORD answered him. 10 As Samuel was offering up the burnt offering, the Phĭlĭs'tĭneş drew near to attack Israel; but the LORD thundered with a mighty voice that day against the Philistines and threw them into confusion; and they were routed before Israel. 11 And the men of Israel went out of Mĭzpăh and pursued the Phĭlĭs'tĭneş, and smote them, as far as below Bĕth-car.

c. *The Ebenezer*

12 Then Samuel took a stone and set it up between Mĭzpăh and Jĕshā'năh,[l] and called its name Ēbĕnē'zĕr;[m] for he said, "Hitherto the LORD has helped us." 13 So the Phĭlĭs'tĭneş were subdued and did not again enter the territory of Israel. And the hand of the LORD was against the Philistines all the days of Samuel. 14 The cities which the Phĭlĭs'tĭneş had taken from Israel were restored to Israel, from Ēkrŏn to Găth; and Israel rescued their territory from the hand of the Philistines. There was peace also between Israel and the Ăm'ŏrĭtes.

d. *Samuel's circuit*

15 Samuel judged Israel all the days of his life. 16 And he went

l Gk Syr: Heb Shĕn   m That is *Stone of help*

6.20
Lev 11.44, 45;
2 Sam 6.9
6.21
Josh 9.17;
15.9,60
7.1
2 Sam 6.3,4

7.3
Joel 2.2;
Josh 24.14;
Judg 2.13;
Deut 6.13;
Mt 4.10

7.6
Ps 62.8;
Neh 9.1;
Judg 10.10
7.7
1 Sam 17.11

7.8
Isa 37.4

7.9
Ps 99.6;
Jer 15.1
7.10
Josh 10.10;
1 Sam 2.10;
2 Sam 22.14,15

7.12
Gen 35.14;
Josh 4.9
7.13
Judg 13.1;
1 Sam 13.5

7.15
ver 6;
1 Sam 12.11

★7.17
1 Sam 1.19;
7.5
Judg 20.1;
1 Sam 8.6

on a circuit year by year to Bĕthĕl, Gĭlgăl, and Mĭzpáh; and he judged Israel in all these places. 17 Then he would come back to Rāmáh, for his home was there, and there also he administered justice to Israel. And he built there an altar to the LORD.

II. The reign of Saul 8.1–31.13

A. The appointment of Saul as king

1. Israel demands a king

8.1
Deut 16.18,
19
8.3
Ex 23.6,8;
Deut 16.19;
Ps 15.5
8.4
1 Sam 7.17
★8.5ff
Deut 17.14,
15
8.6
1 Sam 15.11
8.7
1 Sam
10.19;
Ex 16.8

8 When Samuel became old, he made his sons judges over Israel. 2 The name of his first-born son was Jōĕl, and the name of his second, Ăbī'jáh; they were judges in Beër-shē'bá. 3 Yet his sons did not walk in his ways, but turned aside after gain; they took bribes and perverted justice.

4 Then all the elders of Israel gathered together and came to Samuel at Rāmáh, 5 and said to him, "Behold, you are old and your sons do not walk in your ways; now appoint for us a king to govern us like all the nations." 6 But the thing displeased Samuel when they said, "Give us a king to govern us." And Samuel prayed to the LORD. 7And the LORD said to Samuel, "Hearken to the voice of the people in all that they say to you; for they have not rejected you, but they have rejected me from being king over them. 8According to all the deeds which they have done to me,ⁿ from the day I brought them up out of Egypt even to this day, forsaking me and serving other gods, so they are also doing to you.

8.9
ver 11

9 Now then, hearken to their voice; only, you shall solemnly warn them, and show them the ways of the king who shall reign over them."

10 So Samuel told all the words of the LORD to the people who were asking a king from him. 11 He said, "These will be the ways of the king who will reign over you: he will take your sons and appoint them to his chariots and to be his horsemen, and to run before his chariots; 12 and he will appoint for himself commanders of thousands and commanders of fifties, and some to plow his ground and to reap his harvest, and to make his implements of war and the equipment of his chariots. 13 He will take your daughters to be perfumers and cooks and bakers. 14 He will take the best of your fields and vineyards and olive orchards and give them to

8.11
1 Sam
14.52;
2 Sam 15.1
8.12
1 Sam 22.7
8.14
1 Ki 21.7;
Ezek 46.18

ⁿ Gk: Heb lacks *to me*

7.17 *back to Ramah.* Shiloh was in ruins so Samuel made his headquarters at Ramah, his home town, where he built an altar. Ramah is also known as Ramathaim-zophim (1 Sam 1.1).

8.5-7 At Sinai the Israelites ratified a covenant in which God would rule (theocracy) directly through Moses (Ex 19.8). The theocracy was continued through Joshua and Judges. Samuel functioned as prophet, judge, and priest; but when his sons perverted justice, the people demanded a king. The request greatly displeased Samuel, nevertheless the LORD informed him to comply. Theoretically a monarchy with an obedient king could have been more theocratic than rule by Samuel's wicked sons, but the people

were warned of what was in store. They refused to heed the warning, however, and Samuel prepared to anoint Saul as the new king. While this was unquestionably within the plan of God (as a step towards the Davidic kingdom), the sin of Israel's rejection of the theocracy was nonetheless heinous. God predicted that certain unpleasant results would ensue from the establishment of the kingship, and this prophecy was fulfilled to the letter under the rule of the more ungodly kings of Judah and Israel. At the end of the age God once again will govern immediately through Christ His Son, and His theocratic rule shall endure forever (Lk 1.32, 33; 1 Tim 1.17; 6.14–16).

his servants. 15 He will take the tenth of your grain and of your
vineyards and give it to his officers and to his servants. 16 He will
take your menservants and maidservants, and the best of your
cattle*o* and your asses, and put them to his work. 17 He will take
the tenth of your flocks, and you shall be his slaves. 18 And in that
day you will cry out because of your king, whom you have chosen
for yourselves; but the LORD will not answer you in that day."

19 But the people refused to listen to the voice of Samuel; and
they said, "No! but we will have a king over us, 20 that we also
may be like all the nations, and that our king may govern us and
go out before us and fight our battles." 21And when Samuel had
heard all the words of the people, he repeated them in the ears of
the LORD. 22And the LORD said to Samuel, "Hearken to their
voice, and make them a king." Samuel then said to the men of
Israel, "Go every man to his city."

2. *God selects Saul*
a. *The family of Saul*

9 There was a man of Benjamin whose name was Kĭsh, the
son of Ā'bĭĕl, son of Zĕror, son of Bĕcō'rắth, son of Ăphī'ăh,
a Benjaminite, a man of wealth; 2 and he had a son whose name
was Saul, a handsome young man. There was not a man among the
people of Israel more handsome than he; from his shoulders upward he was taller than any of the people.

b. *The search for his father's asses*

3 Now the asses of Kĭsh, Saul's father, were lost. So Kĭsh said
to Saul his son, "Take one of the servants with you, and arise, go
and look for the asses." 4And they*p* passed through the hill country of Ē'phrăim and passed through the land of Shălĭsh'ăh, but
they did not find them. And they passed through the land of Shā'-
ălĭm, but they were not there. Then they passed through the land
of Benjamin, but did not find them.

5 When they came to the land of Zŭph, Saul said to his servant
who was with him, "Come, let us go back, lest my father cease to
care about the asses and become anxious about us." 6 But he said
to him, "Behold, there is a man of God in this city, and he is a man
that is held in honor; all that he says comes true. Let us go there;
perhaps he can tell us about the journey on which we have set
out." 7 Then Saul said to his servant, "But if we go, what can we
bring the man? For the bread in our sacks is gone, and there is no
present to bring to the man of God. What have we?" 8 The servant
answered Saul again, "Here, I have with me the fourth part of a
shekel of silver, and I will give it to the man of God, to tell us our
way." 9 (Formerly in Israel, when a man went to inquire of God,
he said, "Come, let us go to the seer"; for he who is now called a
prophet was formerly called a seer.) 10And Saul said to his serv-

o Gk: Heb *young men*   *p* Gk Vg: Heb *he*

	8.18 Prov 1.25– 28; Mic 3.4
	8.20 ver 5
	8.22 ver 7
	9.1 1 Sam 14.51; 1 Chr 9.36– 39
	9.2 1 Sam 10.23,24
	9.4 Josh 24.33; 2 Ki 4.42; Josh 19.42
	9.5 1 Sam 10.2
	*9.6 Deut 33.1; 1 Sam 3.19
	9.7 1 Ki 14.3; 2 Ki 8.8
	*9.9 2 Sam 24.11; 1 Chr 26.28; Isa 30.10

9.6 *this city*, presumably Ramah, Samuel's
headquarters. *all that he says comes true.* This
test of a true prophet is set forth in Deut
18.21, 22.
9.9 This explanatory note of the compiler
would seem to be more appropriate after

verse 11 where the word *seer* appears for the
first time. Many prophets of Samuel's day
were ecstatics who tended to rove around the
country in bands (10.5, 6), but Samuel the
seer, like the prophets of the compiler's day,
spoke the clear word of the LORD.

ant, "Well said; come, let us go." So they went to the city where the man of God was.

c. *God reveals His choice to Samuel:*
He and Saul talk and eat together

11 As they went up the hill to the city, they met young maidens coming out to draw water, and said to them, "Is the seer here?" 12 They answered, "He is; behold, he is just ahead of you. Make haste; he has come just now to the city, because the people have a sacrifice today on the high place. 13As soon as you enter the city, you will find him, before he goes up to the high place to eat; for the people will not eat till he comes, since he must bless the sacrifice; afterward those eat who are invited. Now go up, for you will meet him immediately." 14 So they went up to the city. As they were entering the city, they saw Samuel coming out toward them on his way up to the high place.

15 Now the day before Saul came, the LORD had revealed to Samuel: 16 "Tomorrow about this time I will send to you a man from the land of Benjamin, and you shall anoint him to be prince over my people Israel. He shall save my people from the hand of the Philis'tines; for I have seen the affliction of*q* my people, because their cry has come to me." 17 When Samuel saw Saul, the LORD told him, "Here is the man of whom I spoke to you! He it is who shall rule over my people." 18 Then Saul approached Samuel in the gate, and said, "Tell me where is the house of the seer?" 19 Samuel answered Saul, "I am the seer; go up before me to the high place, for today you shall eat with me, and in the morning I will let you go and will tell you all that is on your mind. 20As for your asses that were lost three days ago, do not set your mind on them, for they have been found. And for whom is all that is desirable in Israel? Is it not for you and for all your father's house?" 21 Saul answered, "Am I not a Benjaminite, from the least of the tribes of Israel? And is not my family the humblest of all the families of the tribe of Benjamin? Why then have you spoken to me in this way?"

22 Then Samuel took Saul and his servant and brought them into the hall and gave them a place at the head of those who had been invited, who were about thirty persons. 23And Samuel said to the cook, "Bring the portion I gave you, of which I said to you, 'Put it aside.' " 24 So the cook took up the leg and the upper portion*r* and set them before Saul; and Samuel said, "See, what was kept is set before you. Eat; because it was kept for you until the hour appointed, that you might eat with the guests."*s*

So Saul ate with Samuel that day. 25And when they came down from the high place into the city, a bed was spread for Saul*t* upon the roof, and he lay down to sleep. 26 Then at the break of dawn*u* Samuel called to Saul upon the roof, "Up, that I may send you on your way." So Saul arose, and both he and Samuel went out into the street.

q Gk: Heb lacks *the affliction of*   *r* Heb obscure
s Cn: Heb *saying, I have invited the people*   *t* Gk: Heb *and he spoke with Saul*
u Gk: Heb *and they arose early and at break of dawn*

9.12 *the high place.* With Shiloh in ruins, the altar Samuel built on a hilltop became the center of worship. This was according to custom. (See note to 7.17.)

Marginal references:

9.11
Gen 24.15

*9.12
Num 28.11–15;
1 Sam 7.17;
10.5

9.16
1 Sam 10.1;
Ex 3.7,9

9.17
1 Sam 16.12

9.20
ver 3;
1 Sam 8.5;
12.13

9.21
1 Sam
15.17;
Judg 20.46,
48

9.24
Lev 7.32,
33;
Num 18.18

9.25
Deut 22.8;
Acts 10.9

27 As they were going down to the outskirts of the city, Samuel said to Saul, "Tell the servant to pass on before us, and when he has passed on stop here yourself for a while, that I may make known to you the word of God."

3. Saul's coronation
a. Saul anointed by Samuel; his father's asses found

10 Then Samuel took a vial of oil and poured it on his head, and kissed him and said, "Has not the LORD anointed you to be prince over his people Israel? And you shall reign over the people of the LORD and you will save them from the hand of their enemies round about. And this shall be the sign to you that the LORD has anointed you to be prince[w] over his heritage. 2 When you depart from me today you will meet two men by Rachel's tomb in the territory of Benjamin at Zĕlzăh, and they will say to you, 'The asses which you went to seek are found, and now your father has ceased to care about the asses and is anxious about you, saying, "What shall I do about my son?" ' 3 Then you shall go on from there further and come to the oak of Tābŏr; three men going up to God at Bĕthĕl will meet you there, one carrying three kids, another carrying three loaves of bread, and another carrying a skin of wine. 4And they will greet you and give you two loaves of bread, which you shall accept from their hand. 5After that you shall come to Gĭb'ĕăth-ĕlō'hĭm,[x] where there is a garrison of the Phĭlĭs'tĭneş; and there, as you come to the city, you will meet a band of prophets coming down from the high place with harp, tambourine, flute, and lyre before them, prophesying. 6 Then the spirit of the LORD will come mightily upon you, and you shall prophesy with them and be turned into another man. 7 Now when these signs meet you, do whatever your hand finds to do, for God is with you. 8And you shall go down before me to Gĭlgăl; and behold, I am coming to you to offer burnt offerings and to sacrifice peace offerings. Seven days you shall wait, until I come to you and show you what you shall do."

9 When he turned his back to leave Samuel, God gave him another heart; and all these signs came to pass that day. 10 When they came to Gĭb'ĕ-ăh,[z] behold, a band of prophets met him; and the spirit of God came mightily upon him, and he prophesied among them. 11And when all who knew him before saw how he prophesied with the prophets, the people said to one another, "What has come over the son of Kĭsh? Is Saul also among the prophets?" 12And a man of the place answered, "And who is their father?" Therefore it became a proverb, "Is Saul also among the prophets?" 13 When he had finished prophesying, he came to the high place.

14 Saul's uncle said to him and to his servant, "Where did you go?" And he said, "To seek the asses; and when we saw they were not to be found, we went to Samuel." 15And Saul's uncle said,

---

Cross-references (margin):

*10.1 1 Sam 16.13; 2 Ki 9.3,6; Ps 2.12; Deut 32.9; Ps 78.71

10.2 Gen 35.19, 20; 1 Sam 9.3–5

10.3 Gen 28.22; 35.1,3,7,8

10.5 1 Sam 13.3; 9.12;19.20; 2 Ki 3.15

10.6 Num 11.25, 29; ver 10; 1 Sam 19.23,24

10.7 Josh 1.5; Judg 6.12

10.8 1 Sam 11.15; 13.8

*10.9 ver 6

10.10 ver 5,6; 1 Sam 19.20

10.11 1 Sam 19.24; Mt 13.54, 55; Jn 7.15

*10.14

---

w Gk: Heb lacks *over his people Israel? And you shall . . . to be prince*
x Or *the hill of God*   z Or *the hill*

10.1 *the LORD has anointed you.* Two signs are given Saul to assure him that he is the LORD's choice: he will be given two loaves of bread and he will prophesy.

10.9 *God gave him another heart.* This was apparently an experience which prepared Saul to rule Israel.

10.14 *Saul's uncle.* This may have been Ner.

10.16
1 Sam 9.20
"Pray, tell me what Samuel said to you." ¹⁶And Saul said to his uncle, "He told us plainly that the asses had been found." But about the matter of the kingdom, of which Samuel had spoken, he did not tell him anything.

b. Saul accepted and crowned by Israel

10.17
1 Sam 7.5,6
10.18
Judg 6.8,9
17 Now Samuel called the people together to the LORD at Mizpah; 18 and he said to the people of Israel, "Thus says the LORD, the God of Israel, 'I brought up Israel out of Egypt, and I delivered you from the hand of the Egyptians and from the hand of all the kingdoms that were oppressing you.' 10.19
1 Sam 8.6,7;
Josh 24.1 19 But you have this day rejected your God, who saves you from all your calamities and your distresses; and you have said, 'No! but set a king over us.' Now therefore present yourselves before the LORD by your tribes and by your thousands."

10.20
Josh 7.14,
16,17
20 Then Samuel brought all the tribes of Israel near, and the tribe of Benjamin was taken by lot. 21 He brought the tribe of Benjamin near by its families, and the family of the Matrites was taken by lot; finally he brought the family of the Matrites near man by man,ᵃ and Saul the son of Kish was taken by lot. But when they sought him, he could not be found. 10.22
1 Sam 23.2,
4,9–11
10.23
1 Sam 9.2 22 So they inquired again of the LORD, "Did the man come hither?"ᵇ and the LORD said, "Behold, he has hidden himself among the baggage." 23 Then they ran and fetched him from there; and when he stood among the people, he was taller than any of the people from his shoulders upward. *10.24
2 Sam 21.6;
1 Ki 1.25,39 24And Samuel said to all the people, "Do you see him whom the LORD has chosen? There is none like him among all the people." And all the people shouted, "Long live the king!"

10.25
1 Sam 8.11–
18;
Deut 17.14–
20
25 Then Samuel told the people the rights and duties of the kingship; and he wrote them in a book and laid it up before the LORD. Then Samuel sent all the people away, each one to his home. 10.26
1 Sam 11.4 26 Saul also went to his home at Gib'ë-ah, and with him went men of valor whose hearts God had touched. 27 But some 10.27
1 Ki 10.25;
2 Chr 17.5 worthless fellows said, "How can this man save us?" And they despised him, and brought him no present. But he held his peace.

B. The early kingship of Saul

1. The Ammonites defeated

11.1
1 Sam
12.12;
Judg 21.8;
1 Ki 20.34;
Ezek 17.13
11.2
Num 16.14;
1 Sam 17.26
11 Then Nāhăsh the Ăm'mónīte went up and besieged Jābĕsh-gĭl'ĕad; and all the men of Jābĕsh said to Nahash, "Make a treaty with us, and we will serve you." 2 But Nāhăsh the Ăm'mónīte said to them, "On this condition I will make a treaty with you, that I gouge out all your right eyes, and thus put disgrace upon all Israel." 3 The elders of Jābĕsh said to him, "Give us seven days respite that we may send messengers through all the territory of Israel. Then, if there is no one to save us, we

a Gk: Heb lacks *finally . . . man by man* b Gk: Heb *Is there yet a man to come hither?*

10.24 The choice of Saul, a Benjamite, as king presents something of a problem, since Jacob's blessing had designated Judah as the kingly tribe (Gen 49.10). Why then was Saul chosen to be king? While one cannot be dogmatic, the following observations may be helpful: (1) Just as God used Samson and the other judges in a period of temporary distress, so he used Saul until David was old enough to serve as theocratic king; (2) Saul's reign paved the way for David's conquest of the full territory promised to Abraham in Gen 15.18 and his consolidation of the kingdom on a permanent basis.

will give ourselves up to you." 4 When the messengers came to Gĭb´e-äh of Saul, they reported the matter in the ears of the people; and all the people wept aloud.

5 Now Saul was coming from the field behind the oxen; and Saul said, "What ails the people, that they are weeping?" So they told him the tidings of the men of Jābĕsh. 6And the spirit of God came mightily upon Saul when he heard these words, and his anger was greatly kindled. 7 He took a yoke of oxen, and cut them in pieces and sent them throughout all the territory of Israel by the hand of messengers, saying, "Whoever does not come out after Saul and Samuel, so shall it be done to his oxen!" Then the dread of the LORD fell upon the people, and they came out as one man. 8 When he mustered them at Bēzĕk, the men of Israel were three hundred thousand, and the men of Judah thirty thousand. 9And they said to the messengers who had come, "Thus shall you say to the men of Jā´bĕsh-gĭl´ĕäd: 'Tomorrow, by the time the sun is hot, you shall have deliverance.' " When the messengers came and told the men of Jābĕsh, they were glad. 10 Therefore the men of Jābĕsh said, "Tomorrow we will give ourselves up to you, and you may do to us whatever seems good to you." 11And on the morrow Saul put the people in three companies; and they came into the midst of the camp in the morning watch, and cut down the Ăm´-mŏnītes until the heat of the day; and those who survived were scattered, so that no two of them were left together.

12 Then the people said to Samuel, "Who is it that said, 'Shall Saul reign over us?' Bring the men, that we may put them to death." 13 But Saul said, "Not a man shall be put to death this day, for today the LORD has wrought deliverance in Israel." 14 Then Samuel said to the people, "Come, let us go to Gĭlgăl and there renew the kingdom." 15 So all the people went to Gĭlgăl, and there they made Saul king before the LORD in Gilgal. There they sacrificed peace offerings before the LORD, and there Saul and all the men of Israel rejoiced greatly.

2. *Samuel lays down his office as judge*

12 And Samuel said to all Israel, "Behold, I have hearkened to your voice in all that you have said to me, and have made a king over you. 2And now, behold, the king walks before you; and I am old and gray, and behold, my sons are with you; and I have walked before you from my youth until this day. 3 Here I am; testify against me before the LORD and before his anointed. Whose ox have I taken? Or whose ass have I taken? Or whom have I defrauded? Whom have I oppressed? Or from whose hand have I taken a bribe to blind my eyes with it? Testify against me[c] and I will restore it to you." 4 They said, "You have not defrauded us or oppressed us or taken anything from any man's hand." 5And he said to them, "The LORD is witness against you, and his anointed is witness this day, that you have not found anything in my hand." And they said, "He is witness."

6 And Samuel said to the people, "The LORD is witness,[d] who

[c] Gk: Heb lacks *Testify against me*   [d] Gk: Heb lacks *is witness*

11.15 *they made Saul king.* Saul was chosen by lot and presented to the people at Mizpah (10.24) but he was not fully accepted by the people until his dramatic summoning of the tribes (11.7) and his victory over the Ammonites.

11.4	1 Sam 10.26; 15.34; 30.4; Judg 2.4
11.6	Judg 3.10; 6.34; 13.25; 14.6; 1 Sam 10.10; 16.13
11.7	Judg 19.29; 21.5,8,10
11.8	Judg 1.5; 20.2
11.10	ver 3
11.11	Judg 7.16
11.12	1 Sam 10.27; Lk 19.27
11.13	2 Sam 19.22; Ex 14.13; 1 Sam 19.5
11.14	1 Sam 10.8, 25
★11.15	1 Sam 10.8, 17
12.1	1 Sam 8.7, 9,22; 10.24; 11.14,15
12.2	1 Sam 8.1, 5,20
12.3	1 Sam 10.1; 24.6; 2 Sam 1.14; Num 16.15; Acts 20.33; Deut 16.19
12.5	Acts 23.9; 24.20; Ex 22.4
12.6	Ex 6.26

appointed Moses and Aaron and brought your fathers up out of the land of Egypt. 7 Now therefore stand still, that I may plead with you before the LORD concerning all the saving deeds of the LORD which he performed for you and for your fathers. 8 When Jacob went into Egypt and the Egyptians oppressed them,*e* then your fathers cried to the LORD and the LORD sent Moses and Aaron, who brought forth your fathers out of Egypt, and made them dwell in this place. 9 But they forgot the LORD their God; and he sold them into the hand of Sis'era, commander of the army of Jābin king of*f* Hāzor, and into the hand of the Philis'tines, and into the hand of the king of Mōăb; and they fought against them. 10And they cried to the LORD, and said, 'We have sinned, because we have forsaken the LORD, and have served the Bāăls and the Ăsh'tăroth; but now deliver us out of the hand of our enemies, and we will serve thee.' 11And the LORD sent Jĕrŭbbā'ăl and Bărăk,*g* and Jĕphthăh, and Samuel, and delivered you out of the hand of your enemies on every side; and you dwelt in safety. 12And when you saw that Nāhăsh the king of the Ăm'mŏnītes came against you, you said to me, 'No, but a king shall reign over us,' when the LORD your God was your king. 13And now behold the king whom you have chosen, for whom you have asked; behold, the LORD has set a king over you. 14 If you will fear the LORD and serve him and hearken to his voice and not rebel against the commandment of the LORD, and if both you and the king who reigns over you will follow the LORD your God, it will be well; 15 but if you will not hearken to the voice of the LORD, but rebel against the commandment of the LORD, then the hand of the LORD will be against you and your king.*h* 16 Now therefore stand still and see this great thing, which the LORD will do before your eyes. 17 Is it not wheat harvest today? I will call upon the LORD, that he may send thunder and rain; and you shall know and see that your wickedness is great, which you have done in the sight of the LORD, in asking for yourselves a king." 18 So Samuel called upon the LORD, and the LORD sent thunder and rain that day; and all the people greatly feared the LORD and Samuel.

19 And all the people said to Samuel, "Pray for your servants to the LORD your God, that we may not die; for we have added to all our sins this evil, to ask for ourselves a king." 20And Samuel said to the people, "Fear not; you have done all this evil, yet do not turn aside from following the LORD, but serve the LORD with all your heart; 21 and do not turn aside after*i* vain things which cannot profit or save, for they are vain. 22 For the LORD will not cast away his people, for his great name's sake, because it has pleased the LORD to make you a people for himself. 23 Moreover as for me, far be it from me that I should sin against the LORD by ceasing to pray for you; and I will instruct you in the good and the right way. 24 Only fear the LORD, and serve him faithfully with all your heart; for consider what great things he has done for you. 25 But if you still do wickedly, you shall be swept away, both you and your king."

---

e Gk: Heb lacks *and the Egyptians oppressed them*
f Gk: Heb lacks *Jabin king of*
g Gk Syr: Heb *Bēdān*   *h* Gk: Heb *fathers*   *i* Gk Syr Tg Vg: Heb *because after*

12.14 The monarchy was an acceptable form of rule as long as the king and the people followed the precepts of the LORD, their real King.

Cross references (left margin):

12.7 Isa 1.18; Mic 6.1–5
12.8 Ex 2.23; 3.10; 4.16
12.9 Judg 3.7; 4.2; 10.7; 13.1; 3.12
12.10 Judg 10.10; 2.13; 10.15
12.11 Judg 6.14, 32; 4.6; 11.1
12.12 1 Sam 11.1; 8.6,19; Judg 8.23
12.13 1 Sam 10.24; 8.5; Hos 13.11
*12.14 Josh 24.14
12.15 Josh 24.20
12.16 Ex 14.13,31
12.17 Prov 26.1; 1 Sam 7.9, 10; 8.7
12.18 Ex 14.31
12.19 ver 23; Ex 9.28; Jas 5.15
12.21 Deut 11.16; Jer 16.19; Hab 2.18
12.22 1 Ki 6.13; Josh 7.9; Deut 7.7,8
12.23 Rom 1.9; Col 1.9; 2 Tim 1.3; 1 Ki 8.36
12.24 Ecc 12.13; Deut 10.21
12.25 Josh 24.20; 1 Sam 31.1–5

3. Saul's war against the Philistines
a. Opening battles against the Philistines

13 Saul was . . . *j* years old when he began to reign; and he reigned . . . and two*k* years over Israel.

2 Saul chose three thousand men of Israel; two thousand were with Saul in Michmash and the hill country of Bethel, and a thousand were with Jonathan in Gib'ë-àh of Benjamin; the rest of the people he sent home, every man to his tent. 3 Jonathan defeated the garrison of the Philis'tines which was at Geba; and the Philistines heard of it. And Saul blew the trumpet throughout all the land, saying, "Let the Hebrews hear." 4And all Israel heard it said that Saul had defeated the garrison of the Philis'tines, and also that Israel had become odious to the Philistines. And the people were called out to join Saul at Gilgal.

5 And the Philis'tines mustered to fight with Israel, thirty thousand chariots, and six thousand horsemen, and troops like the sand on the seashore in multitude; they came up and encamped in Michmash, to the east of Beth-ä'ven. 6 When the men of Israel saw that they were in straits (for the people were hard pressed), the people hid themselves in caves and in holes and in rocks and in tombs and in cisterns, 7 or crossed the fords of the Jordan*l* to the land of Gad and Gil'ëäd. Saul was still at Gilgal, and all the people followed him trembling.

b. Saul intrudes into the priest's office

8 He waited seven days, the time appointed by Samuel; but Samuel did not come to Gilgal, and the people were scattering from him. 9 So Saul said, "Bring the burnt offering here to me, and the peace offerings." And he offered the burnt offering. 10As soon as he had finished offering the burnt offering, behold, Samuel came; and Saul went out to meet him and salute him. 11 Samuel said, "What have you done?" And Saul said, "When I saw that the people were scattering from me, and that you did not come within the days appointed, and that the Philis'tines had mustered at Michmash, 12 I said, 'Now the Philis'tines will come down upon me at Gilgal, and I have not entreated the favor of the LORD'; so I forced myself, and offered the burnt offering." 13And Samuel said to Saul, "You have done foolishly; you have not kept the commandment of the LORD your God, which he commanded you; for now the LORD would have established your kingdom over Israel for ever. 14 But now your kingdom shall not continue; the LORD has sought out a man after his own heart; and the LORD has appointed him to be prince over his people, because you have not kept what the LORD commanded you." 15And Samuel arose, and went up from Gilgal to Gib'ë-àh of Benjamin.

c. Saul's nondescript army

And Saul numbered the people who were present with him,

j The number is lacking in Heb
k *Two* is not the entire number. Something has dropped out.
l Cn: Heb *Hebrews crossed the Jordan*

13.3 The Israelites were subjugated by Philistine garrisons throughout the country.
13.13 *You have done foolishly.* To forestall corruption, the rights and duties of the kingship prohibited the king from acting as the religious leader as well. Even though the people were beginning to desert him, Saul had no right to function as a priest.

Margin references:
13.2 / 1 Sam 10.26
*13.3 / 1 Sam 10.5
13.5 / Josh 11.4
13.6 / Judg 6.2
13.8 / 1 Sam 10.8
13.9 / 2 Sam 24.25
13.10 / 1 Sam 15.13
13.11 / ver 2,5,16,23
*13.13 / 2 Chr 16.9; 1 Sam 15.11,22
13.14 / 1 Sam 15.28; Acts 13.22
13.15 / 1 Sam 14.2

about six hundred men. 16And Saul, and Jonathan his son, and the people who were present with them, stayed in Gēbā of Benjamin; but the Phĭlĭs′tĭneṣ encamped in Mĭchmăsh. 17And raiders came out of the camp of the Phĭlĭs′tĭneṣ in three companies; one company turned toward Ŏphrăh, to the land of Shuăl, 18 another company turned toward Bĕth-hor′ŏn, and another company turned toward the border that looks down upon the valley of Zĕbō′ĭm toward the wilderness.

19 Now there was no smith to be found throughout all the land of Israel; for the Phĭlĭs′tĭneṣ said, "Lest the Hebrews make themselves swords or spears"; 20 but every one of the Israelites went down to the Phĭlĭs′tĭneṣ to sharpen his plowshare, his mattock, his axe, or his sickle;m 21 and the charge was a pim for the plowshares and for the mattocks, and a third of a shekel for sharpening the axes and for setting the goads.n 22 So on the day of the battle there was neither sword nor spear found in the hand of any of the people with Saul and Jonathan; but Saul and Jonathan his son had them. 23And the garrison of the Phĭlĭs′tĭneṣ went out to the pass of Mĭchmăsh.

d. Jonathan's exploit at Michmash
(1) JONATHAN ATTACKS

14 One day Jonathan the son of Saul said to the young man who bore his armor, "Come, let us go over to the Phĭlĭs′tĭne garrison on yonder side." But he did not tell his father. 2 Saul was staying in the outskirts of Gĭb′ĕ-ăh under the pomegranate tree which is at Mĭgrŏn; the people who were with him were about six hundred men, 3 and Ăhī′jăh the son of Ăhī′tŭb, Ĭch′ăbŏd′ṣ brother, son of Phĭn′ĕhăs, son of Ēlī, the priest of the LORD in Shīlōh, wearing an ephod. And the people did not know that Jonathan had gone. 4 In the pass,o by which Jonathan sought to go over to the Phĭlĭs′tĭne garrison, there was a rocky crag on the one side and a rocky crag on the other side; the name of the one was Bōzĕz, and the name of the other Sēnĕh. 5 The one crag rose on the north in front of Mĭchmăsh, and the other on the south in front of Gēbā.

6 And Jonathan said to the young man who bore his armor, "Come, let us go over to the garrison of these uncircumcised; it may be that the LORD will work for us; for nothing can hinder the LORD from saving by many or by few." 7And his armor-bearer said to him, "Do all that your mind inclines to;p behold, I am with you, as is your mind so is mine."q 8 Then said Jonathan, "Behold, we will cross over to the men, and we will show ourselves to them. 9 If they say to us, 'Wait until we come to you,' then we will stand still in our place, and we will not go up to them. 10 But if they say, 'Come up to us,' then we will go up; for the LORD has given them into our hand. And this shall be the sign to us." 11 So both of them showed themselves to the garrison of the Phĭlĭs′tĭneṣ; and the Philistines said, "Look, Hebrews are coming out of the holes where they have hid themselves." 12And the men of the

Cross-references (margin)
13.17 1 Sam 14.15
13.18 Josh 18.13, 14; Neh 11.34
*13.19 2 Ki 24.14
13.22 Judg 5.8
14.2 1 Sam 13.15
14.3 1 Sam 22.9–12, 20; 4.21; 2.28
14.4 1 Sam 13.23
14.6 Judg 7.4,7; 1 Sam 17.46,47
14.10 Gen 24.14; Judg 6.36, 37
14.11 1 Sam 13.6
14.12 1 Sam 17.43,44; 2 Sam 5.24

---

m Gk: Heb plowshare   n The Heb of this verse is obscure   o Heb between the passes
p Gk: Heb Do all that is in your mind. Turn   q Gk: Heb lacks so is mine

---

13.19 no smith. A basic reason for Philistine supremacy over Israel was their monopoly over the smelting and working of iron. The Israelites were helpless without arms.

garrison hailed Jonathan and his armor-bearer, and said, "Come up to us, and we will show you a thing." And Jonathan said to his armor-bearer, "Come up after me; for the LORD has given them into the hand of Israel." 13 Then Jonathan climbed up on his hands and feet, and his armor-bearer after him. And they fell before Jonathan, and his armor-bearer killed them after him; 14 and that first slaughter, which Jonathan and his armor-bearer made, was of about twenty men within as it were half a furrow's length in an acre*r* of land. 15And there was a panic in the camp, in the field, and among all the people; the garrison and even the raiders trembled; the earth quaked; and it became a very great panic.

14.15
2 Ki 7.6,7;
1 Sam
13.17

(2) THE PHILISTINES FLEE

16 And the watchmen of Saul in Gĭb'ë-äh of Benjamin looked; and behold, the multitude was surging hither and thither.*s* 17 Then Saul said to the people who were with him, "Number and see who has gone from us." And when they had numbered, behold, Jonathan and his armor-bearer were not there. 18And Saul said to Ahī'jäh, "Bring hither the ark of God." For the ark of God went at that time with the people of Israel. 19And while Saul was talking to the priest, the tumult in the camp of the Phĭlĭs'tĭneṣ increased more and more; and Saul said to the priest, "Withdraw your hand." 20 Then Saul and all the people who were with him rallied and went into the battle; and behold, every man's sword was against his fellow, and there was very great confusion. 21 Now the Hebrews who had been with the Phĭlĭs'tĭneṣ before that time and who had gone up with them into the camp, even they also turned to be with*t* the Israelites who were with Saul and Jonathan. 22 Likewise, when all the men of Israel who had hid themselves in the hill country of Ē'phräim heard that the Phĭlĭs'tĭneṣ were fleeing, they too followed hard after them in the battle. 23 So the LORD delivered Israel that day; and the battle passed beyond Bĕth-ā'vĕn.

14.16
2 Sam
18.24

14.19
Num 27.21

14.20
Judg 7.22;
2 Chr 20.23

14.22
1 Sam 13.6

14.23
Ex 14.30;
Ps 44.6,7;
1 Sam 13.5

(3) JONATHAN UNWITTINGLY TRANSGRESSES SAUL'S OATH

24 And the men of Israel were distressed that day; for Saul laid an oath on the people, saying, "Cursed be the man who eats food until it is evening and I am avenged on my enemies." So none of the people tasted food. 25And all the people*u* came into the forest; and there was honey on the ground. 26And when the people entered the forest, behold, the honey was dropping, but no man put his hand to his mouth; for the people feared the oath. 27 But Jonathan had not heard his father charge the people with the oath; so he put forth the tip of the staff that was in his hand, and dipped it in the honeycomb, and put his hand to his mouth; and his eyes became bright. 28 Then one of the people said, "Your father strictly charged the people with an oath, saying, 'Cursed be the man who eats food this day.'" And the people were faint. 29 Then Jonathan said, "My father has troubled the land; see how my eyes have become bright, because I tasted a little of this honey. 30 How much better if the people had eaten freely today of the spoil of their enemies which they found; for now the slaughter among the Phĭlĭs'tĭneṣ has not been great."

14.24
Josh 6.26

14.27
1 Sam
30.12

14.29
1 Ki 18.18

r Heb yoke *s* Gk: Heb they went and thither
t Gk Syr Vg Tg: Heb round about, they also, to be with *u* Heb land

31 They struck down the Phĭlĭs'tĭneş that day from Mĭchmăsh
to Āi'jälŏn. And the people were very faint; 32 the people flew
upon the spoil, and took sheep and oxen and calves, and slew
them on the ground; and the people ate them with the blood.
33 Then they told Saul, "Behold, the people are sinning against
the LORD, by eating with the blood." And he said, "You have
dealt treacherously; roll a great stone to me here."ᵛ 34And Saul
said, "Disperse yourselves among the people, and say to them,
'Let every man bring his ox or his sheep, and slay them here, and
eat; and do not sin against the LORD by eating with the blood.' "
So every one of the people brought his ox with him that night,
and slew them there. 35And Saul built an altar to the LORD; it was
the first altar that he built to the LORD.

(4) JONATHAN'S GUILT DISCOVERED

36 Then Saul said, "Let us go down after the Phĭlĭs'tĭneş by
night and despoil them until the morning light; let us not leave a
man of them." And they said, "Do whatever seems good to you."
But the priest said, "Let us draw near hither to God." 37And Saul
inquired of God, "Shall I go down after the Phĭlĭs'tĭneş? Wilt
thou give them into the hand of Israel?" But he did not answer
him that day. 38And Saul said, "Come hither, all you leaders of
the people; and know and see how this sin has arisen today. 39 For
as the LORD lives who saves Israel, though it be in Jonathan my
son, he shall surely die." But there was not a man among all the
people that answered him. 40 Then he said to all Israel, "You shall
be on one side, and I and Jonathan my son will be on the other
side." And the people said to Saul, "Do what seems good to you."
41 Therefore Saul said, "O LORD God of Israel, why hast thou not
answered thy servant this day? If this guilt is in me or in Jonathan
my son, O LORD, God of Israel, give Ūrĭm; but if this guilt is in
thy people Israel,ʷ give Thŭmmĭm." And Jonathan and Saul were
taken, but the people escaped. 42 Then Saul said, "Cast the lot
between me and my son Jonathan." And Jonathan was taken.

(5) JONATHAN SAVED BY THE PEOPLE

43 Then Saul said to Jonathan, "Tell me what you have done."
And Jonathan told him, "I tasted a little honey with the tip of
the staff that was in my hand; here I am, I will die." 44And Saul
said, "God do so to me and more also; you shall surely die, Jonathan." 45 Then the people said to Saul, "Shall Jonathan die, who
has wrought this great victory in Israel? Far from it! As the LORD
lives, there shall not one hair of his head fall to the ground; for
he has wrought with God this day." So the people ransomed Jonathan, that he did not die. 46 Then Saul went up from pursuing the
Phĭlĭs'tĭneş; and the Philistines went to their own place.

e. Saul wars against other nations

47 When Saul had taken the kingship over Israel, he fought
against all his enemies on every side, against Mōăb, against the

---

Marginal references (left column):

14.32
1 Sam
15.19;
Lev 17.10–
14

★14.34f

14.35
1 Sam 7.17

14.37
1 Sam
10.22;
28.6

14.38
Josh 7.14;
1 Sam
10.19

14.39
2 Sam 12.5

★14.41
Prov 16.33;
Acts 1.24

14.43
Josh 7.19;
ver 23

14.44
Ruth 1.17;
ver 39

14.45
2 Sam
14.11;
1 Ki 1.52;
Acts 27.34

14.47
1 Sam 11.1–
13;
2 Sam 10.6;
ver 52

ᵛ Gk: Heb this day   ʷ Vg Compare Gk: Heb Saul said to the LORD, the God of Israel

---

14.34, 35 To protect the people from the
sin of eating blood (Lev 7.26, 27; 17.12)
Saul built the first of his altars to the LORD

and supervised the sacrifices.
14.41 Urim . . . Thummim. See note to Ex
28.30.

Ăm'mŏnītes, against Ēdòm, against the kings of Zōbáh, and
against the Phĭlĭs'tĭnes; wherever he turned he put them to the
worse. 48And he did valiantly, and smote the Ȧmăl'ēkītes, and delivered Israel out of the hands of those who plundered them.

f. *Saul's family and army*

49 Now the sons of Saul were Jonathan, Ĭshvī, and Măl̦chĭsh'uȧ;
and the names of his two daughters were these: the name of the
first-born was Mērăb, and the name of the younger Mĭchȧl; 50 and
the name of Saul's wife was Ȧhĭn'ō-ȧm the daughter of Ȧhĭm'ä-äz.
And the name of the commander of his army was Abner the son
of Nĕr, Saul's uncle; 51 Kĭsh was the father of Saul, and Nĕr the
father of Abner was the son of Ā'bĭèl.

52 There was hard fighting against the Phĭlĭs'tĭnes all the days
of Saul; and when Saul saw any strong man, or any valiant man, he
attached him to himself.

C. God rejects Saul

1. *The war with the Amalekites*
a. *God's command to destroy*

15 And Samuel said to Saul, "The LORD sent me to anoint
you king over his people Israel; now therefore hearken to
the words of the LORD. 2 Thus says the LORD of hosts, 'I will
punish what Ăm'ălĕk did to Israel in opposing them on the way,
when they came up out of Egypt. 3 Now go and smite Ăm'ălĕk, and
utterly destroy all that they have; do not spare them, but kill
both man and woman, infant and suckling, ox and sheep, camel
and ass.' "

b. *Saul's disobedience*

4 So Saul summoned the people, and numbered them in Tèlā'-
ĭm, two hundred thousand men on foot, and ten thousand men of
Judah. 5And Saul came to the city of Ăm'ălĕk, and lay in wait in
the valley. 6And Saul said to the Kēnītes, "Go, depart, go down
from among the Ȧmăl'ēkītes, lest I destroy you with them; for you
showed kindness to all the people of Israel when they came up out
of Egypt." So the Kenites departed from among the Amalekites.
7And Saul defeated the Ȧmăl'ēkītes, from Hăv'ĭláh as far as Shŭr,
which is east of Egypt. 8And he took Āgăg the king of the Ȧmăl'-
ēkītes alive, and utterly destroyed all the people with the edge of
the sword. 9 But Saul and the people spared Āgăg, and the best of
the sheep and of the oxen and of the fatlings, and the lambs, and
all that was good, and would not utterly destroy them; all that was
despised and worthless they utterly destroyed.

c. *Samuel delivers God's sentence*

10 The word of the LORD came to Samuel: 11"I repent that I
have made Saul king; for he has turned back from following me,
and has not performed my commandments." And Samuel was
angry; and he cried to the LORD all night. 12And Samuel rose early

Margin references:
14.48 / 1 Sam 15.3,7
14.49 / 1 Sam 31.2; 1 Chr 8.33; 1 Sam 18.17-20
14.50 / 2 Sam 2.8
14.51 / 1 Sam 9.1
14.52 / 1 Sam 8.11
15.1 / 1 Sam 9.16
15.2 / Ex 17.8-14; Num 24.20; Deut 25.17-19
*15.3 / Num 24.20; Deut 20.16-18; 1 Sam 22.19
15.6 / Judg 1.16; 4.11; Ex 18.10,19; Num 10.29-32
15.7 / 1 Sam 14.48; Gen 16.7; 25.17,18; Ex 15.22
*15.8 / 1 Ki 20.34ff; 1 Sam 30.1
15.9 / ver 3,15
15.11 / Gen 6.6,7; 2 Sam 24.16; 1 Ki 9.6,7; 1 Sam 16.1
15.12 / Josh 15.55

15.3 *utterly destroy.* The Amalekites were
devoted to the LORD; see note to Deut 2.34.
15.8 *all the people.* This cannot mean all
of the Amalekites because they were a strong
group in David's reign (27.8; 30.1, 18;
2 Sam 1.1). There were undoubtedly other
Amalekites not included in this account. Also
see note to Est 3.1 on Amalekites.

to meet Saul in the morning; and it was told Samuel, "Saul came to Carmel, and behold, he set up a monument for himself and turned, and passed on, and went down to Gilgal." 13And Samuel came to Saul, and Saul said to him, "Blessed be you to the LORD; I have performed the commandment of the LORD." 14And Samuel said, "What then is this bleating of the sheep in my ears, and the lowing of the oxen which I hear?" 15 Saul said, "They have brought them from the Amal'ekites; for the people spared the best of the sheep and of the oxen, to sacrifice to the LORD your God; and the rest we have utterly destroyed." 16 Then Samuel said to Saul, "Stop! I will tell you what the LORD said to me this night." And he said to him, "Say on."

17 And Samuel said, "Though you are little in your own eyes, are you not the head of the tribes of Israel? The LORD anointed you king over Israel. 18And the LORD sent you on a mission, and said, 'Go, utterly destroy the sinners, the Amal'ekites, and fight against them until they are consumed.' 19 Why then did you not obey the voice of the LORD? Why did you swoop on the spoil, and do what was evil in the sight of the LORD?" 20And Saul said to Samuel, "I have obeyed the voice of the LORD, I have gone on the mission on which the LORD sent me, I have brought Agag the king of Am'alek, and I have utterly destroyed the Amal'ekites. 21 But the people took of the spoil, sheep and oxen, the best of the things devoted to destruction, to sacrifice to the LORD your God in Gilgal." 22And Samuel said,

"Has the LORD as great delight in burnt offerings and sacrifices,
as in obeying the voice of the LORD?
Behold, to obey is better than sacrifice,
and to hearken than the fat of rams.
23 For rebellion is as the sin of divination,
and stubbornness is as iniquity and idolatry.
Because you have rejected the word of the LORD,
he has also rejected you from being king."

d. Saul appears penitent

24 And Saul said to Samuel, "I have sinned; for I have transgressed the commandment of the LORD and your words, because I feared the people and obeyed their voice. 25 Now therefore, I pray, pardon my sin, and return with me, that I may worship the LORD." 26And Samuel said to Saul, "I will not return with you; for you have rejected the word of the LORD, and the LORD has rejected you from being king over Israel." 27As Samuel turned to go away, Saul laid hold upon the skirt of his robe, and it tore. 28And Samuel said to him, "The LORD has torn the kingdom of Israel from you this day, and has given it to a neighbor of yours, who is better than you. 29And also the Glory of Israel will not lie or repent; for he is not a man, that he should repent." 30 Then he said, "I have sinned; yet honor me now before the elders of my people and before Israel, and return with me, that I may worship the LORD your God." 31 So Samuel turned back after Saul; and Saul worshiped the LORD.

Cross-references: 15.13 Gen 14.19; Judg 17.2 • 1.15 ver 21; Ger 3.12 • 15.17 1 Sam 9.21 • 15.18 ver 3 • 15.19 1 Sam 14.32 • 15.20 ver 13 • *15.21 ver 15 • 15.22 Isa 1.11–13; Mic 6.6–8; Heb 10.6–9; Hos 6.6; Mk 12.33 • *15.23 1 Sam 13.14 • 15.24 2 Sam 12.13; Prov 29.25; Isa 51.12,13 • 15.26 1 Sam 13.14 • 15.27 1 Ki 11.30,31 • 15.28 1 Sam 28.17 • *15.29 1 Chr 29.11; Num 23.19; Ezek 24.14 • 15.30 Jn 12.43; Isa 29.13

15.21 *the people took.* Saul, like Aaron (Ex 32.22–24), blamed the people, but back of his act was covetousness.

15.23 *divination.* See notes to Deut 18.10 and Ezek 21.21.

15.29 *Glory of Israel,* another name for God.

e. *Samuel slays Agag and sees Saul no more*

32 Then Samuel said, "Bring here to me Āgăg the king of the Amǎl'ĕkītes." And Agag came to him cheerfully. Agag said, "Surely the bitterness of death is past." ³³And Samuel said, "As your sword has made women childless, so shall your mother be childless among women." And Samuel hewed Āgăg in pieces before the LORD in Gĭlgăl.

34 Then Samuel went to Rāmáh; and Saul went up to his house in Gĭb'ĕ-áh of Saul. ³⁵And Samuel did not see Saul again until the day of his death, but Samuel grieved over Saul. And the LORD repented that he had made Saul king over Israel.

2. *David chosen to be king*
a. *God sends Samuel to Jesse's house*

16 The LORD said to Samuel, "How long will you grieve over Saul, seeing I have rejected him from being king over Israel? Fill your horn with oil, and go; I will send you to Jĕssĕ the Bĕth'lĕhĕmīte', for I have provided for myself a king among his sons." ²And Samuel said, "How can I go? If Saul hears it, he will kill me." And the LORD said, "Take a heifer with you, and say, 'I have come to sacrifice to the LORD.' ³And invite Jĕssĕ to the sacrifice, and I will show you what you shall do; and you shall anoint for me him whom I name to you." ⁴ Samuel did what the LORD commanded, and came to Bĕth'lĕhĕm. The elders of the city came to meet him trembling, and said, "Do you come peaceably?" ⁵And he said, "Peaceably; I have come to sacrifice to the LORD; consecrate yourselves, and come with me to the sacrifice." And he consecrated Jĕssĕ and his sons, and invited them to the sacrifice.

b. *David selected and anointed king*

6 When they came, he looked on Ĕlī'ăb and thought, "Surely the LORD's anointed is before him." ⁷ But the LORD said to Samuel, "Do not look on his appearance or on the height of his stature, because I have rejected him; for the LORD sees not as man sees; man looks on the outward appearance, but the LORD looks on the heart." ⁸ Then Jĕssĕ called Abĭn'ădăb, and made him pass before Samuel. And he said, "Neither has the LORD chosen this one." ⁹ Then Jĕssĕ made Shămmăh pass by. And he said, "Neither has the LORD chosen this one." ¹⁰And Jĕssĕ made seven of his sons pass before Samuel. And Samuel said to Jesse, "The LORD has not chosen these." ¹¹And Samuel said to Jĕssĕ, "Are all your sons here?" And he said, "There remains yet the youngest, but behold, he is keeping the sheep." And Samuel said to Jesse, "Send and fetch him; for we will not sit down till he comes here." ¹²And he sent, and brought him in. Now he was ruddy, and had beautiful eyes, and was handsome. And the LORD said, "Arise, anoint him; for this is he." ¹³ Then Samuel took the horn of oil, and anointed

*15.32

15.33
Gen 9.6;
Judg 1.7

15.34
1 Sam
7.17; 11.4
15.35
1 Sam
19.24; 16.1

16.1
1 Sam
15.23,35;
9.16;
2 Ki 9.1;
Ps 78.70;
Acts 13.22
16.2
1 Sam
20.29
16.3
Ex 4.15;
1 Sam 9.16
16.4
Lk 2.4;
1 Ki 2.13;
2 Ki 9.22
16.5
Ex 19.10

16.6
1 Sam
17.13
16.7
Isa 55.8;
1 Ki 8.39;
1 Chr 28.9
16.8
1 Sam 17.13

16.9
1 Sam
17.13

16.11
1 Sam
17.12
16.12
1 Sam
17.42; 9.17
*16.13
1 Sam 10.1,
6,9,10;
Judg 11.29

15.32 See note to Est 3.1 on Amalekites.
16.13 David, the shepherd-king, is a type of Christ. David was taken from responsibility over sheep to become king over Israel. Christ came as the good shepherd who gives His life for His sheep (Jn 10.11). This shepherd has been raised from the dead for us (Heb 13.20) and is now exalted at the right hand of the Father (Acts 5.31). Like David, who was made king, so Christ the shepherd is now King of kings, sitting upon the heavenly counterpart of the throne of His father David. He is indeed great David's greater son (Lk 1.32; Acts 2.30). (See also 1 Chr 17.7; 2 Sam 8.15; Ezek 37.24; Ps 89.19, 20; Phil 2.9.)

him in the midst of his brothers; and the Spirit of the LORD came mightily upon David from that day forward. And Samuel rose up, and went to Rāmáh.

3. Saul overtaken by an evil spirit; David joins his court

14 Now the Spirit of the LORD departed from Saul, and an evil spirit from the LORD tormented him. 15And Saul's servants said to him, "Behold now, an evil spirit from God is tormenting you. 16 Let our lord now command your servants, who are before you, to seek out a man who is skilful in playing the lyre; and when the evil spirit from God is upon you, he will play it, and you will be well." 17 So Saul said to his servants, "Provide for me a man who can play well, and bring him to me." 18 One of the young men answered, "Behold, I have seen a son of Jĕssë the Bĕth′lĕhĕmīte′, who is skilful in playing, a man of valor, a man of war, prudent in speech, and a man of good presence; and the LORD is with him." 19 Therefore Saul sent messengers to Jĕssë, and said, "Send me David your son, who is with the sheep." 20And Jĕssë took an ass laden with bread, and a skin of wine and a kid, and sent them by David his son to Saul. 21And David came to Saul, and entered his service. And Saul loved him greatly, and he became his armor-bearer. 22And Saul sent to Jĕssë, saying, "Let David remain in my service, for he has found favor in my sight." 23And whenever the evil spirit from God was upon Saul, David took the lyre and played it with his hand; so Saul was refreshed, and was well, and the evil spirit departed from him.

D. The rise of David and his persecutions by Saul

1. Goliath the Philistine

17 Now the Philĭs′tĭneṣ gathered their armies for battle; and they were gathered at Sōcōh, which belongs to Judah, and encamped between Socoh and Azē′káh, in Ē′phĕs-dăm′mĭm. 2And Saul and the men of Israel were gathered, and encamped in the valley of Ēláh, and drew up in line of battle against the Philĭs′tĭneṣ. 3And the Philĭs′tĭneṣ stood on the mountain on the one side, and Israel stood on the mountain on the other side, with a valley between them. 4And there came out from the camp of the Philĭs′tĭneṣ a champion named Gōlĭ′áth, of Găth, whose height was six cubits and a span. 5 He had a helmet of bronze on his head, and he was armed with a coat of mail, and the weight of the coat was five thousand shekels of bronze. 6And he had greaves of bronze upon his legs, and a javelin of bronze slung between his shoulders. 7And the shaft of his spear was like a weaver's beam, and his spear's head weighed six hundred shekels of iron; and his shield-bearer went before him. 8 He stood and shouted to the ranks of Israel, "Why have you come out to draw up for battle? Am I not a Philĭs′tĭne, and are you not servants of Saul? Choose a man for yourselves, and let him come down to me. 9 If he is able to fight with me and kill me, then we will be your servants; but if I prevail against him and kill him, then you shall be our servants and serve us." 10And the

---

Cross references (left margin):

*16.14
Judg 16.20;
1 Sam
18.10

16.16
ver 23;
1 Sam
18.10;
19.9;
2 Ki 3.15

16.18
1 Sam
17.32–36;
3.19

16.20
1 Sam
10.27;
Prov 18.16
*16.21f
Gen 41.46;
Prov 22.29
16.23
ver 14–16

17.1
1 Sam 13.5;
2 Chr 28.18
17.2
1 Sam 21.9

17.4
2 Sam
21.19;
Josh 11.21,
22

17.6
ver 45
17.7
2 Sam
21.19;
ver 41
17.8
1 Sam
8.17

17.10
ver 26,36,45

16.14 *evil spirit from the* LORD. Saul's disorder is described as punishment initiated by God.

16.21, 22 This close relationship between Saul and David does not make impossible the apparent unfamiliarity noted in 17.55–58.

Phĭlĭs′tĭne said, "I defy the ranks of Israel this day; give me a man, that we may fight together." 11 When Saul and all Israel heard these words of the Phĭlĭs′tĭne, they were dismayed and greatly afraid.

2. David slays Goliath

12 Now David was the son of an Ĕph′răthĭte of Bĕth′lĕhĕm in Judah, named Jĕssë, who had eight sons. In the days of Saul the man was already old and advanced in years.ˣ 13 The three eldest sons of Jĕssë had followed Saul to the battle; and the names of his three sons who went to the battle were Ĕlĭ′ăb the first-born, and next to him Abĭn′ădăb, and the third Shămmăh. 14 David was the youngest; the three eldest followed Saul, 15 but David went back and forth from Saul to feed his father's sheep at Bĕth′lĕhĕm. 16 For forty days the Phĭlĭs′tĭne came forward and took his stand, morning and evening.

17 And Jĕssë said to David his son, "Take for your brothers an ephah of this parched grain, and these ten loaves, and carry them quickly to the camp to your brothers; 18 also take these ten cheeses to the commander of their thousand. See how your brothers fare, and bring some token from them."

19 Now Saul, and they, and all the men of Israel, were in the valley of Ĕlăh, fighting with the Phĭlĭs′tĭnes. 20 And David rose early in the morning, and left the sheep with a keeper, and took the provisions, and went, as Jĕssë had commanded him; and he came to the encampment as the host was going forth to the battle line, shouting the war cry. 21 And Israel and the Phĭlĭs′tĭnes drew up for battle, army against army. 22 And David left the things in charge of the keeper of the baggage, and ran to the ranks, and went and greeted his brothers. 23 As he talked with them, behold, the champion, the Phĭlĭs′tĭne of Găth, Gŏlĭ′ăth by name, came up out of the ranks of the Phĭlĭs′tĭnes, and spoke the same words as before. And David heard him.

24 All the men of Israel, when they saw the man, fled from him, and were much afraid. 25 And the men of Israel said, "Have you seen this man who has come up? Surely he has come up to defy Israel; and the man who kills him, the king will enrich with great riches, and will give him his daughter, and make his father's house free in Israel." 26 And David said to the men who stood by him, "What shall be done for the man who kills this Phĭlĭs′tĭne, and takes away the reproach from Israel? For who is this uncircumcised Philistine, that he should defy the armies of the living God?" 27 And the people answered him in the same way, "So shall it be done to the man who kills him."

28 Now Ĕlĭ′ăb his eldest brother heard when he spoke to the men; and Ĕlĭ′ăb's anger was kindled against David, and he said, "Why have you come down? And with whom have you left those few sheep in the wilderness? I know your presumption, and the evil of your heart; for you have come down to see the battle." 29 And David said, "What have I done now? Was it not but a word?" 30 And he turned away from him toward another, and spoke in the same way; and the people answered him again as before.

ˣ Gk Syr: Heb *among men*

17.12 Ruth 4.22; 1 Sam 16.18; Gen 35.19; 1 Sam 16.10,11; 1 Chr 2.13–15
17.13 1 Sam 16.6,8,9
17.15 1 Sam 16.19
17.18 Gen 37.14
17.23 ver 8–10
17.25 Josh 15.16
17.26 1 Sam 11.2; 14.6; ver 10; Deut 5.26
17.27 ver 25
17.28 Gen 37.4ff
17.29 ver 17
17.30 ver 26,27

17.32
Deut 20.1–
4;
1 Sam
16.18

31 When the words which David spoke were heard, they repeated them before Saul; and he sent for him. 32And David said to Saul, "Let no man's heart fail because of him; your servant will go and fight with this Philis'tine." 33And Saul said to David, "You are not able to go against this Philis'tine to fight with him; for you are but a youth, and he has been a man of war from his youth." 34 But David said to Saul, "Your servant used to keep sheep for his father; and when there came a lion, or a bear, and took a lamb from the flock, 35 I went after him and smote him and delivered it out of his mouth; and if he arose against me, I caught him by his beard, and smote him and killed him. 36 Your servant has killed both lions and bears; and this uncircumcised Philis'tine shall be like one of them, seeing he has defied the armies of the living God." 37And David said, "The LORD who delivered me from the paw of the lion and from the paw of the bear, will deliver me from the hand of this Philis'tine." And Saul said to David, "Go, and the LORD be with you!" 38 Then Saul clothed David with his armor; he put a helmet of bronze on his head, and clothed him with a coat of mail. 39And David girded his sword over his armor, and he tried in vain to go, for he was not used to them. Then David said to Saul, "I cannot go with these; for I am not used to them." And David put them off. 40 Then he took his staff in his hand, and chose five smooth stones from the brook, and put them in his shepherd's bag or wallet; his sling was in his hand, and he drew near to the Philis'tine.

17.37
2 Tim 4.17;
1 Sam
20.13;
1 Chr
22.11,16

41 And the Philis'tine came on and drew near to David, with his shield-bearer in front of him. 42And when the Philis'tine looked, and saw David, he disdained him; for he was but a youth, ruddy and comely in appearance. 43And the Philis'tine said to David, "Am I a dog, that you come to me with sticks?" And the Philistine cursed David by his gods. 44 The Philis'tine said to David, "Come to me, and I will give your flesh to the birds of the air and to the beasts of the field." 45 Then David said to the Philis'-tine, "You come to me with a sword and with a spear and with a javelin; but I come to you in the name of the LORD of hosts, the God of the armies of Israel, whom you have defied. 46 This day the LORD will deliver you into my hand, and I will strike you down, and cut off your head; and I will give the dead bodies of the host of the Philis'tines this day to the birds of the air and to the wild beasts of the earth; that all the earth may know that there is a God in Israel, 47 and that all this assembly may know that the LORD saves not with sword and spear; for the battle is the LORD's and he will give you into our hand."

17.42
Prov 16.18;
Ps 123.3,4;
1 Sam
16.12
17.43
1 Sam
24.14;
2 Sam 3.8
17.44
1 Ki 20.10
17.45
2 Chr 32.8;
Ps 124.8;
Heb 11.34
17.46
1 Ki 18.36;
2 Ki 19.19;
Isa 52.10
17.47
1 Sam 14.6;
2 Chr 14.11;
Ps 44.6,7

48 When the Philis'tine arose and came and drew near to meet David, David ran quickly toward the battle line to meet the Philistine. 49And David put his hand in his bag and took out a stone, and slung it, and struck the Philis'tine on his forehead; the stone sank into his forehead, and he fell on his face to the ground.

50 So David prevailed over the Philis'tine with a sling and with a stone, and struck the Philistine, and killed him; there was no sword in the hand of David. 51 Then David ran and stood over the Philis'tine, and took his sword and drew it out of its sheath, and killed him, and cut off his head with it. When the Philis'tines saw that their champion was dead, they fled. 52And the men of Israel and Judah rose with a shout and pursued the Philis'tines as far

17.51
1 Sam 21.9;
Heb 11.34
17.52
Josh 15.36

as Găth^y and the gates of Ĕkrŏn, so that the wounded Philistines
fell on the way from Shă-ără'ĭm as far as Gath and Ekron. ⁵³And
the Israelites came back from chasing the Phĭlĭs'tĭneṣ, and they
plundered their camp. ⁵⁴And David took the head of the Phĭlĭs'-
tĭne and brought it to Jerusalem; but he put his armor in his tent.

55 When Saul saw David go forth against the Phĭlĭs'tĭne, he
said to Abner, the commander of the army, "Abner, whose son
is this youth?" And Abner said, "As your soul lives, O king, I cannot tell." ⁵⁶And the king said, "Inquire whose son the stripling
is." ⁵⁷And as David returned from the slaughter of the Phĭlĭs'tĭne,
Abner took him, and brought him before Saul with the head of the
Philistine in his hand. ⁵⁸And Saul said to him, "Whose son are
you, young man?" And David answered, "I am the son of your
servant Jĕssë the Bĕth'lĕhĕmīte'."

3. The friendship of David and Jonathan

18 When he had finished speaking to Saul, the soul of Jonathan was knit to the soul of David, and Jonathan loved
him as his own soul. ²And Saul took him that day, and would not
let him return to his father's house. ³ Then Jonathan made a covenant with David, because he loved him as his own soul. ⁴And
Jonathan stripped himself of the robe that was upon him, and gave
it to David, and his armor, and even his sword and his bow and
his girdle. ⁵And David went out and was successful wherever Saul
sent him; so that Saul set him over the men of war. And this was
good in the sight of all the people and also in the sight of Saul's
servants.

4. The hatred of Saul

6 As they were coming home, when David returned from slaying the Phĭlĭs'tĭne, the women came out of all the cities of Israel,
singing and dancing, to meet King Saul, with timbrels, with songs
of joy, and with instruments^z of music. ⁷And the women sang to
one another as they made merry,
"Saul has slain his thousands,
    and David his ten thousands."
⁸And Saul was very angry, and this saying displeased him; he said,
"They have ascribed to David ten thousands, and to me they have
ascribed thousands; and what more can he have but the kingdom?" ⁹And Saul eyed David from that day on.

10 And on the morrow an evil spirit from God rushed upon
Saul, and he raved within his house, while David was playing the
lyre, as he did day by day. Saul had his spear in his hand; ¹¹ and
Saul cast the spear, for he thought, "I will pin David to the wall."
But David evaded him twice.

12 Saul was afraid of David, because the LORD was with him
but had departed from Saul. ¹³ So Saul removed him from his
presence, and made him a commander of a thousand; and he went
out and came in before the people. ¹⁴And David had success in all his
undertakings; for the LORD was with him. ¹⁵And when Saul saw
that he had great success, he stood in awe of him. ¹⁶ But all Israel
and Judah loved David; for he went out and came in before them.

^{y} Gk: Heb Gā'i
^{z} Or triangles, or three-stringed instruments

17.55
1 Sam
16.21,22

17.57
ver 54

17.58
ver 12

18.1
Gen 44.30;
Deut 13.6;
1 Sam
20.17;
2 Sam 1.26
18.2
1 Sam
17.15

18.6
Ex 15.20;
Judg 11.34;
Ps 68.25
18.7
Ex 15.21;
1 Sam 21.11
18.8
1 Sam 15.8
18.10
1 Sam
16.14,23;
19.9,23,24
18.11
1 Sam
19.10;
20.33
18.12
ver 15,29;
1 Sam
16.13,
14,18
18.13
ver 16;
2 Sam 5.2
18.14
1 Sam
16.18;
Gen 39.2,3,
23

18.16
ver 5

5. David loses Merab but marries Michal

18.17
1 Sam
17.25;
25.28;
ver 21,25

17 Then Saul said to David, "Here is my elder daughter Mērăb; I will give her to you for a wife; only be valiant for me and fight the LORD's battles." For Saul thought, "Let not my hand be upon him, but let the hand of the Phĭlĭs'tĭneṣ be upon him."

18.18
ver 23;
1 Sam 9.21;
2 Sam 7.18

18And David said to Saul, "Who am I, and who are my kinsfolk, my father's family in Israel, that I should be son-in-law to the king?" 19 But at the time when Mērăb, Saul's daughter, should have been given to David, she was given to Ā'drĭĕl the Mĕhō'-lăthīte for a wife.

18.19
2 Sam 21.8;
Judg 7.22

18.20
ver 28

20 Now Saul's daughter Mĭchăl loved David; and they told Saul, and the thing pleased him. 21 Saul thought, "Let me give her to him, that she may be a snare for him, and that the hand of the Phĭlĭs'tĭneṣ may be against him." Therefore Saul said to David a second time,*a* "You shall now be my son-in-law." 22And Saul commanded his servants, "Speak to David in private and say, 'Behold, the king has delight in you, and all his servants love you; now then become the king's son-in-law.' " 23And Saul's servants spoke those words in the ears of David. And David said, "Does it seem to you a little thing to become the king's son-in-law, seeing that I am a poor man and of no repute?" 24And the servants of Saul told him, "Thus and so did David speak." 25 Then Saul said, "Thus shall you say to David, 'The king desires no marriage present except a hundred foreskins of the Phĭlĭs'tĭneṣ, that he may be avenged of the king's enemies.' " Now Saul thought to make David fall by the hand of the Philistines. 26And when his servants told David these words, it pleased David well to be the king's son-in-law. Before the time had expired, 27 David arose and went, along with his men, and killed two hundred of the Phĭlĭs'tĭneṣ; and David brought their foreskins, which were given in full number to the king, that he might become the king's son-in-law. And Saul gave him his daughter Mĭchăl for a wife. 28 But when Saul saw and knew that the LORD was with David, and that all Israel*b* loved him, 29 Saul was still more afraid of David. So Saul was David's enemy continually.

18.21
ver 17,26

*18.25
Ex 22.17;
1 Sam
14.24;
ver 17

18.26
ver 21

18.27
ver 13;
2 Sam 3.14

18.30
ver 5

30 Then the princes of the Phĭlĭs'tĭneṣ came out to battle, and as often as they came out David had more success than all the servants of Saul; so that his name was highly esteemed.

6. Saul seeks to kill David

a. Jonathan's effort to placate Saul

19.1
1 Sam 18.1–
3,8,9

19 And Saul spoke to Jonathan his son and to all his servants, that they should kill David. But Jonathan, Saul's son, delighted much in David. 2And Jonathan told David, "Saul my father seeks to kill you; therefore take heed to yourself in the morning, stay in a secret place and hide yourself; 3 and I will go out and stand beside my father in the field where you are, and I

19.3
1 Sam 20.9,
13

a Heb *by two*   *b* Gk: Heb *Mĭchăl, Saul's daughter*

18.25 Here the figure one hundred is used. David brought back two hundred, according to verse 27. In 2 Sam 3.14 it is stated in David's own words ". . . *I betrothed at the price of a hundred foreskins . . .*" This appears to be a discrepancy. Two possibilities exist. Either some scribe in the course of textual transmission miscopied his original at verse 27 or else David brought back twice as many as were required of him. When indicating what he had done in 2 Sam 3.14 he simply stated the price originally demanded by Saul.

will speak to my father about you; and if I learn anything I will tell you." ⁴And Jonathan spoke well of David to Saul his father, and said to him, "Let not the king sin against his servant David; because he has not sinned against you, and because his deeds have been of good service to you; ⁵ for he took his life in his hand and he slew the Phĭlĭs′tĭne, and the LORD wrought a great victory for all Israel. You saw it, and rejoiced; why then will you sin against innocent blood by killing David without cause?" ⁶And Saul hearkened to the voice of Jonathan; Saul swore, "As the LORD lives, he shall not be put to death." ⁷And Jonathan called David, and Jonathan showed him all these things. And Jonathan brought David to Saul, and he was in his presence as before.

19.4
1 Sam
20.32;
Gen 42.22

19.5
1 Sam
17.49,50;
11.13;
20.32

19.7
1 Sam
16.21;
18.2,13

b. *Saul tries to kill David*

8 And there was war again; and David went out and fought with the Phĭlĭs′tĭnes, and made a great slaughter among them, so that they fled before him. ⁹ Then an evil spirit from the LORD came upon Saul, as he sat in his house with his spear in his hand; and David was playing the lyre. ¹⁰And Saul sought to pin David to the wall with the spear; but he eluded Saul, so that he struck the spear into the wall. And David fled, and escaped.

19.9
1 Sam
16.14;
18.10,11

19.10
1 Sam
18.11

c. *Michal helps David escape*

11 That night Saulˣ sent messengers to David's house to watch him, that he might kill him in the morning. But Mĭchăl, David's wife, told him, "If you do not save your life tonight, tomorrow you will be killed." ¹² So Mĭchăl let David down through the window; and he fled away and escaped. ¹³ Mĭchăl took an imageᶜ and laid it on the bed and put a pillowᵈ of goats' hair at its head, and covered it with the clothes. ¹⁴And when Saul sent messengers to take David, she said, "He is sick." ¹⁵ Then Saul sent the messengers to see David, saying, "Bring him up to me in the bed, that I may kill him." ¹⁶And when the messengers came in, behold, the imageᶜ was in the bed, with the pillowᵈ of goats' hair at its head. ¹⁷ Saul said to Mĭchăl, "Why have you deceived me thus, and let my enemy go, so that he has escaped?" And Michal answered Saul, "He said to me, 'Let me go; why should I kill you?'"

19.12
Josh 2.15;
Acts 9.24,
25

19.14
Josh 2.5

d. *Saul goes to Naioth and prophesies*

18 Now David fled and escaped, and he came to Samuel at Rāmăh, and told him all that Saul had done to him. And he and Samuel went and dwelt at Nāi′ŏth. ¹⁹And it was told Saul, "Behold, David is at Nāi′ŏth in Rāmăh." ²⁰ Then Saul sent messengers to take David; and when they saw the company of the prophets prophesying, and Samuel standing as head over them, the Spirit of God came upon the messengers of Saul, and they also prophesied. ²¹ When it was told Saul, he sent other messengers, and they also prophesied. And Saul sent messengers again the third time, and they also prophesied. ²² Then he himself went to Rāmăh, and came to the great well that is in Sēcū; and he asked, "Where are Samuel and David?" And one said, "Behold, they are at Nāi′ŏth in Ramah." ²³And he went fromᶠ there to Nāi′ŏth in Rāmăh; and the Spirit of God came upon him also, and as he

19.18
1 Sam 7.17

19.20
ver 11,14;
1 Sam
10.5,6;
Num 11.25

19.23
Isa 20.2;
1 Sam
10.10–12

ˣ Gk Old Latin: Heb *escaped that night.* ¹¹*And Saul*
ᶜ Heb *teraphim* ᵈ The meaning of the Hebrew word is uncertain ᶠ Gk: Heb lacks *from*

went he prophesied, until he came to Naioth in Ramah. ²⁴And he too stripped off his clothes, and he too prophesied before Samuel, and lay naked all that day and all that night. Hence it is said, "Is Saul also among the prophets?"

7. Jonathan delivers David
a. The discussion of the problem

20 Then David fled from Nāi'óth in Rāmàh, and came and said before Jonathan, "What have I done? What is my guilt? And what is my sin before your father, that he seeks my life?" ²And he said to him, "Far from it! You shall not die. Behold, my father does nothing either great or small without disclosing it to me; and why should my father hide this from me? It is not so." ³ But David replied,ᵍ "Your father knows well that I have found favor in your eyes; and he thinks, 'Let not Jonathan know this, lest he be grieved.' But truly, as the LORD lives and as your soul lives, there is but a step between me and death." ⁴ Then said Jonathan to David, "Whatever you say, I will do for you." ⁵ David said to Jonathan, "Behold, tomorrow is the new moon, and I should not fail to sit at table with the king; but let me go, that I may hide myself in the field till the third day at evening. ⁶ If your father misses me at all, then say, 'David earnestly asked leave of me to run to Bĕth'lĕhĕm his city; for there is a yearly sacrifice there for all the family.' ⁷ If he says, 'Good!' it will be well with your servant; but if he is angry, then know that evil is determined by him. ⁸ Therefore deal kindly with your servant, for you have brought your servant into a sacred covenantʰ with you. But if there is guilt in me, slay me yourself; for why should you bring me to your father?" ⁹And Jonathan said, "Far be it from you! If I knew that it was determined by my father that evil should come upon you, would I not tell you?" ¹⁰ Then said David to Jonathan, "Who will tell me if your father answers you roughly?" ¹¹And Jonathan said to David, "Come, let us go out into the field." So they both went out into the field.

b. The covenant of David and Jonathan

12 And Jonathan said to David, "The LORD, the God of Israel, be witness!ⁱ When I have sounded my father, about this time tomorrow, or the third day, behold, if he is well disposed toward David, shall I not then send and disclose it to you? ¹³ But should it please my father to do you harm, the LORD do so to Jonathan, and more also, if I do not disclose it to you, and send you away, that you may go in safety. May the LORD be with you, as he has been with my father. ¹⁴ If I am still alive, show me the loyal love of the LORD, that I may not die;ʲ ¹⁵ and do not cut off your loyalty from my house for ever. When the LORD cuts off every one of the enemies of David from the face of the earth, ¹⁶ let not the name of Jonathan be cut off from the house of David.ᵏ And may the LORD take vengeance on David's enemies." ¹⁷And Jonathan made David

Margin references:
20.1
1 Sam 24.9

*20.5
Num 10.10;
28.11;
1 Sam 19.2

20.6
1 Sam
17.58;
Deut 12.5

20.8
1 Sam 18.3;
23.18;
2 Sam
14.32

20.13
1 Sam 3.17;
Ruth 1.17;
1 Sam
17.37

*20.15
2 Sam 9.1

20.17
1 Sam 18.1

ᵍ Gk: Heb swore again   ʰ Heb a covenant of the LORD
ⁱ Heb lacks be witness   ʲ Heb uncertain
ᵏ Gk: Heb earth, and Jonathan made a covenant with the house of David

---

20.5 new moon. The first day of the lunar month was a feast day with work suspended.

20.15 David did what Jonathan asked by showing kindness to his son Mephibosheth.

swear again by his love for him; for he loved him as he loved his own soul.

c. *The signal arranged*

18 Then Jonathan said to him, "Tomorrow is the new moon; and you will be missed, because your seat will be empty. 19And on the third day you will be greatly missed;[l] then go to the place where you hid yourself when the matter was in hand, and remain beside yonder stone heap.[m] 20And I will shoot three arrows to the side of it, as though I shot at a mark. 21And behold, I will send the lad, saying, 'Go, find the arrows.' If I say to the lad, 'Look, the arrows are on this side of you, take them,' then you are to come, for, as the LORD lives, it is safe for you and there is no danger. 22But if I say to the youth, 'Look, the arrows are beyond you,' then go; for the LORD has sent you away. 23And as for the matter of which you and I have spoken, behold, the LORD is between you and me for ever."

d. *Jonathan's plea to Saul for David*

24 So David hid himself in the field; and when the new moon came, the king sat down to eat food. 25 The king sat upon his seat, as at other times, upon the seat by the wall; Jonathan sat opposite,[n] and Abner sat by Saul's side, but David's place was empty. 26 Yet Saul did not say anything that day; for he thought, "Something has befallen him; he is not clean, surely he is not clean." 27 But on the second day, the morrow after the new moon, David's place was empty. And Saul said to Jonathan his son, "Why has not the son of Jĕssĕ come to the meal, either yesterday or today?" 28 Jonathan answered Saul, "David earnestly asked leave of me to go to Bĕth'lĕhĕm; 29 he said, 'Let me go; for our family holds a sacrifice in the city, and my brother has commanded me to be there. So now, if I have found favor in your eyes, let me get away, and see my brothers.' For this reason he has not come to the king's table."

e. *Saul's anger at Jonathan*

30 Then Saul's anger was kindled against Jonathan, and he said to him, "You son of a perverse, rebellious woman, do I not know that you have chosen the son of Jĕssĕ to your own shame, and to the shame of your mother's nakedness? 31 For as long as the son of Jĕssĕ lives upon the earth, neither you nor your kingdom shall be established. Therefore send and fetch him to me, for he shall surely die." 32 Then Jonathan answered Saul his father, "Why should he be put to death? What has he done?" 33 But Saul cast his spear at him to smite him; so Jonathan knew that his father was determined to put David to death. 34And Jonathan rose from the table in fierce anger and ate no food the second day of the month, for he was grieved for David, because his father had disgraced him.

f. *Jonathan warns David*

35 In the morning Jonathan went out into the field to the appointment with David, and with him a little lad. 36And he said to his lad, "Run and find the arrows which I shoot." As the lad ran,

20.18	ver 5,25
20.19	1 Sam 19.2
20.22	ver 37
20.23	ver 14,15; Gen 31.49, 53
20.25	ver 18
20.26	1 Sam 16.5; Lev 7.20,21
20.28	ver 6
20.30	Deut 21.20
20.32	1 Sam 19.5; Mt 27.23; Lk 23.22
20.33	ver 7
20.36	ver 20,21

l Gk: Heb *go down quickly*   *m* Gk: Heb *the stone Ĕzĕl*   *n* Cn See Gk: Heb *stood up*

20.37
ver 22

he shot an arrow beyond him. ³⁷And when the lad came to the place of the arrow which Jonathan had shot, Jonathan called after the lad and said, "Is not the arrow beyond you?" ³⁸And Jonathan called after the lad, "Hurry, make haste, stay not." So Jonathan's lad gathered up the arrows, and came to his master. ³⁹ But the lad knew nothing; only Jonathan and David knew the matter. ⁴⁰And Jonathan gave his weapons to his lad, and said to him, "Go and carry them to the city." ⁴¹And as soon as the lad had gone, David rose from beside the stone heap*o* and fell on his face to the ground, and bowed three times; and they kissed one another, and wept with one another, until David recovered himself.*p* ⁴²Then Jonathan said to David, "Go in peace, forasmuch as we have sworn both of us in the name of the LORD, saying, 'The LORD shall be between me and you, and between my descendants and your descendants, for ever.' " And he rose and departed; and Jonathan went into the city.*q*

20.42
1 Sam 1.17;
ver 22

8. David's flight from Saul
a. Ahimelech the priest and the holy bread

21.1
1 Sam
22.19;
14.3; 16.4

21 *r* Then came David to Nŏb to Ȧhĭm′ĕlĕch the priest; and Ahimelech came to meet David trembling, and said to him, "Why are you alone, and no one with you?" ²And David said to Ȧhĭm′ĕlĕch the priest, "The king has charged me with a matter, and said to me, 'Let no one know anything of the matter about which I send you, and with which I have charged you.' I have made an appointment with the young men for such and such a place. ³ Now then, what have you at hand? Give me five loaves of bread, or whatever is here." ⁴And the priest answered David, "I have no common bread at hand, but there is holy bread; if only the young men have kept themselves from women." ⁵And David answered the priest, "Of a truth women have been kept from us as always when I go on an expedition; the vessels of the young men are holy, even when it is a common journey; how much more today will their vessels be holy?" ⁶ So the priest gave him the holy bread; for there was no bread there but the bread of the Presence, which is removed from before the LORD, to be replaced by hot bread on the day it is taken away.

21.4
Lev 24.5–9;
Mt 12.4
21.5
Ex 19.14,15

21.6
Mt 12.3,4;
Mk 2.25,
26;
Lev 24.8,9

7 Now a certain man of the servants of Saul was there that day, detained before the LORD; his name was Dŏēg the Ē′dŏmīte, the chief of Saul's herdsmen.

21.7
1 Sam 22.9

b. David takes Goliath's sword

8 And David said to Ȧhĭm′ĕlĕch, "And have you not here a spear or a sword at hand? For I have brought neither my sword nor my weapons with me, because the king's business required haste." ⁹And the priest said, "The sword of Gŏlī′ăth the Phĭlĭs′-tīne, whom you killed in the valley of Ēlăh, behold, it is here wrapped in a cloth behind the ephod; if you will take that, take it, for there is none but that here." And David said, "There is none like that; give it to me."

21.9
1 Sam
17.2,51

c. David goes to Achish, king of Gath

10 And David rose and fled that day from Saul, and went to

---

o Gk: Heb *from beside the south*   *p* Or *exceeded*
q This sentence is 21.1 in Heb   *r* Ch 21.2 in Heb

Āchǐsh the king of Gǎth. 11And the servants of Āchǐsh said to him,
"Is not this David the king of the land? Did they not sing to one
another of him in dances,
　'Saul has slain his thousands,
　　and David his ten thousands'?"
12And David took these words to heart, and was much afraid of
Āchǐsh the king of Gǎth. 13 So he changed his behavior before
them, and feigned himself mad in their hands, and made marks on
the doors of the gate, and let his spittle run down his beard.
14 Then said Āchǐsh to his servants, "Lo, you see the man is mad;
why then have you brought him to me? 15 Do I lack madmen, that
you have brought this fellow to play the madman in my presence?
Shall this fellow come into my house?"

d. David in the cave of Adullam

22 David departed from there and escaped to the cave of
Ādǔl'lǎm; and when his brothers and all his father's house
heard it, they went down there to him. 2And every one who was in
distress, and every one who was in debt, and every one who was
discontented, gathered to him; and he became captain over them.
And there were with him about four hundred men.

e. David flees to Mizpeh in Moab

3 And David went from there to Mǐzpěh of Mōǎb; and he said
to the king of Moab, "Pray let my father and my mother stay⁵
with you, till I know what God will do for me." 4And he left them
with the king of Mōǎb, and they stayed with him all the time that
David was in the stronghold. 5 Then the prophet Gǎd said to
David, "Do not remain in the stronghold; depart, and go into the
land of Judah." So David departed, and went into the forest of
Hěrěth.

f. Doeg the Edomite betrays Ahimelech to Saul

6 Now Saul heard that David was discovered, and the men who
were with him. Saul was sitting at Gǐb'ë-ǎh, under the tamarisk
tree on the height, with his spear in his hand, and all his servants
were standing about him. 7And Saul said to his servants who stood
about him, "Hear now, you Benjaminites; will the son of Jěssě
give every one of you fields and vineyards, will he make you all
commanders of thousands and commanders of hundreds, 8 that
all of you have conspired against me? No one discloses to me
when my son makes a league with the son of Jěssě, none of you is
sorry for me or discloses to me that my son has stirred up my servant against me, to lie in wait, as at this day." 9 Then answered
Dōěg the Ē'dȯmīte, who stood by the servants of Saul, "I saw the
son of Jěssě coming to Nōb, to Ăhǐm'ělěch the son of Ăhī'tǔb,
10 and he inquired of the LORD for him, and gave him provisions,
and gave him the sword of Gȯlī'ǎth the Phǐlǐs'tǐne."

g. Saul slays Ahimelech and the priests

11 Then the king sent to summon Ăhǐm'ělěch the priest, the
son of Ăhī'tǔb, and all his father's house, the priests who were at
Nōb; and all of them came to the king. 12And Saul said, "Hear
now, son of Ăhī'tǔb." And he answered, "Here I am, my lord."

⁵ Syr Vg: Heb come out

Marginal references:
21.11 1 Sam 18.7; 29.5
21.12 1 Sam 2.19
22.1 2 Sam 23.13
22.2 1 Sam 23.13; 25.13
22.5 2 Sam 24.11; 1 Chr 29.29; 2 Chr 29.25
22.7 1 Sam 8.14
22.8 1 Sam 18.3; 20.16
22.9 1 Sam 21.1; 14.3
22.10 1 Sam 10.22; 21.6,9

13And Saul said to him, "Why have you conspired against me, you and the son of Jĕssĕ, in that you have given him bread and a sword, and have inquired of God for him, so that he has risen against me, to lie in wait, as at this day?" 14 Then Ăhĭm'ĕlĕch answered the king, "And who among all your servants is so faithful as David, who is the king's son-in-law, and captain over^t your bodyguard, and honored in your house? 15 Is today the first time that I have inquired of God for him? No! Let not the king impute anything to his servant or to all the house of my father; for your servant has known nothing of all this, much or little." 16And the king said, "You shall surely die, Ăhĭm'ĕlĕch, you and all your father's house." 17And the king said to the guard who stood about him, "Turn and kill the priests of the LORD; because their hand also is with David, and they knew that he fled, and did not disclose it to me." But the servants of the king would not put forth their hand to fall upon the priests of the LORD. 18 Then the king said to Dŏĕg, "You turn and fall upon the priests." And Doeg the Ē'dŏmīte turned and fell upon the priests, and he killed on that day eighty-five persons who wore the linen ephod. 19And Nŏb, the city of the priests, he put to the sword; both men and women, children and sucklings, oxen, asses and sheep, he put to the sword.

h. *Abiathar escapes to David*

20 But one of the sons of Ăhĭm'ĕlĕch the son of Ăhī'tŭb, named Ăbī'ăthăr, escaped and fled after David. 21And Ăbī'ăthăr told David that Saul had killed the priests of the LORD. 22And David said to Ăbī'ăthăr, "I knew on that day, when Dŏĕg the Ē'dŏmīte was there, that he would surely tell Saul. I have occasioned the death of all the persons of your father's house. 23 Stay with me, fear not; for he that seeks my life seeks your life; with me you shall be in safekeeping."

i. *David at Keilah*

23 Now they told David, "Behold, the Phĭlĭs'tĭnĕs are fighting against Keīlăh, and are robbing the threshing floors." 2 Therefore David inquired of the LORD, "Shall I go and attack these Phĭlĭs'tĭnĕs?" And the LORD said to David, "Go and attack the Philistines and save Keīlăh." 3 But David's men said to him, "Behold, we are afraid here in Judah; how much more then if we go to Keīlăh against the armies of the Phĭlĭs'tĭnĕs?" 4 Then David inquired of the LORD again. And the LORD answered him, "Arise, go down to Keīlăh; for I will give the Phĭlĭs'tĭnĕs into your hand." 5And David and his men went to Keīlăh, and fought with the Phĭlĭs'tĭnĕs, and brought away their cattle, and made a great slaughter among them. So David delivered the inhabitants of Keilah.

6 When Ăbī'ăthăr the son of Ăhĭm'ĕlĕch fled to David to Keīlăh, he came down with an ephod in his hand. 7 Now it was

---

t Gk Tg: Heb *and has turned aside to*

Marginal references:

22.14
1 Sam 19.4, 5

22.17
Ex 1.17

22.18
1 Sam 2.18, 31

22.20
1 Sam 23.6,9; 2.33

22.22
1 Sam 21.7

22.23
1 Ki 2.26

23.1
Josh 15.44

23.2
ver 4,6,9; 2 Sam 5.19, 23

23.4
Josh 8.7; Judg 7.7

23.6
1 Sam 22.20

★23.7

23.7 It is easily possible for men to be mistaken about providences which seem to be from God. Thus Saul falsely supposed that God had providentially delivered David into his hands. Righteous David, in turn, was there only because it was the will of God. However, God brings to nought the counsels and designs of men which run counter to His divine will. Neh 4.15, 2 Sam 17.14, and Job 5.12 are eloquent illustrations.

told Saul that David had come to Keīlăh. And Saul said, "God has given him into my hand; for he has shut himself in by entering a town that has gates and bars." 8And Saul summoned all the people to war, to go down to Keīlăh, to besiege David and his men. 9 David knew that Saul was plotting evil against him; and he said to Ăbī´ăthăr the priest, "Bring the ephod here." 10 Then said David, "O LORD, the God of Israel, thy servant has surely heard that Saul seeks to come to Keīlăh, to destroy the city on my account. 11 Will the men of Keīlăh surrender me into his hand? Will Saul come down, as thy servant has heard? O LORD, the God of Israel, I beseech thee, tell thy servant." And the LORD said, "He will come down." 12 Then said David, "Will the men of Keīlăh surrender me and my men into the hand of Saul?" And the LORD said, "They will surrender you." 13 Then David and his men, who were about six hundred, arose and departed from Keīlăh, and they went wherever they could go. When Saul was told that David had escaped from Keilah, he gave up the expedition. 14And David remained in the strongholds in the wilderness, in the hill country of the Wilderness of Zīph. And Saul sought him every day, but God did not give him into his hand.

j. The treachery of the Ziphites

15 And David was afraid becauseᵘ Saul had come out to seek his life. David was in the Wilderness of Zīph at Horĕsh. 16And Jonathan, Saul's son, rose, and went to David at Horĕsh, and strengthened his hand in God. 17And he said to him, "Fear not; for the hand of Saul my father shall not find you; you shall be king over Israel, and I shall be next to you; Saul my father also knows this." 18And the two of them made a covenant before the LORD; David remained at Horĕsh, and Jonathan went home.

19 Then the Zīphītes went up to Saul at Gĭb´ĕ-ăh, saying, "Does not David hide among us in the strongholds at Horĕsh, on the hill of Hăchī´lăh, which is south of Jĕsh´ĭmŏn? 20 Now come down, O king, according to all your heart's desire to come down; and our part shall be to surrender him into the king's hand." 21And Saul said, "May you be blessed by the LORD; for you have had compassion on me. 22 Go, make yet more sure; know and see the place where his haunt is, and who has seen him there; for it is told me that he is very cunning. 23 See therefore, and take note of all the lurking places where he hides, and come back to me with sure information. Then I will go with you; and if he is in the land, I will search him out among all the thousands of Judah." 24And they arose, and went to Zīph ahead of Saul.

Now David and his men were in the wilderness of Māŏn, in the Ạr´ăbăh to the south of Jĕsh´ĭmŏn. 25And Saul and his men went to seek him. And David was told; therefore he went down to the rock which isᵛ in the wilderness of Māŏn. And when Saul heard that, he pursued after David in the wilderness of Maon. 26 Saul went on one side of the mountain, and David and his men on the other side of the mountain; and David was making haste to get away from Saul, as Saul and his men were closing in upon David and his men to capture them, 27 when a messenger came to Saul, saying, "Make haste and come; for the Phĭlĭs´tĭneṣ have made a raid upon the land." 28 So Saul returned from pursuing after

ᵘ Or saw that   ᵛ Gk: Heb and dwelt

23.9
ver 6;
1 Sam 30.7

23.12
ver 20

23.13
1 Sam 22.2;
25.13

23.14
Josh 15.15;
Ps 54.3,4

23.16
1 Sam 30.6

23.17
1 Sam
20.31;
24.20

23.18
1 Sam 18.3;
20.16,42;
2 Sam 9.1;
21.7

23.19
1 Sam 26.1

23.20
ver 12

23.21
1 Sam 22.8

23.24
Josh 15.55;
1 Sam 25.2

23.26
Ps 17.9

David, and went against the Philis'tines; therefore that place was called the Rock of Escape. 29wAnd David went up from there, and dwelt in the strongholds of En-ge'di.

k. David cuts off Saul's skirt at En-gedi

24 When Saul returned from following the Philis'tines, he was told, "Behold, David is in the wilderness of En-ge'di." 2 Then Saul took three thousand chosen men out of all Israel, and went to seek David and his men in front of the Wildgoats' Rocks. 3And he came to the sheepfolds by the way, where there was a cave; and Saul went in to relieve himself. Now David and his men were sitting in the innermost parts of the cave. 4And the men of David said to him, "Here is the day of which the LORD said to you, 'Behold, I will give your enemy into your hand, and you shall do to him as it shall seem good to you.'" Then David arose and stealthily cut off the skirt of Saul's robe. 5And afterward David's heart smote him, because he had cut off Saul's skirt. 6 He said to his men, "The LORD forbid that I should do this thing to my lord, the LORD's anointed, to put forth my hand against him, seeing he is the LORD's anointed." 7 So David persuaded his men with these words, and did not permit them to attack Saul. And Saul rose up and left the cave, and went upon his way.

l. David rebukes Saul

8 Afterward David also arose, and went out of the cave, and called after Saul, "My lord the king!" And when Saul looked behind him, David bowed with his face to the earth, and did obeisance. 9And David said to Saul, "Why do you listen to the words of men who say, 'Behold, David seeks your hurt'? 10 Lo, this day your eyes have seen how the LORD gave you today into my hand in the cave; and some bade me kill you, but Ix spared you. I said, 'I will not put forth my hand against my lord; for he is the LORD's anointed.' 11 See, my father, see the skirt of your robe in my hand; for by the fact that I cut off the skirt of your robe, and did not kill you, you may know and see that there is no wrong or treason in my hands. I have not sinned against you, though you hunt my life to take it. 12 May the LORD judge between me and you, may the LORD avenge me upon you; but my hand shall not be against you. 13As the proverb of the ancients says, 'Out of the wicked comes forth wickedness'; but my hand shall not be against you. 14After whom has the king of Israel come out? After whom do you pursue? After a dead dog! After a flea! 15 May the LORD therefore be judge, and give sentence between me and you, and see to it, and plead my cause, and deliver me from your hand."

m. Saul's seeming repentance

16 When David had finished speaking these words to Saul,

w Ch 24.1 in Heb   x Gk Syr Tg: Heb you

Marginal references:

23.29 / 2 Chr 20.2

24.1 / 1 Sam 23.28,29
24.2 / 1 Sam 26.2
24.3 / Judg 3.24
*24.4 / 1 Sam 23.17; 25.28-30
24.5 / 2 Sam 24.10
24.6 / 1 Sam 26.11
24.8 / 1 Sam 25.23,24
24.11 / Ps 7.3; 35.7; 1 Sam 23.14,23; 26.20
24.12 / Gen 31.53; Judg 11.27; 1 Sam 26.10; Job 5.8
24.13 / Mt 7.16-20
24.14 / 1 Sam 17.43; 26.20
24.15 / ver 12; Ps 35.1; Mic 7.9
24.16 / 1 Sam 26.17

24.4 David had several opportunities to kill Saul. On each occasion he refrained from taking his life on the ground that Saul had been anointed king by God's command. He was willing to wait for the fulfilment of God's will in God's way. He did not practice the kind of ethics which supposes that "the end justifies the means." Good ends must be attained by good means. David preferred to wait on God rather than to seize the reins of government by murder. Every believer should learn this valuable lesson that it is God's will done in God's way which leads to God's blessing.

Saul said, "Is this your voice, my son David?" And Saul lifted up his voice and wept. 17 He said to David, "You are more righteous than I; for you have repaid me good, whereas I have repaid you evil. 18And you have declared this day how you have dealt well with me, in that you did not kill me when the LORD put me into your hands. 19 For if a man finds his enemy, will he let him go away safe? So may the LORD reward you with good for what you have done to me this day. 20And now, behold, I know that you shall surely be king, and that the kingdom of Israel shall be established in your hand. 21 Swear to me therefore by the LORD that you will not cut off my descendants after me, and that you will not destroy my name out of my father's house." 22And David swore this to Saul. Then Saul went home; but David and his men went up to the stronghold.

n. David and Abigail
(1) NABAL'S REFUSAL OF HELP

25 Now Samuel died; and all Israel assembled and mourned for him, and they buried him in his house at Rāmäh.

Then David rose and went down to the wilderness of Pārän. 2And there was a man in Mäön, whose business was in Carmel. The man was very rich; he had three thousand sheep and a thousand goats. He was shearing his sheep in Carmel. 3 Now the name of the man was Nābāl, and the name of his wife Ăb'ïgäil. The woman was of good understanding and beautiful, but the man was churlish and ill-behaved; he was a Cālëbïte. 4 David heard in the wilderness that Nābäl was shearing his sheep. 5 So David sent ten young men; and David said to the young men, "Go up to Carmel, and go to Nābál, and greet him in my name. 6And thus you shall salute him: 'Peace be to you, and peace be to your house, and peace be to all that you have. 7 I hear that you have shearers; now your shepherds have been with us, and we did them no harm, and they missed nothing, all the time they were in Carmel. 8Ask your young men, and they will tell you. Therefore let my young men find favor in your eyes; for we come on a feast day. Pray, give whatever you have at hand to your servants and to your son David.' "

9 When David's young men came, they said all this to Nābál in the name of David; and then they waited. 10And Nābäl answered David's servants, "Who is David? Who is the son of Jësse? There are many servants nowadays who are breaking away from their masters. 11 Shall I take my bread and my water and my meat that I have killed for my shearers, and give it to men who come from I do not know where?" 12 So David's young men turned away, and came back and told him all this. 13And David said to his men, "Every man gird on his sword!" And every man of them girded on his sword; David also girded on his sword; and about four hundred men went up after David, while two hundred remained with the baggage.

(2) ABIGAIL PLACATES DAVID

14 But one of the young men told Ăb'ïgäil, Nābál's wife, "Behold, David sent messengers out of the wilderness to salute our master; and he railed at them. 15 Yet the men were very good to us,

24.17
1 Sam
26.21;
Mt 5.44
24.18
1 Sam 26.23

24.20
1 Sam 23.17
24.21
Gen 21.23;
2 Sam
21.6–8
24.22
1 Sam 23.29

25.1
1 Sam 28.3;
Deut 34.8;
2 Chr
33.20;
Gen 21.21
25.2
1 Sam
23.24;
Josh 15.55

25.6
1 Chr 12.18

25.7
2 Sam
13.23,24;
ver 15,21
25.8
Neh 8.10–
12

25.10
Judg 9.28

25.13
1 Sam
23.13;
30.24

25.15
ver 7

and we suffered no harm, and we did not miss anything when we were in the fields, as long as we went with them; 16 they were a wall to us both by night and by day, all the while we were with them keeping the sheep. 17 Now therefore know this and consider what you should do; for evil is determined against our master and against all his house, and he is so ill-natured that one cannot speak to him."

18 Then Ăb'ĭgāil made haste, and took two hundred loaves, and two skins of wine, and five sheep ready dressed, and five measures of parched grain, and a hundred clusters of raisins, and two hundred cakes of figs, and laid them on asses. 19And she said to her young men, "Go on before me; behold, I come after you." But she did not tell her husband Nābăl. 20And as she rode on the ass, and came down under cover of the mountain, behold, David and his men came down toward her; and she met them. 21 Now David had said, "Surely in vain have I guarded all that this fellow has in the wilderness, so that nothing was missed of all that belonged to him; and he has returned me evil for good. 22 God do so to David*y* and more also, if by morning I leave so much as one male of all who belong to him."

23 When Ăb'ĭgāil saw David, she made haste, and alighted from the ass, and fell before David on her face, and bowed to the ground. 24 She fell at his feet and said, "Upon me alone, my lord, be the guilt; pray let your handmaid speak in your ears, and hear the words of your handmaid. 25 Let not my lord regard this ill-natured fellow, Nābăl; for as his name is, so is he; Nabal*z* is his name, and folly is with him; but I your handmaid did not see the young men of my lord, whom you sent. 26 Now then, my lord, as the LORD lives, and as your soul lives, seeing the LORD has restrained you from bloodguilt, and from taking vengeance with your own hand, now then let your enemies and those who seek to do evil to my lord be as Nābăl. 27And now let this present which your servant has brought to my lord be given to the young men who follow my lord. 28 Pray forgive the trespass of your handmaid; for the LORD will certainly make my lord a sure house, because my lord is fighting the battles of the LORD; and evil shall not be found in you so long as you live. 29 If men rise up to pursue you and to seek your life, the life of my lord shall be bound in the bundle of the living in the care of the LORD your God; and the lives of your enemies he shall sling out as from the hollow of a sling. 30And when the LORD has done to my lord according to all the good that he has spoken concerning you, and has appointed you prince over Israel, 31 my lord shall have no cause of grief, or pangs of conscience, for having shed blood without cause or for my lord taking vengeance himself. And when the LORD has dealt well with my lord, then remember your handmaid."

32 And David said to Ăb'ĭgāil, "Blessed be the LORD, the God of Israel, who sent you this day to meet me! 33 Blessed be your discretion, and blessed be you, who have kept me this day from bloodguilt and from avenging myself with my own hand! 34 For as surely as the LORD the God of Israel lives, who has restrained me from hurting you, unless you had made haste and come to meet me, truly by morning there had not been left to Nābăl so much as one male." 35 Then David received from her hand what she had

y Gk Compare Syr: Heb *the enemies of David*   *z* That is *fool*

brought him; and he said to her, "Go up in peace to your house;
see, I have hearkened to your voice, and I have granted your
petition."

(3) NABAL'S DEATH

36 And Ăb'ĭgāil came to Nābăl; and, lo, he was holding a feast
in his house, like the feast of a king. And Nābăl's heart was merry
within him, for he was very drunk; so she told him nothing at all
until the morning light. 37And in the morning, when the wine had
gone out of Nābăl, his wife told him these things, and his heart
died within him, and he became as a stone. 38And about ten days
later the LORD smote Nābăl; and he died.

39 When David heard that Nābăl was dead, he said, "Blessed
be the LORD who has avenged the insult I received at the hand
of Nabal, and has kept back his servant from evil; the LORD has
returned the evil-doing of Nabal upon his own head." Then David
sent and wooed Ăb'ĭgāil, to make her his wife. 40And when the
servants of David came to Ăb'ĭgāil at Carmĕl, they said to her,
"David has sent us to you to take you to him as his wife." 41And
she rose and bowed with her face to the ground, and said, "Behold, your handmaid is a servant to wash the feet of the servants of
my lord." 42And Ăb'ĭgāil made haste and rose and mounted on an
ass, and her five maidens attended her; she went after the messengers of David, and became his wife.

43 David also took Ahĭn'ō-ăm of Jĕzreĕl'; and both of them
became his wives. 44 Saul had given Mĭchăl his daughter, David's
wife, to Păltī the son of Lā'ĭsh, who was of Găllĭm.

o. David spares Saul again

26 Then the Zĭphītes came to Saul at Gĭb'e-äh, saying, "Is
not David hiding himself on the hill of Hăchĭ'läh, which is
on the east of Jĕsh'ĭmŏn?" 2 So Saul arose and went down to the
wilderness of Zĭph, with three thousand chosen men of Israel,
to seek David in the wilderness of Ziph. 3And Saul encamped on
the hill of Hăchĭ'läh, which is beside the road on the east of
Jĕsh'ĭmŏn. But David remained in the wilderness; and when he
saw that Saul came after him into the wilderness, 4 David sent
out spies, and learned of a certainty that Saul had come. 5 Then
David rose and came to the place where Saul had encamped; and
David saw the place where Saul lay, with Abner the son of Nĕr,
the commander of his army; Saul was lying within the encampment, while the army was encamped around him.

6 Then David said to Ăhĭm'ĕlĕch the Hĭttīte, and to Jŏăb'ş
brother Ăbĭsh'āi the son of Zĕru'jăh, "Who will go down with me
into the camp to Saul?" And Abishai said, "I will go down with
you." 7 So David and Ăbĭsh'āi went to the army by night; and
there lay Saul sleeping within the encampment, with his spear
stuck in the ground at his head; and Abner and the army lay
around him. 8 Then said Abĭsh'āi to David, "God has given your
enemy into your hand this day; now therefore let me pin him to
the earth with one stroke of the spear, and I will not strike him
twice." 9 But David said to Ăbĭsh'āi, "Do not destroy him; for
who can put forth his hand against the LORD's anointed, and be
guiltless?" 10And David said, "As the LORD lives, the LORD will
smite him; or his day shall come to die; or he shall go down into

25.36
2 Sam 13.23

25.39
1 Sam
24.15;
ver 26,34;
1 Ki 2.44

25.41
Ruth 2.10,
13;
Mk 1.7

25.42
Gen 24.61–
67

25.43
Josh 15.56;
1 Sam 27.3

25.44
2 Sam 3.14;
Isa 10.30

26.1
1 Sam 23.19

26.2
1 Sam 13.2;
24.2

26.5
1 Sam
14.50;
17.55

26.6
1 Chr 2.16;
Judg 7.10,
11

26.9
1 Sam
24.6,7;
2 Sam 1.16
26.10
1 Sam
25.38;
Deut 31.14;
1 Sam 31.6

26.11
1 Sam
24.6,12
26.12
Gen 2.21;
16.12

battle and perish. 11 The LORD forbid that I should put forth my
hand against the LORD's anointed; but take now the spear that is
at his head, and the jar of water, and let us go." 12 So David took
the spear and the jar of water from Saul's head; and they went
away. No man saw it, or knew it, nor did any awake; for they
were all asleep, because a deep sleep from the LORD had fallen
upon them.

13 Then David went over to the other side, and stood afar off
on the top of the mountain, with a great space between them;
14 and David called to the army, and to Abner the son of Nĕr,
saying, "Will you not answer, Abner?" Then Abner answered,
"Who are you that calls to the king?" 15And David said to Abner,
"Are you not a man? Who is like you in Israel? Why then have you
not kept watch over your lord the king? For one of the people came
in to destroy the king your lord. 16 This thing that you have done
is not good. As the LORD lives, you deserve to die, because you
have not kept watch over your lord, the LORD's anointed. And now
see where the king's spear is, and the jar of water that was at
his head."

26.17
1 Sam 24.16

26.18
1 Sam 24.9,
11–14
26.19
2 Sam 16.11

17 Saul recognized David's voice, and said, "Is this your voice,
my son David?" And David said, "It is my voice, my lord, O
king." 18And he said, "Why does my lord pursue after his servant? For what have I done? What guilt is on my hands? 19 Now
therefore let my lord the king hear the words of his servant. If it is
the LORD who has stirred you up against me, may he accept an
offering; but if it is men, may they be cursed before the LORD, for
they have driven me out this day that I should have no share in
the heritage of the LORD, saying, 'Go, serve other gods.' 20 Now

26.20
1 Sam 24.14

therefore, let not my blood fall to the earth away from the presence
of the LORD; for the king of Israel has come out to seek my life,ᵃ
like one who hunts a partridge in the mountains."

26.21
1 Sam
15.24;
24.17

21 Then Saul said, "I have done wrong; return, my son David,
for I will no more do you harm, because my life was precious in
your eyes this day; behold, I have played the fool, and have erred

26.22
1 Sam
24.12,19

exceedingly." 22And David made answer, "Here is the spear,
O king! Let one of the young men come over and fetch it. 23 The
LORD rewards every man for his righteousness and his faithfulness; for the LORD gave you into my hand today, and I would not
put forth my hand against the LORD's anointed. 24 Behold, as your

26.24
Ps 54.7

life was precious this day in my sight, so may my life be precious
in the sight of the LORD, and may he deliver me out of all tribulation." 25 Then Saul said to David, "Blessed be you, my son
David! You will do many things and will succeed in them." So
David went his way, and Saul returned to his place.

E. Saul's death in the Philistine war

1. David's flight to the Philistines
a. David joins Achish

27 And David said in his heart, "I shall now perish one day
by the hand of Saul; there is nothing better for me than
that I should escape to the land of the Philis'tines; then Saul will
despair of seeking me any longer within the borders of Israel, and
I shall escape out of his hand." 2 So David arose and went over,

27.2
1 Sam
25.13;
21.10

ᵃ Gk: Heb a flea (as in 24.14)

he and the six hundred men who were with him, to Ắchĭsh the
son of Mằŏch, king of Găth. ³And David dwelt with Ắchĭsh at
Găth, he and his men, every man with his household, and David
with his two wives, Ăhĭn'ō-ăm of Jĕzreĕl', and Ăb'ĭgāil of Carmĕl,
Nābăl's widow. ⁴And when it was told Saul that David had fled
to Găth, he sought for him no more.

b. Achish gives David Ziklag

5 Then David said to Ắchĭsh, "If I have found favor in your
eyes, let a place be given me in one of the country towns, that I
may dwell there; for why should your servant dwell in the royal
city with you?" ⁶ So that day Ắchĭsh gave him Zĭklăg; therefore
Ziklag has belonged to the kings of Judah to this day. ⁷And the
number of the days that David dwelt in the country of the Phĭlĭs'-
tĭneş was a year and four months.

2. David's raids

8 Now David and his men went up, and made raids upon the
Gĕsh'ŭrĭtes, the Gĭr'zītes, and the Ămăl'ĕkītes; for these were the
inhabitants of the land from of old, as far as Shŭr, to the land of
Egypt. ⁹And David smote the land, and left neither man nor
woman alive, but took away the sheep, the oxen, the asses, the
camels, and the garments, and came back to Ắchĭsh. ¹⁰ When
Ắchĭsh asked, "Against whomᵇ have you made a raid today?"
David would say, "Against the Nĕgĕb of Judah," or "Against the
Negeb of the Jĕrah'meĕlītes," or, "Against the Negeb of the
Kēnītes." ¹¹And David saved neither man nor woman alive, to
bring tidings to Găth, thinking, "Lest they should tell about us,
and say, 'So David has done.' " Such was his custom all the while
he dwelt in the country of the Phĭlĭs'tĭnes. ¹²And Ắchĭsh trusted
David, thinking, "He has made himself utterly abhorred by his
people Israel; therefore he shall be my servant always."

3. The Philistine plan to battle Israel

28 In those days the Phĭlĭs'tĭnes gathered their forces for
war, to fight against Israel. And Ắchĭsh said to David,
"Understand that you and your men are to go out with me in the
army." ² David said to Ắchĭsh, "Very well, you shall know what
your servant can do." And Achish said to David, "Very well, I
will make you my bodyguard for life."

4. Saul and the medium at Endor
a. God does not answer Saul

3 Now Samuel had died, and all Israel had mourned for him and
buried him in Rāmăh, his own city. And Saul had put the mediums
and the wizards out of the land. ⁴ The Phĭlĭs'tĭneş assembled, and
came and encamped at Shunĕm; and Saul gathered all Israel, and
they encamped at Gĭlbō'ă. ⁵ When Saul saw the army of the
Phĭlĭs'tĭneş, he was afraid, and his heart trembled greatly. ⁶And

ᵇ Gk Vg: Heb lacks whom

27.3
1 Sam 30.3;
25.42,43

27.6
Josh 15.31;
19.5
27.7
1 Sam 29.3

27.8
Josh 13.2,
13;
Ex 17.8;
1 Sam
15.7,8;
Ex 15.22
27.9
1 Sam 15.3
27.10
1 Chr 2.9,
25;
Judg 1.16

*28.1f
1 Sam 29.1

28.3
1 Sam 25.1;
7.17;
15.23;
Lev 19.31;
Deut 18.10,
11
28.4
2 Ki 4.8;
1 Sam 31.1
28.6
1 Chr
10.13,14;
Prov 1.28;
Ex 28.30

28.1, 2 When David first went to Achish
(21.10) he apparently wanted to enlist under
this leader, but his reception made him fearful
and thus he pretended madness. Later Achish
comes to trust David and in these verses
commands him to join him in battle against
Israel. David agrees to do so. However, the
lords of the Philistines object to his presence
(29.3ff) and Achish is forced to dismiss David
so he does not fight against Saul and his army.

1 Samuel 28.7–21

434

when Saul inquired of the LORD, the LORD did not answer him, either by dreams, or by Ūrīm, or by prophets. 7 Then Saul said to his servants, "Seek out for me a woman who is a medium, that I may go to her and inquire of her." And his servants said to him, "Behold, there is a medium at Endor."

28.7 — Acts 16.16; Josh 17.11

b. Saul visits the medium

8 So Saul disguised himself and put on other garments, and went, he and two men with him; and they came to the woman by night. And he said, "Divine for me by a spirit, and bring up for me whomever I shall name to you." 9 The woman said to him, "Surely you know what Saul has done, how he has cut off the mediums and the wizards from the land. Why then are you laying a snare for my life to bring about my death?" 10 But Saul swore to her by the LORD, "As the LORD lives, no punishment shall come upon you for this thing." 11 Then the woman said, "Whom shall I bring up for you?" He said, "Bring up Samuel for me." 12 When the woman saw Samuel, she cried out with a loud voice; and the woman said to Saul, "Why have you deceived me? You are Saul." 13 The king said to her, "Have no fear; what do you see?" And the woman said to Saul, "I see a god coming up out of the earth." 14 He said to her, "What is his appearance?" And she said, "An old man is coming up; and he is wrapped in a robe." And Saul knew that it was Samuel, and he bowed with his face to the ground, and did obeisance.

28.8 — Isa 8.19; Deut 18.10,11

28.9 — ver 3

28.14 — 1 Sam 15.27; 24.8

c. The medium conjures up Samuel

15 Then Samuel said to Saul, "Why have you disturbed me by bringing me up?" Saul answered, "I am in great distress; for the Philis'tines are warring against me, and God has turned away from me and answers me no more, either by prophets or by dreams; therefore I have summoned you to tell me what I shall do." 16 And Samuel said, "Why then do you ask me, since the LORD has turned from you and become your enemy? 17 The LORD has done to you as he spoke by me; for the LORD has torn the kingdom out of your hand, and given it to your neighbor, David. 18 Because you did not obey the voice of the LORD, and did not carry out his fierce wrath against Ăm'ălĕk, therefore the LORD has done this thing to you this day. 19 Moreover the LORD will give Israel also with you into the hand of the Philis'tines; and tomorrow you and your sons shall be with me; the LORD will give the army of Israel also into the hand of the Philistines."

28.15 — 1 Sam 18.12; ver 6

28.17 — 1 Sam 15.28

28.18 — 1 Sam 15.9,20,26

28.19 — 1 Sam 31.2

d. The medium feeds Saul

20 Then Saul fell at once full length upon the ground, filled with fear because of the words of Samuel; and there was no strength in him, for he had eaten nothing all day and all night. 21 And the woman came to Saul, and when she saw that he was

28.21 — 1 Sam 19.5; Judg 12.3

28.7 Even though Saul had tried to root out divination (28.9), in accordance with Deut 18.10, 11, he finally resorted to this illegal means of discerning God's will. Surely Samuel would give him instructions even though God had refused to answer by a private dream, the priestly lot, or the prophetic word. But the spirit of Samuel has only words of doom. Due to the many regulations, both Old and New Testament, against divination of all sorts, some doubt that the medium actually brought up the spirit of Samuel. But the text makes it clear that Saul had no doubts as to the reality of the apparition. In any case, this episode is no justification for modern attempts to contact the spirits of the dead.

terrified, she said to him, "Behold, your handmaid has hearkened to you; I have taken my life in my hand, and have hearkened to what you have said to me. 22 Now therefore, you also hearken to your handmaid; let me set a morsel of bread before you; and eat, that you may have strength when you go on your way." 23 He refused, and said, "I will not eat." But his servants, together with the woman, urged him; and he hearkened to their words. So he arose from the earth, and sat upon the bed. 24 Now the woman had a fatted calf in the house, and she quickly killed it, and she took flour, and kneaded it and baked unleavened bread of it, 25 and she put it before Saul and his servants; and they ate. Then they rose and went away that night.

28.23
2 Ki 5.13

5. The Philistines dismiss David
a. The question raised

29 Now the Philis'tines gathered all their forces at Āphĕk; and the Israelites were encamped by the fountain which is in Jĕzreēl'. 2 As the lords of the Philis'tines were passing on by hundreds and by thousands, and David and his men were passing on in the rear with Āchish, 3 the commanders of the Philis'tines said, "What are these Hebrews doing here?" And Āchish said to the commanders of the Philistines, "Is not this David, the servant of Saul, king of Israel, who has been with me now for days and years, and since he deserted to me I have found no fault in him to this day." 4 But the commanders of the Philis'tines were angry with him; and the commanders of the Philistines said to him, "Send the man back, that he may return to the place to which you have assigned him; he shall not go down with us to battle, lest in the battle he become an adversary to us. For how could this fellow reconcile himself to his lord? Would it not be with the heads of the men here? 5 Is not this David, of whom they sing to one another in dances,

'Saul has slain his thousands,
and David his ten thousands'?"

29.1
1 Sam 28.1;
4.1;
Josh 12.18
29.2
1 Sam
28.1,2
29.3
1 Sam 27.7;
Dan 6.5

29.4
1 Chr
12.19;
1 Sam 14.21

29.5
1 Sam 18.7;
21.11

b. Achish sends David away

6 Then Āchish called David and said to him, "As the LORD lives, you have been honest, and to me it seems right that you should march out and in with me in the campaign; for I have found nothing wrong in you from the day of your coming to me to this day. Nevertheless the lords do not approve of you. 7 So go back now; and go peaceably, that you may not displease the lords of the Philis'tines." 8 And David said to Āchish, "But what have I done? What have you found in your servant from the day I entered your service until now, that I may not go and fight against the enemies of my lord the king?" 9 And Āchish made answer to David, "I know that you are as blameless in my sight as an angel of God; nevertheless the commanders of the Philis'tines have said, 'He shall not go up with us to the battle.' 10 Now then rise early in the morning with the servants of your lord who came with you; and start early in the morning, and depart as soon as you have light." 11 So David set out with his men early in the morning, to return to the land of the Philis'tines. But the Philistines went up to Jĕzreēl'.

29.6
ver 3

29.9
2 Sam
14.17,20;
19.27;
ver 4
29.10
1 Chr
12.19,22

6. David destroys Amalek
a. Amalekites raid Ziklag

30 Now when David and his men came to Zĭklăg on the third day, the Ȧmäl′ĕkītes had made a raid upon the Nĕgĕb and upon Ziklag. They had overcome Ziklag, and burned it with fire, 2 and taken captive the women and all^c who were in it, both small and great; they killed no one, but carried them off, and went their way. 3And when David and his men came to the city, they found it burned with fire, and their wives and sons and daughters taken captive. 4 Then David and the people who were with him raised their voices and wept, until they had no more strength to weep. 5 David's two wives also had been taken captive, Ȧhĭn′ō-ȧm of Jĕzreēl′, and Ȧb′ĭgāil the widow of Nābál of Carmĕl. 6And David was greatly distressed; for the people spoke of stoning him, because all the people were bitter in soul, each for his sons and daughters. But David strengthened himself in the LORD his God.

b. God orders David to pursue the Amalekites

7 And David said to Ȧbī′áthȧr the priest, the son of Ȧhĭm′ĕlĕch, "Bring me the ephod." So Abiathar brought the ephod to David. 8And David inquired of the LORD, "Shall I pursue after this band? Shall I overtake them?" He answered him, "Pursue; for you shall surely overtake and shall surely rescue." 9 So David set out, and the six hundred men who were with him, and they came to the brook Bēsor, where those stayed who were left behind. 10 But David went on with the pursuit, he and four hundred men; two hundred stayed behind, who were too exhausted to cross the brook Bēsor.

c. An Egyptian leads David to the Amalekites

11 They found an Egyptian in the open country, and brought him to David; and they gave him bread and he ate, they gave him water to drink, 12 and they gave him a piece of a cake of figs and two clusters of raisins. And when he had eaten, his spirit revived; for he had not eaten bread or drunk water for three days and three nights. 13And David said to him, "To whom do you belong? And where are you from?" He said, "I am a young man of Egypt, servant to an Ȧmäl′ĕkīte; and my master left me behind because I fell sick three days ago. 14 We had made a raid upon the Nĕgĕb of the Çhĕr′ĕthītes and upon that which belongs to Judah and upon the Negeb of Cālĕb; and we burned Zĭklăg with fire." 15And David said to him, "Will you take me down to this band?" And he said, "Swear to me by God, that you will not kill me, or deliver me into the hands of my master, and I will take you down to this band."

d. David smites the Amalekites

16 And when he had taken him down, behold, they were spread abroad over all the land, eating and drinking and dancing, because of all the great spoil they had taken from the land of the Phĭlĭs′-

---

c Gk: Heb lacks *and all*

30.14 *Negeb of the Cherethites.* In David's time the Negeb, parched land of southern Canaan, was apparently divided into five sections (see also 27.10). One of these belonged to the Cherethites, a people related to the Philistines and possibly another group of the sea peoples who settled along the seacoast of Canaan.

Margin references:

30.1   1 Sam 29.4,11; 15.7; 27.8

30.5   1 Sam 25.42,43

30.6   Ex 17.4; Ps 27.14; 56.3,4,11

30.7   1 Sam 23.9

30.8   1 Sam 23.2,4; ver 18

30.9   1 Sam 27.2

30.10   ver 9,21

30.12   Judg 15.19

*30.14   ver 1,16; 2 Sam 8.18; Ezek 25.16; Josh 14.13

30.16   ver 14

tĭneṣ and from the land of Judah. ¹⁷And David smote them from twilight until the evening of the next day; and not a man of them escaped, except four hundred young men, who mounted camels and fled. ¹⁸ David recovered all that the Amǎl'ĕkītes had taken; and David rescued his two wives. ¹⁹ Nothing was missing, whether small or great, sons or daughters, spoil or anything that had been taken; David brought back all. ²⁰ David also captured all the flocks and herds; and the people drove those cattle before him,ᵈ and said, "This is David's spoil."

e. David divides the spoil

21 Then David came to the two hundred men, who had been too exhausted to follow David, and who had been left at the brook Bēsor; and they went out to meet David and to meet the people who were with him; and when David drew near to the people he saluted them. ²² Then all the wicked and base fellows among the men who had gone with David said, "Because they did not go with us, we will not give them any of the spoil which we have recovered, except that each man may lead away his wife and children, and depart." ²³ But David said, "You shall not do so, my brothers, with what the LORD has given us; he has preserved us and given into our hand the band that came against us. ²⁴ Who would listen to you in this matter? For as his share is who goes down into the battle, so shall his share be who stays by the baggage; they shall share alike." ²⁵And from that day forward he made it a statute and an ordinance for Israel to this day.

f. David sends spoil to Judah

26 When David came to Zĭklăg, he sent part of the spoil to his friends, the elders of Judah, saying, "Here is a present for you from the spoil of the enemies of the LORD"; ²⁷ it was for those in Bĕthĕl, in Rāmŏth of the Nĕgĕb, in Jǎttĭr, ²⁸ in Ărŏ'ĕr, in Sĭphmŏth, in Ĕshtĕmŏ'ă, ²⁹ in Rācăl, in the cities of the Jĕrah'mĕēlītes, in the cities of the Kēnītes, ³⁰ in Hormăh, in Bor'ăshăn, in Ā'thăçh, ³¹ in Hēbrŏn, for all the places where David and his men had roamed.

7. The death of Saul

31   Now the Phĭlĭs'tĭneṣ fought against Israel; and the men of Israel fled before the Philistines, and fell slain on Mount Gĭlbō'ă. ²And the Phĭlĭs'tĭneṣ overtook Saul and his sons; and the Philistines slew Jonathan and Abĭn'ădăb and Mǎlçhĭsh'uă, the sons of Saul. ³ The battle pressed hard upon Saul, and the archers found him; and he was badly wounded by the archers. ⁴ Then Saul said to his armor-bearer, "Draw your sword, and thrust me through with it, lest these uncircumcised come and thrust me through, and make sport of me." But his armor-bearer would not; for he feared greatly. Therefore Saul took his own sword, and fell upon it. ⁵And when his armor-bearer saw that Saul was dead, he also fell upon his sword, and died with him. ⁶ Thus Saul died, and his three sons, and his armor-bearer, and all his men, on the same

ᵈ Cn: Heb they drove before those cattle

31.4 took his own sword, and fell . . . . Compare this with the report of Saul's death brought by an Amalekite (2 Sam 1.9, 10). **31.6** Jonathan left a son, Mephibosheth.

30.17
1 Sam 15.3

30.19
ver 8

30.20
ver 26–31

30.21
ver 10

30.24
Num 31.27;
Josh 22.8

30.27
Josh 15.30;
19.8;
15.48
30.28
Josh 13.16;
15.50
30.29
1 Sam
27.10;
15.16
30.30
Judg 1.17
30.31
Josh 14.13

31.1
1 Chr 10.1–
12;
1 Sam 28.4

31.3
2 Sam 1.6
*31.4
Judg 9.54;
2 Sam
1.6,10

*31.6

day together. 7And when the men of Israel who were on the other side of the valley and those beyond the Jordan saw that the men of Israel had fled and that Saul and his sons were dead, they forsook their cities and fled; and the Philis′tines came and dwelt in them.

8. Saul decapitated

8 On the morrow, when the Philis′tines came to strip the slain, they found Saul and his three sons fallen on Mount Gilbō′a. 9And they cut off his head, and stripped off his armor, and sent messengers throughout the land of the Philis′tines, to carry the good news to their idolsᵉ and to the people. 10 They put his armor in the temple of Ash′tàrŏth; and they fastened his body to the wall of Bĕth-shăn. 11 But when the inhabitants of Jābĕsh-gĭl′ĕăd heard what the Philis′tines had done to Saul, 12 all the valiant men arose, and went all night, and took the body of Saul and the bodies of his sons from the wall of Bĕth-shăn; and they came to Jābĕsh and burnt them there. 13And they took their bones and buried them under the tamarisk tree in Jābĕsh, and fasted seven days.

ᵉ Gk Compare 1 Chron 10.9: Heb *to the house of their idols*

Marginal references:
31.9
2 Sam 1.20
31.10
1 Sam 7.3;
Judg 2.13;
2 Sam 21.12;
Josh 17.11
31.11
1 Sam 11.3, 9,11
31.12
2 Sam 2.4-7;
2 Chr 16.14
31.13
2 Sam 21.12-14;
1 Sam 22.6;
2 Sam 1.12

INTRODUCTION TO
THE SECOND BOOK OF
SAMUEL

Authorship and Background: See 1 Samuel

Characteristics: See 1 Samuel

Contents:

I. David enters into his kingship. 1.1—4.12: David learns of the death of Saul and Jonathan. He slays the Amalekite. He is anointed king. He wars against Israel. Abner and Ishbosheth are defeated; they divide company. Joab murders Abner. David mourns for Abner. Ishbosheth is murdered by two Beerothites.

II. The consolidation of David's kingship. 5.1—10.19: David becomes king over all Israel. The Ark is brought to Mt. Zion. David purposes to build a temple for the Ark; God forbids him to do so. He wars successfully against Philistia, Moab, Zobah, Damascus, Hamath, and Edom. David displays kindness toward Mephibosheth. He wars against the Ammonites.

III. The sin of David. 11.1—12.31: David's sin with Bathsheba; the death of Uriah. Nathan's message and David's repentance; the death of the child.

IV. David's troubles. 13.1—18.33: Amon's incest with Tamar; his death at the hand of Absalom. Absalom revolts against David who flees. Absalom reigns in Jerusalem; he wars against his father and is killed.

V. David restored to his kingdom. 19.1—20.26: David returns from Gilead. He pardons Shimei; Mephibosheth apologizes, Barzillai is blessed. Joab murders Amasa and defeats Sheba's insurrection. Sheba is slain.

VI. The later years of David's kingdom. 21.1—24.25: The famine caused by Saul's crime against the Gibeonites. Victory over the giants of the Philistines. David's Psalm of praise to God. The list of the warrior heroes. David orders a census and is convicted of his sin. He chooses the plague as punishment, confesses his sin, and prays. The altar is erected, and the plague stayed.

THE SECOND BOOK OF
SAMUEL

I. David enters into his kingship 1.1–4.12

A. The news of Saul's death

1.1
1 Sam 31.6;
30.17,26
1.2
1 Sam
4.10,12

1 After the death of Saul, when David had returned from the slaughter of the Amăl′ekītes, David remained two days in Zĭklăg; 2 and on the third day, behold, a man came from Saul's camp, with his clothes rent and earth upon his head. And when he came to David, he fell to the ground and did obeisance. 3 David said to him, "Where do you come from?" And he said to him, "I have escaped from the camp of Israel." 4And David said to him, "How did it go? Tell me." And he answered, "The people have fled from the battle, and many of the people also have fallen and are dead; and Saul and his son Jonathan are also dead." 5 Then David said to the young man who told him, "How do you know that Saul and his son Jonathan are dead?" 6And the young man who told him said, "By chance I happened to be on Mount Gilbō′ȧ; and there was Saul leaning upon his spear; and lo, the chariots and the horsemen were close upon him. 7And when he looked behind him, he saw me, and called to me. And I answered, 'Here I am.' 8And he said to me, 'Who are you?' I answered him, 'I am an Amăl′ekīte.' 9And he said to me, 'Stand beside me and slay me; for anguish has seized me, and yet my life still lingers.' 10 So I stood beside him, and slew him, because I was sure that he could not live after he had fallen; and I took the crown which was on his head and the armlet which was on his arm, and I have brought them here to my lord."

1.6
1 Sam
31.2–4

1.8
1 Sam 15.3
1.10
Judg 9.54

1.11
2 Sam 3.31;
13.31
1.12
2 Sam 3.35
1.13
ver 8
1.14
1 Sam 24.6;
26.9
1.15
2 Sam
4.10,12
1.16
2 Sam
3.28,29;
ver 10

11 Then David took hold of his clothes, and rent them; and so did all the men who were with him; 12 and they mourned and wept and fasted until evening for Saul and for Jonathan his son and for the people of the LORD and for the house of Israel, because they had fallen by the sword. 13And David said to the young man who told him, "Where do you come from?" And he answered, "I am the son of a sojourner, an Amăl′ekīte." 14 David said to him, "How is it you were not afraid to put forth your hand to destroy the LORD's anointed?" 15 Then David called one of the young men and said, "Go, fall upon him." And he smote him so that he died. 16And David said to him, "Your blood be upon your head; for your own mouth has testified against you, saying, 'I have slain the LORD's anointed.'"

B. David's lamentation over Saul and Jonathan

1.17
2 Chr 35.25
*1.18
1 Sam 31.3;
Josh 10.13

17 And David lamented with this lamentation over Saul and Jonathan his son, 18 and he said it*a* should be taught to the people of Judah; behold, it is written in the Book of Jăshȧr.*b* He said:

a Gk: Heb *the Bow*   *b* Or *The upright*

1.18 *Book of Jashar*, an old source which is said to be a collection of poems. Other quota-tions attributed to it may be found in Josh 10.12, 13 and Judg ch 5.

¹⁹ "Thy glory, O Israel, is slain upon thy high places!
    How are the mighty fallen!

²⁰ Tell it not in Găth,
    publish it not in the streets of Ăsh'kĕlon;
lest the daughters of the Phĭlĭs'tĭneş rejoice,
    lest the daughters of the uncircumcised exult.

²¹ "Ye mountains of Gĭlbō'ă,
    let there be no dew or rain upon you,
    nor upsurging of the deep!^c
For there the shield of the mighty was defiled,
    the shield of Saul, not anointed with oil.

²² "From the blood of the slain,
    from the fat of the mighty,
the bow of Jonathan turned not back,
    and the sword of Saul returned not empty.

²³ "Saul and Jonathan, beloved and lovely!
    In life and in death they were not divided;
they were swifter than eagles,
    they were stronger than lions.

²⁴ "Ye daughters of Israel, weep over Saul,
    who clothed you daintily in scarlet,
    who put ornaments of gold upon your apparel.

²⁵ "How are the mighty fallen
    in the midst of the battle!

"Jonathan lies slain upon thy high places.
²⁶   I am distressed for you, my brother Jonathan;
very pleasant have you been to me;
    your love to me was wonderful,
    passing the love of women.

²⁷ "How are the mighty fallen,
    and the weapons of war perished!"

C. David anointed king over Judah

2 After this David inquired of the LORD, "Shall I go up into any of the cities of Judah?" And the LORD said to him, "Go up." David said, "To which shall I go up?" And he said, "To Hēbrón." ² So David went up there, and his two wives also, Ahĭn'ō-ăm of Jĕzreĕl', and Ăb'ĭgăil the widow of Nābál of Carmĕl. ³And David brought up his men who were with him, every one with his household; and they dwelt in the towns of Hēbrón. ⁴And the men of Judah came, and there they anointed David king over the house of Judah.

^c Cn: Heb *fields of offerings*

Side references:

1.19 ver 27
1.20 1 Sam 31.9; Mic 1.10; Ex 15.20; 1 Sam 18.6; 31.4
1.21 1 Sam 31.1; Job 3.3,4; Isa 21.5
1.22 Isa 34.6; 1 Sam 18.4
1.23 Jer 4.13; Judg 14.18
1.25 ver 19.27
1.26 1 Sam 18.1-4
1.27 ver 19,25; 1 Sam 2.4
*2.1 1 Sam 23.2, 4,9-12; 30.31
2.2 1 Sam 30.5
2.3 1 Sam 30.9; 1 Chr 12.1
2.4 2 Sam 5.3,5; 1 Sam 31.11-13

2.1 *Shall I go up . . .?* David seeks guidance from the LORD as he contemplates conquering the kingdom over which he was secretly anointed to rule (16.1–13).

When they told David, "It was the men of Jābësh-gĭl'ëäd who
buried Saul," 5 David sent messengers to the men of Jābësh-
gĭl'ëäd, and said to them, "May you be blessed by the LORD, because you showed this loyalty to Saul your lord, and buried him!
6 Now may the LORD show steadfast love and faithfulness to you!
And I will do good to you because you have done this thing. 7 Now
therefore let your hands be strong, and be valiant; for Saul your
lord is dead, and the house of Judah has anointed me king over
them."

D. The civil war with Israel

1. Abner makes Ish-bosheth king of Israel

8 Now Abner the son of Nër, commander of Saul's army, had
taken Ĭsh-bō'shëth the son of Saul, and brought him over to
Māhảnā'ĭm; 9 and he made him king over Gĭl'ëäd and the Ăsh'-
ûrītes and Jĕzreēl' and Ē'phräĭm and Benjamin and all Israel.
10 Ĭsh-bō'shëth, Saul's son, was forty years old when he began to
reign over Israel, and he reigned two years. But the house of Judah
followed David. 11And the time that David was king in Hēbrón
over the house of Judah was seven years and six months.

2. Abner defeated

12 Abner the son of Nër, and the servants of Ĭsh-bō'shëth the
son of Saul, went out from Māhảnā'ĭm to Gĭb'ëön. 13And Jōāb the
son of Zėru'ĭạh, and the servants of David, went out and met them
at the pool of Gĭb'ëön; and they sat down, the one on the one side
of the pool, and the other on the other side of the pool. 14And
Abner said to Jōāb, "Let the young men arise and play before us."
And Joab said, "Let them arise." 15 Then they arose and passed
over by number, twelve for Benjamin and Ĭsh-bō'shëth the son of
Saul, and twelve of the servants of David. 16And each caught his
opponent by the head, and thrust his sword in his opponent's
side; so they fell down together. Therefore that place was called
Hĕl'kăth-hăzzu'rĭm,*d* which is at Gĭb'ëön. 17And the battle was
very fierce that day; and Abner and the men of Israel were beaten
before the servants of David.

3. Abner slays Asahel

18 And the three sons of Zėru'ĭạh were there, Jōāb, Ȧbĭsh'äī,
and Ăs'ảhĕl. Now Asahel was as swift of foot as a wild gazelle;
19 and Ăs'ảhĕl pursued Abner, and as he went he turned neither
to the right hand nor to the left from following Abner. 20 Then
Abner looked behind him and said, "Is it you, Ăs'ảhĕl?" And he
answered, "It is I." 21Abner said to him, "Turn aside to your right
hand or to your left, and seize one of the young men, and take his
spoil." But Ăs'ảhĕl would not turn aside from following him.
22And Abner said again to Ăs'ảhĕl, "Turn aside from following

d That is *the field of sword-edges*

2.5
1 Sam 23.21

*2.8
2 Sam 14.50

2.9
Judg 1.32;
1 Sam 29.1

2.11
2 Sam 5.5

2.12
Josh 18.25
*2.13
1 Chr 2.16

2.17
2 Sam 3.1

2.18
1 Chr 2.16;
12.8

2.22
2 Sam 3.27

2.8 *Ish-bosheth*, that is, "Man of Shame."
This may not have been his original name.
According to 1 Chr 8.33 his name was
Eshbaal (Ishbaal), "Man of Baal," but the
use of Baal in the proper name of an Israelite
was so revolting that someone may have
substituted *bosheth* (shame) in place of *baal*.
2.13 *pool of Gibeon*. This pool was found
in 1956 by excavators at El-jib, the site of
ancient Gibeon.

me; why should I smite you to the ground? How then could I lift up my face to your brother Jŏăb?" ²³But he refused to turn aside; therefore Abner smote him in the belly with the butt of his spear, so that the spear came out at his back; and he fell there, and died where he was. And all who came to the place where Ăs′ăhĕl had fallen and died, stood still.

2.23
2 Sam 3.27;
4.6; 20.10

4. *Abner and Joab declare a truce*

24 But Jŏăb and Ăbĭsh′ăī pursued Abner; and as the sun was going down they came to the hill of Ămmăh, which lies before Gīăh on the way to the wilderness of Gĭb′ĕŏn. ²⁵And the Benjaminites gathered themselves together behind Abner, and became one band, and took their stand on the top of a hill. ²⁶ Then Abner called to Jŏăb, "Shall the sword devour for ever? Do you not know that the end will be bitter? How long will it be before you bid your people turn from the pursuit of their brethren?" ²⁷And Jŏăb said, "As God lives, if you had not spoken, surely the men would have given up the pursuit of their brethren in the morning." ²⁸ So Jŏăb blew the trumpet; and all the men stopped, and pursued Israel no more, nor did they fight any more.

2.24
Josh 10.41

2.27
ver 14

29 And Abner and his men went all that night through the Ăr′ăbăh; they crossed the Jordan, and marching the whole forenoon they came to Măhănă′im. ³⁰ Jŏăb returned from the pursuit of Abner; and when he had gathered all the people together, there were missing of David's servants nineteen men besides Ăs′ăhĕl. ³¹ But the servants of David had slain of Benjamin three hundred and sixty of Abner's men. ³²And they took up Ăs′ăhĕl, and buried him in the tomb of his father, which was at Bĕth′lĕhĕm. And Jŏăb and his men marched all night, and the day broke upon them at Hēbrŏn.

2.29
ver 8

5. *Abner and Ish-bosheth quarrel*

3 There was a long war between the house of Saul and the house of David; and David grew stronger and stronger, while the house of Saul became weaker and weaker.

2 And sons were born to David at Hēbrŏn: his first-born was Ămnŏn, of Ăhĭn′ō-ăm of Jĕzreēl′; ³ and his second, Chĭl′ē-ăb, of Ăbĭ′gāil the widow of Nābăl of Carmĕl; and the third, Ăb′sălŏm the son of Mā′ăcăh the daughter of Tălmaī king of Gĕshŭr; ⁴ and the fourth, Ădŏnĭ′jăh the son of Hăggĭth; and the fifth, Shĕphătĭ′-ăh the son of Ăb′ĭtăl; ⁵ and the sixth, Ĭth′rē-ăm, of Ĕglăh, David's wife. These were born to David in Hēbrŏn.

3.2
1 Chr
3.1–3;
1 Sam
25.42,43
3.3
1 Sam 27.8;
2 Sam 13.37
3.4
1 Ki 1.5

6 While there was war between the house of Saul and the house of David, Abner was making himself strong in the house of Saul. ⁷ Now Saul had a concubine, whose name was Rĭzpăh, the daughter of Ā′ĭăh; and Ĭsh-bō′shĕth said to Abner, "Why have you gone in to my father's concubine?" ⁸ Then Abner was very angry over the words of Ĭsh-bō′shĕth, and said, "Am I a dog's head of Judah? This day I keep showing loyalty to the house of Saul your father, to his brothers, and to his friends, and have not given you into the hand of David; and yet you charge me today with a fault concerning a woman. ⁹ God do so to Abner, and more also, if I do not accomplish for David what the LORD has sworn to him, ¹⁰ to transfer the kingdom from the house of Saul, and set up the throne of David over Israel and over Judah, from Dan to Beër-

3.7
2 Sam
21.8–11;
16.21
3.8
1 Sam
24.14;
2 Sam 9.8

3.9
1 Ki 19.2;
1 Sam 15.8
3.10
Judg 20.1;
1 Sam 3.20

shē'bȧ." ¹¹And Ĭsh-bō'shĕth could not answer Abner another word, because he feared him.

12 And Abner sent messengers to David at Hēbrȯn,ᵉ saying, "To whom does the land belong? Make your covenant with me, and behold, my hand shall be with you to bring over all Israel to you." ¹³And he said, "Good; I will make a covenant with you; but one thing I require of you; that is, you shall not see my face, unless you first bring Mĭchȧl, Saul's daughter, when you come to see my face." ¹⁴ Then David sent messengers to Ĭsh-bō'shĕth Saul's son, saying, "Give me my wife Mĭchȧl, whom I betrothed at the price of a hundred foreskins of the Phĭlĭs'tĭnes." ¹⁵And Ĭsh-bō'shĕth sent, and took her from her husband Pȧl'tĭ-ĕl the son of Lā'ĭsh. ¹⁶ But her husband went with her, weeping after her all the way to Bȧhu'rĭm. Then Abner said to him, "Go, return"; and he returned.

6. Joab murders Abner
a. Abner visits David

17 And Abner conferred with the elders of Israel, saying, "For some time past you have been seeking David as king over you. ¹⁸ Now then bring it about; for the LORD has promised David, saying, 'By the hand of my servant David I will save my people Israel from the hand of the Phĭlĭs'tĭnes, and from the hand of all their enemies.'" ¹⁹Abner also spoke to Benjamin; and then Abner went to tell David at Hēbrȯn all that Israel and the whole house of Benjamin thought good to do.

20 When Abner came with twenty men to David at Hēbrȯn, David made a feast for Abner and the men who were with him. ²¹And Abner said to David, "I will arise and go, and will gather all Israel to my lord the king, that they may make a covenant with you, and that you may reign over all that your heart desires." So David sent Abner away; and he went in peace.

b. Joab learns of Abner's visit

22 Just then the servants of David arrived with Jōȧb from a raid, bringing much spoil with them. But Abner was not with David at Hēbrȯn, for he had sent him away, and he had gone in peace. ²³ When Jōȧb and all the army that was with him came, it was told Joab, "Abner the son of Nĕr came to the king, and he has let him go, and he has gone in peace." ²⁴ Then Jōȧb went to the king and said, "What have you done? Behold, Abner came to you; why is it that you have sent him away, so that he is gone? ²⁵ You know that Abner the son of Nĕr came to deceive you, and to know your going out and your coming in, and to know all that you are doing."

c. The slaying of Abner

26 When Jōȧb came out from David's presence, he sent messengers after Abner, and they brought him back from the cistern of Sīrȧh; but David did not know about it. ²⁷And when Abner returned to Hēbrȯn, Jōȧb took him aside into the midst of the gate

ᵉ Gk: Heb where he was

3.13 Undoubtedly David thought that the restoration of Michal, his former wife, would enhance his chances for unity with the house of Saul. According to Deut 24.4 a man was not to take back his former wife after she had had another husband.

Margin references: *3.13 Gen 43.3; 1 Sam 18.20 · 3.14 1 Sam 18.25,27 · 3.15 see 1 Sam 25.44 · 3.16 2 Sam 16.5 · 3.18 1 Sam 9.16; 15.28 · 3.19 1 Sam 10.20,21 · 3.21 ver 10.12; 1 Ki 11.37 · 3.22 1 Sam 27.8 · 3.25 1 Sam 29.6; Isa 37.28 · 3.27 2 Sam 2.23; 4.6; 20.9,10; 1 Ki 2.5

to speak with him privately, and there he smote him in the belly, so
that he died, for the blood of Ăs′ăhĕl his brother. 28Afterward,
when David heard of it, he said, "I and my kingdom are for ever
guiltless before the LORD for the blood of Abner the son of Nĕr.
29 May it fall upon the head of Jŏăb, and upon all his father's
house; and may the house of Joab never be without one who has a
discharge, or who is leprous, or who holds a spindle, or who is
slain by the sword, or who lacks bread!" 30 So Jŏăb and Ăbĭsh′ăĭ
his brother slew Abner, because he had killed their brother
Ăs′ăhĕl in the battle at Gĭb′ĕŏn.

d. *David's grief over Abner's death*

31 Then David said to Jŏăb and to all the people who were with
him, "Rend your clothes, and gird on sackcloth, and mourn
before Abner." And King David followed the bier. 32 They buried
Abner at Hēbrŏn; and the king lifted up his voice and wept at the
grave of Abner; and all the people wept. 33And the king lamented
for Abner, saying,
"Should Abner die as a fool dies?
34 Your hands were not bound,
    your feet were not fettered;
as one falls before the wicked
    you have fallen."
And all the people wept again over him. 35 Then all the people
came to persuade David to eat bread while it was yet day; but
David swore, saying, "God do so to me and more also, if I taste
bread or anything else till the sun goes down!" 36And all the people took notice of it, and it pleased them; as everything that the
king did pleased all the people. 37 So all the people and all Israel
understood that day that it had not been the king's will to slay
Abner the son of Nĕr. 38And the king said to his servants, "Do you
not know that a prince and a great man has fallen this day in
Israel? 39And I am this day weak, though anointed king; these men
the sons of Zĕru′ĭăh are too hard for me. The LORD requite the
evildoer according to his wickedness!"

7. *The murder of Ish-bosheth*

4 When Ĭsh-bō′shĕth, Saul's son, heard that Abner had died
at Hēbrŏn, his courage failed, and all Israel was dismayed.
2 Now Saul's son had two men who were captains of raiding bands;
the name of the one was Bā′ănăh, and the name of the other Rēchăb, sons of Rĭmmŏn a man of Benjamin from Be-ĕr′ŏth (for
Be-eroth also is reckoned to Benjamin; 3 the Be-ĕr′ŏthītes fled to
Gĭttā′ĭm, and have been sojourners there to this day).
4 Jonathan, the son of Saul, had a son who was crippled in his
feet. He was five years old when the news about Saul and Jonathan came from Jĕzreēl′; and his nurse took him up, and fled; and,
as she fled in her haste, he fell, and became lame. And his name
was Mĕphĭb′ŏshĕth.
5 Now the sons of Rĭmmŏn the Be-ĕr′ŏthīte, Rēchăb and Bā′-
ănăh, set out, and about the heat of the day they came to the house
of Ĭsh-bō′shĕth, as he was taking his noonday rest. 6And behold,

3.29
1 Ki 2.32,
33;
Lev 15.2
3.30
2 Sam 2.23

3.31
Gen 37.34;
2 Sam 1.2,
11

3.33
2 Sam 1.17

3.35
2 Sam
12.17;
1 Sam 3.17;
2 Sam 1.12

3.39
2 Sam
19.5-7;
1 Ki 2.5,6,
33,34

4.1
2 Sam 3.27;
Ezra 4.4
4.2
Josh 18.25

4.3
Neh 11.33

*4.4
2 Sam
9.3,6;
1 Sam
31.1-4

4.5
2 Sam 2.8
4.6
2 Sam 2.23

4.4 *Mephibosheth*. This name, like Ishbosheth, has been changed. According to 1 Chr

8.34 his name was *Meribbaal*, which means
"my lord is Baal."

the doorkeeper of the house had been cleaning wheat, but she grew drowsy and slept; so Rēchăb and Bā'ănăh his brother slipped in.*f* 7 When they came into the house, as he lay on his bed in his bedchamber, they smote him, and slew him, and beheaded him.

4.8
1 Sam
23.15;
25.29

They took his head, and went by the way of the Ạr'ăbăh all night, 8 and brought the head of Ĭsh-bō'shĕth to David at Hēbrŏn. And they said to the king, "Here is the head of Ish-bosheth, the son of Saul, your enemy, who sought your life; the LORD has avenged my lord the king this day on Saul and on his offspring." 9 But David

4.9
1 Ki 1.29

answered Rēchăb and Bā'ănăh his brother, the sons of Rĭmmŏn the Bĕ-ĕr'ŏthīte, "As the LORD lives, who has redeemed my life out of every adversity, 10 when one told me, 'Behold, Saul is dead,'

4.10
2 Sam 1.2,
4,15

and thought he was bringing good news, I seized him and slew him at Zĭklăg, which was the reward I gave him for his news. 11 How much more, when wicked men have slain a righteous man

4.11
Gen 9.5,6

in his own house upon his bed, shall I not now require his blood at your hand, and destroy you from the earth?" 12And David

4.12
2 Sam 1.15;
3.32

commanded his young men, and they killed them, and cut off their hands and feet, and hanged them beside the pool at Hēbrŏn. But they took the head of Ĭsh-bō'shĕth, and buried it in the tomb of Abner at Hebron.

II. *The consolidation of David's kingship 5.1–10.18*

A. *David made king over all Israel*

5.1
1 Chr 11.1;
2 Sam 19.13
5.2
1 Sam
18.13;
16.1,12;
25.30
5.3
1 Chr 11.3;
2 Sam 3.21;
2.4
5.4
Num 4.3;
Lk 3.23;
1 Chr 26.31
5.5
2 Sam 2.11

5 Then all the tribes of Israel came to David at Hēbrŏn, and said, "Behold, we are your bone and flesh. 2 In times past, when Saul was king over us, it was you that led out and brought in Israel; and the LORD said to you, 'You shall be shepherd of my people Israel, and you shall be prince over Israel.'" 3 So all the elders of Israel came to the king at Hēbrŏn; and King David made a covenant with them at Hebron before the LORD, and they anointed David king over Israel. 4 David was thirty years old when he began to reign, and he reigned forty years. 5At Hēbrŏn he reigned over Judah seven years and six months; and at Jerusalem he reigned over all Israel and Judah thirty-three years.

B. *The capture of Jerusalem*

*5.6
Josh 15.63;
Judg 1.8,21

6 And the king and his men went to Jerusalem against the Jĕb'ūsītes, the inhabitants of the land, who said to David, "You will not come in here, but the blind and the lame will ward you off"— thinking, "David cannot come in here." 7 Nevertheless David

5.8
ver 9;
2 Sam
6.12,16;
1 Ki 2.10
*5.9
ver 7

took the stronghold of Zion, that is, the city of David. 8And David said on that day, "Whoever would smite the Jĕb'ūsītes, let him get up the water shaft to attack the lame and the blind, who are hated by David's soul." Therefore it is said, "The blind and the lame shall not come into the house." 9And David dwelt in the

---

f Gk: Heb 6*And hither they came into the midst of the house fetching wheat; and they smote him in the belly; and Rechab and Baanah his brother escaped*

5.6 *Jebusites*, read also Judg 1.21.
5.9 *the Millo*, that is, "the Filling." The nature of this structure is unknown. Appar- ently it was part of the defenses of the Jebu- site city. Solomon rebuilt the Millo (1 Ki 11.27).

stronghold, and called it the city of David. And David built the
city round about from the Mĭllō inward. [10]And David became
greater and greater, for the LORD, the God of hosts, was with him.

5.10
2 Sam 3.1

11 And Hiram king of Tȳre sent messengers to David, and
cedar trees, also carpenters and masons who built David a house.
[12]And David perceived that the LORD had established him king
over Israel, and that he had exalted his kingdom for the sake of his
people Israel.

5.11
1 Chr 14.1

13 And David took more concubines and wives from Jerusalem,
after he came from Hēbrŏn; and more sons and daughters were
born to David. [14]And these are the names of those who were born
to him in Jerusalem: Shămʹmū-à, Shōbăb, Nathan, Solomon,
[15] Ĭbhar, Ĕlĭshʹu-à, Nĕphĕg, Jăphĭʹà, [16] Ĕlĭʹshămà, Ĕlĭʹàdà, and
Ĕlĭphʹĕlĕt.

5.13
Deut 17.17;
1 Chr 3.9
5.14
1 Chr 3.5–8

C. David defeats the Philistines

17 When the Phĭlĭsʹtĭneş heard that David had been anointed
king over Israel, all the Philistines went up in search of David;
but David heard of it and went down to the stronghold. [18] Now
the Phĭlĭsʹtĭneş had come and spread out in the valley of Rĕphʹ-
àïm. [19]And David inquired of the LORD, "Shall I go up against the
Phĭlĭsʹtĭneş? Wilt thou give them into my hand?" And the LORD
said to David, "Go up; for I will certainly give the Philistines into
your hand." [20]And David came to Bāʹàl-pĕrāʹzĭm, and David defeated them there; and he said, "The LORD has broken through[g]
my enemies before me, like a bursting flood." Therefore the name
of that place is called Baal-perazim.[h] [21]And the Phĭlĭsʹtĭneş left
their idols there, and David and his men carried them away.

5.17
2 Sam 23.14

5.18
Josh 15.18;
17.15;
18.16

5.19
1 Sam 23.2;
2 Sam 2.1

5.20
Isa 28.21

5.21
1 Chr 14.12

22 And the Phĭlĭsʹtĭneş came up yet again, and spread out in the
valley of Rĕphʹàïm. [23]And when David inquired of the LORD, he
said, "You shall not go up; go around to their rear, and come upon
them opposite the balsam trees. [24]And when you hear the sound
of marching in the tops of the balsam trees, then bestir yourself;
for then the LORD has gone out before you to smite the army of the
Phĭlĭsʹtĭneş." [25]And David did as the LORD commanded him, and
smote the Phĭlĭsʹtĭneş from Gēbà to Gēzĕr.

5.22
ver 18
5.23
ver 19
*5.24
2 Ki 7.6;
Judg 4.14
5.25
Josh 12.12;
see 1 Chr
14.16

D. Bringing the ark to Jerusalem

1. The journey commenced

6 David again gathered all the chosen men of Israel, thirty thousand. [2]And David arose and went with all the people who were
with him from Bāʹàlë-juʹdàh, to bring up from there the ark of
God, which is called by the name of the LORD of hosts who sits
enthroned on the cherubim. [3]And they carried the ark of God

*6.2
1 Chr 13.5,
6;
Lev 24.16;
1 Sam 4.4
*6.3
1 Sam 6.7

g Heb paraz   h That is Lord of breaking through

5.24 Here is an instance of guidance by
outward circumstances.
6.2 Baale-judah, that is, Kiriath-jearim
(Josh 15.9; Chr 13.6). on the cherubim. See
note to Ex 25.22.
6.3 God had given specific instructions to
Israel about how to carry the ark of God

(Num 4.15). It was to be carried by four
priests, placing the carrying-poles upon their
shoulders; it was not to be transported by any
vehicle. David failed to obey God's express
instructions in carrying out his pious purpose.
Disaster followed, as it always does when
God's will is disregarded.

upon a new cart, and brought it out of the house of Åbĭn′ådåb which was on the hill; and Ŭzzåh and Åhĭ′ō,ⁱ the sons of Abinadab, were driving the new cartʲ 4 with the ark of God; and Åhĭ′ōⁱ went before the ark. 5And David and all the house of Israel were making merry before the LORD with all their might, with songsᵏ and lyres and harps and tambourines and castanets and cymbals.

6.4
1 Sam 7.1
6.5
1 Sam 18.6,7;
1 Chr 13.8

2. The sin of Uzzah

6 And when they came to the threshing floor of Nācŏn, Ŭzzåh put out his hand to the ark of God and took hold of it, for the oxen stumbled. 7And the anger of the LORD was kindled against Ŭzzåh; and God smote him there because he put forth his hand to the ark;ˡ and he died there beside the ark of God. 8And David was angry because the LORD had broken forth upon Ŭzzåh; and that place is called Pē′rĕz-ŭz′zåh,ᵐ to this day. 9And David was afraid of the LORD that day; and he said, "How can the ark of the LORD come to me?" 10 So David was not willing to take the ark of the LORD into the city of David; but David took it aside to the house of Ō′bĕd-ē′dŏm the Gĭttīte. 11And the ark of the LORD remained in the house of Ō′bĕd-ē′dŏm the Gĭttīte three months; and the LORD blessed Obed-edom and all his household.

6.6
1 Chr 13.9;
Num 4.15,
19,20
6.7
1 Sam 6.19
6.10
1 Chr 13.13
6.11
1 Chr 13.14

3. The ark brought to Jerusalem

12 And it was told King David, "The LORD has blessed the household of Ō′bĕd-ē′dŏm and all that belongs to him, because of the ark of God." So David went and brought up the ark of God from the house of Obed-edom to the city of David with rejoicing; 13 and when those who bore the ark of the LORD had gone six paces, he sacrificed an ox and a fatling. 14And David danced before the LORD with all his might; and David was girded with a linen ephod. 15 So David and all the house of Israel brought up the ark of the LORD with shouting, and with the sound of the horn.

16 As the ark of the LORD came into the city of David, Mĭçhål the daughter of Saul looked out of the window, and saw King David leaping and dancing before the LORD; and she despised him in her heart. 17And they brought in the ark of the LORD, and set it in its place, inside the tent which David had pitched for it; and David offered burnt offerings and peace offerings before the LORD. 18And when David had finished offering the burnt offerings and the peace offerings, he blessed the people in the name of the LORD of hosts, 19 and distributed among all the people, the whole multitude of Israel, both men and women, to each a cake of bread, a portion of meat,ⁿ and a cake of raisins. Then all the people departed, each to his house.

6.12
1 Chr 15.25;
1 Ki 8.1
6.14
Ex 15.20;
1 Sam 2.18
6.15
1 Chr 15.28
*6.16
1 Chr 15.29
6.17
1 Chr 15.1;
16.1;
1 Ki 8.62–65
6.18
1 Ki 8.14,15

4. Michal's sin

20 And David returned to bless his household. But Mĭçhål the

6.20
ver 14,16;
1 Sam 19.24

i Or and his brother
j Compare Gk: Heb the new cart, and brought it out of the house of Abinadab which was on the hill k Gk 1 Chron 13.8: Heb fir-trees l 1 Chron 13.10: Heb uncertain
m That is The breaking forth upon Uzzah n Vg: Heb uncertain

6.16 she despised him. Michal's contempt can hardly be completely explained by David's   unbecoming dance. Evidently she resented him for taking her from Paltiel (3.16).

daughter of Saul came out to meet David, and said, "How the king of Israel honored himself today, uncovering himself today before the eyes of his servants' maids, as one of the vulgar fellows shamelessly uncovers himself!" 21And David said to Michal, "It was before the LORD, who chose me above your father, and above all his house, to appoint me as prince over Israel, the people of the LORD—and I will make merry before the LORD. 22 I will make myself yet more contemptible than this, and I will be abased in your*o* eyes; but by the maids of whom you have spoken, by them I shall be held in honor." 23And Michal the daughter of Saul had no child to the day of her death.

E. David's desire to build the Temple

1. Nathan's approval

7 Now when the king dwelt in his house, and the LORD had given him rest from all his enemies round about, 2 the king said to Nathan the prophet, "See now, I dwell in a house of cedar, but the ark of God dwells in a tent." 3And Nathan said to the king, "Go, do all that is in your heart; for the LORD is with you."

2. God's intervention and disapproval

4 But that same night the word of the LORD came to Nathan, 5 "Go and tell my servant David, 'Thus says the LORD: Would you build me a house to dwell in? 6 I have not dwelt in a house since the day I brought up the people of Israel from Egypt to this day, but I have been moving about in a tent for my dwelling. 7 In all places where I have moved with all the people of Israel, did I speak a word with any of the judges*p* of Israel, whom I commanded to shepherd my people Israel, saying, "Why have you not built me a house of cedar?"' 8 Now therefore thus you shall say to my servant David, 'Thus says the LORD of hosts, I took you from the pasture, from following the sheep, that you should be prince over my people Israel; 9 and I have been with you wherever you went, and have cut off all your enemies from before you; and I will make for you a great name, like the name of the great ones of the earth. 10And I will appoint a place for my people Israel, and will plant them, that they may dwell in their own place, and be disturbed no more; and violent men shall afflict them no more, as formerly, 11from the time that I appointed judges over my people Israel; and I will give you rest from all your enemies. Moreover the LORD declares to you that the LORD will make you a house. 12 When your

o Gk: Heb *my*   *p* 1 Chron 17.6: Heb *tribes*

Reference column:
6.21 1 Sam 13.14; 15.28
7.1 1 Chr 17.1ff
7.2 2 Sam 5.11; Acts 7.46; Ex 26.1
7.3 1 Ki 8.17,18 ★7.4ff
7.5 1 Ki 5.3,4; 8.19
7.6 1 Ki 8.16; Ex 40.18,34
7.7 Lev 26.11,12; Deut 23.14; 2 Sam 5.2
7.8 1 Sam 16.11,12; Ps 78.70; 2 Sam 6.21
7.9 1 Sam 18.14; 2 Sam 5.10; Ps 18.37-42
7.10 Ex 15.17; Isa 5.2,7; Ps 89.22; Isa 60.18
7.11 Judg 2.16; 1 Sam 12.9-11; ver 1,27; 1 Sam 25.28
7.12 1 Ki 2.1

7.4ff The Davidic covenant (ver 4–16) was a phase of the original Abrahamic covenant (Gen 17.6). It was made between God and David in anticipation of the kingly rule of Christ. It was both conditional and unconditional: conditional in the sense that disobedience would result in punishment; unconditional in the sense that even if there were disobedience, the covenant itself would not be abolished. Four elements made up this agreement: (1) the promise of a dynasty; (2) the promise of a kingdom to rule over, including land and people; (3) the promise of regal authority; (4) the promise that this house, ruling over this kingdom, would endure forever. Christ, of course, was the goal of this covenant and He was to be the lineal descendant of the house of David. Note that the fulfilment of this covenant was announced to His mother in Lk 1.31ff. The spiritual fulfilment of the Davidic promise is referred to in Acts 2.25ff, for Christ has been, since the resurrection, exalted to supreme rule over the kingdom of God.

days are fulfilled and you lie down with your fathers, I will raise
up your offspring after you, who shall come forth from your body,
and I will establish his kingdom. 13 He shall build a house for my
name, and I will establish the throne of his kingdom for ever.
14 I will be his father, and he shall be my son. When he commits
iniquity, I will chasten him with the rod of men, with the stripes
of the sons of men; 15 but I will not take*q* my steadfast love from
him, as I took it from Saul, whom I put away from before you.
16And your house and your kingdom shall be made sure for ever
before me; your throne shall be established for ever.' " 17 In accordance with all these words, and in accordance with all this
vision, Nathan spoke to David.

3. David's prayer of yieldingness

18 Then King David went in and sat before the LORD, and said,
"Who am I, O Lord GOD, and what is my house, that thou hast
brought me thus far? 19And yet this was a small thing in thy eyes,
O Lord GOD; thou hast spoken also of thy servant's house for a
great while to come, and hast shown me future generations,*r* O
Lord GOD! 20And what more can David say to thee? For thou
knowest thy servant, O Lord GOD! 21 Because of thy promise, and
according to thy own heart, thou hast wrought all this greatness,
to make thy servant know it. 22 Therefore thou art great, O LORD
God; for there is none like thee, and there is no God besides thee,
according to all that we have heard with our ears. 23 What other*s*
nation on earth is like thy people Israel, whom God went to redeem to be his people, making himself a name, and doing for
them*t* great and terrible things, by driving out*u* before his people
a nation and its gods?*v* 24And thou didst establish for thyself thy
people Israel to be thy people for ever; and thou, O LORD, didst
become their God. 25And now, O LORD God, confirm for ever the
word which thou hast spoken concerning thy servant and concerning his house, and do as thou hast spoken; 26 and thy name will be
magnified for ever, saying, 'The LORD of hosts is God over Israel,'
and the house of thy servant David will be established before thee.
27 For thou, O LORD of hosts, the God of Israel, hast made this
revelation to thy servant, saying, 'I will build you a house'; therefore thy servant has found courage to pray this prayer to thee.
28And now, O Lord GOD, thou art God, and thy words are true,
and thou hast promised this good thing to thy servant; 29 now
therefore may it please thee to bless the house of thy servant, that
it may continue for ever before thee; for thou, O Lord GOD, hast
spoken, and with thy blessing shall the house of thy servant be
blessed for ever."

F. David's military victories: Philistines, Moabites, Zobah, Syrians, Edomites, and Ammonites (ch 10)

8 After this David defeated the Philis′tines and subdued them,
and David took Měth′eg-ăm′mah out of the hand of the
Philistines.

Cross references (margin):

7.13
1 Ki 5.5;
Ps 89.4,29;
36.37;
Isa 9.7
7.14
Ps 89.26,27;
Heb 1.5;
Ps 89.30–33
7.15
1 Sam 15.23,
28
7.16
Ps 89.36,37

7.18
Ex 3.11;
1 Sam 18.18
7.19
Isa 55.8

7.20
1 Sam 16.7;
Jn 21.17

7.22
Ps 48.1;
86.10;
Ex 15.11;
Deut 3.24;
Ps 44.1
7.23
Deut 4.7,
32–38;
10.21;
15.15; 9.26
7.24
Deut 26.18;
Ps 48.14

7.26
Ps 72.18,19

7.27
ver 13

7.28
Jn 17.17
7.29
Num 6.24–
26

---

q Gk Syr Vg 1 Chron 17.13: Heb *shall not depart*
r Cn: Heb *this is the law for man*
s Gk: Heb *one*   *t* Heb *you*
u Gk 1 Chron 17.21: Heb *for your land*
v Heb *before thy people, whom thou didst redeem for thyself from Egypt, nations and its gods*

2 And he defeated Mōăb, and measured them with a line, making them lie down on the ground; two lines he measured to be put to death, and one full line to be spared. And the Mōăbītes became servants to David and brought tribute.

8.2
Num 24.17

3 David also defeated Hădădē'zĕr the son of Rēhŏb, king of Zōbăh, as he went to restore his power at the river Eūphrā'tēṣ. ⁴And David took from him a thousand and seven hundred horsemen, and twenty thousand foot soldiers; and David hamstrung all the chariot horses, but left enough for a hundred chariots. ⁵And when the Syrians of Damascus came to help Hădădē'zĕr king of Zōbăh, David slew twenty-two thousand men of the Syrians. ⁶ Then David put garrisons in Ạrăm of Damascus; and the Syrians became servants to David and brought tribute. And the LORD gave victory to David wherever he went. ⁷And David took the shields of gold which were carried by the servants of Hădădē'zĕr, and brought them to Jerusalem. ⁸And from Bētăh and from Bērō'thaī, cities of Hădădē'zĕr, King David took very much bronze.

*8.3
2 Sam
10.15–19
*8.4
Josh 11.6,9
8.5
1 Ki 11.23–25
8.6
ver 14;
2 Sam 7.9
8.7
1 Ki 10.16

9 When Tō'ī king of Hāmăth heard that David had defeated the whole army of Hădădē'zĕr, ¹⁰ Tō'ī sent his son Jōrăm to King David, to greet him, and to congratulate him because he had fought against Hădădē'zĕr and defeated him; for Hadadezer had often been at war with Toi. And Joram brought with him articles of silver, of gold, and of bronze; ¹¹ these also King David dedicated to the LORD, together with the silver and gold which he dedicated from all the nations he subdued, ¹² from Ēdŏm, Mōăb, the Ăm'mŏnītes, the Philĭs'tĭneṣ, Ăm'ălĕk, and from the spoil of Hădădē'zĕr the son of Rēhŏb, king of Zōbăh.

8.10
1 Chr 18.10
8.11
1 Ki 7.51;
1 Chr 18.11;
26.25

13 And David won a name for himself. When he returned, he slew eighteen thousand Ē'dŏmītesʷ in the Valley of Salt. ¹⁴And he put garrisons in Ēdŏm; throughout all Edom he put garrisons, and all the Ē'dŏmītes became David's servants. And the LORD gave victory to David wherever he went.

*8.13
2 Ki 14.7
8.14
Gen 27.29,
37,40;
Num 24.17,
18;
ver 6

15 So David reigned over all Israel; and David administered justice and equity to all his people. ¹⁶And Jōăb the son of Zēru'jăh was over the army; and Jĕhŏsh'ăphăt the son of Ahī'lŭd was re-

8.16
2 Sam
19.13; 1 Ki
4.3; 2 Ki
18.18,37

ʷ Gk: Heb returned from smiting eighteen thousand Syrians

8.3 Ironically, David's victory over Hadadezer made it easier for Assyria, the future enemy of Israel and Judah, to rise to power.

8.4 Compare this with 1 Chr 18.4 where it is stated that David took *a thousand chariots, seven thousand horsemen, and twenty thousand foot soldiers.* For this reason the KJV in 2 Sam 8.4 inserts the word *chariots* after *thousand* so as to bring it into closer harmony with the parallel passage in Chronicles. Since quite a few words have been dropped out of the Hebrew text of Samuel here and there (cf. 1 Sam 13.1, where the entire number has been lost), it is more than likely that *chariots* dropped out here, although it was preserved in 1 Chr 18.4. Of course the number of horsemen in Chronicles is ten times larger also (7000, rather than the 700 here). The number must originally have been written in tallies of some sort, and it may be that here again Samuel was indistinct and the copyist could only see 700, rather than 7000.

The RSV keeps faithfully to the text as we have it and omits the word *chariots*.

8.13 The parallel account in 1 Chr 18.12 names the Edomites as the ones defeated in this engagement (the difference between the Hebrew spelling of "Edom" and of "Syria" or "Aram" consists of but one letter—a letter *d* which greatly resembles the Hebrew *r*) and hence the reading here ("Edomites" rather than the KJV's "Syrians") seems well founded. Since the Valley of Salt was located at the southern extremity of the Dead Sea, it is more likely that Edomites were the enemies fought there rather than the Syrians who dwelt to the north of Israel. 1 Chr 18.12 contributes the detail that Abishai was in immediate command of the victorious Israelite army, although of course, acting under David's authority. The heading of Ps 60 indicates that Joab, as chief of staff, masterminded the campaign and therefore deserved credit for the victory.

*8.17
1 Chr 24.3
*8.18
1 Sam 30.14

corder; 17 and Zādŏk the son of Ȧhī'tŭb and Ȧhĭm'ėlĕçh the son of Ȧbī'ȧthȧr were priests; and Sėrāi'ȧh was secretary; 18 and Bėnāi'ȧh the son of Jėhoi'ȧdȧ was over[x] the Çhĕr'ėthītes and the Pĕl'-ėthītes; and David's sons were priests.

G. David's kindness to Mephibosheth

*9.1
1 Sam
20.14–17,42
9.2
2 Sam 16.1–
4; 19.17,29
9.3
1 Sam
20.14;
2 Sam 4.4
9.4
2 Sam 17.27

9 And David said, "Is there still any one left of the house of Saul, that I may show him kindness for Jonathan's sake?" 2 Now there was a servant of the house of Saul whose name was Zībȧ, and they called him to David; and the king said to him, "Are you Ziba?" And he said, "Your servant is he." 3And the king said, "Is there not still some one of the house of Saul, that I may show the kindness of God to him?" Zībȧ said to the king, "There is still a son of Jonathan; he is crippled in his feet." 4 The king said to him, "Where is he?" And Zībȧ said to the king, "He is in the house of Māchir the son of Ȧm'mĭĕl, at Lō'-dėbar." 5 Then King David sent and brought him from the house of Māchir the son of Ȧm'mĭĕl, at Lō'-dėbar.

9.6
2 Sam 16.4;
19.24–30

6And Mėphĭb'óshĕth the son of Jonathan, son of Saul, came to David, and fell on his face and did obeisance. And David said, "Mephibosheth!" And he answered, "Behold, your servant." 7And David said to him, "Do not fear; for I will

9.7
ver 1,3;
2 Sam 12.8;
19.28

show you kindness for the sake of your father Jonathan, and I will restore to you all the land of Saul your father; and you shall eat at my table always." 8And he did obeisance, and said, "What is your

9.8
2 Sam 16.9

servant, that you should look upon a dead dog such as I?"

9.9
2 Sam 16.4;
19.29

9 Then the king called Zībȧ, Saul's servant, and said to him, "All that belonged to Saul and to all his house I have given to your master's son. 10And you and your sons and your servants shall till

9.10
ver 7,11,13;
2 Sam 19.28

the land for him, and shall bring in the produce, that your master's son may have bread to eat; but Mėphĭb'óshĕth your master's son shall always eat at my table." Now Zībȧ had fifteen sons and twenty servants. 11 Then Zībȧ said to the king, "According to all that my lord the king commands his servant, so will your servant do." So Mėphĭb'óshĕth ate at David's[y] table, like one of the king's

9.12
1 Chr 8.34

sons. 12And Mėphĭb'óshĕth had a young son, whose name was Mīcȧ. And all who dwelt in Zībȧ's house became Mėphĭb'óshĕth's servants. 13 So Mėphĭb'óshĕth dwelt in Jerusalem; for he ate al-

9.13
ver 3,7,10

ways at the king's table. Now he was lame in both his feet.

x Syr Tg Vg 20.23; 1 Chron 18.17: Heb lacks was over
y Gk: Heb my

8.17 The Hebrew word for scribe is sophĕr, meaning "one who numbers" or "who writes." RSV translators sometimes use secretary (ies) (as here, 2 Ki 12.10; 18.18, etc.) and other times, scribe(s) (1 Chr 2.55; 27.32; 2 Chr 34.13). In Old Testament times they were (1) usually men of great wisdom (1 Chr 27.32); (2) able and facile writers (Ps 45.1); (3) learned in the law (Ezra 7.6); (4) secretaries to kings (20.25; 2 Ki 12.10); (5) notaries (Jer 32.11, 12); (6) writers of state records (1 Chr 24.6); (7) secretaries to prophets (Jer 36.4, 26); (8) secretaries who kept the army rolls for the commanders (2 Ki 25.19; 2 Chr 26.11; Jer 52.25).
Zadok. This is the first mention of the priest who was to become the progenitor of

the recognized priesthood (1 Ki 2.35). In 1 Chr 6.8 he is in the priestly line of Aaron, Eleazar, and Phinehas, but aside from this genealogical data there is nothing in biblical history to show where his father Ahitub and previous ancestors served as priests.
8.18 David's sons were priests. If David's non-Levitical sons actually served as priests, there is no other passage to bear it out. There is reason to question the text here because 20.26 has: Ira the Jairite was also David's priest, while 1 Chr 18.17 reads: David's sons were the chief officials in the service of the king.
9.1 for Jonathan's sake. David did not forget his covenant with Jonathan (compare this with 1 Sam 20.14–17).

H. David's victory over the Ammonites

1. The mistreatment of David's ambassadors

10 After this the king of the Ăm′mŏnītes died, and Hānŭn his son reigned in his stead. ²And David said, "I will deal loyally with Hānŭn the son of Nāhăsh, as his father dealt loyally with me." So David sent by his servants to console him concerning his father. And David's servants came into the land of the Ăm′mŏnītes. ³ But the princes of the Ăm′mŏnītes said to Hānŭn their lord, "Do you think, because David has sent comforters to you, that he is honoring your father? Has not David sent his servants to you to search the city, and to spy it out, and to overthrow it?" ⁴ So Hānŭn took David's servants, and shaved off half the beard of each, and cut off their garments in the middle, at their hips, and sent them away. ⁵ When it was told David, he sent to meet them, for the men were greatly ashamed. And the king said, "Remain at Jĕr′ĭçhō until your beards have grown, and then return."

2. The flight of the Syrians and the Ammonites

6 When the Ăm′mŏnītes saw that they had become odious to David, the Ammonites sent and hired the Syrians of Bĕth-rē′hŏb, and the Syrians of Zōbáh, twenty thousand foot soldiers, and the king of Mā′ăcáh with a thousand men, and the men of Tŏb, twelve thousand men. ⁷And when David heard of it, he sent Jŏáb and all the host of the mighty men. ⁸And the Ăm′mŏnītes came out and drew up in battle array at the entrance of the gate; and the Syrians of Zōbáh and of Rēhŏb, and the men of Tŏb and Mā′-ácáh, were by themselves in the open country.

9 When Jŏáb saw that the battle was set against him both in front and in the rear, he chose some of the picked men of Israel, and arrayed them against the Syrians; 10 the rest of his men he put in the charge of Ăbĭsh′äï his brother, and he arrayed them against the Ăm′mŏnītes. ¹¹And he said, "If the Syrians are too strong for me, then you shall help me; but if the Ăm′mŏnītes are too strong for you, then I will come and help you. ¹² Be of good courage, and let us play the man for our people, and for the cities of our God; and may the LORD do what seems good to him." ¹³ So Jŏáb and the people who were with him drew near to battle against the Syrians; and they fled before him. ¹⁴And when the Ăm′mŏnītes saw that the Syrians fled, they likewise fled before Ăbĭsh′äï, and entered the city. Then Jŏáb returned from fighting against the Ammonites, and came to Jerusalem.

3. The defeat of the Ammonites and Syrians at Helam

15 But when the Syrians saw that they had been defeated by Israel, they gathered themselves together. ¹⁶And Hădădē′zèr sent, and brought out the Syrians who were beyond the Eūphrā′tēs;ᶻ and they came to Hēlám, with Shōbăch the commander of the army of Hadadezer at their head. ¹⁷And when it was told David, he gathered all Israel together, and crossed the Jordan, and came

ᶻ Heb *river*

10.1 king of the Ammonites, that is, Nahash.   **10.16** See note to 2 Sam 8.3.

Margin: ⋆10.1 1 Chr 19.1ff · 10.4 Isa 15.2; 20.4 · 10.6 Gen 34.30; 2Sam 8.3,5; Judg 18.28 · 10.8 1 Chr 19.9; Judg 11.3,5 · 10.12 Deut 31.6; 1 Cor 16.13; 1 Sam 3.18 · 10.13 1 Ki 20.13-21 · ⋆10.16 2 Sam 8.3; 1 Chr 19.16

to Hēlăm. And the Syrians arrayed themselves against David, and fought with him. 18And the Syrians fled before Israel; and David slew of the Syrians the men of seven hundred chariots, and forty thousand horsemen, and wounded Shōbăch the commander of their army, so that he died there. 19And when all the kings who were servants of Hădădē′zĕr saw that they had been defeated by Israel, they made peace with Israel, and became subject to them. So the Syrians feared to help the Ăm′mŏnītes any more.

III. The sin of David 11.1–12.31

A. David commits adultery with Bathsheba

11 In the spring of the year, the time when kings go forth to battle, David sent Jōăb, and his servants with him, and all Israel; and they ravaged the Ăm′mŏnītes, and besieged Răbbăh. But David remained at Jerusalem.

2 It happened, late one afternoon, when David arose from his couch and was walking upon the roof of the king's house, that he saw from the roof a woman bathing; and the woman was very beautiful. 3And David sent and inquired about the woman. And one said, "Is not this Băthshē′bā, the daughter of Ĕli′ăm, the wife of Ūrī′ăh the Hĭttīte?" 4 So David sent messengers, and took her; and she came to him, and he lay with her. (Now she was purifying herself from her uncleanness.) Then she returned to her house. 5And the woman conceived; and she sent and told David, "I am with child."

B. David sends for Uriah; his plan fails

6 So David sent word to Jōăb, "Send me Ūrī′ăh the Hĭttīte." And Joab sent Uriah to David. 7 When Ūrī′ăh came to him, David asked how Jōăb was doing, and how the people fared, and how the war prospered. 8 Then David said to Ūrī′ăh, "Go down to your house, and wash your feet." And Uriah went out of the king's house, and there followed him a present from the king. 9 But Ūrī′ăh slept at the door of the king's house with all the servants of his lord, and did not go down to his house. 10 When they told David, "Ūrī′ăh did not go down to his house," David said to Uriah, "Have you not come from a journey? Why did you not go down to your house?" 11 Ūrī′ăh said to David, "The ark and Israel and Judah dwell in booths; and my lord Jōăb and the servants of my lord are camping in the open field; shall I then go to my house, to eat and to drink, and to lie with my wife? As you live, and as your soul lives, I will not do this thing." 12 Then David said to Ūrī′ăh, "Remain here today also, and tomorrow I will let you depart." So Uriah remained in Jerusalem that day, and the next. 13And David invited him, and he ate in his presence and drank, so

---

*10.18
1 Chr 19.18;
2 Sam 8.6

11.1
1 Chr 20.1;
1 Ki 20.22,
26;
2 Sam
12.26–28

11.2
Deut 22.8;
Mt 5.28

11.3
2 Sam 23.39

11.4
Lev 15.19,
28; 18.19

11.5
Lev 20.10

11.8
Gen 43.24;
Lk 7.44

11.10
2 Sam 7.2,6;
20.6

11.13
ver 9

10.18 The number *seven hundred* chariots here appears as *seven thousand* in the parallel account in 1 Chr 19.18, but the larger figure seems less likely (in view of the resources of the armies engaged) and was probably derived from a confusion in one of the digits in the decimal system originally used for computation. A second copyist's error appears, for the account states forty thousand *horsemen* in this verse as against forty thousand *foot soldiers* in 1 Chr 19.18. Most scribal errors derive from two basic faults: (1) illegibility of worn or torn manuscripts, and (2) inaccurate copying due either to weariness or carelessness.

that he made him drunk; and in the evening he went out to lie
on his couch with the servants of his lord, but he did not go down
to his house.

C. David has Uriah slain

14 In the morning David wrote a letter to Jŏăb, and sent it by
the hand of Ūrī'ăh. ¹⁵ In the letter he wrote, "Set Ūrī'ăh in the
forefront of the hardest fighting, and then draw back from him,
that he may be struck down, and die." ¹⁶And as Jŏăb was besieging
the city, he assigned Ūrī'ăh to the place where he knew there were
valiant men. ¹⁷And the men of the city came out and fought with
Jŏăb; and some of the servants of David among the people fell.
Ūrī'ăh the Hĭttīte was slain also. ¹⁸ Then Jŏăb sent and told David
all the news about the fighting; ¹⁹ and he instructed the messenger,
"When you have finished telling all the news about the fighting
to the king, ²⁰ then, if the king's anger rises, and if he says to you,
'Why did you go so near the city to fight? Did you not know that
they would shoot from the wall? ²¹ Who killed Ăbĭm'ĕlĕch the son
of Jĕrŭb'bĕshĕth? Did not a woman cast an upper millstone upon
him from the wall, so that he died at Thĕbĕz? Why did you go so
near the wall?' then you shall say, 'Your servant Ūrī'ăh the Hĭttīte
is dead also.'"

22 So the messenger went, and came and told David all that
Jŏăb had sent him to tell. ²³ The messenger said to David, "The
men gained an advantage over us, and came out against us in the
field; but we drove them back to the entrance of the gate. ²⁴ Then
the archers shot at your servants from the wall; some of the king's
servants are dead; and your servant Ūrī'ăh the Hĭttīte is dead
also." ²⁵ David said to the messenger, "Thus shall you say to
Jŏăb, 'Do not let this matter trouble you, for the sword devours
now one and now another; strengthen your attack upon the city,
and overthrow it.' And encourage him."

D. David marries Bathsheba

26 When the wife of Ūrī'ăh heard that Uriah her husband was
dead, she made lamentation for her husband. ²⁷And when the
mourning was over, David sent and brought her to his house, and
she became his wife, and bore him a son. But the thing that David
had done displeased the LORD.

E. Nathan and David

1. Nathan's parable

12 And the LORD sent Nathan to David. He came to him,
and said to him, "There were two men in a certain city,
the one rich and the other poor. ² The rich man had very many
flocks and herds; ³ but the poor man had nothing but one little
ewe lamb, which he had bought. And he brought it up, and it grew
up with him and with his children; it used to eat of his morsel, and

Margin references:

11.14
1 Ki 21.8–10
11.15
2 Sam 12.9

11.17
ver 21

*11.21
Judg 9.50–54

11.26
Deut 34.8;
1 Sam 31.13
11.27
2 Sam 12.9;
Ps 51.4,5

12.1
2 Sam
14.4–7;
1 Ki 20.35–41

11.21 *Jerubbesheth*, a reference to Gideon.
Even though Gideon was named Jerubbaal
because he opposed Baal worship (Judg 6.32),
some scribe probably substituted *baal* for
besheth (*bosheth*), "shame"; hence Gideon is
sometimes called Jerubbesheth.

drink from his cup, and lie in his bosom, and it was like a daughter to him. 4 Now there came a traveler to the rich man, and he was unwilling to take one of his own flock or herd to prepare for the wayfarer who had come to him, but he took the poor man's lamb, and prepared it for the man who had come to him." 5 Then David's anger was greatly kindled against the man; and he said to Nathan, "As the LORD lives, the man who has done this deserves to die; 6 and he shall restore the lamb fourfold, because he did this thing, and because he had no pity."

2. *The parable applied to David who repents*

7 Nathan said to David, "You are the man. Thus says the LORD, the God of Israel, 'I anointed you king over Israel, and I delivered you out of the hand of Saul; 8 and I gave you your master's house, and your master's wives into your bosom, and gave you the house of Israel and of Judah; and if this were too little, I would add to you as much more. 9 Why have you despised the word of the LORD, to do what is evil in his sight? You have smitten Ūrī′ah the Hittīte with the sword, and have taken his wife to be your wife, and have slain him with the sword of the Am′-mônītes. 10 Now therefore the sword shall never depart from your house, because you have despised me, and have taken the wife of Ūrī′ah the Hittīte to be your wife.' 11 Thus says the LORD, 'Behold, I will raise up evil against you out of your own house; and I will take your wives before your eyes, and give them to your neighbor, and he shall lie with your wives in the sight of this sun. 12 For you did it secretly; but I will do this thing before all Israel, and before the sun.' " 13 David said to Nathan, "I have sinned against the LORD." And Nathan said to David, "The LORD also has put away your sin; you shall not die. 14 Nevertheless, because by this deed you have utterly scorned the LORD,ᵃ the child that is born to you shall die." 15 Then Nathan went to his house.

3. *The death of the child*

And the LORD struck the child that Ūrī′ah's wife bore to David, and it became sick. 16 David therefore besought God for the child; and David fasted, and went in and lay all night upon the ground. 17And the elders of his house stood beside him, to raise him from the ground; but he would not, nor did he eat food with them. 18 On the seventh day the child died. And the servants of David feared to tell him that the child was dead; for they said, "Behold, while the child was yet alive, we spoke to him, and he did not listen to us; how then can we say to him the child is dead? He may do himself some harm." 19 But when David saw that his servants were whispering together, David perceived that the child was dead; and David said to his servants, "Is the child dead?" They said, "He is dead." 20 Then David arose from the earth, and washed, and anointed himself, and changed his clothes; and he went into the house of the LORD, and worshiped; he then went to his own house; and when he asked, they set food before him, and he ate. 21 Then his servants said to him, "What is this thing that you have done? You fasted and wept for the child while it was alive; but when the child died, you arose and ate food." 22 He said,

a Heb *the enemies of the* LORD

The marginal cross-references, top to bottom:

12.5
1 Ki 20.39, 40

12.6
Ex 22.1;
Lk 19.8

12.7
1 Ki 20.42;
1 Sam 16.13

12.9
1 Sam 15.19;
2 Sam 11.15–17,27

12.10
2 Sam 13.28;
18.14;
1 Ki 2.25

12.11
Deut 28.30;
2 Sam 16.22

12.12
2 Sam 11.4–15; 16.22

12.13
1 Sam 15.24;
2 Sam 24.10;
Prov 28.13;
Mic 7.18

12.14
Isa 52.5;
Rom 2.24

12.15
1 Sam 25.38

12.16
2 Sam 13.31

12.20
Job 1.20

12.22
Isa 38.1,5;
Jon 3.9

"While the child was still alive, I fasted and wept; for I said, 'Who knows whether the LORD will be gracious to me, that the child may live?' ²³ But now he is dead; why should I fast? Can I bring him back again? I shall go to him, but he will not return to me."

4. *The birth of Solomon*

24 Then David comforted his wife, Băthshē′bà, and went in to her, and lay with her; and she bore a son, and he called his name Solomon. And the LORD loved him, ²⁵ and sent a message by Nathan the prophet; so he called his name Jĕdĭdī′àh,ᵇ because of the LORD.

5. *The victory over the Ammonites*

26 Now Jōăb fought against Răbbàh of the Ăm′mónītes, and took the royal city. ²⁷And Jōăb sent messengers to David, and said, "I have fought against Răbbàh; moreover, I have taken the city of waters. ²⁸ Now, then, gather the rest of the people together, and encamp against the city, and take it; lest I take the city, and it be called by my name." ²⁹ So David gathered all the people together and went to Răbbàh, and fought against it and took it. ³⁰And he took the crown of their kingᶜ from his head; the weight of it was a talent of gold, and in it was a precious stone; and it was placed on David's head. And he brought forth the spoil of the city, a very great amount. ³¹And he brought forth the people who were in it, and set them to labor with saws and iron picks and iron axes, and made them toil atᵈ the brickkilns; and thus he did to all the cities of the Ăm′mónītes. Then David and all the people returned to Jerusalem.

IV. *David's troubles 13.1–18.33*

A. Amnon and Tamar

1. *The incest of Amnon*

13 Now Ăb′sálóm, David's son, had a beautiful sister, whose name was Tāmar; and after a time Ămnón, David's son, loved her. ²And Ămnón was so tormented that he made himself ill because of his sister Tāmar; for she was a virgin, and it seemed impossible to Amnon to do anything to her. ³ But Ămnón had a friend, whose name was Jŏn′ádăb, the son of Shĭm′ë-àh, David's brother; and Jonadab was a very crafty man. ⁴And he said to him, "O son of the king, why are you so haggard morning after morning? Will you not tell me?" Ămnón said to him, "I love Tāmar, my brother Ăb′sálóm's sister." ⁵ Jŏn′ádăb said to him, "Lie down on your bed, and pretend to be ill; and when your father comes to see you, say to him, 'Let my sister Tāmar come and give me bread to eat, and prepare the food in my sight, that I may see it, and eat it from her hand.' " ⁶ So Ămnón lay down, and pretended to be ill; and when the king came to see him, Amnon said to the king, "Pray let my sister Tāmar come and make a couple of cakes in my sight, that I may eat from her hand."

7 Then David sent home to Tāmar, saying, "Go to your brother Ămnón's house, and prepare food for him." ⁸ So Tāmar went to her brother Ămnón's house, where he was lying down. And she

12.23 Gen 37.35; Job 7.8–10

12.24 Mt 1.6; 1 Chr 22.9

12.26 1 Chr 20.1–3

12.30 1 Chr 20.2

13.1 2 Sam 3.2,3; 1 Chr 3.9

13.3 1 Sam 16.9

13.6 Gen 18.6

ᵇThat is *beloved of the* LORD   ᶜOr *Milcóm* See Zeph 1.5   ᵈCn: Heb *pass through*

13.9
Gen 45.1

13.11
Gen 39.12

13.12
Lev 20.17;
Judg 19.23;
20.6

13.13
Gen 20.12;
Lev 18.9,11

13.14
Deut 22.25

13.18
Gen 37.3;
Judg 5.30

13.19
1 Sam 4.12;
2 Sam 1.2;
Jer 2.37

13.20
2 Sam 14.24

13.22
Gen 31.24;
Lev 19.17,
18

13.28
Judg 19.6,9,
22;
1 Sam 25.36

13.29
2 Sam
18.9;
1 Ki 1.33,38

took dough, and kneaded it, and made cakes in his sight, and baked the cakes. ⁹And she took the pan and emptied it out before him, but he refused to eat. And Amnon said, "Send out every one from me." So every one went out from him. ¹⁰ Then Amnon said to Tamar, "Bring the food into the chamber, that I may eat from your hand." And Tamar took the cakes she had made, and brought them into the chamber to Amnon her brother. ¹¹ But when she brought them near him to eat, he took hold of her, and said to her, "Come, lie with me, my sister." ¹² She answered him, "No, my brother, do not force me; for such a thing is not done in Israel; do not do this wanton folly. ¹³As for me, where could I carry my shame? And as for you, you would be as one of the wanton fools in Israel. Now therefore, I pray you, speak to the king; for he will not withhold me from you." ¹⁴ But he would not listen to her; and being stronger than she, he forced her, and lay with her.

15 Then Amnon hated her with very great hatred; so that the hatred with which he hated her was greater than the love with which he had loved her. And Amnon said to her, "Arise, be gone." ¹⁶ But she said to him, "No, my brother; for this wrong in sending me away is greater than the other which you did to me."ᵉ But he would not listen to her. ¹⁷ He called the young man who served him and said, "Put this woman out of my presence, and bolt the door after her." ¹⁸ Now she was wearing a long robe with sleeves; for thus were the virgin daughters of the king clad of old.ᶠ So his servant put her out, and bolted the door after her. ¹⁹And Tamar put ashes on her head, and rent the long robe which she wore; and she laid her hand on her head, and went away, crying aloud as she went.

2. *Absalom murders Amnon*

20 And her brother Ab'salom said to her, "Has Amnon your brother been with you? Now hold your peace, my sister; he is your brother; do not take this to heart." So Tamar dwelt, a desolate woman, in her brother Ab'salom's house. ²¹ When King David heard of all these things, he was very angry. ²² But Ab'salom spoke to Amnon neither good nor bad; for Absalom hated Amnon, because he had forced his sister Tamar.

23 After two full years Ab'salom had sheepshearers at Ba'al-ha'zor, which is near E'phraim, and Absalom invited all the king's sons. ²⁴And Ab'salom came to the king, and said, "Behold, your servant has sheepshearers; pray let the king and his servants go with your servant." ²⁵ But the king said to Ab'salom, "No, my son, let us not all go, lest we be burdensome to you." He pressed him, but he would not go but gave him his blessing. ²⁶ Then Ab'-salom said, "If not, pray let my brother Amnon go with us." And the king said to him, "Why should he go with you?" ²⁷ But Ab'-salom pressed him until he let Amnon and all the king's sons go with him. ²⁸ Then Ab'salom commanded his servants, "Mark when Amnon's heart is merry with wine, and when I say to you, 'Strike Amnon,' then kill him. Fear not; have I not commanded you? Be courageous and be valiant." ²⁹ So the servants of Ab'-salom did to Amnon as Absalom had commanded. Then all the king's sons arose, and each mounted his mule and fled.

e Cn Compare Gk Vg: Heb *No, for this great wrong in sending me away is (worse) than the other which you did to me*   *f* Cn: Heb *clad in robes*

30 While they were on the way, tidings came to David, "Ăb'-sàlòm has slain all the king's sons, and not one of them is left." 31 Then the king arose, and rent his garments, and lay on the earth; and all his servants who were standing by rent their garments. 32 But Jŏn'ădăb the son of Shĭm'ĕ-ăh, David's brother, said, "Let not my lord suppose that they have killed all the young men the king's sons, for Ămnŏn alone is dead, for by the command of Ăb'sàlòm this has been determined from the day he forced his sister Tāmar. 33 Now therefore let not my lord the king so take it to heart as to suppose that all the king's sons are dead; for Ămnŏn alone is dead."

3. Absalom flees to Geshur

34 But Ăb'sàlòm fled. And the young man who kept the watch lifted up his eyes, and looked, and behold, many people were coming from the Horónā'ĭm road[g] by the side of the mountain. 35And Jŏn'ădăb said to the king, "Behold, the king's sons have come; as your servant said, so it has come about." 36And as soon as he had finished speaking, behold, the king's sons came, and lifted up their voice and wept; and the king also and all his servants wept very bitterly.

37 But Ăb'sàlòm fled, and went to Tălmaī the son of Ămmī'-hŭd, king of Gĕshŭr. And David mourned for his son day after day. 38 So Ăb'sàlòm fled, and went to Gĕshŭr, and was there three years. 39And the spirit[h] of the king longed to go forth to Ăb'sàlòm; for he was comforted about Ămnŏn, seeing he was dead.

B. Joab secures Absalom's return

1. The woman of Tekoa

14 Now Jŏăb the son of Zĕru'iăh perceived that the king's heart went out to Ăb'sàlòm. 2And Jŏăb sent to Tĕkō'ă, and fetched from there a wise woman, and said to her, "Pretend to be a mourner, and put on mourning garments; do not anoint yourself with oil, but behave like a woman who has been mourning many days for the dead; 3 and go to the king, and speak thus to him." So Jŏăb put the words in her mouth.

4 When the woman of Tĕkō'ă came to the king, she fell on her face to the ground, and did obeisance, and said, "Help, O king." 5And the king said to her, "What is your trouble?" She answered, "Alas, I am a widow; my husband is dead. 6And your handmaid had two sons, and they quarreled with one another in the field; there was no one to part them, and one struck the other and killed

g Cn Compare Gk: Heb the road behind him
h Gk: Heb David

Cross-references (margin):

13.31 · 2 Sam 1.11; 12.16
13.32 · ver 3
13.33 · 2 Sam 19.19
13.34 · ver 37,38; 2 Sam 18.24
*13.37 · ver 34; 2 Sam 3.3; 14.23,32
13.39 · 2 Sam 12.19–23
14.1 · 2 Sam 13.39
14.2 · 2 Chr 11.6; 1 Ki 20.35–43; 2 Sam 12.20
14.3 · ver 19
14.4 · 2 Sam 1.2; 2 Ki 6.26–28
14.5 · 2 Sam 12.1–7

13.37 The story of Absalom has a threefold lesson for the Christian. First it demonstrates the truth that men reap as they have sown, not only in their own lives but also in the lives of their children. David could behold in Absalom the very defects of character which God had mastered in him, but which ran wild in his son. Secondly, the life of Absalom was a fulfilment of the word spoken by Nathan the prophet at the time of David's sin with Bathsheba, that God would raise up evil against David out of his own house (12.11). David's intense grief upon the death of Absalom was more than sorrow for the sins of his son; it expressed in part his own sense of guilt. The third lesson derived from the life of Absalom is that repentance does not necessarily imply that the temporal consequences of sin can be avoided. David repented of his sin with Bathsheba, but Absalom was the instrument of God for the chastisement of David, his father.

14.7
Num 35.19;
Deut 19.12;
Mt 21.38

him. 7And now the whole family has risen against your handmaid, and they say, 'Give up the man who struck his brother, that we may kill him for the life of his brother whom he slew'; and so they would destroy the heir also. Thus they would quench my coal which is left, and leave to my husband neither name nor remnant upon the face of the earth.'"

8 Then the king said to the woman, "Go to your house, and I will give orders concerning you." 9And the woman of Tëkō´a said to the king, "On me be the guilt, my lord the king, and on my father's house; let the king and his throne be guiltless." 10 The king said, "If any one says anything to you, bring him to me, and he shall never touch you again." 11 Then she said, "Pray let the king invoke the LORD your God, that the avenger of blood slay no more, and my son be not destroyed." He said, "As the LORD lives, not one hair of your son shall fall to the ground."

14.9
1 Sam
25.24;
Mt 27.25;
1 Ki 2.33

14.11
Num 35.19;
1 Sam 14.45

2. *The plea for Absalom*

12 Then the woman said, "Pray let your handmaid speak a word to my lord the king." He said, "Speak." 13And the woman said, "Why then have you planned such a thing against the people of God? For in giving this decision the king convicts himself, inasmuch as the king does not bring his banished one home again. 14 We must all die, we are like water spilt on the ground, which cannot be gathered up again; but God will not take away the life of him who devises*i* means not to keep his banished one an outcast. 15 Now I have come to say this to my lord the king because the people have made me afraid; and your handmaid thought, 'I will speak to the king; it may be that the king will perform the request of his servant. 16 For the king will hear, and deliver his servant from the hand of the man who would destroy me and my son together from the heritage of God.' 17And your handmaid thought, 'The word of my lord the king will set me at rest'; for my lord the king is like the angel of God to discern good and evil. The LORD your God be with you!'"

14.13
2 Sam 12.7;
1 Ki 20.40–
42;
2 Sam
13.37,38

14.14
Job 34.15;
Heb 9.27;
Num 35.15,
25,28

14.17
ver 20;
2 Sam 19.27

3. *David implicates Joab*

18 Then the king answered the woman, "Do not hide from me anything I ask you." And the woman said, "Let my lord the king speak." 19 The king said, "Is the hand of Jōăb with you in all this?" The woman answered and said, "As surely as you live, my lord the king, one cannot turn to the right hand or to the left from anything that my lord the king has said. It was your servant Jōăb who bade me; it was he who put all these words in the mouth of your handmaid. 20 In order to change the course of affairs your servant Jōăb did this. But my lord has wisdom like the wisdom of the angel of God to know all things that are on the earth."

14.19
ver 3

14.20
ver 17;
2 Sam 19.27

4. *David brings Absalom back*

21 Then the king said to Jōăb, "Behold now, I grant this; go, bring back the young man Ăb´sàlôm." 22And Jōăb fell on his face to the ground, and did obeisance, and blessed the king; and Joab said, "Today your servant knows that I have found favor in your

i Cn: Heb *and he devises*

sight, my lord the king, in that the king has granted the request of his servant." 23 So Jŏăb arose and went to Gĕshŭr, and brought Ăb′sálŏm to Jerusalem. 24And the king said, "Let him dwell apart in his own house; he is not to come into my presence." So Ăb′sálŏm dwelt apart in his own house, and did not come into the king's presence.

14.23
2 Sam
13.37,38
14.24
2 Sam 3.13

C. Absalom's revolt

1. Absalom's beauty and children

25 Now in all Israel there was no one so much to be praised for his beauty as Ăb′sálŏm; from the sole of his foot to the crown of his head there was no blemish in him. 26And when he cut the hair of his head (for at the end of every year he used to cut it; when it was heavy on him, he cut it), he weighed the hair of his head, two hundred shekels by the king's weight. 27 There were born to Ăb′-sálŏm three sons, and one daughter whose name was Tāmar; she was a beautiful woman.

14.25
Isa 1.6

14.26
Ezek 44.20

*14.27
2 Sam 18.18

2. Absalom's haughtiness

28 So Ăb′sálŏm dwelt two full years in Jerusalem, without com-ing into the king's presence. 29 Then Ăb′sálŏm sent for Jŏăb, to send him to the king; but Joab would not come to him. And he sent a second time, but Joab would not come. 30 Then he said to his servants, "See, Jŏăb′ş field is next to mine, and he has barley there; go and set it on fire." So Ăb′sálŏm's servants set the field on fire. 31 Then Jŏăb arose and went to Ăb′sálŏm at his house, and said to him, "Why have your servants set my field on fire?" 32Ăb′sálŏm answered Jŏăb, "Behold, I sent word to you, 'Come here, that I may send you to the king, to ask, "Why have I come from Gĕshŭr? It would be better for me to be there still." Now therefore let me go into the presence of the king; and if there is guilt in me, let him kill me.' " 33 Then Jŏăb went to the king, and told him; and he summoned Ăb′sálŏm. So he came to the king, and bowed himself on his face to the ground before the king; and the king kissed Absalom.

14.28
ver 24

14.32
1 Sam 20.8

14.33
Gen 33.4;
Lk 15.20

3. Absalom's revolt

15 After this Ăb′sálŏm got himself a chariot and horses, and fifty men to run before him. 2And Ăb′sálŏm used to rise early and stand beside the way of the gate; and when any man had a suit to come before the king for judgment, Absalom would call to him, and say, "From what city are you?" And when he said, "Your servant is of such and such a tribe in Israel," 3 Ăb′sálŏm would say to him, "See, your claims are good and right; but there is no man deputed by the king to hear you." 4Ăb′sálŏm said more-over, "Oh that I were judge in the land! Then every man with a suit or cause might come to me, and I would give him justice." 5And whenever a man came near to do obeisance to him, he would put out his hand, and take hold of him, and kiss him. 6 Thus

15.1
2 Sam
12.11;
1 Ki 1.5
15.2
2 Sam 19.8

15.4
Judg 9.29

15.6
Rom 16.18

14.27 Compare this account with 18.18. A discrepancy has been imagined. One of two possibilities exists. Either the setting up of the pillar took place *before* his three sons were born, or it took place *after* the premature death of all three of his sons. In either event, Absalom was left without male heirs and no mention of them is made in the genealogies.

Ab′sălŏm did to all of Israel who came to the king for judgment; so Absalom stole the hearts of the men of Israel.

7 And at the end of four*ʲ* years Ăb′sălŏm said to the king, "Pray let me go and pay my vow, which I have vowed to the LORD, in Hēbrŏn. 8 For your servant vowed a vow while I dwelt at Gĕshŭr in Arăm, saying, 'If the LORD will indeed bring me back to Jerusalem, then I will offer worship to the LORD.' " 9 The king said to him, "Go in peace." So he arose, and went to Hēbrŏn. 10 But Ăb′sălŏm sent secret messengers throughout all the tribes of Israel, saying, "As soon as you hear the sound of the trumpet, then say, 'Absalom is king at Hēbrŏn!' " 11 With Ăb′sălŏm went two hundred men from Jerusalem who were invited guests, and they went in their simplicity, and knew nothing. 12And while Ăb′sălŏm was offering the sacrifices, he sent for*ᵏ* Ăhĭth′ŏphĕl the Gĭ′lŏnīte, David's counselor, from his city Gĭlŏh. And the conspiracy grew strong, and the people with Absalom kept increasing.

4. The flight of David

13 And a messenger came to David, saying, "The hearts of the men of Israel have gone after Ăb′sălŏm." 14 Then David said to all his servants who were with him at Jerusalem, "Arise, and let us flee; or else there will be no escape for us from Ăb′sălŏm; go in haste, lest he overtake us quickly, and bring down evil upon us, and smite the city with the edge of the sword." 15And the king's servants said to the king, "Behold, your servants are ready to do whatever my lord the king decides." 16 So the king went forth, and all his household after him. And the king left ten concubines to keep the house. 17And the king went forth, and all the people after him; and they halted at the last house. 18And all his servants passed by him; and all the Chĕr′ĕthītes, and all the Pĕl′ĕthītes, and all the six hundred Gĭttītes who had followed him from Găth, passed on before the king.

5. The faithfulness of Ittai the Gittite

19 Then the king said to Ĭttaī the Gĭttīte, "Why do you also go with us? Go back, and stay with the king; for you are a foreigner, and also an exile from*ˡ* your home. 20 You came only yesterday, and shall I today make you wander about with us, seeing I go I know not where? Go back, and take your brethren with you; and may the LORD show*ᵐ* steadfast love and faithfulness to you." 21 But Ĭttaī answered the king, "As the LORD lives, and as my lord the king lives, wherever my lord the king shall be, whether for death or for life, there also will your servant be." 22And David said to Ĭttaī, "Go then, pass on." So Ittai the Gĭttīte passed on, with all his men and all the little ones who were with him. 23And all the country wept aloud as all the people passed by, and the king crossed the brook Kĭdrŏn, and all the people passed on toward the wilderness.

ʲ Gk Syr: Heb *forty*   *ᵏ* Or *sent*
ˡ Gk Syr Vg: Heb *to*
ᵐ Gk: Heb lacks *may the* LORD *show*

15.7ff Absalom used deceit and treachery to steal the hearts of the people away from his father. Yet David continued to love him.

15.18 *Cherethites . . . Pelethites . . . Gittites,* constituted David's personal bodyguard. See 8.18 in this connection.

★15.7ff
2 Sam 3.2,3

15.8
2 Sam
13.37,38;
Gen 28.20,
21

15.11
1 Sam 9.13;
22.15
15.12
ver 31;
Josh 15.51;
Ps 3.1

15.13
ver 6;
Judg 9.3
15.14
2 Sam
12.11; 19.9

15.16
2 Sam
16.21,22

★15.18
2 Sam 8.18

15.19
2 Sam 18.2

15.20
1 Sam 23.13

15.21
Ruth 1.16,
17

6. *The return of the ark*

24 And Ȧbī́áthàr came up, and lo, Zādŏk came also, with all the Lēvītes, bearing the ark of the covenant of God; and they set down the ark of God, until the people had all passed out of the city. 25 Then the king said to Zādŏk, "Carry the ark of God back into the city. If I find favor in the eyes of the LORD, he will bring me back and let me see both it and his habitation; 26 but if he says, 'I have no pleasure in you,' behold, here I am, let him do to me what seems good to him." 27The king also said to Zādŏk the priest, "Look,ⁿ go back to the city in peace, you and Abī́áthàr,ᵒ with your two sons, Ȧhĭḿä-ăz your son, and Jonathan the son of Abiathar. 28 See, I will wait at the fords of the wilderness, until word comes from you to inform me." 29 So Zādŏk and Abī́áthàr carried the ark of God back to Jerusalem; and they remained there.

7. *The treachery of Ahithophel*

30 But David went up the ascent of the Mount of Olives, weeping as he went, barefoot and with his head covered; and all the people who were with him covered their heads, and they went up, weeping as they went. 31And it was told David, "Ȧhĭth́ŏphĕl is among the conspirators with Ȧb́sálŏm." And David said, "O LORD, I pray thee, turn the counsel of Ahithophel into foolishness."

8. *Hushai returns to Jerusalem*

32 When David came to the summit, where God was worshiped, behold, Hūshaī the Arçhīte came to meet him with his coat rent and earth upon his head. 33 David said to him, "If you go on with me, you will be a burden to me. 34 But if you return to the city, and say to Ȧb́sálŏm, 'I will be your servant, O king; as I have been your father's servant in time past, so now I will be your servant,' then you will defeat for me the counsel of Ahĭth́ŏphĕl. 35Are not Zādŏk and Ȧbī́áthàr the priests with you there? So whatever you hear from the king's house, tell it to Zadok and Abiathar the priests. 36 Behold, their two sons are with them there, Ȧhĭḿä-ăz, Zādŏk's son, and Jonathan, Ȧbī́áthàr's son; and by them you shall send to me everything you hear." 37 So Hūshaī, David's friend, came into the city, just as Ȧb́sálŏm was entering Jerusalem.

9. *Zība's lie against Mephibosheth*

16 When David had passed a little beyond the summit, Zībä the servant of Mĕphĭb́ŏshĕth met him, with a couple of asses saddled, bearing two hundred loaves of bread, a hundred bunches of raisins, a hundred of summer fruits, and a skin of wine. 2And the king said to Zībä, "Why have you brought these?" Ziba answered, "The asses are for the king's household to ride on, the bread and summer fruit for the young men to eat, and the wine for those who faint in the wilderness to drink." 3And the king said, "And where is your master's son?" Zībä said to the king, "Behold, he remains in Jerusalem; for he said, 'Today the house of Israel will give me back the kingdom of my father.' " 4 Then the king said to Zībä, "Behold, all that belonged to Mĕphĭb́-

---

ⁿ Gk: Heb *Are you a seer* or *Do you see?*   ᵒ Cn: Heb lacks *and Abiathar*

Cross-references (margin)

15.24
2 Sam 8.17;
Num 4.15;
1 Sam 22.20

15.25
Ps 43.3;
Jer 25.30

15.26
2 Sam
22.20; 1 Ki
10.9; 1 Sam
3.18

15.27
1 Sam
9.6–9;
2 Sam 17.17

15.28
2 Sam 17.16

15.30
Est 6.12;
2 Sam 19.4;
Isa 20.2–4;
Ps 126.6

15.31
ver 12;
2 Sam
16.23;
17.14,23

15.32
Josh 16.2;
2 Sam 1.2

15.33
2 Sam 19.35

15.34
2 Sam 16.19

15.35
2 Sam
17.15,16

15.36
ver 27;
2 Sam 17.17

15.37
2 Sam
16.16,17;
1 Chr 27.33

16.1
2 Sam
15.32; 9.2–13

16.2
2 Sam 17.29

16.3
2 Sam 9.9,
10; 19.26,27

óshĕth is now yours." And Ziba said, "I do obeisance; let me ever
find favor in your sight, my lord the king."

10. *Shimei curses David*

16.5
2 Sam 3.16–
18; 19.16–
23; 1 Ki 2.8

5 When King David came to Báhu'rĭm, there came out a man
of the family of the house of Saul, whose name was Shĭm'ĕ-ī, the
son of Gērá; and as he came he cursed continually. 6And he threw
stones at David, and at all the servants of King David; and all the
people and all the mighty men were on his right hand and on his

16.7
2 Sam 12.9

left. 7And Shĭm'ĕ-ī said as he cursed, "Begone, begone, you man
of blood, you worthless fellow! 8 The LORD has avenged upon you

16.8
2 Sam
21.1–9

all the blood of the house of Saul, in whose place you have reigned;
and the LORD has given the kingdom into the hand of your son
Ăb'sálŏm. See, your ruin is on you; for you are a man of blood."

16.9
2 Sam
19.21; 9.8;
Ex 22.28

9 Then Abĭsh'äī the son of Zèru'iäh said to the king, "Why
should this dead dog curse my lord the king? Let me go over and

16.10
2 Sam
19.22;
1 Pet 2.23;
2 Ki 18.25;
Rom 9.20

take off his head." 10 But the king said, "What have I to do with
you, you sons of Zèru'iäh? If he is cursing because the LORD has
said to him, 'Curse David,' who then shall say, 'Why have you done
so?' " 11And David said to Abĭsh'äī and to all his servants, "Behold, my own son seeks my life; how much more now may this

16.11
2 Sam
12.11;
Gen 45.5

Benjaminite! Let him alone, and let him curse; for the LORD has
bidden him. 12 It may be that the LORD will look upon my affliction,p and that the LORD will repay me with good for this cursing

16.12
Rom 8.28

of me today." 13 So David and his men went on the road, while
Shĭm'ĕ-ī went along on the hillside opposite him and cursed as he
went, and threw stones at him and flung dust. 14And the king, and
all the people who were with him, arrived weary at the Jordan;q
and there he refreshed himself.

11. *The rule of Absalom in Jerusalem*
a. *Hushai pretends to serve Absalom*

16.15
2 Sam 15.37

15 Now Ăb'sálŏm and all the people, the men of Israel, came to
Jerusalem, and Ahĭth'óphĕl with him. 16And when Hūshaī the

16.16
2 Sam 15.37

Arçhīte, David's friend, came to Ăb'sálŏm, Hushai said to Absalom, "Long live the king! Long live the king!" 17And Ăb'sálŏm

16.17
2 Sam 19.25

said to Hūshaī, "Is this your loyalty to your friend? Why did you
not go with your friend?" 18And Hūshaī said to Ăb'sálŏm, "No;
for whom the LORD and this people and all the men of Israel have
chosen, his I will be, and with him I will remain. 19And again,

16.19
2 Sam 15.34

whom should I serve? Should it not be his son? As I have served
your father, so I will serve you."

b. *Ahithophel's counsel about the concubines*

20 Then Ăb'sálŏm said to Ahĭth'óphĕl, "Give your counsel;

16.21
2 Sam
15.16;
1 Sam 13.4;
2 Sam 2.7

what shall we do?" 21Ahĭth'óphĕl said to Ăb'sálŏm, "Go in to your
father's concubines, whom he has left to keep the house; and all
Israel will hear that you have made yourself odious to your father,
and the hands of all who are with you will be strengthened." 22 So

16.22
2 Sam
12.11,12

they pitched a tent for Ăb'sálŏm upon the roof; and Absalom went
in to his father's concubines in the sight of all Israel. 23 Now in

16.23
2 Sam 15.12

those days the counsel which Ahĭth'óphĕl gave was as if one consulted the oracler of God; so was all the counsel of Ahithophel
esteemed, both by David and by Ăb'sálŏm.

p Gk Vg: Heb *iniquity*   *q* Gk: Heb lacks *at the Jordan*   *r* Heb *word*

c. Ahithophel's counsel to pursue David

17 Moreover Ăhĭth'ŏphĕl said to Ăb'sălŏm, "Let me choose twelve thousand men, and I will set out and pursue David tonight. [2] I will come upon him while he is weary and discouraged, and throw him into a panic; and all the people who are with him will flee. I will strike down the king only, [3] and I will bring all the people back to you as a bride comes home to her husband. You seek the life of only one man,[s] and all the people will be at peace." [4]And the advice pleased Ăb'sălŏm and all the elders of Israel.

d. Hushai's diverse counsel

[5] Then Ăb'sălŏm said, "Call Hūshaī the Arçhīte also, and let us hear what he has to say." [6]And when Hūshaī came to Ab'sălŏm, Absalom said to him, "Thus has Ăhĭth'ŏphĕl spoken; shall we do as he advises? If not, you speak." [7] Then Hūshaī said to Ăb'sălŏm, "This time the counsel which Ăhĭth'ŏphĕl has given is not good." [8] Hūshaī said moreover, "You know that your father and his men are mighty men, and that they are enraged, like a bear robbed of her cubs in the field. Besides, your father is expert in war; he will not spend the night with the people. [9] Behold, even now he has hidden himself in one of the pits, or in some other place. And when some of the people fall[t] at the first attack, whoever hears it will say, 'There has been a slaughter among the people who follow Ăb'sălŏm.' [10] Then even the valiant man, whose heart is like the heart of a lion, will utterly melt with fear; for all Israel knows that your father is a mighty man, and that those who are with him are valiant men. [11] But my counsel is that all Israel be gathered to you, from Dan to Beër-shē'bå, as the sand by the sea for multitude, and that you go to battle in person. [12] So we shall come upon him in some place where he is to be found, and we shall light upon him as the dew falls on the ground; and of him and all the men with him not one will be left. [13] If he withdraws into a city, then all Israel will bring ropes to that city, and we shall drag it into the valley, until not even a pebble is to be found there." [14]And Ăb'sălŏm and all the men of Israel said, "The counsel of Hūshaī the Arçhīte is better than the counsel of Ăhĭth'ŏphĕl." For the Lord had ordained to defeat the good counsel of Ahithophel, so that the Lord might bring evil upon Absalom.

e. Hushai reports to David

[15] Then Hūshaī said to Zādŏk and Ăbī'äthår the priests, "Thus and so did Ăhĭth'ŏphĕl counsel Ăb'sălŏm and the elders of Israel; and thus and so have I counseled. [16] Now therefore send quickly and tell David, 'Do not lodge tonight at the fords of the wilderness, but by all means pass over; lest the king and all the people who are with him be swallowed up.'" [17] Now Jonathan and Ahĭm'ä-ăz were waiting at Ĕn-rŏ'gĕl; a maidservant used to go and tell them, and they would go and tell King David; for they must not be seen entering the city. [18] But a lad saw them, and told Ăb'sălŏm; so both of them went away quickly, and came to the house of a man at Băhū'rĭm, who had a well in his courtyard; and they went down into it. [19]And the woman took and spread a covering over the well's mouth, and scattered grain upon it; and nothing

	17.2 2 Sam 16.14; 1 Ki 22.31
	17.5 2 Sam 15.32–34
	17.8 Hos 13.8; 1 Sam 16.18
	17.10 Josh 2.11
	17.14 2 Sam 15.31,34
	17.15 2 Sam 15.35
	17.16 2 Sam 15.28
	17.17 2 Sam 15.27,36; Josh 15.7; 18.16
	17.18 2 Sam 16.5
	17.19 Josh 2.4–6

---

[s] Gk: Heb *like the return of the whole (is) the man whom you seek*
[t] Or *when he falls upon them*

17.20
Josh 2.3–5;
1 Sam
19.12–17

was known of it. 20 When Ăb'sălŏm's servants came to the woman at the house, they said, "Where are Ăhĭm'ă-ăz and Jonathan?" And the woman said to them, "They have gone over the brook[u] of water." And when they had sought and could not find them, they returned to Jerusalem.

17.21
ver 15,16

21 After they had gone, the men came up out of the well, and went and told King David. They said to David, "Arise, and go quickly over the water; for thus and so has Ăhĭth'ŏphĕl counseled against you." 22 Then David arose, and all the people who were with him, and they crossed the Jordan; by daybreak not one was left who had not crossed the Jordan.

f. Ahithophel commits suicide

17.23
2 Sam
15.12;
2 Ki 20.1;
Mt 27.5

23 When Ăhĭth'ŏphĕl saw that his counsel was not followed, he saddled his ass, and went off home to his own city. And he set his house in order, and hanged himself; and he died, and was buried in the tomb of his father.

D. The war between David and Absalom

1. The background

17.24
Gen 32.2;
2 Sam 2.8
17.25
2 Sam
19.13;
20.9–12

24 Then David came to Māhănā'ĭm. And Ăb'sălŏm crossed the Jordan with all the men of Israel. 25 Now Ăb'sălŏm had set Ămă'să over the army instead of Jŏăb. Amasa was the son of a man named Ĭthră the Ĭsh'măĕlīte,[v] who had married Ăb'ĭgăl the daughter of Nāhăsh, sister of Zĕru'ĭăh, Jŏăb's mother. 26And Israel and Ăb'sălŏm encamped in the land of Gĭl'ĕăd.

17.27
2 Sam 10.1,
2; 12.26,29;
19.31,32;
1 Ki 2.7
17.29
2 Sam 16.2

27 When David came to Māhănā'ĭm, Shōbī the son of Nāhăsh from Răbbăh of the Ăm'mŏnītes, and Māchĭr the son of Ăm'-mĭ-ĕl from Lō'-dĕbăr, and Barzĭl'laī the Gĭl'ĕădīte from Rō'gĕlĭm, 28 brought beds, basins, and earthen vessels, wheat, barley, meal, parched grain, beans and lentils,[w] 29 honey and curds and sheep and cheese from the herd, for David and the people with him to eat; for they said, "The people are hungry and weary and thirsty in the wilderness."

2. The battle in the forest of Ephraim

18.1
Ex 18.25;
1 Sam 22.7
18.2
1 Sam
11.11;
2 Sam 15.19
18.3
2 Sam 21.17

18 Then David mustered the men who were with him, and set over them commanders of thousands and commanders of hundreds. 2And David sent forth the army, one third under the command of Jŏăb, one third under the command of Ăbĭsh'ăī the son of Zĕru'ĭăh, Jŏăb's brother, and one third under the command of Ĭttaī the Gĭttīte. And the king said to the men, "I myself will also go out with you." 3 But the men said, "You shall not go out. For if we flee, they will not care about us. If half of us die, they will not care about us. But you are worth ten thousand of us;[x] therefore it is better that you send us help from the city." 4 The king said to them, "Whatever seems best to you I will do." So the king stood at the side of the gate, while all the army marched out by hundreds and by thousands. 5And the king ordered Jŏăb and Ăbĭsh'ăī and Ĭttaī, "Deal gently for my sake with the young man Ăb'sălŏm." And all the people heard when the king gave orders to all the commanders about Absalom.

18.4
ver 24
18.5
ver 12

u The meaning of the Hebrew word is uncertain   v 1 Chron 2.17: Heb Israelite
w Heb lentils and parched grain
x Gk Vg Symmachus: Heb for now there are ten thousand such as we

6 So the army went out into the field against Israel; and the battle was fought in the forest of Ē'phrāïm. 7And the men of Israel were defeated there by the servants of David, and the slaughter there was great on that day, twenty thousand men. 8 The battle spread over the face of all the country; and the forest devoured more people that day than the sword.

3. *Absalom slain by Joab*

9 And Ăb'sàlòm chanced to meet the servants of David. Absalom was riding upon his mule, and the mule went under the thick branches of a great oak, and his head caught fast in the oak, and he was left hanging*y* between heaven and earth, while the mule that was under him went on. 10And a certain man saw it, and told Jōăb, "Behold, I saw Ăb'sàlòm hanging in an oak." 11 Jōăb said to the man who told him, "What, you saw him! Why then did you not strike him there to the ground? I would have been glad to give you ten pieces of silver and a girdle." 12 But the man said to Jōăb, "Even if I felt in my hand the weight of a thousand pieces of silver, I would not put forth my hand against the king's son; for in our hearing the king commanded you and Abĭsh'āī and Ĭttaī, 'For my sake protect the young man Ăb'sàlòm.' 13 On the other hand, if I had dealt treacherously against his life*z* (and there is nothing hidden from the king), then you yourself would have stood aloof." 14 Jōăb said, "I will not waste time like this with you." And he took three darts in his hand, and thrust them into the heart of Ăb'sàlòm, while he was still alive in the oak. 15And ten young men, Jōăb's armor-bearers, surrounded Ăb'sàlòm and struck him, and killed him.

16 Then Jōăb blew the trumpet, and the troops came back from pursuing Israel; for Joab restrained them. 17And they took Ăb'sàlòm, and threw him into a great pit in the forest, and raised over him a very great heap of stones; and all Israel fled every one to his own home. 18 Now Ăb'sàlòm in his lifetime had taken and set up for himself the pillar which is in the King's Valley, for he said, "I have no son to keep my name in remembrance"; he called the pillar after his own name, and it is called Ăb'sàlòm's monument to this day.

4. *Ahimaaz brings the tidings to David*

19 Then said Ăhĭm'ä-ăz the son of Zādŏk, "Let me run, and carry tidings to the king that the LORD has delivered him from the power of his enemies." 20And Jōăb said to him, "You are not to carry tidings today; you may carry tidings another day, but today you shall carry no tidings, because the king's son is dead." 21 Then Jōăb said to the Cŭshīte, "Go, tell the king what you have seen." The Cushite bowed before Joab, and ran. 22 Then Ăhĭm'ä-ăz the son of Zādŏk said again to Jōăb, "Come what may, let me also run after the Cŭshīte." And Joab said, "Why will you run, my son, seeing that you will have no reward for the tidings?" 23 "Come what may," he said, "I will run." So he said to him, "Run." Then Ăhĭm'ä-ăz ran by the way of the plain, and outran the Cŭshīte.

24 Now David was sitting between the two gates; and the watchman went up to the roof of the gate by the wall, and when he lifted

y Gk Syr Tg: Heb *was put*
z Another reading is *at the risk of my life*

18.6
Josh 17.15, 18

18.9
2 Sam 14.26

18.12
ver 5

18.14
2 Sam 14.30

18.16
2 Sam 2.28; 20.22
18.17
Josh 7.26; 8.29;
2 Sam 19.8
18.18
1 Sam 12.12;
Gen 14.17;
2 Sam 14.27

18.19
2 Sam 15.36;
ver 31

18.24
2 Sam 19.8;
13.34;
2 Ki 9.17

up his eyes and looked, he saw a man running alone. 25And the watchman called out and told the king. And the king said, "If he is alone, there are tidings in his mouth." And he came apace, and drew near. 26And the watchman saw another man running; and the watchman called to the gate and said, "See, another man running alone!" The king said, "He also brings tidings." 27And the watchman said, "I think the running of the foremost is like the running of Ahĭm′ä-ăz the son of Zādŏk." And the king said, "He is a good man, and comes with good tidings."

28 Then Ahĭm′ä-ăz cried out to the king, "All is well." And he bowed before the king with his face to the earth, and said, "Blessed be the LORD your God, who has delivered up the men who raised their hand against my lord the king." 29And the king said, "Is it well with the young man Ăb′sălŏm?" Ahĭm′ä-ăz answered, "When Jōăb sent your servant,[b] I saw a great tumult, but I do not know what it was." 30And the king said, "Turn aside, and stand here." So he turned aside, and stood still.

31 And behold, the Cŭshīte came; and the Cushite said, "Good tidings for my lord the king! For the LORD has delivered you this day from the power of all who rose up against you." 32 The king said to the Cŭshīte, "Is it well with the young man Ăb′sălŏm?" And the Cushite answered, "May the enemies of my lord the king, and all who rise up against you for evil, be like that young man." 33 c And the king was deeply moved, and went up to the chamber over the gate, and wept; and as he went, he said, "O my son Ăb′sălŏm, my son, my son Absalom! Would I had died instead of you, O Absalom, my son, my son!"

V. David restored to his kingdom 19.1–20.26

A. Joab rebukes David

19 It was told Jōăb, "Behold, the king is weeping and mourning for Ăb′sălŏm." 2 So the victory that day was turned into mourning for all the people; for the people heard that day, "The king is grieving for his son." 3And the people stole into the city that day as people steal in who are ashamed when they flee in battle. 4 The king covered his face, and the king cried with a loud voice, "O my son Ăb′sălŏm, O Absalom, my son, my son!" 5 Then Jōăb came into the house to the king, and said, "You have today covered with shame the faces of all your servants, who have this day saved your life, and the lives of your sons and your daughters, and the lives of your wives and your concubines, 6 because you love those who hate you and hate those who love you. For you have made it clear today that commanders and servants are nothing to you; for today I perceive that if Ăb′sălŏm were alive and all of us were dead today, then you would be pleased. 7 Now therefore arise, go out and speak kindly to your servants; for I swear by the LORD, if you do not go, not a man will stay with you this night; and this will be worse for you than all the evil that has come upon you from your youth until now." 8 Then the king arose, and took his seat in the gate. And the people were all told, "Behold, the king is sitting in the gate"; and all the people came before the king.

18.28
2 Sam 14.4;
1 Sam
25.23;
17.46
18.29
ver 22

18.31
ver 19;
Judg 5.31
18.32
1 Sam 25.26

18.33
2 Sam
19.4;
Ex 32.32;
Rom 9.3

19.1
2 Sam 18.33

19.4
2 Sam
15.30;
18.33

19.6
Mt 5.46

19.8
2 Sam 15.2;
18.4

b Heb *the king's servant, your servant*
c Ch 19.1 in Heb

B. *David's return to Jerusalem*

1. *The elders invite David back*

Now Israel had fled every man to his own home. 9And all the
people were at strife throughout all the tribes of Israel, saying,
"The king delivered us from the hand of our enemies, and saved
us from the hand of the Philis′tines; and now he has fled out of the
land from Ab′salom. 10 But Ab′salom, whom we anointed over us,
is dead in battle. Now therefore why do you say nothing about
bringing the king back?"

11 And King David sent this message to Zadok and Abi′athar
the priests, "Say to the elders of Judah, 'Why should you be the
last to bring the king back to his house, when the word of all Israel
has come to the king?*d* 12 You are my kinsmen, you are my bone
and my flesh; why then should you be the last to bring back the
king?' 13And say to Amā′sa, 'Are you not my bone and my flesh? God
do so to me, and more also, if you are not commander of my army
henceforth in place of Joab.' " 14And he swayed the heart of all
the men of Judah as one man; so that they sent word to the king,
"Return, both you and all your servants." 15 So the king came back
to the Jordan; and Judah came to Gilgal to meet the king and to
bring the king over the Jordan.

2. *The repentance and forgiveness of Shimei*

16 And Shim′e-i the son of Gera, the Benjaminite, from Bahu′-
rim, made haste to come down with the men of Judah to meet
King David; 17 and with him were a thousand men from Benjamin. And Ziba the servant of the house of Saul, with his fifteen
sons and his twenty servants, rushed down to the Jordan before
the king, 18 and they crossed the ford*e* to bring over the king's
household, and to do his pleasure. And Shim′e-i the son of Gera
fell down before the king, as he was about to cross the Jordan,
19 and said to the king, "Let not my lord hold me guilty or remember how your servant did wrong on the day my lord the king
left Jerusalem; let not the king bear it in mind. 20 For your servant
knows that I have sinned; therefore, behold, I have come this
day, the first of all the house of Joseph to come down to meet my
lord the king." 21Abish′ai the son of Zeru′iah answered, "Shall
not Shim′e-i be put to death for this, because he cursed the
LORD's anointed?" 22 But David said, "What have I to do with you,
you sons of Zeru′iah, that you should this day be as an adversary
to me? Shall any one be put to death in Israel this day? For do I
not know that I am this day king over Israel?" 23And the king
said to Shim′e-i, "You shall not die." And the king gave him
his oath.

3. *The explanation of Mephibosheth*

24 And Mephib′osheth the son of Saul came down to meet the
king; he had neither dressed his feet, nor trimmed his beard, nor

d Gk: Heb *to the king, to his house*   *e* Cn: Heb *the ford crossed*

	19.9
	2 Sam 8.1–
	14; 5.20;
	15.14
	19.12
	2 Sam 5.1
	*19.13
	2 Sam
	17.25;
	1 Ki 19.2;
	8.16;
	ver 5–7
	19.14
	Judg 20.1
	19.15
	Josh 5.9
	19.16
	2 Sam
	16.5;
	1 Ki 2.8
	19.17
	2 Sam
	16.1,2
	19.19
	1 Sam
	22.15;
	2 Sam
	16.6–8;
	13.33
	19.20
	2 Sam 16.5
	19.21
	2 Sam 16.7,
	8; Ex 22.28
	19.22
	2 Sam
	16.10;
	1 Sam 11.13
	19.23
	1 Ki 2.8
	19.24
	2 Sam 9.6–
	10

19.13 Joab had fought faithfully over the
years for David's best interests. He ignored
David's sentimental request to protect
Absalom because he knew the kingdom was
at stake. Yet for this one act of disobedience
David rashly promised to elevate Amasa,
chief of Absalom's army, as commander of
the army in place of Joab.

washed his clothes, from the day the king departed until the day
he came back in safety. 25And when he came from*f* Jerusalem to
meet the king, the king said to him, "Why did you not go with me,
Mephib'osheth?" 26 He answered, "My lord, O king, my servant
deceived me; for your servant said to him, 'Saddle an ass for me,*g*
that I may ride upon it and go with the king.' For your servant is
lame. 27 He has slandered your servant to my lord the king. But
my lord the king is like the angel of God; do therefore what seems
good to you. 28 For all my father's house were but men doomed
to death before my lord the king; but you set your servant among
those who eat at your table. What further right have I, then, to
cry to the king?" 29And the king said to him, "Why speak any
more of your affairs? I have decided: you and Ziba shall divide the
land." 30And Mephib'osheth said to the king, "Oh, let him take it
all, since my lord the king has come safely home."

4. *The blessing by Barzillai*

31 Now Barzil'lai the Gil'eadite had come down from Ro'-
gelim; and he went on with the king to the Jordan, to escort him
over the Jordan. 32 Barzil'lai was a very aged man, eighty years
old; and he had provided the king with food while he stayed at
Mahana'im; for he was a very wealthy man. 33And the king said
to Barzil'lai, "Come over with me, and I will provide for you with
me in Jerusalem." 34 But Barzil'lai said to the king, "How many
years have I still to live, that I should go up with the king to
Jerusalem? 35 I am this day eighty years old; can I discern what
is pleasant and what is not? Can your servant taste what he eats
or what he drinks? Can I still listen to the voice of singing men and
singing women? Why then should your servant be an added burden to my lord the king? 36 Your servant will go a little way over
the Jordan with the king. Why should the king recompense me
with such a reward? 37 Pray let your servant return, that I may die
in my own city, near the grave of my father and my mother. But
here is your servant Chimham; let him go over with my lord the
king; and do for him whatever seems good to you." 38And the king
answered, "Chimham shall go over with me, and I will do for him
whatever seems good to you; and all that you desire of me I will do
for you." 39 Then all the people went over the Jordan, and the
king went over; and the king kissed Barzil'lai and blessed him, and
he returned to his own home. 40 The king went on to Gilgal, and
Chimham went on with him; all the people of Judah, and also half
the people of Israel, brought the king on his way.

5. *Israel's jealousy*

41 Then all the men of Israel came to the king, and said to the
king, "Why have our brethren the men of Judah stolen you away,
and brought the king and his household over the Jordan, and all
David's men with him?" 42All the men of Judah answered the men
of Israel, "Because the king is near of kin to us. Why then are you
angry over this matter? Have we eaten at all at the king's expense?
Or has he given us any gift?" 43And the men of Israel answered
the men of Judah, "We have ten shares in the king, and in David
also we have more than you. Why then did you despise us? Were

f Heb *to*
g Gk Syr Vg: Heb *said, I will saddle an ass for myself*

Side references: 19.25 / 2 Sam 16.17; 19.26 / 2 Sam 9.3; 19.27 / 2 Sam 16.3; 14.17,20; 19.28 / 2 Sam 21.6–9; 9.7,10,13; 19.31 / 1 Ki 2.7; 19.32 / 2 Sam 17.27; 19.35 / Ps 90.10; Isa 5.11,12; 19.37 / ver 40; 1 Ki 2.7; Jer 41.17; 19.39 / Gen 31.55; 19.41 / ver 15; 19.42 / ver 12; 19.43 / 1 Ki 11.30,31

we not the first to speak of bringing back our king?" But the words
of the men of Judah were fiercer than the words of the men of
Israel.

C. Sheba's revolt

1. Sheba calls for rebellion

20 Now there happened to be there a worthless fellow, whose
name was Shēbă, the son of Bĭçhrĭ, a Benjaminite; and he
blew the trumpet, and said,
"We have no portion in David,
    and we have no inheritance in the son of Jĕssĕ;
    every man to his tents, O Israel!"
2 So all the men of Israel withdrew from David, and followed
Shēbă the son of Bĭçhrĭ; but the men of Judah followed their king
steadfastly from the Jordan to Jerusalem.

3 And David came to his house at Jerusalem; and the king took
the ten concubines whom he had left to care for the house, and
put them in a house under guard, and provided for them, but did
not go in to them. So they were shut up until the day of their
death, living as if in widowhood.

2. Amasa slain by Joab

4 Then the king said to Ămā′să, "Call the men of Judah together to me within three days, and be here yourself." 5 So Amā′să
went to summon Judah; but he delayed beyond the set time which
had been appointed him. 6And David said to Ăbĭsh′äĭ, "Now
Shēbă the son of Bĭçhrĭ will do us more harm than Ăb′sălŏm; take
your lord's servants and pursue him, lest he get himself fortified
cities, and cause us trouble."ʰ 7And there went out after Ăbĭsh′äĭ,
Jōăbⁱ and the Çhĕr′ĕthītes and the Pĕl′ĕthītes, and all the mighty
men; they went out from Jerusalem to pursue Shēbă the son of
Bĭçhrĭ. 8 When they were at the great stone which is in Gĭb′ëŏn,
Ămā′să came to meet them. Now Jōăb was wearing a soldier's
garment, and over it was a girdle with a sword in its sheath fastened upon his loins, and as he went forward it fell out. 9And Jōăb
said to Ămā′să, "Is it well with you, my brother?" And Joab took
Amasa by the beard with his right hand to kiss him. 10 But Ămā′să
did not observe the sword which was in Jōăb′ş hand; so Jōăb struck
him with it in the body, and shed his bowels to the ground, without striking a second blow; and he died.

3. Joab pursues Sheba

Then Joab and Ăbĭsh′äĭ his brother pursued Shēbă the son of
Bĭçhrĭ. 11And one of Jōăb′ş men took his stand by Ămā′să, and
said, "Whoever favors Jōăb, and whoever is for David, let him
follow Joab." 12And Amā′să lay wallowing in his blood in the highway. And any one who came by, seeing him, stopped;ⁱ and when
the man saw that all the people stopped, he carried Amasa out of
the highway into the field, and threw a garment over him. 13 When

Marginal references:

*20.1
2 Sam
19.43;
1 Ki 12.16;
2 Chr 10.16

20.3
2 Sam
15.16;
16.21,22

20.4
2 Sam 19.13
*20.5

20.6
2 Sam
11.11;
1 Ki 1.33

20.7
2 Sam 8.18;
1 Ki 1.38;
2 Sam 15.18

20.9
Mt 26.49

20.10
2 Sam 2.23;
3.27;
1 Ki 2.5

ʰ Tg: Heb *snatch away our eyes*   ⁱ Cn Compare Gk: Heb *after him Jōăb's men*
ⁱ This clause is transposed from the end of the verse

20.1 Sheba took advantage of old hatreds
between north and south to rally the northern
tribes against David and the tribe of Judah.
20.5 *Amasa*, a poor successor to Joab.

he was taken out of the highway, all the people went on after Jōăb to pursue Shēbă the son of Bĭchrī.

4. *The slaying of Sheba*

14 And Shēbă passed through all the tribes of Israel to Abel of Bĕth-mā'ăcăh;*k* and all the Bĭchrītes*l* assembled, and followed him in. ¹⁵And all the men who were with Jōăb came and besieged him in Abel of Bĕth-mā'ăcăh; they cast up a mound against the city, and it stood against the rampart; and they were battering the wall, to throw it down. ¹⁶ Then a wise woman called from the city, "Hear! Hear! Tell Jōăb, 'Come here, that I may speak to you.'" ¹⁷And he came near her; and the woman said, "Are you Jōăb?" He answered, "I am." Then she said to him, "Listen to the words of your maidservant." And he answered, "I am listening." ¹⁸ Then she said, "They were wont to say in old time, 'Let them but ask counsel at Abel'; and so they settled a matter. ¹⁹ I am one of those who are peaceable and faithful in Israel; you seek to destroy a city which is a mother in Israel; why will you swallow up the heritage of the LORD?" ²⁰ Jōăb answered, "Far be it from me, far be it, that I should swallow up or destroy! ²¹ That is not true. But a man of the hill country of Ē'phrăĭm, called Shēbă the son of Bĭchrī, has lifted up his hand against King David; give up him alone, and I will withdraw from the city." And the woman said to Jōăb, "Behold, his head shall be thrown to you over the wall." ²² Then the woman went to all the people in her wisdom. And they cut off the head of Shēbă the son of Bĭchrī, and threw it out to Jōăb. So he blew the trumpet, and they dispersed from the city, every man to his home. And Joab returned to Jerusalem to the king.

23 Now Jōăb was in command of all the army of Israel; and Bĕnāi'ăh the son of Jĕhoi'ădă was in command of the Chĕr'ĕthītes and the Pĕl'ĕthītes; ²⁴ and Adō'răm was in charge of the forced labor; and Jĕhōsh'ăphăt the son of Ahī'lŭd was the recorder; ²⁵ and Shēvă was secretary; and Zādŏk and Abī'ăthăr were priests; ²⁶ and Ira the Jā'ĭrīte was also David's priest.

VI. *The later years of David's kingdom 21.1–24.25*

A. *The famine*

1. *The bloodguilt of Saul*

21 Now there was a famine in the days of David for three years, year after year; and David sought the face of the LORD. And the LORD said, "There is bloodguilt on Saul and on his house, because he put the Gĭb'ĕŏnītes to death." ² So the king called the Gĭb'ĕŏnītes.*m* Now the Gibeonites were not of the people of Israel, but of the remnant of the Ăm'ŏrītes; although the people of Israel had sworn to spare them, Saul had sought to slay them in his zeal for the people of Israel and Judah. ³And David

k With 20.15: Heb *and Beth-maacah* *l* Heb *Bērites*
m Heb *the Gibeonites and said to them*

20.15 *Abel of Beth-maacah*, in the northernmost part of what is now Palestine, was held by the people of Naphtali.

20.19 *a mother in Israel*. Abel was a fortress city with dependent villages, known as daughters, round about the countryside.

Side references (left margin):

*20.15
1 Ki 15.20;
2 Ki 19.32

20.16
2 Sam 14.2

*20.19
1 Sam
26.19;
2 Sam 21.3

20.21
ver 2

20.22
Ecc 9.13–
16; ver 1

20.23
2 Sam 8.16–
18

20.25
2 Sam 8.17
20.26
2 Sam 23.38

21.2
Josh 9.3,
15–17

21.3
2 Sam 20.19

said to the Gĭb'ëŏnītes, "What shall I do for you? And how shall I make expiation, that you may bless the heritage of the LORD?" 4 The Gĭb'ëŏnītes said to him, "It is not a matter of silver or gold between us and Saul or his house; neither is it for us to put any man to death in Israel." And he said, "What do you say that I shall do for you?" 5 They said to the king, "The man who consumed us and planned to destroy us, so that we should have no place in all the territory of Israel, 6 let seven of his sons be given to us, so that we may hang them up before the LORD at Gĭb'ëŏn on the mountain of the LORD."ⁿ And the king said, "I will give them."

2. *The hanging of seven of Saul's kin*

7 But the king spared Mĕphĭb'ŏshĕth, the son of Saul's son Jonathan, because of the oath of the LORD which was between them, between David and Jonathan the son of Saul. 8 The king took the two sons of Rĭzpáh the daughter of Ā'iáh, whom she bore to Saul, Armō'ni and Mĕphĭb'ŏshĕth; and the five sons of Mērābᵒ the daughter of Saul, whom she bore to Ā'drĭ-ĕl the son of Barzĭl'-laī the Mĕhō'láthīte; 9 and he gave them into the hands of the Gĭb'ëŏnītes, and they hanged them on the mountain before the LORD, and the seven of them perished together. They were put to death in the first days of harvest, at the beginning of barley harvest.

3. *David's burial of Saul and Jonathan and the seven*

10 Then Rĭzpáh the daughter of Ā'iáh took sackcloth, and spread it for herself on the rock, from the beginning of harvest until rain fell upon them from the heavens; and she did not allow the birds of the air to come upon them by day, or the beasts of the field by night. 11 When David was told what Rĭzpáh the daughter of A'iáh, the concubine of Saul, had done, 12 David went and took the bones of Saul and the bones of his son Jonathan from the men of Jā'bĕsh-gĭl'ëăd, who had stolen them from the public square of Bĕth-shän, where the Phĭlĭs'tīneş had hanged them, on the day the Philistines killed Saul on Gĭlbō'á; 13 and he brought up from there the bones of Saul and the bones of his son Jonathan; and they gathered the bones of those who were hanged. 14And they buried the bones of Saul and his son Jonathan in the land of Benjamin in Zēlá, in the tomb of Kĭsh his father; and they did all that the king commanded. And after that God heeded supplications for the land.

B. *Victories over the Philistines*

15 The Phĭlĭs'tīneş had war again with Israel, and David went down together with his servants, and they fought against the Philistines; and David grew weary. 16And Ĭshbĭ-bē'nŏb, one of the descendants of the giants, whose spear weighed three hundred shekels of bronze, and who was girded with a new sword, thought to kill David. 17 But Ábĭsh'äī the son of Zĕru'iáh came to his aid, and attacked the Phĭlĭs'tīne and killed him. Then David's men adjured him, "You shall no more go out with us to battle, lest you quench the lamp of Israel." 18 After this there was again war with the Phĭlĭs'tīneş at Gŏb;

Cross references (right margin):
21.4 Num 35.31, 32
21.5 1 Sam 10.24,26
21.7 2 Sam 4.4; 9.10; 1 Sam 18.3; 20.8,15; 23.18
21.8 2 Sam 3.7
21.10 ver 8; Deut 21.23; 1 Sam 17.44,46
21.12 1 Sam 31.10–13
21.14 Josh 18.28; 7.26; 2 Sam 24.25
21.17 2 Sam 18.3; 6.17
21.18 1 Chr 20.4; 11.29

ⁿ Cn Compare Gk and 21.9: Heb *at Gibëah of Saul, the chosen of the LORD*
ᵒ Two Hebrew Mss Gk: Heb *Mĭchàl*

*21.19
1 Chr 20.5

21.20
1 Chr 20.6

21.21
see 1 Sam
16.9
21.22
1 Chr 20.8

then Sĭb′bĕcaī the Hū′shȧthīte slew Săph, who was one of the descendants of the giants. [19]And there was again war with the Phĭlĭs′tīneş at Gŏb; and Ĕlhā′nȧn the son of Jȧ′ȧrĕor′ĕgĭm, the Bĕth′lĕhĕmīte, slew Gŏlī′ȧth the Gĭttīte, the shaft of whose spear was like a weaver's beam. [20]And there was again war at Găth, where there was a man of great stature, who had six fingers on each hand, and six toes on each foot, twenty-four in number; and he also was descended from the giants. [21]And when he taunted Israel, Jonathan the son of Shĭm′ĕ-ī, David's brother, slew him. [22] These four were descended from the giants in Găth; and they fell by the hand of David and by the hand of his servants.

C. David's psalm of praise

22.1
Ex 15.1;
Judg 5.1;
Ps 18.2–50
22.2
Deut 32.4;
Ps 31.3;
71.3; 91.2;
144.2
22.3
Heb 2.13;
Gen 15.1;
Lk 1.69;
Ps 9.9;
14.6;
Jer 16.19
22.4
Ps 48.1
22.5
Ps 93.4;
Jon 2.3;
Ps 69.14,15
22.6
Ps 116.3
22.7
Ps 116.4;
120.1;
34.6,15

22.8
Judg 5.4;
Ps 77.18;
Job 26.11
22.9
Ps 97.3;
Heb 12.29
22.10
Ex 19.16;
1 Ki 8.12;
Ps 97.2
22.11
Ps 104.3
22.12
Ps 97.2
22.13
ver 9

22 And David spoke to the LORD the words of this song on the day when the LORD delivered him from the hand of all his enemies, and from the hand of Saul. [2] He said,
"The LORD is my rock, and my fortress, and my deliverer,
[3] my[p] God, my rock, in whom I take refuge,
    my shield and the horn of my salvation,
        my stronghold and my refuge,
            my savior; thou savest me from violence.
[4] I call upon the LORD, who is worthy to be praised,
    and I am saved from my enemies.

[5] "For the waves of death encompassed me,
    the torrents of perdition assailed me;
[6] the cords of Shēōl entangled me,
    the snares of death confronted me.

[7] "In my distress I called upon the LORD;
    to my God I called.
From his temple he heard my voice,
    and my cry came to his ears.

[8] "Then the earth reeled and rocked;
    the foundations of the heavens trembled
    and quaked, because he was angry.
[9] Smoke went up from his nostrils,
    and devouring fire from his mouth;
    glowing coals flamed forth from him.
[10] He bowed the heavens, and came down;
    thick darkness was under his feet.
[11] He rode on a cherub, and flew;
    he was seen upon the wings of the wind.
[12] He made darkness around him
    his canopy, thick clouds, a gathering of water.
[13] Out of the brightness before him

p Gk Ps 18.2: Heb lacks my

21.19 Elhanan . . . slew Goliath. The Hebrew text of this verse presents some difficulties. The parallel passage in 1 Chr 20.5 says that Elhanan slew Lahmi the brother of Goliath. In 1 Sam 17.4; 21.9 the death of Goliath himself is attributed to David, and it would appear that this tradition is to be preferred.

coals of fire flamed forth.

14 The LORD thundered from heaven,
   and the Most High uttered his voice.

15 And he sent out arrows, and scattered them;
   lightning, and routed them.

16 Then the channels of the sea were seen,
   the foundations of the world were laid bare,
   at the rebuke of the LORD,
   at the blast of the breath of his nostrils.

17 "He reached from on high, he took me,
   he drew me out of many waters.

18 He delivered me from my strong enemy,
   from those who hated me;
   for they were too mighty for me.

19 They came upon me in the day of my calamity;
   but the LORD was my stay.

20 He brought me forth into a broad place;
   he delivered me, because he delighted in me.

21 "The LORD rewarded me according to my righteousness;
   according to the cleanness of my hands he recompensed me.

22 For I have kept the ways of the LORD,
   and have not wickedly departed from my God.

23 For all his ordinances were before me,
   and from his statutes I did not turn aside.

24 I was blameless before him,
   and I kept myself from guilt.

25 Therefore the LORD has recompensed me according to my
   righteousness,
   according to my cleanness in his sight.

26 "With the loyal thou dost show thyself loyal;
   with the blameless man thou dost show thyself blameless;

27 with the pure thou dost show thyself pure,
   and with the crooked thou dost show thyself perverse.

28 Thou dost deliver a humble people,
   but thy eyes are upon the haughty to bring them down.

29 Yea, thou art my lamp, O LORD,
   and my God lightens my darkness.

30 Yea, by thee I can crush a troop,
   and by my God I can leap over a wall.

31 This God—his way is perfect;
   the promise of the LORD proves true;
   he is a shield for all those who take refuge in him.

32 "For who is God, but the LORD?
   And who is a rock, except our God?

33 This God is my strong refuge,
   and has made^r my^s way safe.

34 He made my^s feet like hinds' feet,
   and set me secure on the heights.

35 He trains my hands for war,
   so that my arms can bend a bow of bronze.

^{r} Ps 18.32: Heb *set free* ^{s} Another reading is *his*

22.14
1 Sam 2.10

22.16
Hab 3.11

22.17
Ps 144.7;
32.6

22.19
Ps 23.4

22.20
Ps 31.8;
22.8

22.21
1 Ki 8.32;
Ps 24.4
22.22
Gen 18.19;
Ps 128.1
22.23
Deut 6.6–9
22.24
Gen 7.1;
17.1;
Eph 1.4
22.25
ver 21

22.26
Mt 5.7

22.27
Lev 26.23

22.28
Ps 72.12;
Isa 2.11,12,
17
22.29
Ps 27.1

22.31
Deut 32.4;
Mt 5.48;
Ps 12.6;
ver 3

23.32
1 Sam 2.2;
ver 2
22.33
Ps 27.1;
Ps 101.2,6
22.34
Hab 3.19;
Deut 32.13
22.35
Ps 144.1

36 Thou hast given me the shield of thy salvation,
  and thy help*t* made me great.

22.37
Prov 4.12

37 Thou didst give a wide place for my steps under me,
  and my feet*u* did not slip;
38 I pursued my enemies and destroyed them,
  and did not turn back until they were consumed.

22.39
Mal 4.3

39 I consumed them; I thrust them through, so that they did not
    rise;
  they fell under my feet.

22.40
Ps 44.5

40 For thou didst gird me with strength for the battle;
  thou didst make my assailants sink under me.

22.41
Ex 23.27;
Josh 10.24

41 Thou didst make my enemies turn their backs to me,
  those who hated me, and I destroyed them.

22.42
Ps 50.22;
1 Sam 28.6

42 They looked, but there was none to save;
  they cried to the LORD, but he did not answer them.

22.43
Ps 18.42;
Isa 10.6

43 I beat them fine as the dust of the earth,
  I crushed them and stamped them down like the mire of the
    streets.

22.44
2 Sam 3.1;
Deut 28.13;
Isa 55.5

44 "Thou didst deliver me from strife with the peoples;*v*
  thou didst keep me as the head of the nations;
  people whom I had not known served me.

22.45
Ps 66.3

45 Foreigners came cringing to me;
  as soon as they heard of me, they obeyed me.

22.46
Mic 7.17

46 Foreigners lost heart,
  and came trembling*w* out of their fastnesses.

22.47
Ps 89.26

47 "The LORD lives; and blessed be my rock,
  and exalted be my God, the rock of my salvation,

22.48
Ps 94.1;
144.2

48 the God who gave me vengeance
  and brought down peoples under me,

22.49
Ps 44.5;
140.1

49 who brought me out from my enemies;
  thou didst exalt me above my adversaries,
  thou didst deliver me from men of violence.

22.50
Rom 15.9

50 "For this I will extol thee, O LORD, among the nations,
  and sing praises to thy name.

22.51
Ps 144.10;
89.20,29;
2 Sam
7.12-16

51 Great triumphs he gives*x* to his king,
  and shows steadfast love to his anointed,
  to David, and his descendants for ever."

D. David's testament

23.1
2 Sam
7.8,9;
Ps 78.70;
89.27;
1 Sam
16.12,13;
Ps 89.20

23 Now these are the last words of David:
  The oracle of David, the son of Jĕssë,
  the oracle of the man who was raised on high,
the anointed of the God of Jacob,
  the sweet psalmist of Israel:*y*

23.2
2 Pet 1.21
23.3
Deut 32.4;
2 Sam 22.2,
32;
Ex 18.21;
2 Chr 19.7,
9

2 "The Spirit of the LORD speaks by me,
  his word is upon my tongue.
3 The God of Israel has spoken,

t Or *gentleness*   *u* Heb *ankles*
v Gk: Heb *from strife with my people*   *w* Ps 18.45: Heb *girded themselves*
x Another reading is *He is a tower of salvation*   *y* Or *the favorite of the songs of Israel*

the Rock of Israel has said to me:
When one rules justly over men,
    ruling in the fear of God,
4 he dawns on them like the morning light,
    like the sun shining forth upon a cloudless morning,
    like rain^z that makes grass to sprout from the earth.
5 Yea, does not my house stand so with God?
    For he has made with me an everlasting covenant,
    ordered in all things and secure.
For will he not cause to prosper all my help and my desire?
6 But godless men^a are all like thorns that are thrown away;
    for they cannot be taken with the hand;
7 but the man who touches them
    arms himself with iron and the shaft of a spear,
    and they are utterly consumed with fire."^b

Margin references:
23.4 Judg 5.31; Ps 89.36
23.5 Ps 89.29; Isa 55.3
23.6 Mt 13.42

E. *The deeds of David's mighty men*

8 These are the names of the mighty men whom David had: Jōshĕb-bàsshĕ'bèth a Tah-chĕ'mónīte; he was chief of the three;^c he wielded his spear^d against eight hundred whom he slew at one time.

9 And next to him among the three mighty men was Ĕlëä'zàr the son of Dōdō, son of Áhō'hī. He was with David when they defied the Phḷlĭs'tĭnes who were gathered there for battle, and the men of Israel withdrew. 10 He rose and struck down the Phḷlĭs'tĭnes until his hand was weary, and his hand cleaved to the sword; and the LORD wrought a great victory that day; and the men returned after him only to strip the slain.

11 And next to him was Shămmáh, the son of Āǵeē the Hā'rárīte. The Phḷlĭs'tĭnes gathered together at Lĕhī, where there was a plot of ground full of lentils; and the men fled from the Philistines. 12 But he took his stand in the midst of the plot, and defended it, and slew the Phḷlĭs'tĭnes; and the LORD wrought a great victory.

13 And three of the thirty chief men went down, and came about harvest time to David at the cave of Ádŭl'làm, when a band of Phḷlĭs'tĭnes was encamped in the valley of Rĕph'aïm. 14 David was then in the stronghold; and the garrison of the Phḷlĭs'tĭnes was then at Bĕth'lehĕm. 15And David said longingly, "O that some one would give me water to drink from the well of Bĕth'lehĕm which is by the gate!" 16 Then the three mighty men broke through the camp of the Phḷlĭs'tĭnes, and drew water out of the well of Bĕth'lehĕm which was by the gate, and took and brought it to David. But he would not drink of it; he poured it out to the LORD, 17and said, "Far be it from me, O LORD, that I should do this. Shall I drink the blood of the men who went at the risk of their lives?" Therefore he would not drink it. These things did the three mighty men.

Margin references:
*23.8
23.9 1 Chr 27.4
23.10 1 Chr 11.12–14
23.11 1 Chr 11.27
23.13 1 Sam 22.1; 2 Sam 5.18
23.14 1 Sam 22.4, 5
23.17 Lev 17.10

^z Heb *from rain*   ^a Heb *worthlessness*
^b Heb *fire in the sitting*   ^c Or *captains*   ^d 1 Chron 11.11: Heb obscure

23.8 Compare this verse with 1 Chr 11.11 where the figure used is *three hundred*. The first letter of the Hebrew words for three and eight is the same, and in a marred original might have been read incorrectly. Since the two preceding words in the extant Hebrew text of verse 8 are unintelligible, it is possible that the obscurity in the original continued on through the number itself. Chronicles is more likely to be the correct one.

23.18
2 Sam
10,10,14;
1 Chr 11.20

23.20
2 Sam 8.18;
20,33;
Josh 15.21

23.23
2 Sam 8.18;
20.23

23.24
2 Sam 2.18
23.25
1 Chr 11.27

23.38
2 Sam 20.26
23.39
2 Sam
11.3,6

*24.1
2 Sam
20.1,2;
1 Chr 27.23,
24
24.2
2 Sam 3.10;
Judg 20.1

24.5
Deut 2.36;
Josh 13.9,
16;
Num 32.1,3

18 Now Ábǐsh'äī, the brother of Jōäb, the son of Zêru'ịäh, was chief of the thirty.*e* And he wielded his spear against three hundred men and slew them, and won a name beside the three. 19 He was the most renowned of the thirty,*f* and became their commander; but he did not attain to the three.

20 And Bĕnāi'äh the son of Jėhoi'ádá was a valiant man*g* of Käbzeēl, a doer of great deeds; he smote two ariels*h* of Mōäb. He also went down and slew a lion in a pit on a day when snow had fallen. 21And he slew an Egyptian, a handsome man. The Egyptian had a spear in his hand; but Bĕnāi'äh went down to him with a staff, and snatched the spear out of the Egyptian's hand, and slew him with his own spear. 22 These things did Bĕnāi'äh the son of Jėhoi'ádá, and won a name beside the three mighty men. 23 He was renowned among the thirty, but he did not attain to the three. And David set him over his bodyguard.

24 Ãs'áhĕl the brother of Jōäb was one of the thirty; Ĕlhā'nán the son of Dōdō of Bĕth'lĕhĕm, 25 Shămmäh of Härōd, Ĕlī'kà of Harod, 26 Hēlĕz the Pältīte, Ira the son of Ĭkkĕsh of Tĕkō'à, 27 Ãbī-ē'zĕr, of Ãn'áthōth, Mĕbûn'naī the Hū'shäthīte, 28 Zälmŏn the Ahō'hīte, Mā'háraī of Nĕtō'phäh, 29 Hēlĕb the son of Bā'ánäh of Nĕtō'phäh, Ĭttaī the son of Rĭb'äī of Gĭb'ë-äh of the Benjaminites, 30 Bĕnāi'äh of Pĭr'áthŏn, Hĭd'daī of the brooks of Gääsh, 31Ãbī-äl'bŏn the Ar'báthīte, Ãzmā'vĕth of Báhu'rĭm, 32 Ĕlī'áhbà of Shà-äl'bŏn, the sons of Jāshĕn, Jonathan, 33 Shămmäh the Hā'rárīte, Ãhī'ám the son of Shärár the Hararite, 34Ĕlĭph'-ĕlĕt the son of Ãhás'baī of Mā'ácàh, Ĕlī'ám the son of Ãhĭth'ŏphĕl of Gīlō, 35 Hĕzrō*i* of Carmĕl, Pā'áraī the Arbīte, 36 Ĭgäl the son of Nathan of Zōbäh, Bäni the Gädīte, 37 Zĕlĕk the Ăm'mŏnīte, Nā'háraī of Be-ër'ŏth, the armor-bearer of Jōäb the son of Zêru'ịäh, 38 Ira the Ĭthrīte, Gárĕb the Ithrite, 39 Ūrī'äh the Hĭttīte: thirty-seven in all.

F. David's census and punishment

1. The numbering of the people

24 Again the anger of the LORD was kindled against Israel, and he incited David against them, saying, "Go, number Israel and Judah." 2 So the king said to Jōäb and the commanders of the army,*j* who were with him, "Go through all the tribes of Israel, from Dan to Beër-shē'bà, and number the people, that I may know the number of the people." 3 But Jōäb said to the king, "May the LORD your God add to the people a hundred times as many as they are, while the eyes of my lord the king still see it; but why does my lord the king delight in this thing?" 4 But the king's word prevailed against Jōäb and the commanders of the army. So Joab and the commanders of the army went out from the presence of the king to number the people of Israel. 5 They crossed the Jor-

e Two Hebrew Mss Syr: MT *three*
f 1 Chron 11.25: Heb *Was he the most renowned of the three?*
g Another reading is *the son of Ish-hai*   *h* The meaning of the word *ariel* is unknown
i Another reading is *Hĕzraī*   *j* 1 Chron 21.2 Gk: Heb *to Joab the commander of the army*

24.1 the LORD . . . incited David. The census had fearful consequences, perhaps because it was an indication of David's trust in men rather than in God. Here the LORD is said to have incited David. In 1 Chr 21.1 Satan incited him. Both are true. God was the ultimate cause in the sense that he permitted Satan to incite David.

dan, and began from Arō'ėr,[k] and from the city that is in the
middle of the valley, toward Gắd and on to Jāzėr. 6 Then they
came to Gǐl'ĕäd, and to Kādësh in the land of the Hĭttītes;[l] and
they came to Dan, and from Dan[m] they went around to Sidón,
7 and came to the fortress of Tȳre and to all the cities of the
Hǐvītes and Cā'naánītes; and they went out to the Nĕgĕb of Judah
at Beër-shē'bá. 8 So when they had gone through all the land, they
came to Jerusalem at the end of nine months and twenty days.
9 And Jōắb gave the sum of the numbering of the people to the
king: in Israel there were eight hundred thousand valiant men
who drew the sword, and the men of Judah were five hundred
thousand.

2. David's choice of punishment

10 But David's heart smote him after he had numbered the
people. And David said to the LORD, "I have sinned greatly in
what I have done. But now, O LORD, I pray thee, take away the
iniquity of thy servant; for I have done very foolishly." 11 And
when David arose in the morning, the word of the LORD came to
the prophet Gắd, David's seer, saying, 12 "Go and say to David,
'Thus says the LORD, Three things I offer[n] you; choose one of
them, that I may do it to you.' " 13 So Gắd came to David and
told him, and said to him, "Shall three[o] years of famine come to
you in your land? Or will you flee three months before your foes
while they pursue you? Or shall there be three days' pestilence in
your land? Now consider, and decide what answer I shall return
to him who sent me." 14 Then David said to Gắd, "I am in great
distress; let us fall into the hand of the LORD, for his mercy is
great; but let me not fall into the hand of man."

3. The pestilence

15 So the LORD sent a pestilence upon Israel from the morning
until the appointed time; and there died of the people from Dan
to Beër-shē'bä seventy thousand men. 16 And when the angel
stretched forth his hand toward Jerusalem to destroy it, the LORD
repented of the evil, and said to the angel who was working destruction among the people, "It is enough; now stay your hand."
And the angel of the LORD was by the threshing floor of Arau'náh
the Jĕb'ūsīte. 17 Then David spoke to the LORD when he saw the
angel who was smiting the people, and said, "Lo, I have sinned,
and I have done wickedly; but these sheep, what have they done?
Let thy hand, I pray thee, be against me and against my father's
house."

4. The altar on the threshing floor of Araunah

18 And Gắd came that day to David, and said to him, "Go up,
rear an altar to the LORD on the threshing floor of Arau'náh the

24.6
Josh 19.28

24.7
Josh 11.3;
Gen 21.22–
33

★24.9
1 Chr 21.5

24.10
1 Sam 24,5;
2 Sam
12.13;
1 Sam 13.13
24.11
1 Sam 22.5;
9.9;
1 Chr 29.29
24.12
1 Chr 21.12

24.14
Ps 103.8,13,
14

24.15
1 Chr
21.14;
27.24
24.16
Ex 12.23;
Gen 6.6;
1 Sam 15.11

24.17
ver 10;
1 Chr 21.17

24.18
1 Chr
21.18ff

---

k Gk: Heb encamped in Aroer *l* Gk: Heb to the land of Tah'tim-hŏd'shī
m Cn Compare Gk: Heb they came to Dăn-jä'än and *n* Or hold over
o 1 Chron 21.12 Gk: Heb seven

24.9 Cf. 1 Chr 21.5. The numbers given
in the two accounts vary. There have been
three possible explanations advanced for the
discrepancy: (1) that the statements were
taken from oral tradition and not from written
records; (2) that there have been copyists'
errors in either one or both accounts; (3) that
the difference is due to the exclusion or
inclusion of the men in the standing army.
Either (2) or (3) is preferred.

Jĕb'ūsīte." 19 So David went up at Găd'ş word, as the LORD commanded. 20And when Ȧrau'năh looked down, he saw the king and his servants coming on toward him; and Araunah went forth, and did obeisance to the king with his face to the ground. 21And Ȧrau'năh said, "Why has my lord the king come to his servant?" David said, "To buy the threshing floor of you, in order to build an altar to the LORD, that the plague may be averted from the people." 22 Then Ȧrau'năh said to David, "Let my lord the king take and offer up what seems good to him; here are the oxen for the burnt offering, and the threshing sledges and the yokes of the oxen for the wood. 23All this, O king, Ȧrau'năh gives to the king." And Araunah said to the king, "The LORD your God accept you." 24 But the king said to Ȧrau'năh, "No, but I will buy it of you for a price; I will not offer burnt offerings to the LORD my God which cost me nothing." So David bought the threshing floor and the oxen for fifty shekels of silver. 25And David built there an altar to the LORD, and offered burnt offerings and peace offerings. So the LORD heeded supplications for the land, and the plague was averted from Israel.

24.21
Num 16.48,
50

24.22
1 Ki 19.21

24.23
Ezek 20.40,
41
24.24
1 Chr 21.24,
25

24.25
2 Sam
21.14;
ver 21

INTRODUCTION TO
THE FIRST BOOK OF THE
KINGS

Authorship and Background: 1 and 2 Kings, like the two books of Samuel, were originally a single book. The Septuagint translators considered these two larger books a complete history of the kingdoms of Israel and Judah, and after dividing them into four books they named them "Books of Kingdoms" instead of the Hebrew titles "Samuel" and "Kings." Jerome followed the same division in his Latin Vulgate, but he changed the title to "Books of Kings." The various English Bibles have retained the Hebrew titles while following the divisions of the Septuagint and Vulgate. In some instances the four books are subtitled "First, Second, Third, and Fourth Book of Kings," as in the Vulgate.

1 and 2 Kings cover the period from Adonijah's revolt against David to the release of Jehoiachin from prison in Babylonia about 561 B.C. Jewish tradition attributed the books to Jeremiah. While this cannot be verified, the evidence indicates that the author, whoever he was, did most of his work after Josiah's reform in 621 B.C. with subsequent events being added at various times later on. The fact that David's reign closes in 1 and 2 Kings indicates that Samuel-Kings were probably a consecutive history composed by the same individual. As in the case of Samuel, the writer of Kings used early source materials: for example, the court records of Solomon and of the various kings of Israel and Judah, as well as oral or written narratives concerning Elijah and Elisha.

Characteristics: The author of 1 and 2 Kings gives no chronological data as he covers the last days of the reign of David and the reign of Solomon. After Solomon's day, when the kingdom is divided, he presents in a chronological framework the king or kings of one kingdom and then of the other. Even though each successive king is mentioned in order, chronological problems are numerous because the two kingdoms figured their dates differently: part of a year was reckoned as a full year in some instances; sons shared the throne with their fathers in co-regencies.

The author's primary aim is not to chronicle all events of national significance of Solomon's reign and of the Divided Kingdom. He selects incidents from this era for the purpose of showing that the chosen people can endure only as bearers of God's promise and therefore in the measure that they remain faithful to the covenant and keep its commandments. He reinforces the idea that Jerusalem is the only place of worship and he does not hesitate to criticize the kings who erected other shrines or engaged in idolatrous worship. He approves every reform which tended to stamp out idolatry. His work is sweeping and panoramic for he deals with the history of the people of God generally and as a whole. Only two of the kings are given his unqualified endorsement, Hezekiah and Josiah (2 Ki 18.3; 22.2). For those who are criticized, the recurring phrase, "did what was evil in the sight of the LORD" appears.

Introduction to 1 Kings

Contents:

THE FIRST BOOK OF THE

KINGS

I. *The end of David's reign 1.1–2.46*

A. *The struggle for the succession*

1. *David's declining strength*

1 Now King David was old and advanced in years; and although they covered him with clothes, he could not get warm. 2 Therefore his servants said to him, "Let a young maiden be sought for my lord the king, and let her wait upon the king, and be his nurse; let her lie in your bosom, that my lord the king may be warm." 3 So they sought for a beautiful maiden throughout all the territory of Israel, and found Ăb'ĭshăg the Shu'nămmĭte, and brought her to the king. 4 The maiden was very beautiful; and she became the king's nurse and ministered to him; but the king knew her not.

2. *Adonijah seeks to be king*

5 Now Ădŏnī'jăh the son of Hăggĭth exalted himself, saying, "I will be king"; and he prepared for himself chariots and horsemen, and fifty men to run before him. 6 His father had never at any time displeased him by asking, "Why have you done thus and so?" He was also a very handsome man; and he was born next after Ăb'sălŏm. 7 He conferred with Jŏăb the son of Zĕru'ĭăh and with Ăbī'ăthăr the priest; and they followed Ădŏnī'jăh and helped him. 8 But Zādŏk the priest, and Bĕnāi'ăh the son of Jĕhoi'ădă, and Nathan the prophet, and Shĭm'ĕ-ī, and Rē'ī, and David's mighty men were not with Ădŏnī'jăh.

9 Ădŏnī'jăh sacrificed sheep, oxen, and fatlings by the Serpent's Stone, which is beside Ĕn-rŏ'gĕl, and he invited all his brothers, the king's sons, and all the royal officials of Judah, 10 but he did not invite Nathan the prophet or Bĕnāi'ăh or the mighty men or Solomon his brother.

3. *Nathan advises Bathsheba*

11 Then Nathan said to Băthshē'bă the mother of Solomon, "Have you not heard that Ădŏnī'jăh the son of Hăggĭth has become king and David our lord does not know it? 12 Now therefore come, let me give you counsel, that you may save your own life and the life of your son Solomon. 13 Go in at once to King David, and say to him, 'Did you not, my lord the king, swear to your maidservant, saying, "Solomon your son shall reign after me, and he shall sit upon my throne"? Why then is Ădŏnī'jăh king?' 14 Then while you are still speaking with the king, I also will come in after you and confirm your words."

1.3
Josh 19.18

*1.5
2 Sam 3.4;
15.1
1.6
2 Sam 3.3,4

1.7
1 Chr 11.6;
2 Sam
20.25;
1 Ki 2.22,28
1.8
2 Sam
20.25;
8.18; 12.1;
23.8
*1.9
2 Sam 17.17
1.10
2 Sam 12.24

1.11
2 Sam 3.4

*1.13
ver 30;
1 Chr 22.9–
13

1.5 Since the death of Absalom the right of succession, according to ancient custom, fell on Adonijah the next eldest. But David did not inform him that the custom (see 2.15) was to be ignored. Thus Adonijah was not totally at fault in seeking the throne.
1.9 Adonijah was celebrating his anticipated seizure of the throne.
1.13 Secretly David had promised Bathsheba that Solomon was to reign next.

4. *Bathsheba talks to David*

1.15
ver 1

1.17
ver 13,30

1.19
ver 9

1.21
Deut 31.16;
1 Ki 2.10

1.25
ver 9;
1 Sam 10.24

1.26
ver 8,10

1.29
2 Sam 4.9
1.30
ver 13,17

1.31
Neh 2.3;
Dan 2.4

1.33
2 Sam
20.6,7
1.34
1 Sam 10.1;
16.3,12;
2 Sam
15.10;
ver 25

15 So Băthshē′bà went to the king into his chamber (now the king was very old, and Ăb′ĭshăg the Shu′nămmīte was ministering to the king). 16 Băthshē′bà bowed and did obeisance to the king, and the king said, "What do you desire?" 17 She said to him, "My lord, you swore to your maidservant by the LORD your God, saying, 'Solomon your son shall reign after me, and he shall sit upon my throne.' 18And now, behold, Ădŏnī′jàh is king, although you, my lord the king, do not know it. 19 He has sacrificed oxen, fatlings, and sheep in abundance, and has invited all the sons of the king, Abī′àthàr the priest, and Jŏăb the commander of the army; but Solomon your servant he has not invited. 20And now, my lord the king, the eyes of all Israel are upon you, to tell them who shall sit on the throne of my lord the king after him. 21 Otherwise it will come to pass, when my lord the king sleeps with his fathers, that I and my son Solomon will be counted offenders."

5. *Nathan speaks for Solomon*

22 While she was still speaking with the king, Nathan the prophet came in. 23And they told the king, "Here is Nathan the prophet." And when he came in before the king, he bowed before the king, with his face to the ground. 24And Nathan said, "My lord the king, have you said, 'Ădŏnī′jàh shall reign after me, and he shall sit upon my throne'? 25 For he has gone down this day, and has sacrificed oxen, fatlings, and sheep in abundance, and has invited all the king's sons, Jŏăb the commander*a* of the army, and Abī′àthàr the priest; and behold, they are eating and drinking before him, and saying, 'Long live King Ădŏnī′jàh!' 26 But me, your servant, and Zădŏk the priest, and Bĕnāi′àh the son of Jĕhoi′àdà, and your servant Solomon, he has not invited. 27 Has this thing been brought about by my lord the king and you have not told your servants who should sit on the throne of my lord the king after him?"

6. *David decides for Solomon*
a. *Bathsheba informed*

28 Then King David answered, "Call Băthshē′bà to me." So she came into the king's presence, and stood before the king. 29And the king swore, saying, "As the LORD lives, who has redeemed my soul out of every adversity, 30 as I swore to you by the LORD, the God of Israel, saying, 'Solomon your son shall reign after me, and he shall sit upon my throne in my stead'; even so will I do this day." 31 Then Băthshē′bà bowed with her face to the ground, and did obeisance to the king, and said, "May my lord King David live for ever!"

b. *Zadok and Nathan instructed*

32 King David said, "Call to me Zădŏk the priest, Nathan the prophet, and Bĕnāi′àh the son of Jĕhoi′àdà." So they came before the king. 33And the king said to them, "Take with you the servants of your lord, and cause Solomon my son to ride on my own mule, and bring him down to Gīhŏn; 34 and let Zădŏk the priest and Nathan the prophet there anoint him king over Israel; then blow the trumpet, and say, 'Long live King Solomon!' 35 You

a Gk: Heb *commanders*

shall then come up after him, and he shall come and sit upon my throne; for he shall be king in my stead; and I have appointed him to be ruler over Israel and over Judah." ³⁶And Bĕnāi'ah the son of Jĕhoi'ádá answered the king, "Amen! May the LORD, the God of my lord the king, say so. ³⁷As the LORD has been with my lord the king, even so may he be with Solomon, and make his throne greater than the throne of my lord King David."

c. Solomon anointed

38 So Zādŏk the priest, Nathan the prophet, and Bĕnāi'ah the son of Jĕhoi'ádá, and the Chĕr'ĕthītes and the Pĕl'ĕthītes, went down and caused Solomon to ride on King David's mule, and brought him to Gīhŏn. ³⁹ There Zādŏk the priest took the horn of oil from the tent, and anointed Solomon. Then they blew the trumpet; and all the people said, "Long live King Solomon!" ⁴⁰And all the people went up after him, playing on pipes, and rejoicing with great joy, so that the earth was split by their noise.

7. The submission of Adonijah

41 Ădŏni'jáh and all the guests who were with him heard it as they finished feasting. And when Jŏăb heard the sound of the trumpet, he said, "What does this uproar in the city mean?" ⁴² While he was still speaking, behold, Jonathan the son of Ăbī'-áthär the priest came; and Ădŏni'jáh said, "Come in, for you are a worthy man and bring good news." ⁴³ Jonathan answered Ădŏni'jáh, "No, for our lord King David has made Solomon king; ⁴⁴ and the king has sent with him Zādŏk the priest, Nathan the prophet, and Bĕnāi'ah the son of Jĕhoi'ádá, and the Chĕr'ĕthītes and the Pĕl'ĕthītes; and they have caused him to ride on the king's mule; ⁴⁵ and Zādŏk the priest and Nathan the prophet have anointed him king at Gīhŏn; and they have gone up from there rejoicing, so that the city is in an uproar. This is the noise that you have heard. ⁴⁶ Solomon sits upon the royal throne. ⁴⁷ Moreover the king's servants came to congratulate our lord King David, saying, 'Your God make the name of Solomon more famous than yours, and make his throne greater than your throne.' And the king bowed himself upon the bed. ⁴⁸And the king also said, 'Blessed be the LORD, the God of Israel, who has granted one of my offspring^b to sit on my throne this day, my own eyes seeing it.' "

49 Then all the guests of Ădŏni'jáh trembled, and rose, and each went his own way. ⁵⁰And Ădŏni'jáh feared Solomon; and he arose, and went, and caught hold of the horns of the altar. ⁵¹And it was told Solomon, "Behold, Ădŏni'jáh fears King Solomon; for, lo, he has laid hold of the horns of the altar, saying, 'Let King Solomon swear to me first that he will not slay his servant with the sword.' " ⁵²And Solomon said, "If he prove to be a worthy man, not one of his hairs shall fall to the earth; but if wickedness is found in him, he shall die." ⁵³ So King Solomon sent, and they brought him down from the altar. And he came and did obeisance to King Solomon; and Solomon said to him, "Go to your house."

^b Gk: Heb one

Cross references (margin)

1.37 Josh 1.5,17; 1 Sam 20.13; ver 47

1.38 ver 8,33; 2 Sam 8.18

1.39 Ex 30.23–32; Ps 89.20; 1 Chr 29.22; ver 34

1.42 2 Sam 15.27,36; 18.27

1.45 ver 40

1.46 1 Chr 29.23
1.47 ver 37; Gen 47.31

1.48 1 Ki 3.6; 2 Sam 7.12

*1.50 1 Ki 2.28

1.52 1 Sam 14.45; 2 Sam 14.11

1.50 *horns of the altar*, attached to the corners of the altar. By this act Adonijah was appealing for sanctuary until his cause could be heard in court.

B. David's last words and death

1. The charge to Solomon

2.1
Gen 47.29;
Deut 31.14
2.2
Josh 23.14;
Deut 31.7,
23;
Josh 1.6,7
2.3
Josh 1.7;
1 Chr 22.12,
13
2.4
2 Sam 7.25;
Ps 132.12;
2 Ki 20.3;
2 Sam 7.12,
13

2 When David's time to die drew near, he charged Solomon his son, saying, 2 "I am about to go the way of all the earth. Be strong, and show yourself a man, 3 and keep the charge of the LORD your God, walking in his ways and keeping his statutes, his commandments, his ordinances, and his testimonies, as it is written in the law of Moses, that you may prosper in all that you do and wherever you turn; 4 that the LORD may establish his word which he spoke concerning me, saying, 'If your sons take heed to their way, to walk before me in faithfulness with all their heart and with all their soul, there shall not fail you a man on the throne of Israel.'

2. David's last orders

2.5
2 Sam 18.5,
12,14;
3.27; 20.10
2.6
ver 6
2.7
2 Sam
19.31,
38; 9.7,10;
17.27
2.8
2 Sam 16.5–
8; 19.18–23
2.9
ver 6

5 "Moreover you know also what Jŏăb the son of Zĕruʹiăh did to me, how he dealt with the two commanders of the armies of Israel, Abner the son of Nĕr, and Ămăʹsă the son of Jĕthĕr, whom he murdered, avenging^c in time of peace blood which had been shed in war, and putting innocent blood^d upon the girdle about my^e loins, and upon the sandals on my^e feet. 6 Act therefore according to your wisdom, but do not let his gray head go down to Shĕōl in peace. 7 But deal loyally with the sons of Barzĭlʹlaī the Gĭlʹëădīte, and let them be among those who eat at your table; for with such loyalty they met me when I fled from Ăbʹsălŏm your brother. 8 And there is also with you Shĭmʹëʹī the son of Gĕră, the Benjaminite from Băhuʹrĭm, who cursed me with a grievous curse on the day when I went to Māhănāʹĭm; but when he came down to meet me at the Jordan, I swore to him by the LORD, saying, 'I will not put you to death with the sword.' 9 Now therefore hold him not guiltless, for you are a wise man; you will know what you ought to do to him, and you shall bring his gray head down with blood to Shĕōl."

3. David's death

2.10
Acts 2.29;
2 Sam 5.7
2.11
2 Sam 5.4;
1 Chr
29.26,27
2.12
1 Chr
29.23;
2 Chr 1.1

10 Then David slept with his fathers, and was buried in the city of David. 11 And the time that David reigned over Israel was forty years; he reigned seven years in Hĕbrŏn, and thirty-three years in Jerusalem. 12 So Solomon sat upon the throne of David his father; and his kingdom was firmly established.

C. Solomon executes David's orders

1. Adonijah put to death

2.13
1 Sam 16.4
2.15
1 Ki 1.5;
1 Chr 22.9,
10; 28.5–7
2.17
1 Ki 1.3,4

13 Then Ădŏnĭʹjăh the son of Hăggĭth came to Băthshĕʹbă the mother of Solomon. And she said, "Do you come peaceably?" He said, "Peaceably." 14 Then he said, "I have something to say to you." She said, "Say on." 15 He said, "You know that the kingdom was mine, and that all Israel fully expected me to reign; however the kingdom has turned about and become my brother's, for it was his from the LORD. 16 And now I have one request to make of you; do not refuse me." She said to him, "Say on." 17 And he said,

c Gk: Heb placing   d Gk: Heb blood of war   e Gk: Heb his

"Pray ask King Solomon—he will not refuse you—to give me Ăb'ĭshăg the Shu'nămmĭte as my wife." 18 Băthshē'bă said, "Very well; I will speak for you to the king."

19 So Băthshē'bă went to King Solomon, to speak to him on behalf of Ădŏnī'jăh. And the king rose to meet her, and bowed down to her; then he sat on his throne, and had a seat brought for the king's mother; and she sat on his right. 20 Then she said, "I have one small request to make of you; do not refuse me." And the king said to her, "Make your request, my mother; for I will not refuse you." 21 She said, "Let Ăb'ĭshăg the Shu'nămmĭte be given to Ădŏnī'jăh your brother as his wife." 22 King Solomon answered his mother, "And why do you ask Ăb'ĭshăg the Shu'nămmĭte for Ădŏnī'jăh? Ask for him the kingdom also; for he is my elder brother, and on his side are Ăbī'ăthăr f the priest and Jōăb the son of Zĕru'jăh." 23 Then King Solomon swore by the LORD, saying, "God do so to me and more also if this word does not cost Ădŏnī'jăh his life! 24 Now therefore as the LORD lives, who has established me, and placed me on the throne of David my father, and who has made me a house, as he promised, Ădŏnī'jăh shall be put to death this day." 25 So King Solomon sent Bĕnāi'ăh the son of Jĕhoi'ădă; and he struck him down, and he died.

2. *Abiathar banished*

26 And to Ăbī'ăthăr the priest the king said, "Go to Ăn'ăthŏth, to your estate; for you deserve death. But I will not at this time put you to death, because you bore the ark of the Lord GOD before David my father, and because you shared in all the affliction of my father." 27 So Solomon expelled Ăbī'ăthăr from being priest to the LORD, thus fulfilling the word of the LORD which he had spoken concerning the house of Ēlī in Shīlōh.

3. *Joab slain*

28 When the news came to Jōăb—for Joab had supported Ădŏnī'jăh although he had not supported Ăb'sălŏm—Joab fled to the tent of the LORD and caught hold of the horns of the altar. 29 And when it was told King Solomon, "Jōăb has fled to the tent of the LORD, and behold, he is beside the altar," Solomon sent Bĕnāi'ăh the son of Jĕhoi'ădă, saying, "Go, strike him down." 30 So Bĕnāi'ăh came to the tent of the LORD, and said to him, "The king commands, 'Come forth.'" But he said, "No, I will die here." Then Benaiah brought the king word again, saying, "Thus said Jōăb, and thus he answered me." 31 The king replied to him, "Do as he has said, strike him down and bury him; and thus take away from me and from my father's house the guilt for the blood

2.19 Ps 45.9
2.20 ver 16
*2.21 1 Ki 1.3,4
2.22 2 Sam 12.8; 1 Ki 1.6,7
2.23 Ruth 1.17
2.24 2 Sam 7.11, 13; 1 Chr 22.10
2.26 Josh 21.18; 1 Sam 23.6; 2 Sam 15.24–29; 1 Sam 22.20–23
*2.27 1 Sam 2.31-35
*2.28 1 Ki 1.7,50
2.29 ver 25
2.31 Ex 21.14; Num 35.33; Deut 19.13

f Gk Syr Vg: Heb *and for him and for Abiathar*

2.21 The request that Abishag the Shunammite be given to Adonijah, the older brother of Solomon, to be his wife had sinister implications. Adonijah might later renew his claim for the throne of David (in preference to Solomon) on the ground that he had married David's last wife. Solomon sensed these dangerous potentialities, saying ironically to Bathsheba, "...*Ask for him the kingdom also* ..." (ver 22). Naturally he refused the request and took energetic measures against his treasonous brother.

2.27 Because Abiathar, the great-grandson of Eli, had defended the right of Adonijah to the throne, Solomon expelled him to Anathoth. This was interpreted as the fulfilment of 1 Sam 2.31–36. The prophet Jeremiah was a descendant of the priests at Anathoth (Jer 1.1).

2.28 Joab's appeal for sanctuary was rejected by Solomon because he was a murderer.

2.32
Judg 9.24,
57;
Ps 7.16;
2 Chr
21.13;
2 Sam 3.27;
20.10
2.33
2 Sam
3.29;
Prov 25.5

*2.35
1 Ki 4.4;
1 Chr
29.22;
ver 27

2.36
ver 8
2.37
2 Sam
15.23;
Lev 20.9;
2 Sam 1.16

2.39
1 Sam 27.2

2.40
2 Sam
19.16–23

2.44
2 Sam
16.5–13;
1 Sam
25.39;
Ezek 17.19
2.45
2 Sam 7.13
2.46
ver 12,25,
34;
2 Chr 1.1

*3.1
1 Ki 7.8;
9.24;
2 Sam 5.7;
1 Ki 7.1;
ch 6;
9.15,19

which Jōǎb shed without cause. 32 The LORD will bring back his bloody deeds upon his own head, because, without the knowledge of my father David, he attacked and slew with the sword two men more righteous and better than himself, Abner the son of Nĕr, commander of the army of Israel, and Ama'sà the son of Jĕthĕr, commander of the army of Judah. 33 So shall their blood come back upon the head of Jōǎb and upon the head of his descendants for ever; but to David, and to his descendants, and to his house, and to his throne, there shall be peace from the LORD for evermore." 34 Then Bĕnāi'ah the son of Jĕhoi'ǎdà went up, and struck him down and killed him; and he was buried in his own house in the wilderness. 35 The king put Bĕnāi'ah the son of Jĕhoi'ǎdà over the army in place of Jōǎb, and the king put Zādŏk the priest in the place of Àbi'áthár.

4. Shimei's broken oath and death

36 Then the king sent and summoned Shĭm'ĕ-ī, and said to him, "Build yourself a house in Jerusalem, and dwell there, and do not go forth from there to any place whatever. 37 For on the day you go forth, and cross the brook Kĭdrón, know for certain that you shall die; your blood shall be upon your own head." 38And Shĭm'ĕ-ī said to the king, "What you say is good; as my lord the king has said, so will your servant do." So Shime-i dwelt in Jerusalem many days.

39 But it happened at the end of three years that two of Shĭm'-ĕ-ī's slaves ran away to Āchĭsh, son of Mā'ǎcàh, king of Găth. And when it was told Shĭm'ĕ-ī, "Behold, your slaves are in Gath," 40 Shĭm'ĕ-ī arose and saddled an ass, and went to Găth to Āchĭsh, to seek his slaves; Shime-i went and brought his slaves from Gath. 41And when Solomon was told that Shĭm'ĕ-ī had gone from Jerusalem to Găth and returned, 42 the king sent and summoned Shĭm'ĕ-ī, and said to him, "Did I not make you swear by the LORD, and solemnly admonish you, saying, 'Know for certain that on the day you go forth and go to any place whatever, you shall die'? And you said to me, 'What you say is good; I obey.' 43 Why then have you not kept your oath to the LORD and the commandment with which I charged you?" 44 The king also said to Shĭm'-ĕ-ī, "You know in your own heart all the evil that you did to David my father; so the LORD will bring back your evil upon your own head. 45 But King Solomon shall be blessed, and the throne of David shall be established before the LORD for ever." 46 Then the king commanded Bĕnāi'ah the son of Jĕhoi'ǎdà; and he went out and struck him down, and he died.

So the kingdom was established in the hand of Solomon.

II. The Solomonic reign 3.1–11.43

A. Solomon's early years: marriage to Pharaoh's daughter

3 Solomon made a marriage alliance with Phạraōh king of Egypt; he took Phạraōh's daughter, and brought her into the

---

2.35 Zadok ... in the place of Abiathar. From this point on, Zadok and his descendants constitute the legitimate priestly line.
3.1 marriage alliance with Pharaoh. This

political marriage secured peace with Egypt. It was the first of many such marriages whereby Solomon attempted to ensure a peaceful reign.

city of David, until he had finished building his own house and
the house of the LORD and the wall around Jerusalem. ² The
people were sacrificing at the high places, however, because no
house had yet been built for the name of the LORD.

3.2
Lev 17.3–5;
Deut 12.2,
4,5

B. Prayer for wisdom granted

3 Solomon loved the LORD, walking in the statutes of David his
father; only, he sacrificed and burnt incense at the high places.
⁴And the king went to Gĭb'ë̈on to sacrifice there, for that was the
great high place; Solomon used to offer a thousand burnt offerings
upon that altar. ⁵At Gĭb'ë̈on the LORD appeared to Solomon in a
dream by night; and God said, "Ask what I shall give you." ⁶And
Solomon said, "Thou hast shown great and steadfast love to thy
servant David my father, because he walked before thee in faithfulness, in righteousness, and in uprightness of heart toward thee; and
thou hast kept for him this great and steadfast love, and hast given
him a son to sit on his throne this day. ⁷And now, O LORD my
God, thou hast made thy servant king in place of David my father,
although I am but a little child; I do not know how to go out or
come in. ⁸And thy servant is in the midst of thy people whom thou
hast chosen, a great people, that cannot be numbered or counted
for multitude. ⁹ Give thy servant therefore an understanding mind
to govern thy people, that I may discern between good and evil;
for who is able to govern this thy great people?"

*3.3f
Deut 6.5;
Ps 31.23;
1 Ki 2.3;
9.4; 11.4,6,
38

3.4
2 Chr 1.3;
1 Chr 16.39

3.5
1 Ki 9.2;
2 Chr 1.7;
Num 12.6;
Mt 1.20

3.6
2 Chr 1.8ff;
1 Ki 2.4;
9.4; 1.48

3.7
1 Chr 22.9–
13; 29.1;
Num 27.17

3.8
Deut 7.6;
Gen 13.16;
15.5

10 It pleased the Lord that Solomon had asked this. ¹¹And
God said to him, "Because you have asked this, and have not
asked for yourself long life or riches or the life of your enemies,
but have asked for yourself understanding to discern what is
right, ¹² behold, I now do according to your word. Behold, I give
you a wise and discerning mind, so that none like you has been
before you and none like you shall arise after you. ¹³ I give you
also what you have not asked, both riches and honor, so that no
other king shall compare with you, all your days. ¹⁴And if you
will walk in my ways, keeping my statutes and my commandments, as your father David walked, then I will lengthen your
days."

3.9
2 Chr 1.10;
Prov 2.3–9;
Jas 1.5;
Ps 72.1,2

3.11
Jas 4.3

3.12
1 Jn 5.14,
15;
1 Ki 4.29–
31

3.13
Mt 6.33;
1 Ki 4.21–
24

3.14
ver 6

15 And Solomon awoke, and behold, it was a dream. Then he
came to Jerusalem, and stood before the ark of the covenant of the
LORD, and offered up burnt offerings and peace offerings, and
made a feast for all his servants.

3.15
Gen 41.7;
1 Ki 8.65;
Est 1.3;
Dan 5.1;
Mk 6.21

C. Solomon's wise decision

16 Then two harlots came to the king, and stood before him.
¹⁷ The one woman said, "Oh, my lord, this woman and I dwell
in the same house; and I gave birth to a child while she was in the
house. ¹⁸ Then on the third day after I was delivered, this woman
also gave birth; and we were alone; there was no one else with us in
the house, only we two were in the house. ¹⁹And this woman's son
died in the night, because she lay on it. ²⁰And she arose at midnight, and took my son from beside me, while your maidservant

3.17
Num 27.2

3.20
Ruth 4.16

3.3,4 *high places . . . great high place.*
Clearly, Solomon did not recognize Jerusalem
as the central shrine even though David

brought the ark there. He preferred to sacrifice at various of the shrines around Jerusalem, directly in violation of Deut 12.13, 14.

slept, and laid it in her bosom, and laid her dead son in my bosom.
21 When I rose in the morning to nurse my child, behold, it was
dead; but when I looked at it closely in the morning, behold, it
was not the child that I had borne." 22 But the other woman said,
"No, the living child is mine, and the dead child is yours." The
first said, "No, the dead child is yours, and the living child is
mine." Thus they spoke before the king.

23 Then the king said, "The one says, 'This is my son that is
alive, and your son is dead'; and the other says, 'No; but your son
is dead, and my son is the living one.'" 24And the king said,
"Bring me a sword." So a sword was brought before the king.
25And the king said, "Divide the living child in two, and give half
to the one, and half to the other." 26 Then the woman whose
son was alive said to the king, because her heart yearned for her
son, "Oh, my lord, give her the living child, and by no means
slay it." But the other said, "It shall be neither mine nor yours;
divide it." 27 Then the king answered and said, "Give the living
child to the first woman, and by no means slay it; she is its
mother." 28And all Israel heard of the judgment which the king
had rendered; and they stood in awe of the king, because they perceived that the wisdom of God was in him, to render justice.

D. The appointment of court officials

4 King Solomon was king over all Israel, 2 and these were his
high officials: Ăzări′ăh the son of Zādŏk was the priest; 3 Ĕlĭ-
hor′ĕph and Ăhī′jăh the sons of Shīshȧ were secretaries; Jĕhŏsh′-
ȧphăt the son of Ăhī′lŭd was recorder; 4Bĕnāi′ȧh the son of Jĕhoi′-
ȧdȧ was in command of the army; Zādŏk and Ăbī′ȧthȧr were
priests; 5Ăzări′ȧh the son of Nathan was over the officers; Zābŭd
the son of Nathan was priest and king's friend; 6Ăhī′shar was in
charge of the palace; and Ădŏnī′răm the son of Ăbdȧ was in charge
of the forced labor.

7 Solomon had twelve officers over all Israel, who provided
food for the king and his household; each man had to make provision for one month in the year. 8 These were their names: Ben-
hur, in the hill country of Ē′phrȧim; 9 Bĕn-dĕk′ĕr, in Mākȧz,
Shȧ-ăl′bĭm, Bĕth-she′mĕsh, and Ē′lŏnbĕth-hā′nȧn; 10 Bĕn-hĕs′ĕd,
in Ărŭb′bŏth (to him belonged Sōcōh and all the land of Hĕpher);
11 Bĕn-ȧbĭn′ȧdȧb, in all Nā′phăth-dor′ (he had Tāphăth the
daughter of Solomon as his wife); 12 Bā′ȧnȧ the son of Ăhī′lŭd, in
Tā′ȧnȧch, Mĕgĭd′dō, and all Bĕth-shē′ȧn which is beside Zȧr′-
ĕthȧn below Jĕzreĕl′, and from Beth-shean to Ā′bĕl-mĕhō′lȧh, as
far as the other side of Jŏk′mĕȧm; 13 Bĕn-gĕ′bĕr, in Rā′mŏth-
gĭl′ĕȧd (he had the villages of Jāir the son of Mȧnȧs′sĕh, which are
in Gĭl′ĕȧd, and he had the region of Argŏb, which is in Bāshȧn,
sixty great cities with walls and bronze bars); 14Ăhĭn′ȧdȧb the son
of Ĭddō, in Māhȧnā′ĭm; 15Ăhĭm′ȧ-ăz, in Năph′tȧlī (he had taken
Bȧs′emȧth the daughter of Solomon as his wife); 16 Bā′ȧnȧ the son
of Hūshaī, in Ăshĕr and Bĕ′ȧlŏth; 17 Jĕhŏsh′ȧphăt the son of
Pȧru′ȧh, in Ĭs′sȧchar; 18 Shĭm′ĕ-ī the son of Ēlȧ, in Benjamin;

3.26
Gen 43.30;
Isa 49.15;
Jer 31.20

*3.28
ver 9,11,12

4.5
ver 7
*4.7
4.8
Josh 24.33
4.9
Josh 1.35;
21.16
4.10
Josh 15.35;
12.17
4.11
Josh 11.1,2
4.12
Josh 5.19;
17.11;
3.16;
1 Ki 19.16;
1 Chr 6.68
4.13
Num 32.41;
Deut 3.4
4.14
Josh 13.26
4.15
2 Sam 15.27
4.16
2 Sam 15.32
4.18
1 Ki 1.8

3.28 Fulfilment of verses 9, 11, and 12.
4.7 *twelve officers*. It has been inferred that
Solomon divided Israel into twelve adminis-
trative districts, varying somewhat from the
old tribal boundaries, in order to support his
elaborate building and military programs.

19 Gēbēr the son of Ūrī, in the land of Gil'ëàd, the country of
Sihón king of the Ăm'ŏr'ītes and of Ŏg king of Bāshàn. And there
was one officer in the land of Judah.

E. The household provisions

20 Judah and Israel were as many as the sand by the sea; they
ate and drank and were happy. 21g Solomon ruled over all the
kingdoms from the Eūphrā'tēs to the land of the Phĭlĭs'tĭnes and
to the border of Egypt; they brought tribute and served Solomon
all the days of his life.

22 Solomon's provision for one day was thirty cors of fine flour,
and sixty cors of meal, 23 ten fat oxen, and twenty pasture-fed
cattle, a hundred sheep, besides harts, gazelles, roebucks, and
fatted fowl. 24 For he had dominion over all the region west of the
Eūphrā'tēs from Tiphsàh to Gazà, over all the kings west of the
Euphrates; and he had peace on all sides round about him. 25And
Judah and Israel dwelt in safety, from Dan even to Beër-shē'bà,
every man under his vine and under his fig tree, all the days of
Solomon. 26 Solomon also had forty thousand stalls of horses for
his chariots, and twelve thousand horsemen. 27And those officers
supplied provisions for King Solomon, and for all who came to
King Solomon's table, each one in his month; they let nothing be
lacking. 28 Barley also and straw for the horses and swift steeds
they brought to the place where it was required, each according
to his charge.

F. Solomon's great wisdom

29 And God gave Solomon wisdom and understanding beyond
measure, and largeness of mind like the sand on the seashore, 30 so
that Solomon's wisdom surpassed the wisdom of all the people
of the east, and all the wisdom of Egypt. 31 For he was wiser than
all other men, wiser than Ēthàn the Ĕz'ràhīte, and Hēmàn, Călcŏl,
and Dardà, the sons of Māhŏl; and his fame was in all the nations
round about. 32 He also uttered three thousand proverbs; and his
songs were a thousand and five. 33 He spoke of trees, from the
cedar that is in Lebanon to the hyssop that grows out of the wall;
he spoke also of beasts, and of birds, and of reptiles, and of fish.
34And men came from all peoples to hear the wisdom of Solomon,
and from all the kings of the earth, who had heard of his wisdom.

G. The building of the Temple

1. Preparations for building

5h Now Hiram king of Tyre sent his servants to Solomon, when
  he heard that they had anointed him king in place of his
father; for Hiram always loved David. 2And Solomon sent word

g Ch 5.1 in Heb   h Ch 5.15 in Heb

4.19
Deut 3.8–10

*4.20
Gen 32.12;
1 Ki 3.8
4.21
2 Chr 9.26;
Gen 15.18;
Ps 68.29;
72.10,11

4.24
Ps 72.11;
1 Chr 22.9
4.25
Jer 23.6;
Mic 4.4;
Zech 3.10;
Judg 20.1
*4.26
1 Ki 10.26;
2 Chr 1.14
4.27
ver 7

4.29
1 Ki 3.12
4.30
Gen 25.6;
Acts 7.22
4.31
1 Ki 3.12;
1 Chr
15.19;2.6;
6.33
4.32
Prov 1.1;
Ecc 12.9;
Sol 1.1
4.34
1 Ki 10.1;
2 Chr 9.23

5.1
ver 10,18;
2 Chr 2.3;
2 Sam 5.11;
1 Chr 14.1

4.20 *were happy.* This happiness was short-
lived because, as 12.10 indicates, Solomon
put a heavy yoke on the people.
4.26 Compare this figure with the parallel
account in 2 Chr 9.25 where it is given as
four thousand rather than *forty thousand*.

The copyist misread the Hebrew cipher for
four as the Hebrew cipher for *forty*. The
lower number was probably the right one,
especially in view of the modest total of 1400
chariots mentioned in 10.26. Some of these
stalls have been found at Megiddo.

*5.3
1 Chr 22.8;
28.3

5.4
1 Ki 4.24;
1 Chr 22.9

5.5
2 Sam 7.12,
13;
1 Chr
17.12;
22.10

5.9
2 Chr 2.16;
Ezra 3.7;
Ezek 27.17;
Acts 12.20

5.11
cf 2 Chr
2.10

5.12
1 Ki 3.12

5.14
1 Ki 4.6

5.15
1 Ki 9.20–
22;
2 Chr 2.17,
18

5.17
1 Chr 22.2

*6.1
2 Chr 3.1,2;
Acts 7.47

6.2
cf Ezek
41.1ff

to Hiram, 3 "You know that David my father could not build a house for the name of the LORD his God because of the warfare with which his enemies surrounded him, until the LORD put them under the soles of his feet. 4 But now the LORD my God has given me rest on every side; there is neither adversary nor misfortune. 5And so I purpose to build a house for the name of the LORD my God, as the LORD said to David my father, 'Your son, whom I will set upon your throne in your place, shall build the house for my name.' 6 Now therefore command that cedars of Lebanon be cut for me; and my servants will join your servants, and I will pay you for your servants such wages as you set; for you know that there is no one among us who knows how to cut timber like the Sīdō'nĭăns.''

7 When Hiram heard the words of Solomon, he rejoiced greatly, and said, "Blessed be the LORD this day, who has given to David a wise son to be over this great people." 8And Hiram sent to Solomon, saying, "I have heard the message which you have sent to me; I am ready to do all you desire in the matter of cedar and cypress timber. 9 My servants shall bring it down to the sea from Lebanon; and I will make it into rafts to go by sea to the place you direct, and I will have them broken up there, and you shall receive it; and you shall meet my wishes by providing food for my household." 10 So Hiram supplied Solomon with all the timber of cedar and cypress that he desired, 11 while Solomon gave Hiram twenty thousand cors of wheat as food for his household, and twenty thousand^i cors of beaten oil. Solomon gave this to Hiram year by year. 12And the LORD gave Solomon wisdom, as he promised him; and there was peace between Hiram and Solomon; and the two of them made a treaty.

13 King Solomon raised a levy of forced labor out of all Israel; and the levy numbered thirty thousand men. 14And he sent them to Lebanon, ten thousand a month in relays; they would be a month in Lebanon and two months at home; Ădŏnĭ'răm was in charge of the levy. 15 Solomon also had seventy thousand burden-bearers and eighty thousand hewers of stone in the hill country, 16 besides Solomon's three thousand three hundred chief officers who were over the work, who had charge of the people who carried on the work. 17At the king's command, they quarried out great, costly stones in order to lay the foundation of the house with dressed stones. 18 So Solomon's builders and Hiram's builders and the men of Gē'băl did the hewing and prepared the timber and the stone to build the house.

2. The description of the Temple

6 In the four hundred and eightieth year after the people of Israel came out of the land of Egypt, in the fourth year of Solomon's reign over Israel, in the month of Zĭv, which is the second month, he began to build the house of the LORD. 2 The

^{i} Gk: Heb twenty

5.3 under the soles of his feet, a reference to the symbolic act of putting a foot on the neck of the defeated king. See note to Josh 10.24.
6.1 four hundred and eightieth year. If literally true, then Exodus occurred about 1440 B.C. But other evidence (see note to Ex

1.11, for example) points to a later date. The figure 480 may represent the 12 generations between Exodus and Solomon, figured at the round number of 40 years a generation, or it may have derived from adding the reigns of the judges plus the other periods involved.

house which King Solomon built for the LORD was sixty cubits long, twenty cubits wide, and thirty cubits high. 3 The vestibule in front of the nave of the house was twenty cubits long, equal to the width of the house, and ten cubits deep in front of the house. 4And he made for the house windows with recessed frames. 5 He also built a structure against the wall of the house, running round the walls of the house, both the nave and the inner sanctuary; and he made side chambers all around. 6 The lowest story^j was five cubits broad, the middle one was six cubits broad, and the third was seven cubits broad; for around the outside of the house he made offsets on the wall in order that the supporting beams should not be inserted into the walls of the house.

7 When the house was built, it was with stone prepared at the quarry; so that neither hammer nor axe nor any tool of iron was heard in the temple, while it was being built.

8 The entrance for the lowest^k story was on the south side of the house; and one went up by stairs to the middle story, and from the middle story to the third. 9 So he built the house, and finished it; and he made the ceiling of the house of beams and planks of cedar. 10 He built the structure against the whole house, each story^l five cubits high, and it was joined to the house with timbers of cedar.

11 Now the word of the LORD came to Solomon, 12 "Concerning this house which you are building, if you will walk in my statutes and obey my ordinances and keep all my commandments and walk in them, then I will establish my word with you, which I spoke to David your father. 13And I will dwell among the children of Israel, and will not forsake my people Israel."

14 So Solomon built the house, and finished it. 15 He lined the walls of the house on the inside with boards of cedar; from the floor of the house to the rafters^m of the ceiling, he covered them on the inside with wood; and he covered the floor of the house with boards of cypress. 16 He built twenty cubits of the rear of the house with boards of cedar from the floor to the rafters,^{m} and he built this within as an inner sanctuary, as the most holy place. 17 The house, that is, the nave in front of the inner sanctuary, was forty cubits long. 18 The cedar within the house was carved in the form of gourds and open flowers; all was cedar, no stone was seen. 19 The inner sanctuary he prepared in the innermost part of the house, to set there the ark of the covenant of the LORD. 20 The inner sanctuary^n was twenty cubits long, twenty cubits wide, and twenty cubits high; and he overlaid it with pure gold. He also made^o an altar of cedar. 21And Solomon overlaid the inside of the house with pure gold, and he drew chains of gold across, in front of the inner sanctuary, and overlaid it with gold. 22And he overlaid the whole house with gold, until all the house was finished. Also the whole altar that belonged to the inner sanctuary he overlaid with gold.

*6.3

6.4
Ezek 40.16;
41.16
6.5
Ezek 41.6;
ver 16,19–
21,31

6.7
Deut 27.5,6

6.9
ver 14.38

6.12
1 Ki 2.4;
9.4

6.13
Ex 25.8;
Deut 31.6
6.14
ver 9,38

6.16
Ex 26.33;
Lev 16.2;
1 Ki 8.6;
2 Chr 3.8

6.18
1 Ki 7.24

6.22
Ex 30.1,3,6

^{j} Gk: Heb structure ^{k} Gk Tg: Heb middle ^{l} Heb lacks each story
^{m} Gk: Heb walls ^{n} Vg: Heb and before the inner sanctuary ^{o} Gk: Heb covered

6.3 The Solomonic Temple was built about four hundred years after the "tent" or "tabernacle," and was to stand about four hundred years. It took 30,000 Israelites and 150,000 Canaanites seven years at forced labor to complete the Temple. Materials were prepared at a distance and quietly assembled. It was destroyed by the Babylonians in 586 B.C.

*6.23
2 Chr 3.10–
12

23 In the inner sanctuary he made two cherubim of olivewood, each ten cubits high. 24 Five cubits was the length of one wing of the cherub, and five cubits the length of the other wing of the cherub; it was ten cubits from the tip of one wing to the tip of the other. 25 The other cherub also measured ten cubits; both cherubim had the same measure and the same form. 26 The height of one cherub was ten cubits, and so was that of the other cherub.

6.27
Ex 25.20;
37.9;
1 Ki 8.7;
2 Chr 5.8

27 He put the cherubim in the innermost part of the house; and the wings of the cherubim were spread out so that a wing of one touched the one wall, and a wing of the other cherub touched the other wall; their other wings touched each other in the middle of the house. 28 And he overlaid the cherubim with gold.

29 He carved all the walls of the house round about with carved figures of cherubim and palm trees and open flowers, in the inner and outer rooms. 30 The floor of the house he overlaid with gold in the inner and outer rooms.

31 For the entrance to the inner sanctuary he made doors of olivewood; the lintel and the doorposts formed a pentagon.ᵖ 32 He covered the two doors of olivewood with carvings of cherubim, palm trees, and open flowers; he overlaid them with gold, and spread gold upon the cherubim and upon the palm trees.

6.34
Ezek 41.23–
25

33 So also he made for the entrance to the nave doorposts of olivewood, in the form of a square, 34 and two doors of cypress wood; the two leaves of the one door were folding, and the two leaves of the other door were folding. 35 On them he carved cherubim and palm trees and open flowers; and he overlaid them with gold evenly applied upon the carved work. 36 He built the inner

6.36
1 Ki 7.12

court with three courses of hewn stone and one course of cedar beams.

6.37
ver 1

37 In the fourth year the foundation of the house of the LORD was laid, in the month of Ziv. 38 And in the eleventh year, in the month of Bul, which is the eighth month, the house was finished in all its parts, and according to all its specifications. He was seven years in building it.

3. The description of the palace buildings

7.1
1 Ki 9.10;
2 Chr 8.1

7 Solomon was building his own house thirteen years, and he finished his entire house.

7.2
1 Ki 10.17,
21

2 He built the House of the Forest of Lebanon; its length was a hundred cubits, and its breadth fifty cubits, and its height thirty cubits, and it was built upon threeᵍ rows of cedar pillars, with cedar beams upon the pillars. 3 And it was covered with cedar above the chambers that were upon the forty-five pillars, fifteen in each row. 4 There were window frames in three rows, and window opposite window in three tiers. 5 All the doorways and windowsʳ had square frames, and window was opposite window in three tiers.

6 And he made the Hall of Pillars; its length was fifty cubits, and

ᵖ Heb obscure   ᵍ Gk: Heb four   ʳ Gk: Heb posts

6.23 two cherubim. These composite representations, winged lions with human heads, had a wingspread of 15 feet. God was considered as invisibly enthroned on the cherubim (see note to Ex 25.22). This concept led the people in Jeremiah's time to trust in the deceptive words, This is the temple of the LORD (Jer 7.4), that is, God resides there and he will never permit the Temple to be destroyed.

its breadth thirty cubits; there was a porch in front with pillars, and a canopy before them.

7 And he made the Hall of the Throne where he was to pronounce judgment, even the Hall of Judgment; it was finished with cedar from floor to rafters.^{s}

8 His own house where he was to dwell, in the other court back of the hall, was of like workmanship. Solomon also made a house like this hall for Pharaōh's daughter whom he had taken in marriage.

9 All these were made of costly stones, hewn according to measure, sawed with saws, back and front, even from the foundation to the coping, and from the court of the house of the LORD^t to the great court. 10 The foundation was of costly stones, huge stones, stones of eight and ten cubits. 11And above were costly stones, hewn according to measurement, and cedar. 12 The great court had three courses of hewn stone round about, and a course of cedar beams; so had the inner court of the house of the LORD, and the vestibule of the house.

4. The employment of Hiram

13 And King Solomon sent and brought Hiram from Tȳre. 14 He was the son of a widow of the tribe of Năph'tálī, and his father was a man of Tȳre, a worker in bronze; and he was full of wisdom, understanding, and skill, for making any work in bronze. He came to King Solomon, and did all his work.

5. The casting of the bronze pillars

15 He cast two pillars of bronze. Eighteen cubits was the height of one pillar, and a line of twelve cubits measured its circumference; it was hollow, and its thickness was four fingers; the second pillar was the same.^{u} 16 He also made two capitals of molten bronze, to set upon the tops of the pillars; the height of the one capital was five cubits, and the height of the other capital was five cubits. 17 Then he made two^v nets of checker work with wreaths of chain work for the capitals upon the tops of the pillars; a net^w for the one capital, and a net^w for the other capital. 18 Likewise he made pomegranates;^{x} in two rows round about upon the one network, to cover the capital that was upon the top of the pillar; and he did the same with the other capital. 19 Now the capitals that were upon the tops of the pillars in the vestibule were of lily-work, four cubits. 20 The capitals were upon the two pillars and also above the rounded projection which was beside the network; there were two hundred pomegranates, in two rows round about; and so with the other capital. 21 He set up the pillars at the vestibule of the temple; he set up the pillar on the south and called its name Jāchĭn; and he set up the pillar on the north and called its

7.7 1 Ki 6.15,16
7.8 1 Ki 3.1; 2 Chr 8.11
7.12 1 Ki 6.36; ver 6
★7.13 2 Chr 4.11
★7.14 2 Chr. 2.14; 4.16; Ex 31.3–5; 35.31
7.15 2 Ki 25.17; 2 Chr 3.15
7.20 2 Chr 3.16; 4.13; Jer 52.23
★7.21 2 Chr 3.17; 1 Ki 6.3

^{s} Syr Vg: Heb *floor*　^{t} With 7.12: Heb *from the outside*
^{u} Tg Syr Compare Gk and Jer 52.21: Heb *and a line of twelve cubits measured the circumference of the second pillar*　^{v} Gk: Heb lacks *he made two*　^{w} Gk: Heb *seven*
^{x} With 2 Mss Compare Gk: Heb *pillars*

7.13 *Hiram*, not the king noted in 5.1, but the architect and chief craftsman for Solomon.
7.14 *Naphtali*. See 2 Chr 2.14, where Hiram's mother is assigned to the daughters of Dan.

7.21 Apparently these pillars were free-standing as in Phoenician architecture, and not a structural part of the Temple. The names *Jachin* and *Boaz* may represent the first words of inscriptions placed on the pillars.

name Bōăz. 22And upon the tops of the pillars was lily-work. Thus the work of the pillars was finished.

6. *The molten sea*

23 Then he made the molten sea; it was round, ten cubits from brim to brim, and five cubits high, and a line of thirty cubits measured its circumference. 24 Under its brim were gourds, for thirty^y cubits, compassing the sea round about; the gourds were in two rows, cast with it when it was cast. 25 It stood upon twelve oxen, three facing north, three facing west, three facing south, and three facing east; the sea was set upon them, and all their hinder parts were inward. 26 Its thickness was a handbreadth; and its brim was made like the brim of a cup, like the flower of a lily; it held two thousand baths.

7. *The ten brass lavers*

27 He also made the ten stands of bronze; each stand was four cubits long, four cubits wide, and three cubits high. 28 This was the construction of the stands: they had panels, and the panels were set in the frames 29 and on the panels that were set in the frames were lions, oxen, and cherubim. Upon the frames, both above and below the lions and oxen, there were wreaths of beveled work. 30 Moreover each stand had four bronze wheels and axles of bronze; and at the four corners were supports for a laver. The supports were cast, with wreaths at the side of each. 31 Its opening was within a crown which projected upward one cubit; its opening was round, as a pedestal is made, a cubit and a half deep. At its opening there were carvings; and its panels were square, not round. 32And the four wheels were underneath the panels; the axles of the wheels were of one piece with the stands; and the height of a wheel was a cubit and a half. 33 The wheels were made like a chariot wheel; their axles, their rims, their spokes, and their hubs, were all cast. 34 There were four supports at the four corners of each stand; the supports were of one piece with the stands. 35And on the top of the stand there was a round band half a cubit high; and on the top of the stand its stays and its panels were of one piece with it. 36And on the surfaces of its stays and on its panels, he carved cherubim, lions, and palm trees, according to the space of each, with wreaths round about. 37After this manner he made the ten stands; all of them were cast alike, of the same measure and the same form.

38 And he made ten lavers of bronze; each laver held forty baths, each laver measured four cubits, and there was a laver for each of the ten stands. 39And he set the stands, five on the south side of the house, and five on the north side of the house; and he set the sea on the southeast corner of the house.

^y Heb *ten*

7.23 The filling of the molten sea with water was the work of the Gibeonites or Nethinim who were responsible for drawing water for the house of God.
7.26 Compare 2 Chr 4.5 where it is stated that the molten sea held three thousand baths as against two thousand in Kings. Different Hebrew verbs are used and the probable answer is that the molten sea normally contained two thousand baths, but if it were filled to the brim it would hold three thousand. Others have held that the similarity between the figures in the Hebrew indicates a transmissional error by copyists. Calculations based on the dimensions suggest a capacity of about 10,000 gallons.

8. *Other castings*

40 Hiram also made the pots, the shovels, and the basins. So Hiram finished all the work that he did for King Solomon on the house of the LORD: 41 the two pillars, the two bowls of the capitals that were on the tops of the pillars, and the two networks to cover the two bowls of the capitals that were on the tops of the pillars; 42 and the four hundred pomegranates for the two networks, two rows of pomegranates for each network, to cover the two bowls of the capitals that were upon the pillars; 43 the ten stands, and the ten lavers upon the stands; 44 and the one sea, and the twelve oxen underneath the sea.

45 Now the pots, the shovels, and the basins, all these vessels in the house of the LORD, which Hiram made for King Solomon, were of burnished bronze. 46 In the plain of the Jordan the king cast them, in the clay ground between Sùccôth and Zạr'ẻthản. 47And Solomon left all the vessels unweighed, because there were so many of them; the weight of the bronze was not found out.

9. *The golden vessels*

48 So Solomon made all the vessels that were in the house of the LORD: the golden altar, the golden table for the bread of the Presence, 49 the lampstands of pure gold, five on the south side and five on the north, before the inner sanctuary; the flowers, the lamps, and the tongs, of gold; 50 the cups, snuffers, basins, dishes for incense, and firepans, of pure gold; and the sockets of gold, for the doors of the innermost part of the house, the most holy place, and for the doors of the nave of the temple.

51 Thus all the work that King Solomon did on the house of the LORD was finished. And Solomon brought in the things which David his father had dedicated, the silver, the gold, and the vessels, and stored them in the treasuries of the house of the LORD.

H. *The dedication of the Temple*

1. *The ark brought to the Temple*

8 Then Solomon assembled the elders of Israel and all the heads of the tribes, the leaders of the fathers' houses of the people of Israel, before King Solomon in Jerusalem, to bring up the ark of the covenant of the LORD out of the city of David, which is Zion. 2And all the men of Israel assembled to King Solomon at the feast in the month Ẻth'ảnĭm, which is the seventh month. 3And all the elders of Israel came, and the priests took up the ark. 4And they brought up the ark of the LORD, the tent of meeting, and all the holy vessels that were in the tent; the priests and the Lẻvītes brought them up. 5And King Solomon and all the congregation of Israel, who had assembled before him, were with him before the ark, sacrificing so many sheep and oxen that they could not be counted or numbered. 6 Then the priests brought the ark of the covenant of the LORD to its place, in the inner sanctuary of the house, in the most holy place, underneath the wings of the cherubim. 7 For the cherubim spread out their wings over the place of the ark, so that the cherubim made a covering above the ark and its poles. 8And the poles were so long that the ends of the poles were seen from the holy place before the inner sanctuary; but they could not be seen from outside; and they are there to this day.

7.41
ver 17,18

7.42
ver 20

7.44
ver 23,25

7.45
2 Chr 4.16

7.46
2 Chr 4.17;
Josh 13.27;
3.16

7.48
Ex 37.10ff

7.49
Ex 31–38

7.51
2 Sam 8.11;
2 Chr 5.1

8.1
2 Chr 5.2;
2 Sam 6.17;
5.7,9

8.2
Lev 23.34;
2 Chr 7.8
8.3
Num 7.9
8.4
1 Ki 3.4;
2 Chr 1.3
8.5
2 Sam 6.13

8.6
2 Sam 6.17;
1 Ki 6.19,27

8.8
Ex 25.14

8.9
Ex 25.21;
Deut 10.2–
5; Heb 9.4;
Ex 24.7,8
8.10
Ex 40.34,
35;
2 Chr 7.1,2

9 There was nothing in the ark except the two tables of stone which Moses put there at Horĕb, where the LORD made a covenant with the people of Israel, when they came out of the land of Egypt. 10And when the priests came out of the holy place, a cloud filled the house of the LORD, 11 so that the priests could not stand to minister because of the cloud; for the glory of the LORD filled the house of the LORD.

8.12
2 Chr 6.1;
Ps 97.2

12 Then Solomon said,
"The LORD has set the sun in the heavens,
  but[z] has said that he would dwell in thick darkness.

8.13
2 Sam 7.13;
Ps 132.14

13 I have built thee an exalted house,
  a place for thee to dwell in for ever."

2. Solomon's speech

8.14
2 Sam 6.18
8.15
1 Chr 29.10,
20;
Neh 9.5;
2 Sam 7.12,
13
8.16
2 Sam
7.4–6;
Deut 12.11;
1 Sam 16.1;
2 Sam 7.8
8.17
2 Sam 7.2;
1 Chr 17.1
8.19
2 Sam 7.5;
12.13;
1 Ki 5.3,5
8.20
1 Chr 28.5,6
8.21
ver 9

14 Then the king faced about, and blessed all the assembly of Israel, while all the assembly of Israel stood. 15And he said, "Blessed be the LORD, the God of Israel, who with his hand has fulfilled what he promised with his mouth to David my father, saying, 16 'Since the day that I brought my people Israel out of Egypt, I chose no city in all the tribes of Israel in which to build a house, that my name might be there; but I chose David to be over my people Israel.' 17 Now it was in the heart of David my father to build a house for the name of the LORD, the God of Israel. 18 But the LORD said to David my father, 'Whereas it was in your heart to build a house for my name, you did well that it was in your heart; 19 nevertheless you shall not build the house, but your son who shall be born to you shall build the house for my name.' 20 Now the LORD has fulfilled his promise which he made; for I have risen in the place of David my father, and sit on the throne of Israel, as the LORD promised, and I have built the house for the name of the LORD, the God of Israel. 21And there I have provided a place for the ark, in which is the covenant of the LORD which he made with our fathers, when he brought them out of the land of Egypt."

3. Solomon's prayer

8.22
2 Chr
6.12ff;
Ex 9.33;
Ezra 9.5
8.23
1 Sam 2.2;
2 Sam 7.22;
Deut 7.9;
Neh 1.5,
9,32
8.25
2 Sam 7.12,
16;
1 Ki 2.4
8.26
2 Sam 7.25
8.27
2 Chr 2.6;
Isa 66.1;
Jer 23.24;
Acts 7.49

22 Then Solomon stood before the altar of the LORD in the presence of all the assembly of Israel, and spread forth his hands toward heaven; 23 and said, "O LORD, God of Israel, there is no God like thee, in heaven above or on earth beneath, keeping covenant and showing steadfast love to thy servants who walk before thee with all their heart; 24 who hast kept with thy servant David my father what thou didst declare to him; yea, thou didst speak with thy mouth, and with thy hand hast fulfilled it this day. 25 Now therefore, O LORD, God of Israel, keep with thy servant David my father what thou hast promised him, saying, 'There shall never fail you a man before me to sit upon the throne of Israel, if only your sons take heed to their way, to walk before me as you have walked before me.' 26 Now therefore, O God of Israel, let thy word be confirmed, which thou hast spoken to thy servant David my father.

27 "But will God indeed dwell on the earth? Behold, heaven and the highest heaven cannot contain thee; how much less this house which I have built! 28 Yet have regard to the prayer of thy

z Gk: Heb lacks *has set the sun in the heavens, but*

servant and to his supplication, O LORD my God, hearkening to the cry and to the prayer which thy servant prays before thee this day; 29 that thy eyes may be open night and day toward this house, the place of which thou hast said, 'My name shall be there,' that thou mayest hearken to the prayer which thy servant offers toward this place. 30And hearken thou to the supplication of thy servant and of thy people Israel, when they pray toward this place; yea, hear thou in heaven thy dwelling place; and when thou hearest, forgive.

31 "If a man sins against his neighbor and is made to take an oath, and comes and swears his oath before thine altar in this house, 32 then hear thou in heaven, and act, and judge thy servants, condemning the guilty by bringing his conduct upon his own head, and vindicating the righteous by rewarding him according to his righteousness.

33 "When thy people Israel are defeated before the enemy because they have sinned against thee, if they turn again to thee, and acknowledge thy name, and pray and make supplication to thee in this house; 34 then hear thou in heaven, and forgive the sin of thy people Israel, and bring them again to the land which thou gavest to their fathers.

35 "When heaven is shut up and there is no rain because they have sinned against thee, if they pray toward this place, and acknowledge thy name, and turn from their sin, when thou dost afflict them, 36 then hear thou in heaven, and forgive the sin of thy servants, thy people Israel, when thou dost teach them the good way in which they should walk; and grant rain upon thy land, which thou hast given to thy people as an inheritance.

37 "If there is famine in the land, if there is pestilence or blight or mildew or locust or caterpillar; if their enemy besieges them in any*a* of their cities; whatever plague, whatever sickness there is; 38 whatever prayer, whatever supplication is made by any man or by all thy people Israel, each knowing the affliction of his own heart and stretching out his hands toward this house; 39 then hear thou in heaven thy dwelling place, and forgive, and act, and render to each whose heart thou knowest, according to all his ways (for thou, thou only, knowest the hearts of all the children of men); 40 that they may fear thee all the days that they live in the land which thou gavest to our fathers.

41 "Likewise when a foreigner, who is not of thy people Israel, comes from a far country for thy name's sake 42 (for they shall hear of thy great name, and thy mighty hand, and of thy outstretched arm), when he comes and prays toward this house, 43 hear thou in heaven thy dwelling place, and do according to all for which the foreigner calls to thee; in order that all the peoples of the earth may know thy name and fear thee, as do thy people Israel, and that they may know that this house which I have built is called by thy name.

44 "If thy people go out to battle against their enemy, by whatever way thou shalt send them, and they pray to the LORD toward the city which thou hast chosen and the house which I have built for thy name, 45 then hear thou in heaven their prayer and their supplication, and maintain their cause.

a Gk Syr: Heb *the land*

8.29
Deut 12.11;
Dan 6.10

8.30
Neh 1.6

8.31
Ex 22.11

8.32
Deut 25.1

8.33
Lev 26.17;
Deut 28.25;
Lev 26.39

8.35
Lev 26.19;
Deut 28.23

8.36
1 Sam
12.23;
Ps 27.11;
94.12

8.37
Lev 26.16,
25,26;
Deut 28.21–
23,38–42

8.39
1 Sam 16.7;
1 Chr 28.9;
Ps 11.4;
Jer 17.10

8.40
Ps 130.4

8.42
Deut 3.24

8.43
1 Sam
17.46;
2 Ki 19.19;
Ps 102.15

8.46
2 Chr 6.36;
Prov 20.9;
1 Jn 1.8–10;
Lev 26.34–
39;
Deut 28.36,
64
8.47
Lev 26.40;
Neh 1.6;
Ps 106.6;
Dan 9.5
8.48
Jer 29.12–
14;
Dan 6.10
8.50
2 Chr 30.9;
Ps 106.46
8.51
Deut 9.29;
Neh 1.10;
Deut 4.20;
Jer 11.4
8.53
Ex 19.5;
Deut 9.26–
29

46 "If they sin against thee—for there is no man who does not sin—and thou art angry with them, and dost give them to an enemy, so that they are carried away captive to the land of the enemy, far off or near; 47 yet if they lay it to heart in the land to which they have been carried captive, and repent, and make supplication to thee in the land of their captors, saying, 'We have sinned, and have acted perversely and wickedly'; 48 if they repent with all their mind and with all their heart in the land of their enemies, who carried them captive, and pray to thee toward their land, which thou gavest to their fathers, the city which thou hast chosen, and the house which I have built for thy name; 49 then hear thou in heaven thy dwelling place their prayer and their supplication, and maintain their cause 50 and forgive thy people who have sinned against thee, and all their transgressions which they have committed against thee; and grant them compassion in the sight of those who carried them captive, that they may have compassion on them 51 (for they are thy people, and thy heritage, which thou didst bring out of Egypt, from the midst of the iron furnace). 52 Let thy eyes be open to the supplication of thy servant, and to the supplication of thy people Israel, giving ear to them whenever they call to thee. 53 For thou didst separate them from among all the peoples of the earth, to be thy heritage, as thou didst declare through Moses, thy servant, when thou didst bring our fathers out of Egypt, O Lord GOD."

4. Solomon's benediction

8.55
ver 14
8.56
Josh 21.45;
23.14
8.57
Josh 1.5;
Rom 8.28;
Heb 13.5
8.58
Ps 119.36
8.60
1 Ki 18.39;
Jer 10.10–
12
8.61
1 Ki 11.4;
15.3,14;
2 Ki 20.3

54 Now as Solomon finished offering all this prayer and supplication to the LORD, he arose from before the altar of the LORD, where he had knelt with hands outstretched toward heaven; 55 and he stood, and blessed all the assembly of Israel with a loud voice, saying, 56 "Blessed be the LORD who has given rest to his people Israel, according to all that he promised; not one word has failed of all his good promise, which he uttered by Moses his servant. 57 The LORD our God be with us, as he was with our fathers; may he not leave us or forsake us; 58 that he may incline our hearts to him, to walk in all his ways, and to keep his commandments, his statutes, and his ordinances, which he commanded our fathers. 59 Let these words of mine, wherewith I have made supplication before the LORD, be near to the LORD our God day and night, and may he maintain the cause of his servant, and the cause of his people Israel, as each day requires; 60 that all the peoples of the earth may know that the LORD is God; there is no other. 61 Let your heart therefore be wholly true to the LORD our God, walking in his statutes and keeping his commandments, as at this day."

5. The offerings and feast

8.62
2 Chr 7.4ff
*8.63
8.64
2 Chr 7.7;
4.1

62 Then the king, and all Israel with him, offered sacrifice before the LORD. 63 Solomon offered as peace offerings to the LORD twenty-two thousand oxen and a hundred and twenty thousand sheep. So the king and all the people of Israel dedicated the house of the LORD. 64 The same day the king consecrated the middle of

---

8.63 *Twenty-two thousand oxen and a hundred and twenty thousand sheep.* These figures seem high. If Solomon spread the sacrifices out over 14 days: 7 days to dedicate the altar and 7 days of feasting (2 Chr 7.9), it would have meant a daily sacrifice of 1571 oxen and 8571 sheep, an amazing feat for the priests in the middle court of the Temple.

the court that was before the house of the LORD; for there he
offered the burnt offering and the cereal offering and the fat pieces
of the peace offerings, because the bronze altar that was before
the LORD was too small to receive the burnt offering and the cereal
offering and the fat pieces of the peace offerings.

65 So Solomon held the feast at that time, and all Israel with
him, a great assembly, from the entrance of Hāmáth to the Brook
of Egypt, before the LORD our God, seven days.[b] 66 On the
eighth day he sent the people away; and they blessed the king, and
went to their homes joyful and glad of heart for all the goodness
that the LORD had shown to David his servant and to Israel his
people.

I. God's conditional covenant with Solomon

9 When Solomon had finished building the house of the LORD
and the king's house and all that Solomon desired to build,
2 the LORD appeared to Solomon a second time, as he had appeared to him at Gïb′ëön. 3And the LORD said to him, "I have
heard your prayer and your supplication, which you have made
before me; I have consecrated this house which you have built, and
put my name there for ever; my eyes and my heart will be there for
all time. 4And as for you, if you will walk before me, as David your
father walked, with integrity of heart and uprightness, doing according to all that I have commanded you, and keeping my statutes
and my ordinances, 5 then I will establish your royal throne over
Israel for ever, as I promised David your father, saying, 'There
shall not fail you a man upon the throne of Israel.' 6 But if you
turn aside from following me, you or your children, and do not
keep my commandments and my statutes which I have set before
you, but go and serve other gods and worship them, 7 then I will
cut off Israel from the land which I have given them; and the house
which I have consecrated for my name I will cast out of my sight;
and Israel will become a proverb and a byword among all peoples.
8And this house will become a heap of ruins;[c] everyone passing by
it will be astonished, and will hiss; and they will say, 'Why has the
LORD done thus to this land and to this house?' 9 Then they will
say, 'Because they forsook the LORD their God who brought their
fathers out of the land of Egypt, and laid hold on other gods, and
worshiped them and served them; therefore the LORD has brought
all this evil upon them.'"

J. Incidental details about Solomon

10 At the end of twenty years, in which Solomon had built the
two houses, the house of the LORD and the king's house, 11 and
Hiram king of Tȳre had supplied Solomon with cedar and cypress
timber and gold, as much as he desired, King Solomon gave to
Hiram twenty cities in the land of Găl′ileē. 12 But when Hiram
came from Tȳre to see the cities which Solomon had given him,
they did not please him. 13 Therefore he said, "What kind of cities

b Gk: Heb seven days and seven days, fourteen days   *c* Syr Old Latin: Heb high

9.11 In 2 Chr 8.2 Hiram gives the cities to Solomon, who then settles the people of Israel in them. (Hiram is spelled *Huram* in 2 Chr 8.2.)

are these which you have given me, my brother?" So they are called the land of Cābul to this day. 14 Hiram had sent to the king one hundred and twenty talents of gold.

15 And this is the account of the forced labor which King Solomon levied to build the house of the LORD and his own house and the Millō and the wall of Jerusalem and Hāzor and Mègid'dō and Gēzèr 16 (Phàraōh king of Egypt had gone up and captured Gēzèr and burnt it with fire, and had slain the Cā'naànītes who dwelt in the city, and had given it as dowry to his daughter, Solomon's wife; 17 so Solomon rebuilt Gēzèr) and Lower Bĕth-hor'òn 18 and Bā'àlàth and Tāmar in the wilderness, in the land of Judah,*d* 19 and all the store-cities that Solomon had, and the cities for his chariots, and the cities for his horsemen, and whatever Solomon desired to build in Jerusalem, in Lebanon, and in all the land of his dominion. 20All the people who were left of the Ăm'òrītes, the Hĭttītes, the Pĕr'izzītes, the Hīvītes, and the Jĕb'ùsītes, who were not of the people of Israel— 21 their descendants who were left after them in the land, whom the people of Israel were unable to destroy utterly—these Solomon made a forced levy of slaves, and so they are to this day. 22 But of the people of Israel Solomon made no slaves; they were the soldiers, they were his officials, his commanders, his captains, his chariot commanders and his horsemen.

23 These were the chief officers who were over Solomon's work: five hundred and fifty, who had charge of the people who carried on the work.

24 But Phàraōh's daughter went up from the city of David to her own house which Solomon had built for her; then he built the Millō.

25 Three times a year Solomon used to offer up burnt offerings and peace offerings upon the altar which he built to the LORD, burning incense*e* before the LORD. So he finished the house.

26 King Solomon built a fleet of ships at Ēz'ìōn-gē'bèr, which is near Ēlōth on the shore of the Red Sea, in the land of Ēdòm. 27And Hiram sent with the fleet his servants, seamen who were familiar with the sea, together with the servants of Solomon; 28 and they went to Ōphir, and brought from there gold, to the amount of four hundred and twenty talents; and they brought it to King Solomon.

K. The visit of the queen of Sheba

10 Now when the queen of Shēbà heard of the fame of Solomon concerning the name of the LORD, she came to test him with hard questions. 2 She came to Jerusalem with a very great retinue, with camels bearing spices, and very much gold, and

*9.15
1 Ki 5.13;
ver 24;
2 Sam 5.9;
Josh 19.36;
17.11;
16.10
9.16
Josh 16.10
9.17
Josh 16.3;
2 Chr 8.5
9.19
1 Ki 4.26;
ver 1

9.20
2 Chr 8.7

9.21
Judg 1.21,
27,29;
Josh 15.63;
17.12;
Judg 1.21;
Gen 9.25,
26;
Ezra 2.55,
58
9.22
Lev 25.39
9.23
2 Chr 8.10
9.24
1 Ki 3.1;
7,8;11.27;
2 Chr 32.5
9.25
2 Chr 8.12,
13,16

*9.26
2 Chr 8.17,
18;
Num 33.35;
Deut 2.8;
1 Ki 22.48
9.27
1 Ki 10.11
*9.28
1 Chr 29.4

*10.1
2 Chr 9.1ff;
Mt 12.42;
Judg 14.12

d Heb lacks *of Judah*
e Gk: Heb *burning incense with it which*

9.15 *the Millo*, that is, "the Filling," but its exact nature is not known. *Hazor, Megiddo, Gezer*. Solomonic construction has been found in each of these Canaanite fortresses.

9.26 *Ezion-geber*. Evidences of the port have not been found, but an extensive copper smelting refinery, almost certainly the work of Solomon, has been unearthed there.

9.28 *Ophir*. Some locate it in southern

Arabia, but more likely it was along the African coast somewhere near modern Somaliland.

10.1 *Sheba*, that is, the land of the Sabeans in southwestern Arabia. This region, the eastern part of modern Yemen, controlled the caravan routes via which incense and spice were brought from southern Arabia to Palestine.

precious stones; and when she came to Solomon, she told him all that was on her mind. ³And Solomon answered all her questions; there was nothing hidden from the king which he could not explain to her. ⁴And when the queen of Shēbá had seen all the wisdom of Solomon, the house that he had built, ⁵ the food of his table, the seating of his officials, and the attendance of his servants, their clothing, his cupbearers, and his burnt offerings which he offered at the house of the LORD, there was no more spirit in her.

*10.5
1 Chr 26.16

6 And she said to the king, "The report was true which I heard in my own land of your affairs and of your wisdom, ⁷ but I did not believe the reports until I came and my own eyes had seen it; and, behold, the half was not told me; your wisdom and prosperity surpass the report which I heard. ⁸ Happy are your wives!ᶠ Happy are these your servants, who continually stand before you and hear your wisdom! ⁹ Blessed be the LORD your God, who has delighted in you and set you on the throne of Israel! Because the LORD loved Israel for ever, he has made you king, that you may execute justice and righteousness." ¹⁰ Then she gave the king a hundred and twenty talents of gold, and a very great quantity of spices, and precious stones; never again came such an abundance of spices as these which the queen of Shēbá gave to King Solomon.

10.9
1 Ki 5.7;
2 Sam 8.15

10.10
ver 2

11 Moreover the fleet of Hiram, which brought gold from Ōphĭr, brought from Ophir a very great amount of almug wood and precious stones. ¹²And the king made of the almug wood supports for the house of the LORD, and for the king's house, lyres also and harps for the singers; no such almug wood has come or been seen, to this day.

10.11
1 Ki 9.27,28

10.12
2 Chr 9.10,
11

13 And King Solomon gave to the queen of Shēbá all that she desired, whatever she asked besides what was given her by the bounty of King Solomon. So she turned and went back to her own land, with her servants.

L. *The material splendor of Solomon*

14 Now the weight of gold that came to Solomon in one year was six hundred and sixty-six talents of gold, ¹⁵ besides that which came from the traders and from the traffic of the merchants, and from all the kings of Arabia and from the governors of the land. ¹⁶ King Solomon made two hundred large shields of beaten gold; six hundred shekels of gold went into each shield. ¹⁷And he made three hundred shields of beaten gold; three minas of gold went into each shield; and the king put them in the House of the Forest of Lebanon. ¹⁸ The king also made a great ivory throne, and overlaid it with the finest gold. ¹⁹ The throne had six steps, and at the back of the throne was a calf's head, and on each side of the seat were arm rests and two lions standing beside the arm rests, ²⁰ while twelve lions stood there, one on each end of a step on the six steps. The like of it was never made in any kingdom. ²¹All King Solomon's drinking vessels were of gold, and all the vessels of the House of the Forest of Lebanon were of pure gold; none were of silver, it was not considered as anything in the days of

10.14
2 Chr 9.13–
28

10.16
1 Ki 14.26–
28

10.17
1 Ki 7.2

10.18
2 Chr 9.17ff

ᶠ Gk Syr: Heb *men*

10.5 *there was no more spirit in her.* This simply means that she was so overwhelmed by all the opulence and wisdom that there was no energy left in her to cope with it.

*10.22
1 Ki 9.26–
28; 22.48;
2 Chr 20.36

10.23
1 Ki 3.12,
13; 4.30
10.24
1 Ki 3.9,
12,28

10.26
1 Ki 4.26;
2 Chr 1.14;
9.25;
1 Ki 9.19

*10.28
2 Chr 1.16;
9.28
10.29
2 Ki 7.6,7

Solomon. 22 For the king had a fleet of ships of Tarshish at sea with the fleet of Hiram. Once every three years the fleet of ships of Tarshish used to come bringing gold, silver, ivory, apes, and peacocks.g

23 Thus King Solomon excelled all the kings of the earth in riches and in wisdom. 24And the whole earth sought the presence of Solomon to hear his wisdom, which God had put into his mind. 25 Every one of them brought his present, articles of silver and gold, garments, myrrh, spices, horses, and mules, so much year by year.

26 And Solomon gathered together chariots and horsemen; he had fourteen hundred chariots and twelve thousand horsemen, whom he stationed in the chariot cities and with the king in Jerusalem. 27And the king made silver as common in Jerusalem as stone, and he made cedar as plentiful as the sycamore of the Shephē'lāh. 28And Solomon's import of horses was from Egypt and Kū'e, and the king's traders received them from Kue at a price. 29A chariot could be imported from Egypt for six hundred shekels of silver, and a horse for a hundred and fifty; and so through the king's traders they were exported to all the kings of the Hittites and the kings of Syria.

M. Solomon breaks God's covenant

1. He takes strange wives

11.1
Neh 13.26;
Deut 17.17
11.2
Ex 34.16;
Deut 7.3,4

*11.3

11.4
1 Ki 8.61;
9.4
*11.5
ver 33;
Judg 2.13;
2 Ki 23.13

11.7
Num 21.29;
Judg 11.24;
2 Ki 23.13

11 Now King Solomon loved many foreign women: the daughter of Pharaōh, and Mō'ābīte, Ăm'mŏnīte, Ē'dŏmīte, Sīdō'nĭăn, and Hittīte women, 2 from the nations concerning which the LORD had said to the people of Israel, "You shall not enter into marriage with them, neither shall they with you, for surely they will turn away your heart after their gods"; Solomon clung to these in love. 3 He had seven hundred wives, princesses, and three hundred concubines; and his wives turned away his heart. 4 For when Solomon was old his wives turned away his heart after other gods; and his heart was not wholly true to the LORD his God, as was the heart of David his father. 5 For Solomon went after Ash'tŏrĕth the goddess of the Sīdō'nĭăns, and after Mĭlcŏm the abomination of the Ăm'mŏnītes. 6 So Solomon did what was evil in the sight of the LORD, and did not wholly follow the LORD, as David his father had done. 7 Then Solomon built a high place for Chēmŏsh the abomination of Mōăb, and for Mōlĕch the abomination of the Ăm'mŏnītes, on the mountain east of Jerusalem. 8And so he did for all his foreign wives, who burned incense and sacrificed to their gods.

g Or baboons

10.22 *ships of Tarshish.* Apparently this expression was used of large ships such as those employed in trade with Tarshish, a colony somewhere in Sardinia or southern Spain. However, W. F. Albright holds that *Tarshish* may mean "refinery." The Phoenicians controlled the Mediterranean commerce. Solomon's fleets operated in the Red Sea. Then *ships of Tarshish* would mean that the port of origin was the "refinery" at

Ezion-geber.

10.28 *Kue,* that is, Cilicia in Asia Minor.
11.3 Solomon's many wives and his multiplying of horses, silver, and gold were flagrant violations of Deut 17.16–17.
11.5 *Ashtoreth,* that is, Astarte, the Canaanite goddess of fertility. *Milcom.* Another designation for Molech, noted in verse 7, the god to whom children were sacrificed (Lev 20.1–5). See also note to Zeph 1.5.

2. *God warns Solomon*

9 And the LORD was angry with Solomon, because his heart had turned away from the LORD, the God of Israel, who had appeared to him twice, 10 and had commanded him concerning this thing, that he should not go after other gods; but he did not keep what the LORD commanded. 11 Therefore the LORD said to Solomon, "Since this has been your mind and you have not kept my covenant and my statutes which I have commanded you, I will surely tear the kingdom from you and will give it to your servant. 12 Yet for the sake of David your father I will not do it in your days, but I will tear it out of the hand of your son. 13 However I will not tear away all the kingdom; but I will give one tribe to your son, for the sake of David my servant and for the sake of Jerusalem which I have chosen."

*11.9
ver 2,3;
1 Ki 3.5;
9.2
11.10
1 Ki 6.12;
9.6,7
11.11
ver 31;
1 Ki 12.15,
16

11.13
2 Sam 7.15;
1 Ki 12.20;
Deut 12.11

3. *God raises up adversaries against Solomon*
a. *Hadad*

14 And the LORD raised up an adversary against Solomon, Hădăd the Ē′dŏmīte; he was of the royal house in Ēdŏm. 15 For when David was in Ēdŏm, and Jŏăb the commander of the army went up to bury the slain, he slew every male in Edom 16 (for Jŏăb and all Israel remained there six months, until he had cut off every male in Ēdŏm); 17 but Hădăd fled to Egypt, together with certain Ē′dŏmītes of his father's servants, Hadad being yet a little child. 18 They set out from Mĭd′ïăn and came to Părăn, and took men with them from Paran and came to Egypt, to Phăraōh king of Egypt, who gave him a house, and assigned him an allowance of food, and gave him land. 19 And Hădăd found great favor in the sight of Phăraōh, so that he gave him in marriage the sister of his own wife, the sister of Tah′pĕnĕṣ the queen. 20 And the sister of Tah′pĕnĕṣ bore him Gĕnu′băth his son, whom Tahpenes weaned in Phăraōh'ṣ house; and Genubath was in Pharaoh's house among the sons of Phăraōh. 21 But when Hădăd heard in Egypt that David slept with his fathers and that Jŏăb the commander of the army was dead, Hadad said to Phăraōh, "Let me depart, that I may go to my own country." 22 But Phăraōh said to him, "What have you lacked with me that you are now seeking to go to your own country?" And he said to him, "Only let me go."

11.15
2 Sam 8.14;
1 Chr
18.12,13

11.21
1 Ki 2.10

b. *Rezon*

23 God also raised up as an adversary to him, Rĕzŏn the son of Ēlĭ′ădă, who had fled from his master Hădădĕ′zĕr king of Zŏbăh. 24 And he gathered men about him and became leader of a marauding band, after the slaughter by David; and they went to Damascus, and dwelt there, and made him king in Damascus. 25 He was an adversary of Israel all the days of Solomon, doing mischief as Hădăd did; and he abhorred Israel, and reigned over Syria.

11.23
ver 14;
2 Sam 8.3
11.24
2 Sam 8.3;
10.8,18

11.9 "Backsliding" is a turning away from God which prevents any genuine fellowship. It is spoken of as leaving one's first love (Rev 2.4). Backsliding may take many forms. It may involve an overt breach of the moral law, as in the case of David who committed adultery and murder (2 Sam 11). It may involve a verbal denial of Christ, as in the case of Peter (Mt 26.70–74). It may be dis-obedience to a command of God, as in the case of Saul (1 Sam 15.11). Backsliding is not irremediable. Repentance, confession, and restitution will bring a true believer back into fellowship with God. Thus Samson repented before his death (Judg 16.28); David repented of his sin with Bathsheba (2 Sam 12.13); Peter repented and became a transformed man after Pentecost (Acts 2.14ff).

c. Jeroboam

11.26
1 Ki 12.2;
2 Chr 13.6;
2 Sam 20.21

26 Jĕrobō'ăm the son of Nēbăt, an Ē'phräїmīte of Zĕr'ĕdăh, a servant of Solomon, whose mother's name was Zĕru'ăh, a widow, also lifted up his hand against the king. 27And this was the reason

11.27
1 Ki 9.24

why he lifted up his hand against the king. Solomon built the Mīllō, and closed up the breach of the city of David his father. 28 The man Jĕrobō'ăm was very able, and when Solomon saw that the young man was industrious he gave him charge over all the

11.29
1 Ki 14.2

forced labor of the house of Joseph. 29And at that time, when Jĕrobō'ăm went out of Jerusalem, the prophet Ahī'jăh the Shī'-lŏnīte found him on the road. Now Ahijah had clad himself with a new garment; and the two of them were alone in the open country. 30 Then Ahī'jăh laid hold of the new garment that was

11.30
1 Sam
15.27,28
11.31
ver 11–13
★**11.32**

on him, and tore it into twelve pieces. 31And he said to Jĕrobō'ăm, "Take for yourself ten pieces; for thus says the LORD, the God of Israel, 'Behold, I am about to tear the kingdom from the hand of Solomon, and will give you ten tribes 32 (but he shall have one tribe, for the sake of my servant David and for the sake of Jeru-salem, the city which I have chosen out of all the tribes of Israel),

11.33
ver 5–7

33 because he has[h] forsaken me, and worshiped Ăsh'tŏrĕth the goddess of the Sīdō'nïănṣ, Çhĕmŏsh the god of Mōăb, and Mīl-cŏm the god of the Ăm'mŏnītes, and has[h] not walked in my ways, doing what is right in my sight and keeping my statutes and my ordinances, as David his father did. 34 Nevertheless I will not take the whole kingdom out of his hand; but I will make him ruler all the days of his life, for the sake of David my servant whom I

11.35
1 Ki 12.16,
17
11.36
ver 13;
1 Ki 15.4;
2 Ki 8.19

chose, who kept my commandments and my statutes; 35 but I will take the kingdom out of his son's hand, and will give it to you, ten tribes. 36 Yet to his son I will give one tribe, that David my serv-ant may always have a lamp before me in Jerusalem, the city where I have chosen to put my name. 37And I will take you, and you shall reign over all that your soul desires, and you shall be king over Israel. 38And if you will hearken to all that I command you, and

11.38
Josh 1.5;
2 Sam 7.11,
27

will walk in my ways, and do what is right in my eyes by keeping my statutes and my commandments, as David my servant did, I will be with you, and will build you a sure house, as I built for David, and I will give Israel to you. 39And I will for this afflict the descendants of David, but not for ever.'" 40 Solomon sought therefore to kill Jĕrobō'ăm; but Jeroboam arose, and fled into Egypt, to Shīshăk king of Egypt, and was in Egypt until the death of Solomon.

N. *The death of Solomon*

11.41
2 Chr 9.29

41 Now the rest of the acts of Solomon, and all that he did, and his wisdom, are they not written in the book of the acts of Solo-mon? 42And the time that Solomon reigned in Jerusalem over all

11.42
2 Chr 9.30
11.43
2 Chr 9.31;
1 Ki 14.21

Israel was forty years. 43And Solomon slept with his fathers, and was buried in the city of David his father; and Rĕhobō'ăm his son reigned in his stead.

h Gk Syr Vg: Heb *they have*

11.32 one tribe, a reference to Judah. But inasmuch as Benjamin had been assimilated by its more numerous and powerful neighbor, two tribes were involved. *Jerusalem . . . which I have chosen.* This identifies the place referred to in Deut 12.5–14.

III. *The divided kingdom 12.1–22.53*

A. *The division of the kingdom*

1. *The revolt of the ten tribes*

12 Rĕhŏbō′ăm went to Shĕçhĕm, for all Israel had come to Shechem to make him king. ²And when Jĕrŏbō′ăm the son of Nēbăt heard of it (for he was still in Egypt, whither he had fled from King Solomon), then Jeroboam returned from^i Egypt. ³And they sent and called him; and Jĕrŏbō′ăm and all the assembly of Israel came and said to Rĕhŏbō′ăm, ⁴ "Your father made our yoke heavy. Now therefore lighten the hard service of your father and his heavy yoke upon us, and we will serve you." ⁵ He said to them, "Depart for three days, then come again to me." So the people went away.

6 Then King Rĕhŏbō′ăm took counsel with the old men, who had stood before Solomon his father while he was yet alive, saying, "How do you advise me to answer this people?" ⁷And they said to him, "If you will be a servant to this people today and serve them, and speak good words to them when you answer them, then they will be your servants for ever." ⁸ But he forsook the counsel which the old men gave him, and took counsel with the young men who had grown up with him and stood before him. ⁹And he said to them, "What do you advise that we answer this people who have said to me, 'Lighten the yoke that your father put upon us'?" ¹⁰And the young men who had grown up with him said to him, "Thus shall you speak to this people who said to you, 'Your father made our yoke heavy, but do you lighten it for us'; thus shall you say to them, 'My little finger is thicker than my father's loins. ¹¹And now, whereas my father laid upon you a heavy yoke, I will add to your yoke. My father chastised you with whips, but I will chastise you with scorpions.' "

12 So Jĕrŏbō′ăm and all the people came to Rĕhŏbō′ăm the third day, as the king said, "Come to me again the third day." ¹³And the king answered the people harshly, and forsaking the counsel which the old men had given him, ¹⁴ he spoke to them according to the counsel of the young men, saying, "My father made your yoke heavy, but I will add to your yoke; my father chastised you with whips, but I will chastise you with scorpions." ¹⁵ So the king did not hearken to the people; for it was a turn of affairs brought about by the LORD that he might fulfil his word, which the LORD spoke by Ahī′jăh the Shī′lōnīte to Jĕrŏbō′ăm the son of Nēbăt.

16 And when all Israel saw that the king did not hearken to them, the people answered the king,
"What portion have we in David?
We have no inheritance in the son of Jĕssë.
To your tents, O Israel!
Look now to your own house, David."
So Israel departed to their tents. ¹⁷ But Rĕhŏbō′ăm reigned over

^{i} Gk Vg Compare 2 Chron 10.2: Heb *dwelt in*

12.1 To conciliate the northern tribes Rehoboam went to Shechem, but his haughty attitude and harsh words alienated them all the more (ver 16).

*12.1
2 Chr 10.1ff
12.2
1 Ki 11.26, 40
12.4
1 Sam 8.11–18;
1 Ki 4.7
12.5
ver 12
12.7
2 Chr 10.7
12.8
Lev 19.32
12.12
ver 5
12.14
Ex 1.13,14;
5.5–9,16–18
12.15
ver 24;
Judg 14.4;
2 Chr 10.15;
22.7;
25.20;
1 Ki 11.11, 31
12.16
2 Sam 20.1
12.17
1 Ki 11.13, 36

12.18
1 Ki 4.6;
5.14

12.19
2 Ki 17.21
12.20
1 Ki 11.13,
32

12.21
2 Chr 11.1ff

12.24
ver 15

*12.25
Judg 9.45;
8.17

12.27
Deut 12.5,6

*12.28
2 Ki 10.29;
17.16;
Ex 32.4,8
12.29
Gen 28.19;
Judg 18.29
12.30
1 Ki 13.34;
2 Ki 17.21
12.31
1 Ki 13.32,
33;
Num 3.10;
2 Ki 17.32
12.32
Lev 23.33,
34;
Num 29.12;
Amos 7.13
12.33
1 Ki 13.1

the people of Israel who dwelt in the cities of Judah. 18 Then King Rēhóbō′ám sent Àdō′rám, who was taskmaster over the forced labor, and all Israel stoned him to death with stones. And King Rehoboam made haste to mount his chariot, to flee to Jerusalem. 19 So Israel has been in rebellion against the house of David to this day. 20And when all Israel heard that Jĕrōbō′ám had returned, they sent and called him to the assembly and made him king over all Israel. There was none that followed the house of David, but the tribe of Judah only.

2. God forbids Rehoboam to war against Jeroboam

21 When Rēhóbō′ám came to Jerusalem, he assembled all the house of Judah, and the tribe of Benjamin, a hundred and eighty thousand chosen warriors, to fight against the house of Israel, to restore the kingdom to Rehoboam the son of Solomon. 22 But the word of God came to Shĕmāi′áh the man of God: 23 "Say to Rēhóbō′ám the son of Solomon, king of Judah, and to all the house of Judah and Benjamin, and to the rest of the people, 24 'Thus says the LORD, You shall not go up or fight against your kinsmen the people of Israel. Return every man to his home, for this thing is from me.' " So they hearkened to the word of the LORD, and went home again, according to the word of the LORD.

3. The institution of calf worship at Bethel and Dan

25 Then Jĕrōbō′ám built Shĕçhém in the hill country of Ē′phräïm, and dwelt there; and he went out from there and built Pênû′êl. 26And Jĕrōbō′ám said in his heart, "Now the kingdom will turn back to the house of David; 27 if this people go up to offer sacrifices in the house of the LORD at Jerusalem, then the heart of this people will turn again to their lord, to Rēhóbō′ám king of Judah, and they will kill me and return to Rehoboam king of Judah." 28 So the king took counsel, and made two calves of gold. And he said to the people, "You have gone up to Jerusalem long enough. Behold your gods, O Israel, who brought you up out of the land of Egypt." 29And he set one in Bĕthĕl, and the other he put in Dan. 30And this thing became a sin, for the people went to the one at Bĕthĕl and to the other as far as Dan.ʲ 31 He also made houses on high places, and appointed priests from among all the people, who were not of the Lĕvītes. 32And Jĕrōbō′ám appointed a feast on the fifteenth day of the eighth month like the feast that was in Judah, and he offered sacrifices upon the altar; so he did in Bĕthĕl, sacrificing to the calves that he had made. And he placed in Bethel the priests of the high places that he had made. 33 He went up to the altar which he had made in Bĕthĕl on the fifteenth day in the eighth month, in the month which he had devised of his

ʲ Gk: Heb went to the one as far as Dan

12.25 built, that is, fortified and rebuilt.
12.28 In order to have places of worship so the people would not have to go to Jerusalem, Jeroboam set up a calf in Bethel, not far from Jerusalem, and the other in Dan, far to the north. The statement, "Behold your gods . . ." is a quotation from Ex 32.4, implying that these calves were the same as the golden calf made by Aaron. Some, how-ever, contend that Jeroboam intended the calves only as pedestals, much like the cherubim, over which the invisible God was enthroned. Later on, of course, the people transferred their worship to the visible objects. In any case, this form of worship resulted in the vilest form of apostasy and set the tone for the ten tribes until their melancholy end in 722 B.C.

own heart; and he ordained a feast for the people of Israel, and went up to the altar to burn incense.

B. A man of God from Judah

1. The prophecy about Josiah

13 And behold, a man of God came out of Judah by the word of the LORD to Bĕthĕl. Jĕrŏbō'ăm was standing by the altar to burn incense. 2And the man cried against the altar by the word of the LORD, and said, "O altar, altar, thus says the LORD: 'Behold, a son shall be born to the house of David, Jōsī'ăh by name; and he shall sacrifice upon you the priests of the high places who burn incense upon you, and men's bones shall be burned upon you.' " 3And he gave a sign the same day, saying, "This is the sign that the LORD has spoken: 'Behold, the altar shall be torn down, and the ashes that are upon it shall be poured out.' " 4And when the king heard the saying of the man of God, which he cried against the altar at Bĕthĕl, Jĕrŏbō'ăm stretched out his hand from the altar, saying, "Lay hold of him." And his hand, which he stretched out against him, dried up, so that he could not draw it back to himself. 5 The altar also was torn down, and the ashes poured out from the altar, according to the sign which the man of God had given by the word of the LORD. 6And the king said to the man of God, "Entreat now the favor of the LORD your God, and pray for me, that my hand may be restored to me." And the man of God entreated the LORD; and the king's hand was restored to him, and became as it was before. 7And the king said to the man of God, "Come home with me, and refresh yourself, and I will give you a reward." 8And the man of God said to the king, "If you give me half your house, I will not go in with you. And I will not eat bread or drink water in this place; 9 for so was it commanded me by the word of the LORD, saying, 'You shall neither eat bread, nor drink water, nor return by the way that you came.' " 10 So he went another way, and did not return by the way that he came to Bĕthĕl.

2. The lying prophet

11 Now there dwelt an old prophet in Bĕthĕl. And his sons[k] came and told him all that the man of God had done that day in Bethel; the words also which he had spoken to the king, they told to their father. 12And their father said to them, "Which way did he go?" And his sons showed him the way which the man of God who came from Judah had gone. 13And he said to his sons, "Saddle the ass for me." So they saddled the ass for him and he mounted it. 14And he went after the man of God, and found him sitting under an oak; and he said to him, "Are you the man of God who came from Judah?" And he said, "I am." 15 Then he said to him, "Come home with me and eat bread." 16And he said, "I may not return with you, or go in with you; neither will I eat bread nor drink water with you in this place; 17 for it was said to me by the word of the LORD, 'You shall neither eat bread nor drink water there, nor return by the way that you came.' " 18And he said to him, "I also am a prophet as you are, and an angel spoke to me by the word of the LORD, saying, 'Bring him back with you into your

k Gk Syr Vg: Heb son

13.1
2 Ki 23.17;
1 Ki 12.32,
33

13.2
2 Ki 23.15,
16

13.3
Isa 7.14;
Judg 6.17

13.6
Ex 8.8;
9.28;
Acts 8.24;
Lk 6.27,28

13.7
1 Sam
9.7,8;
2 Ki 5.15

13.8
ver 16,17;
Num 22.18;
24.13

13.11
ver 25

13.16
ver 8,9

13.17
1 Ki 20.35

house that he may eat bread and drink water.' " But he lied to him. 19 So he went back with him, and ate bread in his house, and drank water.

3. *The man of God killed by a lion for disobedience*

20 And as they sat at the table, the word of the LORD came to the prophet who had brought him back; 21 and he cried to the man of God who came from Judah, "Thus says the LORD, 'Because you have disobeyed the word of the LORD, and have not kept the commandment which the LORD your God commanded you, 22 but have come back, and have eaten bread and drunk water in the place of which he said to you, "Eat no bread, and drink no water"; your body shall not come to the tomb of your fathers.' " 23 And after he had eaten bread and drunk, he saddled the ass for the prophet whom he had brought back. 24 And as he went away a lion met him on the road and killed him. And his body was thrown in the road, and the ass stood beside it; the lion also stood beside the body. 25 And behold, men passed by, and saw the body thrown in the road, and the lion standing by the body. And they came and told it in the city where the old prophet dwelt.

26 And when the prophet who had brought him back from the way heard of it, he said, "It is the man of God, who disobeyed the word of the LORD; therefore the LORD has given him to the lion, which has torn him and slain him, according to the word which the LORD spoke to him." 27 And he said to his sons, "Saddle the ass for me." And they saddled it. 28 And he went and found his body thrown in the road, and the ass and the lion standing beside the body. The lion had not eaten the body or torn the ass. 29 And the prophet took up the body of the man of God and laid it upon the ass, and brought it back to the city,*j* to mourn and to bury him. 30 And he laid the body in his own grave; and they mourned over him, saying, "Alas, my brother!" 31 And after he had buried him, he said to his sons, "When I die, bury me in the grave in which the man of God is buried; lay my bones beside his bones. 32 For the saying which he cried by the word of the LORD against the altar in Běthěl, and against all the houses of the high places which are in the cities of Sămạr'ĭä, shall surely come to pass."

4. *The continuing apostasy of Jeroboam*

33 After this thing Jĕrŏbō'ăm did not turn from his evil way, but made priests for the high places again from among all the people; any who would, he consecrated to be priests of the high places. 34 And this thing became sin to the house of Jĕrŏbō'ăm, so as to cut it off and to destroy it from the face of the earth.

C. The house of Jeroboam

1. *Ahijah prophesies the death of Jeroboam's son*

14 At that time Ăbī'jăh the son of Jĕrŏbō'ăm fell sick. 2 And Jĕrŏbō'ăm said to his wife, "Arise, and disguise yourself,

---

Margin references (left column):

13.21
1 Sam 15.26

13.24
1 Ki 20.36

13.25
ver 11

13.26
ver 21

13.30
Jer 22.18

13.31
2 Ki 23.17,
18

*13.32
ver 2;
2 Ki 23.16,
17,19;
see 1 Ki
16.24

13.33
1 Ki 12.31;
32;
2 Chr
11.15;
13.9

13.34
1 Ki 12.30;
14.10

14.2
1 Sam 28.8;
2 Sam 14.2;
1 Ki 11.29—
31

---

j Gk: Heb *he came to the city of the old prophet*

13.32 *cities of Samaria.* The northern kingdom is designated by the name of the capital city subsequently built *and called the name . . . Samaria* (16.24).

that it be not known that you are the wife of Jeroboam, and go to Shīlōh; behold, Ahī'jăh the prophet is there, who said of me that I should be king over this people. ³ Take with you ten loaves, some cakes, and a jar of honey, and go to him; he will tell you what shall happen to the child."

4 Jĕróbō'ăm's wife did so; she arose, and went to Shīlōh, and came to the house of Ahī'jăh. Now Ahijah could not see, for his eyes were dim because of his age. ⁵And the LORD said to Ahī'jăh, "Behold, the wife of Jĕróbō'ăm is coming to inquire of you concerning her son; for he is sick. Thus and thus shall you say to her."

When she came, she pretended to be another woman. 6 But when Ahī'jăh heard the sound of her feet, as she came in at the door, he said, "Come in, wife of Jĕróbō'ăm; why do you pretend to be another? For I am charged with heavy tidings for you. 7 Go, tell Jĕróbō'ăm, 'Thus says the LORD, the God of Israel: "Because I exalted you from among the people, and made you leader over my people Israel, 8 and tore the kingdom away from the house of David and gave it to you; and yet you have not been like my servant David, who kept my commandments, and followed me with all his heart, doing only that which was right in my eyes, 9 but you have done evil above all that were before you and have gone and made for yourself other gods, and molten images, provoking me to anger, and have cast me behind your back; 10 therefore behold, I will bring evil upon the house of Jĕróbō'ăm, and will cut off from Jeroboam every male, both bond and free in Israel, and will utterly consume the house of Jeroboam, as a man burns up dung until it is all gone. 11Any one belonging to Jĕróbō'ăm who dies in the city the dogs shall eat; and any one who dies in the open country the birds of the air shall eat; for the LORD has spoken it." ' 12Arise therefore, go to your house. When your feet enter the city, the child shall die. 13And all Israel shall mourn for him, and bury him; for he only of Jĕróbō'ăm shall come to the grave, because in him there is found something pleasing to the LORD, the God of Israel, in the house of Jeroboam. 14 Moreover the LORD will raise up for himself a king over Israel, who shall cut off the house of Jĕróbō'ăm today. And henceforth*m* 15 the LORD will smite Israel, as a reed is shaken in the water, and root up Israel out of this good land which he gave to their fathers, and scatter them beyond the Eūphrā'tēṣ, because they have made their Ashē'rĭm, provoking the LORD to anger. 16And he will give Israel up because of the sins of Jĕróbō'ăm, which he sinned and which he made Israel to sin."

2. The death of Jeroboam

17 Then Jĕróbō'ăm's wife arose, and departed, and came to Tīrzăh. And as she came to the threshold of the house, the child died. 18And all Israel buried him and mourned for him, according to the word of the LORD, which he spoke by his servant Ahī'jăh the prophet. 19 Now the rest of the acts of Jĕróbō'ăm, how he

m Heb obscure

14.3 1 Sam 9.7,8
14.4 1 Ki 11.29; 1 Sam 3.2; 4.15
14.5 2 Sam 14.2
14.7 1 Ki 11.28–31; 16.2
14.8 1 Ki 11.31ff
14.9 1 Ki 12.28; 2 Chr 11.15; Ps 50.17; Ex 34.17; Ezek 23.35
14.10 1 Ki 15.29; 21.21; 2 Ki 9.8; Deut 32.36; 2 Ki 14.26
14.11 1 Ki 16.4; 21.24
14.12 ver 17
14.13 2 Chr 12.12
14.14 1 Ki 15.27–29
★14.15 2 Ki 17.6; Josh 23.15, 16; 2 Ki 15.29; Ex 34.13; Deut 12.3,4
14.16 1 Ki 12.30; 13.34; 15.30,34
★14.17 1 Ki 16.6–9
14.18 ver 13
★14.19 2 Chr 13.2–20

14.15 *Asherim*, see note to Ex 34.13.
14.17 *Tirzah*. The first capital of northern Israel.
14.19 *Book of the Chronicles*, court records of the northern kingdom. Similar annals were kept in Judah (ver 29). These records constituted the main sources for our books of Kings and Chronicles.

warred and how he reigned, behold, they are written in the Book
of the Chronicles of the Kings of Israel. 20And the time that Jĕrobō'ám reigned was twenty-two years; and he slept with his fathers,
and Nādăb his son reigned in his stead.

D. The kingdom of Judah

1. Rehoboam, son of Solomon

a. Judah's apostasy

21 Now Rĕhŏbō'ám the son of Solomon reigned in Judah. Rehoboam was forty-one years old when he began to reign, and he
reigned seventeen years in Jerusalem, the city which the LORD
had chosen out of all the tribes of Israel, to put his name there.
His mother's name was Nā'ámáh the Ămmŏnīt'ĕss. 22And Judah
did what was evil in the sight of the LORD, and they provoked him
to jealousy with their sins which they committed, more than all
that their fathers had done. 23 For they also built for themselves
high places, and pillars, and Ăshē'rĭm on every high hill and under
every green tree; 24 and there were also male cult prostitutes in the
land. They did according to all the abominations of the nations
which the LORD drove out before the people of Israel.

b. Defeat by Shishak of Egypt

25 In the fifth year of King Rĕhŏbō'ám, Shĭshăk king of Egypt
came up against Jerusalem; 26 he took away the treasures of the
house of the LORD and the treasures of the king's house; he took
away everything. He also took away all the shields of gold which
Solomon had made; 27 and King Rĕhŏbō'ám made in their stead
shields of bronze, and committed them to the hands of the officers
of the guard, who kept the door of the king's house. 28And as often
as the king went into the house of the LORD, the guard bore them
and brought them back to the guardroom.

c. Death of Rehoboam

29 Now the rest of the acts of Rĕhŏbō'ám, and all that he did,
are they not written in the Book of the Chronicles of the Kings
of Judah? 30And there was war between Rĕhŏbō'ám and Jĕrŏbō'ám
continually. 31And Rĕhŏbō'ám slept with his fathers and was buried with his fathers in the city of David. His mother's name was
Nā'ámáh the Ămmŏnīt'ĕss. And Ăbī'jám his son reigned in his
stead.

2. Abijam, king of Judah

15 Now in the eighteenth year of King Jĕrŏbō'ám the son of
Nĕbăt, Ăbī'jám began to reign over Judah. 2 He reigned
for three years in Jerusalem. His mother's name was Mā'ácáh the
daughter of Ăbĭsh'álŏm. 3And he walked in all the sins which his
father did before him; and his heart was not wholly true to the
LORD his God, as the heart of David his father. 4 Nevertheless for
David's sake the LORD his God gave him a lamp in Jerusalem,
setting up his son after him, and establishing Jerusalem; 5 because
David did what was right in the eyes of the LORD, and did not turn
aside from anything that he commanded him all the days of his
life, except in the matter of Ūrī'áh the Hĭttīte. 6 Now there was
war between Rĕhŏbō'ám and Jĕrŏbō'ám all the days of his life.

Marginal references:

14.21
2 Chr 12.13;
1 Ki 11.32, 36;
ver 31

14.22
2 Chr 12.1;
Deut 32.21

14.23
Deut 12.2;
Ezek 16.24, 25;
2 Ki 17.9, 10;
Isa 57.5

14.24
Deut 23.17;
1 Ki 15.12;
2 Ki 23.7

14.25
1 Ki 11.40;
2 Chr 12.2, 9–11

14.26
1 Ki 15.18;
10.17

14.29
2 Chr 12.15

14.30
1 Ki 12.21–24; 15.6

14.31
2 Chr 12.16;
ver 21

15.1
2 Chr 13.1,2

15.3
1 Ki 11.4

15.4
1 Ki 11.36;
2 Chr 21.7

15.5
1 Ki 14.8;
2 Sam 11.4, 15–17; 12.9

15.6
1 Ki 14.30

7 The rest of the acts of Ăbī′jăm, and all that he did, are they not written in the Book of the Chronicles of the Kings of Judah? And there was war between Abijam and Jĕrŏbō′ăm. 8And Ăbī′jăm slept with his fathers; and they buried him in the city of David. And Āsă his son reigned in his stead.

3. Asa, king of Judah
a. The reforms of Asa

9 In the twentieth year of Jĕrŏbō′ăm king of Israel Āsă began to reign over Judah, 10 and he reigned forty-one years in Jerusalem. His mother's name was Mā′ăcäh the daughter of Ăbĭsh′-ălŏm. 11And Āsă did what was right in the eyes of the LORD, as David his father had done. 12 He put away the male cult prostitutes out of the land, and removed all the idols that his fathers had made. 13 He also removed Mā′ăcäh his mother from being queen mother because she had an abominable image made for Ăshē′räh; and Āsă cut down her image and burned it at the brook Kĭdrŏn. 14 But the high places were not taken away. Nevertheless the heart of Āsă was wholly true to the LORD all his days. 15And he brought into the house of the LORD the votive gifts of his father and his own votive gifts, silver, and gold, and vessels.

b. War between Asa and Baasha; death of Asa

16 And there was war between Āsă and Bā′ăshă king of Israel all their days. 17 Bā′ăshă king of Israel went up against Judah, and built Rāmăh, that he might permit no one to go out or come in to Āsă king of Judah. 18 Then Āsă took all the silver and the gold that were left in the treasures of the house of the LORD and the treasures of the king's house, and gave them into the hands of his servants; and King Asa sent them to Bĕn-hā′dăd the son of Tăbrĭm′mŏn, the son of Hĕz′ĭ-ŏn, king of Syria, who dwelt in Damascus, saying, 19 "Let there be a league between me and you, as between my father and your father: behold, I am sending to you a present of silver and gold; go, break your league with Bā′ăshă king of Israel, that he may withdraw from me." 20And Bĕn-hā′dăd hearkened to King Āsă, and sent the commanders of his armies against the cities of Israel, and conquered Ĭjŏn, Dan, Ā′bĕl-bĕth-mā′ăcäh, and all Chĭn′nĕrŏth, with all the land of Năph′tălī. 21And when Bā′ăshă heard of it, he stopped building Rāmăh, and he dwelt in Tĭrzăh. 22 Then King Āsă made a proclamation to all Judah, none was exempt, and they carried away the stones of Rāmăh and its timber, with which Bā′ăshă had been building; and with them King Asa built Gēbă of Benjamin and Mĭzpăh. 23 Now the rest of all the acts of Āsă, all his might, and all that he did, and the cities which he built, are they not written in the Book of the Chronicles of the Kings of Judah? But in his old age he was diseased in his feet. 24And Āsă slept with his fathers, and was buried with his fathers in the city of David his father; and Jĕhŏsh′ăphăt his son reigned in his stead.

Cross-references (right margin):

15.7 / 2 Chr 13.2, 3,22
15.8 / 2 Chr 14.1
15.10 / ver 2
15.11 / 2 Chr 14.2
15.12 / 1 Ki 14.24; 22.46
15.13 / 2 Chr 15.16–18; Ex 32.20
15.14 / 1 Ki 22.43; 2 Chr 15.17, 18; ver 3
15.15 / 1 Ki 7.51
15.16 / ver 32
15.17 / 2 Chr 16.1ff; Josh 18.25; 1 Ki 12.27
*15.18 / ver 15; 2 Chr 16.2; 1 Ki 11.23, 24
15.20 / 2 Ki 15.29; Judg 18.29; 2 Sam 20.14
15.22 / 2 Chr 16.6; Josh 21.17
15.23 / 2 Chr 16.11–14
15.24 / 2 Chr 17.1

15.18 Scripture mentions three kings of Damascus, all of whose names were Ben-hadad. The first Ben-hadad is mentioned here. The second one was his son, Ben-hadad II, who warred against Ahab and unsuccessfully sieged Samaria. He was defeated by Ahab at Aphek, and was smothered by Hazael who seized the crown. Accounts of his life may be found in 1 Ki 20 and 2 Ki 7, 8. The third Ben-hadad was the son of Hazael and is mentioned in 2 Ki 13.24. It was this last Ben-hadad who lost his father's Israelite conquests.

E. *The immediate successors to Jeroboam in the Northern Kingdom*

1. *Nadab*

25 Nādăb the son of Jĕrŏbō′ăm began to reign over Israel in the second year of Āsă king of Judah; and he reigned over Israel two years. 26 He did what was evil in the sight of the LORD, and walked in the way of his father, and in his sin which he made Israel to sin.

27 Bā′ăshă the son of Ăhī′jăh, of the house of Ĭs′săchar, conspired against him; and Baasha struck him down at Gĭb′bĕthŏn, which belonged to the Phĭlĭs′tĭneṣ; for Nādăb and all Israel were laying siege to Gibbethon. 28 So Bā′ăshă killed him in the third year of Āsă king of Judah, and reigned in his stead. 29And as soon as he was king, he killed all the house of Jĕrŏbō′ăm; he left to the house of Jeroboam not one that breathed, until he had destroyed it, according to the word of the LORD which he spoke by his servant Ăhī′jăh the Shī′lŏnīte; 30 it was for the sins of Jĕrŏbō′ăm which he sinned and which he made Israel to sin, and because of the anger to which he provoked the LORD, the God of Israel.

31 Now the rest of the acts of Nādăb, and all that he did, are they not written in the Book of the Chronicles of the Kings of Israel? 32And there was war between Āsă and Bā′ăshă king of Israel all their days.

2. *Baasha*

33 In the third year of Āsă king of Judah, Bā′ăshă the son of Ăhī′jăh began to reign over all Israel at Tĭrzăh, and reigned twenty-four years. 34 He did what was evil in the sight of the LORD, and walked in the way of Jĕrŏbō′ăm and in his sin which he made Israel to sin.

16 And the word of the LORD came to Jēhū the son of Hănā′nī against Bā′ăshă, saying, 2 "Since I exalted you out of the dust and made you leader over my people Israel, and you have walked in the way of Jĕrŏbō′ăm, and have made my people Israel to sin, provoking me to anger with their sins, 3 behold, I will utterly sweep away Bā′ăshă and his house, and I will make your house like the house of Jĕrŏbō′ăm the son of Nēbăt. 4Any one belonging to Bā′ăshă who dies in the city the dogs shall eat; and any one of his who dies in the field the birds of the air shall eat."

5 Now the rest of the acts of Bā′ăshă, and what he did, and his might, are they not written in the Book of the Chronicles of the Kings of Israel? 6And Bā′ăshă slept with his fathers, and was buried at Tĭrzăh; and Ēlăh his son reigned in his stead. 7 Moreover the word of the LORD came by the prophet Jēhū the son of Hănā′nī against Bā′ăshă and his house, both because of all the evil that he did in the sight of the LORD, provoking him to anger with the work of his hands, in being like the house of Jĕrŏbō′ăm, and also because he destroyed it.

3. *Elah*

8 In the twenty-sixth year of Āsă king of Judah, Ēlăh the son of Bā′ăshă began to reign over Israel in Tĭrzăh, and reigned two years. 9 But his servant Zĭmrī, commander of half his chariots,

15.25
1 Ki 14.20

15.26
1 Ki 12.30;
14.16

15.27
1 Ki 14.14;
Josh 19.44;
21.23

15.29
1 Ki 14.10,
14

15.30
1 Ki 14.9,16

15.31
ver 16

15.34
1 Ki 12.28,
29; 13.33;
14.16

16.1
ver 7;
2 Chr 19.2;
20.34

16.2
1 Ki 14.7;
15.34

16.3
ver 11;
1 Ki 14.10;
15.29

16.4
1 Ki 14.11

16.5
1 Ki 14.19;
15.31

16.6
1 Ki 14.17;
15.21

16.7
ver 1;
1 Ki 15.27,
29

16.9
2 Ki 9.30–
33

conspired against him. When he was at Tirzah, drinking himself drunk in the house of Arza, who was over the household in Tirzah, 10 Zimri came in and struck him down and killed him, in the twenty-seventh year of Asa king of Judah, and reigned in his stead.

4. Zimri

11 When he began to reign, as soon as he had seated himself on his throne, he killed all the house of Ba'asha; he did not leave him a single male of his kinsmen or his friends. 12 Thus Zimri destroyed all the house of Ba'asha, according to the word of the LORD, which he spoke against Baasha by Jehu the prophet, 13 for all the sins of Ba'asha and the sins of Elah his son which they sinned, and which they made Israel to sin, provoking the LORD God of Israel to anger with their idols. 14 Now the rest of the acts of Elah, and all that he did, are they not written in the Book of the Chronicles of the Kings of Israel?

15 In the twenty-seventh year of Asa king of Judah, Zimri reigned seven days in Tirzah. Now the troops were encamped against Gib'bethon, which belonged to the Philis'tines, 16 and the troops who were encamped heard it said, "Zimri has conspired, and he has killed the king"; therefore all Israel made Omri, the commander of the army, king over Israel that day in the camp. 17 So Omri went up from Gib'bethon, and all Israel with him, and they besieged Tirzah. 18 And when Zimri saw that the city was taken, he went into the citadel of the king's house, and burned the king's house over him with fire, and died, 19 because of his sins which he committed, doing evil in the sight of the LORD, walking in the way of Jerobo'am, and for his sin which he committed, making Israel to sin. 20 Now the rest of the acts of Zimri, and the conspiracy which he made, are they not written in the Book of the Chronicles of the Kings of Israel?

5. Omri

21 Then the people of Israel were divided into two parts; half of the people followed Tibni the son of Ginath, to make him king, and half followed Omri. 22 But the people who followed Omri overcame the people who followed Tibni the son of Ginath; so Tibni died, and Omri became king. 23 In the thirty-first year of Asa king of Judah, Omri began to reign over Israel, and reigned for twelve years; six years he reigned in Tirzah. 24 He bought the hill of Samar'ia from Shemer for two talents of silver; and he fortified the hill, and called the name of the city which he built, Samaria, after the name of Shemer, the owner of the hill.

25 Omri did what was evil in the sight of the LORD, and did more evil than all who were before him. 26 For he walked in all the way of Jerobo'am the son of Nebat, and in the sins which he made Israel to sin, provoking the LORD, the God of Israel, to anger by their idols. 27 Now the rest of the acts of Omri which he did, and the might that he showed, are they not written in the Book of the

16.12
ver 3;
2 Chr 19.2;
20.34
16.13
Deut 32.21;
1 Sam
12.21;
Isa 41.29
16.14
ver 5

16.15
1 Ki 15.27

16.18
1 Sam 31.4,
5;
2 Sam 17.23
16.19
1 Ki 12.28;
15.26,34
16.20
ver 5,14,27

16.23
1 Ki 15.21
*16.24
1 Ki 13.32;
Jn 4.4

16.26
Mic 6.16;
ver 19

16.24 *Samaria.* The new capital was remarkably well built. While Omri was very wicked and his activities are mentioned in just six verses (23–28), he was a very important person from the secular point of view, and for about a century the Assyrians designated the land of Israel as the House of Omri. (See Mic 6.16 for testimony to his importance.)

Chronicles of the Kings of Israel? 28And Ŏmrī slept with his fathers, and was buried in Sàmạr'ïà; and Āhāb his son reigned in his stead.

F. Ahab of Israel and Elijah the prophet

1. Ahab of Israel and Jezebel his wife

29 In the thirty-eighth year of Āsà king of Judah, Āhāb the son of Ŏmrī began to reign over Israel, and Ahab the son of Ŏmrī reigned over Israel in Sàmạr'ïà twenty-two years. 30And Āhāb the son of Ŏmrī did evil in the sight of the LORD more than all that were before him. 31And as if it had been a light thing for him to walk in the sins of Jĕrŏbō'ầm the son of Nēbăt, he took for wife Jĕz'ĕbĕl the daughter of Ĕthbā'ál king of the Sīdō'nïànṣ, and went and served Bāál, and worshiped him. 32 He erected an altar for Bāál in the house of Baal, which he built in Sàmạr'ïà. 33And Āhāb made an Ashē'rah. Ahab did more to provoke the LORD, the God of Israel, to anger than all the kings of Israel who were before him. 34 In his days Hĩel of Bĕthĕl built Jĕr'ĭchō; he laid its foundation at the cost of Ábĩ'rầm his first-born, and set up its gates at the cost of his youngest son Sĕgub, according to the word of the LORD, which he spoke by Joshua the son of Nún.

2. Elijah fed
a. The ravens at Cherith

17 Now Ĕlī'jäh the Tĩshbīte, of Tĩshbën in Gĩl'ëầd, said to Āhāb, "As the LORD the God of Israel lives, before whom I stand, there shall be neither dew nor rain these years, except by my word." 2And the word of the LORD came to him, 3 "Depart from here and turn eastward, and hide yourself by the brook Chĕrïth, that is east of the Jordan. 4 You shall drink from the brook, and I have commanded the ravens to feed you there." 5 So he went and did according to the word of the LORD; he went and dwelt by the brook Chĕrïth that is east of the Jordan. 6And the ravens brought him bread and meat in the morning, and bread and meat in the evening; and he drank from the brook. 7And after a while the brook dried up, because there was no rain in the land.

b. The widow at Zarephath

8 Then the word of the LORD came to him, 9 "Arise, go to Zạr'ĕpháth, which belongs to Sĩdòn, and dwell there. Behold, I have commanded a widow there to feed you." 10 So he arose and went to Zạr'ĕpháth; and when he came to the gate of the city, behold, a widow was there gathering sticks; and he called to her and said, "Bring me a little water in a vessel, that I may drink." 11And as she was going to bring it, he called to her and said, "Bring me a morsel of bread in your hand." 12And she said, "As the LORD your God lives, I have nothing baked, only a handful of meal in a jar, and a little oil in a cruse; and now, I am gathering a couple of sticks, that I may go in and prepare it for myself and

n Gk: Heb *of the settlers*

Marginal references:

16.30
ver 25;
1 Ki 14.9
*16.31
Deut 7.3;
2 Ki 10.18;
17.16
16.32
2 Ki 10.21,
26,27
16.33
2 Ki 13.6;
ver 29,30
*16.34
Josh 6.26

17.1
2 Ki 3.14;
Deut 10.8;
1 Ki 18.1;
Jas 5.17;
Lk 4.25

17.9
Obad 20;
Lk 4.26

17.12
ver 1;
2 Ki 4.2–7

16.31 Ahab's marriage alliance with Jezebel led to official support for the immoral Baal worship fanatically practiced by his wife. **16.34** This was the curse of Joshua (6.26).

my son, that we may eat it, and die." ¹³And Ēlī′jáh said to her, "Fear not; go and do as you have said; but first make me a little cake of it and bring it to me, and afterward make for yourself and your son. ¹⁴ For thus says the LORD the God of Israel, 'The jar of meal shall not be spent, and the cruse of oil shall not fail, until the day that the LORD sends rain upon the earth.' " ¹⁵And she went and did as Ēlī′jáh said; and she, and he, and her household ate for many days. ¹⁶ The jar of meal was not spent, neither did the cruse of oil fail, according to the word of the LORD which he spoke by Ēlī′jáh.

17.14
Lk 4.25,26

*17.16

c. The widow's dead son brought to life

17 After this the son of the woman, the mistress of the house, became ill; and his illness was so severe that there was no breath left in him. ¹⁸And she said to Ēlī′jáh, "What have you against me, O man of God? You have come to me to bring my sin to remembrance, and to cause the death of my son!" ¹⁹And he said to her, "Give me your son." And he took him from her bosom, and carried him up into the upper chamber, where he lodged, and laid him upon his own bed. ²⁰And he cried to the LORD, "O LORD my God, hast thou brought calamity even upon the widow with whom I sojourn, by slaying her son?" ²¹ Then he stretched himself upon the child three times, and cried to the LORD, "O LORD my God, let this child's soul come into him again." ²²And the LORD hearkened to the voice of Ēlī′jáh; and the soul of the child came into him again, and he revived. ²³And Ēlī′jáh took the child, and brought him down from the upper chamber into the house, and delivered him to his mother; and Elijah said, "See, your son lives." ²⁴And the woman said to Ēlī′jáh, "Now I know that you are a man of God, and that the word of the LORD in your mouth is truth."

17.18
2 Ki 3.13

17.21
2 Ki 4.34, 35;
see Acts 20.10
17.22
Heb 11.25

17.24
Jn 3.2;
16.30

3. Elijah at Mount Carmel
a. Obadiah seeks water

18 After many days the word of the LORD came to Ēlī′jáh, in the third year, saying, "Go, show yourself to Āhăb; and I will send rain upon the earth." ² So Ēlī′jáh went to show himself to Āhăb. Now the famine was severe in Sàmar′ĭà. ³And Āhăb called Ōbàdī′áh, who was over the household. (Now Obadiah revered the LORD greatly; ⁴ and when Jĕz′ébèl cut off the prophets of the LORD, Ōbàdī′áh took a hundred prophets and hid them by fifties in a cave, and fed them with bread and water.) ⁵And Āhăb said to Ōbàdī′áh, "Go through the land to all the springs of water and to all the valleys; perhaps we may find grass and save the horses and mules alive, and not lose some of the animals." ⁶ So they divided the land between them to pass through it; Āhăb went

18.1
1 Ki 17.1;
Lk 4.25;
Jas 5.17

18.4
ver 13

17.16 More miracles were performed by Elijah and Elisha than any other two men after Israel came into the land. According to the Scriptural record, Elijah performed five, and Elisha no less than twelve miracles. The total number of miracles recorded in the Old Testament is small when balanced against the number of years over which they were performed. It is to be observed that they were granted by God only at times of major national crisis, especially: (1) at the time of Israel's deliverance from Egypt and their establishment in the Promised Land (Ex 7.10–12; 7.20; 8.6; 14.21; Josh 3.15–17); (2) about the middle of the ninth century when the kingdom of Israel was at the crossroads of decision (18.25ff; 2 Ki 5.1ff; 7.1ff); (3) during the Babylonian exile when the survival of the nation was at stake (Dan 3.19–27; 6.16–23).

in one direction by himself, and Ōbádī'áh went in another direction by himself.

b. *Elijah and Obadiah meet*

18.7
2 Ki 1.6–8

7 And as Ōbádī'áh was on the way, behold, Ēlī'jáh met him; and Obadiah recognized him, and fell on his face, and said, "Is it you, my lord Elijah?" 8And he answered him, "It is I. Go, tell your lord, 'Behold, Ēlī'jáh is here.' " 9And he said, "Wherein have I sinned, that you would give your servant into the hand of Ahǎb, to kill me?

18.10
1 Ki 17.1

10As the LORD your God lives, there is no nation or kingdom whither my lord has not sent to seek you; and when they would say, 'He is not here,' he would take an oath of the kingdom or nation, that they had not found you. 11And now you say, 'Go, tell your lord, "Behold, Ēlī'jáh is here." '

18.12
2 Ki 2.16;
Ezek 3.12,
14;
Acts 8.39

12And as soon as I have gone from you, the Spirit of the LORD will carry you whither I know not; and so, when I come and tell Āhǎb and he cannot find you, he will kill me, although I your servant have revered the LORD from my youth.

18.13
ver 4

13 Has it not been told my lord what I did when Jěz'ébél killed the prophets of the LORD, how I hid a hundred men of the LORD's prophets by fifties in a cave, and fed them with bread and water? 14And now you say, 'Go, tell your lord, "Behold, Ēlī'jáh is here" '; and he will kill me."

18.15
1 Ki 17.1

15And Ēlī'jáh said, "As the LORD of hosts lives, before whom I stand, I will surely show myself to him today." 16 So Ōbádī'áh went to meet Āhǎb, and told him; and Ahab went to meet Ēlī'jáh.

c. *Ahab and Elijah meet*

18.17
1 Ki 21.20;
Josh 7.25;
Acts 16.20

17 When Āhǎb saw Ēlī'jáh, Ahab said to him, "Is it you, you troubler of Israel?"

18.18
2 Chr 15.2;
1 Ki 16.31;
21.25,26

18And he answered, "I have not troubled Israel; but you have, and your father's house, because you have forsaken the commandments of the LORD and followed the Bāǎls.

✶18.19
Josh 19.26;
1 Ki 16.33

19 Now therefore send and gather all Israel to me at Mount Carmèl, and the four hundred and fifty prophets of Bāǎl and the four hundred prophets of Ashē'ráh, who eat at Jěz'ébél's table."

d. *The priests of Baal fail*

20 So Āhǎb sent to all the people of Israel, and gathered the prophets together at Mount Carmèl.

18.21
2 Ki 17.41;
Mt 6.24;
Josh 24.15

21And Ēlī'jáh came near to all the people, and said, "How long will you go limping with two different opinions? If the LORD is God, follow him; but if Bāǎl, then follow him." And the people did not answer him a word.

18.22
1 Ki 19.10,
14;
ver 19

22 Then Ēlī'jáh said to the people, "I, even I only, am left a prophet of the LORD; but Bāǎl's prophets are four hundred and fifty men. 23 Let two bulls be given to us; and let them choose one bull for themselves, and cut it in pieces and lay it on the wood, but put no fire to it; and I will prepare the other bull and lay it on the wood, and put no fire to it.

18.24
ver 38;
see 1 Chr
21.26;
Acts 20.10

24And you call on the name of your god and I will call on the name of the LORD; and the God who answers by fire, he is God." And all the people answered, "It is well spoken."

18.26
Ps 115.5;
Jer 10.5;
1 Cor 8.4;
12.2

25 Then Ēlī'jáh said to the prophets of Bāǎl, "Choose for yourselves one bull and prepare it first, for you are many; and call on the name of your god, but put no fire to it." 26And they took

---

18.19 The *four hundred prophets of Asherah* do not appear in the rest of the story. (For more information on Asherah, see note to Ex 34.13 on *Asherim*.)

the bull which was given them, and they prepared it, and called on the name of Bāál from morning until noon, saying, "O Baal, answer us!" But there was no voice, and no one answered. And they limped about the altar which they had made. 27And at noon Ēlī'jāh mocked them, saying, "Cry aloud, for he is a god; either he is musing, or he has gone aside, or he is on a journey, or perhaps he is asleep and must be awakened." 28And they cried aloud, and cut themselves after their custom with swords and lances, until the blood gushed out upon them. 29And as midday passed, they raved on until the time of the offering of the oblation, but there was no voice; no one answered, no one heeded.

e. Elijah's sacrifice burns: fire from heaven

30 Then Ēlī'jāh said to all the people, "Come near to me"; and all the people came near to him. And he repaired the altar of the LORD that had been thrown down; 31 Ēlī'jāh took twelve stones, according to the number of the tribes of the sons of Jacob, to whom the word of the LORD came, saying, "Israel shall be your name"; 32 and with the stones he built an altar in the name of the LORD. And he made a trench about the altar, as great as would contain two measures of seed. 33And he put the wood in order, and cut the bull in pieces and laid it on the wood. And he said, "Fill four jars with water, and pour it on the burnt offering, and on the wood." 34And he said, "Do it a second time"; and they did it a second time. And he said, "Do it a third time"; and they did it a third time. 35And the water ran round about the altar, and filled the trench also with water.

36 And at the time of the offering of the oblation, Ēlī'jāh the prophet came near and said, "O LORD, God of Abraham, Isaac, and Israel, let it be known this day that thou art God in Israel, and that I am thy servant, and that I have done all these things at thy word. 37Answer me, O LORD, answer me, that this people may know that thou, O LORD, art God, and that thou hast turned their hearts back." 38 Then the fire of the LORD fell, and consumed the burnt offering, and the wood, and the stones, and the dust, and licked up the water that was in the trench. 39And when all the people saw it, they fell on their faces; and they said, "The LORD, he is God; the LORD, he is God." 40And Ēlī'jāh said to them, "Seize the prophets of Bāál; let not one of them escape." And they seized them; and Elijah brought them down to the brook Kīshòn, and killed them there.

f. The coming of the rain

41 And Ēlī'jāh said to Āhǎb, "Go up, eat and drink; for there is a sound of the rushing of rain." 42 So Āhǎb went up to eat and to drink. And Ēlī'jāh went up to the top of Carmėl; and he bowed himself down upon the earth, and put his face between his knees. 43And he said to his servant, "Go up now, look toward the sea." And he went up and looked, and said, "There is nothing." And he said, "Go again seven times." 44And at the seventh time he said, "Behold, a little cloud like a man's hand is rising out of the sea." And he said, "Go up, say to Āhǎb, 'Prepare your chariot and go down, lest the rain stop you.'" 45And in a little while the heavens grew black with clouds and wind, and there was a great rain. And Āhǎb rode and went to Jėzreėl'. 46And the hand of the

18.28 Lev 19.28; Deut 14.1
18.29 ver 26
18.30 1 Ki 19.10, 14
18.31 Gen 32.28; 35.10; 2 Ki 17.34
18.32 Col 3.17
18.33 Gen 22.9; Lev 1.6–8
18.36 Ex 3.6; 1 Ki 8.43; 2 Ki 19.19; Num 16.28
18.38 Lev 9.24; 1 Chr 21.26; 2 Chr 7.1
18.39 ver 21,24
18.40 Deut 13.5; 18.20; 2 Ki 10.24, 25
18.42 ver 19,20; Jas 5.17,18
18.46 2 Ki 3.15; 4.29

LORD was on Ēlī'jäh; and he girded up his loins and ran before
Āhăb to the entrance of Jĕzreēl'.

4. Elijah goes to Horeb
a. Jezebel's intention

19.1
1 Ki 18.40
19.2
1 Ki 20.10;
2 Ki 6.31

19 Āhăb told Jĕz'ĕbĕl all that Ēlī'jäh had done, and how he
had slain all the prophets with the sword. 2 Then Jĕz'ĕbĕl
sent a messenger to Ēlī'jäh, saying, "So may the gods do to me,
and more also, if I do not make your life as the life of one of them
by this time tomorrow." 3 Then he was afraid, and he arose and
went for his life, and came to Beër-shē'bá, which belongs to
Judah, and left his servant there.

b. Elijah's flight

19.4
Num 11.15;
Jon 4.3,8

4 But he himself went a day's journey into the wilderness, and
came and sat down under a broom tree; and he asked that he
might die, saying, "It is enough; now, O LORD, take away my life;
for I am no better than my fathers." 5And he lay down and slept
under a broom tree; and behold, an angel touched him, and said to
him, "Arise and eat." 6And he looked, and behold, there was at his
head a cake baked on hot stones and a jar of water. And he ate and
drank, and lay down again. 7And the angel of the LORD came again
a second time, and touched him, and said, "Arise and eat, else the
journey will be too great for you." 8And he arose, and ate and
drank, and went in the strength of that food forty days and forty
nights to Horĕb the mount of God.

*19.8
Ex 34.28;
Deut 9.9–
11,18;
Mt 4.2;
Ex 3.1

c. God meets with Elijah

19.10
Rom 11.3;
1 Ki 18.4,22

9 And there he came to a cave, and lodged there; and behold,
the word of the LORD came to him, and he said to him, "What are
you doing here, Ēlī'jäh?" 10 He said, "I have been very jealous for
the LORD, the God of hosts; for the people of Israel have forsaken
thy covenant, thrown down thy altars, and slain thy prophets with
the sword; and I, even I only, am left; and they seek my life, to
take it away." 11And he said, "Go forth, and stand upon the mount

19.11
Ex 24.12;
Ezek 1.4;
37.7

before the LORD." And behold, the LORD passed by, and a great
and strong wind rent the mountains, and broke in pieces the rocks
before the LORD, but the LORD was not in the wind; and after the
wind an earthquake, but the LORD was not in the earthquake;
12 and after the earthquake a fire, but the LORD was not in the fire;
and after the fire a still small voice. 13And when Ēlī'jäh heard it,
he wrapped his face in his mantle and went out and stood at
the entrance of the cave. And behold, there came a voice to him,

19.13
Ex 3.6;
ver 9

and said, "What are you doing here, Elijah?" 14 He said, "I have
been very jealous for the LORD, the God of hosts; for the people of
Israel have forsaken thy covenant, thrown down thy altars, and
slain thy prophets with the sword; and I, even I only, am left; and
they seek my life, to take it away." 15And the LORD said to him,
"Go, return on your way to the wilderness of Damascus; and when
you arrive, you shall anoint Hăz'ä'ĕl to be king over Syria; 16 and

19.14
ver 10
19.15
2 Ki 8.12,13

19.16
2 Ki 9.1–3;
ver 19–21;
2 Ki 2.9,15

Jĕhū the son of Nĭmshī you shall anoint to be king over Israel; and
Ēlī'shă the son of Shāphăt of Ā'bĕl-mĕhō'läh you shall anoint to be

---

19.8 Horeb, Mt. Sinai. Apparently Elijah   order to be renewed by the God of Israel who
went to this sacred spot in his despondency in   spoke to Moses.

prophet in your place. [17]And him who escapes from the sword of Hăz´áēl shall Jēhū slay; and him who escapes from the sword of Jehu shall Ēlī´shá slay. [18] Yet I will leave seven thousand in Israel, all the knees that have not bowed to Bāál, and every mouth that has not kissed him."

d. Elijah casts his mantle on Elisha

19 So he departed from there, and found Ēlī´shá the son of Shāphăt, who was plowing, with twelve yoke of oxen before him, and he was with the twelfth. Ēlī´jáh passed by him and cast his mantle upon him. [20]And he left the oxen, and ran after Ēlī´jáh, and said, "Let me kiss my father and my mother, and then I will follow you." And he said to him, "Go back again; for what have I done to you?" [21]And he returned from following him, and took the yoke of oxen, and slew them, and boiled their flesh with the yokes of the oxen, and gave it to the people, and they ate. Then he arose and went after Ēlī´jáh, and ministered to him.

5. Ahab's first Syrian campaign
a. Ben-hadad's demands

20 Bĕn-hā´dăd the king of Syria gathered all his army together; thirty-two kings were with him, and horses and chariots; and he went up and besieged Sámăr´ïă, and fought against it. [2]And he sent messengers into the city to Āhăb king of Israel, and said to him, "Thus says Bĕn-hā´dăd: [3] 'Your silver and your gold are mine; your fairest wives and children also are mine.' " [4]And the king of Israel answered, "As you say, my lord, O king, I am yours, and all that I have." [5] The messengers came again, and said, "Thus says Bĕn-hā´dăd: 'I sent to you, saying, "Deliver to me your silver and your gold, your wives and your children"; [6] nevertheless I will send my servants to you tomorrow about this time, and they shall search your house and the houses of your servants, and lay hands on whatever pleases them,[o] and take it away.' "

b. Ahab's reply

7 Then the king of Israel called all the elders of the land, and said, "Mark, now, and see how this man is seeking trouble; for he sent to me for my wives and my children, and for my silver and my gold, and I did not refuse him." [8]And all the elders and all the people said to him, "Do not heed or consent." [9] So he said to the messengers of Bĕn-hā´dăd, "Tell my lord the king, 'All that you first demanded of your servant I will do; but this thing I cannot do.' " And the messengers departed and brought him word again. [10] Bĕn-hā´dăd sent to him and said, "The gods do so to me, and more also, if the dust of Sámăr´ïă shall suffice for handfuls for all the people who follow me." [11]And the king of Israel answered, "Tell him, 'Let not him that girds on his armor boast himself as he that puts it off.' " [12] When Bĕn-hā´dăd heard this message as he was drinking with the kings in the booths, he said to his men, "Take your positions." And they took their positions against the city.

o Gk Syr Vg: Heb you

19.17
2 Ki 8.12;
9.14ff;
13.3,22
*19.18
Rom 11.4;
Hos 13.2

19.19
2 Ki 2.8,13

19.20
Mt 8.21,22;
Lk 9.61,62

19.21
2 Sam 24.22

20.1
1 Ki 15.18,
20;
2 Ki 6.24;
1 Ki 22.31;
2 Ki 6.24–
29

20.7
2 Ki 5.7

20.10
1 Ki 19.2
20.11
Prov 27.1
20.12
ver 16

19.18 *seven thousand in Israel.* Notwithstanding Elijah's pessimism "*. . . even I only,* *am left . . .*" (18.22) God has his remnant in Israel.

c. *God's promise of victory*

20.13
ver 28

13 And behold, a prophet came near to Āhăb king of Israel and said, "Thus says the LORD, Have you seen all this great multitude? Behold, I will give it into your hand this day; and you shall know that I am the LORD." 14And Āhăb said, "By whom?" He said, "Thus says the LORD, By the servants of the governors of the districts." Then he said, "Who shall begin the battle?" He answered, "You." 15 Then he mustered the servants of the governors of the districts, and they were two hundred and thirty-two; and after them he mustered all the people of Israel, seven thousand.

d. *Ahab's victory*

20.16
ver 12

16 And they went out at noon, while Běn-hā′dăd was drinking himself drunk in the booths, he and the thirty-two kings who helped him. 17 The servants of the governors of the districts went out first. And Běn-hā′dăd sent out scouts, and they reported to him, "Men are coming out from Sàmạr′ïà." 18 He said, "If they have come out for peace, take them alive; or if they have come out for war, take them alive."

20.18
2 Ki 14.8–
12

19 So these went out of the city, the servants of the governors of the districts, and the army which followed them. 20And each killed his man; the Syrians fled and Israel pursued them, but Běn-hā′dăd king of Syria escaped on a horse with horsemen. 21And the king of Israel went out, and captured*p* the horses and chariots, and killed the Syrians with a great slaughter.

e. *A second invasion prophesied*

20.22
ver 13,26;
2 Sam 11.1

22 Then the prophet came near to the king of Israel, and said to him, "Come, strengthen yourself, and consider well what you have to do; for in the spring the king of Syria will come up against you."

6. *Ahab's second Syrian campaign*
a. *Ben-hadad defeated*

*20.23
1 Ki 14.23

23 And the servants of the king of Syria said to him, "Their gods are gods of the hills, and so they were stronger than we; but let us fight against them in the plain, and surely we shall be stronger than they. 24And do this: remove the kings, each from his post, and put commanders in their places; 25 and muster an army like the army that you have lost, horse for horse, and chariot for chariot; then we will fight against them in the plain, and surely we shall be stronger than they." And he hearkened to their voice, and did so.

*20.26
ver 22;
2 Ki 13.7

26 In the spring Běn-hā′dăd mustered the Syrians, and went up to Āphěk, to fight against Israel. 27And the people of Israel were mustered, and were provisioned, and went against them; the people of Israel encamped before them like two little flocks of goats, but the Syrians filled the country. 28And a man of God came near and said to the king of Israel, "Thus says the LORD, 'Because the Syrians have said, "The LORD is a god of the hills but he is not a god of the valleys," therefore I will give all this

20.28
ver 13

p Gk: Heb *smote*

20.23 See note to Judg 1.19.   **20.26** *Aphek*, city in Bashan.

great multitude into your hand, and you shall know that I am the LORD.' " 29And they encamped opposite one another seven days. Then on the seventh day the battle was joined; and the people of Israel smote of the Syrians a hundred thousand foot soldiers in one day. 30And the rest fled into the city of Āphĕk; and the wall fell upon twenty-seven thousand men that were left.

20.30
ver 26;
1 Ki 22.25;
2 Chr 18.24

b. Ahab spares Ben-hadad

Bĕn-hā´dăd also fled, and entered an inner chamber in the city. 31And his servants said to him, "Behold now, we have heard that the kings of the house of Israel are merciful kings; let us put sackcloth on our loins and ropes upon our heads, and go out to the king of Israel; perhaps he will spare your life." 32 So they girded sackcloth on their loins, and put ropes on their heads, and went to the king of Israel and said, "Your servant Bĕn-hā´dăd says, 'Pray, let me live.' " And he said, "Does he still live? He is my brother." 33 Now the men were watching for an omen, and they quickly took it up from him and said, "Yes, your brother Bĕn-hā´dăd." Then he said, "Go and bring him." Then Ben-hadad came forth to him; and he caused him to come up into the chariot. 34And Bĕn-hā´dăd said to him, "The cities which my father took from your father I will restore; and you may establish bazaars for yourself in Damascus, as my father did in Sămạr´ĭă." And Āhăb said, "I will let you go on these terms." So he made a covenant with him and let him go.

20.31
Gen 37.34

20.32
ver 3-6

20.34
1 Ki 15.20

c. The judgment of God against Ahab
for sparing Ben-hadad

35 And a certain man of the sons of the prophets said to his fellow at the command of the LORD, "Strike me, I pray." But the man refused to strike him. 36 Then he said to him, "Because you have not obeyed the voice of the LORD, behold, as soon as you have gone from me, a lion shall kill you." And as soon as he had departed from him, a lion met him and killed him. 37 Then he found another man, and said, "Strike me, I pray." And the man struck him, smiting and wounding him. 38 So the prophet departed, and waited for the king by the way, disguising himself with a bandage over his eyes. 39And as the king passed, he cried to the king and said, "Your servant went out into the midst of the battle; and behold, a soldier turned and brought a man to me, and said, 'Keep this man; if by any means he be missing, your life shall be for his life, or else you shall pay a talent of silver.' 40And as your servant was busy here and there, he was gone." The king of Israel said to him, "So shall your judgment be; you yourself have decided it." 41 Then he made haste to take the bandage away from his eyes; and the king of Israel recognized him as one of the prophets. 42And he said to him, "Thus says the LORD, 'Because you have let go out of your hand the man whom I had devoted to destruction, therefore your life shall go for his life, and your people for his people.' "

20.35
2 Ki 2.3-7;
1 Ki 13.17,
18

20.36
1 Ki 13.24

20.39
2 Ki 10.24

*20.40

20.42
ver 39;
1 Ki 22.31-
37

20.40 God's prophet who rebuked Ahab for his sin of sparing Ben-hadad, used an illustration which has a spiritual relevance for every believer. Busyness is by itself no virtue; it may involve choosing the good in preference to the best. Believers are to be busy at work for God, but they are to seek His guidance in all things and to put first things first (Jas 4.15; Mt 6.10; Rom 1.10; 15.32; Acts 21.14; Deut 28.1ff; Ps 25.9; Jer 32.6-8; Mt 6.33).

43And the king of Israel went to his house resentful and sullen, and came to Sȧmạr'iȧ.

7. Naboth's vineyard
a. Ahab covets the vineyard

21 Now Nābŏth the Jĕz'reēlīte had a vineyard in Jĕzreēl', beside the palace of Ahȧb king of Sȧmạr'iȧ. 2And after this Āhȧb said to Nābŏth, "Give me your vineyard, that I may have it for a vegetable garden, because it is near my house; and I will give you a better vineyard for it; or, if it seems good to you, I will give you its value in money." 3 But Nābŏth said to Āhȧb, "The Lord forbid that I should give you the inheritance of my fathers." 4And Āhȧb went into his house vexed and sullen because of what Nābŏth the Jĕz'reēlīte had said to him; for he had said, "I will not give you the inheritance of my fathers." And he lay down on his bed, and turned away his face, and would eat no food.

b. Jezebel seizes the vineyard

5 But Jĕz'ėbėl his wife came to him, and said to him, "Why is your spirit so vexed that you eat no food?" 6And he said to her, "Because I spoke to Nābŏth the Jĕz'reēlīte, and said to him, 'Give me your vineyard for money; or else, if it please you, I will give you another vineyard for it'; and he answered, 'I will not give you my vineyard.'" 7And Jĕz'ėbėl his wife said to him, "Do you now govern Israel? Arise, and eat bread, and let your heart be cheerful; I will give you the vineyard of Nābŏth the Jĕz'reēlīte."

8 So she wrote letters in Āhȧb's name and sealed them with his seal, and she sent the letters to the elders and the nobles who dwelt with Nābŏth in his city. 9And she wrote in the letters, "Proclaim a fast, and set Nābŏth on high among the people; 10 and set two base fellows opposite him, and let them bring a charge against him, saying, 'You have cursed God and the king.' Then take him out, and stone him to death." 11And the men of his city, the elders and the nobles who dwelt in his city, did as Jĕz'ėbėl had sent word to them. As it was written in the letters which she had sent to them, 12 they proclaimed a fast, and set Nābŏth on high among the people. 13And the two base fellows came in and sat opposite him; and the base fellows brought a charge against Nābŏth, in the presence of the people, saying, "Naboth cursed God and the king." So they took him outside the city, and stoned him to death with stones. 14 Then they sent to Jĕz'ėbėl, saying, "Nābŏth has been stoned; he is dead."

15 As soon as Jĕz'ėbėl heard that Nābŏth had been stoned and was dead, Jezebel said to Āhȧb, "Arise, take possession of the vineyard of Naboth the Jĕz'reēlīte, which he refused to give you for money; for Naboth is not alive, but dead." 16And as soon as Āhȧb heard that Nābŏth was dead, Ahab arose to go down to the vineyard of Naboth the Jĕz'reēlīte, to take possession of it.

c. Elijah pronounces doom on Ahab and Jezebel

17 Then the word of the Lord came to Ëli'jȧh the Tīshbīte, saying, 18 "Arise, go down to meet Āhȧb king of Israel, who is in Sȧmạr'iȧ; behold, he is in the vineyard of Nābŏth, where he has gone to take possession. 19And you shall say to him, 'Thus says

the LORD, "Have you killed, and also taken possession?" ' And
you shall say to him, 'Thus says the LORD: "In the place where
dogs licked up the blood of Nābŏth shall dogs lick your own
blood." ' "

20 Āhăb said to Ēlī'jăh, "Have you found me, O my enemy?"
He answered, "I have found you, because you have sold yourself
to do what is evil in the sight of the LORD. 21 Behold, I will bring
evil upon you; I will utterly sweep you away, and will cut off from
Āhăb every male, bond or free, in Israel; 22 and I will make your
house like the house of Jĕrŏbŏ'ăm the son of Nēbăt, and like the
house of Bā'ăshă the son of Ăhī'jăh, for the anger to which you
have provoked me, and because you have made Israel to sin. 23And
of Jĕz'ĕbĕl the LORD also said, 'The dogs shall eat Jezebel within
the bounds of Jĕzreēl'.' 24Any one belonging to Āhăb who dies in
the city the dogs shall eat; and any one of his who dies in the open
country the birds of the air shall eat."

25 (There was none who sold himself to do what was evil in the
sight of the LORD like Āhăb, whom Jĕz'ĕbĕl his wife incited. 26 He
did very abominably in going after idols, as the Ăm'ŏrītes had
done, whom the LORD cast out before the people of Israel.)

d. Ahab's repentance

27 And when Āhăb heard those words, he rent his clothes, and
put sackcloth upon his flesh, and fasted and lay in sackcloth, and
went about dejectedly. 28And the word of the LORD came to Ēlī'jăh
the Tĭshbīte, saying, 29 "Have you seen how Āhăb has humbled
himself before me? Because he has humbled himself before me, I
will not bring the evil in his days; but in his son's days I will bring
the evil upon his house."

8. Ahab's third Syrian campaign
a. Ahab's agreement with Jehoshaphat of Judah

22 For three years Syria and Israel continued without war.
2 But in the third year Jĕhŏsh'ăphăt the king of Judah came
down to the king of Israel. 3And the king of Israel said to his
servants, "Do you know that Rā'mŏth-gĭl'ĕăd belongs to us, and
we keep quiet and do not take it out of the hand of the king of
Syria?" 4And he said to Jĕhŏsh'ăphăt, "Will you go with me to
battle at Rā'mŏth-gĭl'ĕăd?" And Jehoshaphat said to the king of
Israel, "I am as you are, my people as your people, my horses as
your horses."

b. The lying prophets prophesy victory

5 And Jĕhŏsh'ăphăt said to the king of Israel, "Inquire first
for the word of the LORD." 6 Then the king of Israel gathered the
prophets together, about four hundred men, and said to them,
"Shall I go to battle against Rā'mŏth-gĭl'ĕăd, or shall I forbear?"
And they said, "Go up; for the Lord will give it into the hand of
the king." 7 But Jĕhŏsh'ăphăt said, "Is there not here another
prophet of the LORD of whom we may inquire?" 8And the king of
Israel said to Jĕhŏsh'ăphăt, "There is yet one man by whom we
may inquire of the LORD, Mĭcāi'ăh the son of Ĭmlăh; but I hate
him, for he never prophesies good concerning me, but evil." And
Jehoshaphat said, "Let not the king say so." 9 Then the king of
Israel summoned an officer and said, "Bring quickly Mĭcāi'ăh the

21.20
1 Ki 18.17;
ver 25
21.21
1 Ki 14.10;
2 Ki 9.8
21.22
1 Ki 15.29
21.23
2 Ki 9.10,
30–37
21.24
1 Ki 14.11;
16.4
21.25
ver 20;
1 Ki 16.30–
33
21.26
Gen 15.16;
Lev 18.25–
30

21.27
2 Sam 3.31;
2 Ki 6.30

21.29
2 Ki 9.25

22.2
2 Chr
18.2ff;
1 Ki 15.24
22.3
Deut 4.43;
Josh 21.38
22.4
2 Ki 3.7

22.6
1 Ki 18.19

22.7
2 Ki 3.11

son of Ĭmláh." 10 Now the king of Israel and Jĕhŏsh'áphät the king of Judah were sitting on their thrones, arrayed in their robes, at the threshing floor at the entrance of the gate of Sámạr'ĭä; and all the prophets were prophesying before them. 11And Zĕdĕkī'áh the son of Chĕnā'ánáh made for himself horns of iron, and said, "Thus says the LORD, 'With these you shall push the Syrians until they are destroyed.'" 12And all the prophets prophesied so, and said, "Go up to Rā'mŏth-gĭl'ëäd and triumph; the LORD will give it into the hand of the king."

c. Micaiah's true prophecy

13 And the messenger who went to summon Mĭcāi'áh said to him, "Behold, the words of the prophets with one accord are favorable to the king; let your word be like the word of one of them, and speak favorably." 14 But Mĭcāi'áh said, "As the LORD lives, what the LORD says to me, that I will speak." 15And when he had come to the king, the king said to him, "Mĭcāi'áh, shall we go to Rā'mŏth-gĭl'ëäd to battle, or shall we forbear?" And he answered him, "Go up and triumph; the LORD will give it into the hand of the king." 16 But the king said to him, "How many times shall I adjure you that you speak to me nothing but the truth in the name of the LORD?" 17And he said, "I saw all Israel scattered upon the mountains, as sheep that have no shepherd; and the LORD said, 'These have no master; let each return to his home in peace.'" 18And the king of Israel said to Jĕhŏsh'áphät, "Did I not tell you that he would not prophesy good concerning me, but evil?" 19And Mĭcāi'áh said, "Therefore hear the word of the LORD: I saw the LORD sitting on his throne, and all the host of heaven standing beside him on his right hand and on his left; 20 and the LORD said, 'Who will entice Āhăb, that he may go up and fall at Rā'mŏth-gĭl'ëäd?' And one said one thing, and another said another. 21 Then a spirit came forward and stood before the LORD, saying, 'I will entice him.' 22And the LORD said to him, 'By what means?' And he said, 'I will go forth, and will be a lying spirit in the mouth of all his prophets.' And he said, 'You are to entice him, and you shall succeed; go forth and do so.' 23 Now therefore behold, the LORD has put a lying spirit in the mouth of all these your prophets; the LORD has spoken evil concerning you."

24 Then Zĕdĕkī'áh the son of Chĕnā'ánáh came near and struck Mĭcāi'áh on the cheek, and said, "How did the Spirit of the LORD go from me to speak to you?" 25And Mĭcāi'áh said, "Behold, you shall see on that day when you go into an inner chamber to hide yourself." 26And the king of Israel said, "Seize Mĭcāi'áh, and take him back to Āmòn the governor of the city and to Jō'ásh the king's son; 27 and say, 'Thus says the king, "Put this fellow in prison, and feed him with scant fare of bread and water, until I come in peace."'" 28And Mĭcāi'áh said, "If you return in peace, the LORD has not spoken by me." And he said, "Hear, all you peoples!"

d. Ahab's defeat and death

29 So the king of Israel and Jĕhŏsh'áphät the king of Judah went up to Rā'mŏth-gĭl'ëäd. 30And the king of Israel said to Jĕhŏsh'áphät, "I will disguise myself and go into battle, but you wear your robes." And the king of Israel disguised himself and

went into battle. 31 Now the king of Syria had commanded the
thirty-two captains of his chariots, "Fight with neither small nor
great, but only with the king of Israel." 32And when the captains
of the chariots saw Jehŏsh′áphăt, they said, "It is surely the king of
Israel." So they turned to fight against him; and Jehoshaphat cried
out. 33And when the captains of the chariots saw that it was not
the king of Israel, they turned back from pursuing him. 34 But a
certain man drew his bow at a venture, and struck the king of Israel between the scale armor and the breastplate; therefore he said
to the driver of his chariot, "Turn about, and carry me out of the
battle, for I am wounded." 35And the battle grew hot that day,
and the king was propped up in his chariot facing the Syrians,
until at evening he died; and the blood of the wound flowed into
the bottom of the chariot. 36And about sunset a cry went through
the army, "Every man to his city, and every man to his country!"

37 So the king died, and was brought to Sàmar′iä; and they
buried the king in Samaria. 38And they washed the chariot by the
pool of Sàmar′iä, and the dogs licked up his blood, and the harlots
washed themselves in it, according to the word of the LORD which
he had spoken. 39 Now the rest of the acts of Āhăb, and all that he
did, and the ivory house which he built, and all the cities that he
built, are they not written in the Book of the Chronicles of the
Kings of Israel? 40 So Āhăb slept with his fathers; and Āhàzī′áh
his son reigned in his stead.

9. Judah under Jehoshaphat

41 Jehŏsh′áphăt the son of Āsà began to reign over Judah in the
fourth year of Āhăb king of Israel. 42 Jehŏsh′áphăt was thirty-five
years old when he began to reign, and he reigned twenty-five years
in Jerusalem. His mother's name was Àzu′báh the daughter of
Shĭlhĭ. 43 He walked in all the way of Āsà his father; he did not
turn aside from it, doing what was right in the sight of the LORD;
yet the high places were not taken away, and the people still sacrificed and burned incense on the high places. 44 Jehŏsh′áphăt also
made peace with the king of Israel.

45 Now the rest of the acts of Jehŏsh′áphăt, and his might that
he showed, and how he warred, are they not written in the Book of
the Chronicles of the Kings of Judah? 46And the remnant of the
male cult prostitutes who remained in the days of his father Āsà,
he exterminated from the land.

47 There was no king in Ēdŏm; a deputy was king. 48 Jehŏsh′-
áphăt made ships of Tarshĭsh to go to Ōphĭr for gold; but they did
not go, for the ships were wrecked at Ēz′ĭon-gē′bĕr. 49 Then
Āhàzī′áh the son of Āhăb said to Jehŏsh′áphăt, "Let my servants
go with your servants in the ships," but Jehoshaphat was not
willing. 50And Jehŏsh′áphăt slept with his fathers, and was buried
with his fathers in the city of David his father; and Jehō′rám
his son reigned in his stead.

22.31	2 Chr 18.30
22.32	2 Chr 18.31
*22.34	
22.38	1 Ki 21.19
22.39	Amos 3.15
22.41	2 Chr 20.31
22.43	2 Chr 17.3; 1 Ki 15.14; 2 Ki 12.3
22.44	2 Chr 19.2
22.45	2 Chr 20.34
22.46	1 Ki 14.24; 15.12
22.47	2 Sam 8.14; 2 Ki 3.9
*22.48	2 Chr 20.35ff; 1 Ki 10.22
22.50	2 Chr 21.1

22.34 *bow at a venture.* Ahab sought to secure himself against the Syrians by assuming
the garb of a common soldier, and was shot by
a Syrian soldier who was not aiming at anyone
in particular. But God directed the arrow so
that it hit the man who was marked for destruction. Moreover, Ahab was hit in the
abdomen, the place where his armor was no
shield against the dart of divine vengeance.
Man cannot hide himself from the judgment
of God; what appears to be casual and accidental bespeaks the finger of God.

22.48 Jehoshaphat was not successful in these
operations as was Solomon (1 Ki 9.26–28).

10. *The Northern Kingdom under Ahaziah*

★22.51
ver 40

22.52
1 Ki 15.26;
21.25

22.53
1 Ki 16.30–
32

51 Āházī'áh the son of Āhāb began to reign over Israel in Sámar'iä in the seventeenth year of Jĕhŏsh'áphăt king of Judah, and he reigned two years over Israel. 52 He did what was evil in the sight of the LORD, and walked in the way of his father, and in the way of his mother, and in the way of Jĕrŏbŏ'ăm the son of Nĕbăt, who made Israel to sin. 53 He served Bāal and worshiped him, and provoked the LORD, the God of Israel, to anger in every way that his father had done.

22.51 Ahaziah followed his father who was the worst of all the kings of Israel. All of the nineteen kings of Israel served either the calf or Baal. Baal worship continued for some thirty years and was finally exterminated through the efforts of Elijah, Elisha, and Jehu. Jezebel, of course, was the one who was responsible for its introduction into Israel, and her daughter Athaliah, who married Jehoram, king of Judah, followed in her mother's footsteps, propagating Baalism among the people of Judah. The wicked influence of Jezebel and Athaliah upon both kingdoms staggers the imagination.

THE SECOND BOOK OF THE
KINGS

INTRODUCTION TO
THE SECOND BOOK OF THE
KINGS

Authorship and Background: See 1 Kings

Characteristics: See 1 Kings

Contents:

THE SECOND BOOK OF THE
KINGS

III. *The divided kingdom continued, 1.1–17.41*

G. *The ending of Elijah's ministry*

1. *Ahaziah's (Israel) embassy to Baal-zebub*

1.1
2 Sam 8.2;
2 Ki 3.5
*1.2
ver 3,6;
Mt 10.25;
see 2 Ki
8.7–10

1 After the death of Āhăb, Mŏăb rebelled against Israel. 2 Now Āhăzī'ăh fell through the lattice in his upper chamber in Sămăr'ĭă, and lay sick; so he sent messengers, telling them, "Go, inquire of Bā'ăl-zĕbŭb, the god of Ĕkrŏn, whether I shall recover from this sickness." 3 But the angel of the LORD said to Ĕlī'jăh the Tĭshbīte, "Arise, go up to meet the messengers of the king of Sămăr'ĭă, and say to them, 'Is it because there is no God in Israel that you are going to inquire of Bā'ăl-zĕbŭb, the god of Ĕkrŏn?'

1.4
ver 6,16

4 Now therefore thus says the LORD, 'You shall not come down from the bed to which you have gone, but you shall surely die.'" So Ĕlī'jăh went.

5 The messengers returned to the king, and he said to them, "Why have you returned?" 6And they said to him, "There came a man to meet us, and said to us, 'Go back to the king who sent you, and say to him, Thus says the LORD, Is it because there is no God in Israel that you are sending to inquire of Bā'ăl-zĕbŭb, the god of Ĕkrŏn? Therefore you shall not come down from the bed to which you have gone, but shall surely die.'" 7 He said to them, "What kind of man was he who came to meet you and told you these

1.8
Zech 13.4;
Mt 3.4

things?" 8 They answered him, "He wore a garment of haircloth, with a girdle of leather about his loins." And he said, "It is Ĕlī'jăh the Tĭshbīte."

2. *The attempts to seize Elijah*

9 Then the king sent to him a captain of fifty men with his fifty. He went up to Ĕlī'jăh, who was sitting on the top of a hill, and said to him, "O man of God, the king says, 'Come down.'" 10 But

1.10
1 Ki 18.36–
38;
Lk 9.54

Ĕlī'jăh answered the captain of fifty, "If I am a man of God, let fire come down from heaven and consume you and your fifty." Then fire came down from heaven, and consumed him and his fifty.

11 Again the king sent to him another captain of fifty men with his fifty. And he went up*a* and said to him, "O man of God, this is the king's order, 'Come down quickly!'" 12 But Ĕlī'jăh answered them, "If I am a man of God, let fire come down from heaven and consume you and your fifty." Then the fire of God came down from heaven and consumed him and his fifty.

1.13
1 Sam
26.21;
Ps 72.14

13 Again the king sent the captain of a third fifty with his fifty. And the third captain of fifty went up, and came and fell on his knees before Ĕlī'jăh, and entreated him, "O man of God, I pray

a Gk Compare verses 9, 13: Heb *answered*

1.2 *Baal-zebub*, "Lord of flies," is probably a scribal change intended to ridicule the original name, Baal-zebul, "Lord Prince." One of the Canaanite titles for Baal was "Prince (Zabul), Lord of the Earth." This name occurs in the New Testament as Beelzebul (or, Beelzebub in KJV), but it has the specific meaning, *the prince of demons* (Mt 12.24).

you, let my life, and the life of these fifty servants of yours, be precious in your sight. 14 Lo, fire came down from heaven, and consumed the two former captains of fifty men with their fifties; but now let my life be precious in your sight." 15 Then the angel of the LORD said to Ĕlī′jăh, "Go down with him; do not be afraid of him." So he arose and went down with him to the king, 16 and said to him, "Thus says the LORD, 'Because you have sent messengers to inquire of Bā′ăl-zĕbúb, the god of Ĕkròn,—is it because there is no God in Israel to inquire of his word?—therefore you shall not come down from the bed to which you have gone, but you shall surely die.'"

3. Jehoram, successor to Ahaziah

17 So he died according to the word of the LORD which Ĕlī′jăh had spoken. Jĕhō′răm, his brother,[b] became king in his stead in the second year of Jehoram the son of Jĕhōsh′ăphăt, king of Judah, because Āhăzī′áh had no son. 18 Now the rest of the acts of Āhăzī′áh which he did, are they not written in the Book of the Chronicles of the Kings of Israel?

H. The reign of Jehoram (Israel)

1. Elijah's translation

2 Now when the LORD was about to take Ĕlī′jáh up to heaven by a whirlwind, Elijah and Ĕlī′shá were on their way from Gĭlgăl. 2 And Ĕlī′jáh said to Ĕlī′shá, "Tarry here, I pray you; for the LORD has sent me as far as Bĕthĕl." But Elisha said, "As the LORD lives, and as you yourself live, I will not leave you." So they went down to Bethel. 3 And the sons of the prophets who were in Bĕthĕl came out to Ĕlī′shá, and said to him, "Do you know that today the LORD will take away your master from over you?" And he said, "Yes, I know it; hold your peace."

4 Ĕlī′jáh said to him, "Ĕlī′shá, tarry here, I pray you; for the LORD has sent me to Jĕr′ĭchō." But he said, "As the LORD lives, and as you yourself live, I will not leave you." So they came to Jericho. 5 The sons of the prophets who were at Jĕr′ĭchō drew near to Ĕlī′shá, and said to him, "Do you know that today the LORD will take away your master from over you?" And he answered, "Yes, I know it; hold your peace."

6 Then Ĕlī′jáh said to him, "Tarry here, I pray you; for the LORD has sent me to the Jordan." But he said, "As the LORD lives, and as you yourself live, I will not leave you." So the two of them went on. 7 Fifty men of the sons of the prophets also went, and stood at some distance from them, as they both were standing by the Jordan. 8 Then Ĕlī′jáh took his mantle, and rolled it up, and struck the water, and the water was parted to the one side and to the other, till the two of them could go over on dry ground.

9 When they had crossed, Ĕlī′jáh said to Ĕlī′shá, "Ask what I shall do for you, before I am taken from you." And Eli′sha said,

b Gk Syr: Heb lacks his brother

Marginal references:

1.15 ver 3
1.16 ver 3
1.17 2 Ki 3.1; 8.16
*2.1 Gen 5.24; Heb 11.5; 1 Ki 19.21
2.2 Ruth 1.15, 16; ver 4,6; 1 Sam 1.26; 2 Ki 4.30
*2.3 ver 5,7,15; 2 Ki 4.1,38
2.4 ver 2; Josh 6.26
2.5 ver 3
2.6 ver 3; Josh 3.8, 15–17
2.7 ver 15,16
2.8 1 Ki 19.13, 19; ver 14; Ex 14.21,22
*2.9

2.1 Gilgal, possibly the one in southwest Samaria.
2.3 sons of the prophets. The bands or guilds of prophets which were active at this time.

2.9 inherit a double share. This is not a request to be twice as spiritual as Elijah. Rather, a double share was the portion of the first-born, the heir. Thus, Elisha is asking to be Elijah's heir.

"I pray you, let me inherit a double share of your spirit." 10And he said, "You have asked a hard thing; yet, if you see me as I am being taken from you, it shall be so for you; but if you do not see me, it shall not be so." 11And as they still went on and talked, behold, a chariot of fire and horses of fire separated the two of them. And Ĕlī′jäh went up by a whirlwind into heaven. 12And Ĕlī′shä saw it and he cried, "My father, my father! the chariots of Israel and its horsemen!" And he saw him no more.

2.11
2 Ki 6.17;
Ps 104.4
2.12
2 Ki 13.14

2. The beginning of Elisha's ministry

Then he took hold of his own clothes and rent them in two pieces. 13And he took up the mantle of Ĕlī′jäh that had fallen from him, and went back and stood on the bank of the Jordan. 14 Then he took the mantle of Ĕlī′jäh that had fallen from him, and struck the water, saying, "Where is the LORD, the God of Elijah?" And when he had struck the water, the water was parted to the one side and to the other; and Ĕlī′shä went over.

2.14
ver 8

15 Now when the sons of the prophets who were at Jĕr′ĭchō saw him over against them, they said, "The spirit of Ĕlī′jäh rests on Ĕlī′shä." And they came to meet him, and bowed to the ground before him. 16And they said to him, "Behold now, there are with your servants fifty strong men; pray, let them go, and seek your master; it may be that the Spirit of the LORD has caught him up and cast him upon some mountain or into some valley." And he said, "You shall not send." 17 But when they urged him till he was ashamed, he said, "Send." They sent therefore fifty men; and for three days they sought him but did not find him. 18And they came back to him, while he tarried at Jĕr′ĭchō, and he said to them, "Did I not say to you, Do not go?"

2.15
ver 7
2.16
1 Ki 18.12;
Acts 8.39
2.17
2 Ki 8.11

19 Now the men of the city said to Ĕlī′shä, "Behold, the situation of this city is pleasant, as my lord sees; but the water is bad, and the land is unfruitful." 20 He said, "Bring me a new bowl, and put salt in it." So they brought it to him. 21 Then he went to the spring of water and threw salt in it, and said, "Thus says the LORD, I have made this water wholesome; henceforth neither death nor miscarriage shall come from it." 22 So the water has been wholesome to this day, according to the word which Ĕlī′shä spoke.

2.21
Ex 15.25;
2 Ki 4.41;
6.6

23 He went up from there to Bĕth′ĕl; and while he was going up on the way, some small boys came out of the city and jeered at him, saying, "Go up, you baldhead! Go up, you baldhead!" 24And he turned around, and when he saw them, he cursed them in the name of the LORD. And two she-bears came out of the woods and tore forty-two of the boys. 25 From there he went on to Mount Carmĕl, and thence he returned to Sămar′ĭä.

2.24
see Neh
13.25–27
2.25
2 Ki 4.25;
1 Ki 18.19,
20

3. Jehoram's campaign against Moab

3 In the eighteenth year of Jĕhŏsh′ăphăt king of Judah, Jĕhō′-răm the son of Āhăb became king over Israel in Sămar′ĭä, and he reigned twelve years. 2 He did what was evil in the sight of the LORD, though not like his father and mother, for he put away the pillar of Bāäl which his father had made. 3 Nevertheless he clung to the sin of Jĕrŏbō′äm the son of Nēbăt, which he made Israel to sin; he did not depart from it.
4 Now Mēshä king of Mōäb was a sheep breeder; and he had to

3.1
2 Ki 1.17
3.2
2 Ki 10.18,
26–28;
1 Ki 16.31,
32
3.3
1 Ki 12.28–
32;
14.9,16
3.4
2 Sam 8.2;
Isa 16.1

deliver annually[c] to the king of Israel a hundred thousand lambs, and the wool of a hundred thousand rams. 5 But when Āhăb died, the king of Mōăb rebelled against the king of Israel. 6 So King Jehō'răm marched out of Sàmạr'iă at that time and mustered all Israel. 7And he went and sent word to Jehōsh'àphăt king of Judah, "The king of Mōăb has rebelled against me; will you go with me to battle against Moab?" And he said, "I will go; I am as you are, my people as your people, my horses as your horses." 8 Then he said, "By which way shall we march?" Jehō'răm answered, "By the way of the wilderness of Ēdóm."

9 So the king of Israel went with the king of Judah and the king of Ēdóm. And when they had made a circuitous march of seven days, there was no water for the army or for the beasts which followed them. 10 Then the king of Israel said, "Alas! The LORD has called these three kings to give them into the hand of Mōăb." 11And Jehōsh'àphăt said, "Is there no prophet of the LORD here, through whom we may inquire of the LORD?" Then one of the king of Israel's servants answered, "Ēlī'shà the son of Shāphăt is here, who poured water on the hands of Ēlī'jàh." 12And Jehōsh'-àphăt said, "The word of the LORD is with him." So the king of Israel and Jehoshaphat and the king of Ēdóm went down to him.

13 And Ēlī'shà said to the king of Israel, "What have I to do with you? Go to the prophets of your father and the prophets of your mother." But the king of Israel said to him, "No; it is the LORD who has called these three kings to give them into the hand of Mōăb." 14And Ēlī'shà said, "As the LORD of hosts lives, whom I serve, were it not that I have regard for Jehōsh'àphăt the king of Judah, I would neither look at you, nor see you. 15 But now bring me a minstrel." And when the minstrel played, the power of the LORD came upon him. 16And he said, "Thus says the LORD, 'I will make this dry stream-bed full of pools.' 17For thus says the LORD, 'You shall not see wind or rain, but that stream-bed shall be filled with water, so that you shall drink, you, your cattle, and your beasts.' 18 This is a light thing in the sight of the LORD; he will also give the Mō'àbītes into your hand, 19 and you shall conquer every fortified city, and every choice city, and shall fell every good tree, and stop up all springs of water, and ruin every good piece of land with stones." 20 The next morning, about the time of offering the sacrifice, behold, water came from the direction of Ēdóm, till the country was filled with water.

21 When all the Mō'àbītes heard that the kings had come up to fight against them, all who were able to put on armor, from the youngest to the oldest, were called out, and were drawn up at the frontier. 22And when they rose early in the morning, and the sun shone upon the water, the Mō'àbītes saw the water opposite them as red as blood. 23And they said, "This is blood; the kings have surely fought together, and slain one another. Now then, Mōăb, to the spoil!" 24 But when they came to the camp of Israel, the Israelites rose and attacked the Mō'àbītes, till they fled before them; and they went forward, slaughtering the Moabites as they went.[d] 25And they overthrew the cities, and on every good piece

*3.5
2 Ki 1.1

3.7
1 Ki 22.4

3.9
ver 1,7;
1 Ki 22.47

3.11
1 Ki 22.7;
19.21

3.13
Ezek 14.3-5;
1 Ki 18.19

3.14
1 Ki 17.1;
2 Ki 5.16

3.15
1 Sam 16.23;
Ezek 1.3

3.19
ver 25

3.20
Ex 29.39,40

3.21
Gen 19.37

3.25
ver 19;
Isa 16.7,11;
Jer 48.31, 36

c Tg: Heb lacks annually   d Gk: Heb uncertain

3.5 A stone inscription describing Mesha's revolt against Israel has been found. It was discovered by a Prussian missionary about a century ago and is known as the Moabite Stone.

of land every man threw a stone, until it was covered; they stopped every spring of water, and felled all the good trees; till only its stones were left in Kĭr-har'ĕsĕth, and the slingers surrounded and conquered it. 26 When the king of Mōăb saw that the battle was going against him, he took with him seven hundred swordsmen to break through, opposite the king of Ēdŏm; but they could not. 27 Then he took his eldest son who was to reign in his stead, and offered him for a burnt offering upon the wall. And there came great wrath upon Israel; and they withdrew from him and returned to their own land.

*3.27
Amos 2.1;
Mic 6.7

4. Some of Elisha's miracles
a. The increase of the widow's oil

4.1
2 Ki 2.3;
Lev 25.39;
Mt 18.25

4 Now the wife of one of the sons of the prophets cried to Ēlī'shà, "Your servant my husband is dead; and you know that your servant feared the LORD, but the creditor has come to take my two children to be his slaves." 2 And Ēlī'shà said to her, "What shall I do for you? Tell me; what have you in the house?" And she said, "Your maidservant has nothing in the house, except a jar of oil." 3 Then he said, "Go outside, borrow vessels of all your neighbors, empty vessels and not too few. 4 Then go in, and shut the door upon yourself and your sons, and pour into all these vessels; and when one is full, set it aside." 5 So she went from him and shut the door upon herself and her sons; and as she poured they brought the vessels to her. 6 When the vessels were full, she said to her son, "Bring me another vessel." And he said to her, "There is not another." Then the oil stopped flowing. 7 She came and told the man of God, and he said, "Go, sell the oil and pay your debts, and you and your sons can live on the rest."

*4.7
1 Ki 12.22

b. The promise of a son to the Shunammite woman

4.8
Josh 19.18

4.9
ver 7

8 One day Ēlī'shà went on to Shunĕm, where a wealthy woman lived, who urged him to eat some food. So whenever he passed that way, he would turn in there to eat food. 9 And she said to her husband, "Behold now, I perceive that this is a holy man of God, who is continually passing our way. 10 Let us make a small roof chamber with walls, and put there for him a bed, a table, a chair, and a lamp, so that whenever he comes to us, he can go in there."

4.12
ver 29–31;
2 Ki 5.20–
27;
8.4,5

11 One day he came there, and he turned into the chamber and rested there. 12 And he said to Gĕhā'zī his servant, "Call this Shu'nămmīte." When he had called her, she stood before him. 13 And he said to him, "Say now to her, See, you have taken all this trouble for us; what is to be done for you? Would you have a word spoken on your behalf to the king or to the commander of the army?" She answered, "I dwell among my own people." 14 And he said, "What then is to be done for her?" Gĕhā'zī answered, "Well, she has no son, and her husband is old." 15 He said, "Call her." And when he had called her, she stood in the doorway.

4.16
Gen 18.10,
14;
ver 28

16 And he said, "At this season, when the time comes round, you shall embrace a son." And she said, "No, my lord, O man of God; do not lie to your maidservant." 17 But the woman conceived, and she bore a son about that time the following spring, as Ēlī'shà had said to her.

3.27 Mesha's sacrifice of his eldest son to Molech revolted the Israelites.

4.7 The *man of God* was Shemaiah, a prophet. (See 1 Ki 12.22.)

c. *Elisha raises the dead son of the Shunammite*

18 When the child had grown, he went out one day to his father among the reapers. [19]And he said to his father, "Oh, my head, my head!" The father said to his servant, "Carry him to his mother." [20]And when he had lifted him, and brought him to his mother, the child sat on her lap till noon, and then he died. [21]And she went up and laid him on the bed of the man of God, and shut the door upon him, and went out. 22 Then she called to her husband, and said, "Send me one of the servants and one of the asses, that I may quickly go to the man of God, and come back again." [23]And he said, "Why will you go to him today? It is neither new moon nor sabbath." She said, "It will be well." 24 Then she saddled the ass, and she said to her servant, "Urge the beast on; do not slacken the pace for me unless I tell you." 25 So she set out, and came to the man of God at Mount Carmel.

When the man of God saw her coming, he said to Gēhā'zī his servant, "Look, yonder is the Shu'nåmmīte; 26 run at once to meet her, and say to her, Is it well with you? Is it well with your husband? Is it well with the child?" And she answered, "It is well." [27]And when she came to the mountain to the man of God, she caught hold of his feet. And Gēhā'zī came to thrust her away. But the man of God said, "Let her alone, for she is in bitter distress; and the LORD has hidden it from me, and has not told me." 28 Then she said, "Did I ask my lord for a son? Did I not say, Do not deceive me?" 29 He said to Gēhā'zī, "Gird up your loins, and take my staff in your hand, and go. If you meet any one, do not salute him; and if any one salutes you, do not reply; and lay my staff upon the face of the child." 30 Then the mother of the child said, "As the LORD lives, and as you yourself live, I will not leave you." So he arose and followed her. 31 Gēhā'zī went on ahead and laid the staff upon the face of the child, but there was no sound or sign of life. Therefore he returned to meet him, and told him, "The child has not awaked."

32 When Ēlī'shå came into the house, he saw the child lying dead on his bed. 33 So he went in and shut the door upon the two of them, and prayed to the LORD. 34 Then he went up and lay upon the child, putting his mouth upon his mouth, his eyes upon his eyes, and his hands upon his hands; and as he stretched himself upon him, the flesh of the child became warm. 35 Then he got up again, and walked once to and fro in the house, and went up, and stretched himself upon him; the child sneezed seven times, and the child opened his eyes. 36 Then he summoned Gēhā'zī and said, "Call this Shu'nåmmīte." So he called her. And when she came to him, he said, "Take up your son." 37 She came and fell at his feet, bowing to the ground; then she took up her son and went out.

d. *The poisonous pottage made harmless*

38 And Ēlī'shå came again to Gĭlgăl when there was a famine in the land. And as the sons of the prophets were sitting before him, he said to his servant, "Set on the great pot, and boil pottage for the sons of the prophets." 39 One of them went out into the field to gather herbs, and found a wild vine and gathered from it his lap full of wild gourds, and came and cut them up into the pot of pottage, not knowing what they were. [40]And they poured out

4.21
ver 7,32

4.23
Num 10.10;
28.11;
1 Chr 23.31

4.25
2 Ki 2.25

4.28
ver 16
4.29
1 Ki 18.46;
2 Ki 9.1;
Lk 10.4;
Ex 7.19;
14.16;
2 Ki 2.8,14
4.30
2 Ki 2.2

4.33
ver 4;
Mt 6.6;
1 Ki 17.20
4.34
1 Ki 17.21;
Acts 20.10
4.35
1 Ki 17.21;
2 Ki 8.1,5

4.37
1 Ki 17.23;
Heb 11.35

4.38
2 Ki 2.1,3;
8.1;
Lk 10.39;
Acts 22.3

for the men to eat. But while they were eating of the pottage, they cried out, "O man of God, there is death in the pot!" And they could not eat it. 41 He said, "Then bring meal." And he threw it into the pot, and said, "Pour out for the men, that they may eat." And there was no harm in the pot.

4.41
Ex 15.25;
2 Ki 2.21

e. The miraculous feeding of the hundred men

4.42
1 Sam 9.4,7

42 A man came from Bā′al-shăl′ĭshăh, bringing the man of God bread of the first fruits, twenty loaves of barley, and fresh ears of grain in his sack. And Ĕlĭ′shá said, "Give to the men, that they may eat." 43 But his servant said, "How am I to set this before a hundred men?" So he repeated, "Give them to the men, that they may eat, for thus says the LORD, 'They shall eat and have some left.'" 44 So he set it before them. And they ate, and had some left, according to the word of the LORD.

4.44
Mt 14.16–
21;
15.32–38

5. Naaman the leper and Elisha
a. The testimony of the Israelitish girl

5.1
Lk 4.27

5 Nā′ámàn, commander of the army of the king of Syria, was a great man with his master and in high favor, because by him the LORD had given victory to Syria. He was a mighty man of valor, but he was a leper. 2 Now the Syrians on one of their raids had carried off a little maid from the land of Israel, and she waited on Nā′ámàn's wife. 3 She said to her mistress, "Would that my lord were with the prophet who is in Sámạr′ĭä! He would cure him of his leprosy." 4 So Nā′ámàn went in and told his lord, "Thus and so spoke the maiden from the land of Israel." 5And the king of Syria said, "Go now, and I will send a letter to the king of Israel."

5.5
1 Sam 9.8;
2 Ki 8.8,9

b. The message of the Syrian king to Jehoram

So he went, taking with him ten talents of silver, six thousand shekels of gold, and ten festal garments. 6And he brought the letter to the king of Israel, which read, "When this letter reaches you, know that I have sent to you Nā′ámàn my servant, that you may cure him of his leprosy." 7And when the king of Israel read the letter, he rent his clothes and said, "Am I God, to kill and to make alive, that this man sends word to me to cure a man of his leprosy? Only consider, and see how he is seeking a quarrel with me."

5.7
Gen 37.29;
30.2;
Deut 32.39;
1 Sam 2.6;
1 Ki 20.7

c. Elisha gives orders to Naaman, who is healed

5.8
1 Ki 12.22

8 But when Ĕlĭ′shá the man of God heard that the king of Israel had rent his clothes, he sent to the king, saying, "Why have you rent your clothes? Let him come now to me, that he may know that there is a prophet in Israel." 9 So Nā′ámàn came with his horses and chariots, and halted at the door of Ĕlĭ′shá′ṣ house. 10And Ĕlĭ′shá sent a messenger to him, saying, "Go and wash in the Jordan seven times, and your flesh shall be restored, and you shall be clean." 11 But Nā′ámàn was angry, and went away, saying, "Behold, I thought that he would surely come out to me, and stand, and call on the name of the LORD his God, and wave his hand over the place, and cure the leper. 12Are not Abā′nàe and Pharpar, the rivers of Damascus, better than all the waters of Israel? Could I not wash in them, and be clean?" So he turned and

5.10
Jn 9.7

e Another reading is Ámā′ná

went away in a rage. 13 But his servants came near and said to him, "My father, if the prophet had commanded you to do some great thing, would you not have done it? How much rather, then, when he says to you, 'Wash, and be clean'?" 14 So he went down and dipped himself seven times in the Jordan, according to the word of the man of God; and his flesh was restored like the flesh of a little child, and he was clean.

d. *Elisha refuses a reward*

15 Then he returned to the man of God, he and all his company, and he came and stood before him; and he said, "Behold, I know that there is no God in all the earth but in Israel; so accept now a present from your servant." 16 But he said, "As the LORD lives, whom I serve, I will receive none." And he urged him to take it, but he refused. 17 Then Nā´amàn said, "If not, I pray you, let there be given to your servant two mules' burden of earth; for henceforth your servant will not offer burnt offering or sacrifice to any god but the LORD. 18 In this matter may the LORD pardon your servant: when my master goes into the house of Rimmòn to worship there, leaning on my arm, and I bow myself in the house of Rimmon, when I bow myself in the house of Rimmon, the LORD pardon your servant in this matter." 19 He said to him, "Go in peace."

e. *Gehazi's covetousness and punishment*

But when Nā´amàn had gone from him a short distance, 20 Gè-hā´zī, the servant of Ēlī´shà the man of God, said, "See, my master has spared this Nā´amàn the Syrian, in not accepting from his hand what he brought. As the LORD lives, I will run after him, and get something from him." 21 So Gèhā´zī followed Nā´amàn. And when Naaman saw some one running after him, he alighted from the chariot to meet him, and said, "Is all well?" 22And he said, "All is well. My master has sent me to say, 'There have just now come to me from the hill country of É´phräim two young men of the sons of the prophets; pray, give them a talent of silver and two festal garments.'" 23And Nā´amàn said, "Be pleased to accept two talents." And he urged him, and tied up two talents of silver in two bags, with two festal garments, and laid them upon two of his servants; and they carried them before Gèhā´zī. 24And when he came to the hill, he took them from their hand, and put them in the house; and he sent the men away, and they departed. 25 He went in, and stood before his master, and Ēlī´shà said to him, "Where have you been, Gèhā´zī?" And he said, "Your servant went nowhere." 26 But he said to him, "Did I not go with you in spirit when the man turned from his chariot to meet you? Was it a time to accept money and garments, olive orchards and vineyards, sheep and oxen, menservants and maidservants? 27 Therefore the leprosy of Nā´amàn shall cleave to you, and to your descendants for ever." So he went out from his presence a leper, as white as snow.

6. *The further ministry of Elisha*
a. *The recovery of the lost axe head*

6 Now the sons of the prophets said to Ēlī´shà, "See, the place where we dwell under your charge is too small for us. 2 Let us

---

5.13
2 Ki 6.21;
8.9;
1 Sam 28.23

5.14
ver 10;
Job 33.25;
Lk 4.27

5.15
1 Sam
15.46,47;
Dan 2.47;
3.29;
1 Sam 25.27

5.16
2 Ki 3.14;
ver 20,26;
Gen 14.22,
23

5.18
2 Ki 7.2,17

5.20
2 Ki 4.12,
31,36

5.22
2 Ki 4.26;
Josh 24.33

5.25
ver 22

5.26
ver 16

5.27
Ex 4.6;
Num 12.10;
2 Ki 15.5

6.1
2 Ki 4.38

go to the Jordan and each of us get there a log, and let us make a place for us to dwell there." And he answered, "Go." 3 Then one of them said, "Be pleased to go with your servants." And he answered, "I will go." 4 So he went with them. And when they came to the Jordan, they cut down trees. 5 But as one was felling a log, his axe head fell into the water; and he cried out, "Alas, my master! It was borrowed." 6 Then the man of God said, "Where did it fall?" When he showed him the place, he cut off a stick, and threw it in there, and made the iron float. 7And he said, "Take it up." So he reached out his hand and took it.

b. *Elisha discloses Ben-hadad's plans to Jehoram*

8 Once when the king of Syria was warring against Israel, he took counsel with his servants, saying, "At such and such a place shall be my camp." 9 But the man of God sent word to the king of Israel, "Beware that you do not pass this place, for the Syrians are going down there." 10And the king of Israel sent to the place of which the man of God told him. Thus he used to warn him, so that he saved himself there more than once or twice.

c. *Elisha strikes the Syrians blind*

11 And the mind of the king of Syria was greatly troubled because of this thing; and he called his servants and said to them, "Will you not show me who of us is for the king of Israel?" 12And one of his servants said, "None, my lord, O king; but Ĕlī′shȧ, the prophet who is in Israel, tells the king of Israel the words that you speak in your bedchamber." 13And he said, "Go and see where he is, that I may send and seize him." It was told him, "Behold, he is in Dōthȧn." 14 So he sent there horses and chariots and a great army; and they came by night, and surrounded the city.

15 When the servant of the man of God rose early in the morning and went out, behold, an army with horses and chariots was round about the city. And the servant said, "Alas, my master! What shall we do?" 16 He said, "Fear not, for those who are with us are more than those who are with them." 17 Then Ĕlī′shȧ prayed, and said, "O LORD, I pray thee, open his eyes that he may see." So the LORD opened the eyes of the young man, and he saw; and behold, the mountain was full of horses and chariots of fire round about Elisha. 18And when the Syrians came down against him, Ĕlī′shȧ prayed to the LORD, and said, "Strike this people, I pray thee, with blindness." So he struck them with blindness in accordance with the prayer of Elisha. 19And Ĕlī′shȧ said to them, "This is not the way, and this is not the city; follow me, and I will bring you to the man whom you seek." And he led them to Sȧmar′iȧ.

d. *The blind Syrians led to Samaria*

20 As soon as they entered Sȧmar′iȧ, Ĕlī′shȧ said, "O LORD, open the eyes of these men, that they may see." So the LORD opened their eyes, and they saw; and lo, they were in the midst of Samaria. 21 When the king of Israel saw them he said to Ĕlī′shȧ, "My father, shall I slay them? Shall I slay them?" 22 He answered, "You shall not slay them. Would you slay those whom you have taken captive with your sword and with your bow? Set bread and water before them, that they may eat and drink and go to their

6.6
2 Ki 2.21

6.9
ver 12

6.13
Gen 37.17

6.16
2 Chr 32.7,
8;
Ps 55.18;
Rom 8.31
6.17
2 Ki 2.11;
Ps 68.17;
Zech 6.1–7
6.18
Gen 19.11

6.20
ver 17

6.21
2 Ki 2.12;
5.13; 8.9
6.22
Deut 20.11–
16;
Rom 12.20

master." 23 So he prepared for them a great feast; and when they had eaten and drunk, he sent them away, and they went to their master. And the Syrians came no more on raids into the land of Israel.

6.23
ver 8,9;
2 Ki 5.2

e. Elisha and the siege of Samaria

24 Afterward Bĕn-hā´dăd king of Syria mustered his entire army, and went up, and besieged Sămar´iă. 25And there was a great famine in Sămar´iă, as they besieged it, until an ass's head was sold for eighty shekels of silver, and the fourth part of a kab of dove's dung for five shekels of silver. 26 Now as the king of Israel was passing by upon the wall, a woman cried out to him, saying, "Help, my lord, O king!" 27And he said, "If the LORD will not help you, whence shall I help you? From the threshing floor, or from the wine press?" 28And the king asked her, "What is your trouble?" She answered, "This woman said to me, 'Give your son, that we may eat him today, and we will eat my son tomorrow.' 29 So we boiled my son, and ate him. And on the next day I said to her, 'Give your son, that we may eat him'; but she has hidden her son." 30 When the king heard the words of the woman he rent his clothes—now he was passing by upon the wall—and the people looked, and behold, he had sackcloth beneath upon his body— 31 and he said, "May God do so to me, and more also, if the head of Ĕlī´shá the son of Shāphăt remains on his shoulders today."

6.24
1 Ki 20.1

6.29
Lev 26.27–
29;
Deut 28.52,
53,57
6.30
1 Ki 21.27
6.31
Ruth 1.17;
1 Ki 19.2

32 Ĕlī´shá was sitting in his house, and the elders were sitting with him. Now the king had dispatched a man from his presence; but before the messenger arrived Elisha said to the elders, "Do you see how this murderer has sent to take off my head? Look, when the messenger comes, shut the door, and hold the door fast against him. Is not the sound of his master's feet behind him?" 33And while he was still speaking with them, the king^f came down to him and said, "This trouble is from the LORD! Why should I wait 7 for the LORD any longer?" 1 But Ĕlī´shá said, "Hear the word of the LORD: thus says the LORD, Tomorrow about this time a measure of fine meal shall be sold for a shekel, and two measures of barley for a shekel, at the gate of Sămar´iă." 2 Then the captain on whose hand the king leaned said to the man of God, "If the LORD himself should make windows in heaven, could this thing be?" But he said, "You shall see it with your own eyes, but you shall not eat of it."

6.32
Ezek 8.1;
20.1;
1 Ki 18.4,
13,14

6.33
Job 2.9

7.1
ver 18

7.2
ver 17,19,
20;
Mal 3.10

3 Now there were four men who were lepers at the entrance to the gate; and they said to one another, "Why do we sit here till we die? 4 If we say, 'Let us enter the city,' the famine is in the city, and we shall die there; and if we sit here, we die also. So now come, let us go over to the camp of the Syrians; if they spare our lives we shall live, and if they kill us we shall but die." 5 So they arose at twilight to go to the camp of the Syrians; but when they came to the edge of the camp of the Syrians, behold, there was no one there. 6 For the Lord had made the army of the Syrians hear the sound of chariots, and of horses, the sound of a great army, so that

7.3
Lev 13.46

7.4
2 Ki 6.24

*7.6
2 Sam 5.24;
19.7;
1 Ki 10.29

^{f} See 7.2: Heb messenger

7.6 Egypt (Hebrew misraim) may be a confusion with muzrim, a district in Asia Minor. Kings of this region, not the kings of Egypt, would most likely have been hired along with the Hittites in Asia Minor to attack the Syrians.

they said to one another, "Behold, the king of Israel has hired against us the kings of the Hīttītes and the kings of Egypt to come upon us." 7 So they fled away in the twilight and forsook their tents, their horses, and their asses, leaving the camp as it was, and fled for their lives. 8And when these lepers came to the edge of the camp, they went into a tent, and ate and drank, and they carried off silver and gold and clothing, and went and hid them; then they came back, and entered another tent, and carried off things from it, and went and hid them.

9 Then they said to one another, "We are not doing right. This day is a day of good news; if we are silent and wait until the morning light, punishment will overtake us; now therefore come, let us go and tell the king's household." 10 So they came and called to the gatekeepers of the city, and told them, "We came to the camp of the Syrians, and behold, there was no one to be seen or heard there, nothing but the horses tied, and the asses tied, and the tents as they were." 11 Then the gatekeepers called out, and it was told within the king's household. 12And the king rose in the night, and said to his servants, "I will tell you what the Syrians have prepared against us. They know that we are hungry; therefore they have gone out of the camp to hide themselves in the open country, thinking, 'When they come out of the city, we shall take them alive and get into the city.'" 13And one of his servants said, "Let some men take five of the remaining horses, seeing that those who are left here will fare like the whole multitude of Israel that have already perished; let us send and see." 14 So they took two mounted men, and the king sent them after the army of the Syrians, saying, "Go and see." 15 So they went after them as far as the Jordan; and, lo, all the way was littered with garments and equipment which the Syrians had thrown away in their haste. And the messengers returned, and told the king.

16 Then the people went out, and plundered the camp of the Syrians. So a measure of fine meal was sold for a shekel, and two measures of barley for a shekel, according to the word of the LORD. 17 Now the king had appointed the captain on whose hand he leaned to have charge of the gate; and the people trod upon him in the gate, so that he died, as the man of God had said when the king came down to him. 18 For when the man of God had said to the king, "Two measures of barley shall be sold for a shekel, and a measure of fine meal for a shekel, about this time tomorrow in the gate of Samar'ia," 19 the captain had answered the man of God, "If the LORD himself should make windows in heaven, could such a thing be?" And he had said, "You shall see it with your own eyes, but you shall not eat of it." 20And so it happened to him, for the people trod upon him in the gate and he died.

7. The Shunammite woman comes home

8 Now Eli'sha had said to the woman whose son he had restored to life, "Arise, and depart with your household, and sojourn wherever you can; for the LORD has called for a famine, and it will come upon the land for seven years." 2 So the woman arose, and did according to the word of the man of God; she went with her household and sojourned in the land of the Philis'tines seven years. 3And at the end of the seven years, when the woman returned from the land of the Philis'tines, she went forth to appeal

Marginal references

7.7
Ps 48.4–6

7.9
2 Sam 18.27

7.12
2 Ki 6.25–29

7.16
ver 1

7.17
ver 2;
2 Ki 6.32

7.18
ver 1

7.19
ver 2

8.1
2 Ki 4.35;
Ps 105.16;
Hag 1.11

to the king for her house and her land. 4 Now the king was talking with Gēhā'zī the servant of the man of God, saying, "Tell me all the great things that Ēlī'shá has done." 5And while he was telling the king how Ēlī'shá had restored the dead to life, behold, the woman whose son he had restored to life appealed to the king for her house and her land. And Gēhā'zī said, "My lord, O king, here is the woman, and here is her son whom Elisha restored to life." 6And when the king asked the woman, she told him. So the king appointed an official for her, saying, "Restore all that was hers, together with all the produce of the fields from the day that she left the land until now."

8. *Elisha anoints Hazael king of Syria*

7 Now Ēlī'shá came to Damascus. Bĕn-hā'dăd the king of Syria was sick; and when it was told him, "The man of God has come here," 8 the king said to Hăz'äël, "Take a present with you and go to meet the man of God, and inquire of the LORD through him, saying, 'Shall I recover from this sickness?' " 9 So Hăz'äël went to meet him, and took a present with him, all kinds of goods of Damascus, forty camel loads. When he came and stood before him, he said, "Your son Bĕn-hā'dăd the king of Syria has sent me to you, saying, 'Shall I recover from this sickness?' " 10And Ēlī'shá said to him, "Go, say to him, 'You shall certainly recover'; but the LORD has shown me that he shall certainly die." 11And he fixed his gaze and stared at him, until he was ashamed. And the man of God wept. 12And Hăz'äël said, "Why does my lord weep?" He answered, "Because I know the evil that you will do to the people of Israel; you will set on fire their fortresses, and you will slay their young men with the sword, and dash in pieces their little ones, and rip up their women with child." 13And Hăz'äël said, "What is your servant, who is but a dog, that he should do this great thing?" Ēlī'shá answered, "The LORD has shown me that you are to be king over Syria." 14 Then he departed from Ēlī'shá, and came to his master, who said to him, "What did Elisha say to you?" And he answered, "He told me that you would certainly recover." 15 But on the morrow he took the coverlet and dipped it in water and spread it over his face, till he died. And Hăz'äël became king in his stead.

I. *The reign of Jehoram (Judah)* (cf. 2 Chr 21.2–20)

16 In the fifth year of Jōrám the son of Āhăb, king of Israel,g Jēhō'rám the son of Jēhŏsh'áphăt, king of Judah, began to reign. 17 He was thirty-two years old when he became king, and he reigned eight years in Jerusalem. 18And he walked in the way of the kings of Israel, as the house of Āhăb had done, for the daughter of Ahab was his wife. And he did what was evil in the sight of the LORD. 19 Yet the LORD would not destroy Judah, for the sake of David his servant, since he promised to give a lamp to him and to his sons for ever.

20 In his days Ēdŏm revolted from the rule of Judah, and set up a king of their own. 21 Then Jōrám passed over to Zā'ir with all his chariots, and rose by night, and he and his chariot commanders smote the Ē'dŏmītes who had surrounded him; but his

g Gk Syr: Heb *Israel, Jehoshaphat being king of Judah*

8.4
2 Ki 4.12;
5.20–27
8.5
2 Ki 4.35

8.7
1 Ki 11.24;
2 Ki 6.24
8.8
1 Ki 19.15;
14.3;
2 Ki 1.2

8.10
ver 14,15

8.12
2 Ki 10.32;
12.17;
13.3,7;
15.16;
Hos 13.16;
Amos 1.13
8.13
1 Sam
17.43;
1 Ki 19.15

8.15
ver 10

8.16
2 Ki 1.17;
3.1;
2 Chr 21.3,4
8.17
2 Chr 21.5–10
8.18
ver 27
8.19
2 Sam 7.13;
1 Ki 11.36;
2 Chr 21.7
8.20
1 Ki 22.4;
2 Ki 3.27;
2 Chr 21.8–10
8.21
2 Sam
18.17; 19.8

army fled home. 22 So Ēdŏm revolted from the rule of Judah to this day. Then Lĭbnăh revolted at the same time. 23 Now the rest of the acts of Jōrăm, and all that he did, are they not written in the Book of the Chronicles of the Kings of Judah? 24 So Jōrăm slept with his fathers, and was buried with his fathers in the city of David; and Āhăzī'ăh his son reigned in his stead.

J. The reign of Ahaziah (Judah)

25 In the twelfth year of Jōrăm the son of Āhăb, king of Israel, Āhăzī'ăh the son of Jĕhŏ'răm, king of Judah, began to reign. 26Āhăzī'ăh was twenty-two years old when he began to reign, and he reigned one year in Jerusalem. His mother's name was Āthălī'ăh; she was a granddaughter of Ŏmrĭ king of Israel. 27 He also walked in the way of the house of Āhăb, and did what was evil in the sight of the LORD, as the house of Ahab had done, for he was son-in-law to the house of Ahab.

28 He went with Jōrăm the son of Āhăb to make war against Hăz'ăĕl king of Syria at Rā'mŏth-gĭl'ĕăd, where the Syrians wounded Joram. 29And King Jōrăm returned to be healed in Jĕzreĕl' of the wounds which the Syrians had given him at Rāmăh, when he fought against Hăz'ăĕl king of Syria. And Āhăzī'ăh the son of Jĕhŏ'răm king of Judah went down to see Joram the son of Āhăb in Jezreel, because he was sick.

K. The reign of Jehu (Israel)

1. Jehu anointed king

9 Then Ĕlī'shă the prophet called one of the sons of the prophets and said to him, "Gird up your loins, and take this flask of oil in your hand, and go to Rā'mŏth-gĭl'ĕăd. 2And when you arrive, look there for Jēhū the son of Jĕhŏsh'ăphăt, son of Nĭmshī; and go in and bid him rise from among his fellows, and lead him to an inner chamber. 3 Then take the flask of oil, and pour it on his head, and say, 'Thus says the LORD, I anoint you king over Israel.' Then open the door and flee; do not tarry."

4 So the young man, the prophet,h went to Rā'mŏth-gĭl'ĕăd. 5And when he came, behold, the commanders of the army were in council; and he said, "I have an errand to you, O commander." And Jēhū said, "To which of us all?" And he said, "To you, O commander." 6 So he arose, and went into the house; and the young man poured the oil on his head, saying to him, "Thus says the LORD the God of Israel, I anoint you king over the people of the LORD, over Israel. 7And you shall strike down the house of Āhăb your master, that I may avenge on Jĕz'ĕbĕl the blood of my servants the prophets, and the blood of all the servants of the LORD. 8 For the whole house of Āhăb shall perish; and I will cut off from Ahab every male, bond or free, in Israel. 9And I will make the house of Āhăb like the house of Jĕrŏbō'ăm the son of Nēbăt, and like the house of Bā'ăshă the son of Āhī'jăh. 10And the dogs

h Gk Syr: Heb the young man, the young man, the prophet

8.26 It was through Athaliah, daughter of Ahab and Jezebel, and granddaughter of Omri, that the idolatrous worship of Israel was carried to Judah. As the wife of king Jehoram of Judah, she exercised great influence in the religious realm.

shall eat Jĕz'ĕbĕl in the territory of Jĕzreĕl', and none shall bury
her." Then he opened the door, and fled.

11 When Jēhū came out to the servants of his master, they said
to him, "Is all well? Why did this mad fellow come to you?" And
he said to them, "You know the fellow and his talk." 12And they
said, "That is not true; tell us now." And he said, "Thus and so he
spoke to me, saying, 'Thus says the LORD, I anoint you king over
Israel.' " 13 Then in haste every man of them took his garment,
and put it under him on the bare*i* steps, and they blew the trumpet, and proclaimed, "Jēhū is king."

2. Jehoram (Joram of Israel) defeated and slain

14 Thus Jēhū the son of Jĕhŏsh'áphät the son of Nĭmshī conspired against Jōrám. (Now Joram with all Israel had been on
guard at Rā'mŏth-gĭl'ĕàd against Hăz'äĕl king of Syria; 15 but
King Jōrám had returned to be healed in Jĕzreĕl' of the wounds
which the Syrians had given him, when he fought with Hăz'äĕl
king of Syria.) So Jēhū said, "If this is your mind, then let no one
slip out of the city to go and tell the news in Jezreel." 16 Then
Jēhū mounted his chariot, and went to Jĕzreĕl', for Jōrám lay
there. And Āházī'áh king of Judah had come down to visit Joram.

17 Now the watchman was standing on the tower in Jĕzreĕl',
and he spied the company of Jēhū as he came, and said, "I see a
company." And Jōrám said, "Take a horseman, and send to meet
them, and let him say, 'Is it peace?' " 18 So a man on horseback
went to meet him, and said, "Thus says the king, 'Is it peace?' "
And Jēhū said, "What have you to do with peace? Turn round
and ride behind me." And the watchman reported, saying, "The
messenger reached them, but he is not coming back." 19 Then he
sent out a second horseman, who came to them, and said, "Thus
the king has said, 'Is it peace?' " And Jēhū answered, "What have
you to do with peace? Turn round and ride behind me." 20Again
the watchman reported, "He reached them, but he is not coming
back. And the driving is like the driving of Jēhū the son of Nĭmshī; for he drives furiously."

21 Jōrám said, "Make ready." And they made ready his chariot.
Then Joram king of Israel and Āházī'áh king of Judah set out, each
in his chariot, and went to meet Jēhū, and met him at the property
of Nábŏth the Jĕz'reĕlite. 22And when Jōrám saw Jēhū, he said,
"Is it peace, Jehu?" He answered, "What peace can there be, so
long as the harlotries and the sorceries of your mother Jĕz'ĕbĕl are
so many?" 23 Then Jōrám reined about and fled, saying to Āházī'-
áh, "Treachery, O Ahaziah!" 24And Jēhū drew his bow with his
full strength, and shot Jōrám between the shoulders, so that the
arrow pierced his heart, and he sank in his chariot. 25 Jēhū said to
Bĭdkar his aide, "Take him up, and cast him on the plot of ground
belonging to Nábŏth the Jĕz'reĕlite; for remember, when you and
I rode side by side behind Āhăb his father, how the LORD uttered
this oracle against him: 26 'As surely as I saw yesterday the blood
of Nábŏth and the blood of his sons—says the LORD—I will requite you on this plot of ground.' Now therefore take him up and
cast him on the plot of ground, in accordance with the word of the
LORD."

---

i The meaning of the Hebrew word is uncertain

9.11
Jer 29.26;
Jn 10.20;
Acts 26.24

9.13
Mt 21.7;
2 Sam
15.10;
1 Ki 1.34,39

9.14
2 Ki 8.28

9.15
2 Ki 8.29

9.16
2 Ki 8.29

9.18
ver 19,22

9.20
2 Sam
18.27;
1 Ki 19.17

9.21
2 Chr 22.7;
ver 26;
1 Ki 21.1-7,
15-19

9.22
1 Ki 16.30-
33; 18.19;
2 Chr 21.13

9.23
2 Ki 11.24

9.24
1 Ki 22.34

9.25
1 Ki 21.1,
19,24-29

9.26
1 Ki 21.19

3. Ahaziah (Judah) defeated and slain

9.27
2 Chr 22.9

27 When Āhăzī′ăh the king of Judah saw this, he fled in the direction of Bĕth-hăg′găn. And Jēhū pursued him, and said, "Shoot him also"; and they shot him[j] in the chariot at the ascent of Gŭr, which is by Ĭb′lĕ-ăm. And he fled to Mĕgĭd′dō, and died there. 28 His servants carried him in a chariot to Jerusalem, and

9.28
2 Ki 23.30

buried him in his tomb with his fathers in the city of David. 29 In the eleventh year of Jōrăm the son of Āhăb, Āhăzī′ăh began to reign over Judah.

4. Jehu's massacre of the house of Ahab
a. Jezebel slain

9.30
Jer 4.30;
Ezek 23.40
9.31
1 Ki 16.9–
20

30 When Jēhū came to Jĕzreēl′, Jĕz′ebĕl heard of it; and she painted her eyes, and adorned her head, and looked out of the window. 31And as Jēhū entered the gate, she said, "Is it peace, you Zĭmrī, murderer of your master?" 32And he lifted up his face to the window, and said, "Who is on my side? Who?" Two or three eunuchs looked out at him. 33 He said, "Throw her down." So they threw her down; and some of her blood spattered on the wall and on the horses, and they trampled on her. 34 Then he went in

9.34
1 Ki 21.25;
16.31

and ate and drank; and he said, "See now to this cursed woman, and bury her; for she is a king's daughter." 35 But when they went to bury her, they found no more of her than the skull and the feet and the palms of her hands. 36 When they came back and told him,

9.36
1 Ki 21.23

he said, "This is the word of the LORD, which he spoke by his servant Ēlī′jăh the Tĭshbīte, 'In the territory of Jĕzreēl′ the dogs shall eat the flesh of Jĕz′ebĕl; 37 and the corpse of Jĕz′ebĕl shall be

9.37
Jer 8.1–3

as dung upon the face of the field in the territory of Jĕzreēl′, so that no one can say, This is Jezebel.' "

b. Ahab's seventy sons beheaded

10.1
1 Ki 16.24–
29

10 Now Āhăb had seventy sons in Sămăr′ĭă. So Jēhū wrote letters, and sent them to Samaria, to the rulers of the city,[k] to the elders, and to the guardians of the sons of Ahab, saying, 2 "Now then, as soon as this letter comes to you, seeing your master's sons are with you, and there are with you chariots and horses, fortified cities also, and weapons, 3 select the best and fittest of your master's sons and set him on his father's throne, and fight for your master's house." 4 But they were exceedingly afraid, and said, "Behold, the two kings could not stand before him; how then

10.5
see 1 Ki
20.4,32

can we stand?" 5 So he who was over the palace, and he who was over the city, together with the elders and the guardians, sent to Jēhū, saying, "We are your servants, and we will do all that you bid us. We will not make any one king; do whatever is good in your eyes." 6 Then he wrote to them a second letter, saying, "If you are on my side, and if you are ready to obey me, take the heads of your master's sons, and come to me at Jĕzreēl′ tomorrow at this time." Now the king's sons, seventy persons, were with the great men of the city, who were bringing them up. 7And when the letter

10.7
1 Ki 21.21

came to them, they took the king's sons, and slew them, seventy persons, and put their heads in baskets, and sent them to him at Jĕzreēl′. 8 When the messenger came and told him, "They have brought the heads of the king's sons," he said, "Lay them in two

---

[j] Syr Vg Compare Gk: Heb lacks *and they shot him*   [k] Gk Vg: Heb *Jĕzreēl′*

heaps at the entrance of the gate until the morning." 9 Then in the morning, when he went out, he stood, and said to all the people, "You are innocent. It was I who conspired against my master, and slew him; but who struck down all these? 10 Know then that there shall fall to the earth nothing of the word of the LORD, which the LORD spoke concerning the house of Āhăb; for the LORD has done what he said by his servant Ēlī′jáh." 11 So Jēhū slew all that remained of the house of Āhăb in Jĕzreēl′, all his great men, and his familiar friends, and his priests, until he left him none remaining.

10.9
2 Ki 9.14–24;
ver 6
10.10
2 Ki 9.7–10;
1 Ki 21.19–29

c. Forty-two princes of Ahaziah slain

12 Then he set out and went to Sàmạr′ĭà. On the way, when he was at Bĕth-ē′kĕd of the Shepherds, 13 Jēhū met the kinsmen of Āházī′áh king of Judah, and he said, "Who are you?" And they answered, "We are the kinsmen of Ahaziah, and we came down to visit the royal princes and the sons of the queen mother." 14 He said, "Take them alive." And they took them alive, and slew them at the pit of Bĕth-ē′kĕd, forty-two persons, and he spared none of them.

10.13
2 Ki 8.24, 29;
2 Chr 22.8

d. Jehonadab slays the rest of the house of Ahab

15 And when he departed from there, he met Jéhŏn′ádăb the son of Rēchăb coming to meet him; and he greeted him, and said to him, "Is your heart true to my heart as mine is to yours?"*l* And Jehonadab answered, "It is." Jēhū said,*m* "If it is, give me your hand." So he gave him his hand. And Jehu took him up with him into the chariot. 16And he said, "Come with me, and see my zeal for the LORD." So he*n* had him ride in his chariot. 17And when he came to Sàmạr′ĭà, he slew all that remained to Āhăb in Samaria, till he had wiped them out, according to the word of the LORD which he spoke to Ēlī′jáh.

*10.15
Jer 35.6ff;
1 Chr 2.55;
Ezra 10.19

10.16
1 Ki 19.10
10.17
2 Ki 9.8;
2 Chr 22.8;
ver 10

e. The massacre of the Baal worshipers

18 Then Jēhū assembled all the people, and said to them, "Āhăb served Bāăl a little; but Jehu will serve him much. 19 Now therefore call to me all the prophets of Bāăl, all his worshipers and all his priests; let none be missing, for I have a great sacrifice to offer to Baal; whoever is missing shall not live." But Jēhū did it with cunning in order to destroy the worshipers of Baal. 20And Jēhū ordered, "Sanctify a solemn assembly for Bāăl." So they proclaimed it. 21And Jēhū sent throughout all Israel; and all the worshipers of Bāăl came, so that there was not a man left who did not come. And they entered the house of Baal, and the house of Baal was filled from one end to the other. 22 He said to him who was in charge of the wardrobe, "Bring out the vestments for all the worshipers of Bāăl." So he brought out the vestments for them. 23 Then Jēhū went into the house of Bāăl with Jéhŏn′ádăb the son of Rechăb; and he said to the worshipers of Baal, "Search, and see that there is no servant of the LORD here among you, but

10.18
1 Ki 16.31, 32
10.19
1 Ki 22.6

10.20
Joel 1.14;
Ex 32.4–6
10.21
1 Ki 16.32;
2 Ki 11.18

l Gk: Heb Is it right with your heart, as my heart is with your heart?
m Gk: Heb lacks Jehu said   *n* Gk Syr Tg: Heb they

10.15 *Jehonadab.* This ascetic is mentioned in Jer 35.6 where his descendants, the Recha-   bites, are put to the test by Jeremiah. Jehu accepted Jehonadab as an honorable man.

10.24
1 Ki 20.39

only the worshipers of Baal." 24 Then he[o] went in to offer sacrifices and burnt offerings.

Now Jēhū had stationed eighty men outside, and said, "The man who allows any of those whom I give into your hands to escape shall forfeit his life." 25 So as soon as he had made an end of offering the burnt offering, Jēhū said to the guard and to the officers, "Go in and slay them; let not a man escape." So when they put them to the sword, the guard and the officers cast them out and went into the inner room[p] of the house of Bāal 26 and they brought out the pillar that was in the house of Bāal, and burned it. 27And they demolished the pillar of Bāal, and demolished the house of Baal, and made it a latrine to this day.

10.25
1 Ki 18.40

10.26
1 Ki 14.23

10.27
Ezra 6.11;
Dan 2.5;
3.29

f. Resumé of Jehu's reign

10.29
1 Ki 12.28,
29

28 Thus Jēhū wiped out Bāal from Israel. 29 But Jēhū did not turn aside from the sins of Jĕrŏbō'ăm the son of Nēbăt, which he made Israel to sin, the golden calves that were in Bĕthĕl, and in Dan. 30And the LORD said to Jēhū, "Because you have done well in carrying out what is right in my eyes, and have done to the house of Āhăb according to all that was in my heart, your sons of the fourth generation shall sit on the throne of Israel." 31 But Jēhū was not careful to walk in the law of the LORD the God of Israel with all his heart; he did not turn from the sins of Jĕrŏbō'-ăm, which he made Israel to sin.

10.30
ver 35;
2 Ki 15.8,
12

10.31
ver 29

32 In those days the LORD began to cut off parts of Israel. Hăz'ăĕl defeated them throughout the territory of Israel: 33 from the Jordan eastward, all the land of Gĭl'ĕăd, the Gădītes, and the Reu'bĕnītes, and the Mănăs'sītes, from Ărŏ'ĕr, which is by the valley of the Arnŏn, that is, Gilead and Băshăn. 34 Now the rest of the acts of Jēhū, and all that he did, and all his might, are they not written in the Book of the Chronicles of the Kings of Israel? 35 So Jēhū slept with his fathers, and they buried him in Sămăr'ĭă. And Jēhŏ'ăhăz his son reigned in his stead. 36 The time that Jēhū reigned over Israel in Sămăr'ĭă was twenty-eight years.

10.32
2 Ki 8.12

10.34
Amos 1.3–5

L. The reign of Athaliah (Judah)

1. Athaliah seizes control

11.1
2 Chr
22.10–12

11.2
ver 21;
2 Ki 12.1

11 Now when Ăthălī'ăh the mother of Āhăzī'ăh saw that her son was dead, she arose and destroyed all the royal family. 2 But Jĕhŏsh'ĕbă, the daughter of King Jŏrăm, sister of Āhăzī'ăh, took Jŏ'ăsh the son of Ahaziah, and stole him away from among the king's sons who were about to be slain, and she put[q] him and his nurse in a bedchamber. Thus she[r] hid him from Ăthălī'ăh, so that he was not slain; 3 and he remained with her six years, hid in the house of the LORD, while Ăthălī'ăh reigned over the land.

2. Jehoiada the priest overthrows Athaliah

*11.4
2 Chr
23.1ff;
ver 19

4 But in the seventh year Jĕhoi'ădă sent and brought the captains of the Carītes and of the guards, and had them come to him

---

o Gk Compare verse 25: Heb *they*
p Cn: Heb *city*   q With 2 Chron 22.11: Heb lacks *and she put*
r Gk Syr Vg Compare 2 Chron 22.11: Heb *they*

11.4 *Carites*, another designation for the Cherethites, the foreign mercenaries hired as the royal bodyguard. Note to 2 Sam 15.18 also explains this.

in the house of the LORD; and he made a covenant with them and
put them under oath in the house of the LORD, and he showed
them the king's son. [5]And he commanded them, "This is the
thing that you shall do: one third of you, those who come off duty
on the sabbath and guard the king's house [6] (another third being
at the gate Sûr and a third at the gate behind the guards), shall
guard the palace; [7] and the two divisions of you, which come on
duty in force on the sabbath and guard the house of the LORD,[s]
[8] shall surround the king, each with his weapons in his hand; and
whoever approaches the ranks is to be slain. Be with the king when
he goes out and when he comes in."

[9] The captains did according to all that Jëhoi'ádà the priest
commanded, and each brought his men who were to go off duty
on the sabbath, with those who were to come on duty on the sabbath, and came to Jehoiada the priest. [10]And the priest delivered
to the captains the spears and shields that had been King David's,
which were in the house of the LORD; [11] and the guards stood,
every man with his weapons in his hand, from the south side of
the house to the north side of the house, around the altar and the
house.[t] [12] Then he brought out the king's son, and put the crown
upon him, and gave him the testimony; and they proclaimed him
king, and anointed him; and they clapped their hands, and said,
"Long live the king!"

[13] When Äthäli'äh heard the noise of the guard and of the
people, she went into the house of the LORD to the people; [14] and
when she looked, there was the king standing by the pillar, according to the custom, and the captains and the trumpeters beside
the king, and all the people of the land rejoicing and blowing
trumpets. And Äthäli'äh rent her clothes, and cried, "Treason!
Treason!" [15] Then Jëhoi'ádà the priest commanded the captains
who were set over the army, "Bring her out between the ranks; and
slay with the sword any one who follows her." For the priest said,
"Let her not be slain in the house of the LORD." [16] So they laid
hands on her; and she went through the horses' entrance to the
king's house, and there she was slain.

[17] And Jëhoi'ádà made a covenant between the LORD and the
king and people, that they should be the LORD's people; and also
between the king and the people. [18] Then all the people of the
land went to the house of Bāäl, and tore it down; his altars and his
images they broke in pieces, and they slew Mättän the priest of
Baal before the altars. And the priest posted watchmen over the
house of the LORD. [19]And he took the captains, the Carïtes, the
guards, and all the people of the land; and they brought the king
down from the house of the LORD, marching through the gate of
the guards to the king's house. And he took his seat on the throne
of the kings. [20] So all the people of the land rejoiced; and the
city was quiet after Äthäli'äh had been slain with the sword at the
king's house.

[21][u] Jëhõ'äsh was seven years old when he began to reign.

[s] Heb the LORD to the king   [t] Heb the house to the king   [u] Ch 12.1 in Heb

11.5	1 Chr 9.25
11.9	2 Chr 23.8
11.10	2 Sam 8.7; 1 Chr 18.7
11.12	1 Sam 10.24
11.13	2 Chr 23.12ff
11.14	2 Ki 23.3; 2 Chr 34.31; 1 Ki 1.39, 40; 2 Ki 9.23
*11.16	
11.17	2 Chr 23.16; 15.12–14; 2 Sam 5.3
11.18	2 Ki 10.26; Deut 12.3; 2 Chr 23.17ff
11.19	ver 4,6
11.21	2 Chr 24.1

11.16 The tragic end of Athaliah was the
logical consequence of her hybrid background. Born of Ahab, a nominal Yahweh
worshiper, and Jezebel, an outright Baal
worshiper, she followed in the footsteps of her
idolatrous mother. Just as Jezebel had done
before her, Athaliah also evilly influenced a
spiritually spineless husband (king of Judah).

M. The reign of Jehoash (Joash:Judah)

1. Faithful Jehoash

12 In the seventh year of Jēhū Jéhō'ăsh began to reign, and he reigned forty years in Jerusalem. His mother's name was Zĭb'ĭăh of Beër-shē'bá. 2And Jéhō'ăsh did what was right in the eyes of the LORD all his days, because Jéhoi'ádá the priest instructed him. 3 Nevertheless the high places were not taken away; the people continued to sacrifice and burn incense on the high places.

2. Jehoash repairs the Temple

4 Jéhō'ăsh said to the priests, "All the money of the holy things which is brought into the house of the LORD, the money for which each man is assessed—the money from the assessment of persons —and the money which a man's heart prompts him to bring into the house of the LORD, 5 let the priests take, each from his acquaintance; and let them repair the house wherever any need of repairs is discovered." 6 But by the twenty-third year of King Jéhō'ăsh the priests had made no repairs on the house. 7 Therefore King Jéhō'ăsh summoned Jéhoi'ádá the priest and the other priests and said to them, "Why are you not repairing the house? Now therefore take no more money from your acquaintances, but hand it over for the repair of the house." 8 So the priests agreed that they should take no more money from the people, and that they should not repair the house.

9 Then Jéhoi'ádá the priest took a chest, and bored a hole in the lid of it, and set it beside the altar on the right side as one entered the house of the LORD; and the priests who guarded the threshold put in it all the money that was brought into the house of the LORD. 10And whenever they saw that there was much money in the chest, the king's secretary and the high priest came up and they counted and tied up in bags the money that was found in the house of the LORD. 11 Then they would give the money that was weighed out into the hands of the workmen who had the oversight of the house of the LORD; and they paid it out to the carpenters and the builders who worked upon the house of the LORD, 12 and to the masons and the stonecutters, as well as to buy timber and quarried stone for making repairs on the house of the LORD, and for any outlay upon the repairs of the house. 13 But there were not made for the house of the LORD basins of silver, snuffers, bowls, trumpets, or any vessels of gold, or of silver, from the money that was brought into the house of the LORD, 14 for that was given to the workmen who were repairing the house of the LORD with it. 15And they did not ask an accounting from the men into whose hand they delivered the money to pay out to the workmen, for they dealt honestly. 16 The money from the guilt offerings and the money from the sin offerings was not brought into the house of the LORD; it belonged to the priests.

3. Jehoash pays off Hazael with Temple money

17 At that time Hăz'áël king of Syria went up and fought against Găth, and took it. But when Hazael set his face to go up against Jerusalem, 18 Jéhō'ăsh king of Judah took all the votive gifts that Jéhŏsh'ăphăt and Jéhō'răm and Ăhăzī'ăh, his fathers, the kings of

12.3 2 Ki 14.4; 15.35

12.4 2 Ki 22.4; Ex 35.5; 1 Chr 29.3–9

12.6 2 Chr 24.5
12.7 2 Chr 24.6

12.9 2 Chr 24.8; Mk 12.41; Lk 21.1

12.10 2 Ki 19.2

12.12 2 Ki 22.5,6

12.13 2 Chr 24.14; 1 Ki 7.48, 50

12.15 2 Ki 22.7

12.16 Lev 5.15-18; 4.24,29; Num 18.9, 19

12.17 2 Ki 8.12; 2 Chr 24.23
12.18 1 Ki 15.18; 2 Ki 18.15, 16

Judah, had dedicated, and his own votive gifts, and all the gold that was found in the treasuries of the house of the LORD and of the king's house, and sent these to Häz′äel king of Syria. Then Hazael went away from Jerusalem.

4. Jehoash succeeded by Amaziah

19 Now the rest of the acts of Jō′äsh, and all that he did, are they not written in the Book of the Chronicles of the Kings of Judah? 20 His servants arose and made a conspiracy, and slew Jō′äsh in the house of Mīllō, on the way that goes down to Sīllä. 21 It was Jōz′ȧcar the son of Shǐm′ë-ȧth and Jěhō′zȧbȧd the son of Shōmer, his servants, who struck him down, so that he died. And they buried him with his fathers in the city of David, and Ȧmȧzī′ȧh his son reigned in his stead.

N. Jehoahaz, king of Israel

13 In the twenty-third year of Jō′äsh the son of Āhȧzī′ȧh, king of Judah, Jěhō′ȧhȧz the son of Jěhū began to reign over Israel in Sȧmȧr′ïä, and he reigned seventeen years. 2 He did what was evil in the sight of the LORD, and followed the sins of Jěrŏbō′-ȧm the son of Nēbȧt, which he made Israel to sin; he did not depart from them. 3And the anger of the LORD was kindled against Israel, and he gave them continually into the hand of Häz′äel king of Syria and into the hand of Běn-hā′dȧd the son of Hazael. 4 Then Jěhō′ȧhȧz besought the LORD, and the LORD hearkened to him; for he saw the oppression of Israel, how the king of Syria oppressed them. 5 (Therefore the LORD gave Israel a savior, so that they escaped from the hand of the Syrians; and the people of Israel dwelt in their homes as formerly. 6 Nevertheless they did not depart from the sins of the house of Jěrŏbō′ȧm, which he made Israel to sin, but walked[v] in them; and the Ȧshē′räh also remained in Sȧmȧr′ïä.) 7 For there was not left to Jěhō′ȧhȧz an army of more than fifty horsemen and ten chariots and ten thousand footmen; for the king of Syria had destroyed them and made them like the dust at threshing. 8 Now the rest of the acts of Jěhō′ȧhȧz and all that he did, and his might, are they not written in the Book of the Chronicles of the Kings of Israel? 9 So Jěhō′ȧhȧz slept with his fathers, and they buried him in Sȧmȧr′ïä; and Jō′äsh his son reigned in his stead.

O. Jehoash (Joash), king of Israel

1. The wickedness of Jehoash

10 In the thirty-seventh year of Jō′äsh king of Judah Jěhō′äsh the son of Jěhō′ȧhȧz began to reign over Israel in Sȧmȧr′ïä, and he reigned sixteen years. 11 He also did what was evil in the sight of the LORD; he did not depart from all the sins of Jěrŏbō′ȧm the son of Nēbȧt, which he made Israel to sin, but he walked in them. 12 Now the rest of the acts of Jō′äsh, and all that he did, and the

v Gk Syr Tg Vg: Heb he walked

12.20
2 Ki 14.5;
2 Chr
24.25;
1 Ki 11.27
*12.21
2 Chr
24.26,27;
2 Ki 14.1

13.2
1 Ki 12.26–33

13.3
Judg 2.14;
2 Ki 8.12;
12.17
13.4
Num 21.7–9; Ps 78.34;
Ex 3.7;
2 Ki 14.26
*13.5
ver 25;
2 Ki 14.25,
27
13.6
ver 2;
1 Ki 16.33
13.7
Amos 1.3

13.9
2 Ki 10.35

13.12
ver 14–19;
2 Ki 14.8–15;
2 Chr
25.17ff

12.21 Read 2 Chr 24.25–27.
13.5 a savior may be a reference to the Assyrians, who were threatening the Syrians, thereby giving Israel a respite.

might with which he fought against Ămăzī'ăh king of Judah, are they not written in the Book of the Chronicles of the Kings of Israel? 13 So Jō'ăsh slept with his fathers, and Jĕróbō'ăm sat upon his throne; and Joash was buried in Sámạr'ĭă with the kings of Israel.

2. *Elisha and the* LORD'S *arrow of victory*

13.14
2 Ki 2.12

14 Now when Ēlī'shă had fallen sick with the illness of which he was to die, Jō'ăsh king of Israel went down to him, and wept before him, crying, "My father, my father! The chariots of Israel and its horsemen!" 15And Ēlī'shă said to him, "Take a bow and arrows"; so he took a bow and arrows. 16 Then he said to the king of Israel, "Draw the bow"; and he drew it. And Ēlī'shă laid his hands upon the king's hands. 17And he said, "Open the window eastward"; and he opened it. Then Ēlī'shă said, "Shoot"; and he shot. And he said, "The LORD's arrow of victory, the arrow of victory over Syria! For you shall fight the Syrians in Āphĕk until you have made an end of them." 18And he said, "Take the arrows"; and he took them. And he said to the king of Israel, "Strike the ground with them"; and he struck three times, and stopped. 19 Then the man of God was angry with him, and said, "You should have struck five or six times; then you would have struck down Syria until you had made an end of it, but now you will strike down Syria only three times."

13.17
1 Ki 20.26

13.19
ver 25

3. *The miracle at Elisha's tomb*

13.20
see 2 Ki
3.7; 24.2

20 So Ēlī'shă died, and they buried him. Now bands of Mō'-ăbītes used to invade the land in the spring of the year. 21And as a man was being buried, lo, a marauding band was seen and the man was cast into the grave of Ēlī'shă; and as soon as the man touched the bones of Elisha, he revived, and stood on his feet.

4. *The victories of Israel*

13.22
2 Ki 8.12
13.23
2 Ki 14.27;
Ex 2.24,25;
Gen 13.16,
17

22 Now Hăz'ăĕl king of Syria oppressed Israel all the days of Jĕhō'ăhăz. 23 But the LORD was gracious to them and had compassion on them, and he turned toward them, because of his covenant with Abraham, Isaac, and Jacob, and would not destroy them; nor has he cast them from his presence until now.

13.25
2 Ki 10.32,
33; 14.25;
ver 18,19

24 When Hăz'ăĕl king of Syria died, Bĕn-hă'dăd his son became king in his stead. 25 Then Jĕhō'ăsh the son of Jĕhō'ăhăz took again from Bĕn-hă'dăd the son of Hăz'ăĕl the cities which he had taken from Jehoahaz his father in war. Three times Jō'ăsh defeated him and recovered the cities of Israel.

P. Amaziah, king of Judah

1. *Events of Amaziah's reign*

14.1
2 Ki 13.10;
2 Chr 25.1

14 In the second year of Jō'ăsh the son of Jō'ăhaz, king of Israel, Ămăzī'ăh the son of Joash, king of Judah, began to reign. 2 He was twenty-five years old when he began to reign, and he reigned twenty-nine years in Jerusalem. His mother's name was Jĕhō'-ăddĭn of Jerusalem. 3And he did what was right in the eyes of the LORD, yet not like David his father; he did in all things as Jō'-ăsh his father had done. 4 But the high places were not removed; the people still sacrificed and burned incense on the high places.

14.4
2 Ki 12.3;
16.4

5And as soon as the royal power was firmly in his hand he killed his servants who had slain the king his father. 6 But he did not put to death the children of the murderers; according to what is written in the book of the law of Moses, where the LORD commanded, "The fathers shall not be put to death for the children, or the children be put to death for the fathers; but every man shall die for his own sin."

14.5
2 Ki 12.20
14.6
Deut 24.16;
Ezek 18.4,
20

7 He killed ten thousand Ē′dōmītes in the Valley of Salt and took Sēlā by storm, and called it Jōkthe-ēl, which is its name to this day.

*14.7
2 Chr
25.11;
2 Sam 8.13;
Josh 15.38

2. Amaziah wars against Israel (Jehoash)

8 Then Ămăzī′áh sent messengers to Jĕhō′ăsh the son of Jĕhō′áhăz, son of Jēhū, king of Israel, saying, "Come, let us look one another in the face." 9And Jĕhō′ăsh king of Israel sent word to Ămăzī′áh king of Judah, "A thistle on Lebanon sent to a cedar on Lebanon, saying, 'Give your daughter to my son for a wife'; and a wild beast of Lebanon passed by and trampled down the thistle. 10 You have indeed smitten Ēdŏm, and your heart has lifted you up. Be content with your glory, and stay at home; for why should you provoke trouble so that you fall, you and Judah with you?"

14.8
2 Chr
25.17–24
14.9
Judg 9.8–15

14.10
ver 7;
Deut 8.14;
2 Chr
26.16;
32.25

11 But Ămăzī′áh would not listen. So Jĕhō′ăsh king of Israel went up, and he and Amaziah king of Judah faced one another in battle at Bĕth-shĕ′mĕsh, which belongs to Judah. 12And Judah was defeated by Israel, and every man fled to his home. 13And Jĕhō′ăsh king of Israel captured Ămăzī′áh king of Judah, the son of Jehoash, son of Āhăzī′áh, at Bĕth-shĕ′mĕsh, and came to Jerusalem, and broke down the wall of Jerusalem for four hundred cubits, from the Ē′phrăim Gate to the Corner Gate. 14And he seized all the gold and silver, and all the vessels that were found in the house of the LORD and in the treasuries of the king's house, also hostages, and he returned to Sămăr′ĭá.

14.11
Josh 19.38
14.12
2 Sam 18.17
14.13
Neh 8.16;
12.39;
2 Chr 25.23

14.14
2 Ki 12.18

3. Death of Jehoash

15 Now the rest of the acts of Jĕhō′ăsh which he did, and his might, and how he fought with Ămăzī′áh king of Judah, are they not written in the Book of the Chronicles of the Kings of Israel? 16And Jĕhō′ăsh slept with his fathers, and was buried in Sămăr′ĭá with the kings of Israel; and Jĕrŏbŏ′ăm his son reigned in his stead.

14.15
2 Ki 13.12

4. Amaziah replaced by Azariah (Uzziah)

17 Ămăzī′áh the son of Jō′ăsh, king of Judah, lived fifteen years after the death of Jĕhō′ăsh son of Jĕhō′áhăz, king of Israel. 18 Now the rest of the deeds of Ămăzī′áh, are they not written in the Book of the Chronicles of the Kings of Judah? 19And they made a conspiracy against him in Jerusalem, and he fled to Lăchĭsh. But they sent after him to Lachish, and slew him there. 20And they brought him upon horses; and he was buried in Jerusalem with his fathers in the city of David. 21And all the people of Judah took Ăzărī′áh, who was sixteen years old, and made him king instead of his father Ămăzī′áh. 22 He built Ēlăth and restored it to Judah, after the king slept with his fathers.

14.17
2 Chr
25.25–28

14.19
Josh 10.31;
2 Ki 18.14,
17

*14.21

14.22
2 Ki 16.6;
2 Chr 26.2

14.7 Sela, "Rock," the capital city of Edom.   14.21 Azariah, known also as Uzziah.

Q. Reign of Jeroboam II (Israel)

23 In the fifteenth year of Ămázī'áh the son of Jō'ásh, king of Judah, Jĕróbō'ám the son of Joash, king of Israel, began to reign in Sàmạr'iá, and he reigned forty-one years. 24And he did what was evil in the sight of the LORD; he did not depart from all the sins of Jĕróbō'ám the son of Nēbăt, which he made Israel to sin. 25 He restored the border of Israel from the entrance of Hāmáth as far as the Sea of the Ar'ábàh, according to the word of the LORD, the God of Israel, which he spoke by his servant Jonah the son of Ămĭt'taī, the prophet, who was from Găth-hē'phèr. 26 For the LORD saw that the affliction of Israel was very bitter, for there was none left, bond or free, and there was none to help Israel. 27 But the LORD had not said that he would blot out the name of Israel from under heaven, so he saved them by the hand of Jĕróbō'ám the son of Jō'ásh.

28 Now the rest of the acts of Jĕróbō'ám, and all that he did, and his might, how he fought, and how he recovered for Israel Damascus and Hāmáth, which had belonged to Judah, are they not written in the Book of the Chronicles of the Kings of Israel? 29And Jĕróbō'ám slept with his fathers, the kings of Israel, and Zĕchărī'áh his son reigned in his stead.

R. Judah under Azariah (Uzziah)

15 In the twenty-seventh year of Jĕróbō'ám king of Israel Ăzárī'áh the son of Ămázī'áh, king of Judah, began to reign. 2 He was sixteen years old when he began to reign, and he reigned fifty-two years in Jerusalem. His mother's name was Jĕcólī'áh of Jerusalem. 3And he did what was right in the eyes of the LORD, according to all that his father Ămázī'áh had done. 4Nevertheless the high places were not taken away; the people still sacrificed and burned incense on the high places. 5And the LORD smote the king, so that he was a leper to the day of his death, and he dwelt in a separate house. And Jōthám the king's son was over the household, governing the people of the land. 6 Now the rest of the acts of Ăzárī'áh, and all that he did, are they not written in the Book of the Chronicles of the Kings of Judah? 7And Ăzárī'áh slept with his fathers, and they buried him with his fathers in the city of David, and Jōthám his son reigned in his stead.

S. Reign of Zechariah (Israel)

8 In the thirty-eighth year of Ăzárī'áh king of Judah Zĕchărī'áh the son of Jĕróbō'ám reigned over Israel in Sàmạr'iá six months. 9And he did what was evil in the sight of the LORD, as his fathers had done. He did not depart from the sins of Jĕróbō'ám the son of Nēbăt, which he made Israel to sin. 10 Shăllúm the son of Jábĕsh conspired against him, and struck him down at Ĭb'lĕ-ám,*w* and killed him, and reigned in his stead. 11 Now the rest of the deeds of Zĕchărī'áh, behold, they are written in the Book of the Chronicles of the Kings of Israel. 12 (This was the promise of the LORD which he gave to Jēhū, "Your sons shall sit upon the throne of Israel to the fourth generation." And so it came to pass.)

w Gk Compare 9.27: Heb *before the people*

14.25
2 Ki 10.32;
1 Ki 8.65;
Deut 3.17;
Jon 1.1;
Mt 12.39,
40;
Josh 19.13

14.26
2 Ki 13.4;
Deut 32.36

14.27
2 Ki 13.5,
23

14.28
2 Sam 8.6;
1 Ki 11.24;
2 Chr 8.3

14.29
2 Ki 15.8

15.1
2 Ki 14.21;
2 Chr
26.1,3,4
Uzziah

15.2
2 Chr
26.3,4

15.4
2 Ki 12.3;
14.4

15.5
2 Chr
26.19–21

15.7
2 Chr 26.23

15.10
Amos 7.9

15.12
2 Ki 10.30

T. Reign of Shallum (Israel)

13 Shăllúm the son of Jābĕsh began to reign in the thirty-ninth
year of Úzzí'áh king of Judah, and he reigned one month in
Sámạr'íȧ. 14 Then Mĕn'áhĕm the son of Gādī came up from Tịrzȧh and came to Sámạr'íȧ, and he struck down Shăllúm the son of
Jābĕsh in Samaria and slew him, and reigned in his stead. 15 Now
the rest of the deeds of Shăllúm, and the conspiracy which he
made, behold, they are written in the Book of the Chronicles of the
Kings of Israel. 16At that time Mĕn'áhĕm sacked Táppū'áh x and
all who were in it and its territory from Tịrzȧh on; because they
did not open it to him, therefore he sacked it, and he ripped up all
the women in it who were with child.

15.13
ver 1,8

15.14
1 Ki 14.17

15.16
1 Ki 4.24;
2 Ki 8.12

U. Reign of Menahem (Israel)

17 In the thirty-ninth year of Ăzȧrí'áh king of Judah Mĕn'áhĕm
the son of Gādī began to reign over Israel, and he reigned ten years
in Sámạr'íȧ. 18And he did what was evil in the sight of the
LORD; he did not depart all his days from all the sins of
Jĕróbō'ám the son of Nēbăt, which he made Israel to sin. 19 Púl
the king of Assyria came against the land; and Mĕn'áhĕm gave Pul
a thousand talents of silver, that he might help him to confirm his
hold of the royal power. 20 Mĕn'áhĕm exacted the money from
Israel, that is, from all the wealthy men, fifty shekels of silver from
every man, to give to the king of Assyria. So the king of Assyria
turned back, and did not stay there in the land. 21 Now the rest
of the deeds of Mĕn'áhĕm, and all that he did, are they not written
in the Book of the Chronicles of the Kings of Israel? 22And Mĕn'-
áhĕm slept with his fathers, and Pĕkáhī'áh his son reigned in his
stead.

15.17
ver 1,8,13

*15.19
1 Chr 5.26

V. Reign of Pekahiah (Israel)

23 In the fiftieth year of Ăzȧrí'áh king of Judah Pĕkáhí'áh the
son of Mĕn'áhĕm began to reign over Israel in Sámạr'íȧ, and he
reigned two years. 24And he did what was evil in the sight of the
LORD; he did not turn away from the sins of Jĕróbō'ám the son of
Nēbăt, which he made Israel to sin. 25And Pēkáh the son of
Rĕmálí'áh, his captain, conspired against him with fifty men of the
Gïl'ĕădītes, and slew him in Sámạr'íȧ, in the citadel of the king's
house;y he slew him, and reigned in his stead. 26 Now the rest of
the deeds of Pĕkáhī'áh, and all that he did, behold, they are written
in the Book of the Chronicles of the Kings of Israel.

15.23
ver 1,8,
13,17

15.25
1 Ki 16.18

W. Reign of Pekah (Israel)

27 In the fifty-second year of Ăzȧrí'áh king of Judah Pēkáh the
son of Rĕmálí'áh began to reign over Israel in Sámạr'íȧ, and

*15.27
ver 23;
Isa 7.1

x Compare Gk: Heb Tiphsáh
y Heb adds Argób and Á'riĕh, which probably belong to the list of places in verse 29

15.19 Pul, another name for Tiglath-
pileser III (744–727 B.C.). His inscriptions
note Menahem's payment of tribute.
15.27 twenty years. Pekah actually reigned

only 8 years, but he evidently had the court
records include the 12 years he had assisted
Pekahiah and Menahem, the two previous
kings. See note to 18.1 for further discussion.

reigned twenty years. 28And he did what was evil in the sight of
the LORD; he did not depart from the sins of Jĕróbō'ám the son of
Nēbăt, which he made Israel to sin.

*15.29
ver 19;
2 Ki 17.6;
1 Chr 5.26

29 In the days of Pēkáh king of Israel Tĭg'lăth-pĭlē'şĕr king of
Assyria came and captured Ījón, Ābĕl-bĕth-mā'ácáh, Jánō'áh,
Kĕdĕsh, Hāzor, Gil'ëád, and Găl'ĭleē, all the land of Năph'tălī;
and he carried the people captive to Assyria. 30 Then Hōshĕ'á the
son of Ēláh made a conspiracy against Pēkáh the son of Rĕmálī'áh,
and struck him down, and slew him, and reigned in his stead, in
the twentieth year of Jōthám the son of Ŭzzī'áh. 31 Now the rest
of the acts of Pēkáh, and all that he did, behold, they are written
in the Book of the Chronicles of the Kings of Israel.

X. *Reign of Jotham (Judah)*

15.32
2 Chr
27.1ff
*15.33

32 In the second year of Pēkáh the son of Rĕmálī'áh, king of
Israel, Jōthám the son of Ŭzzī'áh, king of Judah, began to reign.
33 He was twenty-five years old when he began to reign, and he
reigned sixteen years in Jerusalem. His mother's name was Jĕru'-
shá the daughter of Zādŏk. 34And he did what was right in the eyes
of the LORD, according to all that his father Ŭzzī'áh had done.
35 Nevertheless the high places were not removed; the people still
sacrificed and burned incense on the high places. He built the
upper gate of the house of the LORD. 36 Now the rest of the acts
of Jōthám, and all that he did, are they not written in the Book of
the Chronicles of the Kings of Judah? 37 In those days the LORD
began to send Rēzĭn the king of Syria and Pēkáh the son of
Rĕmálī'áh against Judah. 38 Jōthám slept with his fathers, and was
buried with his fathers in the city of David his father; and Āhăz his
son reigned in his stead.

15.34
ver 3;
2 Chr 26.4,5
15.35
ver 4;
2 Chr 27.3

15.37
2 Ki 16.5;
Isa 7.1;
ver 27

Y. *Reign of Ahaz (Judah)*

1. *Description of Ahaz's reign*

16.1
2 Chr 28.1ff

16 In the seventeenth year of Pēkáh the son of Rĕmálī'áh,
Āhăz the son of Jōthám, king of Judah, began to reign.
2Āhăz was twenty years old when he began to reign, and he
reigned sixteen years in Jerusalem. And he did not do what was
right in the eyes of the LORD his God, as his father David had
done, 3 but he walked in the way of the kings of Israel. He even
burned his son as an offering,z according to the abominable practices of the nations whom the LORD drove out before the people
of Israel. 4And he sacrificed and burned incense on the high
places, and on the hills, and under every green tree.

16.3
Lev 18.21;
2 Ki 17.17;
21.6;
Deut 12.31;
2 Ki 21.2,11
16.4
Deut 12.2;
2 Ki 14.4

2. *Ahaz delivered from Syria and Israel by Tiglath-pileser*

16.5
2 Ki 15.37;
Isa 7.1;
2 Chr 28.5,6
16.6
2 Ki 14.22;
2 Chr 26.2

5 Then Rēzĭn king of Syria and Pēkáh the son of Rĕmálī'áh,
king of Israel, came up to wage war on Jerusalem, and they besieged Āhăz but could not conquer him. 6At that timea the king of
Ēdŏmb recovered Ēláth for Edom,b and drove the men of Judah

z Or *made his son to pass through the fire*
a Heb *At that time Rēzĭn*   b Heb *Aram (Syria)*

15.29 Read 16.5–9 for more details.
15.33 *sixteen years.* Four years of co-regency

with Azariah have not been included as was
done in verse 30.

from Elath; and the Ē'dómîtes came to Elath, where they dwell
to this day. 7 So Āhäz sent messengers to Tĭg'läth-pĭlḗ'ṣêr king of
Assyria, saying, "I am your servant and your son. Come up, and
rescue me from the hand of the king of Syria and from the hand of
the king of Israel, who are attacking me." 8Āhäz also took the
silver and gold that was found in the house of the LORD and in the
treasures of the king's house, and sent a present to the king of
Assyria. 9And the king of Assyria hearkened to him; the king of
Assyria marched up against Damascus, and took it, carrying its
people captive to Kîr, and he killed Rĕzin.

16.7
2 Chr
28.16ff;
2 Ki 15.29

16.8
2 Ki 12.17,
18

16.9
2 Chr
28.21;
Amos 1.3–5

3. Ahaz and the strange altar

10 When King Āhäz went to Damascus to meet Tĭg'läth-pĭlḗ'-
ṣêr king of Assyria, he saw the altar that was at Damascus. And
King Ahaz sent to Ūrī'áh the priest a model of the altar, and its
pattern, exact in all its details. 11And Ūrī'áh the priest built the
altar; in accordance with all that King Āhäz had sent from Damascus, so Uriah the priest made it, before King Ahaz arrived from
Damascus. 12And when the king came from Damascus, the king
viewed the altar. Then the king drew near to the altar, and went
up on it, 13 and burned his burnt offering and his cereal offering,
and poured his drink offering, and threw the blood of his peace
offerings upon the altar. 14And the bronze altar which was before
the LORD he removed from the front of the house, from the place
between his altar and the house of the LORD, and put it on the
north side of his altar. 15And King Āhäz commanded Ūrī'áh the
priest, saying, "Upon the great altar burn the morning burnt
offering, and the evening cereal offering, and the king's burnt
offering, and his cereal offering, with the burnt offering of all the
people of the land, and their cereal offering, and their drink offering; and throw upon it all the blood of the burnt offering, and all
the blood of the sacrifice; but the bronze altar shall be for me to
inquire by." 16 Ūrī'áh the priest did all this, as King Āhäz commanded.

16.10
2 Ki 15.29;
Isa 8.2

16.14
2 Chr 4.1

16.15
Ex 29.39–41

17 And King Āhäz cut off the frames of the stands, and removed
the laver from them, and he took down the sea from off the bronze
oxen that were under it, and put it upon a pediment of stone.
18And the covered way for the sabbath which had been built inside
the palace, and the outer entrance for the king he removed from^c

16.17
1 Ki 7.23–
28

4. Ahaz's death and the succession

the house of the LORD, because of the king of Assyria. 19 Now the
rest of the acts of Āhäz which he did, are they not written in the
Book of the Chronicles of the Kings of Judah? 20And Āhäz slept
with his fathers, and was buried with his fathers in the city of
David; and Hĕzĕkī'áh his son reigned in his stead.

16.20
2 Chr 28.27

Z. The end of Israel

1. Samaria captured by Assyria

17 In the twelfth year of Āhäz king of Judah Hōshĕ'á the son
of Ēlâh began to reign in Sămạr'iä over Israel, and he
reigned nine years. 2And he did what was evil in the sight of the
LORD, yet not as the kings of Israel who were before him. 3Against

17.1
2 Ki 15.30

17.3
2 Ki 18.9–
12

^c Cn: Heb turned to

him came up Shălmănē'ṣẹr king of Assyria; and Hōshẹ'å became his vassal, and paid him tribute. 4 But the king of Assyria found treachery in Hōshẹ'å; for he had sent messengers to So, king of Egypt, and offered no tribute to the king of Assyria, as he had done year by year; therefore the king of Assyria shut him up, and bound him in prison. 5 Then the king of Assyria invaded all the land and came to Sȧmạr'ïȧ, and for three years he besieged it. 6 In the ninth year of Hōshẹ'å the king of Assyria captured Sȧmạrï'ȧ, and he carried the Israelites away to Assyria, and placed them in Hālȧh, and on the Hābor, the river of Gōzȧn, and in the cities of the Mēdes.

2. The sins of Israel which brought judgment

7 And this was so, because the people of Israel had sinned against the LORD their God, who had brought them up out of the land of Egypt from under the hand of Phạraōh king of Egypt, and had feared other gods 8 and walked in the customs of the nations whom the LORD drove out before the people of Israel, and in the customs which the kings of Israel had introduced.[d] 9And the people of Israel did secretly against the LORD their God things that were not right. They built for themselves high places at all their towns, from watchtower to fortified city; 10 they set up for themselves pillars and Ȧshē'rïm on every high hill and under every green tree; 11 and there they burned incense on all the high places, as the nations did whom the LORD carried away before them. And they did wicked things, provoking the LORD to anger, 12 and they served idols, of which the LORD had said to them, "You shall not do this." 13 Yet the LORD warned Israel and Judah by every prophet and every seer, saying, "Turn from your evil ways and keep my commandments and my statutes, in accordance with all the law which I commanded your fathers, and which I sent to you by my servants the prophets." 14 But they would not listen, but were stubborn, as their fathers had been, who did not believe in the LORD their God. 15 They despised his statutes, and his covenant that he made with their fathers, and the warnings which he gave them. They went after false idols, and became false, and they followed the nations that were round about them, concerning whom the LORD had commanded them that they should not do like them. 16And they forsook all the commandments of the LORD their God, and made for themselves molten images of two calves; and they made an Ashē'rȧh, and worshiped all the host of heaven, and served Bȧȧl. 17And they burned their sons and their daughters as offerings,[e] and used divination and sorcery, and sold themselves to do evil in the sight of the LORD, provoking him to anger.

Marginal references: 17.5 Hos 13.16; *17.6 Hos 13.16; Deut 28.64; 29.27,28; 1 Chr 5.26; 2 Ki 18.10,11; *17.7 Josh 23.16; Ex 14.15–30; Judg 6.10; 17.8 Lev 18.3; Deut 18.9; 2 Ki 16.3; 17.9 2 Ki 18.8; 17.10 Ex 34.12–14; 1 Ki 14.23; Mic 5.14; 17.12 Ex 20.3,4; 17.13 1 Sam 9.9; Jer 18.11; 25.5;35.15; 17.14 Ex 32.9; Deut 31.27; Acts 7.51; 17.15 Jer 8.9; Deut 29.25; 32.21; Deut 12.30,31; 17.16 1 Ki 12.28; 14.15,23; 2 Ki 21.3; 1 Ki 16.31; 17.17 Lev 19.26; 2 Ki 16.3; Deut 18.10–12; 1 Ki 21.20

d Heb obscure   e Or made their sons and their daughters pass through the fire

17.6 king of Assyria. Shalmaneser (727–722 B.C.) initiated the siege of Samaria, but he died before the city capitulated. His successor, Sargon II (722–705 B.C.), claimed to have captured Samaria and taken the people captive. Thus, the Northern Kingdom ceased late in 722 or early in 721 B.C.

17.7 The captivity of Israel (the ten tribes) was an inevitable penalty for their wickedness. That captivity has never been ended. When some of the people of God returned from the seventy years' captivity, they were largely descendants of the southern tribes of the kingdom of Judah, although there were also individuals from Israel who returned with them. Hosea predicted that the northern tribes would never return as a nation and set up their kingdom again in the Promised Land (Hos 1.6, 9). Apparently (judging from the way Paul quotes and interprets Hos 2.23 in Rom 9.22–26) their ranks were to be filled by Gentile converts in the church of Christ.

18 Therefore the LORD was very angry with Israel, and removed them out of his sight; none was left but the tribe of Judah only. 19 Judah also did not keep the commandments of the LORD their God, but walked in the customs which Israel had introduced. 20And the LORD rejected all the descendants of Israel, and afflicted them, and gave them into the hand of spoilers, until he had cast them out of his sight. 21 When he had torn Israel from the house of David they made Jĕróbō'ám the son of Nēbăt king. And Jeroboam drove Israel from following the LORD and made them commit great sin. 22 The people of Israel walked in all the sins which Jĕróbō'ám did; they did not depart from them, 23 until the LORD removed Israel out of his sight, as he had spoken by all his servants the prophets. So Israel was exiled from their own land to Assyria until this day.

3. *Israel resettled: the origin of the Samaritans*

24 And the king of Assyria brought people from Babylon, Cŭtháh, Āvvá, Hāmáth, and Sëpharvá'ím, and placed them in the cities of Sámar'iä instead of the people of Israel; and they took possession of Samaria, and dwelt in its cities. 25And at the beginning of their dwelling there, they did not fear the LORD; therefore the LORD sent lions among them, which killed some of them. 26 So the king of Assyria was told, "The nations which you have carried away and placed in the cities of Sámar'iä do not know the law of the god of the land; therefore he has sent lions among them, and behold, they are killing them, because they do not know the law of the god of the land." 27 Then the king of Assyria commanded, "Send there one of the priests whom you carried away thence; and let him*ƒ* go and dwell there, and teach them the law of the god of the land." 28 So one of the priests whom they had carried away from Sámar'iä came and dwelt in Bĕthĕl, and taught them how they should fear the LORD.

29 But every nation still made gods of its own, and put them in the shrines of the high places which the Sámar'ítáns had made, every nation in the cities in which they dwelt; 30 the men of Babylon made Súc'cóth-bē'nóth, the men of Cŭth made Nĕrgal, the men of Hāmáth made Āsh'imá, 31 and the Av'vítes made Nĭbhăz and Tartăk; and the Sëphar'vítes burned their children in the fire to Ádrăm'mĕlĕch and Anăm'mĕlĕch, the gods of Sëpharvá'ím. 32 They also feared the LORD, and appointed from among themselves all sorts of people as priests of the high places, who sacrificed for them in the shrines of the high places. 33 So they feared the LORD but also served their own gods, after the manner of the nations from among whom they had been carried away. 34 To this day they do according to the former manner.

They do not fear the LORD, and they do not follow the statutes or the ordinances or the law or the commandment which the LORD commanded the children of Jacob, whom he named Israel. 35 The

ƒ Syr Vg: Heb *them*

17.18
ver 6;
1 Ki 11.13,
32,36
17.19
1 Ki 14.22,
23;
2 Ki 16.3
17.20
2 Ki 15.29
17.21
1 Ki 11.11,
31;
12.20,28–
33
17.23
ver 6,13

★17.24
Ezra 4.2,10;
2 Ki 18.34

17.27
Mic 3.11

★17.29

17.30
ver 24
17.31
ver 17,24

17.32
1 Ki 12.31
17.33
Zeph 1.5

17.34
Gen 32.28;
35.10
17.35
Judg 6.10;
Ex 20.5

17.24 This policy of interchanging minority groups was carried on by Sargon's grandson Esarhaddon (681–669 B.C.; see Ezra 4.2), and great-grandson Ashurbanipal (669–633 B.C.), called *Osnapper* in Ezra 4.10.
17.29 *Samaritans.* This is the first appear-ance of the name which the people of Judah gave to the mixed peoples in central and northern Palestine. While they served the LORD in name so as to insure their safety, they persisted in worshiping their own gods. See note to Jn 4.5.

LORD made a covenant with them, and commanded them, "You
shall not fear other gods or bow yourselves to them or serve them
or sacrifice to them; ³⁶ but you shall fear the LORD, who brought
you out of the land of Egypt with great power and with an outstretched arm; you shall bow yourselves to him, and to him you
shall sacrifice. ³⁷And the statutes and the ordinances and the law
and the commandment which he wrote for you, you shall always
be careful to do. You shall not fear other gods, ³⁸ and you shall not
forget the covenant that I have made with you. You shall not fear
other gods, ³⁹ but you shall fear the LORD your God, and he will
deliver you out of the hand of all your enemies." ⁴⁰ However they
would not listen, but they did according to their former manner.

41 So these nations feared the LORD, and also served their
graven images; their children likewise, and their children's children—as their fathers did, so they do to this day.

IV. The kingdom of Judah to the captivity 18.1–25.30

A. The reign of Hezekiah

1. Summary of the acts of Hezekiah

18 In the third year of Hŏshḗ'á son of Ēláh, king of Israel,
Hĕzĕkī'áh the son of Āhăz, king of Judah, began to reign.
² He was twenty-five years old when he began to reign, and he
reigned twenty-nine years in Jerusalem. His mother's name was
Ābī the daughter of Zĕchárī'áh. ³And he did what was right in the
eyes of the LORD, according to all that David his father had done.
⁴ He removed the high places, and broke the pillars, and cut down
the Ăshḗ'ráh. And he broke in pieces the bronze serpent that
Moses had made, for until those days the people of Israel had
burned incense to it; it was called Nĕhŭsh'tán. ⁵ He trusted in the
LORD the God of Israel; so that there was none like him among all
the kings of Judah after him, nor among those who were before him.
⁶ For he held fast to the LORD; he did not depart from following
him, but kept the commandments which the LORD commanded
Moses. ⁷And the LORD was with him; wherever he went forth,
he prospered. He rebelled against the king of Assyria, and would
not serve him. ⁸ He smote the Philĭs'tĭnĕş as far as Gazá and its
territory, from watchtower to fortified city.

2. The end of the Northern Kingdom (Israel)

9 In the fourth year of King Hĕzĕkī'áh, which was the seventh
year of Hŏshḗ'á son of Ēláh, king of Israel, Shălmánḗ'şĕr king of
Assyria came up against Sàmăr'iă and besieged it ¹⁰ and at the end
of three years he took it. In the sixth year of Hĕzĕkī'áh, which was
the ninth year of Hŏshḗ'á king of Israel, Sàmăr'iă was taken. ¹¹The

Cross-references (left margin)

17.36
Ex 6.6;
Deut 10.20

17.37
Deut 5.32

17.38
Deut 4.23

17.41
ver 32,33

*18.1
2 Ki 17.1;
2 Chr 28.27
*18.2
2 Chr 29.1,2

18.4
2 Chr 31.1;
Num 21.8,9
18.5
2 Ki 19.10;
23.25
18.6
Deut 10.20
18.7
Gen 39.2,3;
1 Sam
18.14;
2 Ki 16.7
18.8
1 Chr 4.41;
Isa 14.29;
2 Ki 17.9

18.9
2 Ki 17.3
18.10
2 Ki 17.6
18.11
2 Ki 17.6

18.1 Hoshea ... Hezekiah. Here and in
verses 9 and 10 the reigns of these two kings are
synchronized. According to verse 13 the
Assyrian king Sennacherib invaded Judah in
the fourteenth year of Hezekiah. Since this
invasion can be dated accurately at 701 B.C.,
Hezekiah should have begun his reign in
715 B.C. But Hoshea, the last king of the
Northern Kingdom, ceased to reign in 722
B.C. Several explanations are possible. One is
that Hezekiah began a twelve year co-
regency in the third year of Hoshea. A second
is that the scribe allowed Pekah the twenty
years assigned him (2 Ki 15.27), thus pushing
Hoshea down twelve years later.
18.2 Abi is Abijah in 2 Chr 29.1.

king of Assyria carried the Israelites away to Assyria, and put them in Hālàh, and on the Hābor, the river of Gōzàn, and in the cities of the Mēdes, 12 because they did not obey the voice of the LORD their God but transgressed his covenant, even all that Moses the servant of the LORD commanded; they neither listened nor obeyed.

3. *Sennacherib's invasion*
a. *Hezekiah pays tribute*

13 In the fourteenth year of King Hĕzĕkī'áh Sĕnnăch'ĕrïb king of Assyria came up against all the fortified cities of Judah and took them. 14And Hĕzĕkī'áh king of Judah sent to the king of Assyria at Lāchĭsh, saying, "I have done wrong; withdraw from me; whatever you impose on me I will bear." And the king of Assyria required of Hezekiah king of Judah three hundred talents of silver and thirty talents of gold. 15And Hĕzĕkī'áh gave him all the silver that was found in the house of the LORD, and in the treasuries of the king's house. 16At that time Hĕzĕkī'áh stripped the gold from the doors of the temple of the LORD, and from the doorposts which Hezekiah king of Judah had overlaid and gave it to the king of Assyria. 17And the king of Assyria sent the Tartàn, the Răbsā'rïs, and the Răbshā'kĕh with a great army from Lāchĭsh to King Hĕzĕkī'áh at Jerusalem. And they went up and came to Jerusalem. When they arrived, they came and stood by the conduit of the upper pool, which is on the highway to the Fuller's Field. 18And when they called for the king, there came out to them Ĕlī'ákĭm the son of Hĭlkī'áh, who was over the household, and Shĕbnàh the secretary, and Jōàh the son of Āsăph, the recorder.

b. *The Assyrian threats*

19 And the Răbshā'kĕh said to them, "Say to Hĕzĕkī'áh, 'Thus says the great king, the king of Assyria: On what do you rest this confidence of yours? 20 Do you think that mere words are strategy and power for war? On whom do you now rely, that you have rebelled against me? 21 Behold, you are relying now on Egypt, that broken reed of a staff, which will pierce the hand of any man who leans on it. Such is Pharaōh king of Egypt to all who rely on him. 22 But if you say to me, "We rely on the LORD our God," is it not he whose high places and altars Hĕzĕkī'áh has removed, saying to Judah and to Jerusalem, "You shall worship before this altar in Jerusalem"? 23 Come now, make a wager with my master the king of Assyria: I will give you two thousand horses, if you are able on your part to set riders upon them. 24 How then can you repulse a single captain among the least of my master's servants, when you rely on Egypt for chariots and for horsemen? 25 Moreover, is it without the LORD that I have come up against this place to destroy it? The LORD said to me, Go up against this land, and destroy it.' "

26 Then Ĕlī'ákĭm the son of Hĭlkī'áh, and Shĕbnàh, and Jōàh, said to the Răbshā'kĕh, "Pray, speak to your servants in the Ârámā'ïc language, for we understand it; do not speak to us in the language of Judah within the hearing of the people who are on the wall." 27 But the Răbshā'kĕh said to them, "Has my master sent me to speak these words to your master and to you, and not to the

18.13 / 2 Chr 32.1ff; / Isa 36.1ff

18.15 / 2 Ki 16.8

*18.17 / Isa 20.1; / 7.3

18.18 / 2 Ki 19.2; / Isa 22.15,20

18.19 / 2 Chr 32.10ff

18.21 / Ezek 29.6,7

18.22 / ver 4; / 2 Chr 31.1; / 32.12

18.24 / Isa 31.1

18.26 / Ezra 4.7

18.17a *Tartan, Rabsaris,* and *Rabshakeh* are titles of Assyrian officers.   18.17b *conduit of the upper pool.* Read Isa 7.3 where it is also mentioned.

men sitting on the wall, who are doomed with you to eat their own dung and to drink their own urine?"

18.29
2 Chr 32.15
28 Then the Răbshă'kĕh stood and called out in a loud voice in the language of Judah: "Hear the word of the great king, the king of Assyria! 29 Thus says the king: 'Do not let Hĕzĕkī'ăh deceive you, for he will not be able to deliver you out of my hand. 30 Do not let Hĕzĕkī'ăh make you to rely on the LORD by saying, The LORD will surely deliver us, and this city will not be given into the hand of the king of Assyria.'

18.31
1 Ki 4.20,25
31 Do not listen to Hĕzĕkī'ăh; for thus says the king of Assyria: 'Make your peace with me and come out to me; then every one of you will eat of his own vine, and every one of his own fig tree, and every one of you will drink the water of his

18.32
Deut 8.7–9
own cistern; 32 until I come and take you away to a land like your own land, a land of grain and wine, a land of bread and vineyards, a land of olive trees and honey, that you may live, and not die. And do not listen to Hĕzĕkī'ăh when he misleads you by saying, The LORD will deliver us.

18.33
2 Ki 19.12;
2 Chr
32.14;
Isa 10.10,11
18.34
2 Ki 19.13;
17.24
33 Has any of the gods of the nations ever delivered his land out of the hand of the king of Assyria? 34 Where are the gods of Hămăth and Arpăd? Where are the gods of Sĕphar-vā'ĭm, Hĕnă, and Ĭvvăh? Have they delivered Săma̢r'ĭă out of my hand? 35 Who among all the gods of the countries have delivered their countries out of my hand, that the LORD should deliver Jerusalem out of my hand?'"

36 But the people were silent and answered him not a word, for the king's command was, "Do not answer him."

18.37
ver 18,26;
2 Ki 6.30
37 Then Ĕlī'ăkĭm the son of Hĭlkī'ăh, who was over the household, and Shĕbnă the secretary, and Jōăh the son of Ăsăph, the recorder, came to Hĕzĕkī'ăh with their clothes rent, and told him the words of the Răbshă'kĕh.

c. Hezekiah sends to Isaiah for a word from God

19.1
2 Chr
32.20–22;
Isa 37.1–38;
2 Ki 18.37;
1 Ki 21.27
19.2
Isa 1.1; 2.1
19 When King Hĕzĕkī'ăh heard it, he rent his clothes, and covered himself with sackcloth, and went into the house of the LORD. 2And he sent Ĕlī'ăkĭm, who was over the household, and Shĕbnă the secretary, and the senior priests, covered with sackcloth, to the prophet Ĭşăī'ăh the son of Ămŏz. 3 They said to him, "Thus says Hĕzĕkī'ăh, This day is a day of distress, of rebuke, and of disgrace; children have come to the birth, and there is no strength to bring them forth.

19.4
2 Sam
16.12;
2 Ki 18.35;
1.9
4 It may be that the LORD your God heard all the words of the Răbshă'kĕh, whom his master the king of Assyria has sent to mock the living God, and will rebuke the words which the LORD your God has heard; therefore lift up your prayer for the remnant that is left."

19.6
Isa 37.6ff;
2 Ki 18.17ff
5 When the servants of King Hĕzĕkī'ăh came to Ĭşăī'ăh, 6 Ĭşăī'ăh said to them, "Say to your master, 'Thus says the LORD: Do not be afraid because of the words that you have heard, with which the servants of the king of Assyria have reviled me.

19.7
ver 35–37
7 Behold, I will put a spirit in him, so that he shall hear a rumor and return to his own land; and I will cause him to fall by the sword in his own land.'"

19.8
Josh 10.29;
2 Ki 18.14
8 The Răbshă'kĕh returned, and found the king of Assyria fighting against Lĭbnăh; for he heard that the king had left Lăchĭsh. 9And when the king heard concerning Tĭrhă'kăh king of Ethiopia, "Behold, he has set out to fight against you," he sent messengers again to Hĕzĕkī'ăh, saying,

19.10
2 Ki 18.5,30
10 "Thus shall you speak to Hĕzĕkī'ăh king of Judah: 'Do not let your God on whom you rely deceive you

by promising that Jerusalem will not be given into the hand of the king of Assyria. 11 Behold, you have heard what the kings of Assyria have done to all lands, destroying them utterly. And shall you be delivered? 12 Have the gods of the nations delivered them, the nations which my fathers destroyed, Gōzán, Hārán, Rězěph, and the people of Eden who were in Těl-ăs´sár? 13 Where is the king of Hāmàth, the king of Arpăd, the king of the city of Sěpharvā´ím, the king of Hēnà, or the king of Ĭvvàh?' "

19.12
2 Ki 18.33

19.13
2 Ki 18.34

d. *Hezekiah at prayer*

14 Hězěkī´áh received the letter from the hand of the messengers, and read it; and Hezekiah went up to the house of the LORD, and spread it before the LORD. 15And Hězěkī´áh prayed before the LORD, and said: "O LORD the God of Israel, who art enthroned above the cherubim, thou art the God, thou alone, of all the kingdoms of the earth; thou hast made heaven and earth. 16 Incline thy ear, O LORD, and hear; open thy eyes, O LORD, and see; and hear the words of Sěnnăçh´ěrĭb, which he has sent to mock the living God. 17 Of a truth, O LORD, the kings of Assyria have laid waste the nations and their lands, 18 and have cast their gods into the fire; for they were no gods, but the work of men's hands, wood and stone; therefore they were destroyed. 19 So now, O LORD our God, save us, I beseech thee, from his hand, that all the kingdoms of the earth may know that thou, O LORD, art God alone.'

19.14
Isa 37.14

19.15
1 Sam 4.4;
1 Ki 18.39

19.16
Ps 31.2;
2 Chr 6.40;
ver 4

19.18
Ps 115.4;
Jer 10.3

19.19
Ps 83.18;
ver 15

e. *Isaiah brings an answer to Hezekiah's prayer*

20 Then Ĭṣāi´áh the son of Āmóz sent to Hězěkī´áh, saying, "Thus says the LORD, the God of Israel: Your prayer to me about Sěnnăçh´ěrĭb king of Assyria I have heard. 21 This is the word that the LORD has spoken concerning him:

19.20
2 Ki 20.5;
Isa 37.21

19.21
Lam 2.13;
Job 16.4;
Ps 22.7,8

"She despises you, she scorns you—
  the virgin daughter of Zion;
she wags her head behind you—
  the daughter of Jerusalem.

22 "Whom have you mocked and reviled?
  Against whom have you raised your voice
and haughtily lifted your eyes?
  Against the Holy One of Israel!

19.22
ver 4,6;
Ps 71.22;
Isa 5.24

23 By your messengers you have mocked the Lord,
  and you have said, 'With my many chariots
I have gone up the heights of the mountains,
  to the far recesses of Lebanon;
I felled its tallest cedars,
  its choicest cypresses;
I entered its farthest retreat,
  its densest forest.

19.23
2 Ki 18.17;
Ps 20.7;
Isa 10.18

24 I dug wells
  and drank foreign waters,

19.24
Isa 19.6

19.14 See 1 Sam 1.10. The same principles which were illustrated in the prayer of Hannah are also involved in this petition. A sincere believer who was prepared to trust God implicitly in the face of impossible odds and whose ardent desire was for the glory of God made Him a specific request. No matter how adverse the circumstances, he believed that God was able and willing to display His redeeming grace, and he embraced the promise as though it had already been fulfilled.

and I dried up with the sole of my foot
    all the streams of Egypt.'

19.25
Isa 45.7;
10.5

25 "Have you not heard
    that I determined it long ago?
I planned from days of old
    what now I bring to pass,
that you should turn fortified cities
    into heaps of ruins,

19.26
Ps 129.6

26 while their inhabitants, shorn of strength,
    are dismayed and confounded,
and have become like plants of the field,
    and like tender grass,
like grass on the housetops;
    blighted before it is grown?

27 "But I know your sitting down
    and your going out and coming in,
    and your raging against me.

19.28
Job 41.2;
Ezek 29.4;
ver 33,36

28 Because you have raged against me
    and your arrogance has come into my ears,
I will put my hook in your nose
    and my bit in your mouth,
and I will turn you back on the way
    by which you came.

19.29
1 Sam 2.34;
2 Ki 20.8,9;
Lk 2.12

29 "And this shall be the sign for you: this year you shall eat
what grows of itself, and in the second year what springs of the
same; then in the third year sow, and reap, and plant vineyards,

19.30
2 Chr
32.22,23

and eat their fruit. 30And the surviving remnant of the house of
Judah shall again take root downward, and bear fruit upward;

19.31
Isa 9.7

31 for out of Jerusalem shall go forth a remnant, and out of Mount
Zion a band of survivors. The zeal of the LORD will do this.
    32 "Therefore thus says the LORD concerning the king of
Assyria, He shall not come into this city or shoot an arrow there,
or come before it with a shield or cast up a siege mound against

19.33
ver 28
19.34
2 Ki 20.6;
1 Ki 11.12,
13

it. 33 By the way that he came, by the same he shall return, and he
shall not come into this city, says the LORD. 34 For I will defend
this city to save it, for my own sake and for the sake of my servant
David."

f. The divine deliverance

*19.35
2 Chr
32.21;
Isa 37.36

35 And that night the angel of the LORD went forth, and slew a
hundred and eighty-five thousand in the camp of the Assyrians;
and when men arose early in the morning, behold, these were all

19.36
ver 7,28,33;
Jon 1.2

dead bodies. 36 Then Sĕnnăch'ĕrĭb king of Assyria departed, and
went home, and dwelt at Nĭn'ĕvĕh. 37And as he was worshiping

*19.37
2 Chr
32.21;
ver 7;
Ezra 4.2

in the house of Nĭsrŏch his god, Ădrăm'mĕlĕch and Shărē'zẽr,
his sons, slew him with the sword, and escaped into the land of
Ar'ărăt. And Ēsarhăd'dŏn his son reigned in his stead.

19.35 The account does not say whether
the soldiers died of plague or by the exercise
of divine wrath, although the latter is suggested by the phrase, the angel . . . slew.

19.37 Sennacherib, like David, bypassed
his eldest son, and chose Esarhaddon, his
favorite, to succeed him. Esarhaddon's reign
lasted twelve years.

4. *The sickness of Hezekiah*
a. *His prayer and Isaiah's answer*

20 In those days Hĕzĕkī′áh became sick and was at the point of death. And Ĭşāi′áh the prophet the son of Āmŏz came to him, and said to him, "Thus says the LORD, 'Set your house in order; for you shall die, you shall not recover.' " 2 Then Hĕzĕkī′áh turned his face to the wall, and prayed to the LORD, saying, 3 "Remember now, O LORD, I beseech thee, how I have walked before thee in faithfulness and with a whole heart, and have done what is good in thy sight." And Hĕzĕkī′áh wept bitterly. 4And before Ĭşāi′áh had gone out of the middle court, the word of the LORD came to him: 5 "Turn back, and say to Hĕzĕkī′áh the prince of my people, Thus says the LORD, the God of David your father: I have heard your prayer, I have seen your tears; behold, I will heal you; on the third day you shall go up to the house of the LORD. 6And I will add fifteen years to your life. I will deliver you and this city out of the hand of the king of Assyria, and I will defend this city for my own sake and for my servant David's sake." 7And Ĭşāi′áh said, "Bring a cake of figs. And let them take and lay it on the boil, that he may recover."

b. *The sign of the shadow*

8 And Hĕzĕkī′áh said to Ĭşāi′áh, "What shall be the sign that the LORD will heal me, and that I shall go up to the house of the LORD on the third day?" 9And Ĭşāi′áh said, "This is the sign to you from the LORD, that the LORD will do the thing that he has promised: shall the shadow go forward ten steps, or go back ten steps?" 10And Hĕzĕkī′áh answered, "It is an easy thing for the shadow to lengthen ten steps; rather let the shadow go back ten steps." 11And Ĭşāi′áh the prophet cried to the LORD; and he brought the shadow back ten steps, by which the sun*g* had declined on the dial of Āhăz.

5. *Hezekiah's foolishness before Merodach-baladan*

12 At that time Mĕr′ŏdăch-băl′ádăn the son of Băl′ádăn, king of Babylon, sent envoys with letters and a present to Hĕzĕkī′áh; for he heard that Hezekiah had been sick. 13And Hĕzĕkī′áh welcomed them, and he showed them all his treasure house, the silver, the gold, the spices, the precious oil, his armory, all that was found in his storehouses; there was nothing in his house or in all his realm that Hezekiah did not show them. 14 Then Ĭşāi′áh the prophet came to King Hĕzĕkī′áh, and said to him, "What did these men say? And whence did they come to you?" And Hezekiah said, "They have come from a far country, from Babylon." 15 He said, "What have they seen in your house?" And Hĕzĕkī′áh answered, "They have seen all that is in my house; there is nothing in my storehouses that I did not show them."

16 Then Ĭşāi′áh said to Hĕzĕkī′áh, "Hear the word of the LORD: 17 Behold, the days are coming, when all that is in your house, and that which your fathers have stored up till this day, shall be carried to Babylon; nothing shall be left, says the LORD. 18And some of your own sons, who are born to you, shall be taken away; and they shall be eunuchs in the palace of the king of Babylon." 19 Then said Hĕzĕkī′áh to Ĭşāi′áh, "The word of the LORD which you have

g Syr See Is 38.8 and Tg: Heb lacks *the sun*

Marginal references:
20.1 2 Chr 32.24; Isa 38.1; see 2 Sam 17.23
20.3 Neh 13.22; 2 Ki 18.3–6
20.5 1 Sam 9.16; 10.1; 2 Ki 19.20; Ps 39.12
20.6 2 Ki 19.34
20.7 Isa 38.21
20.11 Josh 10.12–14
20.12 Isa 39.1ff
20.13 2 Chr 32.27
20.15 ver 13
20.17 2 Ki 24.13; 25.13; Jer 52.17
20.18 2 Ki 24.12; 2 Chr 33.11; Dan 1.3–7
20.19 1 Sam 3.18

spoken is good." For he thought, "Why not, if there will be peace and security in my days?"

20 The rest of the deeds of Hĕzĕkī′ăh, and all his might, and how he made the pool and the conduit and brought water into the city, are they not written in the Book of the Chronicles of the Kings of Judah? 21And Hĕzĕkī′ăh slept with his fathers; and Mănăs′sĕh his son reigned in his stead.

B. The reign of Manasseh

1. His wickedness

21 Mănăs′sĕh was twelve years old when he began to reign, and he reigned fifty-five years in Jerusalem. His mother's name was Hĕph′zĭbăh. 2And he did what was evil in the sight of the LORD, according to the abominable practices of the nations whom the LORD drove out before the people of Israel. 3 For he rebuilt the high places which Hĕzĕkī′ăh his father had destroyed; and he erected altars for Bāăl, and made an Ăshē′răh, as Āhăb king of Israel had done, and worshiped all the host of heaven, and served them. 4And he built altars in the house of the LORD, of which the LORD had said, "In Jerusalem will I put my name." 5And he built altars for all the host of heaven in the two courts of the house of the LORD. 6And he burned his son as an offering, and practiced soothsaying and augury, and dealt with mediums and with wizards. He did much evil in the sight of the LORD, provoking him to anger. 7And the graven image of Ăshē′răh that he had made he set in the house of which the LORD said to David and to Solomon his son, "In this house, and in Jerusalem, which I have chosen out of all the tribes of Israel, I will put my name for ever; 8 and I will not cause the feet of Israel to wander any more out of the land which I gave to their fathers, if only they will be careful to do according to all that I have commanded them, and according to all the law that my servant Moses commanded them." 9 But they did not listen, and Mănăs′sĕh seduced them to do more evil than the nations had done whom the LORD destroyed before the people of Israel.

2. The fall of Jerusalem predicted

10 And the LORD said by his servants the prophets, 11 "Because Mănăs′sĕh king of Judah has committed these abominations, and has done things more wicked than all that the Ăm′ŏrītes did, who were before him, and has made Judah also to sin with his idols; 12 therefore thus says the LORD, the God of Israel, Behold, I am bringing upon Jerusalem and Judah such evil that the ears of every one who hears of it will tingle. 13And I will stretch over Jerusalem the measuring line of Sămăr′ĭă, and the plummet of the house of Āhăb; and I will wipe Jerusalem as one wipes a dish, wiping it and turning it upside down. 14And I will cast off the remnant of my heritage, and give them into the hand of their enemies, and they shall become a prey and a spoil to all their enemies, 15 because they have done what is evil in my sight and have provoked me to

Marginal references

*20.20
2 Chr 32.32;
Neh 3.16
20.21
2 Chr 32.33

*21.1
2 Chr 33.1ff
21.2
2 Ki 16.3
21.3
2 Ki 18.4;
1 Ki 16.32,
33;
2 Ki 17.16;
Deut 17.3
21.4
Jer 32.34;
2 Sam 7.13;
1 Ki 8.29
21.6
Lev 18.21;
2 Ki 16.3;
17.17;
Lev 19.26,
31;
Deut 18.10,
11
21.7
1 Ki 8.29;
9.3;
2 Ki 23.27;
Jer 32.34
21.8
2 Sam 7.10
21.9
Prov 29.12

21.11
2 Ki 24.3,4;
1 Ki 21.26;
ver 16
21.12
1 Sam 3.11;
Jer 19.3
21.13
Isa 34.11;
Amos 7.7,8

20.20 Hezekiah's tunnel was dug through solid rock by two crews, one working from the spring Gihon, and the other from the pool of Siloam. An inscription found in the tunnel near the Siloam end tells of the tense moment when the two crews met.

21.1 Ten years of Manasseh's 55 year reign were in co-regency with Hezekiah.

anger, since the day their fathers came out of Egypt, even to this day."

3. *Summary of Manasseh's reign*

16 Moreover Mánás′séh shed very much innocent blood, till he had filled Jerusalem from one end to another, besides the sin which he made Judah to sin so that they did what was evil in the sight of the LORD.

17 Now the rest of the acts of Mánás′séh, and all that he did, and the sin that he committed, are they not written in the Book of the Chronicles of the Kings of Judah? 18And Mánás′séh slept with his fathers, and was buried in the garden of his house, in the garden of Úzzá; and Āmón his son reigned in his stead.

C. *The reign of Amon*

19 Āmón was twenty-two years old when he began to reign, and he reigned two years in Jerusalem. His mother's name was Mèshŭl′lèmèth the daughter of Hāruz of Jótbáh. 20And he did what was evil in the sight of the LORD, as Mánás′séh his father had done. 21 He walked in all the way in which his father walked, and served the idols that his father served, and worshiped them; 22 he forsook the LORD, the God of his fathers, and did not walk in the way of the LORD. 23And the servants of Āmón conspired against him, and killed the king in his house. 24 But the people of the land slew all those who had conspired against King Āmón, and the people of the land made Jōsī′áh his son king in his stead. 25 Now the rest of the acts of Āmón which he did, are they not written in the Book of the Chronicles of the Kings of Judah? 26And he was buried in his tomb in the garden of Úzzá; and Jōsī′áh his son reigned in his stead.

D. *The reign of Josiah*

1. *Faithful Josiah*

22 Jōsī′áh was eight years old when he began to reign, and he reigned thirty-one years in Jerusalem. His mother's name was Jèdī′dáh the daughter of Ádáī′áh of Bŏzkáth. 2And he did what was right in the eyes of the LORD, and walked in all the way of David his father, and he did not turn aside to the right hand or to the left.

2. *The repair of the Temple*

3 In the eighteenth year of King Jōsī′áh, the king sent Shāphán the son of Ázálī′áh, son of Mèshŭl′lám, the secretary, to the house of the LORD, saying, 4 "Go up to Hílkī′áh the high priest, that he may reckon the amount of the money which has been brought into the house of the LORD, which the keepers of the threshold have collected from the people; 5 and let it be given into the hand of the workmen who have the oversight of the house of the LORD; and let them give it to the workmen who are at the house of the LORD, repairing the house, 6 that is, to the carpenters, and to the builders, and to the masons, as well as for buying timber and quarried stone to repair the house. 7 But no accounting shall be asked from them for the money which is delivered into their hand, for they deal honestly."

Marginal references:

21.16
2 Ki 24.4

21.17
2 Chr 33.11–19
21.18
2 Chr 33.20

21.19
2 Chr 33.21–23
21.20
ver 2–6, 11,16

21.22
1 Ki 11.33

21.23
2 Chr 33.24,25

21.26
ver 18

22.1
2 Chr 34.1; Josh 15.39
22.2
Deut 5.32

22.3
2 Chr 34.8ff
22.4
2 Ki 12.4, 9,10

22.5
2 Ki 12.11–14

22.7
2 Ki 12.15

3. The finding of the Book of the Law

*22.8
Deut 31.24–
26;
2 Chr
34.14,15

8 And Hĭlkī′áh the high priest said to Shāphán the secretary, "I have found the book of the law in the house of the LORD." And Hilkiah gave the book to Shaphan, and he read it. 9And Shāphán the secretary came to the king, and reported to the king, "Your servants have emptied out the money that was found in the house, and have delivered it into the hand of the workmen who have the oversight of the house of the LORD." 10 Then Shāphán the secretary told the king, "Hĭlkī′áh the priest has given me a book." And Shaphan read it before the king.

4. The reaction of Josiah

22.12
2 Ki 25.22;
2 Chr 34.20

22.13
Deut 29.27

11 And when the king heard the words of the book of the law, he rent his clothes. 12And the king commanded Hĭlkī′áh the priest, and Ăhī′kàm the son of Shāphán, and Ăchbor the son of Mĭcāi′áh, and Shaphan the secretary, and Ăsāi′áh the king's servant, saying, 13 "Go, inquire of the LORD for me, and for the people, and for all Judah, concerning the words of this book that has been found; for great is the wrath of the LORD that is kindled against us, because our fathers have not obeyed the words of this book, to do according to all that is written concerning us."

5. The words of Huldah the prophetess

*22.14
2 Chr 34.22

22.17
Deut 29.25–
27

22.19
Ps 51.17;
Isa 57.15;
1 Ki 21.29;
Lev 26.31;
Jer 26.6

14 So Hĭlkī′áh the priest, and Ăhī′kàm, and Ăchbor, and Shāphán, and Ăsāi′áh went to Hŭldáh the prophetess, the wife of Shăllúm the son of Tĭkváh, son of Harhăs, keeper of the wardrobe (now she dwelt in Jerusalem in the Second Quarter); and they talked with her. 15And she said to them, "Thus says the LORD, the God of Israel: 'Tell the man who sent you to me, 16 Thus says the LORD, Behold, I will bring evil upon this place and upon its inhabitants, all the words of the book which the king of Judah has read. 17 Because they have forsaken me and have burned incense to other gods, that they might provoke me to anger with all the work of their hands, therefore my wrath will be kindled against this place, and it will not be quenched. 18 But as to the king of Judah, who sent you to inquire of the LORD, thus shall you say to him, Thus says the LORD, the God of Israel: Regarding the words which you have heard, 19 because your heart was penitent, and you humbled yourself before the LORD, when you heard how I spoke against this place, and against its inhabitants, that they should become a desolation and a curse, and you have rent your clothes and wept before me, I also have heard you, says the LORD. 20 Therefore, behold, I will gather you to your fathers, and you shall be gathered to your grave in peace, and your eyes shall not see all the evil which I will bring upon this place.' " And they brought back word to the king.

23.1
2 Chr
34.29–32
23.2
Deut 31.10–
13;
2 Ki 22.8

6. The renewal of the covenant

23 Then the king sent, and all the elders of Judah and Jerusalem were gathered to him. 2And the king went up to the

---

22.8 *book of the law.* On the basis of details noted in Josiah's reform and also some of the material in Jeremiah, it is evident that the Book of the Law constituted much of the material contained in Deuteronomy.
22.14 Hilkiah the priest went to Huldah the prophetess, although the LORD had called Jeremiah in 626 B.C., five years previously.

house of the LORD, and with him all the men of Judah and all the inhabitants of Jerusalem, and the priests and the prophets, all the people, both small and great; and he read in their hearing all the words of the book of the covenant which had been found in the house of the LORD. ³And the king stood by the pillar and made a covenant before the LORD, to walk after the LORD and to keep his commandments and his testimonies and his statutes, with all his heart and all his soul, to perform the words of this covenant that were written in this book; and all the people joined in the covenant.

23.3
2 Ki 11.14,
17;
Deut 13.4

7. The reforms of Josiah

4 And the king commanded Hĭlkī′äh, the high priest, and the priests of the second order, and the keepers of the threshold, to bring out of the temple of the LORD all the vessels made for Bāál, for Ashē′räh, and for all the host of heaven; he burned them outside Jerusalem in the fields of the Kĭdròn, and carried their ashes to Bĕthèl. ⁵And he deposed the idolatrous priests whom the kings of Judah had ordained to burn incense in the high places at the cities of Judah and round about Jerusalem; those also who burned incense to Bāál, to the sun, and the moon, and the constellations, and all the host of the heavens. ⁶And he brought out the Ashē′räh from the house of the LORD, outside Jerusalem, to the brook Kĭdròn, and burned it at the brook Kĭdròn, and beat it to dust and cast the dust of it upon the graves of the common people. ⁷And he broke down the houses of the male cult prostitutes which were in the house of the LORD, where the women wove hangings for the Ashē′räh. ⁸And he brought all the priests out of the cities of Judah, and defiled the high places where the priests had burned incense, from Gēbá to Beër-shē′bá; and he broke down the high places of the gates that were at the entrance of the gate of Joshua the governor of the city, which were on one's left at the gate of the city. ⁹ However, the priests of the high places did not come up to the altar of the LORD in Jerusalem, but they ate unleavened bread among their brethren. ¹⁰And he defiled Tōphèth, which is in the valley of the sons of Hĭnnòm, that no one might burn his son or his daughter as an offering to Mōlĕch. ¹¹And he removed the horses that the kings of Judah had dedicated to the sun, at the entrance to the house of the LORD, by the chamber of Nāthán-mĕl′ĕçh the chamberlain, which was in the precincts;ʰ and he burned the chariots of the sun with fire. ¹²And the altars on the roof of the upper chamber of Āhăz, which the kings of Judah had made, and the altars which Mánăs′sèh had made in the two courts of the house of the LORD, he pulled down and broke in pieces,ⁱ and cast the dust of them into the brook Kĭdròn. ¹³And the king defiled the high places that were east of Jerusalem, to the south of the mount of corruption, which Solomon the king of Israel had built for Ăsh′tòrĕth the abomination of the Sīdō′nïàns, and for Çhĕmòsh the abomination of Mōáb, and for Milcòm the abomination of the Am′mònītes. ¹⁴And he broke in pieces the pillars, and cut down the Ashē′rïm, and filled their places with the bones of men.

*23.4ff
2 Ki 21.3,7

23.7
1 Ki 14.24;
15.12;
Ezek 16.16
23.8
1 Ki 15.22

23.9
Ezek 44.10–
14
23.10
Isa 30.33;
Jer 7.31;
Lev 18.21;
Deut 18.10

23.12
Jer 19.13;
Zeph 1.5;
2 Ki 21.5;
ver 4,6

23.13
1 Ki 11.7

23.14
Ex 23.24;
Deut 7.5,25

ʰ The meaning of the Hebrew word is uncertain
ⁱ Heb pieces from there

23.4-14 This passage indicates the appalling and rapid degradation to which Judah had sunk after having enjoyed a brilliant and powerful kingdom.

8. *The bones of the man of God*

23.15
1 Ki 12.28–33

15 Moreover the altar at Běthěl, the high place erected by Jěrŏbō'ăm the son of Nēbăt, who made Israel to sin, that altar with the high place he pulled down and he broke in pieces its stones,ʲ crushing them to dust; also he burned the Ăshē'răh.

23.16
1 Ki 13.2

16And as Jōsī'ăh turned, he saw the tombs there on the mount; and he sent and took the bones out of the tombs, and burned them upon the altar, and defiled it, according to the word of the LORD which the man of God proclaimed, who had predicted these things.

23.17
1 Ki 13.1,30

17 Then he said, "What is yonder monument that I see?" And the men of the city told him, "It is the tomb of the man of God who came from Judah and predicted these things which you have done against the altar at Běthěl."

23.18
1 Ki 13.31

18And he said, "Let him be; let no man move his bones." So they let his bones alone, with the bones of the prophet who came out of Sămar'ĭă.

23.19
2 Chr 34.6,7

19And all the shrines also of the high places that were in the cities of Sămar'ĭă, which kings of Israel had made, provoking the LORD to anger, Jōsī'ăh removed; he did to them according to all that he had done at Běthěl.

23.20
2 Ki 10.25;
11.18;
2 Chr 34.5

20And he slew all the priests of the high places who were there, upon the altars, and burned the bones of men upon them. Then he returned to Jerusalem.

9. *The keeping of the Passover*

23.21
2 Chr 35.1;
Ex 12.3;
Num 9.2;
Deut 16.2
23.22
2 Chr 35.18,
19

21 And the king commanded all the people, "Keep the passover to the LORD your God, as it is written in this book of the covenant." 22 For no such passover had been kept since the days of the judges who judged Israel, or during all the days of the kings of Israel or of the kings of Judah; 23 but in the eighteenth year of King Jōsī'ăh this passover was kept to the LORD in Jerusalem.

10. *The zeal of Josiah*

23.24
2 Ki 21.6,
11,21;
Deut 18.10–12
23.25
2 Ki 18.5

24 Moreover Jōsī'ăh put away the mediums and the wizards and the teraphim and the idols and all the abominations that were seen in the land of Judah and in Jerusalem, that he might establish the words of the law which were written in the book that Hĭlkī'ăh the priest found in the house of the LORD. 25 Before him there was no king like him, who turned to the LORD with all his heart and with all his soul and with all his might, according to all the law of Moses; nor did any like him arise after him.

11. *The continued anger of God against Judah*

23.26
2 Ki 21.11,
12;
Jer 15.4
23.27
2 Ki 18.11;
21.13,14

26 Still the LORD did not turn from the fierceness of his great wrath, by which his anger was kindled against Judah, because of all the provocations with which Mănăs'sěh had provoked him. 27And the LORD said, "I will remove Judah also out of my sight, as I have removed Israel, and I will cast off this city which I have chosen, Jerusalem, and the house of which I said, My name shall be there."

12. *The death of Josiah and the succession*

28 Now the rest of the acts of Jōsī'ăh, and all that he did, are they not written in the Book of the Chronicles of the Kings of

ʲ Gk: Heb *he burned the high place*

Judah? 29 In his days Phạraōh Nĕcō king of Egypt went up to the king of Assyria to the river Eūphrā′tēṣ. King Jōsī′áh went to meet him; and Pharaoh Neco slew him at Mĕgĭd′dō, when he saw him. 30And his servants carried him dead in a chariot from Mĕgĭd′dō, and brought him to Jerusalem, and buried him in his own tomb. And the people of the land took Jĕhō′áhăz the son of Jōsī′áh, and anointed him, and made him king in his father's stead.

E. The reign of Jehoahaz; his captivity by Pharaoh Neco

31 Jĕhō′áhăz was twenty-three years old when he began to reign, and he reigned three months in Jerusalem. His mother's name was Hámū′tál the daughter of Jĕrĕmī′áh of Lĭbnáh. 32And he did what was evil in the sight of the LORD, according to all that his fathers had done. 33And Phạraōh Nĕcō put him in bonds at Rĭbláh in the land of Hāmáth, that he might not reign in Jerusalem, and laid upon the land a tribute of a hundred talents of silver and a talent of gold. 34And Phạraōh Nĕcō made Ĕlī′ákĭm the son of Jōsī′áh king in the place of Josiah his father, and changed his name to Jĕhoi′ákim. But he took Jĕhō′áhăz away; and he came to Egypt, and died there. 35And Jĕhoi′ákĭm gave the silver and the gold to Phạraōh, but he taxed the land to give the money according to the command of Pharaoh. He exacted the silver and the gold of the people of the land, from every one according to his assessment, to give it to Pharaoh Nĕcō.

F. The reign of Jehoiakim: first capture of Jerusalem by Nebuchadnezzar

36 Jĕhoi′ákĭm was twenty-five years old when he began to reign, and he reigned eleven years in Jerusalem. His mother's name was Zĕbī′dáh the daughter of Pĕdāi′áh of Rumáh. 37And he did what was evil in the sight of the LORD, according to all that his fathers had done.

24 In his days Nĕbŭchádnĕz′zár king of Babylon came up, and Jĕhoi′ákĭm became his servant three years; then he turned and rebelled against him. 2And the LORD sent against him bands of the Chạldē′áns, and bands of the Syrians, and bands of the Mō′ábītes, and bands of the Ăm′mŏnītes, and sent them against Judah to destroy it, according to the word of the LORD which he spoke by his servants the prophets. 3 Surely this came upon Judah at the command of the LORD, to remove them out of his sight, for the sins of Mánăs′sĕh, according to all that he had done, 4 and also for the innocent blood that he had shed; for he filled Jerusalem with innocent blood, and the LORD would not pardon. 5 Now the rest of the deeds of Jĕhoi′ákĭm, and all that he did, are they not written in the Book of the Chronicles of the Kings of Judah? 6 So Jĕhoi′ákĭm slept with his fathers, and Jĕhoi′áchĭn his son reigned in his stead. 7And the king of Egypt did not come again out of his land, for the

★23.29 2 Chr 35.20; Zech 12.11
★23.30 2 Chr 35.24; 36.1
23.31 1 Chr 3.15; Jer 22.11; 2 Ki 24.18
23.33 2 Ki 25.6; Jer 52.27; 2 Chr 36.3
23.34 2 Chr 36.4; 2 Ki 24.17; Ezek 19.3,4
23.35 ver 33
23.36 2 Chr 36.5
24.1 2 Chr 36.6; Jer 25.1
★24.2 Jer 25.9; 35.11; 2 Ki 23.27
24.3 2 Ki 18.25; 23.26
24.4 2 Ki 21.16
24.6 Jer 22.18,19
24.7 Jer 37.5-7; 46.2

23.29 Pharaoh Neco was rushing to the aid of the Assyrians, whose capital, Nineveh, fell to the Babylonians in 612 B.C. He did not wish to molest Josiah, but with foolish zeal Josiah insisted on an encounter. His death in 609/8 B.C. hastened the downfall of Judah. **23.30** *people . . . took Jehoahaz.* The people passed up Eliakim (Jehoiakim) the eldest son, and made Jehoahaz, two years his junior, king. **24.2** *Chaldeans,* that is, Babylonians.

king of Babylon had taken all that belonged to the king of Egypt
from the Brook of Egypt to the river Eūphrā'tēṣ.

G. The reign of Jehoiachin: the second capture of Jerusalem

8 Jĕhoi'ạchĭn was eighteen years old when he became king, and
he reigned three months in Jerusalem. His mother's name was
Nĕhŭsh'tȧ the daughter of Ĕlnȧ'thȧn of Jerusalem. 9And he did
what was evil in the sight of the LORD, according to all that his
father had done.

10 At that time the servants of Nĕbŭchȧdnĕz'zȧr king of
Babylon came up to Jerusalem, and the city was besieged. 11And
Nĕbŭchȧdnĕz'zȧr king of Babylon came to the city, while his
servants were besieging it; 12 and Jĕhoi'ạchĭn the king of Judah
gave himself up to the king of Babylon, himself, and his mother,
and his servants, and his princes, and his palace officials. The king
of Babylon took him prisoner in the eighth year of his reign, 13 and
carried off all the treasures of the house of the LORD, and the
treasures of the king's house, and cut in pieces all the vessels of
gold in the temple of the LORD, which Solomon king of Israel had
made, as the LORD had foretold. 14 He carried away all Jerusalem,
and all the princes, and all the mighty men of valor, ten thousand
captives, and all the craftsmen and the smiths; none remained,
except the poorest people of the land. 15And he carried away
Jĕhoi'ạchĭn to Babylon; the king's mother, the king's wives, his
officials, and the chief men of the land, he took into captivity from
Jerusalem to Babylon. 16And the king of Babylon brought captive
to Babylon all the men of valor, seven thousand, and the craftsmen
and the smiths, one thousand, all of them strong and fit for war.
17And the king of Babylon made Mȧttȧnī'ȧh, Jĕhoi'ạchĭn's uncle,
king in his stead, and changed his name to Zĕdĕkī'ȧh.

H. The reign of Zedekiah

1. The rebellion against Babylon

18 Zĕdĕkī'ȧh was twenty-one years old when he became king,
and he reigned eleven years in Jerusalem. His mother's name was
Hȧmū'tȧl the daughter of Jĕrĕmīȧh of Lĭbnȧh. 19And he did what
was evil in the sight of the LORD, according to all that Jĕhoi'ȧkĭm
had done. 20 For because of the anger of the LORD it came to the
point in Jerusalem and Judah that he cast them out from his
presence.

And Zĕdĕkī'ȧh rebelled against the king of Babylon. 1And in the
ninth year of his reign, in the tenth month, on the tenth day
of the month, Nĕbŭchȧdnĕz'zȧr king of Babylon came with
all his army against Jerusalem, and laid siege to it; and they built
siegeworks against it round about. 2 So the city was besieged till
the eleventh year of King Zĕdĕkī'ȧh. 3 On the ninth day of the
fourth month the famine was so severe in the city that there was no
food for the people of the land. 4 Then a breach was made in the
city; the king with all the men of war fled^k by night by the way of
the gate between the two walls, by the king's garden, though the

---

k Gk Compare Jer 39.4; 52.7: Heb lacks the king and fled

Margin references:

24.8
1 Chr 3.16;
2 Chr 36.9

24.10
Dan 1.1
24.12
Jer 24.1;
29.1,2;
25.1;
2 Ki 25.27;
Jer 52.28
24.13
2 Ki 20.17;
Isa 39.6;
2 Ki 25.13–
15;
Jer 20.5
24.14
Jer 24.1;
52.28;
2 Ki 25.12;
Jer 40.7
24.15
2 Chr
36.10;
Jer 22.24–
28
24.16
Jer 52.28
24.17
Jer 37.1;
1 Chr 3.15;
2 Chr 36.4,
10

24.18
2 Chr
36.11;
Jer 52.1ff;
2 Ki 23.31
24.19
2 Chr 36.12
24.20
2 Chr 36.13

25.1
2 Chr 36.13,
17–20;
Jer 39.1–7;
Ezek 24.1,2

25.3
Jer 39.1,2
25.4
Jer 39.4–7

Chǎldē'āns were around the city. And they went in the direction
of the Ar'ábàh. 5 But the army of the Chǎldē'āns pursued the king,
and overtook him in the plains of Jěr'ïchō; and all his army was
scattered from him. 6 Then they captured the king, and brought
him up to the king of Babylon at Rïblàh, who passed sentence
upon him. 7 They slew the sons of Zěděkï'àh before his eyes, and
put out the eyes of Zedekiah, and bound him in fetters, and took
him to Babylon.

25.6
Jer 34.21,
22;
2 Ki 23.33
25.7
Jer 39.6,7;
Ezek 12.13

2. *The destruction of Jerusalem and the Temple*

8 In the fifth month, on the seventh day of the month—which
was the nineteenth year of King Něbǔchǎdněz'zàr, king of Babylon—Něbǔzar'ádàn, the captain of the bodyguard, a servant of
the king of Babylon, came to Jerusalem. 9And he burned the house
of the LORD, and the king's house and all the houses of Jerusalem;
every great house he burned down. 10And all the army of the
Chǎldē'āns, who were with the captain of the guard, broke down
the walls around Jerusalem. 11And the rest of the people who were
left in the city and the deserters who had deserted to the king of
Babylon, together with the rest of the multitude, Něbǔzar'ádàn
the captain of the guard carried into exile. 12 But the captain of the
guard left some of the poorest of the land to be vinedressers and
plowmen.

25.8
Jer 52.12–
14; 39.9
25.9
2 Chr
36.19;
Ps 74.3–7;
Amos 2.5
25.10
Neh 1.3;
Jer 52.14
25.11
2 Chr
36.20;
Jer 39.9;
52.15
25.12
2 Ki 24.14;
Jer 40.7

13 And the pillars of bronze that were in the house of the LORD,
and the stands and the bronze sea that were in the house of the
LORD, the Chǎldē'āns broke in pieces, and carried the bronze to
Babylon. 14And they took away the pots, and the shovels, and the
snuffers, and the dishes for incense and all the vessels of bronze
used in the temple service, 15 the firepans also, and the bowls.
What was of gold the captain of the guard took away as gold, and
what was of silver, as silver. 16As for the two pillars, the one sea,
and the stands, which Solomon had made for the house of the
LORD, the bronze of all these vessels was beyond weight. 17 The
height of the one pillar was eighteen cubits, and upon it was a
capital of bronze; the height of the capital was three cubits; a network and pomegranates, all of bronze, were upon the capital round
about. And the second pillar had the like, with the network.

25.13
2 Chr 36.18
25.14
1 Ki 7.47–
50

25.16
1 Ki 7.47
25.17
1 Ki 7.15–
22

3. *The killing of the leaders*

18 And the captain of the guard took Sěrāi'àh the chief priest,
and Zěphánï'àh the second priest, and the three keepers of the
threshold; 19 and from the city he took an officer who had been in
command of the men of war, and five men of the king's council
who were found in the city; and the secretary of the commander of
the army who mustered the people of the land; and sixty men of
the people of the land who were found in the city. 20And Někǔzar'-
ádàn the captain of the guard took them, and brought them to the
king of Babylon at Rïblàh. 21And the king of Babylon smote them,
and put them to death at Rïblàh in the land of Hàmàth. So Judah
was taken into exile out of its land.

25.18
1 Chr 6.14;
Ezra 7.1;
Jer 21.1;
29.25

25.21
Deut 28.64;
2 Ki 23.27

4. *The appointment of Gedaliah as governor: his murder*

22 And over the people who remained in the land of Judah,
whom Něbǔchǎdněz'zàr king of Babylon had left, he appointed
Gědálï'àh the son of Ahï'kàm, son of Shàphàn, governor. 23 Now

25.22
Jer 40.5
25.23
Jer 40.7–9

when all the captains of the forces in the open country[l] and their men heard that the king of Babylon had appointed Gĕdáliʹáh governor, they came with their men to Gedaliah at Mĭzpáh, namely, Ĭshʹmäel the son of Nĕtháníʹáh, and Jōhănʹán the son of Kárēʹáh, and Sērãiʹáh the son of Tánhúʹmĕth the Nĕtŏphʹáthīte, and Já-ázáníʹáh the son of the Má-ăcʹáthīte. 24And Gĕdáliʹáh swore to them and their men, saying, "Do not be afraid because of the Chăldēʹán officials; dwell in the land, and serve the king of Babylon, and it shall be well with you." 25 But in the seventh month, Ĭshʹmäel the son of Nĕtháníʹáh, son of Ēlĭʹshámá, of the royal family, came with ten men, and attacked and killed Gĕdáliʹáh and the Jews and the Chăldēʹánș who were with him at Mĭzpáh. 26 Then all the people, both small and great, and the captains of the forces arose, and went to Egypt; for they were afraid of the Chăldēʹánș.

25.25
Jer 41.1,2

25.26
Jer 43.4–7

5. Jehoiachin set free in Babylon

27 And in the thirty-seventh year of the exile of Jĕhoiʹáchĭn king of Judah, in the twelfth month, on the twenty-seventh day of the month, Ēvĭl-mĕrʹódăch king of Babylon, in the year that he began to reign, graciously freed Jehoiachin king of Judah from prison; 28 and he spoke kindly to him, and gave him a seat above the seats of the kings who were with him in Babylon. 29 So Jĕhoiʹáchĭn put off his prison garments. And every day of his life he dined regularly at the king's table; 30 and for his allowance, a regular allowance was given him by the king, every day a portion, as long as he lived.

*25.27
Jer 52.31–34;
Gen 40.13,20

25.29
2 Sam 9.7

l With Jer 40.7: Heb lacks *in the open country*

25.27 *Evil-merodach*, the son of Nebuchadnezzar, reigned 561–560 B.C. His Babylonian name was Amel-Marduk, "Man of Marduk," but a variant form was Awel-Marduk, the source of the Hebrew form Evil-merodach. Thus, the segment "Evil" is an accident of transliteration and it has no relation in meaning to the adjective "evil." *graciously freed Jehoiachin.* The Babylonians always considered Jehoiachin as the legitimate king of Judah and so they took good care of him and his family. Some clay tablets found in Babylon mention Jehoiachin and five of his sons in connection with rations supplied the captives.

INTRODUCTION TO
THE FIRST BOOK OF THE
CHRONICLES

Authorship and Background: While the English title "Chronicles" derives from Jerome's suggestion, it is fairly close in meaning to the Hebrew title, "Words (events) of the Days." The Septuagint title, "Things Passed Over," indicates that the translators thought of Chronicles primarily as a supplement which included materials neglected by Samuel-Kings. 1 and 2 Chronicles were originally one book, but it was separated into two units by the Septuagint translators. The Book of Ezra was also a part of this history (Ezra 1.1–3a is a repetition of 2 Chr 36.22, 23). In the Hebrew Bible, Chronicles appears as the last book, while in the Septuagint and the Vulgate, it was placed after Kings.

Some scholars date the Chronicler's work about 300 B.C. on the basis of the genealogies in 1 Chr 3.17–24 and Neh 12.10, 11, 22, but these lists permit a different interpretation. The remarkable similarity in language between Chronicles and the memoirs of Ezra (7.27—9.15) suggests that Ezra was the Chronicler. This view, held by tradition, has the further support of the Aramaic letters from Elephantine (modern Aswan) in Egypt. These date from the fifth century B.C. and mention persons named in Ezra and Nehemiah. Although some material may have been added to the Chronicles later, a date somewhere between 425 and 400 B.C. is most probable for the compilation of this history. Many old sources were employed, such as genealogies, court records of Israel and Judah, and writings of the prophets Samuel, Nathan, Gad, Ahijah, Shemaiah, Iddo, Jehu, and Isaiah.

Characteristics: The Chronicler uses some material in common with Samuel and Kings, but there are also basic differences: (1) Israel, the Northern Kingdom, is virtually ignored; (2) most of the references to the defects and the sins of David and Solomon are omitted; (3) the numbers generally are in round figures and larger than those in the other books. The author records events from the vantage point of religious concern and pays particular attention to the Temple and the Davidic line. Apparently he wishes the post-exilic Jews to understand that their community was a continuation of the former Davidic kingdom. Undoubtedly that is why the first nine chapters consist almost entirely of genealogies, which trace the progenitors of the Israelites back to the first man, Adam. He wishes the people to know that God is with those who are faithful to the covenant. His history is a warning and an encouragement both for the people of his day and for every generation since then. Following the genealogies the writer commences his history with the death of Saul and continues through the accession of David, his preparations for building the Temple, the arrangements concerning the Levites, his conduct of the government, and last instructions to Solomon before his death.

Contents:

THE FIRST BOOK OF THE

CHRONICLES

I. The genealogies 1.1–9.44

A. The ancestral lines in the patriarchal period

1 Adam, Sĕth, Ēnόsh; ² Kēnán, Má-há′lálĕl, Jārĕd; ³ Enoch, Mĕthu′ṣĕláh, Lāmĕch; ⁴ Noah, Shĕm, Ham, and Jāphĕth.

5 The sons of Jāphĕth: Gōmĕr, Māgŏg, Mādaī, Jāván, Tubál, Mĕshĕch, and Tīrás. ⁶ The sons of Gōmĕr: Ăsh′kĕnăz, Dī′pháth, and Tógar′máh. ⁷ The sons of Jāvàn: Ēlī′sháh, Tarshīsh, Kĭttīm, and Rōdā′nĭm.

8 The sons of Ham: Cŭsh, Egypt, Put, and Cānaán. ⁹ The sons of Cŭsh: Sēbá, Hăv′ĭláh, Săbtá, Rā′ámá, and Săb′tĕcá. The sons of Rā′ámáh: Shēbá and Dēdán. ¹⁰ Cŭsh was the father of Nĭmrŏd; he began to be a mighty one in the earth.

11 Egypt was the father of Ludĭm, Ăn′ámĭm, Lĕhā′bĭm, Năphtu′hĭm, ¹² Păthru′sĭm, Căslu′hĭm (whence came the Phĭlĭs′tĭneṣ), and Căph′tórĭm.

13 Cānaán was the father of Sīdόn his first-born, and Hĕth, ¹⁴ and the Jĕb′ūsītes, the Ăm′όrītes, the Gĭr′gáshītes, ¹⁵ the Hīvītes, the Arkītes, the Sīnītes, ¹⁶ the Ar′vádītes, the Zĕm′árītes, and the Hā′máthītes.

17 The sons of Shĕm: Ēlám, Ăsshŭr, Arpăch′shăd, Lŭd, Arám, Ŭz, Hŭl, Gĕthĕr, and Mĕshĕch. ¹⁸Arpăch′shăd was the father of Shēláh; and Shelah was the father of Ē′bĕr. ¹⁹ To Ē′bĕr were born two sons: the name of the one was Pĕlĕg (for in his days the earth was divided), and the name of his brother Jŏktán. ²⁰ Jŏktán was the father of Ălmō′dád, Shĕlĕph, Hā′zarmā′vĕth, Jĕráh, ²¹Hádor′-ám, Ŭzál, Dĭkláh, ²² Ēbál, Ăbĭm′ä-ĕl, Shēbá, ²³ Ōphĭr, Hăv′ĭláh, and Jōbăb; all these were the sons of Jŏktán.

24 Shĕm, Arpăch′shăd, Shēláh; ²⁵ Ē′bĕr, Pĕlĕg, Rĕ′ū; ²⁶Sĕrŭg, Nāhor, Tēráh; ²⁷ Abram, that is, Abraham.

28 The sons of Abraham: Isaac and Ĭsh′mäĕl. ²⁹ These are their genealogies: the first-born of Ĭsh′mäĕl, Nĕbāi′όth; and Kē-dar, Ădbeēl, Mĭbsăm, ³⁰ Mĭshmá, Dumáh, Măssá, Hādád, Tēmá, ³¹ Jētŭr, Náphĭsh, and Kĕd′ēmáh. These are the sons of Ĭsh′mäĕl.

32 The sons of Kĕtu′ráh, Abraham's concubine: she bore Zĭmrán, Jŏkshán, Mēdán, Mĭd′ĭán, Ĭshbăk, and Shuáh. The sons of Jokshan: Shēbá and Dēdán. ³³ The sons of Mĭd′ĭán: Ēpháh, Ēphĕr, Hānŏch, Ábĭ′dá, and Ĕldā′áh. All these were the descendants of Kĕtu′ráh.

34 Abraham was the father of Isaac. The sons of Isaac: Ēsau and Israel. ³⁵ The sons of Ēsau: Ēl′ĭpházᴢ, Reu′ĕl, Jē′ŭsh, Jālám, and Kōráh. ³⁶ The sons of Ēl′ĭpházᴢ: Tēmán, Ōmar, Zēphī, Gătám, Kēnăz, Tĭmná, and Ăm′álĕk. ³⁷ The sons of Reu′ĕl: Nāhăth, Zēráh, Shămmáh, and Mĭzzáh.

38 The sons of Sēĭr: Lōtán, Shōbál, Zĭb′ëon, Ānáh, Dīshόn, Ēzĕr, and Dīshăn. ³⁹ The sons of Lōtán: Hōrī and Hōmăm; and Lōtán'ṣ sister was Tīmná. ⁴⁰ The sons of Shōbál: Ăl′ĭán, Mánā′-háth, Ēbál, Shĕphī, and Ōnám. The sons of Zĭb′ëon: Ā′ĭáh and Ānáh. ⁴¹ The sons of Ānáh: Dīshόn. The sons of Dishon: Hămrán, Ēshbán, Ĭthrăn, and Chērán. ⁴² The sons of Ēzĕr: Bĭlhán, Zā′áván, and Jā′ákán. The sons of Dīshán: Ŭz and Ārán.

1.1
Gen 4.25;
5.32
1.5
Gen 10.2–4

1.8
Gen 10.6ff

1.10
Gen 10.8,
13ff

1.17
Gen 10.22ff

1.24
Gen 11.10ff

1.29
Gen 25.13–
16

1.32
Gen 25.1–4

1.34
Gen 21.2,3;
25.25,26
1.35
Gen 36.9,10

1.38
Gen 36.20–
28

1.43
Gen 36.31–
43

43 These are the kings who reigned in the land of Ēdŏm before any king reigned over the Israelites: Bēlă the son of Bēor, the name of whose city was Dĭnhă′băh. 44 When Bēlă died, Jōbăb the son of Zērăh of Bŏzrăh reigned in his stead. 45 When Jōbăb died, Hūshăm of the land of the Tē′mănītes reigned in his stead. 46 When Hūshăm died, Hădăd the son of Bĕdăd, who defeated Mĭd′iăn in the country of Mŏăb, reigned in his stead; and the name of his city was Āvĭth. 47 When Hădăd died, Sămlăh of Măsrē′kăh reigned in his stead. 48 When Sămlăh died, Shaul of Rēhŏ′bŏth on the Eŭphră′tēs reigned in his stead. 49 When Shaul died, Bā′al-hā′năn, the son of Ąchbor, reigned in his stead. 50 When Bā′al-hā′năn died, Hădăd reigned in his stead; and the name of his city was Pā′ī, and his wife's name Mĕhĕt′ăbĕl the daughter of Mātrĕd, the daughter of Mē′zăhăb. 51 And Hădăd died.

The chiefs of Ēdŏm were: chiefs Tĭmnă, Ăl′iăh, Jēthĕth, 52 Ŏhŏlĭbă′măh, Ēlăh, Pīnŏn, 53 Kēnăz, Tēmăn, Mĭbzar, 54 Măg′-dĭ-ĕl, and Īrăm; these are the chiefs of Ēdŏm.

B. The descendants of Judah to David

2.1
Gen 35.23–
26;
46.8–25
2.2
Gen 38.2–
10
2.4
Gen 38.29,
30
2.5
Gen 46.12
2.6
Josh 7.1;
1 Ki 4.31
2.7
Josh 6.18;
7.1
2.10
Ruth 4.19,
20;
Mt 1.4
2.13
1 Sam
16.6,9
2.16
2 Sam 2.18
2.17
2 Sam 17.25

2 These are the sons of Israel: Reubĕn, Sĭm′ĕŏn, Lēvī, Judah, Ĭs′săchar, Zĕb′ŭlŭn, 2 Dan, Joseph, Benjamin, Năph′tălī, Găd, and Ăshĕr. 3 The sons of Judah: Ēr, Ōnăn, and Shēlăh; these three Băth-shu′ă the Că′naănī′tĕss bore to him. Now Er, Judah's firstborn, was wicked in the sight of the LORD, and he slew him. 4 His daughter-in-law Tāmar also bore him Pĕrĕz and Zērăh. Judah had five sons in all.

5 The sons of Pĕrĕz: Hĕzrŏn and Hāmŭl. 6 The sons of Zērăh: Zĭmrī, Ēthăn, Hēmăn, Călcŏl, and Dāră, five in all. 7 The sons of Carmī: Ąchar, the troubler of Israel, who transgressed in the matter of the devoted thing; 8 and Ēthăn′ș son was Ăzărī′ăh.

9 The sons of Hĕzrŏn, that were born to him: Jĕrah′meēl, Ram, and Chĕlu′baī. 10 Ram was the father of Ąmmin′ădăb, and Amminadab was the father of Nahshŏn, prince of the sons of Judah. 11 Nahshŏn was the father of Sălmă, Salma of Bŏăz, 12 Bŏăz of Ōbĕd, Obed of Jĕssĕ. 13 Jĕssĕ was the father of Ēlī′ăb his firstborn, Ăbĭn′ădăb the second, Shĭm′ĕă the third, 14 Nĕthăn′ĕl the fourth, Răd′daī the fifth, 15 Ōzĕm the sixth, David the seventh; 16 and their sisters were Zĕru′iăh and Ăb′ĭgăil. The sons of Zeruiah: Ăbĭsh′ăī, Jŏăb, and Ăs′ăhĕl, three. 17 Ăb′ĭgăil bore Ămă′să, and the father of Amasa was Jēthĕr the Ĭsh′măĕlīte.

18 Călĕb the son of Hĕzrŏn had children by his wife Ăzu′băh, and by Jĕr′iŏth; and these were her sons: Jĕshĕr, Shŏbăb, and Ardŏn. 19 When Ăzu′băh died, Călĕb married Ēphrăth, who bore him Hŭr. 20 Hŭr was the father of Ūrī, and Uri was the father of Bĕz′ălĕl.

2.19
ver 50
2.20
Ex 31.2
2.21
Num 27.1
2.23
Num 32.41;
Deut 3.14;
Josh 13.30
2.24
1 Chr 4.5

21 Afterward Hĕzrŏn went in to the daughter of Māchĭr the father of Gĭl′ĕăd, whom he married when he was sixty years old; and she bore him Sĕgŭb; 22 and Sĕgŭb was the father of Jāir, who had twenty-three cities in the land of Gĭl′ĕăd. 23 But Gĕshŭr and Ąrăm took from them Hăvvŏth-jā′ir, Kēnăth and its villages, sixty towns. All these were descendants of Māchĭr, the father of Gil′ĕăd. 24 After the death of Hĕzrŏn, Călĕb went in to Ēph′răthăh,ᵃ the

a Gk Vg: Heb in Caleb Ephrathah

wife of Hezron his father, and she bore him Ashhur, the father
of Tëkō′á.

25 The sons of Jerah′meēl, the first-born of Hēzrón: Ram, his
first-born, Būnáh, Ōrėn, Ōzĕm, and Áhī′jáh. 26 Jėrah′meēl also
had another wife, whose name was Át′áráh; she was the mother
of Ōnám. 27 The sons of Rám, the first-born of Jėrah′meēl: Má′ăz,
Jámìn, and Ēkėr. 28 The sons of Ōnám: Shăm′mäī and Jádá. The
sons of Shammai: Nādăb and Ábī′shúr. 29 The name of Ábī′shúr′s
wife was Áb′ïhāil, and she bore him Ahbán and Mōlïd. 30 The
sons of Nādăb: Sėlĕd and Áp′pá-ìm; and Seled died childless.
31 The sons of Áp′pá-ìm: Ìshī. The sons of Ishi: Shēshăn. The
sons of Sheshan: Ahlaī. 32 The sons of Jádá, Shăm′mäī′ş brother:
Jēthėr and Jonathan; and Jether died childless. 33 The sons of
Jonathan: Pĕlĕth and Zāzá. These were the descendants of Jėrah′-
meēl. 34 Now Shēshăn had no sons, only daughters; but Sheshan
had an Egyptian slave, whose name was Jarhá. 35 So Shēshăn gave
his daughter in marriage to Jarhá his slave; and she bore him
Āttaī. 36Āttaī was the father of Nathan and Nathan of Zābăd.
37 Zābăd was the father of Ēphlăl, and Ephlal of Ōbėd. 38Ōbėd
was the father of Jēhū, and Jehu of Ázárī′áh. 39Ázárī′áh was the
father of Hēlėz, and Helez of Ēlë-ā′sáh. 40 Ēlë-ā′sáh was the father
of Sïsmaī, and Sismai of Shăllûm. 41 Shăllûm was the father of
Jĕkámī′áh, and Jekamiah of Ēlī′shámá.

42 The sons of Cálėb the brother of Jėrah′meēl: Márē′sháh[b]
his first-born, who was the father of Zïph. The sons of Mareshah:
Hēbrón.[c] 43 The sons of Hēbrón: Kōráh, Táppū′áh, Rĕkĕm, and
Shēmá. 44 Shēmá was the father of Rāhăm, the father of Jor′kë-
ám; and Rĕkĕm was the father of Shăm′mäī. 45 The son of Shăm′-
mäī: Máón; and Maon was the father of Bĕth-zúr. 46 Ēpháh also,
Cálėb′s concubine, bore Hārán, Mōzá, and Gāzĕz; and Haran was
the father of Gazez. 47 The sons of Jah′däī: Rĕgĕm, Jōthám,
Gēshán, Pĕlĕt, Ēpháh, and Shá′ăph. 48 Má′ácáh, Cálėb′s concubine, bore Shēbėr and Tïrhá′náh. 49 She also bore Shá′ăph the
father of Mădmăn′náh, Shēvá the father of Máchbē′náh and the
father of Gïb′ë-á; and the daughter of Cálėb was Áchsáh. 50 These
were the descendants of Cálėb.

The sons[d] of Húr the first-born of Ēph′ráthá: Shōbăl the father
of Kïr′iăth-jē′árìm, 51 Sálmá, the father of Bĕth′lëhĕm, and
Hārėph the father of Bĕth-gā′dėr. 52 Shōbăl the father of Kïr′iăth-
jē′árìm had other sons: Háró′ėh, half of the Mėnū′hóth. 53And the
families of Kïr′iăth-jē′árìm: the Ìthrïtes, the Pūthïtes, the Shu′-
máthïtes, and the Mïsh′rä-ītes; from these came the Zor′áthïtes
and the Ēshtā′ólïtes. 54 The sons of Sálmá: Bĕth′lëhĕm, the Nē-
tōph′áthïtes, Át′róth-bĕth-jō′ăb, and half of the Mánā′háthïtes,
the Zorïtes. 55 The families also of the scribes that dwelt at Jābĕz:
the Tï′ráthïtes, the Shïm′ë-áthïtes, and the Su′cáthïtes. These are
the Kēnïtes who came from Hămmáth, the father of the house
of Rēchăb.

*2.25

2.31
ver 34,35

2.36
1 Chr 11.41

2.42
see 1 Chr
2.18,19

2.50
1 Chr 4.4

*2.55
Judg 1.16;
Jer 35.2

b Gk: Heb Mēshá
c Heb the father of Hebron d Gk Vg: Heb son

2.25 Jerahmeel means "may God have compassion." Some non-Israelites, subjects of
David, called themselves Jerahmeelites. They
are mentioned in 1 Sam 27.10; 30.29.

2.55 scribes. These were non-Levitical
scribes, although some of the Levites were
scribes as well (2 Chr 34.13 specifically states
this).

C. The descendants of David

3.1
2 Sam
3.2,3;
Josh 15.56

3.3
2 Sam 3.5

3.4
2 Sam 2.11;
5.5
*3.5
2 Sam
5.14–16;
2 Sam
12.24; 11.3
3.9
2 Sam 13.1

3.10
1 Ki 11.43

*3.15

*3.16
Mt 1.11
*3.17

*3.19

3.22
Ezek 8.2

4.1
Gen 46.12

4.4
1 Chr 2.50

3 These are the sons of David that were born to him in Hēbrŏn: the first-born Ămnŏn, by Ăhĭn'ō-ăm the Jĕz'reēlĭt'ĕss; the second Daniel, by Ăb'ĭgāil the Car'mĕlĭt'ĕss, 2 the third Ăb'sălŏm, whose mother was Mā'ăcăh, the daughter of Tălmaĭ, king of Gĕshŭr; the fourth Ădŏnī'jăh, whose mother was Hăggĭth; 3 the fifth Shĕphătī'ăh, by Ăb'ītăl; the sixth Ĭth'rĕăm, by his wife Ĕglăh; 4 six were born to him in Hēbrŏn, where he reigned for seven years and six months. And he reigned thirty-three years in Jerusalem 5 These were born to him in Jerusalem: Shĭm'ē-ă, Shōbăb, Nathan, and Solomon, four by Băth-shu'ă, the daughter of Ăm'mĭ-ĕl; 6 then Ĭbhar, Ĕlī'shămă, Ĕlĭph'ĕlĕt, 7 Nōgăh, Nĕphĕg, Jăphī'ă, 8 Ĕlī'shămă, Ĕlī'ădă, and Ĕlĭph'ĕlĕt, nine. 9All these were David's sons, besides the sons of the concubines; and Tāmar was their sister.

10 The descendants of Solomon: Rĕhŏbō'ăm, Ăbī'jăh his son, Āsă his son, Jĕhŏsh'ăphăt his son, 11 Jōrăm his son, Āhăzī'ăh his son, Jō'ăsh his son, 12Ămăzī'ăh his son, Ăzărī'ăh his son, Jōthăm his son, 13Āhăz his son, Hĕzĕkī'ăh his son, Mănăs'sĕh his son, 14Āmŏn his son, Jōsī'ăh his son. 15 The sons of Jōsī'ăh: Jōhăn'ăn the first-born, the second Jĕhoi'ăkĭm, the third Zĕdĕkī'ăh, the fourth Shăllŭm. 16 The descendants of Jĕhoi'ăkĭm: Jĕcŏnī'ăh his son, Zĕdĕkī'ăh his son; 17 and the sons of Jĕcŏnī'ăh, the captive: Shē-ăl'tī-ĕl his son, 18Mălchī'răm, Pĕdāi'ăh, Shĕnăz'zăr, Jĕkămī'ăh, Hŏsh'ămă, and Nĕdăbī'ăh; 19 and the sons of Pĕdāi'ăh: Zĕrŭb'băbĕl and Shĭm'ē-ĭ; and the sons of Zerubbabel: Mĕshŭl'lăm and Hănănī'ăh, and Shĕlō'mĭth was their sister; 20 and Hăshu'băh, Ōhĕl, Bĕrĕchī'ăh, Hăsădī'ăh, and Jushăb-hĕs'ĕd, five. 21 The sons of Hănănī'ăh: Pĕlătī'ăh and Jĕshāi'ăh, his son*e* Rĕphāi'ăh, his son*e* Arnăn, his son*e* Ōbădī'ăh, his son*e* Shĕcănī'ăh. 22 The sons of Shĕcănī'ăh: Shĕmāi'ăh. And the sons of Shemaiah: Hăttŭsh, Īgăl, Bărī'ăh, Nĕărī'ăh, and Shăphăt, six. 23 The sons of Nĕărī'ăh: Ĕl'ĭ-ō-ē'naī, Hĭzkī'ăh, and Ăzrī'kăm, three. 24 The sons of Ĕl'ĭ-ō-ē'naī: Hōdăvī'ăh, Ĕlī'ăshĭb, Pĕlāi'ăh, Ăkkŭb, Jōhăn'ăn, Dĕlāi'ăh, and Ănā'nī, seven.

D. The family of Judah

4 The sons of Judah: Pērĕz, Hĕzrŏn, Carmī, Hŭr, and Shōbăl. 2 Rĕ-āi'ăh the son of Shōbăl was the father of Jāhăth, and Jahath was the father of Ăhu'maī and Lāhăd. These were the families of the Zor'ăthītes. 3 These were the sons*f* of Ētăm: Jĕzreēl', Ĭshmă, and Ĭdbăsh; and the name of their sister was Hăz'zĕlĕlpō'nī, 4 and Pĕnū'ĕl was the father of Gĕdor, and Ēzĕr the father of Hūshăh. These were the sons of Hŭr, the first-born of

e Gk Compare Syr Vg: Heb *sons of*   *f* Gk Compare Vg: Heb *father*

3.5 *Bath-shua*, that is, Bath-sheba.
3.15 *Johanan.* Apparently he died as a youth. He never reigned and is never mentioned in the historical accounts. *Shallum*, that is, Jehoahaz. See Jer 22.11.
3.16 *Jeconiah*, that is, Jehoiachin. He is also called Coniah in Jer 22.24.
3.17 *the captive.* The KJV took this word

as a proper name, listing it as Assir.
3.19 *Zerubbabel.* The Zerubbabel who led the captives back to Palestine was called *the son of Shealtiel* (Ezra 3.2; Neh 12.1). Evidently both Shealtiel and Pedaiah had sons named Zerubbabel. Thus, the descendants listed after Zerubbabel here are most likely from the line of Shealtiel, not Pedaiah.

Ĕph'rȧthȧh, the father of Bĕth'lĕhĕm. 5Ăshhŭr, the father of
Tĕkō'ȧ, had two wives, Hēlȧh and Nā'ȧrȧh; 6 Nā'ȧrȧh bore him
Ȧhŭz'zȧm, Hēphèr, Tē'mĕnī, and Hā'-ȧhȧsh'tȧrī. These were the
sons of Naarah. 7 The sons of Hēlȧh: Zĕrĕth, Ĭzhar, and Ĕthnăn.
8 Kŏz was the father of Ānŭb, Zōbē'bȧh, and the families of
Ahar'hĕl the son of Hārŭm. 9 Jȧbĕz was more honorable than his
brothers; and his mother called his name Jabez, saying, "Because
I bore him in pain." 10 Jȧbĕz called on the God of Israel, saying,
"Oh that thou wouldst bless me and enlarge my border, and that
thy hand might be with me, and that thou wouldst keep me from
harm so that it might not hurt me!" And God granted what he
asked. 11 Chĕlŭb, the brother of Shuhȧh, was the father of Mēhĭr,
who was the father of Ĕshtȯn. 12 Ĕshtȯn was the father of Bĕthrā'-
phȧ, Pȧsē'ȧh, and Tĕhĭn'nȧh the father of Ĭrnā'hȧsh. These are the
men of Rēcȧh. 13 The sons of Kēnȧz: Ŏth'nĭ-ĕl and Sĕrāi'ȧh; and
the sons of Othni-el: Hāthȧth and Mĕȯ'nȯthaī.g 14 Mĕȯ'nȯthaī was
the father of Ŏphrȧh; and Sĕrāi'ȧh was the father of Jŏȧb the father
of Gè-har'ȧshĭm,h so-called because they were craftsmen. 15 The
sons of Cālĕb the son of Jĕphŭn'nĕh: Īru, Ēlȧh, and Nā'ȧm; and
the sons of Elah: Kēnȧz. 16 The sons of Jĕhȧl'lĕlĕl: Zĭph, Zĭphȧh,
Tĭr'ĭ-ȧ, and Ăs'ȧrĕl. 17 The sons of Ĕzrȧh: Jĕthèr, Mĕrĕd, Ĕphèr,
and Jālȯn. These are the sons of Bĭthī'-ȧh, the daughter of
Phȧraōh, whom Mered married;i and she conceived and borej
Miriam, Shăm'māī, and Ĭshbȧh, the father of Ĕshtĕmō'ȧ. 18And
his Jewish wife bore Jĕrĕd the father of Gĕdor, Hēbèr the father of
Sōcō, and Jēkū'thĭĕl the father of Zȧnō'ȧh. 19 The sons of the wife
of Hōdī'ȧh, the sister of Nāhăm, were the fathers of Keīlȧh the
Garmīte and Ĕshtĕmō'ȧ the Mā-ȧc'ȧthīte. 20 The sons of Shĭmȯn:
Ȧmnȯn, Rĭnnȧh, Bĕn-hā'nȧn, and Tīlȯn. The sons of Ĭshī:
Zōhĕth and Bĕn-zō'hĕth. 21 The sons of Shēlȧh the son of Judah:
Ĕr the father of Lēcȧh, Lā'ȧdȧh the father of Mȧrē'shȧh, and the
families of the house of linen workers at Bĕth-ȧshbē'ȧ; 22 and
Jōkĭm, and the men of Cōzē'bȧ, and Jō'ȧsh, and Sārȧph, who
ruled in Mōȧb and returned to Lĕhĕmk (now the recordsl are
ancient). 23 These were the potters and inhabitants of Nĕtā'ĭm and
Gĕdē'rȧh; they dwelt there with the king for his work.

E. The family of Simeon

24 The sons of Sĭm'ĕȯn: Nĕm'ū-ĕl, Jāmĭn, Jā'rĭb, Zĕrȧh, Shaul;
25 Shăllŭm was his son, Mĭbsȧm his son, Mĭshmá his son. 26 The
sons of Mĭshmá: Hăm'mū-ĕl his son, Zăccŭr his son, Shĭm'ĕ-ī his
son. 27 Shĭm'ĕ-ī had sixteen sons and six daughters; but his brothers had not many children, nor did all their family multiply like the
men of Judah. 28 They dwelt in Beĕr-shē'bȧ, Mōlā'dȧh, Hā'zar-
shu'ȧl, 29 Bĭlhȧh, Ēzĕm, Tōlȧd, 30 Bĕthu'ĕl, Hormȧh, Zĭklȧg,
31 Bĕth-mar'cȧbȯth, Hā'zar-su'sĭm, Bĕth-bĭr'ī, and Shā-ȧrā'ĭm.
These were their cities until David reigned. 32And their villages

4.5
1 Chr 2.24

*4.9
Gen 34.19

4.13
Josh 15.17
4.14
Neh 11.35

4.21
Gen 38.1,5

*4.23

4.24
Gen 29.33

4.28
Josh 19.2
4.30
1 Chr 12.1

g Gk Vg: Heb lacks *Meonothai* h That is *Valley of craftsmen*
i The clause: *These are . . . married* is transposed from verse 18
j Heb lacks *and bore* k Vg Compare Gk: Heb *and Jā'shūbī-lā'hèm* l Or *matters*

4.9 *Jabez . . . pain.* If "pain" was the basis
for naming the child, then his name should
have been *Jazeb*, otherwise the last two
consonants are interchanged.

4.23 *potters.* Stamped jar handles found in
excavations by archaeologists have verified
that there were royal potters who worked for
the king.

were Ētàm, Ā'ĭn, Rĭmmòn, Tōçhèn, and Āshàn, five cities, 33 along with all their villages which were round about these cities as far as Bāal. These were their settlements, and they kept a genealogical record.

34 Mèshō'băb, Jămlĕch, Jōshàh the son of Ămàzī'àh, 35 Jōèl, Jēhū the son of Jōshĭbī'àh, son of Sèrāi'àh, son of Ā'sĭ-èl, 36 Ĕl'ĭ-ò-ē'naī, Jā-àkō'bàh, Jĕshòhāi'àh, Àṣāi'àh, Ā'dĭ-èl, Jĕsĭm'ĭèl, Bènāi'àh, 37 Zīzà the son of Shīphī, son of Āllòn, son of Jèdāi'àh, son of Shĭmrī, son of Shèmāi'àh—38 these mentioned by name were princes in their families, and their fathers' houses increased greatly. 39 They journeyed to the entrance of Gēdor, to the east side of the valley, to seek pasture for their flocks, 40 where they found rich, good pasture, and the land was very broad, quiet, and peaceful; for the former inhabitants there belonged to Ham. 41 These, registered by name, came in the days of Hèzĕkī'àh, king of Judah, and destroyed their tents and the Mè-ū'nĭm who were found there, and exterminated them to this day, and settled in their place, because there was pasture there for their flocks. 42 And some of them, five hundred men of the Sĭm'ĕönītes, went to Mount Sēir, having as their leaders Pĕlàtī'àh, Nē-àrī'àh, Rĕphāi'-àh, and Uzzī'èl, the sons of Ĭshī; 43 and they destroyed the remnant of the Àmàl'èkītes that had escaped, and they have dwelt there to this day.

F. The family of Reuben

5 The sons of Reubën the first-born of Israel (for he was the first-born; but because he polluted his father's couch, his birthright was given to the sons of Joseph the son of Israel, so that he is not enrolled in the genealogy according to the birthright; 2 though Judah became strong among his brothers and a prince was from him, yet the birthright belonged to Joseph), 3 the sons of Reubën, the first-born of Israel: Hānoch, Pāllu, Hĕzròn, and Carmī. 4 The sons of Jōèl: Shèmāi'àh his son, Gŏg his son, Shĭm'ĕ-ī his son, 5 Mīcàh his son, Rè-āi'àh his son, Bāal his son, 6 Be-ër'àh his son, whom Tĭl'gàth-pĭlnē'ṣèr king of Assyria carried away into exile; he was a chieftain of the Reu'bènītes. 7 And his kinsmen by their families, when the genealogy of their generations was reckoned: the chief, Je-ī'èl, and Zĕchàrī'àh, 8 and Bēlà the son of Āzàz, son of Shēmà, son of Jōèl, who dwelt in Àrō'èr, as far as Nēbō and Bā'àl-mē'òn. 9 He also dwelt to the east as far as the entrance of the desert this side of the Eūphrā'tēs, because their cattle had multiplied in the land of Gĭl'ĕàd. 10 And in the days of Saul they made war on the Hăgrītes, who fell by their hand; and they dwelt in their tents throughout all the region east of Gĭl'ĕàd.

G. The family of Gad

11 The sons of Găd dwelt over against them in the land of Bāshàn as far as Săl'ĕcàh: 12 Jōèl the chief, Shāphàm the second, Jānaī, and Shāphàt in Bāshàn. 13 And their kinsmen according to

*4.40
Judg 18.7–10

4.41
2 Ki 18.8

4.43
1 Sam 15.8;
30.17;
2 Sam 8.12

*5.1f
Gen 29.32;
35.22;
49.4;
48.15,22

5.2
Gen 49.8,
10;
Mic 5.2;
Mt 2.6

5.3
Gen 46.9;
Num 26.5

5.7
ver 17

5.8
Josh 13.15,
16

5.9
Josh 22.9

5.10
ver 18–21

5.11
Josh 13.11,
24

4.40 to Ham, that is, to the Canaanites, who were listed under Ham (Gen 10.6).
5.1, 2 While the birthright was passed on to Ephraim and Manasseh, leadership came into the hands of Judah, the most powerful tribe.

their fathers' houses: Michael, Mĕshŭl'lăm, Shēba, Jōraī, Jācàn, Zīà, and Ē'bĕr, seven. 14 These were the sons of Ăb'ĭhāil the son of Hūrī, son of Jàrō'àh, son of Gĭl'ĕăd, son of Michael, son of Jĕshĭsh'āī, son of Jahdō, son of Bŭz; 15Ăhī the son of Ăb'dĭ-ĕl, son of Gunī, was chief in their fathers' houses; 16 and they dwelt in Gĭl'ĕăd, in Bāshàn and in its towns, and in all the pasture lands of Shàròn to their limits. 17All of these were enrolled by genealogies in the days of Jōthàm king of Judah, and in the days of Jĕrŏbō'ám king of Israel.

5.16
1 Chr 27.29

5.17
2 Ki 15.5,
32;
14.16,28

18 The Reu'bĕnītes, the Gădītes, and the half-tribe of Mànăs'-sĕh had valiant men, who carried shield and sword, and drew the bow, expert in war, forty-four thousand seven hundred and sixty, ready for service. 19 They made war upon the Hăgrītes, Jĕtùr, Năphĭsh, and Nōdăb; 20 and when they received help against them, the Hăgrītes and all who were with them were given into their hands, for they cried to God in the battle, and he granted their entreaty because they trusted in him. 21 They carried off their livestock: fifty thousand of their camels, two hundred and fifty thousand sheep, two thousand asses, and a hundred thousand men alive. 22 For many fell slain, because the war was of God. And they dwelt in their place until the exile.

5.19
ver 10;
1 Chr 1.31
5.20
2 Chr
4.11–13;
Ps 22.4,5

5.22
2 Ki 15.29;
17.6

H. The half-tribe of Manasseh

23 The members of the half-tribe of Mànăs'sĕh dwelt in the land; they were very numerous from Bāshàn to Bā'àl-hĕr'mòn, Sēnĭr, and Mount Hèrmòn. 24 These were the heads of their fathers' houses: Ēphèr,[m] Ĭshī, Ĕlī'ĕl, Ăz'rĭ-ĕl, Jĕrĕmī'áh, Hōdàvī'-áh, and Jah'dĭ-ĕl, mighty warriors, famous men, heads of their fathers' houses. 25 But they transgressed against the God of their fathers, and played the harlot after the gods of the peoples of the land, whom God had destroyed before them. 26 So the God of Israel stirred up the spirit of Pŭl king of Assyria, the spirit of Tĭl'gàth-pĭlnē'sèr king of Assyria, and he carried them away, namely, the Reu'bĕnītes, the Gădītes, and the half-tribe of Mà-năs'sĕh, and brought them to Hālàh, Hābor, Hārà, and the river Gōzàn, to this day.

*5.23

5.25
2 Ki 17.7

*5.26
2 Ki 15.19,
29; 17.6;
18.11

I. The family of Levi

6[n] The sons of Lēvī: Gèrshóm, Kōhăth, and Mĕrar'ĭ. 2 The sons of Kōhăth: Ămrăm, Ĭzhar, Hēbròn, and Ŭzzī'ĕl. 3 The children of Ămrăm: Aaron, Moses, and Miriam. The sons of Aaron: Nādăb, Abī'hū, Ĕlĕ-ā'zàr, and Ĭth'àmar. 4 Ĕlĕ-ā'zàr was the father of Phĭn'ĕhás, Phinehas of Ăbĭsh'uà, 5Abĭsh'uà of Bŭkkī, Bukki of Ŭzzī, 6 Ŭzzī of Zĕrăhī'áh, Zerahiah of Mèrāī'óth, 7 Mèrāī'óth of Ămàrī'áh, Amariah of Ăhī'tŭb, 8Ăhī'tŭb of Zādŏk, Zadok of Ăhĭm'ä-ăz, 9Ahĭm'ä-ăz of Ăzàrī'áh, Azariah of Jōhăn'àn, 10 and Jōhăn'àn of Ăzàrī'áh (it was he who served as priest in the house that Solomon built in Jerusalem). 11Ăzàrī'áh was the father of

6.1
Ex 6.16;
Num 26.57;
1 Chr 23.6
6.3
Lev 10.1

6.8
2 Sam 8.17;
15.27

---

[m] Gk Vg: Heb and Epher   [n] Ch 5.27 in Heb

5.23 Mount Hermon is probably a scribal explanation of Senir, which was the Amorite name for Mt. Hermon (Deut 3.9).

5.26 Pul and Tilgath-pilneser (Tiglath-pileser) were different names for the same Assyrian king. See note to 2 Ki 15.19.

6.14
Neh 11.11
6.15
2 Ki 25.18

6.16
Ex 6.16

6.20
ver 42

6.25
ver 35,36
6.26
ver 34

*6.31
1 Chr
15.16–16.6

6.37
Ex 6.24

6.41
ver 21

*6.49
Ex 27.1–8;
30.1–7,10

6.50
ver 4–8

Ămărī'áh, Amariah of Åhī'tŭb, 12 Åhī'tŭb of Zādŏk, Zadok of Shăllŭm, 13 Shăllŭm of Hĭlkī'áh, Hilkiah of Ăzărī'áh, 14Ăzărī'áh of Sërāi'áh, Seraiah of Jĕhŏ'zădăk; 15 and Jĕhŏ'zădăk went into exile when the LORD sent Judah and Jĕrusalem into exile by the hand of Nĕbŭchădnĕz'zăr.

16ᵒ The sons of Lēvī: Gĕrshŏm, Kōhăth, and Mĕrar'ī. 17And these are the names of the sons of Gĕrshŏm: Lĭbnī and Shĭm'ĕ-ī. 18 The sons of Kōhăth: Ămrăm, Ĭzhar, Hēbrŏn, and Ŭzzī'ĕl. 19 The sons of Mĕrar'ī: Mahlī and Mushī. These are the families of the Lēvītes according to their fathers. 20 Of Gĕrshŏm: Lĭbnī his son, Jăhăth his son, Zĭmmăh his son, 21 Jŏáh his son, Ĭddŏ his son, Zēráh his son, Jĕ-ăth'ĕraī his son. 22 The sons of Kōhăth: Ammĭn'ădăb his son, Kōráh his son, Ăssĭr his son, 23 Ĕlkā'náh his son, Ĕbī'ăsăph his son, Ăssĭr his son, 24 Tăhăth his son, Ŭ'rĭĕl his son, Ŭzzī'áh his son, and Shaul his son. 25 The sons of Elkā'náh: Ămā'säi and Ahī'mŏth, 26 Ĕlkā'náh his son, Zōphaī his son, Nāhăth his son, 27 Ĕlī'áb his son, Jĕrŏ'hăm his son, Ĕlkā'náh his son. 28 The sons of Samuel: Jŏĕlᵖ his first-born, the second Abī'-jáh.�q 29 The sons of Mĕrar'ī: Mahlī, Lĭbnī his son, Shĭm'ĕ-ī his son, Ŭzzáh his son, 30 Shĭm'ĕ-à his son, Hăggī'áh his son, and Ăsāi'áh his son.

31 These are the men whom David put in charge of the service of song in the house of the LORD, after the ark rested there. 32 They ministered with song before the tabernacle of the tent of meeting, until Solomon had built the house of the LORD in Jerusalem; and they performed their service in due order. 33 These are the men who served and their sons. Of the sons of the Kō'hăthītes: Hēmăn the singer the son of Jŏĕl, son of Samuel, 34 son of Ĕlkā'náh, son of Jĕrŏ'hăm, son of Ĕlī'ĕl, son of Tōáh, 35 son of Zúph, son of Ĕlkā'-náh, son of Māhăth, son of Ămă'säi, 36 son of Ĕlkā'náh, son of Jŏĕl, son of Ăzărī'áh, son of Zēphănī'áh, 37 son of Tăhăth, son of Ăssĭr, son of Ĕbī'ăsăph, son of Kōráh, 38 son of Ĭzhar, son of Kōhăth, son of Lēvī, son of Israel; 39 and his brother Āsăph, who stood on his right hand, namely, Asaph the son of Bĕrĕchī'áh, son of Shĭm'ĕ-à, 40 son of Michael, son of Bā-ăseī'áh, son of Mălchī'-jáh, 41 son of Ĕthnī, son of Zēráh, son of Ădāi'áh, 42 son of Ĕthăn, son of Zĭmmáh, son of Shĭm'ĕ-ī, 43 son of Jăhăth, son of Gĕrshŏm, son of Lēvī. 44 On the left hand were their brethren the sons of Mĕrar'ī: Ĕthăn the son of Kĭshī, son of Ăbdī, son of Măllŭch, 45 son of Hăshăbī'áh, son of Ămāzī'áh, son of Hĭlkī'áh, 46 son of Ămzī, son of Bānī, son of Shĕmĕr, 47 son of Mahlī, son of Mushī, son of Mĕrar'ī, son of Lēvī; 48 and their brethren the Lēvītes were appointed for all the service of the tabernacle of the house of God.

49 But Aaron and his sons made offerings upon the altar of burnt offering and upon the altar of incense for all the work of the most holy place, and to make atonement for Israel, according to all that Moses the servant of God had commanded. 50 These are the sons of Aaron: Ĕlë-ā'zăr his son, Phĭn'ĕhăs his son, Ăbĭsh'uá

ᵒ Ch 6.1 in Heb   ᵖ Gk Syr Compare verse 33 and 1 Sam 8.2: Heb lacks *Joel*
�q Heb *and Abijah*

6.31 In the realm of song and Temple ritual David has an authority equal to that of Moses in the realm of law. The names of some of the singers and musicians are Canaanite in form, causing some to suggest that outwardly the Temple ritual, as well as the architecture, was of Canaanite origin.
6.49 They were entirely within their rights.

his son, 51 Bŭkkĭ his son, Ŭzzī his son, Zĕráhĭ'áh his son, 52 Mĕrāi'ŏth his son, Ămárĭ'áh his son, Ăhĭ'tŭb his son, 53 Zādŏk his
son, Ăhĭm'ä-ăz his son.

54 These are their dwelling places according to their settlements within their borders: to the sons of Aaron of the families
of Kō'hăthītes, for theirs was the lot, 55 to them they gave Hēbrón
in the land of Judah and its surrounding pasture lands, 56 but the
fields of the city and its villages they gave to Cālĕb the son of
Jĕphŭn'nĕh. 57 To the sons of Aaron they gave the cities of refuge:
Hēbrón, Lĭbnáh with its pasture lands, Jăttĭr, Ĕshtĕmō'á with
its pasture lands, 58 Hĭlĕn with its pasture lands, Dēbĭr with its
pasture lands, 59 Āshán with its pasture lands, and Bĕth-shĕ'mĕsh
with its pasture lands; 60 and from the tribe of Benjamin, Gēbá
with its pasture lands, Ăl'ĕmĕth with its pasture lands, and Ăn'-
áthŏth with its pasture lands. All their cities throughout their
families were thirteen.

61 To the rest of the Kō'hăthītes were given by lot out of the
family of the tribe, out of the half-tribe, the half of Mánăs'sĕh,
ten cities. 62 To the Gĕr'shŏmītes according to their families were
allotted thirteen cities out of the tribes of Ĭs'sáchar, Ăshĕr, Năph'-
tálī, and Mánăs'sĕh in Bāshán. 63 To the Mĕrar'ītes according
to their families were allotted twelve cities out of the tribes of
Reubĕn, Găd, and Zĕb'ŭlŭn. 64 So the people of Israel gave the
Lēvītes the cities with their pasture lands. 65 They also gave them
by lot out of the tribes of Judah, Sĭm'ëón, and Benjamin these
cities which are mentioned by name.

66 And some of the families of the sons of Kōhăth had cities of
their territory out of the tribe of Ē'phráĭm. 67 They were given the
cities of refuge: Shĕchĕm with its pasture lands in the hill country
of Ē'phráĭm, Gēzĕr with its pasture lands, 68 Jŏk'mĕ-ăm with its
pasture lands, Bĕth-hor'ón with its pasture lands, 69 Āi'jálón with
its pasture lands, Găth-rĭm'món with its pasture lands, 70 and out
of the half-tribe of Mánăs'sĕh, Ānĕr with its pasture lands, and
Bĭl'ĕ-ám with its pasture lands, for the rest of the families of the
Kō'hăthītes.

71 To the Gĕr'shŏmītes were given out of the half-tribe of
Mánăs'sĕh: Gōlán in Bāshán with its pasture lands and Ăsh'-
tárŏth with its pasture lands; 72 and out of the tribe of Ĭs'sáchar:
Kĕdĕsh with its pasture lands, Dăb'ĕráth with its pasture lands,
73 Rāmŏth with its pasture lands, and Ānĕm with its pasture lands;
74 out of the tribe of Ăshĕr: Māshál with its pasture lands, Ăbdón
with its pasture lands, 75 Hūkŏk with its pasture lands, and Rēhŏb
with its pasture lands; 76 and out of the tribe of Năph'tálī: Kĕdĕsh
in Găl'ĭleē with its pasture lands, Hămmón with its pasture lands,
and Kĭr'ĭáthā'ĭm with its pasture lands. 77 To the rest of the
Mĕrar'ītes were allotted out of the tribe of Zĕb'ŭlŭn: Rĭmmō'nō
with its pasture lands, Tābŏr with its pasture lands, 78 and beyond
the Jordan at Jĕr'ĭchō, on the east side of the Jordan, out of the
tribe of Reubĕn: Bēzĕr in the steppe with its pasture lands, Jahzáh
with its pasture lands, 79 Kĕd'ĕmŏth with its pasture lands, and
Mēphā-áth with its pasture lands; 80 and out of the tribe of Găd:

6.54
Josh 21.4,
10
6.55
Josh 21.11,
12
6.56
Josh 14.13;
15.13
*6.57
Josh 21.13

6.61
ver 66–70;
Josh 21.5

6.63
Josh 21.7,
34
6.64
Josh 21.3,
41,42
6.65
ver 57–60

6.66
ver 61
6.67
Josh 21.21
6.68
see Josh
21.22–35
where some
names are
differently
given

6.73
see Josh
21.29;
19.21

6.76
ver 62

6.77
ver 63

6.57 *cities of refuge.* Of the cities listed,
only Hebron was a city of refuge. Two letters
of the Hebrew text have been interchanged
and need to be inverted. Then the passage
would read, as in Josh 21.13, *city of refuge,*
which explains the apparent discrepancy.

Rāmoth in Gĭl'ëăd with its pasture lands, Māhănā'ĭm with its pasture lands, 81 Hĕshbŏn with its pasture lands, and Jāzĕr with its pasture lands.

J. The family of Issachar

7.1
Gen 46.13;
Num 26.23
7.2
2 Sam 24.1,
2

7 The sons*r* of Ĭs'săchar: Tōlā, Pūăh, Jāshŭb, and Shĭmrŏn, four. 2 The sons of Tōlā: Ŭzzī, Rĕphāi'ăh, Jĕ'rĭ-ĕl, Jah'mäï, Ĭbsăm, and Shĕm'ūĕl, heads of their fathers' houses, namely of Tola, mighty warriors of their generations, their number in the days of David being twenty-two thousand six hundred. 3 The sons of Ŭzzī: Ĭzrăhī'ăh. And the sons of Izrahiah: Michael, Ōbădī'ăh, Jōĕl, and Ĭsshī'ăh, five, all of them chief men; 4 and along with them, by their generations, according to their fathers' houses, were units of the army for war, thirty-six thousand, for they had many wives and sons. 5 Their kinsmen belonging to all the families of Ĭs'săchar were in all eighty-seven thousand mighty warriors, enrolled by genealogy.

7.5
1 Chr 6.62,
72

K. The family of Benjamin

*7.6
Gen 46.21;
Num 26.38;
1 Chr 8.1–
40

6 The sons of Benjamin: Bēlă, Bēchĕr, and Jĕdiā'-ĕl, three. 7 The sons of Bēlă: Ĕzbŏn, Ŭzzī, Ŭzzī'ĕl, Jĕr'ĭmŏth, and Irī, five, heads of fathers' houses, mighty warriors; and their enrollment by genealogies was twenty-two thousand and thirty-four. 8 The sons of Bēchĕr: Zĕmī'răh, Jō'ăsh, Ĕlīĕ'zĕr, Ĕl'ĭ-ō-ē'naī, Ōmrī, Jĕr'ĕmŏth, Ăbī'jăh, Ăn'ăthŏth, and Ăl'ĕmĕth. All these were the sons of Bēchĕr; 9 and their enrollment by genealogies, according to their generations, as heads of their fathers' houses, mighty warriors, was twenty thousand two hundred. 10 The sons of Jĕdiā'-ĕl: Bĭlhăn. And the sons of Bilhan: Jĕ'ŭsh, Benjamin, Ēhŭd, Chĕnă'ănăh, Zēthăn, Tarshĭsh, and Ăhĭsh'ăhar. 11All these were the sons of Jĕdiā'-ĕl according to the heads of their fathers' houses, mighty warriors, seventeen thousand and two hundred, ready for service in war. 12And Shŭppĭm and Hŭppĭm were the sons of Ĭr, Hūshĭm the sons of Āhĕr.

*7.12
Num 26.39

L. The family of Naphtali

7.13
Gen 46.24

13 The sons of Năph'tălī: Jah'zĭ-ĕl, Gunī, Jēzĕr, and Shăllŭm, the offspring of Bĭlhăh.

14 The sons of Mănăs'sĕh: Ăs'rĭ-ĕl, whom his Ărămēăn concubine bore; she bore Māchĭr the father of Gĭl'ëăd. 15And Māchĭr took a wife for Hŭppĭm and for Shŭppĭm. The name of his sister was Mā'ăcăh. And the name of the second was Zēlō'phĕhăd; and Zelophehad had daughters. 16And Mā'ăcăh the wife of Māchĭr bore a son, and she called his name Pĕrĕsh; and the name of his

r Syr Compare Vg: Heb *and to the sons*

7.6 *sons of Benjamin.* It is most likely that Benjamin was a very early scribal mistake for Zebulun. In Hebrew the similarity of names is much closer. Further evidence for this conclusion is that the genealogy for Zebulun is missing, whereas the legitimate genealogy of Benjamin occurs in 8.1–40.

7.12 *the sons of Ir, Hushim the sons of Aher.* Inasmuch as the genealogy of Dan is completely missing, some scholars think the Hebrew text originally read "the sons of Dan, Hushim his one son." This is in accord with Gen 46.23 (*The sons of Dan: Hushim*). Both Chronicles have a number of textual problems.

brother was Shĕrĕsh; and his sons were Ūlȧm and Rākĕm. 17 The
sons of Ūlȧm: Bēdän. These were the sons of Gĭl'ĕȧd the son of
Mȧchĭr, son of Mȧnȧs'sĕh. 18And his sister Hȧmmȯlĕch'ĕth bore
Ĭshhȯd, Ăbĭ-ē'zĕr, and Mȧhlȧh. 19 The sons of Shĕmĭ'dȧ were
Ȧhĭ'ȧn, Shĕchĕm, Lĭkhĭ, and Anĭ'ȧm.

7.17
1 Sam 12.11

M. The family of Ephraim

20 The sons of Ē'phräĭm: Shŭthē'lȧh, and Bĕrĕd his son,
Tāhȧth his son, Ĕlë-ā'dȧh his son, Tahath his son, 21 Zābȧd his
son, Shŭthē'lȧh his son, and Ēzĕr and Ĕl'ĕ-ȧd, whom the men of
Gȧth who were born in the land slew, because they came down to
raid their cattle. 22And Ē'phräĭm their father mourned many days,
and his brothers came to comfort him. 23And Ē'phräĭm went in to
his wife, and she conceived and bore a son; and he called his name
Bĕrĭ'ȧh, because evil had befallen his house. 24 His daughter was
Sheĕrȧh, who built both Lower and Upper Bĕth-hor'ȯn, and
Ŭz'zĕn-sheĕ'rȧh. 25 Rēphȧh was his son, Rĕshĕph his son, Tēlȧh
his son, Tāhȧn his son, 26 Lādȧn his son, Ȧmmĭ'hŭd his son,
Ĕlĭ'shȧmȧ his son, 27 Nŭn his son, Joshua his son. 28 Their pos-
sessions and settlements were Bĕthĕl and its towns, and eastward
Nā'ȧrȧn, and westward Gēzĕr and its towns, Shĕchĕm and its
towns, and Ayyȧh and its towns; 29 also along the borders of the
Mȧnȧs'sītes, Bĕth-shē'ȧn and its towns, Tā'ȧnȧch and its towns,
Mĕgĭd'dō and its towns, Dor and its towns. In these dwelt the
sons of Joseph the son of Israel.

7.20
Num 26.35

7.24
Josh 16.3,5

7.27
Ex 17.9–14;
24.13
7.28
Josh 16.7

N. The family of Asher

30 The sons of Ăshĕr: Ĭmnȧh, Ĭshvȧh, Ĭshvĭ, Bĕrĭ'ȧh, and their
sister Sĕrȧh. 31 The sons of Bĕrĭ'ȧh: Hēbĕr and Mȧl'chĭĕl, who
was the father of Bĭrzā'ĭth. 32 Hēbĕr was the father of Jȧphlĕt,
Shōmĕr, Hōthȧm, and their sister Shua. 33 The sons of Japhlet:
Pāsȧch, Bĭmhȧl, and Ăshvȧth. These are the sons of Japhlet.
34 The sons of Shĕmĕr his brother: Rōhgȧh, Jĕhŭb'bȧh, and Ȧrȧm.
35 The sons of Hēlĕm his brother: Zōphȧh, Ĭmnȧ, Shĕlĕsh, and
Āmȧl. 36 The sons of Zōphȧh: Suȧh, Har'nĕphĕr, Shuȧl, Bĕrĭ,
Ĭmrȧh, 37 Bēzĕr, Hȯd, Shȧmmȧ, Shĭlshȧh, Ĭthrȧn, and Bë-ē'rȧ.
38 The sons of Jēthĕr: Jĕphŭn'nĕh, Pĭspȧ, and Ārȧ. 39 The sons of
Ŭllȧ: Ārȧh, Hȧn'nĭĕl, and Rĭzĭ'ȧ. 40All of these were men of Ăshĕr,
heads of fathers' houses, approved, mighty warriors, chief of the
princes. Their number enrolled by genealogies, for service in war,
was twenty-six thousand men.

7.30
Gen 46.17;
Num 26.44

7.40
ver 30

O. The family of Benjamin

8 Benjamin was the father of Bēlȧ his first-born, Ăshbĕl the
second, Ȧhar'ȧh the third, 2 Nōhȧh the fourth, and Rāphȧ the
fifth. 3And Bēlȧ had sons: Ȧddar, Gērȧ, Ȧbĭ'hŭd, 4Ȧbĭsh'uȧ, Nā'-
ȧmȧn, Ȧhō'ȧh, 5 Gērȧ, Shĕphu'phȧn, and Hūrȧm. 6 These are the
sons of Ēhŭd (they were heads of fathers' houses of the inhabitants
of Gēbȧ, and they were carried into exile to Mȧna'hȧth): 7 Nā'-
ȧmȧn,s Ȧhĭ'jȧh, and Gērȧ, that is, Hĕglȧm,t who was the father of
Ŭzzȧ and Ȧhĭ'hŭd. 8And Shāhȧrā'ĭm had sons in the country of

8.1
Gen 46.21;
1 Chr 7.6

8.6
1 Chr 2.52

s Heb and Naaman   t Or he carried them into exile

Mōáb after he had sent away Hūshǐm and Bā'árá his wives. 9 He had sons by Hōdĕsh his wife: Jōbáb, Zǐb'ǐ-á, Mēshá, Mǎlcám, 10 Jē'ŭz, Sáchī'á, and Mǐrmáh. These were his sons, heads of fathers' houses. 11 He also had sons by Hūshǐm: Abī'tŭb and Ēlpā'ál. 12 The sons of Ēlpā'ál: Ē'bĕr, Mīshám, and Shĕmĕd, who built Ōnō and Lŏd with its towns, 13 and Bĕrī'áh and Shēmá (they were heads of fathers' houses of the inhabitants of Āi'jálón, who put to flight the inhabitants of Gáth); 14 and Ahī'ō, Shāshǎk, and Jĕr'émôth. 15 Zĕbádī'áh, Arád, Ēdĕr, 16 Michael, Ishpáh, and Jōhá were sons of Bĕrī'áh. 17 Zĕbádī'áh, Mĕshŭl'lám, Hǐzkǐ, Hēbĕr, 18 Ish'mĕraī, Izlī'áh, and Jōbáb were the sons of Ēlpā'ál. 19 Jākǐm, Zǐchrī, Zábdī, 20 Ēlǐ-ē'naī, Zǐl'lĕthaī, Ēlī'ĕl, 21 Adāi'áh, Bĕrāi'áh, and Shǐmráth were the sons of Shǐm'ē-ī. 22 Ishpăn, Ē'bĕr, Ēlī'ĕl, 23 Abdón, Zǐchrī, Hānán, 24 Hánánī'áh, Ēlám, Ănthôthī'jáh, 25 Iphdeī'áh, and Pénū'ĕl were the sons of Shāshǎk. 26 Shám'-shĕraī, Shēhárī'áh, Āthálī'áh, 27 Jā'-árĕshī'áh, Ēlī'jáh, and Zǐchrī were the sons of Jĕrō'hám. 28 These were the heads of fathers' houses, according to their generations, chief men. These dwelt in Jerusalem.

29 Je-ī'ĕl[u] the father of Gǐb'ëón dwelt in Gibeon, and the name of his wife was Mā'ácáh. 30 His first-born son: Abdón, then Zúr, Kǐsh, Bāál, Nādăb, 31 Gēdor, Ahī'ō, Zĕchĕr, 32 and Mǐklôth (he was the father of Shǐm'ē-áh). Now these also dwelt opposite their kinsmen in Jerusalem, with their kinsmen. 33 Nĕr was the father of Kǐsh, Kish of Saul, Saul of Jonathan, Mǎlchīsh'uá, Abǐn'ádáb, and Ēshbā'ál; 34 and the son of Jonathan was Mĕrǐb-bā'ál; and Merib-baal was the father of Mīcáh. 35 The sons of Mīcáh: Pīthón, Mĕlĕch, Tā'rëá, and Āhăz. 36 Āhăz was the father of Jĕhō'áddáh; and Jehoaddah was the father of Al'ĕmĕth, Azmā'-vĕth, and Zǐmrī; Zimri was the father of Mōzá. 37 Mōzá was the father of Bǐn'ë-á; Rápháh was his son, Ēlë-ā'sáh his son, Āzĕl his son. 38 Āzĕl had six sons, and these are their names: Azrī'kám, Bō'chĕru, Ish'mäĕl, Shē-árī'áh, Ōbádī'áh, and Hānán. All these were the sons of Azel. 39 The sons of Ēshĕk his brother: Ūlám his first-born, Jē'ush the second, and Ēlǐph'ĕlĕt the third. 40 The sons of Ūlám were men who were mighty warriors, bowmen, having many sons and grandsons, one hundred and fifty. All these were Benjaminites.

P. The families in Jerusalem

9 So all Israel was enrolled by genealogies; and these are written in the Book of the Kings of Israel. And Judah was taken into exile in Babylon because of their unfaithfulness. 2 Now the first to dwell again in their possessions in their cities were Israel, the priests, the Lēvītes, and the temple servants. 3 And some of the people of Judah, Benjamin, Ē'phráǐm, and Mánăs'sëh dwelt in Jerusalem: 4 Ūthaī the son of Ammī'hŭd, son of Ōmrī, son of Imrī, son of Bānī, from the sons of Pĕrĕz the son of Judah. 5 And of the Shī'lónītes: Așāi'áh the first-born, and his sons. 6 Of the sons of Zĕráh: Jeu'ĕl and their kinsmen, six hundred and ninety. 7 Of the

8.13
ver 21

8.21
ver 13

8.29
1 Chr 9.35

*8.33
1 Chr 9.35–38
*8.34
2 Sam 9.12

9.1
1 Chr 5.25, 26
9.2
Neh 11.3–22;
Ezra 2.43;
8.20
9.3
Neh 11.1

u Compare 9.35: Heb lacks Jeiel

8.33 Eshbaal, see note to 2 Sam 2.8.   8.34 Meribbaal, see note to 2 Sam 4.4.

Benjaminites: Săllu the son of Měshŭl′lăm, son of Hōdăvī′ăh, son of Hăssēnu′ăh, 8 Ĭbneī′ăh the son of Jěrō′hăm, Ēláh the son of Ŭzzī, son of Mĭçhrī, and Měshŭl′lăm the son of Shěphătī′ăh, son of Reu′él, son of Ĭbnī′jăh; 9 and their kinsmen according to their generations, nine hundred and fifty-six. All these were heads of fathers' houses according to their fathers' houses.

10 Of the priests: Jědăi′ăh, Jěhoi′ărĭb, Jăçhĭn, 11 and Ăzărī′ăh the son of Hĭlkī′ăh, son of Měshŭl′lăm, son of Zādŏk, son of Mērāi′óth, son of Ăhī′tŭb, the chief officer of the house of God; 12 and Ădăi′ăh the son of Jěrō′hăm, son of Păshhŭr, son of Mălçhī′jăh, and Mā′ásaī the son of Ă′dĭ-él, son of Jah′zěrăh, son of Měshŭl′lăm, son of Měshĭl′lěmĭth, son of Ĭmmĕr; 13 besides their kinsmen, heads of their fathers' houses, one thousand seven hundred and sixty, very able men for the work of the service of the house of God.

14 Of the Lēvītes: Shěmāi′ăh the son of Hăsshŭb, son of Ăzrī′kăm, son of Hăshăbī′ăh, of the sons of Měrar′ĭ; 15 and Băkbăk′kăr, Hērĕsh, Gălăl, and Măttănī′ăh the son of Mīcà, son of Zĭçhrī, son of Āsăph; 16 and Ōbădī′ăh the son of Shěmāi′ăh, son of Gălăl, son of Jědu′thŭn, and Běrěçhī′ăh the son of Āsà, son of Ĕlkā′năh, who dwelt in the villages of the Nětōph′ăthītes.

17 The gatekeepers were: Shăllŭm, Ăkkŭb, Tălmŏn, Ăhī′măn, and their kinsmen (Shallum being the chief), 18 stationed hitherto in the king's gate on the east side. These were the gatekeepers of the camp of the Lēvītes. 19 Shăllŭm the son of Kō′rĕ, son of Ĕbī′ásăph, son of Kōrăh, and his kinsmen of his fathers' house, the Kō′răhītes, were in charge of the work of the service, keepers of the thresholds of the tent, as their fathers had been in charge of the camp of the LORD, keepers of the entrance. 20 And Phĭn′ĕhăs the son of Ĕleă′zăr was the ruler over them in time past; the LORD was with him. 21 Zěçhărī′ăh the son of Měshělěmī′ăh was gatekeeper at the entrance of the tent of meeting. 22 All these, who were chosen as gatekeepers at the thresholds, were two hundred and twelve. They were enrolled by genealogies in their villages. David and Samuel the seer established them in their office of trust. 23 So they and their sons were in charge of the gates of the house of the LORD, that is, the house of the tent, as guards. 24 The gatekeepers were on the four sides, east, west, north, and south; 25 and their kinsmen who were in their villages were obliged to come in every seven days, from time to time, to be with these; 26 for the four chief gatekeepers, who were Lēvītes, were in charge of the chambers and the treasures of the house of God. 27 And they lodged round about the house of God; for upon them lay the duty of watching, and they had charge of opening it every morning.

28 Some of them had charge of the utensils of service, for they were required to count them when they were brought in and taken out. 29 Others of them were appointed over the furniture, and over all the holy utensils, also over the fine flour, the wine, the oil, the incense, and the spices. 30 Others, of the sons of the priests, prepared the mixing of the spices, 31 and Măttĭthī′ăh, one of the Lēvītes, the first-born of Shăllŭm the Kō′răhīte, was in charge of making the flat cakes. 32 Also some of their kinsmen of the Kō′hăthītes had charge of the showbread, to prepare it every sabbath.

33 Now these are the singers, the heads of fathers' houses of the Lēvītes, dwelling in the chambers of the temple free from other

9.10
Neh 11.10–14

9.14
Neh 11.15–19

9.18
Ezek 46.1,2

9.20
Num 25.7–13
9.21
1 Chr 26.2,14
9.22
1 Chr 26.1,2;
2 Chr 31.15,18

9.25
ver 16;
2 Ki 11.5,7;
2 Chr 23.8

9.27
1 Chr 23.30–32

9.29
1 Chr 23.29
9.30
Ex 30.23–25
9.32
Lev 24.8
9.33
1 Chr 6.31;
25.1;
Ps 134.1

service, for they were on duty day and night. 34 These were heads
of fathers' houses of the Lēvītes, according to their generations,
leaders, who lived in Jerusalem.

Q. *The family of Saul*

9.35
1 Chr 8.29

35 In Gĭb'ëŏn dwelt the father of Gibeon, Je-ī'ĕl, and the name
of his wife was Mā'acăh, 36 and his first-born son Ābdŏn, then
Zŭr, Kĭsh, Bāál, Nĕr, Nādăb, 37 Gēdor, Ăhī'ō, Zĕchārī'ăh, and
Mĭklŏth; 38 and Mĭklŏth was the father of Shĭm'ë-ăm; and these
also dwelt opposite their kinsmen in Jerusalem, with their kinsmen.

*9.39
1 Chr 8.33

39 Nĕr was the father of Kĭsh, Kish of Saul, Saul of Jonathan,
Mălchĭsh'uă, Ăbĭn'adăb, and Ĕshbā'ál; 40 and the son of Jonathan
was Mĕrĭb-bā'ál; and Merib-baal was the father of Mīcăh. 41 The

9.41
1 Chr 8.35

sons of Mīcăh: Pīthŏn, Mĕlĕch, Tah'rë-ă, and Āhăz;[v] 42 and Āhăz
was the father of Jā'răh, and Jarah of Ăl'ëmĕth, Ăzmā'vĕth, and
Zĭmrī; and Zimri was the father of Mōzá. 43 Mōzà was the father of
Bĭn'ë-á; and Rĕphāi'ăh was his son, Ĕlĕ-ā'săh his son, Āzĕl his son.
44 Āzĕl had six sons and these are their names: Āzrī'kăm, Bō'chĕru,
Ĭsh'mäel, Shē-ărī'ăh, Ōbádī'ăh, and Hānăn; these were the sons
of Azel.

II. *The reign of King David 10.1–29.30*

A. *Saul's closing days and death*

10.1
1 Sam
31.1,2

10 Now the Phĭlĭs'tĭnĕş fought against Israel; and the men of
Israel fled before the Philistines, and fell slain on Mount
Gĭlbō'á. 2 And the Phĭlĭs'tĭnĕş overtook Saul and his sons; and the
Philistines slew Jonathan and Ăbĭn'adăb and Mălchĭsh'uă, the
sons of Saul. 3 The battle pressed hard upon Saul, and the archers

10.4
cf. 1 Sam
31.4–7

found him; and he was wounded by the archers. 4 Then Saul said
to his armor-bearer, "Draw your sword, and thrust me through
with it, lest these uncircumcised come and make sport of me."
But his armor-bearer would not; for he feared greatly. Therefore
Saul took his own sword, and fell upon it. 5 And when his armor-
bearer saw that Saul was dead, he also fell upon his sword, and
died. 6 Thus Saul died; he and his three sons and all his house died
together. 7 And when all the men of Israel who were in the valley
saw that the army[w] had fled and that Saul and his sons were dead,
they forsook their cities and fled; and the Phĭlĭs'tĭnĕş came and
dwelt in them.

8 On the morrow, when the Phĭlĭs'tĭnĕş came to strip the slain,
they found Saul and his sons fallen on Mount Gĭlbō'á. 9 And they
stripped him and took his head and his armor, and sent messengers
throughout the land of the Phĭlĭs'tĭnĕş, to carry the good news to
their idols and to the people. 10 And they put his armor in the

*10.10
1 Sam 31.10

temple of their gods, and fastened his head in the temple of Dāgŏn.
11 But when all Jābĕsh-gĭl'ëăd heard all that the Phĭlĭs'tĭnĕş had

---

v Compare 8.35: Heb lacks *and Ahaz*   *w* Heb *they*

9.39 Ner's relationship to Saul is not
always made clear.
10.10 In 1 Sam 31.10, Saul's body was fastened to the wall of Bethshan while his armor

was placed in the temple of Ashtaroth. Here
Saul's head was put in the temple of Dagon. All
this is quite possible. Excavations at Bethshan
have revealed four Canaanite temples.

done to Saul, 12 all the valiant men arose, and took away the body
of Saul and the bodies of his sons, and brought them to Jābĕsh.
And they buried their bones under the oak in Jabesh, and fasted
seven days.

13 So Saul died for his unfaithfulness; he was unfaithful to the
LORD in that he did not keep the command of the LORD, and also
consulted a medium, seeking guidance, 14 and did not seek guidance from the LORD. Therefore the LORD slew him, and turned the
kingdom over to David the son of Jĕssë.

10.13
1 Sam
13.13;
15.23; 28.7

10.14
1 Sam
15.28;
1 Chr 12.23

B. David made king of all Israel

1. The capture of Jerusalem

11 Then all Israel gathered together to David at Hēbrŏn, and
said, "Behold, we are your bone and flesh. 2 In times past,
even when Saul was king, it was you that led out and brought in
Israel; and the LORD your God said to you, 'You shall be shepherd
of my people Israel, and you shall be prince over my people
Israel.'" 3 So all the elders of Israel came to the king at Hēbrŏn;
and David made a covenant with them at Hebron before the LORD,
and they anointed David king over Israel, according to the word of
the LORD by Samuel.

11.1
2 Sam 5.1

11.2
2 Sam 5.2;
Ps 78.71

11.3
2 Sam 5.3;
1 Sam 16.1,
12,13

4 And David and all Israel went to Jerusalem, that is Jēbŭs,
where the Jĕb'ūsītes were, the inhabitants of the land. 5 The inhabitants of Jēbŭs said to David, "You will not come in here."
Nevertheless David took the stronghold of Zion, that is, the city
of David. 6 David said, "Whoever shall smite the Jĕb'ūsītes first
shall be chief and commander." And Jŏăb the son of Zĕru'jăh
went up first, so he became chief. 7And David dwelt in the stronghold; therefore it was called the city of David. 8And he built the
city round about from the Mĭllŏ in complete circuit; and Jŏăb repaired the rest of the city. 9And David became greater and greater,
for the LORD of hosts was with him.

11.4
Judg 1.21;
19.10

11.6
2 Sam 8.16

11.9
2 Sam 3.1

2. David's mighty heroes

10 Now these are the chiefs of David's mighty men, who gave
him strong support in his kingdom, together with all Israel, to
make him king, according to the word of the LORD concerning
Israel. 11 This is an account of David's mighty men: Jáshō'bë-ăm,
a Hăch'mŏnīte, was chief of the three;ˣ he wielded his spear
against three hundred whom he slew at one time.

11.10
2 Sam
23.8–39;
ver 3

11.11
2 Sam 23.8

12 And next to him among the three mighty men was Ĕlëä'zăr
the son of Dōdō, the Ăhō'hīte. 13 He was with David at Păs-dăm'-
mĭm when the Phĭlĭs'tĭnes were gathered there for battle. There
was a plot of ground full of barley, and the men fled from the
Philistines. 14 But heʸ took hisʸ stand in the midst of the plot, and
defended it, and slew the Phĭlĭs'tĭnes; and the LORD saved them
by a great victory.

11.13
2 Sam
23.11,12

15 Three of the thirty chief men went down to the rock to David
at the cave of Ădŭl'lăm, when the army of Phĭlĭs'tĭnes was encamped in the valley of Rĕph'ăim. 16 David was then in the stronghold; and the garrison of the Phĭlĭs'tĭnes was then at Bĕth'lĕhĕm.
17And David said longingly, "O that some one would give me
water to drink from the well of Bĕth'lĕhĕm which is by the gate!"

11.15
2 Sam
23.13;
1 Chr 14.9

ˣ Compare 2 Sam 23.8: Heb *thirty* or *captains*   ʸ Compare 2 Sam 23.12: Heb *they . . . their*

18 Then the three mighty men broke through the camp of the Philis'tines, and drew water out of the well of Bĕth'lĕhĕm which was by the gate, and took and brought it to David. But David would not drink of it; he poured it out to the LORD, 19 and said, "Far be it from me before my God that I should do this. Shall I drink the lifeblood of these men? For at the risk of their lives they brought it." Therefore he would not drink it. These things did the three mighty men.

20 Now Ăbĭsh'āī, the brother of Jōăb, was chief of the thirty.ᶻ And he wielded his spear against three hundred men and slew them, and won a name beside the three. 21 He was the most renowned*a* of the thirty,ᶻ and became their commander; but he did not attain to the three.

22 And Bĕnāi'ăh the son of Jĕhoi'ădă was a valiant man*b* of Kăbzeĕl, a doer of great deeds; he smote two ariels*c* of Mōăb. He also went down and slew a lion in a pit on a day when snow had fallen. 23 And he slew an Egyptian, a man of great stature, five cubits tall. The Egyptian had in his hand a spear like a weaver's beam; but Bĕnāi'ăh went down to him with a staff, and snatched the spear out of the Egyptian's hand, and slew him with his own spear. 24 These things did Bĕnāi'ăh the son of Jĕhoi'ădă, and won a name beside the three mighty men. 25 He was renowned among the thirty, but he did not attain to the three. And David set him over his bodyguard.

26 The mighty men of the armies were Ăs'ăhĕl the brother of Jōăb, Ĕlhā'năn the son of Dōdō of Bĕth'lĕhĕm, 27 Shămmŏth of Hărŏd,*d* Hĕlĕz the Pĕl'ŏnīte, 28 Ira the son of Ĭkkĕsh of Tĕkō'ă, Ăbĭ-ē'zĕr of Ăn'ăthŏth, 29 Sĭb'bĕcaī the Hū'shăthīte, Īlaī the Ăhō'hīte, 30 Mā'hăraī of Nĕto'phăh, Hĕlĕd the son of Bā'ănăh of Netophah, 31 Ĭthaī the son of Rĭb'āī of Gĭb'ĕ-ăh of the Benjaminites, Bĕnāi'ăh of Pĭr'ăthŏn, 32 Hūraī of the brooks of Gāăsh, Ā'bĭĕl the Ar'băthīte, 33 Azmā'vĕth of Băhā'rùm, Ĕli'ăhbă of Shă-ăl'bŏn, 34 Hāshĕm*e* the Gī'zŏnīte, Jonathan the son of Shāgeĕ the Hā'rărīte, 35 Ăhī'ăm the son of Sāchar the Hā'rărīte, Ĕli'phăl the son of Ūr, 36 Hĕphĕr the Mĕchē'răthīte, Ăhī'jăh the Pĕl'ŏnīte, 37 Hĕzrō of Carmel, Nā'ăraī the son of Ĕzbaī, 38 Jōĕl the brother of Nathan, Mĭbhar the son of Hăgrī, 39 Zĕlĕk the Ăm'mŏnīte, Nā'hăraī of Be-ĕr'ŏth, the armor-bearer of Jōăb the son of Zĕru'jăh, 40 Ira the Ĭthrīte, Gărĕb the Ithrite, 41 Ūrī'ăh the Hĭttīte, Zābăd the son of Ahlaī, 42 Ăd'īnă the son of Shīză the Reu'bĕnīte, a leader of the Reu'bĕnītes, and thirty with him, 43 Hānăn the son of Mā'ăcăh, and Jōsh'ăphăt the Mĭthnīte, 44 Ŭzzi'ă the Ăsh'tĕrăthīte, Shāmă and Je-ī'ĕl the sons of Hōthăm the Ărō'ĕrīte, 45 Jĕdiă'-ĕl the son of Shĭmrī, and Jōhă his brother, the Tīzīte, 46 Ĕli'ĕl the Mā'hăvīte, and Jĕr'ībaī, and Jōshăvī'ăh, the sons of Ĕlnā'-ăm, and Ĭthmăh the Mō'ăbīte, 47 Ĕli'ĕl, and Ōbĕd, and Jă-ă'sĭĕl the Mĕzō'bä-īte.

3. The names and numbers of David's supporters

12 Now these are the men who came to David at Zĭklăg, while he could not move about freely because of Saul the son of

---

11.20
2 Sam 23.18

11.21
2 Sam 23.19

11.22
2 Sam 23.20

11.23
1 Sam 17.7

11.26
2 Sam 23.24

11.39
1 Chr 18.15

12.1
1 Sam
27.2–6

---

z Syr: Heb *three*
a Compare 2 Sam 23.19: Heb *more renowned among the two*
b Syr: Heb *the son of a valiant man*   c The meaning of the word *ariel* is unknown
d Compare 2 Sam 23.25: Heb *the Hā'rŏrīte*
e Compare Gk and 2 Sam 23.32: Heb *the sons of Hashem*

Kĭsh; and they were among the mighty men who helped him in war. ² They were bowmen, and could shoot arrows and sling stones with either the right or the left hand; they were Benjaminites, Saul's kinsmen. ³ The chief was Āhī-ē′zėr, then Jō′ăsh, both sons of Shėmā′áh of Gĭb′ë-áh; also Jĕz′ĭ-ėl and Pĕlĕt the sons of Ăz′mā′vėth; Bėrā′cáh, Jēhū of Ăn′áthŏth, ⁴ Ĭshmāi′áh of Gĭb′-ëŏn, a mighty man among the thirty and a leader over the thirty; Jĕrĕmī′áh,ᶠ Jáhā′zĭėl, Jōhăn′án, Jŏz′ábăd of Gėdē′ráh, ⁵ Ēlu′zaī,ᵍ Jĕr′ímŏth, Bėālī′áh, Shĕmārī′áh, Shĕphátī′áh the Háru′phīte; ⁶ Ēlkā′náh, Ĭsshī′áh, Ăz′árėl, Jō-ē′zėr, and Jáshō′bë-ám, the Kō′ráhītes; ⁷ and Jō′-ėláh and Zĕbádī′áh, the sons of Jėrō′hám of Gėdor.

8 From the Gădītes there went over to David at the stronghold in the wilderness mighty and experienced warriors, expert with shield and spear, whose faces were like the faces of lions, and who were swift as gazelles upon the mountains: ⁹ Ēzėr the chief, Ōbádī′áh second, Ēlī′áb third, ¹⁰ Mĭshmăn′náh fourth, Jĕrĕmī′áh fifth, ¹¹Attaī sixth, Ēlī′ėl seventh, ¹² Jōhăn′án eighth, Ēlzā′bád ninth, ¹³ Jĕrĕmī′áh tenth, Măch′bánnaī eleventh. ¹⁴ These Gădītes were officers of the army, the lesser over a hundred and the greater over a thousand. ¹⁵ These are the men who crossed the Jordan in the first month, when it was overflowing all its banks, and put to flight all those in the valleys, to the east and to the west.

16 And some of the men of Benjamin and Judah came to the stronghold to David. ¹⁷ David went out to meet them and said to them, "If you have come to me in friendship to help me, my heart will be knit to you; but if to betray me to my adversaries, although there is no wrong in my hands, then may the God of our fathers see and rebuke you." ¹⁸ Then the Spirit came upon Amā′säī, chief of the thirty, and he said,

"We are yours, O David;
    and with you, O son of Jĕssë!
Peace, peace to you,
    and peace to your helpers!
For your God helps you."

Then David received them, and made them officers of his troops.
19 Some of the men of Mánăs′sėh deserted to David when he came with the Phĭlĭs′tĭneş for the battle against Saul. (Yet he did not help them, for the rulers of the Philistines took counsel and sent him away, saying, "At peril to our heads he will desert to his master Saul.") ²⁰As he went to Zĭklăg these men of Mánăs′sėh deserted to him: Ădnáh, Jŏz′ábăd, Jĕdĭā′-ėl, Michael, Jozabad, Ēlī′hū, and Zĭl′lėthaī, chiefs of thousands in Manasseh. ²¹ They helped David against the band of raiders;ʰ for they were all mighty men of valor, and were commanders in the army. ²² For from day to day men kept coming to David to help him, until there was a great army, like an army of God.

23 These are the numbers of the divisions of the armed troops, who came to David in Hēbrŏn, to turn the kingdom of Saul over to him, according to the word of the LORD. ²⁴ The men of Judah bearing shield and spear were six thousand eight hundred armed troops. ²⁵ Of the Sĭm′ëŏnītes, mighty men of valor for war, seven

12.2
Judg 20.16

12.8
2 Sam 2.18

12.15
Josh 3.15

12.18
Judg 6.34;
2 Sam 17.25

12.19
1 Sam
29.2,4

12.21
1 Sam 30.1,
9,10

12.23
2 Sam
2.3,4;
1 Chr 11.1;
10.14;
1 Sam
16.1,3

ᶠ Heb verse 5 ᵍ Heb verse 6 ʰ Or *as officers of his troops*

thousand one hundred. 26 Of the Lēvītes four thousand six hundred. 27 The prince Jēhoi'àdà, of the house of Aaron, and with him three thousand seven hundred. 28 Zādŏk, a young man mighty in valor, and twenty-two commanders from his own father's house. 29 Of the Benjaminites, the kinsman of Saul, three thousand, of whom the majority had hitherto kept their allegiance to the house of Saul. 30 Of the Ē'phraïmītes twenty thousand eight hundred, mighty men of valor, famous men in their fathers' houses. 31 Of the half-tribe of Mảnås'sẹh eighteen thousand, who were expressly named to come and make David king. 32 Of Is'sảchar men who had understanding of the times, to know what Israel ought to do, two hundred chiefs, and all their kinsmen under their command. 33 Of Zẹb'ụlùn fifty thousand seasoned troops, equipped for battle with all the weapons of war, to help David[i] with singleness of purpose. 34 Of Năph'tảlī a thousand commanders with whom were thirty-seven thousand men armed with shield and spear. 35 Of the Dănītes twenty-eight thousand six hundred men equipped for battle. 36 Of Ashér forty thousand seasoned troops ready for battle. 37 Of the Reu'bênītes and Gădītes and the half-tribe of Mảnås'sẹh from beyond the Jordan, one hundred and twenty thousand men armed with all the weapons of war.

38 All these, men of war, arrayed in battle order, came to Hēbrŏn with full intent to make David king over all Israel; likewise all the rest of Israel were of a single mind to make David king. 39And they were there with David for three days, eating and drinking, for their brethren had made preparation for them. 40And also their neighbors, from as far as Is'sảchar and Zẹb'ụlùn and Năph'tảlī, came bringing food on asses and on camels and on mules and on oxen, abundant provisions of meal, cakes of figs, clusters of raisins, and wine and oil, oxen and sheep, for there was joy in Israel.

C. David and the ark of the covenant

1. The removal of the ark from Kiriath-jearim to Obed-edom

13 David consulted with the commanders of thousands and of hundreds, with every leader. 2And David said to all the assembly of Israel, "If it seems good to you, and if it is the will of the LORD our God, let us send abroad to our brethren who remain in all the land of Israel, and with them to the priests and Lēvītes in the cities that have pasture lands, that they may come together to us. 3 Then let us bring again the ark of our God to us; for we neglected it in the days of Saul." 4All the assembly agreed to do so, for the thing was right in the eyes of all the people.

5 So David assembled all Israel from the Shīhor of Egypt to the entrance of Hāmâth, to bring the ark of God from Kïr'ĭăth-jē'ảrĭm. 6And David and all Israel went up to Bā'ảlàh, that is, to Kïr'ĭăth-jē'ảrĭm which belongs to Judah, to bring up from there the ark of God, which is called by the name of the LORD who sits enthroned above the cherubim. 7And they carried the ark of God upon a new cart, from the house of Abĭn'ảdăb, and Úzzảh and Ahī'ō[j] were driving the cart. 8And David and all Israel were making merry before God with all their might, with song and lyres and harps and tambourines and cymbals and trumpets.

12.28
2 Sam 8.17

12.29
2 Sam 2.8,9

12.32
Est 1.13

12.33
Ps 12.2

12.38
2 Sam 5.1–3

12.40
1 Sam 25.18

13.2
1 Sam 31.1;
Isa 37.4

13.3
1 Sam 7.1,2

13.5
2 Sam 6.1;
1 Chr 15.3;
1 Sam 6.21;
7.1
13.6
Josh 15.9;
2 Ki 19.15
13.7
1 Sam 7.1
13.8
2 Sam 6.5

i Gk: Heb lacks David   j Or and his brother

9 And when they came to the threshing floor of Chidon, Uzzah put out his hand to hold the ark, for the oxen stumbled. 10And the anger of the LORD was kindled against Uzzah; and he smote him because he put forth his hand to the ark; and he died there before God. 11And David was angry because the LORD had broken forth upon Uzzah; and that place is called Pē'rĕz-ŭz'zȧ[k] to this day. 12And David was afraid of God that day; and he said, "How can I bring the ark of God home to me?" 13 So David did not take the ark home into the city of David, but took it aside to the house of Ō'bĕd-ē'dŏm the Gittite. 14And the ark of God remained with the household of Ō'bĕd-ē'dŏm in his house three months; and the LORD blessed the household of Obed-edom and all that he had.

2. The prosperity of David
a. His palace and family

14 And Hiram king of Tȳre sent messengers to David, and cedar trees, also masons and carpenters to build a house for him. 2And David perceived that the LORD had established him king over Israel, and that his kingdom was highly exalted for the sake of his people Israel.

3 And David took more wives in Jerusalem, and David begot more sons and daughters. 4 These are the names of the children whom he had in Jerusalem: Shăm'mūȧ, Shōbăb, Nathan, Solomon, 5 Ībhar, Ĕlĭsh'u-ȧ, Ĕlpē'lĕt, 6 Nōgȧh, Nĕphĕg, Jȧphī'ȧ, 7 Ĕlī'-shȧmȧ, Bēĕlī'ȧdȧ, and Ĕlĭph'ĕlĕt.

b. His defeats of the Philistines

8 When the Philĭs'tĭneş heard that David had been anointed king over all Israel, all the Philistines went up in search of David; and David heard of it and went out against them. 9 Now the Philĭs'tĭneş had come and made a raid in the valley of Rĕph'ȧïm. 10And David inquired of God, "Shall I go up against the Philĭs'-tĭneş? Wilt thou give them into my hand?" And the LORD said to him, "Go up, and I will give them into your hand." 11And he went up to Bā'ȧl-pĕrā'zĭm, and David defeated them there; and David said, "God has broken through[l] my enemies by my hand, like a bursting flood." Therefore the name of that place is called Baal-perazim.[m] 12And they left their gods there, and David gave command, and they were burned.

13 And the Philĭs'tĭneş yet again made a raid in the valley. 14And when David again inquired of God, God said to him, "You shall not go up after them; go around and come upon them opposite the balsam trees. 15And when you hear the sound of marching in the tops of the balsam trees, then go out to battle; for God has gone out before you to smite the army of the Philĭs'tĭneş." 16And David did as God commanded him, and they smote the Philĭs'tĭne army from Gĭb'ĕŏn to Gēzĕr. 17And the fame of David went out into all lands, and the LORD brought the fear of him upon all nations.

k That is The breaking forth upon Uzzah
l Heb paraz
m That is Lord of breaking through

Side references:
13.9 2 Sam 6.6
13.10 1 Chr 15.13, 15
*13.13
13.14 1 Chr 26.4,5
*14.1 2 Sam 5.11
14.4 1 Chr 3.5
14.8 2 Sam 5.17
14.9 1 Chr 11.15
14.13 ver 9; 2 Sam 5.22
14.14 2 Sam 5.23
14.16 2 Sam 5.25
14.17 Josh 6.27; 2 Chr 26.8; Deut 2.25

13.13 Obed-edom. His home was blessed because of the ark David placed there.

14.1 Hiram was devoted to David, hence the generosity mentioned here.

3. The bringing of the ark to Jerusalem
a. The preparations

15.1
1 Chr 16.1

15.2
Num 4.15;
Deut 10.8;
31.9

15.3
1 Ki 8.1;
1 Chr 13.5

15.8
Ex 6.22
15.9
Ex 6.18

15.11
1 Chr
12.28;
1 Sam
22.20–23
15.12
Ex 19.14,
15;
2 Chr 35.6
15.13
2 Sam 6.3;
1 Chr 13.7,
10,11
15.14
ver 12
15.15
Ex 25.14;
Num 4.5

15 David built houses for himself in the city of David; and he prepared a place for the ark of God, and pitched a tent for it. 2 Then David said, "No one but the Lēvītes may carry the ark of God, for the LORD chose them to carry the ark of the LORD and to minister to him for ever." 3And David assembled all Israel at Jerusalem, to bring up the ark of the LORD to its place, which he had prepared for it. 4And David gathered together the sons of Aaron and the Lēvītes: 5 of the sons of Kōhăth, Ū'rĭĕl the chief, with a hundred and twenty of his brethren; 6 of the sons of Mĕrar'ĭ, Ȧṣāi'ăh the chief, with two hundred and twenty of his brethren; 7 of the sons of Gĕrshŏm, Jōĕl the chief, with a hundred and thirty of his brethren; 8 of the sons of Ĕlĭz'ăphăn, Shĕmāi'ăh the chief, with two hundred of his brethren; 9 of the sons of Hēbrŏn, Ĕlĭ'ĕl the chief, with eighty of his brethren; 10 of the sons of Ŭzzĭ'ĕl, Ȧmmĭn'ădăb the chief, with a hundred and twelve of his brethren. 11 Then David summoned the priests Zādŏk and Ȧbĭ'ăthăr, and the Lēvītes Ū'rĭĕl, Ȧṣāi'ăh, Jōĕl, Shĕmāi'ăh, Ĕlĭ'ĕl, and Ȧmmĭn'ădăb, 12 and said to them, "You are the heads of the fathers' houses of the Lēvītes; sanctify yourselves, you and your brethren, so that you may bring up the ark of the LORD, the God of Israel, to the place that I have prepared for it. 13 Because you did not carry it the first time,n the LORD our God broke forth upon us, because we did not care for it in the way that is ordained." 14 So the priests and the Lēvītes sanctified themselves to bring up the ark of the LORD, the God of Israel. 15And the Lēvītes carried the ark of God upon their shoulders with the poles, as Moses had commanded according to the word of the LORD.

b. The appointment of the singers and musicians

*15.16
1 Chr 25.1

15.17
1 Chr 6.33,
39,44

*15.21

15.24
ver 28;
1 Chr 16.6

16 David also commanded the chiefs of the Lēvītes to appoint their brethren as the singers who should play loudly on musical instruments, on harps and lyres and cymbals, to raise sounds of joy. 17 So the Lēvītes appointed Hēmăn the son of Jōĕl; and of his brethren Āsăph the son of Bĕrĕchī'ăh; and of the sons of Mĕrar'ĭ, their brethren, Ēthăn the son of Kūshāi'ăh; 18 and with them their brethren of the second order, Zĕchărī'ăh, Jȧ-ā'zĭĕl, Shĕmĭr'ămŏth, Jĕhī'ĕl, Ŭnnī, Ĕlī'ăb, Bĕnāi'ăh, Mȧ-ȧseī'ăh, Măttĭthī'ăh, Ĕlĭph'ĕlē'hū, and Mĭkneī'ăh, and the gatekeepers Ō'bĕd-ē'dŏm and Je-ī'ĕl. 19 The singers, Hēmăn, Āsăph, and Ēthăn, were to sound bronze cymbals; 20 Zĕchărī'ăh, Ā'zĭ-ĕl, Shĕmĭr'ămŏth, Jĕhī'ĕl, Ŭnnī, Ĕlī'ăb, Mȧ-ȧseī'ăh, and Bĕnāi'ăh were to play harps according to Āl'ămŏth; 21 but Măttĭthī'ăh, Ĕlĭph'ĕlē'hū, Mĭkneī'ăh, Ō'bĕd-ē'dŏm, Je-ī'ĕl, and Ȧzăzī'ăh were to lead with lyres according to the Shĕm'ĭnĭth. 22 Chĕnănī'ăh, leader of the Lēvītes in music, should direct the music, for he understood it. 23 Bĕrĕchī'ăh and Ĕlkā'năh were to be gatekeepers for the ark. 24 Shĕbănī'ăh, Jŏsh'ăphăt, Nĕthăn'ĕl, Ȧmā'săī, Zĕchărī'ăh, Bĕnāi'ăh, and Ĕlĭĕ'-

---

n The meaning of the Hebrew word is uncertain

15.16 David's provision for singers and musical accompaniment began with the historic event of bringing the ark to Jerusalem.

Note the further instructions in 16.4, 7.
  15.21 Sheminith, a musical term, the meaning of which is obscure. See heading, Ps 6.

zér, the priests, should blow the trumpets before the ark of God. Ō'bĕd-ē'dóm and Jĕhī'áh also were to be gatekeepers for the ark.

c. David dancing before the ark

25 So David and the elders of Israel, and the commanders of thousands, went to bring up the ark of the covenant of the LORD from the house of Ō'bĕd-ē'dóm with rejoicing. 26And because God helped the Lēvītes who were carrying the ark of the covenant of the LORD, they sacrificed seven bulls and seven rams. 27 David was clothed with a robe of fine linen, as also were all the Lēvītes who were carrying the ark, and the singers, and Chĕnánī'áh the leader of the music of the singers; and David wore a linen ephod. 28 So all Israel brought up the ark of the covenant of the LORD with shouting, to the sound of the horn, trumpets, and cymbals, and made loud music on harps and lyres.

29 And as the ark of the covenant of the LORD came to the city of David, Mĭchál the daughter of Saul looked out of the window, and saw King David dancing and making merry; and she despised him in her heart.

d. The offerings and the music

16 And they brought in the ark of God, and set it inside the tent which David had pitched for it; and they offered burnt offerings and peace offerings before God. 2And when David had finished offering the burnt offerings and the peace offerings, he blessed the people in the name of the LORD, 3 and distributed to all Israel, both men and women, to each a loaf of bread, a portion of meat,o and a cake of raisins.

4 Moreover he appointed certain of the Lēvītes as ministers before the ark of the LORD, to invoke, to thank, and to praise the LORD, the God of Israel. 5Āsáph was the chief, and second to him were Zĕchárī'áh, Je-ī'él, Shĕmĭr'ámóth, Jĕhī'él, Mättĭthī'áh, Ĕlī'áb, Bĕnāi'áh, Ō'bĕd-ē'dóm, and Je-iel, who were to play harps and lyres; Asaph was to sound the cymbals, 6 and Bĕnāi'áh and Jáhā'zĭĕl the priests were to blow trumpets continually, before the ark of the covenant of God.

e. David's psalm of gratitude

7 Then on that day David first appointed that thanksgiving be sung to the LORD by Āsáph and his brethren.

8 O give thanks to the LORD, call on his name,
　make known his deeds among the peoples!
9 Sing to him, sing praises to him,
　tell of all his wonderful works!
10 Glory in his holy name;
　let the hearts of those who seek the LORD rejoice!
11 Seek the LORD and his strength,
　seek his presence continually!
12 Remember the wonderful works that he has done,
　the wonders he wrought, the judgments he uttered,
13 O offspring of Abraham his servant,
　sons of Jacob, his chosen ones!

o Compare Gk Syr Vg: Heb uncertain

16.14
Isa 26.9

14 He is the LORD our God;
  his judgments are in all the earth.
15 He is mindful of his covenant for ever,
  of the word that he commanded, for a thousand generations,

16.16
Gen 17.2;
26.3;
28.13;
35.11

16 the covenant which he made with Abraham,
  his sworn promise to Isaac,

16.17
Gen 35.11,
12

17 which he confirmed as a statute to Jacob,
  as an everlasting covenant to Israel,
18 saying, "To you I will give the land of Cānaån,
  as your portion for an inheritance."

16.19
Gen 34.30

19 When they were few in number,
  and of little account, and sojourners in it,
20 wandering from nation to nation,
  from one kingdom to another people,

16.21
Gen 12.17;
20.3;
Ex 7.15–18

21 he allowed no one to oppress them;
  he rebuked kings on their account,
22 saying, "Touch not my anointed ones,
  do my prophets no harm!"

16.23
Ps 96.1–13

23 Sing to the LORD, all the earth!
  Tell of his salvation from day to day.
24 Declare his glory among the nations,
  his marvelous works among all the peoples!

16.25
Ps 48.1;
89.7

25 For great is the LORD, and greatly to be praised,
  and he is to be held in awe above all gods.

16.26
Ps 96.5

26 For all the gods of the peoples are idols;
  but the LORD made the heavens.
27 Honor and majesty are before him;
  strength and joy are in his place.

16.28
Ps 29.1,2

28 Ascribe to the LORD, O families of the peoples,
  ascribe to the LORD glory and strength!
29 Ascribe to the LORD the glory due his name;
  bring an offering, and come before him!
  Worship the LORD in holy array;
30   tremble before him, all the earth;
  yea, the world stands firm, never to be moved.

16.31
Isa 49.13;
Ps 93.1

31 Let the heavens be glad, and let the earth rejoice,
  and let them say among the nations, "The LORD reigns!"

16.32
Ps 98.7

32 Let the sea roar, and all that fills it,
  let the field exult, and everything in it!
33 Then shall the trees of the wood sing for joy
  before the LORD, for he comes to judge the earth.

16.34
Ps 106.1

34 O give thanks to the LORD, for he is good;
  for his steadfast love endures for ever!

16.35
Ps 106.47,
48

35 Say also:
"Deliver us, O God of our salvation,
  and gather and save us from among the nations,
that we may give thanks to thy holy name,
  and glory in thy praise.

16.36
1 Ki 8.15;
Deut 27.15

36 Blessed be the LORD, the God of Israel,
  from everlasting to everlasting!"
Then all the people said "Amen!" and praised the LORD.

37 So David left Āsăph and his brethren there before the ark of
the covenant of the LORD to minister continually before the ark as
each day required, 38 and also Ō′bĕd-e′dŏm and his *p* sixty-eight
brethren; while Obed-edom, the son of Jĕdu′thŭn, and Hō§ăh were
to be gatekeepers. 39And he left Zādŏk the priest and his brethren
the priests before the tabernacle of the LORD in the high place that
was at Gĭb′ëŏn, 40 to offer burnt offerings to the LORD upon the
altar of burnt offering continually morning and evening, according
to all that is written in the law of the LORD which he commanded
Israel. 41 With them were Hēmăn and Jĕdu′thŭn, and the rest of
those chosen and expressly named to give thanks to the LORD, for
his steadfast love endures for ever. 42 Hēmăn and Jĕdu′thŭn had
trumpets and cymbals for the music and instruments for sacred
song. The sons of Jeduthun were appointed to the gate.

43 Then all the people departed each to his house, and David
went home to bless his household.

D. David's desire to build the Temple

1. David's wish

17   Now when David dwelt in his house, David said to Nathan
    the prophet, "Behold, I dwell in a house of cedar, but the
ark of the covenant of the LORD is under a tent." 2And Nathan
said to David, "Do all that is in your heart, for God is with you."

2. God's disapproval and covenant

3 But that same night the word of the LORD came to Nathan,
4 "Go and tell my servant David, 'Thus says the LORD: You shall
not build me a house to dwell in. 5 For I have not dwelt in a house
since the day I led up Israel to this day, but I have gone from tent
to tent and from dwelling to dwelling. 6 In all places where I have
moved with all Israel, did I speak a word with any of the judges
of Israel, whom I commanded to shepherd my people, saying,
"Why have you not built me a house of cedar?" ' 7 Now therefore
thus shall you say to my servant David, 'Thus says the LORD of
hosts, I took you from the pasture, from following the sheep, that
you should be prince over my people Israel; 8 and I have been with
you wherever you went, and have cut off all your enemies from
before you; and I will make for you a name, like the name of the
great ones of the earth. 9And I will appoint a place for my people
Israel, and will plant them, that they may dwell in their own place,
and be disturbed no more; and violent men shall waste them no
more, as formerly, 10 from the time that I appointed judges over
my people Israel; and I will subdue all your enemies. Moreover
I declare to you that the LORD will build you a house. 11 When
your days are fulfilled to go to be with your fathers, I will raise
up your offspring after you, one of your own sons, and I will establish his kingdom. 12 He shall build a house for me, and I will
establish his throne for ever. 13 I will be his father, and he shall be
my son; I will not take my steadfast love from him, as I took it

p Heb *their*

16.37
ver 4,5;
2 Chr 8.14
16.38
1 Chr
13.14;
26.10
*16.39
1 Chr
15.11;
1 Ki 3.4
16.40
Ex 29.38;
Num 28.3
16.41
1 Chr 6.33;
25.1–6;
2 Chr 5.13

17.1
2 Sam
7.1–29

17.4
1 Chr
28.2,3
17.5
2 Sam 7.6
17.6
2 Sam 7.7

17.10
Judg 2.16

17.13
2 Sam 7.14,
15;
Heb 1.5

16.39 *tabernacle . . . at Gibeon.* According
to this verse (and 21.29) then, there is every
reason to believe that there were two sanctuaries in David's time; one at Jersualem with
the ark, and the other at Gibeon with the
tabernacle and its furniture.

17.14
Lk 1.33

from him who was before you, 14 but I will confirm him in my house and in my kingdom for ever and his throne shall be established for ever.' " 15 In accordance with all these words, and in accordance with all this vision, Nathan spoke to David.

3. David's prayer

17.16
2 Sam 7.18

16 Then King David went in and sat before the LORD, and said, "Who am I, O LORD God, and what is my house, that thou hast brought me thus far? 17And this was a small thing in thy eyes, O God; thou hast also spoken of thy servant's house for a great while to come, and hast shown me future generations,q O LORD God! 18And what more can David say to thee for honoring thy

17.19
Isa 37.35

servant? For thou knowest thy servant. 19 For thy servant's sake, O LORD, and according to thy own heart, thou hast wrought all this greatness, in making known all these great things. 20 There is none like thee, O LORD, and there is no God besides thee, according to all that we have heard with our ears. 21 What otherr nation on earth is like thy people Israel, whom God went to redeem to be his people, making for thyself a name for great and terrible things, in driving out nations before thy people whom thou didst redeem

17.22
Ex 19.5,6

from Egypt? 22And thou didst make thy people Israel to be thy people for ever; and thou, O LORD, didst become their God. 23And now, O LORD, let the word which thou hast spoken concerning thy servant and concerning his house be established for ever, and do as

17.24
Ps 46.7,11

thou hast spoken; 24 and thy name will be established and magnified for ever, saying, 'The LORD of hosts, the God of Israel, is Israel's God,' and the house of thy servant David will be established before thee. 25 For thou, my God, hast revealed to thy servant that thou wilt build a house for him; therefore thy servant has found courage to pray before thee. 26And now, O LORD, thou art God, and thou hast promised this good thing to thy servant; 27 now therefore may it please thee to bless the house of thy servant, that it may continue for ever before thee; for what thou, O LORD, hast blessed is blessed for ever."

E. The account of David's victories

18.1
2 Sam 8.1–
18

18 After this David defeated the Philis'tines and subdued them, and he took Gath and its villages out of the hand of the Philistines.

2 And he defeated Moab, and the Mo'abites became servants to David and brought tribute.

3 David also defeated Hadade'zer king of Zobah, toward Hamath, as he went to set up his monuments at the river Euphra'tes. 4And David took from him a thousand chariots, seven thousand horsemen, and twenty thousand foot soldiers; and David hamstrung all the chariot horses, but left enough for a hundred

18.5
1 Chr 19.6

chariots. 5And when the Syrians of Damascus came to help Hadade'zer king of Zobah, David slew twenty-two thousand men of the Syrians. 6 Then David put garrisonst in Syria of Damascus; and the Syrians became servants to David, and brought tribute. And the LORD gave victory to David wherever he went. 7 And

---

q Cn: Heb uncertain
r Gk Vg: Heb one   s Heb hand
t Gk Vg 2 Sam 8.6 Compare Syr: Heb lacks garrisons

David took the shields of gold which were carried by the servants of Hădăde′zėr, and brought them to Jerusalem. 8And from Tĭb-hăth and from Cŭn, cities of Hădăde′zėr, David took very much bronze; with it Solomon made the bronze sea and the pillars and the vessels of bronze.

9 When Tō′ū king of Hāmăth heard that David had defeated the whole army of Hădăde′zėr, king of Zōbăh, 10 he sent his son Hădor′ăm to King David, to greet him, and to congratulate him because he had fought against Hădăde′zėr and defeated him; for Hadadezer had often been at war with Tō′ū. And he sent all sorts of articles of gold, of silver, and of bronze; 11 these also King David dedicated to the LORD, together with the silver and gold which he had carried off from all the nations, from Ḗdŏm, Mōăb, the Ăm′-mŏnītes, the Phĭlĭs′tīneṣ, and Ăm′ălĕk.

12 And Ăbĭsh′äï, the son of Zĕru′jăh, slew eighteen thousand Ē′dŏmītes in the Valley of Salt. 13And he put garrisons in Ḗdŏm; and all the Ē′dŏmītes became David's servants. And the LORD gave victory to David wherever he went.

14 So David reigned over all Israel; and he administered justice and equity to all his people. 15And Jōăb the son of Zĕru′jăh was over the army; and Jĕhŏsh′ăphăt the son of Ăhĭ′lŭd was recorder; 16 and Zādŏk the son of Ăhĭ′tŭb and Ăhĭm′ėlĕçh the son of Ăbĭ′-áthăr were priests; and Shăvshă was secretary; 17 and Bĕnāi′ăh the son of Jĕhoi′ădă was over the Çhĕr′ĕthītes and the Pĕl′ĕthītes; and David's sons were the chief officials in the service of the king.

19 Now after this Nāhăsh the king of the Ăm′mŏnītes died, and his son reigned in his stead. 2And David said, "I will deal loyally with Hānŭn the son of Nāhăsh, for his father dealt loyally with me." So David sent messengers to console him con-cerning his father. And David's servants came to Hanun in the land of the Ăm′mŏnītes, to console him. 3 But the princes of the Ăm′mŏnītes said to Hānŭn, "Do you think, because David has sent comforters to you, that he is honoring your father? Have not his servants come to you to search and to overthrow and to spy out the land?" 4 So Hānŭn took David's servants, and shaved them, and cut off their garments in the middle, at their hips, and sent them away; 5 and they departed. When David was told concerning the men, he sent to meet them, for the men were greatly ashamed. And the king said, "Remain at Jĕr′ĭçhō until your beards have grown, and then return."

6 When the Ăm′mŏnītes saw that they had made themselves odious to David, Hānŭn and the Ammonites sent a thousand talents of silver to hire chariots and horsemen from Mĕsŏpŏtā′mĭă, from Ărăm-mā′ăcăh, and from Zōbăh. 7 They hired thirty-two thousand chariots and the king of Mā′ăcăh with his army, who came and encamped before Mĕd′ĕbă. And the Ăm′mŏnītes were mustered from their cities and came to battle. 8 When David heard of it, he sent Jōăb and all the army of the mighty men. 9And the Ăm′mŏnītes came out and drew up in battle array at the entrance of the city, and the kings who had come were by themselves in the open country.

10 When Jōăb saw that the battle was set against him both in front and in the rear, he chose some of the picked men of Israel, and arrayed them against the Syrians; 11 the rest of his men he put in the charge of Ăbĭsh′äï his brother, and they were arrayed

18.8
1 Ki 7.15, 23;
2 Chr 4.12, 15,16

18.10
2 Sam 10.16

18.12
2 Sam 8.13

18.15
1 Chr 11.6

18.17
2 Sam 8.18

19.1
2 Sam 10.1

19.3
2 Sam 10.3

19.4
2 Sam 10.4

19.6
1 Chr 18.5,9

19.7
Num 21.30;
Josh 13.9, 16

19.8
2 Sam 10.7

19.11
2 Sam 10.10

against the Ăm'mŏnītes. 12And he said, "If the Syrians are too strong for me, then you shall help me; but if the Ăm'mŏnītes are too strong for you, then I will help you. 13 Be of good courage, and let us play the man for our people, and for the cities of our God; and may the LORD do what seems good to him." 14 So Jŏăb and the people who were with him drew near before the Syrians for battle; and they fled before him. 15And when the Ăm'mŏnītes saw that the Syrians fled, they likewise fled before Ăbĭsh'ăĭ, Jŏăb's brother, and entered the city. Then Jŏăb came to Jerusalem.

16 But when the Syrians saw that they had been defeated by Israel, they sent messengers and brought out the Syrians who were beyond the Eūphrā'tēs, with Shŏphăch the commander of the army of Hădădē'zĕr at their head. 17And when it was told David, he gathered all Israel together, and crossed the Jordan, and came to them, and drew up his forces against them. And when David set the battle in array against the Syrians, they fought with him. 18And the Syrians fled before Israel; and David slew of the Syrians the men of seven thousand chariots, and forty thousand foot soldiers, and killed also Shŏphăch the commander of their army. 19And when the servants of Hădădē'zĕr saw that they had been defeated by Israel, they made peace with David, and became subject to him. So the Syrians were not willing to help the Ăm'mŏnītes any more.

20 In the spring of the year, the time when kings go forth to battle, Jŏăb led out the army, and ravaged the country of the Ăm'mŏnītes, and came and besieged Răbbăh. But David remained at Jerusalem. And Joab smote Rabbah, and overthrew it. 2And David took the crown of their king u from his head; he found that it weighed a talent of gold, and in it was a precious stone; and it was placed on David's head. And he brought forth the spoil of the city, a very great amount. 3And he brought forth the people who were in it, and set them to labor v with saws and iron picks and axes; w and thus David did to all the cities of the Ăm'mŏnītes. Then David and all the people returned to Jerusalem.

4 And after this there arose war with the Phĭlĭs'tīnĕş at Gēzĕr; then Sĭb'bĕcăĭ the Hū'shăthīte slew Sĭppăĭ, who was one of the descendants of the giants; and the Philistines were subdued. 5And there was again war with the Phĭlĭs'tīnĕş; and Ĕlhă'năn the son of Jāĭr slew Lahmī the brother of Gŏlī'ăth the Gĭttīte, the shaft of whose spear was like a weaver's beam. 6And there was again war

Side references (left margin):

19.12 / 2 Sam 10.11
19.14 / 2 Sam 10.13
19.16 / 2 Sam 10.15
19.17 / 2 Sam 10.17
19.18 / 2 Sam 10.18
19.19 / 2 Sam 10.19
*20.1ff / 2 Sam 11.1; 12.26
20.2 / 2 Sam 12.30,31
20.3 / 2 Sam 12.31
20.4 / 2 Sam 21.18
*20.5 / 2 Sam 21.19; 1 Sam 17.7
20.6 / 2 Sam 21.20

---

u Or *Milcŏm* See 1 Kings 11.5   v Compare 2 Sam 12.31: Heb *he sawed*
w Compare 2 Sam 12.31: Heb *saws*

20.1-3 This unit covers the same period of time as 2 Sam 11.1–12.31. The difference in length occurs because the Chronicler left out the account of David's sin against Bath-sheba and Uriah (2 Sam 11.2–12.25). This story occurred between: *David remained at Jerusalem,* and *Joab smote Rabbah.* The Chronicler's interest lay in the Temple (its rituals, personnel, and importance) and in the law (obedience means blessing; disobedience, cursing). David's difficulties with Saul and his seven years at Hebron fighting for the kingdom are hardly mentioned. The one sin which is clearly depicted is David's census of the people (21.1–29), and this is attributed to the instigation of Satan. Solomon also receives special consideration. The account of his idolatry and punishment (1 Ki 11.1–40), which would appear between 2 Chr 9.28 and 29, has been left out. Israel, considered as apostate from the beginning, is mentioned only where it is entwined with some aspect of Judah's history which the Chronicler wants to stress. Along with David and Solomon, the good kings Asa, Jehoshaphat, Uzziah, Hezekiah, and Josiah are featured, with much material not found in the Books of Kings. But from Rehoboam on, most of the kings' sins and difficulties are noted, and usually there is a seer, prophet, or man of God to confront the wayward king.
20.5 See note to 2 Sam 21.19.

at Gǎth, where there was a man of great stature, who had six fingers on each hand, and six toes on each foot, twenty-four in number; and he also was descended from the giants. 7 And when he taunted Israel, Jonathan the son of Shǐm′ë-à, David's brother, slew him. 8 These were descended from the giants in Gǎth; and they fell by the hand of David and by the hand of his servants.

F. David's numbering of the people

1. The census

21 Satan stood up against Israel, and incited David to number Israel. 2 So David said to Jōǎb and the commanders of the army, "Go, number Israel, from Beër-shē′bà to Dan, and bring me a report, that I may know their number." 3 But Jōǎb said, "May the LORD add to his people a hundred times as many as they are! Are they not, my lord the king, all of them my lord's servants? Why then should my lord require this? Why should he bring guilt upon Israel?" 4 But the king's word prevailed against Jōǎb. So Joab departed and went throughout all Israel, and came back to Jerusalem. 5 And Jōǎb gave the sum of the numbering of the people to David. In all Israel there were one million one hundred thousand men who drew the sword, and in Judah four hundred and seventy thousand who drew the sword. 6 But he did not include Lēvī and Benjamin in the numbering, for the king's command was abhorrent to Jōǎb.

2. The plague as a punishment

7 But God was displeased with this thing, and he smote Israel. 8 And David said to God, "I have sinned greatly in that I have done this thing. But now, I pray thee, take away the iniquity of thy servant; for I have done very foolishly." 9 And the LORD spoke to Gǎd, David's seer, saying, 10 "Go and say to David, 'Thus says the LORD, Three things I offer you; choose one of them, that I may do it to you.'" 11 So Gǎd came to David and said to him, "Thus says the LORD, 'Take which you will: 12 either three years of famine; or three months of devastation by your foes, while the sword of your enemies overtakes you; or else three days of the sword of the LORD, pestilence upon the land, and the angel of the LORD destroying throughout all the territory of Israel.' Now decide what answer I shall return to him who sent me." 13 Then David said to Gǎd, "I am in great distress; let me fall into the hand of the LORD, for his mercy is very great; but let me not fall into the hand of man."

14 So the LORD sent a pestilence upon Israel; and there fell

*21.1
2 Sam 24.1–25

21.2
1 Chr 27.23

21.3
Deut 1.11

21.5
cf. 2 Sam 24.9

21.6
1 Chr 27.24

21.8
2 Sam 24.10; 12.13

21.10
1 Chr 29.29; 1 Sam 9.9

21.12
2 Sam 24.13

21.13
Ps 51.1; 130.4,7

*21.14
1 Chr 27.24

21.1 *Satan* (the Adversary), whose name is specifically given here, is referred to by more than thirty different names and titles in Scripture. Each of these designations brings out some particular phase of his work. Among the most significant are: (1) *the serpent* (Gen 3.4); (2) *ruler of this world* (Jn 14.30; (3) *prince of demons* (Mt 12.24); (4) *god of this world* (2 Cor 4.4); and (5) *the tempter* (1 Thess 3.5).

21.14 Here is an illustration of how punishment sometimes affects also those who, so far as the record shows, had no part in the sin.

(Of course it is possible that David's pride in numbers only reflected a similar attitude on the part of his prosperous and successful nation as a whole. But the Scripture does not make that explicit here.) David chose to number the people in disregard of the will of God. Seventy thousand perished as a result of one man's decision. This illustrates one of the inscrutable mysteries of life. Often many suffer because of the sins of the few. In war, for example, devastation comes to those who want no war but who suffer with those who desire it and bring it to pass.

21.15
2 Sam 24.16

21.16
2 Chr 3.1

21.17
2 Sam 7.8;
Ps 74.1

21.18
2 Chr 3.1

21.21
2 Chr 3.1

21.25
2 Sam 24.24
21.26
Lev 9.24;
Judg 6.21

21.29
1 Chr
16.39;
1 Ki 3.4

seventy thousand men of Israel. ¹⁵And God sent the angel to Jerusalem to destroy it; but when he was about to destroy it, the LORD saw, and he repented of the evil; and he said to the destroying angel, "It is enough; now stay your hand." And the angel of the LORD was standing by the threshing floor of Ornán the Jĕb´ŭsīte. ¹⁶And David lifted his eyes and saw the angel of the LORD standing between earth and heaven, and in his hand a drawn sword stretched out over Jerusalem. Then David and the elders, clothed in sackcloth, fell upon their faces. ¹⁷And David said to God, "Was it not I who gave command to number the people? It is I who have sinned and done very wickedly. But these sheep, what have they done? Let thy hand, I pray thee, O LORD my God, be against me and against my father's house; but let not the plague be upon thy people."

18 Then the angel of the LORD commanded Găd to say to David that David should go up and rear an altar to the LORD on the threshing floor of Ornán the Jĕb´ŭsīte. ¹⁹ So David went up at Găd's word, which he had spoken in the name of the LORD. ²⁰ Now Ornán was threshing wheat; he turned and saw the angel, and his four sons who were with him hid themselves. ²¹As David came to Ornán, Ornan looked and saw David and went forth from the threshing floor, and did obeisance to David with his face to the ground. ²²And David said to Ornán, "Give me the site of the threshing floor that I may build on it an altar to the LORD—give it to me at its full price—that the plague may be averted from the people." 23 Then Ornán said to David, "Take it; and let my lord the king do what seems good to him; see, I give the oxen for burnt offerings, and the threshing sledges for the wood, and the wheat for a cereal offering. I give it all." 24 But King David said to Ornán, "No, but I will buy it for the full price; I will not take for the LORD what is yours, nor offer burnt offerings which cost me nothing." 25 So David paid Ornán six hundred shekels of gold by weight for the site. ²⁶And David built there an altar to the LORD and presented burnt offerings and peace offerings, and called upon the LORD, and he answered him with fire from heaven upon the altar of burnt offering. 27 Then the LORD commanded the angel; and he put his sword back into its sheath.

28 At that time, when David saw that the LORD had answered him at the threshing floor of Ornán the Jĕb´ŭsīte, he made his sacrifices there. 29 For the tabernacle of the LORD, which Moses had made in the wilderness, and the altar of burnt offering were at that time in the high place at Gĭb´ëön; 30 but David could not go before it to inquire of God, for he was afraid of the sword of the angel of

---

21.25 Compare 2 Sam 24.24, where it is stated that David paid fifty silver shekels for the threshing floor and the sacrificial oxen. The explanation of the apparent discrepancy seems to be that he paid six hundred shekels of gold for Ornan's entire property (Heb *māqōm* or "place"), although the *goren* or "threshing floor" was purchased for only fifty shekels of silver. We know that David purchased more than the threshing floor before he was through with Ornan, because it was on this site (2 Chr 3.1) that not only the Temple itself but also several palace buildings were later erected. This entire Mt. Moriah tract must have included much more than the mere threshing floor, and with the development of the nearby city, its real estate value might easily have risen to six hundred shekels of gold. Note that Ornan's name in 2 Sam 24 is given as Araunah. (Actually it is spelled Avarnah, in the M.T in 24.16, Aranvah in verse 18, and Araunah in the rest of the chapter. There was apparently some uncertainty as to the exact pronunciation of this foreign name, but Araunah, which differs from Ornan by only one or two secondary letters in the Hebrew consonants, probably represents the earlier form.)

22 the Lord. ¹ Then David said, "Here shall be the house of the Lord God and here the altar of burnt offering for Israel."

G. Preparations for the building of the Temple

1. Materials gathered

2 David commanded to gather together the aliens who were in the land of Israel, and he set stonecutters to prepare dressed stones for building the house of God. ³ David also provided great stores of iron for nails for the doors of the gates and for clamps, as well as bronze in quantities beyond weighing, ⁴ and cedar timbers without number; for the Sīdō′nĭăns and Tӯr′ĭăns brought great quantities of cedar to David. ⁵ For David said, "Solomon my son is young and inexperienced, and the house that is to be built for the Lord must be exceedingly magnificent, of fame and glory throughout all lands; I will therefore make preparation for it." So David provided materials in great quantity before his death.

2. Solomon instructed

6 Then he called for Solomon his son, and charged him to build a house for the Lord, the God of Israel. ⁷ David said to Solomon, "My son, I had it in my heart to build a house to the name of the Lord my God. ⁸ But the word of the Lord came to me, saying, 'You have shed much blood and have waged great wars; you shall not build a house to my name, because you have shed so much blood before me upon the earth. ⁹ Behold, a son shall be born to you; he shall be a man of peace. I will give him peace from all his enemies round about; for his name shall be Solomon, and I will give peace and quiet to Israel in his days. ¹⁰ He shall build a house for my name. He shall be my son, and I will be his father, and I will establish his royal throne in Israel for ever.' ¹¹ Now, my son, the Lord be with you, so that you may succeed in building the house of the Lord your God, as he has spoken concerning you. ¹² Only, may the Lord grant you discretion and understanding, that when he gives you charge over Israel you may keep the law of the Lord your God. ¹³ Then you will prosper if you are careful to observe the statutes and the ordinances which the Lord commanded Moses for Israel. Be strong, and of good courage. Fear not; be not dismayed. ¹⁴ With great pains I have provided for the house of the Lord a hundred thousand talents of gold, a million talents of silver, and bronze and iron beyond weighing, for there is so much of it; timber and stone too I have provided. To these you must add. ¹⁵ You have an abundance of workmen: stonecutters, masons, carpenters, and all kinds of craftsmen without number, skilled in working ¹⁶ gold, silver, bronze, and iron. Arise and be doing! The Lord be with you!"

3. The leaders charged to help

17 David also commanded all the leaders of Israel to help Solo-

Marginal references:
22.1 1 Chr 21.18–29; 2 Chr 3.1
22.2 1 Ki 9.21; 5.17,18
22.3 1 Chr 29.2,7; ver 14
22.4 1 Ki 5.6
22.5 1 Chr 29.1
22.7 2 Sam 7.2; 1 Chr 17.1; Deut 12.5,11
22.8 1 Ki 5.3; 1 Chr 28.3
22.9 1 Ki 4.20,25; 2 Sam 12.24,25
22.10 2 Sam 7.13; 1 Chr 17.12,13
22.11 ver 16
22.12 1 Ki 3.9–12; 2 Chr 1.10
22.13 1 Chr 28.7; Josh 1.6–9; 1 Chr 28.20
*22.14 ver 3
22.16 ver 11
22.17 1 Chr 28.1–6

22.14 *a hundred thousand talents of gold.* This is a good example of the exceedingly large figures which characterize the Books of Chronicles. The most gold that came to Solomon in one of his prosperous years was *six hundred and sixty-six talents* (1 Ki 10.14; 2 Chr 9.13). That David, a man devoted primarily to war and expansion of the kingdom, could have accumulated 100,000 talents of gold (approximately 3 billion dollars) is highly improbable. Somewhere in transmission the original figures were greatly expanded.

*22.18
2 Sam 7.1;
1 Chr 23.25

22.19
1 Chr 28.9;
1 Ki 8.6;
2 Chr 5.7;
ver 7

mon his son, saying, 18 "Is not the LORD your God with you? And has he not given you peace on every side? For he has delivered the inhabitants of the land into my hand; and the land is subdued before the LORD and his people. 19 Now set your mind and heart to seek the LORD your God. Arise and build the sanctuary of the LORD God, so that the ark of the covenant of the LORD and the holy vessels of God may be brought into a house built for the name of the LORD."

H. The arrangements for the Temple service

1. The Levites

23.1
1 Ki 1.33–
39;
1 Chr
29.28; 28.5
23.3
Num 4.3–
49;
ver 24
23.4
2 Chr 19.8
23.5
1 Chr 15.16
23.6
2 Chr 8.14;
29.25

23 When David was old and full of days, he made Solomon his son king over Israel.

2 David assembled all the leaders of Israel and the priests and the Lēvītes. 3 The Lēvītes, thirty years old and upward, were numbered, and the total was thirty-eight thousand men. 4 "Twenty-four thousand of these," David said, "shall have charge of the work in the house of the LORD, six thousand shall be officers and judges, 5 four thousand gatekeepers, and four thousand shall offer praises to the LORD with the instruments which I have made for praise." 6And David organized them in divisions corresponding to the sons of Lēvī: Gēršhóm, Kōhǎth, and Měrar'ī.

7 The sons of Gēršhóm x were Lādán and Shǐm'ë-ī. 8 The sons of Lādán: Jēhī'ël the chief, and Zēthám, and Jōël, three. 9 The sons of Shǐm'ë-ī: Shēlō'móth, Hā'zǐ-ėl, and Hārán, three. These were the heads of the fathers' houses of Lādán. 10And the sons of Shǐm'ë-ī: Jāháth, Zīná, and Jē'ush, and Běrī'áh. These four were the sons of Shime-i. 11 Jāháth was the chief, and Zīzáh the second; but Jē'ush and Běrī'áh had not many sons, therefore they became a father's house in one reckoning.

23.12
Ex 6.18
23.13
Ex 6.20;
28.1;
30.6–10;
Deut 21.5

23.16
1 Chr
26.24ff

12 The sons of Kōhǎth: Ǎmrǎm, Ǐzhar, Hēbrón, and Ǔzzī'ël, four. 13 The sons of Ǎmrǎm: Aaron and Moses. Aaron was set apart to consecrate the most holy things, that he and his sons for ever should burn incense before the LORD, and minister to him and pronounce blessings in his name for ever. 14 But the sons of Moses the man of God were named among the tribe of Lēvī. 15 The sons of Moses: Gēršhóm and Ĕliē'zėr. 16 The sons of Gēršhóm: Shěb'uël the chief. 17 The sons of Ĕliē'zėr: Rēhábī'áh the chief; Eliezer had no other sons, but the sons of Rehabiah were very many. 18 The sons of Ǐzhar: Shēlō'mǐth the chief. 19 The sons of Hēbrón: Jērī'áh the chief, Ǎmārī'áh the second, Jāhā'zǐël the third, and Jěkámē'ám the fourth. 20 The sons of Ǔzzī'ėl: Mīcáh the chief and Ǐsshī'áh the second.

23.21
1 Chr
24.26ff

21 The sons of Měrar'ī: Mahlī and Mushī. The sons of Mahli: Ělëä'zár and Kǐsh. 22 Ělëä'zár died having no sons, but only daughters; their kinsmen, the sons of Kǐsh, married them. 23 The sons of Mushī: Mahlī, Ēdėr, and Jěr'émóth, three.

x Vg Compare Gk Syr; Heb *to the Gěr'shónīte*

22.18 *the land is subdued before the* LORD *and his people.* Under David and Solomon the kingdom of Israel reaches its greatest heights. Starting from slavery in Egypt, Israel now has a territory, a people, and a stable government. The favor of God is manifest. But, in a few short years this great kingdom will sink into oblivion from which it never recovers.

2. *Their duties*

24 These were the sons of Lēvī by their fathers' houses, the heads of fathers' houses as they were registered according to the number of the names of the individuals from twenty years old and upward who were to do the work for the service of the house of the LORD. 25 For David said, "The LORD, the God of Israel, has given peace to his people; and he dwells in Jerusalem for ever. 26And so the Lēvītes no longer need to carry the tabernacle or any of the things for its service"—27 for by the last words of David these were the number of the Lēvītes from twenty years old and upward—28 "but their duty shall be to assist the sons of Aaron for the service of the house of the LORD, having the care of the courts and the chambers, the cleansing of all that is holy, and any work for the service of the house of God; 29 to assist also with the showbread, the flour for the cereal offering, the wafers of unleavened bread, the baked offering, the offering mixed with oil, and all measures of quantity or size. 30And they shall stand every morning, thanking and praising the LORD, and likewise at evening, 31 and whenever burnt offerings are offered to the LORD on sabbaths, new moons, and feast days, according to the number required of them, continually before the LORD. 32 Thus they shall keep charge of the tent of meeting and the sanctuary, and shall attend the sons of Aaron, their brethren, for the service of the house of the LORD."

3. *The division of the priests*

24 The divisions of the sons of Aaron were these. The sons of Aaron: Nādăb, Ȧbī′hū, Ēlĕä′zȧr, and Ĭth′ȧmar. 2 But Nādăb and Ȧbī′hū died before their father, and had no children, so Ēlĕä′zȧr and Ĭth′ȧmar became the priests. 3 With the help of Zādŏk of the sons of Ēlĕä′zȧr, and Ȧhĭm′ĕlĕch of the sons of Ĭth′ȧmar, David organized them according to the appointed duties in their service. 4 Since more chief men were found among the sons of Ēlĕä′zȧr than among the sons of Ĭth′ȧmar, they organized them under sixteen heads of fathers' houses of the sons of Eleazar, and eight of the sons of Ithamar. 5 They organized them by lot, all alike, for there were officers of the sanctuary and officers of God among both the sons of Ēlĕä′zȧr and the sons of Ĭth′ȧmar. 6And the scribe Shĕmāi′ȧh the son of Nēthăn′ĕl, a Lēvīte, recorded them in the presence of the king, and the princes, and Zādŏk the priest, and Ȧhĭm′ĕlĕch the son of Ȧbī′ȧthȧr, and the heads of the fathers' houses of the priests and of the Lēvītes; one father's house being chosen for Ēlĕä′zȧr and one chosen for Ĭth′ȧmar.

7 The first lot fell to Jĕhoi′ȧrĭb, the second to Jĕdāi′ȧh, 8 the third to Hārĭm, the fourth to Së-ō′rĭm, 9 the fifth to Mălchī′jȧh, the sixth to Mĭj′ȧmĭn, 10 the seventh to Hăkkŏz, the eighth to Ȧbī′jȧh, 11 the ninth to Jĕsh′uȧ, the tenth to Shĕcání′ȧh, 12 the eleventh to Ēlī′ȧshĭb, the twelfth to Jākĭm, 13 the thirteenth to Hŭppȧh, the fourteenth to Jĕshĕb′ĕ-ăb, 14 the fifteenth to Bĭlgȧh, the sixteenth to Ĭmmĕr, 15 the seventeenth to Hēzĭr, the eighteenth to Hăp′pĭzzĕz, 16 the nineteenth to Pĕtháhī′ȧh, the twentieth to Jĕhĕz′kĕl, 17 the twenty-first to Jāchĭn, the twenty-second to

*23.24
Num 10.17, 21;
ver 3

23.25
1 Chr 22.18

23.26
Num 4.5

23.29
Lev 23.5–9;
Ex 25.30;
Lev 6.20;
2.4–7;
19.35

23.31
Isa 1.13,14;
Lev 23.24
23.32
Num 1.53;
1 Chr 9.27;
Num 3.6

24.1
Ex 6.23
24.2
Lev 10.2;
Num 3.4

24.5
ver 31

24.10
Neh 12.4, 17;
Lk 1.5

23.24 Num 4.30; 1 Chr 23.3 give the active years of the Levites as *thirty* to *fifty*. Presumably the reason for lowering it here was a need for more Levites to assist the priests.

Gāmúl, 18 the twenty-third to Dēlāi'áh, the twenty-fourth to Mā-

24.19
1 Chr 9.25
āzī'áh. 19 These had as their appointed duty in their service to come into the house of the LORD according to the procedure established for them by Aaron their father, as the LORD God of Israel had commanded him.

20 And of the rest of the sons of Lēvī: of the sons of Ămrăm,
24.21
1 Chr 23.17
Shu'bä-ĕl; of the sons of Shuba-el, Jĕhdei'áh. 21 Of Rēhābī'áh: of the sons of Rehabiah, Ĭsshī'áh the chief. 22 Of the Ĭz'harītes,
24.23
1 Chr 23.19
Shēlō'mŏth; of the sons of Shelomoth, Jāháth. 23 The sons of Hēbrón:ʸ Jĕrī'áh the chief,ᶻ Ămārī'áh the second, Jāhā'zĭĕl the third, Jĕkámē'ám the fourth. 24 The sons of Ŭzzī'ĕl, Mīcáh; of the sons of Micah, Shāmĭr. 25 The brother of Mīcáh, Ĭsshī'áh; of the
24.26
1 Chr 23.21
sons of Isshiah, Zĕchárī'áh. 26 The sons of Mêrar'ĭ: Mahlī and Mushī. The sons of Jā-ázī'áh: Bēnō. 27 The sons of Mêrar'ĭ: of Jā-ázī'áh, Bēnō, Shōhám, Zăccŭr, and Ĭbrī. 28 Of Mahlī: Ēlëä'zár, who had no sons. 29 Of Kĭsh, the sons of Kish: Jérah'meĕl. 30 The sons of Mushī: Mahlī, Ēdêr, and Jĕr'ĭmóth. These were the sons of the Lēvītes according to their fathers' houses. 31 These also, the
24.31
ver 5,6
head of each father's house and his younger brother alike, cast lots, just as their brethren the sons of Aaron, in the presence of King David, Zādŏk, Ăhĭm'ĕlĕch, and the heads of fathers' houses of the priests and of the Lēvītes.

4. *The arrangements for music*

25.1
1 Chr 6.33,
39; 15.16
25 David and the chiefs of the service also set apart for the service certain of the sons of Āsăph, and of Hēmăn, and of Jédu'thûn, who should prophesy with lyres, with harps, and with cymbals. The list of those who did the work and of their duties was: 2 Of the sons of Āsăph: Zăccŭr, Joseph, Nĕthánī'áh, and Ăshārē'láh, sons of Asaph, under the direction of Asaph, who
25.3
1 Chr
16.41,42
prophesied under the direction of the king. 3 Of Jédu'thûn, the sons of Jeduthun: Gĕdālī'áh, Zērī, Jĕshāi'áh, Shĭm'ĕ-ī̄,ᵃ Hāshābī'-áh, and Măttĭthī'áh, six, under the direction of their father Jeduthun, who prophesied with the lyre in thanksgiving and praise to the LORD. 4 Of Hēmăn, the sons of Heman: Bŭkkī'áh, Mättānī'áh,
*25.4
1 Chr 6.33;
ver 25
Ŭzzī'ĕl, Shĕb'üĕl, and Jĕr'ĭmóth, Hănănī'áh, Hānā'nī, Ēlī'átháh, Gĭddäl'tī, and Rō'mămtĭ-ē'zêr, Jŏshbĕkásh'áh, Măl'lŏthī, Hōthĭr, Māhā'zĭ-ŏth. 5 All these were the sons of Hēmăn the king's seer, according to the promise of God to exalt him; for God had given
25.6
1 Chr
15.16,19
Heman fourteen sons and three daughters. 6 They were all under the direction of their father in the music in the house of the LORD with cymbals, harps, and lyres for the service of the house of God. Āsăph, Jédu'thûn, and Hēmăn were under the order of the king. 7 The number of them along with their brethren, who were trained in singing to the LORD, all who were skilful, was two hun-
25.8
1 Chr 26.13
25.9
1 Chr 6.39
dred and eighty-eight. 8 And they cast lots for their duties, small and great, teacher and pupil alike.

9 The first lot fell for Āsăph to Joseph; the second to Gĕdálī'áh,

---

ʸ See 23.19: Heb lacks *Hebron*   ᶻ See 23.19: Heb lacks *the chief*
ᵃ One Ms: Gk: Heb lacks *Shimei*

25.4 *Hananiah ... Mahazi-oth.* While the first two of the nine names appear as valid proper names elsewhere, the other forms are impossible as individual names. With slight change of vowels and division of consonants the list becomes a fragment of an old poem or prayer. No one knows how it was interpreted as a list of names and incorporated here.

to him and his brethren and his sons, twelve; 10 the third to Zăccûr, his sons and his brethren, twelve; 11 the fourth to Ĭzrī, his sons and his brethren, twelve; 12 the fifth to Nĕthánì'áh, his sons and his brethren, twelve; 13 the sixth to Bŭkkì'áh, his sons and his brethren, twelve; 14 the seventh to Jĕshárē'láh, his sons and his brethren, twelve; 15 the eighth to Jĕshāi'áh, his sons and his brethren, twelve; 16 the ninth to Mӑttánì'áh, his sons and his brethren, twelve; 17 the tenth to Shĭm'ĕ-ī, his sons and his brethren, twelve; 18 the eleventh to Ăz'árĕl, his sons and his brethren, twelve; 19 the twelfth to Hăshàbì'áh, his sons and his brethren, twelve; 20 to the thirteenth, Shu'bä-ĕl, his sons and his brethren, twelve; 21 to the fourteenth, Mӑttĭthì'áh, his sons and his brethren, twelve; 22 to the fifteenth, to Jĕr'ĕmóth, his sons and his brethren, twelve; 23 to the sixteenth, to Hănánì'áh, his sons and his brethren, twelve; 24 to the seventeenth, to Jŏshbĕkásh'áh, his sons and his brethren, twelve; 25 to the eighteenth, to Hánà'nī, his sons and his brethren, twelve; 26 to the nineteenth, to Mӑl'lóthī, his sons and his brethren, twelve; 27 to the twentieth, to Ēlì'átháh, his sons and his brethren, twelve; 28 to the twenty-first, to Hōthịr, his sons and his brethren, twelve; 29 to the twenty-second, to Gĭddál'tī, his sons and his brethren, twelve; 30 to the twenty-third, to Máhà'zĭ-ŏth, his sons and his brethren, twelve; 31 to the twenty-fourth, to Rō'mӑmtĭ-ē'zĕr, his sons and his brethren, twelve.

5. *The arrangements for gatekeepers*

26 As for the divisions of the gatekeepers: of the Kō'ráhītes, Mĕshĕlĕmì'áh the son of Kō'rĕ, of the sons of Āsăph. 2And Mĕshĕlĕmì'áh had sons: Zĕçhárì'áh the first-born, Jĕdiä-ĕl the second, Zĕbádì'áh the third, Játh'nĭ-ĕl the fourth, 3 Ēlám the fifth, Jĕhō'hánän the sixth, Ēl'ĭĕ-hò-ē'naī the seventh. 4And Ō'bĕd-ē'dóm had sons: Shĕmāi'áh the first-born, Jĕhō'zàbăd the second, Jōäh the third, Sáçhar the fourth, Nĕthăn'ĕl the fifth, 5Ăm'mĭ-ĕl the sixth, Ĭs'sáçhar the seventh, Pĕ-ùl'lĕthaī the eighth; for God blessed him. 6Also to his son Shĕmāi'áh were sons born who were rulers in their fathers' houses, for they were men of great ability. 7 The sons of Shĕmái'áh: Othnì, Rĕph'ä-ĕl, Ōbĕd, and Ēlzá'bád, whose brethren were able men, Ēlì'hū and Sĕmáçhī'-áh. 8All these were of the sons of Ō'bĕd-ē'dóm with their sons and brethren, able men qualified for the service; sixty-two of Obed-edom. 9And Mĕshĕlĕmì'áh had sons and brethren, able men, eighteen. 10And Hōṣáh, of the sons of Mĕrar'ĭ, had sons: Shĭmrī the chief (for though he was not the first-born, his father made him chief), 11 Hĭlkì'áh the second, Tĕbálì'áh the third, Zĕçhárì'áh the fourth: all the sons and brethren of Hōṣáh were thirteen.

12 These divisions of the gatekeepers, corresponding to their chief men, had duties, just as their brethren did, ministering in the house of the LORD; 13 and they cast lots by fathers' houses, small and great alike, for their gates. 14 The lot for the east fell to Shĕl-ĕmì'áh. They cast lots also for his son Zĕçhárì'áh, a shrewd counselor, and his lot came out for the north. 15 Ō'bĕd-ē'dóm's came out for the south, and to his sons was allotted the storehouse. 16 For Shŭppĭm and Hōṣáh it came out for the west, at the gate of Shăllĕçh'eth on the road that goes up. Watch corresponded to watch. 17 On the east there were six each day,*b* on the north four

b Gk: Heb *Levites*

25.16
ver 4

25.23
ver 4

25.25
ver 4

26.1
ver 19

26.4
1 Chr 15.18

26.10
1 Chr 16.38

26.12
ver 1

26.13
1 Chr 24.5, 31; 25.8

each day, on the south four each day, as well as two and two at the storehouse; 18 and for the parbar^c on the west there were four at the road and two at the parbar. 19 These were the divisions of the gatekeepers among the Kŏ'rähītes and the sons of Mérar'ī.

6. *The arrangements for the treasuries*

26.20
1 Chr 28.12

20 And of the Lēvītes, Ȧhī'jäh had charge of the treasuries of the house of God and the treasuries of the dedicated gifts. 21 The sons of Lådȧn, the sons of the Gėr'shŏnītes belonging to Ladan, the heads of the fathers' houses belonging to Ladan the Gėr'shŏnīte: Jėhī'ėlī.^d

22 The sons of Jėhī'ėlī, Zētham and Jōėl his brother, were in charge of the treasuries of the house of the LORD. 23 Of the Ȧm'-rȧmītes, the Ĭz'harītes, the Hē'brŏnītes, and the Ŭzzī'ėlītes—

26.24
1 Chr 23.16
26.25
1 Chr 23.18
26.26
2 Sam 8.11

24 and Shĕb'ūėl the son of Gérshóm, son of Moses, was chief officer in charge of the treasuries. 25 His brethren: from Ĕlīē'zėr were his son Rėhȧbī'ȧh, and his son Jėshāi'ȧh, and his son Jōrȧm, and his son Zĭchrī, and his son Shĕlō'möth. 26 This Shĕlō'möth and his brethren were in charge of all the treasuries of the dedicated gifts which David the king, and the heads of the fathers' houses, and the officers of the thousands and the hundreds, and the commanders of the army, had dedicated. 27 From spoil won in battles they dedicated gifts for the maintenance of the house of the LORD. 28 Also all that Samuel the seer, and Saul the son of Kĭsh, and Abner the son of Nĕr, and Jōäb the son of Zėru'jȧh had dedicated—all dedicated gifts were in the care of Shĕlō'möth^e and his brethren.

26.28
1 Sam 9.9

7. *The arrangements for officers and judges*

26.29
Neh 11.16;
1 Chr 23.4
26.30
1 Chr 27.17

29 Of the Ĭz'harītes, Chĕnȧnī'ȧh and his sons were appointed to outside duties for Israel, as officers and judges. 30 Of the Hē'-brŏnītes, Hȧshȧbī'ȧh and his brethren, one thousand seven hundred men of ability, had the oversight of Israel westward of the Jordan for all the work of the LORD and for the service of the king. 31 Of the Hē'brŏnītes, Jėrī'jȧh was chief of the Hebronites of whatever genealogy or fathers' houses. (In the fortieth year of David's reign search was made and men of great ability among them were found at Jāzėr in Gĭl'ėäd.) 32 King David appointed him and his brethren, two thousand seven hundred men of ability, heads of fathers' houses, to have the oversight of the Reu'-bĕnītes, the Gȧdītes, and the half-tribe of the Mȧnȧs'sītes for everything pertaining to God and for the affairs of the king.

26.31
1 Chr 23.19
26.32
2 Chr 19.11

I. *The appointment of the military and civil officials*

27 This is the list of the people of Israel, the heads of fathers' houses, the commanders of thousands and hundreds, and their officers who served the king in all matters concerning the divisions that came and went, month after month throughout the year, each division numbering twenty-four thousand:

27.2
2 Sam
23.8–30;
1 Chr
11.11–31

2 Jȧshō'bëam the son of Zȧb'dĭ-ėl was in charge of the first division in the first month; in his division were twenty-four thousand. 3 He was a descendant of Pērėz, and was chief of all the com-

---

c The meaning of the word *parbar* is unknown
d The Hebrew text of verse 21 is confused   e Heb *Shĕlō'mith*

manders of the army for the first month. 4 Dōdaī the Åhō'hīte*
was in charge of the division of the second month; in his division
were twenty-four thousand. 5 The third commander, for the third
month, was Bĕnāi'ăh, the son of Jĕhoi'ădă the priest, as chief; in
his division were twenty-four thousand. 6 This is the Bĕnāi'ăh
who was a mighty man of the thirty and in command of the thirty;
Ămmĭz'ăbăd his son was in charge of his division.* 7 Ås'ăhĕl the
brother of Jōăb was fourth, for the fourth month, and his son
Zĕbădī'ăh after him; in his division were twenty-four thousand.
8 The fifth commander, for the fifth month, was Shămhŭth, the
Ĭz'răhīte; in his division were twenty-four thousand. 9 Sixth, for
the sixth month, was Ira, the son of Ĭkkĕsh the Tĕkō'īte; in his
division were twenty-four thousand. 10 Seventh, for the seventh
month, was Hĕlĕz the Pĕl'ōnīte, of the sons of Ē'phrāĭm; in his
division were twenty-four thousand. 11 Eighth, for the eighth
month, was Sĭb'bĕcaī the Hū'shăthīte, of the Zĕr'ăhītes; in his
division were twenty-four thousand. 12 Ninth, for the ninth
month, was Ābī-ē'zĕr of Ăn'ăthōth, a Benjaminite; in his division
were twenty-four thousand. 13 Tenth, for the tenth month, was
Mā'hăraī of Nĕtō'phăh, of the Zĕr'ăhītes; in his division were
twenty-four thousand. 14 Eleventh, for the eleventh month, was
Bĕnāi'ăh of Pĭr'ăthōn, of the sons of Ē'phrāĭm; in his division
were twenty-four thousand. 15 Twelfth, for the twelfth month,
was Hĕldaī the Nĕtŏph'ăthīte, of Ŏth'nĭ-ĕl; in his division were
twenty-four thousand.

16 Over the tribes of Israel, for the Reu'bĕnītes Ĕlië'zĕr the son
of Zĭ'chrī was chief officer; for the Sĭm'ĕŏnītes, Shĕphătī'ăh the
son of Mā'ăcăh; 17 for Lĕvī, Hăshăbī'ăh the son of Kĕm'ūĕl;
for Aaron, Zādŏk; 18 for Judah, Ĕlī'hū, one of David's brothers;
for Ĭs'săchar, Ŏmrī the son of Michael; 19 for Zĕb'ŭlŭn, Ĭshmāī'ăh
the son of Ōbădī'ăh; for Năph'tălī, Jĕr'ĕmŏth the son of Ăz'rĭĕl;
20 for the Ē'phrāĭmītes, Hōshĕ'ă the son of Ăzăzī'ăh; for the half-
tribe of Mánăs'sĕh, Jōĕl the son of Pĕdāi'ăh; 21 for the half-tribe
of Mánăs'sĕh in Gĭl'ĕăd, Ĭddō the son of Zĕchărī'ăh; for Benjamin,
Jă-ă'sĭ-ĕl the son of Abner; 22 for Dan, Ăz'ărĕl the son of Jĕrō'-
hăm. These were the leaders of the tribes of Israel. 23 David did
not number those below twenty years of age, for the LORD had
promised to make Israel as many as the stars of heaven. 24 Jōăb
the son of Zĕru'iăh began to number, but did not finish; yet wrath
came upon Israel for this, and the number was not entered in the
chronicles of King David.

25 Over the king's treasuries was Ăzmā'vĕth the son of Ā'dĭ-ĕl;
and over the treasuries in the country, in the cities, in the villages
and in the towers, was Jonathan the son of Ŭzzī'ăh; 26 and over
those who did the work of the field for tilling the soil was Ĕzrī the
son of Chĕlŭb; 27 and over the vineyards was Shĭm'ĕ-ī the Rā'-
măthīte; and over the produce of the vineyards for the wine cellars
was Zăbdī the Shĭphmīte. 28 Over the olive and sycamore trees in
the Shĕphē'lăh was Bā'ăl-hā'năn the Gĕd'ĕrīte; and over the stores
of oil was Jō'ăsh. 29 Over the herds that pastured in Shăron was
Shĭtraī the Shăr'ōnīte; over the herds in the valleys was Shāphăt
the son of Ădlaī. 30 Over the camels was Ōbĭl the Ĭsh'măĕlīte; and
over the she-asses was Jĕhdeī'ăh the Mĕrō'nōthīte. Over the flocks

27.6
1 Chr
11.22ff
27.7
1 Chr 11.26

27.9
1 Chr 11.28
27.10
1 Chr 11.27
27.11
1 Chr 11.29
27.12
1 Chr 11.28
27.13
1 Chr 11.30
27.14
1 Chr 11.31

27.22
1 Chr 28.1
27.23
Gen 15.5
27.24
2 Sam 24.15;
1 Chr 21.7

27.28
1 Ki 10.27;
2 Chr 1.15

---

f Gk: Heb *Ahohite and his division and Mĭklŏth the chief officer*
g Gk Vg: Heb *was his division*

was Jāzĭz the Hăgrīte. ³¹All these were stewards of King David's property.

32 Jonathan, David's uncle, was a counselor, being a man of understanding and a scribe; he and Jėhī'ĕl the son of Hăçh'mónī attended the king's sons. ³³Ăhīth'óphĕl was the king's counselor, and Hūshaī the Arçhīte was the king's friend. ³⁴Ăhīth'óphĕl was succeeded by Jėhoi'ádȧ the son of Bėnāi'áh, and Ȧbī'áthȧr. Jŏȧb was commander of the king's army.

J. David's last words and death

1. The people instructed to assist Solomon

28 David assembled at Jerusalem all the officials of Israel, the officials of the tribes, the officers of the divisions that served the king, the commanders of thousands, the commanders of hundreds, the stewards of all the property and cattle of the king and his sons, together with the palace officials, the mighty men, and all the seasoned warriors. 2 Then King David rose to his feet and said: "Hear me, my brethren and my people. I had it in my heart to build a house of rest for the ark of the covenant of the LORD, and for the footstool of our God; and I made preparations for building. 3 But God said to me, 'You may not build a house for my name, for you are a warrior and have shed blood.' 4 Yet the LORD God of Israel chose me from all my father's house to be king over Israel for ever; for he chose Judah as leader, and in the house of Judah my father's house, and among my father's sons he took pleasure in me to make me king over all Israel. ⁵And of all my sons (for the LORD has given me many sons) he has chosen Solomon my son to sit upon the throne of the kingdom of the LORD over Israel. 6 He said to me, 'It is Solomon your son who shall build my house and my courts, for I have chosen him to be my son, and I will be his father. 7 I will establish his kingdom for ever if he continues resolute in keeping my commandments and my ordinances, as he is today.' 8 Now therefore in the sight of all Israel, the assembly of the LORD, and in the hearing of our God, observe and seek out all the commandments of the LORD your God; that you may possess this good land, and leave it for an inheritance to your children after you for ever.

2. David's instructions to Solomon

9 "And you, Solomon my son, know the God of your father, and serve him with a whole heart and with a willing mind; for the LORD searches all hearts, and understands every plan and thought. If you seek him, he will be found by you; but if you forsake him, he will cast you off for ever. 10 Take heed now, for the LORD has chosen you to build a house for the sanctuary; be strong, and do it."

11 Then David gave Solomon his son the plan of the vestibule of the temple, and of its houses, its treasuries, its upper rooms, and its inner chambers, and of the room for the mercy seat; 12 and the plan of all that he had in mind for the courts of the house of the LORD, all the surrounding chambers, the treasuries of the house of God, and the treasuries for dedicated gifts; 13 for the divisions of the priests and of the Lēvītes, and all the work of the service in the house of the LORD; for all the vessels for the service in the house of

27.33
2 Sam
15.12,
32,37
27.34
1 Ki 1.7;
1 Chr 11.6

28.1
1 Chr 27.1–
31;
11.10–47

28.2
2 Sam 7.2;
1 Chr
17.1,2;
Ps 132.7
28.3
2 Sam
7.5,13;
1 Chr 22.8
28.4
1 Sam
16.6–13;
1 Chr
17.23,
27; 5.2;
Gen 49.8–
10
28.5
1 Chr
3.1–9;
22.9,10
28.6
2 Sam
7.13,14;
1 Chr 22.9,
10
28.7
1 Chr 22.13

28.9
Jer 9.24;
1 Chr
29.17–19;
1 Sam 16.7;
2 Chr 15.2;
Jer 29.13
28.10
1 Chr 22.13
28.11
ver 12,19;
Ex 25.40
28.12
1 Chr 26.20

28.13
1 Chr 24.1;
23.6

the LORD, 14 the weight of gold for all golden vessels for each service, the weight of silver vessels for each service, 15 the weight of the golden lampstands and their lamps, the weight of gold for each lampstand and its lamps, the weight of silver for a lampstand and its lamps, according to the use of each lampstand in the service, 16 the weight of gold for each table for the showbread, the silver for the silver tables, 17 and pure gold for the forks, the basins, and the cups; for the golden bowls and the weight of each; for the silver bowls and the weight of each; 18 for the altar of incense made of refined gold, and its weight; also his plan for the golden chariot of the cherubim that spread their wings and covered the ark of the covenant of the LORD. 19All this he made clear by the writing from the hand of the LORD concerning it,ʰ all the work to be done according to the plan.

20 Then David said to Solomon his son, "Be strong and of good courage, and do it. Fear not, be not dismayed; for the LORD God, even my God, is with you. He will not fail you or forsake you, until all the work for the service of the house of the LORD is finished. 21And behold the divisions of the priests and the Lēvītes for all the service of the house of God; and with you in all the work will be every willing man who has skill for any kind of service; also the officers and all the people will be wholly at your command."

3. David invites the people to give

29 And David the king said to all the assembly, "Solomon my son, whom alone God has chosen, is young and inexperienced, and the work is great; for the palace will not be for man but for the LORD God. 2 So I have provided for the house of my God, so far as I was able, the gold for the things of gold, the silver for the things of silver, and the bronze for the things of bronze, the iron for the things of iron, and wood for the things of wood, besides great quantities of onyx and stones for setting, antimony, colored stones, all sorts of precious stones, and marble. 3 Moreover, in addition to all that I have provided for the holy house, I have a treasure of my own of gold and silver, and because of my devotion to the house of my God I give it to the house of my God: 4 three thousand talents of gold, of the gold of Ōphĭr, and seven thousand talents of refined silver, for overlaying the walls of the house, 5 and for all the work to be done by craftsmen, gold for the things of gold and silver for the things of silver. Who then will offer willingly, consecrating himself today to the LORD?"

6 Then the heads of fathers' houses made their freewill offerings, as did also the leaders of the tribes, the commanders of thousands and of hundreds, and the officers over the king's work. 7 They gave for the service of the house of God five thousand talents and ten thousand darics of gold, ten thousand talents of silver, eighteen thousand talents of bronze, and a hundred thousand talents of iron. 8And whoever had precious stones gave them to the treasury of the house of the LORD, in the care of Jĕhī'ĕl

ʰ Cn: Heb upon me

Margin refs: 28.15 Ex 25.31–39; 28.18 Ex 30.1–10; 25.18–22; 28.19 ver 11,12; 28.20 Josh 1.6,7,9; 1 Chr 22.13; Josh 1.5; 28.21 ver 13; Ex 35.25–35; 36.1,2; 29.1 1 Chr 22.5; ver 19; 29.2 1 Chr 22.3–5; 29.4 1 Chr 22.14; 1 Ki 9.28; 29.6 1 Chr 27.1; 28.1; 27.25ff; ★29.7 Ezra 2.69; Neh 7.70; 29.8 1 Chr 26.21

29.7 darics. The Chronicler has indicated the amount of the freewill offering to David by enumerating part of the gold in terms of darics, Persian coins used in his day.

29.9
1 Ki 8.61;
2 Cor 9.7
the Gĕr′shŏnīte. 9 Then the people rejoiced because these had given willingly, for with a whole heart they had offered freely to the LORD; David the king also rejoiced greatly.

4. David's prayer

10 Therefore David blessed the LORD in the presence of all the assembly; and David said: "Blessed art thou, O LORD, the God of Israel our father, for ever and ever. 11 Thine, O LORD, is the greatness, and the power, and the glory, and the victory, and the majesty; for all that is in the heavens and in the earth is thine; thine is the kingdom, O LORD, and thou art exalted as head above all. 12 Both riches and honor come from thee, and thou rulest over all. In thy hand are power and might; and in thy hand it is to make great and to give strength to all. 13And now we thank thee, our God, and praise thy glorious name.

14 "But who am I, and what is my people, that we should be able thus to offer willingly? For all things come from thee, and of thy own have we given thee. 15 For we are strangers before thee, and sojourners, as all our fathers were; our days on the earth are like a shadow, and there is no abiding.[i] 16 O LORD our God, all this abundance that we have provided for building thee a house for thy holy name comes from thy hand and is all thy own. 17 I know, my God, that thou triest the heart, and hast pleasure in uprightness; in the uprightness of my heart I have freely offered all these things, and now I have seen thy people, who are present here, offering freely and joyously to thee. 18 O LORD, the God of Abraham, Isaac, and Israel, our fathers, keep for ever such purposes and thoughts in the hearts of thy people, and direct their hearts toward thee. 19 Grant to Solomon my son that with a whole heart he may keep thy commandments, thy testimonies, and thy statutes, performing all, and that he may build the palace for which I have made provision."

20 Then David said to all the assembly, "Bless the LORD your God." And all the assembly blessed the LORD, the God of their fathers, and bowed their heads, and worshiped the LORD, and did obeisance to the king. 21And they performed sacrifices to the LORD, and on the next day offered burnt offerings to the LORD, a thousand bulls, a thousand rams, and a thousand lambs, with their drink offerings, and sacrifices in abundance for all Israel; 22 and they ate and drank before the LORD on that day with great gladness.

5. Solomon made king

And they made Solomon the son of David king the second time, and they anointed him as prince for the LORD, and Zādŏk as priest. 23 Then Solomon sat on the throne of the LORD as king instead of David his father; and he prospered, and all Israel obeyed him. 24All the leaders and the mighty men, and also all the

29.11
Mt 6.13;
1 Tim 1.17;
Rev 5.13

29.12
2 Chr 1.12;
Rom 11.36

*29.14

29.15
Lev 25.23;
Ps 39.12;
Heb 11.13;
1 Pet 2.11;
Job 14.2

29.17
1 Chr 28.9;
Prov 11.20

29.19
1 Chr 28.9;
Ps 72.1;
ver 2;
1 Chr 22.14

29.21
1 Ki 8.62,63

29.22
1 Chr 23.1;
1 Ki
1.33–39

i Gk Vg: Heb hope

29.14 David recognized that God is the source of all wealth and the giver of every good gift. Anything we give to God is simply a rendering back of what He has entrusted to us. In that sense any gifts we bring to Him indicate that we are but stewards of the remainder, which is loaned to us for the balance of our earthly existence.

sons of King David, pledged their allegiance to King Solomon.
²⁵And the LORD gave Solomon great repute in the sight of all
Israel, and bestowed upon him such royal majesty as had not been
on any king before him in Israel.

6. *The death of David*

26 Thus David the son of Jĕssë reigned over all Israel. ²⁷ The
time that he reigned over Israel was forty years; he reigned seven
years in Hĕbròn, and thirty-three years in Jerusalem. ²⁸ Then
he died in a good old age, full of days, riches, and honor; and
Solomon his son reigned in his stead. ²⁹ Now the acts of King
David, from first to last, are written in the Chronicles of Samuel
the seer, and in the Chronicles of Nathan the prophet, and in the
Chronicles of Găd the seer, ³⁰ with accounts of all his rule and his
might and of the circumstances that came upon him and upon
Israel, and upon all the kingdoms of the countries.

29.25
2 Chr 1.1,
12;
1 Ki 3.13

29.26
1 Chr 18.14
29.27
2 Sam
5.4,5;
1 Ki 2.11
29.28
Gen 15.15;
25.8;
1 Chr 23.1
29.30
Dan 2.21;
4.23,25

INTRODUCTION TO
THE SECOND BOOK OF THE
CHRONICLES

Authorship and Background: See 1 Chronicles

Characteristics: The Chronicler's selection of events from history for his purpose, which was begun with the reign of David, is continued through the reign of his son. All references to the idolatry and punishment of Solomon are omitted (whereas they may be found in 1 Kings). But Rehoboam and his successors are evaluated according to a definite standard. A good king is approved if he keeps the law of God, destroys the Asherim, removes the places of idolatrous Baal worship, and refrains from making alliances with other powers, Israel included. Evil kings, and even good kings who make a false move, have to reckon sooner or later with a prophet or man of God: king Rehoboam is confronted by Shemaiah the prophet (12.5); good king Asa by Hanani the seer (16.7); good king Jehoshaphat by Jehu the son of Hanani (19.2) and Eliezer (20.37); Jehoram by a letter from Elijah (21.12); Joash by Zechariah the priest (24.20); Amaziah by a man of God (25.7) and a prophet (25.15); good king Uzziah by Azariah the priest (26.17); Manasseh by the LORD (33.10) and a number of seers (33.18); Zedekiah by Jeremiah the prophet (36.12).

The normal pattern of the Chronicler is to summarize the reigns of the evil kings as quickly as possible, pausing only to point out their sins, and to go into some detail about the reigns of the good kings. The religious reforms of Asa, Jehoshaphat, Hezekiah, and Josiah are described quite fully and it is in these sections that much of the material unique to Chronicles appears.

Contents:

I.   The reign of Solomon. 1.1—9.31: Solomon succeeds to the throne. He builds the Temple: preparations for building, selection of the site, the dimensions, and the furniture. The dedication of the Temple: bringing in the treasures and the ark; Solomon's address and prayer; God's confirmation of the dedication. Solomon's prosperity and fame: his house, victories, sacrifices, the visit of the Queen of Sheba; his wealth and wisdom; his death.

II.   The history of Judah from Solomon's death to the captivity. 10.1— 36.23: The division of the kingdom—Israel and Judah. The apostasy under Rehoboam and Abijah: Rehoboam's wicked life; his defeat by Shishak of Egypt; his death and the succession of Abijah; Abijah's war with Jeroboam. Reform period under Asa and Jehoshaphat: Asa's victory over Zerah of Egypt; the attempt at reform; the war with Baasha of Israel; Asa's wickedness and death; Jehoshaphat's early reforms; his prosperity; his alliance with Ahab; the reproof of Jehu;

Jehoshaphat's later reforms; his victories over his enemies; his alliance
with Ahaziah. Apostasy under Jehoram (Joram), Ahaziah, and Athaliah. The reformation under Joash: the restoration of the Temple; his
backsliding; his defeat by the Syrians; his death. Apostasy under Amaziah, Uzziah, Jotham, and Ahaz: Amaziah's victory over the Edomites, his idolatry, war with Jehoash and his death. Uzziah's godly
beginning, his sin and punishment by leprosy, the co-regency of
Jotham his son; Jotham's godly heart, his wars and periods of peace,
his death and successor; Ahaz's idolatry, his military defeats by the
Syrians, Israelites, Edomites, and Assyrians; his death and successor.
The reformation under Hezekiah: his godly start; the cleansing and
reconsecration of the Temple; celebration of the Passover; destruction
of the heathen altars; his deliverance from Sennacherib; his sickness
and new lease on life; his last years and death. The period of apostasy
under Manasseh and Amon: Manasseh's ungodly life, his captivity in
Babylon, his death, and successor; Amon's short and wicked reign. The
reformation under Josiah: his good start; the recovery of the Book of the
Law; the celebration of the Passover; his struggle with Neco. The final
years of apostasy: Jehoahaz's vassalage to Neco; his captivity in
Egypt; Jehoiakim's wickedness and captivity in Babylon; Jehoiachin's
wickedness and captivity in Babylon; Zedekiah's ungodliness, rebellion
against Nebuchadnezzar; the capture and destruction of Jerusalem
and the Temple. The proclamation of Cyrus allowing the Jews to
return to Jerusalem and to rebuild the Temple.

THE SECOND BOOK OF THE

CHRONICLES

I. The reign of Solomon 1.1–9.31

A. The wisdom and wealth of Solomon

1.1
1 Ki 2.12, 46;
Gen 39.2;
1 Chr 29.25

1.2
1 Chr 28.1

*1.3ff
1 Ki 3.4;
Ex 36.8

1.4
2 Sam 6.2, 17;
1 Chr 15.1

1.5
Ex 38.1,2

1.6
1 Ki 3.4

1.7
1 Ki 3.5,6

1.8
1 Chr 28.5

1.9
1 Ki 3.7,8

1.10
1 Ki 3.9

1.11
1 Ki 3.11–13

1.12
1 Chr 29.25;
2 Chr 9.22

*1.14ff
1 Ki 4.26;
10.26–29;
2 Chr 9.25

1.15
1 Ki 10.27;
2 Chr 9.27

*1.16
1 Ki 10.28, 29;
2 Chr 9.28

1 Solomon the son of David established himself in his kingdom, and the LORD his God was with him and made him exceedingly great.

2 Solomon spoke to all Israel, to the commanders of thousands and of hundreds, to the judges, and to all the leaders in all Israel, the heads of fathers' houses. 3And Solomon, and all the assembly with him, went to the high place that was at Gib'ëon; for the tent of meeting of God, which Moses the servant of the LORD had made in the wilderness, was there. 4 (But David had brought up the ark of God from Kir'iăth-jē'árïm to the place that David had prepared for it, for he had pitched a tent for it in Jerusalem.) 5 Moreover the bronze altar that Bĕz'álĕl the son of Ūrī, son of Hûr, had made, was there before the tabernacle of the LORD. And Solomon and the assembly sought the LORD. 6And Solomon went up there to the bronze altar before the LORD, which was at the tent of meeting, and offered a thousand burnt offerings upon it.

7 In that night God appeared to Solomon, and said to him, "Ask what I shall give you." 8And Solomon said to God, "Thou hast shown great and steadfast love to David my father, and hast made me king in his stead. 9 O LORD God, let thy promise to David my father be now fulfilled, for thou hast made me king over a people as many as the dust of the earth. 10 Give me now wisdom and knowledge to go out and come in before this people, for who can rule this thy people, that is so great?" 11 God answered Solomon, "Because this was in your heart, and you have not asked possessions, wealth, honor, or the life of those who hate you, and have not even asked long life, but have asked wisdom and knowledge for yourself that you may rule my people over whom I have made you king, 12 wisdom and knowledge are granted to you. I will also give you riches, possessions, and honor, such as none of the kings had who were before you, and none after you shall have the like." 13 So Solomon came from^a the high place at Gib'ëon, from before the tent of meeting, to Jerusalem. And he reigned over Israel.

14 Solomon gathered together chariots and horsemen; he had fourteen hundred chariots and twelve thousand horsemen, whom he stationed in the chariot cities and with the king in Jerusalem. 15And the king made silver and gold as common in Jerusalem as stone, and he made cedar as plentiful as the sycamore of the Shĕphē'láh. 16And Solomon's import of horses was from Egypt

^{a} Gk Vg: Heb to

1.3–6 Apparently the Chronicler knew of the regulation in Deut 12.13, 14 which prohibited burnt offerings except in Jerusalem. Therefore he explained why Solomon offered a thousand burnt offerings at Gibeon; the tent of meeting (tabernacle) and bronze altar were there.
1.14–17 Of Solomon's multiplying of horses, silver, and gold, see note to 1 Ki 11.3.
1.16 *Kue*. Cilicia in Asia Minor.

and Kū'ĕ, and the king's traders received them from Kue for a price. 17 They imported a chariot from Egypt for six hundred shekels of silver, and a horse for a hundred and fifty; likewise through them these were exported to all the kings of the Hittītes and the kings of Syria.

B. The building of the Temple

1. The preparations for building

2 [b] Now Solomon purposed to build a temple for the name of the LORD, and a royal palace for himself. 2c And Solomon assigned seventy thousand men to bear burdens and eighty thousand to quarry in the hill country, and three thousand six hundred to oversee them. 3And Solomon sent word to Hūrăm the king of Tyre: "As you dealt with David my father and sent him cedar to build himself a house to dwell in, so deal with me. 4 Behold, I am about to build a house for the name of the LORD my God and dedicate it to him for the burning of incense of sweet spices before him, and for the continual offering of the showbread, and for burnt offerings morning and evening, on the sabbaths and the new moons and the appointed feasts of the LORD our God, as ordained for ever for Israel. 5 The house which I am to build will be great, for our God is greater than all gods. 6 But who is able to build him a house, since heaven, even highest heaven, cannot contain him? Who am I to build a house for him, except as a place to burn incense before him? 7 So now send me a man skilled to work in gold, silver, bronze, and iron, and in purple, crimson, and blue fabrics, trained also in engraving, to be with the skilled workers who are with me in Judah and Jerusalem, whom David my father provided. 8 Send me also cedar, cypress, and algum timber from Lebanon, for I know that your servants know how to cut timber in Lebanon. And my servants will be with your servants, 9 to prepare timber for me in abundance, for the house I am to build will be great and wonderful. 10 I will give for your servants, the hewers who cut timber, twenty thousand cors of crushed wheat, twenty thousand cors of barley, twenty thousand baths of wine, and twenty thousand baths of oil."

11 Then Hūrăm the king of Tyre answered in a letter which he sent to Solomon, "Because the LORD loves his people he has made you king over them." 12 Hūrăm also said, "Blessed be the LORD God of Israel, who made heaven and earth, who has given King

*2.1
1 Ki 5.5
2.2
ver 18;
1 Ki 5.15,
16
2.3
1 Ki 5.2–
11;
1 Chr 14.1
2.4
ver 1;
Ex 30.7;
25.30;
Num 28.9,
10
2.5
1 Chr 16.25;
Ps 135.5
2.6
1 Ki 8.27;
2 Chr 6.18
2.7
ver 13,14;
1 Chr 22.15
2.8
2 Chr 9.10,
11
2.10
1 Ki 5.11
2.11
1 Ki 10.9;
2 Chr 9.8
2.12
1 Ki 5.7;
Ps 33.6;
102.25

[b] Ch 1.18 in Heb   [c] Ch 2.1 in Heb

2.1 Israel had three major places of worship during its long history. The first was the tabernacle in the wilderness; the second was the Temple built by Solomon; the third was the second Temple built after the captivity. This latter Temple was much renovated and adorned by Herod the Great over a forty-six-year period (Jn 2.20). David had originally hoped to build the first temple himself, but was forbidden to do so by God (1 Chr 22.8). He did, however, collect costly and choice materials from which his son would be able to construct it (1 Chr 22.2–5, 14–16; 29.2–5). Solomon was seven years in completing the Temple (1 Ki 6.38) and employed thirty thousand Israelites in the work (1 Ki 5.13, 14). The Temple was referred to variously as *the house of the God of Jacob* (Isa 2.3), *Mount Zion* (Ps 74.2), and *Zion* (Ps 84.1–7). When Solomon dedicated it, fire came down from heaven upon its altar and the shekinah cloud of glory filled it (2 Chr 7.2, 3; 1 Ki 8.10, 11; 2 Chr 5.13). The destruction of the Temple by invaders was clearly predicted (Mic 3.12; Jer 26.18), and this prophecy was fulfilled by the Chaldeans under Nebuchadnezzar (2 Ki 25.9, 13–17; 2 Chr 36.18, 19).

David a wise son, endued with discretion and understanding, who will build a temple for the LORD, and a royal palace for himself.

*2.14
1 Ki 7.13,14

13 "Now I have sent a skilled man, endued with understanding, Hūrăm′ăbī, 14 the son of a woman of the daughters of Dan, and his father was a man of Tȳre. He is trained to work in gold, silver, bronze, iron, stone, and wood, and in purple, blue, and crimson fabrics and fine linen, and to do all sorts of engraving and execute any design that may be assigned him, with your craftsmen,

2.15
ver 10

the craftsmen of my lord, David your father. 15 Now therefore the wheat and barley, oil and wine, of which my lord has spoken, let

2.16
1 Ki 5.8,9

him send to his servants; 16 and we will cut whatever timber you need from Lebanon, and bring it to you in rafts by sea to Jŏppă, so that you may take it up to Jerusalem."

2.17
1 Chr 22.2

17 Then Solomon took a census of all the aliens who were in the land of Israel, after the census of them which David his father had taken; and there were found a hundred and fifty-three thousand six hundred. 18 Seventy thousand of them he assigned to bear

2.18
ver 2

burdens, eighty thousand to quarry in the hill country, and three thousand six hundred as overseers to make the people work.

2. The construction of the Temple

a. The site, dimensions, and materials

3.1
1 Ki 6.1ff;
1 Chr 21.18

3 Then Solomon began to build the house of the LORD in Jerusalem on Mount Mòrī′áh, where the LORD had appeared to David his father, at the place that David had appointed, on the threshing floor of Ornàn the Jĕb′ūsīte. 2 He began to build in the second month of the fourth year of his reign. 3 These are Solomon's measurements d for building the house of God: the length, in cubits of the old standard, was sixty cubits, and the breadth twenty cubits. 4 The vestibule in front of the nave of the house was twenty cubits long, equal to the width of the house;e and its height was a hundred and twenty cubits. He overlaid it on the

3.5
1 Ki 6.17

inside with pure gold. 5 The nave he lined with cypress, and covered it with fine gold, and made palms and chains on it. 6 He adorned the house with settings of precious stones. The gold was

3.7
1 Ki 6.20–
22,29–35

gold of Parvā′ĭm. 7 So he lined the house with gold—its beams, its thresholds, its walls, and its doors; and he carved cherubim on the walls.

3.8
1 Ki 6.16

8 And he made the most holy place; its length, corresponding to the breadth of the house, was twenty cubits, and its breadth was twenty cubits; he overlaid it with six hundred talents of fine gold. 9 The weight of the nails was one shekelf to fifty shekels of gold. And he overlaid the upper chambers with gold.

3.10
1 Ki 6.23–
28

10 In the most holy place he made two cherubim of woodg and overlaidh them with gold. 11 The wings of the cherubim together extended twenty cubits: one wing of the one, of five cubits, touched the wall of the house, and its other wing, of five cubits, touched the wing of the other cherub; 12 and of this cherub, one wing, of five cubits, touched the wall of the house, and the other wing, also

---

d Syr: Heb foundations   e 1 Kings 6.3: Heb uncertain
f Compare Gk: Heb lacks one shekel   g Gk: Heb uncertain   h Heb they overlaid

---

2.14 In 1 Ki 7.14 Hiram (the Huramabi of this verse) is said to have been the son of a   widow of the tribe of Naphtali. He was an artist and an architect.

of five cubits, was joined to the wing of the first cherub. 13 The wings of these cherubim extended twenty cubits; the cherubim[i] stood on their feet, facing the nave. 14And he made the veil of blue and purple and crimson fabrics and fine linen, and worked cherubim on it.

3.14
Ex 26.31;
Heb 9.3

15 In front of the house he made two pillars thirty-five cubits high, with a capital of five cubits on the top of each. 16 He made chains like a necklace[j] and put them on the tops of the pillars; and he made a hundred pomegranates, and put them on the chains. 17 He set up the pillars in front of the temple, one on the south, the other on the north; that on the south he called Jāchĭn, and that on the north Bōăz.

*3.15
1 Ki 7.15–20

3.17
1 Ki 7.21

b. *The furnishings of the Temple*

4 He made an altar of bronze, twenty cubits long, and twenty cubits wide, and ten cubits high. 2 Then he made the molten sea; it was round, ten cubits from brim to brim, and five cubits high, and a line of thirty cubits measured its circumference. 3 Under it were figures of gourds,[k] for thirty[l] cubits, compassing the sea round about; the gourds[k] were in two rows, cast with it when it was cast. 4 It stood upon twelve oxen, three facing north, three facing west, three facing south, and three facing east; the sea was set upon them, and all their hinder parts were inward. 5 Its thickness was a handbreadth; and its brim was made like the brim of a cup, like the flower of a lily; it held over three thousand baths. 6 He also made ten lavers in which to wash, and set five on the south side, and five on the north side. In these they were to rinse off what was used for the burnt offering, and the sea was for the priests to wash in.

4.1
Ex 27.1,2;
2 Ki 16.14
4.2
1 Ki 7.23
4.3
1 Ki 7.24–26

*4.5
1 Ki 7.26

4.6
1 Ki 7.38

7 And he made ten golden lampstands as prescribed, and set them in the temple, five on the south side and five on the north. 8 He also made ten tables, and placed them in the temple, five on the south side and five on the north. And he made a hundred basins of gold. 9 He made the court of the priests, and the great court, and doors for the court, and overlaid their doors with bronze; 10 and he set the sea at the southeast corner of the house.

4.7
1 Ki 7.49;
Ex 25.31,40
4.8
1 Ki 7.48
4.9
1 Ki 6.36;
2 Ki 21.5
4.10
1 Ki 7.39

11 Hūrăm also made the pots, the shovels, and the basins. So Huram finished the work that he did for King Solomon on the house of God: 12 the two pillars, the bowls, and the two capitals on the top of the pillars; and the two networks to cover the two bowls of the capitals that were on the top of the pillars; 13 and the four hundred pomegranates for the two networks, two rows of pomegranates for each network, to cover the two bowls of the capitals that were upon the pillars. 14 He made the stands also, and the lavers upon the stands, 15 and the one sea, and the twelve oxen underneath it. 16 The pots, the shovels, the forks, and all the equipment for these Hūrăm′-ăbī made of burnished bronze for King Solomon for the house of the LORD. 17 In the plain of the Jordan the king cast them, in the clay ground between Sŭccŏth and Zĕr′ĕdăh. 18 Solomon made all these things in great quantities, so that the weight of the bronze was not ascertained.

4.11
1 Ki 7.40
4.12
1 Ki 7.41
4.13
1 Ki 7.20

4.14
1 Ki 7.27

4.16
1 Ki 7.14

4.17
1 Ki 7.46
4.18
1 Ki 7.47

---

i Heb *they*   *j* Cn: Heb *in the inner sanctuary*
k 1 Kings 7.24: Heb *oxen*   *l* Compare verse 2: Heb *ten*

3.15 *thirty-five cubits high.* See 1 Ki 7.15.   **4.5** *three thousand.* See note to 1 Ki 7.26.

4.19
1 Ki 7.48–
50;
Ex 25.30
4.20
Ex 25.31–37

19 So Solomon made all the things that were in the house of God: the golden altar, the tables for the bread of the Presence, 20 the lampstands and their lamps of pure gold to burn before the inner sanctuary, as prescribed; 21 the flowers, the lamps, and the tongs, of purest gold; 22 the snuffers, basins, dishes for incense, and firepans, of pure gold; and the sockets*m* of the temple, for the inner doors to the most holy place and for the doors of the nave of the temple were of gold.

5.1
1 Ki 7.51

5 Thus all the work that Solomon did for the house of the LORD was finished. And Solomon brought in the things which David his father had dedicated, and stored the silver, the gold, and all the vessels in the treasuries of the house of God.

C. The dedication of the Temple

1. The bringing of the ark to the Temple

5.2
1 Ki 8.1–9;
2 Sam 6.12

2 Then Solomon assembled the elders of Israel and all the heads of the tribes, the leaders of the fathers' houses of the people of Israel, in Jerusalem, to bring up the ark of the covenant of the LORD out of the city of David, which is Zion. 3And all the men of Israel assembled before the king at the feast which is in the seventh month. 4And all the elders of Israel came, and the Lēvītes took up the ark. 5And they brought up the ark, the tent of meeting, and all the holy vessels that were in the tent; the priests and the Lēvītes brought them up. 6And King Solomon and all the congregation of Israel, who had assembled before him, were before the ark, sacrificing so many sheep and oxen that they could not be counted or numbered. 7 So the priests brought the ark of the covenant of the LORD to its place, in the inner sanctuary of the house, in the most holy place, underneath the wings of the cherubim. 8 For the cherubim spread out their wings over the place of the ark, so that the cherubim made a covering above the ark and its poles. 9And the poles were so long that the ends of the poles were seen from the holy place before the inner sanctuary; but they could not be seen from outside; and they are there to this day. 10 There was nothing in the ark except the two tables which Moses put there at Horĕb, where the LORD made a covenant with the people of Israel, when they came out of Egypt. 11 Now when the priests came out of the holy place (for all the priests who were present had sanctified themselves, without regard to their divisions; 12 and all the Lēvīt′ícăl singers, Āsăph, Hēmăn, and Jĕdu′thŭn, their sons and kinsmen, arrayed in fine linen, with cymbals, harps, and lyres, stood east of the altar with a hundred and twenty priests who were trumpeters; 13 and it was the duty of the trumpeters and singers to make themselves heard in unison in praise and thanksgiving to the LORD), and when the song was raised, with trumpets and cymbals and other musical instruments, in praise to the LORD,

5.4
ver 7
★5.9
1 Ki 8.8,9
5.10
Deut 10.2–
5;
Heb 9.4
5.11
1 Chr
24.1–5
5.12
1 Chr
25.1–4;
15.24
5.13
2 Chr 7.3;
1 Chr
16.34,
42

"For he is good,
    for his steadfast love endures for ever,"

m 1 Kings 7.50: Heb *the door of the house*

5.9 *to this day.* The poles were not in the Temple at the time of the Chronicler because they were destroyed in 586 B.C. This verse was probably taken from a source compiled by the writer of Kings, thus, *this day* refers to the time of that compilation.

the house, the house of the LORD, was filled with a cloud, 14 so that the priests could not stand to minister because of the cloud; for the glory of the LORD filled the house of God.

2. *The address by Solomon*

6 Then Solomon said,
"The LORD has said that he would dwell in thick darkness.
2 I have built thee an exalted house,
a place for thee to dwell in for ever."

3 Then the king faced about, and blessed all the assembly of Israel, while all the assembly of Israel stood. 4 And he said, "Blessed be the LORD, the God of Israel, who with his hand has fulfilled what he promised with his mouth to David my father, saying, 5 'Since the day that I brought my people out of the land of Egypt, I chose no city in all the tribes of Israel in which to build a house, that my name might be there, and I chose no man as prince over my people Israel; 6 but I have chosen Jerusalem that my name may be there and I have chosen David to be over my people Israel.' 7 Now it was in the heart of David my father to build a house for the name of the LORD, the God of Israel. 8 But the LORD said to David my father, 'Whereas it was in your heart to build a house for my name, you did well that it was in your heart; 9 nevertheless you shall not build the house, but your son who shall be born to you shall build the house for my name.' 10 Now the LORD has fulfilled his promise which he made; for I have risen in the place of David my father, and sit on the throne of Israel, as the LORD promised, and I have built the house for the name of the LORD, the God of Israel. 11 And there I have set the ark, in which is the covenant of the LORD which he made with the people of Israel."

3. *Solomon's prayer of dedication*

12 Then Solomon stood before the altar of the LORD in the presence of all the assembly of Israel, and spread forth his hands. 13 Solomon had made a bronze platform five cubits long, five cubits wide, and three cubits high, and had set it in the court; and he stood upon it. Then he knelt upon his knees in the presence of all the assembly of Israel, and spread forth his hands toward heaven; 14 and said, "O LORD, God of Israel, there is no God like thee, in heaven or on earth, keeping covenant and showing steadfast love to thy servants who walk before thee with all their heart; 15 who hast kept with thy servant David my father what thou didst declare to him; yea, thou didst speak with thy mouth, and with thy hand hast fulfilled it this day. 16 Now therefore, O LORD, God of Israel, keep with thy servant David my father what thou hast promised him, saying, 'There shall never fail you a man before me to sit upon the throne of Israel, if only your sons take heed to their way, to walk in my law as you have walked before me.' 17 Now therefore, O LORD, God of Israel, let thy word be confirmed, which thou hast spoken to thy servant David.

18 "But will God dwell indeed with man on the earth? Behold, heaven and the highest heaven cannot contain thee; how much less this house which I have built! 19 Yet have regard to the prayer of thy servant and to his supplication, O LORD my God, hearkening to the cry and to the prayer which thy servant prays before

5.14
1 Ki 8.11;
2 Chr 7.2

6.1
1 Ki 8.12–
50

6.6
2 Chr
12.13;
1 Chr 28.4
6.7
1 Chr 28.2

6.11
2 Chr 5.10

6.12
1 Ki 8.22

6.13
1 Ki 8.54

6.14
Ex 15.11;
Deut 7.9

6.15
1 Chr 22.9,
10
6.16
2 Sam
7.12,16;
1 Ki 2.4;
2 Chr 7.18

6.18
2 Chr 2.6

thee; 20 that thy eyes may be open day and night toward this house, the place where thou hast promised to set thy name, that thou mayest hearken to the prayer which thy servant offers toward this place. 21And hearken thou to the supplications of thy servant and of thy people Israel, when they pray toward this place; yea, hear thou from heaven thy dwelling place; and when thou hearest, forgive.

6.21
Mic 7.18

22 "If a man sins against his neighbor and is made to take an oath, and comes and swears his oath before thy altar in this house, 23 then hear thou from heaven, and act, and judge thy servants, requiting the guilty by bringing his conduct upon his own head, and vindicating the righteous by rewarding him according to his righteousness.

6.22
Mt 5.33

24 "If thy people Israel are defeated before the enemy because they have sinned against thee, when they turn again and acknowledge thy name, and pray and make supplication to thee in this house, 25 then hear thou from heaven, and forgive the sin of thy people Israel, and bring them again to the land which thou gavest to them and to their fathers.

6.24
2 Chr 7.14

26 "When heaven is shut up and there is no rain because they have sinned against thee, if they pray toward this place, and acknowledge thy name, and turn from their sin, when thou dost afflict them, 27 then hear thou in heaven, and forgive the sin of thy servants, thy people Israel, when thou dost teach them the good way[n] in which they should walk; and grant rain upon thy land, which thou hast given to thy people as an inheritance.

6.26
1 Ki 17.1

28 "If there is famine in the land, if there is pestilence or blight or mildew or locust or caterpillar; if their enemies besiege them in any of their cities; whatever plague, whatever sickness there is; 29 whatever prayer, whatever supplication is made by any man or by all thy people Israel, each knowing his own affliction, and his own sorrow and stretching out his hands toward this house; 30 then hear thou from heaven thy dwelling place, and forgive, and render to each whose heart thou knowest, according to all his ways (for thou, thou only, knowest the hearts of the children of men); 31 that they may fear thee and walk in thy ways all the days that they live in the land which thou gavest to our fathers.

6.28
2 Chr 20.9

6.30
1 Sam 16.7;
1 Chr 28.9

32 "Likewise when a foreigner, who is not of thy people Israel, comes from a far country for the sake of thy great name, and thy mighty hand, and thy outstretched arm, when he comes and prays toward this house, 33 hear thou from heaven thy dwelling place, and do according to all for which the foreigner calls to thee; in order that all the peoples of the earth may know thy name and fear thee, as do thy people Israel, and that they may know that this house which I have built is called by thy name.

6.32
Josh 12.20;
Acts 8.27

6.33
2 Chr 7.14

34 "If thy people go out to battle against their enemies, by whatever way thou shalt send them, and they pray to thee toward this city which thou hast chosen and the house which I have built for thy name, 35 then hear thou from heaven their prayer and their supplication, and maintain their cause.

36 "If they sin against thee—for there is no man who does not sin—and thou art angry with them, and dost give them to an enemy, so that they are carried away captive to a land far or near; 37 yet if they lay it to heart in the land to which they have been

6.36
Job 15.14–
16;
Jas 3.2;
1 Jn 1.8–10

6.37
2 Chr 7.14

n Gk Syr Vg: Heb *toward the good way*

carried captive, and repent, and make supplication to thee in the land of their captivity, saying, 'We have sinned, and have acted perversely and wickedly'; 38 if they repent with all their mind and with all their heart in the land of their captivity, to which they were carried captive, and pray toward their land, which thou gavest to their fathers, the city which thou hast chosen, and the house which I have built for thy name, 39 then hear thou from heaven thy dwelling place their prayer and their supplications, and maintain their cause and forgive thy people who have sinned against thee. 40 Now, O my God, let thy eyes be open and thy ears attentive to a prayer of this place.

41 "And now arise, O Lord God, and go to thy resting place,
    thou and the ark of thy might.
Let thy priests, O Lord God, be clothed with salvation,
    and let thy saints rejoice in thy goodness.
42 O Lord God, do not turn away the face of thy anointed one!
    Remember thy steadfast love for David thy servant."

4. God's answer to Solomon's prayer
a. Fire from heaven

7 When Solomon had ended his prayer, fire came down from heaven and consumed the burnt offering and the sacrifices, and the glory of the Lord filled the temple. 2And the priests could not enter the house of the Lord, because the glory of the Lord filled the Lord's house. 3 When all the children of Israel saw the fire come down and the glory of the Lord upon the temple, they bowed down with their faces to the earth on the pavement, and worshiped and gave thanks to the Lord, saying,
"For he is good,
    for his steadfast love endures for ever."

4 Then the king and all the people offered sacrifice before the Lord. 5 King Solomon offered as a sacrifice twenty-two thousand oxen and a hundred and twenty thousand sheep. So the king and all the people dedicated the house of God. 6 The priests stood at their posts; the Levites also, with the instruments for music to the Lord which King David had made for giving thanks to the Lord —for his steadfast love endures for ever—whenever David offered praises by their ministry; opposite them the priests sounded trumpets; and all Israel stood.

7 And Solomon consecrated the middle of the court that was before the house of the Lord; for there he offered the burnt offering and the fat of the peace offerings, because the bronze altar Solomon had made could not hold the burnt offering and the cereal offering and the fat.

8 At that time Solomon held the feast for seven days, and all Israel with him, a very great congregation, from the entrance of Hāmāth to the Brook of Egypt. 9And on the eighth day they held a solemn assembly; for they had kept the dedication of the altar seven days and the feast seven days. 10 On the twenty-third day of the seventh month he sent the people away to their homes, joyful and glad of heart for the goodness that the Lord had shown to David and to Solomon and to Israel his people.

6.40
2 Chr 7.15;
Ps 17.1

6.41
Ps 132.8–
10;
1 Chr 28.2

*7.1
1 Ki 8.54;
18.24,38;
2 Chr
5.13,14

7.2
Deut 12.5,
11

7.3
2 Chr 5.13;
Ps 136.1;
1 Chr 16.41

7.4
1 Ki 8.62,
63

*7.5

7.6
1 Chr
15.16–21;
2 Chr 5.12

7.7
1 Ki 8.64–
66

7.8
1 Ki 8.65

7.9
Lev 23.36

7.10
1 Ki 8.66

7.1 The *glory* did not fill Ezra's temple.   **7.5** *sacrifice*, see note to 1 Ki 8.63.

b. God's appearance and promise

7.11
1 Ki 9.1–9

11 Thus Solomon finished the house of the LORD and the king's house; all that Solomon had planned to do in the house of the LORD and in his own house he successfully accomplished. 12 Then the LORD appeared to Solomon in the night and said to him: "I have heard your prayer, and have chosen this place for myself as a house of sacrifice. 13 When I shut up the heavens so that there is no rain, or command the locust to devour the land, or send pestilence among my people, 14 if my people who are called by my name humble themselves, and pray and seek my face, and turn from their wicked ways, then I will hear from heaven, and will forgive their sin and heal their land. 15 Now my eyes will be open and my ears attentive to the prayer that is made in this place. 16 For now I have chosen and consecrated this house that my name may be there for ever; my eyes and my heart will be there for all time. 17 And as for you, if you walk before me, as David your father walked, doing according to all that I have commanded you and keeping my statutes and my ordinances, 18 then I will establish your royal throne, as I covenanted with David your father, saying, 'There shall not fail you a man to rule Israel.'

7.13
2 Chr
6.26–28
7.14
2 Chr 6.27,
30,37–39
7.15
2 Chr 6.40
7.16
1 Ki 9.3;
2 Chr 6.6;
ver 12
7.17
1 Ki 9.4ff
7.18
2 Chr 6.16

c. God's warning against disobedience

7.19
Lev 26.14,
33;
Deut 28.15
7.20
Deut 29.28
7.21
Deut 29.24

19 "But if you° turn aside and forsake my statutes and my commandments which I have set before you, and go and serve other gods and worship them, 20 then I will pluck you▫ up from the land which I have given you;▫ and this house, which I have consecrated for my name, I will cast out of my sight, and will make it a proverb and a byword among all peoples. 21 And at this house, which is exalted, every one passing by will be astonished, and say, 'Why has the LORD done thus to this land and to this house?' 22 Then they will say, 'Because they forsook the LORD the God of their fathers who brought them out of the land of Egypt, and laid hold on other gods, and worshiped them and served them; therefore he has brought all this evil upon them.'"

D. Solomon's prosperity and fame

1. His buildings, cities, and victories

8.1
1 Ki 9.1–28
*8.2

8 At the end of twenty years, in which Solomon had built the house of the LORD and his own house, 2 Solomon rebuilt the cities which Hūrăm had given to him, and settled the people of Israel in them.

*8.4

3 And Solomon went to Hā′măth-zō′băh, and took it. 4 He built Tădmor in the wilderness and all the store-cities which he built in Hāmăth. 5 He also built Upper Bĕth-hŏr′ŏn and Lower Beth-horon, fortified cities with walls, gates, and bars, 6 and Bā′-ălăth, and all the store-cities that Solomon had, and all the cities for his chariots, and the cities for his horsemen, and whatever

8.5
1 Chr 7.24;
2 Chr 14.7

○ The word you is plural here   ▫ Heb them

8.2 See note to 1 Ki 9.11 where Solomon gives twenty cities to Hiram.

8.4 Tadmor, another name for the oasis Palmyra in the Syrian desert, would hardly

have been under the jurisdiction of Solomon. The correct name was Tamar (as in 1 Ki 9.18), a caravan station in the wilderness southwest of the Dead Sea.

Solomon desired to build in Jerusalem, in Lebanon, and in all the
land of his dominion. 7All the people who were left of the Hĭttītes,
the Ăm′ŏrītes, the Pĕr′izzītes, the Hīvītes, and the Jĕb′ūsītes, who
were not of Israel, 8 from their descendants who were left after
them in the land, whom the people of Israel had not destroyed—
these Solomon made a forced levy and so they are to this day.
9 But of the people of Israel Solomon made no slaves for his work;
they were soldiers, and his officers, the commanders of his chariots,
and his horsemen. 10And these were the chief officers of King
Solomon, two hundred and fifty, who exercised authority over
the people.

2. The house of his Egyptian wife

11 Solomon brought Pharaoh′s daughter up from the city of
David to the house which he had built for her, for he said, "My
wife shall not live in the house of David king of Israel, for the
places to which the ark of the LORD has come are holy."

3. The sacrifices

12 Then Solomon offered up burnt offerings to the LORD upon
the altar of the LORD which he had built before the vestibule, 13 as
the duty of each day required, offering according to the commandment of Moses for the sabbaths, the new moons, and the three
annual feasts—the feast of unleavened bread, the feast of weeks,
and the feast of tabernacles. 14According to the ordinance of David
his father, he appointed the divisions of the priests for their
service, and the Lēvītes for their offices of praise and ministry
before the priests as the duty of each day required, and the gatekeepers in their divisions for the several gates; for so David the
man of God had commanded. 15And they did not turn aside from
what the king had commanded the priests and Lēvītes concerning
any matter and concerning the treasuries.

16 Thus was accomplished all the work of Solomon from*q* the
day the foundation of the house of the LORD was laid until it was
finished. So the house of the LORD was completed.

17 Then Solomon went to Ēz′ĭŏn-gē′bĕr and Ēlŏth on the shore
of the sea, in the land of Ēdŏm. 18And Hūrăm sent him by his
servants ships and servants familiar with the sea, and they went
to Ōphĭr together with the servants of Solomon, and fetched from
there four hundred and fifty talents of gold and brought it to
King Solomon.

4. The visit of the Queen of Sheba

9 Now when the queen of Shēbā heard of the fame of Solomon
she came to Jerusalem to test him with hard questions, having
a very great retinue and camels bearing spices and very much gold
and precious stones. When she came to Solomon, she told him all
that was on her mind. 2And Solomon answered all her questions;
there was nothing hidden from Solomon which he could not explain to her. 3And when the queen of Shēbā had seen the wisdom
of Solomon, the house that he had built, 4 the food of his table,

q Gk Syr Vg: Heb *to*

8.8
1 Ki 4.6;
9.21

8.11
1 Ki 3.1;
7.8

8.12
2 Chr 4.1
8.13
Ex 29.38;
Num 28.3;
Ex 23.14–17
8.14
1 Chr 24.1;
25.1; 26.1;
Neh 12.24,
36

*8.17
1 Ki 9.26
8.18
1 Ki 9.27;
2 Chr
9.10,13

*9.1
1 Ki 10.1–
13;
Mt 12.42;
Lk 11.31

9.3
1 Ki 5.12

the seating of his officials, and the attendance of his servants, and their clothing, his cupbearers, and their clothing, and his burnt offerings which he offered at the house of the LORD, there was no more spirit in her.

9.5
1 Ki 10.6

5 And she said to the king, "The report was true which I heard in my own land of your affairs and of your wisdom, 6 but I did not believe the*r* reports until I came and my own eyes had seen it; and behold, half the greatness of your wisdom was not told me; you surpass the report which I heard. 7 Happy are your wives!*s* Happy are these your servants, who continually stand before you and hear your wisdom! 8 Blessed be the LORD your God, who has delighted in you and set you on his throne as king for the LORD your God!

9.8
1 Chr 28.5;
29.23;
2 Chr 2.11

Because your God loved Israel and would establish them for ever, he has made you king over them, that you may execute justice and righteousness." 9 Then she gave the king a hundred and twenty talents of gold, and a very great quantity of spices, and precious stones: there were no spices such as those which the queen of Shēbá gave to King Solomon.

9.9
1 Ki 10.10

10 Moreover the servants of Hūrám and the servants of Solomon, who brought gold from Ōphĭr, brought algum wood and precious stones. 11And the king made of the algum wood steps*t* for the house of the LORD and for the king's house, lyres also and harps for the singers; there never was seen the like of them before in the land of Judah.

9.10
2 Chr 8.18

12 And King Solomon gave to the queen of Shēbá all that she desired, whatever she asked besides what she had brought to the king. So she turned and went back to her own land, with her servants.

5. The wealth and wisdom of Solomon

9.13
1 Ki 10.14–
28

13 Now the weight of gold that came to Solomon in one year was six hundred and sixty-six talents of gold, 14 besides that which the traders and merchants brought; and all the kings of Arabia and the governors of the land brought gold and silver to Solomon. 15 King Solomon made two hundred large shields of beaten gold; six hundred shekels of beaten gold went into each shield. 16And he made three hundred shields of beaten gold; three hundred shekels of gold went into each shield; and the king put them in the House of the Forest of Lebanon. 17 The king also made a great ivory throne, and overlaid it with pure gold. 18 The throne had six steps and a footstool of gold, which were attached to the throne, and on each side of the seat were arm rests and two lions standing beside the arm rests, 19 while twelve lions stood there, one on each end of a step on the six steps. The like of it was never made in any kingdom. 20All King Solomon's drinking vessels were of gold, and all the vessels of the House of the Forest of Lebanon were of pure gold; silver was not considered as anything in the days of Solomon. 21 For the king's ships went to Tarshish with the servants of Hūrám; once every three years the ships of Tarshish used to come bringing gold, silver, ivory, apes, and peacocks.*x*

9.18
1 Ki 10.18

9.19
1 Ki 10.20

9.21
2 Chr
20.36,37

22 Thus King Solomon excelled all the kings of the earth in riches and in wisdom. 23And all the kings of the earth sought the

9.22
2 Chr 1.12;
1 Ki 3.13

r Heb *their*   *s* Gk Compare 1 Kings 10.8: Heb *men*
t Gk Vg: The meaning of the Hebrew word is uncertain   *x* Or *baboons*

presence of Solomon to hear his wisdom, which God had put into his mind. 24 Every one of them brought his present, articles of silver and of gold, garments, myrrh, spices, horses, and mules, so much year by year. 25And Solomon had four thousand stalls for horses and chariots, and twelve thousand horsemen, whom he stationed in the chariot cities and with the king in Jerusalem. 26And he ruled over all the kings from the Eūphrā′tēṣ to the land of the Philĭs′tīneṣ, and to the border of Egypt. 27And the king made silver as common in Jerusalem as stone, and cedar as plentiful as the sycamore of the Shĕphē′lăh. 28And horses were imported for Solomon from Egypt and from all lands.

6. Solomon's death and the succession

29 Now the rest of the acts of Solomon, from first to last, are they not written in the history of Nathan the prophet, and in the prophecy of Ăhī′jăh the Shī′lŏnīte, and in the visions of Ĭddō the seer concerning Jĕrŏbō′ăm the son of Nĕbăt? 30 Solomon reigned in Jerusalem over all Israel forty years. 31And Solomon slept with his fathers, and was buried in the city of David his father; and Rĕhŏbō′ăm his son reigned in his stead.

II. The history of Judah from Solomon's death to the captivity 10.1–36.23

A. The division of the kingdom

1. Rehoboam's ill-chosen words to the ten tribes

10 Rĕhŏbō′ăm went to Shĕçhĕm, for all Israel had come to Shechem to make him king. 2And when Jĕrŏbō′ăm the son of Nĕbăt heard of it (for he was in Egypt, whither he had fled from King Solomon), then Jeroboam returned from Egypt. 3And they sent and called him; and Jĕrŏbō′ăm and all Israel came and said to Rĕhŏbō′ăm, 4 "Your father made our yoke heavy. Now therefore lighten the hard service of your father and his heavy yoke upon us, and we will serve you." 5 He said to them, "Come to me again in three days." So the people went away.

6 Then King Rĕhŏbō′ăm took counsel with the old men, who had stood before Solomon his father while he was yet alive, saying, "How do you advise me to answer this people?" 7And they said to him, "If you will be kind to this people and please them, and speak good words to them, then they will be your servants for ever." 8 But he forsook the counsel which the old men gave him, and took counsel with the young men who had grown up with him and stood before him. 9And he said to them, "What do you advise that we answer this people who have said to me, 'Lighten the yoke that your father put upon us'?" 10And the young men who had grown up with him said to him, "Thus shall you speak to the people who said to you, 'Your father made our yoke heavy, but do you lighten it for us'; thus shall you say to them, 'My little finger is thicker than my father's loins. 11And now, whereas my father laid upon you a heavy yoke, I will add to your yoke. My

*9.25
1 Ki 4.26;
10.26;
2 Chr 1.14
9.26
1 Ki 4.21;
Ps 72.8
9.27
1 Ki 10.27;
2 Chr 1.15
*9.28
1 Ki 10.28;
2 Chr 1.16

9.29
1 Ki 11.41;
1 Chr 29.29
9.30
1 Ki 11.42, 43
9.31
1 Ki 2.10

10.1
1 Ki 12.1–20
10.2
1 Ki 11.40

10.6
1 Ki 12.6

10.9
1 Ki 12.9

9.25 1 Ki 4.26 says *forty thousand stalls.* There is a copyist's error in one or the other.   9.28 Chronologically, the material contained in 1 Ki 11.1–40 fits here.

father chastised you with whips, but I will chastise you with scorpions.' "

2. *The revolt of the ten tribes*

*10.12
ver 5

12 So Jĕróbō'ám and all the people came to Rĕhŏbō'ám the third day, as the king said, "Come to me again the third day." 13And the king answered them harshly, and forsaking the counsel of the old men, 14 King Rĕhŏbō'ám spoke to them according to the counsel of the young men, saying, "My father made your yoke heavy, but I will add to it; my father chastised you with whips, but I will chastise you with scorpions." 15 So the king did not hearken to the people; for it was a turn of affairs brought about by God that the LORD might fulfil his word, which he spoke by Ăhī'jäh the Shī'lŏnīte to Jĕróbō'ám the son of Nēbăt.

10.15
1 Ki 12.15,
24;
2 Chr
25.16–20;
1 Ki 11.29

16 And when all Israel saw that the king did not hearken to them, the people answered the king,

10.16
2 Sam 20.1;
ver 19

"What portion have we in David?
    We have no inheritance in the son of Jĕssë.
Each of you to your tents, O Israel!
Look now to your own house, David."

So all Israel departed to their tents. 17 But Rĕhŏbō'ám reigned over the people of Israel who dwelt in the cities of Judah. 18 Then King Rĕhŏbō'ám sent Hădŏr'ám, who was taskmaster over the forced labor, and the people of Israel stoned him to death with stones. And King Rehoboam made haste to mount his chariot, to flee to Jerusalem. 19 So Israel has been in rebellion against the house of David to this day.

10.19
1 Ki 12.19

3. *The LORD forbids Judah to war against Israel*

11.1
1 Ki 12.21–
24

11 When Rĕhŏbō'ám came to Jerusalem, he assembled the house of Judah, and Benjamin, a hundred and eighty thousand chosen warriors, to fight against Israel, to restore the kingdom to Rehoboam. 2 But the word of the LORD came to Shĕmāi'ăh the man of God: 3 "Say to Rĕhŏbō'ám the son of Solomon king of Judah, and to all Israel in Judah and Benjamin, 4 'Thus says the LORD, You shall not go up or fight against your brethren. Return every man to his home, for this thing is from me.' " So they hearkened to the word of the LORD, and returned and did not go against Jĕróbō'ám.

11.2
2 Chr 12.15

11.4
2 Chr 10.15

4. *Rehoboam erects fortresses*

5 Rĕhŏbō'ám dwelt in Jerusalem, and he built cities for defense in Judah. 6 He built Bĕth'lĕhĕm, Ētăm, Tĕkō'å, 7 Beth-zŭr, Sōcō, Ădŭl'lăm, 8 Găth, Mărĕ'shăh, Zĭph, 9Ădŏrā'ĭm, Lăchĭsh, Ăzē'kăh, 10 Zŏrăh, Āi'jălŏn, and Hē'brŏn, fortified cities which are in Judah and in Benjamin. 11 He made the fortresses strong, and put commanders in them, and stores of food, oil, and wine. 12And he put shields and spears in all the cities, and made them very strong. So he held Judah and Benjamin.

10.12 Following the death of Solomon, his kingdom was broken up into two divisions: Israel (Northern Kingdom) and Judah (Southern Kingdom). Jeroboam founded the Northern Kingdom. Calf-worship and Baal worship characterized the religion of his people. Approximately two hundred years later the Northern Kingdom was destroyed by Assyria. During this period of two hundred years, there was not a single good king on the throne of Israel, although Judah was blessed by several godly rulers in the Davidic line.

5. The Levites remain with Judah

13 And the priests and the Lēvītes that were in all Israel resorted to him from all places where they lived. 14 For the Lēvītes left their common lands and their holdings and came to Judah and Jerusalem, because Jĕrŏbŏ′ăm and his sons cast them out from serving as priests of the LORD, 15 and he appointed his own priests for the high places, and for the satyrs, and for the calves which he had made. 16And those who had set their hearts to seek the LORD God of Israel came after them from all the tribes of Israel to Jerusalem to sacrifice to the LORD, the God of their fathers. 17 They strengthened the kingdom of Judah, and for three years they made Rēhŏbŏ′ăm the son of Solomon secure, for they walked for three years in the way of David and Solomon.

6. The polygamy of Rehoboam

18 Rēhŏbŏ′ăm took as wife Mā′hălăth the daughter of Jĕr′-imŏth the son of David, and of Ăb′ĭhāil the daughter of Ĕlī′ăb the son of Jĕssë; 19 and she bore him sons, Jĕ′ŭsh, Shĕmărī′ăh, and Zāhăm. 20After her he took Mā′ăcăh the daughter of Ăb′-sălŏm, who bore him Ăbī′jăh, Ăttăī, Zīză, and Shĕlŏ′mĭth. 21 Rēhŏbŏ′ăm loved Mā′ăcăh the daughter of Ăb′sălŏm above all his wives and concubines (he took eighteen wives and sixty concubines, and had twenty-eight sons and sixty daughters); 22 and Rēhŏbŏ′ăm appointed Ăbī′jăh the son of Mā′ăcăh as chief prince among his brothers, for he intended to make him king. 23And he dealt wisely, and distributed some of his sons through all the districts of Judah and Benjamin, in all the fortified cities; and he gave them abundant provisions, and procured wives for them.ᵘ

7. Shishak defeats Rehoboam

12 When the rule of Rēhŏbŏ′ăm was established and was strong, he forsook the law of the LORD, and all Israel with him. 2 In the fifth year of King Rēhŏbŏ′ăm, because they had been unfaithful to the LORD, Shĭshăk king of Egypt came up against Jerusalem 3 with twelve hundred chariots and sixty thousand horsemen. And the people were without number who came with him from Egypt—Lĭbyăns, Sŭk′kĭ-ĭm, and Ethiopians. 4And he took the fortified cities of Judah and came as far as Jerusalem. 5 Then Shĕmăi′ăh the prophet came to Rēhŏbŏ′ăm and to the princes of Judah, who had gathered at Jerusalem because of Shĭshăk, and said to them, "Thus says the LORD, 'You abandoned me, so I have abandoned you to the hand of Shĭshăk.'" 6 Then the princes of Israel and the king humbled themselves and said, "The LORD is righteous." 7 When the LORD saw that they humbled themselves, the word of the LORD came to Shĕmăi′ăh: "They have humbled themselves; I will not destroy them, but I will grant them some deliverance, and my wrath shall not be poured out upon Jerusalem by the hand of Shĭshăk. 8 Nevertheless they shall

ᵘ Cn: Heb sought a multitude of wives

11.14
Num 35.2–5;
2 Chr 13.9

11.15
1 Ki 12.28–33; 13.33;
2 Chr 13.9

11.16
2 Chr 15.9

11.17
2 Chr 12.1

11.18
1 Sam 16.6

11.21
Deut 17.17

11.22
Deut 21.15–17

*12.1
2 Chr 11.17;
1 Ki 14.22–24

12.2
1 Ki 14.24, 25; 11.40

12.3
2 Chr 16.8

12.5
2 Chr 11.2; 15.2;
Deut 28.15

12.6
Ex 9.27;
Dan 9.14

12.7
1 Ki 21.29

12.8
Deut 28.47, 48

12.1 Rehoboam inherited the throne from his father Solomon. He was responsible for the division of the kingdom by his folly. He turned from the LORD and suffered judgment as a consequence (2 Chr 12.2). He was followed upon the throne by nineteen successors, some of whom were good and some evil. The Southern Kingdom lasted slightly over three hundred years, then it was destroyed by Babylon.

be servants to him, that they may know my service and the service
of the kingdoms of the countries.''

12.9
1 Ki 14.25,
26;
2 Chr 9.15,
16

9 So Shīshăk king of Egypt came up against Jerusalem; he took
away the treasures of the house of the LORD and the treasures of
the king's house; he took away everything. He also took away
the shields of gold which Solomon had made; 10 and King Rēhóbō'ám made in their stead shields of bronze, and committed
them to the hands of the officers of the guard, who kept the door
of the king's house. 11 And as often as the king went into the house
of the LORD, the guard came and bore them, and brought them

12.12
2 Chr 19.3

back to the guardroom. 12 And when he humbled himself the
wrath of the LORD turned from him, so as not to make a complete
destruction; moreover, conditions were good in Judah.

8. *Summary of Rehoboam's reign*

12.13
1 Ki 14.21;
2 Chr 6.6

13 So King Rēhóbō'ám established himself in Jerusalem and
reigned. Rehoboam was forty-one years old when he began to
reign, and he reigned seventeen years in Jerusalem, the city which
the LORD had chosen out of all the tribes of Israel to put his name

12.14
2 Chr 19.3

there. His mother's name was Nā'ámăh the Ămmónī'těss. 14 And
he did evil, for he did not set his heart to seek the LORD.

12.15
1 Ki 14.29,
30;
2 Chr 9.29

15 Now the acts of Rēhóbō'ám, from first to last, are they not
written in the chronicles of Shēmāi'áh the prophet and of Ĭddō the
seer?ᵛ There were continual wars between Rehoboam and Jĕróbō'-

12.16
1 Ki 14.31;
2 Chr 11.20

ám. 16 And Rēhóbō'ám slept with his fathers, and was buried in the
city of David; and Ăbī'jáh his son reigned in his stead.

B. *The reign of Abijah*

1. *War between Abijah and Jeroboam*

13.1
1 Ki 15.1,2
13.2
2 Chr
11.20;
1 Ki 15.7

13 In the eighteenth year of King Jĕróbō'ám Ăbī'jáh began to
reign over Judah. 2 He reigned for three years in Jerusalem.
His mother's name was Mĭcāi'áh the daughter of Ū'rĭèl of
Gĭb'ĕ-áh.

Now there was war between Ăbī'jáh and Jĕróbō'ám. 3 Ăbī'jáh
went out to battle having an army of valiant men of war, four hundred thousand picked men; and Jĕróbō'ám drew up his line of
battle against him with eight hundred thousand picked mighty

13.4
Josh 18.22

warriors. 4 Then Ăbī'jáh stood up on Mount Zĕmárā'ĭm which is
in the hill country of Ē'phrăim, and said, "Hear me, O Jĕróbō'ám

13.5
2 Sam 7.12,
13,16;
Num 18.19

and all Israel! 5 Ought you not to know that the LORD God of
Israel gave the kingship over Israel for ever to David and his sons
by a covenant of salt? 6 Yet Jĕróbō'ám the son of Nēbăt, a servant

13.6
1 Ki 11.26

of Solomon the son of David, rose up and rebelled against his lord;
7 and certain worthless scoundrels gathered about him and defied
Rēhóbō'ám the son of Solomon, when Rehoboam was young and
irresolute and could not withstand them.

13.8
1 Ki 12.28;
2 Chr 11.15

8 "And now you think to withstand the kingdom of the LORD
in the hand of the sons of David, because you are a great multitude
and have with you the golden calves which Jĕróbō'ám made you

13.9
2 Chr
11.14;
Ex 29.35;
Jer 2.11;
5.7

for gods. 9 Have you not driven out the priests of the LORD, the
sons of Aaron, and the Lēvītes, and made priests for yourselves
like the peoples of other lands? Whoever comes to consecrate

ᵛ Heb *seer, to enroll oneself*

himself with a young bull or seven rams becomes a priest of what are no gods. 10 But as for us, the Lord is our God, and we have not forsaken him. We have priests ministering to the Lord who are sons of Aaron, and Lēvītes for their service. 11 They offer to the Lord every morning and every evening burnt offerings and incense of sweet spices, set out the showbread on the table of pure gold, and care for the golden lampstand that its lamps may burn every evening; for we keep the charge of the Lord our God, but you have forsaken him. 12 Behold, God is with us at our head, and his priests with their battle trumpets to sound the call to battle against you. O sons of Israel, do not fight against the Lord, the God of your fathers; for you cannot succeed."

2. Defeat of Jeroboam

13 Jĕróbō'ám had sent an ambush around to come on them from behind; thus his troops*w* were in front of Judah, and the ambush was behind them. 14 And when Judah looked, behold, the battle was before and behind them; and they cried to the Lord, and the priests blew the trumpets. 15 Then the men of Judah raised the battle shout. And when the men of Judah shouted, God defeated Jĕróbō'ám and all Israel before Ábī'jáh and Judah. 16 The men of Israel fled before Judah, and God gave them into their hand. 17 Ábī'jáh and his people slew them with a great slaughter; so there fell slain of Israel five hundred thousand picked men. 18 Thus the men of Israel were subdued at that time, and the men of Judah prevailed, because they relied upon the Lord, the God of their fathers. 19 And Ábī'jáh pursued Jĕróbō'ám, and took cities from him, Bēthēl with its villages and Jéshā'náh with its villages and Ēphrŏn*x* with its villages. 20 Jĕróbō'ám did not recover his power in the days of Ábī'jáh; and the Lord smote him, and he died. 21 But Ábī'jáh grew mighty. And he took fourteen wives, and had twenty-two sons and sixteen daughters. 22 The rest of the acts of Ábī'jáh, his ways and his sayings, are written in the story of the prophet Ĭddō.

C. The reign of Asa

1. Faithful Asa blessed of God

14 *y* So Ábī'jáh slept with his fathers, and they buried him in the city of David; and Āsà his son reigned in his stead. In his days the land had rest for ten years. 2 *z* And Āsà did what was good and right in the eyes of the Lord his God. 3 He took away the foreign altars and the high places, and broke down the pillars and hewed down the Ashē'rĭm, 4 and commanded Judah to seek the Lord, the God of their fathers, and to keep the law and the commandment. 5 He also took out of all the cities of Judah the high places and the incense altars. And the kingdom had rest under him. 6 He built fortified cities in Judah, for the land had rest. He had no war in those years, for the Lord gave him peace. 7 And he said to Judah, "Let us build these cities, and surround them with walls and towers, gates and bars; the land is still ours, because we have sought the Lord our God; we have sought him, and he has given us peace on every side." So they built and prospered. 8 And Āsà had an army of three hundred thousand from Judah, armed

---

13.11
2 Chr 2.4;
Lev 24.5–9

13.12
Num 10.8, 9;
Acts 5.39

13.14
2 Chr 14.11

13.15
2 Chr 14.12

13.16
2 Chr 16.8

13.18
1 Chr 5.20;
2 Chr 14.11;
Ps 22.5

13.20
1 Sam 25.38;
1 Ki 14.20

13.22
2 Chr 12.15

14.1
1 Ki 15.8

14.3
Deut 7.5;
1 Ki 15.12–14;
Ex 34.13

14.5
2 Chr 34.4,7

14.6
2 Chr 15.15

---

w Heb *they*   *x* Another reading is *Ēphrāin*   *y* Ch 13.23 in Heb   *z* Ch 14.1 in Heb

with bucklers and spears, and two hundred and eighty thousand men from Benjamin, that carried shields and drew bows; all these were mighty men of valor.

2. Asa defeats Zerah of Ethiopia

*14.9
2 Chr 16.8;
11.8

9 Zērăh the Ethiopian came out against them with an army of a million men and three hundred chariots, and came as far as Mărē'shăh. 10And Āsă went out to meet him, and they drew up their lines of battle in the valley of Zĕph'ăthăh at Mărē'shăh.

14.11
2 Chr 13.14,
18;
1 Sam 14.6;
17.45

11And Āsă cried to the LORD his God, "O LORD, there is none like thee to help, between the mighty and the weak. Help us, O LORD our God, for we rely on thee, and in thy name we have come against this multitude. O LORD, thou art our God; let not man pre-

14.12
2 Chr 13.15
*14.13
Gen 10.19

vail against thee." 12 So the LORD defeated the Ethiopians before Asă and before Judah, and the Ethiopians fled. 13Asă and the people that were with him pursued them as far as Gērar, and the Ethiopians fell until none remained alive; for they were broken before the LORD and his army. The men of Judah*a* carried away

14.14
Gen 35.5;
2 Chr 17.10

very much booty. 14And they smote all the cities round about Gērar, for the fear of the LORD was upon them. They plundered all the cities, for there was much plunder in them. 15And they smote the tents of those who had cattle,*b* and carried away sheep in abundance and camels. Then they returned to Jerusalem.

3. Asa's reform movement

15.1
Num 24.2;
2 Chr
20.14;
24.20
15.2
Jas 4,8;
ver 4,15;
2 Chr 24.20
*15.3
Hos 3.4;
Lev 10.11;
2 Chr 17.9
15.4
Deut 4.29
15.5
Judg 5.6
15.6
Mt 24.7
15.7
Josh 1.7,9
15.8
2 Chr 13.19

15 The Spirit of God came upon Ăzărī'ăh the son of Ōdĕd, 2 and he went out to meet Āsă, and said to him, "Hear me, Asa, and all Judah and Benjamin: The LORD is with you, while you are with him. If you seek him, he will be found by you, but if you forsake him, he will forsake you. 3 For a long time Israel was without the true God, and without a teaching priest, and without law; 4 but when in their distress they turned to the LORD, the God of Israel, and sought him, he was found by them. 5 In those times there was no peace to him who went out or to him who came in, for great disturbances afflicted all the inhabitants of the lands. 6 They were broken in pieces, nation against nation and city against city, for God troubled them with every sort of distress. 7 But you, take courage! Do not let your hands be weak, for your work shall be rewarded."

8 When Āsă heard these words, the prophecy of Ăzărī'ăh the son of Ōdĕd,*c* he took courage, and put away the abominable idols from all the land of Judah and Benjamin and from the cities which he had taken in the hill country of Ē'phrăim, and he repaired the altar of the LORD that was in front of the vestibule of the house of

15.9
2 Chr 11.16

the LORD.*d* 9And he gathered all Judah and Benjamin, and those from Ē'phrăim, Mănăs'sĕh, and Sĭm'ĕŏn who were sojourning with them, for great numbers had deserted to him from Israel when they saw that the LORD his God was with him. 10 They were gathered at Jerusalem in the third month of the fifteenth year of

a Heb *they*   *b* Heb obscure   *c* Compare Syr Vg: Heb *the prophecy, Oded the prophet*
d Heb *the vestibule of the* LORD

14.9 *a million men* is a figure which is either hyperbole or a copyist's error.
14.13 *none remained alive.* The rout of the Ethiopians is pictured with this generalization.
15.3 Indicates how scarce written portions of the law were during much of Judah's history.

the reign of Āsá. 11 They sacrificed to the LORD on that day, from
the spoil which they had brought, seven hundred oxen and seven
thousand sheep. 12And they entered into a covenant to seek the
LORD, the God of their fathers, with all their heart and with all
their soul; 13 and that whoever would not seek the LORD, the God
of Israel, should be put to death, whether young or old, man or
woman. 14 They took oath to the LORD with a loud voice, and with
shouting, and with trumpets, and with horns. 15And all Judah
rejoiced over the oath; for they had sworn with all their heart, and
had sought him with their whole desire, and he was found by
them, and the LORD gave them rest round about.

16 Even Mā'acáh, his mother, King Āsá removed from being
queen mother because she had made an abominable image for
Ashē'ráh. Asa cut down her image, crushed it, and burned it at the
brook Kĭdrón. 17 But the high places were not taken out of Israel.
Nevertheless the heart of Āsá was blameless all his days. 18And
he brought into the house of God the votive gifts of his father and
his own votive gifts, silver, and gold, and vessels. 19And there was
no more war until the thirty-fifth year of the reign of Āsá.

4. Asa's sinful alliance with Ben-hadad

16 In the thirty-sixth year of the reign of Āsá, Bā'ásha king of
Israel went up against Judah, and built Rāmáh, that he might
permit no one to go out or come in to Asa king of Judah. 2 Then
Āsá took silver and gold from the treasures of the house of the
LORD and the king's house, and sent them to Bĕn-hā'dăd king of
Syria, who dwelt in Damascus, saying, 3 "Let there be a league
between me and you, as between my father and your father; behold, I am sending to you silver and gold; go, break your league
with Bā'ásha king of Israel, that he may withdraw from me." 4And
Bĕn-hā'dăd hearkened to King Āsá, and sent the commanders of
his armies against the cities of Israel, and they conquered Ĭjŏn,
Dan, Ā'bĕl-mā'ĭm, and all the store-cities of Năph'tálĭ. 5And when
Bā'ásha heard of it, he stopped building Rāmáh, and let his work
cease. 6 Then King Āsá took all Judah, and they carried away the
stones of Rāmáh and its timber, with which Bā'ásha had been
building, and with them he built Gēbá and Mĭzpáh.

5. Hanani pronounces God's judgment

7 At that time Hănā'nĭ the seer came to Āsá king of Judah, and
said to him, "Because you relied on the king of Syria, and did not
rely on the LORD your God, the army of the king of Syria has
escaped you. 8 Were not the Ethiopians and the Libyans a huge
army with exceedingly many chariots and horsemen? Yet because
you relied on the LORD, he gave them into your hand. 9 For the
eyes of the LORD run to and fro throughout the whole earth, to
show his might in behalf of those whose heart is blameless toward
him. You have done foolishly in this; for from now on you will
have wars." 10 Then Āsá was angry with the seer, and put him in
the stocks, in prison, for he was in a rage with him because of this.
And Asa inflicted cruelties upon some of the people at the same
time.

	15.11 2 Chr 14.13–15
	15.12 2 Chr 23.16; 34.31
	15.13 Ex 22.20; Deut 13.5, 9,15
	15.15 ver 2; 2 Chr 14.7
	*15.16 1 Ki 15.13– 15; Ex 34.13; 2 Chr 14.2–5
	16.1 1 Ki 15.17– 22
	*16.2
	16.4 1 Ki 15.18, 20
	16.7 2 Chr 19.2; 14.11; 32.7,8
	16.8 2 Chr 14.9; 12.3
	16.9 Prov 15.3; Zech 4.10; 1 Sam 13.13

15.16 *Asherah*, see note to Deut 12.3.   **16.2** *Ben-hadad*, see note to 1 Ki 15.18.

6. Asa's sickness and death

16.11
1 Ki 15.23
16.12
Jer 17.5

16.13
1 Ki 15.24
16.14
Gen 50.2;
Jn 19.39,40;
2 Chr 21.19;
Jer 34.5

11 The acts of Āsȧ, from first to last, are written in the Book of the Kings of Judah and Israel. 12 In the thirty-ninth year of his reign Āsȧ was diseased in his feet, and his disease became severe; yet even in his disease he did not seek the LORD, but sought help from physicians. 13And Āsȧ slept with his fathers, dying in the forty-first year of his reign. 14 They buried him in the tomb which he had hewn out for himself in the city of David. They laid him on a bier which had been filled with various kinds of spices prepared by the perfumer's art; and they made a very great fire in his honor.

D. The reign of Jehoshaphat

1. Godly Jehoshaphat

17.1
1 Ki 15.24
17.2
2 Chr 15.8

17.4
1 Ki 12.28

17.5
2 Chr 18.1
17.6
2 Chr 15.17

17 Jėhȯsh'ȧphȧt his son reigned in his stead, and strengthened himself against Israel. 2 He placed forces in all the fortified cities of Judah, and set garrisons in the land of Judah, and in the cities of Ē'phrȧim which Āsȧ his father had taken. 3 The LORD was with Jėhȯsh'ȧphȧt, because he walked in the earlier ways of his father;ᵉ he did not seek the Bāȧls, 4 but sought the God of his father and walked in his commandments, and not according to the ways of Israel. 5 Therefore the LORD established the kingdom in his hand; and all Judah brought tribute to Jėhȯsh'ȧphȧt; and he had great riches and honor. 6 His heart was courageous in the ways of the LORD; and furthermore he took the high places and the Àshē'rȉm out of Judah.

2. The Book of the Law taught

17.7
2 Chr 15.3

17.8
2 Chr 19.8

★17.9
Deut 6.4–9

7 In the third year of his reign he sent his princes, Bĕn-hāil, Ōbȧdī'ȧh, Zĕchȧrī'ȧh, Nėthȧn'ĕl, and Mȉcāi'ȧh, to teach in the cities of Judah; 8 and with them the Lēvītes, Shėmāi'ȧh, Nĕthȧnī'-ȧh, Zĕbȧdī'ȧh, Ȧs'ȧhĕl, Shėmȉr'ȧmȯth, Jėhȯn'ȧthȧn, Ȧdȯnī'jȧh, Tȯbī'jȧh, and Tŏb'ȧdȯnī'jȧh; and with these Levites, the priests Ēlī'shȧmȧ and Jėhȯ'rȧm. 9And they taught in Judah, having the book of the law of the LORD with them; they went about through all the cities of Judah and taught among the people.

3. Jehoshaphat's prosperity

17.10
2 Chr 14.14

17.11
2 Chr 9.14;
26.8

★17.14ff

10 And the fear of the LORD fell upon all the kingdoms of the lands that were round about Judah, and they made no war against Jėhȯsh'ȧphȧt. 11 Some of the Philis'tȉnes brought Jėhȯsh'ȧphȧt presents, and silver for tribute; and the Arabs also brought him seven thousand seven hundred rams and seven thousand seven hundred he-goats. 12And Jėhȯsh'ȧphȧt grew steadily greater. He built in Judah fortresses and store-cities, 13 and he had great stores in the cities of Judah. He had soldiers, mighty men of valor, in Jerusalem. 14 This was the muster of them by fathers' houses:

ᵉ Another reading is his father David

17.9 Jehoshaphat's reform, like all other reforms, was based essentially on the rediscovery and teaching of God's law. The priests were charged with the teaching ministry, but here they are aided considerably by the princes and the Levites.

17.14-19 Besides the soldiers stationed in fortified cities, the standing army of Jehoshaphat (drawn from Judah and Benjamin) totals 1,160,000. This is exactly double the 580,000 of Asa's army (14.8)—a very substantial increase in the few years following Asa's reign.

Of Judah, the commanders of thousands: Ădnáh the commander, with three hundred thousand mighty men of valor, 15 and next to him Jĕhō'hánăn the commander, with two hundred and eighty thousand, 16 and next to him Ămásī'áh the son of Zĭchrī, a volunteer for the service of the LORD, with two hundred thousand mighty men of valor. 17 Of Benjamin: Ĕlī'ádá, a mighty man of valor, with two hundred thousand men armed with bow and shield, 18 and next to him Jĕhō'zábăd with a hundred and eighty thousand armed for war. 19 These were in the service of the king, besides those whom the king had placed in the fortified cities throughout all Judah.

17.16
Judg 5.2,9;
1 Chr 29.9

4. Jehoshaphat's alliances with Ahab
a. Ahab's proposition

18 Now Jĕhŏsh'áphăt had great riches and honor; and he made a marriage alliance with Āhăb. 2After some years he went down to Āhăb in Sàmąr'ĭà. And Ahab killed an abundance of sheep and oxen for him and for the people who were with him, and induced him to go up against Rā'môth-gĭl'ĕăd. 3Āhăb king of Israel said to Jĕhŏsh'áphăt king of Judah, "Will you go with me to Rā'môth-gĭl'ĕăd?" He answered him, "I am as you are, my people as your people. We will be with you in the war."

18.1
2 Chr 17.5
18.2
1 Ki 22.2–35

b. The advice of the false prophets

4 And Jĕhŏsh'áphăt said to the king of Israel, "Inquire first for the word of the LORD." 5 Then the king of Israel gathered the prophets together, four hundred men, and said to them, "Shall we go to battle against Rā'môth-gĭl'ĕăd, or shall I forbear?" And they said, "Go up; for God will give it into the hand of the king." 6 But Jĕhŏsh'áphăt said, "Is there not here another prophet of the LORD of whom we may inquire?" 7And the king of Israel said to Jĕhŏsh'áphăt, "There is yet one man by whom we may inquire of the LORD, Mĭcāi'áh the son of Ĭmláh; but I hate him, for he never prophesies good concerning me, but always evil." And Jehoshaphat said, "Let not the king say so." 8 Then the king of Israel summoned an officer and said, "Bring quickly Mĭcāi'áh the son of Ĭmláh." 9 Now the king of Israel and Jĕhŏsh'áphăt the king of Judah were sitting on their thrones, arrayed in their robes; and they were sitting at the threshing floor at the entrance of the gate of Sàmąr'ĭà; and all the prophets were prophesying before them. 10And Zĕdĕkī'áh the son of Chĕnă'ánáh made for himself horns of iron, and said, "Thus says the LORD, 'With these you shall push the Syrians until they are destroyed.'" 11And all the prophets prophesied so, and said, "Go up to Rā'môth-gĭl'ĕăd and triumph; the LORD will give it into the hand of the king."

18.4
1 Sam 23.2,
4,9;
2 Sam 2.1

18.7
1 Ki 22.8

18.9
Ruth 4.1

18.11
2 Chr 22.5

c. Micaiah's true prophecy

12 And the messenger who went to summon Mĭcāi'áh said to him, "Behold, the words of the prophets with one accord are favorable to the king; let your word be like the word of one of them, and speak favorably." 13 But Mĭcāi'áh said, "As the LORD lives, what my God says, that I will speak." 14And when he had come to the king, the king said to him, "Mĭcāi'áh, shall we go to Rā'môth-gĭl'ĕăd to battle, or shall I forbear?" And he answered, "Go up and triumph; they will be given into your hand." 15 But

18.13
Num
22.18–20,35

2 Chronicles 18.16—19.2

636

the king said to him, "How many times shall I adjure you that you speak to me nothing but the truth in the name of the LORD?" ¹⁶And he said, "I saw all Israel scattered upon the mountains, as sheep that have no shepherd; and the LORD said, 'These have no master; let each return to his home in peace.'" ¹⁷And the king of Israel said to Jĕhŏsh′áphăt, "Did I not tell you that he would not prophesy good concerning me, but evil?" ¹⁸And Mĭcāi′áh said, "Therefore hear the word of the LORD: I saw the LORD sitting on his throne, and all the host of heaven standing on his right hand and on his left; ¹⁹ and the LORD said, 'Who will entice Āhăb the king of Israel, that he may go up and fall at Rā′mŏth-gĭl′ĕăd?' And one said one thing, and another said another. ²⁰ Then a spirit came forward and stood before the LORD, saying, 'I will entice him.' And the LORD said to him, 'By what means?' ²¹And he said, 'I will go forth, and will be a lying spirit in the mouth of all his prophets.' And he said, 'You are to entice him, and you shall succeed; go forth and do so.' ²² Now therefore behold, the LORD has put a lying spirit in the mouth of these your prophets; the LORD has spoken evil concerning you."

²³ Then Zĕdĕkī′áh the son of Ҫhĕnā′ánáh came near and struck Mĭcāi′áh on the cheek, and said, "Which way did the Spirit of the LORD go from me to speak to you?" ²⁴And Mĭcāi′áh said, "Behold, you shall see on that day when you go into an inner chamber to hide yourself." ²⁵And the king of Israel said, "Seize Mĭcāi′áh, and take him back to Āmŏn the governor of the city and to Jō′ăsh the king's son; ²⁶ and say, 'Thus says the king, Put this fellow in prison, and feed him with scant fare of bread and water, until I return in peace.'" ²⁷And Mĭcāi′áh said, "If you return in peace, the LORD has not spoken by me." And he said, "Hear, all you peoples!"

d. The defeat and death of Ahab

²⁸ So the king of Israel and Jĕhŏsh′áphăt the king of Judah went up to Rā′mŏth-gĭl′ĕăd. ²⁹And the king of Israel said to Jĕhŏsh′áphăt, "I will disguise myself and go into battle, but you wear your robes." And the king of Israel disguised himself; and they went into battle. ³⁰ Now the king of Syria had commanded the captains of his chariots, "Fight with neither small nor great, but only with the king of Israel." ³¹And when the captains of the chariots saw Jĕhŏsh′áphăt, they said, "It is the king of Israel." So they turned to fight against him; and Jehoshaphat cried out, and the LORD helped him. God drew them away from him, ³² for when the captains of the chariots saw that it was not the king of Israel, they turned back from pursuing him. ³³ But a certain man drew his bow at a venture, and struck the king of Israel between the scale armor and the breastplate; therefore he said to the driver of his chariot, "Turn about, and carry me out of the battle, for I am wounded." ³⁴And the battle grew hot that day, and the king of Israel propped himself up in his chariot facing the Syrians until evening; then at sunset he died.

e. Jehu reproves Jehoshaphat

19 Jĕhŏsh′áphăt the king of Judah returned in safety to his house in Jerusalem. ² But Jĕhū the son of Hánā′nī the seer went out to meet him, and said to King Jĕhŏsh′áphăt, "Should

18.16
Num 27.17;
Ezek 34.5–8

18.20
Job 1.6

18.22
Job 12.16;
Ezek 14.9

18.23
Jer 20.2;
Mk 14.65;
Acts 23.2

18.25
ver 8

18.26
2 Chr 16.10

18.27
Mic 1.9

18.31
2 Chr
13.14,
15

18.33
1 Ki 22.34

19.2
1 Ki 16.1;
Ps 139.21;
2 Chr 32.25

you help the wicked and love those who hate the LORD? Because of this, wrath has gone out against you from the LORD. 3 Nevertheless some good is found in you, for you destroyed the Ashē′rāhṣ out of the land, and have set your heart to seek God."

19.3
2 Chr 12.12, 14; 17.6; Ezra 7.10

5. *Additional reforms by Jehoshaphat*

4 Jĕhŏsh′ăphăt dwelt at Jerusalem; and he went out again among the people, from Bĕer-shē′bā to the hill country of Ē′phrāịm, and brought them back to the LORD, the God of their fathers. 5 He appointed judges in the land in all the fortified cities of Judah, city by city, 6 and said to the judges, "Consider what you do, for you judge not for man but for the LORD; he is with you in giving judgment. 7 Now then, let the fear of the LORD be upon you; take heed what you do, for there is no perversion of justice with the LORD our God, or partiality, or taking bribes."

19.4
2 Chr 15.8–13

19.6
Deut 1.17

19.7
Gen 18.25;
Deut 32,4;
10.17,18;
Rom 2.11;
Col 3.25

8 Moreover in Jerusalem Jĕhŏsh′ăphăt appointed certain Lē-vītes and priests and heads of families of Israel, to give judgment for the LORD and to decide disputed cases. They had their seat at Jerusalem. 9And he charged them: "Thus you shall do in the fear of the LORD, in faithfulness, and with your whole heart: 10 whenever a case comes to you from your brethren who live in their cities, concerning bloodshed, law or commandment, statutes or ordinances, then you shall instruct them, that they may not incur guilt before the LORD and wrath may not come upon you and your brethren. Thus you shall do, and you will not incur guilt. 11And behold, Ămărī′ăh the chief priest is over you in all matters of the LORD; and Zĕbădī′ăh the son of Ĭsh′māĕl, the governor of the house of Judah, in all the king's matters; and the Lēvītes will serve you as officers. Deal courageously, and may the LORD be with the upright!"

19.8
2 Chr 17.8,9

19.9
2 Sam 23.3

19.10
Deut 17.8;
ver 2

19.11
ver 8;
1 Chr 28.20

6. *Jehoshaphat's victory over the Moabites, Ammonites, and Syrians*
a. *Jehoshaphat seeking the LORD*

20 After this the Mŏ′ăbītes and Ăm′mŏnītes, and with them some of the Mĕ-ū′nītes,ᶠ came against Jĕhŏsh′ăphăt for battle. 2 Some men came and told Jĕhŏsh′ăphăt, "A great multitude is coming against you from Ēdŏm,ᵍ from beyond the sea; and, behold, they are in Hăz′ăzŏn-tā′măr" (that is, Ĕn-gĕ′dī). 3 Then Jĕhŏsh′ăphăt feared, and set himself to seek the LORD, and proclaimed a fast throughout all Judah. 4And Judah assembled to seek help from the LORD; from all the cities of Judah they came to seek the LORD.

20.2
Gen 14.7

20.3
2 Chr 19.3

b. *The prayer of Jehoshaphat for help*

5 And Jĕhŏsh′ăphăt stood in the assembly of Judah and Jerusalem, in the house of the LORD, before the new court, 6 and said, "O LORD, God of our fathers, art thou not God in heaven? Dost thou not rule over all the kingdoms of the nations? In thy hand

*20.6
Deut 4.39;
Mt 6.9;
1 Chr 29.11, 12;
Mt 6.13

ᶠ Compare 26.7: Heb *Ammonites*   ᵍ One Ms: Heb *Aram* (Syria)

20.6 This prayer of Jehoshaphat is instructive as a model for us. He begins with adoration of God and acknowledgment of His divine power (ver 6). He draws attention to the promises God has made to His people. Then he sets forth the problem itself (ver 10), confessing that he does not know what to do and asking God specifically for divine help

are power and might, so that none is able to withstand thee. [7] Didst thou not, O our God, drive out the inhabitants of this land before thy people Israel, and give it for ever to the descendants of Abraham thy friend? [8] And they have dwelt in it, and have built thee in it a sanctuary for thy name, saying, [9] 'If evil comes upon us, the sword, judgment,[h] or pestilence, or famine, we will stand before this house, and before thee, for thy name is in this house, and cry to thee in our affliction, and thou wilt hear and save.' [10] And now behold, the men of Ammon and Moab and Mount Seïr, whom thou wouldest not let Israel invade when they came from the land of Egypt, and whom they avoided and did not destroy—[11] behold, they reward us by coming to drive us out of thy possession, which thou hast given us to inherit. [12] O our God, wilt thou not execute judgment upon them? For we are powerless against this great multitude that is coming against us. We do not know what to do, but our eyes are upon thee."

c. *The message of deliverance by Jahaziel the prophet*

13 Meanwhile all the men of Judah stood before the LORD, with their little ones, their wives, and their children. [14] And the Spirit of the LORD came upon Jahā'ziĕl the son of Zĕchărī'ăh, son of Bĕnāi'ăh, son of Je-ī'ĕl, son of Măttănī'ăh, a Lēvīte of the sons of Āsăph, in the midst of the assembly. [15] And he said, "Hearken, all Judah and inhabitants of Jerusalem, and King Jĕhŏsh'ăphăt: Thus says the LORD to you, 'Fear not, and be not dismayed at this great multitude; for the battle is not yours but God's. [16] Tomorrow go down against them; behold, they will come up by the ascent of Zĭz; you will find them at the end of the valley, east of the wilderness of Jĕru'ĕl. [17] You will not need to fight in this battle; take your position, stand still, and see the victory of the LORD on your behalf, O Judah and Jerusalem.' Fear not, and be not dismayed; tomorrow go out against them, and the LORD will be with you."

18 Then Jĕhŏsh'ăphăt bowed his head with his face to the ground, and all Judah and the inhabitants of Jerusalem fell down before the LORD, worshiping the LORD. [19] And the Lēvītes, of the Kō'hăthītes and the Kō'răhītes, stood up to praise the LORD, the God of Israel, with a very loud voice.

d. *God's deliverance*

20 And they rose early in the morning and went out into the wilderness of Tĕkō'ă; and as they went out, Jĕhŏsh'ăphăt stood and said, "Hear me, Judah and inhabitants of Jerusalem! Believe in the LORD your God, and you will be established; believe his prophets, and you will succeed." [21] And when he had taken counsel with the people, he appointed those who were to sing to the LORD and praise him in holy array, as they went before the army, and say,
"Give thanks to the LORD,
    for his steadfast love endures for ever."

[h] Or *the sword of judgment*

Marginal references:
20.7 Isa 41.8
20.9 1 Ki 8.33, 37; 2 Chr 6.20, 28–30
20.10 ver 1,22; Deut 2.4,9, 19; Num 20.21
20.11 Ps 83.12
20.12 Judg 11.27; Ps 25.15; 121.1,2
20.14 2 Chr 15.1; 24.20
20.15 Ex 14.13, 14; 2 Chr 32.7, 8; 1 Sam 17.47
20.17 Ex 14.13, 14; 2 Chr 15.2
20.18 Ex 4.31; 2 Chr 7.3
20.20 Isa 7.9
20.21 1 Chr 16.29, 34,41; Ps 29.2

(ver 12). His sublime confidence that the LORD has heard his prayer and intends to deliver His people is eloquently expressed in his exhortation in verse 20. He thus encouraged the faithful to praise God as exultantly for His answer as if they had already received it (ver 21). (See note to Lk 11.1, which lists conditions for effectual prayer.)

22And when they began to sing and praise, the LORD set an ambush against the men of Ămmón, Mōăb, and Mount Sēįr, who had come against Judah, so that they were routed. 23 For the men of Ămmón and Mōăb rose against the inhabitants of Mount Sēįr, destroying them utterly, and when they had made an end of the inhabitants of Seir, they all helped to destroy one another. 24 When Judah came to the watchtower of the wilderness, they looked toward the multitude; and behold, they were dead bodies lying on the ground; none had escaped. 25 When Jéhŏsh'áphăt and his people came to take the spoil from them, they found cattle*i* in great numbers, goods, clothing, and precious things, which they took for themselves until they could carry no more. They were three days in taking the spoil, it was so much. 26 On the fourth day they assembled in the Valley of Bĕră'căh,*j* for there they blessed the LORD; therefore the name of that place has been called the Valley of Beracah to this day. 27 Then they returned, every man of Judah and Jerusalem, and Jéhŏsh'áphăt at their head, returning to Jerusalem with joy, for the LORD had made them rejoice over their enemies. 28 They came to Jerusalem, with harps and lyres and trumpets, to the house of the LORD. 29And the fear of God came on all the kingdoms of the countries when they heard that the LORD had fought against the enemies of Israel. 30 So the realm of Jéhŏsh'áphăt was quiet, for his God gave him rest round about.

7. Summary of Jehoshaphat's reign

31 Thus Jéhŏsh'áphăt reigned over Judah. He was thirty-five years old when he began to reign, and he reigned twenty-five years in Jerusalem. His mother's name was Ăzu'băh the daughter of Shĭlhī. 32 He walked in the way of Ăsă his father and did not turn aside from it; he did what was right in the sight of the LORD. 33 The high places, however, were not taken away; the people had not yet set their hearts upon the god of their fathers. 34 Now the rest of the acts of Jéhŏsh'áphăt, from first to last, are written in the chronicles of Jēhū the son of Hánā'nī, which are recorded in the Book of the Kings of Israel. 35 After this Jéhŏsh'áphăt king of Judah joined with Ăhăzī'áh king of Israel, who did wickedly. 36 He joined him in building ships to go to Tarshish, and they built the ships in Ĕz'ĭŏn-gē'bĕr. 37 Then Élĭē'zĕr the son of Dōdăvă'hu of Mărē'shăh prophesied against Jéhŏsh'áphăt, saying, "Because you have joined with Ăhăzī'áh, the LORD will destroy what you have made." And the ships were wrecked and were not able to go to Tarshish.

E. The reign of Jehoram (Joram)

1. The wickedness of Jehoram

21 Jéhŏsh'áphăt slept with his fathers, and was buried with his fathers in the city of David; and Jéhō'răm his son reigned in his stead. 2 He had brothers, the sons of Jéhŏsh'áphăt: Ăzărī'áh,

i Gk: Heb *among them*   *j* That is *Blessing*

20.22
Judg 7.22;
2 Chr 13.13
20.23
1 Sam 14.20

20.27
Neh 12.43

20.29
2 Chr
14.14;
17.10
20.30
2 Chr 14.6,
7; 15.15

20.31
1 Ki 22.41–43

*20.33
2 Chr 17.6;
19.3
20.34
1 Ki 16.1,7

20.35
1 Ki 22.48,
49

20.37
2 Chr 9.21

21.1
1 Ki 22.50

20.33 Whereas 1 Ki 22.43 notes that the people continued sacrificing and burning incense at the high places, the Chronicler tries to explain why Jehoshaphat, a king who *did what was right in the sight of the* LORD (ver 32), did not remove them. Jehoshaphat could not be blamed because the hearts of the people were not ready yet.

Jĕhī'ĕl, Zĕçhārī'ah, Azariah, Michael, and Shĕphătī'ah; all these were the sons of Jehoshaphat king of Judah. ³ Their father gave them great gifts, of silver, gold, and valuable possessions, together with fortified cities in Judah; but he gave the kingdom to Jĕhō'răm, because he was the first-born. ⁴ When Jĕhō'răm had ascended the throne of his father and was established, he slew all his brothers with the sword, and also some of the princes of Israel. ⁵ Jĕhō'răm was thirty-two years old when he became king, and he reigned eight years in Jerusalem. ⁶And he walked in the way of the kings of Israel, as the house of Āhăb had done; for the daughter of Ahab was his wife. And he did what was evil in the sight of the LORD. ⁷ Yet the LORD would not destroy the house of David, because of the covenant which he had made with David, and since he had promised to give a lamp to him and to his sons for ever.

2. The loss of Edom and Libnah

8 In his days Ēdŏm revolted from the rule of Judah, and set up a king of their own. ⁹ Then Jĕhō'răm passed over with his commanders and all his chariots, and he rose by night and smote the Ē'dŏmītes who had surrounded him and his chariot commanders. ¹⁰ So Ēdŏm revolted from the rule of Judah to this day. At that time Lĭbnăh also revolted from his rule, because he had forsaken the LORD, the God of his fathers.

3. Elijah's pronouncement of judgment

11 Moreover he made high places in the hill country of Judah, and led the inhabitants of Jerusalem into unfaithfulness, and made Judah go astray. ¹²And a letter came to him from Ēlī'jăh the prophet, saying, "Thus says the LORD, the God of David your father, 'Because you have not walked in the ways of Jĕhōsh'ăphăt your father, or in the ways of Āsā king of Judah, ¹³ but have walked in the way of the kings of Israel, and have led Judah and the inhabitants of Jerusalem into unfaithfulness, as the house of Āhăb led Israel into unfaithfulness, and also you have killed your brothers, of your father's house, who were better than yourself; ¹⁴ behold, the LORD will bring a great plague on your people, your children, your wives, and all your possessions, ¹⁵ and you yourself will have a severe sickness with a disease of your bowels, until your bowels come out because of the disease, day by day.'"

4. The evil end of Jehoram

16 And the LORD stirred up against Jĕhō'răm the anger of the Phĭlĭs'tĭneş and of the Arabs who are near the Ethiopians; ¹⁷ and they came up against Judah, and invaded it, and carried away all the possessions they found that belonged to the king's house, and also his sons and his wives, so that no son was left to him except Jĕhō'ăhăz, his youngest son.

18 And after all this the LORD smote him in his bowels with an

---

21.6 daughter of Ahab, that is, Athaliah, who was like her wicked mother, Jezebel.

21.12 From the context, the letter came to Jehoram, the son of Jehoshaphat, but from 2 Ki 3.11 it is clear that Elijah was dead in the reign of Jehoshaphat. Elijah's words were probably adapted by some other man of God.

21.17 This incident is not mentioned in Kings. Undoubtedly such a raid occurred. Either some of the wives of Jehoram were recovered, or the writer did not mean that every wife was taken captive, because Athaliah is very much alive, and in charge of affairs after her husband's death.

incurable disease. 19 In course of time, at the end of two years, his bowels came out because of the disease, and he died in great agony. His people made no fire in his honor, like the fires made for his fathers. 20 He was thirty-two years old when he began to reign, and he reigned eight years in Jerusalem; and he departed with no one's regret. They buried him in the city of David, but not in the tombs of the kings.

F. The reign of Ahaziah and Athaliah

1. The wickedness of Ahaziah

22 And the inhabitants of Jerusalem made Āhǎzī'áh his youngest son king in his stead; for the band of men that came with the Arabs to the camp had slain all the older sons. So Ahaziah the son of Jěhō'rám king of Judah reigned. 2 Āhǎzī'áh was forty-two years old when he began to reign, and he reigned one year in Jerusalem. His mother's name was Ăthǎlī'áh, the granddaughter of Ŏmrī. 3 He also walked in the ways of the house of Āhǎb, for his mother was his counselor in doing wickedly. 4 He did what was evil in the sight of the LORD, as the house of Āhǎb had done; for after the death of his father they were his counselors, to his undoing. 5 He even followed their counsel, and went with Jěhō'rám the son of Āhǎb king of Israel to make war against Hǎz'aěl king of Syria at Rā'móth-gǐl'ěǎd. And the Syrians wounded Jōrǎm, 6 and he returned to be healed in Jězreěl' of the wounds which he had received at Rāmáh, when he fought against Hǎz'aěl king of Syria. And Āhǎzī'áh the son of Jěhō'rám king of Judah went down to see Jōrǎm the son of Āhǎb in Jezreel, because he was sick.

2. Jehu murders Ahaziah

7 But it was ordained by God that the downfall of Āhǎzī'áh should come about through his going to visit Jōrǎm. For when he came there he went out with Jěhō'rám to meet Jēhū the son of Nǐmshī, whom the LORD had anointed to destroy the house of Āhǎb. 8 And when Jēhū was executing judgment upon the house of Āhǎb, he met the princes of Judah and the sons of Āhǎzī'áh's brothers, who attended Āhǎzī'áh, and he killed them. 9 He searched for Āhǎzī'áh, and he was captured while hiding in Sámar'iǎ, and he was brought to Jēhū and put to death. They buried him, for they said, "He is the grandson of Jěhōsh'áphǎt, who sought the LORD with all his heart." And the house of Ahaziah had no one able to rule the kingdom.

3. Athaliah seizes the throne
a. The murder of the royal princes except Joash

10 Now when Ăthǎlī'áh the mother of Āhǎzī'áh saw that her son was dead, she arose and destroyed all the royal family of the house of Judah. 11 But Jěhō-shǎb'e-áth, the daughter of the king, took Jō'ásh the son of Āhǎzī'áh, and stole him away from among the king's sons who were about to be slain, and she put him and his nurse in a bedchamber. Thus Jeho-shabe-ath, the daughter of

Margin refs: 21.19 2 Chr 16.14 / 21.20 Jer 22.18,28; 2 Chr 24.25; 28.27 / *22.1 2 Ki 8.24–29; 2 Chr 21.16,17 *22.2 2 Chr 21.6 / 22.5 2 Ki 8.28ff / 22.6 2 Ki 9.15 / 22.7 2 Chr 10.15; 2 Ki 9.6,7,21 / 22.8 2 Ki 10.10–14 / 22.9 2 Ki 9.27,28; 2 Chr 17.4 / 22.10 2 Ki 11.1–3

22.1 *Ahaziah*, an inverted form of the name Jehoahaz (21.17). **22.2** *forty-two* should be *twenty-two* as in 2 Ki 8.26.

King Jèhō'rảm and wife of Jèhoi'ảdả the priest, because she was a sister of Ahaziah, hid him from Ăthảlī'ảh, so that she did not slay him; 12 and he remained with them six years, hid in the house of God, while Ăthảlī'ảh reigned over the land.

b. *The revolt fostered by Jehoiada*

<table>
<tr><td>

23.1
2 Ki 11.4–
20

23.3
2 Sam 7.12;
1 Ki 2.4;
2 Chr 6.16;
7.18; 21.7
23.4
1 Chr 9.25

23.7
1 Chr
23.28–32

23.8
1 Chr 24.1

23.9
ver 1

23.11
Ex 25.16;
1 Sam 10.24

23.12
2 Ki 11.13

23.15
Neh 3.28;
Jer 31.40

</td><td>

23 But in the seventh year Jèhoi'ảdả took courage, and entered into a compact with the commanders of hundreds, Ăzảrī'ảh the son of Jèrō'hảm, Ĭsh'mảĕl the son of Jèhō'hảnản, Azariah the son of Ōbĕd, Mả-ảseī'ảh the son of Ảdāi'ảh, and Ĕlī'shảphảt the son of Zĭchrī. 2And they went about through Judah and gathered the Lèvītes from all the cities of Judah, and the heads of fathers' houses of Israel, and they came to Jerusalem. 3And all the assembly made a covenant with the king in the house of God. And Jèhoi'ảdả¹ said to them, "Behold, the king's son! Let him reign, as the LORD spoke concerning the sons of David. 4 This is the thing that you shall do: of you priests and Lèvītes who come off duty on the sabbath, one third shall be gatekeepers, 5 and one third shall be at the king's house and one third at the Gate of the Foundation; and all the people shall be in the courts of the house of the LORD. 6 Let no one enter the house of the LORD except the priests and ministering Lèvītes; they may enter, for they are holy, but all the people shall keep the charge of the LORD. 7 The Lèvītes shall surround the king, each with his weapons in his hand; and whoever enters the house shall be slain. Be with the king when he comes in, and when he goes out."

8 The Lèvītes and all Judah did according to all that Jèhoi'ảdả the priest commanded. They each brought his men, who were to go off duty on the sabbath, with those who were to come on duty on the sabbath; for Jehoiada the priest did not dismiss the divisions. 9And Jèhoi'ảdả the priest delivered to the captains the spears and the large and small shields that had been King David's, which were in the house of God; 10 and he set all the people as a guard for the king, every man with his weapon in his hand, from the south side of the house to the north side of the house, around the altar and the house. 11 Then he brought out the king's son, and put the crown upon him, and gave him the testimony; and they proclaimed him king, and Jèhoi'ảdả and his sons anointed him, and they said, "Long live the king."

12 When Ăthảlī'ảh heard the noise of the people running and praising the king, she went into the house of the LORD to the people; 13 and when she looked, there was the king standing by his pillar at the entrance, and the captains and the trumpeters beside the king, and all the people of the land rejoicing and blowing trumpets, and the singers with their musical instruments leading in the celebration. And Ăthảlī'ảh rent her clothes, and cried, "Treason! Treason!" 14 Then Jèhoi'ảdả the priest brought out the captains who were set over the army, saying to them, "Bring her out between the ranks; any one who follows her is to be slain with the sword." For the priest said, "Do not slay her in the house of the LORD." 15 So they laid hands on her; and she went into the entrance of the horse gate of the king's house, and they slew her there.

16 And Jèhoi'ảdả made a covenant between himself and all the

</td></tr>
</table>

¹ Heb *he*

people and the king that they should be the LORD's people. 17 Then all the people went to the house of Bāal, and tore it down; his altars and his images they broke in pieces, and they slew Măttán the priest of Baal before the altars. 18And Jĕhoi′ádá posted watchmen for the house of the LORD under the direction of the Lĕvĭt′ĭcăl priests and the Lēvītes whom David had organized to be in charge of the house of the LORD, to offer burnt offerings to the LORD, as it is written in the law of Moses, with rejoicing and with singing, according to the order of David. 19 He stationed the gatekeepers at the gates of the house of the LORD so that no one should enter who was in any way unclean. 20And he took the captains, the nobles, the governors of the people, and all the people of the land; and they brought the king down from the house of the LORD, marching through the upper gate to the king's house. And they set the king upon the royal throne. 21 So all the people of the land rejoiced; and the city was quiet, after Ăthălĭ′áh had been slain with the sword.

G. The reign of Joash

1. The faithfulness of Joash

24 Jō′ăsh was seven years old when he began to reign, and he reigned forty years in Jerusalem; his mother's name was Zĭb′ĭáh of Beër-shē′bá. 2And Jō′ăsh did what was right in the eyes of the LORD all the days of Jĕhoi′ádá the priest. 3 Jĕhoi′ádá got for him two wives, and he had sons and daughters.

2. The repair of the Temple

4 After this Jō′ăsh decided to restore the house of the LORD. 5And he gathered the priests and the Lēvītes, and said to them, "Go out to the cities of Judah, and gather from all Israel money to repair the house of your God from year to year; and see that you hasten the matter." But the Levites did not hasten it. 6 So the king summoned Jĕhoi′ádá the chief, and said to him, "Why have you not required the Lēvītes to bring in from Judah and Jerusalem the tax levied by Moses, the servant of the LORD, on*m* the congregation of Israel for the tent of testimony?" 7 For the sons of Ăthălĭ′áh, that wicked woman, had broken into the house of God; and had also used all the dedicated things of the house of the LORD for the Bāáls.

8 So the king commanded, and they made a chest, and set it outside the gate of the house of the LORD. 9And proclamation was made throughout Judah and Jerusalem, to bring in for the LORD the tax that Moses the servant of God laid upon Israel in the wilderness. 10And all the princes and all the people rejoiced and brought their tax and dropped it into the chest until they had finished. 11And whenever the chest was brought to the king's officers by the Lēvītes, when they saw that there was much money in it, the king's secretary and the officer of the chief priest would come and empty the chest and take it and return it to its place. Thus they did day after day, and collected money in abundance. 12And the king and Jĕhoi′ádá gave it to those who had charge of the work of the house of the LORD, and they hired masons and

m Compare Vg: Heb *and*

Cross references

23.17	Deut 13.9
23.18	2 Chr 5.5; 1 Chr 23.6, 30,31; 25.1,2,6
23.19	1 Chr 9.22
23.20	2 Ki 11.19
24.1	2 Ki 11.21; 12.1–15
24.2	2 Chr 26.5
24.4	ver 7
24.6	Ex 30.12–16
24.7	2 Chr 21.17
24.9	ver 6
24.11	2 Ki 12.10

carpenters to restore the house of the LORD, and also workers in
iron and bronze to repair the house of the LORD. 13 So those who
were engaged in the work labored, and the repairing went forward
in their hands, and they restored the house of God to its proper
condition and strengthened it. 14And when they had finished, they
brought the rest of the money before the king and Jĕhoi′ádá, and
with it were made utensils for the house of the LORD, both for the
service and for the burnt offerings, and dishes for incense, and
vessels of gold and silver. And they offered burnt offerings in the
house of the LORD continually all the days of Jehoiada.

3. *The death of Jehoiada*

15 But Jĕhoi′ádá grew old and full of days, and died; he was a
hundred and thirty years old at his death. 16And they buried him
in the city of David among the kings, because he had done good
in Israel, and toward God and his house.

4. *The apostasy of Joash and Judah*

17 Now after the death of Jĕhoi′ádá the princes of Judah came
and did obeisance to the king; then the king hearkened to them.
18And they forsook the house of the LORD, the God of their fathers,
and served the Àshē′rĭm and the idols. And wrath came upon
Judah and Jerusalem for this their guilt. 19 Yet he sent prophets
among them to bring them back to the LORD; these testified
against them, but they would not give heed.

5. *Joash kills Zechariah the son of Jehoiada*

20 Then the Spirit of God took possession of[n] Zĕchárī′áh the
son of Jĕhoi′ádá the priest; and he stood above the people, and
said to them, "Thus says God, 'Why do you transgress the commandments of the LORD, so that you cannot prosper? Because
you have forsaken the LORD, he has forsaken you.' " 21 But they
conspired against him, and by command of the king they stoned
him with stones in the court of the house of the LORD. 22 Thus
Jō′ásh the king did not remember the kindness which Jĕhoi′ádá,
Zĕchárī′áh's father, had shown him, but killed his son. And when
he was dying, he said, "May the LORD see and avenge!"

6. *The defeat and death of Joash*

23 At the end of the year the army of the Syrians came up
against Jō′ásh. They came to Judah and Jerusalem, and destroyed
all the princes of the people from among the people, and sent all
their spoil to the king of Damascus. 24 Though the army of the
Syrians had come with few men, the LORD delivered into their
hand a very great army, because they had forsaken the LORD, the
God of their fathers. Thus they executed judgment on Jō′ásh.
25 When they had departed from him, leaving him severely
wounded, his servants conspired against him because of the blood
of the son[o] of Jĕhoi′ádá the priest, and slew him on his bed. So he
died; and they buried him in the city of David, but they did not
bury him in the tombs of the kings. 26 Those who conspired
against him were Zābăd the son of Shĭm′ĕ-áth the Ămmŏnīt′ĕss,
and Jĕhō′zábăd the son of Shĭmrĭth the Mōábĭt′ĕss. 27Accounts
of his sons, and of the many oracles against him, and of the re-

24.13
Neh 10.39

24.16
2 Chr 21.2,
20

24.18
ver 4;
Ex 34.12–
14;
1 Ki 14.23;
Josh 22.20;
2 Chr 19.2
24.19
Jer 7.25

24.20
2 Chr
20.14;
Num 14.41;
2 Chr 15.2

24.21
Neh 9.26;
Mt 23.35;
Acts 7.58,
59
24.22
Gen 9.5

24.23
2 Ki 12.17

24.24
Lev 26.25;
Deut 28.25;
2 Chr 22.8;
Isa 10.5

24.25
2 Ki 12.20;
ver 21

24.27
2 Ki 12.18,
21

n Heb *clothed itself with*   *o* Gk Vg: Heb *sons*

building*p* of the house of God are written in the Commentary on the Book of the Kings. And Ămăzī'ăh his son reigned in his stead.

H. *The reign of Amaziah*

1. *Amaziah's early acts*

25 Ămăzī'ăh was twenty-five years old when he began to reign, and he reigned twenty-nine years in Jerusalem. His mother's name was Jĕhō'-ăddăn of Jerusalem. 2And he did what was right in the eyes of the LORD, yet not with a blameless heart. 3And as soon as the royal power was firmly in his hand he killed his servants who had slain the king his father. 4 But he did not put their children to death, according to what is written in the law, in the book of Moses, where the LORD commanded, "The fathers shall not be put to death for the children, or the children be put to death for the fathers; but every man shall die for his own sin."

2. *The defeat of the Edomites in the Valley of Salt*

5 Then Ămăzī'ăh assembled the men of Judah, and set them by fathers' houses under commanders of thousands and of hundreds for all Judah and Benjamin. He mustered those twenty years old and upward, and found that they were three hundred thousand picked men, fit for war, able to handle spear and shield. 6 He hired also a hundred thousand mighty men of valor from Israel for a hundred talents of silver. 7 But a man of God came to him and said, "O king, do not let the army of Israel go with you, for the LORD is not with Israel, with all these Ē'phrāimītes. 8 But if you suppose that in this way you will be strong for war,*q* God will cast you down before the enemy; for God has power to help or to cast down." 9And Ămăzī'ăh said to the man of God, "But what shall we do about the hundred talents which I have given to the army of Israel?" The man of God answered, "The LORD is able to give you much more than this." 10 Then Ămăzī'ăh discharged the army that had come to him from Ē'phrāim, to go home again. And they became very angry with Judah, and returned home in fierce anger. 11 But Ămăzī'ăh took courage, and led out his people, and went to the Valley of Salt and smote ten thousand men of Sēir. 12 The men of Judah captured another ten thousand alive, and took them to the top of a rock and threw them down from the top of the rock; and they were all dashed to pieces. 13 But the men of the army whom Ămăzī'ăh sent back, not letting them go with him to battle, fell upon the cities of Judah, from Sămăr'iă to Bĕth-hor'ŏn, and killed three thousand people in them, and took much spoil.

3. *Amaziah's idolatry*

14 After Ămăzī'ăh came from the slaughter of the Ē'dŏmītes, he brought the gods of the men of Sēir, and set them up as his gods, and worshiped them, making offerings to them. 15 Therefore the LORD was angry with Ămăzī'ăh and sent to him a prophet, who said to him, "Why have you resorted to the gods of a people, which did not deliver their own people from your hand?" 16 But as he was speaking the king said to him, "Have we made you a royal counselor? Stop! Why should you be put to death?" So the

p Heb *founding*　*q* Gk: Heb *But if you go, act, be strong for the battle*

25.1
2 Ki 14.1–6

25.2
ver 14

25.4
Deut 24.16;
2 Ki 14.6

25.5
Num 1.3

25.8
2 Chr
14.11; 20.6

25.11
2 Ki 14.7

25.14
2 Chr
28.23;
Ex 20.3,5
25.15
Ps 96.5;
ver 11,12

prophet stopped, but said, "I know that God has determined to destroy you, because you have done this and have not listened to my counsel."

4. *Amaziah's defeat by Joash of Israel*

25.17
2 Ki 14.8–
14

17 Then Ămăzī'áh king of Judah took counsel and sent to Jō'ăsh the son of Jèhō'áhăz, son of Jèhū, king of Israel, saying, "Come, let us look one another in the face." 18And Jō'ăsh the king of Israel sent word to Ămăzī'áh king of Judah, "A thistle on Lebanon sent to a cedar on Lebanon, saying, 'Give your daughter to my son for a wife'; and a wild beast of Lebanon passed by and trampled down the thistle. 19 You say, 'See, I have smitten Ēdŏm,' and your heart has lifted you up in boastfulness. But now stay at home; why should you provoke trouble so that you fall, you and Judah with you?"

25.18
Judg 9.8–15

25.19
2 Chr
26.16;
32.25

20 But Ămăzī'áh would not listen; for it was of God, in order that he might give them into the hand of their enemies, because they had sought the gods of Ēdŏm. 21 So Jō'ăsh king of Israel went up; and he and Ămăzī'áh king of Judah faced one another in battle at Bĕth-shĕ'mĕsh, which belongs to Judah. 22And Judah was defeated by Israel, and every man fled to his home. 23And Jō'ăsh king of Israel captured Ămăzī'áh king of Judah, the son of Joash, son of Āhăzī'áh, at Bĕth-shĕ'mĕsh, and brought him to Jerusalem, and broke down the wall of Jerusalem for four hundred cubits, from the Ē'phrăjm Gate to the Corner Gate. 24And he seized all the gold and silver, and all the vessels that were found in the house of God, and Ō'bĕd-ē'dŏm with them; he seized also the treasuries of the king's house, and hostages, and he returned to Sămạr'ĭầ.

25.20
1 Ki 12.15;
2 Chr 22.7

25.23
2 Chr
21.17; 22.1

5. *The murder of Amaziah*

25.25
2 Ki 14.17–
22

25 Ămăzī'áh the son of Jō'ăsh king of Judah lived fifteen years after the death of Joash the son of Jèhō'áhăz, king of Israel. 26 Now the rest of the deeds of Ămăzī'áh, from first to last, are they not written in the Book of the Kings of Judah and Israel? 27 From the time when he turned away from the LORD they made a conspiracy against him in Jerusalem, and he fled to Lāchish. But they sent after him to Lachish, and slew him there. 28And they brought him upon horses; and he was buried with his fathers in the city of David.

I. The reign of Uzziah (Azariah)

1. *His godly start*

*26.1
2 Ki 14.21,
22; 15.2,3

26 And all the people of Judah took Ủzzī'áh, who was sixteen years old, and made him king instead of his father Ămăzī'áh. 2 He built Ēlóth and restored it to Judah, after the king slept with his fathers. 3 Ủzzī'áh was sixteen years old when he began to reign, and he reigned fifty-two years in Jerusalem. His mother's name was Jĕcŏlī'áh of Jerusalem. 4And he did what was right in the eyes of the LORD, according to all that his father Ămăzī'áh had done. 5 He set himself to seek God in the days of Zĕchărī'áh, who

*26.5
2 Chr 24.2;
Dan 1.17;
2.19;
2 Chr 15.2

26.1 *Uzziah*, the Azariah of 2 Ki 15.1.
26.5 Uzziah's experience yields a lesson for the believer: obedience brings blessing; pride at God-given success leads to disregard of God's will and tragic failure and loss (ver 19–21).

instructed him in the fear of God; and as long as he sought the LORD, God made him prosper.

2. *His success*

6 He went out and made war against the Phĭlĭs'tĭneş, and broke down the wall of Găth and the wall of Jăbnĕh and the wall of Ăshdŏd; and he built cities in the territory of Ashdod and elsewhere among the Philistines. 7 God helped him against the Phĭlĭs'tĭneş, and against the Arabs that dwelt in Gûrbā'ăl, and against the Mĕ-ū'nītes. 8 The Ăm'mónītes paid tribute to Ŭzzī'ăh, and his fame spread even to the border of Egypt, for he became very strong. 9 Moreover Ŭzzī'ăh built towers in Jerusalem at the Corner Gate and at the Valley Gate and at the Angle, and fortified them. 10And he built towers in the wilderness, and hewed out many cisterns, for he had large herds, both in the Shĕphĕ'lăh and in the plain, and he had farmers and vinedressers in the hills and in the fertile lands, for he loved the soil. 11 Moreover Ŭzzī'ăh had an army of soldiers, fit for war, in divisions according to the numbers in the muster made by Je-ī'ĕl the secretary and Mā-àseī'ăh the officer, under the direction of Hănánī'ăh, one of the king's commanders. 12 The whole number of the heads of fathers' houses of mighty men of valor was two thousand six hundred. 13 Under their command was an army of three hundred and seven thousand five hundred, who could make war with mighty power, to help the king against the enemy. 14And Ŭzzī'ăh prepared for all the army shields, spears, helmets, coats of mail, bows, and stones for slinging. 15 In Jerusalem he made engines, invented by skilful men, to be on the towers and the corners, to shoot arrows and great stones. And his fame spread far, for he was marvelously helped, till he was strong.

3. *His sin and punishment*

16 But when he was strong he grew proud, to his destruction. For he was false to the LORD his God, and entered the temple of the LORD to burn incense on the altar of incense. 17 But Ăzārī'ăh the priest went in after him, with eighty priests of the LORD who were men of valor; 18 and they withstood King Ŭzzī'ăh, and said to him, "It is not for you, Ŭzzī'ăh, to burn incense to the LORD, but for the priests the sons of Aaron, who are consecrated to burn incense. Go out of the sanctuary; for you have done wrong, and it will bring you no honor from the LORD God." 19 Then Ŭzzī'ăh was angry. Now he had a censer in his hand to burn incense, and when he became angry with the priests leprosy broke out on his forehead, in the presence of the priests in the house of the LORD, by the altar of incense. 20And Ăzārī'ăh the chief priest, and all the priests, looked at him, and behold, he was leprous in his forehead! And they thrust him out quickly, and he himself hastened to go out, because the LORD had smitten him. 21And King Ŭzzī'ăh was a leper to the day of his death, and being a leper dwelt in a separate house, for he was excluded from the house of the LORD. And Jōthăm his son was over the king's household, governing the people of the land.

4. *His death and the succession*

22 Now the rest of the acts of Ŭzzī'ăh, from first to last, Ĭşāi'ăh

26.6
Isa 14.29

26.7
2 Chr 21.16
26.8
2 Chr 17.11

26.9
2 Chr 25.23;
Neh 3.13

26.13
2 Chr 25.5

26.16
Deut 32.15;
2 Chr 25.19;
2 Ki 16.12, 13
26.17
1 Chr 6.10
26.18
Num 16.39, 40;
Ex 30.7,8
26.19
2 Ki 5.25–27

26.21
2 Ki 15.5–7;
Lev 13.46;
Num 5.2

26.22
Isa 1.1

26.23
2 Ki 15.7;
Isa 6.1

the prophet the son of Āmóz wrote. 23And Úzzī'áh slept with his fathers, and they buried him with his fathers in the burial field which belonged to the kings, for they said, "He is a leper." And Jōthám his son reigned in his stead.

J. The reign of Jotham

27.1
2 Ki 15.33–
35
27.2
2 Chr 26.16

★27.3
2 Chr
33.14;
Neh 3.26

27 Jōthám was twenty-five years old when he began to reign, and he reigned sixteen years in Jerusalem. His mother's name was Jéru'shàh the daughter of Zādŏk. 2And he did what was right in the eyes of the LORD according to all that his father Úzzī'áh had done—only he did not invade the temple of the LORD. But the people still followed corrupt practices. 3 He built the upper gate of the house of the LORD, and did much building on the wall of Ōphĕl. 4 Moreover he built cities in the hill country of Judah, and forts and towers on the wooded hills. 5 He fought with the king of the Ăm'mónītes and prevailed against them. And the Ammonites gave him that year a hundred talents of silver, and ten thousand cors of wheat and ten thousand of barley. The Ammonites paid him the same amount in the second and the third years.

27.6
2 Chr 26.5
27.7
2 Ki 15.36
27.8
ver 1

6 So Jōthám became mighty, because he ordered his ways before the LORD his God. 7 Now the rest of the acts of Jōthám, and all his wars, and his ways, behold, they are written in the Book of the Kings of Israel and Judah. 8 He was twenty-five years old when he began to reign, and he reigned sixteen years in Jerusalem. 9And Jōthám slept with his fathers, and they buried him in the city of David; and Āhăz his son reigned in his stead.

K. The reign of Ahaz

1. His evil ways

28.1
2 Ki 16.2–4
28.2
2 Chr 22.3;
Ex 34.17
28.3
2 Ki 23.10;
Lev 18.21;
2 Ki 16.3;
2 Chr 33.6
28.4
ver 25

28 Āhăz was twenty years old when he began to reign, and he reigned sixteen years in Jerusalem. And he did not do what was right in the eyes of the LORD, like his father David, 2 but walked in the ways of the kings of Israel. He even made molten images for the Bāálṣ; 3 and he burned incense in the valley of the son of Hĭnnóm, and burned his sons as an offering, according to the abominable practices of the nations whom the LORD drove out before the people of Israel. 4And he sacrificed and burned incense on the high places, and on the hills, and under every green tree.

2. His defeats by Syria and Israel

28.5
Isa 7.1;
2 Ki 16.5,6

28.6
2 Ki 15.27

5 Therefore the LORD his God gave him into the hand of the king of Syria, who defeated him and took captive a great number of his people and brought them to Damascus. He was also given into the hand of the king of Israel, who defeated him with great slaughter. 6 For Pēkáh the son of Rĕmálī'áh slew a hundred and twenty thousand in Judah in one day, all of them men of valor, because they had forsaken the LORD, the God of their fathers. 7And Zĭchrī, a mighty man of Ē'phrăĭm, slew Mā-áseī'áh the king's son and Āzrī'kàm the commander of the palace and Ĕlkā'náh the next in authority to the king.

27.3 Ophel, eastern promontory on which Jerusalem of Old Testament times was situated; 33.14 and Nehemiah also refer to Ophel.

8 The men of Israel took captive two hundred thousand of their kinsfolk, women, sons, and daughters; they also took much spoil from them and brought the spoil to Såmạr′iå. 9 But a prophet of the LORD was there, whose name was Ōdẹd; and he went out to meet the army that came to Såmạr′iå, and said to them, "Behold, because the LORD, the God of your fathers, was angry with Judah, he gave them into your hand, but you have slain them in a rage which has reached up to heaven. 10And now you intend to subjugate the people of Judah and Jerusalem, male and female, as your slaves. Have you not sins of your own against the LORD your God? 11 Now hear me, and send back the captives from your kinsfolk whom you have taken, for the fierce wrath of the LORD is upon you." 12 Certain chiefs also of the men of Ē′phraïm, Ăzărī′åh the son of Jōhän′ạn, Bĕrĕçhī′åh the son of Mĕshĭl′lĕmŏth, Jĕhĭzkī′åh the son of Shăllụm, and Ămā′så the son of Hădlaī, stood up against those who were coming from the war, 13 and said to them, "You shall not bring the captives in here, for you propose to bring upon us guilt against the LORD in addition to our present sins and guilt. For our guilt is already great, and there is fierce wrath against Israel." 14 So the armed men left the captives and the spoil before the princes and all the assembly. 15And the men who have been mentioned by name rose and took the captives, and with the spoil they clothed all that were naked among them; they clothed them, gave them sandals, provided them with food and drink, and anointed them; and carrying all the feeble among them on asses, they brought them to their kinsfolk at Jĕr′içhō, the city of palm trees. Then they returned to Såmạr′iå.

3. His defeats by the Edomites and Assyrians, and his death

16 At that time King Āhăz sent to the kingʳ of Assyria for help. 17 For the Ē′dŏmītes had again invaded and defeated Judah, and carried away captives. 18And the Phĭlĭs′tĭnẹs had made raids on the cities in the Shĕphē′låh and the Nĕgĕb of Judah, and had taken Bĕth-shĕ′mĕsh, Ăī′jålŏn, Gĕd′ĕrŏth, Sōcō with its villages, Tĭmnåh with its villages, and Gĭmzō with its villages; and they settled there. 19 For the LORD brought Judah low because of Āhăz king of Israel, for he had dealt wantonly in Judah and had been faithless to the LORD. 20 So Tĭl′găth-pĭlnē′şĕr king of Assyria came against him, and afflicted him instead of strengthening him. 21 For Āhăz took from the house of the LORD and the house of the king and of the princes, and gave tribute to the king of Assyria; but it did not help him.

22 In the time of his distress he became yet more faithless to the LORD—this same King Āhăz. 23 For he sacrificed to the gods of Damascus which had defeated him, and said, "Because the gods of the kings of Syria helped them, I will sacrifice to them that they may help me." But they were the ruin of him, and of all Israel. 24And Āhăz gathered together the vessels of the house of God and cut in pieces the vessels of the house of God, and he shut up the doors of the house of the LORD; and he made himself altars in every corner of Jerusalem. 25 In every city of Judah he made high places to burn incense to other gods, provoking to anger the LORD, the God of his fathers. 26 Now the rest of his acts and all his ways, from first to last, behold, they are written in the Book of the Kings

28.8 2 Chr 11.4
28.9 2 Chr 25.15; Isa 10.5; 47.6; Ezra 9.6; Rev 18.5
28.10 Lev 25.39, 42,43,46
28.11 ver 8
28.15 ver 12; 2 Ki 6.22; Prov 25.21, 22; Deut 34.3; Judg 1.16
28.16 2 Ki 16.7
28.18 Ezek 16.57
28.19 2 Chr 21.2
28.20 1 Chr 5.26; 2 Ki 16.8,9
28.23 2 Chr 25.14; Jer 44.17. 18
28.24 2 Ki 16.17; 2 Chr 29.7; 30.14; 33.3–5
28.26 2 Ki 16.19, 20

ʳ Gk Syr Vg Compare 2 Kings 16.7: Heb *kings*

of Judah and Israel. 27And Āhăz slept with his fathers, and they
buried him in the city, in Jerusalem, for they did not bring him
into the tombs of the kings of Israel. And Hĕzĕkī′ah his son reigned
in his stead.

L. The reign of Hezekiah

1. The cleansing of the Temple
a. The announcement of his intentions

29 Hĕzĕkī′ah began to reign when he was twenty-five years
old, and he reigned twenty-nine years in Jerusalem. His
mother's name was Ăbī′jah the daughter of Zĕchărī′ah. 2And he
did what was right in the eyes of the LORD, according to all that
David his father had done.

3 In the first year of his reign, in the first month, he opened
the doors of the house of the LORD, and repaired them. 4 He
brought in the priests and the Lēvītes, and assembled them in the
square on the east, 5 and said to them, "Hear me, Lēvītes! Now
sanctify yourselves, and sanctify the house of the LORD, the God of
your fathers, and carry out the filth from the holy place. 6 For our
fathers have been unfaithful and have done what was evil in the
sight of the LORD our God; they have forsaken him, and have
turned away their faces from the habitation of the LORD, and
turned their backs. 7 They also shut the doors of the vestibule and
put out the lamps, and have not burned incense or offered burnt
offerings in the holy place to the God of Israel. 8 Therefore the
wrath of the LORD came on Judah and Jerusalem, and he has
made them an object of horror, of astonishment, and of hissing,
as you see with your own eyes. 9 For lo, our fathers have fallen by
the sword and our sons and our daughters and our wives are in
captivity for this. 10 Now it is in my heart to make a covenant with
the LORD, the God of Israel, that his fierce anger may turn away
from us. 11 My sons, do not now be negligent, for the LORD has
chosen you to stand in his presence, to minister to him, and to be
his ministers and burn incense to him."

b. The sanctifying of the Levites and
the cleansing of the Temple

12 Then the Lēvītes arose, Māhăth the son of Ămā′sāï, and
Jōĕl the son of Ăzărī′ah, of the sons of the Kō′hăthītes; and of the
sons of Mĕrar′ī, Kĭsh the son of Ăbdī, and Azariah the son of
Jĕhăl′lĕlĕl; and of the Gĕr′shonītes, Jōăh the son of Zĭmmăh, and
Eden the son of Joah; 13 and of the sons of Ĕlīz′ăphăn, Shĭmrī
and Jeu′ĕl; and of the sons of Āsăph, Zĕchărī′ah and Măttănī′ah;
14 and of the sons of Hēmăn, Jĕhū′ĕl and Shĭm′ĕ-ī; and of the
sons of Jĕdu′thŭn, Shĕmāi′ah and Ŭzzī′ĕl. 15 They gathered their
brethren, and sanctified themselves, and went in as the king had
commanded, by the words of the LORD, to cleanse the house of the
LORD. 16 The priests went into the inner part of the house of the
LORD to cleanse it, and they brought out all the uncleanness that
they found in the temple of the LORD into the court of the house of
the LORD; and the Lēvītes took it and carried it out to the brook
Kĭdrŏn. 17 They began to sanctify on the first day of the first
month, and on the eighth day of the month they came to the vestibule of the LORD; then for eight days they sanctified the house of

28.27
2 Chr 24.25

29.1
2 Ki 18.1–3
29.2
2 Chr 28.1

29.3
ver 7;
2 Chr 28.24

29.5
ver 15,34;
2 Chr 35.6
29.6
Jer 2.27;
Ezek 8.16

29.8
2 Chr
24.18;
28.5;
Deut 28.25;
Jer 25.9,18
29.9
2 Chr 28.5–
8,17
29.10
2 Chr
15.12;
23.16
29.11
Num 3.6;
8.14

29.15
ver 5;
2 Chr
30.12;
1 Chr 23.28

29.17
ver 3

the Lord, and on the sixteenth day of the first month they finished.
18 Then they went in to Hĕzĕkī′áh the king and said, "We have
cleansed all the house of the Lord, the altar of burnt offering and
all its utensils, and the table for the showbread and all its utensils.
19All the utensils which King Āhăz discarded in his reign when
he was faithless, we have made ready and sanctified; and behold,
they are before the altar of the Lord."

29.19
2 Chr 28.24

c. The consecration of the Temple

20 Then Hĕzĕkī′áh the king rose early and gathered the officials
of the city, and went up to the house of the Lord. 21And they
brought seven bulls, seven rams, seven lambs, and seven he-goats
for a sin offering for the kingdom and for the sanctuary and for
Judah. And he commanded the priests the sons of Aaron to offer
them on the altar of the Lord. 22 So they killed the bulls, and the
priests received the blood and threw it against the altar; and they
killed the rams and their blood was thrown against the altar; and
they killed the lambs and their blood was thrown against the altar.
23 Then the he-goats for the sin offering were brought to the king
and the assembly, and they laid their hands upon them, 24 and
the priests killed them and made a sin offering with their blood
on the altar, to make atonement for all Israel. For the king commanded that the burnt offering and the sin offering should be
made for all Israel.

29.21
Lev 4.3–14

29.22
Lev 4.18;
8.14

29.23
Lev 4.15
29.24
Lev 4.26

25 And he stationed the Lēvītes in the house of the Lord with
cymbals, harps, and lyres, according to the commandment of
David and of Găd the king's seer and of Nathan the prophet; for
the commandment was from the Lord through his prophets.
26 The Lēvītes stood with the instruments of David, and the
priests with the trumpets. 27 Then Hĕzĕkī′áh commanded that
the burnt offering be offered on the altar. And when the burnt
offering began, the song to the Lord began also, and the trumpets,
accompanied by the instruments of David king of Israel. 28 The
whole assembly worshiped, and the singers sang, and the trumpeters sounded; all this continued until the burnt offering was
finished. 29 When the offering was finished, the king and all who
were present with him bowed themselves and worshiped. 30And
Hĕzĕkī′áh the king and the princes commanded the Lēvītes to
sing praises to the Lord with the words of David and of Āsăph the
seer. And they sang praises with gladness, and they bowed down
and worshiped.

29.25
1 Chr 25.6;
2 Chr 8.14;
2 Sam
24.11; 7.2

29.26
1 Chr 23.5;
2 Chr 5.12
29.27
2 Chr 23.18

29.29
2 Chr 20.18

d. The sacrifices at the Temple

31 Then Hĕzĕkī′áh said, "You have now consecrated yourselves to the Lord; come near, bring sacrifices and thank offerings
to the house of the Lord." And the assembly brought sacrifices
and thank offerings; and all who were of a willing heart brought
burnt offerings. 32 The number of the burnt offerings which the
assembly brought was seventy bulls, a hundred rams, and two
hundred lambs; all these were for a burnt offering to the Lord.
33And the consecrated offerings were six hundred bulls and three
thousand sheep. 34 But the priests were too few and could not flay
all the burnt offerings, so until other priests had sanctified themselves their brethren the Lēvītes helped them, until the work was
finished—for the Levites were more upright in heart than the

29.31
2 Chr 13.9;
Ex 35.5,22

29.34
2 Chr
35.11; 30.3

priests in sanctifying themselves. 35 Besides the great number of burnt offerings there was the fat of the peace offerings, and there were the libations for the burnt offerings. Thus the service of the house of the LORD was restored. 36And Hĕzĕkī′äh and all the people rejoiced because of what God had done for the people; for the thing came about suddenly.

2. The celebration of the Passover
a. The invitation to all Israel and Judah

30 Hĕzĕkī′äh sent to all Israel and Judah, and wrote letters also to E′phrä̇ịm and Mȧnăs′sĕh, that they should come to the house of the LORD at Jerusalem, to keep the passover to the LORD the God of Israel. 2 For the king and his princes and all the assembly in Jerusalem had taken counsel to keep the passover in the second month—3 for they could not keep it in its time because the priests had not sanctified themselves in sufficient number, nor had the people assembled in Jerusalem—4 and the plan seemed right to the king and all the assembly. 5 So they decreed to make a proclamation throughout all Israel, from Beër-shē′bȧ to Dan, that the people should come and keep the passover to the LORD the God of Israel, at Jerusalem; for they had not kept it in great numbers as prescribed. 6 So couriers went throughout all Israel and Judah with letters from the king and his princes, as the king had commanded, saying, "O people of Israel, return to the LORD, the God of Abraham, Isaac, and Israel, that he may turn again to the remnant of you who have escaped from the hand of the kings of Assyria. 7 Do not be like your fathers and your brethren, who were faithless to the LORD God of their fathers, so that he made them a desolation, as you see. 8 Do not now be stiff-necked as your fathers were, but yield yourselves to the LORD, and come to his sanctuary, which he has sanctified for ever, and serve the LORD your God, that his fierce anger may turn away from you. 9 For if you return to the LORD, your brethren and your children will find compassion with their captors, and return to this land. For the LORD your God is gracious and merciful, and will not turn away his face from you, if you return to him."

10 So the couriers went from city to city through the country of E′phrä̇ịm and Mȧnăs′sĕh, and as far as Zĕb′ụlün; but they laughed them to scorn, and mocked them. 11 Only a few men of Ăshèr, of Mȧnăs′sĕh, and of Zĕb′ụlün humbled themselves and came to Jerusalem. 12 The hand of God was also upon Judah to give them one heart to do what the king and the princes commanded by the word of the LORD.

b. The keeping of the Passover

13 And many people came together in Jerusalem to keep the feast of unleavened bread in the second month, a very great assembly. 14 They set to work and removed the altars that were in Jerusalem, and all the altars for burning incense they took away

29.35
ver 32;
Lev 3.16;
Num 15.5–
10

30.2
ver 13,15;
Num 9.10,
11
30.3
Ex 12.6,18;
2 Chr 29.34
★30.5
Judg 20.1

30.6
Est 8.14;
Job 9.25;
Jer 51.31;
2 Chr 20.8

30.7
Ezek 20.18;
2 Chr 29.8
30.8
Ex 32.9;
2 Chr 29.10

30.9
Deut 30.2;
Ex 34.6,7;
Mic 7.18;
Isa 55.7

30.10
2 Chr 36.16

30.11
ver 18,21,25

30.13
ver 2

30.14
2 Chr 28.24

30.5 *from Beer-sheba to Dan.* The fact that Hezekiah's invitation covered all of Palestine and that his couriers could go from city to city throughout Ephraim, Manasseh, and Zebulun (30.10) is an indication that the Northern Kingdom had fallen. Jehoshaphat's reform extended only from Beer-sheba to the hill country of Ephraim (19.4) because the officials of the Northern Kingdom were a threat to his activities.

and threw into the Kĭdròn valley. 15And they killed the passover
lamb on the fourteenth day of the second month. And the priests
and the Lēvītes were put to shame, so that they sanctified themselves, and brought burnt offerings into the house of the LORD.
16 They took their accustomed posts according to the law of Moses
the man of God; the priests sprinkled the blood which they received from the hand of the Lēvītes. 17 For there were many in
the assembly who had not sanctified themselves; therefore the
Lēvītes had to kill the passover lamb for every one who was not
clean, to make it holy to the LORD. 18 For a multitude of the people, many of them from Ē′phräįm, Mȧnȧs′sēh, Ĭs′sȧçhar, and
Zĕb′u̇lùn, had not cleansed themselves, yet they ate the passover
otherwise than as prescribed. For Hĕzĕkī′ȧh had prayed for them,
saying, "The good LORD pardon every one 19 who sets his heart to
seek God, the LORD the God of his fathers, even though not according to the sanctuary's rules of cleanness." 20And the LORD heard
Hĕzĕkī′ȧh, and healed the people. 21And the people of Israel that
were present at Jerusalem kept the feast of unleavened bread
seven days with great gladness; and the Lēvītes and the priests
praised the LORD day by day, singing with all their might^s to the
LORD. 22And Hĕzĕkī′ȧh spoke encouragingly to all the Lēvītes
who showed good skill in the service of the LORD. So the people
ate the food of the festival for seven days, sacrificing peace offerings and giving thanks to the LORD the God of their fathers.

c. The feast continued for seven days

23 Then the whole assembly agreed together to keep the feast
for another seven days; so they kept it for another seven days with
gladness. 24 For Hĕzĕkī′ȧh king of Judah gave the assembly a
thousand bulls and seven thousand sheep for offerings, and the
princes gave the assembly a thousand bulls and ten thousand
sheep. And the priests sanctified themselves in great numbers.
25 The whole assembly of Judah, and the priests and the Lēvītes,
and the whole assembly that came out of Israel, and the sojourners
who came out of the land of Israel, and the sojourners who dwelt in
Judah, rejoiced. 26 So there was great joy in Jerusalem, for since
the time of Solomon the son of David king of Israel there had been
nothing like this in Jerusalem. 27 Then the priests and the Lēvītes
arose and blessed the people, and their voice was heard, and their
prayer came to his holy habitation in heaven.

3. Further reforms of Hezekiah
a. The high places destroyed

31 Now when all this was finished, all Israel who were present
went out to the cities of Judah and broke in pieces the pillars
and hewed down the Ȧshē′rĭm and broke down the high places
and the altars throughout all Judah and Benjamin, and in Ē′phrä-
ĭm and Mȧnȧs′sēh, until they had destroyed them all. Then all the
people of Israel returned to their cities, every man to his possession.

b. The Levitical service reformed

2 And Hĕzĕkī′ȧh appointed the divisions of the priests and of
the Lēvītes, division by division, each according to his service,

^{s} Compare 1 Chron 13.8: Heb *with instruments of might*

Marginal references

30.15
ver 2,3;
2 Chr 29.34

30.16
2 Chr
35.10,15

30.17
2 Chr 29.34

30.18
ver 11,25;
Ex 12.43–
49

30.19
2 Chr 19.3

30.21
Ex 12.15;
13.6

30.22
2 Chr 32.6;
Ezra 10.11

30.23
1 Ki 8.65

30.24
2 Chr 35.7,
8; 29.34

30.27
2 Chr
23.18;
Num 6.23;
Deut 26.15;
Ps 68.5

31.1
2 Ki 18.4

31.2
1 Chr 24.1;
23.28–31

the priests and the Levites, for burnt offerings and peace offerings, to minister in the gates of the camp of the LORD and to give thanks and praise. ³ The contribution of the king from his own possessions was for the burnt offerings: the burnt offerings of morning and evening, and the burnt offerings for the sabbaths, the new moons, and the appointed feasts, as it is written in the law of the LORD. ⁴And he commanded the people who lived in Jerusalem to give the portion due to the priests and the Lēvītes, that they might give themselves to the law of the LORD. ⁵As soon as the command was spread abroad, the people of Israel gave in abundance the first fruits of grain, wine, oil, honey, and of all the produce of the field; and they brought in abundantly the tithe of everything. ⁶And the people of Israel and Judah who lived in the cities of Judah also brought in the tithe of cattle and sheep, and the dedicated things ᵗ which had been consecrated to the LORD their God, and laid them in heaps. ⁷ In the third month they began to pile up the heaps, and finished them in the seventh month. ⁸ When Hĕzĕkī′áh and the princes came and saw the heaps, they blessed the LORD and his people Israel. ⁹And Hĕzĕkī′áh questioned the priests and the Lēvītes about the heaps. ¹⁰Ăzărī′áh the chief priest, who was of the house of Zādŏk, answered him, "Since they began to bring the contributions into the house of the LORD we have eaten and had enough and have plenty left; for the LORD has blessed his people, so that we have this great store left."

11 Then Hĕzĕkī′áh commanded them to prepare chambers in the house of the LORD; and they prepared them. ¹²And they faithfully brought in the contributions, the tithes and the dedicated things. The chief officer in charge of them was Cŏnănī′áh the Lēvīte, with Shĭm′ĕ-ī his brother as second; ¹³ while Jĕhī′ĕl, Ăzăzī′áh, Nāhăth, Ăs′áhĕl, Jĕr′ĭmŏth, Jŏz′ábăd, Ĕlī′ĕl, Ĭsmăchī′áh, Māhăth, and Bĕnāi′áh were overseers assisting Cŏnănī′áh and Shĭm′ĕ-ī his brother, by the appointment of Hĕzĕkī′áh the king and Ăzărī′áh the chief officer of the house of God. ¹⁴And Kō′rĕ the son of Ĭmnăh the Lēvīte, keeper of the east gate, was over the freewill offerings to God, to apportion the contribution reserved for the LORD and the most holy offerings. ¹⁵ Eden, Mĭn′jámĭn, Jĕsh′uá, Shĕmāi′áh, Ămărī′áh, and Shĕcănī′áh were faithfully assisting him in the cities of the priests, to distribute the portions to their brethren, old and young alike, by divisions, ¹⁶ except those enrolled by genealogy, males from three years old and upwards, all who entered the house of the LORD as the duty of each day required, for their service according to their offices, by their divisions. ¹⁷ The enrollment of the priests was according to their fathers' houses; that of the Lēvītes from twenty years old and upwards was according to their offices, by their divisions. ¹⁸ The priests were enrolled with all their little children, their wives, their sons, and their daughters, the whole multitude; for they were faithful in keeping themselves holy. ¹⁹And for the sons of Aaron, the priests, who were in the fields of common land belonging to their cities, there were men in the several cities who were designated by name to distribute portions to every male among the priests and to every one among the Lēvītes who was enrolled.

ᵗ Heb the tithe of the dedicated things

c. *The personal faithfulness of Hezekiah*

20 Thus Hĕzĕkī′áh did throughout all Judah; and he did what
was good and right and faithful before the LORD his God. 21And
every work that he undertook in the service of the house of God
and in accordance with the law and the commandments, seeking
his God, he did with all his heart, and prospered.

31.20
2 Ki 20.3;
22.2

4. *The defeat of Sennacherib*
a. *The defense against Sennacherib*

32 After these things and these acts of faithfulness Sĕnnăch′-
erĭb king of Assyria came and invaded Judah and encamped
against the fortified cities, thinking to win them for himself.
2And when Hĕzĕkī′áh saw that Sĕnnăch′erĭb had come and intended to fight against Jerusalem, 3 he planned with his officers
and his mighty men to stop the water of the springs that were
outside the city; and they helped him. 4A great many people were
gathered, and they stopped all the springs and the brook that
flowed through the land, saying, "Why should the kings of
Assyria come and find much water?" 5 He set to work resolutely
and built up all the wall that was broken down, and raised towers
upon it,ᵘ and outside it he built another wall; and he strengthened
the Mĭllō in the city of David. He also made weapons and shields
in abundance. 6And he set combat commanders over the people,
and gathered them together to him in the square at the gate of the
city and spoke encouragingly to them, saying, 7 "Be strong and of
good courage. Do not be afraid or dismayed before the king of
Assyria and all the horde that is with him; for there is one greater
with us than with him. 8 With him is an arm of flesh; but with us is
the LORD our God, to help us and to fight our battles." And the
people took confidence from the words of Hĕzĕkī′áh king of Judah.

32.1
2 Ki 18.13–
19;
Isa 36.1ff

32.4
2 Ki 20.20;
ver 30

32.5
2 Chr
25.23;
1 Ki 9.24

32.6
2 Chr 30.22

32.7
1 Chr
22.13;
2 Ki 6.16
32.8
Jer 17.5;
2 Chr
13.12;
20.17

b. *The message of Sennacherib*

9 After this Sĕnnăch′erĭb king of Assyria, who was besieging
Lăchĭsh with all his forces, sent his servants to Jerusalem to
Hĕzĕkī′áh king of Judah and to all the people of Judah that were
in Jerusalem, saying, 10 "Thus says Sĕnnăch′erĭb king of Assyria,
'On what are you relying, that you stand siege in Jerusalem? 11 Is
not Hĕzĕkī′áh misleading you, that he may give you over to die
by famine and by thirst, when he tells you, "The LORD our God
will deliver us from the hand of the king of Assyria"? 12 Has not
this same Hĕzĕkī′áh taken away his high places and his altars and
commanded Judah and Jerusalem, "Before one altar you shall
worship, and upon it you shall burn your sacrifices"? 13 Do you
not know what I and my fathers have done to all the peoples of
other lands? Were the gods of the nations of those lands at all able
to deliver their lands out of my hand? 14 Who among all the gods
of those nations which my fathers utterly destroyed was able to
deliver his people from my hand, that your God should be able
to deliver you from my hand? 15 Now therefore do not let Hĕzĕkī′-
áh deceive you or mislead you in this fashion, and do not believe
him, for no god of any nation or kingdom has been able to deliver
his people from my hand or from the hand of my fathers. How
much less will your God deliver you out of my hand!' "

32.11
2 Ki 18.30

32.12
2 Ki 18.22;
2 Chr 31.1

32.13
2 Ki
18.33–35

32.14
Isa 10.9–11

32.15
2 Ki 18.29

ᵘ Vg: Heb *and raised upon the towers*

c. *Sennacherib's blasphemy against God*

32.17
2 Ki 19.9,12

16 And his servants said still more against the LORD GOD and against his servant Hĕzĕkī'áh. 17And he wrote letters to cast contempt on the LORD the God of Israel and to speak against him, saying, "Like the gods of the nations of the lands who have not delivered their people from my hands, so the God of Hĕzĕkī'áh will not deliver his people from my hand." 18And they shouted it with a loud voice in the language of Judah to the people of Jerusalem who were upon the wall, to frighten and terrify them, in order that they might take the city. 19And they spoke of the God of Jerusalem as they spoke of the gods of the peoples of the earth, which are the work of men's hands.

32.18
2 Ki 18.26–
28

32.19
2 Ki 19.18

d. *Sennacherib turned back by the angel*

32.20
2 Ki 19.2,
4,15
32.21
2 Ki 19.35ff

20 Then Hĕzĕkī'áh the king and Ĭşāi'áh the prophet, the son of Āmŏz, prayed because of this and cried to heaven. 21And the LORD sent an angel, who cut off all the mighty warriors and commanders and officers in the camp of the king of Assyria. So he returned with shame of face to his own land. And when he came into the house of his god, some of his own sons struck him down there with the sword. 22 So the LORD saved Hĕzĕkī'áh and the inhabitants of Jerusalem from the hand of Sĕnnăch'ĕrĭb king of Assyria and from the hand of all his enemies; and he gave them rest on every side. 23And many brought gifts to the LORD to Jerusalem and precious things to Hĕzĕkī'áh king of Judah, so that he was exalted in the sight of all nations from that time onward.

32.23
2 Chr 17.5

5. *The extension of life granted to Hezekiah*

32.24
2 Ki 20.1–
11;
Isa 38.1–8
32.25
Ps 116.12;
2 Chr
26.16;
24.18
32.26
Jer 26.18,
19

24 In those days Hĕzĕkī'áh became sick and was at the point of death, and he prayed to the LORD; and he answered him and gave him a sign. 25 But Hĕzĕkī'áh did not make return according to the benefit done to him, for his heart was proud. Therefore wrath came upon him and Judah and Jerusalem. 26 But Hĕzĕkī'áh humbled himself for the pride of his heart, both he and the inhabitants of Jerusalem, so that the wrath of the LORD did not come upon them in the days of Hezekiah.

6. *The greatness of Hezekiah*

32.29
1 Chr 29.12

32.30
2 Ki 20.20;
1 Ki 1,33
32.31
2 Ki 20.12;
Isa 39.1;
Deut 8.2,16

27 And Hĕzĕkī'áh had very great riches and honor; and he made for himself treasuries for silver, for gold, for precious stones, for spices, for shields, and for all kinds of costly vessels; 28 storehouses also for the yield of grain, wine, and oil; and stalls for all kinds of cattle, and sheepfolds. 29 He likewise provided cities for himself, and flocks and herds in abundance; for God had given him very great possessions. 30 This same Hĕzĕkī'áh closed the upper outlet of the waters of Gīhŏn and directed them down to the west side of the city of David. And Hezeki'ah prospered in all his works. 31And so in the matter of the envoys of the princes of Babylon, who had been sent to him to inquire about the sign that had been done in the land, God left him to himself, in order to try him and to know all that was in his heart.

7. *Hezekiah's death and the succession*

32 Now the rest of the acts of Hĕzĕkī'áh, and his good deeds, behold, they are written in the vision of Ĭşāi'áh the prophet the son

of Āmŏz, in the Book of the Kings of Judah and Israel. ³³And Hĕzĕkī′áh slept with his fathers, and they buried him in the ascent of the tombs of the sons of David; and all Judah and the inhabitants of Jerusalem did him honor at his death. And Mănăs′sĕh his son reigned in his stead.

M. The reigns of Manasseh and Amon

1. The wickedness of Manasseh

33 Mănăs′sĕh was twelve years old when he began to reign, and he reigned fifty-five years in Jerusalem. ² He did what was evil in the sight of the LORD, according to the abominable practices of the nations whom the LORD drove out before the people of Israel. ³ For he rebuilt the high places which his father Hĕzĕkī′áh had broken down, and erected altars to the Bă̄ăls, and made Ăshē′-ráhs, and worshiped all the host of heaven, and served them. ⁴And he built altars in the house of the LORD, of which the LORD had said, "In Jerusalem shall my name be for ever." ⁵And he built altars for all the host of heaven in the two courts of the house of the LORD. ⁶And he burned his sons as an offering in the valley of the son of Hĭnnŏm, and practiced soothsaying and augury and sorcery, and dealt with mediums and with wizards. He did much evil in the sight of the LORD, provoking him to anger. ⁷And the image of the idol which he had made he set in the house of God, of which God said to David and to Solomon his son, "In this house, and in Jerusalem, which I have chosen out of all the tribes of Israel, I will put my name for ever; ⁸ and I will no more remove the foot of Israel from the land which I appointed for your fathers, if only they will be careful to do all that I have commanded them, all the law, the statutes, and the ordinances given through Moses." ⁹ Mănăs′sĕh seduced Judah and the inhabitants of Jerusalem, so that they did more evil than the nations whom the LORD destroyed before the people of Israel.

2. His imprisonment and release

10 The LORD spoke to Mănăs′sĕh and to his people, but they gave no heed. ¹¹ Therefore the LORD brought upon them the commanders of the army of the king of Assyria, who took Mănăs′sĕh with hooks and bound him with fetters of bronze and brought him to Babylon. ¹²And when he was in distress he entreated the favor of the LORD his God and humbled himself greatly before the God of his fathers. ¹³ He prayed to him, and God received his entreaty and heard his supplication and brought him again to Jerusalem into his kingdom. Then Mănăs′sĕh knew that the LORD was God.

3. The removal of the heathen altars

14 Afterwards he built an outer wall for the city of David west of Gīhŏn, in the valley, and for the entrance into the Fish Gate, and carried it round Ŏphĕl, and raised it to a very great height; he also put commanders of the army in all the fortified cities in Judah. ¹⁵And he took away the foreign gods and the idol from the house of the LORD, and all the altars that he had built on the mountain of the house of the LORD and in Jerusalem, and he threw them

Marginal references

32.33
2 Ki 20.21;
Prov 10.7

★33.1
2 Ki 21.1–9
33.2
Deut 18.9;
2 Chr 28.3
33.3
2 Chr 31.1;
Deut 16.21;
2 Ki 23.5,6;
Deut 17.3
33.4
2 Chr
28.24;
7.16
33.5
2 Chr 4.9
33.6
Lev 18.21;
2 Chr 28.3;
Deut 18.10,
11;
2 Ki 21.6
33.7
2 Ki 21.7;
ver 4,15
33.8
2 Sam 7.10

★33.10
33.11
Deut 28.36;
Ps 107.10,
11
33.12
2 Chr
32.26;
1 Pet 5.6
33.13
1 Chr 5.20;
Ezra 8.23;
Dan 4.25,
32

33.14
1 Ki 1.33;
Neh 3.3;
2 Chr 27.3

33.15
ver 3–7

33.1 *fifty-five years.* Ten years were a coregency with Hezekiah.

33.10 Because wicked Manasseh would not heed God, judgment fell until he was humbled.

outside of the city. 16 He also restored the altar of the LORD and
offered upon it sacrifices of peace offerings and of thanksgiving;
and he commanded Judah to serve the LORD the God of Israel.

33.17
2 Chr 32.12

17 Nevertheless the people still sacrificed at the high places, but
only to the LORD their God.

4. *The summary of Manasseh's reign and death*

33.18
ver 10,12,18

18 Now the rest of the acts of Mánǎs'sëh, and his prayer to his
God, and the words of the seers who spoke to him in the name of
the LORD the God of Israel, behold, they are in the Chronicles

33.19
ver 3,13

of the Kings of Israel. 19And his prayer, and how God received his
entreaty, and all his sin and his faithlessness, and the sites on
which he built high places and set up the Åshē'rïm and the images,
before he humbled himself, behold, they are written in the Chron-

33.20
2 Ki 21.18

icles of the Seers.[v] 20 So Mánǎs'sëh slept with his fathers, and they
buried him in his house; and Åmón his son reigned in his stead.

5. *The reign of Amon*

33.21
**2 Ki 21.19–
24**

21 Åmón was twenty-two years old when he began to reign, and
he reigned two years in Jerusalem. 22 He did what was evil in the

33.22
ver 2–7

sight of the LORD, as Mánǎs'sëh his father had done. Åmón sacrificed to all the images that Manas'sëh his father had made, and

33.23
ver 12

served them. 23And he did not humble himself before the LORD,
as Mánǎs'sëh his father had humbled himself, but this Åmón in-

33.24
**see 2 Chr
25.27**

curred guilt more and more. 24And his servants conspired against
him and killed him in his house. 25 But the people of the land slew
all those who had conspired against King Åmón; and the people
of the land made Jōsī'áh his son king in his stead.

N. *The reign of Josiah*

1. *His removal of the idols and high places*

34.1
2 Ki 22.1,2

34 Jōsī'áh was eight years old when he began to reign, and he
reigned thirty-one years in Jerusalem. 2 He did what was

34.3
**2 Chr
15.2;
1 Ki 13.3;
2 Chr
33.17,22**

right in the eyes of the LORD, and walked in the ways of David his
father; and he did not turn aside to the right or to the left. 3 For in
the eighth year of his reign, while he was yet a boy, he began to
seek the God of David his father; and in the twelfth year he began
to purge Judah and Jerusalem of the high places, the Åshē'rïm,

34.4
**Lev 26.30;
2 Ki 23.4;
Ex 32.20**

and the graven and the molten images. 4And they broke down
the altars of the Bảàḷṣ in his presence; and he hewed down the incense altars which stood above them; and he broke in pieces the
Åshē'rïm and the graven and the molten images, and he made dust
of them and strewed it over the graves of those who had sacrificed

34.5
**1 Ki 13.2;
2 Ki 23.20**

to them. 5 He also burned the bones of the priests on their altars,
and purged Judah and Jerusalem. 6And in the cities of Mánǎs'sëh,

34.6
**2 Ki 23.15,
19**

Ē'phrǎïm, and Sïm'ëön, and as far as Nǎph'tǎlī, in their ruins[w]
round about, 7 he broke down the altars, and beat the Åshē'rïm

34.7
2 Chr 31.1

and the images into powder, and hewed down all the incense
altars throughout all the land of Israel. Then he returned to
Jerusalem.

2. *His repair of the house of the* LORD

34.8
**2 Ki 22.3–
20**

8 Now in the eighteenth year of his reign, when he had purged

---

[v] One Ms: Gk: Heb *of Hōzaï*   [w] Heb uncertain

the land and the house, he sent Shăphán the son of Ăzălī'áh, and Mā-ăseī'áh the governor of the city, and Jōáh the son of Jō'áhăz, the recorder, to repair the house of the LORD his God. 9 They came to Hĭlkī'áh the high priest and delivered the money that had been brought into the house of God, which the Lēvītes, the keepers of the threshold, had collected from Mánăs'sĕh and Ē'phrăjm and from all the remnant of Israel and from all Judah and Benjamin and from the inhabitants of Jerusalem. 10 They delivered it to the workmen who had the oversight of the house of the LORD; and the workmen who were working in the house of the LORD gave it for repairing and restoring the house. 11 They gave it to the carpenters and the builders to buy quarried stone, and timber for binders and beams for the buildings which the kings of Judah had let go to ruin. 12And the men did the work faithfully. Over them were set Jāhăth and Ōbădī'áh the Lēvītes, of the sons of Mèrar'ĭ, and Zĕchárī'áh and Mĕshŭl'lăm, of the sons of the Kō'-hăthītes, to have oversight. The Levites, all who were skilful with instruments of music, 13 were over the burden bearers and directed all who did work in every kind of service; and some of the Lēvītes were scribes, and officials, and gatekeepers.

3. The discovery of the Book of the Law

14 While they were bringing out the money that had been brought into the house of the LORD, Hĭlkī'áh the priest found the book of the law of the LORD given through Moses. 15 Then Hĭlkī'-áh said to Shāphán the secretary, "I have found the book of the law in the house of the LORD"; and Hilkiah gave the book to Shaphan. 16 Shăphán brought the book to the king, and further reported to the king, "All that was committed to your servants they are doing. 17 They have emptied out the money that was found in the house of the LORD and have delivered it into the hand of the overseers and the workmen." 18 Then Shăphán the secretary told the king, "Hĭlkī'áh the priest has given me a book." And Shaphan read it before the king.

19 When the king heard the words of the law he rent his clothes. 20And the king commanded Hĭlkī'áh, Ăhī'kăm the son of Shāphán, Ăbdón the son of Mĭcáh, Shaphan the secretary, and Ăsāi'áh the king's servant, saying, 21 "Go, inquire of the LORD for me and for those who are left in Israel and in Judah, concerning the words of the book that has been found; for great is the wrath of the LORD that is poured out on us, because our fathers have not kept the word of the LORD, to do according to all that is written in this book."

22 So Hĭlkī'áh and those whom the king had sent* went to Hŭldáh the prophetess, the wife of Shăllùm the son of Tŏkháth, son of Hăsráh, keeper of the wardrobe (now she dwelt in Jerusalem in the Second Quarter) and spoke to her to that effect. 23And she said to them, "Thus says the LORD, the God of Israel: 'Tell the man who sent you to me, 24 Thus says the LORD, Behold, I will bring evil upon this place and upon its inhabitants, all the curses that are written in the book which was read before the king of Judah. 25 Because they have forsaken me and have burned incense to other gods, that they might provoke me to anger with all

x Syr Vg: Heb lacks had sent

34.9
2 Chr 35.8

34.11
2 Chr
33.4-7

34.12
1 Chr 25.1

34.13
1 Chr 23.4,5

34.14
ver 9

34.16
ver 8

34.19
Josh 7.6

34.21
2 Chr 29.8

34.22
2 Ki 22.14

34.24
2 Chr
36.14-20;
Deut 28.15-
68
34.25
2 Chr 33.3

the works of their hands, therefore my wrath will be poured out upon this place and will not be quenched. 26 But to the king of Judah, who sent you to inquire of the LORD, thus shall you say to him, Thus says the LORD, the God of Israel: Regarding the words which you have heard, 27 because your heart was penitent and you humbled yourself before God when you heard his words against this place and its inhabitants, and you have humbled yourself before me, and have rent your clothes and wept before me, I also have heard you, says the LORD. 28 Behold, I will gather you to your fathers, and you shall be gathered to your grave in peace, and your eyes shall not see all the evil which I will bring upon this place and its inhabitants.' " And they brought back word to the king.

4. The reading of the Law and the renewal of the covenant

29 Then the king sent and gathered together all the elders of Judah and Jerusalem. 30And the king went up to the house of the LORD, with all the men of Judah and the inhabitants of Jerusalem and the priests and the Lēvītes, all the people both great and small; and he read in their hearing all the words of the book of the covenant which had been found in the house of the LORD. 31And the king stood in his place and made a covenant before the LORD, to walk after the LORD and to keep his commandments and his testimonies and his statutes, with all his heart and all his soul, to perform the words of the covenant that were written in this book. 32 Then he made all who were present in Jerusalem and in Benjamin stand to it. And the inhabitants of Jerusalem did according to the covenant of God, the God of their fathers. 33And Jōsī´áh took away all the abominations from all the territory that belonged to the people of Israel, and made all who were in Israel serve the LORD their God. All his days they did not turn away from following the LORD the God of their fathers.

5. The keeping of the Passover

35 Jōsī´áh kept a passover to the LORD in Jerusalem; and they killed the passover lamb on the fourteenth day of the first month. 2 He appointed the priests to their offices and encouraged them in the service of the house of the LORD. 3And he said to the Lēvītes who taught all Israel and who were holy to the LORD, "Put the holy ark in the house which Solomon the son of David, king of Israel, built; you need no longer carry it upon your shoulders. Now serve the LORD your God and his people Israel. 4 Prepare yourselves according to your fathers' houses by your divisions, following the directions of David king of Israel and the directions of Solomon his son. 5And stand in the holy place according to the groupings of the fathers' houses of your brethren the lay people, and let there be for each a part of a father's house of the Lēvītes.ʸ 6And kill the passover lamb, and sanctify yourselves, and prepare for your brethren, to do according to the word of the LORD by Moses."

7 Then Jōsī´áh contributed to the lay people, as passover offerings for all that were present, lambs and kids from the flock to the number of thirty thousand, and three thousand bulls; these were from the king's possessions. 8And his princes contributed

34.27
2 Chr 12.7;
32.26

34.29
2 Ki 23.1–3
34.30
Neh 8.1–3

34.31
2 Ki 11.14;
23.3;
2 Chr 23.3,
16; 29.10

34.33
ver 3–7;
2 Chr 33.2–
7

35.1
2 Ki 23.21,
22;
Ex 12.6;
Num 9.3
35.2
2 Chr
23.18;
29.11
35.3
Deut 33.10;
2 Chr 5.7;
1 Chr 23.26
35.4
1 Chr
9.10–13;
2 Chr 8.14
35.5
Ps 134.1
35.6
ver 1;
2 Chr 29.5,
15;
Ezra 6.20
35.7
2 Chr 30.24

ʸ Heb obscure

willingly to the people, to the priests, and to the Lēvītes. Hĭlkī'ȧh, Zĕchȧrī'ȧh, and Jĕhī'ĕl, the chief officers of the house of God, gave to the priests for the passover offerings two thousand six hundred lambs and kids and three hundred bulls. 9 Cŏnȧnī'ȧh also, and Shĕmāi'ȧh and Nĕthȧn'ĕl his brothers, and Hȧshȧbī'ȧh and Je-ī'ĕl and Jŏz'ȧbȧd, the chiefs of the Lēvītes, gave to the Levites for the passover offerings five thousand lambs and kids and five hundred bulls.

35.9
2 Chr 31.12

10 When the service had been prepared for, the priests stood in their place, and the Lēvītes in their divisions according to the king's command. 11And they killed the passover lamb, and the priests sprinkled the blood which they received from them while the Lēvītes flayed the victims. 12And they set aside the burnt offerings that they might distribute them according to the groupings of the fathers' houses of the lay people, to offer to the LORD, as it is written in the book of Moses. And so they did with the bulls. 13And they roasted the passover lamb with fire according to the ordinance; and they boiled the holy offerings in pots, in caldrons, and in pans, and carried them quickly to all the lay people. 14And afterward they prepared for themselves and for the priests, because the priests the sons of Aaron were busied in offering the burnt offerings and the fat parts until night; so the Lēvītes prepared for themselves and for the priests the sons of Aaron. 15 The singers, the sons of Āsȧph, were in their place according to the command of David, and Asaph, and Hēmȧn, and Jĕdu'thŭn the king's seer; and the gatekeepers were at each gate; they did not need to depart from their service, for their brethren the Lēvītes prepared for them.

35.10
ver 5;
Ezra 6.18
35.11
ver 1,6;
2 Chr
29.22,34

35.13
Ex 12.8,9;
Lev 6.25;
1 Sam 2.13–
15

35.15
1 Chr 25.1;
26.12–19

16 So all the service of the LORD was prepared that day, to keep the passover and to offer burnt offerings on the altar of the LORD, according to the command of King Jŏsī'ȧh. 17And the people of Israel who were present kept the passover at that time, and the feast of unleavened bread seven days. 18 No passover like it had been kept in Israel since the days of Samuel the prophet; none of the kings of Israel had kept such a passover as was kept by Jŏsī'ȧh, and the priests and the Lēvītes, and all Judah and Israel who were present, and the inhabitants of Jerusalem. 19 In the eighteenth year of the reign of Jŏsī'ȧh this passover was kept.

35.17
Ex 12.15;
2 Chr 30.21
*35.18
2 Ki 23.21–
23

6. Josiah's battle against Neco of Egypt, and his death

20 After all this, when Jŏsī'ȧh had prepared the temple, Nĕcō king of Egypt went up to fight at Car'chĕmĭsh on the Eūphrā'tēs and Josiah went out against him. 21 But he sent envoys to him, saying, "What have we to do with each other, king of Judah? I am not coming against you this day, but against the house with which I am at war; and God has commanded me to make haste. Cease opposing God, who is with me, lest he destroy you." 22 Never-

35.20
2 Ki 23.29,
30;
Isa 10.9;
Jer 46.2

*35.22
2 Chr
18.29;
Judg 5.19

35.18 While there was nothing like Hezekiah's celebration of the Passover in Jerusalem since the time of Solomon (30.26), Josiah's Passover was greater still. There had been nothing like it since the days of Samuel or *since the days of the judges* (2 Ki 23.22).
35.22 *plain of Megiddo.* The fortress of Megiddo, rising above the plain in the southern reaches of the Esdraelon or Jezreel Valley,

acquired the name *Har-megiddo*, "The Hill of Megiddo." It guarded the pass on the best north-south route in Canaan, and it was here that many of the great battles of ancient history were fought, even from the 15th century B.C. during the campaigns of Thutmose III of Egypt. It is also here that the Armageddon, the climactic battle between good and evil forces, is ultimately to take place (Rev 16.16).

theless Jōsī'áh would not turn away from him, but disguised himself in order to fight with him. He did not listen to the words of Nĕcō from the mouth of God, but joined battle in the plain of Mĕgĭd'dō. 23And the archers shot King Jōsī'áh; and the king said to his servants, "Take me away, for I am badly wounded." 24 So his servants took him out of the chariot and carried him in his second chariot and brought him to Jerusalem. And he died, and was buried in the tombs of his fathers. All Judah and Jerusalem mourned for Jōsī'áh. 25 Jĕrĕmī'áh also uttered a lament for Jōsī'áh; and all the singing men and singing women have spoken of Josiah in their laments to this day. They made these an ordinance in Israel; behold, they are written in the Laments. 26 Now the rest of the acts of Jōsī'áh, and his good deeds according to what is written in the law of the LORD, 27 and his acts, first and last, behold, they are written in the Book of the Kings of Israel and Judah.

*35.23

35.24
2 Ki 23.30;
Zech 12.11

35.25
Lam 4.20;
Jer 22.20

O. From Josiah to the captivity

1. Jehoahaz captive in Egypt

36 The people of the land took Jĕhō'áhăz the son of Jōsī'áh and made him king in his father's stead in Jerusalem. 2 Jĕhō'-áhăz was twenty-three years old when he began to reign; and he reigned three months in Jerusalem. 3 Then the king of Egypt deposed him in Jerusalem and laid upon the land a tribute of a hundred talents of silver and a talent of gold. 4And the king of Egypt made Ĕlī'ákĭm his brother king over Judah and Jerusalem, and changed his name to Jĕhoi'ákĭm; but Nĕcō took Jĕhō'áhăz his brother and carried him to Egypt.

36.1
2 Ki 23.30–
34;
Jer 22.11

2. Jehoiakim captive in Babylon

5 Jĕhoi'ákĭm was twenty-five years old when he began to reign, and he reigned eleven years in Jerusalem. He did what was evil in the sight of the LORD his God. 6Against him came up Nĕbŭchádnĕz'zár king of Babylon, and bound him in fetters to take him to Babylon. 7 Nĕbŭchádnĕz'zár also carried part of the vessels of the house of the LORD to Babylon and put them in his palace in Babylon. 8 Now the rest of the acts of Jĕhoi'ákĭm, and the abominations which he did, and what was found against him, behold, they are written in the Book of the Kings of Israel and Judah; and Jĕhoi'-áchĭn his son reigned in his stead.

36.5
2 Ki 23.36,
37
36.6
2 Ki 24.1;
2 Chr 33.11
36.7
2 Ki 24.13
36.8
2 Ki 24.5;
see 1 Chr
3.16

3. Jehoiachin captive in Babylon

9 Jĕhoi'áchĭn was eight years old when he began to reign, and he reigned three months and ten days in Jerusalem. He did what was evil in the sight of the LORD. 10 In the spring of the year King Nĕbŭchádnĕz'zár sent and brought him to Babylon, with the precious vessels of the house of the LORD, and made his brother Zĕdĕkī'áh king over Judah and Jerusalem.

*36.9
2 Ki 24.8–
17
36.10
2 Sam 11.1;
Jer 37.1

35.23 During his lifetime Josiah was to see many religious reforms take place as a result of his efforts.

36.9 *eight* is an error for *eighteen* (2 Ki 24.8 gives the latter figure, which we can assume to be the more reliable one).

4. *Wicked Zedekiah*
a. *His rebellion against Nebuchadnezzar*

11 Zĕdĕkī'ăh was twenty-one years old when he began to reign, and he reigned eleven years in Jerusalem. 12 He did what was evil in the sight of the LORD his God. He did not humble himself before Jĕrĕmī'ăh the prophet, who spoke from the mouth of the LORD. 13 He also rebelled against King Nĕbŭçhădnĕz'zăr, who had made him swear by God; he stiffened his neck and hardened his heart against turning to the LORD, the God of Israel. 14All the leading priests and the people likewise were exceedingly unfaithful, following all the abominations of the nations; and they polluted the house of the LORD which he had hallowed in Jerusalem.

36.11
2 Ki 24.18–20;
Jer 52.1
36.12
2 Chr 33.23;
Jer 21.3–7
36.13
Jer 52.3;
Ezek 17.15;
2 Ki 17.14;
2 Chr 30.8

b. *The mocking of God's messengers*

15 The LORD, the God of their fathers, sent persistently to them by his messengers, because he had compassion on his people and on his dwelling place; 16 but they kept mocking the messengers of God, despising his words, and scoffing at his prophets, till the wrath of the LORD rose against his people, till there was no remedy.

36.15
Jer 25.3,4;
35.15; 44.4
36.16
2 Chr 30.10;
Jer 5.12,13;
Prov 1.25;
Ezra 5.12

c. *The destruction of the Temple and Jerusalem: the captivity*

17 Therefore he brought up against them the king of the Çhăldē'ăns, who slew their young men with the sword in the house of their sanctuary, and had no compassion on young man or virgin, old man or aged; he gave them all into his hand. 18And all the vessels of the house of God, great and small, and the treasures of the house of the LORD, and the treasures of the king and of his princes, all these he brought to Babylon. 19And they burned the house of God, and broke down the wall of Jerusalem, and burned all its palaces with fire, and destroyed all its precious vessels. 20 He took into exile in Babylon those who had escaped from the sword, and they became servants to him and to his sons until the establishment of the kingdom of Persia, 21 to fulfil the word of the LORD by the mouth of Jĕrĕmī'ăh, until the land had enjoyed its sabbaths. All the days that it lay desolate it kept sabbath, to fulfil seventy years.

36.17
2 Ki 25.1–7
36.18
2 Ki 25.13ff
36.19
2 Ki 25.9;
Jer 52.13
36.20
2 Ki 25.11;
Jer 27.7
*36.21
Jer 29.10;
Lev 26.34;
25.4

5. *The return from the captivity prophesied*

22 Now in the first year of Cyrus king of Persia, that the word of the LORD by the mouth of Jĕrĕmī'ăh might be accomplished, the LORD stirred up the spirit of Cyrus king of Persia so that he made a proclamation throughout all his kingdom and also put it in writing: 23 "Thus says Cyrus king of Persia, 'The LORD, the God of heaven, has given me all the kingdoms of the earth, and he has charged me to build him a house at Jerusalem, which is in Judah. Whoever is among you of all his people, may the LORD his God be with him. Let him go up.' "

*36.22
Ezra 1.1;
Jer 25.12;
Isa 44.28
36.23
Ezra 1.2,3

36.21 *mouth of Jeremiah*, a reference to Jer 25.11,12; 29.10 where the seventy years' service to Babylon is mentioned.

36.22 Cyrus was the founder of the Persian Empire, which became the largest empire the world had yet seen.

INTRODUCTION TO
THE BOOK OF
EZRA

Authorship and Background: See 1 Chronicles for a discussion of authorship. The book is named for its principal character, Ezra, the priest and scribe. The compilation includes a number of different sources: documents in Hebrew relating to Zerubbabel's return and subsequent difficulties in Jerusalem (1.1—4.7); extracts from Aramaic records (4.8—6.18); and personal writings of Ezra (7.27—9.15). Two different periods of history are considered: the return of the exiles under Zerubbabel (1–6), and the return under Ezra (7–10). The first return and its results are treated in two phases: the decree of Cyrus to the cessation of Temple construction (539–535 B.C.), and the resumption of construction until the completion of the Temple (520–515 B.C.).

Ezra's return is dated in the seventh year of Artaxerxes (7.7). Some take this to mean Artaxerxes I (465–424 B.C.), in which event Ezra returned in 458 B.C.; others take it to mean Artaxerxes II (404–358 B.C.), which would indicate that Ezra returned in 397 B.C. The traditional fifth century date for Ezra, however, has been reinforced in the writings of W. F. Albright. The Elephantine letter #30, dated 408 B.C., was addressed to Bigvai (Bagoas), governor of Judea, who was apparently Nehemiah's successor. The same letter noted that Johanan (or Jehohanan), the person mentioned in Ezra 6.10 and Neh 12.22, 23, was priest in Jerusalem in 411 B.C. In fact, nothing in the genealogical lists or the narrative of the Chronicler's history is dated after about 400 B.C. A third view dates Ezra's return to Jerusalem in 428 B.C. on the assumption that a scribal error changed the thirty-seventh year to the seventh year of Artaxerxes, something which could easily have occurred because in the Hebrew the words "thirty," "seven," and "year" all begin with the same letter.

Characteristics: A portion of Ezra is personal, being written in the first person; other parts are in the third person. It is a historical book in the Hagiographa (the *holy writings*, together with the *Law* and the *Prophets*, made up the Old Testament canon of Scripture) which emphasizes Israel's obligation as a people of holiness, i.e., chosen and separated by God from other nations for His express purposes. The Jews are to be kept "pure" by dissolving and avoiding foreign contacts. The book describes how Ezra gets the people to bind themselves to the Law of God, and how he successfully completes the mission given by his king when he is allowed to return to Palestine.

Contents:

I.   The first return to the land. 1.1—2.70: Cyrus issues an edict permitting return to Jerusalem. Preparations are made for the return. The returning Israelites are listed. Summaries, and gathering of money for the Temple.

II.   The restoration of worship and dedication of the Temple. 3.1—6.22: The altar rebuilt and the sacrifices commenced. Work on the Temple begun. The Samaritans seek to stop the work. The Temple completed under Darius after an official investigation. The feasts of the Passover and Unleavened Bread celebrated.

III.   The return of Ezra and the reform which followed. 7.1—10.44: The genealogy of Ezra and his career depicted. His commission to return; funds secured. Accompanied by others, he acquires Temple servants, puts a guard over the treasure, and comes to Jerusalem. Upon hearing of the mixed marriages Ezra mourns and prays. The people repent and meet in public assembly. They separate themselves from their foreign spouses; those with foreign wives are listed.

THE BOOK OF

EZRA

I. The first return to the land 1.1–2.70

A. The edict of Cyrus

*1.1ff
2 Chr
36.22,23;
Jer 25.12;
29.10;
Ezra 5.13,
14

1 In the first year of Cyrus king of Persia, that the word of the LORD by the mouth of Jĕrĕmī'ăh might be accomplished, the LORD stirred up the spirit of Cyrus king of Persia so that he made a proclamation throughout all his kingdom and also put it in writing:

1.2
Isa 44.28;
45.1,12,13

2 "Thus says Cyrus king of Persia: The LORD, the God of heaven, has given me all the kingdoms of the earth, and he has charged me to build him a house at Jerusalem, which is in Judah.

1.3
Dan 6.26

3 Whoever is among you of all his people, may his God be with him, and let him go up to Jerusalem, which is in Judah, and rebuild the house of the LORD, the God of Israel—he is the God who is in Jerusalem; 4 and let each survivor, in whatever place he sojourns, be assisted by the men of his place with silver and gold, with goods and with beasts, besides freewill offerings for the house of God which is in Jerusalem."

B. Preparation for the return

1.5
Phil 2.13

5 Then rose up the heads of the fathers' houses of Judah and Benjamin, and the priests and the Lēvītes, every one whose spirit God had stirred to go up to rebuild the house of the LORD which is in Jerusalem; 6 and all who were about them aided them with vessels of silver, with gold, with goods, with beasts, and with costly wares, besides all that was freely offered. 7 Cyrus the king also brought out the vessels of the house of the LORD which Nĕbŭ-chădnĕz'zăr had carried away from Jerusalem and placed in the house of his gods. 8 Cyrus king of Persia brought these out in charge of Mĭth'rĕdăth the treasurer, who counted them out to Shĕsh-băz'zăr the prince of Judah. 9 And this was the number of them: a thousand[a] basins of gold, a thousand basins of silver, twenty-nine censers, 10 thirty bowls of gold, two thousand[b] four hundred and ten bowls of silver, and a thousand other vessels; 11 all the vessels of gold and of silver were five thousand four hundred and sixty-nine.[c] All these did Shĕsh-băz'zăr bring up, when the exiles were brought up from Babylonia to Jerusalem.

1.7
Ezra 5.14;
6.5;
2 Ki 24.13;
2 Chr 36.7
*1.8
Ezra 5.14

---

a 1 Esdras 2.13: Heb thirty   b 1 Esdras 2.13: Heb of a second sort
c 1 Esdras 2.14: Heb five thousand four hundred

1.1 *first year*, being 539 B.C. Cyrus reigned 559–530 B.C., but his control over Babylonia began in 539 B.C.

1.1-3 These verses, a repetition of 2 Chr 36.22, 23, indicate (along with the style, language, and interests of the book) that Ezra may well have been an integral part of the Chronicler's history. See here the Introductions to 1 and 2 Chronicles.

1.8 *Shesh-bazzar*, perhaps the Shenazzar of 1 Chr 3.18. (Some have even considered that Shesh-bazzar was the pseudonym for Zerubbabel.) Being a son of Jehoiachin, he would have been the one entrusted with the priceless vessels of the Temple. In fact, so well thought of was this "prince of Judah" that Cyrus later appointed him governor over the people. (See Ezra 5.14.)

C. The first return under Zerubbabel

2 Now these were the people of the province who came up out of the captivity of those exiles whom Nĕbùchầdnĕz′zàr the king of Babylon had carried captive to Babylonia; they returned to Jerusalem and Judah, each to his own town. 2 They came with Zẽrúb′bábẽl, Jĕsh′uả, Nẽhĕmī′áh, Sẽrāi′áh, Rẽ-ĕl-āi′áh, Mor′- dĕcaī, Bĭlshăn, Mĭspar, Bĭgvaī, Rēhùm, and Bā′ánáh.

The number of the men of the people of Israel: 3 the sons of Pārósh, two thousand one hundred and seventy-two. 4 The sons of Shĕphátī′áh, three hundred and seventy-two. 5 The sons of Ārăh, seven hundred and seventy-five. 6 The sons of Pā′hăth- mō′ăb, namely the sons of Jĕsh′uả and Jō′ăb, two thousand eight hundred and twelve. 7 The sons of Ēlăm, one thousand two hundred and fifty-four. 8 The sons of Zăttu, nine hundred and forty-five. 9 The sons of Zăc′caī, seven hundred and sixty. 10 The sons of Bānī, six hundred and forty-two. 11 The sons of Bēbaī, six hundred and twenty-three. 12 The sons of Ăzgăd, one thousand two hundred and twenty-two. 13 The sons of Ădónī′kàm, six hundred and sixty-six. 14 The sons of Bĭgvaī, two thousand and fifty-six. 15 The sons of Ādĭn, four hundred and fifty-four. 16 The sons of Ātĕr, namely of Hĕzĕkī′áh, ninety-eight. 17 The sons of Bēzaī, three hundred and twenty-three. 18 The sons of Jōráh, one hundred and twelve. 19 The sons of Hāshùm, two hundred and twenty-three. 20 The sons of Gĭbbar, ninety-five. 21 The sons of Bĕth′lĕhĕm, one hundred and twenty-three. 22 The men of Nĕtō′pháh, fifty-six. 23 The men of Ăn′áthŏth, one hundred and twenty-eight. 24 The sons of Ăzmā′vĕth, forty-two. 25 The sons of Kĭr′ĭăthā′rĭm, Chĕphī′ráh, and Be-ĕr′ŏth, seven hundred and forty-three. 26 The sons of Rāmàh and Gēbà, six hundred and twenty-one. 27 The men of Mĭchmàs, one hundred and twenty- two. 28 The men of Bĕthĕl and Āī, two hundred and twenty-three. 29 The sons of Nēbō, fifty-two. 30 The sons of Măgbĭsh, one hun- dred and fifty-six. 31 The sons of the other Ēlăm, one thousand two hundred and fifty-four. 32 The sons of Hārĭm, three hundred and twenty. 33 The sons of Lŏd, Hādĭd, and Ōnō, seven hundred and twenty-five. 34 The sons of Jĕr′ĭchō, three hundred and forty-five. 35 The sons of Sĕnă′áh, three thousand six hundred and thirty.

36 The priests: the sons of Jĕdāi′uả, of the house of Jĕsh′uả, nine hundred and seventy-three. 37 The sons of Immĕr, one thou- sand and fifty-two. 38 The sons of Păshhùr, one thousand two hundred and forty-seven. 39 The sons of Hārĭm, one thousand and seventeen.

40 The Lēvītes: the sons of Jĕsh′uả and Kăd′mĭ-ĕl, of the sons of Hōdávī′áh, seventy-four. 41 The singers: the sons of Āsáph, one hundred and twenty-eight. 42 The sons of the gatekeepers: the sons of Shăllùm, the sons of Ātĕr, the sons of Tălmòn, the sons of Akkùb, the sons of Hătī′tà, and the sons of Shōbaī, in all one hundred and thirty-nine.

2.1
Neh 7.6–
73;
2 Ki 24.14–
16; 25.11;
2 Chr 36.20

*2.5
cf. Neh 7.10
2.6
cf. Neh 7.11

2.16
Neh 7.21

2.21
Neh 7.26

2.31
see ver 7

2.36
1 Chr 24.7-
18
2.38
1 Chr 9.12
2.39
1 Chr 24.8

2.5 Neh 7.10 states that Arah had *six hun- dred and fifty-two* children instead of *seven hundred and seventy-five*. This is undoubtedly a copyist's error. A comparison of 2.6–65 with Neh 7.11–67 will show other differences in numbers. The fact that Jewish letters were used to represent numbers made this con- fusion almost unavoidable.

2.43
1 Chr 9.2

43 The temple servants:*d* the sons of Zīhȧ, the sons of Hȧsu′phȧ, the sons of Tȧbbā′ŏth, 44 the sons of Kērŏs, the sons of Sī′ȧhȧ, the sons of Pādȯn, 45 the sons of Lĕbā′nȧh, the sons of Hăg′ȧbȧh, the sons of Ăkkūb, 46 the sons of Hăg′ȧb, the sons of Shămlaī, the sons of Hānȧn, 47 the sons of Gĭddĕl, the sons of Gāhar, the sons

2.48
Neh 7.50

of Rė-āi′ȧh, 48 the sons of Rĕzĭn, the sons of Nȇkō′dȧ, the sons of Găzzȧm, 49 the sons of Ŭzzȧ, the sons of Pȧsē′ȧh, the sons of Bēsaī, 50 the sons of Ăsnȧh, the sons of Mė-ū′nĭm, the sons of Nĕph′ĭsĭm, 51 the sons of Băkbūk, the sons of Hȧku′phȧ, the sons of Harhúr, 52 the sons of Băzlūth, the sons of Mėhī′dȧ, the sons of Harshȧ, 53 the sons of Barkȯs, the sons of Sĭs′ȇrȧ, the sons of Tēmȧh, 54 the sons of Nėzī′ȧh, and the sons of Hȧtī′phȧ.

2.55
Neh 7.57,
60; 11.3

55 The sons of Solomon's servants: the sons of Sōtaī, the sons of Hȧssȯphĕr′ĕth, the sons of Pĕru′dȧ, 56 the sons of Jȧ′ȧlȧh, the sons of Darkȯn, the sons of Gĭddĕl, 57 the sons of Shĕphȧtī′ȧh, the sons of Hăttil, the sons of Pō′çhĕrĕth-hăzzȇbā′ĭm, and the sons of Āmī.

2.58
ver 55

58 All the temple servants*d* and the sons of Solomon's servants were three hundred and ninety-two.

59 The following were those who came up from Tĕl-mē′lȧh, Tĕl-har′shȧ, Çhĕrúb, Ăddȧn, and Ĭmmȇr, though they could not prove their fathers' houses or their descent, whether they belonged to Israel: 60 the sons of Dĕlāi′ȧh, the sons of Tȯbī′ȧh, and

2.61
2 Sam 17.27

the sons of Nȇkō′dȧ, six hundred and fifty-two. 61 Also, of the sons of the priests: the sons of Hȧbāi′ȧh, the sons of Hăkkȯz, and the sons of Barzĭl′laī (who had taken a wife from the daughters of Barzillai the Gĭl′ĕȧdīte, and was called by their name). 62 These

2.62
Num 3.10;
16.39,40

sought their registration among those enrolled in the genealogies, but they were not found there, and so they were excluded from the priesthood as unclean; 63 the governor told them that they

*2.63
Lev 2.3,10;
Ex 28.30

were not to partake of the most holy food, until there should be a priest to consult Ūrĭm and Thŭmmĭm.

2.64
Neh 7.66ff

64 The whole assembly together was forty-two thousand three hundred and sixty, 65 besides their menservants and maidservants, of whom there were seven thousand three hundred and thirty-seven; and they had two hundred male and female singers. 66 Their horses were seven hundred and thirty-six, their mules were two hundred and forty-five, 67 their camels were four hundred and thirty-five, and their asses were six thousand seven hundred and twenty.

68 Some of the heads of families, when they came to the house of the LORD which is in Jerusalem, made freewill offerings for

*2.69
Ezra 8.25–
34

the house of God, to erect it on its site; 69 according to their ability they gave to the treasury of the work sixty-one thousand darics of gold, five thousand minas of silver, and one hundred priests' garments.

70 The priests, the Lēvītes, and some of the people lived in Jerusalem and its vicinity;*e* and the singers, the gatekeepers, and the temple servants lived in their towns, and all Israel in their towns.

d Heb *nethinim*   *e* 1 Esdras 5.46: Heb lacks *lived in Jerusalem and its vicinity*

2.63 *Urim and Thummim*, see note to Ex 28.30. The last mention of these is in Neh 7.65.

2.69 *darics*, Persian coins. Some suggest "drachma," a Greek coin used in the Persian empire.

II. The restoration of worship and dedication of the Temple 3.1–6.22

A. The altar rebuilt: sacrifices offered

3 When the seventh month came, and the sons of Israel were in the towns, the people gathered as one man to Jerusalem. [3.1 Neh 7.73; 8.1] 2 Then arose Jĕsh′uă the son of Jŏz′ădăk, with his fellow priests, and Zĕrŭb′băbĕl the son of Shĕ-ăl′tĭ-ĕl with his kinsmen, and they built the altar of the God of Israel, to offer burnt offerings upon it, as it is written in the law of Moses the man of God. [★3.2 Neh 12.1,8; Ezra 2.2; 1 Chr 3.17; Deut 12.5,6] 3 They set the altar in its place, for fear was upon them because of the peoples of the lands, and they offered burnt offerings upon it to the LORD, burnt offerings morning and evening. [3.3 Ezra 4.4; Num 28.2–4] 4And they kept the feast of booths, as it is written, and offered the daily burnt offerings by number according to the ordinance, as each day required, [3.4 Neh 8.14; Ex 23.16; Num 29.12] 5 and after that the continual burnt offerings, the offerings at the new moon and at all the appointed feasts of the LORD, and the offerings of every one who made a freewill offering to the LORD. [3.5 Num 28.3, 11,19,26; 29.39] 6 From the first day of the seventh month they began to offer burnt offerings to the LORD. But the foundation of the temple of the LORD was not yet laid. 7 So they gave money to the masons and the carpenters, and food, drink, and oil to the Sĭdō′-nĭăns and the Tўr′ĭăns to bring cedar trees from Lebanon to the sea, to Jŏppå, according to the grant which they had from Cyrus king of Persia. [3.7 2 Chr 2.10, 16; Ezra 1.2; 6.3]

B. Rebuilding of the Temple begun

8 Now in the second year of their coming to the house of God at Jerusalem, in the second month, Zĕrŭb′băbĕl the son of Shĕ-ăl′tĭ-ĕl and Jĕsh′uă the son of Jŏz′ădăk made a beginning, together with the rest of their brethren, the priests and the Lēvītes and all who had come to Jerusalem from the captivity. They appointed the Levites, from twenty years old and upward, to have the oversight of the work of the house of the LORD. [3.8 ver 2; Ezra 4.3; 1 Chr 23.24,27] 9And Jĕsh′uă with his sons and his kinsmen, and Kăd′mĭ-ĕl and his sons, the sons of Judah, together took the oversight of the workmen in the house of God, along with the sons of Hĕn′ădăd and the Lēvītes, their sons and kinsmen. [3.9 Ezra 2.40]

10 And when the builders laid the foundation of the temple of the LORD, the priests in their vestments came forward with trumpets, and the Lēvītes, the sons of Āsăph, with cymbals, to praise the LORD, according to the directions of David king of Israel; [3.10 1 Chr 16.5, 6,42; 6.31; 25.1] 11 and they sang responsively, praising and giving thanks to the LORD, [3.11 Ex 15.21; 2 Chr 7.3; Neh 12.24; 1 Chr 16.34,41]

"For he is good,
  for his steadfast love endures for ever toward Israel."

And all the people shouted with a great shout, when they praised the LORD, because the foundation of the house of the LORD was laid. 12 But many of the priests and Lēvītes and heads of fathers' houses, old men who had seen the first house, wept with a loud

3.2 *son of She-alti-el.* Zerubbabel was the legitimate heir, since his father was the eldest son of Jehoiachin. (See 1 Chr 3.17 and note to 1 Chr 3.19.)

voice when they saw the foundation of this house being laid, though many shouted aloud for joy; 13 so that the people could not distinguish the sound of the joyful shout from the sound of the people's weeping, for the people shouted with a great shout, and the sound was heard afar.

C. Opposition to the rebuilding

1. Help offered and refused

4.1
ver 7–10

4 Now when the adversaries of Judah and Benjamin heard that the returned exiles were building a temple to the LORD, the God of Israel, 2 they approached Zĕrŭb′bábĕl and the heads of fathers' houses and said to them, "Let us build with you; for we worship your God as you do, and we have been sacrificing to him ever since the days of Ē′sar-hăd′dŏn king of Assyria who brought us here." 3 But Zĕrŭb′bábĕl, Jĕsh′uă, and the rest of the heads of fathers' houses in Israel said to them, "You have nothing to do with us in building a house to our God; but we alone will build to the LORD, the God of Israel, as King Cyrus the king of Persia has commanded us."

*4.2
2 Ki 17.24,
32,33;
19.37

4.3
Neh 2.20;
Ezra 1.1–3

4 Then the people of the land discouraged the people of Judah, and made them afraid to build, 5 and hired counselors against them to frustrate their purpose, all the days of Cyrus king of Persia, even until the reign of Dărī′ŭs king of Persia.

4.4
Ezra 3.3

*4.5

2. The letter to Artaxerxes: the work stopped

*4.6ff
Est 1.1;
Dan 9.1

6 And in the reign of Ăhăsŭ-ē′rŭs, in the beginning of his reign, they wrote an accusation against the inhabitants of Judah and Jerusalem.

*4.7
2 Ki 18.26;
Dan 2.4

7 And in the days of Ar-tà-xerx′ĕs, Bĭshlăm and Mĭth′rĕdăth and Tā′bĕĕl and the rest of their associates wrote to Ar-ta-xerxes king of Persia; the letter was written in Ărămā′ĭc and translated.ƒ 8 Rēhŭm the commander and Shĭm′shaï the scribe wrote a letter against Jerusalem to Ar-tà-xerx′ĕs the king as follows—9 then wrote Rēhŭm the commander, Shĭmshaï the scribe, and the rest of their associates, the judges, the governors, the officials, the Persians, the men of Ĕrĕch, the Babylonians, the men of Susà, that is, the Ē′lămītes, 10 and the rest of the nations whom the great and noble Ŏsnăp′păr deported and settled in the cities of Sàmar′ĭă and in the rest of the province Beyond the River, and now 11 this is a copy of the letter that they sent—"To Ar-tà-xerx′ĕs the king: Your servants, the men of the province Beyond the River, send greeting. And now 12 be it known to the king that the Jews who came up from you to us have gone to Jerusalem. They are rebuilding that rebellious and wicked city; they are finishing the walls and repairing the foundations. 13 Now be it known to the king that, if this city is rebuilt and the walls finished, they will not pay tribute,

*4.10
ver 1

4.12
Ezra 5.3,9

4.13
ver 20;
Ezra 7.24

ƒ Heb adds *in Aramaic*, indicating that 4.8–6.18 is in Aramaic. Another interpretation is *The letter was written in the Aramaic script and set forth in the Aramaic language*

4.2 *Esar-haddon*, see note to 2 Ki 17.24.
4.5 *Darius* reigned 522–486 B.C.
4.6-23 Chronologically this unit, concerning the city walls (not the Temple), belongs between chapters 6 and 7.

4.6 *Ahasuerus*, that is Xerxes, (486–465 B.C.).
4.7 *Artaxerxes* reigned 465–423 B.C.
4.10 *Osnapper*, that is, Ashurbanipal. See note to 2 Ki 17.24.

custom, or toll, and the royal revenue will be impaired. 14 Now because we eat the salt of the palace and it is not fitting for us to witness the king's dishonor, therefore we send and inform the king, 15 in order that search may be made in the book of the records of your fathers. You will find in the book of the records and learn that this city is a rebellious city, hurtful to kings and provinces, and that sedition was stirred up in it from of old. That was why this city was laid waste. 16 We make known to the king that, if this city is rebuilt and its walls finished, you will then have no possession in the province Beyond the River."

17 The king sent an answer: "To Rēhùm the commander and Shĭmshaī the scribe and the rest of their associates who live in Sàmar'ĭà and in the rest of the province Beyond the River, greeting. And now 18 the letter which you sent to us has been plainly read before me. 19And I made a decree, and search has been made, and it has been found that this city from of old has risen against kings, and that rebellion and sedition have been made in it. 20And mighty kings have been over Jerusalem, who ruled over the whole province Beyond the River, to whom tribute, custom, and toll were paid. 21 Therefore make a decree that these men be made to cease, and that this city be not rebuilt, until a decree is made by me. 22And take care not to be slack in this matter; why should damage grow to the hurt of the king?"

23 Then, when the copy of King Ar-tà-xèrx'ĕṣ' letter was read before Rēhùm and Shĭmshaī the scribe and their associates, they went in haste to the Jews at Jerusalem and by force and power made them cease. 24 Then the work on the house of God which is in Jerusalem stopped; and it ceased until the second year of the reign of Dàrī'ùs king of Persia.

3. *Rebuilding the Temple under Haggai and Zechariah*
a. *The work begun*

5 Now the prophets, Hăg'gäī and Zĕchàrī'áh the son of Ĭddō, prophesied to the Jews who were in Judah and Jerusalem, in the name of the God of Israel who was over them. 2 Then Zērùb'-bàbèl the son of Shè-ăl'tĭ-èl and Jĕsh'uà the son of Jŏz'ádăk arose and began to rebuild the house of God which is in Jerusalem; and with them were the prophets of God, helping them.

b. *An investigation instituted*

3 At the same time Tăt'tènaī the governor of the province Beyond the River and Shè'thar-bŏz'ènaī and their associates came to them and spoke to them thus, "Who gave you a decree to build this house and to finish this structure?" 4 They[g] also asked them this, "What are the names of the men who are building this building?" 5 But the eye of their God was upon the elders of the Jews, and they did not stop them till a report should reach Dàrī'ùs and then answer be returned by letter concerning it.

c. *Tattenai's letter to Darius*

6 The copy of the letter which Tăt'tènaī the governor of the province Beyond the River and Shè'thar-bŏz'ènaī and his associates the governors who were in the province Beyond the River

4.18
Neh 8.8

4.20
1 Ki 4.21;
Ps 72.8

5.1
Hag 1.1;
Zech 1.1
5.2
Ezra 3.2

5.3
Ezra 6.6;
ver 9;
Ezra 1.3
5.4
ver 10
5.5
Ezra 7.6,28;
Ps 33.18

5.6
Ezra 4.9

g Gk Syr: Aramaic *We*

sent to Dārī'ūs the king; 7 they sent him a report, in which was written as follows: "To Dārī'ūs the king, all peace. 8 Be it known to the king that we went to the province of Judah, to the house of the great God. It is being built with huge stones, and timber is laid in the walls; this work goes on diligently and prospers in their hands. 9 Then we asked those elders and spoke to them thus, 'Who gave you a decree to build this house and to finish this structure?' 10 We also asked them their names, for your information, that we might write down the names of the men at their head. 11And this was their reply to us: 'We are the servants of the God of heaven and earth, and we are rebuilding the house that was built many years ago, which a great king of Israel built and finished. 12 But because our fathers had angered the God of heaven, he gave them into the hand of Nĕbūchādnĕz'zăr king of Babylon, the Chăldē'ăn, who destroyed this house and carried away the people to Babylonia. 13 However in the first year of Cyrus king of Babylon, Cyrus the king made a decree that this house of God should be rebuilt. 14And the gold and silver vessels of the house of God, which Nĕbūchādnĕz'zăr had taken out of the temple that was in Jerusalem and brought into the temple of Babylon, these Cyrus the king took out of the temple of Babylon, and they were delivered to one whose name was Shĕsh-băz'zăr, whom he had made governor; 15 and he said to him, "Take these vessels, go and put them in the temple which is in Jerusalem, and let the house of God be rebuilt on its site." 16 Then this Shĕsh-băz'zăr came and laid the foundations of the house of God which is in Jerusalem; and from that time until now it has been in building, and it is not yet finished.' 17 Therefore, if it seem good to the king, let search be made in the royal archives there in Babylon, to see whether a decree was issued by Cyrus the king for the rebuilding of this house of God in Jerusalem. And let the king send us his pleasure in this matter."

d. Darius' search and reply

6 Then Dārī'ūs the king made a decree, and search was made in Babylonia, in the house of the archives where the documents were stored. 2And in Ĕcbăt'ănă, the capital which is in the province of Mē'dĭă, a scroll was found on which this was written: "A record. 3 In the first year of Cyrus the king, Cyrus the king issued a decree: Concerning the house of God at Jerusalem, let the house be rebuilt, the place where sacrifices are offered and burnt offerings are brought; its height shall be sixty cubits and its breadth sixty cubits, 4 with three courses of great stones and one course of timber; let the cost be paid from the royal treasury. 5And also let the gold and silver vessels of the house of God, which Nĕbūchădnĕz'zăr took out of the temple that is in Jerusalem and brought to Babylon, be restored and brought back to the temple which is in Jerusalem, each to its place; you shall put them in the house of God."

6 "Now therefore, Tăt'tĕnaī, governor of the province Beyond the River, Shē'thar-bŏz'ĕnaī, and your associates the governors who are in the province Beyond the River, keep away; 7 let the work on this house of God alone; let the governor of the Jews and the elders of the Jews rebuild this house of God on its site. 8 Moreover I make a decree regarding what you shall do for these elders

---

Marginal references (left column):

5.9
ver 3,4

5.11
1 Ki 6.1

5.12
2 Chr
36.16,17;
2 Ki 24.2;
25.8,9,11

5.13
Ezra 1.1

5.14
Ezra 1.7;
6.5;
Dan 5.2;
ver 16;
Ezra 1.8

5.16
Ezra 3.8,10;
6.15

5.17
Ezra 6.1,2

6.1
Ezra 5.17

6.3
Ezra 1.1

6.4
1 Ki 6.36

6.5
Ezra 1.7,8;
5.14

6.6
ver 13;
Ezra 5.3

of the Jews for the rebuilding of this house of God; the cost is to
be paid to these men in full and without delay from the royal
revenue, the tribute of the province from Beyond the River. 9And
whatever is needed—young bulls, rams, or sheep for burnt offerings to the God of heaven, wheat, salt, wine, or oil, as the priests
at Jerusalem require—let that be given to them day by day without fail, 10 that they may offer pleasing sacrifices to the God of
heaven, and pray for the life of the king and his sons. 11Also I make
a decree that if any one alters this edict, a beam shall be pulled
out of his house, and he shall be impaled upon it, and his house
shall be made a dunghill. 12 May the God who has caused his
name to dwell there overthrow any king or people that shall put
forth a hand to alter this, or to destroy this house of God which is
in Jerusalem. I Dȧrī′ŭs make a decree; let it be done with all
diligence."

e. The rebuilding of the Temple completed

13 Then, according to the word sent by Dȧrī′ŭs the king, Tȧt′-
tēnaī, the governor of the province Beyond the River, Shē′thar-
bŏz′ēnaī, and their associates did with all diligence what Darius
the king had ordered. 14And the elders of the Jews built and prospered, through the prophesying of Hăg′gäī the prophet and
Zĕchȧrī′ăh the son of Ĭddō. They finished their building by command of the God of Israel and by decree of Cyrus and Dȧrī′ŭs
and Ar-tȧ-xẻrx′ēș king of Persia; 15 and this house was finished on
the third day of the month of Adar′, in the sixth year of the reign
of Dȧrī′ŭs the king.

f. The Temple dedicated: the Passover and Feast
of Unleavened Bread celebrated

16 And the people of Israel, the priests and the Lēvītes, and the
rest of the returned exiles, celebrated the dedication of this house
of God with joy. 17 They offered at the dedication of this house of
God one hundred bulls, two hundred rams, four hundred lambs,
and as a sin offering for all Israel twelve he-goats, according to the
number of the tribes of Israel. 18And they set the priests in their
divisions and the Lēvītes in their courses, for the service of God at
Jerusalem, as it is written in the book of Moses.

19 On the fourteenth day of the first month the returned exiles
kept the passover. 20 For the priests and the Lēvītes had purified
themselves together; all of them were clean. So they killed the
passover lamb for all the returned exiles, for their fellow priests,
and for themselves; 21 it was eaten by the people of Israel who had
returned from exile, and also by every one who had joined them
and separated himself from the pollutions of the peoples of the
land to worship the LORD, the God of Israel. 22And they kept the

6.10 Ezra 7.23
6.11 Ezra 7.26; Dan 2.5; 3.29
6.12 Deut 12.5; 11
6.13 ver 6
*6.14 Ezra 5.1,2; 1.1; ver 12; Ezra 7.1
*6.15
6.16 1 Ki 8.63; 2 Chr 7.5
*6.17 Ezra 8.35
6.18 2 Chr 35.5; 1 Chr 23.6; Num 3.6; 8.9
6.19 Ezra 1.11; Ex 12.6
6.20 2 Chr 29.34; 30.15; 35.11
6.21 Neh 9.2; 10.28; Ezra 9.11
*6.22 Ex 12.15; Ezra 7.27; 1.1; 6.2

6.14 *Artaxerxes* is a later addition. He did not reign until fifty years after the Temple was completed.
6.15 *sixth year,* 515 B.C.
6.17 The return of the remnant was accompanied by the rebuilding of the Temple, which never attained the glory of the Solomonic Temple. Neither was there a restoration of the kingship or of the earlier theocracy.

Nothing in Scripture indicates that the she-kinah glory of God filled this Temple as in the case of Solomon's house of worship. The Temple itself was enlarged and embellished by Herod the Great and his immediate successors. It was finally destroyed in A.D. 70 when Jerusalem fell to the legions of Titus.
6.22 A Persian king is meant. The reason for the Assyrian designation is not clear.

feast of unleavened bread seven days with joy; for the LORD had made them joyful, and had turned the heart of the king of Assyria to them, so that he aided them in the work of the house of God, the God of Israel.

III. The return of Ezra and the reform which followed 7.1–10.44

A. Ezra's genealogy and career

7 Now after this, in the reign of Ar-tá-χẻrx′ẻṣ king of Persia, Ezra the son of Sẻrái′áh, son of Ăzárí′áh, son of Hĭlkí′áh, ²son of Shăllŭm, son of Zādŏk, son of Ăhĭ′tŭb, ³ son of Ămărí′áh, son of Ăzárí′áh, son of Mẻrái′ŏth, ⁴ son of Zẻráhí′áh, son of Ŭzzī, son of Bŭkkī, ⁵ son of Ăbĭsh′uá, son of Phĭn′ëhás, son of Ělëä′zár, son of Aaron the chief priest—⁶ this Ezra went up from Babylonia. He was a scribe skilled in the law of Moses which the LORD the God of Israel had given; and the king granted him all that he asked, for the hand of the LORD his God was upon him.

7 And there went up also to Jerusalem, in the seventh year of Ar-tá-χẻrx′ẻṣ the king, some of the people of Israel, and some of the priests and Lẻvītes, the singers and gatekeepers, and the temple servants. ⁸And he came to Jerusalem in the fifth month, which was in the seventh year of the king; ⁹ for on the first day of the first month he began ʰ to go up from Babylonia, and on the first day of the fifth month he came to Jerusalem, for the good hand of his God was upon him. ¹⁰ For Ezra had set his heart to study the law of the LORD, and to do it, and to teach his statutes and ordinances in Israel.

B. Ezra's commission from Artaxerxes

11 This is a copy of the letter which King Ar-tá-χẻrx′ẻṣ gave to Ezra the priest, the scribe, learned in matters of the commandments of the LORD and his statutes for Israel: ¹² "Ar-tá-χẻrx′ẻṣ, king of kings, to Ezra the priest, the scribe of the law of the God of heaven. ˣAnd now ¹³ I make a decree that any one of the people of Israel or their priests or Lẻvītes in my kingdom, who freely offers to go to Jerusalem, may go with you. ¹⁴ For you are sent by the king and his seven counselors to make inquiries about Judah and Jerusalem according to the law of your God, which is in your hand, ¹⁵ and also to convey the silver and gold which the king and his counselors have freely offered to the God of Israel, whose dwelling is in Jerusalem, ¹⁶ with all the silver and gold which you shall find in the whole province of Babylonia, and with the freewill offerings of the people and the priests, vowed willingly for the house of their God which is in Jerusalem. ¹⁷ With this money, then, you shall with all diligence buy bulls, rams, and lambs, with their cereal offerings and their drink offerings, and you shall offer

Margin references

7.1
1 Chr 6.4–14;
ver 12,21;
Neh 2.1

7.6
ver 9,11,12,
21,28

*7.7
Ezra 8.1–20

7.9
ver 6

7.10
Ps 119.45;
ver 25;
Neh 8.1–8

7.12
Ezek 26.7;
Dan 2.37

7.14
Est 1.14

7.15
2 Chr 6.2;
Ezra 6.12

7.16
Ezra 8.25;
1 Chr 29.6,
9;
Ezra 1.4,6

7.17
Num 15.4–
13;
Deut 12.5–
11

ʰ Vg See Syr: Heb that was the foundation of the going up
ˣ Aram adds a word of uncertain meaning

7.7 seventh year. If Artaxerxes I, 458 B.C.; but if Artaxerxes II, then 397 B.C. Some suggest that the number "thirty" (which begins with the same letter as "seventh" and "year") has accidentally dropped out. If so, then Ezra came in 428 B.C.

them upon the altar of the house of your God which is in Jerusalem. 18 Whatever seems good to you and your brethren to do with the rest of the silver and gold, you may do, according to the will of your God. 19 The vessels that have been given you for the service of the house of your God, you shall deliver before the God of Jerusalem. 20And whatever else is required for the house of your God, which you have occasion to provide, you may provide it out of the king's treasury.

7.20
Ezra 6.4

21 "And I, Ar-tá-xẹrx′ẹṣ the king, make a decree to all the treasurers in the province Beyond the River: Whatever Ezra the priest, the scribe of the law of the God of heaven, requires of you, be it done with all diligence, 22 up to a hundred talents of silver, a hundred cors of wheat, a hundred baths of wine, a hundred baths of oil, and salt without prescribing how much. 23 Whatever is commanded by the God of heaven, let it be done in full for the house of the God of heaven, lest his wrath be against the realm of the king and his sons. 24 We also notify you that it shall not be lawful to impose tribute, custom, or toll upon any one of the priests, the Lēvītes, the singers, the doorkeepers, the temple servants, or other servants of this house of God.

7.21
ver 6

7.23
Ezra 6.10

25 "And you, Ezra, according to the wisdom of your God which is in your hand, appoint magistrates and judges who may judge all the people in the province Beyond the River, all such as know the laws of your God; and those who do not know them, you shall teach. 26 Whoever will not obey the law of your God and the law of the king, let judgment be strictly executed upon him, whether for death or for banishment or for confiscation of his goods or for imprisonment."

7.25
Ex 18.21;
Deut 16.18;
ver 10

C. Ezra's song of praise

27 Blessed be the LORD, the God of our fathers, who put such a thing as this into the heart of the king, to beautify the house of the LORD which is in Jerusalem, 28 and who extended to me his steadfast love before the king and his counselors, and before all the king's mighty officers. I took courage, for the hand of the LORD my God was upon me, and I gathered leading men from Israel to go up with me.

7.27
1 Chr
29.10;
Ezra 6.22
7.28
Ezra 9.9;
ver 6,9

D. The list of the returning remnant

8 These are the heads of their fathers' houses, and this is the genealogy of those who went up with me from Babylonia, in the reign of Ar-tá-xẹrx′ẹṣ the king: 2 Of the sons of Phĭn′ẽhás, Gẹrshóm. Of the sons of Ĭth′ámar, Daniel. Of the sons of David, Hăttŭsh, 3 of the sons of Shẹcắnī′áh. Of the sons of Pārósh, Zẹchárī′áh, with whom were registered one hundred and fifty men. 4 Of the sons of Pā′hăth-mō′ăb, Ĕl′ĭě-hò-ē′naī the son of Zẹráhī′áh, and with him two hundred men. 5 Of the sons of Zăttu,ⁱ Shẹcắnī′áh the son of Jáhá′zĭĕl, and with him three hundred men. 6 Of the sons of Ādĭn, Ēbĕd the son of Jonathan, and with him fifty men. 7 Of the sons of Ēlám, Jẹshāī′áh the son of Āthálī′áh, and with him seventy men. 8 Of the sons of

8.2
1 Chr 3.22

8.3
Ezra 2.3

ⁱ Gk 1 Esdras 8.32: Heb lacks of Zattu

Shĕphátī'áh, Zĕbádī'áh the son of Michael, and with him eighty men. 9 Of the sons of Jōăb, Ōbádī'áh the son of Jéhī'él, and with him two hundred and eighteen men. 10 Of the sons of Bānī,ʲ Shélō'mĭth the son of Jōṣĭphī'áh, and with him a hundred and sixty men. 11 Of the sons of Bēbaī, Zĕchárī'áh, the son of Bebai, and with him twenty-eight men. 12 Of the sons of Āzgăd, Jōhăn'án the son of Hăk'kátăn, and with him a hundred and ten men. 13 Of the sons of Ădónī'kám, those who came later, their names being Ělĭph'élĕt, Jeu'él, and Shĕmāi'áh, and with them sixty men. 14 Of the sons of Bĭgvaī, Ūthaī and Zăccúr, and with them seventy men.

E. The selection of Temple servants

8.15
ver 21,31;
Ezra 7.7

15 I gathered them to the river that runs to Ăhā'vá, and there we encamped three days. As I reviewed the people and the priests, I found there none of the sons of Lēvī. 16 Then I sent for Ĕlīē'zĕr, Ar'ĭ-él, Shĕmāi'áh, Ělnā'thàn, Jā'rĭb, Elnathan, Nathan, Zĕchárī'-áh, and Mĕshŭl'lám, leading men, and for Joi'árĭb and Elnathan,

8.17
Ezra 2.43

who were men of insight, 17 and sent them to Ĭddō, the leading man at the place Cásĭph'ĭá, telling them what to say to Iddo and his brethren the temple servantsᵏ at the place Casiphia, namely,

8.18
Ezra 7.6

to send us ministers for the house of our God. 18And by the good hand of our God upon us, they brought us a man of discretion, of the sons of Mahlī the son of Lēvī, son of Israel, namely Shĕrĕ-bī'áh with his sons and kinsmen, eighteen; 19 also Hăshàbī'áh and with him Jĕshāi'áh of the sons of Mĕrar'ĭ, with his kinsmen and

8.20
Ezra 2.43

their sons, twenty; 20 besides two hundred and twenty of the temple servants, whom David and his officials had set apart to attend the Lēvītes. These were all mentioned by name.

F. The return to the land

1. A fast proclaimed

8.21
2 Chr 20.3;
Isa 58.3,5

21 Then I proclaimed a fast there, at the river Ăhā'vá, that we might humble ourselves before our God, to seek from him a straight way for ourselves, our children, and all our goods. 22 For

8.22
Ezra 7.6,9, 28;
Ps 33.18,19; 34.16;
2 Chr 15.2

I was ashamed to ask the king for a band of soldiers and horsemen to protect us against the enemy on our way; since we had told the king, "The hand of our God is for good upon all that seek him, and the power of his wrath is against all that forsake him." 23 So

8.23
2 Chr 33.13

we fasted and besought our God for this, and he listened to our entreaty.

2. The treasure cared for

24 Then I set apart twelve of the leading priests: Shĕrĕbī'áh,

8.25
Ezra 7.15, 16

Hăshàbī'áh, and ten of their kinsmen with them. 25And I weighed out to them the silver and the gold and the vessels, the offering for the house of our God which the king and his counselors and his

8.26
Ezra 1.9–11

lords and all Israel there present had offered; 26 I weighed out into their hand six hundred and fifty talents of silver, and silver vessels worth a hundred talents, and a hundred talents of gold, 27 twenty bowls of gold worth a thousand darics, and two vessels of fine bright bronze as precious as gold. 28And I said to them, "You are

8.28
Lev 21.6–8; 22.2,3

holy to the LORD, and the vessels are holy; and the silver and the

ʲ Gk 1 Esdras 8.36: Heb lacks *Bani* ᵏ Heb *nethinim*

gold are a freewill offering to the LORD, the God of your fathers. ²⁹ Guard them and keep them until you weigh them before the chief priests and the Lēvītes and the heads of fathers' houses in Israel at Jerusalem, within the chambers of the house of the LORD." ³⁰ So the priests and the Lēvītes took over the weight of the silver and the gold and the vessels, to bring them to Jerusalem, to the house of our God.

8.29
ver 33,34

3. *The departure from Ahava and arrival at Jerusalem*

31 Then we departed from the river Ahā′vä on the twelfth day of the first month, to go to Jerusalem; the hand of our God was upon us, and he delivered us from the hand of the enemy and from ambushes by the way. ³² We came to Jerusalem, and there we remained three days. ³³ On the fourth day, within the house of our God, the silver and the gold and the vessels were weighed into the hands of Mĕr′ĕmŏth the priest, son of Ūrī′äh, and with him was Ĕlëä′zär the son of Phĭn′ëhäs, and with them were the Lēvītes, Jŏz′äbăd the son of Jĕsh′uä and Nō-ădī′äh the son of Bĭn′nūī. ³⁴ The whole was counted and weighed, and the weight of everything was recorded.

8.31
Ezra 7.6,9,
28
8.32
Neh 2.11
8.33
ver 26,30

35 At that time those who had come from captivity, the returned exiles, offered burnt offerings to the God of Israel, twelve bulls for all Israel, ninety-six rams, seventy-seven lambs, and as a sin offering twelve he-goats; all this was a burnt offering to the LORD. ³⁶ They also delivered the king's commissions to the king's satraps and to the governors of the province Beyond the River; and they aided the people and the house of God.

8.35
Ezra 2.1;
6.17
8.36
Ezra 7.21

G. *The reformation of the people*

1. *Ezra bemoans the mixed marriages*

9 After these things had been done, the officials approached me and said, "The people of Israel and the priests and the Lēvītes have not separated themselves from the peoples of the lands with their abominations, from the Cā′naänītes, the Hittītes, the Pĕr′ĭzzītes, the Jĕb′ūsītes, the Ăm′mŏnites, the Mō′äbītes, the Egyptians, and the Ăm′órites. ² For they have taken some of their daughters to be wives for themselves and for their sons; so that the holy race has mixed itself with the peoples of the lands. And in this faithlessness the hand of the officials and chief men has been foremost." ³ When I heard this, I rent my garments and my mantle, and pulled hair from my head and beard, and sat appalled. ⁴ Then all who trembled at the words of the God of Israel, because of the faithlessness of the returned exiles, gathered round me while I sat appalled until the evening sacrifice. ⁵And at the evening sacrifice I rose from my fasting, with my garments and my mantle rent, and fell upon my knees and spread out my hands to the LORD my God, ⁶ saying:

9.1
Ezra 6.21;
Neh 9.2;
Lev 18.24–
30
9.2
Ezra 10.2,
18;
Ex 22.31;
Neh 13.3
9.3
Job 1.20;
Neh 1.4
9.4
Ezra 10.3;
Ex 29.39
9.5
Ex 9.29,33
9.6
Dan 9.7,8;
2 Chr 28.9;
Rev 18.5

2. *Ezra's prayer*

"O my God, I am ashamed and blush to lift my face to thee, my God, for our iniquities have risen higher than our heads, and our guilt has mounted up to the heavens. ⁷ From the days of our fathers to this day we have been in great guilt; and for our iniquities we, our kings, and our priests have been given into the

9.7
Dan 9.5,6;
Deut 28.36,
64;
Dan 9.7,8

hand of the kings of the lands, to the sword, to captivity, to plundering, and to utter shame, as at this day. ⁸ But now for a brief moment favor has been shown by the LORD our God, to leave us a remnant, and to give us a secure hold*l* within his holy place, that our God may brighten our eyes and grant us a little reviving in our bondage. ⁹ For we are bondmen; yet our God has not forsaken us in our bondage, but has extended to us his steadfast love before the kings of Persia, to grant us some reviving to set up the house of our God, to repair its ruins, and to give us protection*m* in Judē´a and Jerusalem.

10 "And now, O our God, what shall we say after this? For we have forsaken thy commandments, ¹¹ which thou didst command by thy servants the prophets, saying, 'The land which you are entering, to take possession of it, is a land unclean with the pollutions of the peoples of the lands, with their abominations which have filled it from end to end with their uncleanness. ¹² Therefore give not your daughters to their sons, neither take their daughters for your sons, and never seek their peace or prosperity, that you may be strong, and eat the good of the land, and leave it for an inheritance to your children for ever.' ¹³And after all that has come upon us for our evil deeds and for our great guilt, seeing that thou, our God, hast punished us less than our iniquities deserved and hast given us such a remnant as this, ¹⁴ shall we break thy commandments again and intermarry with the peoples who practice these abominations? Wouldst thou not be angry with us till thou wouldst consume us, so that there should be no remnant, nor any to escape? ¹⁵ O LORD the God of Israel, thou art just, for we are left a remnant that has escaped, as at this day. Behold, we are before thee in our guilt, for none can stand before thee because of this."

3. Ezra's reform

10 While Ezra prayed and made confession, weeping and casting himself down before the house of God, a very great assembly of men, women, and children, gathered to him out of Israel; for the people wept bitterly. ²And Shĕcănī´ah the son of Jĕhī´el, of the sons of Ēlăm, addressed Ezra: "We have broken faith with our God and have married foreign women from the peoples of the land, but even now there is hope for Israel in spite of this. ³ Therefore let us make a covenant with our God to put away all these wives and their children, according to the counsel of my lord and of those who tremble at the commandment of our God; and let it be done according to the law. ⁴Arise, for it is your task, and we are with you; be strong and do it." ⁵ Then Ezra arose and made the leading priests and Lēvītes and all Israel take oath that they would do as had been said. So they took the oath.

6 Then Ezra withdrew from before the house of God, and went to the chamber of Jĕhō´hānăn the son of Ēlī´ashĭb, where he spent the night,*n* neither eating bread nor drinking water; for he was mourning over the faithlessness of the exiles. ⁷And a proclamation was made throughout Judah and Jerusalem to all the returned

Marginal refs: 9.8 Isa 22.23; Ps 13.3; 34.5 | 9.9 Neh 9.36; Ezra 7.28 | 9.11 Ezra 6.21 | 9.12 Deut 7.3; 23.6; Prov 13.22 | 9.13 ver 6–8 | 9.14 ver 2; Neh 13.23, 27; Deut 9.8,14 | 9.15 Neh 9.33; Dan 9.14; ver 6; Ps 130.3 | 10.1 Dan 9.4,20; 2 Chr 20.9 | *10.2 Ezra 9.2; Neh 13.27 | 10.3 2 Chr 34.31; ver 44; Ezra 9.4; Deut 7.2,3 | 10.4 1 Chr 28.10 | 10.5 Neh 5.12 | *10.6 Deut 9.18

l Heb *nail* or *tent-pin*   *m* Heb *a wall*   *n* 1 Esdras 9.2: Heb *where he went*

10.2 *Shecaniah*, convicted of his sin, evidences true repentance.

10.6 *Jehohanan*. Perhaps Johanan, the grandson of Eliashib (Neh 12.22).

exiles that they should assemble at Jerusalem, 8 and that if any one did not come within three days, by order of the officials and the elders all his property should be forfeited, and he himself banned from the congregation of the exiles.

9 Then all the men of Judah and Benjamin assembled at Jerusalem within the three days; it was the ninth month, on the twentieth day of the month. And all the people sat in the open square before the house of God, trembling because of this matter and because of the heavy rain. 10And Ezra the priest stood up and said to them, "You have trespassed and married foreign women, and so increased the guilt of Israel. 11 Now then make confession to the LORD the God of your fathers, and do his will; separate yourselves from the peoples of the land and from the foreign wives." 12 Then all the assembly answered with a loud voice, "It is so; we must do as you have said. 13 But the people are many, and it is a time of heavy rain; we cannot stand in the open. Nor is this a work for one day or for two; for we have greatly transgressed in this matter. 14 Let our officials stand for the whole assembly; let all in our cities who have taken foreign wives come at appointed times, and with them the elders and judges of every city, till the fierce wrath of our God over this matter be averted from us." 15 Only Jonathan the son of Ăs'ăhĕl and Jahzeī'ăh the son of Tĭkvăh opposed this, and Mĕshŭl'lăm and Shăb'bĕthaī the Lēvīte supported them.

16 Then the returned exiles did so. Ezra the priest selected men,ᵒ heads of fathers' houses, according to their fathers' houses, each of them designated by name. On the first day of the tenth month they sat down to examine the matter; 17 and by the first day of the first month they had come to the end of all the men who had married foreign women.

4. The list of the offending priests

18 Of the sons of the priests who had married foreign women were found Mā-ăseī'ăh, Ĕliē'zĕr, Jā'rĭb, and Gĕdălī'ăh, of the sons of Jĕsh'uá the son of Jŏz'ădăk and his brethren. 19 They pledged themselves to put away their wives, and their guilt offering was a ram of the flock for their guilt. 20Of the sons of Ĭmmĕr: Hānā'nī and Zĕbădī'ăh. 21 Of the sons of Hārĭm: Mā-ăseī'ăh, Ĕlī'jăh, Shĕmāi'ăh, Jĕhī'ĕl, and Ŭzzī'ăh. 22 Of the sons of Păshhúr: Ĕl'ĭ-ô-ē'naī, Mā-ăseī'ăh, Ĭsh'măĕl, Nĕthăn'ĕl, Jŏz'ăbăd, and Ĕlā'săh.

23 Of the Lēvītes: Jŏz'ăbăd, Shĭm'ĕ-ī, Kĕlāi'ăh (that is, Kĕlī'tă), Pĕthăhī'ăh, Judah, and Ĕliē'zĕr. 24 Of the singers: Ĕlī'ăshĭb. Of the gatekeepers: Shăllŭm, Tĕlĕm, and Ūrī.

25 And of Israel: of the sons of Pārŏsh: Rămī'ăh, Ĭzzī'ăh, Mălchī'jăh, Mĭj'ămĭn, Ĕlĕă'zăr, Hăshăbī'ăh,ᵖ and Bĕnāi'ăh. 26 Of the sons of Ēlăm: Măttănī'ăh, Zĕchărī'ăh, Jĕhī'ĕl, Ăbdī, Jĕr'ĕmôth, and Ĕlī'jăh. 27 Of the sons of Zăttu: Ĕl'ĭ-ô-ē'naī, Ĕlī'ăshĭb, Măttănī'ăh, Jĕr'ĕmôth, Zābăd, and Ăzī'ză. 28 Of the sons of Bēbaī were Jĕhō'hănăn, Hănănī'ăh, Zăb'băī, and Ăthlaī. 29 Of the sons of Bānī were Mĕshŭl'lăm, Măllúch, Ădāi'ăh, Jāshŭb, Shĕăl, and Jĕr'ĕmôth. 30 Of the sons of Pā'hăth-mō'ăb: Ădnă, Çhĕlăl,

	10.9
	ver 3;
	Ezra 9.4
	10.11
	Lev 26.40;
	ver 3
	10.14
	2 Chr
	29.10; 30.8
	10.16
	Ezra 4.1
	10.19
	2 Ki 10.15;
	2 Chr 30.8;
	Lev 5.15;
	6.6
	10.23
	Ex 6.25
	10.25
	ver 1

ᵒ 1 Esdras 9.16: Syr: Heb *and there were selected Ezra*, etc.
ᵖ 1 Esdras 9.26: Gk: Heb *Malchijah*

Bėnāi'ȧh, Mā-ȧsei'ȧh, Măttȧnī'ȧh, Bĕz'ȧlėl, Bĭn'nūī, and Mȧnăs'-
sėh. 31 Of the sons of Hārĭm: Ĕlīē'zėr, Ĭsshī'jȧh, Mălçhī'jȧh,
Shėmāi'ȧh, Shĭm'ë-ȯn, 32 Benjamin, Măllŭçh, and Shĕmȧrī'ȧh.
33 Of the sons of Hāshŭm: Măt'tėnaī, Măt'tȧttȧh, Zābăd, Ĕlĭph'-
ėlĕt, Jĕr'ėmaī, Mȧnăs'sėh, and Shĭm'ë-ī. 34 Of the sons of Bānī:
Mā'-ȧdaī, Ămrăm, Ūėl, 35 Bėnāi'ȧh, Bėdeī'ȧh, Çhėlu'hī, 36 Vȧnī'-
ȧh, Mĕr'ėmȯth, Ĕlī'ȧshĭb, 37 Măttȧnī'ȧh, Măt'tėnaī, Jā'ȧsu. 38 Of
the sons of Bĭn'nūī:[q] Shĭm'ë-ī, 39 Shĕlėmī'ȧh, Nathan, Ȧdāi'ȧh,
40 Măçhnăd'ėbaī, Shāshaī, Shā'rāī, 41 Ăz'ȧrėl, Shĕlėmī'ȧh, Shĕmȧrī'ȧh, 42 Shăllŭm, Ămȧrī'ȧh, and Joseph. 43 Of the sons of Nēbō:
Je-ī'ėl, Măttĭthī'ȧh, Zābăd, Zėbī'nȧ, Jăddaī, Jōėl, and Bėnāi'ȧh.
10.44 ver 3 44All these had married foreign women, and they put them away
with their children.[r]

[q] Gk: Heb *Bānī, Binnui* [r] 1 Esdras 9.36: Heb obscure

INTRODUCTION TO
THE BOOK OF
NEHEMIAH

Authorship and Background: The Book of Nehemiah, named for its leading figure, is part of The Book of Ezra in the Hebrew Bible. Internal evidence suggests two separate sources: the material which concludes the Chronicler's history (Ezra 1–10; Neh 8–10) and the memoirs of Nehemiah (1–7, 11–13). External evidence (for example, Elephantine letter #30 noted in the Introduction to Ezra) indicates that very little of the history or the memoirs may be dated after about 400 B.C. The two sources were put together by the author, but just when, it is difficult to say. Scholars have differed as to whether Nehemiah followed Ezra or vice versa. Nehemiah, like Ezra, is one of the five historical books which are part of the Hagiographa, which include the Poetical Books and the Megilloth (the Scrolls).

Nehemiah was a cupbearer for Artaxerxes. His name means "whom God hath comforted." The return of the first remnant occurred almost a hundred years before Nehemiah went back to Jerusalem. His call to service came as the result of a discouraging report brought to him at the Persian court by a kinsman named Hanani. He went to Jerusalem with the permission of Artaxerxes. A man of great energy and self-denial, he was able to cope successfully with plots laid against the Jews by neighboring peoples.

Characteristics: The first part of the book is autobiographical, containing the memoirs of Nehemiah. It is a personal report of his own activities which was incorporated into the book. These memoirs and The Book of Ezra supply most of our knowledge of Jewish history from 538 to 430 B.C. Like Ezra, there are lists found in Nehemiah: one is geographical (Neh 11.25–35); another itemizes the gifts to the Temple (Neh 7.70–72). The portion of the book which contains the memoirs of Nehemiah differs markedly from the remainder of the book. The style is somewhat disjointed and the account disconnected.

Contents:

I.   The rebuilding of the walls and the reform movement of Nehemiah. 1.1—7.73*a*: Nehemiah hears from Jerusalem, prays, and seeks permission to return. He arrives in Jerusalem, inspects the walls, and encourages the people to build. A conflict arises from neighboring officials. The rebuilding of the gates. Sanballat's opposition. Nehemiah defends the poor and stops usury. Sanballat, Shemaiah, and Tobiah fail to halt the work. The wall is finished and Jerusalem resettled. The genealogy of the exiles.

II.   The reading of the Law and the renewing of the covenant. 7.73*b*— 10.39: The people are assembled and the Law read. They are en-

joined to celebrate; the Feast of Booths is held. A penitential psalm is sung praising God as Creator and remembering former mercies in Egypt, the exodus, the wanderings, and in the conquest of Canaan. A plea for mercy and salvation is made. A pledge for reform is drawn up and signed by officials, priests, Levites, and laymen. Its legislative acts include prohibition against mixed marriages, the observance of the Sabbath, the Temple tax, wood offering, first fruits, tithes, and a pledge to support the Temple.

III.   The reconstituting of Jerusalem: Nehemiah's second reform movement. 11.1—13.31: The listing of those who repeopled Jerusalem, and the names of the towns outside Jerusalem which were settled. A list of the priests and Levites. The walls of Jerusalem are dedicated: the Levites and musicians are assembled, rites of purification celebrated, the city circumambulated, and sacrifices offered. The ideal community is described. Nehemiah expels Tobiah, gathers support for the Levites, engages in Sabbath and mixed-marriage reforms.

THE BOOK OF
NEHEMIAH

I. The rebuilding of the walls and the reform movement of Nehemiah 1.1–7.73a

A. Introduction

1. Nehemiah's sorrow

1 The words of Nĕhĕmī′ăh the son of Hăcălī′ăh.
Now it happened in the month of Chĭslĕv, in the twentieth year, as I was in Suṣȧ the capital, ² that Hȧnā′nī, one of my brethren, came with certain men out of Judah; and I asked them concerning the Jews that survived, who had escaped exile, and concerning Jerusalem. ³And they said to me, "The survivors there in the province who escaped exile are in great trouble and shame; the wall of Jerusalem is broken down, and its gates are destroyed by fire."

4 When I heard these words I sat down and wept, and mourned for days; and I continued fasting and praying before the God of heaven. ⁵And I said, "O LORD God of heaven, the great and terrible God who keeps covenant and steadfast love with those who love him and keep his commandments; ⁶ let thy ear be attentive, and thy eyes open, to hear the prayer of thy servant which I now pray before thee day and night for the people of Israel thy servants, confessing the sins of the people of Israel, which we have sinned against thee. Yea, I and my father's house have sinned. ⁷ We have acted very corruptly against thee, and have not kept the commandments, the statutes, and the ordinances which thou didst command thy servant Moses. ⁸ Remember the word which thou didst command thy servant Moses, saying, 'If you are unfaithful, I will scatter you among the peoples; ⁹ but if you return to me and keep my commandments and do them, though your dispersed be under the farthest skies, I will gather them thence and bring them to the place which I have chosen, to make my name dwell there.' ¹⁰ They are thy servants and thy people, whom thou hast redeemed by thy great power and by thy strong hand. ¹¹ O Lord, let thy ear be attentive to the prayer of thy servant, and to the prayer of thy servants who delight to fear thy name; and give success to thy servant today, and grant him mercy in the sight of this man."

2. Nehemiah's request to go to Jerusalem

Now I was cupbearer to the king.

2 In the month of Nĭsăn, in the twentieth year of King Ar-tȧ-xĕrx′ĕṣ, when wine was before him, I took up the wine and gave it to the king. Now I had not been sad in his presence. ²And

---

1.1 *Chislev*, latter part of November and early December; *twentieth year* of Artaxerxes I, that is 445 B.C.
1.11 *cupbearer.* Since ancient monarchs were always in danger of poisoning, the cupbearer had to be the most faithful, trustworthy servant. In most cases he was a eunuch, and such may have been the case with Nehemiah; especially since he was also in contact with the queen (2.6). Deut 23.1 excludes emasculated persons from the Jewish community, but Nehemiah may have been excepted.

683

Marginal references:

*1.1
Neh 10.1;
2.1;
Est 1.2;
Dan 8.2

1.3
Neh 7.6;
2.17; 2.3

1.4
Ezra 9.3;
10.1;
Neh 2.4

1.5
Neh 4.14;
9.32;
Ex 20.6

1.6
Dan 9.17;
Ezra 10.1;
Dan 9.20;
2 Chr 29.6

1.7
Dan 9.5;
Deut 28.14,
15

1.8
Lev 26.33

1.9
Deut 30.2–
4; 12.5

1.10
Deut 9.29;
Dan 9.15

*1.11
ver 6

2.1
Neh 1.1;
Ezra 7.1;
Neh 1.11

2.2
Prov 15.13

the king said to me, "Why is your face sad, seeing you are not sick? This is nothing else but sadness of the heart." Then I was very much afraid. 3 I said to the king, "Let the king live for ever! Why should not my face be sad, when the city, the place of my fathers' sepulchres, lies waste, and its gates have been destroyed by fire?" 4 Then the king said to me, "For what do you make request?" So I prayed to the God of heaven. 5And I said to the king, "If it pleases the king, and if your servant has found favor in your sight, that you send me to Judah, to the city of my fathers' sepulchres, that I may rebuild it." 6And the king said to me (the queen sitting beside him), "How long will you be gone, and when will you return?" So it pleased the king to send me; and I set him a time. 7And I said to the king, "If it pleases the king, let letters be given me to the governors of the province Beyond the River, that they may let me pass through until I come to Judah; 8 and a letter to Āsăph, the keeper of the king's forest, that he may give me timber to make beams for the gates of the fortress of the temple, and for the wall of the city, and for the house which I shall occupy." And the king granted me what I asked, for the good hand of my God was upon me.

3. Nehemiah's journey to Jerusalem: his inspection of the walls

9 Then I came to the governors of the province Beyond the River, and gave them the king's letters. Now the king had sent with me officers of the army and horsemen. 10 But when Săn-băl'lăt the Hor'ŏnīte and Tŏbī'ăh the servant, the Ăm'mŏnite, heard this, it displeased them greatly that some one had come to seek the welfare of the children of Israel.

11 So I came to Jerusalem and was there three days. 12 Then I arose in the night, I and a few men with me; and I told no one what my God had put into my heart to do for Jerusalem. There was no beast with me but the beast on which I rode. 13 I went out by night by the Valley Gate to the Jackal's Well and to the Dung Gate, and I inspected the walls of Jerusalem which were broken down and its gates which had been destroyed by fire. 14 Then I went on to the Fountain Gate and to the King's Pool; but there was no place for the beast that was under me to pass. 15 Then I went up in the night by the valley and inspected the wall; and I turned back and entered by the Valley Gate, and so returned. 16And the officials did not know where I had gone or what I was doing; and I had not yet told the Jews, the priests, the nobles, the officials, and the rest that were to do the work.

4. Nehemiah's determination to rebuild; the opposition of Sanballat and Tobiah

17 Then I said to them, "You see the trouble we are in, how Jerusalem lies in ruins with its gates burned. Come, let us build the wall of Jerusalem, that we may no longer suffer disgrace." 18And I told them of the hand of my God which had been upon me for good, and also of the words which the king had spoken to me. And they said, "Let us rise up and build." So they strengthened their hands for the good work. 19 But when Sănbăl'lăt the Hor'ŏnīte and Tŏbī'ăh the servant, the Ăm'mŏnite, and Gĕshĕm

the Arab heard of it, they derided us and despised us and said, "What is this thing that you are doing? Are you rebelling against the king?" 20 Then I replied to them, "The God of heaven will make us prosper, and we his servants will arise and build; but you have no portion or right or memorial in Jerusalem."

2.20
ver 4

B. The rebuilding of the walls

1. *The workers and the places they worked*

3 Then Ĕlĭ´áshĭb the high priest rose up with his brethren the priests and they built the Sheep Gate. They consecrated it and set its doors; they consecrated it as far as the Tower of the Hundred, as far as the Tower of Hăn´ănĕl. 2And next to him the men of Jĕr´ĭchŏ built. And next to them*a* Zăccŭr the son of Ĭmrĭ built.

3.1
ver 20,32;
Neh 6.1;
7.1; 12.39;
Jer 31.38
3.2
Neh 7.36

3 And the sons of Hăssĕnä´áh built the Fish Gate; they laid its beams and set its doors, its bolts, and its bars. 4And next to them Mĕr´ĕmŏth the son of Ūrĭ´áh, son of Hăkkŏz repaired. And next to them Mĕshŭl´lám the son of Bĕrĕchĭ´áh, son of Mĕshĕz´ábĕl repaired. And next to them Zādŏk the son of Bā´ănä repaired. 5And next to them the Tĕkŏ´ītes repaired; but their nobles did not put their necks to the work of their Lord.*b*

3.3
Neh 12.39

★3.5

6 And Joi´ádá the son of Pásé´áh and Mĕshŭl´lám the son of Bĕsŏdeĭ´áh repaired the Old Gate; they laid its beams and set its doors, its bolts, and its bars. 7And next to them repaired Mĕlátĭ´áh the Gĭb´ëónĭte and Jādŏn the Mĕrŏ´nŏthīte, the men of Gĭb´ëön and of Mĭzpáh, who were under the jurisdiction of the governor of the province Beyond the River. 8 Next to them Ŭzzĭ´ĕl the son of Harhāi´áh, goldsmiths, repaired. Next to him Hănánĭ´áh, one of the perfumers, repaired; and they restored*c* Jerusalem as far as the Broad Wall. 9 Next to them Rĕphāi´áh the son of Hŭr, ruler of half the district of*d* Jerusalem, repaired. 10 Next to them Jĕdāi´áh the son of Háru´máph repaired opposite his house; and next to him Hăttŭsh the son of Hăshăbneĭ´áh repaired. 11 Mălchĭ´jáh the son of Harĭm and Hăsshŭb the son of Pā´hăth-mŏ´áb repaired another section and the Tower of the Ovens. 12 Next to him Shăllŭm the son of Hăllŏ´hĕsh, ruler of half the district of*d* Jerusalem, repaired, he and his daughters.

3.6
Neh 12.39
3.7
Neh 2.7
3.8
ver 31,32;
Neh 12.38
3.9
ver 12,17
3.11
Neh 12.38
3.12
ver 9

13 Hānŭn and the inhabitants of Zánŏ´áh repaired the Valley Gate; they rebuilt it and set its doors, its bolts, and its bars, and repaired a thousand cubits of the wall, as far as the Dung Gate.

3.13
Neh 2.13

14 Mălchĭ´jáh the son of Rĕchăb, ruler of the district of*d* Bĕthhăc´chĕrĕm, repaired the Dung Gate; he rebuilt it and set its doors, its bolts, and its bars.

15 And Shăllŭm the son of Cŏlhŏ´zĕh, ruler of the district of*d* Mĭzpáh, repaired the Fountain Gate; he rebuilt it and covered it and set its doors, its bolts, and its bars; and he built the wall of the Pool of Shĕláh of the king's garden, as far as the stairs that go down from the City of David. 16After him Nĕhĕmĭ´áh the son of Ăzbŭk, ruler of half the district of*d* Beth-zŭr, repaired to a point opposite the sepulchres of David, to the artificial pool, and to the

★3.15
Neh 2.14;
2 Ki 25.4;
Neh 12.37
3.16
ver 9,12,17;
2 Ki 20.20

a Heb *him*   *b* Or *lords*   *c* Or *abandoned*   *d* Or *foreman of half the portion assigned to*

3.5 *Lord* may be a reference to Nehemiah.   3.15 *Shelah*, that is, Siloam.

house of the mighty men. ¹⁷After him the Lēvītes repaired: Rēhùm the son of Bānī; next to him Hăshăbī'ăh, ruler of half the district of^d Keīlăh, repaired for his district. ¹⁸After him their brethren
repaired: Băvvaī the son of Hěn'ădăd, ruler of half the district
of^d Keīlăh; ¹⁹ next to him Ēzĕr the son of Jĕsh'uă, ruler of Mĭzpăh,
repaired another section opposite the ascent to the armory at the
Angle. ²⁰After him Băruch the son of Zăb'băi repaired another
section from the Angle to the door of the house of Ĕlī'ăshĭb the
high priest. ²¹After him Mĕr'ĕmŏth the son of Ūrī'ăh, son of
Hăkkŏz repaired another section from the door of the house of
Ĕlī'ăshĭb to the end of the house of Eliashib. ²²After him the
priests, the men of the Plain, repaired. ²³After them Benjamin
and Hăsshŭb repaired opposite their house. After them Ăzărī'ăh
the son of Mă-ăseī'ăh, son of Ănănī'ăh repaired beside his own
house. ²⁴After him Bĭn'nūī the son of Hěn'ădăd repaired another
section, from the house of Ăzărī'ăh to the Angle ²⁵ and to the
corner. Pălăl the son of Ūzaī repaired opposite the Angle and the
tower projecting from the upper house of the king at the court
of the guard. After him Pĕdāi'ăh the son of Părŏsh ²⁶ and the
temple servants living^e on Ŏphĕl repaired to a point opposite the
Water Gate on the east and the projecting tower. ²⁷After him the
Tĕkō'ītes repaired another section opposite the great projecting
tower as far as the wall of Ŏphĕl.

28 Above the Horse Gate the priests repaired, each one opposite his own house. ²⁹After them Zādŏk the son of Ĭmmĕr repaired opposite his own house. After him Shĕmāi'ăh the son of
Shĕcănī'ăh, the keeper of the East Gate, repaired. ³⁰After him
Hănănī'ăh the son of Shĕlĕmī'ăh and Hānùn the sixth son of
Zālăph repaired another section. After him Mĕshŭl'lăm the son
of Bĕrĕchī'ăh repaired opposite his chamber. ³¹After him Mălchī'-
jăh, one of the goldsmiths, repaired as far as the house of the
temple servants and of the merchants, opposite the Muster
Gate,^f and to the upper chamber of the corner. ³²And between
the upper chamber of the corner and the Sheep Gate the goldsmiths and the merchants repaired.

2. The opposition to the work
a. The stratagems of Sanballat and Tobiah

4^g Now when Sănbăl'lăt heard that we were building the wall,
he was angry and greatly enraged, and he ridiculed the Jews.
²And he said in the presence of his brethren and of the army of
Sămăr'iă, "What are these feeble Jews doing? Will they restore
things? Will they sacrifice? Will they finish up in a day? Will they
revive the stones out of the heaps of rubbish, and burned ones at
that?" ³ Tòbī'ăh the Ăm'mŏnīte was by him, and he said, "Yes,
what they are building—if a fox goes up on it he will break down
their stone wall!" ⁴ Hear, O our God, for we are despised; turn
back their taunt upon their own heads, and give them up to be
plundered in a land where they are captives. ⁵ Do not cover their
guilt, and let not their sin be blotted out from thy sight; for they
have provoked thee to anger before the builders.

6 So we built the wall; and all the wall was joined together to
half its height. For the people had a mind to work.

Margin references:
3.19 ver 15; 2 Chr 26.9
3.20 ver 1; Neh 13.7
3.22 Neh 12.28
3.24 ver 19
3.25 Jer 32.2
3.26 Neh 7.46; 11.21; 8.1
3.28 2 Ki 11.16; 2 Chr 23.15; Jer 31.40
3.31 ver 8,32
3.32 ver 1
4.1 Neh 2.10,19
4.2 ver 10
4.3 Neh 2.10,19
4.4 Ps 123.3,4; 79.12
4.5 Ps 69.27, 28; Jer 18.23

d Or foreman of half the portion assigned to
e Cn: Heb were living   f Or Hămmiph'kăd Gate   g Ch 3.33 in Heb

7[h] But when Sănbăl′lăt and Tŏbī′áh and the Arabs and the Ăm′mŏnītes and the Ăsh′dŏdītes heard that the repairing of the walls of Jerusalem was going forward and that the breaches were beginning to be closed, they were very angry; 8 and they all plotted together to come and fight against Jerusalem and to cause confusion in it. 9And we prayed to our God, and set a guard as a protection against them day and night.

10 But Judah said, "The strength of the burden-bearers is failing, and there is much rubbish; we are not able to work on the wall." 11And our enemies said, "They will not know or see till we come into the midst of them and kill them and stop the work." 12 When the Jews who lived by them came they said to us ten times, "From all the places where they live[i] they will come up against us."[j] 13 So in the lowest parts of the space behind the wall, in open places, I stationed the people according to their families, with their swords, their spears, and their bows. 14And I looked, and arose, and said to the nobles and to the officials and to the rest of the people, "Do not be afraid of them. Remember the Lord, who is great and terrible, and fight for your brethren, your sons, your daughters, your wives, and your homes."

15 When our enemies heard that it was known to us and that God had frustrated their plan, we all returned to the wall, each to his work. 16 From that day on, half of my servants worked on construction, and half held the spears, shields, bows, and coats of mail; and the leaders stood behind all the house of Judah, 17 who were building on the wall. Those who carried burdens were laden in such a way that each with one hand labored on the work and with the other held his weapon. 18And each of the builders had his sword girded at his side while he built. The man who sounded the trumpet was beside me. 19And I said to the nobles and to the officials and to the rest of the people, "The work is great and widely spread, and we are separated on the wall, far from one another. 20 In the place where you hear the sound of the trumpet, rally to us there. Our God will fight for us."

21 So we labored at the work, and half of them held the spears from the break of dawn till the stars came out. 22 I also said to the people at that time, "Let every man and his servant pass the night within Jerusalem, that they may be a guard for us by night and may labor by day." 23 So neither I nor my brethren nor my servants nor the men of the guard who followed me, none of us took off our clothes; each kept his weapon in his hand.[k]

b. *Disaffection among the Jews themselves*

5 Now there arose a great outcry of the people and of their wives against their Jewish brethren. 2 For there were those who said, "With our sons and our daughters, we are many; let us get grain, that we may eat and keep alive." 3 There were also those who said, "We are mortgaging our fields, our vineyards, and our

Marginal references:

4.7 ver 1

*4.9 Ps 50.15

4.13 ver 17,18

4.14 Num 14.9; Deut 1.29; 2 Sam 10.12

4.15 2 Sam 17.14; Job 5.12

4.20 Ex 14.14; Deut 1.30; Josh 23.10

*5.1 Lev 25.35; Deut 15.7

---

[h] Ch 4.1 in Heb   [i] Cn: Heb *you return*
[j] Compare Gk Syr: Heb uncertain   [k] Cn: Heb *each his weapon the water*

4.9 Prayer and works are perfectly illustrated here. We are to pray as though we had never worked and work as though we had never prayed.

5.1 A reason for the *great outcry* was the exaction of interest (ver 7) by the rich when they loaned money to the poor. This was forbidden, according to Deut 23.20.

houses to get grain because of the famine." ⁴And there were those
who said, "We have borrowed money for the king's tax upon our
fields and our vineyards. ⁵ Now our flesh is as the flesh of our
brethren, our children are as their children; yet we are forcing our
sons and our daughters to be slaves, and some of our daughters
have already been enslaved; but it is not in our power to help it,
for other men have our fields and our vineyards."

6 I was very angry when I heard their outcry and these words.
⁷ I took counsel with myself, and I brought charges against the
nobles and the officials. I said to them, "You are exacting interest,
each from his brother." And I held a great assembly against them,
⁸ and said to them, "We, as far as we are able, have bought back
our Jewish brethren who have been sold to the nations; but you
even sell your brethren that they may be sold to us!" They were
silent, and could not find a word to say. ⁹ So I said, "The thing
that you are doing is not good. Ought you not to walk in the fear
of our God to prevent the taunts of the nations our enemies?
¹⁰ Moreover I and my brethren and my servants are lending them
money and grain. Let us leave off this interest. ¹¹ Return to them
this very day their fields, their vineyards, their olive orchards, and
their houses, and the hundredth of money, grain, wine, and oil
which you have been exacting of them." ¹² Then they said, "We
will restore these and require nothing from them. We will do as
you say." And I called the priests, and took an oath of them to
do as they had promised. ¹³ I also shook out my lap and said, "So
may God shake out every man from his house and from his labor
who does not perform this promise. So may he be shaken out and
emptied." And all the assembly said "Amen" and praised the
LORD. And the people did as they had promised.

14 Moreover from the time that I was appointed to be their
governor in the land of Judah, from the twentieth year to the
thirty-second year of Ar-ta-xerx'es the king, twelve years, neither
I nor my brethren ate the food allowance of the governor. ¹⁵ The
former governors who were before me laid heavy burdens upon
the people, and took from them food and wine, besides forty
shekels of silver. Even their servants lorded it over the people.
But I did not do so, because of the fear of God. ¹⁶ I also held to
the work on this wall, and acquired no land; and all my servants
were gathered there for the work. ¹⁷ Moreover there were at my
table a hundred and fifty men, Jews and officials, besides those
who came to us from the nations which were about us. ¹⁸ Now that
which was prepared for one day was one ox and six choice sheep;
fowls likewise were prepared for me, and every ten days skins of
wine in abundance; yet with all this I did not demand the food
allowance of the governor, because the servitude was heavy upon
this people. ¹⁹ Remember for my good, O my God, all that I have
done for this people.

c. The continued difficulties from Sanballat and Tobiah

6 Now when it was reported to Sănbăl'lăt and Tòbĭ'ăh and to
Gĕshĕm the Arab and to the rest of our enemies that I had
built the wall and that there was no breach left in it (although up
to that time I had not set up the doors in the gates), ² Sănbăl'lăt
and Gĕshĕm sent to me, saying, "Come and let us meet together
in one of the villages in the plain of Ōnō." But they intended to do

5.4
Ezra 4.13;
7.24
5.5
Gen 37.27;
Lev 25.39

5.7
Ex 22.25;
Lev 25.36

5.8
Lev 25.48

5.9
2 Sam
12.14;
Neh 4.4;
Rom 2.24

5.12
Ezra 10.5

5.13
Acts 18.6;
Neh 8.6

5.14
Neh 13.6;
Ezra 4.13,
14

5.15
ver 9

5.17
1 Ki 18.19

5.18
1 Ki 4.22,
23;
2 Thess 3.8

5.19
Neh 13.14,
22.31

6.1
Neh 2.10,
19; 4.1.7;
3.1,3

6.2
1 Chr 8.12

me harm. ³And I sent messengers to them, saying, "I am doing a great work and I cannot come down. Why should the work stop while I leave it and come down to you?" ⁴And they sent to me four times in this way and I answered them in the same manner. ⁵ In the same way Sănbăl'lăt for the fifth time sent his servant to me with an open letter in his hand. ⁶ In it was written, "It is reported among the nations, and Gĕshêm*l* also says it, that you and the Jews intend to rebel; that is why you are building the wall; and you wish to become their king, according to this report. ⁷And you have also set up prophets to proclaim concerning you in Jerusalem, 'There is a king in Judah.' And now it will be reported to the king according to these words. So now come, and let us take counsel together." ⁸ Then I sent to him, saying, "No such things as you say have been done, for you are inventing them out of your own mind." ⁹ For they all wanted to frighten us, thinking, "Their hands will drop from the work, and it will not be done." But now, O God, strengthen thou my hands.

6.6
Neh 2.19

10 Now when I went into the house of Shĕmăi'ăh the son of Dĕlăi'ăh, son of Mĕhĕt'ăbĕl, who was shut up, he said, "Let us meet together in the house of God, within the temple, and let us close the doors of the temple; for they are coming to kill you, at night they are coming to kill you." ¹¹ But I said, "Should such a man as I flee? And what man such as I could go into the temple and live?*m* I will not go in." ¹²And I understood, and saw that God had not sent him, but he had pronounced the prophecy against me because Tŏbī'ăh and Sănbăl'lăt had hired him. ¹³ For this purpose he was hired, that I should be afraid and act in this way and sin, and so they could give me an evil name, in order to taunt me. ¹⁴ Remember Tŏbī'ăh and Sănbăl'lăt, O my God, according to these things that they did, and also the prophetess Nō-ădī'ăh and the rest of the prophets who wanted to make me afraid.

6.10
Jer 36.5

6.12
Ezek 13.22

6.13
ver 6

6.14
Neh 13.29;
Ezek 13.17

15 So the wall was finished on the twenty-fifth day of the month Ĕlul', in fifty-two days. ¹⁶And when all our enemies heard of it, all the nations round about us were afraid*n* and fell greatly in their own esteem; for they perceived that this work had been accomplished with the help of our God. ¹⁷ Moreover in those days the nobles of Judah sent many letters to Tŏbī'ăh, and Tŏbī'ăh's letters came to them. ¹⁸ For many in Judah were bound by oath to him, because he was the son-in-law of Shĕcănī'ăh the son of Ărăh: and his son Jĕhō'hănăn had taken the daughter of Mĕshŭl'-lăm the son of Bĕrĕchī'ăh as his wife. ¹⁹Also they spoke of his good deeds in my presence, and reported my words to him. And Tŏbī'ăh sent letters to make me afraid.

*6.15
6.16
Neh 2.10;
4.1,7;
Ex 14.25;
Ps 126.2

C. The new order at Jerusalem and list of returning exiles

1. The appointment of Hanani and Hananiah

7 Now when the wall had been built and I had set up the doors, and the gatekeepers, the singers, and the Lēvītes had been appointed, ² I gave my brother Hănā'nī and Hănănī'ăh the governor of the castle charge over Jerusalem, for he was a more faith-

7.1
Neh 6.1,15

7.2
Neh 2.8

l Heb *Găshmū*   *m* Or *would go into the temple to save his life*   *n* Another reading is *saw*

6.15 *fifty-two days.* This probably refers to the last phase of completion. According to

Josephus, it took two years and four months to rebuild the walls.

ful and God-fearing man than many. ³And I said to them, "Let not the gates of Jerusalem be opened until the sun is hot; and while they are still standing guard° let them shut and bar the doors. Appoint guards from among the inhabitants of Jerusalem, each to his station and each opposite his own house." ⁴ The city was wide and large, but the people within it were few and no houses had been built.

2. *The genealogy of the returning remnant*

5 Then God put it into my mind to assemble the nobles and the officials and the people to be enrolled by genealogy. And I found the book of the genealogy of those who came up at the first, and I found written in it:

6 These were the people of the province who came up out of the captivity of those exiles whom Nĕbŭchădnĕz'zàr the king of Babylon had carried into exile; they returned to Jerusalem and Judah, each to his town. ⁷ They came with Zĕrŭb'bàbĕl, Jĕsh'uà, Nĕhĕmī'àh, Ăzàrī'àh, Rā-àmī'àh, Nāhàmà'nī, Mŏr'dĕcàī, Bĭlshăn, Mĭs'pĕrĕth, Bĭgvaī, Nĕhŭm, Bā'ànàh.

The number of the men of the people of Israel: ⁸ the sons of Pàrŏsh, two thousand a hundred and seventy-two. ⁹ The sons of Shĕphàtī'àh, three hundred and seventy-two. ¹⁰ The sons of Ārăh, six hundred and fifty-two. ¹¹ The sons of Pā'hăth-mō'ăb, namely the sons of Jĕsh'uà and Jŏăb, two thousand eight hundred and eighteen. ¹² The sons of Ēlàm, a thousand two hundred and fifty-four. ¹³ The sons of Zăttu, eight hundred and forty-five. ¹⁴ The sons of Zăc'cāī, seven hundred and sixty. ¹⁵ The sons of Bĭn'nūī, six hundred and forty-eight. ¹⁶ The sons of Bēbaī, six hundred and twenty-eight. ¹⁷ The sons of Āzgăd, two thousand three hundred and twenty-two. ¹⁸ The sons of Ădŏnī'kàm, six hundred and sixty-seven. ¹⁹ The sons of Bĭgvaī, two thousand and sixty-seven. ²⁰ The sons of Ādĭn, six hundred and fifty-five. ²¹ The sons of Ātĕr, namely of Hĕzĕkī'àh, ninety-eight. ²² The sons of Hāshŭm, three hundred and twenty-eight. ²³ The sons of Bēzaī, three hundred and twenty-four. ²⁴ The sons of Hārĭph, a hundred and twelve. ²⁵ The sons of Gĭb'ĕŏn, ninety-five. ²⁶ The men of Bĕth'lĕhĕm and Nĕtō'phàh, a hundred and eighty-eight. ²⁷ The men of Ăn'àthŏth, a hundred and twenty-eight. ²⁸ The men of Bĕth-ăzmā'vĕth, forty-two. ²⁹ The men of Kĭr'iăth-jē'àrĭm, Chĕphī'ràh, and Be-ĕr'ŏth, seven hundred and forty-three. ³⁰ The men of Rāmàh and Gēbà, six hundred and twenty-one. ³¹ The men of Mĭchmăs, a hundred and twenty-two. ³² The men of Bĕthĕl and Āī, a hundred and twenty-three. ³³ The men of the other Nĕbō, fifty-two. ³⁴ The sons of the other Ēlàm, a thousand two hundred and fifty-four. ³⁵ The sons of Hārĭm, three hundred and twenty. ³⁶ The sons of Jĕr'ĭchō, three hundred and forty-five. ³⁷ The sons of Lŏd, Hādĭd, and Ōnō, seven hundred and twenty-one. ³⁸ The sons of Sĕnā'àh, three thousand nine hundred and thirty.

39 The priests: the sons of Jĕdāi'àh, namely the house of Jĕsh'uà, nine hundred and seventy-three. ⁴⁰ The sons of Ĭmmĕr, a thousand and fifty-two. ⁴¹ The sons of Păshhŭr, a thousand two hundred and forty-seven. ⁴² The sons of Hārĭm, a thousand and seventeen.

o Heb obscure

Margin references

7.6
Ezra 2.1–70

7.7
Ezra 2.2

7.12
Ezra 2.7

7.17
see Ezra 2.12

7.23
Ezra 2.17

7.27
Ezra 2.23

7.34
Ezra 2.31

7.39
Ezra 2.36

43 The Lēvītes: the sons of Jĕsh′uȧ, namely of Kăd′mĭ-ėl of the 7.43
sons of Hȯdē′vȧh, seventy-four. 44 The singers: the sons of Ezra 2.40
Āsăph, a hundred and forty-eight. 45 The gatekeepers: the sons
of Shăllȯm, the sons of Ātėr, the sons of Tălmȯn, the sons of
Ăkkŭb, the sons of Hȧtī′tȧ, the sons of Shōbaī, a hundred and
thirty-eight.

46 The temple servants:[p] the sons of Zīhȧ, the sons of Hȧsu′- 7.46
phȧ, the sons of Tȧbbā′ȯth, 47 the sons of Kērȯs, the sons of Sīȧ, Ezra 2.43
the sons of Pādȯn, 48 the sons of Lėbā′nȧ, the sons of Hăg′ȧbȧ,
the sons of Shălmaī, 49 the sons of Hānȧn, the sons of Gĭddėl,
the sons of Gāhar, 50 the sons of Rė-āi′ȧh, the sons of Rĕzĭn, the
sons of Nėkō′dȧ, 51 the sons of Găzzȧm, the sons of Ŭzzȧ, the sons
of Pȧsē′ȧh, 52 the sons of Bēsaī, the sons of Mė-ū′nĭm, the sons
of Nėphŭsh′ėsĭm, 53 the sons of Băkbŭk, the sons of Hȧku′phȧ,
the sons of Harhŭr, 54 the sons of Băzlĭth, the sons of Mėhī′dȧ,
the sons of Harshȧ, 55 the sons of Barkȯs, the sons of Sĭs′ėrȧ, the
sons of Tēmȧh, 56 the sons of Nėzī′ȧh, the sons of Hȧtī′phȧ.

57 The sons of Solomon's servants: the sons of Sōtaī, the sons 7.57
of Sōphĕr′ėth, the sons of Pėrī′dȧ, 58 the sons of Jā′ȧlȧ, the sons of Ezra 2.55
Darkȯn, the sons of Gĭddėl, 59 the sons of Shĕphȧtī′ȧh, the sons
of Hăttĭl, the sons of Pō′çhėrĕth-hăzzėbā′ĭm, the sons of Āmȯn.

60 All the temple servants and the sons of Solomon's servants 7.60
were three hundred and ninety-two. ver 46

61 The following were those who came up from Tĕl-mē′lȧh,
Tĕl-har′shȧ, Çhĕrŭb, Ăddȯn, and Ĭmmėr, but they could not
prove their fathers' houses nor their descent, whether they belonged to Israel: 62 the sons of Dĕlāi′ȧh, the sons of Tȯbī′ȧh, the
sons of Nėkō′dȧ, six hundred and forty-two. 63 Also, of the priests: 7.63
the sons of Hȯbāi′ȧh, the sons of Hăkkȯz, the sons of Barzĭl′laī Ezra 2.61
(who had taken a wife of the daughters of Barzillai the Gĭl′ĕȧdīte
and was called by their name). 64 These sought their registration
among those enrolled in the genealogies, but it was not found
there, so they were excluded from the priesthood as unclean;
65 the governor told them that they were not to partake of the 7.65
most holy food, until a priest with Ūrĭm and Thŭmmĭm should Neh 8.9;
arise. 10.1

66 The whole assembly together was forty-two thousand three
hundred and sixty, 67 besides their menservants and maidservants,
of whom there were seven thousand three hundred and thirty-
seven; and they had two hundred and forty-five singers, male and
female. 68 Their horses were seven hundred and thirty-six, their
mules two hundred and forty-five,[q] 69 their camels four hundred
and thirty-five, and their asses six thousand seven hundred and
twenty.

70 Now some of the heads of fathers' houses gave to the work. 7.70
The governor gave to the treasury a thousand darics of gold, fifty Neh 8.9
basins, five hundred and thirty priests' garments. 71 And some of 7.71
the heads of fathers' houses gave into the treasury of the work Ezra 2.69
twenty thousand darics of gold and two thousand two hundred
minas of silver. 72 And what the rest of the people gave was twenty
thousand darics of gold, two thousand minas of silver, and sixty-
seven priests' garments.

73 So the priests, the Lēvītes, the gatekeepers, the singers, 7.73 Ezra 3.1

[p] Heb *nethinim*
[q] Ezra 2.66 and the margins of some Hebrew Mss: Heb lacks *their horses . . . forty-five*

some of the people, the temple servants, and all Israel, lived in their towns.

II. The reading of the Law and the renewing of the covenant 7.73b–10.39

A. The Law read and explained

8.1
Ezra 3.1;
Neh 3.26;
Ezra 7.6

And when the seventh month had come, the children of Israel 8 were in their towns. [1]And all the people gathered as one man into the square before the Water Gate; and they told Ezra the scribe to bring the book of the law of Moses which the LORD had given to Israel.

8.2
Deut 31.11,
12;
Lev 23.24

[2]And Ezra the priest brought the law before the assembly, both men and women and all who could hear with understanding, on the first day of the seventh month. [3]And he read from it facing the square before the Water Gate from early morning until midday, in the presence of the men and the women and those who could understand; and the ears of all the people were attentive to the book of the law. [4]And Ezra the scribe stood on a wooden pulpit which they had made for the purpose; and beside him stood Mǎttǐthī′áh, Shěmá, Ánāi′áh, Ūrī′áh, Hǐlkī′áh, and Mā-áseī′áh on his right hand; and Pědāi′áh, Mǐsh′ä-ėl, Mǎlçhī′jáh, Hāshùm, Hǎsh-bǎd′dánáh, Zěçhárī′áh, and Měshǔl′- lám on his left hand.

8.6
Neh 5.13;
Gen 14.22;
Ex 4.31

[5]And Ezra opened the book in the sight of all the people, for he was above all the people; and when he opened it all the people stood. [6]And Ezra blessed the LORD, the great God; and all the people answered, "Amen, Amen," lifting up their hands; and they bowed their heads and worshiped the LORD with their faces to the ground.

8.7
2 Chr
17.7–9

[7]Also Jěsh′uá, Bānī, Shěrěbī′áh, Jāmǐn, Ăkkǔb, Shǎb′bethaī, Hǒdī′áh, Mā-áseī′áh, Kělī′tá, Ázárī′áh, Jŏz′- ábǎd, Hānán, Pělāi′áh, the Lēvītes,ʳ helped the people to under- stand the law, while the people remained in their places.

*8.8

[8]And they read from the book, from the law of God, clearly;ˢ and they gave the sense, so that the people understood the reading.

8.9
Neh 7.65,
70; 12.26;
Num 29.1;
Deut 16.14,
15

9 And Něhěmī′áh, who was the governor, and Ezra the priest and scribe, and the Lēvītes who taught the people said to all the people, "This day is holy to the LORD your God; do not mourn or weep." For all the people wept when they heard the words of the law.

8.10
Deut 26.11,
13

10 Then he said to them, "Go your way, eat the fat and drink sweet wine and send portions to him for whom nothing is prepared; for this day is holy to our Lord; and do not be grieved, for the joy of the LORD is your strength." 11 So the Lēvītes stilled all the people, saying, "Be quiet, for this day is holy; do not be grieved."

8.12
ver 10,7,8

12And all the people went their way to eat and drink and to send portions and to make great rejoicing, because they had understood the words that were declared to them.

B. The Feast of Tabernacles celebrated

8.13
Lev 23.34,
42

13 On the second day the heads of fathers' houses of all the

ʳ 1 Esdras 9.48 Vg: Heb and the Levites   ˢ Or with interpretation

---

8.8 *gave the sense.* Since Aramaic was rapidly replacing Hebrew as the language of the average Jew, some interpreters take verses

7, 8 to mean that Ezra's aides gave a Targum, Aramaic translation of the Hebrew text, so that all would clearly understand.

people, with the priests and the Lēvītes, came together to Ezra
the scribe in order to study the words of the law. ¹⁴And they found
it written in the law that the LORD had commanded by Moses that
the people of Israel should dwell in booths during the feast of the
seventh month, ¹⁵and that they should publish and proclaim
in all their towns and in Jerusalem, "Go out to the hills and bring
branches of olive, wild olive, myrtle, palm, and other leafy trees
to make booths, as it is written." ¹⁶So the people went out and
brought them and made booths for themselves, each on his roof,
and in their courts and in the courts of the house of God, and in
the square at the Water Gate and in the square at the Gate of
Ē'phrȧim. ¹⁷And all the assembly of those who had returned from
the captivity made booths and dwelt in the booths; for from the
days of Jĕsh'uȧ the son of Nȯn to that day the people of Israel
had not done so. And there was very great rejoicing. ¹⁸And day
by day, from the first day to the last day, he read from the book
of the law of God. They kept the feast seven days; and on the
eighth day there was a solemn assembly, according to the ordinance.

8.15
Lev 23.4;
Deut 16.16;
Lev 23.40

8.16
Jer 32.29;
Neh 12.39;
2 Ki 14.13

8.17
2 Chr 30.21

8.18
Deut 31.11;
Lev 23.36;
Num 29.35

C. The covenant renewed

1. Separation from unbelievers

9 Now on the twenty-fourth day of this month the people of
Israel were assembled with fasting and in sackcloth, and with
earth upon their heads. ²And the Israelites separated themselves
from all foreigners, and stood and confessed their sins and the
iniquities of their fathers. ³And they stood up in their place and
read from the book of the law of the LORD their God for a fourth
of the day; for another fourth of it they made confession and
worshiped the LORD their God. ⁴Upon the stairs of the Lēvītes
stood Jĕsh'uȧ, Bānī, Kăd'mĭ-ėl, Shĕbȧnī'ȧh, Bŭnnī, Shĕrėbī'ȧh,
Bani, and Chėnȧ'nī; and they cried with a loud voice to the LORD
their God. ⁵Then the Lēvītes, Jĕsh'uȧ, Kăd'mĭ-ėl, Bānī, Hăsh-
ăbnēi'ȧh, Shĕrėbī'ȧh, Hȯdī'ȧh, Shĕbȧnī'ȧh, and Pĕthȧhī'ȧh, said,
"Stand up and bless the LORD your God from everlasting to
everlasting. Blessed be thy glorious name which is exalted above
all blessing and praise."

★9.1
Neh 8.2;
Ezra 8.23;
1 Sam 4.12

9.2
Ezra 10.11;
Neh 13.3,30

9.3
Neh 8.4

9.4
Neh 8.7

9.5
1 Chr 29.13

2. The penitential psalm

6 And Ezra said:ᶦ "Thou art the LORD, thou alone; thou hast
made heaven, the heaven of heavens, with all their host, the earth
and all that is on it, the seas and all that is in them; and thou pre-
servest all of them; and the host of heaven worships thee. ⁷Thou
art the LORD, the God who didst choose Abram and bring him
forth out of Ur of the Chăldē'ȧnṣ and give him the name Abraham; ⁸and thou didst find his heart faithful before thee, and didst
make with him the covenant to give to his descendants the land of
the Cā'naȧnīte, the Hĭttīte, the Ăm'ȯrīte, the Pĕr'ĭzzīte, the
Jĕb'ūsīte, and the Gĭr'gȧshīte; and thou hast fulfilled thy promise,
for thou art righteous.

9.6
2 Ki 19.15;
Gen 1.1;
Ps 36.6;
Col 1.17

★9.7
Gen 11.31;
12.1; 17.5

9.8
Gen 15.6,
18–21;
Josh 21.43–
45

ᶦ Gk: Heb lacks and Ezra said

9.1 *fasting*, see note to Lev 16.29.   **9.7** *Chaldeans*, Babylonians.

9.9
Ex 3.7;
14.10–12
9.10
Ex 5.2;
9.16
9.11
Ex 14.21;
15.5,10

9.12
Ex 13.21,
22

9.13
Ex 19.20;
20.1;
Ps 19.7–9
9.14
Gen 2.3;
Ex 20.8,11
9.15
Ex 16.14;
17.6;
Num 20.7–
13;
Deut 1.8
9.16
Ps 106.6;
Deut 31.27
9.17
Ps 78.11;
Num 14.4;
Ex 34.6,7

9.18
Ex 32.4

9.19
ver 27,31;
12

9.20
Num 11.17;
Isa 63.11–
14;
Ex 16.15;
17.6
9.21
Deut 2.7;
8.4; 29.5
9.22
Num
21.21–35
9.23
Gen 15.5
9.24
Josh 21.43;
18.1

9.25
Deut 3.9;
Num 13.27;
Deut 6.11;
32.15;
1 Ki 8.66
9.26
Judg 2.11;
1 Ki 14.9;
2 Chr
36.16;
ver 30
9.27
Judg 2.14;
Deut 4.29;
Judg 2.16,
18

9 "And thou didst see the affliction of our fathers in Egypt and hear their cry at the Red Sea, 10 and didst perform signs and wonders against Phạraōh and all his servants and all the people of his land, for thou knewest that they acted insolently against our fathers; and thou didst get thee a name, as it is to this day. 11And thou didst divide the sea before them, so that they went through the midst of the sea on dry land; and thou didst cast their pursuers into the depths, as a stone into mighty waters. 12 By a pillar of cloud thou didst lead them in the day, and by a pillar of fire in the night to light for them the way in which they should go. 13 Thou didst come down upon Mount Sī'näï, and speak with them from heaven and give them right ordinances and true laws, good statutes and commandments, 14 and thou didst make known to them thy holy sabbath and command them commandments and statutes and a law by Moses thy servant. 15 Thou didst give them bread from heaven for their hunger and bring forth water for them from the rock for their thirst, and thou didst tell them to go in to possess the land which thou hadst sworn to give them.

16 "But they and our fathers acted presumptuously and stiffened their neck and did not obey thy commandments; 17 they refused to obey, and were not mindful of the wonders which thou didst perform among them; but they stiffened their neck and appointed a leader to return to their bondage in Egypt. But thou art a God ready to forgive, gracious and merciful, slow to anger and abounding in steadfast love, and didst not forsake them. 18 Even when they had made for themselves a molten calf and said, 'This is your God who brought you up out of Egypt,' and had committed great blasphemies, 19 thou in thy great mercies didst not forsake them in the wilderness; the pillar of cloud which led them in the way did not depart from them by day, nor the pillar of fire by night which lighted for them the way by which they should go. 20 Thou gavest thy good Spirit to instruct them, and didst not withhold thy manna from their mouth, and gavest them water for their thirst. 21 Forty years didst thou sustain them in the wilderness, and they lacked nothing; their clothes did not wear out and their feet did not swell. 22And thou didst give them kingdoms and peoples, and didst allot to them every corner; so they took possession of the land of Sīhȯn king of Hĕshbȯn and the land of Ōg king of Bāshȧn. 23 Thou didst multiply their descendants as the stars of heaven, and thou didst bring them into the land which thou hadst told their fathers to enter and possess. 24 So the descendants went in and possessed the land, and thou didst subdue before them the inhabitants of the land, the Cā'naȧnītes, and didst give them into their hands, with their kings and the peoples of the land, that they might do with them as they would. 25And they captured fortified cities and a rich land, and took possession of houses full of all good things, cisterns hewn out, vineyards, olive orchards and fruit trees in abundance; so they ate, and were filled and became fat, and delighted themselves in thy great goodness.

26 "Nevertheless they were disobedient and rebelled against thee and cast thy law behind their back and killed thy prophets, who had warned them in order to turn them back to thee, and they committed great blasphemies. 27 Therefore thou didst give them into the hand of their enemies, who made them suffer; and in the time of their suffering they cried to thee and thou didst

hear them from heaven; and according to thy great mercies thou didst give them saviors who saved them from the hand of their enemies. 28 But after they had rest they did evil again before thee, and thou didst abandon them to the hand of their enemies, so that they had dominion over them; yet when they turned and cried to thee thou didst hear from heaven, and many times thou didst deliver them according to thy mercies. 29And thou didst warn them in order to turn them back to thy law. Yet they acted presumptuously and did not obey thy commandments, but sinned against thy ordinances, by the observance of which a man shall live, and turned a stubborn shoulder and stiffened their neck and would not obey. 30 Many years thou didst bear with them, and didst warn them by thy Spirit through thy prophets; yet they would not give ear. Therefore thou didst give them into the hand of the peoples of the lands. 31 Nevertheless in thy great mercies thou didst not make an end of them or forsake them; for thou art a gracious and merciful God.

32 "Now therefore, our God, the great and mighty and terrible God, who keepest covenant and steadfast love, let not all the hardship seem little to thee that has come upon us, upon our kings, our princes, our priests, our prophets, our fathers, and all thy people, since the time of the kings of Assyria until this day. 33 Yet thou hast been just in all that has come upon us, for thou hast dealt faithfully and we have acted wickedly; 34 our kings, our princes, our priests, and our fathers have not kept thy law or heeded thy commandments and thy warnings which thou didst give them. 35 They did not serve thee in their kingdom, and in thy great goodness which thou gavest them, and in the large and rich land which thou didst set before them; and they did not turn from their wicked works. 36 Behold, we are slaves this day; in the land that thou gavest to our fathers to enjoy its fruit and its good gifts, behold, we are slaves. 37And its rich yield goes to the kings whom thou hast set over us because of our sins; they have power also over our bodies and over our cattle at their pleasure, and we are in great distress."

38u Because of all this we make a firm covenant and write it, and our princes, our Lēvītes, and our priests set their seal to it.

3. Those who signed the covenant

10v Those who set their seal are Nehēmī′ah the governor, the son of Hăcălī′ah, Zĕdĕkī′ah, 2 Sĕrāi′ah, Ăzắrī′ah, Jĕrĕmī′ah, 3 Păshhúr, Ămắrī′ah, Mălchī′jăh, 4 Hằttŭsh, Shĕbằnī′ah, Măl-lúch, 5 Hārĭm, Mĕr′ĕmŏth, Ōbắdī′ah, 6 Daniel, Gĭn′nĕthón, Bᾳrúch, 7 Mĕshŭl′làm, Ăbí′jăh, Mĭj′ămĭn, 8 Mā-ăzĭ′ah, Bĭlgaī, Shĕmāi′ah; these are the priests. 9And the Lēvītes: Jĕsh′uᾳ the son of Ăzằnī′ah, Bĭn′nūī of the sons of Hĕn′ᾳdắd, Kắd′mĭ-ēl; 10 and their brethren, Shĕbằnī′ah, Hŏdī′ah, Kĕlī′tᾳ, Pĕlāi′ah, Hānᾳn, 11 Mīcᾳ, Rĕhŏb, Hăshábī′ah, 12 Zăccúr, Shĕrĕbī′ah, Shĕbằnī′ah, 13 Hŏdī′ah, Bānī, Bĕnī′nu. 14 The chiefs of the people: Pārŏsh, Pᾳ′hăth-mō′ăb, Ēlăm, Zắttu, Bānī, 15 Bŭnnī, Ăzgắd, Bēbaī, 16Ădŏnī′jăh, Bĭgvaī, Ādĭn, 17Ătĕr, Hĕzĕkī′ah, Ăzzúr, 18 Hŏdī′ah, Hāshùm, Bēzaī, 19 Hārĭph, Ăn′ắthŏth, Nēbaī, 20 Măg′pĭăsh, Mĕshŭl′làm, Hēzĭr, 21 Mĕshĕz′ăbĕl, Zādŏk, Jăd′dᾳ-ᾳ, 22 Pĕlắtī′ah,

---

Marginal cross-references:

9.28 Judg 3.11; Ps 106.43

9.29 ver 26,30, 16; Lev 18.5; Zech 7.11

9.30 2 Ki 17.13; Acts 7.51, 52

9.31 Jer 4.27

9.32 Neh 1.5; 2 Ki 15.19; 17.3

9.33 Jer 12.1; Dan 9.5,6,8

9.35 Deut 28.47

9.36 Deut 28.48

9.37 Deut 28.33

9.38 2 Chr 29.10; 34.31

10.1 Neh 9.38

Hānán, Ánāi'áh, 23 Hóshe'á, Hănánī'áh, Hăsshúb, 24 Hăllō'hĕsh,
Pilhá, Shóbĕk, 25 Rēhúm, Háshăb'năh, Mā-áseī'áh, 26Áhī'áh,
Hánán, Ānăn, 27 Măllúch, Hărĭm, Bā'ánáh.

4. *Résumé of the covenant*
a. *Mixed marriages*

10.28
Ezra 2.36-
58;
Neh 9.2

28 The rest of the people, the priests, the Lēvītes, the gate-keepers, the singers, the temple servants, and all who have sepa-rated themselves from the peoples of the lands to the law of God, their wives, their sons, their daughters, all who have knowledge

10.29
Neh 5.12;
2 Chr 34.31

and understanding, 29 join with their brethren, their nobles, and enter into a curse and an oath to walk in God's law which was given by Moses the servant of God, and to observe and do all the

10.30
Ex 34.16;
Deut 7.3

commandments of the LORD our Lord and his ordinances and his statutes. 30 We will not give our daughters to the peoples of the

b. *Observance of the Sabbath*

10.31
Neh 13.15-
22;
Ex 23.10,
11;
Deut 15.1,2

land or take their daughters for our sons; 31 and if the peoples of the land bring in wares or any grain on the sabbath day to sell, we will not buy from them on the sabbath or on a holy day; and we will forego the crops of the seventh year and the exaction of every debt.

c. *The promise to fulfil specific covenant obligations*

*10.32
Ex 30.11-16

32 We also lay upon ourselves the obligation to charge our-selves yearly with the third part of a shekel for the service of the

*10.33

house of our God: 33 for the showbread, the continual cereal offering, the continual burnt offering, the sabbaths, the new moons, the appointed feasts, the holy things, and the sin offerings to make atonement for Israel, and for all the work of the house of

10.34
Neh 11.1;
13.31

our God. 34 We have likewise cast lots, the priests, the Lēvītes, and the people, for the wood offering, to bring it into the house of our God, according to our fathers' houses, at times appointed, year by year, to burn upon the altar of the LORD our God, as it is

10.35
Ex 23.19;
Deut 26.2
10.36
Ex 13.2;
Num 18.15,
16

written in the law. 35 We obligate ourselves to bring the first fruits of our ground and the first fruits of all fruit of every tree, year by year, to the house of the LORD; 36 also to bring to the house of our God, to the priests who minister in the house of our God, the first-born of our sons and of our cattle, as it is written in the law,

10.37
Lev 23.17;
Neh 13.5,9;
Lev 27.30

and the firstlings of our herds and of our flocks; 37 and to bring the first of our coarse meal, and our contributions, the fruit of every tree, the wine and the oil, to the priests, to the chambers of the house of our God; and to bring to the Lēvītes the tithes from our ground, for it is the Levites who collect the tithes in all our

10.38
Num 18.26;
Neh 13.12,
13

rural towns. 38And the priest, the son of Aaron, shall be with the Lēvītes when the Levites receive the tithes; and the Levites shall bring up the tithe of the tithes to the house of our God, to the

10.39
Deut 12.6;
Neh 13.10,
11

chambers, to the storehouse. 39 For the people of Israel and the sons of Lēvī shall bring the contribution of grain, wine, and oil to the chambers, where are the vessels of the sanctuary, and the priests that minister, and the gatekeepers and the singers. We will not neglect the house of our God.

10.32 *third ... shekel.* The *tax levied by Moses* (2 Chr 24.6) in Ex 30.13 is *half a shekel*, the regulation in Jesus' day (Mt 17.24). **10.33** *showbread.* Read Ex 25.30.

III. The reconstituting of Jerusalem: Nehemiah's second reform movement 11.1–13.31

A. The repeopling of Jerusalem

11 Now the leaders of the people lived in Jerusalem; and the rest of the people cast lots to bring one out of ten to live in Jerusalem the holy city, while nine tenths remained in the other towns. ²And the people blessed all the men who willingly offered to live in Jerusalem.

11.1
Neh 10.34;
ver 18;
Isa 48.2

B. The key people in Jerusalem

3 These are the chiefs of the province who lived in Jerusalem; but in the towns of Judah every one lived on his property in their towns: Israel, the priests, the Lēvītes, the temple servants, and the descendants of Solomon's servants. ⁴And in Jerusalem lived certain of the sons of Judah and of the sons of Benjamin. Of the sons of Judah: Āthāi'äh the son of Ŭzzī'äh, son of Zĕchārī'äh, son of Āmārī'äh, son of Shĕphātī'äh, son of Māhā'lálĕl, of the sons of Pērĕz; 5 and Mā-āseī'äh the son of Bărŭch, son of Cŏl-hō'zĕh, son of Házāi'äh, son of Ādāi'äh, son of Joi'ārĭb, son of Zĕchārī'äh, son of the Shī'lōnĭte. ⁶All the sons of Pērĕz who lived in Jerusalem were four hundred and sixty-eight valiant men.

11.3
1 Chr 9.2,3;
ver 20;
Ezra 2.43;
Neh 7.57
11.4
1 Chr 9.3ff

7 And these are the sons of Benjamin: Sāllu the son of Mĕshŭl'-lám, son of Jōĕd, son of Pĕdāi'äh, son of Kŏlāi'äh, son of Mā-āseī'äh, son of Ĭth'ï-ĕl, son of Jĕshāi'äh. ⁸And after him Gābbai, Sāllai, nine hundred and twenty-eight. ⁹ Jōĕl the son of Zĭchrī was their overseer; and Judah the son of Hāssĕnu'-äh was second over the city.

11.7
ver 4

10 Of the priests: Jĕdāi'äh the son of Joi'ārĭb, Jāchĭn, ¹¹ Sĕrāi'äh the son of Hīlkī'äh, son of Mĕshŭl'lám, son of Zādŏk, son of Mĕrāi'ōth, son of Āhī'tŭb, ruler of the house of God, ¹² and their brethren who did the work of the house, eight hundred and twenty-two; and Adāi'äh the son of Jĕrō'hám, son of Pĕlālī'äh, son of Āmzī, son of Zĕchārī'äh, son of Pāshhŭr, son of Mālchī'jäh, ¹³ and his brethren, heads of fathers' houses, two hundred and forty-two; and Āmāsh'säi, the son of Āz'árĕl, son of Ahzai, son of Mĕshĭl'lĕmōth, son of Ĭmmĕr, ¹⁴ and their brethren, mighty men of valor, a hundred and twenty-eight; their overseer was Zāb'dïĕl the son of Hāggĕdō'lïm.

11.10
1 Chr 9.10

15 And of the Lēvītes: Shĕmāi'äh the son of Hāsshŭb, son of Āzrī'kám, son of Hāshābī'äh, son of Bŭnnī; ¹⁶ and Shāb'bĕthai and Jŏz'ábād, of the chiefs of the Lēvītes, who were over the outside work of the house of God; ¹⁷ and Māttánī'äh the son of Mīcá, son of Zābdī, son of Āsäph, who was the leader to begin the thanksgiving in prayer, and Bākbŭkī'äh, the second among his brethren; and Ābdā the son of Shăm'mūá, son of Gālăl, son of Jĕdu'thún. ¹⁸All the Lēvītes in the holy city were two hundred and eighty-four.

11.16
1 Chr 26.29

11.18
ver 1

19 The gatekeepers, Ăkkŭb, Tālmŏn and their brethren, who kept watch at the gates, were a hundred and seventy-two. ²⁰And the rest of Israel, and of the priests and the Lēvītes, were in all the towns of Judah, every one in his inheritance. ²¹ But the temple servants lived on Ōphĕl; and Zīhá and Gīshpa were over the temple servants.

11.21
Neh 3.26

11.22
ver 9,14

11.23
Ezra 6.8;
7.20;
Neh 12.47

22 The overseer of the Lēvītes in Jerusalem was Ŭzzī the son of Bānī, son of Hăshăbī'ăh, son of Măttănī'ăh, son of Mīcă, of the sons of Āsăph, the singers, over the work of the house of God. 23 For there was a command from the king concerning them, and a settled provision for the singers, as every day required. 24And Pĕthăhī'ăh the son of Mĕshĕz'ăbĕl, of the sons of Zĕrăh the son of Judah, was at the king's hand in all matters concerning the people.

C. The villages settled outside Jerusalem

*11.25
Josh 14.15;
13.9,17

25 And as for the villages, with their fields, some of the people of Judah lived in Kĭr'ĭăth-ar'bă and its villages, and in Dībŏn and its villages, and in Jĕkăb'zeēl and its villages, 26 and in Jĕsh'uă and in Mōlā'dăh and Bĕth-pĕl'ĕt, 27 in Hā'zar-shu'ăl, in Beēr-shē'bă and its villages, 28 in Zĭklăg, in Mĕcō'năh and its villages, 29 in Ĕn-rĭm'mŏn, in Zorăh, in Jarmŭth, 30 Zănō'ăh, Ădŭl'lăm, and their villages, Lāchĭsh and its fields, and Ăzē'kăh and its villages. So they encamped from Beēr-shē'bă to the valley of Hĭnnŏm. 31 The people of Benjamin also lived from Gēbă onward, at Mĭchmăsh, Āi'jă, Bĕthĕl and its villages, 32Ăn'ăthŏth, Nŏb, Ănănī'ăh, 33 Hāzor, Rāmăh, Gittā'ĭm, 34 Hādĭd, Zĕbō'ĭm, Nĕbăl'lăt, 35 Lŏd, and Ōnō, the valley of craftsmen. 36And certain divisions of the Lēvītes in Judah were joined to Benjamin.

D. The genealogies of the priests and Levites

12.1
Ezra 2.1,2;
see Neh
10.2–8

12.7
Ezra 3.2

12.8
Neh 11.17

*12.11

12 These are the priests and the Lēvītes who came up with Zĕrŭb'băbĕl the son of Shē-ăl'tĭ-ĕl, and Jĕsh'uă: Sĕrăi'ăh, Jĕrĕmī'ăh, Ezra, 2Ămărī'ăh, Măllŭch, Hăttŭsh, 3 Shĕcănī'ăh, Rĕhŭm, Mĕr'ĕmŏth, 4 Ĭddō, Gĭn'nĕthoi, Ăbī'jăh, 5 Mĭj'ămĭn, Mā-ădī'ăh, Bĭlgăh, 6 Shĕmăi'ăh, Joi'ărĭb, Jĕdăi'ăh, 7 Săllu, Āmŏk, Hĭlkī'ăh, Jĕdăi'ăh. These were the chiefs of the priests and of their brethren in the days of Jĕsh'uă.

8 And the Lēvītes: Jĕsh'uă, Bĭn'nūī, Kăd'mĭ-ĕl, Shĕrĕbī'ăh, Judah, and Măttănī'ăh, who with his brethren was in charge of the songs of thanksgiving. 9And Băkbŭkī'ăh and Ŭnnō their brethren stood opposite them in the service. 10And Jĕsh'uă was the father of Joi'ăkĭm, Joiakim the father of Ĕlī'ăshĭb, Eliashib the father of Joi'ădă, 11 Joi'ădă the father of Jonathan, and Jonathan the father of Jăd'du-ă.

12 And in the days of Joi'ăkĭm were priests, heads of fathers' houses: of Sĕrăi'ăh, Mĕrăi'ăh; of Jĕrĕmī'ăh, Hănănī'ăh; 13 of Ezra, Mĕshŭl'lăm; of Ămărī'ăh, Jĕhō'hănăn; 14 of Măl'lŭchī, Jonathan; of Shĕbănī'ăh, Joseph; 15 of Hārĭm, Ădnă; of Mĕrăi'ŏth, Hĕlkăī; 16 of Ĭddō, Zĕchărī'ăh; of Gĭn'nĕthŏn, Mĕshŭl'lăm; 17 of Ăbī'jăh, Zĭchrī; of Mĭn'jămĭn, of Mōădī'ăh, Pĭltăī; 18 of Bĭlgăh, Shăm'mū-ă; of Shĕmăi'ăh, Jĕhŏn'ăthăn; 19 of Joi'ărĭb, Măt'tĕnăi; of Jĕdăi'ăh, Ŭzzī; 20 of Săllaī, Kăl'lāī; of Āmŏk, Ē'bĕr; 21 of Hĭlkī'ăh, Hăshăbī'ăh; of Jĕdăi'ăh, Nĕthăn'ĕl.

22 As for the Lēvītes, in the days of Ĕlī'ăshĭb, Joi'ădă, Jōhăn'ăn, and Jăd'du-ă, there were recorded the heads of fathers' houses;

11.25 *villages with their fields* probably means the adjoining land.   **12.11** *Jonathan* is a scribal error for *Johanan* (ver 22, 23).

also the priests until the reign of Dǎrī'ŭs the Persian. 23 The sons of Lēvī, heads of fathers' houses, were written in the Book of the Chronicles until the days of Jōhăn'ăn the son of Ēlī'ăshĭb. 24And the chiefs of the Lēvītes: Hăshăbī'ăh, Shērēbī'ăh, and Jĕsh'uǎ the son of Kăd'mĭ-ĕl, with their brethren over against them, to praise and to give thanks, according to the commandment of David the man of God, watch corresponding to watch. 25 Măttănī'ăh, Băkbŭkī'ăh, Ōbădī'ăh, Mĕshŭl'lăm, Tălmŏn, and Ăkkŭb were gatekeepers standing guard at the storehouses of the gates. 26 These were in the days of Joi'ăkĭm the son of Jĕsh'uǎ son of Jŏz'ădăk, and in the days of Nēhĕmī'ăh the governor and of Ezra the priest the scribe.

E. Dedication of the city walls

27 And at the dedication of the wall of Jerusalem they sought the Lēvītes in all their places, to bring them to Jerusalem to celebrate the dedication with gladness, with thanksgivings and with singing, with cymbals, harps, and lyres. 28And the sons of the singers gathered together from the circuit round Jerusalem and from the villages of the Nĕtŏph'ăthītes; 29 also from Bĕth-gĭl'găl and from the region of Gēbà and Ăzmā'vĕth; for the singers had built for themselves villages around Jerusalem. 30And the priests and the Lēvītes purified themselves; and they purified the people and the gates and the wall.

31 Then I brought up the princes of Judah upon the wall, and appointed two great companies which gave thanks and went in procession. One went to the right upon the wall to the Dung Gate; 32 and after them went Hōshāi'ăh and half of the princes of Judah, 33 and Ăzărī'ăh, Ezra, Mĕshŭl'lăm, 34 Judah, Benjamin, Shēmāi'ăh, and Jĕrĕmī'ăh, 35 and certain of the priests' sons with trumpets: Zĕchărī'ăh the son of Jonathan, son of Shēmāi'ăh, son of Măttănī'ăh, son of Mīcāi'ăh, son of Zăccŭr, son of Āsăph; 36 and his kinsmen, Shēmāi'ăh, Ăz'ărĕl, Mĭl'ălaī, Gĭl'ălaī, Mā'aī, Nĕthăn'ĕl, Judah, and Hánā'nī, with the musical instruments of David the man of God; and Ezra the scribe went before them. 37At the Fountain Gate they went up straight before them by the stairs of the city of David, at the ascent of the wall, above the house of David, to the Water Gate on the east.

38 The other company of those who gave thanks went to the left, and I followed them with half of the people, upon the wall, above the Tower of the Ovens, to the Broad Wall, 39 and above the Gate of Ē'phrăĭm, and by the Old Gate, and by the Fish Gate and the Tower of Hăn'ănĕl and the Tower of the Hundred, to the Sheep Gate; and they came to a halt at the Gate of the Guard. 40 So both companies of those who gave thanks stood in the house of God, and I and half of the officials with me; 41 and the priests Ēlī'ăkĭm, Mā-ăseī'ăh, Mĭn'iămĭn, Mīcāi'ăh, Ēlī-ŏ-ē'naī, Zĕchărī'-ăh, and Hănănī'ăh, with trumpets; 42 and Mā-ăseī'ăh, Shēmāi'ăh, Ēlĕā'zăr, Ŭzzī, Jĕhō'hănăn, Mălchī'jăh, Ēlăm, and Ēzĕr. And the singers sang with Jĕzrăhī'ăh as their leader. 43And they offered

*12.23
1 Chr 9.14ff

12.24
Neh 11.17

12.25
1 Chr 26.15

12.26
Neh 8.9;
Ezra 7.6,11

12.27
1 Chr 25.6

12.28
1 Chr 9.16

12.30
Neh 13.22,
30

12.31
ver 38;
Neh 2.13;
3.13

12.35
Num 10.2,8

*12.36
1 Chr 23.5

12.37
Neh 2.14;
3.15; 3.26

12.38
ver 31;
Neh 3.11;
3.8

12.39
Neh 8.16;
3.6; 3.3;
3.1; 3.25

12.23 son, that is, grandson.
12.36 That Ezra and Nehemiah (ver 38) headed the two companies is in accord with

8.9 which indicates that the two were contemporaries during part of their activities: Nehemiah as governor, Ezra as priest.

great sacrifices that day and rejoiced, for God had made them rejoice with great joy; the women and children also rejoiced. And the joy of Jerusalem was heard afar off.

F. The appointment of collectors, singers, and gatekeepers

12.44
Neh 13.5;
12,13

44 On that day men were appointed over the chambers for the stores, the contributions, the first fruits, and the tithes, to gather into them the portions required by the law for the priests and for the Lēvītes according to the fields of the towns; for Judah rejoiced over the priests and the Levites who ministered. 45And they per-

12.45
1 Chr 25.1;
26.1

formed the service of their God and the service of purification, as did the singers and the gatekeepers, according to the command of David and his son Solomon. 46 For in the days of David and

12.46
2 Chr 29.30

Āsăph of old there was a chief of the singers, and there were songs of praise and thanksgiving to God. 47And all Israel in the days of

12.47
Neh 11.23;
Num 18.21

Zĕrŭb'bábĕl and in the days of Nĕhĕmĭ'áh gave the daily portions for the singers and the gatekeepers; and they set apart that which was for the Lēvītes; and the Levites set apart that which was for the sons of Aaron.

G. Nehemiah's final reforms

1. The people separated

★13.1
Neh 9.3;
Deut 23.3–5

13 On that day they read from the book of Moses in the hearing of the people; and in it was found written that no Ăm'mŏnīte or Mō'ábīte should ever enter the assembly of God;

★13.2
Num 22.3–
11; 23.11

2 for they did not meet the children of Israel with bread and water, but hired Bālaám against them to curse them—yet our God turned the curse into a blessing. 3 When the people heard the law,

13.3
Neh 9.2;
Ex 12.38

they separated from Israel all those of foreign descent.

2. Tobiah's furniture cast out of the Temple

13.4
Neh 12.44;
2.10; 6.1,
17,18

4 Now before this, Ĕlĭ'áshĭb the priest, who was appointed over the chambers of the house of our God, and who was connected with Tŏbĭ'áh, 5 prepared for Tŏbĭ'áh a large chamber where they

13.5
Num 18.21

had previously put the cereal offering, the frankincense, the vessels, and the tithes of grain, wine, and oil, which were given by commandment to the Lēvītes, singers, and gatekeepers, and the contributions for the priests. 6 While this was taking place I was

13.6
Neh 5.14;
Ezra 6.22

not in Jerusalem, for in the thirty-second year of Ar-tá-xèrx'ĕṣ king of Babylon I went to the king. And after some time I asked leave of the king 7 and came to Jerusalem, and I then discovered

13.7
ver 5

the evil that Ĕlĭ'áshĭb had done for Tŏbĭ'áh, preparing for him a chamber in the courts of the house of God. 8And I was very angry, and I threw all the household furniture of Tŏbĭ'áh out of the

13.9
2 Chr 29.5,
15,16

chamber. 9 Then I gave orders and they cleansed the chambers; and I brought back thither the vessels of the house of God, with the cereal offering and the frankincense.

3. The support of the priesthood begun

13.10
Neh 10.37;
12.28,29

10 I also found out that the portions of the Lēvītes had not been

---

13.1 written, see Deut 23.3–6. This was not carried out in the case of Ruth.   **13.2** Balaam . . . to curse them. Read Num 22.6 in this connection.

given to them; so that the Levites and the singers, who did the
work, had fled each to his field. 11 So I remonstrated with the
officials and said, "Why is the house of God forsaken?" And I
gathered them together and set them in their stations. 12 Then all
Judah brought the tithe of the grain, wine, and oil into the storehouses. 13And I appointed as treasurers over the storehouses
Shĕlĕmī′ah the priest, Zādŏk the scribe, and Pĕdāi′ah of the
Lēvītes, and as their assistant Hānăn the son of Zăccur, son of
Măttănī′ah, for they were counted faithful; and their duty was to
distribute to their brethren. 14 Remember me, O my God, concerning this, and wipe not out my good deeds that I have done for
the house of my God and for his service.

4. Sabbath reforms instituted

15 In those days I saw in Judah men treading wine presses on
the sabbath, and bringing in heaps of grain and loading them on
asses; and also wine, grapes, figs, and all kinds of burdens, which
they brought into Jerusalem on the sabbath day; and I warned
them on the day when they sold food. 16 Men of Tȳre also, who
lived in the city, brought in fish and all kinds of wares and sold
them on the sabbath to the people of Judah, and in Jerusalem.
17 Then I remonstrated with the nobles of Judah and said to them,
"What is this evil thing which you are doing, profaning the sabbath day? 18 Did not your fathers act in this way, and did not our
God bring all this evil on us and on this city? Yet you bring more
wrath upon Israel by profaning the sabbath."

19 When it began to be dark at the gates of Jerusalem before
the sabbath, I commanded that the doors should be shut and gave
orders that they should not be opened until after the sabbath.
And I set some of my servants over the gates, that no burden
might be brought in on the sabbath day. 20 Then the merchants
and sellers of all kinds of wares lodged outside Jerusalem once or
twice. 21 But I warned them and said to them, "Why do you lodge
before the wall? If you do so again I will lay hands on you." From
that time on they did not come on the sabbath. 22And I commanded the Lēvītes that they should purify themselves and come
and guard the gates, to keep the sabbath day holy. Remember this
also in my favor, O my God, and spare me according to the greatness of thy steadfast love.

5. Marriage reforms

23 In those days also I saw the Jews who had married women
of Ăshdŏd, Ămmŏn, and Mŏăb; 24 and half of their children spoke
the language of Ăshdŏd, and they could not speak the language of
Judah, but the language of each people. 25And I contended with
them and cursed them and beat some of them and pulled out their
hair; and I made them take oath in the name of God, saying, "You
shall not give your daughters to their sons, or take their daughters
for your sons or for yourselves. 26 Did not Solomon king of Israel

---

Cross-references (right margin):

13.11 ver 17,25; Neh 10.39
13.12 Neh 10.37–39; 12.44
13.13 Neh 12.44; 7.2
13.14 ver 22,31; Neh 5.19
*13.15 Ex 20.8,10; Neh 10.31
13.17 ver 11,25
13.18 Jer 17.21–23
13.19 Lev 23.32; Jer 17.21
13.21 ver 15
13.22 Neh 12.30; ver 14,31
13.23 Ezra 9.2
13.25 ver 11,17; Deut 25.2; Ezra 10.29, 30
13.26 1 Ki 11.1; 3.13; 2 Chr 1.12; 1 Ki 11.4ff

13.15 Three of the recurring sins of God's
people were: (1) Sabbath-breaking (Num
15.32–36; Neh 13.17, 18; Isa 58.13, 14; Ezek
20.13; 22.8); (2) intermarriage with the
heathen (Neh 13.23–25; 1 Ki 11.1, 2; Deut
7.3, 4); (3) idolatry (1 Ki 21.26; 2 Ki 17.12;
Ezek 6.1–5; Zech 13.2). These had to be
faced and dealt with by appropriate discipli-
nary measures if the nation was to carry on
its witness.

sin on account of such women? Among the many nations there was no king like him, and he was beloved by his God, and God made him king over all Israel; nevertheless foreign women made even him to sin. 27 Shall we then listen to you and do all this great evil and act treacherously against our God by marrying foreign women?"

28 And one of the sons of Jehoi′ada, the son of Eli′ashib the high priest, was the son-in-law of Sanbal′lat the Hor′onite; therefore I chased him from me. 29 Remember them, O my God, because they have defiled the priesthood and the covenant of the priesthood and the Levites.

6. Conclusion

30 Thus I cleansed them from everything foreign, and I established the duties of the priests and Levites, each in his work; 31 and I provided for the wood offering, at appointed times, and for the first fruits. Remember me, O my God, for good.

13.28 *chased him from me.* Josephus tells how Sanballat arranged for a political marriage of his daughter to Manasseh, a priest. While Josephus dates the event about a century later, he may well have been describing this very expulsion. Evidently the grandson of Eliashib refused to put his wife away and so Nehemiah drove him out. The priest took with him a copy of the Pentateuch (this ancient copy is still in the possession of a small colony of Samaritans) and on Mt. Gerazim the Samaritan temple was erected.

INTRODUCTION TO
THE BOOK OF
ESTHER

Authorship and Background: The name Esther, a Persian word meaning "Star," derives from the principal character of the book. Her Hebrew name was Hadassah, meaning "Myrtle." The book appears in the last section of the Hebrew Bible among the Five Scrolls, *Megilloth,* which also include Ruth, Song of Solomon, Ecclesiastes, and Lamentations. Esther, the last of the five, is considered by Judaism as "the Scroll" par excellence. The events described took place at Shushan (Susa), the Persian capital, in the reign of Ahasuerus (486–465 B.C.), known usually as Xerxes, the Greek spelling of his name. The book is filled with Persian loan words and accurate information about the palace, customs, and history of the Persian Empire. Some scholars suppose the book was composed in the Maccabean period (about 168 B.C.), but the Persian atmosphere argues for a date not later than the conquest of the Persian Empire by Alexander the Great (331 B.C.). Tradition has dated the book within the reign of Artaxerxes Longimanus (465–424 B.C.) as does Josephus. Because 9.20, 23, 29 note that Mordecai wrote certain instructions, some have thought him to be the author (e.g., Clement of Alexandria). Others have ascribed the authorship to Ezra (e.g., Augustine), but in all probability the author was an unknown Jew who lived in Persia and had access to oral and written sources.

Characteristics: Esther contains no reference to Palestine or the return of the exiles from Babylon although it is fervently patriotic. The author stresses God's providential watch-care but the name of God is never mentioned, nor are we told that the Jews offered prayers or supplications to God during their trials. The book explains the origin of the Feast of Purim and it became a Jewish tradition to read the book annually as a part of the Purim ritual. The literary style is one of skilful composition, the story moves smoothly, and the element of suspense is sustained in a developing plot with a final denouement. The author uses no adjectives to describe the characters who are made known by their concrete actions, and through the use of literary techniques he achieves great vividness.

Contents:

I.   Intrigues in the court at Susa. 1.1—2.23: Drunken Ahasuerus asks Vashti to present herself. She refuses and is deposed. Mordecai's cousin Esther is chosen to replace Vashti. Mordecai discovers a plot against Ahasuerus' life which is foiled.

II. The struggle between the houses of Mordecai and Haman. 3.1—9.19: Haman becomes vizier. Mordecai refuses to bow before him. Haman plots to kill all the Jews. Mordecai appeals to Esther for help. She

points out that she may die if she seeks the king without prior permission. She yields to Mordecai, asking the Jews to fast and says, "...if I perish, I perish" (4.16). She approaches Ahasuerus who holds out the golden scepter. She invites the king and Haman to her banquet. Haman prepares the gallows for Mordecai. The king wishes to honor Mordecai and asks Haman what he should do. Haman thinks it is to be for himself and is required to honor Mordecai. Esther pleads with the king for her life and her people's lives. She points the finger of accusation at Haman who is hanged on his own gallows. Mordecai is set over the house of Haman. The Jews defend themselves and slay their enemies.

III.   The Feast of Purim: observance and regulations. 9.20—10.3: The two days' festival instituted. Mordecai is advanced further and the Jews prosper.

THE BOOK OF
ESTHER

I. Intrigues in the court at Susa 1.1–2.23

A. The riches and splendor of Ahasuerus

1 In the days of Ăhăṣŭ-ē'rŭs, the Ahasu-erus who reigned from India to Ethiopia over one hundred and twenty-seven provinces, 2 in those days when King Ăhăṣŭ-ē'rŭs sat on his royal throne in Suṣā the capital, 3 in the third year of his reign he gave a banquet for all his princes and servants, the army chiefs*a* of Persia and Mē'dĭă and the nobles and governors of the provinces being before him, 4 while he showed the riches of his royal glory and the splendor and pomp of his majesty for many days, a hundred and eighty days. 5And when these days were completed, the king gave for all the people present in Suṣā the capital, both great and small, a banquet lasting for seven days, in the court of the garden of the king's palace. 6 There were white cotton curtains and blue hangings caught up with cords of fine linen and purple to silver rings*b* and marble pillars, and also couches of gold and silver on a mosaic pavement of porphyry, marble, mother-of-pearl and precious stones. 7 Drinks were served in golden goblets, goblets of different kinds, and the royal wine was lavished according to the bounty of the king. 8And drinking was according to the law, no one was compelled; for the king had given orders to all the officials of his palace to do as every man desired. 9 Queen Văshtī also gave a banquet for the women in the palace which belonged to King Ăhăṣŭ-ē'rŭs.

B. The removal of Queen Vashti

1. Vashti's refusal

10 On the seventh day, when the heart of the king was merry with wine, he commanded Mêhū'măn, Bĭzthā, Harbō'nă, Bĭgthā and Ăbăg'thā, Zēthar and Carkās, the seven eunuchs who served King Ăhăṣŭ-ē'rŭs as chamberlains, 11 to bring Queen Văshtī before the king with her royal crown, in order to show the peoples and the princes her beauty; for she was fair to behold. 12 But Queen Văshtī refused to come at the king's command conveyed by the eunuchs. At this the king was enraged, and his anger burned within him.

2. Vashti's removal

13 Then the king said to the wise men who knew the times—for this was the king's procedure toward all who were versed in law and judgment, 14 the men next to him being Carshē'nă, Shēthar, Ădmā'thā, Tarshĭsh, Mĕrĕs, Marsē'nă, and Mĕmū'căn, the seven princes of Persia and Mē'dĭă, who saw the king's face, and sat first

a Heb the army   *b* Or rods

1.1 Ahasuerus. He has been identified as Xerxes (486–465 B.C.).

1.12 Vashti's refusal eventually cost her the crown. (See 2.4.)

705

Marginal references:

*1.1
Ezra 4.6;
Dan 9.1;
Est 8.9;
9.30
1.2
Neh 1.1
1.3
Est 2.18

1.5
Est 7.7,8

1.6
Ezek 23.41;
Amos 6.4

1.7
Est 2.18

1.10
Judg 16.25;
Est 7.9

*1.12

1.13
Jer 10.7;
Dan 2.12;
1 Chr 12.32
1.14
2 Ki 25.19

in the kingdom—: 15 "According to the law, what is to be done to Queen Văshtī, because she has not performed the command of King Ăhăşŭ-ē′rŭs conveyed by the eunuchs?" 16 Then Mĕmū′căn said in presence of the king and the princes, "Not only to the king has Queen Văshtī done wrong, but also to all the princes and all the peoples who are in all the provinces of King Ăhăşŭ-ē′rŭs.

1.17
Eph 5.33 17 For this deed of the queen will be made known to all women, causing them to look with contempt upon their husbands, since they will say, 'King Ăhăşŭ-ē′rŭs commanded Queen Văshtī to be brought before him, and she did not come.' 18 This very day the ladies of Persia and Mē′dĭă who have heard of the queen's behavior will be telling it to all the king's princes, and there will be contempt and wrath in plenty. 19 If it please the king, let a royal

*1.19
Est 8.8;
Dan 6.8 order go forth from him, and let it be written among the laws of the Persians and the Mēdes so that it may not be altered, that Văshtī is to come no more before King Ăhăşŭ-ē′rŭs; and let the king give her royal position to another who is better than she.

1.20
Eph 5.22;
Col 3.18 20 So when the decree made by the king is proclaimed throughout all his kingdom, vast as it is, all women will give honor to their husbands, high and low." 21 This advice pleased the king and the

1.22
Est 8.9;
Eph 5.22–
24;
1 Tim 2.12 princes, and the king did as Mĕmū′căn proposed; 22 he sent letters to all the royal provinces, to every province in its own script and to every people in its own language, that every man be lord in his own house and speak according to the language of his people.

C. Esther made Queen

1. The search for a queen

2.1
Est 7.10;
1.19,20 2 After these things, when the anger of King Ăhăşŭ-ē′rŭs had abated, he remembered Văshtī and what she had done and what had been decreed against her. 2 Then the king's servants who attended him said, "Let beautiful young virgins be sought out for

2.3
ver 8,15 the king. 3And let the king appoint officers in all the provinces of his kingdom to gather all the beautiful young virgins to the harem in Suşà the capital, under custody of Hĕg′aī the king's eunuch who is in charge of the women; let their ointments be given them. 4And let the maiden who pleases the king be queen instead of Văshtī." This pleased the king, and he did so.

2. Esther's background

2.5
Est 3.2 5 Now there was a Jew in Suşà the capital whose name was Mor′dĕcaī, the son of Jāïr, son of Shĭm′ĕ-ī, son of Kĭsh, a Ben-

2.6
2 Ki 24.14,
15; 24.6
*2.7
ver 15 jaminite, 6 who had been carried away from Jerusalem among the captives carried away with Jĕcŏnī′ăh king of Judah, whom Nĕbŭchădnĕz′zàr king of Babylon had carried away. 7 He had brought up Hàdăs′sàh, that is Esther, the daughter of his uncle, for she had neither father nor mother; the maiden was beautiful

2.8
ver 3,15 and lovely, and when her father and her mother died, Mor′dĕcaī adopted her as his own daughter. 8 So when the king's order and

---

1.19 *Persians and the Medes*, Medes and Persians in Dan 5.28 which is the correct chronological order. *not be altered*. The idea of immutability is also stated in 8.8 and Dan 6.8.

2.7 *Hadassah*, that is, Myrtle; *Esther*, either from the Persian word "star," or the Babylonian goddess "Ishtar"; *daughter of his uncle*, indicating that Mordecai adopted his cousin as his daughter.

his edict were proclaimed, and when many maidens were gathered in Suṣà the capital in custody of Hĕg´aī, Esther also was taken into the king's palace and put in custody of Hegai who had charge of the women. ⁹And the maiden pleased him and won his favor; and he quickly provided her with her ointments and her portion of food, and with seven chosen maids from the king's palace, and advanced her and her maids to the best place in the harem. ¹⁰ Esther had not made known her people or kindred, for Mor´decai had charged her not to make it known. ¹¹And every day Mor´decai walked in front of the court of the harem, to learn how Esther was and how she fared.

3. *Ahasuerus chooses Esther*

12 Now when the turn came for each maiden to go in to King Ăhăṣŭ-ē´rŭs, after being twelve months under the regulations for the women, since this was the regular period of their beautifying, six months with oil of myrrh and six months with spices and ointments for women— ¹³ when the maiden went in to the king in this way she was given whatever she desired to take with her from the harem to the king's palace. ¹⁴ In the evening she went, and in the morning she came back to the second harem in custody of Shà-ăsh´găz the king's eunuch who was in charge of the concubines; she did not go in to the king again, unless the king delighted in her and she was summoned by name.

15 When the turn came for Esther the daughter of Ăb´ĭhāil the uncle of Mor´decai, who had adopted her as his own daughter, to go in to the king, she asked for nothing except what Hĕg´aī the king's eunuch, who had charge of the women, advised. Now Esther found favor in the eyes of all who saw her. ¹⁶And when Esther was taken to King Ăhăṣŭ-ē´rŭs into his royal palace in the tenth month, which is the month of Tĕbĕth, in the seventh year of his reign, ¹⁷ the king loved Esther more than all the women, and she found grace and favor in his sight more than all the virgins, so that he set the royal crown on her head and made her queen instead of Văshtī. ¹⁸ Then the king gave a great banquet to all his princes and servants; it was Esther's banquet. He also granted a remission of taxes[c] to the provinces, and gave gifts with royal liberality.

D. *The plot to kill Ahasuerus and its failure*

19 When the virgins were gathered together the second time, Mor´decai was sitting at the king's gate. ²⁰ Now Esther had not made known her kindred or her people, as Mor´decai had charged her; for Esther obeyed Mordecai just as when she was brought up by him. ²¹And in those days, as Mor´decai was sitting at the king's gate, Bīgthăn and Tĕrĕsh, two of the king's eunuchs, who guarded the threshold, became angry and sought to lay hands on King Ăhăṣŭ-ē´rŭs. ²²And this came to the knowledge of Mor´decai, and he told it to Queen Esther, and Esther told the king in the

[c] Or *a holiday*

2.9 / ver 3,12
2.10 / ver 20
2.15 / ver 6; Est 9.29
*2.16
2.17 / Est 1.11
2.18 / Est 1.3; 1.7
*2.19
2.20 / ver 10
2.21 / Est 6.2
2.22 / Est 6.1,2

2.16 *seventh year.* Four years after the deposition of Vashti.

2.19 *sitting . . . king's gate.* Mordecai's relationship to Esther had not yet been disclosed.

*2.23
Est 10.2

name of Mordecai. 23 When the affair was investigated and found to be so, the men were both hanged on the gallows. And it was recorded in the Book of the Chronicles in the presence of the king.

II. The struggle between the houses of Mordecai and Haman 3.1—9.19

A. The elevation of Haman: the refusal of Mordecai to bow

*3.1
Est 5.11;
ver 10
3.2
Est 2.19;
ver 5

3 After these things King Ăhăşŭ-ē'rŭs promoted Hāmán the Ăg'ăgīte, the son of Hămmĕdā'thá, and advanced him and set his seat above all the princes who were with him. 2And all the king's servants who were at the king's gate bowed down and did obeisance to Hāmán; for the king had so commanded concerning him. But Mor'dĕcaī did not bow down or do obeisance. 3 Then the king's servants who were at the king's gate said to Mor'dĕcaī, "Why do you transgress the king's command?" 4And when they spoke to him day after day and he would not listen to them, they told Hāmán, in order to see whether Mor'dĕcaī's words would avail; for he had told them that he was a Jew. 5And when Hāmán saw that Mor'dĕcaī did not bow down or do obeisance to him, Haman was filled with fury. 6 But he disdained to lay hands on Mor'dĕcaī alone. So, as they had made known to him the people of Mordecai, Hāmán sought to destroy all the Jews, the people of Mordecai, throughout the whole kingdom of Ăhăşŭ-ē'rŭs.

3.3
ver 2

3.5
ver 2;
Est 5.9
3.6
Ps 83.4

B. Haman's plot against the Jews

3.7
Est 9.24;
Ezra 6.15

3.8
Ezra 4.12–
15;
Acts 16.20

3.10
Est 8.2;
Gen 41.42;
Est 7.6

7 In the first month, which is the month of Nīsăn, in the twelfth year of King Ăhăşŭ-ē'rŭs, they cast Pūr, that is the lot, before Hāmán day after day; and they cast it month after month till the twelfth month, which is the month of Ádar'. 8 Then Hāmán said to King Ăhăşŭ-ē'rŭs, "There is a certain people scattered abroad and dispersed among the peoples in all the provinces of your kingdom; their laws are different from those of every other people, and they do not keep the king's laws, so that it is not for the king's profit to tolerate them. 9 If it please the king, let it be decreed that they be destroyed, and I will pay ten thousand talents of silver into the hands of those who have charge of the king's business, that they may put it into the king's treasuries." 10 So the king took his signet ring from his hand and gave it to Hāmán the Ăg'ăgīte, the son of Hămmĕdā'thá, the enemy of the Jews. 11And the king said to Hāmán, "The money is given to you, the people also, to do with them as it seems good to you."

2.23 *Book of the Chronicles,* the court records of daily events, not the biblical books.

3.1 Haman is here called a descendant of the line of Agag. An Amalekite king named Agag is mentioned in 1 Sam 15 as the last survivor of a tribe which was destroyed by King Saul at God's command. If the old rabbinic tradition is correct in tracing Haman's ancestry from this Agag, we may see in this episode another chapter in the conflict between the line of Jacob and that of Esau (for Esau was an ancestor of Amalek). But a more likely explanation of the term "Agagite" is that it refers to a district in the Persian Empire called Agag (spoken of in an Assyrian inscription of King Sargon). Haman's father, Hammedatha, had a Persian name, and so did all of his sons (9.7–9). This would hardly have been the case in a family of Amalekite descent.

12 Then the king's secretaries were summoned on the thirteenth day of the first month, and an edict, according to all that Hāmàn commanded, was written to the king's satraps and to the governors over all the provinces and to the princes of all the peoples, to every province in its own script and every people in its own language; it was written in the name of King Āhăsŭ-ĕ'rùs and sealed with the king's ring. 13 Letters were sent by couriers to all the king's provinces, to destroy, to slay, and to annihilate all Jews, young and old, women and children, in one day, the thirteenth day of the twelfth month, which is the month of Ādar', and to plunder their goods. 14A copy of the document was to be issued as a decree in every province by proclamation to all the peoples to be ready for that day. 15 The couriers went in haste by order of the king, and the decree was issued in Suşà the capital. And the king and Hāmàn sat down to drink; but the city of Suşà was perplexed.

3.12
Est 8.8–10;
1 Ki 21.8

3.13
Est 8.10–14

3.14
Est 8.13,14

3.15
Est 8.15

C. Mordecai appeals to Esther for help

4 When Mor'dècaī learned all that had been done, Mordecai rent his clothes and put on sackcloth and ashes, and went out into the midst of the city, wailing with a loud and bitter cry; 2 he went up to the entrance of the king's gate, for no one might enter the king's gate clothed with sackcloth. 3And in every province, wherever the king's command and his decree came, there was great mourning among the Jews, with fasting and weeping and lamenting, and most of them lay in sackcloth and ashes.

*4.1ff
Est 3.8–10;
Jon 3.5,6;
Ezek 27.30

4.3
Isa 58.5

4 When Esther's maids and her eunuchs came and told her, the queen was deeply distressed; she sent garments to clothe Mor'-dècaī, so that he might take off his sackcloth, but he would not accept them. 5 Then Esther called for Hāthăch, one of the king's eunuchs, who had been appointed to attend her, and ordered him to go to Mor'dècaī to learn what this was and why it was. 6 Hāthăch went out to Mor'dècaī in the open square of the city in front of the king's gate, 7 and Mor'dècaī told him all that had happened to him, and the exact sum of money that Hāmàn had promised to pay into the king's treasuries for the destruction of the Jews. 8 Mor'dècaī also gave him a copy of the written decree issued in Suşà for their destruction, that he might show it to Esther and explain it to her and charge her to go to the king to make supplication to him and entreat him for her people. 9And Hāthăch went and told Esther what Mor'dècaī had said. 10 Then Esther spoke to Hāthăch and gave him a message for Mor'dècaī, saying, 11 "All the king's servants and the people of the king's provinces know that if any man or woman goes to the king inside the inner court without being called, there is but one law; all alike are to be put to death, except the one to whom the king holds out the golden scepter that he may live. And I have not been called to come in to the king these thirty days." 12And they told Mor'dècaī what Esther had said. 13 Then Mor'dècaī told them to return answer to Esther, "Think not that in the king's palace you will escape any more than all the other Jews. 14 For if you keep silence at such a time as this,

4.7
Est 3.9

4.8
Est 3.14,15

4.11
Est 5.1;
6.4;
Dan 2.9;
Est 5.2; 8.4

4.1 *sackcloth.* A dark-colored garment made of coarse material woven from camels' and goats' hair. It was worn when mourning (as here) in hope of averting national catastrophe.

4.1-3 *rent his clothes.* These were outward signs of mourning. (Today, the tearing of clothes has been modified to the wearing of a black ribbon by some Jews.)

relief and deliverance will rise for the Jews from another quarter, but you and your father's house will perish. And who knows whether you have not come to the kingdom for such a time as this?" 15 Then Esther told them to reply to Mor′decai, 16 "Go, gather all the Jews to be found in Suṣà, and hold a fast on my behalf, and neither eat nor drink for three days, night or day. I and my maids will also fast as you do. Then I will go to the king, though it is against the law; and if I perish, I perish." 17 Mor′-decai then went away and did everything as Esther had ordered him.

D. Esther's intervention

1. Her appeal to Ahasuerus

5 On the third day Esther put on her royal robes and stood in the inner court of the king's palace, opposite the king's hall. The king was sitting on his royal throne inside the palace opposite the entrance to the palace; 2 and when the king saw Queen Esther standing in the court, she found favor in his sight and he held out to Esther the golden scepter that was in his hand. Then Esther approached and touched the top of the scepter. 3And the king said to her, "What is it, Queen Esther? What is your request? It shall be given you, even to the half of my kingdom." 4And Esther said, "If it please the king, let the king and Hāmàn come this day to a dinner that I have prepared for the king." 5 Then said the king, "Bring Hāmàn quickly, that we may do as Esther desires." So the king and Haman came to the dinner that Esther had prepared. 6And as they were drinking wine, the king said to Esther, "What is your petition? It shall be granted you. And what is your request? Even to the half of my kingdom, it shall be fulfilled." 7 But Esther said, "My petition and my request is: 8 If I have found favor in the sight of the king, and if it please the king to grant my petition and fulfil my request, let the king and Hāmàn come tomorrow*d* to the dinner which I will prepare for them, and tomorrow I will do as the king has said."

2. Haman's plan against Mordecai

9 And Hāmàn went out that day joyful and glad of heart. But when Haman saw Mor′decai in the king's gate, that he neither rose nor trembled before him, he was filled with wrath against Mordecai. 10 Nevertheless Hāmàn restrained himself, and went home; and he sent and fetched his friends and his wife Zĕrĕsh. 11And Hāmàn recounted to them the splendor of his riches, the number of his sons, all the promotions with which the king had honored him, and how he had advanced him above the princes and the servants of the king. 12And Hāmàn added, "Even Queen Esther let no one come with the king to the banquet she prepared but myself. And tomorrow also I am invited by her together with the king. 13 Yet all this does me no good, so long as I see Mor′decai the Jew sitting at the king's gate." 14 Then his wife Zĕrĕsh and all his friends said to him, "Let a gallows fifty cubits high be made, and in the morning tell the king to have Mor′decai hanged upon it; then go merrily with the king to the dinner." This counsel pleased Hāmàn, and he had the gallows made.

Marginal references:
4.15 Est 5.1
5.1 Est 4.16; 4.11; 6.4
5.2 Prov 21.1; Est 4.11; 8.4
5.3 Est 7.2; Mk 6.23
5.5 Est 6.14
5.6 Est 7.2; ver 3
5.8 Est 7.3; 8.5; 6.14
5.9 Est 2.19; 3.5
5.10 Est 6.13
5.11 Est 9.7-10; 3.1
5.12 ver 8
5.13 ver 9
5.14 Est 6.4; 7.9,10

d Gk: Heb lacks *tomorrow*

E. *The deliverance of the Jews*

1. *Haman's plot and its failure*

6 On that night the king could not sleep; and he gave orders to bring the book of memorable deeds, the chronicles, and they were read before the king. 2And it was found written how Mor´-dĕcaī had told about Bĭgthā´nȧ and Tērĕsh, two of the king's eunuchs, who guarded the threshold, and who had sought to lay hands upon King Ȧhȧṣ̌u-ē´rȕs. 3And the king said, "What honor or dignity has been bestowed on Mor´dĕcaī for this?" The king's servants who attended him said, "Nothing has been done for him." 4And the king said, "Who is in the court?" Now Hȧmȧn had just entered the outer court of the king's palace to speak to the king about having Mor´dĕcaī hanged on the gallows that he had prepared for him. 5 So the king's servants told him, "Hȧmȧn is there, standing in the court." And the king said, "Let him come in." 6 So Hȧmȧn came in, and the king said to him, "What shall be done to the man whom the king delights to honor?" And Haman said to himself, "Whom would the king delight to honor more than me?" 7And Hȧmȧn said to the king, "For the man whom the king delights to honor, 8 let royal robes be brought, which the king has worn, and the horse which the king has ridden, and on whose head a royal crown is set; 9 and let the robes and the horse be handed over to one of the king's most noble princes; let him[e] array the man whom the king delights to honor, and let him[e] conduct the man on horseback through the open square of the city, proclaiming before him: 'Thus shall it be done to the man whom the king delights to honor.' " 10 Then the king said to Hȧmȧn, "Make haste, take the robes and the horse, as you have said, and do so to Mor´dĕcaī the Jew who sits at the king's gate. Leave out nothing that you have mentioned." 11 So Hȧmȧn took the robes and the horse, and he arrayed Mor´dĕcaī and made him ride through the open square of the city, proclaiming, "Thus shall it be done to the man whom the king delights to honor."

12 Then Mor´dĕcaī returned to the king's gate. But Hȧmȧn hurried to his house, mourning and with his head covered. 13And Hȧmȧn told his wife Zĕrĕsh and all his friends everything that had befallen him. Then his wise men and his wife Zeresh said to him, "If Mor´dĕcaī, before whom you have begun to fall, is of the Jewish people, you will not prevail against him but will surely fall before him."

14 While they were yet talking with him, the king's eunuchs arrived and brought Hȧmȧn in haste to the banquet that Esther had prepared.

2. *The downfall of Haman*

7 So the king and Hȧmȧn went in to feast with Queen Esther. 2And on the second day, as they were drinking wine, the king again said to Esther, "What is your petition, Queen Esther? It shall be granted you. And what is your request? Even to the half of my kingdom, it shall be fulfilled." 3 Then Queen Esther answered, "If I have found favor in your sight, O king, and if it please the king, let my life be given me at my petition, and my people at my request. 4 For we are sold, I and my people, to be

---

[e] Heb *them*

Marginal references:

6.1 Dan 6.18; Est 2.23; 10.2
6.2 Est 2.21,22
6.4 Est 4.11; 5.1; 5.14
6.6 ver 7,9,11
6.8 1 Ki 1.33
6.9 Gen 41.43
6.12 2 Sam 15.30
6.13 Est 5.10
6.14 Est 5.8
7.2 Est 5.6; 5.3
7.3 Est 5.8; 8.5
7.4 Est 3.9,13

destroyed, to be slain, and to be annihilated. If we had been sold merely as slaves, men and women, I would have held my peace; for our affliction is not to be compared with the loss to the king." 5 Then King Ăhăşŭ-ē'rŭs said to Queen Esther, "Who is he, and where is he, that would presume to do this?" 6And Esther said, "A foe and enemy! This wicked Hāmån!" Then Haman was in terror before the king and the queen. 7And the king rose from the feast in wrath and went into the palace garden; but Hāmån stayed to beg his life from Queen Esther, for he saw that evil was determined against him by the king. 8And the king returned from the palace garden to the place where they were drinking wine, as Hāmån was falling on the couch where Esther was; and the king said, "Will he even assault the queen in my presence, in my own house?" As the words left the mouth of the king, they covered Hāmån's face. 9 Then said Harbō'nà, one of the eunuchs in attendance on the king, "Moreover, the gallows which Hāmån has prepared for Mor'dėcaī, whose word saved the king, is standing in Haman's house, fifty cubits high." 10And the king said, "Hang him on that." So they hanged Hāmån on the gallows which he had prepared for Mor'dėcaī. Then the anger of the king abated.

3. *The promotion of Mordecai*

8 On that day King Ăhăşŭ-ē'rŭs gave to Queen Esther the house of Hāmån, the enemy of the Jews. And Mor'dėcaī came before the king, for Esther had told what he was to her; 2 and the king took off his signet ring, which he had taken from Hāmån, and gave it to Mor'dėcaī. And Esther set Mordecai over the house of Haman.

4. *Esther's request and Ahasuerus' decree*

3 Then Esther spoke again to the king; she fell at his feet and besought him with tears to avert the evil design of Hāmån the Ăg'ågīte and the plot which he had devised against the Jews. 4And the king held out the golden scepter to Esther, 5 and Esther rose and stood before the king. And she said, "If it please the king, and if I have found favor in his sight, and if the thing seem right before the king, and I be pleasing in his eyes, let an order be written to revoke the letters devised by Hāmån the Ăg'ågīte, the son of Hămmėdā'thá, which he wrote to destroy the Jews who are in all the provinces of the king. 6 For how can I endure to see the calamity that is coming to my people? Or how can I endure to see the destruction of my kindred?" 7 Then King Ăhăşŭ-ē'rŭs said to Queen Esther and to Mor'dėcaī the Jew, "Behold, I have given Esther the house of Hāmån, and they have hanged him on the gallows, because he would lay hands on the Jews. 8And you may write as you please with regard to the Jews, in the name of the king, and seal it with the king's ring; for an edict written in the name of the king and sealed with the king's ring cannot be revoked."

9 The king's secretaries were summoned at that time, in the third month, which is the month of Sīvan', on the twenty-third day; and an edict was written according to all that Mor'dėcaī com-

7.6
Est 3.10

7.8
Est 1.6

7.9
Est 1.10;
5.14;
Ps 7.16;
Prov 11.5,6

*8.1
Est 7.6; 2.7

8.2
Est 3.10

8.4
Est 4.11;
5.2

8.5
Est 5.8;
7.3; 3.13

8.6
Est 7.4; 9.1

8.7
ver 1

8.8
ver 10;
Est 3.12;
1.19

*8.9
Est 3.12;
1.1; 1.22

8.1 *house of Haman*, that is, his property.
8.9 *their script and their language*, probably

Hebrew in the old script, not the square script of the Aramaic language.

manded concerning the Jews to the satraps and the governors and
the princes of the provinces from India to Ethiopia, a hundred
and twenty-seven provinces, to every province in its own script
and to every people in its own language, and also to the Jews in
their script and their language. 10 The writing was in the name of
King Ăhăṣŭ-ē′rŭs and sealed with the king's ring, and letters were
sent by mounted couriers riding on swift horses that were used in
the king's service, bred from the royal stud. 11 By these the king
allowed the Jews who were in every city to gather and defend
their lives, to destroy, to slay, and to annihilate any armed force
of any people or province that might attack them, with their children and women, and to plunder their goods, 12 upon one day
throughout all the provinces of King Ăhăṣŭ-ē′rŭs, on the thirteenth day of the twelfth month, which is the month of Ădar′.
13A copy of what was written was to be issued as a decree in every
province, and by proclamation to all peoples, and the Jews were
to be ready on that day to avenge themselves upon their enemies.
14 So the couriers, mounted on their swift horses that were used
in the king's service, rode out in haste, urged by the king's command; and the decree was issued in Suṣà the capital.

5. *The victory of the Jews*

15 Then Mor′dēcaī went out from the presence of the king in
royal robes of blue and white, with a great golden crown and a
mantle of fine linen and purple, while the city of Suṣà shouted and
rejoiced. 16 The Jews had light and gladness and joy and honor.
17And in every province and in every city, wherever the king's
command and his edict came, there was gladness and joy among
the Jews, a feast and a holiday. And many from the peoples of the
country declared themselves Jews, for the fear of the Jews had
fallen upon them.

9 Now in the twelfth month, which is the month of Ădar′, on
the thirteenth day of the same, when the king's command and
edict were about to be executed, on the very day when the enemies
of the Jews hoped to get the mastery over them, but which had
been changed to a day when the Jews should get the mastery over
their foes, 2 the Jews gathered in their cities throughout all the
provinces of King Ăhăṣŭ-ē′rŭs to lay hands on such as sought their
hurt. And no one could make a stand against them, for the fear
of them had fallen upon all peoples. 3All the princes of the provinces and the satraps and the governors and the royal officials also
helped the Jews, for the fear of Mor′dēcaī had fallen upon them.
4 For Mor′dēcaī was great in the king's house, and his fame
spread throughout all the provinces; for the man Mordecai grew
more and more powerful. 5 So the Jews smote all their enemies
with the sword, slaughtering, and destroying them, and did as
they pleased to those who hated them. 6 In Suṣà the capital itself
the Jews slew and destroyed five hundred men, 7 and also slew
Păr-shăn-dā′thă and Dălphŏn and Ăspā′thă 8 and Porā′thă and
Ădā′lĭa and Ărīdā′thă 9 and Parmăsh′tà and Ăr′īsaī and Ăr′īdaī and
Vaīzā′thă, 10 the ten sons of Hāmàn the son of Hămmĕdā′thă, the
enemy of the Jews; but they laid no hand on the plunder.

6. *The hanging of Haman's sons*

11 That very day the number of those slain in Suṣà the capital

8.10
1 Ki 21.8;
Est 3.12,13

8.11
Est 9.2,10,
15,16; 3.13

8.13
Est 3.14

8.15
Est 3.15

8.17
Est 9.2,
19,27

9.1
Est 8.12;
ver 17;
Est 3.13

9.2
ver 15–18;
Est 8.11;
Ps 71.13,24;
Est 8.17
9.3
Ezra 8.36

9.5
2 Sam 3.1;
Prov 4.18

9.10
Est 5.11;
8.11

9.12
Est 7.2
was reported to the king. 12And the king said to Queen Esther, "In Suṣā the capital the Jews have slain five hundred men and also the ten sons of Hāmàn. What then have they done in the rest of the king's provinces! Now what is your petition? It shall be granted you. And what further is your request? It shall be fulfilled."

9.13
Est 8.11
13And Esther said, "If it please the king, let the Jews who are in Suṣā be allowed tomorrow also to do according to this day's edict. And let the ten sons of Hāmàn be hanged on the gallows." 14 So the king commanded this to be done; a decree was issued in Suṣā,

9.15
ver 10
and the ten sons of Hāmàn were hanged. 15 The Jews who were in Suṣā gathered also on the fourteenth day of the month of Àdar' and they slew three hundred men in Suṣā; but they laid no hands on the plunder.

7. The Feast of Purim commenced

9.16
ver 2,10,15
16 Now the other Jews who were in the king's provinces also gathered to defend their lives, and got relief from their enemies, and slew seventy-five thousand of those who hated them; but they

9.17
ver 1,21
laid no hands on the plunder. 17 This was on the thirteenth day of the month of Àdar', and on the fourteenth day they rested and

9.18
ver 2,21
made that a day of feasting and gladness. 18 But the Jews who were in Suṣā gathered on the thirteenth day and on the fourteenth, and rested on the fifteenth day, making that a day of feasting and glad-

9.19
Deut 16.11,
14;
ver 22;
Neh 8.10
ness. 19 Therefore the Jews of the villages, who live in the open towns, hold the fourteenth day of the month of Àdar' as a day for gladness and feasting and holiday-making, and a day on which they send choice portions to one another.

III. The Feast of Purim: observance and regulations 9.20–10.3

A. The permanent establishment of Purim

20 And Mor'dècaï recorded these things, and sent letters to all the Jews who were in all the provinces of King Ăhăṣŭ-ë'rŭs, both near and far, 21 enjoining them that they should keep the four-teenth day of the month Àdar' and also the fifteenth day of the

9.22
ver 19
same, year by year, 22 as the days on which the Jews got relief from their enemies, and as the month that had been turned for them from sorrow into gladness and from mourning into a holiday; that they should make them days of feasting and gladness, days for sending choice portions to one another and gifts to the poor.

23 So the Jews undertook to do as they had begun, and as Mor'-dècaï had written to them. 24 For Hāmàn the Ăg'àgite, the son of

9.24
Est 3.6,7
Hămmèdà'thà, the enemy of all the Jews, had plotted against the Jews to destroy them, and had cast Pūr, that is the lot, to crush

9.25
Est 7.4–10;
3.6–15;
Ps 7.16
and destroy them; 25 but when Esther came before the king, he gave orders in writing that his wicked plot which he had devised against the Jews should come upon his own head, and that he and his sons should be hanged on the gallows. 26 Therefore they called

*9.26
ver 20
these days Pūrìm, after the term Pūr. And therefore, because of all

---

9.26 *Purim.* The first mention of this feast outside of Scripture is in 2 Maccabees 15.36 where it is called "the day before Mordecai's (Mardocheus in the KJV) day."

that was written in this letter, and of what they had faced in this
matter, and of what had befallen them, 27 the Jews ordained and
took it upon themselves and their descendants and all who joined
them, that without fail they would keep these two days according
to what was written and at the time appointed every year, 28 that
these days should be remembered and kept throughout every
generation, in every family, province, and city, and that these days
of Pūrĭm should never fall into disuse among the Jews, nor should
the commemoration of these days cease among their descendants.

9.27
Est 8.17;
ver 20,21

B. The approval of Esther

29 Then Queen Esther, the daughter of Ăb'ĭhāil, and Mor'-
dĕcaī the Jew gave full written authority, confirming this second
letter about Pūrĭm. 30 Letters were sent to all the Jews, to the
hundred and twenty-seven provinces of the kingdom of Ăhăsŭ-
ē'rŭs, in words of peace and truth, 31 that these days of Pūrĭm
should be observed at their appointed seasons, as Mor'dĕcaī the
Jew and Queen Esther enjoined upon the Jews, and as they had
laid down for themselves and for their descendants, with regard
to their fasts and their lamenting. 32 The command of Queen
Esther fixed these practices of Pūrĭm, and it was recorded in
writing.

9.29
Est 2.15;
ver 20,21
9.30
Est 1.1

*9.31
Est 4.3

*9.32
ver 26

C. The power and might of Mordecai

10 King Ăhăsŭ-ē'rŭs laid tribute on the land and on the coastlands of the sea. 2And all the acts of his power and might,
and the full account of the high honor of Mor'dĕcaī, to which the
king advanced him, are they not written in the Book of the
Chronicles of the kings of Mē'dĭä and Persia? 3 For Mor'dĕcaī the
Jew was next in rank to King Ăhăsŭ-ē'rŭs, and he was great
among the Jews and popular with the multitude of his brethren,
for he sought the welfare of his people and spoke peace to all his
people.

10.1
Isa 24.15
10.2
Est 8.15;
9.4; 2.23
10.3
Gen 41.40;
Neh 2.10

9.31 *fasts.* The thirteenth day of Adar
became Esther's Fast, a prelude to the joyous
days of Purim.
9.32 The Feast of Purim was inaugurated
by Mordecai (9.20) to commemorate the
deliverance of the Jews from wicked Haman

(3.7–15; 9.24–26). It commenced on the
fourteenth day of the twelfth month and
lasted two days. It is thought that Jn 5.1
may refer to the celebration of this feast. The
Jews bound themselves and their descendants
to keep this feast forever (9.27, 28).

INTRODUCTION TO
THE BOOK OF
JOB

Authorship and Background: The book derives its title from the central character, Job, whose name some have taken to mean "he who turns to God". Other meanings have been proposed, but the evidence is not clear. The author of the book is unknown, although Jewish tradition suggested writers from Moses to the time of Ahasuerus. It was probably written during the Solomonic age.

Sometimes regarded as a parable, the book appears to be a historical poem describing real events which took place during the patriarchal age, in the land of Uz, which probably lay in southeastern Edom. Job was a wealthy man, living a semi-nomadic life, free from worldly cares, when sudden catastrophe struck and he was faced with the problem of human suffering. The book was written for the purpose of seeking an answer to questions concerning the reason for human suffering and why a loving God allows it.

Characteristics: This epic poem has been acknowledged by many as one of the great literary works of all time. It has a magnificence and sublimity which defy analysis. In scope and treatment it moves majestically through the problem of suffering, seeking to resolve the dilemma in terms of human understanding. The friends of Job are skilfully depicted and their arguments cogently presented. Through their words, as well as through the words of Job himself, one is able to classify the characters who, in some sense, are representative of men everywhere. The author does not find his solution in the dogmatic assertions of Job's friends, who shortsightedly suppose that Job has personally sinned; rather he comes, full circle, back to God and bows in acceptance of the will of God which he may not always understand, for "we see through a glass darkly."

Contents:

I. The prologue. 1.1—2.13: Job is depicted as a pious and prosperous man. At the prompting of Satan, the LORD agrees to try Job. He loses children, wealth, and health. Job's friends come to comfort him. They remain silent for seven days.

II. Job's discussions with his friends. 3.1—31.40: Job speaks of his misery and despair. Eliphaz accuses Job of guilt. Job pleads for pity. Bildad accuses him of hypocrisy. Job denies the charge and pleads for divine relief. Zophar condemns Job as a liar and hypocrite. He responds that their words are platitudes; he knows God's power and his own innocence. Eliphaz repeats his platitudes. Job argues that his friends are confusing him with words. Bildad depicts the terrors of the wicked. Job charges his friends with persecution and slander. Zophar pictures the punishment of the wicked. Job points out the fallacies.

Eliphaz speaks the third time and urges Job to repent. Job says that God is just and renders justice. Bildad utters words of protest. Job claims that Bildad's words are without meaning. He insists that he is speaking the truth, and that ultimate knowledge is in God, not in man. He protests his innocence and commits his way unto God in answer to Eliphaz's earlier charges.

III.   The speeches of Elihu. 32.1—37.24: Elihu enters the controversy because Job's friends have failed him. He denounces Job's reaction to his plight. He summarizes Job's complaints and refutes them in order. He argues that man, in his finiteness, must lean not on his own intelligence but upon his fear of God.

IV.   The voice of God. 38.1—42.6: God calls Job to account. He rehearses the marvels of the inanimate world, the animal world, and his own mighty power. Job responds to the divine Word in repentance and confession, renouncing human words and wisdom. He rejoices in his experience of God.

V.   Epilogue. 42.7–17: Poetry gives way to prose as Job's friends are condemned. Job's spiritual blessings are recounted. His material possessions are restored, a new family is given him, and at last he dies in fulness of age.

THE BOOK OF
JOB

I. The prologue 1.1–2.13

A. Job and his background

*1.1
Jer 25.20;
Ezek 14.14;
Jas 5.11;
Gen 6.9;
17.1;
Ex 18.21
1.2
Job 42.13
1.3
Job 42.12
1.5
Ex 19.10;
Gen 8.20;
1 Ki 21.10,
13

1 There was a man in the land of Úz, whose name was Jōb; and that man was blameless and upright, one who feared God, and turned away from evil. 2 There were born to him seven sons and three daughters. 3 He had seven thousand sheep, three thousand camels, five hundred yoke of oxen, and five hundred she-asses, and very many servants; so that this man was the greatest of all the people of the east. 4 His sons used to go and hold a feast in the house of each on his day; and they would send and invite their three sisters to eat and drink with them. 5 And when the days of the feast had run their course, Jōb would send and sanctify them, and he would rise early in the morning and offer burnt offerings according to the number of them all; for Job said, "It may be that my sons have sinned, and cursed God in their hearts." Thus Job did continually.

B. The controversy of Satan with God

1. God grants Satan permission to test Job

*1.6
Job 38.7;
1 Chr 21.1
1.7
1 Pet 5.8
1.8
Job 42.7,8;
ver 1
*1.9
1 Tim 6.5
1.10
Job 29.2–6;
Ps 128.1,2;
Job 31.25
1.11
Job 2.5;
19.21
*1.12

6 Now there was a day when the sons of God came to present themselves before the LORD, and Satan[a] also came among them. 7 The LORD said to Satan, "Whence have you come?" Satan answered the LORD, "From going to and fro on the earth, and from walking up and down on it." 8 And the LORD said to Satan, "Have you considered my servant Jōb, that there is none like him on the earth, a blameless and upright man, who fears God and turns away from evil?" 9 Then Satan answered the LORD, "Does Jōb fear God for nought? 10 Hast thou not put a hedge about him and his house and all that he has, on every side? Thou hast blessed the work of his hands, and his possessions have increased in the land. 11 But put forth thy hand now, and touch all that he has, and he will curse thee to thy face." 12 And the LORD said to Satan, "Behold, all that he has is in your power; only upon himself do not put forth your hand." So Satan went forth from the presence of the LORD.

2. Satan takes away Job's wealth and children

13 Now there was a day when his sons and daughters were eating

a Heb the adversary

1.1 *the land of Uz*, probably located in Edom (cf. Lam 4.21), east of the territory occupied by Israel.
1.6 *the sons of God*, i.e., the angels. Among the angels we meet *Satan* (the adversary).
1.9 *Does Job fear God for nought?* The question of Job's motivation was a subtle attack on God's providence. The accuser implies that love and loyalty can always be bought.
1.12 *in your power* suggests that God had delegated a limited jurisdiction to Satan. God explicitly forbade any harm to Job's person, however.

and drinking wine in their eldest brother's house; 14 and there came a messenger to Jōb, and said, "The oxen were plowing and the asses feeding beside them; 15 and the Sābē'ăns fell upon them and took them, and slew the servants with the edge of the sword; and I alone have escaped to tell you." 16 While he was yet speaking, there came another, and said, "The fire of God fell from heaven and burned up the sheep and the servants, and consumed them; and I alone have escaped to tell you." 17 While he was yet speaking, there came another, and said, "The Chăldē'ăns formed three companies, and made a raid upon the camels and took them, and slew the servants with the edge of the sword; and I alone have escaped to tell you." 18 While he was yet speaking, there came another, and said, "Your sons and daughters were eating and drinking wine in their eldest brother's house; 19 and behold, a great wind came across the wilderness, and struck the four corners of the house, and it fell upon the young people, and they are dead; and I alone have escaped to tell you."

3. Job exhibits patience

20 Then Jōb arose, and rent his robe, and shaved his head, and fell upon the ground, and worshiped. 21And he said, "Naked I came from my mother's womb, and naked shall I return; the LORD gave, and the LORD has taken away; blessed be the name of the LORD."

22 In all this Jōb did not sin or charge God with wrong.

C. Satan's second request of God

1. Satan's request granted

2 Again there was a day when the sons of God came to present themselves before the LORD, and Satan also came among them to present himself before the LORD. 2And the LORD said to Satan, "Whence have you come?" Satan answered the LORD, "From going to and fro on the earth, and from walking up and down on it." 3And the LORD said to Satan, "Have you considered my servant Jōb, that there is none like him on the earth, a blameless and upright man, who fears God and turns away from evil? He still holds fast his integrity, although you moved me against him, to destroy him without cause." 4 Then Satan answered the LORD, "Skin for skin! All that a man has he will give for his life. 5 But put forth thy hand now, and touch his bone and his flesh, and he will curse thee to thy face." 6And the LORD said to Satan, "Behold, he is in your power; only spare his life."

2. Satan afflicts Job physically

7 So Satan went forth from the presence of the LORD, and

Cross-references (margin):

*1.14
1.15 Job 6.19
1.16 Gen 19.24; Lev 10.2; Num 11.1–3; 2 Ki 1.10
1.17 Gen 11.28, 31
1.18 ver 4,13
1.19 Jer 4.11; 13.24
1.20 Gen 37.29; 1 Pet 5.6
1.21 Ecc 5.15; 1 Tim 6.7; Job 2.10; Eph 5.20; 1 Thess 5.18
*1.22 Job 2.10
2.1 Job 1.6
2.2 Job 1.7
2.3 Job 1.1,8; 27.5,6; 9.17
*2.4
2.5 Job 1.11
2.6 Job 1.12
2.7 Job 7.5

1.14 Job lost his wealth (ver 14–17); he lost his children (ver 18, 19); he lost his health (2.1–8). Since these are among life's most precious possessions, the loss of them was designed to lead to defection from God. Having lost all of these things, his own life seemed hardly worth preserving.
1.22 *charge God with wrong* is, literally, "reproach God." Job did not understand the reason for the calamities which he experienced but he did not question God's sovereign rights over His creatures.
2.4 *Skin for skin* is probably a proverbial expression (used by tradesmen). The loss of possessions and loved ones may be regarded as secondary. Satan insists that Job will renounce his loyalty to God if He will bring affliction on his body.

afflicted Jōb with loathsome sores from the sole of his foot to the crown of his head. ⁸And he took a potsherd with which to scrape himself, and sat among the ashes.

2.8
Job 42.6;
Ezek 27.30;
Mt 11.21

3. *Job's continued patience*

*2.9
2.10
Job 1.21,
22; Ps 39.1

9 Then his wife said to him, "Do you still hold fast your integrity? Curse God, and die." ¹⁰ But he said to her, "You speak as one of the foolish women would speak. Shall we receive good at the hand of God, and shall we not receive evil?" In all this Jōb did not sin with his lips.

D. *The friends of Job*

*2.11
1 Chr 1.45;
Gen 25.2;
Job 42.11

11 Now when Jōb's three friends heard of all this evil that had come upon him, they came each from his own place, Ĕl'ĭphăz the Tē'mánĭte, Bĭldăd the Shuhĭte, and Zōphar the Nā'ámáthĭte. They made an appointment together to come to condole with him and comfort him. ¹²And when they saw him from afar, they did not recognize him; and they raised their voices and wept; and they rent their robes and sprinkled dust upon their heads toward heaven. ¹³And they sat with him on the ground seven days and seven nights, and no one spoke a word to him, for they saw that his suffering was very great.

2.12
Josh 7.6;
Lam 2.10;
Ezek 27.30

2.13
Gen 50.10;
Ezek 3.15

II. *Job's discussions with his friends 3.1–31.40*

A. *Job's lament of misery and despair*

1. *He curses the day of his birth*

3 After this Jōb opened his mouth and cursed the day of his birth. ² And Jōb said:

*3.3
Job 10.18;
Jer 20.14

3 "Let the day perish wherein I was born,
  and the night which said,
'A man-child is conceived.'
⁴ Let that day be darkness!
  May God above not seek it,
  nor light shine upon it.

3.5
Job 10.21;
Ps 23.4;
Jer 2.6

⁵ Let gloom and deep darkness claim it.
  Let clouds dwell upon it;
  let the blackness of the day terrify it.

3.6
Job 23.17

⁶ That night—let thick darkness seize it!
  let it not rejoice among the days of the year,
  let it not come into the number of the months.
⁷ Yea, let that night be barren;

2.9 *Curse God, and die.* Afflicted with a loathsome disease, Job might well think life intolerable. His wife suggests that he curse God and accept the penalty, death (cf. Lev 24.10–16).
2.11 *when Job's three friends heard.* There is no reason to question the good intent of Job's friends. They learned that their friend was afflicted and they came to be of help. Their homes appear to have been in northern

Arabia. *Teman* is the name of an Edomite clan (Gen 36.4, 11), and the Shuhites appear to be a brother tribe to Midian (cf. Gen 25.2; 1 Chron 1.32). There are no other references to the Naamathites than those in the Book of Job.
3.3 Although he would not curse God, Job did curse the day of his birth. He wished that he had never been born (3.3–10) or that he might have been born dead (3.11–19.)

let no joyful cry be heard[b] in it.
8 Let those curse it who curse the day,
   who are skilled to rouse up Lēvī′áthán.
9 Let the stars of its dawn be dark;
   let it hope for light, but have none,
   nor see the eyelids of the morning;
10 because it did not shut the doors of my mother's womb,
   nor hide trouble from my eyes.

2. He asks why he did not die

11 "Why did I not die at birth,
   come forth from the womb and expire?
12 Why did the knees receive me?
   Or why the breasts, that I should suck?
13 For then I should have lain down and been quiet;
   I should have slept; then I should have been at rest,
14 with kings and counselors of the earth
   who rebuilt ruins for themselves,
15 or with princes who had gold,
   who filled their houses with silver.
16 Or why was I not as a hidden untimely birth,
   as infants that never see the light?
17 There the wicked cease from troubling,
   and there the weary are at rest.
18 There the prisoners are at ease together;
   they hear not the voice of the taskmaster.
19 The small and the great are there,
   and the slave is free from his master.

3. He cries out in his agony

20 "Why is light given to him that is in misery,
   and life to the bitter in soul,
21 who long for death, but it comes not,
   and dig for it more than for hid treasures;
22 who rejoice exceedingly,
   and are glad, when they find the grave?
23 Why is light given to a man whose way is hid,
   whom God has hedged in?
24 For my sighing comes as[c] my bread,
   and my groanings are poured out like water.
25 For the thing that I fear comes upon me,
   and what I dread befalls me.
26 I am not at ease, nor am I quiet;
   I have no rest; but trouble comes."

b Heb come   c Heb before

Marginal references:
*3.8 Job 41.10
3.9 Job 41.18
*3.11 Job 10.18
3.12 Gen 30.3; Isa 66.12
3.14 Job 12.17, 18; 15.28
3.16 Ecc 6.3
3.17 Job 17.16
*3.20 1 Sam 1.10; Prov 31.6; Isa 38.15; Ezek 27.31
3.21 Rev 9.6
3.23 Job 19.6,8, 12; Lam 3.7
3.24 Ps 42.3,4

3.8 *Leviathan*, the legendary sea monster, was thought to swallow up the sun in times of eclipse. Had Leviathan been aroused, the day of Job's birth might never have dawned!
3.11 *Why did I not die at birth . . . ?* Job wished that he had never been born or that he had died as soon as he was born. Jesus said, *"Blessed are the barren . . . and the breasts that never gave suck!"* (Lk 23.29), but in blessing the barren womb He never cursed the fruitful one. Job here curses life and welcomes death and the grave as the greatest boon. He was sadly mistaken and unwilling to make the most of affliction.
3.20 *the bitter in soul* describes Job during the days following his affliction. Conscious that he has not committed some great sin, he cannot understand the reason for his suffering. He had refused to "curse God," but in his distress questions the reason for his trials.

B. The first cycle of speeches

1. The speech of Eliphaz

a. God does not punish the righteous

4 Then Ĕl′íphăz the Tē′mànīte answered:

2 "If one ventures a word with you, will you be offended?
  Yet who can keep from speaking?
3 Behold, you have instructed many,
  and you have strengthened the weak hands.
4 Your words have upheld him who was stumbling,
  and you have made firm the feeble knees.
5 But now it has come to you, and you are impatient;
  it touches you, and you are dismayed.
6 Is not your fear of God your confidence,
  and the integrity of your ways your hope?

7 "Think now, who that was innocent ever perished?
  Or where were the upright cut off?
8 As I have seen, those who plow iniquity
  and sow trouble reap the same.
9 By the breath of God they perish,
  and by the blast of his anger they are consumed.
10 The roar of the lion, the voice of the fierce lion,
  the teeth of the young lions, are broken.
11 The strong lion perishes for lack of prey,
  and the whelps of the lioness are scattered.

b. Sinful man must perish

12 "Now a word was brought to me stealthily,
  my ear received the whisper of it.
13 Amid thoughts from visions of the night,
  when deep sleep falls on men,
14 dread came upon me, and trembling,
  which made all my bones shake.
15 A spirit glided past my face;
  the hair of my flesh stood up.
16 It stood still,
  but I could not discern its appearance.

Cross references (left margin):

*4.1
*4.2 Job 32.18–20
*4.3 Isa 35.3; Heb 12.12
4.4 Isa 35.3; Heb 12.12
4.5 Job 6.14; 19.21
4.6 Job 1.1
*4.7 Ps 37.25
4.8 Prov 22.8; Hos 10.13; Gal 6.7,8
4.9 Job 15.30; Isa 30.33; Ps 59.13
4.10 Ps 58.6
4.11 Ps 34.10
4.12 Job 26.14
4.14 Jer 23.9
*4.15

4.1 The speeches of Eliphaz, Bildad, Zophar, and Elihu are poetic in form. They constitute a true record of what was said, but this does not mean that what Job's friends said was necessarily true. God himself passes adverse judgment on Eliphaz, Bildad, and Zophar (42.7–9). Nevertheless, some of the statements made by these men are true and are quoted as Scripture in the New Testament (e.g., the statements of Eliphaz in 5.11–13, echoed in Lk 1.52 and quoted in 1 Cor 3.19).

4.2 In substance, the argument of Eliphaz is as follows: (1) If Job had been a righteous man he would have had confidence in God rather than wishing to die; (2) Job's suffering could be explained by the maxim that as a man sows so shall he reap (4.8, 9); (3) Job should submit to God's chastening with a humble repentance which would enable him to regain his former prosperity. Eliphaz's maxims contain truth, but unfortunately they

did not apply to Job's case, for he was not being punished for any secret sin he had committed, as the three comforters (Eliphaz, Bildad, and Zophar) implied.

4.3 *you have instructed many* is a tribute to the godly influence of Job in earlier times. Eliphaz implies that the godly Job who has helped others so often is now in need of help himself.

4.7 *who that was innocent ever perished?* This expresses the philosophy of Job's friends. They assure him that only the wicked suffer. The logic of their position is that since Job is suffering, he must be wicked. Therefore they consider it their duty to urge Job to confess his sin and to trust in the mercy of God.

4.15 *A spirit glided past my face.* Eliphaz made his appeal to Job on the basis of a night vision. His mystical experience is deemed sufficient to accuse Job of sin.

A form was before my eyes;
   there was silence, then I heard a voice:

17 'Can mortal man be righteous before*d* God?
   Can a man be pure before*d* his Maker?

18 Even in his servants he puts no trust,
   and his angels he charges with error;

19 how much more those who dwell in houses of clay,
   whose foundation is in the dust,
   who are crushed before the moth.

20 Between morning and evening they are destroyed;
   they perish for ever without any regarding it.

21 If their tent-cord is plucked up within them,
   do they not die, and that without wisdom?'

c. Punishment the fruit of unrighteousness

5 "Call now; is there any one who will answer you?
   To which of the holy ones will you turn?

2 Surely vexation kills the fool,
   and jealousy slays the simple.

3 I have seen the fool taking root,
   but suddenly I cursed his dwelling.

4 His sons are far from safety,
   they are crushed in the gate,
   and there is no one to deliver them.

5 His harvest the hungry eat,
   and he takes it even out of thorns;*e*
   and the thirsty*f* pant after his*g* wealth.

6 For affliction does not come from the dust,
   nor does trouble sprout from the ground;

7 but man is born to trouble
   as the sparks fly upward.

d. Eliphaz implores Job to seek God

8 "As for me, I would seek God,
   and to God would I commit my cause;

9 who does great things and unsearchable,
   marvelous things without number:

10 he gives rain upon the earth
   and sends waters upon the fields;

11 he sets on high those who are lowly,
   and those who mourn are lifted to safety.

12 He frustrates the devices of the crafty,
   so that their hands achieve no success.

13 He takes the wise in their own craftiness;
   and the schemes of the wily are brought to a quick end.

14 They meet with darkness in the daytime,
   and grope at noonday as in the night.

15 But he saves the fatherless from their mouth,*h*
   the needy from the hand of the mighty.

16 So the poor have hope,
   and injustice shuts her mouth.

17 "Behold, happy is the man whom God reproves;

Marginal references:

4.17 Job 9.2; 35.10
4.18 Job 15.15
4.19 Job 10.9; 22.16
4.20 Ps 90.5,6; Job 20.7
4.21 Job 36.12
5.1 Job 15.15
5.2 Prov 12.16
5.3 Ps 37.35
5.4 Amos 5.12
5.5 Job 18.8–10
5.7 Job 14.1
5.8 Ps 35.23
5.9 Ps 40.5; 72.18
5.10 Ps 65.9
5.11 1 Sam 2.7; Ps 113.7
5.12 Neh 4.15; Ps 33.10; Isa 8.10
5.14 Job 12.25; Deut 28.29
5.15 Ps 35.10
5.16 Ps 107.42
5.17 Ps 94.12; Jas 1.12; Heb 12.5-11

d Or *more than*   *e* Heb obscure   *f* Aquila Symmachus Syr Vg: Heb *snare*
g Heb *their*   *h* Cn: Heb uncertain

therefore despise not the chastening of the Almighty.

5.18
Isa 30.26
18 For he wounds, but he binds up;
   he smites, but his hands heal.

5.19
Ps 34.19;
91.10
19 He will deliver you from six troubles;
   in seven there shall no evil touch you.

5.20
Ps 33.19;
144.10
20 In famine he will redeem you from death,
   and in war from the power of the sword.

5.21
Ps 31.20;
91.5,6
21 You shall be hid from the scourge of the tongue,
   and shall not fear destruction when it comes.

5.22
Ps 91.13;
Ezek 34.25
22 At destruction and famine you shall laugh,
   and shall not fear the beasts of the earth.

5.23
Ps 91.12;
Isa 11.6–9
23 For you shall be in league with the stones of the field,
   and the beasts of the field shall be at peace with you.

5.24
Job 8.6;
21.9
24 You shall know that your tent is safe,
   and you shall inspect your fold and miss nothing.

5.25
Ps 72.16;
112.2
25 You shall know also that your descendants shall be many,
   and your offspring as the grass of the earth.

5.26
Gen 15.15;
Prov 9.11
26 You shall come to your grave in ripe old age,
   as a shock of grain comes up to the threshing floor in its season.

27 Lo, this we have searched out; it is true.
   Hear, and know it for your good." *i*

2. Job's reply to Eliphaz
a. He complains that God will not let him die

6 Then Jōb answered:

6.2
Job 31.6
2 "O that my vexation were weighed,
   and all my calamity laid in the balances!

6.3
Prov 27.3
3 For then it would be heavier than the sand of the sea;
   therefore my words have been rash.

6.4
Ps 38.2;
Job 21.20;
Ps 88.15
4 For the arrows of the Almighty are in me;
   my spirit drinks their poison;
   the terrors of God are arrayed against me.

5 Does the wild ass bray when he has grass,
   or the ox low over his fodder?

6 Can that which is tasteless be eaten without salt,
   or is there any taste in the slime of the purslane? *j*

7 My appetite refuses to touch them;
   they are as food that is loathsome to me. *k*

6.8
Job 14.13
8 "O that I might have my request,
   and that God would grant my desire;

6.9
1 Ki 19.4
9 that it would please God to crush me,
   that he would let loose his hand and cut me off!

6.10
Job 23.11,
12;
Lev 19.2;
Isa 57.15;
Hos 11.9
10 This would be my consolation;
   I would even exult *l* in pain unsparing;
   for I have not denied the words of the Holy One.

6.11
Job 21.4
11 What is my strength, that I should wait?
   And what is my end, that I should be patient?

12 Is my strength the strength of stones,
   or is my flesh bronze?

6.13
Job 26.2,3
13 In truth I have no help in me,
   and any resource is driven from me.

---

i Heb *for yourself*   *j* The meaning of the Hebrew word is uncertain
k Heb obscure   *l* The meaning of the Hebrew word is uncertain

b. Job calls his friends unfaithful

14 "He who withholds[m] kindness from a friend
    forsakes the fear of the Almighty.
15 My brethren are treacherous as a torrent-bed,
    as freshets that pass away,
16 which are dark with ice,
    and where the snow hides itself.
17 In time of heat they disappear;
    when it is hot, they vanish from their place.
18 The caravans turn aside from their course;
    they go up into the waste, and perish.
19 The caravans of Tēmā look,
    the travelers of Shēbā hope.
20 They are disappointed because they were confident;
    they come thither and are confounded.

6.15 Ps 38.11; Jer 15.18
6.17 Job 24.19
6.19 Gen 25.15; Isa 21.14; 1 Ki 10.1
6.20 Jer 14.3

c. He asks for evidences of his sins

21 Such you have now become to me;[n]
    you see my calamity, and are afraid.
22 Have I said, 'Make me a gift'?
    Or, 'From your wealth offer a bribe for me'?
23 Or, 'Deliver me from the adversary's hand'?
    Or, 'Ransom me from the hand of oppressors'?

24 "Teach me, and I will be silent;
    make me understand how I have erred.
25 How forceful are honest words!
    But what does reproof from you reprove?
26 Do you think that you can reprove words,
    when the speech of a despairing man is wind?
27 You would even cast lots over the fatherless,
    and bargain over your friend.

6.25 Ecc 12.10, 11
6.26 Job 8.2
6.27 Joel 3.3; 2 Pet 3.3

28 "But now, be pleased to look at me;
    for I will not lie to your face.
29 Turn, I pray, let no wrong be done.
    Turn now, my vindication is at stake.
30 Is there any wrong on my tongue?
    Cannot my taste discern calamity?

6.28 Job 27.4
6.30 Job 27.4; 12.11

d. He argues against hope

7 "Has not man a hard service upon earth,
    and are not his days like the days of a hireling?
2 Like a slave who longs for the shadow,
    and like a hireling who looks for his wages,
3 so I am allotted months of emptiness,
    and nights of misery are apportioned to me.
4 When I lie down I say, 'When shall I arise?'
    But the night is long,
    and I am full of tossing till the dawn.
5 My flesh is clothed with worms and dirt;
    my skin hardens, then breaks out afresh.
6 My days are swifter than a weaver's shuttle,
    and come to their end without hope.

7.1 Job 10.17; 14.14; Isa 40.2; Job 14.6
7.2 Lev 19.13
7.3 Lam 1.7; Ps 6.6
7.4 Deut 28.67
7.6 Job 9.25; 13.15; 17.15,16

m Syr Vg Compare Tg: Heb obscure   n Cn Compare Gk Syr: Heb obscure

e. *He prays to his God*

7.7
Ps 78.39;
Job 9.25

7.8
Job 20.9;
ver 21

7.9
Job 30.15;
11.8;
2 Sam 12.23

7.10
Job 10.21;
Ps 103.16

7.11
Ps 40.9;
1 Sam 1.10

7.12
Ezek 32.2,3

7.13
Job 9.27

7.14
Job 9.34

7.15
1 Ki 19.4

7.16
Job 10.1;
Ecc 7.15

7.17
Ps 8.4;
144.3;
Heb 2.6

7.20
Job 35.3,6;
ver 12;
Job 16.12

★**7.21**
Job 10.14;
Ps 104.29;
ver 8

★**8.1**

8.3
Gen 18.25;
Deut 32.4;
2 Chr 19.7;
Dan 9.14;
Rom 3.5

8.4
Job 1.5,18,
19

8.5
Job 5.8;
11.13; 9.15

7 "Remember that my life is a breath;
　　my eye will never again see good.
8 The eye of him who sees me will behold me no more;
　　while thy eyes are upon me, I shall be gone.
9 As the cloud fades and vanishes,
　　so he who goes down to Shēōl does not come up;
10 he returns no more to his house,
　　nor does his place know him any more.

11 "Therefore I will not restrain my mouth;
　　I will speak in the anguish of my spirit;
　　I will complain in the bitterness of my soul.
12 Am I the sea, or a sea monster,
　　that thou settest a guard over me?
13 When I say, 'My bed will comfort me,
　　my couch will ease my complaint,'
14 then thou dost scare me with dreams
　　and terrify me with visions,
15 so that I would choose strangling
　　and death rather than my bones.
16 I loathe my life; I would not live for ever.
　　Let me alone, for my days are a breath.
17 What is man, that thou dost make so much of him,
　　and that thou dost set thy mind upon him,
18 dost visit him every morning,
　　and test him every moment?
19 How long wilt thou not look away from me,
　　nor let me alone till I swallow my spittle?
20 If I sin, what do I do to thee, thou watcher of men?
　　Why hast thou made me thy mark?
　　Why have I become a burden to thee?
21 Why dost thou not pardon my transgression
　　and take away my iniquity?
　　For now I shall lie in the earth;
　　thou wilt seek me, but I shall not be."

3. *The speech of Bildad: Bildad calls Job a hypocrite*
and urges repentance

8 Then Bĭldăd the Shuhīte answered:
2 "How long will you say these things,
　　and the words of your mouth be a great wind?
3 Does God pervert justice?
　　Or does the Almighty pervert the right?
4 If your children have sinned against him,
　　he has delivered them into the power of their transgression.
5 If you will seek God
　　and make supplication to the Almighty,

7.21 *Why dost thou not pardon my trans-*
gression? Job insists that no sin he has committed has harmed God. Let God forgive
Job, for he does not merit the sore chastisement he has experienced. The words represent a "reasoning with God" and need not

be deemed irreverent.

8.1 Bildad presents much the same argument as Eliphaz. He contends that if Job will
stop rebelling against his suffering and
acknowledge the justice of God's dealings
with him, he will soon regain his prosperity.

6 if you are pure and upright,
  surely then he will rouse himself for you
  and reward you with a rightful habitation.

8.6
Ps 7.6

7 And though your beginning was small,
  your latter days will be very great.

8.7
Job 42.12

8 "For inquire, I pray you, of bygone ages,
  and consider what the fathers have found;

★8.8
Deut 4.32;
32.7;
Job 15.18

9 for we are but of yesterday, and know nothing,
  for our days on earth are a shadow.

8.9
Gen 47.9;
1 Chr 29.15;
Job 7.6

10 Will they not teach you, and tell you,
   and utter words out of their understanding?

11 "Can papyrus grow where there is no marsh?
   Can reeds flourish where there is no water?

12 While yet in flower and not cut down,
   they wither before any other plant.

8.12
Ps 129.6;
Jer 17.6

13 Such are the paths of all who forget God;
   the hope of the godless man shall perish.

8.13
Ps 9.17;
Job 11.20;
Prov 10.28

14 His confidence breaks in sunder,
   and his trust is a spider's web.*o*

8.14
Isa 59.5,6

15 He leans against his house, but it does not stand;
   he lays hold of it, but it does not endure.

8.15
Job 27.18

16 He thrives before the sun,
   and his shoots spread over his garden.

8.16
Ps 37.35;
80.11

17 His roots twine about the stone-heap;
   he lives among the rocks.*p*

18 If he is destroyed from his place,
   then it will deny him, saying, 'I have never seen you.'

8.18
Job 7.10;
Ps 37.36

19 Behold, this is the joy of his way;
   and out of the earth others will spring.

8.19
Job 20.5;
Ecc 1.4

20 "Behold, God will not reject a blameless man,
   nor take the hand of evildoers.

8.20
Job 4.7;
21.30

21 He will yet fill your mouth with laughter,
   and your lips with shouting.

8.21
Ps 126.2;
132.16

22 Those who hate you will be clothed with shame,
   and the tent of the wicked will be no more."

8.22
Ps 35.26;
109.29;
ver 15

4. *Job answers Bildad*
a. *The doctrine and proof of God's justice*

9 Then Jōb answered:
2 "Truly I know that it is so:
  But how can a man be just before God?

9.2
Ps 143.2;
Rom 3.20

3 If one wished to contend with him,
  one could not answer him once in a thousand times.

4 He is wise in heart, and mighty in strength
  —who has hardened himself against him, and succeeded?—

9.4
Job 36.5;
2 Chr 13.12

5 he who removes mountains, and they know it not,
  when he overturns them in his anger;

9.5
Mic 1.4

o Heb *house*   *p* Gk Vg: Heb uncertain

8.8 *consider what the fathers have found.*
Bildad appeals to history and tradition in
seeking to convince Job of his error. Bildad's
philosophy is similar to that of Eliphaz, but
his appeal is on the basis of scholarship rather
than mystical experience.

9.6 Isa 2.19,21; Hag 2.6; Heb 12.26; Job 26.11	6 who shakes the earth out of its place, and its pillars tremble;
	7 who commands the sun, and it does not rise; who seals up the stars;
9.8 Gen 1.6; Ps 104.2,3	8 who alone stretched out the heavens, and trampled the waves of the sea;^q
9.9 Gen 1.16; Job 38.31; Amos 5.8	9 who made the Bear and Ōrī′on, the Plēī′adēṣ and the chambers of the south;
9.10 Ps 71.15	10 who does great things beyond understanding, and marvelous things without number.
9.11 Job 23.8,9; 35.14	11 Lo, he passes by me, and I see him not; he moves on, but I do not perceive him.
9.12 Isa 45.9; Rom 9.20; Job 11.10	12 Behold, he snatches away; who can hinder him? Who will say to him, 'What doest thou'?

b. *Job acknowledges himself a sinner*

*9.13 Job 26.12; Isa 30.7	13 "God will not turn back his anger; beneath him bowed the helpers of Rāhăb.
9.14 ver 3,32	14 How then can I answer him, choosing my words with him?
9.15 Job 10.15; 8.5	15 Though I am innocent, I cannot answer him; I must appeal for mercy to my accuser.^r
	16 If I summoned him and he answered me, I would not believe that he was listening to my voice.
9.17 Job 16.12, 14; 2.3	17 For he crushes me with a tempest, and multiplies my wounds without cause;
9.18 Job 27.2	18 he will not let me get my breath, but fills me with bitterness.
	19 If it is a contest of strength, behold him! If it is a matter of justice, who can summon him?^s
9.20 ver 15,29	20 Though I am innocent, my own mouth would condemn me; though I am blameless, he would prove me perverse.
9.21 Job 1.1; 7.16	21 I am blameless; I regard not myself; I loathe my life.
9.22 Ecc 9.2,3; Ezek 21.3	22 It is all one; therefore I say, he destroys both the blameless and the wicked.
9.23 Ps 64.4; Heb 11.36; 1 Pet 1.7	23 When disaster brings sudden death, he mocks at the calamity^t of the innocent.

9.24
Job 10.3;
12.6; 12.17
	24 The earth is given into the hand of the wicked;
	    he covers the faces of its judges—
	    if it is not he, who then is it?

c. *Job's complaint against God*

9.25 Job 7.6,7	25 "My days are swifter than a runner; they flee away, they see no good.
9.26 Hab 1.8	26 They go by like skiffs of reed, like an eagle swooping on the prey.

q Or trampled the back of the sea dragon   *r Or* for my right
s Compare Gk: Heb me.   *The text of the verse is uncertain*
t The meaning of the Hebrew word is uncertain

9.13 *the helpers of Rahab.* Rahab is a mythological figure who symbolizes the power of evil over which Yahweh, Israel's God, gained a significant victory in primordial times (cf. Isa 51.9). Job depicts God as gaining a victory over Rahab's helpers. The Babylonian Creation Epic (*Enuma Elish*, iv, 105ff) describes the victory of Marduk, god of Babylon, over Tiâmat, an evil deity who likewise had helpers "who marched at her side."

27 If I say, 'I will forget my complaint,
   I will put off my sad countenance, and be of good cheer,'
28 I become afraid of all my suffering,
   for I know thou wilt not hold me innocent.
29 I shall be condemned;
   why then do I labor in vain?
30 If I wash myself with snow,
   and cleanse my hands with lye,
31 yet thou wilt plunge me into a pit,
   and my own clothes will abhor me.
32 For he is not a man, as I am, that I might answer him,
   that we should come to trial together.
33 There is no u umpire between us,
   who might lay his hand upon us both.
34 Let him take his rod away from me,
   and let not dread of him terrify me.
35 Then I would speak without fear of him,
   for I am not so in myself.

d. Job's persistence in complaint

10 "I loathe my life;
   I will give free utterance to my complaint;
   I will speak in the bitterness of my soul.
2 I will say to God, Do not condemn me;
   let me know why thou dost contend against me.
3 Does it seem good to thee to oppress,
   to despise the work of thy hands
   and favor the designs of the wicked?
4 Hast thou eyes of flesh?
   Dost thou see as man sees?
5 Are thy days as the days of man,
   or thy years as man's years,
6 that thou dost seek out my iniquity
   and search for my sin,
7 although thou knowest that I am not guilty,
   and there is none to deliver out of thy hand?

e. Job acknowledges God as creator and preserver

8 Thy hands fashioned and made me;
   and now thou dost turn about and destroy me. v
9 Remember that thou hast made me of clay; w
   and wilt thou turn me to dust again?
10 Didst thou not pour me out like milk
   and curdle me like cheese?
11 Thou didst clothe me with skin and flesh,
   and knit me together with bones and sinews.
12 Thou hast granted me life and steadfast love;
   and thy care has preserved my spirit.
13 Yet these things thou didst hide in thy heart;
   I know that this was thy purpose.

f. Job again complains against God

14 If I sin, thou dost mark me,

Reference column:
9.27 Job 7.13
9.28 Ps 119.120; Job 7.21
9.29 ver 20
9.30 Jer 2.22
9.32 Ecc 6.10; Rom 9.20; ver 3; Ps 143.2
9.33 1 Sam 2.25
9.34 Job 13.21; Ps 39.10
9.35 Job 13.22
10.1 1 Ki 19.4; Job 7.16; 7.11
10.2 Job 9.29; Hos 4.1
10.3 ver 8; Job 21.16; 22.18
10.4 1 Sam 16.7
10.5 Ps 90.4; 2 Pet 3.8
10.7 Job 9.21; 9.12
10.8 Ps 119.73
10.9 Gen 2.7; 3.19; Isa 64.8
10.10 Ps 139.14–16
10.12 Job 33.4
10.14 Job 13.27; 9.28

u Another reading is *Would that there were*
v Cn Compare Gk Syr: Heb *made me together round about and thou dost destroy me*
w Gk: Heb *like clay*

and dost not acquit me of my iniquity.

10.15
Isa 3.11;
Job 9.12,15;
Ps 25.8

15 If I am wicked, woe to me!
    If I am righteous, I cannot lift up my head,
for I am filled with disgrace
    and look upon my affliction.

10.16
Isa 38.13;
Lam 3.10;
Job 5.9

16 And if I lift myself up,ˣ thou dost hunt me like a lion,
    and again work wonders against me;

10.17
Job 16.8;
7.1

17 thou dost renew thy witnesses against me,
    and increase thy vexation toward me;
    thou dost bring fresh hosts against me.ʸ

10.18
Job 3.11

18 "Why didst thou bring me forth from the womb?
    Would that I had died before any eye had seen me,
19 and were as though I had not been,
    carried from the womb to the grave.

10.20
Job 14.1;
7.16,19;
9.27

20 Are not the days of my life few?ᶻ
    Let me alone, that I may find a little comfortᵃ
21 before I go whence I shall not return,
    to the land of gloom and deep darkness,

10.21
Ps 88.12;
23.4

22 the land of gloomᵇ and chaos,
    where light is as darkness."

5. The speech of Zophar
a. He accuses Job of lying and hypocrisy

★11.1
11.2
Job 8.2

11 Then Zōphar the Nāʹámáthīte answered:
2 "Should a multitude of words go unanswered,
    and a man full of talk be vindicated?

11.3
Jas 3.5;
Job 17.2;
21.3

3 Should your babble silence men,
    and when you mock, shall no one shame you?

11.4
Job 6.10;
10.7

4 For you say, 'My doctrine is pure,
    and I am clean in God's eyes.'
5 But oh, that God would speak,
    and open his lips to you,

★11.6
Job 28.21;
Ezra 9.13

6 and that he would tell you the secrets of wisdom!
    For he is manifold in understanding.ᶜ
Know then that God exacts of you less than your guilt deserves.

b. He argues for God's sovereignty and infinity

11.7
Ecc 3.11;
Rom 11.33

7 "Can you find out the deep things of God?
    Can you find out the limit of the Almighty?

11.8
Job 22.12;
17.16

8 It is higher than heavenᵈ—what can you do?
    Deeper than Shēōl—what can you know?

11.10
Job 9.12;
Rev 3.7

9 Its measure is longer than the earth,
    and broader than the sea.
10 If he passes through, and imprisons,
    and calls to judgment, who can hinder him?

11.11
Job 34.21–
25;
Ps 10.14

11 For he knows worthless men;

---

x Syr: Heb *he lifts himself up*   y Cn Compare Gk: Heb *changes and a host are with me*
z Cn Compare Gk Syr: Heb *Are not my days few? Let him cease*   a Heb *brighten up*
b Heb *gloom as darkness, deep darkness*   c Heb *obscure*   d Heb *The heights of heaven*

11.1 Zophar repeats the same arguments of Bildad and Eliphaz. He thinks Job is a liar and a hypocrite and his evil plight is the just consequence of his sins.
11.6 *God exacts of you less than your guilt*

deserves. Zophar dogmatically insists that Job is a hypocrite who deserves more, not less, suffering. His appeal is neither to mysticism (Eliphaz) nor scholarship (Bildad), but to his own conviction of right and wrong.

when he sees iniquity, will he not consider it?
12 But a stupid man will get understanding,
   when a wild ass's colt is born a man.

c. *He assures Job of restoration upon repentance and reformation*

13 "If you set your heart aright,
   you will stretch out your hands toward him.
14 If iniquity is in your hand, put it far away,
   and let not wickedness dwell in your tents.
15 Surely then you will lift up your face without blemish;
   you will be secure, and will not fear.
16 You will forget your misery;
   you will remember it as waters that have passed away.
17 And your life will be brighter than the noonday;
   its darkness will be like the morning.
18 And you will have confidence, because there is hope;
   you will be protected*e* and take your rest in safety.
19 You will lie down, and none will make you afraid;
   many will entreat your favor.
20 But the eyes of the wicked will fail;
   all way of escape will be lost to them,
   and their hope is to breathe their last."

6. Job's reply to Zophar
a. Job denies the accusations

12 Then Jōb answered:
2 "No doubt you are the people,
   and wisdom will die with you.
3 But I have understanding as well as you;
   I am not inferior to you.
   Who does not know such things as these?
4 I am a laughingstock to my friends;
   I, who called upon God and he answered me,
   a just and blameless man, am a laughingstock.
5 In the thought of one who is at ease there is contempt for mis-
      fortune;
   it is ready for those whose feet slip.
6 The tents of robbers are at peace,
   and those who provoke God are secure,
   who bring their god in their hand.*f*

b. He argues that God is watching over all

7 "But ask the beasts, and they will teach you;
   the birds of the air, and they will tell you;
8 or the plants of the earth,*g* and they will teach you;
   and the fish of the sea will declare to you.
9 Who among all these does not know
   that the hand of the LORD has done this?
10 In his hand is the life of every living thing

---

e Or *you will look around*   *f* Hebrew uncertain   *g* Or *speak to the earth*

11.13
Ps 78.8;
88.9
11.14
Job 22.23;
Ps 101.3
11.15
1 Jn 3.21;
Ps 27.3
11.16
Isa 65.16;
Job 22.11
11.17
Ps 37.6;
112.4;
Isa 58.8,10
11.18
Ps 3.5;
Prov 3.24
11.19
ver 18
11.20
Deut 28.65;
Jer 15.9

★**12.2**

12.3
Job 13.2

12.4
Job 6.10,20;
21.3;
Ps 91.15;
Job 6.29
12.5
Ps 123.4

12.6
Job 9.24;
21.9; 22.18

★**12.7**

12.9
Isa 41.20
12.10
Acts 17.28;
Job 27.3;
33.4

12.2 *wisdom will die with you.* Job resorts to irony in conceding that his friends are the embodiment of wisdom. They "know it all" and when they are gone, wisdom will be dead also!

12.7 *But ask the beasts.* Although Job's friends profess wisdom, Job insists that they can learn from beast and bird.

and the breath of all mankind.

12.11
Job 34.3
11 Does not the ear try words
    as the palate tastes food?

12.12
Job 32.7
12 Wisdom is with the aged,
    and understanding in length of days.

c. *He enlarges on God's providences*

12.13
Job 9.4;
11.6
13 "With God[h] are wisdom and might;
    he has counsel and understanding.

12.14
Job 19.10;
37.7
14 If he tears down, none can rebuild;
    if he shuts a man in, none can open.

12.15
1 Ki 8.35;
Gen 7.11
15 If he withholds the waters, they dry up;
    if he sends them out, they overwhelm the land.

12.16
ver 13;
Job 13.7,9
16 With him are strength and wisdom;
    the deceived and the deceiver are his.

12.17
Job 3.14;
19.9; 9.24
17 He leads counselors away stripped,
    and judges he makes fools.

12.18
Ps 116.16
18 He looses the bonds of kings,
    and binds a waistcloth on their loins.

12.20
Job 32.9
19 He leads priests away stripped,
    and overthrows the mighty.

12.21
Ps 107.40;
ver 18
20 He deprives of speech those who are trusted,
    and takes away the discernment of the elders.

12.22
Dan 2.22;
1 Cor 4.5;
Job 3.5
21 He pours contempt on princes,
    and looses the belt of the strong.

12.23
Ps 107.38;
Isa 9.3;
Jer 25.9;
Deut 12.20;
Ps 78.61
22 He uncovers the deeps out of darkness,
    and brings deep darkness to light.

23 He makes nations great, and he destroys them:
    he enlarges nations, and leads them away.

12.24
ver 20;
Ps 107.40
24 He takes away understanding from the chiefs of the people of
        the earth,
    and makes them wander in a pathless waste.

12.25
Job 5.14;
Ps 107.27
25 They grope in the dark without light;
    and he makes them stagger like a drunken man.

d. *Job's resentment of his friends*

13.1
Job 12.9
13 "Lo, my eye has seen all this,
    my ear has heard and understood it.

13.2
Job 12.3
2 What you know, I also know;
    I am not inferior to you.

13.3
Job 23.3,4;
ver 15
3 But I would speak to the Almighty,
    and I desire to argue my case with God.

13.4
Ps 119.69;
Jer 23.32
4 As for you, you whitewash with lies;
    worthless physicians are you all.

13.5
Prov 17.28
5 Oh that you would keep silent,
    and it would be your wisdom!

6 Hear now my reasoning,
    and listen to the pleadings of my lips.

13.7
Job 36.4
7 Will you speak falsely for God,
    and speak deceitfully for him?

8 Will you show partiality toward him,
    will you plead the case for God?

13.9
Ps 44.21;
Gal 6.7
9 Will it be well with you when he searches you out?
    Or can you deceive him, as one deceives a man?

h Heb *him*

¹⁰ He will surely rebuke you
  if in secret you show partiality.
¹¹ Will not his majesty terrify you,
  and the dread of him fall upon you?
¹² Your maxims are proverbs of ashes,
  your defenses are defenses of clay.

e. Job's defense of his own integrity

¹³ "Let me have silence, and I will speak,
  and let come on me what may.
¹⁴ I will take*ⁱ* my flesh in my teeth,
  and put my life in my hand.
¹⁵ Behold, he will slay me; I have no hope;
  yet I will defend my ways to his face.
¹⁶ This will be my salvation,
  that a godless man shall not come before him.
¹⁷ Listen carefully to my words,
  and let my declaration be in your ears.
¹⁸ Behold, I have prepared my case;
  I know that I shall be vindicated.
¹⁹ Who is there that will contend with me?
  For then I would be silent and die.
²⁰ Only grant two things to me,
  then I will not hide myself from thy face:
²¹ withdraw thy hand far from me,
  and let not dread of thee terrify me.
²² Then call, and I will answer;
  or let me speak, and do thou reply to me.

f. Job asks for the number of his sins and complains of God's severe dealings

²³ How many are my iniquities and my sins?
  Make me know my transgression and my sin.
²⁴ Why dost thou hide thy face,
  and count me as thy enemy?
²⁵ Wilt thou frighten a driven leaf
  and pursue dry chaff?
²⁶ For thou writest bitter things against me,
  and makest me inherit the iniquities of my youth.
²⁷ Thou puttest my feet in the stocks,
  and watchest all my paths;
  thou settest a bound to the soles of my feet.
²⁸ Man*ʲ* wastes away like a rotten thing,
  like a garment that is moth-eaten.

g. Job speaks to God

14 "Man that is born of a woman
  is of few days, and full of trouble.
² He comes forth like a flower, and withers;
  he flees like a shadow, and continues not.

ⁱ Gk: Heb *Why should I take?* ʲ Heb *He*

13.19 Job here claims that he is righteous, guiltless of any such unconfessed sin as would warrant his present sufferings. Therefore he can only suppose that God is treating him capriciously and arbitrarily, and is at a loss to understand why.

14.3
Ps 144.3;
143.2
14.4
Ps 51.2,10;
Jn 3.6;
Rom 5.12;
Eph 2.3
*14.5
Ps 139.16;
Job 21.21;
Acts 17.26
14.6
Job 7.19;
7.1

14.9
Isa 55.10
14.10
Job 13.19
14.11
Isa 19.5
14.12
Ps 102.26;
Acts 3.21;
Rev 20.11;
21.1
14.13
Isa 26.20

14.14
Job 7.1

14.15
Job 13.22
14.16
Job 10.6;
31.4;
34.21;
Prov 5.21;
Jer 32.19
14.17
Deut 32.34;
Hos 13.12
14.18
Job 18.4
14.19
Job 7.6

*14.20
Job 34.20;
Jas 1.10
14.21
Ecc 9.5;
Isa 63.16

3 And dost thou open thy eyes upon such a one
   and bring him[k] into judgment with thee?
4 Who can bring a clean thing out of an unclean?
   There is not one.
5 Since his days are determined,
   and the number of his months is with thee,
   and thou hast appointed his bounds that he cannot pass,
6 look away from him, and desist,[l]
   that he may enjoy, like a hireling, his day.

7 "For there is hope for a tree,
   if it be cut down, that it will sprout again,
   and that its shoots will not cease.
8 Though its root grow old in the earth,
   and its stump die in the ground,
9 yet at the scent of water it will bud
   and put forth branches like a young plant.
10 But man dies, and is laid low;
   man breathes his last, and where is he?
11 As waters fail from a lake,
   and a river wastes away and dries up,
12 so man lies down and rises not again;
   till the heavens are no more he will not awake,
   or be roused out of his sleep.
13 Oh that thou wouldest hide me in Shēōl,
   that thou wouldest conceal me until thy wrath be past,
   that thou wouldest appoint me a set time, and remember me!
14 If a man die, shall he live again?
   All the days of my service I would wait,
   till my release should come.
15 Thou wouldest call, and I would answer thee;
   thou wouldest long for the work of thy hands.
16 For then thou wouldest number my steps,
   thou wouldest not keep watch over my sin;
17 my transgression would be sealed up in a bag,
   and thou wouldest cover over my iniquity.

18 "But the mountain falls and crumbles away,
   and the rock is removed from its place;
19 the waters wear away the stones;
   the torrents wash away the soil of the earth;
   so thou destroyest the hope of man.
20 Thou prevailest for ever against him, and he passes;
   thou changest his countenance, and sendest him away.
21 His sons come to honor, and he does not know it;
   they are brought low, and he perceives it not.
22 He feels only the pain of his own body,
   and he mourns only for himself."

k Gk Syr Vg: Heb me   l Cn: Heb that he may desist

14.5 Man's days: (1) are numbered, not
numberless; (2) are set by the will of God who
has determined how long he shall live and
when he shall die; (3) cannot be increased or
diminished.

14.20 Thou prevailest for ever against him.
Man is an unequal match against God, and he
cannot hope to defeat the divine purposes.

C. The second cycle of speeches

1. Eliphaz's second speech

a. Job's own words condemn him

15 ¹ Then Ĕl′ĭphăz the Tē′mănīte answered:
² "Should a wise man answer with windy knowledge,
and fill himself with the east wind?
³ Should he argue in unprofitable talk,
or in words with which he can do no good?
⁴ But you are doing away with the fear of God,
and hindering meditation before God.
⁵ For your iniquity teaches your mouth,
and you choose the tongue of the crafty.
⁶ Your own mouth condemns you, and not I;
your own lips testify against you.

b. Job is deluding himself

⁷ "Are you the first man that was born?
Or were you brought forth before the hills?
⁸ Have you listened in the council of God?
And do you limit wisdom to yourself?
⁹ What do you know that we do not know?
What do you understand that is not clear to us?
¹⁰ Both the gray-haired and the aged are among us,
older than your father.
¹¹ Are the consolations of God too small for you,
or the word that deals gently with you?

c. Job is condemned before God

¹² Why does your heart carry you away,
and why do your eyes flash,
¹³ that you turn your spirit against God,
and let such words go out of your mouth?
¹⁴ What is man, that he can be clean?
Or he that is born of a woman, that he can be righteous?
¹⁵ Behold, God puts no trust in his holy ones,
and the heavens are not clean in his sight;
¹⁶ how much less one who is abominable and corrupt,
a man who drinks iniquity like water!

d. The end of an evil man

¹⁷ "I will show you, hear me;
and what I have seen I will declare
¹⁸ (what wise men have told,
and their fathers have not hidden,
¹⁹ to whom alone the land was given,

15.1 Eliphaz (ch 15), Bildad (ch 18) and Zophar (ch 20) paint vivid pictures of the terrors which befall the wicked in this life. They cannot answer Job's rebuttals, for the stubborn fact remains that experience simply does not bear out their dogma that the wicked receive their just retribution in this life, and that no injustice ever befalls those who are righteous. In chapters 27 and 28 Job himself speaks of God's ultimate justice out-side this present visible world. In 29–31 he complains that God deals capriciously with the world at present.

15.2 Should a wise man answer with windy knowledge . . . ? Eliphaz begins the second round of speeches on a more hostile note than his earlier address. Job's friends are angered that Job will not accept their counsel, and their words contain threats as well as rebukes for this terribly tormented man.

Cross references (margin):
★15.1
★15.2
Job 6.26

15.5
Ps 36.3;
Prov 16.23;
Job 5.12,13

15.6
Job 9.20;
Lk 19.22

15.7
Job 38.4,21;
Ps 90.2;
Prov 8.25

15.8
Rom 11.34;
Job 12.2

15.9
Job 13.2

15.10
Job 32.6,7

15.11
Job 36.15,
16;
2 Cor 1.3,4;
Zech 1.13

15.13
Job 33.13

15.14
Job 14.4;
Prov 20.9;
Ecc 7.20;
Job 25.4;
Ps 51.5

15.15
Job 4.18;
25.5

15.16
Ps 14.1,3;
Job 34.7

15.18
Job 8.8

and no stranger passed among them).

20 The wicked man writhes in pain all his days,
  through all the years that are laid up for the ruthless.

21 Terrifying sounds are in his ears;
  in prosperity the destroyer will come upon him.

22 He does not believe that he will return out of darkness,
  and he is destined for the sword.

23 He wanders abroad for bread, saying, 'Where is it?'
  He knows that a day of darkness is ready at his hand;
24 distress and anguish terrify him;
  they prevail against him, like a king prepared for battle.

25 Because he has stretched forth his hand against God,
  and bids defiance to the Almighty,
26 running stubbornly against him
  with a thick-bossed shield;

27 because he has covered his face with his fat,
  and gathered fat upon his loins,
28 and has lived in desolate cities,
  in houses which no man should inhabit,
  which were destined to become heaps of ruins;

29 he will not be rich, and his wealth will not endure,
  nor will he strike root in the earth;m

30 he will not escape from darkness;
  the flame will dry up his shoots,
  and his blossomn will be swept awayo by the wind.

31 Let him not trust in emptiness, deceiving himself;
  for emptiness will be his recompense.

32 It will be paid in full before his time,
  and his branch will not be green.

33 He will shake off his unripe grape, like the vine,
  and cast off his blossom, like the olive tree.

34 For the company of the godless is barren,
  and fire consumes the tents of bribery.

35 They conceive mischief and bring forth evil
  and their heart prepares deceit."

2. Job's second reply to Eliphaz
a. He charges his friends with unkindness

16 Then Jōb answered:

2 "I have heard many such things;
  miserable comforters are you all.

3 Shall windy words have an end?
  Or what provokes you that you answer?

4 I also could speak as you do,
  if you were in my place;
  I could join words together against you,
  and shake my head at you.
5 I could strengthen you with my mouth,
  and the solace of my lips would assuage your pain.

m Vg: Heb obscure   n Gk: Heb mouth   o Cn: Heb will depart

15.20 The wicked man. Here Eliphaz refers
to Job, supposing that he (Job) will see himself in this description.

16.2 miserable comforters are you all expresses Job's opinion of those who professed
to be friends but acted like enemies.

b. *He alleges that God is angry with him*

6 "If I speak, my pain is not assuaged,
　and if I forbear, how much of it leaves me?
7 Surely now God has worn me out;
　he has[p] made desolate all my company.
8 And he has[p] shriveled me up,
　which is a witness against me;
and my leanness has risen up against me,
　it testifies to my face.
9 He has torn me in his wrath, and hated me;
　he has gnashed his teeth at me;
　my adversary sharpens his eyes against me.
10 Men have gaped at me with their mouth,
　they have struck me insolently upon the cheek,
　they mass themselves together against me.
11 God gives me up to the ungodly,
　and casts me into the hands of the wicked.
12 I was at ease, and he broke me asunder;
　he seized me by the neck and dashed me to pieces;
　he set me up as his target,
13 　his archers surround me.
He slashes open my kidneys, and does not spare;
　he pours out my gall on the ground.
14 He breaks me with breach upon breach;
　he runs upon me like a warrior.
15 I have sewed sackcloth upon my skin,
　and have laid my strength in the dust.
16 My face is red with weeping,
　and on my eyelids is deep darkness;
17 although there is no violence in my hands,
　and my prayer is pure.

c. *His conscience is clear*

18 "O earth, cover not my blood,
　and let my cry find no resting place.
19 Even now, behold, my witness is in heaven,
　and he that vouches for me is on high.
20 My friends scorn me;
　my eye pours out tears to God,
21 that he would maintain the right of a man with God,
　like[q] that of a man with his neighbor.
22 For when a few years have come
　I shall go the way whence I shall not return.

d. *Job's appeal to God against the verdict of his friends*

17 My spirit is broken, my days are extinct,
　the grave is ready for me.
2 Surely there are mockers about me,
　and my eye dwells on their provocation.

3 "Lay down a pledge for me with thyself;
　who is there that will give surety for me?
4 Since thou hast closed their minds to understanding,

---

p Heb *thou hast*　　*q* Syr Vg Tg: Heb *and*

Marginal references

16.7　Job 7.3; ver 20
16.8　Job 10.17; 19.20
16.9　Ps 35.16; Job 13.24
16.10　Ps 22.13; Lam 3.30; Mic 5.1; Ps 35.15
16.11　Job 1.15,17
16.12　Job 9.17
16.13　Job 19.12; 27.22; 20.25
16.14　Job 9.17; Joel 2.7
16.15　Gen 37.34; Job 30.19
16.16　ver 20
16.17　Job 27.4
16.18　Isa 26.21; Ps 66.18,19
16.19　Rom 1.9
16.20　ver 7; Lam 2.19
16.21　1 Ki 8.45; Ps 9.4
16.22　Ecc 12.5
17.1　Ps 88.3,4
17.2　ver 6; 1 Sam 1.6,7
17.3　Ps 119.122; Prov 6.1
17.4　Job 12.20

therefore thou wilt not let them triumph.

5 He who informs against his friends to get a share of their
     property,
    the eyes of his children will fail.

6 "He has made me a byword of the peoples,
    and I am one before whom men spit.
7 My eye has grown dim from grief,
    and all my members are like a shadow.
8 Upright men are appalled at this,
    and the innocent stirs himself up against the godless.
9 Yet the righteous holds to his way,
    and he that has clean hands grows stronger and stronger.
10 But you, come on again, all of you,
    and I shall not find a wise man among you.
11 My days are past, my plans are broken off,
    the desires of my heart.
12 They make night into day,
    'The light,' they say, 'is near to the darkness.'ʳ
13 If I look for Shēōl as my house,
    if I spread my couch in darkness,
14 if I say to the pit, 'You are my father,'
    and to the worm, 'My mother,' or 'My sister,'
15 where then is my hope?
    Who will see my hope?
16 Will it go down to the bars of Shēōl?
    Shall we descend together into the dust?"

3. *Bildad's second speech*
a. *He reproves Job as haughty and obstinate*

18 Then Bĭldăd the Shuhīte answered:
2 "How long will you hunt for words?
Consider, and then we will speak.
3 Why are we counted as cattle?
    Why are we stupid in your sight?
4 You who tear yourself in your anger,
    shall the earth be forsaken for you,
    or the rock be removed out of its place?

b. *He describes the misery and ruin of the wicked*

5 "Yea, the light of the wicked is put out,
    and the flame of his fire does not shine.
6 The light is dark in his tent,
    and his lamp above him is put out.
7 His strong steps are shortened
    and his own schemes throw him down.
8 For he is cast into a net by his own feet,
    and he walks on a pitfall.
9 A trap seizes him by the heel,
    a snare lays hold of him.
10 A rope is hid for him in the ground,
    a trap for him in the path.
11 Terrors frighten him on every side,
    and chase him at his heels.

r Heb obscure

17.5
Lev 19.16;
Job 11.20

17.6
Job 30.9,10

17.7
Job 16.16;
16.8

17.8
Job 22.19

17.9
Prov 4.18;
Job 22.30

17.10
Job 12.2

17.11
Job 7.6

17.13
Job 3.13

17.14
Ps 16.10;
Job 21.26;
24.20

17.15
Job 7.6

17.16
Jon 2.6;
Job 3.17–
19

18.3
Ps 73.22;
Job 36.14

18.4
Job 13.14;
14.18

18.5
Prov 13.9;
20.20;
24.20

18.7
Prov 4.12;
Job 5.13

18.8
Job 22.10;
Ps 9.15;
35.8

18.9
Ps 140.5;
Job 5.5

18.10
Ps 69.22

18.11
Job 15.21;
Jer 6.25;
20.3

12 His strength is hunger-bitten,
    and calamity is ready for his stumbling.
13 By disease his skin is consumed,[s]
    the first-born of death consumes his limbs.
14 He is torn from the tent in which he trusted,
    and is brought to the king of terrors.
15 In his tent dwells that which is none of his;
    brimstone is scattered upon his habitation.
16 His roots dry up beneath,
    and his branches wither above.
17 His memory perishes from the earth,
    and he has no name in the street.
18 He is thrust from light into darkness,
    and driven out of the world.
19 He has no offspring or descendant among his people,
    and no survivor where he used to live.
20 They of the west are appalled at his day,
    and horror seizes them of the east.
21 Surely such are the dwellings of the ungodly,
    such is the place of him who knows not God."

4. Job's second reply to Bildad
a. Job reproves his friends

19   Then Jōb answered:
   2 "How long will you torment me,
    and break me in pieces with words?
3 These ten times you have cast reproach upon me;
    are you not ashamed to wrong me?
4 And even if it be true that I have erred,
    my error remains with myself.
5 If indeed you magnify yourselves against me,
    and make my humiliation an argument against me,
6 know then that God has put me in the wrong,
    and closed his net about me.
7 Behold, I cry out, 'Violence!' but I am not answered;
    I call aloud, but there is no justice.

b. God the author of his afflictions

8 He has walled up my way, so that I cannot pass,
    and he has set darkness upon my paths.
9 He has stripped from me my glory,
    and taken the crown from my head.
10 He breaks me down on every side, and I am gone,
    and my hope has he pulled up like a tree.
11 He has kindled his wrath against me,
    and counts me as his adversary.
12 His troops come on together;
    they have cast up siegeworks[t] against me,
    and encamp round about my tent.

c. He is deserted of men

13 "He has put my brethren far from me,
    and my acquaintances are wholly estranged from me.
14 My kinsfolk and my close friends have failed me;

[s] Cn: Heb it consumes the limbs of his skin   [t] Heb their way

---

18.12
Isa 8.21

18.14
Job 8.22;
15.21

18.15
Ps 11.6

18.16
Isa 5.24;
Hos 9.1–16;
Amos 2.9;
Mal 4.1;
Job 15.30,
32

18.17
Ps 34.16;
Prov 2.22;
10.7

18.18
Job 5.14;
27.21–23

18.19
Isa 14.22;
Jer 22.30

18.21
Jer 9.3;
1 Thess 4.5

19.4
Job 6.24

19.5
Ps 35.26;
38.16

19.6
Job 27.2;
18.8–10

19.7
Job 30.20

19.8
Job 3.23;
30.26

19.9
Ps 89.44;
89.39

19.10
Job 12.14;
7.6; 24.20

19.11
Job 16.9;
13.24

19.12
Job 30.12

19.14
ver 19

19.15
Gen 14.14;
Ecc 2.7

15 the guests in my house have forgotten me;
    my maidservants count me as a stranger;
      I have become an alien in their eyes.
16 I call to my servant, but he gives me no answer;
    I must beseech him with my mouth.
17 I am repulsive to my wife,
    loathsome to the sons of my own mother.

19.18
2 Ki 2.23

18 Even young children despise me;
    when I rise they talk against me.

19.19
Ps 38.11;
55.13

19 All my intimate friends abhor me,
    and those whom I loved have turned against me.

d. *His plea for pity*

19.20
Job 33.21;
Ps 102.5

20 My bones cleave to my skin and to my flesh,
    and I have escaped by the skin of my teeth.

19.21
Job 6.14;
Ps 38.2

21 Have pity on me, have pity on me, O you my friends,
    for the hand of God has touched me!

19.22
Job 16.11

22 Why do you, like God, pursue me?
    Why are you not satisfied with my flesh?

19.23
Isa 30.8

23 "Oh that my words were written!
    Oh that they were inscribed in a book!

19.24
Jer 17.1

24 Oh that with an iron pen and lead
    they were graven in the rock for ever!

e. *His unshakable confidence in the living Redeemer*

*19.25
Job 16.19;
Ps 78.35;
Isa 43.14;
Jer 50.34

25 For I know that my Redeemer^u lives,
    and at last he will stand upon the earth;^{v}
26 and after my skin has been thus destroyed,
    then from^w my flesh I shall see God,^{x}

*19.26
Mt 5.8;
1 Cor
13.12;
1 Jn 3.2

27 whom I shall see on my side,^{y}
    and my eyes shall behold, and not another.
    My heart faints within me!

19.27
Ps 73.26

28 If you say, 'How we will pursue him!'
    and, 'The root of the matter is found in him';

19.28
Ps 69.26

29 be afraid of the sword,
    for wrath brings the punishment of the sword,
    that you may know there is a judgment."

19.29
Job 22.4

^{u} Or *Vindicator* ^{v} Or *dust* ^{w} Or *without*
^{x} The meaning of this verse is uncertain ^{y} Or *for myself*

19.25 *I know that my Redeemer lives.* As Job's friends had been unable to convince him of his guilt, so he was unable to convince them of his innocence. In the agony of the hour, however, Job gave expression to the great assurance that God was his vindicator (or Redeemer).

19.26 The doctrine of the resurrection is latent in the Old Testament and clearly revealed in the New Testament teaching. Old Testament references include Ps 16.10, 49.15, Isa 26.19, Dan 12.2, and Hos 13.14. In Apostolic times the Jews in general expected a resurrection of the body (Jn 11.24; Heb 6.1, 2). While it was denied by the Sadducees it was basic in the thinking of the Pharisees (Acts 23.6–8). Jesus taught and accepted the bodily resurrection as an indisputable fact (Mt 22.29–32; Lk 14.14; Jn 5.28, 29). His Apostles preached it constantly (Acts 4.2; 17.18; 24.15). Believers embrace the truth of a resurrection with hope and look forward to it with anticipation (Dan 12.13; Phil 3.11; 2 Cor 5.1). The credibility of a resurrection is attested to by the Resurrection of Christ Himself and of others (Mt 9.25; Lk 7.14; Jn 11.44; Heb 11.35). It should be noted that *from my flesh I shall see God* is a better translation of the Hebrew here than the rendering in the footnote (w), and it makes the doctrine of the resurrection of the body more explicit. But even if we construe it as *without my flesh* (which is not linguistically legitimate), the following verse, *my eyes shall behold*, makes mention of the possession and use of a body after death.

*5. Zophar's second discourse: the misery and ruin
which await the wicked*

20 Then Zōphar the Nā′ámáthīte answered:
2 "Therefore my thoughts answer me,
because of my haste within me.
3 I hear censure which insults me,
and out of my understanding a spirit answers me.
4 Do you not know this from of old,
since man was placed upon earth,
5 that the exulting of the wicked is short,
and the joy of the godless but for a moment?
6 Though his height mount up to the heavens,
and his head reach to the clouds,
7 he will perish for ever like his own dung;
those who have seen him will say, 'Where is he?'
8 He will fly away like a dream, and not be found;
he will be chased away like a vision of the night.
9 The eye which saw him will see him no more,
nor will his place any more behold him.
10 His children will seek the favor of the poor,
and his hands will give back his wealth.
11 His bones are full of youthful vigor,
but it will lie down with him in the dust.

12 "Though wickedness is sweet in his mouth,
though he hides it under his tongue,
13 though he is loath to let it go,
and holds it in his mouth,
14 yet his food is turned in his stomach;
it is the gall of asps within him.
15 He swallows down riches and vomits them up again;
God casts them out of his belly.
16 He will suck the poison of asps;
the tongue of a viper will kill him.
17 He will not look upon the rivers,
the streams flowing with honey and curds.
18 He will give back the fruit of his toil,
and will not swallow it down;
from the profit of his trading
he will get no enjoyment.
19 For he has crushed and abandoned the poor,
he has seized a house which he did not build.

20 "Because his greed knew no rest,
he will not save anything in which he delights.
21 There was nothing left after he had eaten;
therefore his prosperity will not endure.
22 In the fulness of his sufficiency he will be in straits;
all the force of misery will come upon him.
23 To fill his belly to the full
God z will send his fierce anger into him,
and rain it upon him as his food. a

z Heb *he*   a Cn: Heb *in his flesh*

Cross-references: 20.3 Job 19.3; 20.4 Deut 4.32; 20.5 Ps 37.35; 73.19; 20.6 Isa 14.13,14; Obad 3,4; 20.7 Job 4.20; 7.10; 8.18; 20.8 Ps 73.20; 90.5; Job 18.18; 27.21–23; 20.9 Job 7.8,10; 20.10 Job 5.4; 27.16,17; 20.11 Job 13.26; 21.26; 20.12 Prov 20.17; Ps 10.7; 20.16 Deut 32.24,33; 20.17 Job 29.6; Deut 32.13,14; 20.18 ver 10,15; 20.19 Job 24.2–4; 35.9; 20.20 Ecc 5.13,14; 20.21 Job 15.29; 20.23 Ps 78.30,31

20.24 Isa 24.18; Jer 48.43; Amos 5.19	24 He will flee from an iron weapon; a bronze arrow will strike him through.

20.25
Job 16.13;
18.11
	25 It is drawn forth and comes out of his body,
	   the glittering point comes out of his gall;
	   terrors come upon him.

20.26
Job 18.18;
Ps 21.9
	26 Utter darkness is laid up for his treasures;
	   a fire not blown upon will devour him;
	   what is left in his tent will be consumed.

20.27 Deut 31.28	27 The heavens will reveal his iniquity, and the earth will rise up against him.
20.28 Deut 28.31; Job 21.30	28 The possessions of his house will be carried away, dragged off in the day of God's*b* wrath.
20.29 Job 27.13	29 This is the wicked man's portion from God, the heritage decreed for him by God."

6. Job's second reply to Zophar
a. He pleads to speak without interruption

21 Then Jōb answered:
2 "Listen carefully to my words,
   and let this be your consolation.

21.3 Job 16.10	3 Bear with me, and I will speak, and after I have spoken, mock on.
21.4 Job 6.11	4 As for me, is my complaint against man? Why should I not be impatient?

21.5
Judg 18.19;
Job 29.9;
40.4
	5 Look at me, and be appalled,
	   and lay your hand upon your mouth.
	6 When I think of it I am dismayed,
	   and shuddering seizes my flesh.

b. The wicked often prosper in this life

21.7 Job 12.6; Ps 73.3,12; Jer 12.1	7 Why do the wicked live, reach old age, and grow mighty in power?
21.8 Ps 17.14	8 Their children are established in their presence, and their offspring before their eyes.
21.9 Ps 73.5	9 Their houses are safe from fear, and no rod of God is upon them.

21.10
Ex 23.26
	10 Their bull breeds without fail;
	   their cow calves, and does not cast her calf.
	11 They send forth their little ones like a flock,
	   and their children dance.

21.12 Ps 81.2; Job 30.31	12 They sing to the tambourine and the lyre, and rejoice to the sound of the pipe.
21.13 Job 36.11	13 They spend their days in prosperity, and in peace they go down to Shēōl.
21.14 Job 22.17; Prov 1.29	14 They say to God, 'Depart from us! We do not desire the knowledge of thy ways.
21.15 Ex 5.2; Job 34.9; Mal 3.14	15 What is the Almighty, that we should serve him? And what profit do we get if we pray to him?'
21.16 Job 22.18	16 Behold, is not their prosperity in their hand? The counsel of the wicked is far from me.

c. A sovereign God does as He pleases
with righteous and wicked alike

21.17 Job 18.5,6, 12	17 "How often is it that the lamp of the wicked is put out?

b Heb *his*

That their calamity comes upon them?
That God^c distributes pains in his anger?

¹⁸ That they are like straw before the wind,
and like chaff that the storm carries away?

21.18
Ps 1.4

¹⁹ You say, 'God stores up their iniquity for their sons.'
Let him recompense it to themselves, that they may know it.

21.19
Ex 20.5

²⁰ Let their own eyes see their destruction,
and let them drink of the wrath of the Almighty.

21.20
Ps 75.8;
Isa 51.17;
Jer 25.15;
Rev 14.10

²¹ For what do they care for their houses after them,
when the number of their months is cut off?

21.21
Job 14.5

²² Will any teach God knowledge,
seeing that he judges those that are on high?

21.22
Isa 40.13,
14;
Rom 11.34

²³ One dies in full prosperity,
being wholly at ease and secure,

²⁴ his body^d full of fat
and the marrow of his bones moist.

²⁵ Another dies in bitterness of soul,
never having tasted of good.

²⁶ They lie down alike in the dust,
and the worms cover them.

21.26
Ecc 9.2;
Job 24.20

d. *Job admits that his friends will not agree with him*

²⁷ "Behold, I know your thoughts,
and your schemes to wrong me.

²⁸ For you say, "Where is the house of the prince?
Where is the tent in which the wicked dwelt?'

21.28
Job 12.21;
8.22

²⁹ Have you not asked those who travel the roads,
and do you not accept their testimony

³⁰ that the wicked man is spared in the day of calamity,
that he is rescued in the day of wrath?

21.30
Prov 16.4;
2 Pet 2.9;
Job 20.28;
Rom 2.5

³¹ Who declares his way to his face,
and who requites him for what he has done?

³² When he is borne to the grave,
watch is kept over his tomb.

³³ The clods of the valley are sweet to him;
all men follow after him,
and those who go before him are innumerable.

21.33
Job 3.22;
17.16;
3.19; 24.24

³⁴ How then will you comfort me with empty nothings?
There is nothing left of your answers but falsehood."

21.34
Job 16.2

D. The third cycle of speeches

1. *Eliphaz's third speech*
a. *He charges that Job has accused God of unjustness*

22 Then Ĕl'ĭphăz the Tē'mánīte answered:
² "Can a man be profitable to God?
Surely he who is wise is profitable to himself.

22.2
Lk 17.10

³ Is it any pleasure to the Almighty if you are righteous,
or is it gain to him if you make your ways blameless?

⁴ Is it for your fear of him that he reproves you,
and enters into judgment with you?

22.4
Job 14.3;
Ps 143.2

⁵ Is not your wickedness great?
There is no end to your iniquities.

22.5
Job 11.6;
15.5

---

^c Heb *he*   ^d The meaning of the Hebrew word is uncertain

b. *He catalogs Job's sins*

6 For you have exacted pledges of your brothers for nothing,
    and stripped the naked of their clothing.
7 You have given no water to the weary to drink,
    and you have withheld bread from the hungry.
8 The man with power possessed the land,
    and the favored man dwelt in it.
9 You have sent widows away empty,
    and the arms of the fatherless were crushed.
10 Therefore snares are round about you,
    and sudden terror overwhelms you;
11 your light is darkened, so that*e* you cannot see,
    and a flood of water covers you.

12 "Is not God high in the heavens?
    See the highest stars, how lofty they are!
13 Therefore you say, 'What does God know?
    Can he judge through the deep darkness?
14 Thick clouds enwrap him, so that he does not see,
    and he walks on the vault of heaven.'

c. *He would awaken Job to repentance*

15 Will you keep to the old way
    which wicked men have trod?
16 They were snatched away before their time;
    their foundation was washed away.
17 They said to God, 'Depart from us,'
    and 'What can the Almighty do to us?'*f*
18 Yet he filled their houses with good things—
    but the counsel of the wicked is far from me.
19 The righteous see it and are glad;
    the innocent laugh them to scorn,
20 saying, 'Surely our adversaries are cut off,
    and what they left the fire has consumed.'

d. *He urges Job to repent and be restored*

21 "Agree with God, and be at peace;
    thereby good will come to you.
22 Receive instruction from his mouth,
    and lay up his words in your heart.
23 If you return to the Almighty and humble yourself,*g*
    if you remove unrighteousness far from your tents,
24 if you lay gold in the dust,
    and gold of Ōphir among the stones of the torrent bed,
25 and if the Almighty is your gold,
    and your precious silver;
26 then you will delight yourself in the Almighty,
    and lift up your face to God.
27 You will make your prayer to him, and he will hear you;
    and you will pay your vows.
28 You will decide on a matter, and it will be established for you,
    and light will shine on your ways.
29 For God abases the proud,*h*
    but he saves the lowly.

---

e Cn Compare Gk: Heb *or darkness* *f* Gk Syr: Heb *them*
g Gk: Heb *you will be built up* *h* Cn: Heb *when they abased you said, Proud*

Cross references (margin):
22.6 Ex 22.26; Deut 24.6, 17; Ezek 18.12, 16
22.7 Mt 10.42; Job 31.31
22.9 Job 24.3; Isa 10.2
22.11 Job 5.14; Ps 69.2
22.12 Job 11.7–9
22.13 Ps 10.11
22.14 Job 26.9
22.16 Job 15.32; 14.19; Mt 7.26,27
22.18 Job 12.6; 21.16
22.19 Ps 58.10; 107.42
22.20 Ps 18.39; Job 15.30
22.21 Jer 9.24; Gal 4.9
22.22 Ps 138.4
22.23 Job 8.5; Isa 19.22; Acts 20.32; Job 11.14
22.24 Ps 19.10
22.25 Isa 33.6; Mt 6.20
22.26 Job 27.10; Isa 58.14
22.27 Job 33.26; Isa 58.9; Job 34.28; Ps 22.25
22.28 Ps 145.19
22.29 Prov 29.23; Mt 23.12; 1 Pet 5.5

30 He delivers the innocent man;*i*
    you will be delivered through the cleanness of your hands."

2. *Job's third reply to Eliphaz*
a. *He would find God and be tried of Him*

23 Then Jōb answered:
2 "Today also my complaint is bitter,*j*
    his*k* hand is heavy in spite of my groaning.
3 Oh, that I knew where I might find him,
    that I might come even to his seat!
4 I would lay my case before him
    and fill my mouth with arguments.
5 I would learn what he would answer me,
    and understand what he would say to me.
6 Would he contend with me in the greatness of his power?
    No; he would give heed to me.
7 There an upright man could reason with him,
    and I should be acquitted for ever by my judge.

8 "Behold, I go forward, but he is not there;
    and backward, but I cannot perceive him;
9 on the left hand I seek him,*l* but I cannot behold him;
    I*m* turn to the right hand, but I cannot see him.
10 But he knows the way that I take;
    when he has tried me, I shall come forth as gold.
11 My foot has held fast to his steps;
    I have kept his way and have not turned aside.
12 I have not departed from the commandment of his lips;
    I have treasured in*n* my bosom the words of his mouth.
13 But he is unchangeable and who can turn him?
    What he desires, that he does.
14 For he will complete what he appoints for me;
    and many such things are in his mind.
15 Therefore I am terrified at his presence;
    when I consider, I am in dread of him.
16 God has made my heart faint;
    the Almighty has terrified me;
17 for I am*o* hemmed in by darkness,
    and thick darkness covers my face.*p*

23.2
Job 7.11;
6.2,3
23.3
Deut 4.29;
Ps 9.4
23.4
Job 13.18

23.6
Job 9.4
23.7
Job 13.3,16

23.8
Job 9.11

23.10
Ps 139.1–3
23.11
Ps 44.18
23.12
Jn 4.32,34
23.13
Job 9.12;
12.14;
Ps 115.3
23.14
1 Thess 3.3

23.16
Ps 22.14;
Jer 51.46
23.17
Job 10.18,
19; 19.8

b. *The punishment of the wicked is not always seen*

24 "Why are not times of judgment kept by the Almighty,
    and why do those who know him never see his days?
2 Men remove landmarks;
    they seize flocks and pasture them.
3 They drive away the ass of the fatherless;
    they take the widow's ox for a pledge.
4 They thrust the poor off the road;
    the poor of the earth all hide themselves.
5 Behold, like wild asses in the desert
    they go forth to their toil,

24.1
Ps 31.15;
Jer 46.10
24.2
Deut 19.14;
27.17;
28.31
24.3
Ex 22.26;
Deut 24.6,
10,12,17;
Job 22.6
24.4
Deut 24.14;
Prov 28.28
24.5
Job 39.5–8;
Ps 104.23

---

i Gk Syr Vg: Heb *him that is not innocent*
j Syr Vg Tg: Heb *rebellious*   *k* Gk Syr: Heb *my*
l Compare Syr: Heb *on the left hand when he works*   *m* Syr Vg: Heb *he*
n Gk Vg: Heb *from*   *o* With one Ms: Heb *am not*   *p* Vg: Heb *from my face*

Job 24.6–25

as food^q for their children.

6 They gather their^r fodder in the field
and they glean the vineyard of the wicked man.

7 They lie all night naked, without clothing,
and have no covering in the cold.

8 They are wet with the rain of the mountains,
and cling to the rock for want of shelter.

9 (There are those who snatch the fatherless child from the breast,
and take in pledge the infant of the poor.)

10 They go about naked, without clothing;
hungry, they carry the sheaves;

11 among the olive rows of the wicked^s they make oil;
they tread the wine presses, but suffer thirst.

12 From out of the city the dying groan,
and the soul of the wounded cries for help;
yet God pays no attention to their prayer.

13 "There are those who rebel against the light,
who are not acquainted with its ways,
and do not stay in its paths.

14 The murderer rises in the dark,^{t}
that he may kill the poor and needy;
and in the night he is as a thief.

15 The eye of the adulterer also waits for the twilight,
saying, 'No eye will see me';
and he disguises his face.

16 In the dark they dig through houses;
by day they shut themselves up;
they do not know the light.

17 For deep darkness is morning to all of them;
for they are friends with the terrors of deep darkness.

18 "You say, 'They are swiftly carried away upon the face of the
waters;
their portion is cursed in the land;
no treader turns toward their vineyards.

19 Drought and heat snatch away the snow waters;
so does Sheōl those who have sinned.

20 The squares of the town^u forget them;
their name^v is no longer remembered;
so wickedness is broken like a tree.'

21 "They feed on the barren childless woman,
and do no good to the widow.

22 Yet God^w prolongs the life of the mighty by his power;
they rise up when they despair of life.

23 He gives them security, and they are supported;
and his eyes are upon their ways.

24 They are exalted a little while, and then are gone;
they wither and fade like the mallow;^{x}
they are cut off like the heads of grain.

25 If it is not so, who will prove me a liar,

---

^{q} Heb *food to him* ^{r} Heb *his* ^{s} Heb *their olive rows* ^{t} Cn: Heb *at the light*
^{u} Cn: Heb obscure ^{v} Cn: Heb *a worm* ^{w} Heb *he* ^{x} Gk: Heb *all*

Cross references (margin):
24.7 Ex 22.26; Job 22.6 · 24.8 Lam 4.5 · 24.9 Deut 24.17 · 24.12 Jer 51.52; Ezek 26.15; Job 9.23,24 · 24.13 Isa 5.20; Jn 3.19 · 24.14 Mic 2.1; Ps 10.8 · 24.15 Prov 7.9; Ps 10.11 · 24.16 Ex 22.2 · 24.17 Ps 91.5 · 24.18 Job 9.26; Ps 90.5 · 24.19 Job 6.16,17; 21.13 · 24.20 Ps 31.12; Prov 10.7 · 24.21 Job 22.9 · 24.22 Deut 28.66 · 24.23 Job 12.6; 11.11 · 24.24 Ps 37.10; Job 14.21; Isa 17.5 · 24.25 Job 6.28; 27.4

746

and show that there is nothing in what I say?"

3. Bildad's third speech: no one is righteous before God

25 Then Bildăd the Shuhīte answered:
² "Dominion and fear are with God;*y*
he makes peace in his high heaven.
³ Is there any number to his armies?
Upon whom does his light not arise?
⁴ How then can man be righteous before God?
How can he who is born of woman be clean?
⁵ Behold, even the moon is not bright
and the stars are not clean in his sight;
⁶ how much less man, who is a maggot,
and the son of man, who is a worm!"

4. Job's third reply to Bildad:
he knows the greatness and majesty of God

26 Then Jōb answered:
² "How you have helped him who has no power!
How you have saved the arm that has no strength!
³ How you have counseled him who has no wisdom,
and plentifully declared sound knowledge!
⁴ With whose help have you uttered words,
and whose spirit has come forth from you?
⁵ The shades below tremble,
the waters and their inhabitants.
⁶ Shēōl is naked before God,
and Ăbăd′dŏn has no covering.
⁷ He stretches out the north over the void,
and hangs the earth upon nothing.
⁸ He binds up the waters in his thick clouds,
and the cloud is not rent under them.
⁹ He covers the face of the moon,*z*
and spreads over it his cloud.
¹⁰ He has described a circle upon the face of the waters
at the boundary between light and darkness.
¹¹ The pillars of heaven tremble,
and are astounded at his rebuke.
¹² By his power he stilled the sea;
by his understanding he smote Rāhăb.
¹³ By his wind the heavens were made fair;
his hand pierced the fleeing serpent.
¹⁴ Lo, these are but the outskirts of his ways;
and how small a whisper do we hear of him!
But the thunder of his power who can understand?"

5. Job's last reply to his friends
a. He avers that he speaks the truth

27 And Jōb again took up his discourse, and said:
² "As God lives, who has taken away my right,

y Heb *him*   *z* Or *his throne*

Marginal references:
25.2 Job 9.4; Rev 1.6; Job 22.12
25.3 Jas 1.17
25.4 Job 4.17; Ps 143.2; Job 14.4
25.5 Job 31.26; 15.15
25.6 Job 7.17; Ps 22.6
26.2 Ps 71.9
*26.6 Ps 139.8,11; Heb 4.13
26.7 Job 9.8
26.8 Prov 30.4
26.9 Ps 97.2
26.10 Job 38.8–11; Prov 8.29; Job 38.19, 20,24
26.12 Ex 14.21; Isa 51.15; Jer 31.35
26.13 Job 9.8; Isa 27.1
26.14 Job 36.29
27.1 Job 13.12; 29.1
27.2 Job 34.5; 9.18

26.6 *Abaddon* means "destruction." Here it is used as a parallel to Sheol (cf. Prov 15.11). In Rev 9.11 it is used as a name for Satan himself, the prince of the bottomless pit.

and the Almighty, who has made my soul bitter;

27.3
Job 32.8;
33.4
3 as long as my breath is in me,
  and the spirit of God is in my nostrils;

27.4
Job 6.28
4 my lips will not speak falsehood,
  and my tongue will not utter deceit.

27.5
Job 2.9;
13.15
5 Far be it from me to say that you are right;
  till I die I will not put away my integrity from me.

27.6
Job 2.3;
13.18;
Acts 23.1
6 I hold fast my righteousness, and will not let it go;
  my heart does not reproach me for any of my days.

b. *His detestation of the wicked*

7 "Let my enemy be as the wicked,
  and let him that rises up against me be as the unrighteous.

27.8
Job 8.13;
11.20
8 For what is the hope of the godless when God cuts him off,
  when God takes away his life?

27.9
Job 35.12;
Prov 1.28;
Isa 1.15;
Jer 14.12;
Mic 3.4
9 Will God hear his cry,
  when trouble comes upon him?

10 Will he take delight in the Almighty?
  Will he call upon God at all times?

27.10
Job 22.26,
27
11 I will teach you concerning the hand of God;
  what is with the Almighty I will not conceal.

12 Behold, all of you have seen it yourselves;
  why then have you become altogether vain?

27.13
Job 20.29;
15.20
13 "This is the portion of a wicked man with God,
  and the heritage which oppressors receive from the Almighty:

27.14
Deut 28.41;
Hos 9.13;
Job 20.10
14 If his children are multiplied, it is for the sword;
  and his offspring have not enough to eat.

27.15
Ps 78.64
15 Those who survive him the pestilence buries,
  and their widows make no lamentation.

27.16
Zech 9.3
16 Though he heap up silver like dust,
  and pile up clothing like clay;

27.17
Prov 28.8;
Ecc 2.26
17 he may pile it up, but the just will wear it,
  and the innocent will divide the silver.

18 The house which he builds is like a spider's web, *a*
  like a booth which a watchman makes.

27.19
Ezek 29.5;
Job 7.8,21
19 He goes to bed rich, but will do so no more; *b*
  he opens his eyes, and his wealth is gone.

27.20
Job 15.21;
20.8
20 Terrors overtake him like a flood;
  in the night a whirlwind carries him off.

27.21
Job 21.18;
7.10
21 The east wind lifts him up and he is gone;
  it sweeps him out of his place.

27.22
Jer 13.14;
Ezek 5.11;
Job 11.20
22 It *c* hurls at him without pity;
  he flees from its *d* power in headlong flight.

27.23
Lam 2.15;
Job 18.18
23 It *c* claps its *d* hands at him,
  and hisses at him from its *d* place.

c. *How and where true wisdom is to be acquired*

28 "Surely there is a mine for silver,
   and a place for gold which they refine.

28.2
Deut 8.9
2 Iron is taken out of the earth,
  and copper is smelted from the ore.

3 Men put an end to darkness,

---

a Cn Compare Gk Syr: Heb *He builds his house like the moth*
b Gk Compare Syr: Heb *shall not be gathered*   *c* Or *he* (that is God)   *d* Or *his*

and search out to the farthest bound
    the ore in gloom and deep darkness.
4 They open shafts in a valley away from where men live;
    they are forgotten by travelers,
    they hang afar from men, they swing to and fro.
5 As for the earth, out of it comes bread;
    but underneath it is turned up as by fire.
6 Its stones are the place of sapphires,*e*
    and it has dust of gold.

7 "That path no bird of prey knows,
    and the falcon's eye has not seen it.
8 The proud beasts have not trodden it;
    the lion has not passed over it.

9 "Man puts his hand to the flinty rock,
    and overturns mountains by the roots.
10 He cuts out channels in the rocks,
    and his eye sees every precious thing.
11 He binds up the streams so that they do not trickle,
    and the thing that is hid he brings forth to light.

12 "But where shall wisdom be found?
    And where is the place of understanding?
13 Man does not know the way to it,*f*
    and it is not found in the land of the living.
14 The deep says, 'It is not in me,'
    and the sea says, 'It is not with me.'
15 It cannot be gotten for gold,
    and silver cannot be weighed as its price.
16 It cannot be valued in the gold of Ōphir,
    in precious onyx or sapphire.*g*
17 Gold and glass cannot equal it,
    nor can it be exchanged for jewels of fine gold.
18 No mention shall be made of coral or of crystal;
    the price of wisdom is above pearls.
19 The topaz of Ethiopia cannot compare with it,
    nor can it be valued in pure gold.

20 "Whence then comes wisdom?
    And where is the place of understanding?
21 It is hid from the eyes of all living,
    and concealed from the birds of the air.
22 Ābăd'dŏn and Death say,
    'We have heard a rumor of it with our ears.'

23 "God understands the way to it,
    and he knows its place.
24 For he looks to the ends of the earth,
    and sees everything under the heavens.
25 When he gave to the wind its weight,
    and meted out the waters by measure;
26 when he made a decree for the rain,

e Or *lapis lazuli*   *f* Gk: Heb *its price*   *g* Or *lapis lazuli*

Marginal references:
28.5 Ps 104.14
28.9 Deut 8.15; 32.13
28.12 ver 23,28
28.13 Prov 3.15
28.17 Prov 8.10; 16.16
28.18 Prov 3.15; 8.11
28.19 Prov 8.19
28.20 ver 23,28
28.22 Job 26.6
28.23 ver 23–28
28.24 Ps 33.13; Prov 15.3
28.25 Ps 135.7; Job 12.15
28.26 Job 37.6,11, 12; 37.3; 38.25

and a way for the lightning of the thunder;
27 then he saw it and declared it;
    he established it, and searched it out.

28.28
Deut 4.6;
Ps 111.10;
Prov 1.7;
  9.10

28 And he said to man,
    'Behold, the fear of the Lord, that is wisdom;
    and to depart from evil is understanding.' "

d. *Job sums up his life*
(1) HIS EARLIER PROSPERITY

29.1
Job 13.12;
  27.1
29.2
Jer 31.28
29.3
Job 11.17
29.4
Ps 25.14

29 And Jōb again took up his discourse, and said:
2 "Oh, that I were as in the months of old,
    as in the days when God watched over me;
3 when his lamp shone upon my head,
    and by his light I walked through darkness;
4 as I was in my autumn days,
    when the friendship of God was upon my tent;
5 when the Almighty was yet with me,
    when my children were about me;

29.6
Job 20.17;
Deut 32.13,
  14

6 when my steps were washed with milk,
    and the rock poured out for me streams of oil!
7 When I went out to the gate of the city,
    when I prepared my seat in the square,
8 the young men saw me and withdrew,
    and the aged rose and stood;

29.9
ver 21;
Job 21.5
29.10
ver 22

9 the princes refrained from talking,
    and laid their hand on their mouth;
10 the voice of the nobles was hushed,
    and their tongue cleaved to the roof of their mouth.
11 When the ear heard, it called me blessed,
    and when the eye saw, it approved;

29.12
Job 31.16,
  17,21
29.13
Job 31.19,
  20
29.14
Ps 132.9;
Isa 59.17;
  61.10;
Eph 6.14

12 because I delivered the poor who cried,
    and the fatherless who had none to help him.
13 The blessing of him who was about to perish came upon me,
    and I caused the widow's heart to sing for joy.
14 I put on righteousness, and it clothed me;
    my justice was like a robe and a turban.
15 I was eyes to the blind,
    and feet to the lame.

29.16
Prov 29.7

16 I was a father to the poor,
    and I searched out the cause of him whom I did not know.

29.17
Ps 3.7

17 I broke the fangs of the unrighteous,
    and made him drop his prey from his teeth.

29.18
Ps 30.6

18 Then I thought, 'I shall die in my nest,
    and I shall multiply my days as the sand,

29.19
Job 18.16;
Jer 17.8

19 my roots spread out to the waters,
    with the dew all night on my branches,

29.20
Gen 49.24;
Ps 18.34

20 my glory fresh with me,
    and my bow ever new in my hand.'

29.21
ver 9

21 "Men listened to me, and waited,
    and kept silence for my counsel.

29.22
ver 10;
Job 32.2

22 After I spoke they did not speak again,
    and my word dropped upon them.
23 They waited for me as for the rain;
    and they opened their mouths as for the spring rain.

24 I smiled on them when they had no confidence;
   and the light of my countenance they did not cast down.
25 I chose their way, and sat as chief,
   and I dwelt like a king among his troops,
   like one who comforts mourners.

29.25
Job 1.3;
31.37; 4.4

(2) HIS PRESENT SUFFERING

30 "But now they make sport of me,
      men who are younger than I,
   whose fathers I would have disdained
      to set with the dogs of my flock.
2 What could I gain from the strength of their hands,
   men whose vigor is gone?
3 Through want and hard hunger
   they gnaw the dry and desolate ground;*h*
4 they pick mallow and the leaves of bushes,
   and to warm themselves the roots of the broom.
5 They are driven out from among men;
   they shout after them as after a thief.
6 In the gullies of the torrents they must dwell,
   in holes of the earth and of the rocks.
7 Among the bushes they bray;
   under the nettles they huddle together.
8 A senseless, a disreputable brood,
   they have been whipped out of the land.

30.1
Job 12.4

9 "And now I have become their song,
   I am a byword to them.
10 They abhor me, they keep aloof from me;
   they do not hesitate to spit at the sight of me.
11 Because God has loosed my cord and humbled me,
   they have cast off restraint in my presence.
12 On my right hand the rabble rise,
   they drive me*i* forth,
   they cast up against me their ways of destruction.
13 They break up my path,
   they promote my calamity;
   no one restrains*j* them.
14 As through*k* a wide breach they come;
   amid the crash they roll on.
15 Terrors are turned upon me;
   my honor is pursued as by the wind,
   and my prosperity has passed away like a cloud.

30.9
Job 12.4;
17.6
30.10
Num 12.14;
Deut 25.9;
Isa 50.6;
Mt 26.67
30.11
Ruth 1.21;
Ps 88.7
30.12
Ps 140.4,5;
Job 19.12

30.15
Job 3.25;
31.23;
Hos 13.3

16 "And now my soul is poured out within me;
   days of affliction have taken hold of me.
17 The night racks my bones,
   and the pain that gnaws me takes no rest.
18 With violence it seizes my garment;*l*
   it binds me about like the collar of my tunic.
19 God has cast me into the mire,
   and I have become like dust and ashes.
20 I cry to thee and thou dost not answer me;

30.16
Ps 22.14;
42.4
30.17
ver 30

30.19
Ps 69.2,14
30.20
Ps 19.7

h Heb *ground yesterday waste*
i Heb *my feet* *j* Cn: Heb *helps* *k* Cn: Heb *like* *l* Gk: Heb *my garment is disfigured*

I stand, and thou dost not[m] heed me.

30.21
Job 10.3;
16.9,14;
19.6,22
21 Thou hast turned cruel to me;
with the might of thy hand thou dost persecute me.

30.22
Job 9.17;
27.21
22 Thou liftest me up on the wind, thou makest me ride on it,
and thou tossest me about in the roar of the storm.

30.23
Job 9.22;
10.8; 3.19;
17.13
23 Yea, I know that thou wilt bring me to death,
and to the house appointed for all living.

30.24
Job 19.7
24 "Yet does not one in a heap of ruins stretch out his hand,
and in his disaster cry for help?[n]

30.25
Ps 35.13,14;
Rom 12.15
25 Did not I weep for him whose day was hard?
Was not my soul grieved for the poor?

30.26
Job 3.25,26;
Jer 8.15;
Job 19.8
26 But when I looked for good, evil came;
and when I waited for light, darkness came.
27 My heart is in turmoil, and is never still;
days of affliction come to meet me.

30.28
Ps 38.6;
42.9; 43.2;
Job 19.7
28 I go about blackened, but not by the sun;
I stand up in the assembly, and cry for help.

30.29
Mic 1.8
29 I am a brother of jackals,
and a companion of ostriches.

30.30
Ps 119.83;
Lam 4.8;
Ps 102.3
30 My skin turns black and falls from me,
and my bones burn with heat.

30.31
Ps 107.1,2
31 My lyre is turned to mourning,
and my pipe to the voice of those who weep.

(3) HIS VINDICATION OF HIMSELF

*31.1
Mt 5.28
31 "I have made a covenant with my eyes;
how then could I look upon a virgin?

31.2
Job 20.29
2 What would be my portion from God above,
and my heritage from the Almighty on high?

31.3
Job 21.30;
34.22
3 Does not calamity befall the unrighteous,
and disaster the workers of iniquity?

31.4
2 Chr 16.9;
Prov 5.21
4 Does not he see my ways,
and number all my steps?

31.5
Mic 2.11
5 "If I have walked with falsehood,
and my foot has hastened to deceit;

31.6
Job 6.2,3;
27.5,6
6 (Let me be weighed in a just balance,
and let God know my integrity!)

*31.7
Job 23.11;
9.30
7 if my step has turned aside from the way,
and my heart has gone after my eyes,
and if any spot has cleaved to my hands;

31.8
Lev 26.16;
Job 20.18
8 then let me sow, and another eat;
and let what grows for me be rooted out.

31.9
Job 24.15
9 "If my heart has been enticed to a woman,
and I have lain in wait at my neighbor's door;

31.10
Jer 8.10
10 then let my wife grind for another,

m One Heb Ms and Vg: Heb lacks *not*   *n* Cn: Heb obscure

31.1 *I have made a covenant with my eyes.* Here Job utters a declaration of his ethical standard. He asserts his purity of act and motivation in the matters of sexual morality (31.1–6); receiving bribes (7, 8; also see note to 31.7); adultery (9–12); treat-

ment of slaves (13–15); benevolence (16–23); proper use of money (24, 25); idolatry (26–28); attitude toward enemies (29, 30); hospitality (31, 32); admission of transgression (33, 34).

31.7 *any spot* is otherwise "any thing." Job has been honest in all his relationships.

and let others bow down upon her.

11 For that would be a heinous crime;
   that would be an iniquity to be punished by the judges;
12 for that would be a fire which consumes unto Àbăd′dŏn,
   and it would burn to the root all my increase.

13 "If I have rejected the cause of my manservant or my maid-
      servant,
   when they brought a complaint against me;
14 what then shall I do when God rises up?
   When he makes inquiry, what shall I answer him?
15 Did not he who made me in the womb make him?
   And did not one fashion us in the womb?

16 "If I have withheld anything that the poor desired,
   or have caused the eyes of the widow to fail,
17 or have eaten my morsel alone,
   and the fatherless has not eaten of it
18 (for from his youth I reared him as a father,
   and from his mother's womb I guided him);o
19 if I have seen any one perish for lack of clothing,
   or a poor man without covering;
20 if his loins have not blessed me,
   and if he was not warmed with the fleece of my sheep;
21 if I have raised my hand against the fatherless,
   because I saw help in the gate;
22 then let my shoulder blade fall from my shoulder,
   and let my arm be broken from its socket.
23 For I was in terror of calamity from God,
   and I could not have faced his majesty.

24 "If I have made gold my trust,
   or called fine gold my confidence;
25 if I have rejoiced because my wealth was great,
   or because my hand had gotten much;
26 if I have looked at the sunp when it shone,
   or the moon moving in splendor,
27 and my heart has been secretly enticed,
   and my mouth has kissed my hand;
28 this also would be an iniquity to be punished by the judges,
   for I should have been false to God above.

29 "If I have rejoiced at the ruin of him that hated me,
   or exulted when evil overtook him
30 (I have not let my mouth sin
   by asking for his life with a curse);
31 if the men of my tent have not said,
   'Who is there that has not been filled with his meat?'
32 (the sojourner has not lodged in the street;
   I have opened my doors to the wayfarer);
33 if I have concealed my transgressions from men,q
   by hiding my iniquity in my bosom,
34 because I stood in great fear of the multitude,

31.11
Gen 38.24;
Deut 22.22-
24
31.12
Job 15.30;
26.6;
20.28
31.13
Deut 24.14,
15

31.15
Mal 2.10

31.16
Job 20.19;
22.7,9
31.17
Job 22.7;
29.12

31.19
Job 22.6;
29.13
31.20
Deut 31.20
31.21
Job 22.9
31.22
Job 38.15
31.23
ver 3;
Job 13.11

31.24
Mk 10.24
31.25
Ps 62.10
31.26
Deut 4.19;
Ezek 8.16

31.28
ver 11

31.29
Prov 17.5
31.30
Mt 5.44
31.31
Job 22.7
31.32
Gen 19.2,3;
Rom 12.13
31.33
Gen 3.8;
Prov 28.13
31.34
Ex 23.2

o Cn: Heb for from my youth he grew up to me as a father, and from my mother's womb I
guided her   p Heb the light   q Cn: Heb like men or like Adam

and the contempt of families terrified me,
so that I kept silence, and did not go out of doors—
35 Oh, that I had one to hear me!
    (Here is my signature! let the Almighty answer me!)
    Oh, that I had the indictment written by my adversary!
36 Surely I would carry it on my shoulder;
    I would bind it on me as a crown;
37 I would give him an account of all my steps;
    like a prince I would approach him.

38 "If my land has cried out against me,
    and its furrows have wept together;
39 if I have eaten its yield without payment,
    and caused the death of its owners;
40 let thorns grow instead of wheat,
    and foul weeds instead of barley."

The words of Jōb are ended.

III. The speeches of Elihu 32.1–37.24

A. Elihu's anger at Job for his justification of self

32 So these three men ceased to answer Jōb, because he was righteous in his own eyes. ² Then Ēlī′hū the son of Băr′ăchĕl the Būzīte, of the family of Ram, became angry. He was angry at Jōb because he justified himself rather than God; ³ he was angry also at Jōb's three friends because they had found no answer, although they had declared Jōb to be in the wrong. ⁴ Now Ēlī′hū had waited to speak to Jōb because they were older than he. ⁵And when Ēlī′hū saw that there was no answer in the mouth of these three men, he became angry.

6 And Ēlī′hū the son of Băr′ăchĕl the Būzīte answered:
"I am young in years,
    and you are aged;
therefore I was timid and afraid
    to declare my opinion to you.
7 I said, 'Let days speak,
    and many years teach wisdom.'
8 But it is the spirit in a man,
    the breath of the Almighty, that makes him understand.
9 It is not the old^r that are wise,
    nor the aged that understand what is right.
10 Therefore I say, 'Listen to me;
    let me also declare my opinion.'

11 "Behold, I waited for your words,

^r Gk Syr Vg: Heb *many*

Marginal references:
31.35 — Job 19.7; 30.20,24, 28; 35.14
31.37 — ver 4; Job 1.3; 29.25
31.38 — Gen 4.10,11
31.39 — Lev 19.13; 1 Ki 21.19; Jas 5.4
31.40 — Gen 3.18
32.1 — Job 33.9
★32.2 — Gen 22.21; Jer 25.23
32.3 — Job 11.6; 15.16; 22.5
32.6 — Job 15.10
32.8 — Job 27.3; 33.4; 1 Ki 3.12; Prov 2.6
32.9 — 1 Cor 1.26
32.11 — Job 5.27

32.2 Elihu enters into the discussion between Job and his friends because he is dissatisfied with Job's contention that God deals capriciously with men in this life. On the other hand, he realizes that Job's three friends have not won the argument with Job because they have defended too narrow a viewpoint. The substance of Elihu's argument is that God permitted Job's sufferings in order to achieve beneficial results in Job's life and faith. 36.6–15 contains the clearest statement of the theory of Elihu on suffering.

I listened for your wise sayings,
while you searched out what to say.
12 I gave you my attention,
and, behold, there was none that confuted Jōb,
or that answered his words, among you.
13 Beware lest you say, 'We have found wisdom;
God may vanquish him, not man.'

32.13
Jer 9.23

14 He has not directed his words against me,
and I will not answer him with your speeches.

15 "They are discomfited, they answer no more;
they have not a word to say.
16 And shall I wait, because they do not speak,
because they stand there, and answer no more?
17 I also will give my answer;
I also will declare my opinion.
18 For I am full of words,
the spirit within me constrains me.

32.18
Acts 18.5

19 Behold, my heart is like wine that has no vent;
like new wineskins, it is ready to burst.

32.19
Acts 9.17

20 I must speak, that I may find relief;
I must open my lips and answer.
21 I will not show partiality to any person
or use flattery toward any man.

32.21
Lev 19.15;
Mt 22.16

22 For I do not know how to flatter,
else would my Maker soon put an end to me.

32.22
1 Thess 2.5

B. God uses pain to chasten men

33 "But now, hear my speech, O Jōb,
and listen to all my words.
2 Behold, I open my mouth;
the tongue in my mouth speaks.
3 My words declare the uprightness of my heart,
and what my lips know they speak sincerely.

33.3
Job 6.28;
27.4; 36.4

4 The spirit of God has made me,
and the breath of the Almighty gives me life.

*33.4
Gen 2.7;
Job 27.3

5 Answer me, if you can;
set your words in order before me; take your stand.

33.5
ver 32;
Job 13.18

6 Behold, I am toward God as you are;
I too was formed from a piece of clay.
7 Behold, no fear of me need terrify you;
my pressure will not be heavy upon you.

33.7
Job 9.34;
13.21;
2 Cor 2.5

8 "Surely, you have spoken in my hearing,
and I have heard the sound of your words.
9 You say, 'I am clean, without transgression;
I am pure, and there is no iniquity in me.

33.9
Job 10.7;
13.23;
16.17

33.4 The Holy Spirit is referred to by more than thirty names or titles in Scripture. Job here speaks of Him as the *spirit of God* and the *breath of the Almighty*. Many of the names given indicate attributes or characteristics of the Holy Spirit. He is called the *Spirit of life* (Rom 8.2), *spirit of wis-* dom . . . *understanding* . . . *counsel and might* . . . *knowledge* (Isa 11.2), *Spirit of truth* (Jn 14.17), and *Spirit of holiness* (Rom 1.4), among others. An exhaustive study of these titles would reveal much about the person and work of the Holy Spirit, the third person of the Trinity.

Job 33.10–32

756

33.10
Job 13.24
10 Behold, he finds occasions against me,
he counts me as his enemy;

33.11
Job 13.27;
14.16
11 he puts my feet in the stocks,
and watches all my paths.'

12 "Behold, in this you are not right. I will answer you.
God is greater than man.

33.13
Job 15.25;
Isa 45.9
13 Why do you contend against him,
saying, 'He will answer none of my^s words'?

33.14
Ps 62.11
14 For God speaks in one way,
and in two, though man does not perceive it.

33.15
Num 12.6;
Job 4.13
15 In a dream, in a vision of the night,
when deep sleep falls upon men,
while they slumber on their beds,

33.16
Job 36.10,
15
16 then he opens the ears of men,
and terrifies them with warnings,
17 that he may turn man aside from his deed,
and cut off^t pride from man;

33.18
ver 24,28,30
18 he keeps back his soul from the Pit,
his life from perishing by the sword.

33.19
Job 30.17
19 "Man is also chastened with pain upon his bed,
and with continual strife in his bones;

33.20
Ps 107.18
20 so that his life loathes bread,
and his appetite dainty food.

33.21
Job 16.8;
19.20
21 His flesh is so wasted away that it cannot be seen;
and his bones which were not seen stick out.

33.22
Ps 88.3
22 His soul draws near the Pit,
and his life to those who bring death.

33.23
Mic 6.8
23 If there be for him an angel,
a mediator, one of the thousand,
to declare to man what is right for him;

33.24
Isa 38.17
24 and he is gracious to him, and says,
'Deliver him from going down into the Pit,
I have found a ransom;

33.25
2 Ki 5.14
25 let his flesh become fresh with youth;
let him return to the days of his youthful vigor';

33.26
Job 22.27;
34.28;
22.26;
Ps 51.12
26 then man prays to God, and he accepts him,
he comes into his presence with joy.
He recounts^u to men his salvation,

33.27
Lk 15.21;
Rom 6.21
27 and he sings before men, and says:
'I sinned, and perverted what was right,
and it was not requited to me.

33.28
Ps 103.14;
Job 22.28
28 He has redeemed my soul from going down into the Pit,
and my life shall see the light.'

33.29
Eph 1.11;
1 Cor 12.6;
Phil 2.13
29 "Behold, God does all these things,
twice, three times, with a man,

33.30
Ps 56.13
30 to bring back his soul from the Pit,
that he may see the light of life.^v
31 Give heed, O Jōb, listen to me;
be silent, and I will speak.
32 If you have anything to say, answer me;

^s Compare Gk: Heb his   ^t Cn: Heb hide
^u Cn: Heb returns   ^v Syr: Heb to be lighted with the light of life

speak, for I desire to justify you.
33 If not, listen to me;
   be silent, and I will teach you wisdom."

C. God is not unjust

34 Then Ēlī′hū said:
2 "Hear my words, you wise men,
   and give ear to me, you who know;
3 for the ear tests words
   as the palate tastes food.
4 Let us choose what is right;
   let us determine among ourselves what is good.
5 For Jōb has said, 'I am innocent,
   and God has taken away my right;
6 in spite of my right I am counted a liar;
   my wound is incurable, though I am without transgression.'
7 What man is like Jōb,
   who drinks up scoffing like water,
8 who goes in company with evildoers
   and walks with wicked men?
9 For he has said, 'It profits a man nothing
   that he should take delight in God.'

10 "Therefore, hear me, you men of understanding,
   far be it from God that he should do wickedness,
   and from the Almighty that he should do wrong.
11 For according to the work of a man he will requite him,
   and according to his ways he will make it befall him.
12 Of a truth, God will not do wickedly,
   and the Almighty will not pervert justice.
13 Who gave him charge over the earth
   and who laid on him[w] the whole world?
14 If he should take back his spirit[x] to himself,
   and gather to himself his breath,
15 all flesh would perish together,
   and man would return to dust.

16 "If you have understanding, hear this;
   listen to what I say.
17 Shall one who hates justice govern?
   Will you condemn him who is righteous and mighty,
18 who says to a king, 'Worthless one,'
   and to nobles, 'Wicked man';
19 who shows no partiality to princes,
   nor regards the rich more than the poor,
   for they are all the work of his hands?
20 In a moment they die;
   at midnight the people are shaken and pass away,
   and the mighty are taken away by no human hand.

21 "For his eyes are upon the ways of a man,
   and he sees all his steps.
22 There is no gloom or deep darkness

---

w Heb lacks on him   x Heb his heart his spirit

Cross references (right column):

33.33 Ps 34.11

34.3 Job 12.11
34.4 1 Thess 5.21
34.5 Job 33.9; 27.2
34.6 Jer 15.18; 30.12
34.7 Job 15.16
34.8 Ps 50.18
34.9 Job 21.15; 35.3

34.10 Job 8.3

34.11 Ps 62.12; Mt 16.27; Rom 2.6; 2 Cor 5.10; Rev 22.12
34.12 Job 8.3
34.13 Job 38.5,6
34.14 Ps 104.29
34.15 Isa 40.6,7; Gen 3.19

34.17 2 Sam 23.3

34.18 Ex 22.28

34.19 Deut 10.17; Gal 2.6; Job 31.15

34.20 Ex 12.29; Job 12.19

34.21 Job 31.4
34.22 Ps 139.12; Amos 9.2,3

where evildoers may hide themselves.
23 For he has not appointed a time[y] for any man
   to go before God in judgment.

34.24
Dan 2.21
24 He shatters the mighty without investigation,
   and sets others in their place.

34.25
ver 11,20
25 Thus, knowing their works,
   he overturns them in the night, and they are crushed.

34.26
Job 26.12
26 He strikes them for their wickedness
   in the sight of men,

34.27
1 Sam
15.11;
Ps 28.5;
Isa 5.12
27 because they turned aside from following him,
   and had no regard for any of his ways,
28 so that they caused the cry of the poor to come to him,
   and he heard the cry of the afflicted—

34.28
Job 35.9;
Jas 5.4;
Ex 22.23
29 When he is quiet, who can condemn?
   When he hides his face, who can behold him,
   whether it be a nation or a man?—

34.29
1 Chr 22.9
34.30
ver 17
30 that a godless man should not reign,
   that he should not ensnare the people.

31 "For has any one said to God,
   'I have borne chastisement; I will not offend any more;

34.32
Job 35.11;
Ps 25.4
32 teach me what I do not see;
   if I have done iniquity, I will do it no more'?
33 Will he then make requital to suit you,
   because you reject it?
   For you must choose, and not I;
   therefore declare what you know.[z]
34 Men of understanding will say to me,
   and the wise man who hears me will say:

34.35
Job 35.16
35 'Jōb speaks without knowledge,
   his words are without insight.'

34.36
Job 23.10;
22.15
36 Would that Jōb were tried to the end,
   because he answers like wicked men.
37 For he adds rebellion to his sin;
   he claps his hands among us,
   and multiplies his words against God."

35   And Ēlī′hū said:
35.2
Job 32.2
2 "Do you think this to be just?
   Do you say, 'It is my right before God,'

35.3
Job 34.9;
9.30,31
3 that you ask, 'What advantage have I?
   How am I better off than if I had sinned?'
4 I will answer you
   and your friends with you.

35.5
Job 22.12
5 Look at the heavens, and see;
   and behold the clouds, which are higher than you.

35.6
Prov 8.36;
Jer 7.19
6 If you have sinned, what do you accomplish against him?
   And if your transgressions are multiplied, what do you do
      to him?

35.7
Job 22.2,3;
Prov 9.12;
Lk 17.10
7 If you are righteous, what do you give to him;
   or what does he receive from your hand?
8 Your wickedness concerns a man like yourself,
   and your righteousness a son of man.

─────────────────────────
[y] Cn: Heb yet   [z] The Hebrew of verses 29-33 is obscure

9 "Because of the multitude of oppressions people cry out;
  they call for help because of the arm of the mighty.
10 But none says, 'Where is God my Maker,
  who gives songs in the night,
11 who teaches us more than the beasts of the earth,
  and makes us wiser than the birds of the air?'
12 There they cry out, but he does not answer,
  because of the pride of evil men.
13 Surely God does not hear an empty cry,
  nor does the Almighty regard it.
14 How much less when you say that you do not see him,
  that the case is before him, and you are waiting for him!
15 And now, because his anger does not punish,
  and he does not greatly heed transgression,[a]
16 Jōb opens his mouth in empty talk,
  he multiplies words without knowledge."

D. The justice of God whose ways are inscrutable

36 And Ēlī'hū continued, and said:
  2 "Bear with me a little, and I will show you,
  for I have yet something to say on God's behalf.
3 I will fetch my knowledge from afar,
  and ascribe righteousness to my Maker.
4 For truly my words are not false;
  one who is perfect in knowledge is with you.

5 "Behold, God is mighty, and does not despise any;
  he is mighty in strength of understanding.
6 He does not keep the wicked alive,
  but gives the afflicted their right.
7 He does not withdraw his eyes from the righteous,
  but with kings upon the throne
  he sets them for ever, and they are exalted.
8 And if they are bound in fetters
  and caught in the cords of affliction,
9 then he declares to them their work
  and their transgressions, that they are behaving arrogantly.
10 He opens their ears to instruction,
  and commands that they return from iniquity.
11 If they hearken and serve him,
  they complete their days in prosperity,
  and their years in pleasantness.
12 But if they do not hearken, they perish by the sword,
  and die without knowledge.

13 "The godless in heart cherish anger;
  they do not cry for help when he binds them.
14 They die in youth,
  and their life ends in shame.[b]
15 He delivers the afflicted by their affliction,
  and opens their ear by adversity.
16 He also allured you out of distress

Marginal references:
35.9 Ex 2.23; Job 12.19
35.10 Job 27.10; Ps 42.8; 149.5; Acts 16.25
35.11 Ps 94.12; Lk 12.24
35.12 Prov 1.28
35.13 Job 27.9; Prov 15.29; Isa 1.15; Jer 11.11
35.14 Ps 37.5,6
35.15 Ecc 8.11
35.16 Job 34.37, 35
36.3 Job 8.3; 37.23
36.4 Job 33.3; 37.16
36.5 Ps 22.24; Job 12.13
36.6 Job 8.22; 5.15
36.7 Ps 33.18; 113.8
36.8 Ps 107.10; ver 15,21
36.9 Job 15.25
36.10 Job 33.16; 2 Ki 17.13
36.11 Isa 1.19,20
36.12 Job 15.22; 4.21
36.13 Rom 2.5
36.14 Job 15.32; 22.16
36.15 Ps 119.67; ver 10
36.16 Hos 2.14; Ps 118.5; 23.5

---

a Theodotion Symmachus Compare Vg: The meaning of the Hebrew word is uncertain
b Heb *among the cult prostitutes*

into a broad place where there was no cramping,
and what was set on your table was full of fatness.

17 "But you are full of the judgment on the wicked;
judgment and justice seize you.

36.18
Job 34.33;
Jon 4.9;
Job 33.24
18 Beware lest wrath entice you into scoffing;
and let not the greatness of the ransom turn you aside.

19 Will your cry avail to keep you from distress,
or all the force of your strength?

36.20
Job
34.20,25
20 Do not long for the night,
when peoples are cut off in their place.

36.21
Ps 66.18;
Heb 11.25
21 Take heed, do not turn to iniquity,
for this you have chosen rather than affliction.

36.22
Isa 40.13;
1 Cor 2.16
22 Behold, God is exalted in his power;
who is a teacher like him?

36.23
Job 34.13;
Job 8.3
23 Who has prescribed for him his way,
or who can say, 'Thou hast done wrong'?

36.24
2 Sam 7.26;
Ps 35.27;
59.16
24 "Remember to extol his work,
of which men have sung.

25 All men have looked on it;
man beholds it from afar.

*36.26
Ps 102.24
26 Behold, God is great, and we know him not;
the number of his years is unsearchable.

36.27
Ps 147.8
27 For he draws up the drops of water,
he[c] distils his mist in rain

28 which the skies pour down,
and drop upon man abundantly.

36.29
Job 37.11,
16; 26.14
29 Can any one understand the spreading of the clouds,
the thunderings of his pavilion?

30 Behold, he scatters his lightning about him,
and covers the roots of the sea.

36.31
Job 37.13;
Ps 136.25
31 For by these he judges peoples;
he gives food in abundance.

36.32
Job 37.15
32 He covers his hands with the lightning,
and commands it to strike the mark.

36.33
Job 37.2
33 Its crashing declares concerning him,
who is jealous with anger against iniquity.

37 "At this also my heart trembles,
and leaps out of its place.

*37.2
Job 36.33
2 Hearken to the thunder of his voice
and the rumbling that comes from his mouth.

37.3
ver 12
3 Under the whole heaven he lets it go,
and his lightning to the corners of the earth.

37.4
Ps 29.3
4 After it his voice roars;
he thunders with his majestic voice
and he does not restrain the lightnings[d] when his voice is
heard.

c Cn: Heb *they distil*   d Heb *them*

36.26 *we know him not*, i.e., God is infinite and unsearchable. Man knows that God is, but he does not know who or what God is, save as God chooses to reveal himself.
37.2 *thunder* (ver 2) and *lightning* (ver 3) go together. They bespeak the power and the glory of God. One witnesses to the ear and the other to the eye. They are designed by God to attract the attention of men. Elihu here speaks as though these natural phenomena happened while he was engaged in conversation with Job.

5 God thunders wondrously with his voice;
   he does great things which we cannot comprehend.
6 For to the snow he says, 'Fall on the earth';
   and to the shower and the rain,ᵉ 'Be strong.'
7 He seals up the hand of every man,
   that all men may know his work.ᶠ
8 Then the beasts go into their lairs,
   and remain in their dens.
9 From its chamber comes the whirlwind,
   and cold from the scattering winds.
10 By the breath of God ice is given,
   and the broad waters are frozen fast.
11 He loads the thick cloud with moisture;
   the clouds scatter his lightning.
12 They turn round and round by his guidance,
   to accomplish all that he commands them
   on the face of the habitable world.
13 Whether for correction, or for his land,
   or for love, he causes it to happen.

14 "Hear this, O Jōb;
   stop and consider the wondrous works of God.
15 Do you know how God lays his command upon them,
   and causes the lightning of his cloud to shine?
16 Do you know the balancings of the clouds,
   the wondrous works of him who is perfect in knowledge,
17 you whose garments are hot
   when the earth is still because of the south wind?
18 Can you, like him, spread out the skies,
   hard as a molten mirror?
19 Teach us what we shall say to him;
   we cannot draw up our case because of darkness.
20 Shall it be told him that I would speak?
   Did a man ever wish that he would be swallowed up?

21 "And now men cannot look on the light
   when it is bright in the skies,
   when the wind has passed and cleared them.
22 Out of the north comes golden splendor;
   God is clothed with terrible majesty.
23 The Almighty—we cannot find him;
   he is great in power and justice,
   and abundant righteousness he will not violate.
24 Therefore men fear him;
   he does not regard any who are wise in their own conceit."

37.5
Job 5.9;
36.26
37.6
Job 38.22;
36.27
★37.7
Job 12.14
37.8
Ps 104.22
37.9
Job 9.9;
Ps 147.17
37.10
Job 38.29;
Ps 147.17
37.11
Job 36.27,
29;
ver 15
37.12
Ps 148.8;
Isa 14.21;
27.6;
Prov 8.31
37.13
Ex 9.18;
1 Sam
12.18;
Job 38.26;
1 Ki 18.45
37.14
Ps 111.2
37.16
ver 5,14,23;
Job 36.4
37.18
Job 9.8;
Ps 104.2;
Isa 44.24
37.23
1 Tim 6.16;
Job 9.4;
8.3;
Isa 63.9
★37.24
Mt 10.28;
11.25;
1 Cor 1.26

ᵉ Cn Compare Syr: Heb *shower of rain and shower of rains*
ᶠ Vg Compare Syr Tg: Heb *that all men whom he has made may know it*

37.7 *He seals up the hand of every man.* Through His control of the elements God is able to control the actions of men. Thus in winter the farmer cannot plough, and in blizzards salesmen stay at home.
37.24 Elihu argued that God cannot be charged with injustice (ver 23). Job's suffering was first designed to uphold God's glory before the cynicism of Satan. Job's suffering was also to serve the purpose of perfecting his sanctification. God's glory was upheld, to be sure, but God then permitted the trial to continue that Job might be conformed more to God's image.

IV. *The voice of God 38.1–42.6*

A. *God challenges Job*

38.1
Job 40.6

*38.2
Job 42.3;
35.16;
1 Tim 1.7

38.3
Job 40.7

38 Then the LORD answered Jōb out of the whirlwind:
2 "Who is this that darkens counsel by words without knowledge?
3 Gird up your loins like a man,
    I will question you, and you shall declare to me.

B. *God's creation*

38.4
Ps 104.5;
Prov 8.29

4 "Where were you when I laid the foundation of the earth?
    Tell me, if you have understanding.
5 Who determined its measurements—surely you know!
    Or who stretched the line upon it?

38.6
Job 26.7

6 On what were its bases sunk,
    or who laid its cornerstone,

38.7
Job 1.6

7 when the morning stars sang together,
    and all the sons of God shouted for joy?

38.8
Gen 1.9

8 "Or who shut in the sea with doors,
    when it burst forth from the womb;

38.9
Prov 30.4

9 when I made clouds its garment,
    and thick darkness its swaddling band,

38.10
Job 26.10

10 and prescribed bounds for it,
    and set bars and doors,

38.11
Ps 89.9

11 and said, 'Thus far shall you come, and no farther,
    and here shall your proud waves be stayed'?

38.12
Ps 74.16

12 "Have you commanded the morning since your days began,
    and caused the dawn to know its place,

38.13
Ps 104.35

13 that it might take hold of the skirts of the earth,
    and the wicked be shaken out of it?
14 It is changed like clay under the seal,
    and it is dyed[g] like a garment.

38.15
Job 18.5;
Ps 10.15

15 From the wicked their light is withheld,
    and their uplifted arm is broken.

C. *Man's inability to probe the mystery of God's creation*

38.16
Ps 77.19

16 "Have you entered into the springs of the sea,
    or walked in the recesses of the deep?

38.17
Ps 9.13

17 Have the gates of death been revealed to you,
    or have you seen the gates of deep darkness?

38.18
Job 28.24

18 Have you comprehended the expanse of the earth?
    Declare, if you know all this.

g Cn: Heb *they stand forth*

38.2 *words without knowledge.* Job's three friends could not get him to confess sin, and Elihu was only partially helpful in the solution of the problem. Although Job was correct in insisting that his suffering was not the result of sin, he erred in thinking too highly of his own ability to rationalize the Creator's actions. The climax of the book is reached when God appears in theophany to show Job the greatness of creation and underscore man's ignorance and finiteness. This is done by a series of questions in chapters 38—41.

19 "Where is the way to the dwelling of light,
　　and where is the place of darkness,
20 that you may take it to its territory
　　and that you may discern the paths to its home?
21 You know, for you were born then,
　　and the number of your days is great!

22 "Have you entered the storehouses of the snow,
　　or have you seen the storehouses of the hail,
23 which I have reserved for the time of trouble,
　　for the day of battle and war?
24 What is the way to the place where the light is distributed,
　　or where the east wind is scattered upon the earth?

25 "Who has cleft a channel for the torrents of rain,
　　and a way for the thunderbolt,
26 to bring rain on a land where no man is,
　　on the desert in which there is no man;
27 to satisfy the waste and desolate land,
　　and to make the ground put forth grass?

28 "Has the rain a father,
　　or who has begotten the drops of dew?
29 From whose womb did the ice come forth,
　　and who has given birth to the hoarfrost of heaven?
30 The waters become hard like stone,
　　and the face of the deep is frozen.

31 "Can you bind the chains of the Plēi′adēs,
　　or loose the cords of Ōri′on?
32 Can you lead forth the Măz′zărŏth in their season,
　　or can you guide the Bear with its children?
33 Do you know the ordinances of the heavens?
　　Can you establish their rule on the earth?

34 "Can you lift up your voice to the clouds,
　　that a flood of waters may cover you?
35 Can you send forth lightnings, that they may go
　　and say to you, 'Here we are'?
36 Who has put wisdom in the clouds,[h]
　　or given understanding to the mists?[h]
37 Who can number the clouds by wisdom?
　　Or who can tilt the waterskins of the heavens,
38 when the dust runs into a mass
　　and the clods cleave fast together?

D. Man's inability to probe the mysteries of animal and bird life

39 "Can you hunt the prey for the lion,
　　or satisfy the appetite of the young lions,
40 when they crouch in their dens,
　　or lie in wait in their covert?

h The meaning of the Hebrew word is uncertain

38.20
Job 26.10;
24.13

38.21
Job 15.7

38.22
Job 37.6

38.23
Ex 9.18;
Josh 10.11;
Isa 30.30;
Ezek 13.11,
13;
Rev 16.21

38.24
Job 26.10;
27.21

38.25
Job 28.26

38.26
Job 36.27;
Ps 107.35

38.27
Ps 104.13,14

38.28
Ps 147.8;
Jer 14.22

38.29
Ps 147.16,
17

38.31
Job 9.9;
Amos 5.8

38.33
Job 31.35

38.34
ver 37;
Job 22.11;
36.27,28

38.35
Job 36.32;
37.3

38.36
Job 32.8;
Ps 51.6;
Ecc 2.26;
Job 32.8

38.39
Ps 104.21

38.40
Job 38.8;
Ps 17.12

38.41
Ps 147.9;
Mt 6.26
41 Who provides for the raven its prey,
  when its young ones cry to God,
    and wander about for lack of food?

39.1
Ps 29.9

39 "Do you know when the mountain goats bring forth?
  Do you observe the calving of the hinds?
2 Can you number the months that they fulfil,
  and do you know the time when they bring forth,

39.3
1 Sam 4.19
3 when they crouch, bring forth their offspring,
  and are delivered of their young?
4 Their young ones become strong, they grow up in the open;
  they go forth, and do not return to them.

39.5
Job 6.5;
11.12; 24.5
39.6
Job 24.5;
Jer 2.24;
Hos 8.9;
Ps 107.34
5 "Who has let the wild ass go free?
  Who has loosed the bonds of the swift ass,
6 to whom I have given the steppe for his home,
  and the salt land for his dwelling place?
7 He scorns the tumult of the city;
  he hears not the shouts of the driver.
8 He ranges the mountains as his pasture,
  and he searches after every green thing.

39.9
Num 23.22;
Deut 33.17
9 "Is the wild ox willing to serve you?
  Will he spend the night at your crib?
10 Can you bind him in the furrow with ropes,
  or will he harrow the valleys after you?
11 Will you depend on him because his strength is great,
  and will you leave to him your labor?
12 Do you have faith in him that he will return,
  and bring your grain to your threshing floor?[i]

13 "The wings of the ostrich wave proudly;
  but are they the pinions and plumage of love?[j]
14 For she leaves her eggs to the earth,
  and lets them be warmed on the ground,
15 forgetting that a foot may crush them,
  and that the wild beast may trample them.

39.16
Lam 4.3;
ver 22
39.17
Job 35.11
16 She deals cruelly with her young, as if they were not hers;
  though her labor be in vain, yet she has no fear;
17 because God has made her forget wisdom,
  and given her no share in understanding.
18 When she rouses herself to flee,[k]
  she laughs at the horse and his rider.

39.19
Ps 147.10
39.20
Joel 2.5;
Jer 8.16
39.21
Jer 8.6
19 "Do you give the horse his might?
  Do you clothe his neck with strength?[l]
20 Do you make him leap like the locust?
  His majestic snorting is terrible.
21 He paws[m] in the valley, and exults in his strength;
  he goes out to meet the weapons.
22 He laughs at fear, and is not dismayed;

i Heb your grain and your threshing floor
j Heb obscure   k Heb obscure
l Tg: The meaning of the Hebrew word is obscure   m Gk Syr Vg: Heb they dig

he does not turn back from the sword.
23 Upon him rattle the quiver,
   the flashing spear and the javelin.
24 With fierceness and rage he swallows the ground;
   he cannot stand still at the sound of the trumpet.
25 When the trumpet sounds, he says 'Aha!'
   He smells the battle from afar,
   the thunder of the captains, and the shouting.

26 "Is it by your wisdom that the hawk soars,
   and spreads his wings toward the south?
27 Is it at your command that the eagle mounts up
   and makes his nest on high?
28 On the rock he dwells and makes his home
   in the fastness of the rocky crag.
29 Thence he spies out the prey;
   his eyes behold it afar off.
30 His young ones suck up blood;
   and where the slain are, there is he."

E. Job's penitent submission

40 And the LORD said to Jōb:
2 "Shall a faultfinder contend with the Almighty?
   He who argues with God, let him answer it."

3 Then Jōb answered the LORD:
4 "Behold, I am of small account; what shall I answer thee?
   I lay my hand on my mouth.
5 I have spoken once, and I will not answer;
   twice, but I will proceed no further."

F. God's second speech

1. God challenges Job

6 Then the LORD answered Jōb out of the whirlwind:
7 "Gird up your loins like a man;
   I will question you, and you declare to me.
8 Will you even put me in the wrong?
   Will you condemn me that you may be justified?
9 Have you an arm like God,
   and can you thunder with a voice like his?

10 "Deck yourself with majesty and dignity;
   clothe yourself with glory and splendor.
11 Pour forth the overflowings of your anger,
   and look on every one that is proud, and abase him.
12 Look on every one that is proud, and bring him low;
   and tread down the wicked where they stand.
13 Hide them all in the dust together;
   bind their faces in the world below.[n]
14 Then will I also acknowledge to you,
   that your own right hand can give you victory.

n Heb *hidden place*

39.24
Jer 4.19;
Ezek 7.14;
Amos 3.6
39.25
Josh 6.5;
Amos 1.14;
2.2

39.27
Jer 46.16;
Obad 4

39.30
Mt 24.28;
Lk 17.37

40.1
Job 33.13;
13.3; 23.4;
31.35

40.4
Job 42.6;
29.9
40.5
Job 9.3,15

40.6
Job 38.1
40.7
Job 38.3;
42.4
40.8
Isa 14.27;
Rom 3.4
40.9
2 Chr 32.8;
Jer 17.5;
Job 37.5
40.10
Ps 93.1;
104.1
40.11
Isa 42.25;
2.12;
Dan 4.37
40.12
1 Sam 2.7;
Isa 13.11;
63.3;
Job 36.20
40.14
Ps 20.6;
60.5; 108.6

2. *The God who made Behemoth cannot be overcome by man*

40.15
ver 19
15 "Behold, Bĕhē'mŏth,°
  which I made as I made you;
  he eats grass like an ox.
16 Behold, his strength in his loins,
  and his power in the muscles of his belly.
17 He makes his tail stiff like a cedar;
  the sinews of his thighs are knit together.
18 His bones are tubes of bronze,
  his limbs like bars of iron.

40.19
Job 41.33;
ver 15
19 "He is the first of the works*p* of God;
  let him who made him bring near his sword!
40.20
Ps 104.26
20 For the mountains yield food for him
  where all the wild beasts play.
21 Under the lotus plants he lies,
  in the covert of the reeds and in the marsh.
40.22
Isa 44.4
22 For his shade the lotus trees cover him;
  the willows of the brook surround him.
23 Behold, if the river is turbulent he is not frightened;
  he is confident though Jordan rushes against his mouth.
40.24
Prov 1.17
24 Can one take him with hooks,*q*
  or pierce his nose with a snare?

3. *The God who made Leviathan is superior to man*

*41.1
Ps 104.26;
Isa 27.1
41 *r* "Can you draw out Lĕvī'áthán*s* with a fishhook,
  or press down his tongue with a cord?
41.2
Isa 37.29
2 Can you put a rope in his nose,
  or pierce his jaw with a hook?
3 Will he make many supplications to you?
  Will he speak to you soft words?
4 Will he make a covenant with you
  to take him for your servant for ever?
5 Will you play with him as with a bird,
  or will you put him on leash for your maidens?
6 Will traders bargain over him?
  Will they divide him up among the merchants?
7 Can you fill his skin with harpoons,
  or his head with fishing spears?
8 Lay hands on him;
  think of the battle; you will not do it again!
41.10
Job 3.8
9*t* Behold, the hope of a man is disappointed;
  he is laid low even at the sight of him.
41.11
Rom 11.35;
Ex 19.5;
Deut 10.14;
Ps 24.1;
50.12;
1 Cor 10.26
10 No one is so fierce that he dares to stir him up.
  Who then is he that can stand before me?
11 Who has given to me,*u* that I should repay him?
  Whatever is under the whole heaven is mine.

o Or *the hippopotamus*   *p* Heb *ways*
q Cn: Heb *in his eyes*   *r* Ch 40.25 in Heb
s Or *the crocodile*   *t* Ch 41.1 in Heb
u The meaning of the Hebrew is uncertain

41.1 *Leviathan,* identified often with the crocodile, may here be the mythological sea monster mentioned in 3.8: *Let those curse it ... rouse up Leviathan.*

12 "I will not keep silence concerning his limbs,
    or his mighty strength, or his goodly frame.
13 Who can strip off his outer garment?
    Who can penetrate his double coat of mail?*v*
14 Who can open the doors of his face?
    Round about his teeth is terror.
15 His back*w* is made of rows of shields,
    shut up closely as with a seal.
16 One is so near to another
    that no air can come between them.
17 They are joined one to another;
    they clasp each other and cannot be separated.
18 His sneezings flash forth light,
    and his eyes are like the eyelids of the dawn.
19 Out of his mouth go flaming torches;
    sparks of fire leap forth.
20 Out of his nostrils comes forth smoke,
    as from a boiling pot and burning rushes.
21 His breath kindles coals,
    and a flame comes forth from his mouth.
22 In his neck abides strength,
    and terror dances before him.
23 The folds of his flesh cleave together,
    firmly cast upon him and immovable.
24 His heart is hard as a stone,
    hard as the nether millstone.
25 When he raises himself up the mighty*x* are afraid;
    at the crashing they are beside themselves.
26 Though the sword reaches him, it does not avail;
    nor the spear, the dart, or the javelin.
27 He counts iron as straw,
    and bronze as rotten wood.
28 The arrow cannot make him flee;
    for him slingstones are turned to stubble.
29 Clubs are counted as stubble;
    he laughs at the rattle of javelins.
30 His underparts are like sharp potsherds;
    he spreads himself like a threshing sledge on the mire.
31 He makes the deep boil like a pot;
    he makes the sea like a pot of ointment.
32 Behind him he leaves a shining wake;
    one would think the deep to be hoary.
33 Upon earth there is not his like,
    a creature without fear.
34 He beholds everything that is high;
    he is king over all the sons of pride."

4. Job repentant

42 Then Jōb answered the Lord:
2 "I know that thou canst do all things,
    and that no purpose of thine can be thwarted.

v Gk: Heb *bridle*   *w* Cn Compare Gk Vg: Heb *pride*   *x* Or *gods*

41.12ff Tells of an indomitable monster.   **42.1** Job now understands God's purpose.

(marginal references:)
*41.12ff
41.18
Job 3.9
41.33
Job 40.19
*42.1
42.2
Gen 18.14;
Mt 19.26;
Mk 10.27;
Lk 18.27;
2 Chr 20.6;
Isa 14.27

*42.3
Job 38.2;
Ps 40.5;
131.1;
139.6
42.4
Job 38.3;
40.7
42.5
Job 26.14;
Judg 13.22;
Isa 6.5
42.6
Ezra 9.6;
Job 40.4

3 'Who is this that hides counsel without knowledge?'
  Therefore I have uttered what I did not understand,
    things too wonderful for me, which I did not know.
4 'Hear, and I will speak;
  I will question you, and you declare to me.'
5 I had heard of thee by the hearing of the ear,
  but now my eye sees thee;
6 therefore I despise myself,
  and repent in dust and ashes."

V. Epilogue 42.7–17

A. Job's prayer for his friends

*42.7
Job 32.3;
ver 1–6;
40.3–5
42.8
Num 23.1;
Job 1.5;
Jas 5.15,16

7 After the LORD had spoken these words to Jōb, the LORD said to Ĕl'ĭphăz the Tē'mănīte: "My wrath is kindled against you and against your two friends; for you have not spoken of me what is right, as my servant Job has. 8 Now therefore take seven bulls and seven rams, and go to my servant Jōb, and offer up for yourselves a burnt offering; and my servant Job shall pray for you, for I will accept his prayer not to deal with you according to your folly; for you have not spoken of me what is right, as my servant Job has." 9 So Ĕl'ĭphăz the Tē'mănīte and Bĭldăd the Shuhīte and Zōphar the Nā'ămăthīte went and did what the LORD had told them; and the LORD accepted Jōb's prayer.

B. The latter end of Job

*42.10
Ps 14.7;
126.1
42.11
Job 19.13

42.12
Job 1.10;
8.7; 1.3

42.13
Job 1.2

42.16
Job 5.26;
Prov 3.16
42.17
Gen 25.8

10 And the LORD restored the fortunes of Jōb, when he had prayed for his friends; and the LORD gave Job twice as much as he had before. 11 Then came to him all his brothers and sisters and all who had known him before, and ate bread with him in his house; and they showed him sympathy and comforted him for all the evil that the LORD had brought upon him; and each of them gave him a piece of moneyʸ and a ring of gold. 12And the LORD blessed the latter days of Jōb more than his beginning; and he had fourteen thousand sheep, six thousand camels, a thousand yoke of oxen, and a thousand she-asses. 13 He had also seven sons and three daughters. 14And he called the name of the first Jĕmī'măh; and the name of the second Kĕzī'ăh; and the name of the third Kĕrĕn-hăp'pŭch. 15And in all the land there were no women so fair as Jōb's daughters; and their father gave them inheritance among their brothers. 16And after this Jōb lived a hundred and forty years, and saw his sons, and his sons' sons, four generations. 17And Jōb died, an old man, and full of days.

ʸ Heb qesitah

42.3 *I . . . did not understand.* Job's vision of God did not provide a full answer to the problem of his suffering, but it did bring satisfaction to the sufferer. God's wisdom and power, contrasted with Job's ignorance and weakness, brought Job to humility and penitence.

42.7 *not spoken . . . as my servant Job has.* Job's repentance did not mean that the friends were right in their charges. God tells them that they were wrong. They are instructed to offer appropriate sacrifices and are assured that Job will pray for them. This would involve Job's forgiving them for their hard words. God heard Job's prayer on behalf of his friends (ver 9) and Job's own renewed prosperity followed (ver 10).

42.10 *The LORD restored the fortunes of Job.* The number of sheep, camels, oxen, and she-asses at the end of Job's career is double that which he had before his trials (1.3).

INTRODUCTION TO
THE PSALMS

Authorship and Background: The Hebrew name for this book was "The Book of Praises." The present name derives from the Latin Vulgate, which followed the Septuagint. The authorship is varied and includes David, Solomon, Asaph, Moses, and others who are anonymous. The final editing probably took place in the time of Ezra. Thus the dates when the individual Psalms were written, range through many centuries. The Psalter was closely associated with the Pentateuch. The repeated reading of the latter led to the choice of certain Psalms which were used on specific occasions and festivals such as the Feast of Booths. This would indicate that the Psalms were used liturgically in ancient times, just as they have been in the life of the church.

Characteristics: The Psalms have a unique place in Scripture. They cover the gamut of human emotions from imprecatory cries to heavenly praises. They are marked by spiritual intensity springing out of personal experience in the worship of God. God, nature, history, sin, animals, and heavenly constellations find their way naturally into these exalted acts of worship and devotion. The book itself is divided into five sections or "books," each of which ends with a doxology. The last Psalm is entirely given over to doxology. Eight categories of Psalms may be distinguished: (1) personal Psalms; (2) penitential Psalms; (3) Psalms of praise; (4) prayer Psalms; (5) Messianic Psalms; (6) historical Psalms; (7) liturgical Psalms; (8) Psalms which attribute majesty and power to God. Many of the Psalms have features of more than one of these categories although some have been identified more nearly with one group than any other. Thus Psalms 120 and 135 are often thought of as liturgical; Psalms 2, 22, 45, and 110 as Messianic; Psalms 18, 100, and 103 as Psalms of praise; Psalms 23, 27, 34, and 37 as personal; and Psalms 32, 51, and 130 as penitential.

Contents: The five books in the Psalter divide the Psalms thus:

I.   Psalms 1—41
II.   Psalms 42—72
III.   Psalms 73—89
IV.   Psalms 90—106
V.   Psalms 107—150

Note: The word *Selah* (Heb *sālal*, "to lift up") occurs seventy-one times in The Psalms, as well as three times in Habakkuk. It is generally agreed that the word is a liturgical or musical sign, although its precise meaning remains uncertain. In all probability, Selah was a direction to the orchestra who had been playing softly in accompaniment to the singers' voices to "lift up loud" their music. Some suggest that the word was not in the original text, but first appeared as a marginal gloss and gradually found its way into the main body of the book over the centuries.

THE PSALMS

BOOK I

I. *The happiness of the godly 1.1–3*

1.1
Prov 4.14;
Job 21.16;
Ps 17.4;
26.5;
Jer 15.17

1 Blessed is the man
who walks not in the counsel of the wicked,
nor stands in the way of sinners,
nor sits in the seat of scoffers;

1.2
Ps 119.35;
Josh 1.8;
Ps 119.1

2 but his delight is in the law of the LORD,
and on his law he meditates day and night.

1.3
Jer 17.8;
Ezek 47.12;
Gen 39.3;
Ps 128.2

3 He is like a tree
planted by streams of water,
that yields its fruit in its season,
and its leaf does not wither.
In all that he does, he prospers.

II. *The misery of the wicked 1.4–6*

1.4
Job 21.18;
Isa 17.13

4 The wicked are not so,
but are like chaff which the wind drives away.

1.5
Ps 5.5; 9.7;
8.16;
111.1;
149.1

5 Therefore the wicked will not stand in the judgment,
nor sinners in the congregation of the righteous;

1.6
Ps 37.18;
2 Tim 2.19;
Ps 9.3–6

6 for the LORD knows the way of the righteous,
but the way of the wicked will perish.

I. *The Messiah's Psalm 2.1–11*

A. *The Messiah rejected*

＊2.1ff
Acts 4.25;
Ps 21.11

2 Why do the nations conspire,
and the peoples plot in vain?

2.2
Ps 48.4–6;
74.18,23;
Jn 1.41

2 The kings of the earth set themselves,
and the rulers take counsel together,
against the LORD and his anointed, saying,

2.3
Jer 5.5

3 "Let us burst their bonds asunder,
and cast their cords from us."

2.1-11 Many of the Psalms were written almost a thousand years before the advent of Jesus Christ. Yet some of these evidently refer to Him, as the Apostles made clear at Pentecost, and thereafter in the sermons of Acts. They could not fully apply to David himself or to any other person who has ever lived. It is possible, of course, to read Messianic implications into some Psalms where such implications are, to say the least, doubtful. On the other hand, it is not unusual for a Psalm to refer to David as a type of the Messianic king. Among the Psalms which are clearly Messianic are: 2, 8, 16, 22, 45, 69, 72, 89, 110, 132.

Psalm 2 probably has as its historical background some rebellion of the nations against David or some ruler of the Davidic line. A revolt is described as futile, however, for God has willed that His Anointed (the Davidic king) should rule all nations. Jesus as

the Messiah (i.e., the Anointed One, the Son of David) brings ultimate fulfilment to words which could apply only in a limited sense to others who claimed descent from David.

This is a Messianic Psalm. The *anointed* of verse 2 is, in its ultimate application, Christ. Verse 6 uses historical language (*my king on Zion, my holy hill*) which may be employed to depict Christ ascended to the right hand of the Father. This same Christ shall reign over a reconstituted Zion in the future. *You are my son* (ver 7), while applicable to human kings who are chosen of God, looks forward to the incarnation for its ultimate fulfilment. These words were to be confirmed at Christ's baptism: *This is my beloved Son, with whom I am well pleased* (Mt 3.17). The note sounded in verse 12 sets blessing and happiness for the faithful against anger and judgment for the unbelieving.

B. The LORD's derision

⁴ He who sits in the heavens laughs;
   the LORD has them in derision.
⁵ Then he will speak to them in his wrath,
   and terrify them in his fury, saying,
⁶ "I have set my king
   on Zion, my holy hill."

C. The Messiah triumphant

⁷ I will tell of the decree of the LORD:
   He said to me, "You are my son,
   today I have begotten you.
⁸ Ask of me, and I will make the nations your heritage,
   and the ends of the earth your possession.
⁹ You shall break them with a rod of iron,
   and dash them in pieces like a potter's vessel."

D. The LORD's counsel to kings

¹⁰ Now therefore, O kings, be wise;
    be warned, O rulers of the earth.
¹¹ Serve the LORD with fear,
    with trembling ¹² kiss his feet,ᵃ
   lest he be angry, and you perish in the way;
    for his wrath is quickly kindled.

   Blessed are all who take refuge in him.

A Psalm of David, when he fled from Ăb′sȧlŏm his son.

I. David in distress 3.1–8

A. His complaint

3 O LORD, how many are my foes!
   Many are rising against me;
² many are saying of me,
   there is no help for him in God.   *Sēlȧh*

ᵃ Cn: The Hebrew of 11b and 12a is uncertain.

2.4	Ps 59.8; 37.13; Prov 1.26
2.5	Ps 21.8,9; 78.49,50
2.6	Ps 3.4
★2.7	Acts 13.33; Heb 1.5
2.8	Ps 22.27
2.9	Ps 89.23; Rev 2.27; 12.5
2.11	Heb 12.28; Ps 119.119, 120
★2.12	Jn 5.23; Rev 6.16; Ps 34.8; Rom 9.33
3.1	2 Sam 15.12
3.2	Ps 71.11

2.7 Scripture records more than sixty prophecies relating to Christ which were fulfilled by His earthly ministry and crucifixion. Many of them concern Christ's birth, ministry, and death on the cross. Among the prophecies which have been partially fulfilled, or are yet to be fulfilled, may be included: (1) the conversion of the Gentiles to Him (Isa 11.10; 42.1; Jn 10.16; Acts 10.45, 47); (2) Christ's universal dominion (72.8; Dan 7.14); (3) Christ as king in Zion (2.6); (4) His eternal and righteous government (45.6, 7).

2.12 The wording of the Hebrew presents some difficulties here. The KJV renders the verse, "Kiss the Son, lest he be angry . . ." which is a reasonable translation of the text as we have it. No ancient manuscript, Hebrew or non-Hebrew, contains the words, "Kiss his feet," and this translation is conjectural. The LXX renders it "accept correction," a sense followed by the Latin Vulgate. The word translated *son* (*bar*) is an Aramaic word, rather than the usual Hebrew *ben* (which occurs in verse 7), but it also occurs in the Hebrew of Prov 31.2, and it would be appropriate in a prophetic reference to an Aramaic-speaking Messiah who constantly used this word of Himself in the title "the Son of man." The translation should not be regarded as crucial for the Messianic understanding of the Psalm, for kings of the Davidic dynasty were looked upon as "sons" of God (2 Sam 7.12–14).

B. *His confidence*

3.3
Ps 28.7;
27.6
3.4
Ps 34.4;
99.9

3 But thou, O Lord, art a shield about me,
    my glory, and the lifter of my head.
4 I cry aloud to the Lord,
    and he answers me from his holy hill.   *Sēlāh*

C. *His security*

3.5
Lev 26.6;
Ps 139.18
3.6
Ps 27.3

5 I lie down and sleep;
    I wake again, for the Lord sustains me.
6 I am not afraid of ten thousands of people
    who have set themselves against me round about.

D. *His prayer and rejoicing*

3.7
Ps 7.6; 6.4;
Job 16.10;
Ps 58.6

7 Arise, O Lord!
    Deliver me, O my God!
For thou dost smite all my enemies on the cheek,
    thou dost break the teeth of the wicked.

3.8
Isa 43.11;
Jer 3.23;
Num
6.23–27

8 Deliverance belongs to the Lord;
    thy blessing be upon thy people!   *Sēlàh*

To the choirmaster: with stringed instruments. A Psalm of David.

I. *Thoughts in the night 4.1–8*

A. *Prayer for help*

4.1
Ps 27.7;
18.6; 24.5;
18.18;
25.16;
17.6

4 Answer me when I call, O God of my right!
Thou hast given me room when I was in distress.
Be gracious to me, and hear my prayer.

B. *Reproof of his enemies*

4.2
Ps 31.6,18

2 O men, how long shall my honor suffer shame?
    How long will you love vain words, and seek after lies?
                                          Sēlàh

4.3
Ps 31.23;
6.8,9

3 But know that the Lord has set apart the godly for himself;
    the Lord hears when I call to him.

C. *His enemies exhorted*

4.4
Ps 33.8;
Eph 4.26;
Ps 77,6

4 Be angry, but sin not;
    commune with your own hearts on your beds, and be silent.
                                          Sēlàh

4.5
Deut 33.19;
Ps 50.14;
37.3

5 Offer right sacrifices,
    and put your trust in the Lord.

D. *His confidence in God*

4.6
Num 6.26

6 There are many who say, "Oh that we might see some good!
    Lift up the light of thy countenance upon us, O Lord!"

7 Thou hast put more joy in my heart
   than they have when their grain and wine abound.

4.7
Acts 14.17;
Isa 9.3

8 In peace I will both lie down and sleep;
   for thou alone, O LORD, makest me dwell in safety.

4.8
Ps 3.5;
Lev 25.18

To the choirmaster: for the flutes. A Psalm of David.

I. *A morning prayer 5.1–12*

A. *God hears prayer*

5 Give ear to my words, O LORD;
   give heed to my groaning.

5.1
Ps 54.2;
19.14

2 Hearken to the sound of my cry,
   my King and my God,
   for to thee do I pray.

5.2
Ps 3.4; 84.3

3 O LORD, in the morning thou dost hear my voice;
   in the morning I prepare a sacrifice for thee, and watch.

5.3
Ps 88.13;
Hab 2.1

B. *God hates wickedness*

4 For thou art not a God who delights in wickedness;
   evil may not sojourn with thee.

5.4
Ps 11.5;
92.15

5 The boastful may not stand before thy eyes;
   thou hatest all evildoers.

5.5
Ps 73.3;
1.5; 11.5

6 Thou destroyest those who speak lies;
   the LORD abhors bloodthirsty and deceitful men.

5.6
Rev 21.8;
Ps 55.23

C. *God blesses the righteous*

7 But I through the abundance of thy steadfast love
   will enter thy house,
 I will worship toward thy holy temple
   in the fear of thee.

5.7
Ps 69.13;
28.2

8 Lead me, O LORD, in thy righteousness
   because of my enemies;
   make thy way straight before me.

5.8
Ps 27.11;
31.1

9 For there is no truth in their mouth;
   their heart is destruction,
 their throat is an open sepulchre,
   they flatter with their tongue.

5.9
Deut 32.20;
Lk 11.44;
Rom 3.13;
Ps 12.2

10 Make them bear their guilt, O God;
   let them fall by their own counsels;
 because of their many transgressions cast them out,
   for they have rebelled against thee.

5.10
Ps 9.16;
Lam 1.5;
Ps107.10,11

11 But let all who take refuge in thee rejoice,
   let them ever sing for joy;
 and do thou defend them,
   that those who love thy name may exult in thee.

5.11
Ps 2.12;
Isa 65.13;
Zech 9.15;
Ps 69.36

12 For thou dost bless the righteous, O LORD;
   thou dost cover him with favor as with a shield.

5.12
Ps 112.2;
32.7,10

To the choirmaster: with stringed instruments; according to
The Shĕm′inith. A Psalm of David.

I. *Prayer for mercy in time of trouble 6.1–10*

A. *Prayer for mercy*

6.1 6 O LORD, rebuke me not in thy anger,
Ps 38.1; 2.5   nor chasten me in thy wrath.
6.2   2 Be gracious to me, O LORD, for I am languishing;
Ps 51.1;   O LORD, heal me, for my bones are troubled.
102.4,11;   3 My soul also is sorely troubled.
41.4;   But thou, O LORD—how long?
22.14

6.3   4 Turn, O LORD, save my life;
Jn 12.27;   deliver me for the sake of thy steadfast love.
Ps 90.13   5 For in death there is no remembrance of thee;
6.4   in Shēol who can give thee praise?
Ps 17.13

6.5
Ps 30.9;
Isa 38.18

6.6   6 I am weary with my moaning;
Ps 69.3;   every night I flood my bed with tears;
22.1; 42.3   I drench my couch with my weeping.
6.7   7 My eye wastes away because of grief,
Ps 31.9   it grows weak because of all my foes.

B. *Assurance of a good answer*

6.8   8 Depart from me, all you workers of evil;
Ps 119.115;   for the LORD has heard the sound of my weeping.
Lk 13.27;   9 The LORD has heard my supplication;
Ps 5.5; 28.6   the LORD accepts my prayer.
6.9   10 All my enemies shall be ashamed and sorely troubled;
Ps 116.1;   they shall turn back, and be put to shame in a moment.
66.19,20
6.10
Ps 71.24;
40.14;
73.19

A Shĭggāi′on of David, which he sang to the LORD
concerning Cŭsh a Benjaminite.

I. *The prayer of a wronged man 7.1–17*

A. *David turns to God*

7.1   7 O LORD my God, in thee do I take refuge;
Ps 11.1;   save me from all my pursuers, and deliver me,
31.15   2 lest like a lion they rend me,
7.2   dragging me away, with none to rescue.
Ps 17.12;
50.22

B. *He pleads his innocence*

7.3   3 O LORD my God, if I have done this,
2 Sam 16.7;   if there is wrong in my hands,
1 Sam 24.11   4 if I have requited my friend with evil
7.4   or plundered my enemy without cause,
1 Sam 24.7   5 let the enemy pursue me and overtake me,
                     and let him trample my life to the ground,
                     and lay my soul in the dust.   *Sēlah*

C. *He cries for justice*

6 Arise, O Lord, in thy anger,
   lift thyself up against the fury of my enemies;
   awake, O my God;[b] thou hast appointed a judgment.
7 Let the assembly of the peoples be gathered about thee;
   and over it take thy seat[c] on high.
8 The Lord judges the peoples;
   judge me, O Lord, according to my righteousness
   and according to the integrity that is in me.

9 O let the evil of the wicked come to an end,
   but establish thou the righteous,
   thou who triest the minds and hearts,
   thou righteous God.

D. *The fate of the wicked*

10 My shield is with God,
   who saves the upright in heart.
11 God is a righteous judge,
   and a God who has indignation every day.

12 If a man[d] does not repent, God[d] will whet his sword;
   he has bent and strung his bow;
13 he has prepared his deadly weapons,
   making his arrows fiery shafts.
14 Behold, the wicked man conceives evil,
   and is pregnant with mischief,
   and brings forth lies.
15 He makes a pit, digging it out,
   and falls into the hole which he has made.
16 His mischief returns upon his own head,
   and on his own pate his violence descends.

E. *Praise to a righteous God*

17 I will give to the Lord the thanks due to his righteousness,
   and I will sing praise to the name of the Lord, the Most High.

To the choirmaster: according to The Gittith. A Psalm of David.

I. *God's glory and man's honor 8.1–9*

A. *God the great creator*

8 O Lord, our Lord,
   how majestic is thy name in all the earth!

   Thou whose glory above the heavens is chanted
2 by the mouth of babes and infants,
   thou hast founded a bulwark because of thy foes,
   to still the enemy and the avenger.

b Or for me   c Cn: Heb return   d Heb he

7.6
Ps 3.7;
94.2; 44.23

7.7
Ps 68.18

7.8
Ps 96.13;
18.20;
35.24

7.9
Ps 34.21;
Isa 54.14;
I Chr 28.9;
Jer 11.20;
Rev 2.23

7.10
Ps 18.2;
125.4
7.11
Ps 50.6;
Isa 34.2

7.12
Ezek 3.19;
33.9;
Deut 32.41;
Ps 21.12
7.13
Ps 64.7
7.14
Isa 59.4;
Jas 1.15
7.15
Job 4.8;
Ps 9.15;
Ecc 10.8
7.16
Ps 140.9;
Est 9.25

7.17
Ps 71.15,16;
9.2

8.1
Ps 66.2;
148.13;
57.5,11;
113.4

8.2
Mt 21.16;
Ps 44.16

3 When I look at thy heavens, the work of thy fingers,
    the moon and the stars which thou hast established;
4 what is man that thou art mindful of him,
    and the son of man that thou dost care for him?

B. Man the chief agent of God

5 Yet thou hast made him little less than God,
    and dost crown him with glory and honor.
6 Thou hast given him dominion over the works of thy hands;
    thou hast put all things under his feet,
7 all sheep and oxen,
    and also the beasts of the field,
8 the birds of the air, and the fish of the sea,
    whatever passes along the paths of the sea.

9 O Lord, our Lord,
    how majestic is thy name in all the earth!

To the choirmaster: according to Mŭth-lăb′bĕn. A Psalm of David.

I. Praise to God for deliverance 9.1–20

A. Hymn of thanksgiving

9 I will give thanks to the Lord with my whole heart;
    I will tell of all thy wonderful deeds.
2 I will be glad and exult in thee,
    I will sing praise to thy name, O Most High.

3 When my enemies turned back,
    they stumbled and perished before thee.
4 For thou hast maintained my just cause;
    thou hast sat on the throne giving righteous judgment.

5 Thou hast rebuked the nations, thou hast destroyed the wicked;
    thou hast blotted out their name for ever and ever.
6 The enemy have vanished in everlasting ruins;
    their cities thou hast rooted out;
    the very memory of them has perished.

B. Faith in God's righteousness

7 But the Lord sits enthroned for ever,
    he has established his throne for judgment;
8 and he judges the world with righteousness,
    he judges the peoples with equity.

9 The Lord is a stronghold for the oppressed,
    a stronghold in times of trouble.

Marginal references:

8.3 Ps 89.11; 102.5; 136.9
8.4 Job 7.17; Ps 144.3; Heb 2.6
*8.5 Ps 103.4; 21.5; Heb 2.9
8.6 Gen 1.26; Heb 2.8
8.9 ver 1
9.1 Ps 86.12; 26.7
9.2 Ps 5.11; 83.18
9.3 Ps 56.9; 27.2
9.4 Ps 140.12; 47.8; 67.4; 1 Pet 2.23
9.5 Deut 9.14
9.6 Ps 40.15; 34.16
9.7 Ps 29.10; 89.14
9.8 Ps 96.13
9.9 Ps 18.2; 32.7; 37.39

8.5 Psalm 8 contains a paradox—man is very little in comparison with the vastness of creation (3, 4), yet God has given him a position of glory and honor (5–8). Jesus, who as Son of God is sovereign over all creation, in humility became man, taking upon Himself the title "Son of man" as an expression of His identification with mankind.

10 And those who know thy name put their trust in thee,
   for thou, O LORD, hast not forsaken those who seek thee.

9.10
Ps 91.14;
37.28

11 Sing praises to the LORD, who dwells in Zion!
   Tell among the peoples his deeds!
12 For he who avenges blood is mindful of them;
   he does not forget the cry of the afflicted.

9.11
Ps 76.2;
105.1
9.12
Gen 9.5;
ver 18

C. A prayer for help

13 Be gracious to me, O LORD!
   Behold what I suffer from those who hate me,
   O thou who liftest me up from the gates of death,
14 that I may recount all thy praises,
   that in the gates of the daughter of Zion
   I may rejoice in thy deliverance.

9.13
Ps 30.10;
25.18;
38.19; 30.3
9.14
Ps 106.2;
87.2; 13.5

D. A testimony to God's past judgments

15 The nations have sunk in the pit which they made;
   in the net which they hid has their own foot been caught.
16 The LORD has made himself known, he has executed judgment;
   the wicked are snared in the work of their own hands.
                                          Higg'āi'ŏn. Sĕlāh

9.15
Ps 7.15;
35.8
9.16
Isa 64.2;
ver 4

E. Assurance of, and prayer for, justice

17 The wicked shall depart to Shēōl,
   all the nations that forget God.

9.17
Ps 49.14;
50.22;
Job 8.13

18 For the needy shall not always be forgotten,
   and the hope of the poor shall not perish for ever.

9.18
ver 12;
Ps 74.19

19 Arise, O LORD! Let not man prevail;
   let the nations be judged before thee!
20 Put them in fear, O LORD!
   Let the nations know that they are but men!   *Sĕlāh*

9.19
Ps 3.7;
2 Chr 14.11;
Ps 110.6
9.20
Ps 83.15;
Isa 31.3

I. When judgment is delayed 10.1–18

A. The evil acts of the wicked

10 Why dost thou stand afar off, O LORD?
    Why dost thou hide thyself in times of trouble?
2 In arrogance the wicked hotly pursue the poor;
   let them be caught in the schemes which they have devised.

10.1
Ps 22.1;
13.1
10.2
Ps 109.16;
7.15; 9.16

3 For the wicked boasts of the desires of his heart,
   and the man greedy for gain curses and renounces the LORD.
4 In the pride of his countenance the wicked does not seek him;
   all his thoughts are, "There is no God."

10.3
Ps 94.4;
Job 1.5,11;
ver 13
10.4
ver 13;
Ps 14.1

5 His ways prosper at all times;
   thy judgments are on high, out of his sight;
   as for all his foes, he puffs at them.

6 He thinks in his heart, "I shall not be moved;
   throughout all generations I shall not meet adversity."

7 His mouth is filled with cursing and deceit and oppression;
   under his tongue are mischief and iniquity.
8 He sits in ambush in the villages;
   in hiding places he murders the innocent.

His eyes stealthily watch for the hapless,
9   he lurks in secret like a lion in his covert;
he lurks that he may seize the poor,
   he seizes the poor when he draws him into his net.

10 The hapless is crushed, sinks down,
   and falls by his might.
11 He thinks in his heart, "God has forgotten,
   he has hidden his face, he will never see it."

B. A prayer for relief and confidence of an answer

12 Arise, O LORD; O God, lift up thy hand;
   forget not the afflicted.
13 Why does the wicked renounce God,
   and say in his heart, "Thou wilt not call to account"?

14 Thou dost see; yea, thou dost note trouble and vexation,
   that thou mayest take it into thy hands;
the hapless commits himself to thee;
   thou hast been the helper of the fatherless.

15 Break thou the arm of the wicked and evildoer;
   seek out his wickedness till thou find none.
16 The LORD is king for ever and ever;
   the nations shall perish from his land.

17 O LORD, thou wilt hear the desire of the meek;
   thou wilt strengthen their heart, thou wilt incline thy ear
18 to do justice to the fatherless and the oppressed,
   so that man who is of the earth may strike terror no more.

To the choirmaster. Of David.

I. The LORD our refuge and defense 11.1–7

A. Temptation to distrust in trial

11 In the LORD I take refuge;
   how can you say to me,
"Flee like a bird to the mountains;[e]
2 for lo, the wicked bend the bow,
   they have fitted their arrow to the string,
   to shoot in the dark at the upright in heart;

[e] Gk Syr Jerome Tg: Heb *flee to your mountain, O bird*

³ if the foundations are destroyed,
    what can the righteous do"?

11.3
Ps 82.5

B. Affirmation of faith in the LORD

⁴ The LORD is in his holy temple,
    the LORD's throne is in heaven;
    his eyes behold, his eyelids test, the children of men.
⁵ The LORD tests the righteous and the wicked,
    and his soul hates him that loves violence.
⁶ On the wicked he will rain coals of fire and brimstone;
    a scorching wind shall be the portion of their cup.
⁷ For the LORD is righteous, he loves righteous deeds;
    the upright shall behold his face.

11.4
Ps 18.6;
103.19;
33.13;
34.15,16
11.5
Gen 22.1;
Jas 1.12;
Ps 5.5
11.6
Ezek 38.22;
Jer 4.11,12;
Ps 75.8
11.7
Ps 7.9,11;
33.5; 17.15

To the choirmaster: according to The Shĕm'ĭnĭth.
A Psalm of David.

I. Good thoughts for bad times 12.1–8

A. Prayer for help amidst the ungodly

12 Help, LORD; for there is no longer any that is godly;
      for the faithful have vanished from among the sons of men.
² Every one utters lies to his neighbor;
    with flattering lips and a double heart they speak.

12.1
Isa 57.1

12.2
Ps 41.6;
55.21;
1 Chr 12.33

³ May the LORD cut off all flattering lips,
    the tongue that makes great boasts,
⁴ those who say, "With our tongue we will prevail,
    our lips are with us; who is our master?"

12.3
Ps 73.8,9

B. Assurance of the LORD'S deliverance

⁵ "Because the poor are despoiled, because the needy groan,
    I will now arise," says the LORD;
"I will place him in the safety for which he longs."
⁶ The promises of the LORD are promises that are pure,
    silver refined in a furnace on the ground,
    purified seven times.

12.5
Ps 10.18;
3.7; 34.6

12.6
Ps 18.30;
Prov 30.5

⁷ Do thou, O LORD, protect us,
    guard us ever from this generation.
⁸ On every side the wicked prowl,
    as vileness is exalted among the sons of men.

12.7
Ps 37.28

12.8
Ps 55.10,11

To the choirmaster. A Psalm of David.

I. The deserted soul 13.1–6

A. His desperate plight

13 How long, O LORD? Wilt thou forget me for ever?
      How long wilt thou hide thy face from me?

13.1
Job 13.24;
Ps 44.24;
88.14

13.2
Ps 42.4,9;
94.3

2 How long must I bear pain^f in my soul,
  and have sorrow in my heart all the day?
How long shall my enemy be exalted over me?

B. *His prayer for help*

13.3
Ps 5.1;
Ezra 9.8;
Jer 51.39
13.4
Jer 20.10;
Ps 25.2

3 Consider and answer me, O LORD my God;
  lighten my eyes, lest I sleep the sleep of death;
4 lest my enemy say, "I have prevailed over him";
  lest my foes rejoice because I am shaken.

C. *His assurance of deliverance*

13.5
Ps 52.8;
9.14
13.6
Ps 59.16;
116.7

5 But I have trusted in thy steadfast love;
  my heart shall rejoice in thy salvation.
6 I will sing to the LORD,
  because he has dealt bountifully with me.

To the choirmaster. Of David.

I. *The principles and practices of the wicked 14.1-7*

*14.1
Ps 10.4;
53.1-6;
73.8;
Rom 3.10-
12

14 The fool says in his heart,
  "There is no God."
They are corrupt, they do abominable deeds,
there is none that does good.

14.2
Ps 33.13;
92.6;
Ezra 6.21

2 The LORD looks down from heaven upon the children of men,
  to see if there are any that act wisely,
  that seek after God.

14.3
Ps 58.3;
2 Pet 2.7;
Rev 22.11;
Ps 143.2

3 They have all gone astray, they are all alike corrupt;
  there is none that does good,
  no, not one.

14.4
Ps 82.5;
27.2; 79.6;
Isa 64.7

4 Have they no knowledge, all the evildoers
  who eat up my people as they eat bread,
  and do not call upon the LORD?

14.5
Ps 73.15

5 There they shall be in great terror,
  for God is with the generation of the righteous.

14.6
Ps 9.9;
40.17

6 You would confound the plans of the poor,
  but the LORD is his refuge.

14.7
Ps 53.6;
Job 42.10

7 O that deliverance for Israel would come out of Zion!
  When the LORD restores the fortunes of his people,
  Jacob shall rejoice, Israel shall be glad.

^{f} Syr: Heb *hold counsels*

14.1 In Mt 5.22 Christ says that to call a brother a fool provokes danger of hell fire. Yet He Himself reproaches the Pharisees as *fools* (using the same word as in 5.22) when He exposes their shallow legalism in Mt 23.17, 19. Here in 14.1 God calls the atheist a fool. The distinction between passages of this type and the injunction in Mt 5.22 lies in the attitude and authority of the one speaking. As the surrounding verses in Mt 5 show, what Christ forbade was passing judgment upon another in a spirit of contempt or hatred.

A Psalm of David.

I. *The happiness of the holy 15.1–5*

15 O LORD, who shall sojourn in thy tent?
Who shall dwell on thy holy hill?

2 He who walks blamelessly, and does what is right,
 and speaks truth from his heart;
3 who does not slander with his tongue,
 and does no evil to his friend,
 nor takes up a reproach against his neighbor;
4 in whose eyes a reprobate is despised,
 but who honors those who fear the LORD;
 who swears to his own hurt and does not change;
5 who does not put out his money at interest,
 and does not take a bribe against the innocent.

He who does these things shall never be moved.

A Mĭktăm of David.

I. *A Messianic prophecy 16.1–11*

A. *Faith evidenced*

16 Preserve me, O God, for in thee I take refuge.
 2 I say to the LORD, "Thou art my Lord;
 I have no good apart from thee."*g*

3 As for the saints in the land, they are the noble,
 in whom is all my delight.

4 Those who choose another god multiply their sorrows;*h*
 their libations of blood I will not pour out
 or take their names upon my lips.

B. *Calvary predicted*

5 The LORD is my chosen portion and my cup;
 thou holdest my lot.
6 The lines have fallen for me in pleasant places;
 yea, I have a goodly heritage.

7 I bless the LORD who gives me counsel;
 in the night also my heart instructs me.
8 I keep the LORD always before me;
 because he is at my right hand, I shall not be moved.

Cross references (right margin):

*15.1
Ps 24.3–5;
27.5,6; 2.6

15.2
Ps 24.4;
51.6;
Eph 4.25

15.3
Lev 19.16;
Ex 23.1

15.4
2 Tim 3.8;
Acts 28.10;
Judg 11.35

15.5
Ex 22.25;
23.8;
Deut 16.19;
Ps 112.6

16.1
Ps 17.8; 7.1

16.2
Ps 73.25

16.3
Deut 33.3;
Ps 101.6

16.4
Ps 32.10;
106.37,38;
Ex 23.13

16.5
Ps 73.26;
23.5; 125.3

16.6
Ps 78.55;
Jer 3.19

16.7
Ps 73.24;
77.6

16.8
Ps 54.3;
73.23; 62.2*

---

g Jerome Tg: The meaning of the Hebrew is uncertain
h Cn: The meaning of the Hebrew is uncertain

15.1 *thy tent.* The tabernacle (tent of meeting) and later, the Temple were structures in which God made manifest His presence in the midst of His people. The Psalmist asks, "Who is qualified to dwell in fellowship with God?"

C. *The resurrection assured*

16.9
Ps 4.7;
30.12; 4.8

9 Therefore my heart is glad, and my soul rejoices;
   my body also dwells secure.

*16.10
Acts 2.27;
13.35;
Ps 49.9

10 For thou dost not give me up to Shēōl,
   or let thy godly one see the Pit.

16.11
Mt 7.14;
Ps 17.15;
36,7,8

11 Thou dost show me the path of life;
   in thy presence there is fulness of joy,
   in thy right hand are pleasures for evermore.

A Prayer of David.

I. *David's desire for deliverance 17.1–15*

A. *He pleads his integrity*

17.1
Ps 9.4;
61.1; 55.1;
Isa 29.13
17.2
1 Chr 29.17

17 Hear a just cause, O LORD; attend to my cry!
   Give ear to my prayer from lips free of deceit!
2 From thee let my vindication come!
   Let thy eyes see the right!

17.3
Ps 26.2;
66.10;
Job 23.10;
Jer 50.20;
Ps 39.1
17.4
Prov 1.15
17.5
Ps 44.18;
18.36

3 If thou triest my heart, if thou visitest me by night,
   if thou testest me, thou wilt find no wickedness in me;
   my mouth does not transgress.
4 With regard to the works of men, by the word of thy lips
   I have avoided the ways of the violent.
5 My steps have held fast to thy paths,
   my feet have not slipped.

B. *He prays to be preserved*

17.6
Ps 86.7;
88.2
17.7
Ps 31.21;
20.6

6 I call upon thee, for thou wilt answer me, O God;
   incline thy ear to me, hear my words.
7 Wondrously show thy steadfast love,
   O savior of those who seek refuge
   from their adversaries at thy right hand.

17.8
Deut 32.10;
Ps 36.7
17.9
Ps 31.20;
38.12;
109.3

8 Keep me as the apple of the eye;
   hide me in the shadow of thy wings,
9 from the wicked who despoil me,
   my deadly enemies who surround me.

C. *He describes his enemies*

17.10
Ps 73.7;
1 Sam 2.3;
Ps 31.18

10 They close their hearts to pity;
   with their mouths they speak arrogantly.

16.10 This is a Messianic Psalm in which the Resurrection of Christ is predicted. Words which were of comfort to David and the righteous of all ages are quoted in Acts 2.27, 31 as being fulfilled in Christ at His Resurrection. Some prefer the ASV translation, "thou wilt not leave my soul to Sheol" rather than *thou dost not give me up to Sheol*. In Acts 2.27 it is translated *thou wilt not abandon my soul to Hades*. However, the Hebrew word *nephesh* does not mean "soul" as distinct from "body," but often refers to the whole person, so that *thou dost not give me up* is an accurate translation.

11 They track me down; now they surround me;
    they set their eyes to cast me to the ground.
12 They are like a lion eager to tear,
    as a young lion lurking in ambush.

17.11
Ps 88.17;
37.14
17.12
Ps 7.2; 10.9

D. He expresses his confidence in the LORD

13 Arise, O LORD! confront them, overthrow them!
    Deliver my life from the wicked by thy sword,
14 from men by thy hand, O LORD,
    from men whose portion in life is of the world.
  May their belly be filled with what thou hast stored up for them;
    may their children have more than enough;
    may they leave something over to their babes.

17.13
Ps 73.18;
22.20; 7.12
17.14
Lk 16.8;
Ps 73.3–7;
Isa 2.7;
Job 21.11

15 As for me, I shall behold thy face in righteousness;
    when I awake, I shall be satisfied with beholding thy form.

17.15
1 Jn 3.2;
Ps 4.6,7;
16.11

To the choirmaster. A Psalm of David the servant of the LORD,
who addressed the words of this song to the LORD on the day when
the LORD delivered him from the hand of all his enemies, and from
the hand of Saul. He said:

I. Hymn of deliverance 18.1–50

A. He glories in the LORD

18   I love thee, O LORD, my strength.
  2 The LORD is my rock, and my fortress, and my deliverer,
  my God, my rock, in whom I take refuge,
  my shield, and the horn of my salvation, my stronghold.
3 I call upon the LORD, who is worthy to be praised,
    and I am saved from my enemies.

18.1
Ps 27.1
18.2
Ps 19.14;
91.2;
40.17;
11.1;59.11;
75.10; 9.9
18.3
Ps 48.1;
Num 10.9

B. He testifies to His deliverances

4 The cords of death encompassed me,
    the torrents of perdition assailed me;
5 the cords of Shēōl entangled me,
    the snares of death confronted me.

18.4
Ps 116.3;
124.3,4
18.5
Ps 116.3;
Prov 14.27

6 In my distress I called upon the LORD;
    to my God I cried for help.
From his temple he heard my voice,
    and my cry to him reached his ears.

18.6
Ps 86.7;
11.4;
34.15

7 Then the earth reeled and rocked;
    the foundations also of the mountains trembled
    and quaked, because he was angry.
8 Smoke went up from his nostrils,
    and devouring fire from his mouth;
    glowing coals flamed forth from him.
9 He bowed the heavens, and came down;
    thick darkness was under his feet.

18.7
Ps 68.7,8;
114.4,6
18.8
Deut 29.20;
Hab 3.5
18.9
Ps 144.5;
Ex 20.21

18.10 Ps 80.1; 104.3	10 He rode on a cherub, and flew; he came swiftly upon the wings of the wind.
18.11 Ps 97.2	11 He made darkness his covering around him, his canopy thick clouds dark with water.

18.12
Ps 104.2;
Isa 30.30;
Ps 140.10
	12 Out of the brightness before him
	    there broke through his clouds
	    hailstones and coals of fire.

18.13
Ps 29.3;
104.7
	13 The LORD also thundered in the heavens,
	    and the Most High uttered his voice,
	    hailstones and coals of fire.

18.14 Ps 7.13; 144.6; Ex 14.24; Judg 4.15	14 And he sent out his arrows, and scattered them; he flashed forth lightnings, and routed them.

18.15
Ps 106.9;
76.6;
Ex 15.8
	15 Then the channels of the sea were seen,
	    and the foundations of the world were laid bare,
	  at thy rebuke, O LORD,
	    at the blast of the breath of thy nostrils.

18.16 Ps 144.7	16 He reached from on high, he took me, he drew me out of many waters.

18.17
ver 48;
Ps 35.10
	17 He delivered me from my strong enemy,
	    and from those who hated me;
	    for they were too mighty for me.

18.18 Ps 59.16; Isa 10.20	18 They came upon me in the day of my calamity; but the LORD was my stay.
18.19 Ps 31.8; 118.5; 37.23	19 He brought me forth into a broad place; he delivered me, because he delighted in me.

C. *He justifies his integrity*

18.20 Ps 7.8; 1 Ki 8.32; Ps 24.4	20 The LORD rewarded me according to my righteousness; according to the cleanness of my hands he recompensed me.
18.21 Ps 119.33; 2 Chr 34.33; Ps 119.102	21 For I have kept the ways of the LORD, and have not wickedly departed from my God.

18.22
Ps 119.30,
83
	22 For all his ordinances were before me,
	    and his statutes I did not put away from me.
	23 I was blameless before him,
	    and I kept myself from guilt.

18.24
1 Sam 26.23
	24 Therefore the LORD has recompensed me according to my right-
	        eousness,
	    according to the cleanness of my hands in his sight.

18.25 Ps 62.12; Mt 5.7	25 With the loyal thou dost show thyself loyal; with the blameless man thou dost show thyself blameless;
18.26 Job 25.5; Prov 3.34	26 with the pure thou dost show thyself pure; and with the crooked thou dost show thyself perverse.
18.27 Ps 72.12; Prov 6.17	27 For thou dost deliver a humble people; but the haughty eyes thou dost bring down.
18.28 Job 18.6; Ps 27.1; Job 29.3	28 Yea, thou dost light my lamp; the LORD my God lightens my darkness.
18.29 2 Cor 12.9; Heb 11.34	29 Yea, by thee I can crush a troop; and by my God I can leap over a wall.

18.30
Deut 32.4;
Ps 12.6;
17.7
	30 This God—his way is perfect;
	    the promise of the LORD proves true;
	    he is a shield for all those who take refuge in him.

D. He acknowledges that God has delivered him

31 For who is God, but the LORD?
  And who is a rock, except our God?—
32 the God who girded me with strength,
  and made my way safe.
33 He made my feet like hinds' feet,
  and set me secure on the heights.
34 He trains my hands for war,
  so that my arms can bend a bow of bronze.
35 Thou hast given me the shield of thy salvation,
  and thy right hand supported me,
  and thy help*i* made me great.
36 Thou didst give a wide place for my steps under me,
  and my feet did not slip.
37 I pursued my enemies and overtook them;
  and did not turn back till they were consumed.
38 I thrust them through, so that they were not able to rise;
  they fell under my feet.
39 For thou didst gird me with strength for the battle;
  thou didst make my assailants sink under me.
40 Thou didst make my enemies turn their backs to me,
  and those who hated me I destroyed.
41 They cried for help, but there was none to save,
  they cried to the LORD, but he did not answer them.
42 I beat them fine as dust before the wind;
  I cast them out like the mire of the streets.

E. He expresses confidence in the future

43 Thou didst deliver me from strife with the peoples;*j*
  thou didst make me the head of the nations;
  people whom I had not known served me.
44 As soon as they heard of me they obeyed me;
  foreigners came cringing to me.
45 Foreigners lost heart,
  and came trembling out of their fastnesses.

46 The LORD lives; and blessed be my rock,
  and exalted be the God of my salvation,
47 the God who gave me vengeance
  and subdued peoples under me;
48 who delivered me from my enemies;
  yea, thou didst exalt me above my adversaries;
  thou didst deliver me from men of violence.

49 For this I will extol thee, O LORD, among the nations,
  and sing praises to thy name.
50 Great triumphs he gives to his king,
  and shows steadfast love to his anointed,
  to David and his descendants for ever.

i Or *gentleness*   *j* Gk Tg: Heb *people*

18.31 *rock.* In a symbolic sense, this word expresses the firm foundation of God.   **18.33** *hinds' feet.* Hind is a female member of the deer family.

*18.31
Deut 32.31,
39;
Ps 86.8–10;
Isa 45.5

18.32
Isa 45.5;
Heb 13.21;
1 Pet 5.10

*18.33
Hab 3.19;
Deut 32.13

18.34
Ps 144.1;
Job 20.24

18.35
Deut 33.29;
Ps 119.117;
138.6

18.36
Ps 31.8;
71.5

18.37
Ps 44.5;
37.20

18.38
Ps 110.6;
36.12; 47.3

18.39
ver 32,47

18.40
Ps 21.21;
94.23

18.41
Ps 50.22;
Prov 1.28

18.42
Ps 83.13

18.43
Ps 35.1;
Isa 52.15;
55.5

18.44
Ps 66.3

18.46
Ps 42.2;
51.14

18.47
Ps 94.1;
47.3

18.48
Ps 143.9;
27.6; 140.1,
4

18.49
Rom 15.9;
Ps 108.1

18.50
Ps 144.10;
28.8; 89.4,
29

To the choirmaster. A Psalm of David.

I. *The works and Word of God 19.1–14*

A. *The revelation of God in creation*

19.1
Gen 1.6;
Isa 40.22;
Rom 1.19,
20
19.2
Ps 74.16

19 The heavens are telling the glory of God;
and the firmament proclaims his handiwork.
2 Day to day pours forth speech,
and night to night declares knowledge.
3 There is no speech, nor are there words;
their voice is not heard;

19.4
Rom 10.18

4 yet their voice*k* goes out through all the earth,
and their words to the end of the world.

In them he has set a tent for the sun,

19.5
Ecc 1.5

5 which comes forth like a bridegroom leaving his chamber,
and like a strong man runs its course with joy.

★19.6
Ps 113.3;
Deut 30.4

6 Its rising is from the end of the heavens,
and its circuit to the end of them;
and there is nothing hid from its heat.

B. *The revelation of God in the Word of God*

19.7
Ps 119.142;
23.3; 93.5;
111.7;
119.98–100

7 The law of the LORD is perfect,
reviving the soul;
the testimony of the LORD is sure,
making wise the simple;

19.8
Ps 119.128;
12.6;
119.30

8 the precepts of the LORD are right,
rejoicing the heart;
the commandment of the LORD is pure,
enlightening the eyes;

19.9
Ps 119.42

9 the fear of the LORD is clean,
enduring for ever;
the ordinances of the LORD are true,
and righteous altogether.

19.10
Prov 8.10;
16.24

10 More to be desired are they than gold,
even much fine gold;
sweeter also than honey
and drippings of the honeycomb.

19.11
Ps 17.4;
Prov 29.18
19.12
Ps 139.6;
51.1,2; 90.8
19.13
Ps 119.33;
32.2; 25.11

11 Moreover by them is thy servant warned;
in keeping them there is great reward.
12 But who can discern his errors?
Clear thou me from hidden faults.
13 Keep back thy servant also from presumptuous sins;
let them not have dominion over me!
Then I shall be blameless,
and innocent of great transgression.

19.14
Ps 104.34;
18.2;
Isa 41.14;
43.14

14 Let the words of my mouth and the meditation of my heart
be acceptable in thy sight,
O LORD, my rock and my redeemer.

k Gk Jerome Compare Syr: Heb *line*

19.6 *its circuit*. The sun appears to run a course from east to west across the sky. Scrip-ture does not teach that the sun revolves around the earth.

To the choirmaster. A Psalm of David.

I. *A liturgy for the king 20.1–9*

A. *Prayer for victory*

20 The LORD answer you in the day of trouble!
   The name of the God of Jacob protect you!
2 May he send you help from the sanctuary,
   and give you support from Zion!
3 May he remember all your offerings,
   and regard with favor your burnt sacrifices!   *Selâh*

4 May he grant you your heart's desire,
   and fulfil all your plans!
5 May we shout for joy over your victory,
   and in the name of our God set up our banners!
   May the LORD fulfil all your petitions!

B. *Assurance of divine help*

6 Now I know that the LORD will help his anointed;
   he will answer him from his holy heaven
   with mighty victories by his right hand.
7 Some boast of chariots, and some of horses;
   but we boast of the name of the LORD our God.
8 They will collapse and fall;
   but we shall rise and stand upright.

9 Give victory to the king, O LORD;
   answer us when we call.[1]

To the choirmaster. A Psalm of David.

I. *Praise for deliverance 21.1–13*

A. *Thanksgiving for past victories*

21 In thy strength the king rejoices, O LORD;
   and in thy help how greatly he exults!
2 Thou hast given him his heart's desire,
   and hast not withheld the request of his lips.   *Selâh*
3 For thou dost meet him with goodly blessings;
   thou dost set a crown of fine gold upon his head.
4 He asked life of thee; thou gavest it to him,
   length of days for ever and ever.
5 His glory is great through thy help;
   splendor and majesty thou dost bestow upon him.
6 Yea, thou dost make him most blessed for ever;
   thou dost make him glad with the joy of thy presence.
7 For the king trusts in the LORD;
   and through the steadfast love of the Most High he shall not
   be moved.

[1] Gk: Heb *give victory, O* LORD, *let the King answer us when we call*

Marginal references:

20.1 Ps 102.2; 91.14; 36.7,11; 59.1
20.2 Ps 3.4; 119.28
20.3 Ps 51.19
20.4 Ps 21.2; 145.19
20.5 Ps 9.14; 1 Sam 1.17
20.6 Ps 41.11; Isa 58.9; Ps 28.8
20.7 Isa 36.9; 31.1; 2 Chr 32.8
20.8 Ps 37.24
20.9 Ps 3.7
21.1 Ps 59.16,17; 9.14
21.2 Ps 37.4
21.3 Ps 59.10
21.4 Ps 133.3; 91.16
21.5 Ps 18.50; 45.3,4
21.6 1 Chr 17.27; Ps 16.11
21.7 2 Ki 18.5; Ps 16.8

B. *Assurance of future victories*

21.8
Isa 10.10

8 Your hand will find out all your enemies;
  your right hand will find out those who hate you.

21.9
Mal 4.1;
Lam 2.2

9 You will make them as a blazing oven
    when you appear.
The LORD will swallow them up in his wrath;
  and fire will consume them.

21.10
Deut 28.18;
Ps 37.28

10 You will destroy their offspring from the earth,
    and their children from among the sons of men.

21.11
Ps 2.1–3;
10.2

11 If they plan evil against you,
    if they devise mischief, they will not succeed.

21.12
Ps 18.40;
7.12,13

12 For you will put them to flight;
    you will aim at their faces with your bows.

21.13
Ps 57.5;
81.1

13 Be exalted, O LORD, in thy strength!
    We will sing and praise thy power.

To the choirmaster: according to The Hind of the Dawn.
A Psalm of David.

I. *The suffering and the glory of Messiah predicted*
22.1–31

A. *Forsaken of God*

★22.1
Mt 27.46;
Ps 10.1

22 My God, my God, why hast thou forsaken me?
   Why art thou so far from helping me, from the words of my
   groaning?

22.2
Ps 42.3

2 O my God, I cry by day, but thou dost not answer;
    and by night, but find no rest.

22.3
Ps 99.9;
35.8

3 Yet thou art holy,
    enthroned on the praises of Israel.
4 In thee our fathers trusted;
    they trusted, and thou didst deliver them.

22.5
Ps 107.6;
25.2,3;
Rom 9.33

5 To thee they cried, and were saved;
    in thee they trusted, and were not disappointed.

B. *Scorned by men*

★22.6
Job 25.6;
Isa 41.14;
Ps 31.11;
Isa 49.7

6 But I am a worm, and no man;
    scorned by men, and despised by the people.

22.7
Mt 27.39;
Mk 15.29

7 All who see me mock at me,
    they make mouths at me, they wag their heads;

22.8
Mt 27.43;
Mk 1.11

8 "He committed his cause to the LORD; let him deliver him,
    let him rescue him, for he delights in him!"

22.1 In language which expresses the thoughts of God's suffering people of all ages, Psalm 22 prophetically sets forth Christ's agonizing emotions on the cross. Verses 14–17 are graphic representations of the suffering He endured through crucifixion. Moreover, two specific details are foretold in this Psalm.

In verse 1 the fourth saying of Christ on the cross is enunciated for the first time (Mt 27.46). In verse 18 the prophecy of the soldiers casting lots over Christ's seamless robe is foretold (Mt 27.35; Lk 23.34; Jn 19.23, 24).
22.6 A *worm* is trodden underfoot and treated with contempt.

9 Yet thou art he who took me from the womb;
   thou didst keep me safe upon my mother's breasts.
10 Upon thee was I cast from my birth,
   and since my mother bore me thou hast been my God.
11 Be not far from me,
   for trouble is near
   and there is none to help.

C. Encompassed by animals

12 Many bulls encompass me,
   strong bulls of Bāshán surround me;
13 they open wide their mouths at me,
   like a ravening and roaring lion.

14 I am poured out like water,
   and all my bones are out of joint;
   my heart is like wax,
   it is melted within my breast;
15 my strength is dried up like a potsherd,
   and my tongue cleaves to my jaws;
   thou dost lay me in the dust of death.

D. They pierce his hands; they cast lots for his raiment

16 Yea, dogs are round about me;
   a company of evildoers encircle me;
   they have pierced[m] my hands and feet—
17 I can count all my bones—
   they stare and gloat over me;
18 they divide my garments among them,
   and for my raiment they cast lots.

E. His prayer for deliverance

19 But thou, O LORD, be not far off!
   O thou my help, hasten to my aid!
20 Deliver my soul from the sword,
   my life[n] from the power of the dog!
21 Save me from the mouth of the lion,
   my afflicted soul[o] from the horns of the wild oxen!

F. Praise to the LORD

22 I will tell of thy name to my brethren;
   in the midst of the congregation I will praise thee:
23 You who fear the LORD, praise him!
   all you sons of Jacob, glorify him,
   and stand in awe of him, all you sons of Israel!
24 For he has not despised or abhorred
   the affliction of the afflicted;
   and he has not hid his face from him,
   but has heard, when he cried to him.

25 From thee comes my praise in the great congregation;
   my vows I will pay before those who fear him.

m Gk Syr Jerome: Heb like a lion   n Heb my only one   o Gk Syr: Heb thou hast answered me

Cross-references (right margin):

22.9 Ps 71.6
22.10 Isa 46.3
22.11 Ps 72.12
22.12 Ps 68.30; Deut 32.14
22.13 Ps 35.21; 17.12
22.14 Job 30.16; Ps 31.10; 107.26
22.15 Ps 38.10; 137.6; 104.29
22.16 Ps 59.6; Mt 27.35
22.18 Mt 27.35
22.19 ver 11; Ps 70.5
22.20 Ps 35.17
22.21 ver 13; Ps 34.4
22.22 Heb 2.12
22.23 Ps 135.19; 86.12; 33.8
22.24 Ps 102.17; 69.17; Heb 5.7
22.25 Ps 35.18; 66.13

G. Salvation offered to all

22.26
Ps 107.9;
40.16;
69.32

26 The afflicted*p* shall eat and be satisfied;
    those who seek him shall praise the LORD!
    May your hearts live for ever!

22.27
Ps 2.8; 86.9

27 All the ends of the earth shall remember
    and turn to the LORD;
and all the families of the nations
    shall worship before him.*q*

22.28
Ps 47.7,8;
Mt 6.13

28 For dominion belongs to the LORD,
    and he rules over the nations.

22.29
Ps 47.7;
Isa 27.13;
Ps 95.6

29 Yea, to him*r* shall all the proud of the earth bow down;
    before him shall bow all who go down to the dust,
    and he who cannot keep himself alive.

22.30
Ps 102.28;
71.18

30 Posterity shall serve him;
    men shall tell of the Lord to the coming generation,

22.31
Ps 78.6

31 and proclaim his deliverance to a people yet unborn,
    that he has wrought it.

A Psalm of David.

I. The LORD my shepherd 23.1–6

A. He feeds and guides His sheep

*23.1
Isa 40.11;
Jer 23.4;
Jn 10.11;
1 Pet 2.25;
Phil 4.19

23   The LORD is my shepherd, I shall not want;
    2 he makes me lie down in green pastures.
He leads me beside still waters;*s*

23.2
Ezek 34.14;
Rev 7.17

3   he restores my soul.*t*
He leads me in paths of righteousness*u*
    for his name's sake.

23.3
Ps 19.7;
5.8;
85.13;
143.11

4 Even though I walk through the valley of the shadow of death,*v*
    I fear no evil;
for thou art with me;
    thy rod and thy staff,
    they comfort me.

23.4
Ps 138.7;
Job 3.5;
Ps 27.1;
Isa 43.2

B. He is host to His people forever

23.5
Ps 78.19;
31.19;
92.10; 16.5

5 Thou preparest a table before me
    in the presence of my enemies;
thou anointest my head with oil,
    my cup overflows.

23.6
Ps 25.7,10;
27.4–6

6 Surely*w* goodness and mercy*x* shall follow me

p Or *poor*   *q* Gk Syr Jerome: Heb *thee*
r Cn: Heb *they have eaten and*
s Heb *the waters of rest*   *t* Or *life*
u Or *right paths*   *v* Or *the valley of deep darkness*
w Or *Only*   *x* Or *kindness*

23.1 This, the most famous of all the Psalms, has been identified as Messianic, picturing Jesus as the *good shepherd* (Jn 10.11) and the *great shepherd* (Heb 13.20).

all the days of my life;
and I shall dwell in the house of the LORD
for ever.*y*

A Psalm of David.

I. *Psalm to the King of glory 24.1–10*

A. *The LORD the creator*

24 The earth is the LORD's and the fulness thereof,
the world and those who dwell therein;
2 for he has founded it upon the seas,
and established it upon the rivers.

B. *The character of the LORD'S people*

3 Who shall ascend the hill of the LORD?
And who shall stand in his holy place?
4 He who has clean hands and a pure heart,
who does not lift up his soul to what is false,
and does not swear deceitfully.
5 He will receive blessing from the LORD,
and vindication from the God of his salvation.
6 Such is the generation of those who seek him,
who seek the face of the God of Jacob.*z*   *Sēlāh*

C. *The entry of the King of glory*

7 Lift up your heads, O gates!
and be lifted up, O ancient doors!
that the King of glory may come in.
8 Who is the King of glory?
The LORD, strong and mighty,
the LORD, mighty in battle!
9 Lift up your heads, O gates!
and be lifted up,*a* O ancient doors!
that the King of glory may come in.
10 Who is this King of glory?
The LORD of hosts,
he is the King of glory!   *Sēlāh*

A Psalm of David.

I. *Prayer for guidance and protection 25.1–22*

A. *God's way sought*

25 2 To thee, O LORD, I lift up my soul.
2 O my God, in thee I trust,

y Or *as long as I live*   *z* Gk Syr: Heb *thy face, O Jacob*
a Gk Syr Jerome Tg Compare verse 7: Heb *lift up*

Marginal references:

24.1
Ex 9.29;
Job 41.11;
1 Cor
10.26;
Ps 89.11

24.3
Ps 15.1;
2.6; 65.4
24.4
Job 17.9;
Mt 5.8;
Ps 15.4
24.5
Deut
11.26,27;
Isa 46.13;
Ps 25.5
24.6
Ps 27.8

24.7
Isa 26.2;
1 Cor 2.8

24.8
Ps 89.13;
76.3–6

24.9
Zech 9.9;
Mt 21.5

25.1
Ps 86.4
25.2
Ps 31.6;
41.11

let me not be put to shame;
let not my enemies exult over me.

3 Yea, let none that wait for thee be put to shame;
let them be ashamed who are wantonly treacherous.

25.3
Isa 49.23;
33.1

4 Make me to know thy ways, O LORD;
teach me thy paths.

★**25.4**
Ps 5.8;
86.11

5 Lead me in thy truth, and teach me,
for thou art the God of my salvation;
for thee I wait all the day long.

25.5
Jn 16.13;
Ps 24.5;
40.1

6 Be mindful of thy mercy, O LORD, and of thy steadfast love,
for they have been from of old.

25.6
Ps 103.17;
Isa 63.15

7 Remember not the sins of my youth, or my transgressions;
according to thy steadfast love remember me,
for thy goodness' sake, O LORD!

25.7
Job 13.26;
Jer 3.25;
Ps 51.1

B. God's way made plain

8 Good and upright is the LORD;
therefore he instructs sinners in the way.

25.8
Ps 106.1;
92.15; 32.8

9 He leads the humble in what is right,
and teaches the humble his way.

25.9
Ps 23.3;
27.11

10 All the paths of the LORD are steadfast love and faithfulness,
for those who keep his covenant and his testimonies.

25.10
Ps 40.11;
103.18

11 For thy name's sake, O LORD,
pardon my guilt, for it is great.

25.11
Ps 31.1;
Rom 5.20

12 Who is the man that fears the LORD?
Him will he instruct in the way that he should choose.

13 He himself shall abide in prosperity,
and his children shall possess the land.

25.13
Prov 19.23;
Ps 37.11

14 The friendship of the LORD is for those who fear him,
and he makes known to them his covenant.

25.14
Prov 3.32;
Jn 7.17

15 My eyes are ever toward the LORD,
for he will pluck my feet out of the net.

25.15
Ps 141.8

C. Prayer for deliverance

16 Turn thou to me, and be gracious to me;
for I am lonely and afflicted.

25.16
Ps 69.16

17 Relieve the troubles of my heart,
and bring me[b] out of my distresses.

25.17
Ps 88.3;
107.6

18 Consider my affliction and my trouble,
and forgive all my sins.

25.18
2 Sam 16.12

19 Consider how many are my foes,
and with what violent hatred they hate me.

25.19
Ps 3.1;
27.12

b Or The troubles of my heart are enlarged; bring me

25.4 Scripture everywhere affirms that God has a perfect will for every believer. Here, and in verse 5, David, whose trust is in God, prays that God will reveal that will to him. Then he exclaims triumphantly that God will guide him in the way he should go (ver 9, 10). This same truth is set forth in Col 1.9 and Isa 30.20, 21. Rom 12.2 implies that a total self-surrender will enable the believer to experience God's perfect will for his life.

20 Oh guard my life, and deliver me;
    let me not be put to shame, for I take refuge in thee.
21 May integrity and uprightness preserve me,
    for I wait for thee.

22 Redeem Israel, O God,
    out of all his troubles.

A Psalm of David.

I. A plea for vindication 26.1–12

A. Prayer for divine help

26 Vindicate me, O LORD,
    for I have walked in my integrity,
and I have trusted in the LORD without wavering.
2 Prove me, O LORD, and try me;
    test my heart and my mind.
3 For thy steadfast love is before my eyes,
    and I walk in faithfulness to thee.^c

B. David's defense of himself

4 I do not sit with false men,
    nor do I consort with dissemblers;
5 I hate the company of evildoers,
    and I will not sit with the wicked.

6 I wash my hands in innocence,
    and go about thy altar, O LORD,
7 singing aloud a song of thanksgiving,
    and telling all thy wondrous deeds.

C. His final plea for help

8 O LORD, I love the habitation of thy house,
    and the place where thy glory dwells.
9 Sweep me not away with sinners,
    nor my life with bloodthirsty men,
10 men in whose hands are evil devices,
    and whose right hands are full of bribes.

11 But as for me, I walk in my integrity;
    redeem me, and be gracious to me.
12 My foot stands on level ground;
    in the great congregation I will bless the LORD.

^c Or *in thy faithfulness*

Marginal references: 25.20 Ps 86.2 | 25.21 Ps 41.12; ver 3 | 25.22 Ps 130.8 | *26.1 Ps 7.8; Prov 20.7; Ps 25.2; Heb 10.23 | 26.2 Ps 7.9; 66.10 | 26.3 2 Ki 20.3 | 26.4 Ps 1.1 | 26.5 Ps 139.21; 1.1 | 26.6 Ps 73.13 | 26.7 Ps 35.18; 9.1 | 26.8 Ps 27.4 | 26.9 Ps 28.3 | 26.10 1 Sam 8.3 | 26.11 ver 1; Ps 69.18 | 26.12 Ps 40.2; 27.11; 22.22

26.1 False accusations, slander, and defamation are the lot of those who seek to serve God. In Mt 5.11 and Jn 15.20 Jesus warned His disciples to expect this kind of treatment. David here appeals to the judgment of God over against the judgment of men, and is willing to let God examine and prove him, confident that his prayer is heard and he is safe.

A Psalm of David.

I. *David's song of confidence 27.1–6*

<table>
<tr><td>27.1
Isa 60.19;
Ex 15.2;
Ps 62.2</td><td>27 The LORD is my light and my salvation;
    whom shall I fear?
The LORD is the stronghold^d of my life;
    of whom shall I be afraid?</td></tr>
</table>

27.1
Isa 60.19;
Ex 15.2;
Ps 62.2

27 The LORD is my light and my salvation;
    whom shall I fear?
The LORD is the stronghold[d] of my life;
    of whom shall I be afraid?

27.2
Ps 14.4

2 When evildoers assail me,
    uttering slanders against me,[e]
my adversaries and foes,
    they shall stumble and fall.

27.3
Ps 3.6

3 Though a host encamp against me,
    my heart shall not fear;
though war arise against me,
    yet I will be confident.

27.4
Ps 26.8;
90.17

4 One thing have I asked of the LORD,
    that will I seek after;
that I may dwell in the house of the LORD
    all the days of my life,
to behold the beauty of the LORD,
    and to inquire in his temple.

27.5
Ps 31.20;
40.2

5 For he will hide me in his shelter
    in the day of trouble;
he will conceal me under the cover of his tent,
    he will set me high upon a rock.

27.6
Ps 3.3

6 And now my head shall be lifted up
    above my enemies round about me;
and I will offer in his tent
    sacrifices with shouts of joy;
I will sing and make melody to the LORD.

II. *David's prayer for help 27.7–14*

27.7
Ps 39.12;
13.3
27.8
Ps 24.6

7 Hear, O LORD, when I cry aloud,
    be gracious to me and answer me!
8 Thou hast said, "Seek ye my face."
    My heart says to thee,
"Thy face, LORD, do I seek."

27.9
Ps 69.17

9   Hide not thy face from me.

Turn not thy servant away in anger,
    thou who hast been my help.
Cast me not off, forsake me not,
    O God of my salvation!

27.10
Isa 49.15;
40.11

10 For my father and my mother have forsaken me,
    but the LORD will take me up.

d Or refuge
e Heb to eat up my flesh

11 Teach me thy way, O LORD;
    and lead me on a level path
    because of my enemies.
12 Give me not up to the will of my adversaries;
    for false witnesses have risen against me,
    and they breathe out violence.

13 I believe that I shall see the goodness of the LORD
    in the land of the living!
14 Wait for the LORD;
    be strong, and let your heart take courage;
    yea, wait for the LORD!

A Psalm of David.

I. The prayer for help 28.1–5

28 To thee, O LORD, I call;
    my rock, be not deaf to me,
lest, if thou be silent to me,
    I become like those who go down to the Pit.
2 Hear the voice of my supplication,
    as I cry to thee for help,
    as I lift up my hands
    toward thy most holy sanctuary.*f*

3 Take me not off with the wicked,
    with those who are workers of evil,
who speak peace with their neighbors,
    while mischief is in their hearts.
4 Requite them according to their work,
    and according to the evil of their deeds;
requite them according to the work of their hands;
    render them their due reward.
5 Because they do not regard the works of the LORD,
    or the work of his hands,
he will break them down and build them up no more.

II. The assurance of an answer 28.6–9

6 Blessed be the LORD!
    for he has heard the voice of my supplications.
7 The LORD is my strength and my shield;
    in him my heart trusts;
so I am helped, and my heart exults,
    and with my song I give thanks to him.

8 The LORD is the strength of his people,
    he is the saving refuge of his anointed.
9 O save thy people, and bless thy heritage;
    be thou their shepherd, and carry them for ever.

f Heb *thy innermost sanctuary*

Cross-references (right margin):

27.11 Ps 25.4; 86.11; 5.8
27.12 Ps 41.2; 35.11; Mt 26.60; Acts 9.1
27.13 Ps 31.19; Jer 11.19
27.14 Ps 40.1; Josh 1.6
28.1 Ps 83.1; 88.4
28.2 Ps 140.6; 5.7; 138.2
28.3 Ps 26.9; 12.2; Jer 9.8
28.4 Rev 18.6
28.5 Isa 5.12
28.6 Ps 116.1
28.7 Ps 18.2; 13.5
28.8 Ps 20.6
28.9 Deut 9.29; Ezra 1.4

A Psalm of David.

I. *The* LORD *of the thunderstorm 29.1–11*

A. *Summons to give glory to God*

29 Ascribe to the LORD, O heavenly beings,[g]
ascribe to the LORD glory and strength.
2 Ascribe to the LORD the glory of his name;
worship the LORD in holy array.

B. *God's power in the storm*

3 The voice of the LORD is upon the waters;
the God of glory thunders,
the LORD, upon many waters.
4 The voice of the LORD is powerful,
the voice of the LORD is full of majesty.

5 The voice of the LORD breaks the cedars,
the LORD breaks the cedars of Lebanon.
6 He makes Lebanon to skip like a calf,
and Sïr'ïŏn like a young wild ox.

7 The voice of the LORD flashes forth flames of fire.
8 The voice of the LORD shakes the wilderness,
the LORD shakes the wilderness of Kādësh.

9 The voice of the LORD makes the oaks to whirl,[h]
and strips the forests bare;
and in his temple all cry, "Glory!"

C. *Prayer for the blessing of the* LORD *of the storm*

10 The LORD sits enthroned over the flood;
the LORD sits enthroned as king for ever.
11 May the LORD give strength to his people!
May the LORD bless his people with peace!

A Psalm of David. A Song at the dedication of the Temple.

I. *Song of deliverance 30.1–12*

A. *Praise for deliverance*

30 I will extol thee, O LORD, for thou hast drawn me up,
and hast not let my foes rejoice over me.
2 O LORD my God, I cried to thee for help,
and thou hast healed me.
3 O LORD, thou hast brought up my soul from Shēōl,
restored me to life from among those gone down to the Pit.[i]

g Heb *sons of gods* h Or *makes the hinds to calve*
i Or *that I should not go down to the Pit*

Side references: 29.1 / 1 Chr 16.28,29; Ps 96.7–9; 29.2 / 2 Chr 20.21; 29.3 / Job 37.4,5; 29.4 / Ps 68.33; 29.5 / Isa 2.13; 29.6 / Ps 114.4; Deut 3.9; 29.8 / Num 13.26; 29.9 / Ps 26.8; 29.10 / Ps 10.16; 29.11 / Ps 28.8; 37.11; 30.1 / Ps 28.9; 25.2; 30.2 / Ps 88.13; 6.2; 30.3 / Ps 86.13; 28.1

B. *Exhortation for others to praise the* LORD

4 Sing praises to the LORD, O you his saints,
    and give thanks to his holy name.
5 For his anger is but for a moment,
    and his favor is for a lifetime.
Weeping may tarry for the night,
    but joy comes with the morning.

6 As for me, I said in my prosperity,
    "I shall never be moved."
7 By thy favor, O LORD,
    thou hadst established me as a strong mountain;
thou didst hide thy face,
    I was dismayed.

8 To thee, O LORD, I cried;
    and to the LORD I made supplication:
9 "What profit is there in my death,
    if I go down to the Pit?
Will the dust praise thee?
    Will it tell of thy faithfulness?
10 Hear, O LORD, and be gracious to me!
    O LORD, be thou my helper!"

11 Thou hast turned for me my mourning into dancing;
    thou hast loosed my sackcloth
    and girded me with gladness,
12 that my soul*j* may praise thee and not be silent.
    O LORD my God, I will give thanks to thee for ever.

To the choirmaster. A Psalm of David.

I. *"My times are in thy hand."* 31.1–24

A. *Trust in God and prayer for deliverance*

31 In thee, O LORD, do I seek refuge;
    let me never be put to shame;
    in thy righteousness deliver me!
2 Incline thy ear to me,
    rescue me speedily!
Be thou a rock of refuge for me,
    a strong fortress to save me!

3 Yea, thou art my rock and my fortress;
    for thy name's sake lead me and guide me,
4 take me out of the net which is hidden for me,
    for thou art my refuge.
5 Into thy hand I commit my spirit;
    thou hast redeemed me, O LORD, faithful God.

j Heb *that glory*

Marginal references:

★30.4
Ps 149.1;
50.5; 97.12

30.5
Ps 103.9;
63.3

30.7
Ps 104.29

30.9
Ps 6.5

30.11
Ps 6.8;
Jer 31.4,13;
Ps 4.7
30.12
Ps 16.9;
44.8

31.1
Ps 22.5;
Isa 49.23

★31.2
Ps 71.2

31.3
Ps 18.2;
23.3
31.4
Ps 25.15;
28.8
31.5
Lk 23.46;
Acts 7.59

30.4 *his saints,* i.e., his pious ones.   **31.2** *rock,* i.e., strength and impregnability.

31.6 Jon 2.8	6 Thou hatest^k those who pay regard to vain idols; 　but I trust in the LORD.
31.7 Ps 90.14; 10.14; Jn 10.27	7 I will rejoice and be glad for thy steadfast love, 　because thou hast seen my affliction, 　thou hast taken heed of my adversities,
31.8 Deut 32.30; Ps 4.1	8 and hast not delivered me into the hand of the enemy; 　thou hast set my feet in a broad place.

B. Complaints which require deliverance

31.9 Ps 6.7	9 Be gracious to me, O LORD, for I am in distress; 　my eye is wasted from grief, 　my soul and my body also.
31.10 Ps 13.2; 39.11; 38.3	10 For my life is spent with sorrow, 　and my years with sighing; 　my strength fails because of my misery,^l 　and my bones waste away.
31.11 Isa 53.4; Ps 38.11; 64.8	11 I am the scorn of all my adversaries, 　a horror^m to my neighbors, 　an object of dread to my acquaintances; 　those who see me in the street flee from me.
31.12 Ps 88.4,5	12 I have passed out of mind like one who is dead; 　I have become like a broken vessel.
31.13 Jer 20.10; Lam 2.20; Mt 27.1	13 Yea, I hear the whispering of many— 　terror on every side!— 　as they scheme together against me, 　as they plot to take my life.
31.14 Ps 140.6	14 But I trust in thee, O LORD, 　I say, "Thou art my God."
31.15 Job 24.1; Ps 143.9	15 My times are in thy hand; 　deliver me from the hand of my enemies and persecutors!
31.16 Num 6.25; Ps 4.6	16 Let thy face shine on thy servant; 　save me in thy steadfast love!
31.17 Ps 25.2,3	17 Let me not be put to shame, O LORD, 　for I call on thee; 　let the wicked be put to shame, 　let them go dumbfounded to Sheōl.
31.18 Ps 120.2; 94.4	18 Let the lying lips be dumb, 　which speak insolently against the righteous 　in pride and contempt.

C. Praise to a delivering LORD

31.19 Isa 64.4; Rom 11.22; Ps 5.11	19 O how abundant is thy goodness, 　which thou hast laid up for those who fear thee, 　and wrought for those who take refuge in thee, 　in the sight of the sons of men!
31.20 Ps 27.5; Job 5.21	20 In the covert of thy presence thou hidest them 　from the plots of men; 　thou holdest them safe under thy shelter 　from the strife of tongues.

---

k With one Heb Ms Gk Syr Jerome: Heb *I hate*
l Gk Syr: Heb *iniquity*　m Cn: Heb *exceedingly*

21 Blessed be the LORD,
    for he has wondrously shown his steadfast love to me
        when I was beset as in a besieged city.

31.21
Ps 17.7;
1 Sam 23.7

22 I had said in my alarm,
    "I am driven far[n] from thy sight."
    But thou didst hear my supplications,
        when I cried to thee for help.

31.22
Ps 116.11;
Lam 3.54

23 Love the LORD, all you his saints!
    The LORD preserves the faithful,
        but abundantly requites him who acts haughtily.
24 Be strong, and let your heart take courage,
    all you who wait for the LORD!

31.23
Ps 34.9;
145.20;
94.2

31.24
Ps 27.14

A Psalm of David. A Mäskil.

I. *The penitent's Psalm 32.1–11*

A. *The blessedness of the forgiven*

32 Blessed is he whose transgression is forgiven,
    whose sin is covered.
2 Blessed is the man to whom the LORD imputes no iniquity,
    and in whose spirit there is no deceit.

32.1
Ps 85.2

32.2
2 Cor 5.19;
Jn 1.47

B. *Sin confessed and forgiven*

3 When I declared not my sin, my body wasted away
    through my groaning all day long.
4 For day and night thy hand was heavy upon me;
    my strength was dried up[o] as by the heat of summer. *Sēlāh*

32.3
Ps 39.2,3;
31.10; 38.8

32.4
Job 33.7

5 I acknowledged my sin to thee,
    and I did not hide my iniquity;
    I said, "I will confess my transgressions to the LORD";
        then thou didst forgive the guilt of my sin. *Sēlāh*

32.5
Lev 26.40;
Job 31.33;
Prov 28.13;
Ps 103.12

6 Therefore let every one who is godly
    offer prayer to thee;
    at a time of distress,[p] in the rush of great waters,
        they shall not reach him.
7 Thou art a hiding place for me,
    thou preservest me from trouble;
    thou dost encompass me with deliverance.[q]   *Sēlāh*

32.6
Ps 69.13;
144.7;
Isa 43.2

32.7
Ps 31.20;
121.7;
Ex 15.1

C. *Exhortation to sinners to repent*

8 I will instruct you and teach you
    the way you should go;
    I will counsel you with my eye upon you.
9 Be not like a horse or a mule, without understanding,
    which must be curbed with bit and bridle,
        else it will not keep with you.

32.8
Ps 25.8;
33.18

32.9
Jas 3.3

---

[n] Another reading is *cut off*   [o] Heb obscure   [p] Cn: Heb *at a time of finding only*
[q] Cn: Heb *shouts of deliverance*

10 Many are the pangs of the wicked;
   but steadfast love surrounds him who trusts in the LORD.
11 Be glad in the LORD, and rejoice, O righteous,
   and shout for joy, all you upright in heart!

I. Praise to the LORD who provides and delivers 33.1–22

A. Exhortation to praise the LORD

33 Rejoice in the LORD, O you righteous!
   Praise befits the upright.
2 Praise the LORD with the lyre,
   make melody to him with the harp of ten strings!
3 Sing to him a new song,
   play skilfully on the strings, with loud shouts.

B. Reasons for praising the LORD

1. He is the LORD the creator

4 For the word of the LORD is upright;
   and all his work is done in faithfulness.
5 He loves righteousness and justice;
   the earth is full of the steadfast love of the LORD.

6 By the word of the LORD the heavens were made,
   and all their host by the breath of his mouth.
7 He gathered the waters of the sea as in a bottle;
   he put the deeps in storehouses.

8 Let all the earth fear the LORD,
   let all the inhabitants of the world stand in awe of him!
9 For he spoke, and it came to be;
   he commanded, and it stood forth.

2. He is the LORD of providence

10 The LORD brings the counsel of the nations to nought;
   he frustrates the plans of the peoples.
11 The counsel of the LORD stands for ever,
   the thoughts of his heart to all generations.
12 Blessed is the nation whose God is the LORD,
   the people whom he has chosen as his heritage!

13 The LORD looks down from heaven,
   he sees all the sons of men;
14 from where he sits enthroned he looks forth
   on all the inhabitants of the earth,
15 he who fashions the hearts of them all,
   and observes all their deeds.
16 A king is not saved by his great army;
   a warrior is not delivered by his great strength.
17 The war horse is a vain hope for victory,
   and by its great might it cannot save.

3. He is the deliverer of His people

18 Behold, the eye of the LORD is on those who fear him,

Cross-references: 32.10 Rom 2.9; Prov 16.20; 32.11 Ps 64.10; 33.1 Ps 32.11; 147.1; 33.2 Ps 92.3; 33.3 Ps 96.1; 98.4; 33.4 Ps 19.8; 119.90; 33.5 Ps 11.7; 119.64; 33.6 Gen 11.3; Job 23.13; 33.7 Ps 78.13; 33.8 Ps 67.7; 96.9; 33.9 Gen 1.3; Ps 148.5; 33.10 Isa 8.10; 19.3; 33.11 Job 23.13; Prov 19.21; Ps 40.5; 33.12 Ps 144.15; Ex 19.5; Deut 7.6; 33.13 Job 28.24; Ps 11.4; 33.15 Jer 32.19; 33.16 Ps 44.6; 33.17 Ps 20.7; Prov 21.31; 33.18 Job 36.7; Ps 34.15; 147.11

on those who hope in his steadfast love,
19 that he may deliver their soul from death,
    and keep them alive in famine.

20 Our soul waits for the LORD;
    he is our help and shield.
21 Yea, our heart is glad in him,
    because we trust in his holy name.
22 Let thy steadfast love, O LORD, be upon us,
    even as we hope in thee.

A Psalm of David, when he feigned madness before
Abĭm'ĕlĕch, so that he drove him out, and he went away.

I. A Psalm of praise and trust 34.1–22

A. Praise for God's goodness

34 I will bless the LORD at all times;
      his praise shall continually be in my mouth.
2 My soul makes its boast in the LORD;
    let the afflicted hear and be glad.
3 O magnify the LORD with me,
    and let us exalt his name together!

4 I sought the LORD, and he answered me,
    and delivered me from all my fears.
5 Look to him, and be radiant;
    so your[r] faces shall never be ashamed.
6 This poor man cried, and the LORD heard him,
    and saved him out of all his troubles.

B. Exhortation to trust and seek the LORD

7 The angel of the LORD encamps
    around those who fear him, and delivers them.
8 O taste and see that the LORD is good!
    Happy is the man who takes refuge in him!
9 O fear the LORD, you his saints,
    for those who fear him have no want!
10 The young lions suffer want and hunger;
    but those who seek the LORD lack no good thing.

C. Warning against sin

11 Come, O sons, listen to me,
    I will teach you the fear of the LORD.
12 What man is there who desires life,
    and covets many days, that he may enjoy good?
13 Keep your tongue from evil,
    and your lips from speaking deceit.
14 Depart from evil, and do good;
    seek peace, and pursue it.

[r] Gk Syr Jerome: Heb *their*

Side references:
33.19 Ps 37.19
33.20 Ps 130.6; 115.9
33.21 Zech 10.7; Jn 16.22
34.1 Eph 5.20; Ps 71.6
34.2 Jer 9.24; Ps 119.74
34.3 Lk 1.46
34.4 Mt 7.7; ver 6,17,19
34.5 Ps 36.9; 25.3
34.6 ver 4,17,19
34.7 Dan 6.22; 2 Ki 6.17
34.8 1 Pet 2.3; Ps 2.12
34.9 Ps 23.1
34.10 Ps 84.11
34.11 Ps 111.10
34.12 1 Pet 3.10
34.13 1 Pet 2.22
34.14 Ps 37.27; Heb 12.14

D. *The righteous delivered: the wicked condemned*

34.15
Job 36.7;
Ps 33.18

15 The eyes of the LORD are toward the righteous,
    and his ears toward their cry.

34.16
Jer 44.11;
Prov 10.7

16 The face of the LORD is against evildoers,
    to cut off the remembrance of them from the earth.

34.17
Ps 145.19;
ver 19

17 When the righteous cry for help, the LORD hears,
    and delivers them out of all their troubles.

34.18
Ps 145.18;
Isa 57.15

18 The LORD is near to the brokenhearted,
    and saves the crushed in spirit.

34.19
Prov 24.16;
ver 4,6,17

19 Many are the afflictions of the righteous;
    but the LORD delivers him out of them all.

34.20
Jn 19.36

20 He keeps all his bones;
    not one of them is broken.

34.21
Ps 94.23

21 Evil shall slay the wicked;
    and those who hate the righteous will be condemned.

34.22
1 Ki 1.29;
Ps 71.23

22 The LORD redeems the life of his servants;
    none of those who take refuge in him will be condemned.

A Psalm of David.

I. *A prayer for help 35.1–28*

A. *From persecution*

35.1
Ps 43.1

35 Contend, O LORD, with those who contend with me;
    fight against those who fight against me!
2 Take hold of shield and buckler,
    and rise for my help!

35.3
Ps 62.2

3 Draw the spear and javelin
    against my pursuers!
Say to my soul,
"I am your deliverance!"

35.4
Ps 70.2,3

4 Let them be put to shame and dishonor
    who seek after my life!
Let them be turned back and confounded
    who devise evil against me!

35.5
Job 21.18;
Ps 1.4;
Isa 29.5

5 Let them be like chaff before the wind,
    with the angel of the LORD driving them on!

35.6
Ps 73.18;
Jer 23.12

6 Let their way be dark and slippery,
    with the angel of the LORD pursuing them!

35.7
Ps 9.15

7 For without cause they hid their net for me;
    without cause they dug a pit*s* for my life.

35.8
I Thess 5.3

8 Let ruin come upon them unawares!
And let the net which they hid ensnare them;
    let them fall therein to ruin!

35.9
Isa 61.10;
Lk 1.47

9 Then my soul shall rejoice in the LORD,
    exulting in his deliverance.

35.10
Ex 15.11;
Ps 18.17;
37.14

10 All my bones shall say,

---

s The word pit is transposed from the preceding line

"O LORD, who is like thee,
thou who deliverest the weak
   from him who is too strong for him,
   the weak and needy from him who despoils him?"

B. *From slanderers*

11 Malicious witnesses rise up;
   they ask me of things that I know not.

12 They requite me evil for good;
   my soul is forlorn.

13 But I, when they were sick—
   I wore sackcloth,
   I afflicted myself with fasting.
I prayed with head bowed *t* on my bosom,
14 as though I grieved for my friend or my brother;
I went about as one who laments his mother,
   bowed down and in mourning.

15 But at my stumbling they gathered in glee,
   they gathered together against me;
cripples whom I knew not
   slandered me without ceasing;
16 they impiously mocked more and more, *u*
   gnashing at me with their teeth.

17 How long, O LORD, wilt thou look on?
   Rescue me from their ravages,
   my life from the lions!
18 Then I will thank thee in the great congregation;
   in the mighty throng I will praise thee.

C. *From haters*

19 Let not those rejoice over me
   who are wrongfully my foes,
and let not those wink the eye
   who hate me without cause.
20 For they do not speak peace,
   but against those who are quiet in the land
   they conceive words of deceit.

21 They open wide their mouths against me;
   they say, "Aha, Aha!
   our eyes have seen it!"

22 Thou hast seen, O LORD; be not silent!
   O Lord, be not far from me!
23 Bestir thyself, and awake for my right,
   for my cause, my God and my Lord!
24 Vindicate me, O LORD, my God, according to thy righteousness;
   and let them not rejoice over me!
25 Let them not say to themselves,
   "Aha, we have our heart's desire!"

t Or *My prayer turned back*
u Cn Compare Gk: Heb *like the profanest of mockers of a cake*

Marginal references:

35.11 Ps 27.12
35.12 Jn 10.32
35.13 Job 30.25; Ps 69.10
35.15 Job 30.1,8
35.16 Lam 2.16
35.17 Hab 1.13; Ps 22.20
35.18 Ps 22.22,25
35.19 Ps 13.4; 38.19; Prov 6.13; Ps 69.4; Jn 15.25
35.21 Ps 22.13; 40.15
35.22 Ex 3.7; Ps 28.1; 10.1
35.23 Ps 44.23
35.24 Ps 9.4; ver 19
35.25 Lam 2.16

Let them not say, "We have swallowed him up."

35.26
Ps 40.14;
38.16
26 Let them be put to shame and confusion altogether
    who rejoice at my calamity!
Let them be clothed with shame and dishonor
    who magnify themselves against me!

35.27
Ps 32.11;
9.4; 40.16;
147.11
27 Let those who desire my vindication
    shout for joy and be glad,
    and say evermore,
"Great is the LORD,
    who delights in the welfare of his servant!"

35.28
Ps 51.14
28 Then my tongue shall tell of thy righteousness
    and of thy praise all the day long.

To the choirmaster. A Psalm of David,
the servant of the LORD.

I. The sinfulness of sin 36.1–4

36.1
Rom 3.18
36 Transgression speaks to the wicked
    deep in his heart;
there is no fear of God
    before his eyes.
2 For he flatters himself in his own eyes
    that his iniquity cannot be found out and hated.

36.3
Jer 4.22
3 The words of his mouth are mischief and deceit;
    he has ceased to act wisely and do good.

36.4
Prov 4.16;
Mic 2.1;
Isa 65.2
4 He plots mischief while on his bed;
    he sets himself in a way that is not good;
    he spurns not evil.

II. The goodness and graciousness of God 36.5–12

5 Thy steadfast love, O LORD, extends to the heavens,
    thy faithfulness to the clouds.

36.6
Job 11.8;
Ps 77.19;
Rom 11.33
6 Thy righteousness is like the mountains of God,
    thy judgments are like the great deep;
    man and beast thou savest, O LORD.

36.7
Ruth 2.12
7 How precious is thy steadfast love, O God!
    The children of men take refuge in the shadow of thy wings.

36.8
Ps 65.4;
Job 20.17;
Rev 22.1
8 They feast on the abundance of thy house,
    and thou givest them drink from the river of thy delights.

36.9
Jer 2.13;
1 Pet 2.9
9 For with thee is the fountain of life;
    in thy light do we see light.

10 O continue thy steadfast love to those who know thee,
    and thy salvation to the upright of heart!
11 Let not the foot of arrogance come upon me,
    nor the hand of the wicked drive me away.

36.12
Ps 140.10
12 There the evildoers lie prostrate,
    they are thrust down, unable to rise.

A Psalm of David.

I. The wisdom of an aged man 37.1–40

A. The righteous will prosper: the wicked cut off

37 Fret not yourself because of the wicked,
be not envious of wrongdoers!

²For they will soon fade like the grass,
and wither like the green herb.

³Trust in the LORD, and do good;
so you will dwell in the land, and enjoy security.

⁴Take delight in the LORD,
and he will give you the desires of your heart.

⁵Commit your way to the LORD;
trust in him, and he will act.

⁶He will bring forth your vindication as the light,
and your right as the noonday.

⁷Be still before the LORD, and wait patiently for him;
fret not yourself over him who prospers in his way,
over the man who carries out evil devices!

⁸Refrain from anger, and forsake wrath!
Fret not yourself; it tends only to evil.

⁹For the wicked shall be cut off;
but those who wait for the LORD shall possess the land.

¹⁰Yet a little while, and the wicked will be no more;
though you look well at his place, he will not be there.

¹¹But the meek shall possess the land,
and delight themselves in abundant prosperity.

B. The comparison between the wicked and the righteous

¹²The wicked plots against the righteous,
and gnashes his teeth at him;

¹³but the LORD laughs at the wicked,
for he sees that his day is coming.

¹⁴The wicked draw the sword and bend their bows,
to bring down the poor and needy,
to slay those who walk uprightly;

¹⁵their sword shall enter their own heart,
and their bows shall be broken.

¹⁶Better is a little that the righteous has
than the abundance of many wicked.

37.1	Ps 73.3; Prov 23.17
37.2	Ps 90.5,6
37.3	Ps 62.8; Deut 30.20; Isa 40.11
37.4	Isa 58.14
*37.5	Ps 55.22; Prov 16.3; 1 Pet 5.7
37.6	Job 11.17; Mic 7.9
37.7	Ps 62.5; 40.1; ver 1,8
37.8	Ps 73.3; Eph 4.26
37.9	Isa 60.21
37.10	Job 24.24; 7.10
37.11	Mt 5.5
37.12	Ps 35.16
37.13	Ps 2.4; 1 Sam 26.10
37.14	Ps 11.2; 35.10
37.15	Ps 9.16
37.16	Prov 15.16

37.5 Anxiety or care is a form of sin in the believer. We are earnestly warned against it (Lk 21.34). Anxiety about earthly things is forbidden (Mt 6.25; Lk 12.22, 29; Jn 6.27) and may be conquered by: (1) trusting in God (Jer 17.7, 8; Dan 3.15–18); (2) casting care upon God (55.22; Prov 16.3; 1 Pet 5.7); (3) claiming the promises of God (Heb 13.6); (4) thanking Him in advance for His answer to prayer (Phil 4.6).

37.17
Job 38.15;
Ps 10.15

17 For the arms of the wicked shall be broken;
   but the LORD upholds the righteous.

37.18
Ps 1.6

18 The LORD knows the days of the blameless,
   and their heritage will abide for ever;

37.19
Job 5.20;
Ps 33.19

19 they are not put to shame in evil times,
   in the days of famine they have abundance.

37.20
Ps 72.27;
102.3

20 But the wicked perish;
   the enemies of the LORD are like the glory of the pastures,
   they vanish—like smoke they vanish away.

37.21
Ps 112.5,9

21 The wicked borrows, and cannot pay back,
   but the righteous is generous and gives;

37.22
Prov 3.33;
Job 5.3

22 for those blessed by the LORD shall possess the land,
   but those cursed by him shall be cut off.

C. *The sure deliverance and security of the righteous*

37.23
1 Sam 2.9;
Ps 147.11

23 The steps of a man are from the LORD,
   and he establishes him in whose way he delights;

37.24
Prov 24.16;
Ps 147.6

24 though he fall, he shall not be cast headlong,
   for the LORD is the stay of his hand.

*37.25
Heb 13.5;
Job 15.23

25 I have been young, and now am old;
   yet I have not seen the righteous forsaken
   or his children begging bread.

37.26
ver 21;
Ps 147.13

26 He is ever giving liberally and lending,
   and his children become a blessing.

37.27
Ps 34.14;
ver 18

27 Depart from evil, and do good;
   so shall you abide for ever.

37.28
Ps 11.7;
21.10;
Isa 14.20

28 For the LORD loves justice;
   he will not forsake his saints.
   The righteous shall be preserved for ever,
   but the children of the wicked shall be cut off.

37.29
ver 9,18

29 The righteous shall possess the land,
   and dwell upon it for ever.

37.30
Mt 12.35

30 The mouth of the righteous utters wisdom,
   and his tongue speaks justice.

37.31
Ps 40.8;
Isa 51.7;
ver 23

31 The law of his God is in his heart;
   his steps do not slip.

37.32
Ps 10.8

32 The wicked watches the righteous,
   and seeks to slay him.

37.33
2 Pet 2.9;
Ps 109.31

33 The LORD will not abandon him to his power,
   or let him be condemned when he is brought to trial.

37.25 Scripture abounds with promises for the supply of the material needs of God's people (e.g., Phil 4.19; Eph 3.20). What we *think* we need may differ from what God *knows* we need. Depending upon his gifts and circumstances, the quantity for each believer varies. But every believer may claim God's promises for that legitimate supply which he may secure from God in his particular situation.

34 Wait for the LORD, and keep to his way,
    and he will exalt you to possess the land;
    you will look on the destruction of the wicked.

> 37.34
> Ps 27.14;
> 52.5,6

35 I have seen a wicked man overbearing,
    and towering like a cedar of Lebanon.ᵛ

> 37.35
> Job 5.3

36 Again Iʷ passed by, and, lo, he was no more;
    though I sought him, he could not be found.

> 37.36
> Job 20.5

37 Mark the blameless man, and behold the upright,
    for there is posterity for the man of peace.

> 37.37
> Isa 57.1,2

38 But transgressors shall be altogether destroyed;
    the posterity of the wicked shall be cut off.

> 37.38
> Ps 1.4;
> ver 9,20,28

39 The salvation of the righteous is from the LORD;
    he is their refuge in the time of trouble.

> 37.39
> Ps 3.8; 9.9

40 The LORD helps them and delivers them;
    he delivers them from the wicked, and saves them,
    because they take refuge in him.

> 37.40
> Isa 31.5;
> 1 Chr 5.20

A Psalm of David, for the memorial offering.

I. *The penitent's plea for mercy 38.1—22*

A. *The extremity of his condition*

38 O LORD, rebuke me not in thy anger,
    nor chasten me in thy wrath!

> 38.1
> Ps 6.1

2 For thy arrows have sunk into me,
    and thy hand has come down on me.

> 38.2
> Job 6.4;
> Ps 32.4

3 There is no soundness in my flesh
    because of thy indignation;
there is no health in my bones
    because of my sin.

> 38.3
> Isa 1.6;
> Ps 6.2

4 For my iniquities have gone over my head;
    they weigh like a burden too heavy for me.

> 38.4
> Ezra 9.6

5 My wounds grow foul and fester
    because of my foolishness,

> 38.5
> Ps 69.5

6 I am utterly bowed down and prostrate;
    all the day I go about mourning.

> 38.6
> Ps 35.14;
> 42.9

7 For my loins are filled with burning,
    and there is no soundness in my flesh.

> 38.7
> Ps 102.3;
> ver 3

8 I am utterly spent and crushed;
    I groan because of the tumult of my heart.

> 38.8
> Job 3.24;
> Ps 22.1

B. *His desire for deliverance*

> 38.9
> Ps 10.17;
> 6.6

9 Lord, all my longing is known to thee,
    my sighing is not hidden from thee.
10 My heart throbs, my strength fails me;

> 38.10
> Ps 31.10;
> 6.7

ᵛ Gk: Heb obscure   ʷ Gk Syr Jerome: Heb *he*

and the light of my eyes—it also has gone from me.

38.11
Ps 31.11;
Lk 23.49
11 My friends and companions stand aloof from my plague,
  and my kinsmen stand afar off.

38.12
Ps 54.3;
140.5;
35.4,20
12 Those who seek my life lay their snares,
  those who seek my hurt speak of ruin,
  and meditate treachery all the day long.

38.13
Ps 39.2,9
13 But I am like a deaf man, I do not hear,
  like a dumb man who does not open his mouth.
14 Yea, I am like a man who does not hear,
  and in whose mouth are no rebukes.

C. *His confidence in God*

38.15
Ps 39.7;
17.6
15 But for thee, O Lord, do I wait;
  it is thou, O Lord my God, who wilt answer.
38.16
Ps 13.4;
35.26
16 For I pray, "Only let them not rejoice over me,
  who boast against me when my foot slips!"

38.17
Ps 13.2
17 For I am ready to fall,
  and my pain is ever with me.
★38.18
Ps 32.5;
2 Cor 7.9
18 I confess my iniquity,
  I am sorry for my sin.
38.19
Ps 18.17;
35.19
19 Those who are my foes without cause^x are mighty,
  and many are those who hate me wrongfully.
38.20
Ps 35.12;
1 Jn 3.12
20 Those who render me evil for good
  are my adversaries because I follow after good.

38.21
Ps 35.22
21 Do not forsake me, O Lord!
  O my God, be not far from me!
38.22
Ps 40.13,17;
27.1
22 Make haste to help me,
  O Lord, my salvation!

To the choirmaster: to Jĕdu'thŭn. A Psalm of David.

I. *In time of trouble 39.1–13*

A. *Silence in trouble*

★39.1
1 Ki 2.4;
Job 2.10;
Jas 3.2
39 I said, "I will guard my ways,
  that I may not sin with my tongue;
I will bridle^y my mouth,
  so long as the wicked are in my presence."
39.2
Ps 38.13
2 I was dumb and silent,
  I held my peace to no avail;
my distress grew worse,
3   my heart became hot within me.
As I mused, the fire burned;
  then I spoke with my tongue:

x Cn: Heb *living*   y Heb *muzzle*

38.18 The penitent are patient under affliction.

39.1 God's providences sometimes occasion doubt.

B. *Desire for enlightenment*

4 "LORD, let me know my end,
   and what is the measure of my days;
   let me know how fleeting my life is!

5 Behold, thou hast made my days a few handbreadths,
   and my lifetime is as nothing in thy sight.
   Surely every man stands as a mere breath!   *Selāh*

6   Surely man goes about as a shadow!
   Surely for nought are they in turmoil;
   man heaps up, and knows not who will gather!

C. *Prayer for deliverance*

7 "And now, Lord, for what do I wait?
   My hope is in thee.

8 Deliver me from all my transgressions.
   Make me not the scorn of the fool!

9 I am dumb, I do not open my mouth;
   for it is thou who hast done it.

10 Remove thy stroke from me;
   I am spent by the blows^z of thy hand.

11 When thou dost chasten man
   with rebukes for sin,
   thou dost consume like a moth what is dear to him;
   surely every man is a mere breath!   *Selāh*

12 "Hear my prayer, O LORD,
   and give ear to my cry;
   hold not thy peace at my tears!
   For I am thy passing guest,
   a sojourner, like all my fathers.

13 Look away from me, that I may know gladness,
   before I depart and be no more!"

To the choirmaster. A Psalm of David.

I. *Delight in the will of the LORD 40.1–17*

A. *His acknowledgment of God's delivering goodness*

40 I waited patiently for the LORD;
    he inclined to me and heard my cry.

2 He drew me up from the desolate pit,^{a}
   out of the miry bog,
   and set my feet upon a rock,
   making my steps secure.

3 He put a new song in my mouth,
   a song of praise to our God.
   Many will see and fear,
   and put their trust in the LORD.

^{z} Heb *hostility*
^{a} Cn: Heb *pit of tumult*

39.4	Ps 90.12; 103.14
39.5	Ps 89.47; 144.4; 62.9
39.6	1 Pet 1.24; Ps 127.2; Job 27.17; Lk 12.20
39.7	Ps 38.15
39.8	Ps 51.9; 44.13
39.9	ver 2; Job 2.10
39.10	Job 9.34; Ps 32.4
39.11	2 Pet 2.16; Job 13.28; ver 5
39.12	Ps 102.1; 56.8; Heb 11.13; 1 Pet 2.11
39.13	Job 10.20; 14.10
40.1	Ps 27.14; 34.15
40.2	Ps 69.2; 27.5
40.3	Ps 33.3

<table>
<tr><td>40.4
Ps 84.12</td><td>4 Blessed is the man who makes
    the LORD his trust,
who does not turn to the proud,
    to those who go astray after false gods!</td></tr>
</table>

<table>
<tbody>
<tr><td>40.4
Ps 84.12</td><td>4 Blessed is the man who makes
the LORD his trust,
who does not turn to the proud,
to those who go astray after false gods!</td></tr>
</tbody>
</table>

40.4
Ps 84.12

4 Blessed is the man who makes
    the LORD his trust,
who does not turn to the proud,
    to those who go astray after false gods!

40.5
Ps 136.4;
Isa 55.8;
Ps 139.18

5 Thou hast multiplied, O LORD my God,
    thy wondrous deeds and thy thoughts toward us;
    none can compare with thee!
Were I to proclaim and tell of them,
    they would be more than can be numbered.

B. His grateful obedience

*40.6
1 Sam 15.22

6 Sacrifice and offering thou dost not desire;
    but thou hast given me an open ear.[b]
Burnt offering and sin offering
    thou hast not required.

*40.7

7 Then I said, "Lo, I come;
    in the roll of the book it is written of me;

40.8
Jn 4.34;
Rom 7.22;
Ps 37.31

8 I delight to do thy will, O my God;
    thy law is within my heart."

40.9
Ps 22.22;
119.13

9 I have told the glad news of deliverance
    in the great congregation;
lo, I have not restrained my lips,
    as thou knowest, O LORD.

40.10
Acts 20.20;
Ps 89.1

10 I have not hid thy saving help within my heart,
    I have spoken of thy faithfulness and thy salvation;
I have not concealed thy steadfast love and thy faithfulness
    from the great congregation.

C. His prayer for mercy and grace

40.11
Ps 43.3

11 Do not thou, O LORD, withhold
    thy mercy from me,
let thy steadfast love and thy faithfulness
    ever preserve me!

40.12
Ps 116.3;
38.4; 69.4;
73.26

12 For evils have encompassed me
    without number;
my iniquities have overtaken me,
    till I cannot see;
they are more than the hairs of my head;
    my heart fails me.

40.13
Ps 70.1

13 Be pleased, O LORD, to deliver me!
    O LORD, make haste to help me!

40.14
Ps 35.4;
63.9

14 Let them be put to shame and confusion altogether
    who seek to snatch away my life;
let them be turned back and brought to dishonor
    who desire my hurt!

40.15
Ps 70.3

15 Let them be appalled because of their shame
    who say to me, "Aha, Aha!"

---

b Heb *ears thou hast dug for me*

40.6 *open ear.* The Psalmist speaks of the ear as open and ready to hear and act upon God's Word.

40.7 *the roll of the book*, the Law of God.

16 But may all who seek thee
   rejoice and be glad in thee;
 may those who love thy salvation
   say continually, "Great is the LORD!"
17 As for me, I am poor and needy;
   but the Lord takes thought for me.
 Thou art my help and my deliverer;
   do not tarry, O my God!

40.16
Ps 70.4;
35.27

40.17
Ps 70.5

To the choirmaster. A Psalm of David.

I. The Psalm of the compassionate 41.1–13

A. The blessedness of the compassionate

41 Blessed is he who considers the poor!*c*
   The LORD delivers him in the day of trouble;
 2 the LORD protects him and keeps him alive;
   he is called blessed in the land;
   thou dost not give him up to the will of his enemies.
 3 The LORD sustains him on his sickbed;
   in his illness thou healest all his infirmities.*d*

41.1
Ps 82.3,4;
Prov 14.21
41.2
Ps 37.22,28;
27.12

41.3
Ps 6.6

B. The malice of false friends

4 As for me, I said, "O LORD, be gracious to me;
   heal me, for I have sinned against thee!"
 5 My enemies say of me in malice:
   "When will he die, and his name perish?"
 6 And when one comes to see me, he utters empty words,
   while his heart gathers mischief;
   when he goes out, he tells it abroad.
 7 All who hate me whisper together about me;
   they imagine the worst for me.

41.4
Ps 6.2; 51.4

41.5
Ps 38.12

41.6
Ps 12.2

41.7
Ps 56.5

8 They say, "A deadly thing has fastened upon him;
   he will not rise again from where he lies."
 9 Even my bosom friend in whom I trusted,
   who ate of my bread, has lifted his heel against me.
10 But do thou, O LORD, be gracious to me,
   and raise me up, that I may requite them!

41.8
Ps 71.10,11

*41.9
Job 19.19;
Ps 55.12;
Jn 13.18
41.10
Ps 3.3

C. Integrity vindicated

11 By this I know that thou art pleased with me,
   in that my enemy has not triumphed over me.
12 But thou hast upheld me because of my integrity,
   and set me in thy presence for ever.

41.11
Ps 147.11;
25.2
41.12
Ps 37.17;
Job 36.7

c Or *weak*   *d* Heb *thou changest all his bed*

41.9 The Psalmist's note that he is betrayed by a friend suggests the betrayal of
Christ by Judas. Christ quoted this verse as
He prophesied of His own betrayal in Jn
13.18, 19: *He who ate my bread has lifted his
heel against me.*

D. Doxology

41.13
Ps 106.48

13 Blessed be the LORD, the God of Israel,
    from everlasting to everlasting!
  Amen and Amen.

BOOK II

To the choirmaster. A Măskĭl of the Sons of Kōrăh.

I. The sorrow and consolation of the godly 42.1–11

A. The sorrow of separation

42.1
Ps 119.131

42 As a hart longs
    for flowing streams,
  so longs my soul
    for thee, O God.

42.2
Ps 63.1;
Jer 10.10;
Ps 43.4

2 My soul thirsts for God,
    for the living God.
  When shall I come and behold
    the face of God?

42.3
Ps 80.5;
79.10

3 My tears have been my food
    day and night,
  while men say to me continually,
    "Where is your God?"

42.4
Ps 62.8;
Isa 30.29;
Ps 100.4

4 These things I remember,
    as I pour out my soul:
  how I went with the throng,
    and led them in procession to the house of God,
  with glad shouts and songs of thanksgiving,
    a multitude keeping festival.

42.5
Ps 38.6;
77.3;
Lam 3.24;
Ps 44.3

5 Why are you cast down, O my soul,
    and why are you disquieted within me?
  Hope in God; for I shall again praise him,
    my help 6 and my God.

B. The consolation and hope of the godly

My soul is cast down within me,
    therefore I remember thee
  from the land of Jordan and of Hèrmòn,
    from Mount Mĭzar.

42.7
Ps 88.7;
Jon 2.3

7 Deep calls to deep
    at the thunder of thy cataracts;
  all thy waves and thy billows
    have gone over me.

42.8
Ps 57.3;
Job 35.10;
Ps 63.6;
149.5

8 By day the LORD commands his steadfast love;
    and at night his song is with me,
    a prayer to the God of my life.

42.9
Ps 38.6

9 I say to God, my rock:
    "Why hast thou forgotten me?

Why go I mourning
　　because of the oppression of the enemy?"
10 As with a deadly wound in my body,
　　my adversaries taunt me,
while they say to me continually,
　　"Where is your God?"

	42.10
	ver 3

11 Why are you cast down, O my soul,
　　and why are you disquieted within me?
Hope in God; for I shall again praise him,
　　my help and my God.

	42.11
	ver 5

I. *A plea for vindication 43.1–5*

43 Vindicate me, O God, and defend my cause
　　against an ungodly people;
from deceitful and unjust men
　　deliver me!

	43.1
	Ps 26.1;
	1Sam 24.15;
	Ps 5.6

2 For thou art the God in whom I take refuge;
　　why hast thou cast me off?
Why go I mourning
　　because of the oppression of the enemy?

	43.2
	Ps 18.1;
	44.9; 42.9

3 Oh send out thy light and thy truth;
　　let them lead me,
let them bring me to thy holy hill
　　and to thy dwelling!

	43.3
	Ps 36.9;
	42.4; 84.1

4 Then I will go to the altar of God,
　　to God my exceeding joy;
and I will praise thee with the lyre,
　　O God, my God.

	43.4
	Ps 26.6;
	33.2

5 Why are you cast down, O my soul,
　　and why are you disquieted within me?
Hope in God; for I shall again praise him,
　　my help and my God.

	43.5
	Ps 42.5,11

To the choirmaster. A Măskĭl of the Sons of Kōrăh.

I. *A prayer for deliverance 44.1–26*

A. *Acknowledgment of past mercies*

44 We have heard with our ears, O God,
　　our fathers have told us,
what deeds thou didst perform in their days,
　　in the days of old:

	44.1
	Ex 12.26;
	Ps 78.3,12

2 thou with thy own hand didst drive out the nations,
　　but them thou didst plant;
thou didst afflict the peoples,
　　but them thou didst set free;

	44.2
	Ex 15.17;
	Ps 78.55;
	80.8

3 for not by their own sword did they win the land,
　　nor did their own arm give them victory;

	44.3
	Josh 24.12;
	Ps 77.15;
	Deut 4.37;
	7.7,8

but thy right hand, and thy arm,
  and the light of thy countenance;
  for thou didst delight in them.

4 Thou art my King and my God,
  who ordainest[e] victories for Jacob.
5 Through thee we push down our foes;
  through thy name we tread down our assailants.
6 For not in my bow do I trust,
  nor can my sword save me.
7 But thou hast saved us from our foes,
  and hast put to confusion those who hate us.
8 In God we have boasted continually,
  and we will give thanks to thy name for ever.   *Sēlàh*

B. *Statement of present complaints*

9 Yet thou hast cast us off and abased us,
  and hast not gone out with our armies.
10 Thou hast made us turn back from the foe;
  and our enemies have gotten spoil.
11 Thou hast made us like sheep for slaughter,
  and hast scattered us among the nations.
12 Thou hast sold thy people for a trifle,
  demanding no high price for them.

13 Thou hast made us the taunt of our neighbors;
  the derision and scorn of those about us.
14 Thou hast made us a byword among the nations,
  a laughingstock[f] among the peoples.
15 All day long my disgrace is before me,
  and shame has covered my face,
16 at the words of the taunters and revilers,
  at the sight of the enemy and the avenger.

C. *Appeal to God for deliverance*

17 All this has come upon us,
    though we have not forgotten thee,
    or been false to thy covenant.
18 Our heart has not turned back,
    nor have our steps departed from thy way,
19 that thou shouldst have broken us in the place of jackals,
    and covered us with deep darkness.

20 If we had forgotten the name of our God,
    or spread forth our hands to a strange god,
21 would not God discover this?
    For he knows the secrets of the heart.
22 Nay, for thy sake we are slain all the day long,
    and accounted as sheep for the slaughter.

23 Rouse thyself! Why sleepest thou, O Lord?
    Awake! Do not cast us off for ever!

e Gk Syr: Heb *Thou art my King, O God; ordain*   *f* Heb *a shaking of the head*

Marginal references:

44.4
Ps 74.12;
79.9
44.5
Dan 8.4;
Ps 108.13
44.6
Ps 33.16
44.7
Ps 136.24;
53.5
44.8
Ps 34.2;
30.12
44.9
Ps 60.1,10;
74.1
44.10
Lev 26.17;
Josh 7.8;
Ps 89.41
44.11
ver 22;
Deut 4.27;
28.64;
Ps 106.27
44.12
Isa 52.3,4;
Jer 15.13
44.13
Ps 79.4;
80.6
44.14
Jer 24.9;
Ps 109.25
44.16
Ps 74.10;
8.2
44.17
Dan 9.13;
Ps 78.7,57
44.18
Ps 78.57;
Job 23.11
44.19
Ps 51.8;
Job 3.5
44.20
Ps 78.11;
68.31;81.9
44.21
Ps 139.1,2;
Jer 17.10
44.22
Rom 8.36;
Isa 53.7
44.23
Ps 7.6;
78.65;77.7

24 Why dost thou hide thy face?
Why dost thou forget our affliction and oppression?
25 For our soul is bowed down to the dust;
our body cleaves to the ground.
26 Rise up, come to our help!
Deliver us for the sake of thy steadfast love!

To the choirmaster: according to Lilies.
A Măskĭl of the Sons of Kōráh; a love song.

I. The king's marriage 45.1–17

A. The king and his rule

45 My heart overflows with a goodly theme;
I address my verses to the king;
my tongue is like the pen of a ready scribe.

2 You are the fairest of the sons of men;
grace is poured upon your lips;
therefore God has blessed you for ever.
3 Gird your sword upon your thigh, O mighty one,
in your glory and majesty!

4 In your majesty ride forth victoriously
for the cause of truth and to defend[g] the right;
let your right hand teach you dread deeds!
5 Your arrows are sharp
in the heart of the king's enemies;
the peoples fall under you.

6 Your divine throne[h] endures for ever and ever.
Your royal scepter is a scepter of equity;
7 you love righteousness and hate wickedness.
Therefore God, your God, has anointed you
with the oil of gladness above your fellows;
8 your robes are all fragrant with myrrh and aloes and cassia.
From ivory palaces stringed instruments make you glad;
9 daughters of kings are among your ladies of honor;
at your right hand stands the queen in gold of Ōphĭr.

B. The bride and the wedding

10 Hear, O daughter, consider, and incline your ear;
forget your people and your father's house;
11 and the king will desire your beauty.

g Cn: Heb and the meekness of
h Or Your throne is a throne of God, or Thy throne, O God

Marginal references:
44.24 Job 13.24; Ps 42.9
44.25 Ps 119.25
44.26 Ps 35.2; 25.22
*45.1 Ezra 7.6
45.2 Lk 4.22
45.3 Isa 9.6
45.4 Rev 6.2
45.6 Ps 93.2; Heb 1.8,9; Ps 98.9
45.7 Ps 33.5; Isa 61.1; Ps 79.4; 21.6
45.8 Sol 1.3
45.9 Sol 6.8; 1 Ki 2.19
45.10 Deut 21.13
45.11 Ps 95.6; Isa 54.5

45.1 This Psalm, describing in glowing terms the marriage of an ancient king, and elaborating upon the beauties of the bride and the bridegroom, is considered by many to describe the relationship of Christ to His church. The words in verse 6 when applied to an ancient king of the line of David imply that he rules in behalf of God over Israel. As applied to Christ the words are: *Thy throne, O God, is for ever and ever* (Heb 1.8).

Since he is your lord, bow to him;

*45.12
Ps 22.29
45.13
Isa 61.10

12 the people[i] of Tȳre will sue your favor with gifts,
    the richest of the people 13 with all kinds of wealth.

The princess is decked in her chamber with gold-woven robes;[j]

45.14
Sol 1.4;
ver 9

14 in many-colored robes she is led to the king,
    with her virgin companions, her escort,[k] in her train.
15 With joy and gladness they are led along
    as they enter the palace of the king.

C. The conclusion

45.16
1 Pet 2.9;
Rev 1.6;
20.6
45.17
Mal 1.11;
Ps 138.4

16 Instead of your fathers shall be your sons;
    you will make them princes in all the earth.
17 I will cause your name to be celebrated in all generations;
    therefore the peoples will praise you for ever and ever.

To the choirmaster. A Psalm of the Sons of Kōrah.
According to Ăl'ămŏth. A Song.

I. God our refuge and strength 46.1–11

A. God our refuge

46.1
Ps 14.6;
Deut 4.7;
Ps 9.9
46.2
Ps 23.4;
82.5; 18.7
46.3
Ps 93.3,4

46 God is our refuge and strength,
    a very present[l] help in trouble.
2 Therefore we will not fear though the earth should change,
    though the mountains shake in the heart of the sea;
3 though its waters roar and foam,
    though the mountains tremble with its tumult.   *Sēlăh*

B. God our strength

46.4
Isa 8.7;
Ps 48.1,8;
Isa 60.14
46.5
Isa 12.6;
Ps 37.40
46.6
Ps 2.1;
68.33;
Mic 1.4
46.7
2 Chr
13.12;
Ps 9.9

4 There is a river whose streams make glad the city of God,
    the holy habitation of the Most High.
5 God is in the midst of her, she shall not be moved;
    God will help her right early.
6 The nations rage, the kingdoms totter;
    he utters his voice, the earth melts.
7 The LORD of hosts is with us;
    the God of Jacob is our refuge.[m]   *Sēlăh*

C. God our victory

46.8
Ps 66.5;
Isa 61.4
46.9
Isa 2.4;
Ps 76.3;
Ezek 39.9

8 Come, behold the works of the LORD,
    how he has wrought desolations in the earth.
9 He makes wars cease to the end of the earth;

i Heb *daughter*
j Or *people. All glorious is the princess within, gold embroidery is her clothing*
k Heb *those brought to you*   l Or *well proved*   m Or *fortress*

45.12 *Tyre*, the wealthy maritime state, is pictured bringing her gift to the bride. Hiram of Tyre assisted both David and Solomon in their building projects.

he breaks the bow, and shatters the spear,
he burns the chariots with fire!
10 "Be still, and know that I am God.
I am exalted among the nations,
I am exalted in the earth!"
11 The LORD of hosts is with us;
the God of Jacob is our refuge.*m*   Selàh

46.10
Ps 100.3;
Isa 2.11,17

To the choirmaster. A Psalm of the Sons of Kōràh.

I. God the king of the earth 47.1–9

A. The nations subdued

47 Clap your hands, all peoples!
Shout to God with loud songs of joy!
2 For the LORD, the Most High, is terrible,
a great king over all the earth.
3 He subdued peoples under us,
and nations under our feet.
4 He chose our heritage for us,
the pride of Jacob whom he loves.   Selàh

47.1
Ps 98.8;
Isa 55.12;
Ps 106.47
47.2
Deut 7.21
47.3
Ps 18.47
47.4
1 Pet 1.4

B. God reigns over all the earth

5 God has gone up with a shout,
the LORD with the sound of a trumpet.
6 Sing praises to God, sing praises!
Sing praises to our King, sing praises!
7 For God is the king of all the earth;
sing praises with a psalm!*n*

8 God reigns over the nations;
God sits on his holy throne.
9 The princes of the peoples gather
as the people of the God of Abraham.
For the shields of the earth belong to God;
he is highly exalted!

47.5
Ps 68.33;
98.6
47.6
Ps 68.4;
89.18
47.7
1 Cor 14.15
47.8
1 Chr 16.31
47.9
Ps 72.11;
Rom 4.11,
12;
Ps 89.18;
97.9

A Song. A Psalm of the Sons of Kōràh

I. A song of Zion 48.1–14

A. Zion, city of our God

48 Great is the LORD and greatly to be praised
in the city of our God!
His holy mountain, 2 beautiful in elevation,
is the joy of all the earth,
Mount Zion, in the far north,
the city of the great King.

48.1
Ps 96.4;
Zech 8.3
48.2
Ps 50.2;
Lam 2.15;
Mt 5.35

m Or *fortress*   *n* Heb *Màskil*

<table>
<tr><td>48.3
Ps 46.7</td><td>3 Within her citadels God
   has shown himself a sure defense.</td></tr>
</table>

B. *Zion established*

48.4
2 Sam
10.6–19

4 For lo, the kings assembled,
   they came on together.

48.5
Ex 15.15

5 As soon as they saw it, they were astounded,
   they were in panic, they took to flight;
6 trembling took hold of them there,
   anguish as of a woman in travail.

*48.7
Jer 18.17

7 By the east wind thou didst shatter the ships of Tarshish.
8 As we have heard, so have we seen
   in the city of the LORD of hosts,

48.8
Ps 87.5

in the city of our God,
   which God establishes for ever.   *Sēlàh*

C. *Zion praising God*

48.9
Ps 26.3

9 We have thought on thy steadfast love, O God,
   in the midst of thy temple.

48.10
Josh 7.9;
Isa 41.10

10 As thy name, O God,
   so thy praise reaches to the ends of the earth.
Thy right hand is filled with victory;

48.11
Ps 97.8

11   let Mount Zion be glad!
Let the daughters of Judah rejoice
   because of thy judgments!

12 Walk about Zion, go round about her,
   number her towers,

48.13
Ps 122.7;
78.5–7

13 consider well her ramparts,
   go through her citadels;
that you may tell the next generation

48.14
Ps 23.4

14   that this is God,
our God for ever and ever.
He will be our guide for ever.

To the choirmaster. A Psalm of the Sons of Kōràh.

I. *A sermon on the foolishness of trusting in riches*
49.1–20

A. *The summons to hear*

*49.1
Ps 78.1;
33.8

49
Hear this, all peoples!
   Give ear, all inhabitants of the world,
2 both low and high,
   rich and poor together!

49.3
Ps 37.30;
119.130

3 My mouth shall speak wisdom;
   the meditation of my heart shall be understanding.

49.4
Ps 78.2;
Num 12.8

4 I will incline my ear to a proverb;
   I will solve my riddle to the music of the lyre.

48.7 *ships of Tarshish,* see note to 1 Ki 10.22.

49.1 These thoughts have universal application.

B. *The limitations of wealth*

5 Why should I fear in times of trouble,
　　when the iniquity of my persecutors surrounds me,
6 men who trust in their wealth
　　and boast of the abundance of their riches?
7 Truly no man can ransom himself,*o*
　　or give to God the price of his life,
8 for the ransom of his*p* life is costly,
　　and can never suffice,
9 that he should continue to live on for ever,
　　and never see the Pit.

10 Yea, he shall see that even the wise die,
　　the fool and the stupid alike must perish
　　and leave their wealth to others.
11 Their graves*q* are their homes for ever,
　　their dwelling places to all generations,
　　though they named lands their own.
12 Man cannot abide in his pomp,
　　he is like the beasts that perish.

C. *The end of those who trust in wealth*

13 This is the fate of those who have foolish confidence,
　　the end of those*r* who are pleased with their portion. *Selah*
14 Like sheep they are appointed for Sheōl;
　　Death shall be their shepherd;
　straight to the grave they descend,*s*
　　and their form shall waste away;
　　Sheol shall be their home.*t*
15 But God will ransom my soul from the power of Sheōl,
　　for he will receive me. *Selah*

D. *The final exhortation*

16 Be not afraid when one becomes rich,
　　when the glory*u* of his house increases.
17 For when he dies he will carry nothing away;
　　his glory*u* will not go down after him.
18 Though, while he lives, he counts himself happy,
　　and though a man gets praise when he does well for himself,
19 he will go to the generation of his fathers,
　　who will never more see the light.
20 Man cannot abide in his pomp,
　　he is like the beasts that perish.

Cross references:
49.5 Ps 23.4 · *49.6 Job 31.24 · 49.7 Mt 25.8,9; Job 36.18 · 49.8 Mt 16.26 · 49.9 Ps 22.29; 89.48 · 49.10 Ecc 2.16,18 · 49.11 Ps 64.6; 10.6; Deut 3.14 · 49.12 ver 20 · *49.13 Lk 12.20 · 49.14 Ps 9.17; Dan 7.18; Mal 4.3; 1 Cor 6.2; Rev 2.26; Job 24.19 · 49.15 Ps 56.13; 73.24 · 49.16 Ps 37.7 · 49.17 Ps 17.14 · 49.18 Lk 12.19 · 49.19 Gen 15.15; Job 33.30 · 49.20 ver 12

o Another reading is *no man can ransom his brother*　*p* Gk: Heb *their*
q Gk Syr Compare Tg: Heb *their inward* (thought)　*r* Tg: Heb *after them*
s Cn: Heb *the upright shall have dominion over them in the morning*
t Heb uncertain　*u* Or *wealth*

49.6 Wealthy worldlings are guilty of three sins: (1) they trust in their wealth; (2) they boast of their wealth; (3) they think they can keep their wealth forever.
49.13 The power of wealth is limited. It cannot: (1) keep one's dearest friend from death; (2) keep oneself from death at the appointed hour; (3) affect one's condition after death. The poor of this world, rich in faith, are better off than the wealthy without faith.

A Psalm of Āsăph.

I. *True and false religion 50.1–23*

A. *God is the true judge*

50.1
Josh 22.22;
Ps 113.3

50 The Mighty One, God the LORD,
    speaks and summons the earth
  from the rising of the sun to its setting.

50.2
Ps 48.2;
Deut 33.2

2 Out of Zion, the perfection of beauty,
    God shines forth.

50.3
Ps 96.13;
97.3;
Dan 7.10

3 Our God comes, he does not keep silence,
    before him is a devouring fire,
    round about him a mighty tempest.

50.4
Deut 4.26;
Isa 1.2

4 He calls to the heavens above
    and to the earth, that he may judge his people:

50.5
Ps 30.4;
Ex 24.7;
ver 8

5 "Gather to me my faithful ones,
    who made a covenant with me by sacrifice!"

50.6
Ps 89.5;
75.7

6 The heavens declare his righteousness,
    for God himself is judge!   *Sēlàh*

B. *God judges the intent, not the outward form*

50.7
Ps 81.8;
Ex 20.2

7 "Hear, O my people, and I will speak,
    O Israel, I will testify against you.
  I am God, your God.

50.8
Ps 40.6;
Hos 6.6

8 I do not reprove you for your sacrifices;
    your burnt offerings are continually before me.

50.9
Ps 69.31

9 I will accept no bull from your house,
    nor he-goat from your folds.

50.10
Ps 104.24

10 For every beast of the forest is mine,
    the cattle on a thousand hills.
11 I know all the birds of the air,[v]
    and all that moves in the field is mine.

50.12
Ex 19.5

12 "If I were hungry, I would not tell you;
    for the world and all that is in it is mine.
13 Do I eat the flesh of bulls,
    or drink the blood of goats?

50.14
Heb 13.15;
Deut 23.21

14 Offer to God a sacrifice of thanksgiving,[w]
    and pay your vows to the Most High;

50.15
Ps 91.15;
81.7; 22.23

15 and call upon me in the day of trouble;
    I will deliver you, and you shall glorify me."

C. *Hypocrisy rebuked*

50.16
Isa 29.13

16 But to the wicked God says:
    "What right have you to recite my statutes,
    or take my covenant on your lips?

50.17
Rom 2.21,
22;
Neh 9.26

17 For you hate discipline,
    and you cast my words behind you.

50.18
Rom 1.32;
1 Tim 5.22

18 If you see a thief, you are a friend of his;

v Gk Syr Tg: Heb *mountains* *w* Or *make thanksgiving your sacrifice to God*

and you keep company with adulterers.

19 "You give your mouth free rein for evil,
   and your tongue frames deceit.
20 You sit and speak against your brother;
   you slander your own mother's son.
21 These things you have done and I have been silent;
   you thought that I was one like yourself.
But now I rebuke you, and lay the charge before you.

D. The conclusion stated

22 "Mark this, then, you who forget God,
   lest I rend, and there be none to deliver!
23 He who brings thanksgiving as his sacrifice honors me;
   to him who orders his way aright
   I will show the salvation of God!"

To the choirmaster. A Psalm of David, when Nathan
the prophet came to him, after he had gone in to Băthshē'bȧ.

I. The penitent's Psalm 51.1–19

A. David's prayer for forgiveness and confession of sin

51 Have mercy on me, O God,
   according to thy steadfast love;
   according to thy abundant mercy blot out my transgressions.
2 Wash me thoroughly from my iniquity,
   and cleanse me from my sin!

3 For I know my transgressions,
   and my sin is ever before me.
4 Against thee, thee only, have I sinned,
   and done that which is evil in thy sight,
so that thou art justified in thy sentence
   and blameless in thy judgment.
5 Behold, I was brought forth in iniquity,
   and in sin did my mother conceive me.

6 Behold, thou desirest truth in the inward being;
   therefore teach me wisdom in my secret heart.
7 Purge me with hyssop, and I shall be clean;
   wash me, and I shall be whiter than snow.
8 Fill[x] me with joy and gladness;
   let the bones which thou hast broken rejoice.

x Syr: Heb *Make to hear*

Marginal references:

50.19 Ps 10.7; 52.2
50.20 Mt 10.21
50.21 Ecc 8.11; Isa 42.14; Ps 90.8
50.22 Job 8.13; Ps 9.17; 7.2
50.23 ver 14; Ps 85.13; 91.16
*51.1 Ps 4.1; 106.45; Isa 43.25; Acts 3.19
51.2 Heb 9.14; 1 Jn 1.7
51.3 Isa 59.12
51.4 Gen 20.6; Lk 15.21; Rom 3.4
51.5 Ps 58.3; Job 14.4
51.6 Ps 15.2; Prov 2.6
*51.7 Lev 14.4; Heb 9.19; Isa 1.18
51.8 Ps 35.10

51.1 This Psalm is one of the great biblical passages on confession and cleansing from the defilement of sin. David's repentance includes: (1) a godly sorrow for his sin; (2) confession of that sin; (3) a turning from sin; (4) forgiveness; (5) restoration; (6) rejoicing; (7) a readiness to witness to others of the grace of God.
51.7 The leaves and heads of the hyssop plant are used as a spice or condiment. David uses it in connection with cleansing from the defilement of sin. Here it cannot mean the inward use of the plant, but rather its use as specified in Ex 12.22, where the plant was dipped in the blood of the slain animal and the blood sprinkled upon the lintel and two doorposts. See also Lev 14.4–8 and Num 19.17, 18.

9 Hide thy face from my sins,
　　and blot out all my iniquities.

B. David's prayer and vow

10 Create in me a clean heart, O God,
　　and put a new and right*y* spirit within me.
11 Cast me not away from thy presence,
　　and take not thy holy Spirit from me.
12 Restore to me the joy of thy salvation,
　　and uphold me with a willing spirit.

13 Then I will teach transgressors thy ways,
　　and sinners will return to thee.
14 Deliver me from bloodguiltiness,*z* O God,
　　thou God of my salvation,
　　and my tongue will sing aloud of thy deliverance.

C. God's acceptance of the broken and contrite heart

15 O Lord, open thou my lips,
　　and my mouth shall show forth thy praise.
16 For thou hast no delight in sacrifice;
　　were I to give a burnt offering, thou wouldst not be pleased.
17 The sacrifice acceptable to God*a* is a broken spirit;
　　a broken and contrite heart, O God, thou wilt not despise.

D. David's prayer for Zion

18 Do good to Zion in thy good pleasure;
　　rebuild the walls of Jerusalem,
19 then wilt thou delight in right sacrifices,
　　in burnt offerings and whole burnt offerings;
　　then bulls will be offered on thy altar.

To the choirmaster. A Măskĭl of David, when Dōëg, the Ē′dŏmīte,
came and told Saul, "David has come to the house of Ăhĭm′ĕlĕch."

I. The fate of the wicked 52.1–9

A. The portrait of the wicked

52 Why do you boast, O mighty man,
　　of mischief done against the godly?*b*
　　All the day 2 you are plotting destruction.

---

y Or *steadfast*　*z* Or *death*
a Or *My sacrifice, O God*　*b* Cn Compare Syr: Heb *the kindness of God*

Side references (left margin):

51.9
Jer 16.17

51.10
Acts 15.9;
Eph 2.10;
Ps 78.37
*51.11
2 Ki 13.23;
Eph 4.30
51.12
Ps 13.5;
2 Cor 3.17
51.13
Acts 9.21,
22;
Ps 22.27
51.14
2 Sam 12.9;
Ps 25.5;
35.28

51.15
Ps 9.14

51.16
1 Sam
15.22;
Ps 40.6
51.17
Ps 34.18

51.18
Isa 51.3;
Ps 102.16
51.19
Ps 4.5;
66.13,15

52.1
1 Sam 22.9;
Ps 94.4
52.2
Ps 50.19;
57.4; 59.7

51.11 The *holy Spirit* dwelt in the heart of David. This verse, therefore, does not mean that David is apprehensive that the indwelling Spirit may actually be withdrawn from him. But he does fear that the Holy Spirit may be so quenched within him that he may lose all sense of the presence of God. Thus David earnestly begs that the sense of God's presence not be removed, but that he may remain responsive to His leading and will, and that his blessed fellowship with Him may not be forever lost.

Your tongue is like a sharp razor,
>   you worker of treachery.
3 You love evil more than good,
>   and lying more than speaking the truth.   *Sēlàh*   52.3
>   Jer 9.4,5
4 You love all words that devour,   52.4
>   O deceitful tongue.   Ps 120.3

B. *The end of the wicked*

5 But God will break you down for ever;   52.5
>   he will snatch and tear you from your tent;   Prov 2.22;
>   he will uproot you from the land of the living. *Sēlàh* Ps 27.13
6 The righteous shall see, and fear,   52.6
>   and shall laugh at him, saying,   Job 22.19;
7 "See the man who would not make   Ps 37.34;
>   God his refuge,   40.3
> but trusted in the abundance of his riches,   52.7
>   and sought refuge in his wealth!"*c*   Ps 49.6

C. *The praise of the righteous*

8 But I am like a green olive tree   52.8
>   in the house of God.   Jer 11.16;
> I trust in the steadfast love of God   Ps 13.5
>   for ever and ever.
9 I will thank thee for ever,   52.9
>   because thou hast done it.   Ps 30.12;
> I will proclaim*d* thy name, for it is good,   54.6
>   in the presence of the godly.

To the choirmaster: according to Mā'hàlàth. A Màskìl of David.

I. *The folly and wickedness of men 53.1–6*

A. *The depravity of men*

53 The fool says in his heart,   *53.1
>   "There is no God."   Ps 14.1–7;
> They are corrupt, doing abominable iniquity;   Rom 3.10
>   there is none that does good.

2 God looks down from heaven   53.2
>   upon the sons of men   Ps 33.13
> to see if there are any that are wise,
>   that seek after God.

3 They have all fallen away;   53.3
>   Rom 3.12

c Syr Tg: Heb *his destruction*   *d* Cn: Heb *wait for*

53.1 See note to 14.1 on *fool*. The Hebrew word is *nabal*, which means senseless or foolish; having no perception of ethical and religious values (with the collateral idea of ignoble or disgraceful).
This Psalm should be compared with Psalm 14 with which it is closely related. It is thought by some scholars that Book II of The Psalms (ch 42—47) may have been used in the Northern Kingdom and that the differences reflect local usage. Psalms were adapted to liturgical usage, and thus, minor alterations in form occurred during their long history.

they are all alike depraved;
there is none that does good,
no, not one.

B. *The punishment by God*

53.4
Jer 4.22

4 Have those who work evil no understanding,
who eat up my people as they eat bread,
and do not call upon God?

53.5
Lev 26.17,36;
Ezek 6.5

5 There they are, in great terror,
in terror such as has not been!
For God will scatter the bones of the ungodly;[e]
they will be put to shame,[f] for God has rejected them.

C. *The prayer for salvation*

53.6
Ps 14.7

6 O that deliverance for Israel would come from Zion!
When God restores the fortunes of his people,
Jacob will rejoice and Israel be glad.

To the choirmaster: with stringed instruments. A Măskĭl of
David, when the Zĭphītes went and told Saul,
"David is in hiding among us."

I. *A song for the distressed 54.1–7*

A. *Complaint and prayer for help*

54.1
Ps 20.1;
2 Chr 20.6

54 Save me, O God, by thy name,
and vindicate me by thy might.

54.2
Ps 55.1; 5.1

2 Hear my prayer, O God;
give ear to the words of my mouth.

54.3
Ps 86.14;
40.14; 36.1

3 For insolent[g] men have risen against me,
ruthless men seek my life;
they do not set God before them.   *Sĕlăh*

B. *Assurance of God's favor and deliverance*

54.4
Ps 118.7;
41.12

4 Behold, God is my helper;
the Lord is the upholder[h] of my life.

54.5
Ps 94.23;
143.12;
89.49

5 He will requite my enemies with evil;
in thy faithfulness put an end to them.

54.6
Ps 50.14;
52.9

6 With a freewill offering I will sacrifice to thee;
I will give thanks to thy name, O LORD, for it is good.

54.7
Ps 34.6;
59.10

7 For thou hast delivered me from every trouble,
and my eye has looked in triumph on my enemies.

e Cn Compare Gk Syr: Heb *him who encamps against you*
f Gk: Heb *you will put to shame*
g Another reading is *strangers*
h Gk Syr Jerome: Heb *of* or *with those who uphold*

To the choirmaster: with stringed instruments. A Măskĭl of David.

I. A song for those who have been betrayed 55.1–23

A. David describes his distress

55 Give ear to my prayer, O God;
and hide not thyself from my supplication!

2 Attend to me, and answer me;
I am overcome by my trouble.
I am distraught 3 by the noise of the enemy,
because of the oppression of the wicked.
For they bring[i] trouble upon me,
and in anger they cherish enmity against me.

4 My heart is in anguish within me,
the terrors of death have fallen upon me.

5 Fear and trembling come upon me,
and horror overwhelms me.

6 And I say, "O that I had wings like a dove!
I would fly away and be at rest;

7 yea, I would wander afar,
I would lodge in the wilderness,   *Sēlàh*

8 I would haste to find me a shelter
from the raging wind and tempest."

B. The treachery of a friend

9 Destroy their plans,[j] O Lord, confuse their tongues;
for I see violence and strife in the city.

10 Day and night they go around it
on its walls;
and mischief and trouble are within it,

11   ruin is in its midst;
oppression and fraud
do not depart from its market place.

12 It is not an enemy who taunts me—
then I could bear it;
it is not an adversary who deals insolently with me—
then I could hide from him.

13 But it is you, my equal,
my companion, my familiar friend.

14 We used to hold sweet converse together;
within God's house we walked in fellowship.

15 Let death[k] come upon them;
let them go down to Shēōl alive;
let them go away in terror into their graves.[l]

C. David's confidence in God

16 But I call upon God;
and the LORD will save me.

Reference column:

55.1
Ps 61.1;
27.9
55.2
Ps 66.19;
77.3;
Isa 38.14
55.3
Ps 17.9;
2 Sam
16.7,8;
Ps 71.11
55.4
Ps 116.3
55.5
Ps 119.120;
Job 21.6
55.6
Job 3.13
55.8
Isa 4.6
55.9
Jer 6.7
55.11
Ps 5.9;10.7
55.12
Ps 41.9
55.13
2 Sam
15.12;
Ps 41.9;
Jer 9.4
55.14
Ps 42.4
55.15
Ps 64.7;
Num
16.30,33
55.16
Ps 57.2,3

---

[i] Cn Compare Gk: Heb *they cause to totter*   [j] Tg: Heb lacks *their plans*
[k] Or *desolations*   [l] Cn: Heb *evils are in their habitation, in their midst*

55.17
Ps 141.2;
Dan 6.10;
Acts 3.1;
Ps 5.3
	17 Evening and morning and at noon
	   I utter my complaint and moan,
	   and he will hear my voice.

55.18
Ps 103.4;
2 Chr 32.7,
8
	18 He will deliver my soul in safety
	   from the battle that I wage,
	   for many are arrayed against me.

55.19
Ps 78.59;
Deut 33.27
	19 God will give ear, and humble them,
	   he who is enthroned from of old;
	because they keep no law,*m*
	   and do not fear God. *Sēlàh*

55.20 Ps 7.4; 89.34	20 My companion stretched out his hand against his friends, he violated his covenant.

55.21
Ps 28.3;
57.4;
Prov 5.3;
Ps 59.7
	21 His speech was smoother than butter,
	   yet war was in his heart;
	his words were softer than oil,
	   yet they were drawn swords.

55.22
Ps 37.5;
Mt 6.25;
1 Pet 5.7;
Ps 37.24
	22 Cast your burden*n* on the LORD,
	   and he will sustain you;
	he will never permit
	   the righteous to be moved.

55.23
Ps 73.18;
5.6;
Job 15.32;
Prov 10.27;
Ps 25.2
	23 But thou, O God, wilt cast them down
	   into the lowest pit;
	men of blood and treachery
	   shall not live out half their days.
	But I will trust in thee.

To the choirmaster: according to The Dove on Far-off Tĕr′ebĭnths.
A Mĭktăm of David, when the Phĭlis′tĭnes seized him in Găth.

I. *A prayer for deliverance 56.1–13*

A. *His petition for help*

56.1 Ps 57.1,3	**56** Be gracious to me, O God, for men trample upon me; all day long foemen oppress me;
56.2 Ps 57.3; 35.1	2 my enemies trample upon me all day long, for many fight against me proudly.
56.3 Ps 55.4,5; 11.1	3 When I am afraid, I put my trust in thee.
56.4 Ps 118.6; Heb 13.6	4 In God, whose word I praise, in God I trust without a fear. What can flesh do to me?

B. *The malice of his enemies*

56.5 Ps 41.7	5 All day long they seek to injure my cause; all their thoughts are against me for evil.
56.6 Ps 59.3; 140.2; 19.10,11	6 They band themselves together, they lurk, they watch my steps. As they have waited for my life,

m Or do not change   n Or what he has given you

7 so recompense^o them for their crime;
   in wrath cast down the peoples, O God!

56.7
Ps 36.12;
55.23

C. His trust in God without a fear

8 Thou hast kept count of my tossings;
   put thou my tears in thy bottle!
   Are they not in thy book?

56.8
Ps 139.3;
39.12;
Mal 3.16

9 Then my enemies will be turned back
   in the day when I call.
   This I know, that^p God is for me.
10 In God, whose word I praise,
   in the LORD, whose word I praise,
11 in God I trust without a fear.
   What can man do to me?

56.9
Ps 9.3;
102.2;
Rom 8.31

D. His gratitude for deliverance

12 My vows to thee I must perform, O God;
   I will render thank offerings to thee.

56.12
Ps 50.14

13 For thou hast delivered my soul from death,
   yea, my feet from falling,
   that I may walk before God
   in the light of life.

56.13
Ps 116.8;
Job 33.30

To the choirmaster: according to Do Not Destroy. A Miktăm of
David, when he fled from Saul, in the cave.

I. David's deliverance from Saul 57.1–11

A. A prayer and a complaint

57 Be merciful to me, O God, be merciful to me,
   for in thee my soul takes refuge;
in the shadow of thy wings I will take refuge,
   till the storms of destruction pass by.

57.1
Ps 2.12;
17.8;
Isa 26.20

2 I cry to God Most High,
   to God who fulfils his purpose for me.

57.2
Ps 138.8

3 He will send from heaven and save me,
   he will put to shame those who trample upon me.   Sélâh
God will send forth his steadfast love and his faithfulness!

57.3
Ps 18.16;
56.2; 40.11

4 I lie in the midst of lions
   that greedily devour^q the sons of men;
their teeth are spears and arrows,
   their tongues sharp swords.

57.4
Ps 35.17;
Prov 30.14;
Ps 55.21

5 Be exalted, O God, above the heavens!
   Let thy glory be over all the earth!

57.5
Ps 108.5

6 They set a net for my steps;
   my soul was bowed down.

57.6
Ps 35.7;
145.14;
7.15;
Prov 28.10

^{o} Cn: Heb deliver ^{p} Or because ^{q} Cn: Heb are aflame

They dug a pit in my way,
  but they have fallen into it themselves.   *Selah*

B. *Praise and thanksgiving*

57.7
Ps 108.1

7 My heart is steadfast, O God,
  my heart is steadfast!
I will sing and make melody!

57.8
Ps 16.9;
30.12;
150.3

8 Awake, my soul!
Awake, O harp and lyre!
I will awake the dawn!

57.9
Ps 108.3

9 I will give thanks to thee, O Lord, among the peoples;
  I will sing praises to thee among the nations.

57.10
Ps 36.5

10 For thy steadfast love is great to the heavens,
  thy faithfulness to the clouds.

57.11
ver 5

11 Be exalted, O God, above the heavens!
Let thy glory be over all the earth!

To the choirmaster: according to Do Not Destroy.
A Mĭktăm of David.

I. *The punishment of the wicked 58.1–11*

A. *Their sins*

58.1
Ps 82.2

58   Do you indeed decree what is right, you gods?*s*
    Do you judge the sons of men uprightly?

58.2
Mal 3.15;
Ps 94.20

2 Nay, in your hearts you devise wrongs;
  your hands deal out violence on earth.

58.3
Ps 51.5;
Isa 48.8;
Ps 53.3

3 The wicked go astray from the womb,
  they err from their birth, speaking lies.

58.4
Ps 140.3;
Ecc 10.11

4 They have venom like the venom of a serpent,
  like the deaf adder that stops its ear,

58.5
Ps 81.11

5 so that it does not hear the voice of charmers
  or of the cunning enchanter.

B. *Their judgment*

58.6
Job 4.10;
Ps 3.7

6 O God, break the teeth in their mouths;
  tear out the fangs of the young lions, O Lord!

58.7
Josh 7.5;
Ps 112.10;
64.3

7 Let them vanish like water that runs away;
  like grass let them be trodden down and wither.*t*

58.8
Job 3.16

8 Let them be like the snail which dissolves into slime,
  like the untimely birth that never sees the sun.

58.9
Ps 118.12;
Prov 10.25

9 Sooner than your pots can feel the heat of thorns,
  whether green or ablaze, may he sweep them away!

58.10
Ps 64.10;
91.8; 68.23

10 The righteous will rejoice when he sees the vengeance;
  he will bathe his feet in the blood of the wicked.

58.11
Ps 18.20;
9.8

11 Men will say, "Surely there is a reward for the righteous;
  surely there is a God who judges on earth."

s Or *mighty lords*   *t* Cn: Heb uncertain

To the choirmaster: according to Do Not Destroy. A Mĭktăm of
David, when Saul sent men to watch his house in order to kill him.

I. *David's deliverance from Saul 59.1–17*

A. *David's prayer for deliverance*

59 Deliver me from my enemies, O my God,
  protect me from those who rise up against me,
2 deliver me from those who work evil,
  and save me from bloodthirsty men.

3 For, lo, they lie in wait for my life;
  fierce men band themselves against me.
For no transgression or sin of mine, O LORD,
4 for no fault of mine, they run and make ready.

Rouse thyself, come to my help, and see!
5 Thou, LORD God of hosts, art God of Israel.
Awake to punish all the nations;
  spare none of those who treacherously plot evil.   *Sēlâh*

B. *David's trust in God*

6 Each evening they come back,
  howling like dogs
  and prowling about the city.
7 There they are, bellowing with their mouths,
  and snarling with[u] their lips—
  for "Who," they think, "will hear us?"

8 But thou, O LORD, dost laugh at them;
  thou dost hold all the nations in derision.
9 O my Strength, I will sing praises to thee;[v]
  for thou, O God, art my fortress.
10 My God in his steadfast love will meet me;
  my God will let me look in triumph on my enemies.

C. *Prayer for defeat of the enemy*

11 Slay them not, lest my people forget;
  make them totter by thy power, and bring them down,
  O Lord, our shield!
12 For the sin of their mouths, the words of their lips,
  let them be trapped in their pride.
For the cursing and lies which they utter,
13 consume them in wrath,
  consume them till they are no more,
that men may know that God rules over Jacob
to the ends of the earth.   *Sēlâh*

14 Each evening they come back,
  howling like dogs
  and prowling about the city.

Side references:
59.1 Ps 143.9
59.2 Ps 28.3; 139.19
59.3 Ps 56.6
59.4 Ps 35.19,23
59.5 Ps 9.5; Jer 18.23
59.6 ver 14
59.7 Ps 57.4; 10.11
59.8 Ps 37.13; 2.4
59.9 Ps 9.9
59.10 Ps 21.3; 54.7
59.11 Deut 4.9; Ps 106.27; 84.9
59.12 Prov 12.13; Zeph 3.11; Ps 10.7
59.13 Ps 104.35; 83.18
59.14 ver 6

u Cn: Heb *swords in*   v Syr: Heb *I will watch for thee*

15 They roam about for food,
  and growl if they do not get their fill.

D. *David's song of praise*

59.16
Ps 21.13;
101.1;
88.13;
ver 9;
Ps 46.1

16 But I will sing of thy might;
  I will sing aloud of thy steadfast love in the morning.
For thou hast been to me a fortress
  and a refuge in the day of my distress.

59.17
ver 9,10

17 O my Strength, I will sing praises to thee,
  for thou, O God, art my fortress,
  the God who shows me steadfast love.

To the choirmaster: according to Shu'shăn Ē'dŭth. A Mĭktăm of
David; for instruction; when he strove with Ạrăm-nahărā'ĭm and
with Ạrăm-zō'băh, and when Jōăb on his return killed twelve
thousand of Ēdŏm in the Valley of Salt.

I. *A prayer for national deliverance 60.1–12*

A. *Israel's distress*

60.1
Ps 44.9;
2 Sam 5.20;
Ps 79.5;
80.3
60.2
Ps 18.7;
2 Chr 7.14
60.3
Ps 71.20;
Isa 51.17,22
60.4
Ps 20.5
60.5
Ps 108.6;
127.2; 17.7

60 O God, thou hast rejected us, broken our defenses;
  thou hast been angry; oh, restore us.
2 Thou hast made the land to quake, thou hast rent it open;
  repair its breaches, for it totters.
3 Thou hast made thy people suffer hard things;
  thou hast given us wine to drink that made us reel.

4 Thou hast set up a banner for those who fear thee,
  to rally to it from the bow.*w*   *Sĕlah*
5 That thy beloved may be delivered,
  give victory by thy right hand and answer us!

B. *Claiming God's promise*

60.6
Ps 89.35;
Josh 1.6;
Gen 12.6
60.7
Josh 13.31;
Deut
33.17;
Gen 49.10
60.8
2 Sam 8.1

6 God has spoken in his sanctuary:*x*
  "With exultation I will divide up Shĕçhĕm
  and portion out the Vale of Sŭccŏth.
7 Gĭl'ĕăd is mine; Mănăs'sĕh is mine;
  Ē'phrăĭm is my helmet;
  Judah is my scepter.
8 Mōăb is my washbasin;
  upon Ēdŏm I cast my shoe;
  over Phĭlĭs'tĭă I shout in triumph."

C. *Plea for aid*

60.10
ver 1;
Ps 44.9

9 Who will bring me to the fortified city?
  Who will lead me to Ēdŏm?
10 Hast thou not rejected us, O God?
  Thou dost not go forth, O God, with our armies.

w Gk Syr Jerome: Heb *truth*   *x* Or *by his holiness*

11 O grant us help against the foe,
   for vain is the help of man!
12 With God we shall do valiantly;
   it is he who will tread down our foes.

60.11
Ps 146.3

60.12
Num 24.18;
Ps 44.5

To the choirmaster: with stringed instruments. A Psalm of David.

I. *The prayer of the troubled heart 61.1–8*

A. *The prayer of faith*

61 Hear my cry, O God,
    listen to my prayer;
2 from the end of the earth I call to thee,
   when my heart is faint.

61.1
Ps 64.1;
86.6

61.2
Ps 77.3;
18.2

   Lead thou me
   to the rock that is higher than I;
3 for thou art my refuge,
   a strong tower against the enemy.

61.3
Ps 62.7;
Prov 18.10

4 Let me dwell in thy tent for ever!
   Oh to be safe under the shelter of thy wings!   *Sēlāh*

61.4
Ps 23.6;
91.4

B. *The song of praise*

5 For thou, O God, hast heard my vows,
   thou hast given me the heritage of those who fear thy name.

61.5
Ps 56.12;
86.11

6 Prolong the life of the king;
   may his years endure to all generations!
7 May he be enthroned for ever before God;
   bid steadfast love and faithfulness watch over him!

61.6
Ps 21.4

61.7
Ps 41.12;
40.11

8 So will I ever sing praises to thy name,
   as I pay my vows day after day.

61.8
Ps 71.22;
65.1

To the choirmaster: according to Jĕdu'thùn. A Psalm of David.

I. *The trial of faith 62.1–4*

62 For God alone my soul waits in silence;
    from him comes my salvation.
2 He only is my rock and my salvation,
   my fortress; I shall not be greatly moved.

62.1
Ps 33.20

62.2
Ps 89.26;
ver 6

3 How long will you set upon a man
   to shatter him, all of you,
   like a leaning wall, a tottering fence?
4 They only plan to thrust him down from his eminence.
   They take pleasure in falsehood.
They bless with their mouths,
   but inwardly they curse.   *Sēlāh*

62.3
Isa 30.13

62.4
Ps 4.2; 28.3

II. *The confidence of faith 62.5–7*

5 For God alone my soul waits in silence,
  for my hope is from him.

6 He only is my rock and my salvation,
  my fortress; I shall not be shaken.

7 On God rests my deliverance and my honor;
  my mighty rock, my refuge is God.

III. *The exhortation to faith 62.8–12*

8 Trust in him at all times, O people;
  pour out your heart before him;
  God is a refuge for us.   *Selah*

9 Men of low estate are but a breath,
  men of high estate are a delusion;
  in the balances they go up;
  they are together lighter than a breath.

10 Put no confidence in extortion,
  set no vain hopes on robbery;
  if riches increase, set not your heart on them.

11 Once God has spoken;
  twice have I heard this:
  that power belongs to God;

12   and that to thee, O Lord, belongs steadfast love.
  For thou dost requite a man
  according to his work.

A Psalm of David, when he was in the Wilderness of Judah.

I. *The thirsty soul 63.1–11*

A. *The soul that thirsts for God*

63 O God, thou art my God, I seek thee,
  my soul thirsts for thee;
my flesh faints for thee,
  as in a dry and weary land where no water is.

2 So I have looked upon thee in the sanctuary,
  beholding thy power and glory.

3 Because thy steadfast love is better than life,
  my lips will praise thee.

4 So I will bless thee as long as I live;
  I will lift up my hands and call on thy name.

B. *The soul whose thirst is quenched by God*

5 My soul is feasted as with marrow and fat,
  and my mouth praises thee with joyful lips,

6 when I think of thee upon my bed,
  and meditate on thee in the watches of the night;

7 for thou hast been my help,

62.6
ver 2

62.7
Ps 85.9;
46.1

62.8
Ps 37.3;
1 Sam 1.15;
Ps 42.4;
Lam 2.19

62.9
Ps 39.5,11;
Isa 40.15,
17; Rom 3.4

62.10
Isa 30.12;
61.8;
Job 31.25;
Ps 52.7;
1 Tim 6.7

62.11
Job 33.14;
1 Chr 29.11

62.12
Job 34.11;
Mt 16.27;
Col 3.25

63.1
Ps 42.2;
84.2

63.2
Ps 27.4

63.3
Ps 69.16

63.4
Ps 104.33;
28.2

63.5
Ps 36.8;
71.23

63.6
Ps 42.8

63.7
Ps 27.9

and in the shadow of thy wings I sing for joy.
8 My soul clings to thee;
   thy right hand upholds me.

63.8
Ps 18.35

9 But those who seek to destroy my life
   shall go down into the depths of the earth;
10 they shall be given over to the power of the sword,
   they shall be prey for jackals.

*63.9ff
Ps 40.14;
55.15

11 But the king shall rejoice in God;
   all who swear by him shall glory;
   for the mouths of liars will be stopped.

63.11
Ps 21.1;
Deut 6.13;
Isa 45.23

To the choirmaster. A Psalm of David.

I. A prayer for help against secret enemies 64.1–10

A. The appeal for aid: the enemies described

64 Hear my voice, O God, in my complaint;
   preserve my life from dread of the enemy,
2 hide me from the secret plots of the wicked,
   from the scheming of evildoers,
3 who whet their tongues like swords,
   who aim bitter words like arrows,
4 shooting from ambush at the blameless,
   shooting at him suddenly and without fear.
5 They hold fast to their evil purpose;
   they talk of laying snares secretly,
   thinking, "Who can see us?"y
6 Who can search out our crimes?z
   We have thought out a cunningly conceived plot."
   For the inward mind and heart of a man are deep!

64.1
Ps 55.2;
140.1
64.2
Ps 56.6;
59.2
64.3
Ps 58.7
64.4
Ps 11.2;
55.19
64.5
Ps 10.11
64.6
Ps 49.11

B. God's judgment of the wicked

7 But God will shoot his arrow at them;
   they will be wounded suddenly.

*64.7

8 Because of their tongue he will bring them to ruin;a
   all who see them will wag their heads.
9 Then all men will fear;
   they will tell what God has wrought,
   and ponder what he has done.

64.8
Ps 9.3;
Prov 18.7;
Ps 22.7
64.9
Jer 50.28

10 Let the righteous rejoice in the LORD,
   and take refuge in him!
   Let all the upright in heart glory!

64.10
Ps 32.11;
25.20

y Syr: Heb *them* z Cn: Heb *they search out crimes*
a Cn: Heb *They will bring him to ruin, their tongue being against them*

63.9ff What a man is, finds its expression in what he does. What he does, determines his destiny.
64.7 What the righteous man has at life's worst is infinitely better than what the wicked man has at life's best. Therefore choose righteousness, however unprepossessing it may appear at first glance.

To the choirmaster. A Psalm of David. A Song.

I. *The power and goodness of God 65.1–13*

A. *God's praise required*

65.1
Ps 116.18

65 Praise is due to thee,
O God, in Zion;
and to thee shall vows be performed,

65.2
Isa 66.23

2 O thou who hearest prayer!
To thee shall all flesh come

65.3
Ps 38.4;
Heb 9.14

3 on account of sins.
When our transgressions prevail over us,[b]
thou dost forgive them.

★65.4
Ps 33.12;
4.3; 36.8

4 Blessed is he whom thou dost choose and bring near,
to dwell in thy courts!
We shall be satisfied with the goodness of thy house,
thy holy temple!

B. *God's power manifested*

65.5
Ps 66.3;
85.4;22.27;
107.23

5 By dread deeds thou dost answer us with deliverance,
O God of our salvation,
who art the hope of all the ends of the earth,
and of the farthest seas;

★65.6
Ps 93.1

6 who by thy strength hast established the mountains,
being girded with might;

65.7
Mt 8.26;
Isa 17.12

7 who dost still the roaring of the seas,
the roaring of their waves,
the tumult of the peoples;
8 so that those who dwell at earth's farthest bounds
are afraid at thy signs;
thou makest the outgoings of the morning and the evening
to shout for joy.

C. *God's bounty displayed*

65.9
Ps 68.9,10;
46.4;
104.14

9 Thou visitest the earth and waterest it,
thou greatly enrichest it;
the river of God is full of water;
thou providest their grain,
for so thou hast prepared it.
10 Thou waterest its furrows abundantly,
settling its ridges,
softening it with showers,
and blessing its growth.
11 Thou crownest the year with thy bounty;
the tracks of thy chariot drip with fatness.

b Gk: Heb *me*

65.4 Every believer has access to God. Scripture reveals various truths about this: (1) it is possible through Christ alone (Jn 10.7, 9; Rom 5.2; Heb 10.19); (2) it is by the Holy Spirit (Eph 2.18); (3) it is secured by the believer through personal faith (Rom 5.2; Eph 3.12; Heb 11.6); (4) mercy and grace are fruits which flow to the believer as a consequence of it (Heb 4.16).
65.6 *girded with might.* See Ps 93.1.

12 The pastures of the wilderness drip,
    the hills gird themselves with joy,
13 the meadows clothe themselves with flocks,
    the valleys deck themselves with grain,
    they shout and sing together for joy.

65.12
Job
38.26,27;
Ps 98.8
65.13
Ps 144.13;
72.16;98.8

To the choirmaster. A Song. A Psalm.

I. A Psalm of thanksgiving 66.1–20

A. For national deliverances

66 Make a joyful noise to God, all the earth;
    2 sing the glory of his name;
    give to him glorious praise!
3 Say to God, "How terrible are thy deeds!
    So great is thy power that thy enemies cringe before thee.
4 All the earth worships thee;
    they sing praises to thee,
    sing praises to thy name."   *Sēlāh*

5 Come and see what God has done:
    he is terrible in his deeds among men.
6 He turned the sea into dry land;
    men passed through the river on foot.
    There did we rejoice in him,
7   who rules by his might for ever,
    whose eyes keep watch on the nations—
    let not the rebellious exalt themselves.   *Sēlāh*

8 Bless our God, O peoples,
    let the sound of his praise be heard,
9 who has kept us among the living,
    and has not let our feet slip.
10 For thou, O God, hast tested us;
    thou hast tried us as silver is tried.
11 Thou didst bring us into the net;
    thou didst lay affliction on our loins;
12 thou didst let men ride over our heads;
    we went through fire and through water;
    yet thou hast brought us forth to a spacious place.*c*

B. For personal help

13 I will come into thy house with burnt offerings;
    I will pay thee my vows,
14 that which my lips uttered
    and my mouth promised when I was in trouble.
15 I will offer to thee burnt offerings of fatlings,
    with the smoke of the sacrifice of rams;
    I will make an offering of bulls and goats.   *Sēlāh*

*66.1
Ps 100.1
66.2
Ps 81.1;
79.9
66.3
Ps 65.5;
18.44
66.4
Ps 22.27;
67.3,4
66.5
Ps 46.8;
106.22
66.6
Ex 14.21;
Josh 3.6;
Ps 105.43
66.7
Ps 145.13;
11.4;140.8
66.8
Ps 98.4
66.9
Ps 121.3
66.10
Ps 17.3;
Isa 48.10;
Zech 13.9;
1 Pet 1.6,7
66.11
Lam 1.13
66.12
Isa 51.23;
43.2
*66.13
Ecc 5.4
66.14
Ps 18.6
66.15
Ps 51.19;
Num 6.14

c Cn Compare Gk Syr Jerome Tg: Heb *saturation*

66.1 He calls on all peoples to praise God.   **66.13** A vow once made must be fulfilled.

66.16
Ps 34.11;
71.15,24

16 Come and hear, all you who fear God,
      and I will tell what he has done for me.
17 I cried aloud to him,
      and he was extolled with my tongue.

*66.18
Job 36.21;
Isa 1.15;
Jas 4.3

18 If I had cherished iniquity in my heart,
      the Lord would not have listened.

66.19
Ps 116.1,2

19 But truly God has listened;
      he has given heed to the voice of my prayer.

66.20
Ps 68.35;
22.24

20 Blessed be God,
      because he has not rejected my prayer
      or removed his steadfast love from me!

To the choirmaster: with stringed instruments. A Psalm. A Song.

I. *A missionary Psalm 67.1–7*

67.1
Num 6:25;
Ps 4.6

67 May God be gracious to us and bless us
      and make his face to shine upon us,   *Sēlàh*

67.2
Acts 18.25;
Tit 2.11

2 that thy way may be known upon earth,
      thy saving power among all nations.
3 Let the peoples praise thee, O God;
      let all the peoples praise thee!

67.4
Ps 96.10;
98.9

4 Let the nations be glad and sing for joy,
      for thou dost judge the peoples with equity
      and guide the nations upon earth.   *Sēlàh*

67.5
ver 3

5 Let the peoples praise thee, O God;
      let all the peoples praise thee!

67.6
Lev 26.4;
Ps 85.12;
Ezek 34.27

6 The earth has yielded its increase;
      God, our God, has blessed us.

67.7
Ps 33.8

7 God has blessed us;
      let all the ends of the earth fear him!

To the choirmaster. A Psalm of David. A Song.

I. *The God of the whole earth 68.1–35*

A. *The God of the exodus*

68.1
Num 10.35;
Isa 33.3

68 Let God arise, let his enemies be scattered;
      let those who hate him flee before him!

68.2
Isa 9.18;
Hos 13.3;
Ps 97.5;
Mic 1.4

2 As smoke is driven away, so drive them away;
      as wax melts before fire,
      let the wicked perish before God!

68.3
Ps 32.11

3 But let the righteous be joyful;
      let them exult before God;
      let them be jubilant with joy!

66.18 Sin (cherishing iniquity in the heart) is one of the reasons that prayers of believers remain unanswered. The first ques- tion the believer should ask himself is, "Is there any known, unconfessed sin in my life?"

4 Sing to God, sing praises to his name;
  lift up a song to him who rides upon the clouds;*d*
  his name is the LORD, exult before him!

68.4
Ps 66.2;
Isa 57.14;
40.3;
Ps 83.18

5 Father of the fatherless and protector of widows
  is God in his holy habitation.
6 God gives the desolate a home to dwell in;
  he leads out the prisoners to prosperity;
  but the rebellious dwell in a parched land.

68.5
Ps 146.9;
Deut 10.18;
26.15

68.6
Ps 113.9;
Acts 21.6;
Ps 107.34

B. The God of the wilderness

7 O God, when thou didst go forth before thy people,
  when thou didst march through the wilderness,   *Selah*
8 the earth quaked, the heavens poured down rain,
  at the presence of God;
  yon Si'naï quaked at the presence of God,
  the God of Israel.
9 Rain in abundance, O God, thou didst shed abroad;
  thou didst restore thy heritage as it languished;
10 thy flock found a dwelling in it;
  in thy goodness, O God, thou didst provide for the needy.

68.7
Ex 13.21;
Judg 4.14

68.8
Ex 19.16,
18;
Judg 5.4

68.9
Deut 11.11

68.10
Deut 26.5;
Ps 74.19

C. The God of Canaan conquest

11 The Lord gives the command;
  great is the host of those who bore the tidings:
12 "The kings of the armies, they flee, they flee!"
  The women at home divide the spoil,
13   though they stay among the sheepfolds—
  the wings of a dove covered with silver,
  its pinions with green gold.
14 When the Almighty scattered kings there,
  snow fell on Zǎlmon.

★68.12
Ps 135.11;
1 Sam 30.24

68.13
Gen 49.14

★68.14
Josh 10.10

D. The God of Zion

15 O mighty mountain, mountain of Bāshàn;
  O many-peaked mountain, mountain of Bashan!
16 Why look you with envy, O many-peaked mountain,
  at the mount which God desired for his abode,
  yea, where the LORD will dwell for ever?

68.16
Deut 12.5;
Ps 87.1,2

17 With mighty chariotry, twice ten thousand,
  thousands upon thousands,
  the Lord came from Si'naï into the holy place.*e*
18 Thou didst ascend the high mount,
  leading captives in thy train,
  and receiving gifts among men,
  even among the rebellious, that the LORD God may dwell there.

68.17
Deut 33.2;
Dan 7.10

68.18
Acts 1.9;
Eph 4.8;
Judg 5.12;
1 Tim 1.13

d Or *cast up a highway for him who rides through the deserts*
e Cn: Heb *The Lord among them Sinai in the holy place*

68.12 *divide the spoil.* The spoil of battle was brought home by the victorious army. The wives would share the booty.

68.14 *Zalmon* was a mountain near Shechem (Judg 9.48). Possibly a snowstorm there was used by God in routing Israel's foes.

E. The God of salvation

68.19
Ps 55.22;
65.5

19 Blessed be the Lord,
who daily bears us up;
God is our salvation.   *Sēlāh*

68.20
Ps 49.15;
56.13

20 Our God is a God of salvation;
and to GOD, the Lord, belongs escape from death.

68.21
Ps 110.6;
55.23

21 But God will shatter the heads of his enemies,
the hairy crown of him who walks in his guilty ways.

68.22
Num 21.33;
Ex 14.22

22 The Lord said,
"I will bring them back from Bāshăn,
I will bring them back from the depths of the sea,

68.23
Ps 58.10;
1 Ki 21.19

23 that you may bathe*f* your feet in blood,
that the tongues of your dogs may have their portion from
the foe."

F. The God of the sanctuary

1. *The Temple procession*

68.24
Ps 77.13;
63.2

24 Thy solemn processions are seen,*g* O God,
the processions of my God, my King, into the sanctuary—

68.25
1 Chr 13.8;
Judg 11.34

25 the singers in front, the minstrels last,
between them maidens playing timbrels:

68.26
Ps 26.12;
Deut 33.28;
Isa 48.1

26 "Bless God in the great congregation,
the LORD, O you who are of Israel's fountain!"

68.27
1 Sam 9.21

27 There is Benjamin, the least of them, in the lead,
the princes of Judah in their throng,
the princes of Zĕb'ŭlŭn, the princes of Năph'tălĭ.

2. *The nations acknowledge Him*

28 Summon thy might, O God;
show thy strength, O God, thou who has wrought for us.

68.29
Ps 72.10

29 Because of thy temple at Jerusalem
kings bear gifts to thee.

★68.30
Ps 22.12;
89.10

30 Rebuke the beasts that dwell among the reeds,
the herd of bulls with the calves of the peoples.
Trample*h* under foot those who lust after tribute;
scatter the peoples who delight in war.*i*

68.31
Isa 19.19;
45.14

31 Let bronze be brought from Egypt;
let Ethiopia hasten to stretch out her hands to God.

3. *Praise to the God of the whole earth*

★68.32

32 Sing to God, O kingdoms of the earth;
sing praises to the Lord,   *Sēlāh*

68.33
Ps 18.10;
Deut 10.14;
Ps 44.6;
29.4

33 to him who rides in the heavens, the ancient heavens;
lo, he sends forth his voice, his mighty voice.

68.34
Ps 29.1

34 Ascribe power to God,
whose majesty is over Israel,
and his power is in the skies.

---

f Gk Syr Tg: Heb *shatter*   *g* Or *have been seen*   *h* Cn: Heb *trampling*
i The Hebrew of verse 30 is obscure

68.30 *the beasts that dwell among the reeds*
are the hippopotamuses, symbolic of Egypt.

68.32 Verses 32–35 speak of a sovereign,
omnipotent, and majestic God.

35 Terrible is God in his^j sanctuary,
   the God of Israel,
   he gives power and strength to his people.

   68.35
   Ps 47.2;
   29.11;
   66.20

Blessed be God!

To the choirmaster: according to Lilies. A Psalm of David.

I. A plea for deliverance: a Messianic Psalm 69.1–36

A. The prayer and problem of the Psalmist

69 Save me, O God!
   For the waters have come up to my neck.

   *69.1
   ver 14,15

2 I sink in deep mire,
   where there is no foothold;
 I have come into deep waters,
   and the flood sweeps over me.

   69.2
   Ps 40.2;
   Jon 2.3

3 I am weary with my crying;
   my throat is parched.
 My eyes grow dim
   with waiting for my God.

   69.3
   Ps 6.6;
   119.82;
   Isa 38.14

4 More in number than the hairs of my head
   are those who hate me without cause;
 mighty are those who would destroy me,
   those who attack me with lies.
 What I did not steal
   must I now restore?

   69.4
   Ps 35.19;
   Jn 15.25;
   Ps 38.19;
   35.11

5 O God, thou knowest my folly;
   the wrongs I have done are not hidden from thee.

   69.5
   Ps 38.5;
   44.21

6 Let not those who hope in thee be put to shame through me,
   O Lord GOD of hosts;
 let not those who seek thee be brought to dishonor through me,
   O God of Israel.

   69.6
   2 Sam 12.14

7 For it is for thy sake that I have borne reproach,
   that shame has covered my face.

   69.7
   Jer 15.15;
   Ps 44.15

8 I have become a stranger to my brethren,
   an alien to my mother's sons.

   69.8
   Ps 31.11;
   Isa 53.3

9 For zeal for thy house has consumed me,
   and the insults of those who insult thee have fallen on me.

   69.9
   Jn 2.17;
   Ps 89.50

10 When I humbled^k my soul with fasting,
   it became my reproach.

   69.10
   Ps 35.13

^{j} Gk: Heb *from thy*
^{k} Gk Syr: Heb *I wept with fasting my soul* or *I made my soul mourn with fasting*

69.1 This is a Psalm with Messianic implications. In all probability it serves a dual purpose: it refers to some experience in the life of David, yet at the same time it has typical reference to Jesus Christ. Mt 27.34, 48 is a literal fulfilment of verse 21. The strongest argument against the view which holds that it had direct reference to the Messiah is found in verse 5 where sin is confessed. Christ was the sinless one to whom this could hardly apply. Yet David, though imperfect, could in certain respects serve as a type of the Messiah. See also note to 1 Sam 16.13.

69.11
Ps 35.13;
Jer 24.9
69.12
Job 30.9

11 When I made sackcloth my clothing,
    I became a byword to them.
12 I am the talk of those who sit in the gate,
    and the drunkards make songs about me.

B. *The prayer for deliverance renewed*

69.13
Isa 49.8;
2 Cor 6.2;
Ps 51.1
69.14
ver 2;
Ps 144.7

13 But as for me, my prayer is to thee, O LORD.
    At an acceptable time, O God,
    in the abundance of thy steadfast love answer me.
With thy faithful help 14 rescue me
    from sinking in the mire;
let me be delivered from my enemies
    and from the deep waters.

69.15
Ps 124.4,5;
Num 16.33

15 Let not the flood sweep over me,
    or the deep swallow me up,
    or the pit close its mouth over me.

69.16
Ps 63.3;
51.1; 25.16

16 Answer me, O LORD, for thy steadfast love is good;
    according to thy abundant mercy, turn to me.

69.17
Ps 27.9;
66.14

17 Hide not thy face from thy servant;
    for I am in distress, make haste to answer me.

69.18
Ps 49.15

18 Draw near to me, redeem me,
    set me free because of my enemies!

69.19
Ps 22.6,7;
Isa 53.3

19 Thou knowest my reproach,
    and my shame and my dishonor;
    my foes are all known to thee.

69.20
Jer 23.9;
Isa 63.5;
Job 16.2

20 Insults have broken my heart,
    so that I am in despair.
I looked for pity, but there was none;
    and for comforters, but I found none.

69.21
Mt 27.34;
Jn 19.29

21 They gave me poison for food,
    and for my thirst they gave me vinegar to drink.

C. *Imprecation on his enemies*

69.22
Rom 11.9,
10

22 Let their own table before them become a snare;
    let their sacrificial feasts[l] be a trap.

69.23
Isa 6.9,10;
Dan 5.6

23 Let their eyes be darkened, so that they cannot see;
    and make their loins tremble continually.

69.24
Ps 79.6

24 Pour out thy indignation upon them,
    and let thy burning anger overtake them.

69.25
Mt 23.38;
Acts 1.20

25 May their camp be a desolation,
    let no one dwell in their tents.

69.26
Isa 53.4

26 For they persecute him whom thou hast smitten,
    and him[m] whom thou hast wounded, they afflict still more.[n]
27 Add to them punishment upon punishment;
    may they have no acquittal from thee.

69.28
Ex 32.32;
Phil 4.3;
Lk 10.20

28 Let them be blotted out of the book of the living;
    let them not be enrolled among the righteous.

---

l Tg: Heb *for security*
m One Ms Tg Compare Syr: Heb *those*
n Gk Syr: Heb *recount the pain of*

D. Concluding song of praise and assurance

29 But I am afflicted and in pain;
   let thy salvation, O God, set me on high!

30 I will praise the name of God with a song;
   I will magnify him with thanksgiving.
31 This will please the LORD more than an ox
   or a bull with horns and hoofs.
32 Let the oppressed see it and be glad;
   you who seek God, let your hearts revive.
33 For the LORD hears the needy,
   and does not despise his own that are in bonds.

34 Let heaven and earth praise him,
   the seas and everything that moves therein.
35 For God will save Zion
   and rebuild the cities of Judah;
   and his servants shall dwell[o] there and possess it;
36   the children of his servants shall inherit it,
   and those who love his name shall dwell in it.

To the choirmaster. A Psalm of David, for the memorial offering.

I. Appeal for deliverance from persecutors 70.1–5

70 Be pleased, O God, to deliver me!
   O LORD, make haste to help me!
2 Let them be put to shame and confusion
   who seek my life!
Let them be turned back and brought to dishonor
   who desire my hurt!
3 Let them be appalled because of their shame
   who say, "Aha, Aha!"

4 May all who seek thee
   rejoice and be glad in thee!
May those who love thy salvation
   say evermore, "God is great!"
5 But I am poor and needy;
   hasten to me, O God!
Thou art my help and my deliverer;
   O LORD, do not tarry!

I. The prayer of an aged man for deliverance 71.1–24

A. The plea for help

71 In thee, O LORD, do I take refuge;
   let me never be put to shame!
2 In thy righteousness deliver me and rescue me;
   incline thy ear to me, and save me!
3 Be thou to me a rock of refuge,

o Syr: Heb *and they shall dwell*

69.29	Ps 70.5; 59.1
69.30	Ps 28.7; 34.3; 50.14
69.31	Ps 50.13,14
69.32	Ps 34.2; 22.26
69.33	Ps 12.5; 68.6
69.34	Ps 96.11; 148.1; Isa 44.23; 49.13
69.35	Ps 51.18; Isa 44.26
69.36	Ps 102.28; 37.29
70.1	Ps 40.13
70.2	Ps 35.4,26
70.3	Ps 40.15
70.5	Ps 40.17; 141.1
71.1	Ps 25.2,3
71.2	Ps 31.1; 17.6
71.3	Ps 31.2,3; 44.4

a strong fortress,[p] to save me,
for thou art my rock and my fortress.

71.4
Ps 140.1,4

4 Rescue me, O my God, from the hand of the wicked,
from the grasp of the unjust and cruel man.

71.5
Jer 17.7

5 For thou, O Lord, art my hope,
my trust, O Lord, from my youth.

71.6
Ps 22.9,10;
Isa 46.3;
Ps 34.1

6 Upon thee I have leaned from my birth;
thou art he who took me from my mother's womb.
My praise is continually of thee.

71.7
1 Cor 4.9;
Ps 61.3

7 I have been as a portent to many;
but thou art my strong refuge.

71.8
Ps 35.28

8 My mouth is filled with thy praise,
and with thy glory all the day.

71.9
ver 18

9 Do not cast me off in the time of old age;
forsake me not when my strength is spent.

71.10
Ps 56.6;
Mt 27.1

10 For my enemies speak concerning me,
those who watch for my life consult together,

71.11
Ps 3.2; 7.2

11 and say, "God has forsaken him;
pursue and seize him,
for there is none to deliver him."

71.12
Ps 35.22;
70.1

12 O God, be not far from me;
O my God, make haste to help me!

71.13
Ps 35.4;
109.29;
ver 24

13 May my accusers be put to shame and consumed;
with scorn and disgrace may they be covered
who seek my hurt.

14 But I will hope continually,
and will praise thee yet more and more.

71.15
Ps 35.28;
40.5

15 My mouth will tell of thy righteous acts,
of thy deeds of salvation all the day,
for their number is past my knowledge.

71.16
Ps 106.2;
51.14

16 With the mighty deeds of the Lord God I will come,
I will praise thy righteousness, thine alone.

71.17
Deut 4.5;
6.7;
Ps 26.7
71.18
ver 9

17 O God, from my youth thou hast taught me,
and I still proclaim thy wondrous deeds.
18 So even to old age and gray hairs,
O God, do not forsake me,
till I proclaim thy might
to all the generations to come.[q]

71.19
Ps 57.10;
35.10

Thy power 19 and thy righteousness, O God,
reach the high heavens.

B. Song of assurance and praise for deliverance

Thou who hast done great things,
O God, who is like thee?

71.20
Ps 60.3;
Hos 6.1,2

20 Thou who hast made me see many sore troubles
wilt revive me again;
from the depths of the earth
thou wilt bring me up again.

[p] Gk Compare 31.3: Heb *to come continually thou hast commanded*
[q] Gk Compare Syr: Heb *to a generation, to all that come*

21 Thou wilt increase my honor,
and comfort me again.

22 I will also praise thee with the harp
for thy faithfulness, O my God;
I will sing praises to thee with the lyre,
O Holy One of Israel.
23 My lips will shout for joy,
when I sing praises to thee;
my soul also, which thou hast rescued.
24 And my tongue will talk of thy righteous help
all the day long,
for they have been put to shame and disgraced
who sought to do me hurt.

71.22
Ps 33.2;
78.41

71.23
Ps 5.11;
103.4

71.24
Ps 35.28;
ver 13

A Psalm of Solomon.

I. A prayer for the king 72.1–20

A. For justice

72 Give the king thy justice, O God,
and thy righteousness to the royal son!
2 May he judge thy people with righteousness,
and thy poor with justice!
3 Let the mountains bear prosperity for the people,
and the hills, in righteousness!
4 May he defend the cause of the poor of the people,
give deliverance to the needy,
and crush the oppressor!

*72.1
Ps 24.5

72.2
Isa 9.7;
Ps 82.3

72.3
Ps 85.10;
Isa 32.17

72.4
Isa 11.4

B. For length of days

5 May he liver while the sun endures,
and as long as the moon, throughout all generations!
6 May he be like rain that falls on the mown grass,
like showers that water the earth!
7 In his days may righteousness flourish,
and peace abound, till the moon be no more!

72.5
Ps 89.36

72.6
2 Sam 23.4;
Hos 6.3

72.7
Ps 92.12

C. For dominion

8 May he have dominion from sea to sea,
and from the River to the ends of the earth!
9 May his foess bow down before him,

72.8
Ex 23.31;
Zech 9.10
72.9
Ps 74.14;
Isa 49.23;
Mic 7.17

r Gk: Heb *may they fear thee*   s Cn: Heb *those who dwell in the wilderness*

72.1 This Solomonic Psalm depicts the reign and kingdom of God's ideal King, hence finds fulfilment in Christ, the true Messiah. It goes far beyond any human empire. Messiah's kingdom goes from sea to sea, and from the river to the ends of the earth (ver 8). All kings of the earth fall before Him; all nations do Him homage (ver 11). His kingdom shall endure forever (ver 17). The King is immortal, omnipotent, and omniscient. The Hebrew text makes possible the use of the subjunctive mood (identified by the word "may"), or the declarative "he shall," in the KJV. Since Solomon speaks of one who goes beyond human proportions, it is perfectly proper to accept the Messianic implications of the Psalm as portraying what has come and will surely come to fruition in Jesus Christ.

and his enemies lick the dust!

72.10
2 Chr 9.21;
Ps 68.29

10 May the kings of Tarshĭsh and of the isles
    render him tribute,
  may the kings of Shēbà and Sēbà
    bring gifts!

72.11
Ps 49.23

11 May all kings fall down before him,
    all nations serve him!

D. *For compassion*

72.12
Job 29.12

12 For he delivers the needy when he calls,
    the poor and him who has no helper.
13 He has pity on the weak and the needy,
    and saves the lives of the needy.

72.14
Ps 116.15

14 From oppression and violence he redeems their life;
    and precious is their blood in his sight.

E. *For an enduring name*

72.15
Isa 60.6

15 Long may he live,
    may gold of Shēbà be given to him!
  May prayer be made for him continually,
    and blessings invoked for him all the day!

72.16
Ps 104.16;
Job 5.25

16 May there be abundance of grain in the land;
    on the tops of the mountains may it wave;
    may its fruit be like Lebanon;
  and may men blossom forth from the cities
    like the grass of the field!

72.17
Ps 89.36;
Gen 12.3;
22.18;
Lk 1.48

17 May his name endure for ever,
    his fame continue as long as the sun!
  May men bless themselves by him,
    all nations call him blessed!

F. *Benediction*

72.18
Ps 41.13;
106.48;
77.14
72.19
Neh 9.5;
Zech 14.9

18 Blessed be the LORD, the God of Israel,
    who alone does wondrous things.
19 Blessed be his glorious name for ever;
    may his glory fill the whole earth! Amen and Amen!

20 The prayers of David, the son of Jĕssë, are ended.

BOOK III

A Psalm of Āsăph.

I. *The end of the prosperous wicked 73.1–28*

A. *The temptation to envy the wicked*

73.1
Ps 86.5;
51.10

73 Truly God is good to the upright,
   to those who are pure in heart.*t*

t Or Truly God is good to Israel, to those who are pure in heart

2 But as for me, my feet had almost stumbled,
    my steps had well nigh slipped.
3 For I was envious of the arrogant,
    when I saw the prosperity of the wicked.

73.2
Ps 94.18

73.3
Ps 37.1;
Jer 12.1

B. *The prosperity of the wicked*

4 For they have no pangs;
    their bodies are sound and sleek.
5 They are not in trouble as other men are;
    they are not stricken like other men.
6 Therefore pride is their necklace;
    violence covers them as a garment.
7 Their eyes swell out with fatness,
    their hearts overflow with follies.
8 They scoff and speak with malice;
    loftily they threaten oppression.
9 They set their mouths against the heavens,
    and their tongue struts through the earth.

73.5
Job 21.9

73.6
Ps 109.18

73.7
Job 15.27;
Ps 17.10
73.8
Ps 53.1;
Jude 16

C. *The lament of the righteous*

10 Therefore the people turn and praise them;*u*
    and find no fault in them.*v*
11 And they say, "How can God know?
    Is there knowledge in the Most High?"
12 Behold, these are the wicked;
    always at ease, they increase in riches.
13 All in vain have I kept my heart clean
    and washed my hands in innocence.
14 For all the day long I have been stricken,
    and chastened every morning.

73.11
Job 22.13

73.12
Ps 49.6;
Jer 49.31
73.13
Job 21.15;
34.9; 35.3;
Ps 26.6
73.14
Ps 38.6;
118.18

D. *The solution to the dilemma*

15 If I had said, "I will speak thus,"
    I would have been untrue to the generation of thy children.
16 But when I thought how to understand this,
    it seemed to me a wearisome task,
17 until I went into the sanctuary of God;
    then I perceived their end.
18 Truly thou dost set them in slippery places;
    thou dost make them fall to ruin.
19 How they are destroyed in a moment,
    swept away utterly by terrors!
20 They are*w* like a dream when one awakes,
    on awaking you despise their phantoms.

73.16
Ecc 8.17

73.17
Ps 77.13;
37.38
73.18
Ps 35.6,8

73.19
Num 16.21;
Job 18.11
73.20
Job 20.8;
Ps 78.65;
1 Sam 2.30

E. *The assurance that God delivers the righteous*

21 When my soul was embittered,
    when I was pricked in heart,
22 I was stupid and ignorant,
    I was like a beast toward thee.

74.22
Ps 49.10;
Job 18.3

u Cn: Heb *his people return hither*
v Cn: Heb *abundant waters are drained by them*   *w* Cn: Heb *Lord*

23 Nevertheless I am continually with thee;
    thou dost hold my right hand.

73.24
Ps 32.8;
48.14

24 Thou dost guide me with thy counsel,
    and afterward thou wilt receive me to glory.x

73.25
Phil 3.8

25 Whom have I in heaven but thee?
    And there is nothing upon earth that I desire besides thee.

73.26
Ps 84.2;
16.5

26 My flesh and my heart may fail,
    but God is the strengthy of my heart and my portion for ever.

73.27
Ps 37.20;
119.155

27 For lo, those who are far from thee shall perish;
    thou dost put an end to those who are false to thee.

73.28
Heb 10.22;
Ps 71.7;
40.5

28 But for me it is good to be near God;
    I have made the Lord GOD my refuge,
    that I may tell of all thy works.

A Măskĭl of Āsăph.

I. Complaint over a devastated land 74.1–23

A. Appeal for help against the enemy

74.1
Ps 44.9,23;
Deut 29.20;
Ps 95.7

74 O God, why dost thou cast us off for ever?
    Why does thy anger smoke against the sheep of thy pasture?

74.2
Deut 32.6;
Ps 77.15;
68.16

2 Remember thy congregation, which thou hast gotten of old,
    which thou hast redeemed to be the tribe of thy heritage!
    Remember Mount Zion, where thou hast dwelt.

74.3
Isa 61.4;
Ps 79.1

3 Direct thy steps to the perpetual ruins;
    the enemy has destroyed everything in the sanctuary!

74.4
Lam 2.7;
Num 2.2

4 Thy foes have roared in the midst of thy holy place;
    they set up their own signs for signs.

74.5
Jer 46.22

5 At the upper entrance they hacked
    the wooden trellis with axes.z

6 And then all its carved wood
    they broke down with hatchets and hammers.

74.7
2 Ki 25.9

7 They set thy sanctuary on fire;
    to the ground they desecrated the dwelling place of thy name.

74.8
Ps 83.4

8 They said to themselves, "We will utterly subdue them";
    they burned all the meeting places of God in the land.

74.9
Ps 78.43;
1 Sam 3.1;
Ps 79.5

9 We do not see our signs;
    there is no longer any prophet,
    and there is none among us who knows how long.

74.10
Ps 44.16;
Lev 24.16

10 How long, O God, is the foe to scoff?
    Is the enemy to revile thy name for ever?

74.11
Lam 2.3;
Ps 59.13

11 Why dost thou hold back thy hand,
    why dost thou keep thy right hand ina thy bosom?

B. Assurance of a sovereign God's power

74.12
Ps 44.4

12 Yet God my King is from of old,

x Or honor   y Heb rock   z Cn Compare Gk Syr: Heb uncertain
a Cn: Heb consume thy right hand from

working salvation in the midst of the earth.
13 Thou didst divide the sea by thy might;
    thou didst break the heads of the dragons on the waters.
14 Thou didst crush the heads of Lêvī'áthàn,
    thou didst give him as food[b] for the creatures of the wilderness.
15 Thou didst cleave open springs and brooks;
    thou didst dry up ever-flowing streams.
16 Thine is the day, thine also the night;
    thou hast established the luminaries and the sun.
17 Thou hast fixed all the bounds of the earth;
    thou hast made summer and winter.

C. Final appeal for help

18 Remember this, O LORD, how the enemy scoffs,
    and an impious people reviles thy name.
19 Do not deliver the soul of thy dove to the wild beasts;
    do not forget the life of thy poor for ever.

20 Have regard for thy[c] covenant;
    for the dark places of the land are full of the habitations of
        violence.
21 Let not the downtrodden be put to shame;
    let the poor and needy praise thy name.

22 Arise, O God, plead thy cause;
    remember how the impious scoff at thee all the day!
23 Do not forget the clamor of thy foes,
    the uproar of thy adversaries which goes up continually!

To the choirmaster: according to Do Not Destroy.
A Psalm of Asăph. A Song.

I. The justice of God 75.1–10

A. Invocation

75 We give thanks to thee, O God; we give thanks;
we call on thy name and recount[d] thy wondrous deeds.

B. Assurance of judgment

2 At the set time which I appoint
    I will judge with equity.
3 When the earth totters, and all its inhabitants,
    it is I who keep steady its pillars.   *Sēlàh*
4 I say to the boastful, "Do not boast,"
    and to the wicked, "Do not lift up your horn;

b Heb *food for the people* *c* Gk Syr: Heb *the*
d Syr Compare Gk: Heb *and near is thy name. They recount*

Cross references (margin):

74.13 Ex 14.21; Isa 51.9
★74.14
74.15 Ex 17.5,6; Num 20.11; Josh 3.13
74.16 Ps 104.19
74.17 Gen 8.22
74.18 ver 10; Ps 39.8
74.19 Sol 2.14; Ps 9.18
74.20 Gen 17.7; Ps 106.45; 88.6
74.21 Ps 103.6; 35.10
74.22 Ps 43.1; ver 18
74.23 ver 10; Ps 65.7
75.1 Ps 79.13; 145.18; 44.1
75.3 Ps 46.6; 1 Sam 2.8
75.4 Zech 1.21

74.14 *Leviathan* was a many-headed mythological sea monster who became a symbol of evil throughout the Bible. (Leviathan is probably the *dragons* of verse 13.)

75.5 Ps 94.4	5 do not lift up your horn on high, or speak with insolent neck.''

C. God is the judge

75.6 Ps 3.3	6 For not from the east or from the west and not from the wilderness comes lifting up;
75.7 Ps 50.6; 1 Sam 2.7; Dan 2.21	7 but it is God who executes judgment, putting down one and lifting up another.

75.8
Job 21.20;
Ps 60.3;
Jer 25.15;
Prov 23.30;
Ps 73.10
	8 For in the hand of the LORD there is a cup,
	  with foaming wine, well mixed;
	and he will pour a draught from it,
	  and all the wicked of the earth
	  shall drain it down to the dregs.

D. Praise to Him

75.9 Ps 40.10	9 But I will rejoice^e for ever, I will sing praises to the God of Jacob.
75.10 Ps 89.17; 148.14	10 All the horns of the wicked he^f will cut off, but the horns of the righteous shall be exalted.

To the choirmaster: with stringed instruments.
A Psalm of Āsăph. A Song.

I. The victorious power of God 76.1–12

76.1 Ps 48.3	**76** In Judah God is known, his name is great in Israel.
76.2 Ps 27.5; 9.11	2 His abode has been established in Sālêm, his dwelling place in Zion.
76.3 Ps 46.9	3 There he broke the flashing arrows, the shield, the sword, and the weapons of war. *Sēlăh*
	4 Glorious art thou, more majestic than the everlasting mountains.^{g}

76.5
Isa 46.12;
Ps 13.3
	5 The stouthearted were stripped of their spoil;
	  they sank into sleep;
	all the men of war
	  were unable to use their hands.

76.6 Ex 15.1,21; Ps 78.53	6 At thy rebuke, O God of Jacob, both rider and horse lay stunned.

76.7
Ps 96.4;
Nah 1.6
	7 But thou, terrible art thou!
	  Who can stand before thee
	  when once thy anger is roused?

76.8 Ezek 38.20; 2 Chr 20.29, 30	8 From the heavens thou didst utter judgment; the earth feared and was still,
76.9 Ps 9.7–9; 72.4	9 when God arose to establish judgment to save all the oppressed of the earth. *Sēlăh*
76.10 Ex 9.16; Rom 9.17	10 Surely the wrath of men shall praise thee; the residue of wrath thou wilt gird upon thee.

e Gk: Heb *declare*   *f* Heb *I*   *g* Gk: Heb *the mountains of prey*

11 Make your vows to the LORD your God, and perform them;
    let all around him bring gifts
    to him who is to be feared,
12 who cuts off the spirit of princes,
    who is terrible to the kings of the earth.

To the choirmaster: according to Jẻdu'thùn. A Psalm of Āsăph.

I. Comfort in the memory of God's mighty deeds 77.1–20

A. The call for help

77 I cry aloud to God,
    aloud to God, that he may hear me.
2 In the day of my trouble I seek the Lord;
    in the night my hand is stretched out without wearying;
    my soul refuses to be comforted.

3 I think of God, and I moan;
    I meditate, and my spirit faints.   *Sẻlâh*
4 Thou dost hold my eyelids from closing;
    I am so troubled that I cannot speak.
5 I consider the days of old,
    I remember the years long ago.
6 I commune[h] with my heart in the night;
    I meditate and search my spirit:[i]
7 "Will the Lord spurn for ever,
    and never again be favorable?
8 Has his steadfast love for ever ceased?
    Are his promises at an end for all time?
9 Has God forgotten to be gracious?
    Has he in anger shut up his compassion?"   *Sẻlâh*
10 And I say, "It is my grief
    that the right hand of the Most High has changed."

B. God's former wonders

11 I will call to mind the deeds of the LORD;
    yea, I will remember thy wonders of old.
12 I will meditate on all thy work,
    and muse on thy mighty deeds.
13 Thy way, O God, is holy.
    What god is great like our God?
14 Thou art the God who workest wonders,
    who hast manifested thy might among the peoples.
15 Thou didst with thy arm redeem thy people,
    the sons of Jacob and Joseph.   *Sẻlâh*
16 When the waters saw thee, O God,
    when the waters saw thee, they were afraid,
    yea, the deep trembled.
17 The clouds poured out water;

---

h Gk Syr: Heb *my music*   *i* Syr Jerome: Heb *my spirit searches*

76.11 Ps 50.14; 68.29
76.12 Ps 68.35
77.1 Ps 3.4
77.2 Ps 50.15; Isa 26.9,16
77.3 Ps 142.3; 143.4
77.5 Deut 32.7; Ps 143.5; Isa 51.9
77.6 Ps 42.8; 4.4
77.7 Ps 74.1; 85.1
77.8 Ps 89.49; 2 Pet 3.9
77.9 Isa 49.15; Ps 25.6
77.10 Ps 31.22; 44.2,3
77.11 Ps 143.5
77.13 Ps 73.17; Ex 15.11
77.15 Ex 6.6; Deut 9.29
77.16 Ex 14.21
77.17 Judg 5.4; Ps 68.33; 2 Sam 22.15

the skies gave forth thunder;
    thy arrows flashed on every side.

77.18
2 Sam 22.8

18 The crash of thy thunder was in the whirlwind;
    thy lightnings lighted up the world;
    the earth trembled and shook.

77.19
Hab 3.15;
Ex 14.28

19 Thy way was through the sea,
    thy path through the great waters;
    yet thy footprints were unseen.

77.20
Ex 13.21;
Isa 63.11–
13;
Ex 6.26

20 Thou didst lead thy people like a flock
    by the hand of Moses and Aaron.

A Măskĭl of Āsăph.

I. *God's guidance despite His people's unfaithfulness* 78.1–72

A. *The call to hear and heed*

78.1
Isa 51.4

78 Give ear, O my people, to my teaching;
    incline your ears to the words of my mouth!

78.2
Mt 13.35

2 I will open my mouth in a parable;
    I will utter dark sayings from of old,

78.3
Ps 44.1

3 things that we have heard and known,
    that our fathers have told us.

78.4
Ex 12.26;
Ps 22.30;
71.17

4 We will not hide them from their children,
    but tell to the coming generation
the glorious deeds of the LORD, and his might,
    and the wonders which he has wrought.

78.5
Ps 147.19;
Deut 4.9

5 He established a testimony in Jacob,
    and appointed a law in Israel,
which he commanded our fathers
    to teach to their children;

78.6
Ps 102.18

6 that the next generation might know them,
    the children yet unborn,
and arise and tell them to their children,

78.7
Deut 6.12;
27.1

7   so that they should set their hope in God,
    and not forget the works of God,
    but keep his commandments;

78.8
Ezek 20.18;
Ex 32.9;
ver 37

8 and that they should not be like their fathers,
    a stubborn and rebellious generation,
a generation whose heart was not steadfast,
    whose spirit was not faithful to God.

B. *The sins of Israel*

1. *The Ephraimites' disobedience*

78.9
1 Chr 12.2;
Judg 20.39

9 The Ē'phraïmītes, armed with[j] the bow,
    turned back on the day of battle.

78.10
2 Ki 18.12;
Ps 119.1

10 They did not keep God's covenant,
    but refused to walk according to his law.

78.11
Ps 106.13

11 They forgot what he had done,

j Heb *armed with shooting*

and the miracles that he had shown them.
12 In the sight of their fathers he wrought marvels
    in the land of Egypt, in the fields of Zŏan.
13 He divided the sea and let them pass through it,
    and made the waters stand like a heap.
14 In the daytime he led them with a cloud,
    and all the night with a fiery light.
15 He cleft rocks in the wilderness,
    and gave them drink abundantly as from the deep.
16 He made streams come out of the rock,
    and caused waters to flow down like rivers.

2. Lusting for flesh in the wilderness

17 Yet they sinned still more against him,
    rebelling against the Most High in the desert.
18 They tested God in their heart
    by demanding the food they craved.
19 They spoke against God, saying,
    "Can God spread a table in the wilderness?
20 He smote the rock so that water gushed out
    and streams overflowed.
    Can he also give bread,
    or provide meat for his people?"

21 Therefore, when the LORD heard, he was full of wrath;
    a fire was kindled against Jacob,
    his anger mounted against Israel;
22 because they had no faith in God,
    and did not trust his saving power.
23 Yet he commanded the skies above,
    and opened the doors of heaven;
24 and he rained down upon them manna to eat,
    and gave them the grain of heaven.
25 Man ate of the bread of the angels;
    he sent them food in abundance.
26 He caused the east wind to blow in the heavens,
    and by his power he led out the south wind;
27 he rained flesh upon them like dust,
    winged birds like the sand of the seas;
28 he let them fall in the midst of their camp,
    all around their habitations.
29 And they ate and were well filled,
    for he gave them what they craved.
30 But before they had sated their craving,
    while the food was still in their mouths,
31 the anger of God rose against them
    and he slew the strongest of them,
    and laid low the picked men of Israel.

3. Israel's sinful waywardness

32 In spite of all this they still sinned;
    despite his wonders they did not believe.
33 So he made their days vanish like a breath,
    and their years in terror.
34 When he slew them, they sought for him;

78.12 Ex 7–12; Num 13.22; Isa 19.11, 13; Ezek 30.14
78.13 Ex 14.21; 15.8
78.14 Ex 13.21
78.15 Num 20.11; 1 Cor 10.4
78.17 Deut 9.22; Heb 3.16
78.18 Ex 16.2; 1 Cor 10.9
78.19 Num 11.4
78.20 Num 20.11
78.21 Num 11.1
78.22 Heb 3.18
78.23 Mal 3.10
78.24 Jn 6.31
78.26 Num 11.31
78.27 Ps 105.40
78.29 Num 11.20
78.31 Num 11.33
78.32 Num 14,16, 17; ver 22
78.33 Num 14.29, 35
78.34 Hos 5.15

they repented and sought God earnestly.

35 They remembered that God was their rock,
   the Most High God their redeemer.

36 But they flattered him with their mouths;
   they lied to him with their tongues.

37 Their heart was not steadfast toward him;
   they were not true to his covenant.

38 Yet he, being compassionate,
   forgave their iniquity,
   and did not destroy them;
 he restrained his anger often,
   and did not stir up all his wrath.

39 He remembered that they were but flesh,
   a wind that passes and comes not again.

4. Israel's forgetfulness of past mercies

40 How often they rebelled against him in the wilderness
   and grieved him in the desert!

41 They tested him again and again,
   and provoked the Holy One of Israel.

42 They did not keep in mind his power,
   or the day when he redeemed them from the foe;

43 when he wrought his signs in Egypt,
   and his miracles in the fields of Zōän.

44 He turned their rivers to blood,
   so that they could not drink of their streams.

45 He sent among them swarms of flies, which devoured them,
   and frogs, which destroyed them.

46 He gave their crops to the caterpillar,
   and the fruit of their labor to the locust.

47 He destroyed their vines with hail,
   and their sycamores with frost.

48 He gave over their cattle to the hail,
   and their flocks to thunderbolts.

49 He let loose on them his fierce anger,
   wrath, indignation, and distress,
   a company of destroying angels.

50 He made a path for his anger;
   he did not spare them from death,
   but gave their lives over to the plague.

51 He smote all the first-born in Egypt,
   the first issue of their strength in the tents of Ham.

52 Then he led forth his people like sheep,
   and guided them in the wilderness like a flock.

53 He led them in safety, so that they were not afraid;
   but the sea overwhelmed their enemies.

54 And he brought them to his holy land,
   to the mountain which his right hand had won.

55 He drove out nations before them;
   he apportioned them for a possession
   and settled the tribes of Israel in their tents.

5. Israel's idolatry in Canaan

56 Yet they tested and rebelled against the Most High God,
   and did not observe his testimonies,

Cross-references (margin):

78.35 Deut 32.4; Isa 41.14
78.36 Ezek 33.31; Ex 32.7,8
78.38 Num 14.18; Isa 48.9; 1 Ki 21.29
78.39 Ps 103.14; Gen 6.3; Job 7.7,16
78.40 Ps 95.8–10; Heb 3.16
78.41 Num 14.22; Ps 89.18
78.44 Ex 7.20
78.45 Ex 8.24; Ps 105.31; Ex 8.6
78.47 Ex 9.25
78.48 Ex 9.23
78.49 Ex 15.7
78.51 Ex 12.29; Ps 106.22
78.52 Ps 77.20
78.53 Ex 14.19,27
78.54 Ex 15.17; Ps 44.3
78.55 Ps 44.2; 105.11
78.56 ver 18,40

57 but turned away and acted treacherously like their fathers;
    they twisted like a deceitful bow.
58 For they provoked him to anger with their high places;
    they moved him to jealousy with their graven images.
59 When God heard, he was full of wrath,
    and he utterly rejected Israel.
60 He forsook his dwelling at Shīlōh,
    the tent where he dwelt among men,
61 and delivered his power to captivity,
    his glory to the hand of the foe.
62 He gave his people over to the sword,
    and vented his wrath on his heritage.
63 Fire devoured their young men,
    and their maidens had no marriage song.
64 Their priests fell by the sword,
    and their widows made no lamentation.
65 Then the Lord awoke as from sleep,
    like a strong man shouting because of wine.
66 And he put his adversaries to rout;
    he put them to everlasting shame.

C. Judah and David chosen

67 He rejected the tent of Joseph,
    he did not choose the tribe of Ē'phräįm;
68 but he chose the tribe of Judah,
    Mount Zion, which he loves.
69 He built his sanctuary like the high heavens,
    like the earth, which he has founded for ever.
70 He chose David his servant,
    and took him from the sheepfolds;
71 from tending the ewes that had young he brought him
    to be the shepherd of Jacob his people,
    of Israel his inheritance.
72 With upright heart he tended them,
    and guided them with skilful hand.

A Psalm of Āsăph.

I. Lament over the destruction of Jerusalem 79.1–13

A. The evil described

79 O God, the heathen have come into thy inheritance;
    they have defiled thy holy temple;
    they have laid Jerusalem in ruins.
2 They have given the bodies of thy servants
    to the birds of the air for food,
    the flesh of thy saints to the beasts of the earth.
3 They have poured out their blood like water
    round about Jerusalem,
    and there was none to bury them.
4 We have become a taunt to our neighbors,
    mocked and derided by those round about us.

78.57
Ezek 20.27,
28;
Hos 7.16
78.58
Deut 32.16,
21; 12.2;
1 Ki 11.7
78.60
1 Sam 4.11
78.61
Judg 18.30
78.62
1 Sam 4.10
78.63
Jer 7.34
78.64
1 Sam
22.18;
Job 27.15
78.65
Isa 42.13
78.66
1 Sam 5.6

78.68
Ps 87.2
78.69
1 Sam 6.1–
38
78.70
1 Sam
16.11,12
78.71
2 Sam 7.8;
Gen 33.13;
2 Sam 5.2;
1 Chr 11.2
78.72
1 Ki 9.4

79.1
Ex 15.17;
Ps 74.2;
2 Ki 25.9;
Mic 3.12
79.2
Jer 7.33
79.3
Jer 14.16
79.4
Ps 44.13

B. *The help of God besought*

79.5
Ps 74.1,9;
Zeph 3.8

5 How long, O LORD? Wilt thou be angry for ever?
  Will thy jealous wrath burn like fire?

79.6
Jer 10.25;
Rev 16.1;
Isa 45.4,5;
2 Thess 1.8

6 Pour out thy anger on the nations
    that do not know thee,
  and on the kingdoms
    that do not call on thy name!
7 For they have devoured Jacob,
    and laid waste his habitation.

79.8
Isa 64.9

8 Do not remember against us the iniquities of our forefathers;
    let thy compassion come speedily to meet us,
  for we are brought very low.

79.9
2 Chr 14.11;
Jer 14.7

9 Help us, O God of our salvation,
    for the glory of thy name;
  deliver us, and forgive our sins,
    for thy name's sake!

79.10
Ps 42.10;
94.1,2

10 Why should the nations say,
   "Where is their God?"
  Let the avenging of the outpoured blood of thy servants
    be known among the nations before our eyes!

79.11
Ps 102.20

11 Let the groans of the prisoners come before thee;
    according to thy great power preserve those doomed to die!

79.12
Isa 65.6,7;
Jer 32.18;
Lk 6.38;
Ps 74.18,22

12 Return sevenfold into the bosom of our neighbors
    the taunts with which they have taunted thee, O Lord!
13 Then we thy people, the flock of thy pasture,
    will give thanks to thee for ever;
  from generation to generation we will recount thy praise.

79.13
Ps 74.1;
95.7;
Isa 43.21

To the choirmaster: according to Lilies.
A Testimony of Āsăph. A Psalm.

I. *Israel's prayer for deliverance from calamities 80.1–19*

A. *The call for help*

80.1
Ps 23.1;
77.20; 99.1

80 Give ear, O Shepherd of Israel,
  thou who leadest Joseph like a flock!
Thou who art enthroned upon the cherubim, shine forth

80.2
Ps 35.23

2 before Ē′phrăim and Benjamin and Mănăs′sĕh!
Stir up thy might,
    and come to save us!

80.3
Lam 5.21;
Num 6.25

3 Restore us, O God;
    let thy face shine, that we may be saved!

B. *Israel's problem*

80.4
Ps 85.5

4 O LORD God of hosts,
    how long wilt thou be angry with thy people's prayers?

80.5
Ps 42.3;
102.9

5 Thou hast fed them with the bread of tears,
    and given them tears to drink in full measure.

⁶ Thou dost make us the scorn^k of our neighbors;
and our enemies laugh among themselves.

80.6
Ps 44.13;
79.4

⁷ Restore us, O God of hosts;
let thy face shine, that we may be saved!

C. Israel a wasted vine

⁸ Thou didst bring a vine out of Egypt;
thou didst drive out the nations and plant it.
⁹ Thou didst clear the ground for it;
it took deep root and filled the land.

80.8
Isa 5.1,7;
Jer 2.21;
Ezek 15.6;
Ps 44.2

¹⁰ The mountains were covered with its shade,
the mighty cedars with its branches;

80.9
Hos 14.5

¹¹ it sent out its branches to the sea,
and its shoots to the River.
¹² Why then hast thou broken down its walls,
so that all who pass along the way pluck its fruit?

80.12
Ps 89.40;
Nah 2.2

¹³ The boar from the forest ravages it,
and all that move in the field feed on it.

80.13
Jer 5.6

D. The call for help repeated

¹⁴ Turn again, O God of hosts!
Look down from heaven, and see;
have regard for this vine,
¹⁵ the stock which thy right hand planted.^l

80.14
Isa 63.15

¹⁶ They have burned it with fire, they have cut it down;
may they perish at the rebuke of thy countenance!

80.16
Ps 39.11;
76.6

¹⁷ But let thy hand be upon the man of thy right hand,
the son of man whom thou hast made strong for thyself!

80.17
Ps 89.21

¹⁸ Then we will never turn back from thee;
give us life, and we will call on thy name!

80.18
Isa 50.5;
Ps 71.20

¹⁹ Restore us, O LORD God of hosts!
let thy face shine, that we may be saved!

To the choirmaster: according to The Gĭttĭth. A Psalm of Āsăph.

I. The goodness of God and the waywardness of Israel
81.1–16

A. The call to praise

81 Sing aloud to God our strength;
shout for joy to the God of Jacob!

81.1
Ps 59.16;
66.1

² Raise a song, sound the timbrel,
the sweet lyre with the harp.
³ Blow the trumpet at the new moon,
at the full moon, on our feast day.

81.3
Num 10.10;
Lev 23.24

⁴ For it is a statute for Israel,
an ordinance of the God of Jacob.

k Syr: Heb strife l Heb planted and upon the son whom thou hast reared for thyself

81.5
Ex 11.4

5 He made it a decree in Joseph,
  when he went out over*m* the land of Egypt.

B. *The goodness of God to Israel*

I hear a voice I had not known:

81.6
Isa 9.4;
10.27

6 "I relieved your*n* shoulder of the burden;
  your*n* hands were freed from the basket.

81.7
Ex 2.23;
Ps 50.15;
Ex 19.19;
17.6,7

7 In distress you called, and I delivered you;
  I answered you in the secret place of thunder;
  I tested you at the waters of Mĕr'ĭbah.   *Sēlåh*

81.8
Ps 50.7

8 Hear, O my people, while I admonish you!
  O Israel, if you would but listen to me!

81.9
Deut 32.12;
Isa 43.12

9 There shall be no strange god among you;
  you shall not bow down to a foreign god.

81.10
Ex 20.2;
Ps 103.5

10 I am the LORD your God,
  who brought you up out of the land of Egypt.
  Open your mouth wide, and I will fill it.

C. *God's yearning for a backslidden people*

81.11
Ex 32.1

11 "But my people did not listen to my voice;
  Israel would have none of me.

81.12
Acts 7.42;
Rom 1.24

12 So I gave them over to their stubborn hearts,
  to follow their own counsels.

81.13
Deut 5.29;
Isa 48.18;
Ps 128.1

13 O that my people would listen to me,
  that Israel would walk in my ways!

81.14
Ps 47.3;
Amos 1.8

14 I would soon subdue their enemies,
  and turn my hand against their foes.

15 Those who hate the LORD would cringe toward him,
  and their fate would last for ever.

81.16
Deut 32.13;
Ps 147.14

16 I would feed you*o* with the finest of the wheat,
  and with honey from the rock I would satisfy you."

A Psalm of Āsăph.

I. *Unjust judgments rebuked 82.1–8*

82.1
Isa 3.13;
Ex 21.6

82 God has taken his place in the divine council;
  in the midst of the gods he holds judgment:

82.2
Ps 58.1;
Deut 1.17;
Prov 18.5

2 "How long will you judge unjustly
  and show partiality to the wicked?   *Sēlåh*

82.3
Deut 24.17

3 Give justice to the weak and the fatherless;
  maintain the right of the afflicted and the destitute.

82.4
Job 29.12

4 Rescue the weak and the needy;
  deliver them from the hand of the wicked."

82.5
Mic 3.1;
Ps 11.3

5 They have neither knowledge nor understanding,
  they walk about in darkness;
  all the foundations of the earth are shaken.

82.6
Jn 10.34;
Ps 89.26

6 I say, "You are gods,
  sons of the Most High, all of you;

m Or *against*   *n* Heb *his*   *o* Cn Compare verse 16b: Heb *he would feed him*

7 nevertheless, you shall die like men,
   and fall like any prince."p

82.7
Ps 49.12;
Ezek 31.14

8 Arise, O God, judge the earth;
   for to thee belong all the nations!

82.8
Ps 12.5;
Mic 7.2,7;
Ps 2.8;
Rev 11.15

A Song. A Psalm of Āsăph.

I. A prayer for God to confound the enemies 83.1–18

A. Prayer to judge Israel's enemies

83   O God, do not keep silence;
     do not hold thy peace or be still, O God!
2 For lo, thy enemies are in tumult;
   those who hate thee have raised their heads.
3 They lay crafty plans against thy people;
   they consult together against thy protected ones.
4 They say, "Come, let us wipe them out as a nation;
   let the name of Israel be remembered no more!"
5 Yea, they conspire with one accord;
   against thee they make a covenant—
6 the tents of Ēdóm and the Ĭsh'mäelĭtes,
   Mŏăb and the Hăgrītes,
7 Gēbăl and Ămmŏn and Ăm'ălĕk,
   Phĭlĭs'tĭä with the inhabitants of Tȳre;
8 Assyria also has joined them;
   they are the strong arm of the children of Lot.   Sēlăh

83.1
Ps 28.1;
109.1
83.2
Ps 2.1;
81.15
83.3
Ps 27.5
83.4
Est 3.6
83.5
Ps 2.2
83.6
2 Chr 20.1,
10,11

B. The prayer of imprecation

9 Do to them as thou didst to Mĭd'ĭăn,
   as to Sĭs'ĕra and Jābĭn at the river Kĭshŏn,
10 who were destroyed at Ĕn-dor,
   who became dung for the ground.
11 Make their nobles like Ōrĕb and Zeēb,
   all their princes like Zēbăh and Zălmún'nă,
12 who said, "Let us take possession for ourselves
   of the pastures of God."

83.9
Judg 4.22,
23

83.11
Judg 8.12,
21
83.12
2 Chr 20.11;
Ps 132.13

13 O my God, make them like whirling dust,q
   like chaff before the wind.
14 As fire consumes the forest,
   as the flame sets the mountains ablaze,
15 so do thou pursue them with thy tempest
   and terrify them with thy hurricane!
16 Fill their faces with shame,
   that they may seek thy name, O LORD.
17 Let them be put to shame and dismayed for ever;
   let them perish in disgrace.
18 Let them know that thou alone,
   whose name is the LORD,
   art the Most High over all the earth.

83.13
Isa 17.13;
Ps 35.5
83.14
Deut 32.22
83.15
Job 9.17

83.17
Ps 70.2
83.18
Ps 59.13;
Ex 6.3;
Ps 92.8

p Or fall as one man, O princes   q Or a tumbleweed

To the choirmaster: according to The Gĭttĭth.
A Psalm of the Sons of Kōrăh.

I. Longing to be in the sanctuary 84.1–12

A. Longing for the courts of the LORD

84.1
Ps 27.4

84 How lovely is thy dwelling place,
O LORD of hosts!

84.2
Ps 42.1,2

2 My soul longs, yea, faints
    for the courts of the LORD;
my heart and flesh sing for joy
    to the living God.

B. Blessedness in the LORD'S house

84.3
Ps 43.4; 5.2

3 Even the sparrow finds a home,
    and the swallow a nest for herself,
    where she may lay her young,
at thy altars, O LORD of hosts,
    my King and my God.

84.4
Ps 65.4

4 Blessed are those who dwell in thy house,
    ever singing thy praise!   *Sēlăh*

C. Blessedness of this pilgrim journey

84.5
Ps 81.1

5 Blessed are the men whose strength is in thee,
    in whose heart are the highways to Zion.[r]

★84.6
2 Sam 5.23;
Ps 107.35

6 As they go through the valley of Bācă
    they make it a place of springs;
    the early rain also covers it with pools.

84.7
Prov 4.18;
2 Cor 3.18;
Deut 16.16;
Ps 42.2

7 They go from strength to strength;
    the God of gods will be seen in Zion.

D. Expression of petition and trust

8 O LORD God of hosts, hear my prayer;
    give ear, O God of Jacob!   *Sēlăh*

84.9
Gen 15.1;
Ps 2.2

9 Behold our shield, O God;
    look upon the face of thine anointed!

84.10
1 Chr 23.5

10 For a day in thy courts is better
    than a thousand elsewhere.
I would rather be a doorkeeper in the house of my God
    than dwell in the tents of wickedness.

★84.11
Isa 60.19;
Rev 21.23;
Ps 34.10

11 For the LORD God is a sun and shield;
    he bestows favor and honor.
No good thing does the LORD withhold
    from those who walk uprightly.

84.12
Ps 2.12

12 O LORD of hosts,
    blessed is the man who trusts in thee!

r Heb lacks *to Zion*

84.6 *valley of Baca,* a normally dry valley
in which the balsam tree flourishes.

84.11 *sun,* a source of light, life, and
fruitfulness.

To the choirmaster. A Psalm of the Sons of Kōràh.

I. *Prayer for mercy to Israel 85.1–13*

A. *The LORD'S past mercies*

85 LORD, thou wast favorable to thy land;
thou didst restore the fortunes of Jacob.
2 Thou didst forgive the iniquity of thy people;
thou didst pardon all their sin.   *Sēlàh*
3 Thou didst withdraw all thy wrath;
thou didst turn from thy hot anger.

B. *The prayer for revival*

4 Restore us again, O God of our salvation,
and put away thy indignation toward us!
5 Wilt thou be angry with us for ever?
Wilt thou prolong thy anger to all generations?
6 Wilt thou not revive us again,
that thy people may rejoice in thee?
7 Show us thy steadfast love, O LORD,
and grant us thy salvation.

C. *The steadfast love and faithfulness of the LORD*

8 Let me hear what God the LORD will speak,
for he will speak peace to his people,
to his saints, to those who turn to him in their hearts.[s]
9 Surely his salvation is at hand for those who fear him,
that glory may dwell in our land.

10 Steadfast love and faithfulness will meet;
righteousness and peace will kiss each other.
11 Faithfulness will spring up from the ground,
and righteousness will look down from the sky.
12 Yea, the LORD will give what is good,
and our land will yield its increase.
13 Righteousness will go before him,
and make his footsteps a way.

A Prayer of David.

I. *A prayer for deliverance from trouble 86.1–17*

A. *Appeal for help in trouble*

86 Incline thy ear, O LORD, and answer me,
for I am poor and needy.
2 Preserve my life, for I am godly;
save thy servant who trusts in thee.
Thou art my God; 3 be gracious to me, O Lord,

[s] Gk: Heb *but let them not turn back to folly*

85.1	Ezra 1.11; Jer 30.18; Ezek 39.25
85.2	Ps 103.3; 32.1
85.3	Ps 78.38; Deut 13.17
85.4	Ps 80.3,7
85.5	Ps 74.1; 79.5; 80.4
85.6	Hab 3.2
85.7	Ps 106.4
85.8	Hab 2.1; Zech 9.10
85.9	Isa 46.13; Zech 2.5; Jn 1.14
85.10	Ps 72.3; Isa 32.17; Lk 2.14
85.12	Ps 84.11; Jas 1.17
85.13	Ps 89.14
86.1	Ps 17.6; 40.17
86.2	Ps 25.20; 4.3; 31.14
86.3	Ps 57.1; 88.9

for to thee do I cry all the day.

86.4
Ps 25.1;
143.8
4 Gladden the soul of thy servant,
    for to thee, O Lord, do I lift up my soul.

86.5
Ps 130.7;
145.9;
Joel 2.13
5 For thou, O Lord, art good and forgiving,
    abounding in steadfast love to all who call on thee.

86.6
Ps 55.1
6 Give ear, O LORD, to my prayer;
    hearken to my cry of supplication.

86.7
Ps 50.15;
17.6
7 In the day of my trouble I call on thee,
    for thou dost answer me.

B. Adoration of God

86.8
Ex 15.11;
Ps 89.6;
Deut 3.24
8 There is none like thee among the gods, O Lord,
    nor are there any works like thine.

86.9
Ps 22.31;
Isa 43.7;
Rev 15.4
9 All the nations thou hast made shall come
    and bow down before thee, O Lord,
    and shall glorify thy name.

86.10
Ex 15.11;
Ps 72.18;
Deut 6.4;
Mk 12.29
10 For thou art great and doest wondrous things,
    thou alone art God.

C. Petition and thanksgiving

86.11
Ps 25.4
11 Teach me thy way, O LORD,
    that I may walk in thy truth;
    unite my heart to fear thy name.

86.12
Ps 111.1
12 I give thanks to thee, O Lord my God, with my whole heart,
    and I will glorify thy name for ever.

86.13
Ps 30.3
13 For great is thy steadfast love toward me;
    thou hast delivered my soul from the depths of Shēōl.

D. Assurance of God's mercy and grace

86.14
Ps 54.3
14 O God, insolent men have risen up against me;
    a band of ruthless men seek my life,
    and they do not set thee before them.

86.15
Ex 34.6;
Neh 9.17;
Ps 103.8;
Joel 2.13
15 But thou, O Lord, art a God merciful and gracious,
    slow to anger and abounding in steadfast love and faithfulness.

86.16
Ps 25.16;
68.35;
116.16
16 Turn to me and take pity on me;
    give thy strength to thy servant,
    and save the son of thy handmaid.

86.17
Ps 112.10;
118.13
17 Show me a sign of thy favor,
    that those who hate me may see and be put to shame
    because thou, LORD, hast helped me and comforted me.

A Psalm of the Sons of Kōráh. A Song.

I. The privileges of citizenship in Zion 87.1–7

87 On the holy mount stands the city he founded;
2 the LORD loves the gates of Zion
    more than all the dwelling places of Jacob.

87.2
Ps 78.67

87.3
Isa 60.1
3 Glorious things are spoken of you,
    O city of God.   *Sēláh*

4 Among those who know me I mention Rāhăb and Babylon;
   behold, Phĭlis′tĭă and Tŷre, with Ethiopia—
   "This one was born there," they say.

5 And of Zion it shall be said,
   "This one and that one were born in her";
   for the Most High himself will establish her.

6 The LORD records as he registers the peoples,
   "This one was born there."   *Sĕlâh*

7 Singers and dancers alike say,
   "All my springs are in you."

*87.4
87.5 Ps 48.8
87.6 Ezek 13.9
87.7 Ps 36.9

A Song. A Psalm of the Sons of Kōrăh.
To the choirmaster: according to Mă′hălăth Lĕăn′nŏth.
A Măskĭl of Hēmăn the Ĕz′răhīte.

I. A petition to be saved from death 88.1–18

A. The Psalmist's petition

88 O LORD, my God, I call for help *t* by day;
   I cry out in the night before thee.
2 Let my prayer come before thee,
   incline thy ear to my cry!

B. The Psalmist's troubles

3 For my soul is full of troubles,
   and my life draws near to Shēōl.
4 I am reckoned among those who go down to the Pit;
   I am a man who has no strength,
5 like one forsaken among the dead,
   like the slain that lie in the grave,
   like those whom thou dost remember no more,
   for they are cut off from thy hand.
6 Thou hast put me in the depths of the Pit,
   in the regions dark and deep.
7 Thy wrath lies heavy upon me,
   and thou dost overwhelm me with all thy waves.   *Sĕlâh*
8 Thou hast caused my companions to shun me;
   thou hast made me a thing of horror to them.
   I am shut in so that I cannot escape;
9   my eye grows dim through sorrow.
   Every day I call upon thee, O LORD;
   I spread out my hands to thee.

C. The Psalmist's questions

10 Dost thou work wonders for the dead?
   Do the shades rise up to praise thee?   *Sĕlâh*

88.1 Ps 27.9; 51.14
88.2 Ps 18.6; 86.1
88.3 Ps 107.18, 26
88.4 Ps 28.1
88.5 Isa 53.8
88.6 Ps 86.13; 143.3; 69.15
88.7 Ps 42.7
88.8 Job 19.13; Ps 31.11; 142.4; Lam 3.7
88.9 Ps 38.10; 86.3; Job 11.13; Ps 143.6
88.10 Ps 6.5; Isa 38.18

t Cn: Heb *O* LORD, *God of my salvation*

87.4 *Rahab*, the name of a mythological monster used symbolically of Egypt. The word means "the haughty," "arrogant." See also Isa 30.7.

11 Is thy steadfast love declared in the grave,
   or thy faithfulness in Àbăd'dòn?

88.12
Job 10.21

12 Are thy wonders known in the darkness,
   or thy saving help in the land of forgetfulness?

88.13
Ps 5.3;
119.147

13 But I, O LORD, cry to thee;
   in the morning my prayer comes before thee.

88.14
Job 13.24;
Ps 13.1

14 O LORD, why dost thou cast me off?
   Why dost thou hide thy face from me?

D. The Psalmist's closing complaints

88.15
Job 6.4

15 Afflicted and close to death from my youth up,
   I suffer thy terrors; I am helpless. *u*
16 Thy wrath has swept over me;
   thy dread assaults destroy me.

88.17
Ps 22.16

17 They surround me like a flood all day long;
   they close in upon me together.

88.18
Job 19.13;
Ps 31.11;
38.11

18 Thou hast caused lover and friend to shun me;
   my companions are in darkness.

A Măskĭl of Ēthăn the Ĕz'răhīte

I. God's covenant with David and Israel's afflictions
89.1—52

A. The covenant with David

*89.1
Ps 101.1

89 I will sing of thy steadfast love, O LORD, *v* for ever;
   with my mouth I will proclaim thy faithfulness to all
   generations.

89.2
Ps 103.17;
36.5

2 For thy steadfast love was established for ever,
   thy faithfulness is firm as the heavens.

89.3
1 Ki 8.16;
Ps 132.11

3 Thou hast said, "I have made a covenant with my chosen one,
   I have sworn to David my servant:

89.4
2 Sam 7.16;
Isa 9.7;
Lk 1.33

4 'I will establish your descendants for ever,
   and build your throne for all generations.' "   *Sēlàh*

B. Praise to a faithful and mighty God

89.5
Ps 19.1;
149.1

5 Let the heavens praise thy wonders, O LORD,
   thy faithfulness in the assembly of the holy ones!

u The meaning of the Hebrew word is uncertain   *v* Gk: Heb *the steadfast love of the* LORD

89.1 This Psalm is related to the Davidic covenant (see note to 2 Sam 7.4 on the subject). It reaffirms the divine promise of a line which will be established and will endure forever (ver 36). The Psalm has Messianic implications and this prophetic word looks to the rule of Jesus Christ. After the fall of Jerusalem in 587 B.C., which resulted in the loss of Jewish independence, there was no throne to be occupied by a descendant of David. This may be explained simply by observing that the purpose and plan of God was not changed by the changing fortunes of the royal house. An unbroken line of those who would have been eligible for the throne continued. The suspension of royal authority during these centuries was the consequence of chastening for sin. In a spiritual sense, the Lord Jesus Christ fulfilled the covenant promise by occupying the glorious heavenly counterpart of David's throne after His ascension.

6 For who in the skies can be compared to the LORD?
  Who among the heavenly beings[w] is like the LORD,
7 a God feared in the council of the holy ones,
  great and terrible[x] above all that are round about him?
8 O LORD God of hosts,
  who is mighty as thou art, O LORD,
  with thy faithfulness round about thee?
9 Thou dost rule the raging of the sea;
  when its waves rise, thou stillest them.
10 Thou didst crush Rāhāb like a carcass,
  thou didst scatter thy enemies with thy mighty arm.
11 The heavens are thine, the earth also is thine;
  the world and all that is in it, thou hast founded them.
12 The north and the south, thou hast created them;
  Tābôr and Hérmòn joyously praise thy name.
13 Thou hast a mighty arm;
  strong is thy hand, high thy right hand.
14 Righteousness and justice are the foundation of thy throne;
  steadfast love and faithfulness go before thee.
15 Blessed are the people who know the festal shout,
  who walk, O LORD, in the light of thy countenance,
16 who exult in thy name all the day,
  and extol[y] thy righteousness.
17 For thou art the glory of their strength;
  by thy favor our horn is exalted.
18 For our shield belongs to the LORD,
  our king to the Holy One of Israel.

C. God's promises to David and his seed

19 Of old thou didst speak in a vision
  to thy faithful one, and say:
"I have set the crown[z] upon one who is mighty,
  I have exalted one chosen from the people.
20 I have found David, my servant;
  with my holy oil I have anointed him;
21 so that my hand shall ever abide with him,
  my arm also shall strengthen him.
22 The enemy shall not outwit him,
  the wicked shall not humble him.
23 I will crush his foes before him
  and strike down those who hate him.
24 My faithfulness and my steadfast love shall be with him,
  and in my name shall his horn be exalted.
25 I will set his hand on the sea
  and his right hand on the rivers.

89.6
Mic 7.18;
Ps 29.1
89.7
Ps 47.2;
96.4
89.8
Ps 71.19

89.9
Ps 65.7

89.10
Ps 87.4;
Isa 51.9;
Ps 68.1
89.11
1 Chr 29.11;
Ps 24.1,2
89.12
Josh 19.22;
12.1
89.13
Ps 98.1
89.14
Ps 97.2;
85.13
89.15
Num 10.10

89.17
Ps 28.8;
75.10
89.18
Ps 47.9;
71.22

★89.19
1 Ki 11.34

89.20
Acts 13.22;
1 Sam 16.1,
12

89.22
2 Sam 7.10

89.23
2 Sam 7.9

89.24
2 Sam 7.15

w Or *sons of gods*   *x* Gk Syr: Heb *greatly terrible*   *y* Cn: Heb *are exalted in*   *z* Cn: Heb *help*

89.19 Visions (like this one granted to Nathan, cf. 1 Chr 17.15) were often the means by which God made known His will to men, both in the Old and New Testaments (Num 12.6; Acts 16.9). These visions sometimes: (1) occurred at night (Gen 46.2; Dan 2.19); (2) occurred when the recipient was in a trance (Num 24.16; Acts 11.5); (3) were not fully understood by the recipient (Dan 7.15; Acts 10.17); (4) were claimed by false prophets (Jer 14.14; 23.16). Examples of those who experienced dreams include: (1) Abraham (Gen 15.1); (2) Moses (Ex 3.2, 3); (3) Samuel (1 Sam 3.2–15); (4) Paul (Acts 9.3, 6, 12; 16.9); (5) Peter (Acts 10.9–17); (6) John (Rev 1.12ff).

26 He shall cry to me, 'Thou art my Father,
   my God, and the Rock of my salvation.'
27 And I will make him the first-born,
   the highest of the kings of the earth.
28 My steadfast love I will keep for him for ever,
   and my covenant will stand firm for him.
29 I will establish his line for ever
   and his throne as the days of the heavens.
30 If his children forsake my law
   and do not walk according to my ordinances,
31 if they violate my statutes
   and do not keep my commandments,
32 then I will punish their transgression with the rod
   and their iniquity with scourges;
33 but I will not remove from him my steadfast love,
   or be false to my faithfulness.
34 I will not violate my covenant,
   or alter the word that went forth from my lips.
35 Once for all I have sworn by my holiness;
   I will not lie to David.
36 His line shall endure for ever,
   his throne as long as the sun before me.
37 Like the moon it shall be established for ever;
   it shall stand firm while the skies endure."[a]   *Selâh*

D. A plea for renewal of the covenant

1. *The punishment of the* LORD

38 But now thou hast cast off and rejected,
   thou art full of wrath against thy anointed.
39 Thou hast renounced the covenant with thy servant;
   thou hast defiled his crown in the dust.
40 Thou hast breached all his walls;
   thou hast laid his strongholds in ruins.
41 All that pass by despoil him;
   he has become the scorn of his neighbors.
42 Thou hast exalted the right hand of his foes;
   thou hast made all his enemies rejoice.
43 Yea, thou hast turned back the edge of his sword,
   and thou hast not made him stand in battle.
44 Thou hast removed the scepter from his hand,[b]
   and cast his throne to the ground.
45 Thou hast cut short the days of his youth;
   thou hast covered him with shame.   *Selâh*

2. *The prayer for renewal*

46 How long, O LORD? Wilt thou hide thyself for ever?
   How long will thy wrath burn like fire?
47 Remember, O Lord,[c] what the measure of life is,
   for what vanity thou hast created all the sons of men!
48 What man can live and never see death?
   Who can deliver his soul from the power of Shĕōl?   *Selâh*

---

a Cn: Heb *the witness in the skies is sure*
b Cn: Heb *removed his cleanness*   *c* Cn: Heb *I*

89.26
2 Sam 7.14;
22.47
89.27
Col 1.15;
Num 24.7;
Rev 1.5
89.28
Isa 55.3
89.29
Isa 9.7;
Jer 33.17;
Deut 11.21
89.30
2 Sam 7.14
89.32
2 Sam 7.14
89.33
2 Sam 7.15
89.34
Deut 7.9;
Num 23.19
89.35
Amos 4.2
89.36
Ps 72.5

89.38
1 Chr 28.9;
Deut 32.19
89.39
Lam 5.16
89.40
Ps 80.12;
Lam 2.2,5
89.41
Ps 44.13
89.42
Ps 13.2;
80.6
89.43
Ps 44.10
89.44
Ezek 28.7
89.45
Ps 102.23;
44.15

89.46
Ps 79.5
89.47
Job 7.7;
10.9; 14.1;
Ps 39.5
89.48
Ps 49.9;
Heb 11.5

49 Lord, where is thy steadfast love of old,
     which by thy faithfulness thou didst swear to David?
50 Remember, O Lord, how thy servant is scorned;
     how I bear in my bosom the insults^d of the peoples,
51 with which thy enemies taunt, O LORD,
     with which they mock the footsteps of thy anointed.

52 Blessed be the LORD for ever!
     Amen and Amen.

BOOK IV

A Prayer of Moses, the man of God.

I. God's eternity and man's transitoriness 90.1–17

A. Eternal God and transitory man

90 Lord, thou hast been our dwelling place^e
     in all generations.
2 Before the mountains were brought forth,
     or ever thou hadst formed the earth and the world,
     from everlasting to everlasting thou art God.

3 Thou turnest man back to the dust,
     and sayest, "Turn back, O children of men!"
4 For a thousand years in thy sight
     are but as yesterday when it is past,
     or as a watch in the night.

5 Thou dost sweep men away; they are like a dream,
     like grass which is renewed in the morning:
6 in the morning it flourishes and is renewed;
     in the evening it fades and withers.

7 For we are consumed by thy anger;
     by thy wrath we are overwhelmed.
8 Thou hast set our iniquities before thee,
     our secret sins in the light of thy countenance.

9 For all our days pass away under thy wrath,
     our years come to an end^f like a sigh.
10 The years of our life are threescore and ten,
     or even by reason of strength fourscore;
   yet their span^g is but toil and trouble;
     they are soon gone, and we fly away.

Reference column:
★89.49 / 2 Sam 7.15; Ps 54.5
89.50 / Ps 69.9,19
89.51 / Ps 74.10
89.52 / Ps 41.13
90.1 / Deut 33.27; Ezek 11.16
90.2 / Prov 8.25; Ps 102.25; 93.2
90.3 / Gen 3.19
90.4 / 2 Pet 3.8; Ps 39.5
90.5 / Job 27.20; Ps 73.20; 103.15; Isa 40.6
90.6 / Job 14.2; Ps 92.7
90.8 / Ps 50.21; Jer 16.17; Ps 19.12
90.9 / Ps 78.33
90.10 / Ecc 12.2–7

^d Cn: Heb all of many ^e Another reading is refuge
^f Syr: Heb we bring our years to an end ^g Cn Compare Gk Syr Jerome Tg: Heb pride

89.49 The word here translated *faithfulness* ('emunah) has to do with truth. God is a God of truth, that is, He keeps His own word and preserves the integrity of His own character. This is also said of Christ, who is the truth (Jn 14.6; 7.18). The Holy Spirit is correspondingly called the Spirit of truth (Jn 14.17). The word of God is itself called the truth (Jn 17.17). Believers are called upon to serve and worship God and walk according to truth (1 Sam 12.24; Josh 24.14; Jn 4.24). God's truth should be known, believed in, and obeyed from the heart (2 Tim 2.25; 1 Tim 4.3; 2 Thess 2.12, 13; Rom 2.8). Of particular significance is the injunction to handle aright the word of truth (2 Tim 2.15).

90.11
Ps 76.7
11 Who considers the power of thy anger,
   and thy wrath according to the fear of thee?

90.12
Ps 39.4
12 So teach us to number our days
   that we may get a heart of wisdom.

B. A prayer for God's favor

*90.13
Deut 32.26;
Ps 135.14
13 Return, O LORD! How long?
   Have pity on thy servants!

90.14
Ps 65.4;
85.6
14 Satisfy us in the morning with thy steadfast love,
   that we may rejoice and be glad all our days.
15 Make us glad as many days as thou hast afflicted us,
   and as many years as we have seen evil.

90.16
Hab 3.2;
1 Ki 8.11
16 Let thy work be manifest to thy servants,
   and thy glorious power to their children.

90.17
Ps 27.4;
Isa 26.12
17 Let the favor of the Lord our God be upon us,
   and establish thou the work of our hands upon us,
   yea, the work of our hands establish thou it.

I. The security of the godly 91.1–16

A. The promise of security

*91.1
Ps 27.5;
31.20; 17.8
91 He who dwells in the shelter of the Most High,
   who abides in the shadow of the Almighty,

91.2
Ps 142.5
2 will say to the LORD, "My refuge and my fortress;
   my God, in whom I trust."

91.3
Ps 124.7
3 For he will deliver you from the snare of the fowler
   and from the deadly pestilence;

91.4
Isa 51.16;
Ps 57.1;
40.11; 35.2
4 he will cover you with his pinions,
   and under his wings you will find refuge;
   his faithfulness is a shield and buckler.

91.5
Ps 23.4;
Sol 3.8;
Ps 64.4
5 You will not fear the terror of the night,
   nor the arrow that flies by day,

91.6
ver 10;
Job 5.22
6 nor the pestilence that stalks in darkness,
   nor the destruction that wastes at noonday.

7 A thousand may fall at your side,
   ten thousand at your right hand;
   but it will not come near you.

91.8
Ps 37.34;
Mal 1.5
8 You will only look with your eyes
   and see the recompense of the wicked.

B. The witness of the Psalmist

9 Because you have made the LORD your refuge,[h]
   the Most High your habitation,

91.10
Prov 12.21
10 no evil shall befall you,
   no scourge come near your tent.

91.11
Ps 34.7;
Mt 4.6;
Lk 4.10;
Heb 1.14
11 For he will give his angels charge of you
   to guard you in all your ways.

h Cn: Heb *Because thou*, LORD, *art my refuge; you have made*

12 On their hands they will bear you up,
    lest you dash your foot against a stone.
13 You will tread on the lion and the adder,
    the young lion and the serpent you will trample under foot.

91.13
Lk 10.19

C. The witness of the LORD

14 Because he cleaves to me in love, I will deliver him;
    I will protect him, because he knows my name.
15 When he calls to me, I will answer him;
    I will be with him in trouble,
    I will rescue him and honor him.
16 With long life I will satisfy him,
    and show him my salvation.

91.14
Ps 145.20;
59.1; 9.10
91.15
Ps 50.15;
1 Sam 2.30;
Jn 12.26
91.16
Ps 21.4;
50.23

A Psalm. A Song for the Sabbath.

I. Praise for the LORD'S goodness 92.1–15

A. The command to give thanks

92 It is good to give thanks to the LORD,
    to sing praises to thy name, O Most High;
2 to declare thy steadfast love in the morning,
    and thy faithfulness by night,
3 to the music of the lute and the harp,
    to the melody of the lyre.
4 For thou, O LORD, hast made me glad by thy work;
    at the works of thy hands I sing for joy.

92.1
Ps 147.1
92.2
Ps 89.1
92.3
1 Chr 23.5;
Ps 33.2

B. The end of the wicked

5 How great are thy works, O LORD!
    Thy thoughts are very deep!
6 The dull man cannot know,
    the stupid cannot understand this:
7 that, though the wicked sprout like grass
    and all evildoers flourish,
they are doomed to destruction for ever,
8   but thou, O LORD, art on high for ever.
9 For, lo, thy enemies, O LORD,
    for, lo, thy enemies shall perish;
    all evildoers shall be scattered.

92.5
Ps 40.5;
Isa 28.29;
Rom 11.33
92.6
Ps 73.22
92.7
Ps 90.5;
94.4;
37.38; 93.4
92.8
Ps 83.18
92.9
Ps 68.1;
89.10

10 But thou hast exalted my horn like that of the wild ox;
    thou hast poured over me[i] fresh oil.
11 My eyes have seen the downfall of my enemies,
    my ears have heard the doom of my evil assailants.

92.10
Ps 89.17;
23.5
92.11
Ps 54.7;
59.10

C. The end of the righteous

12 The righteous flourish like the palm tree,
    and grow like a cedar in Lebanon.

92.12
Ps 52.8;
Isa 65.22;
Hos 14.5,6;
Ps 104.16

i Syr: Heb uncertain

13 They are planted in the house of the LORD,
 they flourish in the courts of our God.
14 They still bring forth fruit in old age,
 they are ever full of sap and green,
15 to show that the LORD is upright;
 he is my rock, and there is no unrighteousness in him.

I. *The majesty of the* LORD *93.1–5*

93 The LORD reigns; he is robed in majesty;
 the LORD is robed, he is girded with strength.
Yea, the world is established; it shall never be moved;
2 thy throne is established from of old;
 thou art from everlasting.

3 The floods have lifted up, O LORD,
 the floods have lifted up their voice,
 the floods lift up their roaring.
4 Mightier than the thunders of many waters,
 mightier than the waves^j of the sea,
 the LORD on high is mighty!

5 Thy decrees are very sure;
 holiness befits thy house,
 O LORD, for evermore.

I. *An appeal to avenge 94.1–23*

A. *The cry for vengeance on the wicked*

94 O LORD, thou God of vengeance,
 thou God of vengeance, shine forth!
2 Rise up, O judge of the earth;
 render to the proud their deserts!
3 O LORD, how long shall the wicked,
 how long shall the wicked exult?

4 They pour out their arrogant words,
 they boast, all the evildoers.
5 They crush thy people, O LORD,
 and afflict thy heritage.
6 They slay the widow and the sojourner,
 and murder the fatherless;
7 and they say, "The LORD does not see;
 the God of Jacob does not perceive."

8 Understand, O dullest of the people!
 Fools, when will you be wise?
9 He who planted the ear, does he not hear?
 He who formed the eye, does he not see?
10 He who chastens the nations, does he not chastise?
 He who teaches men knowledge,
11 the LORD, knows the thoughts of man,
 that they are but a breath.

---

j Cn: Heb *mighty the waves*

Marginal references:

92.13 — Ps 80.15; 100.4
92.14 — Isa 37.31
92.15 — Ps 25.8; Deut 32.4; Rom 9.14
93.1 — Ps 96.10; 97.1; 99.1; 104.1; 65.6
93.2 — Ps 45.6; 90.2
93.3 — Ps 98.7,8
93.4 — Ps 65.7; 89.9
93.5 — Ps 19.7; 1 Cor 3.17
94.1 — Deut 32.35; Nah 1.2; Ps 50.2
94.2 — Ps 7.6; Gen 18.25; Ps 31.23
94.3 — Job 20.5
94.4 — Ps 31.18; 10.3
94.6 — Isa 10.2
94.7 — Ps 10.11
94.8 — Ps 92.6
94.9 — Ex 4.11; Prov 20.12
94.10 — Ps 44.2; Job 35.11; Isa 28.26
94.11 — 1 Cor 3.20

B. *The* LORD *will not forsake His people*

12 Blessed is the man whom thou dost chasten, O LORD,
    and whom thou dost teach out of thy law
13 to give him respite from days of trouble,
    until a pit is dug for the wicked.
14 For the LORD will not forsake his people;
    he will not abandon his heritage;
15 for justice will return to the righteous,
    and all the upright in heart will follow it.

C. *The Psalmist seeks the* LORD

16 Who rises up for me against the wicked?
    Who stands up for me against evildoers?
17 If the LORD had not been my help,
    my soul would soon have dwelt in the land of silence.
18 When I thought, "My foot slips,"
    thy steadfast love, O LORD, held me up.
19 When the cares of my heart are many,
    thy consolations cheer my soul.
20 Can wicked rulers be allied with thee,
    who frame mischief by statute?
21 They band together against the life of the righteous,
    and condemn the innocent to death.
22 But the LORD has become my stronghold,
    and my God the rock of my refuge.
23 He will bring back on them their iniquity
    and wipe them out for their wickedness;
    the LORD our God will wipe them out.

I. *A call to praise the* LORD *95.1–11*

A. *The praise to be sung*

95   O come, let us sing to the LORD;
    let us make a joyful noise to the rock of our salvation!
2 Let us come into his presence with thanksgiving;
    let us make a joyful noise to him with songs of praise!
3 For the LORD is a great God,
    and a great King above all gods.
4 In his hand are the depths of the earth;
    the heights of the mountains are his also.
5 The sea is his, for he made it;
    for his hands formed the dry land.

6 O come, let us worship and bow down,
    let us kneel before the LORD, our Maker!
7 For he is our God,
    and we are the people of his pasture,
    and the sheep of his hand.

B. *The warning to be followed*

O that today you would hearken to his voice!
8   Harden not your hearts, as at Mĕr′ĭbah,

Cross-references (margin):

94.12 Job 5.17; Heb 12.5
94.13 Ps 49.5; 9.15
94.14 1 Sam 12.22; Rom 11.1,2
94.16 Isa 28.21; Ps 59.2
94.17 Ps 124.1
94.18 Ps 38.16
94.19 Isa 66.13
94.20 Amos 6.3; Isa 10.1
94.21 Ps 56.6; Mt 27.1; Prov 17.15
94.22 Ps 59.9; 71.7
94.23 Ps 7.16
95.1 Ps 100.1; Deut 32.15; 2 Sam 22.47
95.2 Mic 6.6; Ps 100.4; 81.2
95.3 Ps 96.4; 97.9; 135.5
95.5 Gen 1.9,10
95.6 Ps 99.5,9; 2 Chr 6.13; Ps 100.3
95.7 Ps 79.13; 100.3; Heb 3.7–11
95.8 Ex 17.2,7; Deut 6.16

as on the day at Mässäh in the wilderness,

95.9
Ps 78.18;
1 Cor 10.9

9 when your fathers tested me,
   and put me to the proof, though they had seen my work.

95.10
Heb 3.10,17

10 For forty years I loathed that generation
    and said, "They are a people who err in heart,
    and they do not regard my ways."

95.11
Heb 4.3,5

11 Therefore I swore in my anger
    that they should not enter my rest.

I. A call to worship the LORD 96.1–13

A. The call to praise the LORD

96.1
1 Chr
16.23–33
96.2
Ps 71.15

96 O sing to the LORD a new song;
      sing to the LORD, all the earth!
2 Sing to the LORD, bless his name;
   tell of his salvation from day to day.

96.3
Ps 145.12

3 Declare his glory among the nations,
   his marvelous works among all the peoples!

96.4
Ps 145.3;
18.3; 95.3

4 For great is the LORD, and greatly to be praised;
   he is to be feared above all gods.

96.5
1 Chr
16.26;
Ps 115.15

5 For all the gods of the peoples are idols;
   but the LORD made the heavens.

96.6
Ps 104.1

6 Honor and majesty are before him;
   strength and beauty are in his sanctuary.

B. All the earth to praise the LORD

96.7
Ps 29.1,2

7 Ascribe to the LORD, O families of the peoples,
   ascribe to the LORD glory and strength!

96.8
Ps 79.9

8 Ascribe to the LORD the glory due his name;
   bring an offering, and come into his courts!

96.9
Ps 29.2

9 Worship the LORD in holy array;
   tremble before him, all the earth!

C. The LORD the righteous judge

96.10
Ps 93.1;
67.4

10 Say among the nations, "The LORD reigns!
    Yea, the world is established, it shall never be moved;
    he will judge the peoples with equity."

96.11
Ps 97.1;
98.7

11 Let the heavens be glad, and let the earth rejoice;
    let the sea roar, and all that fills it;
12 let the field exult, and everything in it!
    Then shall all the trees of the wood sing for joy

96.13
Ps 67.4;
Rev 19.11

13 before the LORD, for he comes,
    for he comes to judge the earth.
    He will judge the world with righteousness,
    and the peoples with his truth.

I. The power and dominion of the LORD 97.1–12

A. The reign of the LORD

97.1
96.10,11

97 The LORD reigns; let the earth rejoice;
      let the many coastlands be glad!

2 Clouds and thick darkness are round about him;
   righteousness and justice are the foundation of his throne.
3 Fire goes before him,
   and burns up his adversaries round about.
4 His lightnings lighten the world;
   the earth sees and trembles.
5 The mountains melt like wax before the LORD,
   before the Lord of all the earth.

B. *The exaltation of the* LORD

6 The heavens proclaim his righteousness;
   and all the peoples behold his glory.
7 All worshipers of images are put to shame,
   who make their boast in worthless idols;
   all gods bow down before him.
8 Zion hears and is glad,
   and the daughters of Judah rejoice,
   because of thy judgments, O God.
9 For thou, O LORD, art most high over all the earth;
   thou art exalted far above all gods.

C. *The deliverance of the righteous by the* LORD

10 The LORD loves those who hate evil;[k]
   he preserves the lives of his saints;
   he delivers them from the hand of the wicked.
11 Light dawns[l] for the righteous,
   and joy for the upright in heart.
12 Rejoice in the LORD, O you righteous,
   and give thanks to his holy name!

A Psalm.

I. *A call to praise the righteous* LORD 98.1-9

A. *The song of salvation*

98 O sing to the LORD a new song,
   for he has done marvelous things!
His right hand and his holy arm
   have gotten him victory.
2 The LORD has made known his victory,
   he has revealed his vindication in the sight of the nations.
3 He has remembered his steadfast love and faithfulness
   to the house of Israel.
All the ends of the earth have seen
   the victory of our God.

B. *The summons of men to praise*

4 Make a joyful noise to the LORD, all the earth;
   break forth into joyous song and sing praises!

---

k Cn: Heb *You who love the* LORD *hate evil*   *l* Gk Syr Jerome: Heb *is sown*

Marginal references:

97.2 — 1 Ki 8.12; Ps 18.11; 89.14
97.3 — Ps 18.8; Dan 7.10; Hab 3.5; Heb 12.29
97.4 — Ps 77.18
97.5 — Mic 1.4; Josh 3.11
97.6 — Ps 50.6
97.7 — Ex 20.4; Lev 26.1; Heb 1.6
97.8 — Ps 48.11
97.9 — Ps 83.18; Ex 18.11; Ps 95.3
97.10 — Ps 34.14; Amos 5.15; Prov 2.8; Ps 37.39; Dan 3.28
97.11 — Job 22.28; Ps 112.4
97.12 — Ps 32.11; 30.4
98.1 — Ps 33.3; 40.5; Ex 15.6; Isa 52.10
98.2 — Rom 3.25
98.3 — Lk 1.54; Isa 49.6
98.4 — Ps 100.1

5 Sing praises to the LORD with the lyre,
  with the lyre and the sound of melody!
6 With trumpets and the sound of the horn
  make a joyful noise before the King, the LORD!

C. *The summons of nature to praise*

7 Let the sea roar, and all that fills it;
  the world and those who dwell in it!
8 Let the floods clap their hands;
  let the hills sing for joy together
9 before the LORD, for he comes
  to judge the earth.
He will judge the world with righteousness,
  and the peoples with equity.

I. *Praise to a holy God 99.1–9*

A. *The summons to praise*

99 The LORD reigns; let the peoples tremble!
   He sits enthroned upon the cherubim; let the earth quake!
2 The LORD is great in Zion;
  he is exalted over all the peoples.
3 Let them praise thy great and terrible name!
  Holy is he!
4 Mighty King,[m] lover of justice,
  thou hast established equity;
thou hast executed justice
  and righteousness in Jacob.
5 Extol the LORD our God;
  worship at his footstool!
  Holy is he!

B. *Reasons for praise*

6 Moses and Aaron were among his priests,
  Samuel also was among those who called on his name.
  They cried to the LORD, and he answered them.
7 He spoke to them in the pillar of cloud;
  they kept his testimonies,
  and the statutes that he gave them.

8 O LORD our God, thou didst answer them;
  thou wast a forgiving God to them,
  but an avenger of their wrongdoings.
9 Extol the LORD our God,
  and worship at his holy mountain;
  for the LORD our God is holy!

m Cn: Heb *and the king's strength*

Side references

98.6 Num 10.10
★98.7 Ps 96.11; 24.1
98.8 Ps 93.3; 65.12
98.9 Ps 96.10,13
99.1 Ex 25.22
99.2 Ps 97.9
99.4 Ps 11.7; 17.2;103.6
★99.5 Ps 132.7; Lev 19.2
★99.6 Jer 15.1; Ex 14.15; 1 Sam 7.9
99.7 Ex 33.9
99.8 Ps 106.44; Num 14.20; Deut 9.20
99.9 Ps 34.3

98.7 As the whole creation has groaned under sin, so shall it exult when it is delivered.
99.5 *Holy is he!* Holiness sums up all of ~d's moral perfections. Therefore we should all worship Him.
99.6 These great saints worshiped the LORD God in: (1) their earnest prayers (ver 6); (2) their holy lives (ver 7).

A Psalm for the thank offering.

I. *All men exhorted to praise God 100.1–5*

100 Make a joyful noise to the LORD, all the lands![n]
2 Serve the LORD with gladness!
Come into his presence with singing!

3 Know that the LORD is God!
It is he that made us, and we are his;[o]
we are his people, and the sheep of his pasture.

4 Enter his gates with thanksgiving,
and his courts with praise!
Give thanks to him, bless his name!

5 For the LORD is good;
his steadfast love endures for ever,
and his faithfulness to all generations.

100.1
Ps 98.4

100.3
Ps 46.10;
95.6,7

100.4
Ps 95.2;
96.2

100.5
Ps 25.8;
119.90

A Psalm of David.

I. *A profession of integrity 101.1–8*

A. *David's desire for personal integrity*

101 I will sing of loyalty and of justice;
to thee, O LORD, I will sing.
2 I will give heed to the way that is blameless.
Oh when wilt thou come to me?

I will walk with integrity of heart
within my house;
3 I will not set before my eyes
anything that is base.

I hate the work of those who fall away;
it shall not cleave to me.
4 Perverseness of heart shall be far from me;
I will know nothing of evil.

101.1
Ps 89.1

101.2
1 Sam
18.14;
1 Ki 9.4

101.3
Deut 15.9;
Ps 40.4

101.4
Prov 11.20

B. *David's desire for integrity in others*

5 Him who slanders his neighbor secretly
I will destroy.
The man of haughty looks and arrogant heart
I will not endure.

6 I will look with favor on the faithful in the land,
that they may dwell with me;
he who walks in the way that is blameless
shall minister to me.

101.5
Ps 50.20;
Prov 6.17

101.6
Ps 119.1

[n] Heb *land* or *earth*   [o] Another reading is *and not we ourselves*

7 No man who practices deceit
   shall dwell in my house;
no man who utters lies
   shall continue in my presence.

101.8
Ps 75.10;
118.10-12

8 Morning by morning I will destroy
   all the wicked in the land,
cutting off all the evildoers
   from the city of the LORD.

A prayer of one afflicted, when he is faint and pours out
his complaint before the LORD.

I. *Appeal for mercy and for Zion 102.1–28*

A. *The sufferings of the Psalmist*

102.1
Ex 2.23;
1 Sam 9.16
102.2
Ps 69.17;
71.2

102   Hear my prayer, O LORD;
      let my cry come to thee!
2 Do not hide thy face from me
   in the day of my distress!
Incline thy ear to me;
   answer me speedily in the day when I call!

102.3
Jas 4.14;
Job 30.30;
Ps 31.10
102.4
Ps 37.2
102.5
Lam 4.8

3 For my days pass away like smoke,
   and my bones burn like a furnace.
4 My heart is smitten like grass, and withered;
   I forget to eat my bread.
5 Because of my loud groaning
   my bones cleave to my flesh.

102.6
Isa 34.11
102.7
Ps 77.4;
38.11
102.8
Acts 26.11;
23.12
102.9
Ps 42.3
102.10
Ps 38.3;
Job 30.22
102.11
Job 14.2;
ver 4

6 I am like a vulture*p* of the wilderness,
   like an owl of the waste places;
7 I lie awake,
   I am like a lonely bird on the housetop.
8 All the day my enemies taunt me,
   those who deride me use my name for a curse.
9 For I eat ashes like bread,
   and mingle tears with my drink,
10 because of thy indignation and anger;
   for thou hast taken me up and thrown me away.
11 My days are like an evening shadow;
   I wither away like grass.

B. *The eternal God the refuge of Zion*

102.12
Ps 9.7;
Lam 5.19;
Ps 135.13
102.13
Isa 60.10;
Zech 1.12;
Ps 75.2

12 But thou, O LORD, art enthroned for ever;
   thy name endures to all generations.
13 Thou wilt arise and have pity on Zion;
   it is the time to favor her;
   the appointed time has come.
14 For thy servants hold her stones dear,
   and have pity on her dust.

p The meaning of the Hebrew word is uncertain

15 The nations will fear the name of the LORD,
and all the kings of the earth thy glory.
16 For the LORD will build up Zion,
he will appear in his glory;
17 he will regard the prayer of the destitute,
and will not despise their supplication.

18 Let this be recorded for a generation to come,
so that a people yet unborn may praise the LORD:
19 that he looked down from his holy height,
from heaven the LORD looked at the earth,
20 to hear the groans of the prisoners,
to set free those who were doomed to die;
21 that men may declare in Zion the name of the LORD,
and in Jerusalem his praise,
22 when peoples gather together,
and kingdoms, to worship the LORD.

C. The assurance of deliverance

23 He has broken my strength in midcourse;
he has shortened my days.
24 "O my God," I say, "take me not hence
in the midst of my days,
thou whose years endure
throughout all generations!"

25 Of old thou didst lay the foundation of the earth,
and the heavens are the work of thy hands.
26 They will perish, but thou dost endure;
they will all wear out like a garment.
Thou changest them like raiment, and they pass away;
27 but thou art the same, and thy years have no end.
28 The children of thy servants shall dwell secure;
their posterity shall be established before thee.

A Psalm of David.

I. An exhortation to bless the LORD 103.1–22

A. The exhortation to self

103 Bless the LORD, O my soul;
and all that is within me, bless his holy name!
2 Bless the LORD, O my soul,
and forget not all his benefits,
3 who forgives all your iniquity,
who heals all your diseases,
4 who redeems your life from the Pit,
who crowns you with steadfast love and mercy,
5 who satisfies you with good as long as you live*a*
so that your youth is renewed like the eagle's.

a Heb uncertain

Reference column: 102.15 1 Ki 8.43; Ps 138.4 | 102.16 Isa 60.1,2 | 102.17 Neh 1.6 | 102.18 Rom 15.4; Ps 22.31 | 102.19 Deut 26.15; Ps 33.13 | 102.20 Ps 79.11 | 102.21 Ps 22.22 | 102.22 Ps 86.9 | 102.23 Job 21.21 | 102.24 Isa 38.10; Ps 90.2; Hab 1.12 | 102.25 Gen 1.1; Heb 1.10; Ps 96.5 | 102.26 Isa 34.4; Mt 24.35; 2 Pet 3.7,10; Rev 20.11 | 102.27 Mal 3.6; Heb 13.8; Jas 1.17 | 102.28 Ps 69.36; 89.4 | 103.1 Ps 104.1; 33.21 | 103.3 Ps 130.8; Isa 43.25; Ex 15.26 | 103.4 Ps 49.15; 5.12 | 103.5 Isa 40.31

B. *God's mercies a reason to bless Him*

6 The LORD works vindication
  and justice for all who are oppressed.
7 He made known his ways to Moses,
  his acts to the people of Israel.
8 The LORD is merciful and gracious,
  slow to anger and abounding in steadfast love.
9 He will not always chide,
  nor will he keep his anger for ever.
10 He does not deal with us according to our sins,
  nor requite us according to our iniquities.
11 For as the heavens are high above the earth,
  so great is his steadfast love toward those who fear him;
12 as far as the east is from the west,
  so far does he remove our transgressions from us.
13 As a father pities his children,
  so the LORD pities those who fear him.

C. *God's everlasting love*

14 For he knows our frame;
  he remembers that we are dust.

15 As for man, his days are like grass;
  he flourishes like a flower of the field;
16 for the wind passes over it, and it is gone,
  and its place knows it no more.
17 But the steadfast love of the LORD is from everlasting to everlasting
  upon those who fear him,
  and his righteousness to children's children,
18 to those who keep his covenant
  and remember to do his commandments.

D. *The universal call to bless God's name*

19 The LORD has established his throne in the heavens,
  and his kingdom rules over all.
20 Bless the LORD, O you his angels,
  you mighty ones who do his word,
  hearkening to the voice of his word!
21 Bless the LORD, all his hosts,
  his ministers that do his will!
22 Bless the LORD, all his works,
  in all places of his dominion.
  Bless the LORD, O my soul!

I. *Praise to God the creator and sustainer 104.1–35*

A. *The beginning of creation*

104 Bless the LORD, O my soul!
  O LORD my God, thou art very great!
  Thou art clothed with honor and majesty,

Marginal references (left column):

103.8
Ex 34.6;
Neh 9.17;
Ps 145.8

103.9
Ps 30.5;
Isa 57.16;
Jer 3.5

103.10
Ezra 9.13

103.11
Ps 36.5

103.12
2 Sam
12.13;
Isa 38.17;
Heb 9.26

103.13
Mal 3.17

103.14
Isa 29.16;
Gen 3.19

103.15
1 Pet 1.24;
Job 14.1,2

103.16
Job 7.10

103.18
Deut 7.9

103.19
Ps 11.4;
47.2

103.20
Ps 148.2;
Mt 6.10;
Heb 1.14

103.21
Ps 148.2

104.1
Ps 103.1

2 who coverest thyself with light as with a garment,
  who hast stretched out the heavens like a tent,
3   who hast laid the beams of thy chambers on the waters,
  who makest the clouds thy chariot,
    who ridest on the wings of the wind,
4 who makest the winds thy messengers,
    fire and flame thy ministers.

	104.2 Dan 7.9; Isa 40.22
	104.3 Amos 9.6; Isa 19.1; Ps 18.10
	104.4 Heb 1.7

B. *The foundations of the earth*

5 Thou didst set the earth on its foundations,
  so that it should never be shaken.
6 Thou didst cover it with the deep as with a garment;
  the waters stood above the mountains.
7 At thy rebuke they fled;
  at the sound of thy thunder they took to flight.
8 The mountains rose, the valleys sank down
  to the place which thou didst appoint for them.
9 Thou didst set a bound which they should not pass,
  so that they might not again cover the earth.

	104.5 Job 26.7; Ps 24.2
	104.6 Gen 7.19
	104.8 Ps 33.7
	104.9 Job 38.10, 11; Jer 5.22

C. *The springs in the valleys*

10 Thou makest springs gush forth in the valleys;
  they flow between the hills,
11 they give drink to every beast of the field;
  the wild asses quench their thirst.
12 By them the birds of the air have their habitation;
  they sing among the branches.
13 From thy lofty abode thou waterest the mountains;
  the earth is satisfied with the fruit of thy work.

	104.10 Ps 107.35
	104.11 Job 39.5
	104.12 Mt 8.20
	104.13 Ps 65.9; 147.8

D. *The fruitfulness of the earth*

14 Thou dost cause the grass to grow for the cattle,
  and plants for man to cultivate,ʳ
  that he may bring forth food from the earth,
15   and wine to gladden the heart of man,
  oil to make his face shine,
  and bread to strengthen man's heart.
16 The trees of the LORD are watered abundantly,
  the cedars of Lebanon which he planted.
17 In them the birds build their nests;
  the stork has her home in the fir trees.
18 The high mountains are for the wild goats;
  the rocks are a refuge for the badgers.

	104.14 Ps 147.8; Job 38.27; Gen 1.29; Job 28.5
	104.15 Judg 9.13; Ps 23.5
	104.18 Prov 30.26

E. *The moon and the sun*

19 Thou hast made the moon to mark the seasons;
  the sun knows its time for setting.
20 Thou makest darkness, and it is night,
  when all the beasts of the forest creep forth.
21 The young lions roar for their prey,

	104.19 Gen 1.14
	104.20 Isa 45.7
	104.21 Job 38.39

ʳ Or *fodder for the animals that serve man*

seeking their food from God.
22 When the sun rises, they get them away
and lie down in their dens.

104.23
Gen 3.19

23 Man goes forth to his work
and to his labor until the evening.

F. The creatures of the sea

104.24
Ps 40.5;
Prov 3.19;
Ps 65.9

24 O LORD, how manifold are thy works!
In wisdom hast thou made them all;
the earth is full of thy creatures.
25 Yonder is the sea, great and wide,
which teems with things innumerable,
living things both small and great.

104.26
Ps 107.23;
Job 41.1

26 There go the ships,
and Lēvī'áthán which thou didst form to sport in it.

G. God the sustainer of life

104.27
Ps 136.25;
145.15

27 These all look to thee,
to give them their food in due season.
28 When thou givest to them, they gather it up;
when thou openest thy hand, they are filled with good things.

104.29
Job 34.14;
Ps 146.4;
Ecc 12.7

29 When thou hidest thy face, they are dismayed;
when thou takest away their breath, they die
and return to their dust.

104.30
Isa 32.15;
Ezek 37.9

30 When thou sendest forth thy Spirit,^{s} they are created;
and thou renewest the face of the ground.

H. Concluding praise to a mighty God

104.31
Gen 1.31

31 May the glory of the LORD endure for ever,
may the LORD rejoice in his works,

104.32
Ps 97.4,5;
144.5

32 who looks on the earth and it trembles,
who touches the mountains and they smoke!

104.33
Ps 63.4;
146.2

33 I will sing to the LORD as long as I live;
I will sing praise to my God while I have being.
34 May my meditation be pleasing to him,
for I rejoice in the LORD.

104.35
Ps 59.13;
37.10;
ver 1

35 Let sinners be consumed from the earth,
and let the wicked be no more!
Bless the LORD, O my soul!
Praise the LORD!

I. Praise to a covenant-keeping God 105.1—45

A. The call to thanksgiving

105.1
1 Chr 16.8;
Ps 145.12

105 O give thanks to the LORD, call on his name,
make known his deeds among the peoples!

105.2
Ps 77.12

2 Sing to him, sing praises to him,
tell of all his wonderful works!

105.3
Ps 33.21

3 Glory in his holy name;
let the hearts of those who seek the LORD rejoice!

^{s} Or breath

4 Seek the LORD and his strength,
    seek his presence continually!

5 Remember the wonderful works that he has done,
    his miracles, and the judgments he uttered,

6 O offspring of Abraham his servant,
    sons of Jacob, his chosen ones!

B. *The Abrahamic covenant*

7 He is the LORD our God;
    his judgments are in all the earth.

8 He is mindful of his covenant for ever,
    of the word that he commanded, for a thousand generations,

9 the covenant which he made with Abraham,
    his sworn promise to Isaac,

10 which he confirmed to Jacob as a statute,
    to Israel as an everlasting covenant,

11 saying, "To you I will give the land of Cānaán
    as your portion for an inheritance."

12 When they were few in number,
    of little account, and sojourners in it,

13 wandering from nation to nation,
    from one kingdom to another people,

14 he allowed no one to oppress them;
    he rebuked kings on their account,

15 saying, "Touch not my anointed ones,
    do my prophets no harm!"

C. *God sends Joseph to Egypt*

16 When he summoned a famine on the land,
    and broke every staff of bread,

17 he had sent a man ahead of them,
    Joseph, who was sold as a slave.

18 His feet were hurt with fetters,
    his neck was put in a collar of iron;

19 until what he had said came to pass
    the word of the LORD tested him.

20 The king sent and released him,
    the ruler of the peoples set him free;

21 he made him lord of his house,
    and ruler of all his possessions,

22 to instruct*t* his princes at his pleasure,
    and to teach his elders wisdom.

D. *Israel in Egypt*

23 Then Israel came to Egypt;
    Jacob sojourned in the land of Ham.

24 And the LORD made his people very fruitful,
    and made them stronger than their foes.

25 He turned their hearts to hate his people,
    to deal craftily with his servants.

t Gk Syr Jerome: Heb *to bind*

Marginal references:

105.4 Ps 27.8
105.5 Ps 77.11
105.7 Isa 26.9
105.8 Lk 1.72
105.9 Gen 17.2; 22.16; 26.3
105.10 Gen 28.13–15
105.11 Gen 13.15; 15.18
105.12 Gen 34.30; Deut 7.7; Heb 11.9
105.14 Gen 35.5; 12.17
105.16 Gen 41.54; Lev 26.26; Isa 3.1; Ezek 4.16
105.17 Gen 45.5; 37.28,36
105.18 Gen 39.20
105.19 Gen 40.20, 21; Ps 66.10
105.20 Gen 41.14
105.21 Gen 41.40
105.23 Gen 46.6; Acts 13.17
105.24 Ex 1.7
105.25 Ex 1.8,10

E. Moses and the plagues

*105.26
Ex 3.10;
Num 16.5

26 He sent Moses his servant,
  and Aaron whom he had chosen.

105.27
Ex 7–12;
Ps 78.43

27 They wrought his signs among them,
  and miracles in the land of Ham.

105.28
Ex 10.22;
Ps 99.7

28 He sent darkness, and made the land dark;
  they rebelled[u] against his words.

105.29
Ex 7.20

29 He turned their waters into blood,
  and caused their fish to die.

105.30
Ex 8.6

30 Their land swarmed with frogs,
  even in the chambers of their kings.

105.31
Ex 8.16,21

31 He spoke, and there came swarms of flies,
  and gnats throughout their country.

105.32
Ex 9.23

32 He gave them hail for rain,
  and lightning that flashed through their land.

33 He smote their vines and fig trees,
  and shattered the trees of their country.

105.34
Ex 10.4;
Ps 78.46

34 He spoke, and the locusts came,
  and young locusts without number;

35 which devoured all the vegetation in their land,
  and ate up the fruit of their ground.

105.36
Ex 12.29;
Ps 78.51

36 He smote all the first-born in their land,
  the first issue of all their strength.

F. The exodus and the wanderings

*105.37
Ex 12.35

37 Then he led forth Israel with silver and gold,
  and there was none among his tribes who stumbled.

105.38
Ex 12.33

38 Egypt was glad when they departed,
  for dread of them had fallen upon it.

105.39
Ex 13.21;
Neh 9.12

39 He spread a cloud for a covering,
  and fire to give light by night.

105.40
Ex 16.12ff;
Ps 78.24ff

40 They asked, and he brought quails,
  and gave them bread from heaven in abundance.

105.41
Ex 17.6;
Ps 78.15,16;
1 Cor 10.4

41 He opened the rock, and water gushed forth;
  it flowed through the desert like a river.

105.42
ver 8

42 For he remembered his holy promise,
  and Abraham his servant.

G. The settlement of Canaan

43 So he led forth his people with joy,
  his chosen ones with singing.

105.44
Deut 6–10;
Josh 13.7

44 And he gave them the lands of the nations;
  and they took possession of the fruit of the peoples' toil,

105.45
Deut 6.21–
25

45 to the end that they should keep his statutes,
  and observe his laws.
  Praise the LORD!

u Cn Compare Gk Syr: Heb *they did not rebel*

105.26 God delivered Israel from Egypt: (1) by human instrumentalities (Moses and Aaron); (2) by overcoming Pharaoh's resistance; (3) by circumstances which gave Israel wealth, health, respect, and joy.

105.37 *. . . he led forth Israel.* God's guidance was provided: (1) by His Holy Word; (2) by His Spirit; (3) by circumstances.

I. Praise to God who has mercy on a sinful people
106.1–48

A. The prayer for mercy

106 Praise the LORD!
O give thanks to the LORD, for he is good;
for his steadfast love endures for ever!

2 Who can utter the mighty doings of the LORD,
or show forth all his praise?

3 Blessed are they who observe justice,
who do righteousness at all times!

4 Remember me, O LORD, when thou showest favor to thy people;
help me when thou deliverest them;

5 that I may see the prosperity of thy chosen ones,
that I may rejoice in the gladness of thy nation,
that I may glory with thy heritage.

B. Israel's sin at the Red Sea (cf. Ex 14.10–12)

6 Both we and our fathers have sinned;
we have committed iniquity, we have done wickedly.

7 Our fathers, when they were in Egypt,
did not consider thy wonderful works;
they did not remember the abundance of thy steadfast love,
but rebelled against the Most High[v] at the Red Sea.

8 Yet he saved them for his name's sake,
that he might make known his mighty power.

9 He rebuked the Red Sea, and it became dry;
and he led them through the deep as through a desert.

10 So he saved them from the hand of the foe,
and delivered them from the power of the enemy.

11 And the waters covered their adversaries;
not one of them was left.

12 Then they believed his words;
they sang his praise.

C. Israel's sins in the wilderness (cf. Num 11)

13 But they soon forgot his works;
they did not wait for his counsel.

14 But they had a wanton craving in the wilderness,
and put God to the test in the desert;

15 he gave them what they asked,
but sent a wasting disease among them.

[v] Cn Compare 78.17, 56: Heb *at the sea*

	*106.1 Ps 105.1; 100.5; 1 Chr 16.34
	106.2 Ps 145.4,12
	106.3 Ps 15.2
	106.4 Ps 119.132
	106.5 Ps 1.3; 118.15; 105.3
	106.6 Dan 9.5
	106.7 Ps 78.11,42; Ex 14.11
	106.8 Ex 9.16
	106.9 Ex 14.21; Ps 18.15; 78.11,42; Isa 63.11–14
	106.10 Ex 14.30; Ps 107.2
	106.11 Ex 14.28; 15.5
	106.12 Ex 14.31; 15.1–21
	106.13 Ex 15.24
	106.14 1 Cor 10.6,9
	*106.15 Num 11.31; Isa 10.16

106.1 This is the first of what has been called the "Hallelujah Psalms," for the word "Hallelujah" is, as it were, the inscription. The others are Ps 106, 111–113, 117, 135, 146–50.
106.15 Here a spiritual principle is laid down which has value for all ages. In the instance cited, the children of Israel insisted upon having meat when God provided manna. It was not His will for them to have meat, but since they insisted on obtaining what they wanted, God gave it to them. In return for meat they received spiritual poverty. Insistence on having our own preference (rather than God's) can lead only to unfortunate consequences at a cost higher than the anticipated benefits.

D. The sin of Dathan and Abiram (cf. Num 16; Deut 11.6)

106.16
Num 16.1–3

16 When men in the camp were jealous of Moses
  and Aaron, the holy one of the LORD,

106.17
Deut 11.6

17 the earth opened and swallowed up Dāthăn,
  and covered the company of Àbī'răm.

106.18
Num 16.35

18 Fire also broke out in their company;
  the flame burned up the wicked.

E. The golden calf at Horeb (cf. Ex 32; Deut 9.8–21)

106.19
Ex 32.14

19 They made a calf in Horĕb
  and worshiped a molten image.

106.20
Jer 2.11;
Rom 1.23

20 They exchanged the glory of God
  for the image of an ox that eats grass.

106.21
Ps 78.11;
Deut 10.21

21 They forgot God, their Savior,
  who had done great things in Egypt,

106.22
Ps 105.27

22 wondrous works in the land of Ham,
  and terrible things by the Red Sea.

106.23
Ex 32.10;
32.11–14

23 Therefore he said he would destroy them—
  had not Moses, his chosen one,
stood in the breach before him,
  to turn away his wrath from destroying them.

F. The refusal to enter Canaan (cf. Num 13–14)

106.24
Deut 8.7;
Heb 3.18,19

24 Then they despised the pleasant land,
  having no faith in his promise.

106.25
Num 14.2

25 They murmured in their tents,
  and did not obey the voice of the LORD.

106.26
Num 14.28–
35;
Heb 11.3

26 Therefore he raised his hand and swore to them
  that he would make them fall in the wilderness,
27 and would disperse[w] their descendants among the nations,

106.27
Ps 44.11

  scattering them over the lands.

G. Baal of Peor (cf. Num 25)

★106.28
Num 25.2,3

28 Then they attached themselves to the Bāăl of Pē'or,
  and ate sacrifices offered to the dead;
29 they provoked the LORD to anger with their doings,
  and a plague broke out among them.

106.30
Num 25.7

30 Then Phĭn'ĕhăs stood up and interposed,
  and the plague was stayed.

106.31
Num 25.11–
13

31 And that has been reckoned to him as righteousness
  from generation to generation for ever.

H. Israel's sin at Meribah (cf. Num 20.2–13)

106.32
Num 20.3,
13;
Ps 81.7

32 They angered him at the waters of Mĕr'ĭbah,
  and it went ill with Moses on their account;

106.33
Num 20.10

33 for they made his spirit bitter,
  and he spoke words that were rash.

w Syr Compare Ezek 20.23: Heb *cause to fall*

106.28 *sacrifices offered to the dead.* Heathen sacrifices are offered to dead gods in contrast to the living God of Israel. This was one of Israel's recurring sins.

I. *Israel's idolatry in Canaan*

³⁴ They did not destroy the peoples,
  as the LORD commanded them,
³⁵ but they mingled with the nations
  and learned to do as they did.
³⁶ They served their idols,
  which became a snare to them.
³⁷ They sacrificed their sons
  and their daughters to the demons;
³⁸ they poured out innocent blood,
  the blood of their sons and daughters,
whom they sacrificed to the idols of Cānaàn;
  and the land was polluted with blood.
³⁹ Thus they became unclean by their acts,
  and played the harlot in their doings.

J. *Israel's punishment*

⁴⁰ Then the anger of the LORD was kindled against his people,
  and he abhorred his heritage;
⁴¹ he gave them into the hand of the nations,
  so that those who hated them ruled over them.
⁴² Their enemies oppressed them,
  and they were brought into subjection under their power.
⁴³ Many times he delivered them,
  but they were rebellious in their purposes,
  and were brought low through their iniquity.

K. *God's mercy*

⁴⁴ Nevertheless he regarded their distress,
  when he heard their cry.
⁴⁵ He remembered for their sake his covenant,
  and relented according to the abundance of his steadfast love.
⁴⁶ He caused them to be pitied
  by all those who held them captive.

L. *Final appeal and doxology*

⁴⁷ Save us, O LORD our God,
  and gather us from among the nations,
that we may give thanks to thy holy name
  and glory in thy praise.

⁴⁸ Blessed be the LORD, the God of Israel,
  from everlasting to everlasting!
And let all the people say, "Amen!"
  Praise the LORD!

Cross-references: *106.34 Judg 1.21; Deut 7.2,16; 106.35 Judg 3.5,6; 106.36 Judg 2.12; 106.37 2 Ki 17.7; 106.38 Ps 94.21; Num 35.33; 106.39 Ezek 20.18; Lev 17.7; Num 15.39; 106.40 Ps 78.59; 106.41 Judg 2.14; Neh 9.27; 106.43 Judg 2.16–18; *106.44 Judg 3.9; 10.10; 106.45 Ps 105.8; Judg 2.18; 106.46 Ezra 9.9; Jer 42.12; 106.47 1 Chr 16.35,36; Ps 147.2; 106.48 Ps 41.13

106.34 Israel sinned against God in that: (1) they disobeyed and did not destroy the nations as God commanded them; (2) they intermarried with the heathen and took over their evil practices; (3) they served their idols which became a snare to them; (4) they even went so far as to offer human sacrifices, which were explicitly forbidden.

106.44 God visited them with His anger, but He did not forget them. This grace is ever displayed toward those whom God has redeemed, however far they stray from the fold.

BOOK V

I. Thanksgiving to a delivering God 107.1–43

A. The call to praise

107 O give thanks to the LORD, for he is good;
for his steadfast love endures for ever!

2 Let the redeemed of the LORD say so,
whom he has redeemed from trouble

3 and gathered in from the lands,
from the east and from the west,
from the north and from the south.

B. Deliverance from the desert

4 Some wandered in desert wastes,
finding no way to a city to dwell in;

5 hungry and thirsty,
their soul fainted within them.

6 Then they cried to the LORD in their trouble,
and he delivered them from their distress;

7 he led them by a straight way,
till they reached a city to dwell in.

8 Let them thank the LORD for his steadfast love,
for his wonderful works to the sons of men!

9 For he satisfies him who is thirsty,
and the hungry he fills with good things.

C. Deliverance from the prison

10 Some sat in darkness and in gloom,
prisoners in affliction and in irons,

11 for they had rebelled against the words of God,
and spurned the counsel of the Most High.

12 Their hearts were bowed down with hard labor;
they fell down, with none to help.

13 Then they cried to the LORD in their trouble,
and he delivered them from their distress;

14 he brought them out of darkness and gloom,
and broke their bonds asunder.

15 Let them thank the LORD for his steadfast love,
for his wonderful works to the sons of men!

16 For he shatters the doors of bronze,
and cuts in two the bars of iron.

D. Deliverance of the sick

17 Some were sick[x] through their sinful ways,

x Cn: Heb *fools*

107.1 The recurring sequence expressed in this Psalm is as follows: (1) men ought to praise the Lord for His goodness and His delivering mercies; (2) men soon forget what they ought to remember; (3) men turn from God to sin; (4) God uses judgment to bring them to repentance; (5) men sense their need for deliverance and call upon God; (6) God delivers them; (7) they then praise God for His deliverance.

Margin references:

*107.1 Ps 106.1
107.2 Ps 106.10
107.3 Ps 106.47; Isa 43.5,6
107.4 Num 14.33; 32.13
107.6 Ps 50.15
107.7 Ezra 8.21
107.8 ver 15,21,31
107.9 Ps 22.26; Lk 1.53
107.10 Lk 1.79; Job 36.8
107.11 Ps 106.7; 2 Chr 36.16
107.12 Ps 22.11
107.13 ver 6
107.14 Ps 116.16; Lk 13.16; Acts 12.7
107.15 ver 8,21,31
107.16 Isa 45.2
107.17 Isa 65.6,7*

and because of their iniquities suffered affliction;
18 they loathed any kind of food,
     and they drew near to the gates of death.
19 Then they cried to the LORD in their trouble,
     and he delivered them from their distress;
20 he sent forth his word, and healed them,
     and delivered them from destruction.
21 Let them thank the LORD for his steadfast love,
     for his wonderful works to the sons of men!
22 And let them offer sacrifices of thanksgiving,
     and tell of his deeds in songs of joy!

E. *Deliverance from the sea*

23 Some went down to the sea in ships,
     doing business on the great waters;
24 they saw the deeds of the LORD,
     his wondrous works in the deep.
25 For he commanded, and raised the stormy wind,
     which lifted up the waves of the sea.
26 They mounted up to heaven, they went down to the depths;
     their courage melted away in their evil plight;
27 they reeled and staggered like drunken men,
     and were at their wits' end.
28 Then they cried to the LORD in their trouble,
     and he delivered them from their distress;
29 he made the storm be still,
     and the waves of the sea were hushed.
30 Then they were glad because they had quiet,
     and he brought them to their desired haven.
31 Let them thank the LORD for his steadfast love,
     for his wonderful works to the sons of men!
32 Let them extol him in the congregation of the people,
     and praise him in the assembly of the elders.

F. *The LORD who blesses the earth*

33 He turns rivers into a desert,
     springs of water into thirsty ground,
34 a fruitful land into a salty waste,
     because of the wickedness of its inhabitants.
35 He turns a desert into pools of water,
     a parched land into springs of water.
36 And there he lets the hungry dwell,
     and they establish a city to live in;
37 they sow fields, and plant vineyards,
     and get a fruitful yield.
38 By his blessing they multiply greatly;
     and he does not let their cattle decrease.

G. *The steadfast love of the LORD*

39 When they are diminished and brought low
     through oppression, trouble, and sorrow,
40 he pours contempt upon princes

107.18
Job 33.20,
22;
Ps 9.13;
88.3

107.20
Mt 8.8;
Ps 30.2;
103.3

107.22
Lev 7.12;
Ps 50.14;
9.11;
73.28;
118.17

107.25
Ps 105.31,
34;
Jon 1.4;
Ps 93.3,4
107.26
Ps 22.14;
119.28
107.27
Job 12.25
107.28
ver 6,13,19
107.29
Ps 89.9;
Mt 8.26

107.31
ver 8,15,21
107.32
Ps 22.22,
25; 35.18

107.33
Ps 74.15
107.34
Gen 13.10;
14.3; 19.25
107.35
Ps 114.8;
Isa 41.18

107.37
Isa 65.21
107.38
Gen 12.2;
17.16,20;
Ex 1.7

107.39
Ezek 5.11;
Ps 57.6
107.40
Job 12.21,
24

and makes them wander in trackless wastes;
41 but he raises up the needy out of affliction,
  and makes their families like flocks.
42 The upright see it and are glad;
  and all wickedness stops its mouth.
43 Whoever is wise, let him give heed to these things;
  let men consider the steadfast love of the LORD.

A Song. A Psalm of David.

I. A song of confidence in God 108.1–13

(cf. Ps 57.7–11; 60.5–12)

A. Thanksgiving to the LORD

108 My heart is steadfast, O God, my heart is steadfast!
  I will sing and make melody!
  Awake, my soul!
2 Awake, O harp and lyre!
  I will awake the dawn!
3 I will give thanks to thee, O LORD, among the peoples,
  I will sing praises to thee among the nations.
4 For thy steadfast love is great above the heavens,
  thy faithfulness reaches to the clouds.

5 Be exalted, O God, above the heavens!
  Let thy glory be over all the earth!

B. Pleading God's promises

6 That thy beloved may be delivered,
  give help by thy right hand, and answer me!

7 God has promised in his sanctuary:[y]
  "With exultation I will divide up Shĕçhĕm,
  and portion out the Vale of Sùccóth.
8 Gĭl'ĕăd is mine; Mănăs'sĕh is mine;
  Ē'phrăịm is my helmet;
  Judah my scepter.
9 Mŏăb is my washbasin;
  upon Ēdŏm I cast my shoe;
  over Phĭlĭs'tĭă I shout in triumph."

C. The cry for help

10 Who will bring me to the fortified city?
  Who will lead me to Ēdŏm?
11 Hast thou not rejected us, O God?
  Thou dost not go forth, O God, with our armies.
12 O grant us help against the foe,
  for vain is the help of man!

y Or by his holiness

Marginal references:

107.41
1 Sam 2.8;
Ps 113.7–9
107.42
Job 22.19;
Ps 52.6;
Job 5.16;
Ps 63.11;
Rom 3.19
107.43
Ps 64.9;
Jer 9.12;
Hos 14.9

108.1
Ps 57.7

108.2
Ps 57.8–11

108.4
Ps 113.4

108.6
Ps 60.5–12

108.8
Ps 60.7

108.11
Ps 44.9

13 With God we shall do valiantly;
 it is he who will tread down our foes.

To the choirmaster. A Psalm of David.

I. *A Psalm of anathema 109.1–31*

A. *The cry for help*

109 Be not silent, O God of my praise!
   2 For wicked and deceitful mouths are opened against me,
  speaking against me with lying tongues.
3 They beset me with words of hate,
 and attack me without cause.
4 In return for my love they accuse me,
 even as I make prayer for them.[z]
5 So they reward me evil for good,
 and hatred for my love.

109.1	Ps 83.1
109.2	Ps 52.4; 120.2
109.3	Ps 69.4
109.4	Ps 38.20; 69.13
109.5	Ps 35.12; 38.20

B. *The imprecation*

6 Appoint a wicked man against him;
 let an accuser bring him to trial.[a]
7 When he is tried, let him come forth guilty;
 let his prayer be counted as sin!
8 May his days be few;
 may another seize his goods!
9 May his children be fatherless,
 and his wife a widow!
10 May his children wander about and beg;
 may they be driven out of[b] the ruins they inhabit!
11 May the creditor seize all that he has;
 may strangers plunder the fruits of his toil!
12 Let there be none to extend kindness to him,
 nor any to pity his fatherless children!
13 May his posterity be cut off;
 may his name be blotted out in the second generation!
14 May the iniquity of his fathers be remembered before the LORD,
 and let not the sin of his mother be blotted out!
15 Let them be before the LORD continually;
 and may his[c] memory be cut off from the earth!
16 For he did not remember to show kindness,
 but pursued the poor and needy
 and the brokenhearted to their death.
17 He loved to curse; let curses come on him!
 He did not like blessing; may it be far from him!
18 He clothed himself with cursing as his coat,
 may it soak into his body like water,
 like oil into his bones!
19 May it be like a garment which he wraps round him,
 like a belt with which he daily girds himself!

109.6	Zech 3.1
109.7	Prov 28.9
109.8	Acts 1.20
109.9	Ex 22.24
109.11	Job 5.5; 18.9
109.12	Isa 9.17
109.13	Ps 37.28; Prov 10.7
109.14	Ex 20.5; Neh 4.5; Jer 18.23
109.15	Ps 34.16
109.16	Ps 37.14,32
109.17	Prov 14.14; Ezek 35.6
109.18	Ps 73.6; Num 5.22

z Syr: Heb *I prayer* *a* Heb *stand at his right hand*
b Gk: Heb *and seek* *c* Gk: Heb *their*

109.20
Ps 94.23;
2 Tim 4.14;
Ps 71.10

20 May this be the reward of my accusers from the LORD,
  of those who speak evil against my life!

C. The cry for help continued

109.21
Ps 79.9;
69.16

21 But thou, O GOD my Lord,
  deal on my behalf for thy name's sake;
  because thy steadfast love is good, deliver me!

109.22
Ps 40.17;
143.4

22 For I am poor and needy,
  and my heart is stricken within me.

109.23
Ps 102.11

23 I am gone, like a shadow at evening;
  I am shaken off like a locust.

109.24
Heb 12.12

24 My knees are weak through fasting;
  my body has become gaunt.

109.25
Ps 22.6,7;
Mt 27.39;
Mk 15.29

25 I am an object of scorn to my accusers;
  when they see me, they wag their heads.

109.26
Ps 119.86

26 Help me, O LORD my God!
  Save me according to thy steadfast love!

109.27
Job 37.7

27 Let them know that this is thy hand;
  thou, O LORD, hast done it!

109.28
2 Sam
16.11,12;
Isa 65.14

28 Let them curse, but do thou bless!
  Let my assailants be put to shame;[d] may thy servant be glad!

109.29
Ps 35.26;
132.18

29 May my accusers be clothed with dishonor;
  may they be wrapped in their own shame as in a mantle!

109.30
Ps 35.18

30 With my mouth I will give great thanks to the LORD;
  I will praise him in the midst of the throng.

109.31
Ps 16.8;
121.5

31 For he stands at the right hand of the needy,
  to save him from those who condemn him to death.

A Psalm of David.

I. A Messianic Psalm (Messiah's dominion) 110.1–7

A. Messiah the king

*110.1
Mt 22.44;
Mk 12.36;
Lk 20.42;
Acts 2.34;
1 Cor 15.25

110 The LORD says to my lord:
  "Sit at my right hand,
till I make your enemies
  your footstool."

110.2
Ps 45.6;
2.9

2 The LORD sends forth from Zion
  your mighty scepter.
  Rule in the midst of your foes!

B. Messiah the priest

110.3
Judg 5.2;
Ps 96.9

3 Your people will offer themselves freely

d Gk: Heb *they have arisen and have been put to shame*

110.1 The New Testament makes use of this Psalm in a direct Messianic sense. Christ Himself employs verse 1 to confound His critics and to substantiate His claim to deity (Mt 22.44). Hebrews quotes verse 4 to endorse the eternal priesthood of Christ (Heb 5.6). The Psalm itself looks forward to that day when Christ will reign over the nations of the earth.

on the day you lead your host
    upon the holy mountains.*e*
From the womb of the morning
    like dew your youth*f* will come to you.

4 The LORD has sworn
    and will not change his mind,
"You are a priest for ever
    after the order of Mĕlchĭz'ĕdĕk."

110.4
Heb 5.6,10;
6.20; 7.11,
15,21

5 The Lord is at your right hand;
    he will shatter kings on the day of his wrath.

110.5
Ps 16.8;
2.5,12;
Rom 2.5;
Rev 11.18

C. Messiah the victor

6 He will execute judgment among the nations,
    filling them with corpses;
he will shatter chiefs*g*
    over the wide earth.

110.6
Isa 2.4;
66.24;
Ps 68.21

7 He will drink from the brook by the way;
    therefore he will lift up his head.

110.7
Ps 27.6

I. Praise of the LORD 111.1–10

A. The call to praise

111 Praise the LORD.
    I will give thanks to the LORD with my whole heart,
in the company of the upright, in the congregation.

111.1
Ps 138.1;
149.1

B. The cause for praise

2 Great are the works of the LORD,
    studied by all who have pleasure in them.

111.2
Ps 92.5

3 Full of honor and majesty is his work,
    and his righteousness endures for ever.

111.3
Ps 145.5

4 He has caused his wonderful works to be remembered;
    the LORD is gracious and merciful.

111.4
Ps 86.5;
103.8

5 He provides food for those who fear him;
    he is ever mindful of his covenant.

111.5
Mt 6.26,33

6 He has shown his people the power of his works,
    in giving them the heritage of the nations.

7 The works of his hands are faithful and just;
    all his precepts are trustworthy,

111.7
Rev 15.3;
Ps 19.7

8 they are established for ever and ever,
    to be performed with faithfulness and uprightness.

111.8
Mt 5.18;
Ps 19.9

9 He sent redemption to his people;
    he has commanded his covenant for ever.
    Holy and terrible is his name!

111.9
Lk 1.68;
Ps 99.3

C. The spirit of praise

10 The fear of the LORD is the beginning of wisdom;
    a good understanding have all those who practice it.
    His praise endures for ever!

111.10
Prov 9.10;
3.4;
Ps 145.2

e Another reading is *in holy array*   *f* Cn: Heb *the dew of your youth*   *g* Or *the head*

I. *The excellence and reward of the pious 112.1–10*

112.1
Ps 128.1;
119.16

112.2
Ps 25.13

112.3
Prov 3.16;
8.18

112.4
Job 11.17;
Ps 97.11

112.5
Ps 37.26

112.6
Prov 10.7

112.7
Prov 1.33;
Ps 57.7

112.8
Ps 59.10;
118.7

112.9
2 Cor 9.9;
Deut 24.13;
Ps 75.10

112.10
Ps 86.17;
37.12;
58.7,8;
Prov 10.28;
11.7

112
Praise the LORD.
Blessed is the man who fears the LORD,
who greatly delights in his commandments!

2 His descendants will be mighty in the land;
the generation of the upright will be blessed.

3 Wealth and riches are in his house;
and his righteousness endures for ever.

4 Light rises in the darkness for the upright;
the LORD*h* is gracious, merciful, and righteous.

5 It is well with the man who deals generously and lends,
who conducts his affairs with justice.

6 For the righteous will never be moved;
he will be remembered for ever.

7 He is not afraid of evil tidings;
his heart is firm, trusting in the LORD.

8 His heart is steady, he will not be afraid,
until he sees his desire on his adversaries.

9 He has distributed freely, he has given to the poor;
his righteousness endures for ever;
his horn is exalted in honor.

10 The wicked man sees it and is angry;
he gnashes his teeth and melts away;
the desire of the wicked man comes to nought.

I. *A hymn of praise to God 113.1–9*

113.1
Ps 135.1

113.2
Dan 2.20

113.3
Ps 50.1

113.4
Ps 97.9;
99.2; 8.1

113.5
Ps 89.6;
103.19

113.6
Ps 11.4;
138.6;
Isa 57.15

113.7
1 Sam 2.8;
Ps 107.41

113.8
Job 36.7

113.9
1 Sam 2.5;
Ps 68.6;
Isa 54.1

113
Praise the LORD!
Praise, O servants of the LORD,
praise the name of the LORD!

2 Blessed be the name of the LORD
from this time forth and for evermore!

3 From the rising of the sun to its setting
the name of the LORD is to be praised!

4 The LORD is high above all nations,
and his glory above the heavens!

5 Who is like the LORD our God,
who is seated on high,

6 who looks far down
upon the heavens and the earth?

7 He raises the poor from the dust,
and lifts the needy from the ash heap,

8 to make them sit with princes,
with the princes of his people.

9 He gives the barren woman a home,
making her the joyous mother of children.
Praise the LORD!

I. *In remembrance of Israel's delivering God 114.1–8*

114.1
Ex 13.3

114
When Israel went forth from Egypt,
the house of Jacob from a people of strange language,

h Gk: Heb lacks *the* LORD

² Judah became his sanctuary,
  Israel his dominion.

114.2
Ex 19.6;
29.45,46

³ The sea looked and fled,
  Jordan turned back.

114.3
Ex 14.21;
Josh 3.13,16

⁴ The mountains skipped like rams,
  the hills like lambs.

114.4
Ps 29.6;
Hab 3.6

⁵ What ails you, O sea, that you flee?
  O Jordan, that you turn back?

114.5
Hab 3.8

⁶ O mountains, that you skip like rams?
  O hills, like lambs?

⁷ Tremble, O earth, at the presence of the LORD,
  at the presence of the God of Jacob,

114.7
Ps 96.9

⁸ who turns the rock into a pool of water,
  the flint into a spring of water.

114.8
Ex 17.6;
Num 20.11;
Ps 107.35;
Deut 8.15

I. Give glory to God 115.1–18

A. To God alone belongs glory

115 Not to us, O LORD, not to us,
    but to thy name give glory,
  for the sake of thy steadfast love and thy faithfulness!

115.1
Isa 48.11;
Ezek 36.32;
Ps 96.8

² Why should the nations say,
  "Where is their God?"

*115.2
Ps 42.3;
79.10

B. The evil of idols

³ Our God is in the heavens;
  he does whatever he pleases.

115.3
Ps 103.19;
135.6;
Dan 4.35

⁴ Their idols are silver and gold,
  the work of men's hands.

115.4
Deut 4.28;
Ps 135.15–
17;
Jer 10.3ff

⁵ They have mouths, but do not speak;
  eyes, but do not see.
⁶ They have ears, but do not hear;
  noses, but do not smell.

115.5
Jer 10.5

⁷ They have hands, but do not feel;
  feet, but do not walk;
  and they do not make a sound in their throat.
⁸ Those who make them are like them;
  so are all who trust in them.

115.8
Ps 135.18

C. Israel enjoined to trust the LORD

⁹ O Israel, trust in the LORD!
  He is their help and their shield.

115.9
Ps 118.2–4;
33.20

¹⁰ O house of Aaron, put your trust in the LORD!
   He is their help and their shield.
¹¹ You who fear the LORD, trust in the LORD!
   He is their help and their shield.

115.11
Ps 135.20

115.2 *Where is their God?* This is asked by those whose hearts are full of human folly, who do not believe in an invisible God beyond the reach of man's sense perceptions.

D. *The LORD will bless Israel*

12 The LORD has been mindful of us; he will bless us;
  he will bless the house of Israel;
  he will bless the house of Aaron;

115.13
Ps 128.1,4

13 he will bless those who fear the LORD,
  both small and great.

115.14
Deut 1.11

14 May the LORD give you increase,
  you and your children!

115.15
Gen 14.19;
1.1;
Ps 96.5

15 May you be blessed by the LORD,
  who made heaven and earth!

115.16
Ps 89.11;
8.6

16 The heavens are the LORD's heavens,
  but the earth he has given to the sons of men.

115.17
Ps 6.5;
31.17

17 The dead do not praise the LORD,
  nor do any that go down into silence.

115.18
Ps 113.2

18 But we will bless the LORD
  from this time forth and for evermore.
Praise the LORD!

I. *Hymn of thanksgiving for deliverance 116.1–19*

A. *Acknowledgment of God's deliverance*

116.1
Ps 18.1;
66.19

116 I love the LORD, because he has heard
  my voice and my supplications.

116.2
Ps 40.1

2 Because he inclined his ear to me,
  therefore I will call on him as long as I live.

116.3
Ps 18.4–6

3 The snares of death encompassed me;
  the pangs of Shēōl laid hold on me;
  I suffered distress and anguish.

116.4
Ps 118.5;
22.20

4 Then I called on the name of the LORD:
  "O LORD, I beseech thee, save my life!"

116.5
Ps 103.8;
Ezra 9.15;
Neh 9.8;
Ps 145.17;
Ex 34.6

5 Gracious is the LORD, and righteous;
  our God is merciful.

116.6
Ps 19.7;
79.8

6 The LORD preserves the simple;
  when I was brought low, he saved me.

7 Return, O my soul, to your rest;
  for the LORD has dealt bountifully with you.

116.7
Jer 6.16;
Mt 11.29;
Ps 13.6

8 For thou hast delivered my soul from death,
  my eyes from tears,
  my feet from stumbling;

116.8
Ps 56.13

116.9
Ps 27.13

9 I walk before the LORD
  in the land of the living.

116.10
2 Cor 4.13

10 I kept my faith, even when I said,
  "I am greatly afflicted";

116.11
Ps 31.22;
Rom 3.4

11 I said in my consternation,
  "Men are all a vain hope."

B. *Resolve to pay his vows*

12 What shall I render to the LORD
  for all his bounty to me?

13 I will lift up the cup of salvation
   and call on the name of the LORD,
14 I will pay my vows to the LORD
   in the presence of all his people.
15 Precious in the sight of the LORD
   is the death of his saints.
16 O LORD, I am thy servant;
   I am thy servant, the son of thy handmaid.
   Thou hast loosed my bonds.
17 I will offer to thee the sacrifice of thanksgiving
   and call on the name of the LORD.
18 I will pay my vows to the LORD
   in the presence of all his people,
19 in the courts of the house of the LORD,
   in your midst, O Jerusalem.
   Praise the LORD!

I. Extol Him for His steadfast love 117.1, 2

117 Praise the LORD, all nations!
    Extol him, all peoples!
2 For great is his steadfast love toward us;
   and the faithfulness of the LORD endures for ever.
   Praise the LORD!

I. Thanks to the LORD 118.1–29

A. The LORD's mercy

118 O give thanks to the LORD, for he is good;
    his steadfast love endures for ever!

2 Let Israel say,
   "His steadfast love endures for ever."
3 Let the house of Aaron say,
   "His steadfast love endures for ever."
4 Let those who fear the LORD say,
   "His steadfast love endures for ever."

B. The LORD's answer to prayer

5 Out of my distress I called on the LORD;
   the LORD answered me and set me free.
6 With the LORD on my side I do not fear.
   What can man do to me?
7 The LORD is on my side to help me;
   I shall look in triumph on those who hate me.
8 It is better to take refuge in the LORD
   than to put confidence in man.
9 It is better to take refuge in the LORD
   than to put confidence in princes.

C. The LORD's deliverance

10 All nations surrounded me;
   in the name of the LORD I cut them off!

116.13 Ps 16.5; 80.18
116.14 Ps 22.25; Jon 2.9
116.15 Ps 72.14
116.16 Ps 119.125; 143.12; 86.16
116.17 Ps 50.14; ver 13
116.18 ver 14
116.19 Ps 96.8; 135.2
117.1 Rom 15.11
117.2 Ps 100.5
118.1 Ps 106.1; 136.1
118.2 Ps 115.9
118.5 Ps 120.1; 18.19
118.6 Ps 27.1; Heb 13.6; Ps 56.4,11
118.7 Ps 54.4; 59.10
118.8 Ps 40.4; Jer 17.5
118.9 Ps 146.3
118.10 Ps 3.6; 18.40

11 They surrounded me, surrounded me on every side;
   in the name of the LORD I cut them off!

118.12
Deut 1.44;
Ps 58.9

12 They surrounded me like bees,
   they blazed*i* like a fire of thorns;
   in the name of the LORD I cut them off!

118.13
Ps 140.4;
86.17
118.14
Ex 15.2;
Isa 12.2

13 I was pushed hard,*j* so that I was falling,
   but the LORD helped me.
14 The LORD is my strength and my song;
   he has become my salvation.

D. The LORD'S *mighty right hand*

118.15
Ps 68.3;
89.13

15 Hark, glad songs of victory
   in the tents of the righteous:
"The right hand of the LORD does valiantly,

118.16
Ex 15.6

16   the right hand of the LORD is exalted,
   the right hand of the LORD does valiantly!"

118.17
Hab 1.12;
Ps 73.28
118.18
2 Cor 6.9

17 I shall not die, but I shall live,
   and recount the deeds of the LORD.
18 The LORD has chastened me sorely,
   but he has not given me over to death.

118.19
Isa 26.2

19 Open to me the gates of righteousness,
   that I may enter through them
   and give thanks to the LORD.

118.20
Ps 24.7;
Isa 35.8;
Rev 22.14

20 This is the gate of the LORD;
   the righteous shall enter through it.

118.21
Ps 116.1;
ver 14

21 I thank thee that thou hast answered me
   and hast become my salvation.

E. The LORD'S *wisdom*

118.22
Mt 21.42;
Mk 12.10;
Lk 20.17;
Acts 4.11;
Eph 2.20;
1 Pet 2.4,7

22 The stone which the builders rejected
   has become the head of the corner.
23 This is the LORD's doing;
   it is marvelous in our eyes.
24 This is the day which the LORD has made;
   let us rejoice and be glad in it.
25 Save us, we beseech thee, O LORD!
   O LORD, we beseech thee, give us success!

118.26
Mt 21.9;
Mk 11.9;
Lk 13.35;
19.38;
Jn 12.13
118.27
1 Ki 18.39;
Est 8.16;
1 Pet 2.9

26 Blessed be he who enters in the name of the LORD!
   We bless you from the house of the LORD.
27 The LORD is God,
   and he has given us light.
Bind the festal procession with branches,
   up to the horns of the altar!

F. The doxology

118.28
Ex 15.2;
Isa 25.1

28 Thou art my God, and I will give thanks to thee;
   thou art my God, I will extol thee.

i Gk: Heb *were extinguished*   *j* Gk Syr Jerome: Heb *thou didst push me hard*

29 O give thanks to the LORD, for he is good;
  for his steadfast love endures for ever!

118.29
ver 1

I. The law of the LORD 119.1–176

A. The blessedness of those who keep His law

119 Blessed are those whose way is blameless,
       who walk in the law of the LORD!
2 Blessed are those who keep his testimonies,
  who seek him with their whole heart,
3 who also do no wrong,
  but walk in his ways!
4 Thou hast commanded thy precepts
  to be kept diligently.
5 O that my ways may be steadfast
  in keeping thy statutes!
6 Then I shall not be put to shame,
  having my eyes fixed on all thy commandments.
7 I will praise thee with an upright heart,
  when I learn thy righteous ordinances.
8 I will observe thy statutes;
  O forsake me not utterly!

*119.1
Ps 101.2,6;
128.1
119.2
ver 22,10;
Deut 6.5
119.3
1 Jn 3.9;
5.18

119.6
ver 80

119.7
ver 62

B. Holiness the fruit of keeping God's law

9 How can a young man keep his way pure?
  By guarding it according to thy word.
10 With my whole heart I seek thee;
   let me not wander from thy commandments!
11 I have laid up thy word in my heart,
   that I might not sin against thee.
12 Blessed be thou, O LORD;
   teach me thy statutes!
13 With my lips I declare
   all the ordinances of thy mouth.
14 In the way of thy testimonies I delight
   as much as in all riches.
15 I will meditate on thy precepts,
   and fix my eyes on thy ways.
16 I will delight in thy statutes;
   I will not forget thy word.

119.9
2 Chr 6.16
119.10
2 Chr
15.15;
ver 21,118
*119.11
Ps 37.31;
Lk 2.19,51
119.12
ver 26,64,
68,108,124,
135,171
119.13
Ps 40.9;
ver 72
119.15
ver 23,48,
78;
Ps 1.2
119.16
Ps 1.2

119.1 This Psalm has twenty-two sections arranged according to the Hebrew alphabet.

119.11 Why do believers say the Bible is the Word of God? (See also note to 2 Tim 3.16.) The reasons are as follows: (1) The Old Testament writers affirmed that they were speaking the Word of God and not the word of man. "Thus says the LORD," or an equivalent, is found more than 2000 times in the Old Testament (2 Sam 23.1–3; Isa 8.1, 11; Jer 1.9; 5.14; 7.27; 13.12; Ezek 3.4; Mic 5.10; Hab 2.2, etc.); (2) the apostles regarded the whole of Scripture as the infallible Word of God (2 Tim 3.16; 2 Pet 1.21; 1 Cor 14.37; 1 Thess 2.13; Gal 1.11, 12); (3) Jesus Christ unqualifiedly endorsed the Scriptures as the inspired Word of God (Jn 10.35; Mt 5.18; etc.); (4) fulfilled prophecy unmistakably demonstrates the authoritativeness of Scripture (Deut 28.63–65; 28.37; Lk 21.24; Nah 3.1, 4–6; Zeph 2.13, 14; Isa 13.19–22; Jer 51.37; Ezek 29.15; 30.6; Jer 46.19, 20); (5) archaeology confirms the accuracy of Scripture; (6) the pragmatic test, the fact that it performs what it promises (that it works in actual human experience in response to faith), also shows the Bible to be the Word of God (34.8; Jn 7.17).

C. *Eyes to behold the truth of God's law*

119.17
Ps 13.6

17 Deal bountifully with thy servant,
    that I may live and observe thy word.
18 Open my eyes, that I may behold
    wondrous things out of thy law.

119.19
Gen 47.9;
1 Chr
29.15;
Ps 39.12;
2 Cor 5.6;
Heb 11.13

19 I am a sojourner on earth;
    hide not thy commandments from me!
20 My soul is consumed with longing
    for thy ordinances at all times.

119.20
Ps 42.1,2

21 Thou dost rebuke the insolent, accursed ones,
    who wander from thy commandments;

119.21
ver 10,118

22 take away from me their scorn and contempt,
    for I have kept thy testimonies.

119.22
Ps 39.8

23 Even though princes sit plotting against me,
    thy servant will meditate on thy statutes.

119.23
ver 15

24 Thy testimonies are my delight,
    they are my counselors.

119.24
ver 16

D. *Prayer to understand God's precepts*

119.25
Ps 44.25;
ver 37

25 My soul cleaves to the dust;
    revive me according to thy word!
26 When I told of my ways, thou didst answer me;
    teach me thy statutes!

119.26
ver 12

27 Make me understand the way of thy precepts,
    and I will meditate on thy wondrous works.

119.27
Ps 145.5

28 My soul melts away for sorrow;
    strengthen me according to thy word!

119.28
Ps 107.26;
20.2;
1 Pet 5.10

29 Put false ways far from me;
    and graciously teach me thy law!
30 I have chosen the way of faithfulness,
    I set thy ordinances before me.

119.31
Deut 11.22

31 I cleave to thy testimonies, O LORD;
    let me not be put to shame!

119.32
1 Ki 4.29;
Isa 60.5;
2 Cor 6.11

32 I will run in the way of thy commandments
    when thou enlargest my understanding!

E. *Perseverance based on God's promises*

119.33
ver 5,12

33 Teach me, O LORD, the way of thy statutes;
    and I will keep it to the end.

119.34
ver 73;
Prov 2.6;
Jas 1.5

34 Give me understanding, that I may keep thy law
    and observe it with my whole heart.

119.35
ver 16

35 Lead me in the path of thy commandments,
    for I delight in it.

119.36
1 Ki 8.58;
Lk 12.15

36 Incline my heart to thy testimonies,
    and not to gain!

119.37
Isa 33.15;
Ps 71.20

37 Turn my eyes from looking at vanities;
    and give me life in thy ways.

119.38
2 Sam 7.25

38 Confirm to thy servant thy promise,
    which is for those who fear thee.
39 Turn away the reproach which I dread;
    for thy ordinances are good.

119.40
ver 20,25

40 Behold, I long for thy precepts;
    in thy righteousness give me life!

F. Salvation through the law of the LORD

41 Let thy steadfast love come to me, O LORD,
    thy salvation according to thy promise;
42 then shall I have an answer for those who taunt me,
    for I trust in thy word.
43 And take not the word of truth utterly out of my mouth,
    for my hope is in thy ordinances.
44 I will keep thy law continually,
    for ever and ever;
45 and I shall walk at liberty,
    for I have sought thy precepts.
46 I will also speak of thy testimonies before kings,
    and shall not be put to shame;
47 for I find my delight in thy commandments,
    which I love.
48 I revere thy commandments, which I love,
    and I will meditate on thy statutes.

G. The law of the LORD a source of hope and comfort

49 Remember thy word to thy servant,
    in which thou hast made me hope.
50 This is my comfort in my affliction
    that thy promise gives me life.
51 Godless men utterly deride me,
    but I do not turn away from thy law.
52 When I think of thy ordinances from of old,
    I take comfort, O LORD.
53 Hot indignation seizes me because of the wicked,
    who forsake thy law.
54 Thy statutes have been my songs
    in the house of my pilgrimage.
55 I remember thy name in the night, O LORD,
    and keep thy law.
56 This blessing has fallen to me,
    that I have kept thy precepts.

H. The LORD our portion

57 The LORD is my portion;
    I promise to keep thy words.
58 I entreat thy favor with all my heart;
    be gracious to me according to thy promise.
59 When I think of thy ways,
    I turn my feet to thy testimonies;
60 I hasten and do not delay
    to keep thy commandments.
61 Though the cords of the wicked ensnare me,
    I do not forget thy law.
62 At midnight I rise to praise thee,
    because of thy righteous ordinances.
63 I am a companion of all who fear thee,
    of those who keep thy precepts.
64 The earth, O LORD, is full of thy steadfast love;
    teach me thy statutes!

119.41 ver 77,116
119.42 Prov 27.11
119.46 Mt 10.18; Acts 26.1,2
119.47 ver 16
119.48 ver 15
119.50 Rom 15.4
119.51 Jer 20.7; ver 157; Job 23.11; Ps 44.18
119.52 Ps 103.18
119.53 Ezra 9.3; Ps 89.30
119.55 Ps 63.6
119.57 Ps 16.5; Deut 33.9
119.58 1 Ki 13.6; ver 41
119.59 Lk 15.17,18
119.61 Ps 140.5; ver 83
119.62 Acts 16.25
119.63 Ps 101.6
119.64 Ps 33.5; ver 12

I. *The law of the LORD taught by affliction*

65 Thou hast dealt well with thy servant,
   O LORD, according to thy word.
66 Teach me good judgment and knowledge,
   for I believe in thy commandments.
67 Before I was afflicted I went astray;
   but now I keep thy word.
68 Thou art good and doest good;
   teach me thy statutes.
69 The godless besmear me with lies,
   but with my whole heart I keep thy precepts;
70 their heart is gross like fat,
   but I delight in thy law.
71 It is good for me that I was afflicted,
   that I might learn thy statutes.
72 The law of thy mouth is better to me
   than thousands of gold and silver pieces.

J. *Fellowship based upon the law of the LORD*

73 Thy hands have made and fashioned me;
   give me understanding that I may learn thy commandments.
74 Those who fear thee shall see me and rejoice,
   because I have hoped in thy word.
75 I know, O LORD, that thy judgments are right,
   and that in faithfulness thou hast afflicted me.
76 Let thy steadfast love be ready to comfort me
   according to thy promise to thy servant.
77 Let thy mercy come to me, that I may live;
   for thy law is my delight.
78 Let the godless be put to shame,
   because they have subverted me with guile;
   as for me, I will meditate on thy precepts.
79 Let those who fear thee turn to me,
   that they may know thy testimonies.
80 May my heart be blameless in thy statutes,
   that I may not be put to shame!

K. *A longing for peace*

81 My soul languishes for thy salvation;
   I hope in thy word.
82 My eyes fail with watching for thy promise;
   I ask, "When wilt thou comfort me?"
83 For I have become like a wineskin in the smoke,
   yet I have not forgotten thy statutes.
84 How long must thy servant endure?
   When wilt thou judge those who persecute me?
85 Godless men have dug pitfalls for me,
   men who do not conform to thy law.
86 All thy commandments are sure;
   they persecute me with falsehood; help me!
87 They have almost made an end of me on earth;
   but I have not forsaken thy precepts.

119.67
ver 71;
Jer 31.18,
19;
Heb 12.11
119.68
Ps 106.1;
Deut 8.16;
ver 12
119.69
Job 13.4;
ver 56
119.70
Ps 17.10;
Isa 6.10;
ver 16
119.72
ver 127;
Ps 19.10;
Prov 8.10,
11,19

119.73
Job 10.8;
Ps 138.8;
ver 34
119.74
Ps 34.2;
ver 43
119.75
Heb 12.10

119.77
ver 41,47

119.78
Jer 50.32;
ver 86,15

119.80
ver 1,46

119.81
Ps 84.2

119.82
Ps 69.3

119.83
Job 30.30

119.84
Ps 39.4;
Rev 6.10
119.85
Ps 35.7
119.86
ver 78;
Ps 35.19;
109.26
119.87
Isa 58.2

88 In thy steadfast love spare my life,
   that I may keep the testimonies of thy mouth.

L. *The immutability of the law of the* LORD

89 For ever, O LORD, thy word
   is firmly fixed in the heavens.
90 Thy faithfulness endures to all generations;
   thou hast established the earth, and it stands fast.
91 By thy appointment they stand this day;
   for all things are thy servants.
92 If thy law had not been my delight,
   I should have perished in my affliction.
93 I will never forget thy precepts;
   for by them thou hast given me life.
94 I am thine, save me;
   for I have sought thy precepts.
95 The wicked lie in wait to destroy me;
   but I consider thy testimonies.
96 I have seen a limit to all perfection,
   but thy commandment is exceedingly broad.

M. *The love of the law of the* LORD

97 Oh, how I love thy law!
   It is my meditation all the day.
98 Thy commandment makes me wiser than my enemies,
   for it is ever with me.
99 I have more understanding than all my teachers,
   for thy testimonies are my meditation.
100 I understand more than the aged,
    for I keep thy precepts.
101 I hold back my feet from every evil way,
    in order to keep thy word.
102 I do not turn aside from thy ordinances,
    for thou hast taught me.
103 How sweet are thy words to my taste,
    sweeter than honey to my mouth!
104 Through thy precepts I get understanding;
    therefore I hate every false way.

N. *The law of the* LORD *a lamp to the feet*

105 Thy word is a lamp to my feet
    and a light to my path.
106 I have sworn an oath and confirmed it,
    to observe thy righteous ordinances.
107 I am sorely afflicted;
    give me life, O LORD, according to thy word!
108 Accept my offerings of praise, O LORD,
    and teach me thy ordinances.
109 I hold my life in my hand continually,
    but I do not forget thy law.
110 The wicked have laid a snare for me,
    but I do not stray from thy precepts.

119.89
Mt 24.34,
35;
1 Pet 1.25
119.90
Ps 36.5;
148.6;
Ecc 1.4
119.91
Jer 33.25
119.92
ver 16,50
119.93
ver 16,25
119.94
ver 146,45

119.97
Ps 1.2
119.98
ver 130;
Deut 4.6
119.99
ver 15
119.100
Job 32.7–9
119.101
Prov 1.15

119.103
Ps 19.10
119.104
ver 128,130

119.105
Prov 6.23
119.106
Neh 10.29
119.107
ver 25
119.108
Hos 14.2;
Heb 13.15;
ver 12
119.109
Job 13.14;
ver 16
119.110
Ps 140.5;
141.9;
ver 10

119.111 Deut 33.4; ver 14,162	111 Thy testimonies are my heritage for ever; yea, they are the joy of my heart.
119.112 ver 33	112 I incline my heart to perform thy statutes for ever, to the end.

O. *The law of the* LORD *a hiding place*

119.113 Jas 1.8; ver 47	113 I hate double-minded men, but I love thy law.
119.114 Ps 32.7; 91.1; ver 74	114 Thou art my hiding place and my shield; I hope in thy word.
	115 Depart from me, you evildoers, that I may keep the commandments of my God.
119.115 Ps 6.8; 139.19; Mt 7.23	116 Uphold me according to thy promise, that I may live, and let me not be put to shame in my hope!
119.116 Ps 54.4; 25.2; Rom 5.5; 9.33	117 Hold me up, that I may be safe and have regard for thy statutes continually!
	118 Thou dost spurn all who go astray from thy statutes; yea, their cunning is in vain.
119.118 ver 21	119 All the wicked of the earth thou dost count as dross; therefore I love thy testimonies.
119.119 Ezek 22.18	120 My flesh trembles for fear of thee, and I am afraid of thy judgments.
119.120 Hab 3.16	

P. *The Psalmist has kept the law of the* LORD

	121 I have done what is just and right; do not leave me to my oppressors.
119.122 Job 17.3	122 Be surety for thy servant for good; let not the godless oppress me.
119.123 ver 81,82	123 My eyes fail with watching for thy salvation, and for the fulfilment of thy righteous promise.
119.124 ver 12	124 Deal with thy servant according to thy steadfast love, and teach me thy statutes.
119.125 Ps 116.16	125 I am thy servant; give me understanding, that I may know thy testimonies!
	126 It is time for the LORD to act, for thy law has been broken.
119.127 Ps 19.10	127 Therefore I love thy commandments above gold, above fine gold.
119.128 ver 104	128 Therefore I direct my steps by all thy precepts;[k] I hate every false way.

Q. *Prayer for grace to keep the law of the* LORD

119.129 ver 18,22	129 Thy testimonies are wonderful; therefore my soul keeps them.
119.130 Prov 6.23; Ps 19.7	130 The unfolding of thy words gives light; it imparts understanding to the simple.
119.131 Ps 42.1; ver 20	131 With open mouth I pant, because I long for thy commandments.
119.132 Ps 25.16	132 Turn to me and be gracious to me, as is thy wont toward those who love thy name.

k Gk Jerome: Heb uncertain

133 Keep steady my steps according to thy promise,
and let no iniquity get dominion over me.
134 Redeem me from man's oppression,
that I may keep thy precepts.
135 Make thy face shine upon thy servant,
and teach me thy statutes.
136 My eyes shed streams of tears,
because men do not keep thy law.

119.133
Ps 17.15;
19.13
119.134
Ps 142.6
119.135
Ps 4.6;
ver 12
119.136
Jer 9.1;
Ezek 9.4

R. *The LORD and His law are righteous*

137 Righteous art thou, O LORD,
and right are thy judgments.
138 Thou hast appointed thy testimonies in righteousness
and in all faithfulness.
139 My zeal consumes me,
because my foes forget thy words.
140 Thy promise is well tried,
and thy servant loves it.
141 I am small and despised,
yet I do not forget thy precepts.
142 Thy righteousness is righteous for ever,
and thy law is true.
143 Trouble and anguish have come upon me,
but thy commandments are my delight.
144 Thy testimonies are righteous for ever;
give me understanding that I may live.

119.137
Ezra 9.15;
Neh 9.13;
Jer 12.1
119.138
Ps 19.7–9
119.139
Ps 69.9
119.140
Ps 12.6

119.142
Ps 19.9;
ver 151,160
119.143
ver 24,77
119.144
Ps 19.9;
ver 34,73

S. *A cry for salvation*

145 With my whole heart I cry; answer me, O LORD!
I will keep thy statutes.
146 I cry to thee; save me,
that I may observe thy testimonies.
147 I rise before dawn and cry for help;
I hope in thy words.
148 My eyes are awake before the watches of the night,
that I may meditate upon thy promise.
149 Hear my voice in thy steadfast love;
O LORD, in thy justice preserve my life.
150 They draw near who persecute me with evil purpose;
they are far from thy law.
151 But thou art near, O LORD,
and all thy commandments are true.
152 Long have I known from thy testimonies
that thou hast founded them for ever.

119.145
ver 10,22,55

119.148
Ps 5.3

119.149
ver 40,154

119.151
Ps 145.18;
ver 142
119.152
Lk 21.33

T. *Keeping the law of the LORD in adversity*

153 Look on my affliction and deliver me,
for I do not forget thy law.
154 Plead my cause and redeem me;
give me life according to thy promise!
155 Salvation is far from the wicked,
for they do not seek thy statutes.

119.153
ver 50;
Prov 3.1
119.154
1 Sam
24.15;
ver 134
119.155
Job 5.4

Psalms 119.156–176

902

156 Great is thy mercy, O LORD;
  give me life according to thy justice.
157 Many are my persecutors and my adversaries,
  but I do not swerve from thy testimonies.
158 I look at the faithless with disgust,
  because they do not keep thy commands.
159 Consider how I love thy precepts!
  Preserve my life according to thy steadfast love.
160 The sum of thy word is truth;
  and every one of thy righteous ordinances endures for ever.

U. Prayer for deliverance from persecution

161 Princes persecute me without cause,
  but my heart stands in awe of thy words.
162 I rejoice at thy word
  like one who finds great spoil.
163 I hate and abhor falsehood,
  but I love thy law.
164 Seven times a day I praise thee
  for thy righteous ordinances.
165 Great peace have those who love thy law;
  nothing can make them stumble.
166 I hope for thy salvation, O LORD,
  and I do thy commandments.
167 My soul keeps thy testimonies;
  I love them exceedingly.
168 I keep thy precepts and testimonies,
  for all my ways are before thee.

V. The closing general petition

169 Let my cry come before thee, O LORD;
  give me understanding according to thy word!
170 Let my supplication come before thee;
  deliver me according to thy word.
171 My lips will pour forth praise
  that thou dost teach me thy statutes.
172 My tongue will sing of thy word,
  for all thy commandments are right.
173 Let thy hand be ready to help me,
  for I have chosen thy precepts.
174 I long for thy salvation, O LORD,
  and thy law is my delight.
175 Let me live, that I may praise thee,
  and let thy ordinances help me.
176 I have gone astray like a lost sheep; seek thy servant,
  for I do not forget thy commandments.

119.156 2 Sam 24.14
119.157 Ps 7.1; ver 51
119.158 Ps 139.21
119.159 ver 47,88
119.160 Ps 139.17; ver 142
119.161 1 Sam 24.11
119.162 1 Sam 30.16
★119.164 ver 7,160
119.165 Prov 3.2; Isa 26.3; 32.17
119.166 ver 174; Gen 49.18
119.168 ver 22; Prov 5.21
119.169 Ps 18.6; ver 27,65
119.170 Ps 28.2; 31.2
119.171 Ps 51.15; 94.12
119.173 Ps 37.24
119.174 ver 166,24
119.175 Isa 55.3
★119.176 Isa 53.6; ver 16

119.164 *seven times a day,* i.e., again and again, according to some interpreters. Rabbi Solomon understood it literally: men should praise God twice in the morning before reading the Ten Commandments, and once after; twice in the evening before reading them and twice after.

119.176 Men, like sheep, display folly and ingratitude as they go astray. God, the shepherd, through love, searches for, and finds, the lost sheep—a fitting climax to this, the longest of the Psalms.

A Song of Ascents.

I. *A prayer for deliverance 120.1–7*

A. *From lying lips*

120 In my distress I cry to the LORD,
      that he may answer me:
2 "Deliver me, O LORD,
  from lying lips,
  from a deceitful tongue."

3 What shall be given to you?
  And what more shall be done to you,
    you deceitful tongue?
4 A warrior's sharp arrows,
  with glowing coals of the broom tree!

B. *From haters of peace*

5 Woe is me, that I sojourn in Měshěch,
  that I dwell among the tents of Kēdar!
6 Too long have I had my dwelling
  among those who hate peace.
7 I am for peace;
  but when I speak,
  they are for war!

A Song of Ascents.

I. *The LORD my keeper 121.1–8*

121 I lift up my eyes to the hills.
      From whence does my help come?
2 My help comes from the LORD,
  who made heaven and earth.

3 He will not let your foot be moved,
  he who keeps you will not slumber.
4 Behold, he who keeps Israel
  will neither slumber nor sleep.

5 The LORD is your keeper;
  the LORD is your shade
    on your right hand.
6 The sun shall not smite you by day,
  nor the moon by night.

7 The LORD will keep you from all evil;
  he will keep your life.
8 The LORD will keep

Cross-references (margin):

120.1 Ps 102.2; Jon 2.2
120.2 Prov 12.22; Ps 52.4
120.4 Ps 45.5; 140.10
★120.5 Gen 10.2; Ezek 27.13; Gen 25.13; Jer 49.28
120.7 Ps 55.21
121.2 Ps 124.8; 115.15
121.3 Ps 66.9; 127.1
121.5 Isa 25.4; Ps 16.8
121.6 Ps 91.5; Isa 49.10; Rev 7.16
121.7 Ps 91.10–12
121.8 Deut 28.6

120.5 *Meshech ... Kedar* (cf. Gen 10.2; 25.13). The reference is to the Gentile peoples among whom the Psalmist lived. *Kedar* refers both to the region and the people.

your going out and your coming in
from this time forth and for evermore.

A Song of Ascents. Of David.

I. *The peace of Jerusalem 122.1–9*

A. *The house of the LORD*

122.1
Isa 2.3;
Zech 8.21

122 I was glad when they said to me,
          "Let us go to the house of the LORD!"
² Our feet have been standing
          within your gates, O Jerusalem!

122.3
Ps 48.13

³ Jerusalem, built as a city
          which is bound firmly together,

122.4
Deut 16.16;
Ex 16.34

⁴ to which the tribes go up,
          the tribes of the LORD,
     as was decreed for Israel,
          to give thanks to the name of the LORD.

122.5
Deut 17.8;
2 Chr 19.8

⁵ There thrones for judgment were set,
          the thrones of the house of David.

B. *The prayer for its peace and prosperity*

122.6
Ps 51.18

⁶ Pray for the peace of Jerusalem!
          "May they prosper who love you!"
⁷ Peace be within your walls,
          and security within your towers!"
⁸ For my brethren and companions' sake
          I will say, "Peace be within you!"

122.9
Neh 2.10

⁹ For the sake of the house of the LORD our God,
          I will seek your good.

A Song of Ascents.

I. *A song of confidence in God 123.1–4*

A. *Looking to the LORD*

123.1
Ps 121.1;
141.8; 2.4;
11.4

123 To thee I lift up my eyes,
          O thou who art enthroned in the heavens!
² Behold, as the eyes of servants
          look to the hand of their master,

123.2
Prov 27.18;
Ps 25.15

     as the eyes of a maid
          to the hand of her mistress,
     so our eyes look to the LORD our God,
          till he have mercy upon us.

B. *Prayer for mercy*

123.3
Ps 4.1;
51.1

³ Have mercy upon us, O LORD, have mercy upon us,

for we have had more than enough of contempt.
4 Too long our soul has been sated
     with the scorn of those who are at ease,
     the contempt of the proud.

123.4
Ps 79.4

A Song of Ascents. Of David.

I. *Thanksgiving for a supernatural deliverance 124.1–8*

A. *God alone the deliverer*

124 If it had not been the LORD who was on our side,
        let Israel now say—
2 if it had not been the LORD who was on our side,
     when men rose up against us,
3 then they would have swallowed us up alive,
     when their anger was kindled against us;
4 then the flood would have swept us away,
     the torrent would have gone over us;
5 then over us would have gone
     the raging waters.

124.1
Ps 94.17;
129.1

124.3
Ps 56.1;
57.3;
Prov 1.12

124.5
Ps 69.2

B. *Praise to the deliverer*

6 Blessed be the LORD,
     who has not given us
     as prey to their teeth!
7 We have escaped as a bird
     from the snare of the fowlers;
the snare is broken,
     and we have escaped!

8 Our help is in the name of the LORD,
     who made heaven and earth.

124.6
Ps 27.2

124.7
Prov 6.5;
Ps 91.3

124.8
Ps 121.2;
Gen 1.1

A Song of Ascents.

I. *The* LORD *the protector of His people 125.1–5*

125 Those who trust in the LORD are like Mount Zion,
        which cannot be moved, but abides for ever.
2 As the mountains are round about Jerusalem,
     so the LORD is round about his people,
     from this time forth and for evermore.
3 For the scepter of wickedness shall not rest
     upon the land allotted to the righteous,
lest the righteous put forth
     their hands to do wrong.
4 Do good, O LORD, to those who are good,
     and to those who are upright in their hearts!
5 But those who turn aside upon their crooked ways
     the LORD will lead away with evildoers!
     Peace be in Israel!

125.1
Ps 46.5

125.2
Zech 2.5;
Ps 121.8

125.3
Prov 22.8;
Isa 14.5;
Ps 55.20

125.4
Ps 119.68;
7.10;94.15
125.5
Prov 2.15;
Ps 128.6

A Song of Ascents.

I. A song of thanks for God's deliverance 126.1–6

126 When the LORD restored the fortunes of Zion,[1]
we were like those who dream.
2 Then our mouth was filled with laughter,
and our tongue with shouts of joy;
then they said among the nations,
"The LORD has done great things for them."
3 The LORD has done great things for us;
we are glad.

4 Restore our fortunes, O LORD,
like the watercourses in the Něgěb!
5 May those who sow in tears
reap with shouts of joy!
6 He that goes forth weeping,
bearing the seed for sowing,
shall come home with shouts of joy,
bringing his sheaves with him.

A Song of Ascents. Of Solomon.

I. The vanity of work without God 127.1–5

127 Unless the LORD builds the house,
those who build it labor in vain.
Unless the LORD watches over the city,
the watchman stays awake in vain.
2 It is in vain that you rise up early
and go late to rest,
eating the bread of anxious toil;
for[m] he gives to his beloved sleep.

3 Lo, sons are a heritage from the LORD,
the fruit of the womb a reward.
4 Like arrows in the hand of a warrior
are the sons of one's youth.
5 Happy is the man who has
his quiver full of them!
He shall not be put to shame
when he speaks with his enemies in the gate.

Cross references (left margin):

*126.1 Ps 85.1; Acts 12.9
126.2 Job 8.21; Ps 51.14; 71.19
126.3 Isa 25.9
126.4 Isa 35.6; 43.19
126.5 Jer 31.16; Isa 35.10
*127.1 Ps 78.69; 121.4
127.2 Gen 3.17; Job 11.18, 19
*127.3 Gen 33.5; Josh 24.3, 4; Deut 28.4
127.5 Job 5.4; Prov 27.11*

---

l Or *brought back those who returned to Zion*   *m* Another reading is *so*

126.1 Many commentators think this Psalm refers to some great deliverance of Israel out of difficulty and bondage, in all probability their return to the land from Babylon in Ezra's time. Israel's liberation is directly attributed to God when the weeping (ver 6) of the captives turns to shouts of joy upon deliverance.

127.1 Men are ambitious to found a family and to continue the family name. But to found a family and to leave God out of the picture is to labor futilely.
127.3 Children are the gift of God and should be trained as such. They are a source of great joy to their parents and are their strength and defense.

A Song of Ascents.

I. The family that fears the LORD is blessed 128.1–6

A. The blessedness of the individual

128 Blessed is every one who fears the LORD,
who walks in his ways!
2 You shall eat the fruit of the labor of your hands;
you shall be happy, and it shall be well with you.

*128.1
Ps 112.1;
119.3
128.2
Isa 3.10;
Ezek 23.29;
Ecc 8.12

B. The blessedness of the home

3 Your wife will be like a fruitful vine
within your house;
your children will be like olive shoots
around your table.
4 Lo, thus shall the man be blessed
who fears the LORD.

128.3
Ezek 19.10;
Ps 52.8;
144.12

C. The blessedness of the nation

5 The LORD bless you from Zion!
May you see the prosperity of Jerusalem
all the days of your life!
6 May you see your children's children!
Peace be upon Israel!

128.5
Ps 134.3;
20.2; 122.9
128.6
Gen 50.23;
Job 42.16;
Ps 125.5

A Song of Ascents.

I. A prayer for the shame of Israel's enemies 129.1–8

129 "Sorely have they afflicted me from my youth,"
let Israel now say—
2 "Sorely have they afflicted me from my youth,
yet they have not prevailed against me.
3 The plowers plowed upon my back;
they made long their furrows."
4 The LORD is righteous;
he has cut the cords of the wicked.
5 May all who hate Zion
be put to shame and turned backward!
6 Let them be like the grass on the housetops,
which withers before it grows up,
7 with which the reaper does not fill his hand
or the binder of sheaves his bosom,
8 while those who pass by do not say,
"The blessing of the LORD be upon you!
We bless you in the name of the LORD!"

*129.1
Ps 88.15;
Hos 2.15;
Ps 124.1
129.2
Mt 16.18

129.4
Ps 119.137

129.5
Mic 4.11;
Ps 71.13
129.6
Ps 37.2

129.8
Ruth 2.4;
Ps 118.26

128.1 This Psalm is one which has been thought by many to have been sung at Israelite marriages. It teaches that family prosperity depends on the blessing of God.

129.1 This Psalm was penned after the captivity began. The writer refers to the many tribulations endured by Israel even as far back as the bondage in Egypt.

A Song of Ascents.

I. *The soul that waits on God 130.1–8*

A. *The cry for help*

130 Out of the depths I cry to thee, O LORD!
2 Lord, hear my voice!
Let thy ears be attentive
    to the voice of my supplications!

3 If thou, O LORD, shouldst mark iniquities,
    Lord, who could stand?
4 But there is forgiveness with thee,
    that thou mayest be feared.

B. *The patient waiting*

5 I wait for the LORD, my soul waits,
    and in his word I hope;
6 my soul waits for the LORD
    more than watchmen for the morning,
    more than watchmen for the morning.

C. *Exhortation to hope*

7 O Israel, hope in the LORD!
    For with the LORD there is steadfast love,
    and with him is plenteous redemption.
8 And he will redeem Israel
    from all his iniquities.

A Song of Ascents. Of David.

I. *The song of a humble and a quiet heart 131.1–3*

131 O LORD, my heart is not lifted up,
    my eyes are not raised too high;
I do not occupy myself with things
    too great and too marvelous for me.
2 But I have calmed and quieted my soul,
    like a child quieted at its mother's breast;
    like a child that is quieted is my soul.

3 O Israel, hope in the LORD
    from this time forth and for evermore.

Margin references:

*130.1 Ps 42.7; 69.2
130.2 Ps 64.1; 2 Chr 6.40; Ps 28.2
130.3 Ps 76.7
130.4 Ex 34.7; Isa 55.7; 1 Ki 8.40; Jer 33.8
130.5 Ps 33.20; Isa 8.17; Ps 119.81
130.6 Ps 63.6; 119.147
130.7 Ps 131.3; Isa 55.7
130.8 Lk 1.68
*131.1 Ps 101.5; Isa 5.15; Rom 12.16
131.2 Ps 62.1; Mt 18.3; 1 Cor 14.20
131.3 Ps 130.7*

130.1 Man can expect no help apart from God; but no soul is beyond God's help. Each helpless soul should prayerfully seek the help of God for deliverance.

131.1 The humility of David is expressed by the absence of a proud heart, of the "high look" (*my eyes are not raised too high*), and of overweening ambition to strive after things beyond his ken and reach. Rather, he takes on the humility characteristic of a little child at its mother's breast. This is the opposite of the proud who are always fretful and discontented, never satisfied or even at rest.

A Song of Ascents.

I. *David and the ark of the* LORD *132.1–18*

A. *David's vow*

132 Remember, O LORD, in David's favor,
all the hardships he endured;
2 how he swore to the LORD
and vowed to the Mighty One of Jacob,
3 "I will not enter my house
or get into my bed;
4 I will not give sleep to my eyes
or slumber to my eyelids,
5 until I find a place for the LORD,
a dwelling place for the Mighty One of Jacob."

B. *The fulfilment of David's vow*

6 Lo, we heard of it in Ĕph'ráthàh,
we found it in the fields of Jā'ar.
7 "Let us go to his dwelling place;
let us worship at his footstool!"

8 Arise, O LORD, and go to thy resting place,
thou and the ark of thy might.
9 Let thy priests be clothed with righteousness,
and let thy saints shout for joy.
10 For thy servant David's sake
do not turn away the face of thy anointed one.

C. *The promise of the* LORD *to David and to Zion*

11 The LORD swore to David a sure oath
from which he will not turn back:
"One of the sons of your body
I will set on your throne.
12 If your sons keep my covenant
and my testimonies which I shall teach them,
their sons also for ever
shall sit upon your throne."

13 For the LORD has chosen Zion;
he has desired it for his habitation:
14 "This is my resting place for ever;
here I will dwell, for I have desired it.
15 I will abundantly bless her provisions;
I will satisfy her poor with bread.
16 Her priests I will clothe with salvation,
and her saints will shout for joy.
17 There I will make a horn to sprout for David;
I have prepared a lamp for my anointed.

132.2 Gen 49.24
132.4 Prov 6.4
132.5 Acts 7.46
*132.6 1 Sam 17.12; 7.1; 1 Chr 13.5
132.7 Ps 5.7; 99.5
132.8 Num 10.35; 2 Chr 6.41; Ps 78.61
132.9 ver 16; Job 29.14; Isa 61.10
132.11 Ps 89.3,4; 2 Sam 7.12; 2 Chr 6.16
132.12 Lk 1.32; Acts 2.30
132.13 Ps 48.1,2; 68.16
132.14 ver 8
132.15 Ps 147.14; 107.9
132.16 ver 9
132.17 Ezek 29.21; Lk 1.69; 1 Ki 11.36; 15.4; 2 Chr 21.7

132.6 *Ephrathah* means "fruitful land."
Although usually used of Bethlehem (Gen 35.19), here it appears to refer to Kiriath-jearim (1 Sam 7.1, 2).

132.18
Ps 35.26;
109.29

18 His enemies I will clothe with shame,
but upon himself his crown will shed its luster."

A Song of Ascents.

I. *Brotherly unity 133.1–3*

133.1
Gen 13.8;
Heb 13.1
*133.2
Ex 30.25;
39.24

133 Behold, how good and pleasant it is
when brothers dwell in unity!
2 It is like the precious oil upon the head,
running down upon the beard,
upon the beard of Aaron,
running down on the collar of his robes!

133.3
Deut 4.48;
Lev 25.21;
Deut 28.8;
Ps 42.8

3 It is like the dew of Hèrmòn,
which falls on the mountains of Zion!
For there the LORD has commanded the blessing,
life for evermore.

A Song of Ascents.

I. *An exhortation for the night watch 134.1–3*

*134.1
Ps 103.21;
135.1,2;
1 Chr 9.33

134 Come, bless the LORD,
all you servants of the LORD,
who stand by night in the house of the LORD!

134.2
Ps 28.2;
1 Tim 2.8

2 Lift up your hands to the holy place,
and bless the LORD!

134.3
Ps 124.8;
128.5

3 May the LORD bless you from Zion,
he who made heaven and earth!

I. *Praise to the LORD 135.1–21*

A. *The exhortation to praise*

135.1
Ps 113.1;
134.1

135 Praise the LORD.
Praise the name of the LORD,
give praise, O servants of the LORD,

135.2
Lk 2.37;
Ps 92.13

2 you that stand in the house of the LORD,
in the courts of the house of our God!

135.3
Ps 119.68;
147.1

3 Praise the LORD, for the LORD is good;
sing to his name, for he is gracious!

135.4
Deut 7.6,7;
10.15;
Ex 19.5;
1 Pet 2.9

4 For the LORD has chosen Jacob for himself,
Israel as his own possession.

B. *The greatness of the LORD*

135.5
Ps 48.1;
97.9

5 For I know that the LORD is great,
and that our Lord is above all gods.

135.6
Ps 115.3

6 Whatever the LORD pleases he does,

133.2 *precious oil* was used for anointing the priests.

134.1 The greeting is to the priests and Levites who had the night watch in the Temple.

in heaven and on earth,
in the seas and all deeps.
7 He it is who makes the clouds rise at the end of the earth,
who makes lightnings for the rain
and brings forth the wind from his storehouses.

135.7
Jer 10.13;
Job 28.25;
Zech 10.1;
Job 38.22

C. The deliverances of the LORD

8 He it was who smote the first-born of Egypt,
both of man and of beast;
9 who in thy midst, O Egypt,
sent signs and wonders
against Phạraōh and all his servants;
10 who smote many nations
and slew mighty kings,
11 Sīhȯn, king of the Ăm'ȯrītes,
and Og, king of Bāshản,
and all the kingdoms of Cānaản,
12 and gave their land as a heritage,
a heritage to his people Israel.

135.8
Ex 12.12;
Ps 78.51
135.9
Ps 78.43;
136.15
135.10
Num 21.24;
Ps 136.17
135.11
Num 21.21–
26,33–35;
Josh 12.7
135.12
Ps 78.55

D. The vindication of the LORD

13 Thy name, O LORD, endures for ever,
thy renown, O LORD, throughout all ages.
14 For the LORD will vindicate his people,
and have compassion on his servants.

135.13
Ex 3.15;
Ps 102.12
135.14
Deut 32.36;
Ps 106.45

E. The idolatry of the nations

15 The idols of the nations are silver and gold,
the work of men's hands.
16 They have mouths, but they speak not,
they have eyes, but they see not,
17 they have ears, but they hear not,
nor is there any breath in their mouths.
18 Like them be those who make them!—
yea, every one who trusts in them!

135.15
Ps 115.4–8

F. Concluding exhortation to praise

19 O house of Israel, bless the LORD!
O house of Aaron, bless the LORD!
20 O house of Lēvī, bless the LORD!
You that fear the LORD, bless the LORD!
21 Blessed be the LORD from Zion,
he who dwells in Jerusalem!
Praise the LORD!

135.19
Ps 115.9
135.20
Ps 118.4
135.21
Ps 134.3;
132.14

I. Praise to the God of eternal mercy 136.1–26

A. The exhortation to give thanks

136 O give thanks to the LORD, for he is good,
for his steadfast love endures for ever.

136.1
Ps 106.1;
107.1;
118.1;
1 Chr
16.34;
2 Chr 20.21

2 O give thanks to the God of gods,
  for his steadfast love endures for ever.
3 O give thanks to the Lord of lords,
  for his steadfast love endures for ever;

B. Praise to God the creator

4 to him who alone does great wonders,
  for his steadfast love endures for ever;
5 to him who by understanding made the heavens,
  for his steadfast love endures for ever;
6 to him who spread out the earth upon the waters,
  for his steadfast love endures for ever;
7 to him who made the great lights,
  for his steadfast love endures for ever;
8 the sun to rule over the day,
  for his steadfast love endures for ever;
9 the moon and stars to rule over the night,
  for his steadfast love endures for ever;

C. Praise to God the deliverer of Israel

10 to him who smote the first-born of Egypt,
  for his steadfast love endures for ever;
11 and brought Israel out from among them,
  for his steadfast love endures for ever;
12 with a strong hand and an outstretched arm,
  for his steadfast love endures for ever;
13 to him who divided the Red Sea in sunder,
  for his steadfast love endures for ever;
14 and made Israel pass through the midst of it,
  for his steadfast love endures for ever;
15 but overthrew Pharaōh and his host in the Red Sea,
  for his steadfast love endures for ever;
16 to him who led his people through the wilderness,
  for his steadfast love endures for ever;
17 to him who smote great kings,
  for his steadfast love endures for ever;
18 and slew famous kings,
  for his steadfast love endures for ever;
19 Sihón, king of the Ăm'órītes,
  for his steadfast love endures for ever;
20 and Ŏg, king of Bāshán,
  for his steadfast love endures for ever;
21 and gave their land as a heritage,
  for his steadfast love endures for ever;
22 a heritage to Israel his servant,
  for his steadfast love endures for ever.

D. Praise to the God of steadfast love

23 It is he who remembered us in our low estate,
  for his steadfast love endures for ever;
24 and rescued us from our foes,
  for his steadfast love endures for ever;

Margin references: 136.2 Deut 10.17; 136.4 Ps 72.18; 136.5 Gen 1.1; Prov 3.19; Jer 51.15; 136.6 Gen 1.9; Ps 24.2; Jer 10.12; 136.7 Gen 1.14,16; 136.8 Gen 1.16; 136.10 Ex 12.29; Ps 135.8; 136.11 Ex 12.51; 136.12 Ex 6.6; Ps 44.3; Deut 4.34; 136.13 Ex 14.21; Ps 78.13; 136.14 Ex 14.22; 136.15 Ex 14.27; Ps 135.9; 136.16 Ex 13.18; 15.22; Deut 8.15; 136.17 Ps 135.10-12; 136.21 Josh 12.1; 136.23 Ps 113.7; 136.24 Ps 107.2

25 he who gives food to all flesh,
     for his steadfast love endures for ever.

136.25
Ps 104.27;
145.15

E. *Closing thanksgiving*

26 O give thanks to the God of heaven,
     for his steadfast love endures for ever.

I. *A hymn of the exiles in Babylon 137.1–9*

A. *Their present plight*

137 By the waters*o* of Babylon,
          there we sat down and wept,
when we remembered Zion.
2 On the willows*p* there
     we hung up our lyres.
3 For there our captors
     required of us songs,
and our tormentors, mirth, saying,
"Sing us one of the songs of Zion!"

137.1
Ezek 1.1,3;
Neh 1.4

137.3
Ps 80.6

B. *Their remembrance of Zion*

4 How shall we sing the LORD's song
     in a foreign land?
5 If I forget you, O Jerusalem,
     let my right hand wither!
6 Let my tongue cleave to the roof of my mouth,
     if I do not remember you,
if I do not set Jerusalem
     above my highest joy!

137.6
Ezek 3.26

C. *Their cry for vengeance*

7 Remember, O LORD, against the Ē′dòmītes
     the day of Jerusalem,
how they said, "Rase it, rase it!
     Down to its foundations!"
8 O daughter of Babylon, you devastator!*q*
     Happy shall he be who requites you
     with what you have done to us!
9 Happy shall he be who takes your little ones
     and dashes them against the rock!

137.7
Jer 49.7;
Lam 4.22;
Ezek 25.12;
Obad 10–14

137.8
Isa 13.1,6;
Jer 25.12;
50.15;
Rev 18.6

137.9
2 Ki 8.12;
Isa 13.16

A Psalm of David.

I. *The LORD the faithful God 138.1–8*

A. *David's acknowledgment of God's faithfulness*

138 I give thee thanks, O LORD, with my whole heart;
          before the gods I sing thy praise;

138.1
Ps 111.1;
95.3; 96.4

o Heb *streams*   *p* Or *poplars*   *q* Or *you who are devastated*

138.2
Ps 28.2;
1 Ki 8.29,
30;
Isa 42.21

2 I bow down toward thy holy temple
  and give thanks to thy name for thy steadfast love and thy
    faithfulness;
for thou hast exalted above everything
  thy name and thy word.[r]

138.3
Ps 118.5;
28.7; 46.1

3 On the day I called, thou didst answer me,
  my strength of soul thou didst increase.[s]

B. *All the kings shall praise the* LORD

138.4
Ps 102.15

4 All the kings of the earth shall praise thee, O LORD,
  for they have heard the words of thy mouth;
5 and they shall sing of the ways of the LORD,
  for great is the glory of the LORD.

138.6
Ps 113.5,6;
Isa 57.15;
Prov 3.34;
Jas 4.6

6 For though the LORD is high, he regards the lowly;
  but the haughty he knows from afar.

C. *David's confidence in God's faithfulness*

138.7
Ps 23.3,4;
71.20;
Jer 51.25;
Ps 20.6

7 Though I walk in the midst of trouble,
  thou dost preserve my life;
thou dost stretch out thy hand against the wrath of my enemies,
  and thy right hand delivers me.

138.8
Ps 57.2;
Phil 1.6;
Ps 136.1;
27.9;
Job 10.3,8;
14.15

8 The LORD will fulfil his purpose for me;
  thy steadfast love, O LORD, endures for ever.
  Do not forsake the work of thy hands.

To the choirmaster. A Psalm of David.

I. *The prayer of a believing heart 139.1–24*

A. *The omniscient God*

*139.1
Ps 17.3;
Jer 12.3

139 O LORD, thou hast searched me and known me!
2 Thou knowest when I sit down and when I rise up;
  thou discernest my thoughts from afar.

139.2
2 Ki 19.27;
Mt 9.4;
Jn 2.24

3 Thou searchest out my path and my lying down,
  and art acquainted with all my ways.

139.3
Job 31.4

4 Even before a word is on my tongue,
  lo, O LORD, thou knowest it altogether.

139.4
Heb 4.13

5 Thou dost beset me behind and before,
  and layest thy hand upon me.

139.5
Ps 34.7;
Job 9.33

6 Such knowledge is too wonderful for me;
  it is high, I cannot attain it.

139.6
Rom 11.33;
Job 42.3

B. *The omnipresent God*

139.7
Jer 23.24;
Jon 1.3

7 Whither shall I go from thy Spirit?
  Or whither shall I flee from thy presence?

r Cn: Heb *thou hast exalted thy word above all thy name*
s Syr Compare Gk Tg: Heb *thou didst make me arrogant in my soul* with *strength*

139.1 In this Psalm, the omniscience and omnipresence of God are emphasized. Verses 1, 2, 4, 6 stress that God is all-knowing; 7–13 present God as being everywhere present and affirm that man cannot find a refuge too hidden or remote from His presence; 15, 16 deal with God's foreknowledge of men before they are fashioned in human form.

8 If I ascend to heaven, thou art there!
  If I make my bed in Shēōl, thou art there!
9 If I take the wings of the morning
  and dwell in the uttermost parts of the sea,
10 even there thy hand shall lead me,
  and thy right hand shall hold me.
11 If I say, "Let only darkness cover me,
  and the light about me be night,"
12 even the darkness is not dark to thee,
  the night is bright as the day;
  for darkness is as light with thee.

C. The God of creation

13 For thou didst form my inward parts,
  thou didst knit me together in my mother's womb.
14 I praise thee, for thou art fearful and wonderful.*
  Wonderful are thy works!
  Thou knowest me right well;
15   my frame was not hidden from thee,
  when I was being made in secret,
  intricately wrought in the depths of the earth.
16 Thy eyes beheld my unformed substance;
  in thy book were written, every one of them,
  the days that were formed for me,
  when as yet there was none of them.
17 How precious to me are thy thoughts, O God!
  How vast is the sum of them!
18 If I would count them, they are more than the sand.
  When I awake, I am still with thee.*

D. Concluding prayer for the wicked and for self

19 O that thou wouldst slay the wicked, O God,
  and that men of blood would depart from me,
20 men who maliciously defy thee,
  who lift themselves up against thee for evil!*
21 Do I not hate them that hate thee, O LORD?
  And do I not loathe them that rise up against thee?
22 I hate them with perfect hatred;
  I count them my enemies.
23 Search me, O God, and know my heart!
  Try me and know my thoughts!
24 And see if there be any wicked* way in me,
  and lead me in the way everlasting!*

139.8ff
Amos 9.2–4;
Job 26.6;
Prov 15.11

139.10
Ps 23.2,3

139.11
Job 22.13

139.12
Job 34.22;
Dan 2.22;
Heb 4.13

139.13ff
Ps 119.73;
Job 10.11

139.14
Ps 40.5

139.15
Job 10.8–10; Ps 63.9

139.17
Ps 40.5

139.19
Isa 11.4;
Ps 119.115

139.20
Jude 15

139.21
Ps 119.158

139.23
Job 31.6;
Ps 26.2;
Jer 11.20

139.24
Prov 15.9;
Ps 5.8;
143.10

t Cn Compare Gk Syr Jerome: Heb *fearful things I am wonderful*
u Or *were I to come to the end I would still be with thee*   *v* Cn: Heb uncertain
w Heb *hurtful*   *x* Or *the ancient way*. Compare Jer 6.16

139.8ff Even though the Psalmist speaks of God as being everywhere, yet he is not a pantheist. God is distinct from His creation. He fills His creation and sustains it, but He is independent of it and cannot be mingled with it.

139.13ff This God who is the creator also made man according to His own desire, under His inquiring eye, and by His own power. The marvelous body of man, his rational faculties, and the composite nature of his being—body and soul—show the work of God.

To the choirmaster. A Psalm of David.

I. *Prayer for protection against enemies 140.1–13*

A. *Petition for deliverance from the wicked*

<table>
<tr><td>140.1
Ps 17.13;
18.48</td><td>140 Deliver me, O LORD, from evil men;
    preserve me from violent men,</td></tr>
</table>

140.1
Ps 17.13;
18.48

140 Deliver me, O LORD, from evil men;
preserve me from violent men,

140.2
Ps 36.4;
56.6

2 who plan evil things in their heart,
and stir up wars continually.

140.3
Ps 57.4;
58.4;
Jas 3.8

3 They make their tongue sharp as a serpent's,
and under their lips is the poison of vipers.   *Sēlàh*

140.4
Ps 71.4

4 Guard me, O LORD, from the hands of the wicked;
preserve me from violent men,
who have planned to trip up my feet.

140.5
Ps 35.7;
31.4;
141.9

5 Arrogant men have hidden a trap for me,
and with cords they have spread a net,*y*
by the wayside they have set snares for me.   *Sēlàh*

B. *A cry for God to hear*

140.6
Ps 16.2;
143.1;
116.1

6 I say to the LORD, Thou art my God;
give ear to the voice of my supplications, O LORD!

140.7
Ps 28.8;
144.10

7 O LORD, my Lord, my strong deliverer,
thou hast covered my head in the day of battle.

140.8
Ps 112.10;
10.2

8 Grant not, O LORD, the desires of the wicked;
do not further his evil plot!   *Sēlàh*

C. *A prayer of imprecation*

140.9
Ps 7.16

9 Those who surround me lift up their head,*z*
let the mischief of their lips overwhelm them!

140.10
Ps 11.6;
21.9; 36.12

10 Let burning coals fall upon them!
Let them be cast into pits, no more to rise!

140.11
Ps 34.21

11 Let not the slanderer be established in the land;
let evil hunt down the violent man speedily!

D. *Expression of confidence in the LORD*

140.12
Ps 9.4;
35.10

12 I know that the LORD maintains the cause of the afflicted,
and executes justice for the needy.

140.13
Ps 97.12;
11.7

13 Surely the righteous shall give thanks to thy name;
the upright shall dwell in thy presence.

A Psalm of David.

I. *The conduct of a good man in trouble 141.1–10*

A. *The appeal to the LORD*

141.1
Ps 22.19;
70.5;
143.1

141 I call upon thee, O LORD; make haste to me!
Give ear to my voice, when I call to thee!

y Or *they have spread cords as a net*
z Cn Compare Gk: Heb *those who surround me are uplifted in head*

2 Let my prayer be counted as incense before thee,
    and the lifting up of my hands as an evening sacrifice!

141.2
Rev 5.8;
8.3;
Ps 134.2;
Ex 29.39

B. *The prayer for an upright heart*

3 Set a guard over my mouth, O LORD,
    keep watch over the door of my lips!
4 Incline not my heart to any evil,
    to busy myself with wicked deeds
in company with men who work iniquity;
    and let me not eat of their dainties!

141.4
Ps 119.36;
Prov 23.6

C. *The end of the wicked*

5 Let a good man strike or rebuke me in kindness,
    but let the oil of the wicked never anoint my head;*a*
    for my prayer is continually*b* against their wicked deeds.
6 When they are given over to those who shall condemn them,
    then they shall learn that the word of the LORD is true.
7 As a rock which one cleaves and shatters on the land,
    so shall their bones be strewn at the mouth of Shēōl.*c*

141.5
Prov 9.8;
Ps 23.5;
35.14

141.7
Ps 53.5

D. *His eyes are upon God*

8 But my eyes are toward thee, O LORD God;
    in thee I seek refuge; leave me not defenseless!
9 Keep me from the trap which they have laid for me,
    and from the snares of evildoers!
10 Let the wicked together fall into their own nets,
    while I escape.

141.8
Ps 25.15;
2.12; 27.9
141.9
Ps 38.12;
140.5
141.10
Ps 35.8

A Măskĭl of David, when he was in the cave. A Prayer.

I. *The prisoner's prayer 142.1–7*

A. *The appeal of the prisoner*

142 I cry with my voice to the LORD,
    with my voice I make supplication to the LORD,
2 I pour out my complaint before him,
    I tell my trouble before him.
3 When my spirit is faint,
    thou knowest my way!

142.1
Ps 77.1;
30.8
142.2
Isa 26.16
142.3
Ps 143.4;
140.5

B. *The plight of the prisoner*

In the path where I walk
    they have hidden a trap for me.
4 I look to the right and watch,*d*
    but there is none who takes notice of me;
no refuge remains to me,
    no man cares for me.

142.4
Ps 31.11;
Job 11.20;
Jer 30.17

---

a Gk: Heb obscure   *b* Cn: Heb *for continually and my prayer*
c The Hebrew of verses 5–7 is obscure   *d* Or *Look to the right and watch*

C. *The prayer for deliverance*

142.5
Ps 46.1;
16.5; 27.13

5 I cry to thee, O Lᴏʀᴅ;
  I say, Thou art my refuge,
    my portion in the land of the living.

142.6
Ps 17.1;
79.8;
116.6

6 Give heed to my cry;
    for I am brought very low!

Deliver me from my persecutors;
    for they are too strong for me!

142.7
Ps 146.7;
13.6

7 Bring me out of prison,
    that I may give thanks to thy name!
The righteous will surround me;
    for thou wilt deal bountifully with me.

A Psalm of David.

I. *The prayer of a soul in distress 143.1–12*

A. *The complaint of the Psalmist*

143.1
Ps 140.6;
89.1,2;
71.2

143 Hear my prayer, O Lᴏʀᴅ;
        give ear to my supplications!
In thy faithfulness answer me, in thy righteousness!

143.2
Job 14.3;
4.17;
Ps 130.3;
Ecc 7.20;
Rom 3.20

2 Enter not into judgment with thy servant;
    for no man living is righteous before thee.

3 For the enemy has pursued me;
    he has crushed my life to the ground;
    he has made me sit in darkness like those long dead.

143.4
Ps 142.3;
Lam 3.11

4 Therefore my spirit faints within me;
    my heart within me is appalled.

143.5
Ps 77.5;
77.12;
105.2

5 I remember the days of old,
    I meditate on all that thou hast done;
    I muse on what thy hands have wrought.

143.6
Ps 88.9;
63.1

6 I stretch out my hands to thee;
    my soul thirsts for thee like a parched land.   *Sēlâh*

B. *The prayer for deliverance*

143.7
Ps 69.17;
27.9; 28.1

7 Make haste to answer me, O Lᴏʀᴅ!
    My spirit fails!
Hide not thy face from me,
    lest I be like those who go down to the Pit.

143.8
Ps 90.14;
25.2;
27.11; 25.1

8 Let me hear in the morning of thy steadfast love,
    for in thee I put my trust.
Teach me the way I should go,
    for to thee I lift up my soul.

143.9
Ps 31.15
143.10
Ps 25.4,5;
Neh 9.20;
Ps 23.3

9 Deliver me, O Lᴏʀᴅ, from my enemies!
    I have fled to thee for refuge!ᵉ
10 Teach me to do thy will,

---

e One Heb Ms Gk: Heb *to thee I have hidden*

for thou art my God!
Let thy good spirit lead me
  on a level path!

11 For thy name's sake, O LORD, preserve my life!
  In thy righteousness bring me out of trouble!
12 And in thy steadfast love cut off my enemies,
  and destroy all my adversaries,
  for I am thy servant.

143.11
Ps 119.25;
31.1

143.12
Ps 54.5;
52.5;
116.16

A Psalm of David.

I. The warrior's Psalm 144.1–15

A. Praise to a great God

144 Blessed be the LORD, my rock,
  who trains my hands for war,
  and my fingers for battle;
2 my rock^f and my fortress,
  my stronghold and my deliverer,
  my shield and he in whom I take refuge,
  who subdues the peoples under him.^{g}

144.1
Ps 18.2,34

144.2
Ps 91.2;
59.9; 84.9;
18.39

3 O LORD, what is man that thou dost regard him,
  or the son of man that thou dost think of him?
4 Man is like a breath,
  his days are like a passing shadow.

144.3
Ps 8.4;
Heb 2.6

144.4
Ps 39.11;
102.11

B. Prayer for help and deliverance

5 Bow thy heavens, O LORD, and come down!
  Touch the mountains that they smoke!
6 Flash forth the lightning and scatter them,
  send out thy arrows and rout them!
7 Stretch forth thy hand from on high,
  rescue me and deliver me from the many waters,
  from the hand of aliens,
8 whose mouths speak lies,
  and whose right hand is a right hand of falsehood.

144.5
Ps 18.9;
Isa 64.1;
Ps 104.32

144.6
Ps 18.13,14;
7.13

144.7
Ps 69.1,14;
18.44

144.8
Ps 12.2;
Isa 44.20

9 I will sing a new song to thee, O God;
  upon a ten-stringed harp I will play to thee,
10 who givest victory to kings,
  who rescuest David thy^h servant.
11 Rescue me from the cruel sword,
  and deliver me from the hand of aliens,
whose mouths speak lies,
  and whose right hand is a right hand of falsehood.

144.9
Ps 33.2,3

144.10
Ps 18.50;
140.7

144.11
Ps 12.2;
Isa 44.20

C. Prayer for prosperity for the people of God

12 May our sons in their youth

144.12
Ps 128.3

^{f} With 18.2 2 Sam. 22.2: Heb _my steadfast love_
^{g} Another reading is _my people under me_ ^{h} Heb _his_

be like plants full grown,
 our daughters like corner pillars
  cut for the structure of a palace;
13 may our garners be full,
 providing all manner of store;
may our sheep bring forth thousands
 and ten thousands in our fields;
14 may our cattle be heavy with young,
 suffering no mischance or failure in bearing;
may there be no cry of distress in our streets!

144.15
Ps 33.12

15 Happy the people to whom such blessings fall!
 Happy the people whose God is the LORD!

A Song of Praise. Of David.

I. *The goodness of God 145.1–21*

A. *The greatness of the* LORD

145.1
Ps 30.1;
5.2; 34.1

145 I will extol thee, my God and King,
  and bless thy name for ever and ever.

145.2
Ps 71.6

2 Every day I will bless thee,
 and praise thy name for ever and ever.

145.3
Ps 96.4;
Job 5.9;
Rom 11.33

3 Great is the LORD, and greatly to be praised,
 and his greatness is unsearchable.

145.4
Isa 38.19

4 One generation shall laud thy works to another,
 and shall declare thy mighty acts.

145.5
ver 12;
Ps 119.27

5 On the glorious splendor of thy majesty,
 and on thy wondrous works, I will meditate.

145.6
Ps 66.3;
Deut 32.3

6 Men shall proclaim the might of thy terrible acts,
 and I will declare thy greatness.

145.7
Isa 63.7;
Ps 51.14

7 They shall pour forth the fame of thy abundant goodness,
 and shall sing aloud of thy righteousness.

B. *The graciousness of the* LORD

145.8
Ex 34.6;
Ps 86.5,15

8 The LORD is gracious and merciful,
 slow to anger and abounding in steadfast love.

145.9
Ps 100.5;
Nah 1.7

9 The LORD is good to all,
 and his compassion is over all that he has made.

145.10
Ps 19.1;
68.26

10 All thy works shall give thanks to thee, O LORD,
 and all thy saints shall bless thee!
11 They shall speak of the glory of thy kingdom,
 and tell of thy power,

145.12
Ps 105.1;
ver 5

12 to make known to the sons of men thy*h* mighty deeds,
 and the glorious splendor of thy*h* kingdom.

145.13
Ps 146.10;
2 Pet 1.11

13 Thy kingdom is an everlasting kingdom,
 and thy dominion endures throughout all generations.

The LORD is faithful in all his words,
 and gracious in all his deeds.*i*

---

h Heb *his* *i* These two lines are supplied by one Hebrew Ms, Gk and Syr

C. *The goodness of the* LORD

14 The LORD upholds all who are falling,
    and raises up all who are bowed down.
15 The eyes of all look to thee,
    and thou givest them their food in due season.
16 Thou openest thy hand,
    thou satisfiest the desire of every living thing.
17 The LORD is just in all his ways,
    and kind in all his doings.
18 The LORD is near to all who call upon him,
    to all who call upon him in truth.
19 He fulfils the desire of all who fear him,
    he also hears their cry, and saves them.
20 The LORD preserves all who love him;
    but all the wicked he will destroy.

21 My mouth will speak the praise of the LORD,
    and let all flesh bless his holy name for ever and ever.

I. *An exhortation to trust God* 146.1–10

A. *The vanity of trusting men*

146 Praise the LORD!
    Praise the LORD, O my soul!
2 I will praise the LORD as long as I live;
    I will sing praises to my God while I have being.

3 Put not your trust in princes,
    in a son of man, in whom there is no help.
4 When his breath departs he returns to his earth;
    on that very day his plans perish.

B. *The wisdom of trusting God*

5 Happy is he whose help is the God of Jacob,
    whose hope is in the LORD his God,
6 who made heaven and earth,
    the sea, and all that is in them;
who keeps faith for ever;
7   who executes justice for the oppressed;
    who gives food to the hungry.

The LORD sets the prisoners free;
8   the LORD opens the eyes of the blind.
The LORD lifts up those who are bowed down;
    the LORD loves the righteous.
9 The LORD watches over the sojourners,
    he upholds the widow and the fatherless;
    but the way of the wicked he brings to ruin.

10 The LORD will reign for ever,
    thy God, O Zion, to all generations.
    Praise the LORD!

Marginal references

145.14 Ps 37.24; 146.8
145.15 Ps 104.27
145.16 Ps 124.28
145.18 Deut 4.7; Jn 4.24
145.19 Ps 37.4; Prov 15.29
145.20 Ps 31.23; 97.10; 9.5
145.21 Ps 71.8; 65.2; ver 1,2
146.1 Ps 103.1
146.2 Ps 104.33
146.3 Ps 118.8; Isa 2.22
146.4 Ps 104.29; Ecc 12.7; Ps 33.10
146.5 Ps 144.15; 71.5
146.6 Ps 115.15; Acts 14.15; Ps 117.2
146.7 Ps 103.6; 107.9; 68.6
146.8 Mt 9.30; Jn 9.7; Ps 145.14; 11.7
146.9 Ex 22.21; Deut 10.18; Ps 68.5; 147.6
146.10 Ex 15.18; Ps 10.16; Rev 11.15

I. The LORD of might and grace 147.1–20

A. The God of might in history

147.1
Ps 135.3;
33.1

★147.2
Ps 102.16;
Deut 30.3

147.3
Isa 61.1;
30.26

★147.4
Isa 40.26

147.5
Ps 48.1;
Isa 40.28

147.6
Ps 146.8,9

147 Praise the LORD!
For it is good to sing praises to our God;
for he is gracious, and a song of praise is seemly.

2 The LORD builds up Jerusalem;
he gathers the outcasts of Israel.

3 He heals the brokenhearted,
and binds up their wounds.

4 He determines the number of the stars,
he gives to all of them their names.

5 Great is our LORD, and abundant in power;
his understanding is beyond measure.

6 The LORD lifts up the downtrodden,
he casts the wicked to the ground.

B. The God who sustains life

147.7
Ps 33.2

147.8
Job 38.26;
Ps 104.13

147.9
Ps 104.27;
Job 38.41

147.10
Ps 33.16,17;
1 Sam 16.7

148.11
Ps 102.15

7 Sing to the LORD with thanksgiving;
make melody to our God upon the lyre!

8 He covers the heavens with clouds,
he prepares rain for the earth,
he makes grass grow upon the hills.

9 He gives to the beasts their food,
and to the young ravens which cry.

10 His delight is not in the strength of the horse,
nor his pleasure in the legs of a man;

11 but the LORD takes pleasure in those who fear him,
in those who hope in his steadfast love.

C. Israel exhorted to praise God

12 Praise the LORD, O Jerusalem!
Praise your God, O Zion!

147.13
Ps 37.26

147.14
Isa 60.17;
Ps 132.15

147.15
Job 37.12;
Ps 104.4

147.16
Job 37.6;
38.29

147.18
Ps 33.9;
107.25

147.19
Deut 33.2;
Mal 4.4

147.20
Deut 4.32

13 For he strengthens the bars of your gates;
he blesses your sons within you.

14 He makes peace in your borders;
he fills you with the finest of the wheat.

15 He sends forth his command to the earth;
his word runs swiftly.

16 He gives snow like wool;
he scatters hoarfrost like ashes.

17 He casts forth his ice like morsels;
who can stand before his cold?

18 He sends forth his word, and melts them;
he makes his wind blow, and the waters flow.

19 He declares his word to Jacob,
his statutes and ordinances to Israel.

20 He has not dealt thus with any other nation;
they do not know his ordinances.
Praise the LORD!

147.2 See Neh 12.27 in this connection.   **147.4** God has infinite power and knowledge.

I. Nature's praise of the LORD 148.1–14

A. The heavens to praise the LORD

148 Praise the LORD!
Praise the LORD from the heavens,
praise him in the heights!
2 Praise him, all his angels,
praise him, all his host!

3 Praise him, sun and moon,
praise him, all you shining stars!
4 Praise him, you highest heavens,
and you waters above the heavens!

5 Let them praise the name of the LORD!
For he commanded and they were created.
6 And he established them for ever and ever;
he fixed their bounds which cannot be passed.*j*

B. The earth to praise the LORD

7 Praise the LORD from the earth,
you sea monsters and all deeps,
8 fire and hail, snow and frost,
stormy wind fulfilling his command!

9 Mountains and all hills,
fruit trees and all cedars!
10 Beasts and all cattle,
creeping things and flying birds!

11 Kings of the earth and all peoples,
princes and all rulers of the earth!
12 Young men and maidens together,
old men and children!

13 Let them praise the name of the LORD,
for his name alone is exalted;
his glory is above earth and heaven.
14 He has raised up a horn for his people,
praise for all his saints,
for the people of Israel who are near to him.
Praise the LORD!

I. The LORD'S love of Israel 149.1–9

A. Exhortation to sing a new song

149 Praise the LORD!
Sing to the LORD a new song,
his praise in the assembly of the faithful!
2 Let Israel be glad in his Maker,
let the sons of Zion rejoice in their King!

j Or *he set a law which cannot pass away*

148.2
Ps 103.20,
21

148.4
1 Ki 8.27;
Gen 1.7

148.5
Gen 1.1;
Ps 33.6,9
148.6
Ps 89.37;
Jer 33.25;
Job 38.33

148.7
Ps 74.13

148.8
Ps 147.15–
18

148.9
Isa 44.23;
49.13;
55.12

148.13
Ps 8.1;
Isa 12.4;
Ps 113.4
148.14
Ps 75.10;
Deut 10.21;
Eph 2.17

149.1
Ps 33.3;
35.18

149.2
Ps 95.6;
47.6

149.3
Ps 150.4;
81.2
149.4
Ps 35.27;
132.16

3 Let them praise his name with dancing,
  making melody to him with timbrel and lyre!
4 For the LORD takes pleasure in his people;
  he adorns the humble with victory.

B. *Exhortation to wreak vengeance on the nations*

149.5
Ps 132.16;
Job 35.10
149.6
Ps 66.17;
Heb 4.12;
Rev 1.16

5 Let the faithful exult in glory;
  let them sing for joy on their couches.
6 Let the high praises of God be in their throats
  and two-edged swords in their hands,
7 to wreak vengeance on the nations
  and chastisement on the peoples,
8 to bind their kings with chains
  and their nobles with fetters of iron,

149.9
Ezek 28.26;
Ps 148.14

9 to execute on them the judgment written!
  This is glory for all his faithful ones.
  Praise the LORD!

I. *Let everything praise the* LORD *150.1–6*

150.1
Ps 102.19;
19.1

150 Praise the LORD!
  Praise God in his sanctuary;
  praise him in his mighty firmament!

150.2
Ps 145.5,6;
Deut 3.24

2 Praise him for his mighty deeds;
  praise him according to his exceeding greatness!

150.3
Ps 149.3

3 Praise him with trumpet sound;
  praise him with lute and harp!

150.4
Ex 15.20;
Isa 38.20
150.5
1 Chr 13.8;
15.16

4 Praise him with timbrel and dance;
  praise him with strings and pipe!
5 Praise him with sounding cymbals;
  praise him with loud clashing cymbals!

150.6
Ps 145.21

6 Let everything that breathes praise the LORD!
  Praise the LORD!

INTRODUCTION TO
THE PROVERBS

Authorship and Background: Solomon was the author of much of the Book of Proverbs. The book itself, however, does not derive completely from Solomon's day. Some of the proverbs are said to be "the words of the wise" (22.17; 24.23); others were copied out by the scribes of Hezekiah's day, and the last two chapters of the book were composed by Agur and Lemuel. Thus the final arrangement of the book cannot be dated before 700 B.C. In 1 Ki 4.30, Solomon's wisdom is compared with that of Egypt and the "people of the east." Archaeology has brought to light a large body of wisdom literature from the ancient Near East. The Egyptian "Wisdom of Amenemope" has many parallels to the section of Proverbs (22.17—24.23) called "the words of the wise."

Characteristics: A proverb is a short, pithy saying centering in an antithesis or comparison. There is no necessary connection between the proverbs in the order in which they are given. They are aimed primarily at giving an outline of ethical regulations for daily life. The sayings are of practical import and cover a diversity of subjects such as knowledge, morality, chastity, control of the tongue, association with others, laziness, and justice. The contents do not yield to an orderly analysis. The book is cast in poetic form, usually in couplets. The sayings are a distillation of the wisdom of that age. There are stern warnings against sin, and ultimate punishment is promised. The source of wisdom is "the fear of the LORD."

Contents:

I.   Wisdom. 1.1—9.18: Introduction. Wisdom is to be sought. Listeners are exhorted to seek it. The benefits and blessings of wisdom are described. It is commended to students. Marriage is commended and warnings against licentiousness, and exhortation to faithfulness follow. Warnings about suretyship, indolence, perversity, and the seven sins. Warnings against adultery. Men are exhorted to follow wisdom which occupies an exalted position. Wisdom and folly are contrasted.

II.   Proverbs of Solomon. 10.1—22.16: The rewards of righteous and unrighteous living. Certain aspects of wickedness are dealt with. The conduct of good and bad men contrasted. Conduct and paternal discipline. The fear of God in the life of man. The secret of the happy. How God watches over life. The perils and blessings of life described. Thumbnail sketches in character. Sundry teachings: wine and strong drink; hearing ear and seeing eye; deceit, the spirit of man. Man finds no victory apart from God. The law of cause and effect stated.

III.   Sundry sayings. 22.17—24.34: Things men should avoid: exploiting the poor; temper; suretyship. Instruction on table manners, miserli-

ness, the rights of the helpless. Folly and wisdom are compared. Sayings of the wise.

IV. Miscellaneous sayings of Solomon. 25.1—29.27: Law courts and litigation. Fools and scoundrels described; sluggards. Human relationships. Conduct in the light of pure religion. God and society; rulers and justice.

V. The words of Agur. 30.1–33: Agur records his personal reflections on life. His varied sayings: unfilial conduct; the four ways; the four intolerable things; the four tiny things; the four comely things; the closing admonition.

VI. The words of Lemuel: the folly of lust and strong drink. 31.1–9: The duties of kingship; warnings against lust and intemperance. He urges righteous rule and justice for the needy.

VII. The virtuous woman. 31.10–31: The perfect wife and mother is praised by her husband and children.

THE PROVERBS

I. *Wisdom 1.1–9.18*

A. *Authorship*

1 The proverbs of Solomon, son of David, king of Israel:

*1.1
1 Ki 4.32;
Ecc 12.9

B. *The purpose*

2 That men may know wisdom and instruction,
   understand words of insight,
3 receive instruction in wise dealing,
   righteousness, justice, and equity;
4 that prudence may be given to the simple,
   knowledge and discretion to the youth—
5 the wise man also may hear and increase in learning,
   and the man of understanding acquire skill,
6 to understand a proverb and a figure,
   the words of the wise and their riddles.

1.3
Prov 19.20;
2.9
1.4
Prov 8.5,12;
2.10,11
1.5
Prov 9.9;
14.6
1.6
Ps 78.2

C. *The major theme*

7 The fear of the LORD is the beginning of knowledge;
   fools despise wisdom and instruction.

1.7
Job 28.28;
Ps 111.10;
Ecc 12.13

D. *Warnings against violence*

8 Hear, my son, your father's instruction,
   and reject not your mother's teaching;
9 for they are a fair garland for your head,
   and pendants for your neck.
10 My son, if sinners entice you,
   do not consent.
11 If they say, "Come with us, let us lie in wait for blood,
   let us wantonly ambush the innocent;
12 like Sheōl let us swallow them alive
   and whole, like those who go down to the Pit;
13 we shall find all precious goods,
   we shall fill our houses with spoil;
14 throw in your lot among us,
   we will all have one purse"—
15 my son, do not walk in the way with them,
   hold back your foot from their paths;
16 for their feet run to evil,
   and they make haste to shed blood.
17 For in vain is a net spread
   in the sight of any bird;
18 but these men lie in wait for their own blood,
   they set an ambush for their own lives.
19 Such are the ways of all who get gain by violence;
   it takes away the life of its possessors.

1.8
Prov 4.1;
6.20
1.9
Prov 4.9;
Gen 41.42
1.10
Deut 13.8;
Eph 5.11
1.11
Prov 12.6;
ver 18
1.12
Ps 124.3;
28.1
1.15
Ps 1.1;
119.101
1.16
Isa 59.7
1.19
Prov 15.27

1.1 *The proverbs of Solomon.* Although Solomon is credited with the proverbs, not all of them originated with him. (See Introduction for authorship and background.)

E. *Warning against the neglect of wisdom*

1.20
Prov 8.1

20 Wisdom cries aloud in the street;
  in the markets she raises her voice;
21 on the top of the walls*a* she cries out;
  at the entrance of the city gates she speaks:

1.22
ver 4.32;
Ps 1.1;
ver 29

22 "How long, O simple ones, will you love being simple?
  How long will scoffers delight in their scoffing
    and fools hate knowledge?

1.23
Joel 2.28

23 Give heed*b* to my reproof;
  behold, I will pour out my thoughts*c* to you;
  I will make my words known to you.

1.24
Isa 65.12;
Zech 7.11;
Rom 10.21

24 Because I have called and you refused to listen,
  have stretched out my hand and no one has heeded,

1.25
Ps 107.11;
Lk 7.30;
Prov 15.10

25 and you have ignored all my counsel
  and would have none of my reproof,

1.26
Ps 2.4;
Prov 6.15;
10.24

26 I also will laugh at your calamity;
  I will mock when panic strikes you,
27 when panic strikes you like a storm,
  and your calamity comes like a whirlwind,
  when distress and anguish come upon you.

1.28
Isa 1.15;
Ezek 8.18;
Mic 3.4;
Zech 7.13

28 Then they will call upon me, but I will not answer;
  they will seek me diligently but will not find me.
29 Because they hated knowledge
  and did not choose the fear of the LORD,

1.30
Ps 81.11

30 would have none of my counsel,
  and despised all my reproof,

1.31
Job 4.8;
Prov 14.14;
Isa 3.11;
Jer 6.19

31 therefore they shall eat the fruit of their way
  and be sated with their own devices.
32 For the simple are killed by their turning away,
  and the complacence of fools destroys them;

1.32
Jer 2.19

1.33
Ps 25.12

33 but he who listens to me will dwell secure
  and will be at ease, without dread of evil."

F. *The reward of seeking wisdom*

2.1
Prov 4.10

2 My son, if you receive my words
  and treasure up my commandments with you,

2.2
Prov 3.1

2 making your ear attentive to wisdom
  and inclining your heart to understanding;
3 yes, if you cry out for insight
  and raise your voice for understanding,

2.4
Prov 3.14;
Mt 13.44

4 if you seek it like silver
  and search for it as for hidden treasures;

2.5
Prov 1.7

5 then you will understand the fear of the LORD
  and find the knowledge of God.

2.6
1 Ki 3.9,12;
Jas 1.5

6 For the LORD gives wisdom;
  from his mouth come knowledge and understanding;

2.7
Ps 84.11

7 he stores up sound wisdom for the upright;
  he is a shield to those who walk in integrity,

2.8
1 Sam 2.9;
Ps 66.9

8 guarding the paths of justice
  and preserving the way of his saints.

2.9
Prov 8.20;
4.18

9 Then you will understand righteousness and justice
  and equity, every good path;

a Heb uncertain   *b* Heb *Turn*   *c* Heb *spirit*

10 for wisdom will come into your heart,
 and knowledge will be pleasant to your soul;
11 discretion will watch over you;
 understanding will guard you;
12 delivering you from the way of evil,
 from men of perverted speech,
13 who forsake the paths of uprightness
 to walk in the ways of darkness,
14 who rejoice in doing evil
 and delight in the perverseness of evil;
15 men whose paths are crooked,
 and who are devious in their ways.

16 You will be saved from the loose[d] woman,
 from the adventuress[e] with her smooth words,
17 who forsakes the companion of her youth
 and forgets the covenant of her God;
18 for her house sinks down to death,
 and her paths to the shades;
19 none who go to her come back
 nor do they regain the paths of life.

G. Walking in the way of wisdom

20 So you will walk in the way of good men
 and keep to the paths of the righteous.
21 For the upright will inhabit the land,
 and men of integrity will remain in it;
22 but the wicked will be cut off from the land,
 and the treacherous will be rooted out of it.

H. The blessing of wisdom

3 My son, do not forget my teaching,
 but let your heart keep my commandments;
2 for length of days and years of life
 and abundant welfare will they give you.

3 Let not loyalty and faithfulness forsake you;
 bind them about your neck,
 write them on the tablet of your heart.
4 So you will find favor and good repute[f]
 in the sight of God and man.

5 Trust in the LORD with all your heart,
 and do not rely on your own insight.
6 In all your ways acknowledge him,
 and he will make straight your paths.
7 Be not wise in your own eyes;
 fear the LORD, and turn away from evil.
8 It will be healing to your flesh[g]
 and refreshment[h] to your bones.

---

d Heb strange   e Heb foreign woman
f Cn: Heb understanding
g Heb navel   h Or medicine

2.10	Prov 14.33; 22.18
2.11	Prov 6.22
2.13	Jn 3.19
2.14	Prov 10.23; Jer 11.15
2.15	Ps 125.5
2.16	Prov 6.24; 23.27
2.17	Mal 2.14,15
2.18	Prov 7.27
2.21	Ps 37.29; 28.10
2.22	Ps 37.38; Deut 28.63
3.1	Prov 4.5; Ex 20.6; Deut 30.16
3.2	Prov 4.10; Ps 119.165
3.3	2 Sam 15.20; Prov 1.9; 7.3
3.4	Prov 8.5; Ps 111.10
3.5	Ps 37.3,5; Jer 9.23
3.6	1 Chr 28.9; Isa 45.13
3.7	Rom 12.16; Prov 16.6
3.8	Job 21.24

3.9 Isa 43.23; Ex 23.19	9 Honor the LORD with your substance and with the first fruits of all your produce;
3.10 Deut 28.8	10 then your barns will be filled with plenty, and your vats will be bursting with wine.
3.11 Heb 12.5,6	11 My son, do not despise the LORD's discipline or be weary of his reproof,
3.12 Deut 8.5	12 for the LORD reproves him whom he loves, as a father the son in whom he delights.

I. Wisdom more precious than wealth

3.13 Prov 8.32, 34	13 Happy is the man who finds wisdom, and the man who gets understanding,
3.14 Job 28.13; Prov 8.10, 19	14 for the gain from it is better than gain from silver and its profit better than gold.
3.15 Job 28.18; Prov 8.11	15 She is more precious than jewels, and nothing you desire can compare with her.
3.16 Prov 8.18	16 Long life is in her right hand; in her left hand are riches and honor.
3.17 Prov 16.7	17 Her ways are ways of pleasantness, and all her paths are peace.
3.18 Prov 11.30; Gen 2.9	18 She is a tree of life to those who lay hold of her; those who hold her fast are called happy.
3.19 Ps 104.24	19 The LORD by wisdom founded the earth; by understanding he established the heavens;
3.20 Gen 7.11; Job 36.28	20 by his knowledge the deeps broke forth, and the clouds drop down the dew.

J. The wise inherit honor

	21 My son, keep sound wisdom and discretion; let them not escape from your sight,[i]
3.22 Prov 4.22; 1.9	22 and they will be life for your soul and adornment for your neck.
3.23 Prov 4.12	23 Then you will walk on your way securely and your foot will not stumble.
3.24 Ps 3.5	24 If you sit down,[j] you will not be afraid; when you lie down, your sleep will be sweet.
3.25 Ps 91.5; Job 5.21	25 Do not be afraid of sudden panic, or of the ruin[k] of the wicked, when it comes;
	26 for the LORD will be your confidence and will keep your foot from being caught.
3.27 Rom 13.7; Gal 6.10	27 Do not withhold good from those to whom it[l] is due, when it is in your power to do it.
3.28 Lev 19.13	28 Do not say to your neighbor, "Go, and come again, tomorrow I will give it"—when you have it with you.
3.29 Prov 14.22	29 Do not plan evil against your neighbor who dwells trustingly beside you.
3.30 Rom 12.18	30 Do not contend with a man for no reason, when he has done you no harm.

i Reversing the order of the clauses j Gk: Heb lie down k Heb storm
l Heb Do not withhold good from its owners

31 Do not envy a man of violence
    and do not choose any of his ways;   *3.31*
Ps 37.1;
Prov 24.1
32 for the perverse man is an abomination to the LORD,
    but the upright are in his confidence.   *3.32*
Prov 11.20;
Ps 25.14
33 The LORD'S curse is on the house of the wicked,
    but he blesses the abode of the righteous.   *3.33*
Deut 11.28;
Mal 2.2;
Job 8.6
34 Toward the scorners he is scornful,
    but to the humble he shows favor.   *3.34*
Jas 4.6;
1 Pet 5.5
35 The wise will inherit honor,
    but fools get*m* disgrace.

K. *Admonitions of a father to his son*

1. *The command to obtain wisdom*

4 Hear, O sons, a father's instruction,
    and be attentive, that you may gain*n* insight;   *4.1*
Prov 1.8;
2.2
2 for I give you good precepts:
    do not forsake my teaching.
3 When I was a son with my father,
    tender, the only one in the sight of my mother,   *4.3*
1 Chr 22.5
4 he taught me, and said to me,   *4.4*
1 Chr 28.9;
Prov 7.2
  "Let your heart hold fast my words;
    keep my commandments, and live;
5 do not forget, and do not turn away from the words of my mouth.   *4.5*
ver 7;
Prov 16.16
  Get wisdom; get insight.*o*
6 Do not forsake her, and she will keep you;   *4.6*
2 Thess 2.10
    love her, and she will guard you.
7 The beginning of wisdom is this: Get wisdom,   *4.7*
Prov 23.23
    and whatever you get, get insight.
8 Prize her highly,*p* and she will exalt you;   *4.8*
1 Sam 2.30
    she will honor you if you embrace her.
9 She will place on your head a fair garland;   *4.9*
Prov 1.9
    she will bestow on you a beautiful crown."

2. *Contrast of the wise and the wicked*

10 Hear, my son, and accept my words,   *4.10*
Prov 2.1;
3.2
    that the years of your life may be many.
11 I have taught you the way of wisdom;   *4.11*
1 Sam 12.23
    I have led you in the paths of uprightness.
12 When you walk, your step will not be hampered;   *4.12*
Ps 18.36;
Prov 3.23
    and if you run, you will not stumble.
13 Keep hold of instruction, do not let go;
    guard her, for she is your life.
14 Do not enter the path of the wicked,   *4.14*
Ps 1.1;
Prov 1.15
    and do not walk in the way of evil men.
15 Avoid it; do not go on it;
    turn away from it and pass on.
16 For they cannot sleep unless they have done wrong;   *4.16*
Ps 36.4;
Mic 2.1
    they are robbed of sleep unless they have made some one
    stumble.
17 For they eat the bread of wickedness   *4.18*
Isa 26.7;
2 Sam 23.4;
Dan 12.3
    and drink the wine of violence.
18 But the path of the righteous is like the light of dawn,

---

m Cn: Heb *exalt*   *n* Heb *know*
o Reversing the order of the lines   *p* The meaning of the Hebrew is uncertain

which shines brighter and brighter until full day.

4.19
Job 18.5;
Isa 59.9,10;
Jer 23.12;
Jn 12.35

19 The way of the wicked is like deep darkness;
   they do not know over what they stumble.

3. Positive instructions to a son

20 My son, be attentive to my words;
   incline your ear to my sayings.

4.21
Prov 3.21;
7.1,2

21 Let them not escape from your sight;
   keep them within your heart.

4.22
Prov 3.8;
12.18

22 For they are life to him who finds them,
   and healing to all his flesh.

4.23
Mt 12.34;
Mk 7.21;
Lk 6.45

23 Keep your heart with all vigilance;
   for from it flow the springs of life.

24 Put away from you crooked speech,
   and put devious talk far from you.

4.24
Prov 6.12;
19.1

25 Let your eyes look directly forward,
   and your gaze be straight before you.

4.26
Heb 12.13;
Ps 119.5

26 Take heed to*q* the path of your feet,
   then all your ways will be sure.

4.27
Deut 5.32;
28.14;
Prov 1.15

27 Do not swerve to the right or to the left;
   turn your foot away from evil.

L. Instruction on marriage

1. Warning against unchastity

5.1
Prov 4.20;
22.17

5 My son, be attentive to my wisdom,
   incline your ear to my understanding;

2 that you may keep discretion,
   and your lips may guard knowledge.

5.2
Mal 2.7

5.3
Prov 2.16;
Ps 55.21

3 For the lips of a loose woman drip honey,
   and her speech*r* is smoother than oil;

5.4
Ecc 7.26;
Ps 57.4

4 but in the end she is bitter as wormwood,
   sharp as a two-edged sword.

5.5
Prov 7.27

5 Her feet go down to death;
   her steps follow the path to*s* Shēōl;

6 she does not take heed to*t* the path of life;
   her ways wander, and she does not know it.

5.7
Prov 7.24;
Ps 119.102

7 And now, O sons, listen to me,
   and do not depart from the words of my mouth.

5.8
Prov 7.25;
9.14

8 Keep your way far from her,
   and do not go near the door of her house;

9 lest you give your honor to others
   and your years to the merciless;

10 lest strangers take their fill of your strength,*u*
   and your labors go to the house of an alien;

11 and at the end of your life you groan,
   when your flesh and body are consumed,

5.12
Prov 1.29;
12.1

12 and you say, "How I hated discipline,
   and my heart despised reproof!

13 I did not listen to the voice of my teachers
   or incline my ear to my instructors.

---

q The meaning of the Hebrew word is uncertain
r Heb *palate*   *s* Heb *lay hold of*
t The meaning of the Hebrew word is uncertain   *u* Or *wealth*

¹⁴ I was at the point of utter ruin
　　in the assembled congregation."

2. *Marital joys and responsibilities*

¹⁵ Drink water from your own cistern,
　　flowing water from your own well.
¹⁶ Should your springs be scattered abroad,
　　streams of water in the streets?
¹⁷ Let them be for yourself alone,
　　and not for strangers with you.
¹⁸ Let your fountain be blessed,
　　and rejoice in the wife of your youth,
¹⁹ 　　a lovely hind, a graceful doe.
　　Let her affection fill you at all times with delight,
　　be infatuated always with her love.
²⁰ Why should you be infatuated, my son, with a loose woman
　　and embrace the bosom of an adventuress?
²¹ For a man's ways are before the eyes of the LORD,
　　and he watches[v] all his paths.
²² The iniquities of the wicked ensnare him,
　　and he is caught in the toils of his sin.
²³ He dies for lack of discipline,
　　and because of his great folly he is lost.

M. *Warning against suretyship*

6 My son, if you have become surety for your neighbor,
　　have given your pledge for a stranger;
² if you are snared in the utterance of your lips,[w]
　　caught in the words of your mouth;
³ then do this, my son, and save yourself,
　　for you have come into your neighbor's power:
　　go, hasten,[x] and importune your neighbor.
⁴ Give your eyes no sleep
　　and your eyelids no slumber;
⁵ save yourself like a gazelle from the hunter,[y]
　　like a bird from the hand of the fowler.

N. *Warning against idleness*

⁶ Go to the ant, O sluggard;
　　consider her ways, and be wise.
⁷ Without having any chief,
　　officer or ruler,
⁸ she prepares her food in summer,
　　and gathers her sustenance in harvest.
⁹ How long will you lie there, O sluggard?
　　When will you arise from your sleep?
¹⁰ A little sleep, a little slumber,
　　a little folding of the hands to rest,
¹¹ and poverty will come upon you like a vagabond,
　　and want like an armed man.

Margin references:

5.16 Prov 9.17
5.18 Ecc 9.9; Mal 2.14
5.19 Sol 2.9; 4.5; 7.3
5.20 Prov 2.16; 7.5
5.21 Job 31.4; 34.21; Prov 15.3; Jer 16.17; 32.19; Hos 7.2; Heb 4.13
5.22 Ps 9.15
5.23 Job 4.21; 36.12
6.1 Prov 11.15; 17.18; 20.16; 22.26; 27.13
6.4 Ps 132.4
6.5 Ps 91.3
6.6 Prov 30.24, 25
6.8 Prov 10.5
6.9 Prov 24.33
6.11 Prov 10.4; 13.4; 20.4

---

v The meaning of the Hebrew word is uncertain
w Cn Compare Gk Syr: Heb *the words of your mouth*
x Or *humble yourself*　y Cn: Heb *hand*

O. *Warning against sowing discord*

6.12
Prov 16.27;
10.32
6.13
Ps 35.19;
Prov 10.10
6.14
Mic 2.1;
ver 19
6.15
Prov 24.22;
Jer 19.11;
2 Chr 36.16

12 A worthless person, a wicked man,
    goes about with crooked speech,
13 winks with his eyes, scrapes[z] with his feet,
    points with his finger,
14 with perverted heart devises evil,
    continually sowing discord;
15 therefore calamity will come upon him suddenly;
    in a moment he will be broken beyond healing.

P. *Warning against seven sins*

6.17
Ps 18.27;
120.2;
Isa 1.15
6.18
Gen 6.5;
Prov 1.16
6.19
Ps 27.12;
ver 4

16 There are six things which the LORD hates,
    seven which are an abomination to him:
17 haughty eyes, a lying tongue,
    and hands that shed innocent blood,
18 a heart that devises wicked plans,
    feet that make haste to run to evil,
19 a false witness who breathes out lies,
    and a man who sows discord among brothers.

Q. *Warning against adultery*

6.20
Prov 7.1;
1.8
6.21
Prov 3.3
6.22
Prov 3.23,
24
6.23
Ps 19.8
6.24
Prov 2.16;
5.3
6.25
Mt 5.28
6.26
Prov 29.3;
7.23;
Ezek 13.18
6.29
Ezek 18.6;
33.26
6.31
Ex 22.1–4
6.32
Prov 7.7

20 My son, keep your father's commandment,
    and forsake not your mother's teaching.
21 Bind them upon your heart always;
    tie them about your neck.
22 When you walk, they[a] will lead you;
    when you lie down, they[a] will watch over you;
    and when you awake, they[a] will talk with you.
23 For the commandment is a lamp and the teaching a light,
    and the reproofs of discipline are the way of life,
24 to preserve you from the evil woman,
    from the smooth tongue of the adventuress.
25 Do not desire her beauty in your heart,
    and do not let her capture you with her eyelashes;
26 for a harlot may be hired for a loaf of bread,[b]
    but an adulteress[c] stalks a man's very life.
27 Can a man carry fire in his bosom
    and his clothes not be burned?
28 Or can one walk upon hot coals
    and his feet not be scorched?
29 So is he who goes in to his neighbor's wife;
    none who touches her will go unpunished.
30 Do not men despise[d] a thief if he steals
    to satisfy his appetite when he is hungry?
31 And if he is caught, he will pay sevenfold;
    he will give all the goods of his house.
32 He who commits adultery has no sense;
    he who does it destroys himself.
33 Wounds and dishonor will he get,
    and his disgrace will not be wiped away.

z Or *taps*   a Heb *it*
b Cn Compare Gk Syr Vg Tg: Heb *for because of a harlot to a piece of bread*
c Heb *a man's wife*   d Or *Men do not despise*

34 For jealousy makes a man furious,
and he will not spare when he takes revenge.
35 He will accept no compensation,
nor be appeased though you multiply gifts.

R. *The folly of yielding to a harlot*

7 My son, keep my words
and treasure up my commandments with you;
2 keep my commandments and live,
keep my teachings as the apple of your eye;
3 bind them on your fingers,
write them on the tablet of your heart.
4 Say to wisdom, "You are my sister,"
and call insight your intimate friend;
5 to preserve you from the loose woman,
from the adventuress with her smooth words.

6 For at the window of my house
I have looked out through my lattice,
7 and I have seen among the simple,
I have perceived among the youths,
a young man without sense,
8 passing along the street near her corner,
taking the road to her house
9 in the twilight, in the evening,
at the time of night and darkness.

10 And lo, a woman meets him,
dressed as a harlot, wily of heart.[e]
11 She is loud and wayward,
her feet do not stay at home;
12 now in the street, now in the market,
and at every corner she lies in wait.
13 She seizes him and kisses him,
and with impudent face she says to him:
14 "I had to offer sacrifices,
and today I have paid my vows;
15 so now I have come out to meet you,
to seek you eagerly, and I have found you.
16 I have decked my couch with coverings,
colored spreads of Egyptian linen;
17 I have perfumed my bed with myrrh,
aloes, and cinnamon.
18 Come, let us take our fill of love till morning;
let us delight ourselves with love.
19 For my husband is not at home;

e The meaning of the Hebrew is uncertain

Marginal references:
6.34 Prov 27.4; 11.4
7.1 Prov 2.1
7.2 Prov 4.4; Deut 32.10
7.3 Deut 6.8; Prov 3.3
7.5 Prov 2.16; 5.3; 6.24
*7.6ff
7.7 Prov 1.22; 6.32
7.8 ver 12,27
7.9 Job 24.15
7.11 Prov 9.13; 1 Tim 5.13
7.12 Prov 23.28
*7.14 Prov 7.11, 16
7.16 Prov 31.22; Isa 19.9

7.6ff Proverbs are frequently addressed to the young to warn them of the pitfalls into which they may be led by sin. The youth will assuredly hear the voice of the temptress (7.21), but he must spurn her entreaty and heed the call of wisdom (8.1).
7.14 *I had to offer sacrifices.* The flesh of sacrificial peace offerings had to be eaten the day on which they were offered, or the following day. The temptress told her intended victim that she had just offered her sacrifices, which would mean that a plentiful supply of meat was in her house. She would prepare a sumptuous feast with it.

he has gone on a long journey;
20 he took a bag of money with him;
   at full moon he will come home."

7.21
Prov 5.3
21 With much seductive speech she persuades him;
   with her smooth talk she compels him.
22 All at once he follows her,
   as an ox goes to the slaughter,
   or as a stag is caught fast*f*

7.23
Ecc 9.12
23   till an arrow pierces its entrails;
   as a bird rushes into a snare;
   he does not know that it will cost him his life.

7.24
Prov 5.7
24 And now, O sons, listen to me,
   and be attentive to the words of my mouth.

7.25
Prov 5.8
25 Let not your heart turn aside to her ways,
   do not stray into her paths;

7.26
Prov 9.18
26 for many a victim has she laid low;
   yea, all her slain are a mighty host.

7.27
Prov 2.18;
5.5;9.18
27 Her house is the way to Shēōl,
   going down to the chambers of death.

S. *Wisdom personified*

1. *The call of wisdom*

8.1
Prov 1.20;
9.3
8 Does not wisdom call,
   does not understanding raise her voice?
2 On the heights beside the way,
   in the paths she takes her stand;

8.3
Job 29.7
3 beside the gates in front of the town,
   at the entrance of the portals she cries aloud:
4 "To you, O men, I call,
   and my cry is to the sons of men.

8.5
Prov 1.4,
22,32
5 O simple ones, learn prudence;
   O foolish men, pay attention.

8.6
Prov 22.20;
23.16
6 Hear, for I will speak noble things,
   and from my lips will come what is right;

8.7
Ps 37.30
7 for my mouth will utter truth;
   wickedness is an abomination to my lips.
8 All the words of my mouth are righteous;
   there is nothing twisted or crooked in them.

8.9
Prov 14.6;
3.13
9 They are all straight to him who understands
   and right to those who find knowledge.

8.10
Prov 3.14,
15
10 Take my instruction instead of silver,
   and knowledge rather than choice gold;

8.11
Job 28.18;
Prov 3.15
11 for wisdom is better than jewels,
   and all that you may desire cannot compare with her.

8.12
ver 5;
Prov 1.4
12 I, wisdom, dwell in prudence,*g*
   and I find knowledge and discretion.

8.13
Prov 16.6;
16.18;15.9;
6.12
13 The fear of the LORD is hatred of evil.
   Pride and arrogance and the way of evil
   and perverted speech I hate.

8.14
Prov 1.25;
2.7;
Ecc 7.19
14 I have counsel and sound wisdom,
   I have insight, I have strength.

---

f Cn Compare Gk: Heb uncertain   *g* Heb obscure

15 By me kings reign,
   and rulers decree what is just;
16 by me princes rule,
   and nobles govern[h] the earth.
17 I love those who love me,
   and those who seek me diligently find me.
18 Riches and honor are with me,
   enduring wealth and prosperity.
19 My fruit is better than gold, even fine gold,
   and my yield than choice silver.
20 I walk in the way of righteousness,
   in the paths of justice,
21 endowing with wealth those who love me,
   and filling their treasuries.

2. The eternity of wisdom

22 The LORD created me at the beginning of his work,[i]
   the first of his acts of old.
23 Ages ago I was set up,
   at the first, before the beginning of the earth.
24 When there were no depths I was brought forth,
   when there were no springs abounding with water.
25 Before the mountains had been shaped,
   before the hills, I was brought forth;
26 before he had made the earth with its fields,[j]
   or the first of the dust[j] of the world.
27 When he established the heavens, I was there,
   when he drew a circle on the face of the deep,
28 when he made firm the skies above,
   when he established[j] the fountains of the deep,
29 when he assigned to the sea its limit,
   so that the waters might not transgress his command,
   when he marked out the foundations of the earth,
30   then I was beside him, like a master workman;[l]
   and I was daily his[m] delight,
   rejoicing before him always,
31 rejoicing in his inhabited world
   and delighting in the sons of men.

3. The invitation to wisdom

32 And now, my sons, listen to me:
   happy are those who keep my ways.
33 Hear instruction and be wise,
   and do not neglect it.
34 Happy is the man who listens to me,
   watching daily at my gates,
   waiting beside my doors.

---

h Gk: Heb all the governors of   i Heb way
j The meaning of the Hebrew is uncertain   l Another reading is little child
m Gk: Heb lacks his

Cross references

8.15 Dan 2.21; Rom 13.1
8.17 1 Sam 2.30; Ps 91.14; Jn 14.21; Jas 1.5
8.18 Prov 3.16; Mt 6.33
8.19 Prov 3.14; 10.20
8.21 Prov 24.4
*8.22 Prov 3.19
8.23 Jn 17.5
8.25 Ps 90.2
8.27 Prov 3.19; Job 26.10
8.29 Job 38.10; Ps 104.9; Job 38.6
8.30 Jn 1.1–3
8.31 Ps 16.3
8.32 Prov 5.7; Ps 119.1,2; Lk 11.28
8.33 Prov 4.1
8.34 Prov 3.13, 18

8.22 Wisdom is personified in the passage from verse 22 to the end of the chapter. Wisdom is depicted as having been with God from the time of creation, thus having a claim on all men who would know life in its fulness (8.35, 36). The New Testament writers looked upon Christ as the Incarnate Wisdom (cf. Jn 8.51 with Prov 8.35, 36; Rom 1.24–30).

<table>
<tr><td>

8.35
Prov 4.22;
12.2
8.36
Prov 20.2

</td><td>

35 For he who finds me finds life
    and obtains favor from the LORD;
36 but he who misses me injures himself;
    all who hate me love death."

</td></tr>
</table>

T. Wisdom and folly contrasted

1. The invitation of wisdom

<table>
<tr><td>

9.1
Mt 16.18;
Eph 2.20,
22;
1 Pet 2.5
9.2
Mt 22.4;
Lk 14.16,
17
9.3
Ps 68.11;
Mt 22.3;
Prov 8.1,2
9.4
Prov 8.5;
6.32
9.5
Sol 5.1;
Isa 55.1;
Jn 6.27
9.6
Ezek 11.20;
37.24

</td><td>

9 Wisdom has built her house,
    she has set up^n her seven pillars.
2 She has slaughtered her beasts, she has mixed her wine,
    she has also set her table.
3 She has sent out her maids to call
    from the highest places in the town,
4 "Whoever is simple, let him turn in here!"
    To him who is without sense she says,
5 "Come, eat of my bread
    and drink of the wine I have mixed.
6 Leave simpleness,^{o} and live,
    and walk in the way of insight."

</td></tr>
</table>

2. Interlude

<table>
<tr><td>

9.7
Prov 23.9
9.8
Mt 7.6;
Ps 141.5
9.9
Prov 1.5
9.10
Job 28.28;
Prov 1.7
9.11
Prov 3.16;
10.27
9.12
Prov 19.29

</td><td>

7 He who corrects a scoffer gets himself abuse,
    and he who reproves a wicked man incurs injury.
8 Do not reprove a scoffer, or he will hate you;
    reprove a wise man, and he will love you.
9 Give instruction^p to a wise man, and he will be still wiser;
    teach a righteous man and he will increase in learning.
10 The fear of the LORD is the beginning of wisdom,
    and the knowledge of the Holy One is insight.
11 For by me your days will be multiplied,
    and years will be added to your life.
12 If you are wise, you are wise for yourself;
    if you scoff, you alone will bear it.

</td></tr>
</table>

3. The invitation of the foolish woman

<table>
<tr><td>

*9.13
Prov 7.11;
5.6
9.14
ver 3

9.16
ver 4

9.17
Prov 20.17

9.18
Prov 7.27

</td><td>

13 A foolish woman is noisy;
    she is wanton^q and knows no shame.^{r}
14 She sits at the door of her house,
    she takes a seat on the high places of the town,
15 calling to those who pass by,
    who are going straight on their way,
16 "Whoever is simple, let him turn in here!"
    And to him who is without sense she says,
17 "Stolen water is sweet,
    and bread eaten in secret is pleasant."
18 But he does not know that the dead^s are there,
    that her guests are in the depths of Sheōl.

</td></tr>
</table>

n Gk Syr Tg: Heb *hewn* o Gk Syr Vg Tg: Heb *simple ones*
p Heb lacks *instruction* q Cn Compare Syr Vg: The meaning of the Hebrew is uncertain
r Gk Syr: The meaning of the Hebrew is uncertain s Heb *shades*

9.13 Verses 13–18 describe the feast of folly in which the guests wrong themselves, wrong God, and wrong their fellow-men by sitting down at her wicked table.

II. The wealth in wisdom 10.1–22.16

A. The upright and the wicked

10   The proverbs of Solomon.

A wise son makes a glad father,
   but a foolish son is a sorrow to his mother.
2 Treasures gained by wickedness do not profit,
   but righteousness delivers from death.
3 The LORD does not let the righteous go hungry,
   but he thwarts the craving of the wicked.
4 A slack hand causes poverty,
   but the hand of the diligent makes rich.
5 A son who gathers in summer is prudent,
   but a son who sleeps in harvest brings shame.
6 Blessings are on the head of the righteous,
   but the mouth of the wicked conceals violence.
7 The memory of the righteous is a blessing,
   but the name of the wicked will rot.
8 The wise of heart will heed commandments,
   but a prating fool will come to ruin.
9 He who walks in integrity walks securely,
   but he who perverts his ways will be found out.
10 He who winks the eye causes trouble,
   but he who boldly reproves makes peace.[t]
11 The mouth of the righteous is a fountain of life,
   but the mouth of the wicked conceals violence.
12 Hatred stirs up strife,
   but love covers all offenses.
13 On the lips of him who has understanding wisdom is found,
   but a rod is for the back of him who lacks sense.
14 Wise men lay up knowledge,
   but the babbling of a fool brings ruin near.
15 A rich man's wealth is his strong city;
   the poverty of the poor is their ruin.
16 The wage of the righteous leads to life,
   the gain of the wicked to sin.
17 He who heeds instruction is on the path to life,
   but he who rejects reproof goes astray.
18 He who conceals hatred has lying lips,
   and he who utters slander is a fool.
19 When words are many, transgression is not lacking,
   but he who restrains his lips is prudent.
20 The tongue of the righteous is choice silver;
   the mind of the wicked is of little worth.
21 The lips of the righteous feed many,
   but fools die for lack of sense.
22 The blessing of the LORD makes rich,
   and he adds no sorrow with it.[u]

B. Fear of the LORD prolongs life

23 It is like sport to a fool to do wrong,
   but wise conduct is pleasure to a man of understanding.

10.1 Prov 1.1; 15.20; 29.3,15
10.2 Ps 49.6; Prov 11.4; Lk 12.19, 20; Prov 11.4,6
10.3 Ps 34.9,10; Mt 6.33; Ps 112.10
10.4 Prov 12.24; 13.4
10.5 Prov 6.8; 17.2
10.6 Est 7.8
10.7 Ps 9.5,6; Ecc 8.10
10.8 Prov 13.3
10.9 Ps 23.4; Prov 28.18; Isa 33.15; Prov 26.26
10.10 Prov 6.13
10.11 Ps 37.30
10.12 1 Pet 4.8
10.13 Prov 26.3
10.14 Prov 9.9; 18.7
10.15 Job 31.24; Ps 52.7; Prov 18.11; 19.7
10.17 Prov 6.23
10.18 Prov 26.24; Ps 15.3
10.19 Prov 18.21; Ecc 5.3; Jas 3.2
10.20 Prov 8.19
10.21 ver 11; Prov 5.23
10.22 Gen 24.35; Ps 37.22
10.23 Prov 15.21

---

t Gk: Heb *but a prating fool will come to ruin*   u Or *and toil adds nothing to it*

10.24
Ps 145.19;
Mt 5.6;
1 Jn 5.14,15
24 What the wicked dreads will come upon him,
　　but the desire of the righteous will be granted.

10.25
Prov 12.7;
Ps 15.5;
Mt 7.24;
16.18
25 When the tempest passes, the wicked is no more,
　　but the righteous is established for ever.
26 Like vinegar to the teeth, and smoke to the eyes,
　　so is the sluggard to those who send him.

10.26
Prov 26.6
27 The fear of the LORD prolongs life,
　　but the years of the wicked will be short.

10.27
Prov 9.11;
Ps 55.23
28 The hope of the righteous ends in gladness,
　　but the expectation of the wicked comes to nought.

10.29
Ps 28.8;
Prov 21.15
29 The LORD is a stronghold to him whose way is upright,
　　but destruction to evildoers.

10.30
Ps 37.29
30 The righteous will never be removed,
　　but the wicked will not dwell in the land.

10.31
Ps 37.30;
Prov 17.20
31 The mouth of the righteous brings forth wisdom,
　　but the perverse tongue will be cut off.
32 The lips of the righteous know what is acceptable,
　　but the mouth of the wicked, what is perverse.

C. The godless and the upright

11.1
Lev 19.35;
Deut 25.13–
16
11 A false balance is an abomination to the LORD,
　　but a just weight is his delight.

11.2
Prov 16.18
2 When pride comes, then comes disgrace;
　　but with the humble is wisdom.

11.3
Prov 13.6
3 The integrity of the upright guides them,
　　but the crookedness of the treacherous destroys them.

11.4
Ezek 7.19;
Zeph 1.18;
Gen 7.1
4 Riches do not profit in the day of wrath,
　　but righteousness delivers from death.
5 The righteousness of the blameless keeps his way straight,
　　but the wicked falls by his own wickedness.

11.6
Ecc 10.8
6 The righteousness of the upright delivers them,
　　but the treacherous are taken captive by their lust.

11.7
Prov 10.28
7 When the wicked dies, his hope perishes,
　　and the expectation of the godless comes to nought.

11.8
Prov 21.18
8 The righteous is delivered from trouble,
　　and the wicked gets into it instead.
9 With his mouth the godless man would destroy his neighbor,
　　but by knowledge the righteous are delivered.

11.10
Prov 28.12
10 When it goes well with the righteous, the city rejoices;
　　and when the wicked perish there are shouts of gladness.

11.11
Prov 29.8
11 By the blessing of the upright a city is exalted,
　　but it is overthrown by the mouth of the wicked.

D. The trustworthy and the talebearer

11.12
Prov 14.21;
10.19
12 He who belittles his neighbor lacks sense,
　　but a man of understanding remains silent.

11.13
Lev 19.16;
Prov 20.19;
1 Tim 5.13;
Prov 19.11
13 He who goes about as a talebearer reveals secrets,
　　but he who is trustworthy in spirit keeps a thing hidden.

11.14
Prov 15.22;
20.18;
24.6
14 Where there is no guidance, a people falls;
　　but in an abundance of counselors there is safety.
15 He who gives surety for a stranger will smart for it,
　　but he who hates suretyship is secure.

11.16
Prov 31.30
16 A gracious woman gets honor,

and violent men get riches.
17 A man who is kind benefits himself,
   but a cruel man hurts himself.
18 A wicked man earns deceptive wages,
   but one who sows righteousness gets a sure reward.
19 He who is steadfast in righteousness will live,
   but he who pursues evil will die.
20 Men of perverse mind are an abomination to the LORD,
   but those of blameless ways are his delight.
21 Be assured, an evil man will not go unpunished,
   but those who are righteous will be delivered.
22 Like a gold ring in a swine's snout
   is a beautiful woman without discretion.
23 The desire of the righteous ends only in good;
   the expectation of the wicked in wrath.

E. *The man who gives freely*

24 One man gives freely, yet grows all the richer;
   another withholds what he should give, and only suffers want.
25 A liberal man will be enriched,
   and one who waters will himself be watered.
26 The people curse him who holds back grain,
   but a blessing is on the head of him who sells it.
27 He who diligently seeks good seeks favor,
   but evil comes to him who searches for it.
28 He who trusts in his riches will wither,^{v}
   but the righteous will flourish like a green leaf.
29 He who troubles his household will inherit wind,
   and the fool will be servant to the wise.
30 The fruit of the righteous is a tree of life,
   but lawlessness^w takes away lives.
31 If the righteous is requited on earth,
   how much more the wicked and the sinner!

F. *The discipline of knowledge*

12 Whoever loves discipline loves knowledge,
   but he who hates reproof is stupid.
2 A good man obtains favor from the LORD,
   but a man of evil devices he condemns.
3 A man is not established by wickedness,
   but the root of the righteous will never be moved.
4 A good wife is the crown of her husband,
   but she who brings shame is like rottenness in his bones.
5 The thoughts of the righteous are just;
   the counsels of the wicked are treacherous.
6 The words of the wicked lie in wait for blood,
   but the mouth of the upright delivers men.
7 The wicked are overthrown and are no more,
   but the house of the righteous will stand.
8 A man is commended according to his good sense,
   but one of perverse mind is despised.

^{v} Cn: Heb *fall* ^{w} Cn Compare Gk Syr: Heb *a wise man*

Marginal references:

11.17 Mt 5.7; 25.34–36
11.18 Hos 10.12; Gal 6.8,9
11.20 Prov 12.22; Ps 119.1
11.21 Prov 16.5; Ps 112.2
11.23 Rom 2.8,9
11.24 Prov 13.7; 19.17
11.25 2 Cor 9.6–10; Mt 5.7
11.26 Amos 8.5,6; Job 29.13
11.27 Est 7.10; Ps 7.15; 10.2
11.28 Ps 52.7; Mk 10.24; 1 Tim 6.17; Ps 1.3; Jer 17.8
11.30 1 Cor 9.19; Jas 5.20
11.31 Prov 13.21; 2 Sam 22.21,25
12.1 Prov 9.8; 15.10
12.2 Prov 8.35
12.3 Prov 10.25
12.4 Prov 31.23; 1 Cor 11.7; Prov 14.30
12.6 Prov 1.11; 14.3
12.7 Ps 37.36; Mt 7.24

G. Care for life and land

9 Better is a man of humble standing who works for himself
   than one who plays the great man but lacks bread.

10 A righteous man has regard for the life of his beast,
   but the mercy of the wicked is cruel.

11 He who tills his land will have plenty of bread,
   but he who follows worthless pursuits has no sense.

12 The strong tower of the wicked comes to ruin,
   but the root of the righteous stands firm.*x*

13 An evil man is ensnared by the transgression of his lips,
   but the righteous escapes from trouble.

14 From the fruit of his words a man is satisfied with good,
   and the work of a man's hand comes back to him.

H. The wise and the foolish

15 The way of a fool is right in his own eyes,
   but a wise man listens to advice.

16 The vexation of a fool is known at once,
   but the prudent man ignores an insult.

17 He who speaks the truth gives honest evidence,
   but a false witness utters deceit.

18 There is one whose rash words are like sword thrusts,
   but the tongue of the wise brings healing.

19 Truthful lips endure for ever,
   but a lying tongue is but for a moment.

20 Deceit is in the heart of those who devise evil,
   but those who plan good have joy.

21 No ill befalls the righteous,
   but the wicked are filled with trouble.

22 Lying lips are an abomination to the LORD,
   but those who act faithfully are his delight.

23 A prudent man conceals his knowledge,
   but fools*y* proclaim their folly.

24 The hand of the diligent will rule,
   while the slothful will be put to forced labor.

25 Anxiety in a man's heart weighs him down,
   but a good word makes him glad.

26 A righteous man turns away from evil,*z*
   but the way of the wicked leads them astray.

27 A slothful man will not catch his prey,*a*
   but the diligent man will get precious wealth.*b*

28 In the path of righteousness is life,
   but the way of error leads to death.*c*

I. The source of great wealth

13 A wise son hears his father's instruction,
   but a scoffer does not listen to rebuke.

2 From the fruit of his mouth a good man eats good,
   but the desire of the treacherous is for violence.

---

x Cn: The Hebrew of verse 12 is obscure
y Heb *the heart of fools*   *z* Cn: The meaning of the Hebrew is uncertain
a Cn Compare Gk Syr: The meaning of the Hebrew is uncertain
b Cn: The meaning of the Hebrew is uncertain
c Cn: The meaning of the Hebrew is uncertain

3 He who guards his mouth preserves his life;
   he who opens wide his lips comes to ruin.
4 The soul of the sluggard craves, and gets nothing,
   while the soul of the diligent is richly supplied.
5 A righteous man hates falsehood,
   but a wicked man acts shamefully and disgracefully.
6 Righteousness guards him whose way is upright,
   but sin overthrows the wicked.
7 One man pretends to be rich, yet has nothing;
   another pretends to be poor, yet has great wealth.
8 The ransom of a man's life is his wealth,
   but a poor man has no means of redemption.^{d}
9 The light of the righteous rejoices,
   but the lamp of the wicked will be put out.
10 By insolence the heedless make strife,
   but with those who take advice is wisdom.
11 Wealth hastily gotten^e will dwindle,
   but he who gathers little by little will increase it.

J. The source of hope

12 Hope deferred makes the heart sick,
   but a desire fulfilled is a tree of life.
13 He who despises the word brings destruction on himself,
   but he who respects the commandment will be rewarded.
14 The teaching of the wise is a fountain of life,
   that one may avoid the snares of death.
15 Good sense wins favor,
   but the way of the faithless is their ruin.^{f}
16 In everything a prudent man acts with knowledge,
   but a fool flaunts his folly.
17 A bad messenger plunges men into trouble,
   but a faithful envoy brings healing.
18 Poverty and disgrace come to him who ignores instruction,
   but he who heeds reproof is honored.
19 A desire fulfilled is sweet to the soul;
   but to turn away from evil is an abomination to fools.
20 He who walks with wise men becomes wise,
   but the companion of fools will suffer harm.
21 Misfortune pursues sinners,
   but prosperity rewards the righteous.
22 A good man leaves an inheritance to his children's children,
   but the sinner's wealth is laid up for the righteous.
23 The fallow ground of the poor yields much food,
   but it is swept away through injustice.
24 He who spares the rod hates his son,
   but he who loves him is diligent to discipline him.
25 The righteous has enough to satisfy his appetite,
   but the belly of the wicked suffers want.

^{d} Cn: Heb *does not hear rebuke* ^{e} Gk Vg: Heb *from vanity*
^{f} Cn Compare Gk Syr Vg Tg: Heb *is enduring*

13.12 Hope includes a desire for the thing wanted and also an expectation that it will come. If the desire is present but not the expectation, it is not true hope.

Cross-references: 13.3 Ps 39.1; Jas 3.2 — 13.4 Prov 10.4 — 13.6 Prov 11.3,5 — 13.7 Prov 11.24; Lk 12.20, 21,33; 2 Cor 6.10 — 13.9 Job 18.5; Prov 24.20 — 13.10 Prov 11.14 — 13.11 Prov 10.2; 14.23 — *13.12 ver 19 — 13.13 2 Chr 36.16 — 13.14 Prov 10.11; Ps 18.5 — 13.15 Prov 3.4; 21.8 — 13.16 Prov 12.23; 15.2 — 13.17 Prov 25.13 — 13.18 Prov 15.5, 31,32 — 13.20 Prov 15.31; 28.19 — 13.21 Ps 32.10 — 13.22 Job 27.16,17; Prov 28.8; Ecc 2.26 — 13.23 Prov 12.11 — 13.24 Prov 19.18; 22.15; 29.15,17 — 13.25 Ps 34.10; 37.3

K. *The upright and the wicked*

14 Wisdom[g] builds her house,
   but folly with her own hands tears it down.

2 He who walks in uprightness fears the LORD,
   but he who is devious in his ways despises him.

3 The talk of a fool is a rod for his back,[h]
   but the lips of the wise will preserve them.

4 Where there are no oxen, there is no[i] grain;
   but abundant crops come by the strength of the ox.

5 A faithful witness does not lie,
   but a false witness breathes out lies.

6 A scoffer seeks wisdom in vain,
   but knowledge is easy for a man of understanding.

7 Leave the presence of a fool,
   for there you do not meet words of knowledge.

8 The wisdom of a prudent man is to discern his way,
   but the folly of fools is deceiving.

9 God scorns the wicked,[j]
   but the upright enjoy his favor.

10 The heart knows its own bitterness,
   and no stranger shares its joy.

11 The house of the wicked will be destroyed,
   but the tent of the upright will flourish.

12 There is a way which seems right to a man,
   but its end is the way to death.[k]

13 Even in laughter the heart is sad,
   and the end of joy is grief.

14 A perverse man will be filled with the fruit of his ways,
   and a good man with the fruit of his deeds.[l]

15 The simple believes everything,
   but the prudent looks where he is going.

16 A wise man is cautious and turns away from evil,
   but a fool throws off restraint and is careless.

17 A man of quick temper acts foolishly,
   but a man of discretion is patient.[m]

18 The simple acquire folly,
   but the prudent are crowned with knowledge.

19 The evil bow down before the good,
   the wicked at the gates of the righteous.

L. *The rich and the poor*

20 The poor is disliked even by his neighbor,
   but the rich has many friends.

21 He who despises his neighbor is a sinner,
   but happy is he who is kind to the poor.

22 Do they not err that devise evil?
   Those who devise good meet loyalty and faithfulness.

23 In all toil there is profit,
   but mere talk tends only to want.

24 The crown of the wise is their wisdom,[n]
   but folly is the garland[o] of fools.

---

g Heb *Wisdom of women* h Cn: Heb *a rod of pride* i Cn: Heb *a manger of*
j Cn: Heb obscure k Heb *ways of death* l Cn: Heb *from upon him* m Gk: Heb *is hated*
n Cn Compare Gk: Heb *riches* o Cn: Heb *folly*

Cross-references (margin)
14.1 Prov 24.3
14.2 Prov 19.1; Rom 2.4
14.3 Prov 12.6
14.5 Ex 20.16; Prov 6.19; 12.17
14.6 Prov 24.7; 8.9; 17.24
14.8 Prov 15.21; ver 24
14.11 Prov 3.33; 12.7; 15.25
14.12 Prov 16.25; Rom 6.21
14.13 Prov 5.4; Ecc 2.2
14.14 Prov 1.31; 12.14
14.16 Prov 22.3
14.17 ver 29
14.18 Prov 18.15
14.19 Prov 11.29
14.20 Prov 19.7
14.21 Prov 11.12; Ps 41.1

25 A truthful witness saves lives,
but one who utters lies is a betrayer.
26 In the fear of the LORD one has strong confidence,
and his children will have a refuge.
27 The fear of the LORD is a fountain of life,
that one may avoid the snares of death.
28 In a multitude of people is the glory of a king,
but without people a prince is ruined.
29 He who is slow to anger has great understanding,
but he who has a hasty temper exalts folly.
30 A tranquil mind gives life to the flesh,
but passion makes the bones rot.
31 He who oppresses a poor man insults his Maker,
but he who is kind to the needy honors him.
32 The wicked is overthrown through his evil-doing,
but the righteous finds refuge through his integrity.[p]
33 Wisdom abides in the mind of a man of understanding,
but it is not[q] known in the heart of fools.
34 Righteousness exalts a nation,
but sin is a reproach to any people.
35 A servant who deals wisely has the king's favor,
but his wrath falls on one who acts shamefully.

M. *The tongue of the wise*

15 A soft answer turns away wrath,
but a harsh word stirs up anger.
2 The tongue of the wise dispenses knowledge,[r]
but the mouths of fools pour out folly.
3 The eyes of the LORD are in every place,
keeping watch on the evil and the good.
4 A gentle tongue is a tree of life,
but perverseness in it breaks the spirit.
5 A fool despises his father's instruction,
but he who heeds admonition is prudent.
6 In the house of the righteous there is much treasure,
but trouble befalls the income of the wicked.
7 The lips of the wise spread knowledge;
not so the minds of fools.
8 The sacrifice of the wicked is an abomination to the LORD,
but the prayer of the upright is his delight.
9 The way of the wicked is an abomination to the LORD,
but he loves him who pursues righteousness.
10 There is severe discipline for him who forsakes the way;
he who hates reproof will die.
11 Shēōl and Ȧbăd′dȯn lie open before the LORD,
how much more the hearts of men!
12 A scoffer does not like to be reproved;
he will not go to the wise.

[p] Gk Syr: Heb *in his death* [q] Gk Syr: Heb lacks *not* [r] Cn: Heb *makes knowledge good*

14.25 ver 5
14.26 Prov 19.23; Isa 33.6
14.27 Prov 13.14
★14.29 Prov 16.32; Jas 1.19; Prov 29.20
14.30 Prov 12.4
14.31 Prov 17.5; ver 21
14.32 Job 13.15; Ps 23.4; 2 Cor 1.9; 2 Tim 4.18
14.33 Prov 2.10; 12.16
14.34 Prov 11.11
14.35 Mt 24.45
15.1 Judg 8.1–3; 1 Sam 25.10–13
15.2 Prov 12.23; 13.16
15.3 Job 34.21; Heb 4.13
15.5 Prov 13.1, 18
15.8 Isa 1.11; Jer 6.20; Mic 6.7
15.9 Prov 21.21; 1 Tim 6.11
15.10 Prov 1.29–32; 5.12
15.11 Job 26.6; Ps 139.8; 2 Chr 6.30
15.12 Prov 13.1; Amos 5.10

14.29 Anger may be either sinful or righteous, depending on the reason for the anger. As an expression of mere human passion, it is a work of the flesh (Gal 5.20) and is forbidden to the Christian. Illustrations of justifiable anger were furnished by: (1) Jesus (Mk 3.5); (2) Moses (Ex 11.8); (3) Nehemiah (Neh 5.6). Sinful anger was illustrated by: (1) Cain (Gen 4.5, 6); (2) Jonah (Jon 4.4); (3) the priests who condemned Stephen (Acts 7.54).

N. *The reward of a cheerful heart*

15.13
Prov 17.22;
12.25

13 A glad heart makes a cheerful countenance,
   but by sorrow of heart the spirit is broken.
14 The mind of him who has understanding seeks knowledge,
   but the mouths of fools feed on folly.

15.15
ver 13

15 All the days of the afflicted are evil,
   but a cheerful heart has a continual feast.

15.16
Ps 37.16;
Prov 16.8;
1 Tim 6.6

16 Better is a little with the fear of the LORD
   than great treasure and trouble with it.

15.17
Prov 17.1

17 Better is a dinner of herbs where love is
   than a fatted ox and hatred with it.

15.18
Prov 26.21;
29.22;
14.29

18 A hot-tempered man stirs up strife,
   but he who is slow to anger quiets contention.

15.19
Prov 22.5

19 The way of a sluggard is overgrown with thorns,
   but the path of the upright is a level highway.

15.20
Prov 10.1;
30.17

20 A wise son makes a glad father,
   but a foolish man despises his mother.

O. *Instruction in wisdom*

15.21
Prov 10.23;
Eph 5.15

21 Folly is a joy to him who has no sense,
   but a man of understanding walks aright.

15.22
Prov 11.14;
20.18

22 Without counsel plans go wrong,
   but with many advisers they succeed.

15.23
Prov 25.11

23 To make an apt answer is a joy to a man,
   and a word in season, how good it is!

15.24
Prov 4.18

24 The wise man's path leads upward to life,
   that he may avoid Shēōl beneath.

15.25
Prov 12.7;
Ps 68.5,6

25 The LORD tears down the house of the proud,
   but maintains the widow's boundaries.

15.26
Prov 6.16–
19; 16.24

26 The thoughts of the wicked are an abomination to the LORD,
   the words of the pure are pleasing to him.ˢ

15.27
Prov 28.25;
1 Tim 6.10;
Isa 33.15

27 He who is greedy for unjust gain makes trouble for his household,
   but he who hates bribes will live.

15.28
1 Pet 3.15

28 The mind of the righteous ponders how to answer,
   but the mouth of the wicked pours out evil things.

15.29
Ps 34.16;
145.18

29 The LORD is far from the wicked,
   but he hears the prayer of the righteous.

30 The light of the eyes rejoices the heart,
   and good news refreshesᵗ the bones.

15.31
ver 5

31 He whose ear heeds wholesome admonition
   will abide among the wise.

15.32
Prov 1.7;
8.36; 15.5

32 He who ignores instruction despises himself,
   but he who heeds admonition gains understanding.

15.33
Prov 1.7;
18.12

33 The fear of the LORD is instruction in wisdom,
   and humility goes before honor.

P. *The LORD weighs the way of man*

16.1
Prov 19.21

16 The plans of the mind belong to man,
   but the answer of the tongue is from the LORD.

16.2
Prov 21.2

2 All the ways of a man are pure in his own eyes,

ˢ Cn Compare Gk: Heb *pleasant words are pure*   ᵗ Heb *makes fat*

but the LORD weighs the spirit.
3 Commit your work to the LORD,
    and your plans will be established.

16.3
Ps 37.5

4 The LORD has made everything for its purpose,
    even the wicked for the day of trouble.

16.4
Isa 43.7;
Job 21.30

5 Every one who is arrogant is an abomination to the LORD;
    be assured, he will not go unpunished.

16.5
Prov 6.17;
11.21

6 By loyalty and faithfulness iniquity is atoned for,
    and by the fear of the LORD a man avoids evil.

16.6
Dan 4.27;
Prov 14.16

7 When a man's ways please the LORD,
    he makes even his enemies to be at peace with him.

16.7
2 Chr 17.10

8 Better is a little with righteousness
    than great revenues with injustice.

9 A man's mind plans his way,
    but the LORD directs his steps.

16.9
Ps 37.23;
Prov 20.24;
Jer 10.23

10 Inspired decisions are on the lips of a king;
    his mouth does not sin in judgment.

11 A just balance and scales are the LORD's;
    all the weights in the bag are his work.

16.11
Prov 11.1

Q. Wisdom the fountain of life

12 It is an abomination to kings to do evil,
    for the throne is established by righteousness.

16.12
Prov 25.5

13 Righteous lips are the delight of a king,
    and he loves him who speaks what is right.

16.13
Prov 14.35

14 A king's wrath is a messenger of death,
    and a wise man will appease it.

16.14
Prov 19.12

15 In the light of a king's face there is life,
    and his favor is like the clouds that bring the spring rain.

16.15
Job 29.23

16 To get wisdom is better^u than gold;
    to get understanding is to be chosen rather than silver.

16.16
Prov 8.10,
19

17 The highway of the upright turns aside from evil;
    he who guards his way preserves his life.

18 Pride goes before destruction,
    and a haughty spirit before a fall.

16.18
Prov 11.2

19 It is better to be of a lowly spirit with the poor
    than to divide the spoil with the proud.

20 He who gives heed to the word will prosper,
    and happy is he who trusts in the LORD.

16.20
Ps 2.12;
34.8;
Jer 17.7

21 The wise of heart is called a man of discernment,
    and pleasant speech increases persuasiveness.

22 Wisdom is a fountain of life to him who has it,
    but folly is the chastisement of fools.

16.22
Prov 13.14;
7.22

23 The mind of the wise makes his speech judicious,
    and adds persuasiveness to his lips.

16.23
Prov 37.30

24 Pleasant words are like a honeycomb,
    sweetness to the soul and health to the body.

R. The wicked ways of man

25 There is a way which seems right to a man,
    but its end is the way to death.^{v}

16.25
Prov 14.12

^{u} Gk Syr Vg Tg: Heb *how much better*
^{v} Heb *ways of death*

26 A worker's appetite works for him;
    his mouth urges him on.

16.27
Prov 6.12,
14,18;
Jas 3.6
27 A worthless man plots evil,
    and his speech is like a scorching fire.

16.28
Prov 15.18;
17.9
28 A perverse man spreads strife,
    and a whisperer separates close friends.

16.29
Prov 1.10
29 A man of violence entices his neighbor
    and leads him in a way that is not good.

30 He who winks his eyes plans _w_ perverse things,
    he who compresses his lips brings evil to pass.

16.31
Prov 20.29
31 A hoary head is a crown of glory;
    it is gained in a righteous life.

16.32
Prov 19.11
32 He who is slow to anger is better than the mighty,
    and he who rules his spirit than he who takes a city.

*16.33
33 The lot is cast into the lap,
    but the decision is wholly from the LORD.

S. Fine speech and false speech

17.1
Prov 15.17
17 Better is a dry morsel with quiet
    than a house full of feasting with strife.

17.2
Prov 10.5
2 A slave who deals wisely will rule over a son who acts shamefully,
    and will share the inheritance as one of the brothers.

17.3
Prov 27.21;
Ps 26.2
3 The crucible is for silver, and the furnace is for gold,
    and the LORD tries hearts.

4 An evildoer listens to wicked lips;
    and a liar gives heed to a mischievous tongue.

17.5
Prov 14.31;
Job 31.29
5 He who mocks the poor insults his Maker;
    he who is glad at calamity will not go unpunished.

17.6
Prov 13.22
6 Grandchildren are the crown of the aged,
    and the glory of sons is their fathers.

7 Fine speech is not becoming to a fool;
    still less is false speech to a prince.

17.8
Prov 21.14;
Isa 1.23;
Amos 5.12
8 A bribe is like a magic stone in the eyes of him who gives it;
    wherever he turns he prospers.

17.9
Prov 10.12;
Jas 5.20;
1 Pet 4.8;
Prov 16.28
9 He who forgives an offense seeks love,
    but he who repeats a matter alienates a friend.

10 A rebuke goes deeper into a man of understanding
    than a hundred blows into a fool.

11 An evil man seeks only rebellion,
    and a cruel messenger will be sent against him.

_w_ Gk Syr Vg Tg: Heb _to plan_

16.33 God's providence is that foresight and arrangement in advance of actual happenings by which God accomplishes the ends He has purposed beforehand. The preservation of God's creation continues through His providence. Thus it may be said that nature serves the purposes of God, and man is likewise subject to His providence. For example: (1) the days of our years are numbered by His providence (Gen 6.3); (2) God saves or destroys life at His pleasure (Gen 8.1,21; Ps 18.17; Gen 7.23; 19.29); (3) nothing can befall man without God's knowledge (Mt 10.29, 30); (4) the flowers of the field and birds of the air are subject to His providence (Mt 6.25–33). At the same time, man's freedom and responsibility are taught (Isa 1.16; Jer 21.8). The existence of problems connected with this doctrine in no way destroys its truth; and the solutions are often given by God in Scripture. Thus the answer to the question, "Does not the suffering of the righteous contradict that moral order which requires the wicked to be punished and the righteous rewarded?" is given in Job by the conclusion that the suffering of the righteous is a needful discipline which purifies the life and demonstrates the true believer's love for God.

12 Let a man meet a she-bear robbed of her cubs,
    rather than a fool in his folly.

17.12
Hos 13.8

T. *The price of wisdom*

13 If a man returns evil for good,
    evil will not depart from his house.

17.13
Ps 109.4,5;
Jer 18.20

14 The beginning of strife is like letting out water;
    so quit before the quarrel breaks out.

17.14
Prov 20.3

15 He who justifies the wicked and he who condemns the righteous
    are both alike an abomination to the LORD.

17.15
Ex 23.7;
Isa 5.23

16 Why should a fool have a price in his hand to buy wisdom,
    when he has no mind?

17 A friend loves at all times,
    and a brother is born for adversity.

17.17
Ruth 1.16;
Prov 18.24

18 A man without sense gives a pledge,
    and becomes surety in the presence of his neighbor.

17.18
Prov 6.1

19 He who loves transgression loves strife;
    he who makes his door high seeks destruction.

17.19
Prov 29.22;
16.18

20 A man of crooked mind does not prosper,
    and one with a perverse tongue falls into calamity.

17.20
Jas 3.8

21 A stupid son is a grief to a father;
    and the father of a fool has no joy.

17.21
Prov 10.1;
19.13

22 A cheerful heart is a good medicine,
    but a downcast spirit dries up the bones.

17.22
Prov 15.13;
Ps 22.15

23 A wicked man accepts a bribe from the bosom
    to pervert the ways of justice.

17.23
Ex 23.8

24 A man of understanding sets his face toward wisdom,
    but the eyes of a fool are on the ends of the earth.

17.24
Ecc 2.14

25 A foolish son is a grief to his father
    and bitterness to her who bore him.

17.25
Prov 10.1

26 To impose a fine on a righteous man is not good;
    to flog noble men is wrong.

17.26
Prov 18.5

27 He who restrains his words has knowledge,
    and he who has a cool spirit is a man of understanding.

17.27
Jas 1.19

28 Even a fool who keeps silent is considered wise;
    when he closes his lips, he is deemed intelligent.

17.28
Job 13.5

U. *Words of the wise and the foolish*

18 He who is estranged[x] seeks pretexts[y]
    to break out against all sound judgment.

2 A fool takes no pleasure in understanding,
    but only in expressing his opinion.

18.2
Prov 12.23

3 When wickedness comes, contempt comes also;
    and with dishonor comes disgrace.

4 The words of a man's mouth are deep waters;
    the fountain of wisdom is a gushing stream.

18.4
Prov 20.5;
10.11

5 It is not good to be partial to a wicked man,
    or to deprive a righteous man of justice.

18.5
Lev 19.15;
Deut 1.17;
Prov 24.23

6 A fool's lips bring strife,
    and his mouth invites a flogging.

7 A fool's mouth is his ruin,
    and his lips are a snare to himself.

18.7
Prov 10.14;
Ecc 10.12

x Heb *separated* y Gk Vg: Heb *desire*

18.8 Prov 26.22	8 The words of a whisperer are like delicious morsels; they go down into the inner parts of the body.
18.9 Prov 28.24	9 He who is slack in his work is a brother to him who destroys.
18.10 2 Sam 22.3; Ps 18.2	10 The name of the LORD is a strong tower; the righteous man runs into it and is safe.
18.11 Prov 10.15	11 A rich man's wealth is his strong city, and like a high wall protecting him.ᶻ
18.12 Prov 11.2	12 Before destruction a man's heart is haughty, but humility goes before honor.
18.13 Jn 7.51	13 If one gives answer before he hears, it is his folly and shame.
	14 A man's spirit will endure sickness; but a broken spirit who can bear?
	15 An intelligent mind acquires knowledge, and the ear of the wise seeks knowledge.
18.16 Gen 32.20; 1 Sam 25.27	16 A man's gift makes room for him and brings him before great men.
	17 He who states his case first seems right, until the other comes and examines him.
18.18 Prov 16.33	18 The lot puts an end to disputes and decides between powerful contenders.
★18.19	19 A brother helped is like a strong city,ᵃ but quarreling is like the bars of a castle.
18.20 Prov 12.14	20 From the fruit of his mouth a man is satisfied; he is satisfied by the yield of his lips.
18.21 Mt 12.37	21 Death and life are in the power of the tongue, and those who love it will eat its fruits.
18.22 Prov 19.14; 8.35	22 He who finds a wife finds a good thing, and obtains favor from the LORD.
★18.23 Jas 2.3	23 The poor use entreaties, but the rich answer roughly.
18.24 Prov 17.17	24 There areᵇ friends who pretend to be friends,ᶜ but there is a friend who sticks closer than a brother.

V. Contrasts of wealth and poverty

19.1 Prov 28.6	**19** Better is a poor man who walks in his integrity than a man who is perverse in speech, and is a fool.
	2 It is not good for a man to be without knowledge, and he who makes haste with his feet misses his way.
19.3 Prov 11.3; Ps 37.7	3 When a man's folly brings his way to ruin, his heart rages against the LORD.
19.4 Prov 14.20	4 Wealth brings many new friends, but a poor man is deserted by his friend.
19.5 Ex 23.1; Prov 6.19	5 A false witness will not go unpunished, and he who utters lies will not escape.
19.6 Prov 29.26; 17.8	6 Many seek the favor of a generous man, and every one is a friend to a man who gives gifts.

z Or *in his imagination*
a Gk Syr Vg Tg: The meaning of the Hebrew is uncertain
b Syr Tg: Heb *A man of*   c Cn Compare Syr Vg Tg: Heb *to be broken*

18.19 *quarreling is like the bars of a castle.* It is as difficult to settle the problems of brethren who quarrel, as to storm a castle.

18.23 This stresses man's fallen condition.

7 All a poor man's brothers hate him;
  how much more do his friends go far from him!
He pursues them with words, but does not have them. *d*

8 He who gets wisdom loves himself;
  he who keeps understanding will prosper.

9 A false witness will not go unpunished,
  and he who utters lies will perish.

10 It is not fitting for a fool to live in luxury,
  much less for a slave to rule over princes.

11 Good sense makes a man slow to anger,
  and it is his glory to overlook an offense.

12 A king's wrath is like the growling of a lion,
  but his favor is like dew upon the grass.

13 A foolish son is ruin to his father,
  and a wife's quarreling is a continual dripping of rain.

14 House and wealth are inherited from fathers,
  but a prudent wife is from the LORD.

15 Slothfulness casts into a deep sleep,
  and an idle person will suffer hunger.

16 He who keeps the commandment keeps his life;
  he who despises the word *e* will die.

17 He who is kind to the poor lends to the LORD,
  and he will repay him for his deed.

W. *Advice and instruction*

18 Discipline your son while there is hope;
  do not set your heart on his destruction.

19 A man of great wrath will pay the penalty;
  for if you deliver him, you will only have to do it again. *f*

20 Listen to advice and accept instruction,
  that you may gain wisdom for the future.

21 Many are the plans in the mind of a man,
  but it is the purpose of the LORD that will be established.

22 What is desired in a man is loyalty,
  and a poor man is better than a liar.

23 The fear of the LORD leads to life;
  and he who has it rests satisfied;
  he will not be visited by harm.

24 The sluggard buries his hand in the dish,
  and will not even bring it back to his mouth.

25 Strike a scoffer, and the simple will learn prudence;
  reprove a man of understanding, and he will gain knowledge.

26 He who does violence to his father and chases away his mother
  is a son who causes shame and brings reproach.

27 Cease, my son, to hear instruction
  only to stray from the words of knowledge.

28 A worthless witness mocks at justice,
  and the mouth of the wicked devours iniquity.

29 Condemnation is ready for scoffers,
  and flogging for the backs of fools.

d Heb uncertain   *e* Cn Compare 13.13: Heb *his ways*   *f* Heb obscure

---

19.7 ver 4; Ps 38.11
19.8 Prov 16.20
19.9 ver 5
19.10 Ecc 10.6,7
19.11 Jas 1.19; Prov 16.32
19.12 Prov 16.14; Hos 14.5
19.13 Prov 10.1; 21.9
19.14 2 Cor 12.14; Prov 18.22
*19.15 Prov 6.9; 10.4
*19.16 Lk 10.28
19.17 Ecc 11.1; Mt 10.42; 2 Cor 9.6–8; Heb 6.10
19.18 Prov 13.24
19.20 Prov 8.33
19.21 Prov 16.1,9; Ps 33.10,11
19.23 1 Tim 4.8; Ps 25.13; Prov 12.21
19.24 Prov 26.15
19.25 Prov 21.11; 9.8
19.26 Prov 28.24; 17.2
19.28 Job 15.16
19.29 Prov 10.13; 26.3

19.15 This has the same meaning as verse 24.

19.16 *the word*, i.e., the divine commandments.

X. *The integrity of the righteous*

20 Wine is a mocker, strong drink a brawler;
and whoever is led astray by it is not wise.

2 The dread wrath of a king is like the growling of a lion;
he who provokes him to anger forfeits his life.

3 It is an honor for a man to keep aloof from strife;
but every fool will be quarreling.

4 The sluggard does not plow in the autumn;
he will seek at harvest and have nothing.

5 The purpose in a man's mind is like deep water,
but a man of understanding will draw it out.

6 Many a man proclaims his own loyalty,
but a faithful man who can find?

7 A righteous man who walks in his integrity—
blessed are his sons after him!

8 A king who sits on the throne of judgment
winnows all evil with his eyes.

9 Who can say, "I have made my heart clean;
I am pure from my sin"?

10 Diverse weights and diverse measures
are both alike an abomination to the LORD.

11 Even a child makes himself known by his acts,
whether what he does is pure and right.

12 The hearing ear and the seeing eye,
the LORD has made them both.

13 Love not sleep, lest you come to poverty;
open your eyes, and you will have plenty of bread.

14 "It is bad, it is bad," says the buyer;
but when he goes away, then he boasts.

Y. *The hastily-gotten inheritance*

15 There is gold, and abundance of costly stones;
but the lips of knowledge are a precious jewel.

16 Take a man's garment when he has given surety for a stranger,
and hold him in pledge when he gives surety for foreigners.

17 Bread gained by deceit is sweet to a man,
but afterward his mouth will be full of gravel.

18 Plans are established by counsel;
by wise guidance wage war.

19 He who goes about gossiping reveals secrets;
therefore do not associate with one who speaks foolishly.

20 If one curses his father or his mother,
his lamp will be put out in utter darkness.

21 An inheritance gotten hastily in the beginning
will in the end not be blessed.

22 Do not say, "I will repay evil";
wait for the LORD, and he will help you.

23 Diverse weights are an abomination to the LORD,
and false scales are not good.

24 A man's steps are ordered by the LORD;
how then can man understand his way?

25 It is a snare for a man to say rashly, "It is holy,"
and to reflect only after making his vows.

20.1
Gen 9.21;
Isa 5.22
20.2
Prov 19.12;
8.36;
1 Ki 2.23
20.3
Prov 17.14
20.4
Prov 10.4;
19.15,24
20.5
Prov 18.4
20.6
Prov 25.14;
Mt 6.2;
Lk 18.11;
Ps 12.1;
Lk 18.8
20.7
2 Cor 1.12;
Ps 37.26
20.8
ver 26
20.9
1 Ki 8.46;
1 Jn 1.8
20.10
Deut 25.13;
ver 23
20.11
Mt 7.16
20.12
Ex 4.11
20.13
Prov 6.9,10;
Rom 12.11

20.16
Prov 27.13
20.17
Prov 9.17
20.18
Prov 15.22;
24.6;
Lk 14.31
20.19
Prov 11.13;
Rom 16.18
20.20
Mt 15.4;
Job 18.5
20.21
Prov 28.20
20.22
Rom 12.17;
1 Pet 3.9;
Ps 27.14
20.24
Ps 37.23;
Prov 16.9;
Jer 10.23
20.25
Ecc 5.4,5

26 A wise king winnows the wicked,
 and drives the wheel over them.
27 The spirit of man is the lamp of the LORD,
 searching all his innermost parts.
28 Loyalty and faithfulness preserve the king,
 and his throne is upheld by righteousness.g
29 The glory of young men is their strength,
 but the beauty of old men is their gray hair.
30 Blows that wound cleanse away evil;
 strokes make clean the innermost parts.

Z. The treasures of the wicked

21 The king's heart is a stream of water in the hand of
 the LORD;
 he turns it wherever he will.
2 Every way of a man is right in his own eyes,
 but the LORD weighs the heart.
3 To do righteousness and justice
 is more acceptable to the LORD than sacrifice.
4 Haughty eyes and a proud heart,
 the lamp of the wicked, are sin.
5 The plans of the diligent lead surely to abundance,
 but every one who is hasty comes only to want.
6 The getting of treasures by a lying tongue
 is a fleeting vapor and a snare of death.
7 The violence of the wicked will sweep them away,
 because they refuse to do what is just.
8 The way of the guilty is crooked,
 but the conduct of the pure is right.
9 It is better to live in a corner of the housetop
 than in a house shared with a contentious woman.
10 The soul of the wicked desires evil;
 his neighbor finds no mercy in his eyes.
11 When a scoffer is punished, the simple becomes wise;
 when a wise man is instructed, he gains knowledge.
12 The righteous observes the house of the wicked;
 the wicked are cast down to ruin.

AA. The treasures of the wise

13 He who closes his ear to the cry of the poor
 will himself cry out and not be heard.
14 A gift in secret averts anger;
 and a bribe in the bosom, strong wrath.

g Gk: Heb loyalty

20.26	ver 8
*20.27	1 Cor 2.11
20.28	Prov 29.14
20.29	Prov 16.31
21.2	Prov 16.2; 24.12; Lk 16.15
21.3	1 Sam 15.22; Prov 15.8; Isa 1.11–17; Hos 6.6; Mic 6.7,8
*21.4	Prov 6.17
21.5	Prov 10.4; 28.22
21.6	2 Pet 2.3
21.7	Prov 10.25
21.9	Prov 25.24
21.10	Prov 2.14; 14.21
21.11	Prov 19.25
21.12	Prov 14.11
21.13	Mt 18.30–34; 1 Jn 3.17; Jas 2.13
21.14	Prov 18.16; 19.6

20.27 *The spirit of man is the lamp of the* LORD. The spirit which God has placed in man illuminates his thoughts and motives, bringing to light all that is unworthy, and making it possible for man to attain to the purposes for which he was created.
21.4 The pride of man is a great sin which is condemned in Scripture (Prov 6.16, 17; 16.5; 1 Sam 2.3; Ps 131.1; 101.5). It is characteristic of: (1) false teachers (1 Tim 6.3, 4); (2) the wicked (Hab 2.4, 5; Rom 1.30); (3) Satan (1 Tim 3.6); (4) those who love the world (1 Jn 2.16). Pride leads to anger, contentiousness towards others, and deception of oneself (Prov 21.24; 28.25; Jer 49.16); its fruits are shame, debasement, and punishment (Prov 11.2; 29.23; Zeph 2.10, 11). Believers should avoid it because God resists the proud (Jas 4.6; 1 Pet 5.5) and bestows no blessing upon them except chastisement.

15 When justice is done, it is a joy to the righteous,
  but dismay to evildoers.

16 A man who wanders from the way of understanding
  will rest in the assembly of the dead.

17 He who loves pleasure will be a poor man;
  he who loves wine and oil will not be rich.

18 The wicked is a ransom for the righteous,
  and the faithless for the upright.

19 It is better to live in a desert land
  than with a contentious and fretful woman.

20 Precious treasure remains *h* in a wise man's dwelling,
  but a foolish man devours it.

21 He who pursues righteousness and kindness
  will find life *i* and honor.

22 A wise man scales the city of the mighty
  and brings down the stronghold in which they trust.

23 He who keeps his mouth and his tongue
  keeps himself out of trouble.

24 "Scoffer" is the name of the proud, haughty man
  who acts with arrogant pride.

25 The desire of the sluggard kills him
  for his hands refuse to labor.

26 All day long the wicked covets, *j*
  but the righteous gives and does not hold back.

27 The sacrifice of the wicked is an abomination;
  how much more when he brings it with evil intent.

28 A false witness will perish,
  but the word of a man who hears will endure.

29 A wicked man puts on a bold face,
  but an upright man considers *k* his ways.

30 No wisdom, no understanding, no counsel,
  can avail against the LORD.

31 The horse is made ready for the day of battle,
  but the victory belongs to the LORD.

BB. *The value of a good name*

22 A good name is to be chosen rather than great riches,
  and favor is better than silver or gold.

2 The rich and the poor meet together;
  the LORD is the maker of them all.

3 A prudent man sees danger and hides himself;
  but the simple go on, and suffer for it.

4 The reward for humility and fear of the LORD
  is riches and honor and life.

5 Thorns and snares are in the way of the perverse;
  he who guards himself will keep far from them.

6 Train up a child in the way he should go,
  and when he is old he will not depart from it.

7 The rich rules over the poor,
  and the borrower is the slave of the lender.

8 He who sows injustice will reap calamity,
  and the rod of his fury will fail.

---

h Gk: Heb *and oil*   *i* Gk: Heb *life and righteousness*
j Gk: Heb *all day long he covets covetously*   *k* Another reading is *establishes*

21.16
Ps 49.14

21.18
Prov 11.8
21.19
ver 9
21.20
Prov 22.4;
Job 20.15,
18
21.21
Mt 5.6
21.22
Ecc 9.15,16
21.23
Prov 12.13;
Jas 3.2
21.24
Ps 1.1;
Prov 1.22;
Isa 16.6;
Jer 48.29
21.25
Prov 13.4;
20.4
21.26
Ps 37.26;
Mt 5.42;
Eph 4.28
21.27
Isa 66.3;
Jer 6.20;
Amos 5.22
21.28
Prov 19.5,9
21.29
Ecc 8.1
21.30
Isa 8.9,10;
Jer 9.23;
Acts 5.39
21.31
Isa 31.1;
Ps 3.8;
1 Cor 15.28

22.1
Ecc 7.1

22.3
Prov 14.16;
27.12

22.5
Prov 15.19

22.6
Eph 6.4
22.7
Prov 18.23;
Jas 2.6
22.8
Prov 24.16;
Ps 125.3

9 He who has a bountiful eye will be blessed,
   for he shares his bread with the poor.
10 Drive out a scoffer, and strife will go out,
   and quarreling and abuse will cease.
11 He who loves purity of heart,
   and whose speech is gracious, will have the king as his friend.
12 The eyes of the LORD keep watch over knowledge,
   but he overthrows the words of the faithless.
13 The sluggard says, "There is a lion outside!
   I shall be slain in the streets!"
14 The mouth of a loose woman is a deep pit;
   he with whom the LORD is angry will fall into it.
15 Folly is bound up in the heart of a child,
   but the rod of discipline drives it far from him.
16 He who oppresses the poor to increase his own wealth,
   or gives to the rich, will only come to want.

III. Sundry sayings 22.17–24.34

A. Hear the words of the wise

17 Incline your ear, and hear the words of the wise,
   and apply your mind to my knowledge;
18 for it will be pleasant if you keep them within you,
   if all of them are ready on your lips.
19 That your trust may be in the LORD,
   I have made them known to you today, even to you.

20 Have I not written for you thirty sayings
   of admonition and knowledge,
21 to show you what is right and true,
   that you may give a true answer to those who sent you?

22 Do not rob the poor, because he is poor,
   or crush the afflicted at the gate;
23 for the LORD will plead their cause
   and despoil of life those who despoil them.
24 Make no friendship with a man given to anger,
   nor go with a wrathful man,
25 lest you learn his ways
   and entangle yourself in a snare.
26 Be not one of those who give pledges,
   who become surety for debts.
27 If you have nothing with which to pay,
   why should your bed be taken from under you?
28 Remove not the ancient landmark
   which your fathers have set.
29 Do you see a man skilful in his work?
   he will stand before kings;
   he will not stand before obscure men.

Cross-references: 22.9 2 Cor 9.6; 22.10 Prov 18.6; 26.20; 22.11 Mt 5.8; Prov 16.13; 22.12 Prov 21.12; 22.13 Prov 26.13; 22.14 Prov 2.16; 5.3; 23.27; Ecc 7.26; ★22.15 Prov 13.24; 23.14; 22.17 Prov 5.1; 23.12; 22.18 Prov 2.10; 22.19 Prov 3.5; 22.20 Prov 8.6,10; 22.21 Lk 1.3,4; 22.22 Zech 7.10; Mal 3.5; 22.23 1 Sam 25.39; Ps 12.5; 35.10; Prov 23.11; 22.26 Prov 11.15; ★22.28 Prov 23.10; 22.29 Rom 12.11; 1 Ki 10.8

22.15 *Folly*, or delinquency, comes naturally to youth. Correction and discipline are a virtual necessity if the young are to come to live useful lives.

22.28 *landmark* refers to the marker which designated the boundaries of property. To remove the landmark was to encroach on the property of a neighbor.

B. *The desire for delicacies*

23 When you sit down to eat with a ruler,
observe carefully what¹ is before you;

2 and put a knife to your throat
if you are a man given to appetite.

3 Do not desire his delicacies,
for they are deceptive food.

4 Do not toil to acquire wealth;
be wise enough to desist.

5 When your eyes light upon it, it is gone;
for suddenly it takes to itself wings,
flying like an eagle toward heaven.

6 Do not eat the bread of a man who is stingy;
do not desire his delicacies;

7 for he is like one who is inwardly reckoning.ᵐ
"Eat and drink!" he says to you;
but his heart is not with you.

8 You will vomit up the morsels which you have eaten,
and waste your pleasant words.

9 Do not speak in the hearing of a fool,
for he will despise the wisdom of your words.

10 Do not remove an ancient landmark
or enter the fields of the fatherless;

11 for their Redeemer is strong;
he will plead their cause against you.

12 Apply your mind to instruction
and your ear to words of knowledge.

13 Do not withhold discipline from a child;
if you beat him with a rod, he will not die.

14 If you beat him with the rod
you will save his life from Shēōl.

C. *Wise words to a son*

15 My son, if your heart is wise,
my heart too will be glad.

16 My soul will rejoice
when your lips speak what is right.

17 Let not your heart envy sinners,
but continue in the fear of the LORD all the day.

18 Surely there is a future,
and your hope will not be cut off.

19 Hear, my son, and be wise,
and direct your mind in the way.

20 Be not among winebibbers,
or among gluttonous eaters of meat;

21 for the drunkard and the glutton will come to poverty,
and drowsiness will clothe a man with rags.

¹ Or *who*
ᵐ Heb obscure

23.11 their *Redeemer* was the next of kin who had the responsibility for repurchasing the family estate which had become alienated (Lev 25.25).

Cross references:
23.2 ver 20; 23.3 ver 6; Ps 141.4; 23.4 Prov 28.20; 1 Tim 6.9, 10; Rom 12.16; 23.5 Prov 27.24; 23.6 Ps 141.4; 23.7 Prov 26.24, 25; 23.9 Mt 7.6; Prov 1.7; 23.10 Prov 22.28; Jer 22.3; Zech 7.10; *23.11 Prov 22.23; 23.12 Prov 22.17; 23.13 Prov 13.24; 19.18; 22.15; 23.16 ver 24,25; Prov 27.11; 23.17 Ps 37.1; Prov 28.14; 23.20 Isa 5.22; Mt 24.49; Lk 21.34; Rom 13.13; Eph 5.18; 23.21 Prov 21.17; 6.10,11

22 Hearken to your father who begot you,
  and do not despise your mother when she is old.
23 Buy truth, and do not sell it;
  buy wisdom, instruction, and understanding.
24 The father of the righteous will greatly rejoice;
  he who begets a wise son will be glad in him.
25 Let your father and mother be glad,
  let her who bore you rejoice.

26 My son, give me your heart,
  and let your eyes observe[n] my ways.
27 For a harlot is a deep pit;
  an adventuress is a narrow well.
28 She lies in wait like a robber
  and increases the faithless among men.

29 Who has woe? Who has sorrow?
  Who has strife? Who has complaining?
  Who has wounds without cause?
  Who has redness of eyes?
30 Those who tarry long over wine,
  those who go to try mixed wine.
31 Do not look at wine when it is red,
  when it sparkles in the cup
  and goes down smoothly.
32 At the last it bites like a serpent,
  and stings like an adder.
33 Your eyes will see strange things,
  and your mind utter perverse things.
34 You will be like one who lies down in the midst of the sea,
  like one who lies on the top of a mast.[o]
35 "They struck me," you will say,[p] "but I was not hurt;
  they beat me, but I did not feel it.
  When shall I awake?
  I will seek another drink."

24 Be not envious of evil men,
  nor desire to be with them;
2 for their minds devise violence,
  and their lips talk of mischief.

D. Wisdom weighed

3 By wisdom a house is built,
  and by understanding it is established;
4 by knowledge the rooms are filled
  with all precious and pleasant riches.
5 A wise man is mightier than a strong man,[q]
  and a man of knowledge than he who has strength;
6 for by wise guidance you can wage your war,
  and in abundance of counselors there is victory.
7 Wisdom is too high for a fool;
  in the gate he does not open his mouth.

Cross references: 23.22 Prov 1.8; 30.17; Eph 6.1; 23.23 Prov 4.5,7; Mt 13.44; 23.24 Prov 10.1; 15.20; 23.26 Prov 3.1; 4.4; Ps 1.2; 23.27 Prov 22.14; 23.28 Prov 7.12; Ecc 7.26; 23.29 Isa 5.11,22; 23.30 Eph 5.18; Ps 75.8; 23.33 Prov 2.12; 23.35 Jer 5.3; 24.1 Ps 37.1; 73.3; Prov 3.31; 24.2 Jer 22.17; Job 15.35; 24.3 Prov 9.1; 24.5 Prov 21.22; 24.6 Lk 14.31; 24.7 Ps 10.5

n Another reading is *delight in*   o Heb obscure
p Gk Syr Vg Tg: Heb lacks *you will say*
q Gk Compare Syr Tg: Heb *is in strength*

24.8
Prov 6.14;
Rom 1.30
8 He who plans to do evil
    will be called a mischief-maker.
9 The devising of folly is sin,
    and the scoffer is an abomination to men.

24.10
Jer 51.46;
Heb 12.3
10 If you faint in the day of adversity,
    your strength is small.
24.11
Ps 82.4;
Isa 58.6,7
11 Rescue those who are being taken away to death;
    hold back those who are stumbling to the slaughter.
24.12
Prov 21.2;
Ecc 5.8;
Ps 121.3–8;
94.9–11;
Prov 12.14
12 If you say, "Behold, we did not know this,"
    does not he who weighs the heart perceive it?
Does not he who keeps watch over your soul know it,
    and will he not requite man according to his work?

E. Counsel to a son

24.13
Sol 5.1
13 My son, eat honey, for it is good,
    and the drippings of the honeycomb are sweet to your taste.
24.14
Prov 2.10
14 Know that wisdom is such to your soul;
    if you find it, there will be a future,
    and your hope will not be cut off.

24.15
Ps 10.9,10
15 Lie not in wait as a wicked man against the dwelling of the
    righteous;
    do not violence to his home;
24.16
Ps 34.19;
Mic 7.8;
ver 22
16 for a righteous man falls seven times, and rises again;
    but the wicked are overthrown by calamity.

24.17
Job 31.29;
Obad 12
17 Do not rejoice when your enemy falls,
    and let not your heart be glad when he stumbles;
18 lest the LORD see it, and be displeased,
    and turn away his anger from him.

24.19
Ps 37.1
19 Fret not yourself because of evildoers,
    and be not envious of the wicked;
24.20
Prov 13.9
20 for the evil man has no future;
    the lamp of the wicked will be put out.

24.21
Rom 13.1–
7;
1 Pet 2.17
21 My son, fear the LORD and the king,
    and do not disobey either of them;[r]
22 for disaster from them will rise suddenly,
    and who knows the ruin that will come from them both?

F. Sayings of the wise

24.23
Prov 1.6;
18.5;
Lev 19.15;
Deut 1.17
23   These also are sayings of the wise.

Partiality in judging is not good.
24.24
Prov 17.15
24 He who says to the wicked, "You are innocent,"
    will be cursed by peoples, abhorred by nations;
24.25
Prov 28.23
25 but those who rebuke the wicked will have delight,
    and a good blessing will be upon them.
26 He who gives a right answer
    kisses the lips.

---

r Gk: Heb do not associate with those who change

27 Prepare your work outside,
    get everything ready for you in the field;
    and after that build your house.

28 Be not a witness against your neighbor without cause,
    and do not deceive with your lips.
29 Do not say, "I will do to him as he has done to me;
    I will pay the man back for what he has done."

30 I passed by the field of a sluggard,
    by the vineyard of a man without sense;
31 and lo, it was all overgrown with thorns;
    the ground was covered with nettles,
    and its stone wall was broken down.
32 Then I saw and considered it;
    I looked and received instruction.
33 A little sleep, a little slumber,
    a little folding of the hands to rest,
34 and poverty will come upon you like a robber,
    and want like an armed man.

IV. *Miscellaneous sayings of Solomon 25.1–29.27*

A. *Counsel for the king's presence*

25 These also are proverbs of Solomon which the men of Hĕzĕkī´áh king of Judah copied.

2 It is the glory of God to conceal things,
    but the glory of kings is to search things out.
3 As the heavens for height, and the earth for depth,
    so the mind of kings is unsearchable.
4 Take away the dross from the silver,
    and the smith has material for a vessel;
5 take away the wicked from the presence of the king,
    and his throne will be established in righteousness.
6 Do not put yourself forward in the king's presence
    or stand in the place of the great;
7 for it is better to be told, "Come up here,"
    than to be put lower in the presence of the prince.

What your eyes have seen
8   do not hastily bring into court;
for*s* what will you do in the end,
    when your neighbor puts you to shame?
9 Argue your case with your neighbor himself,
    and do not disclose another's secret;
10 lest he who hears you bring shame upon you,
    and your ill repute have no end.

11 A word fitly spoken
    is like apples of gold in a setting of silver.
12 Like a gold ring or an ornament of gold
    is a wise reprover to a listening ear.

s Cn: Heb *lest*

Marginal references:

24.28 Prov 25.18; Eph 4.25
24.29 Prov 20.22; Mt 5.39; Rom 12.17
24.30 Prov 6.6–11
24.33 Prov 6.9; 20.13
25.1 Prov 1.1
25.2 Deut 29.29; Ezra 6.1
25.4 2 Tim 2.21
25.5 Prov 20.8; 16.12
25.7 Lk 14.7–11
25.8 Mt 5.25
25.9 Mt 18.15; Prov 11.13
25.11 Prov 15.23
25.12 Prov 15.31; 20.12

25.13
ver 25;
Prov 13.17
13 Like the cold of snow in the time of harvest
    is a faithful messenger to those who send him,
    he refreshes the spirit of his masters.

25.14
Prov 20.6;
Jude 12
14 Like clouds and wind without rain
    is a man who boasts of a gift he does not give.

B. The neighbor and the enemy

25.15
Gen 32.4;
1 Sam
25.24;
Prov 15.1;
16.14
15 With patience a ruler may be persuaded,
    and a soft tongue will break a bone.
16 If you have found honey, eat only enough for you,
    lest you be sated with it and vomit it.

25.16
ver 27
17 Let your foot be seldom in your neighbor's house,
    lest he become weary of you and hate you.

25.18
Ps 57.4;
Prov 12.18
18 A man who bears false witness against his neighbor
    is like a war club, or a sword, or a sharp arrow.
19 Trust in a faithless man in time of trouble
    is like a bad tooth or a foot that slips.
20 He who sings songs to a heavy heart
    is like one who takes off a garment on a cold day,
    and like vinegar on a wound.[t]

25.21
Ex 23.4,5;
Mt 5.44;
Rom 12.20
21 If your enemy is hungry, give him bread to eat;
    and if he is thirsty, give him water to drink;

25.22
2 Sam 16.12
22 for you will heap coals of fire on his head,
    and the LORD will reward you.

25.23
Ps 101.5
23 The north wind brings forth rain;
    and a backbiting tongue, angry looks.

25.24
Prov 21.9
24 It is better to live in a corner of the housetop
    than in a house shared with a contentious woman.

25.25
ver 13;
Prov 15.30
25 Like cold water to a thirsty soul,
    so is good news from a far country.

25.26
Ezek 32.2;
34.18,19
26 Like a muddied spring or a polluted fountain
    is a righteous man who gives way before the wicked.

25.27
ver 16;
Prov 27.2
27 It is not good to eat much honey,
    so be sparing of complimentary words.[u]

25.28
Prov 16.32
28 A man without self-control
    is like a city broken into and left without walls.

C. The fool and his folly

26.1
1 Sam 12.17
26 Like snow in summer or rain in harvest,
      so honor is not fitting for a fool.

26.2
Num 23.8;
Deut 23.5
2 Like a sparrow in its flitting, like a swallow in its flying,
    a curse that is causeless does not alight.

26.3
Ps 32.9
3 A whip for the horse, a bridle for the ass,
    and a rod for the back of fools.

26.4
Prov 23.9;
29.9
4 Answer not a fool according to his folly,
    lest you be like him yourself.

26.5
Mt 16.1-4;
21.24-27
5 Answer a fool according to his folly,
    lest he be wise in his own eyes.
6 He who sends a message by the hand of a fool
    cuts off his own feet and drinks violence.

26.7
ver 9
7 Like a lame man's legs, which hang useless,
    is a proverb in the mouth of fools.

[t] Gk: Heb lye   [u] Cn Compare Gk Syr Tg: Heb searching out their glory is glory

8 Like one who binds the stone in the sling
   is he who gives honor to a fool.

9 Like a thorn that goes up into the hand of a drunkard
   is a proverb in the mouth of fools.

10 Like an archer who wounds everybody
   is he who hires a passing fool or drunkard.ᵛ

11 Like a dog that returns to his vomit
   is a fool that repeats his folly.

12 Do you see a man who is wise in his own eyes?
   There is more hope for a fool than for him.

D. The lazy man and the lying tongue

13 The sluggard says, "There is a lion in the road!
   There is a lion in the streets!"

14 As a door turns on its hinges,
   so does a sluggard on his bed.

15 The sluggard buries his hand in the dish;
   it wears him out to bring it back to his mouth.

16 The sluggard is wiser in his own eyes
   than seven men who can answer discreetly.

17 He who meddles in a quarrel not his own
   is like one who takes a passing dog by the ears.

18 Like a madman who throws firebrands,
   arrows, and death,

19 is the man who deceives his neighbor
   and says, "I am only joking!"

20 For lack of wood the fire goes out;
   and where there is no whisperer, quarreling ceases.

21 As charcoal to hot embers and wood to fire,
   so is a quarrelsome man for kindling strife.

22 The words of a whisperer are like delicious morsels;
   they go down into the inner parts of the body.

23 Like the glazeʷ covering an earthen vessel
   are smoothˣ lips with an evil heart.

24 He who hates, dissembles with his lips
   and harbors deceit in his heart;

25 when he speaks graciously, believe him not,
   for there are seven abominations in his heart;

26 though his hatred be covered with guile,
   his wickedness will be exposed in the assembly.

27 He who digs a pit will fall into it,
   and a stone will come back upon him who starts it rolling.

28 A lying tongue hates its victims,
   and a flattering mouth works ruin.

E. Wisdom for today and tomorrow

27 Do not boast about tomorrow,
   for you do not know what a day may bring forth.

2 Let another praise you, and not your own mouth;
   a stranger, and not your own lips.

3 A stone is heavy, and sand is weighty,
   but a fool's provocation is heavier than both.

ᵛ The Hebrew text of this verse is uncertain   ʷ Cn: Heb *silver of dross*   ˣ Gk: Heb *burning*

Cross-references (right margin)

26.8   ver 1
26.9   ver 7
26.11   2 Pet 2.22; Ex 8.15
26.12   ver 5; Prov 3.7; 29.20
26.13   Prov 22.13
26.15   Prov 19.24
26.17   Prov 3.30
26.18   Isa 50.11
26.19   Prov 24.28
26.20   Prov 16.28; 22.10
26.21   Prov 15.18
26.22   Prov 18.8
26.24   Prov 10.18; 12.20
26.25   Ps 28.3; Jer 9.8
26.26   Mt 23.28; Lk 8.17
26.27   Ps 7.15; Prov 28.10; Ecc 10.8
26.28   Prov 29.5
27.1   Lk 12.19, 20; Jas 4.14
27.2   Prov 25.27; 2 Cor 10.12, 18
27.3   Prov 12.16

4 Wrath is cruel, anger is overwhelming;
  but who can stand before jealousy?

27.5
Prov 28.23
5 Better is open rebuke
  than hidden love.

6 Faithful are the wounds of a friend;
  profuse are the kisses of an enemy.

27.7
Prov 25.16
7 He who is sated loathes honey,
  but to one who is hungry everything bitter is sweet.

8 Like a bird that strays from its nest,
  is a man who strays from his home.

9 Oil and perfume make the heart glad,
  but the soul is torn by trouble.y

27.10
2 Chr 10.6–
8;
Prov 17.17;
18.24
10 Your friend, and your father's friend, do not forsake;
   and do not go to your brother's house in the day of your
     calamity.
   Better is a neighbor who is near
     than a brother who is far away.

27.11
Prov 10.1;
23.15;
Ps 119.42
11 Be wise, my son, and make my heart glad,
   that I may answer him who reproaches me.

27.12
Prov 22.3
12 A prudent man sees danger and hides himself;
   but the simple go on, and suffer for it.

27.13
Prov 20.16
13 Take a man's garment when he has given surety for a stranger,
   and hold him in pledge when he gives surety for foreigners.z

14 He who blesses his neighbor with a loud voice,
   rising early in the morning,
   will be counted as cursing.

27.15
Prov 19.13
15 A continual dripping on a rainy day
   and a contentious woman are alike;
16 to restrain her is to restrain the winda
   or to grasp oil in his right hand.

F. Man never satisfied

17 Iron sharpens iron,
   and one man sharpens another.

27.18
1 Cor 9.7;
Lk 12.42–
44;
19.17
18 He who tends a fig tree will eat its fruit,
   and he who guards his master will be honored.

19 As in water face answers to face,
   so the mind of man reflects the man.

27.20
Hab 2.5;
Ecc 1.8
20 Shēōl and Ăbăd'dón are never satisfied,
   and never satisfied are the eyes of man.

27.21
Lk 6.26
21 The crucible is for silver, and the furnace is for gold,
   and a man is judged by his praise.

27.22
Prov 23.35;
Jer 5.3
22 Crush a fool in a mortar with a pestle
   along with crushed grain,
   yet his folly will not depart from him.

23 Know well the condition of your flocks,
   and give attention to your herds;

27.24
Prov 23.5;
Job 19.9
24 for riches do not last for ever;
   and does a crown endure to all generations?

27.25
Ps 104.14
25 When the grass is gone, and the new growth appears,
   and the herbage of the mountains is gathered,

y Gk: Heb the sweetness of his friend from hearty counsel
z Vg and 20.16: Heb a foreign woman   a Heb obscure

26 the lambs will provide your clothing,
   and the goats the price of a field;
27 there will be enough goats' milk for your food,
   for the food of your household
   and maintenance for your maidens.

G. *The wicked and the righteous*

28 The wicked flee when no one pursues,
   but the righteous are bold as a lion.

28.1
Lev 26.17;
Ps 53.5

2 When a land transgresses
   it has many rulers;
   but with men of understanding and knowledge
   its stability will long continue.

28.2
Prov 11.11

3 A poor man who oppresses the poor
   is a beating rain that leaves no food.

28.3
Mt 18.28

4 Those who forsake the law praise the wicked,
   but those who keep the law strive against them.

28.4
Rom 1.32;
1 Ki 18.18

5 Evil men do not understand justice,
   but those who seek the LORD understand it completely.

28.5
Ps 92.6;
Jn 7.17;
1 Cor 2.15

6 Better is a poor man who walks in his integrity
   than a rich man who is perverse in his ways.

28.6
Prov 19.1;
ver 18

7 He who keeps the law is a wise son,
   but a companion of gluttons shames his father.

28.7
Prov 23.20

8 He who augments his wealth by interest and increase
   gathers it for him who is kind to the poor.

28.8
Lev 25.36;
Prov 13.22;
14.31

9 If one turns away his ear from hearing the law,
   even his prayer is an abomination.

28.9
Ps 66.18;
Prov 15.8

10 He who misleads the upright into an evil way
   will fall into his own pit;
   but the blameless will have a goodly inheritance.

28.10
Prov 26.27;
Mt 6.33;
Heb 6.12

11 A rich man is wise in his own eyes,
   but a poor man who has understanding will find him out.

28.11
Prov 26.5,
12; 18.17

12 When the righteous triumph, there is great glory;
   but when the wicked rise, men hide themselves.

28.12
Prov 11.10;
Ecc 10.5,6

13 He who conceals his transgressions will not prosper,
   but he who confesses and forsakes them will obtain mercy.

28.13
Ps 32.3,5

14 Blessed is the man who fears the LORD always;
   but he who hardens his heart will fall into calamity.

28.14
Ps 16.8;
Rom 2.5

15 Like a roaring lion or a charging bear
   is a wicked ruler over a poor people.

28.15
1 Pet 5.8;
Mt 2.16

16 A ruler who lacks understanding is a cruel oppressor;
   but he who hates unjust gain will prolong his days.

17 If a man is burdened with the blood of another,
   let him be a fugitive until death;
   let no one help him.

28.17
Gen 9.6;
Ex 21.14

18 He who walks in integrity will be delivered,
   but he who is perverse in his ways will fall into a pit.*b*

28.18
Prov 10.9,
25;
ver 6

19 He who tills his land will have plenty of bread,
   but he who follows worthless pursuits will have plenty of
   poverty.

28.19
Prov 12.11

20 A faithful man will abound with blessings,
   but he who hastens to be rich will not go unpunished.

28.20
Prov 10.6;
ver 22;
1 Tim 6.9

21 To show partiality is not good;

28.21
Prov 18.5;
Ezek 13.19

b Syr: Heb *in one*

but for a piece of bread a man will do wrong.

28.22
Prov 23.6;
ver 20
22 A miserly man hastens after wealth,
  and does not know that want will come upon him.

28.23
Prov 27.5,6
23 He who rebukes a man will afterward find more favor
  than he who flatters with his tongue.

28.24
Prov 19.26;
18.9
24 He who robs his father or his mother
  and says, "That is no transgression,"
  is the companion of a man who destroys.

28.25
Prov 15.27;
29.25
25 A greedy man stirs up strife,
  but he who trusts in the LORD will be enriched.

28.26
Prov 3.5;
ver 18
26 He who trusts in his own mind is a fool;
  but he who walks in wisdom will be delivered.

28.27
Deut 15.7;
Prov 19.17;
21.13
27 He who gives to the poor will not want,
  but he who hides his eyes will get many a curse.

28.28
ver 12
28 When the wicked rise, men hide themselves,
  but when they perish, the righteous increase.

H. *The reign of the righteous*

29.1
1 Sam 2.25;
2 Chr
36.16;
Prov 6.15
29 He who is often reproved, yet stiffens his neck
  will suddenly be broken beyond healing.

29.2
Est 8.15;
Prov 28.15
2 When the righteous are in authority, the people rejoice;
  but when the wicked rule, the people groan.

29.3
Prov 10.1;
5.9,10;
Lk 15.13
3 He who loves wisdom makes his father glad,
  but one who keeps company with harlots squanders
    his substance.

4 By justice a king gives stability to the land,
  but one who exacts gifts ruins it.

29.5
Ps 5.9
5 A man who flatters his neighbor
  spreads a net for his feet.

29.6
Prov 22.5;
Ex 15.1
6 An evil man is ensnared in his transgression,
  but a righteous man sings and rejoices.

29.7
Job 29.16;
Ps 41.1
7 A righteous man knows the rights of the poor;
  a wicked man does not understand such knowledge.

29.8
Prov 11.11;
16.14
8 Scoffers set a city aflame,
  but wise men turn away wrath.

9 If a wise man has an argument with a fool,
  the fool only rages and laughs, and there is no quiet.

29.10
1 Jn 3.12
10 Bloodthirsty men hate one who is blameless,
  and the wicked[c] seek his life.

29.11
Prov 12.16;
19.11
11 A fool gives full vent to his anger,
  but a wise man quietly holds it back.

12 If a ruler listens to falsehood,
  all his officials will be wicked.

29.13
Ps 13.3
13 The poor man and the oppressor meet together;
  the LORD gives light to the eyes of both.

29.14
Ps 72.4;
Isa 11.4;
Prov 16.12;
25.5
14 If a king judges the poor with equity
  his throne will be established for ever.

29.15
Prov 13.24;
10.1
15 The rod and reproof give wisdom,
  but a child left to himself brings shame to his mother.

29.16
Ps 37.36;
58.10;
91.8; 92.11
16 When the wicked are in authority, transgression increases;
  but the righteous will look upon their downfall.

29.17
ver 15;
Prov 10.1
17 Discipline your son, and he will give you rest;
  he will give delight to your heart.

c Cn: Heb *upright*

18 Where there is no prophecy the people cast off restraint,
   but blessed is he who keeps the law.
19 By mere words a servant is not disciplined,
   for though he understands, he will not give heed.
20 Do you see a man who is hasty in his words?
   There is more hope for a fool than for him.
21 He who pampers his servant from childhood,
   will in the end find him his heir.*d*
22 A man of wrath stirs up strife,
   and a man given to anger causes much transgression.
23 A man's pride will bring him low,
   but he who is lowly in spirit will obtain honor.
24 The partner of a thief hates his own life;
   he hears the curse, but discloses nothing.
25 The fear of man lays a snare,
   but he who trusts in the LORD is safe.
26 Many seek the favor of a ruler,
   but from the LORD a man gets justice.
27 An unjust man is an abomination to the righteous,
   but he whose way is straight is an abomination to the wicked.

V. The words of Agur 30.1–33

A. Personal observations

30 The words of Āgŭr son of Jākĕh of Măssá.*e*

   The man says to Ĭth'ĭ-ĕl,
      to Ithi-el and Ŭcăl:*f*
2 Surely I am too stupid to be a man.
   I have not the understanding of a man.
3 I have not learned wisdom,
   nor have I knowledge of the Holy One.
4 Who has ascended to heaven and come down?
   Who has gathered the wind in his fists?
Who has wrapped up the waters in a garment?
   Who has established all the ends of the earth?
What is his name, and what is his son's name?
   Surely you know!

5 Every word of God proves true;
   he is a shield to those who take refuge in him.
6 Do not add to his words,
   lest he rebuke you, and you be found a liar.

7 Two things I ask of thee;
   deny them not to me before I die:
8 Remove far from me falsehood and lying;
   give me neither poverty nor riches;
   feed me with the food that is needful for me,

d The meaning of the Hebrew word is uncertain   *e* Or *the oracle*
f The Hebrew of this verse is obscure

Cross references:
29.18 1 Sam 3.1; Amos 8.11, 12; Jn 13.17
29.20 Jas 1.19; Prov 26.12
29.22 Prov 15.18; 17.19
29.23 Job 22.29; Isa 66.2; Dan 4.30; Mt 23.12
29.24 Lev 5.1
29.25 Gen 12.12; Ps 91.1–16
29.26 Isa 49.4
★30.1 Prov 31.1
30.2 Ps 73.22
30.3 Prov 9.10
30.4 Jn 3.13; Ps 104.3; Isa 40.12; Job 38.8,9; Isa 45.18
30.5 Ps 12.6; 18.30; 84.11
30.6 Deut 4.2; 12.32; Rev 22.18
30.8 Mt 6.11

30.1 *words of Agur.* Agur and Lemuel (31.1) left writings incorporated into the Book of Proverbs. We know nothing about them otherwise.

30.9
Deut 8.12;
Neh 9.25;
Job 31.24;
Hos 13.6

9 lest I be full, and deny thee,
   and say, "Who is the LORD?"
or lest I be poor, and steal,
   and profane the name of my God.

B. *Numerical proverbs*

30.10
Ecc 7.21

10 Do not slander a servant to his master,
   lest he curse you, and you be held guilty.

30.11
Prov 20.20

11 There are those who curse their fathers
   and do not bless their mothers.

30.12
Lk 18.11

12 There are those who are pure in their own eyes
   but are not cleansed of their filth.

30.13
Ps 131.1;
Prov 6.17

13 There are those—how lofty are their eyes,
   how high their eyelids lift!

30.14
Job 29.17;
Ps 52.2;
14.4;
Amos 8.4

14 There are those whose teeth are swords,
   whose teeth are knives,
to devour the poor from off the earth,
   the needy from among men.

15 The leech*g* has two daughters;
   "Give, give," they cry.
Three things are never satisfied;
   four never say, "Enough":

30.16
Prov 27.20

16 Shēōl, the barren womb,
   the earth ever thirsty for water,
   and the fire which never says, "Enough."*h*

30.17
Gen 9.22;
Prov 23.22;
Deut 28.26

17 The eye that mocks a father
   and scorns to obey a mother
will be picked out by the ravens of the valley
   and eaten by the vultures.

18 Three things are too wonderful for me;
   four I do not understand:
19 the way of an eagle in the sky,
   the way of a serpent on a rock,
the way of a ship on the high seas,
   and the way of a man with a maiden.

30.20
Prov 5.6

20 This is the way of an adulteress:
   she eats, and wipes her mouth,
   and says, "I have done no wrong."

21 Under three things the earth trembles;
   under four it cannot bear up:

30.22
Prov 19.10

22 a slave when he becomes king,
   and a fool when he is filled with food;
23 an unloved woman when she gets a husband,
   and a maid when she succeeds her mistress.

24 Four things on earth are small,
   but they are exceedingly wise:

---

g The meaning of the Hebrew word is uncertain   h Heb obscure

25 the ants are a people not strong,
    yet they provide their food in the summer;
26 the badgers are a people not mighty,
    yet they make their homes in the rocks;
27 the locusts have no king,
    yet all of them march in rank;
28 the lizard you can take in your hands,
    yet it is in kings' palaces.

29 Three things are stately in their tread;
    four are stately in their stride:
30 the lion, which is mightiest among beasts
    and does not turn back before any;
31 the strutting cock,[i] the he-goat,
    and a king striding before[j] his people.

32 If you have been foolish, exalting yourself,
    or if you have been devising evil,
    put your hand on your mouth.
33 For pressing milk produces curds,
    pressing the nose produces blood,
    and pressing anger produces strife.

VI. *The words of Lemuel: the folly of lust and strong drink 31.1–9*

31 The words of Lĕm′ūĕl, king of Măssă,[k] which his mother
    taught him:

2 What, my son? What, son of my womb?
    What, son of my vows?
3 Give not your strength to women,
    your ways to those who destroy kings.
4 It is not for kings, O Lĕm′ūĕl,
    it is not for kings to drink wine,
    or for rulers to desire[l] strong drink;
5 lest they drink and forget what has been decreed,
    and pervert the rights of all the afflicted.
6 Give strong drink to him who is perishing,
    and wine to those in bitter distress;
7 let them drink and forget their poverty,
    and remember their misery no more.
8 Open your mouth for the dumb,
    for the rights of all who are left desolate.[m]
9 Open your mouth, judge righteously,
    maintain the rights of the poor and needy.

VII. *The virtuous woman 31.10–31*

10 A good wife who can find?
    She is far more precious than jewels.
11 The heart of her husband trusts in her,

---

i Gk Syr Tg Compare Vg: Heb obscure　*j* The meaning of the Hebrew is uncertain
k Or *King Lemuel, the oracle*　*l* Cn: Heb *where*　*m* Heb *are sons of passing away*

30.25
Prov 6.6–8

30.26
Ps 104.18

30.30
Judg 14.18;
Mic 5.8

30.32
Job 21.5;
40.4;
Mic 7.16
30.33
Prov 10.12;
29.22

31.1
Prov 30.1

31.2
Isa 49.15

31.3
Prov 5.9;
Deut 17.17;
1 Ki 11.1;
Neh 13.26
31.4
Ecc 10.17;
Prov 20.1
31.5
Hos 4.11

31.8
Job 29.12–
17
31.9
Lev 19.15;
Deut 1.16

31.10
Prov 12.4;
19.14

and he will have no lack of gain.

12 She does him good, and not harm,
    all the days of her life.

31.13
ver 21–24

13 She seeks wool and flax,
    and works with willing hands.

14 She is like the ships of the merchant,
    she brings her food from afar.

31.15
Rom 12.11;
Lk 12.42

15 She rises while it is yet night
    and provides food for her household
    and tasks for her maidens.

16 She considers a field and buys it;
    with the fruit of her hands she plants a vineyard.

17 She girds her loins with strength and makes her arms strong.

18 She perceives that her merchandise is profitable.
    Her lamp does not go out at night.

19 She puts her hands to the distaff,
    and her hands hold the spindle.

31.20
Eph 4.28;
Heb 13.16

20 She opens her hand to the poor,
    and reaches out her hands to the needy.

31.21
1 Sam 1.24

21 She is not afraid of snow for her household,
    for all her household are clothed in scarlet.

22 She makes herself coverings;
    her clothing is fine linen and purple.

31.23
Ruth 4.1,
11;
Prov 12.4

23 Her husband is known in the gates,
    when he sits among the elders of the land.

24 She makes linen garments and sells them;
    she delivers girdles to the merchant.

31.25
ver 17

25 Strength and dignity are her clothing,
    and she laughs at the time to come.

31.26
Prov 10.31

26 She opens her mouth with wisdom,
    and the teaching of kindness is on her tongue.

31.27
Prov 19.15

27 She looks well to the ways of her household,
    and does not eat the bread of idleness.

28 Her children rise up and call her blessed;
    her husband also, and he praises her:

31.29
Prov 12.4

29 "Many women have done excellently,
    but you surpass them all."

31.30
Prov 6.25;
22.4

30 Charm is deceitful, and beauty is vain,
    but a woman who fears the LORD is to be praised.

31 Give her of the fruit of her hands,
    and let her works praise her in the gates.

INTRODUCTION TO
ECCLESIASTES
OR THE PREACHER

Authorship and Background: Traditionally, Ecclesiastes has been ascribed to
Solomon, and it is thought to be the expression of the thinking of his later years.
Actually, only the first section of the book gives any evidence of Solomonic authorship, and even there Solomon is not specifically named. Many scholars
suggest a postexilic date for the book (ca. 430–400 B.C. or later). Since Luther's
time, it has been thought that Ecclesiastes was composed by a later writer who
put Solomon's thoughts in the form in which we now have them. The title
"Ecclesiastes" is derived from the Septuagint title signifying "The Preacher."
The Hebrew name is *Qoheleth*.

Characteristics: This is one of the most difficult Old Testament books. The
vocabulary contains obscure, perplexing words, and the style is disjointed.
References are made to customs, incidents, circumstances, and sayings easily
understood by those to whom the work was addressed but lost to the modern
mind. The material is not logically connected, which suggests that it is a
collection of diverse fragments brought together in one book. Despite all
of this, and the fact that the book cannot be outlined adequately, a message of tremendous significance is to be found in its critique of religion which has been secu-
larized, and of men whose thoughts have been misguided. Stressing that search
for happiness and satisfaction in earthly pursuits apart from God always ends
in "vanity of vanities" (1.2; 12.8), Ecclesiastes bears witness to the climactic
statement that while man cannot reconcile all of his problems in this life, he
can safely trust God who knows the end from the beginning and who will
ultimately justify His ways.

Contents:

I.   First discourse: the vanity of human wisdom. 1.1—2.26: All is vanity.
      This is shown in experience as men seek wisdom, pleasure, and wealth.
      Neither philosophy, pleasure, nor a middle pathway between them solves
      the problem. In life, man's days are pain; in death, he leaves it
      all behind him.

II.   Second discourse: the disappointing experiences of life. 3.1—5.20:
      There is a time and a season for all things; but ultimately all must go
      the same way. Society has its evils of oppression, and industry
      governed by envy. Idleness and contentment are no solution. Success
      produces enemies. The desire to possess and loneliness are common
      ills. Ambition is to strive after wind. Worship and service are vain.
      Government oppresses, avarice is evil, and wealth is a gift of God to
      be enjoyed by those fortunate enough to experience it.

III. Third discourse: the vanity of wealth and honor. 6.1—8.17: It is vain to have wealth which cannot be enjoyed; life itself is vanity. There is wisdom in death. Asceticism and excess are harmful. Moral pride is sin. Man opposes himself because of sin. Man knows not the hour of his death and cannot avert it; he has power over others to hurt them. The ends of the righteous and the wicked are often the same, yet man cannot know the answer.

IV. Fourth discourse: leaving with God the injustices of this life. 9.1—12.8: Look for death which is inevitable. Enjoy life while you can. Time and chance happen to all men. Be wise. Cultivate wisdom and avoid folly. Revere those in authority over you. Perform charitable works. Days of darkness will be many. Rejoice in God. Man is a creature of time; remember thy Creator in the days of thy youth.

V. Conclusion: considering life in the light of eternity. 12.9–14: The preacher has taught men well. The sum of it all is this: "Fear God, and keep his commandments, for this is the whole duty of man."

ECCLESIASTES

OR THE PREACHER

I. *First discourse: the vanity of human wisdom 1.1–2.26*

A. *The theme advanced: the vanity of human effort and experience*

1 The words of the Preacher,*a* the son of David, king in
Jerusalem.
2 Vanity of vanities, says the Preacher,
vanity of vanities! All is vanity.
3 What does man gain by all the toil
at which he toils under the sun?

B. *The theme demonstrated*

1. *The meaningless cycle of life*

4 A generation goes, and a generation comes,
but the earth remains for ever.
5 The sun rises and the sun goes down,
and hastens to the place where it rises.
6 The wind blows to the south,
and goes round to the north;
round and round goes the wind,
and on its circuits the wind returns.
7 All streams run to the sea,
but the sea is not full;
to the place where the streams flow,
there they flow again.
8 All things are full of weariness;
a man cannot utter it;
the eye is not satisfied with seeing,
nor the ear filled with hearing.
9 What has been is what will be,
and what has been done is what will be done;
and there is nothing new under the sun.
10 Is there a thing of which it is said,
"See, this is new"?
It has been already,
in the ages before us.
11 There is no remembrance of former things,
nor will there be any remembrance
of later things yet to happen
among those who come after.

a Heb *Kōhĕl'ĕth*

Cross-references (margin):

*1.1
ver 12;
Ecc 7.27;
12.8–10
*1.2
Ps 39.5,6;
62.9;144.4;
Ecc 12.8
1.3
Ecc 2.22;
3.9

1.4
Ps 104.5;
119.90
1.5
Ps 19.5,6
1.6
Ecc 11.5;
Jn 3.8

1.8
Prov 27.20

1.9
Ecc 2.12;
3.15

1.11
Ecc 2.16;
9.5

1.1 The author of Ecclesiastes uses the
name Qoheleth, traditionally rendered *The
Preacher*. The word means "the gatherer"
and can refer to the gatherer of people,
or of wise sayings and proverbs. The fact
that the name of Solomon is not used has
led many to suggest that the writer, while
drawing on Solomon's experiences in his
opening discourse, did not wish to identify
himself specifically with the king. The words
of Solomon may be incorporated into a work
written some time after Solomon's reign.
1.2 *Vanity* as used here alludes to the uselessness and emptiness of life which is not
lived in fellowship with God and in accord
with the divine will. The solution to this
problem of life's vanity is forcibly stated by
the orator in 12.13, 14.

2. *The vanity of human wisdom*

1.12
ver 1
1.13
ver 17;
Ecc 3.10
1.14
Ecc 2.11,17
1.15
Ecc 7.13
1.16
1 Ki 3.12,
13; 4.30;
10.23;
Ecc 2.9
1.17
Ecc 2.3,12;
7.23,25
1.18
Ecc 12.12

12 I the Preacher have been king over Israel in Jerusalem. 13And I applied my mind to seek and to search out by wisdom all that is done under heaven; it is an unhappy business that God has given to the sons of men to be busy with. 14 I have seen everything that is done under the sun; and behold, all is vanity and a striving after wind.*b*

15 What is crooked cannot be made straight,
    and what is lacking cannot be numbered.

16 I said to myself, "I have acquired great wisdom, surpassing all who were over Jerusalem before me; and my mind has had great experience of wisdom and knowledge." 17And I applied my mind to know wisdom and to know madness and folly. I perceived that this also is but a striving after wind.

18 For in much wisdom is much vexation,
    and he who increases knowledge increases sorrow.

3. *The vanity of pleasure and wealth*

2.1
Lk 12.19;
Ecc 1.2
2.2
Prov 14.13;
Ecc 7.6

2.4
1 Ki 7.1–12;
Sol 8.10,11
2.5
Sol 4.16;
5.1;
Neh 2.8

2.8
1 Ki 9.28;
10.10,14,
21; 4.21;
20.14;
2 Sam 19.35
2.9
Ecc 1.16
2.10
Ecc 3.22;
5.18; 9.9
2.11
Ecc 1.3,14

2 I said to myself, "Come now, I will make a test of pleasure; enjoy yourself." But behold, this also was vanity. 2 I said of laughter, "It is mad," and of pleasure, "What use is it?" 3 I searched with my mind how to cheer my body with wine—my mind still guiding me with wisdom—and how to lay hold on folly, till I might see what was good for the sons of men to do under heaven during the few days of their life. 4 I made great works; I built houses and planted vineyards for myself; 5 I made myself gardens and parks, and planted in them all kinds of fruit trees. 6 I made myself pools from which to water the forest of growing trees. 7 I bought male and female slaves, and had slaves who were born in my house; I had also great possessions of herds and flocks, more than any who had been before me in Jerusalem. 8 I also gathered for myself silver and gold and the treasure of kings and provinces; I got singers, both men and women, and many concubines,*c* man's delight.

9 So I became great and surpassed all who were before me in Jerusalem; also my wisdom remained with me. 10And whatever my eyes desired I did not keep from them; I kept my heart from no pleasure, for my heart found pleasure in all my toil, and this was my reward for all my toil. 11 Then I considered all that my hands had done and the toil I had spent in doing it, and behold, all was vanity and a striving after wind, and there was nothing to be gained under the sun.

4. *Both the fool and the wise must die*

2.12
Ecc 1.17;
7.25
2.13
Ecc 7.11,12
2.14
Prov 17.24;
Ps 49.10;
Ecc 9.2,3,11
2.15
Ecc 6.8,11
2.16
Ecc 1.11;
9.5; ver 14

12 So I turned to consider wisdom and madness and folly; for what can the man do who comes after the king? Only what he has already done. 13 Then I saw that wisdom excels folly as light excels darkness. 14 The wise man has his eyes in his head, but the fool walks in darkness; and yet I perceived that one fate comes to all of them. 15 Then I said to myself, "What befalls the fool will befall me also; why then have I been so very wise?" And I said to myself that this also is vanity. 16 For of the wise man as of the fool there is

b Or a feeding on wind. See Hos 12.1
c The meaning of the Hebrew word is uncertain

no enduring remembrance, seeing that in the days to come all will have been long forgotten. How the wise man dies just like the fool! 17 So I hated life, because what is done under the sun was grievous to me; for all is vanity and a striving after wind.

5. *The futility of leaving fruit of toil to undeserving heirs*

18 I hated all my toil in which I had toiled under the sun, seeing that I must leave it to the man who will come after me; 19 and who knows whether he will be a wise man or a fool? Yet he will be master of all for which I toiled and used my wisdom under the sun. This also is vanity. 20 So I turned about and gave my heart up to despair over all the toil of my labors under the sun, 21 because sometimes a man who has toiled with wisdom and knowledge and skill must leave all to be enjoyed by a man who did not toil for it. This also is vanity and a great evil. 22 What has a man from all the toil and strain with which he toils beneath the sun? 23 For all his days are full of pain, and his work is a vexation; even in the night his mind does not rest. This also is vanity.

6. *The godly must be content with what God gives them*

24 There is nothing better for a man than that he should eat and drink, and find enjoyment in his toil. This also, I saw, is from the hand of God; 25 for apart from him*d* who can eat or who can have enjoyment? 26 For to the man who pleases him God gives wisdom and knowledge and joy; but to the sinner he gives the work of gathering and heaping, only to give to one who pleases God. This also is vanity and a striving after wind.

II. Second discourse: the disappointing experiences of life 3.1–5.20

A. The prudent attitude toward life

1. *A time for everything*

3 For everything there is a season, and a time for every matter under heaven:

2 a time to be born, and a time to die;
a time to plant, and a time to pluck up what is planted;
3 a time to kill, and a time to heal;
a time to break down, and a time to build up;
4 a time to weep, and a time to laugh;
a time to mourn, and a time to dance;
5 a time to cast away stones, and a time to gather stones together;
a time to embrace, and a time to refrain from embracing;
6 a time to seek, and a time to lose;
a time to keep, and a time to cast away;
7 a time to rend, and a time to sew;
a time to keep silence, and a time to speak;
8 a time to love, and a time to hate;
a time for war, and a time for peace.
9 What gain has the worker from his toil?

d Gk Syr: Heb *apart from me*

Marginal references:

2.17 Ecc 4.2; ver 22,23

2.18 ver 11; Ps 39.6; 49.10

2.20 ver 11
2.21 Ecc 4.4; ver 18
2.22 Ecc 1.3; 3.9
2.23 Job 5.7; 14.1; Ecc 1.18; Ps 127.2

2.24 Ecc 3.12,13, 22; 5.18; 8.15
2.26 Job 32.8; 27.16,17; Ecc 1.14

3.1 ver 17; Ecc 8.6
3.2 Heb 9.27

3.4 Rom 12.15; Ps 126.2; Ex 15.20
3.5 1 Cor 7.5

3.7 Amos 5.13
3.8 Lk 14.26
3.9 Ecc 1.3

2. *Uselessness of human striving*

10 I have seen the business that God has given to the sons of men to be busy with. 11 He has made everything beautiful in its time; also he has put eternity into man's mind, yet so that he cannot find out what God has done from the beginning to the end. 12 I know that there is nothing better for them than to be happy and enjoy themselves as long as they live; 13 also that it is God's gift to man that every one should eat and drink and take pleasure in all his toil. 14 I know that whatever God does endures for ever; nothing can be added to it, nor anything taken from it; God has made it so, in order that men should fear before him. 15 That which is, already has been; that which is to be, already has been; and God seeks what has been driven away.

3. *Man must make the best of this present life*

16 Moreover I saw under the sun that in the place of justice, even there was wickedness, and in the place of righteousness, even there was wickedness. 17 I said in my heart, God will judge the righteous and the wicked, for he has appointed a time for every matter, and for every work. 18 I said in my heart with regard to the sons of men that God is testing them to show them that they are but beasts. 19 For the fate of the sons of men and the fate of beasts is the same; as one dies, so dies the other. They all have the same breath, and man has no advantage over the beasts; for all is vanity. 20 All go to one place; all are from the dust, and all turn to dust again. 21 Who knows whether the spirit of man goes upward and the spirit of the beast goes down to the earth? 22 So I saw that there is nothing better than that a man should enjoy his work, for that is his lot; who can bring him to see what will be after him?

B. *The disappointments of earthly life*

1. *Oppression makes life a dubious blessing*

4 Again I saw all the oppressions that are practiced under the sun. And behold, the tears of the oppressed, and they had no one to comfort them! On the side of their oppressors there was power, and there was no one to comfort them. 2 And I thought the dead who are already dead more fortunate than the living who are still alive; 3 but better than both is he who has not yet been, and has not seen the evil deeds that are done under the sun.

2. *Life's trials better faced by partners than alone*

4 Then I saw that all toil and all skill in work come from a man's envy of his neighbor. This also is vanity and a striving after wind. 5 The fool folds his hands, and eats his own flesh. 6 Better is a handful of quietness than two hands full of toil and a striving after wind. 7 Again, I saw vanity under the sun: 8 a person who has no one, either son or brother, yet there is no end to all his toil, and his eyes are never satisfied with riches, so that he never asks, "For whom am I toiling and depriving myself of pleasure?" This also is vanity and an unhappy business. 9 Two are better than one, because they have a good reward for their toil. 10 For if they fall, one will lift up his fellow; but woe to him who is alone when he falls and has not another to lift him

3.10 Ecc 1.13
3.11 Gen 1.31; Ecc 8.17; Rom 11.33
3.13 Ecc 2.24; 5.19
3.14 Jas 1.17; Ecc 5.7; 1.3; 3.9
3.15 Ecc 1.9; 6.10
3.17 Mt 16.27; Rom 2.6–8; 2 Cor 5.10; 2 Thess 1.6, 7; ver 1
3.19 Ps 73.22; Ecc 9.12
3.20 Gen 3.19; Ecc 12.7
3.21 Ecc 12.7
3.22 Ecc 2.24; 5.18; 6.12; 8.7; 10.14
4.1 Ecc 3.16; 5.8; Isa 5.7; Lam 1.9
4.2 Job 3.11–26; Ecc 2.17
4.3 Ecc 6.3
4.4 Ecc 2.21; 1.14
4.5 Prov 6.10; Isa 9.20
4.6 Prov 15.16, 17; 16.8
4.8 Prov 27.20; 1 Jn 2.16

up. 11Again, if two lie together, they are warm; but how can one be warm alone? 12And though a man might prevail against one who is alone, two will withstand him. A threefold cord is not quickly broken.

3. *Instability of political fame*

13 Better is a poor and wise youth than an old and foolish king, who will no longer take advice, 14 even though he had gone from prison to the throne or in his own kingdom had been born poor. 15 I saw all the living who move about under the sun, as well as that*f* youth, who was to stand in his place; 16 there was no end of all the people; he was over all of them. Yet those who come later will not rejoice in him. Surely this also is vanity and a striving after wind.

C. *The futility of the self-seeking life*

1. *Warnings against certain sins*

5*g* Guard your steps when you go to the house of God; to draw near to listen is better than to offer the sacrifice of fools; for they do not know that they are doing evil. 2*h* Be not rash with your mouth, nor let your heart be hasty to utter a word before God, for God is in heaven, and you upon earth; therefore let your words be few.

3 For a dream comes with much business, and a fool's voice with many words.

4 When you vow a vow to God, do not delay paying it; for he has no pleasure in fools. Pay what you vow. 5 It is better that you should not vow than that you should vow and not pay. 6 Let not your mouth lead you into sin, and do not say before the messenger*i* that it was a mistake; why should God be angry at your voice, and destroy the work of your hands?

7 For when dreams increase, empty words grow many:*j* but do you fear God.

2. *The end of the oppressor and the covetous*

8 If you see in a province the poor oppressed and justice and right violently taken away, do not be amazed at the matter; for the high official is watched by a higher, and there are yet higher ones over them. 9 But in all, a king is an advantage to a land with cultivated fields.*k*

10 He who loves money will not be satisfied with money; nor he who loves wealth, with gain: this also is vanity.

11 When goods increase, they increase who eat them; and what gain has their owner but to see them with his eyes?

12 Sweet is the sleep of a laborer, whether he eats little or much; but the surfeit of the rich will not let him sleep.

13 There is a grievous evil which I have seen under the sun: riches were kept by their owner to his hurt, 14 and those riches were lost in a bad venture; and he is father of a son, but he has

---

f Heb *the second*   *g* Ch 4.17 in Heb   *h* Ch 5.1 in Heb   *i* Or *angel*
j Or *For in a multitude of dreams there is futility, and ruin in a flood of words*
k Or *The profit of the land is among all of them; a cultivated field has a king*

5.4 See note to Num 6.2 on vows.   **5.10** See note to 1 Tim 6.10 on money.

Cross-references

4.11 1 Ki 1.1

4.13 Ecc 9.15
4.14 Gen 41.14, 41–43

4.16 Ecc 1.14

5.1 Ex 3.5; Isa 1.12; 1 Sam 15.22; Prov 15.8; 21–27; Hos 6.6
5.2 Prov 20.25; 10.19; Mt 6.7
*5.4 Deut 23.21–23; Ps 50.14; 76.11; 66.13,14
5.5 Prov 20.25; Acts 5.4
5.7 Ecc 3.14; 12.13

5.8 Ecc 4.1; Ps 12.5; 58.11; 82.1

*5.10 Ecc 2.10,11
5.11 Ecc 2.9
5.12 Prov 3.24
5.13 Ecc 6.1,2

nothing in his hand. 15As he came from his mother's womb he shall go again, naked as he came, and shall take nothing for his toil, which he may carry away in his hand. 16 This also is a grievous evil: just as he came, so shall he go; and what gain has he that he toiled for the wind, 17 and spent all his days in darkness and grief,[1] in much vexation and sickness and resentment?

3. Making the best of what God gives

18 Behold, what I have seen to be good and to be fitting is to eat and drink and find enjoyment in all the toil with which one toils under the sun the few days of his life which God has given him, for this is his lot. 19 Every man also to whom God has given wealth and possessions and power to enjoy them, and to accept his lot and find enjoyment in his toil—this is the gift of God. 20 For he will not much remember the days of his life because God keeps him occupied with joy in his heart.

III. Third discourse: the vanity of wealth and honor 6.1–8.17

A. Ambition and desire frustrated

6 There is an evil which I have seen under the sun, and it lies heavy upon men: 2 a man to whom God gives wealth, possessions, and honor, so that he lacks nothing of all that he desires, yet God does not give him power to enjoy them, but a stranger enjoys them; this is vanity; it is a sore affliction. 3 If a man begets a hundred children, and lives many years, so that the days of his years are many, but he does not enjoy life's good things, and also has no burial, I say that an untimely birth is better off than he. 4 For it comes into vanity and goes into darkness, and in darkness its name is covered; 5 moreover it has not seen the sun or known anything; yet it finds rest rather than he. 6 Even though he should live a thousand years twice told, yet enjoy no good—do not all go to the one place?

7 All the toil of man is for his mouth, yet his appetite is not satisfied. 8 For what advantage has the wise man over the fool? And what does the poor man have who knows how to conduct himself before the living? 9 Better is the sight of the eyes than the wandering of desire; this also is vanity and a striving after wind.

10 Whatever has come to be has already been named, and it is known what man is, and that he is not able to dispute with one stronger than he. 11 The more words, the more vanity, and what is man the better? 12 For who knows what is good for man while he lives the few days of his vain life, which he passes like a shadow? For who can tell man what will be after him under the sun?

B. Counsels of prudence in a sin-corrupted world

1. Choosing the better

7 A good name is better than precious ointment;
    and the day of death, than the day of birth.
2 It is better to go to the house of mourning
    than to go to the house of feasting;

---

[1] Gk: Heb all his days also he eats in darkness

5.15
Job 1.21;
Ps 49.17;
1 Tim 6.7
5.16
Ecc 1.3;
Prov 11.29
5.17
Ecc 2.23
5.18
Ecc 2.10,24;
3.22
5.19
2 Chr 1.12;
Ecc 2.24;
3.13; 6.2
6.1
Ecc 5.13
6.2
1 Ki 3.13;
Ps 17.14;
73.7
6.3
2 Ki 9.35;
Isa 14.19,
20;
Jer 22.19;
Ecc 4.3
6.7
Prov 16.26
6.8
Ecc 2.15
6.9
Ecc 11.9;
1.14
6.10
Ecc 1.9;
Job 9.32;
Isa 45.9;
Jer 49.19
6.12
Jas 4.14;
Ps 39.6;
Ecc 8.7
7.1
Prov 15.30;
22.1;
Ecc 4.2
7.2
Ecc 2.16;
Ps 90.12

for this is the end of all men,
  and the living will lay it to heart.
³ Sorrow is better than laughter,
  for by sadness of countenance the heart is made glad.
⁴ The heart of the wise is in the house of mourning;
  but the heart of fools is in the house of mirth.
⁵ It is better for a man to hear the rebuke of the wise
  than to hear the song of fools.
⁶ For as the crackling of thorns under a pot,
  so is the laughter of the fools;
  this also is vanity.
⁷ Surely oppression makes the wise man foolish,
  and a bribe corrupts the mind.
⁸ Better is the end of a thing than its beginning;
  and the patient in spirit is better than the proud in spirit.

2. *The value of wisdom over wealth*

⁹ Be not quick to anger,
  for anger lodges in the bosom of fools.
¹⁰ Say not, "Why were the former days better than these?"
  For it is not from wisdom that you ask this.
¹¹ Wisdom is good with an inheritance,
  an advantage to those who see the sun.
¹² For the protection of wisdom is like the protection of money;
  and the advantage of knowledge is that wisdom preserves the
  life of him who has it.
¹³ Consider the work of God;
  who can make straight what he has made crooked?
14 In the day of prosperity be joyful, and in the day of adversity consider; God has made the one as well as the other, so that man may not find out anything that will be after him.

3. *Asceticism and excess contrasted*

15 In my vain life I have seen everything; there is a righteous man who perishes in his righteousness, and there is a wicked man who prolongs his life in his evil-doing. 16 Be not righteous overmuch, and do not make yourself overwise; why should you destroy yourself? 17 Be not wicked overmuch, neither be a fool; why should you die before your time? 18 It is good that you should take hold of this, and from that withhold not your hand; for he who fears God shall come forth from them all.

4. *The value of wisdom and wickedness of folly*

19 Wisdom gives strength to the wise man more than ten rulers that are in a city.
20 Surely there is not a righteous man on earth who does good and never sins.
21 Do not give heed to all the things that men say, lest you hear your servant cursing you; 22 your heart knows that many times you have yourself cursed others.
23 All this I have tested by wisdom; I said, "I will be wise"; but it was far from me. 24 That which is, is far off, and deep, very deep; who can find it out? 25 I turned my mind to know and to search out and to seek wisdom and the sum of things, and to know the wickedness of folly and the foolishness which is madness.

7.3
2 Cor 7.10

7.5
Ps 141.5;
Prov 13.18;
15.31,32
7.6
Ps 118.12;
Ecc 2.2
7.7
Ex 23.8;
Deut 16.19
7.8
ver 1;
Prov 14.29;
Gal 5.22;
Eph 4.2

7.9
Prov 14.17;
Jas 1.19

7.11
Prov 8.10,
11
7.12
Ecc 9.18;
Prov 3.18;
8.35
7.13
Ecc 3.11;
8.17; 1.15;
Isa 14.27
7.14
Ecc 3.4;
Deut 8.5

7.15
Ecc 6.12;
8.14
7.16
Rom 12.3

7.17
Job 15.32;
Ps.55.23;
Prov 10.27

7.19
Ecc 9.13–18

7.20
1 Ki 8.46;
2 Chr 6.36;
Prov 20.9;
Rom 3.23

7.23
Rom 1.22
7.24
Job 28.12;
Rom 11.33
7.25
Ecc 1.17;
2.12

5. *Wicked womanhood discussed*

26And I found more bitter than death the woman whose heart is snares and nets, and whose hands are fetters; he who pleases God escapes her, but the sinner is taken by her. 27 Behold, this is what I found, says the Preacher, adding one thing to another to find the sum, 28 which my mind has sought repeatedly, but I have not found. One man among a thousand I found, but a woman among all these I have not found. 29 Behold, this alone I found, that God made man upright, but they have sought out many devices.

C. *Expediency in an imperfect world*

1. *The acceptance of authority*

8 Who is like the wise man?
   And who knows the interpretation of a thing?
A man's wisdom makes his face shine,
   and the hardness of his countenance is changed.

2 Keep*m* the king's command, and because of your sacred oath be not dismayed; 3 go from his presence, do not delay when the matter is unpleasant, for he does whatever he pleases. 4 For the word of the king is supreme, and who may say to him, "What are you doing?" 5 He who obeys a command will meet no harm, and the mind of a wise man will know the time and way. 6 For every matter has its time and way, although man's trouble lies heavy upon him. 7 For he does not know what is to be, for who can tell him how it will be? 8 No man has power to retain the spirit, or authority over the day of death; there is no discharge from war, nor will wickedness deliver those who are given to it. 9All this I observed while applying my mind to all that is done under the sun, while man lords it over man to his hurt.

2. *The judgment of the wicked*

10 Then I saw the wicked buried; they used to go in and out of the holy place, and were praised in the city where they had done such things. This also is vanity. 11 Because sentence against an evil deed is not executed speedily, the heart of the sons of men is fully set to do evil. 12 Though a sinner does evil a hundred times and prolongs his life, yet I know that it will be well with those who fear God, because they fear before him; 13 but it will not be well with the wicked, neither will he prolong his days like a shadow, because he does not fear before God.

3. *Injustices in this life*

14 There is a vanity which takes place on earth, that there are righteous men to whom it happens according to the deeds of the wicked, and there are wicked men to whom it happens according to the deeds of the righteous. I said that this also is vanity. 15And I commend enjoyment, for man has no good thing under the sun but to eat, and drink, and enjoy himself, for this will go with him in his toil through the days of life which God gives him under the sun.

m Heb inserts an *I*

8.1 Compare with the words in Deut 28.50.   **8.8** Man cannot prevent the inevitable.

4. The ways of God are inscrutable

16 When I applied my mind to know wisdom, and to see the business that is done on earth, how neither day nor night one's eyes see sleep; 17 then I saw all the work of God, that man cannot find out the work that is done under the sun. However much man may toil in seeking, he will not find it out; even though a wise man claims to know, he cannot find it out.

IV. Fourth discourse: leaving with God the injustices of this life 9.1–12.8

A. Make the best of this life

1. Death inevitable for both the good and the evil

9 But all this I laid to heart, examining it all, how the righteous and the wise and their deeds are in the hand of God; whether it is love or hate man does not know. Everything before them is vanity,[n] 2 since one fate comes to all, to the righteous and the wicked, to the good and the evil,[o] to the clean and the unclean, to him who sacrifices and him who does not sacrifice. As is the good man, so is the sinner; and he who swears is as he who shuns an oath. 3 This is an evil in all that is done under the sun, that one fate comes to all; also the hearts of men are full of evil, and madness is in their hearts while they live, and after that they go to the dead. 4 But he who is joined with all the living has hope, for a living dog is better than a dead lion. 5 For the living know that they will die, but the dead know nothing, and they have no more reward; but the memory of them is lost. 6 Their love and their hate and their envy have already perished, and they have no more for ever any share in all that is done under the sun.

2. Enjoy life while you can

7 Go, eat your bread with enjoyment, and drink your wine with a merry heart; for God has already approved what you do.

8 Let your garments be always white; let not oil be lacking on your head.

9 Enjoy life with the wife whom you love, all the days of your vain life which he has given you under the sun, because that is your portion in life and in your toil at which you toil under the sun. 10 Whatever your hand finds to do, do it with your might; for there

[n] Syr Compare Gk: Heb Everything before them is everything
[o] Gk Syr Vg: Heb lacks and the evil

Cross references (margin):

8.16 Ecc 1.13,14; 2.23
8.17 Job 5.9; Ecc 3.11; Rom 11.33; Ecc 8.7; Ps 73.16

9.1 Deut 33.3; Job 12.10; Ps 119.109; ver 6; Ecc 10.14
9.2 Job 9.22; Ecc 6.6; 7.2
9.3 ver 2; Ecc 8.11; 1.17
*9.5 Job 14.21; Ecc 1.11; 2.16; Ps 88.12; Isa 26.14
9.6 Ecc 3.22

9.7 Ecc 8.15
*9,8 Rev 3.4; Ps 23.5
9.9 Ecc 6.12; 7.15
9.10 Rom 12.11; Col 3.23; Isa 38.10

9.5 From this verse some have adduced the dogma of *soul sleep* for the dead until the resurrection. The doctrine of soul sleep is not biblical. The problem is solved when one understands that the Bible is a book of *progressive revelation*. The Old Testament does not have the full-orbed biblical doctrine of the intermediate state after death. The person and nature of God are not fully disclosed in the Pentateuch. The mystery of the New Testament church is by no means fully revealed in the Old Testament. Since revela-tion is progressive it is important that the principle of interpretation known as the analogy of Scripture be employed; that the Old Testament be interpreted by the New Testament; that the clear portions of Scripture take precedence over the obscure. In brief, no single portion of the Bible should be interpreted apart from its relation to the totality of the Word of God.

9.8 *white* garments would be worn on festive occasions; *oil* on the head produced a cooling and refreshing effect.

is no work or thought or knowledge or wisdom in Shēōl, to which you are going.

3. *Chance operates for all*

9.11
Amos 2.14,
15;
Deut 8.17,
18;
1 Sam 6.9
9.12
Ecc 8.7;
Prov 29.6;
Isa 24.18;
Lk 21.34,35

11 Again I saw that under the sun the race is not to the swift, nor the battle to the strong, nor bread to the wise, nor riches to the intelligent, nor favor to the men of skill; but time and chance happen to them all. 12 For man does not know his time. Like fish which are taken in an evil net, and like birds which are caught in a snare, so the sons of men are snared at an evil time, when it suddenly falls upon them.

4. *Wisdom is superior*

9.15
Ecc 4.13;
2.16; 8.10
9.16
Prov 21.22;
Ecc 7.19
9.17
Ecc 7.5;
10.12
9.18
ver 16;
Josh 7.1,11,
12

13 I have also seen this example of wisdom under the sun, and it seemed great to me. 14 There was a little city with few men in it; and a great king came against it and beseiged it, building great siegeworks against it. 15 But there was found in it a poor wise man, and he by his wisdom delivered the city. Yet no one remembered that poor man. 16 But I say that wisdom is better than might, though the poor man's wisdom is despised, and his words are not heeded.

17 The words of the wise heard in quiet are better than the shouting of a ruler among fools. 18 Wisdom is better than weapons of war, but one sinner destroys much good.

B. *Life is uncertain and folly baneful*

1. *Folly hurtful; wisdom helpful*

10 Dead flies make the perfumer's ointment give off an evil odor;
 so a little folly outweighs wisdom and honor.
2 A wise man's heart inclines him toward the right,
 but a fool's heart toward the left.

10.3
Prov 13.16;
18.2
10.4
Ecc 8.3;
1 Sam
25.24–33;
Prov 25.15
10.5
Ecc 5.6
10.6
Est 3.1
10.7
Prov 19.10;
Est 6.8
10.8
Ps 7.15;
Prov 26.27

3 Even when the fool walks on the road, he lacks sense,
 and he says to every one that he is a fool.
4 If the anger of the ruler rises against you, do not leave your place,
 for deference will make amends for great offenses.
5 There is an evil which I have seen under the sun, as it were an error proceeding from the ruler: 6 folly is set in many high places, and the rich sit in a low place. 7 I have seen slaves on horses, and princes walking on foot like slaves.
8 He who digs a pit will fall into it;
 and a serpent will bite him who breaks through a wall.
9 He who quarries stones is hurt by them;
 and he who splits logs is endangered by them.
10 If the iron is blunt, and one does not whet the edge,
 he must put forth more strength;
 but wisdom helps one to succeed.

10.11
Ps 58.4,5;
Jer 8.17

11 If the serpent bites before it is charmed,
 there is no advantage in a charmer.

2. *The folly of empty talk*

10.12
Prov 10.32;
Lk 4.22;
Prov 10.14;
18.7

12 The words of a wise man's mouth win him favor,
 but the lips of a fool consume him.

13 The beginning of the words of his mouth is foolishness,
   and the end of his talk is wicked madness.
14 A fool multiplies words,
   though no man knows what is to be,
   and who can tell him what will be after him?
15 The toil of a fool wearies him,
   so that he does not know the way to the city.

3. Concluding maxims

16 Woe to you, O land, when your king is a child,
   and your princes feast in the morning!
17 Happy are you, O land, when your king is the son of free men,
   and your princes feast at the proper time,
   for strength, and not for drunkenness!
18 Through sloth the roof sinks in,
   and through indolence the house leaks.
19 Bread is made for laughter,
   and wine gladdens life,
   and money answers everything.
20 Even in your thought, do not curse the king,
   nor in your bedchamber curse the rich;
   for a bird of the air will carry your voice,
   or some winged creature tell the matter.

C. How to invest a life

1. Works of charity

11 Cast your bread upon the waters,
   for you will find it after many days.
2 Give a portion to seven, or even to eight,
   for you know not what evil may happen on earth.
3 If the clouds are full of rain,
   they empty themselves on the earth;
   and if a tree falls to the south or to the north,
   in the place where the tree falls, there it will lie.
4 He who observes the wind will not sow;
   and he who regards the clouds will not reap.
5 As you do not know how the spirit comes to the bones in the
womb *p* of a woman with child, so you do not know the work of God
who makes everything.
6 In the morning sow your seed, and at evening withhold not

p Or *As you do not know the way of the wind, or how the bones grow in the womb*

Marginal references:

10.13 Ecc 7.25

*10.14 Prov 15.2; Ecc 3.22; 6.12; 8.7

*10.16 Isa 3.4,5,12; 5.11

10.17 Prov 31.4; Isa 5.11

*10.18 Prov 24.30–34

10.19 Ps 104.15; Ecc 7.12

*10.20 Ex 22.28; Acts 23.5; 2 Ki 6.12; Lk 12.3

11.1 Isa 32.20; Deut 15.10; Prov 19.17; Mt 10.42; 2 Cor 9.8; Gal 6.9,10; Heb 6.10

*11.2 Ps 112.9; Lk 6.30; 1 Tim 6.18,19; Ecc 12.1

11.5 Jn 3.8; Ps 139.14, 15

11.6 Ecc 9.10

10.14 *A fool multiplies words*, but the wide use of words does not necessarily make a man a fool. The value of speech is obvious, and right speech is a powerful instrument for good even as foolish words are a powerful instrument for evil or for folly. Even the wise man must be dextrous in the use of words which reveal what the heart really is like. Everywhere Scripture warns men about the use of words.

10.16 Israel experienced this in a painful way in the lives of men like Absalom and Rehoboam who were absurd and self-willed, destitute of those virtues which make for a good ruler.

10.18 *sloth* results in deterioration of soul and home.

10.20 Men may become vocal because of indignation over evil, but prudence often dictates silence. Even the words one thinks are spoken in secret may come to light most unexpectedly, as, for example, *Elisha . . . tells the king of Israel the words that you speak in your bedchamber* (2 Ki 6.12).

11.2 *seven, or even to eight*. This is a Hebrew idiom to indicate an indefinite number. The climactic use of numbers adds emphasis and is a common poetic device in the Near East.

your hand; for you do not know which will prosper, this or that, or whether both alike will be good.

7 Light is sweet, and it is pleasant for the eyes to behold the sun.

8 For if a man lives many years, let him rejoice in them all; but let him remember that the days of darkness will be many. All that comes is vanity.

2. A misspent youth brings retribution

9 Rejoice, O young man, in your youth, and let your heart cheer you in the days of your youth; walk in the ways of your heart and the sight of your eyes. But know that for all these things God will bring you into judgment.

10 Remove vexation from your mind, and put away pain from your body; for youth and the dawn of life are vanity.

3. Injunction to live for God

12 Remember also your Creator in the days of your youth, before the evil days come, and the years draw nigh, when you will say, "I have no pleasure in them"; 2 before the sun and the light and the moon and the stars are darkened and the clouds return after the rain; 3 in the day when the keepers of the house tremble, and the strong men are bent, and the grinders cease because they are few, and those that look through the windows are dimmed, 4 and the doors on the street are shut; when the sound of the grinding is low, and one rises up at the voice of a bird, and all the daughters of song are brought low; 5 they are afraid also of what is high, and terrors are in the way; the almond tree blossoms, the grasshopper drags itself along*q* and desire fails; because man goes to his eternal home, and the mourners go about the streets; 6 before the silver cord is snapped,*r* or the golden bowl is broken, or the pitcher is broken at the fountain, or the wheel broken at the cistern, 7 and the dust returns to the earth as it was, and the spirit returns to God who gave it. 8 Vanity of vanities, says the Preacher; all is vanity.

V. Conclusion: considering life in the light of eternity 12.9–14

A. The Preacher's purpose

9 Besides being wise, the Preacher also taught the people knowledge, weighing and studying and arranging proverbs with great care. 10 The Preacher sought to find pleasing words, and uprightly he wrote words of truth.

q Or is a burden   r Syr Vg Compare Gk: Heb is removed

Marginal references:

11.7 Ecc 7.11
11.8 Ecc 9.7; 12.1
11.9 Ecc 2.10; Num 15.39; Ecc 3.17; 12.14; Rom 14.10
*11.10 2 Cor 7.1; 2 Tim 2.22
*12.1ff Ps 63.6; 119.55; Ecc 11.8; 2 Sam 19.35
12.4 Jer 25.10; 2 Sam 19.35
12.5 Job 17.13; Jer 9.17
*12.7 Gen 3.19; Job 34.15; Ps 90.3; Job 34.14; Isa 57.16; Zech 12.1
12.8 Ecc 1.2
12.9 1 Ki 4.32
*12.10 Prov 10.32; 22.20,21

11.10 Life has both inward and outward troubles: pain which comes to the flesh and to the mind. All must experience some of both, but one can infer that obedience to the commandments of a loving God will save man from many of these afflictions and he will be abundantly supplied with a full measure of grace to endure those things which cannot be avoided.

12.1ff This is a superb narrative (figuratively speaking) on the advent of old age, its effect on our mind, body, and soul; and the gradual deterioration of all.

12.7 Man's spirit returns to God neither to sleep nor to perish, but to be judged.

12.10 Truth is often harsh but it can be stated so as to cause the least possible offense. Regard for truth should not keep men from clothing it in garments of beauty.

B. The value of the Preacher's words

11 The sayings of the wise are like goads, and like nails firmly
fixed are the collected sayings which are given by one Shepherd.
12 My son, beware of anything beyond these. Of making many
books there is no end, and much study is a weariness of the flesh.

12.11
Ecc 7.5;
Acts 2.37;
Ezra 9.8;
Isa 22.23

C. The concluding injunction

13 The end of the matter; all has been heard. Fear God, and
keep his commandments; for this is the whole duty of man.[s]
14 For God will bring every deed into judgment, with[t] every
secret thing, whether good or evil.

*12.13
Deut 4.2;
Ecc 8.5;
Mic 6.8
12.14
Mt 10.26;
12.36;
1 Cor 4.5

[s] Or *the duty of all men*   [t] Or *into the judgment on*

12.13 Ecclesiastes has depicted the spiritual
pilgrimage of a man concerned with the meaning of life. He has entertained many and
frequently contradictory thoughts in his quest
for the highest good. He could not solve the
riddle of life by anything he discovered or
observed "under the sun." The end of his
quest did not provide a philosophical answer
to the questions which plagued him, but it
did provide a brief summary of that which

makes life, with all its bewildering facets,
meaningful. It does not take worldly wisdom
to *fear God*, i.e., walk in reverence before
the LORD, and *keep his commandments*,
i.e., bring the totality of life into subjection
to His will. This is a summary of God's
demands upon His people—His law which
served as a custodian until Christ came (Gal
3.24). In any age, and at any time, man may
safely trust God.

Ecclesiastes 12.11—14

B. The value of the Preacher's words.

11 The sayings of the wise are like goads, and like nails firmly
fixed are the collected sayings which are given by one Shepherd.
12 My son, beware of anything beyond these. Of making many
books there is no end, and much study is a weariness of the flesh.
13 The end of the matter; all has been heard. Fear God, and
keep his commandments; for this is the whole duty of man.
14 For God will bring every deed into judgment, with every
secret thing, whether good or evil.

INTRODUCTION TO
THE SONG OF SOLOMON

Authorship and Background: The opening verse of the book ascribes the
Song to Solomon, who is known to have composed songs as well as proverbs
(1 Ki 4.32). Internal evidence suggests that the book was written before the division of the kingdom. Assuming the Solomonic authorship, the book must
have been written in the tenth century B.C., although some of its phraseology
was changed at a later date. This would account for the Greek and Persian
words in it. The English versions prefer the title "Song of Solomon"; the Greek
and Latin versions follow the Hebrew title "The Song of Songs," which signifies
"The Best of Songs."

Love songs were popular in all ancient lands. The Chester Beatty Papyrus
No. 1 is an entire book of love songs in seven long cantos (called "houses")
which are put alternately into the mouths of two sweethearts who address each
other as "brother" and "sister" (cf. 5.1, 2; 8.1). Lovesickness plays a great part
in both.

Characteristics: The Song of Solomon is rich in oriental imagery and filled
with beautiful descriptions of local scenery. Accepted in its best sense, it is an
idyll of love and courtship. Various interpretations have been given to this remarkable book. It is regarded by some as a type of allegory, while others look
upon it is a drama. According to the Shepherd Hypothesis, Solomon seeks to
alienate the affections of the young lady from her lover, but she resists his temptations and the king finally allows her to return home. Perhaps the view which
is most acceptable is that the book presents love and marriage in the proper
biblical framework, since marriage is ordained of God for man. It avoids both
the error of lust and of asceticism. The highest, purest, and most lofty elements
of this honorable relationship are expressed. The marriage tie is used to illustrate the relationship of Yahweh to Israel in the Old Testament, and of
Christ to the church in the New Testament. If this book is taken as an
allegory, Solomon is a type of Christ and the bride is a type of the church.

Contents:

I. The bride and bridegroom. 1.1—2.7: The bride speaks of her love
for her beloved. She describes his beauty as she sees it. He praises her.
She delights in his fellowship.

II. The praise of her beloved. 2.8—3.5: The bridegroom takes the initiative. He invites her to come with him. She acknowledges her submission to his love. Her beloved disappears; she seeks and finds him.

III. In praise of the bride. 3.6—5.1: Solomon draws near; betrothal and
marriage are discussed. Solomon breaks forth into song twice. The
Shulammite appeals to him and he responds.

IV.   A troubled love. 5.2—7.9: Her beloved comes and departs. She searches for him and depicts what he is like. She claims him for herself. When she finds him, he praises her. She recounts for him her recent experience. He praises her as the daughter of a prince. She asks him to join her in the open fields and countryside.

V.   The unbroken communion. 7.10—8.14: The Shulammite declares her love and devotion to her beloved. Before leaving he asks to hear her voice. She looks for his early return.

THE SONG OF SOLOMON

I. *The bride and bridegroom 1.1–2.7*

A. *Inscription*

1.1
1 Ki 4.32

1 The Song of Songs, which is Solomon's.

B. *The bride awaits her lover*

1.2
Sol 4.10

2 O that you^a would kiss me with the kisses of your^b mouth!
  For your love is better than wine,

1.3
Sol 4.10;
Ecc 7.1

3   your anointing oils are fragrant,
  your name is oil poured out;
    therefore the maidens love you.

1.4
Ps 45.14,15

4 Draw me after you, let us make haste.
  The king has brought me into his chambers.
We will exult and rejoice in you;
  we will extol your love more than wine;
  rightly do they love you.

1.5
Sol 2.14;
4.3; 2.7;
5.8

5 I am very dark, but comely,
  O daughters of Jerusalem,
like the tents of Kēdar,
  like the curtains of Solomon.

1.6
Ps 69.8;
Sol 8.11

6 Do not gaze at me because I am swarthy,
  because the sun has scorched me.
My mother's sons were angry with me,
  they made me keeper of the vineyards;
  but, my own vineyard I have not kept!

1.7
Sol 3.1–4;
2.16; 8.13

7 Tell me, you whom my soul loves,
  where you pasture your flock,
  where you make it lie down at noon;
for why should I be like one who wanders^c
  beside the flocks of your companions?

1.8
Sol 5.9; 6.1

8 If you do not know,
  O fairest among women,
follow in the tracks of the flock,
  and pasture your kids
  beside the shepherds' tents.

C. *Bride and bridegroom meet*

1.9
Sol 2.2,10,
13;
2 Chr 1.16

9 I compare you, my love,
  to a mare of Pharaōh's chariots.

1.10
5.13

10 Your cheeks are comely with ornaments,
  your neck with strings of jewels.
11 We will make you ornaments of gold,
  studded with silver.

12 While the king was on his couch,
  my nard gave forth its fragrance.
13 My beloved is to me a bag of myrrh,

---

a Heb *he* *b* Heb *his* *c* Gk Syr Vg: Heb *is veiled*

that lies between my breasts.

14 My beloved is to me a cluster of henna blossoms
 in the vineyards of Ĕn-gĕ′dī.

               1.14
               Sol 4.13

15 Behold, you are beautiful, my love;
 behold, you are beautiful;
 your eyes are doves.

               1.15
               Sol 4.1;
               5.12

16 Behold, you are beautiful, my beloved,
 truly lovely.
 Our couch is green;
17 the beams of our house are cedar,
 our rafters[d] are pine.

               1.17
               1 Ki 6.9,10;
               2 Chr 3.5

2 I am a rose[e] of Shạrọn,
 a lily of the valleys.

2 As a lily among brambles,
 so is my love among maidens.

               2.1
               Isa 35.1,2;
               Sol 5.13;
               7.2

3 As an apple tree among the trees of the wood,
 so is my beloved among young men.
With great delight I sat in his shadow,
 and his fruit was sweet to my taste.

               2.3
               Sol 8.5;
               4.13

4 He brought me to the banqueting house,
 and his banner over me was love.

               2.4
               Ps 20.5

5 Sustain me with raisins,
 refresh me with apples;
 for I am sick with love.

               2.5
               Sol 7.8; 5.8

6 O that his left hand were under my head,
 and that his right hand embraced me!

               2.6
               Sol 8.3

7 I adjure you, O daughters of Jerusalem,
 by the gazelles or the hinds of the field,
that you stir not up nor awaken love
 until it please.

               2.7
               Sol 3.5; 8.4

II. *The praise of her beloved 2.8–3.5*

A. *Her praise by day*

8 The voice of my beloved!
 Behold, he comes,
leaping upon the mountains,
 bounding over the hills.

               2.8
               ver 17

9 My beloved is like a gazelle,
 or a young stag.
Behold, there he stands
 behind our wall,
gazing in at the windows,
 looking through the lattice.

               2.9
               ver 17

10 My beloved speaks and says to me:
"Arise, my love, my fair one,
 and come away;
11 for lo, the winter is past,

               2.10
               ver 13

---

[d] The meaning of the Hebrew word is uncertain [e] Heb *crocus*

the rain is over and gone.

2.12
Ps 74.19

12 The flowers appear on the earth,
  the time of singing has come,
and the voice of the turtledove
  is heard in our land.

2.13
Mt 24.32;
Sol 7.12;
ver 10

13 The fig tree puts forth its figs,
  and the vines are in blossom;
  they give forth fragrance.
Arise, my love, my fair one,
  and come away.

2.14
Sol 5.2;
Jer 48.28;
Sol 8.13;
1.5

14 O my dove, in the clefts of the rock,
  in the covert of the cliff,
let me see your face,
  let me hear your voice,
for your voice is sweet,
  and your face is comely.

2.15
Ezek 13.4

15 Catch us the foxes,
  the little foxes,
that spoil the vineyards,
  for our vineyards are in blossom."

2.16
Sol 6.3;
7.10

16 My beloved is mine and I am his,
  he pastures his flock among the lilies.

2.17
Sol 4.6;
ver 8,9

17 Until the day breathes
  and the shadows flee,
turn, my beloved, be like a gazelle,
  or a young stag upon rugged^f mountains.

B. *Her praise by night*

*3.1
Isa 26.9;
Sol 1.7; 5.6

3 Upon my bed by night
  I sought him whom my soul loves;
I sought him, but found him not;
  I called him, but he gave no answer.^g

3.2
Jer 5.1

2 "I will rise now and go about the city,
  in the streets and in the squares;
I will seek him whom my soul loves."
  I sought him, but found him not.

3.3
Sol 5.7

3 The watchmen found me,
  as they went about in the city.
"Have you seen him whom my soul loves?"

3.4
Sol 8.2

4 Scarcely had I passed them,
  when I found him whom my soul loves.
I held him, and would not let him go
  until I had brought him into my mother's house,
  and into the chamber of her that conceived me.

3.5
Sol 2.7; 8.4

5 I adjure you, O daughters of Jerusalem,
  by the gazelles or the hinds of the field,
that you stir not up nor awaken love
  until it please.

---

^f The meaning of the Hebrew word is unknown   ^g Gk: Heb lacks this line

---

3.1 Verses 1–5 are probably a song in which Shulammite (the bride) relates a dream. Her sleeping as well as her waking hours are always centered in her beloved.

III. *In praise of the bride 3.6–5.1*

A. *The bridegroom comes*

6 What is that coming up from the wilderness,
  like a column of smoke,
 perfumed with myrrh and frankincense,
  with all the fragrant powders of the merchant?
7 Behold, it is the litter of Solomon!
  About it are sixty mighty men
  of the mighty men of Israel,
8 all girt with swords
  and expert in war,
 each with his sword at his thigh,
  against alarms by night.
9 King Solomon made himself a palanquin
  from the wood of Lebanon.
10 He made its posts of silver,
  its back of gold, its seat of purple;
 it was lovingly wrought within*h*
  by the daughters of Jerusalem.
11 Go forth, O daughters of Zion,
  and behold King Solomon,
 with the crown with which his mother crowned him
  on the day of his wedding,
  on the day of the gladness of his heart.

3.6
Sol 8.5;
1.13; 4.6,14

3.8
Jer 50.9;
Ps 45.3;
91.5

3.10
Sol 1.5

3.11
Sol 3.16,17

B. *His proposal accepted*

4 Behold, you are beautiful, my love,
  behold, you are beautiful!
 Your eyes are doves
  behind your veil.
 Your hair is like a flock of goats,
  moving down the slopes of Gil'ëãd.
2 Your teeth are like a flock of shorn ewes
  that have come up from the washing,
 all of which bear twins,
  and not one among them is bereaved.
3 Your lips are like a scarlet thread,
  and your mouth is lovely.
 Your cheeks are like halves of a pomegranate
  behind your veil.
4 Your neck is like the tower of David,
  built for an arsenal,*i*
 whereon hang a thousand bucklers,
  all of them shields of warriors.
5 Your two breasts are like two fawns,
  twins of a gazelle,
  that feed among the lilies.
6 Until the day breathes
  and the shadows flee,
 I will hie me to the mountain of myrrh
  and the hill of frankincense.

4.1
Sol 1.15;
5.12; 6.5,7

4.2
Sol 6.6

4.3
Sol 6.7

4.4
Sol 7.4;
Neh 3.19

4.5
Sol 7.3;
2.16; 6.2,3

4.6
Sol 2.17;
ver 14

---

h The meaning of the Hebrew is uncertain
i The meaning of the Hebrew word is uncertain

4.7
Sol 1.15
7 You are all fair, my love;
  there is no flaw in you.

4.8
Sol 5.1;
Deut 3.9
8 Come with me from Lebanon, my bride;
  come with me from Lebanon.
Depart[j] from the peak of Amā′nă,
  from the peak of Sēnĭr and Hĕrmŏn,
from the dens of lions,
  from the mountains of leopards.

4.9
ver 10,12;
Prov 1,9;
Ezek 16.11
9 You have ravished my heart, my sister, my bride,
  you have ravished my heart with a glance of your eyes,
  with one jewel of your necklace.

4.10
Sol 1.2–4
10 How sweet is your love, my sister, my bride!
   how much better is your love than wine,
   and the fragrance of your oils than any spice!

4.11
Prov 5.3;
24.13;
Gen 27.27;
Hos 14.6
11 Your lips distil nectar, my bride;
   honey and milk are under your tongue;
   the scent of your garments is like the scent of Lebanon.

4.12
Prov 5.15–
18;
Gen 29.3
12 A garden locked is my sister, my bride,
   a garden locked, a fountain sealed.

4.13
Ecc 2.5;
Sol 6.11;
7.12;
ver 16;
Sol 1.14
13 Your shoots are an orchard of pomegranates
   with all choicest fruits,
   henna with nard,

4.14
Sol 1.12;
Ex 30.23;
ver 6;
Sol 3.6;
Jn 19.39
14 nard and saffron, calamus and cinnamon,
   with all trees of frankincense,
   myrrh and aloes,
   with all chief spices—

4.15
Jn 4.10;
7.38
15 a garden fountain, a well of living water,
   and flowing streams from Lebanon.

4.16
Sol 5.1;6.2
16 Awake, O north wind,
   and come, O south wind!
Blow upon my garden,
   let its fragrance be wafted abroad.
Let my beloved come to his garden,
   and eat its choicest fruits.

5.1
Sol 6.2;
4.9,11,14;
Lk 15.7,10;
Jn 3.29
5 I come to my garden, my sister, my bride,
  I gather my myrrh with my spice,
  I eat my honeycomb with my honey,
  I drink my wine with my milk.

Eat, O friends, and drink:
  drink deeply, O lovers!

IV. A troubled love 5.2—7.9

A. Her disturbing dream

5.2
Sol 4.9;
6.9;
ver 11
2 I slept, but my heart was awake.
Hark! my beloved is knocking.
"Open to me, my sister, my love,
  my dove, my perfect one;

j Or *Look*

for my head is wet with dew,
  my locks with the drops of the night."

3 I had put off my garment,
  how could I put it on?
I had bathed my feet,
  how could I soil them?
4 My beloved put his hand to the latch,
  and my heart was thrilled within me.

5 I arose to open to my beloved,
  and my hands dripped with myrrh,
my fingers with liquid myrrh,
  upon the handles of the bolt.
6 I opened to my beloved,
  but my beloved had turned and gone.
My soul failed me when he spoke.
I sought him, but found him not;
  I called him, but he gave no answer.
7 The watchmen found me,
  as they went about in the city;
they beat me, they wounded me,
  they took away my mantle,
  those watchmen of the walls.
8 I adjure you, O daughters of Jerusalem,
  if you find my beloved,
that you tell him
  I am sick with love.

9 What is your beloved more than another beloved,
  O fairest among women?
What is your beloved more than another beloved,
  that you thus adjure us?

10 My beloved is all radiant and ruddy,
  distinguished among ten thousand.
11 His head is the finest gold;
  his locks are wavy,
  black as a raven.
12 His eyes are like doves
  beside springs of water,
bathed in milk,
  fitly set.^{k}
13 His cheeks are like beds of spices,
  yielding fragrance.
His lips are lilies,
  distilling liquid myrrh.
14 His arms are rounded gold,
  set with jewels.
His body is ivory work,^{l}
  encrusted with sapphires.^{m}
15 His legs are alabaster columns,
  set upon bases of gold.

5.3
Lk 11.7;
Gen 19.2

5.5
ver 13

5.6
Sol 6.1; 3.1;
Prov 1.28

5.7
Sol 3.3

5.8
Sol 2.7;
3.5; 2.5

5.9
Sol 1.8; 6.1

5.12
Sol 1.15;
4.1

5.13
Sol 6.2; 2.1

---

k The meaning of the Hebrew is uncertain
l The meaning of the Hebrew word is uncertain
m Heb lapis lazuli

His appearance is like Lebanon,
    choice as the cedars.

5.16
Sol 7.9;
2 Sam 1.23
16 His speech is most sweet,
    and he is altogether desirable.
This is my beloved and this is my friend,
    O daughters of Jerusalem.

6.1
Sol 5.6;
1.8
6 Whither has your beloved gone,
    O fairest among women?
Whither has your beloved turned,
    that we may seek him with you?

6.2
Sol 4.16;
5.1,13;
1.7; 2.1
2 My beloved has gone down to his garden,
    to the beds of spices,
to pasture his flock in the gardens,
    and to gather lilies.

6.3
Sol 2.16;
7.10
3 I am my beloved's and my beloved is mine;
    he pastures his flock among the lilies.

B. The bridegroom's inner thoughts of his beloved

*6.4
Sol 1.15;
ver 10
4 You are beautiful as Tịrzạh, my love,
    comely as Jerusalem,
    terrible as an army with banners.

6.5
Sol 4.1
5 Turn away your eyes from me,
    for they disturb me—
Your hair is like a flock of goats,
    moving down the slopes of Gịl'ëäd.

6.6
Sol 4.2
6 Your teeth are like a flock of ewes,
    that have come up from the washing,
all of them bear twins,
    not one among them is bereaved.

6.7
Sol 4.3
7 Your cheeks are like halves of a pomegranate
    behind your veil.

6.8
1 Ki 11.3;
Sol 1.3
8 There are sixty queens and eighty concubines,
    and maidens without number.

6.9
Sol 2.14;
5.2;
Gen 30.13
9 My dove, my perfect one, is only one,
    the darling of her mother,
    flawless to her that bore her.
The maidens saw her and called her happy;
    the queens and concubines also, and they praised her.

6.10
ver 4
10 "Who is this that looks forth like the dawn,
    fair as the moon, bright as the sun,
    terrible as an army with banners?"

6.11
Sol 7.12
11 I went down to the nut orchard,
    to look at the blossoms of the valley,
to see whether the vines had budded,
    whether the pomegranates were in bloom.
12 Before I was aware, my fancy set me
    in a chariot beside my prince.[n]

n Cn: The meaning of the Hebrew is uncertain

6.4 *Tirzah* was the capital of the Northern Kingdom until the time of Omri who built Samaria (1 Ki 16.15–24). Here the beauty of Tirzah is compared to that of Jerusalem.

13 o Return, return, O Shu′lămmīte,
    return, return, that we may look upon you.

Why should you look upon the Shulammite,
    as upon a dance before two armies?p

*6.13
Judg 21.21;
Gen 32.2

7 How graceful are your feet in sandals,
    O queenly maiden!
Your rounded thighs are like jewels,
    the work of a master hand.
2 Your navel is a rounded bowl
    that never lacks mixed wine.
Your belly is a heap of wheat,
    encircled with lilies.
3 Your two breasts are like two fawns,
    twins of a gazelle.
4 Your neck is like an ivory tower.
Your eyes are pools in Hĕshbŏn,
    by the gate of Băth-răb′bĭm.
Your nose is like a tower of Lebanon,
    overlooking Damascus.
5 Your head crowns you like Carmĕl,
    and your flowing locks are like purple;
    a king is held captive in the tresses.q

7.1
Ps 45.13

7.3
Sol 4.5

7.4
Sol 4.4

7.5
Isa 35.2

6 How fair and pleasant you are,
    O loved one, delectable maiden!r
7 You are statelys as a palm tree,
    and your breasts are like its clusters.
8 I say I will climb the palm tree
    and lay hold of its branches.
Oh, may your breasts be like clusters of the vine,
    and the scent of your breath like apples,
9 and your kissest like the best wine
    that goes downu smoothly,
    gliding over lips and teeth.v

7.6
Sol 1.15,16

7.8
Sol 2.5

V. The unbroken communion 7.10—8.14

A. The bride gives her love

10 I am my beloved's,
    and his desire is for me.
11 Come, my beloved,
    let us go forth into the fields,
    and lodge in the villages;
12 let us go out early to the vineyards,
    and see whether the vines have budded,

7.10
Sol 2.16;
6.3;
Ps 45.11

7.12
Sol 6.11

o Ch 7.1 in Heb p Or dance of Māhănă′ĭm
q The meaning of the Hebrew word is uncertain r Syr: Heb in delights
s Heb This your stature is t Heb palate u Heb down for my lover
v Gk Syr Vg: Heb lips of sleepers

6.13 The Shulammite came from Shulem
(probably a variant of Shunem), a village in
the Plain of Esdraelon (check here 1 Sam
28.4 and 2 Ki 4.8).

whether the grape blossoms have opened
and the pomegranates are in bloom.
There I will give you my love.

*7.13
Gen 30.14;
Sol 2.3;
4.13,16

13 The mandrakes give forth fragrance,
and over our doors are all choice fruits,
new as well as old,
which I have laid up for you, O my beloved.

8 O that you were like a brother to me,
that nursed at my mother's breast!
If I met you outside, I would kiss you,
and none would despise me.

8.2
Sol 3.4

2 I would lead you and bring you
into the house of my mother,
and into the chamber of her that conceived me. *w*
I would give you spiced wine to drink,
the juice of my pomegranates.

8.3
Sol 2.6

3 O that his left hand were under my head,
and that his right hand embraced me!

8.4
Sol 2.7; 3.5

4 I adjure you, O daughters of Jerusalem,
that you stir not up nor awaken love
until it please.

B. The beauty of love

8.5
Sol 3.6; 2.3

5 Who is that coming up from the wilderness,
leaning upon her beloved?

Under the apple tree I awakened you.
There your mother was in travail with you,
there she who bore you was in travail.

8.6
Isa 49.16;
Jer 22.24;
Hag 2.23;
Prov 6.34

6 Set me as a seal upon your heart,
as a seal upon your arm;
for love is strong as death,
jealousy is cruel as the grave.
Its flashes are flashes of fire,
a most vehement flame.
7 Many waters cannot quench love,
neither can floods drown it.
If a man offered for love
all the wealth of his house,
it would be utterly scorned.

8.8
Ezek 16.7

8 We have a little sister,
and she has no breasts.
What shall we do for our sister,
on the day when she is spoken for?

*8.9

9 If she is a wall,
we will build upon her a battlement of silver;

w Gk Syr: Heb *mother; she* (or *you*) *will teach me*

7.13 *mandrakes* were thought to produce feelings of love (cf. Gen 30.14–16). Mandrakes were also associated with magic.

8.9 *a wall* is here symbolic of resistance to attack. The brothers think of their sister as resisting any who attack her innocence.

but if she is a door,
    we will enclose her with boards of cedar.
10 I was a wall,
    and my breasts were like towers;
  then I was in his eyes
    as one who brings^x peace.

11 Solomon had a vineyard at Bā′ăl-hā′mŏn;
    he let out the vineyard to keepers;
    each one was to bring for its fruit a thousand pieces of silver.
12 My vineyard, my very own, is for myself;
    you, O Solomon, may have the thousand,
    and the keepers of the fruit two hundred.

13 O you who dwell in the gardens,
    my companions are listening for your voice;
    let me hear it.

14 Make haste, my beloved,
    and be like a gazelle
  or a young stag
    upon the mountains of spices.

^{x} Or *finds*

8.11
Ecc 2.4;
Mt 21.33;
Sol 1.6;
2.3;
Isa 7.23

8.13
Sol 1.7;
2.14

8.14
Sol 2.17;
4.6

INTRODUCTION TO
THE BOOK OF
ISAIAH

Authorship and Background: This book contains the prophecies of Isaiah (whose name means "Yahweh is salvation"), the son of Amoz, who lived in Jerusalem and prophesied mainly about Judah and Jerusalem. He took up his prophetic office in the year King Uzziah died and continued that ministry during the reigns of Jotham, Ahaz, and Hezekiah. Hosea and Micah were among his contemporaries. Isaiah's ministry lasted over fifty years (ca. 740–687 B.C.), after which, according to tradition, he was sawn in pieces during the persecutions which raged after the accession of Manasseh (cf. Heb 11.37).

The authorship of the latter half of Isaiah, beginning with chapter 40, has been the subject of much dispute. Unquestionably, there is a distinct break at the end of chapter 39. The difference may be explained in one of two ways. The traditional view holds that 40–66 were composed later in Isaiah's life and are predictive prophecy. Others assume that because of the Babylonian setting of this unit, it was composed by some great unknown prophet who wrote *after* the events occurred rather than before. A variant of this view suggests a school of Isaiah in which the prophet's disciples spoke in the name of their teacher after his death. Once prediction is regarded as a fundamental part of the prophet's message, there is no compelling reason for denying the unity of the book, although, as in other books, later editing probably took place.

Characteristics: By Isaiah's time, Solomon's kingdom had been divided into Northern and Southern Kingdoms for many years. The Southern Kingdom (ca. 740 B.C.) faced attack by Israel (Northern Kingdom) and Syria. Assyria overcame Syria and threatened Israel. Samaria fell and Israel was taken captive (722 B.C.). Assyria now threatened Judah (Southern Kingdom) which looked toward Egypt for help. Isaiah wrote historically and prophetically. Chapters 36–39 are a record of his own life and activity during the days of Hezekiah. The remainder of the first half is devoted to prophecies concerning Judah and Jerusalem, and Judah with respect to Egypt and Assyria. The language of Isaiah is energetic and forceful. Beginning with chapter 40, the language becomes solemn, filled with pathos and marked by poetical outbursts of moving grandeur. The latter half of the book is replete with his messages of redemption and Messianic hope. Employing figures of rocks, forests, mountains, flocks of rams, trees of cedar and acacia, and moving torrents of flowing waters, Isaiah paints a graphic picture. In no other place in the Old Testament is there to be found a more realistic view of Calvary than in Isaiah 53.

Contents:

I.   Volume of rebuke and promise. 1.1—6.13: Isaiah arraigns the people

of Judah, charging them with sin and rebellion. He exhorts them to repent and promises forgiveness, pronouncing ultimate judgment if they do not. He prophesies about a glorious future for Judah in the last days and sketches the present sins of the people. The parable of the vineyard follows with a prophecy of invasion. Isaiah delineates his own call and commission.

II.   Volume of Immanuel. 7.1—12.6: Isaiah prophesies the coming of Immanuel to Ahaz. He speaks of the impending Assyrian invasion. Two other signs are given: one is the sign of Shear-jashub; the other the sign of Maher-shalal-hash-baz.

III.   Volume of burdens upon heathen nations. 13.1—23.18: Isaiah prophesies: the fall of Babylon; the defeat of Assyria; Palestine to have worse oppressors; Moab to be judged; Syria (Damascus) to become a heap; Israel to be doomed; Ethiopia to be trodden down; a confused and fearful Egypt to be taken captive; Sennacherib to invade Judah; the visions of Edom (Dumah) and Arabia; Jerusalem to be overcome and Shebna removed; Tyre to be overthrown and restored.

IV.   First volume of general rebuke and promise. 24.1—27.13: The whole world to be judged. The song of praise for judgment. It is the righteous God who must judge and whose mercy brings salvation.

V.   Volume of woes upon the unbelievers of Israel. 28.1—33.24: Isaiah prophesies that Judah's alliance with Egypt is death; it is a shame. Egypt itself will fall. Jerusalem also shall fall but will be restored. Her salvation is of God.

VI.   Second volume of general rebuke and promise. 34.1—35.10: The destruction of the hostile nations is prophesied, and the restoration of Zion promised. The desert shall blossom, the sick to be made well, the ground to bring forth fruit, and the captives to return with singing.

VII.   The volume of Hezekiah. 36.1—39.8: Sennacherib's invasion. Isaiah prophesies his defeat. The Babylonian captivity foretold. Hezekiah recovers from sickness and foolishly displays his wealth.

VIII. Volume of comfort and assurance. 40.1—66.24: The deliverance of God's people announced. God has power to save them. The agent of deliverance is God's Servant. Israel is His servant-nation. Cyrus is God's servant-king who shall bring to pass God's will. Babylon falls and the people go back to Jerusalem. The coming Servant King is pictured followed by a description of His reign and kingdom. It shall be permanent; men are invited to enter into it; the rules and requirements of the kingdom are laid down; there shall be judgment upon its foes. At last there shall be a sifting at the final day of judgment.

THE BOOK OF
ISAIAH

I. Volume of rebuke and promise 1.1–6.13

A. Rebellion confronted with judgment and grace

1. Superscription

*1.1
Num 12.6;
Isa 2.1;
2 Ki 15.1,
13,32; 16.1;
18.1

1 The vision of Īṣāi′áh the son of Āmóz, which he saw concerning Judah and Jerusalem in the days of Úzzī′áh, Jōthám, Āház, and Hĕzĕkī′áh, kings of Judah.

2. Judah's ingratitude

1.2
Deut 23.1

2 Hear, O heavens, and give ear, O earth;
    for the LORD has spoken:
"Sons have I reared and brought up,
    but they have rebelled against me.

1.3
Jer 8.7;
9.3,6

3 The ox knows its owner,
    and the ass its master's crib;
but Israel does not know,
    my people does not understand."

1.4
Isa 14.20;
ver 28;
Isa 5.24

4 Ah, sinful nation,
    a people laden with iniquity,
offspring of evildoers,
    sons who deal corruptly!
They have forsaken the LORD,
    they have despised the Holy One of Israel,
    they are utterly estranged.

*1.5
Isa 31.6;
33.24

5 Why will you still be smitten,
    that you continue to rebel?
The whole head is sick,
    and the whole heart faint.

1.6
Job 2.7;
Ps 38.3;
Isa 30.26;
Lk 10.34

6 From the sole of the foot even to the head,
    there is no soundness in it,
but bruises and sores
    and bleeding wounds;

1.1 Isaiah was a prophet. "The Hebrew word for 'prophet' means literally 'one who is inspired by God.' The prophets . . . all felt themselves to be spiritual leaders commissioned by God to warn their contemporaries of the perils of wickedness, to point the way to true religion, and to give guidance on moral issues. . . . Though prophecy was primarily concerned with current situations, the prophets realized that tomorrow is inherent in today. They foresaw the outcome of Israel's national crises and her evil patterns of living. Time and again their predictions of impending doom were fulfilled. When Jerusalem fell in 587 B.C., as prophets had warned for generations, people saw prophecy fulfilled in history. This gave the post-Exilic prophets great prestige." (Madelaine S. and J. Lane Miller, HARPER'S BIBLE DICTIONARY, Harper and Row, p. 582.)

Scripture reveals that all three Persons of the Trinity cooperate in the bestowal of the prophetic gift (Jer 1.5; Jon 1.2; 3.2; Eph 4.11; Rev 11.3; 1 Cor 12.10,11). The New Testament letters are striking examples of the exercise of the prophetic gift as it relates to instruction, reproof, and exhortation. Only occasionally (as in Rom 9.23–26; 1 Thess 4.13–17; 2 Thess 2.3,4) do they contain predictive material. Whether the New Testament gift of prophecy in the post-apostolic age includes the gift of prediction is not clear. At best, it would be rare and more often simulated than real.

1.5 The whole head is sick. In 701 B.C., Sennacherib of Assyria invaded Judah and despoiled the countryside. Jerusalem alone was spared (2 Ki 18.13–16). Isa 1.5–9 describes the plight of Judah following Sennacherib's invasion.

they are not pressed out, or bound up,
 or softened with oil.

7 Your country lies desolate,
 your cities are burned with fire;
in your very presence
 aliens devour your land;
 it is desolate, as overthrown by aliens.

1.7
Isa 6.11;
Jer 44.6

8 And the daughter of Zion is left
 like a booth in a vineyard,
like a lodge in a cucumber field,
 like a besieged city.

1.8
Job 27.18

9 If the LORD of hosts
 had not left us a few survivors,
we should have been like Sŏdŏm,
 and become like Gŏmor′răh.

1.9
Rom 9.29;
Isa 10.20–22

3. God's requirement of a holy life

10 Hear the word of the LORD,
 you rulers of Sŏdŏm!
Give ear to the teaching of our God,
 you people of Gŏmor′răh!

1.10
Isa 28.14;
3.9;
Ezek 16.46;
Rev 11.8

11 "What to me is the multitude of your sacrifices?
 says the LORD;
I have had enough of burnt offerings of rams
 and the fat of fed beasts;
I do not delight in the blood of bulls,
 or of lambs, or of he-goats.

1.11
1 Sam
15.22;
Jer 6.20;
Mic 6.7

12 "When you come to appear before me,
 who requires of you
 this trampling of my courts?

1.12
Ex 23.17

13 Bring no more vain offerings;
 incense is an abomination to me.
New moon and sabbath and the calling of assemblies—
 I cannot endure iniquity and solemn assembly.

★1.13
Isa 66.3;
1 Chr 23.31;
Ex 12.16;
Jer 7.9,10

14 Your new moons and your appointed feasts
 my soul hates;
they have become a burden to me,
 I am weary of bearing them.

1.14
Num 28.11;
Lev 23.2;
Isa 7.13;
43.24

15 When you spread forth your hands,
 I will hide my eyes from you;
even though you make many prayers,
 I will not listen;
your hands are full of blood.

1.15
1 Ki 8.22;
Isa 8.17;
59.2;
Mic 3.4;
Isa 59.3

16 Wash yourselves; make yourselves clean;
 remove the evil of your doings
 from before my eyes;
cease to do evil,
17 learn to do good;

1.16
Jer 4.14;
Isa 52.11;
55.7;
Jer 25.5

1.17
Jer 22.3;
Isa 58.6;
Ps 82.3

1.13 *vain offerings* were sacrifices devoid of any spiritual content. The forms of religion might be observed by those who had no real love of God or their fellow man. In verse 15 Isaiah complains that some who make religious profession are actually murderers.

seek justice,
correct oppression;
defend the fatherless,
plead for the widow.

4. The choice: repentance or destruction

1.18
Isa 43.26;
Ps 51.7;
Rev 7.14

18 "Come now, let us reason together,
says the LORD:
though your sins are like scarlet,
they shall be as white as snow;
though they are red like crimson,
they shall become like wool.

∗1.19
Deut 30.15,
16
1.20
Isa 3.25;
34.16

19 If you are willing and obedient,
you shall eat the good of the land;
20 But if you refuse and rebel,
you shall be devoured by the sword;
for the mouth of the LORD has spoken."

5. The promise to redeem Zion after judgment

1.21
Jer 2.20;
Isa 59.7

21 How the faithful city
has become a harlot,
she that was full of justice!
Righteousness lodged in her,
but now murderers.

1.22
Ezek 22.18

22 Your silver has become dross,
your wine mixed with water.

1.23
Hos 9.15;
Ex 23.8;
Mic 7.3;
Jer 5.28;
Zech 7.10

23 Your princes are rebels
and companions of thieves.
Every one loves a bribe
and runs after gifts.
They do not defend the fatherless,
and the widow's cause does not come to them.

1.24
Isa 49.26;
35.4

24 Therefore the Lord says,
the LORD of hosts,
the Mighty One of Israel:
"Ah, I will vent my wrath on my enemies,
and avenge myself on my foes.

1.25
Mal 3.3

25 I will turn my hand against you
and will smelt away your dross as with lye
and remove all your alloy.

∗1.26
Jer 33.7;
Zech 8.3

26 And I will restore your judges as at the first,
and your counselors as at the beginning.
Afterward you shall be called the city of righteousness,
the faithful city."

27 Zion shall be redeemed by justice,
and those in her who repent, by righteousness.

1.19 *If you are willing and obedient* expresses the condition for renewed blessing. Isaiah makes it clear that a formal relationship of the people (i.e., Israel) to God is not enough to insure God's favor.
1.26 *Afterward you shall be called the city of righteousness.* The immediate future of Judah might involve victory or defeat, depending upon the attitude of its people to God's revealed will. The prophet, however, looks to the more remote future and envisions a purged and restored nation. Once-faithful Jerusalem had become a harlot (1.21), but Isaiah here envisions her full restoration.

28 But rebels and sinners shall be destroyed together,
    and those who forsake the LORD shall be consumed.
29 For you shall be ashamed of the oaks
    in which you delighted;
  and you shall blush for the gardens
    which you have chosen.
30 For you shall be like an oak
    whose leaf withers,
  and like a garden without water.
31 And the strong shall become tow,
    and his work a spark,
  and both of them shall burn together,
    with none to quench them.

B. Present judgment will lead to future glory

1. *Promise of the triumph of God's kingdom on earth*

2 The word which Īṣāi'âh the son of Āmóz saw concerning Judah and Jerusalem.
2 It shall come to pass in the latter days
    that the mountain of the house of the LORD
  shall be established as the highest of the mountains,
    and shall be raised above the hills;
  and all the nations shall flow to it,
3   and many peoples shall come, and say:
"Come, let us go up to the mountain of the LORD,
    to the house of the God of Jacob;
  that he may teach us his ways
    and that we may walk in his paths."
For out of Zion shall go forth the law,
    and the word of the LORD from Jerusalem.
4 He shall judge between the nations,
    and shall decide for many peoples;
  and they shall beat their swords into plowshares,
    and their spears into pruning hooks;
  nation shall not lift up sword against nation,
    neither shall they learn war any more.

2. *Sin to be judged before the goal is attained*
a. *The house of Jacob urged to repent*

5 O house of Jacob,
  come, let us walk
    in the light of the LORD.

6 For thou hast rejected thy people,
  the house of Jacob,
because they are full of diviners*a* from the east
  and of soothsayers like the Philis'tines,

a Cn: Heb lacks *of diviners*

Cross-references (margin):

1.28 Isa 24.20; Ps 9.5; 2 Thess 1.8,9
1.29 Isa 57.5; 65.3
1.31 Isa 5.24; 66.24; Mt 3.12
*2.1ff Isa 1.1
*2.2 Mic 4.1–3; Isa 27.13; 66.20; 56.7
2.3 Isa 55.5; 66.18; Zech 8.20–23; Lk 24.47
2.4 Isa 32.17, 18; Hos 2.18
2.5 Isa 58.1; 60.1,2,19; 18.14
2.6 Deut 31.17; 2 Ki 16.7,8

2.1-4 This passage should be closely linked with chapter 1, combined with which it furnishes a noble prelude to a great symphony in which the composer first introduces the theme of his entire production before return- ing to a development and expansion of the individual parts. Taken in this context, verses 1–4 refer to Christ's kingdom.

    2.2 *the mountain of the house of the* LORD is the Temple Mount, Mount Moriah.

and they strike hands with foreigners.

2.7
Deut 17.16

7 Their land is filled with silver and gold,
and there is no end to their treasures;
their land is filled with horses,
and there is no end to their chariots.

2.8
Isa 10.11;
17.8

8 Their land is filled with idols;
they bow down to the work of their hands,
to what their own fingers have made.

2.9
Isa 5.15;
Neh 4.5

9 So man is humbled,
and men are brought low—
forgive them not!

2.10
Rev 6.15;
2 Thess 1.9

10 Enter into the rock,
and hide in the dust
from before the terror of the LORD,
and from the glory of his majesty.

2.11
Isa 13.11;
Zech 9.16

11 The haughty looks of man shall be brought low,
and the pride of men shall be humbled;
and the LORD alone will be exalted
in that day.

b. *Human pride to be humbled in judgment*

*2.12
Isa 24.4,21

12 For the LORD of hosts has a day
against all that is proud and lofty,
against all that is lifted up and high;[b]

2.13
Isa 10.33;
34;
Zech 11.2

13 against all the cedars of Lebanon,
lofty and lifted up;
and against all the oaks of Bāshàn;

2.14
Isa 30.25

14 against all the high mountains,
and against all the lofty hills;

15 against every high tower,
and against every fortified wall;

2.16
1 Ki 10.22

16 against all the ships of Tarshish,
and against all the beautiful craft.

2.17
ver 11

17 And the haughtiness of man shall be humbled,
and the pride of men shall be brought low;
and the LORD alone will be exalted in that day.

2.18
Isa 21.9
2.19
Hos 10.8;
Rev 9.6;
2 Thess 1.9;
Heb 12.26

18 And the idols shall utterly pass away.
19 And men shall enter the caves of the rocks
and the holes of the ground,
from before the terror of the LORD,
and from the glory of his majesty,
when he rises to terrify the earth.

2.20
Isa 30.22

20 In that day men will cast forth
their idols of silver and their idols of gold,
which they made for themselves to worship,
to the moles and to the bats,

2.21
ver 10,19

21 to enter the caverns of the rocks
and the clefts of the cliffs,

b Cn Compare Gk: Heb *low*

2.12 *For the* LORD *of hosts has a day.* The prophet speaks of a day of judgment and humiliation in which proud, rebellious man is confronted with the majestic glory of Israel's God. At this time, human pride shall be judged and brought to nought.

from before the terror of the LORD,
   and from the glory of his majesty,
   when he rises to terrify the earth.
22 Turn away from man
   in whose nostrils is breath,
   for of what account is he?

2.22
Ps 146.3;
Job 27.3;
Jas 4.14

c. *All classes to be punished for their guilt*

3 For, behold, the Lord, the LORD of hosts,
   is taking away from Jerusalem and from Judah
stay and staff,
   the whole stay of bread,
   and the whole stay of water;

*3.1
Jer 37.21;
Lev 26.26

2 the mighty man and the soldier,
   the judge and the prophet,
   the diviner and the elder,

3.2
2 Ki 24.14

3 the captain of fifty
   and the man of rank,
the counselor and the skilful magician
   and the expert in charms.

4 And I will make boys their princes,
   and babes shall rule over them.

*3.4
Ecc 10.16

5 And the people will oppress one another,
   every man his fellow
   and every man his neighbor;
the youth will be insolent to the elder,
   and the base fellow to the honorable.

3.5
Mic 7.3–6;
Isa 9.19

6 When a man takes hold of his brother
   in the house of his father, saying:
"You have a mantle;
   you shall be our leader,
and this heap of ruins
   shall be under your rule";

3.6
Isa 4.1

7 in that day he will speak out, saying:
"I will not be a healer;
   in my house there is neither bread nor mantle;
you shall not make me
   leader of the people."

3.7
Ezek 34.4

8 For Jerusalem has stumbled,
   and Judah has fallen;
because their speech and their deeds are against the LORD,
   defying his glorious presence.

3.8
Isa 1.7;
6.11; 9.17;
65.3,5

9 Their partiality witnesses against them;
   they proclaim their sin like Sŏdŏm,
   they do not hide it.
Woe to them!
   For they have brought evil upon themselves.

3.9
Isa 1.10;
Gen 13.13

10 Tell the righteous that it shall be well with them,
   for they shall eat the fruit of their deeds.

3.10
Deut 28.1–
14

3.1 *stay and staff*, i.e., everything that could be looked upon as a means of support for one.

3.4 *I will make boys their princes*, i.e., they shall have youthful, inexperienced rulers, adding to their problems.

3.11
Isa 65.6,7

*3.12
ver 4;
Isa 9.16

3.13
Isa 66.16;
Mic 6.2
3.14
Ezek 20.35,
36;
Isa 10.1,2;
Jas 2.6

3.15
Ps 94.5

3.16
Isa 4.4

3.17
Isa 47.3

3.18
Judg 8.21
3.20
Ex 39.28
3.21
Ezek 16.12

3.24
Prov 31.24;
Isa 22.12;
15.3

3.25
Isa 1.20;
65.12
3.26
Jer 14.2;
Lam 2.10
*4.1
Isa 13.12;
2 Thess
3.12;
Isa 54.4

11 Woe to the wicked! It shall be ill with him,
  for what his hands have done shall be done to him.
12 My people—children are their oppressors,
  and women rule over them.
O my people, your leaders mislead you,
  and confuse the course of your paths.

13 The LORD has taken his place to contend,
  he stands to judge his people.^{d}
14 The LORD enters into judgment
  with the elders and princes of his people:
"It is you who have devoured the vineyard,
  the spoil of the poor is in your houses.
15 What do you mean by crushing my people,
  by grinding the face of the poor?"
  says the Lord GOD of hosts.

16 The LORD said:
Because the daughters of Zion are haughty
  and walk with outstretched necks,
  glancing wantonly with their eyes,
mincing along as they go,
  tinkling with their feet;
17 the Lord will smite with a scab
  the heads of the daughters of Zion,
  and the LORD will lay bare their secret parts.

18 In that day the Lord will take away the finery of the anklets,
the headbands, and the crescents; 19 the pendants, the bracelets,
and the scarfs; 20 the headdresses, the armlets, the sashes, the
perfume boxes, and the amulets; 21 the signet rings and nose
rings; 22 the festal robes, the mantles, the cloaks, and the hand-
bags; 23 the garments of gauze, the linen garments, the turbans,
and the veils.
24 Instead of perfume there will be rottenness;
  and instead of a girdle, a rope;
and instead of well-set hair, baldness;
  and instead of a rich robe, a girding of sackcloth;
  instead of beauty, shame.^{e}
25 Your men shall fall by the sword
  and your mighty men in battle.
26 And her gates shall lament and mourn;
  ravaged, she shall sit upon the ground.

4 And seven women shall take hold of one man in that day,
  saying, "We will eat our own bread and wear our own clothes,
only let us be called by your name; take away our reproach."

^{d} Gk Syr: Heb judge peoples ^{e} One ancient Ms: Heb lacks shame

---

3.12 women rule over them. In 3.16, 17 the
prophet describes the haughty and wanton
women of Jerusalem. Although the prophetess
Deborah served as a judge in Israel (Judg
4.4), the only woman ruler during the
monarchy was the wicked Athaliah (2 Ki
11.1–16).

4.1 seven women shall take hold of one man,
i.e., they shall need a protector in a time of
anarchy. The men will have been decimated
in battle. Seven is a conventional number,
meaning "many" in a context such as this.
take away our reproach, i.e., shame or
contempt here.

d. *Blessedness of revived Israel under Messiah*

2 In that day the branch of the LORD shall be beautiful and glorious, and the fruit of the land shall be the pride and glory of the survivors of Israel. ³And he who is left in Zion and remains in Jerusalem will be called holy, every one who has been recorded for life in Jerusalem, ⁴ when the Lord shall have washed away the filth of the daughters of Zion and cleansed the bloodstains of Jerusalem from its midst by a spirit of judgment and by a spirit of burning. ⁵ Then the LORD will create over the whole site of Mount Zion and over her assemblies a cloud by day, and smoke and the shining of a flaming fire by night; for over all the glory there will be a canopy and a pavilion. ⁶ It will be for a shade by day from the heat, and for a refuge and a shelter from the storm and rain.

C. Judah to be exiled for unfaithfulness

1. *The parable of the vineyard*

5   Let me sing for my beloved
         a love song concerning his vineyard:
   My beloved had a vineyard
         on a very fertile hill.

² He digged it and cleared it of stones,
         and planted it with choice vines;
   he built a watchtower in the midst of it,
         and hewed out a wine vat in it;
   and he looked for it to yield grapes,
         but it yielded wild grapes.

³ And now, O inhabitants of Jerusalem
         and men of Judah,
   judge, I pray you, between me
         and my vineyard.

⁴ What more was there to do for my vineyard,
         that I have not done in it?
   When I looked for it to yield grapes,
         why did it yield wild grapes?

⁵ And now I will tell you
         what I will do to my vineyard.
   I will remove its hedge,

★4.2
Isa 11.1;
Zech 3.8;
6.12;
Ps 72.16;
Isa 10.20
★4.3
Isa 28.5;
60.21;
52.1;
Lk 10.20
4.4
Isa 3.16,24;
1.15; 28.6;
Mal 3.2,3
4.5
Ex 13.21;
Isa 60.1,2
4.6
Isa 25.4

★5.1
Ps 80.8;
Mt 21.33;
Mk 12.1;
Lk 20.9

5.2
Jer 2.21;
Mt 21.19;
Mk 11.13;
Lk 13.6

5.3
Mt 21.40

★5.4
Mt 23.37

★5.5
Ps 89.40;
Isa 6.13;
Ps 80.12;
Isa 10.6;
Lk 21.24;
Rev 11.2

4.2 The *branch* is an Old Testament name for Christ. It is a reference to the Messianic king as the descendant of the promised line of David. The word itself comes from the Hebrew *tsemach*, meaning a "sprout." In Jer 23.5 and 33.15 it is referred to as the *righteous Branch*, and finally, as the personal name of the Messiah in Zech 3.8 and 6.12. In Isaiah Christ is the *branch of the LORD*. In Jeremiah He is David's *righteous Branch*. In Zechariah He is *the man...Branch*. (Cf. the closely related title in 11.1 of the *shoot from the stump of Jesse*.)
4.3 *he who is left in Zion*. The prophet has depicted the judgment of God which would fall upon the wicked. Here he depicts the righteous remnant protected by the presence of God in the cloud (by day) and fire (by

night), reminiscent of the period of wilderness wandering.
5.1 *My beloved had a vineyard*. The prophet uses a parable to show God's care for Israel, and their ingratitude and disobedience. God cared for the vineyard (Israel), but received in return wild grapes (5.4).
5.4 *What more was there to do ...?* Israel is given opportunity to answer the charge. There must be some reason for the wild grapes. What had the beloved failed to do?
5.5 *I will remove its hedge*. The hedge was built to protect the vineyard and insure a good vintage. It had failed in its purpose. God too had placed a protecting hedge around Israel. When removed, Israel's powerful enemies could quickly devastate her.

and it shall be devoured;
I will break down its wall,
    and it shall be trampled down.

5.6
Isa 24.1,3;
Heb 6.8;
1 Ki 8.35

6 I will make it a waste;
    it shall not be pruned or hoed,
    and briers and thorns shall grow up;
I will also command the clouds
    that they rain no rain upon it.

5.7
Ps 80.8–11;
Isa 3.14,15

7 For the vineyard of the LORD of hosts
    is the house of Israel,
and the men of Judah
    are his pleasant planting;
and he looked for justice,
    but behold, bloodshed;
for righteousness,
    but behold, a cry!

2. *Judah guilty of seven sins*

a. *Selfish greed*

5.8
Mic 2.2

8 Woe to those who join house to house,
    who add field to field,
until there is no more room,
    and you are made to dwell alone
    in the midst of the land.

5.9
Isa 22.14;
6.11,12

9 The LORD of hosts has sworn in my hearing:
"Surely many houses shall be desolate,
    large and beautiful houses, without inhabitant.

5.10
Isa 7.23;
Ezek 45.11

10 For ten acres of vineyard shall yield but one bath,
    and a homer of seed shall yield but an ephah."

b. *Self-indulgence*

5.11
Prov 23.29,
30;
Ecc 10.16

11 Woe to those who rise early in the morning,
    that they may run after strong drink,
who tarry late into the evening
    till wine inflames them!

5.12
Amos 6.5,
6;
Job 34.27;
Ps 28.5

12 They have lyre and harp,
    timbrel and flute and wine at their feasts;
but they do not regard the deeds of the LORD,
    or see the work of his hands.

5.13
Hos 4.6;
Isa 1.3; 3.3;
9.14,15

13 Therefore my people go into exile
    for want of knowledge;
their honored men are dying of hunger,
    and their multitude is parched with thirst.

*5.14
Prov 30.16;
Num 16.30–
34;
Ps 141.7

14 Therefore Shĕōl has enlarged its appetite
    and opened its mouth beyond measure,
and the nobility of Jerusalem[f] and her multitude go down,
    her throng and he who exults in her.

5.15
Isa 2.9,11

15 Man is bowed down, and men are brought low,

f Heb *her nobility*

5.14 *Sheol has enlarged its appetite.* The nether world is personified and portrayed as a monster which opens its mouth and swallows the proud inhabitants of Jerusalem.

and the eyes of the haughty are humbled.
16 But the LORD of hosts is exalted in justice,
and the Holy God shows himself holy in righteousness.
17 Then shall the lambs graze as in their pasture,
fatlings and kids^g shall feed among the ruins.

c. *Cynical materialism*

18 Woe to those who draw iniquity with cords of falsehood,
who draw sin as with cart ropes,
19 who say: "Let him make haste,
let him speed his work
that we may see it;
let the purpose of the Holy One of Israel draw near,
and let it come, that we may know it!"

d. *Perversion of the standards of morality*

20 Woe to those who call evil good
and good evil,
who put darkness for light
and light for darkness,
who put bitter for sweet
and sweet for bitter!

e. *Intellectual pride and self-sufficiency*

21 Woe to those who are wise in their own eyes,
and shrewd in their own sight!

f. *Intemperance*

22 Woe to those who are heroes at drinking wine,
and valiant men in mixing strong drink,

g. *Loss of integrity*

23 who acquit the guilty for a bribe,
and deprive the innocent of his right!

3. *God's judgment against Judah*

24 Therefore, as the tongue of fire devours the stubble,
and as dry grass sinks down in the flame,
so their root will be as rottenness,
and their blossom go up like dust;
for they have rejected the law of the LORD of hosts,
and have despised the word of the Holy One of Israel.
25 Therefore the anger of the LORD was kindled against his people,
and he stretched out his hand against them and smote them,
and the mountains quaked;
and their corpses were as refuse
in the midst of the streets.
For all this his anger is not turned away
and his hand is stretched out still.

26 He will raise a signal for a nation afar off,

g Cn Compare Gk: Heb *aliens*

5.16	Isa 2.11,17; 8.13; 29.23
5.18	Isa 59.4–8
5.19	Ezek 12.22; 2 Pet 3.3,4
5.20	Prov 17.15; Mt 6.22,23; Lk 11.34,35
5.21	Rom 12.16
5.22	ver 11
5.23	Isa 10.1,2; Ps 94.21
5.24	Isa 9.18,19; Job 18.16; Hos 5.12; Acts 13.41
5.25	2 Ki 22.13; Jer 4.24; Isa 14.19; 9.12,17,21; 23.11
*5.26	Isa 13.2,3; 7.18; Deut 28.49; Isa 13.4,5

5.26 *He will raise a signal.* God will signal for a distant nation of warriors (probably Assyria) to punish sinful Israel. This is but one of the many threats to be found in Isaiah.

and whistle for it from the ends of the earth;
and lo, swiftly, speedily it comes!

5.27
Joel 2.7,8;
Dan 5.6

27 None is weary, none stumbles,
none slumbers or sleeps,
not a waistcloth is loose,
not a sandal-thong broken;

5.28
Ps 7.12,13;
Jer 4.13

28 their arrows are sharp,
all their bows bent,
their horses' hoofs seem like flint,
and their wheels like the whirlwind.

5.29
Jer 51.38;
Isa 10.6;
42.22

29 Their roaring is like a lion,
like young lions they roar;
they growl and seize their prey,
they carry it off, and none can rescue.

5.30
Isa 17.12;
8.22

30 They will growl over it on that day,
like the roaring of the sea.
And if one look to the land,
behold, darkness and distress;
and the light is darkened by its clouds.

D. Isaiah cleansed and commissioned

1. God's holiness revealed

*6.1
Isa 1.1;
2 Ki 15.7;
1 Ki 22.9

6 In the year that King Uzzi'ah died I saw the Lord sitting upon a throne, high and lifted up; and his train filled the temple.

*6.2
Rev 4.8;
Ezek 1.11

2Above him stood the seraphim; each had six wings: with two he covered his face, and with two he covered his feet, and with two he flew.

6.3
Rev 4.8;
Ps 72.19

3And one called to another and said:
"Holy, holy, holy is the LORD of hosts;
the whole earth is full of his glory."

4And the foundations of the thresholds shook at the voice of him who called, and the house was filled with smoke. 5And I said:

2. Isaiah's repentance, confession, and cleansing

6.5
Ex 33.20;
Jer 9.3–8;
51.57

"Woe is me! For I am lost; for I am a man of unclean lips, and I dwell in the midst of a people of unclean lips; for my eyes have seen the King, the LORD of hosts!"

6.7
Jer 1.9;
Isa 40.2;
1 Jn 1.7

6 Then flew one of the seraphim to me, having in his hand a burning coal which he had taken with tongs from the altar. 7And he touched my mouth, and said: "Behold, this has touched your lips; your guilt is taken away, and your sin forgiven." 8And I

6.8
Ezek 10.5;
Acts 9.4;
26.19

3. His commission to preach

6.9
Ezek 3.11;
Mt 13.14,
15;
Mk 4.12;
Lk 8.10;
Jn 12.40;
Rom 11.8

heard the voice of the Lord saying, "Whom shall I send, and who will go for us?" Then I said, "Here am I! Send me." 9And he said, "Go, and say to this people:
'Hear and hear, but do not understand;
see and see, but do not perceive.'

6.1 Here, and in verses 5–8, the prophet recalls Uzziah's horrible death from leprosy. Israel's king dies, but Israel's God lives forever.

6.2 *seraphim* in Hebrew signifies that which is burning and dazzling. The word is used of angelic beings only in Isaiah, and no explana-

tion of the term is given in the Bible. The Jews generally believed that the seraphim were a higher order of celestial beings, a theory supported by the fact that they worship and glorify God. This would certainly imply that they are moral beings rather than mere symbolic figures of some sort.

10 Make the heart of this people fat,
    and their ears heavy,
    and shut their eyes;
    lest they see with their eyes,
    and hear with their ears,
    and understand with their hearts,
    and turn and be healed."
11 Then I said, "How long, O Lord?"
And he said:
"Until cities lie waste
    without inhabitant,
    and houses without men,
    and the land is utterly desolate,
12 and the LORD removes men far away,
    and the forsaken places are many in the midst of the land.
13 And though a tenth remain in it,
    it will be burned again,
    like a terebinth or an oak,
    whose stump remains standing
    when it is felled."
The holy seed is its stump.

*6.10
Ps 119.70;
Jer 5.21

6.11
Mic 3.12

6.12
Jer 4.29

*6.13
Isa 1.9;
Job 14.7;
Ezra 9.2

II. The volume of Immanuel 7.1–12.6

A. Immanuel rejected by the wisdom of this world

1. The northern coalition

7 In the days of Āhǎz the son of Jōthǎm, son of Ŭzzī'ǎh, king of Judah, Rězin the king of Syria and Pēkǎh the son of Rěmǎli'ǎh the king of Israel came up to Jerusalem to wage war against it, but they could not conquer it. 2 When the house of David was told, "Syria is in league with Ē'phrǎim," his heart and the heart of his people shook as the trees of the forest shake before the wind.

7.1
2 Ki 16.1;
15.37;
15.25

7.2
ver 13;
Isa 8.12

2. God's answer on behalf of His people

3 And the LORD said to Ĭşǎi'ǎh, "Go forth to meet Āhǎz, you and Shē'ǎr-jǎsh'ǔb[h] your son, at the end of the conduit of the upper pool on the highway to the Fuller's Field, 4 and say to him, 'Take heed, be quiet, do not fear, and do not let your heart be faint because of these two smoldering stumps of firebrands, at the fierce anger of Rězin and Syria and the son of Rěmǎli'ǎh. 5 Because Syria, with Ē'phrǎim and the son of Rěmǎli'ǎh, has devised evil against you, saying, 6 "Let us go up against Judah and terrify it, and let us conquer it for ourselves, and set up the son of

*7.3
Isa 10.21;
2 Ki 18.17

7.4
Isa 30.15;
10.24; 35.4

*7.6

---

h That is A remnant shall return

6.10 Make the heart of this people fat. Isaiah was to declare the purposes of God even though the people would reject his ministry. His faithful proclamation would result in rebellion—hardness of heart.

6.13 The holy seed is its stump. From the stump that is left after the tree is cut down, a new nation will arise. Attention is on the faithful remnant with whom God will work.

7.3 the conduit of the upper pool. Ahaz,

threatened by an alliance of Israel and Syria, checked the water supplies of Jerusalem. In the event of a siege, water was necessary for survival. Ephraim was one of the tribes of Israel (the Northern Kingdom) and Ephraim and Israel are used synonymously (ver 2).

7.6 Ahaz had refused to join Israel and Syria in opposing Assyria. The two states to the north determined to depose Ahaz and place their own puppet on the throne of Jerusalem.

7.7
Isa 8.10

Tā'bë-ėl as king in the midst of it," 7 thus says the Lord GOD:
It shall not stand,
and it shall not come to pass.

7.8
Isa 17.1–3

8 For the head of Syria is Damascus,
and the head of Damascus is Rĕzĭn.
(Within sixty-five years Ē'phräįm will be broken to pieces so
that it will no longer be a people.)

*7.9
2 Chr 20.20

9 And the head of Ē'phräįm is Sámạr'ĭä,
and the head of Samaria is the son of Rĕmáli'äh.
If you will not believe,
surely you shall not be established.' "

3. *The sign of Immanuel and the child who will typify Him*

7.11
Isa 37.30;
38.7,8;
2 Ki 19.29

10 Again the LORD spoke to Āhăz, 11 "Ask a sign of the LORD
your God; let it be deep as Shĕōl or high as heaven." 12 But Āhăz
said, "I will not ask, and I will not put the LORD to the test."
13 And he said, "Hear then, O house of David! Is it too little for
you to weary men, that you weary my God also? 14 Therefore the

*7.14
Mt 1.23;
Lk 1.31;
Isa 9.6; 8.8

Lord himself will give you a sign. Behold, a young woman*i* shall
conceive and bear*j* a son, and shall call his name Ĭmmă'ū-ėl.*k*

7.15
ver 22
7.16
Isa 8.4

15 He shall eat curds and honey when he knows how to refuse the
evil and choose the good. 16 For before the child knows how to
refuse the evil and choose the good, the land before whose two

7.17
2 Chr 28.19;
1 Ki 12.16

kings you are in dread will be deserted. 17 The LORD will bring
upon you and upon your people and upon your father's house such
days as have not come since the day that Ē'phräįm departed from
Judah—the king of Assyria."

7.18
Isa 5.26

18 In that day the LORD will whistle for the fly which is at the
sources of the streams of Egypt, and for the bee which is in the

7.19
Isa 2.19;
Jer 16.16

land of Assyria. 19 And they will all come and settle in the steep
ravines, and in the clefts of the rocks, and on all the thornbushes,
and on all the pastures.

i Or *virgin*
j Or *is with child and shall bear*
k That is *God is with us*

7.9 *If you will not believe, surely you shall
not be established.* At this time of crisis, Ahaz
was weak in faith. Isaiah urged him to trust
the LORD, assuring him that this was the only
basis for confidence. Although stated in the
negative, the positive is implied, "If you
believe, surely you shall be established" and
you need not fear your enemies.

7.14 *Behold, a young woman shall conceive.*
When Ahaz refused to ask for a sign to
strengthen his faith, at the explicit command
of the LORD through Isaiah (7.10–12), he was
given a sign which would indicate that the
enemy would soon be removed (7.16). The
word rendered *young woman* denotes an
adolescent of marriageable age. The *sign* is
that such a young woman will give birth
to a child to be named *Immanuel*, "with
us, God." This, itself, would be an expression of faith, which was lacking in
Ahaz. During the childhood of Immanuel
there will be no agricultural crops because of
the devastation wrought by invading armies,
so his diet will be limited to *curds and honey*
(7.15) before he reaches the age of discern-

ment between good and evil (7.16). About
three years later Damascus fell (732 B.C.), followed a decade later by Samaria (722 B.C.).
Immanuel was intended to serve as a sign to
the people. It may be compared with *Shear-
jashub* (7.3), meaning "a remnant shall return"
and *Maher-shalal-hash-baz* (8.3), "The spoil
speedeth, the prey hasteth." Ch 8.18 depicts
Isaiah and his sons as *signs and portents in
Israel from the LORD of hosts.* Although it is
clear that Immanuel lived in the days of
Ahaz and his immediate successors, we cannot identify him with certainty. The young
woman, his mother, may have been the wife
of Isaiah, a woman of the royal family, or any
woman of Judah. This deliverance promised
to Ahaz is declared to be typical in Mt 1.23.
The antitype of the "young woman" is the
Virgin Mary, who miraculously gives birth to
Immanuel, a name or title for Jesus, God manifest in the flesh, (see Lk 1.26–38). The
deliverance to be achieved by Him transcends the national problems of ancient
Judah and her neighbors, the salvation which
He brings is from sin, man's greatest enemy.

20 In that day the Lord will shave with a razor which is hired beyond the River—with the king of Assyria—the head and the hair of the feet, and it will sweep away the beard also.

21 In that day a man will keep alive a young cow and two sheep; 22 and because of the abundance of milk which they give, he will eat curds; for every one that is left in the land will eat curds and honey.

23 In that day every place where there used to be a thousand vines, worth a thousand shekels of silver, will become briers and thorns. 24 With bow and arrows men will come there, for all the land will be briers and thorns; 25 and as for all the hills which used to be hoed with a hoe, you will not come there for fear of briers and thorns; but they will become a place where cattle are let loose and where sheep tread.

B. *The coming war and the future deliverer*

1. *Sign of Maher-shalal-hash-baz*

8 Then the LORD said to me, "Take a large tablet and write upon it in common characters, 'Belonging to Mā′hèr-shălăl-hăsh′-băz.' "¹ 2And I got reliable witnesses, Ūrī′áh the priest and Zĕchărī′áh the son of Jĕbĕr′ĕchī′áh, to attest for me. 3And I went to the prophetess, and she conceived and bore a son. Then the LORD said to me, "Call his name Mā′hĕr-shălăl-hăsh′-băz; 4 for before the child knows how to cry 'My father' or 'My mother,' the wealth of Damascus and the spoil of Sàmạr′iả will be carried away before the king of Assyria."

2. *The river overflowing its banks*

5 The LORD spoke to me again: 6 "Because this people have refused the waters of Shĭlō′áh that flow gently, and melt in fear beforeᵐ Rĕzĭn and the son of Rĕmăli′áh; 7 therefore, behold, the Lord is bringing up against them the waters of the River, mighty and many, the king of Assyria and all his glory; and it will rise over all its channels and go over all its banks; 8 and it will sweep on into Judah, it will overflow and pass on, reaching even to the neck; and its outspread wings will fill the breadth of your land, O Ĭmmăn′ū-ĕl."

3. *The stone of stumbling*

9 Be broken, you peoples, and be dismayed;
   give ear, all you far countries;

Cross-references (margin):

7.20 Isa 24.1; Ezek 5.1–4; Isa 10.5,15; 8.7
7.23 Isa 5.6
7.25 Isa 5.17
8.1 Isa 30.8; Hab 2.2
8.2 2 Ki 16.10
*8.3
8.4 Isa 7.16; 7.8,9
*8.6 Neh 3.15; Jn 9.7; Isa 7.1,2,6
8.7 Isa 17.12, 13; 7.20; 10.5,6;
8.8 Isa 10.6; 30.28; 7.14

---

l That is *The spoil speeds, the prey hastes*   *m* Cn: Heb *rejoices in*

8.3 The sign given to Ahaz has a double fulfilment. The first fulfilment is here specified. The birth of this son was not a virgin birth in the same sense that the birth of Christ was. The prophetess, who may have been a virgin at the time 7.14 was spoken, after entering into a normal marriage relationship with Isaiah, gave birth to Maher-shalal-hash-baz. Some hold that this little boy with the long name was therefore a type of the Messianic Immanuel. Others do not. The second fulfilment of this sign occurred in the birth of Christ, who was Himself the true Immanuel. (See also note to 7.14.)

The prophetess is the wife of Isaiah. She bears her title because of her relationship to the prophet, not because of any prophetic gift of her own.

8.6 *the waters of Shiloah*, the modern Ain Silwan, are located southwest of Mount Moriah. The quiet waters of Shiloah are contrasted with the turbulent *waters of the River* (Euphrates) of 8.7. Since Judah has rejected Shiloah, symbolic of God's rule, she would be overwhelmed by the King of Assyria, from beyond the Euphrates.

gird yourselves and be dismayed;
gird yourselves and be dismayed.

10 Take counsel together, but it will come to nought;
speak a word, but it will not stand,
for God is with us.[x]

11 For the LORD spoke thus to me with his strong hand upon me, and warned me not to walk in the way of this people, saying: 12 "Do not call conspiracy all that this people call conspiracy, and do not fear what they fear, nor be in dread. 13 But the LORD of hosts, him you shall regard as holy; let him be your fear, and let him be your dread. 14And he will become a sanctuary, and a stone of offense, and a rock of stumbling to both houses of Israel, a trap and a snare to the inhabitants of Jerusalem. 15And many shall stumble thereon; they shall fall and be broken; they shall be snared and taken."

4. *Command to trust the* LORD

16 Bind up the testimony, seal the teaching among my disciples. 17 I will wait for the LORD, who is hiding his face from the house of Jacob, and I will hope in him. 18 Behold, I and the children whom the LORD has given me are signs and portents in Israel from the LORD of hosts, who dwells on Mount Zion. 19And when they say to you, "Consult the mediums and the wizards who chirp and mutter," should not a people consult their God? Should they consult the dead on behalf of the living? 20 To the teaching and to the testimony! Surely for this word which they speak there is no dawn. 21 They will pass through the land,[n] greatly distressed and hungry; and when they are hungry, they will be enraged and will curse[o] their king and their God, and turn their faces upward; 22 and they will look to the earth, but behold, distress and darkness, the gloom of anguish; and they will be thrust into thick darkness.

5. *The birth of the Messianic king*

9[p] But there will be no gloom for her that was in anguish. In the former time he brought into contempt the land of Zĕb′-ŭlŭn and the land of Năph′tălī, but in the latter time he will make glorious the way of the sea, the land beyond the Jordan, Găl′ĭleē of the nations.

2[q] The people who walked in darkness
have seen a great light;
those who dwelt in a land of deep darkness,
on them has light shined.
3 Thou hast multiplied the nation,
thou hast increased its joy;
they rejoice before thee
as with joy at the harvest,
as men rejoice when they divide the spoil.
4 For the yoke of his burden,

x Heb *immanu el*   n Heb *it*   o Or *curse by*   p Ch 8.23 in Heb   q Ch 9.1 in Heb

---

9.1 *In the former time,* 734 B.C., Tiglath-pileser III deprived Israel of Ephraim, Zebulun, and Naphtali (2 Ki 15.29); *in the* *latter time,* looks forward to a time of restoration. Mt 4.13–17 sees a fulfilment of these words in Jesus' preaching in Galilee.

8.10
Job 5.12;
Isa 7.7;
Rom 8.31
8.11
Ezek 3.14;
2.8
8.12
Isa 7.2;
1 Pet 3.14,
15
8.13
Isa 5.16;
29.23;
Num 20.12
8.14
Ezek 11.16;
Lk 2.34;
Rom 9.33;
1 Pet 2.8
8.15
Isa 28.13;
Mt 21.44;
Lk 20.18;
Rom 9.32
8.16
ver 1,2;
Dan 12.4
8.17
Isa 54.8;
Hab 2.3
8.18
Heb 2.13;
Ps 71.7;
Zech 3.8
8.19
1 Sam 28.8;
Isa 19.3;
30.2; 45.11
8.20
Lk 16.29;
Mic 3.6
8.21
Isa 9.20,21;
Rev 16.11
8.22
Isa 5.30;
9.1
*9.1
2 Ki 15.29;
2 Chr 16.4
9.2
Mt 4.15,16
9.3
Isa 26.15;
35.10;
1 Sam 30.16
9.4
Isa 10.27;
14.4; 10.26

and the staff for his shoulder,
the rod of his oppressor,
thou hast broken as on the day of Mĭd'ĭăn.

5 For every boot of the tramping warrior in battle tumult
and every garment rolled in blood
will be burned as fuel for the fire.

6 For to us a child is born,
to us a son is given;
and the government will be upon his shoulder,
and his name will be called
"Wonderful Counselor, Mighty God,
Everlasting Father, Prince of Peace."

7 Of the increase of his government and of peace
there will be no end,
upon the throne of David, and over his kingdom,
to establish it, and to uphold it
with justice and with righteousness
from this time forth and for evermore.
The zeal of the LORD of hosts will do this.

C. The doom of boastful (Ephraim) Samaria

1. Samaria's pride

8 The Lord has sent a word against Jacob,
and it will light upon Israel;

9 and all the people will know,
Ē'phrăĭm and the inhabitants of Să·mar'ĭă,
who say in pride and in arrogance of heart:

10 "The bricks have fallen,
but we will build with dressed stones;
the sycamores have been cut down,
but we will put cedars in their place."

11 So the LORD raises adversaries[r] against them,
and stirs up their enemies.

12 The Syrians on the east and the Phĭlĭs'tĭnĕṣ on the west
devour Israel with open mouth.
For all this his anger is not turned away
and his hand is stretched out still.

2. Samaria's hypocrisy

13 The people did not turn to him who smote them,
nor seek the LORD of hosts.

14 So the LORD cut off from Israel head and tail,
palm branch and reed in one day—

r Cn: Heb the adversaries of Rĕzin

9.5	Isa 2.4
*9.6	Isa 7.14; Lk 2.11; Jn 3.16; Mt 28.18; 1 Cor 15.25; Isa 28.29; 10.21; 63.16; Eph 2.14
9.7	Dan 2.44; Lk 1.32,33; Isa 16.15; 11.4,5; 37.32
9.9	Isa 7.8,9; 46.12
9.11	Isa 7.1,8
9.12	2 Ki 16.6; 2 Chr 28.18; Ps 79.7; Isa 5.25
9.13	Jer 5.3; Hos 7.10; Isa 31.1
9.14	Isa 19.15; Rev 18.8

9.6 *For to us a child is born.* Although some commentators see this as a prophecy of Hezekiah's birth, it is more probable that the words express hope for a future deliverance. This would take place in *the latter time* of 9.1. This proclamation of the birth of the Messiah king undoubtedly refers to the Lord Jesus Christ as the God-Man. The title *Everlasting Father* is more literally "Father of Eternity" in the sense that He, as Creator, begot all things. Thus it does not involve any confusion between the Father and the Son in the Holy Trinity. The title *Prince of Peace* refers to the spiritual peace of the regenerate believer. The titles applied to Christ in this verse are only a few of the many ascribed to Him in Scripture. Among the others are: *God* (Isa 40.9; Jn 20.28), *the Almighty* (Rev 1.8), *the bread of life* (Jn 6.35), *good shepherd* (Jn 10.14), *Lord of glory* (1 Cor 2.8), *Son of David* (Mt 9.27), *King of kings* (Rev 17.14), and *Lamb* (Rev 13.8).

9.15
Isa 3.2,3;
28.15

15 the elder and honored man is the head,
  and the prophet who teaches lies is the tail;

9.16
Isa 3.12

16 for those who lead this people lead them astray,
  and those who are led by them are swallowed up.

9.17
Jer 18.21;
Isa 27.11;
10.6;
Mic 7.2;
Isa 5.25

17 Therefore the Lord does not rejoice over their young men,
  and has no compassion on their fatherless and widows;
for every one is godless and an evildoer,
  and every mouth speaks folly.
For all this his anger is not turned away
  and his hand is stretched out still.

3. *The self-destructiveness of sin*

9.18
Isa 10.17;
Mal 4.1

18 For wickedness burns like a fire,
  it consumes briers and thorns;
it kindles the thickets of the forest,
  and they roll upward in a column of smoke.

9.19
Isa 10.6;
Joel 2.3;
Isa 1.31;
24.6;
Mic 7.2,6

19 Through the wrath of the LORD of hosts
  the land is burned,
and the people are like fuel for the fire;
  no man spares his brother.

9.20
Isa 8.21,22;
49.26

20 They snatch on the right, but are still hungry,
  and they devour on the left, but are not satisfied;
each devours his neighbor's⁵ flesh,

9.21
Isa 5.25

21 Mȧnăsˊsĕh Ēˊphrȧïm, and Ephraim Manasseh,
  and together they are against Judah.
For all this his anger is not turned away
  and his hand is stretched out still.

4. *The oppressors doomed to captivity*

10.1
Ps 94.20

10 Woe to those who decree iniquitous decrees,
  and the writers who keep writing oppression,

10.2
Isa 5.23;
1.23

2 to turn aside the needy from justice
  and to rob the poor of my people of their right,
that widows may be their spoil,
  and that they may make the fatherless their prey!

10.3
Job 31.14;
Hos 9.7;
Lk 19.44;
Isa 5.26;
20.6

3 What will you do on the day of punishment,
  in the storm which will come from afar?
To whom will you flee for help,
  and where will you leave your wealth?

10.4
Isa 24.22;
22.2; 5.25

4 Nothing remains but to crouch among the prisoners
  or fall among the slain.
For all this his anger is not turned away
  and his hand is stretched out still.

D. *The false empire vanquished: a glorious empire to come*

1. *God's instrument of judgment shall in turn be judged*
a. *Assyria, the rod, to be destroyed*

★10.5
Jer 51.20

5 Ah, Assyria, the rod of my anger,
  the staff of my fury!ᵗ

⁵ Tg Compare Gk: Heb *the flesh of his arm*   ᵗ Heb *a staff it is in their hand my fury*

10.5 *Assyria, the rod of my anger.* God used Assyria to humble sinful Israel and Judah. The proud Assyrian, however, would be humbled in due time (10.12).

6 Against a godless nation I send him,
  and against the people of my wrath I command him,
to take spoil and seize plunder,
  and to tread them down like the mire of the streets.
7 But he does not so intend,
  and his mind does not so think;
but it is in his mind to destroy,
  and to cut off nations not a few;
8 for he says:
"Are not my commanders all kings?
9 Is not Cälnō like Car′çhĕmĭsh?
  Is not Hāmáth like Arpăd?
  Is not Sâmạr′ĭá like Damascus?
10 As my hand has reached to the kingdoms of the idols
  whose graven images were greater than those of Jerusalem
    and Sâmạr′ĭá,
11 shall I not do to Jerusalem and her idols
  as I have done to Sâmạr′ĭá and her images?"

12 When the Lord has finished all his work on Mount Zion
and on Jerusalem he[u] will punish the arrogant boasting of the
king of Assyria and his haughty pride. 13 For he says:
"By the strength of my hand I have done it,
  and by my wisdom, for I have understanding;
I have removed the boundaries of peoples,
  and have plundered their treasures;
like a bull I have brought down those who sat on thrones.
14 My hand has found like a nest
  the wealth of the peoples;
and as men gather eggs that have been forsaken
  so I have gathered all the earth;
and there was none that moved a wing,
  or opened the mouth, or chirped."

15 Shall the axe vaunt itself over him who hews with it,
  or the saw magnify itself against him who wields it?
As if a rod should wield him who lifts it,
  or as if a staff should lift him who is not wood!
16 Therefore the Lord, the LORD of hosts,
  will send wasting sickness among his stout warriors,
and under his glory a burning will be kindled,
  like the burning of fire.
17 The light of Israel will become a fire,
  and his Holy One a flame;
and it will burn and devour
  his thorns and briers in one day.
18 The glory of his forest and of his fruitful land
  the LORD will destroy, both soul and body,
and it will be as when a sick man wastes away.
19 The remnant of the trees of his forest will be so few
  that a child can write them down.

b. A remnant of Israel to be saved

20 In that day the remnant of Israel and the survivors of the

[Marginal references:]
10.6 Isa 9.17,19; Jer 34.22; Isa 5.25,29
10.7 Gen 50.20
10.8 2 Ki 18.24, 34; 19.10ff
10.9 Amos 6.2; 2 Chr 35.20; 2 Ki 16.9
10.10 2 Ki 19.17, 18
10.12 2 Ki 19.31; Jer 50.18; Isa 37.23
10.13 Isa 37.24; Ezek 28.4; Dan 4.30
10.14 Job 31.25
10.15 Jer 51.20; Rom 9.20, 21; ver 5
10.16 Isa 17.4; Ps 106.15; ver 18
10.17 Isa 30.33; 37.23; 27.4
10.18 Jer 21.14
10.19 Isa 21.17
10.20 2 Ki 16.7; 2 Chr 28.20; Isa 17.7,8

[u] Heb I

10.21
Isa 6.13;
9.6

10.22
Rom 9.27,
28;
Isa 28.22
10.23
Dan 9.27
10.24
Ps 87.5,6;
Isa 37.6;
Ex 5.14–16
10.25
Isa 17.14;
ver 5
10.26
Isa 37.36–
38;
Judg 7.25;
Ex 14.16,27
10.27
Isa 9.4;
30.23

10.28
1 Sam 14.2;
13.2,5;
17.22
10.29
Josh 21.17;
18.25;
1 Sam 10.26

10.30
1 Sam
25.44;
Josh 21.18
10.31
Josh 15.31

10.32
1 Sam 21.1;
Neh 11.32;
Isa 13.2;
37.22

10.33
Amos 2.9

*11.1
Zech 6.12;
Rev 5.5;
Acts 13.23;
Isa 4.2

house of Jacob will no more lean upon him that smote them, but will lean upon the LORD, the Holy One of Israel, in truth. ²¹A remnant will return, the remnant of Jacob, to the mighty God. ²² For though your people Israel be as the sand of the sea, only a remnant of them will return. Destruction is decreed, overflowing with righteousness. ²³ For the Lord, the LORD of hosts, will make a full end, as decreed, in the midst of all the earth.

24 Therefore thus says the Lord, the LORD of hosts: "O my people, who dwell in Zion, be not afraid of the Assyrians when they smite with the rod and lift up their staff against you as the Egyptians did. ²⁵ For in a very little while my indignation will come to an end, and my anger will be directed to their destruction. ²⁶And the LORD of hosts will wield against them a scourge, as when he smote Mĭd'ĭăn at the rock of Ō'rĕb; and his rod will be over the sea, and he will lift it as he did in Egypt. ²⁷ And in that day his burden will depart from your shoulder, and his yoke will be destroyed from your neck."

He has gone up from Rĭmmŏn,ᵛ
28   he has come to Ā'ĭăth;
     he has passed through Mĭgrŏn,
         at Mĭchmăsh he stores his baggage;
29   they have crossed over the pass,
         at Gē'bă they lodge for the night;
     Rā'măh trembles,
     Gĭb'ë-ăh of Saul has fled.
30 Cry aloud, O daughter of Găllĭm!
     Hearken, O Lā'ĭshăh!
     Answer her, O Ăn'ăthŏth!
31 Mădmē'năh is in flight,
         the inhabitants of Gēbĭm flee for safety.
32 This very day he will halt at Nŏb,
     he will shake his fist
         at the mount of the daughter of Zion,
         the hill of Jerusalem.

33 Behold, the Lord, the LORD of hosts
         will lop the boughs with terrifying power;
     the great in height will be hewn down,
         and the lofty will be brought low.
34 He will cut down the thickets of the forest with an axe,
     and Lebanon with its majestic treesʷ will fall.

2. The age of Messiah

a. The Branch out of Jesse

11   There shall come forth a shoot from the stump of Jĕssë,
     and a branch shall grow out of his roots.

ᵛ Cn: Heb and his yoke from your neck, and a yoke will be destroyed because of fatness
ʷ Cn Compare Gk Vg: Heb with a majestic one

11.1 a shoot from the stump of Jesse. Jesse, the father of David, is likened unto a tree. Judgment upon Israel may be likened to the felling of the tree. The judgment is not final, however, for the stump will produce a new shoot. Thus God's covenant with David is fulfilled. This description of the ideal king of David's line is interpreted in the New Testament as fulfilled in Christ. (See especially Rev 5.5.)

2 And the Spirit of the LORD shall rest upon him,
  the spirit of wisdom and understanding,
  the spirit of counsel and might,
  the spirit of knowledge and the fear of the LORD.
3 And his delight shall be in the fear of the LORD.

He shall not judge by what his eyes see,
  or decide by what his ears hear;
4 but with righteousness he shall judge the poor,
  and decide with equity for the meek of the earth;
and he shall smite the earth with the rod of his mouth,
  and with the breath of his lips he shall slay the wicked.
5 Righteousness shall be the girdle of his waist,
  and faithfulness the girdle of his loins.

6 The wolf shall dwell with the lamb,
  and the leopard shall lie down with the kid,
and the calf and the lion and the fatling together,
  and a little child shall lead them.
7 The cow and the bear shall feed;
  their young shall lie down together;
and the lion shall eat straw like the ox.
8 The sucking child shall play over the hole of the asp,
  and the weaned child shall put his hand on the adder's den.
9 They shall not hurt or destroy
  in all my holy mountain;
for the earth shall be full of the knowledge of the LORD
  as the waters cover the sea.

b. *Messiah to restore Israel*

10 In that day the root of Jĕssë shall stand as an ensign to the peoples; him shall the nations seek, and his dwellings shall be glorious.
11 In that day the Lord will extend his hand yet a second time to recover the remnant which is left of his people, from Assyria, from Egypt, from Păthrŏs, from Ethiopia, from Ēlăm, from Shīnar, from Hāmăth, and from the coastlands of the sea.
12 He will raise an ensign for the nations,
  and will assemble the outcasts of Israel,
and gather the dispersed of Judah
  from the four corners of the earth.
13 The jealousy of Ē′phraĭm shall depart,
  and those who harass Judah shall be cut off;
Ephraim shall not be jealous of Judah,
  and Judah shall not harass Ephraim.
14 But they shall swoop down upon the shoulder of the Phĭlĭs′tĭnĕş
  in the west,
  and together they shall plunder the people of the east.
They shall put forth their hand against Ēdŏm and Mōăb,
  and the Ăm′mŏnītes shall obey them.
15 And the LORD will utterly destroy

Cross-references (right margin):

11.2 Isa 61.1; Mt 3.16; Jn 1.32
11.3 Jn 2.25; 7.24
11.4 Isa 9.7; 3.14; 29.19; Mal 4.6; Job 4.9; 2 Thess 2.8
11.5 Eph 6.14; Isa 25.1
11.6 Isa 65.25
11.7 Isa 65.25
11.9 Job 5.23; Hab 2.14
11.10 Rom 15.12; Jn 3.14,15; Lk 2.32; Isa 14.3
11.11 Zech 10.10; Mic 7.12; Isa 66.19
11.12 ver 10; Zech 10.6; Isa 24.16
11.13 Jer 3.18; Ezek 37.16, 17,22; Hos 1.11
11.14 Dan 11.41; Joel 3.19; Isa 16.14; 25.10
*11.15 Isa 43.16; 19.16; 7.20; 8.7

11.15 *the tongue of the sea of Egypt* is the gulf of Suez. God is depicted as providing a passageway for the safe return of His people as He did at the Exodus.

the tongue of the sea of Egypt;
and will wave his hand over the River
    with his scorching wind,
and smite it into seven channels
    that men may cross dryshod.

11.16
Isa 19.23;
62.10;
Ex 14.26–
29;
Isa 51.10;
63.12,13

16 And there will be a highway from Assyria
    for the remnant which is left of his people,
as there was for Israel
    when they came up from the land of Egypt.

3. *Thanksgiving for God's salvation*

12.1
Isa 26.1;
25.1;40.1,2

12 You will say in that day:
    "I will give thanks to thee, O LORD,
    for though thou wast angry with me,
thy anger turned away,
    and thou didst comfort me.

12.2
Isa 33.2;
26.3;
Ex 15.2;
Ps 118.14

2 "Behold, God is my salvation;
    I will trust, and will not be afraid;
for the LORD GOD is my strength and my song,
    and he has become my salvation."

12.3
Jn 4.10;
7.37,38;
Isa 41.18

3 With joy you will draw water from the wells of salvation. 4And
you will say in that day:
"Give thanks to the LORD,
    call upon his name;
make known his deeds among the nations,
    proclaim that his name is exalted.

12.5
Isa 24.14;
Ex 15.1;
Ps 98.1

12.6
Zeph 3.14;
Isa 49.26

5 "Sing praises to the LORD, for he has done gloriously;
    let this be known*x* in all the earth.
6 Shout, and sing for joy, O inhabitant of Zion,
    for great in your midst is the Holy One of Israel."

III. *Volume of burdens upon heathen nations 13.1–23.18*

A. *First burden of Babylon*

1. *The doom of Babylon*

13.1
Jer ch 50,51

13 The oracle concerning Babylon which Īṣāi′áh the son of
    Āmóz saw.

13.2
Jer 50.2;
51.25;
Isa 10.32

2 On a bare hill raise a signal,
    cry aloud to them;
wave the hand for them to enter
    the gates of the nobles.

13.3
Joel 3.11;
Ps 149.2

3 I myself have commanded my consecrated ones,
    have summoned my mighty men to execute my anger,
    my proudly exulting ones.

13.4
Isa 5.30

4 Hark, a tumult on the mountains
    as of a great multitude!
Hark, an uproar of kingdoms,

x Or this is made known

of nations gathering together!
The LORD of hosts is mustering
  a host for battle.

5 They come from a distant land,
  from the end of the heavens,
the LORD and the weapons of his indignation,
  to destroy the whole earth.

	13.5
	Isa 5.26;
	42.13;
	10.5; 24.1

6 Wail, for the day of the LORD is near;
  as destruction from the Almighty it will come!
7 Therefore all hands will be feeble,
  and every man's heart will melt,
8   and they will be dismayed.
Pangs and agony will seize them;
  they will be in anguish like a woman in travail.
They will look aghast at one another;
  their faces will be aflame.

	13.6
	Zeph 1.7;
	Isa 10.25;
	Joel 1.15
	13.7
	Ezek 7.17;
	21.7
	13.8
	Isa 21.3;
	26.17

9 Behold, the day of the LORD comes,
  cruel, with wrath and fierce anger,
to make the earth a desolation
  and to destroy its sinners from it.

	13.9
	Isa 66.15,16

10 For the stars of the heavens and their constellations
  will not give their light;
the sun will be dark at its rising
  and the moon will not shed its light.
11 I will punish the world for its evil,
  and the wicked for their iniquity;
I will put an end to the pride of the arrogant,
  and lay low the haughtiness of the ruthless.
12 I will make men more rare than fine gold,
  and mankind than the gold of Ōphir.
13 Therefore I will make the heavens tremble,
  and the earth will be shaken out of its place,
at the wrath of the LORD of hosts
  in the day of his fierce anger.
14 And like a hunted gazelle,
  or like sheep with none to gather them,
every man will turn to his own people,
  and every man will flee to his own land.
15 Whoever is found will be thrust through,
  and whoever is caught will fall by the sword.
16 Their infants will be dashed in pieces
  before their eyes;
their houses will be plundered
  and their wives ravished.

	13.10
	Isa 5.30;
	Joel 2.10;
	Mt 24.29;
	Mk 13.24;
	Lk 21.25
	13.11
	Isa 26.21;
	11.4; 2.11;
	Jer 48.29
	13.12
	Isa 4.1;
	6.11,12
	13.13
	Isa 34.4;
	51.6;
	Jer 10.10;
	Amos 8.8;
	Hag 2.6
	13.14
	1 Ki 22.17;
	Jer 50.16;
	51.9
	13.15
	Isa 14.19
	13.16
	Ps 137.9;
	Nah 3.10;
	Zech 14.2

17 Behold, I am stirring up the Mēdes against them,
  who have no regard for silver
  and do not delight in gold.

	*13.17
	Isa 21.2;
	Jer 51.11;
	Dan 5.28

13.17 *the Medes*, an ancient, Aryan (Iranian) people located southwest of the Caspian Sea, joined forces with the Babylonians (Chaldeans) to bring about the destruction of Nineveh (612 B.C.). Subsequently, however, the Medes were incorporated into the Persian Empire which, under Cyrus, captured Babylon (539 B.C.).

18 Their bows will slaughter the young men;
    they will have no mercy on the fruit of the womb;
    their eyes will not pity children.

19 And Babylon, the glory of kingdoms,
    the splendor and pride of the Chăldē′ănṣ,
  will be like Sŏdŏm and Gòmor′răh
    when God overthrew them.

20 It will never be inhabited
    or dwelt in for all generations;
  no Arab will pitch his tent there,
    no shepherds will make their flocks lie down there.

21 But wild beasts will lie down there,
    and its houses will be full of howling creatures;
  there ostriches will dwell,
    and there satyrs will dance.

22 Hyenas will cry in its towers,
    and jackals in the pleasant palaces;
  its time is close at hand
    and its days will not be prolonged.

2. Taunt against the king of Babylon

14 The LORD will have compassion on Jacob and will again choose Israel, and will set them in their own land, and aliens will join them and will cleave to the house of Jacob. ²And the peoples will take them and bring them to their place, and the house of Israel will possess them in the LORD's land as male and female slaves; they will take captive those who were their captors, and rule over those who oppressed them.

3 When the LORD has given you rest from your pain and turmoil and the hard service with which you were made to serve, ⁴ you will take up this taunt against the king of Babylon:

"How the oppressor has ceased,
    the insolent fury^y ceased!

5 The LORD has broken the staff of the wicked,
    the scepter of rulers,

6 that smote the peoples in wrath
    with unceasing blows,
  that ruled the nations in anger
    with unrelenting persecution.

7 The whole earth is at rest and quiet;
    they break forth into singing.

8 The cypresses rejoice at you,
    the cedars of Lebanon, saying,
  'Since you were laid low,
    no hewer comes up against us.'

9 Shē̄ol beneath is stirred up
    to meet you when you come,
  it rouses the shades to greet you,

^y One ancient Ms Compare Gk Syr Vg: The meaning of the Hebrew word is uncertain

---

13.18
2 Ki 8.12;
Ezek 9.5,10

13.19
Isa 21.9;
Dan 4.30;
Gen 19.24;
Deut 29.23;
Jer 49.18

★**13.20**
Jer 51.37–43

★**13.21**
Isa 34.11–15

13.22
Jer 51.33

14.1
Ps 102.13;
Zech 1.17;
2.12;
Isa 60.4,5,
10;
Eph 2.12–19

14.2
Isa 49.22;
60.9,10;
66.20;
60.14

14.3
Isa 40.2

14.4
Isa 13.19;
Hab 2.6;
Rev 18.6

14.6
Isa 10.14;
47.6

14.8
Isa 55.12

14.9
Ezek 32.21

13.20 Scripture foretold the utter ruin of Babylon and prophesied that it should never be rebuilt. It never has to this day. Consonant with the prophecy, then, it is proper to conclude that the Babylon of the Apocalypse (Rev 17) is not a literal one. Undoubtedly it is a political and ecclesiastical combination of which the Old Testament Babylon is a prophetic type and example.

13.21 *satyr*. In myth, part goat, part man.

all who were leaders of the earth;
it raises from their thrones
all who were kings of the nations.
10 all of them will speak
and say to you:
'You too have become as weak as we!
You have become like us!'
11 Your pomp is brought down to Shēōl,
the sound of your harps;
maggots are the bed beneath you,
and worms are your covering.

> **14.11**
> Isa 5.14;
> Ezek 28.13;
> Isa 51.8

12 "How you are fallen from heaven,
O Day Star, son of Dawn!
How you are cut down to the ground,
you who laid the nations low!

> **★14.12**
> Isa 34.4;
> Lk 10.18

13 You said in your heart,
'I will ascend to heaven;
above the stars of God
I will set my throne on high;
I will sit on the mount of assembly
in the far north;

> **14.13**
> Ezek 28.2;
> Dan 8.10

14 I will ascend above the heights of the clouds,
I will make myself like the Most High.'

> **14.14**
> Isa 47.8;
> 2 Thess 2.4

15 But you are brought down to Shēōl,
to the depths of the Pit.

> **14.15**
> Mt 11.23

16 Those who see you will stare at you,
and ponder over you:
'Is this the man who made the earth tremble,
who shook kingdoms,

> **14.16**
> Jer 50.23

17 who made the world like a desert
and overthrew its cities,

> **14.17**
> Joel 2.3;
> Isa 45.13

14.12 Scripture uses many names for Satan. Among them are (1) *liar* (Jn 8.44); (2) *prince of the power of the air* (Eph 2.2); (3) *your adversary the Devil* (1 Pet 5.8); (4) *the dragon, that ancient serpent, who is the Devil and Satan* (Rev 20.2). His origin is obscure, but 14.12–15, Ezek 28.12–19, and Lk 10.18 throw light on it. Satan is (1) very wicked (1 Jn 3.8); (2) very shrewd and cunning (Rev 12.9; 2 Cor 11.3; 13–15); (3) the great enemy of God who has many helpers (Eph 6.12; Lk 11.15; 8.30). Actually Satan is already a defeated foe (Jn 12.31). His destiny and doom are sure. At last he will be cast into the lake of fire and there be tormented day and night forever (Rev 20.10). Satan's works are numerous and various: (1) he tempts the servants of God (1 Thess 3.5; 2 Cor 2.11); (2) he blinds men's eyes (2 Cor 4.3, 4); (3) he seeks to destroy the Word of God (Mk 4.15); (4) he becomes regnant in individuals or takes up his abode in their hearts (Jn 13.27); (5) he accuses believers before God (Rev 12.10); (6) he seeks to harass and molest the servants of God (1 Thess 2.18; 1 Pet 5.8). Christians are commanded to resist the devil (Jas 4.7); to watch and pray (Mt 26.41); and to employ the shield of faith (Eph 6.16). Satan is responsible for sin, having led Adam and Eve to sin in the Garden.

In this particular passage (14.12) the title *Day Star* (or, Lucifer) is used. This taunt is addressed by the denizens of Sheol to the *king of Babylon* (ver 4), but the dimensions of the God-defying ambition expressed in verses 13, 14 surpass anything that could be put into the mouth of a mere human being (even hyperbolically). No human king is ever represented in any ancient Semitic literature, either Hebrew or pagan, as vaunting himself to set his throne above the heights of the clouds like the Most High God. Therefore the best interpretation of this passage is to see in the human king of Babylon a tool in the hand of the devil himself, who has empowered and directed him in his opposition to God's people and cause.

O Day Star, son of Dawn! As the morning star quickly disappears when the sun rises, so the Babylonian king, brilliant in his hour, will soon be removed from his place. The Babylonian worship of Ishtar, later equated with Venus, an astral deity, may have occasioned the figure of speech used of the Babylonian ruler.

who did not let his prisoners go home?"

18 All the kings of the nations lie in glory,
   each in his own tomb;

14.19
Isa 22.16–
18;
Jer 41.7,9;
Isa 5.25

19 but you are cast out, away from your sepulchre,
   like a loathed untimely birth,[z]
clothed with the slain, those pierced by the sword,
   who go down to the stones of the Pit,
   like a dead body trodden under foot.

14.20
Job 18.19;
Ps 21.10;
37.28;
Isa 31.2

20 You will not be joined with them in burial,
   because you have destroyed your land,
   you have slain your people.

"May the descendants of evildoers
   nevermore be named!

14.21
Ex 20.5;
Isa 13.16;
Mt 23.35;
Isa 27.6

21 Prepare slaughter for his sons
   because of the guilt of their fathers,
lest they rise and possess the earth,
   and fill the face of the world with cities."

14.22
Isa 26.14;
Prov 10.7;
Isa 47.9

22 "I will rise up against them," says the LORD of hosts, "and will cut off from Babylon name and remnant, offspring and posterity, says the LORD. 23And I will make it a possession of the hedgehog, and pools of water, and I will sweep it with the broom of destruction, says the LORD of hosts."

14.23
Isa 34.11–
15;
Zeph 2.14;
Isa 13.6

B. *The overthrow of Assyria*

14.24
Isa 45.23;
55.8,9;
Acts 4.28

24 The LORD of hosts has sworn:
"As I have planned,
   so shall it be,
and as I have purposed,
   so shall it stand,

14.25
Isa 10.12,
27

25 that I will break the Assyrian in my land,
   and upon my mountains trample him under foot;
and his yoke shall depart from them,
   and his burden from their shoulder."

14.26
Isa 23.9;
Ex 15.12

26 This is the purpose that is purposed
   concerning the whole earth;
and this is the hand that is stretched out
   over all the nations.

14.27
2 Chr 20.6;
Isa 43.13;
Dan 4.31,35

27 For the LORD of hosts has purposed,
   and who will annul it?
His hand is stretched out,
   and who will turn it back?

C. *Burden of Philistia*

14.28
2 Ki 16.20

28 In the year that King Āhăz died came this oracle:

14.29
Jer 47.1–7;
2 Chr 26.6

29 "Rejoice not, O Phĭlis′tĭă, all of you,
   that the rod which smote you is broken,
for from the serpent's root will come forth an adder,
   and its fruit will be a flying serpent.

14.30
Isa 3.14,15;
7.21; 8.21;
Jer 25.16,20

30 And the first-born of the poor will feed,
   and the needy lie down in safety;

z Cn Compare Tg Symmachus: Heb *a loathed branch*

but I will kill your root with famine,
and your remnant I[a] will slay.

31 Wail, O gate; cry, O city;
melt in fear, O Phĭlĭs′tĭă, all of you!
For smoke comes out of the north,
and there is no straggler in his ranks.''

14.31
Isa 3.26;
ver 29;
Jer 1.14;
Isa 34.16

32 What will one answer the messengers of the nation?
''The LORD has founded Zion,
and in her the afflicted of his people find refuge.''

14.32
Isa 37.9;
Ps 87.1,5;
Zeph 3.12;
Zech 11.11

D. Burden of Moab

1. Scenes of her coming devastation

15 An oracle concerning Mō̆ăb.
Because Ar is laid waste in a night
Moab is undone;
because Kĭr is laid waste in a night
Moab is undone.

15.1
Isa 11.14;
Jer 48;
Ezek 25.8–
11;
Jer 48.41

2 The daughter of Dībŏn[b] has gone up
to the high places to weep;
over Nē̆bō and over Mĕd′ĕbá
Mō̆ăb wails.
On every head is baldness,
every beard is shorn;

15.2
Lev 21.5

3 in the streets they gird on sackcloth;
on the housetops and in the squares
every one wails and melts in tears.

15.3
Jon 3.6– 8;
Jer 48.38;
Isa 22.4

4 Hĕshbŏn and Ĕlĕ-ā′lĕh cry out,
their voice is heard as far as Jāhăz;
therefore the armed men of Mō̆ăb cry aloud;
his soul trembles.

5 My heart cries out for Mō̆ăb;
his fugitives flee to Zō′ar,
to Ĕg′lăth-shĕlĭshī′yáh.
For at the ascent of Luhĭth
they go up weeping;
on the road to Horŏnā′ĭm
they raise a cry of destruction;

15.5
Jer 48.5,
31,34;
Isa 59.7

6 the waters of Nimrĭm
are a desolation;
the grass is withered, the new growth fails,
the verdure is no more.

15.6
Isa 19.5–7;
Joel 1.10–
12

7 Therefore the abundance they have gained
and what they have laid up
they carry away
over the Brook of the Willows.

15.7
Isa 30.6

8 For a cry has gone
round the land of Mō̆ăb;
the wailing reaches to Ĕglā′ĭm,
the wailing reaches to Beĕr-ē′lĭm.

9 For the waters of Dībŏn[c] are full of blood;

15.9
2 Ki 17.25;
Jer 50.17

---

[a] One ancient Ms Vg: Heb *he*   [b] Cn: Heb *the house and Dibon*
[c] One ancient Ms Vg Compare Syr: Heb *Dīmŏn*

yet I will bring upon Dibon^c even more,
a lion for those of Mōăb who escape,
for the remnant of the land.

2. *Moab's pride and fall*

16.1
2 Ki 3.4;
14.7;
Isa 10.32

16 They have sent lambs
      to the ruler of the land,
from Sēlă, by way of the desert,
   to the mount of the daughter of Zion.

16.2
Num 21.13,
14

2 Like fluttering birds,
      like scattered nestlings,
so are the daughters of Mōăb
   at the fords of the Arnŏn.

16.3
Isa 25.4

3 "Give counsel,
      grant justice;
make your shade like night
   at the height of noon;
hide the outcasts,
   betray not the fugitive;

16.4
Isa 9.4;
54.14

4 let the outcasts of Mōăb
      sojourn among you;
be a refuge to them
   from the destroyer.
When the oppressor is no more,
   and destruction has ceased,
and he who tramples under foot
   has vanished from the land,

16.5
Dan 7.14;
Mic 4.7;
Lk 1.33;
Isa 9.7

5 then a throne will be established in steadfast love
      and on it will sit in faithfulness
         in the tent of David
one who judges and seeks justice
   and is swift to do righteousness."

16.6
Jer 48.29,
30;
Zeph 2.8,10

6 We have heard of the pride of Mōăb,
      how proud he was;
of his arrogance, his pride, and his insolence—
   his boasts are false.

16.7
1 Chr 16.3;
2 Ki 3.25;
Jer 48.31

7 Therefore let Mōăb wail,
      let every one wail for Moab.
Mourn, utterly stricken,
   for the raisin-cakes of Kĭr-har′ĕsĕth.

16.8
Isa 15.4;
Num 32.38;
Jer 48.32

8 For the fields of Hĕshbŏn languish,
      and the vine of Sĭbmăh;
the lords of the nations
   have struck down its branches,
which reach to Jāzĕr
   and strayed to the desert;
its shoots spread abroad
   and passed over the sea.

16.9
Jer 48.32;
Isa 15.4;
Jer 40.10,12

9 Therefore I weep with the weeping of Jāzĕr
      for the vine of Sĭbmăh;
I drench you with my tears,

^{c} One ancient Ms Vg Compare Syr: Heb *Dĭmŏn*

O Hĕshbŏn and Ĕlĕ-ā'lĕh;
for upon your fruit and your harvest
    the battle shout has fallen.
10 And joy and gladness are taken away
    from the fruitful field;
and in the vineyards no songs are sung,
    no shouts are raised;
no treader treads out wine in the presses;
    the vintage shout is hushed.*d*

11 Therefore my soul moans like a lyre for Mōăb,
    and my heart for Kĭr-hĕr'ĕs.

12 And when Mōăb presents himself, when he wearies himself
upon the high place, when he comes to his sanctuary to pray, he
will not prevail.

13 This is the word which the LORD spoke concerning Mōăb in
the past. 14 But now the LORD says, "In three years, like the years
of a hireling, the glory of Mōăb will be brought into contempt,
in spite of all his great multitude, and those who survive will be
very few and feeble."

E. Burden of Damascus and Samaria

1. The crushing of Damascus and Ephraim

17 An oracle concerning Damascus.
    Behold, Damascus will cease to be a city,
and will become a heap of ruins.
2 Her cities will be deserted for ever;*e*
    they will be for flocks,
which will lie down, and none will make them afraid.
3 The fortress will disappear from Ē'phrăĭm,
    and the kingdom from Damascus;
and the remnant of Syria will be
    like the glory of the children of Israel,
                    says the LORD of hosts.

2. Survival of an idol-hating remnant

4 And in that day
    the glory of Jacob will be brought low,
and the fat of his flesh will grow lean.
5 And it shall be as when the reaper gathers standing grain
    and his arm harvests the ears,
and as when one gleans the ears of grain
    in the Valley of Rĕph'ăĭm.
6 Gleanings will be left in it,
    as when an olive tree is beaten—
two or three berries
    in the top of the highest bough,
four or five
    on the branches of a fruit tree,
              says the LORD God of Israel.

d Gk: Heb *I have hushed*   *e* Cn Compare Gk: Heb *the cities of Arŏ'ĕr are deserted*

16.10
Isa 24.7,8;
Jer 48.33;
Job 24.11

16.11
Isa 15.5;
63.15;
Jer 48.36

16.12
Jer 48.35;
1 Ki 18.29;
Isa 15.2;
2 Ki 19.12

★**16.14**
Isa 21.16;
25.10

17.1
2 Ki 16.9;
Jer 49.23;
Amos 1.3;
Zech 9.1;
Isa 8.4;
10.9

17.2
Jer 7.33

17.3
Isa 7.16;
8.4

17.4
Isa 10.3,16

17.5
Jer 51.33;
2 Sam 5.18,
22

17.6
Isa 24.13;
27.12

16.14 *the years of a hireling.* A hireling
labors only as long as he must. The simile
means "no more than three years," as is indicated at the start of the verse.

17.7
Isa 10.20;
Mic 7.7
17.8
Isa 27.9;
30.22;
31.7;
Ex 34.13;
Deut 7.5

7 In that day men will regard their Maker, and their eyes will look to the Holy One of Israel; 8 they will not have regard for the altars, the work of their hands, and they will not look to what their own fingers have made, either the Ashēʹrĭm or the altars of incense.

3. The imminent horrors of invasion

17.9
Isa 7.25

9 In that day their strong cities will be like the deserted places of the Hīʹvītes and the Ămʹŏrītes,ᶠ which they deserted because of the children of Israel, and there will be desolation.

17.10
Isa 51.13;
Ps 68.19;
Isa 26.4;
30.29

10 For you have forgotten the God of your salvation,
    and have not remembered the Rock of your refuge;
therefore, though you plant pleasant plants
    and set out slips of an alien god,

17.11
Ps 90.6;
Job 4.8

11 though you make them grow on the day that you plant them,
    and make them blossom in the morning that you sow;
yet the harvest will flee away
    in a day of grief and incurable pain.

17.12
Jer 6.23;
Ezek 43.2;
Ps 18.4

12 Ah, the thunder of many peoples,
    they thunder like the thundering of the sea!
Ah, the roar of nations,
    they roar like the roaring of mighty waters!

17.13
Isa 33.3;
Ps 9.5;
Isa 13.14;
29.5;
41.15,16

13 The nations roar like the roaring of many waters,
    but he will rebuke them, and they will flee far away,
chased like chaff on the mountains before the wind
    and whirling dust before the storm.

17.14
Isa 41.12;
2 Ki 19.35

14 At evening time, behold, terror!
    Before morning, they are no more!
This is the portion of those who despoil us,
    and the lot of those who plunder us.

F. Burden of Ethiopia

*18.1
Isa 20.3–5;
Ezek 30.4,
5,9;
Zeph 2.12;
3.10

18 Ah, land of whirring wings
    which is beyond the rivers of Ethiopia;
2 which sends ambassadors by the Nile,
    in vessels of papyrus upon the waters!
Go, you swift messengers,
    to a nation, tall and smooth,

18.2
Ex 2.3;
ver 7;
2 Chr 12.2–
4

to a people feared near and far,
    a nation mighty and conquering,
    whose land the rivers divide.

18.3
Ps 49.1;
Isa 5.26;
26.11

3 All you inhabitants of the world,
    you who dwell on the earth,
when a signal is raised on the mountains, look!
    When a trumpet is blown, hear!

18.4
Isa 26.21;
2 Sam 23.4;
Isa 26.19

4 For thus the LORD said to me:
"I will quietly look from my dwelling

ᶠ Cn Compare Gk: Heb the wood and the highest bough

18.1 land of whirring wings refers to the numerous insects of the Nile Valley. Ethiopia. An Ethiopian dynasty was ruling Egypt during the lifetime of Isaiah.

like clear heat in sunshine,
  like a cloud of dew in the heat of harvest."

5 For before the harvest, when the blossom is over,
  and the flower becomes a ripening grape,
he will cut off the shoots with pruning hooks,
  and the spreading branches he will hew away.

6 They shall all of them be left
  to the birds of prey of the mountains
  and to the beasts of the earth.
And the birds of prey will summer upon them,
  and all the beasts of the earth will winter upon them.

7 At that time gifts will be brought to the LORD of hosts
from a people tall and smooth,
  from a people feared near and far,
a nation mighty and conquering,
  whose land the rivers divide,
to Mount Zion, the place of the name of the LORD of hosts.

G. Burden of Egypt

1. The doom of Egypt

19 An oracle concerning Egypt.
  Behold, the LORD is riding on a swift cloud
and comes to Egypt;
and the idols of Egypt will tremble at his presence,
  and the heart of the Egyptians will melt within them.
2 And I will stir up Egyptians against Egyptians,
  and they will fight, every man against his brother
  and every man against his neighbor,
  city against city, kingdom against kingdom;
3 and the spirit of the Egyptians within them will be emptied out,
  and I will confound their plans;
and they will consult the idols and the sorcerers,
  and the mediums and the wizards;
4 and I will give over the Egyptians
  into the hand of a hard master;
and a fierce king will rule over them,
          says the Lord, the LORD of hosts.

5 And the waters of the Nile will be dried up,
  and the river will be parched and dry;
6 and its canals will become foul,
  and the branches of Egypt's Nile will diminish and dry up,
  reeds and rushes will rot away.
7 There will be bare places by the Nile,
  on the brink of the Nile,
and all that is sown by the Nile will dry up,
  be driven away, and be no more.
8 The fishermen will mourn and lament,

Marginal references: 18.5 Ezek 17.6–10; Isa 27.11 · 18.6 Isa 46.11; 56.9; Jer 7.33 · 18.7 Ps 68.31; Isa 45.14; Zeph 3.10; Zech 14.16,17 · *19.1 Isa 13.1; Jer 46.13–26; Ezek ch 29, 30; Ps 18.10; 104.3; Ex 12.12; Jer 43.12 · 19.2 Judg 7.22; 1 Sam 14.16,20; 2 Chr 20.23; Mt 10.21,36 · 19.3 ver 11–14; Isa 8.19 · 19.4 Isa 20.4; Jer 46.26; Ezek 29.19 · 19.5 Jer 51.36; Ezek 30.12 · 19.6 Ex 7.18; Isa 37.25; 15.6 · 19.7 Isa 23.3,10

19.1 *the LORD is riding on a swift cloud.* The Canaanite Baal was a god of fertility who was described as the rider of the clouds. The figure of speech is used of the God of Israel (cf. Ps 18.10; 104.3) who brings fertility to the land and hastens to bring blessing to His faithful people and to execute judgment upon the wicked.

all who cast hook in the Nile;
and they will languish
who spread nets upon the water.

19.9
Prov 7.16;
Ezek 27.7
9 The workers in combed flax will be in despair,
and the weavers of white cotton.

19.10
Ps 11.3
10 Those who are the pillars of the land will be crushed,
and all who work for hire will be grieved.

19.11
Num 13.22;
1 Ki 4.30;
Acts 7.22
11 The princes of Zōan are utterly foolish;
the wise counselors of Phạraōh give stupid counsel.
How can you say to Pharaoh,
"I am a son of the wise,
a son of ancient kings"?

19.12
1 Cor 1.20;
Isa 14.24;
Rom 9.17
12 Where then are your wise men?
Let them tell you and make known
what the Lord of hosts has purposed against Egypt.

19.13
Jer 2.16;
Ezek 30.13;
Zech 10.4
13 The princes of Zōan have become fools,
and the princes of Memphis are deluded;
those who are the cornerstones of her tribes
have led Egypt astray.

19.14
Isa 29.10;
Mt 17.17;
Isa 3.12;
9.16; 28.7
14 The Lord has mingled within her
a spirit of confusion;
and they have made Egypt stagger in all her doings
as a drunken man staggers in his vomit.

19.15
Isa 9.14,
15
15 And there will be nothing for Egypt
which head or tail, palm branch or reed, may do.

2. *God's people will triumph over Egypt*

19.16
Jer 51.30;
Isa 2.19;
11.15;
30.32
16 In that day the Egyptians will be like women, and tremble
with fear before the hand which the Lord of hosts shakes over
them. 17And the land of Judah will become a terror to the Egyptians; every one to whom it is mentioned will fear because of the
19.17
Isa 14.24
purpose which the Lord of hosts has purposed against them.
★19.18
Isa 45.23;
65.16
18 In that day there will be five cities in the land of Egypt which
speak the language of Cānaàn and swear allegiance to the Lord of
hosts. One of these will be called the City of the Sun.

3. *The final conversion and deliverance of Egypt*

★19.19
Isa 56.7;
Gen 28.18;
Ex 24.4;
Josh 22.10,
26,27
19 In that day there will be an altar to the Lord in the midst of
the land of Egypt, and a pillar to the Lord at its border. 20 It will
be a sign and a witness to the Lord of hosts in the land of Egypt;
19.20
Isa 43.3,11;
49.25
when they cry to the Lord because of oppressors he will send
them a savior, and will defend and deliver them. 21And the Lord
will make himself known to the Egyptians; and the Egyptians will
19.21
Isa 11.9;
Mal 1.11;
Isa 44.5
know the Lord in that day and worship with sacrifice and burnt
offering, and they will make vows to the Lord and perform them.
19.22
Isa 30.26;
27.13;
45.14
22And the Lord will smite Egypt, smiting and healing, and they
will return to the Lord, and he will heed their supplications and
heal them.

19.18 *the language of Canaan* (Hebrew),
was the language adopted by the Israelite
patriarchs after their entrance into Canaan.
19.19 *an altar to the* Lord *in the midst of
the land of Egypt.* The prophet depicts a
future day when Egypt will call upon the
Lord and worship Him at an altar in Egypt.
Josephus once stated that Onias IV, who
built an altar at Leontopolis (154 B.C.), appealed
to this text.

23 In that day there will be a highway from Egypt to Assyria, and the Assyrian will come into Egypt, and the Egyptian into Assyria, and the Egyptians will worship with the Assyrians. 24 In that day Israel will be the third with Egypt and Assyria, a blessing in the midst of the earth, 25 whom the LORD of hosts has blessed, saying, "Blessed be Egypt my people, and Assyria the work of my hands, and Israel my heritage."

4. Egypt to be conquered by Assyria

20 In the year that the commander in chief, who was sent by Sargon the king of Assyria, came to Ăshdŏd and fought against it and took it,—2 at that time the LORD had spoken by Iṣāi'áh the son of Āmŏz, saying, "Go, and loose the sackcloth from your loins and take off your shoes from your feet," and he had done so, walking naked and barefoot—3 the LORD said, "As my servant Iṣāi'áh has walked naked and barefoot for three years as a sign and a portent against Egypt and Ethiopia, 4 so shall the king of Assyria lead away the Egyptians captives and the Ethiopians exiles, both the young and the old, naked and barefoot, with buttocks uncovered, to the shame of Egypt. 5 Then they shall be dismayed and confounded because of Ethiopia their hope and of Egypt their boast. 6And the inhabitants of this coastland will say in that day, 'Behold, this is what has happened to those in whom we hoped and to whom we fled for help to be delivered from the king of Assyria! And we, how shall we escape?' "

H. The defeat of Babylon by Medo-Persia

21 The oracle concerning the wilderness of the sea.
As whirlwinds in the Nĕgĕb sweep on,
   it comes from the desert,
   from a terrible land.
2 A stern vision is told to me;
   the plunderer plunders,
   and the destroyer destroys.
Go up, O Ēlám,
   lay siege, O Mē'dĭa;
all the sighing she has caused
   I bring to an end.
3 Therefore my loins are filled with anguish;
   pangs have seized me,
   like the pangs of a woman in travail;
I am bowed down so that I cannot hear,
   I am dismayed so that I cannot see.
4 My mind reels, horror has appalled me;
   the twilight I longed for
has been turned for me into trembling.
5 They prepare the table,
   they spread the rugs,
   they eat, they drink.
Arise, O princes,
   oil the shield!

19.23
Isa 11.16;
27.13

19.25
Isa 45.14;
Hos 2.23;
Eph 2.10

★20.1
2 Ki 18.17;
1 Sam 5.1
20.2
Zech 13.4;
Ezek 24.17,
23;
1 Sam
19.24;
Mic 1.8
20.3
Isa 8.18;
37.9; 43.3
20.4
Isa 19.4;
3.17;
Jer 13.22,26
20.5
2 Ki 18.21;
Isa 30.3,5,7;
Ezek 29.6,7
20.6
Isa 10.3;
30.7;
Mt 23.33;
Heb 2.3

21.1
Isa 31.1;
Jer 51.42;
Zech 9.14

21.2
Isa 33.1;
13.17;
Jer 49.34

21.3
Isa 15.5;
16.11; 13.8

21.4
Deut 28.67

21.5
Jer 51.39,
57;
Dan 5.1–4

20.1 Ashdod, a Philistine city, was allied with Egypt against Assyria. Sargon's com- mander took the city in 711 B.C., and was later besieged by Sennacherib and other aggressors.

6 For thus the Lord said to me:
"Go, set a watchman,
        let him announce what he sees.

21.7
ver 9

7 When he sees riders, horsemen in pairs,
        riders on asses, riders on camels,
    let him listen diligently,
        very diligently."

21.8
Hab 2.1

8 Then he who saw[g] cried:
"Upon a watchtower I stand, O Lord,
        continually by day,
    and at my post I am stationed
        whole nights.

21.9
Jer 51.8;
Rev 14.8;
18.2;
Isa 46.1;
Jer 50.2;
51.44

9 And, behold, here come riders,
        horsemen in pairs!"
    And he answered,
        "Fallen, fallen is Babylon;
    and all the images of her gods
        he has shattered to the ground."

21.10
Jer 51.33

10 O my threshed and winnowed one,
        what I have heard from the LORD of hosts,
        the God of Israel, I announce to you.

I. Burden of (Edom) Dumah

*21.11
Gen 25.14;
32.3

11 The oracle concerning Dumáh.
    One is calling to me from Sẹir,
    "Watchman, what of the night?
    Watchman, what of the night?"
12 The watchman says:
"Morning comes, and also the night.
    If you will inquire, inquire;
    come back again."

J. Burden of Arabia

*21.13
Isa 13.1;
Jer 49.28;
1 Chr 1.9,32

13 The oracle concerning Arabia.
    In the thickets in Arabia you will lodge,
        O caravans of Dẽ'dànītes.

21.14
Gen 25.15;
Job 6.19

14 To the thirsty bring water,
        meet the fugitive with bread,
        O inhabitants of the land of Tẽmå.

21.15
Isa 13.14,
15; 17.13

15 For they have fled from the swords,
        from the drawn sword,
    from the bent bow,
        and from the press of battle.

*21.16
Isa 16.14;
17.4;
Ps 120.5;
Isa 60.7

16 For thus the Lord said to me, "Within a year, according to
the years of a hireling, all the glory of Kẽdar will come to an end;

21.17
Isa 10.19;
Num 23.19;
Zech 1.6

17 and the remainder of the archers of the mighty men of the sons
of Kẽdar will be few; for the LORD, the God of Israel, has spoken."

g One ancient Ms: Heb a lion

21.11 Dumah (Edom) means silence.
21.13 The Dedanites were apparently a commercial people who carried on an extensive trade with Tyre and Damascus.
    21.16 Isaiah's prophecy concerning Kedar was quickly fulfilled.

K. *Burden of Jerusalem, the valley of vision*

1. *Heedless of warning, the city to fall*

22 The oracle concerning the valley of vision.
　What do you mean that you have gone up,
　　all of you, to the housetops,

2 you who are full of shoutings,
　tumultuous city, exultant town?
Your slain are not slain with the sword
　or dead in battle.

3 All your rulers have fled together,
　without the bow they were captured.
All of you who were found were captured,
　though they had fled far away.*h*

4 Therefore I said:
"Look away from me,
　let me weep bitter tears;
do not labor to comfort me
　for the destruction of the daughter of my people."

5 For the Lord GOD of hosts has a day
　of tumult and trampling and confusion
　in the valley of vision,
a battering down of walls
　and a shouting to the mountains.

6 And Ēlām bore the quiver
　with chariots and horsemen,*i*
　and Kĭr uncovered the shield.

7 Your choicest valleys were full of chariots,
　and the horsemen took their stand at the gates.

8 He has taken away the covering of Judah.

In that day you looked to the weapons of the House of the Forest, 9 and you saw that the breaches of the city of David were many, and you collected the waters of the lower pool, 10 and you counted the houses of Jerusalem, and you broke down the houses to fortify the wall. 11 You made a reservoir between the two walls for the water of the old pool. But you did not look to him who did it, or have regard for him who planned it long ago.

12 In that day the Lord GOD of hosts
　called to weeping and mourning,
　to baldness and girding with sackcloth;

13 and behold, joy and gladness,
　slaying oxen and killing sheep,
　eating flesh and drinking wine.
"Let us eat and drink,
　for tomorrow we die."

14 The LORD of hosts has revealed himself in my ears:
"Surely this iniquity will not be forgiven you
　till you die,"
　　says the Lord GOD of hosts.

h Gk Syr Vg: Heb *from far away*
i The Hebrew of this line is obscure

22.1 Isa 13.1; Joel 3.12, 14; Isa 15.3
22.2 Isa 32.13; Jer 14.18; Lam 2.20
22.3 Isa 21.15
22.4 Isa 15.3; Jer 4.19; 9.1
22.5 Isa 37.3; 63.3; Lam 1.5; 2.2; ver 1
22.6 Jer 49.35; 2 Ki 16.9
22.7 2 Chr 32.1
22.8 2 Chr 32.3–5,30; 1 Ki 7.2; 10.17
22.9 Neh 3.16
22.11 2 Ki 25.4; 20.20; 2 Chr 32.3, 4; Isa 37.26
22.12 Joel 1.13; Isa 15.2; Mic 1.16
22.13 Isa 5.11,22; 56.12; 1 Cor 15.32
22.14 Isa 5.9; 65.7,20

2. Corrupt Shebna to be replaced by Eliakim

22.15
2 Ki 18.37;
Isa 36.3
15 Thus says the Lord GOD of hosts, "Come, go to this steward, to Shĕbnă, who is over the household, and say to him: 16 What

22.16
2 Sam
18.18;
2 Chr
16.14;
Mt 27.60
have you to do here and whom have you here, that you have hewn here a tomb for yourself, you who hew a tomb on the height, and carve a habitation for yourself in the rock? 17 Behold, the LORD will hurl you away violently, O you strong man. He will seize firm hold on you, 18 and whirl you round and round, and throw you

22.18
Isa 17.13;
Job 18.18
like a ball into a wide land; there you shall die, and there shall be your splendid chariots, you shame of your master's house. 19 I will

22.19
Job 40.11,
12;
Ezek 17.24
thrust you from your office, and you will be cast down from your station. 20 In that day I will call my servant Ĕlĭ'ăkĭm the son of

*22.20
2 Ki 18.18;
Isa 36.3
Hĭlkī'ăh, 21 and I will clothe him with your robe, and will bind your girdle on him, and will commit your authority to his hand; and he shall be a father to the inhabitants of Jerusalem and to the house of Judah. 22And I will place on his shoulder the key of the

*22.22
Rev 3.7;
Isa 7.2,13;
Job 12.14
house of David; he shall open, and none shall shut; and he shall shut, and none shall open. 23And I will fasten him like a peg in a sure place, and he will become a throne of honor to his father's

22.23
Ezra 9.8;
Job 36.7
house. 24And they will hang on him the whole weight of his father's house, the offspring and issue, every small vessel, from the cups to all the flagons. 25 In that day, says the LORD of hosts,

22.25
ver 23;
Isa 46.11;
Mic 4.4
the peg that was fastened in a sure place will give way; and it will be cut down and fall, and the burden that was upon it will be cut off, for the LORD has spoken."

L. The burden of Tyre

1. The fall of Tyre predicted

*23.1
Jer 25.22;
47.4;
Ezek ch 26,
27, 28;
ver 12
23 The oracle concerning Tyre.
Wail, O ships of Tarshish,
   for Tyre is laid waste, without house or haven!
From the land of Cyprus
   it is revealed to them.

23.2
Isa 47.5
2 Be still, O inhabitants of the coast,
      O merchants of Sidon;
   your messengers passed over the sea[j]

23.3
Jer 2.18;
Ezek 27.3–
23
3   and were on many waters;
   your revenue was the grain of Shĭhor,
      the harvest of the Nile;
   you were the merchant of the nations.

23.4
Ezek 28.21,
22
4 Be ashamed, O Sidon, for the sea has spoken,
      the stronghold of the sea, saying:

---

j One ancient Ms: Heb *who passed over the sea, they replenished you*

22.20 Eliakim (whose name means "God will establish") is a type of Christ. As a leader and representative of the godly remnant of Isaiah's day who still believed and obeyed God, he stood in contrast to the worldly-minded Shebna (who doubtless advocated ignoring Isaiah's warnings against alliance with idolatrous Egypt). To Eliakim the key of the house of David was to be given. He was granted power to open and to shut; and no man would shut what he had opened or open what he had shut. The type is fulfilled in

Rev. 3.7, where Christ holds the key of David. *my servant Eliakim* contrasts his person and work with Shebna, who sought his own ends.

22.22 *the key of the house of David* was the symbol of royal authority (cf. Rev 3.7 where Christ holds the key of David).

23.1 *ships of Tarshish* is a term used of merchant ships in the Old Testament. Tarshish probably refers to Tartesus, a city on the Quadalquivir River in Spain (cf. 2.16), which had been colonized by Tyrians. See also note to 1 Ki 10.22.

"I have neither travailed nor given birth,
  I have neither reared young men
    nor brought up virgins."
5 When the report comes to Egypt,
  they will be in anguish over the report about Tyre.
6 Pass over to Tarshish,
  wail, O inhabitants of the coast!
7 Is this your exultant city
  whose origin is from days of old,
whose feet carried her
  to settle afar?
8 Who has purposed this
  against Tyre, the bestower of crowns,
whose merchants were princes,
  whose traders were the honored of the earth?
9 The LORD of hosts has purposed it,
  to defile the pride of all glory,
  to dishonor all the honored of the earth.
10 Overflow your land like the Nile,
  O daughter of Tarshish;
  there is no restraint any more.
11 He has stretched out his hand over the sea,
  he has shaken the kingdoms;
the LORD has given command concerning Cānaàn
  to destroy its strongholds.
12 And he said:
  "You will no more exult,
    O oppressed virgin daughter of Sīdòn;
  arise, pass over to Cyprus,
    even there you will have no rest."

13 Behold the land of the Chǎldē′ànş! This is the people; it was
not Assyria. They destined Tyre for wild beasts. They erected
their siege towers, they razed her palaces, they made her a ruin. *k*
14 Wail, O ships of Tarshish,
  for your stronghold is laid waste.

2. Tyre to be restored after seventy years

15 In that day Tyre will be forgotten for seventy years, like the
days of one king. At the end of seventy years, it will happen to
Tyre as in the song of the harlot:
16 "Take a harp,
  go about the city,
  O forgotten harlot!
Make sweet melody,
  sing many songs,
  that you may be remembered."
17 At the end of seventy years, the LORD will visit Tyre, and she
will return to her hire, and will play the harlot with all the kingdoms of the world upon the face of the earth. 18 Her merchandise
and her hire will be dedicated to the LORD; it will not be stored
or hoarded, but her merchandise will supply abundant food and fine
clothing for those who dwell before the LORD.

k The Hebrew of this verse is obscure

23.7
Isa 22.2;
32.13

23.9
Isa 2.11;
13.11;
Job 40.11,
12;
Isa 5.13;
9.15

23.11
Isa 14.26;
50.2; 25.2

23.12
Rev 18.22;
Isa 47.1;
ver 1

23.13
Isa 10.5,7

23.14
ver 1

23.15
Jer 25.11,22

23.17
Rev 17.2

23.18
Isa 60.5–9;
Zech 14.20

IV. *First volume of general rebuke and promise*
24.1–27.13

A. *Sermon I: universal judgment for universal sin*

1. *Devouring judgment meted out to all classes*

*24 Behold, the LORD will lay waste the earth and make it desolate,
and he will twist its surface and scatter its inhabitants.

2 And it shall be, as with the people, so with the priest;
as with the slave, so with his master;
as with the maid, so with her mistress;
as with the buyer, so with the seller;
as with the lender, so with the borrower;
as with the creditor, so with the debtor.

3 The earth shall be utterly laid waste and utterly despoiled;
for the LORD has spoken this word.

4 The earth mourns and withers,
the world languishes and withers;
the heavens languish together with the earth.

5 The earth lies polluted
under its inhabitants;
for they have transgressed the laws,
violated the statutes,
broken the everlasting covenant.

6 Therefore a curse devours the earth,
and its inhabitants suffer for their guilt;
therefore the inhabitants of the earth are scorched,
and few men are left.

7 The wine mourns,
the vine languishes,
all the merry-hearted sigh.

8 The mirth of the timbrels is stilled,
the noise of the jubilant has ceased,
the mirth of the lyre is stilled.

9 No more do they drink wine with singing;
strong drink is bitter to those who drink it.

10 The city of chaos is broken down,
every house is shut up so that none can enter.

11 There is an outcry in the streets for lack of wine;
all joy has reached its eventide;
the gladness of the earth is banished.

12 Desolation is left in the city,
the gates are battered into ruins.

13 For thus it shall be in the midst of the earth
among the nations,
as when an olive tree is beaten,
as at the gleaning when the vintage is done.

Cross references (left margin):

*24.1 ver 19,20; Isa 13.13,14
24.2 Hos 4.9; Lev 25.36,37; Deut 23.19,20
24.3 Isa 6.11,12
24.4 Isa 33.9; 2.12
*24.5 Gen 3.17; Num 35.33; Isa 59.12
24.6 Isa 34.5; Mal 4.6; Isa 5.24; 9.19
24.7 Isa 16.8–10; Joel 1.10–12
24.8 Jer 7.34; 16.9; 25.10; Ezek 26.13; Hos 2.11; Rev 18.22
24.9 Isa 5.11,20,22
24.10 Isa 23.1
24.11 Jer 14.2; 46.12; Isa 16.10; 32.13
24.12 Isa 14.31; 45.2
24.13 Isa 17.5,6

24.1 *the* LORD *will lay waste the earth.* In apocalyptic form the prophet envisions a guilty world in chaos.

24.5 Three sins are mentioned: (1) they *transgressed the laws* of creation; (2) they *violated the statutes* of revealed religion; (3) they broke the *covenant* of God's agreement with them.

2. *The grateful remnant praise God*

14 They lift up their voices, they sing for joy;
   over the majesty of the LORD they shout from the west.
15 Therefore in the east give glory to the LORD;
   in the coastlands of the sea, to the name of the LORD, the
   God of Israel.
16 From the ends of the earth we hear songs of praise,
   of glory to the Righteous One.

3. *Sure judgment and a new age*

But I say, "I pine away,
   I pine away. Woe is me!
For the treacherous deal treacherously,
   the treacherous deal very treacherously."

17 Terror, and the pit, and the snare
   are upon you, O inhabitant of the earth!
18 He who flees at the sound of the terror
      shall fall into the pit;
   and he who climbs out of the pit
      shall be caught in the snare.
For the windows of heaven are opened,
   and the foundations of the earth tremble.
19 The earth is utterly broken,
      the earth is rent asunder,
      the earth is violently shaken.
20 The earth staggers like a drunken man,
      it sways like a hut;
   its transgression lies heavy upon it,
      and it falls, and will not rise again.

21 On that day the LORD will punish
      the host of heaven, in heaven,
      and the kings of the earth, on the earth.
22 They will be gathered together
      as prisoners in a pit;
   they will be shut up in a prison,
      and after many days they will be punished.
23 Then the moon will be confounded,
      and the sun ashamed;
   for the LORD of hosts will reign
      on Mount Zion and in Jerusalem
   and before his elders he will manifest his glory.

B. *Sermon II: praise to the* LORD

1. *For past judgments*

25 O LORD, thou art my God;
   I will exalt thee, I will praise thy name;
for thou hast done wonderful things,
   plans formed of old, faithful and sure.
2 For thou hast made the city a heap,
      the fortified city a ruin;
   the palace of aliens is a city no more,
      it will never be rebuilt.

24.14
Isa 12.6;
42.10

24.15
Isa 25.3;
Mal 1.11;
Isa 66.19

24.16
Isa 11.12;
28.5;
Jer 5.11

24.17
1 Ki 19.17

24.18
Jer 48.43,
44;
Gen 7.11;
Ps 18.7

24.19
ver 1;
Jer 4.23

24.20
Isa 19.14;
66.24;
Dan 11.19;
Amos 8.14

24.21
Isa 10.12;
ver 4;
Ps 76.12

24.22
Isa 10.4;
42.22;
Ezek 38.8;
Zech 9.11,
12

24.23
Isa 13.10;
60.19;
Zech 14.6,
7;
Mic 4.7;
Heb 12.22

25.1
Ps 118.28;
98.1;
Num 23.19

25.2
Isa 17.1;
13.22;
32.14

3 Therefore strong peoples will glorify thee;
  cities of ruthless nations will fear thee.

25.4
Isa 14.32;
11.4;
32.2; 49.25

4 For thou hast been a stronghold to the poor,
  a stronghold to the needy in his distress,
  a shelter from the storm and a shade from the heat;
for the blast of the ruthless is like a storm against a wall,

25.5
Jer 51.54—
56

5   like heat in a dry place.
  Thou dost subdue the noise of the aliens;
    as heat by the shade of a cloud,
    so the song of the ruthless is stilled.

2. For salvation yet to come

*25.6
Isa 2.2—4;
Prov 9.2;
Mt 22.4;
Dan 7.14;
Mt 8.11
*25.8
Hos 13.14;
1 Cor
15.54;
Rev 7.17;
21.4;
Isa 54.4

6 On this mountain the LORD of hosts will make for all peoples
a feast of fat things, a feast of wine on the lees, of fat things full of
marrow, of wine on the lees well refined. 7And he will destroy
on this mountain the covering that is cast over all peoples, the
veil that is spread over all nations. 8 He will swallow up death for
ever, and the Lord GOD will wipe away tears from all faces, and
the reproach of his people he will take away from all the earth; for
the LORD has spoken.

25.9
Isa 40.9;
30.18;
33.22;
66.10;
Ps 20.5

9 It will be said on that day, "Lo, this is our God; we have
waited for him, that he might save us. This is the LORD; we have
waited for him; let us be glad and rejoice in his salvation."

25.10
Isa 16.14

10 For the hand of the LORD will rest on this mountain, and
Mōăb shall be trodden down in his place, as straw is trodden
down in a dung-pit. 11And he will spread out his hands in the
midst of it as a swimmer spreads his hands out to swim; but the
LORD will lay low his pride together with the skill[l] of his hands.
12And the high fortifications of his walls he will bring down, lay
low, and cast to the ground, even to the dust.

C. Sermon III: song of rejoicing

1. Praise to the LORD as Israel's defender

26.1
Isa 4.2;
12.1;14.31;
60.18

26 In that day this song will be sung in the land of Judah:
   "We have a strong city;
     he sets up salvation
     as walls and bulwarks.

26.2
Isa 60.11,
18;61.3;
62.1,2

2 Open the gates,
    that the righteous nation which keeps faith
    may enter in.
3 Thou dost keep him in perfect peace,
    whose mind is stayed on thee,
    because he trusts in thee.

26.4
Isa 12.2;
17.10

4 Trust in the LORD for ever,
    for the LORD GOD
    is an everlasting rock.

26.5
Isa 25.12;
Job 40.11—
13

5 For he has brought low
    the inhabitants of the height,
    the lofty city.

---

[l] The meaning of the Hebrew word is uncertain

25.6 *a feast.* The prophet envisions a great
victory banquet on Mt. Zion. God has
delivered His people (25.4, 5).

25.8 *swallow up death.* Death is forever
abolished. God's presence with His people
transcends time. Tears are washed away.

He lays it low, lays it low to the ground,
 casts it to the dust.
6 The foot tramples it,
 the feet of the poor,
 the steps of the needy."

26.6
Isa 28.3;
3.14,15

7 The way of the righteous is level;
 thou^m dost make smooth the path of the righteous.

26.7
Isa 57.2;
42.16

8 In the path of thy judgments,
 O LORD, we wait for thee;
thy memorial name
 is the desire of our soul.

26.8
Isa 51.4;
56.1;
ver 13;
Ex 3.15

9 My soul yearns for thee in the night,
 my spirit within me earnestly seeks thee.
For when thy judgments are in the earth,
 the inhabitants of the world learn righteousness.

26.9
Ps 63.6;
Isa 55.6;
Hos 5.15

2. The doom of persistent wrongdoers

10 If favor is shown to the wicked,
 he does not learn righteousness;
in the land of uprightness he deals perversely
 and does not see the majesty of the LORD.

26.10
Rom 2.4;
Isa 22.12,
13;
Hos 11.7;
Jn 5.37,38

11 O LORD, thy hand is lifted up,
 but they see it not.
Let them see thy zeal for thy people, and be ashamed.
 Let the fire for thy adversaries consume them.

26.11
Isa 5.12;
9.7; 10.17;
66.15,24

12 O LORD, thou wilt ordain peace for us,
 thou hast wrought for us all our works.

★26.12
ver 3;
Isa 64.8

13 O LORD our God,
 other lords besides thee have ruled over us,
 but thy name alone we acknowledge.

★26.13
Isa 2.8;
10.11; 63.7

14 They are dead, they will not live;
 they are shades, they will not arise;
to that end thou hast visited them with destruction
 and wiped out all remembrance of them.

26.14
Isa 8.19;
Hab 2.19;
Isa 10.3

3. Israel's prayer for deliverance answered

15 But thou hast increased the nation, O LORD,
 thou hast increased the nation; thou art glorified;
 thou hast enlarged all the borders of the land.

26.15
Isa 9.3;
33.17

16 O LORD, in distress they sought thee,

26.16
Hos 5.15

^m Cn Compare Gk: Heb thou (that art) upright

26.12 The word *peace* is used in different ways in Scripture. The root idea of the word denotes prosperity and well-being such as was enjoyed during Solomon's reign (1 Ki 4.20, 25), an earthly state of blessedness, wholeness, and right relations which will be permanently enjoyed under Messiah's rule (Mic 4.3, 4). A second use of *peace* is the absence of war. This kind of peace can come only after the Second Advent of Christ. Until that time Christ revealed that there would be *wars and rumors of wars* (Mt 24.6–14). Two other uses of *peace* in Scripture have spiritual connotations and refer to the relationship of saints to God. The first kind of spiritual *peace* concerns justification of believers. Having been justified by faith, *we have peace with God* (Rom 5.1). This is a matter of legal status in which all charges against believers have been completely discharged and they have been acquitted for Christ's sake. The other kind of spiritual *peace* is the *peace of God, which passes all understanding* (Phil 4.7). This condition is one of inner tranquility amid vicissitude and trouble.

26.13 *other lords besides thee*, i.e., other gods.

they poured out a prayer[n]
when thy chastening was upon them.

26.17
Isa 13.8;
Jn 16.21
17 Like a woman with child,
who writhes and cries out in her pangs,
when she is near her time,
so were we because of thee, O LORD;

26.18
Isa 33.11;
Ps 17.14
18 we were with child, we writhed,
we have as it were brought forth wind.
We have wrought no deliverance in the earth,
and the inhabitants of the world have not fallen.

*26.19
Ezek 37.1–
14;
Dan 12.2
19 Thy dead shall live, their bodies[o] shall rise.
O dwellers in the dust, awake and sing for joy!
For thy dew is a dew of light,
and on the land of the shades thou wilt let it fall.

4. Appeal to take refuge in God alone

*26.20
Ex 12.22,
23;
Ps 30.5;
Isa 54.7,8;
2 Cor 4.17
20 Come, my people, enter your chambers,
and shut your doors behind you;
hide yourselves for a little while
until the wrath is past.

26.21
Mic 1.3;
Jude 14;
Isa 13.11;
Job 16.18
21 For behold, the LORD is coming forth out of his place
to punish the inhabitants of the earth for their iniquity,
and the earth will disclose the blood shed upon her,
and will no more cover her slain.

*27.1
Isa 34.5,6;
Job 3.8;
Ps 74.14;
Isa 51.9
27 In that day the LORD with his hard and great and strong sword will punish Lēvī´áthán the fleeing serpent, Leviathan the twisting serpent, and he will slay the dragon that is in the sea.

D. Sermon IV: punishment for oppressors; preservation of God's people

1. Future prosperity of Israel

27.2
Ps 5.7;
80.8;
Jer 2.21
2 In that day:
"A pleasant vineyard, sing of it!

27.3
Isa 58.11;
31.5;
1 Sam 2.9
3 I, the LORD, am its keeper;
every moment I water it.
Lest any one harm it,
I guard it night and day;

27.4
2 Sam 23.6;
Isa 33.12
4 I have no wrath.
Would that I had thorns and briers to battle!
I would set out against them,
I would burn them up together.

27.5
Isa 25.4;
Job 22.21
5 Or let them lay hold of my protection,
let them make peace with me,
let them make peace with me."

27.6
Isa 37.31;
Hos 14.5,6
6 In days to come[q] Jacob shall take root,
Israel shall blossom and put forth shoots,
and fill the whole world with fruit.

[n] Heb uncertain [o] Cn Compare Syr Tg: Heb *my body* [q] Heb *Those to come*

26.19 *Thy dead*, i.e., God's faithful people, Israel.
26.20 See especially Ps 30.5.

27.1 *Leviathan* was a mythological sea monster which became the symbol of evil which must be destroyed.

2. Exile a means of purging Israel

7 Has he smitten them as he smote those who smote them?
  Or have they been slain as their slayers were slain?
8 Measure by measure,ʳ by exile thou didst contend with them;
  he removed them with his fierce blast in the day of the east
    wind.
9 Therefore by this the guilt of Jacob will be expiated,
  and this will be the full fruit of the removal of his sin:
when he makes all the stones of the altars
  like chalkstones crushed to pieces,
  no Ashḗrim or incense altars will remain standing.
10 For the fortified city is solitary,
  a habitation deserted and forsaken, like the wilderness;
there the calf grazes,
  there he lies down, and strips its branches.
11 When its boughs are dry, they are broken;
  women come and make a fire of them.
For this is a people without discernment;
  therefore he who made them will not have compassion on
    them,
  he that formed them will show them no favor.

3. The future regathering of Israel

12 In that day from the river Ēuphrā́tēṣ to the Brook of Egypt
the LORD will thresh out the grain, and you will be gathered one
by one, O people of Israel. 13And in that day a great trumpet will
be blown, and those who were lost in the land of Assyria and those
who were driven out to the land of Egypt will come and worship
the LORD on the holy mountain at Jerusalem.

V. Volumes of woes upon the unbelievers of Israel 28.1–33.24

A. Sermon I: God's dealing with drunkards and scoffers

1. Woe upon the drunkards of Samaria

28 Woe to the proud crown of the drunkards of Ē′phraim,
  and to the fading flower of its glorious beauty,
  which is on the head of the rich valley of those overcome with
    wine!
2 Behold, the Lord has one who is mighty and strong;
  like a storm of hail, a destroying tempest,
like a storm of mighty, overflowing waters,
  he will cast down to the earth with violence.
3 The proud crown of the drunkards of Ē′phraim
  will be trodden under foot;
4 and the fading flower of its glorious beauty,
  which is on the head of the rich valley,
will be like a first-ripe fig before the summer:
  when a man sees it, he eats it up
  as soon as it is in his hand.

Marginal references:
27.7 Isa 10.12,17
27.8 Job 23.6; Jer 10.23; Ps 78.38
27.9 Isa 1.25; Rom 11.27; Isa 17.8
27.10 Isa 32.13,14; Jer 26.6,18
27.11 Deut 32.28; Isa 1.3; Jer 8.7; Deut 32.18; Isa 43.1,7; 44.2,21,24
27.12 Isa 11.11; Gen 15.18; Deut 30.3,4
27.13 Lev 25.9; Mt 24.31; Rev 11.15; Isa 19.23–25
28.1 ver 3,4,7
28.2 Isa 40.10; 30.30; Ezek 13.11; Isa 29.6; 30.28
28.3 ver 1,18
28.4 Hos 9.10; Mic 7.1; Nah 3.12

ʳ Compare Syr Vg Tg: The meaning of the Hebrew word is unknown

28.5
Isa 41.16;
62.3; 4.2

5 In that day the LORD of hosts will be a crown of glory,
  and a diadem of beauty, to the remnant of his people;

28.6
Isa 11.2;
32.15; 25.4

6 and a spirit of justice to him who sits in judgment,
  and strength to those who turn back the battle at the gate.

28.7
Prov 20.1;
Hos 4.11;
Isa 56.10,12

7 These also reel with wine
  and stagger with strong drink;
the priest and the prophet reel with strong drink,
  they are confused with wine,
  they stagger with strong drink;
they err in vision,
  they stumble in giving judgment.

28.8
Jer 48.26

8 For all tables are full of vomit,
  no place is without filthiness.

2. Scoffers to be scourged by Assyria

28.9
ver 26;
Ps 131.2;
Heb 5.12,
13

9 "Whom will he teach knowledge,
  and to whom will he explain the message?
Those who are weaned from the milk,
  those taken from the breast?

28.10
Neh 9.30

10 For it is precept upon precept, precept upon precept,
  line upon line, line upon line,
  here a little, there a little."

28.11
1 Cor 14.21

11 Nay, but by men of strange lips
  and with an alien tongue
the LORD will speak to this people,

28.12
Jer 6.16;
Mt 11.28,29

12 to whom he has said,
"This is rest;
  give rest to the weary;
and this is repose";
  yet they would not hear.

28.13
Mt 21.44

13 Therefore the word of the LORD will be to them
precept upon precept, precept upon precept,
  line upon line, line upon line,
  here a little, there a little;
that they may go, and fall backward,
  and be broken, and snared, and taken.

28.14
ver 22;
Isa 29.20

14 Therefore hear the word of the LORD, you scoffers,
  who rule this people in Jerusalem!

*28.15
ver 18,2;
Isa 59.3,4;
29.15

15 Because you have said, "We have made a covenant with death,
  and with Shēol we have an agreement;
when the overwhelming scourge passes through
  it will not come to us;
for we have made lies our refuge,
  and in falsehood we have taken shelter";

*28.16
Ps 118.22;
Mt 21.42;
Acts 4.11;
Rom 9.33;
10.11;
Eph 2.20;
1 Pet 2.4-6

16 therefore thus says the Lord GOD,
  "Behold, I am laying in Zion for a foundation

28.15 *a covenant with death, and with Sheol.*
The proud in Israel insist that they have no
fear of the future because they have entered
into alliance with Egypt against Assyria.
Allusion may be to the Egyptian gods of the
nether world.
28.16 Scripture often makes reference to
Christ as the stone of protection, deliverance,
and judgment. One should use caution in the
use of typology, but in this case analogies

a stone, a tested stone,
a precious cornerstone, of a sure foundation:
'He who believes will not be in haste.'

17 And I will make justice the line,
  and righteousness the plummet;
and hail will sweep away the refuge of lies,
  and waters will overwhelm the shelter."

18 Then your covenant with death will be annulled,
  and your agreement with Shēōl will not stand;
when the overwhelming scourge passes through
  you will be beaten down by it.

19 As often as it passes through it will take you;
  for morning by morning it will pass through,
  by day and by night;
and it will be sheer terror to understand the message.

20 For the bed is too short to stretch oneself on it,
  and the covering too narrow to wrap oneself in it.

21 For the LORD will rise up as on Mount Perā'zim,
  he will be wroth as in the valley of Gib'ëön;
to do his deed—strange is his deed!
  and to work his work—alien is his work!

22 Now therefore do not scoff,
  lest your bonds be made strong;
for I have heard a decree of destruction
  from the Lord GOD of hosts upon the whole land.

3. Parable of the farmer

23 Give ear, and hear my voice;
  hearken, and hear my speech.

24 Does he who plows for sowing plow continually?
  does he continually open and harrow his ground?

25 When he has leveled its surface,
  does he not scatter dill, sow cummin,
and put in wheat in rows
  and barley in its proper place,
  and spelt as the border?

26 For he is instructed aright;
  his God teaches him.

27 Dill is not threshed with a threshing sledge,
  nor is a cart wheel rolled over cummin;
but dill is beaten out with a stick,
  and cummin with a rod.

28 Does one crush bread grain?
  No, he does not thresh it for ever;
when he drives his cart wheel over it
  with his horses, he does not crush it.

28.17
Isa 5.16;
ver 2

28.18
ver 15

28.19
Isa 50.4;
Ps 88.15;
Jer 15.8

*28.21
2 Sam 5.20;
1 Chr 14.11;
Josh 10.10,
12;
2 Sam 5.25;
1 Chr
14.16;
Lam 3.33
28.22
ver 14;
Isa 10.22,23

28.27
Amos 1.3

---

should be carefully studied: (1) Christ the
Rock was smitten for our sins (Ex 17.6;
Num 20.8, see also 1 Cor 10.4); (2) Christ is
the smiting stone which destroys the final
world-power (Dan 2.34); (3) the stone of the
Messianic kingdom becomes a great mountain
and fills the whole earth (Dan 2.35); (4)
Christ is here (28.16) the chief cornerstone
and also in Eph 2.20 and 1 Pet 2.6; (5)

Christ is a stone of stumbling and a rock
of judgment over which men will fall (1 Pet
2.8; Rom 9.32, 33; 1 Cor 1.23).
  a stone. God Himself provides the only sure
foundation on which Israel may build. *be in
haste,* i.e., be anxious.
  28.21 *Mount Perazim* was the site of a
Philistine defeat (2 Sam 5.20). *the valley of
Gibeon,* cf. 1 Chr 14.16.

28.29
Isa 9.6;
31.2;
Rom 11.33

29 This also comes from the LORD of hosts;
  he is wonderful in counsel,
  and excellent in wisdom.

B. Sermon II: the doom of blind hypocrites

1. *The careless Jews are to be humbled*

★29.1
2 Sam 5.9;
ver 9,13

29 Ho Ar′iël, Ariel,
  the city where David encamped!
Add year to year;
  let the feasts run their round.

29.2
Isa 3.26;
Lam 2.5

2 Yet I will distress Ar′iël,
  and there shall be moaning and lamentation,
  and she shall be to me like an Ariel.

29.3
Lk 19.43,44

3 And I will encamp against you round about,
  and will besiege you with towers
  and I will raise siegeworks against you.

29.4
Isa 8.19;
Lev 20.6;
Deut 18.10,
11;
1 Sam 28.8,
15;
2 Chr 33.6

4 Then deep from the earth you shall speak,
  from low in the dust your words shall come;
your voice shall come from the ground like the voice of a ghost,
  and your speech shall whisper out of the dust.

2. *Sudden destruction of Israel's foes*

29.5
Isa 17.13,
14;
25.3–5;
30.13;
1 Thess 5.3
29.6
Isa 28.2;
Mt 24.7;
Mk 13.8;
Lk 21.11;
Rev 11.13,
19; 16.18

5 But the multitude of your foes^s shall be like small dust,
  and the multitude of the ruthless like passing chaff.
And in an instant, suddenly,
6   you will be visited by the LORD of hosts
with thunder and with earthquake and great noise,
  with whirlwind and tempest, and the flame of a devouring
    fire.

29.7
Mic 4.11,
12;
Zech 12.9;
Job 20.8;
Ps 73.20
★29.8
Isa 54.17

7 And the multitude of all the nations that fight against Ar′iël,
  all that fight against her and her stronghold and distress her,
  shall be like a dream, a vision of the night.
8 As when a hungry man dreams he is eating
  and awakes with his hunger not satisfied,
or as when a thirsty man dreams he is drinking
  and awakes faint, with his thirst not quenched,
so shall the multitude of all the nations be
  that fight against Mount Zion.

3. *The folly of trying to deceive God with a sham faith*

29.9
Isa 51.17,
21,22

9 Stupefy yourselves and be in a stupor,
  blind yourselves and be blind!
Be drunk, but not with wine;
  stagger, but not with strong drink!

29.10
Rom 11.8;
Ps 69.23;
Isa 6.9,10;
Mic 3.6

10 For the LORD has poured out upon you
  a spirit of deep sleep,
and has closed your eyes, the prophets,
  and covered your heads, the seers.

^s Cn: Heb *strangers*

29.1 *Ariel*, a poetic name for Jerusalem. The Targum defines Ariel here and in Ezek 43.15,16 as *altar*.

29.8 The Assyrians dreamed of conquering Jerusalem, but awakened from their dreams in great disappointment and failure.

11 And the vision of all this has become to you like the words
of a book that is sealed. When men give it to one who can read,
saying, "Read this," he says, "I cannot, for it is sealed." 12And
when they give the book to one who cannot read, saying, "Read
this," he says, "I cannot read."

29.11
Isa 27.7;
8.16;
Dan 12.4,9;
Mt 13.11

13 And the Lord said:
"Because this people draw near with their mouth
    and honor me with their lips,
    while their hearts are far from me,
and their fear of me is a commandment of men learned by rote;
14 therefore, behold, I will again
    do marvelous things with this people,
    wonderful and marvelous;
and the wisdom of their wise men shall perish,
    and the discernment of their discerning men shall be hid."

29.13
Ezek 33.31;
Mt 15.8,9;
Mk 7.6,7

29.14
Hab 1.5;
Jer 8.9;
49.7;
1 Cor 1.19

15 Woe to those who hide deep from the LORD their counsel,
    whose deeds are in the dark,
    and who say, "Who sees us? Who knows us?"
16 You turn things upside down!
    Shall the potter be regarded as the clay;
that the thing made should say of its maker,
    "He did not make me";
or the thing formed say of him who formed it,
    "He has no understanding"?

29.15
Isa 30.1;
57.12;
Ps 94.7

29.16
Isa 45.9;
Jer 18.1–6;
Rom 9.19–
21

4. *Future deliverance of God's people from blindness*

17 Is it not yet a very little while
    until Lebanon shall be turned into a fruitful field,
    and the fruitful field shall be regarded as a forest?
18 In that day the deaf shall hear
    the words of a book,
and out of their gloom and darkness
    the eyes of the blind shall see.
19 The meek shall obtain fresh joy in the LORD,
    and the poor among men shall exult in the Holy One of Israel.
20 For the ruthless shall come to nought and the scoffer cease,
    and all who watch to do evil shall be cut off,
21 who by a word make a man out to be an offender,
    and lay a snare for him who reproves in the gate,
    and with an empty plea turn aside him who is in the right.

29.17
Isa 32.15

29.18
Isa 35.5;
ver 11

29.19
Isa 61.1;
Mt 11.5;
Jas 2.5

29.20
ver 5;
Isa 28.14,
22; 59.4

29.21
Amos 5.10,
12;
Prov 28.21

5. *Jacob's reproach rolled away*

22 Therefore thus says the LORD, who redeemed Abraham,
concerning the house of Jacob:
"Jacob shall no more be ashamed,
    no more shall his face grow pale.
23 For when he sees his children,
    the work of my hands, in his midst,
    they will sanctify my name;
they will sanctify the Holy One of Jacob,
    and will stand in awe of the God of Israel.
24 And those who err in spirit will come to understanding,
    and those who murmur will accept instruction."

29.22
Isa 41.8;
45.17; 54.4

29.23
Isa 49.20–
26; 45.11;
5.16; 8.13

29.24
Isa 28.7

C. Sermon III: trust in man versus trust in God

1. Sinful reliance upon Egypt

30 "Woe to the rebellious children," says the LORD,
  "who carry out a plan, but not mine;
and who make a league, but not of my spirit,
  that they may add sin to sin;
2 who set out to go down to Egypt,
  without asking for my counsel,
to take refuge in the protection of Phạraōh,
  and to seek shelter in the shadow of Egypt!
3 Therefore shall the protection of Phạraōh turn to your shame,
  and the shelter in the shadow of Egypt to your humiliation.
4 For though his officials are at Zōăn
  and his envoys reach Hānēṣ,
5 every one comes to shame
  through a people that cannot profit them,
that brings neither help nor profit,
  but shame and disgrace."

2. The embassy to Egypt of no avail

6 An oracle on the beasts of the Něgěb.
Through a land of trouble and anguish,
  from where come the lioness and the lion,
  the viper and the flying serpent,
they carry their riches on the backs of asses,
  and their treasures on the humps of camels,
  to a people that cannot profit them.
7 For Egypt's help is worthless and empty,
  therefore I have called her
  "Rāhăb who sits still."

3. Rebellious Judah to be crushed

8 And now, go, write it before them on a tablet,
  and inscribe it in a book,
that it may be for the time to come
  as a witness for ever.
9 For they are a rebellious people,
  lying sons,
sons who will not hear
  the instruction of the LORD;
10 who say to the seers, "See not";
  and to the prophets, "Prophesy not to us what is right;

Marginal references:
30.1 ver 9; Isa 29.15; 8.11,12
*30.2 Isa 31.1; Num 27.21; Josh 9.14; 1 Ki 22.7; Jer 21.2
30.3 Isa 20.5; Jer 37.3,5
30.4 Isa 19.11
30.5 Jer 2.36; ver 7
*30.6 Isa 46.1,2; 8.22; 14.29; 15.7
*30.7 Jer 37.7; ver 15
30.8 Isa 8.1; Hab 2.2
30.9 ver 1; Isa 28.15; 24.5
30.10 Isa 29.10; 5.20; 1 Ki 22.8,13

30.2 *set out to go down to Egypt*, i.e., seek to make an alliance with the Egyptians. In a time of national crisis Judah preferred to lean on the arm of flesh rather than to put trust in God. The sin was that of making an alliance with idol-worshiping Egypt without seeking God. Had they sought God and been told to make an alliance it would have been a different matter entirely. The grossness of their sin lay in the fact that they seemed to have greater confidence in Egypt than they had in God. They are told: (1) their strength lies in resting and waiting expectantly for God

to intervene for them (ver 15); (2) Egypt's help is sure to prove worthless and empty (ver 7); (3) God is willing and eager to be gracious to His sinning people when they turn to Him with repentant faith (ver 18).
30.6 *beasts of the Negeb*. The wilderness must be traversed en route to Egypt.
30.7 *Rahab who sits still* is an allusion to a primordial sea monster familiar from Semitic mythology. There is irony in the prophet's charge. Egypt is arrogant, like Rahab, but sits still and fails to help her allies. Judah should not trust her. Cf. 51.9.

speak to us smooth things,
    prophesy illusions,
11 leave the way, turn aside from the path,
    let us hear no more of the Holy One of Israel."

12 Therefore thus says the Holy One of Israel,
  "Because you despise this word,
    and trust in oppression and perverseness,
    and rely on them;
13 therefore this iniquity shall be to you
    like a break in a high wall, bulging out, and about to collapse,
    whose crash comes suddenly, in an instant;
14 and its breaking is like that of a potter's vessel
    which is smashed so ruthlessly
that among its fragments not a sherd is found
    with which to take fire from the hearth,
    or to dip up water out of the cistern."

15 For thus said the Lord GOD, the Holy One of Israel,
  "In returning and rest you shall be saved;
    in quietness and in trust shall be your strength."
And you would not, 16 but you said,
"No! We will speed upon horses,"
    therefore you shall speed away;
and, "We will ride upon swift steeds,"
    therefore your pursuers shall be swift.
17 A thousand shall flee at the threat of one,
    at the threat of five you shall flee,
till you are left
    like a flagstaff on the top of a mountain,
    like a signal on a hill.

4. God's promise to a repentant people

18 Therefore the LORD waits to be gracious to you;
    therefore he exalts himself to show mercy to you.
For the LORD is a God of justice;
    blessed are all those who wait for him.
19 Yea, O people in Zion who dwell at Jerusalem; you shall weep no more. He will surely be gracious to you at the sound of your cry; when he hears it, he will answer you. 20And though the Lord give you the bread of adversity and the water of affliction, yet your Teacher will not hide himself any more, but your eyes shall see your Teacher. 21And your ears shall hear a word behind you, saying, "This is the way, walk in it," when you turn to the right or when you turn to the left. 22 Then you will defile your silver-covered graven images and your gold-plated molten images. You will scatter them as unclean things; you will say to them, "Begone!"
23 And he will give rain for the seed with which you sow the ground, and grain, the produce of the ground, which will be rich and plenteous. In that day your cattle will graze in large pastures; 24 and the oxen and the asses that till the ground will eat salted provender, which has been winnowed with shovel and fork. 25And upon every lofty mountain and every high hill there will be brooks running with water, in the day of the great slaughter, when the towers fall. 26 Moreover the light of the moon will be as the light

30.11 Job 21.14
30.12 Isa 5.24; 59.13
30.13 Isa 26.21; Ps 62.3; Isa 29.5
30.14 Ps 2.9; Jer 19.10,11
30.15 Isa 7.4; 28.12; 32.17
30.16 Isa 31.1,3
30.17 Lev 26.8; Deut 28.25; 32.30; Josh 23.10
30.18 Isa 42.14; 33.5; 5.16; 25.9
30.19 Isa 65.9; 60.20; 61.1–3; Mt 7.7–11
30.20 1 Ki 22.27; Ps 80.5; 74.9; Amos 8.11
30.21 Isa 35.8,9; Prov 3.6; Isa 29.24
30.22 Isa 2.20; 31.7; 46.2; Mt 4.10
30.23 Ps 65.9–13; Isa 65.21, 22; 32.20
30.26 Isa 60.19, 20; Rev 21.23; 22.5; Isa 61.1; 1.6; Jer 33.6

of the sun, and the light of the sun will be sevenfold, as the light of seven days, in the day when the LORD binds up the hurt of his people, and heals the wounds inflicted by his blow.

5. *Israel's enemies to be smitten*

27 Behold, the name of the LORD comes from far,
    burning with his anger, and in thick rising smoke;
his lips are full of indignation,
    and his tongue is like a devouring fire;
28 his breath is like an overflowing stream
    that reaches up to the neck;
to sift the nations with the sieve of destruction,
    and to place on the jaws of the peoples a bridle that leads
    astray.

29 You shall have a song as in the night when a holy feast is kept; and gladness of heart, as when one sets out to the sound of the flute to go to the mountain of the LORD, to the Rock of Israel. 30 And the LORD will cause his majestic voice to be heard and the descending blow of his arm to be seen, in furious anger and a flame of devouring fire, with a cloudburst and tempest and hailstones. 31 The Assyrians will be terror-stricken at the voice of the LORD, when he smites with his rod. 32 And every stroke of the staff of punishment which the LORD lays upon them will be to the sound of timbrels and lyres; battling with brandished arm he will fight with them. 33 For a burning place ^{t} has long been prepared; yea, for the king ^{u} it is made ready, its pyre made deep and wide, with fire and wood in abundance; the breath of the LORD, like a stream of brimstone, kindles it.

D. *Sermon IV: Israel's deliverance by divine intervention*

1. *Folly of reliance on Egypt*

31 Woe to those who go down to Egypt for help
    and rely on horses,
who trust in chariots because they are many
    and in horsemen because they are very strong,
but do not look to the Holy One of Israel
    or consult the LORD!
2 And yet he is wise and brings disaster,
    he does not call back his words,
but will arise against the house of the evildoers,
    and against the helpers of those who work iniquity.
3 The Egyptians are men, and not God;
    and their horses are flesh, and not spirit.
When the LORD stretches out his hand,
    the helper will stumble, and he who is helped will fall,
    and they will all perish together.

2. *The call to trust in the LORD*

4 For thus the LORD said to me,
    As a lion or a young lion growls over his prey,

30.27
Isa 59.19;
10.5,13,17;
66.15

30.28
Isa 11.4;
2 Thess 2.8;
Isa 8.8;
37.29

30.29
Ps 42.4;
Isa 2.3;
17.10

30.30
Isa 28.2;
32.19

30.31
Isa 31.8

30.32
Isa 10.24;
Jer 31.4;
Ezek 32.10

30.33
Jer 7.3;
19.6;
ver 27,28;
Isa 34.9

31.1
Isa 30.2;
Ezek 17.15;
Isa 2.7;
Ps 20.7;
Dan 9.13;
Isa 10.17

31.2
Isa 28.29;
Rom 16.27;
Isa 45.7;
Num 23.19;
Isa 14.20;
22.14

31.3
Ezek 28.9;
Isa 36.9;
9.17; 30.5,7

31.4
Hos 11.10;
Amos 3.8;
Isa 42.13

---

^{t} Or *Tōphĕth* ^{u} Or *Mōlĕch*

and when a band of shepherds is called forth against him
is not terrified by their shouting
   or daunted at their noise,
so the LORD of hosts will come down
   to fight upon Mount Zion and upon its hill.
5 Like birds hovering, so the LORD of hosts
   will protect Jerusalem;
he will protect and deliver it,
   he will spare and rescue it.

31.5
Ps 91.4;
Isa 17.13

6 Turn to him from whom you[v] have deeply revolted, O people
of Israel. 7 For in that day every one shall cast away his idols of
silver and his idols of gold, which your hands have sinfully
made for you.
8 "And the Assyrian shall fall by a sword, not of man;
   and a sword, not of man, shall devour him;
and he shall flee from the sword,
   and his young men shall be put to forced labor.
9 His rock shall pass away in terror,
   and his officers desert the standard in panic,"
says the LORD, whose fire is in Zion,
   and whose furnace is in Jerusalem.

31.6
Isa 44.22;
1.2,5
31.7
Isa 2.20

31.8
Isa 10.12;
66.16;
21.15; 14.2

31.9
Deut 32.31,
37;
Isa 5.26;
10.16

3. *Israel's ultimate deliverance*

32 Behold, a king will reign in righteousness,
   and princes will rule in justice.
2 Each will be like a hiding place from the wind,
   a covert from the tempest,
like streams of water in a dry place,
   like the shade of a great rock in a weary land.
3 Then the eyes of those who see will not be closed,
   and the ears of those who hear will hearken.
4 The mind of the rash will have good judgment,
   and the tongue of the stammerers will speak readily and
   distinctly.
5 The fool will no more be called noble,
   nor the knave said to be honorable.
6 For the fool speaks folly,
   and his mind plots iniquity:
to practice ungodliness,
   to utter error concerning the LORD,
to leave the craving of the hungry unsatisfied,
   and to deprive the thirsty of drink.
7 The knaveries of the knave are evil;
   he devises wicked devices
to ruin the poor with lying words,
   even when the plea of the needy is right.
8 But he who is noble devises noble things,
   and by noble things he stands.

*32.1
Isa 9.6,7;
Jer 23.5;
Zech 9.9

32.2
Isa 4.6;
35.6;
41.18;
43.19,20
32.3
Isa 29.18

32.4
Isa 29.24

32.5
1 Sam 25.25

32.6
Isa 59.7,13;
10.6;
9.15,16;
3.15

32.7
Jer 5.26–28;
Isa 11.4;
5.23

32.8
2 Cor 9.6–
11

[v] Heb *they*

32.1 *a king will reign in righteousness*
expresses the hope of the Old Testament
saints. Surrounded by oppression, and often
ruled by weak, unworthy kings, the godly in
Israel looked to the day when a righteous king
would reign.

4. *After calamity, restoration*

32.9
Isa 47.8;
28.23

9 Rise up, you women who are at ease, hear my voice;
you complacent daughters, give ear to my speech.

32.10
Isa 5.5,6

10 In little more than a year
you will shudder, you complacent women;
for the vintage will fail,
the fruit harvest will not come.

32.11
Isa 22.12;
47.2

11 Tremble, you women who are at ease,
shudder, you complacent ones;
strip, and make yourselves bare,
and gird sackcloth upon your loins.

32.12
Nah 2.7

12 Beat upon your breasts for the pleasant fields,
for the fruitful vine,

32.13
Isa 34.13;
22.2

13 for the soil of my people
growing up in thorns and briers;
yea, for all the joyous houses
in the joyful city.

32.14
Isa 13.22;
6.11; 13.21

14 For the palace will be forsaken,
the populous city deserted;
the hill and the watchtower
will become dens for ever,
a joy of wild asses,
a pasture of flocks;

32.15
Isa 11.2;
Ezek 39.29;
Joel 2.28;
Isa 29.17;
35.2

15 until the Spirit is poured upon us from on high,
and the wilderness becomes a fruitful field,
and the fruitful field is deemed a forest.

32.16
Isa 33.5

16 Then justice will dwell in the wilderness,
and righteousness abide in the fruitful field.

★32.17
Rom 14.17;
Jas 3.18;
Isa 30.15

17 And the effect of righteousness will be peace,
and the result of righteousness, quietness and trust for ever.

18 My people will abide in a peaceful habitation,
in secure dwellings, and in quiet resting places.

32.19
Isa 30.30;
Zech 11.2

19 And the forest will utterly go down,[w]
and the city will be utterly laid low.

32.20
Isa 30.24

20 Happy are you who sow beside all waters,
who let the feet of the ox and the ass range free.

E. *Sermon V: the punishment of the treacherous and the triumph of the LORD*

1. *Treacherous Gentiles will be spoiled*

33.1
Isa 21.2;
Hab 2.8;
Isa 24.16;
Jer 25.12–
14;
Mt 7.2

33 Woe to you, destroyer,
who yourself have not been destroyed;
you treacherous one,
with whom none has dealt treacherously!
When you have ceased to destroy,
you will be destroyed;

[w] Cn: Heb *And it will hail when the forest comes down*

32.17 Assurance is the Christian's firm conviction that he has been saved, and will be kept by faith through the power of the Holy Spirit. The basis of all assurance derives from the promises of God. It is the product of faith (Eph 3.12; 2 Tim 1.12; Heb 10.22). Believers can be assured of: (1) salvation (12.2; Jn 3.17; Acts 16.30, 31); (2) eternal life (1 Jn 5.13); (3) peace with God (Rom 5.1); (4) a glorious resurrection (Phil 3.21); (5) a kingdom (Heb 12.28); (6) a crown (2 Tim 4.7, 8; Jas 1.12).

and when you have made an end of dealing treacherously,
    you will be dealt with treacherously.

2 O LORD, be gracious to us; we wait for thee.
    Be our arm every morning,
      our salvation in the time of trouble.
3 At the thunderous noise peoples flee,
    at the lifting up of thyself nations are scattered;
4 and spoil is gathered as the caterpillar gathers;
    as locusts leap, men leap upon it.

5 The LORD is exalted, for he dwells on high;
    he will fill Zion with justice and righteousness;
6 and he will be the stability of your times,
    abundance of salvation, wisdom, and knowledge;
      the fear of the LORD is his treasure.

2. Judah's distress described

7 Behold, the valiant ones[y] cry without;
    the envoys of peace weep bitterly.
8 The highways lie waste,
    the wayfaring man ceases.
Covenants are broken,
    witnesses[z] are despised,
    there is no regard for man.
9 The land mourns and languishes;
    Lebanon is confounded and withers away;
Sharon is like a desert;
    and Bashan and Carmel shake off their leaves.

3. Prediction of God's vengeance

10 "Now I will arise," says the LORD,
    "now I will lift myself up;
    now I will be exalted.
11 You conceive chaff, you bring forth stubble;
    your breath is a fire that will consume you.
12 And the peoples will be as if burned to lime,
    like thorns cut down, that are burned in the fire."

13 Hear, you who are far off, what I have done;
    and you who are near, acknowledge my might.
14 The sinners in Zion are afraid;
    trembling has seized the godless:
"Who among us can dwell with the devouring fire?
    Who among us can dwell with everlasting burnings?"
15 He who walks righteously and speaks uprightly,
    who despises the gain of oppressions,
who shakes his hands, lest they hold a bribe,
    who stops his ears from hearing of bloodshed
    and shuts his eyes from looking upon evil,
16 he will dwell on the heights;
    his place of defense will be the fortresses of rocks;
    his bread will be given him, his water will be sure.

---

y The meaning of the Hebrew word is uncertain   z One ancient Ms: Heb cities

33.2
Isa 25.9

33.3
Isa 17.13;
Jer 25.30,31

33.5
Ps 97.9

33.6
ver 20;
Isa 45.17;
11.9;
Mt 6.33

33.7
2 Ki 18.18,
37

33.8
Isa 35.8;
24.5

33.9
Isa 24.4;
2.13; 35.2

33.10
Ps 12.5

33.11
Ps 7.14;
Isa 59.4

33.12
Isa 9.18;
10.17

33.13
Isa 49.1

33.14
Isa 32.11;
30.27,30;
9.18,19

33.15
Ps 15.2;
24.4;
119.37

33.16
Isa 25.4;
26.1; 49.10

4. Promise of safety and joy under Messiah

33.17
ver 21,22;
Isa 26.15

17 Your eyes will see the king in his beauty;
　　they will behold a land that stretches afar.

33.18
Isa 17.14;
1 Cor 1.20

18 Your mind will muse on the terror:
　　"Where is he who counted, where is he who weighed the
　　　tribute?
　　Where is he who counted the towers?"

33.19
2 Ki 19.32;
Deut
28.49,50;
Jer 5.15

19 You will see no more the insolent people,
　　the people of an obscure speech which you cannot com-
　　　prehend,
　　stammering in a tongue which you cannot understand.

33.20
Ps 48.12;
46.5;
125.1,2;
Isa 37.33;
54.2

20 Look upon Zion, the city of our appointed feasts!
　　Your eyes will see Jerusalem,
　　a quiet habitation, an immovable tent,
　　whose stakes will never be plucked up,
　　　nor will any of its cords be broken.

33.21
Isa 41.18

21 But there the LORD in majesty will be for us
　　a place of broad rivers and streams,
　　where no galley with oars can go,
　　　nor stately ship can pass.

33.22
Isa 2.4;
Jas 4.12;
ver 17;
Zech 9.9;
Isa 35.4

22 For the LORD is our judge, the LORD is our ruler,
　　the LORD is our king; he will save us.

33.23
2 Ki 7.8,16

23 Your tackle hangs loose;
　　it cannot hold the mast firm in its place,
　　or keep the sail spread out.

Then prey and spoil in abundance will be divided;
　　even the lame will take the prey.

33.24
Jer 30.17;
50.20

24 And no inhabitant will say, "I am sick";
　　the people who dwell there will be forgiven their iniquity.

VI. Second volume of general rebuke and promise 34.1–35.10

A. Sermon I: destruction of the nations who are enemies of God

1. The judgment on the nations

34.1
Ps 49.1;
Deut 32.1

34 Draw near, O nations, to hear,
　　　and harken, O peoples!
Let the earth listen, and all that fills it;
　　the world, and all that comes from it.

34.2
Isa 26.20,
21; 13.5;
30.25

2 For the LORD is enraged against all the nations,
　　and furious against all their host,
　　he has doomed them, has given them over for slaughter.

34.3
Joel 2.20;
Ezek 14.19

3 Their slain shall be cast out,
　　and the stench of their corpses shall rise;
　　the mountains shall flow with their blood.

34.4
Ezek 32.7,
8;
Joel 2.31;
Mt 24.29;
2 Pet 3.10;
Rev 6.13,14

4 All the host of heaven shall rot away,
　　and the skies roll up like a scroll.
All their host shall fall,
　　as leaves fall from the vine,
　　like leaves falling from the fig tree.

2. The example of Edom

5 For my sword has drunk its fill in the heavens;
  behold, it descends for judgment upon Ēdŏm,
  upon the people I have doomed.

34.5
Jer 46.10;
49.7;
Mal 1.4

6 The LORD has a sword; it is sated with blood,
  it is gorged with fat,
  with the blood of lambs and goats,
  with the fat of the kidneys of rams.
For the LORD has a sacrifice in Bŏzràh,
  a great slaughter in the land of Ēdŏm.

34.6
Jer 49.13;
Isa 63.1

7 Wild oxen shall fall with them,
  and young steers with the mighty bulls.
Their land shall be soaked with blood,
  and their soil made rich with fat.

34.7
Ps 22.21;
68.30;
Isa 29.9;
49.26

8 For the LORD has a day of vengeance,
  a year of recompense for the cause of Zion.

34.8
Isa 63.4

9 And the streams of Ēdŏm[a] shall be turned into pitch,
  and her soil into brimstone;
  her land shall become burning pitch.

34.9
Deut 29.23

10 Night and day it shall not be quenched;
  its smoke shall go up for ever.
From generation to generation it shall lie waste;
  none shall pass through it for ever and ever.

34.10
Isa 66.24;
Rev 14.11;
19.3;
Mal 1.4;
Ezek 29.11

11 But the hawk and the porcupine shall possess it,
  the owl and the raven shall dwell in it.
He shall stretch the line of confusion over it,
  and the plummet of chaos over[b] its nobles.

34.11
Isa 14.23;
Zeph 2.14;
Rev 18.2;
2 Ki 21.13;
Lam 2.8

12 They shall name it No Kingdom There,
  and all its princes shall be nothing.

13 Thorns shall grow over its strongholds,
  nettles and thistles in its fortresses.
It shall be the haunt of jackals,
  an abode for ostriches.

34.13
Isa 13.22;
32.13;
Jer 9.11;
10.22

14 And wild beasts shall meet with hyenas,
  the satyr shall cry to his fellow;
yea, there shall the night hag alight,
  and find for herself a resting place.

34.14
Isa 13.21

15 There shall the owl nest and lay
  and hatch and gather her young in her shadow;
yea, there shall the kites be gathered,
  each one with her mate.

34.15
Deut 14.13

16 Seek and read from the book of the LORD:
  Not one of these shall be missing;
  none shall be without her mate.
For the mouth of the LORD has commanded,
  and his Spirit has gathered them.

*34.16
Isa 30.8;
40.5

a Heb *her streams*   b Heb lacks *over*

34.16 *the book of the* LORD. The fulfilment may be compared with its prophecy in Scripture where it will be seen that the thing prophesied has come to pass.

34.17
Jer 13.25;
ver 10,11
	17 He has cast the lot for them,
	    his hand has portioned it out to them with the line;
	they shall possess it for ever,
	    from generation to generation they shall dwell in it.

B. Sermon II: the return to Zion promised

*35.1f
Isa 55.12;
51.3
35.2
Isa 32.15;
ver 10;
Isa 60.13;
25.9
	35 The wilderness and the dry land shall be glad,
	    the desert shall rejoice and blossom;
	like the crocus 2 it shall blossom abundantly,
	    and rejoice with joy and singing.
	The glory of Lebanon shall be given to it,
	    the majesty of Carmel and Sharon.
	They shall see the glory of the LORD,
	    the majesty of our God.

35.3
Job 4.3,4;
Heb 12.12
35.4
Isa 1.24;
34.8;
Ps 145.19
	3 Strengthen the weak hands,
	    and make firm the feeble knees.
	4 Say to those who are of a fearful heart,
	    "Be strong, fear not!
	Behold, your God
	    will come with vengeance,
	with the recompense of God.
	    He will come and save you."

35.5
Isa 29.18;
Mt 11.5;
Jn 9.6,7
35.6
Mt 15.30;
Jn 5.8,9;
Acts 3.8;
Mt 9.32;
Isa 41.18;
43.19;
Jn 7.38
35.7
Isa 49.10;
34.13
	5 Then the eyes of the blind shall be opened,
	    and the ears of the deaf unstopped;
	6 then shall the lame man leap like a hart,
	    and the tongue of the dumb sing for joy.
	For waters shall break forth in the wilderness,
	    and streams in the desert;
	7 the burning sand shall become a pool,
	    and the thirsty ground springs of water;
	the haunt of jackals shall become a swamp,[c]
	    the grass shall become reeds and rushes.

35.8
Isa 62.10;
Mt 7.13,14;
Jer 14.8
	8 And a highway shall be there,
	    and it shall be called the Holy Way;
	the unclean shall not pass over it,[d]
	    and fools shall not err therein.

35.9
Isa 30.6;
34.14;
62.12
	9 No lion shall be there,
	    nor shall any ravenous beast come up on it;
	they shall not be found there,
	    but the redeemed shall walk there.

35.10
Isa 51.11;
25.8;65.19;
Rev 7.17;
21.4
	10 And the ransomed of the LORD shall return,
	    and come to Zion with singing;
	everlasting joy shall be upon their heads;
	    they shall obtain joy and gladness,
	    and sorrow and sighing shall flee away.

c Cn: Heb in the haunt of jackals is her resting place   d Heb it and he is for them a wayfarer

---

35.1, 2 The contrast in these opening verses is conspicuous. From wilderness and dry land there shall come: (1) gladness and rejoicing; (2) fertility, for the desert shall blossom; (3) beauty, after dryness and sterility; (4) glory and majesty; (5) *the glory of the LORD*.

VII. The volume of Hezekiah 36.1–39.8

A. Sennacherib's challenge to the people of God

1. His demand for Judah to submit

36 In the fourteenth year of King Hĕzĕkī'ăh, Sĕnnăch'ĕrĭb king of Assyria came up against all the fortified cities of Judah and took them. 2And the king of Assyria sent the Răbshā'kĕh from Lāchĭsh to King Hĕzĕkī'ăh at Jerusalem, with a great army. And he stood by the conduit of the upper pool on the highway to the Fuller's Field. 3And there came out to him Ĕlī'ăkĭm the son of Hĭlkī'ăh, who was over the household, and Shĕbnă the secretary, and Jōăh the son of Āsăph, the recorder.

4 And the Răbshā'kĕh said to them, "Say to Hĕzĕkī'ăh, 'Thus says the great king, the king of Assyria: On what do you rest this confidence of yours? 5 Do you think that mere words are strategy and power for war? On whom do you now rely, that you have rebelled against me? 6 Behold, you are relying on Egypt, that broken reed of a staff, which will pierce the hand of any man who leans on it. Such is Phăraōh king of Egypt to all who rely on him. 7 But if you say to me, "We rely on the LORD our God," is it not he whose high places and altars Hĕzĕkī'ăh has removed, saying to Judah and to Jerusalem, "You shall worship before this altar"? 8 Come now, make a wager with my master the king of Assyria: I will give you two thousand horses, if you are able on your part to set riders upon them. 9 How then can you repulse a single captain among the least of my master's servants, when you rely on Egypt for chariots and for horsemen? 10 Moreover, is it without the LORD that I have come up against this land to destroy it? The LORD said to me, Go up against this land, and destroy it.' "

2. Direct summons to the people to surrender

11 Then Ĕlī'ăkĭm, Shĕbnă, and Jōăh said to the Răbshā'kĕh, "Pray, speak to your servants in Ărămā'ĭc, for we understand it; do not speak to us in the language of Judah within the hearing of the people who are on the wall." 12 But the Răbshā'kĕh said, "Has my master sent me to speak these words to your master and to you, and not to the men sitting on the wall, who are doomed with you to eat their own dung and drink their own urine?"

13 Then the Răbshā'kĕh stood and called out in a loud voice in the language of Judah: "Hear the words of the great king, the king of Assyria! 14 Thus says the king: 'Do not let Hĕzĕkī'ăh deceive you, for he will not be able to deliver you. 15 Do not let Hĕzĕkī'ăh make you rely on the LORD by saying, "The LORD will surely deliver us; this city will not be given into the hand of the king of Assyria." 16 Do not listen to Hĕzĕkī'ăh; for thus says the king of Assyria: Make your peace with me and come out to me; then every one of you will eat of his own vine, and every one of his own fig tree, and every one of you will drink the water of his own

36.1
2 Ki 18.13;
Isa 1.1
★36.2
2 Ki 18.17–
20;
Isa 7.3
36.3
Isa 22.15,20

36.4
2 Ki 18.19
36.5
2 Ki 18.7
36.6
Ezek 29.6,7;
Isa 30.3,5,7
★36.7
2 Ki 18.4,5

36.9
Isa 37.29;
20.5

★36.11
Ezra 4.7;
ver 13

36.13
2 Chr 32.18
36.14
Isa 37.10
36.15
ver 18

36.16
Zech 3.10;
Prov 5.15

36.2 *the Rabshakeh,* i.e., the chief officer of the Assyrian army.
36.7 *Hezekiah has removed.* The reforms of Hezekiah are interpreted as sacrilege. The Rabshakeh implies that Israel's God is displeased at Hezekiah's conduct.

36.11 *in Aramaic,* the official language which the courtiers could understand. It was only at the exile that Aramaic became the vernacular language of the Jews.

cistern; 17 until I come and take you away to a land like your own land, a land of grain and wine, a land of bread and vineyards. 18 Beware lest Hĕzĕkī′ăh mislead you by saying, "The LORD will deliver us." Has any of the gods of the nations delivered his land out of the hand of the king of Assyria? 19 Where are the gods of Hā′măth and Arpăd? Where are the gods of Sĕpharvā′ĭm? Have they delivered Săma̧r′ĭă out of my hand? 20 Who among all the gods of these countries have delivered their countries out of my hand, that the LORD should deliver Jerusalem out of my hand?' "

21 But they were silent and answered him not a word, for the king's command was, "Do not answer him." 22 Then Ĕlī′ăkĭm the son of Hĭlkī′ăh, who was over the household, and Shĕbnă the secretary, and Jŏăh the son of Āsăph, the recorder, came to Hĕzĕkī′ăh with their clothes rent, and told him the words of the Răbshā′kĕh.

B. God's answer to Sennacherib

1. Hezekiah's appeal to God

37 When King Hĕzĕkī′ăh heard it, he rent his clothes, and covered himself with sackcloth, and went into the house of the LORD. 2 And he sent Ĕlī′ăkĭm, who was over the household, and Shĕbnă the secretary, and the senior priests, clothed with sackcloth, to the prophet Ĭṣāi′ăh the son of Āmŏz. 3 They said to him, "Thus says Hĕzĕkī′ăh, 'This day is a day of distress, of rebuke, and of disgrace; children have come to the birth, and there is no strength to bring them forth. 4 It may be that the LORD your God heard the words of the Răbshā′kĕh, whom his master the king of Assyria has sent to mock the living God, and will rebuke the words which the LORD your God has heard; therefore lift up your prayer for the remnant that is left.' "

2. God's first assurance of deliverance

5 When the servants of King Hĕzĕkī′ăh came to Ĭṣāi′ăh, 6 Ĭṣāi′ăh said to them, "Say to your master, 'Thus says the LORD: Do not be afraid because of the words that you have heard, with which the servants of the king of Assyria have reviled me. 7 Behold, I will put a spirit in him, so that he shall hear a rumor, and return to his own land; and I will make him fall by the sword in his own land.' "

3. Blasphemous challenge from Assyria

8 The Răbshā′kĕh returned, and found the king of Assyria fighting against Lĭbnăh; for he had heard that the king had left Lāchĭsh. 9 Now the king heard concerning Tĭrhā′kăh king of Ethiopia, "He has set out to fight against you." And when he heard it, he sent messengers to Hĕzĕkī′ăh, saying, 10 "Thus shall you speak to Hĕzĕkī′ăh king of Judah: 'Do not let your God on whom you rely deceive you by promising that Jerusalem will not be given into the hand of the king of Assyria. 11 Behold, you have heard what the kings of Assyria have done to all lands, destroying

36.18
ver 15

36.19
Isa 37.11–
13;
2 Ki 17.6

36.20
1 Ki 20.23,
28;
ver 15

36.22
ver 3;
Isa 22.15,20

37.1
2 Ki 19.1–
37

37.2
Isa 22.15,20

37.3
Isa 26.16–
18

37.4
Isa 36.15,
18,20

37.6
Isa 7.4;
35.4
37.7
ver 9,37,38

*37.9
ver 7;
Isa 18.1;
20.5
37.10
Isa 36.15

37.11
Isa 10.9–11;
36.18–20

37.9 *Tirhakah* is known in history as "Taharkah", the next to the last king of the   Twenty-fifth (or Ethiopian) Dynasty in Egypt.

them utterly. And shall you be delivered? 12 Have the gods of the
nations delivered them, the nations which my fathers destroyed,
Gōzȧn, Hārȧn, Rĕzĕph, and the people of Eden who were in
Tĕlȧs'sȧr? 13 Where is the king of Hāmȧth, the king of Arpăd, the
king of the city of Sĕpharvā'ĭm, the king of Hēnȧ, or the king
of Ĭvvȧh?' "

4. *Hezekiah's prayer to the* LORD

14 Hĕzĕkī'ȧh received the letter from the hand of the messengers, and read it; and Hezekiah went up to the house of the LORD,
and spread it before the LORD. 15And Hĕzĕkī'ȧh prayed to the
LORD: 16 "O LORD of hosts, God of Israel, who art enthroned
above the cherubim, thou art the God, thou alone, of all the kingdoms of the earth; thou hast made heaven and earth. 17 Incline thy
ear, O LORD, and hear; open thy eyes, O LORD, and see; and hear
all the words of Sĕnnȧch'ĕrĭb, which he has sent to mock the
living God. 18 Of a truth, O LORD, the kings of Assyria have laid
waste all the nations and their lands, 19 and have cast their gods
into the fire; for they were no gods, but the work of men's hands,
wood and stone; therefore they were destroyed. 20 So now, O
LORD our God, save us from his hand, that all the kingdoms of the
earth may know that thou alone art the LORD."

5. *God's second answer: Sennacherib shall be crushed*

21 Then Ĭṣāi'ȧh the son of Āmŏz sent to Hĕzĕkī'ȧh, saying,
"Thus says the LORD, the God of Israel: Because you have prayed
to me concerning Sĕnnȧch'ĕrĭb king of Assyria, 22 this is the word
that the LORD has spoken concerning him:
'She despises you, she scorns you—
    the virgin daughter of Zion;
she wags her head behind you—
    the daughter of Jerusalem.

23 'Whom have you mocked and reviled?
    Against whom have you raised your voice
and haughtily lifted your eyes?
    Against the Holy One of Israel!
24 By your servants you have mocked the Lord,
    and you have said, With my many chariots
I have gone up the heights of the mountains,
    to the far recesses of Lebanon;
I felled its tallest cedars,
    its choicest cypresses;
I came to its remotest height,
    its densest forest.
25 I dug wells
    and drank waters,
and I dried up with the sole of my foot
    all the streams of Egypt.

26 'Have you not heard
    that I determined it long ago?
I planned from days of old
    what now I bring to pass,
that you should make fortified cities

37.12
2 Ki 17.6;
18.11;
Gen 11.31;
12.1–4;
Acts 7.2

37.16
Ex 25.22;
Deut 10.17;
Isa 42.5;
45.12
37.17
Dan 9.18;
Ps 74.22;
ver 4
37.18
2 Ki 15.29;
1 Chr 5.26;
Nah 2.11,12
37.19
Isa 2.8;
26.14
37.20
Isa 25.9;
Ps 46.10;
Ezek 36.23

37.21
ver 2

37.22
Jer 14.17;
Lam 2.13;
Zech 2.10;
Job 16.4

37.23
ver 4;
Isa 2.11;
5.15,21;
Ezek 39.7;
Hab 1.12
37.24
Isa 8.7,8;
10.18,33,
34; 14.8

37.26
Isa 40.21,
28;
Acts 2.23;
4.27,28;
Isa 46.11;
10.6; 17.1

crash into heaps of ruins,
27 while their inhabitants, shorn of strength,
    are dismayed and confounded,
and have become like plants of the field
    and like tender grass,
like grass on the housetops,
    blighted*e* before it is grown.

28 'I know your sitting down
    and your going out and coming in,
    and your raging against me.
29 Because you have raged against me
    and your arrogance has come to my ears,
I will put my hook in your nose
    and my bit in your mouth,
and I will turn you back on the way
    by which you came.'

30 "And this shall be the sign for you: this year eat what grows
of itself, and in the second year what springs of the same; then
in the third year sow and reap, and plant vineyards, and eat their
fruit. 31And the surviving remnant of the house of Judah shall
again take root downward, and bear fruit upward; 32 for out of
Jerusalem shall go forth a remnant, and out of Mount Zion a band
of survivors. The zeal of the LORD of hosts will accomplish this.
33 "Therefore thus says the LORD concerning the king of Assyria: He shall not come into this city, or shoot an arrow there, or
come before it with a shield, or cast up a siege mound against it.
34 By the way that he came, by the same he shall return, and he
shall not come into this city, says the LORD. 35 For I will defend
this city to save it, for my own sake and for the sake of my servant David."

6. *The fulfilment of God's promise*

36 And the angel of the LORD went forth, and slew a hundred
and eighty-five thousand in the camp of the Assyrians; and when
men arose early in the morning, behold, these were all dead
bodies. 37 Then Sënnăch'ĕrīb king of Assyria departed, and went
home and dwelt at Nĭn'ĕvĕh. 38And as he was worshiping in the
house of Nĭsrŏch his god, Ădrăm'mĕlĕch and Shărē'zĕr, his sons,
slew him with the sword, and escaped into the land of Ar'ărăt.
And Ēsar-hăd'dŏn his son reigned in his stead.

C. *Hezekiah's sickness and recovery*

1. *His prayer: God's answer*

38 In those days Hĕzĕkī'ah became sick and was at the point of
death. And Ĭşaī'ah the prophet the son of Āmŏz came to him,
and said to him, "Thus says the LORD: Set your house in order;
for you shall die, you shall not recover." 2 Then Hĕzĕkī'ah turned
his face to the wall, and prayed to the LORD, 3 and said, "Remember now, O LORD, I beseech thee, how I have walked before
thee in faithfulness and with a whole heart, and have done what

e With 2 Kings 19.26: Heb *field*

is good in thy sight." And Hĕzĕkī'áh wept bitterly. 4 Then the word of the LORD came to Ĭṣai'áh: 5 "Go and say to Hĕzĕkī'áh, Thus says the LORD, the God of David your father: I have heard your prayer, I have seen your tears; behold, I will add fifteen years to your life. 6 I will deliver you and this city out of the hand of the king of Assyria, and defend this city.

7 "This is the sign to you from the LORD, that the LORD will do this thing that he has promised: 8 Behold, I will make the shadow cast by the declining sun on the dial of Āhăz turn back ten steps." So the sun turned back on the dial the ten steps by which it had declined.ᶠ

2. *His psalm of praise*

9 A writing of Hĕzĕkī'áh king of Judah, after he had been sick and had recovered from his sickness:

10 I said, In the noontide of my days
　　I must depart;
I am consigned to the gates of Shēōl
　　for the rest of my years.
11 I said, I shall not see the LORD
　　in the land of the living;
I shall look upon man no more
　　among the inhabitants of the world.
12 My dwelling is plucked up and removed from me
　　like a shepherd's tent;
like a weaver I have rolled up my life;
　　he cuts me off from the loom;
from day to night thou dost bring me to an end;ᵍ
13 　I cry for helpʰ until morning;
like a lion he breaks all my bones;
　　from day to night thou dost bring me to an end.ᵍ

14 Like a swallow or a craneⁱ I clamor,
　　I moan like a dove.
My eyes are weary with looking upward.
　　O Lord, I am oppressed; be thou my security!
15 But what can I say? For he has spoken to me,
　　and he himself has done it.
All my sleep has fledʲ
　　because of the bitterness of my soul.

16 O Lord, by these things men live,
　　and in all these is the life of my spirit.ᵏ
Oh, restore me to health and make me live!
17 Lo, it was for my welfare
　　that I had great bitterness;
but thou hast held backˡ my life
　　from the pit of destruction,
for thou hast cast all my sins
　　behind thy back.
18 For Shēōl cannot thank thee,
　　death cannot praise thee;

38.5 2 Ki 18.2,13
38.6 Isa 37.35
38.7 Isa 7.11
38.8 2 Ki 20.9–11; Josh 10.12–14
38.10 Ps 102.24; 107.18; Job 17.11, 15; 2 Cor 1.9
38.11 Ps 27.13; 116.9
38.12 2 Cor 5.1,4; Heb 1.12; Job 7.6; 6.9; Ps 73.14
38.13 Job 10.16; 16.12; Ps 51.8; 32.4
38.14 Isa 59.11; Ps 119.122, 123
38.15 Ps 39.9; 1 Ki 21.27; Job 7.11; 10.1
38.16 Ps 119.71, 75; 39.13
38.17 Ps 30.3; Isa 43.25; Jer 31.34; Mic 7.19
38.18 Ps 6.5; 88.11; 115.17; Ecc 9.10; Ps 28.1

ᶠ The Hebrew of this verse is obscure　ᵍ Heb uncertain　ʰ Cn: Heb obscure　ⁱ Heb uncertain
ʲ Cn Compare Syr: Heb *I will walk slowly all my years*　ᵏ Heb uncertain
ˡ Cn Compare Gk Vg: Heb *loved*

those who go down to the pit cannot hope
   for thy faithfulness.

38.19
Ps 118.17;
Deut 6.7;
Ps 78.5–7

19 The living, the living, he thanks thee,
      as I do this day;
   the father makes known to the children
      thy faithfulness.

38.20
Ps 86.5;
33.1–3;
104.33;
116.17–19

20 The LORD will save me,
      and we will sing to stringed instruments*m*
   all the days of our life,
      at the house of the LORD.

38.21
2 Ki 20.7,8

21 Now Īṣāi′áh had said, "Let them take a cake of figs, and apply it to the boil, that he may recover." 22 Hĕzĕkī′áh also had said, "What is the sign that I shall go up to the house of the LORD?"

D. *Hezekiah's folly*

1. *His display of his wealth*

39.1
2 Ki 20.12–
19;
2 Chr 32.31

39 At that time Mĕr′ŏdăch-băl′ădăn the son of Băl′ădăn, king of Babylon, sent envoys with letters and a present to Hĕzĕkī′áh, for he heard that he had been sick and had recovered. 2 And

39.2
2 Chr 32.25,
31;
2 Ki 18.15,
16

Hĕzĕkī′áh welcomed them; and he showed them his treasure house, the silver, the gold, the spices, the precious oil, his whole armory, all that was found in his storehouses. There was nothing in his house or in all his realm that Hezekiah did not show them.

39.3
2 Sam 12.1;
2 Chr 16.7;
Jer 5.15

3 Then Īṣāi′áh the prophet came to King Hĕzĕkī′áh, and said to him, "What did these men say? And whence did they come to you?" Hezekiah said, "They have come to me from a far country, from Babylon." 4 He said, "What have they seen in your house?" Hĕzĕkī′áh answered, "They have seen all that is in my house; there is nothing in my storehouses that I did not show them."

2. *God's sentence of exile*

39.5
1 Sam
13.13,14;
15.16

5 Then Īṣāi′áh said to Hĕzĕkī′áh, "Hear the word of the LORD of hosts: 6 Behold, the days are coming, when all that is in your house, and that which your fathers have stored up till this day, shall be carried to Babylon; nothing shall be left, says the LORD.

39.6
Jer 20.5

39.7
Dan 1.2–7

7 And some of your own sons, who are born to you, shall be taken away; and they shall be eunuchs in the palace of the king of Babylon." 8 Then said Hĕzĕkī′áh to Īṣāi′áh, "The word of the

39.8
2 Chr 32.26;
1 Sam 3.18;
2 Chr 34.28

LORD which you have spoken is good." For he thought, "There will be peace and security in my days."

VIII. *The volume of comfort and assurance* 40.1–66.24

A. *Part I: the salvation of the LORD*

1. *The majesty of the LORD the comforter*
a. *The messenger of the LORD to come*

40.1
Isa 12.1

40.2
Isa 35.4;
41.11–13;
33.24;
Jer 16.18

40 Comfort, comfort my people,
      says your God.
   2 Speak tenderly to Jerusalem,

---

m Heb *my stringed instruments*

and cry to her
that her warfare[n] is ended,
    that her iniquity is pardoned,
that she has received from the LORD's hand
    double for all her sins.

3 A voice cries:
"In the wilderness prepare the way of the LORD,
    make straight in the desert a highway for our God.
4 Every valley shall be lifted up,
    and every mountain and hill be made low;
the uneven ground shall become level,
    and the rough places a plain.
5 And the glory of the LORD shall be revealed,
    and all flesh shall see it together,
    for the mouth of the LORD has spoken."

6 A voice says, "Cry!"
    And I said, "What shall I cry?"
All flesh is grass,
    and all its beauty is like the flower of the field.
7 The grass withers, the flower fades,
    when the breath of the LORD blows upon it;
    surely the people is grass.
8 The grass withers, the flower fades;
    but the word of our God will stand for ever.

9 Get you up to a high mountain,
    O Zion, herald of good tidings;[o]
lift up your voice with strength,
    O Jerusalem, herald of good tidings,[p]
lift it up, fear not;
say to the cities of Judah,
    "Behold your God!"
10 Behold, the Lord GOD comes with might,
    and his arm rules for him;
behold, his reward is with him,
    and his recompense before him.
11 He will feed his flock like a shepherd,
    he will gather the lambs in his arms,
he will carry them in his bosom,
    and gently lead those that are with young.

b. *Infinite power and wisdom of the* LORD

12 Who has measured the waters in the hollow of his hand
    and marked off the heavens with a span,
enclosed the dust of the earth in a measure

Cross references:
40.3 Mt 3.3; Mk 1.3; Lk 3.4–6; Jn 1.23; Mal 3.1
40.4 Isa 45.2
40.5 Isa 6.3; 52.10
40.6 Job 14.2; Ps 102.11; 103.15; 1 Pet 1.24, 25
40.7 Ps 90.5,6; ver 24
40.8 Isa 55.11; Mt 5.18; 1 Pet 1.24, 25
40.9 Isa 60.1; 52.7; Acts 10.36; Rom 10.15
40.10 Isa 59.16, 18; 62.11; Rev 22.7,12
★40.11 Ezek 34.23; Mic 5.4; Jn 10.11; Heb 13.20
40.12 Isa 48.13; Job 38.8–11; Heb 1.10–12

n Or *time of service*   o Or *O herald of good tidings to Zion*
p Or *O herald of good tidings to Jerusalem*

40.11 Christ is the divine shepherd here portrayed by Isaiah (see also Gen 49.24; Ezek 34.23 and 37.24). In Scripture He is called the *good shepherd* (Jn 10.11, 14); the *chief Shepherd* (1 Pet 5.4); the *great shepherd* (Heb 13.20; Mic 5.4). As shepherd He was to lay down His life for His sheep (Jn 10.11, 15; Acts 20.28). He gives His sheep eternal life (Jn 10.28). His sheep are known to Him and they know Him. He calls them, guides and preserves them, and He cherishes and feeds them. (See Jn 10; Isa 40; Ps 23.)

and weighed the mountains in scales
and the hills in a balance?

40.13
Rom 11.34;
1 Cor 2.16
13 Who has directed the Spirit of the LORD,
or as his counselor has instructed him?

40.14
Job 38.4;
21.22
14 Whom did he consult for his enlightenment,
and who taught him the path of justice,
and taught him knowledge,
and showed him the way of understanding?

40.15
Jer 10.10;
Isa 17.13;
29.5
15 Behold, the nations are like a drop from a bucket,
and are accounted as the dust on the scales;
behold, he takes up the isles like fine dust.

16 Lebanon would not suffice for fuel,
nor are its beasts enough for a burnt offering.

40.17
Isa 29.7;
30.28
17 All the nations are as nothing before him,
they are accounted by him as less than nothing and emptiness.

c. Contrast between idols and the living God

40.18
ver 25;
Isa 46.5;
Mic 7.18;
Acts 17.29
18 To whom then will you liken God,
or what likeness compare with him?

40.19
Isa 41.6,7;
44.12;
Jer 10.3
19 The idol! a workman casts it,
and a goldsmith overlays it with gold,
and casts for it silver chains.

40.20
Isa 41.7;
Jer 10.3–5
20 He who is impoverished[q] chooses for an offering
wood that will not rot;
he seeks out a skilful craftsman
to set up an image that will not move.

40.21
Ps 19.1;
Acts 14.17;
Rom 1.19
21 Have you not known? Have you not heard?
Has it not been told you from the beginning?
Have you not understood from the foundations of the earth?

40.22
Job 22.14;
Num 13.33;
Isa 42.5;
44.24;
Ps 104.2
22 It is he who sits above the circle of the earth,
and its inhabitants are like grasshoppers;
who stretches out the heavens like a curtain,
and spreads them like a tent to dwell in;

40.23
Job 12.21;
Ps 107.40;
Isa 5.21
23 who brings princes to nought,
and makes the rulers of the earth as nothing.

40.24
Isa 17.10,
11;
ver 7;
Isa 17.13;
41.16
24 Scarcely are they planted, scarcely sown,
scarcely has their stem taken root in the earth,
when he blows upon them, and they wither,
and the tempest carries them off like stubble.

40.25
ver 18
25 To whom then will you compare me,
that I should be like him? says the Holy One.

40.26
Isa 51.6;
42.5;
Ps 147.4;
89.11–13;
Isa 34.16
26 Lift up your eyes on high and see:
who created these?
He who brings out their host by number,
calling them all by name;
by the greatness of his might,
and because he is strong in power
not one is missing.

d. God's faithfulness and empowering grace

40.27
Isa 49.4,14;
54.8;
Lk 18.7,
8;
Isa 25.1
27 Why do you say, O Jacob,

---

[q] Heb uncertain

and speak, O Israel,
"My way is hid from the LORD,
    and my right is disregarded by my God"?
28 Have you not known? Have you not heard?
    The LORD is the everlasting God,
        the Creator of the ends of the earth.
    He does not faint or grow weary,
        his understanding is unsearchable.
29 He gives power to the faint,
    and to him who has no might he increases strength.
30 Even youths shall faint and be weary,
    and young men shall fall exhausted;
31 but they who wait for the LORD shall renew their strength,
    they shall mount up with wings like eagles,
their shall run and not be weary,
    they shall walk and not faint.

2. *The God of providence challenges unbelievers*
    a. *God's providence based on omnipotence*

41 Listen to me in silence, O coastlands;
        let the peoples renew their strength;
    let them approach, then let them speak;
        let us together draw near for judgment.

2 Who stirred up one from the east
    whom victory meets at every step?
He gives up nations before him,
    so that he tramples kings under foot;
he makes them like dust with his sword,
    like driven stubble with his bow.
3 He pursues them and passes on safely,
    by paths his feet have not trod.
4 Who has performed and done this,
    calling the generations from the beginning?
I, the LORD, the first,
    and with the last; I am He.

5 The coastlands have seen and are afraid,
    the ends of the earth tremble;
    they have drawn near and come.
6 Every one helps his neighbor,
    and says to his brother, "Take courage!"
7 The craftsman encourages the goldsmith,
    and he who smooths with the hammer him who strikes the
        anvil,
saying of the soldering, "It is good";
    and they fasten it with nails so that it cannot be moved.

    b. *God's servant, Israel, an instrument of His providence*
8 But you, Israel, my servant,
    Jacob, whom I have chosen,
        the offspring of Abraham, my friend;
9 you whom I took from the ends of the earth,
    and called from its farthest corners,
saying to you, "You are my servant,

40.28
Ps 90.2;
147.5;
Rom 11.33

40.29
Isa 50.4;
Jer 31.25;
Isa 41.10

40.30
Jer 6.11;
Isa 9.17

40.31
Ps 103.5;
2 Cor 4.8–
10,16;
Deut 32.11;
2 Cor 4.1;
Heb 12.3

41.1
Zech 2.13;
Isa 40.31;
34.1; 43.26

41.2
Isa 45.1–3;
46.11;
42.6;
2 Chr
36.23;
Isa 29.5;
40.24

41.4
Isa 44.7;
46.10;
43.10;
44.6;
Rev 1.17;
22.13

41.5
Ps 67.7

41.6
Isa 40.19

41.7
Isa 40.19,20

41.8
Isa 44.1;
2 Chr 20.7;
Jas 2.23

41.9
Isa 11.11;
43.5–7;
42.1;
Ps 135.4

I have chosen you and not cast you off";

41.10
Isa 43.5;
Rom 8.31;
Isa 44.2

10 fear not, for I am with you,
   be not dismayed, for I am your God;
I will strengthen you, I will help you,
   I will uphold you with my victorious right hand.

c. His chosen people will overcome their foes

*41.11
Isa 45.24;
17.13

11 Behold, all who are incensed against you
   shall be put to shame and confounded;
those who strive against you
   shall be as nothing and shall perish.

41.12
Isa 17.14;
29.20

12 You shall seek those who contend with you,
   but you shall not find them;
those who war against you
   shall be as nothing at all.

41.13
Isa 42.6;
ver 10

13 For I, the LORD your God,
   hold your right hand;
it is I who say to you, "Fear not,
   I will help you."

*41.14
Job 25.6;
Isa 43.14

14 Fear not, you worm Jacob,
   you men of Israel!
I will help you, says the LORD;
   your Redeemer is the Holy One of Israel.

41.15
Mic 4.13

15 Behold, I will make of you a threshing sledge,
   new, sharp, and having teeth;
you shall thresh the mountains and crush them,
   and you shall make the hills like chaff;

41.16
Jer 51.2;
Isa 45.25

16 you shall winnow them and the wind shall carry them away,
   and the tempest shall scatter them.
And you shall rejoice in the LORD;
   in the Holy One of Israel you shall glory.

d. God will deliver and prosper His people

41.17
Isa 43.20;
30.19;
42.16

17 When the poor and needy seek water,
   and there is none,
   and their tongue is parched with thirst,
I the LORD will answer them,
   I the God of Israel will not forsake them.

41.18
Isa 35.6,7;
43.19

18 I will open rivers on the bare heights,
   and fountains in the midst of the valleys;
I will make the wilderness a pool of water,
   and the dry land springs of water.

19 I will put in the wilderness the cedar,
   the acacia, the myrtle, and the olive;
I will set in the desert the cypress,
   the plane and the pine together;

41.11 The Christian life is a warfare. There is no release from it until death. There are biblical principles which throw light on this problem. The warfare is directed against known enemies such as: (1) Satan (2 Cor 2.11; Eph 6.11, 12); (2) the flesh (Rom 7.23; Gal 5.17; 1 Pet 2.11); (3) the world (Jn 16.33; 1 Jn 5.4, 5); and (4) death (1 Cor 15.26; Heb 2.14, 15). Saints are exhorted: (1) to be spiritually armed (Eph 6.14–18); (2) to be watchful (1 Pet 5.8); (3) to be sober (1 Thess 5.6); (4) to exercise faith (1 Tim 1.18, 19). There are assurances of victory (Rom 16.20; Gal 5.24; 1 Jn 5.4, 5; Rom 8.37); also the certainty of rewards (Rev 2.17; 3.5; 21.7).

41.14 *you worm Jacob* is actually a term of compassion and love. A worm on the ground is at the mercy of any who might trample upon it. God will help his helpless worm, Jacob-Israel.

20 that men may see and know,
     may consider and understand together,
that the hand of the LORD has done this,
     the Holy One of Israel has created it.

     e. *God's omnipotence shown by foretelling the future*

21 Set forth your case, says the LORD;
     bring your proofs, says the King of Jacob.
22 Let them bring them, and tell us
     what is to happen.
Tell us the former things, what they are,
     that we may consider them,
that we may know their outcome;
     or declare to us the things to come.
23 Tell us what is to come hereafter,
     that we may know that you are gods;
do good, or do harm,
     that we may be dismayed and terrified.
24 Behold, you are nothing,
     and your work is nought;
an abomination is he who chooses you.

25 I stirred up one from the north, and he has come,
     from the rising of the sun, and he shall call on my name;
he shall trample*r* on rulers as on mortar,
     as the potter treads clay.
26 Who declared it from the beginning, that we might know,
     and beforetime, that we might say, "He is right"?
There was none who declared it, none who proclaimed,
     none who heard your words.
27 I first have declared it to Zion,*s*
     and I give to Jerusalem a herald of good tidings.
28 But when I look there is no one;
     among these there is no counselor
who, when I ask, gives an answer.
29 Behold, they are all a delusion;
     their works are nothing;
their molten images are empty wind.

     3. *God's servant: individual and national*
         a. *The mission of the servant*

42 Behold my servant, whom I uphold,
     my chosen, in whom my soul delights;
I have put my Spirit upon him,
     he will bring forth justice to the nations.
2 He will not cry or lift up his voice,
     or make it heard in the street;
3 a bruised reed he will not break,
     and a dimly burning wick he will not quench;
he will faithfully bring forth justice.
4 He will not fail*t* or be discouraged*u*
     till he has established justice in the earth;
and the coastlands wait for his law.

---

r Cn: Heb *come*
s Cn: Heb *first to Zion, Behold, behold them*
t Or *burn dimly*   *u* Or *bruised*

41.20
Isa 40.5;
Job 12.9

41.21
ver 1;
Isa 43.15

41.22
Isa 45.21;
43.9

41.23
Isa 42.9;
44.7,8;
45.3;
Jn 13.19;
Jer 10.5

41.24
Ps 115.8;
Isa 44.9;
1 Cor 8.4;
ver 29

41.25
ver 2;
Isa 10.6

41.26
Isa 44.7;
45.21;
Hab 2.18,19

41.27
ver 4;
Isa 40.9

41.28
Isa 63.5;
40.13,14;
46.7

41.29
ver 24;
Isa 44.9;
Jer 5.13

42.1
Isa 43.10;
53.11;
Mt 12.18–
20;
3.16,17;
17.5;
Isa 2.4

42.3
Isa 57.15;
Ps 72.2

42.4
Isa 40.28;
ver 10,12

b. *The servant a light to the nations*

42.5
Isa 44.24;
Zech 12.1;
Acts 17.25

5 Thus says God, the LORD,
    who created the heavens and stretched them out,
    who spread forth the earth and what comes from it,
  who gives breath to the people upon it
    and spirit to those who walk in it:

42.6
Isa 43.1;
49.6,8;
Lk 2.32;
Acts 13.47

6 "I am the LORD, I have called you in righteousness,
    I have taken you by the hand and kept you;
  I have given you as a covenant to the people,
    a light to the nations,

42.7
Isa 35.5;
61.1;
Lk 4.18;
2 Tim 2.26;
Heb 2.14

7   to open the eyes that are blind,
  to bring out the prisoners from the dungeon,
    from the prison those who sit in darkness.

42.8
Isa 48.11

8 I am the LORD, that is my name;
  my glory I give to no other,
    nor my praise to graven images.

42.9
Isa 48.3,6

9 Behold, the former things have come to pass,
  and new things I now declare;
  before they spring forth
    I tell you of them."

c. *Song of praise to the* LORD

42.10
Isa 33.3;
40.3; 98.1;
107.23

10 Sing to the LORD a new song,
  his praise from the end of the earth!
  Let the sea roar^v and all that fills it,
    the coastlands and their inhabitants.

*42.11

11 Let the desert and its cities lift up their voice,
    the villages that Kēdar inhabits;
  let the inhabitants of Sēlā sing for joy,
    let them shout from the top of the mountains.

42.12
Isa 24.15;
ver 4

12 Let them give glory to the LORD,
  and declare his praise in the coastlands.

42.13
Isa 9.7;
Ex 15.3;
Hos 11.10;
Isa 66.14–
16

13 The LORD goes forth like a mighty man,
  like a man of war he stirs up his fury;
  he cries out, he shouts aloud,
    he shows himself mighty against his foes.

d. *Idolators to be punished; backsliders restored*

42.14
Isa 57.11

14 For a long time I have held my peace,
  I have kept still and restrained myself;
  now I will cry out like a woman in travail,
    I will gasp and pant.

42.15
Isa 2.12–16;
44.27

15 I will lay waste mountains and hills,
  and dry up all their herbage;
  I will turn the rivers into islands,
    and dry up the pools.

42.16
Isa 29.18;
Lk 1.78,79;
3.5;
Isa 41.17

16 And I will lead the blind
  in a way that they know not,
  in paths that they have not known
    I will guide them.

^{v} Cn Compare Ps 96.11; 98.7: Heb *Those who go down to the sea*

42.11 *the villages that Kedar inhabits* were occupied by nomads of the Syrian desert. They would see the glory of Israel's God as He brings His people back from exile.

I will turn the darkness before them into light,
   the rough places into level ground.
These are the things I will do,
   and I will not forsake them.
17 They shall be turned back and utterly put to shame,
   who trust in graven images,
who say to molten images,
   "You are our gods."

42.17
Ps 97.7;
Isa 1.29;
44.11;
45.16

e. *Blindness of the servant-nation and its punishment*

18 Hear, you deaf;
   and look, you blind, that you may see!
19 Who is blind but my servant,
   or deaf as my messenger whom I send?
Who is blind as my dedicated one,
   or blind as the servant of the LORD?

42.19
Isa 43.8;
Ezek 12.2

20 He sees*w* many things, but does not observe them;
   his ears are open, but he does not hear.

42.20
Jer 6.10

21 The LORD was pleased, for his righteousness' sake,
   to magnify his law and make it glorious.

42.21
Isa 58.13

22 But this is a people robbed and plundered,
   they are all of them trapped in holes
   and hidden in prisons;
they have become a prey with none to rescue,
   a spoil with none to say, "Restore!"

42.22
Isa 24.18,
22; 10.6

23 Who among you will give ear to this,
   will attend and listen for the time to come?
24 Who gave up Jacob to the spoiler,
   and Israel to the robbers?
Was it not the LORD, against whom we have sinned,
   in whose ways they would not walk,
   and whose law they would not obey?

42.24
Isa 30.15;
48.18

25 So he poured upon him the heat of his anger
   and the might of battle;
it set him on fire round about, but he did not understand;
   it burned him, but he did not take it to heart.

42.25
Isa 5.25;
2 Ki 25.9;
Hos 7.9

4. *Redemption by grace*
a. *God's love will support, redeem, and restore His people*

43 But now thus says the LORD,
   he who created you, O Jacob,
he who formed you, O Israel:
"Fear not, for I have redeemed you;
   I have called you by name, you are mine.

43.1
ver 7,15,21;
Isa 44.2,6,
21

2 When you pass through the waters I will be with you;
   and through the rivers, they shall not overwhelm you;
when you walk through fire you shall not be burned,
   and the flame shall not consume you.

43.2
Ps 66.12;
Deut 31.6,
8;
Dan 3.25,27

3 For I am the LORD your God,
   the Holy One of Israel, your Savior.
I give Egypt as your ransom,

43.3
Ex 20.2;
ver 11;
Prov 11.8;
21.18

w Heb *you see*

43.3 *Egypt as your ransom.* Persia is compensated for the loss of the Israelites by being assigned Egypt, Ethiopia, and Seba (conquered by Cambyses, son of Cyrus).

Ethiopia and Sēbä in exchange for you.

43.4
Isa 63.9

4 Because you are precious in my eyes,
    and honored, and I love you,
I give men in return for you,
    peoples in exchange for your life.

43.5
Isa 41.10,
14;
44.2;
Jer 30.10,
11;
46.27,28

5 Fear not, for I am with you;
    I will bring your offspring from the east,
    and from the west I will gather you;

43.6
Ps 107.3;
Isa 14.2

6 I will say to the north, Give up,
    and to the south, Do not withhold;
bring my sons from afar
    and my daughters from the end of the earth,

43.7
Ps 100.3;
Isa 29.23;
Eph 2.10;
ver 1

7 every one who is called by my name,
    whom I created for my glory,
    whom I formed and made."

b. *The servant-nation a witness to the world*

43.8
Isa 6.9;
42.19;
Ezek 12.2

8 Bring forth the people who are blind, yet have eyes,
    who are deaf, yet have ears!

43.9
Isa 41.21,
22,26

9 Let all the nations gather together,
    and let the peoples assemble.
Who among them can declare this,
    and show us the former things?
Let them bring their witnesses to justify them,
    and let them hear and say, It is true.

43.10
Isa 44.8;
42.1; 41.4;
44.6

10 "You are my witnesses," says the LORD,
    "and my servant whom I have chosen,
that you may know and believe me
    and understand that I am He.
Before me no god was formed,
    nor shall there be any after me.

43.11
Isa 45.21

11 I, I am the LORD,
    and besides me there is no savior.

43.12
Deut 32.16;
Ps 81.9;
ver 10;
Isa 44.8

12 I declared and saved and proclaimed,
    when there was no strange god among you;
    and you are my witnesses," says the LORD.

43.13
Ps 90.2;
Job 9.12;
Isa 14.27

13 "I am God, and also henceforth I am He;
    there is none who can deliver from my hand;
    I work and who can hinder it?"

c. *The Redeemer will restore His people from Babylon*

43.14
Isa 41.14;
13.14,15

14 Thus says the LORD,
    your Redeemer, the Holy One of Israel:
"For your sake I will send to Babylon
    and break down all the bars,
    and the shouting of the Chäldē′ans will be turned to lamen-
        tations.ˣ

15 I am the LORD, your Holy One,
    the Creator of Israel, your King."

43.16
Ex 14.16;
Ps 77.19;
Isa 51.10;
Josh 3.13

16 Thus says the LORD,
    who makes a way in the sea,
    a path in the mighty waters,

43.17
Ex 14.4–9,
25

17 who brings forth chariot and horse,
    army and warrior;

ˣ Heb obscure

they lie down, they cannot rise,
   they are extinguished, quenched like a wick:
18 "Remember not the former things,
   nor consider the things of old.

> 43.18
> Jer 16.14

19 Behold, I am doing a new thing;
   now it springs forth, do you not perceive it?
I will make a way in the wilderness
   and rivers in the desert.

> 43.19
> 2 Cor 5.17;
> Rev 21.5;
> Ex 17.6;
> Num 20.11;
> Isa 35.6

20 The wild beasts will honor me,
   the jackals and the ostriches;
for I give water in the wilderness,
   rivers in the desert,
to give drink to my chosen people,

> 43.20
> Isa 48.21

21   the people whom I formed for myself
that they might declare my praise.

> 43.21
> ver 1;
> Ps 102.18;
> Lk 1.74,75

d. Israel's sin was ingratitude

22 "Yet you did not call upon me, O Jacob;
   but you have been weary of me, O Israel!

> 43.22
> Isa 30.9–11;
> Mal 1.13

23 You have not brought me your sheep for burnt offerings,
   or honored me with your sacrifices.
I have not burdened you with offerings,
   or wearied you with frankincense.

> 43.23
> Amos 5.25;
> Mal 1.6–8

24 You have not bought me sweet cane with money,
   or satisfied me with the fat of your sacrifices.
But you have burdened me with your sins,
   you have wearied me with your iniquities.

> 43.24
> Ex 30.23;
> Isa 1.14;
> Mal 2.17

25 "I, I am He
   who blots out your transgressions for my own sake,
   and I will not remember your sins.

> 43.25
> Isa 44.23;
> Ezek 36.22;
> Jer 31.34

26 Put me in remembrance, let us argue together;
   set forth your case, that you may be proved right.

> 43.26
> Isa 1.18;
> ver 9

27 Your first father sinned,
   and your mediators transgressed against me.
28 Therefore I profaned the princes of the sanctuary,
   I delivered Jacob to utter destruction
   and Israel to reviling.

> 43.28
> Isa 47.6;
> Lam 2.2,6;
> Zech 8.13

e. The servant-nation shall yet be converted

44 "But now hear, O Jacob my servant,
   Israel whom I have chosen!

> 44.1
> Isa 41.8;
> Jer 30.10;
> 46.27,28

2 Thus says the LORD who made you,
   who formed you from the womb and will help you:
Fear not, O Jacob my servant,
   Jĕsh'úrùn whom I have chosen.

> 44.2
> Isa 43.1,7;
> Deut 32.15

3 For I will pour water on the thirsty land,
   and streams on the dry ground;
I will pour my Spirit upon your descendants,
   and my blessing on your offspring.

> 44.3
> Isa 35.7;
> Joel 2.28;
> Jn 7.38;
> Acts 2.18

4 They shall spring up like grass amid waters,[y]
   like willows by flowing streams.

5 This one will say, 'I am the LORD's,'
   another will call himself by the name of Jacob,

> 44.5
> Isa 19.21;
> Zech 8.20–22

[y] Gk Compare Tg: Heb *They shall spring up in among grass*

and another will write on his hand, 'The LORD's,'
and surname himself by the name of Israel."

5. *God's judgment upon idolatrous polytheism*
a. *Yahweh as the incomparable God*

44.6
Isa 43.1,14;
41.4;
48.12;
Rev 1.8,17;
22.13

6 Thus says the LORD, the King of Israel
  and his Redeemer, the LORD of hosts:
"I am the first and I am the last;
  besides me there is no god.

44.7
Isa 41.4,22

7 Who is like me? Let him proclaim it,
  let him declare and set it forth before me.
Who has announced from of old the things to come?ᶻ
  Let them tell usᵃ what is yet to be.

44.8
Isa 41.22;
43.10;
Deut 4.35;
1 Sam 2.2;
Isa 26.4

8 Fear not, nor be afraid;
  have I not told you from of old and declared it?
  And you are my witnesses!
Is there a God besides me?
  There is no Rock; I know not any."

b. *The folly of worshiping idols*

44.9
Isa 41.24;
66.3; 43.9;
42.17

9 All who make idols are nothing, and the things they delight
in do not profit; their witnesses neither see nor know, that they

44.10
Jer 10.5;
Hab 2.18

may be put to shame. 10 Who fashions a god or casts an image,
that is profitable for nothing? 11 Behold, all his fellows shall be put

44.11
Isa 1.29;
42.17

to shame, and the craftsmen are but men; let them all assemble,
let them stand forth, they shall be terrified, they shall be put to
shame together.

44.12
Isa 40.19;
41.6;
Jer 10.3–5

12 The ironsmith fashions itᵇ and works it over the coals; he
shapes it with hammers, and forges it with his strong arm; he becomes hungry and his strength fails, he drinks no water and is

44.13
Isa 41.7;
Ps 115.5–7

faint. 13 The carpenter stretches a line, he marks it out with a
pencil; he fashions it with planes, and marks it with a compass; he
shapes it into the figure of a man, with the beauty of a man, to
dwell in a house. 14 He cuts down cedars; or he chooses a holm
tree or an oak and lets it grow strong among the trees of the
forest; he plants a cedar and the rain nourishes it. 15 Then it be-

44.15
ver 17,19;
2 Chr 25.14

comes fuel for a man; he takes a part of it and warms himself, he
kindles a fire and bakes bread; also he makes a god and worships
it, he makes it a graven image and falls down before it. 16 Half of
it he burns in the fire; over the half he eats flesh, he roasts meat
and is satisfied; also he warms himself and says, "Aha, I am warm,
I have seen the fire!" 17And the rest of it he makes into a god, his

44.17
ver 15;
Isa 45.20;
1 Ki 18.26,
28

idol; and falls down to it and worships it; he prays to it and says,
"Deliver me, for thou art my god!"

44.18
Isa 1.3;
6.9,10

18 They know not, nor do they discern; for he has shut their
eyes, so that they cannot see, and their minds, so that they cannot

44.19
Isa 5.13;
45.20;
27.11;
Deut 27.15

understand. 19 No one considers, nor is there knowledge or discernment to say, "Half of it I burned in the fire, I also baked
bread on its coals, I roasted flesh and have eaten; and shall I make
the residue of it an abomination? Shall I fall down before a block

44.20
Ps 102.9;
Job 15.31;
Isa 57.11

of wood?" 20 He feeds on ashes; a deluded mind has led him
astray, and he cannot deliver himself or say, "Is there not a lie
in my right hand?"

ᶻ Cn: Heb *from my placing an eternal people and things to come*
ᵃ Tg: Heb *them*   ᵇ Cn: Heb *an axe*

c. Monotheistic Israel shall be redeemed

21 Remember these things, O Jacob,
    and Israel, for you are my servant;
 I formed you, you are my servant;
    O Israel, you will not be forgotten by me.

22 I have swept away your transgressions like a cloud,
    and your sins like mist;
 return to me, for I have redeemed you.

23 Sing, O heavens, for the LORD has done it;
    shout, O depths of the earth;
 break forth into singing, O mountains,
    O forest, and every tree in it!
 For the LORD has redeemed Jacob,
    and will be glorified in Israel.

6. The sovereign God employing and converting the heathen

a. God's decree to restore Jerusalem through Cyrus

24 Thus says the LORD, your Redeemer,
    who formed you from the womb:
 "I am the LORD, who made all things,
    who stretched out the heavens alone,
    who spread out the earth—Who was with me?c—

25 who frustrates the omens of liars,
    and makes fools of diviners;
 who turns wise men back,
    and makes their knowledge foolish;

26 who confirms the word of his servant,
    and performs the counsel of his messengers;
 who says of Jerusalem, 'She shall be inhabited,'
    and of the cities of Judah, 'They shall be built,
    and I will raise up their ruins';

27 who says to the deep, 'Be dry,
    I will dry up your rivers';

28 who says of Cyrus, 'He is my shepherd,
    and he shall fulfil all my purpose';
 saying of Jerusalem, 'She shall be built,'
    and of the temple, 'Your foundation shall be laid.' "

b. Promise of victory to Cyrus

45 Thus says the LORD to his anointed, to Cyrus,
    whose right hand I have grasped,
 to subdue nations before him

c Another reading is *who spread out the earth by myself*

Marginal references:

44.21
Isa 46.8;
ver 1,2;
Isa 49.15

44.22
Isa 43.25;
55.7; 43.1;
1 Pet 1.18,
19

44.23
Isa 42.10;
55.12;
43.1; 61.3

44.24
Isa 43.14;
ver 2;
Isa 40.14,22

44.25
Isa 40.14;
29.14;
1 Cor 1.20,
27

44.26
Isa 55.11;
49.7–20;
Jer 32.15,44

44.27
Isa 43.16;
42.15

★44.28
Isa 45.1;
14.32;
45.13

45.1
Isa 44.28;
41.13;
Jer 50.3,35;
ver 5

44.28 This prediction of the rebuilding of the Temple at Jerusalem was made one hundred and fifty years before Cyrus' decree to rebuild it was promulgated. His decree was given in the first year of his reign over Babylon, about 538 B.C. (Ezra 1.1, 2; 6.3). The new Temple was known as the second Temple and it remained as the center of Jewish worship until the fall of Jerusalem in A.D. 70. It was desecrated by Antiochus Epiphanes in 168 B.C., an event which was predicted by Daniel (Dan 9.27; 11.31). In New Testament days the Temple was repaired and improved by Herod the Great and his successors over a period of forty-six years (Jn 2.20). Jesus often taught in this Temple (Mk 14.49) and He predicted its utter destruction (Mt 24.2; Mk 13.2; Lk 21.6). It was the curtain (veil) of this Temple that was rent in two at Christ's death (Mt 27.51). No Gentile was ever permitted to enter its inner courts (Acts 21.27–30).

and ungird the loins of kings,
to open doors before him
that gates may not be closed:

45.2
Isa 40.4;
Ps 107.16;
Jer 51.30

2 "I will go before you
and level the mountains,*d*
I will break in pieces the doors of bronze
and cut asunder the bars of iron,

45.3
Jer 41.8;
Isa 43.1

3 I will give you the treasures of darkness
and the hoards in secret places,
that you may know that it is I, the LORD,
the God of Israel, who call you by your name.

45.4
Isa 41.8;
43.1;
Acts 17.23

4 For the sake of my servant Jacob,
and Israel my chosen,
I call you by your name,
I surname you, though you do not know me.

45.5
ver 6;
Isa 44.6,8;
Ps 18.39

5 I am the LORD, and there is no other,
besides me there is no God;
I gird you, though you do not know me,

45.6
Mal 1.11;
Isa 43.5;
ver 5

6 that men may know, from the rising of the sun
and from the west, that there is none besides me;
I am the LORD, and there is no other.

c. *The folly of striving with God*

★45.7
Isa 42.16;
Ps 104.20;
Amos 3.6

7 I form light and create darkness,
I make weal and create woe,
I am the LORD, who do all these things.

45.8
Ps 72.6;
85.11;
Isa 12.3;
60.21

8 "Shower, O heavens, from above,
and let the skies rain down righteousness;
let the earth open, that salvation may sprout forth,*c*
and let it cause righteousness to spring up also;
I the LORD have created it.

45.9
Isa 29.16;
Rom 9.20,
21

9 "Woe to him who strives with his Maker,
an earthen vessel with the potter!*f*
Does the clay say to him who fashions it, 'What are you making'?
or 'Your work has no handles'?
10 Woe to him who says to a father, 'What are you begetting?'
or to a woman, 'With what are you in travail?' "

45.11
Isa 43.15;
54.5; 8.19;
Jer 31.9;
60.21

11 Thus says the LORD,
the Holy One of Israel, and his Maker:
"Will you question me*g* about my children,
or command me concerning the work of my hands?

45.12
ver 18;
Isa 42.5;
Neh 9.6

12 I made the earth,
and created man upon it;
it was my hands that stretched out the heavens,

---

d One ancient Ms Gk: Heb *the swellings*
e One ancient Ms: Heb *that they may bring forth salvation*
f Cn: Heb *potsherds* or *potters*   *g* Cn: Heb *Ask me of things to come*

45.7 The King James translation, "I make peace, and create evil," has led to the idea that God is the author of sin. The RSV translation is more accurate, since this word for "evil" (*ra*‘) is often used of physical evil or calamity, rather than moral evil. God is not the author of sin. Man has the power of free will and contrary choice. Since all sin is basically rebellion against God, it is impossible for Him to have created it.

and I commanded all their host.
13 I have aroused him in righteousness,
   and I will make straight all his ways;
  he shall build my city
   and set my exiles free,
not for price or reward,"
  says the LORD of hosts.

45.13
Isa 41.2;
ver 2;
Isa 44.28;
52.3

d. *The future conversion of the Gentiles*

14 Thus says the LORD:
"The wealth of Egypt and the merchandise of Ethiopia,
   and the Sábē'áns, men of stature,
shall come over to you and be yours,
   they shall follow you;
  they shall come over in chains and bow down to you.
They will make supplication to you, saying:
  'God is with you only, and there is no other,
  no god besides him.' "
15 Truly, thou art a God who hidest thyself,
  O God of Israel, the Savior.
16 All of them are put to shame and confounded,
  the makers of idols go in confusion together.
17 But Israel is saved by the LORD
  with everlasting salvation;
you shall not be put to shame or confounded
  to all eternity.

45.14
Isa 14.1,2;
Ps 149.8;
Isa 49.23;
Jer 16.19;
1 Cor 14.25;
ver 5

45.15
Isa 8.17;
43.3

45.16
Isa 44.9,11

45.17
Isa 26.4;
Rom 11.26;
Isa 49.23

18 For thus says the LORD,
  who created the heavens
   (he is God!),
who formed the earth and made it
   (he established it;
he did not create it a chaos,
  he formed it to be inhabited!):
"I am the LORD, and there is no other.
19 I did not speak in secret,
  in a land of darkness;
I did not say to the offspring of Jacob,
  'Seek me in chaos.'
I the LORD speak the truth,
  I declare what is right.

45.18
Isa 42.5;
ver 12;
Gen 1.2,26;
ver 5

45.19
Isa 48.16;
41.8;
Jer 29.13,
14;
Isa 63.1;
44.8

e. *The heathen invited to be saved by faith in the* LORD

20 "Assemble yourselves and come,
  draw near together,
  you survivors of the nations!
They have no knowledge
  who carry about their wooden idols,
and keep on praying to a god
  that cannot save.
21 Declare and present your case;
  let them take counsel together!
Who told this long ago?
  Who declared it of old?
Was it not I, the LORD?

45.20
Isa 43.9;
44.18,19;
Jer 10.5;
Isa 46.6,7

45.21
Isa 41.23,
26;
ver 5;
Isa 43.3,11

And there is no other god besides me,
a righteous God and a Savior;
there is none besides me.

*45.22
Num 21.8,
9;
Isa 30.15;
49.6,12

22 "Turn to me and be saved,
all the ends of the earth!
For I am God, and there is no other.

45.23
Isa 62.8;
Rom 14.11;
Isa 55.11;
65.16

23 By myself I have sworn,
from my mouth has gone forth in righteousness
a word that shall not return:
'To me every knee shall bow,
every tongue shall swear.'

45.24
Isa 54.17;
41.11

24 "Only in the LORD, it shall be said of me,
are righteousness and strength;
to him shall come and be ashamed,
all who were incensed against him.

45.25
Isa 53.11;
60.19

25 In the LORD all the offspring of Israel
shall triumph and glory."

7. Lessons from Babylon's fall and Israel's preservation
a. Babylon's helpless idols and the omnipotent God

*46.1
Jer 50.2–4;
Isa 45.20

46 Bĕl bows down, Nēbō stoops,
their idols are on beasts and cattle;
these things you carry are loaded
as burdens on weary beasts.

46.2
Jer 43.12,13

2 They stoop, they bow down together,
they cannot save the burden,
but themselves go into captivity.

46.3
ver 12;
Isa 45.19;
10.21,22;
63.9

3 "Hearken to me, O house of Jacob,
all the remnant of the house of Israel,
who have been borne by me from your birth,
carried from the womb;

46.4
Isa 43.13;
Ps 71.18

4 even to your old age I am He,
and to gray hairs I will carry you.
I have made, and I will bear;
I will carry and will save.

46.5
Isa 40.18,
25
46.6
Isa 40.19;
44.15,17

5 "To whom will you liken me and make me equal,
and compare me, that we may be alike?
6 Those who lavish gold from the purse,
and weigh out silver in the scales,
hire a goldsmith, and he makes it into a god;
then they fall down and worship!

46.7
ver 1;
Isa 40.20;
44.17;
41.26,28;
45.20

7 They lift it upon their shoulders, they carry it,
they set it in its place, and it stands there;
it cannot move from its place.
If one cries to it, it does not answer
or save him from his trouble.

45.22 Verse 20 speaks of great idolatry. But a loving God extends a universal call to all men. It is clear that all need to be saved and that all who come can be saved.

46.1 *Bel bows down, Nebo stoops.* Bel-Marduk was the principal God of Babylon; Nebo the Babylon god of writing and patron of Borsippa.

8 "Remember this and consider,
  recall it to mind, you transgressors,
9   remember the former things of old;
  for I am God, and there is no other;
  I am God, and there is none like me,
10 declaring the end from the beginning
  and from ancient times things not yet done,
  saying, 'My counsel shall stand,
  and I will accomplish all my purpose,'
11 calling a bird of prey from the east,
  the man of my counsel from a far country.
  I have spoken, and I will bring it to pass;
  I have purposed, and I will do it.

12 "Hearken to me, you stubborn of heart,
  you who are far from deliverance:
13 I bring near my deliverance, it is not far off,
  and my salvation will not tarry;
  I will put salvation in Zion,
  for Israel my glory."

b. Judgment against merciless Babylon

47 Come down and sit in the dust,
  O virgin daughter of Babylon;
sit on the ground without a throne,
  O daughter of the Chăldē′ăns!
For you shall no more be called
  tender and delicate.
2 Take the millstones and grind meal,
  put off your veil,
strip off your robe, uncover your legs,
  pass through the rivers.
3 Your nakedness shall be uncovered,
  and your shame shall be seen.
I will take vengeance,
  and I will spare no man.
4 Our Redeemer—the LORD of hosts is his name—
  is the Holy One of Israel.

5 Sit in silence, and go into darkness,
  O daughter of the Chăldē′ăns;
for you shall no more be called
  the mistress of kingdoms.
6 I was angry with my people,
  I profaned my heritage;
I gave them into your hand,
  you showed them no mercy;
on the aged you made your yoke
  exceedingly heavy.
7 You said, "I shall be mistress for ever,"
  so that you did not lay these things to heart
  or remember their end.

c. Babylon's false security amid wickedness
8 Now therefore hear this, you lover of pleasures,

46.8
Isa 44.19,
21; 48.8
46.9
Isa 45.5,21;
41.26,27

46.10
Isa 45.21;
14.24;
Acts 5.39

46.11
Isa 18.6;
41.2,25;
37.26

46.12
ver 3;
Isa 48.4;
Jer 2.5
46.13
Isa 61.11;
43.7; 44.23

47.1
Jer 48.18;
46.11;
51.33

47.3
Ezek 16.37;
Isa 34.8;
63.4

47.4
Isa 41.14

47.5
Isa 23.2;
13.10;
ver
Isa 13.19;
Dan 2.37
47.6
Zech 1.15;
Isa 43.28;
10.14;
Deut 28.50

47.7
ver 5;
Isa 42.25;
45.21

47.8
Isa 32.9,11;
Zeph 2.15;
Rev 18.7

who sit securely,
who say in your heart,
"I am, and there is no one besides me;
I shall not sit as a widow
or know the loss of children":

47.9
Isa 13.16,
18;
1 Thess 5.3;
Nah 3.4

9 These two things shall come to you
in a moment, in one day;
the loss of children and widowhood
shall come upon you in full measure,
in spite of your many sorceries
and the great power of your enchantments.

47.10
Ps 52.7;
Isa 29.15;
44.20;
ver 8

10 You felt secure in your wickedness,
you said, "No one sees me";
your wisdom and your knowledge
led you astray,
and you said in your heart,
"I am, and there is no one besides me."

47.11
Isa 57.1;
1 Thess 5.3;
ver 9

11 But evil shall come upon you,
for which you cannot atone;
disaster shall fall upon you,
which you will not be able to expiate;
and ruin shall come on you suddenly,
of which you know nothing.

d. *Helplessness of Babylon to avert her fall*

47.12
ver 9

12 Stand fast in your enchantments
and your many sorceries,
with which you have labored from your youth;
perhaps you may be able to succeed,
perhaps you may inspire terror.

47.13
Isa 57.10;
Dan 2.2

13 You are wearied with your many counsels;
let them stand forth and save you,
those who divide the heavens,
who gaze at the stars,
who at the new moons predict
what[h] shall befall you.

47.14
Nah 1.10;
Mal 4.1

14 Behold, they are like stubble,
the fire consumes them;
they cannot deliver themselves
from the power of the flame.
No coal for warming oneself is this,
no fire to sit before!

47.15
Rev 18.11;
Isa 43.13;
46.7

15 Such to you are those with whom you have labored,
who have trafficked with you from your youth;
they wander about each in his own direction;
there is no one to save you.

8. *Israel punished and returned to her land*
a. *The prophecy of captivity fulfilled*

48.1
Isa 46.12;
Num 24.7;
Ps 68.26;
Isa 45.23

48 Hear this, O house of Jacob,
who are called by the name of Israel,
and who came forth from the loins[i] of Judah;

h Gk Syr Compare Vg: Heb *from what*   *i* Cn: Heb *waters*

who swear by the name of the LORD,
  and confess the God of Israel,
    but not in truth or right.

2 For they call themselves after the holy city,
  and stay themselves on the God of Israel;
    the LORD of hosts is his name.

> **48.2**
> Isa 52.1;
> Mic 3.11;
> Rom 2.17

3 "The former things I declared of old,
  they went forth from my mouth and I made them known;
    then suddenly I did them and they came to pass.

> **48.3**
> Isa 41.22;
> 42.9; 43.9;
> 44.7,8;
> 45.21;
> Josh 21.45

4 Because I know that you are obstinate,
  and your neck is an iron sinew
    and your forehead brass,

> **48.4**
> Ezek 2.4;
> Ex 32.9;
> Deut 31.27;
> Ezek 3.7–9

5 I declared them to you from of old,
  before they came to pass I announced them to you,
lest you should say, 'My idol did them,
  my graven image and my molten image commanded them.'

> **48.5**
> Ezek 2.4;
> 3.7

6 "You have heard; now see all this;
  and will you not declare it?
From this time forth I make you hear new things,
  hidden things which you have not known.

> **48.6**
> Isa 42.9;
> 43.19

7 They are created now, not long ago;
  before today you have never heard of them,
    lest you should say, 'Behold, I knew them.'

8 You have never heard, you have never known,
  from of old your ear has not been opened.
For I knew that you would deal very treacherously,
  and that from birth you were called a rebel.

> **48.8**
> Isa 42.25;
> 46.8;
> Ps 58.3

b. *God's glory upheld by Israel's affliction*

9 "For my name's sake I defer my anger,
  for the sake of my praise I restrain it for you,
    that I may not cut you off.

> **48.9**
> ver 11;
> Ps 78.38;
> Isa 30.18

10 Behold, I have refined you, but not like^j silver;
  I have tried you in the furnace of affliction.

> **48.10**
> Jer 9.7;
> Ezek 22.18–
> 22;
> Jer 11.4

11 For my own sake, for my own sake, I do it,
  for how should my name^k be profaned?
  My glory I will not give to another.

> **48.11**
> ver 9;
> Deut 32.26;
> Ezek 20.9;
> Isa 42.8

c. *God to send Cyrus against Babylon*

12 "Hearken to me, O Jacob,
  and Israel, whom I called!
I am He, I am the first,
  and I am the last.

> **48.12**
> Deut 32.39;
> Isa 41.4;
> Rev 1.17;
> 22.13

13 My hand laid the foundation of the earth,
  and my right hand spread out the heavens;
when I call to them,
  they stand forth together.

> **48.13**
> Ps 102.25;
> Isa 40.26

14 "Assemble, all of you, and hear!
  Who among them has declared these things?
The LORD loves him;
  he shall perform his purpose on Babylon,

> **48.14**
> Isa 43.9;
> 45.21;
> 46.10,11;
> Jer 50.21–
> 29

j Cn: Heb *with* *k* Gk Old Latin: Heb lacks *my name*

and his arm shall be against the Chăldē´ăns.

48.15
Isa 41.2;
45.1,2

15 I, even I, have spoken and called him,
 I have brought him, and he will prosper in his way.

48.16
Isa 41.1;
45.19;
43.13;
Zech 2.9,11

16 Draw near to me, hear this:
 from the beginning I have not spoken in secret,
 from the time it came to be I have been there."
And now the Lord God has sent me and his Spirit.

   d. A chastened Israel to flee from Babylon and return home

48.17
Isa 43.14;
Ps 32.8

17 Thus says the Lord,
 your Redeemer, the Holy One of Israel:
"I am the Lord your God,
 who teaches you to profit,
 who leads you in the way you should go.

48.18
Deut 32.29;
Ps 119.165;
Isa 61.10,11

18 O that you had hearkened to my commandments!
 Then your peace would have been like a river,
 and your righteousness like the waves of the sea;

48.19
Gen 22.17;
Jer 33.22;
Isa 56.5;
66.22

19 your offspring would have been like the sand,
 and your descendants like its grains;
their name would never be cut off
 or destroyed from before me."

48.20
Jer 50.8;
Isa 42.10;
62.11; 43.1

20 Go forth from Babylon, flee from Chăldē a,
 declare this with a shout of joy, proclaim it,
send it forth to the end of the earth;
 say, "The Lord has redeemed his servant Jacob!"

48.21
Isa 41.17;
Ex 17.6;
Ps 105.41

21 They thirsted not when he led them through the deserts;
 he made water flow for them from the rock;
 he cleft the rock and the water gushed out.

48.22
Isa 57.21

22 "There is no peace," says the Lord, "for the wicked."

B. Part II: God's servant-king Redeemer

1. *God's servant-king to restore Israel and bring light to the Gentiles*
  a. *Messiah's call and commission; message
   to Israel and the heathen*

49.1
Isa 42.4;
66.19;
44.2,24;
Isa 7.14;
9.6;
Mt 1.20;
Gal 1.15

49
Listen to me, O coastlands,
 and hearken, you peoples from afar.
The Lord called me from the womb,
 from the body of my mother he named my name.

49.2
Isa 11.4;
Heb 4.12;
Isa 51.16;
Hab 3.11

2 He made my mouth like a sharp sword,
 in the shadow of his hand he hid me;
he made me a polished arrow,
 in his quiver he hid me away.

49.3
Isa 42.1;
44.23

3 And he said to me, "You are my servant,
 Israel, in whom I will be glorified."

49.4
Isa 65.23

4 But I said, "I have labored in vain,
 I have spent my strength for nothing and vanity;
yet surely my right is with the Lord,
 and my recompense with my God."

49.5
Isa 44.2,23;
27.12;
43.4; 12.2

5 And now the Lord says,
 who formed me from the womb to be his servant,
 to bring Jacob back to him,
 and that Israel might be gathered to him,

for I am honored in the eyes of the LORD,
    and my God has become my strength—
6 he says:
"It is too light a thing that you should be my servant
    to raise up the tribes of Jacob
    and to restore the preserved of Israel;
I will give you as a light to the nations,
    that my salvation may reach to the end of the earth."

7 Thus says the LORD,
    the Redeemer of Israel and his Holy One,
to one deeply despised, abhorred by the nations,
    the servant of rulers:
"Kings shall see and arise;
    princes, and they shall prostrate themselves;
because of the LORD, who is faithful,
    the Holy One of Israel, who has chosen you."

b. God's deliverance and care of His redeemed

8 Thus says the LORD:
"In a time of favor I have answered you,
    in a day of salvation I have helped you;
I have kept you and given you
    as a covenant to the people,
to establish the land,
    to apportion the desolate heritages;
9 saying to the prisoners, 'Come forth,'
    to those who are in darkness, 'Appear.'
They shall feed along the ways,
    on all bare heights shall be their pasture;
10 they shall not hunger or thirst,
    neither scorching wind nor sun shall smite them,
for he who has pity on them will lead them,
    and by springs of water will guide them.
11 And I will make all my mountains a way,
    and my highways shall be raised up.
12 Lo, these shall come from afar,
    and lo, these from the north and from the west,
    and these from the land of Sȳē'nē."[l]
13 Sing for joy, O heavens, and exult, O earth;
    break forth, O mountains, into singing!
For the LORD has comforted his people,
    and will have compassion on his afflicted.

c. Zion assured of God's continuing love

14 But Zion said, "The LORD has forsaken me,
    my Lord has forgotten me."
15 "Can a woman forget her sucking child,
    that she should have no compassion on the son of her womb?
Even these may forget,
    yet I will not forget you.
16 Behold, I have graven you on the palms of my hands;
    your walls are continually before me.
17 Your builders outstrip your destroyers,

[l] Cn: Heb Sinim

49.6
Isa 42.6;
Lk 2.32;
Acts 13.47;
26.23

49.7
Isa 48.17;
53.3;
Ps 22.6–8;
Isa 52.15;
66.23

49.8
Ps 69.13;
2 Cor 6.2;
Isa 42.6;
44.26

49.9
Isa 42.7;
Lk 4.18;
Isa 41.18

49.10
Rev 7.16;
Ps 121.6;
Isa 14.1;
40.11;
41.17

49.11
Isa 40.4;
62.10

49.12
Isa 43.5,6

49.13
Isa 44.23;
40.1;
54.7,8,10;
Rev 12.12;
18.20

49.14
Isa 40.27

49.15
Isa 44.21

49.16
Sol 8.6;
Isa 62.6,7

49.17
ver 19

and those who laid you waste go forth from you.

49.18
Isa 60.4;
43.5;45.23;
52.1

18 Lift up your eyes round about and see;
  they all gather, they come to you.
As I live, says the LORD,
  you shall put them all on as an ornament,
  you shall bind them on as a bride does.

49.19
Isa 51.3;
54.1,2;
Zech 10.10;
Ps 56.1,2

19 "Surely your waste and your desolate places
    and your devastated land—
surely now you will be too narrow for your inhabitants,
    and those who swallowed you up will be far away.

49.20
Isa 54.1–3

20 The children born in the time of your bereavement
    will yet say in your ears:
'The place is too narrow for me;
    make room for me to dwell in.'

49.21
Isa 54.6,7;
27.10;
5.13;1.8

21 Then you will say in your heart:
  'Who has borne me these?
I was bereaved and barren,
    exiled and put away,
but who has brought up these?
Behold, I was left alone;
    whence then have these come?'"

d. Glorious restoration of Israel along with converted Gentiles

49.22
Isa 62.10;
60.4; 66.20

22 Thus says the Lord GOD:
"Behold, I will lift up my hand to the nations,
    and raise my signal to the peoples;
and they shall bring your sons in their bosom,
    and your daughters shall be carried on their shoulders.

★49.23
Isa 60.16;
45.14;
Ps 72.9;
Mic 7.17;
Isa 43.10;
25.9;
Ps 25.3

23 Kings shall be your foster fathers,
    and their queens your nursing mothers.
With their faces to the ground they shall bow down to you,
    and lick the dust of your feet.
Then you will know that I am the LORD;
    those who wait for me shall not be put to shame."

24 Can the prey be taken from the mighty,
    or the captives of a tyrant*m* be rescued?

49.25
Isa 14.1,2;
25.9

25 Surely, thus says the LORD:
"Even the captives of the mighty shall be taken,
    and the prey of the tyrant be rescued,
for I will contend with those who contend with you,
    and I will save your children.

49.26
Isa 9.4,20;
45.6; 43.3;
ver 7

26 I will make your oppressors eat their own flesh,
    and they shall be drunk with their own blood as with wine.
Then all flesh shall know
    that I am the LORD your Savior,
    and your Redeemer, the Mighty One of Jacob."

m One ancient Ms Syr Vg: Heb righteous man

49.23 *those who wait for me.* Men are always impatient and in haste. God is never in a hurry. Thus a long time elapsed between the promise of the Redeemer and His advent. A long time has passed between the First Advent of Jesus and His second return which has not yet taken place. There is the sure promise of God, however, that those who wait for Him *shall not be put to shame,* i.e., God will justify their confidence for having waited.

2. *Sinfulness of Israel contrasted with obedience of the servant*

a. *The* LORD *separated from His wife, Israel, by sin*

50 Thus says the LORD:
"Where is your mother's bill of divorce,
    with which I put her away?
Or which of my creditors is it
    to whom I have sold you?
Behold, for your iniquities you were sold,
    and for your transgressions your mother was put away.

⋆50.1
Deut 24.1,3;
Jer 3.8;
Isa 54.6,7;
Deut 32.30;
Isa 52.3;
48.8

2 Why, when I came, was there no man?
    When I called, was there no one to answer?
Is my hand shortened, that it cannot redeem?
    Or have I no power to deliver?
Behold, by my rebuke I dry up the sea,
    I make the rivers a desert;
their fish stink for lack of water,
    and die of thirst.

⋆50.2
Isa 65.12;
66.4;
Num 11.23;
Isa 59.1;
Ex 14.21;
Josh 3.16

3 I clothe the heavens with blackness,
    and make sackcloth their covering."

50.3
Isa 13.10;
Rev 6.12

b. *Obedient response of the servant, the true Israel*

4 The Lord GOD has given me
    the tongue of those who are taught,
that I may know how to sustain with a word
    him that is weary.
Morning by morning he wakens,
    he wakens my ear
to hear as those who are taught.

50.4
Isa 54.13;
Jer 31.25;
Ps 143.8

5 The Lord GOD has opened my ear,
    and I was not rebellious,
    I turned not backward.

50.5
Ps 40.6;
Mt 26.39;
Jn 8.29;
14.31;
Phil 2.8

6 I gave my back to the smiters,
    and my cheeks to those who pulled out the beard;
I hid not my face
    from shame and spitting.

50.6
Isa 53.5;
Mt 26.67;
Lk 22.63

7 For the Lord GOD helps me;
    therefore I have not been confounded;
therefore I have set my face like a flint,
    and I know that I shall not be put to shame;

50.7
Isa 49.8;
54.4;
Ezek 3.8,9

8   he who vindicates me is near.
Who will contend with me?
    Let us stand up together.
Who is my adversary?
    Let him come near to me.

50.8
Rom 8.32–34

9 Behold, the Lord GOD helps me;
    who will declare me guilty?
Behold, all of them will wear out like a garment;
    the moth will eat them up.

50.9
Isa 41.10;
54.17; 5.18

50.1 *Where . . . ?* The question is rhetorical. The implied answer is that there is no bill of divorcement. Israel was never divorced, never sold to creditors, still the beloved of God although estranged from Him by sin.

50.2 *Is my hand shortened . . . ?* Israel had been taken captive, not because God was unable to deliver her, but because of her sins. Yet a sovereign God still could easily fulfil His promise of deliverance.

c. *Exhortation to trust the* LORD

50.10
Isa 49.2,3;
9.2;
Eph 5.8;
Isa 12.2

10 Who among you fears the LORD
    and obeys the voice of his servant,
who walks in darkness
    and has no light,
yet trusts in the name of the LORD
    and relies upon his God?

50.11
Ps 35.8;
Isa 65.13—
15

11 Behold, all you who kindle a fire,
    who set brands alight![n]
Walk by the light of your fire,
    and by the brands which you have kindled!
This shall you have from my hand:
    you shall lie down in torment.

3. *Encouragement to trust in God, not fearing man*

a. *God's mercy to Abraham bestowed on his descendants*

51.1
ver 7;
Ps 94.15

51 "Hearken to me, you who pursue deliverance,
        you who seek the LORD;
look to the rock from which you were hewn,
    and to the quarry from which you were digged.

51.2
Rom 4.16;
Heb 11.11,
12;
Gen 12.1;
24.35

2 Look to Abraham your father
    and to Sarah who bore you;
for when he was but one I called him,
    and I blessed him and made him many.

51.3
Isa 40.1;
52.9;
Joel 2.3;
Gen 13.10;
Isa 66.10

3 For the LORD will comfort Zion;
    he will comfort all her waste places,
and will make her wilderness like Eden,
    her desert like the garden of the LORD;
joy and gladness will be found in her,
    thanksgiving and the voice of song.

b. *Trust in the eternal Creator, not fearing man*

51.4
Ps 50.7;
Isa 2.3;
42.4,6

4 "Listen to me, my people,
    and give ear to me, my nation;
for a law will go forth from me,
    and my justice for a light to the peoples.

51.5
Isa 46.13;
40.10;
42.4; 63.5

5 My deliverance draws near speedily,
    my salvation has gone forth,
    and my arms will rule the peoples;
the coastlands wait for me,
    and for my arm they hope.

51.6
Isa 40.26;
Ps 102.26;
Mt 24.35;
2 Pet 3.10;
Isa 45.17

6 Lift up your eyes to the heavens,
    and look at the earth beneath;
for the heavens will vanish like smoke,
    the earth will wear out like a garment,
    and they who dwell in it will die like gnats;[o]
but my salvation will be for ever,
    and my deliverance will never be ended.

51.7
ver 1;
Ps 37.31;
Mt 5.11;
Acts 5.41

7 "Hearken to me, you who know righteousness,
    the people in whose heart is my law;
fear not the reproach of men,
    and be not dismayed at their revilings.

---

n Syr: Heb *gird yourselves with brands*   o Or *in like manner*

8 For the moth will eat them up like a garment,
    and the worm will eat them like wool;
but my deliverance will be for ever,
    and my salvation to all generations."

51.8
Isa 50.9;
ver 6

c. *Prayer that God will again deliver Israel*

9 Awake, awake, put on strength,
    O arm of the LORD;
awake, as in days of old,
    the generations of long ago.
Was it not thou that didst cut Rāhăb in pieces,
    that didst pierce the dragon?

51.9
Isa 52.1;
Deut 4.34;
Ps 89.10;
74.13;
Ezek 29.3

10 Was it not thou that didst dry up the sea,
    the waters of the great deep;
that didst make the depths of the sea a way
    for the redeemed to pass over?

51.10
Ex 14.21;
Isa 43.16;
63.9,16

11 And the ransomed of the LORD shall return,
    and come to Zion with singing;
everlasting joy shall be upon their heads;
    they shall obtain joy and gladness,
    and sorrow and sighing shall flee away.

51.11
Isa 35.10;
60.19;
Rev 7.17;
22.3

d. *The* LORD *the Maker will faithfully deliver His people*

12 "I, I am he that comforts you;
    who are you that you are afraid of man who dies,
    of the son of man who is made like grass,

51.12
ver 3;
2 Cor 1.3;
Ps 118.6;
Isa 40.6,7;
1 Pet 1.24

13 and have forgotten the LORD, your Maker,
    who stretched out the heavens
    and laid the foundations of the earth,
and fear continually all the day
    because of the fury of the oppressor,
when he sets himself to destroy?
    And where is the fury of the oppressor?

51.13
Isa 17.10;
Job 9.8;
Ps 104.2;
Isa 40.22;
7.4; 49.26

14 He who is bowed down shall speedily be released;
    he shall not die and go down to the Pit,
    neither shall his bread fail.

51.14
Isa 52.2;
38.18;
49.10

15 For I am the LORD your God,
    who stirs up the sea so that its waves roar—
    the LORD of hosts is his name.

51.15
Jer 31.35

16 And I have put my words in your mouth,
    and hid you in the shadow of my hand,
stretching out*p* the heavens
    and laying the foundations of the earth,
    and saying to Zion, 'You are my people.'"

51.16
Deut 18.18;
Isa 59.21;
49.2; 65.17

4. *Israel summoned to awaken and return*
a. *Her cup of wrath has been drunk*

17 Rouse yourself, rouse yourself,
    stand up, O Jerusalem,
you who have drunk at the hand of the LORD
    the cup of his wrath,
who have drunk to the dregs
    the bowl of staggering.

51.17
Isa 52.1;
Job 21.20;
Jer 25.15

18 There is none to guide her

51.18
Isa 59.21

p Syr: Heb *plant*

among all the sons she has borne;
there is none to take her by the hand
among all the sons she has brought up.

51.19
Isa 9.20

19 These two things have befallen you—
who will condole with you?—
devastation and destruction, famine and sword;
who will comfort you?*q*

51.20
Isa 5.25;
42.25;
66.15

20 Your sons have fainted,
they lie at the head of every street
like an antelope in a net;
they are full of the wrath of the LORD,
the rebuke of your God.

51.21
Isa 54.11;
29.9

21 Therefore hear this, you who are afflicted,
who are drunk, but not with wine:

51.22
Jer 50.34;
ver 17

22 Thus says your Lord, the LORD,
your God who pleads the cause of his people:
"Behold, I have taken from your hand
the cup of staggering;
the bowl of my wrath
you shall drink no more;

51.23
Jer 25.15–
17,26,28;
Zech 12.2;
Josh 10.24

23 and I will put it into the hand of your tormentors,
who have said to you,
'Bow down, that we may pass over';
and you have made your back like the ground
and like the street for them to pass over."

b. *God will restore Jerusalem for His own glory*

52.1
Isa 51.9,17;
Neh 11.1;
Mt 4.5;
Rev 21.2,27

52 Awake, awake,
put on your strength, O Zion;
put on your beautiful garments,
O Jerusalem, the holy city;
for there shall no more come into you
the uncircumcised and the unclean.

52.2
Isa 29.4;
9.4; 51.14

2 Shake yourself from the dust, arise,
O captive*r* Jerusalem;
loose the bonds from your neck,
O captive daughter of Zion.

52.3
Ps 44.12;
Isa 63.4;
45.13

3 For thus says the LORD: "You were sold for nothing, and you shall be redeemed without money. 4 For thus says the Lord GOD: My people went down at the first into Egypt to sojourn there, and the Assyrian oppressed them for nothing. 5 Now therefore what have I here, says the LORD, seeing that my people are taken away for nothing? Their rulers wail, says the LORD, and continually all the day my name is despised. 6 Therefore my people shall know my name; therefore in that day they shall know that it is I who speak; here am I."

52.4
Gen 46.6

52.5
Ezek 36.20;
Rom 2.24

52.6
Isa 49.23

c. *Exultant response of the captives*

52.7
Nah 1.15;
Rom 10.15;
Ps 93.1

7 How beautiful upon the mountains
are the feet of him who brings good tidings,
who publishes peace, who brings good tidings of good,
who publishes salvation,

---

q One ancient Ms Gk Syr Vg: Heb *how may I comfort you*   *r* Cn: Heb *sit*

who says to Zion, "Your God reigns."

8 Hark, your watchmen lift up their voice,
    together they sing for joy;
for eye to eye they see
    the return of the LORD to Zion.

52.8
Isa 62.6

9 Break forth together into singing,
    you waste places of Jerusalem;
for the LORD has comforted his people,
    he has redeemed Jerusalem.

52.9
Isa 44.23,
26; 48.20

10 The LORD has bared his holy arm
    before the eyes of all the nations;
and all the ends of the earth shall see
    the salvation of our God.

52.10
Ps 98.2,3;
Isa 45.22;
48.20;
Lk 3.6

11 Depart, depart, go out thence,
    touch no unclean thing;
go out from the midst of her, purify yourselves,
    you who bear the vessels of the LORD.

52.11
Jer 50.8;
2 Cor 6.17;
2 Tim 2.19;
Isa 1.16

12 For you shall not go out in haste,
    and you shall not go in flight,
for the LORD will go before you,
    and the God of Israel will be your rear guard.

52.12
Ex 12.33;
Isa 42.16;
58.8

5. The triumph of the servant through atoning death
a. His amazing exaltation through humiliation

13 Behold, my servant shall prosper,
    he shall be exalted and lifted up,
    and shall be very high.

52.13
Isa 42.1;
Phil 2.9

14 As many were astonished at him[s]—
    his appearance was so marred, beyond human semblance,
    and his form beyond that of the sons of men—

52.14
Ps 22.6,7;
Isa 53.2,3

15 so shall he startle[t] many nations;
    kings shall shut their mouths because of him;
for that which has not been told them they shall see,
    and that which they have not heard they shall understand.

52.15
Ezek 36.25;
Rom 15.21

b. The servant as seen by man: despised and rejected

53 Who has believed what we have heard?
    And to whom has the arm of the LORD been revealed?
2 For he grew up before him like a young plant,
    and like a root out of dry ground;
he had no form or comeliness that we should look at him,
    and no beauty that we should desire him.

53.1
Jn 12.38;
Rom 10.16
53.2
Isa 11.1;
52.14

3 He was despised and rejected[u] by men;
    a man of sorrows,[v] and acquainted with grief;[w]
and as one from whom men hide their faces
    he was despised, and we esteemed him not.

53.3
Ps 22.6;
ver 10;
Jn 1.10,11

c. The servant as seen by God: the Redeemer

4 Surely he has borne our griefs[x]
    and carried our sorrows;[y]
yet we esteemed him stricken,
    smitten by God, and afflicted.

53.4
Mt 8.17;
Heb 9.28;
1 Pet 2.24

---

s Syr Tg: Heb you   t The meaning of the Hebrew word is uncertain
u Or forsaken   v Or pains   w Or sickness   x Or sicknesses   y Or pains

*53.5
Rom 4.25;
1 Cor 15.3;
1 Pet 2.24

5 But he was wounded for our transgressions,
    he was bruised for our iniquities;
upon him was the chastisement that made us whole,
    and with his stripes we are healed.

*53.6
ver 11

6 All we like sheep have gone astray;
    we have turned every one to his own way;
and the LORD has laid on him
    the iniquity of us all.

d. *His death as seen by man: tragic failure*

53.7
Mt 26.63;
Acts 8.32

7 He was oppressed, and he was afflicted,
    yet he opened not his mouth;
like a lamb that is led to the slaughter,
    and like a sheep that before its shearers is dumb,
so he opened not his mouth.

*53.8
ver 5,12

8 By oppression and judgment he was taken away;
    and as for his generation, who considered
that he was cut off out of the land of the living,
    stricken for the trangression of my people?

53.9
Mt 27.57;
1 Pet 2.22

9 And they made his grave with the wicked
    and with a rich man in his death,
although he had done no violence,
    and there was no deceit in his mouth.

e. *His death as seen by God: glorious success*

53.10
ver 3–6;
Isa 54.3;
46.10

10 Yet it was the will of the LORD to bruise him;
    he has put him to grief;^z
when he makes himself^a an offering for sin,
    he shall see his offspring, he shall prolong his days;
the will of the LORD shall prosper in his hand;

53.11
Jn 10.14–
18;
Rom 5.18,
19;
ver 5,6

11 he shall see the fruit of the travail of his soul and be satisfied;
by his knowledge shall the righteous one, my servant,
    make many to be accounted righteous;
    and he shall bear their iniquities.

53.12
Isa 52.13;
Mt 26.38,
39,42;
Lk 22.37;
2 Cor 5.21

12 Therefore I will divide him a portion with the great,
    and he shall divide the spoil with the strong;
because he poured out his soul to death,
    and was numbered with the transgressors;
yet he bore the sin of many,
    and made intercession for the transgressors.

^z Heb *made him sick*   ^a Vg: Heb *thou makest his soul*

53.5 See note to 1 Pet 2.24 on substitution. Verses 5 and 6 support the New Testament doctrine that Christ died in the place and stead of sinners.

53.6 Men, like sheep, do go astray and are ready to follow any evil example. As lost sheep cannot find their way home, so sinners cannot find the right way. The Good Shepherd saves the sheep, i.e., lost sinners.

53.8 The manner of Christ's death is here foretold (i.e., by a judicial murder). Other aspects of that death which are taught by Scripture are: (1) that it was necessary for our redemption (Acts 17.3; Lk 24.46); (2) that it was ordained of God (Acts 2.23); (3) that it was a voluntary act on Christ's part (Mt 26.53; Jn 10.17, 18); (4) that His death was acceptable to God as a true and saving sacrifice (Eph 5.2; 1 Thess 5.10). His death itself was a literal fulfilment of many prophetic Scriptures. Among them are: (1) He should be crucified so that His hands and feet would be pierced (Ps 22.14–17; Zech 12.10 and 13.6); (2) He should be offered gall and vinegar (Ps 69.21); (3) He should be crucified with malefactors (53.9, 12); (4) not a bone of His body should be broken (Ps 34.20); (5) they should cast lots for His garments (Ps 22.18); (6) He should be buried with a rich man (53.9).

6. Israel's blessing through the servant
a. Captive Israel multiplied and enlarged

54 "Sing, O barren one, who did not bear;
    break forth into singing and cry aloud,
you who have not been in travail!
For the children of the desolate one will be more
    than the children of her that is married, says the LORD.

2 Enlarge the place of your tent,
    and let the curtains of your habitations be stretched out;
hold not back, lengthen your cords
    and strengthen your stakes.

3 For you will spread abroad to the right and to the left,
    and your descendants will possess the nations
    and will people the desolate cities.

b. The LORD's exiled wife restored

4 "Fear not, for you will not be ashamed;
    be not confounded, for you will not be put to shame;
for you will forget the shame of your youth,
    and the reproach of your widowhood you will remember no
    more.

5 For your Maker is your husband,
    the LORD of hosts is his name;
and the Holy One of Israel is your Redeemer,
    the God of the whole earth he is called.

6 For the LORD has called you
    like a wife forsaken and grieved in spirit,
like a wife of youth when she is cast off,
    says your God.

7 For a brief moment I forsook you,
    but with great compassion I will gather you.

8 In overflowing wrath for a moment
    I hid my face from you,
but with everlasting love I will have compassion on you,
    says the LORD, your Redeemer.

c. Promise of God's unchanging favor

9 "For this is like the days of Noah to me:
    as I swore that the waters of Noah
    should no more go over the earth,
so I have sworn that I will not be angry with you
    and will not rebuke you.

10 For the mountains may depart
    and the hills be removed,
but my steadfast love shall not depart from you,
    and my covenant of peace shall not be removed,
    says the LORD, who has compassion on you.

d. Future radiance of the new Jerusalem

11 "O afflicted one, storm-tossed, and not comforted,
    behold, I will set your stones in antimony,
    and lay your foundations with sapphires.[b]

12 I will make your pinnacles of agate,
    your gates of carbuncles,

Cross-references:
54.1 Gal 4.27; 1 Sam 2.5; Isa 62.4
54.2 Isa 49.19,20
54.3 Isa 43.5,6; 49.19,23
54.4 Isa 45.17; Jer 31.19; Isa 4.1; 25.8
54.5 Jer 3.14; Isa 43.14; 48.17; 6.3
54.6 Isa 62.4
54.7 Isa 26.20; 43.5
54.8 Isa 60.10; ver 10; Isa 49.10,13; ver 5
54.9 Gen 9.11; Isa 12.1
54.10 Isa 51.6; Ps 89.33,34; ver 8
54.11 1 Chr 29.2; Rev 21.18

b Or lapis lazuli

and all your wall of precious stones.

54.13
Jer 31.34;
Jn 6.45;
Ps 119.165

13 All your sons shall be taught by the LORD,
and great shall be the prosperity of your sons.

54.14
Isa 62.1;
9.4; 14.4;
ver 4

14 In righteousness you shall be established;
you shall be far from oppression, for you shall not fear;
and from terror, for it shall not come near you.

54.15
Isa 41.11–
16

15 If any one stirs up strife,
it is not from me;
whoever stirs up strife with you
shall fall because of you.

16 Behold, I have created the smith
who blows the fire of coals,
and produces a weapon for its purpose.
I have also created the ravager to destroy;

54.17
Isa 29.8;
50.8,9;
45.24

17 no weapon that is fashioned against you shall prosper,
and you shall confute every tongue that rises against you in judgment.
This is the heritage of the servants of the LORD
and their vindication from me, says the LORD."

7. *Grace for trusting sinners*
a. *The repentant to be blessed*

55.1
Isa 41.17;
Jn 4.14;
7.37;
Mt 13.44;
Rev 3.18

55 "Ho, every one who thirsts,
come to the waters;
and he who has no money,
come, buy and eat!
Come, buy wine and milk
without money and without price.

55.2
Hos 8.7;
Isa 62.8,9;
25.6

2 Why do you spend your money for that which is not bread,
and your labor for that which does not satisfy?
Hearken diligently to me, and eat what is good,
and delight yourselves in fatness.

55.3
Isa 51.4;
Rom 10.5;
Isa 61.8;
Acts 13.34

3 Incline your ear, and come to me;
hear, that your soul may live;
and I will make with you an everlasting covenant,
my steadfast, sure love for David.

55.4
Jer 30.9;
Ezek 34.23,
24;
Dan 9.25

4 Behold, I made him a witness to the peoples,
a leader and commander for the peoples.

55.5
Isa 49.6,12,
23;
Zech 8.22;
Isa 60.9

5 Behold, you shall call nations that you know not,
and nations that knew you not shall run to you,
because of the LORD your God, and of the Holy One of Israel,
for he has glorified you.

b. *Repentant sinners commanded to seek the LORD*

55.6
Ps 32.6;
Isa 49.8;
2 Cor 6.1,2

6 "Seek the LORD while he may be found,
call upon him while he is near;

★55.7
Isa 1.16;
59.7; 31.6;
54.8,10;
44.22

7 let the wicked forsake his way,

55.7 A pardon is an official warrant of remission of penalty. God alone can grant a pardon, although the assurance of such pardon may be communicated to men by God's agents. Several conditions inhere when a pardon is granted: (1) the person to whom the pardon is granted is acknowledgedly guilty of transgression (Ps 51.3, 4; Lk 15.18; 18.13); (2) the guilty transgressor must forsake his wickedness, i.e., repent (Acts 3.19; 17.30); (3) the guilty transgressor must turn to God who alone can grant pardon (1 Thess 1.9; Isa 55.6; Acts 26.20); (4) God's mercy is available in a pardon when the guilty transgressor repents and turns to God (55.7; Lk 24.47; Jer 33.3, 8).

and the unrighteous man his thoughts;
let him return to the LORD, that he may have mercy on him,
    and to our God, for he will abundantly pardon.
8 For my thoughts are not your thoughts,
    neither are your ways my ways, says the LORD.
9 For as the heavens are higher than the earth,
    so are my ways higher than your ways   **55.9**
    and my thoughts than your thoughts.   Ps 103.11

c. *The efficacy of God's word*

10 "For as the rain and the snow come down from heaven,   **55.10**
    and return not thither but water the earth,   Isa 30.23;
making it bring forth and sprout,   2 Cor 9.10
    giving seed to the sower and bread to the eater,
11 so shall my word be that goes forth from my mouth;   **55.11**
    it shall not return to me empty,   Isa 45.23;
but it shall accomplish that which I purpose,   59.21;
    and prosper in the thing for which I sent it.   46.10

d. *The joyous return of the redeemed*

12 "For you shall go out in joy,   **55.12**
    and be led forth in peace;   Isa 51.11;
the mountains and the hills before you   54.10,13;
    shall break forth into singing,   44.23;
    and all the trees of the field shall clap their hands. 1 Chr 16.33
13 Instead of the thorn shall come up the cypress;   **55.13**
    instead of the brier shall come up the myrtle;   Isa 41.19;
and it shall be to the LORD for a memorial,   32.13;
    for an everlasting sign which shall not be cut off."   63.12,14;
                                                           19.20

8. *Gentiles included in Israel's blessing*
a. *Admonition to maintain a godly witness*

56 Thus says the LORD:
    "Keep justice, and do righteousness,   **56.1**
for soon my salvation will come,   Isa 61.8;
    and my deliverance be revealed.   46.13
2 Blessed is the man who does this,   **56.2**
    and the son of man who holds it fast,   Isa 58.13
who keeps the sabbath, not profaning it,
    and keeps his hand from doing any evil."

b. *Promised blessing to childless believers*

3 Let not the foreigner who has joined himself to the LORD say,   **56.3**
    "The LORD will surely separate me from his people";   ver 6;
and let not the eunuch say,   Acts 8.27
    "Behold, I am a dry tree."
4 For thus says the LORD: **56.4**
"To the eunuchs who keep my sabbaths,   ver 2,6
    who choose the things that please me
    and hold fast my covenant,
5 I will give in my house and within my walls   **56.5**
    a monument and a name   ver 7;
    better than sons and daughters;   Isa 66.20;
I will give them an everlasting name   26.1; 62.2;
    which shall not be cut off.   48.19

c. *Believing Gentiles included in God's covenant people*

56.6
Isa 60.10;
61.5;
ver 2,4

6 "And the foreigners who join themselves to the LORD,
   to minister to him, to love the name of the LORD,
   and to be his servants,
every one who keeps the sabbath, and does not profane it,
   and holds fast my covenant—

*56.7
Isa 11.9;
65.25;
Rom 12.1;
Heb 13.15;
Mt 21.13;
Mk 11.17;
Lk 19.46

7 these I will bring to my holy mountain,
   and make them joyful in my house of prayer;
their burnt offerings and their sacrifices
   will be accepted on my altar;
for my house shall be called a house of prayer
   for all peoples.

56.8
Isa 11.12;
60.3–11;
Jn 10.16

8 Thus says the Lord GOD,
   who gathers the outcasts of Israel,
I will gather yet others to him
   besides those already gathered."[c]

9. *Condemnation of the wicked rulers of Israel*
a. *Israel's wicked prophets*

56.9
Jer 12.9

9 All you beasts of the field, come to devour—
   all you beasts in the forest.

56.10
Isa 29.9–
14;
Nah 3.18

10 His watchmen are blind,
   they are all without knowledge;
they are all dumb dogs,
   they cannot bark;
dreaming, lying down,
   loving to slumber.

11 The dogs have a mighty appetite;
   they never have enough.
The shepherds also have no understanding;
   they have all turned to their own way,
   each to his own gain, one and all.

12 "Come," they say, "let us[d] get wine,
   let us fill ourselves with strong drink;
and tomorrow will be like this day,
   great beyond measure."

b. *Heavenly reward of persecuted believers*

57.1
Ps 12.1;
Isa 42.25;
47.7,11

57 The righteous man perishes,
   and no one lays it to heart;
devout men are taken away,
   while no one understands.
For the righteous man is taken away from calamity,

57.2
Isa 26.7

2   he enters into peace;
they rest in their beds
   who walk in their uprightness.

c. *The wicked Jews sacrifice their children to idols*

57.3
Mt 16.4;
Isa 1.21

3 But you, draw near hither,
   sons of the sorceress,

c Heb *his gathered ones*   *d* One ancient Ms Syr Vg Tg: Heb *me*

56.7 Private and family prayers do not exhaust our responsibility to God. Public prayer is also required of believers. We are exhorted so to pray (Heb 10.25) and God promises to hear and to answer this kind of prayer (2 Chr 7.14, 16; Mt 18.19). Scripture abounds in examples of godly people who engaged in public prayer.

offspring of the adulterer and the harlot.

4 Of whom are you making sport?
  Against whom do you open your mouth wide
  and put out your tongue?
Are you not children of transgression,
  the offspring of deceit,
5 you who burn with lust among the oaks,
  under every green tree;
who slay your children in the valleys,
  under the clefts of the rocks?
6 Among the smooth stones of the valley is your portion;
  they, they, are your lot;
to them you have poured out a drink offering,
  you have brought a cereal offering.
  Shall I be appeased for these things?

d. *Idolatrous worship on the "high places"*

7 Upon a high and lofty mountain
  you have set your bed,
  and thither you went up to offer sacrifice.
8 Behind the door and the doorpost
  you have set up your symbol;
for, deserting me, you have uncovered your bed,
  you have gone up to it,
  you have made it wide;
and you have made a bargain for yourself with them,
  you have loved their bed,
  you have looked on nakedness.^e
9 You journeyed to Mōlĕch^f with oil
  and multiplied your perfumes;
you sent your envoys far off,
  and sent down even to Shĕōl.
10 You were wearied with the length of your way,
  but you did not say, "It is hopeless";
you found new life for your strength,
  and so you were not faint.

e. *Idols are helpless to deliver*

11 Whom did you dread and fear,
  so that you lied,
and did not remember me,
  did not give me a thought?
Have I not held my peace, even for a long time,
  and so you do not fear me?
12 I will tell of your righteousness and your doings,
  but they will not help you.
13 When you cry out, let your collection of idols deliver you!
  The wind will carry them off,
  a breath will take them away.
But he who takes refuge in me shall possess the land,
  and shall inherit my holy mountain.

f. *Compassion for the repentant, but no peace for the wicked*

14 And it shall be said,

57.4	Isa 48.8
57.5	2 Ki 16.4; Lev 18.21; 2 Ki 16.3; Jer 7.31
57.6	Jer 3.9; 7.18; 5.9,29
57.7	Ezek 16.16; 23.41
57.8	Ezek 23.7, 18; 16.26,28
57.9	Ezek 23.16, 40
57.10	Isa 47.13; Jer 2.25
57.11	Isa 51.12; Jer 2.32; ver 1; Ps 50.21
57.13	Jer 22.20; Isa 25.4; 60.21; 65.9
57.14	Isa 62.10; Jer 18.15

---

^e The meaning of the Hebrew is uncertain. ^f Or *the king*

"Build up, build up, prepare the way,
    remove every obstruction from my people's way."

57.15
Isa 52.13;
40.28;66.1;
Ps 34.18;
51.17;
14.2,3;
Isa 61.1

15 For thus says the high and lofty One
    who inhabits eternity, whose name is Holy:
"I dwell in the high and holy place,
    and also with him who is of a contrite and humble spirit,
to revive the spirit of the humble,
    and to revive the heart of the contrite.

57.16
Gen 6.3;
Ps 85.5;
103.9;
Mic 7.18;
Job 34.14;
Isa 42.5

16 For I will not contend for ever,
    nor will I always be angry;
for from me proceeds the spirit,
    and I have made the breath of life.

57.17
Jer 6.13;
Isa 1.4

17 Because of the iniquity of his covetousness I was angry,
    I smote him, I hid my face and was angry;
    but he went on backsliding in the way of his own heart.

57.18
Isa 53.5;
52.12;
61.1–3

18 I have seen his ways, but I will heal him;
    I will lead him and requite him with comfort,
    creating for his mourners the fruit of the lips.

57.19
Heb 13.15;
Acts 2.39;
Eph 2.17

19 Peace, peace, to the far and to the near, says the LORD;
    and I will heal him.

57.20
Job 18.5–14

20 But the wicked are like the tossing sea;
    for it cannot rest,
    and its waters toss up mire and dirt.

57.21
Isa 48.22

21 There is no peace, says my God, for the wicked."

C. Part III: the program of peace

1. Contrast between true and false worship
a. Right and wrong fasting

58.1
Isa 48.8;
50.1;59.12

58 "Cry aloud, spare not,
    lift up your voice like a trumpet;
declare to my people their transgression,
    to the house of Jacob their sins.

58.2
Isa 1.11;
48.1;59.13;
29.13

2 Yet they seek me daily,
    and delight to know my ways,
as if they were a nation that did righteousness
    and did not forsake the ordinance of their God;
they ask of me righteous judgments,
    they delight to draw near to God.

58.3
Mal 3.14;
Isa 22.12,13

3 'Why have we fasted, and thou seest it not?
    Why have we humbled ourselves, and thou takest no
        knowledge of it?'
Behold, in the day of your fast you seek your own pleasure,[g]
    and oppress all your workers.

58.4
1 Ki 21.9,
12,13;
Isa 59.2

4 Behold, you fast only to quarrel and to fight
    and to hit with wicked fist.
Fasting like yours this day
    will not make your voice to be heard on high.

58.5
Zech 7.5;
Est 4.3;
Job 2.8

5 Is such the fast that I choose,
    a day for a man to humble himself?
Is it to bow down his head like a rush,
    and to spread sackcloth and ashes under him?
Will you call this a fast,
    and a day acceptable to the LORD?

g Or pursue your own business

6 "Is not this the fast that I choose:
    to loose the bonds of wickedness,
    to undo the thongs of the yoke,
to let the oppressed go free,
    and to break every yoke?

7 Is it not to share your bread with the hungry,
    and bring the homeless poor into your house;
when you see the naked, to cover him,
    and not to hide yourself from your own flesh?

b. Protection and blessing for the righteous

8 Then shall your light break forth like the dawn,
    and your healing shall spring up speedily;
your righteousness shall go before you,
    the glory of the LORD shall be your rear guard.

9 Then you shall call, and the LORD will answer;
    you shall cry, and he will say, Here I am.

"If you take away from the midst of you the yoke,
    the pointing of the finger, and speaking wickedness,

10 if you pour yourself out for the hungry
    and satisfy the desire of the afflicted,
then shall your light rise in the darkness
    and your gloom be as the noonday.

11 And the LORD will guide you continually,
    and satisfy your desire with good things,[h]
    and make your bones strong;
and you shall be like a watered garden,
    like a spring of water,
    whose waters fail not.

12 And your ancient ruins shall be rebuilt;
    you shall raise up the foundations of many generations;
you shall be called the repairer of the breach,
    the restorer of streets to dwell in.

c. The reward for keeping the Sabbath

13 "If you turn back your foot from the sabbath,
    from doing your pleasure[i] on my holy day,
and call the sabbath a delight
    and the holy day of the LORD honorable;
if you honor it, not going your own ways,
    or seeking your own pleasure,[j] or talking idly;

14 then you shall take delight in the LORD,
    and I will make you ride upon the heights of the earth;
I will feed you with the heritage of Jacob your father,
    for the mouth of the LORD has spoken."

Cross references (right margin):

58.6 Neh 5.10–12; Jer 34.9
58.7 Ezek 18.7, 16; Mt 25.35; Job 31.19; Gen 29.14; Neh 5.5
58.8 ver 10; Isa 30.26; 62.1; Ex 14.19; Isa 52.12
58.9 Isa 55.6; ver 6; Ps 12.2
58.10 ver 7; Ps 37.6
58.11 Isa 49.10; 41.17; 66.14; Jn 4.14; 7.38
58.12 Isa 49.8; 44.28; 30.13; Amos 9.11
*58.13 Isa 56.2; Ps 84.2,10; Isa 55.8; 59.13
58.14 Isa 61.10; Deut 32.13; Isa 1.19,20

---

h The meaning of the Hebrew word is uncertain   i Or business
i Or pursuing your own business

58.13 Mt 28.1 talks about the Christian Sabbath. The principle of the Sabbath is to set a day apart in a special way for God's service and fellowship, rather than to use it for personal recreation and pleasure. There is no reason to suppose that the same blessings promised for faithful adherence to the Old Testament Sabbath will not be accorded to those who faithfully and regularly gather to worship him in divine services and in private devotions. Historically, profanation of the Lord's Day leads to spiritual decline and withdrawal of God's blessing. (See Neh 13.17, 18.)

2. Confessing national wickedness, Israel is rescued by God's grace
a. Iniquity keeps Israel from God's deliverance

59 Behold, the LORD's hand is not shortened, that it cannot save,
or his ear dull, that it cannot hear;

2 but your iniquities have made a separation
between you and your God,
and your sins have hid his face from you
so that he does not hear.

3 For your hands are defiled with blood
and your fingers with iniquity;
your lips have spoken lies,
your tongue mutters wickedness.

4 No one enters suit justly,
no one goes to law honestly;
they rely on empty pleas, they speak lies,
they conceive mischief and bring forth iniquity.

5 They hatch adders' eggs,
they weave the spider's web;
he who eats their eggs dies,
and from one which is crushed a viper is hatched.

6 Their webs will not serve as clothing;
men will not cover themselves with what they make.
Their works are works of iniquity,
and deeds of violence are in their hands.

7 Their feet run to evil,
and they make haste to shed innocent blood;
their thoughts are thoughts of iniquity,
desolation and destruction are in their highways.

8 The way of peace they know not,
and there is no justice in their paths;
they have made their roads crooked,
no one who goes in them knows peace.

b. Israel's confession of sins

9 Therefore justice is far from us,
and righteousness does not overtake us;
we look for light, and behold, darkness,
and for brightness, but we walk in gloom.

10 We grope for the wall like the blind,
we grope like those who have no eyes;
we stumble at noon as in the twilight,
among those in full vigor we are like dead men.

11 We all growl like bears,
we moan and moan like doves;
we look for justice, but there is none;
for salvation, but it is far from us.

12 For our transgressions are multiplied before thee,
and our sins testify against us;
for our transgressions are with us,
and we know our iniquities:

13 transgressing, and denying the LORD,
and turning away from following our God,
speaking oppression and revolt,
conceiving and uttering from the heart lying words.

Cross references (margin):

59.1 — Num 11.23; Isa 50.2; 58.9

59.2 — Isa 1.15; 58.4

59.3 — Isa 1.15; Jer 2.30; ver 13; Isa 28.15

59.4 — ver 14,15; Isa 30.12; Job 15.35; Ps 7.14

59.5 — Isa 14.29; Job 8.14

59.6 — Isa 28.20; 57.12; 58.4

59.7 — Rom 3.15–17; Isa 65.2

59.8 — ver 9,11; Ps 125.5; ver 14

59.9 — ver 14; Isa 5.30; 8.21,22

59.10 — Deut 28.29; Job 5.14; Amos 8.9; Isa 8.14,15

59.11 — Isa 38.14; Ezek 7.16; ver 9,14

59.12 — Isa 58.1; Jer 14.7

59.13 — Josh 24.27; Tit 1.16; Isa 30.12; ver 3,4

¹⁴ Justice is turned back,
     and righteousness stands afar off;
for truth has fallen in the public squares,
     and uprightness cannot enter.

¹⁵ Truth is lacking,
     and he who departs from evil makes himself a prey.

> 59.14
> Isa 1.21;
> 46.12; 48.1

> 59.15
> Isa 5.23;
> 1.21–23

c. *God intervenes to redeem Zion*

The LORD saw it, and it displeased him
     that there was no justice.
¹⁶ He saw that there was no man,
     and wondered that there was no one to intervene;
then his own arm brought him victory,
     and his righteousness upheld him.

> 59.16
> Isa 63.5;
> Ezek 22.30;
> Ps 98.1

¹⁷ He put on righteousness as a breastplate,
     and a helmet of salvation upon his head;
he put on garments of vengeance for clothing,
     and wrapped himself in fury as a mantle.

> 59.17
> Eph 6.14;
> 1 Thess 5.8;
> Isa 63.2,3

¹⁸ According to their deeds, so will he repay,
     wrath to his adversaries, requital to his enemies;
     to the coastlands he will render requital.

> 59.18
> Isa 65.6,7;
> 66.6

¹⁹ So they shall fear the name of the LORD from the west,
     and his glory from the rising of the sun;
for he will come like a rushing stream,
     which the wind of the LORD drives.

> 59.19
> Ps 113.3;
> Isa 66.12

²⁰ "And he will come to Zion as Redeemer,
     to those in Jacob who turn from transgression, says the LORD.
²¹ "And as for me, this is my covenant with them, says the LORD:
my spirit which is upon you, and my words which I have put in
your mouth, shall not depart out of your mouth, or out of the
mouth of your children, or out of the mouth of your children's
children, says the LORD, from this time forth and for evermore."

> 59.20
> Rom 11.26,
> 27;
> Ezek 18.30,
> 31;
> Acts 2.38,39
> 59.21
> Jer 31.31–
> 34;
> Isa 44.3,26;
> 54.10;
> Jer 32.40

3. *The future glory of Zion*
a. *The dawn of Zion's glory*

60 Arise, shine; for your light has come,
     and the glory of the LORD has risen upon you.
² For behold, darkness shall cover the earth,
     and thick darkness the peoples;
but the LORD will arise upon you,
     and his glory will be seen upon you.

> 60.1
> Eph 5.14;
> Mal 4.2
> 60.2
> Col 1.13;
> Isa 4.5

³ And nations shall come to your light,
     and kings to the brightness of your rising.

> 60.3
> Isa 49.6,23;
> ver 11

b. *Converted Gentiles to adore Israel's God*

⁴ Lift up your eyes round about, and see;
     they all gather together, they come to you;
your sons shall come from far,
     and your daughters shall be carried in the arms.

> 60.4
> Isa 49.18,
> 20–22

⁵ Then you shall see and be radiant,
     your heart shall thrill and rejoice;^k
because the abundance of the sea shall be turned to you,
     the wealth of the nations shall come to you.

> 60.5
> Ps 34.5;
> Isa 23.18;
> 24.14; 61.6

---

k Heb *be enlarged*

60.6
Gen 25.4;
Ps 72.10;
Isa 43.23;
42.10

6 A multitude of camels shall cover you,
   the young camels of Mĭd'ĭän and Ēphåh;
   all those from Shēbá shall come.
   They shall bring gold and frankincense,
   and shall proclaim the praise of the LORD.

*60.7
Gen 25.13;
Isa 56.7;
Hag 2.7,9

7 All the flocks of Kēdar shall be gathered to you,
   the rams of Nēbāi'óth shall minister to you;
   they shall come up with acceptance on my altar,
   and I will glorify my glorious house.

8 Who are these that fly like a cloud,
   and like doves to their windows?

60.9
Isa 66.19;
2.16;
49.22; 55.5

9 For the coastlands shall wait for me,
   the ships of Tarshish first,
   to bring your sons from far,
   their silver and gold with them,
   for the name of the LORD your God,
   and for the Holy One of Israel,
   because he has glorified you.

c. *Millennial peace and supremacy of God's people*

60.10
Zech 6.15;
Isa 49.23;
54.8

10 Foreigners shall build up your walls,
   and their kings shall minister to you;
   for in my wrath I smote you,
   but in my favor I have had mercy on you.

60.11
ver 18,5;
Ps 149.8

11 Your gates shall be open continually;
   day and night they shall not be shut;
   that men may bring to you the wealth of the nations,
   with their kings led in procession.

60.12
Zech 14.17

12 For the nation and kingdom
   that will not serve you shall perish;
   those nations shall be utterly laid waste.

60.13
Isa 35.2;
41.19;
1 Chr 28.2;
Ps 132.7

13 The glory of Lebanon shall come to you,
   the cypress, the plane, and the pine,
   to beautify the place of my sanctuary;
   and I will make the place of my feet glorious.

60.14
Isa 49.23;
Heb 12.22;
Rev 3.9

14 The sons of those who oppressed you
   shall come bending low to you;
   and all who despised you
   shall bow down at your feet;
   they shall call you the City of the LORD,
   the Zion of the Holy One of Israel.

d. *Prosperity and peace of the Messianic kingdom*

*60.15
Jer 30.17;
Isa 66.5;
33.8,9;
65.18

15 Whereas you have been forsaken and hated,
   with no one passing through,
   I will make you majestic for ever,
   a joy from age to age.

60.16
Isa 49.23;
66.11;
63.8,16

16 You shall suck the milk of nations,
   you shall suck the breast of kings;
   and you shall know that I, the LORD, am your Savior
   and your Redeemer, the Mighty One of Jacob.

60.7 *Kedar ... Nebaioth,* tribes of nomadic
Ishmaelites.

60.15 The persecution and hatred of the
Jews, still God's people, at last shall cease.

17 Instead of bronze I will bring gold,
      and instead of iron I will bring silver;
   instead of wood, bronze,
      instead of stones, iron.
   I will make your overseers peace
      and your taskmasters righteousness.
18 Violence shall no more be heard in your land,   **60.18**
      devastation or destruction within your borders;   Isa 54.14;
   you shall call your walls Salvation,   51.19;26.1;
      and your gates Praise.   ver 11

19 The sun shall be no more   **60.19**
      your light by day,   Rev 21.23;
   nor for brightness shall the moon   22.5;
      give light to you by night;[1]   Isa 9.2;
                                                          Zech 2.5
   but the LORD will be your everlasting light,
      and your God will be your glory.
20 Your sun shall no more go down,   **60.20**
      nor your moon withdraw itself;   Isa 30.26;
   for the LORD will be your everlasting light,   65.19
      and your days of mourning shall be ended.
21 Your people shall all be righteous;   **60.21**
      they shall possess the land for ever,   Isa 52.1;
   the shoot of my planting, the work of my hands,   Ps 37.11,22;
      that I might be glorified.   Isa 29.23;
                                                          45.11
22 The least one shall become a clan,   **60.22**
      and the smallest one a mighty nation;   Isa 51.2
   I am the LORD;
      in its time I will hasten it.

4. *Good tidings of salvation*

a. *The commission to preach the good tidings*

61   The Spirit of the Lord GOD is upon me,   ***61.1f**
        because the LORD has anointed me   Isa 11.2;
     to bring good tidings to the afflicted;[m]   Lk 4.18;
        he has sent me to bind up the brokenhearted,   Ps 45.7;
     to proclaim liberty to the captives,   Isa 57.15;
        and the opening of the prison[n] to those who are bound;   42.7
 2 to proclaim the year of the LORD's favor,   **61.2**
      and the day of vengeance of our God;   Isa 49.8;
   to comfort all who mourn;   34.8;57.18;
                                                          Mt 5.4
 3 to grant to those who mourn in Zion—   **61.3**
      to give them a garland instead of ashes,   Isa 60.20;
   the oil of gladness instead of mourning,   Ps 45.7;
      the mantle of praise instead of a faint spirit;   Isa 60.21

[1] One ancient Ms Gk Old Latin Tg: Heb lacks *by night*
[m] Or *poor*
[n] Or *the opening of the eyes*: Heb *the opening*

61.1, 2 This Scripture is quoted by Jesus Christ and applied to Himself (Lk 4.18, 19). It must have been for a definite reason that He stopped in the middle of verse 2. He ended with: *to proclaim the . . . year of the Lord* as designating the age of grace which would continue until His coming again. With His Second Advent *the day of vengeance of our God* (ver 2) is to take place. Christ stated that the very day He quoted this Scripture was the day it was fulfilled in their hearing. The remainder of it will be fully and inexorably fulfilled when He returns to earth the second time.

that they may be called oaks of righteousness,
    the planting of the LORD, that he may be glorified.

b. *Exaltation of Zion in the final age*

61.4
Isa 49.8;
Ezek 36.33

4 They shall build up the ancient ruins,
    they shall raise up the former devastations;
they shall repair the ruined cities,
    the devastations of many generations.

61.5
Isa 60.10

5 Aliens shall stand and feed your flocks,
    foreigners shall be your plowmen and vinedressers;

61.6
Isa 66.21;
60.5,11

6 but you shall be called the priests of the LORD,
    men shall speak of you as the ministers of our God;
you shall eat the wealth of the nations,
    and in their riches you shall glory.

61.7
Isa 54.4;
40.2;
Zech 9.12;
Isa 60.15;
Ps 16.11

7 Instead of your shame you shall have a double portion,
    instead of dishonor you*o* shall rejoice in your*p* lot;
therefore in your*p* land you*o* shall possess a double portion;
    yours*q* shall be everlasting joy.

61.8
Isa 30.18;
55.3

8 For I the LORD love justice,
    I hate robbery and wrong;*r*
I will faithfully give them their recompense,
    and I will make an everlasting covenant with them.

61.9
Isa 54.3;
44.3

9 Their descendants shall be known among the nations,
    and their offspring in the midst of the peoples;
all who see them shall acknowledge them,
    that they are a people whom the LORD has blessed.

c. *Song of praise for God's redemptive love*

61.10
Isa 12.1,2;
49.4,18;
Rev 21.2

10 I will greatly rejoice in the LORD,
    my soul shall exult in my God;
for he has clothed me with the garments of salvation,
    he has covered me with the robe of righteousness,
as a bridegroom decks himself with a garland,
    and as a bride adorns herself with her jewels.

61.11
Isa 55.10;
45.23,24;
Ps 72.3;
85.11;
Isa 60.18

11 For as the earth brings forth its shoots,
    and as a garden causes what is sown in it to spring up,
so the Lord GOD will cause righteousness and praise
    to spring forth before all the nations.

5. *Zion restored and glorified*
a. *God's promise to honor Israel as a wife*

62.1
Isa 61.11;
52.10

62 For Zion's sake I will not keep silent,
    and for Jerusalem's sake I will not rest,
until her vindication goes forth as brightness,
    and her salvation as a burning torch.

62.2
Isa 60.3;
ver 4,12;
Isa 65.15

2 The nations shall see your vindication,
    and all the kings your glory;
and you shall be called by a new name
    which the mouth of the LORD will give.

62.3
Zech 9.16

3 You shall be a crown of beauty in the hand of the LORD,
    and a royal diadem in the hand of your God.

62.4
Hos 1.10;
Isa 54.6,7;
Jer 32.41;
3.14

4 You shall no more be termed Forsaken,*s*

---

o Heb they   p Heb their   q Heb theirs   r Or robbery with a burnt offering   s Heb Azu'băh

and your land shall no more be termed Desolate;[t]
but you shall be called My delight is in her,[u]
and your land Married;[v]
for the LORD delights in you,
and your land shall be married.

5 For as a young man marries a virgin,
so shall your sons marry you,
and as the bridegroom rejoices over the bride,
so shall your God rejoice over you.

> **62.5**
> Isa 65.19

b. *Zion to have rest without fear*

6 Upon your walls, O Jerusalem,
I have set watchmen;
all the day and all the night
they shall never be silent.
You who put the LORD in remembrance,
take no rest,

> **62.6**
> Isa 52.8;
> Jer 6.17;
> Ezek 3.17;
> Ps 74.2

7 and give him no rest
until he establishes Jerusalem
and makes it a praise in the earth.

> **62.7**
> Mt 15.21–
> 28;
> Lk 18.1–8;
> Jer 33.9

8 The LORD has sworn by his right hand
and by his mighty arm:
"I will not again give your grain
to be food for your enemies,
and foreigners shall not drink your wine
for which you have labored;

> **62.8**
> Isa 45.23;
> Deut 28.31,
> 33;
> Jer 5.17

9 but those who garner it shall eat it
and praise the LORD,
and those who gather it shall drink it
in the courts of my sanctuary."

> **62.9**
> Isa 65.13,
> 21–23

c. *God's favor upon His holy people*

10 Go through, go through the gates,
prepare the way for the people;
build up, build up the highway,
clear it of stones,
lift up an ensign over the peoples.

> **62.10**
> Isa 57.14;
> 49.11;
> 11.10,12

11 Behold, the LORD has proclaimed
to the end of the earth:
Say to the daughter of Zion,
"Behold, your salvation comes;
behold, his reward is with him,
and his recompense before him."

> **62.11**
> Isa 49.6;
> Zech 9.9;
> Mt 21.5;
> Isa 51.1;
> 40.10

12 And they shall be called The holy people,
The redeemed of the LORD;
and you shall be called Sought out,
a city not forsaken.

> **62.12**
> Isa 4.3;
> 51.10;
> ver 4

d. *God's wrath on Zion's foes*

63 Who is this that comes from Ēdŏm,
in crimsoned garments from Bŏzräh,

> ***63.1**
> Isa 34.5,6;
> Amos 1.12;
> Zeph 3.17

[t] Heb *Shémă'măh* [u] Heb *Hĕph'zĭbăh* [v] Heb *Beulah*

63.1 *Edom* had acted treacherously against Israel at the time of the fall of Jerusalem.

Isaiah pictures the judgment upon his people's foe.

he that is glorious in his apparel,
   marching in the greatness of his strength?

"It is I, announcing vindication,
   mighty to save."

63.2
Rev 19.13,
15

2 Why is thy apparel red,
   and thy garments like his that treads in the wine press?

63.3
Isa 22.5;
28.3;
Mic 7.10;
Rev 19.15

3 "I have trodden the wine press alone,
   and from the peoples no one was with me;
I trod them in my anger
   and trampled them in my wrath;
their lifeblood is sprinkled upon my garments,
   and I have stained all my raiment.

63.4
Isa 34.8;
61.2

4 For the day of vengeance was in my heart,
   and my year of redemption[w] has come.

63.5
Isa 59.16;
Ps 98.1;
Isa 52.10

5 I looked, but there was no one to help;
   I was appalled, but there was no one to uphold;
so my own arm brought me victory,
   and my wrath upheld me.

63.6
Isa 65.12;
51.17,21,
22; 34.3

6 I trod down the peoples in my anger,
   I made them drunk in my wrath,
   and I poured out their lifeblood on the earth."

6. Remembering past mercies, repentant Israel pleads to God for deliverance

a. Israel the elect of God

★63.7
Isa 54.8,10;
1 Ki 8.66;
Ps 51.1

7 I will recount the steadfast love of the LORD,
   the praises of the LORD,
according to all that the LORD has granted us,
   and the great goodness to the house of Israel
which he has granted them according to his mercy,
   according to the abundance of his steadfast love.
8 For he said, Surely they are my people,
   sons who will not deal falsely;
   and he became their Savior.

63.9
Judg 10.16;
Ex 23.20–
23;
Deut 7.7,8;
Ex 19.4;
Deut 1.31

9 In all their affliction he was afflicted,[x]
   and the angel of his presence saved them;
in his love and in his pity he redeemed them;
   he lifted them up and carried them all the days of old.

b. God's deliverance in Moses' day

63.10
Ps 78.40;
Acts 7.51;
Eph 4.30;
Ps 106.40

10 But they rebelled
   and grieved his holy Spirit;
therefore he turned to be their enemy,
   and himself fought against them.

63.11
Ps 106.44,
45;
Ex 14.30;
Isa 51.9,10;
Num 11.17

11 Then he remembered the days of old,
   of Moses his servant.
Where is he who brought up out of the sea

w Or the year of my redeemed   x Another reading is he did not afflict

---

63.7 *steadfast love.* God's vindication of His
people and judgment on their enemies is
evidence of His love, a love which continues
even in their disobedience.

the shepherds of his flock?
Where is he who put in the midst of them
    his holy Spirit,
12 who caused his glorious arm
    to go at the right hand of Moses,
who divided the waters before them
    to make for himself an everlasting name,
13   who led them through the depths?
Like a horse in the desert,
    they did not stumble.
14 Like cattle that go down into the valley,
    the Spirit of the LORD gave them rest.
So thou didst lead thy people,
    to make for thyself a glorious name.

c. *Chastened Judah appeals to her Father and Redeemer*

15 Look down from heaven and see,
    from thy holy and glorious habitation.
Where are thy zeal and thy might?
    The yearning of thy heart and thy compassion
are withheld from me.
16 For thou art our Father,
    though Abraham does not know us
and Israel does not acknowledge us;
    thou, O LORD, art our Father,
our Redeemer from of old is thy name.
17 O LORD, why dost thou make us err from thy ways
    and harden our heart, so that we fear thee not?
Return for the sake of thy servants,
    the tribes of thy heritage.
18 Thy holy people possessed thy sanctuary a little while;
    our adversaries have trodden it down.
19 We have become like those over whom thou hast never ruled,
    like those who are not called by thy name.

d. *God is besought for help against the heathen*

64 O that thou wouldst rend the heavens and come down,
    that the mountains might quake at thy presence—
2y as when fire kindles brushwood
    and the fire causes water to boil—
to make thy name known to thy adversaries,
    and that the nations might tremble at thy presence!
3 When thou didst terrible things which we looked not for,
    thou camest down, the mountains quaked at thy presence.
4 From of old no one has heard
    or perceived by the ear,
no eye has seen a God besides thee,
    who works for those who wait for him.

e. *Confession of iniquity*

5 Thou meetest him that joyfully works righteousness,
    those that remember thee in thy ways.
Behold, thou wast angry, and we sinned;
    in our sins we have been a long time, and shall we be saved?z

y Ch 64.1 in Heb   z Hebrew obscure

63.12
Ex 15.6;
14.21;
Isa 50.10,11

63.13
Ps 106.9

63.14
Deut 32.12

63.15
Deut 26.15;
Ps 80.14;
Jer 31.20;
Hos 11.8

63.16
Isa 64.8;
51.2; 44.6;
60.16

63.17
Ezek 14.7–
9;
Isa 29.13,
14;
Num 10.36
63.18
Deut 7.6;
Ps 74.3–7
63.19
Lam 3.43–
45

64.1
Ps 144.5;
Judg 5.5
64.2
Jer 5.22

64.3
Ps 65.5;
66.3,5;
106.22
64.4
1 Cor 2.9;
Isa 40.31

64.5
Ex 20.24;
Isa 56.1;
63.7,10

64.6
Isa 6.5;
46.12;
Ps 90.5,6;
Isa 50.1

6 We have all become like one who is unclean,
  and all our righteous deeds are like a polluted garment.
We all fade like a leaf,
  and our iniquities, like the wind, take us away.

64.7
Isa 59.4;
27.5; 54.8;
9.18

7 There is no one that calls upon thy name,
  that bestirs himself to take hold of thee;
for thou hast hid thy face from us,
  and hast delivered*a* us into the hand of our iniquities.

f. *Appeal for pardon and restoration*

64.8
Isa 63.16;
29.16;
60.21

8 Yet, O LORD, thou art our Father;
  we are the clay, and thou art our potter;
  we are all the work of thy hand.

64.9
Isa 60.10;
43.25; 63.8

9 Be not exceedingly angry, O LORD,
  and remember not iniquity for ever.
Behold, consider, we are all thy people.

64.10
Isa 6.11

10 Thy holy cities have become a wilderness,
  Zion has become a wilderness,
  Jerusalem a desolation.

64.11
Isa 63.18;
Ps 74.5-7;
Isa 7.23

11 Our holy and beautiful house,
  where our fathers praised thee,
has been burned by fire,
  and all our pleasant places have become ruins.

64.12
Isa 42.14;
Ps 83.1

12 Wilt thou restrain thyself at these things, O LORD?
  Wilt thou keep silent, and afflict us sorely?

7. *The judgment and redemption of God's people*
a. *Retribution for idolatrous, hypocritical Israel*

65.1
Rom 10.20;
Hos 1.10

65 I was ready to be sought by those who did not ask for me;
  I was ready to be found by those who did not seek me.
I said, "Here am I, here am I,"
  to a nation that did not call on my name.

65.2
Rom 10.21;
Isa 30.1,9;
59.7

2 I spread out my hands all the day
  to a rebellious people,
who walk in a way that is not good,
  following their own devices;

65.3
Isa 3.8;
66.3,17

3 a people who provoke me
  to my face continually,
sacrificing in gardens
  and burning incense upon bricks;

65.4
Lev 11.7;
Isa 66.3,17

4 who sit in tombs,
  and spend the night in secret places;
who eat swine's flesh,
  and broth of abominable things is in their vessels;

65.5
Mt 9.11;
Lk 18.9-12

5 who say, "Keep to yourself,
  do not come near me, for I am set apart from you."
These are a smoke in my nostrils,
  a fire that burns all the day.

65.6
Ps 50.3;
79.12;
Jer 16.18

6 Behold, it is written before me:
  "I will not keep silent, but I will repay,
yea, I will repay into their bosom

65.7
Isa 30.13,
14;
57.7;
Ezek 20.27,
28;
Jer 5.29

7 their*b* iniquities and their*b* fathers' iniquities together,
                                            says the LORD;
because they burned incense upon the mountains

a Gk Syr Old Latin Tg: Heb *melted*   *b* Gk Syr: Heb *your*

and reviled me upon the hills,
I will measure into their bosom
    payment for their former doings.''

b. *The righteous to have an inheritance
but apostates to be destroyed*

8 Thus says the LORD:
"As the wine is found in the cluster,
    and they say, 'Do not destroy it,
    for there is a blessing in it,'
so I will do for my servants' sake,
    and not destroy them all.
9 I will bring forth descendants from Jacob,
    and from Judah inheritors of my mountains;
my chosen shall inherit it,
    and my servants shall dwell there.
10 Sharon shall become a pasture for flocks,
    and the Valley of Achor a place for herds to lie down,
    for my people who have sought me.
11 But you who forsake the LORD,
    who forget my holy mountain,
who set a table for Fortune
    and fill cups of mixed wine for Destiny;
12 I will destine you to the sword,
    and all of you shall bow down to the slaughter;
because, when I called, you did not answer,
    when I spoke, you did not listen,
but you did what was evil in my eyes,
    and chose what I did not delight in.''

c. *The obedient blessed; the disobedient punished*

13 Therefore thus says the Lord GOD:
"Behold, my servants shall eat,
    but you shall be hungry;
behold, my servants shall drink,
    but you shall be thirsty;
behold, my servants shall rejoice,
    but you shall be put to shame;
14 behold, my servants shall sing for gladness of heart,
    but you shall cry out for pain of heart,
    and shall wail for anguish of spirit.
15 You shall leave your name to my chosen for a curse,
    and the Lord GOD will slay you;
    but his servants he will call by a different name.
16 So that he who blesses himself in the land
    shall bless himself by the God of truth,
and he who takes an oath in the land
    shall swear by the God of truth;
because the former troubles are forgotten
    and are hid from my eyes.

d. *Messianic bliss in the new age*

17 "For behold, I create new heavens

Marginal references:

*65.9f
Isa 45.19,
25;
49.8;57.13;
32.18

65.10
Isa 33.9;
Josh 7.24;
Hos 2.15

65.11
Deut 29.24,
25;
Isa 56.7

65.12
Isa 34.5,6;
63.6;
2 Chr 36.15,
16;
Prov 1.24;
Jer 7.13

65.13
Isa 1.19;
8.21;41.17,
18; 5.13;
66.5,14

65.14
Mt 8.12;
Lk 13.28

65.15
Zech 8.13;
Isa 62.2

65.16
Ps 72.17;
31.5;
Isa 45.23;
Jer 31.12

*65.17
2 Pet 3.13;
Isa 43.18

65.9,10 God's chosen people shall dwell in Palestine.

65.17 Isaiah here seems to be speaking of the era described by John in Rev 21.1.

and a new earth;
and the former things shall not be remembered
or come into mind.

65.18
Isa 61.10

18 But be glad and rejoice for ever
in that which I create;
for behold, I create Jerusalem a rejoicing,
and her people a joy.

65.19
Isa 62.5;
35.10;
Rev 7.17

19 I will rejoice in Jerusalem,
and be glad in my people;
no more shall be heard in it the sound of weeping
and the cry of distress.

65.20
Deut 4.40;
Ecc 8.12,13

20 No more shall there be in it
an infant that lives but a few days,
or an old man who does not fill out his days,
for the child shall die a hundred years old,
and the sinner a hundred years old shall be accursed.

65.21
Amos 9.14;
Isa 37.30

21 They shall build houses and inhabit them;
they shall plant vineyards and eat their fruit.

65.22
Isa 62.8,9;
Ps 92.12–
14;
Deut 32.46,
47

22 They shall not build and another inhabit;
they shall not plant and another eat;
for like the days of a tree shall the days of my people be,
and my chosen shall long enjoy the work of their hands.

65.23
Isa 55.2;
61.9

23 They shall not labor in vain,
or bear children for calamity;c
for they shall be the offspring of the blessed of the LORD,
and their children with them.

65.24
Dan 9.27

24 Before they call I will answer,
while they are yet speaking I will hear.

65.25
Isa 11.6,7,9;
Gen 3.14

25 The wolf and the lamb shall feed together,
the lion shall eat straw like the ox;
and dust shall be the serpent's food.
They shall not hurt or destroy
in all my holy mountain,
says the LORD."

8. The final judgments of the LORD
a. God's doom upon the unrepentant

66.1
1 Ki 8.27;
2 Chr 6.18;
Mt 5.34,35;
Jer 7.4;
Acts 7.49,50

66 Thus says the LORD:
"Heaven is my throne
and the earth is my footstool;
what is the house which you would build for me,
and what is the place of my rest?

66.2
Isa 40.26;
57.15;
Mt 5.3,4;
ver 5

2 All these things my hand has made,
and so all these things are mine,d
says the LORD.
But this is the man to whom I will look,
he that is humble and contrite in spirit,
and trembles at my word.

66.3
Isa 1.11,13;
65.2,4

3 "He who slaughters an ox is like him who kills a man;
he who sacrifices a lamb, like him who breaks a dog's neck;
he who presents a cereal offering, like him who offers swine's
blood;

c Or sudden terror
d Gk Syr: Heb came to be

he who makes a memorial offering of frankincense, like him
　　　who blesses an idol.
These have chosen their own ways,
　　　and their soul delights in their abominations;
4 I also will choose affliction for them,
　　　and bring their fears upon them;
because, when I called, no one answered,
　　　when I spoke they did not listen;
but they did what was evil in my eyes,
　　　and chose that in which I did not delight."

b. *The deliverance of the believing remnant*

5 Hear the word of the LORD,
　　　you who tremble at his word:
"Your brethren who hate you
　　　and cast you out for my name's sake
have said, 'Let the LORD be glorified,
　　　that we may see your joy';
but it is they who shall be put to shame.

6 "Hark, an uproar from the city!
　　　A voice from the temple!
The voice of the LORD,
　　　rendering recompense to his enemies!

7 "Before she was in labor
　　　she gave birth;
before her pain came upon her
　　　she was delivered of a son.
8 Who has heard such a thing?
　　　Who has seen such things?
Shall a land be born in one day?
　　　Shall a nation be brought forth in one moment?
For as soon as Zion was in labor
　　　she brought forth her sons.
9 Shall I bring to the birth and not cause to bring forth?
　　　says the LORD;
shall I, who cause to bring forth, shut the womb?
　　　says your God.

c. *Comfort and prosperity in the Messianic age*

10 "Rejoice with Jerusalem, and be glad for her,
　　　all you who love her;
rejoice with her in joy,
　　　all you who mourn over her;
11 that you may suck and be satisfied
　　　with her consoling breasts;
that you may drink deeply with delight
　　　from the abundance of her glory."

12 For thus says the LORD:
"Behold, I will extend prosperity to her like a river,
　　　and the wealth of the nations like an overflowing stream;
and you shall suck, you shall be carried upon her hip,
　　　and dandled upon her knees.

66.4
Prov 1.24;
Isa 65.12;
Jer 7.13

66.5
ver 2;
Isa 60.15;
Mt 5.10–12;
Lk 13.17

66.6
Isa 6.1,8;
65.6

66.7
Isa 37.3

66.8
Isa 64.4

66.10
Isa 65.18;
Ps 26.8;
137.6

66.11
Isa 60.16

66.12
Isa 48.18;
60.4,5

66.13
2 Cor 1.3,4

13 As one whom his mother comforts,
  so I will comfort you;
 you shall be comforted in Jerusalem.

66.14
Isa 33.20;
Zech 10.7;
Isa 58.11;
Ezra 7.9;
Isa 34.2

14 You shall see, and your heart shall rejoice;
  your bones shall flourish like the grass;
 and it shall be known that the hand of the LORD is with his
  servants,
 and his indignation is against his enemies.

d. *The wicked consigned to judgment*

66.15
Isa 31.9;
2 Thess 1.8;
Ps 78.16

15 "For behold, the LORD will come in fire,
  and his chariots like the stormwind,
 to render his anger in fury,
  and his rebuke with flames of fire.

66.16
Isa 30.30;
65.12; 34.3

16 For by fire will the LORD execute judgment,
  and by his sword, upon all flesh;
 and those slain by the LORD shall be many.

66.17
Isa 65.3,4;
Ps 37.20

17 "Those who sanctify and purify themselves to go into the gardens, following one in the midst, eating swine's flesh and the abomination and mice, shall come to an end together, says the LORD.

e. *God glorified in Israel and Gentile converts*

66.18
Isa 59.7;
45.22–25

66.19
Isa 62.10;
42.12

18 "For I know[e] their works and their thoughts, and I am[f] coming to gather all nations and tongues; and they shall come and shall see my glory, 19 and I will set a sign among them. And from them I will send survivors to the nations, to Tarshish, Put,[g] and Lud, who draw the bow, to Tubal and Javan, to the coastlands afar off, that have not heard my fame or seen my glory; and they shall declare my glory among the nations. 20And they shall bring all your brethren from all the nations as an offering to the LORD, upon horses, and in chariots, and in litters, and upon mules, and upon dromedaries, to my holy mountain Jerusalem, says the LORD, just as the Israelites bring their cereal offering in a clean vessel to the house of the LORD. 21And some of them also I will take for priests and for Levites, says the LORD.

66.20
Isa 60.4;
65.11,25;
52.11

66.21
Isa 61.6;
1 Pet 2.5,9

f. *Heaven for the righteous; eternal fire for the wicked*

66.22
Isa 65.17;
2 Pet 3.13;
Rev 21.1;
Isa 65.22,
23; 56.5

22 "For as the new heavens and the new earth
  which I will make
 shall remain before me, says the LORD;
  so shall your descendants and your name remain.

66.23
Isa 1.13,14;
49.7

23 From new moon to new moon,
  and from sabbath to sabbath,
 all flesh shall come to worship before me,
  says the LORD.

66.24
Isa 5.25;
24.20;
Mk 9.48;
Isa 1.31;
Dan 12.2

24 "And they shall go forth and look on the dead bodies of the men that have rebelled against me; for their worm shall not die, their fire shall not be quenched, and they shall be an abhorrence to all flesh."

---

e Gk Syr: Heb lacks *know*
f Gk Syr Vg Tg: Heb *it is*   *g* Gk: Heb *Pul*

INTRODUCTION TO

THE BOOK OF

JEREMIAH

Authorship and Background: This book is named after Jeremiah the prophet, who was the son of Hilkiah. He was born in the priest-city of Anathoth and called to be a prophet around 627 B.C. when he was but twenty years of age. He began his ministry in the reign of Josiah and continued in his office for about fifty years. The Northern Kingdom had already fallen. Judah, the Southern Kingdom, had suffered many reverses and was declining. Jeremiah prophesied during the closing days of that kingdom and lived through the invasion of Nebuchadnezzar, who destroyed Jerusalem. The international situation of that time involved a threefold battle for world supremacy among Assyria, Babylon, and Egypt. Assyria was broken under the heel of Babylon, and Babylon, in the battle of Carchemish in 605 B.C., crushed Egypt too. Judah was caught between the upper and nether millstones in the struggle, only to fall under the hand of the Babylonian oppressor.

The prophecies in the Book of Jeremiah are not arranged in chronological order. The book itself was written by Baruch who was Jeremiah's faithful amanuensis. Jeremiah dictated much of the work to him. In Jer 36.32 it is stated that "many similar words were added to them," i.e., to the dictated words of Jeremiah. This has led some to conclude that the book contains more than the words of Jeremiah. Chapter 52 is almost identical with 2 Ki 24, 25. The problem has been further complicated by the fact that the Septuagint version of Jeremiah differs markedly from the Hebrew text in arrangement and length (it is more than 2500 words shorter). The Septuagint translators seem to have edited the Hebrew text in the process of translation.

Characteristics: Jeremiah predicts the fall of Judah and the seventy-year captivity. He regards himself as the true spokesman of Yahweh against false prophets like Hananiah. He claims that they are not sent by Yahweh even though they think themselves to be sincere. They hate him fiercely and bring pressure to bear upon the king. Jeremiah records his personal history in all of these political and religious intrigues of the day. He loses politically, but wins spiritually. He feels his sense of aloneness, agonizing over the sins of the people and the sure judgment to come. While he shrinks from his task, he is unable to remain silent. He speaks in parables, warns of apostasy, and employs burning words of rebuke, contempt, and doom. Beneath them lies the aching heart of the patriot who senses that Israel's security cannot be divorced from faith in God and a right covenantal relationship and obedience.

Contents:

I.   Prophecies under Josiah and Jehoiakim. 1.1—20.18: Jeremiah's call.
       His prophecy that Jerusalem will fall because the people are immoral

Introduction to Jeremiah

and wicked. Judgment lies before them. Their sinful impenitence in their religious worship threatens them with judgment. They are idolatrous and obdurate, and this too calls for judgment. God must judge them because He punishes those who refuse to repent; nor will He hear Jeremiah's prayer of intercession. He strengthens His prophet for the task He has given him. The parable of the potter and the clay illustrating the breaking of Jerusalem by the breaking of the pottery. Jeremiah is placed in stocks and offers his complaint to God.

II. Prophecies under Jehoiakim and Zedekiah. 21.1—39.18: Zedekiah asks about Nebuchadnezzar; Jeremiah suggests surrender. He calls for the people to amend their ways, and urges them not to lament over Shallum. He rebukes Jehoiakim (Eliakim) and pronounces judgment on Coniah (Jehoiachin). He warns against the false prophets. He uses the vision of the two baskets of figs as a symbol: the good figs represent the people in captivity; the bad figs Zedekiah and the judgment to come. He prophesies the seventy-year captivity, the fall of Babylon, and the destruction of the Temple. Jeremiah's trial, his warning against false prophets. He promises a return from captivity and speaks of the new covenant. As a token he buys land in Anathoth. Jerusalem shall be restored and they shall have a new king—the Branch. He describes the siege of Jerusalem. Zedekiah destroys Jeremiah's roll. He asks for prayer. Jeremiah is imprisoned. He and Zedekiah consult secretly. Jerusalem is captured.

III. Prophecies after the fall of Jerusalem. 40.1—45.5: Jeremiah returns to Gedaliah at Mizpah. Ishmael conspires against Gedaliah who is murdered. Jeremiah warns against flight to Egypt. He is abducted and prophesies in Egypt against Egypt and Judah. He encourages Baruch.

IV. Prophecies against heathen nations. 46.1—51.64: Jeremiah pronounces doom on Egypt by the Chaldeans. He also prophesies the doom of Philistia, Moab, Ammon, Edom, Damascus (Syria), Kedar (Arabia), Hazor, Elam, and Babylon.

V. Historical appendix. 52.1–34: The fall of Jerusalem described again: the rebellion, capture, destruction, the booty, the slain, the captives, and the disposition of Jehoiachin.

THE BOOK OF

JEREMIAH

I. Prophecies under Josiah and Jehoiakim 1.1–20.18

A. The prophet's call and commission

1. Superscription

1 The words of Jĕrĕmī′ăh, the son of Hĭlkī′ăh, of the priests who were in Ăn′ăthŏth in the land of Benjamin, 2 to whom the word of the LORD came in the days of Jōsī′ăh the son of Āmŏn, king of Judah, in the thirteenth year of his reign. 3 It came also in the days of Jĕhoi′ăkĭm the son of Jōsī′ăh, king of Judah, and until the end of the eleventh year of Zĕdĕkī′ăh, the son of Josiah, king of Judah, until the captivity of Jerusalem in the fifth month.

2. His personal call from God

4 Now the word of the LORD came to me saying,
5 "Before I formed you in the womb I knew you,
   and before you were born I consecrated you;
   I appointed you a prophet to the nations."
6 Then I said, "Ah, Lord GOD! Behold, I do not know how to speak, for I am only a youth." 7 But the LORD said to me,
   "Do not say, 'I am only a youth';
   for to all to whom I send you you shall go,
   and whatever I command you you shall speak.
8 Be not afraid of them,
   for I am with you to deliver you,
                    says the LORD."
9 Then the LORD put forth his hand and touched my mouth; and the LORD said to me,
   "Behold, I have put my words in your mouth.
10 See, I have set you this day over nations and over kingdoms,
   to pluck up and to break down,
   to destroy and to overthrow,
   to build and to plant."

3. Vision of the almond rod and the boiling pot

11 And the word of the LORD came to me, saying, "Jĕrĕmī′ăh, what do you see?" And I said, "I see a rod of almond." *a* 12 Then the LORD said to me, "You have seen well, for I am watching *b* over my word to perform it."
13 The word of the LORD came to me a second time, saying, "What do you see?" And I said, "I see a boiling pot, facing away

---

a Heb shaqed   *b* Heb shoqed

1.1
2 Chr 35.25;
1 Chr 6.60;
Isa 32.7–9
1.2
1 Ki 13.2;
2 Ki 21.18, 24
1.3
Jer 25.1;
39.2; 52.12

★1.5
Ps 139.15, 16;
Isa 49.1,5
1.6
Ex 4.10;
Isa 6.5

1.8
Ezek 2.6;
Jer 15.20

1.9
Isa 6.7;
Ex 4.11–16
1.10
Jer 18.7;
2 Cor 10.4,5

★1.11
Jer 24.3

1.13
Zech 4.2;
Ezek 11.3,7;
24.3

1.5 From this Scripture we may learn much about the operation of God's will: (1) God had a master plan for the life of Jeremiah before he was even born; (2) God's call in connection with this will was effectual— Jeremiah voluntarily became what God wanted; (3) God provided the means by which it was possible for Jeremiah to do the will of God; (4) Jeremiah's excuses for avoid-

ing the divine call were puerile and unworthy; (5) Jeremiah was not able to stay silent even when he wanted to do so (20.9).
1.11 *almond.* Jeremiah uses a word play based on the fact that the Hebrew word for almond (*shaqed*) is formed on the root of the verb "to be wakeful," "to watch." The almond is so named because it awakens early, i.e., blossoms in January–February.

1.14
Jer 4.6; 6.1
1.15
Isa 22.7;
Jer 9.11

1.16
Deut 28.20;
Jer 17.13;
7.9; 10.3–5
1.17
1 Ki 18.46;
Ex 3.12;
Ezek 2.6
1.18
Isa 50.7;
Jer 6.27;
15.20
1.19
Jer 11.19;
15.10,11;
ver 8

2.1
Jer 1.2,11
2.2
Jer 7.2;
11.6;
Ezek 16.8;
Deut 2.7

★2.3
Ex 19.5,6;
Jer 30.16;
50.7

2.5
Isa 5.4;
Mic 6.3;
Jer 8.19;
2 Ki 17.15

2.6
Ex 20.2;
Isa 63.11;
Hos 13.4;
Deut 8.15;
32.10

2.7
Num 13.27;
Lev 18.25;
Ps 78.58
2.8
Jer 10.21;
Mal 2.6,7;
Rom 2.20;
Jer 23.13;
16.19

from the north." 14 Then the LORD said to me, "Out of the north evil shall break forth upon all the inhabitants of the land. 15 For, lo, I am calling all the tribes of the kingdoms of the north, says the LORD; and they shall come and every one shall set his throne at the entrance of the gates of Jerusalem, against all its walls round about, and against all the cities of Judah. 16And I will utter my judgments against them, for all their wickedness in forsaking me; they have burned incense to other gods, and worshiped the works of their own hands. 17 But you, gird up your loins; arise, and say to them everything that I command you. Do not be dismayed by them, lest I dismay you before them. 18And I, behold, I make you this day a fortified city, an iron pillar, and bronze walls, against the whole land, against the kings of Judah, its princes, its priests, and the people of the land. 19 They will fight against you; but they shall not prevail against you, for I am with you, says the LORD, to deliver you."

B. First movement: God's summons to Judah for judgment

1. Sermon I: unfaithful Israel
a. Israel's early fidelity

2 The word of the LORD came to me, saying, 2 "Go and proclaim in the hearing of Jerusalem, Thus says the LORD,
I remember the devotion of your youth,
　　your love as a bride,
how you followed me in the wilderness,
　　in a land not sown.
3 Israel was holy to the LORD,
　　the first fruits of his harvest.
All who ate of it became guilty;
　　evil came upon them,

　　　　　　　　　　says the LORD."

b. Israel forsakes the LORD

4 Hear the word of the LORD, O house of Jacob, and all the families of the house of Israel. 5 Thus says the LORD:
"What wrong did your fathers find in me
　　that they went far from me,
and went after worthlessness, and became worthless?
6 They did not say, 'Where is the LORD
　　who brought us up from the land of Egypt,
who led us in the wilderness,
　　in a land of deserts and pits,
in a land of drought and deep darkness,
　　in a land that none passes through,
　　where no man dwells?'
7 And I brought you into a plentiful land
　　to enjoy its fruits and its good things.
But when you came in you defiled my land,
　　and made my heritage an abomination.
8 The priests did not say, 'Where is the LORD?'
　　Those who handle the law did not know me;

2.3 *the first fruits.* As the first fruits, Israel was consecrated to God. The metaphor, how-ever, suggests that there would be a later harvest extending beyond Israel.

the rulers[c] transgressed against me;
the prophets prophesied by Bāāl,
and went after things that do not profit.

9 "Therefore I still contend with you,
                    says the LORD,
and with your children's children I will contend.
10 For cross to the coasts of Cyprus and see,
or send to Kēdar and examine with care;
see if there has been such a thing.
11 Has a nation changed its gods,
even though they are no gods?
But my people have changed their glory
for that which does not profit.
12 Be appalled, O heavens, at this,
be shocked, be utterly desolate,
                    says the LORD,
13 for my people have committed two evils;
they have forsaken me,
the fountain of living waters,
and hewed out cisterns for themselves,
broken cisterns,
that can hold no water.

c. Consequences of Israel's apostasy

14 "Is Israel a slave? Is he a homeborn servant?
Why then has he become a prey?
15 The lions have roared against him,
they have roared loudly.
They have made his land a waste;
his cities are in ruins, without inhabitant.
16 Moreover, the men of Memphis and Tah′pȧnhēs
have broken the crown of your head.
17 Have you not brought this upon yourself
by forsaking the LORD your God,
when he led you in the way?
18 And now what do you gain by going to Egypt,
to drink the waters of the Nile?
Or what do you gain by going to Assyria,
to drink the waters of the Euphrā′tēs?
19 Your wickedness will chasten you,
and your apostasy will reprove you.
Know and see that it is evil and bitter
for you to forsake the LORD your God;
the fear of me is not in you,
                    says the Lord GOD of hosts.

d. Israel to be punished for her idolatry

20 "For long ago you broke your yoke

c Heb shepherds

2.9	Ezek 20.35, 36; Mic 6.2
2.10	Isa 23.12; Jer 49.28
★2.11	Mic 4.5; Ps 106.20; Rom 1.23
2.13	Ps 36.9; Jer 17.13; Jn 4.14; Jer 14.3
2.14	Ex 4.22; Jer 5.19
2.15	Jer 50.17; 4.7
2.16	Jer 44.1; 43.7–9; 48.45
2.17	Jer 4.18; Deut 32.10
2.18	Isa 30.1,2; Josh 13.3; Jer 50.17
2.19	Isa 3.9; Hos 5.5; 11.7; Jer 5.24; Ps 36.1
★2.20	Lev 26.13; ver 25; Deut 12.2; Isa 57.5,7

2.11 a nation here means "a heathen nation." The heathen remain true to their idols, but Israel has rejected the true God.
2.20 every high hill. Idolatrous Baal worship took place at "high places." Israel adopted this heathen custom for the worship of Baal, and also in her worship of Yahweh, adopted the idolatries of Baal worship.

and burst your bonds;
and you said, 'I will not serve.'
Yea, upon every high hill
and under every green tree
you bowed down as a harlot.

2.21
Ex 15.17;
Isa 5.4

21 Yet I planted you a choice vine,
wholly of pure seed.
How then have you turned degenerate
and become a wild vine?

2.22
Jer 4.14

22 Though you wash yourself with lye
and use much soap,
the stain of your guilt is still before me,

says the Lord GOD.

*2.23
Prov 30.12;
Jer 9.14;
7.31

23 How can you say, 'I am not defiled,
I have not gone after the Bāāļs'?
Look at your way in the valley;
know what you have done—
a restive young camel interlacing her tracks,

2.24
Jer 14.6

24 a wild ass used to the wilderness,
in her heat sniffing the wind!
Who can restrain her lust?
None who seek her need weary themselves;
in her month they will find her.

2.25
Jer 18.12;
14.10;
Deut 32.16

25 Keep your feet from going unshod
and your throat from thirst.
But you said, 'It is hopeless,
for I have loved strangers,
and after them I will go.'

2.26
Jer 48.27

26 "As a thief is shamed when caught,
so the house of Israel shall be shamed:
they, their kings, their princes,
their priests, and their prophets,

2.27
Jer 3.9;
18.17;
22.23;
Isa 26.16

27 who say to a tree, 'You are my father,'
and to a stone, 'You gave me birth.'
For they have turned their back to me,
and not their face.
But in the time of their trouble they say,
'Arise and save us!'

2.28
Deut 32.37;
Isa 45.20;
Jer 11.13

28 But where are your gods
that you made for yourself?
Let them arise, if they can save you,
in your time of trouble;
for as many as your cities
are your gods, O Judah.

e. *The punishment is at hand*

2.29
Jer 5.1;
6.13

29 "Why do you complain against me?
You have all rebelled against me,

says the LORD.

2.30
Isa 1.5;
Jer 26.20–
24

30 In vain have I smitten your children,
they took no correction;

2.23 the *valley*, i.e., the "Valley of Hinnom" where infants were sacrificed in the
Molech cult. This valley is located southwest
of Jerusalem.

your own sword devoured your prophets
  like a ravening lion.
³¹ And you, O generation, heed the word of the LORD.
  Have I been a wilderness to Israel,
    or a land of thick darkness?
  Why then do my people say, 'We are free,
    we will come no more to thee'?
³² Can a maiden forget her ornaments,
    or a bride her attire?
  Yet my people have forgotten me
    days without number.

³³ "How well you direct your course
    to seek lovers!
  So that even to wicked women
    you have taught your ways.
³⁴ Also on your skirts is found
    the lifeblood of guiltless poor;
  you did not find them breaking in.
  Yet in spite of all these things
³⁵ you say, 'I am innocent;
    surely his anger has turned from me.'
  Behold, I will bring you to judgment
    for saying, 'I have not sinned.'
³⁶ How lightly you gad about,
    changing your way!
  You shall be put to shame by Egypt
    as you were put to shame by Assyria.
³⁷ From it too you will come away
    with your hands upon your head,
  for the LORD has rejected those in whom you trust,
    and you will not prosper by them.

f. Let Judah repent and turn to the LORD

3 "If*d* a man divorces his wife and she goes from him
    and becomes another man's wife,
  will he return to her?
  Would not that land be greatly polluted?
  You have played the harlot with many lovers;
    and would you return to me?
                                    says the LORD.
² Lift up your eyes to the bare heights, and see!
    Where have you not been lain with?
  By the waysides you have sat awaiting lovers
    like an Arab in the wilderness.
  You have polluted the land
    with your vile harlotry.

d Gk Syr: Heb *Saying, If*

2.31 Isa 45.19; Deut 32.15
2.32 Isa 17.10; Hos 8.14
2.34 Jer 19.4; Ex 22.2
2.35 ver 23; Jer 25.31; 1 Jn 1.8,10
2.36 ver 23; Hos 12.1; Isa 30.3; 2 Chr 28.16,20,21
2.37 2 Sam 13.19; Jer 37.7-10
★3.1 Deut 24.4; Jer 2.20; Ezek 16.26,28,29; Zech 1.3
★3.2 Deut 12.2; Jer 2.20; Prov 23.28; Jer 2.7

3.1 God knew that the captivity was about to occur. He knew what Judah would do. Yet verses 1–5 bespeak the mercy of God. He urges repentance and a return to Himself in the light of imminent judgment. Had Judah obeyed God, the judgment would have been delayed or averted. Once again the inevitability of ultimate judgment for disobedience is made plain.
3.2 *like an Arab in the wilderness.* The Arab was free to approach or attack any who passed through his wilderness abode. Israel was equally ready to embrace her *lovers*, the gods of the land.

3.3
Lev 26.19;
Jer 6.15;
Ezek 3.7

3 Therefore the showers have been withheld,
and the spring rain has not come;
yet you have a harlot's brow,
you refuse to be ashamed.

3.4
ver 19;
Ps 71.17

4 Have you not just now called to me,
'My father, thou art the friend of my youth—

3.5
ver 12;
Isa 57.16

5 will he be angry for ever,
will he be indignant to the end?'
Behold, you have spoken,
but you have done all the evil that you could.''

2. *Sermon II: the warning example of exiled Samaria*
a. *The ten tribes dispersed but urged to repent*

*3.6
Jer 7.24;
17.2

6 The LORD said to me in the days of King Jōsī′äh: "Have you
seen what she did, that faithless one, Israel, how she went up on
every high hill and under every green tree, and there played the

3.7
Ezek 16.46,
47

harlot? 7And I thought, 'After she has done all this she will return
to me'; but she did not return, and her false sister Judah saw it.

3.8
2 Ki 17.6;
Isa 50.1;
Ezek 23.11

8 She saw that for all the adulteries of that faithless one, Israel, I
had sent her away with a decree of divorce; yet her false sister
Judah did not fear, but she too went and played the harlot. 9 Be-

3.9
Jer 2.7,27
3.10
Hos 7.14

cause harlotry was so light to her, she polluted the land, committing adultery with stone and tree. 10 Yet for all this her false sister
Judah did not return to me with her whole heart, but in pretense,
says the LORD.''

3.11
Ezek 16.51;
ver 7
3.12
2 Ki 17.6;
Ps 86.15

11 And the LORD said to me, "Faithless Israel has shown herself less guilty than false Judah. 12 Go, and proclaim these words
toward the north, and say,
'Return, faithless Israel,
says the LORD.
I will not look on you in anger,
for I am merciful,
says the LORD;
I will not be angry for ever.

3.13
Deut 30.1–
3;
Jer 2.20,25;
Deut 12.2

13 Only acknowledge your guilt,
that you rebelled against the LORD your God
and scattered your favors among strangers under every green
tree,
and that you have not obeyed my voice,
says the LORD.

3.14
Hos 2.19;
Jer 50.4,5

14 Return, O faithless children,
says the LORD;
for I am your master;
I will take you, one from a city and two from a family,
and I will bring you to Zion.

3.15
Jer 23.4;
Acts 20.28

15 " 'And I will give you shepherds after my own heart, who
will feed you with knowledge and understanding. 16And when you

3.16
Isa 65.17

have multiplied and increased in the land, in those days, says the
LORD, they shall no more say, "The ark of the covenant of the
LORD." It shall not come to mind, or be remembered, or missed; it

---

3.6 Scripture repeatedly warns men of impending judgment. Here Jeremiah uses
Samaria (already dispersed) as a warning to
Judah that a similar judgment will fall upon
her. But men seem all too prone to disregard
such warnings, as the Apostle Peter pointed
out, using the illustrations of Noah, Sodom
and Gomorrah, and Balaam (2 Pet 2.1–16).

shall not be made again. ¹⁷At that time Jerusalem shall be called the throne of the LORD, and all nations shall gather to it, to the presence of the LORD in Jerusalem, and they shall no more stubbornly follow their own evil heart. ¹⁸ In those days the house of Judah shall join the house of Israel, and together they shall come from the land of the north to the land that I gave your fathers for a heritage.

¹⁹ " 'I thought
    how I would set you among my sons,
and give you a pleasant land,
    a heritage most beauteous of all nations.
And I thought you would call me, My Father,
    and would not turn from following me.
²⁰ Surely, as a faithless wife leaves her husband,
    so have you been faithless to me, O house of Israel,
                                says the LORD.' "

²¹ A voice on the bare heights is heard,
    the weeping and pleading of Israel's sons,
because they have perverted their way,
    they have forgotten the LORD their God.
²² "Return, O faithless sons,
    I will heal your faithlessness."
"Behold, we come to thee;
    for thou art the LORD our God.
²³ Truly the hills are a delusion,
    the orgies on the mountains.
Truly in the LORD our God
    is the salvation of Israel.

²⁴ "But from our youth the shameful thing has devoured all for which our fathers labored, their flocks and their herds, their sons and their daughters. ²⁵ Let us lie down in our shame, and let our dishonor cover us; for we have sinned against the LORD our God, we and our fathers, from our youth even to this day; and we have not obeyed the voice of the LORD our God."

4 "If you return, O Israel,
                    says the LORD,
    to me you should return.
If you remove your abominations from my presence,
    and do not waver,
² and if you swear, 'As the LORD lives,'
    in truth, in justice, and in uprightness,
then nations shall bless themselves in him,
    and in him shall they glory."

b. *Judah promised a similar judgment*
(1) JUDGMENT TO COME FROM THE NORTH

³ For thus says the LORD to the men of Judah and to the inhabitants of Jerusalem:
"Break up your fallow ground,
    and sow not among thorns.

3.17
Jer 17.12;
ver 19;
Isa 60.9;
Jer 11.8
3.18
Isa 11.13;
Hos 1.11;
Jer 31.8;
Amos 9.15
3.19
Dan 8.9;
Ps 16.6;
Isa 63.16

3.20
ver 6,7;
Isa 48.8

3.21
Isa 15.2;
Jer 2,32

3.22
ver 14;
Hos 6.1;
14.4;
Jer 31.6

*3.23
Ps 121.1,2;
3.8

3.24
Jer 8.16

3.25
Ezra 9.7;
Jer 22.21

4.1
Jer 3.1,22;
Joel 2.12;
Jer 7.3,7

4.2
Deut 10.20;
Gen 22.18;
Gal 3.8;
Isa 45.25;
1 Cor 1.31

4.3
Hos 10.12;
Mt 13.7,22

3.23 *the hills are a delusion*, i.e., no help will come from the idolatrous worship associated with the high places, whereas Israel can find real help in *the* LORD *our God*.

4.4
Deut 10.16;
30.6;
Jer 9.26;
Rom 2.28,
29;
Jer 21.12;
Mk 9.43,48

4.5
Jer 6.1;
8.14

4.6
Jer 1.13-15;
6.1,22

★4.7
2 Ki 24.1;
Jer 5.6;
Dan 7.4;
Jer 25.9;
Isa 1.7;
Jer 2.15

4.8
Isa 22.12;
Jer 6.26;
30.24

4.9
Isa 22.3-5;
29.9,10

4.10
Ezek 14.9;
2 Thess
2.11;
Jer 5.12;
14.13

4.11
Jer 51.1;
Ezek 17.10;
Hos 13.15

4.12
Jer 1.16

4.13
Isa 19.1;
5.28;
Deut 28.49;
Lam 4.19;
Isa 3.8

4.14
Isa 1.16;
Jas 4.8;
Jer 6.19;
13.27

★4.15
Jer 8.16

4.16
Jer 5.6,15;
Isa 39.3;
Ezek 21.22

4 Circumcise yourselves to the Lord,
  remove the foreskin of your hearts,
    O men of Judah and inhabitants of Jerusalem;
lest my wrath go forth like fire,
  and burn with none to quench it,
    because of the evil of your doings."

5 Declare in Judah, and proclaim in Jerusalem, and say,
"Blow the trumpet through the land;
  cry aloud and say,
'Assemble, and let us go
  into the fortified cities!'
6 Raise a standard toward Zion,
  flee for safety, stay not,
for I bring evil from the north,
  and great destruction.
7 A lion has gone up from his thicket,
  a destroyer of nations has set out;
he has gone forth from his place
to make your land a waste;
  your cities will be ruins
    without inhabitant.
8 For this gird you with sackcloth,
  lament and wail;
for the fierce anger of the Lord
  has not turned back from us."

9 "In that day, says the Lord, courage shall fail both king and
princes; the priests shall be appalled and the prophets astounded."
10 Then I said, "Ah, Lord God, surely thou hast utterly deceived
this people and Jerusalem, saying, 'It shall be well with you';
whereas the sword has reached their very life."

11 At that time it will be said to this people and to Jerusalem,
"A hot wind from the bare heights in the desert toward the daughter of my people, not to winnow or cleanse, 12 a wind too full for
this comes for me. Now it is I who speak in judgment upon
them."
13 Behold, he comes up like clouds,
  his chariots like the whirlwind;
his horses are swifter than eagles—
  woe to us, for we are ruined!
14 O Jerusalem, wash your heart from wickedness,
  that you may be saved.
How long shall your evil thoughts
  lodge within you?
15 For a voice declares from Dan
  and proclaims evil from Mount E′phra̅im.
16 Warn the nations that he is coming;
  announce to Jerusalem,
"Besiegers come from a distant land;

4.7 *A lion* here is a metaphor for Nebuchadnezzar, the king who destroyed Jerusalem.
4.15 *Dan* was in the far north of Palestine.

The enemy would first be seen at Dan as he
moved from the east through the Fertile
Crescent.

they shout against the cities of Judah.

17 Like keepers of a field are they against her round about,
  because she has rebelled against me,
                              says the LORD.

4.17
2 Ki 25.1,4;
Jer 5.23

18 Your ways and your doings
    have brought this upon you.
  This is your doom, and it is bitter;
    it has reached your very heart."

4.18
Ps 107.17;
Isa 50.1;
Jer 2.17,19

19 My anguish, my anguish! I writhe in pain!
    Oh, the walls of my heart!
  My heart is beating wildly;
    I cannot keep silent;
  for I hear the sound of the trumpet,
    the alarm of war.

4.19
Isa 15.5;
16.11;21.3;
22.4;
Jer 9.1,10

20 Disaster follows hard on disaster,
    the whole land is laid waste.
  Suddenly my tents are destroyed,
    my curtains in a moment.

4.20
Ps 42.7;
Ezek 7.26;
Jer 10.20

21 How long must I see the standard,
    and hear the sound of the trumpet?
22 "For my people are foolish,
    they know me not;
  they are stupid children,
    they have no understanding.
  They are skilled in doing evil,
    but how to do good they know not."

4.22
Jer 10.8;
2.8;
Rom 16.19

23 I looked on the earth, and lo, it was waste and void;
    and to the heavens, and they had no light.
24 I looked on the mountains, and lo, they were quaking,
    and all the hills moved to and fro.
25 I looked, and lo, there was no man,
    and all the birds of the air had fled.
26 I looked, and lo, the fruitful land was a desert,
    and all its cities were laid in ruins
    before the LORD, before his fierce anger.
27 For thus says the LORD, "The whole land shall be a desolation; yet I will not make a full end.
28 For this the earth shall mourn,
    and the heavens above be black;
  for I have spoken, I have purposed;
    I have not relented nor will I turn back."

4.23
Gen 1.2;
Isa 24.19
4.24
Isa 5.25;
Ezek 38.20
4.25
Zeph 1.3
4.26
Jer 9.10
4.27
Jer 12.11,
12;
5.10,18;
30.11;
46.28
4.28
Hos 4.3;
Isa 5.30;
50.3;
Num 23.19;
Jer 7.16

29 At the noise of horseman and archer
    every city takes to flight;
  they enter thickets; they climb among rocks;
    all the cities are forsaken,
    and no man dwells in them.

4.29
Jer 6.23;
16.16

30 And you, O desolate one,
  what do you mean that you dress in scarlet,
    that you deck yourself with ornaments of gold,
    that you enlarge your eyes with paint?
  In vain you beautify yourself.
    Your lovers despise you;

4.30
Jer 13.21;
2 Ki 9.30;
Ezek 23.40;
Jer 22.20,22

they seek your life.

4.31
Jer 13.21;
Isa 42.14;
  1.15;
Lam 1.17

31 For I heard a cry as of a woman in travail,
    anguish as of one bringing forth her first child,
the cry of the daughter of Zion gasping for breath,
    stretching out her hands,
"Woe is me! I am fainting before murderers."

(2) FUTILE SEARCH FOR AN UPRIGHT MAN

5.1
2 Chr 16.9;
Ezek 22.30;
Gen 18.23,
    26,32

5 Run to and fro through the streets of Jerusalem,
    look and take note!
Search her squares to see
    if you can find a man,
one who does justice
    and seeks truth;
that I may pardon her.

5.2
Tit 1.16;
Jer 4.2; 7.9

2 Though they say, "As the LORD lives,"
    yet they swear falsely.

5.3
Isa 1.5;
  9.13;
Jer 2.30;
Zeph 3.2;
Jer 7.26;
  19.15

3 O LORD, do not thy eyes look for truth?
Thou hast smitten them,
    but they felt no anguish;
thou hast consumed them,
    but they refused to take correction.
They have made their faces harder than rock;
    they have refused to repent.

5.4
Jer 4.22;
  8.7

4 Then I said, "These are only the poor,
    they have no sense;
for they do not know the way of the LORD,
    the law of their God.

5.5
Mic 3.1;
Ps 2.3

5 I will go to the great,
    and will speak to them;
for they know the way of the LORD,
    the law of their God."
But they all alike had broken the yoke,
    they had burst the bonds.

5.6
Hab 1.8;
Zeph 3.3;
Hos 13.7;
Jer 30.14,15

6 Therefore a lion from the forest shall slay them,
    a wolf from the desert shall destroy them.
A leopard is watching against their cities,
    every one who goes out of them shall be torn in pieces;
because their transgressions are many,
    their apostasies are great.

5.7
Josh 23.7;
Zeph 1.5;
Deut 32.21;
Gal 4.8;
Jer 7.9;
Num 25.1–3

7 "How can I pardon you?
    Your children have forsaken me,
    and have sworn by those who are no gods.
When I fed them to the full,
    they committed adultery
    and trooped to the houses of harlots.

5.8
Ezek 22.11;
Jer 13.27

8 They were well-fed lusty stallions,
    each neighing for his neighbor's wife.

5.9
Jer 9.9;
  44.22

9 Shall I not punish them for these things?
                                        says the LORD;
    and shall I not avenge myself
    on a nation such as this?

(3) SUMMONS TO INVADE JUDAH

10 "Go up through her vine-rows and destroy,
    but make not a full end;
strip away her branches,
    for they are not the LORD's.
11 For the house of Israel and the house of Judah
    have been utterly faithless to me,
                says the LORD.
12 They have spoken falsely of the LORD,
    and have said, 'He will do nothing;
no evil will come upon us,
    nor shall we see sword or famine.
13 The prophets will become wind;
    the word is not in them.
Thus shall it be done to them!' "

14 Therefore thus says the LORD, the God of hosts:
"Because they*e* have spoken this word,
behold, I am making my words in your mouth a fire,
    and this people wood, and the fire shall devour them.
15 Behold, I am bringing upon you
    a nation from afar, O house of Israel,
               says the LORD.
It is an enduring nation,
    it is an ancient nation,
a nation whose language you do not know,
    nor can you understand what they say.
16 Their quiver is like an open tomb,
    they are all mighty men.
17 They shall eat up your harvest and your food;
    they shall eat up your sons and your daughters;
they shall eat up your flocks and your herds;
    they shall eat up your vines and your fig trees;
your fortified cities in which you trust
    they shall destroy with the sword."

(4) JUDGMENT DUE TO STUBBORNNESS AND REBELLION

18 "But even in those days, says the LORD, I will not make a full end of you. 19 And when your people say, 'Why has the LORD our God done all these things to us?' you shall say to them, 'As you have forsaken me and served foreign gods in your land, so you shall serve strangers in a land that is not yours.' "

20 Declare this in the house of Jacob,
    proclaim it in Judah:
21 "Hear this, O foolish and senseless people,
    who have eyes, but see not,
    who have ears, but hear not.
22 Do you not fear me? says the LORD;
    Do you not tremble before me?
I placed the sand as the bound for the sea,
    a perpetual barrier which it cannot pass;
though the waves toss, they cannot prevail,
    though they roar, they cannot pass over it.

e Heb *you*

5.10 Jer 39.8; ver 18; Jer 4.27
5.11 Jer 3.20
5.12 2 Chr 36.16; Isa 28.15; Jer 23.17; 14.13
5.13 Jer 14.13,15
5.14 Jer 1.9; 23.29
5.15 Deut 28.49; Isa 5.26; Jer 1.15; 6.22; 4.16; Isa 39.3
5.16 Isa 5.28; 13.18
5.17 Lev 26.16; Deut 28.31, 33; Jer 8.13; Hos 8.14
5.18 Jer 4.27
5.19 Deut 29.24–26; 1 Ki 9.8,9; Jer 16.10–13; Deut 28.48
5.21 ver 4; Isa 6.9; Ezek 12.2; Mt 13.14; Jer 6.10
5.22 Jer 2.19; Job 26.10; Ps 104.9

23 But this people has a stubborn and rebellious heart;
    they have turned aside and gone away.
24 They do not say in their hearts,
    'Let us fear the LORD our God,
who gives the rain in its season,
    the autumn rain and the spring rain,
and keeps for us
    the weeks appointed for the harvest.'
25 Your iniquities have turned these away,
    and your sins have kept good from you.
26 For wicked men are found among my people;
    they lurk like fowlers lying in wait.*f*
They set a trap;
    they catch men.
27 Like a basket full of birds,
    their houses are full of treachery;
therefore they have become great and rich,
28   they have grown fat and sleek.
They know no bounds in deeds of wickedness;
    they judge not with justice
the cause of the fatherless, to make it prosper,
    and they do not defend the rights of the needy.
29 Shall I not punish them for these things?
                                        says the LORD,

    and shall I not avenge myself
    on a nation such as this?"

30 An appalling and horrible thing
    has happened in the land:
31 the prophets prophesy falsely,
    and the priests rule at their direction;
my people love to have it so,
    but what will you do when the end comes?

(5) THE FAITHFUL ENJOINED TO FLEE BEFORE THE SIEGE

6 Flee for safety, O people of Benjamin,
    from the midst of Jerusalem!
Blow the trumpet in Tĕkō´á,
    and raise a signal on Bĕth-hăc´chĕrĕm;
for evil looms out of the north,
    and great destruction.
2 The comely and delicately bred I will destroy,
    the daughter of Zion.
3 Shepherds with their flocks shall come against her;
    they shall pitch their tents around her,
    they shall pasture, each in his place.
4 "Prepare war against her;
    up, and let us attack at noon!"
"Woe to us, for the day declines,
    for the shadows of evening lengthen!"
5 "Up, and let us attack by night,
    and destroy her palaces!"

f Heb uncertain

5.31 *the prophets* as a class were opposed
to Jeremiah's ministry. History knows them
as false prophets who were without inspiration, although they were influential.

(6) THE BESIEGERS ENCOURAGED AGAINST JERUSALEM

6 For thus says the LORD of hosts:
"Hew down her trees;
    cast up a siege mound against Jerusalem.
This is the city which must be punished;
    there is nothing but oppression within her.
7 As a well keeps its water fresh,
    so she keeps fresh her wickedness;
violence and destruction are heard within her;
    sickness and wounds are ever before me.
8 Be warned, O Jerusalem,
    lest I be alienated from you;
lest I make you a desolation,
    an uninhabited land."

9 Thus says the LORD of hosts:
"Glean[g] thoroughly as a vine
    the remnant of Israel;
like a grape-gatherer pass your hand again
    over its branches."
10 To whom shall I speak and give warning,
    that they may hear?
Behold, their ears are closed,[h]
    they cannot listen;
behold, the word of the LORD is to them an object of scorn,
    they take no pleasure in it.
11 Therefore I am full of the wrath of the LORD;
    I am weary of holding it in.
"Pour it out upon the children in the street,
    and upon the gatherings of young men, also;
both husband and wife shall be taken,
    the old folk and the very aged.
12 Their houses shall be turned over to others,
    their fields and wives together;
for I will stretch out my hand
    against the inhabitants of the land,"
                  says the LORD.
13 "For from the least to the greatest of them,
    every one is greedy for unjust gain;
and from prophet to priest,
    every one deals falsely.
14 They have healed the wound of my people lightly,
    saying, 'Peace, peace,'
    when there is no peace.
15 Were they ashamed when they committed abomination?
    No, they were not at all ashamed;
    they did not know how to blush.
Therefore they shall fall among those who fall;
    at the time that I punish them, they shall be overthrown,"
                  says the LORD.

(7) REFUSAL TO REPENT DESPITE IMPENDING RUIN

16 Thus says the LORD:
"Stand by the roads, and look,

g Cn: Heb *they shall glean*   h Heb *uncircumcised*

6.6 Deut 20.19, 20; Jer 32.24; 22.17

6.7 Isa 57.20; Ps 55.9–11; Jer 20.8; Ezek 7.11, 23

6.8 Jer 7.28; Ezek 23.18; Hos 9.12

6.9 Jer 49.9; 8.3

6.10 Jer 7.26; Acts 7.51; Jer 20.8

6.11 Job 32.18, 19; Jer 20.9; 9.21

6.12 Deut 28.30; Jer 8.10; 15.6

6.13 Isa 56.11; Jer 8.10; 22.17; Mic 3.5,11

6.14 Jer 8.11; Ezek 13.10; Jer 4.10; 23.17

6.15 Jer 3.3; 8.12

6.16 Isa 8.20; Jer 18.15; Mal 4.4; Lk 16.29; Mt 11.29

and ask for the ancient paths,
　　where the good way is; and walk in it,
　　and find rest for your souls.
But they said, 'We will not walk in it.'

6.17
Isa 21.11;
58.1;
Jer 25.4;
Ezek 3.17;
Hab 2.1

17 I set watchmen over you, saying,
　　'Give heed to the sound of the trumpet!'
But they said, 'We will not give heed.'

18 Therefore hear, O nations,
　　and know, O congregation, what will happen to them.

6.19
Isa 1.2;
Jer 19.3,15;
Prov 1.31;
Jer 8.9

19 Hear, O earth; behold, I am bringing evil upon this people,
　　the fruit of their devices,
because they have not given heed to my words;
　　and as for my law, they have rejected it.

6.20
Isa 1.11;
Amos 5.21;
Mic 6.6;
Isa 60.6;
Jer 7.21

20 To what purpose does frankincense come to me from Shébá,
　　or sweet cane from a distant land?
Your burnt offerings are not acceptable,
　　nor your sacrifices pleasing to me.

6.21
Isa 8.14;
Jer 13.16;
9.21,22

21 Therefore thus says the LORD:
'Behold, I will lay before this people
　　stumbling blocks against which they shall stumble;
fathers and sons together,
　　neighbor and friend shall perish.' "

(8) THE INVADER WILL SUDDENLY DESTROY

6.22
Jer 1.15;
5.15;10.22;
50.41–43;
Neh 1.9

22 Thus says the LORD:
"Behold, a people is coming from the north country,
　　a great nation is stirring from the farthest parts of the earth.

6.23
Jer 4.29;
50.42;
Isa 5.30

23 They lay hold on bow and spear,
　　they are cruel and have no mercy,
　　the sound of them is like the roaring sea;
they ride upon horses,
　　set in array as a man for battle,
　　against you, O daughter of Zion!"

6.24
Jer 4.31;
13.21;
49.24;
50.43

24 We have heard the report of it,
　　our hands fall helpless;
anguish has taken hold of us,
　　pain as of a woman in travail.

6.25
Jer 14.18;
12.12;
20.10

25 Go not forth into the field,
　　nor walk on the road;
for the enemy has a sword,
　　terror is on every side.

6.26
Jer 4.8;
25.34;
Mic 1.10;
Zech 12.10

26 O daughter of my people, gird on sackcloth,
　　and roll in ashes;
make mourning as for an only son,
　　most bitter lamentation;
for suddenly the destroyer
　　will come upon us.

6.27
Jer 1.18;
15.20; 9.7

27 "I have made you an assayer and tester among my people,
　　that you may know and assay their ways.

6.28
Jer 5.23;
9.4;
Ezek 22.18

28 They are all stubbornly rebellious,
　　going about with slanders;
they are bronze and iron,
　　all of them act corruptly.

6.29
Jer 15.19

29 The bellows blow fiercely,

the lead is consumed by the fire;
in vain the refining goes on,
  for the wicked are not removed.
30 Refuse silver they are called,
  for the LORD has rejected them."

C. Second movement: Sermon III: the great Temple-sermon

1. First indictment: idolatry and immorality

7 The word that came to Jĕrĕmī´äh from the LORD: 2 "Stand in the gate of the LORD's house, and proclaim there this word, and say, Hear the word of the LORD, all you men of Judah who enter these gates to worship the LORD. 3 Thus says the LORD of hosts, the God of Israel, Amend your ways and your doings, and I will let you dwell in this place. 4 Do not trust in these deceptive words: 'This is the temple of the LORD, the temple of the LORD, the temple of the LORD.'

5 "For if you truly amend your ways and your doings, if you truly execute justice one with another, 6 if you do not oppress the alien, the fatherless or the widow, or shed innocent blood in this place, and if you do not go after other gods to your own hurt, 7 then I will let you dwell in this place, in the land that I gave of old to your fathers for ever.

8 "Behold, you trust in deceptive words to no avail. 9 Will you steal, murder, commit adultery, swear falsely, burn incense to Bāäl, and go after other gods that you have not known, 10 and then come and stand before me in this house, which is called by my name, and say, 'We are delivered!'—only to go on doing all these abominations? 11 Has this house, which is called by my name, become a den of robbers in your eyes? Behold, I myself have seen it, says the LORD. 12 Go now to my place that was in Shīlōh, where I made my name dwell at first, and see what I did to it for the wickedness of my people Israel. 13And now, because you have done all these things, says the LORD, and when I spoke to you persistently you did not listen, and when I called you, you did not answer, 14 therefore I will do to the house which is called by my name, and in which you trust, and to the place which I gave to you and to your fathers, as I did to Shīlōh. 15And I will cast you out of my sight, as I cast out all your kinsmen, all the offspring of Ē´phräim.

16 "As for you, do not pray for this people, or lift up cry or prayer for them, and do not intercede with me, for I do not hear you. 17 Do you not see what they are doing in the cities of Judah and in the streets of Jerusalem? 18 The children gather wood, the fathers kindle fire, and the women knead dough, to make cakes for the queen of heaven; and they pour out drink offerings to other gods, to provoke me to anger. 19 Is it I whom they provoke? says

6.30	Jer 7.29
★7.1f	Jer 26.1,2
7.2	Jer 17.19; 2.4
7.3	Jer 18.11; 26.13
★7.4	Mic 3.11
7.5	Jer 4.1,2; 22.3
7.6	Deut 6.14, 15; 8.19; Jer 13.10
7.8	Jer 13.25
7.9	Ex 20.3; Jer 11.13, 17; 19.4
7.10	Ezek 23.39; Jer 32.34; 2.23,35
7.11	Mt 21.13; Mk 11.17; Lk 19.46
★7.12	Jer 26.6; 1 Sam 4.10, 11
7.13	2 Chr 36.15; Jer 35.17; Isa 65.12
7.14	1 Ki 9.7; ver 4,12
7.15	Jer 15.1; 2 Ki 17.23; Ps 78.67
7.16	Ex 32.10; Jer 11.14; 15.1
★7.18	Jer 44.17; 19.13; 11.17
7.19	Deut 32.16, 21

7.1, 2 Here, as elsewhere in Scripture, the writer professes that the words which he speaks are not his own words but originate with God. This is characteristic of the Old Testament prophets who often preface their message with, *"Thus says the* LORD*"* or some similar phrase. *Hear the word of the* LORD is Jeremiah's way of introducing a message which had been directly given to him by God. This is the essence of revelation.

7.4 *the temple of the* LORD. The false prophets insisted that God would never allow the heathen Babylonians to defile His Temple.

7.12 *Shiloh* had been the site of a sanctuary to Israel's God, but it was destroyed by the Philistines (cf. 1 Sam 4.10). Jerusalem could not expect its iniquities to be overlooked.

7.18 *the queen of heaven* was Ishtar, the Babylonian fertility goddess, later identified with Venus.

7.20
Jer 6.11,12;
8.13; 11.16

7.21
Isa 1.11;
Amos 5.21;
Hos 8.13

7.22
1 Sam
15.22;
Ps 51.16;
Hos 6.6

7.23
Ex 15.26;
Lev 26.12;
Isa 3.10

7.24
Ps 81.11,12;
Jer 15.6

7.25
Jer 25.4;
Lk 11.49

7.26
Jer 19.15;
16.12

7.27
Ezek 2.7;
3.7;
Isa 50.2

7.28
Jer 6.17;
5.3; 9.5

7.29
Job 1.20;
Isa 15.2;
Jer 16.6;
Mic 1.16;
Jer 3.21;
14.19

7.30
2 Ki 21.4;
2 Chr 33.4,
5,7;
Jer 23.11;
Ezek 7.20;
Dan 9.27

*7.31
2 Ki 23.10;
Jer 19.5;
Ps 106.38;
Deut 17.3

7.32
Jer 19.6,7,
11;
2 Ki 23.10

7.34
Isa 24.7,8;
Ezek 26.13;
Hos 2.11;
Rev 18.23;
Isa 1.7

8.1
Ezek 6.5

8.2
Acts 7.42;
Jer 22.19

8.3
Job 3.21;
7.15,16;
Rev 9.6;
Jer 23.3,8

the LORD. Is it not themselves, to their own confusion? 20 Therefore thus says the Lord GOD: Behold, my anger and my wrath will be poured out on this place, upon man and beast, upon the trees of the field and the fruit of the ground; it will burn and not be quenched."

21 Thus says the LORD of hosts, the God of Israel: "Add your burnt offerings to your sacrifices, and eat the flesh. 22 For in the day that I brought them out of the land of Egypt, I did not speak to your fathers or command them concerning burnt offerings and sacrifices. 23 But this command I gave them, 'Obey my voice, and I will be your God, and you shall be my people; and walk in all the way that I command you, that it may be well with you.' 24 But they did not obey or incline their ear, but walked in their own counsels and the stubbornness of their evil hearts, and went backward and not forward. 25 From the day that your fathers came out of the land of Egypt to this day, I have persistently sent all my servants the prophets to them, day after day; 26 yet they did not listen to me, or incline their ear, but stiffened their neck. They did worse than their fathers.

27 "So you shall speak all these words to them, but they will not listen to you. You shall call to them, but they will not answer you. 28 And you shall say to them, 'This is the nation that did not obey the voice of the LORD their God, and did not accept discipline; truth has perished; it is cut off from their lips.

29 Cut off your hair and cast it away;
    raise a lamentation on the bare heights,
for the LORD has rejected and forsaken
    the generation of his wrath.'

30 "For the sons of Judah have done evil in my sight, says the LORD; they have set their abominations in the house which is called by my name, to defile it. 31 And they have built the high place[i] of Tōpheth, which is in the valley of the son of Hinnom, to burn their sons and their daughters in the fire; which I did not command, nor did it come into my mind. 32 Therefore, behold, the days are coming, says the LORD, when it will no more be called Tōpheth, or the valley of the son of Hinnom, but the valley of Slaughter: for they will bury in Topheth, because there is no room elsewhere. 33 And the dead bodies of this people will be food for the birds of the air, and for the beasts of the earth; and none will frighten them away. 34 And I will make to cease from the cities of Judah and from the streets of Jerusalem the voice of mirth and the voice of gladness, the voice of the bridegroom and the voice of the bride; for the land shall become a waste.

8 "At that time, says the LORD, the bones of the kings of Judah, the bones of its princes, the bones of the priests, the bones of the prophets, and the bones of the inhabitants of Jerusalem shall be brought out of their tombs; 2 and they shall be spread before the sun and the moon and all the host of heaven, which they have loved and served, which they have gone after, and which they have sought and worshiped; and they shall not be gathered or buried; they shall be as dung on the surface of the ground. 3 Death shall be

---

i Gk Tg: Heb high places

7.31 *I did not command.* Human sacrifice such as that practiced at Hinnom was explic- itly contrary to God's command. Indeed, note: *nor did it come into my mind.*

preferred to life by all the remnant that remains of this evil family
in all the places where I have driven them, says the LORD of hosts.

2. *Second indictment: stubbornly unrepentant,*
they must be exiled

4 "You shall say to them, Thus says the LORD:
   When men fall, do they not rise again?
   If one turns away, does he not return?

8.4
Prov 24.16

5 Why then has this people turned away
   in perpetual backsliding?
They hold fast to deceit,
   they refuse to return.

8.5
Jer 5.6;
7.24; 5.27;
9.6

6 I have given heed and listened,
   but they have not spoken aright;
no man repents of his wickedness,
   saying, 'What have I done?'
Every one turns to his own course,
   like a horse plunging headlong into battle.

8.6
Ps 14.2;
Ezek 22.30;
Rev 9.20;
Job 39.21–
25

7 Even the stork in the heavens
   knows her times;
and the turtledove, swallow, and crane[j]
   keep the time of their coming;
but my people know not
   the ordinance of the LORD.

8.7
Isa 1.3;
Sol 2.12;
Jer 5.4,5

8 "How can you say, 'We are wise,
   and the law of the LORD is with us'?
But, behold, the false pen of the scribes
   has made it into a lie.

8.8
Jer 4.22;
Rom 2.17

9 The wise men shall be put to shame,
   they shall be dismayed and taken;
lo, they have rejected the word of the LORD,
   and what wisdom is in them?

8.9
Jer 6.15,19

10 Therefore I will give their wives to others
   and their fields to conquerors,
because from the least to the greatest
   every one is greedy for unjust gain;
from prophet to priest
   every one deals falsely.

8.10
Deut 28.30;
Isa 56.11

11 They have healed the wound of my people lightly,
   saying, 'Peace, peace,'
   when there is no peace.

*8.11
Jer 6.14;
Ezek 13.10

12 Were they ashamed when they committed abomination?
   No, they were not at all ashamed;
   they did not know how to blush.
Therefore they shall fall among the fallen;
   when I punish them, they shall be overthrown,
               says the LORD.

8.12
Jer 3.3;
6.21; 10.15

8.13
Jer 14.12;
Ezek 22.20,
21;

13 When I would gather them, says the LORD,
   there are no grapes on the vine,

Isa 5.2;
Joel 1.7;
Mt 21.19

---

j The meaning of the Hebrew word is uncertain

8.11 *lightly* here conveys the idea, "super-
ficially." False prophets sought to encourage
the people with assurances of peace, when
actually the sins of the Israelites were to lead
them to the judgment of the exile. (Also see
note to 5.31 on false prophets.)

nor figs on the fig tree;
   even the leaves are withered,
      and what I gave them has passed away from them."*k*

8.14
Jer 4.5;
35.11;9.15;
Mt 27.34;
Jer 3.25;
14.20

14 Why do we sit still?
   Gather together, let us go into the fortified cities
      and perish there;
   for the LORD our God has doomed us to perish,
      and has given us poisoned water to drink,
   because we have sinned against the LORD.

8.15
Jer 14.19

15 We looked for peace, but no good came,
      for a time of healing, but behold, terror.

*8.16
Jer 4.15;
Judg 5.22;
Jer 3.24;
10.25

16 "The snorting of their horses is heard from Dan;
      at the sound of the neighing of their stallions
         the whole land quakes.
   They come and devour the land and all that fills it,
      the city and those who dwell in it.

8.17
Num 21.6;
Ps 58.4,5

17 For behold, I am sending among you serpents,
      adders which cannot be charmed,
         and they shall bite you,"
                           says the LORD.

18 My grief is beyond healing,*l*
      my heart is sick within me.

8.19
Jer 4.16;
Isa 39.3;
Jer 14.9;
Deut 32.21;
Ps 31.6

19 Hark, the cry of the daughter of my people
      from the length and breadth of the land:
   "Is the LORD not in Zion?
      Is her King not in her?"
   "Why have they provoked me to anger with their graven images,
      and with their foreign idols?"

20 "The harvest is past, the summer is ended,
      and we are not saved."

8.21
Jer 14.17;
Joel 2.6;
Nah 2.10

21 For the wound of the daughter of my people is my heart
         wounded,
   I mourn, and dismay has taken hold on me.

*8.22
Gen 37.25;
Jer 14.19;
30.13

22 Is there no balm in Gil'ë*ă*d?
      Is there no physician there?
   Why then has the health of the daughter of my people
      not been restored?

3. *Third indictment: faithless and truthless, they must be scattered and slain*

9.1
Isa 22.4;
Lam 2.11;
Jer 6.26;
8.21,22

9*m* O that my head were waters,
      and my eyes a fountain of tears,
   that I might weep day and night
      for the slain of the daughter of my people!

9.2
Isa 55.6,7;
Jer 5,7,8,11;
12.1,6

2*n* O that I had in the desert
      a wayfarers' lodging place,

k Heb uncertain   *l* Cn Compare Gk: Heb uncertain
m Ch 8.23 in Heb   *n* Ch 9.1 in Heb

8.16 *Dan,* see note to Jer 4.15.
8.22 *balm.* Gilead produced a medicinal
balm. Israel's sickness could not be healed by
such balm, however.

that I might leave my people
and go away from them!
For they are all adulterers,
a company of treacherous men.
3 They bend their tongue like a bow;
falsehood and not truth has grown strong*o* in the land;
for they proceed from evil to evil,
and they do not know me, says the LORD.

9.3
Ps 64.3;
Isa 59.4;
Jer 4.22;
1 Sam 2.12;
Hos 4.1

4 Let every one beware of his neighbor,
and put no trust in any brother;
for every brother is a supplanter,
and every neighbor goes about as a slanderer.

9.4
ver 8;
Jer 12.6;
Gen 27.35;
Jer 6.28

5 Every one deceives his neighbor,
and no one speaks the truth;
they have taught their tongue to speak lies;
they commit iniquity and are too weary to repent.*p*

9.5
Mic 6.12;
Jer 12.13;
51.58,64

6 Heaping oppression upon oppression, and deceit upon deceit,
they refuse to know me, says the LORD.

9.6
Jer 5.27;
11.10;
Jn 3.19,20

7 Therefore thus says the LORD of hosts:
"Behold, I will refine them and test them,
for what else can I do, because of my people?

9.7
Isa 1.25;
Mal 3.3;
Hos 11.8

8 Their tongue is a deadly arrow;
it speaks deceitfully;
with his mouth each speaks peaceably to his neighbor,
but in his heart he plans an ambush for him.

9.8
Ps 12.2;
28.3;
Jer 5.26

9 Shall I not punish them for these things? says the LORD;
and shall I not avenge myself
on a nation such as this?

9.9
Jer 5.9,29

10 "Take up*q* weeping and wailing for the mountains,
and a lamentation for the pastures of the wilderness,
because they are laid waste so that no one passes through,
and the lowing of cattle is not heard;
both the birds of the air and the beasts
have fled and are gone.

9.10
Jer 4.24–26;
Hos 4.3;
Ezek 14.15

11 I will make Jerusalem a heap of ruins,
a lair of jackals;
and I will make the cities of Judah a desolation,
without inhabitant."

9.11
Isa 25.2;
13.22;
34.13;
Jer 4.27;
26.9

9.12
Ps 107.43;
Hos 14.9;
Jer 23.10,16

12 Who is the man so wise that he can understand this? To whom has the mouth of the LORD spoken, that he may declare it? Why is the land ruined and laid waste like a wilderness, so that no one passes through? 13And the LORD says: "Because they have forsaken my law which I set before them, and have not obeyed my voice, or walked in accord with it, 14 but have stubbornly followed their own hearts and have gone after the Baals, as their fathers taught them. 15 Therefore thus says the LORD of hosts, the God of Israel: Behold, I will feed this people with wormwood, and give them poisonous water to drink. 16 I will scatter them among the nations whom neither they nor their fathers have known; and I will send the sword after them, until I have consumed them."

9.13
Jer 5.19;
Ps 89.30

9.14
Rom 1.21–24;
Gal 1.14;
1 Pet 1.18

9.15
Jer 8.14;
23.15

9.16
Lev 26.33;
Deut 28.64;
Jer 44.27;
Ezek 5.2

---

o Gk: Heb *and not for truth they have grown strong*
p Cn Compare Gk: Heb *your dwelling*   *q* Gk Syr: Heb *I will take up*

Jeremiah 9.17—10.4

9.17
2 Chr 35.25;
Ecc 12.5;
Amos 5.16

17 Thus says the LORD of hosts:
"Consider, and call for the mourning women to come;
    send for the skilful women to come;

9.18
Jer 14.17

18 let them make haste and raise a wailing over us,
    that our eyes may run down with tears,
    and our eyelids gush with water.

9.19
Jer 4.13;
7.15; 15.1

19 For a sound of wailing is heard from Zion:
    'How we are ruined!
We are utterly shamed,
because we have left the land,
    because they have cast down our dwellings.' "

9.20
Isa 32.9

20 Hear, O women, the word of the LORD,
    and let your ear receive the word of his mouth;
teach to your daughters a lament,
    and each to her neighbor a dirge.

9.21
Jer 15.7;
18.21; 6.11

21 For death has come up into our windows,
    it has entered our palaces,
cutting off the children from the streets
    and the young men from the squares.

4. *Conclusion: true wisdom is knowing the LORD; idolatry brings destruction*

9.22
Jer 8.2;
16.4

22 Speak, "Thus says the LORD:
'The dead bodies of men shall fall
    like dung upon the open field,
like sheaves after the reaper,
    and none shall gather them.' "

9.23
Ecc 9.11;
Isa 10.8–12;
Ps 49.6–9
9.24
1 Cor 1.31;
2 Cor 10.17;
Gal 6.14;
Ps 36.5,7;
Mic 7.18

23 Thus says the LORD: "Let not the wise man glory in his wisdom, let not the mighty man glory in his might, let not the rich man glory in his riches; 24 but let him who glories glory in this, that he understands and knows me, that I am the LORD who practice steadfast love, justice, and righteousness in the earth; for in these things I delight, says the LORD."

*9.25
Rom 2.8,9
9.26
Jer 25.23;
Lev 26.41;
Ezek 44.7;
Rom 2.28

25 "Behold, the days are coming, says the LORD, when I will punish all those who are circumcised but yet uncircumcised— 26 Egypt, Judah, Ēdóm, the sons of Ămmòn, Mòãb, and all who dwell in the desert that cut the corners of their hair; for all these nations are uncircumcised, and all the house of Israel is uncircumcised in heart."

10.2
Lev 18.3;
Isa 47.12–
14

10 Hear the word which the LORD speaks to you, O house of Israel. 2 Thus says the LORD:
"Learn not the way of the nations,
    nor be dismayed at the signs of the heavens
    because the nations are dismayed at them,

10.3
Isa 40.19;
45.20

3 for the customs of the peoples are false.
A tree from the forest is cut down,
    and worked with an axe by the hands of a craftsman.

10.4
ver 14;
Isa 41.7

4 Men deck it with silver and gold;

9.25 *circumcised but yet uncircumcised.* Yahweh makes a distinction between the external rite of circumcision and the Israelite motivated by spiritual considerations. The external mark was not enough. The words stipulate that spiritual devotion is necessary.

they fasten it with hammer and nails
   so that it cannot move.
5 Their idols[r] are like scarecrows in a cucumber field,
   and they cannot speak;
they have to be carried,
   for they cannot walk.
Be not afraid of them,
   for they cannot do evil,
   neither is it in them to do good."

6 There is none like thee, O LORD;
   thou art great, and thy name is great in might.
7 Who would not fear thee, O King of the nations?
   For this is thy due;
for among all the wise ones of the nations
   and in all their kingdoms
   there is none like thee.
8 They are both stupid and foolish;
   the instruction of idols is but wood!
9 Beaten silver is brought from Tarshĭsh,
   and gold from Ūphâz.
They are the work of the craftsman and of the hands of the goldsmith;
   their clothing is violet and purple;
   they are all the work of skilled men.
10 But the LORD is the true God;
   he is the living God and the everlasting King.
At his wrath the earth quakes,
   and the nations cannot endure his indignation.

11 Thus shall you say to them: "The gods who did not make
the heavens and the earth shall perish from the earth and from
under the heavens."[s]

12 It is he who made the earth by his power,
   who established the world by his wisdom,
   and by his understanding stretched out the heavens.
13 When he utters his voice there is a tumult of waters in the
   heavens,
   and he makes the mist rise from the ends of the earth.
He makes lightnings for the rain,
   and he brings forth the wind from his storehouses.
14 Every man is stupid and without knowledge;
   every goldsmith is put to shame by his idols;
for his images are false,
   and there is no breath in them.
15 They are worthless, a work of delusion;
   at the time of their punishment they shall perish.
16 Not like these is he who is the portion of Jacob,
   for he is the one who formed all things,

[r] Heb *They*   [s] This verse is in Aramaic

Marginal references:

10.5
Ps 115.5;
1 Cor 12.2;
Isa 46.1,7;
41.23

10.6
Deut 33.26;
Isa 12.6;
Jer 32.18

10.7
Ps 22.28;
Dan 2.27,
28;
1 Cor 1.19,
20

10.8
ver 14;
Jer 4.22;
2.27

*10.9
Isa 40.19;
Ps 72.10;
Dan 10.5;
Ps 115.4

10.10
Isa 65.16;
Jer 4.2;
50.46;
Ps 76.7

10.11
Ps 96.5;
Isa 2.18;
Zeph 2.11

10.12
Jer 51.15–
19;
Ps 78.69;
Job 9.8;
Isa 40.22

10.13
Ps 29.3–9;
Job 36.27–
29;
Ps 135.7

10.14
Jer 51.17;
Isa 42.17;
Hab 2.18

10.15
Jer 8.19;
51.18

10.16
Ps 73.26;
Jer 51.19;
Isa 45.7;
Deut 32.9;
Jer 31.35

10.9 *Uphaz* may be a variant of Ophir, the
more modern rendering. This would place
it in southwest Arabia. Dan 10.5 also refers
to Uphaz in connection with gold.

and Israel is the tribe of his inheritance;
the LORD of hosts is his name.

10.17
Ezek 12.3–12

17 Gather up your bundle from the ground,
O you who dwell under siege!

10.18
1 Sam 25.29;
Ezek 6.10

18 For thus says the LORD:
"Behold, I am slinging out the inhabitants of the land
at this time,
and I will bring distress on them,
that they may feel it."

10.19
Jer 4.19,31;
14.17;
Mic 7.9

19 Woe is me because of my hurt!
My wound is grievous.
But I said, "Truly this is an affliction,
and I must bear it."

10.20
Jer 4.20;
31.15;
Isa 51.18

20 My tent is destroyed,
and all my cords are broken;
my children have gone from me,
and they are not;
there is no one to spread my tent again,
and to set up my curtains.

10.21
Jer 2.8;
23.2

21 For the shepherds are stupid,
and do not inquire of the LORD;
therefore they have not prospered,
and all their flock is scattered.

*10.22
Jer 4.15;
1.14; 9.11

22 Hark, a rumor! Behold, it comes!—
a great commotion out of the north country
to make the cities of Judah a desolation,
a lair of jackals.

10.23
Prov 20.24;
Isa 26.7
10.24
Ps 6.1

23 I know, O LORD, that the way of man is not in himself,
that it is not in man who walks to direct his steps.
24 Correct me, O LORD, but in just measure;
not in thy anger, lest thou bring me to nothing.

10.25
Ps 79.6,7;
Job 18.21;
Jer 8.16;
50.7,17

25 Pour out thy wrath upon the nations that know thee not,
and upon the peoples that call not on thy name;
for they have devoured Jacob;
they have devoured him and consumed him,
and have laid waste his habitation.

D. *Third movement: signs of judgments and deliverances
to come*

1. *Sermon IV: the broken covenant and the marred waistcloth*
a. *Judah has broken the covenant*

11 The word that came to Jĕrémī'áh from the LORD: 2 "Hear
the words of this covenant, and speak to the men of Judah
and the inhabitants of Jerusalem. 3 You shall say to them, Thus
says the LORD, the God of Israel: Cursed be the man who does not

*11.3
Deut 27.26;
Gal 3.10

10.22 *the north country* first hears the report
of the advance of Nebuchadnezzar's armies.
11.3 Jeremiah here is speaking of the
broken covenant (see note to Deut 29.1).

The failure of Israel to keep the terms
and conditions of this covenant could lead
only to judgment and dispersion, according to
the promises of God in that covenant.

heed the words of this covenant 4 which I commanded your fathers when I brought them out of the land of Egypt, from the iron furnace, saying, Listen to my voice, and do all that I command you. So shall you be my people, and I will be your God, 5 that I may perform the oath which I swore to your fathers, to give them a land flowing with milk and honey, as at this day." Then I answered, "So be it, LORD."

6 And the LORD said to me, "Proclaim all these words in the cities of Judah, and in the streets of Jerusalem: Hear the words of this covenant and do them. 7 For I solemnly warned your fathers when I brought them up out of the land of Egypt, warning them persistently, even to this day, saying, Obey my voice. 8 Yet they did not obey or incline their ear, but every one walked in the stubbornness of his evil heart. Therefore I brought upon them all the words of this covenant, which I commanded them to do, but they did not."

9 Again the LORD said to me, "There is revolt among the men of Judah and the inhabitants of Jerusalem. 10 They have turned back to the iniquities of their forefathers, who refused to hear my words; they have gone after other gods to serve them; the house of Israel and the house of Judah have broken my covenant which I made with their fathers. 11 Therefore, thus says the LORD, Behold, I am bringing evil upon them which they cannot escape; though they cry to me, I will not listen to them. 12 Then the cities of Judah and the inhabitants of Jerusalem will go and cry to the gods to whom they burn incense, but they cannot save them in the time of their trouble. 13 For your gods have become as many as your cities, O Judah; and as many as the streets of Jerusalem are the altars you have set up to shame, altars to burn incense to Bāäl.

14 "Therefore do not pray for this people, or lift up a cry or prayer on their behalf, for I will not listen when they call to me in the time of their trouble. 15 What right has my beloved in my house, when she has done vile deeds? Can vows' and sacrificial flesh avert your doom? Can you then exult? 16 The LORD once called you, 'A green olive tree, fair with goodly fruit'; but with the roar of a great tempest he will set fire to it, and its branches will be consumed. 17 The LORD of hosts, who planted you, has pronounced evil against you, because of the evil which the house of Israel and the house of Judah have done, provoking me to anger by burning incense to Bāäl."

b. Her corruption makes doom inevitable

18 The LORD made it known to me and I knew;
then thou didst show me their evil deeds.
19 But I was like a gentle lamb
led to the slaughter.
I did not know it was against me
they devised schemes, saying,
"Let us destroy the tree with its fruit,
let us cut him off from the land of the living,
that his name be remembered no more."
20 But, O LORD of hosts, who judgest righteously,
who triest the heart and the mind,

' Gk: Heb many

11.4 Ex 24.3–8; Deut 4.20; 1 Ki 8.51; Jer 7.23; 24.7
11.5 Ex 13.5; Deut 7.12; Jer 32.22; 28.6
11.6 Jer 3.12; ver 2; Rom 2.13
11.7 1 Sam 8.9; Jer 7.13,25
11.8 Jer 7.26; Mic 7.9; Lev 26.14–43
11.9 Ezek 22.25; Hos 6.9
11.10 1 Sam 15.11; Jer 13.10; Judg 2.11–13; Jer 3.6–11
11.11 ver 17; Jer 35.35; ver 14; Jer 14.12
11.12 Deut 32.37; Jer 44.17
11.13 Jer 2.28; 3.24; 7.9
11.14 Ex 32.10; ver 11; Ps 66.18
11.15 Jer 12.7; 13.27; 4.22
11.16 Ps 52.8; 83.2; Jer 21.14
11.17 Jer 12.2; 16.10,11; 32.27
11.18 1 Sam 23.11,12
11.19 Isa 53.7; Jer 18.18; Ps 83.4; 52.5; 109.13
11.20 Jer 20.12; Ps 7.9

let me see thy vengeance upon them,
for to thee have I committed my cause.

21 Therefore thus says the LORD concerning the men of Ăn'-
ăthŏth, who seek your life, and say, "Do not prophesy in the name
of the LORD, or you will die by our hand"—22 therefore thus says
the LORD of hosts: "Behold, I will punish them; the young men
shall die by the sword; their sons and their daughters shall die by
famine; 23 and none of them shall be left. For I will bring evil upon
the men of Ăn'ăthŏth, the year of their punishment."

12 Righteous art thou, O LORD,
    when I complain to thee;
  yet I would plead my case before thee.
Why does the way of the wicked prosper?
  Why do all who are treacherous thrive?

2 Thou plantest them, and they take root;
    they grow and bring forth fruit;
  thou art near in their mouth
    and far from their heart.

3 But thou, O LORD, knowest me;
    thou seest me, and triest my mind toward thee.
  Pull them out like sheep for the slaughter,
    and set them apart for the day of slaughter.

4 How long will the land mourn,
    and the grass of every field wither?
  For the wickedness of those who dwell in it
    the beasts and the birds are swept away,
  because men said, "He will not see our latter end."

5 "If you have raced with men on foot, and they have wearied you,
    how will you compete with horses?
  And if in a safe land you fall down,
    how will you do in the jungle of the Jordan?
6 For even your brothers and the house of your father,
    even they have dealt treacherously with you;
    they are in full cry after you;
  believe them not,
    though they speak fair words to you."

7 "I have forsaken my house,
    I have abandoned my heritage;
  I have given the beloved of my soul
    into the hands of her enemies.
8 My heritage has become to me
    like a lion in the forest,
  she has lifted up her voice against me;
    therefore I hate her.
9 Is my heritage to me like a speckled bird of prey?
    Are the birds of prey against her round about?
  Go, assemble all the wild beasts;
    bring them to devour.

Cross references (left margin):
11.21: Jer 12.5,6; Amos 2.12; Jer 26.8; 38.4
11.22: Jer 21.14; 18.21
11.23: Jer 6.9; 23.12; 48.44
*12.1: Jer 11.20; Job 13.3; Jer 5.27,28; 20.5,11
12.2: Jer 11.17; Isa 29.13; Ezek 33.31
12.3: Ps 139.1-4; Jer 11.20; 17.18
12.4: Jer 9.10; Joel 1.10-17; Hos 4.3; Jer 4.25
*12.5: Jer 26.8; 38.4-6; 49.19; 50.44
12.6: Jer 9.4; Ps 12.2; Prov 26.25
12.7: Jer 7.29; 11.15; Lam 2.1
12.8: Isa 59.13; Hos 9.15
12.9: 2 Ki 24.2; Isa 56.9

12.1 *when I complain to thee.* The prophet was disturbed at the prosperity of the wicked and brought his complaint to God.
12.5 *horses.* Jeremiah is told that his trials will become greater rather than less. Instead of competing with *men on foot* he will have to race horses! *the jungle* was the place where lions and other wild beasts lurked.

¹⁰ Many shepherds have destroyed my vineyard,
　they have trampled down my portion,
they have made my pleasant portion
　a desolate wilderness.
¹¹ They have made it a desolation;
　desolate, it mourns to me.
The whole land is made desolate,
　but no man lays it to heart.
¹² Upon all the bare heights in the desert
　destroyers have come;
for the sword of the LORD devours
　from one end of the land to the other;
　no flesh has peace.
¹³ They have sown wheat and have reaped thorns,
　they have tired themselves out but profit nothing.
They shall be ashamed of their^u harvests
　because of the fierce anger of the LORD."

14 Thus says the LORD concerning all my evil neighbors who touch the heritage which I have given my people Israel to inherit: "Behold, I will pluck them up from their land, and I will pluck up the house of Judah from among them. ¹⁵And after I have plucked them up, I will again have compassion on them, and I will bring them again each to his heritage and each to his land. ¹⁶And it shall come to pass, if they will diligently learn the ways of my people, to swear by my name, 'As the LORD lives,' even as they taught my people to swear by Bāal, then they shall be built up in the midst of my people. ¹⁷ But if any nation will not listen, then I will utterly pluck it up and destroy it, says the LORD."

c. Five warnings to Judah: the marred waistcloth in the mud

13 Thus said the LORD to me, "Go and buy a linen waistcloth, and put it on your loins, and do not dip it in water." ² So I bought a waistcloth according to the word of the LORD, and put it on my loins. ³And the word of the LORD came to me a second time, ⁴ "Take the waistcloth which you have bought, which is upon your loins, and arise, go to the Eūphrā′tēṣ, and hide it there in a cleft of the rock." ⁵ So I went, and hid it by the Eūphrā′tēṣ, as the LORD commanded me. ⁶And after many days the LORD said to me, "Arise, go to the Eūphrā′tēṣ, and take from there the waistcloth which I commanded you to hide there." ⁷ Then I went to the Eūphrā′tēṣ, and dug, and I took the waistcloth from the place where I had hidden it. And behold, the waistcloth was spoiled; it was good for nothing.

⁸ Then the word of the LORD came to me: ⁹ "Thus says the LORD: Even so will I spoil the pride of Judah and the great pride of Jerusalem. ¹⁰ This evil people, who refuse to hear my words, who stubbornly follow their own heart and have gone after other gods to serve them and worship them, shall be like this waistcloth, which is good for nothing. ¹¹ For as the waistcloth clings to the loins of a man, so I made the whole house of Israel and the whole house of Judah cling to me, says the LORD, that they might be for me a people, a name, a praise, and a glory, but they would not listen.

^u Heb your

12.10 Jer 23.1; Isa 5.1–7; 63.18; Jer 3.19
12.11 Jer 4.20,27; Isa 42.25
12.12 Jer 3.2,21; Isa 34.6; Jer 16.5; 30.5
12.13 Lev 26.16; Deut 28.38; Mic 6.15; Hag 1.6; Jer 9.5; 17.10
12.14 Zech 2.8–10; Deut 30.3; Isa 11.11–16
12.15 Ezek 28.25; Jer 48.47; 49.6,39; Amos 9.14
12.16 Isa 42.6; Jer 4.2; 5.7; Eph 2.20,21
12.17 Isa 60.12
13.1 ver 11
13.2 Isa 20.2
13.4 Jer 51.63
13.5 Ex 39.42, 43; 40.16
13.9 Lev 26.19; ver 15–17
13.10 Jer 9.14; 11.8; 16.12
13.11 Ex 19.5,6; Jer 7.23; 32.20; 33.9

*13.12

13.13
Isa 51.17;
21; 63.6;
Jer 25.27;
51.7
13.14
Jer 19.9–11;
6.21; 16.5;
Isa 27.11

13.15
Prov 16.5

13.16
Ps 96.8;
Isa 59.9;
Jer 23.12;
2.6

13.17
Mal 2.2;
Jer 9.1;
14.17;
23.1,2

*13.18
2 Chr
33.12,19;
Isa 3.20;
Ezek 24.17,
23
13.19
Jer 32.44;
20.4;
52.27–30

13.20
Jer 6.22;
ver 17

13.21
Jer 5.31;
2,25; 4.31

13.22
Deut 7.17;
Jer 5.19;
16.10

13.23
Prov 27.22;
Jer 4.22

12 "You shall speak to them this word: 'Thus says the LORD, the God of Israel, "Every jar shall be filled with wine."' And they will say to you, 'Do we not indeed know that every jar will be filled with wine?' 13 Then you shall say to them, 'Thus says the LORD: Behold, I will fill with drunkenness all the inhabitants of this land: the kings who sit on David's throne, the priests, the prophets, and all the inhabitants of Jerusalem. 14 And I will dash them one against another, fathers and sons together, says the LORD. I will not pity or spare or have compassion, that I should not destroy them.' "

15 Hear and give ear; be not proud,
    for the LORD has spoken.
16 Give glory to the LORD your God
    before he brings darkness,
    before your feet stumble
    on the twilight mountains,
and while you look for light
    he turns it into gloom
    and makes it deep darkness.
17 But if you will not listen,
    my soul will weep in secret for your pride;
my eyes will weep bitterly and run down with tears,
    because the LORD's flock has been taken captive.

18 Say to the king and the queen mother:
    "Take a lowly seat,
for your beautiful crown
    has come down from your head."ᵛ
19 The cities of the Nĕgĕb are shut up,
    with none to open them;
all Judah is taken into exile,
    wholly taken into exile.

20 "Lift up your eyes and see
    those who come from the north.
Where is the flock that was given you,
    your beautiful flock?
21 What will you say when they set as head over you
    those whom you yourself have taught
    to be friends to you?
Will not pangs take hold of you,
    like those of a woman in travail?
22 And if you say in your heart,
    'Why have these things come upon me?'
it is for the greatness of your iniquity
    that your skirts are lifted up,
    and you suffer violence.
23 Can the Ethiopian change his skin
    or the leopard his spots?
Then also you can do good

ᵛ Gk Syr Vg: Heb obscure

13.12 *Every jar shall be filled with wine,* i.e., everything gets what it is fitted for.   **13.18** *the king,* Jehoiachin. *the queen mother,* Nehushta (2 Ki 24.8).

who are accustomed to do evil.
24 I will scatter you^w like chaff
  driven by the wind from the desert.
25 This is your lot,
  the portion I have measured out to you, says the LORD,
because you have forgotten me
  and trusted in lies.
26 I myself will lift up your skirts over your face,
  and your shame will be seen.
27 I have seen your abominations,
  your adulteries and neighings, your lewd harlotries,
  on the hills in the field.
Woe to you, O Jerusalem!
  How long will it be
  before you are made clean?"

2. Sermon V: the exile inevitable, yet Judah will some day be restored

a. Judah beyond deliverance: drought, sword, famine must come

14 The word of the LORD which came to Jĕrĕmī'áh concerning the drought:

2 "Judah mourns
  and her gates languish;
her people lament on the ground,
  and the cry of Jerusalem goes up.
3 Her nobles send their servants for water;
  they come to the cisterns,
they find no water,
  they return with their vessels empty;
they are ashamed and confounded
  and cover their heads.
4 Because of the ground which is dismayed,
  since there is no rain on the land,
the farmers are ashamed,
  they cover their heads.
5 Even the hind in the field forsakes her newborn calf
  because there is no grass.
6 The wild asses stand on the bare heights,
  they pant for air like jackals;
their eyes fail
  because there is no herbage.

7 "Though our iniquities testify against us,
  act, O LORD, for thy name's sake;
for our backslidings are many,
  we have sinned against thee.
8 O thou hope of Israel,
  its savior in time of trouble,
why shouldst thou be like a stranger in the land,
  like a wayfarer who turns aside to tarry for a night?
9 Why shouldst thou be like a man confused,
  like a mighty man who cannot save?
Yet thou, O LORD, art in the midst of us,

^w Heb them

Marginal references:
13.24 Jer 9.16; 4.11; 18.17
13.25 Ps 11.6; Jer 2.32; 3.21
13.26 Ezek 16.37; Hos 2.10
13.27 Jer 5.7,8; 11.15; 2.20; 4.14; Hos 8.5
14.1 Jer 17.8
14.2 Isa 3.26; Jer 8.21; 11.11; 46.12
14.3 1 Ki 18.5; 2 Ki 18.31; 2 Sam 15.30
14.4 Joel 1.19, 20; Jer 3.3; Joel 1.11
14.5 Isa 15.6
14.6 Jer 2.24; Joel 1.18
14.7 Isa 59.12; Jer 5.6; 8.5
14.8 Jer 17.13; Isa 43.3; 63.8; Ps 50.15
14.9 Isa 50.2; Jer 8.19; 15.16; Isa 63.19

and we are called by thy name;
    leave us not."

14.10
Jer 2.25;
6.20;
Hos 8.13

10 Thus says the LORD concerning this people:
"They have loved to wander thus,
    they have not restrained their feet;
therefore the LORD does not accept them,
    now he will remember their iniquity
    and punish their sins."

14.11
Ex 32.10;
Jer 7.16
14.12
Isa 1.15;
Jer 11.11;
6.20; 7.21;
9.16; 21.9

11 The LORD said to me: "Do not pray for the welfare of this people. 12 Though they fast, I will not hear their cry, and though they offer burnt offering and cereal offering, I will not accept them; but I will consume them by the sword, by famine, and by pestilence."

14.13
Jer 5.12;
23.17; 6.14
14.14
Jer 5.31;
27.15;
23.16,26;
Ezek 12.24
14.15
Jer 5.12,13;
Ezek 14.10

13 Then I said: "Ah, Lord GOD, behold, the prophets say to them, 'You shall not see the sword, nor shall you have famine, but I will give you assured peace in this place.'" 14And the LORD said to me: "The prophets are prophesying lies in my name; I did not send them, nor did I command them or speak to them. They are prophesying to you a lying vision, worthless divination, and the deceit of their own minds. 15 Therefore thus says the LORD concerning the prophets who prophesy in my name although I did not send them, and who say, 'Sword and famine shall not come on this land': By sword and famine those prophets shall be consumed.

14.16
Isa 9.16;
Jer 7.33;
8.1,2;
13.22–25

16And the people to whom they prophesy shall be cast out in the streets of Jerusalem, victims of famine and sword, with none to bury them—them, their wives, their sons, and their daughters. For I will pour out their wickedness upon them.

14.17
Jer 9.1;
Lam 1.15,
16;
Jer 10.19;
30.14,15

17 "You shall say to them this word:
'Let my eyes run down with tears night and day,
    and let them not cease,
for the virgin daughter of my people is smitten with a great
        wound,
    with a very grievous blow.

14.18
Jer 6.25;
Ezek 7.15;
Jer 6.13;
2.8; 5.5

18 If I go out into the field,
    behold, those slain by the sword!
And if I enter the city,
    behold, the diseases of famine!
For both prophet and priest ply their trade through the land,
    and have no knowledge.'"

14.19
Jer 6.30;
30.13; 8.15;
1 Thess 5.3

19 Hast thou utterly rejected Judah?
    Does thy soul loathe Zion?
Why hast thou smitten us
    so that there is no healing for us?
We looked for peace, but no good came;
    for a time of healing, but behold, terror.

14.20
Jer 3.25;
8.14

20 We acknowledge our wickedness, O LORD,
    and the iniquity of our fathers,
    for we have sinned against thee.

14.21
ver 7;
Jer 3.17;
17.12

21 Do not spurn us, for thy name's sake;
    do not dishonor thy glorious throne;
    remember and do not break thy covenant with us.

22 Are there any among the false gods of the nations that can
    bring rain?
  Or can the heavens give showers?
Art thou not he, O LORD our God?
  We set our hope on thee,
  for thou doest all these things.

b. *Not even the intercession of Moses or Samuel could avert judgment*

15 Then the LORD said to me, "Though Moses and Samuel
stood before me, yet my heart would not turn toward this
people. Send them out of my sight, and let them go! 2And when
they ask you, 'Where shall we go?' you shall say to them, 'Thus
says the LORD:

"Those who are for pestilence, to pestilence,
  and those who are for the sword, to the sword;
those who are for famine, to famine,
  and those who are for captivity, to captivity." '

3 "I will appoint over them four kinds of destroyers, says the
LORD: the sword to slay, the dogs to tear, and the birds of the air
and the beasts of the earth to devour and destroy. 4And I will make
them a horror to all the kingdoms of the earth because of what
Mȧnăs′sėh the son of Hĕzĕkī′ȧh, king of Judah, did in Jerusalem.

5 "Who will have pity on you, O Jerusalem,
  or who will bemoan you?
Who will turn aside
  to ask about your welfare?
6 You have rejected me, says the LORD,
  you keep going backward;
so I have stretched out my hand against you and destroyed
  you;—
  I am weary of relenting.
7 I have winnowed them with a winnowing fork
  in the gates of the land;
I have bereaved them, I have destroyed my people;
  they did not turn from their ways.
8 I have made their widows more in number
  than the sand of the seas;
I have brought against the mothers of young men
  a destroyer at noonday;
I have made anguish and terror
  fall upon them suddenly.
9 She who bore seven has languished;
  she has swooned away;
her sun went down while it was yet day;
  she has been shamed and disgraced.
And the rest of them I will give to the sword
  before their enemies,

                says the LORD."

10 Woe is me, my mother, that you bore me, a man of strife
and contention to the whole land! I have not lent, nor have I borrowed, yet all of them curse me. 11 So let it be, O LORD,ˣ if I have

x Gk Old Latin: Heb *the* LORD *said*

Marginal references:

14.22 Isa 41.29; Jer 10.3; 5.24; Isa 41.4; 43.10; Lam 3.26

15.1 Ezek 14.14, 20; Ex 32.11, 12; 1 Sam 7.9; 12.23; 2 Ki 17.20; Jer 7.15; 10.20

15.2 Jer 43.11; Ezek 5.2, 12; Zech 11.9

15.3 Lev 26.16; 1 Ki 21.23, 24; Deut 28.26; Jer 7.33

15.4 Deut 28.25; 2 Ki 21.11ff; 23.26

15.5 Ps 69.20; Isa 51.19; Jer 16.5

15.6 Jer 6.19; 7.24; 6.11, 12; 7.16

15.7 Jer 51.2; 18.21; 5.3

15.8 Isa 3.25,26; Jer 22.7; 6.4

15.9 1 Sam 2.5; Isa 47.9; Jer 6.4; Amos 8.9; Jer 50.12; 21.7

15.10 Job 3.1; Jer 20.14; Deut 23.19

15.11 Isa 41.10; Jer 39.11, 12; 40.4,5

not entreated^y thee for their good, if I have not pleaded with thee
on behalf of the enemy in the time of trouble and in the time of
distress! 12 Can one break iron, iron from the north, and bronze?

13 "Your wealth and your treasures I will give as spoil, without
price, for all your sins, throughout all your territory. 14 I will make
you serve your enemies in a land which you do not know, for in
my anger a fire is kindled which shall burn for ever."

c. Jeremiah encouraged to persevere

15 O LORD, thou knowest;
     remember me and visit me,
     and take vengeance for me on my persecutors.
   In thy forbearance take me not away;
     know that for thy sake I bear reproach.
16 Thy words were found, and I ate them,
     and thy words became to me a joy
     and the delight of my heart;
   for I am called by thy name,
     O LORD, God of hosts.
17 I did not sit in the company of merrymakers,
     nor did I rejoice;
   I sat alone, because thy hand was upon me,
     for thou hadst filled me with indignation.
18 Why is my pain unceasing,
     my wound incurable,
     refusing to be healed?
   Wilt thou be to me like a deceitful brook,
     like waters that fail?

19 Therefore thus says the LORD:
   "If you return, I will restore you,
     and you shall stand before me.
   If you utter what is precious, and not what is worthless,
     you shall be as my mouth.
   They shall turn to you,
     but you shall not turn to them.
20 And I will make you to this people
     a fortified wall of bronze;
   they will fight against you,
     but they shall not prevail over you,
   for I am with you
     to save you and deliver you,
                                   says the LORD.
21 I will deliver you out of the hand of the wicked,
     and redeem you from the grasp of the ruthless."

3. Sermon VI: the sign of Jeremiah's unmarried state

a. Command to remain unmarried lest his children should perish

16 The word of the LORD came to me: 2 "You shall not take a
wife, nor shall you have sons or daughters in this place.
3 For thus says the LORD concerning the sons and daughters who
are born in this place, and concerning the mothers who bore them

^y Cn: Heb obscure

15.12
Jer 28.14
15.13
Ps 44.12;
Jer 17.3;
Isa 52.3,5
15.14
Jer 16.13;
17.4;
Deut 32.22
15.15
Jer 12.3;
20.11;
Ps 69.7–9
15.16
Ezek 3.1–3;
Ps 119.72;
Jer 14.9
15.17
Jer 16.8;
Ezek 3.24,
25
15.18
Jer 30.15;
Mic 1.9;
Jer 14.3
15.19
Jer 4.1;
Ezek 22.26
15.20
Jer 1.18,19;
20.11;
Isa 41.10
15.21
Jer 20.13;
31.11
16.1
Jer 1.2,4
16.2
1 Cor 7.26
16.3
Jer 6.11;
15.8; 6.21

and the fathers who begot them in this land: 4 They shall die of deadly diseases. They shall not be lamented, nor shall they be buried; they shall be as dung on the surface of the ground. They shall perish by the sword and by famine, and their dead bodies shall be food for the birds of the air and for the beasts of the earth.

5 "For thus says the LORD: Do not enter the house of mourning, or go to lament, or bemoan them; for I have taken away my peace from this people, says the LORD, my steadfast love and mercy. 6 Both great and small shall die in this land; they shall not be buried, and no one shall lament for them or cut himself or make himself bald for them. 7 No one shall break bread for the mourner, to comfort him for the dead; nor shall any one give him the cup of consolation to drink for his father or his mother. 8 You shall not go into the house of feasting to sit with them, to eat and drink. 9 For thus says the LORD of hosts, the God of Israel: Behold, I will make to cease from this place, before your eyes and in your days, the voice of mirth and the voice of gladness, the voice of the bridegroom and the voice of the bride.

10 "And when you tell this people all these words, and they say to you, 'Why has the LORD pronounced all this great evil against us? What is our iniquity? What is the sin that we have committed against the LORD our God?' 11 then you shall say to them: 'Because your fathers have forsaken me, says the LORD, and have gone after other gods and have served and worshiped them, and have forsaken me and have not kept my law, 12 and because you have done worse than your fathers, for behold, every one of you follows his stubborn evil will, refusing to listen to me; 13 therefore I will hurl you out of this land into a land which neither you nor your fathers have known, and there you shall serve other gods day and night, for I will show you no favor.'

14 "Therefore, behold, the days are coming, says the LORD, when it shall no longer be said, 'As the LORD lives who brought up the people of Israel out of the land of Egypt,' 15 but 'As the LORD lives who brought up the people of Israel out of the north country and out of all the countries where he had driven them.' For I will bring them back to their own land which I gave to their fathers.

16 "Behold, I am sending for many fishers, says the LORD, and they shall catch them; and afterwards I will send for many hunters, and they shall hunt them from every mountain and every hill, and out of the clefts of the rocks. 17 For my eyes are upon all their ways; they are not hid from me, nor is their iniquity concealed from my eyes. 18 And*z* I will doubly recompense their iniquity and their sin, because they have polluted my land with the carcasses of their detestable idols, and have filled my inheritance with their abominations."

19 O LORD, my strength and my stronghold,
    my refuge in the day of trouble,
to thee shall the nations come
    from the ends of the earth and say:
"Our fathers have inherited nought but lies,
    worthless things in which there is no profit.
20 Can man make for himself gods?
    Such are no gods!"

z Gk: Heb *And first*

16.4
Ps 83.10;
Jer 9.22;
15.3; 34.20

16.5
Ezek 24.16–23;
Jer 12.12;
13.14

16.6
Ezek 9.6;
Jer 41.5;
47.5

16.7
Ezek 24.17;
Hos 9.4

16.8
Jer 15.17

16.9
Jer 7.34;
25.10;
Hos 2.11;
Rev 18.23

16.10
Deut 29.24;
1 Ki 9.8,9;
Jer 5.19

16.11
Jer 22.9;
Ezek 11.21;
1 Pet 4.3

16.12
Jer 7.26;
13.10;
Ecc 9.3

16.13
Deut 4.26–28; 28.36;
Jer 15.4;
5.19

16.14
Isa 43.18;
Jer 23.7,8;
Ex 20.2

16.15
Ps 106.47;
Isa 11.11–16;
Jer 24.6

16.16
Amos 4.2;
Hab 1.14,15;
Mic 7.2;
Isa 2.21

16.17
Ps 90.8;
1 Cor 4.5;
Heb 4.13;
Jer 2.22

16.18
Rev 18.6;
Ezek 11.18,21

16.19
Jer 15.11;
Ps 14.6;
Hab 2.18,19

16.20
Isa 37.19;
Jer 2.11;
Gal 4.8

21 "Therefore, behold, I will make them know, this once I will make them know my power and my might, and they shall know that my name is the LORD."

b. *Idolatry Judah's sin: her only hope, the* LORD

17 "The sin of Judah is written with a pen of iron; with a point of diamond it is engraved on the tablet of their heart, and on the horns of their altars, 2 while their children remember their altars and their Ashē′rĭm, beside every green tree, and on the high hills, 3 on the mountains in the open country. Your wealth and all your treasures I will give for spoil as the price of your sin*a* throughout all your territory. 4 You shall loosen your hand*b* from your heritage which I gave to you, and I will make you serve your enemies in a land which you do not know, for in my anger a fire is kindled which shall burn for ever."

5 Thus says the LORD:
"Cursed is the man who trusts in man
    and makes flesh his arm,
    whose heart turns away from the LORD.
6 He is like a shrub in the desert,
    and shall not see any good come.
He shall dwell in the parched places of the wilderness,
    in an uninhabited salt land.

7 "Blessed is the man who trusts in the LORD,
    whose trust is the LORD.
8 He is like a tree planted by water,
    that sends out its roots by the stream,
and does not fear when heat comes,
    for its leaves remain green,
and is not anxious in the year of drought,
    for it does not cease to bear fruit."

9 The heart is deceitful above all things,
    and desperately corrupt;
    who can understand it?
10 "I the LORD search the mind
    and try the heart,
to give to every man according to his ways,
    according to the fruit of his doings."

11 Like the partridge that gathers a brood which she did not hatch,
    so is he who gets riches but not by right;
in the midst of his days they will leave him,
    and at his end he will be a fool.

12 A glorious throne set on high from the beginning
    is the place of our sanctuary.
13 O LORD, the hope of Israel,
    all who forsake thee shall be put to shame;

a Cn: Heb *your high places for sin*   *b* Cn: Heb *and in you*

17.1 *pen of iron*, for use on rock. Jeremiah suggests that no ordinary pen would do.

Israel's sin cannot be effaced, and punishment must be imposed upon her.

Cross references (left margin):

16.21
Ps 9.16;
Jer 33.2;
Amos 5.8

*17.1
Jer 2.22;
Job 19.24;
Prov 3.3;
2 Cor 3.3
17.2
Jer 7.18;
Ex 34.13;
Jer 3.6
17.3
Jer 26.18;
15.13
17.4
Jer 12.7;
15.14; 7.20

17.5
Isa 30.1–3;
2 Chr 32.8

17.6
Jer 48.6;
Deut 29.23

17.7
Ps 34.8;
84.12; 40.4;
Prov 16.20
17.8
Ps 1.3;
Jer 14.1–6

17.9
Mk 7.21,
22;
Rom 7.11;
Eph 4.22
17.10
1 Sam 16.7;
Jer 11.20;
20.12;
Rom 8.27;
Jer 32.19;
Rom 2.6
17.11
Jer 6.13;
8.10;
22.13,17

17.12
Jer 3.17;
14.21
17.13
Jer 14.8;
Ps 73.27;
Isa 1.28;
Jer 2.13,17

those who turn away from thee^c shall be written in the earth,
    for they have forsaken the LORD, the fountain of living water.

14 Heal me, O LORD, and I shall be healed;
    save me, and I shall be saved;
    for thou art my praise.
15 Behold, they say to me,
    "Where is the word of the LORD?
    Let it come!"
16 I have not pressed thee to send evil,
    nor have I desired the day of disaster,
    thou knowest;
that which came out of my lips
    was before thy face.
17 Be not a terror to me;
    thou art my refuge in the day of evil.
18 Let those be put to shame who persecute me,
    but let me not be put to shame;
let them be dismayed,
    but let me not be dismayed;
bring upon them the day of evil;
    destroy them with double destruction!

4. Sabbath observance stressed

19 Thus said the LORD to me: "Go and stand in the Benjamin^d Gate, by which the kings of Judah enter and by which they go out, and in all the gates of Jerusalem, 20 and say: 'Hear the word of the LORD, you kings of Judah, and all Judah, and all the inhabitants of Jerusalem, who enter by these gates. 21 Thus says the LORD: Take heed for the sake of your lives, and do not bear a burden on the sabbath day or bring it in by the gates of Jerusalem. 22 And do not carry a burden out of your houses on the sabbath or do any work, but keep the sabbath day holy, as I commanded your fathers. 23 Yet they did not listen or incline their ear, but stiffened their neck, that they might not hear and receive instruction.

24 " 'But if you listen to me, says the LORD, and bring in no burden by the gates of this city on the sabbath day, but keep the sabbath day holy and do no work on it, 25 then there shall enter by the gates of this city kings^e who sit on the throne of David, riding in chariots and on horses, they and their princes, the men of Judah and the inhabitants of Jerusalem; and this city shall be inhabited for ever. 26 And people shall come from the cities of Judah and the places round about Jerusalem, from the land of Benjamin, from the Shĕphē'lăh, from the hill country, and from the Nĕgĕb, bringing burnt offerings and sacrifices, cereal offerings and frankincense, and bringing thank offerings to the house of the LORD. 27 But if you do not listen to me, to keep the sabbath day holy, and not to bear a burden and enter by the gates of Jerusalem on the sabbath day, then I will kindle a fire in its gates, and it shall devour the palaces of Jerusalem and shall not be quenched.' "

^{c} Heb me ^{d} Cn: Heb sons of people ^{e} Cn: Heb kings and princes

17.14
Jer 30.17;
Ps 54.1;
Deut 10.21;
Ps 109.1
17.15
Isa 5.19;
Amos 5.18
17.16
Jer 1.6;
12.3
17.17
Ps 88.15;
Jer 16.19
17.18
Ps 35.4,26;
35.8;
Jer 16.18
17.19
Jer 7.2;
26.2
17.20
Jer 19.3;
22.2;
Hos 5.1
*17.21
Deut 4.9,
15,23;
Num 15.32–
36;
Neh 13.15–
21
17.22
Ex 20.8;
23.12;
31.13;
Ezek 20.12
17.23
Jer 7.24,26;
11.10;
19.15
17.24
Deut 11.13;
Ex 20.8–11;
Ezek 20.20
17.25
Jer 22.4;
Isa 9.7;
Lk 1.32;
Heb 12.22
17.26
Zech 7.7;
Ps 107.22
17.27
Jer 22.5;
Isa 9.18,19;
Jer 11.16;
Amos 2.5;
7.20

17.21 The Sabbath was made for the man, not man for the Sabbath. Israel, by breaking the Sabbath, was helping to break herself. Moreover, judgment must follow.

5. *Sermon VII: the sign of the potter's house and the broken vessel*
   a. *First symbol: the potter and the clay*

18.2
Jer 19.1,2;
23.22

18 The word that came to Jĕrĕmī'áh from the LORD: 2 "Arise, and go down to the potter's house, and there I will let you hear my words." 3 So I went down to the potter's house, and there he was working at his wheel. 4 And the vessel he was making of clay was spoiled in the potter's hand, and he reworked it into another vessel, as it seemed good to the potter to do.

18.6
Isa 45.9;
Mt 20.15;
Rom 9.20,
21
18.7
Jer 1.10
18.8
Ezek 18.21;
Jer 26.3;
Jon 3.10
18.9
Jer 1.10;
31.28
18.10
Jer 7.24-28;
Ezek 33.18
18.11
Jer 4.6;
2 Ki 17.13;
Isa 1.16-19;
Acts 26.20
18.12
Jer 2.25;
7.24;16.12

5 Then the word of the LORD came to me: 6 "O house of Israel, can I not do with you as this potter has done? says the LORD. Behold, like the clay in the potter's hand, so are you in my hand, O house of Israel. 7 If at any time I declare concerning a nation or a kingdom, that I will pluck up and break down and destroy it, 8 and if that nation, concerning which I have spoken, turns from its evil, I will repent of the evil that I intended to do to it. 9 And if at any time I declare concerning a nation or a kingdom that I will build and plant it, 10 and if it does evil in my sight, not listening to my voice, then I will repent of the good which I had intended to do to it. 11 Now, therefore, say to the men of Judah and the inhabitants of Jerusalem: 'Thus says the LORD, Behold, I am shaping evil against you and devising a plan against you. Return, every one from his evil way, and amend your ways and your doings.'

12 "But they say, 'That is in vain! We will follow our own plans, and will every one act according to the stubbornness of his evil heart.'

18.13
Jer 2.10,11;
14.17;5.30;
23.14

13 "Therefore thus says the LORD:
   Ask among the nations,
      who has heard the like of this?
   The virgin Israel
      has done a very horrible thing.
14 Does the snow of Lebanon leave
      the crags of Sïr'ïón?*f*
   Do the mountain*g* waters run dry,*h*
      the cold flowing streams?

18.15
Isa 65.7;
Jer 7.9;
6.16;
Isa 57.14;
62.10

15 But my people have forgotten me,
      they burn incense to false gods;
   they have stumbled*i* in their ways,
      in the ancient roads,
   and have gone into bypaths,
      not the highway,

18.16
Jer 25.9;
50.13;
48.27

16 making their land a horror,
      a thing to be hissed at for ever.
   Every one who passes by it is horrified
      and shakes his head.

18.17
Job 27.21;
Jer 13.24;
2.27; 46.21

17 Like the east wind I will scatter them
      before the enemy.
   I will show them my back, not my face,
      in the day of their calamity."

18.18
Jer 11.19;
Mal 2.7;
Jer 8.8;
5.13;
20.10;43.2

18 Then they said, "Come, let us make plots against Jĕrĕmī'áh, for the law shall not perish from the priest, nor counsel from the

f Cn: Heb *the field*   *g* Cn: Heb *foreign*
h Cn: Heb *Are . . . plucked up?*   *i* Gk Syr Vg: Heb *they made them stumble*

wise, nor the word from the prophet. Come, let us smite him with the tongue, and let us not heed any of his words."

19 Give heed to me, O LORD,
and hearken to my plea.ʲ
20 Is evil a recompense for good?
Yet they have dug a pit for my life.
Remember how I stood before thee
to speak good for them,
to turn away thy wrath from them.
21 Therefore deliver up their children to famine;
give them over to the power of the sword,
let their wives become childless and widowed.
May their men meet death by pestilence,
their youths be slain by the sword in battle.
22 May a cry be heard from their houses,
when thou bringest the marauder suddenly upon them!
For they have dug a pit to take me,
and laid snares for my feet.
23 Yet, thou, O LORD, knowest
all their plotting to slay me.
Forgive not their iniquity,
nor blot out their sin from thy sight.
Let them be overthrown before thee;
deal with them in the time of thine anger.

b. Second symbol: the broken flask

19 Thus said the LORD, "Go, buy a potter's earthen flask, and take some of the elders of the people and some of the senior priests, 2 and go out to the valley of the son of Hïnnöm at the entry of the Potsherd Gate, and proclaim there the words that I tell you. 3 You shall say, 'Hear the word of the LORD, O kings of Judah and inhabitants of Jerusalem. Thus says the LORD of hosts, the God of Israel, Behold, I am bringing such evil upon this place that the ears of every one who hears of it will tingle. 4 Because the people have forsaken me, and have profaned this place by burning incense in it to other gods whom neither they nor their fathers nor the kings of Judah have known; and because they have filled this place with the blood of innocents, 5 and have built the high places of Bāäl to burn their sons in the fire as burnt offerings to Baal, which I did not command or decree, nor did it come into my mind; 6 therefore, behold, days are coming, says the LORD, when this place shall no more be called Töphëth, or the valley of the son of Hïnnöm, but the valley of Slaughter. 7And in this place I will make void the plans of Judah and Jerusalem, and will cause their people to fall by the sword before their enemies, and by the hand of those who seek their life. I will give their dead bodies for food to the birds of the air and to the beasts of the earth. 8And I will make this city a horror, a thing to be hissed at; every one who passes by it will be horrified and will hiss because of all its disasters. 9And I will make them eat the flesh of their sons and their daughters, and every one shall eat the flesh of his neighbor in the siege and in the distress, with which their enemies and those who seek their life afflict them.'

ʲ Gk Compare Syr Tg: Heb *my adversaries*

18.20
Ps 35.7;
57.6;
106.23

18.21
Ps 109.9,10;
Isa 13.18;
Jer 15.8;
Ezek 22.25;
Jer 9.21;
11.22

18.22
Jer 6.26;
Ps 140.5

18.23
Ps 109.14;
Isa 2.9;
Jer 6.15,21;
7.20

19.1
Jer 18.2;
ver 10;
Num 11.16;
2 Ki 19.2
19.2
Josh 15.8;
Jer 7.31
19.3
Jer 17.20;
1 Sam 3.11;
4.18
19.4
Deut 28.20;
Isa 65.11;
2 Ki 21.6;
Jer 2.34
19.5
Jer 32.35;
2 Ki 17.17;
Lev 18.21
19.6
Jer 7.32;
Josh 15.8
19.7
Jer 15.2,9;
Ps 79.2;
Jer 16.4
19.8
Jer 18.16;
49.13;
1 Ki 9.8;
2 Chr 7.21
19.9
Deut 28.53,
55;
Isa 9.20;
Lam 4.10

10 "Then you shall break the flask in the sight of the men who go with you, 11 and shall say to them, 'Thus says the LORD of hosts: So will I break this people and this city, as one breaks a potter's vessel, so that it can never be mended. Men shall bury in Tōphĕth because there will be no place else to bury. 12 Thus will I do to this place, says the LORD, and to its inhabitants, making this city like Tōphĕth. 13 The houses of Jerusalem and the houses of the kings of Judah—all the houses upon whose roofs incense has been burned to all the host of heaven, and drink offerings have been poured out to other gods—shall be defiled like the place of Tōphĕth.' "

14 Then Jĕrĕmī'ăh came from Tōphĕth, where the LORD had sent him to prophesy, and he stood in the court of the LORD's house, and said to all the people: 15 "Thus says the LORD of hosts, the God of Israel, Behold, I am bringing upon this city and upon all its towns all the evil that I have pronounced against it, because they have stiffened their neck, refusing to hear my words."

c. Jeremiah must preach despite persecution

20 Now Păshhŭr the priest, the son of Ĭmmĕr, who was chief officer in the house of the LORD, heard Jĕrĕmī'ăh prophesying these things. 2 Then Păshhŭr beat Jĕrĕmī'ăh the prophet, and put him in the stocks that were in the upper Benjamin Gate of the house of the LORD. 3 On the morrow, when Păshhŭr released Jĕrĕmī'ăh from the stocks, Jeremiah said to him, "The LORD does not call your name Pashhur, but Terror on every side. 4 For thus says the LORD: Behold, I will make you a terror to yourself and to all your friends. They shall fall by the sword of their enemies while you look on. And I will give all Judah into the hand of the king of Babylon; he shall carry them captive to Babylon, and shall slay them with the sword. 5 Moreover, I will give all the wealth of the city, all its gains, all its prized belongings, and all the treasures of the kings of Judah into the hand of their enemies, who shall plunder them, and seize them, and carry them to Babylon. 6And you, Păshhŭr, and all who dwell in your house, shall go into captivity; to Babylon you shall go; and there you shall die, and there you shall be buried, you and all your friends, to whom you have prophesied falsely."

7 O LORD, thou hast deceived me,
    and I was deceived;
thou art stronger than I,
    and thou hast prevailed.
I have become a laughingstock all the day;
    every one mocks me.
8 For whenever I speak, I cry out,
    I shout, "Violence and destruction!"
For the word of the LORD has become for me
    a reproach and derision all day long.

19.10
ver 1
19.11
Ps 2.9;
Isa 30.14;
Rev 2.27;
Jer 7.32

19.13
Jer 52.13;
7.18;
Ezek 20.28;
Acts 7.42

19.14
Jer 26.2

19.15
Jer 7.26;
17.23;
Ps 58.4

20.1
1 Chr 24.14;
2 Ki 25.18
*20.2
Jer 1.19;
Job 13.27;
Jer 37.13;
38.7
20.3
ver 10
20.4
Job 18.11–
21;
Jer 29.21;
21.4–10;
52.27
20.5
Jer 15.13;
17.3;
2 Ki 20.17;
2 Chr 36.10;
Jer 3.24
20.6
ver 1;
Jer 28.15–
17;
14.13–15;
29.21

20.7
Jer 1.6–8;
Mic 3.8;
Jer 38.19

20.8
Jer 6.7,10;
2 Chr 36.16

20.2 Jeremiah is often called the "weeping prophet." His ministry had to be carried on in the midst of apostasy without repentance. He suffered persecution because of his faithful preaching. His life is a shining example of a stalwart prophet who faithfully proclaimed a message which his people did not wish to hear and which they rejected. Here Jeremiah is flogged for his faithfulness to God and then placed in stocks.

9 If I say, "I will not mention him,
    or speak any more in his name,"
there is in my heart as it were a burning fire
    shut up in my bones,
and I am weary with holding it in,
    and I cannot.

*20.9
1 Ki 19.3,4;
Ps 39.3;
Job 32.18–
20;
Acts 4.20

10 For I hear many whispering.
    Terror is on every side!
"Denounce him! Let us denounce him!"
    say all my familiar friends,
    watching for my fall.
"Perhaps he will be deceived,
    then we can overcome him,
    and take our revenge on him."

20.10
Ps 31.13;
41.9;
Lk 11.53,54

11 But the LORD is with me as a dread warrior;
    therefore my persecutors will stumble,
    they will not overcome me.
They will be greatly shamed,
    for they will not succeed.
Their eternal dishonor
    will never be forgotten.

20.11
Jer 1.8,19;
15.20;
17.18;
23.40

12 O LORD of hosts, who triest the righteous,
    who seest the heart and the mind,
let me see thy vengeance upon them,
    for to thee have I committed my cause.

20.12
Jer 11.20;
17.10;
Ps 54.7;
59.10

13 Sing to the LORD;
    praise the LORD!
For he has delivered the life of the needy
    from the hand of evildoers.

20.13
Jer 31.7;
Ps 35.9,10;
Jer 15.21

14 Cursed be the day
    on which I was born!
The day when my mother bore me,
    let it not be blessed!

20.14
Job 3.3;
Jer 15.10

15 Cursed be the man
    who brought the news to my father,
"A son is born to you,"
    making him very glad.

20.15
Gen 21.6,7

16 Let that man be like the cities
    which the LORD overthrew without pity;
let him hear a cry in the morning
    and an alarm at noon,

*20.16
Gen 19.25;
Jer 18.22

17 because he did not kill me in the womb;
    so my mother would have been my grave,
    and her womb for ever great.

20.17
Job 3.10,
11; 10.18,19

18 Why did I come forth from the womb
    to see toil and sorrow,
    and spend my days in shame?

20.18
Job 3.20;
Ps 90.9;
Jer 3.25

20.9 Jeremiah was crushed and in great distress of spirit before God, but he stood before the people heroically warning the princes, the priests, and the people of the consequences of their sins. He would have preferred to be silent and not to *speak any more in his name*, but there was the feeling of the *burning fire*. He had to speak out for God.

20.16 *the cities*, in this verse, refer to Sodom and Gomorrah.

II. *Prophecies under Jehoiakim and Zedekiah 21.1–39.18*

A. *Nebuchadnezzar is God's instrument to punish Jerusalem*

1. *Sermon I: God's judgment upon the wicked kings and prophets of Judah*

a. *Zedekiah's prayer for deliverance and God's negative answer*

21 This is the word which came to Jĕrĕmī′áh from the LORD, when King Zĕdĕkī′áh sent to him Păshhŭr the son of Mălchī′áh and Zĕphánī′áh the priest, the son of Mā-áseī′áh, saying, 2 "Inquire of the LORD for us, for Nĕbŭchádrĕz′zár king of Babylon is making war against us; perhaps the LORD will deal with us according to all his wonderful deeds, and will make him withdraw from us."

3 Then Jĕrĕmī′áh said to them: 4 "Thus you shall say to Zĕdĕkī′áh, 'Thus says the LORD, the God of Israel: Behold, I will turn back the weapons of war which are in your hands and with which you are fighting against the king of Babylon and against the Chăldē′áns who are besieging you outside the walls; and I will bring them together into the midst of this city. 5 I myself will fight against you with outstretched hand and strong arm, in anger, and in fury, and in great wrath. 6 And I will smite the inhabitants of this city, both man and beast; they shall die of a great pestilence. 7 Afterward, says the LORD, I will give Zĕdĕkī′áh king of Judah, and his servants, and the people in this city who survive the pestilence, sword, and famine, into the hand of Nĕbŭchádrĕz′zár king of Babylon and into the hand of their enemies, into the hand of those who seek their lives. He shall smite them with the edge of the sword; he shall not pity them, or spare them, or have compassion.'

8 "And to this people you shall say: 'Thus says the LORD: Behold, I set before you the way of life and the way of death. 9 He who stays in this city shall die by the sword, by famine, and by pestilence; but he who goes out and surrenders to the Chăldē′áns who are besieging you shall live and shall have his life as a prize of war. 10 For I have set my face against this city for evil and not for good, says the LORD: it shall be given into the hand of the king of Babylon, and he shall burn it with fire.'

11 "And to the house of the king of Judah say, 'Hear the word of the LORD, 12 O house of David! Thus says the LORD:

" 'Execute justice in the morning,
        and deliver from the hand of the oppressor
        him who has been robbed,
lest my wrath go forth like fire,
        and burn with none to quench it,
        because of your evil doings.' "

13 "Behold, I am against you, O inhabitant of the valley,
        O rock of the plain,
                        says the LORD;

Cross-references (margin)

21.1 — 2 Ki 24.17, 18; Jer 38.1; 2 Ki 25.18; Jer 29.25; 37.3
21.2 — Jer 37.3,7
21.4 — Zech 14.2
21.5 — Isa 63.10; Jer 32.37
21.6 — Jer 7.20; 14.12
21.7 — Jer 37.17; 39.5; 52.9; 13.14
21.8 — Deut 30.15, 19
★21.9 — Jer 38.2,17, 18; 14.12; 39.18; 45.5
21.10 — Jer 44.11, 27; 39.16; 32.28,29; 38.18,23; 52.13
21.11 — Jer 13.18; 17.20
21.12 — Isa 7.2,13; Jer 22.3; Zech 7.9; Jer 7.20
★21.13 — Ezek 13.8; Jer 49.4

21.9 Jeremiah foretold the fall of Judah at the hands of Nebuchadnezzar (Nebuchadrezzar) and forthrightly warned the people to capitulate to Babylon. He said that those who failed to do so would die. Although he preached this as the Word of God, it was looked upon as treason by the leaders of Judah, and he was later to be punished accordingly.

21.13 *the valley*, in this verse, is used of Jerusalem.

you who say, 'Who shall come down against us,
  or who shall enter our habitations?'
14 I will punish you according to the fruit of your doings,
                                        says the LORD;
  I will kindle a fire in her forest,
  and it shall devour all that is round about her."

b. *Woe pronounced upon the four evil kings and their dishonest prophets*

(1) THE WICKED KINGS, AND MESSIAH THE TRUE KING

22 Thus says the LORD: "Go down to the house of the king of Judah, and speak there this word, 2 and say, 'Hear the word of the LORD, O King of Judah, who sit on the throne of David, you, and your servants, and your people who enter these gates. 3 Thus says the LORD: Do justice and righteousness, and deliver from the hand of the oppressor him who has been robbed. And do no wrong or violence to the alien, the fatherless, and the widow, nor shed innocent blood in this place. 4 For if you will indeed obey this word, then there shall enter the gates of this house kings who sit on the throne of David, riding in chariots and on horses, they, and their servants, and their people. 5 But if you will not heed these words, I swear by myself, says the LORD, that this house shall become a desolation. 6 For thus says the LORD concerning the house of the king of Judah:

" 'You are as Gĭl'ĕäd to me,
  as the summit of Lebanon,
yet surely I will make you a desert,
  an uninhabited city.*k*

7 I will prepare destroyers against you,
  each with his weapons;
and they shall cut down your choicest cedars,
  and cast them into the fire.

8 " 'And many nations will pass by this city, and every man will say to his neighbor, "Why has the LORD dealt thus with this great city?" 9 And they will answer, "Because they forsook the covenant of the LORD their God, and worshiped other gods and served them." ' "

10 Weep not for him who is dead,
  nor bemoan him;
but weep bitterly for him who goes away,
  for he shall return no more
  to see his native land.

11 For thus says the LORD concerning Shăllŭm the son of Jōsī'-äh, king of Judah, who reigned instead of Josiah his father, and who went away from this place: "He shall return here no more, 12 but in the place where they have carried him captive, there shall he die, and he shall never see this land again."

13 "Woe to him who builds his house by unrighteousness,
  and his upper rooms by injustice;

k Cn: Heb *cities*

21.14
Isa 3.10,11;
Ezek 20.46,
48;
2 Chr 36.19;
Jer 52.13

22.1
Jer 21.11;
2 Chr 25.15,
16
22.2
Jer 19.3;
29.20
22.3
Jer 21.12;
Ps 72.4;
Ex 22.21–24
22.4
Jer 17.25

22.5
Jer 17.27;
26.4;
Heb 6.13;
Jer 7.14;
26.6,9
★22.6
Jer 7.34

22.7
Isa 10.3–6;
Jer 4.6,7;
Isa 10.33,34

22.8
Deut 29.24,
25;
1 Ki 9.8,9;
Jer 16.10
22.9
2 Ki 22.17;
2 Chr 34.25

★22.10
2 Ki 22.20;
ver 18;
Jer 16.7;
44.14

★22.11
2 Ki 23.30,
34

22.13
Mic 3.10;
Hab 2.9;
Jas 5.4

22.6 *as Gilead*, a place of beauty.
22.10 *him who is dead*, viz., Josiah who was   killed at Megiddo. (Read 2 Ki 23.29.)
22.11 *Shallum*, also known as Jehoahaz.

who makes his neighbor serve him for nothing,
and does not give him his wages;

22.14
Isa 5.8,9;
2 Sam 7.2

14 who says, 'I will build myself a great house
with spacious upper rooms,'
and cuts out windows for it,
paneling it with cedar,
and painting it with vermilion.

22.15
2 Ki 23.25;
Jer 7.5;
42.6

15 Do you think you are a king
because you compete in cedar?
Did not your father eat and drink
and do justice and righteousness?
Then it was well with him.

22.16
Ps 72.1–4,
12,13;
1 Chr 28.9;
Jer 9.24

16 He judged the cause of the poor and needy;
then it was well.
Is not this to know me?
says the LORD.

22.17
Jer 6.13;
8.10; 6.6

17 But you have eyes and heart
only for your dishonest gain,
for shedding innocent blood,
and for practicing oppression and violence."

22.18
1 Ki 13.30;
Jer 34.5

18 Therefore thus says the LORD concerning Jĕhoi′ăkim the son
of Jōsī′ăh, king of Judah:
"They shall not lament for him, saying,
'Ah my brother!' or 'Ah sister!'
They shall not lament for him, saying,
'Ah lord!' or 'Ah his majesty!'

22.19
Jer 36.30

19 With the burial of an ass he shall be buried,
dragged and cast forth beyond the gates of Jerusalem."

22.20
Deut 32.49;
Jer 2.25;
3.1

20 "Go up to Lebanon, and cry out,
and lift up your voice in Bāshán;
cry from Āb′ărĭm,
for all your lovers are destroyed.

22.21
Jer 13.10;
19.15;
3.24,25;
32.30

21 I spoke to you in your prosperity,
but you said, 'I will not listen.'
This has been your way from your youth,
that you have not obeyed my voice.

22.22
Jer 5.13;
30.14;
Isa 65.13;
Jer 20.11

22 The wind shall shepherd all your shepherds,
and your lovers shall go into captivity;
then you will be ashamed and confounded
because of all your wickedness.

22.23
Jer 4.31;
6.24

23 O inhabitant of Lebanon,
nested among the cedars,
how you will groan¹ when pangs come upon you,
pain as of a woman in travail!"

22.24
Jer 37.1;
Sol 8.6;
Hag 2.23

22.25
2 Ki 24.15,
16;
Jer 34.20

22.26
2 Ki 24.15;
2 Chr
36.10;
2 Ki 24.8

24 "As I live, says the LORD, though Cŏnī′ăh the son of Jĕhoi′-
ăkĭm, king of Judah, were the signet ring on my right hand, yet I
would tear you off 25 and give you into the hand of those who seek
your life, into the hand of those of whom you are afraid, even into
the hand of Nĕbúchádrĕz′zár king of Babylon and into the hand of
the Chăldē′ăns. 26 I will hurl you and the mother who bore you
into another country, where you were not born, and there you

_l_ Gk Vg Syr: Heb _be pitied_

shall die. 27 But to the land to which they will long to return, there they shall not return."

28 Is this man Cŏnĭ'áh a despised, broken pot,
     a vessel no one cares for?
Why are he and his children hurled and cast
     into a land which they do not know?

29 O land, land, land,
     hear the word of the LORD!

30 Thus says the LORD:
"Write this man down as childless,
     a man who shall not succeed in his days;
for none of his offspring shall succeed
     in sitting on the throne of David,
     and ruling again in Judah."

23 "Woe to the shepherds who destroy and scatter the sheep of my pasture!" says the LORD. 2 Therefore thus says the LORD, the God of Israel, concerning the shepherds who care for my people: "You have scattered my flock, and have driven them away, and you have not attended to them. Behold, I will attend to you for your evil doings, says the LORD. 3 Then I will gather the remnant of my flock out of all the countries where I have driven them, and I will bring them back to their fold, and they shall be fruitful and multiply. 4 I will set shepherds over them who will care for them, and they shall fear no more, nor be dismayed, neither shall any be missing, says the LORD.

5 "Behold, the days are coming, says the LORD, when I will raise up for David a righteous Branch, and he shall reign as king and deal wisely, and shall execute justice and righteousness in the land. 6 In his days Judah will be saved, and Israel will dwell securely. And this is the name by which he will be called: 'The LORD is our righteousness.'

7 "Therefore, behold, the days are coming, says the LORD, when men shall no longer say, 'As the LORD lives who brought up the people of Israel out of the land of Egypt,' 8 but 'As the LORD lives who brought up and led the descendants of the house of Israel out of the north country and out of all the countries where he[m] had driven them.' Then they shall dwell in their own land."

(2) FALSE PROPHETS SHALL DIE IN MISERY AND SHAME

9 Concerning the prophets:
My heart is broken within me,
     all my bones shake;
I am like a drunken man,
     like a man overcome by wine,
because of the LORD
     and because of his holy words.

10 For the land is full of adulterers;
     because of the curse the land mourns,

m Gk: Heb *I*

★22.28
Ps 31.12;
Jer 48.38;
Hos 8.8;
Jer 15.1;
17.4

22.29
Deut 32.1;
Jer 6.19;
Mic 1.2

22.30
1 Chr 3.16;
17;
Mt 1.12

23.1
Ezek 13.3;
Jer 10.21;
50.6;
Ezek 34.31

23.3
Isa 11.11–16;
Jer 32.37;
Ezek 34.13–16

23.4
Jer 3.15;
Ezek 34.23;
Jer 30.10;
Jn 6.39;
10.28

★23.5
Isa 4.2;
11.1; 53.2;
Jer 33.14–16;
Zech 3.8;
6.12;
Isa 9.7;
Lk 1.32,33

23.6
Deut 33.28;
Zech 14.11;
Isa 7.14;
9.6;
Mt 1.21–23;
Jer 33.16;
Rom 3.22;
1 Cor 1.30

23.7
Isa 43.18,
19;
Jer 16.14,15

23.9
Hab 3.16;
Jer 20.8,9

23.10
Jer 5.7,8;
Hos 4.2,3;
Jer 9.10;
12.4

22.28 *Coniah*, another name for Jehoiachin.
23.5 *a righteous Branch*, or a true shoot from the old stock of David. Kings of the Davidic line had become guilty of injustice and oppression. The godly in Israel looked, however, to the prophetic promise that a righteous king would one day arise as the LORD's anointed (or Messiah).

and the pastures of the wilderness are dried up.
Their course is evil,
and their might is not right.

23.11
Jer 6.13;
8.10;7.9,
10;32.3411 "Both prophet and priest are ungodly;
even in my house I have found their wickedness,
says the LORD.

23.12
Ps 35.6;
Jn 12.35;
Jer 11.2312 Therefore their way shall be to them
like slippery paths in the darkness,
into which they shall be driven and fall;
for I will bring evil upon them
in the year of their punishment,
says the LORD.

23.13
Hos 9.7,8;
Jer 2.813 In the prophets of Samar′iä
I saw an unsavory thing:
they prophesied by Bāäl
and led my people Israel astray.

23.14
Jer 5.30;
29.23;
Ezek 13.22;
Isa 1.9,10;
Jer 20.1614 But in the prophets of Jerusalem
I have seen a horrible thing:
they commit adultery and walk in lies;
they strengthen the hands of evildoers,
so that no one turns from his wickedness;
all of them have become like Sŏdŏm to me,
and its inhabitants like Gŏmor′räh."

23.15
Jer 8.14;
9.1515 Therefore thus says the LORD of hosts concerning the prophets:
"Behold, I will feed them with wormwood,
and give them poisoned water to drink;
for from the prophets of Jerusalem
ungodliness has gone forth into all the land."

23.16
Jer 27.9,10;
14.14;
9.12,20
23.17
Jer 8.11;
13.10;
18.12;
5.12;
Mic 3.1116 Thus says the LORD of hosts: "Do not listen to the words of the prophets who prophesy to you, filling you with vain hopes; they speak visions of their own minds, not from the mouth of the LORD. 17 They say continually to those who despise the word of the LORD, 'It shall be well with you'; and to every one who stubbornly follows his own heart, they say, 'No evil shall come upon you.'"

23.18
Job 15.8;
33.3118 For who among them has stood in the council of the LORD
to perceive and to hear his word,
or who has given heed to his word and listened?

23.19
Jer 25.32;
30.2319 Behold, the storm of the LORD!
Wrath has gone forth,
a whirling tempest;
it will burst upon the head of the wicked.

23.20
Jer 30.24;
Gen 49.120 The anger of the LORD will not turn back
until he has executed and accomplished
the intents of his mind.
In the latter days you will understand it clearly.

23.21
Jer 14.14;
27.15;29.9
23.22
Jer 9.12;
35.15;
1 Thess 1.9,
1021 "I did not send the prophets,
yet they ran;
I did not speak to them,
yet they prophesied.
22 But if they had stood in my council,
then they would have proclaimed my words to my people,

and they would have turned them from their evil way,
  and from the evil of their doings.

23 "Am I a God at hand, says the LORD, and not a God afar off? 24 Can a man hide himself in secret places so that I cannot see him? says the LORD. Do I not fill heaven and earth? says the LORD. 25 I have heard what the prophets have said who prophesy lies in my name, saying, 'I have dreamed, I have dreamed!' 26 How long shall there be lies[n] in the heart of the prophets who prophesy lies, and who prophesy the deceit of their own heart, 27 who think to make my people forget my name by their dreams which they tell one another, even as their fathers forgot my name for Bāál? 28 Let the prophet who has a dream tell the dream, but let him who has my word speak my word faithfully. What has straw in common with wheat? says the LORD. 29 Is not my word like fire, says the LORD, and like a hammer which breaks the rock in pieces? 30 Therefore, behold, I am against the prophets, says the LORD, who steal my words from one another. 31 Behold, I am against the prophets, says the LORD, who use their tongues and say, 'Says the LORD.' 32 Behold, I am against those who prophesy lying dreams, says the LORD, and who tell them and lead my people astray by their lies and their recklessness, when I did not send them or charge them; so they do not profit this people at all, says the LORD.

33 "When one of this people, or a prophet, or a priest asks you, 'What is the burden of the LORD?' you shall say to them, 'You are the burden,[o] and I will cast you off, says the LORD.' 34 And as for the prophet, priest, or one of the people who says, 'The burden of the LORD,' I will punish that man and his household. 35 Thus shall you say, every one to his neighbor and every one to his brother, 'What has the LORD answered?' or 'What has the LORD spoken?' 36 But 'the burden of the LORD' you shall mention no more, for the burden is every man's own word, and you pervert the words of the living God, the LORD of hosts, our God. 37 Thus you shall say to the prophet, 'What has the LORD answered you?' or 'What has the LORD spoken?' 38 But if you say, 'The burden of the LORD,' thus says the LORD, 'Because you have said these words, "The burden of the LORD," when I sent to you, saying, "You shall not say, 'The burden of the LORD,'" 39 therefore, behold, I will surely lift you up and cast you away from my presence, you and the city which I gave to you and your fathers. 40 And I will bring upon you ever-lasting reproach and perpetual shame, which shall not be forgotten.' "

c. The sign of the good and the bad figs

24 After Nĕbúchádrĕz'zár king of Babylon had taken into exile from Jerusalem Jĕcóní'áh the son of Jĕhoi'ákĭm, king of Judah, together with the princes of Judah, the craftsmen, and the smiths, and had brought them to Babylon, the LORD showed me this vision: Behold, two baskets of figs placed before the temple of the LORD. 2 One basket had very good figs, like first-ripe figs, but the other basket had very bad figs, so bad that they

[n] Cn Compare Syr: Heb obscure   [o] Gk Vg: Heb What burden

23.28 *Let the prophet who has a dream tell the dream.* The dreams, however, were not to   be confused with true prophecy, i.e., the *word* handed down by the LORD.

23.23
Ps 139.1–10;
Jer 50.51

23.24
Ps 139.7–12;
Isa 29.15;
Amos 9.2;
1 Ki 8.27

23.25
Jer 8.6;
14.14;
29.8

23.27
Judg 3.7;
8.33,34

★23.28
Jer 9.12,20

23.29
Jer 5.14;
20.9;
2 Cor 10.4,5

23.30
Ezek 13.8

23.31
ver 17

23.32
ver 25,28

23.33
Isa 13.1;
Hab 1.1;
Mal 1.1;
ver 39

23.34
Lam 2.14;
Zech 13.3

23.35
Jer 33.3;
42.4

23.36
Jer 10.10

23.38
ver 36

23.39
Jer 7.14,15;
Ezek 8.18

23.40
Jer 20.11

24.1
Amos 8.1;
2 Ki 24.10–16;
2 Chr 36.10;
Jer 22.24;
29.2

24.2
Nah 3.12;
Jer 27.19

could not be eaten. ³And the LORD said to me, "What do you see, Jĕrĕmī′áh?" I said, "Figs, the good figs very good, and the bad figs very bad, so bad that they cannot be eaten."

4 Then the word of the LORD came to me: ⁵ "Thus says the LORD, the God of Israel: Like these good figs, so I will regard as good the exiles from Judah, whom I have sent away from this place to the land of the Chăldē′áns. ⁶ I will set my eyes upon them for good, and I will bring them back to this land. I will build them up, and not tear them down; I will plant them, and not uproot them. ⁷ I will give them a heart to know that I am the LORD; and they shall be my people and I will be their God, for they shall return to me with their whole heart.

8 "But thus says the LORD: Like the bad figs which are so bad they cannot be eaten, so will I treat Zĕdĕkī′áh the king of Judah, his princes, the remnant of Jerusalem who remain in this land, and those who dwell in the land of Egypt. ⁹ I will make them a horrorᵖ to all the kingdoms of the earth, to be a reproach, a byword, a taunt, and a curse in all the places where I shall drive them. ¹⁰And I will send sword, famine, and pestilence upon them, until they shall be utterly destroyed from the land which I gave to them and their fathers."

2. Sermon II: the vision of the end coming upon Judah and the heathen

a. The captivity of Judah and the end of Babylon

25 The word that came to Jĕrĕmī′áh concerning all the people of Judah, in the fourth year of Jĕhoi′ákim the son of Jōsī′áh, king of Judah (that was the first year of Nĕbúchădrĕz′zăr king of Babylon), ² which Jĕrĕmī′áh the prophet spoke to all the people of Judah and all the inhabitants of Jerusalem: ³ "For twenty-three years, from the thirteenth year of Jōsī′áh the son of Āmon, king of Judah, to this day, the word of the LORD has come to me, and I have spoken persistently to you, but you have not listened. ⁴ You have neither listened nor inclined your ears to hear, although the LORD persistently sent to you all his servants the prophets, ⁵ saying, 'Turn now, every one of you, from his evil way and wrong doings, and dwell upon the land which the LORD has given to you and your fathers from of old and for ever; ⁶ do not go after other gods to serve and worship them, or provoke me to anger with the work of your hands. Then I will do you no harm.' ⁷ Yet you have not listened to me, says the LORD, that you might provoke me to anger with the work of your hands to your own harm.

8 "Therefore thus says the LORD of hosts: Because you have not obeyed my words, ⁹ behold, I will send for all the tribes of the north, says the LORD, and for Nĕbúchădrĕz′zăr the king of Babylon, my servant, and I will bring them against this land and its inhabitants, and against all these nations round about; I will utterly destroy them, and make them a horror, a hissing, and an everlasting reproach.�q ¹⁰ Moreover, I will banish from them the voice of mirth and the voice of gladness, the voice of the bridegroom and the voice of the bride, the grinding of the millstones and the

24.3
Jer 1.11,13

24.5
Nah 1.7;
Zech 13.9

24.6
Jer 29.10;
Ezek 11.17;
Jer 33.7;
42.10

24.7
Jer 31.33;
32.40;
Zech 8.8;
Heb 8.10;
Jer 29.13

24.8
Jer 29.17;
39.5,9;
44.26-30

24.9
Jer 15.4;
29.18;
34.17;
1 Ki 9.7;
Ps 44.13,14;
Isa 65.15

24.10
Isa 51.19;
Jer 21.9;
27.8

25.1
Jer 36.1;
2 Ki 24.1,2

25.2
Jer 18.11

25.3
Jer 1.2;
2 Chr 34.1-
3,8;
Jer 36.2;
7.13; 22.21

25.4
Jer 7.13,25;
26.5

25.5
Isa 55.6,7;
Jer 4.1; 7.7

25.6
Deut 6.14;
8.19;
Jer 35.15

25.7
Deut 32.21;
2 Ki 17.17;
21.15;
Jer 7.19

★25.8

★25.9
Jer 1.15;
27.6;
18.16

25.10
Isa 24.7;
Ezek 26.13;
Ecc 12.4;
Isa 47.2

ᵖ Compare Gk: Heb horror for evil   q Gk Compare Syr: Heb desolations

---

25.8 Even flight to Egypt provided no safety.   **25.9** my servant, i.e., under God's control.

light of the lamp. ¹¹ This whole land shall become a ruin and a waste, and these nations shall serve the king of Babylon seventy years. ¹² Then after seventy years are completed, I will punish the king of Babylon and that nation, the land of the Chǎldē'ǎns, for their iniquity, says the LORD, making the land an everlasting waste. ¹³ I will bring upon that land all the words which I have uttered against it, everything written in this book, which Jěrěmī'ǎh prophesied against all the nations. ¹⁴ For many nations and great kings shall make slaves even of them; and I will recompense them according to their deeds and the work of their hands."

b. *The cup of wrath visited on the nations*

¹⁵ Thus the LORD, the God of Israel, said to me: "Take from my hand this cup of the wine of wrath, and make all the nations to whom I send you drink it. ¹⁶ They shall drink and stagger and be crazed because of the sword which I am sending among them."

¹⁷ So I took the cup from the LORD's hand, and made all the nations to whom the LORD sent me drink it: ¹⁸ Jerusalem and the cities of Judah, its kings and princes, to make them a desolation and a waste, a hissing and a curse, as at this day; ¹⁹ Phǎraōh king of Egypt, his servants, his princes, all his people, ²⁰ and all the foreign folk among them; all the kings of the land of Ûz and all the kings of the land of the Phǐlǐs'tǐneș (Ăsh'kělòn, Gazȧ, Ĕkrón, and the remnant of Ăshdŏd); ²¹ Ēdŏm, Mōǎb, and the sons of Ămmòn; ²² all the kings of Tȳre, all the kings of Sīdòn, and the kings of the coastland across the sea; ²³ Dēdȧn, Tēmȧ, Bùz, and all who cut the corners of their hair; ²⁴ all the kings of Arabia and all the kings of the mixed tribes that dwell in the desert; ²⁵ all the kings of Zǐmrī, all the kings of Ēlȧm, and all the kings of Mē'dǐȧ; ²⁶ all the kings of the north, far and near, one after another, and all the kingdoms of the world which are on the face of the earth. And after them the king of Babylonʳ shall drink.

²⁷ "Then you shall say to them, 'Thus says the LORD of hosts, the God of Israel: Drink, be drunk and vomit, fall and rise no more, because of the sword which I am sending among you.'

²⁸ "And if they refuse to accept the cup from your hand to drink, then you shall say to them, 'Thus says the LORD of hosts: You must drink! ²⁹ For behold, I begin to work evil at the city which is called by my name, and shall you go unpunished? You shall not go unpunished, for I am summoning a sword against all the inhabitants of the earth, says the LORD of hosts.'

c. *The vengeance of the LORD*

³⁰ "You, therefore, shall prophesy against them all these words, and say to them:
'The LORD will roar from on high,

ʳ Heb *Shēshǎch*, a cipher for Babylon

25.11
Jer 4.27;
12.11,12;
Dan 9.2
25.12
Ezra 1.1;
Jer 29.10;
Isa 13.14;
13.19;
14.23
25.14
Jer 50.9;
51.27,28;
50.41;
51.6,24
25.15
Ps 75.8;
Isa 51.17
25.16
Jer 51.7;
Nah 3.11
25.17
ver 28;
Ezek 43.3
25.18
Isa 51.17;
Jer 24.9;
44.22
25.19
Jer 46.2-28
25.20
Job 1.1;
Jer 47.1-7;
Isa 20.1
25.21
Jer 49.1-22;
48.1-47
25.22
Jer 47.4;
49.23
25.23
Jer 49.7,8;
9.26; 49.32
25.24
2 Chr 9.14
25.26
Jer 50.9
25.27
Hab 2.16;
Ezek 21.4,5
25.29
Ezek 9.6;
1 Pet 4.17;
1 Ki 8.43;
ver 31
25.30
Isa 42.13;
Joel 3.16;
Amos 1.2;
Isa 16.9

25.11 Jeremiah states the length of the captivity (seventy years). Some compute it from 605 B.C., when the first deportation took place (2 Ki 24.10-15); others start with 586 B.C., when the final deportation occurred and the Temple was destroyed (2 Chr 36.17-20). In the former case, the captivity terminated in 538 B.C. with the decree of Cyrus for the return of the remnant to the land (Ezra 1.1-3); in the latter case, the terminating date would be 516 B.C. when the second Temple was completed. Seventy may, on the other hand, be a conventional round number (ten times seven). In this instance it would not be necessary to press for the exact length of time the Jews were in servitude to Babylon.

and from his holy habitation utter his voice;
   he will roar mightily against his fold,
      and shout, like those who tread grapes,
      against all the inhabitants of the earth.

25.31
Hos 4.1;
Mic 6.2;
Joel 3.2

31 The clamor will resound to the ends of the earth,
   for the LORD has an indictment against the nations;
he is entering into judgment with all flesh,
   and the wicked he will put to the sword,

                    says the LORD.'

25.32
Isa 34.2;
Jer 29.19;
30.23

32 "Thus says the LORD of hosts:
Behold, evil is going forth
   from nation to nation,
and a great tempest is stirring
   from the farthest parts of the earth!

25.33
Isa 66.16;
Ps 79.3;
Jer 16.4;
Isa 5.25

33 "And those slain by the LORD on that day shall extend from
one end of the earth to the other. They shall not be lamented, or
gathered, or buried; they shall be dung on the surface of the
ground.

25.34
Jer 6.26;
Ezek 27.30;
Isa 34.7;
Jer 50.27

34 "Wail, you shepherds, and cry,
   and roll in ashes, you lords of the flock,
for the days of your slaughter and dispersion have come,
   and you shall fall like choice rams.*s*

25.35
Jer 11.11

35 No refuge will remain for the shepherds,
   nor escape for the lords of the flock.

25.36
ver 34

36 Hark, the cry of the shepherds,
   and the wail of the lords of the flock!

25.37
Isa 27.10,
11;
Jer 5.17;
13.10

For the LORD is despoiling their pasture,
37   and the peaceful folds are devastated,
   because of the fierce anger of the LORD.

25.38
Jer 4.7

38 Like a lion he has left his covert,
   for their land has become a waste
because of the sword of the oppressor,
   and because of his fierce anger."

26.1
2 Ki 23.36;
2 Chr 36.4,
5;
Jer 7.1,2

3. *Four contests between Jeremiah and the false prophets*

26.2
Jer 19.14;
Lk 19.47,
48;
Jer 1.17;
Acts 20.20,
27;
Deut 4.2

a. *Jeremiah arrested and released: Uriah murdered*

26 In the beginning of the reign of Jĕhoi´ăkĭm the son of
Jŏsī´ăh, king of Judah, this word came from the LORD,
2 "Thus says the LORD: Stand in the court of the LORD's house,
and speak to all the cities of Judah which come to worship in the
house of the LORD all the words that I command you to speak to

26.3
Jer 36.3–7;
18.8

them; do not hold back a word. 3 It may be they will listen, and
every one turn from his evil way, that I may repent of the evil

26.4
Lev 26.14;
Deut 28.15;
Jer 17.27;
32.23;
44.10,23

which I intend to do to them because of their evil doings. 4 You
shall say to them, 'Thus says the LORD: If you will not listen to
me, to walk in my law which I have set before you, 5 and to heed

26.5
2 Ki 9.7;
Jer 25.3,4

the words of my servants the prophets whom I send to you urgently, though you have not heeded, 6 then I will make this house

26.6
1 Sam 4.10,
11;
Isa 65.15;
Jer 24.9

like Shīlŏh, and I will make this city a curse for all the nations of
the earth.' "

26.8
Jer 20.1,2;
11.19;
18.23

7 The priests and the prophets and all the people heard Jĕrĕmī´-
ăh speaking these words in the house of the LORD. 8 And when

---

s Gk: Heb *a choice vessel*

Jĕrĕmī'ăh had finished speaking all that the LORD had commanded him to speak to all the people, then the priests and the prophets and all the people laid hold of him, saying, "You shall die! 9 Why have you prophesied in the name of the LORD, saying, 'This house shall be like Shīlōh, and this city shall be desolate, without inhabitant'?" And all the people gathered about Jĕrĕmī'ăh in the house of the LORD.

10 When the princes of Judah heard these things, they came up from the king's house to the house of the LORD and took their seat in the entry of the New Gate of the house of the LORD. 11 Then the priests and the prophets said to the princes and to all the people, "This man deserves the sentence of death, because he has prophesied against this city, as you have heard with your own ears."

12 Then Jĕrĕmī'ăh spoke to all the princes and all the people, saying, "The LORD sent me to prophesy against this house and this city all the words you have heard. 13 Now therefore amend your ways and your doings, and obey the voice of the LORD your God, and the LORD will repent of the evil which he has pronounced against you. 14 But as for me, behold, I am in your hands. Do with me as seems good and right to you. 15 Only know for certain that if you put me to death, you will bring innocent blood upon yourselves and upon this city and its inhabitants, for in truth the LORD sent me to you to speak all these words in your ears."

16 Then the princes and all the people said to the priests and the prophets, "This man does not deserve the sentence of death, for he has spoken to us in the name of the LORD our God." 17And certain of the elders of the land arose and spoke to all the assembled people, saying, 18 "Mīcăh of Mō'rĕshĕth prophesied in the days of Hĕzĕkī'ăh king of Judah, and said to all the people of Judah: 'Thus says the LORD of hosts,

    Zion shall be plowed as a field;
      Jerusalem shall become a heap of ruins,
    and the mountain of the house a wooded height.'

19 Did Hĕzĕkī'ăh king of Judah and all Judah put him to death? Did he not fear the LORD and entreat the favor of the LORD, and did not the LORD repent of the evil which he had pronounced against them? But we are about to bring great evil upon ourselves."

20 There was another man who prophesied in the name of the LORD, Ūrī'ăh the son of Shĕmāi'ăh from Kīr'ĭăth-jĕ'ărĭm. He prophesied against this city and against this land in words like those of Jĕrĕmī'ăh. 21And when King Jĕhoi'ăkĭm, with all his warriors and all the princes, heard his words, the king sought to put him to death; but when Ūrī'ăh heard of it, he was afraid and fled and escaped to Egypt. 22 Then King Jĕhoi'ăkĭm sent to Egypt certain men, Ĕlnā'thăn the son of Ăchbor and others with him, 23 and they fetched Ūrī'ăh from Egypt and brought him to King Jĕhoi'ăkĭm, who slew him with the sword and cast his dead body into the burial place of the common people.

24 But the hand of Ăhī'kăm the son of Shāphăn was with Jĕrĕmī'ăh so that he was not given over to the people to be put to death.

26.9 *Shiloh*, cf. 7.12. Jeremiah cited Shiloh as an example of the fact that even a sanctuary of the LORD could be destroyed when God brings judgment on His people. The false prophets insisted that the Temple was inviolable.
26.10 *the princes.* These were officials of the palace, not to be mistaken for royalty.

Cross-references (margin):

★26.9
Jer 9.11;
33.10

★26.10
Jer 36.10

26.11
Jer 18.23;
Deut 18.20;
Mt 26.66;
Jer 38.4;
Acts 6.11–
14

26.12
Jer 1.17,18;
5.6; 46.16

26.13
Jer 7.3,5;
18.11;
Joel 2.14;
Jon 3.9; 4.2

26.14
Jer 38.5

26.15
Prov 6.16,
17;
Jer 7.6

26.16
ver 11;
Acts 5.34–
39;
23.9,29;
25.25;
26.31

26.18
Mic 1.1;
Ps 79.1;
Mic 3.12;
Zech 8.3

26.19
2 Chr 29.6–
11; 32.26;
2 Sam
24.16;
Acts 5.39

26.20
Josh 9.17;
1 Sam 6.21;
7.2

26.21
1 Ki 19.2–
4;
Mt 10.23,28

26.22
Jer 36.12

26.23
Jer 2.30

26.24
2 Ki 22.12–
14;
Jer 39.14

b. Jeremiah testifies again that Nebuchadnezzar will conquer

27 In the beginning of the reign of Zĕdĕkī'áh[u] the son of Jōsī'-
áh, king of Judah, this word came to Jĕrĕmī'áh from the
LORD. 2 Thus the LORD said to me: "Make yourself thongs and
yoke-bars, and put them on your neck. 3 Send word[v] to the king
of Ēdŏm, the king of Mōăb, the king of the sons of Ămmŏn, the
king of Tȳre, and the king of Sīdŏn by the hand of the envoys
who have come to Jerusalem to Zĕdĕkī'áh king of Judah. 4 Give
them this charge for their masters: 'Thus says the LORD of hosts,
the God of Israel: This is what you shall say to your masters:
5 "It is I who by my great power and my outstretched arm have
made the earth, with the men and animals that are on the earth,
and I give it to whomever it seems right to me. 6 Now I have
given all these lands into the hand of Nĕbùchádnĕz'zăr, the king
of Babylon, my servant, and I have given him also the beasts of
the field to serve him. 7 All the nations shall serve him and his son
and his grandson, until the time of his own land comes; then many
nations and great kings shall make him their slave.

8 " ' "But if any nation or kingdom will not serve this Nĕbùchádnĕz'zăr king of Babylon, and put its neck under the yoke of
the king of Babylon, I will punish that nation with the sword, with
famine, and with pestilence, says the LORD, until I have consumed
it by his hand. 9 So do not listen to your prophets, your diviners,
your dreamers,[w] your soothsayers, or your sorcerers, who are saying to you, 'You shall not serve the king of Babylon.' 10 For it is
a lie which they are prophesying to you, with the result that you
will be removed far from your land, and I will drive you out, and
you will perish. 11 But any nation which will bring its neck under
the yoke of the king of Babylon and serve him, I will leave on its
own land, to till it and dwell there, says the LORD." ' "

12 To Zĕdĕkī'áh king of Judah I spoke in like manner: "Bring
your necks under the yoke of the king of Babylon, and serve him
and his people, and live. 13 Why will you and your people die by
the sword, by famine, and by pestilence, as the LORD has spoken
concerning any nation which will not serve the king of Babylon?
14 Do not listen to the words of the prophets who are saying to you,
'You shall not serve the king of Babylon,' for it is a lie which they
are prophesying to you. 15 I have not sent them, says the LORD,
but they are prophesying falsely in my name, with the result that
I will drive you out and you will perish, you and the prophets who
are prophesying to you."

16 Then I spoke to the priests and to all this people, saying,
"Thus says the LORD: Do not listen to the words of your prophets
who are prophesying to you, saying, 'Behold, the vessels of the
LORD's house will now shortly be brought back from Babylon,' for
it is a lie which they are prophesying to you. 17 Do not listen to
them; serve the king of Babylon and live. Why should this city
become a desolation? 18 If they are prophets, and if the word of the
LORD is with them, then let them intercede with the LORD of hosts,
that the vessels which are left in the house of the LORD, in the
house of the king of Judah, and in Jerusalem may not go to Babylon. 19 For thus says the LORD of hosts concerning the pillars, the
sea, the stands, and the rest of the vessels which are left in this

27.1
Jer 26.1

27.2
Jer 28.10,
13
27.3
Jer 25.21,22

27.5
Jer 10.12;
51.15;
Ps 115.15,
16;
Acts 17.26
27.6
Ezek 29.18–
20;
Jer 25.9;
28.14
27.7
Jer 44.30;
46.13;
25.12;
Isa 14.4–6
27.8
Jer 38.17–
19;
Ezek 17.19–
21;
Jer 29.17,
18;
Ezek 14.21
27.9
Ex 22.18;
Deut 18.10;
Isa 8.19;
Mal 3.5
27.10
Jer 23.25;
8.19;
32.31
27.11
Jer 21.9
27.12
Jer 28.1
27.13
Ezek 18.31
27.14
Jer 14.14;
Ezek 13.22
27.15
Jer 23.21,
25;
6.13–15;
14.15,16
27.16
2 Chr 36.7,
10;
Jer 28.3;
Dan 1.2;
ver 10
27.17
ver 13
27.18
1 Sam 7.8;
12.19,23
27.19
2 Ki 25.13,
17;
Jer 52,17–23

u Another reading is Jĕhoi'ăkim   v Cn: Heb send them   w Gk Syr Vg: Heb dreams

city, 20 which Nĕbúçhàdnĕz'zár king of Babylon did not take away, when he took into exile from Jerusalem to Babylon Jĕcònĭ'áh the son of Jĕhòi'ákĭm, king of Judah, and all the nobles of Judah and Jerusalem—21 thus says the LORD of hosts, the God of Israel, concerning the vessels which are left in the house of the LORD, in the house of the king of Judah, and in Jerusalem: 22 They shall be carried to Babylon and remain there until the day when I give attention to them, says the LORD. Then I will bring them back and restore them to this place."

c. Jeremiah exposes Hananiah and foretells his death

28 In that same year, at the beginning of the reign of Zĕdĕ-kì'áh king of Judah, in the fifth month of the fourth year, Hănánĭ'áh the son of Ázzúr, the prophet from Gĭb'ëön, spoke to me in the house of the LORD, in the presence of the priests and all the people, saying, 2 "Thus says the LORD of hosts, the God of Israel: I have broken the yoke of the king of Babylon. 3 Within two years I will bring back to this place all the vessels of the LORD's house, which Nĕbúçhàdnĕz'zár king of Babylon took away from this place and carried to Babylon. 4 I will also bring back to this place Jĕcònĭ'áh the son of Jĕhòi'ákĭm, king of Judah, and all the exiles from Judah who went to Babylon, says the LORD, for I will break the yoke of the king of Babylon."

5 Then the prophet Jĕrĕmì'áh spoke to Hănánĭ'áh the prophet in the presence of the priests and all the people who were standing in the house of the LORD; 6 and the prophet Jĕrĕmì'áh said, "Amen! May the LORD do so; may the LORD make the words which you have prophesied come true, and bring back to this place from Babylon the vessels of the house of the LORD, and all the exiles. 7 Yet hear now this word which I speak in your hearing and in the hearing of all the people. 8 The prophets who preceded you and me from ancient times prophesied war, famine, and pestilence against many countries and great kingdoms. 9 As for the prophet who prophesies peace, when the word of that prophet comes to pass, then it will be known that the LORD has truly sent the prophet."

10 Then the prophet Hănánĭ'áh took the yoke-bars from the neck of Jĕrĕmì'áh the prophet, and broke them. 11 And Hănánĭ'áh spoke in the presence of all the people, saying, "Thus says the LORD: Even so will I break the yoke of Nĕbúçhàdnĕz'zár king of Babylon from the neck of all the nations within two years." But Jĕrĕmì'áh the prophet went his way.

28.1 Every age of history has both its true and its false prophets. Wherever there is the real there is sure to be the counterfeit. Jeremiah found in Hananiah the antithesis of all he stood for. Probably the people were in doubt as to whose prophecies they should accept, although they might have inclined toward those of Hananiah as being far more to their liking. But God did not long leave them without a sign to confirm the truth of Jeremiah's message. Jeremiah prophesied the death of Hananiah himself, and in the very year of the prophecy it came to pass. This sign should have convinced the people, but it did not. (See 28.1–17.) It should be noted that while God is consistent with Himself, His dealings with His people vary from generation to generation. The false prophets of Jeremiah's day prophesied that God would spare Jerusalem and protect His Temple. This had been God's word through Isaiah at the time of Sennacherib's invasion (Isa 37.6, 7), but God's word through Jeremiah was one of victory for Nebuchadnezzar and the enemies of Judah. (Read 32.26–35.)

28.3 Hananiah insisted that Temple treasures and captives from Jerusalem would be returned from Babylon within two years.

Marginal refs: 27.20 2 Ki 24.14–16; Jer 24.1 · 27.22 2 Ki 25.13; 2 Chr 36.18; Jer 29.10; 32.5; Ezra 1.7; 7.19 · *28.1 Jer 27.1,3,12; Josh 9.3; 10.12 · *28.3 2 Ki 24.13; 2 Chr 36.10; Jer 27.12 · 28.4 Jer 22.24, 26,27; 27.8 · 28.5 ver 1 · 28.6 1 Ki 1.36; Jer 11.5 · 28.7 1 Ki 22.28 · 28.8 1 Ki 14.15; Isa 5.5–7; Joel 1.20; Amos 1.2; Nah 1.2 · 28.9 Deut 18.22 · 28.10 Jer 27.2 · 28.11 Jer 14.14; 27.10

28.12
Jer 1.2

28.13
Ps 107.16;
Isa 45.2

28.14
Deut 28.48;
Jer 27.6-8;
25.11

28.15
Jer 29.31;
Ezek 13.22

28.16
Deut 6.15;
13.5;
Jer 29.32

12 Sometime after the prophet Hănănī'ăh had broken the yoke-bars from off the neck of Jĕrĕmī'ăh the prophet, the word of the LORD came to Jeremiah: 13 "Go, tell Hănănī'ăh, 'Thus says the LORD: You have broken wooden bars, but Iˣ will make in their place bars of iron. 14 For thus says the LORD of hosts, the God of Israel: I have put upon the neck of all these nations an iron yoke of servitude to Nĕbŭchădnĕz'zăr king of Babylon, and they shall serve him, for I have given to him even the beasts of the field.'" 15And Jĕrĕmī'ăh the prophet said to the prophet Hănănī'ăh, "Listen, Hananiah, the LORD has not sent you, and you have made this people trust in a lie. 16 Therefore thus says the LORD: 'Behold, I will remove you from the face of the earth. This very year you shall die, because you have uttered rebellion against the LORD.'"

17 In that same year, in the seventh month, the prophet Hănănī'ăh died.

d. Jeremiah assures the captives they are safer in Babylon, for Jerusalem will be destroyed

29.1
ver 25,29

29.2
2 Ki 24.12-
16;
Jer 22.24-
28; 24.1;
28.4

*29.4ff
Isa 10.5,6;
Jer 24.5

29.6
Jer 16.2-4

29.7
Ezra 6.10;
Dan 4.19;
1 Tim 2.2

29.8
Jer 27.9;
14.14;
23.21,25,27

29.9
Jer 27.15;
ver 31

29.10
2 Chr 36.21,
22;
Jer 25.12;
27.22;
Dan 9.2

29.11
Isa 40.9-
11;
Jer 30.18-
22; 31.17

29.12
Ps 50.15;
Jer 33.3;
Ps 145.19

29 These are the words of the letter which Jĕrĕmī'ăh the prophet sent from Jerusalem to the eldersʸ of the exiles, and to the priests, the prophets, and all the people, whom Nĕbŭchădnĕz'zăr had taken into exile from Jerusalem to Babylon. 2 This was after King Jĕcŏnī'ăh, and the queen mother, the eunuchs, the princes of Judah and Jerusalem, the craftsmen, and the smiths had departed from Jerusalem. 3 The letter was sent by the hand of Ĕlā'săh the son of Shāphăn and Gĕmărī'ăh the son of Hĭlkī'ăh, whom Zĕdĕkī'ăh king of Judah sent to Babylon to Nĕbŭchădnĕz'-zăr king of Babylon. It said: 4 "Thus says the LORD of hosts, the God of Israel, to all the exiles whom I have sent into exile from Jerusalem to Babylon: 5 Build houses and live in them; plant gardens and eat their produce. 6 Take wives and have sons and daughters; take wives for your sons, and give your daughters in marriage, that they may bear sons and daughters; multiply there, and do not decrease. 7 But seek the welfare of the city where I have sent you into exile, and pray to the LORD on its behalf, for in its welfare you will find your welfare. 8 For thus says the LORD of hosts, the God of Israel: Do not let your prophets and your diviners who are among you deceive you, and do not listen to the dreams which they dream,ᶻ 9 for it is a lie which they are prophesying to you in my name; I did not send them, says the LORD.

10 "For thus says the LORD: When seventy years are completed for Babylon, I will visit you, and I will fulfil to you my promise and bring you back to this place. 11 For I know the plans I have for you, says the LORD, plans for welfare and not for evil, to give you a future and a hope. 12 Then you will call upon me and come and

x Gk: Heb you   y Gk: Heb the rest of the elders
z Cn: Heb your dreams which you cause to dream

29.4-23 In his letter to the captives in Babylon, Jeremiah sought to counteract two errors: (1) False prophets had assured them of a speedy return. Jeremiah stated that they would be in Babylon a long time. They should build houses, marry, raise families, and pray for the well-being of the land in which they were exiles. (2) Discouragement might lead them to think their exile would be endless. It would indeed be long: *seventy years* (29.10), but when God's people sought Him whole-heartedly (29.13), they would find Him. The exile was brought about because of sin, but when sin was forsaken by the people, God's purposes in mercy would then be realized.

pray to me, and I will hear you. 13 You will seek me and find me; when you seek me with all your heart, 14 I will be found by you, says the LORD, and I will restore your fortunes and gather you from all the nations and all the places where I have driven you, says the LORD, and I will bring you back to the place from which I sent you into exile.

15 "Because you have said, 'The LORD has raised up prophets for us in Babylon,'—16 Thus says the LORD concerning the king who sits on the throne of David, and concerning all the people who dwell in this city, your kinsmen who did not go out with you into exile: 17 'Thus says the LORD of hosts, Behold, I am sending on them sword, famine, and pestilence, and I will make them like vile figs which are so bad they cannot be eaten. 18 I will pursue them with sword, famine, and pestilence, and will make them a horror to all the kingdoms of the earth, to be a curse, a terror, a hissing, and a reproach among all the nations where I have driven them, 19 because they did not heed my words, says the LORD, which I persistently sent to you by my servants the prophets, but you would not listen, says the LORD.'—20 Hear the word of the LORD, all you exiles whom I sent away from Jerusalem to Babylon: 21 'Thus says the LORD of hosts, the God of Israel, concerning Āhǎb the son of Kōlāi'ah and Zědėkī'ah the son of Mā-ásei'ah, who are prophesying a lie to you in my name: Behold, I will deliver them into the hand of Něbuchǎdrěz'zar king of Babylon, and he shall slay them before your eyes. 22 Because of them this curse shall be used by all the exiles from Judah in Babylon: "The LORD make you like Zědėkī'ah and Āhǎb, whom the king of Babylon roasted in the fire," 23 because they have committed folly in Israel, they have committed adultery with their neighbors' wives, and they have spoken in my name lying words which I did not command them. I am the one who knows, and I am witness, says the LORD.' "

24 To Shěmāi'ah of Nėhěl'ám you shall say: 25 "Thus says the LORD of hosts, the God of Israel: You have sent letters in your name to all the people who are in Jerusalem, and to Zěphāni'ah the son of Mā-ásei'ah the priest, and to all the priests, saying, 26 'The LORD has made you priest instead of Jěhoi'ádá the priest, to have charge in the house of the LORD over every madman who prophesies, to put him in the stocks and collar. 27 Now why have you not rebuked Jěrěmī'ah of Ăn'áthŏth who is prophesying to you? 28 For he has sent to us in Babylon, saying, "Your exile will be long; build houses and live in them, and plant gardens and eat their produce." ' "

29 Zěphāni'ah the priest read this letter in the hearing of Jěrěmī'ah the prophet. 30 Then the word of the LORD came to Jěrěmī'ah: 31 "Send to all the exiles, saying, 'Thus says the LORD concerning Shěmāi'ah of Nėhěl'ám: Because Shemaiah has prophesied to you when I did not send him, and has made you trust in a lie, 32 therefore thus says the LORD: Behold, I will punish Shěmāi'ah of Nėhěl'ám and his descendants; he shall not have any one living among this people to see[a] the good that I will do to my people, says the LORD, for he has talked rebellion against the LORD.' "

_____
a Gk: Heb *and he shall not see*

29.13 1 Chr 22.19; 2 Chr 22.9; Jer 24.7
29.14 Deut 30.1–10; Jer 30.3; Isa 43.5,6; Jer 3.14
29.16 Jer 38.2,3, 17–23
29.17 Jer 27.8; 32.24; 24.3,8–10
29.18 Isa 65.15; Jer 42.18; 25.9
29.19 Jer 6.19; 25.4; 26.5
29.20 Jer 24.5
29.21 ver 8,9
29.22 Isa 65.15; Dan 3.6
29.23 2 Sam 13.12; Prov 5.21; Jer 16.17
29.24 ver 31,32
29.25 ver 1,29; 2 Ki 25.18; Jer 21.1
29.26 Jer 20.1; 2 Ki 9.11; Acts 26.24; Jer 20.2
29.28 ver 1,5,10
29.29 ver 25
29.31 ver 20,24; Jer 14.14, 15; 28.15
29.32 Jer 36.31; 22.30;17.6; 28.16

B. The glorious future of latter-day Israel and their new covenant

1. Sermon III: ultimate deliverance and blessing of the reunited kingdom
a. Israel restored; the heathen judged

30 The word that came to Jĕrĕmī′ăh from the LORD: 2 "Thus says the LORD, the God of Israel: Write in a book all the words that I have spoken to you. 3 For behold, days are coming, says the LORD, when I will restore the fortunes of my people, Israel and Judah, says the LORD, and I will bring them back to the land which I gave to their fathers, and they shall take possession of it."

4 These are the words which the LORD spoke concerning Israel and Judah:

5 "Thus says the LORD:
We have heard a cry of panic,
   of terror, and no peace.
6 Ask now, and see,
   can a man bear a child?
Why then do I see every man
   with his hands on his loins like a woman in labor?
   Why has every face turned pale?
7 Alas! that day is so great
      there is none like it;
   it is a time of distress for Jacob;
      yet he shall be saved out of it.

8 "And it shall come to pass in that day, says the LORD of hosts, that I will break the yoke from off their[b] neck, and I will burst their[b] bonds, and strangers shall no more make servants of them.[c] 9 But they shall serve the LORD their God and David their king, whom I will raise up for them.

10 "Then fear not, O Jacob my servant, says the LORD,
      nor be dismayed, O Israel;
   for lo, I will save you from afar,
      and your offspring from the land of their captivity.
   Jacob shall return and have quiet and ease,
      and none shall make him afraid.
11 For I am with you to save you,
                            says the LORD;
   I will make a full end of all the nations
      among whom I scattered you,
      but of you I will not make a full end.
   I will chasten you in just measure,
      and I will by no means leave you unpunished.

12 "For thus says the LORD:
   Your hurt is incurable,
      and your wound is grievous.

b Gk Old Latin: Heb *your*   *c* Heb *make a servant of him*

Cross references (margin):

30.2 — Jer 25.13; Hab 2.2
30.3 — Jer 29.10; Ps 53.6; Zeph 3.20; Jer 16.15; Ezek 20.42
30.5 — Isa 5.30; Amos 5.16-18
30.6 — Jer 4.31; 6.24
*30.7 — Isa 2.12; Joel 2.11; Lam 1.12; Jer 2.27,28; ver 10
30.8 — Isa 9.4; Jer 27.2; Ezek 34.27
*30.9 — Isa 55.3,4; Ezek 34.23; 37.24; Hos 3.5; Lk 1.69; Acts 2.30; 13.23
30.10 — Isa 43.5; 44.2; Jer 46.27, 28; Isa 60.4; Jer 33.16; Mic 4.4
30.11 — Jer 46.28; 4.27; 10.24
30.12 — ver 15; Jer 15.18

30.7 *he shall be saved out of it.* The exile, while long, will not be permanent. God will deliver His people from their affliction.

30.9 With the restoration, Jeremiah promised a Davidic king, a future ideal ruler who would inherit the promises made to David.

13 There is none to uphold your cause,
    no medicine for your wound,
    no healing for you.

14 All your lovers have forgotten you;
    they care nothing for you;
for I have dealt you the blow of an enemy,
    the punishment of a merciless foe,
because your guilt is great,
    because your sins are flagrant.

15 Why do you cry out over your hurt?
    Your pain is incurable.
Because your guilt is great,
    because your sins are flagrant,
    I have done these things to you.

16 Therefore all who devour you shall be devoured,
    and all your foes, every one of them, shall go into captivity;
those who despoil you shall become a spoil,
    and all who prey on you I will make a prey.

17 For I will restore health to you,
    and your wounds I will heal,
                  says the LORD,
because they have called you an outcast:
    'It is Zion, for whom no one cares!'

18 "Thus says the LORD:
Behold, I will restore the fortunes of the tents of Jacob,
    and have compassion on his dwellings;
the city shall be rebuilt upon its mound,
    and the palace shall stand where it used to be.

19 Out of them shall come songs of thanksgiving,
    and the voices of those who make merry.
I will multiply them, and they shall not be few;
    I will make them honored, and they shall not be small.

20 Their children shall be as they were of old,
    and their congregation shall be established before me;
    and I will punish all who oppress them.

21 Their prince shall be one of themselves,
    their ruler shall come forth from their midst;
I will make him draw near, and he shall approach me,
    for who would dare of himself to approach me?
                  says the LORD.

22 And you shall be my people,
    and I will be your God."

23 Behold the storm of the LORD!
    Wrath has gone forth,
    a whirling tempest;
    it will burst upon the head of the wicked.

24 The fierce anger of the LORD will not turn back
    until he has executed and accomplished
    the intents of his mind.
In the latter days you will understand this.

Cross-references (right column):

30.13 Jer 14.19; 46.11

30.14 Lam 1.2; 2.4,5; Jer 5.6; 32.30–35

30.16 Isa 33.1; 41.11; Jer 10.25; 50.10

30.17 Jer 8.22; 22.33; 33.24

★30.18 Jer 31.23; Ps 102.13; Jer 31.4, 38–40

30.19 Isa 35.10; Jer 31.4,12, 13; 33.10, 11,22

30.20 Isa 54.13; Jer 31.17; Isa 54.14

30.21 Num 16.5; Jer 50.44

30.22 Jer 32.38; Ezek 11.20; 36.28; Zech 13.9

★30.23f Jer 23.19, 20; 25.32

30.24 Jer 4.8; 23.20

30.18 *rebuilt upon its mound.* Assurance that Jerusalem would be rebuilt.   **30.23, 24** Except for two words, these verses repeat 23.19,20 verbatim.

b. *Restoration and blessing of both Ephraim and Judah*

31.1
Jer 30.22,
24;
Isa 41.10;
Rom 11.26–
28
*31.2
Num 14.20;
Josh 1.13;
Isa 63.14
31.3
Deut 7.8;
Ps 25.6;
Hos 11.4
31.4
Jer 30.19

31 "At that time, says the LORD, I will be the God of all the families of Israel, and they shall be my people."

2 Thus says the LORD:
"The people who survived the sword
    found grace in the wilderness;
when Israel sought for rest,
3   the LORD appeared to him *d* from afar.
I have loved you with an everlasting love;
    therefore I have continued my faithfulness to you.
4 Again I will build you, and you shall be built,
    O virgin Israel!
Again you shall adorn yourself with timbrels,
    and shall go forth in the dance of the merrymakers.

31.5
Isa 65.21;
Jer 50.19

5 Again you shall plant vineyards
    upon the mountains of Sȧmạr′ĭȧ;
the planters shall plant,
    and shall enjoy the fruit.

31.6
Isa 2.3;
Mic 4.2

6 For there shall be a day when watchmen will call
    in the hill country of Ē′phrä̈im:
'Arise, and let us go up to Zion,
    to the LORD our God.' "

31.7
Ps 14.7;
Deut 28.13;
Isa 61.9;
Ps 28.9;
Isa 37.31

7 For thus says the LORD:
"Sing aloud with gladness for Jacob,
    and raise shouts for the chief of the nations;
proclaim, give praise, and say,
    'The LORD has saved his people,
    the remnant of Israel.'

31.8
Jer 3.18;
23.8;
Isa 43.6;
Ezek 20.34,
41;
Isa 42.16;
40.11
31.9
Isa 43.19;
49.10,11;
64.8;
Jer 3,4,19

8 Behold, I will bring them from the north country,
    and gather them from the farthest parts of the earth,
among them the blind and the lame,
    the woman with child and her who is in travail, together;
    a great company, they shall return here.
9 With weeping they shall come,
    and with consolations *e* I will lead them back,
I will make them walk by brooks of water,
    in a straight path in which they shall not stumble;
for I am a father to Israel,
    and Ē′phrä̈im is my first-born.

31.10
Isa 66.19;
Jer 50.19;
Isa 40.11
31.11
Isa 44.23;
48.20;
Jer 50.34;
Isa 49.24,25
31.12
Ezek 17.23;
Hos 3.5;
Isa 58.11;
35.10;
65.19;
Rev 21.4

10 "Hear the word of the LORD, O nations,
    and declare it in the coastlands afar off;
say, 'He who scattered Israel will gather him,
    and will keep him as a shepherd keeps his flock.'
11 For the LORD has ransomed Jacob,
    and has redeemed him from hands too strong for him.
12 They shall come and sing aloud on the height of Zion,
    and they shall be radiant over the goodness of the LORD,
over the grain, the wine, and the oil,

---

d Gk: Heb *me*
e Gk Compare Vg Tg: Heb *supplications*

31.2 *grace in the wilderness,* cf. Hos 2.14, 15. Away from the land of "milk and honey," the remnant of Israel would find grace, for God loves them with an everlasting love (ver 3).

and over the young of the flock and the herd;
their life shall be like a watered garden,
and they shall languish no more.
13 Then shall the maidens rejoice in the dance,
and the young men and the old shall be merry.
I will turn their mourning into joy,
I will comfort them, and give them gladness for sorrow.
14 I will feast the soul of the priests with abundance,
and my people shall be satisfied with my goodness,
says the LORD."

15 Thus says the LORD:
"A voice is heard in Rāmah,
lamentation and bitter weeping.
Rachel is weeping for her children;
she refuses to be comforted for her children,
because they are not."

16 Thus says the LORD:
"Keep your voice from weeping,
and your eyes from tears;
for your work shall be rewarded,
says the LORD,
and they shall come back from the land of the enemy.
17 There is hope for your future,
says the LORD,
and your children shall come back to their own country.
18 I have heard Ē'phraïm bemoaning
'Thou hast chastened me, and I was chastened,
like an untrained calf;
bring me back that I may be restored,
for thou art the LORD my God.
19 For after I had turned away I repented;
and after I was instructed, I smote upon my thigh;
I was ashamed, and I was confounded,
because I bore the disgrace of my youth.'
20 Is Ē'phraïm my dear son?
Is he my darling child?
For as often as I speak against him,
I do remember him still.
Therefore my heart yearns for him;
I will surely have mercy on him,
says the LORD.

21 "Set up waymarks for yourself,
make yourself guideposts;
consider well the highway,
the road by which you went.
Return, O virgin Israel,
return to these your cities.

31.13	Ps 30.11; Zech 8.4,5; Isa 61.3; 51.11
31.14	ver 25; Jer 50.19
*31.15	Mt 2.17,18; Gen 37.35; Ps 77.2; Jer 10.20
31.16	Isa 25.8; 30.19; Heb 6.10; ver 4,5; Jer 30.3; Ezek 11.17
31.17	Jer 29.11
31.18	Job 5.17; Ps 94.12; Hos 4.16; Ps 80.3,7, 19; Jer 17.14; Acts 3.26
31.19	Ezek 36.31; Zech 12.10; Ezek 21.12; Jer 3.25; Ps 25.7; Jer 22.21
31.20	Hos 11.8; Gen 43.30; Isa 63.15; 55.7; Hos 14.4
31.21	Jer 6.16; 50.5; Isa 48.20; ver 4

31.15 The mother of Joseph (and thus of the tribes of Ephraim and Manasseh) and Benjamin is depicted weeping because her children are taken into exile. Verses 16 and 17 are filled with a promise of their return, however. The Northern Kingdom which fell to Assyria in 722 B.C. was in large measure descended from Rachel. The words are also applied to the horrors of Herod's massacre of male children near Bethlehem (Mt 2.17, 18).

31.22
Jer 2.18,23,
36; 49.4

22 How long will you waver,
    O faithless daughter?
For the LORD has created a new thing on the earth:
    a woman protects a man.' '

31.23
Jer 30.18;
32.44;
Isa 1.26;
Jer 50.7;
Zech 8.3

23 Thus says the LORD of hosts, the God of Israel: "Once more they shall use these words in the land of Judah and in its cities, when I restore their fortunes:
'The LORD bless you, O habitation of righteousness,
    O holy hill!'

31.24
Jer 33.12,
13

24 And Judah and all its cities shall dwell there together, and the farmers and those who wander*f* with their flocks. 25 For I will satisfy the weary soul, and every languishing soul I will replenish."

31.25
Mt 5.6

26 Thereupon I awoke and looked, and my sleep was pleasant to me.

31.27
Ezek 36.9–
11;
Hos 2.23

27 "Behold, the days are coming, says the LORD, when I will sow the house of Israel and the house of Judah with the seed of man and the seed of beast. 28 And it shall come to pass that as I have watched over them to pluck up and break down, to overthrow, destroy, and bring evil, so I will watch over them to build and to plant, says the LORD. 29 In those days they shall no longer say:

31.28
Jer 44.27;
1.10

31.29
Ezek 18.2

'The fathers have eaten sour grapes,
    and the children's teeth are set on edge.'

31.30
Deut 24.16;
Ezek 18.4,
20;
Gal 6.5,7

30 But every one shall die for his own sin, each man who eats sour grapes, his teeth shall be set on edge.

*31.31
Jer 32.40;
Ezek 37.26;
Heb 8.8–12

31 "Behold, the days are coming, says the LORD, when I will make a new covenant with the house of Israel and the house of Judah, 32 not like the covenant which I made with their fathers when I took them by the hand to bring them out of the land of Egypt, my covenant which they broke, though I was their husband, says the LORD. 33 But this is the covenant which I will make with the house of Israel after those days, says the LORD: I will put my law within them, and I will write it upon their hearts; and I will be their God, and they shall be my people. 34 And no longer shall each man teach his neighbor and each his brother, saying, 'Know the LORD,' for they shall all know me, from the least of them to the greatest, says the LORD; for I will forgive their iniquity, and I will remember their sin no more."

31.32
Ex 19.5;
24.6–8;
Deut 1.31;
Jer 11.7,8;
3.14

31.33
Jer 32.40;
24.7;
32.38

31.34
1 Thess 4.9;
Isa 54.13;
Jn 6.45;
Mic 7.18;
Rom 11.27

31.35
Gen 1.16;
Ps 19.1–6;
Jer 10.16

35 Thus says the LORD,
    who gives the sun for light by day
        and the fixed order of the moon and the stars for light by
            night,
    who stirs up the sea so that its waves roar—
        the LORD of hosts is his name:

31.36
Isa 54.9,10;
Jer 33.20;
Amos 9.8,9

36 "If this fixed order departs

f Cn Compare Syr Vg Tg: Heb *and they shall wander*

31.31 Jeremiah here speaks of *a new covenant*. Reference is made to this in Rom 11.26–36 and Heb 8.8–12. The contrast here is between the tables of the law written on stones and the law of God written in the hearts of men. It is "new," not in the sense that it has no continuity with the past, but rather in that the graciousness of God would then be fully revealed, bestowing upon man what he could not earn by his own effort or good works.

from before me, says the LORD,
then shall the descendants of Israel cease
from being a nation before me for ever."

37 Thus says the LORD:
"If the heavens above can be measured,
    and the foundations of the earth below can be explored,
then I will cast off all the descendants of Israel
    for all that they have done,
                                            says the LORD."

38 "Behold, the days are coming, says the LORD, when the city shall be rebuilt for the LORD from the tower of Hăn′ănĕl to the Corner Gate. 39And the measuring line shall go out farther, straight to the hill Gărĕb, and shall then turn to Gōäh. 40 The whole valley of the dead bodies and the ashes, and all the fields as far as the brook Kidrŏn, to the corner of the Horse Gate toward the east, shall be sacred to the LORD. It shall not be uprooted or overthrown any more for ever."

2. Sermon IV: the glorious restoration of Israel after the captivity

a. Jeremiah's land-purchase a sign of restoration to the land

32 The word that came to Jĕrĕmī′ăh from the LORD in the tenth year of Zĕdĕkī′ăh king of Judah, which was the eighteenth year of Nĕbúchădrĕz′zàr. 2At that time the army of the king of Babylon was besieging Jerusalem, and Jĕrĕmī′ăh the prophet was shut up in the court of the guard which was in the palace of the king of Judah. 3 For Zĕdĕkī′ăh king of Judah had imprisoned him, saying, "Why do you prophesy and say, 'Thus says the LORD: Behold, I am giving this city into the hand of the king of Babylon, and he shall take it; 4 Zĕdĕkī′ăh king of Judah shall not escape out of the hand of the Chăldē′ăns, but shall surely be given into the hand of the king of Babylon, and shall speak with him face to face and see him eye to eye; 5 and he shall take Zĕdĕkī′ăh to Babylon, and there he shall remain until I visit him, says the LORD; though you fight against the Chăldē′ăns, you shall not succeed'?"

6 Jĕrĕmī′ăh said, "The word of the LORD came to me: 7 Behold, Hăn′ămĕl the son of Shăllŭm your uncle will come to you and say, 'Buy my field which is at Ăn′áthŏth, for the right of redemption by purchase is yours.' 8 Then Hăn′ámĕl my cousin came to me in the court of the guard, in accordance with the word of the LORD, and said to me, 'Buy my field which is at Ăn′áthŏth in the land of Benjamin, for the right of possession and redemption is yours; buy it for yourself.' Then I knew that this was the word of the LORD.

9 "And I bought the field at Ăn′áthŏth from Hăn′ámĕl my cousin, and weighed out the money to him, seventeen shekels of silver. 10 I signed the deed, sealed it, got witnesses, and weighed

---

Marginal references:

31.37
Jer 33.22–26

31.38
Neh 3.1;
Zech 14.10;
2 Ki 14.13

31.40
Jer 7.32;
2 Sam 15.23;
2 Ki 23.6;
Joel 3.17

32.1
2 Ki 25.1, 2;
Jer 39.1;
25.1

32.2
Neh 3.25;
Jer 37.21;
39.14

32.3
2 Ki 6.31, 32;
Jer 26.8,9;
34.2,3

32.4
Jer 38.18, 23; 39.5

32.5
Jer 39.7;
27.22;
34.4,5;
21.4

★32.6

32.7
Jer 1.1;
Lev 25.25;
Ruth 4.4

32.8
ver 2,7,25

★32.9
Gen 23.16;
24.22;
Ex 21.32

32.10
Ruth 4.1,9

32.6, 9 Somehow the Holy Spirit conveyed to Jeremiah the will of God. *For all who are led by the Spirit of God are the sons of God* (Rom 8.14), then as now. But it is important to observe that the spoken word of 32.7 was con-firmed by circumstances in 32.8: *Then I knew that this was the word of the LORD.* The purchase of the field by Jeremiah was simply a token from God that there would be a restoration of that land after the captivity.

32.11
Lk 2.27
32.12
Jer 36.4;
51.59

*32.14
ver 10–12

32.15
Jer 33.12,
13;
Zech 3.10

32.17
Jer 1.6;
4.10;
2 Ki 19.15;
Isa 40.26–
28
32.18
Ex 34.7;
Jer 20.11;
10.16
*32.19
Isa 28.29;
Jer 16.17;
17.10
32.20
Ex 9.16;
Dan 9.15
32.21
Ex 6.6;
1 Chr 17.21
32.22
Ex 3.8,17;
Jer 11.5
32.23
Jer 2.7;
26.4;
44.10;
Neh 9.26;
Jer 11.8;
Dan 9.10–
14
32.24
Jer 33.4;
Ezek 14.21;
Deut 4.26;
Zech 1.6
32.25
ver 8,24

32.27
Num 16.22
32.28
Jer 34.2,3
32.29
Jer 21.10;
37.8,10;
52.13;
19.13
32.30
Jer 2.7;
22.21;
25.7

the money on scales. 11 Then I took the sealed deed of purchase, containing the terms and conditions, and the open copy; 12 and I gave the deed of purchase to Bąrúch the son of Nėrī'áh son of Mahṣeī'áh, in the presence of Hăn'ámĕl my cousin, in the presence of the witnesses who signed the deed of purchase, and in the presence of all the Jews who were sitting in the court of the guard. 13 I charged Bąrúch in their presence, saying, 14 'Thus says the LORD of hosts, the God of Israel: Take these deeds, both this sealed deed of purchase and this open deed, and put them in an earthenware vessel, that they may last for a long time. 15 For thus says the LORD of hosts, the God of Israel: Houses and fields and vineyards shall again be bought in this land.'

16 "After I had given the deed of purchase to Bąrúch the son of Nėrī'áh, I prayed to the LORD, saying: 17 'Ah Lord GOD! It is thou who hast made the heavens and the earth by thy great power and by thy outstretched arm! Nothing is too hard for thee, 18 who showest steadfast love to thousands, but dost requite the guilt of fathers to their children after them, O great and mighty God whose name is the LORD of hosts, 19 great in counsel and mighty in deed; whose eyes are open to all the ways of men, rewarding every man according to his ways and according to the fruit of his doings; 20 who hast shown signs and wonders in the land of Egypt, and to this day in Israel and among all mankind, and hast made thee a name, as at this day. 21 Thou didst bring thy people Israel out of the land of Egypt with signs and wonders, with a strong hand and outstretched arm, and with great terror; 22 and thou gavest them this land, which thou didst swear to their fathers to give them, a land flowing with milk and honey; 23 and they entered and took possession of it. But they did not obey thy voice or walk in thy law; they did nothing of all thou didst command them to do. Therefore thou hast made all this evil come upon them. 24 Behold, the siege mounds have come up to the city to take it, and because of sword and famine and pestilence the city is given into the hands of the Chăldē'ánṣ who are fighting against it. What thou didst speak has come to pass, and behold, thou seest it. 25 Yet thou, O Lord GOD, hast said to me, "Buy the field for money and get witnesses"—though the city is given into the hands of the Chăldē'ánṣ.' "

26 The word of the LORD came to Jĕrĕmī'áh: 27 "Behold, I am the LORD, the God of all flesh; is anything too hard for me? 28 Therefore, thus says the LORD: Behold, I am giving this city into the hands of the Chăldē'ánṣ and into the hand of Nĕbúchăd-rĕz'zăr king of Babylon, and he shall take it. 29 The Chăldē'ánṣ who are fighting against this city shall come and set this city on fire, and burn it, with the houses on whose roofs incense has been offered to Bāál and drink offerings have been poured out to other gods, to provoke me to anger. 30 For the sons of Israel and the sons

---

32.14 *an earthenware vessel.* This served as a safe deposit box. The Dead Sea Scrolls from Qumran were preserved in large jars for two thousand years.
32.19 God is sovereign over His universe. His purposes do not change and His counsels are true. Of His purposes and counsels Scripture says: (1) they are wise and wonder-

ful (Isa 28.29); (2) they are great (32.19); (3) they are immutable or unchangeable (Heb 6.17); (4) they are eternal (Eph 3.11); (5) they cannot be disannulled (Isa 14.27). Furthermore, the counsels and purposes of God: (1) are not understood by evil men (Mic 4.12); (2) are rejected by unregenerate men, even those of a religious profession (Lk 7.30).

of Judah have done nothing but evil in my sight from their youth; the sons of Israel have done nothing but provoke me to anger by the work of their hands, says the LORD. ³¹ This city has aroused my anger and wrath, from the day it was built to this day, so that I will remove it from my sight ³² because of all the evil of the sons of Israel and the sons of Judah which they did to provoke me to anger—their kings and their princes, their priests and their prophets, the men of Judah and the inhabitants of Jerusalem. ³³ They have turned to me their back and not their face; and though I have taught them persistently they have not listened to receive instruction. ³⁴ They set up their abominations in the house which is called by my name, to defile it. ³⁵ They built the high places of Bāǎl in the valley of the son of Hǐnnòm, to offer up their sons and daughters to Mōlěch, though I did not command them, nor did it enter into my mind, that they should do this abomination, to cause Judah to sin.

36 "Now therefore thus says the LORD, the God of Israel, concerning this city of which you say, 'It is given into the hand of the king of Babylon by sword, by famine, and by pestilence': ³⁷ Behold, I will gather them from all the countries to which I drove them in my anger and my wrath and in great indignation; I will bring them back to this place, and I will make them dwell in safety. ³⁸And they shall be my people, and I will be their God. ³⁹ I will give them one heart and one way, that they may fear me for ever, for their own good and the good of their children after them. ⁴⁰ I will make with them an everlasting covenant, that I will not turn away from doing good to them; and I will put the fear of me in their hearts, that they may not turn from me. ⁴¹ I will rejoice in doing them good, and I will plant them in this land in faithfulness, with all my heart and all my soul.

42 "For thus says the LORD: Just as I have brought all this great evil upon this people, so I will bring upon them all the good that I promise them. ⁴³ Fields shall be bought in this land of which you are saying, It is a desolation, without man or beast; it is given into the hands of the Chǎldē'ǎns. ⁴⁴ Fields shall be bought for money, and deeds shall be signed and sealed and witnessed, in the land of Benjamin, in the places about Jerusalem, and in the cities of Judah, in the cities of the hill country, in the cities of the Shěphē'lǎh, and in the cities of the Nĕgĕb; for I will restore their fortunes, says the LORD."

b. Beyond the exile: restoration of Jerusalem under the righteous Branch

33 The word of the LORD came to Jĕrĕmi'ǎh a second time, while he was still shut up in the court of the guard: ² "Thus says the LORD who made the earth,^g the LORD who formed it to establish it—the LORD is his name: ³ Call to me and I will answer you, and will tell you great and hidden things which you have not known. ⁴ For thus says the LORD, the God of Israel, concerning the houses of this city and the houses of the kings of Judah which were torn down to make a defense against the siege mounds and before the sword:^h ⁵ The Chǎldē'ǎns are coming in to fightⁱ and to fill them with the dead bodies of men whom I shall smite in my

g Gk: Heb *it* h Heb obscure
i Cn: Heb *They are coming in to fight against the Chaldeans*

Reference column:
32.31 2 Ki 23.27; 24.3
32.32 Isa 1.4–6; Dan 9.8
32.33 Jer 2.27; Ezek 8.16; Jer 35.15
32.34 Jer 7.30,31; Ezek 8.5,6
32.35 Jer 7.31; 19.5; Lev 18.21; 1 Ki 11.33
32.37 Deut 30.3; Jer 23.3,6; Zech 14.11
32.38 Jer 30.22; 31.33
32.39 Jer 24.7; Ezek 11.19,20; 37.25
32.40 Isa 55.3; 31.31,33; Ezek 39.29
32.41 Deut 30.9; Zeph 3.17; Amos 9.15
32.42 Jer 31.28; Zech 8.14,15; Jer 33.14
32.43 ver 15,25
32.44 Jer 17.26; 33.7,11,26
33.1 Jer 32.2,3
33.2 Jer 10.16; 51.19; Ex 15.3
33.3 Ps 50.15; Jer 29.12; 32.17,27; Isa 48.6
33.4 Jer 32.13, 14,24
33.5 Isa 8.17; Jer 21.10

anger and my wrath, for I have hidden my face from this city because of all their wickedness. 6 Behold, I will bring to it health and healing, and I will heal them and reveal to them abundance[j] of prosperity and security. 7 I will restore the fortunes of Judah and the fortunes of Israel, and rebuild them as they were at first. 8 I will cleanse them from all the guilt of their sin against me, and I will forgive all the guilt of their sin and rebellion against me. 9 And this city[k] shall be to me a name of joy, a praise and a glory before all the nations of the earth who shall hear of all the good that I do for them; they shall fear and tremble because of all the good and all the prosperity I provide for it.

10 "Thus says the LORD: In this place of which you say, 'It is a waste without man or beast,' in the cities of Judah and the streets of Jerusalem that are desolate, without man or inhabitant or beast, there shall be heard again 11 the voice of mirth and the voice of gladness, the voice of the bridegroom and the voice of the bride, the voices of those who sing, as they bring thank offerings to the house of the LORD:

'Give thanks to the LORD of hosts,
    for the LORD is good,
    for his steadfast love endures for ever!'

For I will restore the fortunes of the land as at first, says the LORD.

12 "Thus says the LORD of hosts: In this place which is waste, without man or beast, and in all of its cities, there shall again be habitations of shepherds resting their flocks. 13 In the cities of the hill country, in the cities of the Shĕphē'lăh, and in the cities of the Nĕgĕb, in the land of Benjamin, the places about Jerusalem, and in the cities of Judah, flocks shall again pass under the hands of the one who counts them, says the LORD.

14 "Behold, the days are coming, says the LORD, when I will fulfil the promise I made to the house of Israel and the house of Judah. 15 In those days and at that time I will cause a righteous Branch to spring forth for David; and he shall execute justice and righteousness in the land. 16 In those days Judah will be saved and Jerusalem will dwell securely. And this is the name by which it will be called: 'The LORD is our righteousness.'

17 "For thus says the LORD: David shall never lack a man to sit on the throne of the house of Israel, 18 and the Lĕvĭt'ĭcăl priests shall never lack a man in my presence to offer burnt offerings, to burn cereal offerings, and to make sacrifices for ever."

19 The word of the LORD came to Jĕrĕmī'ăh: 20 "Thus says the LORD: If you can break my covenant with the day and my covenant with the night, so that day and night will not come at their appointed time, 21 then also my covenant with David my servant

---

33.6
Isa 66.12;
Gal 5.22,23
33.7
Jer 32.44;
Amos 9.14,
15
33.8
Mic 7.18;
Zech 13.1;
Heb 9.13,14
33.9
Isa 62.7;
Jer 13.11;
Isa 60.5
33.10
Jer 32.43;
26.9;
34.22
33.11
Isa 35.10;
51.3,11;
1 Chr 16.8,
34;
2 Chr 5.13;
Lev 7.12
33.12
Isa 65.10;
Ezek 34.12–
14
33.13
Jer 17.26;
Lev 27.32;
Lk 15.4
33.14
Jer 23.5;
Ezek 34.23–
25
33.15
Isa 4.2;
11.1;
Zech 3.8;
Ps 72.1–5
33.16
Jer 23.6;
Isa 45.24,
25;
Phil 3.9
★33.17
2 Sam 7.16;
1 Ki 2.4;
Lk 1.32,33
33.18
Deut 18.1;
24.8;
Heb 13.15
33.20
Ps 89.37;
Isa 54.9;
Jer 31.36
33.21
Ps 89.34

---

[j] Heb uncertain   [k] Heb and it

33.17 *David shall never lack a man*, i.e., the Davidic dynasty shall be permanent. (See here footnote on the Davidic covenant, 2 Sam 7.4.) 33.17 does not necessarily imply that there would always be an occupant on the throne of David, but only that the Davidic line would never die out, and that the descendants of David would never be permanently cut off from royal authority in the Holy Land. So understood, the Davidic covenant allowed for a temporary discontinuance of effective royal authority on the part of his dynasty, but at the same time it did guarantee that his posterity would ultimately exercise permanent and enduring sovereignty. At the annunciation to the Virgin Mary, the angel made it clear that Jesus Christ was the fulfilment of this covenant-promise (Lk 1.32).

may be broken, so that he shall not have a son to reign on his throne, and my covenant with the Lêvĭt′ĭcăl priests my ministers. ²²As the host of heaven cannot be numbered and the sands of the sea cannot be measured, so I will multiply the descendants of David my servant, and the Lêvĭt′ĭcăl priests who minister to me."

23 The word of the LORD came to Jĕrĕmī′ăh: 24 "Have you not observed what these people are saying, 'The LORD has rejected the two families which he chose'? Thus they have despised my people so that they are no longer a nation in their sight. 25 Thus says the LORD: If I have not established my covenant with day and night and the ordinances of heaven and earth, 26 then I will reject the descendants of Jacob and David my servant and will not choose one of his descendants to rule over the seed of Abraham, Isaac, and Jacob. For I will restore their fortunes, and will have mercy upon them."

C. Encounters between Jeremiah and the kings of Judah

1. Zedekiah condemned for breaking his promise to slaves

34 The word which came to Jĕrĕmī′ăh from the LORD, when Nĕbŭchădrĕz′zăr king of Babylon and all his army and all the kingdoms of the earth under his dominion and all the peoples were fighting against Jerusalem and all of its cities: 2 "Thus says the LORD, the God of Israel: Go and speak to Zĕdĕkī′ăh king of Judah and say to him, 'Thus says the LORD: Behold, I am giving this city into the hand of the king of Babylon, and he shall burn it with fire. 3 You shall not escape from his hand, but shall surely be captured and delivered into his hand; you shall see the king of Babylon eye to eye and speak with him face to face; and you shall go to Babylon.' 4 Yet hear the word of the LORD, O Zĕdĕkī′ăh king of Judah! Thus says the LORD concerning you: 'You shall not die by the sword. 5 You shall die in peace. And as spices were burned for your fathers, the former kings who were before you, so men shall burn spices for you and lament for you, saying, "Alas, lord!" ' For I have spoken the word, says the LORD."

6 Then Jĕrĕmī′ăh the prophet spoke all these words to Zĕdĕkī′ăh king of Judah, in Jerusalem, 7 when the army of the king of Babylon was fighting against Jerusalem and against all the cities of Judah that were left, Lā́chĭsh and Ăzē′kăh; for these were the only fortified cities of Judah that remained.

8 The word which came to Jĕrĕmī′ăh from the LORD, after King Zĕdĕkī′ăh had made a covenant with all the people in Jerusalem to make a proclamation of liberty to them, 9 that every one should set free his Hebrew slaves, male and female, so that no one should enslave a Jew, his brother. 10And they obeyed, all the princes and all the people who had entered into the covenant that every one would set free his slave, male or female, so that they would not be enslaved again; they obeyed and set them free. 11 But afterward they turned around and took back the male and female slaves they had set free, and brought them into subjection as slaves. 12 The word of the LORD came to Jĕrĕmī′ăh from the LORD: 13 "Thus says the LORD, the God of Israel: I made a covenant with your fathers when I brought them out of the land of Egypt, out of the house of bondage, saying, 14 'At the end of six*l* years each of you

l Gk: Heb *seven*

Cross references (marginal)

33.22
Gen 15.5;
22.17;
Jer 30.19

33.24
Neh 4.2–4;
Ezek 36.2

33.25
Ps 74.16,17;
Jer 31.35,36

33.26
Jer 31.37;
Isa 14.1;
Hos 1.7;
2.23

34.1
2 Ki 25.1ff;
Jer 39.1;
1.15;
Dan 2.37,
38

34.2
Jer 22.1,2;
37.1–4;
Jer 32.29

34.3
Jer 32.4;
2 Ki 25.6,
7;
Jer 39.6,7

34.5
2 Chr
16.14;
21.19;
Jer 22.18

34.7
2 Chr 11.9;
2 Ki 18.13;
19.8

34.8
Ex 21.2;
Lev 25.10

34.9
Neh 5.11;
Lev 25.39–
46

34.11
ver 21;
Jer 37.5;
Hos 6.4

34.13
Ex 24.3,7,8;
Deut 15.22

34.14
Ex 21.2;
23.10;
Deut 15.12;
1 Sam 8.7,
8;
2 Ki 17.13,
14

must set free the fellow Hebrew who has been sold to you and has served you six years; you must set him free from your service.' But your fathers did not listen to me or incline their ears to me. 15 You recently repented and did what was right in my eyes by proclaiming liberty, each to his neighbor, and you made a covenant before me in the house which is called by my name; 16 but then you turned around and profaned my name when each of you took back his male and female slaves, whom you had set free according to their desire, and you brought them into subjection to be your slaves. 17 Therefore, thus says the LORD: You have not obeyed me by proclaiming liberty, every one to his brother and to his neighbor; behold, I proclaim to you liberty to the sword, to pestilence, and to famine, says the LORD. I will make you a horror to all the kingdoms of the earth. 18And the men who transgressed my covenant and did not keep the terms of the covenant which they made before me, I will make like[m] the calf which they cut in two and passed between its parts—19 the princes of Judah, the princes of Jerusalem, the eunuchs, the priests, and all the people of the land who passed between the parts of the calf; 20 and I will give them into the hand of their enemies and into the hand of those who seek their lives. Their dead bodies shall be food for the birds of the air and the beasts of the earth. 21And Zĕdĕkī'ăh king of Judah, and his princes I will give into the hand of their enemies and into the hand of those who seek their lives, into the hand of the army of the king of Babylon which has withdrawn from you. 22 Behold, I will command, says the LORD, and will bring them back to this city; and they will fight against it, and take it, and burn it with fire. I will make the cities of Judah a desolation without inhabitant."

2. The faithfulness of the Rechabites emphasizes the guilt of Judah

35 The word which came to Jĕrĕmī'ăh from the LORD in the days of Jĕhoi'ăkĭm the son of Jōsī'ăh, king of Judah: 2 "Go to the house of the Rĕch'ăbītes, and speak with them, and bring them to the house of the LORD, into one of the chambers; then offer them wine to drink." 3 So I took Jā-ăzănī'ăh the son of Jĕrĕmī'ăh, son of Hăb'ăzzĭnī'ăh, and his brothers, and all his sons, and the whole house of the Rĕch'ăbītes. 4 I brought them to the house of the LORD into the chamber of the sons of Hānăn the son of Ĭgdălī'ăh, the man of God, which was near the chamber of the princes, above the chamber of Mā-ăseī'ăh the son of Shăllŭm, keeper of the threshold. 5 Then I set before the Rĕch'ăbītes pitchers full of wine, and cups; and I said to them, "Drink wine." 6 But they answered, "We will drink no wine, for Jŏn'ădăb the son of Rĕchăb, our father, commanded us, 'You shall not drink wine, neither you nor your sons for ever; 7 you shall not build a house; you shall not sow seed; you shall not plant or have a vineyard; but you shall live in tents all your days, that you may live many days in the land where you sojourn.' 8 We have obeyed the voice of Jŏn'ădăb the son of Rĕchăb, our father, in all that he com-

[Left margin cross-references:]

34.15
2 Ki 23.3;
Neh 10.29;
Jer 7.10,11;
32.34
34.16
Ex 20.7;
Lev 19.12

34.17
Mt 7.2;
Gal 6.7;
Deut 28.25,
64

34.18
Deut 17.2;
Hos 6.7;
Gen 15.10,
17
34.19
ver 10
34.20
Jer 11.21;
7.33; 19.7

34.21
Jer 37.5,11

34.22
Jer 37.8,10;
4.7; 33.10;
44.22

35.1
2 Ki 24.1;
Jer 1.3;
27.20
★35.2
2 Ki 10.15;
1 Chr 2.55;
1 Ki 6.5
35.4
Deut 33.1;
1 Ki 12.22;
2 Ki 12.9;
25.18;
1 Chr 9.18,
19
35.5
Amos 2.12
35.6
2 Ki 10.15;
1 Chr 2.55;
Lev 10.9;
Lk 1.15
35.7
Gen 25.27;
Heb 11.9;
Ex 20.12;
Eph 6.2,3
35.8
Prov 1.8,9;
Eph 6.1;
Col 3.20

m Cn: Heb lacks *like*

35.2 *Rechabites.* A nomadic tribe of Kenite descent which refused to take part in urban culture and vowed not to drink intoxicating beverages.

manded us, to drink no wine all our days, ourselves, our wives,
our sons, or our daughters, 9 and not to build houses to dwell in.
We have no vineyard or field or seed; 10 but we have lived in tents,
and have obeyed and done all that Jŏn'ådăb our father commanded
us. 11 But when Nĕbüçhådrĕz'zår king of Babylon came up against
the land, we said, 'Come, and let us go to Jerusalem for fear of the
army of the Çhåldē'åns and the army of the Syrians.' So we are
living in Jerusalem."

12 Then the word of the LORD came to Jĕrĕmī'åh: 13 "Thus
says the LORD of hosts, the God of Israel: Go and say to the men
of Judah and the inhabitants of Jerusalem, Will you not receive
instruction and listen to my words? says the LORD. 14 The command which Jŏn'ådăb the son of Rēçhăb gave to his sons, to drink
no wine, has been kept; and they drink none to this day, for they
have obeyed their father's command. I have spoken to you persistently, but you have not listened to me. 15 I have sent to you all
my servants the prophets, sending them persistently, saying,
'Turn now every one of you from his evil way, and amend your
doings, and do not go after other gods to serve them, and then
you shall dwell in the land which I gave to you and your fathers.'
But you did not incline your ear or listen to me. 16 The sons of
Jŏn'ådăb the son of Rēçhăb have kept the command which their
father gave them, but this people has not obeyed me. 17 Therefore,
thus says the LORD, the God of hosts, the God of Israel: Behold,
I am bringing on Judah and all the inhabitants of Jerusalem all
the evil that I have pronounced against them; because I have
spoken to them and they have not listened, I have called to them
and they have not answered."

18 But to the house of the Rēch'åbītes Jĕrĕmī'åh said, "Thus
says the LORD of hosts, the God of Israel: Because you have obeyed
the command of Jŏn'ådăb your father, and kept all his precepts,
and done all that he commanded you, 19 therefore thus says the
LORD of hosts, the God of Israel: Jŏn'ådăb the son of Rēçhăb shall
never lack a man to stand before me."

3. Jehoiakim's arrogance in burning the scroll; the scroll rewritten

36 In the fourth year of Jĕhoi'åkĭm the son of Jōsī'åh, king of
Judah, this word came to Jĕrĕmī'åh from the LORD: 2 "Take
a scroll and write on it all the words that I have spoken to you
against Israel and Judah and all the nations, from the day I spoke
to you, from the days of Jōsī'åh until today. 3 It may be that the
house of Judah will hear all the evil which I intend to do to them,
so that every one may turn from his evil way, and that I may forgive their iniquity and their sin."

4 Then Jĕrĕmī'åh called Bąrŭch the son of Nērī'åh, and Baruch
wrote upon a scroll at the dictation of Jeremiah all the words of the
LORD which he had spoken to him. 5 And Jĕrĕmī'åh ordered
Bąrŭch, saying, "I am debarred from going to the house of the
LORD; 6 so you are to go, and on a fast day in the hearing of all
the people in the LORD's house you shall read the words of the
LORD from the scroll which you have written at my dictation.
You shall read them also in the hearing of all the men of Judah
who come out of their cities. 7 It may be that their supplication
will come before the LORD, and that every one will turn from his

35.9
ver 7
35.10
ver 6,7
35.11
2 Ki 24.1,2;
Jer 4.5–7;
8.14
35.13
Isa 28.9–12;
Jer 32.33
35.14
2 Chr
36.15;
Jer 7.13;
25.3;
Isa 30.9;
50.2
35.15
Jer 26.5;
32.33;
Isa 1.16,17;
Jer 4.1;
18.11;7.6;
13.10;22.4;
34.14
35.16
ver 14
35.17
Jer 19.3,15;
Mic 3.12;
Prov 1.24;
Isa 65.12;
66.4;
Jer 7.13
35.19
Jer 33.17;
15.19
36.1
2 Ki 24.1;
Jer 25.1,3
36.2
ver 6,23,28;
Zech 5.1;
Jer 1.9,10;
25.9–29;
25.3
36.3
ver 7;
Jer 26.3;
Isa 55.7;
Jer 18.8;
Jon 3.8;
Mk 4.12;
Acts 3.19
36.4
ver 18;
Jer 32.12;
ver 14;
Ezek 2.9
36.5
Jer 32.2;
33.1
36.7
2 Ki 22.13;
Jer 4.4;
21.5

evil way, for great is the anger and wrath that the LORD has pronounced against this people." ⁸And Bạrŭch the son of Nĕrī'ạh did
all that Jĕrĕmī'ạh the prophet ordered him about reading from the
scroll the words of the LORD in the LORD's house.

9 In the fifth year of Jĕhoi'ạkĭm the son of Jōsī'ạh, king of
Judah, in the ninth month, all the people in Jerusalem and all the
people who came from the cities of Judah to Jerusalem proclaimed
a fast before the LORD. ¹⁰ Then, in the hearing of all the people,
Bạrŭch read the words of Jĕrĕmī'ạh from the scroll, in the house
of the LORD, in the chamber of Gĕmạrī'ạh the son of Shāphạn the
secretary, which was in the upper court, at the entry of the New
Gate of the LORD's house.

11 When Mĭcāi'ạh the son of Gĕmạrī'ạh, son of Shāphạn, heard
all the words of the LORD from the scroll, ¹² he went down to the
king's house, into the secretary's chamber; and all the princes were
sitting there: Ĕlī'shạmá the secretary, Dĕlāi'ạh the son of Shĕmāi'-
ạh, Ĕlnā'thạn the son of Ăchbor, Gĕmạrī'ạh the son of Shāphạn,
Zĕdĕkī'ạh the son of Hănănī'ạh, and all the princes. ¹³And Mĭcāi'-
ạh told them all the words that he had heard, when Bạrŭch read the
scroll in the hearing of the people. ¹⁴ Then all the princes sent
Jĕhū'dī the son of Nĕthănī'ạh, son of Shĕlĕmī'ạh, son of Cŭshī,
to say to Bạrŭch, "Take in your hand the scroll that you read in
the hearing of the people, and come." So Baruch the son of
Nĕrī'ạh took the scroll in his hand and came to them. ¹⁵And they
said to him, "Sit down and read it." So Bạrŭch read it to them.
¹⁶ When they heard all the words, they turned one to another in
fear; and they said to Bạrŭch, "We must report all these words to
the king." ¹⁷ Then they asked Bạrŭch, "Tell us, how did you write
all these words? Was it at his dictation?" ¹⁸ Bạrŭch answered them,
"He dictated all these words to me, while I wrote them with ink
on the scroll." ¹⁹ Then the princes said to Bạrŭch, "Go and hide,
you and Jĕrĕmī'ạh, and let no one know where you are."

20 So they went into the court to the king, having put the scroll
in the chamber of Ĕlī'shạmá the secretary; and they reported all
the words to the king. ²¹ Then the king sent Jĕhū'dī to get the
scroll, and he took it from the chamber of Ĕlī'shạmá the secretary;
and Jehudi read it to the king and all the princes who stood beside
the king. ²² It was the ninth month, and the king was sitting in the
winter house and there was a fire burning in the brazier before
him. ²³As Jĕhū'dī read three or four columns, the king would
cut them off with a penknife and throw them into the fire in the
brazier, until the entire scroll was consumed in the fire that was in
the brazier. ²⁴ Yet neither the king, nor any of his servants who
heard all these words, was afraid, nor did they rend their garments.
²⁵ Even when Ĕlnā'thạn and Dĕlāi'ạh and Gĕmạrī'ạh urged the
king not to burn the scroll, he would not listen to them. ²⁶And
the king commanded Jĕrah'meĕl the king's son and Sĕrāi'ạh the
son of Ăz'rĭ-ĕl and Shĕlĕmī'ạh the son of Ăbdeĕl to seize Bạrŭch
the secretary and Jĕrĕmī'ạh the prophet, but the LORD hid them.

27 Now, after the king had burned the scroll with the words
which Bạrŭch wrote at Jĕrĕmī'ạh's dictation, the word of the LORD
came to Jĕrĕmī'ạh: ²⁸ "Take another scroll and write on it all the
former words that were in the first scroll, which Jĕhoi'ạkĭm the
king of Judah has burned. ²⁹And concerning Jĕhoi'ạkĭm king of
Judah you shall say, 'Thus says the LORD, You have burned this

36.8
ver 6

36.9
ver 6;
Est 4.16;
Jon 3.5

36.10
Jer 26.10

36.11
ver 13
36.12
ver 20,25;
Jer 26.22

36.13
2 Ki 22.10;
36.14;
ver 21

36.15
ver 21
36.16
ver 24;
Acts 24.25;
Jer 13.18;
Amos 7.10,
11
36.18
ver 4
36.19
ver 26;
Jer 26.20–
24
36.20
ver 12
36.21
ver 14;
2 Chr 34.18
36.22
Amos 3.15
36.23
ver 29
36.24
2 Ki 19.1,2;
22.11;
Isa 36.22;
37.1
36.25
Acts 5.34–
39
36.26
1 Ki 19.1ff;
Jer 15.20,21
36.27
ver 23,4,18
36.28
Jer 28.13,14
36.29
Job 15.24,
25;
Isa 45.9;
30.10;
Jer 26.9;
32.3;
25.9–11

scroll, saying, "Why have you written in it that the king of Babylon will certainly come and destroy this land, and will cut off from
it man and beast?" 30 Therefore thus says the LORD concerning
Jěhoi'ǎkǐm king of Judah, He shall have none to sit upon the
throne of David, and his dead body shall be cast out to the heat by
day and the frost by night. 31And I will punish him and his offspring and his servants for their iniquity; I will bring upon them,
and upon the inhabitants of Jerusalem, and upon the men of
Judah, all the evil that I have pronounced against them, but they
would not hear.' "

32 Then Jěrěmī'ǎh took another scroll and gave it to Bạrúch the
scribe, the son of Něrī'ǎh, who wrote on it at the dictation of
Jeremiah all the words of the scroll which Jěhoi'ǎkǐm king of
Judah had burned in the fire; and many similar words were added
to them.

4. *Jeremiah's arrest and imprisonment*

37 Zěděkī'ǎh the son of Jōsī'ǎh, whom Něbùchǎdrěz'zǎr king
of Babylon made king in the land of Judah, reigned instead
of Cǒnī'ǎh the son of Jěhoi'ǎkǐm. 2 But neither he nor his servants
nor the people of the land listened to the words of the LORD which
he spoke through Jěrěmī'ǎh the prophet.

3 King Zěděkī'ǎh sent Jěhū'cǎl the son of Shělěmī'ǎh, and
Zěphǎnī'ǎh the priest, the son of Mā-àseī'ǎh, to Jěrěmī'ǎh the
prophet, saying, "Pray for us to the LORD our God." 4 Now Jěrěmī'ǎh was still going in and out among the people, for he had not
yet been put in prison. 5 The army of Phạraōh had come out of
Egypt; and when the Chǎlděáns who were besieging Jerusalem
heard news of them, they withdrew from Jerusalem.

6 Then the word of the LORD came to Jěrěmī'ǎh the prophet:
7 "Thus says the LORD, God of Israel: Thus shall you say to the
king of Judah who sent you to me to inquire of me, 'Behold,
Phạraōh's army which came to help you is about to return to
Egypt, to its own land. 8And the Chǎlděáns shall come back and
fight against this city; they shall take it and burn it with fire.
9 Thus says the LORD, Do not deceive yourselves, saying, "The
Chǎlděáns will surely stay away from us," for they will not stay
away. 10 For even if you should defeat the whole army of Chǎlděáns who are fighting against you, and there remained of them only
wounded men, every man in his tent, they would rise up and burn
this city with fire.' "

11 Now when the Chǎlděán army had withdrawn from Jerusalem at the approach of Phạraōh's army, 12 Jěrěmī'ǎh set out from
Jerusalem to go to the land of Benjamin to receive his portion[n]
there among the people. 13 When he was at the Benjamin Gate, a
sentry there named Īrī'jǎh the son of Shělěmī'ǎh, son of Hǎnǎnī'-
ǎh, seized Jěrěmī'ǎh the prophet, saying, "You are deserting to the
Chǎlděáns." 14And Jěrěmī'ǎh said, "It is false; I am not deserting
to the Chǎlděáns." But Īrī'jǎh would not listen to him, and seized
Jeremiah and brought him to the princes. 15And the princes were
enraged at Jěrěmī'ǎh, and they beat him and imprisoned him in
the house of Jonathan the secretary, for it had been made a prison.

16 When Jěrěmī'ǎh had come to the dungeon cells, and remained there many days, 17 King Zěděkī'ǎh sent for him, and re-

n Heb obscure

36.30
2 Ki 24.12–
15;
Jer 22.30;
22.19
36.31
Jer 23.34;
Deut 28.15;
Jer 19.15

36.32
ver 28,4,23

37.1
2 Ki 24.17;
2 Chr 36.10;
Jer 22.24;
Ezek 17.12–
21
37.2
2 Chr 36.12,
14
37.3
Jer 21.1,2;
29.25;
52.24;
1 Ki 13.6;
Acts 8.24
37.4
ver 15
37.5
2 Ki 24.7;
Ezek 17.15;
Jer 34.21
37.7
Jer 21.2;
Isa 30.1–3;
31.1–3;
Ezek 17.17
37.8
Jer 34.22
37.9
Jer 29.8
37.10
Jer 21.4,5;
Joel 2.11
37.11
ver 5
37.13
Jer 38.7;
Zech 14.10;
Jer 18.18;
20.10;
Lk 23.2;
Acts 24.5–
9,13
37.14
Jer 40.4–6;
Mt 5.11,12
37.15
Jer 18.23;
2 Chr 16.10;
18.26
37.16
Jer 38.6
37.17
Jer 38.5,14–
16,24–27

ceived him. The king questioned him secretly in his house, and said, "Is there any word from the LORD?" Jĕrĕmī′ah said, "There is." Then he said, "You shall be delivered into the hand of the king of Babylon." 18 Jĕrĕmī′ah also said to King Zĕdĕkī′ah, "What wrong have I done to you or your servants or this people, that you have put me in prison? 19 Where are your prophets who prophesied to you, saying, 'The king of Babylon will not come against you and against this land'? 20 Now hear, I pray you, O my lord the king: let my humble plea come before you, and do not send me back to the house of Jonathan the secretary, lest I die there." 21 So King Zĕdĕkī′ah gave orders, and they committed Jĕrĕmī′ah to the court of the guard; and a loaf of bread was given him daily from the bakers' street, until all the bread of the city was gone. So Jeremiah remained in the court of the guard.

5. Jeremiah cast into the miry pit; rescued by Ebedmelech

38 Now Shĕphătī′ah the son of Măttăn, Gĕdălī′ah the son of Păshhŭr, Jucăl the son of Shĕlĕmī′ah, and Pashhur the son of Mălchī′ah heard the words that Jĕrĕmī′ah was saying to all the people, 2 "Thus says the LORD, He who stays in this city shall die by the sword, by famine, and by pestilence; but he who goes out to the Chăldē′ăns shall live; he shall have his life as a prize of war, and live. 3 Thus says the LORD, This city shall surely be given into the hand of the army of the king of Babylon and be taken." 4 Then the princes said to the king, "Let this man be put to death, for he is weakening the hands of the soldiers who are left in this city, and the hands of all the people, by speaking such words to them. For this man is not seeking the welfare of this people, but their harm." 5 King Zĕdĕkī′ah said, "Behold, he is in your hands; for the king can do nothing against you." 6 So they took Jĕrĕmī′ah and cast him into the cistern of Mălchī′ah, the king's son, which was in the court of the guard, letting Jeremiah down by ropes. And there was no water in the cistern, but only mire, and Jeremiah sank in the mire.

7 When Ĕ′bĕd-mĕl′ĕch the Ethiopian, a eunuch, who was in the king's house, heard that they had put Jĕrĕmī′ah into the cistern— the king was sitting in the Benjamin Gate—8 Ĕ′bĕd-mĕl′ĕch went from the king's house and said to the king, 9 "My lord the king, these men have done evil in all that they did to Jĕrĕmī′ah the prophet by casting him into the cistern; and he will die there of hunger, for there is no bread left in the city." 10 Then the king commanded Ĕ′bĕd-mĕl′ĕch, the Ethiopian, "Take three men with you from here, and lift Jĕrĕmī′ah the prophet out of the cistern before he dies." 11 So Ĕ′bĕd-mĕl′ĕch took the men with him and went to the house of the king, to a wardrobe of *o* the storehouse, and

o Cn: Heb to under

37.18
Dan 6.22;
Jn 10.32;
Acts 25.8,
11,25
37.19
Jer 2.28;
6.14; 29.31
37.20
Jer 36.7;
38.26;
18.23
37.21
Jer 32.3;
38.13,28;
Isa 33.16;
Jer 38.9;
52.6;
39.14,15

38.1
Jer 37.3;
21.1,8

38.2
Jer 21.9;
42.17;45.5

38.3
Jer 21.10;
32.3
★**38.4**
Jer 18.23;
26.11;
1 Ki 18.17,
18; 21.20;
Amos 7.10;
Acts 16.20;
Jer 29.7
38.5
2 Sam 3.39
38.6
Jer 37.21;
Acts 16.24;
Zech 9.11

★**38.7**
Jer 39.16;
37.13;
Amos 5.10
38.9
Jer 37.21;
52.6

38.11
ver 6

38.4 Jeremiah appeared to his nationalistic compatriots to be guilty of treason and betrayal of the nation to Nebuchadnezzar, and for that reason his enemies sought to have him killed. Jeremiah himself knew that he was only fulfilling his God-given mission, and yet it resulted in his being cast into a vile dungeon where he sank into the mire (ver 6, 11–13). Scripture nowhere affirms that God's servants will be exempted from persecution

and tribulation as a reward for their faithfulness. On the contrary, it implies that affliction and hardship may be their portion (Heb 11.32–37). But God does promise grace and strength sufficient to triumph in adversity (Phil 4.6, 7, 19; 2 Cor 1.3–7; 9.8; Eph 3.20).

38.7 *a eunuch.* The word may be rendered simply "an officer." Eunuchs were frequently employed in oriental courts where some attained considerable power.

took from there old rags and worn-out clothes, which he let down to Jĕrĕmī′áh in the cistern by ropes. 12 Then Ĕ′bĕd-mĕl′ĕçh the Ethiopian said to Jĕrĕmī′áh, "Put the rags and clothes between your armpits and the ropes." Jeremiah did so. 13 Then they drew Jĕrĕmī′áh up with ropes and lifted him out of the cistern. And Jeremiah remained in the court of the guard.

14 King Zĕdĕkī′áh sent for Jĕrĕmī′áh the prophet and received him at the third entrance of the temple of the LORD. The king said to Jeremiah, "I will ask you a question; hide nothing from me." 15 Jĕrĕmī′áh said to Zĕdĕkī′áh, "If I tell you, will you not be sure to put me to death? And if I give you counsel, you will not listen to me." 16 Then King Zĕdĕkī′áh swore secretly to Jĕrĕmī′áh, "As the LORD lives, who made our souls, I will not put you to death or deliver you into the hand of these men who seek your life."

17 Then Jĕrĕmī′áh said to Zĕdĕkī′áh, "Thus says the LORD, the God of hosts, the God of Israel, If you will surrender to the princes of the king of Babylon, then your life shall be spared, and this city shall not be burned with fire, and you and your house shall live. 18 But if you do not surrender to the princes of the king of Babylon, then this city shall be given into the hand of the Çhăldē′-ănṣ, and they shall burn it with fire, and you shall not escape from their hand." 19 King Zĕdĕkī′áh said to Jĕrĕmī′áh, "I am afraid of the Jews who have deserted to the Çhăldē′ánṣ, lest I be handed over to them and they abuse me." 20 Jĕrĕmī′áh said, "You shall not be given to them. Obey now the voice of the LORD in what I say to you, and it shall be well with you, and your life shall be spared. 21 But if you refuse to surrender, this is the vision which the LORD has shown to me: 22 Behold, all the women left in the house of the king of Judah were being led out to the princes of the king of Babylon and were saying,

'Your trusted friends have deceived you
　　and prevailed against you;
now that your feet are sunk in the mire,
　　they turn away from you.'

23 All your wives and your sons shall be led out to the Çhăldē′ánṣ, and you yourself shall not escape from their hand, but shall be seized by the king of Babylon; and this city shall be burned with fire."

24 Then Zĕdĕkī′áh said to Jĕrĕmī′áh, "Let no one know of these words and you shall not die. 25 If the princes hear that I have spoken with you and come to you and say to you, 'Tell us what you said to the king and what the king said to you; hide nothing from us and we will not put you to death,' 26 then you shall say to them, 'I made a humble plea to the king that he would not send me back to the house of Jonathan to die there.' " 27 Then all the princes came to Jĕrĕmī′áh and asked him, and he answered them as the king had instructed him. So they left off speaking with him, for the conversation had not been overheard. 28 And Jĕrĕmī′áh remained in the court of the guard until the day that Jerusalem was taken.

6. The fall of Jerusalem and the capture of Zedekiah; special blessing for Ebedmelech

39 In the ninth year of Zĕdĕkī′áh king of Judah, in the tenth month, Nĕbùçhădrĕz′zàr king of Babylon and all his army

38.13
Jer 37.21;
39.14,15

38.14
Jer 21.1,2;
37.17;
15.11;
42.2–5,20

38.15
Lk 22.67,
68

38.16
Jer 37.17;
Isa 57.16;
Zech 12.1;
ver 4–6

38.17
Ps 80.7,14;
1 Chr 17.24;
Ezek 8.4;
2 Ki 24.12;
26.27–30

38.18
Jer 27.8;
32.4;
34.3

38.19
Isa 51.12,
13;
Jn 12.42;
19.12,13;
Jer 39.9;
2 Chr
30.10;
Neh 4.1

38.20
Jer 11.4,8;
7.23;
Isa 55.3

38.22
Jer 6.12;
8.10;43.6

38.23
Jer 39.6;
41.10

38.25
ver 4–6,27

38.26
Jer 37.15,20

38.27
1 Sam
10.15,16;
16.2–5

38.28
Jer 37.21;
39.14

39.1
2 Ki 25.1–
4;
Jer 52.4–7;
Ezek 24.1,2

39.2
2 Ki 25.4;
Jer 52.7
39.3
Jer 38.17

39.4
2 Ki 25.4;
Jer 52.7;
Amos 2.14;
2 Chr 32.5
39.5
Jer 32.4;
38.18,23;
Josh 4.13;
2 Ki 23.33
39.6
2 Ki 25.7;
Jer 34.19–21
39.7
2 Ki 25.7;
Jer 52.11;
Ezek 12.13;
Jer 32.5
39.8
2 Ki 25.9,
10;
Jer 38.18;
52.13
39.9
2 Ki 25.11,
20;
Jer 52.12–
16; 24.8;
38.19
39.10
2 Ki 25.12;
Jer 52.16
39.11
Jer 1.8;
15.20,21;
Acts 24.23
39.14
Jer 38.28;
40.1–6;
2 Ki 22.12,
14;
2 Chr 34.20
39.16
Jer 38.7,12;
21.10;
Dan 9.12;
Zech 1.6
39.17
Ps 41.1,2;
50.15
39.18
Jer 21.9;
45.5;
Ps 34.22;
Jer 17.7,8

came against Jerusalem and besieged it; 2 in the eleventh year of Zĕdĕkī′áh, in the fourth month, on the ninth day of the month, a breach was made in the city. 3 When Jerusalem was taken,*p* all the princes of the king of Babylon came and sat in the middle gate: Nēr′gal-shárē′zĕr, Săm′gar-nē′bō, Sar′sĕchĭm the Răbsā′rĭs, Ner-gal-sharezer the Răbmăg, with all the rest of the officers of the king of Babylon. 4 When Zĕdĕkī′áh king of Judah and all the soldiers saw them, they fled, going out of the city at night by way of the king's garden through the gate between the two walls; and they went toward the Ar′ábáh. 5 But the army of the Chăldē′áns pursued them, and overtook Zĕdĕkī′áh in the plains of Jĕr′ĭchō; and when they had taken him, they brought him up to Nĕbŭchádrĕz′-zár king of Babylon, at Rĭblăh, in the land of Hāmáth; and he passed sentence upon him. 6 The king of Babylon slew the sons of Zĕdĕkī′áh at Rĭblăh before his eyes; and the king of Babylon slew all the nobles of Judah. 7 He put out the eyes of Zĕdĕkī′áh, and bound him in fetters to take him to Babylon. 8 The Chăldē′áns burned the king's house and the house of the people, and broke down the walls of Jerusalem. 9 Then Nĕbŭzar′ádán, the captain of the guard, carried into exile to Babylon the rest of the people who were left in the city, those who had deserted to him, and the people who remained. 10 Nĕbŭzar′ádán, the captain of the guard, left in the land of Judah some of the poor people who owned nothing, and gave them vineyards and fields at the same time.

11 Nĕbŭchádrĕz′zár king of Babylon gave command concerning Jĕrĕmī′áh through Nĕbŭzar′ádán, the captain of the guard, saying, 12 "Take him, look after him well and do him no harm, but deal with him as he tells you." 13 So Nĕbŭzar′ádán the captain of the guard, Nĕbŭshăz′bán the Răbsā′rĭs, Nēr′gal-shárē′zĕr the Răbmăg, and all the chief officers of the king of Babylon 14 sent and took Jĕrĕmī′áh from the court of the guard. They entrusted him to Gĕdálī′áh the son of Ăhī′kám, son of Shāphán, that he should take him home. So he dwelt among the people.

15 The word of the Lord came to Jĕrĕmī′áh while he was shut up in the court of the guard: 16 "Go, and say to Ē′bĕd-mĕl′ĕch the Ethiopian, 'Thus says the Lord of hosts, the God of Israel: Behold, I will fulfil my words against this city for evil and not for good, and they shall be accomplished before you on that day. 17 But I will deliver you on that day, says the Lord, and you shall not be given into the hand of the men of whom you are afraid. 18 For I will surely save you, and you shall not fall by the sword; but you shall have your life as a prize of war, because you have put your trust in me, says the Lord.'"

III. Prophecies after the fall of Jerusalem 40.1–45.5

A. Jeremiah's ministry among the remnant in Judah

1. Released by Nebuzaradan, Jeremiah lives in Mizpah with Governor Gedaliah

40.1
Jer 39.9,11,
14; 31.15;
Eph 6.20

40 The word that came to Jĕrĕmī′áh from the Lord after Nĕbŭzar′ádán the captain of the guard had let him go from Rāmáh, when he took him bound in chains along with all the cap-

p This clause has been transposed from the end of Chapter 38

tives of Jerusalem and Judah who were being exiled to Babylon.
2 The captain of the guard took Jĕrĕmī'äh and said to him, "The
LORD your God pronounced this evil against this place; 3 the LORD
has brought it about, and has done as he said. Because you sinned
against the LORD, and did not obey his voice, this thing has come
upon you. 4 Now, behold, I release you today from the chains on
your hands. If it seems good to you to come with me to Babylon,
come, and I will look after you well; but if it seems wrong to you
to come with me to Babylon, do not come. See, the whole land is
before you; go wherever you think it good and right to go. 5 If you
remain,q then return to Gĕdálī'äh the son of Ȧhī'käm, son of
Shāphän, whom the king of Babylon appointed governor of the
cities of Judah, and dwell with him among the people; or go
wherever you think it right to go." So the captain of the guard
gave him an allowance of food and a present, and let him go.
6 Then Jĕrĕmī'äh went to Gĕdálī'äh the son of Ȧhī'käm, at
Mĭzpäh, and dwelt with him among the people who were left
in the land.

7 When all the captains of the forces in the open country and
their men heard that the king of Babylon had appointed Gĕdálī'äh
the son of Ȧhī'käm governor in the land, and had committed to
him men, women, and children, those of the poorest of the land
who had not been taken into exile to Babylon, 8 they went to
Gĕdálī'äh at Mĭzpäh—Ĭsh'mäël the son of Nĕthánī'äh, Jōhän'än
the son of Kȧrē'äh, Sĕrāi'äh the son of Tănhū'mĕth, the sons of
Ēphaī the Nĕtŏph'äthīte, Jĕzánī'äh the son of the Mā-ăc'äthīte,
they and their men. 9 Gĕdálī'äh the son of Ȧhī'käm, son of
Shāphän, swore to them and their men, saying, "Do not be
afraid to serve the Chăldē'änṣ. Dwell in the land, and serve the
king of Babylon, and it shall be well with you. 10As for me, I will
dwell at Mĭzpäh, to stand for you before the Chăldē'änṣ who will
come to us; but as for you, gather wine and summer fruits and oil,
and store them in your vessels, and dwell in your cities that you
have taken." 11 Likewise, when all the Jews who were in Mōäb and
among the Ȧm'mónītes and in Ēdôm and in other lands heard that
the king of Babylon had left a remnant in Judah and had appointed
Gĕdálī'äh the son of Ȧhī'käm, son of Shāphän, as governor over
them, 12 then all the Jews returned from all the places to which
they had been driven and came to the land of Judah, to Gĕdálī'äh
at Mĭzpäh; and they gathered wine and summer fruits in great
abundance.

13 Now Jōhän'än the son of Kȧrē'äh and all the leaders of the
forces in the open country came to Gĕdálī'äh at Mĭzpäh 14 and said
to him, "Do you know that Bā'álís the king of the Ȧm'mónītes has
sent Ĭsh'mäël the son of Nĕthánī'äh to take your life?" But
Gĕdálī'äh the son of Ahī'käm would not believe them. 15 Then
Jōhän'än the son of Kȧrē'äh spoke secretly to Gĕdálī'äh at Mĭzpäh,
"Let me go and slay Ish'mäël the son of Nĕthánī'äh, and no one
will know it. Why should he take your life, so that all the Jews
who are gathered about you would be scattered, and the remnant
of Judah would perish?" 16 But Gĕdálī'äh the son of Ȧhī'käm said
to Jōhän'än the son of Kȧrē'äh, "You shall not do this thing, for
you are speaking falsely of Ish'mäël."

q Syr: Heb obscure

40.2
Jer 22.8,9;
50.7
40.3
Deut 29.24,
25;
Dan 9.11
40.4
Jer 39.11,
12;
Gen 20.15

40.5
Jer 39.14;
2 Ki 25.23;
ver 4;
Jer 52.34

40.6
Jer 39.14;
Judg 20.1

40.7
2 Ki 25.23,
24;
Jer 39.10;
52.16

40.8
Jer 41.1

40.9
2 Ki 25.24;
Jer 27.11;
38.17–20

40.10
ver 6;
Jer 35.19;
39.10;
ver 12;
Jer 48.32

40.11
Isa 16.4;
1 Sam 11.1;
12.12;
Isa 11.14

40.12
Jer 43.5;
ver 10

40.13
ver 8
40.14
Jer 41.10

40.15
1 Sam 26.8;
2 Sam
21.17;
Jer 42.2

40.16
Mt 10.16

2. *After murdering Gedaliah, Ishmael is routed by Johanan*

41.1
2 Ki 25.25;
Jer 40.6,8,
14

41 In the seventh month, Ĭsh'mä̇el the son of Nĕthänī'ȧh, son of Ĕlī'shȧmȧ, of the royal family, one of the chief officers of the king, came with ten men to Gĕdȧlī'ȧh the son of Ȧhī'kȧm, at Mĭzpȧh. As they ate bread together there at Mizpah, 2 Ĭsh'mä̇el the son of Nĕthänī'ȧh and the ten men with him rose up and struck down Gĕdȧlī'ȧh the son of Ȧhī'kȧm, son of Shäphȧn, with the sword, and killed him, whom the king of Babylon had appointed governor in the land. 3 Ĭsh'mä̇el also slew all the Jews who were with Gĕdȧlī'ȧh at Mĭzpȧh, and the Chȧldē'ȧn soldiers who happened to be there.

41.2
2 Ki 25.25;
Jer 40.5

4 On the day after the murder of Gĕdȧlī'ȧh, before any one knew of it, 5 eighty men arrived from Shĕçhĕm and Shīlōh and Sȧmȧr'ĭȧ, with their beards shaved and their clothes torn, and their bodies gashed, bringing cereal offerings and incense to present at the temple of the LORD. 6 And Ĭsh'mä̇el the son of Nĕthänī'ȧh came out from Mĭzpȧh to meet them, weeping as he came. As he met them, he said to them, "Come in to Gĕdȧlī'ȧh the son of Ȧhī'kȧm." 7 When they came into the city, Ĭsh'mä̇el the son of Nĕthänī'ȧh and the men with him slew them, and cast them into a cistern. 8 But there were ten men among them who said to Ĭsh'mä̇el, "Do not kill us, for we have stores of wheat, barley, oil, and honey hidden in the fields." So he refrained and did not kill them with their companions.

41.5
Gen 33.18;
Josh 18.1;
1 Ki 16.24,
29;
Jer 16.6;
2 Ki 25.9
41.6
Jer 50.4
41.7
Isa 59.7;
Ezek 22.27

9 Now the cistern into which Ĭsh'mä̇el cast all the bodies of the men whom he had slain was the large cistern[r] which King Äsȧ had made for defense against Bä'ȧshȧ king of Israel; Ishmael the son of Nĕthänī'ȧh filled it with the slain. 10 Then Ĭsh'mä̇el took captive all the rest of the people who were in Mĭzpȧh, the king's daughters and all the people who were left at Mizpah, whom Nĕbŭzȧr'ȧdȧn, the captain of the guard, had committed to Gĕdȧlī'ȧh the son of Ȧhī'kȧm. Ishmael the son of Nĕthänī'ȧh took them captive and set out to cross over to the Äm'mȯnītes.

41.9
1 Ki 15.22;
2 Chr 16.6

41.10
Jer 40.11,
12; 43.6;
40.7,14

11 But when Jōhȧn'ȧn the son of Kȧrē'ȧh and all the leaders of the forces with him heard of all the evil which Ĭsh'mä̇el the son of Nĕthänī'ȧh had done, 12 they took all their men and went to fight against Ĭsh'mä̇el the son of Nĕthänī'ȧh. They came upon him at the great pool which is in Gĭb'ēȯn. 13 And when all the people who were with Ĭsh'mä̇el saw Jōhȧn'ȧn the son of Kȧrē'ȧh and all the leaders of the forces with him, they rejoiced. 14 So all the people whom Ĭsh'mä̇el had carried away captive from Mĭzpȧh turned about and came back, and went to Jōhȧn'ȧn the son of Kȧrē'ȧh. 15 But Ĭsh'mä̇el the son of Nĕthänī'ȧh escaped from Jōhȧn'ȧn with eight men, and went to the Äm'mȯnītes. 16 Then Jōhȧn'ȧn the son of Kȧrē'ȧh and all the leaders of the forces with him took all the rest of the people whom Ĭsh'mä̇el the son of Nĕthänī'ȧh had carried away captive[s] from Mĭzpȧh after he had slain Gĕdȧlī'ȧh the son of Ȧhī'kȧm—soldiers, women, children, and eunuchs, whom Johanan brought back from Gĭb'ēȯn. 17 And they went and stayed at Gēruth Chĭmhȧm near Bĕth'lĕhĕm, intending to go to Egypt 18 because of the Chȧldē'ȧns; for they were afraid of them, because Ĭsh'mä̇el the son of Nĕthänī'ȧh had slain Gĕdȧlī'ȧh the son of

41.11
Jer 40.7,8,
13–16
41.12
2 Sam 2.13

41.13
ver 10,14

41.15
ver 2
41.16
Jer 42.8;
43.4–7
41.17
2 Sam
19.37,38;
Jer 42.14
41.18
Jer 42.11,
16;
Lk 12.4,5;
Jer 40.5

---

r Gk: Heb *he had slain by the hand of Gĕdȧlī'ȧh*
s Cn: Heb *whom he recovered from Ĭsh'mä̇el*

Åhĭ′kȧm, whom the king of Babylon had made governor over the land.

3. Jeremiah warns the remnant not to flee to Egypt

42 Then all the commanders of the forces, and Jōhăn′ȧn the son of Kȧrē′ȧh and Āzȧrī′ȧh[t] the son of Hōshāi′ȧh, and all the people from the least to the greatest, came near ² and said to Jĕrĕmī′ȧh the prophet, "Let our supplication come before you, and pray to the LORD your God for us, for all this remnant (for we are left but a few of many, as your eyes see us), ³ that the LORD your God may show us the way we should go, and the thing that we should do." ⁴ Jĕrĕmī′ȧh the prophet said to them, "I have heard you; behold, I will pray to the LORD your God according to your request, and whatever the LORD answers you I will tell you; I will keep nothing back from you." ⁵ Then they said to Jĕrĕmī′ȧh, "May the LORD be a true and faithful witness against us if we do not act according to all the word with which the LORD your God sends you to us. ⁶ Whether it is good or evil, we will obey the voice of the LORD our God to whom we are sending you, that it may be well with us when we obey the voice of the LORD our God."

⁷ At the end of ten days the word of the LORD came to Jĕrĕmī′ȧh. ⁸ Then he summoned Jōhăn′ȧn the son of Kȧrē′ȧh and all the commanders of the forces who were with him, and all the people from the least to the greatest, ⁹ and said to them, "Thus says the LORD, the God of Israel, to whom you sent me to present your supplication before him: ¹⁰ If you will remain in this land, then I will build you up and not pull you down; I will plant you, and not pluck you up; for I repent of the evil which I did to you. ¹¹ Do not fear the king of Babylon, of whom you are afraid; do not fear him, says the LORD, for I am with you, to save you and to deliver you from his hand. ¹² I will grant you mercy, that he may have mercy on you and let you remain in your own land. ¹³ But if you say, 'We will not remain in this land,' disobeying the voice of the LORD your God ¹⁴ and saying, 'No, we will go to the land of Egypt, where we shall not see war, or hear the sound of the trumpet, or be hungry for bread, and we will dwell there,' ¹⁵ then hear the word of the LORD, O remnant of Judah. Thus says the LORD of hosts, the God of Israel: If you set your faces to enter Egypt and go to live there, ¹⁶ then the sword which you fear shall overtake you there in the land of Egypt; and the famine of which you are afraid shall follow hard after you to Egypt; and there you shall die. ¹⁷All the men who set their faces to go to Egypt to live there shall die by the sword, by famine, and by pestilence; they shall have no remnant or survivor from the evil which I will bring upon them.

¹⁸ "For thus says the LORD of hosts, the God of Israel: As my anger and my wrath were poured out on the inhabitants of Jerusalem, so my wrath will be poured out on you when you go to Egypt. You shall become an execration, a horror, a curse, and a taunt. You shall see this place no more. ¹⁹ The LORD has said to you, O remnant of Judah, 'Do not go to Egypt.' Know for a certainty that I have warned you this day ²⁰ that you have gone astray at the cost of your lives. For you sent me to the LORD your

t Gk: Heb Jĕzȧnī′ȧh

42.1 Jer 40.8,13; 41.11
42.2 Jer 36.7; 37.20; ver 20; 1 Ki 13.6; Acts 8.24; Deut 28.62; Lam 1.1
42.3 Ps 86.11; Mic 4.2
42.4 1 Sam 12.23; 1 Ki 22.14; Jer 23.28; 1 Sam 3.17,18; Ps 40.10
42.5 Gen 31.50; Mic 1.2
42.6 Deut 6.3; Jer 7.23
42.8 ver 1
42.9 2 Ki 19.4,6, 20; 22.15
42.10 Jer 24.6; 31.28; Ezek 36.36; Jon 3.10; 4.2
42.11 Jer 41.18; Isa 43.5; Rom 8.31
42.12 Ps 106.45, 46
42.13 Jer 44.16
42.14 Jer 41.17; 4.19,21
42.15 Jer 44.12–14
42.16 Jer 44.13, 27; Ezek 11.8
42.17 Jer 44.13, 14,28
42.18 Jer 7.20; 33.5; Isa 65.15; Jer 29.18; 22.10,27
42.19 Deut 17.16; Isa 30.1–7; Neh 9.26, 29,30
42.20 ver 2

God, saying, 'Pray for us to the LORD our God, and whatever the LORD our God says declare to us and we will do it.' 21And I have this day declared it to you, but you have not obeyed the voice of the LORD your God in anything that he sent me to tell you. 22 Now therefore know for a certainty that you shall die by the sword, by famine, and by pestilence in the place where you desire to go to live."

B. *Jeremiah's ministry among the refugees in Egypt*

1. *God's warning rejected, the Jews migrate to Tahpanhes*

43 When Jĕrĕmī'ăh finished speaking to all the people all these words of the LORD their God, with which the LORD their God had sent him to them, 2Ăzărī'ăh the son of Hōshāi'ăh and Jōhăn'ăn the son of Kărē'ăh and all the insolent men said to Jĕrĕmī'ăh, "You are telling a lie. The LORD our God did not send you to say, 'Do not go to Egypt to live there'; 3 but Bărŭch the son of Nĕrī'ăh has set you against us, to deliver us into the hand of the Chăldē'ănş, that they may kill us or take us into exile in Babylon." 4 So Jōhăn'ăn the son of Kărē'ăh and all the commanders of the forces and all the people did not obey the voice of the LORD, to remain in the land of Judah. 5 But Jōhăn'ăn the son of Kărē'ăh and all the commanders of the forces took all the remnant of Judah who had returned to live in the land of Judah from all the nations to which they had been driven—6 the men, the women, the children, the princesses, and every person whom Nĕbŭzar'ădăn the captain of the guard had left with Gĕdălī'ăh the son of Ăhī'kăm, son of Shāphăn; also Jĕrĕmī'ăh the prophet and Bărŭch the son of Nĕrī'ăh. 7And they came into the land of Egypt, for they did not obey the voice of the LORD. And they arrived at Tah'pănhĕş.

2. *Prophecy of the invasion of Egypt by Chaldea*

8 Then the word of the LORD came to Jĕrĕmī'ăh in Tah'pănhĕş: 9 "Take in your hands large stones, and hide them in the mortar in the pavement which is at the entrance to Pharaōh'ş palace in Tah'pănhĕş, in the sight of the men of Judah, 10 and say to them, 'Thus says the LORD of hosts, the God of Israel: Behold, I will send and take Nĕbŭchădrĕz'zăr the king of Babylon, my servant, and he[u] will set his throne above these stones which I have hid, and he will spread his royal canopy over them. 11 He shall come and smite the land of Egypt, giving to the pestilence those who are doomed to the pestilence, to captivity those who are doomed to captivity, and to the sword those who are doomed to the sword. 12 He[v] shall kindle a fire in the temples of the gods of Egypt; and he shall burn them and carry them away captive; and he shall clean the land of Egypt, as a shepherd cleans his cloak of vermin; and he shall go away from there in peace. 13 He shall break the obelisks of Hēliŏp'ŏlĭs which is in the land of Egypt; and the temples of the gods of Egypt he shall burn with fire.' "

3. *The refugees to perish in Egypt*

44 The word that came to Jĕrĕmī'ăh concerning all the Jews that dwelt in the land of Egypt, at Mĭgdŏl, at Tah'pănhĕş, at

Cross-references (margin)

42.21
Jer 43.1;
Ezek 2.7;
Jer 43.4

42.22
Jer 43.11;
Hos 9.6

43.1
Jer 26.8;
51.63;
42.10–18

43.2
Jer 42.1;
2 Chr 36.13;
Jer 42.5

43.3
Jer 38.4

43.4
Jer 42.5,6,
10–12

43.5
Jer 40.11,12

43.6
Jer 41.10;
39.10; 40.7

43.7
Jer 44.1

43.8
Jer 2.16;
44.1; 46.14

43.10
Jer 25.9,11;
27.5,6;
31.20

43.11
Isa 19.1–25;
Jer 44.13;
46.13;
Ezek 29.19,
20;
Jer 15.2

43.12
Isa 19.1;
Jer 46.25;
Ezek 30.13

44.1
Jer 46.14;
43.7;
Isa 19.13

u Gk Syr: Heb *I*   *v* Gk Syr Vg: Heb *I*

Memphis, and in the land of Păthrŏs, 2 "Thus says the LORD of hosts, the God of Israel: You have seen all the evil that I brought upon Jerusalem and upon all the cities of Judah. Behold, this day they are a desolation, and no one dwells in them, 3 because of the wickedness which they committed, provoking me to anger, in that they went to burn incense and serve other gods that they knew not, neither they, nor you, nor your fathers. 4 Yet I persistently sent to you all my servants the prophets, saying, 'Oh, do not do this abominable thing that I hate!' 5 But they did not listen or incline their ear, to turn from their wickedness and burn no incense to other gods. 6 Therefore my wrath and my anger were poured forth and kindled in the cities of Judah and in the streets of Jerusalem; and they became a waste and a desolation, as at this day. 7 And now thus says the LORD God of hosts, the God of Israel: Why do you commit this great evil against yourselves, to cut off from you man and woman, infant and child, from the midst of Judah, leaving you no remnant? 8 Why do you provoke me to anger with the works of your hands, burning incense to other gods in the land of Egypt where you have come to live, that you may be cut off and become a curse and a taunt among all the nations of the earth? 9 Have you forgotten the wickedness of your fathers, the wickedness of the kings of Judah, the wickedness of their *w* wives, your own wickedness, and the wickedness of your wives, which they committed in the land of Judah and in the streets of Jerusalem? 10 They have not humbled themselves even to this day, nor have they feared, nor walked in my law and my statutes which I set before you and before your fathers.

11 "Therefore thus says the LORD of hosts, the God of Israel: Behold, I will set my face against you for evil, to cut off all Judah. 12 I will take the remnant of Judah who have set their faces to come to the land of Egypt to live, and they shall all be consumed; in the land of Egypt they shall fall; by the sword and by famine they shall be consumed; from the least to the greatest, they shall die by the sword and by famine; and they shall become an execration, a horror, a curse, and a taunt. 13 I will punish those who dwell in the land of Egypt, as I have punished Jerusalem, with the sword, with famine, and with pestilence, 14 so that none of the remnant of Judah who have come to live in the land of Egypt shall escape or survive or return to the land of Judah, to which they desire to return to dwell there; for they shall not return, except some fugitives."

15 Then all the men who knew that their wives had offered incense to other gods, and all the women who stood by, a great assembly, all the people who dwelt in Păthrŏs in the land of Egypt, answered Jĕrĕmī'áh: 16 "As for the word which you have spoken to us in the name of the LORD, we will not listen to you. 17 But we will do everything that we have vowed, burn incense to the queen of heaven and pour out libations to her, as we did, both we and our fathers, our kings and our princes, in the cities of Judah and in the streets of Jerusalem; for then we had plenty of food, and prospered, and saw no evil. 18 But since we left off burning incense to the queen of heaven and pouring out libations to her, we have lacked everything and have been consumed by the

44.2
Jer 9.11;
34.22;
Mic 3.12
44.3
Ezek 8.17,
18;
Dan 9.5;
Isa 3.8;
Jer 19.4;
32.17
44.4
2 Chr
36.15;
Jer 7.25;
25.4; 26.5;
Ezek 8.10
44.5
Jer 11.8,10;
13.10
44.6
Jer 42.18
44.7
Jer 26.19;
Ezek 33.11;
Jer 9.21;
51.22
44.8
2 Ki 17.15-
17;
Jer 25.6,7;
42.18
44.9
Jer 7.9,10,
17,18
44.10
Jer 6.15;
8.12;
26.4; 32.23
44.11
Lev 26.17;
Jer 21.10;
Amos 9.4
44.12
Jer 42.15-
18,22

44.13
Jer 11.22;
21.9; 24.10;
42.17,22
44.14
Jer 22.26,
27;
Isa 4.2;
10.20;
ver 28;
Rom 9.27
*44.15
Jer 5.1-5
44.16
Jer 8.6,12;
13.10
*44.17
2 Ki 17.16;
Jer 7.18;
Hos 2.5-9;
Phil 3.19
44.18
Jer 40.12

w Heb *his*

44.15 *Pathros*, a section of Upper Egypt.　　　　**44.17** *the queen of heaven*, cf. 7.18.

Jeremiah 44.19—45.5

Jeremiah 44.19—45.5

Jeremiah 44.19—45.5 1180

burned incense to the queen of heaven and poured out libations
to her, was it without our husbands' approval that we made cakes
for her bearing her image and poured out libations to her?"

20 Then Jĕrĕmī′ăh said to all the people, men and women, all
the people who had given him this answer: 21 "As for the incense
that you burned in the cities of Judah and in the streets of Jerusalem, you and your fathers, your kings and your princes, and the
people of the land, did not the LORD remember it?ʸ Did it not
come into his mind? 22 The LORD could no longer bear your evil
doings and the abominations which you committed; therefore your
land has become a desolation and a waste and a curse, without inhabitant, as it is this day. 23 It is because you burned incense, and
because you sinned against the LORD and did not obey the voice of
the LORD or walk in his law and in his statutes and in his testimonies, that this evil has befallen you, as at this day."

24 Jĕrĕmī′ăh said to all the people and all the women, "Hear
the word of the LORD, all you of Judah who are in the land of
Egypt, 25 Thus says the LORD of hosts, the God of Israel: You
and your wives have declared with your mouths, and have fulfilled
it with your hands, saying, 'We will surely perform our vows that
we have made, to burn incense to the queen of heaven and to pour
out libations to her.' Then confirm your vows and perform your
vows! 26 Therefore hear the word of the LORD, all you of Judah
who dwell in the land of Egypt: Behold, I have sworn by my great
name, says the LORD, that my name shall no more be invoked by
the mouth of any man of Judah in all the land of Egypt, saying, 'As
the Lord GOD lives.' 27 Behold, I am watching over them for evil
and not for good; all the men of Judah who are in the land of
Egypt shall be consumed by the sword and by famine, until there
is an end of them. 28And those who escape the sword shall return
from the land of Egypt to the land of Judah, few in number; and
all the remnant of Judah, who came to the land of Egypt to live,
shall know whose word will stand, mine or theirs. 29 This shall be
the sign to you, says the LORD, that I will punish you in this place,
in order that you may know that my words will surely stand against
you for evil: 30 Thus says the LORD, Behold, I will give Phạrăŏh
Hŏphrā′ king of Egypt into the hand of his enemies and into the
hand of those who seek his life, as I gave Zĕdĕkī′ăh king of Judah
into the hand of Nĕbŭchădrĕz′zăr king of Babylon, who was his
enemy and sought his life."

C. Encouragement to Baruch, Jeremiah's secretary

45 The word that Jĕrĕmī′ăh the prophet spoke to Bạrŭch the
son of Nĕrī′ăh, when he wrote these words in a book at the
dictation of Jeremiah, in the fourth year of Jĕhoi′ăkim the son of
Jōsī′ăh, king of Judah: 2 "Thus says the LORD, the God of Israel,
to you, O Bạrŭch: 3 You said, 'Woe is me! for the LORD has added
sorrow to my pain; I am weary with my groaning, and I find no
rest.' 4 Thus shall you say to him, Thus says the LORD: Behold,
what I have built I am breaking down, and what I have planted I
am plucking up—that is, the whole land. 5And do you seek great
things for yourself? Seek them not; for, behold, I am bringing evil

ˣ Compare Syr: Heb lacks *And the women said* ʸ Syr: Heb *them*

upon all flesh, says the LORD; but I will give you your life as a
prize of war in all places to which you may go."

IV. *Prophecies against heathen nations 46.1–51.64*

A. *Prophecies against Egypt*

1. *Nebuchadrezzar will crush Neco at Carchemish*

46 The word of the LORD which came to Jĕrĕmī'ăh the prophet
concerning the nations.

2 About Egypt. Concerning the army of Phạraōh Nĕcō, king of
Egypt, which was by the river Eūphrā'tĕş at Car'chĕmĭsh and
which Nĕbúchădrĕz'zăr king of Babylon defeated in the fourth
year of Jĕhoi'ăkĭm the son of Jōsī'ăh, king of Judah:

3 "Prepare buckler and shield,
    and advance for battle!
4 Harness the horses;
    mount, O horsemen!
Take your stations with your helmets,
    polish your spears,
    put on your coats of mail!
5 Why have I seen it?
They are dismayed
    and have turned backward.
Their warriors are beaten down,
    and have fled in haste;
they look not back—
    terror on every side!
                    says the LORD.
6 The swift cannot flee away,
    nor the warrior escape;
in the north by the river Eūphrā'tĕş
    they have stumbled and fallen.

7 "Who is this, rising like the Nile,
    like rivers whose waters surge?
8 Egypt rises like the Nile,
    like rivers whose waters surge.
He said, I will rise, I will cover the earth,
    I will destroy cities and their inhabitants.
9 Advance, O horses,
    and rage, O chariots!
Let the warriors go forth:
    men of Ethiopia and Put who handle the shield,
    men of Lúd, skilled in handling the bow.
10 That day is the day of the Lord GOD of hosts,
    a day of vengeance,
    to avenge himself on his foes.
The sword shall devour and be sated,
    and drink its fill of their blood.
For the Lord GOD of hosts holds a sacrifice
    in the north country by the river Eūphrā'tĕş.
11 Go up to Gĭl'ĕăd, and take balm,
    O virgin daughter of Egypt!
In vain you have used many medicines;

46.1
Jer 25.15–
38
46.2
2 Ki 23.29;
2 Chr 35.20;
Jer 45.1
46.3
Jer 51.11,
12;
Nah 2.1;
3.14
46.4
Ezek 21.9–
11;
Jer 51.3
46.5
Isa 42.17;
Ezek 39.18;
Jer 6.25;
49.29
46.6
Isa 30.16;
Dan 11.19
46.7
Jer 47.2
46.8
Isa 37.24;
10.13
46.9
Jer 47.3;
Nah 2.4;
3.9;
Isa 66.19
46.10
Isa 13.6;
Joel 1.15;
2.1;
Jer 50.15,
28;
Isa 34.6;
Zeph 1.7
46.11
Jer 8.22;
51.8;
Isa 47.1;
Jer 31.4,21;
30.13;
Ezek 30.21

there is no healing for you.

46.12
Jer 2.36;
Nah 3.8–10;
Jer 14.2

12 The nations have heard of your shame,
  and the earth is full of your cry;
for warrior has stumbled against warrior;
  they have both fallen together."

2. *Nebuchadrezzar will ravage Memphis and Thebes*

46.13
Isa 19.1;
Jer 43.10,11

13 The word which the LORD spoke to Jĕrĕmī′ăh the prophet about the coming of Nĕbŭchădrĕz′zăr king of Babylon to smite the land of Egypt:

*46.14
Jer 44.1;
43.8;
Nah 2.13

14 "Declare in Egypt, and proclaim in Mĭgdŏl;
  proclaim in Memphis and Tăh′pănhĕş;
Say, 'Stand ready and be prepared,
  for the sword shall devour round about you.'

*46.15

15 Why has Āpĭs fled?ᶻ
  Why did not your bull stand?
  Because the LORD thrust him down.

46.16
Lev 26.36,
37;
Jer 51.9;
50.16

16 Your multitudeᵃ stumbled and fell,
  and they said one to another,
'Arise, and let us go back to our own people
  and to the land of our birth,
because of the sword of the oppressor.'

46.17
Isa 19.11–
16

17 Call the name of Phₐraōh, king of Egypt,
  'Noisy one who lets the hour go by.'

46.18
Jer 48.15;
Ps 89.12;
1 Ki 18.42

18 "As I live, says the King,
  whose name is the LORD of hosts,
like Tābór among the mountains,
  and like Carmĕl by the sea, shall one come.

46.19
Jer 48.18;
Isa 20.4;
ver 4;
Ezek 30.13

19 Prepare yourselves baggage for exile,
  O inhabitants of Egypt!
For Memphis shall become a waste,
  a ruin, without inhabitant.

46.20
Jer 50.11;
ver 24
46.21
ver 5;
Ps 37.13;
Jer 50.27

20 "A beautiful heifer is Egypt,
  but a gadfly from the north has come upon her.
21 Even her hired soldiers in her midst
  are like fatted calves;
yea, they have turned and fled together,
  they did not stand;
for the day of their calamity has come upon them,
  the time of their punishment.

46.22
Isa 29.4

22 "She makes a sound like a serpent gliding away;
  for her enemies march in force,
and come against her with axes,
  like those who fell trees.

46.23
Isa 10.34;
Jer 21.14;
Judg 6.5;
Joel 2.25

23 They shall cut down her forest,
                                    says the LORD,
  though it is impenetrable,
because they are more numerous than locusts;

ᶻ Gk: Heb *Why was it swept away*   ᵃ Gk: Heb *He made many stumble*

46.14 *Migdol . . . Memphis and Tahpanhes,* all cities of Egypt.   **46.15** *Apis* was the sacred bull of the Egyptian god Ptah.

they are without number.

24 The daughter of Egypt shall be put to shame,
    she shall be delivered into the hand of a people from the
       north."

25 The LORD of hosts, the God of Israel, said: "Behold, I am
bringing punishment upon Āmȯn of Thēbeṣ, and Pḫaraōh, and
Egypt and her gods and her kings, upon Pharaoh and those who
trust in him. 26 I will deliver them into the hand of those who seek
their life, into the hand of Nĕbŭçhȧdrĕz′zȧr king of Babylon and
his officers. Afterward Egypt shall be inhabited as in the days of
old, says the LORD.

3. Israel will be restored, and the enemy powers will be destroyed

27 "But fear not, O Jacob my servant,
    nor be dismayed, O Israel;
for lo, I will save you from afar,
    and your offspring from the land of their captivity.
Jacob shall return and have quiet and ease,
    and none shall make him afraid.
28 Fear not, O Jacob my servant,
                                says the LORD,
    for I am with you.
I will make a full end of all the nations
    to which I have driven you,
    but of you I will not make a full end.
I will chasten you in just measure,
    and I will by no means leave you unpunished."

B. Prophecy against Philistia

47 The word of the LORD that came to Jĕrĕmī′áh the prophet
concerning the Pḫilĭs′tīneṣ, before Pḫaraōh smote Gazȧ.
2 "Thus says the LORD:
Behold, waters are rising out of the north,
    and shall become an overflowing torrent;
they shall overflow the land and all that fills it,
    the city and those who dwell in it.
Men shall cry out,
    and every inhabitant of the land shall wail.
3 At the noise of the stamping of the hoofs of his stallions,
    at the rushing of his chariots, at the rumbling of their wheels,
the fathers look not back to their children,
    so feeble are their hands,
4 because of the day that is coming to destroy
    all the Pḫilĭs′tīneṣ,
to cut off from Tȳre and Sīdȯn
    every helper that remains.
For the LORD is destroying the Philistines,
    the remnant of the coastland of Cȧphtor.
5 Baldness has come upon Gazȧ,
    Ăsh′kĕlȯn has perished.
O remnant of the Ăn′ȧkĭm,[b]

---

[b] Gk: Heb *their valley*

Marginal references:

46.24 — ver 19; Jer 1.15

46.25 — Jer 43.12; Ezek 30.14–16;
46.25 — Jer 44.30; Ezek 30.13; Isa 20.5
46.26 — Jer 44.30; Ezek 32.11; 29.11–14

46.27 — Isa 41.13; 43.5; Jer 30.10, 11; 23.3,4, 6; 50.19

46.28 — Isa 8.9,10; Jer 1.19; 4.27; Amos 9.8,9; Jer 10.24; 30.11

47.1 — Jer 25.17, 20; Amos 1.6; Zeph 2.4
47.2 — Isa 14.31; Jer 46.20, 24; Isa 8.7; 15.2–5; Jer 46.12

47.3 — Jer 8.16; Nah 3.2

47.4 — Isa 14.31; 23.5,6,11; Joel 3.4; Zech 9.2–4; Gen 10.14

47.5 — Mic 1.16; Jer 25.20; 16.6; 41.5

how long will you gash yourselves?

47.6
Jer 12.12;
4.21

6 Ah, sword of the LORD!
How long till you are quiet?
Put yourself into your scabbard,
rest and be still!

47.7
Ezek 14.17;
Mic 6.9

7 How can it*c* be quiet,
when the LORD has given it a charge?
Against Ash′kelon and against the seashore
he has appointed it.”

C. *Prophecy against Moab*

48.1
Isa 15.2;
ver 22,23;
Num 32.37

48 Concerning Mōăb.
Thus says the LORD of hosts, the God of Israel:
“Woe to Nēbō, for it is laid waste!
Kīrĭăthă′ĭm is put to shame, it is taken;
the fortress is put to shame and broken down;

48.2
Isa 16.14;
15.4;
Jer 49.3

2   the renown of Mōăb is no more.
In Hĕshbŏn they planned evil against her:
‘Come, let us cut her off from being a nation!’
You also, O Madmen, shall be brought to silence;
the sword shall pursue you.

48.3
Isa 15.5;
ver 5,34

3 “Hark! a cry from Horōnă′ĭm,
‘Desolation and great destruction!’
4 Mōăb is destroyed;
a cry is heard as far as Zō′ar.*d*

*48.5
Isa 15.5

5 For at the ascent of Luhĭth
they go up weeping;*e*
for at the descent of Horōnă′ĭm
they have heard the cry*f* of destruction.

48.6
Jer 51.6;
17.6

6 Flee! Save yourselves!
Be like a wild ass*g* in the desert!

*48.7
Jer 9.23;
Num 21.29;
1 Ki 11.33;
Jer 49.3

7 For, because you trusted in your strongholds*h* and your treasures,
you also shall be taken;
and Chēmŏsh shall go forth into exile,
with his priests and his princes.

48.8
Jer 6.26

8 The destroyer shall come upon every city,
and no city shall escape;
the valley shall perish,
and the plain shall be destroyed,
as the LORD has spoken.

48.9
Isa 16.2;
Jer 44.22

9 “Give wings to Mōăb,
for she would fly away;
her cities shall become a desolation,
with no inhabitant in them.

48.10
Jer 11.3;
1 Sam 15.3,
9;
1 Ki 20.42;
Jer 47.6,7

10 “Cursed is he who does the work of the LORD with slackness;
and cursed is he who keeps back his sword from bloodshed.

c Gk Vg: Heb *you*   *d* Gk: Heb *her little ones*
e Cn: Heb *weeping goes up with weeping*   *f* Gk Compare Is 15.5: Heb *the distress of the cry*
g Gk Aquila: Heb *like Arō′ēr*   *h* Gk: Heb *works*

48.5 Similar to the lament in Isa 15.5.   **48.7** *Chemosh* was the god of Moab.

11 "Mōăb has been at ease from his youth
    and has settled on his lees;
he has not been emptied from vessel to vessel,
    nor has he gone into exile;
so his taste remains in him,
    and his scent is not changed.
12 "Therefore, behold, the days are coming, says the LORD,
when I shall send to him tilters who will tilt him, and empty his
vessels, and break his *i* jars in pieces. 13 Then Mōăb shall be
ashamed of Çhēmŏsh, as the house of Israel was ashamed of
Bĕthĕl, their confidence.

14 "How do you say, 'We are heroes
    and mighty men of war'?
15 The destroyer of Mōăb and his cities has come up,
    and the choicest of his young men have gone down to
      slaughter,
says the King, whose name is the LORD of hosts.
16 The calamity of Mōăb is near at hand
    and his affliction hastens apace.
17 Bemoan him, all you who are round about him,
    and all who know his name;
say, 'How the mighty scepter is broken,
    the glorious staff.'

18 "Come down from your glory,
    and sit on the parched ground,
O inhabitant of Dībŏn!
For the destroyer of Mōăb has come up against you;
    he has destroyed your strongholds.
19 Stand by the way and watch,
    O inhabitant of Ârŏ'ĕr!
Ask him who flees and her who escapes;
    say, 'What has happened?'
20 Mōăb is put to shame, for it is broken;
    wail and cry!
Tell it by the Arnŏn,
    that Moab is laid waste.

21 "Judgment has come upon the tableland, upon Hōlŏn, and
Jahzăh, and Mĕphā'-ăth, 22 and Dībŏn, and Nēbō, and Bĕth-
dĭblăthā'ĭm, 23 and Kĭrĭăthā'ĭm, and Bĕth-gā'mŭl, and Bĕth-
mē'ŏn, 24 and Kĕr'ĭ-ŏth, and Bŏzrăh, and all the cities of the land
of Mōăb, far and near. 25 The horn of Mōăb is cut off, and his arm
is broken, says the LORD.
26 "Make him drunk, because he magnified himself against the
LORD; so that Mōăb shall wallow in his vomit, and he too shall be
held in derision. 27 Was not Israel a derision to you? Was he found
among thieves, that whenever you spoke of him you wagged
your head?

28 "Leave the cities, and dwell in the rock,
    O inhabitants of Mōăb!
Be like the dove that nests

i Gk Aquila: Heb *their*

48.11
Jer 22.21;
Zech 1.15;
Zeph 1.12;
Nah 2.2

48.13
Isa 45.16;
ver 39;
Hos 10.6;
1 Ki 12.29

48.14
Isa 10.13–
16
48.15
Jer 50.27;
46.18

48.16
Isa 13.22

48.17
Jer 9.17–20;
Isa 14.5

48.18
Isa 47.1;
Jer 46.19;
ver 8

48.19
Deut 2.36;
1 Sam 4.13,
16

48.20
Isa 16.7;
Num 21.13

48.21
ver 8,34;
Josh 13.18

48.24
Amos 2.2
48.25
Ps 75.10;
Ezek 30.21
48.26
Jer 25.15,27
48.27
Zeph 2.8;
Jer 2.26;
18.16

48.28
Jer 49.16;
Ps 55.6,7;
Sol 2.14

in the sides of the mouth of a gorge.

48.29
Isa 16.6;
Zeph 2.8;
Ps 138.6

29 We have heard of the pride of Mōăb—
   he is very proud—
of his loftiness, his pride, and his arrogance,
   and the haughtiness of his heart.

48.30
Isa 37.28;
16.6

30 I know his insolence, says the LORD;
   his boasts are false,
   his deeds are false.

48.31
Isa 15.5;
16.7,11

31 Therefore I wail for Mōăb;
   I cry out for all Moab;
   for the men of Kir-hĕr′ĕs I mourn.

48.32
Isa 16.8,9;
Num 21.32

32 More than for Jāzĕr I weep for you,
   O vine of Sĭbmăh!
Your branches passed over the sea,
   reached as far as Jazer;*j*
upon your summer fruits and your vintage
   the destroyer has fallen.

48.33
Isa 16.10;
Joel 1.12;
Isa 5.10;
Hag 2.16

33 Gladness and joy have been taken away
   from the fruitful land of Mōăb;
I have made the wine cease from the wine presses;
   no one treads them with shouts of joy;
   the shouting is not the shout of joy.

48.34
Isa 15.4–6

34 "Hĕshbŏn and Ēlë-ā′lĕh cry out;*k* as far as Jāhăz they utter their voice, from Zō′ar to Horŏnā′ĭm and Ĕg′lăth-shĕlĭshī′yăh. For the waters of Nĭmrĭm also have become desolate. 35And I will

48.35
Isa 15.2;
16.12;
Jer 7.9;
11.13

bring to an end in Mōăb, says the LORD, him who offers sacrifice in the high place and burns incense to his god. 36 Therefore my heart moans for Mōăb like a flute, and my heart moans like a flute

48.36
Isa 16.11;
15.7

for the men of Kir-hĕr′ĕs; therefore the riches they gained have perished.

48.37
Isa 15.2,3;
Jer 47.5

37 "For every head is shaved and every beard cut off; upon all the hands are gashes, and on the loins is sackcloth. 38 On all the

48.38
Jer 22.28;
25.34

housetops of Mōăb and in the squares there is nothing but lamentation; for I have broken Moab like a vessel for which no one cares, says the LORD. 39 How it is broken! How they wail! How Mōăb has

48.39
Ezek 26.16

turned his back in shame! So Moab has become a derision and a horror to all that are round about him."

40 For thus says the LORD:

48.40
Jer 49.22;
Dan 7.4;
Hos 8.1;
Isa 8.8

"Behold, one shall fly swiftly like an eagle,
   and spread his wings against Mōăb;

41 the cities shall be taken
   and the strongholds seized.

48.41
Isa 21.3;
Jer 30.6;
49.22,24;
Mic 4.9

The heart of the warriors of Mōăb shall be in that day
   like the heart of a woman in her pangs;

48.42
ver 2;
Ps 83.4;
ver 26;
Isa 37.23

42 Mōăb shall be destroyed and be no longer a people,
   because he magnified himself against the LORD.

43 Terror, pit, and snare
   are before you, O inhabitant of Mōăb!
                    says the LORD.

48.43
Isa 24.17,
18;
Lam 3.47

48.44
1 Ki 19.17;
Jer 11.23;
46.21

44 He who flees from the terror
   shall fall into the pit,
and he who climbs out of the pit
   shall be caught in the snare.

---

j Cn: Heb *the sea of Jazer*   *k* Cn: Heb *From the cry of Heshbon to Elealeh*

For I will bring these things[l] upon Mōăb
in the year of their punishment,
says the LORD.

45 "In the shadow of Hĕshbŏn
fugitives stop without strength;
for a fire has gone forth from Heshbon,
a flame from the house of Sīhŏn;
it has destroyed the forehead of Mōăb,
the crown of the sons of tumult.
46 Woe to you, O Mōăb!
The people of Chĕmŏsh is undone;
for your sons have been taken captive,
and your daughters into captivity.
47 Yet I will restore the fortunes of Mōăb
in the latter days, says the LORD."
Thus far is the judgment on Moab.

D. *Prophecies against Ammon, Edom, Kedar, and Elam*

1. *The Ammonites to go into captivity*

49 Concerning the Ăm′mŏnītes.
Thus says the LORD:
"Has Israel no sons?
Has he no heir?
Why then has Mĭlcŏm dispossessed Găd,
and his people settled in its cities?
2 Therefore, behold, the days are coming,
says the LORD,
when I will cause the battle cry to be heard
against Răbbăh of the Ăm′mŏnītes;
it shall become a desolate mound,
and its villages shall be burned with fire;
then Israel shall dispossess those who dispossessed him,
says the LORD.

3 "Wail, O Hĕshbŏn, for Āī is laid waste!
Cry, O daughters of Răbbăh!
Gird yourselves with sackcloth,
lament, and run to and fro among the hedges!
For Mĭlcŏm shall go into exile,
with his priests and his princes.
4 Why do you boast of your valleys,[m]
O faithless daughter,
who trusted in her treasures, saying,
'Who will come against me?'
5 Behold, I will bring terror upon you,
says the Lord GOD of hosts,
from all who are round about you,
and you shall be driven out, every man straight before him,
with none to gather the fugitives.

[l] Gk Syr: Heb *to her*   [m] Heb *valleys, your valley flows*

49.1 *Milcom* was the god of Ammon.   **49.2** *Rabbah*, the capital of the Ammonites.

Cross-references (right margin):

48.45
ver 2;
Num 21.21,
26,28,29;
24.17

48.46
Num 21.29;
ver 7

48.47
Jer 49.6,39

*49.1
Ezek 21.28;
25.2;
Amos 1.13;
Zeph 2.8,9

*49.2
Jer 4.19;
Ezek 21.20;
Isa 14.2

49.3
Jer 48.2;
Josh 7.2–5;
8.1–29;
Isa 32.11;
Jer 4.8;
48.7

49.4
Jer 9.23;
31.22;
Ps 62.10;
Ezek 28.4,5

49.5
Jer 48.43,
44; 16.16;
46.5;
Lam 4.15

<table>
<tr><td>

49.6
ver 39;
Jer 48.47

</td><td>

6 But afterward I will restore the fortunes of the Ăm′mónītes, says the Lord.”

</td></tr>
</table>

2. *Edom to be devastated and dispossessed*

<table>
<tr><td>

49.7
Isa 34.5,6;
Ezek 25.12;
Amos 1.11,
12;
Jer 8.9;
ver 20

</td><td>

7 Concerning Ēdóm.
Thus says the Lord of hosts:
“Is wisdom no more in Tēmàn?
    Has counsel perished from the prudent?
    Has their wisdom vanished?

</td></tr>
<tr><td>

49.8
ver 30;
Jer 25.23;
46.21

</td><td>

8 Flee, turn back, dwell in the depths,
    O inhabitants of Dēdàn!
For I will bring the calamity of Ēsau upon him,
    the time when I punish him.

</td></tr>
<tr><td>

49.9
Obad 5

</td><td>

9 If grape-gatherers came to you,
    would they not leave gleanings?
If thieves came by night,
    would they not destroy only enough for themselves?

</td></tr>
<tr><td>

49.10
Jer 13.26;
Mal 1.3;
Isa 17.14

</td><td>

10 But I have stripped Ēsau bare,
    I have uncovered his hiding places,
    and he is not able to conceal himself.
His children are destroyed, and his brothers,
    and his neighbors; and he is no more.

</td></tr>
<tr><td>

49.11
Ps 68.5

</td><td>

11 Leave your fatherless children, I will keep them alive;
    and let your widows trust in me.”

</td></tr>
<tr><td>

49.12
Jer 25.28,
29;
1 Pet 4.17

</td><td>

12 For thus says the Lord: “If those who did not deserve to drink the cup must drink it, will you go unpunished? You shall not go unpunished, but you must drink.

</td></tr>
<tr><td>

49.13
Jer 44.26;
Isa 34.6;
34.9-15

</td><td>

13 For I have sworn by myself, says the Lord, that Bŏzràh shall become a horror, a taunt, a waste, and a curse; and all her cities shall be perpetual wastes.”

</td></tr>
<tr><td>

49.14
Obad 1-4;
Isa 18.2;
30.4;
Jer 50.14

</td><td>

14 I have heard tidings from the Lord,
    and a messenger has been sent among the nations:
“Gather yourselves together and come against her,
    and rise up for battle!”

</td></tr>
<tr><td></td><td>

15 For behold, I will make you small among the nations,
    despised among men.

</td></tr>
<tr><td>

49.16
Isa 25.5;
14.13-15;
Amos 9.2

</td><td>

16 The horror you inspire has deceived you,
    and the pride of your heart,
you who live in the clefts of the rock,*n*
    who hold the height of the hill.
Though you make your nest as high as the eagle’s,
    I will bring you down from there,
                    says the Lord.

</td></tr>
<tr><td>

49.17
Jer 50.13;
1 Ki 9.8;
Jer 51.37

</td><td>

17 “Ēdóm shall become a horror; every one who passes by it will be horrified and will hiss because of all its disasters. 18As when

</td></tr>
<tr><td>

49.18
Gen 19.25;
Deut 29.23;
Amos 4.11

</td><td>

Sŏdóm and Gòmor′ràh and their neighbor cities were overthrown, says the Lord, no man shall dwell there, no man shall sojourn in her.

</td></tr>
<tr><td>

49.19
Jer 50.44;
12.5;
Isa 46.9

</td><td>

19 Behold, like a lion coming up from the jungle of the Jordan against a strong sheepfold, I will suddenly make them*o* run away from her; and I will appoint over her whomever I choose. For who is like me? Who will summon me? What shepherd can stand before me?

</td></tr>
<tr><td>

49.20
Jer 50.45;
Mal 1.3,4

</td><td>

20 Therefore hear the plan which the Lord has made against Ēdóm and the purposes which he has formed against the inhabitants of Tēmàn: Even the little ones of the flock shall be dragged

</td></tr>
</table>

n Or *Sēlà*   *o* Gk Syr: Heb *him*

away; surely their fold shall be appalled at their fate. 21 At the
sound of their fall the earth shall tremble; the sound of their cry
shall be heard at the Red Sea. 22 Behold, one shall mount up and
fly swiftly like an eagle, and spread his wings against Bŏzrȧh, and
the heart of the warriors of Ēdȯm shall be in that day like the heart
of a woman in her pangs."

23 Concerning Damascus.
"Hāmȧth and Arpăd are confounded,
for they have heard evil tidings;
they melt in fear, they are troubled like the sea[p]
which cannot be quiet.
24 Damascus has become feeble, she turned to flee,
and panic seized her;
anguish and sorrows have taken hold of her,
as of a woman in travail.
25 How the famous city is forsaken,[q]
the joyful city![r]
26 Therefore her young men shall fall in her squares,
and all her soldiers shall be destroyed in that day,
says the LORD of hosts.
27 And I will kindle a fire in the wall of Damascus,
and it shall devour the strongholds of Běn-hā'dăd."

3. *Kedar and Hazor to be ravaged by Nebuchadrezzar*

28 Concerning Kēdar and the kingdoms of Hāzor which Něbůçhȧdrěz'zȧr king of Babylon smote.
Thus says the LORD:
"Rise up, advance against Kedar!
Destroy the people of the east!
29 Their tents and their flocks shall be taken,
their curtains and all their goods;
their camels shall be borne away from them,
and men shall cry to them: 'Terror on every side!'
30 Flee, wander far away, dwell in the depths,
O inhabitants of Hāzor!
says the LORD.
For Něbůçhȧdrěz'zȧr king of Babylon
has made a plan against you,
and formed a purpose against you.

31 "Rise up, advance against a nation at ease,
that dwells securely,
says the LORD,
that has no gates or bars,
that dwells alone.
32 Their camels shall become booty,
their herds of cattle a spoil.
I will scatter to every wind
those who cut the corners of their hair,
and I will bring their calamity
from every side of them,
says the LORD.

49.21 Jer 50.46; Ezek 26.15, 18
49.22 Jer 4.13; 48.40,41
49.23 2 Chr 16.2; Jer 39.5; Isa 10.9; 57.20
49.24 ver 22; Jer 6.24; 30.6; 48.41
49.25 Jer 33.9; 51.41
49.26 Jer 50.30; 51.4; Amos 4.10
49.27 Jer 43.12; Amos 1.3–5; 1 Ki 15.18–20
49.28 Isa 21.16, 17; Jer 2.10; Ezek 27.21; Isa 11.14
49.29 Jer 6.25; 20.3,10; 46.5
49.30 Jer 25.9
49.31 Isa 47.8; Ezek 38.11; Deut 33.28
49.32 Ezek 12.14, 15; Jer 9.26; 25.23

[p] Cn: Heb *there is trouble in the sea*
[q] Vg: Heb *not forsaken* [r] Syr Vg Tg: Heb *city of my joy*

49.33
Jer 10.22;
Zeph 2.9,
13–15

33 Hāzor shall become a haunt of jackals,
   an everlasting waste;
no man shall dwell there,
   no man shall sojourn in her."

4. The Elamites to be dispersed and their rulers slain; a remnant to return

49.34
Ezek 32.24;
2 Ki 24.17,
18;
Jer 28.1

34 The word of the LORD that came to Jĕrĕmī'ăh the prophet concerning Ēlăm, in the beginning of the reign of Zĕdĕkī'ăh king of Judah.

49.35
Isa 22.6;
Jer 51.56

35 Thus says the LORD of hosts: "Behold, I will break the bow of Ēlăm, the mainstay of their might; 36 and I will bring upon

49.36
Rev 7.1;
Ezek 5.10;
Amos 9.9

Ēlăm the four winds from the four quarters of heaven; and I will scatter them to all those winds, and there shall be no nation to which those driven out of Elam shall not come. 37 I will terrify

49.37
Jer 8.9;
17.18;
6.19;
30.24;
9.16

Ēlăm before their enemies, and before those who seek their life; I will bring evil upon them, my fierce anger, says the LORD. I will send the sword after them, until I have consumed them; 38 and I will set my throne in Ēlăm, and destroy their king and princes, says the LORD.

49.39
Jer 48.47

39 "But in the latter days I will restore the fortunes of Ēlăm, says the LORD."

E. Prophecies against Babylon

1. Babylon to become an uninhabited waste; the Jews to return home

50.1
Isa 13.1;
Rev 14.8

50 The word which the LORD spoke concerning Babylon, concerning the land of the Çhăldē'ăns, by Jĕrĕmī'ăh the prophet:

*50.2
Jer 51.27,
31;
Isa 46.1;
Jer 51.44,47

2 "Declare among the nations and proclaim,
   set up a banner and proclaim,
   conceal it not, and say:
'Babylon is taken,
   Bĕl is put to shame,
   Mĕr'ŏdăch is dismayed.
Her images are put to shame,
   her idols are dismayed.'

*50.3
Jer 51.48;
9.10;
Zeph 1.3

3 "For out of the north a nation has come up against her, which shall make her land a desolation, and none shall dwell in it; both man and beast shall flee away.

50.4
Hos 1.11;
Ezra 3.12,
13;
Jer 31.9;
Zech 12.10;
Hos 3.5

4 "In those days and in that time, says the LORD, the people of Israel and the people of Judah shall come together, weeping as they come; and they shall seek the LORD their God. 5 They shall ask the way to Zion, with faces turned toward it, saying, 'Come, let us join ourselves to the LORD in an everlasting covenant which will never be forgotten.'

50.6
Isa 53.6;
Ezek 34.15,
16;
Jer 23.11–
14; 2.20;
3.6,23;
33.12

50.7
Jer 40.2,3;
31.23;
14.8; 17.13

6 "My people have been lost sheep; their shepherds have led them astray, turning them away on the mountains; from mountain to hill they have gone, they have forgotten their fold. 7 All

---

50.2 Bel . . . Merodach, names of the god of Babylon, Bel-Marduk.

50.3 out of the north. Here the reference is to Media, north of Babylon.

who found them have devoured them, and their enemies have said, 'We are not guilty, for they have sinned against the LORD, their true habitation, the LORD, the hope of their fathers.'

8 "Flee from the midst of Babylon, and go out of the land of the Chăldē´ăns, and be as he-goats before the flock. 9 For behold, I am stirring up and bringing against Babylon a company of great nations, from the north country; and they shall array themselves against her; from there she shall be taken. Their arrows are like a skilled warrior who does not return empty-handed. 10 Chăldē´á shall be plundered; all who plunder her shall be sated, says the LORD.

11 "Though you rejoice, though you exult,
    O plunderers of my heritage,
though you are wanton as a heifer at grass,
    and neigh like stallions,
12 your mother shall be utterly shamed,
    and she who bore you shall be disgraced.
Lo, she shall be the last of the nations,
    a wilderness dry and desert.
13 Because of the wrath of the LORD she shall not be inhabited,
    but shall be an utter desolation;
every one who passes by Babylon shall be appalled,
    and hiss because of all her wounds.
14 Set yourselves in array against Babylon round about,
    all you that bend the bow;
shoot at her, spare no arrows,
    for she has sinned against the LORD.
15 Raise a shout against her round about,
    she has surrendered;
her bulwarks have fallen,
    her walls are thrown down.
For this is the vengeance of the LORD:
    take vengeance on her,
    do to her as she has done.
16 Cut off from Babylon the sower,
    and the one who handles the sickle in time of harvest;
because of the sword of the oppressor,
    every one shall turn to his own people,
    and every one shall flee to his own land.

17 "Israel is a hunted sheep driven away by lions. First the king of Assyria devoured him, and now at last Nĕbúchădrĕz´zăr king of Babylon has gnawed his bones. 18 Therefore, thus says the LORD of hosts, the God of Israel: Behold, I am bringing punishment on the king of Babylon and his land, as I punished the king of Assyria. 19 I will restore Israel to his pasture, and he shall feed on Carmĕl and in Bāshăn, and his desire shall be satisfied on the hills of Ē´phrăim and in Gil´ĕăd. 20 In those days and in that time, says the LORD, iniquity shall be sought in Israel, and there shall be none; and sin in Judah, and none shall be found; for I will pardon those whom I leave as a remnant.

50.8	Jer 51.6,45; Rev 18.4
50.9	Jer 51.1,2
*50.10	Jer 51.24, 35; Rev 17.16
50.11	Jer 12.14; 46.20
50.12	Jer 22.6; 51.43
50.13	Jer 25.12; 49.17
50.14	Jer 49.35; Hab 2.8,17
50.15	Jer 51.14; 1 Chr 29.24; Ezek 17.18; Jer 51.44, 58; 46.10
50.16	Joel 1.11; Jer 51.9
50.17	Jer 2.15; 2 Ki 17.6; 24.10,14
50.18	Isa 10.12; Ezek 31.3, 11,12
*50.19	Jer 31.10; 33.12; 31.5
50.20	Jer 31.34; Mic 7.19; Isa 1.9; Jer 33.8

50.10 Destroyed Babylon will never be rebuilt. (Read 50.39)

50.19 This is a promise of Israel's ultimate return.

*50.21
Ezek 23.23;
Isa 10.6;
44.28;
48.14;
Jer 34.22

21 "Go up against the land of Měrǎthā'ǐm,ˢ
     and against the inhabitants of Pěkŏd.ᵗ
   Slay, and utterly destroy after them,
                                    says the LORD,
     and do all that I have commanded you.

50.22
Jer 51.54–
56

22 The noise of battle is in the land,
     and great destruction!

50.23
Isa 14.6;
Jer 51.20–
24

23 How the hammer of the whole earth
     is cut down and broken!
   How Babylon has become
     a horror among the nations!

50.24
Jer 48.43,
44; 51.8,
31,39,57;
Dan 5.30,31

24 I set a snare for you and you were taken, O Babylon,
     and you did not know it;
   you were found and caught,
     because you strove against the LORD.

50.25
Isa 13.5;
Jer 51.12,
25,55

25 The LORD has opened his armory,
     and brought out the weapons of his wrath,
   for the Lord GOD of hosts has a work to do
     in the land of the Chǎldē'ǎns.

50.26
ver 41;
Isa 14.23

26 Come against her from every quarter;
     open her granaries;
   pile her up like heaps of grain, and destroy her utterly;
     let nothing be left of her.

50.27
Isa 34.7;
Ezek 7.7;
Jer 48.44

27 Slay all her bulls,
     let them go down to the slaughter.
   Woe to them, for their day has come,
     the time of their punishment.

50.28
Isa 48.20;
Jer 51.6;
51.10,11

28 "Hark! they flee and escape from the land of Babylon, to declare in Zion the vengeance of the LORD our God, vengeance for his temple.

*50.29
Jer 51.56;
Rev 18.6;
Isa 47.10

29 "Summon archers against Babylon, all those who bend the bow. Encamp round about her; let no one escape. Requite her according to her deeds, do to her according to all that she has done; for she has proudly defied the LORD, the Holy One of Israel.

50.30
Isa 13.17,
18;
Jer 49.26;
51.56,57

30 Therefore her young men shall fall in her squares, and all her soldiers shall be destroyed on that day, says the LORD.

50.31
Jer 21.13;
Nah 2.13

31 "Behold, I am against you, O proud one,
     says the Lord GOD of hosts;
   for your day has come,
     the time when I will punish you.

50.32
Isa 10.12–
15;
Jer 21.14;
49.27

32 The proud one shall stumble and fall,
     with none to raise him up,
   and I will kindle a fire in his cities,
     and it will devour all that is round about him.

50.33
Isa 14.17;
58.6

33 "Thus says the LORD of hosts: The people of Israel are op-

ˢ Or Double Rebellion   ᵗ Or Punishment

50.21 Merathaim, "double rebellion," a reference to southern Babylonia. Pekod, "punishment," a reference to a people in eastern Babylonia.

50.29 Babylon has defied the true God. Therefore she shall be requited.

pressed, and the people of Judah with them; all who took them captive have held them fast, they refuse to let them go. 34 Their Redeemer is strong; the LORD of hosts is his name. He will surely plead their cause, that he may give rest to the earth, but unrest to the inhabitants of Babylon.

35 "A sword upon the Chăldē′ăns, says the LORD,
    and upon the inhabitants of Babylon,
    and upon her princes and her wise men!
36 A sword upon the diviners,
    that they may become fools!
A sword upon her warriors,
    that they may be destroyed!
37 A sword upon her horses and upon her chariots,
    and upon all the foreign troops in her midst,
    that they may become women!
A sword upon all her treasures,
    that they may be plundered!
38 A drought upon her waters,
    that they may be dried up!
For it is a land of images,
    and they are mad over idols.

39 "Therefore wild beasts shall dwell with hyenas in Babylon, and ostriches shall dwell in her; she shall be peopled no more for ever, nor inhabited for all generations. 40As when God overthrew Sŏdŏm and Gŏmor′răh and their neighbor cities, says the LORD, so no man shall dwell there, and no son of man shall sojourn in her.

41 "Behold, a people comes from the north;
    a mighty nation and many kings
    are stirring from the farthest parts of the earth.
42 They lay hold of bow and spear;
    they are cruel, and have no mercy.
The sound of them is like the roaring of the sea;
    they ride upon horses,
arrayed as a man for battle
    against you, O daughter of Babylon!

43 "The king of Babylon heard the report of them,
    and his hands fell helpless;
anguish seized him,
    pain as of a woman in travail.

44 "Behold, like a lion coming up from the jungle of the Jordan against a strong sheepfold, I will suddenly make them run away from her; and I will appoint over her whomever I choose. For who is like me? Who will summon me? What shepherd can stand before me? 45 Therefore hear the plan which the LORD has made against Babylon, and the purposes which he has formed against the land of the Chăldē′ăns: Surely the little ones of their flock shall be dragged away; surely their fold shall be appalled at their fate. 46At the sound of the capture of Babylon the earth shall tremble, and her cry shall be heard among the nations."

50.34
Isa 43.14;
Jer 15.21;
31.11;
32.18;
51.19,36;
Isa 14.3–7

50.35
Dan 5.1,2,
7,8,30

50.36
Isa 44.25;
Jer 49.22

50.37
Jer 51.21,
22; 25.30;
Ezek 30.5;
Jer 51.30;
Nah 3.13

50.38
Jer 51.32,
36,42,47,52

50.39
Isa 13.21,
22;
Jer 51.37;
Isa 13.20

59,40
Gen 19.25;
Jer 49.18;
Lk 17.28–30

50.41
cf. ver 3;
Jer 6.22;
Rev 17.16

50.42
Jer 6.23;
Isa 13.18;
5.30

50.43
Jer 51.31;
49.24

50.44
Jer 49.19–
21;
Isa 46.9;
Job 41.10;
Jer 49.19

50.45
Isa 14.24;
Jer 51.11
49.20

50.46
Rev 18.9;
Ezek 27.28

2. Babylon to be destroyed by the Medes

51.1
Jer 4.11;
Hos 13.15

51 Thus says the LORD:
   "Behold, I will stir up the spirit of a destroyer
      against Babylon,
      against the inhabitants of Chăldē′å;[u]

51.2
Isa 41.16;
Jer 15.7;
Mt 3.12

2 and I will send to Babylon winnowers,
      and they shall winnow her,
   and they shall empty her land,
      when they come against her from every side
      on the day of trouble.

51.3
Jer 50.14;
46.4;
50.21

3 Let not the archer bend his bow,
      and let him not stand up in his coat of mail.
   Spare not her young men;
      utterly destroy all her host.

51.4
Jer 49.26;
50.30,37

4 They shall fall down slain in the land of the Chăldē′ăns,
      and wounded in her streets.

51.5
Isa 54.7,8;
Jer 33.24–26

5 For Israel and Judah have not been forsaken
      by their God, the LORD of hosts;
   but the land of the Chăldē′ăns[v] is full of guilt
      against the Holy One of Israel.

51.6
Jer 50.8;
Rev 18.4;
Num 16.26;
Jer 50.15;
25.14

6 "Flee from the midst of Babylon,
      let every man save his life!
   Be not cut off in her punishment,
      for this is the time of the LORD's vengeance,
      the requital he is rendering her.

51.7
Rev 17.4;
Jer 25.15;
Rev 14.8;
18.3;
Jer 25.16

7 Babylon was a golden cup in the LORD's hand,
      making all the earth drunken;
   the nations drank of her wine,
      therefore the nations went mad.

51.8
Isa 21.9;
Rev 14.8;
18.2;
Jer 48.20;
Rev 18.9,
11,19

8 Suddenly Babylon has fallen and been broken;
      wail for her!
   Take balm for her pain;
      perhaps she may be healed.

51.9
Isa 13.14;
Jer 50.16;
Rev 18.5

9 We would have healed Babylon,
      but she was not healed.
   Forsake her, and let us go
      each to his own country;
   for her judgment has reached up to heaven
      and has been lifted up even to the skies.

51.10
Ps 37.6;
Mic 7.9;
Isa 40.2;
Jer 50.28

10 The LORD has brought forth our vindication;
      come, let us declare in Zion
      the work of the LORD our God.

51.11
Jer 46.4;
Joel 3.9,10;
Jer 50.3,9,
28

11 "Sharpen the arrows!
      Take up the shields!
   The LORD has stirred up the spirit of the kings of the Mēdes, because his purpose concerning Babylon is to destroy it, for that is
the vengeance of the LORD, the vengeance for his temple.

51.12
Isa 13.2;
Jer 50.2

12 Set up a standard against the walls of Babylon;
      make the watch strong;
   set up watchmen;
      prepare the ambushes;

---

[u] Heb Lĕb-qā′maī, a cipher for Chăld′ēă   [v] Heb their land

for the LORD has both planned and done
  what he spoke concerning the inhabitants of Babylon.
¹³ O you who dwell by many waters,
  rich in treasures,
your end has come,
  the thread of your life is cut.

¹⁴ The LORD of hosts has sworn by himself:
  Surely I will fill you with men, as many as locusts,
  and they shall raise the shout of victory over you.

¹⁵ "It is he who made the earth by his power,
  who established the world by his wisdom,
and by his understanding stretched out the heavens.
¹⁶ When he utters his voice there is a tumult of waters in the
    heavens,
  and he makes the mist rise from the ends of the earth.
He makes lightnings for the rain,
  and he brings forth the wind from his storehouses.
¹⁷ Every man is stupid and without knowledge;
  every goldsmith is put to shame by his idols;
for his images are false,
  and there is no breath in them.
¹⁸ They are worthless, a work of delusion;
  at the time of their punishment they shall perish.
¹⁹ Not like these is he who is the portion of Jacob,
  for he is the one who formed all things,
and Israel is the tribe of his inheritance;
  the LORD of hosts is his name.

²⁰ "You are my hammer and weapon of war:
  with you I break nations in pieces;
  with you I destroy kingdoms;
²¹ with you I break in pieces the horse and his rider;
  with you I break in pieces the chariot and the charioteer;
²² with you I break in pieces man and woman;
  with you I break in pieces the old man and the youth;
with you I break in pieces the young man and the maiden;
²³   with you I break in pieces the shepherd and his flock;
with you I break in pieces the farmer and his team;
  with you I break in pieces governors and commanders.

²⁴ "I will requite Babylon and all the inhabitants of Chăldē´à
before your very eyes for all the evil that they have done in Zion,
says the LORD.

²⁵ "Behold, I am against you, O destroying mountain,
                 says the LORD,
  which destroys the whole earth;
I will stretch out my hand against you,
  and roll you down from the crags,
  and make you a burnt mountain.

51.13
Rev 17.1,15

51.14
Jer 49.13;
Amos 6.8;
Nah 3.15;
Jer 50.15

*51.15ff
Gen 1.1,6;
Jer 10.12–16;
Acts 14.15;
Rom 1.20;
Job 9.8;
Ps 104.2;
Isa 40.22
51.16
Ps 18.13;
Jer 10.13;
Ps 135.7
51.17
Jer 10.14;
50.2;
Hab 2.18,19

51.18
Jer 10.15

51.19
Jer 10.16;
50.34

51.20
Isa 10.5,15;
Jer 50.23;
Isa 41.15,16;
Mic 4.12,13

51.22
2 Chr 36.17

51.23
ver 57

51.24
Jer 50.10,15,29

*51.25
Jer 50.31;
Zech 4.7;
Rev 8.8

51.15–19 These verses are borrowed from 10.12–16. (Moffatt eliminates them altogether here in chapter 51.)

51.25 O *destroying mountain*, a symbol of power. *a burnt mountain*, an extinct volcano.

51.26
ver 29;
Jer 50.13

26 No stone shall be taken from you for a corner
    and no stone for a foundation,
but you shall be a perpetual waste,
    says the LORD.

*51.27
Isa 13.2;
Jer 50.2;
25.14;
50.41,42

27 "Set up a standard on the earth,
    blow the trumpet among the nations;
prepare the nations for war against her,
    summon against her the kingdoms,
      Ạr′ạrăt, Minnī, and Ăsh′kĕnăz;
appoint a marshal against her,
    bring up horses like bristling locusts.

51.28
ver 11

28 Prepare the nations for war against her,
    the kings of the Mēdes, with their governors and deputies,
    and every land under their dominion.

51.29
Jer 8.16;
10.10;
50.46;
Amos 8.8;
Isa 13.19,
20; 47.11

29 The land trembles and writhes in pain,
    for the LORD's purposes against Babylon stand,
to make the land of Babylon a desolation,
    without inhabitant.

51.30
Ps 76.5;
Jer 50.36,
37;
Isa 13.7,8;
Lam 2.9;
Amos 1.5;
Nah 3.13

30 The warriors of Babylon have ceased fighting,
    they remain in their strongholds;
their strength has failed,
    they have become women;
her dwellings are on fire,
    her bars are broken.

51.31
2 Chr 30.6;
2 Sam
18.19–31;
Jer 50.24

31 One runner runs to meet another,
    and one messenger to meet another,
to tell the king of Babylon
    that his city is taken on every side;

51.32
Jer 50.37,38

32 the fords have been seized,
    the bulwarks are burned with fire,
    and the soldiers are in panic.

51.33
Isa 21.10;
41.15;
Hab 3.12;
Isa 17.5–7;
Hos 6.11;
Joel 3.13

33 For thus says the LORD of hosts, the God of Israel:
The daughter of Babylon is like a threshing floor
    at the time when it is trodden;
yet a little while
    and the time of her harvest will come."

51.34
Jer 50.17;
Isa 24.1–3;
Amos 8.4

34 "Nĕbúchádrĕz′zăr the king of Babylon has devoured me,
    he has crushed me;
he has made me an empty vessel,
    he has swallowed me like a monster;
he has filled his belly with my delicacies,
    he has rinsed me out.

51.35
Ps 137.8;
ver 24

35 The violence done to me and to my kinsmen be upon Babylon,"
    let the inhabitant of Zion say.
"My blood be upon the inhabitants of Chăldē′á,"
    let Jerusalem say.

51.36
Ps 140.12;
Jer 50.34;
Rom 12.19;
Jer 50.38

36 Therefore thus says the LORD:
"Behold, I will plead your cause
    and take vengeance for you.
I will dry up her sea

51.27 *Ararat, Minni, and Ashkenaz.* Areas north of Babylon: Assyrian Urartu (part of modern Armenia); Mannai (southwest of Lake Van); Ashguzu (south of Lake Urmiah).

and make her fountain dry;
37 and Babylon shall become a heap of ruins,
     the haunt of jackals,
a horror and a hissing,
     without inhabitant.

	51.37 Isa 13.22; Jer 50.39; Rev 18.2; Jer 49.33; 50.13

38 "They shall roar together like lions;
     they shall growl like lions' whelps.
39 While they are inflamed I will prepare them a feast
     and make them drunk, till they swoon away *w*
and sleep a perpetual sleep
     and not wake, says the LORD.

	51.39 Jer 25.27

40 I will bring them down like lambs to the slaughter,
     like rams and he-goats.

	51.40 Jer 50.27

41 "How Babylon *x* is taken,
     the praise of the whole earth seized!
How Babylon has become
     a horror among the nations!

	51.41 Jer 25.26; Isa 13.19; Jer 49.25

42 The sea has come up on Babylon;
     she is covered with its tumultuous waves.
43 Her cities have become a horror,
     a land of drought and a desert,
a land in which no one dwells,
     and through which no son of man passes.

	51.42 Isa 8.7,8; Dan 9.26 **51.43** Jer 50.12; Isa 13.20

44 And I will punish Bĕl in Babylon,
     and take out of his mouth what he has swallowed.
The nations shall no longer flow to him;
     the wall of Babylon has fallen.

	∗51.44 Isa 46.1; Jer 50.2; ver 34,58

45 "Go out of the midst of her, my people!
     Let every man save his life
from the fierce anger of the LORD!
46 Let not your heart faint, and be not fearful
     at the report heard in the land,
when a report comes in one year
     and afterward a report in another year,
and violence is in the land,
     and ruler is against ruler.

	51.45 ver 6; Jer 50.8; Rev 18.4; Acts 2.40 **51.46** Jer 46.27, 28; 2 Ki 19.7; Isa 13.3–5; 19.2

47 "Therefore, behold, the days are coming
     when I will punish the images of Babylon;
her whole land shall be put to shame,
     and all her slain shall fall in the midst of her.
48 Then the heavens and the earth,
     and all that is in them,
shall sing for joy over Babylon;
     for the destroyers shall come against them out of the north,
     says the LORD.

	∗51.47 Isa 46.1,2; ver 52; Jer 50.2; 50.12,35– 37 **51.48** Isa 44.23; 49.13; Rev 12.12; 18.20; ver 11,27

49 Babylon must fall for the slain of Israel,
     as for Babylon have fallen the slain of all the earth.

	51.49 Jer 50.29

w Gk Vg: Heb *rejoice*   *x* Heb *Shēshăch*, a cipher for Babylon

---

51.44 *Bel*, or Bel-Marduk, the god of Babylon.   **51.47** Idolatrous Babylon who has punished Israel shall likewise be punished.

51.50
ver 45;
Ps 137.6

50 "You that have escaped from the sword,
  go, stand not still!
Remember the LORD from afar,
  and let Jerusalem come into your mind:

51.51
Ps 79.4

51 'We are put to shame, for we have heard reproach;
  dishonor has covered our face,
for aliens have come
  into the holy places of the LORD's house.'

51.52
ver 47;
Jer 50.38

52 "Therefore, behold, the days are coming, says the LORD,
  when I will execute judgment upon her images,
and through all her land
  the wounded shall groan.

51.53
Isa 14.12,
  13;
Jer 49.16;
Isa 13.3

53 Though Babylon should mount up to heaven,
  and though she should fortify her strong height,
yet destroyers would come from me upon her,
  says the LORD.

51.54
Jer 50.46

54 "Hark! a cry from Babylon!
  The noise of great destruction from the land of the Chăl-
    dē'ăns!

51.55
ver 42

55 For the LORD is laying Babylon waste,
  and stilling her mighty voice.
Their waves roar like many waters,
  the noise of their voice is raised;

51.56
ver 48;
Hab 2.8;
Ps 94.1,2;
ver 6,24

56 for a destroyer has come upon her,
  upon Babylon;
her warriors are taken,
  their bows are broken in pieces;
for the LORD is a God of recompense,
  he will surely requite.

51.57
ver 39;
Ps 76.5,6;
Jer 46.18;
48.15

57 I will make drunk her princes and her wise men,
  her governors, her commanders, and her warriors;
they shall sleep a perpetual sleep and not wake,
  says the King, whose name is the LORD of hosts.

51.58
ver 44;
Jer 50.15;
Hab 2.13;
ver 64

58 "Thus says the LORD of hosts:
The broad wall of Babylon
  shall be leveled to the ground
and her high gates
  shall be burned with fire.
The peoples labor for nought,
  and the nations weary themselves only for fire."

51.59
Jer 32.12;
  28.1

59 The word which Jĕrĕmī'ăh the prophet commanded Sĕrāi'ăh
the son of Nĕrī'ăh, son of Mahṣeī'ăh, when he went with Zĕdĕkī'-
ăh king of Judah to Babylon, in the fourth year of his reign.

51.60
Jer 30.2,3;
36.2,4,32

Seraiah was the quartermaster. 60 Jĕrĕmī'ăh wrote in a book all the
evil that should come upon Babylon, all these words that are written concerning Babylon. 61And Jĕrĕmī'ăh said to Sĕrāi'ăh: "When

51.62
Jer 25.12;
50.3,39;
ver 43;
Ezek 35.9

you come to Babylon, see that you read all these words, 62 and
say, 'O LORD, thou hast said concerning this place that thou wilt
cut it off, so that nothing shall dwell in it, neither man nor beast,
and it shall be desolate for ever.' 63 When you finish reading this

51.63
Rev 18.21

book, bind a stone to it, and cast it into the midst of the Eūphrā'-

tēṣ, ⁶⁴ and say, 'Thus shall Babylon sink, to rise no more, because of the evil that I am bringing upon her.' "ʸ
Thus far are the words of Jĕrĕmī′áh.

V. Historical appendix 52.1–34

A. Zedekiah's reign

52 Zĕdĕkī′áh was twenty-one years old when he became king; and he reigned eleven years in Jerusalem. His mother's name was Hámū′tál the daughter of Jĕrĕmī′áh of Lĭbnáh. ²And he did what was evil in the sight of the LORD, according to all that Jĕhoi′-ákĭm had done. ³ Surely because of the anger of the LORD things came to such a pass in Jerusalem and Judah that he cast them out from his presence.

B. Siege and fall of Jerusalem

And Zĕdĕkī′áh rebelled against the king of Babylon. ⁴And in the ninth year of his reign, in the tenth month, on the tenth day of the month, Nĕbŭchádrĕz′zár king of Babylon came with all his army against Jerusalem, and they laid siege to it and built siegeworks against it round about. ⁵ So the city was besieged till the eleventh year of King Zĕdĕkī′áh. ⁶ On the ninth day of the fourth month the famine was so severe in the city, that there was no food for the people of the land. ⁷ Then a breach was made in the city; and all the men of war fled and went out from the city by night by the way of a gate between the two walls, by the king's garden, while the Chăldē′áns were round about the city. And they went in the direction of the Ár′ábáh. ⁸ But the army of the Chăldē′áns pursued the king, and overtook Zĕdĕkī′áh in the plains of Jĕr′ĭchō; and all his army was scattered from him. ⁹ Then they captured the king, and brought him up to the king of Babylon at Rĭbláh in the land of Hámáth, and he passed sentence upon him. ¹⁰ The king of Babylon slew the sons of Zĕdĕkī′áh before his eyes, and also slew all the princes of Judah at Rĭbláh. ¹¹ He put out the eyes of Zĕdĕkī′áh, and bound him in fetters, and the king of Babylon took him to Babylon, and put him in prison till the day of his death.

12 In the fifth month, on the tenth day of the month—which was the nineteenth year of King Nĕbŭchádrĕz′zár, king of Babylon—Nĕbŭzar′ádán the captain of the bodyguard who served the king of Babylon, entered Jerusalem. ¹³And he burned the house of the LORD, and the king's house and all the houses of Jerusalem; every great house he burned down. ¹⁴And all the army of the Chăldē′áns, who were with the captain of the guard, broke down all the walls round about Jerusalem. ¹⁵And Nĕbŭzar′ádán the captain of the guard carried away captive some of the poorest of the people and the rest of the people who were left in the city and the deserters who had deserted to the king of Babylon, together with the rest of the artisans. ¹⁶ But Nĕbŭzar′ádán the captain of the guard left some of the poorest of the land to be vinedressers and plowmen.

17 And the pillars of bronze that were in the house of the LORD, and the stands and the bronze sea that were in the house of the LORD, the Chăldē′áns broke in pieces, and carried all the bronze

ʸ Gk: Heb *upon her. And they shall weary themselves*

51.64
Nah 1.8,9;
ver 58

52.1
2 Ki 24.18;
2 Chr
36.11–13
52.2
Jer 36.30,31
52.3
Isa 3.1,4,5;
2 Chr 36.13

52.4
2 Ki 25.1–7;
Jer 39.1;
Ezek 24.1,2;
Jer 32.24

52.6
Jer 38.9

52.7
Jer 39.2;
39.4–7

52.8
Jer 21.7;
32.4; 34.21;
37.17;
38.23
52.9
Jer 32.4;
2 Ki 25.6;
Jer 39.5
52.10
Jer 39.6
52.11
Jer 39.7;
Ezek 12.13
52.12
2 Ki 25.8–
21;
Jer 39.9
52.13
2 Chr 36.19;
Lam 2.7;
Mic 3.12;
Jer 39.8
52.14
2 Ki 25.10
52.15
2 Ki 25.11;
Jer 39.9

52.16
2 Ki 25.12;
Jer 39.10;
40.2–6
52.17
1 Ki 7.15–
36;
Jer 27.19–22

to Babylon. 18And they took away the pots, and the shovels, and the snuffers, and the basins, and the dishes for incense, and all the vessels of bronze used in the temple service; 19 also the small bowls, and the firepans, and the basins, and the pots, and the lampstands, and the dishes for incense, and the bowls for libation. What was of gold the captain of the guard took away as gold, and what was of silver, as silver. 20As for the two pillars, the one sea, the twelve bronze bulls which were under the sea, *z* and the stands, which Solomon the king had made for the house of the LORD, the bronze of all these things was beyond weight. 21As for the pillars, the height of the one pillar was eighteen cubits, its circumference was twelve cubits, and its thickness was four fingers, and it was hollow. 22 Upon it was a capital of bronze; the height of the one capital was five cubits; a network and pomegranates, all of bronze, were upon the capital round about. And the second pillar had the like, with pomegranates. 23 There were ninety-six pomegranates on the sides; all the pomegranates were a hundred upon the network round about.

24 And the captain of the guard took Sērāi′áh the chief priest, and Zĕphȧni′áh the second priest, and the three keepers of the threshold; 25 and from the city he took an officer who had been in command of the men of war, and seven men of the king's council, who were found in the city; and the secretary of the commander of the army who mustered the people of the land; and sixty men of the people of the land, who were found in the midst of the city. 26And Nĕbŭzar′ádán the captain of the guard took them, and brought them to the king of Babylon at Rĭblȧh. 27And the king of Babylon smote them, and put them to death at Rĭblȧh in the land of Hāmȧth. So Judah was carried captive out of its land.

C. The deportations

28 This is the number of the people whom Nĕbŭçhȧdrĕz′zȧr carried away captive: in the seventh year, three thousand and twenty-three Jews; 29 in the eighteenth year of Nĕbŭçhȧdrĕz′zȧr he carried away captive from Jerusalem eight hundred and thirty-two persons; 30 in the twenty-third year of Nĕbŭçhȧdrĕz′zȧr, Nĕbŭzar′ádán the captain of the guard carried away captive of the Jews seven hundred and forty-five persons; all the persons were four thousand and six hundred.

D. The honor accorded Jehoiachin

31 And in the thirty-seventh year of the captivity of Jĕhoi′ȧçhĭn king of Judah, in the twelfth month, on the twenty-fifth day of the month, Ēvĭl-mĕr′ódȧçh king of Babylon, in the year that he became king, lifted up the head of Jehoiachin king of Judah and brought him out of prison; 32 and he spoke kindly to him, and gave him a seat above the seats of the kings who were with him in Babylon. 33 So Jĕhoi′ȧçhĭn put off his prison garments. And every day of his life he dined regularly at the king's table; 34 as for his allowance, a regular allowance was given him by the king according to his daily need, until the day of his death as long as he lived.

z Heb lacks *the sea*

52.18
1 Ki 7.40,45

52.19
1 Ki 7.49,50

52.20
1 Ki 7.47

52.21
1 Ki 7.15

52.22
1 Ki 7.16;
20,42

52.24
2 Ki 25.18;
Jer 21.1;
29.25;
37.3; 35.4

52.26
ver 12,15,
16;
2 Ki 25.20,
21;
ver 9
52.27
Isa 6.11,12;
Jer 13.19;
Ezek 33.28;
Mic 4.10

52.28
2 Ki 24.2,3,
12–16;
Neh 7.6;
Dan 1.1–3

52.30
2 Ki 25.11;
Jer 39.9

52.31
2 Ki 25.27–
30;
Gen 40.13

52.33
Gen 41.14,
42;
2 Sam 9.13;
1 Ki 2.7
52.34
2 Sam 9.10

INTRODUCTION TO
THE LAMENTATIONS
OF JEREMIAH

Authorship and Background: Tradition has assigned the authorship of this book to the prophet Jeremiah. The title of the book appears as The Lamentations of Jeremiah in the Septuagint and Greek uncial manuscripts. However, the rabbinical and Talmud writers referred to it simply as Lamentations. In the Hebrew Bible the book appears in the Writings (Hagiographa) and is the third of the five Megilloth (Scrolls) which include the Song of Solomon, Ruth, Ecclesiastes, and Esther. The style of Lamentations differs from that of Jeremiah. Many believe that the author was a younger contemporary of Jeremiah, an eyewitness, in which event the book was composed around 540 B.C.

Characteristics: The writer pens this elegy in sorrow and lament over the fall of Jerusalem and the destruction of the Temple. His work takes the form of an acrostic in the first four chapters. Each chapter has twenty-two verses except chapter three which has sixty-six. The verses are arranged alphabetically (from *aleph* to *tau*). Chapter three employs the same design but for each letter of the alphabet the author allots three verses instead of one. For some reason the last chapter, which has twenty-two verses, is not in acrostic form.

The author expresses deep grief over the evil which has befallen Jerusalem and the people of God. Throughout there is a sense of horror over what has taken place. The judgment of God for sin is prominently featured in the book, and yet hope is expressed that the people will profit from their experience. The book serves to memorialize for the Jews the destruction of Jerusalem in 587 B.C. To this day they read Lamentations in their synagogues on the ninth of Ab when they mourn the destruction of Jerusalem.

Contents:

I. Jerusalem desolate and forsaken. 1.1–22: The desolation of Jerusalem occasioned by her sin. A cry for compassion.

II. God's judgment explained, and repentance urged. 2.1–22: God has judged His people; He is their enemy. The horrors of famine. Jerusalem's false prophets. A call to supplication.

III. The prophet's lament and hope. 3.1–66: The cry of affliction; the prophet has shared in the suffering. He hopes for the mercies of God, and calls for conversion. Sin has its sorrows. A prayer for Jerusalem.

IV. The condition of Zion, past and present, contrasted. 4.1–22: What Jerusalem was and now is. Consequences of her sin. Edom to be punished.

V. The prayer for mercy amid affliction. 5.1–22: An appeal for mercy and confession of sin. A final plea to God.

THE LAMENTATIONS

OF JEREMIAH

I. *Jerusalem desolate and forsaken 1.1–22*

A. *Description of her desolation*

1.1
Isa 3.26;
54.4;
Ezra 4.20;
Jer 40.9

1 How lonely sits the city
   that was full of people!
How like a widow has she become,
   she that was great among the nations!
She that was a princess among the cities
   has become a vassal.

1.2
Ps 6.6;
Jer 2.25;
4.30

2 She weeps bitterly in the night,
   tears on her cheeks;
among all her lovers
   she has none to comfort her;
all her friends have dealt treacherously with her,
   they have become her enemies.

1.3
Jer 13.19;
Deut 28.64,
65;
2 Ki 25.4,5

3 Judah has gone into exile because of affliction
   and hard servitude;
she dwells now among the nations,
   but finds no resting place;
her pursuers have all overtaken her
   in the midst of her distress.

1.4
Jer 9.11;
10.22;
Joel 1.8–13

4 The roads to Zion mourn,
   for none come to the appointed feasts;
all her gates are desolate,
   her priests groan;
her maidens have been dragged away,*a*
   and she herself suffers bitterly.

1.5
Deut 28.43,
44;
Jer 30.14,
15; 39.9;
52.28

5 Her foes have become the head,
   her enemies prosper,
because the LORD has made her suffer
   for the multitude of her transgressions;
her children have gone away,
   captives before the foe.

1.6
Jer 13.18;
2 Ki 25.4,5

6 From the daughter of Zion has departed
   all her majesty.
Her princes have become like harts
   that find no pasture;
they fled without strength
   before the pursuer.

1.7
Ps 42.4;
Isa 5.1–4;
Jer 37.7;
Lam 4.17;
Jer 48.27

7 Jerusalem remembers
   in the days of her affliction and bitterness*b*
all the precious things
   that were hers from days of old.

a Gk Old Latin: Heb *afflicted*   *b* Cn: Heb *wandering*

When her people fell into the hand of the foe,
    and there was none to help her,
the foe gloated over her,
    mocking at her downfall.

8 Jerusalem sinned grievously,
    therefore she became filthy;
all who honored her despise her,
    for they have seen her nakedness;
yea, she herself groans,
    and turns her face away.

9 Her uncleanness was in her skirts;
    she took no thought of her doom;
therefore her fall is terrible,
    she has no comforter.
"O LORD, behold my affliction,
    for the enemy has triumphed!"

10 The enemy has stretched out his hands
    over all her precious things;
yea, she has seen the nations
    invade her sanctuary,
those whom thou didst forbid
    to enter thy congregation.

11 All her people groan
    as they search for bread;
they trade their treasures for food
    to revive their strength.
"Look, O LORD, and behold,
    for I am despised."

B. Acknowledgment of her sin

12 "Is it nothing to you,c all you who pass by?
    Look and see
if there is any sorrow like my sorrow
    which was brought upon me,
which the LORD inflicted
    on the day of his fierce anger.

13 "From on high he sent fire;
    into my bonesd he made it descend;
he spread a net for my feet;
    he turned me back;
he has left me stunned,
    faint all the day long.

14 "My transgressions were bounde into a yoke;
    by his hand they were fastened together;

c Heb uncertain d Gk: Heb bones and e Cn: Heb uncertain

Cross-references (right margin):

*1.8
1 Ki 8.46;
ver 5,20,17;
Jer 13.22,
26;
ver 4,11,21,
22

*1.9
Ezek 24.13;
Deut 32.29;
Isa 47.7;
Jer 13.17,
18; 16.7

1.10
Isa 64.10,
11;
Jer 51.51;
Deut 23.3

1.11
Jer 38.9;
52.6;
1 Sam 30.12

1.12
Jer 18.16;
48.27;
ver 18;
Jer 30.23,
24; 4.8

1.13
Job 30.30;
Hab 3.16;
Job 19.6;
Jer 44.6

1.14
Deut 28.48;
Isa 47.6;
Jer 28.13,
14; 32.3,5;
Ezek 25.4,7

1.8 *her nakedness.* Sin leaves one without adequate covering.

1.9 *in her skirts,* i.e., for all to see. Her sins are now public knowledge.

they were set upon my neck;
  he caused my strength to fail;
the Lord gave me into the hands
  of those whom I cannot withstand.

1.15
Isa 41.2;
Jer 13.24;
  18.21;
Isa 28.18;
Mic 7.10;
Rev 14.19

15 "The Lord flouted all my mighty men
    in the midst of me;
  he summoned an assembly against me
    to crush my young men;
  the Lord has trodden as in a wine press
    the virgin daughter of Judah.

1.16
Jer 13.17;
  14.17;
Lam 2.18;
ver 2,9

16 "For these things I weep;
    my eyes flow with tears;
  for a comforter is far from me,
    one to revive my courage;
  my children are desolate,
    for the enemy has prevailed."

1.17
Jer 4.31;
2 Ki 24.2–4;
ver 8

17 Zion stretches out her hands,
    but there is none to comfort her;
  the LORD has commanded against Jacob
    that his neighbors should be his foes;
  Jerusalem has become
    a filthy thing among them.

1.18
Jer 12.1;
1 Sam
12.14;
ver 12;
Deut 28.32,
  41

18 "The LORD is in the right,
    for I have rebelled against his word;
  but hear, all you peoples,
    and behold my suffering;
  my maidens and my young men
    have gone into captivity.

1.19
Jer 30.14;
14.15;
Lam 2.20

19 "I called to my lovers
    but they deceived me;
  my priests and elders
    perished in the city,
  while they sought food
    to revive their strength.

1.20
Isa 16.11;
Jer 4.19;
Lam 2.11;
Deut 32.29;
Ezek 7.15

20 "Behold, O LORD, for I am in distress,
    my soul is in tumult,
  my heart is wrung within me,
    because I have been very rebellious.
  In the street the sword bereaves;
    in the house it is like death.

1.21
Lam 2.15;
Isa 14.5,6;
Jer 30.16

21 "Hear^f how I groan;
    there is none to comfort me.
  All my enemies have heard of my trouble;
    they are glad that thou hast done it.
  Bring thou^g the day thou hast announced,
    and let them be as I am.

f Gk Syr: Heb they heard   g Syr: Heb thou hast brought

22 "Let all their evil-doing come before thee;
and deal with them
as thou hast dealt with me
because of all my transgressions;
for my groans are many
and my heart is faint."

II. God's judgment explained and repentance urged
2.1–22

A. The judgment of the LORD

2 How the Lord in his anger
has set the daughter of Zion under a cloud!
He has cast down from heaven to earth
the splendor of Israel;
he has not remembered his footstool
in the day of his anger.

2 The Lord has destroyed without mercy
all the habitations of Jacob;
in his wrath he has broken down
the strongholds of the daughter of Judah;
he has brought down to the ground in dishonor
the kingdom and its rulers.

3 He has cut down in fierce anger
all the might of Israel;
he has withdrawn from them his right hand
in the face of the enemy;
he has burned like a flaming fire in Jacob,
consuming all around.

4 He has bent his bow like an enemy,
with his right hand set like a foe;
and he has slain all the pride of our eyes
in the tent of the daughter of Zion;
he has poured out his fury like fire.

5 The Lord has become like an enemy,
he has destroyed Israel;
he has destroyed all its palaces,
laid in ruins its strongholds;
and he has multiplied in the daughter of Judah
mourning and lamentation.

6 He has broken down his booth like that of a garden,
laid in ruins the place of his appointed feasts;
the LORD has brought to an end in Zion
appointed feast and sabbath,
and in his fierce indignation has spurned
king and priest.

	1.22 Neh 4.4,5; Ps 137.7,8
	★2.1 Lam 3.43, 44; Ezek 28.14–16; Isa 64.11; Ps 99.5; 132.7
	★2.2 Ps 21.9; Lam 3.43; Mic 5.11, 14; Isa 25.12; Ps 89.39
	2.3 Ps 75.5,10; 74.11; Jer 21.4,5; 21.14
	2.4 Lam 3.12, 13; Ezek 24.25; Isa 42.25; Jer 7.20
	2.5 Jer 30.14; 6.26; 9.17–20
	2.6 Jer 7.14; 52.13; Lam 1.4; Zeph 3.18; Lam 4.16, 20; 5.12

2.1 *Zion* here means Jerusalem.   2.2 *Jacob* here is another name for Israel.

2.7
Isa 64.11;
Ezek 7.20–
22;
Jer 33.4,5;
Ps 74.4

7 The Lord has scorned his altar,
  disowned his sanctuary;
he has delivered into the hand of the enemy
  the walls of her palaces;
a clamor was raised in the house of the LORD
  as on the day of an appointed feast.

2.8
Jer 5,10;
2 Ki 21.13;
Isa 34.11;
3.26;
Jer 14.2

8 The LORD determined to lay in ruins
  the wall of the daughter of Zion;
he marked it off by the line;
  he restrained not his hand from destroying;
he caused rampart and wall to lament,
  they languish together.

2.9
Neh 1.3;
Jer 51.30;
Deut 28.36;
2 Ki 24.15;
2 Chr 15.3;
Jer 14.14;
23.16;
Ezek 7.26

9 Her gates have sunk into the ground;
  he has ruined and broken her bars;
her king and princes are among the nations;
  the law is no more,
and her prophets obtain
  no vision from the LORD.

2.10
Job 2.13;
Isa 3.26;
Amos 8.3;
Job 2.12;
Ezek 27.30,
31;
Isa 15.3;
Lam 1.4

10 The elders of the daughter of Zion
  sit on the ground in silence;
they have cast dust on their heads
  and put on sackcloth;
the maidens of Jerusalem
  have bowed their heads to the ground.

2.11
Ps 6.7;
Lam 3.48;
1.20;
Job 16.13;
Ps 22.14;
Lam 4.4

11 My eyes are spent with weeping;
  my soul is in tumult;
my heart is poured out in grief^h
  because of the destruction of the daughter of my people,
because infants and babes faint
  in the streets of the city.

2.12
Jer 5.17;
Lam 4.4;
Job 30.16

12 They cry to their mothers,
  "Where is bread and wine?"
as they faint like wounded men
  in the streets of the city,
as their life is poured out
  on their mothers' bosom.

2.13
Lam 1.12;
Isa 37.22;
Jer 14.17;
8.22;
30.12–15

13 What can I say for you, to what compare you,
  O daughter of Jerusalem?
What can I liken to you, that I may comfort you,
  O virgin daughter of Zion?
For vast as the sea is your ruin;
  who can restore you?

B. The false prophets of Zion

2.14
Jer 2.8;
29.8,9;
Isa 58.1;
Jer 23.36;
Ezek 22.25,
28

14 Your prophets have seen for you
  false and deceptive visions;
they have not exposed your iniquity

h Heb to the ground

to restore your fortunes,
but have seen for you oracles
false and misleading.

15 All who pass along the way
   clap their hands at you;
they hiss and wag their heads
   at the daughter of Jerusalem;
"Is this the city which was called
   the perfection of beauty,
   the joy of all the earth?"

16 All your enemies
   rail against you;
they hiss, they gnash their teeth,
   they cry: "We have destroyed her!
Ah, this is the day we longed for;
   now we have it; we see it!"

17 The LORD has done what he purposed,
   has carried out his threat;
as he ordained long ago,
   he has demolished without pity;
he has made the enemy rejoice over you,
   and exalted the might of your foes.

18 Cry aloud[i] to the Lord!
   O[j] daughter of Zion!
Let tears stream down like a torrent
   day and night!
Give yourself no rest,
   your eyes no respite!

19 Arise, cry out in the night,
   at the beginning of the watches!
Pour out your heart like water
   before the presence of the Lord!
Lift your hands to him
   for the lives of your children,
who faint for hunger
   at the head of every street.

20 Look, O LORD, and see!
   With whom hast thou dealt thus?
Should women eat their offspring,
   the children of their tender care?
Should priest and prophet be slain
   in the sanctuary of the Lord?

21 In the dust of the streets
   lie the young and the old;

*2.15
Jer 19.8;
Zeph 2.15;
Isa 37.22;
Ps 48.2;
50.2

2.16
Ps 22.13;
Lam 3.46;
Ps 37.12;
56.2;
Obad 12-15

2.17
Deut 28.15;
Jer 18.11;
ver 1,2;
Ps 35.24,26;
Lam 1.5

2.18
Hos 7.14;
Jer 9.1;
Lam 1.2,16

2.19
Ps 42.3;
Isa 26.9;
Ps 62.8;
Isa 51.20

*2.20
Jer 19.9;
14.15;
Lam 4.13,
16

2.21
2 Chr 36.17;
Jer 6.11;
Ps 78.62,63;
Jer 13.14;
Zech 11.6

---

[i] Cn: Heb *Their heart cried*   [j] Cn: Heb *O wall of*

2.15 Jerusalem, *the perfection of beauty*, is
desolate and deserted.

2.20 *eat their offspring*. Famine produced
inhuman conditions (cf. 2 Ki 6.26-29).

my maidens and my young men
    have fallen by the sword;
in the day of thy anger thou hast slain them,
    slaughtering without mercy.

22 Thou didst invite as to the day of an appointed feast
    my terrors on every side;
and on the day of the anger of the LORD
    none escaped or survived;
those whom I dandled and reared
    my enemy destroyed.

III. *The prophet's lament and hope 3.1–66*

A. *Lament over Zion's tragic condition*

3 I am the man who has seen affliction
    under the rod of his wrath;

2 he has driven and brought me
    into darkness without any light;

3 surely against me he turns his hand
    again and again the whole day long.

4 He has made my flesh and my skin waste away,
    and broken my bones;

5 he has besieged and enveloped me
    with bitterness and tribulation;

6 he has made me dwell in darkness
    like the dead of long ago.

7 He has walled me about so that I cannot escape;
    he has put heavy chains on me;

8 though I call and cry for help,
    he shuts out my prayer;

9 he has blocked my ways with hewn stones,
    he has made my paths crooked.

10 He is to me like a bear lying in wait,
    like a lion in hiding;

11 he led me off my way and tore me to pieces;
    he has made me desolate;

12 he bent his bow and set me
    as a mark for his arrow.

13 He drove into my heart
    the arrows of his quiver;

14 I have become the laughingstock of all peoples,
    the burden of their songs all day long.

15 He has filled me with bitterness,
    he has sated me with wormwood.

16 He has made my teeth grind on gravel,
    and made me cower in ashes;

17 my soul is bereft of peace,
    I have forgotten what happiness is;

18 so I say, "Gone is my glory,
and my expectation from the LORD."

3.18
Ps 31.22

19 Remember my affliction and my bitterness,[k]
the wormwood and the gall!

3.19
Jer 9.15

20 My soul continually thinks of it
and is bowed down within me.

3.20
Ps 42.5,6,11

B. *The mercies of God recalled and trust expressed*

21 But this I call to mind,
and therefore I have hope:

3.21
Ps 130.7

22 The steadfast love of the LORD never ceases,[l]
his mercies never come to an end;

3.22
Mal 3.6

23 they are new every morning;
great is thy faithfulness.

3.23
Zeph 3.5

24 "The LORD is my portion," says my soul,
"therefore I will hope in him."

3.24
Ps 16.5;
33.18

25 The LORD is good to those who wait for him,
to the soul that seeks him.

3.25
Isa 25.9;
30.18; 26.9

26 It is good that one should wait quietly
for the salvation of the LORD.

3.26
Ps 37.7;
40.1;
Isa 30.15

27 It is good for a man that he bear
the yoke in his youth.

3.27
Ps 94.12

28 Let him sit alone in silence
when he has laid it on him;

3.28
Jer 15.17

29 let him put his mouth in the dust—
there may yet be hope;

3.29
Job 16.15;
Jer 31.17

30 let him give his cheek to the smiter,
and be filled with insults.

3.30
Isa 50.6;
Mt 5.39

31 For the Lord will not
cast off for ever,

3.31
Ps 94.14

32 but, though he cause grief, he will have compassion
according to the abundance of his steadfast love;

3.32
Ps 78.38;
Hos 11.8

33 for he does not willingly afflict
or grieve the sons of men.

3.33
Ezek 33.11;
Heb 12.10

34 To crush under foot
all the prisoners of the earth,

35 to turn aside the right of a man
in the presence of the Most High,

3.35
Ps 140.12

36 to subvert a man in his cause,
the Lord does not approve.

3.36
Hab 1.13

37 Who has commanded and it came to pass,
unless the Lord has ordained it?

3.37
Ps 33.9

38 Is it not from the mouth of the Most High
that good and evil come?

3.38
Job 2.10;
Isa 45.7;
Jer 32.42

39 Why should a living man complain,
a man, about the punishment of his sins?

3.39
Mic 7.9;
Heb 12.5,6

k Cn: Heb *wandering*   *l* Syr Tg: Heb *we are not cut off*

C. Israel exhorted to turn to God

3.40
Ps 119.59;
2 Cor 13.5
40 Let us test and examine our ways,
  and return to the LORD!
3.41
Ps 25.1;
28.2
41 Let us lift up our hearts and hands
  to God in heaven:
3.42
Dan 9.5;
Jer 5.7,9
42 "We have transgressed and rebelled,
  and thou hast not forgiven.

3.43
Lam 2.21;
Ps 83.15
43 "Thou hast wrapped thyself with anger and pursued us,
  slaying without pity;
3.44
Ps 97.2;
ver 8
44 thou hast wrapped thyself with a cloud
  so that no prayer can pass through.
3.45
1 Cor 4.13
45 Thou hast made us offscouring and refuse
  among the peoples.

3.46
Lam 2.16
46 "All our enemies
  rail against us;
3.47
Isa 24.17;
Jer 48.43;
Isa 51.19
47 panic and pitfall have come upon us,
  devastation and destruction;
3.48
Lam 1.16;
2.11,18
48 my eyes flow with rivers of tears
  because of the destruction of the daughter of my people.

3.49
Ps 77.2
49 "My eyes will flow without ceasing,
  without respite,
3.50
Isa 63.15
50 until the LORD from heaven
  looks down and sees;
51 my eyes cause me grief
  at the fate of all the maidens of my city.

3.52
Ps 35.7
52 "I have been hunted like a bird
  by those who were my enemies without cause;
3.53
Jer 37.16
53 they flung me alive into the pit
  and cast stones on me;
3.54
Ps 69.2;
Isa 38.10
54 water closed over my head;
  I said, 'I am lost.'

D. The cry for vengeance against Israel's enemies

3.55
Jon 2.2
55 "I called on thy name, O LORD,
  from the depths of the pit;
3.56
Ps 116.1,2
56 thou didst hear my plea, 'Do not close
  thine ear to my cry for help!'[m]
3.57
Ps 145.18;
Isa 41.10,14
57 Thou didst come near when I called on thee;
  thou didst say, 'Do not fear!'

3.58
Jer 51.36;
Ps 71.23
58 "Thou hast taken up my cause, O Lord,
  thou hast redeemed my life.
3.59
Jer 18.19,
20;
Ps 35.23
59 Thou hast seen the wrong done to me, O LORD;
  judge thou my cause.
3.60
Jer 11.19,
20; 18.18
60 Thou hast seen all their vengeance, all their devices against me.

3.61
Lam 5.1
61 "Thou hast heard their taunts, O LORD,
  all their devices against me.

m Heb uncertain

62 The lips and thoughts of my assailants
    are against me all the day long.
63 Behold their sitting and their rising;
    I am the burden of their songs.

64 "Thou wilt requite them, O Lord,
    according to the work of their hands.
65 Thou wilt give them dullness of heart;
    thy curse will be on them.
66 Thou wilt pursue them in anger and destroy them
    from under thy heavens, O Lord." n

	3.62 Ezek 36.3
	3.63 Ps 139.2
	3.64 Ps 28.4
	3.65 Isa 6.10
	3.66 Ps 8.3

IV. The condition of Zion; past and present contrasted
4.1–22

A. The effects of the siege

4 How the gold has grown dim,
    how the pure gold is changed!
The holy stones lie scattered
    at the head of every street.

  4.1
  Ezek 7.19–
  22;
  Jer 52.13,14

2 The precious sons of Zion,
    worth their weight in fine gold,
how they are reckoned as earthen pots,
    the work of a potter's hands!

  4.2
  Isa 51.18;
  30.14;
  Jer 19.11

3 Even the jackals give the breast
    and suckle their young,
but the daughter of my people has become cruel,
    like the ostriches in the wilderness.

  4.3
  Isa 34.13;
  49.15;
  Job 39.14,
  16

4 The tongue of the nursling cleaves
    to the roof of its mouth for thirst;
the children beg for food,
    but no one gives to them.

  4.4
  Jer 14.3;
  Lam 2.12

5 Those who feasted on dainties
    perish in the streets;
those who were brought up in purple
    lie on ash heaps.

  4.5
  Jer 6.2;
  Amos 6.3–
  7;
  Ps 113.7

6 For the chastisement o of the daughter of my people has been
    greater
    than the punishment p of Sŏdŏm,
which was overthrown in a moment,
    no hand being laid on it. q

  4.6
  Ezek 16.48;
  Gen 19.23;
  Jer 20.16

7 Her princes were purer than snow,
    whiter than milk;
their bodies were more ruddy than coral,
    the beauty of their form r was like sapphire. s

  4.7
  Ps 51.7

---

n Syr Compare Gk Vg: Heb the heavens of the Lord   o Or iniquity
p Or sin   q Heb uncertain
r Heb uncertain   s Heb lapis lazuli

4.8
Job 30.30;
Lam 5.10;
Ps 102.5

8 Now their visage is blacker than soot,
 they are not recognized in the streets;
their skin has shriveled upon their bones,
 it has become as dry as wood.

4.9
Jer 15.2;
Ezek 24.23

9 Happier were the victims of the sword
 than the victims of hunger,
who pined away, stricken
 by want of the fruits of the field.

4.10
Lam 2.20;
2 Ki 6.29;
Deut 28.57

10 The hands of compassionate women
 have boiled their own children;
they became their food
 in the destruction of the daughter of my people.

4.11
Jer 7.20;
ver 22;
Deut 32.22;
Jer 21.14

11 The LORD gave full vent to his wrath,
 he poured out his hot anger;
and he kindled a fire in Zion,
 which consumed its foundations.

4.12
1 Ki 9.8,9;
Jer 21.13

12 The kings of the earth did not believe,
 or any of the inhabitants of the world,
that foe or enemy could enter
 the gates of Jerusalem.

B. *The uselessness of the false prophets*

4.13
Jer 5.31;
6.13;
Ezek 22.26;
Mic 3.11,
12;
Mt 23.31

13 This was for the sins of her prophets
 and the iniquities of her priests,
who shed in the midst of her
 the blood of the righteous.

4.14
Isa 56.10;
59.9,10;
Jer 19.4;
2.34

14 They wandered, blind, through the streets,
 so defiled with blood
that none could touch
 their garments.

4.15
Lev 13.45;
Jer 49.5

15 "Away! Unclean!" men cried at them;
 "Away! Away! Touch not!"
So they became fugitives and wanderers;
 men said among the nations,
"They shall stay with us no longer."

4.16
Lam 5.12

16 The LORD himself has scattered them,
 he will regard them no more;
no honor was shown to the priests,
 no favor to the elders.

C. *The absence of external help*

4.17
2 Ki 24.7;
Isa 20.5;
Jer 37.7;
Ezek 29.16

17 Our eyes failed, ever watching
 vainly for help;
in our watching*t* we watched
 for a nation which could not save.

t Heb uncertain

18 Men dogged our steps
      so that we could not walk in our streets;
   our end drew near; our days were numbered;
      for our end had come.

19 Our pursuers were swifter
      than the vultures in the heavens;
   they chased us on the mountains,
      they lay in wait for us in the wilderness.

20 The breath of our nostrils, the LORD's anointed,
      was taken in their pits,
   he of whom we said, "Under his shadow
      we shall live among the nations."

D. *Closing refrain*

21 Rejoice and be glad, O daughter of Ēdȯm,
      dweller in the land of Ūz;
   but to you also the cup shall pass;
      you shall become drunk and strip yourself bare.

22 The punishment of your iniquity, O daughter of Zion, is ac-
      complished,
      he will keep you in exile no longer;
   but your iniquity, O daughter of Ēdȯm, he will punish,
      he will uncover your sins.

V. *The prayer for mercy amid affliction 5.1–22*

A. *Acknowledgment of their sin and evil condition*

5 Remember, O LORD, what has befallen us;
      behold, and see our disgrace!
2 Our inheritance has been turned over to strangers,
      our homes to aliens.
3 We have become orphans, fatherless;
      our mothers are like widows.
4 We must pay for the water we drink,
      the wood we get must be bought.
5 With a yoke*u* on our necks we are hard driven;
      we are weary, we are given no rest.
6 We have given the hand to Egypt,
      and to Assyria, to get bread enough.
7 Our fathers sinned, and are no more;
      and we bear their iniquities.
8 Slaves rule over us;
      there is none to deliver us from their hand.
9 We get our bread at the peril of our lives,
      because of the sword in the wilderness.

u Symmachus: Heb lacks *with a yoke*

4.21 *O daughter of Edom.* The Edomites side with the Babylonians against Judah in the months before the fall of Jerusalem (587 B.C.). Edom, as a result, profited from Israel's tragedy but was herself punished in the end (cf. Ezek 25.12–14; 35.5; Obad 11–14).

4.18
2 Ki 25.4;
Ezek 7.2,3;
Amos 8.2

4.19
Deut 28.49;
Jer 4.13;
Hab 1.8

4.20
2 Sam 1.14;
19.21;
Ezek 12.13;
19.4,8

★**4.21**
Isa 34.7;
Amos 1.11,
12;
Obad 1,16

4.22
Isa 40.2;
Mal 1.3,4

5.1
Ps 89.50;
44.13–16
5.2
Ps 79.1;
Zeph 1.13
5.3
Jer 15.8;
18.21
5.4
Isa 3.1
5.5
Jer 28.14;
Neh 9.36,37
5.6
Jer 2.36;
Hos 5.13;
7.11; 9.3
5.7
Jer 14.20;
16.12
5.8
Neh 5.15;
Zech 11.6

10 Our skin is hot as an oven
  with the burning heat of famine.
11 Women are ravished in Zion,
  virgins in the towns of Judah.
12 Princes are hung up by their hands;
  no respect is shown to the elders.
13 Young men are compelled to grind at the mill;
  and boys stagger under loads of wood.
14 The old men have quit the city gate,
  the young men their music.
15 The joy of our hearts has ceased;
  our dancing has been turned to mourning.
16 The crown has fallen from our head;
  woe to us, for we have sinned!
17 For this our heart has become sick,
  for these things our eyes have grown dim,
18 for Mount Zion which lies desolate;
  jackals prowl over it.

B. *Their prayer for mercy*

19 But thou, O LORD, dost reign for ever;
  thy throne endures to all generations.
20 Why dost thou forget us for ever,
  why dost thou so long forsake us?
21 Restore us to thyself, O LORD, that we may be restored!
  Renew our days as of old!
22 Or hast thou utterly rejected us?
  Art thou exceedingly angry with us?

5.10 Lam 4.8
5.11 Isa 13.16; Zech 14.2
5.12 Lam 4.16
5.13 Jer 7.18
5.14 Lam 4.8; Jer 7.34
5.15 Jer 25.10
5.16 Ps 89.39; Isa 3.9–11
5.17 Isa 1.5; Ps 6.7
5.18 Ps 74.2,3; Neh 4.3
5.19 Ps 9.7; 102.12,25–27; 45.6
5.20 Ps 13.1
5.21 Jer 31.18
5.22 Jer 7.29; Isa 64.9

INTRODUCTION TO
THE BOOK OF
EZEKIEL

Authorship and Background: This book is the work of Ezekiel, whose name means "God strengtheneth," or "God is strong." Ezekiel belonged to a priestly family and was the son of Buzi. As a young man he was carried away captive to Babylon along with Jehoiachin a decade before the destruction of Jerusalem. In captivity he lived in Telabib on the river Chebar. He was married and had his own home. Ezekiel's call to the prophetic office came in the fourth month of the fifth year of the captivity. He prophesied for more than two decades and undoubtedly knew both Daniel and Jeremiah. On the day that the siege of Jerusalem began, his wife died suddenly. Ezekiel wrote in Babylon but often addressed the Jews in Jerusalem describing situations and events in that city. This has caused some to question whether the book was composed in Babylon at the indicated time despite the internal evidences favoring authorship by Ezekiel in Babylon.

Characteristics: Ezekiel writes as one whose main burden is judgment. In a sense, he closely parallels the writer of The Revelation in the New Testament. No one exposes the sins of the people of God more openly or pronounces judgment more explicitly. Through the use of parables, oratory, and logic he arraigns Judah and does it in language which causes men to draw back in horror. He discloses the wrath of God against sin in the strongest language. Ezekiel uses his vivid imagination and often engages in symbolic actions. Occasionally a ray of hope shines through his utterances in the first half of the book. In the second half he prophesies the doom of Judah's conquerors and neighbors. Following the news of the fall of Jerusalem, people flock to hear the one whose prophecy has been fulfilled. Then it is that he speaks of the restoration of the people of God with hope and assurance. He is the forerunner of the apocalyptic writers of a later day.

Contents:

I.   The divine judgment on Judah and Jerusalem. 1.1—24.27: The call of Ezekiel in the vision of the glory of God enthroned on the four cherubim. He is commissioned to be a watchman, to speak and to be silent as God moves him. He prophesies the fall of Jerusalem by symbolic act and by word of mouth. It will occur because of the unbelief and hypocrisy of the people as illustrated by false prophets, and in spite of the idea that God will not punish His own people. He argues that Jerusalem has become a harlot. Judah has trusted her armies and fails to understand the righteousness of God as shown by the proverb of the sour grapes and the pictures of the lioness and the

Introduction to Ezekiel 1216

vine. God will judge Jerusalem because He wants a holy people. By parables of forest fire and the two harlots, as well as the boiling pot, he shows that God must punish the sins of His people.

II. The prophecies against the surrounding nations. 25.1—32.32: Ezekiel pronounces doom on Ammon, Moab, and Philistia. Tyre is condemned for her pride and insults to Jerusalem. The fall of Tyre is described. Sidon is condemned for not knowing the LORD and shall be destroyed by sword and pestilence. Egypt is guilty of treachery and pride, and Nebuchadnezzar will be the instrument of punishment. Pharaoh will fall.

III. Israel restored. 33.1—39.29: The prophet watchman is described who will warn of danger. There is the promise of a good Shepherd along with a restored land, a new heart among the people, and new life as illustrated in the vision of the valley of dry bones which come to life. In the union of the two sticks Israel and Judah will be joined together once more and there will be a covenant of peace. The defeat of the last enemy is predicted. Gog makes great plans which come to nought and this nation is destroyed. The slain are buried and the birds and beasts eat the flesh of the dead. Israel recognizes God's mercy.

IV. Israel in the land in the kingdom age. 40.1—48.35: Ezekiel describes the new Temple in the latter age with its courts, gateways, interior, measurements, priests' chamber, and dimensions of the Temple area. Yahweh returns to His Temple, and His glory fills it. The priesthood is described and its provisions for sacrifices catalogued. The regulations for worship are announced. The land is seen as fertile, its boundaries are stated, and the allocation of territory to the various tribes made.

THE BOOK OF
EZEKIEL

I. *The divine judgment on Judah and Jerusalem 1.1–24.27*

A. Introduction

1. *Superscription*

1 In the thirtieth year, in the fourth month, on the fifth day of the month, as I was among the exiles by the river Chebar, the heavens were opened, and I saw visions of God. 2 On the fifth day of the month (it was the fifth year of the exile of King Jehoi'achin), 3 the word of the LORD came to Eze'kiel the priest, the son of Buzi, in the land of the Chaldē'ans by the river Chebar; and the hand of the LORD was upon him there.

2. *The vision of the four living creatures and the four wheels*

4 As I looked, behold, a stormy wind came out of the north, and a great cloud, with brightness round about it, and fire flashing forth continually, and in the midst of the fire, as it were gleaming bronze. 5And from the midst of it came the likeness of four living creatures. And this was their appearance: they had the form of men, 6 but each had four faces, and each of them had four wings. 7 Their legs were straight, and the soles of their feet were like the sole of a calf's foot; and they sparkled like burnished bronze. 8 Under their wings on their four sides they had human hands. And the four had their faces and their wings thus: 9 their wings touched one another; they went every one straight forward, without turning as they went. 10As for the likeness of their faces, each had the face of a man in front;*a* the four had the face of a lion on the right side, the four had the face of an ox on the left side, and the four had the face of an eagle at the back.*b* 11 Such were their faces. And their wings were spread out above; each creature had two wings, each of which touched the wing of another, while two covered their bodies. 12And each went straight forward; wherever the spirit would go, they went, without turning as they went. 13 In the midst of*c* the living creatures there was something that looked like burning coals of fire, like torches moving to and fro among the living creatures; and the fire was bright, and out of the fire went forth lightning. 14And the living creatures darted to and fro, like a flash of lightning.

15 Now as I looked at the living creatures, I saw a wheel upon the earth beside the living creatures, one for each of the four of them.*d* 16As for the appearance of the wheels and their construction: their appearance was like the gleaming of a chrysolite; and the four had the same likeness, their construction being as it were a wheel within a wheel. 17 When they went, they went in any of their four directions*e* without turning as they went. 18 The four

---

a Cn: Heb lacks *in front*   *b* Cn: Heb lacks *at the back*
c Gk Old Latin: Heb *And the likeness of*   *d* Heb *of their faces*   *e* Heb *on their four sides*

1.1 *the river Chebar.* The Grand Canal, running southeast of Babylon.

1.5 For the *living creatures* see note to 10.1 on *cherubim*.

1.19
Ezek 10.16,
17,19
1.20
ver 12;
Ezek 10.17
1.21
Ezek 10.17

wheels had rims and they had spokes;*f* and their rims were full of eyes round about. 19And when the living creatures went, the wheels went beside them; and when the living creatures rose from the earth, the wheels rose. 20 Wherever the spirit would go, they went, and the wheels rose along with them; for the spirit of the living creatures was in the wheels. 21 When those went, these went; and when those stood, these stood; and when those rose from the earth, the wheels rose along with them; for the spirit of the living creatures was in the wheels.

1.22
Ezek 10.1

1.23
ver 6,4

1.24
Ezek 10.5;
43.2;
Rev 1.15;
19.6;
2 Ki 7.6

1.25
ver 22

22 Over the heads of the living creatures there was the likeness of a firmament, shining like crystal,*g* spread out above their heads. 23And under the firmament their wings were stretched out straight, one toward another; and each creature had two wings covering its body. 24And when they went, I heard the sound of their wings like the sound of many waters, like the thunder of the Almighty, a sound of tumult like the sound of a host; when they stood still, they let down their wings. 25And there came a voice from above the firmament over their heads; when they stood still, they let down their wings.

1.26
Ezek 10.1;
Ex 24.10;
Ezek 43.6,7;
Rev 1.13

1.27
ver 4;
Ezek 8.2

*1.28
Rev 4.3;
10.1;
Ezek 3.23;
8.4;
Dan 8.17;
Rev 1.17

26 And above the firmament over their heads there was the likeness of a throne, in appearance like sapphire;*h* and seated above the likeness of a throne was a likeness as it were of a human form. 27And upward from what had the appearance of his loins I saw as it were gleaming bronze, like the appearance of fire enclosed round about; and downward from what had the appearance of his loins I saw as it were the appearance of fire, and there was brightness round about him.*i* 28 Like the appearance of the bow that is in the cloud on the day of rain, so was the appearance of the brightness round about.

Such was the appearance of the likeness of the glory of the LORD. And when I saw it, I fell upon my face, and I heard the voice of one speaking.

3. *The commissions of Ezekiel*
a. *To go to the house of Israel*

*2.1
Dan 10.11
*2.2
Dan 8.18;
Ezek 3.24
2.3
Jer 3.25;
Ezek 20.18,
30
2.4
Jer 5.3;
Ezek 3.7
2.5
Ezek 3.11,
26,27;
33.33

2 And he said to me, "Son of man, stand upon your feet, and I will speak with you." 2And when he spoke to me, the Spirit entered into me and set me upon my feet; and I heard him speaking to me. 3And he said to me, "Son of man, I send you to the people of Israel, to a nation*j* of rebels, who have rebelled against me; they and their fathers have transgressed against me to this very day. 4 The people also are impudent and stubborn: I send you to them; and you shall say to them, 'Thus says the Lord GOD.' 5And whether they hear or refuse to hear (for they are a rebellious house) they will know that there has been a prophet among them.

---

f Cn: Heb uncertain   *g* Gk: Heb *awesome crystal*
h Heb *lapis lazuli*   *i* Or *it*   *j* Syr: Heb *nations*

1.28 *the likeness of the glory of the* LORD. Ezekiel saw a vision of Israel's God. Although invisible, He revealed Himself to Ezekiel in the manner described in chapter 1 (cf. Isaiah's vision, Isa ch 6).
2.1 Ezekiel is addressed as *Son of man*, et passim, a term stressing the prophet's humanity. Although given celestial visions,

Ezekiel was but a "son of man," i.e., a human being. The term later came to be used in a Messianic sense to describe the representative man, the Son of man who would establish God's rule over the earth and usher in the Messianic Age (cf. Dan 7.9–13). This usage does not occur in Ezekiel, however.
2.2 *The Spirit.* This is the Spirit of God.

⁶And you, son of man, be not afraid of them, nor be afraid of their words, though briers and thorns are with you and you sit upon scorpions; be not afraid of their words, nor be dismayed at their looks, for they are a rebellious house. ⁷And you shall speak my words to them, whether they hear or refuse to hear; for they are a rebellious house.

b. *To eat the scroll*

8 "But you, son of man, hear what I say to you; be not rebellious like that rebellious house; open your mouth, and eat what I give you." ⁹And when I looked, behold, a hand was stretched out to me, and, lo, a written scroll was in it; ¹⁰ and he spread it before me; and it had writing on the front and on the back, and there were written on it words of lamentation and mourning and woe. 3 ¹And he said to me, "Son of man, eat what is offered to you; eat this scroll, and go, speak to the house of Israel." ² So I opened my mouth, and he gave me the scroll to eat. ³And he said to me, "Son of man, eat this scroll that I give you and fill your stomach with it." Then I ate it; and it was in my mouth as sweet as honey.

c. *To speak God's message to Israel*

4 And he said to me, "Son of man, go, get you to the house of Israel, and speak with my words to them. ⁵ For you are not sent to a people of foreign speech and a hard language, but to the house of Israel—⁶ not to many peoples of foreign speech and a hard language, whose words you cannot understand. Surely, if I sent you to such, they would listen to you. ⁷ But the house of Israel will not listen to you; for they are not willing to listen to me; because all the house of Israel are of a hard forehead and of a stubborn heart. ⁸ Behold, I have made your face hard against their faces, and your forehead hard against their foreheads. ⁹ Like adamant harder than flint have I made your forehead; fear them not, nor be dismayed at their looks, for they are a rebellious house." ¹⁰ Moreover he said to me, "Son of man, all my words that I shall speak to you receive in your heart, and hear with your ears. ¹¹And go, get you to the exiles, to your people, and say to them, 'Thus says the Lord GOD'; whether they hear or refuse to hear."

d. *The visit to Babylon*

12 Then the Spirit lifted me up, and as the glory of the LORD arose[k] from its place, I heard behind me the sound of a great earthquake; ¹³ it was the sound of the wings of the living creatures as they touched one another, and the sound of the wheels beside them, that sounded like a great earthquake. ¹⁴ The Spirit lifted me up and took me away, and I went in bitterness in the heat of my spirit, the hand of the LORD being strong upon me; ¹⁵ and I came to the exiles at Tĕl-ā'bĭb, who dwelt by the river Çhēbar.[l] And I sat there overwhelmed among them seven days.

[k] Cn: Heb *blessed be the glory of the* LORD
[l] Heb *Chebar, and to where they dwelt.* Another reading is *Chebar, and I sat where they sat*

3.5 *foreign speech and a hard language,* i.e., deep of lip and heavy of tongue.
3.14 *in bitterness in the heat of my spirit,* i.e.,

the prophet was both depressed and excited. Insufficient, he was mastered by God's mighty hand.

Cross references (right margin):

2.6 Jer 1.8,17; Isa 9.18; Mic 7.4; Ezek 3.9
2.7 Jer 1.7,17
2.8 Isa 50.5; Rev 10.9
2.9 Ezek 8.3; 3.1
2.10 Rev 8.13
3.1 Ezek 2.8,9
3.3 Rev 10.9, 10; Jer 15.16; Ps 19.10; 119.103
3.4 ver 11
★3.5 Jon 1.2; Isa 28.11; 33.19
3.6 Mt 11.21, 23; Acts 13.46-48
3.7 Jn 15.20; Ezek 2.4
3.8 Jer 1.18; 15.20
3.9 Isa 50.7; Mic 3.8; Ezek 2.6
3.10 ver 1-3
3.11 Ezek 2.5,7
3.12 Ezek 8.3; Acts 8.39; 2.2
3.13 Ezek 1.24; 10.5,16,17
★3.14 Jer 6.11; Ezek 1.3; 8.1
3.15 Ezek 1.1; Job 2.13

e. *The message of the watchman given*

16 And at the end of seven days, the word of the LORD came to me: **17** "Son of man, I have made you a watchman for the house of Israel; whenever you hear a word from my mouth, you shall give them warning from me. **18** If I say to the wicked, 'You shall surely die,' and you give him no warning, nor speak to warn the wicked from his wicked way, in order to save his life, that wicked man shall die in his iniquity; but his blood I will require at your hand. **19** But if you warn the wicked, and he does not turn from his wickedness, or from his wicked way, he shall die in his iniquity; but you will have saved your life. **20** Again, if a righteous man turns from his righteousness and commits iniquity, and I lay a stumbling block before him, he shall die; because you have not warned him, he shall die for his sin, and his righteous deeds which he has done shall not be remembered; but his blood I will require at your hand. **21** Nevertheless if you warn the righteous man not to sin, and he does not sin, he shall surely live, because he took warning; and you will have saved your life."

f. *The commission to confinement*

22 And the hand of the LORD was there upon me; and he said to me, "Arise, go forth into the plain,*m* and there I will speak with you." **23** So I arose and went forth into the plain;*m* and, lo, the glory of the LORD stood there, like the glory which I had seen by the river Chēbar; and I fell on my face. **24** But the Spirit entered into me, and set me upon my feet; and he spoke with me and said to me, "Go, shut yourself within your house. **25** And you, O son of man, behold, cords will be placed upon you, and you shall be bound with them, so that you cannot go out among the people; **26** and I will make your tongue cleave to the roof of your mouth, so that you shall be dumb and unable to reprove them; for they are a rebellious house. **27** But when I speak with you, I will open your mouth, and you shall say to them, 'Thus says the Lord GOD'; he that will hear, let him hear; and he that will refuse to hear, let him refuse; for they are a rebellious house.

B. *The coming destruction of Jerusalem*

1. *The symbol of the siege*

4 "And you, O son of man, take a brick and lay it before you, and portray upon it a city, even Jerusalem; **2** and put siege-works against it, and build a siege wall against it, and cast up a mound against it; set camps also against it, and plant battering rams against it round about. **3** And take an iron plate, and place it as an iron wall between you and the city; and set your face toward it, and let it be in a state of siege, and press the siege against it. This is a sign for the house of Israel.

m Or *valley*

3.16-21 As a watchman, Ezekiel was responsible to sound the alarm of impending catastrophe. Faithlessness on his part would mean the destruction of his people. Faithfulness could not insure safety, for his message might go unheeded. Nevertheless, the prophet must be faithful to his God-appointed task.

4.1 *take a brick.* Ezekiel was ordered to draw a plan of Jerusalem on a clay tablet such as the Babylonians used as writing material. He then would enact a mock battle to depict the coming siege.

Marginal cross-references:

★3.16ff

3.17
Ezek 33.7–9;
Isa 52.8;
56.10;
Jer 6.17

3.18
Gen 2.17;
Ezek 33.6;
Jn 8.21,24

3.19
Ezek 33.3,9;
Acts 18.6;
20.26

3.20
Ezek 18.24;
33.12,13;
Jer 6.21

3.21
Acts 20.31;
ver 19

3.22
ver 14;
Ezek 8.4;
Acts 9.6

3.23
Ezek 1.28;
1.1

3.24
Ezek 2.2

3.25
Ezek 4.8

3.26
Ezek 24.27;
Lk 1.20,22;
Ezek 2.5–7

3.27
Ezek 24.27;
33.22;
ver 11,9,26

★4.1
Isa 20.2;
Ezek 5.1

4.2
Ezek 21.22

4.3
Ezek 5.2;
12.6,11;
24.24,27

2. *The symbol of the punishment*

4 "Then lie upon your left side, and I will lay the punishment of the house of Israel upon you;[n] for the number of the days that you lie upon it, you shall bear their punishment. 5 For I assign to you a number of days, three hundred and ninety days, equal to the number of the years of their punishment; so long shall you bear the punishment of the house of Israel. 6And when you have completed these, you shall lie down a second time, but on your right side, and bear the punishment of the house of Judah; forty days I assign you, a day for each year. 7And you shall set your face toward the siege of Jerusalem, with your arm bared; and you shall prophesy against the city. 8And, behold, I will put cords upon you, so that you cannot turn from one side to the other, till you have completed the days of your siege.

3. *The symbol of the consequences of the siege*

9 "And you, take wheat and barley, beans and lentils, millet and spelt, and put them into a single vessel, and make bread of them. During the number of days that you lie upon your side, three hundred and ninety days, you shall eat it. 10And the food which you eat shall be by weight, twenty shekels a day; once a day you shall eat it. 11And water you shall drink by measure, the sixth part of a hin; once a day you shall drink. 12And you shall eat it as a barley cake, baking it in their sight on human dung." 13And the LORD said, "Thus shall the people of Israel eat their bread unclean, among the nations whither I will drive them." 14 Then I said, "Ah Lord GOD! behold, I have never defiled myself; from my youth up till now I have never eaten what died of itself or was torn by beasts, nor has foul flesh come into my mouth." 15 Then he said to me, "See, I will let you have cow's dung instead of human dung, on which you may prepare your bread." 16 Moreover he said to me, "Son of man, behold, I will break the staff of bread in Jerusalem; they shall eat bread by weight and with fearfulness; and they shall drink water by measure and in dismay. 17 I will do this that they may lack bread and water, and look at one another in dismay, and waste away under their punishment.

4. *The symbol of Jerusalem's fate*
a. *What will happen to the people*

5 "And you, O son of man, take a sharp sword; use it as a barber's razor and pass it over your head and your beard; then take balances for weighing, and divide the hair. 2A third part you shall burn in the fire in the midst of the city, when the days of the siege are completed; and a third part you shall take and strike with the sword round about the city; and a third part you shall scatter to the wind, and I will unsheathe the sword after them. 3And you shall take from these a small number, and bind them in the skirts of your robe. 4And of these again you shall take some, and cast them into the fire, and burn them in the fire; from there

b. *Jerusalem's fate the result of sin (idolatry)*

a fire will come forth into all the house of Israel. 5 Thus says the Lord GOD: This is Jerusalem; I have set her in the center of the

---

Cross-references (margin):

4.4 Lev 10.17; Num 18.1
4.5 Num 14.34
4.7 ver 3; Ezek 21.2
4.8 Ezek 3.25
4.9 ver 5
4.10 ver 16
4.12 Isa 36.12
4.13 Hos 9.3
4.14 Ezek 9.8; Acts 10.14; Ex 22.31; Lev 17.15; Deut 14.3; Isa 65.4
4.16 Lev 26.26; Isa 3.1; Ezek 5.16; 14.13; ver 10,11; Ezek 12.19
4.17 Lev 26.39; Ezek 24.23
5.1 Lev 21.5; Isa 7.20; Ezek 44.20
5.2 ver 12; Ezek 4.2–8; Lev 26.33
5.3 Jer 39.10
5.4 Jer 41.1,2; 44.14
5.5 Ezek 4.1; Lam 1.1

---

[n] Cn: Heb *you shall lay . . . upon it*

nations, with countries round about her. 6And she has wickedly rebelled against my ordinances *o* more than the nations, and against my statutes more than the countries round about her, by rejecting my ordinances and not walking in my statutes. 7 Therefore thus says the Lord GOD: Because you are more turbulent than the nations that are round about you, and have not walked in my statutes or kept my ordinances, but have acted*p* according to the ordinances of the nations that are round about you; 8 therefore thus says the Lord GOD: Behold, I, even I, am against you; and I will execute judgments in the midst of you in the sight of the nations. 9And because of all your abominations I will do with you what I have never yet done, and the like of which I will never do again. 10 Therefore fathers shall eat their sons in the midst of you, and sons shall eat their fathers; and I will execute judgments on you, and any of you who survive I will scatter to all the winds. 11 Wherefore, as I live, says the Lord GOD, surely, because you have defiled my sanctuary with all your detestable things and with all your abominations, therefore I will cut you down;*q* my eye will not spare, and I will have no pity. 12A third part of you shall die of pestilence and be consumed with famine in the midst of you; a third part shall fall by the sword round about you; and a third part I will scatter to all the winds and will unsheathe the sword after them.

13 "Thus shall my anger spend itself, and I will vent my fury upon them and satisfy myself; and they shall know that I, the LORD, have spoken in my jealousy, when I spend my fury upon them. 14 Moreover I will make you a desolation and an object of reproach among the nations round about you and in the sight of all that pass by. 15 You shall be*r* a reproach and a taunt, a warning and a horror, to the nations round about you, when I execute judgments on you in anger and fury, and with furious chastisements— I, the LORD, have spoken—16 when I loose against you*s* my deadly arrows of famine, arrows for destruction, which I will loose to destroy you, and when I bring more and more famine upon you, and break your staff of bread. 17 I will send famine and wild beasts against you, and they will rob you of your children; pestilence and blood shall pass through you; and I will bring the sword upon you. I, the LORD, have spoken."

C. The oracle of the mountains

1. The high places to be destroyed

6 The word of the LORD came to me: 2 "Son of man, set your face toward the mountains of Israel, and prophesy against them, 3 and say, You mountains of Israel, hear the word of the Lord GOD! Thus says the Lord GOD to the mountains and the hills, to the ravines and the valleys: Behold, I, even I, will bring a sword upon you, and I will destroy your high places. 4 Your altars shall become desolate, and your incense altars shall be broken; and I will cast down your slain before your idols. 5And I will lay the dead bodies of the people of Israel before their idols; and I will scatter your bones round about your altars. 6 Wherever

5.6
Ezek 16.47,
48,51;
Jer 11.10;
Zech 7.11
5.7
2 Chr 33.9;
Ezek 16.47
5.8
Ezek 15.7
5.9
Dan 9.12;
Mt 24.21
5.10
Lev 26.29;
Ezek 12.14;
Zech 2.6
5.11
2 Chr 36.14;
Ezek 7.4,9;
8.18
5.12
Jer 43.10,
11;
Ezek 12.14
5.13
Lam 4.11;
Ezek 21.17;
36.6
5.14
Lev 26.31,
32;
Neh 2.17
5.15
Deut 28.37;
1 Ki 9.7;
Jer 24.9;
Ezek 25.17
5.16
Deut 32.23,
24;
Ezek 4.16
5.17
Ezek 14.21;
28.23

6.2
Ezek 36.1
6.3
Ezek 36.4,6
6.4
Lev 26.30
6.5
Jer 8.1,2
6.6
Lev 26.31;
Zech 13.2

o Or *changed my ordinances into wickedness*
p Another reading is *and have not acted*
q Another reading is *I will withdraw*
r Gk Syr Vg Tg: Heb *And it shall be*   *s* Heb *them*

you dwell your cities shall be waste and your high places ruined, so that your altars will be waste and ruined,ᵗ your idols broken and destroyed, your incense altars cut down, and your works wiped out. 7And the slain shall fall in the midst of you, and you shall know that I am the Lord.

2. A remnant to be preserved

8 "Yet I will leave some of you alive. When you have among the nations some who escape the sword, and when you are scattered through the countries, 9 then those of you who escape will remember me among the nations where they are carried captive, when I have brokenᵘ their wanton heart which has departed from me, and blinded their eyes which turn wantonly after their idols; and they will be loathsome in their own sight for the evils which they have committed, for all their abominations. 10And they shall know that I am the Lord; I have not said in vain that I would do this evil to them."

3. Israel to know the Lord by His judgments

11 Thus says the Lord God: "Clap your hands, and stamp your foot, and say, Alas! because of all the evil abominations of the house of Israel; for they shall fall by the sword, by famine, and by pestilence. 12 He that is far off shall die of pestilence; and he that is near shall fall by the sword; and he that is left and is preserved shall die of famine. Thus I will spend my fury upon them. 13And you shall know that I am the Lord, when their slain lie among their idols round about their altars, upon every high hill, on all the mountain tops, under every green tree, and under every leafy oak, wherever they offered pleasing odor to all their idols. 14And I will stretch out my hand against them, and make the land desolate and waste, throughout all their habitations, from the wilderness to Riblah.ᵛ Then they will know that I am the Lord."

D. The oracle of the coming end

1. The disaster in the land

7 The word of the Lord came to me: 2 "And you, O son of man, thus says the Lord God to the land of Israel: An end! The end has come upon the four corners of the land. 3 Now the end is upon you, and I will let loose my anger upon you, and will judge you according to your ways, and I will punish you for all your abominations. 4And my eye will not spare you, nor will I have pity; but I will punish you for your ways, while your abominations are in your midst. Then you will know that I am the Lord.

5 "Thus says the Lord God: Disaster after disaster! Behold, it comes. 6An end has come, the end has come; it has awakened against you. Behold, it comes. 7 Your doomʷ has come to you, O inhabitant of the land; the time has come, the day is near, a day of tumult, and not of joyful shouting upon the mountains. 8 Now I will soon pour out my wrath upon you, and spend my anger against you, and judge you according to your ways; and I will punish you for all your abominations. 9And my eye will not spare, nor will I have pity; I will punish you according to your ways,

6.7 Ezek 11.10, 12
6.8 Jer 44.28; Ezek 5.2, 12; 12.16; 14.22
6.9 Jer 51.50; Ps 78.40; Isa 7.13; Ezek 43.24; 20.7,24; 20.43
6.10 ver 7
6.11 Ezek 21.14; 25.6; 5.12; 7.15
6.12 Dan 9.7; Ezek 5.13
6.13 ver 7; Jer 2.20; Hos 4.13; Isa 57.5
6.14 Isa 5.25; Ezek 14.13; Num 33.46
7.2 Amos 8.2; Ezek 11.13; Rev 7.1; 20.8
7.3 ver 8,9,27
7.4 Ezek 5.11; 8.18;11.21; 6.7
7.5 2 Ki 21.12, 13
7.6 ver 2,10
7.7 ver 12; Isa 22.5
7.8 Ezek 20.8, 21; 6.12; ver 3

ᵗ Syr Vg Tg: Heb and be made guilty   ᵘ Syr Vg Tg: Heb I have been broken
ᵛ Another reading is Diblah   ʷ The meaning of the Hebrew word is uncertain

while your abominations are in your midst. Then you will know that I am the LORD, who smite.

10 "Behold, the day! Behold, it comes! Your doom[w] has come, injustice[x] has blossomed, pride has budded. 11 Violence has grown up into a rod of wickedness; none of them shall remain, nor their abundance, nor their wealth; neither shall there be pre-eminence among them.[y] 12 The time has come, the day draws near. Let not the buyer rejoice, nor the seller mourn, for wrath is upon all their multitude. 13 For the seller shall not return to what he has sold, while they live. For wrath[z] is upon all their multitude; it shall not turn back; and because of his iniquity, none can maintain his life.[a]

2. The desolation of the inhabitants within and without

14 "They have blown the trumpet and made all ready; but none goes to battle, for my wrath is upon all their multitude. 15 The sword is without, pestilence and famine are within; he that is in the field dies by the sword; and him that is in the city famine and pestilence devour. 16And if any survivors escape, they will be on the mountains, like doves of the valleys, all of them moaning, every one over his iniquity. 17All hands are feeble, and all knees weak as water. 18 They gird themselves with sackcloth, and horror covers them; shame is upon all faces, and baldness on all their heads. 19 They cast their silver into the streets, and their gold is like an unclean thing; their silver and gold are not able to deliver them in the day of the wrath of the LORD; they cannot satisfy their hunger or fill their stomachs with it. For it was the stumbling block of their iniquity. 20 Their[b] beautiful ornament they used for vainglory, and they made their abominable images and their detestable things of it; therefore I will make it an unclean thing to them. 21And I will give it into the hands of foreigners for a prey, and to the wicked of the earth for a spoil; and they shall profane it. 22 I will turn my face from them, that they may profane my precious[c] place; robbers shall enter and profane it, 23 and make a desolation.[d]

3. The profanation of the holy places

"Because the land is full of bloody crimes and the city is full of violence, 24 I will bring the worst of the nations to take possession of their houses; I will put an end to their proud might, and their holy places shall be profaned. 25 When anguish comes, they will seek peace, but there shall be none. 26 Disaster comes upon disaster, rumor follows rumor; they seek a vision from the prophet, but the law perishes from the priest, and counsel from the elders. 27 The king mourns, the prince is wrapped in despair, and the hands of the people of the land are palsied by terror. According to their way I will do to them, and according to their own judgments I will judge them; and they shall know that I am the LORD."

E. The vision of abominations in Jerusalem

1. Idolatry in the Temple
a. The background of the vision

8 In the sixth year, in the sixth month, on the fifth day of the month, as I sat in my house, with the elders of Judah sitting

7.10
ver 7;
Isa 10.5
7.11
Jer 6.7;
16.5,6;
Ezek 24.16,
22
7.12
ver 5-7,10;
1 Cor 7.30;
ver 14
7.14
Jer 4.5;
ver 12
7.15
Deut 32.25;
Ezek 5.12
7.16
Ezek 6.8;
14.22;
Isa 38.14;
59.11
7.17
Isa 13.7;
Ezek 21.7;
Heb 12.12
7.18
Isa 15.2,3;
Amos 8.10;
Ezek 27.31
7.19
Isa 30.22;
Prov 11.4;
Zeph 1.18;
Ezek 13.5;
14.3,4
7.20
Jer 7.30
7.21
Ps 74.2-8
7.22
Ezek 39.23,
24
7.23
2 Ki 21.16;
Ezek 9.9;
8.17
7.24
Ezek 21.31;
33.28;
24.21
7.25
Ezek 13.10,
16
7.26
Deut 32.23;
Jer 4.20;
Ezek 21.7;
Ps 74.9;
Ezek 20.1,3
7.27
Ps 35.26;
Ezek 26.16;
ver 3,4,8;
Ezek 18.20
8.1
Ezek 14.1;
20.1;33.31;
1.3; 3.22

w The meaning of the Hebrew word is uncertain   x Or the rod
y The Hebrew of verse 11 is uncertain   z Cn: Heb vision   a Heb obscure
b Syr Symmachus: Heb Its   c Or secret   d Cn: Heb make the chain

before me, the hand of the Lord GOD fell there upon me. 2 Then I beheld, and, lo, a form that had the appearance of a man;*e* below what appeared to be his loins it was fire, and above his loins it was like the appearance of brightness, like gleaming bronze. 3 He put forth the form of a hand, and took me by a lock of my head; and the Spirit lifted me up between earth and heaven, and brought me in visions of God to Jerusalem, to the entrance of the gateway of the inner court that faces north, where was the seat of the image of jealousy, which provokes to jealousy. 4And behold, the glory of the God of Israel was there, like the vision that I saw in the plain.

b. *The image of jealousy*

5 Then he said to me, "Son of man, lift up your eyes now in the direction of the north." So I lifted up my eyes toward the north, and behold, north of the altar gate, in the entrance, was this image of jealousy. 6And he said to me, "Son of man, do you see what they are doing, the great abominations that the house of Israel are committing here, to drive me far from my sanctuary? But you will see still greater abominations."

c. *The worship of idols and pictures*

7 And he brought me to the door of the court; and when I looked, behold, there was a hole in the wall. 8 Then said he to me, "Son of man, dig in the wall"; and when I dug in the wall, lo, there was a door. 9And he said to me, "Go in, and see the vile abominations that they are committing here." 10 So I went in and saw; and there, portrayed upon the wall round about, were all kinds of creeping things, and loathsome beasts, and all the idols of the house of Israel. 11And before them stood seventy men of the elders of the house of Israel, with Jā-ăzănī'ăh the son of Shāphăn standing among them. Each had his censer in his hand, and the smoke of the cloud of incense went up. 12 Then he said to me, "Son of man, have you seen what the elders of the house of Israel are doing in the dark, every man in his room*f* of pictures? For they say, 'The LORD does not see us, the LORD has forsaken the land.'" 13 He said also to me, "You will see still greater abominations which they commit."

d. *The worship of Tammuz*

14 Then he brought me to the entrance of the north gate of the house of the LORD; and behold, there sat women weeping for Tămmŭz. 15 Then he said to me, "Have you seen this, O son of man? You will see still greater abominations than these."

e. *The worship of the sun*

16 And he brought me into the inner court of the house of the LORD; and behold, at the door of the temple of the LORD, between the porch and the altar, were about twenty-five men, with their backs to the temple of the LORD, and their faces toward the east,

e Gk: Heb *fire*   *f* Gk Syr Vg Tg: Heb *rooms*

8.2 Ezek 1.4,27
8.3 Dan 5.5; Ezek 3.12, 14; 11.1; Jer 32.34; Ezek 5.11
8.4 Ezek 1.28
★8.5 Zech 5.5; ver 3
8.6 ver 9,17; Ezek 5.11; 7.22,24; ver 11,14,16
8.10 Ex 20.4; Ezek 14.3
8.11 Jer 19.1; Num 16.17, 35; Ezek 16.18; 23.41
8.12 Ezek 9.9
8.13 Ezek 9.3
★8.14 Ezek 44.4; 46.9
8.16 Ezek 11.1; Jer 2.27; Deut 4.19; Job 31.26; Jer 44.17

8.5 *image of jealousy*, i.e., an image which provokes the LORD to jealousy (cf. Ex 20.5).
8.14 *Tammuz* was a Babylonian vegetation deity who was believed to vanish into the nether world during the dry season when plants withered and streams dried up. Public dirges marked the departure of Tammuz. The women of Jerusalem, taking part in this idolatrous worship, gave evidence of the hold of idolatry in the Holy City.

f. *The call to judgment*

worshiping the sun toward the east. 17 Then he said to me, "Have you seen this, O son of man? Is it too slight a thing for the house of Judah to commit the abominations which they commit here, that they should fill the land with violence, and provoke me further to anger? Lo, they put the branch to their nose. 18 Therefore I will deal in wrath; my eye will not spare, nor will I have pity; and though they cry in my ears with a loud voice, I will not hear them."

2. *The slaughter of the idolaters*
a. *The marking of the innocent*

9 Then he cried in my ears with a loud voice, saying, "Draw near, you executioners of the city, each with his destroying weapon in his hand." 2And lo, six men came from the direction of the upper gate, which faces north, every man with his weapon for slaughter in his hand, and with them was a man clothed in linen, with a writing case at his side. And they went in and stood beside the bronze altar.

3 Now the glory of the God of Israel had gone up from the cherubim on which it rested to the threshold of the house; and he called to the man clothed in linen, who had the writing case at his side. 4And the LORD said to him, "Go through the city, through Jerusalem, and put a mark upon the foreheads of the men who sigh and groan over all the abominations that are committed in

b. *The slaughter of the guilty*

it." 5And to the others he said in my hearing, "Pass through the city after him, and smite; your eye shall not spare, and you shall show no pity; 6 slay old men outright, young men and maidens, little children and women, but touch no one upon whom is the mark. And begin at my sanctuary." So they began with the elders who were before the house. 7 Then he said to them, "Defile the house, and fill the courts with the slain. Go forth." So they went forth, and smote in the city. 8And while they were smiting, and I was left alone, I fell upon my face, and cried, "Ah Lord GOD! wilt thou destroy all that remains of Israel in the outpouring of thy wrath upon Jerusalem?"

9 Then he said to me, "The guilt of the house of Israel and Judah is exceedingly great; the land is full of blood, and the city full of injustice; for they say, 'The LORD has forsaken the land, and the LORD does not see.' 10As for me, my eye will not spare, nor will I have pity, but I will requite their deeds upon their heads."

11 And lo, the man clothed in linen, with the writing case at his side, brought back word, saying, "I have done as thou didst command me."

9.2 *writing case at his side.* It was customary in the East for men to wear the writing case or inkhorn (KJV) in the girdle.

9.3 *the glory of the God of Israel* was the visible manifestation and evidence of God's presence with His people. In vision, Ezekiel saw the Glory leave the Holy of Holies and tarry at the threshold (9.3). Then it hovered over the city and paused on the Mount of Olives (11.23). Slowly, reluctantly, God was leaving His people. After the departure of the Glory of God, the city was defenseless before its enemies.

9.4 *the men who sigh and groan,* i.e., those who disapprove of the city's idolatry. They are marked for safety. All others are to be destroyed.

9.5 *Pass . . . and smite,* i.e., spare neither female nor aged; save only those *upon whom is the mark* (ver 6).

3. *The departure of the* Lord *from the sanctuary*

10 Then I looked, and behold, on the firmament that was over the heads of the cherubim there appeared above them something like a sapphire, in form resembling a throne. 2And he said to the man clothed in linen, "Go in among the whirling wheels underneath the cherubim; fill your hands with burning coals from between the cherubim, and scatter them over the city."

And he went in before my eyes. 3 Now the cherubim were standing on the south side of the house, when the man went in; and a cloud filled the inner court. 4And the glory of the Lord went up from the cherubim to the threshold of the house; and the house was filled with the cloud, and the court was full of the brightness of the glory of the Lord. 5And the sound of the wings of the cherubim was heard as far as the outer court, like the voice of God Almighty when he speaks.

6 And when he commanded the man clothed in linen, "Take fire from between the whirling wheels, from between the cherubim," he went in and stood beside a wheel. 7And a cherub stretched forth his hand from between the cherubim to the fire that was between the cherubim, and took some of it, and put it into the hands of the man clothed in linen, who took it and went out. 8 The cherubim appeared to have the form of a human hand under their wings.

9 And I looked, and behold, there were four wheels beside the cherubim, one beside each cherub; and the appearance of the wheels was like sparkling chrysolite. 10And as for their appearance, the four had the same likeness, as if a wheel were within a wheel. 11 When they went, they went in any of their four directions*g* without turning as they went, but in whatever direction the front wheel faced the others followed without turning as they went. 12And*h* their rims, and their spokes,*i* and the wheels were full of eyes round about—the wheels that the four of them had. 13As for the wheels, they were called in my hearing the whirling wheels. 14And every one had four faces: the first face was the face of the cherub, and the second face was the face of a man, and the third the face of a lion, and the fourth the face of an eagle.

15 And the cherubim mounted up. These were the living creatures that I saw by the river Chēbar. 16And when the cherubim went, the wheels went beside them; and when the cherubim lifted up their wings to mount up from the earth, the wheels did not turn from beside them. 17 When they stood still, these stood still, and when they mounted up, these mounted up with them; for the spirit of the living creatures*j* was in them.

g Heb *on their four sides*   *h* Gk: Heb *And their whole body and*
i Heb *spokes and their wings*   *j* Or *of life*

*10.1
Ezek 1.22, 26;
Rev 4.2
10.2
Ezek 9.2,3;
ver 13;
Isa 6.6;
Rev 8.5
10.3
Ezek 8.3,16
10.4
Ezek 1.28;
9.3;
Ex 40.34,35;
1 Ki 8.10,11
10.5
Ezek 1.24
10.6
ver 2
10.7
Ezek 1.13
10.8
Ezek 1.8
10.9
Ezek 1.15, 16
10.11
Ezek 1.17;
ver 22
10.12
Rev 4.6,8;
Ezek 1.18
10.13
ver 2
10.14
Ezek 1,6,10;
Rev 4.7
10.15
Ezek 1.3,5
10.16
Ezek 1.19
10.17
Ezek 1.12, 20,21

10.1 The Scripture describes the cherubim as winged creatures of great splendor and power in the service of the Lord. In Genesis we are told God placed the cherubim at the east of the Garden of Eden to keep Adam and Eve from the sacred tree (Gen 3.24). Golden figures of two cherubim were on either end of the lid or mercy seat of the ark of the covenant, bowing before the presence of the Lord and touching each other with the tips of their outstretched wings (Ex 25.18–21). Figures of cherubim were also embroidered into the veil or curtain which separated the Holy of Holies from the holy place (Ex 26.31). In The Revelation to John, the cherubim are spoken of as living creatures, four in number, who stand in the midst of and around the throne of God (Rev 4.6, 7). Some hold that the reference in 28.14 to the cherub goes beyond the king of Tyre and speaks of Satan, whose fall may have been described in Isa 14.12–14. (Read also 1.26.)

10.18
ver 4
10.19
11.1,22

10.20
ver 15;
Ezek 1.22;
1.1
10.21
Ezek 1.6,8
10.22
Ezek 1.10,
12

11.1
Ezek 3.12,
14; 8.3;
10.19; 8.16

11.2
Isa 30.1;
Mic 2.1
11.3
Ezek 12.22,
27;
2 Pet 3.4;
Jer 1.13;
Ezek 24.3,6
11.4
Ezek 3.4,17
11.5
Ezek 2.2;
3.24;
Jer 11.20;
Ezek 38.10
11.6
Ezek 7.23;
22.3,4
11.7
Ezek 24.3,
6,10,11;
Mic 3.3;
ver 9
11.9
Ps 106.41;
Ezek 5.8
11.10
2 Ki 25.19–
21;
Jer 52.10;
2 Ki 14.25;
Ezek 6.7
11.11
ver 3
11.12
ver 10;
Ezek 18.8,9;
8.10,14,16
11.13
ver 1;
Ezek 9.8
11.15
Ezek 33.24
11.16
Isa 8.14

18 Then the glory of the LORD went forth from the threshold of the house, and stood over the cherubim. 19And the cherubim lifted up their wings and mounted up from the earth in my sight as they went forth, with the wheels beside them; and they stood at the door of the east gate of the house of the LORD; and the glory of the God of Israel was over them.

20 These were the living creatures that I saw underneath the God of Israel by the river Chēbar; and I knew that they were cherubim. 21 Each had four faces, and each four wings, and underneath their wings the semblance of human hands. 22And as for the likeness of their faces, they were the very faces whose appearance I had seen by the river Chēbar. They went every one straight forward.

4. *The ungodly rulers of the nation to be punished*

11 The Spirit lifted me up, and brought me to the east gate of the house of the LORD, which faces east. And behold, at the door of the gateway there were twenty-five men; and I saw among them Jā-ăzănī'áh the son of Ăzzŭr, and Pĕlătī'áh the son of Bĕnāi'áh, princes of the people. 2And he said to me, "Son of man, these are the men who devise iniquity and who give wicked counsel in this city; 3 who say, 'The time is not near k to build houses; this city is the caldron, and we are the flesh.' 4 Therefore prophesy against them, prophesy, O son of man."

5 And the Spirit of the LORD fell upon me, and he said to me, "Say, Thus says the LORD: So you think, O house of Israel; for I know the things that come into your mind. 6 You have multiplied your slain in this city, and have filled its streets with the slain. 7 Therefore thus says the Lord GOD: Your slain whom you have laid in the midst of it, they are the flesh, and this city is the caldron; but you shall be brought forth out of the midst of it. 8 You have feared the sword; and I will bring the sword upon you, says the Lord GOD. 9And I will bring you forth out of the midst of it, and give you into the hands of foreigners, and execute judgments upon you. 10 You shall fall by the sword; I will judge you at the border of Israel; and you shall know that I am the LORD. 11 This city shall not be your caldron, nor shall you be the flesh in the midst of it; I will judge you at the border of Israel; 12 and you shall know that I am the LORD; for you have not walked in my statutes, nor executed my ordinances, but have acted according to the ordinances of the nations that are round about you."

13 And it came to pass, while I was prophesying, that Pĕlătī'áh the son of Bĕnāi'áh died. Then I fell down upon my face, and cried with a loud voice, and said, "Ah Lord GOD! wilt thou make a full end of the remnant of Israel?"

14 And the word of the LORD came to me: 15 "Son of man, your brethren, even your brethren, your fellow exiles, l the whole house of Israel, all of them, are those of whom the inhabitants of Jerusalem have said, 'They have gone far from the LORD; to us this land is given for a possession.' 16 Therefore say, 'Thus says the Lord GOD: Though I removed them far off among the nations, and though I scattered them among the countries, yet I have been a sanctuary to them for a while m in the countries where they have

---

k Or *Is not the time near . . . ?*
l Gk Syr: Heb *men of your kindred*   m Or *in small measure*

gone.' 17 Therefore say, 'Thus says the Lord GOD: I will gather you from the peoples, and assemble you out of the countries where you have been scattered, and I will give you the land of Israel.' 18And when they come there, they will remove from it all its detestable things and all its abominations. 19And I will give them one*n* heart, and put a new spirit within them; I will take the stony heart out of their flesh and give them a heart of flesh, 20 that they may walk in my statutes and keep my ordinances and obey them; and they shall be my people, and I will be their God. 21 But as for those*o* whose heart goes after their detestable things and their abominations, I will requite their deeds upon their own heads, says the Lord GOD."

5. The glory of the LORD departs from Jerusalem

22 Then the cherubim lifted up their wings, with the wheels beside them; and the glory of the God of Israel was over them. 23And the glory of the LORD went up from the midst of the city, and stood upon the mountain which is on the east side of the city. 24And the Spirit lifted me up and brought me in the vision by the Spirit of God into Chăldē′ȧ, to the exiles. Then the vision that I had seen went up from me. 25And I told the exiles all the things that the LORD had showed me.

F. The reasons for the fall of Jerusalem

1. Unbelief of the people
a. The sign of the exile's baggage

12 The word of the LORD came to me: 2 "Son of man, you dwell in the midst of a rebellious house, who have eyes to see, but see not, who have ears to hear, but hear not; 3 for they are a rebellious house. Therefore, son of man, prepare for yourself an exile's baggage, and go into exile by day in their sight; you shall go like an exile from your place to another place in their sight. Perhaps they will understand, though*p* they are a rebellious house. 4 You shall bring out your baggage by day in their sight, as baggage for exile; and you shall go forth yourself at evening in their sight, as men do who must go into exile. 5 Dig through the wall in their sight, and go*q* out through it. 6 In their sight you shall lift the baggage upon your shoulder, and carry it out in the dark; you shall cover your face, that you may not see the land; for I have made you a sign for the house of Israel."

7 And I did as I was commanded. I brought out my baggage by day, as baggage for exile, and in the evening I dug through the wall with my own hands; I went forth in the dark, carrying my outfit upon my shoulder in their sight.

8 In the morning the word of the LORD came to me: 9 "Son of man, has not the house of Israel, the rebellious house, said to you, 'What are you doing?' 10 Say to them, 'Thus says the Lord GOD: This oracle concerns the prince in Jerusalem and all the house

11.17 Jer 24.5; Ezek 28.25; 34.13
11.18 Ezek 37.23; 5.11
11.19 Jer 32.39; Ezek 36.26, 27; 18.31; Zech 7.12; 2 Cor 3.3
11.20 Ps 105.45; Ezek 14.11
11.21 Ezek 9.10
11.22 Ezek 1.19; 10.19
11.23 Ezek 8.4; 9.3; Zech 14.4
11.24 Ezek 8.3; 1.1,3
11.25 Ezek 2.7
12.2 Ezek 2.6-8; Jer 5.21; Mt 13.13,14
12.3 Jer 26.3; 36.3,7; 2 Tim 2.25
12.4 Jer 39.4; ver 12
12.6 ver 12,13; Isa 8.18; Ezek 4.3; 24.24
12.7 Ezek 24.18; ver 3-6
12.9 Ezek 2.5; 17.12; 24.19
*12.10 Mal 1.1

n Another reading is *a new*
o Cn: Heb *To the heart of their detestable things and their abominations their heart goes*
p Or *will see that*   *q* Gk Syr Vg Tg: Heb *bring*

12.10 *the prince in Jerusalem,* i.e., Zedekiah who was to be blinded before being taken as a prisoner to Babylon. (See Jer 52.11: *He put out the eyes of Zedekiah.*)

12.11
ver 6;
2 Ki 25.4–7
12.12
Jer 39.4

12.13
Isa 24.17,
18;
Hos 7.12;
Jer 52.11;
Ezek 17.16
12.14
2 Ki 25.4,5;
Ezek 5.2,12
12.15
Ezek 6.7,14
12.16
Ezek 6.8–
10;
14.22;
Jer 22.8,9

12.18
Ezek 4.16

12.19
Ezek 4.16;
23.33;
Zech 7.14

12.20
Ezek 5.14;
36.3

12.22
Ezek 16.44;
11.3;
ver 27;
Amos 6.3;
2 Pet 3.4
12.23
Joel 2.1;
Zeph 1.14
12.24
Ezek 13.23;
Zech 13.2–4
12.25
ver 28;
Isa 55.11;
Dan 9.12;
Hab 1.5;
ver 2
12.27
ver 22;
Dan 10.14;
2 Pet 3.4
12.28
ver 25;
Mt 24.48–
50

13.2
Jer 37.19;
ver 17;
Jer 14.14;
23.16,26;
Amos 7.16
13.3
Lam 2.14;
Jer 23.28–32

of Israel who are in it.*r* 11 Say, 'I am a sign for you: as I have done, so shall it be done to them; they shall go into exile, into captivity.' 12And the prince who is among them shall lift his baggage upon his shoulder in the dark, and shall go forth; he*s* shall dig through the wall and go*t* out through it; he shall cover his face, that he may not see the land with his eyes. 13And I will spread my net over him, and he shall be taken in my snare; and I will bring him to Babylon in the land of the Chăldē´ăns, yet he shall not see it; and he shall die there. 14And I will scatter toward every wind all who are round about him, his helpers*u* and all his troops; and I will unsheathe the sword after them. 15And they shall know that I am the LORD, when I disperse them among the nations and scatter them through the countries. 16 But I will let a few of them escape from the sword, from famine and pestilence, that they may confess all their abominations among the nations where they go, and may know that I am the LORD."

b. The sign of eating and drinking with quaking

17 Moreover the word of the LORD came to me: 18 "Son of man, eat your bread with quaking, and drink water with trembling and with fearfulness; 19 and say of the people of the land, Thus says the Lord GOD concerning the inhabitants of Jerusalem in the land of Israel: They shall eat their bread with fearfulness, and drink water in dismay, because their land will be stripped of all it contains, on account of the violence of all those who dwell in it. 20And the inhabited cities shall be laid waste, and the land shall become a desolation; and you shall know that I am the LORD."

c. The word of the LORD to the house of Israel

21 And the word of the LORD came to me: 22 "Son of man, what is this proverb that you have about the land of Israel, saying, 'The days grow long, and every vision comes to nought'? 23 Tell them therefore, 'Thus says the Lord GOD: I will put an end to this proverb, and they shall no more use it as a proverb in Israel.' But say to them, The days are at hand, and the fulfilment*v* of every vision. 24 For there shall be no more any false vision or flattering divination within the house of Israel. 25 But I the LORD will speak the word which I will speak, and it will be performed. It will no longer be delayed, but in your days, O rebellious house, I will speak the word and perform it, says the Lord GOD."

26 Again the word of the LORD came to me: 27 "Son of man, behold, they of the house of Israel say, 'The vision that he sees is for many days hence, and he prophesies of times far off.' 28 Therefore say to them, Thus says the Lord GOD: None of my words will be delayed any longer, but the word which I speak will be performed, says the Lord GOD."

2. Heeding false prophets and prophetesses
a. The prophecy against the false prophets

13 The word of the LORD came to me: 2 "Son of man, prophesy against the prophets of Israel, prophesy*w* and say to those who prophesy out of their own minds: 'Hear the word of the LORD!' 3 Thus says the Lord GOD, Woe to the foolish prophets

who follow their own spirit, and have seen nothing! 4 Your prophets have been like foxes among ruins, O Israel. 5 You have not gone
up into the breaches, or built up a wall for the house of Israel, that
it might stand in battle in the day of the LORD. 6 They have
spoken falsehood and divined a lie; they say, 'Says the LORD,'
when the LORD has not sent them, and yet they expect him to
fulfil their word. 7 Have you not seen a delusive vision, and uttered
a lying divination, whenever you have said, 'Says the LORD,'
although I have not spoken?"

8 Therefore thus says the Lord GOD: "Because you have uttered delusions and seen lies, therefore behold, I am against you,
says the Lord GOD. 9 My hand will be against the prophets who
see delusive visions and who give lying divinations; they shall not
be in the council of my people, nor be enrolled in the register of
the house of Israel, nor shall they enter the land of Israel; and you
shall know that I am the Lord GOD. 10 Because, yea, because they
have misled my people, saying, 'Peace,' when there is no peace;
and because, when the people build a wall, these prophets daub
it with whitewash; 11 say to those who daub it with whitewash that
it shall fall! There will be a deluge of rain,ˣ great hailstones will
fall, and a stormy wind break out; 12 and when the wall falls, will
it not be said to you, 'Where is the daubing with which you daubed
it?' 13 Therefore thus says the Lord GOD: I will make a stormy
wind break out in my wrath; and there shall be a deluge of rain
in my anger, and great hailstones in wrath to destroy it. 14And I
will break down the wall that you have daubed with whitewash,
and bring it down to the ground, so that its foundation will be laid
bare; when it falls, you shall perish in the midst of it; and you shall
know that I am the LORD. 15 Thus will I spend my wrath upon
the wall, and upon those who have daubed it with whitewash; and
I will say to you, The wall is no more, nor those who daubed it,
16 the prophets of Israel who prophesied concerning Jerusalem and
saw visions of peace for her, when there was no peace, says the
Lord GOD.

b. The prophecy against the false prophetesses

17 "And you, son of man, set your face against the daughters of
your people, who prophesy out of their own minds; prophesy
against them 18 and say, Thus says the Lord GOD: Woe to the
women who sew magic bands upon all wrists, and make veils for
the heads of persons of every stature, in the hunt for souls! Will
you hunt down souls belonging to my people, and keep other souls
alive for your profit? 19 You have profaned me among my people
for handfuls of barley and for pieces of bread, putting to death
persons who should not die and keeping alive persons who should
not live, by your lies to my people, who listen to lies.

20 "Wherefore thus says the Lord GOD: Behold, I am against
your magic bands with which you hunt the souls,ʸ and I will tear
them from your arms; and I will let the souls that you hunt go
freeᶻ like birds. 21 Your veils also I will tear off, and deliver my
people out of your hand, and they shall be no more in your hand
as prey; and you shall know that I am the LORD. 22 Because you
have disheartened the righteous falsely, although I have not disheartened him, and you have encouraged the wicked, that he

13.5 Ps 106.23, 30; Ezek 22.30; Isa 58.12; Ezek 7.19
13.6 ver 22; Ezek 22.28; Jer 28.15
13.7 Ezek 22.28
13.8 Ezek 21.29; 5.8
13.9 Ezra 2.59, 62; Neh 7.5; Ps 69.28; Ezek 11.10, 12
13.10 Jer 50.6; 8.11; ver 16; Ezek 22.28
13.11 Ezek 38.22
13.13 ver 11; Isa 30.30; Rev 11.19; 16.21
13.14 Mic 1.6; ver 9; Ezek 14.8
13.16 Ezek 6.14; Isa 57.21
13.17 Ezek 20.46; 21.2; ver 2
13.18 Ezek 22.25; 2 Pet 2.14
13.19 Ezek 20.39; Prov 28.21; Mic 3.5; Jer 23.14,17
13.20 ver 17
13.21 Ps 124.7; ver 9
13.22 Amos 5.12; Jer 23.14; Ezek 33.14–16

ˣ Heb *rain and you*   ʸ Gk Syr: Heb *souls for birds*   ᶻ Cn: Heb *the souls*

13.23
ver 6;
Ezek 12.24;
Mic 3.6;
ver 9;
Ezek 14.8

should not turn from his wicked way to save his life; 23 therefore you shall no more see delusive visions nor practice divination; I will deliver my people out of your hand. Then you will know that I am the LORD."

3. *The idolatry of the elders*
a. *Hypocrisy rebuked*

14.1
Ezek 8.1;
20.1; 33.31
14.3
Ezek 20.16;
7.19;
Jer 11.11;
Ezek 20.3,
31
14.4
ver 7

14 Then came certain of the elders of Israel to me, and sat before me. 2And the word of the LORD came to me: 3 "Son of man, these men have taken their idols into their hearts, and set the stumbling block of their iniquity before their faces; should I let myself be inquired of at all by them? 4 Therefore speak to them, and say to them, Thus says the Lord GOD: Any man of the house of Israel who takes his idols into his heart and sets the stumbling block of his iniquity before his face, and yet comes to the prophet, I the LORD will answer him myself*a* because of the multitude of his idols, 5 that I may lay hold of the hearts of the house of Israel, who are all estranged from me through their idols.

14.5
Isa 1.4;
Jer 2.11;
Zech 11.8

b. *Repentance urged*

14.6
Isa 2.20;
30.22;
Ezek 18.30;
8.6
14.7
Ex 12.48;
20.10;
ver 4

6 "Therefore say to the house of Israel, Thus says the Lord GOD: Repent and turn away from your idols; and turn away your faces from all your abominations. 7 For any one of the house of Israel, or of the strangers that sojourn in Israel, who separates himself from me, taking his idols into his heart and putting the stumbling block of his iniquity before his face, and yet comes to a prophet to inquire for himself of me, I the LORD will answer him myself; 8 and I will set my face against that man, I will make him a sign and a byword and cut him off from the midst of my people; and you shall know that I am the LORD. 9And if the prophet be deceived and speak a word, I, the LORD, have deceived that prophet, and I will stretch out my hand against him, and will destroy him from the midst of my people Israel. 10And they shall bear their punishment—the punishment of the prophet and the punishment of the inquirer shall be alike—11 that the house of Israel may go no more astray from me, nor defile themselves any more with all their transgressions, but that they may be my people and I may be their God, says the Lord GOD."

14.8
Jer 44.11;
Ezek 15.7;
Isa 65.15;
Ezek 5.15;
6.7
14.9
1 Ki 22.23;
Job 12.16;
Jer 4.10;
2 Thess
2.11;
Jer 14.15
14.11
Ezek 44.10,
15; 11.20;
37.27

c. *The presence of some righteous cannot effect the deliverance of the wicked*

14.13
Ezek 15.8;
6.14; 5.16;
ver 17,19,21
*14.14
Jer 15.1;
Gen 6.8;
Dan 1.6;
Job 1.1,5;
ver 16,18,20
14.15
Ezek 5.17

12 And the word of the LORD came to me: 13 "Son of man, when a land sins against me by acting faithlessly, and I stretch out my hand against it, and break its staff of bread and send famine upon it, and cut off from it man and beast, 14 even if these three men, Noah, Daniel, and Jōb, were in it, they would deliver but their own lives by their righteousness, says the Lord GOD. 15 If I cause wild beasts to pass through the land, and they ravage it, and it be made desolate, so that no man may pass through because of the

a Cn Compare Tg: Heb uncertain

14.14 So certain was the fall of Jerusalem as predicted here that not even intercession on the part of Israel's holiest saints would forestall it. The best that Noah, Daniel, and Job could do with their godly petitions would be to save themselves but no one else among their countrymen, so awful was the apostasy of Ezekiel's generation.

beasts; 16 even if these three men were in it, as I live, says the Lord GOD, they would deliver neither sons nor daughters; they alone would be delivered, but the land would be desolate. 17 Or if I bring a sword upon that land, and say, Let a sword go through the land; and I cut off from it man and beast; 18 though these three men were in it, as I live, says the Lord GOD, they would deliver neither sons nor daughters, but they alone would be delivered. 19 Or if I send a pestilence into that land, and pour out my wrath upon it with blood, to cut off from it man and beast; 20 even if Noah, Daniel, and Jōb were in it, as I live, says the Lord GOD, they would deliver neither son nor daughter; they would deliver but their own lives by their righteousness.

21 "For thus says the Lord GOD: How much more when I send upon Jerusalem my four sore acts of judgment, sword, famine, evil beasts, and pestilence, to cut off from it man and beast! 22 Yet, if there should be left in it any survivors to lead out sons and daughters, when they come forth to you, and you see their ways and their doings, you will be consoled for the evil that I have brought upon Jerusalem, for all that I have brought upon it. 23 They will console you, when you see their ways and their doings; and you shall know that I have not done without cause all that I have done in it, says the Lord GOD."

	14.16 ver 14,18,20; Ezek 18.20
	14.17 Ezek 5.12; 21.3,4; 25.13; Zeph 1.3
	14.18 ver 14
	14.19 ver 21; Ezek 38.22; 7.8
	14.20 ver 14
	14.21 Ezek 5.17; Jer 15.2,3; Rev 6.8
	14.22 Ezek 12.16; 7.16;20.43; 16.54
	14.23 Jer 22.8,9

G. The punishment both certain and necessary

1. The example of the vine

15 And the word of the LORD came to me: 2 "Son of man, how does the wood of the vine surpass any wood, the vine branch which is among the trees of the forest? 3 Is wood taken from it to make anything? Do men take a peg from it to hang any vessel on? 4 Lo, it is given to the fire for fuel; when the fire has consumed both ends of it, and the middle of it is charred, is it useful for anything? 5 Behold, when it was whole, it was used for nothing; how much less, when the fire has consumed it and it is charred, can it ever be used for anything! 6 Therefore thus says the Lord GOD: Like the wood of the vine among the trees of the forest, which I have given to the fire for fuel, so will I give up the inhabitants of Jerusalem. 7 And I will set my face against them; though they escape from the fire, the fire shall yet consume them; and you will know that I am the LORD, when I set my face against them. 8 And I will make the land desolate, because they have acted faithlessly, says the Lord GOD."

	15.2 Isa 5.1–7; Jer 2.21; Hos 10.1
	15.4 ver 6; Ezek 19.14; Jn 15.6
	15.6 ver 2; Ezek 17.3–10
	15.7 Lev 17.10; Ezek 14.8; Isa 24.18; 7.4;14.8
	15.8 Ezek 14.13

2. The example of the unfaithful wife
a. The foundling child, Israel

16 Again the word of the LORD came to me: 2 "Son of man, make known to Jerusalem her abominations, 3 and say, Thus says the Lord GOD to Jerusalem: Your origin and your birth are of the land of the Cā′naȧnītes; your father was an Ăm′ȯrīte, and your mother a Hĭttīte. 4 And as for your birth, on the day you were born your navel string was not cut, nor were you washed with water to

	16.2 Ezek 20.4; 22.2; 8.9–17
	*16.3 Ezek 21.30; ver 45
	16.4 Hos 2.3

16.3 of the land of the Canaanites. Ezekiel stresses the non-Israelite origin of Jerusalem. Amorites, Hittites, and Canaanites left their mark upon later Israelite history.

16.5
Deut 32.10

16.6
ver 22;
Ex 19.4
16.7
Ex 1.7;
ver 22

16.8
Ruth 3.9;
Gen 22.16–
18;
Ex 24.7,8;
19.5;
Jer 2.2
16.10
ver 13

16.11
Ezek 23.40;
Gen 24.22,
47;
Prov 1.9
16.13
Deut 32.13,
14;
1 Sam 10.1

16.14
Ps 50.2;
Lam 2.15

16.15
Isa 57.8;
Jer 2.20;
Ezek 23.3,
8,11,12
16.16
ver 10;
Ezek 6.3,6;
Hos 2.8
16.17
Ezek 7.20
16.18
ver 10
16.19
Hos 2.8
16.20
2 Ki 16.3;
Isa 57.5
16.21
2 Ki 17.17;
Jer 19.5
16.22
Hos 11.1;
ver 4–6
16.24
Isa 57.5,7;
Jer 2.20;3.2
16.25
Prov 9.14;
ver 15
16.26
Ezek 8.17;
20.7,8;
23.19–21

cleanse you, nor rubbed with salt, nor swathed with bands. 5 No eye pitied you, to do any of these things to you out of compassion for you; but you were cast out on the open field, for you were abhorred, on the day that you were born.

6 "And when I passed by you, and saw you weltering in your blood, I said to you in your blood, 'Live, 7 and grow up[b] like a plant of the field.' And you grew up and became tall and arrived at full maidenhood;[c] your breasts were formed, and your hair had grown; yet you were naked and bare.

b. *Its rescue by God*

8 "When I passed by you again and looked upon you, behold, you were at the age for love; and I spread my skirt over you, and covered your nakedness: yea, I plighted my troth to you and entered into a covenant with you, says the Lord GOD, and you became mine. 9 Then I bathed you with water and washed off your blood from you, and anointed you with oil. 10 I clothed you also with embroidered cloth and shod you with leather, I swathed you in fine linen and covered you with silk. 11 And I decked you with ornaments, and put bracelets on your arms, and a chain on your neck. 12 And I put a ring on your nose, and earrings in your ears, and a beautiful crown upon your head. 13 Thus you were decked with gold and silver; and your raiment was of fine linen, and silk, and embroidered cloth; you ate fine flour and honey and oil. You grew exceedingly beautiful, and came to regal estate. 14 And your renown went forth among the nations because of your beauty, for it was perfect through the splendor which I had bestowed upon you, says the Lord GOD.

c. *The harlotry of the rescued foundling*

15 "But you trusted in your beauty, and played the harlot because of your renown, and lavished your harlotries on any passerby. 16 You took some of your garments, and made for yourself gaily decked shrines, and on them played the harlot; the like has never been, nor ever shall be. 17 You also took your fair jewels of my gold and of my silver, which I had given you, and made for yourself images of men, and with them played the harlot; 18 and you took your embroidered garments to cover them, and set my oil and my incense before them. 19 Also my bread which I gave you—I fed you with fine flour and oil and honey—you set before them for a pleasing odor, says the Lord GOD.[d] 20 And you took your sons and your daughters, whom you had borne to me, and these you sacrificed to them to be devoured. Were your harlotries so small a matter 21 that you slaughtered my children and delivered them up as an offering by fire to them? 22 And in all your abominations and your harlotries you did not remember the days of your youth, when you were naked and bare, weltering in your blood.

23 "And after all your wickedness (woe, woe to you! says the Lord GOD), 24 you built yourself a vaulted chamber, and made yourself a lofty place in every square; 25 at the head of every street you built your lofty place and prostituted your beauty, offering yourself to any passer-by, and multiplying your harlotry. 26 You

---

b Gk Syr: Heb *I made you a myriad*
c Cn: Heb *ornament of ornaments*
d Syr: Heb *and it was, says the Lord* GOD

also played the harlot with the Egyptians, your lustful neighbors, multiplying your harlotry, to provoke me to anger. 27 Behold, therefore, I stretched out my hand against you, and diminished your allotted portion, and delivered you to the greed of your enemies, the daughters of the Phĭlĭs′tĭneṣ, who were ashamed of your lewd behavior. 28 You played the harlot also with the Assyrians, because you were insatiable; yea, you played the harlot with them, and still you were not satisfied. 29 You multiplied your harlotry also with the trading land of Chăldē′ȧ; and even with this you were not satisfied.

30 "How lovesick is your heart, says the Lord GOD, seeing you did all these things, the deeds of a brazen harlot; 31 building your vaulted chamber at the head of every street, and making your lofty place in every square. Yet you were not like a harlot, because you scorned hire. 32 Adulterous wife, who receives strangers instead of her husband! 33 Men give gifts to all harlots; but you gave your gifts to all your lovers, bribing them to come to you from every side for your harlotries. 34 So you were different from other women in your harlotries: none solicited you to play the harlot; and you gave hire, while no hire was given to you; therefore you were different.

d. The promised punishment for harlotry

35 "Wherefore, O harlot, hear the word of the LORD: 36 Thus says the Lord GOD, Because your shame was laid bare and your nakedness uncovered in your harlotries with your lovers, and because of all your idols, and because of the blood of your children that you gave to them, 37 therefore, behold, I will gather all your lovers, with whom you took pleasure, all those you loved and all those you loathed; I will gather them against you from every side, and will uncover your nakedness to them, that they may see all your nakedness. 38 And I will judge you as women who break wedlock and shed blood are judged, and bring upon you the blood of wrath and jealousy. 39 And I will give you into the hand of your lovers, and they shall throw down your vaulted chamber and break down your lofty places; they shall strip you of your clothes and take your fair jewels, and leave you naked and bare. 40 They shall bring up a host against you, and they shall stone you and cut you to pieces with their swords. 41 And they shall burn your houses and execute judgments upon you in the sight of many women; I will make you stop playing the harlot, and you shall also give hire no more. 42 So will I satisfy my fury on you, and my jealousy shall depart from you; I will be calm, and will no more be angry. 43 Because you have not remembered the days of your youth, but have enraged me with all these things; therefore, behold, I will requite your deeds upon your head, says the Lord GOD.

e. The sin worse than that of Sodom and Samaria

"Have you not committed lewdness in addition to all your abominations? 44 Behold, every one who uses proverbs will use this proverb about you, 'Like mother, like daughter.' 45 You are the daughter of your mother, who loathed her husband and her children; and you are the sister of your sisters, who loathed their husbands and their children. Your mother was a Hĭt′tīte and your father an Ăm′ŏrīte. 46 And your elder sister is Sȧmắr′ĭȧ, who lived

16.27 Ezek 14.13; 20.33,34; 2 Chr 28.18,19

16.28 2 Ki 16.7,10; 2 Chr 28.23

16.29 Ezek 23.14–17

16.30 Jer 3.3

16.31 ver 24; Isa 52.3

16.33 Isa 30.6; Hos 8.9,10

16.36 ver 15; Ezek 23.10,18,29; Jer 19.5

16.37 Jer 13.22,26; Hos 2.10; Nah 3.5; Isa 47.3

16.38 Lev 20.10; Ezek 23.45; Jer 18.21

16.39 Ezek 21.31; ver 24,31; Ezek 23.26

16.40 Ezek 23.46,47; Jn 8.5,7

16.41 Deut 13.16; 2 Ki 25.9; Jer 52.13; Ezek 23.10,27

16.42 Ezek 5.13; Isa 54.9,10; Ezek 39.29

16.43 Ps 78.42; ver 22; Ezek 6.9; 11.21; 22.31

16.44 Ezek 12.22,23

16.46 Gen 13.11–13; Isa 1.10

with her daughters to the north of you; and your younger sister, who lived to the south of you, is Sŏdŏm with her daughters. ⁴⁷ Yet you were not content to walk in their ways, or do according to their abominations; within a very little time you were more corrupt than they in all your ways. ⁴⁸As I live, says the Lord God, your sister Sŏdŏm and her daughters have not done as you and your daughters have done. ⁴⁹ Behold, this was the guilt of your sister Sŏdŏm: she and her daughters had pride, surfeit of food, and prosperous ease, but did not aid the poor and needy. ⁵⁰ They were haughty, and did abominable things before me; therefore I removed them, when I saw it. ⁵¹ Sâmạr′iä has not committed half your sins; you have committed more abominations than they, and have made your sisters appear righteous by all the abominations which you have committed. ⁵² Bear your disgrace, you also, for you have made judgment favorable to your sisters; because of your sins in which you acted more abominably than they, they are more in the right than you. So be ashamed, you also, and bear your disgrace, for you have made your sisters appear righteous.

f. The promise of restoration

53 "I will restore their fortunes, both the fortunes of Sŏdŏm and her daughters, and the fortunes of Sâmạr′iä and her daughters, and I will restore your own fortunes in the midst of them, ⁵⁴ that you may bear your disgrace and be ashamed of all that you have done, becoming a consolation to them. ⁵⁵As for your sisters, Sŏdŏm and her daughters shall return to their former estate, and Sâmạr′iä and her daughters shall return to their former estate; and you and your daughters shall return to your former estate. ⁵⁶ Was not your sister Sŏdŏm a byword in your mouth in the day of your pride, ⁵⁷ before your wickedness was uncovered? Now you have become like her ᵉ an object of reproach for the daughters of Ēdŏm ᶠ and all her neighbors, and for the daughters of the Phĭlĭs′tĭneṣ, those round about who despise you. ⁵⁸ You bear the penalty of your lewdness and your abominations, says the Lord.

59 "Yea, thus says the Lord God: I will deal with you as you have done, who have despised the oath in breaking the covenant, ⁶⁰ yet I will remember my covenant with you in the days of your youth, and I will establish with you an everlasting covenant. ⁶¹ Then you will remember your ways, and be ashamed when I ᵍ take your sisters, both your elder and your younger, and give them to you as daughters, but not on account of the covenant with you. ⁶² I will establish my covenant with you, and you shall know that I am the Lord, ⁶³ that you may remember and be confounded, and never open your mouth again because of your shame, when I forgive you all that you have done, says the Lord God."

ᵉ Cn: Heb uncertain
ᶠ Another reading is *Arâm*   ᵍ Syr: Heb *you*

16.47
2 Ki 21.9;
Ezek 5.6,7

★16.48
Mt 10.15;
11.24

16.49
Isa 3.9;
Gen 13.10;
Lk 12.16–
20;
Ezek 18.7,
12,16

16.50
Ezek 7.10

16.51
Ezek 5.6;
Jer 3.11;
Mt 12.41,42

16.52
ver 54,61,
47,48,51

16.53
ver 60,61;
Isa 19.24,25

16.54
Ezek 14.22,
23

16.55
ver 53;
Ezek 36.11;
Mal 3.4

16.57
2 Ki 16.5;
2 Chr 28.18;
Ezek 5.14

16.58
Ezek 23.49

16.59
Ezek 17.13;
Deut 29.12

★16.60
Jer 2.2;
Hos 2.15;
Jer 32.40;
Ezek 37.26

16.61
Ezek 20.43;
Isa 54.1;
60.4;
Jer 31.31

16.62
Ezek 20.37;
Hos 2.19,
20;
Ezek 20.43,
44

16.63
ver 61;
Rom 3.19

16.48 *Sodom and her daughters have not done.* If God destroyed Sodom because of its awful sins, there is no reason why Israel, whose sins are greater, should be spared.

16.60 Here we see unfolded the amazing grace of a faithful and patient God. He chose Israel and made her great, only to have her rebel against Him. Justice demanded severest punishment, but God's grace and loving-kindness, nevertheless, promised for Israel a future restoration with all the blessings of an enduring covenant. The Scripture seems to teach that His dispersed people will some day be regathered to their ancestral land.

3. *The two eagles and the cedar*
a. *The allegory presented*

17 The word of the LORD came to me: 2 "Son of man, propound a riddle, and speak an allegory to the house of Israel; 3 say, Thus says the Lord GOD: A great eagle with great wings and long pinions, rich in plumage of many colors, came to Lebanon and took the top of the cedar; 4 he broke off the topmost of its young twigs and carried it to a land of trade, and set it in a city of merchants. 5 Then he took of the seed of the land and planted it in fertile soil; he placed it beside abundant waters. He set it like a willow twig, 6 and it sprouted and became a low spreading vine, and its branches turned toward him, and its roots remained where it stood. So it became a vine, and brought forth branches and put forth foliage.

b. *The allegory interpreted*

7 "But there was another great eagle with great wings and much plumage; and behold, this vine bent its roots toward him, and shot forth its branches toward him that he might water it. From the bed where it was planted 8 he transplanted it*h* to good soil by abundant waters, that it might bring forth branches, and bear fruit, and become a noble vine. 9 Say, Thus says the Lord GOD: Will it thrive? Will he not pull up its roots and cut off its branches,*i* so that all its fresh sprouting leaves wither? It will not take a strong arm or many people to pull it from its roots. 10 Behold, when it is transplanted, will it thrive? Will it not utterly wither when the east wind strikes it—wither away on the bed where it grew?"

11 Then the word of the LORD came to me: 12 "Say now to the rebellious house, Do you not know what these things mean? Tell them, Behold, the king of Babylon came to Jerusalem, and took her king and her princes and brought them to him to Babylon. 13And he took one of the seed royal and made a covenant with him, putting him under oath. (The chief men of the land he had taken away, 14 that the kingdom might be humble and not lift itself up, and that by keeping his covenant it might stand.) 15 But he rebelled against him by sending ambassadors to Egypt, that they might give him horses and a large army. Will he succeed? Can a man escape who does such things? Can he break the covenant and yet escape? 16As I live, says the Lord GOD, surely in the place where the king dwells who made him king, whose oath he despised, and whose covenant with him he broke, in Babylon he shall die. 17 Pharaoh with his mighty army and great company will not help him in war, when mounds are cast up and siege walls built to cut off many lives. 18 Because he despised the oath and broke the covenant, because he gave his hand and yet did all these things, he shall not escape. 19 Therefore thus says the Lord GOD: As I live, surely my oath which he despised, and my covenant which he broke, I will requite upon his head. 20 I will spread my net over him, and he shall be taken in my snare, and I will bring him to Babylon and enter into judgment with him there for the treason he has committed against me. 21And all the pick*j* of his troops shall fall by the sword, and the survivors shall be scattered to every wind; and you shall know that I, the LORD, have spoken."

---

h Cn: Heb *it was transplanted*
i Cn: Heb *fruit*   *j* Another reading is *fugitives*

Marginal references:

17.2 Ezek 20.49; 24.3
17.3 Jer 22.23
17.5 Deut 8.7–9; Isa 44.4
17.6 ver 14
17.7 ver 15
17.8 ver 5
17.9 ver 10,15–21
17.10 ver 15; Ezek 19.14; Hos 13.15
17.12 Ezek 2.5; 12.9; ver 3; 2 Ki 24.11–16
17.13 2 Ki 24.15–17; 2 Chr 36.13
17.14 ver 6; Ezek 29.14
17.15 2 Ki 24.20; 2 Chr 36.13
17.16 ver 13,18,19; Jer 52.11; Ezek 12.13
17.17 Jer 37.7; Ezek 29.6,7; 4.2
17.18 Lam 5.6
17.19 Ezek 16.59
17.20 Ezek 12.13; 32.3; 20.36
17.21 2 Ki 25.5, 11; Ezek 12.14; 6.7,10

c. The goodly cedar a type of Messiah

17.22
Isa 11.1;
Jer 23.5;
Zech 3.8;
Ezek 36.36;
20.40
17.23
Isa 2.2,3;
Ezek 20.40;
Hos 14.5–7;
Mt 13.31,32
17.24
Ps 96.12;
Ezek 21.26;
19.12;
22.14;
24.14

22 Thus says the Lord GOD: "I myself will take a sprig from the lofty top of the cedar, and will set it out; I will break off from the topmost of its young twigs a tender one, and I myself will plant it upon a high and lofty mountain; 23 on the mountain height of Israel will I plant it, that it may bring forth boughs and bear fruit, and become a noble cedar; and under it will dwell all kinds of beasts;*k* in the shade of its branches birds of every sort will nest. 24And all the trees of the field shall know that I the LORD bring low the high tree, and make high the low tree, dry up the green tree, and make the dry tree flourish. I the LORD have spoken, and I will do it."

H. The justice of a righteous God

1. The soul that sins shall die

18.2
Jer 31.29;
Lam 5.7

18 The word of the LORD came to me again: 2 "What do you mean by repeating this proverb concerning the land of Israel, 'The fathers have eaten sour grapes, and the children's teeth are set on edge'? 3As I live, says the Lord GOD, this proverb shall no more be used by you in Israel. 4 Behold, all souls are mine; the soul of the father as well as the soul of the son is mine: the soul that sins shall die.

18.3
ver 11,20,30
18.4
Isa 42.5;
ver 20;
Rom 6.23

2. The righteous man shall live

18.6
Ezek 22.9;
ver 12,15;
Lev 18.19;
20.18;
Ezek 22.10
18.7
Ex 22.21;
Lev 19.15;
Deut 24.12,
13;
Lev 19.13
18.8
Ex 22.25;
Lev 25.36,
37;
Deut 23.19;
1.16;
Zech 8.16

5 "If a man is righteous and does what is lawful and right—6 if he does not eat upon the mountains or lift up his eyes to the idols of the house of Israel, does not defile his neighbor's wife or approach a woman in her time of impurity, 7 does not oppress any one, but restores to the debtor his pledge, commits no robbery, gives his bread to the hungry and covers the naked with a garment, 8 does not lend at interest or take any increase, withholds his hand from iniquity, executes true justice between man and man, 9 walks in my statutes, and is careful to observe my ordinances*l*—he is righteous, he shall surely live, says the Lord GOD.

3. The wicked son of a righteous man shall die

18.9
Ezek 20.11;
Amos 5.4
18.10
Ex 21.12;
Num 35.31
18.11
ver 6,15
18.12
Amos 4.1;
Isa 59.6,7;
Ezek 8.6,17

10 "If he begets a son who is a robber, a shedder of blood,*m* 11 who does none of these duties, but eats upon the mountains, defiles his neighbor's wife, 12 oppresses the poor and needy, commits robbery, does not restore the pledge, lifts up his eyes to the idols, commits abomination, 13 lends at interest, and takes increase; shall he then live? He shall not live. He has done all these abominable things; he shall surely die; his blood shall be upon himself.

4. The righteous son of a wicked man shall live

18.13
ver 8,17;
Ezek 33.4,5
18.14
Prov 23.24
18.15
ver 6,11,12
18.16
Ps 41.1

14 "But if this man begets a son who sees all the sins which his father has done, and fears, and does not do likewise, 15 who does not eat upon the mountains or lift up his eyes to the idols of the house of Israel, does not defile his neighbor's wife, 16 does not wrong any one, exacts no pledge, commits no robbery, but gives his bread to the hungry and covers the naked with a garment,

---

k Gk: Heb lacks *all kinds of beasts* *l* Gk: Heb *has kept my ordinances, to deal truly*
m Heb *blood, and he does any one of these things*

17 withholds his hand from iniquity,*n* takes no interest or increase, observes my ordinances, and walks in my statutes; he shall not die for his father's iniquity; he shall surely live. 18 As for his father, because he practiced extortion, robbed his brother, and did what is not good among his people, behold, he shall die for his iniquity.

19 "Yet you say, 'Why should not the son suffer for the iniquity of the father?' When the son has done what is lawful and right, and has been careful to observe all my statutes, he shall surely live. 20 The soul that sins shall die. The son shall not suffer for the iniquity of the father, nor the father suffer for the iniquity of the son; the righteousness of the righteous shall be upon himself, and the wickedness of the wicked shall be upon himself.

5. *The wicked man who repents shall live*

21 "But if a wicked man turns away from all his sins which he has committed and keeps all my statutes and does what is lawful and right, he shall surely live; he shall not die. 22 None of the transgressions which he has committed shall be remembered against him; for the righteousness which he has done he shall live. 23 Have I any pleasure in the death of the wicked, says the Lord GOD, and not rather that he should turn from his way and live? 24 But when a righteous man turns away from his righteousness and commits iniquity and does the same abominable things that the wicked man does, shall he live? None of the righteous deeds which he has done shall be remembered; for the treachery of which he is guilty and the sin he has committed, he shall die.

6. *The way of the LORD is just*

25 "Yet you say, 'The way of the Lord is not just.' Hear now, O house of Israel: Is my way not just? Is it not your ways that are not just? 26 When a righteous man turns away from his righteousness and commits iniquity, he shall die for it; for the iniquity which he has committed he shall die. 27 Again, when a wicked man turns away from the wickedness he has committed and does what is lawful and right, he shall save his life. 28 Because he considered and turned away from all the transgressions which he had committed, he shall surely live, he shall not die. 29 Yet the house of Israel says, 'The way of the Lord is not just.' O house of Israel, are my ways not just? Is it not your ways that are not just?

7. *The command to repent*

30 "Therefore I will judge you, O house of Israel, every one according to his ways, says the Lord GOD. Repent and turn from all your transgressions, lest iniquity be your ruin.*o* 31 Cast away from you all the transgressions which you have committed against me, and get yourselves a new heart and a new spirit! Why will you die, O house of Israel? 32 For I have no pleasure in the death of any one, says the Lord GOD; so turn, and live."

n Gk: Heb *the poor*   *o* Or *so that they shall not be a stumbling block of iniquity to you*

18.17 ver 8,9,13,19,20
18.18 ver 10–13; Ezek 3.18
18.19 Ex 20.5; Deut 5.9; 2 Ki 23.26
18.20 Deut 24.16; Isa 3.10,11; Rom 2.9
18.21 Ezek 33.12,19; 3.21
18.22 Ezek 33.16; Mic 7.19; Ps 18.20–24
18.23 Ezek 33.11; 1 Tim 2.4; 2 Pet 3.9
18.24 Ezek 3.20; 33.12,13,18; 2 Pet 2.20
★18.25 ver 29; Ezek 33.17,20; Zeph 3.5
18.26 ver 24
18.27 ver 21
18.28 ver 22,30,31
18.29 ver 25
18.30 Ezek 7.3; 33.20; Mt 3.2; Rev 2.5
18.31 Isa 1.16,17; 55.7; Ezek 11.19; 36.26
18.32 Ezek 33.11; 2 Pet 3.9

18.25 Sinful men habitually charge God with injustice. This is the normal response of guilty but unrepentant sinners. Scripture does reveal that God's ways are not our ways (Isa 55.8, 9), but it also states that whatever God does is right (Rom 9.20–24). In the final judgment, every mouth will be stopped and all will have to confess that God's judgments are wholly righteous and according to truth (Rev 19.2).

I. *Lamentation over the princes of Israel*

1. *The case of Jehoahaz*

19.1
Ezek 26.17;
27.2
19.2
Nah 2.11,
12;
Isa 5.29;
Zech 11.3

19 And you, take up a lamentation for the princes of Israel,
2 and say:

What a lioness was your mother
  among lions!
She couched in the midst of young lions,
  rearing her whelps.

19.3
2 Ki 23.31,
32;
ver 6

3 And she brought up one of her whelps;
  he became a young lion,
and he learned to catch prey;
  he devoured men.

19.4
2 Ki 23.33;
2 Chr 36.4

4 The nations sounded an alarm against him;
  he was taken in their pit;
and they brought him with hooks
  to the land of Egypt.

2. *The case of Jehoiachin*

19.5
2 Ki 23.34

5 When she saw that she was baffled,[p]
  that her hope was lost,
she took another of her whelps
  and made him a young lion.

19.6
2 Ki 24.9;
ver 3

6 He prowled among the lions;
  he became a young lion,
and he learned to catch prey;
  he devoured men.

19.7
Ezek 12.19;
30.12

7 And he ravaged their strongholds,[q]
  and laid waste their cities;
and the land was appalled and all who were in it
  at the sound of his roaring.

19.8
2 Ki 24.2;
ver 4

8 Then the nations set against him
  snares[r] on every side;
they spread their net over him;
  he was taken in their pit.

19.9
2 Chr 36.6;
Jer 22.18;
Ezek 6.2

9 With hooks they put him in a cage,
  and brought him to the king of Babylon;
  they brought him into custody,
that his voice should no more be heard
  upon the mountains of Israel.

3. *The case of Zedekiah*

19.10
Ps 80.8–11

10 Your mother was like a vine in a vineyard[s]
  transplanted by the water,
fruitful and full of branches
  by reason of abundant water.

19.11
Ezek 31.3;
Dan 4.11

11 Its strongest stem became
  a ruler's scepter;
it towered aloft
  among the thick boughs;
it was seen in its height
  with the mass of its branches.

---

p Heb *had waited*
q Tg Compare Theodotion: Heb *knew his widows*
r Cn: Heb *from the provinces*   *s* Cn: Heb *in your blood*

¹² But the vine was plucked up in fury,
  cast down to the ground;
the east wind dried it up;
  its fruit was stripped off,
its strong stem was withered;
  the fire consumed it.
¹³ Now it is transplanted in the wilderness,
  in a dry and thirsty land.
¹⁴ And fire has gone out from its stem,
  has consumed its branches and fruit,
so that there remains in it no strong stem,
  no scepter for a ruler.

This is a lamentation, and has become a lamentation.

J. The abominations of Israel

1. Ezekiel commanded to answer the elders

20 In the seventh year, in the fifth month, on the tenth day of the month, certain of the elders of Israel came to inquire of the LORD, and sat before me. ²And the word of the LORD came to me: ³"Son of man, speak to the elders of Israel, and say to them, Thus says the Lord GOD, Is it to inquire of me that you come? As I live, says the Lord GOD, I will not be inquired of by you. ⁴ Will you judge them, son of man, will you judge them? Then let them know the abominations of their fathers, ⁵ and say to them,

2. Israel's idolatry in Egypt

Thus says the Lord GOD: On the day when I chose Israel, I swore to the seed of the house of Jacob, making myself known to them in the land of Egypt, I swore to them, saying, I am the LORD your God. ⁶ On that day I swore to them that I would bring them out of the land of Egypt into a land that I had searched out for them, a land flowing with milk and honey, the most glorious of all lands. ⁷And I said to them, Cast away the detestable things your eyes feast on, every one of you, and do not defile yourselves with the idols of Egypt; I am the LORD your God. ⁸ But they rebelled against me and would not listen to me; they did not every man cast away the detestable things their eyes feasted on, nor did they forsake the idols of Egypt.

"Then I thought I would pour out my wrath upon them and spend my anger against them in the midst of the land of Egypt. ⁹ But I acted for the sake of my name, that it should not be profaned in the sight of the nations among whom they dwelt, in whose sight I made myself known to them in bringing them out of

3. Israel's rebellion in the wilderness

the land of Egypt. ¹⁰ So I led them out of the land of Egypt and brought them into the wilderness. ¹¹ I gave them my statutes and showed them my ordinances, by whose observance man shall live. ¹² Moreover I gave them my sabbaths, as a sign between me and them, that they might know that I the LORD sanctify them. ¹³ But the house of Israel rebelled against me in the wilderness; they did not walk in my statutes but rejected my ordinances, by whose observance man shall live; and my sabbaths they greatly profaned.

19.12
Jer 31.28;
Ezek 28.17;
17.10;
Hos 13.15

19.13
Hos 2.3

19.14
Ezek 15.4;
Lam 4.20

20.1
Ezek 8.1,11,
12; 9.6

20.3
ver 31;
Ezek 14.3;
Mic 3.7

20.4
Ezek 16.2;
22.2

20.5
Ex 6.7;
Deut 7.6;
Ex 6.2,3;
20.2

20.6
Ex 3.8,17;
Deut 8.7–9;
Jer 32.22;
Ps 48.2;
Dan 8.9

20.7
Ezek 18.31;
Deut 29.16,
18;
Ex 20.2

20.8
Isa 63.10;
Ezek 7.8

20.9
Ex 32.12;
Num
14.13ff;
Ezek 36.21;
39.7

20.10
Ex 13.18

20.11
Deut 4.8;
Lev 18.5;
Rom 10.5;
Gal 3.12

20.12
Ex 31.13,
17;
ver 20

20.13
Num 14.22;
Ps 78.40;
95.8–10;
Prov 1.25;
Num 14.29;
Ps 106.23

20.14
ver 9,22;
Ezek 36.22,
23
20.15
Num 14.28;
Ps 95.11;
ver 6
20.16
Num 15.39;
Ps 78.37;
Amos 5,25

"Then I thought I would pour out my wrath upon them in the wilderness, to make a full end of them. 14 But I acted for the sake of my name, that it should not be profaned in the sight of the nations, in whose sight I had brought them out. 15 Moreover I swore to them in the wilderness that I would not bring them into the land which I had given them, a land flowing with milk and honey, the most glorious of all lands, 16 because they rejected my ordinances and did not walk in my statutes, and profaned my sabbaths; for their heart went after their idols. 17 Nevertheless my eye spared them, and I did not destroy them or make a full end of them in the wilderness.

20.18
Deut 4.3–6;
Zech 1.4;
ver 7
20.19
Ex 6.7;
20.2;
Deut 5.32
20.20
ver 12
20.21
Num 25.1;
ver 8,13,16

18 "And I said to their children in the wilderness, Do not walk in the statutes of your fathers, nor observe their ordinances, nor defile yourselves with their idols. 19 I the LORD am your God; walk in my statutes, and be careful to observe my ordinances, 20 and hallow my sabbaths that they may be a sign between me and you, that you may know that I the LORD am your God. 21 But the children rebelled against me; they did not walk in my statutes, and were not careful to observe my ordinances, by whose observance man shall live; they profaned my sabbaths.

20.22
ver 17;
Ps 78.38;
ver 9,14
20.23
Lev 26.33;
Deut 28.64;
Ps 106.27;
Jer 15.4
20.24
ver 13,16;
Ezek 6.9
20.25
Ps 81.12;
Rom 1.24;
2 Thess 2.11
20.26
ver 30;
2 Ki 17.17;
2 Chr 28.3;
Ezek 16.20,
21; 6.7

"Then I thought I would pour out my wrath upon them and spend my anger against them in the wilderness. 22 But I withheld my hand, and acted for the sake of my name, that it should not be profaned in the sight of the nations, in whose sight I had brought them out. 23 Moreover I swore to them in the wilderness that I would scatter them among the nations and disperse them through the countries, 24 because they had not executed my ordinances, but had rejected my statutes and profaned my sabbaths, and their eyes were set on their fathers' idols. 25 Moreover I gave them statutes that were not good and ordinances by which they could not have life; 26 and I defiled them through their very gifts in making them offer by fire all their first-born, that I might horrify them; I did it that they might know that I am the LORD.

4. Israel's idolatry in Canaan

20.27
Ezek 2.7;
Rom 2.24;
Ezek 18.24;
39.23,26
20.28
Isa 57.5–7;
Ezek 6.13;
16.19

27 "Therefore, son of man, speak to the house of Israel and say to them, Thus says the Lord GOD: In this again your fathers blasphemed me, by dealing treacherously with me. 28 For when I had brought them into the land which I swore to give them, then wherever they saw any high hill or any leafy tree, there they offered their sacrifices and presented the provocation of their offering; there they sent up their soothing odors, and there they poured out their drink offerings. 29 (I said to them, What is the high place to which you go? So its name is called Bāmáh[t] to this

5. God refuses to be inquired of

20.30
ver 43;
Jer 7.26;
16.12
20.31
Ps 106.37–
39;
Jer 7.31;
Ezek 16.20

day.) 30 Wherefore say to the house of Israel, Thus says the Lord GOD: Will you defile yourselves after the manner of your fathers and go astray after their detestable things? 31 When you offer your gifts and sacrifice your sons by fire, you defile yourselves with all your idols to this day. And shall I be inquired of by you, O house of Israel? As I live, says the Lord GOD, I will not be inquired of by you.

_____

t That is High Place

6. *God to purge Israel*

32 "What is in your mind shall never happen—the thought, 'Let us be like the nations, like the tribes of the countries, and worship wood and stone.'

33 "As I live, says the Lord GOD, surely with a mighty hand and an outstretched arm, and with wrath poured out, I will be king over you. 34 I will bring you out from the peoples and gather you out of the countries where you are scattered, with a mighty hand and an outstretched arm, and with wrath poured out; 35 and I will bring you into the wilderness of the peoples, and there I will enter into judgment with you face to face. 36As I entered into judgment with your fathers in the wilderness of the land of Egypt, so I will enter into judgment with you, says the Lord GOD. 37 I will make you pass under the rod, and I will let you go in by number.*u* 38 I will purge out the rebels from among you, and those who transgress against me; I will bring them out of the land where they sojourn, but they shall not enter the land of Israel. Then you will know that I am the LORD.

39 "As for you, O house of Israel, thus says the Lord GOD: Go serve every one of you his idols, now and hereafter, if you will not listen to me; but my holy name you shall no more profane with your gifts and your idols.

7. *God to show mercy on the obedient*

40 "For on my holy mountain, the mountain height of Israel, says the Lord GOD, there all the house of Israel, all of them, shall serve me in the land; there I will accept them, and there I will require your contributions and the choicest of your gifts, with all your sacred offerings. 41As a pleasing odor I will accept you, when I bring you out from the peoples, and gather you out of the countries where you have been scattered; and I will manifest my holiness among you in the sight of the nations. 42And you shall know that I am the LORD, when I bring you into the land of Israel, the country which I swore to give to your fathers. 43And there you shall remember your ways and all the doings with which you have polluted yourselves; and you shall loathe yourselves for all the evils that you have committed. 44And you shall know that I am the LORD, when I deal with you for my name's sake, not according to your evil ways, nor according to your corrupt doings, O house of Israel, says the Lord GOD."

8. *The prophecy against the south*

45*v* And the word of the LORD came to me: 46 "Son of man, set your face toward the south, preach against the south, and prophesy against the forest land in the Něgěb; 47 say to the forest of the Něgěb, Hear the word of the LORD: Thus says the Lord GOD, Behold, I will kindle a fire in you, and it shall devour every green tree in you and every dry tree; the blazing flame shall not be quenched, and all faces from south to north shall be scorched by it. 48All flesh shall see that I the LORD have kindled it; it shall not be quenched." 49 Then I said, "Ah Lord GOD! they are saying of me, 'Is he not a maker of allegories?'"

u Gk: Heb *bring you into the bond of the covenant*
v Ch 21.1 in Heb

20.32 Ezek 11.5; 16.16; Jer 2.25; 44.17
20.33 Jer 21.5
20.34 ver 38; Jer 42.18; 44.6; Lam 2.4
20.35 Ezek 17.20
20.36 ver 13,21; 1 Cor 10.5–10; Deut 32.10
20.37 Lam 27.32; Jer 33.13; Ezek 16.60, 62
20.38 Ezek 34.17, 20; Amos 9.9, 10; Jer 44.14; Ezek 6.7
20.39 Jer 44.25, 26; Amos 4.4; Isa 1.13; Ezek 23.38, 39
20.40 Ezek 17.23; Mic 4.1; Ezek 37.22, 24; Isa 56.7; 60.7; Mal 3.4
20.41 Eph 5.2; Phil 4.18
20.42 Ezek 34.13; 36.24
20.43 Ezek 16.61; Hos 5.15; Ezek 36.31; Zech 12.10
20.44 Ezek 24.44; 36.22
20.46 Ezek 6.2; 21.2
20.47 Jer 21.14; 17.24; 21.4
20.48 Jer 7.20; 17.27
20.49 Ezek 17.2; Mt 13.13,14

K. The prophecies of the sharpened sword

1. The sword drawn from the sheath

21 ^{w} The word of the LORD came to me: 2 "Son of man, set your face toward Jerusalem and preach against the sanctuaries; prophesy against the land of Israel 3 and say to the land of Israel, Thus says the LORD: Behold, I am against you, and will draw forth my sword out of its sheath, and will cut off from you both righteous and wicked. 4 Because I will cut off from you both righteous and wicked, therefore my sword shall go out of its sheath against all flesh from south to north; 5 and all flesh shall know that I the LORD have drawn my sword out of its sheath; it shall not be sheathed again. 6 Sigh therefore, son of man; sigh with breaking heart and bitter grief before their eyes. 7And when they say to you, 'Why do you sigh?' you shall say, 'Because of the tidings. When it comes, every heart will melt and all hands will be feeble, every spirit will faint and all knees will be weak as water. Behold, it comes and it will be fulfilled,'" says the Lord GOD.

2. The sword sharpened

8 And the word of the LORD came to me: 9 "Son of man, prophesy and say, Thus says the Lord, Say:

A sword, a sword is sharpened
and also polished,

10 sharpened for slaughter,
polished to flash like lightning!

Or do we make mirth? You have despised the rod, my son, with everything of wood. 11 So the sword is given to be polished, that it may be handled; it is sharpened and polished to be given into the hand of the slayer. 12 Cry and wail, son of man, for it is against my people; it is against all the princes of Israel; they are delivered over to the sword with my people. Smite therefore upon your thigh. 13 For it will not be a testing—what could it do if you despise the rod?" says the Lord GOD.

14 "Prophesy therefore, son of man; clap your hands and let the sword come down twice, yea thrice, the sword for those to be slain; it is the sword for the great slaughter, which encompasses them, 15 that their hearts may melt, and many fall at all their gates. I have given the glittering sword; ah! it is made like lightning, it is polished^x for slaughter. 16 Cut sharply to right^y and left where your edge is directed. 17 I also will clap my hands, and I will satisfy my fury; I the LORD have spoken."

3. The sword wielded by Babylon

18 The word of the LORD came to me again: 19 "Son of man, mark two ways for the sword of the king of Babylon to come; both of them shall come forth from the same land. And make a signpost, make it at the head of the way to a city; 20 mark a way for the sword to come to Răbbăh of the Ăm'mŏnītes and to Judah and to^z Jerusalem the fortified. 21 For the king of Babylon stands at the

Cross-references (left margin)

21.2 Ezek 20.46; Amos 7.16
21.3 Jer 21.13; Ezek 5.8; ver 9–11,19; Job 9.22
21.4 Ezek 20.47
21.5 Ezek 20.48; Jer 23.20; Nah 1.9
21.6 Isa 22.4
21.7 Ezek 7.26; Isa 13.7; Ezek 7.17; 22.14
21.9 Deut 32.41
21.10 Isa 34.5,6; ver 15
21.11 ver 15,19
21.12 Jer 31.19
21.14 Num 24.10; Ezek 6.11; Lev 26.21,24; Ezek 30.24
21.15 ver 7,10
21.17 ver 14; Ezek 22.13; 5.13
21.19 Ezek 4.1–3; ver 15
21.20 Jer 49.2; Ezek 25.5; Amos 1.14
*21.21 Num 23.23; Prov 16.33; Judg 17.5

^{w} Ch 21.6 in Heb ^{x} Tg: Heb wrapped up
^{y} Gk Syr Vg: Heb right, set ^{z} Gk Syr: Heb in

21.21 Nebuchadnezzar made use of *divination* to determine whether to march against Rabbah or Jerusalem. The liver of a freshly killed sheep was inspected in seeking omens.

parting of the way, at the head of the two ways, to use divination; he shakes the arrows, he consults the teraphim, he looks at the liver. 22 Into his right hand comes the lot for Jerusalem,*a* to open the mouth with a cry,*b* to lift up the voice with shouting, to set battering rams against the gates, to cast up mounds, to build siege towers. 23 But to them it will seem like a false divination; they have sworn solemn oaths; but he brings their guilt to remembrance, that they may be captured.

24 "Therefore thus says the Lord GOD: Because you have made your guilt to be remembered, in that your transgressions are uncovered, so that in all your doings your sins appear—because you

4. The punishment of the prince of Israel

have come to remembrance, you shall be taken in them.*c* 25And you, O unhallowed wicked one, prince of Israel, whose day has come, the time of your final punishment, 26 thus says the Lord GOD: Remove the turban, and take off the crown; things shall not remain as they are; exalt that which is low, and abase that which is high. 27A ruin, ruin, ruin I will make it; there shall not be even a trace*d* of it until he comes whose right it is; and to him I will give it.

5. The sentence against the Ammonites

28 "And you, son of man, prophesy, and say, Thus says the Lord GOD concerning the Am'monites, and concerning their reproach; say, A sword, a sword is drawn for the slaughter, it is polished to glitter*e* and to flash like lightning—29 while they see for you false visions, while they divine lies for you—to be laid on the necks of the unhallowed wicked, whose day has come, the time of their final punishment. 30 Return it to its sheath. In the place where you were created, in the land of your origin, I will judge you. 31And I will pour out my indignation upon you; I will blow upon you with the fire of my wrath; and I will deliver you into the hands of brutal men, skilful to destroy. 32 You shall be fuel for the fire; your blood shall be in the midst of the land; you shall be no more remembered; for I the LORD have spoken."

L. The sins of Jerusalem

1. The indictment

22 Moreover the word of the LORD came to me, saying, 2 "And you, son of man, will you judge, will you judge the bloody city? Then declare to her all her abominable deeds. 3 You shall say, Thus says the Lord GOD: A city that sheds blood in the midst of her, that her time may come, and that makes idols to defile herself! 4 You have become guilty by the blood which you have shed, and defiled by the idols which you have made; and you have brought your day near, the appointed time*f* of your years has come. Therefore I have made you a reproach to the nations, and a mocking to all the countries. 5 Those who are near and those who are far from you will mock you, you infamous one, full of tumult.

6 "Behold, the princes of Israel in you, every one according to

---

a Heb *Jerusalem, to set battering rams*   *b* Gk: Heb *with slaughter*
c Gk: Heb *with the hand*   *d* Cn: Heb *not even this*   *e* Cn: Heb *to contain*
f Two Mss Gk Syr Vg Tg: Heb *until*

21.22
Jer 51.14;
Ezek 4.2

21.23
Ezek 17.13,
15,16,18;
29.16

21.25
Ezek 7.2,3,
7; 35.5

21.26
Jer 13.18;
Ezek 16.12;
17.24;
Lk 1.52

21.27
Hag 2.21,
22;
Ps 2.6;
Jer 23.5,6;
Ezek 34.24;
37.24

21.28
Jer 49.1;
Ezek 25.2,
3;
Zeph 2.8;
Isa 31.8;
Jer 12.12

21.29
Ezek 13.6–
9; 22.28;
ver 25;
Ezek 35.5

21.30
Jer 47.6,7;
Ezek 16.3

21.31
Ezek 7.8;
14.19;
22.20,21;
Jer 6.22,23;
51.20,21

21.32
Mal 4.1;
Ezek 25.10

22.2
Ezek 20.4;
24.6–9;
Nah 3.1;
Ezek 16.2;
20.4

22.3
ver 6,27;
Ezek 23.37,
45

22.4
2 Ki 21.16;
Ezek 24.7,8;
21.25; 5.14,
15; 16.57

22.5
Isa 22.5

22.6
Isa 1.23

his power, have been bent on shedding blood. 7 Father and mother are treated with contempt in you; the sojourner suffers extortion in your midst; the fatherless and the widow are wronged in you. 8 You have despised my holy things, and profaned my sabbaths. 9 There are men in you who slander to shed blood, and men in you who eat upon the mountains; men commit lewdness in your midst. 10 In you men uncover their fathers' nakedness; in you they humble women who are unclean in their impurity. 11 One commits abomination with his neighbor's wife; another lewdly defiles his daughter-in-law; another in you defiles his sister, his father's daughter. 12 In you men take bribes to shed blood; you take interest and increase and make gain of your neighbors by extortion; and you have forgotten me, says the Lord GOD.

13 "Behold, therefore, I strike my hands together at the dishonest gain which you have made, and at the blood which has been in the midst of you. 14 Can your courage endure, or can your hands be strong, in the days that I shall deal with you? I the LORD have spoken, and I will do it. 15 I will scatter you among the nations and disperse you through the countries, and I will consume your filthiness out of you. 16 And I^g shall be profaned through you in the sight of the nations; and you shall know that I am the LORD."

2. The promise of God's wrath

17 And the word of the LORD came to me: 18 "Son of man, the house of Israel has become dross to me; all of them, silver^h and bronze and tin and iron and lead in the furnace, have become dross. 19 Therefore thus says the Lord GOD: Because you have all become dross, therefore, behold, I will gather you into the midst of Jerusalem. 20 As men gather silver and bronze and iron and lead and tin into a furnace, to blow the fire upon it in order to melt it; so I will gather you in my anger and in my wrath, and I will put you in and melt you. 21 I will gather you and blow upon you with the fire of my wrath, and you shall be melted in the midst of it. 22 As silver is melted in a furnace, so you shall be melted in the midst of it; and you shall know that I the LORD have poured out my wrath upon you."

3. The indictment extended to all classes

23 And the word of the LORD came to me: 24 "Son of man, say to her, You are a land that is not cleansed, or rained upon in the day of indignation. 25 Her princes^i in the midst of her are like a roaring lion tearing the prey; they have devoured human lives; they have taken treasure and precious things; they have made many widows in the midst of her. 26 Her priests have done violence to my law and have profaned my holy things; they have made no distinction between the holy and the common, neither have they taught the difference between the unclean and the clean, and they have disregarded my sabbaths, so that I am profaned among them. 27 Her princes in the midst of her are like wolves tearing the prey, shedding blood, destroying lives to get dishonest gain. 28 And her prophets have daubed for them with whitewash, seeing false visions and divining lies for them, saying, 'Thus says the Lord

---

g Gk Syr Vg: Heb you h Transposed from the end of the verse. Compare verse 20
i Gk: Heb a conspiracy of her prophets

GOD,' when the LORD has not spoken. 29 The people of the land have practiced extortion and committed robbery; they have oppressed the poor and needy, and have extorted from the sojourner without redress. 30And I sought for a man among them who should build up the wall and stand in the breach before me for the land, that I should not destroy it; but I found none. 31 Therefore I have poured out my indignation upon them; I have consumed them with the fire of my wrath; their way have I requited upon their heads, says the Lord GOD."

M. The harlotry of Oholah (Samaria) and Oholibah (Jerusalem)

1. Introduction

23 The word of the LORD came to me: 2 "Son of man, there were two women, the daughters of one mother; 3 they played the harlot in Egypt; they played the harlot in their youth; there their breasts were pressed and their virgin bosoms handled. 4 Ŏhō'lăh was the name of the elder and Ŏhō'lĭbăh the name of her sister. They became mine, and they bore sons and daughters. As for their names, Oholah is Sămăr'ĭă, and Oholibah is Jerusalem.

2. The sin of Oholah

5 "Ŏhō'lăh played the harlot while she was mine; and she doted on her lovers the Assyrians, 6 warriors clothed in purple, governors and commanders, all of them desirable young men, horsemen riding on horses. 7 She bestowed her harlotries upon them, the choicest men of Assyria all of them; and she defiled herself with all the idols of every one on whom she doted. 8 She did not give up her harlotry which she had practiced since her days in Egypt; for in her youth men had lain with her and handled her virgin bosom and poured out their lust upon her. 9 Therefore I delivered her into the hands of her lovers, into the hands of the Assyrians, upon whom she doted. 10 These uncovered her nakedness; they seized her sons and her daughters; and her they slew with the sword; and she became a byword among women, when judgment had been executed upon her.

3. The sin of Oholibah

11 "Her sister Ŏhō'lĭbăh saw this, yet she was more corrupt than she in her doting and in her harlotry, which was worse than that of her sister. 12 She doted upon the Assyrians, governors and commanders, warriors clothed in full armor, horsemen riding on horses, all of them desirable young men. 13And I saw that she was defiled; they both took the same way. 14 But she carried her harlotry further; she saw men portrayed upon the wall, the images of the Chăldē'ăns portrayed in vermilion, 15 girded with belts on their loins, with flowing turbans on their heads, all of them looking like officers, a picture of Babylonians whose native land was Chăldē'ă. 16 When she saw them she doted upon them, and sent messengers to them in Chăldē'ă. 17And the Babylonians came to her into the bed of love, and they defiled her with their lust; and after she was polluted by them, she turned from them in disgust. 18 When she carried on her harlotry so openly and flaunted her

22.29
Isa 5.7;
Amos 3.10;
Ex 22.21;
23.9
22.30
Jer 5.1;
Ezek 13.5;
Ps 106.23
22.31
Isa 13.5;
Ezek 9.10;
11.21;
16.43

23.2
Jer 3.7,8;
Ezek 16.44,
46; 16.3,45
23.3
Josh 24.14;
Ezek 20.8;
16.22
23.4
Ezek 16.8,
20
23.5
1 Ki 12.28–
30;
Ezek 16.28;
Hos 8.9,10
23.6
ver 12,23
23.7
ver 30;
Ezek 16.15;
20.7;
Hos 5.3;
6.10
23.8
Ex 32.4;
ver 3;
Ezek 16.15
23.9
ver 22;
Ezek 16.37;
2 Ki 18.9–
11;
Hos 11.5
23.10
Ezek 16.37;
Hos 2.10;
ver 47;
Ezek 16.57
23.11
Jer 3.8–11;
Ezek 16.47
23.12
2 Ki 16.7–
10;
2 Chr
28.16–23;
ver 6,23
23.14
Ezek 8.10;
16.29;
Jer 22.14
23.15
Isa 22.21
23.16
ver 20
23.17
ver 28,30
23.18
ver 10;
Jer 6.8

nakedness, I turned in disgust from her, as I had turned from her sister. [19] Yet she increased her harlotry, remembering the days of her youth, when she played the harlot in the land of Egypt [20] and doted upon her paramours there, whose members were like those of asses, and whose issue was like that of horses. [21] Thus you longed for the lewdness of your youth, when the Egyptians[j] handled your bosom and pressed[k] your young breasts."

4. *The punishment of Oholibah*

22 Therefore, O Ŏhŏ'lĭbáh, thus says the Lord God: "Behold, I will rouse against you your lovers from whom you turned in disgust, and I will bring them against you from every side: [23] the Babylonians and all the Chăldē'áns, Pēkŏd and Shōá and Kŏá, and all the Assyrians with them, desirable young men, governors and commanders all of them, officers and warriors,[l] all of them riding on horses. [24]And they shall come against you from the north[m] with chariots and wagons and a host of peoples; they shall set themselves against you on every side with buckler, shield, and helmet, and I will commit the judgment to them, and they shall judge you according to their judgments. [25]And I will direct my indignation against you, that they may deal with you in fury. They shall cut off your nose and your ears, and your survivors shall fall by the sword. They shall seize your sons and your daughters, and your survivors shall be devoured by fire. [26] They shall also strip you of your clothes and take away your fine jewels. [27] Thus I will put an end to your lewdness and your harlotry brought from the land of Egypt; so that you shall not lift up your eyes to the Egyptians or remember them any more. [28] For thus says the Lord God: Behold, I will deliver you into the hands of those whom you hate, into the hands of those from whom you turned in disgust; [29] and they shall deal with you in hatred, and take away all the fruit of your labor, and leave you naked and bare, and the nakedness of your harlotry shall be uncovered. Your lewdness and your harlotry [30] have brought this upon you, because you played the harlot with the nations, and polluted yourself with their idols. [31] You have gone the way of your sister; therefore I will give her cup into your hand. [32] Thus says the Lord God:
"You shall drink your sister's cup
    which is deep and large;
you shall be laughed at and held in derision,
    for it contains much;
33 you will be filled with drunkenness and sorrow.
A cup of horror and desolation,
    is the cup of your sister Sámar'ĭá;
34 you shall drink it and drain it out,
    and pluck out your hair,[n]
    and tear your breasts;
for I have spoken, says the Lord God. [35] Therefore thus says the Lord God: Because you have forgotten me and cast me behind your back, therefore bear the consequences of your lewdness and harlotry."

23.19
ver 14,3
23.20
Ezek 16.26
23.21
ver 3

23.22
ver 28;
Ezek 16.37
23.23
Ezek 21.19;
2 Ki 24.2;
Jer 50.21;
ver 6,12
23.24
Ezek 21.15,
19;
Jer 47.3;
Ezek 16.40;
Jer 39.5,6
23.25
Ezek 8.17,
18;
Zeph 1.18;
ver 47;
Ezek 20.47,
48;
22.20,21
23.26
Ezek 16.39
23.27
Ezek 16.41;
22.15;
ver 3,19
23.28
Ezek 16.37
23.29
ver 26;
Ezek 16.39

23.30
ver 7,17;
Jer 2.18–20;
Ezek 6.9
23.32
Isa 51.17;
Jer 25.15;
Ezek 22.4,5

23.33
Jer 25.15,
16,27;
Ezek 4.16
23.34
Ps 75.8;
Isa 51.17

23.35
Jer 3.21;
Hos 8.14;
1 Ki 14.9;
Neh 9.26

---

j Two Mss: Heb *from Egypt*
k Cn: Heb *for the sake of*
l Compare verses 6 and 12: Heb *called*
m Gk: The meaning of the Hebrew word is unknown
n Compare Syr: Heb *gnaw its sherds*

5. *The judgment of the* LORD *on Oholah and Oholibah*

36 The LORD said to me: "Son of man, will you judge Ŏhŏ′lăh and Ŏhŏ′lĭbăh? Then declare to them their abominable deeds. 37 For they have committed adultery, and blood is upon their hands; with their idols they have committed adultery; and they have even offered up to them for food the sons whom they had borne to me. 38 Moreover this they have done to me: they have defiled my sanctuary on the same day and profaned my sabbaths. 39 For when they had slaughtered their children in sacrifice to their idols, on the same day they came into my sanctuary to profane it. And lo, this is what they did in my house. 40 They even sent for men to come from far, to whom a messenger was sent, and lo, they came. For them you bathed yourself, painted your eyes, and decked yourself with ornaments; 41 you sat upon a stately couch, with a table spread before it on which you had placed my incense and my oil. 42 The sound of a carefree multitude was with her; and with men of the common sort drunkards*o* were brought from the wilderness; and they put bracelets upon the hands of the women, and beautiful crowns upon their heads.

43 "Then I said, Do not men now commit adultery*p* when they practice harlotry with her? 44 For they have gone in to her, as men go in to a harlot. Thus they went in to Ŏhŏ′lăh and to Ŏhŏ′lĭbăh to commit lewdness.*q* 45 But righteous men shall pass judgment on them with the sentence of adulteresses, and with the sentence of women that shed blood; because they are adulteresses, and blood is upon their hands."

46 For thus says the Lord GOD: "Bring up a host against them, and make them an object of terror and a spoil. 47And the host shall stone them and dispatch them with their swords; they shall slay their sons and their daughters, and burn up their houses. 48 Thus will I put an end to lewdness in the land, that all women may take warning and not commit lewdness as you have done. 49And your lewdness shall be requited upon you, and you shall bear the penalty for your sinful idolatry; and you shall know that I am the Lord GOD."

N. *The allegory of the boiling pot*

24 In the ninth year, in the tenth month, on the tenth day of the month, the word of the LORD came to me: 2 "Son of man, write down the name of this day, this very day. The king of Babylon has laid siege to Jerusalem this very day. 3And utter an allegory to the rebellious house and say to them, Thus says the Lord GOD:

Set on the pot, set it on,
    pour in water also;
4 put in it the pieces of flesh,
    all the good pieces, the thigh and the shoulder;
    fill it with choice bones.
5 Take the choicest one of the flock,
    pile the logs*r* under it;
boil its pieces,*s*
    seethe*t* also its bones in it.

23.36 Ezek 20.4; 22.2; Isa 58.1
23.37 ver 3,45; Ezek 16.20, 21,36,45
23.38 Ezek 5.11; 7.20; 22.8
23.39 2 Ki 21.4
23.40 Isa 57.9; 2 Ki 9.30; Jer 4.30; Ezek 16.13-16
23.41 Est 1.6; Amos 6.4; Prov 7.17; Hos 2.8
23.42 Ezek 16.49; Jer 51.7; Ezek 16.11, 12
23.45 Ezek 16.38; Hos 6.5; Lev 20.10
23.46 ver 24; Ezek 16.40; 24.9; 29.18
23.47 Ezek 16.40; 2 Chr 36.17, 19; Ezek 24.21; Jer 39.8
23.48 ver 27; Ezek 22.15; 2 Pet 2.6
23.49 ver 35; Ezek 6.7; 20.38,42,44
24.1 Ezek 1.2; 8.1; 20.1; 26.1
24.2 Isa 8.1; 2 Ki 25.1; Jer 39.1; 52.4
24.3 Ezek 17.2; Jer 1.13; Ezek 11.3
24.4 Ezek 22.19-22; Mic 3.2,3
24.5 ver 10

o Heb uncertain   *p* Compare Gk: Heb obscure
q Gk: Heb *a woman of lewdness*   *r* Compare verse 10: Heb *the bones*
s Two Mss: Heb *its boilings*   *t* Cn: Heb *its bones seethe*

6 "Therefore thus says the Lord GOD: Woe to the bloody city, to the pot whose rust is in it, and whose rust has not gone out of it! Take out of it piece after piece, without making any choice.*u* 7 For the blood she has shed is still in the midst of her; she put it on the bare rock, she did not pour it upon the ground to cover it with dust. 8 To rouse my wrath, to take vengeance, I have set on the bare rock the blood she has shed, that it may not be covered. 9 Therefore thus says the Lord GOD: Woe to the bloody city! I also will make the pile great. 10 Heap on the logs, kindle the fire, boil well the flesh, and empty out the broth,*v* and let the bones be burned up. 11 Then set it empty upon the coals, that it may become hot, and its copper may burn, that its filthiness may be melted in it, its rust consumed. 12 In vain I have wearied myself;*w* its thick rust does not go out of it by fire. 13 Its rust is your filthy lewdness. Because I would have cleansed you and you were not cleansed from your filthiness, you shall not be cleansed any more till I have satisfied my fury upon you. 14 I the LORD have spoken; it shall come to pass, I will do it; I will not go back, I will not spare, I will not repent; according to your ways and your doings I will judge you, says the Lord GOD."

O. The death of Ezekiel's wife

15 Also the word of the LORD came to me: 16 "Son of man, behold, I am about to take the delight of your eyes away from you at a stroke; yet you shall not mourn or weep nor shall your tears run down. 17 Sigh, but not aloud; make no mourning for the dead. Bind on your turban, and put your shoes on your feet; do not cover your lips, nor eat the bread of mourners."*x* 18 So I spoke to the people in the morning, and at evening my wife died. And on the next morning I did as I was commanded.

19 And the people said to me, "Will you not tell us what these things mean for us, that you are acting thus?" 20 Then I said to them, "The word of the LORD came to me: 21 'Say to the house of Israel, Thus says the Lord GOD: Behold, I will profane my sanctuary, the pride of your power, the delight of your eyes, and the desire of your soul; and your sons and your daughters whom you left behind shall fall by the sword. 22 And you shall do as I have done; you shall not cover your lips, nor eat the bread of mourners.*x* 23 Your turbans shall be on your heads and your shoes on your feet; you shall not mourn or weep, but you shall pine away in your iniquities and groan to one another. 24 Thus shall Ēzē′kĭĕl be to you a sign; according to all that he has done you shall do. When this comes, then you will know that I am the Lord GOD.'

25 "And you, son of man, on the day when I take from them their stronghold, their joy and glory, the delight of their eyes and their heart's desire, and also their sons and daughters, 26 on that

u Heb *no lot has fallen upon it*   *v* Compare Gk: Heb *mix the spices*
w Cn: Heb uncertain   *x* Vg Tg: Heb *men*

24.16 *the delight of your eyes,* Ezekiel's wife. *at a stroke.* The death of Ezekiel's wife occurred in a sudden and striking manner, making it obvious that it was a providential visitation of God and there was to be no grief. **24.18** Ezekiel here represents the case of the obedient servant who is faithful to God despite personal disappointment and sorrow. This lesson needs to be learned by every servant of God who is called upon to live above life's tragic moments and to find his highest happiness in his Father in heaven.

day a fugitive will come to you to report to you the news. 27 On
that day your mouth will be opened to the fugitive, and you shall
speak and be no longer dumb. So you will be a sign to them; and
they will know that I am the LORD."

II. The prophecies against the surrounding nations
25.1–32.32

A. Ammon

25 The word of the LORD came to me: 2 "Son of man, set your
face toward the Ăm'mŏnītes, and prophesy against them.
3 Say to the Ăm'mŏnītes, Hear the word of the Lord GOD: Thus says
the Lord GOD, Because you said, 'Aha!' over my sanctuary when it
was profaned, and over the land of Israel when it was made desolate, and over the house of Judah when it went into exile; 4 therefore I am handing you over to the people of the East for a possession, and they shall set their encampments among you and make
their dwellings in your midst; they shall eat your fruit, and they
shall drink your milk. 5 I will make Răbbáh a pasture for camels
and the cities of the Ăm'mŏnītes ʸ a fold for flocks. Then you will
know that I am the LORD. 6 For thus says the Lord GOD: Because
you have clapped your hands and stamped your feet and rejoiced
with all the malice within you against the land of Israel, 7 therefore,
behold, I have stretched out my hand against you, and will hand
you over as spoil to the nations; and I will cut you off from the
peoples and will make you perish out of the countries; I will
destroy you. Then you will know that I am the LORD.

B. Moab

8 "Thus says the Lord GOD: Because Mŏăb ᶻ said, Behold, the
house of Judah is like all the other nations, 9 therefore I will lay
open the flank of Mŏăb from the cities ᵃ on its frontier, the glory
of the country, Běth-jěsh'ĭmŏth, Bā'ăl-mē'ŏn, and Kĭ'rĭăthā'ĭm.
10 I will give it along with the Ăm'mŏnītes to the people of the
East as a possession, that it ᵇ may be remembered no more among
the nations, 11 and I will execute judgments upon Mŏăb. Then
they will know that I am the LORD.

C. Edom

12 "Thus says the Lord GOD: Because Ēdŏm acted revengefully
against the house of Judah and has grievously offended in taking

ʸ Cn: Heb lacks the cities of
ᶻ Gk Old Latin: Heb Moab and Seir
ᵃ Heb cities from its cities   ᵇ Cn: Heb the Ammonites

25.2 The Ammonites were descendants of the younger daughter of Lot, who bore her father a son, Ben-ammi, by incest. Ben-ammi was the father of the Ammonites, who turned out to be inveterate enemies of the true people of God. (See Gen 19.33–38.)
25.9 The Moabites were descendants of Moab, the son of Lot's elder daughter. She bore Moab by her father in an incestuous relation. The Moabites and the Ammonites were prohibited by the Mosaic Law from entering the congregation of Israel until the tenth generation. (See Gen 19.33–38; Deut 23.3.)
25.12 See note to Gen 36.9 for information on the Edomites.

24.27 Ezek 3.26, 27; 33.22; ver 24 — *25.2 Jer 27.3; Ezek 21.28; Amos 1.13; Zeph 2.8,9 — 25.3 Prov 17.5; Ezek 26.2 — 25.4 Ezek 21.31 — 25.5 Ezek 21.20; Isa 17.2; Zeph 2.14 — 25.6 Job 27.23; Lam 2.15; Zeph 2.8,10 — 25.7 Ezek 26.5; Amos 1.14,15; Ezek 6.14 — 25.8 Isa ch 15,16; Jer 48.1; Amos 2.1; Ezek 35.2,5 — *25.9 Num 33.49; 32.3,38; 32.37 — 25.10 ver 4; Ezek 21.32 — 25.11 Ezek 5.15; 11.9 — *25.12 Lam 4.21, 22; Ezek 35.2; Amos 1.11; Obad 10–16

vengeance upon them, 13 therefore thus says the Lord GOD, I will stretch out my hand against Ēdòm, and cut off from it man and beast; and I will make it desolate; from Tēmàn even to Dēdàn they shall fall by the sword. 14And I will lay my vengeance upon Ēdòm by the hand of my people Israel; and they shall do in Edom according to my anger and according to my wrath; and they shall know my vengeance, says the Lord GOD.

D. Philistia

15 "Thus says the Lord GOD: Because the Phịlĭs'tĭnẹṣ acted revengefully and took vengeance with malice of heart to destroy in never-ending enmity; 16 therefore thus says the Lord GOD, Behold, I will stretch out my hand against the Phịlĭs'tĭnẹṣ, and I will cut off the Chĕr'ĕthītes, and destroy the rest of the seacoast. 17 I will execute great vengeance upon them with wrathful chastisements. Then they will know that I am the LORD, when I lay my vengeance upon them."

E. Tyre

1. Prediction of its doom

26 In the eleventh year, on the first day of the month, the word of the LORD came to me: 2 "Son of man, because Tȳre said concerning Jerusalem, 'Aha, the gate of the peoples is broken, it has swung open to me; I shall be replenished, now that she is laid waste,' 3 therefore thus says the Lord GOD: Behold, I am against you, O Tȳre, and will bring up many nations against you, as the sea brings up its waves. 4 They shall destroy the walls of Tȳre, and break down her towers; and I will scrape her soil from her, and make her a bare rock. 5 She shall be in the midst of the sea a place for the spreading of nets; for I have spoken, says the Lord GOD; and she shall become a spoil to the nations; 6 and her daughters on the mainland shall be slain by the sword. Then they will know that I am the LORD.

2. Nebuchadrezzar the agent of destruction

7 "For thus says the Lord GOD: Behold, I will bring upon Tȳre from the north Nĕbúchàdrĕz'zàr king of Babylon, king of kings, with horses and chariots, and with horsemen and a host of many soldiers. 8 He will slay with the sword your daughters on the mainland; he will set up a siege wall against you, and throw up a mound against you, and raise a roof of shields against you. 9 He will direct the shock of his battering rams against your walls, and with his axes he will break down your towers. 10 His horses will be

---

26.2 The overthrow of Tyre was predicted by Isaiah long before the time of Ezekiel (see Isa ch 23). The reference here is to Nebuchadnezzar's coming siege and the permanent desolation of this splendid and wealthy maritime city. Old Tyre was located on the shore of the mainland, whereas New Tyre was built on an island one-half mile offshore. Nebuchadnezzar seems to have reduced Old Tyre after a thirteen years' siege, although it is not certain that he was able to storm the island. At any rate, it came under Persian suzerainty under Cyrus the Great and fell for the last time under the attack of Alexander the Great in 332 B.C. Unable to capture it by ships, he built a stone causeway all the way out to the island itself. From that day to this its glory has never been recovered, and it stands as a monument to fulfilled prophecy which declared that it should become a bare uninhabited rock fit only for the spreading of fish nets (26.4, 5, 14, 21; 27.36; 28.2-9).

so many that their dust will cover you; your walls will shake at the noise of the horsemen and wagons and chariots, when he enters your gates as one enters a city which has been breached. 11 With the hoofs of his horses he will trample all your streets; he will slay your people with the sword; and your mighty pillars will fall to the ground. 12 They will make a spoil of your riches and a prey of your merchandise; they will break down your walls and destroy your pleasant houses; your stones and timber and soil they will cast into the midst of the waters. 13And I will stop the music of your songs, and the sound of your lyres shall be heard no more. 14 I will make you a bare rock; you shall be a place for the spreading of nets; you shall never be rebuilt; for I the LORD have spoken, says the Lord GOD.

3. Lamentation of the princes of the sea

15 "Thus says the Lord GOD to Tȳre: Will not the coastlands shake at the sound of your fall, when the wounded groan, when slaughter is made in the midst of you? 16 Then all the princes of the sea will step down from their thrones, and remove their robes, and strip off their embroidered garments; they will clothe themselves with trembling; they will sit upon the ground and tremble every moment, and be appalled at you. 17And they will raise a lamentation over you, and say to you,

'How you have vanished*c* from the seas,
     O city renowned,
that was mighty on the sea,
     you and your inhabitants,
who imposed your terror
     on all the mainland!*d*
18 Now the isles tremble
     on the day of your fall;
yea, the isles that are in the sea
     are dismayed at your passing.'

4. Tyre to go down to the Pit

19 "For thus says the Lord GOD: When I make you a city laid waste, like the cities that are not inhabited, when I bring up the deep over you, and the great waters cover you, 20then I will thrust you down with those who descend into the Pit, to the people of old, and I will make you to dwell in the nether world, among primeval ruins, with those who go down to the Pit, so that you will not be inhabited or have a place*e* in the land of the living. 21 I will bring you to a dreadful end, and you shall be no more; though you be sought for, you will never be found again, says the Lord GOD."

5. The lamentation over Tyre
a. The beauty and wealth of Tyre

27   The word of the LORD came to me: 2 "Now you, son of man, raise a lamentation over Tȳre, 3 and say to Tȳre, who dwells at the entrance to the sea, merchant of the peoples on many coastlands, thus says the Lord GOD:

"O Tyre, you have said,

---

c Gk Old Latin Aquila: Heb *vanished, O inhabited one,*
d Cn: Heb *her inhabitants* *e* Gk: Heb *I will give beauty*

26.11
Hab 1.8;
Isa 26.5;
Jer 43.13

26.12
ver 5

26.13
Isa 14.11;
25.10;
Isa 23.16;
Rev 18.22

26.14
ver 4.5;
Mal 1.4;
Isa 14.27

26.15
ver 18;
Ezek 31.16

26.16
Ezek 27.35;
Jon 3.6;
Job 2.13

26.17
Ezek 27.32;
Rev 18.9;
Isa 23.4;
Ezek 28.2

26.18
ver 15

26.20
Ezek 32.18,
24;
Amos 9.2;
Jer 33.9

26.21
Ezek 27.36;
28.19;
ver 14

27.2
Ezek 28.12
27.3
Ezek 28.2;
ver 33;
Ezek 28.12

'I am perfect in beauty.'

27.4
ver 25–27

4 Your borders are in the heart of the seas;
  your builders made perfect your beauty.

27.5
Deut 3.9

5 They made all your planks
    of fir trees from Sĕnĭr;
  they took a cedar from Lebanon
    to make a mast for you.

27.6
Zech 11.2;
Isa 2.13;
Jer 2.10

6 Of oaks of Bāshán
    they made your oars;
  they made your deck of pines
    from the coasts of Cyprus,
    inlaid with ivory.

7 Of fine embroidered linen from Egypt
    was your sail,
    serving as your ensign;
  blue and purple from the coasts of Ĕlĭ'shàh
    was your awning.

27.8
1 Ki 9.27

8 The inhabitants of Sĭdón and Arvăd
    were your rowers;
  skilled men of Zĕmĕr*f* were in you,
    they were your pilots.

27.9
1 Ki 5.18;
ver 27

9 The elders of Gĕbál and her skilled men were in you,
    caulking your seams;
  all the ships of the sea with their mariners were in you,
    to barter for your wares.

b. *The armies of Tyre*

27.10
Ezek 30.5;
38.5;
ver 11

10 "Persia and Lúd and Put were in your army as your men of war; they hung the shield and helmet in you; they gave you splendor. 11 The men of Arvăd and Hĕlĕch*g* were upon your walls round about, and men of Gāmăd were in your towers; they hung their shields upon your walls round about; they made perfect your beauty.

27.11
ver 3,8,10

c. *The commerce of Tyre*

27.12
2 Chr 20.36;
Isa 23.6,10;
ver 18,33

12 "Tarshĭsh trafficked with you because of your great wealth of every kind; silver, iron, tin, and lead they exchanged for your wares. 13 Jāvăn, Tubăl, and Mĕshĕch traded with you; they exchanged the persons of men and vessels of bronze for your merchandise. 14 Bĕth-tógar'máh exchanged for your wares horses, war horses, and mules. 15 The men of Rhodes*h* traded with you; many coastlands were your own special markets, they brought you in payment ivory tusks and ebony. 16 Ĕdóm*i* trafficked with you because of your abundant goods; they exchanged for your wares emeralds, purple, embroidered work, fine linen, coral, and agate. 17 Judah and the land of Israel traded with you; they exchanged for your merchandise wheat, olives and early figs,*j* honey, oil, and balm. 18 Damascus trafficked with you for your abundant goods, because of your great wealth of every kind; wine of Hĕlbón, and white wool, 19 and wine*k* from Ūzál they exchanged for your wares; wrought iron, cassia, and calamus were bartered for your

27.13
Gen 10.2;
Isa 66.19;
Ezek 38.2;
Joel 3.3;
Rev 18.13

27.14
Gen 10.3;
Ezek 38.6

27.15
Gen 10.7;
Rev 18.12

27.16
Ezek 28.13;
16.13,18

27.17
Judg 11.33;
Jer 8.22

27.18
Jer 49.23;
Ezek 47.16–
18;
ver 12,33

---

f Compare Gen 10.18: Heb *your skilled men, O Tyre*
g Or *and your army*   *h* Gk: Heb *Dĕdán*
i Another reading is *Arám*
j Cn: Heb *wheat of minnith and pannag*
k Gk: Heb *Vĕdăn and Jāvăn*

merchandise. 20 Dēdản traded with you in saddlecloths for riding.
21Arabia and all the princes of Kēdar were your favored dealers in
lambs, rams, and goats; in these they trafficked with you. 22 The
traders of Shēbả and Rả'ảmảh traded with you; they exchanged
for your wares the best of all kinds of spices, and all precious
stones, and gold. 23 Hārản, Cảnnẻh, Eden,*l* Ảsshủr, and Çhỉlmảd
traded with you. 24 These traded with you in choice garments, in
clothes of blue and embroidered work, and in carpets of colored
stuff, bound with cords and made secure; in these they traded with
you.*m* 25 The ships of Tarshỉsh traveled for you with your merchandise.*n*

27.20
ver 15
27.21
Jer 25.24;
49.28;
Isa 60.7
27.22
Gen 10.7;
1 Ki 10.1,2;
Isa 60.6
27.23
Gen 11.31;
2 Ki 19.12;
Amos 1.5
27.25
Isa 2.16;
23.14;
ver 4

d. *The ruin of Tyre*

"So you were filled and heavily laden
  in the heart of the seas.
26 Your rowers have brought you out
  into the high seas.
The east wind has wrecked you
  in the heart of the seas.

27.26
Ezek 26.19;
Ps 48.7;
ver 4,25,27

27 Your riches, your wares, your merchandise,
  your mariners and your pilots,
your caulkers, your dealers in merchandise,
  and all your men of war who are in you,
with all your company
  that is in your midst,
sink into the heart of the seas
  on the day of your ruin.

27.27
Prov 11.4;
Rev 18.9–19

28 At the sound of the cry of your pilots
  the countryside shakes,
29 and down from their ships
  come all that handle the oar.
The mariners and all the pilots of the sea
  stand on the shore

27.28
Ezek 26.15
27.29
Rev 18.17–
19

30 and wail aloud over you,
  and cry bitterly.
They cast dust on their heads
  and wallow in ashes;

27.30
Job 2.12;
Rev 18.19;
Est 4.1,3;
Jer 6.26

31 they make themselves bald for you,
  and gird themselves with sackcloth,
and they weep over you in bitterness of soul,
  with bitter mourning.

27.31
Jer 16.6;
Ezek 29.18;
Isa 22.12;
16.9

32 In their wailing they raise a lamentation for you,
  and lament over you:
'Who was ever destroyed*o* like Tŷre
  in the midst of the sea?

27.32
ver 2;
Ezek 26.17;
Rev 18.18

33 When your wares came from the seas,
  you satisfied many peoples;
with your abundant wealth and merchandise
  you enriched the kings of the earth.

27.33
Rev 18.19

34 Now you are wrecked by the seas,
  in the depths of the waters;
your merchandise and all your crew
  have sunk with you.

27.34
ver 26,27;
Ezek 26.19;
Zech 9.3,4

l Cn: Heb *Eden the traders of Shēbả*   *m* Cn: Heb *in your market*
n Cn: Heb *your travelers your merchandise*   *o* Tg Vg: Heb *like silence*

27.35
Ezek 26.15,
16; 32.10

35 All the inhabitants of the coastlands
    are appalled at you;
  and their kings are horribly afraid,
    their faces are convulsed.

27.36
Jer 18.16;
Zeph 2.15;
Ezek 26.21;
Ps 37.10,36

36 The merchants among the peoples hiss at you;
    you have come to a dreadful end
    and shall be no more for ever.' "

F. Prophecies against Tyre and Sidon

1. The pride of Tyre the reason for its ruin

★28.2
Ezek 27.25–
27;
Isa 31.3;
ver 6

28 The word of the LORD came to me: 2 "Son of man, say to the prince of Tyre, Thus says the Lord GOD:
"Because your heart is proud,
    and you have said, 'I am a god,
  I sit in the seat of the gods,
    in the heart of the seas,'
  yet you are but a man, and no god,
    though you consider yourself as wise as a god—

28.3
Dan 1.20

3 you are indeed wiser than Daniel;
    no secret is hidden from you;

28.4
Ezek 27.33

4 by your wisdom and your understanding
    you have gotten wealth for yourself,
  and have gathered gold and silver
    into your treasuries;

28.5
Ps 62.10;
Zech 9.3;
Hos 13.6

5 by your great wisdom in trade
    you have increased your wealth,
  and your heart has become proud in your wealth—

28.6
ver 2

6 therefore thus says the Lord GOD:
"Because you consider yourself
    as wise as a god,

28.7
Ezek 26.7;
30.11;
31.12;
32.12;
ver 17

7 therefore, behold, I will bring strangers upon you,
    the most terrible of the nations;
  and they shall draw their swords against the beauty of your
    wisdom
  and defile your splendor.

28.8
Ezek 32.30;
27.26,27,34

8 They shall thrust you down into the Pit,
    and you shall die the death of the slain
    in the heart of the seas.

28.9
ver 2

9 Will you still say, 'I am a god,'
    in the presence of those who slay you,
  though you are but a man, and no god,
    in the hands of those who wound you?

28.10
Ezek 31.18;
32.19,21,
25,27

10 You shall die the death of the uncircumcised
    by the hand of foreigners;
  for I have spoken, says the Lord GOD."

2. The lamentation over Tyre

28.12
Ezek 27.2;
ver 3;
Ezek 27.3

11 Moreover the word of the LORD came to me: 12 "Son of man, raise a lamentation over the king of Tyre, and say to him, Thus says the Lord GOD:

28.2 *in the heart of the seas.* Tyre occupied an island one-half mile from the Phoenician coast. From the island stronghold, Tyre was able to withstand Nebuchadnezzar's siege for thirteen years. As an island fortress it was almost impregnable for that day.

"You were the signet of perfection,[p]
　　full of wisdom
　　and perfect in beauty.
13 You were in Eden, the garden of God;
　　every precious stone was your covering,
　　carnelian, topaz, and jasper,
　　　chrysolite, beryl, and onyx,
　　sapphire,[q] carbuncle, and emerald;
　　and wrought in gold were your settings
　　　and your engravings.[r]
On the day that you were created
　　they were prepared.
14 With an anointed guardian cherub I placed you;[s]
　　you were on the holy mountain of God;
　　in the midst of the stones of fire you walked.
15 You were blameless in your ways
　　from the day you were created,
　　till iniquity was found in you.
16 In the abundance of your trade
　　you were filled with violence, and you sinned;
　　so I cast you as a profane thing from the mountain of God,
　　and the guardian cherub drove you out
　　from the midst of the stones of fire.
17 Your heart was proud because of your beauty;
　　you corrupted your wisdom for the sake of your splendor.
　　I cast you to the ground;
　　I exposed you before kings,
　　to feast their eyes on you.
18 By the multitude of your iniquities,
　　in the unrighteousness of your trade
　　you profaned your sanctuaries;
　　so I brought forth fire from the midst of you;
　　it consumed you,
and I turned you to ashes upon the earth
　　in the sight of all who saw you.
19 All who know you among the peoples
　　are appalled at you;
　　you have come to a dreadful end
　　and shall be no more for ever."

3. Sidon to perish by pestilence and the sword

20 The word of the LORD came to me: 21 "Son of man, set your face toward Sīdôn, and prophesy against her 22 and say, Thus says the Lord GOD:

"Behold, I am against you, O Sīdôn,
　　and I will manifest my glory in the midst of you.
And they shall know that I am the LORD
　　when I execute judgments in her,
　　and manifest my holiness in her;
23 for I will send pestilence into her,
　　and blood into her streets;
and the slain shall fall in the midst of her,
　　by the sword that is against her on every side.
Then they will know that I am the LORD.

Marginal references:

28.13 Ezek 31.8, 9; 36.35

28.14 Ex 25.20; ver 16; Ezek 20.40; Rev 18.16

28.15 Ezek 27.3,4; Isa 14.12; ver 17,18

28.16 Ezek 27.12ff; 8.17; Gen 3.24; ver 14

28.17 ver 2,5; Ezek 31.10; 27.3,4; 26.16

28.18 ver 16; Amos 1.9, 10; Mal 4.3

28.19 Ezek 26.21; 27.36; Jer 51.64

28.21 Ezek 6.2; 25.2; Isa 23.4,12; Ezek 32.30

28.22 Ezek 26.3; 39.13; Ps 9.16; ver 26; Ezek 38.16

28.23 Ezek 38.22; Jer 51.52; ver 24,26

---

[p] Heb obscure　　[q] Or lapis lazuli　　[r] Heb uncertain　　[s] Heb uncertain

4. The recovery of the house of Israel

28.24
Num 33.55;
Josh 23.13;
Isa 55.13;
Ezek 25.6;
36.5

24 "And for the house of Israel there shall be no more a brier to prick or a thorn to hurt them among all their neighbors who have treated them with contempt. Then they will know that I am the Lord GOD.

28.25
Isa 11.12;
Jer 32.37;
Ezek 20.41;
Jer 23.8;
27.11;
Ezek 37.25

25 "Thus says the Lord GOD: When I gather the house of Israel from the peoples among whom they are scattered, and manifest my holiness in them in the sight of the nations, then they shall dwell in their own land which I gave to my servant Jacob. 26And they shall dwell securely in it, and they shall build houses and plant vineyards. They shall dwell securely, when I execute judgments upon all their neighbors who have treated them with contempt. Then they will know that I am the Lord their God."

28.26
Jer 23.6;
Isa 65.21;
Amos 9.13,
14

G. The prophecies against Egypt

1. The word against Pharaoh

a. Pharaoh's sin of pride

★29.2
Ezek 28.21;
Jer 44.30;
Isa 19.1;
Jer 25.19;
46.2,25

29 In the tenth year, in the tenth month, on the twelfth day of the month, the word of the LORD came to me: 2 "Son of man, set your face against Pharaōh king of Egypt, and prophesy against him and against all Egypt; 3 speak, and say, Thus says the Lord GOD:

29.3
Jer 44.30;
Ezek 28.22;
Isa 27.1;
51.9;
Ezek 32.2

"Behold, I am against you,
    Pharaōh king of Egypt,
the great dragon that lies
    in the midst of his streams,
that says, 'My Nile is my own;
    I made it.'[t]

29.4
2 Ki 19.28;
Isa 37.29;
Ezek 38.4

4 I will put hooks in your jaws,
    and make the fish of your streams stick to your scales;
and I will draw you up out of the midst of your streams,
    with all the fish of your streams
    which stick to your scales.

29.5
Ezek 32.4–
6;
Jer 7.33;
34.20;
Ezek 39.4

5 And I will cast you forth into the wilderness,
    you and all the fish of your streams;
you shall fall upon the open field,
    and not be gathered and buried.
To the beasts of the earth and to the birds of the air
    I have given you as food.

b. Egypt's judgment

29.6
Isa 36.6
29.7
Jer 37.5–
11;
Ezek 17.17

6 "Then all the inhabitants of Egypt shall know that I am the LORD. Because you[u] have been a staff of reed to the house of Israel; 7 when they grasped you with the hand, you broke, and tore all their shoulders; and when they leaned upon you, you broke, and

t Syr Compare Gk: Heb *I have made myself*
u Gk Syr Vg: Heb *they*

29.2 God plainly foretold the overthrow of Egypt (Jer 43.8–13; Ezek ch 29—31; Isa 19.1–15). This prophecy was later fulfilled by Nebuchadnezzar in his invasions of 572 and 568 B.C., when it was reduced to the status of *the most lowly of the kingdoms* (29.15). From the Persian conquest by Cambyses (ca. 524 B.C.) until the present generation, the Land of the Nile has for the most part been either subject to foreign powers (Alexander the Great, Rome, Arabia, Turkey) or to a foreign dynasty.

made all their loins to shake;[v] 8 therefore thus says the Lord GOD: Behold, I will bring a sword upon you, and will cut off from you man and beast; 9 and the land of Egypt shall be a desolation and a waste. Then they will know that I am the LORD.

c. The desolation and restoration of Egypt

"Because you[w] said, 'The Nile is mine, and I made it,' 10 therefore, behold, I am against you, and against your streams, and I will make the land of Egypt an utter waste and desolation, from Mĭg'dŏl to Sȳē'nē, as far as the border of Ethiopia. 11 No foot of man shall pass through it, and no foot of beast shall pass through it; it shall be uninhabited forty years. 12 And I will make the land of Egypt a desolation in the midst of desolated countries; and her cities shall be a desolation forty years among cities that are laid waste. I will scatter the Egyptians among the nations, and disperse them among the countries.

13 "For thus says the Lord GOD: At the end of forty years I will gather the Egyptians from the peoples among whom they were scattered; 14 and I will restore the fortunes of Egypt, and bring them back to the land of Păth'rŏs, the land of their origin; and there they shall be a lowly kingdom. 15 It shall be the most lowly of the kingdoms, and never again exalt itself above the nations; and I will make them so small that they will never again rule over the nations. 16 And it shall never again be the reliance of the house of Israel, recalling their iniquity, when they turn to them for aid. Then they will know that I am the Lord GOD."

2. Nebuchadrezzar to receive Egypt as his wages

17 In the twenty-seventh year, in the first month, on the first day of the month, the word of the LORD came to me: 18 "Son of man, Nĕb'ŭçhȧdrĕz'zȧr king of Babylon made his army labor hard against Tȳre; every head was made bald and every shoulder was rubbed bare; yet neither he nor his army got anything from Tyre to pay for the labor that he had performed against it. 19 Therefore thus says the Lord GOD: Behold, I will give the land of Egypt to Nĕb'ŭçhȧdrĕz'zȧr king of Babylon; and he shall carry off its wealth[x] and despoil it and plunder it; and it shall be the wages for his army. 20 I have given him the land of Egypt as his recompense for which he labored, because they worked for me, says the Lord GOD.

21 "On that day I will cause a horn to spring forth to the house of Israel, and I will open your lips among them. Then they will know that I am the LORD."

3. The nearness of Egypt's doom
a. The LORD'S vengeance on Egypt

30 The word of the LORD came to me: 2 "Son of man, prophesy, and say, Thus says the Lord GOD:
"Wail, 'Alas for the day!'
3   For the day is near,
        the day of the LORD is near;

[v] Syr: Heb stand   [w] Gk Syr Vg: Heb he   [x] Or multitude

29.18 labor hard against Tyre. Nebuchadnezzar besieged Tyre for thirteen years before it fell in 572 B.C. (See note to 28.2 for location of Tyre.)

29.8
Ezek 14.17;
32.11–13
29.9
ver 10–12,
6,3

29.10
Ezek 30.12,
6

29.11
Jer 43.11,
12;
Ezek 32.13
29.12
Ezek 30.7,
26

29.13
Isa 19.22,
23;
Jer 46.26
29.14
Ezek 30.14;
17.6,14
29.15
ver 14;
Zech 10.11

29.16
Isa 30.2,3;
36.4,6;
Jer 14.10;
Hos 8.13;
ver 6,9,21

★29.18
Jer 27.6;
Ezek 26,7,8;
27.31

29.19
Ezek 30.10;
Jer 43.10–
13;
Ezek 30.4
29.20
Isa 45.1–3;
Jer 25.9
29.21
Ps 132.17;
Ezek 24.27;
33.22;
Lk 21.15;
Ezek 6.7;
ver 6
30.2
Isa 13.6;
Ezek 21.12;
Joel 1.5,11,
13
30.3
Ezek 7.7,12;
Joel 2.1;
Obad 15;
Zeph 1.7;
ver 18

it will be a day of clouds,
a time of doom for the nations.

30.4
ver 11,5,9;
Ezek 29.19

4 A sword shall come upon Egypt,
and anguish shall be in Ethiopia,
when the slain fall in Egypt,
and her wealth is carried away,
and her foundations are torn down.

30.5
Jer 25.20,24

5 Ethiopia, and Put, and Lùd, and all Arabia, and Libya,y and the people of the land that is in league, shall fall with them by the sword.

b. The fall of Egypt's supporters

30.6
Isa 20.3–6;
Ezek 29.10

6 "Thus says the LORD:
Those who support Egypt shall fall,
and her proud might shall come down;
from Mĭgdŏl to Sy̆e'nē
they shall fall within her by the sword,
says the Lord GOD.

30.7
Ezek 29.12

7 And shez shall be desolated in the midst of desolated countries
and her cities shall be in the midst of cities that are laid waste.

30.8
Ezek 29.6;
9.16;
ver 14,16,
5,6

8 Then they will know that I am the LORD,
when I have set fire to Egypt,
and all her helpers are broken.

30.9
Isa 18.1,2;
Ezek 38.11;
32.9,10

9 "On that day swifta messengers shall go forth from me to terrify the unsuspecting Ethiopians; and anguish shall come upon them on the day of Egypt's doom; for, lo, it comes!

c. The advent of Nebuchadrezzar

30.10
Ezek 29.19

10 "Thus says the Lord GOD:
I will put an end to the wealthb of Egypt,
by the hand of Nĕbúchádrĕz'zàr king of Babylon.

30.11
Ezek 28.7;
ver 4

11 He and his people with him, the most terrible of the nations,
shall be brought in to destroy the land;
and they shall draw their swords against Egypt,
and fill the land with the slain.

30.12
Isa 19.5,6;
Ezek 29.3,9

12 And I will dry up the Nile,
and will sell the land into the hand of evil men;
I will bring desolation upon the land and everything in it,
by the hand of foreigners;
I, the LORD, have spoken.

d. The vengeance of the LORD on Egypt

30.13
Isa 19.1;
Zech 13.2;
ver 16;
Zech 10.11;
Isa 19.16

13 "Thus says the Lord GOD:
I will destroy the idols,
and put an end to the images, in Memphis;
there shall no longer be a prince in the land of Egypt;
so I will put fear in the land of Egypt.

30.14
Ezek 29.14;
Ps 78.12,
43;
ver 15,16

14 I will make Păthrŏs a desolation,
and will set fire to Zŏăn,
and will execute acts of judgment upon Thēbĕş.

30.15
Jer 46.25;
ver 16

15 And I will pour my wrath upon Pĕlu'sĭúm,
the stronghold of Egypt,
and cut off the multitude of Thēbĕş.

y Gk Compare Syr Vg: Heb Cub   z Gk: Heb they
a Gk Syr: Heb in ships   b Or multitude

¹⁶ And I will set fire to Egypt;
  Pêlu'sïüm shall be in great agony;
Thēbes shall be breached,
  and its walls broken down.^c
¹⁷ The young men of On and of Pîbē'sèth shall fall by the sword;
  and the women shall go into captivity.
¹⁸ At Tëhăph'nèhēs the day shall be dark,
  when I break there the dominion of Egypt,
and her proud might shall come to an end;
  she shall be covered by a cloud,
  and her daughters shall go into captivity.
¹⁹ Thus I will execute acts of judgment upon Egypt.
  Then they will know that I am the Lord."

e. The arms of Pharaoh to be broken

20 In the eleventh year, in the first month, on the seventh day of the month, the word of the Lord came to me: ²¹ "Son of man, I have broken the arm of Pharaōh king of Egypt; and lo, it has not been bound up, to heal it by binding it with a bandage, so that it may become strong to wield the sword. ²² Therefore thus says the Lord God: Behold, I am against Pharaōh king of Egypt, and will break his arms, both the strong arm and the one that was broken; and I will make the sword fall from his hand. ²³ I will scatter the Egyptians among the nations, and disperse them throughout the lands. ²⁴And I will strengthen the arms of the king of Babylon, and put my sword in his hand; but I will break the arms of Pharaōh, and he will groan before him like a man mortally wounded. ²⁵ I will strengthen the arms of the king of Babylon, but the arms of Pharaōh shall fall; and they shall know that I am the Lord. When I put my sword into the hand of the king of Babylon, he shall stretch it out against the land of Egypt; ²⁶ and I will scatter the Egyptians among the nations and disperse them throughout the countries. Then they will know that I am the Lord."

4. The allegory of the great cedar
a. Egypt likened to a great cedar

31 In the eleventh year, in the third month, on the first day of the month, the word of the Lord came to me: ² "Son of man, say to Pharaōh king of Egypt and to his multitude:
"Whom are you like in your greatness?
³   Behold, I will liken you to^d a cedar in Lebanon,
  with fair branches and forest shade,
  and of great height,
  its top among the clouds.^e
⁴ The waters nourished it,
  the deep made it grow tall,
making its rivers flow^f
  round the place of its planting,
sending forth its streams
  to all the trees of the forest.
⁵ So it towered high
  above all the trees of the forest;

30.16 ver 8,13–15

30.18 Jer 43.8–13; Ezek 34.27; ver 3

30.19 ver 14,25,26

30.21 Ps 10.15; Jer 46.11

30.22 Ezek 29.3; Ps 37.17

30.23 Ezek 29.12; ver 26
30.24 ver 10,25; Zech 10.12; Zeph 2.12; Ezek 26.15; 21.14,25
30.25 ver 24,22,11; Isa 5.25
30.26 Ezek 29.12

31.2 Ezek 29.19; 30.10; ver 18
31.3 Nah 3.1ff; Ezek 17.23; ver 5,10
31.4 Ezek 17.5, 8; Rev 17.1,15

31.5 Ps 37.35; Ezek 17.5

^c Cn: Heb and Memphis, distresses by day   ^d Cn: Heb Behold, Assyria
^e Gk: Heb thick boughs   ^f Gk: Heb going

its boughs grew large
and its branches long,
from abundant water in its shoots.

31.6
Ezek 17.23;
Dan 4.12;
Mt 13.32;
Mk 4.32;
Lk 13.19

6 All the birds of the air
made their nests in its boughs;
under its branches all the beasts of the field
brought forth their young;
and under its shadow
dwelt all great nations.

31.7
ver 2,9

7 It was beautiful in its greatness,
in the length of its branches;
for its roots went down
to abundant waters.

31.8
Gen 2.8;
13.10;
Ezek 28.13;
ver 16,18

8 The cedars in the garden of God could not rival it,
nor the fir trees equal its boughs;
the plane trees were as nothing
compared with its branches;
no tree in the garden of God
was like it in beauty.

31.9
Ezek 16.14

9 I made it beautiful
in the mass of its branches,
and all the trees of Eden envied it,
that were in the garden of God.

b. The fall of the cedar (Egypt) into the Pit

31.10
Isa 14.13,
14;
Ezek 28.17;
Dan 5.20

10 "Therefore thus says the Lord GOD: Because it*g* towered high and set its top among the clouds,*h* and its heart was proud of its height, 11 I will give it into the hand of a mighty one of the nations; he shall surely deal with it as its wickedness deserves. I have cast it out. 12 Foreigners, the most terrible of the nations, will cut it down and leave it. On the mountains and in all the valleys its branches will fall, and its boughs will lie broken in all the watercourses of the land; and all the peoples of the earth will go from its shadow and leave it. 13 Upon its ruin will dwell all the birds of the air, and upon its branches will be all the beasts of the field. 14All this is in order that no trees by the waters may grow to lofty height or set their tops among the clouds,*h* and that no trees that drink water may reach up to them in height; for they are all given over to death, to the nether world among mortal men, with those who go down to the Pit.

31.11
Ezek 30.10,
11;
Nah 3.18
31.12
Ezek 28.7;
Hab 1.6;
Ezek 32.5;
35.8;
Nah 3.17,18
31.13
Isa 18.6;
Ezek 32.4
31.14
ver 16,17;
Ps 63.9;
ver 18;
Ezek 32.24

15 "Thus says the Lord GOD: When it goes down to Shēōl I will make the deep mourn for*i* it, and restrain its rivers, and many waters shall be stopped; I will clothe Lebanon in gloom for it, and all the trees of the field shall faint because of it. 16 I will make the nations quake at the sound of its fall, when I cast it down to Shēōl with those who go down to the Pit; and all the trees of Eden, the choice and best of Lebanon, all that drink water, will be comforted in the nether world. 17 They also shall go down to Shēōl with it, to those who are slain by the sword; yea, those who dwelt under its shadow among the nations shall perish.*j* 18 Whom are you thus like in glory and in greatness among the trees of Eden? You shall be brought down with the trees of Eden to the nether world;

31.15
Ezek 32.7;
Nah 2.10
31.16
Ezek 26.15;
Isa 14.15;
Ezek 32.18;
Isa 14.8;
Ezek 32.31
31.17
Ps 9.17;
Ezek 32.18–
20
31.18
Ezek 32.19;
ver 8,9,14;
Ezek 28.10;
32.19,21

g Syr Vg: Heb *you*
h Gk: Heb *thick boughs*
i Gk: Heb *mourn for, I have covered*
j Compare Gk: Heb obscure

you shall lie among the uncircumcised, with those who are slain by
the sword.

"This is Phạraōh and all his multitude, says the Lord GOD."

5. *The lamentation over Pharaoh*
a. *The evils that shall befall him*

32 In the twelfth year, in the twelfth month, on the first day
of the month, the word of the LORD came to me: 2 "Son of
man, raise a lamentation over Phạraōh king of Egypt, and say to
him:

"You consider yourself a lion among the nations,
but you are like a dragon in the seas;
you burst forth in your rivers,
trouble the waters with your feet,
and foul their rivers.
3 Thus says the Lord GOD:
I will throw my net over you
with a host of many peoples;
and I *k* will haul you up in my dragnet.
4 And I will cast you on the ground,
on the open field I will fling you,
and will cause all the birds of the air to settle on you,
and I will gorge the beasts of the whole earth with you.
5 I will strew your flesh upon the mountains,
and fill the valleys with your carcass.*l*
6 I will drench the land even to the mountains
with your flowing blood;
and the watercourses will be full of you.
7 When I blot you out, I will cover the heavens,
and make their stars dark;
I will cover the sun with a cloud,
and the moon shall not give its light.
8 All the bright lights of heaven
will I make dark over you,
and put darkness upon your land,

says the Lord GOD.

b. *The dispersal of the peoples*

9 "I will trouble the hearts of many peoples, when I carry you
captive*m* among the nations, into the countries which you have
not known. 10 I will make many peoples appalled at you, and their
kings shall shudder because of you, when I brandish my sword
before them; they shall tremble every moment, every one for his
own life, on the day of your downfall. 11 For thus says the Lord
GOD: The sword of the king of Babylon shall come upon you.
12 I will cause your multitude to fall by the swords of mighty ones,
all of them most terrible among the nations.

"They shall bring to nought the pride of Egypt,
and all its multitude shall perish.
13 I will destroy all its beasts
from beside many waters;
and no foot of man shall trouble them any more,
nor shall the hoofs of beasts trouble them.

---

k Gk Vg: Heb *they*
l Symmachus Syr Vg: Heb *your height*   *m* Gk: Heb *bring your destruction*

Marginal references:

32.2
Ezek 27.2;
19.3,6;
38.13;
34.18

32.3
Ezek 12.13;
17.20;
Hos 7.12

32.4
Ezek 29.5;
31.13;
Isa 18.6

32.5
Ezek 35.8

32.6
Ezek 35.6;
Rev 14.20

32.7
Prov 13.9;
Isa 34.4;
13.10;
Joel 2.31;
3.15;
Amos 8.9;
Mt 24.29;
Rev 6.12,13

32.9
Ezek 28.19;
Rev 18.10–
15;
Ex 15.14–16
32.10
Ezek 27.35;
26.16;
Jer 46.10
32.11
Jer 46.26;
Ezek 30.4
32.12
Ezek 28.7;
31.12;
30.18
32.13
Ezek 29.8,
11

14 Then I will make their waters clear,
   and cause their rivers to run like oil, says the Lord GOD.

32.15
Ezek 29.12,
19,20;
Ps 9.16;
Ezek 6.7
15 When I make the land of Egypt desolate
   and when the land is stripped of all that fills it,
when I smite all who dwell in it,
   then they will know that I am the LORD.

32.16
2 Sam 1.17;
2 Chr 35.25;
Ezek 26.17
16 This is a lamentation which shall be chanted; the daughters of the nations shall chant it; over Egypt, and over all her multitude, shall they chant it, says the Lord GOD."

6. The lamentation over Egypt: the nations Egypt will join in the Pit

32.18
ver 2,16;
Mic 1.8;
Ezek 26.20;
31.14;
ver 24
17 In the twelfth year, in the first month,[n] on the fifteenth day of the month, the word of the LORD came to me: 18 "Son of man, wail over the multitude of Egypt, and send them down, her and the daughters of majestic nations, to the nether world, to those who have gone down to the Pit:

32.19
Ezek 31.2,
18; 28.10;
ver 21,24,29
19 'Whom do you surpass in beauty?
   Go down, and be laid with the uncircumcised.'

32.21
Isa 1.31;
14.9,10;
ver 27,31,32
20 They shall fall amid those who are slain by the sword,[o] and with her shall lie all her multitudes.[p] 21 The mighty chiefs shall speak of them, with their helpers, out of the midst of Shēōl: 'They have come down, they lie still, the uncircumcised, slain by the sword.'

32.22
Ezek 31.3,
16
32.23
Isa 14.15;
ver 24–27,32
22 "Assyria is there, and all her company, their graves round about her, all of them slain, fallen by the sword; 23 whose graves are set in the uttermost parts of the Pit, and her company is round about her grave; all of them slain, fallen by the sword, who spread terror in the land of the living.

32.24
Jer 49.34–
39;
Ps 27.13;
Isa 38.11;
Jer 11.19;
ver 25,30
32.25
Ps 139.8;
ver 19,23,24
24 "Ēlám is there, and all her multitude about her grave; all of them slain, fallen by the sword, who went down uncircumcised into the nether world, who spread terror in the land of the living, and they bear their shame with those who go down to the Pit. 25 They have made her a bed among the slain with all her multitude, their graves round about her, all of them uncircumcised, slain by the sword; for terror of them was spread in the land of the living, and they bear their shame with those who go down to the Pit; they are placed among the slain.

32.26
Gen 10.2;
Ezek 27.13;
38.2;
ver 19,32
32.27
Isa 14.18,19,
21,23
26 "Mēshēḥ and Tubál are there, and all their multitude, their graves round about them, all of them uncircumcised, slain by the sword; for they spread terror in the land of the living. 27 And they do not lie with the fallen mighty men of old[q] who went down to Shēōl with their weapons of war, whose swords were laid under their heads, and whose shields[r] are upon their bones; for the terror of the mighty men was in the land of the living. 28 So you shall be broken and lie among the uncircumcised, with those who are slain by the sword.

32.28
ver 19

32.29
Isa 34.5–
15;
Jer 49.7–22;
Ezek 25.13
29 "Ēdóm is there, her kings and all her princes, who for all their might are laid with those who are slain by the sword; they lie with the uncircumcised, with those who go down to the Pit.

32.30
Ezek 38.6,
15; 39.2;
28.21
30 "The princes of the north are there, all of them, and all the Sīdō'nïáns, who have gone down in shame with the slain, for all the terror which they caused by their might; they lie uncircum-

n Gk: Heb lacks in the first month
o Gk Syr: Heb sword, the sword is delivered
p Gk: Heb they have drawn her away and all her multitudes
q Gk Old Latin: Heb of the uncircumcised   r Cn: Heb iniquities

cised with those who are slain by the sword, and bear their shame
with those who go down to the Pit.

31 "When Pharaōh sees them, he will comfort himself for all
his multitude, Pharaoh and all his army, slain by the sword, says
the Lord GOD. 32 For he⁵ spread terror in the land of the living;
therefore he shall be laid among the uncircumcised, with those
who are slain by the sword, Pharaōh and all his multitude, says
the Lord GOD."

III. Israel restored 33.1–39.29

A. The prophet watchman

1. Ezekiel as Israel's watchman

33 The word of the LORD came to me: 2 "Son of man, speak
to your people and say to them, If I bring the sword upon a
land, and the people of the land take a man from among them, and
make him their watchman; 3 and if he sees the sword coming upon
the land and blows the trumpet and warns the people; 4 then if
any one who hears the sound of the trumpet does not take warning, and the sword comes and takes him away, his blood shall be
upon his own head. 5 He heard the sound of the trumpet, and
did not take warning; his blood shall be upon himself. But if he
had taken warning, he would have saved his life. 6 But if the
watchman sees the sword coming and does not blow the trumpet,
so that the people are not warned, and the sword comes, and takes
any one of them; that man is taken away in his iniquity, but his
blood I will require at the watchman's hand.

7 "So you, son of man, I have made a watchman for the house of
Israel; whenever you hear a word from my mouth, you shall give
them warning from me. 8 If I say to the wicked, O wicked man,
you shall surely die, and you do not speak to warn the wicked
to turn from his way, that wicked man shall die in his iniquity,
but his blood I will require at your hand. 9 But if you warn the
wicked to turn from his way, and he does not turn from his way;
he shall die in his iniquity, but you will have saved your life.

2. The watchman's message of righteousness

10 "And you, son of man, say to the house of Israel, Thus have
you said: 'Our transgressions and our sins are upon us, and we
waste away because of them; how then can we live?' 11 Say to them,
As I live, says the Lord GOD, I have no pleasure in the death of
the wicked, but that the wicked turn from his way and live; turn
back, turn back from your evil ways; for why will you die, O house
of Israel? 12And you, son of man, say to your people, The righteousness of the righteous shall not deliver him when he transgresses; and as for the wickedness of the wicked, he shall not fall
by it when he turns from his wickedness; and the righteous shall
not be able to live by his righteousness ᵗ when he sins. 13 Though
I say to the righteous that he shall surely live, yet if he trusts in his
righteousness and commits iniquity, none of his righteous deeds
shall be remembered; but in the iniquity that he has committed
he shall die. 14Again, though I say to the wicked, 'You shall surely

⁵ Cn: Heb *I*   ᵗ Heb *by it*

Marginal references

32.31
ver 18,21;
Ezek 31.16
32.32
ver 19–24

33.2
Ezek 3.11;
Jer 12.12;
Zech 13.7;
2 Sam
18.24,25;
2 Ki 9.17
33.3
Hos 8.1;
Joel 2.1
33.4
Jer 6.17;
Zech 1.4;
Ezek 18.13;
Acts 18.6
33.5
Heb 11.7
33.6
Isa 56.10,
11;
ver 8;
Ezek 3.18,
20
33.7
Ezek 3.17–
21;
Jer 26.2;
Acts 5.20
33.8
ver 14,6
33.9
Acts 13.40,
41,46;
Ezek 3.19,
21

33.10
Ezek 18.2;
24.23;
37.11
33.11
2 Sam
14.14;
Ezek 18.23,
32;
2 Pet 3.9;
Ezek 18.30,
31
33.12
Ezek 3.20;
2 Chr 7.14
33.13
Ezek 3.20;
18.24;
2 Pet 2.20,
21
33.14
Ezek 3.18,
19; 18.27

die,' yet if he turns from his sin and does what is lawful and right, 15 if the wicked restores the pledge, gives back what he has taken by robbery, and walks in the statutes of life, committing no iniquity; he shall surely live, he shall not die. 16 None of the sins that he has committed shall be remembered against him; he has done what is lawful and right, he shall surely live.

17 "Yet your people say, 'The way of the Lord is not just'; when it is their own way that is not just. 18 When the righteous turns from his righteousness, and commits iniquity, he shall die for it. 19And when the wicked turns from his wickedness, and does what is lawful and right, he shall live by it. 20 Yet you say, 'The way of the Lord is not just.' O house of Israel, I will judge each of you according to his ways."

3. *The tidings of Jerusalem's fall*

21 In the twelfth year of our exile, in the tenth month, on the fifth day of the month, a man who had escaped from Jerusalem came to me and said, "The city has fallen." 22 Now the hand of the LORD had been upon me the evening before the fugitive came; and he had opened my mouth by the time the man came to me in the morning; so my mouth was opened, and I was no longer dumb.

4. *The desolation to come upon the remnant*

23 The word of the LORD came to me: 24 "Son of man, the inhabitants of these waste places in the land of Israel keep saying, 'Abraham was only one man, yet he got possession of the land; but we are many; the land is surely given us to possess.' 25 Therefore say to them, Thus says the Lord GOD: You eat flesh with the blood, and lift up your eyes to your idols, and shed blood; shall you then possess the land? 26 You resort to the sword, you commit abominations and each of you defiles his neighbor's wife; shall you then possess the land? 27 Say this to them, Thus says the Lord GOD: As I live, surely those who are in the waste places shall fall by the sword; and him that is in the open field I will give to the beasts to be devoured; and those who are in strongholds and in caves shall die by pestilence. 28And I will make the land a desolation and a waste; and her proud might shall come to an end; and the mountains of Israel shall be so desolate that none will pass through. 29 Then they will know that I am the LORD, when I have made the land a desolation and a waste because of all their abominations which they have committed.

5. *The people will hear but not heed Ezekiel*

30 "As for you, son of man, your people who talk together about you by the walls and at the doors of the houses, say to one another, each to his brother, 'Come, and hear what the word is that comes forth from the LORD.' 31And they come to you as people come, and they sit before you as my people, and they hear what you say but they will not do it; for with their lips they show much love, but their heart is set on their gain. 32And, lo, you are to them like one who sings love songs *u* with a beautiful voice and plays well on an instrument, for they hear what you say, but they will not do it. 33 When this comes—and come it will!—then they will know that a prophet has been among them."

u Cn: Heb *like a love song*

33.15
Lev 6,2,4,
   5;
Num 5.6,7;
Lk 19.8;
Ezek 20.11
33.16
Ezek 18.22
33.17
Ezek 18.25,
   29;
ver 20
33.18
Ezek 18.26
33.19
ver 12,14
33.20
Ezek 18.25;
ver 17

33.21
Ezek 1.2;
   24.26;
2 Ki 25.4
33.22
Ezek 1.3;
   24.27;
Lk 1.64

33.24
Ezek 36.4;
Isa 51.2;
Acts 7.5
33.25
Deut 12.16;
Ezek 20.24;
   22.6,9
33.26
Ezek 18.6;
   22.11
33.27
Ezek 39.4;
1 Sam 13.6;
Isa 2.19
33.28
Jer 44.2,6,
   22;
Ezek 7.24;
   36.34,35
33.29
Ezek 23.33,
   35

33.30
ver 2,17;
Isa 29.13;
   58.2
33.31
Ezek 14.1;
   20.1; 8.1;
Ps 78.36,37;
Isa 29.13;
Mt 13.22

33.33
1 Sam 3.20;
Ezek 2.5

B. The prophecy concerning the shepherds of Israel

1. Indictment of the shepherds who failed to care for their sheep

34 The word of the LORD came to me: 2 "Son of man, prophesy against the shepherds of Israel, prophesy, and say to them, even to the shepherds, Thus says the Lord GOD: Ho, shepherds of Israel who have been feeding yourselves! Should not shepherds feed the sheep? 3 You eat the fat, you clothe yourselves with the wool, you slaughter the fatlings; but you do not feed the sheep. 4 The weak you have not strengthened, the sick you have not healed, the crippled you have not bound up, the strayed you have not brought back, the lost you have not sought, and with force and harshness you have ruled them. 5 So they were scattered, because there was no shepherd; and they became food for all the wild beasts. 6 My sheep were scattered, they wandered over all the mountains and on every high hill; my sheep were scattered over all the face of the earth, with none to search or seek for them.

7 "Therefore, you shepherds, hear the word of the LORD: 8 As I live, says the Lord GOD, because my sheep have become a prey, and my sheep have become food for all the wild beasts, since there was no shepherd; and because my shepherds have not searched for my sheep, but the shepherds have fed themselves, and have not fed my sheep; 9 therefore, you shepherds, hear the word of the LORD: 10 Thus says the Lord GOD, Behold, I am against the shepherds; and I will require my sheep at their hand, and put a stop to their feeding the sheep; no longer shall the shepherds feed themselves. I will rescue my sheep from their mouths, that they may not be food for them.

2. The LORD the shepherd of the sheep

11 "For thus says the Lord GOD: Behold, I, I myself will search for my sheep, and will seek them out. 12 As a shepherd seeks out his flock when some of his sheep*v* have been scattered abroad, so will I seek out my sheep; and I will rescue them from all places where they have been scattered on a day of clouds and thick darkness. 13 And I will bring them out from the peoples, and gather them from the countries, and will bring them into their own land; and I will feed them on the mountains of Israel, by the fountains, and in all the inhabited places of the country. 14 I will feed them with good pasture, and upon the mountain heights of Israel shall be their pasture; there they shall lie down in good grazing land, and on fat pasture they shall feed on the mountains of Israel. 15 I myself will be the shepherd of my sheep, and I will make them lie down, says the Lord GOD. 16 I will seek the lost, and I will bring back the strayed, and I will bind up the crippled, and I will strengthen the weak, and the fat and the strong I will watch over;*w* I will feed them in justice.

3. The LORD's judgment between sheep and sheep

17 "As for you, my flock, thus says the Lord GOD: Behold, I judge between sheep and sheep, rams and he-goats. 18 Is it not enough for you to feed on the good pasture, that you must tread down with your feet the rest of your pasture; and to drink of clear water, that you must foul the rest with your feet? 19 And must

v Cn: Heb *when he is among his sheep*   *w* Gk Syr Vg: Heb *destroy*

34.2 Jer 10.21; ver 8–10, 14,15; Jn 10.11; 21.15–17
34.3 Isa 56.11; Zech 11.16; Ezek 22.25, 27
34.4 Zech 11.16; Mt 9.36; Lk 15.4; 1 Pet 5.3
34.5 Jer 10.21; 50.6,7; Jer 23.2; Mt 9.36
34.8 Acts 20.29; ver 5,6,2
34.10 Ezek 3.18; Heb 13.17; ver 2,8
34.11 Ezek 11.17; 20.41
34.12 Jn 10.16; Ezek 30.3; Joel 2.2
34.13 Isa 65.9,10; Jer 23.3; Ezek 37.22; Isa 30.25
34.14 Ps 23.1,2; Ezek 20.40; 28.25,26
34.16 Mt 18.11; Lk 5.32; Isa 49.26
34.17 Ezek 20.37, 38; Zech 10.3; Mt 25.32,33
34.18 2 Sam 7.19

my sheep eat what you have trodden with your feet, and drink what you have fouled with your feet?

20 "Therefore, thus says the Lord GOD to them: Behold, I, I myself will judge between the fat sheep and the lean sheep. 21 Because you push with side and shoulder, and thrust at all the weak with your horns, till you have scattered them abroad, 22 I will save my flock, they shall no longer be a prey; and I will judge between

4. *The Messiah as the new shepherd*

sheep and sheep. 23And I will set up over them one shepherd, my servant David, and he shall feed them: he shall feed them and be their shepherd. 24And I, the LORD, will be their God, and my servant David shall be prince among them; I, the LORD, have spoken.

5. *The LORD's covenant of peace*

25 "I will make with them a covenant of peace and banish wild beasts from the land, so that they may dwell securely in the wilderness and sleep in the woods. 26And I will make them and the places round about my hill a blessing; and I will send down the showers in their season; they shall be showers of blessing. 27And the trees of the field shall yield their fruit, and the earth shall yield its increase, and they shall be secure in their land; and they shall know that I am the LORD, when I break the bars of their yoke, and deliver them from the hand of those who enslaved them. 28 They shall no more be a prey to the nations, nor shall the beasts of the land devour them; they shall dwell securely, and none shall make them afraid. 29And I will provide for them prosperous*x* plantations so that they shall no more be consumed with hunger in the land, and no longer suffer the reproach of the nations. 30And they shall know that I, the LORD their God, am with them, and that they, the house of Israel, are my people, says the Lord GOD. 31And you are my sheep, the sheep of my pasture,*y* and I am your God, says the Lord GOD."

C. The prophecy against Mount Seir

35 The word of the LORD came to me: 2 "Son of man, set your face against Mount Seir, and prophesy against it, 3 and say to it, Thus says the Lord GOD: Behold, I am against you, Mount Seir, and I will stretch out my hand against you, and I will make you a desolation and a waste. 4 I will lay your cities waste, and you shall become a desolation; and you shall know that I am the LORD. 5 Because you cherished perpetual enmity, and gave over the people of Israel to the power of the sword at the time of their calamity, at the time of their final punishment; 6 therefore, as I live, says the Lord GOD, I will prepare you for blood, and blood shall pursue you; because you are guilty of blood,*z* therefore blood shall pursue you. 7 I will make Mount Seir a waste and a desola-

---

x Gk Syr Old Latin: Heb *for renown*
y Gk Old Latin: Heb *pasture you are men*   *z* Gk: Heb *you have hated blood*

34.23 *one shepherd*. The Davidic king will rule the united kingdom (Israel and Judah, cf. 37.15–18). Israel and Judah are also the *two nations* mentioned in 35.10.

34.20
ver 17
34.21
Deut 33.17;
Dan 8.4
34.22
ver 5,8,10,
17

*34.23
Isa 40.11;
Jer 23.4,5;
30.9;
Hos 3.5
34.24
Ezek 36.28;
37.27;
37.24,25;
Hos 3.5

34.25
Isa 11.6-9;
Hos 2.18;
Jer 23.6
34.26
Isa 56.7;
Zech 8.13
34.27
Ps 85.12;
Isa 4.2;
Jer 2.20
34.28
Jer 30.10

34.29
Isa 60.21;
Ezek 36.29,
3,6
34.30
Ezek 36.28;
37.27
34.31
Ps 100.3;
Jn 10.11

35.2
Jer 49.7,8
35.3
Ezek 21.3;
Jer 6.12;
15.6;
Ezek 25.13;
ver 7
35.4
ver 9;
Mal 1.3,4
35.5
Ezek 25.12;
Obad 10;
Ezek 7.2;
21.25,29
35.6
Ezek 16.38;
32.6
35.7
Ezek 25.13;
29.11

tion; and I will cut off from it all who come and go. 8And I will fill
your mountains with the slain; on your hills and in your valleys
and in all your ravines those slain with the sword shall fall. 9 I will
make you a perpetual desolation, and your cities shall not be inhabited. Then you will know that I am the LORD.

10 "Because you said, 'These two nations and these two countries shall be mine, and we will take possession of them,'—although the LORD was there—11 therefore, as I live, says the Lord
GOD, I will deal with you according to the anger and envy which
you showed because of your hatred against them; and I will make
myself known among you,a when I judge you. 12And you shall
know that I, the LORD, have heard all the revilings which you
uttered against the mountains of Israel, saying, 'They are laid
desolate, they are given us to devour.' 13And you magnified yourselves against me with your mouth, and multiplied your words
against me; I heard it. 14 Thus says the Lord GOD: For the rejoicing of the whole earth I will make you desolate. 15As you rejoiced
over the inheritance of the house of Israel, because it was desolate,
so I will deal with you; you shall be desolate, Mount Sēir, and all
Ēdom, all of it. Then they will know that I am the LORD.

D. The restoration of Israel

1. Judgment on Israel's oppressors

36 "And you, son of man, prophesy to the mountains of Israel,
and say, O mountains of Israel, hear the word of the LORD.
2 Thus says the Lord GOD: Because the enemy said of you, 'Aha!'
and, 'The ancient heights have become our possession,' 3 therefore
prophesy, and say, Thus says the Lord GOD: Because, yea, because
they made you desolate, and crushed you from all sides, so that you
became the possession of the rest of the nations, and you became
the talk and evil gossip of the people; 4 therefore, O mountains of
Israel, hear the word of the Lord GOD: Thus says the Lord GOD to
the mountains and the hills, the ravines and the valleys, the desolate wastes and the deserted cities, which have become a prey and
derision to the rest of the nations round about; 5 therefore thus
says the Lord GOD: I speak in my hot jealousy against the rest
of the nations, and against all Ēdom, who gave my land to themselves as a possession with wholehearted joy and utter contempt,
that they might possessb it and plunder it. 6 Therefore prophesy
concerning the land of Israel, and say to the mountains and hills,
to the ravines and valleys, Thus says the Lord GOD: Behold, I
speak in my jealous wrath, because you have suffered the reproach
of the nations; 7 therefore thus says the Lord GOD: I swear that
the nations that are round about you shall themselves suffer reproach.

2. Israel to be returned

8 "But you, O mountains of Israel, shall shoot forth your
branches, and yield your fruit to my people Israel; for they will
soon come home. 9 For, behold, I am for you, and I will turn to

a Gk: Heb them   b One Ms: Heb drive out

35.8
Isa 34.5,6;
Ezek 31.12;
32.4,5

35.9
Jer 49.13;
Ezek 6.7;
36.11

★35.10
Ezek 36.2,5;
Ps 48.1,3;
Ezek 48.35

35.11
Amos 1.11;
Mt 7.2;
Ps 9.16

35.13
Ezek 36.3;
Jer 7.11;
29.23

35.14
Isa 49.13;
Jer 51.48

35.15
Jer 50.11;
Obad 4,21;
Ezek 6.7

36.1
Ezek 6.2,3

36.2
Ezek 25.3;
Hab 3.19;
Ezek 35.10

36.3
Jer 2.15;
51.34;
18.16;
Ezek 35.13

36.4
Ezek 6.3;
34.28;
Ps 79.4;
Jer 48.27

36.5
Ezek 38.19;
25.12–14;
35.10,12;
Jer 50.11;
Mic 7.8

36.6
Ps 123.3,4;
Ezek 34.29

★36.7
Ezek 20.6,
15,23;
Jer 25.9,15,
29

36.8
ver 4;
Isa 27.6;
Ezek 17.23

35.10 *Two nations*, i.e., Judah and Israel.   36.7 Israel's shame was only temporary.

36.10
Isa 27.6;
Ezek 37.21,
22;
ver 33
36.11
Jer 30.18;
Ezek 16.55;
35.9

36.13
Num 13.32

36.15
Ezek 34.29;
22.4;
Jer 13.16;
18.15

36.17
Lev 18.25,
27,28;
Jer 2.7
36.18
Ezek 22.20;
16.36,38;
23.37
36.19
Amos 9.9;
Ezek 39.24;
Rom 2.6
36.20
Isa 52.5;
Rom 2.24;
Jer 33.24
36.21
Ps 74.18;
Isa 48.9;
Ezek 20.44

36.22
Ps 106.8

36.23
Ezek 20.41;
Ps 126.2;
Ezek 28.25;
39.27
36.24
Ezek 34.13;
37.21
36.25
Isa 52.15;
Heb 10.22;
Zech 13.1
36.26
Ps 51.10;
Ezek 11.19
36.27
Ezek 11.19;
37.14
36.28
Jer 30.22;
Ezek 11.20;
37.27
36.29
Zech 13.1;
36.30
Ezek 34.27,
29;
Hos 2.21–
23

you, and you shall be tilled and sown; 10 and I will multiply men upon you, the whole house of Israel, all of it; the cities shall be inhabited and the waste places rebuilt; 11 and I will multiply upon you man and beast; and they shall increase and be fruitful; and I will cause you to be inhabited as in your former times, and will do more good to you than ever before. Then you will know that I am the LORD. 12 Yea, I will let men walk upon you, even my people Israel; and they shall possess you, and you shall be their inheritance, and you shall no longer bereave them of children. 13 Thus says the Lord GOD: Because men say to you, 'You devour men, and you bereave your nation of children,' 14 therefore you shall no longer devour men and no longer bereave your nation of children, says the Lord GOD; 15 and I will not let you hear any more the reproach of the nations, and you shall no longer bear the disgrace of the peoples and no longer cause your nation to stumble, says the Lord GOD.''

3. *Israel's punishment due to idolatry*

16 The word of the LORD came to me: 17 "Son of man, when the house of Israel dwelt in their own land, they defiled it by their ways and their doings; their conduct before me was like the uncleanness of a woman in her impurity. 18 So I poured out my wrath upon them for the blood which they had shed in the land, for the idols with which they had defiled it. 19 I scattered them among the nations, and they were dispersed through the countries; in accordance with their conduct and their deeds I judged them. 20 But when they came to the nations, wherever they came, they profaned my holy name, in that men said of them, 'These are the people of the LORD, and yet they had to go out of his land.' 21 But I had concern for my holy name, which the house of Israel caused to be profaned among the nations to which they came.

4. *The LORD Himself to regather Israel*

22 "Therefore say to the house of Israel, Thus says the Lord GOD: It is not for your sake, O house of Israel, that I am about to act, but for the sake of my holy name, which you have profaned among the nations to which you came. 23 And I will vindicate the holiness of my great name, which has been profaned among the nations, and which you have profaned among them; and the nations will know that I am the LORD, says the Lord GOD, when through you I vindicate my holiness before their eyes. 24 For I will take you from the nations, and gather you from all the countries, and bring you into your own land. 25 I will sprinkle clean water upon you, and you shall be clean from all your uncleannesses, and from all your idols I will cleanse you. 26 A new heart I will give you, and a new spirit I will put within you; and I will take out of your flesh the heart of stone and give you a heart of flesh. 27 And I will put my spirit within you, and cause you to walk in my statutes and be careful to observe my ordinances. 28 You shall dwell in the land which I gave to your fathers; and you shall be my people, and I will be your God. 29 And I will deliver you from all your uncleannesses; and I will summon the grain and make it abundant and lay no famine upon you. 30 I will make the fruit of the tree and the increase of the field abundant, that you may never again suffer the disgrace of famine among the nations.

31 Then you will remember your evil ways, and your deeds that were not good; and you will loathe yourselves for your iniquities and your abominable deeds. 32 It is not for your sake that I will act, says the Lord GOD; let that be known to you. Be ashamed and confounded for your ways, O house of Israel.

5. *The cities to be inhabited; the waste places rebuilt*

33 "Thus says the Lord GOD: On the day that I cleanse you from all your iniquities, I will cause the cities to be inhabited, and the waste places shall be rebuilt. 34 And the land that was desolate shall be tilled, instead of being the desolation that it was in the sight of all who passed by. 35 And they will say, 'This land that was desolate has become like the garden of Eden; and the waste and desolate and ruined cities are now inhabited and fortified.' 36 Then the nations that are left round about you shall know that I, the LORD, have rebuilt the ruined places, and replanted that which was desolate; I, the LORD, have spoken, and I will do it.

6. *The people to increase in number*

37 "Thus says the Lord GOD: This also I will let the house of Israel ask me to do for them: to increase their men like a flock. 38 Like the flock for sacrifices,*c* like the flock at Jerusalem during her appointed feasts, so shall the waste cities be filled with flocks of men. Then they will know that I am the LORD."

E. *The vision of the dry bones in the valley: Israel to be regathered*

37 The hand of the LORD was upon me, and he brought me out by the Spirit of the LORD, and set me down in the midst of the valley;*d* it was full of bones. 2 And he led me round among them; and behold, there were very many upon the valley;*d* and lo, they were very dry. 3 And he said to me, "Son of man, can these bones live?" And I answered, "O Lord GOD, thou knowest." 4 Again he said to me, "Prophesy to these bones, and say to them, O dry bones, hear the word of the LORD. 5 Thus says the Lord GOD to these bones: Behold, I will cause breath*e* to enter you, and you shall live. 6 And I will lay sinews upon you, and will cause flesh to come upon you, and cover you with skin, and put breath*e* in you, and you shall live; and you shall know that I am the LORD."

7 So I prophesied as I was commanded; and as I prophesied, there was a noise, and behold, a rattling; and the bones came together, bone to its bone. 8 And as I looked, there were sinews on them, and flesh had come upon them, and skin had covered them; but there was no breath in them. 9 Then he said to me, "Prophesy to the breath, prophesy, son of man, and say to the breath,*f* Thus says the Lord GOD: Come from the four winds, O breath,*f* and breathe upon these slain, that they may live." 10 So I prophesied as he commanded me, and the breath came into them, and they lived, and stood upon their feet, an exceedingly great host.

c Heb *flock of holy things*   *d* Or *plain*   *e* Or *spirit*   *f* Or *wind* or *spirit*

37.6 *you shall know that I am the* LORD, i.e., God will prove both His deity and His sover-eignty by reviving Israel which is pictured as dead (dry) bones in need of resurrection.

Marginal references:

36.31 Ezek 16.61–63; 20.43; 6.9
36.32 Ezek 20.44; ver 22
36.33 ver 25; Zech 8.7,8; Isa 58.12; ver 10
36.34 ver 9
36.35 Isa 51.3; Ezek 31.9; Joel 2.3
36.36 Ezek 39.27, 28; 22.14; 37.14
36.38 1 Ki 8.63; ver 33–35; Zech 11.17
37.1 Ezek 1.3; 8.3; 11.24; Lk 4.1; Acts 8.39
37.2 ver 11
37.3 Isa 26.19; Deut 32.39; 1 Sam 2.6
37.4 ver 9,12; Isa 42.18; Ezek 36.1
37.5 Ps 104.29, 30; ver 9,10
★37.6 ver 8–10; Ezek 6.7; 35.12; Joel 2.27; 3.17
37.7 Jer 13.5–7; Ezek 38.19
37.9 Ps 104.30; ver 5; Hos 13.14
37.10 ver 5,6; Rev 11.11

★37.11
Ezek 36.10;
39.25;
Ps 141.7;
Isa 49.14
37.12
Isa 26.19;
Hos 13.14;
ver 25;
Ezek 36.24;
Amos 9.14,
15
37.13
Ezek 6.7;
ver 6,12
37.14
Ezek 36.27;
39.29;
36.36

11 Then he said to me, "Son of man, these bones are the whole house of Israel. Behold, they say, 'Our bones are dried up, and our hope is lost; we are clean cut off.' 12 Therefore prophesy, and say to them, Thus says the Lord GOD: Behold, I will open your graves, and raise you from your graves, O my people; and I will bring you home into the land of Israel. 13And you shall know that I am the LORD, when I open your graves, and raise you from your graves, O my people. 14And I will put my Spirit within you, and you shall live, and I will place you in your own land; then you shall know that I, the LORD, have spoken, and I have done it, says the LORD."

F. The union of the two sticks (Israel and Judah)

37.16
Num 17.2;
2 Chr
11.11–17;
15.9
37.17
ver 22–24
37.18
Ezek 12.9;
24.19
37.19
Zech 10.6;
ver 16,17

15 The word of the LORD came to me: 16 "Son of man, take a stick and write on it, 'For Judah, and the children of Israel associated with him'; then take another stick and write upon it, 'For Joseph (the stick of Ē'phräim) and all the house of Israel associated with him'; 17 and join them together into one stick, that they may become one in your hand. 18And when your people say to you, 'Will you not show us what you mean by these?' 19 say to them, Thus says the Lord GOD: Behold, I am about to take the stick of Joseph (which is in the hand of Ē'phräim) and the tribes of Israel associated with him; and I will joing with it the stick of Judah, and make them one stick, that they may be one in my hand. 20 When the sticks on which you write are in your hand before their eyes,

37.21
Ezek 36.24;
39.27

21 then say to them, Thus says the Lord GOD: Behold, I will take the people of Israel from the nations among which they have gone, and will gather them from all sides, and bring them to their own land; 22 and I will make them one nation in the land, upon

37.22
Isa 11.13;
Jer 3.18;
Hos 1.11;
Ezek 34.23
37.23
Ezek 11.18;
43.7;36.25;
36.28

the mountains of Israel; and one king shall be king over them all; and they shall be no longer two nations, and no longer divided into two kingdoms. 23 They shall not defile themselves any more with their idols and their detestable things, or with any of their transgressions; but I will save them from all the backslidings in which they have sinned, and will cleanse them; and they shall be my people, and I will be their God.

37.24
Jer 30.9;
Isa 40.11;
Hos 3.5;
Ezek 36.27
37.25
Ezek 28.25;
36.28;
Zech 6.12
37.26
Isa 55.3;
Ezek 36.10;
20.40; 43.7
37.27
Lev 26.11;
Jn 1.14
37.28
Ezek 36.23;
20.12

24 "My servant David shall be king over them; and they shall all have one shepherd. They shall follow my ordinances and be careful to observe my statutes. 25 They shall dwell in the land where your fathers dwelt that I gave to my servant Jacob; they and their children and their children's children shall dwell there for ever; and David my servant shall be their prince for ever. 26 I will make a covenant of peace with them; it shall be an everlasting covenant with them; and I will blessh them and multiply them, and will set my sanctuary in the midst of them for evermore. 27 My dwelling place shall be with them; and I will be their God, and they shall be my people. 28 Then the nations will know that I the LORD sanctify Israel, when my sanctuary is in the midst of them for evermore."

g Heb join them   h Tg: Heb give

37.11 Verses 11–14 contain the explanation of the vision of the dry bones. The regathering of Israel is in view here, an event which is still future. The fulfilment of this prophetic promise is guaranteed by the Word of the LORD: I . . . have spoken, and I have done it.

G. The prophecy of Gog and Magog

1. The hordes of Gog to be assembled

38 The word of the LORD came to me: 2 "Son of man, set your
face toward Gŏg, of the land of Māgŏg, the chief prince of
Mĕshĕçh and Tubál, and prophesy against him 3 and say, Thus
says the Lord GOD: Behold, I am against you, O Gŏg, chief prince
of Mĕshĕçh and Tubál; 4 and I will turn you about, and put hooks
into your jaws, and I will bring you forth, and all your army,
horses and horsemen, all of them clothed in full armor, a great
company, all of them with buckler and shield, wielding swords;
5 Persia, Cŭsh, and Put are with them, all of them with shield and
helmet; 6 Gōmĕr and all his hordes; Bĕth-tŏgar'màh from the
uttermost parts of the north with all his hordes—many peoples
are with you.

7 "Be ready and keep ready, you and all the hosts that are assembled about you, and be a guard for them. 8After many days
you will be mustered; in the latter years you will go against the
land that is restored from war, the land where people were gathered from many nations upon the mountains of Israel, which had
been a continual waste; its people were brought out from the nations and now dwell securely, all of them. 9 You will advance,
coming on like a storm, you will be like a cloud covering the land,
you and all your hordes, and many peoples with you.

2. The evil scheme of Gog

10 "Thus says the Lord GOD: On that day thoughts will come
into your mind, and you will devise an evil scheme 11 and say, 'I
will go up against the land of unwalled villages; I will fall upon the
quiet people who dwell securely, all of them dwelling without
walls, and having no bars or gates'; 12 to seize spoil and carry off
plunder; to assail the waste places which are now inhabited, and
the people who were gathered from the nations, who have gotten
cattle and goods, who dwell at the center of the earth. 13 Shēbà and
Dēdàn and the merchants of Tarshìsh and all its villages will say
to you, 'Have you come to seize spoil? Have you assembled your
hosts to carry off plunder, to carry away silver and gold, to take
away cattle and goods, to seize great spoil?'

3. Gog descends on Israel

14 "Therefore, son of man, prophesy, and say to Gŏg, Thus
says the Lord GOD: On that day when my people Israel are dwelling securely, you will bestir yourselfⁱ 15 and come from your
place out of the uttermost parts of the north, you and many peoples with you, all of them riding on horses, a great host, a mighty
army; 16 you will come up against my people Israel, like a cloud
covering the land. In the latter days I will bring you against my

ⁱ Gk: Heb *will you not know?*

★38.2 Ezek 39.1; Rev 20.8
38.3 Ezek 39.1
38.4 2 Ki 19.28; Ezek 39.2
38.5 Ezek 27.10; 30.4,5
38.6 Gen 10.2; Ezek 27.14
38.7 Jer 46.3; 51.12
38.8 Isa 24.22; Ezek 36.24
38.9 Isa 28.2; Joel 2.2
38.10 Mic 2.1
38.11 Zech 2.4; Jer 49.31; ver 8
38.12 Isa 10.6; Ezek 29.19; ver 8
38.13 Ezek 27.22; 27.15; Nah 2.11-13
38.14 Jer 23.6; Zech 2.5,8
38.15 ver 6; Ezek 39.2
38.16 Ezek 36.23; 39.21

38.2 Gog is the ruler of the land called Magog. Magog, Meshech, and Tubal are mentioned in Gen 10.2 as sons of Japheth. They have been identified with the Goths, the Cretans, the Scythians, and the Russians. Although positive identification is not pos-sible, these peoples appear in Rev 20.8 as furnishing leadership for the final rebellion against God. The fearsome dimensions of this cataclysm may be seen by two statistics: (1) the weapons of the defeated enemy will provide fuel enough for seven years (39.9); (2) it will require seven months to bury the innumerable corpses left on the battlefield (39.14).

land, that the nations may know me, when through you, O Gŏg, I
vindicate my holiness before their eyes.

4. The defeat of Gog

17 "Thus says the Lord GOD: Are you he of whom I spoke in
former days by my servants the prophets of Israel, who in those
days prophesied for years that I would bring you against them?
18 But on that day, when Gŏg shall come against the land of Israel, says the Lord GOD, my wrath will be roused. 19 For in my
jealousy and in my blazing wrath I declare, On that day there shall
be a great shaking in the land of Israel; 20 the fish of the sea, and
the birds of the air, and the beasts of the field, and all creeping
things that creep on the ground, and all the men that are upon the
face of the earth, shall quake at my presence, and the mountains
shall be thrown down, and the cliffs shall fall, and every wall shall
tumble to the ground. 21 I will summon every kind of terror^j
against Gŏg,^{k} says the Lord GOD; every man's sword will be
against his brother. 22 With pestilence and bloodshed I will enter
into judgment with him; and I will rain upon him and his hordes
and the many peoples that are with him, torrential rains and hailstones, fire and brimstone. 23 So I will show my greatness and my
holiness and make myself known in the eyes of many nations.
Then they will know that I am the LORD.

5. The slaughtered hordes of Gog to be buried

39 "And you, son of man, prophesy against Gŏg, and say,
Thus says the Lord GOD: Behold, I am against you, O Gog,
chief prince of Mĕshĕch and Tubăl; 2 and I will turn you about
and drive you forward, and bring you up from the uttermost parts
of the north, and lead you against the mountains of Israel; 3 then
I will strike your bow from your left hand, and will make your
arrows drop out of your right hand. 4 You shall fall upon the mountains of Israel, you and all your hordes and the peoples that are
with you; I will give you to birds of prey of every sort and to the
wild beasts to be devoured. 5 You shall fall in the open field; for I
have spoken, says the Lord GOD. 6 I will send fire on Măgŏg and
on those who dwell securely in the coastlands; and they shall
know that I am the LORD.

7 "And my holy name I will make known in the midst of my
people Israel; and I will not let my holy name be profaned any
more; and the nations shall know that I am the LORD, the Holy
One in Israel. 8 Behold, it is coming and it will be brought about,
says the Lord GOD. That is the day of which I have spoken.

9 "Then those who dwell in the cities of Israel will go forth and
make fires of the weapons and burn them, shields and bucklers,
bows and arrows, handpikes and spears, and they will make fires of
them for seven years; 10 so that they will not need to take wood out
of the field or cut down any out of the forests, for they will make
their fires of the weapons; they will despoil those who despoiled
them, and plunder those who plundered them, says the Lord GOD.

11 "On that day I will give to Gŏg a place for burial in Israel,
the Valley of the Travelers^l east of the sea; it will block the travelers, for there Gog and all his multitude will be buried; it will be

38.17
Isa 34.1–6
38.18
ver 2;
Ps 18.8,15
38.19
Ezek 36.5,
6;
Nah 1.2;
Hag 2.6,7;
Rev 16.18
38.20
Jer 4.24;
Hos 4.3;
Nah 1.5,6;
Zech 14.4
38.21
Ezek 14.17;
Judg 7.22;
1 Sam
14.20;
2 Chr 20.23
38.22
Isa 66.16;
Jer 25.31;
Rev 16.21;
Ps 11.6
38.23
Ezek 36.23;
Ps 9.16;
Ezek 37.28

39.1
Ezek 38.2–4

39.2
Ezek 38.15

39.3
Ezek 30.21–
24;
Hos 1.5
39.4
Ezek 38.21;
33.37

39.6
Ezek 38.22;
Amos 1.4;
Ps 72.10;
Jer 25.22
39.7
Ezek 36.20–
22;
ver 25;
Ezek 20.39;
38.16;
Isa 60.9,14
39.8
Ezek 38.17
39.9
Ps 46.9
39.10
Isa 14.2;
Hab 2.8

39.11
Ezek 38.2;
ver 1,15

^{j} Gk: Heb a sword to all my mountains ^{k} Heb him ^{l} Or Ăb'ărim

called the Valley of Hā′mŏn-gŏg′.ᵐ ¹² For seven months the house of Israel will be burying them, in order to cleanse the land. ¹³All the people of the land will bury them; and it will redound to their honor on the day that I show my glory, says the Lord GOD. ¹⁴ They will set apart men to pass through the land continually and buryⁿ those remaining upon the face of the land, so as to cleanse it; at the end of seven months they will make their search. ¹⁵And when these pass through the land and any one sees a man's bone, then he shall set up a sign by it, till the buriers have buried it in the Valley of Hā′mŏn-gŏg′. ¹⁶ (A city Hámō′náhᵒ is there also.) Thus shall they cleanse the land.

6. *The sacrificial feast of the* LORD

¹⁷ "As for you, son of man, thus says the Lord GOD: Speak to the birds of every sort and to all beasts of the field, 'Assemble and come, gather from all sides to the sacrificial feast which I am preparing for you, a great sacrificial feast upon the mountains of Israel, and you shall eat flesh and drink blood. ¹⁸ You shall eat the flesh of the mighty, and drink the blood of the princes of the earth—of rams, of lambs, and of goats, of bulls, all of them fatlings of Bāshán. ¹⁹And you shall eat fat till you are filled, and drink blood till you are drunk, at the sacrificial feast which I am preparing for you. ²⁰And you shall be filled at my table with horses and riders, with mighty men and all kinds of warriors,' says the Lord GOD.

²¹ "And I will set my glory among the nations; and all the nations shall see my judgment which I have executed, and my hand which I have laid on them. ²² The house of Israel shall know that I am the LORD their God, from that day forward. ²³And the nations shall know that the house of Israel went into captivity for their iniquity, because they dealt so treacherously with me that I hid my face from them and gave them into the hand of their adversaries, and they all fell by the sword. ²⁴ I dealt with them according to their uncleanness and their transgressions, and hid my face from them.

7. *The regathering of God's people:*
Israel shall know the LORD

²⁵ "Therefore thus says the Lord GOD: Now I will restore the fortunes of Jacob, and have mercy upon the whole house of Israel; and I will be jealous for my holy name. ²⁶ They shall forget their shame, and all the treachery they have practiced against me, when they dwell securely in their land with none to make them afraid, ²⁷ when I have brought them back from the peoples and gathered them from their enemies' lands, and through them have vindicated my holiness in the sight of many nations. ²⁸ Then they shall know that I am the LORD their God because I sent them into exile among the nations, and then gathered them into their own land. I will leave none of them remaining among the nations any more; ²⁹ and I will not hide my face any more from them, when I pour out my Spirit upon the house of Israel, says the Lord GOD."

39.12	ver 14,16
39.13	Jer 33.9; Ezek 28.22
39.14	Jer 14.16; ver 12
39.15	ver 11
39.16	ver 12
39.17	ver 4; Rev 19.17; Isa 34.6,7; Jer 46.10; Zeph 1.7
39.18	Rev 19.18; Deut 32.14; Ps 22.12; Amos 4.1
39.20	Ps 76.6; Ezek 38.4; Rev 19.18
39.21	Ezek 38.16, 23; ver 13
39.22	ver 7,28
39.23	Ezek 36.18–20,23; 20.27; ver 26; Isa 59.2; ver 29
39.24	Ezek 36.19; ver 23
★39.25	Jer 30.3,18; Ezek 34.13; 36.24; 20.40; Hos 1.11
★39.26	Ezek 34.25–28; Isa 17.2; Mic 4.4
39.27	Ezek 28.25, 26; 36.23, 24; 38.16
39.28	Ezek 34.30; ver 22
39.29	Isa 32.15; Ezek 36.27; 37.14; Joel 2.28; Acts 2.17

ᵐ That is *the multitude of Gog*   ⁿ Gk Syr: Heb *bury the travelers*   ᵒ That is *Multitude*

39.25 *Jacob,* the one whose name was changed to *Israel.*

39.26 *They shall not forget their shame.* "They have borne their shame" in the KJV.

IV. *Israel in the land in the kingdom age 40.1–48.35*

A. *The new Temple arrangements*

1. *Introduction*

40 In the twenty-fifth year of our exile, at the beginning of the year, on the tenth day of the month, in the fourteenth year after the city was conquered, on that very day, the hand of the LORD was upon me, 2 and brought me in the visions of God into the land of Israel, and set me down upon a very high mountain, on which was a structure like a city opposite me.*p* 3 When he brought me there, behold, there was a man, whose appearance was like bronze, with a line of flax and a measuring reed in his hand; and he was standing in the gateway. 4And the man said to me, "Son of man, look with your eyes, and hear with your ears, and set your mind upon all that I shall show you, for you were brought here in order that I might show it to you; declare all that you see to the house of Israel."

5 And behold, there was a wall all around the outside of the temple area, and the length of the measuring reed in the man's hand was six long cubits, each being a cubit and a handbreadth in length; so he measured the thickness of the wall, one reed; and the

2. *The outer court: the east gate*

height, one reed. 6 Then he went into the gateway facing east, going up its steps, and measured the threshold of the gate, one reed deep;*q* 7 and the side rooms, one reed long, and one reed broad; and the space between the side rooms, five cubits; and the threshold of the gate by the vestibule of the gate at the inner end, one reed. 8 Then he measured the vestibule of the gateway, eight cubits; 9 and its jambs, two cubits; and the vestibule of the gate was at the inner end. 10And there were three side rooms on either side of the east gate; the three were of the same size; and the jambs on either side were of the same size. 11 Then he measured the breadth of the opening of the gateway, ten cubits; and the breadth of the gateway, thirteen cubits. 12 There was a barrier before the side rooms, one cubit on either side; and the side rooms were six cubits on either side. 13 Then he measured the gate from the back*r* of the one side room to the back*r* of the other, a breadth of five and twenty cubits, from door to door. 14 He measured also the vestibule, twenty cubits; and round about the vestibule of the gateway was the court.*s* 15 From the front of the gate at the entrance to the end of the inner vestibule of the gate was fifty cubits. 16And the gateway had windows round about, narrowing inwards into their jambs in the side rooms, and likewise the vestibule had windows round about inside, and on the jambs were palm trees.

3. *The thirty chambers about the court*

17 Then he brought me into the outer court; and behold, there were chambers and a pavement, round about the court; thirty chambers fronted on the pavement. 18And the pavement ran along

p Gk: Heb *on the south*   *q* Heb *deep, and one threshold, one reed deep*
r Compare Gk: Heb *roof*
s Compare Gk: Heb *and he made the jambs sixty cubits, and to the jamb of the court was the gateway round about*

Marginal references

40.1 Ezek 33.21; 1.2,3

40.2 Ezek 8.3; Dan 7.1,7; Ezek 17.23; Rev 21.10

40.3 Ezek 1.7; Dan 10.6; Ezek 47.3; Rev 11.1; 21.15

40.4 Ezek 44.5; 43.10; Jer 26.2; Acts 20.27

40.5 Ezek 42.20; ver 3

40.6 ver 20,26

40.7 ver 10–16, 21,29,33,36

40.10 ver 7

40.14 ver 9,16; 1 Chr 28.6; Isa 62.9; Ezek 42.1

40.16 1 Ki 6.4; ver 21,22,26, 31,34,37

40.17 Rev 11.2; 1 Chr 9.26; 2 Chr 31.11; Ezek 41.6; 45.5

the side of the gates, corresponding to the length of the gates; this was the lower pavement. ¹⁹ Then he measured the distance from the inner front of^t the lower gate to the outer front of the inner court, a hundred cubits.

4. *The north gate of the outer court*

Then he went before me to the north, ²⁰ and behold, there was a gate^u which faced toward the north, belonging to the outer court. He measured its length and its breadth. ²¹ Its side rooms, three on either side, and its jambs and its vestibule were of the same size as those of the first gate; its length was fifty cubits, and its breadth twenty-five cubits. ²²And its windows, its vestibule, and its palm trees were of the same size as those of the gate which faced toward the east; and seven steps led up to it; and its vestibule was on the inside. ²³And opposite the gate on the north, as on the east, was a gate to the inner court; and he measured from gate to gate, a hundred cubits.

5. *The south gate of the outer court*

24 And he led me toward the south, and behold, there was a gate on the south; and he measured its jambs and its vestibule; they had the same size as the others. ²⁵And there were windows round about in it and in its vestibule, like the windows of the others; its length was fifty cubits, and its breadth twenty-five cubits. ²⁶And there were seven steps leading up to it, and its vestibule was on the inside; and it had palm trees on its jambs, one on either side. ²⁷And there was a gate on the south of the inner court; and he measured from gate to gate toward the south, a hundred cubits.

6. *The gates of the inner court*

28 Then he brought me to the inner court by the south gate, and he measured the south gate; it was of the same size as the others. ²⁹ Its side rooms, its jambs, and its vestibule were of the same size as the others; and there were windows round about in it and in its vestibule; its length was fifty cubits, and its breadth twenty-five cubits. ³⁰And there were vestibules round about, twenty-five cubits long and five cubits broad. ³¹ Its vestibule faced the outer court, and palm trees were on its jambs, and its stairway had eight steps.

32 Then he brought me to the inner court on the east side, and he measured the gate; it was of the same size as the others. ³³ Its side rooms, its jambs, and its vestibule were of the same size as the others; and there were windows round about in it and in its vestibule; its length was fifty cubits, and its breadth twenty-five cubits. ³⁴ Its vestibule faced the outer court, and it had palm trees on its jambs, one on either side; and its stairway had eight steps.

35 Then he brought me to the north gate, and he measured it; it had the same size as the others. ³⁶ Its side rooms, its jambs, and its vestibule were of the same size as the others;^v and it had windows round about; its length was fifty cubits, and its breadth

	40.19 ver 23,27
	40.20 ver 6
	40.21 ver 7,16,30, 15,13
	40.22 ver 16,6,26, 31,34,37,49
	40.23 ver 19,27
	40.24 ver 21
	40.25 ver 16,22,21, 33
	40.26 ver 6,22,16
	40.27 ver 23,32,19
	40.28 ver 32,35
	40.29 ver 7,10,21, 16,22,25
	40.30 ver 16,21,25
	40.31 ver 16,22,26, 34,37
	40.32 ver 28–31,35
	40.33 ver 29,16,21
	40.34 ver 16,22,37
	40.35 Ezek 44.4; 47.2
	40.36 ver 7,29,16, 21

^t Compare Gk: Heb *from before*
^u Gk: Heb *a hundred cubits on the east and on the north.* 20*And the gate*
^v One Ms Compare verses 29 and 33: Heb lacks *were of the same size as the others*

40.37
ver 16,35

40.38
Ezek 41.10;
42.13;
2 Chr 4.6
40.39
Lev 4.2,3;
5.6; 6.6;
7.1
40.41
ver 39,40
40.42
ver 39;
Ex 20.25

40.44
ver 23,27,
17,38;
1 Chr 6.31;
25.1-7
40.45
ver 17,38;
Lev 8.35;
1 Chr 9.23;
2 Chr 13.11
40.46
ver 17,38;
Num 18.5;
Ezek 44.15;
43.19;
1 Ki 2.35
40.47
ver 19,23,27

40.49
1 Ki 6.3;
2 Ki 7.21;
Jer 52.17-
23;
Rev 3.12

41.1
Ezek 40.2,3,
17;
ver 21,23;
Ezek 40.9
41.2
1 Ki 6.2,17;
2 Chr 3.3

twenty-five cubits. 37 Its vestibule[w] faced the outer court, and it had palm trees on its jambs, one on either side; and its stairway had eight steps.

7. *The tables of sacrifice*

38 There was a chamber with its door in the vestibule of the gate,[x] where the burnt offering was to be washed. 39 And in the vestibule of the gate were two tables on either side, on which the burnt offering and the sin offering and the guilt offering were to be slaughtered. 40 And on the outside of the vestibule[y] at the entrance of the north gate were two tables; and on the other side of the vestibule of the gate were two tables. 41 Four tables were on the inside, and four tables on the outside of the side of the gate, eight tables, on which the sacrifices were to be slaughtered. 42 And there were also four tables of hewn stone for the burnt offering, a cubit and a half long, and a cubit and a half broad, and one cubit high, on which the instruments were to be laid with which the burnt offerings and the sacrifices were slaughtered. 43 And hooks, a handbreadth long, were fastened round about within. And on the tables the flesh of the offering was to be laid.

8. *The chambers for the priests*

44 Then he brought me from without into the inner court, and behold, there were two chambers[z] in the inner court, one[a] at the side of the north gate facing south, the other at the side of the south[b] gate facing north. 45 And he said to me, This chamber which faces south is for the priests who have charge of the temple, 46 and the chamber which faces north is for the priests who have charge of the altar; these are the sons of Zādŏk, who alone among the sons of Lēvī may come near to the LORD to minister to him. 47 And he measured the court, a hundred cubits long, and a hundred cubits broad, foursquare; and the altar was in front of the temple.

9. *The vestibule of the Temple*

48 Then he brought me to the vestibule of the temple and measured the jambs of the vestibule, five cubits on either side; and the breadth of the gate was fourteen cubits; and the sidewalls of the gate were three cubits[c] on either side. 49 The length of the vestibule was twenty cubits, and the breadth twelve[d] cubits; and ten steps led up[e] to it; and there were pillars beside the jambs on either side.

B. *The new Temple*

1. *The nave and the holy place*

41 Then he brought me to the nave, and measured the jambs; on each side six cubits was the breadth of the jambs.[f] 2 And the breadth of the entrance was ten cubits; and the sidewalls of the entrance were five cubits on either side; and he measured the

---

[w] Gk Vg Compare verses 26, 31, 34: Heb *jambs*   [x] Cn: Heb *at the jambs of the gates*
[y] Cn: Heb *to him who goes up*
[z] Gk: Heb *and from without to the inner gate were chambers for singers*
[a] Gk: Heb *which*   [b] Gk: Heb *east*
[c] Gk: Heb *and the breadth of the gate was three cubits*
[d] Gk: Heb *eleven*   [e] Gk: Heb *and by steps which went up*   [f] Compare Gk: Heb *tent*

length of the nave forty cubits, and its breadth, twenty cubits.
3 Then he went into the inner room and measured the jambs of the
entrance, two cubits; and the breadth of the entrance, six cubits;
and the sidewalls*g* of the entrance, seven cubits. 4And he measured
the length of the room, twenty cubits, and its breadth, twenty
cubits, beyond the nave. And he said to me, This is the most holy
place.

2. The side chambers

5 Then he measured the wall of the temple, six cubits thick; and
the breadth of the side chambers, four cubits, round about the
temple. 6And the side chambers were in three stories, one over
another, thirty in each story. There were offsets*h* all around the
wall of the temple to serve as supports for the side chambers, so
that they should not be supported by the wall of the temple. 7And
the side chambers became broader as they rose*i* from story to
story, corresponding to the enlargement of the offset*j* from story
to story round about the temple; on the side of the temple a stairway led upward, and thus one went up from the lowest story to
the top story through the middle story. 8 I saw also that the temple
had a raised platform round about; the foundations of the side
chambers measured a full reed of six long cubits. 9 The thickness
of the outer wall of the side chambers was five cubits; and the part
of the platform which was left free was five cubits.*k* Between the
platform*l* of the temple and the 10 chambers of the court was a
breadth of twenty cubits round about the temple on every side.
11And the doors of the side chambers opened on the part of the
platform that was left free, one door toward the north, and another
door toward the south; and the breadth of the part that was left
free was five cubits round about.

3. The building facing the Temple on the west

12 The building that was facing the temple yard on the west
side was seventy cubits broad; and the wall of the building was
five cubits thick round about, and its length ninety cubits.

4. The measurements of the Temple and the yard

13 Then he measured the temple, a hundred cubits long; and
the yard and the building with its walls, a hundred cubits long;
14 also the breadth of the east front of the temple and the yard, a
hundred cubits.
15 Then he measured the length of the building facing the yard
which was at the west and its walls*m* on either side, a hundred
cubits.

5. The interior decorations

The nave of the temple and the inner room and the outer*n* vestibule 16 were paneled*o* and round about all three had windows with
recessed*p* frames. Over against the threshold the temple was
paneled with wood round about, from the floor up to the windows

---

41.3
Ezek 40.16;
ver 1
41.4
1 Ki 6.20;
2 Chr 3.8

41.5
ver 6–11
41.6
1 Ki 6.5,6

41.7
1 Ki 6.8

41.8
Ezek 40.5
41.9
ver 11

41.10
Ezek 40.17
41.11
ver 9

41.12
ver 13–15;
Ezek 42.1

41.13
Ezek 40.47;
ver 13–15
41.14
Ezek 40.47
41.15
Ezek 42.1,
10,13;
40.6;
ver 25

41.16
ver 25,26;
Ezek 40.16;
ver 15;
Ezek 42.3;
1 Ki 6.15

---

g Gk: Heb *breadth*   *h* Gk Compare 1 Kings 6.6: Heb *they entered*
i Cn: Heb *it was surrounded*   *j* Gk: Heb *for the encompassing of the temple*
k Syr: Heb lacks *five cubits*   *l* Cn: Heb *house of the side chambers*
m Cn: The meaning of the Hebrew term is unknown
n Gk: Heb *of the court*   *o* Gk: Heb *the thresholds*
p Cn Compare Gk 1 Kings 6.4: The meaning of the Hebrew term is unknown

(now the windows were covered), 17 to the space above the door, even to the inner room, and on the outside. And on all the walls round about in the inner room and the nave were carved like-nesses*q* 18 of cherubim and palm trees, a palm tree between cherub and cherub. Every cherub had two faces: 19 the face of a man toward the palm tree on the one side, and the face of a young lion toward the palm tree on the other side. They were carved on the whole temple round about; 20 from the floor to above the door cherubim and palm trees were carved on the wall.*r*

21 The doorposts of the nave were squared; and in front of the holy place was something resembling 22 an altar of wood, three cubits high, two cubits long, and two cubits broad;*s* its corners, its base,*t* and its walls were of wood. He said to me, "This is the table which is before the LORD." 23 The nave and the holy place had each a double door. 24 The doors had two leaves apiece, two swinging leaves for each door. 25 And on the doors of the nave were carved cherubim and palm trees, such as were carved on the walls; and there was a canopy of wood in front of the vestibule outside. 26 And there were recessed windows and palm trees on either side, on the sidewalls of the vestibule.*u*

C. The priests' chambers: north and south

42 Then he led me out into the inner*v* court, toward the north, and he brought me to the chambers which were opposite the temple yard and opposite the building on the north. 2 The length of the building which was on the north side*w* was*x* a hundred cubits, and the breadth fifty cubits. 3 Adjoining the twenty cubits which belonged to the inner court, and facing the pavement which belonged to the outer court, was gallery*y* against gallery*y* in three stories. 4 And before the chambers was a passage inward, ten cubits wide and a hundred cubits long,*z* and their doors were on the north. 5 Now the upper chambers were narrower, for the galleries*y* took more away from them than from the lower and middle chambers in the building. 6 For they were in three stories, and they had no pillars like the pillars of the outer*a* court; hence the upper chambers were set back from the ground more than the lower and the middle ones. 7 And there was a wall outside parallel to the chambers, toward the outer court, opposite the chambers, fifty cubits long. 8 For the chambers on the outer court were fifty cubits long, while those opposite the temple were a hundred cubits long. 9 Below these chambers was an entrance on the east side, as one enters them from the outer court, 10 where the outside wall begins.*b*

On the south*c* also, opposite the yard and opposite the building, there were chambers 11 with a passage in front of them; they were similar to the chambers on the north, of the same length and breadth, with the same exits*d* and arrangements and doors. 12 And below the south chambers was an entrance on the east side, where

Marginal references

41.18
1 Ki 6.29;
7.36;
Ezek 40.16;
2 Chr 3.5

41.19
Ezek 1.10;
10.14

41.20
ver 18

41.21
ver 1;
1 Ki 6.33;
Ezek 40.16,
14,16

41.22
Ex 30.1;
Rev 8.3;
Ezek 44.16;
Mal 1.7,12;
Ex 30.8

41.23
1 Ki 6.31–
35;
ver 1,4

41.25
ver 16

41.26
ver 16;
Ezek 40.9,
16,48

42.1
Ezek 40.17,
28; 41.1,12;
ver 10,13

42.2
Ezek 41.13

42.3
Ezek 41.10,
16

42.4
Ezek 46.19

42.5
ver 3

42.6
Ezek 41.6

42.7
ver 10,12

42.8
Ezek 41.13,
14

42.9
Ezek 44.5;
46.19

42.10
ver 7,1,13;
Ezek 40.17

42.11
ver 4

---

q Cn: Heb *measures and carved*   *r* Cn Compare verse 25: Heb *and the wall*
s Gk: Heb lacks *two cubits broad*   *t* Gk: Heb *length*
u Cn: Heb *vestibule. And the side chambers of the temple and the canopies*
v Gk: Heb *outer*   *w* Gk: Heb *door*   *x* Gk: Heb *before the length*
y The meaning of the Hebrew word is unknown   *z* Gk Syr: Heb *a way of one cubit*
a Gk: Heb lacks *outer*   *b* Cn Compare Gk: Heb *in the breadth of the wall of the court*
c Gk: Heb *east*   *d* Heb *and all their exits*

one enters the passage, and opposite them was a dividing wall.*

13 Then he said to me, "The north chambers and the south chambers opposite the yard are the holy chambers, where the priests who approach the LORD shall eat the most holy offerings; there they shall put the most holy offerings—the cereal offering, the sin offering, and the guilt offering, for the place is holy. 14 When the priests enter the holy place, they shall not go out of it into the outer court without laying there the garments in which they minister, for these are holy; they shall put on other garments before they go near to that which is for the people."

D. The measurements of the Temple area

15 Now when he had finished measuring the interior of the temple area, he led me out by the gate which faced east, and measured the temple area round about. 16 He measured the east side with the measuring reed, five hundred cubits by the measuring reed. 17 Then he turned and measured*f* the north side, five hundred cubits by the measuring reed. 18 Then he turned and measured*f* the south side, five hundred cubits by the measuring reed. 19 Then he turned to the west side and measured, five hundred cubits by the measuring reed. 20 He measured it on the four sides. It had a wall around it, five hundred cubits long and five hundred cubits broad, to make a separation between the holy and the common.

E. The return of the LORD to the Temple

1. His glory enters the Temple

43 Afterward he brought me to the gate, the gate facing east. 2And behold, the glory of the God of Israel came from the east; and the sound of his coming was like the sound of many waters; and the earth shone with his glory. 3And*g* the vision I saw was like the vision which I had seen when he came to destroy the city, and*h* like the vision which I had seen by the river Chēbar; and I fell upon my face. 4As the glory of the LORD entered the temple by the gate facing east, 5 the Spirit lifted me up, and brought me into the inner court; and behold, the glory of the LORD filled the temple.

2. The message of the LORD

6 While the man was standing beside me, I heard one speaking to me out of the temple; 7 and he said to me, "Son of man, this is the place of my throne and the place of the soles of my feet, where I will dwell in the midst of the people of Israel for ever. And the house of Israel shall no more defile my holy name, neither they, nor their kings, by their harlotry, and by the dead bodies*i* of their

Cross references (right margin):

42.13 Lev 7.6; 10.13,14, 17; Lev 6.25, 29; Num 18.9, 10
42.14 Ezek 44.19; Ex 29.4-9; Zech 3.4,5
42.15 Ezek 40.6; 43.1
42.16 Ezek 40.3
42.20 Ezek 40.5; Zech 2.5; Ezek 45.2
43.1 Ezek 10.19; 44.1; 46.1
*43.2 Ezek 11.23; 1.24; Rev 1.15; 18.1; Ezek 10.4
43.3 Ezek 1.4,28; Jer 1.10; Ezek 1.3; 3.23
43.4 Ezek 10.19; 44.2
43.5 Ezek 3.14; 8.3; 1 Ki 8.10, 11; Ezek 44.4
43.6 Ezek 1.26; 40.3
43.7 Ps 47.8; Ezek 1.26; 37.26,28; Jer 16.18; Ezek 6.5,13

---

e Cn: Heb *And according to the entrances of the chambers that were toward the south was an entrance at the head of the way, the way before the dividing wall toward the east as one enters them*   *f* Gk: Heb *measuring reed round about. He measured*
g Gk: Heb *And like the vision*   *h* Syr: Heb *and the visions*   *i* Or *the monuments*

43.2 *the glory of the God of Israel came from the east* (cf. 9.3). It had gone eastward as a token of the fact that God was delivering Jerusalem to its enemies. Its return was a token that God was about to take up His abode in the midst of His people again.

43.8
Ezek 8.3;
23.39; 44.7

43.9
Ezek 18.30,
31
43.10
Ezek 40.4;
ver 11
43.11
Ezek 44.5;
12.3; 11.20;
36.27

43.12
Ezek 40.2

43.13
Ezek 40.5;
41.8

43.14
ver 17,20;
Ezek 45.19

43.15
Ex 27.2;
Lev 9.9;
1 Ki 1.50
43.16
Ex 27.1
43.17
Ex 20.26;
Ezek 40.6

43.18
Ezek 2.1;
Ex 40.29;
Lev 1.5
*43.19
1 Ki 2.35;
Ezek 44.15;
Num 16.5,
40;
ver 23;
Ezek 45.18,
19
43.21
Ex 29.14;
Heb 13.11

kings, 8 by setting their threshold by my threshold and their door-posts beside my doorposts, with only a wall between me and them. They have defiled my holy name by their abominations which they have committed, so I have consumed them in my anger. 9 Now let them put away their idolatry and the dead bodies[i] of their kings far from me, and I will dwell in their midst for ever.

10 "And you, son of man, describe to the house of Israel the temple and its appearance and plan,[j] that they may be ashamed of their iniquities. 11 And if they are ashamed of all that they have done, portray[k] the temple, its arrangement, its exits and its entrances, and its whole form; and make known to them all its ordinances and all its laws; and write it down in their sight, so that they may observe and perform all its laws[l] and all its ordinances.

12 This is the law of the temple: the whole territory round about upon the top of the mountain shall be most holy. Behold, this is the law of the temple.

3. The measurements of the altar of burnt offering

13 "These are the dimensions of the altar by cubits (the cubit being a cubit and a handbreadth): its base shall be one cubit high,[m] and one cubit broad, with a rim of one span around its edge. And this shall be the height[x] of the altar: 14 from the base on the ground to the lower ledge, two cubits, with a breadth of one cubit; and from the smaller ledge to the larger ledge, four cubits, with a breadth of one cubit; 15 and the altar hearth, four cubits; and from the altar hearth projecting upward, four horns, one cubit high.[n] 16 The altar hearth shall be square, twelve cubits long by twelve broad. 17 The ledge also shall be square, fourteen cubits long by fourteen broad, with a rim around it half a cubit broad, and its base one cubit round about. The steps of the altar shall face east."

4. Instructions for the consecration of the altar

18 And he said to me, "Son of man, thus says the Lord GOD: These are the ordinances for the altar: On the day when it is erected for offering burnt offerings upon it and for throwing blood against it, 19 you shall give to the Levit'ical priests of the family of Zādōk, who draw near to me to minister to me, says the Lord GOD, a bull for a sin offering. 20 And you shall take some of its blood, and put it on the four horns of the altar, and on the four corners of the ledge, and upon the rim round about; thus you shall cleanse the altar and make atonement for it. 21 You shall also take

i Or the monuments j Gk: Heb the temple that they may measure the pattern
k Gk: Heb the form of l Compare Gk: Heb its whole form
m Gk: Heb lacks high x Gk: Heb back n Gk: Heb lacks one cubit high

43.19 Ezekiel's prophecy (ch 40—48) is replete with difficulties for interpreters of all schools of thought, whether millennialists or a-millennialists. These chapters are thought to refer to the kingdom-age since they have never found any recognizable fulfilment up to the present day. Interpreters differ as to whether this prophecy is to be taken literally or figuratively. Particularly difficult is the problem of whether there will be a literal restoration of the Old Testament sacrificial offerings which were done away with by the sacrifice of Christ on Calvary. The offerings referred to in these chapters are understood by some scholars as serving as a memorial, corresponding to the Lord's Supper of our present church age. Others, noting that the Letter to the Hebrews (9.26) indicates that the Old Testament sacrifices are completely superseded by the sacrifice of Christ, consider the account in Ezekiel as a description, in Old Testament terms, of the principle that the blood of Christ, the lamb of God, will avail wholly during the kingdom-age.

the bull of the sin offering, and it shall be burnt in the appointed place belonging to the temple, outside the sacred area. 22And on the second day you shall offer a he-goat without blemish for a sin offering; and the altar shall be cleansed, as it was cleansed with the bull. 23 When you have finished cleansing it, you shall offer a bull without blemish and a ram from the flock without blemish. 24 You shall present them before the LORD, and the priests shall sprinkle salt upon them and offer them up as a burnt offering to the LORD. 25 For seven days you shall provide daily a goat for a sin offering; also a bull and a ram from the flock, without blemish, shall be provided. 26 Seven days shall they make atonement for the altar and purify it, and so consecrate it. 27And when they have completed these days, then from the eighth day onward the priests shall offer upon the altar your burnt offerings and your peace offerings; and I will accept you, says the Lord GOD."

43.22
ver 25,20,26

43.23
Ex 29.1
43.24
Lev 2.13;
Mk 9.49,50;
Col 4.6
43.25
Ex 29.35,
36;
Lev 8.33
43.27
Lev 9.1;
3.1; 17.5;
Ezek 20.40

F. The rules of the sanctuary

1. The east gate and the prince

44 Then he brought me back to the outer gate of the sanctuary, which faces east; and it was shut. 2And he*o* said to me, "This gate shall remain shut; it shall not be opened, and no one shall enter by it; for the LORD, the God of Israel, has entered by it; therefore it shall remain shut. 3 Only the prince may sit in it to eat bread before the LORD; he shall enter by way of the vestibule of the gate, and shall go out by the same way."

44.1
Ezek 42.14;
43.1
44.2
Ezek 43.4
44.3
Ezek 37.25;
Gen 31.54;
1 Cor 10.18;
Ezek 46.2,8

2. The exclusion of the uncircumcised

4 Then he brought me by way of the north gate to the front of the temple; and I looked, and behold, the glory of the LORD filled the temple of the LORD; and I fell upon my face. 5And the LORD said to me, "Son of man, mark well, see with your eyes, and hear with your ears all that I shall tell you concerning all the ordinances of the temple of the LORD and all its laws; and mark well those who may be admitted to*p* the temple and all those who are to be excluded from the sanctuary. 6And say to the rebellious house,*q* to the house of Israel, Thus says the Lord GOD: O house of Israel, let there be an end to all your abominations, 7 in admitting foreigners, uncircumcised in heart and flesh, to be in my sanctuary, profaning it,*r* when you offer to me my food, the fat and the blood. You*s* have broken my covenant, in addition to all your abominations. 8And you have not kept charge of my holy things; but you have set foreigners to keep my charge in my sanctuary.

44.4
Ezek 40.20,
40; 3.23;
43.5; 1.28;
Rev 15.8
44.5
Ezek 40.4;
43.10,11
44.6
Ezek 2.5;
3.9; 45.9;
1 Pet 4.3
44.7
Ex 12.43–
49;
Lev 26.41;
Deut 10.16;
Jer 4.4;
9.26;
Lev 22.25;
Gen 17.14
44.8
Num 18.7

3. The exclusion of the idolatrous Levites

9 "Therefore*t* thus says the Lord GOD: No foreigner, uncircumcised in heart and flesh, of all the foreigners who are among the people of Israel, shall enter my sanctuary. 10 But the Lēvītes who went far from me, going astray from me after their idols when Israel went astray, shall bear their punishment. 11 They shall be ministers in my sanctuary, having oversight at the gates of the temple, and serving in the temple; they shall slay the burnt offering and the sacrifice for the people, and they shall attend

44.9
ver 7;
Zech 14.21
44.10
2 Ki 23.8,9;
Ezek 22.26;
Num 18.23
44.11
1 Chr 26.1;
2 Chr 29.34;
Num 16.9

o Cn: Heb the LORD   *p* Cn: Heb the entrance of   *q* Gk: Heb lacks house
r Gk: Heb it my temple   *s* Gk Syr Vg: Heb they   *t* Gk: Heb for you

44.12
2 Ki 16.10–
16;
Ezek 14.3,4;
Ps 106.26
44.13
Num 18.3;
2 Ki 23.9;
Ezek 32.30;
39.26
44.14
Num 18.4;
ver 11

on the people, to serve them. 12 Because they ministered to them before their idols and became a stumbling block of iniquity to the house of Israel, therefore I have sworn concerning them, says the Lord God, that they shall bear their punishment. 13 They shall not come near to me, to serve me as priest, nor come near any of my sacred things and the things that are most sacred; but they shall bear their shame, because of the abominations which they have committed. 14 Yet I will appoint them to keep charge of the temple, to do all its service and all that is to be done in it.

4. The service of the Levitical sons of Zadok: their duties

44.15
Ezek 40.46;
48.11;
Deut 10.8
44.16
Ezek 41.22;
Mal 1.7,12
44.17
Ex 28.39,
40,43;
39.27,28
44.18
Ex 28.40,
42;
Isa 3.20
44.19
Ezek 42.14;
46.20
44.20
Lev 21.5;
Num 6.5
44.21
Lev 10.9
44.22
Lev 21.7,
13,14
44.23
Lev 10.10;
Mal 2.7
44.24
Deut 17.8,
9;
Ezek 20.12,
20
44.25
Lev 21.1–3
44.26
Num 19.13–
19
44.28
Num 18.20;
Deut 10.9;
Josh 13.14,
33
44.29
Num 18.9,
14;
Lev 27.21,
28
44.30
Ex 29.19;
Num 3.13;
15.20;
Neh 10.37;
Mal 3.10
44.31
Ex 22.31;
Lev 22.8

15 "But the Levit′ic̆ăl priests, the sons of Zādŏk, who kept the charge of my sanctuary when the people of Israel went astray from me, shall come near to me to minister to me; and they shall attend on me to offer me the fat and the blood, says the Lord God; 16 they shall enter my sanctuary, and they shall approach my table, to minister to me, and they shall keep my charge. 17 When they enter the gates of the inner court, they shall wear linen garments; they shall have nothing of wool on them, while they minister at the gates of the inner court, and within. 18 They shall have linen turbans upon their heads, and linen breeches upon their loins; they shall not gird themselves with anything that causes sweat. 19 And when they go out into the outer court to the people, they shall put off the garments in which they have been ministering, and lay them in the holy chambers; and they shall put on other garments, lest they communicate holiness to the people with their garments. 20 They shall not shave their heads or let their locks grow long; they shall only trim the hair of their heads. 21 No priest shall drink wine, when he enters the inner court. 22 They shall not marry a widow, or a divorced woman, but only a virgin of the stock of the house of Israel, or a widow who is the widow of a priest. 23 They shall teach my people the difference between the holy and the common, and show them how to distinguish between the unclean and the clean. 24 In a controversy they shall act as judges, and they shall judge it according to my judgments. They shall keep my laws and my statutes in all my appointed feasts, and they shall keep my sabbaths holy. 25 They shall not defile themselves by going near to a dead person; however, for father or mother, for son or daughter, for brother or unmarried sister they may defile themselves. 26 After he is defiled,u he shall count for himself seven days, and then he shall be clean.v 27 And on the day that he goes into the holy place, into the inner court, to minister in the holy place, he shall offer his sin offering, says the Lord God.

28 "They shall have now inheritance; I am their inheritance: and you shall give them no possession in Israel; I am their possession. 29 They shall eat the cereal offering, the sin offering, and the guilt offering; and every devoted thing in Israel shall be theirs. 30 And the first of all the first fruits of all kinds, and every offering of all kinds from all your offerings, shall belong to the priests; you shall also give to the priests the first of your coarse meal, that a blessing may rest on your house. 31 The priests shall not eat of anything, whether bird or beast, that has died of itself or is torn.

u Syr: Heb cleansed
v Syr: Heb lacks and then he shall be clean
w Vg: Heb as an

G. The land for priests and prince

45 "When you allot the land as a possession, you shall set
apart for the LORD a portion of the land as a holy district,
twenty-five thousand cubits long and twenty^x thousand cubits
broad; it shall be holy throughout its whole extent. 2 Of this a
square plot of five hundred by five hundred cubits shall be for the
sanctuary, with fifty cubits for an open space around it. 3 And in
the holy district you shall measure off a section twenty-five thousand cubits long and ten thousand broad, in which shall be the
sanctuary, the most holy place. 4 It shall be the holy portion of the
land; it shall be for the priests, who minister in the sanctuary and
approach the LORD to minister to him; and it shall be a place for
their houses and a holy place for the sanctuary. 5 Another section,
twenty-five thousand cubits long and ten thousand cubits broad,
shall be for the Lēvītes who minister at the temple, as their possession for cities to live in.^y

6 "Alongside the portion set apart as the holy district you shall
assign for the possession of the city an area five thousand cubits
broad, and twenty-five thousand cubits long; it shall belong to the
whole house of Israel.

7 "And to the prince shall belong the land on both sides of the
holy district and the property of the city, alongside the holy district and the property of the city, on the west and on the east, corresponding in length to one of the tribal portions, and extending
from the western to the eastern boundary of the land. 8 It is to be
his property in Israel. And my princes shall no more oppress my
people; but they shall let the house of Israel have the land according to their tribes.

9 "Thus says the Lord GOD: Enough, O princes of Israel! Put
away violence and oppression, and execute justice and righteousness; cease your evictions of my people, says the Lord GOD.

H. Additional instructions

1. Just balances

10 "You shall have just balances, a just ephah, and a just bath.
11 The ephah and the bath shall be of the same measure, the bath
containing one tenth of a homer, and the ephah one tenth of a
homer; the homer shall be the standard measure. 12 The shekel
shall be twenty gerahs; five shekels shall be five shekels, and ten
shekels shall be ten shekels, and your mina shall be fifty shekels.^z

2. The cereal offerings

13 "This is the offering which you shall make: one sixth of an
ephah from each homer of wheat, and one sixth of an ephah from
each homer of barley, 14 and as the fixed portion of oil,^a one tenth
of a bath from each cor (the cor,^b like the homer, contains ten
baths); 15 and one sheep from every flock of two hundred, from
the families^c of Israel. This is the offering for cereal offerings,
burnt offerings, and peace offerings, to make atonement for them,
says the Lord GOD. 16 All the people of the land shall give^d this

45.1
Ezek 47.21,
22; 48.8

45.2
Ezek 42.20

45.3
Ezek 48.10

45.4
ver 1;
Ezek 48.10,
11

45.5
Ezek 48.13

45.6
Ezek 48.15

45.7
Ezek 46.16–
18; 48.21

45.8
Isa 11.3–5;
Jer 23.5;
Ezek 22.27;
46.18;
Josh 11.23

45.9
Ezek 44.6;
Jer 6.7;
22.3;
Neh 5.1–5

45.10
Lev 19.35,
36;
Prov 11.1
45.11
Isa 5.10
45.12
Ex 30.13;
Lev 27.25;
Num 3.47

45.15
ver 17;
Lev 1.4;
6.30

x Gk: Heb *ten*   y Gk: Heb *twenty chambers*
z Gk: Heb *twenty shekels, twenty-five shekels, fifteen shekels shall be your mina*
a Cn: Heb *oil, the bath the oil*   b Vg: Heb *homer*
c Gk: Heb *watering places*   d Gk Compare Syr: Heb *shall be to*

45.17
Ezek 46.4–
12;
1 Ki 8.64;
2 Chr 31.3;
Lev 23.1–
44;
Ezek 43.27

offering to the prince in Israel. 17 It shall be the prince's duty to furnish the burnt offerings, cereal offerings, and drink offerings, at the feasts, the new moons, and the sabbaths, all the appointed feasts of the house of Israel: he shall provide the sin offerings, cereal offerings, burnt offerings, and peace offerings, to make atonement for the house of Israel.

3. *The offerings at sacred seasons*

45.18
Ezek 46.1,3,
6;
Lev 16.16
45.19
Ezek 43.20

18 "Thus says the Lord God: In the first month, on the first day of the month, you shall take a young bull without blemish, and cleanse the sanctuary. 19 The priest shall take some of the blood of the sin offering and put it on the doorposts of the temple, the four corners of the ledge of the altar, and the posts of the gate of the inner court. 20 You shall do the same on the seventh day of the month for any one who has sinned through error or ignorance; so you shall make atonement for the temple.

45.20
Lev 4.27;
16.20;
ver 15,18

45.21
Ex 12.18;
Lev 23.5,6;
Num 9.2,3;
28.16,17

21 "In the first month, on the fourteenth day of the month, you shall celebrate the feast of the passover, and for seven days unleavened bread shall be eaten. 22 On that day the prince shall provide for himself and all the people of the land a young bull for a sin offering. 23And on the seven days of the festival he shall provide as a burnt offering to the Lord seven young bulls and seven rams without blemish, on each of the seven days; and a he-goat daily for a sin offering. 24And he shall provide as a cereal offering an ephah for each bull, an ephah for each ram, and a hin of oil to each ephah. 25 In the seventh month, on the fifteenth day of the month and for the seven days of the feast, he shall make the same provision for sin offerings, burnt offerings, and cereal offerings, and for the oil.

45.22
Lev 4.14
45.23
Lev 23.8;
Num 28.16–
25;
Job 42.8

45.25
Lev 23.34;
Num 29.12;
Deut 16.13

4. *The new moon and Sabbath offerings of the prince*

46.1
Ezek 45.17–
19

46 "Thus says the Lord God: The gate of the inner court that faces east shall be shut on the six working days; but on the sabbath day it shall be opened and on the day of the new moon it shall be opened. 2 The prince shall enter by the vestibule of the gate from without, and shall take his stand by the post of the gate. The priests shall offer his burnt offering and his peace offerings, and he shall worship at the threshold of the gate. Then he shall go out, but the gate shall not be shut until evening. 3 The people of the land shall worship at the entrance of that gate before the Lord on the sabbaths and on the new moons. 4 The burnt offering that the prince offers to the Lord on the sabbath day shall be six lambs without blemish and a ram without blemish; 5 and the cereal offering with the ram shall be an ephah, and the cereal offering with the lambs shall be as much as he is able, together with a hin of oil to each ephah. 6 On the day of the new moon he shall offer a young bull without blemish, and six lambs and a ram, which shall be without blemish; 7 as a cereal offering he shall provide an ephah with the bull and an ephah with the ram, and with the lambs as much as he is able, together with a hin of oil to each ephah. 8 When the prince enters, he shall go in by the vestibule of the gate, and he shall go out by the same way.

46.2
ver 8;
Ezek 44.3;
45.9;
ver 12

46.3
Lk 1.10;
ver 1
46.4
Ezek 45.17

46.5
Ezek 45.24;
ver 7,11

46.6
ver 1

46.7
ver 5

46.8
Ezek 44.3;
ver 2

5. *Entering and leaving the Temple*

46.9
Ex 23.14–
17;
Deut 16.16

9 "When the people of the land come before the Lord at the

appointed feasts, he who enters by the north gate to worship
shall go out by the south gate; and he who enters by the south gate
shall go out by the north gate: no one shall return by way of the
gate by which he entered, but each shall go out straight ahead.
10 When they go in, the prince shall go in with them; and when
they go out, he shall go out.

6. *Rules for sacrifice*

11 "At the feasts and the appointed seasons the cereal offering
with a young bull shall be an ephah, and with a ram an ephah,
and with the lambs as much as one is able to give, together with a
hin of oil to an ephah. 12 When the prince provides a freewill offering, either a burnt offering or peace offerings as a freewill offering
to the LORD, the gate facing east shall be opened for him; and he
shall offer his burnt offering or his peace offerings as he does on
the sabbath day. Then he shall go out, and after he has gone out
the gate shall be shut.

13 "He shall provide a lamb a year old without blemish for a
burnt offering to the LORD daily; morning by morning he shall
provide it. 14And he shall provide a cereal offering with it morning by morning, one sixth of an ephah, and one third of a hin of
oil to moisten the flour, as a cereal offering to the LORD; this is the
ordinance for the continual burnt offering.*e* 15 Thus the lamb and
the meal offering and the oil shall be provided, morning by morning, for a continual burnt offering.

7. *The prince and the laws of inheritance*

16 "Thus says the Lord GOD: If the prince makes a gift to any
of his sons out of*f* his inheritance, it shall belong to his sons, it is
their property by inheritance. 17 But if he makes a gift out of his
inheritance to one of his servants, it shall be his to the year of
liberty; then it shall revert to the prince; only his sons may keep
a gift from his inheritance. 18 The prince shall not take any of the
inheritance of the people, thrusting them out of their property; he
shall give his sons their inheritance out of his own property, so that
none of my people shall be dispossessed of his property."

8. *The kitchens for the Temple*

19 Then he brought me through the entrance, which was at the
side of the gate, to the north row of the holy chambers for the
priests; and there I saw a place at the extreme western end of
them. 20And he said to me, "This is the place where the priests
shall boil the guilt offering and the sin offering, and where they
shall bake the cereal offering, in order not to bring them out into
the outer court and so communicate holiness to the people."

21 Then he brought me forth to the outer court, and led me to
the four corners of the court; and in each corner of the court there
was a court—22 in the four corners of the court were small*g* courts,
forty cubits long and thirty broad; the four were of the same size.
23 On the inside, around each of the four courts was a row of
masonry, with hearths made at the bottom of the rows round
about. 24 Then he said to me, "These are the kitchens where those
who minister at the temple shall boil the sacrifices of the people."

e Cn: Heb *perpetual ordinances continually*   *f* Gk: Heb *it is his inheritance*
g Gk Syr Vg: The meaning of the Hebrew word is uncertain

46.11
Ezek 45.17;
ver 5,7

46.12
2 Chr 29.31;
Ezek 44.3;
ver 2;
Ezek 45.17

46.13
Ex 29.38;
Num 28.3;
Isa 50.4
46.14
Num 28.5

46.15
Ex 29.42;
Num 28.6

46.16
2 Chr 21.3

46.17
Lev 27.10

46.18
Ezek 45.8;
Mic 2.1,2;
Ezek 34.3–
6,21

46.19
Ezek 42.9,
13

46.20
2 Chr 35.13;
Lev 2.4,5,7;
Ezek 44.19

46.24
Ezek 44.11;
ver 20

I. The river flowing from the Temple

47.1
Jer 2.13;
Joel 3.18;
Zech 13.1;
14.8;
Rev 22.1

47.2
Ezek 44.1,
2,4

47.3
Ezek 40.3

47.5
Isa 11.9;
Hab 2.14

47.6
Ezek 2.1;
8.6; 40.4;
44.5

★47.7
ver 12;
Rev 22.2

47.8
Deut 3.17;
Isa 35.6,7;
Josh 3.16

47.9
Jn 4.14;
7.37,38;
Rev 21.7

47.10
Gen 14.7;
2 Chr 20.2;
Ezek 26.5,
14;
Num 34.6;
Josh 23.4;
Ezek 48.28

47.12
ver 7;
Job 8.16;
Ps 1.3;
Jer 17.8;
Rev 22.2

47.13
Num 34.2–
12;
Gen 48.5;
1 Chr 5.1;
Ezek 48.4

47.14
Gen 12.7;
Deut 1.8;
Ezek 20.5,6

47.15
Num 34.8;
Ezek 48.1

47.16
ver 17,20;
Ezek 48.1;
ver 18

47 Then he brought me back to the door of the temple; and behold, water was issuing from below the threshold of the temple toward the east (for the temple faced east); and the water was flowing down from below the south end of the threshold of the temple, south of the altar. 2 Then he brought me out by way of the north gate, and led me round on the outside to the outer gate, that faces toward the east;[h] and the water was coming out on the south side.

3 Going on eastward with a line in his hand, the man measured a thousand cubits, and then led me through the water; and it was ankle-deep. 4Again he measured a thousand, and led me through the water; and it was knee-deep. Again he measured a thousand, and led me through the water; and it was up to the loins. 5Again he measured a thousand, and it was a river that I could not pass through, for the water had risen; it was deep enough to swim in, a river that could not be passed through. 6And he said to me, "Son of man, have you seen this?"

Then he led me back along the bank of the river. 7As I went back, I saw upon the bank of the river very many trees on the one side and on the other. 8And he said to me, "This water flows toward the eastern region and goes down into the Ar'ábáh; and when it enters the stagnant waters of the sea,[i] the water will become fresh. 9And wherever the river[j] goes every living creature which swarms will live, and there will be very many fish; for this water goes there, that the waters of the sea[k] may become fresh; so everything will live where the river goes. 10 Fishermen will stand beside the sea; from En-ge'di to En-eg'läim it will be a place for the spreading of nets; its fish will be of very many kinds, like the fish of the Great Sea. 11 But its swamps and marshes will not become fresh; they are to be left for salt. 12And on the banks, on both sides of the river, there will grow all kinds of trees for food. Their leaves will not wither nor their fruit fail, but they will bear fresh fruit every month, because the water for them flows from the sanctuary. Their fruit will be for food, and their leaves for healing."

J. The boundaries of the land

13 Thus says the Lord GOD: "These are the boundaries by which you shall divide the land for inheritance among the twelve tribes of Israel. Joseph shall have two portions. 14And you shall divide it equally; I swore to give it to your fathers, and this land shall fall to you as your inheritance.

15 "This shall be the boundary of the land: On the north side, from the Great Sea by way of Hĕthlón to the entrance of Hāmáth, and on to Zēdåd,[l] 16 Bĕrō'thåh, Sĭbrā'ĭm (which lies on the border

---

h Heb obscure
i Compare Syr: Heb into the sea to the sea those that were made to issue forth
j Gk Syr Vg Tg: Heb two rivers   k Compare Syr: Heb lacks the waters of the sea
l Gk: Heb the entrance of Zedad, Hamath

47.7 The river which Ezekiel saw bringing refreshment to the parched Judaean wilderness corresponds to that described in Rev 22.1–2 as *flowing from the throne of God and of the Lamb.* Jesus spoke of *rivers of* *living water* flowing from the heart of the believer (Jn 7.37–39). In each instance the symbolic language describes blessing which finds its source in God and which brings refreshment to all it touches.

between Damascus and Hāmáth), as far as Hāzèr-hät′tĭcòn, which is on the border of Hauran. 17 So the boundary shall run from the sea to Hā′zar-ē′nòn, which is on the northern border of Damascus, with the border of Hāmáth to the north.*m* This shall be the north side.

18 "On the east side, the boundary shall run from Hā′zar-ē′nòn*n* between Hauran and Damascus;*m* along the Jordan between Gĭl′ëàd and the land of Israel; to the eastern sea and as far as Tāmar.*o* This shall be the east side.

19 "On the south side, it shall run from Tāmar as far as the waters of Mĕr′ĭbăth-kā′dĕsh, thence along the Brook of Egypt to the Great Sea. This shall be the south side.

20 "On the west side, the Great Sea shall be the boundary to a point opposite the entrance of Hāmáth. This shall be the west side.

21 "So you shall divide this land among you according to the tribes of Israel. 22 You shall allot it as an inheritance for yourselves and for the aliens who reside among you and have begotten children among you. They shall be to you as native-born sons of Israel; with you they shall be allotted an inheritance among the tribes of Israel. 23 In whatever tribe the alien resides, there you shall assign him his inheritance, says the Lord GOD.

K. The division of the land

1. The land allotted to the north

48 "These are the names of the tribes: Beginning at the northern border, from the sea by way*p* of Hĕthlòn to the entrance of Hāmáth, as far as Hā′zar-ē′nòn (which is on the northern border of Damascus over against Hamath), and*q* extending from the east side to the west,*r* Dan, one portion. 2 Adjoining the territory of Dan, from the east side to the west, Āshèr, one portion. 3 Adjoining the territory of Āshèr, from the east side to the west, Năph′tàlī, one portion. 4 Adjoining the territory of Năph′tàlī, from the east side to the west, Mănăs′sèh, one portion. 5 Adjoining the territory of Mănăs′sèh, from the east side to the west, Ē′phräĭm, one portion. 6 Adjoining the territory of Ē′phräĭm, from the east side to the west, Reubën, one portion. 7 Adjoining the territory of Reubën, from the east side to the west, Judah, one portion.

2. The allotment for the priests and Levites

8 "Adjoining the territory of Judah, from the east side to the west, shall be the portion which you shall set apart, twenty-five thousand cubits in breadth, and in length equal to one of the tribal portions, from the east side to the west, with the sanctuary in the midst of it. 9 The portion which you shall set apart for the LORD shall be twenty-five thousand cubits in length, and twenty*s* thousand in breadth. 10 These shall be the allotments of the holy portion: the priests shall have an allotment measuring twenty-five thousand cubits on the northern side, ten thousand cubits in breadth on the western side, ten thousand in breadth on the eastern side, and twenty-five thousand in length on the southern side,

---

47.17
Num 34.9;
Ezek 48.1;
ver 16

47.18
ver 16;
Jer 50.19;
Gen 13.10,
11

47.19
Ezek 48.28;
Deut 32.51;
Isa 27.12

47.20
Num 34.6;
ver 10,15;
Ezek 48.1;
Amos 6.14

47.22
Num 26.55,
56;
Isa 56.6,7;
Rom 10.12;
Eph 2.12–
14; 3.6;
Col 3.11

48.1
Ezek 47.15–
17,20;
Josh 19.40–
48
48.2
Josh 19.24–
31
48.3
Josh 19.32–
39
48.4
Josh 13.29–
31; 17.1–11
48.5
Josh 16.5–9;
17.8–10,
14–18
48.6
Josh 13.15–
21
48.7
Josh 15.1–
63
48.8
Ezek 45.1–6

48.10
Ezek 44.28;
45.4;
ver 8

---

m Heb obscure *n* Cn: Heb lacks *Hazar-enon* *o* Compare Syr: Heb *you shall measure*
p Compare 47.15: Heb *by the side of the way* *q* Cn: Heb *and they shall be his*
r Gk Compare verses 2–8: Heb *the east side the west* *s* Compare 45.1: Heb *ten*

48.11
Ezek 44.15,
10,12

48.12
Ezek 45.4

48.13
Ezek 45.3

48.14
Lev 25.32–
34

48.15
Ezek 42.20;
45.6

48.16
Rev 21.16

48.17
Ezek 45.2

48.18
ver 8

48.19
Ezek 45.6

48.20
ver 16

48.21
Ezek 34.24;
45.7;
ver 22,8,10

48.23
ver 1–7;
Josh 18.21–
28

48.24
Josh 19.1–9

48.25
Josh 19.17–
23

48.26
Josh 19.10–
16

48.27
Josh 13.24–
28

48.28
Ezek 47.19,
20

with the sanctuary of the LORD in the midst of it. 11 This shall be for the consecrated priests, the sons*t* of Zādŏk, who kept my charge, who did not go astray when the people of Israel went astray, as the Lēvītes did. 12And it shall belong to them as a special portion from the holy portion of the land, a most holy place, adjoining the territory of the Lēvītes. 13And alongside the territory of the priests, the Lēvītes shall have an allotment twenty-five thousand cubits in length and ten thousand in breadth. The whole length shall be twenty-five thousand cubits and the breadth twenty*u* thousand. 14 They shall not sell or exchange any of it; they shall not alienate this choice portion of the land, for it is holy to the LORD.

3. The allotment for the city

15 "The remainder, five thousand cubits in breadth and twenty-five thousand in length, shall be for ordinary use for the city, for dwellings and for open country. In the midst of it shall be the city; 16 and these shall be its dimensions: the north side four thousand five hundred cubits, the south side four thousand five hundred, the east side four thousand five hundred, and the west side four thousand and five hundred. 17And the city shall have open land: on the north two hundred and fifty cubits, on the south two hundred and fifty, on the east two hundred and fifty, and on the west two hundred and fifty. 18 The remainder of the length alongside the holy portion shall be ten thousand cubits to the east, and ten thousand to the west, and it shall be alongside the holy portion. Its produce shall be food for the workers of the city. 19And the workers of the city, from all the tribes of Israel, shall till it. 20 The whole portion which you shall set apart shall be twenty-five thousand cubits square, that is, the holy portion together with the property of the city.

4. The allotment for the prince

21 "What remains on both sides of the holy portion and of the property of the city shall belong to the prince. Extending from the twenty-five thousand cubits of the holy portion to the east border, and westward from the twenty-five thousand cubits to the west border, parallel to the tribal portions, it shall belong to the prince. The holy portion with the sanctuary of the temple in its midst, 22 and the property of the Lēvītes and the property of the city,*v* shall be in the midst of that which belongs to the prince. The portion of the prince shall lie between the territory of Judah and the territory of Benjamin.

5. The land allotted to the south of the sacred portion

23 "As for the rest of the tribes: from the east side to the west, Benjamin, one portion. 24Adjoining the territory of Benjamin, from the east side to the west, Sĭm'ĕŏn, one portion. 25Adjoining the territory of Sĭm'ĕŏn, from the east side to the west, Ĭs'săchar, one portion. 26Adjoining the territory of Ĭs'săchar, from the east side to the west, Zĕb'ŭlŭn, one portion. 27Adjoining the territory of Zĕb'ŭlŭn, from the east side to the west, Găd, one portion. 28And adjoining the territory of Găd to the south, the boundary

t One Ms Gk: Heb *of the sons*   *u* Gk: Heb *ten*
v Cn: Heb *and from the property of the Levites and from the property of the city*

shall run from Tāmar to the waters of Mĕr'ībăth-kā'dĕsh, thence along the Brook of Egypt to the Great Sea. 29 This is the land which you shall allot as an inheritance among the tribes of Israel, and these are their several portions, says the Lord GOD.

48.29
Ezek 47.13–20

6. *The city named "The LORD is there"*

30 "These shall be the exits of the city: On the north side, which is to be four thousand five hundred cubits by measure, 31 three gates, the gate of Reubĕn, the gate of Judah, and the gate of Lēvī, the gates of the city being named after the tribes of Israel. 32 On the east side, which is to be four thousand five hundred cubits, three gates, the gate of Joseph, the gate of Benjamin, and the gate of Dan. 33 On the south side, which is to be four thousand five hundred cubits by measure, three gates, the gate of Sĭm'ĕŏn, the gate of Ĭs'sắchar, and the gate of Zĕb'ŭlŭn. 34 On the west side, which is to be four thousand five hundred cubits, three gates,[w] the gate of Gắd, the gate of Ắshĕr, and the gate of Nắph'tālī. 35 The circumference of the city shall be eighteen thousand cubits. And the name of the city henceforth shall be, The LORD is there."

48.30
ver 31–34

48.31
Rev 21.12, 13

48.35
Jer 23.6;
33.16;
3.17;
Joel 3.21;
Zech 2.10;
Rev 21.3;
22.3

w One Ms Gk Syr: Heb *their gates three*

INTRODUCTION TO
THE BOOK OF
DANIEL

Authorship and Background: Conservative scholarship has always acknowledged that Daniel wrote this book as the internal evidences indicate. Daniel was carried away to Babylon as a captive while he was still a boy. According to the traditional view he lived and prophesied when Babylon was the most powerful empire of its day, and himself watched the activities of a number of famous monarchs (of whom Nebuchadnezzar is best known to Bible students) for almost three quarters of a century.

The Jews and early Christians universally accepted the book as genuine, and it was not until Porphyry's day (ca. A.D. 260) that doubt was cast upon the traditional view. Many critical scholars object to a sixth century date, claiming that the book must have been written *after* the events described took place, not before, since the predictions were so specifically fulfilled by the time of the Maccabean struggle for independence (165 B.C.). A mediating viewpoint acknowledges the historical Daniel and the Babylonian setting in the first portion of the book, and attributes the latter part of the book to the Maccabean period, thus assuming a dual authorship. Even if one were to assume that the book was written in the Maccabean period, there are still important prophecies relating to future events such as the time of the end (Dan 11.35, 40, 45) which had not been fulfilled by 165 B.C.

Perhaps more than any other book, Daniel has been used to develop contradictory schemes of prophetic interpretation. Yet no comprehensive Christian world view can be developed without its use. Daniel's panoramic vision includes the period of Gentile ascendancy after Calvary and sweeps on to the end of the age.

Characteristics: Daniel is written in Aramaic and Hebrew: the Aramaic portions pertain to the Gentile nations in general, the Hebrew portions to the Jewish nation in particular. It is an apocalyptic work, rich in symbol and imagery. The author upholds a philosophy of history in which the sovereign God rules and overrules among men and nations. Direct divine intervention in the affairs of men may be seen in the account of the fiery furnace (3.14ff), the degradation of Nebuchadnezzar (4.33ff), Belshazzar's downfall (5.25ff), and Daniel in the lions' den (6.16ff). Daniel's visions of the beasts, the seventy weeks, and the end time require careful study and interpretation. The style of writing is somewhat similar to the Revelation of John in the New Testament.

Contents:

I.   Daniel and his friends. 1.1—6.28: The personal history of Daniel is related and his rise to power noted. Nebuchadnezzar has a dream which cannot be interpreted. Daniel alone is able to tell the king the meaning

of the vision. He reveals the secret of four world-empires, and God's eternal and universal kingdom. Nebuchadnezzar sets up an image of gold. The three Jews refuse to bow before the image and are cast into the fiery furnace from which they are delivered by God. Nebuchadnezzar has another vision which Daniel interprets and the king is degraded and restored. The story of Belshazzar follows in which pride overtakes him and his vision is interpreted by Daniel who prophesies the end of his kingdom which is taken over by Darius. Darius' decree against prayer to God leads to Daniel's being placed in the lions' den from which God delivers him.

II.   The final dream and visions. 7. 1—12. 13: Daniel portrays the beast vision of a lion, a bear, a leopard, and a fourth beast with ten horns. The interpretation is given. Then follows the vision of the ram and the goat with its interpretation. This is succeeded by the vision of the seventy weeks and his vision of the glory of God. He foresees the movement of history from Darius to Antiochus Epiphanes on to the end of the age. The book closes with a prophecy of a "time of trouble" and a command to seal the book, "until the time of the end."

THE BOOK OF
DANIEL

I. Daniel and his friends 1.1–6.28

A. The training and testing of the remnant

1. The hostages captured

1.1
2 Ki 24.1;
2 Chr 36.6
*1.2
Jer 27.19,
20;
Isa 11.11;
Zech 5.11

1 In the third year of the reign of Jéhoi′ákĭm king of Judah, Nĕbúchádnĕz′zár king of Babylon came to Jerusalem and besieged it. ²And the Lord gave Jéhoi′ákĭm king of Judah into his hand, with some of the vessels of the house of God; and he brought them to the land of Shīnar, to the house of his god, and

2. Daniel and his three friends chosen as students

1.3
2 Ki 20.17,
18;
Isa 39.7
*1.4
2 Sam
14.25;
Dan 2.4
*1.5ff
ver 8,18;
1 Ki 10.8;
ver 19
1.6
Ezek 14.14,
20; 28.3
1.7
Dan 4.8;
5.12; 2.49;
3.12

placed the vessels in the treasury of his god. ³ Then the king commanded Ăsh′pĕnăz, his chief eunuch, to bring some of the people of Israel, both of the royal family and of the nobility, ⁴ youths without blemish, handsome and skilful in all wisdom, endowed with knowledge, understanding learning, and competent to serve in the king's palace, and to teach them the letters and language of the Chăldē′ăns. ⁵ The king assigned them a daily portion of the rich food which the king ate, and of the wine which he drank. They were to be educated for three years, and at the end of that time they were to stand before the king. ⁶Among these were Daniel, Hănáni′áh, Mĭsh′á-él, and Ăzári′áh of the tribe of Judah. ⁷And the chief of the eunuchs gave them names: Daniel he called Bĕltéshăz′zár, Hănáni′áh he called Shădrăch, Mĭsh′á-él he called Méshăch, and Ăzári′áh he called Ăbĕd′nĕgō.

3. The trial of their faith

1.8
Deut 32.38;
Ezek 4.13;
Hos 9.3
1.9
Job 5.15,16;
Ps 106.46;
Prov 16.7
1.10
ver 7

8 But Daniel resolved that he would not defile himself with the king's rich food, or with the wine which he drank; therefore he asked the chief of the eunuchs to allow him not to defile himself. ⁹And God gave Daniel favor and compassion in the sight of the chief of the eunuchs; ¹⁰ and the chief of the eunuchs said to Daniel, "I fear lest my lord the king, who appointed your food and your drink, should see that you were in poorer condition than the youths who are of your own age. So you would endanger my head with the king." ¹¹ Then Daniel said to the steward whom the chief of the eunuchs had appointed over Daniel, Hănáni′áh, Mĭsh′á-él, and Ăzári′áh; ¹² "Test your servants for ten days; let us be given vegetables to eat and water to drink. ¹³ Then let our appearance

1.12
ver 16

1.2 Judah was defeated and taken captive by Babylon. Punished by God because of idolatry, the Jews were delivered into the hands of the Babylonian king. In Babylon they were preserved and, having learned the evil of idolatry, were prepared by God to return that they might be the people through whom the Savior of men might come.
Shinar, or Babylonia, a name for the land of the Chaldeans.
1.4 *letters . . . Chaldeans.* The cuneiform writing system and the Semitic Akkadian

(Assyro-Babylonian) language.
1.5-7 The Babylonians sought to win the Jewish captives to loyalty to Nebuchadnezzar and his court. To this end a three-fold program was adopted: (1) the Jewish youths were given new names, suggesting their change in loyalty; (2) they were subjected to a three year training program; (3) they were provided with the best food Babylon could offer. Although cooperative where possible, Daniel determined to be faithful to the Law of God, and God caused him to prosper.

and the appearance of the youths who eat the king's rich food be observed by you, and according to what you see deal with your servants." 14 So he hearkened to them in this matter, and tested them for ten days. 15At the end of ten days it was seen that they were better in appearance and fatter in flesh than all the youths who ate the king's rich food. 16 So the steward took away their rich food and the wine they were to drink, and gave them vegetables.

4. The reward of their faith

17 As for these four youths, God gave them learning and skill in all letters and wisdom; and Daniel had understanding in all visions and dreams. 18At the end of the time, when the king had commanded that they should be brought in, the chief of the eunuchs brought them in before Nĕbŭçhădnĕz′zăr. 19And the king spoke with them, and among them all none was found like Daniel, Hănănî′ăh, Mĭsh′ä-ĕl, and Ăzărî′ăh; therefore they stood before the king. 20And in every matter of wisdom and understanding concerning which the king inquired of them, he found them ten times better than all the magicians and enchanters that were in all his kingdom. 21And Daniel continued until the first year of King Cyrus.

B. Nebuchadnezzar's dream of the image and the stone

1. Nebuchadnezzar's forgotten dream

2 In the second year of the reign of Nĕbŭçhădnĕz′zăr, Nebuchadnezzar had dreams; and his spirit was troubled, and his sleep left him. 2 Then the king commanded that the magicians, the enchanters, the sorcerers, and the Çhăldē′ănş be summoned, to tell the king his dreams. So they came in and stood before the king. 3And the king said to them, "I had a dream, and my spirit is troubled to know the dream." 4 Then the Çhăldē′ănş said to the king,[a] "O king, live for ever! Tell your servants the dream, and we will show the interpretation." 5 The king answered the Çhăldē′ănş, "The word from me is sure: if you do not make known to me the dream and its interpretation, you shall be torn limb from limb, and your houses shall be laid in ruins. 6 But if you show the dream and its interpretation, you shall receive from me gifts and rewards and great honor. Therefore show me the dream and its interpretation." 7 They answered a second time, "Let the king tell his servants the dream, and we will show its interpretation." 8 The king answered, "I know with certainty that you are trying to gain time, because you see that the word from me is sure 9 that if you do not make the dream known to me, there is but one sentence for you. You have agreed to speak lying and corrupt words before me till the times change. Therefore tell me the dream, and I shall know that you can show me its interpretation." 10 The Çhăldē′ănş answered the king, "There is not a man on earth who can meet

a Heb adds in Ărămă′ĭc, indicating that the text from this point to the end of chapter 7 is in Aramaic

Marginal references

1.15 Ex 23.25; Prov 10.22
1.16 ver 12
1.17 1 Ki 3.12; Jas 1.5,17; Dan 2.19; 7.1; 8.1
1.18 ver 5,3,7
1.19 Gen 41.46; 1 Ki 10.8; Jer 15.1
1.20 Dan 2.27, 28,46,48; 2.2
1.21 Dan 6.28; 10.1
2.1 Gen 41.8; Dan 4.5; Est 6.1; Dan 6.18
★2.2 Gen 41.8; Ex 7.11; ver 10,27; Dan 5.7
2.3 Gen 40.8; 41.15; Dan 4.5
★2.4 Isa 36.11; 1 Ki 1.31; Dan 3.9; 5.10; 6.6,21
2.5 Ezra 6.11; ver 12; Dan 3.29
2.6 Dan 5.7,16, 29
2.7 ver 4
2.9 Est 4.11; Isa 41.23
2.10 ver 27

2.2 *Chaldeans.* The term may be used for the Neo-Babylonians who, under Nabopolassar established an empire in Mesopotamia; or for astrologers, because Chaldeans were noted for astral studies. In this verse, however, Chaldeans refers to "wise men."

2.4 *O king.* These words begin the Aramaic section of Daniel which extends to 7.28.

the king's demand; for no great and powerful king has asked such
a thing of any magician or enchanter or Chăldē'ăn. 11 The thing
that the king asks is difficult, and none can show it to the king
except the gods, whose dwelling is not with flesh."

12 Because of this the king was angry and very furious, and
commanded that all the wise men of Babylon be destroyed. 13 So
the decree went forth that the wise men were to be slain, and they

2. Daniel interpreting Nebuchadnezzar's dream
a. His request for God to reveal the dream

sought Daniel and his companions, to slay them. 14 Then Daniel
replied with prudence and discretion to Ăr'ĭ-ŏch, the captain of
the king's guard, who had gone out to slay the wise men of Babylon; 15 he said to Ăr'ĭ-ŏch, the king's captain, "Why is the decree
of the king so severe?" Then Ari-och made the matter known to
Daniel. 16And Daniel went in and besought the king to appoint
him a time, that he might show to the king the interpretation.

17 Then Daniel went to his house and made the matter known
to Hănănī'ăh, Mĭsh'ă-ĕl, and Ăzărī'ăh, his companions, 18 and
told them to seek mercy of the God of heaven concerning this
mystery, so that Daniel and his companions might not perish with
the rest of the wise men of Babylon. 19 Then the mystery was revealed to Daniel in a vision of the night. Then Daniel blessed the
God of heaven. 20 Daniel said:

b. His hymn of thanksgiving

"Blessed be the name of God for ever and ever,
    to whom belong wisdom and might.
21 He changes times and seasons;
    he removes kings and sets up kings;
  he gives wisdom to the wise
    and knowledge to those who have understanding;
22 he reveals deep and mysterious things;
    he knows what is in the darkness,
    and the light dwells with him.
23 To thee, O God of my fathers,
    I give thanks and praise,
  for thou hast given me wisdom and strength,
    and hast now made known to me what we asked of thee,
    for thou hast made known to us the king's matter."

c. Before the king, Daniel glorifies God

24 Therefore Daniel went in to Ăr'ĭ-ŏch, whom the king had
appointed to destroy the wise men of Babylon; he went and said
thus to him, "Do not destroy the wise men of Babylon; bring me
in before the king, and I will show the king the interpretation."
25 Then Ăr'ĭ-ŏch brought in Daniel before the king in haste,
and said thus to him: "I have found among the exiles from Judah
a man who can make known to the king the interpretation."
26 The king said to Daniel, whose name was Bĕltĕshăz'zăr, "Are
you able to make known to me the dream that I have seen and its
interpretation?" 27 Daniel answered the king, "No wise men, enchanters, magicians, or astrologers can show to the king the
mystery which the king has asked, 28 but there is a God in heaven
who reveals mysteries, and he has made known to King Nĕbŭchăd-

2.11 Dan 5.11; Isa 57.15
2.12 ver 5
2.13 Dan 1.19, 20
2.14 ver 24; Jer 52.12,14
2.15 Dan 3.22; ver 1–12
2.16 Dan 1.19
2.18 Isa 37.4; Jer 33.3; Dan 9.9
2.19 ver 22,27–29; Num 12.6; Job 33.15, 16
2.20 Ps 113.2; Jer 32.19; ver 21–23
2.21 Est 1.13; Dan 7.25; Job 12.18; Ps 75.6,7; Jas 1.5
2.22 Job 12.22; Ps 25.14; 139.11,12; Isa 45.7; Jer 23.24; Dan 5.11, 14; Jas 1.17
2.23 Gen 31.42; ver 21; Dan 17; ver 18,29,30
2.24 ver 12–14
2.25 Gen 41.14; Dan 1.6; 5.13; 6.13
2.26 Dan 1.7; ver 3–7
2.27 ver 2,10
2.28 Gen 40.8; 41.16; 49.1; Isa 2.2; Mic 4.1; Dan 4.5

nĕz'zăr what will be in the latter days. Your dream and the visions of your head as you lay in bed are these: 29 To you, O king, as you lay in bed came thoughts of what would be hereafter, and he who reveals mysteries made known to you what is to be. 30 But as for me, not because of any wisdom that I have more than all the living has this mystery been revealed to me, but in order that the interpretation may be made known to the king, and that you may know the thoughts of your mind.

d. Nebuchadnezzar's dream unfolded

31 "You saw, O king, and behold, a great image. This image, mighty and of exceeding brightness, stood before you, and its appearance was frightening. 32 The head of this image was of fine gold, its breast and arms of silver, its belly and thighs of bronze, 33 its legs of iron, its feet partly of iron and partly of clay. 34As you looked, a stone was cut out by no human hand, and it smote the image on its feet of iron and clay, and broke them in pieces; 35 then the iron, the clay, the bronze, the silver, and the gold, all together were broken in pieces, and became like the chaff of the summer threshing floors; and the wind carried them away, so that not a trace of them could be found. But the stone that struck the image became a great mountain and filled the whole earth.

e. The four earthly kingdoms

36 "This was the dream; now we will tell the king its interpretation. 37 You, O king, the king of kings, to whom the God of heaven has given the kingdom, the power, and the might, and the glory, 38 and into whose hand he has given, wherever they dwell, the sons of men, the beasts of the field, and the birds of the air, making you rule over them all—you are the head of gold. 39After you shall arise another kingdom inferior to you, and yet a third kingdom of bronze, which shall rule over all the earth. 40And there shall be a fourth kingdom, strong as iron, because iron breaks to pieces and shatters all things; and like iron which crushes, it shall break and crush all these. 41And as you saw the feet and toes partly of potter's clay and partly of iron, it shall be a divided kingdom; but some of the firmness of iron shall be in it, just as you saw iron mixed with the miry clay. 42And as the toes of the feet were partly iron and partly clay, so the kingdom shall be partly strong and partly brittle. 43As you saw the iron mixed with miry clay, so they

2.29
ver 22,28
2.30
Gen 41.16;
Isa 45.3;
Ps 139.2

*2.31
Dan 7.7;
Hab 1.7
2.32
ver 38,39
2.33
ver 40–43
2.34
Dan 8.25;
Zech 4.6;
Isa 2.9;
60.12
2.35
Ps 1.4;
Hos 13.3;
Ps 37.10,36;
Isa 2.2,3

2.36
ver 24
2.37
Isa 47.5;
Jer 27.6,7;
Ezek 26.7;
Ezra 1.2;
Ps 62.11
2.38
Jer 27.6;
Dan 4.21,
22;
ver 32
2.39
ver 32
2.40
Dan 7.7,23
2.41
ver 33

2.31 Nebuchadnezzar's dream of the image is capable of very certain interpretation, except for those parts of it which have not yet been fulfilled. The four metals comprising the image stand for four empires: the Babylonian Empire of Nebuchadnezzar (2.37, 38); the Medo-Persian Empire (breast and arms of silver as per 2.32, 39 and the leopard of 7.6); the Grecian Empire under Alexander the Great and his successors (2.39); and the Roman Empire, the mightiest of them all (2.40). The Roman Empire was to be divided into two segments, Eastern and Western Empires (the two legs); then ten toes are mentioned. It is concerning these that interpreters disagree. Some hold that the Roman Empire represented by the ten toes will re-appear at the close of the age in the form of a ten-nation confederacy under the leadership of the "Beast" or final world-dictator. This same school usually holds that the *stone* of 2.35 will strike a final blow at the end of the age. To still others it appears that a blow was struck by the death and Resurrection of Christ and that in a sense His kingdom is filling the whole earth. But the final and consummate fulfilment of this prophetic Scripture came in Christ, for the fifth kingdom is said to eradicate the previous empires altogether, and to take their place. In a spiritual form, Christ's kingdom is already present, and He reigns in the hearts of believers and in His church. The consummation of His kingdom awaits His Second Coming.

will mix with one another in marriage,*b* but they will not hold to-

f. God's eternal kingdom

gether, just as iron does not mix with clay. 44And in the days of
those kings the God of heaven will set up a kingdom which shall
never be destroyed, nor shall its sovereignty be left to another
people. It shall break in pieces all these kingdoms and bring them
to an end, and it shall stand for ever; 45 just as you saw that a stone
was cut from a mountain by no human hand, and that it broke in
pieces the iron, the bronze, the clay, the silver, and the gold. A
great God has made known to the king what shall be hereafter.
The dream is certain, and its interpretation sure."

3. Nebuchadnezzar glorifies God and promotes Daniel

46 Then King Nĕbúchádnĕz'zár fell upon his face, and did
homage to Daniel, and commanded that an offering and incense
be offered up to him. 47 The king said to Daniel, "Truly, your
God is God of gods and Lord of kings, and a revealer of mysteries,
for you have been able to reveal this mystery." 48 Then the king
gave Daniel high honors and many great gifts, and made him ruler
over the whole province of Babylon, and chief prefect over all the
wise men of Babylon. 49 Daniel made request of the king, and he
appointed Shădrăch, Mĕshăch, and Ăbĕd'nĕgō over the affairs of
the province of Babylon; but Daniel remained at the king's court.

C. The golden image and the fiery furnace

1. The abomination: the compulsory state religion

3 King Nĕbúchádnĕz'zár made an image of gold, whose height
was sixty cubits and its breadth six cubits. He set it up on the
plain of Dŭrā, in the province of Babylon. 2 Then King Nĕbúchádnĕz'zár sent to assemble the satraps, the prefects, and the
governors, the counselors, the treasurers, the justices, the magistrates, and all the officials of the provinces to come to the dedication of the image which King Nebuchadnezzar had set up. 3 Then
the satraps, the prefects, and the governors, the counselors, the
treasurers, the justices, the magistrates, and all the officials of the
provinces, were assembled for the dedication of the image that
King Nĕbúchádnĕz'zár had set up; and they stood before the
image that Nebuchadnezzar had set up. 4And the herald proclaimed aloud, "You are commanded, O peoples, nations, and
languages, 5 that when you hear the sound of the horn, pipe, lyre,
trigon, harp, bagpipe, and every kind of music, you are to fall
down and worship the golden image that King Nĕbúchádnĕz'zár
has set up; 6 and whoever does not fall down and worship shall
immediately be cast into a burning fiery furnace." 7 Therefore,
as soon as all the peoples heard the sound of the horn, pipe, lyre,

---

b Aram *by the seed of men*

Marginal references:

*2.44
Ps 2.9;
Isa 60.12;
1 Cor 15.24

*2.45
Isa 28.16;
ver 35;
Dan 8.25;
ver 29;
Mal 1.11;
Gen 41.28,
32

2.46
Dan 8.17;
Acts 10.25;
14.13;
28.6;
Rev 19.10

2.47
Dan 11.36;
ver 22,28

2.48
ver 6;
Dan 4.9;
5.11

2.49
Dan 3.12;
Est 2.19,21;
Dan 3.2

3.1
Isa 46.6;
Hab 2.19;
ver 30;
Dan 2.48

3.2
ver 3,27

3.4
Isa 40.9;
58.1;
Rev 18.2;
Dan 4.1;
6.25

3.5
ver 7,10,15

3.6
ver 11,15,
21;
Jer 29.22;
Rev 14.11

3.7
ver 4,5

2.44 See note to 2.31. Some hold that this
verse lends itself well to the millennial interpretation. Nothing in history has yet approx-
imated the ten toes of the image. Therefore,
this aspect of the prophecy appears to be
definitely future. At that time the kingdom
which now exists only in a spiritual sense and
not in a literal one will become dominant in
the world scene, attaining political supremacy
over all the earth. The stone of verse 45 refers
to Christ and His Second Advent.
2.45 *A great God.* The God of Israel.

trigon, harp, bagpipe, and every kind of music, all the peoples, nations, and languages fell down and worshiped the golden image which King Nĕbùçhàdnĕz'zàr had set up.

2. The accusation and trial of Shadrach, Meshach, and Abednego

8 Therefore at that time certain Çhäldē'àns̩ came forward and maliciously accused the Jews. 9 They said to King Nĕbùçhàdnĕz'zàr, "O king, live for ever! 10 You, O king, have made a decree, that every man who hears the sound of the horn, pipe, lyre, trigon, harp, bagpipe, and every kind of music, shall fall down and worship the golden image; 11 and whoever does not fall down and worship shall be cast into a burning fiery furnace. 12 There are certain Jews whom you have appointed over the affairs of the province of Babylon: Shàdrăch, Mēshăch, and Àbĕd'nĕgō. These men, O king, pay no heed to you; they do not serve your gods or worship the golden image which you have set up."

13 Then Nĕbùçhàdnĕz'zàr in furious rage commanded that Shàdrăch, Mēshăch, and Àbĕd'nĕgō be brought. Then they brought these men before the king. 14 Nĕbùçhàdnĕz'zàr said to them, "Is it true, O Shàdrăch, Mēshăch, and Àbĕd'nĕgō, that you do not serve my gods or worship the golden image which I have set up? 15 Now if you are ready when you hear the sound of the horn, pipe, lyre, trigon, harp, bagpipe, and every kind of music, to fall down and worship the image which I have made, well and good; but if you do not worship, you shall immediately be cast into a burning fiery furnace; and who is the god that will deliver you out of my hands?"

16 Shàdrăch, Mēshăch, and Àbĕd'nĕgō answered the king, "O Nĕbùçhàdnĕz'zàr, we have no need to answer you in this matter. 17 If it be so, our God whom we serve is able to deliver us from the burning fiery furnace; and he will deliver us out of your hand, O king.c 18 But if not, be it known to you, O king, that we will not serve your gods or worship the golden image which you have set up."

3. The sentence and its execution

19 Then Nĕbùçhàdnĕz'zàr was full of fury, and the expression of his face was changed against Shàdrăch, Mēshăch, and Àbĕd'nĕgō. He ordered the furnace heated seven times more than it was wont to be heated. 20And he ordered certain mighty men of his army to bind Shàdrăch, Mēshăch, and Àbĕd'nĕgō, and to cast them into the burning fiery furnace. 21 Then these men were bound in their mantles,d their tunics,d their hats, and their other garments, and they were cast into the burning fiery furnace. 22 Because the king's order was strict and the furnace very hot, the flame of the fire slew those men who took up Shàdrăch, Mēshăch, and Àbĕd'nĕgō. 23And these three men, Shàdrăch, Mēshăch, and Àbĕd'nĕgō, fell bound into the burning fiery furnace.

4. The miraculous deliverance and the fourth man

24 Then King Nĕbùçhàdnĕz'zàr was astonished and rose up

3.8
Dan 4.7;
6.12
3.9
Dan 2.4;
5.10
3.10
ver 4–6;
Dan 6.2;
ver 5,7,15
3.12
Dan 2.49;
1.7; 6.13

3.13
Dan 2.12;
ver 19
3.14
Isa 46.1;
Jer 50.2;
ver 1
3.15
ver 5,6;
Ex 5.2;
Isa 36.18–
20;
Dan 2.47

3.16
ver 12
3.17
Ps 27.1,2;
Isa 26.3,4;
Jer 15.20,21
3.18
ver 28

3.19
ver 13;
Dan 5.6;
ver 12
3.20
ver 23–25
3.21
ver 27
3.22
Ex 12.33;
Dan 2.15
3.23
ver 21

c Or Behold, our God . . . king. Or If our God is able to deliver us, he will deliver us from the burning fiery furnace and out of your hand, O king.
d The meaning of the Àràmā'ic word is uncertain

in haste. He said to his counselors, "Did we not cast three men bound into the fire?" They answered the king, "True, O king." 25 He answered, "But I see four men loose, walking in the midst of the fire, and they are not hurt; and the appearance of the fourth is like a son of the gods."

26 Then Nĕbúchâdnĕz'zàr came near to the door of the burning fiery furnace and said, "Shădrăch, Mēshăch, and Ăbĕd'nēgō, servants of the Most High God, come forth, and come here!" Then Shadrach, Meshach, and Abednego came out from the fire. 27And the satraps, the prefects, the governors, and the king's counselors gathered together and saw that the fire had not had any power over the bodies of those men; the hair of their heads was not singed, their mantles[d] were not harmed, and no smell of fire had come

5. *Nebuchadnezzar glorifies God*

upon them. 28 Nĕbúchâdnĕz'zàr said, "Blessed be the God of Shădrăch, Mēshăch, and Ăbĕd'nēgō, who has sent his angel and delivered his servants, who trusted in him, and set at nought the king's command, and yielded up their bodies rather than serve and worship any god except their own God. 29 Therefore I make a decree: Any people, nation, or language that speaks anything against the God of Shădrăch, Mēshăch, and Ăbĕd'nēgō shall be torn limb from limb, and their houses laid in ruins; for there is no other god who is able to deliver in this way." 30 Then the king promoted Shădrăch, Mēshăch, and Ăbĕd'nēgō in the province of Babylon.

D. *Nebuchadnezzar's insanity*

1. *The frightening dream which could not be interpreted*

4e King Nĕbúchâdnĕz'zàr to all peoples, nations, and languages, that dwell in all the earth: Peace be multiplied to you! 2 It has seemed good to me to show the signs and wonders that the Most High God has wrought toward me.

3 How great are his signs,
  how mighty his wonders!
His kingdom is an everlasting kingdom,
  and his dominion is from generation to generation.

4[f] I, Nĕbúchâdnĕz'zàr, was at ease in my house and prospering in my palace. 5 I had a dream which made me afraid; as I lay in bed the fancies and the visions of my head alarmed me. 6 Therefore I made a decree that all the wise men of Babylon should be brought before me, that they might make known to me the interpretation of the dream. 7 Then the magicians, the enchanters, the Chăldē'ăns, and the astrologers came in; and I told them the dream, but they could not make known to me its interpretation.

2. *The king narrates the dream to Daniel*

8At last Daniel came in before me—he who was named Bĕltĕshăz'-

[d] The meaning of the Arama'ic word is uncertain   [e] Ch 3.31 in Aram   [f] Ch 4.1 in Aram

---

Marginal references:

*3.25
Isa 43.2;
ver 28

3.26
ver 17;
Dan 4.2

3.27
ver 2;
Isa 43.2;
Heb 11.34;
ver 21

3.28
ver 15,25;
Acts 5.19;
12.7;
Ps 34.7,8;
Jer 17.7;
ver 18

3.29
Dan 6.26;
ver 12;
Dan 2.5;
2.47; 6.27

3.30
Dan 2.49

4.1
Dan 6.25

4.2
Dan 3.26

4.3
Dan 6.27;
ver 34;
Dan 2.44;
6.26

4.4
Isa 47.7,8

4.5
Dan 2.28,
29; 2.1

4.6
Dan 2.2

4.7
Dan 2.2

4.8
Dan 1.7;
2.26;
Dan 5.11,14

3.25 This may well be a theophany: an appearance of Christ in the Old Testament. The fourth person in the fire appeared to Nebuchadnezzar to be *like a son of the gods.* Spiritually there is a lesson for all believers. In the midst of temporal affliction suffered for the sake of Christ, He promises to go with His people and to succor and help them (Heb 2.18). Christ has promised never to forsake His own (Mt 28.20; Heb 13.5).

zår after the name of my god, and in whom is the spirit of the holy gods*g*—and I told him the dream, saying, 9 "O Bĕltĕshăz'zår, chief of the magicians, because I know that the spirit of the holy gods*g* is in you and that no mystery is difficult for you, here is*h* the dream which I saw; tell me its interpretation. 10 The visions of my head as I lay in bed were these: I saw, and behold, a tree in the midst of the earth; and its height was great. 11 The tree grew and became strong, and its top reached to heaven, and it was visible to the end of the whole earth. 12 Its leaves were fair and its fruit abundant, and in it was food for all. The beasts of the field found shade under it, and the birds of the air dwelt in its branches, and all flesh was fed from it.

13 "I saw in the visions of my head as I lay in bed, and behold, a watcher, a holy one, came down from heaven. 14 He cried aloud and said thus, 'Hew down the tree and cut off its branches, strip off its leaves and scatter its fruit; let the beasts flee from under it and the birds from its branches. 15 But leave the stump of its roots in the earth, bound with a band of iron and bronze, amid the tender grass of the field. Let him be wet with the dew of heaven; let his lot be with the beasts in the grass of the earth; 16 let his mind be changed from a man's, and let a beast's mind be given to him; and let seven times pass over him. 17 The sentence is by the decree of the watchers, the decision by the word of the holy ones, to the end that the living may know that the Most High rules the kingdom of men, and gives it to whom he will, and sets over it the lowliest of men.' 18 This dream I, King Nĕbŭchădnĕz'zår, saw. And you, O Bĕltĕshăz'zår, declare the interpretation, because all the wise men of my kingdom are not able to make known to me the interpretation, but you are able, for the spirit of the holy gods*i* is in you."

3. Daniel's interpretation and warning

19 Then Daniel, whose name was Bĕltĕshăz'zår, was dismayed for a moment, and his thoughts alarmed him. The king said, "Belteshazzar, let not the dream or the interpretation alarm you." Belteshazzar answered, "My lord, may the dream be for those who hate you and its interpretation for your enemies! 20 The tree you saw, which grew and became strong, so that its top reached to heaven, and it was visible to the end of the whole earth; 21 whose leaves were fair and its fruit abundant, and in which was food for all; under which beasts of the field found shade, and in whose branches the birds of the air dwelt—22 it is you, O king, who have grown and become strong. Your greatness has grown and reaches to heaven, and your dominion to the ends of the earth. 23And whereas the king saw a watcher, a holy one, coming down from heaven and saying, 'Hew down the tree and destroy it, but leave the stump of its roots in the earth, bound with a band of iron and bronze, in the tender grass of the field; and let him be wet with the dew of heaven; and let his lot be with the beasts of the field, till seven times pass over him'; 24 this is the interpretation, O king:

g Or *Spirit of the holy God*　*h* Cn: Aram *visions of*　*i* Or *Spirit of the holy God*

★4.9
Dan 2.48;
5.11; 2.47;
2.4,5

4.10
ver 5,20;
Ezek 31.3–6

4.11
ver 20,22

4.12
Ezek 31.6,7;
Lam 4.20;
Mt 13.32;
Lk 13.19

4.13
Dan 7.1;
ver 17,23;
Dan 8.13;
Zech 14.5

4.14
Ezek 31.10–14;
Mt 3.10;
Ezek 31.12,13

4.15
Job 14.7–9;
ver 32

4.16
Dan 7.25;
11.13; 12.7

4.17
Ps 9.16;
ver 2,25;
Dan 5.18,19;
Dan 11.21

4.18
Gen 41.8,15;
Dan 5.8,15;
ver 7–9

4.19
Dan 7.15,28;
2 Sam 18.32;
Jer 29.7

4.20
ver 10–12

4.21
see ver 12

4.22
2 Sam 12.7;
Dan 2.37,38; 5.18,19;
Jer 27.6–8

4.23
ver 13–17;
Dan 5.21

4.24
ver 17,2;
Job 40.11,12;
Ps 107.40

4.9 *the spirit of the holy gods*. Nebuchadnezzar was a polytheist. Thus he could recognize Daniel as a man whose God or gods had showed themselves strong.

It is a decree of the Most High, which has come upon my lord the king, 25 that you shall be driven from among men, and your dwelling shall be with the beasts of the field; you shall be made to eat grass like an ox, and you shall be wet with the dew of heaven, and seven times shall pass over you, till you know that the Most High rules the kingdom of men, and gives it to whom he will. 26And as it was commanded to leave the stump of the roots of the tree, your kingdom shall be sure for you from the time that you know that Heaven rules. 27 Therefore, O king, let my counsel be acceptable to you; break off your sins by practicing righteousness, and your iniquities by showing mercy to the oppressed, that there may perhaps be a lengthening of your tranquillity."

4. The king's punishment for pride

28 All this came upon King Nĕbûchâdnĕz'zăr. 29At the end of twelve months he was walking on the roof of the royal palace of Babylon, 30 and the king said, "Is not this great Babylon, which I have built by my mighty power as a royal residence and for the glory of my majesty?" 31 While the words were still in the king's mouth, there fell a voice from heaven, "O King Nĕbûchâdnĕz'zăr, to you it is spoken: The kingdom has departed from you, 32 and you shall be driven from among men, and your dwelling shall be with the beasts of the field; and you shall be made to eat grass like an ox; and seven times shall pass over you, until you have learned that the Most High rules the kingdom of men and gives it to whom he will." 33 Immediately the word was fulfilled upon Nĕbûchâdnĕz'zăr. He was driven from among men, and ate grass like an ox, and his body was wet with the dew of heaven till his hair grew as long as eagles' feathers, and his nails were like birds' claws.

5. The king's repentance and recovery

34 At the end of the days I, Nĕbûchâdnĕz'zăr, lifted my eyes to heaven, and my reason returned to me, and I blessed the Most High, and praised and honored him who lives for ever;
for his dominion is an everlasting dominion,
    and his kingdom endures from generation to generation;
35 all the inhabitants of the earth are accounted as nothing;
    and he does according to his will in the host of heaven
    and among the inhabitants of the earth;
and none can stay his hand
    or say to him, "What doest thou?"
36At the same time my reason returned to me; and for the glory of my kingdom, my majesty and splendor returned to me. My counselors and my lords sought me, and I was established in my kingdom, and still more greatness was added to me. 37 Now I, Nĕbûchâdnĕz'zăr, praise and extol and honor the King of heaven; for all his works are right and his ways are just; and those who walk in pride he is able to abase.

4.25 Dan 5.21; Ps 83.18; Jer 27.5

4.26 Mt 21.25; Lk 15.18

4.27 Isa 55.6,7; Ezek 18.21, 22; Ps 41.1–3; 1 Ki 21.29

★4.28ff Zech 1.6

4.30 Hab 2.4; ver 25; Dan 5.20, 21; Isa 37.24, 25

4.31 Dan 5.5; ver 13,14,23

4.32 ver 25

4.33 Dan 5.21

★4.34 ver 16,25, 32,36,2; Dan 5.18, 21; 12.7; Rev 4.10; Lk 1.33

4.35 Isa 40.15, 17; Ps 135.6; Isa 43.13; 45.9; Rom 9.20

4.36 ver 34,30; Dan 2.31; ver 26

4.37 Ps 33.4,5; Ex 18.11; Dan 5.20

4.28ff God was patient, waiting twelve months before executing His sentence upon Nebuchadnezzar. Pride was punished as the king became a brute in the shape of a man.

4.34 I blessed the Most High. Nebuchadnezzar could worship Daniel's God, although still remaining loyal to his own gods—the gods of Babylon.

E. *Belshazzar's feast and punishment for defying God*

1. *The profanation of the Temple vessels*

5 King Bĕlshăz'zăr made a great feast for a thousand of his
lords, and drank wine in front of the thousand.
2 Bĕlshăz'zăr, when he tasted the wine, commanded that the
vessels of gold and of silver which Nĕbŭchădnĕz'zăr his father
had taken out of the temple in Jerusalem be brought, that the king
and his lords, his wives, and his concubines might drink from
them. 3 Then they brought in the golden and silver vessels[j] which
had been taken out of the temple, the house of God in Jerusalem;
and the king and his lords, his wives, and his concubines drank
from them. 4 They drank wine, and praised the gods of gold and
silver, bronze, iron, wood, and stone.

2. *The handwriting on the wall*

5 Immediately the fingers of a man's hand appeared and wrote
on the plaster of the wall of the king's palace, opposite the lampstand; and the king saw the hand as it wrote. 6 Then the king's
color changed, and his thoughts alarmed him; his limbs gave way,
and his knees knocked together. 7 The king cried aloud to bring in
the enchanters, the Chăldē'ăns, and the astrologers. The king said
to the wise men of Babylon, "Whoever reads this writing, and
shows me its interpretation, shall be clothed with purple, and have
a chain of gold about his neck, and shall be the third ruler in the
kingdom." 8 Then all the king's wise men came in, but they could
not read the writing or make known to the king the interpretation.
9 Then King Bĕlshăz'zăr was greatly alarmed, and his color
changed; and his lords were perplexed.

3. *The queen mother turns Belshazzar to Daniel*

10 The queen, because of the words of the king and his lords,
came into the banqueting hall; and the queen said, "O king, live
for ever! Let not your thoughts alarm you or your color change.
11 There is in your kingdom a man in whom is the spirit of the
holy gods.[k] In the days of your father light and understanding and
wisdom, like the wisdom of the gods, were found in him, and King
Nĕbŭchădnĕz'zăr, your father, made him chief of the magicians,

j Theodotion Vg: Aram golden vessels   k Or Spirit of the holy God

*5.1 Est 1.3
5.2 Dan 1.2; Jer 52.19; ver 23
5.4 ver 23; Rev 9.20
5.5 Dan 4.31; ver 24
5.6 Dan 4.5,19; Nah 2.10; Ezek 7.17; 21.7
5.7 Isa 47.13; Dan 2.6; Ezek 16.11; Dan 6.2,3
5.8 Dan 2.10, 27; 4.7
5.9 Isa 21.2–4; Jer 6.24; ver 6
*5.10 Dan 2.4; 3.9
*5.11 Dan 2.47, 48; 4.8,9, 18; 1.17

5.1 A few decades ago the historicity of Belshazzar was in doubt. Secular history seemed to give no confirmation of his actual existence. But in the light of cuneiform records more recently discovered, it has been admitted by all that he was a real person who was a viceroy to his father Nabonidus. The historical reliability of Daniel relative to Belshazzar can no longer be seriously questioned. This still leaves unconfirmed the identity of Darius the Mede (who is stated by Daniel to have assumed the rule over Babylonia immediately after the overthrow of the Chaldeans), for whom there were no historical and archaeological evidences. But more recently strong arguments have been advanced which favor his identification with the Gubaru, whom Cyrus appointed as governor of Babylonia after the death of Ugbaru (who survived his brilliant capture of Babylon by only three weeks). Gubaru the Mede continued in office until 521 B.C., although Cyrus himself seems to have assumed the title of king of Babylon within two years after Gubaru's appointment.

5.10 *The queen.* Probably the queen mother, Nebuchadnezzar's widow, is meant.

5.11 *your father.* Actually Belshazzar was the son of Nabonidus, a usurper. It is possible that Nebuchadnezzar was Belshazzar's grandfather on his mother's side. The terms "father" and "son" do not bear the same exact connotation in Hebrew that they do in Western languages. Jesus was termed the "son of David" although many generations intervened between Him and David.

5.12
Dan 6.3;
1.7

5.13
Dan 2.25;
6.13; 1.1,2
5.14
ver 11,12

5.16
Gen 40.8;
ver 7,29

5.17
2 Ki 5.16
5.18
ver 21;
Dan 2.37,
38; 4.17;
Jer 27.5–7
5.19
Dan 3.4;
2.12,13
5.20
Dan 4.30,
37;
2 Ki 17.14;
2 Chr 36.13;
Jer 13.18
5.21
Dan 4.32–
34; 4.16;
Ezek 17.24;
Dan 4.34,
35
5.22
2 Chr 33.23;
36.12
5.23
Jer 50.29;
ver 3,4;
Ps 115.5,6;
Hab 2.18,
19;
Job 12.10;
31.4;
Jer 10.23
5.24
ver 5
*5.25
*5.26
Isa 13.6,17;
Jer 27.7;
50.41–43

enchanters, Chåldē'ảns, and astrologers,¹ 12 because an excellent spirit, knowledge, and understanding to interpret dreams, explain riddles, and solve problems were found in this Daniel, whom the king named Bĕltĕshăz'zăr. Now let Daniel be called, and he will show the interpretation."

13 Then Daniel was brought in before the king. The king said to Daniel, "You are that Daniel, one of the exiles of Judah, whom the king my father brought from Judah. 14 I have heard of you that the spirit of the holy gods* is in you, and that light and understanding and excellent wisdom are found in you. 15 Now the wise men, the enchanters, have been brought in before me to read this writing and make known to me its interpretation; but they could not show the interpretation of the matter. 16 But I have heard that you can give interpretations and solve problems. Now if you can read the writing and make known to me its interpretation, you shall be clothed with purple, and have a chain of gold about your neck, and shall be the third ruler in the kingdom."

4. Daniel announces God's judgment

17 Then Daniel answered before the king, "Let your gifts be for yourself, and give your rewards to another; nevertheless I will read the writing to the king and make known to him the interpretation. 18 O king, the Most High God gave Nĕbûchảdnĕz'zăr your father kingship and greatness and glory and majesty; 19 and because of the greatness that he gave him, all peoples, nations, and languages trembled and feared before him; whom he would he slew, and whom he would he kept alive; whom he would he raised up, and whom he would he put down. 20 But when his heart was lifted up and his spirit was hardened so that he dealt proudly, he was deposed from his kingly throne, and his glory was taken from him; 21 he was driven from among men, and his mind was made like that of a beast, and his dwelling was with the wild asses; he was fed grass like an ox, and his body was wet with the dew of heaven, until he knew that the Most High God rules the kingdom of men, and sets over it whom he will. 22 And you his son, Bĕlshăz'-zăr, have not humbled your heart, though you knew all this, 23 but you have lifted up yourself against the Lord of heaven; and the vessels of his house have been brought in before you, and you and your lords, your wives, and your concubines have drunk wine from them; and you have praised the gods of silver and gold, of bronze, iron, wood, and stone, which do not see or hear or know, but the God in whose hand is your breath, and whose are all your ways, you have not honored.

24 "Then from his presence the hand was sent, and this writing was inscribed. 25 And this is the writing that was inscribed: MĔ'NE, MENE, TĔKĔL, and PARSĬN. 26 This is the interpretation of the matter: MĔ'NE, God has numbered the days of your kingdom and

l Aram repeats *the king your father*   *k* Or *Spirit of the holy God*

5.25 *Mene.* The Aramaic of the weight known as a *maneh.* The verb from which it is derived means "to number." *Tekel.* The Aramaic of the weight known as a "shekel." The related verb means "to weigh." *Parsin.* The Aramaic plural of the half-maneh weight.

The related verb means "to divide."
5.26 Daniel interpreted the names of the weights in terms of their related verbs: "numbered, numbered, weighed, and divided." *Peres,* the singular of *Parsin* also suggests the name Persians (Aramaic, *paras*).

brought it to an end; 27 TĔKĔL, you have been weighed in the balances and found wanting; 28 PĒ′RĔS, your kingdom is divided and given to the Mēdes and Persians.''

5. Daniel rewarded and Belshazzar slain

29 Then Bĕlshăz′zàr commanded, and Daniel was clothed with purple, a chain of gold was put about his neck, and proclamation was made concerning him, that he should be the third ruler in the kingdom.

30 That very night Bĕlshăz′zàr the Chăldē′àn king was slain. ³¹And Dàrī′ùs the Mēde received the kingdom, being about sixty-two years old.

F. Daniel preserved in the lions' den

1. The conspiracy against Daniel

6 It pleased Dàrī′ùs to set over the kingdom a hundred and twenty satraps, to be throughout the whole kingdom; 2 and over them three presidents, of whom Daniel was one, to whom these satraps should give account, so that the king might suffer no loss. 3 Then this Daniel became distinguished above all the other presidents and satraps, because an excellent spirit was in him; and the king planned to set him over the whole kingdom. 4 Then the presidents and the satraps sought to find a ground for complaint against Daniel with regard to the kingdom; but they could find no ground for complaint or any fault, because he was faithful, and no error or fault was found in him. 5 Then these men said, "We shall not find any ground for complaint against this Daniel unless we find it in connection with the law of his God."

6 Then these presidents and satraps came by agreement[m] to the king and said to him, "O King Dàrī′ùs, live for ever! ⁷All the presidents of the kingdom, the prefects and the satraps, the counselors and the governors are agreed that the king should establish an ordinance and enforce an interdict, that whoever makes petition to any god or man for thirty days, except to you, O king, shall be cast into the den of lions. 8 Now, O king, establish the interdict and sign the document, so that it cannot be changed, according to the law of the Mēdes and the Persians, which cannot be revoked." ⁹ Therefore King Dàrī′ùs signed the document and interdict.

[m] Or thronging

Reference column:
5.27 Job 31.6; Ps 62.9
5.29 ver 7,16
★5.30 Isa 21.4–9; Jer 51.31, 39,57
★5.31 Dan 6.1; 9.1
6.1 Est 1.1; Dan 5.31
6.2 Dan 2.48, 49; Ezra 4.22
6.3 Dan 1.20; 5.12,14; Est 10.3
6.4 Gen 43.18; ver 22
6.6 ver 21; Neh 2.3; Dan 2.4
6.7 Dan 3.2,27; Ps 59.3; Dan 3.6; ver 16
6.8 ver 12,15; Est 1.19; 8.8
★6.9 Ps 118.9; 146.3

5.30 At least two ancient historians (Xenophon and Herodotus) have recorded the fall of Babylon. The Euphrates river ran through the city. Under the cover of night it was diverted from its normal channel by the Medo-Persian invaders. While the inhabitants of Babylon, imagining themselves secure behind their mighty walls amused themselves in drunken carousal, two Babylonian deserters led the conquering hosts into the city by the dry bed of the river. The defending garrison found itself attacked from within the city itself and was helpless to withstand the invaders. Belshazzar himself was slain that same night as the Persian troops raged through the city.
5.31 Darius the Mede, probably the one who took the city in the name of Cyrus.
6.9 Some have objected that this episode is of legendary character for the reason that no king would ever have consented to such a decree as this, exalting himself to a position of exclusive worship even in preference to the gods themselves. But the historical situation prevailing at the beginning of the Persian rule over Babylon made it seem a clever stroke of statesmanship. Imposing such a regulation upon the diverse nations of the empire, clinging with superstitious loyalty to their local gods, would have enforced the lesson that Persia was the new sovereign over them all, and no appeal to the gods would avail to challenge the authority of the new conquerors. And so even though the new measure was a foolish and iniquitous one, it might have commended itself to worldly wisdom on purely political grounds.

2. Daniel detected, tried, and sentenced

10 When Daniel knew that the document had been signed, he went to his house where he had windows in his upper chamber open toward Jerusalem; and he got down upon his knees three times a day and prayed and gave thanks before his God, as he had done previously. 11 Then these men came by agreement[m] and found Daniel making petition and supplication before his God. 12 Then they came near and said before the king, concerning the interdict, "O king! Did you not sign an interdict, that any man who makes petition to any god or man within thirty days except to you, O king, shall be cast into the den of lions?" The king answered, "The thing stands fast, according to the law of the Mēdes and Persians, which cannot be revoked." 13 Then they answered before the king, "That Daniel, who is one of the exiles from Judah, pays no heed to you, O king, or the interdict you have signed, but makes his petition three times a day."

14 Then the king, when he heard these words, was much distressed, and set his mind to deliver Daniel; and he labored till the sun went down to rescue him. 15 Then these men came by agreement[m] to the king, and said to the king, "Know, O king, that it is a law of the Mēdes and Persians that no interdict or ordinance which the king establishes can be changed."

16 Then the king commanded, and Daniel was brought and cast into the den of lions. The king said to Daniel, "May your God, whom you serve continually, deliver you!" 17And a stone was brought and laid upon the mouth of the den, and the king sealed it with his own signet and with the signet of his lords, that nothing might be changed concerning Daniel. 18 Then the king went to his palace, and spent the night fasting; no diversions were brought to him, and sleep fled from him.

3. Daniel delivered and his foes punished

19 Then, at break of day, the king arose and went in haste to the den of lions. 20 When he came near to the den where Daniel was, he cried out in a tone of anguish and said to Daniel, "O Daniel, servant of the living God, has your God, whom you serve continually, been able to deliver you from the lions?" 21 Then Daniel said to the king, "O king, live for ever! 22 My God sent his angel and shut the lions' mouths, and they have not hurt me, because I was found blameless before him; and also before you, O king, I have done no wrong." 23 Then the king was exceedingly glad, and commanded that Daniel be taken up out of the den. So Daniel was taken up out of the den, and no kind of hurt was found upon him, because he had trusted in his God. 24And the king commanded, and those men who had accused Daniel were brought and cast into the den of lions—they, their children, and their wives; and before they reached the bottom of the den the lions overpowered them and broke all their bones in pieces.

4. Darius acknowledges Daniel's God

25 Then King Dàrī'ùs wrote to all the peoples, nations, and

m Or *thronging*

6.10
1 Ki 8.48, 49;
Ps 95.6;
55.17;
1 Thess 5.17,18
6.11
ver 6
6.12
Dan 3.8;
Acts 16.19–21
6.13
Dan 1.6;
5.13;
Est 3.8;
Dan 3.12;
Acts 5.29
6.14
Mk 6.26
6.15
Est 8.8;
ver 8
*6.16
Jer 38.5;
ver 7,20;
Ps 37.39, 40
6.17
Lam 3.55;
Mt 27.66
6.18
2 Sam 12.16, 17;
Est 6.1;
Dan 2.1
6.20
ver 26,27;
Jer 32.17;
Dan 3.17
6.21
Dan 2.4;
ver 6
6.22
Acts 12.11;
2 Tim 4.17;
Heb 11.33;
1 Sam 24.10
6.23
ver 14,18;
Dan 3.25, 27;
Isa 26.3;
Heb 11.33
6.24
2 Ki 14.6;
Ps 54.5;
Isa 38.13
6.25
Ezra 1.1,2;
Est 3.12;
8.9;
Dan 4.1;
1 Pet 1.2

6.16 This event occurred when Daniel was an old man (probably over 80). It reveals his unbroken devotion to God and his refusal to compromise conscience for temporal advantage.

languages that dwell in all the earth: "Peace be multiplied to you.
²⁶ I make a decree, that in all my royal dominion men tremble and fear before the God of Daniel,

for he is the living God,
enduring for ever;
his kingdom shall never be destroyed,
and his dominion shall be to the end.
²⁷ He delivers and rescues,
he works signs and wonders
in heaven and on earth,
he who has saved Daniel
from the power of the lions."

²⁸ So this Daniel prospered during the reign of Dári′üs and the reign of Cyrus the Persian.

6.26
Dan 3.29;
Ps 99.1;
Dan 4.34;
Ps 93.1,2;
Dan 4.3;
7.14,27

6.27
ver 22;
Dan 4.3

6.28
Ezra 1.1,2;
Dan 1.21;
10.1

II. The final dream and visions 7.1–12.13

A. The vision of the four beasts

1. The four beasts of Babylon, Persia, Greece, and Rome

7 In the first year of Bělshăz′zàr king of Babylon, Daniel had a dream and visions of his head as he lay in his bed. Then he wrote down the dream, and told the sum of the matter. ² Daniel said, "I saw in my vision by night, and behold, the four winds of heaven were stirring up the great sea. ³And four great beasts came up out of the sea, different from one another. ⁴ The first was like a lion and had eagles' wings. Then as I looked its wings were plucked off, and it was lifted up from the ground and made to stand upon two feet like a man; and the mind of a man was given to it. ⁵And behold, another beast, a second one, like a bear. It was raised up on one side; it had three ribs in its mouth between its teeth; and it was told, 'Arise, devour much flesh.' ⁶After this I looked, and lo, another, like a leopard, with four wings of a bird on its back; and the beast had four heads; and dominion was given to it. ⁷After this I saw in the night visions, and behold, a fourth beast, terrible and dreadful and exceedingly strong; and it had great iron teeth; it devoured and broke in pieces, and stamped the residue with its feet. It was different from all the beasts that were before it; and it had ten horns. ⁸ I considered the horns, and behold, there came up among them another horn, a little one, before which three of the first horns were plucked up by the roots; and behold, in this horn were eyes like the eyes of a man, and a mouth speaking great things. ⁹As I looked,

7.1
Dan 5.1,22,
30; 1.17;
ver 7,13,15;
Jer 36.4,32

7.3
ver 17;
Rev 13.1

★7.4
Jer 48.40;
Ezek 17.3;
Hab 1.8

★7.5
Dan 2.39

7.6
ver 12

7.7
Rev 12.3;
13.1; 17.3

★7.8
ver 20,21;
Rev 9.7;
ver 11,25

★7.9
Mk 9.3;
Rev 1.14;
Ezek 1.13,
26; 10.2,6

7.4 *lion . . . eagles' wings.* Winged lions have been excavated at Nimrud and Babylon. Here they symbolize the Babylonian empire.

7.5 *another beast.* The vision comprised four beasts in all. In additon to the winged lion, Daniel describes a bear, a leopard, and an unnamed *terrible and dreadful* beast (ver 7). These have been interpreted as meaning: Babylon, Media, Persia, and Greece; or Babylon, Medo-Persia, Greece, and Rome.

7.8 *another horn, a little one.* Horns are symbolic of power. In Daniel they are used of kings. Those who interpret the fourth

kingdom as Greece identify the "little horn" with Antiochus Epiphanes, the Seleucid ruler who sought to suppress Jewish worship. Those who identify the fourth kingdom with Rome, interpret the "little horn" as a reference to a future antichrist.

7.9 Verses 9–14 describe future events. The *son of man* is none other than the Lord Jesus Christ whose kingdom is to be eternal and before whom the nations of the earth shall bow. One should not, however, expect precise details in this general statement about the final outcome of world history.

2. *The everlasting kingdom of the Son of man*

thrones were placed
    and one that was ancient of days took his seat;
his raiment was white as snow,
    and the hair of his head like pure wool;
his throne was fiery flames,
    its wheels were burning fire.

10 A stream of fire issued
    and came forth from before him;
a thousand thousands served him,
    and ten thousand times ten thousand stood before him;
the court sat in judgment,
    and the books were opened.

11 I looked then because of the sound of the great words which the horn was speaking. And as I looked, the beast was slain, and its body destroyed and given over to be burned with fire. 12As for the rest of the beasts, their dominion was taken away, but their lives were prolonged for a season and a time. 13 I saw in the night visions,
    and behold, with the clouds of heaven
there came one like a son of man,
and he came to the Ancient of Days
    and was presented before him.

14 And to him was given dominion
    and glory and kingdom,
that all peoples, nations, and languages
    should serve him;
his dominion is an everlasting dominion,
    which shall not pass away,
and his kingdom one
    that shall not be destroyed.

3. *The dream explained*

15 "As for me, Daniel, my spirit within me was anxious and the visions of my head alarmed me. 16 I approached one of those who stood there and asked him the truth concerning all this. So he told me, and made known to me the interpretation of the things. 17 'These four great beasts are four kings who shall arise out of the earth. 18 But the saints of the Most High shall receive the kingdom, and possess the kingdom for ever, for ever and ever.'

19 "Then I desired to know the truth concerning the fourth beast, which was different from all the rest, exceedingly terrible, with its teeth of iron and claws of bronze; and which devoured and broke in pieces, and stamped the residue with its feet; 20 and concerning the ten horns that were on its head, and the other horn which came up and before which three of them fell, the horn which had eyes and a mouth that spoke great things, and which seemed greater than its fellows. 21As I looked, this horn made war with the saints, and prevailed over them, 22 until the Ancient of

7.10
Ps 50.3;
97.3;
Isa 30.33;
Rev 5.11;
20.12

7.11
ver 7,8;
Rev 19.20
7.12
ver 3–6
★7.13
Ezek 1.26;
Mt 24.30;
26.64;
Mk 13.26;
Lk 21.27;
Rev 1.7,13

7.14
Ps 2.6–8;
1 Cor 15.27;
Eph 1.22;
Phil 2.9–
11;
Ps 72.11;
102.22;
Dan 2.44;
Mic 4.7;
Heb 12.28

7.15
ver 1,28
7.16
Rev 5.5;
7.13,14;
Dan 8.16,
17
7.17
ver 3
7.18
Isa 60.12–
14;
Rev 2.26;
20.4
7.19
ver 7,8
7.21
Rev 13.7
7.22
ver 9,13;
1 Cor 6.2,3;
ver 18

7.13 *a son of man.* This is the Hebrew idiom for a human being. The one who appeared in Daniel's vision was human, in contrast to the beasts which represented the nations. The term "Son of man" was later used more generally as a title of the Messiah, and is so used in the New Testament.

The coming of Christ has been repeatedly foretold in the Scriptures of the Old Testament prophets. Jesus Christ Himself spoke of His Second Coming (Mt 25.31; Jn 14.3). So did the Apostles (Acts 2.30; 1 Tim 6.14), and the angels who relayed God's message to the disciples (Acts 1.10, 11).

Days came, and judgment was given for the saints of the Most High, and the time came when the saints received the kingdom. 23 "Thus he said: 'As for the fourth beast,

there shall be a fourth kingdom on earth,
which shall be different from all the kingdoms,
and it shall devour the whole earth,
and trample it down, and break it to pieces.

24 As for the ten horns,
out of this kingdom
ten kings shall arise,
and another shall arise after them;
he shall be different from the former ones,
and shall put down three kings.

25 He shall speak words against the Most High,
and shall wear out the saints of the Most High,
and shall think to change the times and the law;
and they shall be given into his hand
for a time, two times, and half a time.

26 But the court shall sit in judgment,
and his dominion shall be taken away,
to be consumed and destroyed to the end.

27 And the kingdom and the dominion
and the greatness of the kingdoms under the whole heaven
shall be given to the people of the saints of the Most High;
their kingdom shall be an everlasting kingdom,
and all dominions shall serve and obey them.'

28 "Here is the end of the matter. As for me, Daniel, my thoughts greatly alarmed me, and my color changed; but I kept the matter in my mind."

B. The vision of the ram and the he-goat

1. The ram of Medo-Persia and the he-goat of Greece

8 In the third year of the reign of King Bĕlshăz'zăr a vision appeared to me, Daniel, after that which appeared to me at the first. 2And I saw in the vision; and when I saw, I was in Suşā the capital, which is in the province of Ēlăm; and I saw in the vision, and I was at the river Ūlaī. 3 I raised my eyes and saw, and behold, a ram standing on the bank of the river. It had two horns; and both horns were high, but one was higher than the other, and the higher one came up last. 4 I saw the ram charging westward and northward and southward; no beast could stand before him, and there was no one who could rescue from his power; he did as he pleased and magnified himself.

5 As I was considering, behold, a he-goat came from the west across the face of the whole earth, without touching the ground; and the goat had a conspicuous horn between his eyes. 6 He came to the ram with the two horns, which I had seen standing on the

---

7.24 The ten horns (representing ten kings or kingdoms) parallel the earlier vision of the ten toes (ch 2). Verse 27 indicates that the king who shall emerge as ruler over all will ultimately be defeated by Christ's kingdom. The little horn here, who defeats three of the ten kings, is not to be confused with the little horn of 8.9, for he is said to emerge from the fourth kingdom (the latter-day Roman empire), whereas the little horn of chapter 8 comes from the third kingdom (the Greek empire established by Alexander the Great). **8.3** *two horns*, representing Media and Persia (cf. 8.20). **8.5** *he-goat*, i.e., Greece (cf. 8.21). *a conspicuous horn*, Alexander the Great (cf. 8.21).

8.7
Dan 11.11;
7.7

8.8
2 Chr 26.16;
Dan 5.20;
ver 22;
Dan 7.2;
Rev 7.1

*8.9
ver 23;
Dan 11.16,
41
8.10
Rev 12.4
*8.11
Dan 11.36,
37;
Josh 5.14;
Dan 11.31;
12.11;
Ezek 46.13,
14
8.13
Dan 4.13,
23;12.6,8;
Rev 11.2

*8.14

8.15
ver 1;
Dan 7.13
8.16
Dan 9.21;
Lk 1.19,26
8.17
Ezek 1.28;
Rev 1.17
8.18
Dan 10.9,
16,18;
Ezek 2.2
8.19
Hab 2.3
8.21
ver 5;
Dan 10.20
8.22
ver 8

bank of the river, and he ran at him in his mighty wrath. 7 I saw him come close to the ram, and he was enraged against him and struck the ram and broke his two horns; and the ram had no power to stand before him, but he cast him down to the ground and trampled upon him; and there was no one who could rescue the ram from his power. 8 Then the he-goat magnified himself exceedingly; but when he was strong, the great horn was broken, and instead of it there came up four conspicuous horns toward the four winds of heaven.

2. The little horn

9 Out of one of them came forth a little horn, which grew exceedingly great toward the south, toward the east, and toward the glorious land. 10 It grew great, even to the host of heaven; and some of the host of the stars it cast down to the ground, and trampled upon them. 11 It magnified itself, even up to the Prince of the host; and the continual burnt offering was taken away from him, and the place of his sanctuary was overthrown. 12 And the host was given over to it together with the continual burnt offering through transgression;[n] and truth was cast down to the ground, and the horn acted and prospered. 13 Then I heard a holy one speaking; and another holy one said to the one that spoke, "For how long is the vision concerning the continual burnt offering, the transgression that makes desolate, and the giving over of the sanctuary and host to be trampled under foot?"[o] 14 And he said to him,[p] "For two thousand and three hundred evenings and mornings; then the sanctuary shall be restored to its rightful state."

3. Gabriel's explanation of the vision

15 When I, Daniel, had seen the vision, I sought to understand it; and behold, there stood before me one having the appearance of a man. 16 And I heard a man's voice between the banks of the Ūlaī, and it called, "Gabriel, make this man understand the vision." 17 So he came near where I stood; and when he came, I was frightened and fell upon my face. But he said to me, "Understand, O son of man, that the vision is for the time of the end."

18 As he was speaking to me, I fell into a deep sleep with my face to the ground; but he touched me and set me on my feet. 19 He said, "Behold, I will make known to you what shall be at the latter end of the indignation; for it pertains to the appointed time of the end. 20 As for the ram which you saw with the two horns, these are the kings of Mē′dīa and Persia. 21 And the he-goat[q] is the king of Greece; and the great horn between his eyes is the first king. 22 As for the horn that was broken, in place of which four

---

n Heb obscure   o Heb obscure
p Theodotion Gk Syr Vg: Heb me   q Or shaggy he-goat

8.9 In chapter 8 Daniel returns to the ram and the he-goat visions which represent the second and the third of the four great kingdoms. They have been spoken of as the bronze and silver kingdoms of chapter 2 and the bear and leopard kingdoms of 7.5, 6. The two kingdoms here in view are those of Medo-Persia and Greece. The little horn here is identified by some with Antiochus Epiphanes (175–164 B.C.) who in 168 B.C. profaned the Jewish Temple and sought to stamp out the Jewish religion altogether. They also hold that Antiochus was a type of the final world-dictator (the "beast" of Revelation) who is yet to come. For this reason both Antiochus (the type) and the "beast" (the antitype) are called by the same name: the little horn.

8.11 the Prince, God Himself.

8.14 evenings and mornings, i.e., successive evenings and mornings, 1150 days.

others arose, four kingdoms shall arise from his *r* nation, but not
with his power. 23And at the latter end of their rule, when the
transgressors have reached their full measure, a king of bold countenance, one who understands riddles, shall arise. 24 His power
shall be great,*s* and he shall cause fearful destruction, and shall
succeed in what he does, and destroy mighty men and the people
of the saints. 25 By his cunning he shall make deceit prosper under
his hand, and in his own mind he shall magnify himself. Without
warning he shall destroy many; and he shall even rise up against
the Prince of princes; but, by no human hand, he shall be broken.
26 The vision of the evenings and the mornings which has been
told is true; but seal up the vision, for it pertains to many days
hence."

27 And I, Daniel, was overcome and lay sick for some days;
then I rose and went about the king's business; but I was appalled
by the vision and did not understand it.

C. The vision of the seventy weeks

1. Daniel's persistent, promise-claiming prayer

9 In the first year of Dàrī'ús the son of Ăhăşŭ-ē'rús, by birth a
Mēde, who became king over the realm of the Chăldē'áns—
2 in the first year of his reign, I, Daniel, perceived in the books the
number of years which, according to the word of the LORD to
Jĕrĕmī'áh the prophet, must pass before the end of the desolations
of Jerusalem, namely, seventy years.

3 Then I turned my face to the Lord God, seeking him by
prayer and supplications with fasting and sackcloth and ashes.
4 I prayed to the LORD my God and made confession, saying, "O
Lord, the great and terrible God, who keepest covenant and
steadfast love with those who love him and keep his commandments, 5 we have sinned and done wrong and acted wickedly and
rebelled, turning aside from thy commandments and ordinances;
6 we have not listened to thy servants the prophets, who spoke in
thy name to our kings, our princes, and our fathers, and to all the
people of the land. 7 To thee, O Lord, belongs righteousness, but
to us confusion of face, as at this day, to the men of Judah, to the
inhabitants of Jerusalem, and to all Israel, those that are near and
those that are far away, in all the lands to which thou hast driven
them, because of the treachery which they have committed against
thee. 8 To us, O Lord, belongs confusion of face, to our kings, to
our princes, and to our fathers, because we have sinned against
thee. 9 To the Lord our God belong mercy and forgiveness; because we have rebelled against him, 10 and have not obeyed the
voice of the LORD our God by following his laws, which he set
before us by his servants the prophets. 11All Israel has transgressed
thy law and turned aside, refusing to obey thy voice. And the curse
and oath which are written in the law of Moses the servant of God
have been poured out upon us, because we have sinned against
him. 12 He has confirmed his words, which he spoke against us and

Marginal references:

8.24
Dan 11.36

8.25
Dan 11.21;
ver 11;
Dan 2.34,45

8.26
Dan 10.1;
12.4,9;
10.14

8.27
Dan 7.28;
Hab 3.16

9.1
Dan 5.31;
11.1

*9.2
2 Chr 36.21;
Jer 29.10;
Zech 7.5

9.3
Neh 1.4;
Jer 29.12;
Jas 4.8

9.4
Deut 7.21;
Neh 9.32;
Deut 7.9

9.5
Ps 106.6;
Lam 1.18,
20;
ver 11

9.6
2 Chr 36.15,
16;
ver 8

9.7
Jer 23.6;
33.16;
Amos 9.9

9.8
ver 6,5

9.9
Neh 9.17;
Ps 130.4;

9.10
2 Ki 17.13–
15; 18.12

9.11
Isa 1.4–6;
Jer 8.5,10;
Deut 27.15

9.12
Isa 44.26;
Zech 1.6;
Ezek 5.9

---

r Theodotion Gk Vg: Heb *the*
s Theodotion and Beatty papyrus of Gk: Heb repeats *but not with his power* from verse 22

9.2 *the number of years* (cf. Jer 25.11).
Daniel realized (*perceived in the books*) that

the seventy years of exile and devastation
must be nearing an end.

against our rulers who ruled us, by bringing upon us a great calamity; for under the whole heaven there has not been done the like of what has been done against Jerusalem. 13As it is written in the law of Moses, all this calamity has come upon us, yet we have not entreated the favor of the LORD our God, turning from our iniquities and giving heed to thy truth. 14 Therefore the LORD has kept ready the calamity and has brought it upon us; for the LORD our God is righteous in all the works which he has done, and we have not obeyed his voice. 15And now, O Lord our God, who didst bring thy people out of the land of Egypt with a mighty hand, and hast made thee a name, as at this day, we have sinned, we have done wickedly. 16 O Lord, according to all thy righteous acts, let thy anger and thy wrath turn away from thy city Jerusalem, thy holy hill; because for our sins, and for the iniquities of our fathers, Jerusalem and thy people have become a byword among all who are round about us. 17 Now therefore, O our God, hearken to the prayer of thy servant and to his supplications, and for thy own sake, O Lord,^{t} cause thy face to shine upon thy sanctuary, which is desolate. 18 O my God, incline thy ear and hear; open thy eyes and behold our desolations, and the city which is called by thy name; for we do not present our supplications before thee on the ground of our righteousness, but on the ground of thy great mercy. 19 O LORD, hear; O LORD, forgive; O LORD, give heed and act; delay not, for thy own sake, O my God, because thy city and thy people are called by thy name."

2. Gabriel's appearance and the interpretation

20 While I was speaking and praying, confessing my sin and the sin of my people Israel, and presenting my supplication before the LORD my God for the holy hill of my God; 21 while I was speaking in prayer, the man Gabriel, whom I had seen in the vision at the first, came to me in swift flight at the time of the evening sacrifice. 22 He came ^{u} and he said to me, "O Daniel, I have now come out to give you wisdom and understanding. 23At the beginning of your supplications a word went forth, and I have come to tell it to you, for you are greatly beloved; therefore consider the word and understand the vision.

24 "Seventy weeks of years are decreed concerning your people and your holy city, to finish the transgression, to put an end to sin, and to atone for iniquity, to bring in everlasting righteousness,

Cross-references (margin)

9.13 Isa 9.13; Jer 2.30

9.14 Jer 31.28; 44.27; ver 7,10

9.15 Ex 6.1,6; Jer 32.21; Neh 9.10; Jer 32.20

9.16 1 Sam 12.7; Ps 31.1; Zech 8.3

9.17 Num 6.25; Lam 5.18

9.18 Isa 37.17; Jer 25.29; 36.7

9.19 Ps 44.23; 74.10,11

9.20 ver 3; Isa 58.9; 6.5

*9.21 Dan 8.16; Isa 6.2; Dan 8.18; 10.10,16, 18

9.23 Dan 10.12; Lk 1.28; Mt 24.15

*9.24 Isa 55.10; Rom 5.10; Acts 3.14

---

t Theodotion Vg Compare Syr: Heb *for the Lord's sake*
u Gk Syr: Heb *made to understand*

9.21 the man Gabriel. Gabriel appeared in human form.
9.24 The prophecy of the seventy weeks has been variously interpreted. One conclusion seems self-evident. Each *week* or "heptad" must be a period of seven years or a total of 490 years. Daniel divides this period into three parts: the first has seven weeks or forty-nine years, the second has sixty-two weeks or 434 years, and the third has one week or seven years. Some interpreters hold that the entire seventy weeks were to follow one upon another without interruption. This interpretation, however, encounters the difficulty that, according to the received Hebrew text of verse 25, there are to elapse only sixty-nine weeks, after which time (according to verse 26) the anointed one is to be cut off. (Moreover, a full 490 years can hardly be made out between any of the eligible decrees—538, 457, and 445 B.C.—and the cutting off of the Messiah.) Others hold that sixty-nine weeks only were fulfilled by the time the anointed one was cut off at Calvary, and that the last week belongs to the period of the great tribulation. The early church fathers held this view. Some of those who hold to the latter view interpret the New Testament church age as an unrevealed mystery during Old Testament times, constituting a "parenthesis" until the beginning of the seventieth week. (Others who hold to

to seal both vision and prophet, and to anoint a most holy place.^{v}
^{25} Know therefore and understand that from the going forth of the word to restore and build Jerusalem to the coming of an anointed one, a prince, there shall be seven weeks. Then for sixty-two weeks it shall be built again with squares and moat, but in a troubled time. ^{26}And after the sixty-two weeks, an anointed one shall be cut off, and shall have nothing; and the people of the prince who is to come shall destroy the city and the sanctuary. Its^w end shall come with a flood, and to the end there shall be war; desolations are decreed. ^{27}And he shall make a strong covenant with many for one week; and for half of the week he shall cause sacrifice and offering to cease; and upon the wing of abominations shall come one who makes desolate, until the decreed end is poured out on the desolator."

*9.25
Ezra 4.24;
Neh 2.1–8;
3.1;
Jn 1.41;
4.25;
Isa 9.6;
*9.26
Isa 53.8;
Mk 9.12;
Lk 19.43,
44;
Nah 1.8
*9.27
Dan 11.31;
Mt 24.15;
Lk 21.20;
Isa 10.23

D. The vision of the last days

1. Daniel's vision of an angel

10   In the third year of Cyrus king of Persia a word was revealed to Daniel, who was named Bĕltĕshăz'zăr. And the word was true, and it was a great conflict. And he understood the word and had understanding of the vision.

10.1
Dan 6.28;
1.7; 8.26;
2.21

^{v} Or *thing* or *one* ^{w} Or *his*

---

the deferment of the seventieth week acknowledge that the New Testament church was quite frequently alluded to in the Old Testament.) The *terminus a quo* for the commencement of these sixty-nine weeks of years is stated to be *from the going forth of the word* (or decree) *to restore and build Jerusalem* (ver 25). This may refer to the divine decree, or one of three historical edicts: (1) the decree of King Cyrus in 538 B.C. (Ezra 1.1–4); (2) the order of Artaxerxes to Ezra in 457 B.C. (which apparently involved authority to erect the walls of Jerusalem, cf. Ezra 7.6, 7; 9.9); (3) the order to Nehemiah in 445 B.C. to carry through the rebuilding of the walls (which Ezra had not been able to accomplish). Of these choices, (1) must be ruled out as coming nowhere near to the time of Christ's ministry; (3) comes out too late, unless lunar years are used for the computation. Only (2) comes out right according to regular solar years, for it yields the result as A.D. 27, or the commencement of Christ's ministry. Ezra and Nehemiah render an account of the rebuilding of Jerusalem in forty-nine years and troublous times. Then follow the sixty-two weeks, after which Messiah was cut off for sin. One's view of the remaining week is colored by his whole scheme of prophetic interpretation. Still others hold that the numbers are used symbolically, as in 12.11, 12, and that the passage, "covers the whole period of time from Daniel to the consummation of all things," Herbert C. Leupold, EXPOSITION OF DANIEL (Augsburg Publishing House), p. 405.

9.25 *for sixty-two weeks.* The time of rebuilding the city and land subsequent to the return from exile.

9.26 *an anointed one shall be cut off.* Some scholars identify the "anointed one" with

Onias III, the high priest who was deposed by Antiochus Epiphanes in 175 B.C. The KJV translates it "Messiah," identifying the "anointed one" with Jesus, the Christ (anointed). Historically, the Christian church has tended to interpret the passage Messianically. *destroy the city.* If the reference is to Onias III, the destruction is that described in 1 Maccabees 1.31, 32, 38; 3.45. If interpreted Messianically, the reference is to the destruction of Jersualem, A.D. 70.

9.27 *he shall cause sacrifice and offering to cease.* Antiochus outlawed the rites of the Jewish faith. Similarly, in A.D. 70, the Temple was destroyed and sacrifices ended. *the decreed end.* The prophet knows that God holds the ultimate key to history, and even the *desolator* must stand before God. The phrase "abomination that makes desolate" is used variantly three times in Daniel (9.27; 11.31; 12.11) and once in Matthew (24.15). Probably this significant expression has three prophetic references: (1) in 11.31 it refers to Antiochus Epiphanes, whose troops desecrated the Temple in 168 B.C. and suspended the daily burnt offering and other services. He erected an idol-altar in place of the altar of burnt offering (apparently a statue of Zeus Olympus) and entered into the Holy of Holies; (2) in 9.27 and 12.11, and Mk 13.14 it seems to refer to a desecration which shall take place in the end, during the period of the great tribulation; (3) in Mt 24.15 (cf. Lk 21.19–24) it probably refers also to the destruction of Jerusalem in A.D. 70 by Titus, whose legions triumphantly brought their eagle-topped army standards into holy precincts. Others hold that the ninth chapter gives us "a rather comprehensive description of the New Testament Antichrist" (Leupold *op. cit.*, p. 437).

10.2
Ezra 9.4,5;
Neh 1.4
★10.3
10.4
Dan 8.2;
Gen 2.14
10.5
Dan 12.6,7;
Rev 1.13;
Jer 10.9
10.6
Mt 17.2;
Rev 1.16,14;
1.15; 2.18
10.7
2 Ki 6.17;
Acts 9.7;
Ezek 12.18
10.8
Gen 32.24;
Dan 7.28;
8.27
10.9
Dan 8.18

2 In those days I, Daniel, was mourning for three weeks. 3 I ate no delicacies, no meat or wine entered my mouth, nor did I anoint myself at all, for the full three weeks. 4 On the twenty-fourth day of the first month, as I was standing on the bank of the great river, that is, the Tigris, 5 I lifted up my eyes and looked, and behold, a man clothed in linen, whose loins were girded with gold of Ūphăz. 6 His body was like beryl, his face like the appearance of lightning, his eyes like flaming torches, his arms and legs like the gleam of burnished bronze, and the sound of his words like the noise of a multitude. 7And I, Daniel, alone saw the vision, for the men who were with me did not see the vision, but a great trembling fell upon them, and they fled to hide themselves. 8 So I was left alone and saw this great vision, and no strength was left in me; my radiant appearance was fearfully changed, and I retained no strength. 9 Then I heard the sound of his words; and when I heard the sound of his words, I fell on my face in a deep sleep with my face to the ground.

2. Daniel strengthened, encouraged, and promised further revelations

10.10
Jer 1.9;
Dan 9.21;
Rev 1.17
10.11
Dan 9.23
10.12
Rev 1.17;
Dan 9.3,
20–23
★10.13
ver 20,21;
Dan 12.1;
Jude 9;
Rev 12.7
10.14
Dan 2.28;
8.26;
Hab 2.3
10.15
Ezek 24.27;
Lk 1.20
10.16
Dan 8.15;
ver 10;
Jer 1.9;
ver 8
10.17
Isa 6.1–5;
ver 8
10.18
ver 16;
Isa 35.3,4
10.19
ver 11,12;
Judg 6.23
★10.20
ver 13;
Dan 8.21;
11.2

10 And behold, a hand touched me and set me trembling on my hands and knees. 11And he said to me, "O Daniel, man greatly beloved, give heed to the words that I speak to you, and stand upright, for now I have been sent to you." While he was speaking this word to me, I stood up trembling. 12 Then he said to me, "Fear not, Daniel, for from the first day that you set your mind to understand and humbled yourself before your God, your words have been heard, and I have come because of your words. 13 The prince of the kingdom of Persia withstood me twenty-one days; but Michael, one of the chief princes, came to help me, so I left him there with the prince of the kingdom of Persia× 14 and came to make you understand what is to befall your people in the latter days. For the vision is for days yet to come."

15 When he had spoken to me according to these words, I turned my face toward the ground and was dumb. 16And behold, one in the likeness of the sons of men touched my lips; then I opened my mouth and spoke. I said to him who stood before me, "O my lord, by reason of the vision pains have come upon me, and I retain no strength. 17 How can my lord's servant talk with my lord? For now no strength remains in me, and no breath is left in me."

18 Again one having the appearance of a man touched me and strengthened me. 19And he said, "O man greatly beloved, fear not, peace be with you; be strong and of good courage." And when he spoke to me, I was strengthened and said, "Let my lord speak, for you have strengthened me." 20 Then he said, "Do you know why I have come to you? But now I will return to fight against the prince of Persia; and when I am through with him, lo, the prince

---

× Theodotion Compare Gk: Heb I was left there with the kings of Persia

---

10.3 Check Dan 1.8 in this connection.
10.13 The prince of the kingdom of Persia. Each nation is thought to have a guardian angel. Michael, regarded as the guardian of Israel, came to Daniel's aid.

10.20 the prince of Greece. After her difficulties with Persia (I will return to fight against the prince of Persia), Israel faced even greater problems with the Greeks as well as with their successors.

of Greece will come. 21 But I will tell you what is inscribed in the book of truth: there is none who contends by my side against these

10.21
Dan 11.2;
ver 13

3. The interpretation of Daniel's vision
a. From the Persian Empire to the death of Alexander (323 B.C.)

11 except Michael, your prince. ¹And as for me, in the first year of Dărī´ŭs the Mēde, I stood up to confirm and strengthen him.

*11.1ff
Dan 9.1;
5.31

2 "And now I will show you the truth. Behold, three more kings shall arise in Persia; and a fourth shall be far richer than all of them; and when he has become strong through his riches, he shall stir up all against the kingdom of Greece. ³ Then a mighty king shall arise, who shall rule with great dominion and do according to his will. ⁴And when he has arisen, his kingdom shall be broken and divided toward the four winds of heaven, but not to his posterity, nor according to the dominion with which he ruled; for his kingdom shall be plucked up and go to others besides these.

*11.2
Dan 8.26;
8.21
*11.3
Dan 8.4,5,
21
11.4
Dan 8.8,22;
Ezek 37.9;
Zech 2.6;
Rev 7.1

b. Wars between the Ptolemaic and Seleucid Empires

5 "Then the king of the south shall be strong, but one of his princes shall be stronger than he and his dominion shall be a great dominion. ⁶After some years they shall make an alliance, and the daughter of the king of the south shall come to the king of the north to make peace; but she shall not retain the strength of her arm, and he and his offspring shall not endure; but she shall be given up, and her attendants, her child, and he who got possession of ʸ her.

*11.5
ver 9,11,
14,25,40
*11.6
ver 13,15,40

ʸ Or supported

11.1ff This chapter points forward to specific rulers of the Near East during the last few centuries before Christ. The following outline will help to understand the historical fulfilment of this prophecy: (1) the four kings of verse 2 (although this cannot be stated dogmatically) were the Persian rulers Cyrus, Cambyses, Darius Hystaspes, and Xerxes (Ahasuerus) who attempted the conquest of Greece in 480 B.C.; (2) the mighty king of verse 4 was Alexander the Great who conquered the Persian Empire, ca. 330 B.C.; (3) the division of his kingdom after his death into four parts included Greece, the Asiatic Near East, Egypt, and Asia Minor; (4) the king of the south in verse 5 was Ptolemy I of Egypt (323–285 B.C.) and one of his princes, his son Ptolemy II (who reigned during the development of the Septuagint, and who added various islands and seaport cities to the Egyptian realm); (5) in verse 6 the daughter of Ptolemy II (Berenice) was married to Antiochus II of the Asiatic or "Syrian" Empire; but she and her husband were both murdered by his divorced wife; (6) Berenice's brother, Ptolemy III, avenged her death by invading and pillaging the whole realm of Syria (ver 7–9); (7) the two sons of verse 10 were Seleucus III and Antiochus III (grandsons of Antiochus II), who vigorously pushed down to the borders of Egypt (ver 10); (8) Ptolemy IV enjoyed a temporary success

over Antiochus III at the Battle of Raphia (217 B.C.) and recaptured Palestine from him (ver 11, 12); (9) Fifteen years later Antiochus III launched a new and successful counterattack and annexed Palestine (the glorious land) permanently to the Seleucid Empire (ver 13–16); (10) Cleopatra (ver 17) was given in marriage to Ptolemy V by her father Antiochus III; (11) in verses 18, 19 Antiochus invaded Asia Minor and Greece but was defeated by the Romans at Magnesia in 190 B.C.; (12) from verses 21 through 35 the history of Antiochus Epiphanes (175–164 B.C.) is traced; (13) in verses 36 through 45 the primary reference is to Antiochus Epiphanes who was the type of the antichrist yet to come; but many features of this prediction were not fulfilled in the career of the historical Epiphanes and can only find fulfilment in the end time.
11.2 three more kings. The identification of the three kings and the fourth is uncertain. The fourth is probably Xerxes who campaigned against the Greeks.
11.3 a mighty king, Alexander the Great.
11.5 the king of the south, Ptolemy I, Lagi (son of Lagos), of Egypt. one of his princes, Seleucus I, Nicator, founder of the Seleucid kingdom in Syria.
11.6 the daughter of the king of the south (Berenice), was murdered with her child after being supplanted by her husband's first wife. The attempted alliance thus ended in failure.

*11.7
ver 19,38,39

11.8
Isa 37.19;
46.1,2;
Jer 43.12,13
*11.9

*11.10
Isa 8.8;
Jer 46.7,8;
Dan 9.26;
ver 7
*11.11
ver 5;
Dan 8.7;
ver 13,10
*11.12
*11.13
Dan 4.16;
12.7

*11.15
Jer 6.6;
Ezek 4.2;
17.17

*11.16
Dan 8.4,7;
ver 3,36;
Josh 1.5;
ver 41,45
*11.17
2 Ki 12.17;
Ezek 4.3,7

*11.18
Isa 66.19;
Jer 31.10;
Hos 12.14

11.19
Ps 27.2;
Job 20.8;
Ezek 26.21

*11.20
Isa 60.17

7 "In those times a branch[z] from her roots shall arise in his place; he shall come against the army and enter the fortress of the king of the north, and he shall deal with them and shall prevail. 8 He shall also carry off to Egypt their gods with their molten images and with their precious vessels of silver and of gold; and for some years he shall refrain from attacking the king of the north. 9 Then the latter shall come into the realm of the king of the south but shall return into his own land.

10 "His sons shall wage war and assemble a multitude of great forces, which shall come on and overflow and pass through, and again shall carry the war as far as his fortress. 11 Then the king of the south, moved with anger, shall come out and fight with the king of the north; and he shall raise a great multitude, but it shall be given into his hand. 12 And when the multitude is taken, his heart shall be exalted, and he shall cast down tens of thousands, but he shall not prevail. 13 For the king of the north shall again raise a multitude, greater than the former; and after some years[a] he shall come on with a great army and abundant supplies.

14 "In those times many shall rise against the king of the south; and the men of violence among your own people shall lift themselves up in order to fulfil the vision; but they shall fail. 15 Then the king of the north shall come and throw up siegeworks, and take a well-fortified city. And the forces of the south shall not stand, or even his picked troops, for there shall be no strength to stand. 16 But he who comes against him shall do according to his own will, and none shall stand before him; and he shall stand in the glorious land, and all of it shall be in his power. 17 He shall set his face to come with the strength of his whole kingdom, and he shall bring terms of peace[b] and perform them. He shall give him the daughter of women to destroy the kingdom;[c] but it shall not stand or be to his advantage. 18 Afterward he shall turn his face to the coastlands, and shall take many of them; but a commander shall put an end to his insolence; indeed[d] he shall turn his insolence back upon him. 19 Then he shall turn his face back toward the fortresses of his own land; but he shall stumble and fall, and shall not be found.

20 "Then shall arise in his place one who shall send an exactor of tribute through the glory of the kingdom; but within a few

z Gk: Heb from a branch   a Heb at the end of the times years
b Gk: Heb upright ones   c Heb her or it   d Heb obscure

11.7 a branch from her roots. The brother of Berenice became Ptolemy III of Egypt. He marched against Syria and brought home much booty.
11.9 the latter. Seleucus II attempted a counterblow against Egypt.
11.10 His sons. Seleucus III and Antiochus III (the Great).
11.11 the king of the south. Ptolemy IV, Philopater.
11.12 the multitude. The army of Antiochus.
11.13 after some years. Fourteen years after his defeat at Raphia (217 B.C.), Antiochus again campaigned against Egypt.
11.15 a well-fortified city. Antiochus routed the army of Ptolemy at Panion (198 B.C.).

From this time Seleucid control of Palestine was undisputed.
11.16 the glorious land, Palestine.
11.17 the daughter of women, Cleopatra, daughter of Antiochus, was given in marriage to the Egyptian king. Antiochus actually desired to gain control of Egypt for himself, thus to destroy the kingdom. it shall not stand. Egypt did not come under the control of Antiochus.
11.18 a commander. The Roman consul, Scipio, defeated Antiochus at Magnesia near Smyrna (190 B.C.).
11.20 in his place. Antiochus the Great was succeeded by his son Seleucus IV. The exactor of tribute whom he sent was Heliodorus, who ultimately murdered the king.

c. *Antiochus Epiphanes' persecution of the Jews*

days he shall be broken, neither in anger nor in battle. 21 In his place shall arise a contemptible person to whom royal majesty has not been given; he shall come in without warning and obtain the kingdom by flatteries. 22Armies shall be utterly swept away before him and broken, and the prince of the covenant also. 23And from the time that an alliance is made with him he shall act deceitfully; and he shall become strong with a small people. 24 Without warning he shall come into the richest parts*e* of the province; and he shall do what neither his fathers nor his fathers' fathers have done, scattering among them plunder, spoil, and goods. He shall devise plans against strongholds, but only for a time. 25And he shall stir up his power and his courage against the king of the south with a great army; and the king of the south shall wage war with an exceedingly great and mighty army; but he shall not stand, for plots shall be devised against him. 26 Even those who eat his rich food shall be his undoing; his army shall be swept away, and many shall fall down slain. 27And as for the two kings, their minds shall be bent on mischief; they shall speak lies at the same table, but to no avail; for the end is yet to be at the time appointed. 28And he shall return to his land with great substance, but his heart shall be set against the holy covenant. And he shall work his will, and return to his own land.

29 "At the time appointed he shall return and come into the south; but it shall not be this time as it was before. 30 For ships of Kittim shall come against him, and he shall be afraid and withdraw, and shall turn back and be enraged and take action against the holy covenant. He shall turn back and give heed to those who forsake the holy covenant. 31 Forces from him shall appear and profane the temple and fortress, and shall take away the continual burnt offering. And they shall set up the abomination that makes desolate. 32 He shall seduce with flattery those who violate the covenant; but the people who know their God shall stand firm and take action. 33And those among the people who are wise shall make many understand, though they shall fall by sword and flame, by captivity and plunder, for some days. 34 When they fall, they shall receive a little help. And many shall join themselves to them with flattery; 35 and some of those who are wise shall fall, to refine and to cleanse them*f* and to make them white, until the time of the end, for it is yet for the time appointed.

36 "And the king shall do according to his will; he shall exalt himself and magnify himself above every god, and shall speak astonishing things against the God of gods. He shall prosper till the indignation is accomplished; for what is determined shall be done. 37 He shall give no heed to the gods of his fathers, or to the one beloved by women; he shall not give heed to any other god, for

---

e Or *among the richest men*　*f* Gk: Heb *among them*

＊11.21
ver 24,32,34

＊11.22
ver 10;
Dan 8.10,11
11.23
Dan 8.25
11.24
ver 21;
Ezek 34.14

＊11.25

11.26
ver 10,40
11.27
Ps 52.1;
64.6;
Jer 9.3–5;
ver 35,40;
Hab 2.3
＊11.28

＊11.30
Gen 10.4;
Num 24.24;
Jer 2.10
＊11.31
Dan 8.11;
9.27;
Mt 24.15;
Mk 13.14
11.32
ver 21,34;
Mic 5.7–9
11.33
Mt 24.9;
Jn 16.2;
Heb 11.36–38
＊11.34
Mt 7.15;
Rom 16.18
＊11.35
Zech 13.9;
Jn 15.2;
ver 27,40
11.36
2 Thess 2.4;
Rev 13.5,6;
Dan 2.47;
8.12; 8.19;
9.27
＊11.37
ver 36

11.21 *a contemptible person.* Antiochus Epiphanes, son of Antiochus the Great.
11.22 *the prince of the covenant.* The Jewish High Priest, Onias III.
11.25 *the king of the south.* Ptolemy VI, Philometor.
11.28 *the holy covenant.* The Jewish faith.
11.30 *ships of Kittim.* Roman intervention

is described in terms of ships from Kittim.
11.31 *the abomination* is a statue of Zeus.
11.34 *a little help.* The Maccabees who rebelled against Antiochus.
11.35 *shall fall,* i.e., suffer martyrdom.
11.37 *the one beloved by women.* Probably Tammuz-Adonis whose worship was popular with women (cf. Ezek 8.14).

11.38 he shall magnify himself above all. 38 He shall honor the god of
fortresses instead of these; a god whom his fathers did not know
he shall honor with gold and silver, with precious stones and costly
11.39 gifts. 39 He shall deal with the strongest fortresses by the help of a
foreign god; those who acknowledge him he shall magnify with
honor. He shall make them rulers over many and shall divide the
land for a price.

d. The similar career of the antitype of Antiochus at the time of the end

11.40
ver 10,13,15,
26;
Isa 5.28

11.41
Jer 48.47;
49.6

11.43
2 Chr 12.3;
Ezek 30.4,5;
Nah 3.9

11.45
ver 16,41;
Isa 65.25;
66.20;
Dan 9.16,20

40 "At the time of the end the king of the south shall attack[g]
him; but the king of the north shall rush upon him like a whirlwind, with chariots and horsemen, and with many ships; and he
shall come into countries and shall overflow and pass through.
41 He shall come into the glorious land. And tens of thousands shall
fall, but these shall be delivered out of his hand: Ēdóm and Mōäb
and the main part of the Ăm'mònītes. 42 He shall stretch out his
hand against the countries, and the land of Egypt shall not escape.
43 He shall become ruler of the treasures of gold and of silver, and
all the precious things of Egypt; and the Libyans and the Ethiopians shall follow in his train. 44 But tidings from the east and the
north shall alarm him, and he shall go forth with great fury to ex-
terminate and utterly destroy many. 45And he shall pitch his
palatial tents between the sea and the glorious holy mountain; yet
he shall come to his end, with none to help him.

e. The end of the tribulation and the resurrection of the dead

12.1
Dan 10.13,
21; 9.12;
Mt 24.21;
Rev 16.18;
ver 4

12.2
Isa 26.19;
Mt 25.46;
Jn 5.28;
Acts 24.15

12.3
Mt 13.43;
Dan 11.33

12.4
Rev 22.10;
Dan 11.33

12 "At that time shall arise Michael, the great prince who has
charge of your people. And there shall be a time of trouble,
such as never has been since there was a nation till that time; but at
that time your people shall be delivered, every one whose name
shall be found written in the book. 2And many of those who sleep
in the dust of the earth shall awake, some to everlasting life, and
some to shame and everlasting contempt. 3And those who are wise
shall shine like the brightness of the firmament; and those who
turn many to righteousness, like the stars for ever and ever. 4 But
you, Daniel, shut up the words, and seal the book, until the time
of the end. Many shall run to and fro, and knowledge shall
increase."

f. The sealing of the prophecy until the time of the end

12.5
Dan 10.4ff

5 Then I Daniel looked, and behold, two others stood, one on
this bank of the stream and one on that bank of the stream. 6And
I[h] said to the man clothed in linen, who was above the waters of
the stream, "How long shall it be till the end of these wonders?"

g Heb thrust at   h Gk Vg: Heb he

11.38 the god of fortresses. Probably Jupiter
Capitolinus (Zeus), for whom he built a
temple at Antioch.
11.39 a foreign god. Possibly a reference to
the Gentile garrisons in Jerusalem.
11.40 At the time of the end. When the
destined time for Antiochus' end has arrived.

the king of the south. Ptolemy Philometor.
11.41 the glorious land, i.e., Palestine.
12.1 At that time. Following the destruction of Antiochus, Daniel envisions the final
consummation and ushering in of God's
kingdom.
12.5 two others, i.e., angels.

7 The man clothed in linen, who was above the waters of the stream, raised his right hand and his left hand toward heaven; and I heard him swear by him who lives for ever that it would be for a time, two times, and half a time; and that when the shattering of the power of the holy people comes to an end all these things would be accomplished. 8 I heard, but I did not understand. Then I said, "O my lord, what shall be the issue of these things?" 9 He said, "Go your way, Daniel, for the words are shut up and sealed until the time of the end. 10 Many shall purify themselves, and make themselves white, and be refined; but the wicked shall do wickedly; and none of the wicked shall understand; but those who are wise shall understand. 11And from the time that the continual burnt offering is taken away, and the abomination that makes desolate is set up, there shall be a thousand two hundred and ninety days. 12 Blessed is he who waits and comes to the thousand three hundred and thirty-five days. 13 But go your way till the end; and you shall rest, and shall stand in your allotted place at the end of the days."

12.7
Rev 10.5,6;
Dan 4.34;
7.25;
Rev 12.14;
Lk 21.24;
Rev 10.7
12.8
ver 6
12.9
ver 13,4
12.10
Dan 11.35;
Isa 32.6,7
*12.11f
Dan 8.11–
14; 9.27;
11.31;
Mt 24.15
12.12
Isa 30.18;
Rev 11.2;
12.6; 13.5
12.13
ver 9,4;
Rev 14.13

12.11, 12 In these two verses the figures 1290 and 1335 are given. It is impossible to be dogmatic about their precise significance as to the future fulfilment. In all probability, however, they point to the last days and speak of that persecution which the antichrist will direct against the saints of God when he removes the worship of the true God and oppresses believers. The 1290 days reflect the truth that the period of the tribulation and of the rule of antichrist is limited, and the 1335 days indicate that those who maintain their true faith through the period of persecution will emerge into a time of great blessing.

INTRODUCTION TO
THE BOOK OF
HOSEA

Authorship and Background: The name of the author, Hosea, the son of
Beeri, means "salvation" and is related to the root word for Joshua. He lived
in the eighth century B.C. and was a prophet in the Northern Kingdom during
the reign of Jeroboam. His ministry overlapped that of Amos, Isaiah, and
Micah during an age which was marked by religious apostasy. Instead of
putting their trust in God, the leaders of the Northern Kingdom courted the
favor, or by bribery tried to buy the favor, of Assyria and Egypt. In their religious
practices they kept the name of God but took over the ritual and practices of
Baal worship. There was gross immorality, and the priests reaped a rich harvest
by increasing their own incomes from the sin offerings.

Characteristics: Hosea writes out of the acute agony of personal grief. He is
commanded to marry a woman who then proves faithless ("a wife of harlotry").
He reclaims her after she sins and writes in the white heat of severe judgment,
but also with tenderness. These extremes are intermingled in beautiful fashion
as Hosea uses his personal tragedy to illustrate the relationship of Israel to God.
His wife Gomer's three children are given symbolic names which proclaim
Israel's unfaithfulness. The first is Jezreel, so named to signify the avenging of
the blood of Jezreel upon the dynasty of Jehu (2 Ki 10.1–14); Lo-ruhamah
signifies "no (more) mercy" to be extended to the Northern Kingdom; and
Lo-ammi signifies "not my people," a symbol of God's rejection of the apostate
Israelite kingdom.

Contents:

I. Hosea's marital experiences and their fruits. 1.1—3.5: Gomer is a
    symbol of Israel's unfaithfulness. God's judgment is expressed in the
    names of their three children: Jezreel, Lo-ruhamah, and Lo-ammi. He
    describes Gomer's adultery. His pronouncement of judgment, his
    tenderness toward her, and her restoration.

II. Israel's unfaithfulness to the God of covenant love. 4.1—13.16:
    Hosea accuses Israel of adultery. He is severe in judgment and tender
    in mercy looking to restoration. He repeats accusations of her adultery
    and renders severe judgment that her prayers will not be heard, her
    cities will be destroyed, and her people taken captive. He repeats in
    two sequences the cycle of adultery, judgment, tenderness, and restor-
    ation.

III. Forgiveness and blessing in response to repentance. 14.1–9: He en-
    courages repentance and promises blessing in response to repentance.

THE BOOK OF

HOSEA

I. Hosea's marital experiences and their fruits 1.1–3.5

A. Superscription

1 The word of the LORD that came to Hōṣē′á the son of Be-ë′rī, in the days of Ŭzzī′áh, Jōthám, Āhăz, and Hĕzĕkī′áh, kings of Judah, and in the days of Jĕróbō′ám the son of Jō′ásh, king of Israel.

B. Hosea's marriage to Gomer

2 When the LORD first spoke through Hōṣē′á, the LORD said to Hosea, "Go, take to yourself a wife of harlotry and have children of harlotry, for the land commits great harlotry by forsaking the LORD." 3 So he went and took Gōmĕr the daughter of Dĭblā′ĭm, and she conceived and bore him a son.

4 And the LORD said to him, "Call his name Jĕzrĕēl′; for yet a little while, and I will punish the house of Jēhū for the blood of Jezreel, and I will put an end to the kingdom of the house of Israel. 5And on that day, I will break the bow of Israel in the valley of Jĕzrĕēl′."

6 She conceived again and bore a daughter. And the LORD said to him, "Call her name Not pitied, for I will no more have pity on the house of Israel, to forgive them at all. 7 But I will have pity on the house of Judah, and I will deliver them by the LORD their God; I will not deliver them by bow, nor by sword, nor by war, nor by horses, nor by horsemen."

8 When she had weaned Not pitied, she conceived and bore a son. 9And the LORD said, "Call his name Not my people, for you are not my people and I am not your God."*a*

C. The prophecy of restoration

10*b* Yet the number of the people of Israel shall be like the sand of the sea, which can be neither measured nor numbered; and in the place where it was said to them, "You are not my people," it shall be said to them, "Sons of the living God." 11And the people of Judah and the people of Israel shall be gathered together, and they shall appoint for themselves one head; and they shall go up from the land, for great shall be the day of Jĕzrĕēl′.

---

a Heb *I am not yours* *b* Ch 2.1 in Heb

1.1
Rom 9.25;
2 Ki 15.1–7;
2 Chr 27.1–9;
2 Ki 16.1–20;
2 Chr 28.1–27;
2 Ki 18.1–20;
2 Chr 29.1–32;
2 Ki 13.13;
14.23–29
★1.2
Hos 3.1;
Jer 3.1,12,14;
Hos 2.5;
3.5
★1.4
2 Ki 10.1–14; 15.10
1.5
2 Ki 15.29
★1.6
ver 3,9;
Hos 2.4
1.7
Isa 30.18;
Jer 25.5,6;
Zech 9.9,10

★1.9
ver 6

★1.10
Gen 32.12;
Jer 33.22;
Rom 9.25–27;
ver 9;
Isa 63.16;
64.8
1.11
Isa 11.12;
Jer 23.5,6;
Ezek 37.21–24;
Hos 3.5

1.2 *the land commits great harlotry.* Hosea's own domestic unhappiness served as the background for the prophet's message. Just as Gomer had been unfaithful to Hosea, so Israel had been unfaithful to God.

1.4 *the house of Jehu* was responsible for the death of Joram of Israel, Ahaziah of Judah, and Jezebel (2 Ki 9). Jehu's zeal for the extermination of the Baal cult does not justify his murderous acts.

1.6 The familiar name of the KJV for *Not pitied* is Lo-ruhamah.
1.9 The familiar KJV name for *Not my people* is Lo-ammi.
1.10 Hosea prophesied the judgment of God upon faithless Israel but, with the eye of faith, he looked forward to the day when Israel would be restored to a place of honor and blessing. The new name, *Sons of the living God*, indicates that this indeed will come about.

D. Gomer a symbol of Israel

1. Her adultery

2 Say to your brother, "My people," and to your sister, "She has obtained pity."

2 "Plead with your mother, plead—
for she is not my wife,
and I am not her husband—
that she put away her harlotry from her face,
and her adultery from between her breasts;

3 lest I strip her naked
and make her as in the day she was born,
and make her like a wilderness,
and set her like a parched land,
and slay her with thirst.

4 Upon her children also I will have no pity,
because they are children of harlotry.

5 For their mother has played the harlot;
she that conceived them has acted shamefully.
For she said, 'I will go after my lovers,
who give me my bread and my water,
my wool and my flax, my oil and my drink.'

2. Gomer's judgment

6 Therefore I will hedge up her way with thorns;
and I will build a wall against her,
so that she cannot find her paths.

7 She shall pursue her lovers,
but not overtake them;
and she shall seek them,
but shall not find them.
Then she shall say, 'I will go
and return to my first husband,
for it was better with me then than now.'

8 And she did not know
that it was I who gave her
the grain, the wine, and the oil,
and who lavished upon her silver
and gold which they used for Baäl.

9 Therefore I will take back
my grain in its time,
and my wine in its season;
and I will take away my wool and my flax,
which were to cover her nakedness.

10 Now I will uncover her lewdness
in the sight of her lovers,
and no one shall rescue her out of my hand.

11 And I will put an end to all her mirth,
her feasts, her new moons, her sabbaths,
and all her appointed feasts.

12 And I will lay waste her vines and her fig trees,
of which she said,
'These are my hire,

c Ch 2.3 in Heb   d Gk: Heb brothers
e Gk Vg: Heb sisters   f Gk Syr: Heb your

which my lovers have given me.'
I will make them a forest,
and the beasts of the field shall devour them.
13 And I will punish her for the feast days of the Bāǎls
when she burned incense to them
and decked herself with her ring and jewelry,
and went after her lovers,
and forgot me, says the LORD.

3. Her restoration promised

14 "Therefore, behold, I will allure her,
and bring her into the wilderness,
and speak tenderly to her.
15 And there I will give her her vineyards,
and make the Valley of Āchor a door of hope.
And there she shall answer as in the days of her youth,
as at the time when she came out of the land of Egypt.
16 "And in that day, says the LORD, you will call me, 'My husband,' and no longer will you call me, 'My Bāǎl.' 17 For I will
remove the names of the Bāǎls from her mouth, and they shall be
mentioned by name no more. 18 And I will make for youg a covenant on that day with the beasts of the field, the birds of the air,
and the creeping things of the ground; and I will abolishh the bow,
the sword, and war from the land; and I will make you lie down
in safety. 19 And I will betroth you to me for ever; I will betroth
you to me in righteousness and in justice, in steadfast love, and in
mercy. 20 I will betroth you to me in faithfulness; and you shall
know the LORD.
21 "And in that day, says the LORD,
I will answer the heavens
and they shall answer the earth;
22 and the earth shall answer the grain, the wine, and the oil,
and they shall answer Jēzreēl';i
23 and I will sow himj for myself in the land.
And I will have pity on Not pitied,
and I will say to Not my people, 'You are my people';
and he shall say, 'Thou art my God.' "

4. Her restoration accomplished

3 And the LORD said to me, "Go again, love a woman who is
beloved of a paramour and is an adulteress; even as the LORD
loves the people of Israel, though they turn to other gods and love
cakes of raisins." 2 So I bought her for fifteen shekels of silver
and a homer and a lĕthĕch of barley. 3 And I said to her, "You
must dwell as mine for many days; you shall not play the harlot, or
belong to another man; so will I also be to you." 4 For the children
of Israel shall dwell many days without king or prince, without
sacrifice or pillar, without ephod or teraphim. 5 Afterward the

g Heb them   h Heb break   i That is God sows   j Cn: Heb her

2.14 *I will allure her.* God's love for faithless Israel has not changed. In the land of
Canaan she is tempted by the baalim, but God
states his purpose to take his people into the
wilderness where He will be able to *speak*
tenderly (literally, speak to her heart).
2.15 *a door of hope.* There was no hope for
faithless Israel in Canaan. Achor (trouble) in
exile was the only way she could be restored
to her place of favor with God.

children of Israel shall return and seek the LORD their God, and
David their king; and they shall come in fear to the LORD and to
his goodness in the latter days.

II. *Israel's unfaithfulness to the God of covenant love*
4.1–13.16

A. *Israel's adultery*

4 Hear the word of the LORD, O people of Israel;
    for the LORD has a controversy with the inhabitants of the land.
There is no faithfulness or kindness,
    and no knowledge of God in the land;
2 there is swearing, lying, killing, stealing, and committing adul-
        tery;
    they break all bounds and murder follows murder.
3 Therefore the land mourns,
    and all who dwell in it languish,
    and also the beasts of the field,
        and the birds of the air;
    and even the fish of the sea are taken away.

4 Yet let no one contend,
    and let none accuse,
    for with you is my contention, O priest.[k]
5 You shall stumble by day,
    the prophet also shall stumble with you by night;
    and I will destroy your mother.
6 My people are destroyed for lack of knowledge;
    because you have rejected knowledge,
    I reject you from being a priest to me.
And since you have forgotten the law of your God,
    I also will forget your children.

7 The more they increased,
    the more they sinned against me;
    I will change their glory into shame.
8 They feed on the sin of my people;
    they are greedy for their iniquity.
9 And it shall be like people, like priest;
    I will punish them for their ways,
    and requite them for their deeds.
10 They shall eat, but not be satisfied;
    they shall play the harlot, but not multiply;
because they have forsaken the LORD
    to cherish harlotry.

11 Wine and new wine
    take away the understanding.
12 My people inquire of a thing of wood,
    and their staff gives them oracles.
For a spirit of harlotry has led them astray,
    and they have left their God to play the harlot.

k Cn: Heb uncertain

13 They sacrifice on the tops of the mountains,
    and make offerings upon the hills,
under oak, poplar, and terebinth,
    because their shade is good.

Therefore your daughters play the harlot,
    and your brides commit adultery.
14 I will not punish your daughters when they play the harlot,
    nor your brides when they commit adultery;
for the men themselves go aside with harlots,
    and sacrifice with cult prostitutes,
and a people without understanding shall come to ruin.

15 Though you play the harlot, O Israel,
    let not Judah become guilty.
Enter not into Gilgăl,
    nor go up to Bĕth-ā′vĕn,
    and swear not, "As the LORD lives."
16 Like a stubborn heifer,
    Israel is stubborn;
can the LORD now feed them
    like a lamb in a broad pasture?

17 Ē′phräim is joined to idols,
    let him alone.
18 A band*l* of drunkards, they give themselves to harlotry;
    they love shame more than their glory.*m*
19 A wind has wrapped them*n* in its wings,
    and they shall be ashamed because of their altars.*o*

B. God's severity toward Israel

5 Hear this, O priests!
    Give heed, O house of Israel!
Hearken, O house of the king!
    For the judgment pertains to you;
for you have been a snare at Mĭzpáh,
    and a net spread upon Tābór.
2 And they have made deep the pit of Shĭttĭm;*p*
    but I will chastise all of them.

3 I know Ē′phräim,
    and Israel is not hid from me;
for now, O Ephraim, you have played the harlot,
    Israel is defiled.
4 Their deeds do not permit them
    to return to their God.
For the spirit of harlotry is within them,
    and they know not the LORD.

5 The pride of Israel testifies to his face;
    Ē′phräim*q* shall stumble in his guilt;
    Judah also shall stumble with them.

Cross references (right margin):

4.13 Jer 3.6; Ezek 6.13; Hos 2.13; 11.2; Amos 7.17; Rom 1.28

4.14 ver 18; Deut 23.17; ver 6,11

4.15 Amos 4.4; 1 Ki 12.28, 29

4.16 Ps 78.8; Isa 5.17; 7.25

4.17 Ps 81.12; ver 4
4.18 ver 14,7
4.19 Hos 12.1; 13.15; Isa 1.29

5.1 Hos 4.1; 6.9

5.3 Amos 3.2; Hos 6.10

5.4 Hos 4.11,12

5.5 Hos 7.10; 4.5; Ezek 23.31–35

l Cn: Heb uncertain   *m* Cn Compare Gk: Heb of this line uncertain   *n* Heb *her*
o Gk Syr: Heb *sacrifices*   *p* Cn: Heb uncertain   *q* Heb *Israel and Ephraim*

5.6
Mic 6.6,7;
Isa 1.15;
Ezek 8.6
	6 With their flocks and herds they shall go
	    to seek the LORD,
	  but they will not find him;
	    he has withdrawn from them.

5.7
Isa 48.8;
Hos 6.7;
2.4,11,12
	7 They have dealt faithlessly with the LORD;
	    for they have borne alien children.
	  Now the new moon shall devour them with their fields.

5.8
Hos 9.9;
10.9;
Isa 10.29,
30;
Hos 4.15
	8 Blow the horn in Gĭb′ë-ȧh,
	    the trumpet in Rāmȧh.
	  Sound the alarm at Bĕth-ā′vĕn;
	    tremble,ʳ O Benjamin!

5.9
Isa 37.3;
46.10;
Zech 1.6
	9 Ē′phra̤im shall become a desolation
	    in the day of punishment;
	  among the tribes of Israel
	    I declare what is sure.

5.10
Deut 19.14;
Ezek 7.8;
Ps 93.3,4
	10 The princes of Judah have become
	    like those who remove the landmark;
	  upon them I will pour out
	    my wrath like water.

5.11 Hos 9.16	11 Ē′phra̤im is oppressed, crushed in judgment, because he was determined to go after vanity.ˢ
5.12 Ps 39.11; Prov 12.4	12 Therefore I am like a moth to Ē′phra̤im, and like dry rot to the house of Judah.

5.13
Jer 30.12;
Hos 7.11;
8.9; 10.6;
14.3
	13 When Ē′phra̤im saw his sickness,
	    and Judah his wound,
	  then Ephraim went to Assyria,
	    and sent to the great king.ᵗ
	  But he is not able to cure you
	    or heal your wound.

5.14
Hos 13.7,8;
Ps 50.22;
Mic 5.8
	14 For I will be like a lion to Ē′phra̤im,
	    and like a young lion to the house of Judah.
	  I, even I, will rend and go away,
	    I will carry off, and none shall rescue.

C. Repentance and restoration

5.15
Isa 64.7-9;
Jer 2.27;
Hos 3.5
	15 I will return again to my place,
	    until they acknowledge their guilt and seek my face,
	  and in their distress they seek me, saying,

6.1
Jer 50.4,5;
Hos 5.14;
14.4;
Isa 30.26
	6 "Come, let us return to the LORD;
	    for he has torn, that he may heal us;
	  he has stricken, and he will bind us up.

∗6.2
Ps 30.5
	2 After two days he will revive us;
	    on the third day he will raise us up,
	    that we may live before him.

6.3
Isa 2.3;
Mic 4.2;
Ps 19.6;
Mic 5.2;
Joel 2.23
	3 Let us know, let us press on to know the LORD;
	    his going forth is sure as the dawn;
	  he will come to us as the showers,
	    as the spring rains that water the earth."

ʳ Cn Compare Gk: Heb *after you*   ˢ Gk: Heb *a command*   ᵗ Cn: Heb *a king that will contend*

6.2 Israel shall be as dead people during the period of God's wrath. Yet Hosea affirms that within a short time (*after two days*) God will cause His people to live in His sight.

D. *Israel's unfaithfulness restated*

4 What shall I do with you, O Ē'phräïm?
    What shall I do with you, O Judah?
Your love is like a morning cloud,
    like the dew that goes early away.
5 Therefore I have hewn them by the prophets,
    I have slain them by the words of my mouth,
    and my judgment goes forth as the light.ᵘ
6 For I desire steadfast love and not sacrifice,
    the knowledge of God, rather than burnt offerings.

7 But atᵛ Adam they transgressed the covenant;
    there they dealt faithlessly with me.
8 Gil'ëäd is a city of evildoers,
    tracked with blood.
9 As robbers lie in waitʷ for a man,
    so the priests are banded together;ˣ
they murder on the way to Shĕçhĕm,
    yea, they commit villainy.
10 In the house of Israel I have seen a horrible thing;
    Ē'phräïm's harlotry is there, Israel is defiled.

11 For you also, O Judah, a harvest is appointed.

When I would restore the fortunes of my people,
7 ¹ when I would heal Israel,
    the corruption of Ē'phräïm is revealed,
    and the wicked deeds of Såmar'iä;
for they deal falsely,
    the thief breaks in,
    and the bandits raid without.
2 But they do not consider
    that I remember all their evil works.
Now their deeds encompass them,
    they are before my face.
3 By their wickedness they make the king glad,
    and the princes by their treachery.
4 They are all adulterers;
    they are like a heated oven,
whose baker ceases to stir the fire,
    from the kneading of the dough until it is leavened.
5 On the day of our king the princes
    became sick with the heat of wine;
    he stretched out his hand with mockers.
6 For like an oven their hearts burnʸ with intrigue;
    all night their anger smolders;
    in the morning it blazes like a flaming fire.
7 All of them are hot as an oven,
    and they devour their rulers.
All their kings have fallen;
    and none of them calls upon me.

8 Ē'phräïm mixes himself with the peoples;

ᵘ Gk Syr: Heb *thy judgment goes forth*   ᵛ Cn: Heb *like*   ʷ Cn: Heb uncertain
ˣ Syr: Heb *a company*   ʸ Gk Syr: Heb *brought near*

6.4 Hos 7.1; 11.8; 13.3 / 6.5 Jer 1.10,18; Heb 4.12; ver 3 / 6.6 Mt 9.13; Ps 50.8,9; Hos 2.20 / 6.7 Hos 8.1; 5.7 / 6.8 Hos 4.2 / 6.9 Hos 7.1; Jer 7.9,10; Ezek 22.9; 23.27 / 6.10 Jer 5.30,31; Hos 5.3 / 6.11 Joel 3.13; Zeph 2.7 / 7.1 ver 13; Hos 6.4; 11.8; 4.2; 6.9 / 7.2 Hos 8.13; 9.9; Amos 8.7; Jer 2.19; Hos 4.9 / 7.3 ver 5; Mic 7.3; Hos 4.2; 11.12; Rom 1.32 / 7.4 Jer 9.2; 23.10 / 7.5 Isa 28.1,7,8 / 7.7 Ps 21.9; ver 16; Isa 64.7 / 7.8 Ps 106.35; ver 11; Hos 5.13

Ephraim is a cake not turned.

7.9
Isa 1.7;
Hos 4.6

9 Aliens devour his strength,
  and he knows it not;
gray hairs are sprinkled upon him,
  and he knows it not.

7.10
Hos 5.5;
ver 7,14;
Hos 5.4

10 The pride of Israel witnesses against him;
   yet they do not return to the LORD their God,
   nor seek him, for all this.

★7.11
Hos 11.11;
4.6,11,14;
ver 16;
Hos 5.13;
8.9; 12.1

11 Ē′phräim is like a dove,
   silly and without sense,
   calling to Egypt, going to Assyria.

7.12
Ezek 12.13

12 As they go, I will spread over them my net;
   I will bring them down like birds of the air;
   I will chastise them for their wicked deeds.z

7.13
Hos 9.12,
17;
Jer 14.10;
Ezek 34.6;
ver 1;
Mt 23.37

13 Woe to them, for they have strayed from me!
   Destruction to them, for they have rebelled against me!
   I would redeem them,
   but they speak lies against me.

7.14
Jer 3.10;
Amos 2.8;
Mic 2.11;
Hos 13.16

14 They do not cry to me from the heart,
   but they wail upon their beds;
   for grain and wine they gash themselves,
   they rebel against me.

7.15
Hos 11.13;
Nah 1.9

15 Although I trained and strengthened their arms,
   yet they devise evil against me.

7.16
Ps 78.57;
ver 7;
Ezek 23.32

16 They turn to Bāȧl;a
   they are like a treacherous bow,
   their princes shall fall by the sword
   because of the insolence of their tongue.
   This shall be their derision in the land of Egypt.

E. The fruit of Israel's sin

1. God's sentence upon them

8.1
Hos 5.8;
Hab 1.8;
Hos 6.7;
4.6

8 Set the trumpet to your lips,
  forb a vulture is over the house of the LORD,
because they have broken my covenant,
  and transgressed my law.

8.2
Hos 7.14

2 To me they cry,
  My God, we Israel know thee.

3 Israel has spurned the good;
  the enemy shall pursue him.

8.4
Hos 13.10,
11; 2.8

4 They made kings, but not through me.
  They set up princes, but without my knowledge.
With their silver and gold they made idols
  for their own destruction.

8.5
ver 6;
Hos 10.5;
13.2;
Jer 13.27

5 I havec spurned your calf, O Sȧmȧr′iȧ.
  My anger burns against them.

z Cn: Heb *according to the report to their congregation*
a Cn: Heb *uncertain*   b Cn: Heb *as*   c Heb *He has*

7.11 *calling to Egypt, going to Assyria.* These two world powers sought to control Palestine. The Israelite kings and their nobles were torn between the pro-Egyptian and pro-Assyrian factions at court. Hosea sees this vacillation as evidence of distrust in God.

How long will it be
    till they are pure 6 in Israel?*d*

A workman made it;
    it is not God.
The calf of Sămar'ĭă
    shall be broken to pieces.*e*

7 For they sow the wind,
    and they shall reap the whirlwind.
The standing grain has no heads,
    it shall yield no meal;
if it were to yield,
    aliens would devour it.
8 Israel is swallowed up;
    already they are among the nations
    as a useless vessel.
9 For they have gone up to Assyria,
    a wild ass wandering alone;
Ē'phrăĭm has hired lovers.
10 Though they hire allies among the nations,
    I will soon gather them up.
And they shall cease*f* for a little while
    from anointing*g* king and princes.

11 Because Ē'phrăĭm has multiplied altars for sinning,
    they have become to him altars for sinning.
12 Were I to write for him my laws by ten thousands,
    they would be regarded as a strange thing.
13 They love sacrifice;*h*
    they sacrifice flesh and eat it;
    but the LORD has no delight in them.
Now he will remember their iniquity,
    and punish their sins;
    they shall return to Egypt.
14 For Israel has forgotten his Maker,
    and built palaces;
and Judah has multiplied fortified cities;
    but I will send a fire upon his cities,
    and it shall devour his strongholds.

2. Israel's riches to be taken away

9 Rejoice not, O Israel!
    Exult not*i* like the peoples;
for you have played the harlot, forsaking your God.
    You have loved a harlot's hire
    upon all threshing floors.
2 Threshing floor and winevat shall not feed them,
    and the new wine shall fail them.
3 They shall not remain in the land of the LORD;
    but Ē'phrăĭm shall return to Egypt,
    and they shall eat unclean food in Assyria.

d Gk: Heb *for from Israel*   *e* Or *shall go up in flames*   *f* Gk: Heb *begin*
g Gk: Heb *burden*   *h* Cn: Heb uncertain   *i* Gk: Heb *to exultation*

8.6
Hos 13.2

8.7
Hos 10.12,
13;
Isa 66.15;
Nah 1.3

8.8
Jer 51.34;
Hos 13.15

8.9
Hos 7.11;
Jer 2.24;
Ezek 16.33

8.10
Ezek 16.37;
22.20;
Jer 42.2

8.11
Hos 10.1;
12.11

8.12
ver 1;
Hos 4.6

8.13
Jer 7.21;
Hos 7.2;
1 Cor 4.5;
Hos 4.9;
9.7; 9.3,6

8.14
Hos 2.13;
13.6;
Jer 17.27

9.1
Isa 22.12,
13;
Hos 10.5;
4.12;
Jer 44.17

9.2
Hos 2.9

9.3
Jer 2.7;
Hos 8.13;
Ezek 4.13;
Hos 7.11

4 They shall not pour libations of wine to the LORD;
　　and they shall not please him with their sacrifices.
　Their bread[j] shall be like mourners' bread;
　　all who eat of it shall be defiled;
　for their bread shall be for their hunger only;
　　it shall not come to the house of the LORD.

5 What will you do on the day of appointed festival,
　　and on the day of the feast of the LORD?
6 For behold, they are going to Assyria;[k]
　　Egypt shall gather them,
　　Memphis shall bury them.
　Nettles shall possess their precious things of silver;
　　thorns shall be in their tents.

7 The days of punishment have come,
　　the days of recompense have come;
　　Israel shall know it.
　The prophet is a fool,
　　the man of the spirit is mad,
　because of your great iniquity
　　and great hatred.
8 The prophet is the watchman of Ē′phrāim,
　　the people of my God,
　yet a fowler's snare is on all his ways,
　　and hatred in the house of his God.
9 They have deeply corrupted themselves
　　as in the days of Gĭb′ē-ah:
　he will remember their iniquity,
　　he will punish their sins.

3. Israel's population to decline

10 Like grapes in the wilderness,
　　I found Israel.
　Like the first fruit on the fig tree,
　　in its first season,
　　I saw your fathers.
　But they came to Bā′al-pĕor,
　　and consecrated themselves to Bāal,[l]
　　and became detestable like the thing they loved.
11 Ē′phrāim's glory shall fly away like a bird—
　　no birth, no pregnancy, no conception!
12 Even if they bring up children,
　　I will bereave them till none is left.
　Woe to them
　　when I depart from them!
13 Ē′phrāim's sons, as I have seen, are destined for a prey;[m]
　　Ē′phrāim must lead forth his sons to slaughter.

j Cn: Heb *to them*　k Cn: Heb *from destruction*
l Heb *shame*　m Cn Compare Gk: Heb uncertain

Cross-references (left margin):

9.4 — Jer 6.20; Hos 5.6; 8.13; Hag 2.14

9.5 — Isa 10.3; Jer 5.31; Joel 1.13

*9.6 — ver 3; Jer 2.16; Ezek 30.13, 16; Isa 5.6; Hos 10.8

9.7 — Jer 10.15; Mic 7.4; Isa 34.8; Jer 16.18; Ezek 14.9, 10

9.8 — Hos 5.1

9.9 — Isa 31.6; Judg 19.12; Hos 5.8; 10.9; 7.2; 8.13

*9.10 — Mic 7.1; Jer 24.2; Num 25.3; Hos 4.14; Jer 11.13

9.11 — Hos 4.7; 10.5; ver 14

9.12 — ver 16; Hos 7.13

9.13 — Ezek 27.3,4

9.6 *Memphis shall bury them.* The place of refuge to which they will flee will prove to be a place of death. They flee from God, expecting life, but they will discover instead that they will inherit death.

9.10 *they came to Baal-peor.* The Moabites invited the Israelites to their licentious fertility cult at Baal-peor (Num 25.1–4). Baal worship became prevalent in Israel during the time of the Judges (Judg 2.11–13).

14 Give them, O LORD—
   what wilt thou give?
Give them a miscarrying womb
   and dry breasts.

9.14
ver 11;
Lk 23.29

15 Every evil of theirs is in Gĭl′găl;
   there I began to hate them.
Because of the wickedness of their deeds
   I will drive them out of my house.
I will love them no more;
   all their princes are rebels.

9.15
Hos 4.9;
7.2; 12.2;
Isa 1.23

16 Ē′phrä̆im is stricken,
   their root is dried up,
   they shall bear no fruit.
Even though they bring forth,
   I will slay their beloved children.

9.16
Hos 5.11;
8.7;
ver 12

17 My God will cast them off,
   because they have not hearkened to him;
   they shall be wanderers among the nations.

9.17
Hos 4.10;
Deut 28.65

4. *Israel's idols to be destroyed*

10 Israel is a luxuriant vine
   that yields its fruit.
The more his fruit increased
   the more altars he built;
as his country improved
   he improved his pillars.

10.1
Ezek 15.1–
5;
Hos 8.11;
3.4

2 Their heart is false;
   now they must bear their guilt.
The LORD*n* will break down their altars,
   and destroy their pillars.

10.2
1 Ki 18.21;
Mt 6.24;
Hos 13.16;
ver 8

3 For now they will say:
   "We have no king,
for we fear not the LORD,
   and a king, what could he do for us?"

10.3
Ps 12.4

4 They utter mere words;
   with empty oaths they make covenants;
so judgment springs up like poisonous weeds
   in the furrows of the field.

10.4
Ezek 17.13–
19;
Hos 4.2;
Deut 31.16,
17

5 The inhabitants of Sămạr′ĭä tremble
   for the calf*o* of Bĕth-ā′vĕn.
Its people shall mourn for it,
   and its idolatrous priests shall wail*p* over it,
   over its glory which has departed from it.

10.5
Hos 8.5,6;
9.11

6 Yea, the thing itself shall be carried to Assyria,
   as tribute to the great king.*q*
Ē′phrä̆im shall be put to shame,
   and Israel shall be ashamed of his idol.*r*

10.6
Hos 11.5;
5.13; 4.7;
Isa 30.3;
Jer 7.24

7 Sămạr′ĭä′ṣ king shall perish,
   like a chip on the face of the waters.

10.7
Hos 13.11

n Heb *he* *o* Gk Syr: Heb *calves* *p* Cn: Heb *exult*
q Cn: Heb *a king that will contend* *r* Cn: Heb *counsel*

10.8
ver 5;
1 Ki 12.30;
ver 2;
Hos 9.6;
Lk 23.30;
Rev 6.16

8 The high places of Ā′vĕn, the sin of Israel,
  shall be destroyed.
Thorn and thistle shall grow up
  on their altars;
and they shall say to the mountains, Cover us,
  and to the hills, Fall upon us.

5. *Israel's fortresses to be destroyed*

10.9
Hos 5.8;
9.9

9 From the days of Gĭb′ĕ-ăh, you have sinned, O Israel;
  there they have continued.
Shall not war overtake them in Gibe-ah?

10.10
Ezek 5.13;
Hos 4.9

10 I will come[s] against the wayward people to chastise them;
  and nations shall be gathered against them
  when they are chastised[t] for their double iniquity.

10.11
Jer 50.11;
Hos 4.16;
Jer 28.14;
Ps 66.12

11 Ē′phrāim was a trained heifer
  that loved to thresh,
  and I spared her fair neck;
but I will put Ephraim to the yoke,
  Judah must plow,
  Jacob must harrow for himself.

10.12
Prov 11.18;
Jer 4.3;
Hos 12.6;
6.3;
Isa 44.3;
45.8

12 Sow for yourselves righteousness,
  reap the fruit[u] of steadfast love;
  break up your fallow ground,
for it is the time to seek the LORD,
  that he may come and rain salvation upon you.

10.13
Job 4.8;
Gal 6.7,8;
Hos 4.2;
7.3

13 You have plowed iniquity,
  you have reaped injustice,
  you have eaten the fruit of lies.
Because you have trusted in your chariots[v]
  and in the multitude of your warriors,

10.14
Isa 17.3;
Hos 13.16

14 therefore the tumult of war shall arise among your people,
  and all your fortresses shall be destroyed,
as Shăl′măn destroyed Bĕth-ar′bĕl on the day of battle;
  mothers were dashed in pieces with their children.

10.15
ver 7

15 Thus it shall be done to you, O house of Israel,[w]
  because of your great wickedness.
In the storm[x] the king of Israel
  shall be utterly cut off.

6. *Israel to be a captive of Assyria*

11.1
Hos 2.15;
12.9,13;
13.4;
Mt 2.15

11 When Israel was a child, I loved him,
  and out of Egypt I called my son.

11.2
2 Ki 17.13–
15;
Hos 2.13;
Isa 65.7;
Jer 18.15

2 The more I[y] called them,
  the more they went from me;[z]
they kept sacrificing to the Bā′ăls,
  and burning incense to idols.

*11.3
Hos 7.15;
Deut 1.31;
Jer 30.17

3 Yet it was I who taught Ē′phrāim to walk,

---

s Cn Compare Gk: Heb *in my desire* *t* Gk: Heb *bound* *u* Gk: Heb *according to*
v Gk: Heb *way* *w* Gk: Heb *O Bĕthĕl* *x* Cn: Heb *dawn* *y* Gk: Heb *they* *z* Gk: Heb *them*

11.3 God had tenderly cared for Ephraim-Israel in the day of her immaturity. When Israel "grew up" the Baals took the place of God in worship and affection.

I took them up in my^a arms;
  but they did not know that I healed them.
4 I led them with cords of compassion,^b
  with the bands of love,
and I became to them as one
  who eases the yoke on their jaws,
  and I bent down to them and fed them.

11.4
Jer 31.2,3;
Lev 26.13;
Ex 16.32;
Ps 78.25

5 They shall return to the land of Egypt,
  and Assyria shall be their king,
  because they have refused to return to me.
6 The sword shall rage against their cities,
  consume the bars of their gates,
  and devour them in their fortresses.^c
7 My people are bent on turning away from me;^d
  so they are appointed to the yoke,
  and none shall remove it.

*11.5
Hos 10.6;
7.16

11.6
Hos 13.16;
4.16,17

11.7
Jer 8.5;
ver 2

F. God's tenderness toward Israel

8 How can I give you up, O Ē′phräïm!
  How can I hand you over, O Israel!
How can I make you like Ădmäh!
  How can I treat you like Zěboï′im!
My heart recoils within me,
  my compassion grows warm and tender.
9 I will not execute my fierce anger,
  I will not again destroy Ē′phräïm;
for I am God and not man,
  the Holy One in your midst,
  and I will not come to destroy.^e

11.8
Hos 6.4;
Gen 14.8;
Isa 63.15

11.9
Deut 13.17;
Jer 26.3;
Isa 41.14,
16; 55.8,9;
Mal 3.6

G. Israel to be restored

10 They shall go after the LORD,
  he will roar like a lion;
yea, he will roar,
  and his sons shall come trembling from the west;
11 they shall come trembling like birds from Egypt,
  and like doves from the land of Assyria;
  and I will return them to their homes, says the LORD.

11.10
Hos 6.1–3;
Joel 3.16;
Isa 66.2,5

11.11
Isa 11.11;
60.8;
Ezek 28.25,
26

H. Ephraim's unfaithfulness restated; her doom predicted

1. The sin of Ephraim

12 ^fĒ′phräïm has encompassed me with lies,

11.12
Hos 4.2;
7.3

---

^a Gk Syr Vg: Heb *his*   ^b Heb *man*   ^c Cn: Heb *counsels*
^d The meaning of the Hebrew is uncertain   ^e Cn: Heb *into the city*   ^f Ch 12.1 in Heb

---

11.5 The Northern Kingdom lasted for two hundred years. Hosea prophesies its downfall which was accomplished by Shalmaneser V and Sargon II in 722 B.C. Israel was never to be restored as a nation after her expulsion from the Promised Land as Judah was after the Babylonian captivity. There is a sense in which the Northern Kingdom and the Southern Kingdom shall be united in a single realm in the last days (14.4–8; Isa 11.13). Comparison of 2.1, 23 with Rom 9.24, 25 indicates that this prophecy of the restoration of the Ten Tribes was to be fulfilled, at least in part, by the filling in of their vacant ranks by Gentile Christians. Hence, in that sense, the Gentile believers shall become His people.

and the house of Israel with deceit;
but Judah is still known by*g* God,
  and is faithful to the Holy One.

12.1
2 Ki 17.4;
Isa 30.6

12 Ē′phrāïm herds the wind,
     and pursues the east wind all day long;
they multiply falsehood and violence;
they make a bargain with Assyria,
  and oil is carried to Egypt.

2. The judgment on Jacob

12.2
Mic 6.2;
Hos 4.9

2 The LORD has an indictment against Judah,
    and will punish Jacob according to his ways,
    and requite him according to his deeds.

12.3
Gen 25.26;
32.24,28
12.4
Gen 32.26;
28.12–15

3 In the womb he took his brother by the heel,
    and in his manhood he strove with God.
4 He strove with the angel and prevailed,
    he wept and sought his favor.
He met God at Bēthēl,
    and there God spoke with him*h*—

12.5
Ex 3.15

5 the LORD the God of hosts,
    the LORD is his name:

12.6
Mic 6.8;
Hos 6.6;
Mic 7.7

6 "So you, by the help of your God, return,
    hold fast to love and justice,
    and wait continually for your God."

3. Ephraim's sins enlarged upon

12.7
Amos 8.5;
Mic 6.11

7 A trader, in whose hands are false balances,
    he loves to oppress.

12.8
Hos 13.6;
Rev 3.17;
Hos 4.8;
14.1

8 Ē′phrāïm has said, "Ah, but I am rich,
    I have gained wealth for myself";
but all his riches can never offset*i*
    the guilt he has incurred.

12.9
Hos 11.1;
13.4;
Lev 23.42;
Neh 8.17

9 I am the LORD your God
    from the land of Egypt;
I will again make you dwell in tents,
    as in the days of the appointed feast.

12.10
2 Ki 17.13;
Jer 7.25;
Ezek 17.2;
20.49
12.11
Hos 6.8;
4.15;9.15;
10.1,2

10 I spoke to the prophets;
    it was I who multiplied visions,
    and through the prophets gave parables.
11 If there is iniquity in Gil′ëäd
    they shall surely come to nought;
if in Gil′gäl they sacrifice bulls,
    their altars also shall be like stone heaps
    on the furrows of the field.

12.12
Gen 28.5;
29.20

12 (Jacob fled to the land of Arám,
    there Israel did service for a wife,
    and for a wife he herded sheep.)

12.13
Ex 13.3

13 By a prophet the LORD brought Israel up from Egypt,
    and by a prophet he was preserved.

12.14
Ezek 18.10–
13;
Dan 11.18;
Mic 6.16

14 Ē′phrāïm has given bitter provocation;
    so his LORD will leave his bloodguilt upon him,
    and will turn back upon him his reproaches.

g Cn Compare Gk: Heb *roams with*   *h* Gk Syr: Heb *us*   *i* Cn Compare Gk: Heb obscure

4. *Ephraim's doom predicted*

13 When Ē′phrāịm spoke, men trembled;
   he was exalted in Israel;
 but he incurred guilt through Bāál and died.

2 And now they sin more and more,
   and make for themselves molten images,
 idols skilfully made of their silver,
   all of them the work of craftsmen.
 Sacrifice to these, they say.*j*
 Men kiss calves!

3 Therefore they shall be like the morning mist
   or like the dew that goes early away,
 like the chaff that swirls from the threshing floor
   or like smoke from a window.

4 I am the LORD your God
   from the land of Egypt;
 you know no God but me,
   and besides me there is no savior.

5 It was I who knew you in the wilderness,
   in the land of drought;
6 but when they had fed*k* to the full,
   they were filled, and their heart was lifted up;
   therefore they forgot me.

7 So I will be to them like a lion,
   like a leopard I will lurk beside the way.
8 I will fall upon them like a bear robbed of her cubs,
   I will tear open their breast,
 and there I will devour them like a lion,
   as a wild beast would rend them.

9 I will destroy you, O Israel;
   who*l* can help you?
10 Where*m* now is your king, to save you;
   where are all*n* your princes,*o* to defend you*p*—
 those of whom you said,
   "Give me a king and princes"?
11 I have given you kings in my anger,
   and I have taken them away in my wrath.

12 The iniquity of Ē′phrāịm is bound up,
   his sin is kept in store.
13 The pangs of childbirth come for him,
   but he is an unwise son;
 for now he does not present himself
   at the mouth of the womb.

14 Shall I ransom them from the power of Shēōl?
   Shall I redeem them from Death?
 O Death, where*q* are your plagues?
   O Sheol, where*q* is your destruction?
   Compassion is hid from my eyes.

Cross references
13.1 Judg 8.1; 12.1; Hos 2.8–17
13.2 Isa 46.6; Hos 8.6
13.3 Hos 6.4; Dan 2.35; Ps 68.2
13.4 Hos 12.9; Isa 43.11
13.5 Deut 2.7; 8.15; 32.10
13.6 Deut 8.12, 14; 32.15; Hos 2.13; 4.6; 8.14
13.7 Lam 3.10; Jer 5.6
13.8 2 Sam 17.8; Ps 50.22
13.10 2 Ki 17.4; Hos 8.4
13.11 1 Sam 8.7; 1 Ki 14.7–10
13.12 Deut 32.34; Rom 2.5
13.13 Mic 4.9,10; Isa 37.3; 66.9
13.14 Ezek 37.12, 13; 1 Cor 15.54, 55; Rom 11.29

i Gk: Heb *to these they say sacrifices of* *k* Cn: Heb *according to their pasture*
l Gk Syr: Heb *for in me* *m* Gk Syr Vg: Heb *I will be* *n* Cn: Heb *in all*
o Cn: Heb *cities* *p* Cn Compare Gk: Heb *and your judges* *q* Gk Syr: Heb *I will be*

15 Though he may flourish as the reed plant,^{r}
   the east wind, the wind of the LORD, shall come,
   rising from the wilderness;
  and his fountain shall dry up,
   his spring shall be parched;
it shall strip his treasury
  of every precious thing.

16 Samar'ia shall bear her guilt,
   because she has rebelled against her God;
they shall fall by the sword,
  their little ones shall be dashed in pieces,
  and their pregnant women ripped open.

III. *Forgiveness and blessing in response to repentance* 14.1–9

A. *The call to repent*

14 Return, O Israel, to the LORD your God,
for you have stumbled because of your iniquity.
2 Take with you words
  and return to the LORD;
say to him,
"Take away all iniquity;
accept that which is good
  and we will render
  the fruit^t of our lips.
3 Assyria shall not save us,
  we will not ride upon horses;
and we will say no more, 'Our God,'
  to the work of our hands.
In thee the orphan finds mercy."

B. *The promise of blessing*

4 I will heal their faithlessness;
  I will love them freely,
  for my anger has turned from them.
5 I will be as the dew to Israel;
  he shall blossom as the lily,
  he shall strike root as the poplar;^{u}
6 his shoots shall spread out;
  his beauty shall be like the olive,
  and his fragrance like Lebanon.
7 They shall return and dwell beneath my^v shadow,
  they shall flourish as a garden;^{w}
they shall blossom as the vine,
  their fragrance shall be like the wine of Lebanon.

r Cn: Heb *among brothers* *s* Ch 14.1 in Heb
t Gk Syr: Heb *bulls* *u* Cn: Heb *Lebanon*
v Heb *his* *w* Cn: Heb *they shall grow grain*

14.3 *Assyria shall not save us, we will not ride upon horses.* The hope of Israel is neither in Assyria nor Egypt. In reality, Israel is a helpless orphan, dependent upon God for mercy and protection. If there is to be any deliverance it must come from Israel's God.

Cross-references: 13.15 Hos 10.1; Ezek 17.10; 19.12; Jer 51.36; 20.5 · 13.16 Hos 10.2; 7.14; Isa 13.16; Hos 10.14; 2 Ki 15.16 · 14.1 Hos 10.12; 14.6; Joel 2.13 · 14.2 Mic 7.18, 19; Heb 13.15 · *14.3 Hos 5.13; Isa 31.1; Hos 8.6; 13.2; Ps 10.14 · 14.4 Zeph 3.17; Isa 12.1 · 14.5 Job 29.19; Mt 6.28; Isa 35.2 · 14.6 Ps 52.8; Sol 4.11 · 14.7 Ps 91.4; Ezek 17.23; Hos 2.21,22

8 O Ē'phrāim, what have I to do with idols?
  It is I who answer and look after you.ˣ
I am like an evergreen cypress,
  from me comes your fruit.

*14.8
ver 3;
Isa 41.19;
Ezek 17.23

C. The postscript

9 Whoever is wise, let him understand these things;
  whoever is discerning, let him know them;
for the ways of the LORD are right,
  and the upright walk in them,
  but transgressors stumble in them.

14.9
Ps 107.43;
Acts 13.10;
Isa 26.7;
1.28

ˣ Heb him

14.8 *from me comes your fruit.* Israel will enjoy the blessing of fruitfulness when she turns to the Lord in confession and renunciation of sin (14.1, 2).

INTRODUCTION TO

THE BOOK OF

JOEL

Authorship and Background: Joel, the son of Pethuel, is the author of this book. His is a common name often occurring in the Old Testament and means "Yahweh is God." The evidences for the dating of the book are inconclusive. Many conservatives hold that the internal evidence supports the pre-exilic view that it was written before 800 B.C. Other scholars prefer a sixth century date. If the former view is correct, it was probably written during the reign of Joash in the ninth century B.C. In the Jewish canon the book was placed between Hosea and Amos. There are similarities between the prophecies of Amos and Joel (cf. Joel 3.16 and Amos 1.2; Joel 3.18 and Amos 9.13). Joel was intimately acquainted with Judah and Jerusalem. His prophecy deals largely with a locust invasion of the area which God will send as a judgment and as a warning sign of future disaster.

Characteristics: Joel's book has been described as a literary gem which highlights his writing ability and his purity of style. He carefully polishes and beautifies his work as perhaps no other Old Testament writer does. The language is forceful and the description of the locust invasion minutely accurate. He employs a historical incident to foretell the coming judgment of God against Judah, and from there he goes on to the judgments of the "day of the LORD" which are still future. His prophecy of the outpouring of the Spirit (2.28–32) is quoted by Peter in Acts 2.16 as being fulfilled at Pentecost. In all, his work is characterized by strength, tenderness, and sublimity.

Contents:

I.   The plague of locusts. 1.1—2.27: Joel describes the plague of locusts and calls the people to repentance. They are urged to see, mourn, and fast. He further exhorts them to tremble, repent, fast, and pray.

II.   The judgment of God and His blessing in the last days. 2.28—3.21: God's mercy drives away the locusts and sends an abundant harvest. God pours out His Spirit upon all flesh. He blesses His people and punishes their enemies.

THE BOOK OF

JOEL

I. *The plague of locusts 1.1–2.27*

A. *Superscription*

1 The word of the LORD that came to Jōēl, the son of Pĕthu′ĕl:

1.1
Jer 1.2;
Ezek 1.3;
Hos 1.1;
Acts 2.16

2 Hear this, you aged men,
  give ear, all inhabitants of the land!
Has such a thing happened in your days,
  or in the days of your fathers?

1.2
Hos 4.1;
5.1;
ver 14;
Joel 2.2

3 Tell your children of it,
  and let your children tell their children,
  and their children another generation.

1.3
Ps 78.4

B. *The plague and drought described*

4 What the cutting locust left,
  the swarming locust has eaten.
What the swarming locust left,
  the hopping locust has eaten,
and what the hopping locust left,
  the destroying locust has eaten.

1.4
Deut 28.38;
Joel 2.25;
Nah 3.15,
16;
Isa 33.4

5 Awake, you drunkards, and weep;
  and wail, all you drinkers of wine,
because of the sweet wine,
  for it is cut off from your mouth.

1.5
Joel 3.3;
Isa 32.10

6 For a nation has come up against my land,
  powerful and without number;
its teeth are lions' teeth,
  and it has the fangs of a lioness.

1.6
Joel 2.2,11;
Rev 9.8

7 It has laid waste my vines,
  and splintered my fig trees;
it has stripped off their bark and thrown it down;
  their branches are made white.

1.7
Isa 5.6;
Amos 4.9

8 Lament like a virgin girded with sackcloth
  for the bridegroom of her youth.

1.8
ver 13;
Amos 8.10

9 The cereal offering and the drink offering are cut off
  from the house of the LORD.
The priests mourn,
  the ministers of the LORD.

1.9
Joel 2.14,17

10 The fields are laid waste,
  the ground mourns;
because the grain is destroyed,
  the wine fails,
  the oil languishes.

1.10
Isa 24.4,7;
Hos 9.2

11 Be confounded, O tillers of the soil,
  wail, O vinedressers,
for the wheat and the barley;

1.11
Jer 14.3,4;
Isa 17.11;
Jer 9.12

because the harvest of the field has perished.

*1.12
Hab 3.17,
18;
Isa 16.10;
24.11;
Jer 48.33

12 The vine withers,
   the fig tree languishes.
Pomegranate, palm, and apple,
   all the trees of the field are withered;
and gladness fails
   from the sons of men.

1.13
ver 8;
Jer 4.8;
ver 9;
Joel 2.17;
1 Ki 21.27

13 Gird on sackcloth and lament, O priests,
   wail, O ministers of the altar.
Go in, pass the night in sackcloth,
   O ministers of my God!
Because cereal offering and drink offering
   are withheld from the house of your God.

1.14
2 Chr 20.3,
4;
Joel 2.15,
16;
ver 2;
Jon 3.8

14 Sanctify a fast,
   call a solemn assembly.
Gather the elders
   and all the inhabitants of the land
to the house of the LORD your God;
   and cry to the LORD.

*1.15
Jer 30.7;
Isa 13.6,9;
Joel 2.1,11,
31
1.16
Isa 3.7;
Deut 12.6,
7;
Ps 43.4

15 Alas for the day!
For the day of the LORD is near,
   and as destruction from the Almighty it comes.
16 Is not the food cut off
   before our eyes,
joy and gladness
   from the house of our God?

1.17
Isa 17.10,
11

17 The seed shrivels under the clods,[a]
   the storehouses are desolate;
the granaries are ruined
   because the grain has failed.

1.18
1 Ki 18.5;
Jer 14.5,6;
Hos 4.3

18 How the beasts groan!
   The herds of cattle are perplexed
because there is no pasture for them;
   even the flocks of sheep are dismayed.

1.19
Ps 50.15;
Jer 9.10;
Joel 2.3

19 Unto thee, O LORD, I cry.
   For fire has devoured
the pastures of the wilderness,
   and flame has burned
all the trees of the field.

1.20
Job 38.41;
Ps 104.21;
1 Ki 17.7;
18.5

20 Even the wild beasts cry to thee
   because the water brooks are dried up,
and fire has devoured
   the pastures of the wilderness.

a Heb uncertain

1.12 *The vine withers.* Despite all of the labors of the keepers of the field, the earth gives forth no harvest. The husbandmen labored in hope but are disappointed. Then follows the call to the priests to prepare their hearts in private for their public duty of fasting and praying to God for help.

1.15 *Alas for the day!* This is a day of terror because of the evils which come with it due to the sins of the people.

C. *The coming day of the LORD*

2 Blow the trumpet in Zion;
   sound the alarm on my holy mountain!
Let all the inhabitants of the land tremble,
   for the day of the LORD is coming, it is near,
2 a day of darkness and gloom,
   a day of clouds and thick darkness!
Like blackness there is spread upon the mountains
   a great and powerful people;
their like has never been from of old,
   nor will be again after them
   through the years of all generations.

3 Fire devours before them,
   and behind them a flame burns.
The land is like the garden of Eden before them,
   but after them a desolate wilderness,
   and nothing escapes them.

4 Their appearance is like the appearance of horses,
   and like war horses they run.
5 As with the rumbling of chariots,
   they leap on the tops of the mountains,
like the crackling of a flame of fire
   devouring the stubble,
like a powerful army
   drawn up for battle.

6 Before them peoples are in anguish,
   all faces grow pale.
7 Like warriors they charge,
   like soldiers they scale the wall.
They march each on his way,
   they do not swerve[b] from their paths.
8 They do not jostle one another,
   each marches in his path;
they burst through the weapons
   and are not halted.
9 They leap upon the city,
   they run upon the walls;
they climb up into the houses,
   they enter through the windows like a thief.

10 The earth quakes before them,
   the heavens tremble.
The sun and the moon are darkened,
   and the stars withdraw their shining.
11 The LORD utters his voice
   before his army,

b Gk Syr Vg: Heb *take a pledge*

Cross references: *2.1 Jer 4.5; Num 10.9; Zeph 1.14–16; ver 11,31; Joel 1.15; 2.2 Amos 5.18; Joel 1.6; Lam 1.12; Joel 1.2; 2.3 Joel 1.19,20; Gen 2.8; Isa 51.3; Ps 105.34,35; 2.4 Rev 9.7; 2.5 Rev 9.9; Isa 5.24; 30.30; 2.6 Isa 13.8; Nah 2.10; Jer 30.6; 2.7 Isa 5.26,27; ver 9; 2.9 ver 7; Jer 9.21; Jn 10.1; 2.10 Ps 18.7; Isa 13.10; Joel 3.15; Mt 24.29; 2.11 Joel 3.16; Amos 1.2; ver 2,25; Jer 50.34; Rev 18.8; Joel 3.14; Ezek 22.14*

2.1 *The day of the LORD* spoken of by Joel is still in the future. It will come at the end of the age. It must be remembered that the prophets looked in a horizontal direction from one mountain top to another, rather than from a vertical vantage point. This is the way the nearness of which Joel spoke is to be understood in this context.

for his host is exceedingly great;
  he that executes his word is powerful.
For the day of the LORD is great and very terrible;
  who can endure it?

D. The call to repentance

2.12
Jer 4.1;
Hos 12.6

12 "Yet even now," says the LORD,
  "return to me with all your heart,
with fasting, with weeping, and with mourning;

2.13
Ps 34.18;
Isa 57.15;
2 Sam 1.11;
Jon 4.2;
Jer 18.8;
42.10

13   and rend your hearts and not your garments."
Return to the LORD, your God,
  for he is gracious and merciful,
slow to anger, and abounding in steadfast love,
  and repents of evil.

*2.14
Jer 26.3;
Hag 2.19;
Joel 1.9,13

14 Who knows whether he will not turn and repent,
  and leave a blessing behind him,
a cereal offering and a drink offering
  for the LORD, your God?

*2.15
Num 10.3;
ver 1;
Jer 36.9;
Joel 1.14

15 Blow the trumpet in Zion;
  sanctify a fast;
call a solemn assembly;

2.16
Ex 19.10,
22;
Ps 19.5

16   gather the people.
Sanctify the congregation;
  assemble the elders;
gather the children,
  even nursing infants.
Let the bridegroom leave his room,
  and the bride her chamber.

2.17
Ezek 8.16;
Mt 23.35;
Joel 1.9;
Deut 9.26–
29;
Isa 37.20;
Ps 44.13;
42.10

17 Between the vestibule and the altar
  let the priests, the ministers of the LORD, weep
and say, "Spare thy people, O LORD,
  and make not thy heritage a reproach,
  a byword among the nations.
Why should they say among the peoples,
  'Where is their God?' "

E. The promised deliverance following repentance

2.18
Zech 1.14;
Isa 60.10

18 Then the LORD became jealous for his land,
  and had pity on his people.

2.19
Hos 2.21,
22;
Ezek 34.29;
36.15

19 The LORD answered and said to his people,
  "Behold, I am sending to you
grain, wine, and oil,
  and you will be satisfied;
and I will no more make you
  a reproach among the nations.

2.14 *Who knows whether he will not turn and repent.* Joel describes a desolated land in which there is neither food for man nor pasture for beasts (1.17, 18). He calls upon the people to turn to God, with the thought and hope that God might then turn to them in blessing.

2.15 *Blow the trumpet* is a call to humiliation and public fasting, not an uncommon practice for God's people (see 2 Chr 20).

20 "I will remove the northerner far from you,
　and drive him into a parched and desolate land,
his front into the eastern sea,
　and his rear into the western sea;
the stench and foul smell of him will rise,
　for he has done great things.

*2.20
Jer 1.14,15;
Zech 14.8;
Deut 11.24;
Isa 34.3;
Amos 4.10

21 "Fear not, O land;
　be glad and rejoice,
　for the LORD has done great things!

2.21
Jer 30.10;
ver 26

22 Fear not, you beasts of the field,
　for the pastures of the wilderness are green;
the tree bears its fruit,
　the fig tree and vine give their full yield.

2.22
Ps 65.12,13

23 "Be glad, O sons of Zion,
　and rejoice in the LORD, your God;
for he has given the early rain for your vindication,
　he has poured down for you abundant rain,
　the early and the latter rain, as before.

2.23
Ps 149.2;
Isa 41.16;
Deut 11.14;
Jer 5.24;
Hos 6.3

24 "The threshing floors shall be full of grain,
　the vats shall overflow with wine and oil.

2.24
Amos 9.13;
Mal 3.10

25 I will restore to you the years
　which the swarming locust has eaten,
the hopper, the destroyer, and the cutter,
　my great army, which I sent among you.

*2.25
Joel 1.4

26 "You shall eat in plenty and be satisfied,
　and praise the name of the LORD your God,
　who has dealt wondrously with you.
And my people shall never again be put to shame.

2.26
Isa 62.9;
Ps 67.5–7;
Isa 25.1;
45.17

27 You shall know that I am in the midst of Israel,
　and that I, the LORD, am your God and there is none else.
And my people shall never again be
　put to shame.

2.27
Joel 3.17,
21;
Isa 45.5,21;
49.23

II. The judgment of God and His blessing in the last days
2.28–3.21

A. The promised outpouring of the Spirit

28c "And it shall come to pass afterward,
　that I will pour out my spirit on all flesh;

*2.28
Acts 2.17–
21;
Ezek 39.29;
Isa 40.5

c Ch 3.1 in Heb

2.20 the northerner. Israel's enemies habitually came from the north (cf. Jer 1.14).

2.25 I will restore . . . years. After the years of judgment and devastation, God will give a comparable period of blessing and plenty.

2.28 on all flesh. God's Spirit had come upon prophets, priests, and kings during Old Testament times. Joel looked to a future day when the gifts of the Spirit would come to old and young, men and women, without regard to external office or function. In the New Testament, Peter stated that this prophecy was fulfilled on the day of Pentecost when the Holy Spirit baptized the church (Acts 2.17–21). There may be, however, some elements in this prediction which are to find still further fulfilment in the end time, or ultimate phase of the "last days," e.g., the supernatural signs and meteoric phenomena of verse 30.

your sons and your daughters shall prophesy,
  your old men shall dream dreams,
  and your young men shall see visions.

2.29
1 Cor 12.13;
Gal 3.28

29 Even upon the menservants and maidservants
  in those days, I will pour out my spirit.

2.30
Mt 24.29;
Lk 21.11,
25;
Acts 2.19

2.31
Isa 13.9,10;
Mt 24.29;
Mal 4.1,5;
Rev 6.12

2.32
Isa 46.13;
Mic 4.7;
Rom 9.27

30 "And I will give portents in the heavens and on the earth, blood and fire and columns of smoke. 31 The sun shall be turned to darkness, and the moon to blood, before the great and terrible day of the LORD comes. 32And it shall come to pass that all who call upon the name of the LORD shall be delivered; for in Mount Zion and in Jerusalem there shall be those who escape, as the LORD has said, and among the survivors shall be those whom the LORD calls.

B. *The restoration of Judah and the judgment of her enemies*

3.1
Jer 30.3;
Ezek 38.14

★3.2
Isa 66.16;
Ezek 34.6;
35.10;
36.1–5

3.3
Obad 11;
Nah 3.10

3 *d* "For behold, in those days and at that time, when I restore the fortunes of Judah and Jerusalem, 2 I will gather all the nations and bring them down to the valley of Jehosh'aphat, and I will enter into judgment with them there, on account of my people and my heritage Israel, because they have scattered them among the nations, and have divided up my land, 3 and have cast lots for my people, and have given a boy for a harlot, and have sold a girl for wine, and have drunk it.

3.4
Amos 1.9,
10;
Ezek 25.12,
17

3.5
2 Ki 12.18;
2 Chr 21.16,
17

3.7
Isa 43.5,6;
Jer 23.8

3.8
Isa 14.2;
60.14;
Ezek 23.42;
Jer 6.20

4 "What are you to me, O Tyre and Sidon, and all the regions of Philis'tia? Are you paying me back for something? If you are paying me back, I will requite your deed upon your own head swiftly and speedily. 5 For you have taken my silver and my gold, and have carried my rich treasures into your temples. *e* 6 You have sold the people of Judah and Jerusalem to the Greeks, removing them far from their own border. 7 But now I will stir them up from the place to which you have sold them, and I will requite your deed upon your own head. 8 I will sell your sons and your daughters into the hand of the sons of Judah, and they will sell them to the Sabe'ans, to a nation far off; for the LORD has spoken."

3.9
Isa 8.9,10;
Jer 51.27,
28; 6.4;
46.3,4;
Zech 14.2,3

9 Proclaim this among the nations:
  Prepare war,
    stir up the mighty men.
  Let all the men of war draw near,
    let them come up.

3.10
Isa 2.4;
Mic 4.3;
Zech 12.8

10 Beat your plowshares into swords,
    and your pruning hooks into spears;
  let the weak say, "I am a warrior."

3.11
Ezek 38.15,
16;
Isa 13.3

11 Hasten and come,
    all you nations round about,
    gather yourselves there.
  Bring down thy warriors, O LORD.

d Ch 4.1 in Heb   *e* Or *palaces*

3.2 *Jehoshaphat* means "Yahweh has judged." The name expresses the reality of judgment which would be meted out to the godless there.

¹² Let the nations bestir themselves,
    and come up to the valley of Jĕhŏsh'ăphăt;
for there I will sit to judge
    all the nations round about.

¹³ Put in the sickle,
    for the harvest is ripe.
Go in, tread,
    for the wine press is full.
The vats overflow,
    for their wickedness is great.

¹⁴ Multitudes, multitudes,
    in the valley of decision!
For the day of the LORD is near
    in the valley of decision.
¹⁵ The sun and the moon are darkened,
    and the stars withdraw their shining.

¹⁶ And the LORD roars from Zion,
    and utters his voice from Jerusalem,
and the heavens and the earth shake.
But the LORD is a refuge to his people,
    a stronghold to the people of Israel.

C. Everlasting blessing for God's people

¹⁷ "So you shall know that I am the LORD your God,
    who dwell in Zion, my holy mountain.
And Jerusalem shall be holy
    and strangers shall never again pass through it.

¹⁸ "And in that day
    the mountains shall drip sweet wine,
    and the hills shall flow with milk,
and all the stream beds of Judah
    shall flow with water;
and a fountain shall come forth from the house of the LORD
    and water the valley of Shĭttĭm.

¹⁹ "Egypt shall become a desolation
    and Ēdŏm a desolate wilderness,
for the violence done to the people of Judah,
    because they have shed innocent blood in their land.
²⁰ But Judah shall be inhabited for ever,
    and Jerusalem to all generations.
²¹ I will avenge their blood, and I will not clear the guilty,ᵍ
    for the LORD dwells in Zion."

ᵍ Gk Syr: Heb *I will hold innocent their blood which I have not held innocent*

3.12
Isa 2.4;
3.13

3.13
Mt 13.39;
Rev 14.15;
Isa 63.3;
Rev 14.19

3.14
Isa 34.2–8;
Joel 1.15;
2.1

3.15
Joel 2.10,31

3.16
Amos 1.2;
Joel 2.11;
Hag 2.6;
Jer 17.17

3.17
ver 21;
Ezek 20.40;
Obad 17;
Isa 52.1;
Nah 1.15

3.18
Amos 9.13;
Isa 30.25;
35.6;
Ezek 47.1–12;
Rev 22.1

★**3.19**
Obad 10

3.20
Ezek 37.25;
Amos 9.15

3.21
Ezek 36.25;
ver 17

3.19 *Egypt shall become a desolation.* The enemies of Israel shall be confounded when a spiritually revived Israel enjoys God's blessing in the land He has given her (3.18–21).

INTRODUCTION TO
THE BOOK OF
AMOS

Authorship and Background: The author, Amos, a minor prophet whose name means "burden" or "burden-bearer," is not to be confused with Isaiah's father, Amoz. Amos came from Tekoa, a town about six miles southeast of Bethlehem. He was a herdsman and also a cultivator of sycamore trees, the fruit of which was eaten by the poorer people. Some two hundred years before Amos prophesied, the Davidic kingdom had been broken into two parts, the Northern and Southern kingdoms. Although Amos lived in Judah, he spoke for God to the Northern Kingdom from their religious center at Bethel. He prophesied during the reign of Jeroboam II, which dates his writing about the middle of the eighth century B.C.

Characteristics: Amos writes as one accustomed to the perils and hardships of a shepherd's life. He knows the caravan customs and the market-places of his day. He is familiar with the gross inequalities between rich and poor. He sees the rich getting richer and the poor getting poorer. Filled with a sense of his divine call, he champions the oppressed. He is a rugged and a stern man, fearless and dynamic. Judgment and punishment are his familiar themes. He speaks against moral rottenness, selfishness, greed, immorality, and oppression of the poor. He notes the absence of justice for the oppressed. He condemns the idolatry of God's people and arraigns the Gentile nations which shall also experience the judgment of God. His style is simple, yet it is pure and energetic; it is rich in metaphor and vivid in symbol. Nature is the source of his figures and they speak through him with a loud voice.

Contents:

I.   The prediction of judgment on the surrounding nations. 1.1—2.16: Amos prophesies that the nations that sin shall experience divine punishment: this includes Damascus (Syria), Gaza (Philistia), Tyre (Phoenicia), Teman and Bozrah (Edom), Rabbah (Ammon), and Kerioth (Moab). Jerusalem also shall suffer, and Israel is doomed because of her sins and the abuse of her privileges.

II.   The judgment against Israel. 3.1—6.14: Amos elaborates on the judgment against Israel. God has spoken against Israel; Amos must proclaim that message. The judgment must be published among the heathen. It is a just judgment because the rich lived in luxury while oppressing the poor; idolatry is rampant and she is incorrigible. He laments the judgment and exhorts the people to repent. He prophesies exile beyond Damascus and speaks of their coming desolation and want.

III.   The five visions of the coming judgment and blessings to follow.
        7.1—9.15: The locust plague averted by Amos' prayer. The judgment
        of fire also is averted. The plumb line, a symbol of God's determined
        judgment. Amaziah tells Amos to keep out of Israel. Amos cannot
        heed him because God has called him to prophesy. The vision of the
        basket of summer fruit, a sign that judgment is at hand. The LORD
        beside the altar, a sign that awful judgment, sure and just, is upon them.
        Amos foresees the restoration of the booth of David and the blessings
        of the kingdom in the age to come.

THE BOOK OF

AMOS

I. The prediction of judgment on the surrounding nations 1.1–2.16

A. Superscription and theme

1.1
2 Sam 14.2;
2 Ki 14.23–
29;
Zech 14.5
1.2
Jer 25.30;
Joel 3.16;
1.18,19;
Amos 9.3

1 The words of Amos, who was among the shepherds of Tĕkō´à, which he saw concerning Israel in the days of Ŭzzī´áh king of Judah and in the days of Jĕróbō´ám the son of Jō´ăsh, king of Israel, two years *a* before the earthquake. ²And he said:
"The LORD roars from Zion,
  and utters his voice from Jerusalem;
the pastures of the shepherds mourn,
  and the top of Carmél withers."

B. Prophecy against Damascus

*1.3**
Isa 7.8;8.4;
ver 13

³ Thus says the LORD:
"For three transgressions of Damascus,
  and for four, I will not revoke the punishment;*b*
because they have threshed Gĭl´ëàd
  with threshing sledges of iron.

1.4
Jer 49.27;
1 Ki 20.1;
2 Ki 6.24
1.5
Jer 51.30;
2 Ki 16.9;
Amos 9.7

⁴ So I will send a fire upon the house of Hăz´äèl,
  and it shall devour the strongholds of Bĕn-hā´dăd.
⁵ I will break the bar of Damascus,
  and cut off the inhabitants from the Valley of Āvèn,*c*
and him that holds the scepter from Bĕth-e´dèn;
  and the people of Syria shall go into exile to Kĭr,"
                                              says the LORD.

C. Prophecy against Gaza (Philistia)

1.6
1 Sam 6.17;
Jer 47.1,5;
ver 9;
Obad 11

⁶ Thus says the LORD:
"For three transgressions of Gazà,
  and for four, I will not revoke the punishment;*b*
because they carried into exile a whole people
  to deliver them up to Ēdóm.

1.7
Jer 47.1;
ver 6
1.8
Zeph 2.4;
Zech 9.6;
Ps 81.14;
Ezek 25.16

⁷ So I will send a fire upon the wall of Gazà,
  and it shall devour her strongholds.
⁸ I will cut off the inhabitants from Ăshdŏd,
  and him that holds the scepter from Ăsh´kèlòn;
I will turn my hand against Ekròn;
  and the remnant of the Phĭlĭs´tĭnès shall perish,"
                                              says the Lord GOD.

a Or *during two years*   *b* Heb *cause it to return*   *c* Or *On*

1.3 *For three transgressions of Damascus, and for four*. The numbers "three" and "four" are used in a way in which emphasis and climax are presented. Amos was addressing Israel, the Northern Kingdom. He first pro- nounced judgment on Israel's enemies, then her sister kingdom Judah (2.4,5), and fi- nally upon Israel (2.6–16 and the remainder of the book), although in some passages the whole nation is involved.

D. *Prophecy against Tyre (Phoenicia)*

9 Thus says the LORD:
"For three transgressions of Tȳre,
 and for four, I will not revoke the punishment;*b*
because they delivered up a whole people to Ēdŏm,
 and did not remember the covenant of brotherhood.
10 So I will send a fire upon the wall of Tȳre,
 and it shall devour her strongholds."

1.9
Isa 23.1–18;
Ezek 26.2–
4;
1 Ki 5.1;
9.11–14

1.10
Zech 9.4

E. *Prophecy against Edom*

11 Thus says the LORD:
"For three transgressions of Ēdŏm,
 and for four, I will not revoke the punishment;*b*
because he pursued his brother with the sword,
 and cast off all pity,
and his anger tore perpetually,
 and he kept his wrath*d* for ever.
12 So I will send a fire upon Tēmăn,
 and it shall devour the strongholds of Bŏzrăh."

1.11
Isa 34.5,6;
63.1–6;
Jer 49.7–22;
Obad 10–12;
Isa 57.16;
Mic 7.18

1.12
Jer 49.7,20;
Obad 9,10

F. *Prophecy against Ammon*

13 Thus says the LORD:
"For three transgressions of the Ăm′mŏnītes,
 and for four, I will not revoke the punishment;*b*
because they have ripped up women with child in Gĭlĕăd,
 that they might enlarge their border.
14 So I will kindle a fire in the wall of Răbbăh,
 and it shall devour her strongholds,
with shouting in the day of battle,
 with a tempest in the day of the whirlwind;
15 and their king shall go into exile,
 he and his princes together,"
 says the LORD.

1.13
Jer 49.1–6;
Ezek 25.2–
7;
2 Ki 15.16

1.14
Jer 49.2;
Amos 2.2;
Ezek 21.22;
Isa 29.6;
30.30
1.15
Jer 49.3

G. *Prophecy against Moab*

2 Thus says the LORD:
"For three transgressions of Mŏăb,
 and for four, I will not revoke the punishment;*e*
because he burned to lime
 the bones of the king of Ēdŏm.
2 So I will send a fire upon Mŏăb,
 and it shall devour the strongholds of Kĕr′ĭŏth,
and Moab shall die amid uproar,
 amid shouting and the sound of the trumpet;
3 I will cut off the ruler from its midst,
 and will slay all its princes with him,"
 says the LORD.

*2.1
Isa ch 15,16;
Jer ch 48;
Zeph 2.8,9

2.2
Jer 48.41,45

2.3
Amos 5.7,
12; 6.12;
Ps 2.10;
Isa 40.23;
Jer 48.7

b Heb *cause it to return*   *d* Gk Syr Vg: Heb *his wrath kept*   *e* Heb *cause it to return*

2.1 Amos insists that the moral law is applicable to all peoples. Here he describes the atrocity of one Gentile nation (Moab) against a second (Edom).

H. *Prophecies against the chosen people*

1. *Judah*

4 Thus says the LORD:
"For three transgressions of Judah,
    and for four, I will not revoke the punishment;*e*
because they have rejected the law of the LORD,
    and have not kept his statutes,
but their lies have led them astray,
    after which their fathers walked.
5 So I will send a fire upon Judah,
    and it shall devour the strongholds of Jerusalem."

2. *Israel*

6 Thus says the LORD:
"For three transgressions of Israel,
    and for four, I will not revoke the punishment;*e*
because they sell the righteous for silver,
    and the needy for a pair of shoes;
7 they that trample the head of the poor into the dust of the earth,
    and turn aside the way of the afflicted;
a man and his father go in to the same maiden,
    so that my holy name is profaned;
8 they lay themselves down beside every altar
    upon garments taken in pledge;
and in the house of their God they drink
    the wine of those who have been fined.

9 "Yet I destroyed the Ăm′ŏrīte before them,
    whose height was like the height of the cedars,
    and who was as strong as the oaks;
I destroyed his fruit above,
    and his roots beneath.
10 Also I brought you up out of the land of Egypt,
    and led you forty years in the wilderness,
    to possess the land of the Ăm′ŏrīte.
11 And I raised up some of your sons for prophets,
    and some of your young men for Nă′zĭrītes.
Is it not indeed so, O people of Israel?"
                                                      says the LORD.

12 "But you made the Nă′zĭrītes drink wine,
    and commanded the prophets,
    saying, 'You shall not prophesy.'

13 "Behold, I will press you down in your place,
    as a cart full of sheaves presses down.
14 Flight shall perish from the swift,
    and the strong shall not retain his strength,
    nor shall the mighty save his life;

e Heb *cause it to return*

Margin references: 2.4 2 Ki 17.19; Joel 3.2; Jer 6.19; 8.9; Dan 9.11; Isa 28.15; Jer 16.19; Ezek 20.13, 16,18 / 2.5 Jer 17.27; Hos 8.14 / 2.6 2 Ki 18.12; Joel 3.3; Amos 5.11, 12; 8.6 / 2.7 Amos 8.4; 5.12; Lev 20.3; Hos 4.14 / 2.8 1 Cor 8.10; Ex 22.26; Amos 4.1; 6.6 / *2.9 Deut 2.31; Num 13.33; Isa 5.24; Mal 4.1 / 2.10 Ex 12.51; Deut 2.7; Ex 3.8 / 2.11 Jer 7.25; Num 6.2,3 / 2.12 Isa 30.10; Jer 11.21; Amos 7.12, 13; Mic 2.6 / 2.13 Joel 3.13 / 2.14 Isa 30.16, 17; Jer 9.23; Ps 33.16

2.9 *I destroyed the Amorite.* Because of their sins, the Amorites were expelled from Canaan, and the land was given to Israel as an inheritance. Now, Amos asserts, Israel is guilty of sins comparable to those of the Amorites.

15 he who handles the bow shall not stand,
and he who is swift of foot shall not save himself,
nor shall he who rides the horse save his life;
16 and he who is stout of heart among the mighty
shall flee away naked in that day,"
says the LORD.

II. The judgment against Israel 3.1–6.14

A. The relation of Israel to God

3 Hear this word that the LORD has spoken against you, O people of Israel, against the whole family which I brought up out of the land of Egypt:
2 "You only have I known
of all the families of the earth;
therefore I will punish you
for all your iniquities.

3 "Do two walk together,
unless they have made an appointment?
4 Does a lion roar in the forest,
when he has no prey?
Does a young lion cry out from his den,
if he has taken nothing?
5 Does a bird fall in a snare on the earth,
when there is no trap for it?
Does a snare spring up from the ground,
when it has taken nothing?
6 Is a trumpet blown in a city,
and the people are not afraid?
Does evil befall a city,
unless the LORD has done it?
7 Surely the Lord GOD does nothing,
without revealing his secret
to his servants the prophets.
8 The lion has roared;
who will not fear?
The Lord GOD has spoken;
who can but prophesy?"

B. The sins of Samaria

9 Proclaim to the strongholds in Assyria,*f*
and to the strongholds in the land of Egypt,
and say, "Assemble yourselves upon the mountains of Samar'ia,
and see the great tumults within her,
and the oppressions in her midst."
10 "They do not know how to do right," says the LORD,
"those who store up violence and robbery in their strongholds."

f Gk: Heb *Ashdōd*

Marginal references:
2.15 Jer 51.56; Ezek 39.3; Isa 31.3
2.16 Jer 48.41
3.1 Jer 8.3; 13.11; Amos 2.10; 9.7
★3.2 Deut 7.6; Jer 14.20; Ezek 20.36; Lk 12.47; Rom 2.9
3.3 Lev 26.23, 24
3.4 Hos 11.10
3.6 Jer 6.1; Hos 5.8; Isa 14.24–27; 45.7
3.7 Gen 18.17; Jn 15.15; Rev 10.7
3.8 Amos 1.2; Jon 1.1; 3.1; Jer 20.9; Acts 4.20
3.9 Amos 1.8; 4.1; 6.1; 8.6
3.10 Jer 4.22; Amos 5.7; 6.12; Hab 2.8–11; Zeph 1.9; Zech 5.3,4

3.2 *You only have I known.* God's sovereign choice of Israel placed Israel under solemn obligation to serve Him faithfully. Privilege involves responsibility.

3.11
Amos 6.14;
2.14; 2.5

11 Therefore thus says the Lord GOD:
"An adversary shall surround the land,
    and bring down your defenses from you,
    and your strongholds shall be plundered."

*3.12
1 Sam
17.34–37;
Amos 6.4;
Ps 132.3

12 Thus says the LORD: "As the shepherd rescues from the mouth of the lion two legs, or a piece of an ear, so shall the people of Israel who dwell in Sȧmạr′ïȧ be rescued, with the corner of a couch and part^g of a bed."

3.13
Ezek 2.7

13 "Hear, and testify against the house of Jacob,"
    says the Lord GOD, the God of hosts,

3.14
ver 2;
Amos 4.4;
5.5,6

14 "that on the day I punish Israel for his transgressions,
    I will punish the altars of Bḝthḗl,
and the horns of the altar shall be cut off
    and fall to the ground.

3.15
Jer 36.22;
Judg 3.20;
1 Ki 22.39

15 I will smite the winter house with the summer house;
    and the houses of ivory shall perish,
and the great houses^h shall come to an end,"
                                        says the LORD.

*4.1
Ps 22.12;
Ezek 39.18;
Amos 3.9;
6.1; 5.11;
8.6; 2.8;
6.6

4 "Hear this word, you cows of Bȧshȧn,
    who are in the mountain of Sȧmạr′ïȧ,
who oppress the poor, who crush the needy,
    who say to their husbands, 'Bring, that we may drink!'

*4.2
Ps 89.25;
Amos 6.8;
8.7;
Isa 37.29;
Ezek 38.4;
29.4

2 The Lord GOD has sworn by his holiness
    that, behold, the days are coming upon you,
when they shall take you away with hooks,
    even the last of you with fishhooks.

4.3
Jer 52.7;
Ezek 12.5

3 And you shall go out through the breaches,
    every one straight before her;
and you shall be cast forth into Harmȯn,"
                                        says the LORD.

C. Israel's failure to return to God

4.4
Amos 3.14;
5.5;
Hos 4.15;
Num 28.3,
4;
Deut 14.28

4 "Come to Bḝthḗl, and transgress;
    to Gḯlgȧl, and multiply transgression;
bring your sacrifices every morning,
    your tithes every three days;

4.5
Lev 7.13;
22.18,21;
Hos 9.1,10

5 offer a sacrifice of thanksgiving of that which is leavened,
    and proclaim freewill offerings, publish them;
for so you love to do, O people of Israel!"
                                        says the Lord GOD.

4.6
Isa 3.1;
Jer 14.18;
5.3;
Hag 2.17

6 "I gave you cleanness of teeth in all your cities,
    and lack of bread in all your places,
yet you did not return to me,"
                                        says the LORD.

g The meaning of the Hebrew word is uncertain   h Or many houses

---

3.12 *two legs, or a piece of an ear.* Only a very small remnant of Israel shall be spared the coming judgment.
4.1 *you cows of Bashan.* Amos spoke scornfully of the Israelite women who are likened to the fat cows of Bashan. (Bashan was rich, grain-producing land.)
4.2 *they shall take you away with hooks.* Assyrian reliefs depict prisoners actually led along the road with hooks in their lips.

7 "And I also withheld the rain from you
    when there were yet three months to the harvest;
I would send rain upon one city,
    and send no rain upon another city;
one field would be rained upon,
    and the field on which it did not rain withered;

4.7
Deut 11.17;
2 Chr 7.13;
Ex 9.4,26;
10.22,23

8 so two or three cities wandered to one city
    to drink water, and were not satisfied;
yet you did not return to me,"
                    says the LORD.

4.8
Jer 14.4;
Ezek 4.16;
Jer 3.7

9 "I smote you with blight and mildew;
    I laid waste[i] your gardens and your vineyards;
    your fig trees and your olive trees the locust devoured;
yet you did not return to me,"
                    says the LORD.

4.9
Deut 28.22;
Hag 2.17;
Joel 1.4;
2.25;
Jer 3.10

10 "I sent among you a pestilence after the manner of Egypt;
    I slew your young men with the sword;
I carried away your horses;[j]
    and I made the stench of your camp go up into your nostrils;
yet you did not return to me,"
                    says the LORD.

4.10
Ex 9.3,6;
Deut 28.27,
60;
Jer 11.22;
18.21;
48.15;
Joel 2.20;
Isa 9.13

11 "I overthrew some of you,
    as when God overthrew Sŏdŏm and Gŏmor'răh,
    and you were as a brand plucked out of the burning;
yet you did not return to me,"
                    says the LORD.

4.11
Isa 13.19;
Zech 3.2;
Jer 23.14

12 "Therefore thus I will do to you, O Israel;
    because I will do this to you,
    prepare to meet your God, O Israel!"

4.12
ver 2;
Ezek 13.5

13 For lo, he who forms the mountains, and creates the wind,
    and declares to man what is his thought;
who makes the morning darkness,
    and treads on the heights of the earth—
the LORD, the God of hosts, is his name!

4.13
Jer 10.13;
Ps 139.2;
Dan 2.28;
Jer 13.16;
Mic 1.3;
Amos 5.8,
27; 9.6

D. The LORD'S *lamentation over Israel*

5 Hear this word which I take up over you in lamentation,
  O house of Israel:

5.1
Ezek 19.1

2 "Fallen, no more to rise,
    is the virgin Israel;
forsaken on her land,
    with none to raise her up."

5.2
Jer 14.17;
Amos 8.14;
Isa 51.18;
Jer 50.32

3 For thus says the Lord GOD:
"The city that went forth a thousand
    shall have a hundred left,
and that which went forth a hundred
    shall have ten left
    to the house of Israel."

5.3
Isa 6.13;
Amos 6.9

---

[i] Cn: Heb *the multitude of* [j] Heb *with the captivity of your horses*

E. *The call to repentance*

5.4
Jer 29.3;
Isa 55.3
*5.5
Amos 4.4;
1 Sam 7.16;
11.14;
Amos 8.14

4 For thus says the LORD to the house of Israel:
"Seek me and live;
5   but do not seek Bĕthĕl,
   and do not enter into Gĭlgăl
     or cross over to Beër-shĕ′bà;
   for Gilgal shall surely go into exile,
    and Bethel shall come to nought."

5.6
Isa 55.3,6,7;
ver 14;
Deut 4.24;
Amos 3.14
5.7
Amos 6.12

6 Seek the LORD and live,
   lest he break out like fire in the house of Joseph,
    and it devour, with none to quench it for Bĕthĕl,
7 O you who turn justice to wormwood,
   and cast down righteousness to the earth!

*5.8
Job 9.9;
12.22;
Isa 42.16;
Amos 8.9;
Ps 104.6–9;
Amos 9.6;
4.13

8 He who made the Plĕi′ădĕs and Ōrī′ŏn,
   and turns deep darkness into the morning,
   and darkens the day into night,
who calls for the waters of the sea,
   and pours them out upon the surface of the earth,
the LORD is his name,

5.9
Isa 29.5;
Mic 5.11

9 who makes destruction flash forth against the strong,
   so that destruction comes upon the fortress.

5.10
Isa 29.21;
1 Ki 22.8;
Isa 59.15
5.11
Amos 3.9;
8.6; 3.15;
6.11;
Mic 6.15

10 They hate him who reproves in the gate,
   and they abhor him who speaks the truth.
11 Therefore because you trample upon the poor
   and take from him exactions of wheat,
you have built houses of hewn stone,
   but you shall not dwell in them;
you have planted pleasant vineyards,
   but you shall not drink their wine.

5.12
Amos 2.6,7;
Isa 29.21

12 For I know how many are your transgressions,
   and how great are your sins—
you who afflict the righteous, who take a bribe,
   and turn aside the needy in the gate.

5.13
Ecc 3.7

13 Therefore he who is prudent will keep silent in such a time;
   for it is an evil time.

5.14
ver 6;
Mic 3.11

14 Seek good, and not evil,
   that you may live;
and so the LORD, the God of hosts, will be with you,
   as you have said.

5.15
Ps 97.10;
Rom 12.9;
Joel 2.14;
Mic 5.3,7,8

15 Hate evil, and love good,
   and establish justice in the gate;
it may be that the LORD, the God of hosts,
   will be gracious to the remnant of Joseph.

5.16
Jer 9.17;
Joel 1.11;
2 Chr 35.25

16 Therefore thus says the LORD, the God of hosts, the Lord:
"In all the squares there shall be wailing;
   and in all the streets they shall say, 'Alas! alas!'
They shall call the farmers to mourning

5.5 *Beer-sheba*, a sanctuary used by Israel.   **5.8** *Pleiades and Orion*, constellations.

and to wailing those who are skilled in lamentation,
17 and in all vineyards there shall be wailing,
    for I will pass through the midst of you,"
                                    says the LORD.

5.17
Isa 16.10;
Jer 48.33;
Nah 1.2

F. The double woe for Israel

1. Exile beyond Damascus

18 Woe to you who desire the day of the LORD!
    Why would you have the day of the LORD?
    It is darkness, and not light;
19   as if a man fled from a lion,
       and a bear met him;
    or went into the house and leaned with his hand against the wall,
       and a serpent bit him.
20 Is not the day of the LORD darkness, and not light,
    and gloom with no brightness in it?

*5.18
Isa 5.19;
Joel 1.15;
2.1,11,31;
2 Pet 3.4;
Jer 30.7
5.19
Jer 48.44

5.20
Isa 13.10;
Zeph 1.15

21 "I hate, I despise your feasts,
    and I take no delight in your solemn assemblies.
22 Even though you offer me your burnt offerings and cereal
       offerings,
    I will not accept them,
    and the peace offerings of your fatted beasts
    I will not look upon.
23 Take away from me the noise of your songs;
    to the melody of your harps I will not listen.
24 But let justice roll down like waters,
    and righteousness like an everflowing stream.

5.21
Isa 1.11–16;
Lev 26.31
5.22
Isa 66.3;
Mic 6.6,7;
Amos 4.5

5.23
Amos 6.4,5;
8.10
5.24
Jer 22.3;
Ezek 45.9;
Mic 6.8

25 "Did you bring to me sacrifices and offerings the forty years
in the wilderness, O house of Israel? 26 You shall take up Säkküth
your king, and Kāiwan your star-god, your images,k which you
made for yourselves; 27 therefore I will take you into exile beyond
Damascus," says the LORD, whose name is the God of hosts.

5.25
Deut 32.17;
Ezek 20.8,
16,24;
Acts 7.42
5.27
2 Ki 17.6;
Amos 4.13

2. Oppression, desolation, and want predicted

6 "Woe to those who are at ease in Zion,
    and to those who feel secure on the mountain of Sàmar'ĭä,
    the notable men of the first of the nations,
    to whom the house of Israel come!
2 Pass over to Călnëh, and see;
    and thence go to Hāmáth the great;
    then go down to Gãth of the Phĭlĭs'tĭneş.
Are they better than these kingdoms?
    Or is their territory greater than your territory,
3 O you who put far away the evil day,
    and bring near the seat of violence?

*6.1
Isa 32.9–11;
Lk 6.24;
Ex 19.5;
Amos 3.2

6.2
Jer 2.10;
Isa 10.9;
2 Ki 18.34;
2 Chr 26.6;
Nah 3.8

6.3
Isa 56.12;
Amos 9.10

k Heb your images, your star-god

5.18 the day of the LORD, in popular thought,
was the day when Israel's enemies would be
confounded, and the Israelites vindicated before all the world as the LORD's chosen people.
Amos, like other prophets, states that Israel
herself must face judgment.

6.1 at ease. Conscious of God's great acts
of deliverance in Israel's past history, many
took it for granted that no harm could ever
befall the chosen nation.

6.4
Amos 3.15;
3.12;
Ezek 34.2,3
6.5
Isa 5.12;
Amos 5.23;
1 Chr 23.5
6.6
Amos 2.8;
4.1;
Gen 37.25;
Ezek 9.4
6.7
Amos 7.11,
17;
Dan 5.4–6,
30;
ver 4
6.8
Jer 51.14;
Heb 6.13;
Deut 32.19;
Ps 106.40;
Amos 3.10,
11;
Hos 11.6
6.9
Amos 5.3
6.10
Amos 5.13;
8.3
6.11
Isa 55.11;
Amos 3.15
6.12
Isa 59.13,
14;
Hos 10.4;
Amos 5.7
6.13
Ps 75.4,5
6.14
Jer 5.15;
Amos 3.11;
Num 34.8;
1 Ki 8.65
7.1
ver 4,7;
Amos 8.1;
Joel 1.4;
Amos 4.9;
Nah 3.15
7.2
Ex 10.14,15;
Ezek 9.8;
11.13;
Isa 37.4;
Jer 42.2

4 "Woe to those who lie upon beds of ivory,
  and stretch themselves upon their couches,
and eat lambs from the flock,
  and calves from the midst of the stall;
5 who sing idle songs to the sound of the harp,
  and like David invent for themselves instruments of music;
6 who drink wine in bowls,
  and anoint themselves with the finest oils,
  but are not grieved over the ruin of Joseph!
7 Therefore they shall now be the first of those to go into exile,
  and the revelry of those who stretch themselves shall pass
    away."

8 The Lord GOD has sworn by himself
  (says the LORD, the God of hosts):
"I abhor the pride of Jacob,
  and hate his strongholds;
  and I will deliver up the city and all that is in it."

9 And if ten men remain in one house, they shall die. 10And
when a man's kinsman, he who burns him,[l] shall take him up to
bring the bones out of the house, and shall say to him who is in
the innermost parts of the house, "Is there still any one with
you?" he shall say, "No"; and he shall say, "Hush! We must not
mention the name of the LORD."

11 For behold, the LORD commands,
  and the great house shall be smitten into fragments,
  and the little house into bits.
12 Do horses run upon rocks?
  Does one plow the sea with oxen?
But you have turned justice into poison
  and the fruit of righteousness into wormwood—
13 you who rejoice in Lō'-dĕbar,[n]
  who say, "Have we not by our own strength
  taken Karnā'im[o] for ourselves?"
14 "For behold, I will raise up against you a nation,
  O house of Israel," says the LORD, the God of hosts;
"and they shall oppress you from the entrance of Hāmăth
  to the Brook of the Ạr'ăbăh."

III. The five visions of the coming judgment and blessings to follow 7.1–9.15

A. The plague of locusts

7 Thus the Lord GOD showed me: behold, he was forming
  locusts in the beginning of the shooting up of the latter growth;
and lo, it was the latter growth after the king's mowings. 2 When
they had finished eating the grass of the land, I said,
"O Lord GOD, forgive, I beseech thee!
  How can Jacob stand?
  He is so small!"

l Or who makes a burning for him   n Or a thing of nought   o Or horns

3 The LORD repented concerning this;
   "It shall not be," said the LORD.

B. The fire devouring the deep

4 Thus the Lord GOD showed me: behold, the Lord GOD was
calling for a judgment by fire, and it devoured the great deep and
was eating up the land. 5 Then I said,
   "O Lord GOD, cease, I beseech thee!
   How can Jacob stand?
   He is so small!"
6 The LORD repented concerning this;
   "This also shall not be," said the Lord GOD.

C. The vision of the plumb line: Amos told to leave the land

7 He showed me: behold, the Lord was standing beside a wall
built with a plumb line, with a plumb line in his hand. 8And the
LORD said to me, "Amos, what do you see?" And I said, "A
plumb line." Then the Lord said,
   "Behold, I am setting a plumb line
      in the midst of my people Israel;
   I will never again pass by them;
9 the high places of Isaac shall be made desolate,
      and the sanctuaries of Israel shall be laid waste,
   and I will rise against the house of Jĕróbō'ám with the sword."

10 Then Ămázī'áh the priest of Bĕthĕl sent to Jĕróbō'ám king of
Israel, saying, "Amos has conspired against you in the midst of the
house of Israel; the land is not able to bear all his words. 11 For
thus Amos has said,
   'Jĕróbō'ám shall die by the sword,
      and Israel must go into exile
      away from his land.'"
12 And Ămázī'áh said to Amos, "O seer, go, flee away to the land
of Judah, and eat bread there, and prophesy there; 13 but never
again prophesy at Bĕthĕl, for it is the king's sanctuary, and it is a
temple of the kingdom."
14 Then Amos answered Ămázī'áh, "I am no prophet, nor a
prophet's son;ᵖ but I am a herdsman, and a dresser of sycamore
trees, 15 and the LORD took me from following the flock, and the
LORD said to me, 'Go, prophesy to my people Israel.'
16 "Now therefore hear the word of the LORD.
   You say, 'Do not prophesy against Israel,
      and do not preach against the house of Isaac.'
17 Therefore thus says the LORD:
   'Your wife shall be a harlot in the city,

ᵖ Or one of the sons of the prophets

7.3
Deut 32.36;
Jer 26.19;
Jon 3.10
7.4
Isa 66.15,
16;
Amos 2.5
7.5
ver 2
7.6
ver 3
7.8
Amos 8.2;
Isa 28.17;
34.11;
Lam 2.8;
Mic 7.18
7.9
Hos 10.8;
Mic 1.5;
Isa 63.18;
2 Ki 15.10
*7.10
1 Ki 12.32;
2 Ki 14.23;
Jer 26.8–11
7.11
ver 9,17
*7.13
Amos 2.12;
1 Ki 12.32;
13.1
*7.14
1 Ki 20.35;
2 Ki 2.5;
4.38;
2 Chr 19.2;
Amos 1.1
7.15
2 Sam 7.8;
Amos 3.8;
Jer 7.1;
Ezek 2.3,4
7.16
Amos 2.12;
Ezek 21.2;
Mic 2.6
7.17
Jer 29.21;
Hos 4.13,
14;
Jer 14.16;
Ezek 4.13;
Hos 9.3

7.10 *Amos has conspired against you.* Amos, a native of Tekoa in the Southern Kingdom (Judah), was looked upon as a foreigner who was stirring up trouble in the North. He was told that he was not welcome at Bethel, a shrine city of the Northern Kingdom.
7.13 *Bethel,* see note to Gen 28.19.
7.14 *I am no prophet.* Amos insisted that he was not a professional prophet but a layman to whom God had entrusted a message.

and your sons and your daughters shall fall by the sword,
and your land shall be parceled out by line;
you yourself shall die in an unclean land,
and Israel shall surely go into exile away from its land.' "

D. The basket of summer fruit

1. The vision of Israel's ruin

8 Thus the Lord GOD showed me: behold, a basket of summer
fruit.q 2And he said, "Amos, what do you see?" And I said,
"A basket of summer fruit."q Then the LORD said to me,
"The endr has come upon my people Israel;
I will never again pass by them.
3 The songs of the temples shall become wailings in that day,"
says the Lord GOD;
"the dead bodies shall be many;
in every place they shall be cast out in silence."t

2. The lust for money

4 Hear this, you who trample upon the needy,
and bring the poor of the land to an end,
5 saying, "When will the new moon be over,
that we may sell grain?
And the sabbath,
that we may offer wheat for sale,
that we may make the ephah small and the shekel great,
and deal deceitfully with false balances,
6 that we may buy the poor for silver
and the needy for a pair of sandals,
and sell the refuse of the wheat?"

7 The LORD has sworn by the pride of Jacob:
"Surely I will never forget any of their deeds.
8 Shall not the land tremble on this account,
and every one mourn who dwells in it,
and all of it rise like the Nile,
and be tossed about and sink again, like the Nile of Egypt?"

9 "And on that day," says the Lord GOD,
"I will make the sun go down at noon,
and darken the earth in broad daylight.
10 I will turn your feasts into mourning,
and all your songs into lamentation;
I will bring sackcloth upon all loins,
and baldness on every head;
I will make it like the mourning for an only son,
and the end of it like a bitter day.

3. The famine of the Word of God

11 "Behold, the days are coming," says the Lord GOD,
"when I will send a famine on the land;
not a famine of bread, nor a thirst for water,
but of hearing the words of the LORD.

q Heb qayits r Heb qets s Or palace t Or be silent!

Side refs: 8.2 Amos 7.8; Jer 24.3; Ezek 7.2 | 8.3 Amos 5.23; 6.9,10 | 8.4 Ps 14.4; Amos 5.11,12 | 8.5 2 Ki 4.23; Neh 13.15,16; Mic 6.10,11 | 8.6 Amos 2.6 | 8.7 Amos 6.8; Deut 33.26,29; Hos 8.13; 9.9 | 8.8 Isa 5.25; Hos 4.3; Amos 9.5 | 8.9 Isa 13.10; Jer 15.9; Mic 3.6; Amos 4.13; 5.8 | 8.10 Amos 5.21; 6.4,5; Jer 48.37; Ezek 7.18; Jer 6.26; Zech 12.10 | 8.11 1 Sam 3.1; 2 Chr 15.3; Ezek 7.26; Mic 3.6

12 They shall wander from sea to sea,
   and from north to east;
they shall run to and fro, to seek the word of the LORD,
   but they shall not find it.

13 "In that day the fair virgins and the young men
   shall faint for thirst.
14 Those who swear by Ăsh′imăh of Sămăr′ĭă,
   and say, 'As thy god lives, O Dan,'
and, 'As the way of Beër-shē′bă lives,'
   they shall fall, and never rise again."

E. *The destruction of the sanctuary*

9 I saw the LORD standing beside[u] the altar, and he said:
   "Smite the capitals until the thresholds shake,
   and shatter them on the heads of all the people;[v]
and what are left of them I will slay with the sword;
   not one of them shall flee away,
   not one of them shall escape.

2 "Though they dig into Shēōl,
   from there shall my hand take them;
though they climb up to heaven,
   from there I will bring them down.
3 Though they hide themselves on the top of Carmĕl,
   from there I will search out and take them;
and though they hide from my sight at the bottom of the sea,
   there I will command the serpent, and it shall bite them.
4 And though they go into captivity before their enemies,
   there I will command the sword, and it shall slay them;
and I will set my eyes upon them
   for evil and not for good."

5 The Lord, GOD of hosts,
he who touches the earth and it melts,
   and all who dwell in it mourn,
and all of it rises like the Nile,
   and sinks again, like the Nile of Egypt;
6 who builds his upper chambers in the heavens,
   and founds his vault upon the earth;
who calls for the waters of the sea,
   and pours them out upon the surface of the earth—
the LORD is his name.

7 "Are you not like the Ethiopians to me,
   O people of Israel?" says the LORD.
"Did I not bring up Israel from the land of Egypt,
   and the Phĭlĭs′tĭnes from Căphtor and the Syrians from Kĭr?
8 Behold, the eyes of the Lord GOD are upon the sinful kingdom,

---

Cross-references (right column):

8.12 Ezek 20.3, 31

8.13 Lam 1.18; Isa 41.17; Hos 2.3

8.14 Hos 4.15; 1 Ki 12.28, 29; Amos 5.5

9.1 Amos 3.14; Zeph 2.14; Hab 3.13; ver 4; Amos 2.14

9.2 Ps 139.8; Jer 51.53; Obad 4

9.3 Amos 1.2; Jer 16.16, 17; Isa 27.1

9.4 Lev 26.33; Ezek 5.12; Jer 44.11

9.5 Mic 1.4; Amos 8.8

9.6 Ps 104.3; Amos 5.8; 4.13

*9.7 Isa 43.3; Amos 2.10; 3.1; Deut 2.23; Jer 47.4; Amos 1.5

9.8 Jer 44.27; ver 4,10; Jer 30.11; Joel 2.32

---

[u] Or *upon*   [v] Heb *all of them*

9.7 *the Philistines from Caphtor.* Israel gloried in the fact that God had brought her ancestors from Egypt and had given them an inheritance in Canaan. Amos reminded them that Philistines and Syrians were also under the providential care of God.

and I will destroy it from the surface of the ground;
except that I will not utterly destroy the house of Jacob,"
                                                    says the LORD.

9.9
Isa 30.28

9 "For lo, I will command,
    and shake the house of Israel among all the nations
  as one shakes with a sieve,
    but no pebble shall fall upon the earth.

9.10
Amos 8.14;
6.3

10 All the sinners of my people shall die by the sword,
    who say, 'Evil shall not overtake or meet us.'

F. The promise of Messianic blessing

1. Restoration of the Davidic kingdom

*9.11
Acts 15.16,
17;
Ps 80.12;
Isa 63.11;
Jer 46.26

11 "In that day I will raise up
    the booth of David that is fallen
  and repair its breaches,
    and raise up its ruins,
    and rebuild it as in the days of old;

9.12
Obad 19;
Isa 11.14;
43.7

12 that they may possess the remnant of Ēdóm
    and all the nations who are called by my name,"
  says the LORD who does this.

2. The productivity of the earth

9.13
Lev 26.5;
Joel 3.18

13 "Behold, the days are coming," says the LORD,
    "when the plowman shall overtake the reaper
    and the treader of grapes him who sows the seed;
  the mountains shall drip sweet wine,
    and all the hills shall flow with it.

3. Kingdom blessings

9.14
Isa 60.4;
Jer 30.18;
Isa 61.4;
Ezek 36.35;
28.26

14 I will restore the fortunes of my people Israel,
    and they shall rebuild the ruined cities and inhabit them;
  they shall plant vineyards and drink their wine,
    and they shall make gardens and eat their fruit.

9.15
Jer 24.6;
31.28;
Isa 60.21;
Jer 32.41;
Ezek 34.28

15 I will plant them upon their land,
    and they shall never again be plucked up
  out of the land which I have given them,"
                                    says the LORD your God.

9.11 *In that day.* Amos had prophesied the destruction of Israel, but he held forth the hope of a glorious future when the people would be planted again in their own land with God's blessing. In the New Testament, James, in Acts 15.16, 17, quotes this passage as evidence that the call of the Gentiles into the church was in accord with Old Testament prophecy. Some think that Amos also here prophesied the re-establishment of the house of David following the Second Advent of Christ when the Savior will sit upon the throne of David according to promise (Lk 1.32).

INTRODUCTION TO
THE BOOK OF
OBADIAH

Authorship and Background: We know little or nothing about the author of this book which is the shortest in the Old Testament. The name Obadiah means "servant of Yahweh" and is found frequently in the Old Testament. The date of the book is open to question. The traditional view is that it was written before the Book of Jeremiah. Many scholars construe the reference to the captivity of Jerusalem (11–14) as pointing to a date of composition subsequent to 586 B.C. The people of Edom participated in four plunderings of Jerusalem in a three-hundred-year period beginning in the ninth century B.C. It was in connection with these depredations that Obadiah wrote.

The burden of Obadiah's prophecy concerned Edom. The Edomites were descendants of Esau and had always been enemies of the sons of Jacob. The Herods of Jesus' day came from Edomite stock. Following the destruction of Jerusalem in A.D. 70, the Edomites are heard of no more.

Characteristics: Obadiah prophesies the destruction and extinction of Edom. This is a suitable divine judgment upon the nation for its unbrotherly conduct toward the people of God, to whom they have been cruel, and whose goods they have plundered. The latter part of Obadiah's prophecy deals with the day of the LORD when judgment will come upon Edom and other nations, but deliverance will be in Zion. Israel will conquer its conquerors and extend itself to the four points of the compass. The earlier part of the book is unrelieved in its spirit of judgment. There is no hope for Edom and no mention of repentance and salvation. The message is only of doom and destruction. Nations shall reap as they have sown. But the latter part of the prophecy is encouraging to Israel and ends with the promise that "the kingdom shall be the LORD's."

Contents:

I.   The judgment against Edom. 1–14: Edom shall be destroyed. It is guilty of the sin of pride and has wronged its brother, Judah.

II.   The day of the LORD. 15–21: As nations sow so shall they reap. Judgment will come. Judah will be free, holy, and rich. The enemy shall be destroyed. Judah's boundaries shall be enlarged and the nation shall return from dispersion. The kingdom shall be the LORD's.

THE BOOK OF

OBADIAH

I. The judgment against Edom 1–14

A. The fall of Edom predicted

*1
Isa 34.5;
Ezek 25.12;
Joel 3.19;
Jer 49.14;
Isa 30.4;
Jer 6.4,5

1 The vision of Ōbàdĭ'áh.

Thus says the Lord GOD concerning Ēdŏm:
We have heard tidings from the LORD,
    and a messenger has been sent among the nations:
"Rise up! let us rise against her for battle!"
2 Behold, I will make you small among the nations,
    you shall be utterly despised.

*3
Isa 16.6;
Jer 49.16;
2 Ki 14.7;
Isa 14.13–
   15;
Rev 18.7

3 The pride of your heart has deceived you,
    you who live in the clefts of the rock,ᵃ
    whose dwelling is high,
who say in your heart,
    "Who will bring me down to the ground?"

4
Job 20.6;
Hab 2.9;
Isa 14.13–
   15

4 Though you soar aloft like the eagle,
    though your nest is set among the stars,
    thence I will bring you down,
            says the LORD.

B. Edom's destruction to be complete

5
Jer 49.9;
ver 9,10;
Isa 17.6

5 If thieves came to you,
    if plunderers by night—
    how you have been destroyed!—
    would they not steal only enough for themselves?
If grape gatherers came to you,
    would they not leave gleanings?

*6
Jer 49.10

6 How Ēsau has been pillaged,
    his treasures sought out!

7
Jer 30.14;
  38.22;
Ps 41.9;
Jer 49.7

7 All your allies have deceived you,
    they have driven you to the border;
your confederates have prevailed against you;
    your trusted friends have set a trap under you—
    there is no understanding of it.

8
Job 5.12;
Isa 29.14

8 Will I not on that day, says the LORD,
    destroy the wise men out of Ēdŏm,
    and understanding out of Mount Ēsau?

9
Jer 49.22;
Amos 1.12;
Hab 3.3;
ver 5

9 And your mighty men shall be dismayed, O Tēmàn,
    so that every man from Mount Ēsau will be cut off by
    slaughter.

ᵃ Or Sela

---

1 See note to Gen 36.9 on Edomites.
3 Pride of heart is deceptive, fostered in this instance by the fact that Edom was located on a rock that seemed impregnable. Moreover, pride led to presumption, Edom assuming that it was perfectly safe. But God would

bring it to nought anyhow.
6 *How Esau has been pillaged.* Jacob (Israel) and Esau (Edom) were brothers, and the rivalry between the brothers developed into hostility among their descendants (cf. Gen 27.40).

C. Edom's sins laid bare

10 For the violence done to your brother Jacob,
   shame shall cover you,
   and you shall be cut off for ever.

11 On the day that you stood aloof,
   on the day that strangers carried off his wealth,
and foreigners entered his gates
   and cast lots for Jerusalem,
   you were like one of them.

12 But you should not have gloated over the day of your brother
   in the day of his misfortune;
you should not have rejoiced over the people of Judah
   in the day of their ruin;
you should not have boasted
   in the day of distress.

13 You should not have entered the gate of my people
   in the day of his calamity;
you should not have gloated over his disaster
   in the day of his calamity;
you should not have looted his goods
   in the day of his calamity.

14 You should not have stood at the parting of the ways
   to cut off his fugitives;
you should not have delivered up his survivors
   in the day of distress.

II. The day of the LORD 15–21

A. The judgment of all nations

15 For the day of the LORD is near upon all the nations.
   As you have done, it shall be done to you,
   your deeds shall return on your own head.

16 For as you have drunk upon my holy mountain,
   all the nations round about shall drink;
they shall drink, and stagger,[b]
   and shall be as though they had not been.

B. Deliverance in Zion: the kingdom of the LORD

17 But in Mount Zion there shall be those that escape,
   and it shall be holy;
and the house of Jacob shall possess their own possessions.

18 The house of Jacob shall be a fire,
   and the house of Joseph a flame,
   and the house of Esau stubble;
they shall burn them and consume them,

b Cn: Heb swallow

10	Ps 137.7; Joel 3.19; Amos 1.11
*11	Ps 137.7; Joel 3.3; Nah 3.10
12	Mic 4.11; Ezek 35.15; 36.5; Ps 31.18
13	Ezek 35.5, 10; 36.2,3
*14	
15	Ezek 30.3; Joel 1.15; Jer 50.29; Hab 2.8; Ezek 35.11
16	Jer 49.12, 13; 25.15,16
17	Isa 4.2,3; Amos 9.11–15
*18	Isa 10.17; Jer 11.23; Amos 1.8

11 On the day that you stood aloof. When the territory of Israel was attacked, brother Edom should have come to her aid. Instead, Edom rejoiced over the destruction of the Israelite territory.

14 to cut off his fugitives. Edom refused to allow fugitives from Israel to enter Edomite territory.
18 Edom sprang from Esau; Israel from Jacob. Edom shall be consumed, Israel saved.

and there shall be no survivor to the house of Esau;
    for the LORD has spoken.

19 Those of the Nĕgĕb shall possess Mount Ēsau,
    and those of the Shĕphē'lăh the land of the Phĭlĭs'tĭneṣ;
they shall possess the land of Ē'phrăĭm and the land of Sámar'ĭá
    and Benjamin shall possess Gĭl'ĕăd.
20 The exiles in Hālăh*c* who are of the people of Israel
    shall possess*d* Phoĕnī'çĭá as far as Zạr'ĕphăth;
and the exiles of Jerusalem who are in Sĕphar'ăd
    shall possess the cities of the Nĕgĕb.
21 Saviors shall go up to Mount Zion
    to rule Mount Ēsau;
    and the kingdom shall be the LORD'S.

c Cn: Heb this army   d Cn: Heb which

Side references: *19 Amos 9.12; Isa 11.14; Zeph 2.7; Jer 31.5; 32.44. *20 1 Ki 17.9; Jer 32.44; 33.13. 21 Neh 9.27; Ps 22.28; 67.4; Dan 2.44; Zech 14.9.

19 *Negeb*, see note to Gen 12.9. Located south of Judah, Negeb was relatively waterless. It included a series of rolling hills and was the favored home of the early Israelites. *Shephela:* a geographical term for the region between the coastal plain of Philistia and the high central ranges of Palestine.

20 *Halah*, mentioned in 2 Ki 17.6, 18.11, and 1 Chr 5.26 as one of the places to which the Assyrians deported the prisoners from Samaria. This implies that it must have been somewhere in the neighborhood of the city of Nineveh. *Sepharad*, a place to which the Jews were sent as captives, the location of which has never been determined to the satisfaction of all. Locations in Spain, Assyria, etc. have been advanced but there is nothing to substantiate these claims.

INTRODUCTION TO
THE BOOK OF
JONAH

Authorship and Background: Who wrote this book is nowhere plainly stated. The chief character is Jonah, the son of Amittai, whose name means "dove." According to 2 Ki 14.25, he lived in Gath-hepher, just north of Nazareth, during the reign of Jeroboam II, in the eighth century B.C. when Hosea and Amos were also prophesying. The length of his ministry cannot be determined. Conservatives generally accept the book as history since the names and locations are historical. They infer that Jesus' references to Jonah in the New Testament (Mt 12.39, 40; Lk 11.29, 30) imply the historicity of the book. Some scholars suggest that an unknown author attempted to depict the great theological truth of God's universal concern and wove a parabolic story around the historical character of Jonah. Nineveh, the city which is central in Jonah, was the capital of the world empire of Assyria, an empire that stood for three hundred years. It was a brutally militaristic nation, hated by other peoples of western Asia. Proud Assyria represented heathen defiance against God.

Characteristics: The greater part of Jonah is a biographical narrative. No effort is made to disregard Jonah's disobedience. The account is chronologically progressive and straightforward. One event follows upon another. Behind the story lies the truth of God's saving concern for all nations. Its implications for Israel cannot be overlooked. Here is a Gentile nation which, when faced with judgment, was willing to repent. Israel must do no less if she is to escape punishment for her unfaithfulness in the face of much greater blessings of God. Jonah also has prophetic significance relative to the death, burial, and Resurrection of Jesus Christ, typically pointing to the One who is "greater than Jonah" and whose own experience fulfilled the prophetic word (Mt 12.40, 41).

Contents:

I.   The disobedient and suffering prophet. 1.1–17: God calls Jonah to go to Nineveh. He flees toward Tarshish. A storm rises on the sea. Jonah is cast overboard and swallowed by a great fish.

II. The repentant and delivered prophet. 2.1–10: Jonah repents; he prays from the fish's belly and is delivered.

III. The reluctantly obedient prophet. 3.1–10: God calls Jonah the second time to go to Ninevah. He obeys God. He preaches repentance and deferment of judgment. Nineveh repents and judgment is averted.

IV. The God of unlimited mercy. 4.1–11: Jonah is angry because Nineveh is saved. He is sheltered by a plant that withers. He is distressed. God applies this as a parable to Nineveh, the object of His unlimited mercy.

THE BOOK OF

JONAH

I. *The disobedient and suffering prophet 1.1–17*

*1.1
2 Ki 14.25;
Mt 12.39
1.2
Jon 3.2, 3;
4.1;
Ezra 9.6
*1.3
Ps 139.7,9,
10;
Acts 9.36
1.4
Ps 107.25
1.5
Acts 27.18;
1 Sam 24.3

1.6
Ps 107.28;
Jon 3.9

1.7
Josh 7.14;
1 Sam
10.20;
14.41,42;
Acts 1.26
1.8
Josh 7.19;
1 Sam 14.43
*1.9
Ps 146.6;
Acts 17.24
1.10
Job 27.22

1.12
2 Sam
24.17;
Jn 11.50;
1 Chr 21.17
1.13
Prov 21.30
*1.14
ver 16;
Deut 21.8;
Ps 115.3
1.15
Ps 89.9;
107.29;
Lk 8.24
1.16
1 Sam 6.2–
5;
Mk 4.41

1 Now the word of the LORD came to Jonah the son of Ȧmïttaī, saying, 2 "Arise, go to Nȋn'ėvėh, that great city, and cry against it; for their wickedness has come up before me." 3 But Jonah rose to flee to Tarshish from the presence of the LORD. He went down to Jŏppȧ and found a ship going to Tarshish; so he paid the fare, and went on board, to go with them to Tarshish, away from the presence of the LORD.

4 But the LORD hurled a great wind upon the sea, and there was a mighty tempest on the sea, so that the ship threatened to break up. 5 Then the mariners were afraid, and each cried to his god; and they threw the wares that were in the ship into the sea, to lighten it for them. But Jonah had gone down into the inner part of the ship and had lain down, and was fast asleep. 6 So the captain came and said to him, "What do you mean, you sleeper? Arise, call upon your god! Perhaps the god will give a thought to us, that we do not perish."

7 And they said to one another, "Come, let us cast lots, that we may know on whose account this evil has come upon us." So they cast lots, and the lot fell upon Jonah. 8 Then they said to him, "Tell us, on whose account this evil has come upon us? What is your occupation? And whence do you come? What is your country? And of what people are you?" 9 And he said to them, "I am a Hebrew; and I fear the LORD, the God of heaven, who made the sea and the dry land." 10 Then the men were exceedingly afraid, and said to him, "What is this that you have done!" For the men knew that he was fleeing from the presence of the LORD, because he had told them.

11 Then they said to him, "What shall we do to you, that the sea may quiet down for us?" For the sea grew more and more tempestuous. 12 He said to them, "Take me up and throw me into the sea; then the sea will quiet down for you; for I know it is because of me that this great tempest has come upon you." 13 Nevertheless the men rowed hard to bring the ship back to land, but they could not, for the sea grew more and more tempestuous against them. 14 Therefore they cried to the LORD, "We beseech thee, O LORD, let us not perish for this man's life, and lay not on us innocent blood; for thou, O LORD, hast done as it pleased thee." 15 So they took up Jonah and threw him into the sea; and the sea ceased from its raging. 16 Then the men feared the LORD exceedingly, and they offered a sacrifice to the LORD and made vows.

1.1 *Jonah the son of Amittai* was a prophet in Israel during the reign of Jeroboam II (2 Ki 14.25).

1.3 *to Tarshish*, probably Tartessus in southwestern Spain. See also note to 1 Ki 10.22.

1.9 *a Hebrew*. The term is frequently used by Israelites in situations in which they must identify themselves to foreigners (cf. Gen 40.15; Ex 2.6). *fear the LORD* means to have a reverential trust in Him. It also encompasses the idea of a hatred of sin. The common sense of "fear" as apprehension or dread does not exhaust the meaning of the word.

1.14 *let us not perish*, i.e., do not let the innocent suffer with the guilty.

17[a] And the LORD appointed a great fish to swallow up Jonah; and Jonah was in the belly of the fish three days and three nights.

*1.17
Jon 4.6;
Mt 12.40;
16.4;
Lk 11.30

II. The repentant and delivered prophet 2.1–10

2 Then Jonah prayed to the LORD his God from the belly of the fish, 2 saying,

2.1
Ps 130.1

"I called to the LORD, out of my distress,
    and he answered me;
out of the belly of Shēōl I cried,
    and thou didst hear my voice.

2.2
Ps 18.4–6

3 For thou didst cast me into the deep,
    into the heart of the seas,
    and the flood was round about me;
all thy waves and thy billows
    passed over me.

2.3
Ps 88.6;
42.7

4 Then I said, 'I am cast out
    from thy presence;
how shall I again look
    upon thy holy temple?'

2.4
Ps 31.22;
1 Ki 8.38

5 The waters closed in over me,
    the deep was round about me;
weeds were wrapped about my head

2.5
Ps 69.1;
Lam 3.54

6   at the roots of the mountains.
I went down to the land
    whose bars closed upon me for ever;
yet thou didst bring up my life from the Pit,
    O LORD my God.

2.6
Ps 16.10

7 When my soul fainted within me,
    I remembered the LORD;
and my prayer came to thee,
    into thy holy temple.

2.7
Ps 142.3;
77.10,11;
18.6

8 Those who pay regard to vain idols
    forsake their true loyalty.

2.8
2 Ki 17.15;
Ps 31.6;
Jer 10.8;
16.19

9 But I with the voice of thanksgiving
    will sacrifice to thee;
what I have vowed I will pay.
    Deliverance belongs to the LORD!"

*2.9
Ps 50.14;
Hos 14.2;
Heb 13.15;
Job 22.27;
Ps 3.8

10 And the LORD spoke to the fish, and it vomited out Jonah upon the dry land.

2.10
Jon 1.17

[a] Ch 2.1 in Heb

1.17 Jonah and Christ are compared with each other. Christ Himself points out in a simile in Mt 12.40 that as Jonah was in the belly of the fish (the Greek term is *Kētos*, or sea monster) for three days and nights, so would Christ be in the tomb for the same length of time. As Jonah was delivered from his living tomb, so would Christ be raised from the dead on the third day. Some have theorized that Jonah actually died and was resuscitated upon his ejection from the fish's stomach. But since he was as good as dead while in the creature's digestive tract, the typical meaning is in no sense violated by his having been entombed alive in the fish.

Many have been distracted by supposed scientific difficulties in the account of Jonah's preservation in the belly of the fish and have thus lost sight of the true lesson to be learned from Jonah's life and experience. Whether God created a special whale or other huge fish unlike those known to zoology is of no consequence. The God who created all things must retain the power to create a unique specimen for a special purpose if it suits His purpose. Tradition has interpreted Christ's reference to Jonah (Mt 12.39, 40) as implying the historicity of the event.

2.9 *what I have vowed I will pay.* As a prophet, Jonah had vowed obedience. His flight from God's revealed will was a breaking of a solemn vow.

III. *The reluctantly obedient prophet 3.1–10*

3 Then the word of the LORD came to Jonah the second time, saying, 2 "Arise, go to Nĭn'ĕvĕh, that great city, and proclaim to it the message that I tell you." 3 So Jonah arose and went to Nĭn'ĕvĕh, according to the word of the LORD. Now Nineveh was an exceedingly great city, three days' journey in breadth. 4 Jonah began to go into the city, going a day's journey. And he cried, "Yet forty days, and Nĭn'ĕvĕh shall be overthrown!" 5And the people of Nĭn'ĕvĕh believed God; they proclaimed a fast, and put on sackcloth, from the greatest of them to the least of them.

6 Then tidings reached the king of Nĭn'ĕvĕh, and he arose from his throne, removed his robe, and covered himself with sackcloth, and sat in ashes. 7And he made proclamation and published through Nĭn'ĕvĕh, "By the decree of the king and his nobles: Let neither man nor beast, herd nor flock, taste anything; let them not feed, or drink water, 8 but let man and beast be covered with sackcloth, and let them cry mightily to God; yea, let every one turn from his evil way and from the violence which is in his hands. 9 Who knows, God may yet repent and turn from his fierce anger, so that we perish not?"

10 When God saw what they did, how they turned from their evil way, God repented of the evil which he had said he would do to them; and he did not do it.

IV. *The God of unlimited mercy 4.1–11*

4 But it displeased Jonah exceedingly, and he was angry. 2And he prayed to the LORD and said, "I pray thee, LORD, is not this what I said when I was yet in my country? That is why I made haste to flee to Tarshĭsh; for I knew that thou art a gracious God and merciful, slow to anger, and abounding in steadfast love, and repentest of evil. 3 Therefore now, O LORD, take my life from me, I beseech thee, for it is better for me to die than to live." 4And the LORD said, "Do you do well to be angry?" 5 Then Jonah went out of the city and sat to the east of the city, and made a booth for himself there. He sat under it in the shade, till he should see what would become of the city.

6 And the LORD God appointed a plant,ᵇ and made it come up over Jonah, that it might be a shade over his head, to save him from his discomfort. So Jonah was exceedingly glad because of the plant.ᵇ 7 But when dawn came up the next day, God appointed a worm which attacked the plant,ᵇ so that it withered. 8 When the

b Heb *qiqayon*, probably *the castor oil plant*

Cross-references (margin):

*3.1 — Jon 1.1,2
*3.4
3.5 — Dan 9.3; Joel 1.14; Jer 31.34
3.6 — Job 2.8; Jer 6.26; Dan 9.3
3.7 — ver 5; 2 Chr 20.3
3.8 — Ps 130.1; Jon 1.6,13; Isa 55.6,7; Jer 18.11
3.9 — 2 Sam 12.22; Joel 2.14
3.10 — Jer 31.18; Ex 32.14; Jer 18.8; Amos 7.3,6
4.1 — ver 4,9; Mt 20.15; Lk 15.28
*4.2 — Jon 1.3; Ex 34.6; Ps 86.5; Joel 2.13
4.3 — 1 Ki 19.4; ver 8; Job 7.15,16
4.4 — ver 9; Mt 20.11,15
4.5 — 1 Ki 19.9,13
4.7 — Joel 1.12

3.1 The story of Jonah falls naturally into five sections: (1) Jonah commissioned (1.2); (2) Jonah disobedient (1.3); (3) Jonah repentant (2.1–7); (4) Jonah delivered (2.10); (5) Jonah recommissioned (3.1–3).

3.4 "*Yet forty days, and Nineveh shall be overthrown!*" This statement has an implied condition—"unless she repents." As a matter of fact, Nineveh repented and was not overthrown in forty days, much to the displeasure of Jonah.

4.2 *I knew that thou art a gracious God.* Jonah, as a loyal Israelite, wanted the hated Assyrian capital to be destroyed. He did not resist God's first command to go to Nineveh because of fear for his own safety, but because of fear that his message might bring the Ninevites to repentance, and thus insure their deliverance from divine judgment. The Book of Jonah stresses the fact that God's love transcends all national distinctions and embraces the most unlovely.

sun rose, God appointed a sultry east wind, and the sun beat upon
the head of Jonah so that he was faint; and he asked that he might
die, and said, "It is better for me to die than to live." 9 But God
said to Jonah, "Do you do well to be angry for the plant?"[b] And
he said, "I do well to be angry, angry enough to die." 10And the
LORD said, "You pity the plant,[b] for which you did not labor, nor
did you make it grow, which came into being in a night, and
perished in a night. 11And should not I pity Nin′eveh, that great
city, in which there are more than a hundred and twenty thousand
persons who do not know their right hand from their left, and also
much cattle?"

*4.9
ver 4

*4.11
Jon 1.2;
3.2,3;
Deut 1.39;
Ps 36.6

[b] Heb *qiqayon*, probably *the castor oil plant*

4.9 *Do you do well . . . ?* God reasons with
Jonah in order to reprove him, to show him
the error of his ways, and to produce in him
a humble and a contrite spirit. Jonah might
well have resisted this outburst since his
earlier disobedience had resulted in his imprisonment in the belly of the fish. Evidently
he had not learned all that he might have
from his previous experience.

4.11 *And should not I pity Nineveh?* Jonah
was concerned about a plant which grew
quickly, and just as quickly disappeared. This
in itself was not wrong, but Jonah was
reminded that his concern should include the
people of Nineveh who were of greater value
in God's sight than a plant. Even cattle were
spared the suffering which would have fallen
on unrepentant Nineveh.

INTRODUCTION TO
THE BOOK OF
MICAH

Authorship and Background: The author's name, Micah, is an abbreviation of the Hebrew words which mean "Who is like Yahweh?" Micah came from Moresheth, which was located near Gath, some thirty miles from Jerusalem. He ministered during the reigns of Jotham, Ahaz, and Hezekiah (1.1) and was a contemporary of Hosea and Isaiah in the latter half of the eighth century B.C. As a prophet, Micah spoke both to Judah and Israel, usually referring to them by the names of their capital cities. A rural resident, he appears to have been less familiar with the politics of Jerusalem than his contemporary Isaiah, who lived and prophesied in that city. However, Micah lived near the coastal road over which traders, pilgrims, and soldiers had passed for hundreds of years. He must have observed the traffic between Egypt and Jerusalem and noted the corrupting influence of this entangling foreign alliance. His ministry extended over a long period of time.

Characteristics: The contents of this book form blocks of material indicating that the messages were delivered at different times. The style itself is varied. The language of Micah is direct, rugged, indignant, and convincing. Some of it rises to lofty heights and is beautiful. He exhibits great tenderness as he pleads with the people of God. His messages are moral and religious, with little regard for the political situation. He prophesied briefly against Israel and these prophecies were fulfilled within a short period of time. He prophesied similar doom for Judah because of her sins. Amid his gloomy predictions are signs of hope and blessing if the people will repent. Seeing far beyond the moment of his writing, he alludes to God's promise of ultimate salvation through the appearance of the divine Savior and the establishment of God's glorious kingdom. Peculiar to Micah is the statement in 5.2 which Mt 2.5 quotes as being fulfilled by the birth of Christ in Bethlehem of Judea.

Contents:

I.   The pronouncement of judgment on Israel and Judah. 1.1—2.13: Micah records his vision concerning Samaria and Jerusalem. Both are guilty of sinning against God. The fall of each is predicted. He mourns their end which is occasioned by their iniquity and listening to false prophets. A remnant shall be saved.

II.   The judgment followed by restoration and the reign of Messiah. 3.1—5.15: Micah arraigns the cruel princes. He assails the false prophets. He derides them for their false sense of security. There will be a restored Zion with law and peace. There will be victory. A Ruler will come forth from Bethlehem bringing peace to the "ends of the

earth" (5.4). They should trust in their king and not in the idols of men.

III.   Divine punishment followed by divine mercy. 6.1—7.20: The LORD invites His people to reason with Him. He speaks of what He has done for them in the past and appeals to them "to do justice, and to love kindness, and to walk humbly with your God" (6.8). The sin of commercial dishonesty is denounced. Moral barrenness and vicious exploitation and idolatry are lamented. God's judgment is just, but in mercy God will bring them back to Himself. Micah closes with a psalm of praise to the mercy of God who "does not retain his anger for ever because he delights in steadfast love."

THE BOOK OF

MICAH

I. The pronouncement of judgment on Israel and Judah 1.1–2.13

A. Introductory heading

1.1
Jer 26.18;
2 Ki 15.5,
7,32–38;
16.1–20;
18.1–21

1 The word of the LORD that came to Mīcáh of Mō′rěshěth in the days of Jōthám, Āhăz, and Hězěkī′áh, kings of Judah, which he saw concerning Sàmạr′ïá and Jerusalem.

B. God's anger against Samaria and Judah

1.2
Jer 6.19;
22.29;
Ps 50.7;
11.4

2 Hear, you peoples, all of you;
 hearken, O earth, and all that is in it;
and let the Lord GOD be a witness against you,
 the Lord from his holy temple.

1.3
Isa 26.21;
Amos 4.13

3 For behold, the LORD is coming forth out of his place,
 and will come down and tread upon the high places of the
 earth.

1.4
Isa 64.1,2;
Nah 1.5

4 And the mountains will melt under him
 and the valleys will be cleft,
like wax before the fire,
 like waters poured down a steep place.

1.5
Isa 28.1;
Amos 8.14;
2 Chr 34.3,4

5 All this is for the transgression of Jacob
 and for the sins of the house of Israel.
What is the transgression of Jacob?
 Is it not Sàmạr′ïá?
And what is the sin of the house[a] of Judah?
 Is it not Jerusalem?

*1.6
Jer 31.5;
Amos 5.11;
Ezek 13.14

6 Therefore I will make Sàmạr′ïá a heap in the open country,
 a place for planting vineyards;
and I will pour down her stones into the valley,
 and uncover her foundations.

1.7
Deut 9.21;
2 Chr 34.7;
Isa 23.17

7 All her images shall be beaten to pieces,
 all her hires shall be burned with fire,
 and all her idols I will lay waste;
for from the hire of a harlot she gathered them,
 and to the hire of a harlot they shall return.

1.8
Isa 22.4;
32.11;
13.21,22

8 For this I will lament and wail;
 I will go stripped and naked;
I will make lamentation like the jackals,
 and mourning like the ostriches.

1.9
Jer 30.12,
15;
2 Ki 18.13;
ver 12

9 For her wound[b] is incurable;
 and it has come to Judah,
it has reached to the gate of my people,
 to Jerusalem.

---

a Gk Tg Compare Syr: Heb *what are the high places*   *b* Gk Syr Vg: Heb *wounds*

1.6 See 2 Ki 17.1–18 for the literal fulfilment of this prophecy that the Northern Kingdom of Israel would be taken into captivity by Assyria.

10 Tell it not in Găth,
   weep not at all;
in Bĕth-lĕ-ăph′răh
   roll yourselves in the dust.

11 Pass on your way,
   inhabitants of Shāphĭr,
   in nakedness and shame;
the inhabitants of Zā′ánȧn
   do not come forth;
the wailing of Bĕth-e′zėl
   shall take away from you its standing place.

12 For the inhabitants of Marȯth
   wait anxiously for good,
because evil has come down from the LORD
   to the gate of Jerusalem.

13 Harness the steeds to the chariots,
   inhabitants of Lāchĭsh;
you were c the beginning of sin
   to the daughter of Zion,
for in you were found
   the transgressions of Israel.

14 Therefore you shall give parting gifts
   to Mō′rĕshĕth-găth′;
the houses of Ăchzĭb shall be a deceitful thing
   to the kings of Israel.

15 I will again bring a conqueror upon you,
   inhabitants of Mȧre′shȧh;
the glory of Israel
   shall come to Adŭl′lȧm.

16 Make yourselves bald and cut off your hair,
   for the children of your delight;
make yourselves as bald as the eagle,
   for they shall go from you into exile.

C. The cause of God's anger

1. Their sins described

2 Woe to those who devise wickedness
   and work evil upon their beds!
When the morning dawns, they perform it,
   because it is in the power of their hand.

2 They covet fields, and seize them;
   and houses, and take them away;
they oppress a man and his house,
   a man and his inheritance.

2. God's purpose to punish

3 Therefore thus says the LORD:
Behold, against this family I am devising evil,
   from which you cannot remove your necks;
and you shall not walk haughtily,
   for it will be an evil time.

4 In that day they shall take up a taunt song against you,
   and wail with bitter lamentation,

c Cn: Heb it was

Reference column:

1.10
2 Sam 1.20

1.11
Ezek 23.29

1.12
Isa 59.9–11;
Jer 14.19

1.13
2 Ki 14.19;
Isa 36.2

1.14
2 Ki 16.8;
Josh 15.44;
Jer 15.18

1.15
Josh 15.44;
Mic 5.2;
Josh 12.15;
2 Sam 23.13

1.16
Isa 15.2;
22.12;
Lam 4.5;
Amos 7.11,
17

2.1
Isa 32.7;
Nah 1.11;
Hos 7.6,7;
Prov 3.27

2.2
Amos 8.4;
Isa 5.8;
1 Ki 21.1–
15

2.3
Amos 3.1,2;
Deut 28.48;
Jer 18.11;
Isa 2.11,12;
Amos 5.13

2.4
Hab 2.6;
Mic 1.8;
Isa 24.3;
Jer 4.13;
6.12; 8.10

and say, "We are utterly ruined;
he changes the portion of my people;
how he removes it from me!
Among our captors *d* he divides our fields."

2.5
Josh 18.4,10

5 Therefore you will have none to cast the line by lot
in the assembly of the LORD.

2.6
Isa 30.10;
Amos 2.12;
7.16;
Mic 3.6;
6.16

6 "Do not preach"—thus they preach—
"one should not preach of such things;
disgrace will not overtake us."

7 Should this be said, O house of Jacob?
Is the Spirit of the LORD impatient?
Are these his doings?
Do not my words do good
to him who walks uprightly?

2.7
Isa 50.2;
59.1;
Jer 15.16;
Ps 15.2;
84.11

2.8
Jer 12.8;
Mic 3.2,3;
7.2,3;
Ps 120.6,7

8 But you rise against my people *e* as an enemy;
you strip the robe from the peaceful, *f*
from those who pass by trustingly
with no thought of war.

2.9
Jer 10.20

9 The women of my people you drive out
from their pleasant houses;
from their young children you take away
my glory for ever.

2.10
Lev 18.25,
28,29;
Deut 12.9;
Ps 106.38

10 Arise and go,
for this is no place to rest;
because of uncleanness that destroys
with a grievous destruction.

2.11
Jer 5.13,31;
Isa 28.7;
30.10,11

11 If a man should go about and utter wind and lies,
saying, "I will preach to you of wine and strong drink,"
he would be the preacher for this people!

3. God's purpose of future deliverance

2.12
Mic 4.6,7;
5.7,8; 7.18;
Jer 33.22

12 I will surely gather all of you, O Jacob,
I will gather the remnant of Israel;
I will set them together
like sheep in a fold,
like a flock in its pasture,
a noisy multitude of men.

2.13
Hos 3.5;
Isa 52.12

13 He who opens the breach will go up before them;
they will break through and pass the gate,
going out by it.
Their king will pass on before them,
the LORD at their head.

II. The judgment followed by restoration and the reign of Messiah 3.1–5.15

A. Sins denounced and the destruction of Jerusalem foretold

3.1
Jer 5.4,5

3 And I said:
Hear, you heads of Jacob
and rulers of the house of Israel!
Is it not for you to know justice?—

d Cn: Heb *the rebellious*   *e* Cn: Heb *yesterday my people rose*
f Cn: Heb *from before a garment*

2   you who hate the good and love the evil,
who tear the skin from off my people,
and their flesh from off their bones;
3 who eat the flesh of my people,
and flay their skin from off them,
and break their bones in pieces,
and chop them up like meat[g] in a kettle,
like flesh in a caldron.

4 Then they will cry to the LORD,
but he will not answer them;
he will hide his face from them at that time,
because they have made their deeds evil.

5 Thus says the LORD concerning the prophets
who lead my people astray,
who cry "Peace"
when they have something to eat,
but declare war against him
who puts nothing into their mouths.
6 Therefore it shall be night to you, without vision,
and darkness to you, without divination.
The sun shall go down upon the prophets,
and the day shall be black over them;
7 the seers shall be disgraced,
and the diviners put to shame;
they shall all cover their lips,
for there is no answer from God.
8 But as for me, I am filled with power,
with the Spirit of the LORD,
and with justice and might,
to declare to Jacob his transgression
and to Israel his sin.

9 Hear this, you heads of the house of Jacob
and rulers of the house of Israel,
who abhor justice
and pervert all equity,
10 who build Zion with blood
and Jerusalem with wrong.
11 Its heads give judgment for a bribe,
its priests teach for hire,
its prophets divine for money;
yet they lean upon the LORD and say,
"Is not the LORD in the midst of us?
No evil shall come upon us."
12 Therefore because of you
Zion shall be plowed as a field;
Jerusalem shall become a heap of ruins,
and the mountain of the house a wooded height.

g Gk: Heb *as*

3.2	Mic 2.8; 7.2,3; Ezek 22.27
3.3	Ps 14.4; Zeph 3.3; Ezek 34.2,3; 11.3
3.4	Ps 18.41; Prov 1.28; Isa 1.15; Zech 7.13; Isa 59.2; Mic 7.13
3.5	Isa 56.10; Ezek 13.10; Jer 14.14, 15; Mic 2.11; Jer 6.14; Ezek 13.18, 19
3.6	Isa 8.20,22; Ezek 13.23; Amos 8.9
3.7	Zech 13.4; Isa 44.25; Mic 7.16; 1 Sam 28.6; ver 4
3.8	Isa 61.1,2; 58.1
3.9	ver 1; Isa 1.23
3.10	Jer 22.13; Ezek 22.27; Hab 2.12
★3.11	Isa 1.23; Hos 4.18; Jer 6.13; Isa 48.2; Jer 7.4
★3.12	Jer 26.18; Mic 4.1,2

3.11 *No evil shall come upon us.* Past blessings and deliverances gave the people of Israel a false sense of security.

3.12 *Zion shall be plowed as a field,* i.e., all buildings shall be destroyed and it will lose its identity as a city.

B. *Promise of the coming of God's kingdom*

1. *Law and peace*

4 It shall come to pass in the latter days
    that the mountain of the house of the LORD
shall be established as the highest of the mountains,
    and shall be raised up above the hills;
and peoples shall flow to it,
2 and many nations shall come, and say:
"Come, let us go up to the mountain of the LORD,
    to the house of the God of Jacob;
that he may teach us his ways
    and we may walk in his paths."
For out of Zion shall go forth the law,
    and the word of the LORD from Jerusalem.
3 He shall judge between many peoples,
    and shall decide for strong nations afar off;
and they shall beat their swords into plowshares,
    and their spears into pruning hooks;
nation shall not lift up sword against nation,
    neither shall they learn war any more;
4 but they shall sit every man under his vine and under his fig tree,
    and none shall make them afraid;
    for the mouth of the LORD of hosts has spoken.

5 For all the peoples walk
    each in the name of its god,
but we will walk in the name of the LORD our God
    for ever and ever.

2. *God's victorious reign*

6 In that day, says the LORD,
    I will assemble the lame
and gather those who have been driven away,
    and those whom I have afflicted;
7 and the lame I will make the remnant;
    and those who were cast off, a strong nation;
and the LORD will reign over them in Mount Zion
    from this time forth and for evermore.

8 And you, O tower of the flock,
    hill of the daughter of Zion,
to you shall it come,
    the former dominion shall come,
    the kingdom of the daughter of Jerusalem.

9 Now why do you cry aloud?
    Is there no king in you?
Has your counselor perished,
    that pangs have seized you like a woman in travail?

4.1
Isa 2.2–4;
Ezek 17.22;
43.12;
Jer 3.17

★4.2
Zech 2.11;
14.16;
Jer 31.6;
Isa 54.13;
42.1–4;
Zech 14.8,9

4.3
Isa 2.4;
Joel 3.10;
Ps 72.7

4.4
1 Ki 4.25;
Zech 3.10;
Isa 1.20;
40.5

★4.5
2 Ki 17.29;
Isa 26.8,13;
Zech 10.12

★4.6
Ezek 34.16;
Zeph 3.19;
Ps 147.2;
Ezek 34.13

4.7
Mic 2.12;
5.7,8; 7.18;
Isa 9.6;
Dan 7.14;
Lk 1.33;
Rev 11.15

4.8
Mic 2.12;
Isa 1.26;
Zech 9.10

4.9
Jer 8.19;
Isa 13.8;
Jer 30.6

4.2 *out of Zion shall go forth the law.* Micah depicts a restored Zion which shall be a means of blessing to all peoples.
4.5 *each in the name of its god.* All men are religious and will worship some god; if not the true God it will be a false one, an idol.
4.6 God's flock is helpless, afflicted, and scattered, but God will gather them again.

10 Writhe and groan,ʰ O daughter of Zion,
like a woman in travail;
for now you shall go forth from the city
and dwell in the open country;
you shall go to Babylon.
There you shall be rescued,
there the LORD will redeem you
from the hand of your enemies.

11 Now many nations
are assembled against you,
saying, "Let her be profaned,
and let our eyes gaze upon Zion."
12 But they do not know
the thoughts of the LORD,
they do not understand his plan,
that he has gathered them as sheaves to the threshing floor.
13 Arise and thresh,
O daughter of Zion,
for I will make your horn iron
and your hoofs bronze;
you shall beat in pieces many peoples,
and shallⁱ devote their gain to the LORD,
their wealth to the Lord of the whole earth.

5ʲ Now you are walled about with a wall;ᵏ
siege is laid against us;
with a rod they strike upon the cheek
the ruler of Israel.

3. The coming Messiah and his reign

2ˡ But you, O Bĕth′lĕhĕm Ĕph′rȧtȧh,
who are little to be among the clans of Judah,
from you shall come forth for me
one who is to be ruler in Israel,
whose origin is from of old,
from ancient days.
3 Therefore he shall give them up until the time
when she who is in travail has brought forth;
then the rest of his brethren shall return
to the people of Israel.

ʰ Heb uncertain   ⁱ Gk Syr Tg: Heb I will   ʲ Ch 4.14 in Heb
ᵏ Cn Compare Gk: Heb obscure   ˡ Ch 5.1 in Heb

Margin refs: *4.10 Hos 2.14; Isa 45.13; Mic 7.8–12; Isa 48.20; 52.9–12 | 4.11 Lam 2.16; Obad 12; Mic 7.10 | 4.12 Isa 55.8; Rom 11.33; Isa 21.10 | 4.13 Isa 41.15; Dan 2.44; Zech 4.14 | 5.1 Jer 5.7; 1 Ki 22.24; Lam 3.30 | *5.2 Mt 2.6; 1 Sam 17.12; 23.23; Lk 2.4; Isa 9.6; | 5.3 Mic 4.10; Hos 11.8; Isa 10.20–22

4.10 It is significant that Micah, like his great contemporary Isaiah, was granted a revelation of the Babylonian captivity of 586–537 B.C. even in an age when Babylon was only a vassal of Assyria. Thus these two eighth century prophets foresaw events which transpired in the sixth century B.C.

5.2 This verse was not written merely to impress the reader with the fact of predictive prophecy, but it serves to link the Messiah with the Davidic line. As a "Son of David" the Messiah would come from the city of David's birth, Bethlehem. In Mt 2.5 it is apparent that the Jews accepted this prophecy as genuine. A second truth emerges from Micah's prophecy: the Son existed long before His birth in Bethlehem, and was active in the history of redemption. The Hebrew word here translated origin literally means "His goings-forth" and therefore points to the occasions when the LORD "went forth" to reveal His truth to His people or to redeem them from bondage or peril. (The translation from ancient days is probably better than the KJV "from everlasting," since this Hebrew expression refers to events in ancient patriarchal or Davidic history in the three instances where it occurs elsewhere in the Old Testament.)

4 And he shall stand and feed his flock in the strength of the LORD,
   in the majesty of the name of the LORD his God.
And they shall dwell secure, for now he shall be great
   to the ends of the earth.

5.4
Isa 40.11;
Ezek 34.23;
Isa 52.13;
Lk 1.32

5 And this shall be peace,
   when the Assyrian comes into our land
   and treads upon our soil,*m*
that we will raise against him seven shepherds
   and eight princes of men;

5.5
Isa 9.6;
Rev 11.15;
Isa 8.7,8

6 they shall rule the land of Assyria with the sword,
   and the land of Nĭmrŏd with the drawn sword;*n*
and they *o* shall deliver us from the Assyrian
   when he comes into our land
   and treads within our border.

5.6
Nah 2.11–
13;
Zeph 2.13;
Gen 10.8;
Isa 37.36,37

7 Then the remnant of Jacob shall be
   in the midst of many peoples
like dew from the LORD,
   like showers upon the grass,
which tarry not for men
   nor wait for the sons of men.

5.7
Mic 2.12;
Deut 32.2;
Hos 14.5

8 And the remnant of Jacob shall be among the nations,
   in the midst of many peoples,
like a lion among the beasts of the forest,
   like a young lion among the flocks of sheep,
which, when it goes through, treads down
   and tears in pieces, and there is none to deliver.

5.8
Mic 4.13;
Zech 10.5;
Hos 5.14;
Ps 50.22

9 Your hand shall be lifted up over your adversaries,
   and all your enemies shall be cut off.

5.9
Ps 10.12;
21.8;
Isa 26.11

10 And in that day, says the LORD,
   I will cut off your horses from among you
   and will destroy your chariots;

5.10
Isa 2.7;
Hos 14.3;
Zech 9.10

11 and I will cut off the cities of your land
   and throw down all your strongholds;

5.11
Isa 1.7;
Hos 10.14;
Amos 5.9

12 and I will cut off sorceries from your hand,
   and you shall have no more soothsayers;

5.12
Deut 18.10–
12;
Isa 2.6

13 and I will cut off your images
   and your pillars from among you,
and you shall bow down no more
   to the work of your hands;

5.13
Zech 13.2;
Isa 2.8

14 and I will root out your Ăshē′rĭm from among you
   and destroy your cities.

5.14
Ex 34.13;
Isa 17.8;
27.9

15 And in anger and wrath I will execute vengeance
   upon the nations that did not obey.

5.15
Ps 149.7;
Isa 65.12

III. Divine punishment followed by divine mercy 6.1–7.20

A. God's complaint against a rebellious people

6 Hear what the LORD says:
   Arise, plead your case before the mountains,
   and let the hills hear your voice.

6.1
Ps 50.1;
Ezek 6.2,3

m Gk: Heb *in our palaces* *n* Cn: Heb *in its entrances* *o* Heb *he*

2 Hear, you mountains, the controversy of the LORD,
    and you enduring foundations of the earth;
for the LORD has a controversy with his people,
    and he will contend with Israel.

3 "O my people, what have I done to you?
    In what have I wearied you? Answer me!
4 For I brought you up from the land of Egypt,
    and redeemed you from the house of bondage;
and I sent before you Moses,
    Aaron, and Miriam.
5 O my people, remember what Bālák king of Mōăb devised,
    and what Bālaăm the son of Bēor answered him,
and what happened from Shĭttĭm to Gĭlgăl,
    that you may know the saving acts of the LORD."

6 "With what shall I come before the LORD,
    and bow myself before God on high?
Shall I come before him with burnt offerings,
    with calves a year old?
7 Will the LORD be pleased with thousands of rams,
    with ten thousands of rivers of oil?
Shall I give my first-born for my transgression,
    the fruit of my body for the sin of my soul?"

8 He has showed you, O man, what is good;
    and what does the LORD require of you
but to do justice, and to love kindness,[p]
    and to walk humbly with your God?

9 The voice of the LORD cries to the city—
    and it is sound wisdom to fear thy name:
"Hear, O tribe and assembly of the city![q]
10   Can I forget[r] the treasures of wickedness in the house of the
        wicked,
    and the scant measure that is accursed?
11 Shall I acquit the man with wicked scales
    and with a bag of deceitful weights?
12 Your[s] rich men are full of violence;
    your[s] inhabitants speak lies,
    and their tongue is deceitful in their mouth.
13 Therefore I have begun[t] to smite you,
    making you desolate because of your sins.
14 You shall eat, but not be satisfied,

	6.2
	Deut 32.1;
	Hos 12.2;
	Isa 1.8;
	Hos 4.1
	6.3
	Ps 50.7;
	Jer 2.5;
	Isa 43.22,23
	6.4
	Ex 12.51;
	Deut 4.20;
	7.8;
	Ps 77.20;
	Ex 15.20;
	6.5
	Num 22.5,
	6;
	Rev 2.14;
	Num 25.1;
	Josh 4.19;
	5.9,10;
	Judg 5.11;
	1 Sam 12.7
	6.6
	Ps 40.6–8;
	51.16,17
	*6.7
	2 Ki 16.3;
	21.6;
	Jer 7.31
	*6.8
	Deut 10.12;
	1 Sam
	15.22;
	Hos 6.6;
	12.6;
	Isa 56.1;
	57.15; 66.2
	6.10
	Jer 5.26,27;
	Amos 3.10;
	8.5
	6.11
	Hos 12.7
	6.12
	Amos 6.3,4;
	Mic 2.1,2;
	Jer 9.3,5;
	Hos 7.13;
	Amos 2.4;
	Isa 3.8
	6.13
	Mic 1.9;
	Isa 1.7;
	6.11
	6.14
	Lev 26.26;
	Isa 9.20;
	30.6

p Or steadfast love   q Cn Compare Gk: Heb and who has appointed it yet
r Cn: Heb uncertain   s Heb whose   t Gk Syr Vg: Heb have made sick

6.7 *Shall I give my first-born ... ?* Human sacrifice was practiced by apostate Israelites who took part in Molech worship, although it was distinctly forbidden in Israel. Cf. 2 Ki 16.3; 21.2, 6; Jer 7.31; 19.4–6.
6.8 Some have supposed that this passage teaches that God's only requirement for salvation is a virtuous life, religious dogma being comparatively nonessential. But such an interpretation completely overlooks the setting in which this pronouncement is given.

It is addressed not to the heathen or the human race in general, but only to that special section of mankind which stands in a covenant relationship to Him. In Micah's generation the dominant issue was the insufficiency of a dead faith which did not eventuate in a holy life. God lays emphasis here upon the fruits of a sincere belief and trust in Him, as opposed to an empty and hypocritical profession of faith. The same emphasis is found in the New Testament letter of James.

and there shall be hunger in your inward parts;
you shall put away, but not save,
and what you save I will give to the sword.

6.15
Deut 28.38;
Jer 12.13;
Amos 5.11;
Zeph 1.13
*6.16
1 Ki 16.25–
33;
Jer 7.24;
19.8;
29.18;
51.51

15 You shall sow, but not reap;
   you shall tread olives, but not anoint yourselves with oil;
you shall tread grapes, but not drink wine.

16 For you have kept the statutes of Ōmrī,*u*
   and all the works of the house of Āhăb;
   and you have walked in their counsels;
that I may make you a desolation, and your*v* inhabitants a
   hissing;
   so you shall bear the scorn of the peoples."*w*

B. *The confession of sin and the hope of mercy*

7.1
Isa 24.13;
28.4;
Hos 9.10

7 Woe is me! For I have become
   as when the summer fruit has been gathered,
   as when the vintage has been gleaned:
there is no cluster to eat,
   no first-ripe fig which my soul desires.

7.2
Ps 12.1;
Isa 57.1;
59.7;
Jer 5.26;
Hos 5.1

2 The godly man has perished from the earth,
   and there is none upright among men;
they all lie in wait for blood,
   and each hunts his brother with a net.

7.3
Prov 4.16,
17;
Amos 5.12;
Mic 3.11

3 Their hands are upon what is evil, to do it diligently;
   the prince and the judge ask for a bribe,
and the great man utters the evil desire of his soul;
   thus they weave it together.

7.4
Ezek 2.6;
28.24;
Nah 1.10;
Isa 10.3;
Hos 9.7;
Isa 22.5

4 The best of them is like a brier,
   the most upright of them a thorn hedge.
The day of their*x* watchmen, of their*x* punishment, has come;
   now their confusion is at hand.

7.5
Jer 9.4

5 Put no trust in a neighbor,
   have no confidence in a friend;
guard the doors of your mouth
   from her who lies in your bosom;

7.6
Ezek 22.7;
Mt 10.21,
35,36;
Lk 12.53

6 for the son treats the father with contempt,
   the daughter rises up against her mother,
the daughter-in-law against her mother-in-law;
   a man's enemies are the men of his own house.

7.7
Hab 2.1;
Ps 130.5;
4.3

7 But as for me, I will look to the LORD,
   I will wait for the God of my salvation;
   my God will hear me.

7.8
Prov 24.17;
Lam 4.21;
Ps 37.24;
Isa 9.2
7.9
Lam 3.39,
40;
Isa 42.7,16;
56.1

8 Rejoice not over me, O my enemy;
   when I fall, I shall rise;
when I sit in darkness,
   the LORD will be a light to me.

9 I will bear the indignation of the LORD
   because I have sinned against him,

---

u Gk Syr Vg Tg: Heb *the statutes of Omri are kept*   *v* Heb *its*
w Gk: Heb *my people*   *x* Heb *your*

6.16 *the statutes of Omri* enforced the worship of Baal. See 1 Ki 16.25–32 and 1 Ki 18.19–
40 for a description of the life of Omri and of
Elijah's triumphs over Omri's son Ahab.

until he pleads my cause
and executes judgment for me.
He will bring me forth to the light;
I shall behold his deliverance.
10 Then my enemy will see,
and shame will cover her who said to me,
"Where is the LORD your God?"
My eyes will gloat over her;
now she will be trodden down
like the mire of the streets.

11 A day for the building of your walls!
In that day the boundary shall be far extended.
12 In that day they will come to you,
from Assyria to*y* Egypt,
and from Egypt to the River,
from sea to sea and from mountain to mountain.
13 But the earth will be desolate
because of its inhabitants,
for the fruit of their doings.

14 Shepherd thy people with thy staff,
the flock of thy inheritance,
who dwell alone in a forest
in the midst of a garden land;
let them feed in Bāshȧn and Gïl'ëȧd
as in the days of old.

15 As in the days when you came out of the land of Egypt
I will show them*z* marvelous things.

16 The nations shall see and be ashamed
of all their might;
they shall lay their hands on their mouths;
their ears shall be deaf;
17 they shall lick the dust like a serpent,
like the crawling things of the earth;
they shall come trembling out of their strongholds,
they shall turn in dread to the LORD our God,
and they shall fear because of thee.

18 Who is a God like thee, pardoning iniquity
and passing over transgression
for the remnant of his inheritance?
He does not retain his anger for ever
because he delights in steadfast love.
19 He will again have compassion upon us,
he will tread our iniquities under foot.
Thou wilt cast all our*a* sins
into the depths of the sea.
20 Thou wilt show faithfulness to Jacob
and steadfast love to Abraham,
as thou hast sworn to our fathers
from the days of old.

y Cn: Heb *and cities of*   *z* Heb *him*   *a* Gk Syr Vg Tg: Heb *their*

Cross-references:
7.10 Ps 35.26; Isa 51.23; Zech 10.5
7.11 Isa 54.11; Zeph 2.2
7.12 Isa 11.16; 19.23–25
7.13 Jer 25.11; Mic 6.13; Isa 3.10,11; Mic 3.4
7.14 Mic 5.4; Ps 23.4; Jer 50.19; Amos 9.11
7.15 Ex 3.20; 20.34; Ps 78.12
7.16 Job 21.5; Mic 3.7
7.17 Ps 72.9; Isa 49.23; Deut 32.24; Ps 18.45; Isa 59.19
7.18 Ex 34.7,9; Isa 43.25; Jer 32.41
7.19 Jer 50.20; Isa 38.17; 43.25; Jer 31.34
7.20 Lk 1.55,72; Deut 7.8,12

INTRODUCTION TO
THE BOOK OF
NAHUM

Authorship and Background: The writer of this book, Nahum the Elkoshite, apparently was from Judah, but the location of the town of Elkosh is unknown. Nahum means "consolation," "comfort," or "relief." He was a contemporary of Zephaniah, Habakkuk, and Jeremiah. He prophesied during the second half of the seventh century B.C., prior to the destruction of Nineveh in 612 B.C. The exact date of the book is unknown, but it was probably composed around 620 B.C. Since the sack of No (i.e., No-amon or Thebes) is an accomplished fact (ca. 663 B.C. by Ashurbanipal of Assyria), and the sack of Nineveh is impending (612 B.C.), the book can be dated between these two events.

The earlier prophecy of Jonah forecast the divine judgment that would fall upon Nineveh unless its people repented. When Nahum wrote, however, the day of opportunity for Nineveh had passed; there is no mention of repentance. The messages of these two prophecies, separated by a century and a half, illustrate the patience of God in dealing with sinning nations.

Characteristics: Nahum writes in white heat of the downfall of Nineveh. He breathes out a spirit of divine judgment. His prediction in poetic form is vivid and forceful and may be compared favorably with the Song of Deborah in Judg 5. Burning with moral indignation, he speaks with great plainness concerning two major themes. First he points to Nineveh's ruthless military power, stating that "all who take the sword will perish by the sword" (Mt 26.52). God is against such tyrants (2.11–13), and is responsible for their overthrow and destruction. He also denounces dishonest merchantmen who acquire wealth at the expense of morality and honesty. God is also against such (3.5). His only word to Judah is for them to observe their religious feasts and to fulfil their religious obligations (1.15). The language of Nahum in which he describes the siege and final fall of Nineveh is graphic and amazingly accurate in its details.

Contents:

I. The psalm of the LORD's majesty. 1.1–15: Nahum describes the majesty and power of an angry God who will punish His enemies. God's verdict is against Nineveh, and there shall be relief for Judah.

II. The siege and fall of Nineveh. 2.1–13: Nahum describes the coming of the destroyer, the siege and the sacking of the city; its final overthrow.

III. The reasons for Nineveh's destruction. 3.1–19: Nahum describes Nineveh's lies, thievery, harlotry, and witchcraft. God's verdict is righteous. He reminds Nineveh of the fate of Thebes (No-amon). Let Nineveh prepare for war; it will do her no good. She shall be destroyed.

THE BOOK OF
NAHUM

I. *The psalm of the* LORD'S *majesty 1.1–15*

1 An oracle concerning Nĭn'ĕvĕh. The book of the vision of Nāhŭm of Ĕlkósh.

2 The LORD is a jealous God and avenging,
   the LORD is avenging and wrathful;
the LORD takes vengeance on his adversaries
   and keeps wrath for his enemies.
3 The LORD is slow to anger and of great might,
   and the LORD will by no means clear the guilty.

His way is in whirlwind and storm,
   and the clouds are the dust of his feet.
4 He rebukes the sea and makes it dry,
   he dries up all the rivers;
Bāshăn and Carmĕl wither,
   the bloom of Lebanon fades.
5 The mountains quake before him,
   the hills melt;
the earth is laid waste before him,
   the world and all that dwell therein.

6 Who can stand before his indignation?
   Who can endure the heat of his anger?
His wrath is poured out like fire,
   and the rocks are broken asunder by him.
7 The LORD is good,
   a stronghold in the day of trouble;
he knows those who take refuge in him.
8 But with an overflowing flood
   he will make a full end of his adversaries,[a]
   and will pursue his enemies into darkness.
9 What do you plot against the LORD?
   He will make a full end;
   he will not take vengeance[b] twice on his foes.[c]
10 Like entangled thorns they are consumed,[d]
   like dry stubble.

a Gk: Heb *her place* b Gk: Heb *rise up*
c Cn: Heb *distress*
d Heb *are consumed, drunken as with their drink*

*1.1
Isa 13.1;
Hab 1.1;
Nah 2.8;
3.7;
Zeph 2.13
1.2
Ex 20.5;
Deut 4.24;
32.35,41;
Ps 94.1
1.3
Ex 34.6,7;
Ps 103.8;
Isa 29.6;
Ps 104.3
1.4
Ps 106.9;
Isa 33.9
1.5
Ex 19.18;
Mic 1.4;
Isa 24.1,20
1.6
Jer 10.10;
Mal 3.2;
Isa 66.15;
1 Ki 19.11
1.7
1 Chr 16.34;
Ps 28.8
1.8
Isa 28.2,18;
13.9,10
1.9
Ps 2.1;
Isa 28.22
1.10
2 Sam 23.6;
Mal 4.1

1.1 The city of Nineveh was situated on the Tigris River. It was the ancient capital of Assyria. The might of the Assyrian empire seemed absolutely invincible, yet its downfall was here plainly predicted—a prediction later fulfilled in detail. During the age of Jonah (ca. 770 B.C.), judgment had been averted from Nineveh because the city had repented. But now in the seventh century Nahum was prophesying its utter destruction, as did his contemporary, Zephaniah (Zeph 2.13–15). In 612 B.C. the Chaldeans and the Medes finally closed in on Nineveh and laid it under siege for two years before it fell. So complete was its devastation that two hundred years later Xenophon could pass by the ruins without being able to discover its name from the local inhabitants. Alexander the Great later fought the battle of Arbela in 331 B.C., not far from the site where Nineveh had stood. It was not until 1845 that the site was identified and the ruins uncovered. Archaeological investigations there have confirmed the biblical account of its destruction.

1.11
ver 9;
Ezek 11.2

11 Did one not*e* come out from you,
    who plotted evil against the LORD,
    and counseled villainy?

1.12
Isa 10.16–
19,33,34;
54.7,8

12 Thus says the LORD,
"Though they be strong and many,*f*
    they will be cut off and pass away.
Though I have afflicted you,
    I will afflict you no more.

1.13
Isa 9.4;
Jer 2.20

13 And now I will break his yoke from off you
    and will burst your bonds asunder."

1.14
Isa 46.1,2;
Mic 5.13,
14;
Ezek 32.22,
23

14 The LORD has given commandment about you:
"No more shall your name be perpetuated;
from the house of your gods I will cut off
    the graven image and the molten image.
I will make your grave, for you are vile."

1.15
Isa 40.9;
Ps 52.7;
Rom 10.15;
Lev 23.2,4;
Isa 52.1;
Joel 3.17;
Isa 29.7,8

15*g* Behold, on the mountains the feet of him
    who brings good tidings,
    who proclaims peace!
Keep your feasts, O Judah,
    fulfil your vows,
for never again shall the wicked come against you,
    he is utterly cut off.

II. *The siege and fall of Nineveh 2.1–13*

2.1
Jer 51.20–
23;
Nah 3.12,
14

2 The shatterer has come up against you.
    Man the ramparts;
    watch the road;
gird your loins;
    collect all your strength.

2.2
Isa 60.15;
Ezek 37.21–
23

2 (For the LORD is restoring the majesty of Jacob
    as the majesty of Israel,
for plunderers have stripped them
    and ruined their branches.)

2.3
Ezek 23.14,
15;
Job 39.23

3 The shield of his mighty men is red,
    his soldiers are clothed in scarlet.
The chariots flash like flame*h*
    when mustered in array;
    the chargers*i* prance.

2.4
Ezek 26.10;
Jer 4.13

4 The chariots rage in the streets,
    they rush to and fro through the squares;
they gleam like torches,
    they dart like lightning.

2.5
Nah 3.18;
Jer 46.12

5 The officers are summoned,
    they stumble as they go,
they hasten to the wall,
    the mantelet is set up.

2.6
Nah 3.18

6 The river gates are opened,

---

e Cn: Heb *fully*   *f* Heb uncertain   *g* Ch 2.1 in Heb
h Cn: The meaning of the Hebrew word is uncertain
i Cn Compare Gk Syr: Heb *cypresses*

the palace is in dismay;

7 its mistress[j] is stripped, she is carried off,
    her maidens lamenting,
moaning like doves,
    and beating their breasts.

8 Nin′eveh is like a pool
    whose waters[k] run away.
"Halt! Halt!" they cry;
    but none turns back.

9 Plunder the silver,
    plunder the gold!
There is no end of treasure,
    or wealth of every precious thing.

10 Desolate! Desolation and ruin!
    Hearts faint and knees tremble,
anguish is on all loins,
    all faces grow pale!

11 Where is the lions' den,
    the cave[l] of the young lions,
where the lion brought his prey,
    where his cubs were, with none to disturb?

12 The lion tore enough for his whelps
    and strangled prey for his lionesses;
he filled his caves with prey
    and his dens with torn flesh.

13 Behold, I am against you, says the LORD of hosts, and I will burn your[m] chariots in smoke, and the sword shall devour your young lions; I will cut off your prey from the earth, and the voice of your messengers shall no more be heard.

III. The reasons for Nineveh's destruction 3.1–19

A. The sin of Nineveh

3 Woe to the bloody city,
    all full of lies and booty—
no end to the plunder!

2 The crack of whip, and rumble of wheel,
    galloping horse and bounding chariot!

3 Horsemen charging,
    flashing sword and glittering spear,
hosts of slain,
    heaps of corpses,
dead bodies without end—
    they stumble over the bodies!

4 And all for the countless harlotries of the harlot,

Marginal references

2.7	Isa 59.11; 32.12
2.8	Nah 3.7; Jer 46.5; 47.3
2.10	Ps 22.14; Isa 13.7,8; Joel 2.6
2.11	Isa 5.29; Jer 4.7; Nah 3.1
2.12	Isa 10.6–14; Jer 51.34
2.13	Nah 3.5; Ps 46.9; Isa 49.24,25
★3.1	Ezek 24.6,9
3.2	Nah 2.3,4; Jer 47.3
3.3	Hab 3.11; Isa 34.3; 66.16; 2 Ki 19.35
3.4	Isa 23.17; Rev 17.1,2; Isa 47.9; Rev 18.3

j The meaning of the Hebrew is uncertain
k Cn Compare Gk: Heb *from the days that she has become, and they*
l Cn: Heb *pasture*
m Heb *her*

3.1 Nahum states what is constantly taught in Scripture—that as we sow, thus we must reap. The spiritual laws of cause and effect must prevail and vindicate the timeless principles of justice and equity. Sin and wickedness yield a harvest of destruction.

    graceful and of deadly charms,
who betrays nations with her harlotries,
    and peoples with her charms.

3.5
Nah 2.13;
Isa 47.2,3;
Jer 13.22;
Ezek 16.37

5 Behold, I am against you,
    says the LORD of hosts,
    and will lift up your skirts over your face;
and I will let nations look on your nakedness
    and kingdoms on your shame.

3.6
Job 9.31;
Mal 2.9;
Isa 14.16;
Jer 51.37

6 I will throw filth at you
    and treat you with contempt,
    and make you a gazingstock.

3.7
Jer 51.9;
Nah 2.8;
Zeph 2.13;
Isa 51.19;
Jer 15.5

7 And all who look on you will shrink from you and say,
Wasted is Nin′eveh; who will bemoan her?
    whence shall I seek comforters for her?[n]

B. The justness of the judgment

*3.8
Jer 46.25;
Ezek 30.14–
16;
Isa 19.6–8

8 Are you better than Thēbes[o]
    that sat by the Nile,
with water around her,
    her rampart a sea,
    and water her wall?

3.9
Isa 20.5;
Ezek 27.10;
30.5; 38.5;
2 Chr 12.3;
16.8

9 Ethiopia was her strength,
    Egypt too, and that without limit;
    Put and the Libyans were her[p] helpers.

3.10
Isa 20.4;
13.16;
Hos 13.16;
Lam 2.19;
Joel 3.3;
Obad 11

10 Yet she was carried away,
    she went into captivity;
    her little ones were dashed in pieces
    at the head of every street;
for her honored men lots were cast,
    and all her great men were bound in chains.

3.11
Jer 25.27;
Isa 2.10,19

11 You also will be drunken,
    you will be dazed;
you will seek
    a refuge from the enemy.

3.12
Isa 28.4;
Rev 6.13

12 All your fortresses are like fig trees
    with first-ripe figs—
if shaken they fall
    into the mouth of the eater.

3.13
Jer 50.37;
51.30;
Ps 147.13

13 Behold, your troops
    are women in your midst.
The gates of your land
    are wide open to your foes;
    fire has devoured your bars.

3.14
2 Chr 32.3,
4,11;
Nah 2.1

14 Draw water for the siege,
    strengthen your forts;

n Gk: Heb *you*   *o* Heb *Nō-ā′mȯn*   *p* Gk: Heb *your*

3.8 *Are you better than Thebes?* Thebes, or No-amon, located 400 miles south of modern Cairo, was one of the great cities of the ancient world. Nahum probably refers to the destruction of Thebes by Ashurbanipal (663 B.C.). So if Thebes, the Egyptian capital of a brilliant dynasty, could be destroyed, why not Nineveh?

go into the clay,
    tread the mortar,
    take hold of the brick mold!
15 There will the fire devour you,
    the sword will cut you off.
    It will devour you like the locust.

Multiply yourselves like the locust,
    multiply like the grasshopper!
16 You increased your merchants
    more than the stars of the heavens.
    The locust spreads its wings and flies away.

17 Your princes are like grasshoppers,
    your scribes*q* like clouds of locusts
settling on the fences
    in a day of cold—
when the sun rises, they fly away;
    no one knows where they are.

18 Your shepherds are asleep,
    O king of Assyria;
    your nobles slumber.
Your people are scattered on the mountains
    with none to gather them.
19 There is no assuaging your hurt,
    your wound is grievous.
All who hear the news of you
    clap their hands over you.
For upon whom has not come
    your unceasing evil?

q Or marshals

3.15 ver 13; Joel 1.4
3.16 Isa 23.8
3.17 Jer 51.27; Rev 9.7
3.18 Ps 76.5,6; Isa 56.10; Jer 51.57; Nah 2.5; 1 Ki 22.17
*3.19 Mic 1.9; Lam 2.15; Zeph 2.15

3.19 *All who hear the news of you.* The Assyrians sought to rule all of western Asia and they were universally hated. Nineveh was destroyed, never to rise again.

INTRODUCTION TO
THE BOOK OF
HABAKKUK

Authorship and Background: Little is known about the author of this book except his name. The title of the book in the Septuagint is *Ambakoum*. Jerome thought the name Habakkuk came from a Hebrew root meaning "to clasp." There is some reason to think the name may derive from an Assyrian word signifying a vegetable or a plant. Habakkuk probably prophesied just before the invasion of Judah by the Chaldeans, which would place the date of the book close to the end of the seventh century B.C. He was a contemporary of Jeremiah, whose ministry was much longer than his. The national catastrophe, which was imminent and which had been predicted before the prophet's day, had now come, and Habakkuk spoke and lived to see the fulfilment of his words.

Characteristics: Habakkuk engages in a soliloquy between himself and God. He arraigns God rather than Judah, implying that He allows injustice and wickedness to go unchecked. He asks age-old questions: "Why are the wicked ruling classes allowed to oppress the weak in Jewish society?" God answers, "I will punish them by the Chaldean invasion" (cf. Hab 1.1–11). Next he asks how God can allow wicked Judah to be punished by a nation which itself is more wicked than Judah. His sense of justice is violated by such a thought. God replies that this result is in accord with the divine purpose. Habakkuk seeks further light as he acknowledges that the judgment of God against Judah is just. Then it is that God reveals that the Chaldeans in their turn shall be destroyed, and at last the people of God will possess the earth. Habakkuk writes passionately and inquiringly. Some of his phrases: "the righteous shall live by his faith" (2.4); "the earth will be filled with the knowledge of the glory of the LORD, as the waters cover the sea" (2.14); "in wrath remember mercy" (3.2) stand out as precious jewels in splendid array.

Contents:

I.   Habakkuk's first question. 1.1–4: Why does wrong seem to triumph?

II. God's first answer. 1.5–11: Judean wrongdoers will be punished.

III. Habakkuk's second question. 1.12—2.1: Why does God allow the more wicked to punish the less wicked?

IV. God's second answer. 2.2–20: Chaldea, in turn, shall be punished. The righteous shall live by his faith.

V.   The prayer of Habakkuk. 3.1–19: He asks God in wrath to remember mercy. God replies that he is mighty to punish the wicked and to save those who repent. Habakkuk closes with praise, "God, the LORD, is my strength" (3.19).

THE BOOK OF
HABAKKUK

I. *Habakkuk's first question: why does evil go unpunished?*
1.1–4

1 The oracle of God which Hăbăk′kŭk the prophet saw.
2 O LORD, how long shall I cry for help,
and thou wilt not hear?
Or cry to thee "Violence!"
and thou wilt not save?
3 Why dost thou make me see wrongs
and look upon trouble?
Destruction and violence are before me;
strife and contention arise.
4 So the law is slacked
and justice never goes forth.
For the wicked surround the righteous,
so justice goes forth perverted.

II. *God's first answer: he will use the Chaldeans*
to punish 1.5–11

5 Look among the nations, and see;
wonder and be astounded.
For I am doing a work in your days
that you would not believe if told.
6 For lo, I am rousing the Chăldē′ăns,
that bitter and hasty nation,
who march through the breadth of the earth,
to seize habitations not their own.
7 Dread and terrible are they;
their justice and dignity proceed from themselves.
8 Their horses are swifter than leopards,
more fierce than the evening wolves;
their horsemen press proudly on.
Yea, their horsemen come from afar;
they fly like an eagle swift to devour.
9 They all come for violence;
terror[a] of them goes before them.
They gather captives like sand.
10 At kings they scoff,
and of rulers they make sport.
They laugh at every fortress,
for they heap up earth and take it.
11 Then they sweep by like the wind and go on,
guilty men, whose own might is their god!

a Cn: Heb uncertain

1.1
Isa 13.1;
Nah 1.1
1.2
Ps 13.1,2;
22.1,2
1.3
ver 13;
Jer 20.8
★1.4
Ps 119.126;
22.12;
Isa 5.20

1.5
Acts 13.41;
Isa 29.9,14
★1.6
2 Ki 24.2;
Jer 4.11–13;
5.15; 8.10
1.7
Isa 18.2,7;
Jer 39.5–9
1.8
Jer 4.13;
5.6;
Ezek 17.3;
Hos 8.1
1.9
Hab 2.5
★1.10
2 Chr 36.6,
10;
Isa 10.9;
14.16;
Jer 32.24;
Ezek 26.8
1.11
Jer 4.11,12;
2.3;
Dan 4.30

1.4 *the law is slacked*, i.e., the law had lost its authority. It was both disregarded and perverted.
1.6 *the Chaldeans* were a tribe in southern Babylon which, under Nabopolassar, became independent of Assyria and, under Nebuchadnezzar, dominated all of western Asia including Judea, which fell in 586 B.C.
1.10 *They laugh at every fortress*, i.e., every fortress will fall before their attack.

III. *Habakkuk's second question: why will God use the more wicked to punish the less wicked? 1.12–2.1*

1.12
Deut 33.27;
Ps 90.2;
Isa 10.5–7;
Deut 32.4

12 Art thou not from everlasting,
  O LORD my God, my Holy One?
  We shall not die.
O LORD, thou hast ordained them as a judgment;
  and thou, O Rock, hast established them for chastisement.

1.13
Jer 12.1,2;
Isa 24.16;
Ps 50.21;
56.1,2

13 Thou who art of purer eyes than to behold evil
  and canst not look on wrong,
why dost thou look on faithless men,
  and art silent when the wicked swallows up
  the man more righteous than he?

1.14
Ecc 9.12

14 For thou makest men like the fish of the sea,
  like crawling things that have no ruler.

1.15
Jer 16.16;
Amos 4.2;
Ps 10.9

15 He brings all of them up with a hook,
  he drags them out with his net,
he gathers them in his seine;
  so he rejoices and exults.

16 Therefore he sacrifices to his net
  and burns incense to his seine;
for by them he lives in luxury,[b]
  and his food is rich.

1.17
Isa 19.8;
14.5,6

17 Is he then to keep on emptying his net,
  and mercilessly slaying nations for ever?

2.1
Isa 21.8,11;
Ps 5.3; 85.8

2 I will take my stand to watch,
     and station myself on the tower,
  and look forth to see what he will say to me,
     and what I will answer concerning my complaint.

IV. *God's second answer: the Chaldeans shall be punished also 2.2–20*

A. *Chaldea is greedy*

2.2
Deut 27.8;
Isa 8.1;
Rev 1.19

2 And the LORD answered me:
"Write the vision;
  make it plain upon tablets,
  so he may run who reads it.

2.3
Dan 8.17,
19; 10.14;
Ezek 12.25;
Heb 10.37,
38

3 For still the vision awaits its time;
  it hastens to the end—it will not lie.
If it seem slow, wait for it;
  it will surely come, it will not delay.

*2.4
Rom 1.17;
Gal 3.11;
Heb 10.38,
39

4 Behold, he whose soul is not upright in him shall fail,[c]
  but the righteous shall live by his faith.[d]

b Heb *his portion is fat*   *c* Cn: Heb *is puffed up*   *d* Or *faithfulness*

2.4 This verse is quoted three times with some variation in the New Testament (Rom 1.17; Gal 3.11; Heb 10.38, 39) as proof of the proposition that salvation is granted by grace through faith. 2.4 might be rendered, "Behold his soul is puffed up; it is not upright in him; but a righteous man by his faith (or, faithfulness) shall live." The Jewish Talmud states that Habakkuk reduced the 613 commandments of Moses to one: "the righteous shall live by his faith." In effect, this is true.

5 Moreover, wine is treacherous;
    the arrogant man shall not abide.*e*
His greed is as wide as Shēōl;
    like death he has never enough.
He gathers for himself all nations,
    and collects as his own all peoples."

★2.5
Prov 20.1;
21.24;
2 Ki 14.10;
Jer 25.9

6 Shall not all these take up their taunt against him, in scoffing
derision of him, and say,
"Woe to him who heaps up what is not his own—
    for how long?—
    and loads himself with pledges!"
7 Will not your debtors suddenly arise,
    and those awake who will make you tremble?
    Then you will be booty for them.
8 Because you have plundered many nations,
    all the remnant of the peoples shall plunder you,
for the blood of men and violence to the earth,
    to cities and all who dwell therein.

★2.6ff
Jer 50.13;
ver 12;
Ezek 18.12;
Amos 2.8

2.7
Prov 29.1

2.8
Isa 33.1;
Zech 2.8;
ver 17

B. *Chaldea is covetous*

9 Woe to him who gets evil gain for his house,
    to set his nest on high,
    to be safe from the reach of harm!
10 You have devised shame to your house
    by cutting off many peoples;
    you have forfeited your life.
11 For the stone will cry out from the wall,
    and the beam from the woodwork respond.

2.9
Jer 22.13;
Ezek 22.27;
Jer 49.16

2.10
2 Ki 9.26;
ver 16;
Prov 1.18;
Jer 26.19

2.11
Josh 24.27;
Lk 19.40

C. *Chaldea is cruel*

12 Woe to him who builds a town with blood,
    and founds a city on iniquity!
13 Behold, is it not from the LORD of hosts
    that peoples labor only for fire,
    and nations weary themselves for nought?
14 For the earth will be filled
    with the knowledge of the glory of the LORD,
    as the waters cover the sea.

2.12
Mic 3.10;
Nah 3.1

2.13
Isa 50.11;
Jer 51.58

2.14
Isa 11.9;
Zech 14.8,9

15 Woe to him who makes his neighbors drink
    of the cup of his wrath,*f* and makes them drunk,
    to gaze on their shame!
16 You will be sated with contempt instead of glory.
    Drink, yourself, and stagger!*g*
The cup in the LORD's right hand
    will come around to you,
    and shame will come upon your glory!

2.15
Isa 28.7,8;
Hos 7.5

2.16
ver 10;
Lam 4.21;
Jer 25.15,
27;
Nah 3.6

e The Hebrew of these two lines is obscure
f Cn: Heb *joining to your wrath*
g Cn Compare Gk Syr: Heb *be uncircumcised*

2.5 See note to Deut 32.22 on Sheol, the underworld abode.

2.6ff These verses tell of the dooms that will befall evildoers.

2.17
Zech 11.1;
ver 8;
Jer 51.35

17 The violence done to Lebanon will overwhelm you;
  the destruction of the beasts will terrify you,[h]
for the blood of men and violence to the earth,
  to cities and all who dwell therein.

D. *Chaldea is idolatrous*

2.18
Isa 42.17;
Jer 2.27,28;
10.8,14;
Zech 10.2;
Ps 115.4,8

18 What profit is an idol
  when its maker has shaped it,
  a metal image, a teacher of lies?
For the workman trusts in his own creation
  when he makes dumb idols!

2.19
Jer 2.27,28;
I Ki 18.26–
29;
Jer 10.9,14;
Ps 135.17

19 Woe to him who says to a wooden thing, Awake;
  to a dumb stone, Arise!
  Can this give revelation?
Behold, it is overlaid with gold and silver,
  and there is no breath at all in it.

2.20
Mic 1.2;
Zeph 1.7;
Zech 2.13

20 But the LORD is in his holy temple;
  let all the earth keep silence before him.

V. *The prayer of Habakkuk 3.1–19*

A. *"In wrath remember mercy"*

3.2
Job 42.5,6;
Ps 119.120;
Jer 10.7;
Ps 85.6;
Isa 54.8

3 A prayer of Hăbăk'kŭk the prophet, according to Shĭgĭō'nŏth.
  2 O LORD, I have heard the report of thee,
  and thy work, O LORD, do I fear.
In the midst of the years renew it;
  in the midst of the years make it known;
  in wrath remember mercy.

B. *God dooms the wicked and saves the repentant*

*3.3
Amos 1.12;
Deut 33.2;
Ps 113.4;
48.10

3 God came from Tēmăn,
  and the Holy One from Mount Pāràn.
His glory covered the heavens,
  and the earth was full of his praise.   *Sēlàh*

3.4
Ps 18.12;
Job 26.14

4 His brightness was like the light,
  rays flashed from his hand;
  and there he veiled his power.

3.5
Ex 12.29,
30;
Num
16.46–49

5 Before him went pestilence,
  and plague followed close behind.

3.6
Ps 35.5;
114.1–6;
Mic 5.2

6 He stood and measured the earth;
  he looked and shook the nations;
then the eternal mountains were scattered,
  the everlasting hills sank low.
  His ways were as of old.

*3.7
Ex 15.14–
16;
Judg 7.24,
25

7 I saw the tents of Cŭshăn in affliction;
  the curtains of the land of Mĭd'ĭăn did tremble.

h Gk Syr: Heb *them*

3.3 *God came from Teman.* Teman was a district of Edom. The prophet describes the coming of God to deliver his people in language reminiscent of the exodus from Egypt (cf. Deut 33.3).
3.7 *Cushan* was a Bedouin tribe, settled near Edom, as was Midian. Nothing more is known about it.

8 Was thy wrath against the rivers, O LORD?
   Was thy anger against the rivers,
     or thy indignation against the sea,
  when thou didst ride upon thy horses,
    upon thy chariot of victory?
9 Thou didst strip the sheath from thy bow,
   and put the arrows to the string.[i]   *Sēlāh*
   Thou didst cleave the earth with rivers.
10 The mountains saw thee, and writhed;
   the raging waters swept on;
  the deep gave forth its voice,
    it lifted its hands on high.
11 The sun and moon stood still in their habitation[j]
   at the light of thine arrows as they sped,
   at the flash of thy glittering spear.
12 Thou didst bestride the earth in fury,
   thou didst trample the nations in anger.
13 Thou wentest forth for the salvation of thy people,
   for the salvation of thy anointed.
   Thou didst crush the head of the wicked,[k]
   laying him bare from thigh to neck.[l]   *Sēlāh*
14 Thou didst pierce with thy[m] shafts the head of his warriors,[n]
   who came like a whirlwind to scatter me,
   rejoicing as if to devour the poor in secret.
15 Thou didst trample the sea with thy horses,
   the surging of mighty waters.

C. Habakkuk's unwavering faith

16 I hear, and my body trembles,
   my lips quiver at the sound;
rottenness enters into my bones,
   my steps totter[o] beneath me.
I will quietly wait for the day of trouble
  to come upon people who invade us.

17 Though the fig tree do not blossom,
   nor fruit be on the vines,
the produce of the olive fail
  and the fields yield no food,
the flock be cut off from the fold
  and there be no herd in the stalls,
18 yet I will rejoice in the LORD,
   I will joy in the God of my salvation.
19 GOD, the Lord, is my strength;
   he makes my feet like hinds' feet,
   he makes me tread upon my high places.

To the choirmaster: with stringed[p] instruments.

Marginal references:

3.8 Ex 7.19,20; 14.16,21; Deut 33.26; Ps 68.17
3.9 Gen 26.3; Deut 7.8; Ps 78.16; 105.41
3.10 Ps 114.1–6; 98.7,8; Ex 14.22
3.11 Josh 10.12–14; Ps 18.9,11, 14
3.12 Ps 68.7; Isa 41.15; Jer 51.33
3.13 Ex 15.2; Ps 68.19, 20; 110.6; Ezek 13.14
3.14 Judg 7.22; Dan 11.40; Zech 9.14; Ps 10.8; 64.2–5
3.15 Ps 77.19; Ex 15.8
3.16 Jer 23.9; 5.15
*3.17ff Joel 1.18; Jer 5.17
*3.18 Isa 61.10; Ps 46.1–5; Isa 12.2
3.19 2 Sam 22.34; Ps 18.33; Deut 33.29

---

[i] Cn: Heb obscure   [j] Heb uncertain   [k] Cn: Heb *head from the house of the wicked*
[l] Heb obscure   [m] Heb *his*   [n] Vg Compare Gk Syr: Heb uncertain
[o] Cn Compare Gk: Heb *I tremble because*   [p] Heb *my stringed*

3.17–19 These verses are universally quoted.   **3.18** Habakkuk rejoices in the God he knows.

INTRODUCTION TO
THE BOOK OF
ZEPHANIAH

Authorship and Background: This book was written by Zephaniah, whose name means "he whom Yahweh has hidden, or protected." He was the son of Cushi, the son of Gedaliah, the son of Amariah, the son of Hizkiah (which is the same in Hebrew as Hezekiah). If this was King Hezekiah, Zephaniah was of royal blood. In this event, he would have been a prince as well as a prophet. He lived in Jerusalem and wrote during the reign of Josiah, probably around 625 B.C. Nahum was a contemporary. Possibly the reforms made by Josiah were urged on him by Zephaniah.

A knowledge of general world history is helpful to an understanding of the book. For fifty years before Zephaniah's day, Assyria had reigned supreme. That kingdom was apparently at its zenith (although its end came less than twenty years later). Manasseh (ca. 687–642 B.C.) had ruled in Jerusalem for the benefit of Assyria and had wrought much evil. He was followed by his wicked son Amon, who reigned briefly. Then came the godly grandson, Josiah, under whom reforms were instituted. He recovered the Book of the Law given by Moses and enforced its injunctions on the people. During his reign, the power of Assyria declined. The death of Ashurbanipal in 626 B.C. marked the beginning of the end of Assyria. It was replaced shortly thereafter by Babylonia under the Chaldean dynasty.

Characteristics: Zephaniah is the last of the minor prophets before the captivity. He writes to announce the approaching judgment, the impending day of wrath for Judah. He speaks out of youth with vigor and zeal. His pronouncements of judgment are forthright and unsparing. He exhibits his strong convictions along with a moral earnestness and spiritual sensitivity. The book itself bears evidence of his rhetorical powers strengthened by his use of figures of speech. The immediate reference to approaching judgment is to the invasion by Nebuchadnezzar, but the eschatological reference to the day of wrath is as vivid as it is terrible. The author of the medieval hymn, "Dies Irae," got his inspiration from this description by Zephaniah. Zephaniah envisions judgment for the surrounding nations, but he holds forth hope for the people of God foreseeing their ultimate deliverance and the restoration of Israel. God will be in their midst and rejoice over them.

Contents:

I.   The day of the LORD. 1.1—2.3: God will judge Judah. She is guilty of idolatry and of trusting in riches. Their goods shall be plundered and their houses be laid waste. The day of the LORD is near. They are called upon to repent and to seek the LORD that they may be delivered.

II.   The judgment of the nations. 2.4–15: Gaza and the Philistines shall be destroyed; the seacoasts shall be desolate and uninhabited. God will return the land to Judah and be mindful of her. Moab shall become like Sodom; Ammon shall become like Gomorrah; the LORD will be terrible against them. The Ethiopians shall be slain. Nineveh will become a desolation and the nation of Assyria shall be utterly destroyed.

III.   The sin of Jerusalem and the future salvation. 3.1–20: Jerusalem is rebellious; she does not heed, accept correction, trust the LORD, or draw near to her God. She shall be destroyed because of her sins of rebellion, oppression, disobedience, distrust, and the faithlessness of her political leaders and her priests. Deliverance is to come and the LORD calls for the people to wait for him. Blessing is promised to the remnant of Judah and to the whole Israel of God. They may rejoice because the LORD will be in their midst; he will gather them together and promises to "restore your fortunes before your eyes."

THE BOOK OF

ZEPHANIAH

I. *The day of the* LORD *1.1–2.3*

A. *Introduction*

1 The word of the LORD which came to Zěphǎnī´ǎh the son of Cǔshī, son of Gědǎlī´ǎh, son of Ǎmǎrī´ǎh, son of Hězěkī´ǎh, in the days of Jōsī´ǎh the son of Amón, king of Judah.

B. *The judgment upon Judah*

2 "I will utterly sweep away everything
    from the face of the earth," says the LORD.
3 "I will sweep away man and beast;
    I will sweep away the birds of the air
    and the fish of the sea.
I will overthrow[a] the wicked;
    I will cut off mankind
    from the face of the earth," says the LORD.
4 "I will stretch out my hand against Judah,
    and against all the inhabitants of Jerusalem;
and I will cut off from this place the remnant of Bāǎl
    and the name of the idolatrous priests;[b]
5 those who bow down on the roofs
    to the host of the heavens;
those who bow down and swear to the LORD
    and yet swear by Milcòm;
6 those who have turned back from following the LORD,
    who do not seek the LORD or inquire of him."

7 Be silent before the Lord GOD!
    For the day of the LORD is at hand;
the LORD has prepared a sacrifice
    and consecrated his guests.
8 And on the day of the LORD's sacrifice—
"I will punish the officials and the king's sons
    and all who array themselves in foreign attire.
9 On that day I will punish
    every one who leaps over the threshold,
and those who fill their master's house
    with violence and fraud."

---

a Cn: Heb *the stumbling blocks*   *b* Compare Gk: Heb *idolatrous priests with the priests*

1.5 *Milcom* was a god of the Ammonites. He was also called "Molech," or "Moloch," which were simply variants of the name lacking the *-om* ending. He seems to have been identical with the god Baal in his aspect as the "king-god."

1.7 *the* LORD *has prepared a sacrifice*, i.e., a slaughter of people who rebelled against him.

In this verse and 14 the prophet has in mind a double fulfilment. The earlier pre-liminary judgment was inflicted when Nebuchadnezzar invaded Judah. But the final and climactic *day of the* LORD is yet future and remains to be fulfilled at the end of the present age.

1.8 *foreign attire* identifies the wearer as a follower of the foreign idols.

1.9 *every one who leaps over the threshold.* This is a foreign custom associated with pagan superstitions.

Cross-references:
1.1 2 Ki 22.1–23,34; 21.18–26
1.2 Ezek 33.27
1.3 Isa 6.11,12; Jer 9.10; Ezek 7.19
1.4 Ezek 6.14; Mic 5.13; Hos 10.5
*1.5 Jer 19.13; 5.2,7; 49.1
1.6 Isa 1.4; Jer 2.13; Isa 9.13; Hos 7.7
*1.7 Hab 2.20; Zech 2.13; Isa 13.6; ver 14; Isa 34.6; Jer 46.10
*1.8 Isa 24.21; Jer 39.6; Isa 2.6
*1.9 Jer 5.27; Amos 3.10

10 "On that day," says the LORD,
   "a cry will be heard from the Fish Gate,
   a wail from the Second Quarter,
   a loud crash from the hills.

1.10
Amos 8.3;
2 Chr 33.14;
34.22;
Ezek 6.13

11 Wail, O inhabitants of the Mortar!
   For all the traders are no more;
   all who weigh out silver are cut off.

1.11
Jas 5.1;
Zeph 2.5;
Hos 9.6

12 At that time I will search Jerusalem with lamps,
   and I will punish the men
who are thickening upon their lees,
   those who say in their hearts,
'The LORD will not do good,
   nor will he do ill.'

*1.12
Jer 16.16,
17;
Jer 48.11;
Amos 6.1;
Ezek 8.12;
9.9

13 Their goods shall be plundered,
   and their houses laid waste.
Though they build houses,
   they shall not inhabit them;
though they plant vineyards,
   they shall not drink wine from them."

1.13
Deut 28.30,
39;
Amos 5.11;
Mic 6.15

C. The day of wrath

14 The great day of the LORD is near,
   near and hastening fast;
the sound of the day of the LORD is bitter,
   the mighty man cries aloud there.

1.14
Joel 2.1,11

15 A day of wrath is that day,
   a day of distress and anguish,
   a day of ruin and devastation,
   a day of darkness and gloom,
   a day of clouds and thick darkness,
16 a day of trumpet blast and battle cry
against the fortified cities
   and against the lofty battlements.

1.15
Isa 22.5;
Jer 30.7;
Amos 5.18–
20

1.16
Jer 4.19;
Isa 2.12–15

17 I will bring distress on men,
   so that they shall walk like the blind,
   because they have sinned against the LORD;
their blood shall be poured out like dust,
   and their flesh like dung.

1.17
Jer 10.18;
Isa 59.10;
Ps 79.3;
Jer 9.22

18 Neither their silver nor their gold
   shall be able to deliver them
   on the day of the wrath of the LORD.
In the fire of his jealous wrath,
   all the earth shall be consumed;
for a full, yea, sudden end
   he will make of all the inhabitants of the earth.

1.18
Prov 11.4;
Zeph 3.8;
ver 2,3

D. The call to repentance

2 Come together and hold assembly,
   O shameless nation,

2.1
Joel 1.14;
Jer 3.3;
6.15

1.12 The LORD will not do good, nor will he
do ill, i.e., the LORD will do nothing. Those
who have such sentiments live in practical
disregard of God and his claims on their lives.

2.2
Isa 17.13;
Hos 13.3;
Nah 1.6;
Zeph 1.18

2 before you are driven away
    like the drifting chaff,[c]
before there comes upon you
    the fierce anger of the LORD,
before there comes upon you
    the day of the wrath of the LORD.

2.3
Amos 5.6;
Ps 76.9;
Amos 5.14,
15;
Ps 57.1

3 Seek the LORD, all you humble of the land,
    who do his commands;
seek righteousness, seek humility;
    perhaps you may be hidden
    on the day of the wrath of the LORD.

II. The judgment on the nations 2.4–15

A. Gaza and the Philistines

2.4
Amos 1.7,8;
Zech 9.5–7

4 For Gazà shall be deserted,
    and Ăsh′kélón shall become a desolation;
Ăshdŏd′ş people shall be driven out at noon,
    and Ĕkrón shall be uprooted.

*2.5
Ezek 25.16;
Amos 3.1;
Isa 14.29–
31;
Zeph 3.6

5 Woe to you inhabitants of the seacoast,
    you nation of the Çhĕr′ĕthītes!
The word of the LORD is against you,
    O Cānaàn, land of the Phĭlĭs′tĭnes;
    and I will destroy you till no inhabitant is left.

2.6
Isa 17.2

6 And you, O seacoast, shall be pastures,
    meadows for shepherds
    and folds for flocks.

2.7
Mic 4.7;
Isa 32.14;
Ps 80.14;
Lk 1.68;
Ps 126.1,4

7 The seacoast shall become the possession
    of the remnant of the house of Judah,
    on which they shall pasture,
and in the houses of Ăsh′kélón
    they shall lie down at evening.
For the LORD their God will be mindful of them
    and restore their fortunes.

B. Moab and Ammon

*2.8
Ezek 25.3,6,
8;
Jer 49.1

8 "I have heard the taunts of Mŏăb
    and the revilings of the Ăm′mónītes,
how they have taunted my people
    and made boasts against their territory.

2.9
Isa 15.1–16,
14;
Amos 1.13;
Deut 29.23;
Isa 11.14

9 Therefore, as I live," says the LORD of hosts,
    the God of Israel,
"Mŏăb shall become like Sŏdóm,
    and the Ăm′mónītes like Gómor′ràh,
a land possessed by nettles and salt pits,
    and a waste for ever.
The remnant of my people shall plunder them,
    and the survivors of my nation shall possess them."

2.10
Isa 16.6;
Jer 48.29;
ver 8

10 This shall be their lot in return for their pride,

c Cn Compare Gk Syr: Heb before a decree is born; like chaff a day has passed away

---

2.5 Cherethites, i.e., Cretans.   **2.8** See notes to Ezek 25.9; 25.2.

because they scoffed and boasted
    against the people of the LORD of hosts.
11 The LORD will be terrible against them;
    yea, he will famish all the gods of the earth,
and to him shall bow down,
    each in its place,
    all the lands of the nations.

2.11
Joel 2.11;
Zeph 1.4;
3.9;
Mal 1.11;
Isa 24.15

C. *Ethiopia and Assyria*

12 You also, O Ethiopians,
    shall be slain by my sword.

2.12
Isa 18.1

13 And he will stretch out his hand against the north,
    and destroy Assyria;
and he will make Nïn'évèh a desolation,
    a dry waste like the desert.

2.13
Isa 14.26;
10.12;
Nah 3.7

14 Herds shall lie down in the midst of her,
    all the beasts of the field;*d*
the vulture*e* and the hedgehog
    shall lodge in her capitals;
the owl*f* shall hoot in the window,
    the raven*g* croak on the threshold;
for her cedar work will be laid bare.

2.14
ver 6;
Isa 13.21;
34.11,14;
Jer 22.14

15 This is the exultant city
    that dwelt secure,
that said to herself,
    "I am and there is none else."
What a desolation she has become,
    a lair for wild beasts!
Every one who passes by her
    hisses and shakes his fist.

2.15
Isa 22.2;
47.8;32.14;
Jer 18.16;
19.8

III. *The sin of Jerusalem and the future salvation 3.1—20*

A. *The woe upon Jerusalem*

3   Woe to her that is rebellious and defiled,
    the oppressing city!
2 She listens to no voice,
    she accepts no correction.
She does not trust in the LORD,
    she does not draw near to her God.

3.1
Jer 5.23;
Ezek 23.30;
Jer 6.6
3.2
Jer 22.21;
5.3;
Ps 78.22;
73.28

3 Her officials within her
    are roaring lions;
her judges are evening wolves
    that leave nothing till the morning.

3.3
Ezek 22.27;
Hab 1.8

4 Her prophets are wanton,
    faithless men;
her priests profane what is sacred,
    they do violence to the law.
5 The LORD within her is righteous,

3.4
Hos 9.7;
Ezek 22.26
3.5
ver 15,17;
Deut 32.4;
Jer 3.3

---

d Tg Compare Gk: Heb *nation*
e The meaning of the Hebrew word is uncertain
f Cn: Heb *a voice* *g* Gk Vg: Heb *desolation*

he does no wrong;
    every morning he shows forth his justice,
      each dawn he does not fail;
    but the unjust knows no shame.

3.6
Zeph 1.16;
Isa 6.11;
Zeph 2.5

6 "I have cut off nations;
    their battlements are in ruins;
I have laid waste their streets
    so that none walks in them;
their cities have been made desolate,
    without a man, without an inhabitant.

3.7
ver 2;
Jer 7.7;
Hos 9.9

7 I said, 'Surely she will fear me,
    she will accept correction;
she will not lose sight[h]
    of all that I have enjoined upon her.'
But all the more they were eager
    to make all their deeds corrupt."

B. The deliverance which is to come

1. The call to wait

3.8
Ps 27.14;
Zeph 2.2;
Joel 3.2;
Zeph 1.18

8 "Therefore wait for me," says the LORD,
    "for the day when I arise as a witness.
For my decision is to gather nations,
    to assemble kingdoms,
to pour out upon them my indignation,
    all the heat of my anger;
for in the fire of my jealous wrath
    all the earth shall be consumed.

∗3.9
Isa 19.18;
Ps 22.27;
Zeph 2.11

9 "Yea, at that time I will change the speech of the peoples
    to a pure speech,
that all of them may call on the name of the LORD
    and serve him with one accord.

3.10
Ps 68.31;
Isa 18.1,7;
60.6,7

10 From beyond the rivers of Ethiopia
    my suppliants, the daughter of my dispersed ones,
    shall bring my offering.

3.11
Isa 45.17;
Joel 2.26,
27;
Isa 2.12;
5.15;
Ezek 20.40

11 "On that day you shall not be put to shame
    because of the deeds by which you have rebelled against me;
for then I will remove from your midst
    your proudly exultant ones,
and you shall no longer be haughty
    in my holy mountain.

3.12
Isa 14.32;
Nah 1.7
3.13
Mic 4.7;
Isa 60.21;
Zech 8.3,16;
Rev 14.5;
Ezek 34.28;
Mic 4.4

12 For I will leave in the midst of you
    a people humble and lowly.
They shall seek refuge in the name of the LORD,
13   those who are left in Israel;
they shall do no wrong
    and utter no lies,

[h] Gk Syr: Heb *and her dwelling will not be cut off*

3.9 *a pure speech* is one in which God's name is honored. Idolatrous worship is put aside in favor of the purity of the worship of the LORD.

nor shall there be found in their mouth
    a deceitful tongue.
For they shall pasture and lie down,
    and none shall make them afraid."

2. *The call to rejoice*

14 Sing aloud, O daughter of Zion;
    shout, O Israel!
Rejoice and exult with all your heart,
    O daughter of Jerusalem!

3.14
Isa 12.6;
Zech 2.10

15 The LORD has taken away the judgments against you,
    he has cast out your enemies
The King of Israel, the LORD, is in your midst;
    you shall fear evil no more.

3.15
Ezek 37.26–
28;
ver 5;
Isa 54.14

16 On that day it shall be said to Jerusalem:
"Do not fear, O Zion;
    let not your hands grow weak.

3.16
Isa 35.3,4;
Heb 12.12

17 The LORD, your God, is in your midst,
    a warrior who gives victory;
he will rejoice over you with gladness,
    he will renew you[i] in his love;
he will exult over you with loud singing

★3.17
ver 5,15;
Isa 63.1;
62.5

18   as on a day of festival.[j]
"I will remove disaster[k] from you,
    so that you will not bear reproach for it.

19 Behold, at that time I will deal
    with all your oppressors.
And I will save the lame
    and gather the outcast,
and I will change their shame into praise
    and renown in all the earth.

3.19
Isa 60.14;
Ezek 34.16;
Mic 4.6,7

20 At that time I will bring you home,
    at the time when I gather you together;
yea, I will make you renowned and praised
    among all the peoples of the earth,
when I restore your fortunes
    before your eyes," says the LORD.

3.20
Ezek 37.12,
21;
Isa 56.5;
66.22;
Zeph 2.7

---

i Gk Syr: Heb *he will be silent*   *j* Gk Syr: Heb obscure   *k* Cn: Heb *they were*

3.17 God is love (1 Jn 4.8). This pure and holy love is described in Scripture as being: (1) sovereign (Deut 7.8; 10.15); (2) everlasting (Jer 31.3); (3) indissoluble (Rom 8.39); (4) never failing (Isa 49.15, 16). The measure of God's love may be seen in the advent of Jesus and His death on the Cross of Calvary for the sins of the world. God's love, in turn, has been poured into our hearts by the Holy Spirit (Rom 5.5).

INTRODUCTION TO
THE BOOK OF
HAGGAI

Authorship and Background: This book is the work of Haggai, about whom almost nothing is known except his name. The period covered by his life cannot be fixed with accuracy. He may possibly have been a boy at the time of the exile and have seen the Temple of Solomon. Some think he was born during the time of the captivity, and even in the land of the captivity. He returned with the remnant after the exile and, with his contemporary Zechariah, labored toward the common goal of securing the rebuilding of the Temple. He wrote the four discourses which make up this prophecy during a four-month period in the year 520 B.C. The rebuilding of the Temple was his general theme.

From 605 B.C. Judah was under the dominion of Babylon. Her rebellion finally led to the destruction of the Temple and the burning of the city of Jerusalem. Seventy years of captivity ensued. Then, under an edict of King Cyrus of Persia, a remnant numbering some forty thousand returned to the land. Led by Zerubbabel the governor and Joshua the high priest, they began the rebuilding of the city. The foundation of the Temple was laid right away, but the work was thereafter delayed for fifteen years due to the machinations of hostile neighbors. King Darius ascended the Persian throne in 521 B.C. and was favorable to the Jews. The preaching and encouragement of Haggai and Zechariah resulted in the work on the Temple being resumed in 520 B.C. It was finished in 516 or 515 B.C.

Characteristics: Haggai acts as a goad for God. He urges upon the people the task of rebuilding the Temple. He rebukes the people for their indolence and spurs them on to finish the work. There are no lofty flights of oratory. His style appears somewhat dull and prosaic. He speaks plainly and directly, briefly and tersely. His words give no clue to his person. He shrouds himself in his work as a prophet of God, as an intermediary bearing a letter. He is one of the few prophets who has the privilege of seeing his dream fulfilled. In his day the Temple is finished.

Contents:

I.   The call to rebuild the Temple: the first prophecy 1.1–15: Haggai accuses the Jews of building their own homes and neglecting the Temple. God has not blessed them. The path of obedience is to rebuild the Temple. God will help and they will be blessed.

II. Comfort and hope: the second message 2.1–9: Haggai assures Zerubbabel and Joshua that God is present; His Spirit is among them. He will shake the nations and fill His house with His glory. The latter splendor shall be greater than the former.

III.   Holiness versus uncleanness and God's blessing: third message 2.10–19: The Word of the LORD comes to Haggai. Holy flesh in the skirt of the garment will not make other things holy when touched; but an unclean person by touching the same things can make them unholy. God's people are unclean, so their works are unclean. God has withheld his blessing because of disobedience, and the earth does not yield its fruit. If the people will be obedient then immediate blessing will follow.

IV.   Zerubbabel, the servant of Yahweh: fourth message 2.20–23: The Word of the LORD comes the second time. God says to Zerubbabel that he will shake the heavens and earth; he will overthrow the foreign masters; horses and riders will go down. God will make Zerubbabel like a signet ring, for Zerubbabel is God's servant.

THE BOOK OF

HAGGAI

I. *The call to rebuild the Temple: the first prophecy 1.1–15*

A. *Objections and response*

1.1
Zech 1.1;
1 Chr 3.17;
Ezra 3.2;
Zech 6.11

1 In the second year of Dȧrī´ús the king, in the sixth month, on the first day of the month, the word of the LORD came by Hăg´gäï the prophet to Zẽrŭb´bãbẽl the son of Shẽ-ăl´tĭ-ẽl, governor of Judah, and to Joshua the son of Jẽhō´zȧdăk, the high priest, 2 "Thus says the LORD of hosts: This people say the time

1.2
ver 15

has not yet come to rebuild the house of the LORD." 3 Then the word of the LORD came by Hăg´gäï the prophet, 4 "Is it a time for

1.4
2 Sam 7.2;
ver 9
1.5
Lam 3.40
1.6
Deut 28.38;
Mic 6.14;
Zech 8.10

you yourselves to dwell in your paneled houses, while this house lies in ruins? 5 Now therefore thus says the LORD of hosts: Consider how you have fared. 6 You have sown much, and harvested little; you eat, but you never have enough; you drink, but you never have your fill; you clothe yourselves, but no one is warm; and he who earns wages earns wages to put them into a bag with holes.

1.7
ver 1
1.8
Ezra 3.7;
Ps 132.13,
14;
Hag 2.7,9
1.9
ver 6;
Isa 40.7
1.10
Lev 26.19;
Deut 28.23;
1 Ki 8.35
1.11
Mal 3.9–11;
Deut 28.22;
Hag 2.17

7 "Thus says the LORD of hosts: Consider how you have fared. 8 Go up to the hills and bring wood and build the house, that I may take pleasure in it and that I may appear in my glory, says the LORD. 9 You have looked for much, and, lo, it came to little; and when you brought it home, I blew it away. Why? says the LORD of hosts. Because of my house that lies in ruins, while you busy yourselves each with his own house. 10 Therefore the heavens above you have withheld the dew, and the earth has withheld its produce. 11And I have called for a drought upon the land and the hills, upon the grain, the new wine, the oil, upon what the ground brings forth, upon men and cattle, and upon all their labors."

B. *The call to rebuild obeyed*

1.12
Hag 2.2;
Isa 1.19;
50.10

12 Then Zẽrŭb´bãbẽl the son of Shẽ-ăl´tĭ-ẽl, and Joshua the son of Jẽhō´zȧdăk, the high priest, with all the remnant of the people, obeyed the voice of the LORD their God, and the words of Hăg´gäï the prophet, as the LORD their God had sent him; and the people feared before the LORD. 13 Then Hăg´gäï, the messenger

1.13
Mal 2.7;
3.1;
Mt 28.30;
Rom 8.31
1.14
2 Chr 36.22;
Ezra 1.1;
5.2,8

of the LORD, spoke to the people with the LORD's message, "I am with you, says the LORD." 14And the LORD stirred up the spirit of Zẽrŭb´bãbẽl the son of Shẽ-ăl´tĭ-ẽl, governor of Judah, and the spirit of Joshua the son of Jẽhō´zȧdăk, the high priest, and the spirit of all the remnant of the people; and they came and worked on the house of the LORD of hosts, their God, 15 on the twenty-fourth day of the month, in the sixth month.

II. *Comfort and hope: the second message 2.1–9*

2 In the second year of Dȧrī´ús the king, 1 in the seventh month, on the twenty-first day of the month, the word of the LORD came by Hăg´gäï the prophet, 2 "Speak now to Zẽrŭb´bãbẽl the

son of Shĕ-ăl′tĭ-ĕl, governor of Judah, and to Joshua the son of
Jĕhō′zădăk, the high priest, and to all the remnant of the people,
and say, 3 'Who is left among you that saw this house in its former
glory? How do you see it now? Is it not in your sight as nothing?
4 Yet now take courage, O Zĕrŭb′băbĕl, says the LORD; take courage, O Joshua, son of Jĕhō′zădăk, the high priest; take courage,
all you people of the land, says the LORD; work, for I am with you,
says the LORD of hosts, 5 according to the promise that I made you
when you came out of Egypt. My Spirit abides among you; fear
not. 6 For thus says the LORD of hosts: Once again, in a little
while, I will shake the heavens and the earth and the sea and the
dry land; 7 and I will shake all nations, so that the treasures of all
nations shall come in, and I will fill this house with splendor, says
the LORD of hosts. 8 The silver is mine, and the gold is mine, says
the LORD of hosts. 9 The latter splendor of this house shall be
greater than the former, says the LORD of hosts; and in this place
I will give prosperity, says the LORD of hosts.' "

III. Holiness versus uncleanness and God's blessing: third message 2.10–19

10 On the twenty-fourth day of the ninth month, in the second
year of Dărī′ŭs, the word of the LORD came by Hăg′gäī the prophet, 11 "Thus says the LORD of hosts: Ask the priests to decide this
question, 12 'If one carries holy flesh in the skirt of his garment,
and touches with his skirt bread, or pottage, or wine, or oil, or any
kind of food, does it become holy?' " The priests answered, "No."
13 Then said Hăg′gäī, "If one who is unclean by contact with a
dead body touches any of these, does it become unclean?" The
priests answered, "It does become unclean." 14 Then Hăg′gäī said,
"So is it with this people, and with this nation before me, says the
LORD; and so with every work of their hands; and what they offer
there is unclean. 15 Pray now, consider what will come to pass
from this day onward. Before a stone was placed upon a stone in
the temple of the LORD, 16 how did you fare?ᵃ When one came to a
heap of twenty measures, there were but ten; when one came to
the winevat to draw fifty measures, there were but twenty. 17 I
smote you and all the products of your toil with blight and mildew
and hail; yet you did not return to me, says the LORD. 18 Consider
from this day onward, from the twenty-fourth day of the ninth
month. Since the day that the foundation of the LORD's temple
was laid, consider: 19 Is the seed yet in the barn? Do the vine, the
fig tree, the pomegranate, and the olive tree still yield nothing?
From this day on I will bless you."

ᵃ Gk: Heb since they were

Cross-references (right margin):

2.3
Ezra 3.12;
Zech 4.10

2.4
Zech 8.9;
Acts 7.9

2.5
Ex 29.45,
46;
Neh 9.20;
Isa 63.11,14
*2.6
Heb 12.26;
Isa 10.25;
29.17;
ver 21

2.7
Dan 2.44;
Isa 60.4–9

*2.9
Isa 66.12;
Zech 2.5

2.10
ver 1,20

*2.11
Lev 10.10;
Deut 33.10;
Mal 2.7

2.12
Ezek 44.19;
Mt 23.19

2.13
Num 19.11,
22

2.14
Prov 15.8;
Isa 1.11–15

2.15
Hag 1.5;
Ezra 3.10;
4.24

2.16
Hag 1.6,9;
Zech 8.10

2.17
1 Ki 8.37;
Amos 4.9;
Isa 9.13

2.18
Zech 8.9

2.19
Zech 8.12

2.6 *I will shake the heavens.* Political up-
heavals and earthquakes would be used by
God to accomplish His purposes. The earthly
confusion would be but evidence that God
was preparing to act.

2.9 *greater than the former.* This should not
be taken as referring to external splendor, for
in that respect the Temple of Solomon greatly
surpassed this new edifice under construction by Zerubbabel. It refers rather to the
spiritual glory which would be granted it
when Jesus of Nazareth Himself entered its
courts and preached the gospel to Israel in
its precincts.

2.11 *Ask the priests to decide,* i.e., to illustrate from the law. If they do this the people
will learn that: (1) it is impossible for sacred
things to communicate holiness to the things
they touch; (2) any person who is unclean
will contaminate everything he touches.

IV. *Zerubbabel the servant of the* LORD: *fourth message 2.20–23*

★2.20ff
ver 10
2.21
Hag 1.14;
Zech 4.6–
10;
Heb 12.26
2.22
Dan 2.44;
Mic 5.10;
Zech 4.6;
2 Chr 20.23
2.23
Sol 8.6;
Jer 22.24;
Isa 42.1;
43.10

20 The word of the LORD came a second time to Hăg′găï on the twenty-fourth day of the month, 21 "Speak to Zĕrŭb′bábĕl, governor of Judah, saying, I am about to shake the heavens and the earth, 22 and to overthrow the throne of kingdoms; I am about to destroy the strength of the kingdoms of the nations, and overthrow the chariots and their riders; and the horses and their riders shall go down, every one by the sword of his fellow. 23 On that day, says the LORD of hosts, I will take you, O Zĕrŭb′bábĕl my servant, the son of Shĕ-ăl′tĭ-ĕl, says the LORD, and make you like a signet ring; for I have chosen you, says the LORD of hosts."

2.20-23 In Haggai's day the reader probably interpreted this as referring to the overthrow of Darius I who at that moment was dealing with aspirants to his throne. It may be that the sudden disappearance of Zerubbabel was due to some action of the Persian government. The futuristic interpretation applies this prophecy to Christ.

INTRODUCTION TO
THE BOOK OF
ZECHARIAH

Authorship and Background: The author, Zechariah, whose name means "whom Yahweh hath remembered," was the son of Berechiah. His grandfather, Iddo, returned from the exile with Zerubbabel and Joshua (Neh 12.1, 4, 7). In all probability Zechariah was attached to the priesthood. He was a contemporary of Haggai, beginning his prophetic ministry in 520 B.C. The historical background of the book is identical to that of Haggai. The main divisions of Zechariah (1—8, 9—14) are markedly dissimilar in style and subject matter. Some have therefore supposed that the book is the work of different authors. Those who accept the unity of the authorship account for the differences by concluding that the latter section of the prophecy was composed some decades after the first part. The first part is historical and the second apocalyptic, resulting in distinct styles in the two sections of the book.

Characteristics: Zechariah concerns himself with the rebuilding of the Temple in the first part of his prophecy. He aims to encourage the people to continue the work, which has been interrupted for some years. Then he looks into the future, to distant events not yet fulfilled. Whereas his contemporary, Haggai, uses plain and simple language, Zechariah employs symbolic language such as was common to the Babylonians, and to Daniel and Ezekiel. Often it is difficult to determine the precise meaning of what Zechariah says, although the main lines of the book are plain enough. Zechariah contributes more to angelology than any other Old Testament writer, not excluding Daniel.

In the first section he urges the people to repent and warns them not to act as their forefathers, upon whom the judgment of God fell in the captivity. He notes that the consequences of God's judgment are still in force. The question is, how long will this continue? In a series of visions, Zechariah discloses God's plan to pour out His anger upon the nations, but to allow the rebuilding of Jerusalem and the Temple. He teaches the people the meaning of worship.

Beginning with chapter 9, Zechariah looks into the future. This section is filled with Messianic references and passages which deal with the end of the age. He foresees the day of the LORD when the kingdom will be set up, Israel restored, the nations judged, and God and His kingdom triumphant.

Contents:

I.   Messages during the building of the Temple. 1.1–8.23: Zechariah calls upon his people to repent and return to God. He recounts his visions: the red horse speaks of God watching over Judah; the four horns and four smiths show the defeat of Judah's enemies; the measuring line is the vision of what Jerusalem is yet to be; Joshua reclothed

in clean raiment indicates that the promise of God includes removal of sin, and moral and spiritual reformation of the people; the golden lampstand fed by the two olive trees is a message to Zerubbabel that success in rebuilding comes from the Spirit, for the day of small things is not to be despised; the flying scroll vision pronounces a curse upon those who steal and perjure themselves; the vision of the woman sitting in the ephah deals with iniquity "in all the land" (5.6), teaching that even in restored Israel the spirit of lawlessness will exist; the four chariots symbolize God's spirits released for the fulfilment of God's plans for His people. Joshua, who represents the Branch, is crowned. The deputation from Bethel asks whether the fasts are to be kept. Obey God's Law; disobedience the cause of the captivity. God promises to restore His people. Finish rebuilding the Temple. Love truth and peace; fast days will become feast days. The nation will gather at Jerusalem to seek the LORD and pray before Him.

II.   Messages after the building of the Temple. 9.1—14.21: Sidon, Tyre, and Philistia fall. Jerusalem is spared for the coming of its king. Judah is restored. Temporal prosperity is promised. Wickedness will not go unpunished; Jerusalem is destroyed. The shepherd-king is rejected; false shepherds replace the true shepherd. God delivers Jerusalem which becomes penitent, and is restored. The land is cleansed. The shepherd is stricken, and Jerusalem falls. The shepherd comes victoriously; he is enthroned; his enemies are defeated and ultimately the glory of Jerusalem is established and all nations come to worship the king.

THE BOOK OF

ZECHARIAH

I. Messages during the building of the Temple 1.1–8.23

A. First message: call for national repentance

1 In the eighth month, in the second year of Dǎrī′ŭs, the word of the LORD came to Zěchǎrī′ǎh the son of Běrěchī′ǎh, son of Ĭddō, the prophet, saying, 2 "The LORD was very angry with your fathers. 3 Therefore say to them, Thus says the LORD of hosts: Return to me, says the LORD of hosts, and I will return to you, says the LORD of hosts. 4 Be not like your fathers, to whom the former prophets cried out, 'Thus says the LORD of hosts, Return from your evil ways and from your evil deeds.' But they did not hear or heed me, says the LORD. 5 Your fathers, where are they? And the prophets, do they live for ever? 6 But my words and my statutes, which I commanded my servants the prophets, did they not overtake your fathers? So they repented and said, As the LORD of hosts purposed to deal with us for our ways and deeds, so has he dealt with us."

B. Second message: the eight visions of God's care for Israel

1. The horsemen among the myrtles

7 On the twenty-fourth day of the eleventh month which is the month of Shěbǎt′, in the second year of Dǎrī′ŭs, the word of the LORD came to Zěchǎrī′ǎh the son of Běrěchī′ǎh, son of Ĭddō, the prophet; and Zechariah said, 8 "I saw in the night, and behold, a man riding upon a red horse! He was standing among the myrtle trees in the glen; and behind him were red, sorrel, and white horses. 9 Then I said, 'What are these, my lord?' The angel who talked with me said to me, 'I will show you what they are.' 10 So the man who was standing among the myrtle trees answered, 'These are they whom the LORD has sent to patrol the earth.' 11 And they answered the angel of the LORD who was standing among the myrtle trees, 'We have patrolled the earth, and behold, all the earth remains at rest.' 12 Then the angel of the LORD said, 'O LORD of hosts, how long wilt thou have no mercy on Jerusalem and the cities of Judah, against which thou hast had indignation these seventy years?' 13 And the LORD answered gracious and comforting words to the angel who talked with me. 14 So the angel who talked with me said to me, 'Cry out, Thus says the LORD of hosts: I am exceedingly jealous for Jerusalem and for Zion. 15 And I am very angry with the nations that are at ease; for while I was angry but a little they furthered the disaster. 16 Therefore, thus says the LORD, I have returned to Jerusalem with compassion; my house shall be built in it, says the LORD of hosts, and the measuring line shall be stretched out over Jerusalem. 17 Cry again, Thus says the LORD of hosts: My cities shall again overflow

1.1
Ezra 4.24;
Hag 1.1;
Neh 12.4,16
1.3
Isa 31.6;
Mal 3.7;
Jas 4.8
1.4
2 Chr
36.15;
Hos 14.1;
Jer 6.17;
11.7,8
1.6
Jer 12.16,
17;
Lam 2.17

1.8
Josh 5.13;
Rev 6.4;
Zech 6.2–7
1.9
Zech 2.3;
4.5
1.10
Heb 1.14
★**1.11**
Isa 14.7
1.12
Hab 1.2;
Dan 9.2
1.13
Zech 4.1;
Isa 40.1,2
1.14
Zech 8.2
1.15
Ps 123.4;
Amos 1.11
★**1.16**
Isa 54.8;
Zech 2.1,2,
10
1.17
Isa 44.26;
51.3;
Zech 2.12;
3.2

1.11 *all the earth remains at rest.* The earth was at peace but Jerusalem was still oppressed by external foes and troubled by dissident groups within.

1.16 *the measuring line* would be used as a preparation for building.

with prosperity, and the LORD will again comfort Zion and again choose Jerusalem.' "

2. The four horns and the four smiths

18ᵃ And I lifted my eyes and saw, and behold, four horns! ¹⁹And I said to the angel who talked with me, "What are these?" And he answered me, "These are the horns which have scattered Judah, Israel, and Jerusalem." ²⁰ Then the LORD showed me four smiths. ²¹And I said, "What are these coming to do?" He answered, "These are the horns which scattered Judah, so that no man raised his head; and these have come to terrify them, to cast down the horns of the nations who lifted up their horns against the land of Judah to scatter it."

3. The measuring line of Jerusalem

2ᵇ And I lifted my eyes and saw, and behold, a man with a measuring line in his hand! ² Then I said, "Where are you going?" And he said to me, "To measure Jerusalem, to see what is its breadth and what is its length." ³And behold, the angel who talked with me came forward, and another angel came forward to meet him, ⁴ and said to him, "Run, say to that young man, 'Jerusalem shall be inhabited as villages without walls, because of the multitude of men and cattle in it. ⁵ For I will be to her a wall of fire round about, says the LORD, and I will be the glory within her.' "

6 Ho! ho! Flee from the land of the north, says the LORD; for I have spread you abroad as the four winds of the heavens, says the LORD. ⁷ Ho! Escape to Zion, you who dwell with the daughter of Babylon. ⁸ For thus said the LORD of hosts, after his glory sent me to the nations who plundered you, for he who touches you touches the apple of his eye: ⁹ "Behold, I will shake my hand over them, and they shall become plunder for those who served them. Then you will know that the LORD of hosts has sent me. ¹⁰ Sing and rejoice, O daughter of Zion; for lo, I come and I will dwell in the midst of you, says the LORD. ¹¹And many nations shall join themselves to the LORD in that day, and shall be my people; and I will dwell in the midst of you, and you shall know that the LORD of hosts has sent me to you. ¹²And the LORD will inherit Judah as his portion in the holy land, and will again choose Jerusalem."

13 Be silent, all flesh, before the LORD; for he has roused himself from his holy dwelling.

4. Joshua as the symbol of the priestly nation

3 Then he showed me Joshua the high priest standing before the angel of the LORD, and Satan standing at his right hand to accuse him. ²And the LORD said to Satan, "The LORD rebuke you, O Satan! The LORD who has chosen Jerusalem rebuke you! Is not this a brand plucked from the fire?" ³ Now Joshua was standing before the angel, clothed with filthy garments. ⁴And the angel said

a Ch 2.1 in Heb   *b* Ch 2.5 in Heb

Marginal references

1.20
Isa 44.12;
54.16
1.21
Ps 75.10

2.1
Zech 1.18;
Ezek 40.3
2.2
Ezek 40.3;
Rev 21.15–
17
★2.4
Ezek 38.11;
Jer 30.19
2.5
Isa 26.1;
Zech 9.8;
Rev 21.23
2.6
Isa 48.20;
Jer 1.14;
Ezek 17.21
2.8
Isa 60.7–9;
Deut 32.10
2.9
Isa 11.15;
Zech 4.9
2.10
Isa 12.6;
Zeph 3.14;
Lev 26.12;
Ezek 37.27
2.12
Deut 32.9;
Zech 1.17
2.13
Hab 2.20;
Ps 78.65;
Isa 51.9
3.1
Hag 1.1;
Ps 109.6
3.2
Jude 9,23;
Amos 4.11
3.4
Isa 43.25;
Rev 19.8

2.4 This prophecy about Jerusalem points to a future age when it becomes a large and populous city, too large to be contained within walls, and one which will be indwelt by the glory of God. Note particularly that verse 11 refers to the Gentiles who have been grafted into the stock of Israel by faith (Rom 11.13–25).

to those who were standing before him, "Remove the filthy garments from him." And to him he said, "Behold, I have taken your iniquity away from you, and I will clothe you with rich apparel." [5]And I said, "Let them put a clean turban on his head." So they put a clean turban on his head and clothed him with garments; and the angel of the LORD was standing by.

6 And the angel of the LORD enjoined Joshua, 7 "Thus says the LORD of hosts: If you will walk in my ways and keep my charge, then you shall rule my house and have charge of my courts, and I will give you the right of access among those who are standing here. [8] Hear now, O Joshua the high priest, you and your friends who sit before you, for they are men of good omen: behold, I will bring my servant the Branch. [9] For behold, upon the stone which I have set before Joshua, upon a single stone with seven facets, I will engrave its inscription, says the LORD of hosts, and I will remove the guilt of this land in a single day. [10] In that day, says the LORD of hosts, every one of you will invite his neighbor under his vine and under his fig tree."

5. *The lampstand and the two olive trees*

4 And the angel who talked with me came again, and waked me, like a man that is wakened out of his sleep. [2]And he said to me, "What do you see?" I said, "I see, and behold, a lampstand all of gold, with a bowl on the top of it, and seven lamps on it, with seven lips on each of the lamps which are on the top of it. [3]And there are two olive trees by it, one on the right of the bowl and the other on its left." [4]And I said to the angel who talked with me, "What are these, my lord?" [5] Then the angel who talked with me answered me, "Do you not know what these are?" I said, "No, my lord." [6] Then he said to me, "This is the word of the LORD to Zerub'babel: Not by might, nor by power, but by my Spirit, says the LORD of hosts. [7] What are you, O great mountain? Before Zerub'babel you shall become a plain; and he shall bring forward the top stone amid shouts of 'Grace, grace to it!' " [8] Moreover the word of the LORD came to me, saying, [9] "The hands of Zerub'-babel have laid the foundation of this house; his hands shall also complete it. Then you will know that the LORD of hosts has sent me to you. [10] For whoever has despised the day of small things shall rejoice, and shall see the plummet in the hand of Zerub'-babel.

"These seven are the eyes of the LORD, which range through the whole earth." [11] Then I said to him, "What are these two olive trees on the right and the left of the lampstand?" [12]And a second time I said to him, "What are these two branches of the olive trees, which are beside the two golden pipes from which the oil[c] is poured out?" [13] He said to me, "Do you not know what these are?" I said, "No, my lord." [14] Then he said, "These are the two anointed who stand by the Lord of the whole earth."

[c] Cn: Heb *gold*

3.5
Ex 29.6

3.7
1 Ki 3.14;
Ezek 44.16;
Deut 17.9;
Zech 4.14
*3.8
Isa 20.3;
Ezek 12.11;
Isa 4.2;
53.2;
Jer 33.15
3.9
Isa 28.16;
Zech 4.10;
Jer 31.34;
Mic 7.18
3.10
1 Ki 4.25;
Isa 36.16

4.1
Zech 1.9;
2.3;
Dan 8.18
4.2
Ex 25.31;
Rev 1.12;
Ex 25.37;
Rev 4.5
4.3
Rev 11.4
4.5
Zech 1.9
4.6
Hag 2.4,5;
Hos 1.7;
Eph 6.17
4.7
Jer 51.25;
Ps 118.22;
Ezra 3.10,
11
4.9
Ezra 3.10;
6.15;
Zech 2.9,
11; 6.15;
Isa 48.16;
Zech 2.8
4.10
Hag 2.3;
Zech 3.9;
Rev 8.2;
Zech 1.10
4.11
ver 3
4.14
Rev 11.4;
Zech 3.1–7;
Mic 4.13

3.8 *the Branch*, i.e., the Messiah appears here as a Messianic title, referring to Christ as the descendant of David. At His First Advent the Jews were blinded and unable to discern His presence. But at the end of the age He will be received by Israel in faith and submission. But from the time of His Easter victory He will be constantly building up His spiritual temple, the church (cf. 1 Pet 2.5), as is indicated by 6.12–15.

6. The flying scroll

5.1
Ezek 2.9

5 Again I lifted my eyes and saw, and behold, a flying scroll!
² And he said to me, "What do you see?" I answered, "I see a
flying scroll; its length is twenty cubits, and its breadth ten cubits."

5.3
Jer 26.6;
Ex 20.15;
Mal 3.8,9;
ver 4
5.4
Mal 3.5;
Hos 4.2,3;
Lev 14.45;
Hab 2.9–11

³ Then he said to me, "This is the curse that goes out over the face
of the whole land; for every one who steals shall be cut off henceforth according to it, and every one who swears falsely shall be cut
off henceforth according to it. ⁴ I will send it forth, says the LORD of
hosts, and it shall enter the house of the thief, and the house of him
who swears falsely by my name; and it shall abide in his house
and consume it, both timber and stones."

7. The ephah of iniquity carried back to Babylon

5.5
Zech 1.9,18
5.6
Lev 19.36;
Amos 8.5

5 Then the angel who talked with me came forward and said to
me, "Lift your eyes, and see what this is that goes forth." ⁶ And
I said, "What is it?" He said, "This is the ephah that goes forth."
And he said, "This is their iniquity^d in all the land." ⁷ And behold,
the leaden cover was lifted, and there was a woman sitting in the

5.8
Hos 12.7;
Amos 8.5;
Mic 6.11
5.9
ver 5;
Jer 8.7

ephah! ⁸ And he said, "This is Wickedness." And he thrust her
back into the ephah, and thrust down the leaden weight upon its
mouth. ⁹ Then I lifted my eyes and saw, and behold, two women
coming forward! The wind was in their wings; they had wings like
the wings of a stork, and they lifted up the ephah between earth

*5.11
Jer 29.5,28;
Gen 10.10

and heaven. ¹⁰ Then I said to the angel who talked with me,
"Where are they taking the ephah?" ¹¹ He said to me, "To the
land of Shīnar, to build a house for it; and when this is prepared,
they will set the ephah down there on its base."

8. The four chariots of divine judgment

*6.1
Zech 1.18;
5.9;
ver 5
6.2
Rev 6.4,5
6.3
Rev 6.2
6.4
Zech 5.10
6.5
Jer 49.36;
Ezek 37.9;
Mt 24.31;
Rev 7.1
6.6
Jer 1.14;
Ezek 1.4;
Dan 11.5
6.7
Zech 1.10
6.8
Ezek 5.13

6 And again I lifted my eyes and saw, and behold, four chariots
came out from between two mountains; and the mountains
were mountains of bronze. ² The first chariot had red horses, the
second black horses, ³ the third white horses, and the fourth
chariot dappled gray^e horses. ⁴ Then I said to the angel who talked
with me, "What are these, my lord?" ⁵ And the angel answered
me, "These are going forth to the four winds of heaven, after
presenting themselves before the LORD of all the earth. ⁶ The chariot with the black horses goes toward the north country, the white
ones go toward the west country,^f and the dappled ones go toward
the south country." ⁷ When the steeds came out, they were impatient to get off and patrol the earth. And he said, "Go, patrol
the earth." So they patrolled the earth. ⁸ Then he cried to me,
"Behold, those who go toward the north country have set my
Spirit at rest in the north country."

9. Sequel: Joshua crowned as a type of the Branch

6.9
Zech 1.1;
7.1; 8.1
6.10
Jer 28.6

9 And the word of the LORD came to me: ¹⁰ "Take from the
exiles Hĕldaī, Tŏbī′jăh, and Jĕdāi′ăh, who have arrived from
Babylon; and go the same day to the house of Jōsī′ăh, the son of

d Gk Compare Syr: Heb *eye*
e Compare Gk: The meaning of the Hebrew word is uncertain f Cn: Heb *after them*

5.11 *To the land of Shinar* (Babylon). Iniquity was symbolically taken from Judah to
Babylon and left there.
6.1 *four chariots*, i.e., *the four winds* (ver 5).

Zĕphănĭ'áh. ¹¹ Take from them silver and gold, and make a crown,ᵍ and set it upon the head of Joshua, the son of Jĕhō'zădăk, the high priest; ¹² and say to him, 'Thus says the LORD of hosts, "Behold, the man whose name is the Branch: for he shall grow up in his place, and he shall build the temple of the LORD. ¹³ It is he who shall build the temple of the LORD, and shall bear royal honor, and shall sit and rule upon his throne. And there shall be a priest by his throne, and peaceful understanding shall be between them both." ' ¹⁴And the crownʰ shall be in the temple of the LORD as a reminder to Hĕldaī,ⁱ Tôbī'jáh, Jĕdāi'áh, and Jōsī'áh,ʲ the son of Zĕphănĭ'áh.

15 "And those who are far off shall come and help to build the temple of the LORD; and you shall know that the LORD of hosts has sent me to you. And this shall come to pass, if you will diligently obey the voice of the LORD your God."

C. Third message: the meaning of true piety

1. The inquiry about extra fasts

7 In the fourth year of King Dárī'ŭs, the word of the LORD came to Zĕchárī'áh in the fourth day of the ninth month, which is Chĭslĕv. ² Now the people of Bĕthĕl had sent Shárē'zér and Rĕg'ĕm-mĕl'ĕch and their men, to entreat the favor of the LORD, ³ and to ask the priests of the house of the LORD of hosts and the prophets, "Should I mourn and fast in the fifth month, as I have

2. The fourfold answer
a. The hypocrisy of their fasts

done for so many years?" ⁴ Then the word of the LORD of hosts came to me; ⁵ "Say to all the people of the land and the priests, When you fasted and mourned in the fifth month and in the seventh, for these seventy years, was it for me that you fasted? ⁶And when you eat and when you drink, do you not eat for yourselves and drink for yourselves? ⁷ When Jerusalem was inhabited and in prosperity, with her cities round about her, and the South and the lowland were inhabited, were not these the words which the LORD proclaimed by the former prophets?"

b. The exile a result of their oppressions

8 And the word of the LORD came to Zĕchárī'áh, saying, ⁹ "Thus says the LORD of hosts, Render true judgments, show kindness and mercy each to his brother, ¹⁰ do not oppress the widow, the fatherless, the sojourner, or the poor; and let none of you devise evil against his brother in your heart." ¹¹ But they refused to hearken, and turned a stubborn shoulder, and stopped their ears that they might not hear. ¹² They made their hearts like adamant lest they should hear the law and the words which the LORD of hosts had sent by his Spirit through the former prophets. Therefore great wrath came from the LORD of hosts. ¹³ "As I called, and they would not hear, so they called, and I would not

ᵍ Gk Mss: Heb crowns　ʰ Gk: Heb crowns
ⁱ With verse 10: Heb Hēlēm　ʲ With verse 10: Heb Hēn

7.3 fast in the fifth month commemorated the destruction of Jerusalem (587 B.C.).　**7.5** God's people performed the rites and ceremonies, but not for God's glory.

6.11 Ezra 3.2; Hag 1.1 6.12 Isa 11.1; Zech 3.8; Isa 53.2 6.13 Isa 9.6; 22.24; 9.7; Ps 110.1,4 6.14 ver 11 6.15 Isa 57.19; 60.10; Zech 4.9; 3.7 7.1 Zech 1.1,7; Neh 1.1 7.2 Jer 26.19; Zech 8.21 *7.3 Jer 52.12; Zech 8.19; 12.12–14 *7.5 Isa 58.5; Zech 8.19; Jer 41.1; Rom 14.6 7.7 Zech 1.4; Jer 22.21; 17.26 7.9 Ezek 18.8; Zech 8.16; Mic 6.8 7.10 Deut 24.17; Jer 7.6; Mic 2.1 7.11 Jer 11.10; 17.23; 5.21; Acts 7.57 7.12 Ezek 11.19; 36.26; Neh 9.29, 30; Dan 9.11 7.13 Prov 1.24; Isa 1.15; Mic 3.4

hear," says the LORD of hosts, 14 "and I scattered them with a whirlwind among all the nations which they had not known. Thus the land they left was desolate, so that no one went to and fro, and the pleasant land was made desolate."

c. *God's intention to restore Jerusalem*

8 And the word of the LORD of hosts came to me, saying, 2 "Thus says the LORD of hosts: I am jealous for Zion with great jealousy, and I am jealous for her with great wrath. 3 Thus says the LORD: I will return to Zion, and will dwell in the midst of Jerusalem, and Jerusalem shall be called the faithful city, and the mountain of the LORD of hosts, the holy mountain. 4 Thus says the LORD of hosts: Old men and old women shall again sit in the streets of Jerusalem, each with staff in hand for very age. 5 And the streets of the city shall be full of boys and girls playing in its streets. 6 Thus says the LORD of hosts: If it is marvelous in the sight of the remnant of this people in these days, should it also be marvelous in my sight, says the LORD of hosts? 7 Thus says the LORD of hosts: Behold, I will save my people from the east country and from the west country; 8 and I will bring them to dwell in the midst of Jerusalem; and they shall be my people and I will be their God, in faithfulness and in righteousness."

9 Thus says the LORD of hosts: "Let your hands be strong, you who in these days have been hearing these words from the mouth of the prophets, since the day that the foundation of the house of the LORD of hosts was laid, that the temple might be built. 10 For before those days there was no wage for man or any wage for beast, neither was there any safety from the foe for him who went out or came in; for I set every man against his fellow. 11 But now I will not deal with the remnant of this people as in the former days, says the LORD of hosts. 12 For there shall be a sowing of peace; the vine shall yield its fruit, and the ground shall give its increase, and the heavens shall give their dew; and I will cause the remnant of this people to possess all these things. 13 And as you have been a byword of cursing among the nations, O house of Judah and house of Israel, so will I save you and you shall be a blessing. Fear not, but let your hands be strong."

14 For thus says the LORD of hosts: "As I purposed to do evil to you, when your fathers provoked me to wrath, and I did not relent, says the LORD of hosts, 15 so again have I purposed in these days to do good to Jerusalem and to the house of Judah; fear not. 16 These are the things that you shall do: Speak the truth to one another, render in your gates judgments that are true and make for peace, 17 do not devise evil in your hearts against one another, and love no false oath, for all these things I hate, says the LORD."

d. *The nations to seek the LORD in Jerusalem*

18 And the word of the LORD of hosts came to me, saying, 19 "Thus says the LORD of hosts: The fast of the fourth month, and the fast of the fifth, and the fast of the seventh, and the fast of the tenth, shall be to the house of Judah seasons of joy and gladness, and cheerful feasts; therefore love truth and peace.

20 "Thus says the LORD of hosts: Peoples shall yet come, even the inhabitants of many cities; 21 the inhabitants of one city shall go to another, saying, 'Let us go at once to entreat the favor of the

7.14
Deut 4.27;
Jer 23.19;
44.6;
Isa 60.15

8.2
Zech 1.14
8.3
Zech 1.16;
2.10,11;
Jer 31.23
8.4
Isa 65.20
8.5
Jer 30.19,20
8.6
Ps 118.23;
Jer 32.17,
27
8.7
Isa 11.11;
43.5,6;
Amos 9.14
8.8
Zech 10.10;
Ezek 37.25;
Zech 2.11
8.9
Hag 2.4;
Ezra 5.1
8.10
Hag 1.6

8.11
Ps 103.9;
Isa 12.1
8.12
Joel 2.22;
Hag 1.10;
Isa 61.7
8.13
Jer 42.18;
Gen 12.2;
Ruth 4.11
8.14
Jer 31.28;
Ezek 24.14
8.15
Jer 29.11;
ver 13
8.16
Zech 7.9;
Eph 4.25
8.17
Prov 3.29;
Zech 7.10;
5.4;
Hab 1.13

8.19
Zech 7.3,5;
Jer 39.2;
52.4;
Isa 12.1;
ver 16

8.21
Mic 4.1,2

LORD, and to seek the LORD of hosts; I am going.' 22 Many peoples and strong nations shall come to seek the LORD of hosts in Jerusalem, and to entreat the favor of the LORD. 23 Thus says the LORD of hosts: In those days ten men from the nations of every tongue shall take hold of the robe of a Jew, saying, 'Let us go with you, for we have heard that God is with you.' "

II. Messages after the building of the Temple 9.1–14.21

A. Messiah king rejected, triumphant

1. The coming of the king announced

9   An Oracle

The word of the LORD is against the land of Hādrăch
   and will rest upon Damascus.
For to the LORD belong the cities of Arăm,*k*
   even as all the tribes of Israel;
2 Hāmáth also, which borders thereon,
   Tȳre and Sĭdŏn, though they are very wise.
3 Tȳre has built herself a rampart,
   and heaped up silver like dust,
   and gold like the dirt of the streets.
4 But lo, the Lord will strip her of her possessions
   and hurl her wealth into the sea,
   and she shall be devoured by fire.

5 Ăsh'kĕlŏn shall see it, and be afraid;
   Gază too, and shall writhe in anguish;
   Ekrŏn also, because its hopes are confounded.
The king shall perish from Gaza;
   Ashkelon shall be uninhabited;
6 a mongrel people shall dwell in Ăshdŏd;
   and I will make an end of the pride of Phĭlĭs'tĭă.
7 I will take away its blood from its mouth,
   and its abominations from between its teeth;
it too shall be a remnant for our God;
   it shall be like a clan in Judah,
   and Ekrŏn shall be like the Jĕb'ūsītes.
8 Then I will encamp at my house as a guard,
   so that none shall march to and fro;
no oppressor shall again overrun them,
   for now I see with my own eyes.

9 Rejoice greatly, O daughter of Zion!
   Shout aloud, O daughter of Jerusalem!
Lo, your king comes to you;

k Cn: Heb *the eye of Adam* (or *man*)

8.22
Isa 60.3;
66.23;
ver 21
*8.23
Isa 45.14,
24; 60.14;
1 Cor 14.25;
2 Chr 15.5;
Isa 19.2

9.2
Jer 49.23;
Ezek 28.3–
5,12,21
9.3
2 Sam 24.7;
Ezek 27.33;
1 Ki 10.21,
27
9.4
Isa 23.1;
Ezek 28.18

9.5
Amos 1.6–8

9.6
Amos 1.6–8

9.7
Ezek 25.15–
17

9.8
Zech 2.5;
Isa 52.1;
54.14;
60.18
*9.9
Zeph 3.14,
15;
Isa 9.6,7;
Mt 21.5;
Jn 12.15;
Isa 43.3,11;
57.15

8.23 This prophecy has not been fulfilled as yet. Undoubtedly it awaits the time when Jerusalem shall become the center of the worship of God, and Jewish Christians will be foremost leaders in world evangelism.
9.9 This passage predicts the triumphal

entry of Christ into Jerusalem on the Sunday of Passion Week. Coming as king, Christ was to be acclaimed by the people with shouts of "*Hosanna to the Son of David!* . . . " (Mt 21.9), even though their adulation proved to be short-lived by Good Friday.

triumphant and victorious is he,
humble and riding on an ass,
on a colt the foal of an ass.

10 I will cut off the chariot from E′phra̤im
and the war horse from Jerusalem;
and the battle bow shall be cut off,
and he shall command peace to the nations;
his dominion shall be from sea to sea,
and from the River to the ends of the earth.

2. The program of the king
a. Israel delivered from captivity

11 As for you also, because of the blood of my covenant with you,
I will set your captives free from the waterless pit.
12 Return to your stronghold, O prisoners of hope;
today I declare that I will restore to you double.

b. Triumph over the Greek oppressor

13 For I have bent Judah as my bow;
I have made E′phra̤im its arrow.
I will brandish your sons, O Zion,
over your sons, O Greece,
and wield you like a warrior's sword.

14 Then the LORD will appear over them,
and his arrow go forth like lightning;
the Lord GOD will sound the trumpet,
and march forth in the whirlwinds of the south.

15 The LORD of hosts will protect them,
and they shall devour and tread down the slingers;[l]
and they shall drink their blood[m] like wine,
and be full like a bowl,
drenched like the corners of the altar.

16 On that day the LORD their God will save them
for they are the flock of his people;
for like the jewels of a crown
they shall shine on his land.

17 Yea, how good and how fair it shall be!
Grain shall make the young men flourish,
and new wine the maidens.

c. The complete redemption of God's people

10 Ask rain from the LORD
in the season of the spring rain,
from the LORD who makes the storm clouds,
who gives men showers of rain,
to every one the vegetation in the field.

2 For the teraphim utter nonsense,
and the diviners see lies;
the dreamers tell false dreams,
and give empty consolation.
Therefore the people wander like sheep;
they are afflicted for want of a shepherd.

l Cn: Heb the slingstones   m Gk: Heb be turbulent

3 "My anger is hot against the shepherds,
  and I will punish the leaders;[n]
for the LORD of hosts cares for his flock, the house of Judah,
  and will make them like his proud steed in battle.

10.3
Jer 25.34–
36;
Ezek 34.12,
17

4 Out of them shall come the cornerstone,
  out of them the tent peg,
out of them the battle bow,
  out of them every ruler.

10.4
Zech 9.10

5 Together they shall be like mighty men in battle,
  trampling the foe in the mud of the streets;
they shall fight because the LORD is with them,
  and they shall confound the riders on horses.

10.5
2 Sam
22.43;
Hag 2.22

6 "I will strengthen the house of Judah,
  and I will save the house of Joseph.
I will bring them back because I have compassion on them,
  and they shall be as though I had not rejected them;
for I am the LORD their God and I will answer them.

10.6
ver 12;
Zech 9.16;
8.8; 1.16;
13.9

7 Then Ē'phraïm shall become like a mighty warrior,
  and their hearts shall be glad as with wine.
Their children shall see it and rejoice,
  their hearts shall exult in the LORD.

10.7
Zech 9.13,
15;
Isa 54.13

8 "I will signal for them and gather them in,
  for I have redeemed them,
and they shall be as many as of old.

10.8
Isa 5.26;
Jer 33.22;
Ezek 36.11

9 Though I scattered them among the nations,
  yet in far countries they shall remember me,
and with their children they shall live and return.

10.9
Ezek 6.9

10 I will bring them home from the land of Egypt,
  and gather them from Assyria;
and I will bring them to the land of Gïl'ëäd and to Lebanon,
  till there is no room for them.

10.10
Isa 11.11;
Jer 50.19;
Isa 49.19,20

11 They shall pass through the sea of Egypt,[o]
  and the waves of the sea shall be smitten,
and all the depths of the Nile dried up.
The pride of Assyria shall be laid low,
  and the scepter of Egypt shall depart.

10.11
Isa 51.9,10;
19.5–7;
Zeph 2.13;
Ezek 30.13

12 I will make them strong in the LORD
  and they shall glory[p] in his name,"

                              says the LORD.

10.12
Mic 4.5

3. The rejection of the king
a. The proud in Israel humbled

11 Open your doors, O Lebanon,
    that the fire may devour your cedars!
2 Wail, O cypress, for the cedar has fallen,
  for the glorious trees are ruined!
Wail, oaks of Bāshàn,
  for the thick forest has been felled!

11.1
Jer 22.6,7;
Ezek 31.3
11.2
Isa 32.19

3 Hark, the wail of the shepherds,
  for their glory is despoiled!
Hark, the roar of the lions,
  for the jungle of the Jordan is laid waste!

11.3
Jer 25.34–
36; 50.44

[n] Or he-goats [o] Cn: Heb distress [p] Gk: Heb walk

b. *The good shepherd rejected by his people*

4 Thus said the LORD my God: "Become shepherd of the flock doomed to slaughter. 5 Those who buy them slay them and go unpunished; and those who sell them say, 'Blessed be the LORD, I have become rich'; and their own shepherds have no pity on them. 6 For I will no longer have pity on the inhabitants of this land, says the LORD. Lo, I will cause men to fall each into the hand of his shepherd, and each into the hand of his king; and they shall crush the earth, and I will deliver none from their hand."

7 So I became the shepherd of the flock doomed to be slain for those who trafficked in the sheep. And I took two staffs; one I named Grace, the other I named Union. And I tended the sheep. 8 In one month I destroyed the three shepherds. But I became impatient with them, and they also detested me. 9 So I said, "I will not be your shepherd. What is to die, let it die; what is to be destroyed, let it be destroyed; and let those that are left devour the flesh of one another." 10 And I took my staff Grace, and I broke it, annulling the covenant which I had made with all the peoples. 11 So it was annulled on that day, and the traffickers in the sheep, who were watching me, knew that it was the word of the LORD. 12 Then I said to them, "If it seems right to you, give me my wages; but if not, keep them." And they weighed out as my wages thirty shekels of silver. 13 Then the LORD said to me, "Cast it into the treasury"*q*—the lordly price at which I was paid off by them. So I took the thirty shekels of silver and cast them into the treasury*q* in the house of the LORD. 14 Then I broke my second staff Union, annulling the brotherhood between Judah and Israel.

c. *The false shepherd described*

15 Then the LORD said to me, "Take once more the implements of a worthless shepherd. 16 For lo, I am raising up in the land a shepherd who does not care for the perishing, or seek the wandering,*r* or heal the maimed, or nourish the sound, but devours the flesh of the fat ones, tearing off even their hoofs.

17 Woe to my worthless shepherd,
  who deserts the flock!
May the sword smite his arm
  and his right eye!
Let his arm be wholly withered,
  his right eye utterly blinded!"

B. *The rejected king enthroned*

1. *Repentant Israel triumphant*

a. *Downfall of heathen attackers of Jerusalem*

12

An Oracle

The word of the LORD concerning Israel: Thus says the LORD, who stretched out the heavens and founded the earth and formed the spirit of man within him: 2 "Lo, I am about to make Jerusalem a cup of reeling to all the peoples round about; it will be against Judah also in the siege against Jerusalem. 3 On that day I will make Jerusalem a heavy stone for all the peoples; all who lift it shall

---

q Syr: Heb *to the potter*   *r* Syr Compare Gk Vg: Heb *the youth*

grievously hurt themselves. And all the nations of the earth will come together against it. ⁴ On that day, says the Lord, I will strike every horse with panic, and its rider with madness. But upon the house of Judah I will open my eyes, when I strike every horse of the peoples with blindness. ⁵ Then the clans of Judah shall say to themselves, 'The inhabitants of Jerusalem have strength through the Lord of hosts, their God.'

b. Israel's power to vanquish all foes

6 "On that day I will make the clans of Judah like a blazing pot in the midst of wood, like a flaming torch among sheaves; and they shall devour to the right and to the left all the peoples round about, while Jerusalem shall still be inhabited in its place, in Jerusalem.

7 "And the Lord will give victory to the tents of Judah first, that the glory of the house of David and the glory of the inhabitants of Jerusalem may not be exalted over that of Judah. ⁸ On that day the Lord will put a shield about the inhabitants of Jerusalem so that the feeblest among them on that day shall be like David, and the house of David shall be like God, like the angel of the Lord, at their head. ⁹And on that day I will seek to destroy all the nations that come against Jerusalem.

c. Repentance of Israel for piercing their king

10 "And I will pour out on the house of David and the inhabitants of Jerusalem a spirit of compassion and supplication, so that, when they look on him whom they have pierced, they shall mourn for him, as one mourns for an only child, and weep bitterly over him, as one weeps over a first-born. ¹¹ On that day the mourning in Jerusalem will be as great as the mourning for Hā'dăd'rĭm'mòn in the plain of Mégĭd'dō. ¹² The land shall mourn, each family by itself; the family of the house of David by itself, and their wives by themselves; the family of the house of Nathan by itself, and their wives by themselves; ¹³ the family of the house of Lĕvī by itself, and their wives by themselves; the family of the Shĭm'ĕ-ītes by itself, and their wives by themselves; ¹⁴ and all the families that are left, each by itself, and their wives by themselves.

d. Israel cleansed and evil cut off

13 "On that day there shall be a fountain opened for the house of David and the inhabitants of Jerusalem to cleanse them from sin and uncleanness.

2 "And on that day, says the Lord of hosts, I will cut off the names of the idols from the land, so that they shall be remembered no more; and also I will remove from the land the prophets and the unclean spirit. ³And if any one again appears as a prophet, his father and mother who bore him will say to him, 'You shall not live, for you speak lies in the name of the Lord'; and his father and mother who bore him shall pierce him through when he prophesies. ⁴ On that day every prophet will be ashamed of his vision when he prophesies; he will not put on a hairy mantle in order to deceive, ⁵ but he will say, 'I am no prophet, I am a tiller of the soil; for the land has been my possession* since my youth.' ⁶And if one asks him, 'What are these wounds on your back?' he will say, 'The wounds I received in the house of my friends.' "

_____
* Cn: Heb for man has caused me to possess

12.4 Ps 76.6; Ezek 38.4; Zech 9.10
12.5 Zech 10.6, 12
12.6 Isa 10.17, 18; Obad 18; Zech 2.4; 8.3–5
12.7 Jer 30.18; Amos 9.11
12.8 Zech 9.14, 15; Mic 7.8; Ps 8.5; 82.6
12.9 ver 3; Zech 14.2,3
12.10 Isa 44.3; Ezek 39.29; Joel 2.28; Jn 19.34; Rev 1.7; Jer 6.26; Amos 8.10
12.11 2 Ki 23.29
12.12 Mt 24.30; Rev 1.7
13.1 Jer 2.13; Heb 9.14; Ps 51.2,7; Ezek 36.25
13.2 Ex 23.13; Hos 2.17; Jer 23.14, 15; Ezek 36.25, 29
13.3 Jer 23.34; Deut 18.20; 13.6–11
13.4 Mic 3.6,7; 2 Ki 1.8; Mt 3.4
13.5 Amos 7.14
13.6 2 Ki 9.24

2. *Israel purged, delivered, and triumphant*
a. *Israel chastened after rejecting the king*

13.7
Jer 47.6;
Mic 5.2,4;
Jer 23.5,6;
Isa 53.4,5,
10;
Mt 26.31;
Isa 1.25

7 "Awake, O sword, against my shepherd,
   against the man who stands next to me,"
                              says the LORD of hosts.
"Strike the shepherd, that the sheep may be scattered;
   I will turn my hand against the little ones.

8 In the whole land, says the LORD,
   two thirds shall be cut off and perish,
   and one third shall be left alive.

13.9
Isa 48.10;
1 Pet 1.6;
Zech 10.6;
Jer 30.22;
Hos 2.23

9 And I will put this third into the fire,
   and refine them as one refines silver,
   and test them as gold is tested.
They will call on my name,
   and I will answer them.
I will say, 'They are my people';
   and they will say, 'The LORD is my God.' "

b. *Jerusalem delivered by the* LORD

*14.1
Isa 13.9;
Joel 2.1;
Mal 4.1;
ver 14
14.2
Zech 12.2,3;
Isa 13.6;
Zech 13.8
14.3
Zech 9.14,
15
14.4
Ezek 11.23;
Mic 1.3,4;
Hab 3.6
14.5
Amos 1.1;
Isa 66.15,
16;
Mt 25.31;
Jude 14

14 Behold, a day of the LORD is coming, when the spoil taken from you will be divided in the midst of you. 2 For I will gather all the nations against Jerusalem to battle, and the city shall be taken and the houses plundered and the women ravished; half of the city shall go into exile, but the rest of the people shall not be cut off from the city. 3 Then the LORD will go forth and fight against those nations as when he fights on a day of battle. 4 On that day his feet shall stand on the Mount of Olives which lies before Jerusalem on the east; and the Mount of Olives shall be split in two from east to west by a very wide valley; so that one half of the Mount shall withdraw northward, and the other half southward. 5And the valley of my mountains shall be stopped up, for the valley of the mountains shall touch the side of it; and you shall flee as you fled from the earthquake in the days of Uzzī'ah king of Judah. Then the LORD your[u] God will come, and all the holy ones with him.[v]

6 On that day there shall be neither cold nor frost.[w] 7And there shall be continuous day (it is known to the LORD), not day and not night, for at evening time there shall be light.

8 On that day living waters shall flow out from Jerusalem, half of them to the eastern sea and half of them to the western sea; it shall continue in summer as in winter.

c. *Judah's king supreme over the earth*

*14.9
Rev 11.15;
Isa 45.21–
24;
Eph 4.5,6
14.10
Amos 9.11;
Zech 12.6;
Jer 37.13;
38.7; 31.38

9 And the LORD will become king over all the earth; on that day the LORD will be one and his name one.
10 The whole land shall be turned into a plain from Gēbā to Rimmon south of Jerusalem. But Jerusalem shall remain aloft upon its site from the Gate of Benjamin to the place of the former

u Heb *my* . *v* Gk Syr Vg Tg: Heb *you* . *w* Compare Gk Syr Vg Tg: Heb uncertain

---

14.1 The coming of Christ is here predicted when Jerusalem will be rescued from complete destruction by a miraculous divine interposition.
14.9 This verse assures every believer of an ultimate answer to the prayer, "Thy kingdom come." In its consummation, Christ's kingdom will embrace all the earth and the prayer for the spiritual unity of all believers will be more perfectly fulfilled (Jn 17.21).

gate, to the Corner Gate, and from the Tower of Hăn´ănĕl to the king's wine presses. 11And it shall be inhabited, for there shall be no more curse;x Jerusalem shall dwell in security.

12 And this shall be the plague with which the LORD will smite all the peoples that wage war against Jerusalem: their flesh shall rot while they are still on their feet, their eyes shall rot in their sockets, and their tongues shall rot in their mouths. 13And on that day a great panic from the LORD shall fall on them, so that each will lay hold on the hand of his fellow, and the hand of the one will be raised against the hand of the other; 14 even Judah will fight against Jerusalem. And the wealth of all the nations round about shall be collected, gold, silver, and garments in great abundance. 15And a plague like this plague shall fall on the horses, the mules, the camels, the asses, and whatever beasts may be in those camps.

d. *The nations subjugated and Israel holy*

16 Then every one that survives of all the nations that have come against Jerusalem shall go up year after year to worship the King, the LORD of hosts, and to keep the feast of booths. 17And if any of the families of the earth do not go up to Jerusalem to worship the King, the LORD of hosts, there will be no rain upon them. 18And if the family of Egypt do not go up and present themselves, then upon them shally come the plague with which the LORD afflicts the nations that do not go up to keep the feast of booths. 19 This shall be the punishment to Egypt and the punishment to all the nations that do not go up to keep the feast of booths.

20 And on that day there shall be inscribed on the bells of the horses, "Holy to the LORD." And the pots in the house of the LORD shall be as the bowls before the altar; 21 and every pot in Jerusalem and Judah shall be sacred to the LORD of hosts, so that all who sacrifice may come and take of them and boil the flesh of the sacrifice in them. And there shall no longer be a trader in the house of the LORD of hosts on that day.

x Or *ban of utter destruction*   y Gk Syr: Heb *shall not*

14.11
Zech 2.4;
Rev 22.3;
Jer 23.5,6

14.12
Deut 28.21,
22

14.13
1 Sam
14.15,20;
Zech 11.6;
Ezek 38.21

14.14
Zech 12.2,5;
Isa 23.18

14.15
ver 12

14.16
Isa 60.6,7,
9; 66.23;
ver 9

14.17
ver 9,16;
Amos 4.7

14.18
ver 12

14.19
ver 12

14.20
Ex 28.36–
38;
Zech 9.15

14.21
Neh 8.10;
1 Cor 10.31;
Ezek 44.9;
Zech 9.8

INTRODUCTION TO
THE BOOK OF
MALACHI

Authorship and Background: Almost nothing is known about Malachi, whose name means "my messenger" (3.1). According to synagogue tradition he followed after Zechariah and Haggai and thus came before or during Nehemiah's day. This prophecy, the last book in the canon of the Old Testament Scripture, was written probably in the fifth century either before or during the time of Nehemiah. It was followed by the four hundred "silent years." At the time of the writing the Temple in Jerusalem had been rebuilt, but the glorious kingdom for which the people looked had not yet come. Times were hard because of drought, famine, and blighted crops. These hardships had been met by sloth, indifference, and spiritual lethargy. The people had been in the land after the captivity for almost a hundred years, the walls of Jerusalem had been rebuilt, but present circumstances made them apathetic. They doubted the love of God and wondered whether there was any divine justice. Since the wicked prospered, they questioned whether there was profit in walking penitently before God and obeying His commandments. Against such a background was this book written. Malachi is divided into three chapters in the Hebrew Bible and into four chapters in the English Bible.

Characteristics: Malachi writes as a man of great spiritual force who speaks with the authority of God's Word. His love for the people of God is intense; he has a high conception of the duties of the priesthood and is devoted to the religious ceremonies in the Temple. He speaks his message in the street and the market place. His writing is in the form of a dialogue, of question and answer, both a literary device and also the result of his actual experiences among men. He tries to respond to questions rationally and logically because men demand that their objections be met and his own assertions be justified. Basically, he seeks to answer the question relating to the justice of God. If God is good why do the wicked prosper and the righteous suffer hardship? His first reply is that the people of God have neglected Him and have been disloyal to Him. Secondly, he argues that cruelty and faithlessness do not go unpunished, as the fate of the Edomites indicates.

Malachi reassures the people that the Messiah will surely come, but He will bring judgment upon them because of their sins. The catalogue of their sins is similar to those recorded in the memoirs of Nehemiah, his contemporary. The people offer blemished animals for sacrifice. They neglect to pay their tithes. The priesthood is corrupt, mercenary, and debased. The people have loose marriage morals; divorce is common and intermarriage with the heathen too frequent. Malachi challenges the people to pay their tithes, obey God and see how He will bless them. He foresees a day when God will destroy the wicked and vindicate the righteous. The coming of the prophet Elijah will precede that day.

Contents:

THE BOOK OF
MALACHI

I. *The apostasy and sin of Israel 1.1–2.17*

A. *God's love for Israel shown by the fall of Edom*

1 The oracle of the word of the LORD to Israel by Măl′ȧchī.*a*
2 "I have loved you," says the LORD. But you say, "How hast thou loved us?" "Is not Ēsau Jacob's brother?" says the LORD. "Yet I have loved Jacob 3 but I have hated Ēsau; I have laid waste his hill country and left his heritage to jackals of the desert." 4 If Ēdȯm says, "We are shattered but we will rebuild the ruins," the LORD of hosts says, "They may build, but I will tear down, till they are called the wicked country, the people with whom the LORD is angry for ever." 5 Your own eyes shall see this, and you shall say, "Great is the LORD, beyond the border of Israel!"

B. *The sins of the priesthood*

6 "A son honors his father, and a servant his master. If then I am a father, where is my honor? And if I am a master, where is my fear? says the LORD of hosts to you, O priests, who despise my name. You say, 'How have we despised thy name?' 7 By offering polluted food upon my altar. And you say, 'How have we polluted it?'*b* By thinking that the LORD's table may be despised. 8 When you offer blind animals in sacrifice, is that no evil? And when you offer those that are lame or sick, is that no evil? Present that to your governor; will he be pleased with you or show you favor? says the LORD of hosts. 9 And now entreat the favor of God, that he may be gracious to us. With such a gift from your hand, will he show favor to any of you? says the LORD of hosts. 10 Oh, that there were one among you who would shut the doors, that you might not kindle fire upon my altar in vain! I have no pleasure in you, says the LORD of hosts, and I will not accept an offering from your hand. 11 For from the rising of the sun to its setting my name is great among the nations, and in every place incense is offered to my name, and a pure offering; for my name is great among the nations, says the LORD of hosts. 12 But you profane it when you say that the LORD's table is polluted, and the food for it*c* may be despised. 13 'What a weariness this is,' you say, and you sniff at me,*d* says the LORD of hosts. You bring what has been taken by violence or is lame or sick, and this you bring as your offering! Shall I accept that from your hand? says the LORD. 14 Cursed be the cheat who has a male in his flock, and vows it, and yet sacrifices to the Lord what is blemished; for I am a great King, says the LORD of hosts, and my name is feared among the nations.

C. *The warning to the priesthood*

2 "And now, O priests, this command is for you. 2 If you will not listen, if you will not lay it to heart to give glory to my name, says the LORD of hosts, then I will send the curse upon you

1.1
Nah 1.1;
Hab 1.1
1.2
Isa 41.8,9;
Jer 31.3;
Rom 9.13
1.3
Jer 49.18;
Ezek 35.3–
9
1.5
Ps 35.27;
Job 42.8

1.6
Ex 20.12;
Mal 2.10;
Lk 6.46;
Mal 3.5;
2.1–9
1.7
Lev 21.6,8;
ver 12
1.8
Lev 22.22

1.9
Amos 5.22;
Lev 23.34–
44
1.10
Isa 1.13;
Jer 14.10–
12;
Hos 5.6
1.11
Isa 45.6;
60.3,5,6;
Rev 8.3;
Jer 10.6,7
1.12
Deut 28.15;
ver 7
1.13
Isa 43.22;
61.8;
Lev 22.20
1.14
Lev 22.18–
20;
Zech 14.9;
Zeph 2.11

2.1
ver 7,8
2.2
Lev 26.14;
Deut 28.15–
20

a Or *my messenger*   *b* Gk: Heb *thee*   *c* Heb *its fruit, its food*   *d* Another reading is *it*

and I will curse your blessings; indeed I have already cursed them, because you do not lay it to heart. 3 Behold, I will rebuke your offspring, and spread dung upon your faces, the dung of your offerings, and I will put you out of my presence.*e* 4 So shall you know that I have sent this command to you, that my covenant with Lēvī may hold, says the LORD of hosts. 5 My covenant with him was a covenant of life and peace, and I gave them to him, that he might fear; and he feared me, he stood in awe of my name. 6 True instruction*f* was in his mouth, and no wrong was found on his lips. He walked with me in peace and uprightness, and he turned many from iniquity. 7 For the lips of a priest should guard knowledge, and men should seek instruction*f* from his mouth, for he is the messenger of the LORD of hosts. 8 But you have turned aside from the way; you have caused many to stumble by your instruction;*f* you have corrupted the covenant of Lēvī, says the LORD of hosts, 9 and so I make you despised and abased before all the people, inasmuch as you have not kept my ways but have shown partiality in your instruction."*f*

10 Have we not all one father? Has not one God created us? Why then are we faithless to one another, profaning the covenant of our fathers? 11 Judah has been faithless, and abomination has been committed in Israel and in Jerusalem; for Judah has profaned the sanctuary of the LORD, which he loves, and has married the daughter of a foreign god. 12 May the LORD cut off from the tents of Jacob, for the man who does this, any to witness*g* or answer, or to bring an offering to the LORD of hosts!

13 And this again you do. You cover the LORD's altar with tears, with weeping and groaning because he no longer regards the offering or accepts it with favor at your hand. 14 You ask, "Why does he not?" Because the LORD was witness to the covenant between you and the wife of your youth, to whom you have been faithless, though she is your companion and your wife by covenant. 15 Has not the one God made*h* and sustained for us the spirit of life?*i* And what does he desire? Godly offspring. So take heed to yourselves, and let none be faithless to the wife of his youth. 16 "For I hate*j* divorce, says the LORD the God of Israel, and covering one's garment with violence, says the LORD of hosts. So take heed to yourselves and do not be faithless."

17 You have wearied the LORD with your words. Yet you say, "How have we wearied him?" By saying, "Every one who does evil is good in the sight of the LORD, and he delights in them." Or by asking, "Where is the God of justice?"

II. The judgment for sinners and the blessings for the penitent 3.1–4.6

A. The sending of the Messiah

3 "Behold, I send my messenger to prepare the way before me, and the Lord whom you seek will suddenly come to his temple;

e Cn Compare Gk Syr: Heb *and he shall bear you to it*   *f* Or *law*
g Cn Compare Gk: Heb *arouse*   *h* Or *has he not made one?*
i Cn: Heb *and a remnant of spirit was his*   *j* Cn: Heb *he hates*

Side references:
2.3 Nah 3.6; Ex 29.14
2.4 Num 3.45; 18.21
2.5 Num 25.12; Ezek 34.25; Deut 33.9
2.6 Deut 33.8–10; Jer 23.22; Jas 5.20
2.7 Lev 10.11; Jer 18.18; Num 27.21
2.8 Mal 3.7; Jer 18.15; Ezek 44.10
2.9 1 Sam 2.30; Deut 1.17; Mic 3.11
2.10 Isa 63.16; 1 Cor 8.6; Jer 9.4,5; Ex 19.4–6
★2.11 Jer 3.7–9; Ezra 9.1; Neh 13.23
2.12 Hos 9.12; Mal 1.10,13
2.13 Jer 11.14; 14.12
2.14 Prov 5.18; 2.17
2.15 Gen 2.24; Mt 19.4; Ex 20.14; Lev 20.10
2.16 Deut 24.1; Mt 5.31,32; Ps 73.6; Isa 59.6
2.17 Isa 43.24; 5.19,20
★3.1 Mt 11.10; Mk 1.2; Lk 1.76; 7.27

the messenger of the covenant in whom you delight, behold, he is coming, says the LORD of hosts. 2 But who can endure the day of his coming, and who can stand when he appears?

"For he is like a refiner's fire and like fullers' soap; 3 he will sit as a refiner and purifier of silver, and he will purify the sons of Lēvī and refine them like gold and silver, till they present right offerings to the LORD. 4 Then the offering of Judah and Jerusalem will be pleasing to the LORD as in the days of old and as in former years.

5 "Then I will draw near to you for judgment; I will be a swift witness against the sorcerers, against the adulterers, against those who swear falsely, against those who oppress the hireling in his wages, the widow and the orphan, against those who thrust aside the sojourner, and do not fear me, says the LORD of hosts.

B. The sins of the people

6 "For I the LORD do not change; therefore you, O sons of Jacob, are not consumed. 7 From the days of your fathers you have turned aside from my statutes and have not kept them. Return to me, and I will return to you, says the LORD of hosts. But you say, 'How shall we return?' 8 Will man rob God? Yet you are robbing me. But you say, 'How are we robbing thee?' In your tithes and offerings. 9 You are cursed with a curse, for you are robbing me; the whole nation of you. 10 Bring the full tithes into the storehouse, that there may be food in my house; and thereby put me to the test, says the LORD of hosts, if I will not open the windows of heaven for you and pour down for you an overflowing blessing. 11 I will rebuke the devourer[k] for you, so that it will not destroy the fruits of your soil; and your vine in the field shall not fail to bear, says the LORD of hosts. 12 Then all nations will call you blessed, for you will be a land of delight, says the LORD of hosts.

C. The distinction between the good and the evil

13 "Your words have been stout against me, says the LORD. Yet you say, 'How have we spoken against thee?' 14 You have said, 'It is vain to serve God. What is the good of our keeping his charge or of walking as in mourning before the LORD of hosts? 15 Henceforth we deem the arrogant blessed; evildoers not only prosper but when they put God to the test they escape.'"

16 Then those who feared the LORD spoke with one another; the LORD heeded and heard them, and a book of remembrance was written before him of those who feared the LORD and thought on his name. 17 "They shall be mine, says the LORD of hosts, my special possession on the day when I act, and I will spare them as a man spares his son who serves him. 18 Then once more you shall

k Or devouring locust

3.8 The law of the tithe is set forth in the Mosaic system. But the tithe was already recognized as obligatory before Moses, since even Abraham paid a tenth to Melchizedek (Gen 14.18–20; Heb 7.1–4). The New Testament does not prescribe the tithe as a legal requirement, but the Christian can do no less for God under grace than the Jew did under law. The tithe is therefore an outward evidence of an inward commitment and springs from one's love of God. (See also note to 1 Cor 16.1.)

distinguish between the righteous and the wicked, between one who serves God and one who does not serve him.

4[1] "For behold, the day comes, burning like an oven, when all the arrogant and all evildoers will be stubble; the day that comes shall burn them up, says the LORD of hosts, so that it will leave them neither root nor branch. 2 But for you who fear my name the sun of righteousness shall rise, with healing in its wings. You shall go forth leaping like calves from the stall. 3And you shall tread down the wicked, for they will be ashes under the soles of your feet, on the day when I act, says the LORD of hosts.

4.1
Joel 2.31;
Obad 18;
Amos 2.9

4.2
Mal 3.16;
Lk 1.78;
Eph 5.14

4.3
Mic 7.10;
Zech 10.5

D. Conclusion

1. *The command to obedience*

4 "Remember the law of my servant Moses, the statutes and ordinances that I commanded him at Horĕb for all Israel.

4.4
Ex 20.3

2. *The coming of Elijah before the day of the* LORD

5 "Behold, I will send you Ēlī'jăh the prophet before the great and terrible day of the LORD comes. 6And he will turn the hearts of fathers to their children and the hearts of children to their fathers, lest I come and smite the land with a curse."[m]

*4.5
Mt 11.14;
Mk 9.11;
Lk 1.17

[l] Ch 4.1-6 are Ch 3.19-24 in the Hebrew   [m] Or *ban of utter destruction*

4.5 *Elijah* is depicted as the forerunner, heralding the coming of the day of the LORD. This prophecy of the coming of Elijah envisions two fulfilments, one at the First Advent of Christ and the other in connection with the day of the LORD. Christ identified John the Baptist's coming as a preliminary fulfilment of this prophecy (Mt 11.14; see also Lk 1.17; 9.8, 19; Jn 1.21). The final fulfilment is probably that portrayed in Rev 11.3–6. Elijah also appeared at the Transfiguration of Christ (Mt 17.1–5; Mk 9.2–13; Lk 9.28–36).

HARPER STUDY BIBLE

The New Covenant

COMMONLY CALLED

THE

NEW TESTAMENT

Of Our Lord and Savior Jesus Christ

Revised Standard Version

TRANSLATED FROM THE GREEK
BEING THE VERSION SET FORTH A.D. 1611
REVISED A.D. 1881 AND A.D. 1901
COMPARED WITH THE MOST ANCIENT AUTHORITIES
AND REVISED A.D. 1946
SECOND EDITION 1971

THE

NEW TESTAMENT

Of Our Lord and Savior
Jesus Christ

NAMES AND ORDER

OF THE

BOOKS OF THE NEW TESTAMENT

ABBREVIATIONS

The following abbreviations for the books of the Bible are used in the RSV footnotes: (Where the abbreviations differ in the Introductions, Annotations, and cross references they are indicated in parentheses.)

OLD TESTAMENT

Gen	Genesis	Eccles (Ecc)	Ecclesiastes
Ex	Exodus	Song (Sol)	Song of Solomon
Lev	Leviticus	Is (Isa)	Isaiah
Num	Numbers	Jer	Jeremiah
Deut	Deuteronomy	Lam	Lamentations
Josh	Joshua	Ezek	Ezekiel
Judg	Judges	Dan	Daniel
Ruth	Ruth	Hos	Hosea
1 Sam	1 Samuel	Joel	Joel
2 Sam	2 Samuel	Amos	Amos
1 Kings (1 Ki)	1 Kings	Obad	Obadiah
2 Kings (2 Ki)	2 Kings	Jon	Jonah
1 Chron (1 Chr)	1 Chronicles	Mic	Micah
2 Chron (2 Chr)	2 Chronicles	Nahum (Nah)	Nahum
Ezra	Ezra	Hab	Habakkuk
Neh	Nehemiah	Zeph	Zephaniah
Esther (Est)	Esther	Hag	Haggai
Job	Job	Zech	Zechariah
Ps	Psalms	Mal	Malachi
Prov	Proverbs		

NEW TESTAMENT

Mt	Matthew	1 Tim	1 Timothy
Mk	Mark	2 Tim	2 Timothy
Lk	Luke	Tit	Titus
Jn	John	Philem	Philemon
Acts	Acts of the Apostles	Heb	Hebrews
Rom	Romans	Jas	James
1 Cor	1 Corinthians	1 Pet	1 Peter
2 Cor	2 Corinthians	2 Pet	2 Peter
Gal	Galatians	1 Jn	1 John
Eph	Ephesians	2 Jn	2 John
Phil	Philippians	3 Jn	3 John
Col	Colossians	Jude	Jude
1 Thess	1 Thessalonians	Rev	Revelation
2 Thess	2 Thessalonians		

The
New Testament

INTRODUCTION TO
THE GOSPEL ACCORDING TO
MATTHEW

Authorship and Background: The titles by which the four Gospels are known, "According to Matthew," "According to Mark," "According to Luke," and "According to John" were not composed by the authors, but were added later and represent the thinking of the early church. Any consideration of their authorship must include the fact that in none of them does the author identify himself by name. The first book in the New Testament was accepted and canonized as having for its author the Apostle Matthew, also called Levi, a former tax-gatherer (Mt 9.9; Mk 2.14, 15; Lk 5.27–29). There is no further specific information about him, although later traditions concerning his ministry and death are recorded by different writers.

There is no way of fixing the precise date when the Gospel was written. Some prefer a date between A.D. 60 and 70; others take it to have been written between A.D. 80 and 90.

Characteristics: The importance of this Gospel is shown by the fact that it is placed first, and that the early Christian writers quoted from it more often than they did from any other Gospel. Note that:

(1) The strongly Hebraic character of the book identifies its author as a Jewish Christian writing for Jewish readers. Properly, then, this book should come first in the New Testament, since it connects Jesus Christ with God's promises to, and covenants with, David and Abraham (1.1). Christ's mission to Israel is emphasized and the Old Testament Scriptures are abundantly cited as having been fulfilled in the person and ministry of Jesus. He is "the Son of David," "the King of the Jews," the Messiah whom God had promised to Israel. "The kingdom of heaven" (and its equivalent, "the kingdom of God") is the key phrase and the subject of much of the teaching, especially the parables.

(2) The orderly arrangement of the teachings of Jesus into discourses shows the author to have been a teacher, concerned with the urgent need of preserving and transmitting the lessons of the Great Teacher. There are five great discourses: the Sermon on the Mount (ch 5–7), the Missionary Instructions to the Twelve (ch 10), the Parables of the Kingdom (ch 13), Greatness and Forgiveness in the Christian Community (ch 18), and the Discourse on Last Things (ch 24–25). Much of the material is arranged in groups of threes, fives, and sevens for greater ease in teaching and learning.

(3) Interest in the organized life of the Christian church is shown, for only in this Gospel does the word "church" (*ekklēsia*) appear (16.18; 18.17). Along with this, other teachings emphasize principles and conduct in the Christian fellowship (especially in chapter 18).

(4) Prominence is given to Christ's teachings on the end of the age and the Second Coming, particularly in the parables in chapter 13 and the Olivet Discourse in chapters 24–25.

Introduction to Matthew

Contents:

THE GOSPEL ACCORDING TO

MATTHEW

The genealogy of Jesus (1.1–17; cf. Lk 3.23–38)

1 The book of the genealogy of Jesus Christ, the son of David, the son of Abraham.

2 Abraham was the father of Isaac, and Isaac the father of Jacob, and Jacob the father of Judah and his brothers, 3 and Judah the father of Pĕrĕz and Zĕráh by Tāmar, and Perez the father of Hĕzròn, and Hezron the father of Ram,[a] 4 and Ram[a] the father of Ămmĭn'ădăb, and Amminadab the father of Nahshòn, and Nahshon the father of Sălmòn, 5 and Sălmòn the father of Bōăz by Rāhăb, and Boaz the father of Ōbĕd by Ruth, and Obed the father of Jĕssë, 6 and Jĕssë the father of David the king.

And David was the father of Solomon by the wife of Ūrī'áh, 7 and Solomon the father of Rēhŏbō'ăm, and Rehoboam the father of Ăbī'jáh, and Abijah the father of Āsă,[b] 8 and Āsă[b] the father of Jĕhŏsh'ăphăt, and Jehoshaphat the father of Jōrăm, and Joram the father of Ŭzzī'áh, 9 and Ŭzzī'áh the father of Jōthăm, and Jotham the father of Ăhăz, and Ahaz the father of Hĕzĕkī'áh, 10 and Hĕzĕkī'áh the father of Mănăs'sĕh, and Manasseh the father of Amos,[c] and Amos[c] the father of Jōsī'áh, 11 and Jōsī'áh the father of Jĕchŏnī'áh and his brothers, at the time of the deportation to Babylon.

12 And after the deportation to Babylon: Jĕchŏnī'áh was the father of Shĕ-ăl'tĭ-ĕl,[d] and She-alti-el[d] the father of Zĕrŭb'bábĕl, 13 and Zĕrŭb'bábĕl the father of Abī'ŭd, and Abiud the father of Ĕlī'ăkĭm, and Eliakim the father of Āzor, 14 and Āzor the father of Zādŏk, and Zadok the father of Ăchĭm, and Achim the father of Ĕlī'ŭd, 15 and Ĕlī'ŭd the father of Ĕlĕă'zăr, and Eleazar the father of Mătthàn, and Matthan the father of Jacob, 16 and Jacob the father of Joseph the husband of Mary, of whom Jesus was born, who is called Christ.

17 So all the generations from Abraham to David were fourteen generations, and from David to the deportation to Babylon four-

a Greek *Arăm*   *b* Greek *Ăsăph*   *c* Other authorities read *Āmòn*   *d* Greek *Sălă'thiel*

1.1
Ps 132.11;
Isa 11.1;
Lk 1.32;
Jn 7.42;
Acts 2.30;
13.23;
Rom 1.3;
Gen 12.3;
22.18;
Gal 3.16
1.2
Gen 21.2,3;
25.26;
29.35
1.3
Gen
38.27ff;
Ruth
4.18ff;
1 Chr 2.5,
9ff
*1.5
1.6
1 Sam 16.1;
17.1;
2 Sam 12.24
1.7
1 Chr 3.10
1.10
2 Ki 20.21;
1 Chr 3.13
1.11
2 Ki 24.14–
16;
Jer 27.20;
39.9;
Dan 1.2
1.12
1 Chr 3.17,
19
*1.16
Lk 1.27
*1.17
ver 11,12

1.5 The Davidic line, and thus the line of Christ, was racially mixed in that it included Gentiles as well as Hebrew ancestors. Ruth, the wife of Boaz and great-grandmother of David, was a Moabitess (1.4). Thus there was Gentile blood in the Messianic line. Most interpreters assume that the Rahab of this verse refers to the Gentile harlot of Josh 2.1 (see also Heb 11.31).

1.16 The difference between the accounts of the genealogy of Jesus in Matthew and Luke is usually explained by the fact that Matthew records the genealogy of Joseph as the legal (rather than the natural) father of Jesus. Luke, on the other hand, appears to trace the genealogy of Jesus through Mary, His mother, which accounts for an almost completely different set of ancestors listed from Heli to David (Lk 3.23–31). It is assumed that Heli was Joseph's father-in-law. Mary's name is not mentioned before Heli's because it was not customary among the Jews to trace genealogy through a female.

1.17 The gospel writer divides the forty-two generations from Abraham to Christ into three groups of fourteen generations each: Abraham to David, David to the Babylonian captivity, and from the Babylonian captivity to Christ. In order to maintain the total of forty-two generations, Matthew omitted some names and used others twice, e.g., Jechoniah is the last name in the second group (ver 11) and the first name in the third group (ver 12).

Several generations are omitted, for example; Joash, Amaziah, and Azariah, between Uzziah and Jotham (ver 9).

1437

teen generations, and from the deportation to Babylon to the Christ fourteen generations.

The birth of Jesus (1.18–25; Lk 1.26–35; 2.1–7)

18 Now the birth of Jesus Christ[f] took place in this way. When his mother Mary had been betrothed to Joseph, before they came together she was found to be with child of the Holy Spirit; 19 and her husband Joseph, being a just man and unwilling to put her to shame, resolved to divorce her quietly. 20 But as he considered this, behold, an angel of the Lord appeared to him in a dream, saying, "Joseph, son of David, do not fear to take Mary your wife, for that which is conceived in her is of the Holy Spirit; 21 she will bear a son, and you shall call his name Jesus, for he will save his people from their sins." 22 All this took place to fulfil what the Lord had spoken by the prophet:

23 "Behold, a virgin shall conceive and bear a son,
  and his name shall be called Ëmmăn'ū-él"

(which means, God with us). 24 When Joseph woke from sleep, he did as the angel of the Lord commanded him; he took his wife, 25 but knew her not until she had borne a son; and he called his name Jesus.

The visit of the wise men (2.1–12)

2 Now when Jesus was born in Bĕth'lĕhĕm of Judē'á in the days of Hĕrŏd the king, behold, wise men from the East came to Jerusalem, saying, 2 "Where is he who has been born king of the Jews? For we have seen his star in the East, and have come to worship him." 3 When Hĕrŏd the king heard this, he was troubled, and all Jerusalem with him; 4 and assembling all the chief priests and scribes of the people, he inquired of them where the Christ was to be born. 5 They told him, "In Bĕth'lĕhĕm of Judē'á; for

Margin references (left column):
*1.19 Deut 24.1
1.21 Lk 2.21; 2.11; Jn 1.29; Acts 4.12; 13.23,38
*1.23 Isa 7.14
1.25 Ex 13.2; Lk 2.21
*2.1 Lk 2.4–7; 1.5
2.2 Jer 23.5; Zech 9.9; Mk 15.2; Jn 1.49
2.5 Jn 7.42

_f_ Other ancient authorities read _of the Christ_

1.19 Jewish betrothal could be dissolved only by a formal act in which the man gave the woman a certificate of divorce. Joseph planned to do this quietly, in order to avoid a public scandal.

1.23 This statement stresses the fact that the birth of Christ was a literal fulfilment of Isaiah's prophecy (Isa 7.14). The specific Greek word for _virgin_ (_parthenos_) is quoted here from the standard Greek translation of the Old Testament. The fact that Christ had no human father, but was miraculously conceived in the womb of Mary by the divine act of the Holy Spirit, shows Him to be in a unique sense the Son of God.

2.1a Herod the Great, the son of an Idumean chieftain named Antipater, was a cunning and crafty schemer who ingratiated himself with Julius Caesar. The Romans appointed him procurator of Judea in 47 B.C., and in 37 B.C. elevated him to the rank of king, after which the last reigning descendant of the Maccabean dynasty, Antigonus, was executed. By fawning and flattery he managed to remain in the good graces of Rome through every change of imperial government. In his domestic life he was so ruthless and cruel that even Augustus

could say, "I would rather be Herod's dog than his son." Herod renovated the Temple of the LORD in Jerusalem and was still on the throne when Christ was born in 5 or 4 B.C. He died shortly after the massacre of the infants of Bethlehem.

2.1b The term for _wise men_ is _magoi_, the Greek form of the Old Persian _magav_. These _magoi_ constituted a priestly caste which originated in Media. They specialized in dreams and omens and, according to Herodotus (Book i. 107, 120; Book vii. 19, 37, 113), claimed the gift of prophecy. The term _magos_ came to be applied later to others, not of Median stock, like the Jew Bar-Jesus (Acts 13.6) and the Samaritan Simon (Acts 8.9), who used incantations and magical methods like theirs. But these _magoi_ who visited Bethlehem were Eastern in origin and doubtlessly came from Persia or Media. Having somehow heard of the promise of a Messianic King in Judea, and having observed a new and brilliant star portending His birth, they were ready to be guided by it to His birthplace itself. Their adoration of the Christchild was a token of the later submission of the Gentile world to the Jewish Messiah.

so it is written by the prophet:

6 'And you, O Bĕth'lĕhĕm, in the land of Judah,
are by no means least among the rulers of Judah;
for from you shall come a ruler
who will govern my people Israel.' "

2.6
Mic 5.2;
Jn 21.16

7 Then Hĕrŏd summoned the wise men secretly and ascertained from them what time the star appeared; 8 and he sent them to Bĕth'lĕhĕm, saying, "Go and search diligently for the child, and when you have found him bring me word, that I too may come and worship him." 9 When they had heard the king they went their way; and lo, the star which they had seen in the East went before them, till it came to rest over the place where the child was. 10 When they saw the star, they rejoiced exceedingly with great joy; 11 and going into the house they saw the child with Mary his mother, and they fell down and worshiped him. Then, opening their treasures, they offered him gifts, gold and frankincense and myrrh. 12And being warned in a dream not to return to Hĕrŏd, they departed to their own country by another way.

*2.11
Mt 1.18;
12.46;
Ps 72.10;
Isa 60.2
2.12
Mt 2.22;
Acts 10.22;
Heb 11.7

The flight into Egypt (2.13–18)

13 Now when they had departed, behold, an angel of the Lord appeared to Joseph in a dream and said, "Rise, take the child and his mother, and flee to Egypt, and remain there till I tell you; for Hĕrŏd is about to search for the child, to destroy him." 14And he rose and took the child and his mother by night, and departed to Egypt, 15 and remained there until the death of Hĕrŏd. This was to fulfil what the Lord had spoken by the prophet, "Out of Egypt have I called my son."

2.13
ver 19

2.14
Hos 11.1;
Ex 4.22

16 Then Hĕrŏd, when he saw that he had been tricked by the wise men, was in a furious rage, and he sent and killed all the male children in Bĕth'lĕhĕm and in all that region who were two years old or under, according to the time which he had ascertained from the wise men. 17 Then was fulfilled what was spoken by the prophet Jĕrĕmī'ah:

*2.16

18 "A voice was heard in Rāmah,
wailing and loud lamentation,
Rachel weeping for her children;
she refused to be consoled,
because they were no more."

2.18
Jer 31.15

From Egypt to Nazareth (2.19–23; cf. Mk 1.9; Lk 1.26)

19 But when Hĕrŏd died, behold, an angel of the Lord ap-

2.19
Mt 1.20;
ver 13

2.11 There is no way of determining how long after the birth of Christ the wise men arrived in Bethlehem. That they did not see the babe on the night of his birth is clear from the fact that the family was in a house (2.11), and that King Herod ordered all male children up to two years of age to be slain (2.16), in accordance with the information given him by the wise men concerning the time of the star's appearance (2.7), presumably the night Christ was born.
2.16 Evidently the wise men had indicated to Herod the exact time when they had seen

the natal star in the East, and thus afforded him an idea as to how old the infant king might be when they finally arrived in Palestine and visited Bethlehem. Yet the fact that Herod ordered the execution of all male babies two years of age and under does not necessarily mean that Jesus was as old as two. He may have been not more than twelve months, and Herod may simply have ordered all to be killed within that age-span to make certain that the Messiah Himself should be slain. It is estimated that the number of children slain would not have exceeded forty or fifty.

peared in a dream to Joseph in Egypt, saying, 20 "Rise, take the child and his mother, and go to the land of Israel, for those who sought the child's life are dead." 21And he rose and took the child and his mother, and went to the land of Israel. 22 But when he heard that Arçhēlā'ús reigned over Judē'á in place of his father Hĕrŏd, he was afraid to go there, and being warned in a dream he withdrew to the district of Găl'ilee. 23And he went and dwelt in a city called Năz'ărêth, that what was spoken by the prophets might be fulfilled, "He shall be called a Năz'árĕne."

*2.22
ver 12;
Mt 3.13;
Lk 2.39

2.23
Lk 1.26;
Isa 11.1;
Mk 1.24

The ministry of John the Baptist
(3.1–12; Mk 1.1–8; Lk 3.2–17; Jn 1.6–8,19–28)

*3.1
3.2
Dan 2.44;
Mt 4.7;
10.7
3.3
Isa 40.3;
Mk 1.3;
Lk 3.4;
Jn 1.23;
Lk 1.76
3.4
2 Ki 1.8;
Zech 13.4;
Lev 11.22
3.6
Acts 19.4,
18
*3.7
Mt 12.34;
23.33;
Rom 5.9;
1 Thess 1.10

3 In those days came John the Baptist, preaching in the wilderness of Judē'á, 2 "Repent, for the kingdom of heaven is at hand." 3 For this is he who was spoken of by the prophet Ĭṣāi'áh when he said,

"The voice of one crying in the wilderness:
Prepare the way of the Lord,
make his paths straight."

4 Now John wore a garment of camel's hair, and a leather girdle around his waist; and his food was locusts and wild honey. 5 Then went out to him Jerusalem and all Judē'á and all the region about the Jordan, 6 and they were baptized by him in the river Jordan, confessing their sins.

7 But when he saw many of the Phạr'ịsees and Săd'dụçeēs coming for baptism, he said to them, "You brood of vipers! Who

---

2.22 Archelaus is mentioned here only in the Bible. He was the older of two sons of Herod the Great by Malthace, a Samaritan woman. The Roman Emperor, Caesar Augustus, made him ethnarch (not king) of Judea, Samaria, and Idumea. Archelaus was the worst of all of Herod's sons. During his rule of nine years the people under him suffered greatly and at last appealed to Augustus to depose him. Augustus banished him to Vienna in A.D. 6. Joseph feared Archelaus and for this reason left for Galilee, which was under the control of Antipas. After the deportation of Archelaus, Judea was placed under the rule of Roman procurators until A.D. 41.

3.1 See note to Lk 1.57 on John the Baptist.

3.7a The Pharisees were probably the most influential of the Jewish sects among the people. Their main tenet was separation from everything non-Jewish. They held generally to the following practices and ideas: (1) careful observance of the Law, to which they added many detailed requirements and special interpretations; (2) belief in the immortality of the soul, resurrection of the body, and retribution in the future life; (3) belief in the existence of angels and spirits; (4) belief that God would deliver Israel and restore her to a position of power and prestige; (5) belief in a doctrine of divine providence along with the freedom of the will. But their most characteristic teaching was that the faithful Jew earned merit with God by scrupulously observing the niceties of the Law. They perverted the Law into a system of merit-earning which virtually ex-

cluded the principle of justification by grace through faith. The Pharisees were openly hostile to Christ because he consistently practiced what they rejected and condemned (e.g., Mt 9.3, 11, 14; Lk 5.21). Christ therefore opposed them as legalists and severely condemned their hypocrisy (e.g., 6.2, 5, 16; Mk 7.6; Mt 12.34; 23.33, etc.).

3.7b The Sadducees were one of several Jewish sects. Their name is usually thought to be derived from Zadok, who was a high priest in the reign of David. Their membership came largely from the priestly nobility, whereas the Pharisees enjoyed a wider following among all Jewish social classes. The Sadducees often clashed with the Pharisees both in theological and political matters. They were particularly opposed to the oral law meticulously observed by the Pharisees (known as "the tradition of the elders"), accepting only the written Law of Moses as binding. In their interpretation of Scripture they disagreed with the Pharisees in denying the following doctrines: (1) the bodily resurrection of the dead; (2) the future punishments and rewards of the dead on the day of judgment; (3) the existence of angels and spirits; (4) an overruling divine providence or "fate" as opposed to an unconditional free will. While they are not mentioned in the New Testament as often as the Pharisees, this group opposed Christ just as vigorously as they. Christ refuted and denounced Sadducees on several occasions (16.1–4, 6–12; 22.23–33) although Scripture records His condemnation of them less frequently than His condemnation of the Pharisees (16.6, 11).

warned you to flee from the wrath to come? 8 Bear fruit that befits repentance, 9 and do not presume to say to yourselves, 'We have Abraham as our father'; for I tell you, God is able from these stones to raise up children to Abraham. 10 Even now the axe is laid to the root of the trees; every tree therefore that does not bear good fruit is cut down and thrown into the fire.

11 "I baptize you with water for repentance, but he who is coming after me is mightier than I, whose sandals I am not worthy to carry; he will baptize you with the Holy Spirit and with fire. 12 His winnowing fork is in his hand, and he will clear his threshing floor and gather his wheat into the granary, but the chaff he will burn with unquenchable fire."

The baptism of Jesus (3.13–17; Mk 1.9–11; Lk 3.21,22)

13 Then Jesus came from Găl′ĭleē to the Jordan to John, to be baptized by him. 14 John would have prevented him, saying, "I need to be baptized by you, and do you come to me?" 15 But Jesus answered him, "Let it be so now; for thus it is fitting for us to fulfil all righteousness." Then he consented. 16And when Jesus was baptized, he went up immediately from the water, and behold, the heavens were openedᵍ and he saw the Spirit of God descending like a dove, and alighting on him; 17 and lo, a voice from heaven, saying, "This is my beloved Son,ʰ with whom I am well pleased."

The temptation in the wilderness (4.1–11; Mk 1.12,13; Lk 4.1–13)

4 Then Jesus was led up by the Spirit into the wilderness to be tempted by the devil. 2And he fasted forty days and forty nights, and afterward he was hungry. 3And the tempter came and said to him, "If you are the Son of God, command these stones to become loaves of bread." 4 But he answered, "It is written,

'Man shall not live by bread alone,
but by every word that proceeds from the mouth of God.' "

5 Then the devil took him to the holy city, and set him on the pinnacle of the temple, 6 and said to him, "If you are the Son of God, throw yourself down; for it is written,

'He will give his angels charge of you,'
and
'On their hands they will bear you up,
lest you strike your foot against a stone.' "

7 Jesus said to him, "Again it is written, 'You shall not tempt the Lord your God.'" 8Again, the devil took him to a very high mountain, and showed him all the kingdoms of the world and the glory of them; 9 and he said to him, "All these I will give you, if you will fall down and worship me." 10 Then Jesus said to him, "Begone, Satan! for it is written,

'You shall worship the Lord your God
and him only shall you serve.' "

11 Then the devil left him, and behold, angels came and ministered to him.

ᵍ Other ancient authorities add to him   ʰ Or my Son, my (or the) Beloved

3.17 *This is my beloved Son.* Jesus here begins His public ministry.

4.1 See note to Lk 4.2 on the temptation of Jesus. (This was at the start of His ministry.)

3.8 Acts 26.20
3.9 Jn 8.33,39; Acts 13.26; Rom 4.1,11,16
3.10 Mt 7.19
3.11 Acts 1.5; 11.16; 19.4; Isa 4.4; Acts 2.3,4
3.12 Mal 3.3; Mt 13.30
3.13 Jn 1.31–34
3.16 Isa 11.2; 42.1; Jn 1.32
*3.17 Ps 2.7; Mt 12.18; 17.5; Mk 9.7; Lk 9.35
*4.1
4.2 Ex 34.28; 1 Ki 19.8
4.3 1 Thess 3.5
4.4 Deut 8.3
4.5 Neh 11.1; Dan 9.24; Mt 27.53; Rev 21.10
4.6 Ps 91.11,12
4.7 Deut 6.16
4.10 1 Chr 21.1; Deut 6.13
4.11 Mt 26.53; Lk 22.43; Heb 1.14

The beginning of Jesus' Galilean ministry
(4.12-17; Mk 1.14,15; Lk 4.14,15; Jn 4.43-45)

*4.13

12 Now when he heard that John had been arrested, he withdrew into Găl′ĭleē; 13 and leaving Năz′áreth he went and dwelt in Căpēr′nä-ŭm by the sea, in the territory of Zĕb′ŭlún and Năph′-tălī, 14 that what was spoken by the prophet Īşai′áh might be fulfilled:

4.15
Isa 9.1,2

15 "The land of Zĕb′ŭlún and the land of Năph′tălī,
    toward the sea, across the Jordan,
    Găl′ĭleē of the Gentiles—

4.16
Isa 42.7;
Lk 2.32

16 the people who sat in darkness
    have seen a great light,
    and for those who sat in the region and shadow of death
    light has dawned."

*4.17
Mt 3.2;
10.7

17 From that time Jesus began to preach, saying, "Repent, for the kingdom of heaven is at hand."

The call of James and John
(4.18-25; cf. Mk 1.16-20; Lk 5.1-11)

4.18
Jn 1.35-42

18 As he walked by the Sea of Găl′ĭleē, he saw two brothers, Simon who is called Peter and Andrew his brother, casting a net into the sea; for they were fishermen. 19And he said to them,

4.20
Mt 10.28;
Lk 18.28

"Follow me, and I will make you fishers of men." 20 Immediately they left their nets and followed him. 21And going on from there he saw two other brothers, James the son of Zĕb′ĕdeē and John his brother, in the boat with Zebedee their father, mending their nets, and he called them. 22 Immediately they left the boat and their father, and followed him.

4.23
Mk 1.39;
Lk 4.15,44;
Mt 9.35;
13.54;
Mk 1.21;
1.34

23 And he went about all Găl′ĭleē, teaching in their synagogues and preaching the gospel of the kingdom and healing every disease and every infirmity among the people. 24 So his fame spread

*4.24
Lk 2.2;
Mt 8.16,28,
33;
Mk 1.32;
Lk 8.36;
Mt 17.15;
8.6; 9.2,6

throughout all Syria, and they brought him all the sick, those afflicted with various diseases and pains, demoniacs, epileptics, and paralytics, and he healed them. 25And great crowds followed

4.25
Mk 3.7,8;
Lk 6.17

him from Găl′ĭleē and the Dĕcăp′ólĭs and Jerusalem and Judē′á and from beyond the Jordan.

4.13 From now on Capernaum was Jesus' home in Galilee (cf. Mk 2.1; 3.19). Capernaum, the home town of Simon and Andrew (Mk 1.29), was an important town at the north end of the Sea of Galilee, on the border of the province of Galilee. The international highway ran through there, hence the tax office (9.9; Mk 2.13, 14).

4.17 The phrase *kingdom of heaven* is synonymous with the phrase *kingdom of God,* used in Mark and Luke (although Matthew sometimes uses *the kingdom of God,* cf. 12.28; 19.24; 21.31, 43). Thus, in this particular instance, Matthew quotes Jesus as using the Hebrew or Aramaic phrase, *kingdom of heaven* (where "heaven" is a respectful equivalent to the name of God), whereas Mk 1.15 quotes the identical saying in the form more familiar to Gentile readers, *kingdom of God.* As in many other instances, the

writers express the same truth in a variety of words and phrases.

4.24 Demon possession is presented in Scripture as a dreadful reality. The supposition that the demoniacs of the Gospels were only mentally ill is fallacious, for Mk 1.32 and Lk 6.17 distinguish clearly between demon possession and bodily disease. Christ spoke to the demons themselves as well as to the victims possessed by them, and commanded them to depart (Mk 1.23, 34; 9.25; Mt 8.32; 17.18). In Lk 8.32 the demons are stated to have left those whom they had possessed and to have entered into a herd of swine. In 8.31 and Mk 9.26 the personalities and characteristics of the demons are clearly distinguished from those possessed by them. In Jewish and biblical thought demons are believed to be part of the whole spiritual hierarchy of evil headed by Satan.

The Sermon on the Mount (5.1–7.29; Lk 6.20–49)
1. *The Beatitudes (5.1–12; Lk 6.20–23)*

5 Seeing the crowds, he went up on the mountain, and when he sat down his disciples came to him. ²And he opened his mouth and taught them, saying:

3 "Blessed are the poor in spirit, for theirs is the kingdom of heaven.

4 "Blessed are those who mourn, for they shall be comforted.

5 "Blessed are the meek, for they shall inherit the earth.

6 "Blessed are those who hunger and thirst for righteousness, for they shall be satisfied.

7 "Blessed are the merciful, for they shall obtain mercy.

8 "Blessed are the pure in heart, for they shall see God.

9 "Blessed are the peacemakers, for they shall be called sons of God.

10 "Blessed are those who are persecuted for righteousness' sake, for theirs is the kingdom of heaven.

11 "Blessed are you when men revile you and persecute you and utter all kinds of evil against you falsely on my account. ¹²Rejoice and be glad, for your reward is great in heaven, for so men persecuted the prophets who were before you.

2. *What the believer is like (5.13–16)*

13 "You are the salt of the earth; but if salt has lost its taste, how shall its saltness be restored? It is no longer good for anything except to be thrown out and trodden under foot by men.

14 "You are the light of the world. A city set on a hill cannot be hid. ¹⁵Nor do men light a lamp and put it under a bushel, but on a stand, and it gives light to all in the house. ¹⁶Let your light so shine before men, that they may see your good works and give glory to your Father who is in heaven.

3. *The righteousness required (5.17–20)*

17 "Think not that I have come to abolish the law and the prophets; I have come not to abolish them but to fulfil them. ¹⁸For truly, I say to you, till heaven and earth pass away, not an iota, not a dot, will pass from the law until all is accomplished. ¹⁹Whoever then relaxes one of the least of these commandments and teaches men so, shall be called least in the kingdom of heaven; but he who does them and teaches them shall be called great in the kingdom of heaven. ²⁰For I tell you, unless your righteousness exceeds that of the scribes and Phar′isees, you will never enter the kingdom of heaven.

*5.1
Mk 3.13;
Jn 6.3

5.3
Mk 10.14;
Lk 22.29
5.4
Isa 61.2,3

5.6
Isa 55.1,2

5.8
Heb 12.14;
1 Jn 3.2
5.9
Rom 8.14
5.10
1 Pet 3.14
5.11
1 Pet 4.14
5.12
Acts 7.52;
1 Thess
2.15;
Jas 5.10

5.13
Mk 9.50;
Lk 14.34,35

5.14
Phil 2.15
5.15
Mk 4.21;
Lk 8.16
5.16
1 Pet 2.12

*5.17
Rom 3.31;
Gal 3.24
5.18
Lk 16.17;
5.19
Jas 2.10

5.1 The impression is usually given that the Sermon on the Mount (5–7) was spoken on a single occasion during the early ministry of our Lord. Many hold that these three chapters contain teachings of Jesus which were given on many different occasions. Undoubtedly, much that Jesus said has not been recorded, and many of His utterances were probably repeated in different places and on various occasions.

5.17 Christ was neither lawless nor a lawbreaker. In all things He obeyed God's laws (Jn 8.46; 1 Pet 2.21–23), and in His teaching freed the law from its human accretions and false interpretations. His followers today are not under the yoke of the Mosaic Law with its ceremonial regulations (Acts 15.10; Gal 5.1). They have been redeemed from the curse of the Law by Christ's death (Gal 3.13) and they have been adopted as sons in the household of God; this does not mean, however, that they are free to break whatever God has made binding. The ceremonial law has been rendered obsolete by the Cross, and yet the basic moral law continues in force even for Christians. The children of God must obey its demands, not as a condition of salvation but as the fruit of a transformed life.

4. The sixth commandment (5.21–26)

*5.21f
Ex 20.13;
Deut 5.17

5.22
1 Jn 3.15;
Jas 2.20

5.23
Mt 8.4;
23.19

5.25
Prov 25.8;
Lk 12.57–
59

21 "You have heard that it was said to the men of old, 'You shall not kill; and whoever kills shall be liable to judgment.' 22 But I say to you that every one who is angry with his brother[i] shall be liable to judgment; whoever insults[j] his brother shall be liable to the council, and whoever says, 'You fool!' shall be liable to the hell[k] of fire. 23 So if you are offering your gift at the altar, and there remember that your brother has something against you, 24 leave your gift there before the altar and go; first be reconciled to your brother, and then come and offer your gift. 25 Make friends quickly with your accuser, while you are going with him to court, lest your accuser hand you over to the judge, and the judge to the guard, and you be put in prison; 26 truly, I say to you, you will never get out till you have paid the last penny.

5. The seventh commandment
(5.27–32; cf. 19.9; Mk 10.11; Lk 16.18)

*5.27
Ex 20.14;
Deut 5.18
5.28
Job 31.1;
Prov 6.25
*5.29
Mt 18.9;
Mk 9.43–47

27 "You have heard that it was said, 'You shall not commit adultery.' 28 But I say to you that every one who looks at a woman lustfully has already committed adultery with her in his heart. 29 If your right eye causes you to sin, pluck it out and throw it away; it is better that you lose one of your members than that your whole body be thrown into hell.[k] 30And if your right hand causes you to sin, cut it off and throw it away; it is better that you lose one of your members than that your whole body go into hell.[k]

*5.31
Deut
24.1–4;
Mk 10.11,
12;
Lk 16.18

31 "It was also said, 'Whoever divorces his wife, let him give her a certificate of divorce.' 32 But I say to you that every one who divorces his wife, except on the ground of unchastity, makes her an adulteress; and whoever marries a divorced woman commits adultery.

6. The law of oaths (5.33–37)

5.33
Lev 19.12;
Num 30.2;
Deut 23.21;
Mt 23.16
5.34
Jas 5.12;
Isa 66.1

33 "Again you have heard that it was said to the men of old, 'You shall not swear falsely, but shall perform to the Lord what you have sworn.' 34 But I say to you, Do not swear at all, either by heaven, for it is the throne of God, 35 or by the earth, for it is his footstool, or by Jerusalem, for it is the city of the great King. 36And do not swear by your head, for you cannot make one hair

---

i Other ancient authorities insert without cause
j Greek says Raca to (an obscure term of abuse)   k Greek Gĕhĕn'nä

5.21, 22 Christ did not abolish the Old Testament law concerning murder. Rather, He taught that the righteousness of God's children must exceed that of the scribes and Pharisees (ver 20). These Jewish teachers defined sin as consisting principally in the overt act; Jesus showed that it consists principally in the intention of the heart. Thus murder begins when hatred or hostility rises up in the human heart; such hostility renders a man guilty before God even though the hater or despiser is restrained from murder only by the fear of retribution. The evil desire within the soul is the root of the sin to which it logically leads, and God condemns it as such.
5.27 As with murder, so with adultery. Christ defines the sin as consisting in the evil thought. In Jesus' day the teaching was prevalent that adultery consisted only in the overt act. Thus a man had not broken the law unless and until the act itself was performed. His heart could be filled with adulterous thoughts, but this was not regarded as sinful. Jesus provided the correct interpretation and understanding of what had always been the heart of the moral law relative to adultery, even in the Old Testament.
5.29 This utterance of Jesus is not to be taken literally, for He did not mean for men to pluck out their eyes or cut off their hands. Sin is so dangerous, however, that "it is better to lose the eye and the hand that thus offend than to give way to the sin, and perish eternally in it." (Matthew Henry, COMMENTARY ON THE WHOLE BIBLE, Fleming H. Revell Co. Vol. 5, p. 61.)
5.31 See note to 19.3 on divorce.

white or black. 37 Let what you say be simply 'Yes' or 'No'; anything more than this comes from evil.¹

7. The law of retaliation (5.38–42)

38 "You have heard that it was said, 'An eye for an eye and a tooth for a tooth.' 39 But I say to you, Do not resist one who is evil. But if any one strikes you on the right cheek, turn to him the other also; 40 and if any one would sue you and take your coat, let him have your cloak as well; 41 and if any one forces you to go one mile, go with him two miles. 42 Give to him who begs from you, and do not refuse him who would borrow from you.

8. The law of love (5.43–48)

43 "You have heard that it was said, 'You shall love your neighbor and hate your enemy.' 44 But I say to you, Love your enemies and pray for those who persecute you, 45 so that you may be sons of your Father who is in heaven; for he makes his sun rise on the evil and on the good, and sends rain on the just and on the unjust. 46 For if you love those who love you, what reward have you? Do not even the tax collectors do the same? 47And if you salute only your brethren, what more are you doing than others? Do not even the Gentiles do the same? 48 You, therefore, must be perfect, as your heavenly Father is perfect.

The Sermon on the Mount continued: religious observances (6.1–34)

1. Giving of alms (6.1–4)

6 "Beware of practicing your piety before men in order to be seen by them; for then you will have no reward from your Father who is in heaven.

2 "Thus, when you give alms, sound no trumpet before you, as the hypocrites do in the synagogues and in the streets, that they may be praised by men. Truly, I say to you, they have received their reward. 3 But when you give alms, do not let your left hand know what your right hand is doing, 4 so that your alms may be in secret; and your Father who sees in secret will reward you.

2. Praying (6.5–15; cf. Lk 11.1–4)

5 "And when you pray, you must not be like the hypocrites; for they love to stand and pray in the synagogues and at the street corners, that they may be seen by men. Truly, I say to you, they have received their reward. 6 But when you pray, go into your room and shut the door and pray to your Father who is in secret; and your Father who sees in secret will reward you.

7 "And in praying do not heap up empty phrases as the Gentiles

¹ Or the evil one

5.38 Ex 21.24; Lev 24.20; Deut 19.21
5.39 Prov 24.29; Lk 6.29; Rom 12.17, 19; 1 Cor 6.7; 1 Pet 3.9
5.42 Deut 15.8; Lk 6.30
5.43 Lev 19.18; Deut 23.6; Ps 41.10
5.44 Rom 12.14; Acts 7.60; 1 Cor 4.12; 1 Pet 2.23
5.45 Job 25.3
*5.48 Lev 19.2; Col 1.28; Jas 1.4
6.1 Mt 23.5
6.2 Rom 12.8
6.4 Col 3.23,24
6.5 Mk 11.25; Lk 18.10–14
6.6 2 Ki 4.33
6.7 Ecc 5.2; 1 Ki 18.26, 29

5.48 The word *perfect* (Greek *teleios*) is derived from *telos*, meaning "end," "goal," "limit." It therefore signifies "attaining to the end, complete, mature." But here the comparison is made between God and His children, and so the word must mean more than "mature." From the context we can deduce that the God like quality which must characterize a true believer is the quality of self-disinterested love and kindness for others, even for those who deserve no kindness. This kind of "perfectness" consists in the basic intention or attitude of the believer, rather than in absolute sinlessness. This is perfectly possible for believers who, by faith, draw from Him the grace to maintain that attitude of kindly benevolence and sincere desire for the good of others.

do; for they think that they will be heard for their many words. 8 Do not be like them, for your Father knows what you need before you ask him. 9 Pray then like this:

Our Father who art in heaven,
Hallowed be thy name.
10 Thy kingdom come,
Thy will be done,
On earth as it is in heaven.
11 Give us this day our daily bread;[m]
12 And forgive us our debts,
As we also have forgiven our debtors;
13 And lead us not into temptation,
But deliver us from evil.[n]

14 For if you forgive men their trespasses, your heavenly Father also will forgive you; 15 but if you do not forgive men their trespasses, neither will your Father forgive your trespasses.

3. Fasting (6.16–18)

16 "And when you fast, do not look dismal, like the hypocrites, for they disfigure their faces that their fasting may be seen by men. Truly, I say to you, they have received their reward. 17 But when you fast, anoint your head and wash your face. 18 that your fasting may not be seen by men but by your Father who is in secret; and your Father who sees in secret will reward you.

4. The Christian and the world (6.19–34)
a. True riches (6.19–21)

19 "Do not lay up for yourselves treasures on earth, where moth and rust[o] consume and where thieves break in and steal, 20 but lay up for yourselves treasures in heaven, where neither moth nor rust[o] consumes and where thieves do not break in and steal. 21 For where your treasure is, there will your heart be also.

b. Light or darkness (6.22,23)

22 "The eye is the lamp of the body. So, if your eye is sound, your whole body will be full of light; 23 but if your eye is not sound, your whole body will be full of darkness. If then the light in you is darkness, how great is the darkness!

c. God or mammon (6.24)

24. "No one can serve two masters; for either he will hate the one and love the other, or he will be devoted to the one and despise the other. You cannot serve God and mammon.[x]

---

m Or our bread for the morrow
n Or the evil one. Other authorities, some ancient, add, in some form, For thine is the kingdom and the power and the glory, for ever. Amen.   o Or worm
x Mammon is a Semitic word for money or riches

6.9 This is the model for all true prayer. It begins with adoration and the interests of God's kingdom; then follows the plea for forgiveness and the petition for individual needs. Ever since Christ taught it, this has been the most widely used prayer of the Bible, and it is repeated by millions of Christians every day of the year. Some have imagined that there is an Old Testament legalism in asking for forgiveness as we forgive others (6.12, 14, 15). This is a grave misunderstanding. Our forgiveness is not granted to us upon condition that we furnish God with merit of any kind, not even the merit of forgiving others. It is only that our refusal to forgive others, unavoidably involves our denial of the whole principle of forgiveness as such, and therefore our rejection of God's forgiveness towards us. He who does not forgive his fellow man has not repented of his own sin, and hence cannot find forgiveness for himself.

6.24 See note to Lk 16.9 on mammon.

Margin references:

*6.9
6.10 Mt 26.39,42
6.11 Prov 30.8
6.12 Mt 18.21
6.13 Jn 17.15; 2 Thess 3.3; Jas 1.13
6.14 Mk 11.25, 26; Eph 4.32; Col 3.13
6.15 Mt 18.35
6.16 Isa 58.5
6.18 ver 4,6
6.19 Prov 23.4; 1 Tim 6.17; Heb 13.5; Jas 5.1
6.20 Lk 12.33, 34; 18.22; 1 Tim 6.19; 1 Pet 1.4
6.22 Mt 20.15; Mk 7.22; Lk 11.34–36
6.24 Lk 16.13

d. Trust or anxiety (6.25–34; cf. Lk 12.22–31)

25 "Therefore I tell you, do not be anxious about your life, what you shall eat or what you shall drink, nor about your body, what you shall put on. Is not life more than food, and the body more than clothing? 26 Look at the birds of the air: they neither sow nor reap nor gather into barns, and yet your heavenly Father feeds them. Are you not of more value than they? 27And which of you by being anxious can add one cubit to his span of life?ᵖ 28And why are you anxious about clothing? Consider the lilies of the field, how they grow; they neither toil nor spin; 29 yet I tell you, even Solomon in all his glory was not arrayed like one of these. 30 But if God so clothes the grass of the field, which today is alive and tomorrow is thrown into the oven, will he not much more clothe you, O men of little faith? 31 Therefore do not be anxious, saying, 'What shall we eat?' or 'What shall we drink?' or 'What shall we wear?' 32 For the Gentiles seek all these things; and your heavenly Father knows that you need them all. 33 But seek first his kingdom and his righteousness, and all these things shall be yours as well.

34 "Therefore do not be anxious about tomorrow, for tomorrow will be anxious for itself. Let the day's own trouble be sufficient for the day.

Sermon on the Mount concluded (7.1–29)

1. Censure and reproof (7.1–6; Lk 6.37–42)

7 "Judge not, that you be not judged. 2 For with the judgment you pronounce you will be judged, and the measure you give will be the measure you get. 3 Why do you see the speck that is in your brother's eye, but do not notice the log that is in your own eye? 4 Or how can you say to your brother, 'Let me take the speck out of your eye,' when there is the log in your own eye? 5 You hypocrite, first take the log out of your own eye, and then you will see clearly to take the speck out of your brother's eye.

6 "Do not give dogs what is holy; and do not throw your pearls before swine, lest they trample them under foot and turn to attack you.

2. Prayer and the Golden Rule (7.7–12; cf. Lk 11.9–13)

7 "Ask, and it will be given you; seek, and you will find; knock, and it will be opened to you. 8 For every one who asks receives, and he who seeks finds, and to him who knocks it will be opened. 9 Or what man of you, if his son asks him for bread, will give him a stone? 10 Or if he asks for a fish, will give him a serpent? 11 If you then, who are evil, know how to give good gifts to your children, how much more will your Father who is in heaven give good things to those who ask him! 12 So whatever you wish that men would do to you, do so to them; for this is the law and the prophets.

ᵖ Or to his stature

7.1 This verse cannot be construed as teaching that believers are never to exercise judgment relative to the doctrine or the actions of other men. It does teach that those who do judge, will themselves be judged by the same standards they use in their judgments of others. Therefore one should be careful to employ standards of judgment by which he himself would be happy to be judged in his own conduct and convictions.

7.7 See note to Lk 11.1 on principles of prayer.

Marginal references:

6.25 Ps 55.22; Phil 4.6; 1 Pet 5.7
6.26 Job 38.41; Ps 147.9; Lk 12.24
6.27 Ps 39.5
6.29 1 Ki 10.4-7
6.30 Mt 8.26; 14.31; 16.8
6.32 ver 8
6.33 Mt 19.28; Mk 10.29 30; Lk 18.29,30
*7.1 Mk 4.24; Rom 2.1; 14.10; 1 Cor 4.3
7.6 Prov 9.7,8; Acts 13.45
*7.7 Mk 11.24; Jn 15.7; 16.23,24; Jas 4.3; 1 Jn 3.22; 5.14,15
7.8 Jer 29.12,13
7.12 Lk 6.31; Rom 13.8-10; Gal 5.14

3. *The narrow and the wide gates (7.13,14)*

7.13
Lk 13.24
7.15
Jer 23.16;
Mt 24.11,
24;
Mk 13.22;
2 Pet 2.1;
1 Jn 4.1;
Rev 16.13;
19.20;
20.10;
Acts 20.29
7.16
Mt 12.33;
Mk 3.10;
Jas 3.12
7.19
Mt 3.10;
Lk 3.9;
Jn 15.2,6

13 "Enter by the narrow gate; for the gate is wide and the way is easy,ᵃ that leads to destruction, and those who enter by it are many. 14 For the gate is narrow and the way is hard, that leads to life, and those who find it are few.

4. *The test of false prophets (7.15-20)*

15 "Beware of false prophets, who come to you in sheep's clothing but inwardly are ravenous wolves. 16 You will know them by their fruits. Are grapes gathered from thorns, or figs from thistles? 17 So, every sound tree bears good fruit, but the bad tree bears evil fruit. 18A sound tree cannot bear evil fruit, nor can a bad tree bear good fruit. 19 Every tree that does not bear good fruit is cut down and thrown into the fire. 20 Thus you will know them by their fruits.

5. *Profession versus possession (7.21-29)*

*7.21
Hos 8.2;
Mt 25.11,
12;
Acts 19.13;
Rom 2.13;
Jas 1.22
7.22
Mt 25.12;
Lk 13.25–
27
7.23
Ps 6.8;
Mt 25.12;
Lk 13.25,27
7.24
Lk 6.47–49;
Jas 1.22-25

21 "Not every one who says to me, 'Lord, Lord,' shall enter the kingdom of heaven, but he who does the will of my Father who is in heaven. 22 On that day many will say to me, 'Lord, Lord, did we not prophesy in your name, and cast out demons in your name, and do many mighty works in your name?' 23And then will I declare to them, 'I never knew you; depart from me, you evildoers.'

24 "Every one then who hears these words of mine and does them will be like a wise man who built his house upon the rock; 25 and the rain fell, and the floods came, and the winds blew and beat upon that house, but it did not fall, because it had been founded on the rock. 26And every one who hears these words of mine and does not do them will be like a foolish man who built his house upon the sand; 27 and the rain fell, and the floods came, and the winds blew and beat against that house, and it fell; and great was the fall of it."

7.28
Mt 11.1;
13.53;
19.1; 26.1;
13.54;
Mk 1.22;
6.2;
Lk 4.32;
Jn 7.46
*8.1
8.2
Mt 9.18;
15.25;
18.26;
20.20;
Jn 9.38

28 And when Jesus finished these sayings, the crowds were astonished at his teaching, 29 for he taught them as one who had authority, and not as their scribes.

Miracles of Jesus (1) (8.1-17)

1. *The leper cleansed (8.1-4; Mk 1.40-45; Lk 5.12-16)*

8 When he came down from the mountain, great crowds followed him; 2 and behold, a leper came to him and knelt before

---

ᵃ Other ancient authorities read *for the way is wide and easy*

7.21 The title *Lord* (Greek *kyrios*) is used of Jesus Christ almost seven hundred times. In combination with Jesus and Christ, the title has a threefold significance: Jesus is savior; Christ is the anointed of God; as Lord, He is master of life. The title *kyrios* was also used as an equivalent of Yahweh in the old Greek translation of the Old Testament, and it is so used in the New Testament as well, both in quotations from the Old Testament and in other contexts where God in heaven is referred to as *an angel of the Lord* (2.19), or *the kingdom of our Lord* (Rev 11.15). Therefore

an identification of Jesus Christ with Yahweh Himself is involved in this title of *kyrios* or "Lord."

8.1 Matthew presents Christ as the Savior who manifested His power over nature (8.23–27), death (9.18–26), demons (8.28–34), and disease (8.1–17; 9.27–34). His miracles were only one aspect of His ministry and did not represent the principal goal of His mission. They were evidences which would enable men to know that this was the Son of God and that His authority to forgive and cleanse was of divine origin (cf. 9.1–8).

him, saying, "Lord, if you will, you can make me clean." ³And he stretched out his hand and touched him, saying, "I will; be clean." And immediately his leprosy was cleansed. ⁴And Jesus said to him, "See that you say nothing to any one; but go, show yourself to the priest, and offer the gift that Moses commanded, for a proof to the people."ʳ

2. The centurion's servant healed (8.5–13; Lk 7.1–10)

5 As he entered Cȧpėr′nä-ŭm, a centurion came forward to him, beseeching him ⁶ and saying, "Lord, my servant is lying paralyzed at home, in terrible distress." ⁷And he said to him, "I will come and heal him." ⁸ But the centurion answered him, "Lord, I am not worthy to have you come under my roof; but only say the word, and my servant will be healed. ⁹ For I am a man under authority, with soldiers under me; and I say to one, 'Go,' and he goes, and to another, 'Come,' and he comes, and to my slave, 'Do this,' and he does it." ¹⁰ When Jesus heard him, he marveled, and said to those who followed him, "Truly, I say to you, not evenˢ in Israel have I found such faith. ¹¹ I tell you, many will come from east and west and sit at table with Abraham, Isaac, and Jacob in the kingdom of heaven, ¹² while the sons of the kingdom will be thrown into the outer darkness; there men will weep and gnash their teeth." ¹³And to the centurion Jesus said, "Go; be it done for you as you have believed." And the servant was healed at that very moment.

3. Peter's mother-in-law healed (8.14–17; Mk 1.29–34; Lk 4.28–41)

14 And when Jesus entered Peter's house, he saw his mother-in-law lying sick with a fever; ¹⁵ he touched her hand, and the fever left her, and she rose and served him. ¹⁶ That evening they brought to him many who were possessed with demons; and he cast out the spirits with a word, and healed all who were sick. ¹⁷ This was to fulfil what was spoken by the prophet Iṣāi′äh, "He took our infirmities and bore our diseases."

Impulsive and reluctant followers (8.18–22; Lk 9.57–62)

18 Now when Jesus saw great crowds around him, he gave orders to go over to the other side. ¹⁹And a scribe came up and said to him, "Teacher, I will follow you wherever you go." ²⁰And Jesus said to him, "Foxes have holes, and birds of the air have nests; but the Son of man has nowhere to lay his head." ²¹Another of the disciples said to him, "Lord, let me first go and bury my father." ²² But Jesus said to him, "Follow me, and leave the dead to bury their own dead."

ʳ Greek to them   ˢ Other ancient authorities read with no one

---

8.4
Lev 14.3,4, 10;
Mk 3.12;
5.43; 7.36;
8.30; 9.9

8.8
Ps 107.20

8.11
Isa 49.12;
59.19;
Mal 1.11;
Lk 13.29;
Acts 10.45

8.12
Mt 13.42,
50; 22.13;
25.30;
Lk 13.28

8.14
1 Cor 9.5

8.17
Isa 53.4

8.18
Mk 4.35;
Lk 8.22
*8.20

*8.22
Mt 9.9;
Jn 1.43;
21.19

8.20 Jesus called Himself the *Son of man* about eighty times in the New Testament. That name is used over thirty times in Matthew alone. Jesus used it to describe His office as Messiah, but He tended to avoid the term Messiah itself, because of the improper connotations attached to it by the people of His day. (They conceived of the coming Messiah as an irresistible military conqueror who would restore the political empire of David.) *Son of man* is first used with a Messianic connotation in Dan 7.13 and there is applied to a heavenly figure to whom everlasting dominion over all the earth is granted by the Ancient of Days. By His own person and work, Jesus invested this title with its full Messianic and redemptive significance.

8.22 *Follow me.* Jesus makes it clear that His command takes precedence over all other duties.

Miracles of Jesus (2) (8.23–9.8)

1. *The storm stilled (8.23–27; Mk 4.36–41; Lk 8.22–25)*

23 And when he got into the boat, his disciples followed him. 24And behold, there arose a great storm on the sea, so that the boat was being swamped by the waves; but he was asleep. 25And they went and woke him, saying, "Save, Lord; we are perishing." 26And he said to them, "Why are you afraid, O men of little faith?" Then he rose and rebuked the winds and the sea; and there was a great calm. 27And the men marveled, saying, "What sort of man is this, that even winds and sea obey him?"

2. *Demons cast out (8.28–34; Mk 5.1–20; Lk 8.26–39)*

28 And when he came to the other side, to the country of the Gădărēneṣ,*t* two demoniacs met him, coming out of the tombs, so fierce that no one could pass that way. 29And behold, they cried out, "What have you to do with us, O Son of God? Have you come here to torment us before the time?" 30 Now a herd of many swine was feeding at some distance from them. 31And the demons begged him, "If you cast us out, send us away into the herd of swine." 32And he said to them, "Go." So they came out and went into the swine; and behold, the whole herd rushed down the steep bank into the sea, and perished in the waters. 33 The herdsmen fled, and going into the city they told everything, and what had happened to the demoniacs. 34And behold, all the city came out to meet Jesus; and when they saw him, they begged him to leave their neighborhood.

3. *A paralytic healed and forgiven (9.1–8; Mk 2.1–12; Lk 5.17–26)*

9 And getting into a boat he crossed over and came to his own city. 2And behold, they brought to him a paralytic, lying on his bed; and when Jesus saw their faith he said to the paralytic, "Take heart, my son; your sins are forgiven." 3And behold, some of the scribes said to themselves, "This man is blaspheming." 4 But Jesus, knowing*u* their thoughts, said, "Why do you think evil in your hearts? 5 For which is easier, to say, 'Your sins are forgiven,' or to say, 'Rise and walk'? 6 But that you may know that the Son of man has authority on earth to forgive sins"—he then said to the paralytic—"Rise, take up your bed and go home." 7And he rose and went home. 8 When the crowds saw it, they were afraid, and they glorified God, who had given such authority to men.

Matthew called (9.9–13; Mk 2.13–17; Lk 5.27–32)

9 As Jesus passed on from there, he saw a man called Matthew sitting at the tax office; and he said to him, "Follow me." And he rose and followed him.

t Other ancient authorities read Gĕr′gĕsēneṣ′; some, Gĕr′àsēneṣ′
u Other ancient authorities read *seeing*

8.26 From 8.1 through 9.34 Christ sets forth His credentials in the form of miracles to demonstrate His power to save man from sin and death. Thus He cleansed the leper, healed the sick, cast out demons, raised the dead, and stilled the storm at sea.

9.6 *authority ... to forgive sins* is quite different from the authority to declare that sins have been forgiven. God alone can forgive sins but anyone may declare that a man's sins have been forgiven by God so long as God's requirements have been met.

(marginal references)

*8.26
Mt 6.30;
14.31;
16.8;
Ps 65.7;
89.9;
107.29

8.29
Judg 11.12;
2 Sam
16.10;
Mk 1.24;
Jn 2.4

8.34
See 1.Ki
17.18;
Lk 5.8;
Acts 16.39

9.1
Mt 4.13
9.2
Mt 9.22;
Mk 6.50;
10.49;
Acts 23.11
9.4
Mt 12.25;
Lk 6.8;
9.47; 11.17
*9.6

9.8
Mt 5.16;
15.31;
Lk 7.16;
13.13;
17.15;
23.47;
Jn 15.8;
Acts 4.21;
11.18;
21.20*

10 And as he sat at table^v in the house, behold, many tax collectors and sinners came and sat down with Jesus and his disciples. ¹¹And when the Phar′isees saw this, they said to his disciples, "Why does your teacher eat with tax collectors and sinners?" ¹² But when he heard it, he said, "Those who are well have no need of a physician, but those who are sick. ¹³ Go and learn what this means, 'I desire mercy, and not sacrifice.' For I came not to call the righteous, but sinners."

The question about fasting
(9.14–17; Mk 2.18–22; Lk 5.33–39)

14 Then the disciples of John came to him, saying, "Why do we and the Phar′isees fast,^w but your disciples do not fast?" ¹⁵And Jesus said to them, "Can the wedding guests mourn as long as the bridegroom is with them? The days will come, when the bridegroom is taken away from them, and then they will fast. ¹⁶And no one puts a piece of unshrunk cloth on an old garment, for the patch tears away from the garment, and a worse tear is made. ¹⁷ Neither is new wine put into old wineskins; if it is, the skins burst, and the wine is spilled, and the skins are destroyed; but new wine is put into fresh wineskins, and so both are preserved."

Miracles of Jesus (3) (9.18–34)
1. The issue of blood stopped and the dead raised
(9.18–26; Mk 5.21–43; Lk 8.40–56)

18 While he was thus speaking to them, behold, a ruler came in and knelt before him, saying, "My daughter has just died; but come and lay your hand on her, and she will live." ¹⁹And Jesus rose and followed him, with his disciples. ²⁰And behold, a woman who had suffered from a hemorrhage for twelve years came up behind him and touched the fringe of his garment; ²¹ for she said to herself, "If I only touch his garment, I shall be made well." ²² Jesus turned, and seeing her he said, "Take heart, daughter; your faith has made you well." And instantly the woman was made well. ²³And when Jesus came to the ruler's house, and saw the flute players, and the crowd making a tumult, ²⁴ he said, "Depart; for the girl is not dead but sleeping." And they laughed at him. ²⁵ But when the crowd had been put outside, he went in and took her by the hand, and the girl arose. ²⁶And the report of this went through all that district.

2. Sight to the blind and speech to the dumb (9.27–34)

27 And as Jesus passed on from there, two blind men followed him, crying aloud, "Have mercy on us, Son of David." ²⁸ When

^v Greek reclined ^w Other ancient authorities add much or often

✶9.10
9.11 Mt 11.19; Gal 2.15
9.13 Hos 6.6; Mic 6.6–8; Mt 12.7; 1 Tim 1.15
9.14 Lk 18.12
9.15 Jn 3.29; Acts 13.2,3; 14.23
9.16 Lk 5.36
9.18 Mt 8.2; Jn 9.38
9.20 Mt 14.36; Mk 3.10
9.21 see Lk 6.19
9.22 Mk 10.52; Lk 7.50; 17.19; 18.42; Mt 9.9; 15.28
9.23 see 2 Chr 35.25; Jer 9.17; 16.6; Ezek 24.17
9.24 see Jn 11.13; Acts 20.10
9.27 Mt 15.22; Mk 10.47, 48; Lk 18.38,39

9.10 *tax collectors and sinners.* These *sinners* were not notorious scoundrels or criminals; rather they were ordinary people who did not observe all the minute prescriptions of ceremonial laws prized by the Pharisees, especially laws having to do with food and social relations with non-Jews. Jesus was accused of being a friend of tax collectors and sinners because he associated with them. The Pharisees' attitude may be seen in their contemptuous words (Lk 7.34), which reveal the bitterness of their criticism of Jesus for befriending them. Against such self-righteousness Jesus told the parable of the Pharisee and the tax collector who went to the Temple to pray (Lk 18.9–14).

he entered the house, the blind men came to him; and Jesus said to them, "Do you believe that I am able to do this?" They said to him, "Yes, Lord." 29 Then he touched their eyes, saying, "According to your faith be it done to you." 30And their eyes were opened. And Jesus sternly charged them, "See that no one knows it." 31 But they went away and spread his fame through all that district.

32 As they were going away, behold, a dumb demoniac was brought to him. 33And when the demon had been cast out, the dumb man spoke; and the crowds marveled, saying, "Never was anything like this seen in Israel." 34 But the Phar′isees said, "He casts out demons by the prince of demons."[a]

The need for workers (9.35–38)

35 And Jesus went about all the cities and villages, teaching in their synagogues and preaching the gospel of the kingdom, and healing every disease and every infirmity. 36 When he saw the crowds, he had compassion for them, because they were harassed and helpless, like sheep without a shepherd. 37 Then he said to his disciples, "The harvest is plentiful, but the laborers are few; 38 pray therefore the Lord of the harvest to send out laborers into his harvest."

The names and mission of the Twelve (10.1–15; Mk 6.7–13; Lk 9.1–16)

10 And he called to him his twelve disciples and gave them authority over unclean spirits, to cast them out, and to heal every disease and every infirmity. 2 The names of the twelve apostles are these: first, Simon, who is called Peter, and Andrew his brother; James the son of Zeb′edee, and John his brother; 3 Philip and Barthol′omew; Thomas and Matthew the tax collector; James the son of Alphae′us, and Thad′daeus;[x] 4 Simon the Canana′an, and Judas Iscar′iot, who betrayed him.

5 These twelve Jesus sent out, charging them, "Go nowhere among the Gentiles, and enter no town of the Sama′ritans, 6 but go rather to the lost sheep of the house of Israel. 7And preach as you go, saying, 'The kingdom of heaven is at hand.' 8 Heal the sick, raise the dead, cleanse lepers, cast out demons. You received without paying, give without pay. 9 Take no gold, nor silver, nor copper in your belts, 10 no bag for your journey, nor two tunics, nor sandals, nor a staff; for the laborer deserves his food. 11And whatever town or village you enter, find out who is worthy in it, and stay with him until you depart. 12As you enter the house, salute it. 13And if the house is worthy, let your peace come upon it; but if it is not worthy, let your peace return to you. 14And if any one will not receive you or listen to your words, shake off the dust from your feet as you leave that house or town. 15 Truly, I say to you, it

a Other ancient authorities omit this verse
x Other ancient authorities read Lebbae′us or Lebbaeus called Thaddaeus

10.2 For *apostle* and its definition see note to Lk 6.13.
10.4 The Greek name *Kananaios* represents the Aramaic *kan'an*, meaning "zealous" or "zealot." Here, and in Mk 3.18, it is Cananaean, while Lk 6.15 and Acts 1.13 have *the Zealot*. Perhaps Simon the Zealot had formerly belonged to the extremist party of Zealots who advocated the overthrow of the Roman power by revolution and force.

shall be more tolerable on the day of judgment for the land of
Sŏdŏm and Gŏmor'răh than for that town.

The servant and suffering
(10.16–23; cf. Mk 13.9–13; Lk 21.12–19)

16 "Behold, I send you out as sheep in the midst of wolves; so
be wise as serpents and innocent as doves. 17 Beware of men; for
they will deliver you up to councils, and flog you in their synagogues, 18 and you will be dragged before governors and kings for
my sake, to bear testimony before them and the Gentiles. 19 When
they deliver you up, do not be anxious how you are to speak or
what you are to say; for what you are to say will be given to you
in that hour; 20 for it is not you who speak, but the Spirit of your
Father speaking through you. 21 Brother will deliver up brother
to death, and the father his child, and children will rise against
parents and have them put to death; 22 and you will be hated by all
for my name's sake. But he who endures to the end will be saved.
23 When they persecute you in one town, flee to the next; for truly,
I say to you, you will not have gone through all the towns of
Israel, before the Son of man comes.

The servant's encouragement (10.24–33; cf. Lk 12.2–9)

24 "A disciple is not above his teacher, nor a servant[y] above his
master; 25 it is enough for the disciple to be like his teacher, and
the servant[y] like his master. If they have called the master of the
house Bë-ĕl'zĕbŭl, how much more will they malign those of his
household.
26 "So have no fear of them; for nothing is covered that will not
be revealed, or hidden that will not be known. 27 What I tell you
in the dark, utter in the light; and what you hear whispered, proclaim upon the housetops. 28 And do not fear those who kill the
body but cannot kill the soul; rather fear him who can destroy
both soul and body in hell.[z] 29 Are not two sparrows sold for a
penny? And not one of them will fall to the ground without your
Father's will. 30 But even the hairs of your head are all numbered.
31 Fear not, therefore; you are of more value than many sparrows.
32 So every one who acknowledges me before men, I also will
acknowledge before my Father who is in heaven; 33 but whoever
denies me before men, I also will deny before my Father who is in
heaven.

The servant and the cross (10.34–39)

34 "Do not think that I have come to bring peace on earth; I
have not come to bring peace, but a sword. 35 For I have come to
set a man against his father, and a daughter against her mother,

y Or slave z Greek Gëhĕn'nà

10.16
Lk 10.3;
Rom 16.19

10.18
Acts 25.24–
26

10.20
2 Sam 23.2;
Jn 16.7–11;
Acts 4.8

10.22
Lk 21.17;
Dan 12.12;
Mt 24.13;
Mk 13.13

10.24
Lk 6.40;
Jn 13.16;
15.20
*10.25
Mt 12.24;
Mk 3.22;
Lk 11.15
10.26
Mk 4.22;
Lk 8.17;
12.2,3
10.28
Isa 8.12,13;
Heb 10.31

10.30
Lk 21.18;
Acts 27.34
10.32
Rom 10.9;
2 Tim 2.12;
Rev 3.5

10.34
Lk 12.51–
53;
Mk 13.12
10.35
Mic 7.6

10.25 The Philistine deity *Be-elzebul* was
called by the Old Testament writers *Baal-
zebub* meaning "lord of the flies." (See note to
2 Ki 1.2). In the New Testament Beelzebul
is the name derived from an Aramaic form
which meant, "lord of the high house," or
"lord of the temple." The people of Jesus' day
believed that Beelzebul was the prince of
demons. Therefore it is appropriate to assume,
as most commentators do, that this is another
name for Satan. The Pharisees accused Jesus
of being in league with Beelzebul in exorcis-
ing demons (12.24, 27; Mk 3.22; Lk 11.15,
18, 19).

10.36
Mic 7.6
10.37
Lk 14.26
10.38
Mt 16.24
10.39
Mt 16.25;
Lk 17.33;
Jn 12.25

and a daughter-in-law against her mother-in-law; 36 and a man's foes will be those of his own household. 37 He who loves father or mother more than me is not worthy of me; and he who loves son or daughter more than me is not worthy of me; 38 and he who does not take his cross and follow me is not worthy of me. 39 He who finds his life will lose it, and he who loses his life for my sake will find it.

The servant and the reward (10.40–11.1)

10.40
Lk 9.48;
Jn 12.44;
Gal 4.14

40 "He who receives you receives me, and he who receives me receives him who sent me. 41 He who receives a prophet because he is a prophet shall receive a prophet's reward, and he who receives a righteous man because he is a righteous man shall receive a righteous man's reward. 42And whoever gives to one of these little ones even a cup of cold water because he is a disciple, truly, I say to you, he shall not lose his reward."

10.42
Mt 25.40;
Heb 6.10

11 And when Jesus had finished instructing his twelve disciples, he went on from there to teach and preach in their cities.

John the Baptist's last message (11.2–19; Lk 7.18–35)

11.2
Mt 14.3;
Mk 6.17;
Lk 9.7ff

2 Now when John heard in prison about the deeds of the Christ, he sent word by his disciples 3 and said to him, "Are you he who is to come, or shall we look for another?" 4And Jesus answered them, "Go and tell John what you hear and see: 5 the blind receive their sight and the lame walk, lepers are cleansed and the deaf hear, and the dead are raised up, and the poor have good news preached to them. 6And blessed is he who takes no offense at me."

11.3
Jn 11.27
11.5
Isa 35.4–6;
61.1;
Lk 4.18,19
11.6
Isa 8.14,15;
Rom 9.32;
1 Pet 2.8
11.7
Mt 3.1
11.9
Lk 1.76
11.10
Mal 3.1;
Mk 1.2

7 As they went away, Jesus began to speak to the crowds concerning John: "What did you go out into the wilderness to behold? A reed shaken by the wind? 8 Why then did you go out? To see a mana clothed in soft raiment? Behold, those who wear soft raiment are in kings' houses. 9 Why then did you go out? To see a prophet?b Yes, I tell you, and more than a prophet. 10 This is he of whom it is written,

'Behold, I send my messenger before thy face,
    who shall prepare thy way before thee.'

★11.11

11 Truly, I say to you, among those born of women there has risen no one greater than John the Baptist; yet he who is least in the kingdom of heaven is greater than he. 12 From the days of John the Baptist until now the kingdom of heaven has suffered violence,c and men of violence take it by force. 13 For all the prophets and the law prophesied until John; 14 and if you are willing to accept it,

11.14
Mal 4.5;
Mt 17.12;
Lk 1.17

a Or What then did you go out to see? A man . . .
b Other ancient authorities read What then did you go out to see? A prophet?
c Or has been coming violently

11.11 The statement *he who is least in the kingdom of heaven is greater than he* (John) is enigmatic. Probably Jesus meant that while John was the greatest prophet of the age preceding Calvary and the resurrection, he died before the bestowal of the baptism of the Holy Spirit upon the church at Pentecost. Those who have received this blessed Comforter as their permanent possession— "Christ within you, the hope of glory"— enjoy a more privileged status and a more intimate access to God than even the greatest of the Old Testament saints. According to another interpretation, Jesus was in this phrase referring to Himself, "he who is least in the kingdom of heaven is greater than he (John)."

he is Ēlī'jáh who is to come. 15 He who has ears to hear,^{d} let him hear.

16 "But to what shall I compare this generation? It is like children sitting in the market places and calling to their playmates,
17 'We piped to you, and you did not dance;
    we wailed, and you did not mourn.'
18 For John came neither eating nor drinking, and they say, 'He has a demon'; 19 the Son of man came eating and drinking, and they say, 'Behold, a glutton and a drunkard, a friend of tax collectors and sinners!' Yet wisdom is justified by her deeds."^{e}

The judgment of the unrepentant (11.20–24; cf. Lk 10.12–15)

20 Then he began to upbraid the cities where most of his mighty works had been done, because they did not repent. 21 "Woe to you, Çhŏrā'zĭn! woe to you, Bĕth-sā'ĭdá! for if the mighty works done in you had been done in Tȳre and Sīdón, they would have repented long ago in sackcloth and ashes. 22 But I tell you, it shall be more tolerable on the day of judgment for Tȳre and Sīdón than for you. 23 And you, Cápêr'nä-úm, will you be exalted to heaven? You shall be brought down to Hādēṣ. For if the mighty works done in you had been done in Sŏdóm, it would have remained until this day. 24 But I tell you that it shall be more tolerable on the day of judgment for the land of Sŏdóm than for you."

Jesus who reveals the Father (11.25–30; cf. Lk 10.21,22)

25 At that time Jesus declared, "I thank thee, Father, Lord of heaven and earth, that thou hast hidden these things from the wise and understanding and revealed them to babes; 26 yea, Father, for such was thy gracious will.^{f} 27 All things have been delivered to me by my Father; and no one knows the Son except the Father, and no one knows the Father except the Son and any one to whom the Son chooses to reveal him. 28 Come to me, all who labor and are heavy laden, and I will give you rest. 29 Take my yoke upon you, and learn from me; for I am gentle and lowly in heart, and you will find rest for your souls. 30 For my yoke is easy, and my burden is light."

Jesus the Lord of the Sabbath
(12.1–8; Mk 2.23–28; Lk 6.1–5)

12 At that time Jesus went through the grainfields on the sabbath; his disciples were hungry, and they began to pluck heads of grain and to eat. 2 But when the Phar'isēēs saw it, they said to him, "Look, your disciples are doing what is not lawful to do on the sabbath." 3 He said to them, "Have you not read what

---

^{d} Other ancient authorities omit *to hear* ^{e} Other ancient authorities read *children* (Luke 7.35) ^{f} Or *so it was well-pleasing before thee*

11.15
Mt 13.9,43;
Mk 4.23;
Rev 13.9

11.19
Mt 9.11;
Lk 15.2

11.21
Jonah 3.7,8

11.22
ver 24;
Mt 10.15

11.23
Isa 14.13;
Lam 2.1

11.24
Mt 10.15

11.25
1 Cor 1.26–29

11.27
Mt 28.18;
Jn 3.35;
13.3; 17.2

11.28
see Jer 31.25;
Jn 7.37

11.29
Jn 13.15;
Phil 2.5;
1 Pet 2.21;
1 Jn 2.6;
Jer 6.16

12.1
Deut 23.25

12.2
ver 10;
Lk 13.14;
14.3;
Jn 5.10;
7.23; 9.16

12.3
1 Sam 21.6

12.3 Jesus often answered the criticisms of His opponents by citing Old Testament precedents to explain and justify His own conduct. He cited two incidents: (1) David and his companions, fleeing from Saul, ate the loaves of the Presence which were eaten only by priests (1 Sam 21.1–6): the lesson is that human need takes precedence over ceremonial regulations; (2) priests in the Temple worked on the Sabbath by offering prescribed sacrifices (cf. Num 28.9, 10). If in the service of the Temple they broke the Sabbath law, so could Christ's disciples who served the greater Temple, namely, the Kingdom of God.

*12.4
Ex 25.30;
Lev 24.5,9

12.5
Num
28.9,10
*12.6
ver 41,42
12.7
Hos 6.6;
Mt 9.13

David did, when he was hungry, and those who were with him: 4 how he entered the house of God and ate the bread of the Presence, which it was not lawful for him to eat nor for those who were with him, but only for the priests? 5 Or have you not read in the law how on the sabbath the priests in the temple profane the sabbath, and are guiltless? 6 I tell you, something greater than the temple is here. 7 And if you had known what this means, 'I desire mercy, and not sacrifice,' you would not have condemned the guiltless. 8 For the Son of man is lord of the sabbath."

The healing of the withered hand on the Sabbath (12.9–14; Mk 3.1–6; Lk 6.6–11)

12.10
Lk 13.14;
14.3;
Jn 9.16
12.11
Lk 14.5
12.12
Mt 10.31
12.14
Mt 27.1;
Mk 3.6;
Lk 6.11;
Jn 5.18;
11.53

9 And he went on from there, and entered their synagogue. 10 And behold, there was a man with a withered hand. And they asked him, "Is it lawful to heal on the sabbath?" so that they might accuse him. 11 He said to them, "What man of you, if he has one sheep and it falls into a pit on the sabbath, will not lay hold of it and lift it out? 12 Of how much more value is a man than a sheep! So it is lawful to do good on the sabbath." 13 Then he said to the man, "Stretch out your hand." And the man stretched it out, and it was restored, whole like the other. 14 But the Phar'isees went out and took counsel against him, how to destroy him.

Jesus heals many (12.15–21; Mk 3.7–12; cf. Lk 6.17–19)

12.15
Mt 10.23;
19.2
12.16
Mt 9.30

12.18
Isa 42.1–4

15 Jesus, aware of this, withdrew from there. And many followed him, and he healed them all, 16 and ordered them not to make him known. 17 This was to fulfil what was spoken by the prophet Īṣāi'āh:
18 "Behold, my servant whom I have chosen,
     my beloved with whom my soul is well pleased.
I will put my Spirit upon him,
     and he shall proclaim justice to the Gentiles.
19 He will not wrangle or cry aloud,
     nor will any one hear his voice in the streets;
20 he will not break a bruised reed
     or quench a smoldering wick,
  till he brings justice to victory;
21 and in his name will the Gentiles hope."

Jesus answers the Pharisees' calumny (12.22–37; Mk 3.20–30; Lk 11.14–23)

12.22
Mt 9.32,33
12.23
Mt 9.27
12.24
Mt 9.34;
10.25;
Jn 7.20;
8.52; 10.20
12.25
Mt 9.4
12.27
Mt 9.34;
10.25;
Acts 19.13

22 Then a blind and dumb demoniac was brought to him, and he healed him, so that the dumb man spoke and saw. 23 And all the people were amazed, and said, "Can this be the Son of David?" 24 But when the Phar'isees heard it they said, "It is only by Bē-ĕl'zĕbul, the prince of demons, that this man casts out demons." 25 Knowing their thoughts, he said to them, "Every kingdom divided against itself is laid waste, and no city or house divided against itself will stand; 26 and if Satan casts out Satan, he is divided against himself; how then will his kingdom stand? 27 And

---

12.4 See note to Mk 2.25 for information on the Bread of the Presence.

12.6 *greater than the temple.* This is supported by ver 41, 42.

if I cast out demons by Bë-ĕl′zĕbŭl, by whom do your sons cast them out? Therefore they shall be your judges. 28 But if it is by the Spirit of God that I cast out demons, then the kingdom of God has come upon you. 29 Or how can one enter a strong man's house and plunder his goods, unless he first binds the strong man? Then indeed he may plunder his house. 30 He who is not with me is against me, and he who does not gather with me scatters. 31 Therefore I tell you, every sin and blasphemy will be forgiven men, but the blasphemy against the Spirit will not be forgiven. 32 And whoever says a word against the Son of man will be forgiven; but whoever speaks against the Holy Spirit will not be forgiven, either in this age or in the age to come.

33 "Either make the tree good, and its fruit good; or make the tree bad, and its fruit bad; for the tree is known by its fruit. 34 You brood of vipers! how can you speak good, when you are evil? For out of the abundance of the heart the mouth speaks. 35 The good man out of his good treasure brings forth good, and the evil man out of his evil treasure brings forth evil. 36 I tell you, on the day of judgment men will render account for every careless word they utter; 37 for by your words you will be justified, and by your words you will be condemned."

Warning against seeking signs (12.38–45; Lk 11.29–32)

38 Then some of the scribes and Phar′ĭsēēs said to him, "Teacher, we wish to see a sign from you." 39 But he answered them, "An evil and adulterous generation seeks for a sign; but no sign shall be given to it except the sign of the prophet Jonah. 40 For as Jonah was three days and three nights in the belly of the whale, so will the Son of man be three days and three nights in the heart of the earth. 41 The men of Nĭn′ĕvĕh will arise at the judgment with this generation and condemn it; for they repented at the preaching of Jonah, and behold, something greater than Jonah is here. 42 The queen of the South will arise at the judgment with this generation and condemn it; for she came from the ends of the earth to hear the wisdom of Solomon, and behold, something greater than Solomon is here.

43 "When the unclean spirit has gone out of a man, he passes through waterless places seeking rest, but he finds none. 44 Then he says, 'I will return to my house from which I came.' And when he comes he finds it empty, swept, and put in order. 45 Then he goes and brings with him seven other spirits more evil than himself, and they enter and dwell there; and the last state of that man becomes worse than the first. So shall it be also with this evil generation."

Christ's true kindred (12.46–50; Mk 3.31–35; Lk 8.19–21)

46 While he was still speaking to the people, behold, his mother

12.28	Dan 2.44; 7.14; Lk 1.33; 17.20,21
12.30	Mk 9.40; Lk 9.50
*12.31	Lk 12.10
12.32	Mt 11.19; 13.55; Jn 7.12,52
12.33	Mt 7.17; Lk 6.43,44
12.34	Mt 3.7; 23.33; Lk 6.45
*12.36	
12.38	Mt 16.1; Mk 8.11, 12; Jn 2.18; 6.30; 1 Cor 1.22
*12.39	Mt 16.4
12.40	Jon 1.17
12.41	Jon 1.2; 3.5
12.42	1 Ki 10.2; 2 Chr 9.1
12.45	2 Pet 2.20
12.46	Mt 13.55; Mk 6.3; Jn 2.12; 7.3,5; Acts 1.4; 1 Cor 9.5; Gal 1.19

12.31 See note to Mk 3.29.
12.36 Words are an index to the heart. Careless words inevitably will reap their just reward in the judgment. Words, of course, are neither good nor bad in themselves. The kind of words, the intended meaning, and the

heart intention make them either good or bad. See here the note to 2 Cor 5.10 on the judgment seat of Christ.
12.39 *adulterous*. The sense of the word here is not debasement, but a turning away from God.

and his brothers stood outside, asking to speak to him.*g* 48 But he replied to the man who told him, "Who is my mother, and who are my brothers?" 49And stretching out his hand toward his disciples, he said, "Here are my mother and my brothers! 50 For whoever does the will of my Father in heaven is my brother, and sister, and mother."

12.50
Jn 15.14

Jesus teaches in parables (13.1–52)

1. The sower (13.1–23)
a. The story of the sower (13.1–9; Mk 4.1–9; Lk 8.4–8)

13.2
Lk 5.3

*13.3

13 That same day Jesus went out of the house and sat beside the sea. 2And great crowds gathered about him, so that he got into a boat and sat there; and the whole crowd stood on the beach. 3And he told them many things in parables, saying: "A sower went out to sow. 4And as he sowed, some seeds fell along the path, and the birds came and devoured them. 5 Other seeds fell on rocky ground, where they had not much soil, and immediately they sprang up, since they had no depth of soil, 6 but when the sun rose they were scorched; and since they had no root they withered away. 7 Other seeds fell upon thorns, and the thorns grew up and choked them. 8 Other seeds fell on good soil and brought forth grain, some a hundredfold, some sixty, some thirty. 9 He who has ears,*h* let him hear."

13.8
Gen 26.12

13.9
Mt 11.15

b. The reason for parables (13.10–17; Mk 4.10–12; Lk 8.9–10)

13.11
Mt 11.25;
19.11;
Jn 6.65;
1 Cor 2.10;
1 Jn 2.27

13.12
Mt 25.29;
Lk 19.26

13.13
Jer 5.21;
Ezek 12.2

13.14
Isa 6.9,10;
Ezek 12.2;
Jn 12.40;
Acts 28.26,
27;
Rom 11.8

13.15
Heb 5.11

13.16
Mt 16.17;
Lk 10.23,
24;
Jn 20.29

13.17
Heb 11.13;
1 Pet
1.10,11

10 Then the disciples came and said to him, "Why do you speak to them in parables?" 11And he answered them, "To you it has been given to know the secrets of the kingdom of heaven, but to them it has not been given. 12 For to him who has will more be given, and he will have abundance; but from him who has not, even what he has will be taken away. 13 This is why I speak to them in parables, because seeing they do not see, and hearing they do not hear, nor do they understand. 14 With them indeed is fulfilled the prophecy of Iṣāi'āh which says:
'You shall indeed hear but never understand,
    and you shall indeed see but never perceive.
15 For this people's heart has grown dull,
    and their ears are heavy of hearing,
    and their eyes they have closed,
lest they should perceive with their eyes,
    and hear with their ears,
and understand with their heart,
    and turn for me to heal them.'
16 But blessed are your eyes, for they see, and your ears, for they hear. 17 Truly, I say to you, many prophets and righteous men longed to see what you see, and did not see it, and to hear what you hear, and did not hear it.

g Other ancient authorities insert verse 47, *Some one told him, "Your mother and your brothers are standing outside, asking to speak to you"*
h Other ancient authorities add here and in verse 43 *to hear*

13.3a A *parable* is an earthly story with a heavenly meaning. Spiritual truth is unfolded in everyday language and figures. The details of a parable should not be pressed beyond the principal object of the comparison. Each parable has a main point and was spoken to make that point easily apparent.
13.3b See note to Mk 4.3 on the sower.

c. The parable of the sower explained
(13.18–23; Mk 4.13–20; Lk 8.11–15)

18 "Hear then the parable of the sower. 19 When any one hears the word of the kingdom and does not understand it, the evil one comes and snatches away what is sown in his heart; this is what was sown along the path. 20As for what was sown on rocky ground, this is he who hears the word and immediately receives it with joy; 21 yet he has no root in himself, but endures for a while, and when tribulation or persecution arises on account of the word, immediately he falls away.[i] 22As for what was sown among thorns, this is he who hears the word, but the cares of the world and the delight in riches choke the word, and it proves unfruitful. 23As for what was sown on good soil, this is he who hears the word and understands it; he indeed bears fruit, and yields, in one case a hundredfold, in another sixty, and in another thirty."

2. The wheat and the tares (13.24–30; cf. Mk 4.26–29)

24 Another parable he put before them, saying, "The kingdom of heaven may be compared to a man who sowed good seed in his field; 25 but while men were sleeping, his enemy came and sowed weeds among the wheat, and went away. 26 So when the plants came up and bore grain, then the weeds appeared also. 27And the servants[j] of the householder came and said to him, 'Sir, did you not sow good seed in your field? How then has it weeds?' 28 He said to them, 'An enemy has done this.' The servants[j] said to him, 'Then do you want us to go and gather them?' 29 But he said, 'No; lest in gathering the weeds you root up the wheat along with them. 30 Let both grow together until the harvest; and at harvest time I will tell the reapers, Gather the weeds first and bind them in bundles to be burned, but gather the wheat into my barn.'"

3. The grain of mustard seed
(13.31,32; Mk 4.30–32; Lk 13.18,19)

31 Another parable he put before them, saying, "The kingdom of heaven is like a grain of mustard seed which a man took and sowed in his field; 32 it is the smallest of all seeds, but when it has grown it is the greatest of shrubs and becomes a tree, so that the birds of the air come and make nests in its branches."

---

[i] Or stumbles   [j] Or slaves

13.18   ⋆13.18
13.19
Mt 4.23

13.21   Mt 11.6

13.22   Rom 12.2; 1 Cor 1.20; 2 Cor 4.4; Gal 1.4; Eph 2.2; Mt 19.23; 1 Tim 6.9, 10,17

13.23   ver 8

13.24   Lk 13.18,20

⋆13.29

13.30   Mt 3.12

⋆13.31   see Isa 2.2, 3; Mic 4.1

13.32   Ps 104.12; Ezek 17.23; 31.6; Dan 4.12

13.18 The parable of the sower was readily understood by the listeners, who were quite familiar with the rocky soil from which they wrested their living. The parable would prove very difficult to comprehend for those whose experiences were limited to a fertile non-rocky soil such as would be true in many areas of the world.

13.29 This parable teaches us that there are always true and false believers within the fellowship of those who profess to belong to God. It is not always possible to distinguish the false from the true. While great harm may come from the presence of unbelievers, yet great harm may also come from human efforts to separate the false from the true. Scripture does warrant the exclusion of those who are not true believers if and when they can be positively identified (Tit 3.10). As the interpretation of the parable makes clear (ver 36–43), the final separation is made by the Judge of all, the Son of man.

Indeed, there may be a further lesson that one cannot judge the success or failure of a movement by the smallness of its beginnings. *For whoever has despised the day of small things shall rejoice* (Zech 4.10). The Lord Jesus left behind a small company of despised followers from whom little could be expected. Yet from them came the seeds of history's greatest movement.

13.31 This parable has for its central teaching the growth and spread of the gospel throughout the world. Commencing as a tiny seed it becomes a giant tree. The present-day existence of a world-wide church in some measure represents a fulfilment of this prophetic word.

4. The leaven (13.33–35; Lk 13.20,21)

*13.33
Gen 18.6;
Gal 5.9

33 He told them another parable. "The kingdom of heaven is like leaven which a woman took and hid in three measures of flour, till it was all leavened."

13.34
Mk 4.33, 34
*13.35
Ps 78.2;
Rom 16.25,
26;
1 Cor 2.7;
Eph 3.9;
Col 1.26

34 All this Jesus said to the crowds in parables; indeed he said nothing to them without a parable. 35 This was to fulfil what was spoken by the prophet:*k*

"I will open my mouth in parables,
I will utter what has been hidden since the foundation of the world."

5. The wheat and the tares explained (13.36–43)

13.38
Mt 24.14;
28.19;
Lk 24.47;
Jn 8.44;
1 Jn 3.10
13.39
Joel 3.13;
Mt 24.3;
28.20;
Rev 14.15
13.40
1 Cor
10.11;
Heb 9.26
13.41
Mt 24.31
13.42
Mt 8.12;
ver 50;
Mt 24.51;
25.30;
Lk 13.28
13.43
Dan 12.3;
Mt 11.15

36 Then he left the crowds and went into the house. And his disciples came to him, saying, "Explain to us the parable of the weeds of the field." 37 He answered, "He who sows the good seed is the Son of man; 38 the field is the world, and the good seed means the sons of the kingdom; the weeds are the sons of the evil one, 39 and the enemy who sowed them is the devil; the harvest is the close of the age, and the reapers are angels. 40 Just as the weeds are gathered and burned with fire, so will it be at the close of the age. 41 The Son of man will send his angels, and they will gather out of his kingdom all causes of sin and all evildoers, 42 and throw them into the furnace of fire; there men will weep and gnash their teeth. 43 Then the righteous will shine like the sun in the kingdom of their Father. He who has ears, let him hear.

6. The hidden treasure (13.44)

*13.44
see Phil
3.7,8;
Isa 55.1
*13.45

44 "The kingdom of heaven is like treasure hidden in a field, which a man found and covered up; then in his joy he goes and sells all that he has and buys that field.

7. The pearl (13.45)

45 "Again, the kingdom of heaven is like a merchant in search of fine pearls, 46 who, on finding one pearl of great value, went and sold all that he had and bought it.

k Other ancient authorities read *the prophet Iṣāi'āh*

13.33 In the New Testament *leaven* is used metaphorically in an evil sense: (1) of the doctrines of the Pharisees and Sadducees (16.6, 12; see also Mk 8.15; Lk 12.1); (2) of ungodly professors of the true faith (1 Cor 5.6, 7); (3) of false teachers of Christianity (Gal 5.8, 9); (4) malice and evil (1 Cor 5.8). On the other hand, it seems to be used to illustrate the influence of the gospel here (and in the parallel passage, Lk 13.21). *leaven* suggests permeation and its silent working. Only a small amount of leaven was needed for a large quantity of dough, something like thirty-six quarts. So the kingdom message, apparently insignificant, permeates the whole world.

In the Old Testament: (1) it was forbidden to use leaven during the Passover (Ex 12.15–20); (2) leaven was not to be offered with blood of sacrifice (Ex 34.25); (3) it was not to be offered with cereal offerings which were burned on the altar (Lev 2.11; 10.12). It was permitted, however, with thank-offerings

(Lev 7.13) and with the presentation of the first fruits of wheat (Lev 23.17).

13.35 The parables of Jesus were not understood either by the multitudes or by the disciples of the Lord: *Privately to his own disciples he explained everything* (Mk 4.34).

13.44 This parable has for its central teaching the incomparable value of the gospel, which will cause a man to forsake everything that he may possess the greatest of all. All else when compared to this is of no value whatever (16.26). Another possible interpretation would be the equation of this discoverer with Christ Himself who sacrificed all that He had in order to purchase the treasure of His church.

13.45 The pearl and the hidden treasure are similar in general meaning. In the case of the pearl, Christ suggests that the one who seeks it will find salvation. And when he discovers this one pearl he will gladly sell all else for it. Here again, however, the purchaser may represent the Lord Jesus Himself.

8. The dragnet (13.47–52)

47 "Again, the kingdom of heaven is like a net which was thrown into the sea and gathered fish of every kind; 48 when it was full, men drew it ashore and sat down and sorted the good into vessels but threw away the bad. 49 So it will be at the close of the age. The angels will come out and separate the evil from the righteous, 50 and throw them into the furnace of fire; there men will weep and gnash their teeth.

51 "Have you understood all this?" They said to him, "Yes." 52And he said to them, "Therefore every scribe who has been trained for the kingdom of heaven is like a householder who brings out of his treasure what is new and what is old."

Second rejection of Jesus at Nazareth (13.53–58; Mk 6.1–6; Lk 4.16–30)

53 And when Jesus had finished these parables, he went away from there, 54 and coming to his own country he taught them in their synagogue, so that they were astonished, and said, "Where did this man get this wisdom and these mighty works? 55 Is not this the carpenter's son? Is not his mother called Mary? And are not his brothers James and Joseph and Simon and Judas? 56And are not all his sisters with us? Where then did this man get all this?" 57And they took offense at him. But Jesus said to them, "A prophet is not without honor except in his own country and in his own house." 58And he did not do many mighty works there, because of their unbelief.

Death of John the Baptist (14.1–12; Mk 6.14–29; Lk 9.7–9)

14 At that time Hĕrŏd the tetrarch heard about the fame of Jesus; 2 and he said to his servants, "This is John the Baptist, he has been raised from the dead; that is why these powers are at work in him." 3 For Hĕrŏd had seized John and bound him and put him in prison, for the sake of Hĕrō'dĭ-ăs, his brother Philip's wife;ˡ 4 because John said to him, "It is not lawful for you to have her." 5And though he wanted to put him to death, he feared the people, because they held him to be a prophet. 6 But when Hĕrŏd's birthday came, the daughter of Hĕrō'dĭ-ăs danced before the company, and pleased Hĕrŏd, 7 so that he promised with an oath to give her whatever she might ask. 8 Prompted by her mother, she said, "Give me the head of John the Baptist here on a platter." 9And the king was sorry; but because of his oaths and his guests he commanded it to be given; 10 he sent and had John beheaded in the prison, 11 and his head was brought on a platter and given to the girl, and she brought it to her mother. 12And his disciples came and took the body and buried it; and they went and told Jesus.

ˡ Other ancient authorities read his brother's wife

Marginal references: *13.47 Mt 22.10; 13.49 Mt 25.32; 13.50 ver 42; 13.53 Mt 7.28; 11.1; 19.1; 26.1; 13.54 Mt 4.23; 7.28; *13.55 Lk 3.23; Jn 6.42; 13.57 Jn 4.44; 14.1 Mk 8.15; Lk 3.1,19; 8.3; 13.31; 23.7,8; Acts 4.27; 12.1; *14.3 Lk 3.19,20; 14.4 Lev 18.16; 20.21; 14.5 Mt 21.26; Lk 20.6

13.47 The draw-net represents the kingdom of God. The net is cast into the sea and when drawn to land has in it a mixed company. The good represent the converted, and the bad the unconverted. At the end of the age the righteous will be separated from the unrighteous by the angels of God. Needless to say, this parable precludes the idea of a wholly converted world at the end of the age.
13.55 See note to Mk 6.3 on the family of Jesus.
14.3 See note to Lk 1.57 on John the Baptist. See also note to Mk 6.17 on Philip the brother of Herold Antipas.

The five thousand fed
(14.13–21; Mk 6.30–44; Lk 9.10–17;
Jn 6.1–13; cf. Mt 15.32–38)

13 Now when Jesus heard this, he withdrew from there in a boat to a lonely place apart. But when the crowds heard it, they followed him on foot from the towns. 14As he went ashore he saw a great throng; and he had compassion on them, and healed their sick. 15 When it was evening, the disciples came to him and said, "This is a lonely place, and the day is now over; send the crowds away to go into the villages and buy food for themselves." 16 Jesus said, "They need not go away; you give them something to eat." 17 They said to him, "We have only five loaves here and two fish." 18And he said, "Bring them here to me." 19 Then he ordered the crowds to sit down on the grass; and taking the five loaves and the two fish he looked up to heaven, and blessed, and broke and gave the loaves to the disciples, and the disciples gave them to the crowds. 20And they all ate and were satisfied. And they took up twelve baskets full of the broken pieces left over. 21And those who ate were about five thousand men, besides women and children.

Jesus walks on the sea (14.22–36; Mk 6.45–52; Jn 6.15–21)

22 Then he made the disciples get into the boat and go before him to the other side, while he dismissed the crowds. 23And after he had dismissed the crowds, he went up on the mountain by himself to pray. When evening came, he was there alone, 24 but the boat by this time was many furlongs distant from the land,[m] beaten by the waves; for the wind was against them. 25And in the fourth watch of the night he came to them, walking on the sea. 26 But when the disciples saw him walking on the sea, they were terrified, saying, "It is a ghost!" And they cried out for fear. 27 But immediately he spoke to them, saying, "Take heart, it is I; have no fear."

28 And Peter answered him, "Lord, if it is you, bid me come to you on the water." 29 He said, "Come." So Peter got out of the boat and walked on the water and came to Jesus; 30 but when he saw the wind,[n] he was afraid, and beginning to sink he cried out, "Lord, save me." 31 Jesus immediately reached out his hand and caught him, saying to him, "O man of little faith, why did you doubt?" 32And when they got into the boat, the wind ceased. 33And those in the boat worshiped him, saying, "Truly you are the Son of God."

34 And when they had crossed over, they came to land at Génnes'aret. 35And when the men of that place recognized him, they sent round to all that region and brought to him all that were sick, 36 and besought him that they might only touch the fringe of his garment; and as many as touched it were made well.

m Other ancient authorities read was out on the sea
n Other ancient authorities read strong wind

14.14
Mt 9.36

14.17
Mt 16.9
14.19
1 Sam 9.13;
Mt 15.36;
Mk 14.22;
Lk 24.30

14.23
Lk 6.12;
9.28

*14.25

14.26
see Lk
24.37
14.27
Mt 9.2;
17.7;
28.10;
Rev 1.17

*14.29

14.31
Mt 6.30;
8.26; 16.8

14.33
Ps 2.7;
Mt 16.16;
26.63;
Lk 4.41;
Jn 11.27;
Acts 8.37;
Rom 1.4
14.36
Mt 9.20;
Mk 3.10

14.25 See note to Mk 6.48 on *fourth watch.*
14.29 Peter stepped out of the boat on to the water in faith. Doubt overtook him and

he began to sink. True faith must persevere and does not end when the initial step has been taken. Peter had only beginning faith.

Ceremonial and real defilement (15.1–20; Mk 7.1–23)

15 Then Phar′isees and scribes came to Jesus from Jerusalem
and said, 2 "Why do your disciples transgress the tradition
of the elders? For they do not wash their hands when they eat."
3 He answered them, "And why do you transgress the commandment of God for the sake of your tradition? 4 For God commanded, 'Honor your father and your mother,' and, 'He who
speaks evil of father or mother, let him surely die.' 5 But you say,
'If any one tells his father or his mother, What you would have
gained from me is given to God,[o] he need not honor his father.'
6 So, for the sake of your tradition, you have made void the word[p]
of God. 7 You hypocrites! Well did Īsāi′ah prophesy of you, when
he said:
8 'This people honors me with their lips,
but their heart is far from me;
9 in vain do they worship me,
teaching as doctrines the precepts of men.' "
10 And he called the people to him and said to them, "Hear and
understand: 11 not what goes into the mouth defiles a man, but
what comes out of the mouth, this defiles a man." 12 Then the
disciples came and said to him, "Do you know that the Phar′isees
were offended when they heard this saying?" 13 He answered,
"Every plant which my heavenly Father has not planted will be
rooted up. 14 Let them alone; they are blind guides. And if a blind
man leads a blind man, both will fall into a pit." 15 But Peter said
to him, "Explain the parable to us." 16 And he said, "Are you also
still without understanding? 17 Do you not see that whatever
goes into the mouth passes into the stomach, and so passes on?[q]
18 But what comes out of the mouth proceeds from the heart, and
this defiles a man. 19 For out of the heart come evil thoughts, murder, adultery, fornication, theft, false witness, slander. 20 These
are what defile a man; but to eat with unwashed hands does not
defile a man."

Journey toward Tyre and Sidon (15.21–28; Mk 7.24–30)

21 And Jesus went away from there and withdrew to the district
of Tȳre and Sīdon. 22 And behold, a Cā′naanīte woman from that
region came out and cried, "Have mercy on me, O Lord, Son of
David; my daughter is severely possessed by a demon." 23 But he
did not answer her a word. And his disciples came and begged
him, saying, "Send her away, for she is crying after us." 24 He answered, "I was sent only to the lost sheep of the house of Israel."
25 But she came and knelt before him, saying, "Lord, help me."
26 And he answered, "It is not fair to take the children's bread and
throw it to the dogs." 27 She said, "Yes, Lord, yet even the dogs
eat the crumbs that fall from their masters' table." 28 Then Jesus
answered her, "O woman, great is your faith! Be it done for you as
you desire." And her daughter was healed instantly.

Multitudes healed (15.29–31; Mk 7.31–37)

29 And Jesus went on from there and passed along the Sea of

[o] Or *an offering* [p] Other ancient authorities read *law* [q] Or *is evacuated*

15.2 Lk 11.38
15.4 Ex 20.12; Deut 5.16; Eph 6.2
15.5 Ex 21.17; Lev 20.9; Deut 27.16
15.9 Col 2.18–22
15.11 Acts 10.14, 15; 1 Tim 4.3
15.13 Isa 60.21; Jn 15.2; 1 Cor 3.9ff
15.14 Mt 23.16; Lk 6.39; Rom 2.19
15.15 Mt 13.36
15.16 Mt 16.9
15.18 Mt 12.34; Jas 3.6
15.19 Gal 5.19–21; 1 Cor 6.9, 10; Rom 14.14
15.22 Mt 9.27; 4.24
15.24 Mt 10.6,23
15.25 Mt 8.2; 18.26; 20.20; Jn 9.38
15.28 Mt 9.22,28; Mk 10.52; Lk 7.50; 17.19

15.30
Lk 7.22

Găl'ĭlee. And he went up on the mountain, and sat down there. 30And great crowds came to him, bringing with them the lame, the maimed, the blind, the dumb, and many others, and they put them at his feet, and he healed them, 31 so that the throng wondered,

15.31
Mt 9.8

when they saw the dumb speaking, the maimed whole, the lame walking, and the blind seeing; and they glorified the God of Israel.

The four thousand fed (15.32–39; Mk 8.1–9)

15.32
Mt 9.36

32 Then Jesus called his disciples to him and said, "I have compassion on the crowd, because they have been with me now three days, and have nothing to eat; and I am unwilling to send them away hungry, lest they faint on the way." 33And the disciples said to him, "Where are we to get bread enough in the desert to feed so great a crowd?" 34And Jesus said to them, "How many loaves have you?" They said, "Seven, and a few small fish." 35And com-

15.36
Mt 14.19;
1 Sam 9.13

manding the crowd to sit down on the ground, 36 he took the seven loaves and the fish, and having given thanks he broke them and gave them to the disciples, and the disciples gave them to the crowds. 37And they all ate and were satisfied; and they took up seven baskets full of the broken pieces left over. 38 Those who ate were four thousand men, besides women and children. 39And sending away the crowds, he got into the boat and went to the region of Măg'ádăn.

The Pharisees and Sadducees demand a sign from heaven (16.1–12; Mk 8.11–21)

16.1
Mt 12.38;
Lk 11.16,
29;
12.54–56

16 And the Phạr'ĭsees and Săd'dụçees came, and to test him they asked him to show them a sign from heaven. 2 He answered them,ʳ "When it is evening, you say, 'It will be fair weather; for the sky is red.' 3And in the morning, 'It will be stormy today, for the sky is red and threatening.' You know how to interpret the appearance of the sky, but you cannot interpret the

*16.4
Jon 3.4,
5;
Mt 12.39

signs of the times. 4An evil and adulterous generation seeks for a sign, but no sign shall be given to it except the sign of Jonah." So he left them and departed.

16.6
Lk 12.1

5 When the disciples reached the other side, they had forgotten to bring any bread. 6 Jesus said to them, "Take heed and beware of the leaven of the Phạr'ĭsees and Săd'dụçees." 7And they dis-

16.8
Mt 6.30;
8.26; 14.31

cussed it among themselves, saying, "We brought no bread." 8 But Jesus, aware of this, said, "O men of little faith, why do you

16.9
Mt 14.17–
21

discuss among yourselves the fact that you have no bread? 9 Do you not yet perceive? Do you not remember the five loaves of the five thousand, and how many baskets you gathered? 10 Or the

16.10
Mt 15.34–
38

seven loaves of the four thousand, and how many baskets you gathered? 11 How is it that you fail to perceive that I did not speak

ʳ Other ancient authorities omit the following words to the end of verse 3

16.4 In answer to the request for a sign from heaven, that is, some extraordinary or miraculous act which would prove Jesus' divine authority, Jesus replied that no sign would be given that evil and faithless generation except the sign of Jonah. As Lk 11.29, 30, 32 show, this referred to Jonah's message of imminent destruction unless the people of Nineveh repented: in the same way the Son of man was a sign to his generation.

In 12.39, 40 the sign of Jonah is explained as referring to his three days and nights in the fish's belly, as a type of Christ's burial and resurrection. In Mk 8.11–13 Jesus refused to give any sign (*no sign shall be given to this generation*).

about bread? Beware of the leaven of the Phạr'ịseẹṣ and Săd'-dụ̀çeẹ̄ṣ." 12 Then they understood that he did not tell them to beware of the leaven of bread, but of the teaching of the Phạr'ịseẹ̄ṣ and Săd'dụ̀çeẹ̄ṣ.

Peter's confession (16.13–20; Mk 8.27–30; Lk 9.18–21)

13 Now when Jesus came into the district of Çaẻsȧrẻ'ȧ Phĭl'-ịppī, he asked his disciples, "Who do men say that the Son of man is?" 14And they said, "Some say John the Baptist, others say Ělĭ'jȧh, and others Jěrěmĭ'ȧh or one of the prophets." 15 He said to them, "But who do you say that I am?" 16 Simon Peter replied, "You are the Christ, the Son of the living God." 17And Jesus answered him, "Blessed are you, Simon Bar-Jŏ'nȧ! For flesh and blood has not revealed this to you, but my Father who is in heaven. 18And I tell you, you are Peter,ˢ and on this rockᵗ I will build my church, and the powers of deathᵘ shall not prevail against it. 19 I will give you the keys of the kingdom of heaven, and whatever you bind on earth shall be bound in heaven, and whatever you loose on earth shall be loosed in heaven." 20 Then he strictly charged the disciples to tell no one that he was the Christ.

16.14 Mt 14.2; Jn 1.21
16.16 Mt 14.33; Jn 6.69; 11.27
16.17 1 Cor 15.50; Gal 1.16; Eph 6.12
★16.18 Jn 1.42
★16.19 Mt 18.18; Jn 20.23
16.20 Mk 3.12; 5.43; 7.36; 9.9

Christ foretells his death, resurrection, and second coming (16.21–28; Mk 8.31–9.1; Lk 9.22–27)

21 From that time Jesus began to show his disciples that he must go to Jerusalem and suffer many things from the elders and chief priests and scribes, and be killed, and on the third day be raised. 22And Peter took him and began to rebuke him, saying, "God forbid, Lord! This shall never happen to you." 23 But he turned and said to Peter, "Get behind me, Satan! You are a hindranceᵛ to me; for you are not on the side of God, but of men."

16.21 Mt 17.22, 23; 20.17–19; Lk 17.25
★16.23

ˢ Greek Pĕtrŏs   ᵗ Greek petra
ᵘ Greek the gates of Hādēṣ   ᵛ Greek stumbling block

16.18 Some have interpreted this verse to mean that Christ founded His church on Peter himself. But such an interpretation overlooks some very important elements in this conversation. It is plain that Christ was making a play on words, for Peter and rock are Petros and petra in the Greek. The church is not built on Peter or any other individual as its foundation-stone, for Peter himself makes it clear in 1 Pet 2.4–8 that Christ Himself is the only cornerstone of the church (cf. also Eph 2.20–22). The church, then, is built upon the person of the Lord Jesus and its membership includes only those who have confessed Him as Peter did. The "gates of Hades" cannot prevail against this church, for Christ has risen again from the dead and will keep His body safe from the onslaughts of death.
16.19 The keys of the kingdom were not given to Peter alone. They were for all of the apostles and for the church in all ages (cf. 18.18). Nor is it to be supposed that the power of the keys includes the power of any individual to forgive sins. The Greek tense of the verbs shall be bound and shall be loosed

means "shall have been." Thus men of God have the power to declare that God has forgiven the sins of those who have repented and received Christ by faith. No one may pronounce absolution, but anyone may announce that sins have been forgiven when gospel terms have been met. In 18.18 Jesus uses the same words in speaking to all the apostles. In Jn 20.23 Jesus, in identical language, bestows this "power of the keys" upon all of the apostles and not simply upon Peter alone. Yet Peter made the first significant use of the "keys" in Acts 2 when he preached the gospel to all the pilgrims at Pentecost and proclaimed the message of salvation to them.
16.23 In 16.17 Jesus said to Peter, "Blessed are you." In this verse He rebukes Peter sharply. Peter knew that Jesus was the Christ but apparently he misunderstood the nature of His approaching sacrifice and went so far as to try to deter Jesus from fulfilling His divine mission. Jesus regarded any interference which would take Him out of the will of His Father as satanic. Hence, the rebuke now, after His blessing earlier.

*16.24
Mt 10.38,
39;
Lk 14.27;
17.33;
Jn 12.25
16.27
Mt 10.33;
Lk 12.9;
1 Jn 2.28;
Rom 2.6;
Rev 22.12
16.28
Mt 10.23;
1 Cor
16.22;
1 Thess
4.15–18;
Rev 1.7;
Jas 5.7
17.1
Mt 26.37;
Mk 5.37;
13.2
*17.2
17.5
2 Pet 1.17;
Mt 3.17;
Isa 42.1;
Acts 3.22,
23
17.7
Mt 14.27
17.9
Mt 8.4;
16.20;
Mk 3.12;
5.43; 7.36
17.10
Mal 4.5;
Mt 11.14
*17.11
Mal 4.6;
Lk 1.16,17
17.12
Mt 11.14;
14.3,10;
16.21
17.15
Mt 4.24

24 Then Jesus told his disciples, "If any man would come after me, let him deny himself and take up his cross and follow me. 25 For whoever would save his life will lose it, and whoever loses his life for my sake will find it. 26 For what will it profit a man, if he gains the whole world and forfeits his life? Or what shall a man give in return for his life? 27 For the Son of man is to come with his angels in the glory of his Father, and then he will repay every man for what he has done. 28 Truly, I say to you, there are some standing here who will not taste death before they see the Son of man coming in his kingdom."

The Transfiguration (17.1–13; Mk 9.2–13; Lk 9.28–36)

17 And after six days Jesus took with him Peter and James and John his brother, and led them up a high mountain apart. 2And he was transfigured before them, and his face shone like the sun, and his garments became white as light. 3And behold, there appeared to them Moses and Eli′jah, talking with him. 4And Peter said to Jesus, "Lord, it is well that we are here; if you wish, I will make three booths here, one for you and one for Moses and one for Eli′jah." 5 He was still speaking, when lo, a bright cloud overshadowed them, and a voice from the cloud said, "This is my beloved Son,w with whom I am well pleased; listen to him." 6 When the disciples heard this, they fell on their faces, and were filled with awe. 7 But Jesus came and touched them, saying, "Rise, and have no fear." 8And when they lifted up their eyes, they saw no one but Jesus only.

9 And as they were coming down the mountain, Jesus commanded them, "Tell no one the vision, until the Son of man is raised from the dead." 10And the disciples asked him, "Then why do the scribes say that first Eli′jah must come?" 11 He replied, "Eli′jah does come, and he is to restore all things; 12 but I tell you that Eli′jah has already come, and they did not know him, but did to him whatever they pleased. So also the Son of man will suffer at their hands." 13 Then the disciples understood that he was speaking to them of John the Baptist.

The epileptic boy cured (17.14–21; Mk 9.14–29; Lk 9.37–43)

14 And when they came to the crowd, a man came up to him and kneeling before him said, 15 "Lord, have mercy on my son, for he is an epileptic and he suffers terribly; for often he falls into the fire, and often into the water. 16And I brought him to your disciples, and they could not heal him." 17And Jesus answered, "O faithless and perverse generation, how long am I to be with you? How long am I to bear with you? Bring him here to me."

w Or my Son, my (or the) Beloved

16.24 It is important to notice that Christ does not speak here of self-denial in the sense of denying things to oneself, but rather in the sense of denying self as a life-principle. The self-life belongs to the old, unconverted state of existence. But the new believer renounces the demands of the old ego altogether, for the old ego has been crucified with Christ (cf. Gal 2.20). The true Christian is dead to the world, to the old life, and to the old self; he is alive to God, and Christ is his new life-principle (cf. Rom 6.6–13; Col 3.1–4). The "cross" which he is to take up as he follows Christ is nothing less than the instrument of death, for that is what the cross was to Christ Himself.

17.2 See note to Mk 9.2 on transfiguration.
17.11 See note to Mal 4.5 on Elijah.

18And Jesus rebuked him, and the demon came out of him, and
the boy was cured instantly. 19 Then the disciples came to Jesus
privately and said, "Why could we not cast it out?" 20 He said to
them, "Because of your little faith. For truly, I say to you, if you
have faith as a grain of mustard seed, you will say to this mountain, 'Move from here to there,' and it will move; and nothing
will be impossible to you."x

Jesus again foretells his death and resurrection
(17.22,23; Mk 9.30–32; Lk 9.43–45)

22 As they were gatheringy in Găl'ileē, Jesus said to them, "The
Son of man is to be delivered into the hands of men, 23 and they
will kill him, and he will be raised on the third day." And they
were greatly distressed.

The shekel in the fish's mouth (17.24–27)

24 When they came to Cáper'nä-ùm, the collectors of the half-
shekel tax went up to Peter and said, "Does not your teacher pay
the tax?" 25 He said, "Yes." And when he came home, Jesus spoke
to him first, saying, "What do you think, Simon? From whom do
kings of the earth take toll or tribute? From their sons or from
others?" 26And when he said, "From others," Jesus said to him,
"Then the sons are free. 27 However, not to give offense to them,
go to the sea and cast a hook, and take the first fish that comes up,
and when you open its mouth you will find a shekel; take that and
give it to them for me and for yourself."

Discourse on humility (18.1–9; Mk 9.33–37; Lk 9.46–48)

18 At that time the disciples came to Jesus, saying, "Who is
the greatest in the kingdom of heaven?" 2And calling to him
a child, he put him in the midst of them, 3 and said, "Truly, I say
to you, unless you turn and become like children, you will never
enter the kingdom of heaven. 4 Whoever humbles himself like this
child, he is the greatest in the kingdom of heaven.

5 "Whoever receives one such child in my name receives me;
6 but whoever causes one of these little ones who believe in me to
sin,z it would be better for him to have a great millstone fastened
round his neck and to be drowned in the depth of the sea.

7 "Woe to the world for temptations to sin!a For it is necessary
that temptations come, but woe to the man by whom the temptation comes! 8And if your hand or your foot causes you to sin,x cut
it off and throw it away; it is better for you to enter life maimed
or lame than with two hands or two feet to be thrown into the

x Other ancient authorities insert verse 21, "But this kind never comes out except by prayer
and fasting" y Other ancient authorities read abode z Greek causes . . . to stumble
a Greek stumbling blocks z Greek causes . . . to stumble

*17.20 Mt 21.21; Mk 11.23; 1 Cor 12.9
17.22 Mt 16.21; 20.17; Lk 18.31; 24.6,7
*17.24 Ex 30.13; 38.26
17.25 Rom 13.7; Mt 22.17,19
17.27 Mt 5.29,30; 18.6,8; Lk 17.2; Jn 6.61; 1 Cor 8.13
18.3 Mt 19.14; Mk 10.15; Lk 18.17; 1 Pet 2.2
18.4 Mt 20.27; 23.11
18.5 Mt 10.40; Lk 18.17
18.6 Lk 17.1,2
18.7 Lk 17.1; 1 Cor 11.19
*18.8 Mt 5.29,30; Mk 9.43, 45

17.20 nothing will be impossible cannot be
interpreted without reservation. True faith
is rooted in the conviction that the particular thing anticipated is the will of God.
But many things are not the will of God
and are excluded from this promise.
17.24 The annual temple tax of half-shekel

was paid by all free Jewish males over twenty
years of age (cf. Ex 30.11–16). The Greek
coin equivalent to the Hebrew half-shekel
was the double drachma (didrachma); the
shekel in verse 27 is a stater, worth two di-
drachmas.
18.8 See note to 5.29 explaining this verse.

Matthew 18.9–21

1468

eternal fire. 9And if your eye causes you to sin,ᶻ pluck it out and throw it away; it is better for you to enter life with one eye than with two eyes to be thrown into the hellᵇ of fire.

The lost sheep (18.10–14; Lk 15.4–7)

10 "See that you do not despise one of these little ones; for I tell you that in heaven their angels always behold the face of my Father who is in heaven.ᶜ 12 What do you think? If a man has a hundred sheep, and one of them has gone astray, does he not leave the ninety-nine on the mountains and go in search of the one that went astray? 13And if he finds it, truly, I say to you, he rejoices over it more than over the ninety-nine that never went astray. 14 So it is not the will of myᵈ Father who is in heaven that one of these little ones should perish.

The treatment of offenders (18.15–35)

1. Church discipline (18.15–20)

15 "If your brother sins against you, go and tell him his fault, between you and him alone. If he listens to you, you have gained your brother. 16 But if he does not listen, take one or two others along with you, that every word may be confirmed by the evidence of two or three witnesses. 17 If he refuses to listen to them, tell it to the church; and if he refuses to listen even to the church, let him be to you as a Gentile and a tax collector. 18 Truly, I say to you, whatever you bind on earth shall be bound in heaven, and whatever you loose on earth shall be loosed in heaven. 19Again I say to you, if two of you agree on earth about anything they ask, it will be done for them by my Father in heaven. 20 For where two or three are gathered in my name, there am I in the midst of them."

2. The law of forgiveness (18.21–35)

21 Then Peter came up and said to him, "Lord, how often shall

ᶻ Greek causes . . . to stumble   ᵇ Greek Gēhĕn'nå
ᶜ Other ancient authorities add verse 11, For the Son of man came to save the lost
ᵈ Other ancient authorities read your

18.9 Gehenna (RSV footnote) (spelled Geenna in the Greek) is the Aramaic form of the Hebrew Gehinnom, which means the Valley of Hinnom. This term is used for the place of the eternal punishment of the wicked dead. Body and soul are cast into Gehenna and unquenchable fire is used as the symbol of this unending torment. In the Old Testament, the Valley of Hinnom (Topheth) was the place where, in the idolatrous reigns of Ahaz and Manasseh, helpless infants were immolated by fire and where the gruesome idol of Molech was worshiped. Josiah later defiled Topheth and converted it into the city dump where a smoldering fire was continually burning. Thus it became a very fit symbol for hell itself. Indeed, the KJV usually translates the word for Gehenna as "hell." And yet this is confusing, since it translates the Greek Hades (Hebrew Sheol) as "hell" also. The RSV translates it here in 18.9, and also in 5.22, as the hell of fire, but

renders it simply as hell in 5.29, 30; 10.28; 23.15, 33; Mk 9.43, 45, 47; Lk 12.5; Jas 3.6, always with a footnote indicating that it is the Greek word Gehenna.
18.17 God, who ordained the church, has likewise ordained its government and its order. Order in the church is to be maintained by church discipline, and the effective sanction to enforce discipline is excommunication. Scripture enjoins the churches to maintain sound doctrine (1 Tim 1.3; Tit 1.13) and to see that order prevails (Tit 1.5; 1 Cor 11.34). Offenders are to be dealt with and rebuked (1 Tim 5.20; 2 Tim 4.2). Sincere believers are to submit to discipline (Heb 13.17), which has for its end decency and order (1 Cor 14.40) as well as the correction of the offender (2 Cor 10.8; 13.10). Unrepentant offenders who refuse to accept discipline should be excommunicated from the fellowship (1 Cor 5.3–5, 13), not simply as a penalty, but to bring them to repentance.

my brother sin against me, and I forgive him? As many as seven times?" 22 Jesus said to him, "I do not say to you seven times, but seventy times seven.ᵉ

23 "Therefore the kingdom of heaven may be compared to a king who wished to settle accounts with his servants. 24 When he began the reckoning, one was brought to him who owed him ten thousand talents;ᶠ 25 and as he could not pay, his lord ordered him to be sold, with his wife and children and all that he had, and payment to be made. 26 So the servant fell on his knees, imploring him, 'Lord, have patience with me, and I will pay you everything.' 27And out of pity for him the lord of that servant released him and forgave him the debt. 28 But that same servant, as he went out, came upon one of his fellow servants who owed him a hundred denarii;ᵍ and seizing him by the throat he said, 'Pay what you owe.' 29 So his fellow servant fell down and besought him, 'Have patience with me, and I will pay you.' 30 He refused and went and put him in prison till he should pay the debt. 31 When his fellow servants saw what had taken place, they were greatly distressed, and they went and reported to their lord all that had taken place. 32 Then his lord summoned him and said to him, 'You wicked servant! I forgave you all that debt because you besought me; 33 and should not you have had mercy on your fellow servant, as I had mercy on you?' 34And in anger his lord delivered him to the jailers,ʰ till he should pay all his debt. 35 So also my heavenly Father will do to every one of you, if you do not forgive your brother from your heart."

Jesus goes to Judea (19.1,2)

19 Now when Jesus had finished these sayings, he went away from Găl'ĭleē and entered the region of Judē'á beyond the Jordan; 2 and large crowds followed him, and he healed them there.

Jesus' teaching on marriage (19.3–12; Mk 10.2–12)

3 And Phar'ĭseēṣ came up to him and tested him by asking, "Is it lawful to divorce one's wife for any cause?" 4 He answered, "Have you not read that he who made them from the beginning made them male and female, 5 and said, 'For this reason a man shall leave his father and mother and be joined to his wife, and the two shall become one flesh'? 6 So they are no longer two but one flesh. What therefore God has joined together, let not man put asunder." 7 They said to him, "Why then did Moses command

Cross-references (right margin)
18.22 Mt 6.14; Mk 11.25; Col 3.13
*18.23 Mt 25.19
18.25 Lk 7.42; 2 Ki 4.1; Neh 5.5,8
18.26 Mt 8.2
18.35 Mt 6.14; Mk 11.26; Jas 2.13
19.1 Mk 10.1; Jn 10.40
19.2 Mt 4.23
*19.3 Mt 5.31
19.4 Gen 1.27; 5.2
19.5 Gen 2.24; 1 Cor 6.16; Eph 5.31
19.7 Deut 24.1-4; Mt 5.31

ᵉ Or seventy-seven times ᶠ This talent was more than fifteen years' wages of a laborer
ᵍ The denarius was a day's wage for a laborer ʰ Greek torturers

---

18.23 This parable teaches us the absolute necessity of forgiveness. The unmerciful servant, having been forgiven a debt of unheard-of proportions (for 10,000 talents exceeded the wealth of Croesus himself), refused to forgive a fellow servant for an obligation only one twenty-thousandth of one per cent as great as his own. Since we have been forgiven the heaviest of all debts, it is incumbent upon us to forgive others whose debt to us is nothing compared to that for which we have been forgiven.

19.3 Jesus' teachings on divorce are found in 5.31, 32; 19.3–9; Mk 10.2–12; Lk 16.18. In 1 Cor 7.10, 11 Paul attributes his teaching on divorce to the Lord, by which he means he is reporting the teaching of Jesus. In all these passages divorce is forbidden; in 5.32 and 19.9 a single exception is made, and a man is allowed to divorce his wife in the case of infidelity. (See note to Deut 24.1 on divorce).

one to give a certificate of divorce, and to put her away?" 8 He said to them, "For your hardness of heart Moses allowed you to divorce your wives, but from the beginning it was not so. 9And I say to you: whoever divorces his wife, except for unchastity,^j and marries another, commits adultery."^k

10 The disciples said to him, "If such is the case of a man with his wife, it is not expedient to marry." 11 But he said to them, "Not all men can receive this saying, but only those to whom it is given. 12 For there are eunuchs who have been so from birth, and there are eunuchs who have been made eunuchs by men, and there are eunuchs who have made themselves eunuchs for the sake of the kingdom of heaven. He who is able to receive this, let him receive it."

Jesus blesses little children
(19.13–15; Mk 10.13–16; Lk 18.15–17)

13 Then children were brought to him that he might lay his hands on them and pray. The disciples rebuked the people; 14 but Jesus said, "Let the children come to me, and do not hinder them; for to such belongs the kingdom of heaven." 15And he laid his hands on them and went away.

The rich young ruler
(19.16–30; Mk 10.17–31; Lk 18.18–30)

16 And behold, one came up to him, saying, "Teacher, what good deed must I do, to have eternal life?" 17And he said to him, "Why do you ask me about what is good? One there is who is good. If you would enter life, keep the commandments." 18 He said to him, "Which?" And Jesus said, "You shall not kill, You shall not commit adultery, You shall not steal, You shall not bear false witness, 19 Honor your father and mother, and, You shall love your neighbor as yourself." 20 The young man said to him, "All these I have observed; what do I still lack?" 21 Jesus said to him, "If you would be perfect, go, sell what you possess and give to the poor, and you will have treasure in heaven; and come, follow me." 22 When the young man heard this he went away sorrowful; for he had great possessions.

23 And Jesus said to his disciples, "Truly, I say to you, it will be hard for a rich man to enter the kingdom of heaven. 24Again I tell you, it is easier for a camel to go through the eye of a needle than for a rich man to enter the kingdom of God." 25 When the disciples heard this they were greatly astonished, saying, "Who then can be saved?" 26 But Jesus looked at them and said to them, "With men this is impossible, but with God all things are possible." 27 Then Peter said in reply, "Lo, we have left everything and followed you. What then shall we have?" 28 Jesus said to them, "Truly, I say to you, in the new world, when the Son of man shall sit on his glorious throne, you who have followed me will also sit on twelve thrones, judging the twelve tribes of Israel. 29And every one who has left houses or brothers or sisters or father or mother or children or lands, for my name's sake, will re-

Marginal references:

19.9
Mk 5.32;
Lk 16.18;
1 Cor 7.10–
13

19.11
1 Cor 7.7–9

19.14
Mt 18.3;
1 Cor
14.20;
1 Pet 2.2

19.16
Lev 18.5;
Lk 10.25

19.18
Ex 20.13;
Deut 5.17;
Rom 13.9;
Jas 2.11
19.19
Lev 19.18
Mt 22.39;
Rom 13.9;
Gal 5.14
19.21
Mt 6.20;
Lk 12.33;
16.9;
Acts 2.45;
4.34,35
19.23
Mt 13.22;
1 Cor 1.26;
1 Tim
6.9,10

19.26
Gen 18.14;
Job 42.2;
Jer 32.17;
Zech 8.6
19.27
Mt 4.20;
Lk 5.11
19.28
Mt 20.21;
Lk 22.28–
30;
Rev 3.21

---

j Other ancient authorities, after *unchastity*, read *makes her commit adultery*
k Other ancient authorities insert *and he who marries a divorced woman commits adultery*

ceive a hundredfold,[1] and inherit eternal life. 30 But many that are first will be last, and the last first.

19.30
Mt 20.16;
Lk 13.30

Parable of the householder (20.1–16)

20 "For the kingdom of heaven is like a householder who went out early in the morning to hire laborers for his vineyard. 2After agreeing with the laborers for a denarius[m] a day, he sent them into his vineyard. 3And going out about the third hour he saw others standing idle in the market place; 4 and to them he said, 'You go into the vineyard too, and whatever is right I will give you.' So they went. 5 Going out again about the sixth hour and the ninth hour, he did the same. 6And about the eleventh hour he went out and found others standing; and he said to them, 'Why do you stand here idle all day?' 7 They said to him, 'Because no one has hired us.' He said to them, 'You go into the vineyard too.' 8And when evening came, the owner of the vineyard said to his steward, 'Call the laborers and pay them their wages, beginning with the last, up to the first.' 9And when those hired about the eleventh hour came, each of them received a denarius. 10 Now when the first came, they thought they would receive more; but each of them also received a denarius. 11And on receiving it they grumbled at the householder, 12 saying, 'These last worked only one hour, and you have made them equal to us who have borne the burden of the day and the scorching heat.' 13 But he replied to one of them, 'Friend, I am doing you no wrong; did you not agree with me for a denarius? 14 Take what belongs to you, and go; I choose to give to this last as I give to you. 15Am I not allowed to do what I choose with what belongs to me? Or do you begrudge my generosity?'[n] 16 So the last will be first, and the first last."

*20.1
Mt 13.24;
21.28,33

*20.3

20.8
Lev 19.3;
Deut 24.15

20.12
Jon 4.8;
Lk 12.55;
Jas 1.11
20.13
Mt 22.12;
26.50
20.15
Deut 15.9;
Mt 6.23;
Mk 7.22
20.16
Mt 19.30

Christ foretells his crucifixion and resurrection (20.17–19; Mk 10.32–34; Lk 18.31–34)

17 And as Jesus was going up to Jerusalem, he took the twelve disciples aside, and on the way he said to them, 18 "Behold, we are going up to Jerusalem; and the Son of man will be delivered to the chief priests and scribes, and they will condemn him to death, 19 and deliver him to the Gentiles to be mocked and scourged and crucified, and he will be raised on the third day."

20.18
Mt 16.21
20.19
Mt 16.21;
27.2;
Acts 2.23;
3.13

Ambition of James and John (20.20–28; Mk 10.35–45)

20 Then the mother of the sons of Zĕb′edeē came up to him, with her sons, and kneeling before him she asked him for something. 21And he said to her, "What do you want?" She said to him,

20.20
Mt 4.21;
8.2; 9.18;
Jn 9.38
20.21
Mt 19.28

[1]Other ancient authorities read *manifold* m The denarius was a day's wage for a laborer
n Or *is your eye evil because I am good?*

20.1 The major teaching of this parable is that God bestows His grace of salvation (represented by the denarius) upon all those who respond to His call regardless of human merit. Length of years in the service of the Lord does not insure to the convert any more blessed a heaven than to the sinner who turns to God in faith at the eleventh hour. The

principle in operation here is grace only, and merit has nothing to do with it.

20.3 The working day began at 6:00 A.M., at which time the householder went to the market place to hire workers for the day (ver 1); he returned at 9:00 A.M. (ver 3), 12:00 noon, 3:00 P.M. (ver 5), and at 5:00 P.M. (ver 6) when only one hour of the day was left.

20.22
Mt 26.39,
42;
Lk 22.42;
Jn 18.11
20.23
Acts 12.2;
Rev 1.9;
Mt 25.34
20.24
Lk 22.24,
25
*20.25
Lk 22.25–
27
20.26
Mt 23.11;
Mk 9.35;
Lk 9.48
20.28
Jn 13.4;
Phil 2.7;
Jn 13.14;
Isa 53.10;
1 Tim 2.6;
Tit 2.14;
1 Pet 1.19;
Mt 26.28;
Heb 9.28
20.30
Mt 9.27

"Command that these two sons of mine may sit, one at your right hand and one at your left, in your kingdom." 22 But Jesus answered, "You do not know what you are asking. Are you able to drink the cup that I am to drink?" They said to him, "We are able." 23 He said to them, "You will drink my cup, but to sit at my right hand and at my left is not mine to grant, but it is for those for whom it has been prepared by my Father." 24And when the ten heard it, they were indignant at the two brothers. 25 But Jesus called them to him and said, "You know that the rulers of the Gentiles lord it over them, and their great men exercise authority over them. 26 It shall not be so among you; but whoever would be great among you must be your servant, 27 and whoever would be first among you must be your slave; 28 even as the Son of man came not to be served but to serve, and to give his life as a ransom for many."

Healing two blind men near Jericho
(20.29–34; Mk 10.46–52; Lk 18.35–43)

29 And as they went out of Jĕr'ĭchō, a great crowd followed him. 30And behold, two blind men sitting by the roadside, when they heard that Jesus was passing by, cried out,º "Have mercy on us, Son of David!" 31 The crowd rebuked them, telling them to be silent; but they cried out the more, "Lord, have mercy on us, Son of David!" 32And Jesus stopped and called them, saying, "What do you want me to do for you?" 33 They said to him, "Lord, let our eyes be opened." 34And Jesus in pity touched their eyes, and immediately they received their sight and followed him.

The triumphal entry
(21.1–11; Mk 11.1–11; Lk 19.29–44; Jn 12.12–19)

21 And when they drew near to Jerusalem and came to Bĕth'-phăgė, to the Mount of Olives, then Jesus sent two disciples, 2 saying to them, "Go into the village opposite you, and immediately you will find an ass tied, and a colt with her; untie them and bring them to me. 3 If any one says anything to you, you shall say, 'The Lord has need of them,' and he will send them immediately." 4 This took place to fulfil what was spoken by the prophet, saying,

21.5
Isa 62.11;
Zech 9.9

5 "Tell the daughter of Zion,
   Behold, your king is coming to you,
   humble, and mounted on an ass,
   and on a colt, the foal of an ass."

6 The disciples went and did as Jesus had directed them; 7 they brought the ass and the colt, and put their garments on them, and

º Other ancient authorities insert Lord

20.25 Christ draws a contrast here between the ambition of the natural, once-born man, who covets power and glory for himself, and the ambition of the redeemed, twice-born man, who lives not for self *but for him who for their sake died and was raised.* (2 Cor 5.15). The Christ-centered believer is ambitious only for the performance of God's holy will and the display of His self-sacrificing love. Just as his Savior came to serve rather than to be served (ver 28), so the true Christian lives to bless and serve others rather than himself. Spiritual stature (*whoever would be great among you,* ver 26) will be measured by God according to how close a resemblance the believer bears to the Christ of the cross.

he sat thereon. 8 Most of the crowd spread their garments on the road, and others cut branches from the trees and spread them on the road. 9And the crowds that went before him and that followed him shouted, "Hosanna to the Son of David! Blessed is he who comes in the name of the Lord! Hosanna in the highest!" 10And when he entered Jerusalem, all the city was stirred, saying, "Who is this?" 11And the crowds said, "This is the prophet Jesus from Năz′ărĕth of Găl′ilĕē."

Second cleansing of the Temple
(21.12–17; Mk 11.15–19; Lk 19.45–48; cf. Jn 2.13–22)

12 And Jesus entered the temple of God*p* and drove out all who sold and bought in the temple, and he overturned the tables of the money-changers and the seats of those who sold pigeons. 13 He said to them, "It is written, 'My house shall be called a house of prayer'; but you make it a den of robbers."

14 And the blind and the lame came to him in the temple, and he healed them. 15 But when the chief priests and the scribes saw the wonderful things that he did, and the children crying out in the temple, "Hosanna to the Son of David!" they were indignant; 16 and they said to him, "Do you hear what these are saying?" And Jesus said to them, "Yes; have you never read,

'Out of the mouth of babes and sucklings
    thou hast brought perfect praise'?"

17And leaving them, he went out of the city to Bĕth′ănў and lodged there.

The barren fig tree (21.18–22; Mk 11.12–14, 20–25)

18 In the morning, as he was returning to the city, he was hungry. 19And seeing a fig tree by the wayside he went to it, and found nothing on it but leaves only. And he said to it, "May no fruit ever come from you again!" And the fig tree withered at once. 20 When the disciples saw it they marveled, saying, "How did the fig tree wither at once?" 21And Jesus answered them, "Truly, I say to you, if you have faith and never doubt, you will not only do what has been done to the fig tree, but even if you say to this mountain, 'Be taken up and cast into the sea,' it will be done. 22And whatever you ask in prayer, you will receive, if you have faith."

Christ's authority challenged
(21.23–27; Mk 11.27–33; Lk 20.1–8)

23 And when he entered the temple, the chief priests and the elders of the people came up to him as he was teaching, and said, "By what authority are you doing these things, and who gave you this authority?" 24 Jesus answered them, "I also will ask you a question; and if you tell me the answer, then I also will tell you by what authority I do these things. 25 The baptism of John, whence was it? From heaven or from men?" And they argued with one

p Other ancient authorities omit *of God*

21.8 2 Ki 9.13
★21.9 Ps 118.26; ver 15; Mt 23.39
21.11 Jn 6.14; 7.40; Acts 3.22; Mk 6.15; Lk 13.33
21.12 Ex 30.13; Deut 14.25 21.13 Isa 56.7; Jer 7.11
21.15 ver 9; Lk 19.39
21.16 Ps 8.2
21.21 Mt 17.20; Lk 17.6; Jas 1.6
★21.22 Mt 7.7; Jn 14.13,14; 16.23; Jas 5.16
21.23 Acts 4.7; 7.27

21.9 *Hosanna*, meaning "save we pray thee," occurs six times in the gospels.

21.22 See note to Lk 11.1 on the principles of prayer and faith.

another, "If we say, 'From heaven,' he will say to us, 'Why then did you not believe him?' 26 But if we say, 'From men,' we are afraid of the multitude; for all hold that John was a prophet." 27 So they answered Jesus, "We do not know." And he said to them, "Neither will I tell you by what authority I do these things.

21.26
Mt 14.5;
Mk 6.20

Parable of the two sons (21.28–32)

28 "What do you think? A man had two sons; and he went to the first and said, 'Son, go and work in the vineyard today.' 29And he answered, 'I will not'; but afterward he repented and went. 30And he went to the second and said the same; and he answered, 'I go, sir,' but did not go. 31 Which of the two did the will of his father?" They said, "The first." Jesus said to them, "Truly, I say to you, the tax collectors and the harlots go into the kingdom of God before you. 32 For John came to you in the way of righteousness, and you did not believe him, but the tax collectors and the harlots believed him; and even when you saw it, you did not afterward repent and believe him.

21.28
ver 33;
Mt 20.21

21.31
Lk 7.29,50

21.32
Mt 3.1ff;
Lk 7.29,30;
3.12,13

Parable of the wicked tenants
(21.33–46; Mk 12.1–12; Lk 20.9–19)

33 "Hear another parable. There was a householder who planted a vineyard, and set a hedge around it, and dug a wine press in it, and built a tower, and let it out to tenants, and went into another country. 34 When the season of fruit drew near, he sent his servants to the tenants, to get his fruit; 35 and the tenants took his servants and beat one, killed another, and stoned another. 36Again he sent other servants, more than the first; and they did the same to them. 37Afterward he sent his son to them, saying, 'They will respect my son.' 38 But when the tenants saw the son, they said to themselves, 'This is the heir; come, let us kill him and have his inheritance.' 39And they took him and cast him out of the vineyard, and killed him. 40 When therefore the owner of the vineyard comes, what will he do to those tenants?" 41 They said to him, "He will put those wretches to a miserable death, and let out the vineyard to other tenants who will give him the fruits in their seasons."

*21.33
Ps 80.8;
Isa 5.1–7;
Mt 25.14,15
21.34
Mt 22.3
21.35
2 Chr
24.21;
Mt 23.34,
37;
Heb 11.36,
37
21.38
Ps 2.8;
Heb 1.2;
Mt 26.3;
27.1
21.41
Mt 8.11;
Acts 13.46;
18.6; 28.28

42 Jesus said to them, "Have you never read in the scriptures:
'The very stone which the builders rejected
has become the head of the corner;
this was the Lord's doing,
and it is marvelous in our eyes'?

21.42
Ps 118.22,
23;
Acts 4.11;
1 Pet 2.7

43 Therefore I tell you, the kingdom of God will be taken away from you and given to a nation producing the fruits of it."q

21.43
Mt 8.12

45 When the chief priests and the Phạr'ịseēs heard his parables, they perceived that he was speaking about them. 46 But when they tried to arrest him, they feared the multitudes, because they held him to be a prophet.

*21.46
ver 26,11

q Other ancient authorities add verse 44, "And he who falls on this stone will be broken to pieces; but when it falls on any one, it will crush him"

21.33 See note to Lk 20.9 on the parable of the wicked tenants.

21.46 *multitude*. It was the common people who believed Jesus to be a prophet.

Parable of the marriage feast (22.1–14; Lk 14.15–24)

22 And again Jesus spoke to them in parables, saying, 2 "The kingdom of heaven may be compared to a king who gave a marriage feast for his son, 3 and sent his servants to call those who were invited to the marriage feast; but they would not come. 4Again he sent other servants, saying, 'Tell those who are invited, Behold, I have made ready my dinner, my oxen and my fat calves are killed, and everything is ready; come to the marriage feast.' 5 But they made light of it and went off, one to his farm, another to his business, 6 while the rest seized his servants, treated them shamefully, and killed them. 7 The king was angry, and he sent his troops and destroyed those murderers and burned their city. 8 Then he said to his servants, 'The wedding is ready, but those invited were not worthy. 9 Go therefore to the thoroughfares, and invite to the marriage feast as many as you find.' 10And those servants went out into the streets and gathered all whom they found, both bad and good; so the wedding hall was filled with guests.

11 "But when the king came in to look at the guests, he saw there a man who had no wedding garment; 12 and he said to him, 'Friend, how did you get in here without a wedding garment?' And he was speechless. 13 Then the king said to the attendants, 'Bind him hand and foot, and cast him into the outer darkness; there men will weep and gnash their teeth.' 14 For many are called, but few are chosen."

Three questions by the Jewish rulers (22.15–40)

1. Taxes to Caesar (22.15–22; Mk 12.13–17; Lk 20.19–26)

15 Then the Phạr'iṣeēṣ went and took counsel how to entangle him in his talk. 16And they sent their disciples to him, along with the Hērō'dĭ-ảnṣ, saying, "Teacher, we know that you are true, and teach the way of God truthfully, and care for no man; for you do not regard the position of men. 17. Tell us, then, what you think. Is it lawful to pay taxes to Caesar, or not?" 18 But Jesus, aware of their malice, said, "Why put me to the test, you hypocrites? 19 Show me the money for the tax." And they brought him a coin.ʳ 20And Jesus said to them, "Whose likeness and inscription is this?" 21 They said, "Caesar's." Then he said to them, "Render therefore to Caesar the things that are Caesar's, and to God the things that are God's." 22 When they heard it, they marveled; and they left him and went away.

2. The Sadducees and the resurrection
(22.23–33; Mk 12.18–27; Lk 20.27–38)

23 The same day Săd'dụ̣çeēṣ came to him, who say that there is no resurrection; and they asked him a question, 24 saying, "Teach-

ʳ Greek *a denarius*

Marginal references:

*22.2
Mt 13.24

22.3
Mt 21.34

22.4
Mt 21.36

22.7
Lk 19.27

22.8
Mt 10.11,13

22.10
Mt 13.47

22.11
2 Cor 5.3;
Eph 4.24;
Col 3.10,
12;
Rev 3.4;
16.15; 19.8

22.12
Mt 20.13;
26.50

22.13
Mt 8.12;
Lk 13.28

*22.16
Mk 3.6;
8.15

22.17
Mt 17.25

22.21
Rom 13.7

22.23
Acts 23.8
22.24
Deut 25.5

22.2 See note to Lk 14.16.
22.16 The Herodians are mentioned three times in the New Testament (here and in Mk 3.6; 12.13). Apparently they constituted a political party and were followers of the dynasty of Herod. Archelaus, the son of Herod, became ethnarch of Judea but was deposed (ca. A.D. 6 or 7) and replaced by Roman procurators. The Herodians seem to have favored the return of the old dynasty over Judea. They allied themselves with the Pharisees against Jesus because both of these parties recognized in Christ their greatest opponent. Their differences were subordinated to a temporary alliance until they had disposed of Christ.

*22.25   er, Moses said, 'If a man dies, having no children, his brother must
marry the widow, and raise up children for his brother.' 25 Now
there were seven brothers among us; the first married, and died,
and having no children left his wife to his brother. 26 So too the
second and third, down to the seventh. 27After them all, the
woman died. 28 In the resurrection, therefore, to which of the
seven will she be wife? For they all had her."

22.29   29 But Jesus answered them, "You are wrong, because you
Jn 20.9   know neither the scriptures nor the power of God. 30 For in the
resurrection they neither marry nor are given in marriage, but
are like angels_s_ in heaven. 31And as for the resurrection of the
22.32   dead, have you not read what was said to you by God, 32 'I am the
Ex 3.6,16; God of Abraham, and the God of Isaac, and the God of Jacob'?
Acts 7.32; He is not God of the dead, but of the living." 33And when the
Heb 11.16
22.33   crowd heard it, they were astonished at his teaching.
Mt 7.28

3. The great commandment (22.34–40; Mk 12.28–34)

34 But when the Phar'isees heard that he had silenced the
22.35   Sad'ducees, they came together. 35And one of them, a lawyer,
Lk 7.30;   asked him a question, to test him. 36 "Teacher, which is the great
10.25;   commandment in the law?" 37And he said to him, "You shall love
11.45; 14.3 the Lord your God with all your heart, and with all your soul, and
22.37   with all your mind. 38 This is the great and first commandment.
Deut 6.5
22.39   39And a second is like it, You shall love your neighbor as yourself.
Lev 19.18; 40 On these two commandments depend all the law and the
Mt 19.19; prophets."
Rom 13.9;
Gal 5.14;
Jas 2.8
22.40
Mt 7.12

Christ's unanswerable question
(22.41–46; Mk 12.35–37; Lk 20.41–44)

41 Now while the Phar'isees were gathered together, Jesus
22.42   asked them a question, 42 saying, "What do you think of the
Mt 9.27   Christ? Whose son is he?" They said to him, "The son of David."
43 He said to them, "How is it then that David, inspired by the
Spirit,_t_ calls him Lord, saying,
*22.44   44 'The Lord said to my Lord,
Ps 110.1;   Sit at my right hand,
Acts 2.34;   till I put thy enemies under thy feet'?
Heb 1.13;
10.13   45 If David thus calls him Lord, how is he his son?" 46And no one
22.46   was able to answer him a word, nor from that day did any one dare
Mk 12.34; to ask him any more questions.
Lk 20.40

The warning against Pharisaism
(23.1–12; Mk 12.38–40; Lk 20.45–47)

*23.2   **23** Then said Jesus to the crowds and to his disciples, 2 "The
Ezra 7.6,25;   scribes and the Phar'isees sit on Moses' seat; 3 so practice
Neh 8.4   and observe whatever they tell you, but not what they do; for they
23.4   preach, but do not practice. 4 They bind heavy burdens, hard to
Lk 11.46; bear,_u_ and lay them on men's shoulders; but they themselves will
Acts 15.10;
Gal 6.13

_s_ Other ancient authorities add of God   _t_ Or David in the Spirit
_u_ Other ancient authorities omit hard to bear

22.25 See note to Deut 25.5–10.   means God; the second Lord means Messiah.
22.44 The first use of Lord in this verse   **23.2** See note to 3.7a on Pharisees.

not move them with their finger. 5 They do all their deeds to be seen by men; for they make their phylacteries broad and their fringes long, 6 and they love the place of honor at feasts and the best seats in the synagogues, 7 and salutations in the market places, and being called rabbi by men. 8 But you are not to be called rabbi, for you have one teacher, and you are all brethren. 9And call no man your father on earth, for you have one Father, who is in heaven. 10 Neither be called masters, for you have one master, the Christ. 11 He who is greatest among you shall be your servant; 12 whoever exalts himself will be humbled, and whoever humbles himself will be exalted.

The woes upon the Pharisees (23.13–36)

13 "But woe to you, scribes and Phạr′ịseē̦s, hypocrites! because you shut the kingdom of heaven against men; for you neither enter yourselves, nor allow those who would enter to go in.*v* 15 Woe to you, scribes and Phạr′ịseē̦s, hypocrites! for you traverse sea and land to make a single proselyte, and when he becomes a proselyte, you make him twice as much a child of hell*w* as yourselves.

16 "Woe to you, blind guides, who say, 'If any one swears by the temple, it is nothing; but if any one swears by the gold of the temple, he is bound by his oath.' 17 You blind fools! For which is greater, the gold or the temple that has made the gold sacred? 18And you say, 'If any one swears by the altar, it is nothing; but if any one swears by the gift that is on the altar, he is bound by his oath.' 19 You blind men! For which is greater, the gift or the altar that makes the gift sacred? 20 So he who swears by the altar, swears by it and by everything on it; 21 and he who swears by the temple, swears by it and by him who dwells in it; 22 and he who swears by heaven, swears by the throne of God and by him who sits upon it.

23 "Woe to you, scribes and Phạr′ịseē̦s, hypocrites! for you tithe mint and dill and cummin, and have neglected the weightier matters of the law, justice and mercy and faith; these you ought to have done, without neglecting the others. 24 You blind guides, straining out a gnat and swallowing a camel!

25 "Woe to you, scribes and Phạr′ịseē̦s, hypocrites! for you cleanse the outside of the cup and of the plate, but inside they are full of extortion and rapacity. 26 You blind Phạr′ịseē̦! first cleanse

v Other authorities add here (or after verse 12) verse 14, *Woe to you, scribes and Pharisees, hypocrites! for you devour widows' houses and for a pretense you make long prayers; therefore you will receive the greater condemnation*　*w* Greek *Gĕhĕn′nà*

*23.5
Mt 6.1,2,5, 16;
Deut 6.8
23.6
Lk 11.43;
14.7; 20.46
23.8
Jas 3.1
23.9
Mal 1.6
23.11
Mt 20.26
23.12
Lk 14.11;
18.14;
Jas 4.6;
1 Pet 5.5
23.13
Lk 11.52
*23.16
ver 24;
Mt 5.14;
5.33–35
23.17
Ex 30.29
23.19
Ex 29.37
23.22
Ps 11.4;
Mt 5.34
23.23
Mt 11.42;
Lev 27.30;
Mic 6.8
23.24
ver 16
23.25
Mk 7.4;
Lk 11.39

23.5 *Phylacteries* (sometimes called frontlets) were small leather cases containing strips of vellum on which were written the words from Ex 13.1–10, 11–16; Deut 6.4–9; 11.13–21. Two such cases (called *tephillim*, "prayers") were worn, one on the forehead and one on the arm, in literal obedience to the injunctions of Ex 13.16; Deut 6.8; 11.18.
The *fringes* were the four tassels, one at each corner of the cloak, worn by men as a sign of religious devotion in accordance with Num 15.38–41. To *make their phylacteries broad and their fringes long* was to parade their piety before people.
23.16 Jesus condemns the scribes and

Pharisees because they have made unbiblical distinctions by which they have permitted men to violate their oaths. He who takes an oath by the Temple is exempt from keeping his oath, but if the oath is taken by the gold of the Temple, he is bound to keep it. Jesus teaches that the Temple (or altar) sanctifies the gold, and a vow made there, i.e., swearing *by him that dwelleth therein* (ver 21) is equally binding, despite the casuistry. So also in Mk 7.11 Jesus says that no man has a right to break a commandment on the ground that to keep it is to violate an oath, for wicked men would then use rash oaths to nullify the commandments of the Lord.

the inside of the cup and of the plate, that the outside also may be clean.

27 "Woe to you, scribes and Phaṛ'iseēs, hypocrites! for you are like whitewashed tombs, which outwardly appear beautiful, but within they are full of dead men's bones and all uncleanness. 28 So you also outwardly appear righteous to men, but within you are full of hypocrisy and iniquity.

29 "Woe to you, scribes and Phaṛ'iseēs, hypocrites! for you build the tombs of the prophets and adorn the monuments of the righteous, 30 saying, 'If we had lived in the days of our fathers, we would not have taken part with them in shedding the blood of the prophets.' 31 Thus you witness against yourselves, that you are sons of those who murdered the prophets. 32 Fill up, then, the measure of your fathers. 33 You serpents, you brood of vipers, how are you to escape being sentenced to hell?[w] 34 Therefore I send you prophets and wise men and scribes, some of whom you will kill and crucify, and some you will scourge in your synagogues and persecute from town to town, 35 that upon you may come all the righteous blood shed on earth, from the blood of innocent Abel to the blood of Zĕchāṛi'áh the son of Baṛáchi'áh, whom you murdered between the sanctuary and the altar. 36 Truly, I say to you, all this will come upon this generation.

The lament over Jerusalem (23.37–39; Lk 13.34–35)

37 "O Jerusalem, Jerusalem, killing the prophets and stoning those who are sent to you! How often would I have gathered your children together as a hen gathers her brood under her wings, and you would not! 38 Behold, your house is forsaken and desolate.[x] 39 For I tell you, you will not see me again, until you say, 'Blessed is he who comes in the name of the Lord.' "

The Olivet Discourse (24.1–25.46; Mk ch 13; Lk ch 21)

1. The course of this age (24.1–14; Mk 13.3–13; Lk 21.5–19)

24 Jesus left the temple and was going away, when his disciples came to point out to him the buildings of the temple. 2 But he answered them, "You see all these, do you not? Truly, I say to you, there will not be left here one stone upon another, that will not be thrown down."

3 As he sat on the Mount of Olives, the disciples came to him privately, saying, "Tell us, when will this be, and what will be the sign of your coming and of the close of the age?" 4 And Jesus an-

Marginal references (left column):
23.27 Lk 11.44; Acts 23.3
23.29 Lk 11.47,48
23.31 Acts 7.51, 52
23.32 1 Thess 2.16
23.33 Mt 3.7; 5.22
*23.34 Lk 11.49; 2 Chr 36.15, 16
*23.35 Gen 4.8; Heb 11.4; Zech 1.1; 2 Chr 24.21
23.36 Mt 10.23; 24.34
23.37 2 Chr 24.21
23.39 Ps 118.26; Mt 21.9
24.1 Mk 13.1
*24.2 Mt 26.61; 27.39,40; Lk 19.44; Jn 2.19
*24.3
24.4 Jer 29.8; 2 Thess 2.3

---

w Greek Gĕhĕn'ná   x Other ancient authorities omit and desolate

---

23.35 Zechariah is the Old Testament prophet whose book bears his name. 2 Chr 24.20ff relates the murder of a Zechariah (son of Jehoiada the priest). It may be that this Zechariah is meant. Since the Second Book of Chronicles is last in the Hebrew Bible (Luke does not link Zechariah to anyone), the saying from the blood of Abel to the blood of Zechariah in Lk 11.51 could mean "from the first to the last murder in the Bible."

24.2 The principle of predictive prophecy is exemplified throughout the Scriptures. In the New Testament many prophecies are given concerning the future, some of which have already been fulfilled in subsequent history, and others which await future fulfilment. The Olivet Discourse (ch 23–25) and Revelation contain much prophecy which is yet to come to pass.

24.3 In the Olivet Discourse the disciples of Jesus asked two major questions: (1) When will this be? i.e., the destruction of the buildings of the Temple; (2) What will be the sign of your coming (parousia) and of the close (full end) of the age? All that Jesus had to say to these questions is not recorded in the Gospel of Matthew alone.

swered them, "Take heed that no one leads you astray. 5 For many will come in my name, saying, 'I am the Christ,' and they will lead many astray. 6And you will hear of wars and rumors of wars; see that you are not alarmed; for this must take place, but the end is not yet. 7 For nation will rise against nation, and kingdom against kingdom, and there will be famines and earthquakes in various places; 8 all this is but the beginning of the birth-pangs.

9 "Then they will deliver you up to tribulation, and put you to death; and you will be hated by all nations for my name's sake. 10And then many will fall away,ʸ and betray one another, and hate one another. 11And many false prophets will arise and lead many astray. 12And because wickedness is multiplied, most men's love will grow cold. 13 But he who endures to the end will be saved. 14And this gospel of the kingdom will be preached throughout the whole world, as a testimony to all nations; and then the end will come.

2. The great tribulation (24.15–28; Mk 13.14–23; Lk 21.20–24)

15 "So when you see the desolating sacrilege spoken of by the prophet Daniel, standing in the holy place (let the reader understand), 16 then let those who are in Judē'ả flee to the mountains; 17 let him who is on the housetop not go down to take what is in his house; 18 and let him who is in the field not turn back to take his mantle. 19And alas for those who are with child and for those who give suck in those days! 20 Pray that your flight may not be in winter or on a sabbath. 21 For then there will be great tribulation, such as has not been from the beginning of the world until now, no, and never will be. 22And if those days had not been shortened, no human being would be saved; but for the sake of the elect those days will be shortened. 23 Then if any one says to you, 'Lo, here is the Christ!' or 'There he is!' do not believe it. 24 For false Christs and false prophets will arise and show great signs and wonders, so as to lead astray, if possible, even the elect. 25 Lo, I have told you beforehand. 26 So, if they say to you, 'Lo, he is in the wilderness,' do not go out; if they say, 'Lo, he is in the inner rooms,' do not believe it. 27 For as the lightning comes from the east and shines as far as the west, so will be the coming of the Son of man. 28 Wherever the body is, there the eagles ᶻ will be gathered together.

3. The coming of the Son of man
(24.29–31; Mk 13.24–27; Lk 21.25–28)

29 "Immediately after the tribulation of those days the sun will be darkened, and the moon will not give its light, and the stars will fall from heaven, and the powers of the heavens will be shaken; 30 then will appear the sign of the Son of man in heaven, and then all the tribes of the earth will mourn, and they will see the Son of man coming on the clouds of heaven with power and great glory; 31 and he will send out his angels with a loud trumpet call, and they will gather his elect from the four winds, from one end of heaven to the other.

ʸ Or stumble ᶻ Or vultures

24.5
ver 11,23, 24;
1 Jn 2.18
24.7
Isa 19.2;
Hag 2.22;
Zech 14.13
24.9
Mt 10.17, 22;
Jn 15.18; 16.2
24.10
Mt 11.6
24.11
Mt 7.15;
Acts 20.29;
1 Tim 4.1
24.13
Mt 10.22;
Rev 2.7
★24.14
Rom 10.18;
Col 1.6,23

24.15
Dan 9.27;
11.31;
12.11;
Acts 21.28;
1 Cor 15.52;
1 Thess 4.16

24.21
Dan 12.1;
Joel 2.2
24.22
Isa 65.8,9

24.23
Lk 17.23;
21.8
24.24
2 Thess 2.9–11;
Rev 13.13

24.27
Lk 17.24

24.29
Isa 13.10;
Ezek 32.7;
Joel 2.10;
Rev 8.12
24.30
Dan 7.13;
Mt 16.27;
Rev 1.7
24.31
Isa 27.13;
Zech 9.14

24.14 Prior to the end of the age, the gospel must be preached to all nations for a witness. Since the end has not come, we know that this obligation has not yet been completely fulfilled.

4. *The parable of the fig tree*
(24.32–35; Mk 13.28–31; Lk 21.29–33)

32 "From the fig tree learn its lesson: as soon as its branch becomes tender and puts forth its leaves, you know that summer is near. 33 So also, when you see all these things, you know that he is near, at the very gates. 34 Truly, I say to you, this generation will not pass away till all these things take place. 35 Heaven and earth will pass away, but my words will not pass away.

5. *Watchfulness (24.36–44; Mk 13.32–37; Lk 21.34–36)*

36 "But of that day and hour no one knows, not even the angels of heaven, nor the Son,[a] but the Father only. 37As were the days of Noah, so will be the coming of the Son of man. 38 For as in those days before the flood they were eating and drinking, marrying and giving in marriage, until the day when Noah entered the ark, 39 and they did not know until the flood came and swept them all away, so will be the coming of the Son of man. 40 Then two men will be in the field; one is taken and one is left. 41 Two women will be grinding at the mill; one is taken and one is left. 42 Watch therefore, for you do not know on what day your Lord is coming. 43 But know this, that if the householder had known in what part of the night the thief was coming, he would have watched and would not have let his house be broken into. 44 Therefore you also must be ready; for the Son of man is coming at an hour you do not expect.

6. *Faithful and unfaithful servants (24.45–51; Lk 12.42–46)*

45 "Who then is the faithful and wise servant, whom his master has set over his household, to give them their food at the proper time? 46 Blessed is that servant whom his master when he comes will find so doing. 47 Truly, I say to you, he will set him over all his possessions. 48 But if that wicked servant says to himself, 'My master is delayed,' 49 and begins to beat his fellow servants, and eats and drinks with the drunken, 50 the master of that servant will come on a day when he does not expect him and at an hour he does not know, 51 and will punish[b] him, and put him with the hypocrites; there men will weep and gnash their teeth.

7. *The parable of the ten virgins (25.1–13)*

25 "Then the kingdom of heaven shall be compared to ten maidens who took their lamps and went to meet the bridegroom.[c] 2 Five of them were foolish, and five were wise. 3 For when the foolish took their lamps, they took no oil with them;

a Other ancient authorities omit *nor the Son*   *b* Or *cut him in pieces*
c Other ancient authorities add *and the bride*

24.34 A *generation* in the Old Testament was usually reckoned as forty years. The problem here is whether Jesus was referring to the generation of men who were alive at that time or to the generation of men who would be alive at the time of the Second Advent. In the former case it would mean that He prophesied His Second Advent as taking place within no more than forty years after His death and resurrection. Only in the sense that the destruction of Jerusalem took place in A.D. 70 was it true that any of Christ's contemporaries lived to see the fulfilment of *these things*. In the latter case, the *generation* would refer to those living at the time of the earliest of the signs concerning the end; they will live to see the fulfilment of them all.
25.1 The teaching of this parable is the contrast between watchful preparation and careless security. The whole idea of the parable is that Christians should watch, be ready, be prepared for the coming of the Lord.

4 but the wise took flasks of oil with their lamps. 5As the bridegroom was delayed, they all slumbered and slept. 6 But at midnight there was a cry, 'Behold, the bridegroom! Come out to meet him.' 7 Then all those maidens rose and trimmed their lamps. 8And the foolish said to the wise, 'Give us some of your oil, for our lamps are going out.' 9 But the wise replied, 'Perhaps there will not be enough for us and for you; go rather to the dealers and buy for yourselves.' 10And while they went to buy, the bridegroom came, and those who were ready went in with him to the marriage feast; and the door was shut. 11Afterward the other maidens came also, saying, 'Lord, lord, open to us.' 12 But he replied, 'Truly, I say to you, I do not know you.' 13 Watch therefore, for you know neither the day nor the hour.

8. The parable of the talents (25.14–30)

14 "For it will be as when a man going on a journey called his servants and entrusted to them his property; 15 to one he gave five talents,d to another two, to another one, to each according to his ability. Then he went away. 16 He who had received the five talents went at once and traded with them; and he made five talents more. 17 So also, he who had the two talents made two talents more. 18 But he who had received the one talent went and dug in the ground and hid his master's money. 19 Now after a long time the master of those servants came and settled accounts with them. 20And he who had received the five talents came forward, bringing five talents more, saying, 'Master, you delivered to me five talents; here I have made five talents more.' 21 His master said to him, 'Well done, good and faithful servant; you have been faithful over a little, I will set you over much; enter into the joy of your master.' 22And he also who had the two talents came forward, saying, 'Master, you delivered to me two talents; here I have made two talents more.' 23 His master said to him, 'Well done, good and faithful servant; you have been faithful over a little, I will set you over much; enter into the joy of your master.' 24 He also who had received the one talent came forward, saying, 'Master, I knew you to be a hard man, reaping where you did not sow, and gathering where you did not winnow; 25 so I was afraid, and I went and hid your talent in the ground. Here you have what is yours.' 26 But his master answered him, 'You wicked and slothful servant! You knew that I reap where I have not sowed, and gather where I have not winnowed? 27 Then you ought to have invested my money with the bankers, and at my coming I should have received what was my own with interest. 28 So take the talent from him, and give it to him who has the ten talents. 29 For to every one who has will more be given, and he will have abundance; but from him who has

25.5	1 Thess 5.6
25.7	Lk 12.35
25.10	Lk 13.25; Rev 19.9
25.11	Mt 7.21–23
25.13	Mt 24.42, 44; Mk 13.35; Lk 12.40; 1 Thess 5.6
*25.14	Lk 19.12; Mt 21.33
25.15	Mt 18.23, 24; Lk 19.13
25.19	Mt 18.23
25.21	Mt 24.45, 47; Lk 16.10
25.23	ver 21
25.24	Jn 10.28,29; 2 Thess 2.9–11; 2 Tim 2.19; Rev 13.13
25.27	Lk 17.24
25.29	Mt 13.12; Mk 4.25; Lk 8.18

d This talent was more than fifteen years' wages of a laborer

25.14 Christ here teaches that the use men make of the gifts God has given is vitally important. Responsibility is bestowed in proportion to each person's native endowments, and these may be misused, abused, or properly used. The servant with the one talent was guilty not only of failing to use properly what he had been given, but also of slandering his lord as a greedy and cruel master. (This attitude characterizes those who refuse to accept God's grace as a loving Father, but who project onto Him the smallness and pettiness of their own unconverted nature, and therefore regard Him only as a tyrant who makes impossible demands.) The lord's response to this false and fruitless servant is that by his own estimate of his master he stands condemned. He should have made an effort to measure up to the expectations of his allegedly rapacious master.

25.30
Mt 8.12;
3.42,50;
22.13;
Lk 13.28

not, even what he has will be taken away. 30And cast the worthless servant into the outer darkness; there men will weep and gnash their teeth.'

9. *The judgment* (25.31–46)

25.31
Mt 16.27;
19.28
25.32
Ezek 34.17,
20

31 "When the Son of man comes in his glory, and all the angels with him, then he will sit on his glorious throne. 32 Before him will be gathered all the nations, and he will separate them one from another as a shepherd separates the sheep from the goats, 33 and he will place the sheep at his right hand, but the goats at the left.

25.34
Lk 12.32;
1 Cor 6.9;
15.50;
Gal 5.21;
Rev 13.8;
17.8

34 Then the King will say to those at his right hand, 'Come, O blessed of my Father, inherit the kingdom prepared for you from the foundation of the world; 35 for I was hungry and you gave me food, I was thirsty and you gave me drink, I was a stranger and you welcomed me, 36 I was naked and you clothed me, I was sick and you visited me, I was in prison and you came to me.'

25.35
Isa 58.7;
Ezek 18.7;
Jas 1.27;
Heb 13.2

37 Then the righteous will answer him, 'Lord, when did we see thee hungry and feed thee, or thirsty and give thee drink? 38And when did we see thee a stranger and welcome thee, or naked and clothe thee?

25.36
Jas 2.15,16;
2 Tim 1.16

39And when did we see thee sick or in prison and visit thee?' 40And the King will answer them, 'Truly, I say to you, as you did it to one of the least of these my brethren, you did it to me.'

25.40
Prov 14.31;
19.17;
Mt 10.42;
Heb 6.10

41 Then he will say to those at his left hand, 'Depart from me, you cursed, into the eternal fire prepared for the devil and his angels; 42 for I was hungry and you gave me no food, I was thirsty and you gave me no drink, 43 I was a stranger and you did not welcome me, naked and you did not clothe me, sick and in prison and you did not visit me.'

25.41
Mt 7.23;
Mk 9.48;
Lk 16.24;
Jude 7;
2 Pet 2.4

44 Then they also will answer, 'Lord, when did we see thee hungry or thirsty or a stranger or naked or sick or in prison, and did not minister to thee?' 45 Then he will answer them, 'Truly, I say to you, as you did it not to one of the least of these, you did it not to me.'

25.45
Prov 14.31;
17.5
★25.46
Dan 12.2;
Jn 5.29;
Rom 2.7;
Gal 6.8

46And they will go away into eternal punishment, but the righteous into eternal life."

The trial and condemnation of Jesus (26.1–27.26)

1. *The plot to kill Jesus*
(26.1–5, 14–16; Mk 14.1–2, 10–11; Lk 22.1–6)

26.1
Mt 7.28;
11.1;
13.53;
19.1
26.2
Jn 13.1
26.3
Ps 2.2;
Jn 11.47–53
26.4
Mt 12.14
26.5
Mt 27.24

26 When Jesus had finished all these sayings, he said to his disciples, 2 "You know that after two days the Passover is coming, and the Son of man will be delivered up to be crucified."

3 Then the chief priests and the elders of the people gathered in the palace of the high priest, who was called Cāi'áphàs, 4 and took counsel together in order to arrest Jesus by stealth and kill him. 5 But they said, "Not during the feast, lest there be a tumult among the people."

25.46 Eternal death, or everlasting punishment, is the unavoidable consequence of unforgiven sin (Rom 6.16, 21, 23; 8.13). It differs from the mere physical death which all men, saints and sinners alike, must endure. It assumes its final and most terrible form at the Last Judgment (see note to Rev 20.12). It is variously described in Scripture as *shame and everlasting contempt* (Dan 12.2), *destruction* (Rom 9.22), *second death* (Rev 2.11), *wrath to come* (1 Thess 1.10). It is characterized by unending torment (Rev 20.10; 21.8). Christ Himself says of hell that it is a place *where their worm does not die, and the fire is not quenched* (Mk 9.48). God alone can inflict this eternal death (10.28; Jas 4.12), and Christ alone is the way of escape (Jn 3.16; 8.51; Acts 4.12).

2. Anointing of Jesus by Mary of Bethany
(26.6–13; Mk 14.3–9; Jn 12.1–8)

6 Now when Jesus was at Bĕth′ȧnȳ in the house of Simon the leper, 7 a woman came up to him with an alabaster flask of very expensive ointment, and she poured it on his head, as he sat at table. 8 But when the disciples saw it, they were indignant, saying, "Why this waste? 9 For this ointment might have been sold for a large sum, and given to the poor." 10 But Jesus, aware of this, said to them, "Why do you trouble the woman? For she has done a beautiful thing to me. 11 For you always have the poor with you, but you will not always have me. 12 In pouring this ointment on my body she has done it to prepare me for burial. 13 Truly, I say to you, wherever this gospel is preached in the whole world, what she has done will be told in memory of her."

3. The bargain of Judas Iscariot (26.14–16, ver 1–5)

14 Then one of the twelve, who was called Judas Ĭscar′ĭŏt, went to the chief priests 15 and said, "What will you give me if I deliver him to you?" And they paid him thirty pieces of silver. 16And from that moment he sought an opportunity to betray him.

4. The Last Supper (26.17–35)
a. The Passover prepared (26.17–19; Mk 14.12–16; Lk 22.7–13)

17 Now on the first day of Unleavened Bread the disciples came to Jesus, saying, "Where will you have us prepare for you to eat the passover?" 18 He said, "Go into the city to a certain one, and say to him, 'The Teacher says, My time is at hand; I will keep the passover at your house with my disciples.' " 19And the disciples did as Jesus had directed them, and they prepared the passover.

b. The Passover eaten
(26.20–25; Mk 14.17–21; Lk 22.14–18; see Jn 13.1–30)

20 When it was evening, he sat at table with the twelve disciples;e 21 and as they were eating, he said, "Truly, I say to you, one of you will betray me." 22And they were very sorrowful, and began to say to him one after another, "Is it I, Lord?" 23 He an-

e Other authorities omit disciples

Side references:
26.6 Mt 21.17 ★26.7 / 26.11 Deut 15.11 / 26.12 Jn 19.40 / ★26.14 / 26.15 Ex 21.32 Zech 11.12 / 26.18 Jn 7.6,8; 12.23; 13.1; 17.1 / 26.19 Deut 16.5–8 / 26.23 Ps 41.9; Lk 22.21; Jn 13.18; Isa ch 53; Dan 9.26; Lk 24.25; Acts 17.2,3; 1 Cor 15.3

26.7 a woman, see note to Lk 7.36 for her identity.

26.14 Judas Iscariot secured his ignominious reputation as the betrayer of Jesus Christ. Certain facts connected with his life are of interest. His name Judas is the Greek form of the Hebrew name Judah. Iscariot is taken by some to mean man of Kerioth, a town in Judea. Except for Judas Iscariot, all of the other disciples came from Galilee. Generally, the Judeans looked down upon the Galileans and this may have been a possible cause for alienation between Judas and the other disciples. Judas was called along with the eleven to be an apostle. He is always listed, however, as the last of the Twelve. He was a dishonest coveter who sold Christ for a few pieces of silver. Scripture informs us that Christ knew that Judas would betray Him even before he was chosen as a disciple (see Jn 6.64, 70, 71). It is difficult to reconcile the freedom of choice which Judas exercised in betraying Christ and the divine foreordination which assured that he would do so (Acts 1.15–17, 20). Yet both appear in the Scriptures. Christ announced that it would have been better for that man if he had not been born (26.24). Judas' sin differed from the denial of Peter in that it was deliberate, calculated, and premeditated, whereas the sin of Peter was one of weakness and sudden capitulation in the face of enormous stress. Many have raised the question as to whether Judas Iscariot partook of the bread and the wine at the institution of the Lord's Supper. Most modern interpreters think he did not. The accounts of his death were written by Matthew (27.3–10) and Luke (Acts 1.16–20). A reconciliation of the accounts has been difficult. However, he reaped the just deserts of his wicked actions and his life stands as a constant warning against betrayal of Christ (e.g., see Heb 6.6).

swered, "He who has dipped his hand in the dish with me, will betray me. 24 The Son of man goes as it is written of him, but woe to that man by whom the Son of man is betrayed! It would have been better for that man if he had not been born." 25 Judas, who betrayed him, said, "Is it I, Master?"[f] He said to him, "You have said so."

c. The Lord's Supper instituted
(26.26–29; Mk 14.22–25; Lk 22.19–24)

26 Now as they were eating, Jesus took bread, and blessed, and broke it, and gave it to the disciples and said, "Take, eat; this is my body." 27 And he took a cup, and when he had given thanks he gave it to them, saying, "Drink of it, all of you; 28 for this is my blood of the[g] covenant, which is poured out for many for the forgiveness of sins. 29 I tell you I shall not drink again of this fruit of the vine until that day when I drink it new with you in my Father's kingdom."

d. Peter's denial foretold
(26.30–35; Mk 14.27–31; Lk 22.31–34; see Jn 14–17)

30 And when they had sung a hymn, they went out to the Mount of Olives. 31 Then Jesus said to them, "You will all fall away because of me this night; for it is written, 'I will strike the shepherd, and the sheep of the flock will be scattered.' 32 But after I am raised up, I will go before you to Găl'ĭleē." 33 Peter declared to him, "Though they all fall away because of you, I will never fall away." 34 Jesus said to him, "Truly, I say to you, this very night, before the cock crows, you will deny me three times." 35 Peter said to him, "Even if I must die with you, I will not deny you." And so said all the disciples.

5. Jesus in Gethsemane (26.36–56)
a. Jesus' agony
(26.36–46; Mk 14.32–42; Lk 22.39–46; cf. Jn 18.1)

36 Then Jesus went with them to a place called Gĕthsĕm'ănë, and he said to his disciples, "Sit here, while I go yonder and pray." 37 And taking with him Peter and the two sons of Zĕb'-ĕdeē, he began to be sorrowful and troubled. 38 Then he said to them, "My soul is very sorrowful, even to death; remain here, and watch[h] with me." 39 And going a little farther he fell on his

Margin references:
*26.26 1 Cor 10.16; 11.23–25
*26.28 Ex 24.6–8; Mt 20.28; Mk 1.4; Heb 9.20
26.29 Acts 10.41
26.30 Mk 14.26
26.31 Jn 16.32; Mt 11.6; Zech 13.7
26.32 Mt 28.7,10,16
26.34 Jn 13.38
26.35 Jn 13.37
26.37 Mt 4.21
26.38 Jn 12.27
*26.39 Jn 12.27; Mt 20.22; Jn 6.38; Phil 2.8

---

f Or *Rabbi*   g Other ancient authorities insert *new*   h Or *keep awake*

26.26 See note to Mk 14.22 on the Lord's Supper.

26.28 The mercy of God makes possible the forgiveness of sins (Dan 9.9). The sacrifice of Christ is the ground of forgiveness (Heb 9.22; Acts 13.38; Eph 1.7; 1 Jn 1.7). Forgiveness implies: (1) limitlessness (18.22); (2) infiniteness (Ps 103.12); (3) completeness (Col 2.13); (4) God remembers sins no more (Isa 44.22; Jer 31.34). The only sin which can never be forgiven is the sin of turning away from the Holy Spirit (12.31; 1 Jn 5.16; Mk 3.29), who alone can bring about repentance and faith.

26.39 The *cup* of which Jesus speaks has been the subject of much discussion. Two views prevail generally. The first one suggests

that the God-man in His humanity prayed for some other way to redeem man than Calvary. But since Calvary was the Father's only way, Jesus accepted it in His humanity, for He prayed *not as I will, but as thou wilt*. Those who hold the second view contend that Christ always prayed according to the will of His Father and that in the Garden He feared that Satan would kill Him before He made atonement at Calvary. Thus He prayed for deliverance in the Garden so that He might go to Calvary; but He was willing to die in the Garden if God so willed. In this view His prayer was answered, and He was spared to go to the Cross. Perhaps more plausible than either view is a third explanation that He shrank with a holy abhorrence

face and prayed, "My Father, if it be possible, let this cup pass from me; nevertheless, not as I will, but as thou wilt." ⁴⁰And he came to the disciples and found them sleeping; and he said to Peter, "So, could you not watch*ʰ* with me one hour? ⁴¹ Watch*ʰ* and pray that you may not enter into temptation; the spirit indeed is willing, but the flesh is weak." ⁴²Again, for the second time, he went away and prayed, "My Father, if this cannot pass unless I drink it, thy will be done." ⁴³And again he came and found them sleeping, for their eyes were heavy. ⁴⁴ So, leaving them again, he went away and prayed for the third time, saying the same words. ⁴⁵ Then he came to the disciples and said to them, "Are you still sleeping and taking your rest? Behold, the hour is at hand, and the Son of man is betrayed into the hands of sinners. ⁴⁶ Rise, let us be going; see, my betrayer is at hand."

26.40 ver 38
26.41 Mt 6.13; Lk 11.4
26.42 Jn 4.34; 5.30; 6.38
26.45 ver 18; Jn 12.23,27; 13.1; 17.1

b. Jesus' betrayal and arrest
(26.47–56; Mk 14.43–50; Lk 22.47–53; Jn 18.1–11)

⁴⁷ While he was still speaking, Judas came, one of the twelve, and with him a great crowd with swords and clubs, from the chief priests and the elders of the people. ⁴⁸ Now the betrayer had given them a sign, saying, "The one I shall kiss is the man; seize him." ⁴⁹And he came up to Jesus at once and said, "Hail, Master!" *ⁱ* And he kissed him. ⁵⁰ Jesus said to him, "Friend, why are you here?"*ʲ* Then they came up and laid hands on Jesus and seized him. ⁵¹And behold, one of those who were with Jesus stretched out his hand and drew his sword, and struck the slave of the high priest, and cut off his ear. ⁵² Then Jesus said to him, "Put your sword back into its place; for all who take the sword will perish by the sword. ⁵³ Do you think that I cannot appeal to my Father, and he will at once send me more than twelve legions of angels? ⁵⁴ But how then should the scriptures be fulfilled, that it must be so?" ⁵⁵At that hour Jesus said to the crowds, "Have you come out as against a robber, with swords and clubs to capture me? Day after day I sat in the temple teaching, and you did not seize me. ⁵⁶ But all this has taken place, that the scriptures of the prophets might be fulfilled." Then all the disciples forsook him and fled.

26.49 ver 25
26.50 Mt 20.13; 22.12
26.52 Gen 9.6; Rev 13.10
26.53 2 Ki 6.17; Dan 7.10
26.54 ver 24; Lk 24.25, 44,46
26.56 ver 54

6. Jesus before Caiaphas
(26.57–68; Mk 14.53–65; cf. Lk 22.54; Jn 18.12–14,19–25)

⁵⁷ Then those who had seized Jesus led him to Cāi′aphás the

*26.57

ʰ Or *keep awake*　ⁱ Or *Rabbi*　ʲ Or *do that for which you have come*

---

from the approaching experience of complete identification with the defiling sin of the human race upon the Cross, and the complete forsakenness which this would temporarily entail (*My God, my God, why hast thou forsaken me?*) (27.46). This was the horrid cup from which He shrank; nevertheless, He was willing finally to exalt the Father's will above His own and drink it to the dregs.

26.57 Caiaphas, the high priest, was the son-in-law of Annas who had previously been high priest himself. Caiaphas was appointed to his position by the procurator who preceded Pontius Pilate, Valerius Gratus. He remained as high priest until A.D. 37 when he was removed by Vitellius. As a person, Caiaphas was guilty of hypocrisy and cloaked his hatred

of Christ under the guise of religious pretensions and patriotic loyalty. It was he who recommended the action that would bring Christ to Calvary (Jn 11.49–53). He and his cohorts used Judas Iscariot to further their nefarious scheme (26.3ff). When Christ appeared before Caiaphas He remained silent until pressed to answer the question, "*I adjure you by the living God, tell us if you are the Christ, the Son of God*" (26.63). To this Christ responded that He was (26.64). Having failed to convict Christ on the testimony of perjurers, Caiaphas now condemned Him on the charge of blasphemy, disregarding both religious scruples and common justice. So it was that Christ was sentenced to be crucified.

26.58
Jn 18.15

*26.59

26.60
Ps 27.12;
35.11;
Acts 6.13;
Deut 19.15

26.61
Mt 27.40

26.63
Isa 53.7;
Mt 27.12,
14;
Lev 5.1;
Jn 18.33

26.64
Ps 110.1;
Dan 7.13;
Mt 16.27,28

26.65
Num 14.6;
Acts 14.14;
Lev 24.16

26.66
Jn 19.7

26.67
Isa 53.3;
Mt 27.30;
Jn 19.3

*26.69

26.75
ver 34;
Jn 13.38

high priest, where the scribes and the elders had gathered. 58 But Peter followed him at a distance, as far as the courtyard of the high priest, and going inside he sat with the guards to see the end. 59 Now the chief priests and the whole council sought false testimony against Jesus that they might put him to death, 60 but they found none, though many false witnesses came forward. At last two came forward 61 and said, "This fellow said, 'I am able to destroy the temple of God, and to build it in three days.' " 62And the high priest stood up and said, "Have you no answer to make? What is it that these men testify against you?" 63 But Jesus was silent. And the high priest said to him, "I adjure you by the living God, tell us if you are the Christ, the Son of God." 64 Jesus said to him, "You have said so. But I tell you, hereafter you will see the Son of man seated at the right hand of Power, and coming on the clouds of heaven." 65 Then the high priest tore his robes, and said, "He has uttered blasphemy. Why do we still need witnesses? You have now heard his blasphemy. 66 What is your judgment?" They answered, "He deserves death." 67 Then they spat in his face, and struck him; and some slapped him, 68 saying, "Prophesy to us, you Christ! Who is it that struck you?"

7. Peter's denial of Jesus
(26.69–75; Mk 14.66–72; Lk 22.55–63; Jn 18.15–18,25–27)

69 Now Peter was sitting outside in the courtyard. And a maid came up to him, and said, "You also were with Jesus the Galilē'-án." 70 But he denied it before them all, saying, "I do not know what you mean." 71And when he went out to the porch, another maid saw him, and she said to the bystanders, "This man was with Jesus of Năz'ărĕth." 72And again he denied it with an oath, "I do not know the man." 73After a little while the bystanders came up and said to Peter, "Certainly you are also one of them, for your accent betrays you." 74 Then he began to invoke a curse on himself and to swear, "I do not know the man." And immediately the cock crowed. 75And Peter remembered the saying of Jesus,

---

26.59 The *council*, or *Sanhedrin* (Jewish Supreme Court) of this verse was a familiar institution. The origins of the Sanhedrin are somewhat obscure but it was a firmly developed body during the life of Jesus. The name was applied primarily to the highest court of justice and the supreme council at Jerusalem, but it was also used to designate the lower courts of justice. The Sanhedrin at Jerusalem was called the *Great Sanhedrin*. There were 71 members of this body, although at times the membership was spoken of as 70. Apparently the difference in the figures depended upon whether the president of the body was to be included in the total number. Normally the members of the Sanhedrin were called *elders* and they generally were selected for membership in the body from among the chief priests and the scribes. How the members were elected and how vacancies were filled is not known. In order to be eligible for membership, tradition has it that a man had to be learned, humble, and popular with his people. At the trial of Jesus, the high priest Caiaphas appears to have been the president of the Sanhedrin, but there is no evidence that the presidency belonged to the high priest as such.

The *Little Sanhedrin* with its 23 members passed judgment upon cases other than those which were reserved exclusively for the *Great Sanhedrin*. When the lower courts were unable to reach a decision, the case was taken to the last court of appeal which was the supreme court of justice. Cases involving life and death came before the Little Sanhedrin although important ones were referred to the Great Sanhedrin for judgment. The decisions of the Great Sanhedrin were binding upon all. The court met in the Hall of Hewn Stone in Jerusalem. The members were seated in a semi-circle so that each could see the others. In cases involving life and death, the vote was taken beginning with the younger members so that they could not be influenced by the votes of the older ones. No fewer than 23 members could be in attendance in such cases. In the event a verdict of guilt was reached by a majority of one, the number of members in attendance had to be increased. Only when the full court was assembled could a man be declared guilty of a crime worthy of capital punishment by a majority of one.

26.69 See note to Mk 14.71 for Peter's denial of Christ.

"Before the cock crows, you will deny me three times." And he went out and wept bitterly.

8. *Jesus delivered to Pilate by the Sanhedrin*
(27.1–2; Mk 15.1; Lk 23.1; Jn 18.28)

27 When morning came, all the chief priests and the elders of the people took counsel against Jesus to put him to death; 2 and they bound him and led him away and delivered him to Pilate the governor.

27.2
Mt 20.19;
Acts 3.13

9. *The death of Judas Iscariot (27.3–10; cf. Acts 1.16–20)*

3 When Judas, his betrayer, saw that he was condemned, he repented and brought back the thirty pieces of silver to the chief priests and the elders, 4 saying, "I have sinned in betraying innocent blood." They said, "What is that to us? See to it yourself." 5And throwing down the pieces of silver in the temple, he departed; and he went and hanged himself. 6 But the chief priests, taking the pieces of silver, said, "It is not lawful to put them into the treasury, since they are blood money." 7 So they took counsel, and bought with them the potter's field, to bury strangers in. 8 Therefore that field has been called the Field of Blood to this day. 9 Then was fulfilled what had been spoken by the prophet Jĕrĕmī'ăh, saying, "And they took the thirty pieces of silver, the price of him on whom a price had been set by some of the sons of Israel, 10 and they gave them for the potter's field, as the Lord directed me."

27.3
Mt 26.14,15

27.4
ver 24

27.5
Acts 1.18

27.8
Acts 1.19
*27.9f
Zech 11.12,
13

10. *Jesus before Pontius Pilate*
(27.11–26; Mk 15.2–15; Lk 23.3–25; Jn 18.29–40)
a. *Jesus questioned (27.11–14)*

11 Now Jesus stood before the governor; and the governor asked him, "Are you the King of the Jews?" Jesus said, "You have said so." 12 But when he was accused by the chief priests and elders, he made no answer. 13 Then Pilate said to him, "Do you not hear how many things they testify against you?" 14 But he gave him no answer, not even to a single charge; so that the governor wondered greatly.

27.12
Mt 26.63;
Jn 19.9
27.13
Mt 26.62;
Jn 19.10
27.14
1 Tim 6.13

15 Now at the feast the governor was accustomed to release for the crowd any one prisoner whom they wanted. 16And they had then a notorious prisoner, called Băräb'băs.[k] 17 So when they had gathered, Pilate said to them, "Whom do you want me to release for you, Băräb'băs[k] or Jesus who is called Christ?" 18 For he knew that it was out of envy that they had delivered him up. 19 Besides, while he was sitting on the judgment seat, his wife sent word to him, "Have nothing to do with that righteous man, for I have suf-

27.19
Acts 12.21;
ver 24

[k] Other ancient authorities read *Jesus Barabbas*

27.9, 10 This quotation has largely been taken from Zech 11.12–13, and so its attribution to Jeremiah has been regarded as inaccurate. Actually, however, there is no reference to a *field* in the Zechariah passage; and yet the whole point of the quotation is the field purchased with Judas' money. But Jer 32.6–9 refer to a field which Jeremiah purchased for a certain number of shekels and this field is mentioned as a place for burial. Thus Matthew combines here a reference both to Zechariah and to Jeremiah and assigns the combined quotation to Jeremiah only, both because he was the more prominent prophet of the two, and because the Potter's Field figures so importantly in his prophecy.

27.20
Acts 3.14

fered much over him today in a dream." 20 Now the chief priests and the elders persuaded the people to ask for Bárăb′bàs and destroy Jesus. 21 The governor again said to them, "Which of the two do you want me to release for you?" And they said, "Bárăb′bàs." 22 Pīlâte said to them, "Then what shall I do with Jesus who is called Christ?" They all said, "Let him be crucified." 23And he said, "Why, what evil has he done?" But they shouted all the more, "Let him be crucified."

c. Barabbas released and Jesus delivered (27.24–26)

27.24
Mt 26.5;
Deut 21.6–
8;
Ps 26.6;
ver 19
27.25
Josh 2.19;
Acts 5.28
27.26
Isa 53.5

24 So when Pīlâte saw that he was gaining nothing, but rather that a riot was beginning, he took water and washed his hands before the crowd, saying, "I am innocent of this man's blood;[l] see to it yourselves." 25And all the people answered, "His blood be on us and on our children!" 26 Then he released for them Bárăb′bàs, and having scourged Jesus, delivered him to be crucified.

The Crucifixion and burial of Jesus (27.27–66)

1. Jesus crowned with thorns (27.27–31; Mk 15.16–20; cf. Jn 19.2,3)

27.27
Jn 18.28,33;
Acts 10.1
27.29
Ps 69.19;
Isa 53.3
27.30
Mt 26.67;
Mk 10.34;
14.65
27.31
Isa 53.7

27 Then the soldiers of the governor took Jesus into the praëtor′ïŭm, and they gathered the whole battalion before him. 28And they stripped him and put a scarlet robe upon him, 29 and plaiting a crown of thorns they put it on his head, and put a reed in his right hand. And kneeling before him they mocked him, saying, "Hail, King of the Jews!" 30And they spat upon him, and took the reed and struck him on the head. 31And when they had mocked him, they stripped him of the robe, and put his own clothes on him, and led him away to crucify him.

2. Jesus crucified
(27.32–44; Mk 15.21–32; Lk 23.32–43; Jn 19.17–24)

27.32
Heb 13.12
27.34
Ps 69.21
27.35
Ps 22.18
27.36
ver 54
*27.37
27.38
Isa 53.12

32 As they went out, they came upon a man of Çȳrē′në, Simon by name; this man they compelled to carry his cross. 33And when they came to a place called Gŏl′gòthà (which means the place of a skull), 34 they offered him wine to drink, mingled with gall; but when he tasted it, he would not drink it. 35And when they had crucified him, they divided his garments among them by casting lots; 36 then they sat down and kept watch over him there. 37And over his head they put the charge against him, which read, "This is Jesus the King of the Jews." 38 Then two robbers were crucified

[l] Other authorities read this righteous blood or this righteous man's blood

---

27.37 All four Gospels contain a report of the inscription which specified Jesus' offense: that of presuming to kingly status in opposition to the authority of Rome. The charge on which the accused had been convicted was inscribed on a placard which was normally carried in front of him as he made his way to the place of execution, and then was either affixed to his gallows or hung around his neck. When Christ was crucified it was apparently placed above his head. Each Gospel writer specifies certain elements of the charge on which Christ was crucified. The full inscription seems to have been: This is Jesus of Nazareth the King of the Jews. It was written in Greek, Hebrew, and Latin, representing the universal language of the day, the language of the Jews, and the legal language of the governing power of Rome. One satisfactory reconciliation of the slight variations in the wording of this superscription is as follows: Matthew records the inscription in its Aramaic (Hebrew) form: "This is Jesus the King of the Jews." Mark and Luke record it in its Latin form: "The King of the Jews" (Mark), or "This is the King of the Jews" (Luke). John recalls the Greek version: "Jesus the Nazarene, the King of the Jews." In other words, the versions in the three languages were not absolutely identical, and they contained variations which were faithfully recorded in the four Gospel accounts.

with him, one on the right and one on the left. 39And those who passed by derided him, wagging their heads 40 and saying, "You who would destroy the temple and build it in three days, save yourself! If you are the Son of God, come down from the cross." 41 So also the chief priests, with the scribes and elders, mocked him, saying, 42 "He saved others; he cannot save himself. He is the King of Israel; let him come down now from the cross, and we will believe in him. 43 He trusts in God; let God deliver him now, if he desires him; for he said, 'I am the Son of God.'" 44And the robbers who were crucified with him also reviled him in the same way.

3. The death of Christ
(27.45-50; Mk 15.33-41; Lk 23.41-49; Jn 19.28-37)

45 Now from the sixth hour there was darkness over all the land[m] until the ninth hour. 46And about the ninth hour Jesus cried with a loud voice, "Ēlī, Eli, la'ma sabaçh-tha'nī?" that is, "My God, my God, why hast thou forsaken me?" 47And some of the bystanders hearing it said, "This man is calling Ēlī'jāh." 48And one of them at once ran and took a sponge, filled it with vinegar, and put it on a reed, and gave it to him to drink. 49 But the others said, "Wait, let us see whether Ēlī'jāh will come to save him."[n] 50And Jesus cried again with a loud voice and yielded up his spirit.

4. Redemption completed (27.51-56; Heb 9.8-14; 10.19-20)

51 And behold, the curtain of the temple was torn in two, from top to bottom; and the earth shook, and the rocks were split; 52 the tombs also were opened, and many bodies of the saints who had fallen asleep were raised, 53 and coming out of the tombs after his resurrection they went into the holy city and appeared to many. 54 When the centurion and those who were with him, keeping watch over Jesus, saw the earthquake and what took place, they were filled with awe, and said, "Truly this was the Son[x] of God!"

55 There were also many women there, looking on from afar, who had followed Jesus from Găl'ilee, ministering to him; 56 among whom were Mary Măg'dálēne, and Mary the mother of James and Joseph, and the mother of the sons of Zĕb'ĕdēē.

m Or earth
n Other ancient authorities insert And another took a spear and pierced his side, and out came water and blood   x Or a son

Marginal references:
27.39 Ps 22.7; 109.25
27.40 Mt 26.61; Acts 6.14; Jn 2.19
27.42 Jn 1.49; 12.13
27.43 Ps 22.8
27.45 Amos 8.9
*27.46 Ps 22.1
27.48 Ps 69.21
*27.50
*27.51 Ex 26.31; Heb 9.3; ver 54
*27.52
27.54 Mt 3.17; 17.5
27.55 Lk 8.2,3
27.56 Mk 15.40, 47; Lk 24.10

27.46 See note to Lk 23.34 on the seven last words.

27.50 Christ was not killed by Satan, nor was He overcome by the natural processes of dissolution. He Himself declared that no man could take His life from Him. He stated that He had the power to lay it down and the power to take it up again (Jn 10.14-18). Thus His death was a voluntary one; His act one of free choice in obedience to the Father's will.

27.51 The rending of the *curtain* (veil) signified: (1) that full atonement had been made (Heb 10.19, 20); (2) that Christ had gone through the veil into the most holy place, into the presence of God Himself (Heb 9.12, 24); (3) that Christ as mediating high priest made unnecessary any human priest-hood standing between man and God (Heb 7.23-28); (4) that all believers have immediate access, without the benefit of any priesthood except that of Christ, to the presence and favor of God (Rom 5.2; Eph 2.18; 3.12).

27.52 This miracle is mentioned only by Matthew. There are no simple answers to the many questions which it raises. We do not know which saints rose (the account says *many*), nor do we know whether they continued in resurrection as bodies and eventually died and were again buried. Verse 53 makes it appear that they came out of their graves *after* the resurrection of Christ and entered into the city of Jerusalem where they appeared to many people. Matthew Henry suggests that these resurrected saints ascended with Christ to glory, although this is simply an inference.

5. *Jesus laid in the tomb* (*27.57–61; Mk 15.42–47; Lk 23.50–56; Jn 19.38–42*)

27.57 Acts 13.29
27.60 Mt 28.2 Mk 16.4

57 When it was evening, there came a rich man from Ar̦ịmȧ-
thē'ȧ, named Joseph, who also was a disciple of Jesus. 58 He went
to Pīlȧte and asked for the body of Jesus. Then Pilate ordered it to
be given to him. 59 And Joseph took the body, and wrapped it in a
clean linen shroud, 60 and laid it in his own new tomb, which he
had hewn in the rock; and he rolled a great stone to the door of
the tomb, and departed. 61 Mary Măg'dȧlēne and the other Mary
were there, sitting opposite the sepulchre.

6. *The tomb sealed and guarded* (*27.62–66*)

27.63 Mt 16.21; 17.23; 20.19; Mk 8.31; 10.34; Lk 9.22; 18.33; 24.6,7; Jn 2.19
27.66 ver 60; Mt 28.11–15

62 Next day, that is, after the day of Preparation, the chief
priests and the Phar̦'ịseēș gathered before Pīlȧte 63 and said, "Sir,
we remember how that impostor said, while he was still alive,
'After three days I will rise again.' 64 Therefore order the sepulchre to be made secure until the third day, lest his disciples go and
steal him away, and tell the people, 'He has risen from the dead,'
and the last fraud will be worse than the first." 65 Pīlȧte said to
them, "You have a guard[o] of soldiers; go, make it as secure as you
can."[p] 66 So they went and made the sepulchre secure by sealing
the stone and setting a guard.

The Resurrection of Jesus Christ (28.1–10; Mk 16.1–8; Lk 24.1–11; Jn 20.1–18)

28.1 Lk 8.2; Mt 27.56
28.2 Mt 27.51,60
28.3 Dan 7.9; 10.6; Mk 9.3; Jn 20.12; Acts 1.10
28.5 ver 10; Mt 14.27
★28.6 Mt 12.40; 16.21; 17.23; 20.19
28.7 Mt 26.32; ver 16
28.9 Jn 20.14–18

28 Now after the sabbath, toward the dawn of the first day
of the week, Mary Măg'dȧlēne and the other Mary went to
see the sepulchre. 2 And behold, there was a great earthquake; for
an angel of the Lord descended from heaven and came and rolled
back the stone, and sat upon it. 3 His appearance was like lightning, and his raiment white as snow. 4 And for fear of him the
guards trembled and became like dead men. 5 But the angel said
to the women, "Do not be afraid; for I know that you seek Jesus
who was crucified. 6 He is not here; for he has risen, as he said.
Come, see the place where he[q] lay. 7 Then go quickly and tell his
disciples that he has risen from the dead, and behold, he is going
before you to Găl'ịleē; there you will see him. Lo, I have told
you." 8 So they departed quickly from the tomb with fear and
great joy, and ran to tell his disciples. 9 And behold, Jesus met them
and said, "Hail!" And they came up and took hold of his feet and

[o] Or *Take a guard* [p] Greek *know* [q] Other ancient authorities read *the Lord*

28.6 Christ's Resurrection is spoken of by Peter in Acts 2.25–31 as a fulfilment of David's utterance in Ps 16.10. Christ Himself plainly foretold that He would rise from the dead in 20.19 and Jn 10.18. Other witnesses to the historicity of the Resurrection include: (1) the eleven apostles (Acts 1.3); (2) Paul (1 Cor 15.8; Gal 1.12; Acts 9.3–8); (3) five hundred brethren who met the risen Jesus at one time (1 Cor 15.6); (4) the hard-headed and skeptical Thomas, who would accept no testimony but that of his own fingers and eyes (Jn 20.24–29). Paul demonstrated conclusively (1 Cor 15) that the Christian faith stands or falls on the Resurrection. Without any question he was speaking of a physical resurrection in the same body (although glorified) as that in which Christ was crucified. He appeared in a body which could be seen and felt, and which still bore the prints of the nails. The Resurrection guarantees: (1) that Christ is truly the Son of God (Rom 1.4); (2) that the Father accepted His atoning work and approved it as effective for redemption (Rom 4.25); (3) that the believer has an advocate before the Father (Rom 8.34); (4) that he may enjoy the assurance of eternal life (Jn 14.19; 1 Pet 1.3–5); (5) that believers will also be raised and that they shall be like their risen Lord (1 Cor 15.49; Phil 3.21; 1 Jn 3.2).

worshiped him. 10 Then Jesus said to them, "Do not be afraid; go and tell my brethren to go to Găl'ĭleē, and there they will see me."

28.10
Rom 8.29;
Heb 2.11

The bribing of the soldiers (28.11–15)

11 While they were going, behold, some of the guard went into the city and told the chief priests all that had taken place. 12And when they had assembled with the elders and taken counsel, they gave a sum of money to the soldiers 13 and said, "Tell people, 'His disciples came by night and stole him away while we were asleep.' 14And if this comes to the governor's ears, we will satisfy him and keep you out of trouble." 15 So they took the money and did as they were directed; and this story has been spread among the Jews to this day.

28.11
Mt 27.65,66

28.14
Mt 27.2

The Great Commission: Jesus in Galilee
(28.16–20; Mk 16.15–18)

16 Now the eleven disciples went to Găl'ĭleē, to the mountain to which Jesus had directed them. 17And when they saw him they worshiped him; but some doubted. 18And Jesus came and said to them, "All authority in heaven and on earth has been given to me. 19 Go therefore and make disciples of all nations, baptizing them in the name of the Father and of the Son and of the Holy Spirit, 20 teaching them to observe all that I have commanded you; and lo, I am with you always, to the close of the age."

28.16
ver 7;
Mt 26.32
28.18
Dan 7.13,
14;
Lk 10.22;
Phil 2.9,10;
1 Pet 3.22
*28.19
Lk 24.47;
Acts 1.8
28.20
Acts 2.42;
Mt 18.20;
Acts 18.10

28.19a This Scripture is the warrant for water baptism. Indeed baptism is not optional with a believer; it is, rather, the express command of Christ. To dismiss it as a merely psychological transaction is to do violence to the Word of God. Christians generally have been united in the conviction that baptism is commanded, but they have been divided on almost every other aspect of the subject. Some insist that immersion is the only mode of baptism. Others believe that the Scripture teaches baptism by pouring (affusion) or by sprinkling (aspersion). Some baptize infants on the analogy of Old Testament circumcision (cf. Gen 17; Col 2.11–13); others insist that only those who are old enough to make a personal decision for Christ ought to be baptized. Some call baptism a sacrament and others regard it as an ordinance. The rite is administered in the name of the Father, Son, and Holy Spirit in accordance with Christ's command in this verse.
28.19b The Christian church has always

been trinitarian. This means that God is one in essence, eternally subsisting in three persons: Father, Son, and Holy Spirit. Here the word name is in the singular, intimating that the three persons of the Trinity are one in substance and equality, yet three in person. Biblical evidences for the Trinity include Mt 3.16, 17; Rom 8.9; 1 Cor 12.3–6; 2 Cor 13.14; Eph 4.4–6; 1 Pet 1.2; Jude 20, 21; Rev 1.4, 5. There is no other way of reconciling consistently all that the Bible says about God except by understanding Him as a Trinity (rather than as a mere Unity or as three separate Gods). All of the members of the Trinity are accorded the attributes of deity and each member has an office which He uniquely fulfils. God the Father sent God the Son. It was the Son who died on Calvary. It was the Father and the Son who sent the Holy Spirit who seals and indwells each believer. Salvation is the work of the Trinity, (Father, Son, and Holy Spirit) as stated in Tit 3.4–6 and 2 Thess 2.13, 14.

INTRODUCTION TO
THE GOSPEL ACCORDING TO
MARK

Authorship and Background: From earliest times the second Gospel was ascribed to John Mark, whose name does not appear in the Gospels. Some think
he was the young man present at the arrest of Jesus (14.51, 52). From Acts and
the Epistles it appears that John Mark was the son of Mary, whose home in
Jerusalem was used as a meeting place by the Jerusalem church (Acts 12.12).
His cousin Barnabas (Col 4.10) and Paul took him with them when they returned from Jerusalem to Antioch (Acts 12.25). He went with them on their
first missionary journey as far as Perga, whence he returned to Jerusalem (Acts
13.5, 13). Paul and Barnabas parted company over whether Mark should go
with them on their second journey, Barnabas taking him with him to Cyprus
(Acts 15.37–39). Years later Mark was with Paul when he wrote to the Colossians
and to Philemon (Col 4.10; Philem 24), and later Paul asked for him (2 Tim
4.11). Moreover, he was with Peter in "Babylon" (probably Rome), according
to 1 Pet 5.13.

Mark himself was not one of the Twelve, but his Gospel (claimed by many
to have been the first one to be written as over against the tradition of
Matthew's priority) has all the earmarks of a firsthand witness who was, from
all early accounts, none other than Simon Peter, from whom Mark obtained
his information.

It is generally agreed that the Gospel was written before A.D. 70; some date it as
early as A.D. 50, while others place it around A.D. 65.

Characteristics: This Gospel is the shortest of the four, and most of its contents are also to be found in Matthew or Luke. It presents a vivid, vigorous,
straightforward account of the public ministry of Jesus, culminating in his passion, death, and resurrection. The events of the last week in Jerusalem occupy
over one-third of the book with the climactic end of the ministry dominating the
entire account. From the ministry of John the Baptist to the resurrection of
Jesus, the emphasis is on the mighty acts of the Son of God, vividly described
with an abundance of detail. Comparatively less attention is devoted to the
teachings of Jesus, although there are blocks of teachings, such as the parables
in chapter 4 and the apocalyptic discourse in chapter 13. In this book Jesus is
(1) the Son of God (1.1; 15.39) and (2) the Son of man who is destined to be
betrayed, suffer, and die (8.31; 9.31; 10.33–34; 14.21), and who will come in
the power and glory of the Father (8.38; 13.26; 14.62).

In the key verse of the Gospel, Jesus discloses that the Son of man is the
Suffering Servant of God who will "give his life as a ransom for many" (10.45).

Contents:

THE GOSPEL ACCORDING TO

MARK

The ministry of John the Baptist
(1.1–8; Mt 3.1–12; Lk 3.2–17; Jn 1.6–8, 19–28)

1.1
Mt 4.3

1.2
Mal 3.1;
Mt 11.10;
Lk 7.27

1.3
Isa 40.3

★1.4
Acts 13.24;
Lk 1.77

1.6
Lev 11.22

1.7
Acts 13.25
1.8
Acts 1.5;
Isa 44.3;
Joel 2.28

1.9
Mt 2.23
1.10
Jn 1.32
1.11
Ps 2.7;
Isa 42.1

★1.12
★1.13

1 The beginning of the gospel of Jesus Christ, the Son of God.[a] 2 As it is written in Iṣāiʹáh the prophet,[b]
"Behold, I send my messenger before thy face,
who shall prepare thy way;
3 the voice of one crying in the wilderness:
Prepare the way of the Lord,
make his paths straight—"

4 John the baptizer appeared[c] in the wilderness, preaching a baptism of repentance for the forgiveness of sins. 5And there went out to him all the country of Judēʹá, and all the people of Jerusalem; and they were baptized by him in the river Jordan, confessing their sins. 6 Now John was clothed with camel's hair, and had a leather girdle around his waist, and ate locusts and wild honey. 7And he preached, saying, "After me comes he who is mightier than I, the thong of whose sandals I am not worthy to stoop down and untie. 8 I have baptized you with water; but he will baptize you with the Holy Spirit."

The baptism of Jesus (1.9–11; Mt 3.13–17; Lk 3.21,22)

9 In those days Jesus came from Nāzʹáréth of Gālʹilee and was baptized by John in the Jordan. 10And when he came up out of the water, immediately he saw the heavens opened and the Spirit descending upon him like a dove; 11 and a voice came from heaven, "Thou art my beloved Son;[d] with thee I am well pleased."

The temptation of Jesus (1.12,13; Mt 4.1–11; Lk 4.1–13)

12 The Spirit immediately drove him out into the wilderness. 13And he was in the wilderness forty days, tempted by Satan; and

---

a Other ancient authorities omit the Son of God b Other ancient authorities read in the prophets c Other ancient authorities read John was baptizing
d Or my Son, my (or the) Beloved

1.4 John belonged to the Old Testament dispensation, and his baptism of repentance, though its purpose was the forgiveness of sins, fell short of Christian baptism. The Christian church did not yet exist, and the disciples of John and those who were to be the followers of Jesus were not joined together. John did not administer baptism in the name of the Trinity, nor did he baptize with the Holy Spirit (who had not yet been given to the church, Jn 7.39). Paul felt it necessary to baptize again those who had known only John's baptism (Acts 18.24–19.7).
1.12 See note to Lk 4.2 on the temptation of Jesus.
1.13 Angels are heavenly messengers of God whose purpose is to execute His will or communicate it to mankind. The term angel (both

the Hebrew malʹakh and the Greek angellos) means "messenger," and ordinarily is used to refer to a higher order of spirits who dwell in the very presence of God. But it also refers to the devil's angels (Mt 25.41), and seems to be applied to the pastors who serve as God's messengers to the congregations of the seven churches of Asia (Rev 1–3). In Gen 16.7–14; 22.11–19; Ex 3.2–4; Judg 2.1; 6.11–14; 13.3 the presence of Deity in angelic form is obvious. The Greek word for angel (sometimes translated messenger) is also used for men in passages like Lk 7.24; Jas 2.25. Angels are stated by Scripture to be: (1) created beings (Col 1.16); (2) innumerable (Dan 7.10; Heb 12.22; Rev 5.11); (3) of different orders and ranks (Dan 10.13; Jude 9); (4) powerful (2 Thess 1.7; 2 Ki 19.35;

he was with the wild beasts; and the angels ministered to him.

The beginning of Jesus' Galilean ministry
(1.14,15; Mt 4.12–17; Lk 4.14,15; Jn 4.43–45)

14 Now after John was arrested, Jesus came into Găl'ǐleē, preaching the gospel of God, 15 and saying, "The time is fulfilled, and the
kingdom of God is at hand; repent, and believe in the gospel."

1.14
Mt 4.23
1.15
Gal 4.4;
Eph 1.10;
Acts 20.21

The call of the first four disciples
(1.16–20; Mt 4.18–22; Lk 5.1–11; cf. Jn 1.40–42)

16 And passing along by the Sea of Găli'leē, he saw Simon and
Andrew the brother of Simon casting a net in the sea; for they
were fishermen. 17And Jesus said to them, "Follow me and I will
make you become fishers of men." 18And immediately they left
their nets and followed him. 19And going on a little farther, he saw
James the son of Zĕb'ĕdeē and John his brother, who were in their
boat mending the nets. 20And immediately he called them; and they
left their father Zĕb'ĕdeē in the boat with the hired servants, and
followed him.

1.18
Mt 19.27

The unclean spirit cast out (1.21–28; Lk 4.31–37)

21 And they went into Căpér'nä-ùm; and immediately on the
sabbath he entered the synagogue and taught. 22And they were
astonished at his teaching, for he taught them as one who had
authority, and not as the scribes. 23And immediately there was in
their synagogue a man with an unclean spirit; 24 and he cried out,
"What have you to do with us, Jesus of Năz'ăreth? Have you come
to destroy us? I know who you are, the Holy One of God." 25 But
Jesus rebuked him, saying, "Be silent, and come out of him!"
26And the unclean spirit, convulsing him and crying with a loud
voice, came out of him. 27And they were all amazed, so that they
questioned among themselves, saying, "What is this? A new
teaching! With authority he commands even the unclean spirits,
and they obey him." 28And at once his fame spread everywhere
throughout all the surrounding region of Găl'ǐleē.

1.21
Mt 4.23
1.22
Mt 7.28

1.24
Mt 8.29;
Mk 10.47;
14.67;
Jn 6.69;
Acts 3.14
1.25
ver 34
1.27
Mk 10.24,
32

Peter's mother-in-law healed
(1.29–31; Mt 8.14–17; Lk 4.38–41)

29 And immediately he^e left the synagogue, and entered the

1.29
ver 21,23

e Other ancient authorities read they

Ps 103.20); (5) spirits without material bodies
(Heb 1.14); (6) not bound by physical limitations (Acts 12.5–10); (7) possessed of great
wisdom (2 Sam 14.20); (8) capable of assuming
human form (1 Chr 21.16, 20; Jn 20.12). In
their work angels: (1) guide the destinies of
nations (Dan 10.13, 20); (2) minister to the
people of God (Heb 1.14; 1 Ki 19.5–7; Acts
12.7; Ps 91.10–12); (3) execute God's judgments (2 Ki 19.35; Acts 12.23; Rev 16.1);
(4) will accompany Christ at His Second

Coming (Mt 25.31; 2 Thess 1.7, 8); (5) transmitted the law to Moses and the Israelites
(Ps 68.17; Acts 7.53; Heb 2.2). Aside from
Satan only two are named, one the archangel
Michael and the other Gabriel, to whom
were entrusted special assignments (Dan
10.13, 21; 12.1, 2; 1 Thess 4.16; Jude 9;
Dan 8.16; 9.21; Lk 1.19, 26). Man is said to
be a little lower than the angels and Christ
shared in this low estate in His humiliation
(Heb 2.6–9).

house of Simon and Andrew, with James and John. 30 Now Simon's mother-in-law lay sick with a fever, and immediately they told him of her. 31And he came and took her by the hand and lifted her up, and the fever left her; and she served them.

The sick healed; demons cast out
(1.32–34; Mt 8.16–17; Lk 4.40–41)

32 That evening, at sundown, they brought to him all who were sick or possessed with demons. 33And the whole city was gathered together about the door. 34And he healed many who were sick with various diseases, and cast out many demons; and he would not permit the demons to speak, because they knew him.

First preaching tour in Galilee
(1.35–39; cf. Lk 4.42–44 and see note n)

35 And in the morning, a great while before day, he rose and went out to a lonely place, and there he prayed. 36And Simon and those who were with him pursued him, 37 and they found him and said to him, "Every one is searching for you." 38And he said to them, "Let us go on to the next towns, that I may preach there also; for that is why I came out." 39And he went throughout all Găl'ileē, preaching in their synagogues and casting out demons.

The leper cleansed (1.40–45; Mt 8.1–4; Lk 5.12–16)

40 And a leper came to him beseeching him, and kneeling said to him, "If you will, you can make me clean." 41 Moved with pity, he stretched out his hand and touched him, and said to him, "I will; be clean." 42And immediately the leprosy left him, and he was made clean. 43And he sternly charged him, and sent him away at once, 44 and said to him, "See that you say nothing to any one; but go, show yourself to the priest, and offer for your cleansing what Moses commanded, for a proof to the people."f 45 But he went out and began to talk freely about it, and to spread the news, so that Jesusg could no longer openly enter a town, but was out in the country; and people came to him from every quarter.

A paralytic healed and forgiven
(2.1–12; Mt 9.1–8; Lk 5.17–26)

2 And when he returned to Căpér'nä-üm after some days, it was reported that he was at home. 2And many were gathered together, so that there was no longer room for them, not even about the door; and he was preaching the word to them. 3And they came, bringing to him a paralytic carried by four men. 4And when they could not get near him because of the crowd, they removed the roof above him; and when they had made an opening, they let down the pallet on which the paralytic lay. 5And when Jesus saw their faith, he said to the paralytic, "My son, your sins are forgiven." 6 Now some of the scribes were sitting there, questioning

f Greek *to them*   *g* Greek *he*

Margin refs: 1.32 Mk 4.24; 1.34 Mt 4.23; Mk 3.12; Acts 16.17, 18; 1.35 Mt 14.23; Lk 5.16; 1.38 Isa 61.1; 1.39 Mt 4.23–25; 1.40 Mk 10.17; 1.44 Lev 13.49; 14.2–32; 1.45 Lk 5.15; Mt 28.15; Mk 2.13; Lk 5.17; Jn 6.2; 2.2 ver 13; 2.3 Mt 4.24

in their hearts, 7 "Why does this man speak thus? It is blasphemy! Who can forgive sins but God alone?" 8And immediately Jesus, perceiving in his spirit that they thus questioned within themselves, said to them, "Why do you question thus in your hearts? 9 Which is easier, to say to the paralytic, 'Your sins are forgiven,' or to say, 'Rise, take up your pallet and walk'? 10 But that you may know that the Son of man has authority on earth to forgive sins"— he said to the paralytic—11 "I say to you, rise, take up your pallet and go home." 12And he rose, and immediately took up the pallet and went out before them all; so that they were all amazed and glorified God, saying, "We never saw anything like this!"

Matthew called (2.13–17; Mt 9.9–13; Lk 5.27–32)

13 He went out again beside the sea; and all the crowd gathered about him, and he taught them. 14And as he passed on, he saw Lēvī the son of Ālphaē'ŭs sitting at the tax office, and he said to him, "Follow me." And he rose and followed him.

15 And as he sat at table in his house, many tax collectors and sinners were sitting with Jesus and his disciples; for there were many who followed him. 16And the scribes of[h] the Phar'ĭseēṣ, when they saw that he was eating with sinners and tax collectors, said to his disciples, "Why does he eat[i] with tax collectors and sinners?" 17And when Jesus heard it, he said to them, "Those who are well have no need of a physician, but those who are sick; I came not to call the righteous, but sinners."

The question about fasting (2.18–22; Mt 9.14–17; Lk 5.33–39)

18 Now John's disciples and the Phar'ĭseēṣ were fasting; and people came and said to him, "Why do John's disciples and the disciples of the Pharisees fast, but your disciples do not fast?" 19And Jesus said to them, "Can the wedding guests fast while the bridegroom is with them? As long as they have the bridegroom with them, they cannot fast. 20 The days will come, when the bridegroom is taken away from them, and then they will fast in that day. 21 No one sews a piece of unshrunk cloth on an old garment; if he does, the patch tears away from it, the new from the old, and a worse tear is made. 22And no one puts new wine into old wineskins; if he does, the wine will burst the skins, and the wine is lost, and so are the skins; but new wine is for fresh skins."[j]

*2.7 Isa 43.25
2.12 Mt 9.33
2.13 Mk 1.45
2.14 Mt 8.22
2.16 Acts 23.9
2.17 Lk 19.10; 1 Tim 1.15
*2.18
2.20 Lk 17.22
*2.21

h Other ancient authorities read and i Other ancient authorities add and drink
j Other ancient authorities omit but new wine is for fresh skins

2.7 The scribes asked the right question but came to the wrong conclusion, so far as Christ's authority was concerned. It is true that only God can forgive sins. But as the Son of man Jesus exercised this divine prerogative on earth, of which He gave conclusive proof by healing the paralytic (ver 10–12).
2.18 From the teachings of Jesus and the New Testament record of the practice of the Apostolic Church, it does not appear that early Christians fasted regularly as a religious duty. The answer Jesus gave to the question as to why his disciples did not fast shows he regarded fasting as an expression of sorrow, and thus incompatible with the joy his disciples shared in company with him, like the joy of a wedding feast (a common figure of the Messianic age). In Mt 6.16–18 Jesus teaches that fasting as a religious observance is of value only if practiced without ostentation for the sole purpose of pleasing God.
In the Apostolic Church there are references to fasting on occasions of crisis and decision, particularly in the choosing of leaders for church work (cf. Acts 13.2, 3; 14.23).
2.21 See note to Lk 5.36 on cloth and wine.

Jesus the Lord of the Sabbath
(2.23–28; Mt 12.1–8; Lk 6.1–5)

2.23
Deut 23.25

23 One sabbath he was going through the grainfields; and as they made their way his disciples began to pluck heads of grain.

*2.25

24And the Phar′isee̱s said to him, "Look, why are they doing what is not lawful on the sabbath?" 25And he said to them, "Have you never read what David did, when he was in need and was hungry, he and those who were with him: 26 how he entered the house of

2.26
1 Sam 21.1–
6;
2 Sam 8.17;
Ex 29.32,
33;
Lev 24.9

God, when Ăbi′athar was high priest, and ate the bread of the Presence, which it is not lawful for any but the priests to eat, and also gave it to those who were with him?" 27And he said to them, "The sabbath was made for man, not man for the sabbath; 28 so the Son of man is lord even of the sabbath."

*2.27
Ex 23.12;
Deut 5.14

Jesus heals on the Sabbath (3.1–6; Mt 12.9–14; Lk 6.6–11)

3.1
Mk 1.21,39
3.2
Lk 14.1;
20.20;
Mt 12.10

3 Again he entered the synagogue, and a man was there who had a withered hand. 2And they watched him, to see whether he would heal him on the sabbath, so that they might accuse him. 3And he said to the man who had the withered hand, "Come here." 4And he said to them, "Is it lawful on the sabbath to do good or to do harm, to save life or to kill?" But they were silent. 5And he looked around at them with anger, grieved at their hardness of heart, and said to the man, "Stretch out your hand." He

3.6
Mt 12.14;
22.16;
Mk 12.13

stretched it out, and his hand was restored. 6 The Phar′isee̱s went out, and immediately held counsel with the Hĕrō′di-ăn̯s against him, how to destroy him.

Jesus heals many (3.7–12; Mt 12.15–21; cf. Lk 6.17–19)

3.7
Mt 4.25
3.8
Mt 11.21
3.10
Mt 4.23;
Mk 5.29,
34; 6.56;
8.22

7 Jesus withdrew with his disciples to the sea, and a great multitude from Găl′ilee̱ followed; also from Judē′ă 8 and Jerusalem and Ĭdumē′ă and from beyond the Jordan and from about Tȳre and Sĭdŏn a great multitude, hearing all that he did, came to him. 9And he told his disciples to have a boat ready for him because of the crowd, lest they should crush him; 10 for he had healed many, so that all who had diseases pressed upon him to touch

*3.11
Mk 1.23,
24;
Lk 4.41;
Mt 14.33
3.12
Mk 1.25,34

him. 11And whenever the unclean spirits beheld him, they fell down before him and cried out, "You are the Son of God." 12And he strictly ordered them not to make him known.

2.25 Every week the priests prepared twelve loaves of bread in accordance with instructions in Lev 24.5–9, and laid them on the table on the Sabbath before God (cf. Ex 25.30; 35.13; 39.36). When the twelve fresh loaves were placed on the table, the priests could eat the old loaves if they so desired.

2.27 In Gen 2.2 the statement is made that God rested on the seventh day. That is the first mention of the biblical doctrine of the Sabbath. Among the children of Israel the seventh day, or Saturday, was the Sabbath. Indeed, this was a part of the Mosaic Law (Ex 20.9–11). Eventually it became hedged about by all kinds of artificial and hairsplitting regulations so that in Jesus' day one could not even walk beyond a certain distance without

breaking the Law. The phrase *a sabbath day's journey* (defined as about a thousand yards) illustrates this legal restriction (Acts 1.12). Christ enunciated two major principles concerning the Sabbath: (1) it was made for man, not vice versa (see also Mt 12.1–8; Lk 6.1–5); (2) certain types of work were permissible even on the Sabbath—works of mercy and works of necessity. To pluck grain for food was a work of necessity; and to pull an ox out of a hole was a work of mercy, so also to care for the healing of the sick.

3.11 The unclean spirits had knowledge that Jesus was the Son of God. Yet this knowledge did not issue in salvation. So men may profess belief in all the major doctrines of the Christian faith and still be unregenerate.

The appointing of the Twelve
(3.13–19; Mt 10.1–4; Lk 6.12–16)

13 And he went up on the mountain, and called to him those whom he desired; and they came to him. [14]And he appointed twelve,[k] to be with him, and to be sent out to preach [15] and have authority to cast out demons: [16] Simon[x] whom he surnamed Peter; [17] James the son of Zĕb´edeē and John the brother of James, whom he surnamed Bō-ȧnêr´gēṣ, that is, sons of thunder; [18]Andrew, and Philip, and Barthŏl´ómeẅ, and Matthew, and Thomas, and James the son of Ȧlpha´ēŭs, and Thad´dāēŭs, and Simon the Cȧnȧnaē´ȧn, [19] and Judas Ĭsca̧´rĭŏt, who betrayed him.

3.13
Mt 5.1;
Lk 9.1

3.16
Jn 1.42

Jesus answers the calumny of the Pharisees
(3.20–27; Mt 12.22–45; Lk 11.14–23)

Then he went home; [20] and the crowd came together again, so that they could not even eat. [21]And when his family heard it, they went out to seize him, for people were saying, "He is beside himself." [22]And the scribes who came down from Jerusalem said, "He is possessed by Bĕ-ĕl´zĕbŭl, and by the prince of demons he casts out the demons." [23]And he called them to him, and said to them in parables, "How can Satan cast out Satan? [24] If a kingdom is divided against itself, that kingdom cannot stand. [25]And if a house is divided against itself, that house will not be able to stand. [26]And if Satan has risen up against himself and is divided, he cannot stand, but is coming to an end. [27] But no one can enter a strong man's house and plunder his goods, unless he first binds the strong man; then indeed he may plunder his house.

3.20
Mk 6.31
3.21
Jn 10.20;
Acts 26.24
3.22
Mt 9.34;
10.25;
Jn 7.20;
8.48,52
3.23
Mk 4.2ff

3.27
Isa 49.24,
25

The unforgivable sin (3.28–30)

28 "Truly, I say to you, all sins will be forgiven the sons of men, and whatever blasphemies they utter; [29] but whoever blasphemes against the Holy Spirit never has forgiveness, but is guilty of an eternal sin"—[30] for they had said, "He has an unclean spirit."

3.28
Lk 12.10
*3.29

Christ's true kindred (3.31–35; Mt 12.46–50; Lk 8.19.21)

31 And his mother and his brothers came; and standing outside they sent to him and called him. [32]And a crowd was sitting about him; and they said to him, "Your mother and your brothers[l] are outside, asking for you." [33]And he replied, "Who are my mother and my brothers?" [34]And looking around on those who sat about him, he said, "Here are my mother and my brothers! [35] Whoever does the will of God is my brother, and sister, and mother."

3.31
Mt 12.46;
Lk 8.19

k Other ancient authorities add whom also he named apostles
x Other authorities read demons. 16 So he appointed the twelve: Simon
l Other early authorities add and your sisters

3.29 Blaspheming the Holy Spirit is the unpardonable sin (Mt 12.31, 32; Lk 12.10). To commit this sin one must consciously, persistently, deliberately, and maliciously reject the testimony of the Spirit to the deity and saving power of the Lord Jesus. Since only the Holy Spirit can convince and convert the unsaved, a continuous and final rejection of His wooing and His witness shuts off the only possible avenue whereby the saving work of Christ is applied to the sinner in his need.

Jesus teaches in parables (4.1–34)

1. Parable of the sower (4.1–9; Mt 13.1–9; Lk 8.4–8)

4.1
Mk 2.13;
3.7

4 Again he began to teach beside the sea. And a very large crowd gathered about him, so that he got into a boat and sat in it on the sea; and the whole crowd was beside the sea on the land. 2And he taught them many things in parables, and in his teaching he said to them: 3 "Listen! A sower went out to sow. 4And as he sowed, some seed fell along the path, and the birds came and devoured it. 5 Other seed fell on rocky ground, where it had not much soil, and immediately it sprang up, since it had no depth of soil; 6 and when the sun rose it was scorched, and since it had no root it withered away. 7 Other seed fell among thorns and the thorns grew up and choked it, and it yielded no grain. 8And other seeds fell into good soil and brought forth grain, growing up and increasing and yielding thirtyfold and sixtyfold and a hundredfold." 9And he said, "He who has ears to hear, let him hear."

4.2
Mk 3.23
★4.3

4.8
Jn 15.5;
Col 1.6

4.9
Mt 11.15

2. The reason for parables (4.10–12; Mt 13.10–17; Lk 8.9–10)

10 And when he was alone, those who were about him with the twelve asked him concerning the parables. 11And he said to them, "To you has been given the secret of the kingdom of God, but for those outside everything is in parables; 12 so that they may indeed see but not perceive, and may indeed hear but not understand; lest

4.11
1 Cor 5.12;
Col 4.5;
1 Thess
4.12;
1 Tim 3.7

★4.12
Isa 6.9;
Jn 12.40;
Acts 28.26;
Rom 11.8

3. The parable of the sower explained (4.13–20; Mt 13.18–23; Lk 8.11–15)

they should turn again, and be forgiven." 13And he said to them, "Do you not understand this parable? How then will you understand all the parables? 14 The sower sows the word. 15And these are the ones along the path, where the word is sown; when they hear, Satan immediately comes and takes away the word which is sown in them. 16And these in like manner are the ones sown upon rocky ground, who, when they hear the word, immediately receive it with joy; 17 and they have no root in themselves, but endure for a while; then, when tribulation or persecution arises on account of the word, immediately they fall away.m 18And others are the ones sown among thorns; they are those who hear the word, 19 but the cares of the world, and the delight in riches, and the desire for other things, enter in and choke the word, and it proves unfruitful. 20 But those that were sown upon the good soil are the ones who hear the word and accept it and bear fruit, thirtyfold and sixtyfold and a hundredfold."

4.15
Mk 2.23,26

m Or stumble

4.3 Three elements are significant in this parable: the seed, the sower, and the soil. Note that two of the elements are identical in each instance. It is the same seed and the same sower. The one factor which accounts for the variety of results is the soil. Accepting the principle that the soil means the hearer, then it follows that there are four kinds of people who hear the gospel, and of them only one brings forth enduring or acceptable fruit.

4.12 so that they may indeed see but not perceive, would appear to mean that Jesus used parables in order to hide the truth, not to reveal it. The words of 4.12 are a summary of Isa 6.9, 10 which speak of the prophet's message in terms of its rejection by the people of Israel. The blindness of the people and their unwillingness to repent and receive God's forgiveness came as the result of their wilful rejection of God's message through His prophet. This same pattern of rejection and blindness was repeated in Christ's ministry of teaching, as the lengthier parallel in Mt 13.13–15 makes abundantly clear.

4. The parable of the candle (4.21–25; cf. Mt 5.15; Lk 8.16; 11.33)

21 And he said to them, "Is a lamp brought in to be put under a bushel, or under a bed, and not on a stand? 22 For there is nothing hid, except to be made manifest; nor is anything secret, except to come to light. 23 If any man has ears to hear, let him hear." 24And he said to them, "Take heed what you hear; the measure you give will be the measure you get, and still more will be given you. 25 For to him who has will more be given; and from him who has not, even what he has will be taken away."

4.22
Mt 10.26;
Lk 8.17;
12.2
4.23
Mt 11.15
4.24
Mt 7.2;
Lk 6.38
4.25
Mt 13.12;
25.29;
Lk 8.18;
19.26
*4.26
Mt 13.24

5. The parable of growing grain (4.26–29)

26 And he said, "The kingdom of God is as if a man should scatter seed upon the ground, 27 and should sleep and rise night and day, and the seed should sprout and grow, he knows not how. 28 The earth produces of itself, first the blade, then the ear, then the full grain in the ear. 29 But when the grain is ripe, at once he puts in the sickle, because the harvest has come."

4.29
Rev 14.15

6. The parable of the mustard seed
(4.30–34; Mt 13.31,32; Lk 13.18,19)

30 And he said, "With what can we compare the kingdom of God, or what parable shall we use for it? 31 It is like a grain of mustard seed, which, when sown upon the ground, is the smallest of all the seeds on earth; 32 yet when it is sown it grows up and becomes the greatest of all shrubs, and puts forth large branches, so that the birds of the air can make nests in its shade."

4.30
Mt 13.24

33 With many such parables he spoke the word to them, as they were able to hear it; 34 he did not speak to them without a parable, but privately to his own disciples he explained everything.

4.33
Jn 16.12
4.34
Mt 13.34;
Jn 16.25

The storm stilled (4.35–41; Mt 8.23–27; Lk 8.22–25)

35 On that day, when evening had come, he said to them, "Let us go across to the other side." 36And leaving the crowd, they took him with them in the boat, just as he was. And other boats were with him. 37And a great storm of wind arose, and the waves beat into the boat, so that the boat was already filling. 38 But he was in the stern, asleep on the cushion; and they woke him and said to him, "Teacher, do you not care if we perish?" 39And he awoke and rebuked the wind, and said to the sea, "Peace! Be still!" And the wind ceased, and there was a great calm. 40 He said to them, "Why are you afraid? Have you no faith?" 41And they were filled with awe, and said to one another, "Who then is this, that even wind and sea obey him?"

4.36
Mk 5.2,21
4.40
Mt 14.31,
32;
Mk 16.14

Demons cast out (5.1–20; Mt 8.28–34; Lk 8.26–39)

5 They came to the other side of the sea, to the country of the Gĕr'ȧsēnĕṣ.[n] 2And when he had come out of the boat, there

5.2
Mt 4.1;
1.23

[n] Other ancient authorities read Gĕr'gĕsēnĕṣ', some Găd'ȧrēnĕṣ'

4.26 The law of growth is the central teaching of this parable. The kingdom of God has steadily enlarged itself during the centuries since Christ died and rose again. This growth has not always been perceptible, but in His own way, God knows how to bring forth abundant fruit from the gospel seed which has been planted.

met him out of the tombs a man with an unclean spirit, 3 who lived among the tombs; and no one could bind him any more, even with a chain; 4 for he had often been bound with fetters and chains, but the chains he wrenched apart, and the fetters he broke in pieces; and no one had the strength to subdue him. 5 Night and day among the tombs and on the mountains he was always crying out, and bruising himself with stones. 6And when he saw Jesus from afar, he ran and worshiped him; 7 and crying out with a loud voice, he said, "What have you to do with me, Jesus, Son of the Most High God? I adjure you by God, do not torment me." 8 For he had said to him, "Come out of the man, you unclean spirit!" 9And Jesus° asked him, "What is your name?" He replied, "My name is Legion; for we are many." 10And he begged him eagerly not to send them out of the country. 11 Now a great herd of swine was feeding there on the hillside; 12 and they begged him, "Send us to the swine, let us enter them." 13 So he gave them leave. And the unclean spirits came out, and entered the swine; and the herd, numbering about two thousand, rushed down the steep bank into the sea, and were drowned in the sea.

14 The herdsmen fled, and told it in the city and in the country. And people came to see what it was that had happened. 15And they came to Jesus, and saw the demoniac sitting there, clothed and in his right mind, the man who had had the legion; and they were afraid. 16And those who had seen it told what had happened to the demoniac and to the swine. 17And they began to beg Jesus^p to depart from their neighborhood. 18And as he was getting into the boat, the man who had been possessed with demons begged him that he might be with him. 19 But he refused, and said to him, "Go home to your friends, and tell them how much the Lord has done for you, and how he has had mercy on you." 20And he went away and began to proclaim in the Děcăp'ŏlĭs how much Jesus had done for him; and all men marveled.

The woman with the issue of blood healed and Jairus' daughter raised (5.21–43; Mt 9.18–26; Lk 8.40–56)

21 And when Jesus had crossed again in the boat to the other side, a great crowd gathered about him; and he was beside the sea. 22 Then came one of the rulers of the synagogue, Jaïrŭs by name; and seeing him, he fell at his feet, 23 and besought him, saying, "My little daughter is at the point of death. Come and lay your hands on her, so that she may be made well, and live." 24And he went with him.

And a great crowd followed him and thronged about him. 25And there was a woman who had had a flow of blood for twelve years, 26 and who had suffered much under many physicians, and had spent all that she had, and was no better but rather grew worse. 27 She had heard the reports about Jesus, and came up behind him in the crowd and touched his garment. 28 For she

Margin references:

5.6
Mt 4.9;
18.26

*5.7
Mt 8.29;
4.3;
Lk 8.28;
Acts 16.17;
Heb 7.1

5.15
ver 16,18;
Mt 4.24;
ver 9

5.18
Acts 16.39

5.20
Mk 7.31;
Mt 4.25

5.21
Mt 9.1

5.22
Lk 8.49;
13.14;
Acts 13.15;
18.8,17

5.23
Mk 6.5;
7.32; 8.23;
Acts 9.17;
28.8

5.25
Lev 15.25

o Greek he   p Greek him

5.7 The question "*What have you to do with me . . . ?*" is found also in the parallels, Mt 8.29; Lk 8.28 (see also Mt 27.19; Mk 1.24; Lk 4.34; Jn 2.4). The question is patterned after a Semitic idiom by which the speaker rejects any kind of interference on the part of the person he addresses (in the Old Testament see 2 Sam 16.10; 19.22; also Judg 11.12; 1 Ki 17.18). The question is thus a protest, "What do you want with me?"

said, "If I touch even his garments, I shall be made well." ²⁹And immediately the hemorrhage ceased; and she felt in her body that she was healed of her disease. ³⁰And Jesus, perceiving in himself that power had gone forth from him, immediately turned about in the crowd, and said, "Who touched my garments?" ³¹And his disciples said to him, "You see the crowd pressing around you, and yet you say, 'Who touched me?' " ³²And he looked around to see who had done it. ³³ But the woman, knowing what had been done to her, came in fear and trembling and fell down before him, and told him the whole truth. ³⁴And he said to her, "Daughter, your faith has made you well; go in peace, and be healed of your disease."

35 While he was still speaking, there came from the ruler's house some who said, "Your daughter is dead. Why trouble the Teacher any further?" ³⁶ But ignoring*q* what they said, Jesus said to the ruler of the synagogue, "Do not fear, only believe." ³⁷And he allowed no one to follow him except Peter and James and John the brother of James. ³⁸ When they came to the house of the ruler of the synagogue, he saw a tumult, and people weeping and wailing loudly. ³⁹And when he had entered, he said to them, "Why do you make a tumult and weep? The child is not dead but sleeping." ⁴⁰And they laughed at him. But he put them all outside, and took the child's father and mother and those who were with him, and went in where the child was. ⁴¹ Taking her by the hand he said to her, "Tăli'thă cu'mĭ"; which means, "Little girl, I say to you, arise." ⁴²And immediately the girl got up and walked (she was twelve years of age), and they were immediately overcome with amazement. ⁴³And he strictly charged them that no one should know this, and told them to give her something to eat.

Second rejection of Jesus at Nazareth
(6.1–6; Mt 13.53–58; Lk 4.16–30)

6 He went away from there and came to his own country; and his disciples followed him. ²And on the sabbath he began to teach in the synagogue; and many who heard him were astonished, saying, "Where did this man get all this? What is the wisdom given to him? What mighty works are wrought by his hands! ³ Is not this the carpenter, the son of Mary and brother of James and Jōşĕs and Judas and Simon, and are not his sisters here with us?" And they took offense*r* at him. ⁴And Jesus said to them, "A prophet is not without honor, except in his own country, and among his own kin, and in his own house." ⁵And he could do no mighty work

5.29	ver 34
5.30	Lk 5.17
5.34	Lk 7.50; 8.48; Acts 16.36 Jas 2.16
5.35	ver 22
5.36	Lk 8.50
5.37	Mt 17.1; 26.37
5.38	ver 22
5.39	Jn 11.11
5.41	Lk 7.14; Acts 9.40
5.43	Mt 8.4
6.2	Mt 4.23; 7.28; Mk 1.21
*6.3	Mt 12.46; 11.6
6.4	Jn 4.44
6.5	Mt 5.23; 7.32; 8.23

---

q Or *overhearing.* Other ancient authorities read *hearing*   *r* Or *stumbled*

6.3 Jesus is here called *the carpenter,* and in Mt 13.55, *the carpenter's son;* Lk 4.22 has *Joseph's son.* It is probable that by calling him *the son of Mary* here in 6.3 a slur was intended, since ordinarily a man was called the son of his father, not of his mother.

Jesus' sisters are mentioned here, but no names are given; his brothers are named here and in Mt 13.55: James, Joseph (or, Joses), Simon, and Judas. The brothers are also referred to in Jn 7.3–10 and Acts 1.14. In

Gal 1.19 Paul speaks of James, the Lord's brother, the same James of Acts 12.17; 15.13–21; 1 Cor 15.7. From these references it is surmised that none of Jesus' brothers believed in Him prior to the resurrection.

The way in which the New Testament speaks of the brothers and sisters of Jesus implies that they were the children of Joseph and Mary; there is no New Testament warrant for later theories that they were Joseph's children by a previous marriage, or that they were cousins of Jesus, not brothers and sisters.

there, except that he laid his hands upon a few sick people and healed them. ⁶And he marveled because of their unbelief.

6.6
Mt 9.35;
Lk 13.22

And he went about among the villages teaching.

The mission of the Twelve (6.7–13; Mt 10.1–15; Lk 9.1–6)

6.7
Mk 3.13;
Lk 10.1

7 And he called to him the twelve, and began to send them out two by two, and gave them authority over the unclean spirits. ⁸ He charged them to take nothing for their journey except a staff; no bread, no bag, no money in their belts; ⁹ but to wear sandals and not put on two tunics. ¹⁰And he said to them, "Where you enter a house, stay there until you leave the place. ¹¹And if any place will not receive you and they refuse to hear you, when you leave, shake off the dust that is on your feet for a testimony against them." ¹² So they went out and preached that men should repent. ¹³And they cast out many demons, and anointed with oil many that were sick and healed them.

6.12
Mt 11.1;
Lk 9.6
6.13
Jas 5.14

John the Baptist beheaded (6.14–29; Mt 14.1–12; Lk 9.7–9)

*6.14

14 King Hĕrŏd heard of it; for Jesus'ˢ name had become known. Someᵗ said, "John the baptizer has been raised from the dead; that is why these powers are at work in him." ¹⁵ But others said, "It is Ēlī'jäh." And others said, "It is a prophet, like one of the prophets of old." ¹⁶ But when Hĕrŏd heard of it he said, "John, whom I beheaded, has been raised." ¹⁷ For Hĕrŏd had sent and seized John, and bound him in prison for the sake of Hērō'dĭ-ăs, his brother Philip's wife; because he had married her. ¹⁸ For John said to Hĕrŏd, "It is not lawful for you to have your brother's wife." ¹⁹And Hērō'dĭ-ăs had a grudge against him, and wanted to kill him. But she could not, ²⁰ for Hĕrŏd feared John, knowing that he was a righteous and holy man, and kept him safe. When he heard him, he was much perplexed; and yet he heard him gladly. ²¹ But an opportunity came when Hĕrŏd on his birthday gave a banquet for his courtiers and officers and the leading men of Găl'ĭleē. ²² For when Hērō'dĭ-ăs' daughter came in and danced, she pleased Hĕrŏd and his guests; and the king said to the girl, "Ask me for whatever you wish, and I will grant it." ²³And he vowed to her, "Whatever you ask me, I will give you, even half of my kingdom." ²⁴And she went out, and said to her mother, "What shall I ask?" And she said, "The head of John the baptizer." ²⁵And she came in immediately with haste to the king, and asked, saying, "I want you to give me at once the head of John the Baptist on a platter." ²⁶And the king was exceedingly sorry; but because of his oaths and his guests he did not want to break his word to her. ²⁷And immediately the king sent a soldier of the guard and gave orders to bring his head. He went and beheaded him in the prison, ²⁸ and brought his head on a platter, and gave it to the girl; and the girl gave it to her mother. ²⁹ When his disciples heard of it, they came and took his body, and laid it in a tomb.

6.15
Mt 16.14;
Mk 8.28;
Mt 21.11
6.16
Lk 3.19
*6.17
6.18
Lev 18.16;
20.21
6.20
Mt 21.26
6.21
Est 1.3;
2.18
6.23
Est 5.3,6;
7.2

ˢ Greek his   ᵗ Other ancient authorities read he

6.14 See note to Lk 1.57 on the life of John the Baptist.
6.17 This Philip, brother of Herod Antipas the tetrarch of Galilee and Perea, was not Philip the tetrarch of Iturea (Lk 3.1), but another half-brother of Herod Antipas, the son of Herod the Great and Mariamne, the daughter of Simon the high priest.

The five thousand fed (6.30–44; Mt 14.13–21; Lk 9.10–17; Jn 6.1–13; cf. Mt 15.32–39)

30 The apostles returned to Jesus, and told him all that they had done and taught. 31And he said to them, "Come away by yourselves to a lonely place, and rest a while." For many were coming and going, and they had no leisure even to eat. 32And they went away in the boat to a lonely place by themselves. 33 Now many saw them going, and knew them, and they ran there on foot from all the towns, and got there ahead of them. 34As he went ashore he saw a great throng, and he had compassion on them, because they were like sheep without a shepherd; and he began to teach them many things. 35And when it grew late, his disciples came to him and said, "This is a lonely place, and the hour is now late; 36 send them away, to go into the country and villages round about and buy themselves something to eat." 37 But he answered them, "You give them something to eat." And they said to him, "Shall we go and buy two hundred denarii‹ᵘ› worth of bread, and give it to them to eat?" 38And he said to them, "How many loaves have you? Go and see." And when they had found out, they said, "Five, and two fish." 39 Then he commanded them all to sit down by companies upon the green grass. 40 So they sat down in groups, by hundreds and by fifties. 41And taking the five loaves and the two fish he looked up to heaven, and blessed, and broke the loaves, and gave them to the disciples to set before the people; and he divided the two fish among them all. 42And they all ate and were satisfied. 43And they took up twelve baskets full of broken pieces and of the fish. 44And those who ate the loaves were five thousand men.

6.31 Mk 3.20
6.32 ver 45
6.34 Mt 9.36
6.37 2 Ki 4.42–44
6.38 Mt 15.34; Mk 8.5
6.41 Mt 26.26; Mk 14.22; Lk 24.30,31

Jesus walks on the sea (6.45–52; Mt 14.22–32; Jn 6.15–21)

45 Immediately he made his disciples get into the boat and go before him to the other side, to Bĕth-sā′idȧ, while he dismissed the crowd. 46And after he had taken leave of them, he went up on the mountain to pray. 47And when evening came, the boat was out on the sea, and he was alone on the land. 48And he saw that they were making headway painfully, for the wind was against them. And about the fourth watch of the night he came to them, walking on the sea. He meant to pass by them, 49 but when they saw him walking on the sea they thought it was a ghost, and cried out; 50 for they all saw him, and were terrified. But immediately he spoke to them and said, "Take heart, it is I; have no fear." 51And he got into the boat with them and the wind ceased. And they were utterly astounded, 52 for they did not understand about the loaves, but their hearts were hardened.

6.45 ver 32; Mt 11.21; Mk 8.22
*6.48 Mt 13.35; 24.43
6.50 Mt 9.2
6.51 ver 32
6.52 Mk 8.17, 18; 3.5

Jesus' ministry at Gennesaret (6.53–56; Mt 14.34–36)

53 And when they had crossed over, they came to land at Gĕn-nĕs′ȧrĕt, and moored to the shore. 54And when they got out of the

6.53 Jn 6.24,25

ᵘ The denarius was a day's wage for a laborer

6.48 According to the Graeco-Roman system, the night (6:00 P.M. to 6:00 A.M.) was divided into four watches of three hours each (cf. 13.35).

boat, immediately the people recognized him, 55 and ran about the whole neighborhood and began to bring sick people on their pallets to any place where they heard he was. 56And wherever he came, in villages, cities, or country, they laid the sick in the market places, and besought him that they might touch even the fringe of his garment; and as many as touched it were made well.

Ceremonial and real defilement: the Pharisees rebuked (7.1–23; Mt 15.1–20)

7 Now when the Phar′isees gathered together to him, with some of the scribes, who had come from Jerusalem, 2 they saw that some of his disciples ate with hands defiled, that is, unwashed. 3(For the Phar′isees, and all the Jews, do not eat unless they wash their hands,*v* observing the tradition of the elders; 4 and when they come from the market place, they do not eat unless they purify*w* themselves;*a* and there are many other traditions which they observe, the washing of cups and pots and vessels of bronze.*x*) 5And the Phar′isees and the scribes asked him, "Why do your disciples not live*y* according to the tradition of the elders, but eat with hands defiled?" 6And he said to them, "Well did Īṣāi′ăh prophesy of you hypocrites, as it is written,

'This people honors me with their lips,
    but their heart is far from me;
7 in vain do they worship me,
    teaching as doctrines the precepts of men.'

8 You leave the commandment of God, and hold fast the tradition of men."

9 And he said to them, "You have a fine way of rejecting the commandment of God, in order to keep your tradition! 10 For Moses said, 'Honor your father and your mother'; and, 'He who speaks evil of father or mother, let him surely die'; 11 but you say, 'If a man tells his father or his mother, What you would have gained from me is Corbăn' (that is, given to God)*z*—12 then you no longer permit him to do anything for his father or mother, 13 thus making void the word of God through your tradition which you hand on. And many such things you do."

14 And he called the people to him again, and said to them, "Hear me, all of you, and understand: 15 there is nothing outside a man which by going into him can defile him; but the things which come out of a man are what defile him."*a* 17And when he had entered the house, and left the people, his disciples asked him about the parable. 18And he said to them, "Then are you also without understanding? Do you not see that whatever goes into a man from outside cannot defile him, 19 since it enters, not his

Cross-references (left margin):
6.56 — Mk 3.10; Mt 9.20
*7.1
*7.3 — ver 5; Acts 10.14, 28; 11.8
7.4 — Mt 23.25; Lk 11.39
7.5 — ver 3,8,9,13; Gal 1.14
7.6 — Isa 29.13
7.8 — ver 5,9,13
7.9 — ver 5,8,13
7.10 — Ex 20.12; Deut 5.6; Ex 21.17; Lev 20.9
7.11 — Mt 23.18
7.13 — ver 5,8,9
7.17 — Mk 9.28
7.19 — Rom 14.1–12; Col 2.16; Lk 11.41; Acts 10.15; 11.9

---

v One Greek word is of uncertain meaning and is not translated
w Other ancient authorities read *baptize*
a Other ancient authorities read *and they do not eat anything from the market unless they purify it*
x Other ancient authorities add *and beds*
y Greek *walk*
z Or *an offering*
a Other ancient authorities add verse 16, "*If any man has ears to hear, let him hear*"

7.1 See note to Mt 3.7 on the Pharisees.
7.3 The RSV footnote (*v*) calls attention to the fact that one Greek word has not been translated. The word is *pugme*, "fist," and the statement is literally, "they wash their hands with (or, to) the fist." Some translate "with the fist"; others, "as far as the wrist (or, elbow)"; others, in a more general sense, "carefully." There is no general agreement as to the precise meaning of the word here.

heart but his stomach, and so passes on?"[b] (Thus he declared all foods clean.) 20And he said, "What comes out of a man is what defiles a man. 21 For from within, out of the heart of man, come evil thoughts, fornication, theft, murder, adultery, 22 coveting, wickedness, deceit, licentiousness, envy, slander, pride, foolishness. 23All these evil things come from within, and they defile a man."

7.22
Mt 6.23;
20.15

Journey toward Tyre and Sidon: the Syrophoenician woman's daughter healed (7.24–30; Mt 15.21–28)

24 And from there he arose and went away to the region of Tȳre and Sīdŏn.[c] And he entered a house, and would not have any one know it; yet he could not be hid. 25 But immediately a woman, whose little daughter was possessed by an unclean spirit, heard of him, and came and fell down at his feet. 26 Now the woman was a Greek, a Sȳrŏphoĕnī′çiǎn by birth. And she begged him to cast the demon out of her daughter. 27And he said to her, "Let the children first be fed, for it is not right to take the children's bread and throw it to the dogs." 28 But she answered him, "Yes, Lord; yet even the dogs under the table eat the children's crumbs." 29And he said to her, "For this saying you may go your way; the demon has left your daughter." 30And she went home, and found the child lying in bed, and the demon gone.

7.24
Mt 11.21

A deaf-mute healed (7.31–37; Mt 15.29–31)

31 Then he returned from the region of Tȳre, and went through Sīdŏn to the Sea of Găl′ĭleē, through the region of the Dĕcăp′ŏlĭs. 32And they brought to him a man who was deaf and had an impediment in his speech; and they besought him to lay his hand upon him. 33And taking him aside from the multitude privately, he put his fingers into his ears, and he spat and touched his tongue; 34 and looking up to heaven, he sighed, and said to him, "Ĕph′-phăthá," that is, "Be opened." 35And his ears were opened, his tongue was released, and he spoke plainly. 36And he charged them to tell no one; but the more he charged them, the more zealously they proclaimed it. 37And they were astonished beyond measure, saying, "He has done all things well; he even makes the deaf hear and the dumb speak."

7.32
Mk 5.23;
Mt 9.32;
Lk 11.14
7.33
Mk 8.23
7.34
Mk 6.41;
8.12
7.35
Isa 35.5,6
7.36
Mk 1.44;
5.43

The four thousand fed (8.1–10; Mt 15.32–39)

8 In those days, when again a great crowd had gathered, and they had nothing to eat, he called his disciples to him, and said to them, 2 "I have compassion on the crowd, because they have been with me now three days, and have nothing to eat; 3 and if I send them away hungry to their homes, they will faint on the way; and some of them have come a long way." 4And his disciples answered him, "How can one feed these men with bread here in the desert?" 5And he asked them, "How many loaves have you?" They said, "Seven." 6And he commanded the crowd to sit down on the ground; and he took the seven loaves, and having given thanks he broke them and gave them to his disciples to set before the people; and they set them before the crowd. 7And they had a few small

8.2
Mt 9.36

8.5
Mk 6.38

8.7
Mt 14.19;
Mk 6.41;

[b] Or is evacuated　[c] Other ancient authorities omit and Sidon

fish; and having blessed them, he commanded that these also should be set before them. 8And they ate, and were satisfied; and they took up the broken pieces left over, seven baskets full. 9And

★8.10

there were about four thousand people. 10And he sent them away; and immediately he got into the boat with his disciples, and went to the district of Dălmănu'thá.*d*

The Pharisees seek a sign from heaven (8.11–21; Mt 16.1–10)

8.11
Mt 12.38,
39;
Lk 11.29;
Jn 6.30

8.12
Mk 7.34

11 The Phạr'ịsee̦s came and began to argue with him, seeking from him a sign from heaven, to test him. 12And he sighed deeply in his spirit, and said, "Why does this generation seek a sign? Truly, I say to you, no sign shall be given to this generation." 13And he left them, and getting into the boat again he departed to the other side.

8.15
Lk 12.1;
Mk 16.4;
12.13

8.17
Mk 6.52;
Isa 6.9,10

14 Now they had forgotten to bring bread; and they had only one loaf with them in the boat. 15And he cautioned them, saying, "Take heed, beware of the leaven of the Phạr'ịsee̦s and the leaven of Hěród."*e* 16And they discussed it with one another, saying, "We have no bread." 17And being aware of it, Jesus said to them, "Why do you discuss the fact that you have no bread? Do you not yet perceive or understand? Are your hearts hardened?

8.19
Mt 14.20;
Mk 6.43;
Lk 9.17;
Jn 6.13

8.20
ver 6–9;
Mt 15.37

8.21
Mk 6.52

18 Having eyes do you not see, and having ears do you not hear? And do you not remember? 19 When I broke the five loaves for the five thousand, how many baskets full of broken pieces did you take up?" They said to him, "Twelve." 20 "And the seven for the four thousand, how many baskets full of broken pieces did you take up?" And they said to him, "Seven." 21And he said to them, "Do you not yet understand?"

The blind man healed near Bethsaida (8.22–26)

8.22
Mt 11.21;
Mk 6.45;
Lk 9.10

8.23
Mk 7.33;
5.23

8.26
Mt 8.4

22 And they came to Běth-sā'ịdá. And some people brought to him a blind man, and begged him to touch him. 23And he took the blind man by the hand, and led him out of the village; and when he had spit on his eyes and laid his hands upon him, he asked him, "Do you see anything?" 24And he looked up and said, "I see men; but they look like trees, walking." 25 Then again he laid his hands upon his eyes; and he looked intently and was restored, and saw everything clearly. 26And he sent him away to his home, saying, "Do not even enter the village."

Peter's confession (8.27–30; Mt 16.13–20; Lk 9.18–21)

8.27
Jn 6.66–69

8.28
Mk 6.14

27 And Jesus went on with his disciples, to the villages of Çaěsărē'á Phil'ịppi; and on the way he asked his disciples, "Who do men say that I am?" 28And they told him, "John the Baptist;

d Other ancient authorities read *Măg'ădăn* or *Măg'dálá*
e Other ancient authorities read *the Hěró'diánș*

8.10 This place has not been identified. As the RSV footnote says, some manuscripts of Mark have "Magdala," a town on the west side of the Sea of Galilee; other manuscripts (like the parallel passage in Mt 15.39) have *Magadan*, which is possibly the town of Megiddo, more than twenty miles distant from the Sea of Galilee. It is suggested that the same locality may have been known by two or three different names.

and others say, Ĕlī′jăh; and others one of the prophets." 29And he asked them, "But who do you say that I am?" Peter answered him, "You are the Christ." 30And he charged them to tell no one about him.

Jesus foretells his death, resurrection, and second coming (8.31–9.1; Mt 16.21–28; Lk 9.22–27)

31 And he began to teach them that the Son of man must suffer many things, and be rejected by the elders and the chief priests and the scribes, and be killed, and after three days rise again. 32And he said this plainly. And Peter took him, and began to rebuke him. 33 But turning and seeing his disciples, he rebuked Peter, and said, "Get behind me, Satan! For you are not on the side of God, but of men."

34 And he called to him the multitude with his disciples, and said to them, "If any man would come after me, let him deny himself and take up his cross and follow me. 35 For whoever would save his life will lose it; and whoever loses his life for my sake and the gospel's will save it. 36 For what does it profit a man, to gain the whole world and forfeit his life? 37 For what can a man give in return for his life? 38 For whoever is ashamed of me and of my words in this adulterous and sinful generation, of him will the Son of man also be ashamed, when he comes in the glory of his Father 9 with the holy angels." 1And he said to them, "Truly, I say to you, there are some standing here who will not taste death before they see that the kingdom of God has come with power."

The Transfiguration (9.2–13; Mt 17.1–8; Lk 9.28–36)

2 And after six days Jesus took with him Peter and James and John, and led them up a high mountain apart by themselves; and he was transfigured before them, 3 and his garments became glistening, intensely white, as no fuller on earth could bleach them. 4And there appeared to them Ĕlī′jăh with Moses; and they were talking to Jesus. 5And Peter said to Jesus, "Master,ᶠ it is well that we are here; let us make three booths, one for you and one for Moses and one for Ĕlī′jăh." 6 For he did not know what to say, for they were exceedingly afraid. 7And a cloud overshadowed them, and a voice came out of the cloud, "This is my beloved Son;ᵍ listen to him." 8And suddenly looking around they no longer saw any one with them but Jesus only.

ᶠ Or Rabbi ᵍ Or my Son, my (or the) Beloved

8.29 See note to Mt 16.18 for clarification.
9.2 The Transfiguration of Christ is recorded by Matthew, Mark, and Luke. The accounts supplement each other somewhat, for no single one supplies all the details. Most scholars today believe that the event occurred on Mt. Hermon. Christ called it a vision (Greek *horama*, Mt 17.9) but this does not imply that it was unreal. The clear indication is that Moses and Elijah were actually there in person, since it is said that the three disciples saw the two (Lk 9.32). This solemn interview and donning of the garments of heavenly radiance were intended as a foretaste of Christ's glory. The disciples were greatly strengthened in their faith, as they heard the voice from the cloud declare, *"This is my beloved Son; listen to him"* (ver 7). When Moses and Elijah were suddenly removed from the scene to leave *Jesus only*, the disciples were shown that in Him the Old Testament law and prophecy were fulfilled. Peter always remembered this episode as an event of deep significance and was careful to remind his readers that he was an actual eyewitness of *his majesty* (2 Pet 1.16–18).

9 And as they were coming down the mountain, he charged them to tell no one what they had seen, until the Son of man should have risen from the dead. 10 So they kept the matter to themselves, questioning what the rising from the dead meant. 11And they asked him, "Why do the scribes say that first Ĕlī′jah must come?" 12And he said to them, "Ĕlī′jah does come first to restore all things; and how is it written of the Son of man, that he should suffer many things and be treated with contempt? 13 But I tell you that Ĕlī′jah has come, and they did to him whatever they pleased, as it is written of him."

The demoniac boy cured (9.14–29; Mt 17.14–21; Lk 9.37–43)

14 And when they came to the disciples, they saw a great crowd about them, and scribes arguing with them. 15And immediately all the crowd, when they saw him, were greatly amazed, and ran up to him and greeted him. 16And he asked them, "What are you discussing with them?" 17And one of the crowd answered him, "Teacher, I brought my son to you, for he has a dumb spirit; 18 and wherever it seizes him, it dashes him down; and he foams and grinds his teeth and becomes rigid; and I asked your disciples to cast it out, and they were not able." 19And he answered them, "O faithless generation, how long am I to be with you? How long am I to bear with you? Bring him to me." 20And they brought the boy to him; and when the spirit saw him, immediately it convulsed the boy, and he fell on the ground and rolled about, foaming at the mouth. 21And Jesus[h] asked his father, "How long has he had this?" And he said, "From childhood. 22And it has often cast him into the fire and into the water, to destroy him; but if you can do anything, have pity on us and help us." 23And Jesus said to him, "If you can! All things are possible to him who believes." 24 Immediately the father of the child cried out[i] and said, "I believe; help my unbelief!" 25And when Jesus saw that a crowd came running together, he rebuked the unclean spirit, saying to it, "You dumb and deaf spirit, I command you, come out of him, and never enter him again." 26And after crying out and convulsing him terribly, it came out, and the boy was like a corpse; so that most of them said, "He is dead." 27 But Jesus took him by the hand and lifted him up, and he arose. 28And when he had entered the house, his disciples asked him privately, "Why could we not cast it out?" 29And he said to them, "This kind cannot be driven out by anything but prayer."[j]

h Greek he
i Other ancient authorities add with tears
j Other ancient authorities add and fasting

Cross references
9.9 Mk 5.43; 7.36; 8.30
*9.11 Mt 11.14
9.12 Ps 22.6; Lk 23.11; Phil 2.7
9.13 Mt 11.14; Lk 1.17
9.15 Mk 14.33; 16.5,6
9.20 Mk 1.26
*9.23 Mk 11.23; Lk 17.6; Jn 11.40
9.25 ver 15
9.28 Mk 7.17

9.11 See note to Mal 4.5 on Elijah.

9.23 This statement of Jesus has been misconstrued by well-meaning believers who accept it as an unqualified promise. Believing faith must be based on evidences of the will of God. That which is asked for personal desires or passions (Jas 4.3) is asked amiss and therefore cannot be asked in faith (i.e., in faith that such self-seeking requests are truly the will of God). For a believer to ask God to change the color of his skin, for example, or his sex, or to restore his youth when he is old hardly falls within the purview of this promise. Nor does it imply that deliverance from death is always God's will either, since other Scripture indicates that it is *appointed for men to die once* (Heb 9.27). Unbroken or continued physical existence is not the will of God. But faith which is impelled by a sincere desire for God's glory and is based upon a known promise of Scripture or upon an inward assurance generated by the Holy Spirit, will surely be rewarded with a divine answer.

Jesus again foretells his death and resurrection
(9.30–32; Mt 17.22–23; Lk 9.43–45)

30 They went on from there and passed through Găl'ĭleē. And he would not have any one know it; 31 for he was teaching his disciples, saying to them, "The Son of man will be delivered into the hands of men, and they will kill him; and when he is killed, after three days he will rise." 32 But they did not understand the saying, and they were afraid to ask him.

9.31
Mt 16.21;
Mk 8.31

9.32
Jn 12.16

Discourse on humility (9.33–50; Mt 18.1–5; Lk 9.46–48)

33 And they came to Cápēr'nä-ùm; and when he was in the house he asked them, "What were you discussing on the way?" 34 But they were silent; for on the way they had discussed with one another who was the greatest. 35 And he sat down and called the twelve; and he said to them, "If any one would be first, he must be last of all and servant of all." 36 And he took a child, and put him in the midst of them; and taking him in his arms, he said to them, 37 "Whoever receives one such child in my name receives me; and whoever receives me, receives not me but him who sent me."

9.34
Lk 22.24
9.35
Mt 20.26,
27;
Mk 10.43;
Lk 22.26
9.36
Mk 10.16
9.37
Mt 10.40;
Jn 12.44;
13.20

38 John said to him, "Teacher, we saw a man casting out demons in your name,ᵏ and we forbade him, because he was not following us." 39 But Jesus said, "Do not forbid him; for no one who does a mighty work in my name will be able soon after to speak evil of me. 40 For he that is not against us is for us. 41 For truly, I say to you, whoever gives you a cup of water to drink because you bear the name of Christ, will by no means lose his reward.

★9.38
Num
11.27–29
9.40
Mt 12.30
9.41
Mt 10.42

42 "Whoever causes one of these little ones who believe in me to sin,ˡ it would be better for him if a great millstone were hung round his neck and he were thrown into the sea. 43 And if your hand causes you to sin,ˡ cut it off; it is better for you to enter life maimed than with two hands to go to hell,ᵐ to the unquenchable fire.ⁿ 45 And if your foot causes you to sin,ˡ cut it off; it is better for you to enter life lame than with two feet to be thrown into hell.ᵐ,ⁿ 47 And if your eye causes you to sin,ˡ pluck it out; it is better for you to enter the kingdom of God with one eye than with two eyes to be thrown into hell,ᵐ 48 where their worm does not die, and the fire is not quenched. 49 For every one will be salted with fire.º 50 Salt is good; but if the salt has lost its saltness, how will you season it? Have salt in yourselves, and be at peace with one another."

9.42
Lk 17.1,2;
1 Cor 8.12
★9.43
Mt 5.29,30;
5.22; 25.41
9.45
Mt 5.22
9.47
Mt 5.29
9.48
Isa 66.24
★9.49
Lev 2.13
9.50
Mt 5.13;
Lk 14.34,
35;
Col 4.6;
Rom 12.18;
2 Cor
13.11;
1 Thess 5.13

ᵏ Other ancient authorities add *who does not follow us* ˡ Greek *stumble* ᵐ Greek *Gĕhĕn'nä* ⁿ Verses 44 and 46 (which are identical with verse 48) are omitted by the best ancient authorities º Other ancient authorities add *and every sacrifice will be salted with salt*

9.38 The disciples here fell into the sin of sectarianism. They forbade the man to perform miracles in Christ's name simply because he was not a member of their particular group. Jesus rebuked them for this attitude—an attitude which has been prevalent in the church since then, and which calls for rebuke.
9.43 See here the note to Mt 5.29.
9.49 At least fifteen different explanations

of the meaning of this verse have been proposed. Most commentators see an allusion to Lev 2.13, which contains instructions on seasoning the cereal offerings with the salt of the covenant. Salt generally represents preservation, or dedication, while fire is often used as a figure for purification. Moffatt translates this verse, "Everyone has to be consecrated by the fire of the discipline."

Jesus goes to Judea (10.1)

10.1
Mt 19.1;
Jn 10.40;
11.7

10 And he left there and went to the region of Judē´ā and beyond the Jordan, and crowds gathered to him again; and again, as his custom was, he taught them.

Jesus teaches about marriage (10.2–12; Mt 19.3–12)

2 And Phar´isees came up and in order to test him asked, "Is it lawful for a man to divorce his wife?" 3 He answered them, "What did Moses command you?" 4 They said, "Moses allowed a man to write a certificate of divorce, and to put her away." 5 But Jesus said to them, "For your hardness of heart he wrote you this commandment. 6 But from the beginning of creation, 'God made them male and female.' 7 'For this reason a man shall leave his father and mother and be joined to his wife,*p* 8 and the two shall become one flesh.' So they are no longer two but one flesh. 9 What therefore God has joined together, let not man put asunder."

10.4
Deut 24.1–
4;
Mt 5.31;
19.7
★10.5
10.6
Gen 1.27;
5.2
10.7
Gen 2.24;
1 Cor 6.16

10 And in the house the disciples asked him again about this matter. 11 And he said to them, "Whoever divorces his wife and marries another, commits adultery against her; 12 and if she divorces her husband and marries another, she commits adultery."

★10.11
Mt 5.32;
Lk 16.18;
Rom 7.3;
1 Cor 7.10,
11

Jesus blesses little children (10.13–16; Mt 19.13–15; Lk 18.15–17)

13 And they were bringing children to him, that he might touch them; and the disciples rebuked them. 14 But when Jesus saw it he was indignant, and said to them, "Let the children come to me, do not hinder them; for to such belongs the kingdom of God. 15 Truly, I say to you, whoever does not receive the kingdom of God like a child shall not enter it." 16 And he took them in his arms and blessed them, laying his hands upon them.

10.15
Mt 18.3;
1 Cor
14.20;
1 Pet 2.2
10.16
Mk 9.36

The rich young ruler: the peril of riches (10.17–31; Mt 19.16–30; Lk 18.18–30)

17 And as he was setting out on his journey, a man ran up and knelt before him, and asked him, "Good Teacher, what must I do to inherit eternal life?" 18 And Jesus said to him, "Why do you call me good? No one is good but God alone. 19 You know the commandments: 'Do not kill, Do not commit adultery, Do not steal, Do not bear false witness, Do not defraud, Honor your father and mother.'" 20 And he said to him, "Teacher, all these I have observed from my youth." 21 And Jesus looking upon him loved him, and said to him, "You lack one thing; go, sell what you have, and give to the poor, and you will have treasure in heaven; and come, follow me." 22 At that saying his countenance fell, and he went away sorrowful; for he had great possessions.

23 And Jesus looked around and said to his disciples, "How hard it will be for those who have riches to enter the kingdom of God!" 24 And the disciples were amazed at his words. But Jesus

10.17
Mk 1.40;
Lk 10.25;
Eph 1.18
10.19
Ex 20.12–
16;
Deut 5.16–
20
10.21
Mt 6.20;
Lk 12.33;
Acts 2.35;
4.34,35
10.23
Mt 19.23;
Lk 18.24
10.24
Ps 52.7;
62.10;
1 Tim 6.17

p Other ancient authorities omit *and be joined to his wife*

10.5 See note to Mt 19.3 on divorce.   **10.11** See note to Mt 5.27 on adultery.

said to them again, "Children, how hard it is[r] to enter the kingdom of God! 25 It is easier for a camel to go through the eye of a needle than for a rich man to enter the kingdom of God." 26And they were exceedingly astonished, and said to him,[s] "Then who can be saved?" 27 Jesus looked at them and said, "With men it is impossible, but not with God; for all things are possible with God." 28 Peter began to say to him, "Lo, we have left everything and followed you." 29 Jesus said, "Truly, I say to you, there is no one who has left house or brothers or sisters or mother or father or children or lands, for my sake and for the gospel, 30 who will not receive a hundredfold now in this time, houses and brothers and sisters and mothers and children and lands, with persecutions, and in the age to come eternal life. 31 But many that are first will be last, and the last first."

Christ foretells his crucifixion and resurrection
(10.32–34; Mt 20.17–19; Lk 18.31–34)

32 And they were on the road, going up to Jerusalem, and Jesus was walking ahead of them; and they were amazed, and those who followed were afraid. And taking the twelve again, he began to tell them what was to happen to him, 33 saying, "Behold, we are going up to Jerusalem; and the Son of man will be delivered to the chief priests and the scribes, and they will condemn him to death, and deliver him to the Gentiles; 34 and they will mock him, and spit upon him, and scourge him, and kill him; and after three days he will rise."

Ambition of James and John (10.35–45; Mt 20.20–28)

35 And James and John, the sons of Zĕb′ĕdeē, came forward to him, and said to him, "Teacher, we want you to do for us whatever we ask of you." 36And he said to them, "What do you want me to do for you?" 37And they said to him, "Grant us to sit, one at your right hand and one at your left, in your glory." 38 But Jesus said to them, "You do not know what you are asking. Are you able to drink the cup that I drink, or to be baptized with the baptism with which I am baptized?" 39And they said to him, "We are able." And Jesus said to them, "The cup that I drink you will drink; and with the baptism with which I am baptized, you will be baptized; 40 but to sit at my right hand or at my left is not mine to grant, but it is for those for whom it has been prepared." 41And when the ten heard it, they began to be indignant at James and John. 42And Jesus called them to him and said to them, "You know that those who are supposed to rule over the Gentiles lord it over them, and their great men exercise authority over them. 43 But it shall not be so among you; but whoever would be great among you must be your servant, 44 and whoever would be first among you must be slave of all. 45 For the Son of man also came not to be served but to serve, and to give his life as a ransom for many."

[r] Other ancient authorities add *for those who trust in riches*
[s] Other ancient authorities read *to one another*

10.25 *eye of a needle*, probably a narrow gate through which it was difficult for a camel to pass. Riches often are a hindrance which keep men from the kingdom of God.

Marginal references:

*10.25

10.27
Jer 32.17
10.28
Mt 4.20–22
10.29
Mt 6.33

10.31
Mt 20.16;
Lk 13.30

10.32
Mk 8.31;
9.31;
Lk 9.22

10.34
Mt 26.67;
27.30;
Mk 14.65

10.37
Mt 19.28;
Lk 22.30
10.38
Lk 12.50;
Jn 18.11
10.39
Acts 12.2;
Rev 1.9;
10.41;
Lk 22.25–27

10.43
Mt 9.35

10.45
Jn 13.14;
1 Tim 2.5,6

Bartimaeus receives his sight
(10.46–52; Mt 20.29–34; Lk 18.35–43)

10.47
Mt 9.27

46 And they came to Jĕr′ĭchō; and as he was leaving Jericho with his disciples and a great multitude, Bartĭmaē′ŭs, a blind beggar, the son of Tĭmaē′ŭs, was sitting by the roadside. 47And when he heard that it was Jesus of Năz′ărĕth, he began to cry out and say, "Jesus, Son of David, have mercy on me!" 48And many rebuked him, telling him to be silent; but he cried out all the more, "Son of David, have mercy on me!" 49And Jesus stopped and said, "Call him." And they called the blind man, saying to him, "Take heart; rise, he is calling you." 50And throwing off his mantle he sprang up and came to Jesus. 51And Jesus said to him, "What do you want me to do for you?" And the blind man said to him, "Master,ᵗ let me receive my sight." 52And Jesus said to him, "Go your way; your faith has made you well." And immediately he received his sight and followed him on the way.

10.51
Jn 20.16;
Mt 23.7
10.52
Mt 9.22;
Mk 5.34;
Lk 7.50;
8.48;17.19

The triumphal entry
(11.1–11; Mt 21.1–11; Lk 19.29–44; Jn 12.12–19)

*11.1
Mt 21.17

11 And when they drew near to Jerusalem to Bĕth′phăgē and Bĕth′ănў, at the Mount of Olives, he sent two of his disciples, 2 and said to them, "Go into the village opposite you, and immediately as you enter it you will find a colt tied, on which no one has ever sat; untie it and bring it. 3 If any one says to you, 'Why are you doing this?' say, 'The Lord has need of it and will send it back here immediately.' " 4And they went away, and found a colt tied at the door out in the open street; and they untied it. 5And those who stood there said to them, "What are you doing, untying the colt?" 6And they told them what Jesus had said; and they let them go. 7And they brought the colt to Jesus, and threw their garments on it; and he sat upon it. 8And many spread their garments on the road, and others spread leafy branches which they had cut from the fields. 9And those who went before and those who followed cried out, "Hosanna! Blessed is he who comes in the name of the Lord! 10 Blessed is the kingdom of our father David that is coming! Hosanna in the highest!"

11.4
Mk 14.16

11.9
Ps 118.26;
Mt 23.39

11 And he entered Jerusalem, and went into the temple; and when he had looked round at everything, as it was already late, he went out to Bĕth′ănў with the twelve.

11.11
Mt 21.10,
11,17

The barren fig tree
(11.12–14,20–25; Mt 21.18–22)

11.12
Lk 13.6–9

12 On the following day, when they came from Bĕth′ănў, he was hungry. 13And seeing in the distance a fig tree in leaf, he went to see if he could find anything on it. When he came to it, he found nothing but leaves, for it was not the season for figs. 14And he said

ᵗ Or Rabbi

11.1 Bethany was a village some two miles southeast of Jerusalem (Jn 11.18), the home of Lazarus and his sisters Martha and Mary (Jn 11.1). Bethphage was closer to Jerusalem, probably less than a mile away, somewhat like a suburb of the city.

to it, "May no one ever eat fruit from you again." And his disciples heard it.

Second cleansing of the Temple
(11.15–19; Mt 21.12–17; Lk 19.45–48; cf. Jn 2.13–22)

15 And they came to Jerusalem. And he entered the temple and began to drive out those who sold and those who bought in the temple, and he overturned the tables of the money-changers and the seats of those who sold pigeons; 16 and he would not allow any one to carry anything through the temple. 17And he taught, and said to them, "Is it not written, 'My house shall be called a house of prayer for all the nations'? But you have made it a den of robbers." 18And the chief priests and the scribes heard it and sought a way to destroy him; for they feared him, because all the multitude was astonished at his teaching. 19And when evening came they[u] went out of the city.

*11.17
Isa 56.7;
Jer 7.11

11.18
Mt 21.46;
7.28;
Mk 1.22;
Lk 4.32

The power of faith (11.20–25; note w)

20 As they passed by in the morning, they saw the fig tree withered away to its roots. 21And Peter remembered and said to him, "Master,[v] look! The fig tree which you cursed has withered." 22And Jesus answered them, "Have faith in God. 23 Truly, I say to you, whoever says to this mountain, 'Be taken up and cast into the sea,' and does not doubt in his heart, but believes that what he says will come to pass, it will be done for him. 24 Therefore I tell you, whatever you ask in prayer, believe that you have received[a] it, and it will be yours. 25And whenever you stand praying, forgive, if you have anything against any one; so that your Father also who is in heaven may forgive you your trespasses."[w]

11.20
Mt 21.19
11.21
Mt 23.7
11.22
Mt 17.20
11.23
Mt 21.21;
Lk 17.6
*11.24
Mt 7.7;
Jn 14.13,14;
15.7;
16.23,24;
Jas 1.5,6
11.25
Mt 6.14,15;
Col 3.13

Christ's authority challenged
(11.27–33; Mt 21.23–27; Lk 20.1–8)

27 And they came again to Jerusalem. And as he was walking in the temple, the chief priests and the scribes and the elders came to him, 28 and they said to him, "By what authority are you doing these things, or who gave you this authority to do them?" 29 Jesus said to them, "I will ask you a question; answer me, and I will tell you by what authority I do these things. 30 Was the baptism of John from heaven or from men? Answer me." 31And they argued with one another, "If we say, 'From heaven,' he will say, 'Why

---

[u] Other ancient authorities read he   [v] Or Rabbi
[a] Other ancient authorities read are receiving
[w] Other ancient authorities add verse 26, "But if you do not forgive, neither will your Father who is in heaven forgive your trespasses"

11.17 For the convenience of those who came to the Temple during the great national feasts, the animal vendors provided sacrificial animals which would meet the proper requirements of ritual cleanliness and soundness, while the money-changers exchanged the foreign currency of the Jews of the Dispersion into the proper half-shekel coin required for payment of the annual Temple tax. All this traffic took place in the court of the Gentiles where non-Jews were allowed to come in order to participate in the Temple worship of the Jews. The traders were converting God's house into a bazaar, making it impossible for devout Gentiles to worship in the Temple, thus voiding the words of Isa 56.7, quoted by Jesus, that God's house was a house of prayer for all the nations.

11.24 See note to Lk 11.1 on principles of prayer.

11.32
Mt 14.5
then did you not believe him?' 32 But shall we say, 'From men'?"
—they were afraid of the people, for all held that John was a real
prophet. 33 So they answered Jesus, "We do not know." And Jesus
said to them, "Neither will I tell you by what authority I do
these things."

Parable of the wicked tenants
(12.1–12; Mt 21.33–46; Lk 20.9–19)

*12.1
Isa 5.1–7
12 And he began to speak to them in parables. "A man planted
a vineyard, and set a hedge around it, and dug a pit for the
wine press, and built a tower, and let it out to tenants, and went
into another country. 2 When the time came, he sent a servant to
the tenants, to get from them some of the fruit of the vineyard.
3And they took him and beat him, and sent him away empty-
handed. 4Again he sent to them another servant, and they
wounded him in the head, and treated him shamefully. 5And he
sent another, and him they killed; and so with many others, some
12.6
cf. Heb 1.1–
3
they beat and some they killed. 6 He had still one other, a beloved
son; finally he sent him to them, saying, 'They will respect my
son.' 7 But those tenants said to one another, 'This is the heir;
come, let us kill him, and the inheritance will be ours.' 8And they
took him and killed him, and cast him out of the vineyard. 9 What
will the owner of the vineyard do? He will come and destroy the
12.10
Ps 118.22,
23;
Acts 4.11;
1 Pet 2.7
tenants, and give the vineyard to others. 10 Have you not read this
scripture:
'The very stone which the builders rejected
    has become the head of the corner;
11 this was the Lord's doing,
    and it is marvelous in our eyes'?"
12.12
Mt 21.45,
46;
Mk 11.18;
Mt 22.22
12 And they tried to arrest him, but feared the multitude, for
they perceived that he had told the parable against them; so they
left him and went away.

Three questions by the Jewish rulers (12.13–34)

1. Paying taxes to Caesar
(12.13–17; Mt 22.15–22; Lk 20.20–26)

*12.13
Mk 3.6;
Lk 11.54
13 And they sent to him some of the Phạr′ịseẹṣ and some of the
Hërō′dĭ-ảnṣ, to entrap him in his talk. 14And they came and said
to him, "Teacher, we know that you are true, and care for no man;
for you do not regard the position of men, but truly teach the way
of God. Is it lawful to pay taxes to Caesar, or not? 15 Should we pay
them, or should we not?" But knowing their hypocrisy, he said to
them, "Why put me to the test? Bring me a coin,x and let me look
at it." 16And they brought one. And he said to them, "Whose likeness and inscription is this?" They said to him, "Caesar's."
12.17
Rom 13.7
17 Jesus said to them, "Render to Caesar the things that are Caesar's, and to God the things that are God's." And they were
amazed at him.

x Greek a denarius

12.1 See note to Lk 20.9 on the parable of
the wicked tenants.

12.13 See note to Mt 22.16 for information on the Herodians.

2. *The Sadducees and the resurrection*
(12.18–27; Mt 22.23–33; Lk 20.27–38)

18 And Săd′dụçẹẹṣ came to him, who say that there is no resurrection; and they asked him a question, saying, 19 "Teacher, Moses wrote for us that if a man's brother dies and leaves a wife, but leaves no child, the man*y* must take the wife, and raise up children for his brother. 20 There were seven brothers; the first took a wife, and when he died left no children; 21 and the second took her, and died, leaving no children; and the third likewise; 22 and the seven left no children. Last of all the woman also died. 23 In the resurrection whose wife will she be? For the seven had her as wife."

24 Jesus said to them, "Is not this why you are wrong, that you know neither the scriptures nor the power of God? 25 For when they rise from the dead, they neither marry nor are given in marriage, but are like angels in heaven. 26And as for the dead being raised, have you not read in the book of Moses, in the passage about the bush, how God said to him, 'I am the God of Abraham, and the God of Isaac, and the God of Jacob'? 27 He is not God of the dead, but of the living; you are quite wrong."

3. *The great commandment (12.28–34; Mt 22.34–40)*

28 And one of the scribes came up and heard them disputing with one another, and seeing that he answered them well, asked him, "Which commandment is the first of all?" 29 Jesus answered, "The first is, 'Hear, O Israel: The Lord our God, the Lord is one; 30 and you shall love the Lord your God with all your heart, and with all your soul, and with all your mind, and with all your strength.' 31 The second is this, 'You shall love your neighbor as yourself.' There is no other commandment greater than these." 32And the scribe said to him, "You are right, Teacher; you have truly said that he is one, and there is no other but he; 33 and to love him with all the heart, and with all the understanding, and with all the strength, and to love one's neighbor as oneself, is much more than all whole burnt offerings and sacrifices." 34And when Jesus saw that he answered wisely, he said to him, "You are not far from the kingdom of God." And after that no one dared to ask him any question.

Christ's unanswerable question
(12.35–37; Mt 22.41–46; Lk 20.41–44)

35 And as Jesus taught in the temple, he said, "How can the scribes say that the Christ is the son of David? 36 David himself, inspired by*z* the Holy Spirit, declared,
'The Lord said to my Lord,

y Greek *his brother*   *z* Or *himself, in*

12.19	Deut 25.5
12.25	1 Cor 15.42, 49,52
12.26	Ex 3.6
*12.28	Lk 10.25–28; 20.39
12.29	Deut 6.4
12.31	Lev 19.18; Rom 13.9; Gal 5.14; Jas 2.8
12.32	Deut 4.39; Isa 45.6,14; 46.9
12.33	1 Sam 15.22; Hos 6.6; Mic 6.6–8
12.34	Mt 22.46
12.35	Mt 26.55; 9.27
12.36	Ps 110.1; Acts 2.34, 35; Heb 1.13

12.28 For a discussion of scribes in the Old Testament see 2 Sam 8.17. In Jesus' day the scribes were characterized both by their activities and their attitudes. Of them Scripture says: (1) they were often Pharisees (Acts 23.9); (2) they were doctors of the Old Testament law (check Mt 22.35 with Mk 12.28); (3) they were looked upon as experts in the Old Testament Scriptures (Mt 2.4; 17.10; Mk 12.35); (4) they suffered from the sin of pride (12.38, 39); (5) they sat on Moses' seat (Mt 23.2); (6) they were condemned by Christ (Mt 23.15); (7) they helped to secure Christ's crucifixion (Lk 23.10); (8) they actively persecuted the believers (Acts 4.5, 18, 21; 6.12).

Sit at my right hand,
till I put thy enemies under thy feet.'

12.37
Jn 12.9
37 David himself calls him Lord; so how is he his son?" And the great throng heard him gladly.

Jesus' warning against the scribes
(12.38–40; Mt 23.1–12; Lk 20.45–47)

12.38
Lk 11.43
38 And in his teaching he said, "Beware of the scribes, who like to go about in long robes, and to have salutations in the market places 39 and the best seats in the synagogues and the places of honor at feasts, 40 who devour widows' houses and for a pretense make long prayers. They will receive the greater condemnation."

The widow's penny (12.41–44)

12.41
Jn 8.20;
2 Ki 12.9
*12.42
12.43
2 Cor 8.12
41 And he sat down opposite the treasury, and watched the multitude putting money into the treasury. Many rich people put in large sums. 42And a poor widow came, and put in two copper coins, which make a penny. 43And he called his disciples to him, and said to them, "Truly, I say to you, this poor widow has put in more than all those who are contributing to the treasury. 44 For they all contributed out of their abundance; but she out of her poverty has put in everything she had, her whole living."

The Olivet Discourse (13.1–37; Mt ch 24; Lk ch 21)
1. Course of the present age (13.1–13; Mt 24.1–14; Lk 21.5–19)

13 And as he came out of the temple, one of his disciples said to him, "Look, Teacher, what wonderful stones and what

13.2
Lk 19.44;
Mk 14.58;
15.29;
Acts 6.14
13.3
Mk 5.37;
9.2
*13.4
13.5
Eph 5.6;
1 Thess 2.3
13.6
Jn 8.24
wonderful buildings!" 2And Jesus said to him, "Do you see these great buildings? There will not be left here one stone upon another, that will not be thrown down."

3 And as he sat on the Mount of Olives opposite the temple, Peter and James and John and Andrew asked him privately, 4 "Tell us, when will this be, and what will be the sign when these things are all to be accomplished?" 5And Jesus began to say to them, "Take heed that no one leads you astray. 6 Many will come in my name, saying, 'I am he!' and they will lead many astray. 7And when you hear of wars and rumors of wars, do not be alarmed; this must take place, but the end is not yet. 8 For nation will rise against nation, and kingdom against kingdom; there will be earthquakes in various places, there will be famines; this is but the beginning of the birth-pangs.

13.9
Mt 10.17
9 "But take heed to yourselves; for they will deliver you up to councils; and you will be beaten in synagogues; and you will stand before governors and kings for my sake, to bear testimony before

13.11
Mt 10.19;
Lk 12.11
13.12
Mic 7.6;
Mt 10.21
them. 10And the gospel must first be preached to all nations. 11And when they bring you to trial and deliver you up, do not be anxious beforehand what you are to say; but say whatever is given you in that hour, for it is not you who speak, but the Holy Spirit. 12And brother will deliver up brother to death, and the father his child,

---

12.42 Scripture always treats widows sympathetically.

13.4 See note to Mt 24.3 for information on The Olivet Discourse.

and children will rise against parents and have them put to death; 13 and you will be hated by all for my name's sake. But he who endures to the end will be saved.

2. *The great tribulation (13.14–23; Mt 24.15–28; Lk 21.20–24)*

14 "But when you see the desolating sacrilege set up where it ought not to be (let the reader understand), then let those who are in Judeʹa flee to the mountains; 15 let him who is on the housetop not go down, nor enter his house, to take anything away; 16 and let him who is in the field not turn back to take his mantle. 17And alas for those who are with child and for those who give suck in those days! 18 Pray that it may not happen in winter. 19 For in those days there will be such tribulation as has not been from the beginning of the creation which God created until now, and never will be. 20And if the Lord had not shortened the days, no human being would be saved; but for the sake of the elect, whom he chose, he shortened the days. 21And then if any one says to you, 'Look, here is the Christ!' or 'Look, there he is!' do not believe it. 22 False Christs and false prophets will arise and show signs and wonders, to lead astray, if possible, the elect. 23 But take heed; I have told you all things beforehand.

3. *The Second Advent of Christ*
 (13.24–27; Mt 24.29–31; Lk 21.25–28)

24 "But in those days, after that tribulation, the sun will be darkened, and the moon will not give its light, 25 and the stars will be falling from heaven, and the powers in the heavens will be shaken. 26And then they will see the Son of man coming in clouds with great power and glory. 27And then he will send out the angels, and gather his elect from the four winds, from the ends of the earth to the ends of heaven.

4. *The parable of the fig tree*
 (13.28–31; Mt 24.32–35; Lk 21.29–33)

28 "From the fig tree learn its lesson: as soon as its branch becomes tender and puts forth its leaves, you know that summer is near. 29 So also, when you see these things taking place, you know that he is near, at the very gates. 30 Truly, I say to you, this generation will not pass away before all these things take place. 31 Heaven and earth will pass away, but my words will not pass away.

5. *Watchfulness (13.32–37; Mt 24.32–35; Lk 21.29–33)*

32 "But of that day or that hour no one knows, not even the angels in heaven, nor the Son, but only the Father. 33 Take heed, watch;[a] for you do not know when the time will come. 34 It is like a man going on a journey, when he leaves home and puts his servants in charge, each with his work, and commands the doorkeeper to be on the watch. 35 Watch therefore—for you do not

---

[a] Other ancient authorities add *and pray*

13.14 See note to Dan 9.27 on the abomination of desolation.

13.27 *from the four winds* means "from every direction," "from the four points of the compass." *from the ends of the earth to the ends of heaven* probably means "from one end of the world to the other," i.e., from the whole earth. This saying seems to combine two Old Testament phrases: "from the one end of the earth to the other" (cf. Deut 13.7), and "from one end of heaven to the other" (cf. Deut 4.32).

Marginal references:

13.13 Jn 15.21; Mt 10.22; Rev 2.10

★13.14 Dan 9.27; 11.31; 12.11

13.17 Lk 23.29

13.19 Dan 9.26; 12.1; Joel 2.2

13.21 Lk 17.23; 21.8

13.22 Mt 7.15; Jn 4.48

13.23 2 Pet 3.17

13.24 Zeph 1.15

13.26 Dan 7.13; Mt 16.27; Mk 14.62; 1 Thess 4.16; 2 Thess 1.7,10

★13.27

13.30 Mk 9.1

13.31 Mt 5.18; Lk 16.17

13.32 Acts 1.7

13.33 Eph 6.18; Col 4.2; 1 Thess 5.6

13.34 Mt 25.14

13.35 Lk 12.35–40

*13.37

know when the master of the house will come, in the evening, or at midnight, or at cockcrow, or in the morning—36 lest he come suddenly and find you asleep. 37And what I say to you I say to all: Watch."

The plot to kill Jesus
(14.1,2,10,11; Mt 26.1–5,14–16; Lk 22.1–6)

*14.1
Jn 11.55;
13,1;
Mt 12.14

14 It was now two days before the Passover and the feast of Unleavened Bread. And the chief priests and the scribes were seeking how to arrest him by stealth, and kill him; 2 for they said, "Not during the feast, lest there be a tumult of the people."

Jesus anointed by Mary of Bethany
(14.3–9; Mt 26.6–13; Jn 12.1–8)

*14.3
Lk 7.37–39;
Mt 21.17

3 And while he was at Běth'anỹ in the house of Simon the leper, as he sat at table, a woman came with an alabaster flask of ointment of pure nard, very costly, and she broke the flask and poured it over his head. 4 But there were some who said to themselves indignantly, "Why was the ointment thus wasted? 5 For this ointment might have been sold for more than three hundred denarii,[b] and given to the poor." And they reproached her. 6 But Jesus said, "Let her alone; why do you trouble her? She has done a beautiful thing to me. 7 For you always have the poor with you, and whenever you will, you can do good to them; but you will not always have me. 8 She has done what she could; she has anointed my body beforehand for burying. 9And truly, I say to you, wherever the gospel is preached in the whole world, what she has done will be told in memory of her."

14.7
Deut 15.11

14.8
Jn 19.20

The bargain of Judas Iscariot (14.10,11, 1,2)

*14.10
Lk 22.3,4;
Jn 6.71

10 Then Judas Ĭscar'ĭŏt, who was one of the twelve, went to the chief priests in order to betray him to them. 11And when they heard it they were glad, and promised to give him money. And he sought an opportunity to betray him.

b The denarius was a day's wage for a laborer

13.37 Watchfulness is required of all God's servants (Mt 25.13; Lk 21.36; 1 Thess 5.6; 1 Pet 4.7). (The term used in all these passages is grēgoreō: be awake, keep awake, be alert and on guard, watch out.) They must watch with courage (1 Cor 16.13), with prayer (Lk 21.36; Eph 6.18), and with thanksgiving (Col 4.2). There is blessedness in watching (Lk 12.37; Rev 16.15). Believers are to watch eagerly for Christ's Second Advent since they do not know at what time He may return to earth (Mt 24.42; 25.13; Mk 13.35, 36).
14.1 This feast also celebrated the deliverance from Egypt (cf. Deut 16.3; Ex 12.15). It began on the fifteenth day of Nisan, immediately after Passover, and lasted until the twenty-first. During this time no leavened bread was to be eaten in commemoration of the flight from Egypt when the people ate un

leavened bread only, "the bread of affliction." The feasts of Passover and Unleavened Bread were celebrated as one feast (cf. Lk 22.1).
Passover (Hebrew pesah, from the verb pasah, "pass over") commemorated the ancient Hebrews' deliverance from the Egyptian bondage, in particular the night when the Lord "passed over" the homes of the Hebrews in the slaughter of the first-born of Egypt (cf. Ex 12.13, 23, 27). It was celebrated on the fourteenth day of the month of Nisan (March–April), and was one of the three great religious celebrations of the Jews, at which time all Jewish males over twelve years of age were supposed to go to Jerusalem. (See note to Ex 12.11.)
14.3 See note to Lk 7.36 on the various Marys.
14.10 See note to Mt 26.14 on Judas Iscariot.

The Last Supper (14.12–25)

1. *The Passover prepared (14.12–16; Mt 26.17–19; Lk 22.7–13)*

12 And on the first day of Unleavened Bread, when they sacrificed the passover lamb, his disciples said to him, "Where will you have us go and prepare for you to eat the passover?" 13 And he sent two of his disciples, and said to them, "Go into the city, and a man carrying a jar of water will meet you; follow him, 14 and wherever he enters, say to the householder, 'The Teacher says, Where is my guest room, where I am to eat the passover with my disciples?' 15 And he will show you a large upper room furnished and ready; there prepare for us." 16 And the disciples set out and went to the city, and found it as he had told them; and they prepared the passover.

14.12
Ex 12.11

2. *The Passover eaten*
(14.17–21; Mt 26.20–25; Lk 22.14–18; see Jn 13.1–30)

17 And when it was evening he came with the twelve. 18 And as they were at table eating, Jesus said, "Truly, I say to you, one of you will betray me, one who is eating with me." 19 They began to be sorrowful, and to say to him one after another, "Is it I?" 20 He said to them, "It is one of the twelve, one who is dipping bread into the dish with me. 21 For the Son of man goes as it is written of him, but woe to that man by whom the Son of man is betrayed! It would have been better for that man if he had not been born."

14.18
ver 44,45

3. *The Lord's Supper instituted*
(14.22–25; Mt 26.26–29; Lk 22.19–24)

22 And as they were eating, he took bread, and blessed, and broke it, and gave it to them, and said, "Take; this is my body." 23 And he took a cup, and when he had given thanks he gave it to them, and they all drank of it. 24 And he said to them, "This is my blood of the*c* covenant, which is poured out for many. 25 Truly, I say to you, I shall not drink again of the fruit of the vine until that day when I drink it new in the kingdom of God."

*14.22
Mk 6.41;
8.6;
Lk 24.30;
1 Cor
11.23–25
14.23
1 Cor 10.16
14.24
Ex 24.8;
Heb 9.20

Peter's denial foretold
(14.26–31; Mt 26.30–35; Lk 22.31–34; see Jn 14–17)

26 And when they had sung a hymn, they went out to the Mount of Olives. 27 And Jesus said to them, "You will all fall away; for it is written, 'I will strike the shepherd, and the sheep will be scattered.' 28 But after I am raised up, I will go before you to Găl'-ilee." 29 Peter said to him, "Even though they all fall away, I will

14.26
Mt 21.1
14.27
Zech 13.7
14.28
Mk 16.7
14.29
Jn 13.37,38

c Other ancient authorities insert *new*

14.22 "The Lord's Supper," also known as the *Eucharist* (or Thanksgiving), was instituted by Christ at His last meal before the crucifixion and it is recorded in Matthew and Luke as well as here in Mark. Paul specifically refers to its institution by Christ in 1 Cor 11.23ff. It was prefigured in the Old Testament by the Passover meal (Ex 12.21-28; 1 Cor 5.7, 8). It is to be observed until the Second Advent of Christ and includes the requirement of an earnest self-examination as one partakes of the bread and the wine representing the body and blood of our Lord. The early church practiced this ordinance or sacrament at very frequent intervals (Acts 2.42 and 20.7). Only believers are permitted by Scripture to partake of the Lord's Supper; unworthy partakers are those who do not truly repent and do not discern Christ's body. These are said to be guilty of His shed blood and broken body and will be judged for their sin (1 Cor 11.27-30).

14.30
ver 66–72;
Jn 13.38
not." [30]And Jesus said to him, "Truly, I say to you, this very
night, before the cock crows twice, you will deny me three times."
[31] But he said vehemently, "If I must die with you, I will not deny
you." And they all said the same.

Jesus in Gethsemane (14.32–52)
1. *His agony* (14.32–42; Mt 26.36–46; Lk 22.39–46; cf. Jn 18.1)

32 And they went to a place which was called Gĕthsĕm'ănë; and
he said to his disciples, "Sit here, while I pray." [33]And he took
with him Peter and James and John, and began to be greatly dis-

14.34
Jn 12.27
tressed and troubled. [34]And he said to them, "My soul is very
sorrowful, even to death; remain here, and watch."[d] [35]And going
14.35
ver 41
a little farther, he fell on the ground and prayed that, if it were
14.36
Rom 8.15;
Gal 4.6;
Jn 5.30;
6.38
possible, the hour might pass from him. [36]And he said, "Ăbbá,
Father, all things are possible to thee; remove this cup from me;
yet not what I will, but what thou wilt." [37]And he came and found
them sleeping, and he said to Peter, "Simon, are you asleep?
Could you not watch[d] one hour? [38] Watch[d] and pray that you may
14.38
Mt 6.13;
Lk 11.4;
Rom 7.23;
Gal 5.17
not enter into temptation; the spirit indeed is willing, but the flesh
is weak." [39]And again he went away and prayed, saying the same
words. [40]And again he came and found them sleeping, for their
eyes were very heavy; and they did not know what to answer him.
14.41
ver 35;
Jn 13.1
[41]And he came the third time, and said to them, "Are you still
sleeping and taking your rest? It is enough; the hour has come; the
Son of man is betrayed into the hands of sinners. [42] Rise, let us
be going; see, my betrayer is at hand."

2. *Jesus' betrayal and arrest*
(14.43–52; Mt 26.47–56; Lk 22.47–53; Jn 18.1–11)

43 And immediately, while he was still speaking, Judas came,
one of the twelve, and with him a crowd with swords and clubs,
from the chief priests and the scribes and the elders. [44] Now the
betrayer had given them a sign, saying, "The one I shall kiss is the
man; seize him and lead him away under guard." [45]And when he
14.45
Mt 23.7
came, he went up to him at once, and said, "Master!"[e] And he
kissed him. [46]And they laid hands on him and seized him. [47] But
one of those who stood by drew his sword, and struck the slave of
the high priest and cut off his ear. [48]And Jesus said to them,
"Have you come out as against a robber, with swords and clubs
to capture me? [49] Day after day I was with you in the temple
14.49
Mk 12.35;
Isa 53.7ff;
Lk 19.47;
Jn 18.19–21
teaching, and you did not seize me. But let the scriptures be
fulfilled." [50]And they all forsook him, and fled.
14.50
Ps 88.8;
ver 27
51 And a young man followed him, with nothing but a linen
cloth about his body; and they seized him, [52] but he left the linen
cloth and ran away naked.

Jesus before Caiaphas
(14.53–65; Mt 26.57–68; cf. Lk 22.54; Jn 18.12–14,19–25)

14.54
ver 68;
Mt 26.3;
Jn 18.18
53 And they led Jesus to the high priest; and all the chief priests
and the elders and the scribes were assembled. [54]And Peter had
followed him at a distance, right into the courtyard of the high

d Or *keep awake*   *e* Or *Rabbi*

priest; and he was sitting with the guards, and warming himself at the fire. 55 Now the chief priests and the whole council sought testimony against Jesus to put him to death; but they found none. 56 For many bore false witness against him, and their witness did not agree. 57And some stood up and bore false witness against him, saying, 58 "We heard him say, 'I will destroy this temple that is made with hands, and in three days I will build another, not made with hands.'" 59 Yet not even so did their testimony agree. 60And the high priest stood up in the midst, and asked Jesus, "Have you no answer to make? What is it that these men testify against you?" 61 But he was silent and made no answer. Again the high priest asked him, "Are you the Christ, the Son of the Blessed?" 62And Jesus said, "I am; and you will see the Son of man seated at the right hand of Power, and coming with the clouds of heaven." 63And the high priest tore his garments, and said, "Why do we still need witnesses? 64 You have heard his blasphemy. What is your decision?" And they all condemned him as deserving death. 65And some began to spit on him, and to cover his face, and to strike him, saying to him, "Prophesy!" And the guards received him with blows.

14.58
Mk 15.29;
Jn 2.19;
Acts 6.14

*14.61
Isa 53.7

14.62
Dan 7.13;
Mt 24.30;
Mk 13.26

14.63
Num 14.6;
Acts 14.14

14.64
Lev 24.16

14.65
Mk 10.34;
Est 7.8;
Lk 22.64

Peter's denial of Jesus
(14.66–72; Mt 26.69–75; Lk 22.55–62; Jn 18.15–18,25–27)

66 And as Peter was below in the courtyard, one of the maids of the high priest came; 67 and seeing Peter warming himself, she looked at him, and said, "You also were with the Năz´arēne, Jesus." 68 But he denied it, saying, "I neither know nor understand what you mean." And he went out into the gateway.ƒ 69And the maid saw him, and began again to say to the bystanders, "This man is one of them." 70 But again he denied it. And after a little while again the bystanders said to Peter, "Certainly you are one of them; for you are a Găl̦i̦lē´án." 71 But he began to invoke a curse on himself and to swear, "I do not know this man of whom you speak." 72And immediately the cock crowed a second time. And Peter remembered how Jesus had said to him, "Before the cock crows twice, you will deny me three times." And he broke down and wept.

14.66
ver 30,54
14.67
ver 54;
Mk 1.24
14.68
ver 54

14.70
ver 68;
Acts 2.7
*14.71

14.72
ver 30

Jesus before Pontius Pilate
(15.1–15; Mt 27.11–26; Lk 23.3–25; Jn 18.29–40)

1. Pilate questions Jesus (15.1–5)

15 And as soon as it was morning the chief priests, with the elders and scribes, and the whole council held a consulta-

*15.1
Mt 5.22;
Lk 22.66;
23.1;
Jn 18.28

ƒ Or fore-court. Other ancient authorities add and the cock crowed

---

14.61 This Scripture may be considered to be a fulfilment of the prophecy of Isa 53.7: *He was oppressed, and he was afflicted, yet he opened not his mouth; like a lamb that is led to the slaughter, and like a sheep that before its shearers is dumb, so he opened not his mouth.* (Cf. 1 Pet 2.23.)

14.71 The gravity of Peter's words accentuates the gravity of his sin. He took an oath in the name of Almighty God and called down

upon himself all of the imprecations which attend such an oath. Then he testified to a falsehood when he swore he did not know Jesus Christ. The glory of grace is well illustrated in Peter's later life, for when he repented and was restored he became a flaming evangel for the One he had denied.

15.1 Pontius Pilate was the Roman procurator (called "governor" in the Gospels) of the territory formerly ruled over by Archelaus,

tion; and they bound Jesus and led him away and delivered him to Pīlāte. ²And Pīlāte asked him, "Are you the King of the Jews?" And he answered him, "You have said so." ³And the chief priests accused him of many things. ⁴And Pīlāte again asked him, "Have you no answer to make? See how many charges they bring against you." ⁵ But Jesus made no further answer, so that Pīlāte wondered.

15.5
Isa 53.7

2. Pilate releases Barabbas and delivers Jesus (15.6–15)

15.6
Mt 27.15;
Lk 23.17;
Jn 18.39
*15.7

6 Now at the feast he used to release for them one prisoner for whom they asked. ⁷And among the rebels in prison, who had committed murder in the insurrection, there was a man called Bàrăb'bàs. ⁸And the crowd came up and began to ask Pīlāte to do as he was wont to do for them. ⁹And he answered them, "Do you want me to release for you the King of the Jews?" ¹⁰ For he perceived that it was out of envy that the chief priests had delivered him up.

15.11
Acts 3.14

¹¹But the chief priests stirred up the crowd to have him release for them Bàrăb'bàs instead. ¹²And Pīlāte again said to them, "Then what shall I do with the man whom you call the King of the Jews?" ¹³And they cried out again, "Crucify him." ¹⁴And Pīlāte said to them, "Why, what evil has he done?" But they shouted all the more, "Crucify him." ¹⁵ So Pīlāte, wishing to satisfy the crowd, released for them Bàrăb'bàs; and having scourged Jesus, he delivered him to be crucified.

15.15
Jn 19.1,16

The Crucifixion and burial of Jesus (15.16–47)

1. Jesus crowned with thorns
(15.16–20; Mt 27.27–31; cf. Jn 19.2,3)

15.16
Acts 10.1

16 And the soldiers led him away inside the palace (that is, the praetor'ium); and they called together the whole battalion. ¹⁷And they clothed him in a purple cloak, and plaiting a crown of thorns they put it on him. ¹⁸And they began to salute him, "Hail, King of the Jews!" ¹⁹And they struck his head with a reed, and spat upon him, and they knelt down in homage to him. ²⁰And when they had mocked him, they stripped him of the purple cloak, and put his own clothes on him. And they led him out to crucify him.

---

the son of Herod. It included generally Judea, Idumea, and Samaria. Nothing is known of Pilate's origins although the idea that he was the descendant of a manumitted slave is undoubtedly spurious. Procurators usually came from the Roman equestrian class. Pilate came to Judea about the time John the Baptist began his ministry. He was responsible for the financial administration and collection of taxes for the Roman empire. Normally the subjugated peoples were allowed much freedom to rule themselves. The Sanhedrin was the supreme court of the Jews, but it did not have the power to impose a death sentence without the approval of the governor, who also carried out such executions. Pilate was constantly in some kind of struggle with the Jews, who were themselves turbulent and disaffected. He was capricious, wilful, weak, rude, and overbearing. When Christ appeared before him he intended to release Him but he was outmaneuvered by the Jews and finally capitulated to their demands that Jesus be crucified. Personal and political considerations outweighed his sense of justice and moral obligation. He was finally removed from his procuratorship after ten year's service. Fantastic legends grew up around his later life, none of which seem to have historical certification.

15.7 Barabbas was a well-known insurrectionist (cf. Mt 27.16: *a notorious prisoner*), probably a leader in the insurrection referred to (cf. Lk 23.18, 19, 25). In Jn 18.40 he is called a robber (Greek *lestes*), a word used by Josephus, the Jewish historian, to describe rebels against the Roman power. This is the same word used of the two robbers crucified with Jesus (Mt 27.38; Mk 15.27). Aside from these few verses, nothing else is known about Barabbas. Some manuscripts in Mt 27.16, 17 give his name as "Jesus Barabbas," and Origen of Alexandria, a church father, writer, and teacher of the third century, said this name occurred in some old copies of the Gospel of Matthew.

2. Jesus crucified
(15.21–32; Mt 27.32–44; Lk 23.32–43; Jn 19.17–24)

21 And they compelled a passer-by, Simon of Çȳrē′në, who was coming in from the country, the father of Alexander and Rufus, to carry his cross. ²²And they brought him to the place called Gŏl′-gŏthà (which means the place of a skull). ²³And they offered him wine mingled with myrrh; but he did not take it. ²⁴And they crucified him, and divided his garments among them, casting lots for them, to decide what each should take. ²⁵And it was the third hour, when they crucified him. ²⁶And the inscription of the charge against him read, "The King of the Jews." ²⁷And with him they crucified two robbers, one on his right and one on his left.ᵍ ²⁹And those who passed by derided him, wagging their heads, and saying, "Aha! You who would destroy the temple and build it in three days, ³⁰ save yourself, and come down from the cross!" ³¹ So also the chief priests mocked him to one another with the scribes, saying, "He saved others; he cannot save himself. ³² Let the Christ, the King of Israel, come down now from the cross, that we may see and believe." Those who were crucified with him also reviled him.

15.21
Lk 23.26;
Rom 16.13

*15.23

15.24
Ps 22.18

*15.26

15.29
Ps 22.7;
Mk 13.2;
14.58;
Jn 2.19
15.31
Ps 22.8
15.32
ver 26,27

3. The death of Jesus
(15.33–41; Mt 27.45–50; Lk 23.44–49; Jn 19.28–37)

33 And when the sixth hour had come, there was darkness over the whole landʰ until the ninth hour. ³⁴And at the ninth hour Jesus cried with a loud voice, "Ēlo-i, Elo-i, la′ma sabaçh-tha′nï?" which means, "My God, my God, why hast thou forsaken me?" ³⁵And some of the bystanders hearing it said, "Behold, he is calling Ēlī′jäh." ³⁶And one ran and, filling a sponge full of vinegar, put it on a reed and gave it to him to drink, saying, "Wait, let us see whether Ēlī′jäh will come to take him down." ³⁷And Jesus uttered a loud cry, and breathed his last. ³⁸And the curtain of the temple was torn in two, from top to bottom. ³⁹And when the centurion, who stood facing him, saw that he thusⁱ breathed his last, he said, "Truly this man was the Sonˣ of God!"

40 There were also women looking on from afar, among whom were Mary Măg′dálēne, and Mary the mother of James the younger and of Jōşĕs, and Sálō′më, ⁴¹ who, when he was in Găl′ǐleē, followed him, and ministered to him; and also many other women who came up with him to Jerusalem.

15.34
Ps 22.1

15.36
Ps 69.21

15.38
Heb 10.19,
20
15.39
Mk 1.11;
9.7
15.40
Ps 38.11;
Jn 19.25;
Mk 16.1
15.41
Lk 8.1–3

4. Jesus laid in the tomb
(15.42–47; Mt 27.57–61; Lk 23.50–56; Jn 19.38–42)

42 And when evening had come, since it was the day of Preparation, that is, the day before the sabbath, ⁴³ Joseph of Arǐmăthē′à, a respected member of the council, who was also himself looking for the kingdom of God, took courage and went to Pīláte, and asked for the body of Jesus. ⁴⁴And Pīláte wondered if he were already dead; and summoning the centurion, he asked him whether he was already dead.ʲ ⁴⁵And when he learned from the centurion

15.42
Deut 21.22,
23;
Mt 27.62
15.43
Acts 13.50;
17.12;
Lk 2.25,38

15.45
ver 39

ᵍ Other ancient authorities insert verse 28, *And the scripture was fulfilled which says, "He was reckoned with the transgressors"*   ʰ Or *earth*
ⁱ Other ancient authorities insert *cried out and*   ˣ Or *a son*
ʲ Other ancient authorities read *whether he had been some time dead*

15.23 This was probably intended to ease the pain but Jesus refused such escape.   **15.26** See note to Mt 27.37 for the variations of the superscription on the cross.

that he was dead, he granted the body to Joseph. [46]And he bought a linen shroud, and taking him down, wrapped him in the linen shroud, and laid him in a tomb which had been hewn out of the rock; and he rolled a stone against the door of the tomb. [47] Mary Măg′dålēne and Mary the mother of Jōṣĕs saw where he was laid.

The Resurrection of Jesus Christ
(16.1–8; Mt 28.1–10; Lk 24.1–11; Jn 20.1–18)

16.1
Lk 23.56;
Jn 19.39

16 And when the sabbath was past, Mary Măg′dålēne, and Mary the mother of James, and Săló′mě, bought spices, so that they might go and anoint him. [2]And very early on the first day of the week they went to the tomb when the sun had risen. [3]And they were saying to one another, "Who will roll away the stone for us from the door of the tomb?" [4]And looking up, they saw that the stone was rolled back—it was very large. [5]And entering the tomb, they saw a young man sitting on the right side, dressed in a white robe; and they were amazed. [6]And he said to them, "Do not be amazed; you seek Jesus of Năz′årĕth, who was crucified. He has risen, he is not here; see the place where they laid him. [7] But go, tell his disciples and Peter that he is going before you to Găl′ilēe; there you will see him, as he told you." [8]And they went out and fled from the tomb; for trembling and astonishment had come upon them; and they said nothing to any one, for they were afraid.

16.3
Mk 15.46

16.5
Mk 9.15

16.6
ver 5;
Mk 1.24

16.7
Mk 14.28;
Jn 21.1–23

Appearances and ascension of Jesus Christ (9–20)

16.9
Jn 20.11–18

9 Now when he rose early on the first day of the week, he appeared first to Mary Măg′dålēne, from whom he had cast out seven demons. [10] She went out and told those who had been with him, as they mourned and wept. [11] But when they heard that he was alive and had been seen by her, they would not believe it.

16.12
Lk 24.13–35

12 After this he appeared in another form to two of them, as they were walking into the country. [13]And they went back and told the rest, but they did not believe them.

16.14
Lk 24.36–38
Jn 20.26

14 Afterward he appeared to the eleven themselves as they sat at table; and he upbraided them for their unbelief and hardness of heart, because they had not believed those who saw him after he had risen. [15]And he said to them, "Go into all the world and preach the gospel to the whole creation. [16] He who believes and is baptized will be saved; but he who does not believe will be condemned. [17]And these signs will accompany those who believe: in my name they will cast out demons; they will speak in new tongues; [18] they will pick up serpents, and if they drink any deadly thing, it will not hurt them; they will lay their hands on the sick, and they will recover."

16.15
Mt 28.18–20
Lk 24.47, 48

16.19
Lk 24.50, 51
Acts 1.9–11

19 So then the Lord Jesus, after he had spoken to them, was taken up into heaven, and sat down at the right hand of God. [20]And they went forth and preached everywhere, while the Lord worked with them and confirmed the message by the signs that attended it. Amen.[k]

---

[k] Some of the most ancient authorities bring the book to a close at the end of verse 8. One authority concludes the book by adding after verse 8 the following: *But they reported briefly to Peter and those with him all that they had been told. And after this, Jesus himself sent out by means of them, from east to west, the sacred and imperishable proclamation of eternal salvation.* Other authorities include the preceding passage and continue with verses 9–20. In most authorities verses 9–20 follow immediately after verse 8; a few authorities insert additional material after verse 14.

INTRODUCTION TO
THE GOSPEL ACCORDING TO
LUKE

Authorship and Background: The third Gospel bears the name of Luke, "beloved physician" (Col 4.14), friend and companion of Paul. The earliest references to the third Gospel name Luke as its author, the only known Gentile author in the New Testament. It is clear that the same author wrote the third Gospel and Acts, and according to the accounts in Acts and the Epistles, he joined Paul and his party at Troas, during the second missionary journey, going with them to Philippi (Acts 16.10–41). He apparently remained in Philippi until Paul's return there on the third missionary journey, and went on with him to Jerusalem (Acts 20.5—21.18) and Rome (Acts 27.1—28.16). He was with Paul when he wrote to the Colossians, to Philemon, and to Timothy (Col 4.14; Philem 24; 2 Tim 4.11).

Opinions vary on the exact date of the book: some scholars place it before the destruction of Jerusalem in A.D. 70, while others prefer the period A.D. 80–90.

Characteristics: The nature and purpose of the book is explicitly stated (1.1–4; cf. also Acts 1.1–2). The identity of Theophilus, to whom the work is dedicated, is a matter of surmise. In his "orderly account" (1.3) of the beginning, growth, and spread of the Christian movement, the author writes consciously as a historian, and his work is more nearly akin to history than any of the other Gospels (notice the precise dating of the beginning of John the Baptist's ministry in 3.1–2).

Called by one scholar "the most beautiful book ever written," the Gospel of Luke records the birth of Christ (2.7), and tells with consummate artistry and grace such parables as that of the Good Samaritan (10.29–37), the Rich Man and Lazarus (16.19–31), and the Prodigal Son (15.11–32). The loveliest story of all is the narrative of the Emmaus appearance of the risen Lord (24.13–35).

Beautiful hymns adorn the book: the *Magnificat* of Mary (1.46–55), the *Benedictus* of Zechariah (1.67–79), the *Gloria in Excelsis* of the angels (2.14), and the *Nunc Dimittis* of Simeon (2.29–32).

A strong note of joy runs through the whole narrative, from the angels' song in 2.14 to the end of the story as the disciples return to Jerusalem "with great joy, and were continually in the Temple blessing God" (24.52, 53; cf. also 15.7, 10, 24, 32). Prominence is given to prayer (see 3.21; 5.16; 6.12; 11.1; 22.32; 23.34, 46), and to the work of the Holy Spirit (see 4.1, 14; 10.21; 24.49).

This Gospel sounds the note of universal relevance with its message of "a light for revelation to the Gentiles" (2.32), and God's salvation proffered to all mankind (3.6). Women are accorded a prominent place: Mary, Elizabeth, Anna, Joanna, and Susanna; the women who helped Jesus (8.2, 3); the widow of Nain (7.11, 12); the sinful woman (7.36–50); Mary and Martha (10.38–42); the woman with the spirit of infirmity (13.10–17), and the women who mourned

Introduction to Luke

for Jesus on the way to Golgotha (23.27). Jesus' parables include those of the woman who lost her coin (15.8–10) and the widow who insisted on her rights (18.1–8). His gracious call to salvation embraces society's outcasts also: the "sinners," tax-gatherers, and Samaritans (see 10.29–37; 17.11–19; 18.9–14; 19.1–10).

The narrative reaches its climax in Christ's Passion: before the book is even half finished, Jesus begins his journey to Jerusalem where at Mount Olivet he will be received up into heaven (9.51), in fulfilment of his destiny (9.31). The Passion is the climax and culmination of the whole Gospel, casting its spell over the entire narrative.

Contents:

THE GOSPEL ACCORDING TO

LUKE

Preface (1.1–4)

1 Inasmuch as many have undertaken to compile a narrative of the things which have been accomplished among us, 2 just as they were delivered to us by those who from the beginning were eyewitnesses and ministers of the word, 3 it seemed good to me also, having followed all things closely*a* for some time past, to write an orderly account for you, most excellent Thē-ŏph′ĭlŭs, 4 that you may know the truth concerning the things of which you have been informed.

1.2
Heb 2.3;
1 Pet 5.1;
2 Pet 1.16;
1 Jn 1.1;
Mk 1.1;
Jn 15.27
1.3
Acts 11.4;
18.23; 1.1
1.4
Jn 20.31

Birth of John the Baptist foretold (1.5–25)

5 In the days of Hĕ́rŏd, king of Judē′à, there was a priest named Zĕchàrī′àh,*b* of the division of Àbī′jàh; and he had a wife of the daughters of Aaron, and her name was Elizabeth. 6 And they were both righteous before God, walking in all the commandments and ordinances of the Lord blameless. 7 But they had no child, because Elizabeth was barren, and both were advanced in years.

8 Now while he was serving as priest before God when his division was on duty, 9 according to the custom of the priesthood, it fell to him by lot to enter the temple of the Lord and burn incense. 10 And the whole multitude of the people were praying outside at the hour of incense. 11 And there appeared to him an angel of the Lord standing on the right side of the altar of incense. 12 And Zĕchàrī′àh was troubled when he saw him, and fear fell upon him. 13 But the angel said to him, "Do not be afraid, Zĕchàrī′àh, for your prayer is heard, and your wife Elizabeth will bear you a son, and you shall call his name John.
14 And you will have joy and gladness,
    and many will rejoice at his birth;
15 for he will be great before the Lord,
    and he shall drink no wine nor strong drink,
    and he will be filled with the Holy Spirit,
    even from his mother's womb.
16 And he will turn many of the sons of Israel to the Lord their
    God,
17 and he will go before him in the spirit and power of Ēlī′jàh,
    to turn the hearts of the fathers to the children,
    and the disobedient to the wisdom of the just,
    to make ready for the Lord a people prepared."
18 And Zĕchàrī′àh said to the angel, "How shall I know this? For I am an old man, and my wife is advanced in years." 19 And the angel answered him, "I am Gabriel, who stand in the presence of God; and I was sent to speak to you, and to bring you this good news. 20 And behold, you will be silent and unable to speak until

*1.5
Mt 2.1;
1 Chr 24.10
1.6
Gen 7.1;
1 Ki 9.4;
2 Ki 20.3
1.8
1 Chr
24.19;
2 Chr 8.14
1.9
Ex 30.7,8;
1 Chr
23.13;
2 Chr 29.11
1.10
Lev 16.17
1.13
ver 30,60,63
1.14
ver 58
1.15
Num 6.3;
Judg 13.4;
Lk 7.33;
Jer 1.5;
Gal 1.15
1.16
Mal 4.5,6
*1.17
Mt 11.14;
17.13
1.18
Gen 17.17;
ver 34
1.19
Dan 8.16;
9.21–23;
Mt 18.10
1.20
Ezek 3.26;
24.27

a Or *accurately* *b* Greek *Zăchàrī′às*

1.5 Elizabeth is called *of the daughters of Aaron*, meaning she was of a priestly family.

1.17 See note to Mal 4.5 on the coming of Elijah.

the day that these things come to pass, because you did not believe my words, which will be fulfilled in their time." 21And the people were waiting for Zĕçhări'ăh, and they wondered at his delay in the temple. 22And when he came out, he could not speak to them, and they perceived that he had seen a vision in the temple; and he made signs to them and remained dumb. 23And when his time of service was ended, he went to his home.

24 After these days his wife Elizabeth conceived, and for five months she hid herself, saying, 25 "Thus the Lord has done to me in the days when he looked on me, to take away my reproach among men."

The birth of Jesus foretold: the annunciation
(1.26–38; Mt 1.18–25)

26 In the sixth month the angel Gabriel was sent from God to a city of Găl'ilĕē named Năz'ărĕth, 27 to a virgin betrothed to a man whose name was Joseph, of the house of David; and the virgin's name was Mary. 28And he came to her and said, "Hail, O favored one, the Lord is with you!"c 29 But she was greatly troubled at the saying, and considered in her mind what sort of greeting this might be. 30And the angel said to her, "Do not be afraid, Mary, for you have found favor with God. 31And behold, you will conceive in your womb and bear a son, and you shall call his name Jesus.

32 He will be great, and will be called the Son of the Most High;
   and the Lord God will give to him the throne of his father
      David,
33 and he will reign over the house of Jacob for ever;
   and of his kingdom there will be no end."
34And Mary said to the angel, "How shall this be, since I have no husband?" 35And the angel said to her,

"The Holy Spirit will come upon you,
   and the power of the Most High will overshadow you;
therefore the child to be bornd will be called holy,
   the Son of God.
36And behold, your kinswoman Elizabeth in her old age has also conceived a son; and this is the sixth month with her who was called barren. 37 For with God nothing will be impossible." 38And Mary said, "Behold, I am the handmaid of the Lord; let it be to me according to your word." And the angel departed from her.

Mary visits Elizabeth
(1.39–46a)

39 In those days Mary arose and went with haste into the hill country, to a city of Judah, 40 and she entered the house of Zĕçhări'ăh and greeted Elizabeth. 41And when Elizabeth heard the greeting of Mary, the babe leaped in her womb; and Elizabeth was filled with the Holy Spirit 42 and she exclaimed with a loud cry, "Blessed are you among women, and blessed is the fruit of your womb! 43And why is this granted me, that the mother of my Lord should come to me? 44 For behold, when the voice of your

c Other ancient authorities add "Blessed are you among women!"
d Other ancient authorities add of you

Margin references:

1.22 ver 62

1.25 Gen 30.23; Isa 4.1

1.26 Mt 2.23
1.27 Mt 1.16 ver 19;
1.28 Dan 9.23; 10.19

1.31 Isa 7.14; Lk 2.21

1.32 Mk 5.7; Isa 9.6,7; Jer 23.5; Rev 3.7
1.33 Dan 2.44; 7.14,27; Mt 28.18; Heb 1.8
1.35 ver 32; Mk 1.24; Mt 4.3

1.37 Gen 18.14; Jer 32.17; Mt 19.26; Mk 10.27; Lk 18.27; Rom 4.21

1.39 ver 65
1.41 ver 67

1.42 Judg 5.24; Lk 11.27,28
1.43 Lk 2.11

greeting came to my ears, the babe in my womb leaped for joy.
⁴⁵And blessed is she who believed that there would be[e] a fulfilment of what was spoken to her from the Lord." ⁴⁶And Mary said,

1.46
1 Sam
2.1–10;
Ps 34.2,3

The song of Mary (1.46b–56)

"My soul magnifies the Lord,
⁴⁷ and my spirit rejoices in God my Savior,
⁴⁸ for he has regarded the low estate of his handmaiden.
  For behold, henceforth all generations will call me blessed;
⁴⁹ for he who is mighty has done great things for me,
  and holy is his name.
⁵⁰ And his mercy is on those who fear him
  from generation to generation.
⁵¹ He has shown strength with his arm,
  he has scattered the proud in the imagination of their hearts,
⁵² he has put down the mighty from their thrones,
  and exalted those of low degree;
⁵³ he has filled the hungry with good things,
  and the rich he has sent empty away.
⁵⁴ He has helped his servant Israel,
  in remembrance of his mercy,
⁵⁵ as he spoke to our fathers,
  to Abraham and to his posterity for ever."
⁵⁶And Mary remained with her about three months, and returned
to her home.

1.47
Ps 35.9;
1 Tim 1.1;
2.3;
Tit 2.10;
Jude 25

1.48
Ps 138.6;
Lk 11.27

1.49
Ps 71.19;
111.9

1.50
Ps 103.17

1.51
Ps 98.1;
Isa 40.10;
Ps 33.10;
1 Pet 5.5

1.52
Job 5.11

1.53
Ps 34.10

1.54
Ps 98.3

1.55
Gen 17.19;
Ps 132.11;
Gal 3.16

Birth of John the Baptist (1.57–66)

⁵⁷ Now the time came for Elizabeth to be delivered, and she
gave birth to a son. ⁵⁸And her neighbors and kinsfolk heard that
the Lord had shown great mercy to her, and they rejoiced with
her. ⁵⁹And on the eighth day they came to circumcise the child;
and they would have named him Zĕchàrī'ăh after his father, ⁶⁰ but
his mother said, "Not so; he shall be called John." ⁶¹And they said
to her, "None of your kindred is called by this name." ⁶²And they
made signs to his father, inquiring what he would have him called.
⁶³And he asked for a writing tablet, and wrote, "His name is
John." And they all marveled. ⁶⁴And immediately his mouth was
opened and his tongue loosed, and he spoke, blessing God. ⁶⁵And
fear came on all their neighbors. And all these things were talked
about through all the hill country of Judē'ă; ⁶⁶ and all who heard
them laid them up in their hearts, saying, "What then will this
child be?" For the hand of the Lord was with him.

⋆1.57

1.58
Gen 19.19

1.59
Gen 17.12;
Lev 12.3

1.62
ver 22

1.63
ver 13

1.64
ver 20

1.66
Lk 2.19,51;
Gen 39.2;
Acts 11.21

[e] Or believed, for there will be

1.57 Information about John the Baptist,
other than the New Testament accounts, is
limited to what Josephus, the Jewish historian,
wrote about him. John was the son of Zechariah and Elizabeth, both of whom were descendants of Aaron. He was about six
months older than Jesus. The town of his
birth is unknown, although Luke mentions a
city in the hill country of Judah (1.39). John's
early life may be summarized in several sen-
tences: *the hand of the Lord was with him*
(1.66); he *grew and became strong in spirit . . .*

he was in the wilderness till . . . his manifestation
(1.80); *he will be great before the Lord, and . . .
filled with the Holy Spirit* (1.15). He was imprisoned by Herod prior to his execution, ca.
A.D. 28. John, of course, was the forerunner of
Jesus, and his ministry was prophetic. His
chief preaching burden was the announcement
of the coming kingdom, emphasizing the necessity for repentance and confession of sins
(Mt 3.1–12; Mk 1.4–8; Lk 3.3–18; Jn 1.19–
28). Jesus said that no one born of woman
was greater than John (Mt 11.11).

The song of Zechariah: the "Benedictus" (1.67–80)

1.67 ver 41; Joel 2.28	67 And his father Zĕchărī'ăh was filled with the Holy Spirit, and prophesied, saying,
1.68 Ps 72.18; 111.9; Lk 7.16	68 "Blessed be the Lord God of Israel, for he has visited and redeemed his people,
*1.69 Ps 18.2; 89.17; 132.17; Ezek 29.21	69 and has raised up a horn of salvation for us in the house of his servant David,

1.70
Jer 23.5;
Dan 9.24;
Acts 3.21;
Rom 1.2;
Mic 7.20;
Ps 105.8,9;
106.45;
Ezek 16.60
	70 as he spoke by the mouth of his holy prophets from of old,
	71 that we should be saved from our enemies,
	    and from the hand of all who hate us;
	72 to perform the mercy promised to our fathers,
	    and to remember his holy covenant,
	73 the oath which he swore to our father Abraham, 74 to grant us
	    that we, being delivered from the hand of our enemies,
	    might serve him without fear,

1.74 Rom 6.18; Heb 9.14	75 in holiness and righteousness before him all the days of our life.

1.75
Eph 4.24;
Tit 2.12
	76 And you, child, will be called the prophet of the Most High;
	    for you will go before the Lord to prepare his ways,
	77 to give knowledge of salvation to his people
	    in the forgiveness of their sins,

1.76 Mal 3.1; 4.5; Mt 11.9,10	78 through the tender mercy of our God, when the day shall dawn upon*ʃ* us from on high
1.77 Mk 1.4	79 to give light to those who sit in darkness and in the shadow of death,
1.79 Mt 9.2; Mk 4.16; Acts 26.18	to guide our feet into the way of peace."
1.80 Lk 2.40,52	80And the child grew and became strong in spirit, and he was in the wilderness till the day of his manifestation to Israel.

The birth of Jesus the Christ (2.1–7; Mt 1.18–25)

2.1 Lk 3.1	2 In those days a decree went out from Caesar Augŭs'tŭs that all the world should be enrolled. 2 This was the first enroll-
*2.2	ment, when Quĭrĭn'ĭ-ŭs was governor of Syria. 3And all went to be enrolled, each to his own city. 4And Joseph also went up from
2.4 Lk 1.27	Găl'ĭleē, from the city of Năz'ărĕth, to Judē'ă, to the city of David, which is called Bĕth'lĕhĕm, because he was of the house and line-age of David, 5 to be enrolled with Mary, his betrothed, who was with child. 6And while they were there, the time came for her to be delivered. 7And she gave birth to her first-born son and wrapped him in swaddling cloths, and laid him in a manger, because there was no place for them in the inn.

The angels and the shepherds (2.8–20)

2.9 Lk 1.11; Acts 5.19	8 And in that region there were shepherds out in the field, keeping watch over their flock by night. 9And an angel of the Lord appeared to them, and the glory of the Lord shone around them,

ʃ Or *whereby the dayspring will visit.* Other ancient authorities read *since the dayspring has visited*

1.69 *horn* is often used as a metaphor in the Old Testament, meaning "power," "might" (cf. 1 Sam 2.1, 10; 2 Sam 23.3; Ps 18.2). The phrase *a horn of salvation*, means therefore "a mighty savior" (Goodspeed), "a deliverer of victorious power" (New English Bible).

2.2 While many believe that Quirinius had nothing to do with this enrollment, conservative scholars generally accept Sir W. M. Ramsey's view that he controlled Syria's foreign relations and supervised the census. Luke's accuracy has been vindicated on other points.

and they were filled with fear. 10And the angel said to them, "Be not afraid; for behold, I bring you good news of a great joy which will come to all the people; 11 for to you is born this day in the city of David a Savior, who is Christ the Lord. 12And this will be a sign for you: you will find a babe wrapped in swaddling cloths and lying in a manger." 13And suddenly there was with the angel a multitude of the heavenly host praising God and saying,
14 "Glory to God in the highest,
　　and on earth peace among men with whom he is pleased!"g

15 When the angels went away from them into heaven, the shepherds said to one another, "Let us go over to Bĕth'lĕhĕm and see this thing that has happened, which the Lord has made known to us." 16And they went with haste, and found Mary and Joseph, and the babe lying in a manger. 17And when they saw it they made known the saying which had been told them concerning this child; 18 and all who heard it wondered at what the shepherds told them. 19 But Mary kept all these things, pondering them in her heart. 20And the shepherds returned, glorifying and praising God for all they had heard and seen, as it had been told them.

The circumcision (2.21)

21 And at the end of eight days, when he was circumcised, he was called Jesus, the name given by the angel before he was conceived in the womb.

The presentation in the Temple (2.22–28)

22 And when the time came for their purification according to the law of Moses, they brought him up to Jerusalem to present him to the Lord 23 (as it is written in the law of the Lord, "Every male that opens the womb shall be called holy to the Lord") 24 and to offer a sacrifice according to what is said in the law of the Lord, "a pair of turtledoves, or two young pigeons." 25 Now there was a man in Jerusalem, whose name was Sĭm'ĕŏn, and this man was righteous and devout, looking for the consolation of Israel, and the Holy Spirit was upon him. 26And it had been revealed to him by the Holy Spirit that he should not see death before he had seen the Lord's Christ. 27And inspired by the Spirith he came into the temple; and when the parents brought in the child Jesus, to do for him according to the custom of the law, 28 he took him up in his arms and blessed God and said,

The song of Simeon (2.29–35)

29 "Lord, now lettest thou thy servant depart in peace,

g Other ancient authorities read peace, good will among men　　h Or in the Spirit

Cross-references:
*2.10 Mt 14.27
*2.11 Jn 4.42; Mt 1.16; 16.16; Lk 1.43; Acts 2.36
2.12 1 Sam 2.34; 2 Ki 19.29; Isa 7.14
2.13 Dan 7.10; Rev 5.11
2.14 Isa 57.19; Lk 1.79; Rom 5.1; Eph 1.9; Phil 2.13
2.19 ver 51
2.20 Mt 9.8
2.21 Lk 1.59; 1.31
2.22 Lev 12.2-6
2.23 Ex 13.2,12; Num 3.13
2.25 ver 38; Lk 23.51
2.26 Ps 89.48; Heb 11.5
2.27 ver 22
2.29 ver 26

2.10 The missionary aspect of the gospel and its primacy are stated again and again in Scripture. The message at Jesus' birth was a message for all people (2.30–32). Even Christ's model prayer had a missionary thrust to it: *Thy kingdom come, Thy will be done, On earth as it is in heaven* (Mt 6.10). The first convert, Andrew, became a missionary: *He first found his brother Simon, and said to him, "We have found the Messiah . . . . He brought him to Jesus."* (Jn 1.41, 42). The first apostolic sermon, addressed to representatives of all the language groups of that age, had a strong missionary motif: *For the promise is . . . to all that are far off . . .* (Acts 2.39). The Great Commission of the risen Lord (recorded for us at least three times) gives expression to His all-embracing concern for all men everywhere (Mt 28.18–20; Jn 20.21; Lk.45–49). 2.11 the city of David, Bethlehem.

Luke 2.30–52

2.30
Isa 52.10;
Lk 3.6
30 for mine eyes have seen thy salvation
31 which thou hast prepared in the presence of all peoples,

2.32
Isa 42.6;
49.6;
Acts 13.47;
26.23
32 a light for revelation to the Gentiles,
and for glory to thy people Israel."

2.34
Mt 21.44;
1 Cor 1.23,
24;
2 Cor 2.16;
1 Pet 2.7,8
33 And his father and his mother marveled at what was said about him; 34 and Sĭm'ëön blessed them and said to Mary his mother,
"Behold, this child is set for the fall and rising of many in Israel,
and for a sign that is spoken against
35 (and a sword will pierce through your own soul also),
that thoughts out of many hearts may be revealed."

The adoration of Anna (2.36–40)

2.36
Acts 21.9;
Josh 19.24;
1 Tim 5.9
36 And there was a prophetess, Anna, the daughter of Phăn'ū-ĕl, of the tribe of Ăshĕr; she was of a great age, having lived with her husband seven years from her virginity, 37 and as a widow till she was eighty-four. She did not depart from the temple, worshiping with fasting and prayer night and day. 38And coming up at that very hour she gave thanks to God, and spoke of him to all who were looking for the redemption of Jerusalem.

2.37
Acts 13.3;
1 Tim 5.5

2.38
ver 25;
Lk 24.21

2.39
ver 51
39 And when they had performed everything according to the law of the Lord, they returned into Găl'ĭleē, to their own city, Năz'ărĕth. 40And the child grew and became strong, filled with wisdom; and the favor of God was upon him.

2.40
ver 52;
Lk 1.80

The boy Jesus in the Temple (2.41–52)

2.41
Ex 23.15;
Deut
16.1–6
41 Now his parents went to Jerusalem every year at the feast of the Passover. 42And when he was twelve years old, they went up according to custom; 43 and when the feast was ended, as they were returning, the boy Jesus stayed behind in Jerusalem. His parents did not know it, 44 but supposing him to be in the company they went a day's journey, and they sought him among their kinsfolk and acquaintances; 45 and when they did not find him, they returned to Jerusalem, seeking him. 46After three days they found him in the temple, sitting among the teachers, listening to them and asking them questions; 47 and all who heard him were amazed at his understanding and his answers. 48And when they saw him they were astonished; and his mother said to him, "Son, why have you treated us so? Behold, your father and I have been looking for you anxiously." 49And he said to them, "How is it that you sought me? Did you not know that I must be in my Father's house?" 50And they did not understand the saying which he spoke to them. 51And he went down with them and came to Năz'ărĕth, and was obedient to them; and his mother kept all these things in her heart.
52 And Jesus increased in wisdom and in stature, *i* and in favor with God and man.

*2.46
2.47
Mt 7.28;
Mk 1.22;
Lk 4.22,
32;
Jn 7.15,46
2.48
Mk 3.31–
35
2.49
Jn 2.16
2.50
Mk 9.32;
Lk 9.45
2.51
ver 19,39
*2.52
ver 40;
1 Sam 2.26

i Or years

2.46 *teachers*, authorities on Jewish religion. **2.52** Read ver 40; 1 Sam 2.26.

The ministry of John the Baptist
(3.1–20; Mt 3.1–12; Mk 1.1–8; Jn 1.6–8; 19–28)

3 In the fifteenth year of the reign of Tĭbĕr'ĭ-ŭs Caesar, Pŏnṭiŭs Pīlate being governor of Jŭdē'à, and Hĕrŏd being tetrarch of Găl'ĭlēē, and his brother Philip tetrarch of the region of Ĭturaē'à and Trăchŏnī'tĭs, and Lȳsā'nĭ-às tetrarch of Ăbĭlē'nē, ² in the high-priesthood of Annas and Cāi'áphàs, the word of God came to John the son of Zĕchárī'áh in the wilderness; ³ and he went into all the region about the Jordan, preaching a baptism of repentance for the forgiveness of sins. ⁴As it is written in the book of the words of Ĭṣāi'áh the prophet,
"The voice of one crying in the wilderness:
Prepare the way of the Lord,
make his paths straight.
⁵ Every valley shall be filled,
and every mountain and hill shall be brought low,
and the crooked shall be made straight,
and the rough ways shall be made smooth;
⁶ and all flesh shall see the salvation of God."

7 He said therefore to the multitudes that came out to be baptized by him, "You brood of vipers! Who warned you to flee from the wrath to come? ⁸ Bear fruits that befit repentance, and do not begin to say to yourselves, 'We have Abraham as our father'; for I tell you, God is able from these stones to raise up children to Abraham. ⁹ Even now the axe is laid to the root of the trees; every tree therefore that does not bear good fruit is cut down and thrown into the fire."

10 And the multitudes asked him, "What then shall we do?" ¹¹And he answered them, "He who has two coats, let him share with him who has none; and he who has food, let him do likewise." ¹² Tax collectors also came to be baptized, and said to him, "Teacher, what shall we do?" ¹³And he said to them, "Collect no more than is appointed you." ¹⁴ Soldiers also asked him, "And we, what shall we do?" And he said to them, "Rob no one by violence or by false accusation, and be content with your wages."

15 As the people were in expectation, and all men questioned in their hearts concerning John, whether perhaps he were the Christ, ¹⁶ John answered them all, "I baptize you with water; but he who is mightier than I is coming, the thong of whose sandals I am not worthy to untie; he will baptize you with the Holy Spirit and with fire. ¹⁷ His winnowing fork is in his hand, to clear his threshing floor, and to gather the wheat into his granary, but the chaff he will burn with unquenchable fire."

18 So, with many other exhortations, he preached good news to the people. ¹⁹ But Hĕrŏd the tetrarch, who had been reproved by him for Hĕrŏ'dĭ-às, his brother's wife, and for all the evil things that Herod had done, ²⁰ added this to them all, that he shut up John in prison.

The baptism of Jesus (3.21,22; Mt 3.13–17; Mk 1.9–11)

21 Now when all the people were baptized, and when Jesus also had been baptized and was praying, the heaven was opened, ²² and the Holy Spirit descended upon him in bodily form, as a dove, and

3.1 Mt 27.2; 14.1
3.2 Jn 11.49; 18.13; Acts 4.6; Mt 26.3
3.4 Isa 40.3–5
3.6 Ps 98.2; Isa 52.10; Lk 2.30
3.7 Mt 12.34; 23.33
3.8 Jn 8.33,39
3.9 Mt 7.19; Heb 6.7,8
3.10 Acts 2.37
3.11 Jas 2.15,16
3.12 Lk 7.29
3.13 Lk 19.8
3.14 Ex 23.1; Lev 19.11
3.15 Acts 13.25
3.16 Acts 1.5; 11.16; 19.4
3.17 Isa 30.24; Mic 4.12; Mt 13.30
3.19 Mt 14.3,4; Mk 6.17,18
3.21 Lk 5.16; 6.12; 9.18,28; 11.1
3.22 Ps 2.7; Isa 42.1; Lk 9.35; Acts 10.38; 2 Pet 1.17

a voice came from heaven, "Thou art my beloved Son;*j* with thee I am well pleased."*k*

The genealogy of Jesus (3.23–38; cf. Mt 1.1–17)

*3.23
Mt 4.17;
Acts 1.1;
Jn 8.57;
Lk 1.27

23 Jesus, when he began his ministry, was about thirty years of age, being the son (as was supposed) of Joseph, the son of Hēlī, 24 the son of Mätthăt, the son of Lēvī, the son of Mĕlchī, the son of Jănʹnä-ī, the son of Joseph, 25 the son of Mättathīʹăs, the son of Amos, the son of Nāhùm, the son of Ĕslī, the son of Năgʹgä-ī, 26 the son of Māʹäth, the son of Mättáthīʹăs, the son of Sĕmʹĕ-ĭn, the son of Jōṣĕçh, the son of Jōdá, 27 the son of Jō-ănʹăn, the son of

3.27
Mt 1.12

Rhēsá, the son of Zĕrubʹbábĕl, the son of Shĕ-ălʹtĭ-ĕl,*l* the son of Nērī, 28 the son of Mĕlchī, the son of Ăddī, the son of Cōsäm, the son of Ĕlmäʹdám, the son of Ĕr, 29 the son of Joshua, the son of Ĕliēʹzĕr, the son of Jōrĭm, the son of Mätthăt, the son of Lēvī, 30 the son of Sĭmʹëön, the son of Judah, the son of Joseph, the

3.31
2 Sam 5.14;
1 Chr 3.5
3.32
Ruth
4.18ff;
1 Chr 2.10ff

son of Jōnám, the son of Ĕliʹákim, 31 the son of Mĕʹlĕ-á, the son of Mĕnná, the son of Mätʹtáthá, the son of Nathan, the son of David, 32 the son of Jĕssë, the son of Ōbĕd, the son of Boăz, the son of Sälá, the son of Nahshón, 33 the son of Ămmĭnʹádăb, the son of Ădmĭn, the son of Arnī, the son of Hĕzròn, the son of Pērĕz, the

3.34
Gen 11.24,
26

son of Judah, 34 the son of Jacob, the son of Isaac, the son of Abraham, the son of Tērăh, the son of Nāhor, 35 the son of Sĕrŭg, the son of Rēʹū, the son of Pĕlĕg, the son of Ēʹbĕr, the son of Shĕ-

3.36
Gen 11.12;
5.6ff

läh, 36 the son of Cāʹ-inán, the son of Arphăʹxăd, the son of Shĕm, the son of Noah, the son of Lämĕçh, 37 the son of Mĕthuʹṣĕláh, the son of Enoch, the son of Jārĕd, the son of Máhäʹlále-ēl, the

3.38
Gen 5.1,2

son of Cāʹ-inán, 38 the son of Ēnòs, the son of Sĕth, the son of Adam, the son of God.

The wilderness temptation of Jesus (4.1–13; Mt 4.1–11; Mk 1.12,13)

4.1
ver 14;
Lk 2.27
*4.2
Ex 34.28;
1 Ki 19.8

4 And Jesus, full of the Holy Spirit, returned from the Jordan, and was led by the Spirit 2 for forty days in the wilderness, tempted by the devil. And he ate nothing in those days; and when they were ended, he was hungry. 3 The devil said to him, "If you are the Son of God, command this stone to become bread."

4.4
Deut 8.3
4.6
Jn 12.31;
14.30;
1 Jn 5.19

4And Jesus answered him, "It is written, 'Man shall not live by bread alone.'" 5And the devil took him up, and showed him all the kingdoms of the world in a moment of time, 6 and said to him, "To you I will give all this authority and their glory; for it has been

---

j Or *my Son, my* (or *the*) *Beloved*   *k* Other ancient authorities read *today I have begotten thee* *l* Greek *Sálaʹthiĕl*

3.23 Matthew seems to trace the genealogy of Joseph, whereas Luke seems to record the genealogy of Mary. Joseph is called the *son of Heli* in Luke apparently in order to conform with Jewish legal custom; this can only mean that he was the son of Heli in the sense that he was the husband of Heli's daughter. Luke carefully specifies that Jesus was not *really* Joseph's son. For Luke, a Greek, to trace Mary's genealogy is not inappropriate, for Luke always shows a special interest in the women who followed Jesus. While Matthew

traces the genealogy of Jesus to Abraham, Luke traces it all the way back to Adam.

4.2 The Bible teaches two great truths about Jesus and sin: (1) He was tempted (Mt 4.1; Mk 1.12, 13; Lk 4.1–13); (2) He was sinless (2 Cor 5.21; Heb 4.15; 1 Jn 3.5; cf. Jn 8.46). This means that it was possible for Christ to be tempted without sinning, and that He was sinless although tempted. In His humanity the possibility of sinning existed, yet He resisted temptation and perfectly fulfilled the law and will of God.

delivered to me, and I give it to whom I will. [7] If you, then, will worship me, it shall all be yours." [8]And Jesus answered him, "It is written,

'You shall worship the Lord your God,
    and him only shall you serve.' "

[9]And he took him to Jerusalem, and set him on the pinnacle of the temple, and said to him, "If you are the Son of God, throw yourself down from here; [10] for it is written,

'He will give his angels charge of you, to guard you,'
[11] and
'On their hands they will bear you up,
    lest you strike your foot against a stone.' "

[12]And Jesus answered him, "It is said, 'You shall not tempt the Lord your God.' " [13]And when the devil had ended every temptation, he departed from him until an opportune time.

Jesus returns to Galilee
(4.14,15; Mt 4.12–17; Mk 1.14,15; Jn 4.43–45)

14 And Jesus returned in the power of the Spirit into Găl′ịleē, and a report concerning him went out through all the surrounding country. [15]And he taught in their synagogues, being glorified by all.

Jesus' first rejection at Nazareth (4.16–30)

16 And he came to Năz′ărĕth, where he had been brought up; and he went to the synagogue, as his custom was, on the sabbath day. And he stood up to read; [17] and there was given to him the book of the prophet Iṣāi′ăh. He opened the book and found the place where it was written,

[18] "The Spirit of the Lord is upon me,
    because he has anointed me to preach good news to the poor.
He has sent me to proclaim release to the captives
    and recovering of sight to the blind,
    to set at liberty those who are oppressed,
[19] to proclaim the acceptable year of the Lord."

[20]And he closed the book, and gave it back to the attendant, and sat down; and the eyes of all in the synagogue were fixed on him. [21]And he began to say to them, "Today this scripture has been fulfilled in your hearing." [22]And all spoke well of him, and wondered at the gracious words which proceeded out of his mouth; and they said, "Is not this Joseph's son?" [23]And he said to them, "Doubtless you will quote to me this proverb, 'Physician, heal yourself; what we have heard you did at Căpĕr′nä-ùm, do here also in your own country.' " [24]And he said, "Truly, I say to you, no prophet is acceptable in his own country. 25 But in truth, I tell you, there were many widows in Israel in the days of Ēlī′jăh, when the heaven was shut up three years and six months, when there came a great famine over all the land; 26 and Ēlī′jăh was sent to none of them but only to Zăr′ĕphăth, in the land of Sīdón, to a

4.8
Deut 6.13

4.10
Ps 91.11,12

4.12
Deut 6.16
4.13
Jn 14.30;
Heb 4.15

4.14
Mt 9.26
4.15
Mt 9.35;
11.1

4.16
Mt 13.54;
Mk 6.1;
Acts 13.14–16

4.18
Isa 61.1,2;
Mt 12.18

★4.19
Lev 25.10
4.20
ver 17
4.22
Ps 45.2;
Mt 13.54,
55;
Mk 6.2,3;
Jn 6.42;
7.15
4.23
Mk 1.21ff;
2.1ff;
ver 16
4.24
Mt 13.57;
Mk 6.4;
Jn 4.44
4.25
1 Ki 17.1,
8–16; 18.1;
Jas 5.17,18

4.19 Jesus ended His quotation from Isa 61.1, 2 just before the phrase, *to proclaim . . . the day of vengeance of our God,* although including the phrase *the year of the Lord's favor* (translated here *the acceptable year of the Lord*). Undoubtedly He made this omission purposely, since the "day of vengeance" still awaits His Second Advent, which is yet future. The "acceptable year of the Lord" was related to His First Advent.

woman who was a widow. ²⁷And there were many lepers in Israel
in the time of the prophet Ĕlī'shă; and none of them was cleansed,
but only Nā'ámán the Syrian." ²⁸ When they heard this, all in the
synagogue were filled with wrath. ²⁹And they rose up and put him
out of the city, and led him to the brow of the hill on which their
city was built, that they might throw him down headlong. ³⁰ But
passing through the midst of them he went away.

Jesus performing miracles at Capernaum (4.31–44)

1. The casting out of the unclean spirit (4.31–37; Mk 1.21–28)

31 And he went down to Cȧpėr'nä-ŭm, a city of Găl'ĭleē. And
he was teaching them on the sabbath; ³² and they were astonished
at his teaching, for his word was with authority. ³³And in the
synagogue there was a man who had the spirit of an unclean
demon; and he cried out with a loud voice, ³⁴ "Ah!ᵐ What have
you to do with us, Jesus of Năz'árėth? Have you come to destroy
us? I know who you are, the Holy One of God." ³⁵ But Jesus rebuked him, saying, "Be silent, and come out of him!" And when
the demon had thrown him down in the midst, he came out of
him, having done him no harm. ³⁶And they were all amazed and
said to one another, "What is this word? For with authority and
power he commands the unclean spirits, and they come out."
³⁷And reports of him went out into every place in the surrounding
region.

2. Peter's mother-in-law healed
(4.38, 39; Mt 8.14–17; Mk 1.29–34)

38 And he arose and left the synagogue, and entered Simon's
house. Now Simon's mother-in-law was ill with a high fever, and
they besought him for her. ³⁹And he stood over her and rebuked
the fever, and it left her; and immediately she rose and served
them.

3. Healing the sick; casting out demons
(4.40–44; Mt 8.16–17; Mk 1.32–34)

40 Now when the sun was setting, all those who had any that
were sick with various diseases brought them to him; and he laid
his hands on every one of them and healed them. ⁴¹And demons
also came out of many, crying, "You are the Son of God!" But he
rebuked them, and would not allow them to speak, because they
knew that he was the Christ.

42 And when it was day he departed and went into a lonely
place. And the people sought him and came to him, and would
have kept him from leaving them; ⁴³ but he said to them, "I must
preach the good news of the kingdom of God to the other cities
also; for I was sent for this purpose." ⁴⁴And he was preaching in
the synagogues of Judē'ȧ.ⁿ

The call of the first disciples
(5.1–11; Mt 4.18–22; Mk 1.16–20)

5 While the people pressed upon him to hear the word of God,
he was standing by the lake of Gėnnĕs'ȧrėt. ²And he saw two

4.27
2 Ki 5.1–14

4.29
Num 15.35;
Acts 7.58;
Heb 13.12
4.30
Jn 8.59;
10.39

4.31
Mt 4.13
4.32
Mt 7.28;
Mk 11.18;
Jn 7.46
4.34
ver 41;
Ps 16.10;
Dan 9.24
4.35
ver 39,41;
Mt 8.26;
Mk 4.39;
Lk 8.24
4.36
ver 32
4.37
ver 14

4.39
ver 35,41

4.40
Mk 5.23;
Mt 4.23
4.41
Mt 4.3;
8.4

4.42
Mk 1.35–38
4.44
Mt 4.18–
22;
Mk 1.16–
20;
Jn 1.40–42

ᵐ Or Let us alone   ⁿ Other ancient authorities read Găl'ĭleē

boats by the lake; but the fishermen had gone out of them and were washing their nets. ³ Getting into one of the boats, which was Simon's, he asked him to put out a little from the land. And he sat down and taught the people from the boat. ⁴And when he had ceased speaking, he said to Simon, "Put out into the deep and let down your nets for a catch." ⁵And Simon answered, "Master, we toiled all night and took nothing! But at your word I will let down the nets." ⁶And when they had done this, they enclosed a great shoal of fish; and as their nets were breaking, ⁷ they beckoned to their partners in the other boat to come and help them. And they came and filled both the boats, so that they began to sink. ⁸ But when Simon Peter saw it, he fell down at Jesus' knees, saying, "Depart from me, for I am a sinful man, O Lord." ⁹ For he was astonished, and all that were with him, at the catch of fish which they had taken; ¹⁰ and so also were James and John, sons of Zĕb'ĕdeē, who were partners with Simon. And Jesus said to Simon, "Do not be afraid; henceforth you will be catching men." ¹¹And when they had brought their boats to land, they left everything and followed him.

	5.3
	Mt 13.1,2; Mk 4.1
	5.4
	Jn 21.6
	5.5
	Lk 8.24,45; 9.33,49; 17.13
	5.10
	Mt 14.27
	5.11
	ver 28; Mt 19.29

The leper cleansed (5.12–16; Mt 8.1–4; Mk 1.40–45)

12 While he was in one of the cities, there came a man full of leprosy; and when he saw Jesus, he fell on his face and besought him, "Lord, if you will, you can make me clean." ¹³And he stretched out his hand, and touched him, saying, "I will; be clean." And immediately the leprosy left him. ¹⁴And he charged him to tell no one; but "go and show yourself to the priest, and make an offering for your cleansing, as Moses commanded, for a proof to the people."⁰ ¹⁵ But so much the more the report went abroad concerning him; and great multitudes gathered to hear and to be healed of their infirmities. ¹⁶ But he withdrew to the wilderness and prayed.

	*5.12
	Lk 17.11–19
	5.15
	Mt 9.26; Lk 4.14,37
	5.16
	Mt 14.23; Mk 6.46; Lk 3.21; 6.12; 9.18, 28; 11.1

A paralytic healed and forgiven (5.17–26; Mt 9.1–8; Mk 2.1–12)

17 On one of those days, as he was teaching, there were Phạr'-iseēs and teachers of the law sitting by, who had come from every village of Găl'ileē and Judē'ā and from Jerusalem; and the power of the Lord was with him to heal.ᵖ ¹⁸And behold, men were bringing on a bed a man who was paralyzed, and they sought to bring him in and lay him before Jesus;�q ¹⁹ but finding no way to bring him in, because of the crowd, they went up on the roof and let him down with his bed through the tiles into the midst before Jesus. ²⁰And when he saw their faith he said, "Man, your

	5.17
	Mt 15.1; Mk 5.30; Lk 6.19
	5.19
	Mt 24.17
	5.20
	Lk 7.48,49

o Greek to them   p Other ancient authorities read was present to heal them   q Greek him

---

5.12 Leprosy was a common disease among the Hebrews. It was then almost incurable and was easily transmitted from one person to another. Lepers were: (1) ceremonially unclean (Lev 13.8, 11, 22, 44); (2) cut off from the house of God (2 Chr 26.21); (3) excluded from the office of the priesthood (Lev 22.2–4); (4) forbidden to associate with others (Num 5.2; 12.14, 15); (5) under obligation in public to cry aloud that they were unclean (Lev 13.45). Minute prescriptions were set up to detect and diagnose leprosy as well as rules to govern the cleansing of lepers. Biblically the disease of leprosy is used as a type of the spiritual disease of sin which cuts man off from communion with God until it is cleansed away. Jesus is the only cure for the leprosy of sin.

5.21
Isa 43.25

sins are forgiven you." 21And the scribes and the Phạr'ịseẹ̄ș began to question, saying, "Who is this that speaks blasphemies? Who can forgive sins but God only?" 22 When Jesus perceived their questionings, he answered them, "Why do you question in your hearts? 23 Which is easier, to say, 'Your sins are forgiven you,' or to say, 'Rise and walk'? 24 But that you may know that the Son of man has authority on earth to forgive sins"—he said to the man who was paralyzed—"I say to you, rise, take up your bed and go home." 25And immediately he rose before them, and took up that

5.26
Lk 7.16

on which he lay, and went home, glorifying God. 26And amazement seized them all, and they glorified God and were filled with awe, saying, "We have seen strange things today."

The call of (Matthew) Levi
(5.27–32; Mt 9.9–13; Mk 2.13–17)

★5.27
5.28
ver 11

27 After this he went out, and saw a tax collector, named Lēvī, sitting at the tax office; and he said to him, "Follow me." 28And he left everything, and rose and followed him.

5.29
Lk 15.1

29 And Lēvī made him a great feast in his house; and there was a large company of tax collectors and others sitting at table[r] with

5.30
Acts 23.9

them. 30And the Phạr'ịseẹ̄ș and their scribes murmured against his disciples, saying, "Why do you eat and drink with tax collectors and sinners?" 31And Jesus answered them, "Those who are

5.32
1 Tim 1.15

well have no need of a physician, but those who are sick; 32 I have not come to call the righteous, but sinners to repentance."

The question about fasting
(5.33–39; Mt 9.14–17; Mk 2.18–22)

5.33
Lk 7.18;
Jn 3.25,26

33 And they said to him, "The disciples of John fast often and offer prayers, and so do the disciples of the Phạr'ịseẹ̄ș, but yours eat and drink." 34And Jesus said to them, "Can you make wedding

5.35
Lk 9.22;
17.22

guests fast while the bridegroom is with them? 35 The days will come, when the bridegroom is taken away from them, and then they will fast in those days." 36 He told them a parable also: "No

★5.36

one tears a piece from a new garment and puts it upon an old garment; if he does, he will tear the new, and the piece from the new will not match the old. 37And no one puts new wine into old wineskins; if he does, the new wine will burst the skins and it will be spilled, and the skins will be destroyed. 38 But new wine must be put into fresh wineskins. 39And no one after drinking old wine desires new; for he says, 'The old is good.'"[s]

[r] Greek reclining   [s] Other ancient authorities read better

5.27 The tax collectors (KJV, "publicans") were cordially hated by the Jews and were regarded as extortioners (18.11; 3.13; 19.8). Some of them became quite wealthy (19.2). Christ was condemned for associating with them (Mt 9.11; 11.19). A number of them had already been influenced by John the Baptist (Mt 21.32), and had received his baptism (3.12; 7.29). Many of them now listened to the preaching of Christ and embraced the gospel (Mk 2.15; Lk 15.1; Mt 21.31). The Apostle Matthew was a tax collector (Mt 10.3).

5.36 The parables of the new cloth and the new wine are designed to teach the same general lesson. The unwise bringing together of old and new is self-defeating. To mix the new and living Kingdom of God with the obsolete legalistic system of the old Jewish dispensation is self-defeating. This was shown to be true after Pentecost when it became necessary to separate the Christian church from the Judaistic community which still put its trust in works of religion and merit.

Jesus the Lord of the Sabbath
(6.1–5; Mt 12.1–8; Mk 2.23–28)

6 On a sabbath,^{t} while he was going through the grainfields, his disciples plucked and ate some heads of grain, rubbing them in their hands. 2 But some of the Phar′isees said, "Why are you doing what is not lawful to do on the sabbath?" 3 And Jesus answered, "Have you not read what David did when he was hungry, he and those who were with him: 4 how he entered the house of God, and took and ate the bread of the Presence, which it is not lawful for any but the priests to eat, and also gave it to those with him?" 5 And he said to them, "The Son of man is lord of the sabbath."

*6.1
Deut 23.25
6.2
Ex 20.10;
23.12;
Deut 5.14
*6.3
1 Sam 21.6
6.4
Lev 24.9

Jesus heals on the Sabbath
(6.6–11; Mt 12.9–14; Mk 3.1–6)

6 On another sabbath, when he entered the synagogue and taught, a man was there whose right hand was withered. 7 And the scribes and the Phar′isees watched him, to see whether he would heal on the sabbath, so that they might find an accusation against him. 8 But he knew their thoughts, and he said to the man who had the withered hand, "Come and stand here." And he rose and stood there. 9 And Jesus said to them, "I ask you, is it lawful on the sabbath to do good or to do harm, to save life or to destroy it?" 10 And he looked around on them all, and said to him, "Stretch out your hand." And he did so, and his hand was restored. 11 But they were filled with fury and discussed with one another what they might do to Jesus.

6.6
Lk 13.14;
14.3;
Jn 9.16

6.8
Mt 9.4

The choosing of the Twelve
(6.12–16; Mt 10.1–4; Mk 3.13–19)

12 In these days he went out to the mountain to pray; and all night he continued in prayer to God. 13 And when it was day, he called his disciples, and chose from them twelve, whom he named apostles; 14 Simon, whom he named Peter, and Andrew his brother, and James and John, and Philip, and Barthol′omew, 15 and Matthew, and Thomas, and James the son of Alphae′us, and Simon who was called the Zealot, 16 and Judas the son of James, and Judas Isca′riot, who became a traitor.

*6.12
Mt 14.23;
Lk 9.28
*6.13
Mk 6.30

6.16
Jude 1

^{t} Other ancient authorities read *On the second first sabbath* (on the second sabbath after the first)

6.1 See note to Mk 2.27 for information on the Sabbath.

6.3 See note to Mt 12.3 for further elaboration.

6.12 The prayer life of Jesus shows that important acts were performed only after serious prayer had preceded them. Perhaps the most notable instance is His prayer in Gethsemane.

6.13 An *apostle* (from the Greek *apostolos*) is "one sent forth." He is an ambassador who not only bears a message but also represents the one who sends him. The New Testament office of apostle does not continue today because one of its indispensable qualifications was that an apostle must have actually seen the Lord and thus have become an eye-witness to His Resurrection (24.48; Acts 1.8, 22; 1 Cor 9.1). A second qualification was the special call of the Holy Spirit, for no human authority could invest a man with this office (1 Cor 12.28; Eph 4.11). The apostles often enjoyed the ability to perform signs of an apostolic character, that is wonders and "powers" (or miracles of healing). Incidentally, the number of the apostles was not limited to the twelve disciples. Scripture speaks of Paul, Barnabas, James, and perhaps Andronicus and Junius as apostles (Acts 14.14; Gal 1.19; 1 Cor 15.7; Rom 16.7).

Sermon on the Mount: Beatitudes and other teachings (6.17–26; cf. Mt 5–7)

17 And he came down with them and stood on a level place, with a great crowd of his disciples and a great multitude of people from all Judē'ā and Jerusalem and the seacoast of Tȳre and Sīdòn, who came to hear him and to be healed of their diseases; 18 and those who were troubled with unclean spirits were cured. 19And all the crowd sought to touch him, for power came forth from him and healed them all.

20 And he lifted up his eyes on his disciples, and said: "Blessed are you poor, for yours is the kingdom of God.

21 "Blessed are you that hunger now, for you shall be satisfied. "Blessed are you that weep now, for you shall laugh.

22 "Blessed are you when men hate you, and when they exclude you and revile you, and cast out your name as evil, on account of the Son of man! 23 Rejoice in that day, and leap for joy, for behold, your reward is great in heaven; for so their fathers did to the prophets.

24 "But woe to you that are rich, for you have received your consolation.

25 "Woe to you that are full now, for you shall hunger. "Woe to you that laugh now, for you shall mourn and weep.

26 "Woe to you, when all men speak well of you, for so their fathers did to the false prophets.

The law of love (6.27–36; Mt 5.43–48)

27 "But I say to you that hear, Love your enemies, do good to those who hate you, 28 bless those who curse you, pray for those who abuse you. 29 To him who strikes you on the cheek, offer the other also; and from him who takes away your coat do not withhold even your shirt. 30 Give to every one who begs from you; and of him who takes away your goods do not ask them again. 31And as you wish that men would do to you, do so to them. 32 "If you love those who love you, what credit is that to you? For even sinners love those who love them. 33And if you do good to those who do good to you, what credit is that to you? For even sinners do the same. 34And if you lend to those from whom you hope to receive, what credit is that to you? Even sinners lend to sinners, to receive as much again. 35 But love your enemies, and do good, and lend, expecting nothing in return;^{v} and your reward will be great, and you will be sons of the Most High; for he is kind to the ungrateful and the selfish. 36 Be merciful, even as your Father is merciful.

Censure and reproof (6.37–45; Mt 7.1–5)

37 "Judge not, and you will not be judged; condemn not, and you will not be condemned; forgive, and you will be forgiven; 38 give, and it will be given to you; good measure, pressed down, shaken together, running over, will be put into your lap. For the measure you give will be the measure you get back."

39 He also told them a parable: "Can a blind man lead a blind

Marginal references: 6.17 Mt 4.25; Mk 3.7,8 | 6.19 Mt 9.21; 14.36; Mk 3.10; Lk 5.17 | 6.21 Isa 61.3 | 6.22 1 Pet 4.14; Jn 9.22; 16.2 | 6.23 Acts 5.41; Col 1.24; Mal 4.2; Acts 7.51 | 6.24 Jas 5.1; Lk 16.25 | 6.25 Isa 65.13; Prov 14.13 | 6.26 Jn 15.19 | 6.27 ver 35; Rom 12.20 | 6.28 Lk 23.34; Acts 7.60 | 6.30 Deut 15.7, 8,10; Prov 21.26 | 6.31 Mt 7.12 | 6.35 ver 27,30 | 6.37 Rom 2.1 | 6.38 Mk 4.24; Jas 2.13 | 6.39 Mt 15.4

---

^{v} Other ancient authorities read *despairing of no man*

man? Will they not both fall into a pit? 40A disciple is not above his teacher, but every one when he is fully taught will be like his teacher. 41 Why do you see the speck that is in your brother's eye, but do not notice the log that is in your own eye? 42 Or how can you say to your brother, 'Brother, let me take out the speck that is in your eye,' when you yourself do not see the log that is in your own eye? You hypocrite, first take the log out of your own eye, and then you will see clearly to take out the speck that is in your brother's eye.

43 "For no good tree bears bad fruit, nor again does a bad tree bear good fruit; 44for each tree is known by its own fruit. For figs are not gathered from thorns, nor are grapes picked from a bramble bush. 45 The good man out of the good treasure of his heart produces good, and the evil man out of his evil treasure produces evil; for out of the abundance of the heart his mouth speaks.

The parable of the two houses (6.46–49; Mt 7.24–27)

46 "Why do you call me 'Lord, Lord,' and not do what I tell you? 47 Every one who comes to me and hears my words and does them, I will show you what he is like: 48 he is like a man building a house, who dug deep, and laid the foundation upon rock; and when a flood arose, the stream broke against that house, and could not shake it, because it had been well built.ʷ 49 But he who hears and does not do them is like a man who built a house on the ground without a foundation; against which the stream broke, and immediately it fell, and the ruin of that house was great."

The centurion's servant healed (7.1–10; Mt 8.5–13)

7 After he had ended all his sayings in the hearing of the people he entered Cápêr′nä-ùm. 2 Now a centurion had a slave who was dearˣ to him, who was sick and at the point of death. 3 When he heard of Jesus, he sent to him elders of the Jews, asking him to come and heal his slave. 4And when they came to Jesus, they besought him earnestly, saying, "He is worthy to have you do this for him, 5 for he loves our nation, and he built us our synagogue." 6And Jesus went with them. When he was not far from the house, the centurion sent friends to him, saying to him, "Lord, do not trouble yourself, for I am not worthy to have you come under my roof; 7 therefore I did not presume to come to you. But say the word, and let my servant be healed. 8 For I am a man set under authority, with soldiers under me: and I say to one, 'Go,' and he goes; and to another, 'Come,' and he comes; and to my slave, 'Do this,' and he does it." 9 When Jesus heard this he marveled at him, and turned and said to the multitude that followed him, "I tell you, not even in Israel have I found such faith." 10And when those who had been sent returned to the house, they found the slave well.

ʷ Other ancient authorities read *founded upon the rock*   ˣ Or *valuable*

6.48 The obvious meaning of this parable is the difference between a true and a false profession. The *rock* as a symbol of a true profession is quite appropriate and is analogous to Paul's reference to a solid foundation as a figure for those who live truly in Christ (1 Cor 3.11). Peter's use of the metaphor of the stone is somewhat similar (1 Pet 2.7, 8).

Margin refs: 6.40 Mt 10.24; Jn 13.16; 15.20; 6.43 Mt 7.16,18, 20; 6.44 Mt 12.33; 6.45 Mt 12.34, 35; Mk 7.20; 6.46 Mt 7.21; 6.47 Jas 1.22–25; *6.48; 7.1 Mt 7.28; 7.9 ver 50

The raising of the widow's son (7.11–17)

7.11
1 Ki 17.17–
24;
2 Ki 4.32–
37;
Mk 5.21–
24,35–43;
Jn 11.1–44
7.13
ver 19;
Lk 10.1;
11.1,39;
12.42;
13.15;
17.5,6;
18.6; 19.8;
22.61;
24.34
7.14
Lk 8.54;
Jn 11.43;
Acts 9.40
7.16
Lk 1.65;
Jn 6.14;
Lk 1.68

11 Soon afterwardʸ he went to a city called Nā′in, and his disciples and a great crowd went with him. 12As he drew near to the gate of the city, behold, a man who had died was being carried out, the only son of his mother, and she was a widow; and a large crowd from the city was with her. 13And when the Lord saw her, he had compassion on her and said to her, "Do not weep." 14And he came and touched the bier, and the bearers stood still. And he said, "Young man, I say to you, arise." 15And the dead man sat up, and began to speak. And he gave him to his mother. 16 Fear seized them all; and they glorified God, saying, "A great prophet has arisen among us!" and "God has visited his people!" 17And this report concerning him spread through the whole of Judē′a and all the surrounding country.

John the Baptist's last message (7.18–35; Mt 11.2–19)

7.21
Mt 4.23;
Mk 3.10
7.22
Isa 29.18,
19;35.5,6;
Lk 4.18

18 The disciples of John told him of all these things. 19And John, calling to him two of his disciples, sent them to the Lord, saying, "Are you he who is to come, or shall we look for another?" 20And when the men had come to him, they said, "John the Baptist has sent us to you, saying, 'Are you he who is to come, or shall we look for another?' " 21 In that hour he cured many of diseases and plagues and evil spirits, and on many that were blind he bestowed sight. 22And he answered them, "Go and tell John what you have seen and heard: the blind receive their sight, the lame walk, lepers are cleansed, and the deaf hear, the dead are raised up, the poor have good news preached to them. 23And blessed is he who takes no offense at me."

24 When the messengers of John had gone, he began to speak to the crowds concerning John: "What did you go out into the wilderness to behold? A reed shaken by the wind? 25 What then did you go out to see? A man clothed in soft clothing? Behold, those who are gorgeously appareled and live in luxury are in kings' courts. 26 What then did you go out to see? A prophet? Yes, I tell you, and more than a prophet. 27 This is he of whom it is written,

7.27
Mal 3.1;
Mk 1.2

'Behold, I send my messenger before thy face,
who shall prepare thy way before thee.'
28 I tell you, among those born of women none is greater than John; yet he who is least in the kingdom of God is greater than he." 29 (When they heard this all the people and the tax collectors justified God, having been baptized with the baptism of John; 30 but the Phar′isees and the lawyers rejected the purpose of God for themselves, not having been baptized by him.)

7.29
Mt 21.32;
Lk 3.12
7.30
Mt 22.35;
Acts 20.27

31 "To what then shall I compare the men of this generation, and what are they like? 32 They are like children sitting in the market place and calling to one another,

'We piped to you, and you did not dance;
we wailed, and you did not weep.'
33 For John the Baptist has come eating no bread and drinking no wine; and you say, 'He has a demon.' 34 The Son of man has come eating and drinking; and you say, 'Behold, a glutton and a drunk-

7.33
Lk 1.15
7.34
Lk 5.29;
15.1,2

ʸ Other ancient authorities read *Next day*

ard, a friend of tax collectors and sinners!' 35 Yet wisdom is justified by all her children.''

Jesus anointed: the sinful woman forgiven (7.36–50)

36 One of the Phar'isees asked him to eat with him, and he went
into the Phar'isee's house, and took his place at table. 37 And behold, a woman of the city, who was a sinner, when she learned
that he was at table in the Phar'isee's house, brought an alabaster
flask of ointment, 38 and standing behind him at his feet, weeping,
she began to wet his feet with her tears, and wiped them with the
hair of her head, and kissed his feet, and anointed them with the
ointment. 39 Now when the Phar'isee who had invited him saw it,
he said to himself, "If this man were a prophet, he would have
known who and what sort of woman this is who is touching him,
for she is a sinner." 40 And Jesus answering said to him, "Simon,
I have something to say to you." And he answered, "What is it,
Teacher?" 41 "A certain creditor had two debtors; one owed five
hundred denarii, and the other fifty. 42 When they could not pay,
he forgave them both. Now which of them will love him more?"
43 Simon answered, "The one, I suppose, to whom he forgave
more." And he said to him, "You have judged rightly." 44 Then
turning toward the woman he said to Simon, "Do you see this
woman? I entered your house, you gave me no water for my feet,
but she has wet my feet with her tears and wiped them with her
hair. 45 You gave me no kiss, but from the time I came in she has
not ceased to kiss my feet. 46 You did not anoint my head with oil,
but she has anointed my feet with ointment. 47 Therefore I tell
you, her sins, which are many, are forgiven, for she loved much;
but he who is forgiven little, loves little." 48 And he said to her,
"Your sins are forgiven." 49 Then those who were at table with
him began to say among themselves, "Who is this, who even forgives sins?" 50 And he said to the woman, "Your faith has saved
you; go in peace."

Christ's companions on his second preaching tour (8.1–3)

8 Soon afterward he went on through cities and villages, preaching and bringing the good news of the kingdom of God. And
the twelve were with him, 2 and also some women who had been

*7.36ff
Mt 26.6–
13;
Mk 14.3–9;
Jn 12.1–8

7.39
ver 16;
Lk 24.19;
Jn 6.14

*7.41
Mt 18.28

7.44
Gen 18.4;
19.2;
43.24;
Judg 19.21;
1 Tim 5.10

7.46
Ps 23.5

7.48
Mt 9.2;
Mk 2.5;
Lk 5.20
7.50
Mt 9.22;
Mk 5.34;
Lk 8.48

8.1
Mt 4.23
*8.2
Mt 27.55,56

7.36ff There should not be any confusion
between this incident, during the Galilean
ministry of Christ, and a similar incident
in Bethany of Judea, during the last week of
our Lord's life (Mt 26.6–13; Mk 14.3–9;
Jn 12.1–8). In the one case the woman is
unnamed, in the other she is identified as
Mary, the sister of Martha and Lazarus (Jn
11.1, 2); the host in Galilee was Simon the
Pharisee (7.36, 40); in Bethany he was Simon
the leper (Mt 26.6; Mk 14.3); the concluding
remarks of Jesus are quite dissimilar in the
two incidents. Furthermore, there is no New
Testament evidence for identifying the anonymous *sinner* of 7.37 with Mary Magdalene
(cf. note to 8.2).

7.41 Christ here emphasizes the obligation
of gratitude as incumbent upon those who
have been pardoned. The greater the wickedness from which one has been delivered, the
greater the love he should normally show

toward the person who delivered him. Incidental to this parable is the lesson taught
through the life of the grateful woman. Christ
accepted her outward works as an evidence of
a genuine inner faith. She was saved by faith.
Faith was instrumental in her salvation but
not the ground of it. However, her salvation
was manifested in outward conduct. (See
also Jas 2.14–26; Tit 2.14; 3.4–8.)

8.2 The name *Magdalene* means "of (the
town of) Magdala," a fishing village, also
called Tarichaea, on the west side of the Sea
of Galilee. This verse in Luke contains the
only specific item of information about Mary's
previous life: she had been freed from seven
demons, presumably by Jesus. Nowhere in
the New Testament is demon possession
equated with immorality, or said to be the
cause of immorality, and there is nothing in
the Gospels to support the frequent assertion
that Mary had been a prostitute.

healed of evil spirits and infirmities: Mary, called Măg'dålēne, from whom seven demons had gone out, 3 and Jō-ăn'nà, the wife of Çhuzà, Hĕrŏd'ş steward, and Susanna, and many others, who provided for them^z out of their means.

Parable of the sower (8.4–8; Mt 13.1–8; Mk 4.1–9)

4 And when a great crowd came together and people from town after town came to him, he said in a parable: 5 "A sower went out to sow his seed; and as he sowed, some fell along the path, and was trodden under foot, and the birds of the air devoured it. 6And some fell on the rock; and as it grew up, it withered away, because it had no moisture. 7And some fell among thorns; and the thorns grew with it and choked it. 8And some fell into good soil and grew, and yielded a hundredfold." As he said this, he called out, "He who has ears to hear, let him hear."

The reason for parables (8.9,10; Mt 13.1–17; Mk 4.10–12)

9 And when his disciples asked him what this parable meant, 10 he said, "To you it has been given to know the secrets of the kingdom of God; but for others they are in parables, so that seeing

The parable of the sower explained (8.11–18; Mt 13.18–23; Mk 4.13–20)

they may not see, and hearing they may not understand. 11 Now the parable is this: The seed is the word of God. 12 The ones along the path are those who have heard; then the devil comes and takes away the word from their hearts, that they may not believe and be saved. 13And the ones on the rock are those who, when they hear the word, receive it with joy; but these have no root, they believe for a while and in time of temptation fall away. 14And as for what fell among the thorns, they are those who hear, but as they go on their way they are choked by the cares and riches and pleasures of life, and their fruit does not mature. 15And as for that in the good soil, they are those who, hearing the word, hold it fast in an honest and good heart, and bring forth fruit with patience.

16 "No one after lighting a lamp covers it with a vessel, or puts it under a bed, but puts it on a stand, that those who enter may see the light. 17 For nothing is hid that shall not be made manifest, nor anything secret that shall not be known and come to light. 18 Take heed then how you hear; for to him who has will more be given, and from him who has not, even what he thinks that he has will be taken away."

Christ's true kindred (8.19–21; Mt 12.46–50; Mk 3.31–35)

19 Then his mother and his brothers came to him, but they could not reach him for the crowd. 20And he was told, "Your mother and your brothers are standing outside, desiring to see you." 21 But he said to them, "My mother and my brothers are those who hear the word of God and do it."

z Other ancient authorities read him

8.5 See note to Mk 4.3 for an explanation of the parable of the sower.

8.16 a vessel. Mk 4.21 and Mt 5.15 have a bushel.

margin refs: *8.5 / 8.8 Mt 11.15 / 8.10 Isa 6.9,10; Jer 5.21; Ezek 12.2 / 8.11 1 Thess 2.13; 1 Pet 1.23 / *8.16 Mt 5.15; Mk 4.21; Lk 11.33 / 8.17 Mt 10.26; Mk 4.22; Lk 12.2 / 8.18 Mt 13.12; 25.29; Lk 19.26 / 8.21 Lk 11.28; Jn 15.14

The storm stilled (8.22–25; Mt 8.23–27; Mk 4.36–41)

22 One day he got into a boat with his disciples, and he said to them, "Let us go across to the other side of the lake." So they set out, 23 and as they sailed he fell asleep. And a storm of wind came down on the lake, and they were filling with water, and were in danger. 24And they went and woke him, saying, "Master, Master, we are perishing!" And he awoke and rebuked the wind and the raging waves; and they ceased, and there was a calm. 25 He said to them, "Where is your faith?" And they were afraid, and they marveled, saying to one another, "Who then is this, that he commands even wind and water, and they obey him?"

8.22
Mk 6.47–52;
Jn 6.16–21

8.24
Lk 5.5;
4.39

Demons cast out (8.26–39; Mt 8.28–34; Mk 6.1–20)

26 Then they arrived at the country of the Gĕr′åsēnęs,[a] which is opposite Găl′ịleē. 27And as he stepped out on land, there met him a man from the city who had demons; for a long time he had worn no clothes, and he lived not in a house but among the tombs. 28 When he saw Jesus, he cried out and fell down before him, and said with a loud voice, "What have you to do with me, Jesus, Son of the Most High God? I beseech you, do not torment me." 29 For he had commanded the unclean spirit to come out of the man. (For many a time it had seized him; he was kept under guard, and bound with chains and fetters, but he broke the bonds and was driven by the demon into the desert.) 30 Jesus then asked him, "What is your name?" And he said, "Legion"; for many demons had entered him. 31And they begged him not to command them to depart into the abyss. 32 Now a large herd of swine was feeding there on the hillside; and they begged him to let them enter these. So he gave them leave. 33 Then the demons came out of the man and entered the swine, and the herd rushed down the steep bank into the lake and were drowned.

34 When the herdsmen saw what had happened, they fled, and told it in the city and in the country. 35 Then people went out to see what had happened, and they came to Jesus, and found the man from whom the demons had gone, sitting at the feet of Jesus, clothed and in his right mind; and they were afraid. 36And those who had seen it told them how he who had been possessed with demons was healed. 37 Then all the people of the surrounding country of the Gĕr′åsēnęs[a] asked him to depart from them; for they were seized with great fear; so he got into the boat and returned. 38 The man from whom the demons had gone begged that he might be with him; but he sent him away, saying, 39 "Return to your home, and declare how much God has done for you." And he went away, proclaiming throughout the whole city how much Jesus had done for him.

8.28
Mk 1.24

8.31
Rom 10.7;
Rev 20.1,3

8.33
ver 22,23

8.35
Lk 10.39

8.36
Mt 4.24

8.37
Acts 16.39

The woman with the issue of blood healed and Jairus' daughter raised (8.40–56; Mt 9.18–26; Mk 5.21–43)

40 Now when Jesus returned, the crowd welcomed him, for they were all waiting for him. 41And there came a man named Jaīrŭs, who was a ruler of the synagogue; and falling at Jesus' feet

---

[a] Other ancient authorities read Găd′årēnęs, others Gĕr′gèsēnęs

he besought him to come to his house, 42 for he had an only daughter, about twelve years of age, and she was dying.

As he went, the people pressed round him. 43And a woman who had had a flow of blood for twelve years[b] and could not be healed by any one, 44 came up behind him, and touched the fringe of his garment; and immediately her flow of blood ceased. 45And Jesus said, "Who was it that touched me?" When all denied it, Peter[c] said, "Master, the multitudes surround you and press upon you!" 46 But Jesus said, "Some one touched me; for I perceive that power has gone forth from me." 47And when the woman saw that she was not hidden, she came trembling, and falling down before him declared in the presence of all the people why she had touched him, and how she had been immediately healed. 48And he said to her, "Daughter, your faith has made you well; go in peace."

49 While he was still speaking, a man from the ruler's house came and said, "Your daughter is dead; do not trouble the Teacher any more." 50 But Jesus on hearing this answered him, "Do not fear; only believe, and she shall be well." 51And when he came to the house, he permitted no one to enter with him, except Peter and John and James, and the father and mother of the child. 52And all were weeping and bewailing her; but he said, "Do not weep; for she is not dead but sleeping." 53And they laughed at him, knowing that she was dead. 54 But taking her by the hand he called, saying, "Child, arise." 55And her spirit returned, and she got up at once; and he directed that something should be given her to eat. 56And her parents were amazed; but he charged them to tell no one what had happened.

The mission of the Twelve (9.1–6; Mt 10.1–15; Mk 6.7–13)

9 And he called the twelve together and gave them power and authority over all demons and to cure diseases, 2 and he sent them out to preach the kingdom of God and to heal. 3And he said to them, "Take nothing for your journey, no staff, nor bag, nor bread, nor money; and do not have two tunics. 4And whatever house you enter, stay there, and from there depart. 5And wherever they do not receive you, when you leave that town shake off the dust from your feet as a testimony against them." 6And they departed and went through the villages, preaching the gospel and healing everywhere.

Death of John the Baptist (9.7–9; Mt 14.1–12; Mk 6.14–39)

7 Now Hĕrŏd the tetrarch heard of all that was done, and he was perplexed, because it was said by some that John had been raised from the dead, 8 by some that Ĕlī′jăh had appeared, and by others that one of the old prophets had risen. 9 Hĕrŏd said, "John I be-

b Other ancient authorities add *and had spent all her living upon physicians*
c Other ancient authorities add *and those who were with him*

Marginal references

8.45 Lk 5.5
*8.46 Lk 5.17; 6.19
8.48 Lk 7.50; 17.19; 18.42
8.49 ver 41
8.52 Lk 23.27; Jn 11.11,13
8.54 Lk 7.14; Jn 11.43
8.56 Mt 8.4; Mk 3.12; 7.36; Lk 9.21
9.1 Mk 3.13,14
9.2 Lk 10.1,9
9.3 Lk 10.4; 22.35
9.5 Acts 13.51
9.7 ver 19
9.8 Mt 16.14
9.9 Lk 23.8

8.46 Here, and in the parallel Mk 5.30, reference is made to the *power* (Greek *dunamis*) which went forth from Jesus and healed the woman with the flow of blood. From the account, this took place without any conscious volition on the part of Jesus. In 5.17 it is reported that *the power of the Lord* was with Jesus for him to perform healings, and 6.19 speaks of the power that came forth from Jesus and healed all. These passages point up the truth elsewhere expressed that Jesus healed and expelled demons by the power of God, or the Spirit of God (cf. 4.18; 11.20; Mt 12.28).

headed; but who is this about whom I hear such things?" And he sought to see him.

The five thousand fed (9.10–17; Mt 14.13–21; Mk 6.30–44; Jn 6.1–13; cf. Mt 15.32–38)

10 On their return the apostles told him what they had done. And he took them and withdrew apart to a city called Běth-sā´ĭdă. 11 When the crowds learned it, they followed him; and he welcomed them and spoke to them of the kingdom of God, and cured those who had need of healing. 12 Now the day began to wear away; and the twelve came and said to him, "Send the crowd away, to go into the villages and country round about, to lodge and get provisions; for we are here in a lonely place." 13 But he said to them, "You give them something to eat." They said, "We have no more than five loaves and two fish—unless we are to go and buy food for all these people." 14 For there were about five thousand men. And he said to his disciples, "Make them sit down in companies, about fifty each." 15And they did so, and made them all sit down. 16And taking the five loaves and the two fish he looked up to heaven, and blessed and broke them, and gave them to the disciples to set before the crowd. 17And all ate and were satisfied. And they took up what was left over, twelve baskets of broken pieces.

9.10
ver 17

9.13
2 Ki 4.42–44

9.16
Lk 22.19;
24.30,31;
Acts 2.42;
20.11;
27.35

Peter's confession and Christ's death and resurrection foretold (9.18–27; Mt 16.13–28; Mk 8.27–9.1)

18 Now it happened that as he was praying alone the disciples were with him; and he asked them, "Who do the people say that I am?" 19And they answered, "John the Baptist; but others say, Ĕlī´jȧh; and others, that one of the old prophets has risen." 20And he said to them, "But who do you say that I am?" And Peter answered, "The Christ of God." 21 But he charged and commanded them to tell this to no one, 22 saying, "The Son of man must suffer many things, and be rejected by the elders and chief priests and scribes, and be killed, and on the third day be raised."

9.18
Jn 1.49;
6.66–69;
11.27
9.19
ver 7.8;
Mk 9.11–13
*9.20
Jn 6.69
9.21
Mt 16.20
9.22
ver 43–45;
Lk 18.31–34

23 And he said to all, "If any man would come after me, let him deny himself and take up his cross daily and follow me. 24 For whoever would save his life will lose it; and whoever loses his life for my sake, he will save it. 25 For what does it profit a man if he gains the whole world and loses or forfeits himself? 26 For whoever is ashamed of me and of my words, of him will the Son of man be ashamed when he comes in his glory and the glory of the Father and of the holy angels. 27 But I tell you truly, there are some standing here who will not taste death before they see the kingdom of God."

9.23
Mt 10.38;
Lk 14.27
9.24
Mt 10.39
9.25
Jn 12.25
9.26
Mt 10.33;
Lk 12.9;
2 Tim 2.12;
1 Jn 2.28
9.27
Lk 22.18;
Jn 21.22

The Transfiguration (9.28–36; Mt 17.1–8; Mk 9.2–13)

28 Now about eight days after these sayings he took with him Peter and John and James, and went up on the mountain to pray. 29And as he was praying, the appearance of his countenance was

9.28
Lk 3.21;
5.16; 6.12
*9.29

9.20 See note to Mt 16.18 on Peter and the church.

9.29 See note to Mk 9.2 on the Transfiguration.

altered, and his raiment became dazzling white. 30And behold, two men talked with him, Moses and Eli′jah, 31 who appeared in glory and spoke of his departure, which he was to accomplish at Jerusalem. 32 Now Peter and those who were with him were heavy with sleep, and when they wakened they saw his glory and the two men who stood with him. 33And as the men were parting from him, Peter said to Jesus, "Master, it is well that we are here; let us make three booths, one for you and one for Moses and one for Eli′jah"—not knowing what he said. 34As he said this, a cloud came and overshadowed them; and they were afraid as they entered the cloud. 35And a voice came out of the cloud, saying, "This is my Son, my Chosen;*d* listen to him!" 36And when the voice had spoken, Jesus was found alone. And they kept silence and told no one in those days anything of what they had seen.

The unclean spirit cast out of the boy
(9.37–43a; Mt 17.14–21; Mk 9.14–29)

37 On the next day, when they had come down from the mountain, a great crowd met him. 38And behold, a man from the crowd cried, "Teacher, I beg you to look upon my son, for he is my only child; 39 and behold, a spirit seizes him, and he suddenly cries out; it convulses him till he foams, and shatters him, and will hardly leave him. 40And I begged your disciples to cast it out, but they could not." 41 Jesus answered, "O faithless and perverse generation, how long am I to be with you and bear with you? Bring your son here." 42 While he was coming, the demon tore him and convulsed him. But Jesus rebuked the unclean spirit, and healed the boy, and gave him back to his father. 43And all were astonished at the majesty of God.

Jesus again foretells his death and resurrection
(9.43b–45; Mt 17.22–23; Mk 9.30–32)

But while they were all marveling at everything he did, he said to his disciples, 44 "Let these words sink into your ears; for the Son of man is to be delivered into the hands of men." 45 But they did not understand this saying, and it was concealed from them, that they should not perceive it; and they were afraid to ask him about this saying.

Discourse on humility (9.46–56; Mt 18.1–5; Mk 9.33–37)

46 And an argument arose among them as to which of them was the greatest. 47 But when Jesus perceived the thought of their hearts, he took a child and put him by his side, 48 and said to them, "Whoever receives this child in my name receives me, and whoever receives me receives him who sent me; for he who is least among you all is the one who is great."
49 John answered, "Master, we saw a man casting out demons in your name, and we forbade him, because he does not follow with us." 50 But Jesus said to him, "Do not forbid him; for he that is not against you is for you."

d Other ancient authorities read my Beloved

Marginal cross-references (left column):

9.31 — 2 Pet 1.15
9.32 — Mt 26.43; Mk 14.40
9.33 — Lk 5.8; 8.24,45; 17.13
9.35 — 2 Pet 1.17, 18; Mt 3.17
9.36 — Mt 17.9
9.43 — 2 Pet 1.16
9.44 — ver 22
9.45 — Lk 2.50; 18.34
9.48 — Mt 10.40; Jn 12.44; 13.20; Mt 23.11, 12
9.49 — Mk 9.38
9.50 — Mt 12.30

51 When the days drew near for him to be received up, he set his face to go to Jerusalem. ⁵² And he sent messengers ahead of him, who went and entered a village of the Sámȧr'ĭtȧns, to make ready for him; ⁵³ but the people would not receive him, because his face was set toward Jerusalem. ⁵⁴And when his disciples James and John saw it, they said, "Lord, do you want us to bid fire come down from heaven and consume them?"ᵉ ⁵⁵ But he turned and rebuked them.ᶠ ⁵⁶And they went on to another village.

Impulsive and reluctant followers (9.57-62; Mt 8.18-22)

57 As they were going along the road, a man said to him, "I will follow you wherever you go." ⁵⁸And Jesus said to him, "Foxes have holes, and birds of the air have nests; but the Son of man has no-where to lay his head." ⁵⁹ To another he said, "Follow me." But he said, "Lord, let me first go and bury my father." ⁶⁰ But he said to him, "Leave the dead to bury their own dead; but as for you, go and proclaim the kingdom of God." ⁶¹Another said, "I will follow you, Lord; but let me first say farewell to those at my home." ⁶² Jesus said to him, "No one who puts his hand to the plow and looks back is fit for the kingdom of God."

The mission of the seventy (10.1-24)

10 After this the Lord appointed seventyᵍ others, and sent them on ahead of him, two by two, into every town and place where he himself was about to come. ²And he said to them, "The harvest is plentiful, but the laborers are few; pray therefore the Lord of the harvest to send out laborers into his harvest. ³ Go your way; behold, I send you out as lambs in the midst of wolves. ⁴ Carry no purse, no bag, no sandals; and salute no one on the road. ⁵ Whatever house you enter, first say, 'Peace be to this house!' ⁶And if a son of peace is there, your peace shall rest upon him; but if not, it shall return to you. ⁷And remain in the same house, eating and drinking what they provide, for the laborer deserves his wages; do not go from house to house. ⁸ Whenever you enter a town and they receive you, eat what is set before you; ⁹ heal the sick in it and say to them, 'The kingdom of God has come near to you.' ¹⁰ But whenever you enter a town and they do not receive you, go into its streets and say, ¹¹ 'Even the dust of your town that clings to our feet, we wipe off against you; nevertheless know this, that the kingdom of God has come near.' ¹² I tell you, it shall be more tolerable on that day for Sŏdŏm than for that town.

13 "Woe to you, Çhŏrā'zĭn! woe to you, Bĕth-sā'ĭdá! for if the mighty works done in you had been done in Tȳre and Sĭdón, they would have repented long ago, sitting in sackcloth and ashes. ¹⁴ But it shall be more tolerable in the judgment for Tȳre and Sĭdón than for you. ¹⁵And you, Cápĕr'nä-ùm, will you

Cross-references (margin)
9.51 Lk 13.22; 17.11; 18.31; 19.11,28
9.52 Mt 10.5; Jn 4.4
9.54 Mk 3.17; 1 Ki 1.10,12
9.59 Mt 8.21,22
10.1 Mt 10.1; Mk 6.7; Lk 9.1,2, 51,52
10.2 Mt 9.37,38; Jn 4.35
10.3 Mt 10.16
10.4 Mt 10.9,10; Mk 6.8; Lk 9.3
10.5 Mk 10.12
10.7 Mt 10.10; 1 Cor 9.14; 1 Tim 5.18
10.9 Mt 3.2; 10.7
10.11 Mt 10.14; Mk 6.11; Lk 9.5
10.12 Mt 10.15; 11.24
10.13 Mt 11.21; Lk 6.24-26
★10.15 Mt 11.23

---

e Other ancient authorities add as Ēlĭj'ȧh did
f Other ancient authorities add and he said, "You do not know what manner of spirit you are of; for the Son of man came not to destroy men's lives but to save them".
g Other ancient authorities read seventy-two

10.15 Hades (translated in the KJV as grave or hell; derived from the Greek word hades, or haides, meaning "not to be seen") is the New Testament equivalent of the Old Testament sheol. Progressive revelation throws additional light on the subject, but the New Testament

be exalted to heaven? You shall be brought down to Hādēs.

16 "He who hears you hears me, and he who rejects you rejects me, and he who rejects me rejects him who sent me."

17 The seventy[g] returned with joy, saying, "Lord, even the demons are subject to us in your name!" 18And he said to them, "I saw Satan fall like lightning from heaven. 19 Behold, I have given you authority to tread upon serpents and scorpions, and over all the power of the enemy; and nothing shall hurt you. 20 Nevertheless do not rejoice in this, that the spirits are subject to you; but rejoice that your names are written in heaven."

21 In that same hour he rejoiced in the Holy Spirit and said, "I thank thee, Father, Lord of heaven and earth, that thou hast hidden these things from the wise and understanding and revealed them to babes; yea, Father, for such was thy gracious will.[h] 22All things have been delivered to me by my Father; and no one knows who the Son is except the Father, or who the Father is except the Son and any one to whom the Son chooses to reveal him."

23 Then turning to the disciples he said privately, "Blessed are the eyes which see what you see! 24 For I tell you that many prophets and kings desired to see what you see, and did not see it, and to hear what you hear, and did not hear it."

The good Samaritan (10.25–37)

25 And behold, a lawyer stood up to put him to the test, saying, "Teacher, what shall I do to inherit eternal life?" 26 He said to him, "What is written in the law? How do you read?" 27And he answered, "You shall love the Lord your God with all your heart, and with all your soul, and with all your strength, and with all your mind; and your neighbor as yourself." 28And he said to him, "You have answered right; do this, and you will live."

29 But he, desiring to justify himself, said to Jesus, "And who is my neighbor?" 30 Jesus replied, "A man was going down from Jerusalem to Jěr′ĭchō, and he fell among robbers, who stripped him and beat him, and departed, leaving him half dead. 31 Now by chance a priest was going down that road; and when he saw

Marginal references:
10.16
Mt 10.40;
Mk 9.37;
Lk 9.48;
Jn 13.20
10.17
ver 1
10.18
Jn 12.31;
Rev 9.1;
12.8,9
10.19
Acts 28.5
10.20
Ex 32.32;
Ps 69.28;
Dan 12.1;
Phil 4.3;
Heb 12.23;
Rev 13.8;
21.27
10.21
Mt 11.25;
1 Cor 1.26–29
10.22
Mt 28.18;
Jn 3.35;
17.2
10.23
Mt 13.16
10.24
1 Pet 1.10
10.25
Mt 19.16;
Mk 10.17;
Lk 18.18
10.27
Deut 6.5;
Lev 19.18;
Rom 13.9;
Gal 5.14;
Jas 2.8
10.28
Lev 18.5;
Mt 19.17
10.29
Lk 16.15
★10.30

meaning here must be linked to the Old Testament usage. Sheol was there referred to as the general abode of the dead, but without any clear differentiation as to the dwelling-place of the redeemed and of the damned. In the New Testament, *hades* is used in more than one way. Thus it may refer to an actual place, as in 16.23, or it may mean the state of death itself, rather than the place, as in Acts 2.27–31. When we speak of the wicked as *bound for hell* we should have in mind the biblical sense of the word, either in terms of the *lake of fire* (Rev 20.15) or *Gehenna* (see note to Mt 18.9 on Gehenna).

10.30 The parable of the Good Samaritan cannot be understood apart from its context. A lawyer had asked Jesus what he must do to inherit eternal life. Jesus replied by reciting the first table of the Law: *love the Lord your God* (ver 27). Then Jesus gave the parable of the Good Samaritan which had reference to the second table of the Law: *Love your neighbor as yourself* (ver 27). The Jew, in Jesus' day, acknowledged none as his neighbor except those who were Jews. In the parable the priest and the Levite failed to help one of their own, a fellow Jew. The Samaritan, who was hated by the Jews and who was not regarded as a neighbor, assisted the Jew. Jesus gained an admission from the lawyer that the true neighbor was the Samaritan—although the lawyer could not bring himself to use the word "Samaritan" but rather *the one who showed mercy on him* (ver 37). But, this being true, he had to admit that the Jew must also show mercy to those who were not usually regarded as neighbors. The answer to the question of the lawyer, "... *what shall I do to inherit eternal life?*" (ver 25) was twofold: ... *love the Lord your God with all your heart ... and your neighbor as yourself* (ver 27). This, of course, must be understood as indicating a true and living faith, rather than a way of earning salvation, for Jesus elsewhere made it very clear that salvation was of faith alone, not of good works (Jn 6.28, 29; cf. Mt 7.22, 23).

him he passed by on the other side. 32 So likewise a Lēvīte, when he came to the place and saw him, passed by on the other side. 33 But a Sāmạr'ịtận, as he journeyed, came to where he was; and when he saw him, he had compassion, 34 and went to him and bound up his wounds, pouring on oil and wine; then he set him on his own beast and brought him to an inn, and took care of him. 35And the next day he took out two denarii[i] and gave them to the innkeeper, saying, 'Take care of him; and whatever more you spend, I will repay you when I come back.' 36 Which of these three, do you think, proved neighbor to the man who fell among the robbers?" 37 He said, "The one who showed mercy on him." And Jesus said to him, "Go and do likewise."

10.33
Lk 9.52;
Jn 4.9

Jesus visits Mary and Martha (10.38–42)

38 Now as they went on their way, he entered a village; and a woman named Martha received him into her house. 39And she had a sister called Mary, who sat at the Lord's feet and listened to his teaching. 40 But Martha was distracted with much serving; and she went to him and said, "Lord, do you not care that my sister has left me to serve alone? Tell her then to help me." 41 But the Lord answered her, "Martha, Martha, you are anxious and troubled about many things; 42 one thing is needful.[j] Mary has chosen the good portion, which shall not be taken away from her."

10.38
Jn 11.1;
12.2,3
10.39
Lk 8.35;
Acts 22.3

10.42
Ps 27.4

Jesus' discourse on prayer (11.1–13; cf. Mt 6.5–15)

11 He was praying in a certain place, and when he ceased, one of his disciples said to him, "Lord, teach us to pray, as John taught his disciples." 2And he said to them, "When you pray, say: "Father, hallowed be thy name. Thy kingdom come. 3 Give us each day our daily bread;[k] 4 and forgive us our sins, for we ourselves forgive every one who is indebted to us; and lead us not into temptation."

5 And he said to them, "Which of you who has a friend will go to him at midnight and say to him, 'Friend, lend me three loaves; 6 for a friend of mine has arrived on a journey, and I have nothing to set before him'; 7 and he will answer from within, 'Do not bother me; the door is now shut, and my children are with me in bed; I cannot get up and give you anything'? 8 I tell you, though he will not get up and give him anything because he is his friend, yet because of his importunity he will rise and give him whatever he needs. 9And I tell you, Ask, and it will be given you; seek, and

*11.1
Mk 1.35;
Lk 3.21

11.4
Mt 18.35;
Mk 11.25

*11.8
Lk 18.1–6
11.9
Mt 7.7–11;
18.19;
21.22;
Mk 11.24;
Jas 1.5–8;
1 Jn 5.14,15

---

i The denarius was a day's wage for a laborer
j Other ancient authorities read *few things are needful, or only one*   *k* Or *our bread for the morrow*

11.1 The conditions for effectual prayer include: (1) a right relationship of repentance and faith, for God never promises to answer the prayers of unbelievers although He may occasionally choose to do so (2 Chr 7.14; Jn 14.13, 14); (2) an earnest and spiritual desire (1 Sam 1.10, 11; 2 Ki 19.14–19; Lk 11.5–10); (3) a confidence in God which leads the petitioner to ask in simple trust (Mt 7.7–11; Jas 4.2); (4) a faith which believes that God is both able and willing to answer (Mt 21.22; Heb 11.1; 1 Jn 5.14, 15); (5) a reception of the anticipated answer by faith, as we appropriate or lay hold of that which we have not yet received (Mk 11.24). While there are many hindrances to prayer, all of them may be comprehended under two general classifications: sin (Ps 66.18) and unbelief (Mt 21.22; Jas 1.6–8).

11.8 Here and in Lk 18.1–6 Jesus stresses the necessity for importunity in prayer if one is to prevail before God.

you will find; knock, and it will be opened to you. 10 For every one who asks receives, and he who seeks finds, and to him who knocks it will be opened. 11 What father among you, if his son asks for *l* a fish, will instead of a fish give him a serpent; 12 or if he asks for an egg, will give him a scorpion? 13 If you then, who are evil, know how to give good gifts to your children, how much more will the heavenly Father give the Holy Spirit to those who ask him!"

Jesus answers the calumny of the Pharisees
(11.14–28; Mt 12.22–45; Mk 3.20–30)

14 Now he was casting out a demon that was dumb; when the demon had gone out, the dumb man spoke, and the people marveled. 15 But some of them said, "He casts out demons by Bë-ĕl′zëbùl, the prince of demons"; 16 while others, to test him, sought from him a sign from heaven. 17 But he, knowing their thoughts, said to them, "Every kingdom divided against itself is laid waste, and a divided household falls. 18 And if Satan also is divided against himself, how will his kingdom stand? For you say that I cast out demons by Bë-ĕl′zëbùl. 19 And if I cast out demons by Bë-ĕl′zëbùl, by whom do your sons cast them out? Therefore they shall be your judges. 20 But if it is by the finger of God that I cast out demons, then the kingdom of God has come upon you. 21 When a strong man, fully armed, guards his own palace, his goods are in peace; 22 but when one stronger than he assails him and overcomes him, he takes away his armor in which he trusted, and divides his spoil. 23 He who is not with me is against me, and he who does not gather with me scatters.

24 "When the unclean spirit has gone out of a man, he passes through waterless places seeking rest; and finding none he says, 'I will return to my house from which I came.' 25 And when he comes he finds it swept and put in order. 26 Then he goes and brings seven other spirits more evil than himself, and they enter and dwell there; and the last state of that man becomes worse than the first."

27 As he said this, a woman in the crowd raised her voice and said to him, "Blessed is the womb that bore you, and the breasts that you sucked!" 28 But he said, "Blessed rather are those who hear the word of God and keep it!"

Warning against seeking signs
(11.29–32; Mt 12.38–42)

29 When the crowds were increasing, he began to say, "This generation is an evil generation; it seeks a sign, but no sign shall be given to it except the sign of Jonah. 30 For as Jonah became a sign to the men of Nĭn′ėvėh, so will the Son of man be to this generation. 31 The queen of the South will arise at the judgment with the men of this generation and condemn them; for she came from the ends of the earth to hear the wisdom of Solomon, and behold, something greater than Solomon is here. 32 The men of Nĭn′ėvėh will arise at the judgment with this generation and condemn it; for they repented at the preaching of Jonah, and behold, something greater than Jonah is here.

11.14
Mt 9.32–34

11.16
Mt 16.1;
Mk 8.11

11.17
Jn 2.25

11.20
Ex 8.19

11.23
Lk 9.50

11.26
Heb 10.26;
2 Pet 2.20

11.27
Lk 23.29

11.28
Lk 8.21;
Jn 15.14

11.29
Mt 16.4;
Mk 8.12;
ver 16

11.31
1 Ki 10.1;
2 Chr 9.1

11.32
Jonah 3.5

---

l Other ancient authorities insert *bread, will give him a stone; or if he asks for*

The parable of the lighted lamp (11.33–36)

33 "No one after lighting a lamp puts it in a cellar or under a bushel, but on a stand, that those who enter may see the light. 34 Your eye is the lamp of your body; when your eye is sound, your whole body is full of light; but when it is not sound, your body is full of darkness. 35 Therefore be careful lest the light in you be darkness. 36 If then your whole body is full of light, having no part dark, it will be wholly bright, as when a lamp with its rays gives you light."

Pharisaism exposed and denounced (11.37–54)

37 While he was speaking, a Phạr'ịseē asked him to dine with him; so he went in and sat at table. 38 The Phạr'ịseē was astonished to see that he did not first wash before dinner. 39 And the Lord said to him, "Now you Phạr'ịseēs cleanse the outside of the cup and of the dish, but inside you are full of extortion and wickedness. 40 You fools! Did not he who made the outside make the inside also? 41 But give for alms those things which are within; and behold, everything is clean for you.

42 "But woe to you Phạr'ịseēs! for you tithe mint and rue and every herb, and neglect justice and the love of God; these you ought to have done, without neglecting the others. 43 Woe to you Phạr'ịseēs! for you love the best seat in the synagogues and salutations in the market places. 44 Woe to you! for you are like graves which are not seen, and men walk over them without knowing it."

45 One of the lawyers answered him, "Teacher, in saying this you reproach us also." 46 And he said, "Woe to you lawyers also! for you load men with burdens hard to bear, and you yourselves do not touch the burdens with one of your fingers. 47 Woe to you! for you build the tombs of the prophets whom your fathers killed. 48 So you are witnesses and consent to the deeds of your fathers; for they killed them, and you build their tombs. 49 Therefore also the Wisdom of God said, 'I will send them prophets and apostles, some of whom they will kill and persecute,' 50 that the blood of all the prophets, shed from the foundation of the world, may be required of this generation, 51 from the blood of Abel to the blood of Zĕchạrī'ah, who perished between the altar and the sanctuary. Yes, I tell you, it shall be required of this generation. 52 Woe to you lawyers! for you have taken away the key of knowledge; you did not enter yourselves, and you hindered those who were entering."

53 As he went away from there, the scribes and the Phạr'ịseēs began to press him hard, and to provoke him to speak of many things, 54 lying in wait for him, to catch at something he might say.

Warning against the leaven of the Pharisees (12.1–12)

12 In the meantime, when so many thousands of the multitude had gathered together that they trod upon one another, he began to say to his disciples first, "Beware of the leaven of the Phạr'ịseēs, which is hypocrisy. 2 Nothing is covered up that will not be revealed, or hidden that will not be known. 3 Therefore whatever you have said in the dark shall be heard in the light, and

11.33 Mt 5.15; Mk 4.21; Lk 8.16
11.34 Mt 6.22,23
11.37 Lk 7.36; 14.1
11.38 Mk 7.3,4
11.39 Mt 23.25,26
11.41 Lk 12.33; Mk 7.19; Tit 1.15
11.42 Mt 23.23; Lk 18.12
11.43 Mt 23.6,7; Mk 12.38,39; Lk 20.46
11.44 Mt 23.27
11.46 Mt 23.4
11.47 Mt 23.29–32; Acts 7.51–53
11.49 Mt 23.34–36; 1 Cor 1.24; Col 2.3
11.51 Gen 4.8; 2 Chr 24.20,21
11.52 Mt 23.13
11.54 Mk 12.13
12.1 Mt 16.6; Mk 8.15; Mt 16.12
12.2 Mt 10.26,27; Mk 4.22; Lk 8.17; Eph 5.13

what you have whispered in private rooms shall be proclaimed upon the housetops.

12.4
Mt 10.28–
33;
Jn 15.14,15
12.5
Heb 10.31
12.7
Mt 12.12;
Lk 21.18;
Acts 27.34
12.8
Mk 8.38;
2 Tim 2.12;
1 Jn 2.23
12.10
Mt 12.31,
32;
Mk 3.28,29
12.11
Mt 10.19;
Mk 13.11;
Lk 21.14

4 "I tell you, my friends, do not fear those who kill the body, and after that have no more that they can do. 5 But I will warn you whom to fear: fear him who, after he has killed, has power to cast into hell;*m* yes, I tell you, fear him! 6Are not five sparrows sold for two pennies? And not one of them is forgotten before God. 7 Why, even the hairs of your head are all numbered. Fear not; you are of more value than many sparrows.

8 "And I tell you, every one who acknowledges me before men, the Son of man also will acknowledge before the angels of God; 9 but he who denies me before men will be denied before the angels of God. 10And every one who speaks a word against the Son of man will be forgiven; but he who blasphemes against the Holy Spirit will not be forgiven. 11And when they bring you before the synagogues and the rulers and the authorities, do not be anxious how or what you are to answer or what you are to say; 12 for the Holy Spirit will teach you in that very hour what you ought to say."

Parable of the rich fool: covetousness (12.13–21)

12.14
Mic 6.8;
Rom 2.1,3

*12.16

13 One of the multitude said to him, "Teacher, bid my brother divide the inheritance with me." 14 But he said to him, "Man, who made me a judge or divider over you?" 15And he said to them, "Take heed, and beware of all covetousness; for a man's life does not consist in the abundance of his possessions." 16And he told them a parable, saying, "The land of a rich man brought forth plentifully; 17 and he thought to himself, 'What shall I do, for I have nowhere to store my crops?' 18And he said, 'I will do this: I will pull down my barns, and build larger ones; and there I will store all my grain and my goods. 19And I will say to my soul, Soul, you have ample goods laid up for many years; take your ease, eat, drink, be merry.' 20 But God said to him, 'Fool! This night your soul is required of you; and the things you have prepared, whose will they be?' 21 So is he who lays up treasure for himself, and is not rich toward God."

12.19
Ecc 11.9;
Jas 5.5
12.20
Jer 17.11;
Job 27.8;
Ps 39.6
12.21
ver 33

Trust or anxiety (12.22–34; cf. Mt 6.25–34)

12.24
Job 38.41

12.25
Ps 39.5

22 And he said to his disciples, "Therefore I tell you, do not be anxious about your life, what you shall eat, nor about your body, what you shall put on. 23 For life is more than food, and the body more than clothing. 24 Consider the ravens: they neither sow nor reap, they have neither storehouse nor barn, and yet God feeds them. Of how much more value are you than the birds! 25And which of you by being anxious can add a cubit to his span of life?*n*

m Greek Gĕhĕn'nă   *n* Or to his stature

12.16 Worldly-mindedness, or concern only for this life, is the dominant trait warned against in this parable. Christ here reiterates what He taught in the Sermon on the Mount (Mt 6.20, 32–34). Nowhere did He suggest that being wealthy is wrong or that men should disregard the practical requirements of this life. But when wealth becomes an end in itself and is not used with a sense of holy stewardship unto God, then it becomes a snare and a delusion. Material riches present more temptations than usual to men of wealth, therefore require special precautions. Sometimes wealth must be disposed of altogether if the soul is to be freed for whole-hearted fellowship with Christ (Mt 19.16–24).

26 If then you are not able to do as small a thing as that, why are you anxious about the rest? 27 Consider the lilies, how they grow; they neither toil nor spin;*o* yet I tell you, even Solomon in all his glory was not arrayed like one of these. 28 But if God so clothes the grass which is alive in the field today and tomorrow is thrown into the oven, how much more will he clothe you, O men of little faith! 29And do not seek what you are to eat and what you are to drink, nor be of anxious mind. 30 For all the nations of the world seek these things; and your Father knows that you need them. 31 Instead, seek his*p* kingdom, and these things shall be yours as well.

32 "Fear not, little flock, for it is your Father's good pleasure to give you the kingdom. 33 Sell your possessions, and give alms; provide yourselves with purses that do not grow old, with a treasure in the heavens that does not fail, where no thief approaches and no moth destroys. 34 For where your treasure is, there will your heart be also.

Exhortation to vigilance (12.35–40)

35 "Let your loins be girded and your lamps burning, 36 and be like men who are waiting for their master to come home from the marriage feast, so that they may open to him at once when he comes and knocks. 37 Blessed are those servants whom the master finds awake when he comes; truly, I say to you, he will gird himself and have them sit at table, and he will come and serve them. 38 If he comes in the second watch, or in the third, and finds them so, blessed are those servants! 39 But know this, that if the householder had known at what hour the thief was coming, he*q* would not have left his house to be broken into. 40 You also must be ready; for the Son of man is coming at an unexpected hour."

Faithful and unfaithful servants (12.41–48; Mt 24.45–51)

41 Peter said, "Lord, are you telling this parable for us or for all?" 42And the Lord said, "Who then is the faithful and wise steward, whom his master will set over his household, to give them their portion of food at the proper time? 43 Blessed is that servant whom his master when he comes will find so doing. 44 Truly, I say to you, he will set him over all his possessions. 45 But if that servant says to himself, 'My master is delayed in coming,' and begins to beat the menservants and the maidservants, and to eat and drink and get drunk, 46 the master of that servant will come on a day when he does not expect him and at an hour he does not know, and will punish*r* him, and put him with the unfaithful. 47And that servant who knew his master's will, but did not make ready or act according to his will, shall receive a severe beating. 48 But he

Marginal references:

12.27 1 Ki 10.4–7

12.30 Mt 6.8

12.32 Jn 21.15–17
12.33 Mt 19.21; Mk 6.20
12.34 Mt 6.21

12.35 Mt 25.1–13; Mk 13.33–37; Eph 6.14
12.37 Mt 24.42, 46; Lk 17.8; Jn 13.4
12.39 Mt 24.43; 1 Thess 5.2; 2 Pet 3.10; Rev 3.3; 16.15
12.40 Mt 24.44; Mk 13.33; Lk 21.36

*12.42 Lk 7.13

12.47 Num 15.30; Deut 25.2
12.48 Lev 5.17

---

o Other ancient authorities read *Consider the lilies; they neither spin nor weave*   *p* Other ancient authorities read *God's*
q Other ancient authorities add *would have watched and*   *r* Or *cut him in pieces*

12.42 This parable emphasizes the need of conscientiousness in discharging one's obligations. The thought of possible delay in the return of Christ to earth should dispose no Christian to slothful ease or failure to do God's will. Jesus further indicates here that there is a time of judgment coming for the master's servants when rewards for faithfulness will be handed out, and unfaithfulness will be fittingly punished.

who did not know, and did what deserved a beating, shall receive a light beating. Every one to whom much is given, of him will much be required; and of him to whom men commit much they will demand the more.

Christ the great divider (12.49–59)

49 "I came to cast fire upon the earth; and would that it were already kindled! 50 I have a baptism to be baptized with; and how I am constrained until it is accomplished! 51 Do you think that I have come to give peace on earth? No, I tell you, but rather division; 52 for henceforth in one house there will be five divided, three against two and two against three; 53 they will be divided, father against son and son against father, mother against daughter and daughter against her mother, mother-in-law against her daughter-in-law and daughter-in-law against her mother-in-law."

54 He also said to the multitudes, "When you see a cloud rising in the west, you say at once, 'A shower is coming'; and so it happens. 55And when you see the south wind blowing, you say, 'There will be scorching heat'; and it happens. 56 You hypocrites! You know how to interpret the appearance of earth and sky; but why do you not know how to interpret the present time?

57 "And why do you not judge for yourselves what is right? 58As you go with your accuser before the magistrate, make an effort to settle with him on the way, lest he drag you to the judge, and the judge hand you over to the officer, and the officer put you in prison. 59 I tell you, you will never get out till you have paid the very last copper."

Jesus' call to repentance (13.1–9)

13 There were some present at that very time who told him of the Găḷiḷē′ăṇṣ whose blood Pīlăte had mingled with their sacrifices. 2And he answered them, "Do you think that these Găḷiḷē′ăṇṣ were worse sinners than all the other Galileans, because they suffered thus? 3 I tell you, No; but unless you repent you will all likewise perish. 4 Or those eighteen upon whom the tower in Sīlō′ăm fell and killed them, do you think that they were worse offenders than all the others who dwelt in Jerusalem? 5 I tell you, No; but unless you repent you will all likewise perish."

6 And he told this parable: "A man had a fig tree planted in his vineyard; and he came seeking fruit on it and found none. 7And he said to the vinedresser, 'Lo, these three years I have come seeking fruit on this fig tree, and I find none. Cut it down; why should it use up the ground?' 8And he answered him, 'Let it alone, sir, this year also, till I dig about it and put on manure. 9And if it bears

Marginal references

12.50 Mk 10.38; Jn 12.27
12.51 Mt 10.34–36; ver 49
12.53 Mic 7.6; Mt 10.21
12.54 Mt 16.2
12.55 Mt 20.12
12.56 Mt 16.3
12.58 Mt 5.25,26
12.59 Mk 12.42
*13.1 Mt 27.2
13.2 Jn 9.2,3
13.4 Lk 11.4
*13.6 Mt 21.19
13.7 Mt 3.10; 7.19; Lk 3.9

13.1 There is no further information on this incident. It may be inferred that some Galileans, while in the act of offering sacrifices in the Temple in Jerusalem, were set upon and killed by Pilate's soldiers, so that their blood was mingled with that of their sacrifices. Pilate may have thought that these Galileans were planning an insurrection. An incident like this may explain the enmity which existed between Pilate and Herod Antipas, tetrarch of Galilee (23.12).

13.6 The parable of the barren fig tree had primary reference to the nation of Israel. For centuries God had been expecting Israel to bring forth fruit unto repentance, but there had been none. Now Christ had come, but even He had been rejected; however, as this parable teaches, God who is long-suffering will grant more time for Israel to repent and turn at last to Him. But if the Chosen People persist in their refusal to turn to God, they will finally be cut off.

fruit next year, well and good; but if not, you can cut it down.'"

A woman healed on the Sabbath (13.10–17)

10 Now he was teaching in one of the synagogues on the sabbath. 11And there was a woman who had had a spirit of infirmity for eighteen years; she was bent over and could not fully straighten herself. 12And when Jesus saw her, he called her and said to her, "Woman, you are freed from your infirmity." 13And he laid his hands upon her, and immediately she was made straight, and she praised God. 14 But the ruler of the synagogue, indignant because Jesus had healed on the sabbath, said to the people, "There are six days on which work ought to be done; come on those days and be healed, and not on the sabbath day." 15 Then the Lord answered him, "You hypocrites! Does not each of you on the sabbath untie his ox or his ass from the manger, and lead it away to water it? 16And ought not this woman, a daughter of Abraham whom Satan bound for eighteen years, be loosed from this bond on the sabbath day?" 17As he said this, all his adversaries were put to shame; and all the people rejoiced at all the glorious things that were done by him.

13.11
ver 16

13.13
Mk 5.23

13.14
Ex 20.9;
Lk 6.7;
14.3

13.15
Lk 7.13;
14.5

13.16
Lk 19.9

Parable of the mustard seed
(13.18,19; Mt 13.31,32; Mk 4.30–32)

18 He said therefore, "What is the kingdom of God like? And to what shall I compare it? 19 It is like a grain of mustard seed which a man took and sowed in his garden; and it grew and became a tree, and the birds of the air made nests in its branches."

*13.19

Parable of the leaven (13.20,21; Mt 13.31,32)

20 And again he said, "To what shall I compare the kingdom of God? 21 It is like leaven which a woman took and hid in three measures of flour, till it was all leavened."

*13.21

The narrow door (13.22–30)

22 He went on his way through towns and villages, teaching, and journeying toward Jerusalem. 23And some one said to him, "Lord, will those who are saved be few?" And he said to them, 24 "Strive to enter by the narrow door; for many, I tell you, will seek to enter and will not be able. 25 When once the householder has risen up and shut the door, you will begin to stand outside and to knock at the door, saying, 'Lord, open to us.' He will answer you, 'I do not know where you come from.' 26 Then you will begin to say, 'We ate and drank in your presence, and you taught in our streets.' 27 But he will say, 'I tell you, I do not know where you come from; depart from me, all you workers of iniquity!' 28 There you will weep and gnash your teeth, when you see Abraham and Isaac and Jacob and all the prophets in the kingdom of God and you yourselves thrust out. 29And men will come from

13.22
Lk 9.51

13.24
Mt 7.13

13.25
Mt 25.10–
12; 7.23

13.27
Mt 7.23;
25.41

13.28
Mt 8.11,12

13.19 See note to Mt 13.31 on the parable of the mustard seed.

13.21 See note to Mt 13.33 on the parable of the leaven.

east and west, and from north and south, and sit at table in the
kingdom of God. [30]And behold, some are last who will be first,
and some are first who will be last."

Jesus sends a message to Herod and weeps over Jerusalem (13.31–35)

31 At that very hour some Phar'iseēs came, and said to him,
"Get away from here, for Hĕrŏd wants to kill you." [32]And he said
to them, "Go and tell that fox, 'Behold, I cast out demons and
perform cures today and tomorrow, and the third day I finish my
course. [33] Nevertheless I must go on my way today and tomorrow
and the day following; for it cannot be that a prophet should perish away from Jerusalem.' [34] O Jerusalem, Jerusalem, killing the
prophets and stoning those who are sent to you! How often would
I have gathered your children together as a hen gathers her brood
under her wings, and you would not! [35] Behold, your house is
forsaken. And I tell you, you will not see me until you say,
'Blessed is he who comes in the name of the Lord!' "

Jesus heals on the Sabbath (14.1–6)

14 One sabbath when he went to dine at the house of a ruler
who belonged to the Phar'iseēs, they were watching him.
[2]And behold, there was a man before him who had dropsy. [3]And
Jesus spoke to the lawyers and Phar'iseēs, saying, "Is it lawful to
heal on the sabbath, or not?" [4] But they were silent. Then he took
him and healed him, and let him go. [5]And he said to them, "Which
of you, having a son^s or an ox that has fallen into a well, will not
immediately pull him out on a sabbath day?" [6]And they could
not reply to this.

Parable of the marriage feast (14.7–14)

7 Now he told a parable to those who were invited, when he
marked how they chose the places of honor, saying to them,
[8] "When you are invited by any one to a marriage feast, do not
sit down in a place of honor, lest a more eminent man than you
be invited by him; [9] and he who invited you both will come and
say to you, 'Give place to this man,' and then you will begin with
shame to take the lowest place. [10] But when you are invited, go and
sit in the lowest place, so that when your host comes he may say
to you, 'Friend, go up higher'; then you will be honored in the
presence of all who sit at table with you. [11] For every one who
exalts himself will be humbled, and he who humbles himself will
be exalted."

12 He said also to the man who had invited him, "When you
give a dinner or a banquet, do not invite your friends or your
brothers or your kinsmen or rich neighbors, lest they also invite
you in return, and you be repaid. [13] But when you give a feast,
invite the poor, the maimed, the lame, the blind, [14] and you will be
blessed, because they cannot repay you. You will be repaid at the
resurrection of the just."

s Other ancient authorities read *an ass*

14.1 See note to Mk 2.27 on the Sabbath.   **14.8** Here Jesus gives a lesson on humility.

Margin references:

13.30
Mt 19.30;
Mk 10.31

13.32
Heb 2.10;
7.28

13.34
Mt 23.37–
39;
Lk 19.41

13.35
Ps 118.26;
Mt 21.9;
Lk 19.38

*14.1
Mk 3.2

14.3
Mt 12.10;
Mk 3.4;
Lk 6.9

14.5
Ex 23.5;
Lk 13.15

14.7
Mt 23.6

*14.8
Prov 25.6,7

14.10
Prov 25.6,7

14.11
Mt 23.12;
Lk 18.14;
Jas 4.6;
1 Pet 5.5,6

14.13
ver 21

Parable of the great banquet (14.15–24; Mt 22.1–14)

15 When one of those who sat at table with him heard this, he said to him, "Blessed is he who shall eat bread in the kingdom of God!" 16 But he said to him, "A man once gave a great banquet, and invited many; 17 and at the time for the banquet he sent his servant to say to those who had been invited, 'Come; for all is now ready.' 18 But they all alike began to make excuses. The first said to him, 'I have bought a field, and I must go out and see it; I pray you, have me excused.' 19 And another said, 'I have bought five yoke of oxen, and I go to examine them; I pray you, have me excused.' 20 And another said, 'I have married a wife, and therefore I cannot come.' 21 So the servant came and reported this to his master. Then the householder in anger said to his servant, 'Go out quickly to the streets and lanes of the city, and bring in the poor and maimed and blind and lame.' 22 And the servant said, 'Sir, what you commanded has been done, and still there is room.' 23 And the master said to the servant, 'Go out to the highways and hedges, and compel people to come in, that my house may be filled. 24 For I tell you,*a* none of those men who were invited shall taste my banquet.' "

14.15
Rev 19.9
*14.16
14.17
Prov 9.2,5

14.20
Deut 24.5;
1 Cor 7.33
14.21
ver 13

14.24
Mt 21.43;
Acts 13.46

Counting the cost: (14.25–15.2)

1. Parable of the tower and of the king going to war (14.25-33)

25 Now great multitudes accompanied him; and he turned and said to them, 26 "If any one comes to me and does not hate his own father and mother and wife and children and brothers and sisters, yes, and even his own life, he cannot be my disciple. 27 Whoever does not bear his own cross and come after me, cannot be my disciple. 28 For which of you, desiring to build a tower, does not first sit down and count the cost, whether he has enough to complete it? 29 Otherwise, when he has laid a foundation, and is not able to finish, all who see it begin to mock him, 30 saying, 'This man began to build, and was not able to finish.' 31 Or what king, going to encounter another king in war, will not sit down first and take counsel whether he is able with ten thousand to meet him who comes against him with twenty thousand? 32 And if not, while the other is yet a great way off, he sends an embassy and asks terms of peace. 33 So therefore, whoever of you does not renounce all that he has cannot be my disciple.

14.25
Mt 10.37,38
*14.26

14.27
Mt 16.24;
Mk 8.34;
Lk 9.23

14.33
Lk 18.29,
30;
Phil 3.7;
Heb 11.26

2. Parable of the salt (14.34–15.2)

34 "Salt is good; but if salt has lost its taste, how shall its saltness be restored? 35 It is fit neither for the land nor for the dunghill; men throw it away. He who has ears to hear, let him hear."

15 Now the tax collectors and sinners were all drawing near to hear him. 2 And the Pharisees and the scribes murmured, saying, "This man receives sinners and eats with them."

14.34
Mt 5.13;
Mk 9.50
14.35
Mt 11.15

15.1
Lk 5.29
15.2
Mt 9.11

a The Greek word for *you* here is plural

14.16 See Mt 22.1–14 for a parable which sets forth the same truth. The Jews are the invited guests who decline to come; those gathered from the streets and lanes are the Gentiles who repent and believe. But the call to repentance and salvation is universal to both Jew and Gentile.

14.26 This verse must be understood in the light of Mt 10.37, 38. The meaning is perfectly clear: Neither any person nor anything can be permitted to take precedence over the Lord Jesus.

Three parables of grace: (15.3–32)

1. The lost sheep (15.3–7; Mt 18.10–14)

*15.3

3 So he told them this parable: 4 "What man of you, having a hundred sheep, if he has lost one of them, does not leave the ninety-nine in the wilderness, and go after the one which is lost, until he finds it? 5And when he has found it, he lays it on his shoulders, rejoicing. 6And when he comes home, he calls together his friends and his neighbors, saying to them, 'Rejoice with me, for I have found my sheep which was lost.' 7 Just so, I tell you, there will be more joy in heaven over one sinner who repents than over ninety-nine righteous persons who need no repentance.

15.7
ver 10;
Lk 19.10;
Jas 5.20

2. The lost coin (15.8–10)

*15.8

8 "Or what woman, having ten silver coins,*t* if she loses one coin, does not light a lamp and sweep the house and seek diligently until she finds it? 9And when she has found it, she calls together her friends and neighbors, saying, 'Rejoice with me, for I have found the coin which I had lost.' 10 Just so, I tell you, there is joy before the angels of God over one sinner who repents."

15.10
ver 7

3. The lost son (15.11–32)

*15.11
Mt 21.28
15.12
Deut 21.17

11 And he said, "There was a man who had two sons; 12 and the younger of them said to his father, 'Father, give me the share of property that falls to me.' And he divided his living between them. 13 Not many days later, the younger son gathered all he had and took his journey into a far country, and there he squandered his property in loose living. 14And when he had spent everything, a great famine arose in that country, and he began to be in want. 15 So he went and joined himself to one of the citizens of that country, who sent him into his fields to feed swine. 16And he would gladly have fed on*u* the pods that the swine ate; and no one gave him anything. 17 But when he came to himself he said, 'How

t The drachma, rendered here by *silver coin*, was about a day's wage for a laborer
u Other ancient authorities read *filled his belly with*

15.3 Jesus spoke this parable to the Pharisees and scribes who objected to His association with tax collectors and sinners. Jesus argues that since they considered themselves in the fold they should be glad that He was seeking those who were outside the fold and who obviously, according to their ideas, needed to be brought back. Instead of criticizing Him they should have rejoiced.

15.8 The parable of the lost coin should not be separated from the parable of the lost sheep, for they are intimately connected. Duplicate parables portraying the same truths were not uncommonly used by Christ (5.36–39; 13.19–21). In this parable Jesus tells of the joy of the angels at the conversion of a single lost person. The application is plain. If the angels themselves rejoice, so ought all true believers to rejoice with them when a single soul is converted. By implication these words condemned the Pharisees and scribes for their criticism of Jesus' ministry to despised tax collectors and sinners.

15.11 The parable of the lost son must be understood in the light of the two parables which precede it: the lost sheep and the lost coin. The sheep and the coin are now replaced by a human being. The shepherd and the woman now become our Father in heaven. The son leaves his father's house with disastrous results. When he comes to himself, he returns to his father in repentance and is joyfully received. Here Jesus adds a sidelight which is not found in the two preceding parables. He introduces an elder brother who properly represents the self-righteous Pharisees and scribes, and who is not at all glad that his brother has returned. Instead of rejoicing he is envious and finds fault. Jesus points up the fact that these objectors are like the elder brother, for they are critical of Himself who ate and drank with tax collectors and sinners so that He might bring them back to the Father's house.

many of my father's hired servants have bread enough and to
spare, but I perish here with hunger! 18 I will arise and go to my
father, and I will say to him, "Father, I have sinned against heaven
and before you; 19 I am no longer worthy to be called your son;
treat me as one of your hired servants." ' 20And he arose and came
to his father. But while he was yet at a distance, his father saw him
and had compassion, and ran and embraced him and kissed him.
21And the son said to him, 'Father, I have sinned against heaven
and before you; I am no longer worthy to be called your son.'v
22 But the father said to his servants, 'Bring quickly the best robe,
and put it on him; and put a ring on his hand, and shoes on his
feet; 23 and bring the fatted calf and kill it, and let us eat and make
merry; 24 for this my son was dead, and is alive again; he was lost,
and is found.' And they began to make merry.

25 "Now his elder son was in the field; and as he came and drew
near to the house, he heard music and dancing. 26And he called
one of the servants and asked what this meant. 27And he said to
him, 'Your brother has come, and your father has killed the fatted
calf, because he has received him safe and sound.' 28 But he was
angry and refused to go in. His father came out and entreated him,
29 but he answered his father, 'Lo, these many years I have served
you, and I never disobeyed your command; yet you never gave
me a kid, that I might make merry with my friends. 30 But when
this son of yours came, who has devoured your living with harlots,
you killed for him the fatted calf!' 31And he said to him, 'Son, you
are always with me, and all that is mine is yours. 32 It was fitting
to make merry and be glad, for this your brother was dead, and is
alive; he was lost, and is found.' "

Parable of the unrighteous steward (16.1–13)

16 He also said to the disciples, "There was a rich man who
had a steward, and charges were brought to him that this
man was wasting his goods. 2And he called him and said to him,
'What is this that I hear about you? Turn in the account of your
stewardship, for you can no longer be steward.' 3And the steward
said to himself, 'What shall I do, since my master is taking the
stewardship away from me? I am not strong enough to dig, and I
am ashamed to beg. 4 I have decided what to do, so that people
may receive me into their houses when I am put out of the
stewardship.' 5 So, summoning his master's debtors one by one, he
said to the first, 'How much do you owe my master?' 6 He said, 'A
hundred measures of oil.' And he said to him, 'Take your bill,
and sit down quickly and write fifty.' 7 Then he said to another,
'And how much do you owe?' He said, 'A hundred measures of
wheat.' He said to him, 'Take your bill, and write eighty.' 8 The
master commended the dishonest steward for his shrewdness; for

v Other ancient authorities add *treat me as one of your hired servants*

Marginal references:
15.20 Gen 45.14; 46.29; Acts 20.37
15.21 Ps 51.4
15.22 Zech 3.4; Gen 41.42
15.24 ver 32; 1 Tim 5.6; Eph 2.1; 5.14
15.30 ver 12
15.32 ver 24
*16.1 Lk 15.13
16.8 Jn 12.36; Eph 5.8; 1 Thess 5.5

16.1 The parable of the dishonest steward was spoken to the followers of Jesus, but it was related in the hearing of the Pharisees. The parable taught Jesus' followers the importance of the proper use of this world's goods in the light of eternal values. Jesus did not suggest nor intend to imply that dishonesty is ultimately profitable. Rather He showed that if dishonest people use all of their ingenuity to promote their material welfare, so ought the people of God to use their energies to further their spiritual welfare.

*16.9
Mt 6.19,24;
19.21;
Lk 11.41;
12.33
16.10
Mt 25.21;
Lk 19.17
16.11
ver 9

16.13
Mt 6.24

the sons of this world[w] are more shrewd in dealing with their own generation than the sons of light. 9And I tell you, make friends for yourselves by means of unrighteous mammon,[a] so that when it fails they may receive you into the eternal habitations.

10 "He who is faithful in a very little is faithful also in much; and he who is dishonest in a very little is dishonest also in much. 11 If then you have not been faithful in the unrighteous mammon,[a] who will entrust to you the true riches? 12And if you have not been faithful in that which is another's, who will give you that which is your own? 13 No servant can serve two masters; for either he will hate the one and love the other, or he will be devoted to the one and despise the other. You cannot serve God and mammon."[a]

Jesus answers the Pharisees (16.14–18)

16.14
2 Tim 3.2;
Lk 23.35
16.15
Lk 10.29;
1 Sam 16.7;
Prov 21.2;
Acts 1.24
16.16
Mt 11.12,
13; 4.23
16.17
Isa 40.8;
Mt 5.17,18;
Lk 21.33
*16.18
Mt 5.31,32;
19.19;
Mk 10.11;
1 Cor 7.10,
11

14 The Phạr'ịseēṣ, who were lovers of money, heard all this, and they scoffed at him. 15 But he said to them, "You are those who justify yourselves before men, but God knows your hearts; for what is exalted among men is an abomination in the sight of God.

16 "The law and the prophets were until John; since then the good news of the kingdom of God is preached, and every one enters it violently. 17 But it is easier for heaven and earth to pass away, than for one dot of the law to become void.

18 "Every one who divorces his wife and marries another commits adultery, and he who marries a woman divorced from her husband commits adultery.

The rich man and Lazarus (16.19–31)

*16.19
16.20
Acts 3.2

16.22
Jn 13.23

16.23
Mt 11.23
16.24
ver 30;
Mt 25.41
16.25
Lk 6.24

19 "There was a rich man, who was clothed in purple and fine linen and who feasted sumptuously every day. 20And at his gate lay a poor man named Lăz'ărŭs, full of sores, 21 who desired to be fed with what fell from the rich man's table; moreover the dogs came and licked his sores. 22 The poor man died and was carried by the angels to Abraham's bosom. The rich man also died and was buried; 23 and in Hādēṣ, being in torment, he lifted up his eyes, and saw Abraham far off and Lăz'ărŭs in his bosom. 24And he called out, 'Father Abraham, have mercy upon me, and send Lăz'ărŭs to dip the end of his finger in water and cool my tongue; for I am in anguish in this flame.' 25 But Abraham said, 'Son, remember that you in your lifetime received your good things, and Lăz'ărŭs in like manner evil things; but now he is comforted here, and you are in anguish. 26And besides all this, between us and you a great chasm has been fixed, in order that those who would pass from here to you may not be able, and none may cross from there to us.' 27And he said, 'Then I beg you, father, to send him to my father's house, 28 for I have five brothers, so that he may warn them, lest they also come into this place of torment.' 29 But

16.29
Lk 4.17;
Jn 5.45–47;
Acts 15.21

w Greek age
a Mammon is a Semitic word for money or riches

16.9 mammon means "wealth" or "property." Money or wealth, as such, is neither good nor bad, but it has use in this world, and thus shares in the general nature of unrighteousness. (See also Mt 6.24; Lk 16.11 13.)

16.18 See note to Mt 19.3 on divorce.
16.19 This parable intends to teach two lessons: (1) worldly wealth is no guarantee of eternal bliss; (2) warnings concerning destiny are to be found in Moses and the prophets.

Abraham said, 'They have Moses and the prophets; let them hear them.' 30And he said, 'No, father Abraham; but if some one goes to them from the dead, they will repent.' 31 He said to him, 'If they do not hear Moses and the prophets, neither will they be convinced if some one should rise from the dead.' "

16.30
Lk 3.8;
19.9

Jesus' teaching on forgiveness and faith (17.1–10)

17 And he said to his disciples, "Temptations to sin[x] are sure to come; but woe to him by whom they come! 2 It would be better for him if a millstone were hung round his neck and he were cast into the sea, than that he should cause one of these little ones to sin.[y] 3 Take heed to yourselves; if your brother sins, rebuke him, and if he repents, forgive him; 4 and if he sins against you seven times in the day, and turns to you seven times, and says, 'I repent,' you must forgive him."

17.1
Mt 18.6,7;
Mk 9.42;
1 Cor 11.19
17.2
1 Cor 8.12
17.3
Mt 18.15
17.4
Mt 18.21,22

5 The apostles said to the Lord, "Increase our faith!" 6And the Lord said, "If you had faith as a grain of mustard seed, you could say to this sycamine tree, 'Be rooted up, and be planted in the sea,' and it would obey you.

17.5
Mk 6.30
17.6
Mt 17.20;
21.21;
Mk 9.23;
Lk 7.13

7 "Will any one of you, who has a servant plowing or keeping sheep, say to him when he has come in from the field, 'Come at once and sit down at table'? 8 Will he not rather say to him, 'Prepare supper for me, and gird yourself and serve me, till I eat and drink; and afterward you shall eat and drink'? 9 Does he thank the servant because he did what was commanded? 10 So you also, when you have done all that is commanded you, say, 'We are unworthy servants; we have only done what was our duty.' "

17.8
Lk 12.37

The healing of the ten lepers (17.11–19)

11 On the way to Jerusalem he was passing along between Samar′ia and Gal′ilee. 12And as he entered a village, he was met by ten lepers, who stood at a distance 13 and lifted up their voices and said, "Jesus, Master, have mercy on us." 14 When he saw them he said to them, "Go and show yourselves to the priests." And as they went they were cleansed. 15 Then one of them, when he saw that he was healed, turned back, praising God with a loud voice; 16 and he fell on his face at Jesus' feet, giving him thanks. Now he was a Samar′itan. 17 Then said Jesus, "Were not ten cleansed? Where are the nine? 18 Was no one found to return and give praise to God except this foreigner?" 19And he said to him, "Rise and go your way; your faith has made you well."

17.11
Lk 9.51,52;
Jn 4.3,4
17.12
Lev 13.46
17.14
Lev 13.2;
14.2;
Mt 8.4
17.15
Mt 9.8
17.16
Mt 10.5
17.19
Mt 9.22;
Mk 5.34;
Lk 7.50;
8.48;
18.42

The coming of the kingdom (17.20,21)

20 Being asked by the Phar′isees when the kingdom of God was coming, he answered them, "The kingdom of God is not coming with signs to be observed; 21 nor will they say, 'Lo, here it is!' or 'There!' for behold, the kingdom of God is in the midst of you."[z]

17.20
Lk 19.11;
Acts 1.6
*17.21
ver 23

---

[x] Greek stumbling blocks   [y] Greek stumble   [z] Or within you

---

17.21 The statement that *the kingdom of God is in the midst of you,* or "within you," means that it is already a spiritual reality which exists in the hearts of men. Any external evidence of this kingdom flows from the actions of men who have received Christ within themselves. If they have not done this, any external evidence is spurious. In outward form the kingdom will come fully with the Second Advent of Christ.

Christ's Second Advent (17.22–37)

17.22
Mt 9.15;
Mk 2.20;
Lk 5.35
17.23
Mt 24.23;
Mk 13.21;
Lk 21.8
17.24
Mt 24.27
17.25
Mt 16.21;
Lk 9.22
17.26
Mt 24.37–
39;
Gen ch 7
17.28
Gen 18.20–
33;19.24,25
17.30
2 Thess 1.7
17.31
Mt 24.17,
18;
Mk 13.15,
16
17.32
Gen 19.26
17.33
Mt 10.39;
16.25;
Mk 8.35;
Lk 9.24
17.34
Mt 24.40,41
17.37
Mt 24.28
18.1
Lk 11.5–8;
Rom 12.12;
Eph 6.18;
Col 4.2;
1 Thess
5.17
18.5
Lk 11.8
18.6
Lk 7.13
18.7
Rev 6.10;
Rom 8.33;
Col 3.12;
2 Tim 2.10
*18.9
Lk 16.15
18.11
Mt 6.5;
Mk 11.25

22 And he said to the disciples, "The days are coming when you will desire to see one of the days of the Son of man, and you will not see it. 23And they will say to you, 'Lo, there!' or 'Lo, here!' Do not go, do not follow them. 24 For as the lightning flashes and lights up the sky from one side to the other, so will the Son of man be in his day.[a] 25 But first he must suffer many things and be rejected by this generation. 26As it was in the days of Noah, so will it be in the days of the Son of man. 27 They ate, they drank, they married, they were given in marriage, until the day when Noah entered the ark, and the flood came and destroyed them all. 28 Likewise as it was in the days of Lot—they ate, they drank, they bought, they sold, they planted, they built, 29 but on the day when Lot went out from Sŏdôm fire and sulphur rained from heaven and destroyed them all—30 so will it be on the day when the Son of man is revealed. 31 On that day, let him who is on the housetop, with his goods in the house, not come down to take them away; and likewise let him who is in the field not turn back. 32 Remember Lot's wife. 33 Whoever seeks to gain his life will lose it, but whoever loses his life will preserve it. 34 I tell you, in that night there will be two in one bed; one will be taken and the other left. 35 There will be two women grinding together; one will be taken and the other left."[b] 37And they said to him, "Where, Lord?" He said to them, "Where the body is, there the eagles[c] will be gathered together."

Parable of the widow and the judge (18.1–8)

18 And he told them a parable, to the effect that they ought always to pray and not lose heart. 2 He said, "In a certain city there was a judge who neither feared God nor regarded man; 3 and there was a widow in that city who kept coming to him and saying, 'Vindicate me against my adversary.' 4 For a while he refused; but afterward he said to himself, 'Though I neither fear God nor regard man, 5 yet because this widow bothers me, I will vindicate her, or she will wear me out by her continual coming.'" 6And the Lord said, "Hear what the unrighteous judge says. 7And will not God vindicate his elect, who cry to him day and night? Will he delay long over them? 8 I tell you, he will vindicate them speedily. Nevertheless, when the Son of man comes, will he find faith on earth?"

Parable of the Pharisee and the publican (18.9–14)

9 He also told this parable to some who trusted in themselves that they were righteous and despised others: 10 "Two men went up into the temple to pray, one a Phạr'ịseē and the other a tax collector. 11 The Phạr'ịseē stood and prayed thus with himself,

a Other ancient authorities omit in his day
b Other ancient authorities add verse 36, "Two men will be in the field; one will be taken and the other left"   c Or vultures

18.9 This parable illustrates the difference between those who are trusting in their own works of self-righteousness for salvation, and those who are destitute of any self-righteousness and who seek God's mercy. The Greek word for be merciful in verse 13 is hilaskomai (to be propitiated) and its use indicates the desire of the publican that God be merciful.

'God, I thank thee that I am not like other men, extortioners, unjust, adulterers, or even like this tax collector. 12 I fast twice a week, I give tithes of all that I get.' 13 But the tax collector, standing far off, would not even lift up his eyes to heaven, but beat his breast, saying, 'God, be merciful to me a sinner!' 14 I tell you, this man went down to his house justified rather than the other; for every one who exalts himself will be humbled, but he who humbles himself will be exalted."

Jesus and the little children
(18.15–17; Mt 19.13–15; Mk 10.13–16)

15 Now they were bringing even infants to him that he might touch them; and when the disciples saw it, they rebuked them. 16 But Jesus called them to him, saying, "Let the children come to me, and do not hinder them; for to such belongs the kingdom of God. 17 Truly, I say to you, whoever does not receive the kingdom of God like a child shall not enter it."

The rich young ruler
(18.18–30; Mt 19.16–30; Mk 10.17–31)

18 And a ruler asked him, "Good Teacher, what shall I do to inherit eternal life?" 19 And Jesus said to him, "Why do you call me good? No one is good but God alone. 20 You know the commandments: 'Do not commit adultery, Do not kill, Do not steal, Do not bear false witness, Honor your father and mother.'" 21 And he said, "All these I have observed from my youth." 22 And when Jesus heard it, he said to him, "One thing you still lack. Sell all that you have and distribute to the poor, and you will have treasure in heaven; and come, follow me." 23 But when he heard this he became sad, for he was very rich. 24 Jesus looking at him said, "How hard it is for those who have riches to enter the kingdom of God! 25 For it is easier for a camel to go through the eye of a needle than for a rich man to enter the kingdom of God." 26 Those who heard it said, "Then who can be saved?" 27 But he said, "What is impossible with men is possible with God." 28 And Peter said, "Lo, we have left our homes and followed you." 29 And he said to them, "Truly, I say to you, there is no man who has left house or wife or brothers or parents or children, for the sake of the kingdom of God, 30 who will not receive manifold more in this time, and in the age to come eternal life."

Christ foretells his crucifixion and resurrection
(18.31–34; Mt 20.17–19; Mk 10.32–34)

31 And taking the twelve, he said to them, "Behold, we are going up to Jerusalem, and everything that is written of the Son of man by the prophets will be accomplished. 32 For he will be

*18.12 Mt 9.14; Lk 11.42; 18.13 Lk 23.48; 18.14 Mt 23.12; Lk 14.11; 1 Pet 5.6; 18.17 Mt 18.3; 18.18 Lk 10.25; 18.20 Ex 20.12–16; Deut 5.16–20; Rom 13.9; 18.22 Lk 12.33; Mt 19.21; 18.24 Prov 11.28; 18.27 Gen 18.14; Job 42.2; Jer 32.17; Lk 1.37; 18.28 Lk 5.11; 18.30 Mt 12.32; 18.31 Lk 9.51; Ps 22; 18.32 Mt 16.21; 27.2; Lk 23.1

18.12 The Mosaic Law prescribed only one day of fasting, the day of atonement referred to in Acts 27.9 (cf. Lev 16.29). Although not required by oral traditions, this Pharisee, and probably others like him, fasted two days a week, on Mondays and Thursdays. He went beyond the requirements of the Law and was quite proud of it. Other references to the frequent fasting of the Pharisees and the disciples of John the Baptist are to be found in Mt 9.14; Mk 2.18; Lk 5.33. (See note to Mk 2.18 for Christian fasting.)

delivered to the Gentiles, and will be mocked and shamefully treated and spit upon; 33 they will scourge him and kill him, and on the third day he will rise." 34 But they understood none of these things; this saying was hid from them, and they did not grasp what was said.

18.34
Mk 9.32;
Lk 9.45

Healing the blind man near Jericho
(18.35–43; Mt 20.29–34; Mk 10.46–52)

35 As he drew near to Jĕr'ĭchō, a blind man was sitting by the roadside begging; 36 and hearing a multitude going by, he inquired what this meant. 37 They told him, "Jesus of Năz'ărĕth is passing by." 38And he cried, "Jesus, Son of David, have mercy on me!" 39And those who were in front rebuked him, telling him to be silent; but he cried out all the more, "Son of David, have mercy on me!" 40And Jesus stopped, and commanded him to be brought to him; and when he came near, he asked him, 41 "What do you want me to do for you?" He said, "Lord, let me receive my sight." 42And Jesus said to him, "Receive your sight; your faith has made you well." 43And immediately he received his sight and followed him, glorifying God; and all the people, when they saw it, gave praise to God.

18.38
Mt 9.27
18.39
ver 38

18.42
Mt 9.22;
Mk 5.34;
Lk 17.19
18.43
Mt 9.8;
Lk 13.17

The conversion of Zacchaeus (19.1–10)

19 He entered Jĕr'ĭchō and was passing through. 2And there was a man named Zăcchae'ŭs; he was a chief tax collector, and rich. 3And he sought to see who Jesus was, but could not, on account of the crowd, because he was small of stature. 4 So he ran on ahead and climbed up into a sycamore tree to see him, for he was to pass that way. 5And when Jesus came to the place, he looked up and said to him, "Zăcchae'ŭs, make haste and come down; for I must stay at your house today." 6 So he made haste and came down, and received him joyfully. 7And when they saw it they all murmured, "He has gone in to be the guest of a man who is a sinner." 8And Zăcchae'ŭs stood and said to the Lord, "Behold, Lord, the half of my goods I give to the poor; and if I have defrauded any one of anything, I restore it fourfold." 9And Jesus said to him, "Today salvation has come to this house, since he also is a son of Abraham. 10 For the Son of man came to seek and to save the lost."

19.1
Lk 18.35
19.4
1 Ki 10.27;
1Chr 27.28;
Isa 9.10
19.7
Mt 9.11;
Lk 5.30
19.8
Lk 7.13;
3.14;
Ex 22.1;
Lev 6.5;
Num 5.7;
2 Sam 12.6
19.9
Lk 3.8;
13.16;
Rom 4.16;
Gal 3.7
19.10
Mt 18.11

The parable of the pounds (19.11–27)

11 As they heard these things, he proceeded to tell a parable, because he was near to Jerusalem, and because they supposed that the kingdom of God was to appear immediately. 12 He said therefore, "A nobleman went into a far country to receive a kingdom and then return. 13 Calling ten of his servants, he gave them

*19.11
Acts 1.6
19.12
Mt 25.14–30;
Mk 13.34

19.11 The teaching of this parable is similar to that of the talents in Mt 25.14ff. Christ indicated that diligence receives a fit reward, whereas slothfulness is punished. Undoubtedly He spoke of Himself as the nobleman and the servants as those who belong to Him and to His Kingdom. In His kingdom there are faithful and unfaithful servants to whom appropriate rewards will be given. In this parable those who are not His servants and who refuse to have Him reign over them are slain.

ten pounds,^e and said to them, 'Trade with these till I come.'
14 But his citizens hated him and sent an embassy after him, saying, 'We do not want this man to reign over us.' 15 When he returned, having received the kingdom, he commanded these servants, to whom he had given the money, to be called to him, that he might know what they had gained by trading. 16 The first came before him, saying, 'Lord, your pound has made ten pounds more.' 17And he said to him, 'Well done, good servant! Because you have been faithful in a very little, you shall have authority over ten cities.' 18And the second came, saying, 'Lord, your pound has made five pounds.' 19And he said to him, 'And you are to be over five cities.' 20 Then another came, saying, 'Lord, here is your pound, which I kept laid away in a napkin; 21 for I was afraid of you, because you are a severe man; you take up what you did not lay down, and reap what you did not sow.' 22 He said to him, 'I will condemn you out of your own mouth, you wicked servant! You knew that I was a severe man, taking up what I did not lay down and reaping what I did not sow? 23Why then did you not put my money into the bank, and at my coming I should have collected it with interest?' 24And he said to those who stood by, 'Take the pound from him, and give it to him who has the ten pounds.' 25 (And they said to him, 'Lord, he has ten pounds!') 26 'I tell you, that to every one who has will more be given; but from him who has not, even what he has will be taken away. 27 But as for these enemies of mine, who did not want me to reign over them, bring them here and slay them before me.' "

19.17
Lk 16.10

19.21
Mt 25.24

19.22
2 Sam 1.16;
Job 15.6;
Mt 25.26

19.26
Mt 13.12;
Lk 8.18

The triumphal entry
(19.28–40; Mt 21.1–11; Mk 11.1–11; Jn 12.12–19)

28 And when he had said this, he went on ahead, going up to Jerusalem. 29 When he drew near to Běth'phăge and Běth'ăny̆, at the mount that is called Ol'ĭvĕt, he sent two of the disciples, 30 saying, "Go into the village opposite, where on entering you will find a colt tied, on which no one has ever yet sat; untie it and bring it here. 31 If any one asks you, 'Why are you untying it?' you shall say this, 'The Lord has need of it.' " 32 So those who were sent went away and found it as he had told them. 33And as they were untying the colt, its owners said to them, "Why are you untying the colt?" 34And they said, "The Lord has need of it." 35And they brought it to Jesus, and throwing their garments on the colt they set Jesus upon it. 36And as he rode along, they spread their garments on the road. 37As he was now drawing near, at the descent of the Mount of Olives, the whole multitude of the disciples began to rejoice and praise God with a loud voice for all the mighty works that they had seen, 38 saying, "Blessed is the King who comes in the name of the Lord! Peace in heaven and glory in the highest!" 39And some of the Phạr'ĭsee̱s in the multitude said to him, "Teacher, rebuke your disciples." 40 He answered, "I tell you, if these were silent, the very stones would cry out."

19.28
Mk 10.32;
Mt 21.17;
Lk 21.37

19.32
Lk 22.13

19.36
2 Ki 9.13

19.38
Ps 118.26;
Lk 13.35;
2.14
19.39
Mt 21.15,16
19.40
Hab 2.11

Jesus weeps over Jerusalem (19 41–44)

41 And when he drew near and saw the city he wept over it,

19.41
Lk 13.34,35

e The mina, rendered here by *pound*, was about three months' wages for a laborer

42 saying, "Would that even today you knew the things that make for peace! But now they are hid from your eyes. 43 For the days shall come upon you, when your enemies will cast up a bank about you and surround you, and hem you in on every side, 44 and dash you to the ground, you and your children within you, and they will not leave one stone upon another in you; because you did not know the time of your visitation."

Second cleansing of the Temple
(19.45–48; Mt 21.12–17; Mk 11.15–19; cf. Jn 2.13–22)

45 And he entered the temple and began to drive out those who sold, 46 saying to them, "It is written, 'My house shall be a house of prayer'; but you have made it a den of robbers."

47 And he was teaching daily in the temple. The chief priests and the scribes and the principal men of the people sought to destroy him; 48 but they did not find anything they could do, for all the people hung upon his words.

Christ's authority challenged
(20.1–8; Mt 21.23–27; Mk 11.27–33)

20 One day, as he was teaching the people in the temple and preaching the gospel, the chief priests and the scribes with the elders came up 2 and said to him, "Tell us by what authority you do these things, or who it is that gave you this authority." 3 He answered them, "I also will ask you a question; now tell me, 4 Was the baptism of John from heaven or from men?" 5 And they discussed it with one another, saying, "If we say, 'From heaven,' he will say, 'Why did you not believe him?' 6 But if we say, 'From men,' all the people will stone us; for they are convinced that John was a prophet." 7 So they answered that they did not know whence it was. 8 And Jesus said to them, "Neither will I tell you by what authority I do these things."

Parable of the wicked tenants
(20.9–18; Mt 21.33–46; Mk 12.1–12)

9 And he began to tell the people this parable: "A man planted a vineyard, and let it out to tenants, and went into another country for a long while. 10 When the time came, he sent a servant to the tenants, that they should give him some of the fruit of the vineyard; but the tenants beat him, and sent him away empty-handed. 11 And he sent another servant; him also they beat and treated shamefully, and sent him away empty-handed. 12 And he sent yet a third; this one they wounded and cast out. 13 Then the owner of the vineyard said, 'What shall I do? I will send my beloved son; it may be they will respect him.' 14 But when the tenants saw him, they said to themselves, 'This is the heir; let us kill him, that the inheritance may be ours.' 15 And they cast him out of the vineyard and killed him. What then will the owner of the vineyard do to

Margin references:
19.43 Isa 29.3; Jer 6.6; Ezek 4.2; Lk 21.20
19.44 Mt 24.2; Mk 13.2; Lk 21.6; 1 Pet 2.12
19.46 Isa 56.7
19.47 Mt 26.55; Mk 11.18; Jn 7.19
20.1 Mt 26.55; Lk 8.1
20.2 Jn 2.18; Acts 4.7; 7.27
20.6 Mt 14.5; Lk 7.29
*20.9 Isa 5.1–7; Mt 25.14

20.9 This parable apparently was directed against the Jews as a nation because of their rejection of Christ as their Messiah. He warned them of the dire consequences of their decision, as it related both to judgment upon their nation and to the inclusion of the Gentiles, who would be offered the kingdom they had rejected.

them? 16 He will come and destroy those tenants, and give the vineyard to others." When they heard this, they said, "God forbid!" 17 But he looked at them and said, "What then is this that is written:

'The very stone which the builders rejected
 has become the head of the corner'?

18 Every one who falls on that stone will be broken to pieces; but when it falls on any one it will crush him."

20.16 Lk 19.27; Rom 3.4, 6,31
20.17 Ps 118.22, 23; 1 Pet 2.6
*20.18 Isa 8.14,15

Paying taxes to Caesar
(20.19–26; Mt 22.15–22; Mk 12.13–17)

19 The scribes and the chief priests tried to lay hands on him at that very hour, but they feared the people; for they perceived that he had told this parable against them. 20 So they watched him, and sent spies, who pretended to be sincere, that they might take hold of what he said, so as to deliver him up to the authority and jurisdiction of the governor. 21 They asked him, "Teacher, we know that you speak and teach rightly, and show no partiality, but truly teach the way of God. 22 Is it lawful for us to give tribute to Caesar, or not?" 23 But he perceived their craftiness, and said to them, 24 "Show me a coin.ᶠ Whose likeness and inscription has it?" They said, "Caesar's." 25 He said to them, "Then render to Caesar the things that are Caesar's, and to God the things that are God's." 26And they were not able in the presence of the people to catch him by what he said; but marveling at his answer they were silent.

20.19 Lk 19.47
20.21 Jn 3.2
*20.25 Rom 13.7; Lk 23.2

The Sadducces and the resurrection
(20.27–40; Mt 22.23–33; Mk 12.18–27)

27 There came to him some Săd'dúçēṣ, those who say that there is no resurrection, 28 and they asked him a question, saying, "Teacher, Moses wrote for us that if a man's brother dies, having a wife but no children, the manᵍ must take the wife and raise up children for his brother. 29 Now there were seven brothers; the first took a wife, and died without children; 30 and the second 31 and the third took her, and likewise all seven left no children and died. 32Afterward the woman also died. 33 In the resurrection, therefore, whose wife will the woman be? For the seven had her as wife."

34 And Jesus said to them, "The sons of this age marry and are given in marriage; 35 but those who are accounted worthy to attain to that age and to the resurrection from the dead neither marry nor are given in marriage, 36 for they cannot die any more, because they are equal to angels and are sons of God, being sons of the resurrection. 37 But that the dead are raised, even Moses showed, in the passage about the bush, where he calls the Lord the God of Abraham and the God of Isaac and the God of Jacob. 38 Now he is not God of the dead, but of the living; for all live to him." 39And some of the scribes answered, "Teacher, you have spoken well." 40 For they no longer dared to ask him any question.

20.27 Acts 23.6,8
20.28 Deut 25.5
20.36 Rom 8.16, 17; 1 Jn 3.1,2
20.37 Ex 3.6
20.38 Rom 6.10, 11
20.40 Mt 22.46; Mk 12.34

ᶠ Greek denarius   ᵍ Greek his brother

20.18 A variation of Isa 8.14, 15; Dan 2.34.
20.25 God's due takes precedence over
Caesar's due when one is forced to choose between them.

Christ's unanswerable question
(20.41–44; Mt 22.41–46; Mk 12.35–37)

41 But he said to them, "How can they say that the Christ is David's son? 42 For David himself says in the Book of Psalms,

'The Lord said to my Lord,
Sit at my right hand,
43 till I make thy enemies a stool for thy feet.'
44 David thus calls him Lord; so how is he his son?"

20.42 Ps 110.1; Acts 2.34

Warning against the scribes
(20.45–47; Mt 23.1–12; Mk 12.38–40)

45 And in the hearing of all the people he said to his disciples, 46 "Beware of the scribes, who like to go about in long robes, and love salutations in the market places and the best seats in the synagogues and the places of honor at feasts, 47 who devour widows' houses and for a pretense make long prayers. They will receive the greater condemnation."

20.46 Lk 11.43

The widow's offering (21.1–4)

21 He looked up and saw the rich putting their gifts into the treasury; 2 and he saw a poor widow put in two copper coins. 3 And he said, "Truly I tell you, this poor widow has put in more than all of them; 4 for they all contributed out of their abundance, but she out of her poverty put in all the living that she had."

21.1 Mk 12.41–44
21.2 Mk 12.42

The Olivet Discourse (21.5–38; Mt 24; Mk 13)

1. *The course of this age (21.5–19; Mt 24.1–14; Mk 13.3–13)*

5 And as some spoke of the temple, how it was adorned with noble stones and offerings, he said, 6 "As for these things which you see, the days will come when there shall not be left here one stone upon another that will not be thrown down." 7 And they asked him, "Teacher, when will this be, and what will be the sign when this is about to take place?" 8 And he said, "Take heed that you are not led astray; for many will come in my name, saying, 'I am he!' and, 'The time is at hand!' Do not go after them. 9 And when you hear of wars and tumults, do not be terrified; for this must first take place, but the end will not be at once."

10 Then he said to them, "Nation will rise against nation, and kingdom against kingdom; 11 there will be great earthquakes, and in various places famines and pestilences; and there will be terrors and great signs from heaven. 12 But before all this they will lay their hands on you and persecute you, delivering you up to the synagogues and prisons, and you will be brought before kings and governors for my name's sake. 13 This will be a time for you to bear testimony. 14 Settle it therefore in your minds, not to meditate beforehand how to answer; 15 for I will give you a mouth and wisdom, which none of your adversaries will be able to withstand or contradict. 16 You will be delivered up even by parents and brothers and kinsmen and friends, and some of you they will put to death; 17 you will be hated by all for my name's sake. 18 But not

*21.5 Mk 13.1
21.6 Lk 19.44
*21.7
21.8 Mk 13.21; Lk 17.23
21.10 2 Chr 15.6; Isa 19.2
21.12 Jn 16.2
21.13 Phil 1.12
21.14 Lk 12.11,12
21.15 Lk 12.12
21.16 Lk 12.52,53
21.17 Mt 10.22
21.18 Mt 10.30; Lk 12.7

21.5 *some.* See note to Lk 21.7.
21.7 *they.* Probably the Peter, James, John, and Andrew in Mk 13.3. Also see note to Mt 24.3 on the Olivet Discourse.

a hair of your head will perish. 19 By your endurance you will gain your lives.

2. *The destruction of Jerusalem*
(21.20–24; Mt 24.15–28; Mk 13.14–23)

20 "But when you see Jerusalem surrounded by armies, then know that its desolation has come near. 21 Then let those who are in Judē'á flee to the mountains, and let those who are inside the city depart, and let not those who are out in the country enter it; 22 for these are days of vengeance, to fulfil all that is written. 23Alas for those who are with child and for those who give suck in those days! For great distress shall be upon the earth and wrath upon this people; 24 they will fall by the edge of the sword, and be led captive among all nations; and Jerusalem will be trodden down by the Gentiles, until the times of the Gentiles are fulfilled.

3. *The Second Advent of Christ*
(21.25–28; Mt 24.29–31; Mk 13.24–27)

25 "And there will be signs in sun and moon and stars, and upon the earth distress of nations in perplexity at the roaring of the sea and the waves, 26 men fainting with fear and with foreboding of what is coming on the world; for the powers of the heavens will be shaken. 27And then they will see the Son of man coming in a cloud with power and great glory. 28 Now when these things begin to take place, look up and raise your heads, because your redemption is drawing near."

4. *The parable of the fig tree*
(21.29–33; Mt 24.32–35; Mk 13.28–31)

29 And he told them a parable: "Look at the fig tree, and all the trees; 30 as soon as they come out in leaf, you see for yourselves and know that the summer is already near. 31 So also, when you see these things taking place, you know that the kingdom of God is near. 32 Truly, I say to you, this generation will not pass away till all has taken place. 33 Heaven and earth will pass away, but my words will not pass away.

5. *Watchfulness (21.34–38; Mt 24.36–51; Mk 13.32–37)*

34 "But take heed to yourselves lest your hearts be weighed down with dissipation and drunkenness and cares of this life, and that day come upon you suddenly like a snare; 35 for it will come upon all who dwell upon the face of the whole earth. 36 But watch at all times, praying that you may have strength to escape all these things that will take place, and to stand before the Son of man."

37 And every day he was teaching in the temple, but at night he went out and lodged on the mount called Ol'ĭvĕt. 38And early in the morning all the people came to him in the temple to hear him.

Margin references: 21.19 Rev 2.7; *21.20 Lk 19.43; 21.21 Lk 17.31; 21.22 Isa 63.4; Dan 9.24–27; Zech 11.1; *21.24 Isa 63.18; Dan 8.13; 9.27; 12.7; Rom 11.25; Rev 11.2; 21.25 2 Pet 3.10, 12; 21.27 Rev 1.7; 14.14; 21.28 Lk 18.7; 21.31 Mt 3.2; 21.33 Lk 16.17; 21.34 Mk 4.19; Lk 12.45; 1 Thess 5.6, 7; 21.36 Lk 18.1; 21.37 Lk 19.47; Mk 11.19

21.20 This prophecy about Jerusalem was literally fulfilled in A.D. 70 when the city was destroyed by Roman legions under Titus. Josephus, the Jewish historian, in his WARS OF THE JEWS, Books V and VI, describes the siege and taking of Jerusalem in some detail. From that day to this the city of Jerusalem has been *trodden down by the Gentiles* (ver 24).
21.24 Jesus speaks of the *times of the Gen-* tiles. His prophecy includes the statement that Jerusalem will be trodden down during the length of this period. This implies that the times of the Gentiles will have an end and that then Jerusalem will be restored to the Jews. Rom 11.25 indicates that a hardening has come upon Israel until the *full number of the Gentiles come in*. When this occurs *all Israel will be saved* (Rom 11.26).

The plot to kill Jesus
(22.1–6; Mt 26.1–5, 14–16; Mk 14.1–2,10–11)

22.1
Jn 11.47-53
22.2
Mt 12.14
*22.3
Jn 13.2
22.5
Zech 11.12

22 Now the feast of Unleavened Bread drew near, which is called the Passover. 2And the chief priests and the scribes were seeking how to put him to death; for they feared the people.

3 Then Satan entered into Judas called Iscar′iot, who was of the number of the twelve; 4 he went away and conferred with the chief priests and officers how he might betray him to them. 5And they were glad, and engaged to give him money. 6 So he agreed, and sought an opportunity to betray him to them in the absence of the multitude.

The Last Supper (22.7–30)

1. The Passover prepared (22.7–13; Mt 26.17–19; Mk 14.12–16)

22.7
Ex 12.18-
20;
Deut 16.5-8
22.8
Lk 19.29;
Acts 3.1

7 Then came the day of Unleavened Bread, on which the passover lamb had to be sacrificed. 8 So Jesus[h] sent Peter and John, saying, "Go and prepare the passover for us, that we may eat it." 9 They said to him, "Where will you have us prepare it?" 10 He said to them, "Behold, when you have entered the city, a man carrying a jar of water will meet you; follow him into the house which he enters, 11 and tell the householder, 'The Teacher says to you, Where is the guest room, where I am to eat the passover with my disciples?' 12And he will show you a large upper room furnished; there make ready." 13And they went, and found it as he had told them; and they prepared the passover.

2. The Passover eaten
(22.14–18; Mt 26.20–25; Mk 14.17–21; see Jn 13.1–30)

14 And when the hour came, he sat at table, and the apostles with him. 15And he said to them, "I have earnestly desired to eat this passover with you before I suffer; 16 for I tell you I shall not eat it[i] until it is fulfilled in the kingdom of God." 17And he took a cup, and when he had given thanks he said, "Take this, and divide it among yourselves; 18 for I tell you that from now on I shall not drink of the fruit of the vine until the kingdom of God

22.16
Lk 14.15;
Rev 19.9

*22.19
22.21
Mt 26.21-
24;
Mk 14.18-
21;
Jn 13.21-30
22.22
Acts 2.23;
4.28
22.24
Mk 9.34;
Lk 9.46
22.25
Mt 20.25-
28;
Mk 10.42-
45

3. The Lord's Supper instituted
(22.19–30; Mt 26.26–29; Mk 14.22–25)

comes." 19And he took bread, and when he had given thanks he broke it and gave it to them, saying, "This is my body which is given for you. Do this in remembrance of me." 20And likewise the cup after supper, saying, "This cup which is poured out for you is the new covenant in my blood.[j] 21 But behold the hand of him who betrays me is with me on the table. 22 For the Son of man goes as it has been determined; but woe to that man by whom he is betrayed!" 23And they began to question one another, which of them it was that would do this.

h Greek he i Other ancient authorities read never eat it again
j Other authorities omit, in whole or in part, verses 19b-20 (which is given . . . in my blood).

22.3 See note to Mt 26.14 on Judas Iscariot (cf. also note to Jn 13.27).

22.19 See note to Mk 14.22 on the Lord's Supper.

24 A dispute also arose among them, which of them was to be regarded as the greatest. 25And he said to them, "The kings of the Gentiles exercise lordship over them; and those in authority over them are called benefactors. 26 But not so with you; rather let the greatest among you become as the youngest, and the leader as one who serves. 27 For which is the greater, one who sits at table, or one who serves? Is it not the one who sits at table? But I am among you as one who serves.

28 "You are those who have continued with me in my trials; 29 and I assign to you, as my Father assigned to me, a kingdom, 30 that you may eat and drink at my table in my kingdom, and sit on thrones judging the twelve tribes of Israel.

Peter's denial foretold
(22.31–38; Mt 26.30–35; Mk 14.27–31; see Jn 14–17)

31 "Simon, Simon, behold, Satan demanded to have you,^k that he might sift you^k like wheat, 32 but I have prayed for you that your faith may not fail; and when you have turned again, strengthen your brethren." 33And he said to him, "Lord, I am ready to go with you to prison and to death." 34 He said, "I tell you, Peter, the cock will not crow this day, until you three times deny that you know me."

35 And he said to them, "When I sent you out with no purse or bag or sandals, did you lack anything?" They said, "Nothing." 36 He said to them, "But now, let him who has a purse take it, and likewise a bag. And let him who has no sword sell his mantle and buy one. 37 For I tell you that this scripture must be fulfilled in me, 'And he was reckoned with transgressors'; for what is written about me has its fulfilment." 38And they said, "Look, Lord, here are two swords." And he said to them, "It is enough."

Jesus in Gethsemane (22.39–53)

1. *His agony (22.39–46; Mt 26.36–46; Mk 14.32–43; cf. Jn 18.1)*

39 And he came out, and went, as was his custom, to the Mount of Olives; and the disciples followed him. 40And when he came to the place he said to them, "Pray that you may not enter into temptation." 41And he withdrew from them about a stone's throw, and knelt down and prayed, 42 "Father, if thou art willing, remove this cup from me; nevertheless not my will, but thine, be done."^l 45And when he rose from prayer, he came to the disciples and found them sleeping for sorrow, 46 and he said to them, "Why do you sleep? Rise and pray that you may not enter into temptation."

Cross-references (margin):

22.26 Lk 9.48; 1 Pet 5.5
22.27 Lk 12.37
★22.28 Heb 2.18; 4.15
22.29 Lk 12.32; 2 Tim 2.12
22.30 Lk 14.15; Rev 19.9; Mt 19.28; Rev 3.21
22.31 Job 1.6–12; Amos 9.9
★22.32 Jn 17.9,15; 21.15–17
22.35 Mt 10.9; Lk 9.3; 10.4
22.37 Isa 53.12; Mk 15.28
22.39 Lk 21.37
22.40 Mt 6.13
★22.42 Mk 10.38; Jn 5.30; 18.11
22.46 ver 40

---

k The Greek word for *you* here is plural; in verse 32 it is singular
l Other ancient authorities add verses 43 and 44: 43 *And there appeared to him an angel from heaven, strengthening him. 44 And being in an agony he prayed more earnestly; and his sweat became like great drops of blood falling down upon the ground*

22.28 *trials*, translated *temptation* in Mt 6.13.

22.32 Intercessory prayer is that form of prayer in which believers entreat God on behalf of other people. Like other forms of prayer, it must meet the conditions which govern effective praying. We are commanded to engage in this form of prayer habitually (1 Tim 2.1; Jas 5.14, 16), interceding for: (1) all classes of men, including kings and those in authority (1 Tim 2.1, 2); (2) ministers of the gospel (2 Cor 1.11; Phil 1.19); (3) persecutors (Mt 5.44); (4) friends (Job 42.8).

22.42 *this cup*, see note to Mt 26.39.

2. *Jesus' betrayal and arrest*
(22.47-53; Mt 26.47-56; Mk 14.43-50; Jn 18.1-11)

47 While he was still speaking, there came a crowd, and the man called Judas, one of the twelve, was leading them. He drew near to Jesus to kiss him; 48 but Jesus said to him, "Judas, would you betray the Son of man with a kiss?" 49And when those who were about him saw what would follow, they said, "Lord, shall we strike with the sword?" 50And one of them struck the slave of the high priest and cut off his right ear. 51 But Jesus said, "No more of this!" And he touched his ear and healed him. 52 Then Jesus said to the chief priests and officers of the temple and elders, who had come out against him, "Have you come out as against a robber, with swords and clubs? 53 When I was with you day after day in the temple, you did not lay hands on me. But this is your hour, and the power of darkness."

Peter's denial of Jesus
(22.54-71; Mt 26.69-75; Mk 14.66-72; Jn 18.15-18, 25-27)

54 Then they seized him and led him away, bringing him into the high priest's house. Peter followed at a distance; 55 and when they had kindled a fire in the middle of the courtyard and sat down together, Peter sat among them. 56 Then a maid, seeing him as he sat in the light and gazing at him, said, "This man also was with him." 57 But he denied it, saying, "Woman, I do not know him." 58And a little later someone else saw him and said, "You also are one of them." But Peter said, "Man, I am not." 59And after an interval of about an hour still another insisted, saying, "Certainly this man also was with him; for he is a Galilē'an." 60 But Peter said, "Man, I do not know what you are saying." And immediately, while he was still speaking, the cock crowed. 61And the Lord turned and looked at Peter. And Peter remembered the word of the Lord, how he had said to him, "Before the cock crows today, you will deny me three times." 62And he went out and wept bitterly.

63 Now the men who were holding Jesus mocked him and beat him; 64 they also blindfolded him and asked him, "Prophesy! Who is it that struck you?" 65And they spoke many other words against him, reviling him.

66 When day came, the assembly of the elders of the people gathered together, both chief priests and scribes; and they led him away to their council, and they said, 67 "If you are the Christ, tell us." But he said to them, "If I tell you, you will not believe; 68 and if I ask you, you will not answer. 69 But from now on the Son of man shall be seated at the right hand of the power of God." 70And they all said, "Are you the Son of God, then?" And he said to them, "You say that I am." 71And they said, "What further testimony do we need? We have heard it ourselves from his own lips."

Jesus before Pontius Pilate
(23.1-25; Mt 27.11-26; Mk 15.2-15; Jn 18.29-40)

1. *Pilate questions Jesus (23.1-5)*

23 Then the whole company of them arose, and brought him before Pīlate. 2And they began to accuse him, saying, "We

---

Marginal references:
22.49 ver 38
22.52 ver 4,37
22.53 Jn 12.27
22.54 Mt 26.58; Mk 14.54
22.61 ver 34
22.63 Mt 26.67, 68; Mk 14.65; Jn 18.22,23
*22.66 Mt 27.1; Mk 15.1
22.67 Mt 26.63-66; Mk 14.61-63; Jn 18.19-21
22.70 Mt 27.11; Lk 23.3
*23.1 Mt 27.2; Mk 15.1; Jn 18.28
23.2 Lk 20.22; Jn 19.12

22.66 See note to Mt 26.59 on Sanhedrin.   **23.1** See note to Mk 15.1 on Pilate.

found this man perverting our nation, and forbidding us to give tribute to Caesar, and saying that he himself is Christ a king." ³And Pīlāte asked him, "Are you the King of the Jews?" And he answered him, "You have said so." ⁴And Pīlāte said to the chief priests and the multitudes, "I find no crime in this man." ⁵ But they were urgent, saying, "He stirs up the people, teaching throughout all Judē'á, from Găl'ịleē even to this place."

23.3
Lk 22.70;
1 Tim 6.13
23.4
1 Pet 2.22

2. *Pilate sends Jesus to Herod (23.6–12)*

6 When Pīlāte heard this, he asked whether the man was a Gălịlē'án. ⁷And when he learned that he belonged to Hĕrŏd'ş jurisdiction, he sent him over to Hĕrŏd, who was himself in Jerusalem at that time. ⁸ When Hĕrŏd saw Jesus, he was very glad, for he had long desired to see him, because he had heard about him, and he was hoping to see some sign done by him. ⁹ So he questioned him at some length; but he made no answer. ¹⁰ The chief priests and the scribes stood by, vehemently accusing him. ¹¹And Hĕrŏd with his soldiers treated him with contempt and mocked him; then, arraying him in gorgeous apparel, he sent him back to Pīlāte. ¹²And Hĕrŏd and Pīlāte became friends with each other that very day, for before this they had been at enmity with each other.

23.7
Lk 3.1
23.8
Lk 9.9;
Mt 14.1;
Mk 6.14

23.11
Mk 15.17–
19;
Jn 19.2,3
23.12
Acts 4.27

3. *Pilate would free Jesus (23.13–17)*

13 Pīlāte then called together the chief priests and the rulers and the people, ¹⁴ and said to them, "You brought me this man as one who was perverting the people; and after examining him before you, behold, I did not find this man guilty of any of your charges against him; ¹⁵ neither did Hĕrŏd, for he sent him back to us. Behold, nothing deserving death has been done by him; ¹⁶ I will therefore chastise him and release him." ᵐ

23.14
ver 2,4

23.16
Mt 27.26;
Mk 15.15;
Jn 19.1

4. *Pilate releases Barabbas and delivers Jesus (23.18–25)*

18 But they all cried out together, "Away with this man, and release to us Bàrăb'bàs"—¹⁹ a man who had been thrown into prison for an insurrection started in the city, and for murder. ²⁰ Pīlāte addressed them once more, desiring to release Jesus; ²¹ but they shouted out, "Crucify, crucify him!" ²² A third time he said to them, "Why, what evil has he done? I have found in him no crime deserving death; I will therefore chastise him and release him." ²³ But they were urgent, demanding with loud cries that he should be crucified. And their voices prevailed. ²⁴ So Pīlāte gave sentence that their demand should be granted. ²⁵ He released the man who had been thrown into prison for insurrection and murder, whom they asked for; but Jesus he delivered up to their will.

23.18
Mt 27.20–
23;
Mk 15.11–
14;
Jn 18.38–
40; 19.14,
15;
Acts 3.13,14
23.22
ver 16

The Crucifixion and burial of Jesus (23.26–56)

1. *Jesus on the way to Calvary*
(23.26–31; see Mt 27.32; Mk 15.21)

26 And as they led him away, they seized one Simon of Çȳrē'në, who was coming in from the country, and laid on him the cross, to carry it behind Jesus. ²⁷And there followed him a great multitude of the people, and of women who bewailed and lamented him.

23.26
Jn 19.17
23.27
Lk 8.52

ᵐ Here, or after verse 19, other ancient authorities add verse 17, *Now he was obliged to release one man to them at the festival*

23.28
Lk 19.41–
44; 21.23,24

23.30
Isa 2.19;
Hos 10.8;
Rev 6.16
23.31
Ezek 20.47

23.32
Isa 53.12

*23.34
Ps 22.18;
Acts 7.60
23.35
Ps 22.17

23.36
Ps 69.21;
Mt 27.48

*23.38

23.39
ver 35,37

23.41
ver 4,14,22

*23.43
2 Cor 12.3,
4;
Rev 2.7

23.45
Ex 26.31–
35;
Heb 9.8;
10.19
23.46
Ps 31.5;
1 Pet 2.23
23.47
Mt 27.54

28 But Jesus turning to them said, "Daughters of Jerusalem, do not weep for me, but weep for yourselves and for your children. 29 For behold, the days are coming when they will say, 'Blessed are the barren, and the wombs that never bore, and the breasts that never gave suck!' 30 Then they will begin to say to the mountains, 'Fall on us'; and to the hills, 'Cover us.' 31 For if they do this when the wood is green, what will happen when it is dry?"

2. Jesus crucified
(23.32–38; Mt 27.32–44; Mk 15.21–32; Jn 19.17–24)

32 Two others also, who were criminals, were led away to be put to death with him. 33 And when they came to the place which is called The Skull, there they crucified him, and the criminals, one on the right and one on the left. 34 And Jesus said, "Father, forgive them; for they know not what they do."[n] And they cast lots to divide his garments. 35 And the people stood by, watching; but the rulers scoffed at him, saying, "He saved others; let him save himself, if he is the Christ of God, his Chosen One!" 36 The soldiers also mocked him, coming up and offering him vinegar, 37 and saying, "If you are the King of the Jews, save yourself!" 38 There was also an inscription over him,[o] "This is the King of the Jews."

3. The penitent thief (23.39–43)

39 One of the criminals who were hanged railed at him, saying, "Are you not the Christ? Save yourself and us!" 40 But the other rebuked him, saying, "Do you not fear God, since you are under the same sentence of condemnation? 41 And we indeed justly; for we are receiving the due reward of our deeds; but this man has done nothing wrong." 42 And he said, "Jesus, remember me when you come into[p] your kingdom." 43 And he said to him, "Truly, I say to you, today you will be with me in Paradise."

4. The death of Jesus
(23.44–49; Mt 27.45–50; Mk 15.33–41; Jn 19.28–37)

44 It was now about the sixth hour, and there was darkness over the whole land[q] until the ninth hour, 45 while the sun's light failed;[r] and the curtain of the temple was torn in two. 46 Then Jesus, crying with a loud voice, said, "Father, into thy hands I commit my spirit!" And having said this he breathed his last. 47 Now when

---

n Other ancient authorities omit the sentence And Jesus . . . what they do
o Other ancient authorities add in letters of Greek and Latin and Hebrew
p Other ancient authorities read in
q Or earth   r Or the sun was eclipsed. Other ancient authorities read the sun was darkened

---

23.34 Chronologically, the seven last sayings of Christ on Calvary were spoken in the following order: (1) the word of forgiveness: Father, forgive them (23.34); (2) the word of salvation: today you will be with me in Paradise (23.43); (3) the word of affection: Woman, behold, your son! and Behold; your mother! (Jn 19.26, 27); (4) the word of despair: My God, my God, why hast thou forsaken me? (Mt 27.46; Mk 15.34); (5) the word of physical torment: I thirst (Jn 19.28); (6) the word of triumph: It is finished (Jn 19.30); (7) the word of committal: Father, into thy hands I commit my spirit! (23.46).

Note that Matthew and Mark record only one saying, and Luke and John three each.
23.38 See note to Mt 27.37.
23.43 The Greek word for Paradise (paradeisos) comes from the Persian language as a loan word, and occurs two other times in the New Testament (2 Cor 12.3; Rev 2.7). The original meaning was enclosed park or a pleasure ground, but it came to be used in the Septuagint translation as a term for the Garden of Eden, and in the intertestamental period for a superterrestrial place of blessedness. As it is used here it can mean only heaven or the presence of God.

the centurion saw what had taken place, he praised God, and said, "Certainly this man was innocent!" 48And all the multitudes who assembled to see the sight, when they saw what had taken place, returned home beating their breasts. 49And all his acquaintances and the women who had followed him from Găl'ịleē stood at a distance and saw these things.

23.49
Ps 38.11;
Lk 8.2

5. Jesus laid in the tomb
(23.50–56; Mt 27.57–61; Mk 15.42–47; Jn 19.38–42)

50 Now there was a man named Joseph from the Jewish town of Ạrịmâthē'â. He was a member of the council, a good and righteous man, 51 who had not consented to their purpose and deed, and he was looking for the kingdom of God. 52 This man went to Pīlâte and asked for the body of Jesus. 53 Then he took it down and wrapped it in a linen shroud, and laid him in a rock-hewn tomb, where no one had ever yet been laid. 54 It was the day of Preparation, and the sabbath was beginning.⁵ 55 The women who had come with him from Găl'ịleē followed, and saw the tomb, and how his body was laid; 56 then they returned, and prepared spices and ointments.

On the sabbath they rested according to the commandment.

23.51
Lk 2.25

*23.54
Mt 27.62
23.55
ver 49
23.56
Mk 16.1;
Ex 12.16;
20.10

The Resurrection of Jesus Christ
(24.1–11; note v; Mt 28.1–10; Mk 16.1–8; Jn 20.1–18)

24 But on the first day of the week, at early dawn, they went to the tomb, taking the spices which they had prepared. 2And they found the stone rolled away from the tomb, 3 but when they went in they did not find the body.ᵗ 4 While they were perplexed about this, behold, two men stood by them in dazzling apparel; 5 and as they were frightened and bowed their faces to the ground, the men said to them, "Why do you seek the living among the dead?ᵘ 6 Remember how he told you, while he was still in Găl'ịleē, 7 that the Son of man must be delivered into the hands of sinful men, and be crucified, and on the third day rise." 8And they remembered his words, 9 and returning from the tomb they told all this to the eleven and to all the rest. 10 Now it was Mary Măg'dálēne and Jō-ăn'ná and Mary the mother of James and the other women with them who told this to the apostles; 11 but these words seemed to them an idle tale, and they did not believe them.ᵛ

24.1
Lk 23.56

24.4
Acts 1.10;
12.7

24.6
Mt 17.22,
23;
Mk 9.30,
31;
Lk 9.22
24.8
Jn 2.22
24.9
ver 46
24.10
Lk 8.1–3
24.11
ver 35

The walk to Emmaus (24.13–35)

13 That very day two of them were going to a village named Ĕmmā'ûs, about seven milesʷ from Jerusalem, 14 and talking with each other about all these things that had happened. 15 While

24.15
ver 36

ˢ Greek *was dawning*   ᵗ Other ancient authorities add *of the Lord Jesus*
ᵘ Other ancient authorities add *He is not here, but has risen*
ᵛ Other ancient authorities add verse 12, *But Peter rose and ran to the tomb; stooping and looking in, he saw the linen cloths by themselves; and he went home wondering at what had happened*
ʷ Greek *sixty stadia;* some ancient authorities read *a hundred and sixty stadia*

23.54 The *day of Preparation* was Friday (cf. Mk 15.42; Jn 19.31, 42), the day on which the Jews made the necessary preparations to observe the Sabbath when no work could be done. Sabbath began at sundown on Friday, being thus the day after Preparation (cf. Mt 27.62). The burial of Jesus, therefore, was completed before sundown on Friday.

they were talking and discussing together, Jesus himself drew near and went with them. 16 But their eyes were kept from recognizing him. 17And he said to them, "What is this conversation which you are holding with each other as you walk?" And they stood still, looking sad. 18 Then one of them, named Clē'ŏpȧs, answered him, "Are you the only visitor to Jerusalem who does not know the things that have happened there in these days?" 19And he said to them, "What things?" And they said to him, "Concerning Jesus of Nȧz'ȧrĕth, who was a prophet mighty in deed and word before God and all the people, 20 and how our chief priests and rulers delivered him up to be condemned to death, and crucified him. 21 But we had hoped that he was the one to redeem Israel. Yes, and besides all this, it is now the third day since this happened. 22 Moreover, some women of our company amazed us. They were at the tomb early in the morning 23 and did not find his body; and they came back saying that they had even seen a vision of angels, who said that he was alive. 24 Some of those who were with us went to the tomb, and found it just as the women had said; but him they did not see." 25And he said to them, "O foolish men, and slow of heart to believe all that the prophets have spoken! 26 Was it not necessary that the Christ should suffer these things and enter into his glory?" 27And beginning with Moses and all the prophets, he interpreted to them in all the scriptures the things concerning himself.

28 So they drew near to the village to which they were going. He appeared to be going further, 29 but they constrained him, saying, "Stay with us, for it is toward evening and the day is now far spent." So he went in to stay with them. 30 When he was at table with them, he took the bread and blessed, and broke it, and gave it to them. 31And their eyes were opened and they recognized him; and he vanished out of their sight. 32 They said to each other, "Did not our hearts burn within us while he talked to us on the road, while he opened to us the scriptures?" 33And they rose that same hour and returned to Jerusalem; and they found the eleven gathered together and those who were with them, 34 who said, "The Lord has risen indeed, and has appeared to Simon!" 35 Then they told what had happened on the road, and how he was known to them in the breaking of the bread.

Christ appears to the ten in Jerusalem
(24.36-43; Jn 20.19-25)

36 As they were saying this, Jesus himself stood among them.x 37 But they were startled and frightened, and supposed that they saw a spirit. 38And he said to them, "Why are you troubled, and why do questionings rise in your hearts? 39 See my hands and my feet, that it is I myself; handle me, and see; for a spirit has not flesh and bones as you see that I have."y 41And while they still disbelieved for joy, and wondered, he said to them, "Have you anything here to eat?" 42 They gave him a piece of broiled fish, 43 and he took it and ate before them.

x Other ancient authorities add and said to them, "Peace to you!"
y Other ancient authorities add verse 40, And when he had said this, he showed them his hands and his feet

24.18 Cleopas is not the Clopas of Jn 18.25.   **24.21** Here the reference is to the Messiah.

Cross references (left margin):

24.16 Jn 21.4
*24.18 Jn 19.25
24.19 Mt 21.11; Lk 7.16; 13.33; Acts 3.22
24.20 Lk 23.13
*24.21 Lk 1.68
24.22 ver 9,10
24.24 ver 12
24.26 Heb 2.10; 1 Pet 1.11
24.27 Gen 3.15; Num 21.9; Deut 18.15; Isa 7.14; 9.6; 40.10,11; ch 53; Ezek 34.23; Dan 9.24; Mic 7.20; Mal 3.1
24.28 Mk 6.48
24.30 Mt 14.19
24.33 Acts 1.14
24.34 1 Cor 15.5
24.37 Mk 6.49
24.39 Jn 20.27
24.41 Jn 21.5
24.43 Acts 10.41

The great commission
(24.44-49; cf. Mt 28.18-20; Jn 20.21; Acts 1.8)

44 Then he said to them, "These are my words which I spoke
to you, while I was still with you, that everything written about me
in the law of Moses and the prophets and the psalms must be fulfilled." 45 Then he opened their minds to understand the scriptures, 46 and said to them, "Thus it is written, that the Christ
should suffer and on the third day rise from the dead, 47 and that
repentance and forgiveness of sins should be preached in his name
to all nations,z beginning from Jerusalem. 48 You are witnesses of
these things. 49And behold, I send the promise of my Father upon
you; but stay in the city, until you are clothed with power from
on high."

Christ's ascension
(24.50-53; Mk 16.19-20; cf. Acts 1.9-11)

50 Then he led them out as far as Běth'ǎnў, and lifting up his
hands he blessed them. 51 While he blessed them, he parted from
them, and was carried up into heaven.a 52And theyb returned to
Jerusalem with great joy, 53 and were continually in the temple
blessing God.

Cross references (right column):
24.44 Mt 16.21; Mk 8.31; Lk 9.22; 18.31
*24.46 Isa 50.6; Hos 6.2; 1 Cor 15.3,4
24.47 Acts 5.31; 13.38; Mt 28.19
24.48 Acts 1.8
24.49 Jn 14.16; Acts 1.4
24.50 Acts 1.12
24.51 2 Ki 2.11
24.53 Acts 2.46

z Or nations. Beginning from Jerusalem you are witnesses
a Other ancient authorities omit and was carried up into heaven
b Other ancient authorities add worshiped him, and

24.46 The bodily resurrection of Jesus
Christ is clearly set forth as a historical event
in the New Testament. The Resurrection was
necessary (1) to make possible the forgiveness
of sins (1 Cor 15.17); (2) to fulfil the Scriptures (24.45, 46); (3) to afford justification for
believers (Rom 4.25; 8.34); (4) to furnish a
solid basis for Christian hope (1 Cor 15.19).
The Resurrection was brought to pass: (1) by
the power of God (Acts 2.24; Rom 8.11;
Eph 1.19, 20); (2) by the Lord Jesus Himself
(Jn 2.19; 10.18).

INTRODUCTION TO
THE GOSPEL ACCORDING TO
JOHN

Authorship and Background: Unlike the other Gospels, the Fourth Gospel refers to its author, naming him as "the disciple whom Jesus loved . . . who has written these things" (21.20, 24). This disciple, referred to in 13.23, 19.26, 20.2, and 21.7, 20, is not identified by name. In every instance, except at the cross in 19.26, he is with Simon Peter, and he may be "the other disciple" who was with Peter when they went into the high priest's house at the trial of Jesus (18.15, 16). The early writers who speak of the authorship of this Gospel identify "the beloved disciple" with the Apostle John, the son of Zebedee.

The Gospels reveal that the Apostle John, his father Zebedee, and his brother James were fishermen on Lake Galilee (Mk 1.19–20), partners of Simon Peter (Lk 5.10). The two brothers were called "Boanerges," i.e., "Sons of Thunder" by Jesus (Mk 3.17). Probably their mother was Salome (cf. Mk 15.40 with Mt 27.56). John and Peter were the two disciples sent in advance into Jerusalem to prepare for the Passover meal (Lk 22.8). John, James, and Peter were the only disciples to accompany Jesus at the raising of the daughter of Jairus (Mk 5.37–40), to the Mount of Transfiguration (Mk 9.2), and into the Garden of Gethsemane (Mk 14.33). The three were joined by Andrew when Jesus delivered his discourse on last things on Mount Olivet (Mk 13.3). John and his brother asked for the places of honor in Christ's glory (Mk 10.35–45), and suggested that fire descend from heaven upon the inhospitable Samaritans (Lk 9.54).

After Pentecost, John was associated with Peter in Jerusalem (Acts 3.1—4.22) and on the Samaritan mission (Acts 8.14–25); Paul identified John as one of the three "pillar" apostles whom he saw on his postconversion visit to Jerusalem (Gal 2.9–10).

The date most often suggested for the Fourth Gospel is the last decade of the first century, A.D. 90–100; some date it earlier, near A.D. 70.

Characteristics: The book's purpose is formally stated in 20.30, 31: it is a narrative of some of the signs Jesus performed, written in order that the readers might believe that Jesus is the Christ, the Son of God, and in this faith have life in his name.

The supreme question for faith is, "Who is Jesus?" This Gospel answers: (1) he is the "Word of God" (1.14); (2) the "Lamb of God" (1.29, 36); (3) the "Messiah" (1.41); (4) the "Son of God" (1.49); (5) the "King of Israel" (1.49); (6) the "Savior of the world" (4.42). The climax comes with Thomas' ringing confession, "My Lord and my God!" (20.28). In this Gospel seven "signs" of Jesus are recorded, which reveal the person and mission of Jesus: (1) the turning of water into wine (2.1–11); (2) the cure of the nobleman's son (4.46–54); (3) the cure of the paralytic (5.1–18); (4) the feeding of the multitude (6.6–13); (5)

walking on the water (6.16–21); (6) giving sight to the blind (9.1–7); and (7) the raising of Lazarus (11.1–45). The purpose and effect of these "signs" are disclosed in 12.37–43: they will not believe because their eyes have been blinded.

There are also seven great "I am" sayings: (1) the bread of life (6.35); (2) the light of the world (8.12); (3) the door of the sheep (10.7); (4) the good shepherd (10.11); (5) the resurrection and the life (11.25); (6) the way, and the truth, and the life (14.6); (7) the true vine (15.1).

The ministry of Jesus is controlled by "the hour," the decisive moment when God's purpose will be accomplished (2.4; 4.21, 23; 5.25, 28; 7.30; 8.20; 12.23, 27; 13.1); the decisive climax is reached with the declaration of 17.1, "Father, the hour has come."

Contents:

I.   Prologue. 1.1–18

II.   Revelation to old Israel: the public ministry. 1.19—12.50: John the Baptist; calling of disciples; cleansing of the Temple. Signs. Nicodemus and the woman of Samaria. The climactic sign, the raising of Lazarus; the religious leaders decide to put Jesus to death. The close of the public ministry.

III.   Revelation to new Israel: disclosures to the disciples. 13.1—20.29: The Upper Room: washing the disciples' feet, discourses, and prayer. Gethsemane, arrest, trial, crucifixion, death, burial, resurrection, and appearances of the risen Lord.

IV.   Conclusion of the book. 20.30, 31

V.   Epilogue. 21.1–25

THE GOSPEL ACCORDING TO

JOHN

The eternal Word (1.1–5)

*1.1
Col 1.17;
1 Jn 1.1;
Phil 2.6
1.3
Col 1.16;
Heb 1.2
1.4
Jn 5.26;
11.25; 14.6
1.5
Jn 3.19;
9.5; 12.46

1 In the beginning was the Word, and the Word was with God, and the Word was God. 2 He was in the beginning with God; 3 all things were made through him, and without him was not anything made that was made. 4 In him was life,[a] and the life was the light of men. 5 The light shines in the darkness, and the darkness has not overcome it.

The ministry of John the Baptist (1.6–8; see ver. 19–28; Mt 3.1–12; Mk 1.1–8; Lk 3.2–17)

1.7
Acts 19.4
1.8
ver 20

6 There was a man sent from God, whose name was John. 7 He came for testimony, to bear witness to the light, that all might believe through him. 8 He was not the light, but came to bear witness to the light.

The First Advent of Jesus Christ and his rejection (1.9–13)

1.9
Isa 49.6;
1 Jn 2.8
1.10
Col 1.16;
Heb 1.2
1.12
Gal 3.26;
Jn 3.18;
1 Jn 5.13
1.13
Jn 3.5,6;
Jas 1.18;
1 Pet 1.23

9 The true light that enlightens every man was coming into the world. 10 He was in the world, and the world was made through him, yet the world knew him not. 11 He came to his own home, and his own people received him not. 12 But to all who received him, who believed in his name, he gave power to become children of God; 13 who were born, not of blood nor of the will of the flesh nor of the will of man, but of God.

The witness of John the Baptist to the incarnate Word (1.14–18)

*1.14
Rom 1.3;
Gal 4.4;
1 Tim 3.16;
Heb 2.14

14 And the Word became flesh and dwelt among us, full of

---

a Or was not anything made. That which has been made was life in him

---

1.1 The *Word* (from the Greek *logos*, meaning *reason* or *word*) is a designation for Christ Himself. Scripture makes a distinction between the *Word* of God *written*, the Scriptures, and the *Word* of God *incarnate*, or Jesus Christ in the flesh. John, in his prologue, speaks of Christ as the eternal, pre-existent One who became flesh. We may say: (1) the *Word* existed before the world began; (2) *the Word was with God*, or distinct from, and yet in communion with, God the Father; (3) *the Word was God*, or identical in essence with God the Father; (4) through the Word, God brought into being the entire created universe, both the visible and the invisible (Col 1.16; Heb 1.2; 11.3); (5) the Word is the source of the physical, intellectual, moral, and spiritual life of man (1.4); (6) God the Word became flesh, or incarnate as a true human being (1.14). In essence this is the same teaching as that of Paul, who said that in Christ *the whole fulness of deity dwells bodily* (Col 2.9).

1.14 The incarnation is the fundamental part of the gospel. It is that act whereby the Son of God, being Himself God and of the same substance with the Father, nevertheless condescended to assume human nature for the purpose of man's redemption and restoration. Of the incarnation it may be said: (1) Jesus of Nazareth was and is true God, having a divine nature and all the attributes of deity (Phil 2.6; Col 1.19; Heb 1.8–10); (2) Jesus Christ became true man having a natural human body and exhibiting those attributes which are common to humanity (1 Tim 2.5; Acts 3.22; Gal 4.4; Heb 2.14, 17, 18; 4.15); (3) Jesus Christ was both human and divine (Phil 2.6–11); He was addressed by both divine and human titles, and divine as well as human attributes were ascribed to Him; (4) Jesus Christ shall subsist for ever as the God-man in His resurrected body (cf. Acts 1.11). The truth of the incarnation is so intimately intertwined with every

grace and truth; we have beheld his glory, glory as of the only Son from the Father. [15] (John bore witness to him, and cried, "This was he of whom I said, 'He who comes after me ranks before me, for he was before me.' ") [16]And from his fulness have we all received, grace upon grace. [17] For the law was given through Moses; grace and truth came through Jesus Christ. [18] No one has ever seen God; the only Son,[b] who is in the bosom of the Father, he has made him known.

*1.15
ver 30

1.16
Eph 1.23;
Col 1.19

*1.17
Rom 3.24

*1.18
Ex 33.20;
Jn 6.46;
1 Jn 4.9

John's witness to himself (1.19–28)

[19] And this is the testimony of John, when the Jews sent priests and Lēvītes from Jerusalem to ask him, "Who are you?" [20] He confessed, he did not deny, but confessed, "I am not the Christ." [21]And they asked him, "What then? Are you Ēlī'jáh?" He said, "I am not." "Are you the prophet?" And he answered, "No." [22] They said to him then, "Who are you? Let us have an answer for those who sent us. What do you say about yourself?" [23] He said, "I am the voice of one crying in the wilderness, 'Make straight the way of the Lord,' as the prophet Īṣāi'áh said."

[24] Now they had been sent from the Phar'iseēṣ. [25] They asked him, "Then why are you baptizing, if you are neither the Christ, nor Ēlī'jáh, nor the prophet?" [26] John answered them, "I baptize with water; but among you stands one whom you do not know, [27] even he who comes after me, the thong of whose sandal I am not worthy to untie." [28] This took place in Bĕth'ăny̆ beyond the Jordan, where John was baptizing.

1.20
Jn 3.28;
Lk 3.15, 16

*1.21
Mt 11.14;
16.14;
Deut 18.15

1.23
Mt 3.1;
Mk 1.3;
Lk 3.4;
Isa 40.3

1.26
Acts 1.5
1.27
ver 15.30
1.28
Jn 3.26;
10.40

[b] Other ancient authorities read God

---

other doctrine of the gospel, that if either His true humanity or His true deity is destroyed, Christianity cannot be sustained as genuine. (See 1 Jn 4.2, 3, which emphasizes the necessity of this doctrine.)

Christ, the God-man, was both human and divine. Biblical evidences for the true humanity of Jesus are: (1) He was born of our flesh (Mt 1.16, 25; 2.2; Lk 2.7, 11); (2) He had a human soul (Mt 26.38; Lk 23.46); (3) He was hungry, weary, and required sleep (Mt 4.2; 21.18; Jn 4.6; Mt 8.24; Mk 4.38); (4) He was scourged, nailed to the cross, and His side was pierced (19.1; Lk 23.33; Jn 19.34); (5) He is stated to have been like man in all essentials except that He did not sin (Acts 3.22; Phil 2.7, 8; Jn 8.46; 1 Pet 2.22; Heb 2.14, 17, 18; 4.15).

1.15 See note to Lk 1.57 on the life of John the Baptist.

1.17 *grace* may be defined as the "unmerited favor of God" toward a sinner; it is "everything for nothing to those who deserve the exact opposite." Grace is an attribute of God (Ex 22.27; 33.19; Neh 9.17; 1 Pet 5.10). The supreme revelation of the grace of God is found in the incarnation, ministry, and atoning sacrifice of the Lord Jesus. Scripture teaches that: (1) justification is by grace (Rom 3.24; Tit 3.7); (2) salvation is by grace at every point (Eph 1.7, 8); (3) election is by grace (Rom 11.5, 6); (4) faith is the gift of grace (Acts 18.27; Eph 2.8, 9); (5) spiritual

gifts are of grace (Rom 12.6); (6) comfort, hope, and strength spring from grace (2 Cor 12.9; 2 Thess 2.16).

1.18 Scripture teaches that God is Spirit, hence He is not material and not visible. At the same time there are Scriptures which appear to teach that men have beheld the presence of God (e.g., Gen 32.30; Ex 24.9, 10; Judg 13.22; Isa 6.1; Dan 7.9). Several explanations have been suggested: (1) God may have assumed visible human forms on occasion for the purpose of communicating to men intelligibly (such appearances are called *theophanies*); (2) God may have been represented by proxy, either by a created angelic being who acted for God, or by "the angel of the LORD" (taken by many to be the pre-incarnate Christ); (3) Scripture may have used symbolic language or figures of speech which are not intended literally (e.g., in Isa 6.1 it was evidently a vision; in Num 12.8 God is simply indicating that Moses enjoyed a closer relationship to Him than did the children of Israel). The glory of Judaism lies in its revelation of the unity and spirituality of God; the glory of Christianity, in its revelation of the once-for-all incarnation of God in Jesus Christ.

1.21 The prophet referred to here (also in 1.25; 6.14; 7.40; Acts 3.22, 23; 7.37) is the one spoken of by Moses in Deut 18.15, 18. He is identified in the New Testament, not with John the Baptist, but with Jesus who is also Priest and King.

John's witness to Jesus (1.29–34)

1.29
Isa 53.7;
1 Pet 1.19
1.30
ver 15,27
1.32
Mt 3.16;
Mk 1.10;
Lk 3.22
1.33
Mt 3.11;
Acts 1.5
1.34
ver 49

29 The next day he saw Jesus coming toward him, and said, "Behold, the Lamb of God, who takes away the sin of the world! 30 This is he of whom I said, 'After me comes a man who ranks before me, for he was before me.' 31 I myself did not know him; but for this I came baptizing with water, that he might be revealed to Israel." 32And John bore witness, "I saw the Spirit descend as a dove from heaven, and it remained on him. 33 I myself did not know him; but he who sent me to baptize with water said to me, 'He on whom you see the Spirit descend and remain, this is he who baptizes with the Holy Spirit.' 34And I have seen and have borne witness that this is the Son of God."

Andrew and Peter follow Jesus (1.35–42)

1.35
ver 29
1.36
ver 29
1.38
ver 49

35 The next day again John was standing with two of his disciples; 36 and he looked at Jesus as he walked, and said, "Behold, the Lamb of God!" 37 The two disciples heard him say this, and they followed Jesus. 38 Jesus turned, and saw them following, and said to them, "What do you seek?" And they said to him, "Rābbi" (which means Teacher), "where are you staying?" 39 He said to them, "Come and see." They came and saw where he was staying; and they stayed with him that day, for it was about the tenth hour.

1.40
Mt 4.18–22;
Mk 1.16–
20;
Lk 5.2–11
1.41
Dan 9.25;
Jn 4.25
1.42
Jn 21.15–
17; 1 Cor
15.5;
Mt 16.18

40 One of the two who heard John speak, and followed him, was Andrew, Simon Peter's brother. 41 He first found his brother Simon, and said to him, "We have found the Mèssī'äh" (which means Christ). 42 He brought him to Jesus. Jesus looked at him, and said, "So you are Simon the son of John? You shall be called Çêphås" (which means Peter^c).

Philip and Nathanael follow Jesus (1.43–51)

1.43
Mt 10.3;
Jn 6.5,7;
12.21,22;
14.8,9
1.44
Jn 12.21
1.45
Jn 21.2;
Lk 24.27;
Mt 2.23;
Lk 2.4
1.46
Jn 7.41,42
1.47
Ps 32.2;
73.1;
Rom 9.4,6
1.49
ver 38,34;
Mt 2.2;
Mk 15.32;
Jn 12.13
1.51
Gen 28.12;
Mt 3.16;
Lk 3.21;
Mt 8.20

43 The next day Jesus decided to go to Găl'įleē. And he found Philip and said to him, "Follow me." 44 Now Philip was from Bĕth-sā'idå, the city of Andrew and Peter. 45 Philip found Nåthän'ä-ėl, and said to him, "We have found him of whom Moses in the law and also the prophets wrote, Jesus of Năz'årėth, the son of Joseph." 46 Nåthän'ä-ėl said to him, "Can anything good come out of Năzárėth?" Philip said to him, "Come and see." 47 Jesus saw Nåthän'ä-ėl coming to him, and said of him, "Behold, an Israelite indeed, in whom is no guile!" 48 Nåthän'ä-ėl said to him, "How do you know me?" Jesus answered him, "Before Philip called you, when you were under the fig tree, I saw you." 49 Nåthän'ä-ėl answered him, "Rabbi, you are the Son of God! You are the King of Israel!" 50 Jesus answered him, "Because I said to you, I saw you under the fig tree, do you believe? You shall see greater things than these." 51And he said to him, "Truly, truly, I say to you, you will see heaven opened, and the angels of God ascending and descending upon the Son of man."

The first miracle: water made into wine (2.1–12)

2.1
Jn 4.46;
21.2

2 On the third day there was a marriage at Cānå in Găl'įleē, and the mother of Jesus was there; 2 Jesus also was invited to the

_c From the word for *rock* in Åråmā'īc and Greek, respectively

marriage, with his disciples. 3 When the wine gave out, the mother of Jesus said to him, "They have no wine." 4And Jesus said to her, "O woman, what have you to do with me? My hour has not yet come." 5 His mother said to the servants, "Do whatever he tells you." 6 Now six stone jars were standing there, for the Jewish rites of purification, each holding twenty or thirty gallons. 7 Jesus said to them, "Fill the jars with water." And they filled them up to the brim. 8 He said to them, "Now draw some out, and take it to the steward of the feast." So they took it. 9 When the steward of the feast tasted the water now become wine, and did not know where it came from (though the servants who had drawn the water knew), the steward of the feast called the bridegroom 10 and said to him, "Every man serves the good wine first; and when men have drunk freely, then the poor wine; but you have kept the good wine until now." 11 This, the first of his signs, Jesus did at Cāná in Găl'ilee, and manifested his glory; and his disciples believed in him.

12 After this he went down to Cáper'nä-üm, with his mother and his brothers and his disciples; and there they stayed for a few days.

Cleansing of the Temple
(2.13–25; cf. Mt 21.12–17; Mk 11.15–19; Lk 19.45–48)

13 The Passover of the Jews was at hand, and Jesus went up to Jerusalem. 14 In the temple he found those who were selling oxen and sheep and pigeons, and the money-changers at their business. 15And making a whip of cords, he drove them all, with the sheep and oxen, out of the temple; and he poured out the coins of the money-changers and overturned their tables. 16And he told those who sold the pigeons, "Take these things away; you shall not make my Father's house a house of trade." 17 His disciples remembered that it was written, "Zeal for thy house will consume me." 18 The Jews then said to him, "What sign have you to show us for doing this?" 19 Jesus answered them, "Destroy this temple, and in three days I will raise it up." 20 The Jews then said, "It has taken forty-six years to build this temple, and will you raise it up in three days?" 21 But he spoke of the temple of his body. 22 When therefore he was raised from the dead, his disciples remembered that he had said this; and they believed the scripture and the word which Jesus had spoken.

23 Now when he was in Jerusalem at the Passover feast, many believed in his name when they saw the signs which he did; 24 but Jesus did not trust himself to them, 25 because he knew all men and needed no one to bear witness of man; for he himself knew what was in man.

2.4
Jn 19.26; 7.6,30; 8.20

2.6
Mk 7.3,4; Jn 3.25

2.9
Jn 4.46

*2.11
Jn 1.14

2.12
Mt 4.13; 12.46

2.13
Jn 6.4; 11.55; Deut 16.1-6; Lk 2.41

*2.15

2.16
Lk 2.49

2.17
Ps 69.9

2.18
Mt 12.38

2.19
Mt 26.61; 27.40; Mk 14.58

2.21
1 Cor 6.19

2.22
Lk 24.8; Jn 12.16; 14.26

2.23
ver 13

2.25
Jn 6.61,64; 13.11

2.11 Sign (Greek semeion) is the characteristic word in the Gospel of John used to describe the miracles of Jesus (cf. 2.23; 4.54; 6.2, 14; 7.31; 9.16; 11.47; 12.18). The word stresses the spiritual significance of Christ's miracles, which were intended not simply to alleviate physical suffering and need, but to bring men to the saving knowledge of God. Christ performed his signs before His own people, the Jews, but they did not believe (12.37–40); His disciples, however, believed, and the Gospel of John records Christ's signs in order that the readers themselves might believe that Jesus is the Christ, the Son of God (20.30, 31).

2.15 Jerusalem was crowded with pilgrims at Passover. They traveled far and brought varieties of currency, but no animals for sacrifice. Hence the Temple site became the haunt of money-changers and animal dealers.

Jesus' discourse with Nicodemus: the new birth (3.1–21)

3.1
Jn 7.50;
19.39;
Lk 23.13;
Jn 7.26
3.2
Jn 9.16,33;
Acts 2.22;
10.38
★3.3
Tit 3.5;
Jas 1.18;
1 Pet 1.23;
1 Jn 3.9
3.5
Eph 5.26;
Tit 3.5
3.6
Jn 1.13;
1 Cor 15.50
3.8
1 Cor 2.11
3.9
Jn 6.52,60
3.10
Lk 2.46
3.11
Jn 7.16,17
3.13
Prov 30.4;
Acts 2.34;
Rom 10.6;
Eph 4.9
3.14
Num 21.9;
Jn 8.28;
12.34
3.15
ver 36;
Jn 20.21;
1 Jn 5.11–13
3.16
Rom 5.8;
1 Jn 4.9
3.17
Jn 5.36,38;
8.15;
12.47;
1 Jn 4.14
3.18
Jn 5.24;
1 Jn 4.9
3.19
Jn 1.4;
8.12
3.20
Eph 5.11,13
3.21
1 Jn 1.6
3.22
Jn 4.2

3 Now there was a man of the Phạr'ịseēṣ, named Nĭcŏdē'mŭs, a ruler of the Jews. 2 This man came to Jesus*d* by night and said to him, "Rabbi, we know that you are a teacher come from God; for no one can do these signs that you do, unless God is with him." 3 Jesus answered him, "Truly, truly, I say to you, unless one is born anew,*e* he cannot see the kingdom of God." 4 Nĭcŏdē'mŭs said to him, "How can a man be born when he is old? Can he enter a second time into his mother's womb and be born?" 5 Jesus answered, "Truly, truly, I say to you, unless one is born of water and the Spirit, he cannot enter the kingdom of God. 6 That which is born of the flesh is flesh, and that which is born of the Spirit is spirit.*f* 7 Do not marvel that I said to you, 'You must be born anew.'*e* 8 The wind*f* blows where it wills, and you hear the sound of it, but you do not know whence it comes or whither it goes; so it is with every one who is born of the Spirit." 9 Nĭcŏdē'mŭs said to him, "How can this be?" 10 Jesus answered him, "Are you a teacher of Israel, and yet you do not understand this? 11 Truly, truly, I say to you, we speak of what we know, and bear witness to what we have seen; but you do not receive our testimony. 12 If I have told you earthly things and you do not believe, how can you believe if I tell you heavenly things? 13 No one has ascended into heaven but he who descended from heaven, the Son of man.*g* 14And as Moses lifted up the serpent in the wilderness, so must the Son of man be lifted up, 15 that whoever believes in him may have eternal life."*h*

16 For God so loved the world that he gave his only Son, that whoever believes in him should not perish but have eternal life. 17 For God sent the Son into the world, not to condemn the world, but that the world might be saved through him. 18 He who believes in him is not condemned; he who does not believe is condemned already, because he has not believed in the name of the only Son of God. 19And this is the judgment, that the light has come into the world, and men loved darkness rather than light, because their deeds were evil. 20 For every one who does evil hates the light, and does not come to the light, lest his deeds should be exposed. 21 But he who does what is true comes to the light, that it may be clearly seen that his deeds have been wrought in God.

Jesus baptizes in Judea (3.22–24)

22 After this Jesus and his disciples went into the land of Judē'ä;

d Greek *him*   *e* Or *from above*   *f* The same Greek word means both *wind* and *spirit*
g Other ancient authorities add *who is in heaven*
h Some interpreters hold that the quotation continues through verse 21

3.3 All men are sinners by birth and by choice (Rom 3.23; Jn 8.44). Being "born from above" is a supernatural act involving the impartation of divine life. The basis of the new birth is the sacrificial death of Christ (1 Pet 1.17–23; 1 Cor 15.2, 3; Tit 3.5). The indispensable condition of the new birth is personal faith in Jesus Christ (1.12, 13). Regeneration itself occurs when the Holy Spirit, through the Word of God, convicts, converts, and regenerates the sinner. It is called *the washing of regeneration* in Tit 3.5 (see also 3.5; Jas 1.18; Eph 5.26). At least four benefits accrue to the believer from regeneration: (1) he becomes a child of God (1.12; Gal 3.26; Rom 8.16, 17); (2) he becomes a new creation (2 Cor 5.17; Gal 6.15; Eph 2.10); (3) he partakes *of the divine nature* (2 Pet 1.4); (4) in his own experience he shares in Christ's victory over sin and the world according to the measure of his faith (1 Jn 3.9; 5.4, 18).

there he remained with them and baptized. 23 John also was baptizing at Aē'nŏn near Sālĭm, because there was much water there; and people came and were baptized. 24 For John had not yet been put in prison.

3.24
Mt 4.12;
14.3

John's testimony to Jesus (3.25–36)

25 Now a discussion arose between John's disciples and a Jew over purifying. 26And they came to John, and said to him, "Rabbi, he who was with you beyond the Jordan, to whom you bore witness, here he is, baptizing, and all are going to him." 27 John answered, "No one can receive anything except what is given him from heaven. 28 You yourselves bear me witness, that I said, I am not the Christ, but I have been sent before him. 29 He who has the bride is the bridegroom; the friend of the bridegroom, who stands and hears him, rejoices greatly at the bridegroom's voice; therefore this joy of mine is now full. 30 He must increase, but I must decrease."i

31 He who comes from above is above all; he who is of the earth belongs to the earth, and of the earth he speaks; he who comes from heaven is above all. 32 He bears witness to what he has seen and heard, yet no one receives his testimony; 33 he who receives his testimony sets his seal to this, that God is true. 34 For he whom God has sent utters the words of God, for it is not by measure that he gives the Spirit; 35 the Father loves the Son, and has given all things into his hand. 36 He who believes in the Son has eternal life; he who does not obey the Son shall not see life, but the wrath of God rests upon him.

3.25
Jn 2.6
3.26
Jn 1.7,28
3.27
1 Cor 4.7;
Heb 5.4
3.28
Jn 1.20,23
3.29
Mk 2.19,20;
Mt 25.1;
Jn 15.11;
16.24
3.31
Jn 8.23;
1 Jn 4.5
3.32
ver 11;
Jn 8.26;
15.15
3.33
Rom 4.11;
15.28;
Eph 1.13;
4.30
3.34
Mt 12.18;
Lk 4.18
3.35
Mt 28.18;
Jn 5.20,22;
17.2
3.36
Jn 5.24;
6.47

Jesus in Samaria (4.1–6)

4 Now when the Lord knew that the Phạr'ĭseēș had heard that Jesus was making and baptizing more disciples than John 2 (although Jesus himself did not baptize, but only his disciples), 3 he left Judē'ȧ and departed again to Găl'ĭleē. 4 He had to pass through Sȧmạr'ĭȧ. 5 So he came to a city of Sȧmạr'ĭȧ, called Sȳchar, near the field that Jacob gave to his son Joseph. 6 Jacob's well was there, and so Jesus, wearied as he was with his journey, sat down beside the well. It was about the sixth hour.

4.1
Jn 3.22,26
4.3
Jn 3.22
*4.4
Lk 9.52
*4.5
Gen 33.19;
48.22;
Josh 24.32

i Some interpreters hold that the quotation continues through verse 36

4.4 The Samaritan village of Sychar (modern *Askar*) is on the east slope of Mt. Ebal, not too far removed from Mt. Gerizim. Some of the Syriac texts of the New Testament raise the question whether *Sychar* should not be *Shechem*. Recent excavations at Balatah, between Ebal and Gerizim, have shown it to be ancient Shechem which is nearer to Jacob's well than the site of Askar. The Samaritans had their temple on Mt. Gerizim (although it was destroyed by John Hyrcanus in 128 B.C. and never rebuilt). The Passover was held annually on Mt. Gerizim, not far from the ruins of the temple, but the regular place of worship was probably at the base of Gerizim, not far from Shechem.
4.5 The Samaritans in Jesus' day formed a substantial element in the population. The

Jews hated them and had nothing to do with them. The Samaritans were a mixed people of Assyrian and Jewish blood. When the Northern Kingdom of Samaria had been conquered by the Assyrians and the Jews carried away, their territory was repopulated by Gentiles from the Assyrian Empire. Over the centuries the Assyrians intermarried with Jews to form the hybrid group known as the Samaritans. The Jews did not accept them as their neighbors and it was with this in view that Jesus spoke to the Jews the parable of the Good Samaritan. See also note to Lk 10.30 on the parable of the Good Samaritan.
The fact that Jesus ministered to Samaritans made Him suspect to the Scribes and Pharisees. But Jesus came not to respect position; He came to call all sinners to repentance.

Jesus' discourse with the woman of Samaria (4.7–38)

7 There came a woman of Sȧmar̄'iȧ to draw water. Jesus said to her, "Give me a drink." 8 For his disciples had gone away into the city to buy food. 9 The Sȧmar̄'itȧn woman said to him, "How is it that you, a Jew, ask a drink of me, a woman of Sȧmar̄'iȧ?" For Jews have no dealings with Sȧmar̄'itȧns. 10 Jesus answered her, "If you knew the gift of God, and who it is that is saying to you, 'Give me a drink,' you would have asked him, and he would have given you living water." 11 The woman said to him, "Sir, you have nothing to draw with, and the well is deep; where do you get that living water? 12 Are you greater than our father Jacob, who gave us the well, and drank from it himself, and his sons, and his cattle?" 13 Jesus said to her, "Every one who drinks of this water will thirst again, 14 but whoever drinks of the water that I shall give him will never thirst; the water that I shall give him will become in him a spring of water welling up to eternal life." 15 The woman said to him, "Sir, give me this water, that I may not thirst, nor come here to draw."

16 Jesus said to her, "Go, call your husband, and come here." 17 The woman answered him, "I have no husband." Jesus said to her, "You are right in saying, 'I have no husband'; 18 for you have had five husbands, and he whom you now have is not your husband; this you said truly." 19 The woman said to him, "Sir, I perceive that you are a prophet. 20 Our fathers worshiped on this mountain; and you say that in Jerusalem is the place where men ought to worship." 21 Jesus said to her, "Woman, believe me, the hour is coming when neither on this mountain nor in Jerusalem will you worship the Father. 22 You worship what you do not know; we worship what we know, for salvation is from the Jews. 23 But the hour is coming, and now is, when the true worshipers will worship the Father in spirit and truth, for such the Father seeks to worship him. 24 God is spirit, and those who worship him must worship in spirit and truth." 25 The woman said to him, "I know that Mȇssī'ȧh is coming (he who is called Christ); when he comes, he will show us all things." 26 Jesus said to her, "I who speak to you am he."

27 Just then his disciples came. They marveled that he was talking with a woman, but none said, "What do you wish?" or, "Why are you talking with her?" 28 So the woman left her water jar, and went away into the city, and said to the people, 29 "Come, see a man who told me all that I ever did. Can this be the Christ?" 30 They went out of the city and were coming to him.

31 Meanwhile the disciples besought him, saying, "Rabbi, eat." 32 But he said to them, "I have food to eat of which you do not know." 33 So the disciples said to one another, "Has any one brought him food?" 34 Jesus said to them, "My food is to do the will of him who sent me, and to accomplish his work. 35 Do you not say, 'There are yet four months, then comes the harvest'? I tell you, lift up your eyes, and see how the fields are already white for harvest. 36 He who reaps receives wages, and gathers fruit for eternal life, so that sower and reaper may rejoice together. 37 For here the saying holds true, 'One sows and another reaps.' 38 I sent you to reap that for which you did not labor; others have labored, and you have entered into their labor."

The conversion of Samaritans (4.39–42)

39 Many Samar'itans from that city believed in him because of
the woman's testimony, "He told me all that I ever did." 40 So
when the Samar'itans came to him, they asked him to stay with
them; and he stayed there two days. 41And many more believed
because of his word. 42 They said to the woman, "It is no longer
because of your words that we believe, for we have heard for ourselves, and we know that this is indeed the Savior of the world."

Jesus returns to Galilee
(4.43–45; Mt 4.12–17; Mk 1.14,15; Lk 4.14,15)

43 After the two days he departed to Găl'ĭleē. 44 For Jesus himself testified that a prophet has no honor in his own country.
45 So when he came to Găl'ĭleē, the Găl'ĭlē'ăns welcomed him,
having seen all that he had done in Jerusalem at the feast, for they
too had gone to the feast.

The healing of the official's son (4.46–54)

46 So he came again to Cānă in Găl'ĭleē, where he had made the
water wine. And at Căpėr'nä-ŭm there was an official whose son
was ill. 47 When he heard that Jesus had come from Judē'ă to
Găl'ĭleē, he went and begged him to come down and heal his son,
for he was at the point of death. 48 Jesus therefore said to him,
"Unless you see signs and wonders you will not believe." 49 The
official said to him, "Sir, come down before my child dies."
50 Jesus said to him, "Go; your son will live." The man believed
the word that Jesus spoke to him and went his way. 51As he was
going down, his servants met him and told him that his son was
living. 52 So he asked them the hour when he began to mend, and
they said to him, "Yesterday at the seventh hour the fever left
him." 53 The father knew that was the hour when Jesus had said
to him, "Your son will live"; and he himself believed, and all his
household. 54 This was now the second sign that Jesus did when
he had come from Judē'ă to Găl'ĭleē.

Jesus heals at Bethesda on the Sabbath (5.1–16)

5 After this there was a feast of the Jews, and Jesus went up
to Jerusalem.
2 Now there is in Jerusalem by the Sheep Gate a pool, in
Hebrew called Bĕth-zā'thă,ʲ which has five porticoes. 3 In these
lay a multitude of invalids, blind, lame, paralyzed.ᵏ 5 One man
was there, who had been ill for thirty-eight years. 6 When Jesus
saw him and knew that he had been lying there a long time, he said
to him, "Do you want to be healed?" 7 The sick man answered
him, "Sir, I have no man to put me into the pool when the water
is troubled, and while I am going another steps down before me."
8 Jesus said to him, "Rise, take up your pallet, and walk." 9And

ʲ Other ancient authorities read Bĕthĕṣ'dă, others Bĕth-sā'ĭdă
ᵏ Other ancient authorities insert, wholly or in part, waiting for the moving of the water; ⁴for
an angel of the Lord went down at certain seasons into the pool, and troubled the water:
whoever stepped in first after the troubling of the water was healed of whatever disease
he had

Margin references:

4.39
ver 29

4.42
1 Jn 4.14;
1 Tim 4.10;
2 Tim 1.10

4.43
ver 40
4.44
Mt 13.57;
Mk 6.4;
Lk 4.24
4.45
Jn 2.23

4.46
Jn 2.1–11

4.47
ver 3,54

4.48
Dan 4.2;
Mk 13.22;
Acts 2.19,
22,43; 4.30;
Rom 15.19;
Heb 2.4

4.53
Acts 11.14

4.54
Jn 2.11

5.2
Neh 3.1;
12.39

5.8
Mt 9.6;
Mk 2.11;
Lk 5.24
5.9
Jn 9.14

at once the man was healed, and he took up his pallet and walked.
Now that day was the sabbath. 10 So the Jews said to the man
who was cured, "It is the sabbath, it is not lawful for you to carry
your pallet." 11 But he answered them, "The man who healed me
said to me, 'Take up your pallet, and walk.'" 12 They asked him,
"Who is the man who said to you, 'Take up your pallet, and
walk'?" 13 Now the man who had been healed did not know who
it was, for Jesus had withdrawn, as there was a crowd in the place.
14 Afterward, Jesus found him in the temple, and said to him, "See,
you are well! Sin no more, that nothing worse befall you." 15 The
man went away and told the Jews that it was Jesus who had healed
him. 16 And this was why the Jews persecuted Jesus, because he

Jesus claims to be God (5.17–24)

did this on the sabbath. 17 But Jesus answered them, "My Father
is working still, and I am working." 18 This was why the Jews
sought all the more to kill him, because he not only broke the sabbath but also called God his own Father, making himself equal
with God.
19 Jesus said to them, "Truly, truly, I say to you, the Son can
do nothing of his own accord, but only what he sees the Father
doing; for whatever he does, that the Son does likewise. 20 For the
Father loves the Son, and shows him all that he himself is doing;
and greater works than these will he show him, that you may
marvel. 21 For as the Father raises the dead and gives them life,
so also the Son gives life to whom he will. 22 The Father judges no
one, but has given all judgment to the Son, 23 that all may honor
the Son, even as they honor the Father. He who does not honor
the Son does not honor the Father who sent him. 24 Truly, truly, I
say to you, he who hears my word and believes him who sent
me, has eternal life; he does not come into judgment, but has
passed from death to life.

The two resurrections (5.25–29)

25 "Truly, truly, I say to you, the hour is coming, and now is,
when the dead will hear the voice of the Son of God, and those
who hear will live. 26 For as the Father has life in himself, so he
has granted the Son also to have life in himself, 27 and has given
him authority to execute judgment, because he is the Son of man.
28 Do not marvel at this; for the hour is coming when all who are
in the tombs will hear his voice 29 and come forth, those who have
done good, to the resurrection of life, and those who have done
evil, to the resurrection of judgment.

The Father's witness to the Son (5.30–47)

30 "I can do nothing on my own authority; as I hear, I judge;
and my judgment is just, because I seek not my own will but the

5.10
ver 15,16;
Neh 13.19;
Jer 17.21;
Mt 12.2;
Mk 2.24;
Jn 7.23;
9.16

5.14
Mk 2.5;
Jn 8.11

5.17
Jn 9.4;
14.10
*5.18
Jn 7.1,19;
10.30,33

5.19
Jn 8.28;
12.49;
14.10
5.20
Jn 3.35;
14.12
5.21
Rom 4.17;
8.11;
Jn 11.25
5.22
Jn 9.39;
Acts 17.31
5.23
Lk 10.16;
1 Jn 2.23
5.24
Jn 3.18;
12.44;
20.31;
1 Jn 5.13;
3.14

5.25
Jn 4.21;
6.60; 8.43,
47
5.26
Jn 6.57
5.27
Acts 10.42;
17.31
5.29
Dan 12.2;
Acts 24.15;
Mt 25.46

5.30
Jn 8.16;
4.34; 6.38

5.18 Scripture asserts that on a number
of occasions Jesus claimed to be divine. In
this instance the Jews were perfectly aware
that by the nature of Jesus' claim He made
Himself *equal with God.* Either this was
blasphemy or His claim was true. In the
former case He deserved to die; in the latter
case He was worthy of worship. One's attitude toward the deity of Christ is ever a
dividing line between faith and unbelief.

will of him who sent me. 31 If I bear witness to myself, my testimony is not true; 32 there is another who bears witness to me, and I know that the testimony which he bears to me is true. 33 You sent to John, and he has borne witness to the truth. 34 Not that the testimony which I receive is from man; but I say this that you may be saved. 35 He was a burning and shining lamp, and you were willing to rejoice for a while in his light. 36 But the testimony which I have is greater than that of John; for the works which the Father has granted me to accomplish, these very works which I am doing, bear me witness that the Father has sent me. 37And the Father who sent me has himself borne witness to me. His voice you have never heard, his form you have never seen; 38 and you do not have his word abiding in you, for you do not believe him whom he has sent. 39 You search the scriptures, because you think that in them you have eternal life; and it is they that bear witness to me; 40 yet you refuse to come to me that you may have life. 41 I do not receive glory from men. 42 But I know that you have not the love of God within you. 43 I have come in my Father's name, and you do not receive me; if another comes in his own name, him you will receive. 44 How can you believe, who receive glory from one another and do not seek the glory that comes from the only God? 45 Do not think that I shall accuse you to the Father; it is Moses who accuses you, on whom you set your hope. 46 If you believed Moses, you would believe me, for he wrote of me. 47 But if you do not believe his writings, how will you believe my words?"

The five thousand fed (6.1–14; Mt 14.13–21; Mk 6.30–44; Lk 9.10–17; cf. Mt 15.32–38)

6 After this Jesus went to the other side of the Sea of Găl′ileē, which is the Sea of Tībĕr′ĭ-aŝ. 2And a multitude followed him, because they saw the signs which he did on those who were diseased. 3 Jesus went up on the mountain, and there sat down with his disciples. 4 Now the Passover, the feast of the Jews, was at hand. 5 Lifting up his eyes, then, and seeing that a multitude was coming to him, Jesus said to Philip, "How are we to buy bread, so that these people may eat?" 6 This he said to test him, for he himself knew what he would do. 7 Philip answered him, "Two hundred denarii[l] would not buy enough bread for each of them to get a little." 8 One of his disciples, Andrew, Simon Peter's brother, said to him, 9 "There is a lad here who has five barley loaves and two fish; but what are they among so many?" 10 Jesus said, "Make the people sit down." Now there was much grass in the place; so the men sat down, in number about five thousand. 11 Jesus then took the loaves, and when he had given thanks, he distributed them to those who were seated; so also the fish, as much as they

l The denarius was a day's wage for a laborer

*5.31
Jn 8.14
5.32
Jn 8.18
5.33
Jn 1.7,15,
19,27,32
5.34
1 Jn 5.9
5.35
2 Pet 1.19;
Mt 21.26
5.36
1 Jn 5.9;
Jn 10.25;
14.11;
15.24
5.37
Jn 8.18;
Deut 4.12;
1 Tim 1.17
5.38
Jn 3.17
5.39
Lk 24.25,
27;
Acts 13.27
5.41
ver 44
5.43
Mt 24.5
5.44
Rom 2.29
5.45
Jn 9.28;
Rom 2.17
5.46
Gen 3.15;
Lk 24.27;
Acts 26.22
5.47
Lk 16.29,31
6.2
Jn 2.11
6.3
ver 15
6.4
Jn 2.13
6.5
Jn 1.43
6.6
2 Cor 13.5
6.8
Jn 1.40
6.9
2 Ki 4.43
6.11
ver 23;
Mt 15.36

5.31 In 8.14 Christ affirmed that His witness was in and of itself true and trustworthy and needed no corroborative testimony. In this encounter, however, the context makes it plain that Christ, for purposes of persuasion, yielded to the demands of the rabbis for a verification of His claims. This verse may well be parphrased: "If I bear witness of myself alone, without other witnesses, my testimony is not true," i.e., not measuring up to the requirements of legal evidence. But Christ offered decisive witnesses: (1) the Father Himself (5.32, 37); (2) John the Baptist (5.33); (3) His own miraculous works (5.36); (4) the Word of God (5.39); (5) the prophecy of Moses (5.46; cf. Deut 18.19).

wanted. 12And when they had eaten their fill, he told his disciples, "Gather up the fragments left over, that nothing may be lost." 13 So they gathered them up and filled twelve baskets with fragments from the five barley loaves, left by those who had eaten. 14 When the people saw the sign which he had done, they said, "This is indeed the prophet who is to come into the world!"

Jesus walks on the sea
(6.15–21; Mt 14.22–32; Mk 6.45–52)

15 Perceiving then that they were about to come and take him by force to make him king, Jesus withdrew again to the mountain by himself.
16 When evening came, his disciples went down to the sea, 17 got into a boat, and started across the sea to Cáper'nä-úm. It was now dark, and Jesus had not yet come to them. 18 The sea rose because a strong wind was blowing. 19 When they had rowed about three or four miles,*m* they saw Jesus walking on the sea and drawing near to the boat. They were frightened, 20 but he said to them, "It is I; do not be afraid." 21 Then they were glad to take him into the boat, and immediately the boat was at the land to which they were going.

Jesus' discourse on the bread of life (6.22–40)

22 On the next day the people who remained on the other side of the sea saw that there had been only one boat there, and that Jesus had not entered the boat with his disciples, but that his disciples had gone away alone. 23 However, boats from Tiber'i-ás came near the place where they ate the bread after the LORD had given thanks. 24 So when the people saw that Jesus was not there, nor his disciples, they themselves got into the boats and went to Cáper'nä-úm, seeking Jesus.
25 When they found him on the other side of the sea, they said to him, "Rabbi, when did you come here?" 26 Jesus answered them, "Truly, truly, I say to you, you seek me, not because you saw signs, but because you ate your fill of the loaves. 27 Do not labor for the food which perishes, but for the food which endures to eternal life, which the Son of man will give to you; for on him has God the Father set his seal." 28 Then they said to him, "What must we do, to be doing the works of God?" 29 Jesus answered them, "This is the work of God, that you believe in him whom he has sent." 30 So they said to him, "Then what sign do you do, that we may see, and believe you? What work do you perform? 31 Our fathers ate the manna in the wilderness; as it is written, 'He gave them bread from heaven to eat.'" 32 Jesus then said to them, "Truly, truly, I say to you, it was not Moses who gave you the bread from heaven; my Father gives you the true bread from heaven. 33 For the bread of God is that which comes down from

m Greek twenty-five or thirty stadia

Margin references: 6.14 Gen 49.10; Deut 18.15, 18; Mt 11.3; 21.11 — *6.15 Jn 18.36 — 6.22 ver 2,16ff — 6.23 ver 1,11 — 6.24 Mt 14.34; Mk 6.53 — 6.26 ver 24,30 — 6.27 Isa 55.2; ver 54; Jn 4.14; 3.35 — 6.29 1 Jn 3.23; Jn 3.17 — 6.30 Mt 12.38; Mk 8.11 — 6.31 Ex 16.15; Num 11.8; Neh 9.15; Ps 78.24 — 6.33 ver 50

6.15 The multitude, astonished by the miracle of Christ's feeding them, was swept by a wave of enthusiasm and would have forced Jesus to lead them in their revolt against the Roman power. This information explains why Jesus had to compel his disciples to embark and leave the place, so that He might dismiss the crowds (Mt 14.22; Mk 6.45). Obviously the disciples had been affected by the crowd's delirium and readily went along with them in their attempt to make Jesus their revolutionary leader.

heaven, and gives life to the world." 34 They said to him, "Lord, give us this bread always."

35 Jesus said to them, "I am the bread of life; he who comes to me shall not hunger, and he who believes in me shall never thirst. 36 But I said to you that you have seen me and yet do not believe. 37All that the Father gives me will come to me; and him who comes to me I will not cast out. 38 For I have come down from heaven, not to do my own will, but the will of him who sent me; 39 and this is the will of him who sent me, that I should lose nothing of all that he has given me, but raise it up at the last day. 40 For this is the will of my Father, that every one who sees the Son and believes in him should have eternal life; and I will raise him up at the last day."

The Jews dispute Jesus' claim (6.41–59)

41 The Jews then murmured at him, because he said, "I am the bread which came down from heaven." 42 They said, "Is not this Jesus, the son of Joseph, whose father and mother we know? How does he now say, 'I have come down from heaven'?" 43 Jesus answered them, "Do not murmur among yourselves. 44 No one can come to me unless the Father who sent me draws him; and I will raise him up at the last day. 45 It is written in the prophets, 'And they shall all be taught by God.' Every one who has heard and learned from the Father comes to me. 46 Not that any one has seen the Father except him who is from God; he has seen the Father. 47 Truly, truly, I say to you, he who believes has eternal life. 48 I am the bread of life. 49 Your fathers ate the manna in the wilderness, and they died. 50 This is the bread which comes down from heaven, that a man may eat of it and not die. 51 I am the living bread which came down from heaven; if any one eats of this bread, he will live for ever; and the bread which I shall give for the life of the world is my flesh."

52 The Jews then disputed among themselves, saying, "How can this man give us his flesh to eat?" 53 So Jesus said to them, "Truly, truly, I say to you, unless you eat the flesh of the Son of man and drink his blood, you have no life in you; 54 he who eats my flesh and drinks my blood has eternal life, and I will raise him up at the last day. 55 For my flesh is food indeed, and my blood is drink indeed. 56 He who eats my flesh and drinks my blood abides in me, and I in him. 57As the living Father sent me, and I live because of the Father, so he who eats me will live because of me. 58 This is the bread which came down from heaven, not such as the fathers ate and died; he who eats this bread will live for ever." 59 This he said in the synagogue, as he taught at Ca·per′nä-um.

The questioning disciples (6.60–65)

60 Many of his disciples, when they heard it, said, "This is a

---

6.34
Jn 4.15

★6.35
ver 48,51;
Jn 4.14

6.36
ver 26

6.37
ver 39;
Jn 17.2

6.38
Jn 4.34;
5.30

6.39
Jn 10.28;
17.12;
18.9

6.40
ver 27,47,
54;
Jn 3.15,16

6.42
Lk 4.22;
Jn 7.27,28;
ver 38,62

6.44
Jer 31.3;
Hos 11.4;
Jn 12.32

6.45
Isa 54.13;
Jer 31.34;
Heb 8.10;
10.16

6.46
Jn 1.18;
5.37; 7.29;
8.19

6.47
Jn 3.16,18,
36; 5.24;
11.26

6.48
ver 35,51

6.49
ver 31

6.50
ver 33

6.51
Heb 10.10

6.52
Jn 9.16;
10.19

6.53
Mt 26.26,28

6.54
Jn 4.14

6.56
Jn 15.4;
1 Jn 3.24;
4.15,16

6.57
Jn 3.17

6.58
ver 49–51

6.60
ver 66

6.35 While bread is not exactly a type of Christ, yet it is used metaphorically to illustrate the truth that He is life to the believer. The words *I am the bread of life* are no more to be taken literally than such similar affirmations as *I am the door* and *I am the vine.* Christ only means that as bread and water are necessary to sustain physical life, so He is necessary to sustain the spiritual life of the believer. But the figure goes even beyond this, for He states that those who eat of His bread and drink of the water from His fountain shall never hunger or thirst again. He fully and forever satisfies the heart's needs.

6.61
Mt 11.6

6.62
Jn 3.13;
17.5
6.63
2 Cor 3.6
6.64
Jn 2.25
6.65
ver 37,44;
Jn 3.27

hard saying; who can listen to it?" 61 But Jesus, knowing in himself that his disciples murmured at it, said to them, "Do you take offense at this? 62 Then what if you were to see the Son of man ascending where he was before? 63 It is the spirit that gives life, the flesh is of no avail; the words that I have spoken to you are spirit and life. 64 But there are some of you that do not believe." For Jesus knew from the first who those were that did not believe, and who it was that would betray him. 65And he said, "This is why I told you that no one can come to me unless it is granted him by the Father."

Peter's great affirmation (6.66–71)

6.66
ver 60
6.67
Mt 10.2
6.68
Mt 16.16;
Acts 5.20
6.69
Mk 8.29;
Lk 9.20
6.70
Jn 15.16,
19; 13.27
6.71
Jn 13.26;
Mk 14.10

66 After this many of his disciples drew back and no longer went about with him. 67 Jesus said to the twelve, "Do you also wish to go away?" 68 Simon Peter answered him, "Lord, to whom shall we go? You have the words of eternal life; 69 and we have believed, and have come to know, that you are the Holy One of God." 70 Jesus answered them, "Did I not choose you, the twelve, and one of you is a devil?" 71 He spoke of Judas the son of Simon Iscar'iot, for he, one of the twelve, was to betray him.

Jesus and the Feast of Tabernacles (7.1–13)

7.1
Jn 5.18
*7.2
Lev 23.34;
Deut 16.16
7.3
Mt 12.46;
Mk 3.31
7.5
Mk 3.21
7.6
Mt 26.18;
ver 8,30
7.7
Jn 15.18,
19; 3.19,20
7.8
ver 6
7.11
Jn 11.56
7.12
ver 40–43
7.13
Jn 9.22;
12.42;
19.38

7 After this Jesus went about in Găl'ilee; he would not go about in Judē'ă, because the Jews[n] sought to kill him. 2 Now the Jews' feast of Tabernacles was at hand. 3 So his brothers said to him, "Leave here and go to Judē'ă, that your disciples may see the works you are doing. 4 For no man works in secret if he seeks to be known openly. If you do these things, show yourself to the world." 5 For even his brothers did not believe in him. 6 Jesus said to them, "My time has not yet come, but your time is always here. 7 The world cannot hate you, but it hates me because I testify of it that its works are evil. 8 Go to the feast yourselves; I am not[o] going up to this feast, for my time has not yet fully come." 9 So saying, he remained in Găl'ilee.

10 But after his brothers had gone up to the feast, then he also went up, not publicly but in private. 11 The Jews were looking for him at the feast, and saying, "Where is he?" 12And there was much muttering about him among the people. While some said, "He is a good man," others said, "No, he is leading the people astray." 13 Yet for fear of the Jews no one spoke openly of him.

Jesus teaches in the Temple (7.14–36)

7.14
ver 28
7.15
Mt 13.54;
Mk 6.2;
Lk 4.22
7.16
Jn 3.11;
8.28; 12.49

14 About the middle of the feast Jesus went up into the temple and taught. 15 The Jews marveled at it, saying, "How is it that this man has learning,[p] when he has never studied?" 16 So Jesus answered them, "My teaching is not mine, but his who sent me;

n Or Judē'ăns   o Other ancient authorities add yet   p Or this man knows his letters

---

7.2 The Feast of Tabernacles, starting on the fifteenth day of the seventh month, Tishri (September–October), and lasting eight days, commemorated the wilderness life of the Hebrews in their flight from Egypt. Every day in this period the priests brought water from the pool of Siloam and poured it out in libation upon the altar of the Temple (see the words of Jesus, ver 37–39). (See also note to Ex 23.16.)

17 if any man's will is to do his will, he shall know whether the teaching is from God or whether I am speaking on my own authority. 18 He who speaks on his own authority seeks his own glory; but he who seeks the glory of him who sent him is true, and in him there is no falsehood. 19 Did not Moses give you the law? Yet none of you keeps the law. Why do you seek to kill me?" 20 The people answered, "You have a demon! Who is seeking to kill you?" 21 Jesus answered them, "I did one deed, and you all marvel at it. 22 Moses gave you circumcision (not that it is from Moses, but from the fathers), and you circumcise a man upon the sabbath. 23 If on the sabbath a man receives circumcision, so that the law of Moses may not be broken, are you angry with me because on the sabbath I made a man's whole body well? 24 Do not judge by appearances, but judge with right judgment."

25 Some of the people of Jerusalem therefore said, "Is not this the man whom they seek to kill? 26And here he is, speaking openly, and they say nothing to him! Can it be that the authorities really know that this is the Christ? 27 Yet we know where this man comes from; and when the Christ appears, no one will know where he comes from." 28 So Jesus proclaimed, as he taught in the temple, "You know me, and you know where I come from? But I have not come of my own accord; he who sent me is true, and him you do not know. 29 I know him, for I come from him, and he sent me." 30 So they sought to arrest him; but no one laid hands on him, because his hour had not yet come. 31 Yet many of the people believed in him; they said, "When the Christ appears, will he do more signs than this man has done?"

32 The Phar′isees heard the crowd thus muttering about him, and the chief priests and Pharisees sent officers to arrest him. 33 Jesus then said, "I shall be with you a little longer, and then I go to him who sent me; 34 you will seek me and you will not find me; where I am you cannot come." 35 The Jews said to one another, "Where does this man intend to go that we shall not find him? Does he intend to go to the Dispersion among the Greeks and teach the Greeks? 36 What does he mean by saying, 'You will seek me and you will not find me,' and, 'Where I am you cannot come'?"

The last day of the feast (7.37–52)

37 On the last day of the feast, the great day, Jesus stood up and proclaimed, "If any one thirst, let him come to me and drink. 38 He who believes in me, as^q the scripture has said, 'Out of his heart shall flow rivers of living water.' " 39 Now this he said about the Spirit, which those who believed in him were to receive; for as yet the Spirit had not been given, because Jesus was not yet glorified.

^q Or let him come to me, and let him who believes in me drink. As

7.23 Every male infant was circumcised on the eighth day. If the child had been born on the Sabbath, then the circumcision was performed on the Sabbath, in disregard of the Sabbath laws against work. If the Jews were willing to violate the Sabbath in order to keep the law of circumcision, how could they quarrel with Jesus for having healed the sick man on the Sabbath (5.8–10)?

7.38 No precise source for this quotation is found in the Old Testament. Commentators see parallels in Isa 12.3; 44.3; 58.11; Zech 14.8. Many commentators favor the alternative punctuation found in the RSV footnote.

7.40
Mt 21.11;
Jn 1.21
7.41
Jn 1.46
7.42
Jer 23.5;
Mic 5.2;
Mt 2.5;
Lk 2.4
7.43
Jn 9.16;
10,19
7.44
ver 30
7.46
Mt 7.28,29
7.47
ver 12
7.48
Jn 12.42
7.51
Deut 17.6;
19.15

40 When they heard these words, some of the people said, "This is really the prophet." 41 Others said, "This is the Christ." But some said, "Is the Christ to come from Găl′ilee? 42 Has not the scripture said that the Christ is descended from David, and comes from Bĕth′lĕhĕm, the village where David was?" 43 So there was a division among the people over him. 44 Some of them wanted to arrest him, but no one laid hands on him.

45 The officers then went back to the chief priests and Phar′-isees, who said to them, "Why did you not bring him?" 46 The officers answered, "No man ever spoke like this man!" 47 The Phar′isees answered them, "Are you led astray, you also? 48 Have any of the authorities or of the Phar′isees believed in him? 49 But this crowd, who do not know the law, are accursed." 50 Nīcōdē′-mŭs, who had gone to him before, and who was one of them, said to them, 51 "Does our law judge a man without first giving him a hearing and learning what he does?" 52 They replied, "Are you from Găl′ilee too? Search and you will see that no prophet is to rise from Galilee."

The woman caught in adultery (8.2—11)

8.5
Lev 20.10;
Deut 22.22
8.7
Deut 17.7;
Rom 2.1
8.9
Rom 2.22
8.11
Jn 3.18;
5.14

8 53 They went each to his own house, 1 but Jesus went to the Mount of Olives. 2 Early in the morning he came again to the temple; all the people came to him, and he sat down and taught them. 3 The scribes and the Phar′isees brought a woman who had been caught in adultery, and placing her in the midst 4 they said to him, "Teacher, this woman has been caught in the act of adultery. 5 Now in the law Moses commanded us to stone such. What do you say about her?" 6 This they said to test him, that they might have some charge to bring against him. Jesus bent down and wrote with his finger on the ground. 7And as they continued to ask him, he stood up and said to them, "Let him who is without sin among you be the first to throw a stone at her." 8And once more he bent down and wrote with his finger on the ground. 9 But when they heard it, they went away, one by one, beginning with the eldest, and Jesus was left alone with the woman standing before him. 10 Jesus looked up and said to her, "Woman, where are they? Has no one condemned you?" 11 She said, "No one, Lord." And Jesus said, "Neither do I condemn you; go, and do not sin again."r

Jesus the light of the world: the claim and the testimony (8.12—20)

8.12
Jn 1.4; 9.5;
12.35
8.13
Jn 5.31
8.14
Jn 18.37;
13.3;
16.28;
7.28; 9.29
8.15
Jn 7.24;
3.17
8.16
Jn 5.30
8.17
Deut 17.6;
Mt 18.16

12 Again Jesus spoke to them, saying, "I am the light of the world; he who follows me will not walk in darkness, but will have the light of life." 13 The Phar′isees then said to him, "You are bearing witness to yourself; your testimony is not true." 14 Jesus answered, "Even if I do bear witness to myself, my testimony is true, for I know whence I have come and whither I am going, but you do not know whence I come or whither I am going. 15 You judge according to the flesh, I judge no one. 16 Yet even if I do judge, my judgment is true, for it is not I alone that judge, but I and hes who sent me. 17 In your law it is written that the testimony

r The most ancient authorities omit 7.53-8.11; other authorities add the passage here or after 7.36 or after 21.25 or after Luke 21.38, with variations of text
|s Other ancient authorities read the Father

of two men is true; 18 I bear witness to myself, and the Father who sent me bears witness to me." 19 They said to him therefore, "Where is your Father?" Jesus answered, "You know neither me nor my Father; if you knew me, you would know my Father also." 20 These words he spoke in the treasury, as he taught in the temple; but no one arrested him, because his hour had not yet come.

Jesus warns against unbelief (8.21–30)

21 Again he said to them, "I go away, and you will seek me and die in your sin; where I am going, you cannot come." 22 Then said the Jews, "Will he kill himself, since he says, 'Where I am going, you cannot come'?" 23 He said to them, "You are from below, I am from above; you are of this world, I am not of this world. 24 I told you that you would die in your sins, for you will die in your sins unless you believe that I am he." 25 They said to him, "Who are you?" Jesus said to them, "Even what I have told you from the beginning.[t] 26 I have much to say about you and much to judge; but he who sent me is true, and I declare to the world what I have heard from him." 27 They did not understand that he spoke to them of the Father. 28 So Jesus said, "When you have lifted up the Son of man, then you will know that I am he, and that I do nothing on my own authority but speak thus as the Father taught me. 29 And he who sent me is with me; he has not left me alone, for I always do what is pleasing to him." 30 As he spoke thus, many believed in him.

The true children of Abraham (8.31–59)

31 Jesus then said to the Jews who had believed in him, "If you continue in my word, you are truly my disciples, 32 and you will know the truth, and the truth will make you free." 33 They answered him, "We are descendants of Abraham, and have never been in bondage to any one. How is it that you say, 'You will be made free'?"

34 Jesus answered them, "Truly, truly, I say to you, every one who commits sin is a slave to sin. 35 The slave does not continue in the house for ever; the son continues for ever. 36 So if the Son makes you free, you will be free indeed. 37 I know that you are descendants of Abraham; yet you seek to kill me, because my word finds no place in you. 38 I speak of what I have seen with my Father, and you do what you have heard from your father."

39 They answered him, "Abraham is our father." Jesus said to them, "If you were Abraham's children, you would do what Abraham did, 40 but now you seek to kill me, a man who has told you the truth which I heard from God; this is not what Abraham did. 41 You do what your father did." They said to him, "We were not born of fornication; we have one Father, even God." 42 Jesus said to them, "If God were your Father, you would love me, for I proceeded and came forth from God; I came not of my own accord, but he sent me. 43 Why do you not understand what I say? It is because you cannot bear to hear my word. 44 You are of your father the devil, and your will is to do your father's desires. He was a murderer from the beginning, and has nothing to do with the truth, because there is no truth in him. When he lies, he speaks according to his own nature, for he is a liar and the father of lies.

t Or Why do I talk to you at all?

Cross references

8.18 Jn 5.37
8.19 Jn 14.7; 16.3
8.20 Mk 12.41; Jn 7.30
8.21 Jn 7.34
8.23 Jn 3.31; 17.14
8.24 Mk 13.6; Jn 4.26; 13.19
8.26 Jn 7.28; 3.32; 15.15
8.28 Jn 3.14; 12.32; 5.19; 3.11
8.29 Jn 4.34; 5.30; 6.38
8.30 Jn 7.31; 10.42; 11.45
8.31 Jn 15.7; 2 Jn 9
8.32 Rom 8.2; Jas 2.12
8.33 Mt 3.9
8.34 Rom 6.16; 2 Pet 2.19
8.35 Gal 4.30
8.37 ver 39,40
8.38 Jn 5.19,30; 14.10,24
8.39 Rom 9.7; Gal 3.7
8.40 ver 26
8.41 Isa 63.16; 64.8
8.42 1 Jn 5.1; Jn 16.27, 28; 17.8; 7.28
8.44 1 Jn 3.8; ver 38,41; 1 Jn 2.4; Mt 12.34

45 But, because I tell the truth, you do not believe me. 46 Which of you convicts me of sin? If I tell the truth, why do you not believe me? 47 He who is of God hears the words of God; the reason why you do not hear them is that you are not of God."

48 The Jews answered him, "Are we not right in saying that you are a Sàmạṛ'ịtàn and have a demon?" 49 Jesus answered, "I have not a demon; but I honor my Father, and you dishonor me. 50 Yet I do not seek my own glory; there is One who seeks it and he will be the judge. 51 Truly, truly, I say to you, if any one keeps my word, he will never see death." 52 The Jews said to him, "Now we know that you have a demon. Abraham died, as did the prophets; and you say, 'If any one keeps my word, he will never taste death.' 53Are you greater than our father Abraham, who died? And the prophets died! Who do you claim to be?" 54 Jesus answered, "If I glorify myself, my glory is nothing; it is my Father who glorifies me, of whom you say that he is your God. 55 But you have not known him; I know him. If I said, I do not know him, I should be a liar like you; but I do know him and I keep his word. 56 Your father Abraham rejoiced that he was to see my day; he saw it and was glad." 57 The Jews then said to him, "You are not yet fifty years old, and have you seen Abraham?"u 58 Jesus said to them, "Truly, truly, I say to you, before Abraham was, I am." 59 So they took up stones to throw at him; but Jesus hid himself, and went out of the temple.

Jesus heals the man born blind (9.1–12)

9 As he passed by, he saw a man blind from his birth. 2And his disciples asked him, "Rabbi, who sinned, this man or his parents, that he was born blind?" 3 Jesus answered, "It was not that this man sinned, or his parents, but that the works of God might be made manifest in him. 4 We must work the works of him who sent me, while it is day; night comes, when no one can work. 5As long as I am in the world, I am the light of the world." 6As he said this, he spat on the ground and made clay of the spittle and anointed the man's eyes with the clay, 7 saying to him, "Go, wash in the pool of Sĭlō'ăm" (which means Sent). So he went and washed and came back seeing. 8 The neighbors and those who had seen him before as a beggar, said, "Is not this the man who used to sit and beg?" 9 Some said, "It is he"; others said, "No, but he is like him." He said, "I am the man." 10 They said to him, "Then how were your eyes opened?" 11 He answered, "The man called Jesus made clay and anointed my eyes and said to me, 'Go to Sĭlō'ăm and wash'; so I went and washed and received my sight." 12 They said to him, "Where is he?" He said, "I do not know."

u Other ancient authorities read has Abraham seen you?

Marginal references (left column):

8.47
1 Jn 4.6
8.48
ver 52;
Jn 7.20;
10.20
8.50
Jn 5.41
8.51
Jn 14.23;
15.20;
17.6;
Mt 16.28;
Heb 11.5
8.52
Jn 7.20;
14.23;
15.20;
17.6
8.53
Jn 4.12
8.54
ver 50;
Jn 16.14
8.55
Jn 7.28,29;
15.10
8.56
Mt 13.17;
Heb 11.13
*8.58
Jn 1.1;
17.5,24;
Rev 1.8
8.59
Jn 10.31;
11.8; 12.36
*9.2
ver 34;
Lk 13.2;
Ex 20.5;
Ezek 18.20
9.3
Jn 11.4
9.4
Jn 11.9;
12.35
9.5
Jn 1.4;
8.12; 12.46
9.6
Mk 7.33;
8.23
9.7
ver 11;
Lk 13.4;
Jn 11.37
9.11
ver 7

8.58 The claim of Jesus that *before Abraham was, I am* is one of the evidences of His pre-existence. The instant negative reaction of the Jews to His statement makes it apparent that to accept it was to acknowledge the uniqueness of His person. This they were not prepared to do, for then they would have had to worship Him as God.

9.2 The disciples evidently shared the common Jewish belief that sickness was invariably a penalty for sin. But the fact that this man was blind from birth indicated that personal sin was not the cause of his affliction, and pointed to his parents as the ones responsible. Jesus reiterated what the Book of Job had already taught: that sickness is not always the result of sin either by the individual or, as in this case, by his parents. Note that this is the only recorded case in which Jesus healed one blind from birth.

The Pharisees question the healed man
(9.13-23)

13 They brought to the Phạr'ịsees the man who had formerly been blind. 14 Now it was a sabbath day when Jesus made the clay and opened his eyes. 15 The Phạr'ịsees again asked him how he had received his sight. And he said to them, "He put clay on my eyes, and I washed, and I see." 16 Some of the Phar'isees said, "This man is not from God, for he does not keep the sabbath." But others said, "How can a man who is a sinner do such signs?" There was a division among them. 17 So they again said to the blind man, "What do you say about him, since he has opened your eyes?" He said, "He is a prophet."

18 The Jews did not believe that he had been blind and had received his sight, until they called the parents of the man who had received his sight, 19 and asked them, "Is this your son, who you say was born blind? How then does he now see?" 20 His parents answered, "We know that this is our son, and that he was born blind; 21 but how he now sees we do not know, nor do we know who opened his eyes. Ask him; he is of age, he will speak for himself." 22 His parents said this because they feared the Jews, for the Jews had already agreed that if any one should confess him to be Christ, he was to be put out of the synagogue. 23 Therefore his parents said, "He is of age, ask him."

The Pharisees question the healed man a second time
(9.24-34)

24 So for the second time they called the man who had been blind, and said to him, "Give God the praise; we know that this man is a sinner." 25 He answered, "Whether he is a sinner, I do not know; one thing I know, that though I was blind, now I see." 26 They said to him, "What did he do to you? How did he open your eyes?" 27 He answered them, "I have told you already, and you would not listen. Why do you want to hear it again? Do you too want to become his disciples?" 28 And they reviled him, saying, "You are his disciple, but we are disciples of Moses. 29 We know that God has spoken to Moses, but as for this man, we do not know where he comes from." 30 The man answered, "Why, this is a marvel! You do not know where he comes from, and yet he opened my eyes. 31 We know that God does not listen to sinners, but if any one is a worshiper of God and does his will, God listens to him. 32 Never since the world began has it been heard that any one opened the eyes of a man born blind. 33 If this man were not from God, he could do nothing." 34 They answered him, "You were born in utter sin, and would you teach us?" And they cast him out.

Jesus seeks the outcast (9.35-41)

35 Jesus heard that they had cast him out, and having found him he said, "Do you believe in the Son of man?"*v* 36 He answered, "And who is he, sir, that I may believe in him?" 37 Jesus said to him, "You have seen him, and it is he who speaks to you." 38 He

v Other ancient authorities read *the Son of God*

9.14
Jn 5.9
9.15
ver 10
9.16
Mt 12.2;
Jn 7.43;
10.19
9.17
ver 15;
Mt 21.11
9.18
ver 22
9.22
Jn 7.13;
12.42;
ver 34;
Lk 6.22
9.23
ver 21
9.24
Josh 7.19;
1 Sam 6.5;
ver 16
9.27
ver 15;
Jn 5.25
9.28
Jn 5.45
9.29
Jn 8.14
9.31
Job 27.8,9;
Ps 34.15;
66.18;
Prov 15.29;
28.9;
Isa 1.15;
Jer 11.11;
Zech 7.13
9.33
ver 16
9.34
ver 2
9.35
Mt 14.33;
16.16;
Mk 1.1;
Jn 10.36
9.36
Rom 10.14
9.37
Jn 4.26
9.38
Mt 28.9

9.39
Jn 5.22,27;
3.19;
Mt 13.13;
15.14
9.40
Rom 2.19
9.41
Jn 15.22,24

★10.1

10.2
Mk 6.34;
ver 11,12
10.3
ver 16,27,9
10.4
ver 3
10.6
Jn 16.25
10.7
Jer 23.1,2;
Ezek 34.2
10.10
Jn 5.40
★10.11
Isa 40.11;
Ezek 34.11–
16,23;
Heb 13.20;
1 Pet 5.4;
Rev 7.17;
1 Jn 3.16;
Jn 15.13
10.12
Zech 11.16,
17
10.14
ver 11,27
10.15
Mt 11.27
10.16
Isa 56.8;
Jn 11.52;
Eph 2.14;
1 Pet 2.25
10.17
Isa 53.7,8,12
10.18
Jn 2.19;
15.10;
Heb 5.8

10.19
Jn 7.43;
9.16

said, "Lord, I believe"; and he worshiped him. 39 Jesus said, "For judgment I came into this world, that those who do not see may see, and that those who see may become blind." 40 Some of the Phar′iseēs near him heard this, and they said to him, "Are we also blind?" 41 Jesus said to them, "If you were blind, you would have no guilt; but now that you say, 'We see,' your guilt remains.

Jesus' discourse on the good (true) shepherd (10.1–18)

10 "Truly, truly, I say to you, he who does not enter the sheepfold by the door but climbs in by another way, that man is a thief and a robber; 2 but he who enters by the door is the shepherd of the sheep. 3 To him the gatekeeper opens; the sheep hear his voice, and he calls his own sheep by name and leads them out. 4 When he has brought out all his own, he goes before them, and the sheep follow him, for they know his voice. 5A stranger they will not follow, but they will flee from him, for they do not know the voice of strangers." 6 This figure Jesus used with them, but they did not understand what he was saying to them.

7 So Jesus again said to them, "Truly, truly, I say to you, I am the door of the sheep. 8All who came before me are thieves and robbers; but the sheep did not heed them. 9 I am the door; if any one enters by me, he will be saved, and will go in and out and find pasture. 10 The thief comes only to steal and kill and destroy; I came that they may have life, and have it abundantly. 11 I am the good shepherd. The good shepherd lays down his life for the sheep. 12 He who is a hireling and not a shepherd, whose own the sheep are not, sees the wolf coming and leaves the sheep and flees; and the wolf snatches them and scatters them. 13 He flees because he is a hireling and cares nothing for the sheep. 14 I am the good shepherd; I know my own and my own know me, 15 as the Father knows me and I know the Father; and I lay down my life for the sheep. 16And I have other sheep, that are not of this fold; I must bring them also, and they will heed my voice. So there shall be one flock, one shepherd. 17 For this reason the Father loves me, because I lay down my life, that I may take it again. 18 No one takes it from me, but I lay it down of my own accord. I have power to lay it down, and I have power to take it again; this charge I have received from my Father."

The Jews divided (10.19–21)

19 There was again a division among the Jews because of these

---

10.1 The story of the good shepherd is an *allegory*, not a *parable*. An allegory differs from a parable in one essential regard, and that is that all the details in an allegory are relevant, whereas the details in a parable, for the most part, are incidental to the main idea. For example, in the parable of the mustard seed (Mt 13.31, 32), the connection between the seed, the tree, and the birds is casual. The main idea is the growth of the kingdom. But in the allegory of the good shepherd each detail is important. Thus Jesus is both the shepherd of the sheep and the door. Only through Him can the sheep enter the king-dom. Jesus, the shepherd, died for the sheep. Those who are not true sheep cannot enter the door. (See also the note to Mt 13.3 on the definition of a parable.)

10.11 Christ is called the *good shepherd* here, the *great shepherd* (Heb 13.20), and the *chief Shepherd* (1 Pet 5.4). We need not suppose that these words connote different aspects of the shepherd. They present Jesus as the one whose death on Calvary saves the sheep. The *good* shepherd gave His life; the *great* shepherd did the same through the blood of the eternal covenant; the *chief* shepherd will come again for His sheep.

words. 20 Many of them said, "He has a demon, and he is mad; why listen to him?" 21 Others said, "These are not the sayings of one who has a demon. Can a demon open the eyes of the blind?"

Jesus the Christ the Son of God (10.22–42)

22 It was the feast of the Dedication at Jerusalem; 23 it was winter, and Jesus was walking in the temple, in the portico of Solomon. 24 So the Jews gathered round him and said to him, "How long will you keep us in suspense? If you are the Christ, tell us plainly." 25 Jesus answered them, "I told you, and you do not believe. The works that I do in my Father's name, they bear witness to me; 26 but you do not believe, because you do not belong to my sheep. 27 My sheep hear my voice, and I know them, and they follow me; 28 and I give them eternal life, and they shall never perish, and no one shall snatch them out of my hand. 29 My Father, who has given them to me,^{w} is greater than all, and no one is able to snatch them out of the Father's hand. 30 I and the Father are one."

31 The Jews took up stones again to stone him. 32 Jesus answered them, "I have shown you many good works from the Father; for which of these do you stone me?" 33 The Jews answered him, "It is not for a good work that we stone you but for blasphemy; because you, being a man, make yourself God." 34 Jesus answered them, "Is it not written in your law, 'I said, you are gods'? 35 If he called them gods to whom the word of God came (and scripture cannot be broken), 36 do you say of him whom the Father consecrated and sent into the world, 'You are blas-

*10.20
Jn 7.20;
8.48;
Mk 3.21

10.21
Jn 9.32,33;
Ex 4.11

*10.22

10.23
Acts 3.11;
5.12

10.25
Jn 5.36

10.26
Jn 8.47

10.27
ver 4,14

*10.28
Jn 17.2,3;
1 Jn 2.25;
Jn 6.37,39

10.29
Jn 14.28;
17.2,6ff

10.30
Jn 17.21ff

10.31
Jn 8.59

10.33
Jn 5.18

10.34
Ps 82.6

*10.35

10.36
Jn 6.69;
3.17;
Jn 5.17,18

^{w} Other ancient authorities read What my Father has given to me

10.20 The Gospel of John records no instance of Christ's expelling demons. Several times in this Gospel, however, Jesus Himself is accused of having a demon, as one who imagines things (7.20), or as one who speaks wildly and makes extravagant claims (8.48–52), and appears to be insane (10.20, 21).

10.22 The Feast of the Dedication was instituted long after the time of Moses. After the desecration of the Temple by Antiochus Epiphanes in 168 B.C., Judas Maccabeus recaptured the city and had the sanctuary cleansed of the symbols of idolatry. This feast commemorated the rededication of the Temple to God's worship once the defilement had been removed. It was celebrated for eight days in the winter month of *Chislev* (corresponding to December), according to the apocryphal books of the Maccabees. Dan 11.31 refers to this profanation by Antiochus.

10.28 God promises eternal life to those who receive Christ (1.12) as Savior by faith (Eph 2.8, 9). True believers may know that they possess eternal life (1 Jn 5.13). The Greek word *aionios* means "age lasting." Thus eternal life has a beginning but no end. Believers shall never perish. They are kept by God's power through faith (1 Pet 1.5). This does not mean that believers will never die physically; rather it means that believers will never suffer spiritual death, although their bodies die. The possession of eternal life guarantees to believers a resurrection hope when they will rise in their glorious

resurrection bodies, for mortality and corruption must give way to immortality and to incorruption (1 Cor 15).

10.35 The written Word of God originated in the mind of God, but it was written and compiled by men, humanly speaking. How then did the canon of Scripture come into being? The word *canon* means "rod" or "rule" —a standard of authoritative books containing God's revealed truth. This group of authoritative writings, called the Old Testament, was recognized as God-given. In Jesus' day, the same books we now have in the Old Testament were accepted as sacred Scripture. Jesus himself placed His stamp of approval on the Old Testament and embraced it as the Word of God. The New Testament canon developed gradually as the apostles wrote inspired letters to various churches in Asia Minor, Greece, and Rome. Copies of these wonderful letters were made and distributed to other churches. At the same time, of course, the first three Gospels were being written largely to inform new believers of the content of the gospel message that they might be prepared for baptism and for Christian service. Gradually the church of Jesus Christ recognized and accepted as sacred Scripture those books which now appear in the New Testament. Eventually lists of these canonical letters and Gospels were drawn up, perhaps as a safeguard against the spurious apocryphal "gospels" and letters produced by Gnostics and other heretics.

10.37
Jn 15.24
10.38
Jn 14.10,11;
17.21

10.39
Jn 7.30;
8.59
10.40
Jn 1.28
10.41
Jn 2.11;
3.30
10.42
Jn 7.31;
11.45

11.1
Mk 11.1;
Lk 10.38
11.2
Mk 14.3;
Lk 7.38;
Jn 12.3
11.3
Lk 7.13
11.4
ver 40;
Jn 9.3

11.7
Jn 10.40
11.8
Jn 10.31
11.9
Lk 13.33;
Jn 9.4;
12.35
11.11
ver 3;
Mt 27.52;
Mk 5.39;
Acts 7.60
11.13
Mt 9.24;
Lk 8.52

11.16
Mt 10.3;
Jn 20.24–28

11.17
ver 39
11.18
ver 1
11.19
Job 2.11
11.21
ver 2,32
11.22
Jn 9.31
11.24
Dan 12.2;
Jn 5.28,29;
Acts 24.15
11.25
Jn 1.4;
5.26;
14.6; 3.36

pheming,' because I said, 'I am the Son of God'? 37 If I am not doing the works of my Father, then do not believe me; 38 but if I do them, even though you do not believe me, believe the works, that you may know and understand that the Father is in me and I am in the Father." 39Again they tried to arrest him, but he escaped from their hands.

40 He went away again across the Jordan to the place where John at first baptized, and there he remained. 41And many came to him; and they said, "John did no sign, but everything that John said about this man was true." 42And many believed in him there.

The raising of Lazarus (11.1–57)

1. Jesus hears of Lazarus' death (11.1–4)

11 Now a certain man was ill, Lăz′ărŭs of Bĕth′ănȳ, the village of Mary and her sister Martha. 2 It was Mary who anointed the Lord with ointment and wiped his feet with her hair, whose brother Lăz′ărŭs was ill. 3 So the sisters sent to him, saying, "Lord, he whom you love is ill." 4 But when Jesus heard it he said, "This illness is not unto death; it is for the glory of God, so that the Son of God may be glorified by means of it."

2. Jesus goes to Lazarus' home (11.5–16)

5 Now Jesus loved Martha and her sister and Lăz′ărŭs. 6 So when he heard that he was ill, he stayed two days longer in the place where he was. 7 Then after this he said to the disciples, "Let us go into Judē′ă again." 8 The disciples said to him, "Rabbi, the Jews were but now seeking to stone you, and are you going there again?" 9 Jesus answered, "Are there not twelve hours in the day? If any one walks in the day, he does not stumble, because he sees the light of this world. 10 But if any one walks in the night, he stumbles, because the light is not in him." 11 Thus he spoke, and then he said to them, "Our friend Lăz′ărŭs has fallen asleep, but I go to awake him out of sleep." 12 The disciples said to him, "Lord, if he has fallen asleep, he will recover." 13 Now Jesus had spoken of his death, but they thought that he meant taking rest in sleep. 14 Then Jesus told them plainly, "Lăz′ărŭs is dead; 15 and for your sake I am glad that I was not there, so that you may believe. But let us go to him." 16 Thomas, called the Twin, said to his fellow disciples, "Let us also go, that we may die with him."

3. Jesus talks with Martha: "the resurrection and the life" (11.17–27)

17 Now when Jesus came, he found that Lăz′ărŭs[x] had already been in the tomb four days. 18 Bĕth′ănȳ was near Jerusalem, about two miles[y] off, 19 and many of the Jews had come to Martha and Mary to console them concerning their brother. 20 When Martha heard that Jesus was coming, she went and met him, while Mary sat in the house. 21 Martha said to Jesus, "Lord, if you had been here, my brother would not have died. 22And even now I know that whatever you ask from God, God will give you." 23 Jesus said to her, "Your brother will rise again." 24 Martha said to him, "I know that he will rise again in the resurrection at the last day." 25 Jesus said to her, "I am the resurrection and the life;[z] he who

---

x Greek he   y Greek fifteen stadia   z Other ancient authorities omit and the life

believes in me, though he die, yet shall he live, 26 and whoever
lives and believes in me shall never die. Do you believe this?"
27 She said to him, "Yes, Lord; I believe that you are the Christ,
the Son of God, he who is coming into the world."

4. *Jesus talks with Mary (11.28–37)*

28 When she had said this, she went and called her sister Mary,
saying quietly, "The Teacher is here and is calling for you."
29And when she heard it, she rose quickly and went to him. 30 Now
Jesus had not yet come to the village, but was still in the place
where Martha had met him. 31 When the Jews who were with her
in the house, consoling her, saw Mary rise quickly and go out, they
followed her, supposing that she was going to the tomb to weep
there. 32 Then Mary, when she came where Jesus was and saw
him, fell at his feet, saying to him, "Lord, if you had been here,
my brother would not have died." 33 When Jesus saw her weeping,
and the Jews who came with her also weeping, he was deeply
moved in spirit and troubled; 34 and he said, "Where have you
laid him?" They said to him, "Lord, come and see." 35 Jesus wept.
36 So the Jews said, "See how he loved him!" 37 But some of them
said, "Could not he who opened the eyes of the blind man have
kept this man from dying?"

5. *Jesus raises Lazarus from the dead (11.38–44)*

38 Then Jesus, deeply moved again, came to the tomb; it was a
cave, and a stone lay upon it. 39 Jesus said, "Take away the stone."
Martha, the sister of the dead man, said to him, "Lord, by this
time there will be an odor, for he has been dead four days."
40 Jesus said to her, "Did I not tell you that if you would believe
you would see the glory of God?" 41 So they took away the stone.
And Jesus lifted up his eyes and said, "Father, I thank thee that
thou hast heard me. 42 I knew that thou hearest me always, but I
have said this on account of the people standing by, that they may
believe that thou didst send me." 43 When he had said this, he
cried with a loud voice, "Lăz′à rǔs, come out." 44 The dead man
came out, his hands and feet bound with bandages, and his face
wrapped with a cloth. Jesus said to them, "Unbind him, and
let him go."

6. *The Pharisees plot to kill Jesus (11.45–57)*

45 Many of the Jews therefore, who had come with Mary and
had seen what he did, believed in him; 46 but some of them went
to the Phạr′ịseēṣ and told them what Jesus had done. 47 So the
chief priests and the Phạr′ịseēṣ gathered the council, and said,
"What are we to do? For this man performs many signs. 48 If we
let him go on thus, every one will believe in him, and the Romans
will come and destroy both our holy place*a* and our nation."
49 But one of them, Cā′iȧphȧs, who was high priest that year, said
to them, "You know nothing at all; 50 you do not understand that
it is expedient for you that one man should die for the people,
and that the whole nation should not perish." 51 He did not say
this of his own accord, but being high priest that year he prophesied that Jesus should die for the nation, 52 and not for the nation
only, but to gather into one the children of God who are scattered

a Greek *our place*

11.26	Jn 6.47; 8.51
11.27	Mt 16.16; Jn 6.14
11.28	Mt 26.18; Lk 22.11
11.30	ver 20
11.31	ver 19
11.32	ver 21
11.33	ver 38; Jn 12.27; 13.21
11.35	Lk 19.41
11.37	Jn 9.6,7
11.38	ver 33; Mt 27.60; Mk 15.46; Lk 24.2; Jn 20.1
11.39	ver 17
11.40	ver 4,23
11.41	Jn 17.1; Mt 11.25
11.42	Jn 12.30; 3.17
11.44	Jn 19.40; 20.7
11.45	ver 19; Jn 2.23
11.47	ver 57; Mt 26.3
11.49	Mt 26.3; Jn 18.13,14
11.50	Jn 18.14
11.52	Isa 49.6; Jn 10.16

<table>
</table>

11.53
Mt 26.4

*11.54
Jn 7.1;
2 Chr 13.19

11.55
Mt 26.1,2;
Mk 14.1;
Lk 22.1;
Jn 12.1;
Num 9.10;
2 Chr 30.17,
18
11.56
Jn 7.11

12.1
Lk 7.37–39;
Jn 11.55
12.2
Lk 10.38
*12.3
Jn 11.2;
Mk 14.3
12.4
Jn 6.71
12.6
Jn 13.29;
Lk 8.3
12.7
Jn 19.40
12.8
Mt 26.11;
Mk 14.7
12.9
Mk 12.37;
Mt 11.43,44
12.11
ver 18;
Jn 11.45

12.13
Ps 118.25,
26; Jn 1.49

12.15
Zech 9.9

12.16
Mk 9.32;
Jn 2.22;
14.26; 7.39
12.18
ver 11
12.19
Jn 11.47,48

abroad. 53 So from that day on they took counsel how to put him to death.

54 Jesus therefore no longer went about openly among the Jews, but went from there to the country near the wilderness, to a town called Ē'phraïm; and there he stayed with the disciples.

55 Now the Passover of the Jews was at hand, and many went up from the country to Jerusalem before the Passover, to purify themselves. 56 They were looking for Jesus and saying to one another as they stood in the temple, "What do you think? That he will not come to the feast?" 57 Now the chief priests and the Phar'isees had given orders that if any one knew where he was, he should let them know, so that they might arrest him.

Jesus anointed by Mary of Bethany
(12.1–11; Mt 26.6–13; Mk 14.3–9)

12 Six days before the Passover, Jesus came to Bĕth'anÿ, where Lăz'arŭs was, whom Jesus had raised from the dead. 2 There they made him a supper; Martha served, and Lăz'arŭs was one of those at table with him. 3 Mary took a pound of costly ointment of pure nard and anointed the feet of Jesus and wiped his feet with her hair; and the house was filled with the fragrance of the ointment. 4 But Judas Iscar'iŏt, one of his disciples (he who was to betray him), said, 5 "Why was this ointment not sold for three hundred denarii[b] and given to the poor?" 6 This he said, not that he cared for the poor but because he was a thief, and as he had the money box he used to take what was put into it. 7 Jesus said, "Let her alone, let her keep it for the day of my burial. 8 The poor you always have with you, but you do not always have me."

9 When the great crowd of the Jews learned that he was there, they came, not only on account of Jesus but also to see Lăz'arŭs, whom he had raised from the dead. 10 So the chief priests planned to put Lăz'arŭs also to death, 11 because on account of him many of the Jews were going away and believing in Jesus.

The triumphal entry
(12.12–19; Mt 21.1–11; Mk 11.1–11; Lk 19.29–44)

12 The next day a great crowd who had come to the feast heard that Jesus was coming to Jerusalem. 13 So they took branches of palm trees and went out to meet him, crying, "Hosanna! Blessed is he who comes in the name of the Lord, even the King of Israel!" 14And Jesus found a young ass and sat upon it; as it is written,
15 "Fear not, daughter of Zion;
behold, your king is coming,
sitting on an ass's colt!"
16 His disciples did not understand this at first; but when Jesus was glorified, then they remembered that this had been written of him and had been done to him. 17 The crowd that had been with him when he called Lăz'arŭs out of the tomb and raised him from the dead bore witness. 18 The reason why the crowd went to meet him was that they heard he had done this sign. 19 The Phar'-

b The denarius was a day's wage for a laborer

11.54 Ephraim, a city located north of Jerusalem and possibly east of the Jordan.

12.3 Mary, the sister of Martha and Lazarus. (See note to Lk 7.36.)

isēē̦s then said to one another, "You see that you can do nothing; look, the world has gone after him."

Christ sought by the Gentiles: his last public discourse (12.20–36a)

20 Now among those who went up to worship at the feast were some Greeks. 21 So these came to Philip, who was from Bĕth-sā'idȧ in Găl'ilēē, and said to him, "Sir, we wish to see Jesus." 22 Philip went and told Andrew; Andrew went with Philip and they told Jesus. 23And Jesus answered them, "The hour has come for the Son of man to be glorified. 24 Truly, truly, I say to you, unless a grain of wheat falls into the earth and dies, it remains alone; but if it dies, it bears much fruit. 25 He who loves his life loses it, and he who hates his life in this world will keep it for eternal life. 26 If any one serves me, he must follow me; and where I am, there shall my servant be also; if any one serves me, the Father will honor him.

27 "Now is my soul troubled. And what shall I say? 'Father, save me from this hour'? No, for this purpose I have come to this hour. 28 Father, glorify thy name." Then a voice came from heaven, "I have glorified it, and I will glorify it again." 29 The crowd standing by heard it and said that it had thundered. Others said, "An angel has spoken to him." 30 Jesus answered, "This voice has come for your sake, not for mine. 31 Now is the judgment of this world, now shall the ruler of this world be cast out; 32 and I, when I am lifted up from the earth, will draw all men to myself." 33 He said this to show by what death he was to die. 34 The crowd answered him, "We have heard from the law that the Christ remains for ever. How can you say that the Son of man must be lifted up? Who is this Son of man?" 35 Jesus said to them, "The light is with you for a little longer. Walk while you have the light, lest the darkness overtake you; he who walks in the darkness does not know where he goes. 36 While you have the light, believe in the light, that you may become sons of light."

The cause of unbelief (12.36b–43)

When Jesus had said this, he departed and hid himself from them. 37 Though he had done so many signs before them, yet they did not believe in him; 38 it was that the word spoken by the prophet Īṣāi'äh might be fulfilled:

"Lord, who has believed our report,
   and to whom has the arm of the Lord been revealed?"
39 Therefore they could not believe. For Īṣāi'äh again said,
40 "He has blinded their eyes and hardened their heart,
   lest they should see with their eyes and perceive with their heart,
   and turn for me to heal them."
41 Īṣāi'äh said this because he saw his glory and spoke of him.
42 Nevertheless many even of the authorities believed in him, but

12.20 Jn 7.35; Acts 11.20
12.21 Jn 1.44
12.23 Jn 13.1,32; 17.1; Mk 14.35, 41
12.24 1 Cor 15.36
12.25 Mt 10.39; Mk 8.35; Lk 9.24; 14.26
12.26 Jn 14.3; 17.24; 1 Thess 4.17
12.27 Mt 26.38, 39; Mk 14.34; Jn 11.33
12.28 Mt 3.17; 17.5; Mk 1.11; 9.7; Lk 3.22; 9.35
12.30 Jn 11.42
★12.31 Jn 16.11; 14.30; 2 Cor 4.4; Eph 2.2
12.32 Jn 3.14; 8.28; 6.44
12.33 Jn 18.32
12.34 Ps 110.4; Isa 9.7; Ezek 37.25; Dan 7.14
12.35 Eph 5.8
12.36 Lk 16.8; Jn 8.59
12.37 Jn 2.11
12.38 Isa 53.1; Rom 10.16
12.40 Isa 6.9,10; Mt 13.14
12.41 Isa 6.1
12.42 Jn 7.48,13; 9.22

12.31 Jesus never disputes the fact that Satan has power over this present evil world. (Compare, for example, Mt 4.8–10; Lk 4.5–8; Jn 14.30; 16.11.) Here Jesus proclaims His victory over Satan and the sure end of his earthly reign. Jesus' death (ver 32) not only defeated Satan, but made possible the redemption of man.

12.43
Jn 5.44

for fear of the Phạr'isēēṣ they did not confess it, lest they should be put out of the synagogue: 43 for they loved the praise of men more than the praise of God.

A summary of Jesus' claims (12.44–50)

12.44
Mt 10.40;
Jn 5.24
12.45
Jn 14.9
12.46
Jn 1.4;
3.19;
8.12; 9.5
12.47
Jn 3.17
12.48
Lk 10.16;
Mt 10.15
12.49
Jn 14.31
12.50
Jn 8.28

44 And Jesus cried out and said, "He who believes in me, believes not in me but in him who sent me. 45And he who sees me sees him who sent me. 46 I have come as light into the world, that whoever believes in me may not remain in darkness. 47 If any one hears my sayings and does not keep them, I do not judge him; for I did not come to judge the world but to save the world. 48 He who rejects me and does not receive my sayings has a judge; the word that I have spoken will be his judge on the last day. 49 For I have not spoken on my own authority; the Father who sent me has himself given me commandment what to say and what to speak. 50And I know that his commandment is eternal life. What I say, therefore, I say as the Father has bidden me."

Washing the disciples' feet (13.1–20)

13.1
Jn 11.55;
12.23;
16.28
13.2
Jn 6.70,71;
Mk 14.10
13.3
Mt 28.18;
Heb 2.8;
Jn 8.42;
16.28
13.4
Lk 22.27
13.5
Lk 7.44
13.8
Jn 3.5; 9.7
13.10
Jn 15.3
13.11
Jn 6.64
13.13
Lk 6.46;
Phil 2.11
13.14
1 Pet 5.5
13.15
1 Pet 2.21
13.16
Mt 10.24;
Lk 6.40;
Jn 15.20
13.17
Lk 11.28;
Jas 1.25
13.18
Ps 41.9;
Mt 26.23
13.19
Jn 14.29;
16.4; 8.24
13.20
Mt 10.40;
Lk 10.16

13 Now before the feast of the Passover, when Jesus knew that his hour had come to depart out of this world to the Father, having loved his own who were in the world, he loved them to the end. 2And during supper, when the devil had already put it into the heart of Judas Ĭscạr'ĭŏt, Simon's son, to betray him, 3 Jesus, knowing that the Father had given all things into his hands, and that he had come from God and was going to God, 4 rose from supper, laid aside his garments, and girded himself with a towel. 5 Then he poured water into a basin, and began to wash the disciples' feet, and to wipe them with the towel with which he was girded. 6 He came to Simon Peter; and Peter said to him, "Lord, do you wash my feet?" 7 Jesus answered him, "What I am doing you do not know now, but afterward you will understand." 8 Peter said to him, "You shall never wash my feet." Jesus answered him, "If I do not wash you, you have no part in me." 9 Simon Peter said to him, "Lord, not my feet only but also my hands and my head!" 10 Jesus said to him, "He who has bathed does not need to wash, except for his feet,c but he is clean all over; and youx are clean, but not every one of you." 11 For he knew who was to betray him; that was why he said, "You are not all clean."

12 When he had washed their feet, and taken his garments, and resumed his place, he said to them, "Do you know what I have done to you? 13 You call me Teacher and Lord; and you are right, for so I am. 14 If I then, your Lord and Teacher, have washed your feet, you also ought to wash one another's feet. 15 For I have given you an example, that you also should do as I have done to you. 16 Truly, truly, I say to you, a servantd is not greater than his master; nor is he who is sent greater than he who sent him. 17 If you know these things, blessed are you if you do them. 18 I am not speaking of you all; I know whom I have chosen; it is that the scripture may be fulfilled, 'He who ate my bread has lifted his heel against me.' 19 I tell you this now, before it takes place, that when it does take place you may believe that I am he. 20 Truly, truly, I

---

c Other ancient authorities omit except for his feet   d Or slave

x The Greek word for you here is plural

say to you, he who receives any one whom I send receives me; and he who receives me receives him who sent me."

Jesus dismisses Judas Iscariot his betrayer (13.21–30; Mt 26.21–25; Mk 14.18–21; Lk 22.21–23)

21 When Jesus had thus spoken, he was troubled in spirit, and testified, "Truly, truly, I say to you, one of you will betray me." 22 The disciples looked at one another, uncertain of whom he spoke. 23 One of his disciples, whom Jesus loved, was lying close to the breast of Jesus; 24 so Simon Peter beckoned to him and said, "Tell us who it is of whom he speaks." 25 So lying thus, close to the breast of Jesus, he said to him, "Lord, who is it?" 26 Jesus answered, "It is he to whom I shall give this morsel when I have dipped it." So when he had dipped the morsel, he gave it to Judas, the son of Simon Iscar'iot. 27 Then after the morsel, Satan entered into him. Jesus said to him, "What you are going to do, do quickly." 28 Now no one at the table knew why he said this to him. 29 Some thought that, because Judas had the money box, Jesus was telling him, "Buy what we need for the feast"; or, that he should give something to the poor. 30 So, after receiving the morsel, he immediately went out; and it was night.

13.21
Jn 12.27

13.23
Jn 19.26;
20.2; 21.7,
20

13.25
Jn 21.20

13.26
Jn 6.71

★13.27
Lk 22.3

13.29
Jn 12.5,6

Jesus announces his departure (13.31–35)

31 When he had gone out, Jesus said, "Now is the Son of man glorified, and in him God is glorified; 32 if God is glorified in him, God will also glorify him in himself, and glorify him at once. 33 Little children, yet a little while I am with you. You will seek me; and as I said to the Jews so now I say to you, 'Where I am going you cannot come.' 34 A new commandment I give to you, that you love one another; even as I have loved you, that you also love one another. 35 By this all men will know that you are my disciples, if you have love for one another."

13.31
Jn 7.39;
14.13;
1 Pet 4.11

13.32
Jn 17.1

13.33
Jn 7.33,34

13.34
Lev 19.18;
Jn 15.12;
1 Pet 1.22;
1 Jn 2.7;
3.11; 4.10

13.35
1 Jn 3.14;
4.20

Peter's denial foretold (13.36–38)

36 Simon Peter said to him, "Lord, where are you going?" Jesus answered, "Where I am going you cannot follow me now; but you shall follow afterward." 37 Peter said to him, "Lord, why cannot I follow you now? I will lay down my life for you." 38 Jesus answered, "Will you lay down your life for me? Truly, truly, I say to you, the cock will not crow, till you have denied me three times.

13.36
Jn 21.18;
2 Pet 1.14

13.37
Mt 26.33–
35;
Mk 14.29–
31;
Lk 22.33,34

13.38
Jn 18.27

Christ comforts his disciples (14.1–31)

1. The way, the truth, and the life (14.1–11)

14 "Let not your hearts be troubled; believe^e in God, believe also in me. 2 In my Father's house are many rooms; if it

14.1
Jn 16.23,24

14.2
Jn 13.33

^e Or *you believe*

13.27 The Devil apparently cannot be in more than one place at one time. The Scriptures do not attribute omnipresence to him, yet the number of fallen angels who do his bidding make practically ubiquitous. Here, however, the Devil himself took posses- sion of the person of Judas Iscariot, making his abode in him, since he had allowed himself to be possessed by the Devil. (This is parallel to the experience of true conversion, whereby a repentant believer allows himself to be possessed by the Holy Spirit of Christ.)

14.3
Jn 12.26

14.5
Jn 11.16

14.6
Jn 10.9;
8.32; 1.4;
11.25

14.7
Jn 8.19

14.9
Jn 12.45

14.10
Jn 10.38;
5.19; 12.49

14.11
Jn 5.36;
10.38

14.12
Mt 21.21;
Lk 10.17

14.13
Jn 15.7,16;
16.23;
Jas 1.5

14.15
Jn 15.10;
1 Jn 5.3

*14.16
Jn 15.26;
16.7;
1 Jn 2.1

14.17
Jn 16.13;
1 Jn 4.6;
1 Cor 2.14

14.18
ver 3,28

14.19
Jn 7.33;
16.16; 6.57

14.20
Jn 10.38

14.21
1 Jn 2.5; 5.3

were not so, would I have told you that I go to prepare a place for you? 3And when I go and prepare a place for you, I will come again and will take you to myself, that where I am you may be also. 4And you know the way where I am going."f 5 Thomas said to him, "Lord, we do not know where you are going; how can we know the way?" 6 Jesus said to him, "I am the way, and the truth, and the life; no one comes to the Father, but by me. 7 If you had known me, you would have known my Father also; henceforth you know him and have seen him."

8 Philip said to him, "Lord, show us the Father, and we shall be satisfied." 9 Jesus said to him, "Have I been with you so long, and yet you do not know me, Philip? He who has seen me has seen the Father; how can you say, 'Show us the Father'? 10 Do you not believe that I am in the Father and the Father in me? The words that I say to you I do not speak on my own authority; but the Father who dwells in me does his works. 11 Believe me that I am in the Father and the Father in me; or else believe me for the sake of the works themselves.

2. The promise of greater works (14.12–14)

12 "Truly, truly, I say to you, he who believes in me will also do the works that I do; and greater works than these will he do, because I go to the Father. 13 Whatever you ask in my name, I will do it, that the Father may be glorified in the Son; 14 if you askg anything in my name, I will do it.

3. The promise of the Holy Spirit (14.15–24)

15 "If you love me, you will keep my commandments. 16And I will pray the Father, and he will give you another Counselor, to be with you for ever, 17 even the Spirit of truth, whom the world cannot receive, because it neither sees him nor knows him; you know him, for he dwells with you, and will be in you.

18 "I will not leave you desolate; I will come to you. 19 Yet a little while, and the world will see me no more, but you will see me; because I live, you will live also. 20 In that day you will know that I am in my Father, and you in me, and I in you. 21 He who has my commandments and keeps them, he it is who loves me; and he who loves me will be loved by my Father, and I will love him

---

f Other ancient authorities read where I am going you know, and the way you know
g Other ancient authorities add me

14.16 There are five passages in chapters 14–16 which speak of the ministry of the Holy Spirit: 14.15–17; 14.25, 26; 15.26, 27; 16.7–11, and 16.12–15. In these passages, four times the Holy Spirit is called *parakletos* (14.16, 26; 15.26; 16.7), which the RSV translates *Counselor* (KJV, "Comforter"). The verb *parakaleo*, from which this noun is formed, means "to encourage," "exhort," "comfort," and the noun *parakletos* itself refers to one who is called upon to intercede in behalf of, or to help, someone. In the only other New Testament passage where *parakletos* occurs (1 Jn 2.1) it is used of Christ and translated *advocate*.

In the five passages in the Gospel of John, the Holy Spirit is defined and described both as to origin and as to mission. He is *the Holy Spirit* (14.26), *the Spirit of truth* (14.17; 15.26; 16.13), *another Counselor* (14.16),

who will take the place of Jesus with the disciples (16.7), whom the world cannot receive, but the disciples only (14.17). He proceeds from the Father (15.26), and is sent by the Father at Jesus' request (14.16), and in Jesus' name (14.26); alternately, Jesus Himself sends him from the Father (15.26; 16.7). His ministry as teacher will be: (1) to remain with, and in the disciples forever (14.16, 17); (2) to teach them all things (14.26) and lead them into all the truth (16.13); (3) to speak, not on his own authority, but as directed by Jesus (16.13–15): he will thus bear witness to Jesus (15.26) and glorify Him (16.14), and remind the disciples of what Jesus taught (14.26); (4) to announce future things to the disciples (16.13).

His ministry to the world will be that of convincing it of sin, of righteousness, and of judgment (16.8–11).

and manifest myself to him." 22 Judas (not Ĭscar'ĭŏt) said to him, "Lord, how is it that you will manifest yourself to us, and not to the world?" 23 Jesus answered him, "If a man loves me, he will keep my word, and my Father will love him, and we will come to him and make our home with him. 24 He who does not love me does not keep my words; and the word which you hear is not mine but the Father's who sent me.

4. The promise of peace (14.25–31)

25 "These things I have spoken to you, while I am still with you. 26 But the Counselor, the Holy Spirit, whom the Father will send in my name, he will teach you all things, and bring to your remembrance all that I have said to you. 27 Peace I leave with you; my peace I give to you; not as the world gives do I give to you. Let not your hearts be troubled, neither let them be afraid. 28 You heard me say to you, 'I go away, and I will come to you.' If you loved me, you would have rejoiced, because I go to the Father; for the Father is greater than I. 29And now I have told you before it takes place, so that when it does take place, you may believe. 30 I will no longer talk much with you, for the ruler of this world is coming. He has no power over me; 31 but I do as the Father has commanded me, so that the world may know that I love the Father. Rise, let us go hence.

Christ the true vine (15.1–17)

15 "I am the true vine, and my Father is the vinedresser. 2 Every branch of mine that bears no fruit, he takes away, and every branch that does bear fruit he prunes, that it may bear more fruit. 3 You are already made clean by the word which I have spoken to you. 4Abide in me, and I in you. As the branch cannot bear fruit by itself, unless it abides in the vine, neither· can you, unless you abide in me. 5 I am the vine, you are the branches. He who abides in me, and I in him, he it is that bears much fruit, for apart from me you can do nothing. 6 If a man does not abide in me, he is cast forth as a branch and withers; and the branches are gathered, thrown into the fire and burned. 7 If you abide in me, and my words abide in you, ask whatever you will, and it shall be done for you. 8 By this my Father is glorified, that you bear much fruit, and so prove to be my disciples. 9As the Father has loved me, so have I loved you; abide in my love. 10 If you keep my commandments, you will abide in my love, just as I have kept my Father's commandments and abide in his love. 11 These things I have spoken to you, that my joy may be in you, and that your joy may be full.

14.22
Acts 1.13;
10.14,41
14.23
1 Jn 2.24;
Rev 3.20
14.24
Jn 7.16;
8.28; 12.49
14.26
Jn 15.26;
16.7,13;
1 Jn 2.20,27
14.27
Jn 16.33;
Phil 4.7;
Col 3.15
14.28
ver 3,18;
Jn 5.18;
10.29,30;
Phil 2.6
14.29
Jn 13.19
14.30
Jn 12.31
14.31
Jn 10.18;
12.49; 18.1
15.1
Isa 5.1–7;
Ezek 19.10
*15.2
15.3
Jn 13.10;
17.17;
Eph 5.26
15.4
1 Jn 2.6
15.5
ver 16
15.6
ver 2
15.7
Jn 14.13;
16.23
15.8
Mt 5.16;
Jn 8.31
*15.9
15.10
Jn 14.15 23
15.11
Jn 17.13

15.2 Fruit-bearing is the normal product of regeneration. To be fruitless is abnormal and suggests the possibility of a spurious conversion experience. Christ's statement that fruitless branches shall be removed is in line with James' statement that faith without works is a dead faith (Jas 2.26). At the same time Christ also makes it clear that *fruit* is not the final purpose of the believer's life, but rather a joyous and loving fellowship with God himself. Nevertheless God purges the fruit-bearing Christian (painful though it may be) so that he becomes more fruitful.

15.9 Four relationships of love are expressed here: (1) the Father loves the Son; (2) the Son uses his Father's love for Him as a pattern of His love for the disciples (*as the Father has loved me, so have I loved you*); the measure of His love is expressed by His death for those He loves (15.13); (3) His disciples are to love Him and to abide in His love (15.10); (4) the disciples are likewise to love one another (15.17). Elsewhere, Scripture speaks of Christ's love for His church (Eph 5.25) and affirms that nothing shall separate believers from His love (Rom 8.35).

15.12
Jn 13.34
15.13
Rom 5.7,8;
Jn 10.11
15.14
Mt 12.50
15.15
Jn 8.26
15.16
Jn 6.70;
14.13
15.17
ver 12
15.18
1 Jn 3.13
15.19
Jn 17.14
15.20
Mt 10.24;
Lk 6.40;
Jn 13.16
15.21
Mt 12.24;
Lk 6.40;
Jn 13.16
15.22
Jn 9.41;
Rom 1.20
15.23
1 Jn 2.23
15.24
Jn 5.36
15.25
Ps 35.19;
69.4
15.26
Jn 14.16,17,
26;
1 Jn 2.1; 5.7
15.27
Lk 24.48;
Acts 2.32;
3.15; 5.32;
10.39;
13.31;
1 Jn 4.14
16.1
Jn 15.18–
27; Mt 11.6
16.2
Jn 9.22;
Acts 26.9,
10;
Isa 66.5;
Rev 6.9
16.3
Jn 15.21;
17.25;
1 Jn 3.1
16.4
Jn 13.19;
15.27
16.5
Jn 7.33;
13.36;
14.5
16.7
Jn 7.39;
14.16,26;
15.26
★16.8

12 "This is my commandment, that you love one another as I have loved you. 13 Greater love has no man than this, that a man lay down his life for his friends. 14 You are my friends if you do what I command you. 15 No longer do I call you servants,*h* for the servant*i* does not know what his master is doing; but I have called you friends, for all that I have heard from my Father I have made known to you. 16 You did not choose me, but I chose you and appointed you that you should go and bear fruit and that your fruit should abide; so that whatever you ask the Father in my name, he may give it to you. 17 This I command you, to love one another.

The hatred of the world (15.18–16.4a)

18 "If the world hates you, know that it has hated me before it hated you. 19 If you were of the world, the world would love its own; but because you are not of the world, but I chose you out of the world, therefore the world hates you. 20 Remember the word that I said to you, 'A servant*i* is not greater than his master.' If they persecuted me, they will persecute you; if they kept my word, they will keep yours also. 21 But all this they will do to you on my account, because they do not know him who sent me. 22 If I had not come and spoken to them, they would not have sin; but now they have no excuse for their sin. 23 He who hates me hates my Father also. 24 If I had not done among them the works which no one else did, they would not have sin; but now they have seen and hated both me and my Father. 25 It is to fulfil the word that is written in their law, 'They hated me without a cause.' 26 But when the Counselor comes, whom I shall send to you from the Father, even the Spirit of truth, who proceeds from the Father, he will bear witness to me; 27 and you also are witnesses, because you have been with me from the beginning.

16 "I have said all this to you to keep you from falling away. 2 They will put you out of the synagogues; indeed, the hour is coming when whoever kills you will think he is offering service to God. 3 And they will do this because they have not known the Father, nor me. 4 But I have said these things to you, that when their hour comes you may remember that I told you of them.

The departure of Jesus and the coming of the Holy Spirit (16.4b–11)

"I did not say these things to you from the beginning, because I was with you. 5 But now I am going to him who sent me; yet none of you asks me, 'Where are you going?' 6 But because I have said these things to you, sorrow has filled your hearts. 7 Nevertheless I tell you the truth: it is to your advantage that I go away, for if I do not go away, the Counselor will not come to you; but if I go, I will send him to you. 8 And when he comes, he will con-

h Or slaves   *i* Or slave

16.8 The Holy Spirit's ministry to the world is defined as that of convincing the world of sin, of righteousness, and of judgment: (1) of sin, which is defined basically as the refusal to accept Jesus and His message; (2) of righteousness, inasmuch as the death of Jesus was not the shameful defeat on the cross, but the return of the resurrected Jesus to the Father by which His mission and message were vindicated and shown to be true; (3) of judgment, for the ministry, death, and resurrection of Jesus were the means whereby God condemned the evil ruler of this present age.

vince^x the world concerning sin and righteousness and judgment: 9 concerning sin, because they do not believe in me; 10 concerning righteousness, because I go to the Father, and you will see me no more; 11 concerning judgment, because the ruler of this world is judged.

The illuminating power of the Holy Spirit (16.12–15)

12 "I have yet many things to say to you, but you cannot bear them now. 13 When the Spirit of truth comes, he will guide you into all the truth; for he will not speak on his own authority, but whatever he hears he will speak, and he will declare to you the things that are to come. 14 He will glorify me, for he will take what is mine and declare it to you. 15 All that the Father has is mine; therefore I said that he will take what is mine and declare it to you.

Jesus' farewell to his disciples (16.16–33)

16 "A little while, and you will see me no more; again a little while, and you will see me." 17 Some of his disciples said to one another, "What is this that he says to us, 'A little while, and you will not see me, and again a little while, and you will see me'; and, 'because I go to the Father'?" 18 They said, "What does he mean by 'a little while'? We do not know what he means." 19 Jesus knew that they wanted to ask him; so he said to them, "Is this what you are asking yourselves, what I meant by saying, 'A little while, and you will not see me, and again a little while, and you will see me'? 20 Truly, truly, I say to you, you will weep and lament, but the world will rejoice; you will be sorrowful, but your sorrow will turn into joy. 21 When a woman is in travail she has sorrow, because her hour has come; but when she is delivered of the child, she no longer remembers the anguish, for joy that a child^j is born into the world. 22 So you have sorrow now, but I will see you again and your hearts will rejoice, and no one will take your joy from you. 23 In that day you will ask nothing of me. Truly, truly, I say to you, if you ask anything of the Father, he will give it to you in my name. 24 Hitherto you have asked nothing in my name; ask, and you will receive, that your joy may be full.

25 "I have said this to you in figures; the hour is coming when I shall no longer speak to you in figures but tell you plainly of the Father. 26 In that day you will ask in my name; and I do not say to you that I shall pray the Father for you; 27 for the Father himself loves you, because you have loved me and have believed that I came from the Father. 28 I came from the Father and have come into the world; again, I am leaving the world and going to the Father."

29 His disciples said, "Ah, now you are speaking plainly, not in any figure! 30 Now we know that you know all things, and need none to question you; by this we believe that you came from God."

x Or convict

j Greek a human being

16.9 Jn 15.22
16.10 Acts 3.14; 7.52; 17.31; 1 Pet 3.18
16.11 Jn 12.31
★16.12 Mk 4.33
16.13 Jn 14.17,26
16.14 Jn 7.39
16.15 Jn 17.10
16.16 Jn 7.33; 14.18–24; 13.3
16.17 ver 16,5
16.19 Mk 9.32
16.20 Lk 23.27; Jn 20.20
16.21 1 Thess 5.3
16.22 ver 6,16
16.23 Mt 7.7; Jn 14.13; 15.16
16.24 Jn 15.11
16.25 Jn 10.6; Mt 13.34
16.27 Jn 14.21,23
16.28 Jn 13.3
16.29 ver 25
16.30 Jn 8.42

16.12 God's revelation is progressive. Christ revealed to the disciples only what they were then ready to receive and understand. But He told them to expect further revelation after His ascension at the coming of the Holy Spirit, and to accept this revelation as the Word of God. We may reasonably infer that this promise applies to the additional revealed truths contained in the New Testament.

16.32
Mt 26.31;
Mk 14.27

*16.33
Jn 14.27;
Col 1.20;
Rom 8.37;
Rev 3.21

17.1
Jn 12.23;
13.32
17.2
Dan 7.14;
Heb 2.8;
Jn 6.37
17.3
Jn 5.44;
3.34; 6.29,
57
17.4
Jn 13.31;
4.34; 14.31
17.5
Jn 1.1;
Phil 2.6
17.6
Jn 6.37,39
17.8
Jn 8.28;
16.27
17.9
Lk 22.32;
Jn 14.16
17.10
Jn 16.15
17.11
Jn 13.1;
7.33;
Rev 19.12;
Jn 10.30
17.12
Heb 2.13;
Jn 6.39;
18.9; 6.70
17.14
Jn 15.19;
8.23
17.15
Mt 6.13
17.16
ver 14

31 Jesus answered them, "Do you now believe? 32 The hour is coming, indeed it has come, when you will be scattered, every man to his home, and will leave me alone; yet I am not alone, for the Father is with me. 33 I have said this to you, that in me you may have peace. In the world you have tribulation; but be of good cheer, I have overcome the world."

Christ's intercessory (high priestly) prayer (17.1–26)

1. The prayer to be glorified (17.1–5)

17 When Jesus had spoken these words, he lifted up his eyes to heaven and said, "Father, the hour has come; glorify thy Son that the Son may glorify thee, 2 since thou hast given him power over all flesh, to give eternal life to all whom thou hast given him. 3 And this is eternal life, that they know thee the only true God, and Jesus Christ whom thou hast sent. 4 I glorified thee on earth, having accomplished the work which thou gavest me to do; 5 and now, Father, glorify thou me in thy own presence with the glory which I had with thee before the world was made.

2. The prayer for the disciples (17.6–19)

6 "I have manifested thy name to the men whom thou gavest me out of the world; thine they were, and thou gavest them to me, and they have kept thy word. 7 Now they know that everything that thou hast given me is from thee; 8 for I have given them the words which thou gavest me, and they have received them and know in truth that I came from thee; and they have believed that thou didst send me. 9 I am praying for them; I am not praying for the world but for those whom thou hast given me, for they are thine; 10 all mine are thine, and thine are mine, and I am glorified in them. 11 And now I am no more in the world, but they are in the world, and I am coming to thee. Holy Father, keep them in thy name, which thou hast given me, that they may be one, even as we are one. 12 While I was with them, I kept them in thy name, which thou hast given me; I have guarded them, and none of them is lost but the son of perdition, that the scripture might be fulfilled. 13 But now I am coming to thee; and these things I speak in the world, that they may have my joy fulfilled in themselves. 14 I have given them thy word; and the world has hated them because they are not of the world, even as I am not of the world. 15 I do not pray that thou shouldst take them out of the world, but that thou shouldst keep them from the evil one.k 16 They are not of the

k Or from evil

16.33 The problem of suffering in the Old Testament is dealt with most fully in the Book of Job. In the New Testament, Christ promised His people tribulation (from the Greek word, *thlipsis*, meaning "pressure" or "affliction"). Believers must be careful to distinguish the different forms of pressure and realize the sources from which they come. In general, there are three orders of affliction: (1) that which comes simply because we are alive and share in the fallen nature of the human race (experiences like natural catastrophe, sickness, bereavement, and death); (2) afflictions which (by God's permission) come to us from the malice of Satan because we have been delivered from his power and he strives to bring us back under bondage (1 Pet 5.8); (3) afflictions which come more directly from the hand of God Himself and are designed to purify or refine us (Job 23.10). These often overlap. Thus God can and does use the afflictions in the first two categories to accomplish His work in us. Yet Christians should be careful to avoid attributing to God, or even to Satan, that which they bring upon themselves. Afflictions resulting from our own folly we must face up to as our personal responsibility.

world, even as I am not of the world. 17 Sanctify them in the truth; thy word is truth. 18As thou didst send me into the world, so I have sent them into the world. 19And for their sake I consecrate myself, that they also may be consecrated in truth.

17.17	Jn 15.3
17.18	Jn 20.21
17.19	Jn 15.13

3. The prayer for the church (17.20–26)

20 "I do not pray for these only, but also for those who believe in me through their word, 21 that they may all be one; even as thou, Father, art in me, and I in thee, that they also may be in us, so that the world may believe that thou hast sent me. 22 The glory which thou hast given me I have given to them, that they may be one even as we are one, 23 I in them and thou in me, that they may become perfectly one, so that the world may know that thou hast sent me and hast loved them even as thou hast loved me. 24 Father, I desire that they also, whom thou hast given me, may be with me where I am, to behold my glory which thou hast given me in thy love for me before the foundation of the world. 25 O righteous Father, the world has not known thee, but I have known thee; and these know that thou hast sent me. 26 I made known to them thy name, and I will make it known, that the love with which thou hast loved me may be in them, and I in them."

★17.21	Jn 10.38
17.22	Jn 14.20
17.24	Jn 12.26; Mt 25.34; ver 5
17.25	Jn 15.21; 16.3; 7.29; Jn 16.27
17.26	ver 6; Jn 15.9

Jesus' betrayal and arrest
(18.1–11; Mt 26.47–56; Mk 14.43–50; Lk 22.27–53)

18 When Jesus had spoken these words, he went forth with his disciples across the Kĭdrŏn valley, where there was a garden, which he and his disciples entered. 2 Now Judas, who betrayed him, also knew the place; for Jesus often met there with his disciples. 3 So Judas, procuring a band of soldiers and some officers from the chief priests and the Phăr'ĭsēēṣ, went there with lanterns and torches and weapons. 4 Then Jesus, knowing all that was to befall him, came forward and said to them, "Whom do you seek?" 5 They answered him, "Jesus of Năz'ărĕth." Jesus said to them, "I am he." Judas, who betrayed him, was standing with them. 6 When he said to them, "I am he," they drew back and fell to the ground. 7Again he asked them, "Whom do you seek?" And they said, "Jesus of Năz'ărĕth." 8 Jesus answered, "I told you that I am he; so, if you seek me, let these men go." 9 This was to fulfil the word which he had spoken, "Of those whom thou gavest me I

18.1	2 Sam 15.23
18.2	Lk 21.37; 22.39
18.3	Acts 1.16
18.4	Jn 6.64; 13.1,11; ver 7
18.7	ver 4
18.9	Jn 17.12

17.21 The communion of saints is a central theme in this high-priestly prayer of Christ. It is His will that His people be organically united with one another in life and experience as they are united in Him in spirit. The communion of saints consists in: (1) fellowship with the Father and the Son through the Spirit (1 Jn 1.3); (2) fellow-citizenship with the saints already in glory (Heb 12.22–24); (3) fellowship with other believers here on earth (1 Jn 1.3; Gal 2.9). This organic unity, whereby all regenerate believers belong to the mystical Body of Christ, is here envisioned as a glorious spiritual reality to be brought to pass immediately by the Cross, the Resurrection, and the bestowal of the Spirit. Because of their spiritual solidarity in Christ, the saints partake of both privileges and obligations. On the one hand they enjoy a bond of fellowship far closer than blood. As Christ said (Mk 10.29–30), ". . . there is no one who has left house or brothers or sisters or mother or father or children or lands, for my sake and for the gospel, who will not receive a hundredfold now in this time, houses and brothers and sisters and mothers and children and lands, with persecutions, and in the age to come eternal life." On the other hand, the saints are under obligation to (1) pray for one another (2 Cor 1.11; Eph 6.18); (2) exhort one another (Col 3.16; Heb 10.25); (3) comfort and edify one another (1 Thess 4.18; 5.11). The unity of the saints is expressed in public worship and in the ordinances (or sacraments) of baptism and the Lord's Supper.

*18.10
18.11
Mt 20.22

lost not one." 10 Then Simon Peter, having a sword, drew it and struck the high priest's slave and cut off his right ear. The slave's name was Màlchùs. 11 Jesus said to Peter, "Put your sword into its sheath; shall I not drink the cup which the Father has given me?"

Jesus before the Jewish authorities
(18.12–14; see ver 19–24)

18.13
Mt 26.57;
Mk 14.53;
Lk 22.54
18.14
Jn 11.49–51

12 So the band of soldiers and their captain and the officers of the Jews seized Jesus and bound him. 13 First they led him to Annas; for he was the father-in-law of Càiàphàs, who was high priest that year. 14 It was Càiàphàs who had given counsel to the Jews that it was expedient that one man should die for the people.

Peter's denial of Jesus (18.15–18; ver 25–27; Mt 26.69–75;
Mk 14.66–72; Lk 22.55–62)

*18.15
Mt 26.58;
Mk 14.54;
Lk 22.54

15 Simon Peter followed Jesus, and so did another disciple. As this disciple was known to the high priest, he entered the court of the high priest along with Jesus, 16 while Peter stood outside at the door. So the other disciple, who was known to the high priest, went out and spoke to the maid who kept the door, and brought Peter in. 17 The maid who kept the door said to Peter, "Are not you also one of this man's disciples?" He said, "I am not." 18 Now the servants¹ and officers had made a charcoal fire, because it was cold, and they were standing and warming themselves; Peter also was with them, standing and warming himself.

18.17
ver 25

18.18
Mk 14.54,
67;
Jn 21.9

Jesus before the Jewish authorities
(18.19–27; see ver 12–14)

18.19
Mt 26.59–
68;
Mk 14.55–
65;
Lk 22.63–71
18.20
Mt 26.55;
Jn 7.26
18.22
ver 3;
Jn 19.3
18.23
Mt 5.39;
Acts 23.2–5
*18.24
ver 13

19 The high priest then questioned Jesus about his disciples and his teaching. 20 Jesus answered him, "I have spoken openly to the world; I have always taught in synagogues and in the temple, where all Jews come together; I have said nothing secretly. 21 Why do you ask me? Ask those who have heard me, what I said to them; they know what I said." 22 When he had said this, one of the officers standing by struck Jesus with his hand, saying, "Is that how you answer the high priest?" 23 Jesus answered him, "If I have spoken wrongly, bear witness to the wrong; but if I have spoken rightly, why do you strike me?" 24Annas then sent him bound to Càiàphàs the high priest.

18.25
ver 18
18.26
ver 10

25 Now Simon Peter was standing and warming himself. They said to him, "Are not you also one of his disciples?" He denied it and said, "I am not." 26 One of the servants¹ of the high priest, a kinsman of the man whose ear Peter had cut off, asked, "Did I not see you in the garden with him?" 27 Peter again denied it; and at once the cock crowed.

18.27
Jn 13.38

¹ Or slaves

18.10 Only in John's Gospel is it recorded that it was Peter who cut off the ear of the high priest's servant. Mt 26.51 and Mk 14.47 simply indicate that it was "one of them." Lk 22.50 does say one of them.

18.15 See note to Mk 14.71 on Peter's denial of Christ. See also Introduction to John relative to the term another disciple.

18.24 See note to Mt 26.57 on Caiaphas, high priest.

John 18.28–40

Jesus before Pontius Pilate
(18.28–19.16; Mt 27.11–16; Mk 15.2–15; Lk 23.3–25)

1. Pilate demands the indictment (18.28–32)

28 Then they led Jesus from the house of Cāi′áphás to the praētor′ïüm. It was early. They themselves did not enter the praetorium, so that they might not be defiled, but might eat the passover. 29 So Pīláte went out to them and said, "What accusation do you bring against this man?" 30 They answered him, "If this man were not an evildoer, we would not have handed him over." 31 Pīláte said to them, "Take him yourselves and judge him by your own law." The Jews said to him, "It is not lawful for us to put any man to death." 32 This was to fulfil the word which Jesus had spoken to show by what death he was to die.

2. Pilate's first questioning of Jesus (18.33–38a)

33 Pīláte entered the praētor′ïüm again and called Jesus, and said to him, "Are you the King of the Jews?" 34 Jesus answered, "Do you say this of your own accord, or did others say it to you about me?" 35 Pīláte answered, "Am I a Jew? Your own nation and the chief priests have handed you over to me; what have you done?" 36 Jesus answered, "My kingship is not of this world; if my kingship were of this world, my servants would fight, that I might not be handed over to the Jews; but my kingship is not from the world." 37 Pīláte said to him, "So you are a king?" Jesus answered, "You say that I am a king. For this I was born, and for this I have come into the world, to bear witness to the truth. Every one who is of the truth hears my voice." 38 Pīláte said to him, "What is truth?"

3. The people demand Barabbas (18.38b–40)

After he had said this, he went out to the Jews again, and told them, "I find no crime in him. 39 But you have a custom that I should release one man for you at the Passover; will you have me release for you the King of the Jews?" 40 They cried out again, "Not this man, but Báráb′bás!" Now Barabbas was a robber.

Marginal references:

18.28 Mt 27.1,2; Mk 15.1; Lk 23.1; Jn 11.55; Acts 11.3
*18.29
*18.32 Mt 20.19; Jn 12.32,33
*18.33 ver 28,29; Jn 19.9; Lk 23.3
*18.36 Mt 26.53; Lk 17.21; Jn 6.15
18.37 Jn 8.47; 1 Jn 3.19; 4.6
18.38 Jn 19.4,6
18.39 Mt 27.15–18,20–23; Mk 15.6–15; Lk 23.18–25
18.40 Acts 3.14

18.29 See note to Mk 15.1 on Pontius Pilate.

18.32 The Jewish method of execution was by stoning (cf. 8.5; Acts 7.58, 59). But Jesus had said that He would be *lifted up* (3.14; 8.28; 12.32, 34), which the evangelist here interprets as a prediction of His crucifixion, whereby He was lifted up from the earth.

18.33 *praetorium*, official quarters of Pontius Pilate, praetorian guards and high court officers. Jesus was crowned with thorns in the praetorium (Mk 15.16, 17).

18.36 Christ is King, but His kingdom is not of this present world-system. His is a spiritual and eternal kingdom. According to the interpretation of many, the one-thousand-year reign spoken of in Rev 20.4 refers to a future complete domination of Christ over the world. Although Christ did not come into the world in order to condemn mankind (3.17), His ultimate purpose is to impose God's judgment upon the unrepentant and rebellious world-system and to wrest the

control of world affairs from the grasp of Satan, who constantly aspires to become (for the present) the ruler of this world (12.31). Implicit in the kingship of Christ are three necessary elements: (1) He must have absolute sovereignty; (2) He must have a people to rule over; (3) He must have a definite territory under His domain. In a spiritual sense, Christ has all of these now. He is seated at the right hand of the Father (Acts 2.34; Heb 1.3; Rev 3.21); in His church He certainly has a people to rule over, and the Father has committed to Him all authority in heaven and on earth (Mt 28.18). In the plan of God it was never intended that Christ should set up an earthly kingdom during His First Advent; apart from the Cross He could not have been the *Lamb that was slain* (Rev 13.8), nor could He have taken away the *sin of the world* (1.29). He came the first time in humiliation to die on Calvary. He will come the second time in visible glory and irresistible power as *King of kings* (Rev 19.16), Lord of the whole universe (Phil 2.10, 11).

4. Pilate scourges Jesus, and questions him again (19.1–11)

19 Then Pilāte took Jesus and scourged him. 2And the soldiers plaited a crown of thorns, and put it on his head, and arrayed him in a purple robe; 3 they came up to him, saying, "Hail, King of the Jews!" and struck him with their hands. 4 Pilate went out again, and said to them, "See, I am bringing him out to you, that you may know that I find no crime in him." 5 So Jesus came out, wearing the crown of thorns and the purple robe. Pilāte said to them, "Behold the man!" 6 When the chief priests and the officers saw him, they cried out, "Crucify him, crucify him!" Pilāte said to them, "Take him yourselves and crucify him, for I find no crime in him." 7 The Jews answered him, "We have a law, and by that law he ought to die, because he has made himself the Son of God." 8 When Pilāte heard these words, he was the more afraid; 9 he entered the praētor'ĭum again and said to Jesus, "Where are you from?" But Jesus gave no answer. 10 Pilāte therefore said to him, "You will not speak to me? Do you not know that I have power to release you, and power to crucify you?" 11 Jesus answered him, "You would have no power over me unless it had been given you from above; therefore he who delivered me to you has the greater sin."

5. Pilate delivers Jesus (19.12–16)

12 Upon this Pilāte sought to release him, but the Jews cried out, "If you release this man, you are not Caesar's friend; every one who makes himself a king sets himself against Caesar." 13 When Pilāte heard these words, he brought Jesus out and sat down on the judgment seat at a place called The Pavement, and in Hebrew, Găb'bāthā. 14 Now it was the day of Preparation of the Passover; it was about the sixth hour. He said to the Jews, "Behold your King!" 15 They cried out, "Away with him, away with him, crucify him!" Pilāte said to them, "Shall I crucify your King?" The chief priests answered, "We have no king but Caesar." 16 Then he handed him over to them to be crucified.

The Crucifixion and burial of Jesus (19.17–42)

1. Jesus crucified
(19.17–27; Mt 27.32–44; Mk 15.21–32; Lk 23.32–43)

17 So they took Jesus, and he went out, bearing his own cross, to the place called the place of a skull, which is called in Hebrew Gŏl'gŏthā. 18 There they crucified him, and with him two others, one on either side, and Jesus between them. 19 Pilāte also wrote a title and put it on the cross; it read, "Jesus of Năz'ărĕth, the King of the Jews." 20 Many of the Jews read this title, for the place where Jesus was crucified was near the city; and it was written in Hebrew, in Latin, and in Greek. 21 The chief priests of the Jews then said to Pilāte, "Do not write, 'The King of the Jews,' but, 'This man said, I am King of the Jews.'" 22 Pilāte answered, "What I have written I have written."

Margin references: 19.1 Mt 27.26; 19.2 Mt 27.27–30; Mk 15.16–19; 19.3 Jn 18.22; 19.4 ver 6; Jn 18.38; 19.5 ver 2; 19.6 Acts 3.13; 19.7 Lev 24.16; Mt 26.63–66; Jn 5.18; 10.33; 19.9 Isa 53.7; Mt 27.12,14; *19.11 Rom 13.1; Jn 18.28ff; 19.12 Lk 23.2; 19.13 Mt 27.19; 19.14 Mt 27.62; Mk 15.25; ver 19,21; 19.16 Mt 27.26; Mk 15.15; Lk 23.25; 19.17 Lk 23.26; *19.19; 19.21 ver 14

19.11 *he who delivered me to you* is taken by some to allude to Caiaphas, the high priest under whose leadership the Jews *delivered* (*paradidomi, handed . . . over*, 18.30, 35) Jesus to Pilate. Caiaphas was thus ultimately responsible for Jesus' arrest and condemnation (18.14, 28). Others refer the saying to Judas, who *delivered* (*paradidomi, betrayed*, 6.64, 71; 12.4; 13.2, 11, 21; 18.2, 5) Jesus.

19.19 *cross*, see the note to Mt 27.37.

23 When the soldiers had crucified Jesus they took his garments and made four parts, one for each soldier; also his tunic. But the tunic was without seam, woven from top to bottom; 24 so they said to one another, "Let us not tear it, but cast lots for it to see whose it shall be." This was to fulfil the scripture,

"They parted my garments among them,
and for my clothing they cast lots."

25 So the soldiers did this. But standing by the cross of Jesus were his mother, and his mother's sister, Mary the wife of Clōpàs, and Mary Măg′dàlēne. 26 When Jesus saw his mother, and the disciple whom he loved standing near, he said to his mother, "Woman, behold, your son!" 27 Then he said to the disciple, "Behold, your mother!" And from that hour the disciple took her to his own home.

2. The death of Jesus
(19.28–37; Mt 27.45–50; Mk 15.33–41; Lk 23.44–49)

28 After this Jesus, knowing that all was now finished, said (to fulfil the scripture), "I thirst." 29 A bowl full of vinegar stood there; so they put a sponge full of the vinegar on hyssop and held it to his mouth. 30 When Jesus had received the vinegar, he said, "It is finished"; and he bowed his head and gave up his spirit.

31 Since it was the day of Preparation, in order to prevent the bodies from remaining on the cross on the sabbath (for that sabbath was a high day), the Jews asked Pīlàte that their legs might be broken, and that they might be taken away. 32 So the soldiers came and broke the legs of the first, and of the other who had been crucified with him; 33 but when they came to Jesus and saw that he was already dead, they did not break his legs. 34 But one of the soldiers pierced his side with a spear, and at once there came out blood and water. 35 He who saw it has borne witness—his testimony is true, and he knows that he tells the truth—that you also may believe. 36 For these things took place that the scripture might be fulfilled, "Not a bone of him shall be broken." 37 And again another scripture says, "They shall look on him whom they have pierced."

3. Jesus laid in the tomb
(19.38–42; Mt 27.57–61; Mk 15.42–47; Lk 23.50–56)

38 After this Joseph of Ạrimáthē′ạ, who was a disciple of Jesus, but secretly, for fear of the Jews, asked Pīlàte that he might take away the body of Jesus, and Pīlàte gave him leave. So he came and took away his body. 39 Nĭcōdē′mùs also, who had at first come to him by night, came bringing a mixture of myrrh and aloes, about a hundred pounds' weight. 40 They took the body of Jesus, and bound it in linen cloths with the spices, as is the burial custom of the Jews. 41 Now in the place where he was crucified there was a garden, and in the garden a new tomb where no one had ever been

Cross references:
19.24 Ex 28.32; Ps 22.18
*19.25 Mt 27.55, 56; Mk 15.40, 41; Lk 23.49; 24.18; Jn 20.1,18
19.26 Jn 13.23; 20.2; 21.20; 2.4
*19.28 Jn 13.1; 17.4; Ps 69.21
19.30 Jn 17.4
19.31 Deut 21.23; Ex 12.16
19.32 ver 18
19.34 1 Jn 5.6,8
19.35 Jn 15.27; 21.24
19.36 Ex 12.46; Num 9.12; Ps 34.20
19.37 Zech 12.10
19.39 Jn 3.1; 7.50
19.40 Jn 11.44; Mt 26.12; Jn 20.5,7; Lk 24.12

laid. 42 So because of the Jewish day of Preparation, as the tomb
was close at hand, they laid Jesus there.

The Resurrection of Jesus Christ
(20.1–10; Mt 28.1–10; Mk 16.1–8; Lk 24.1–11)

20 Now on the first day of the week Mary Măg'dálēne came
to the tomb early, while it was still dark, and saw that the
stone had been taken away from the tomb. 2 So she ran, and went
to Simon Peter and the other disciple, the one whom Jesus loved,
and said to them, "They have taken the Lord out of the tomb, and
we do not know where they have laid him." 3 Peter then came out
with the other disciple, and they went toward the tomb. 4 They
both ran, but the other disciple outran Peter and reached the
tomb first; 5 and stooping to look in, he saw the linen cloths lying
there, but he did not go in. 6 Then Simon Peter came, following
him, and went into the tomb; he saw the linen cloths lying, 7 and
the napkin, which had been on his head, not lying with the linen
cloths but rolled up in a place by itself. 8 Then the other disciple,
who reached the tomb first, also went in, and he saw and believed;
9 for as yet they did not know the scripture, that he must rise from
the dead. 10 Then the disciples went back to their homes.

Jesus appears to Mary Magdalene (20.11–18)

11 But Mary stood weeping outside the tomb, and as she wept
she stooped to look into the tomb; 12 and she saw two angels in
white, sitting where the body of Jesus had lain, one at the head
and one at the feet. 13 They said to her, "Woman, why are you
weeping?" She said to them, "Because they have taken away my
Lord, and I do not know where they have laid him." 14 Saying
this, she turned round and saw Jesus standing, but she did not
know that it was Jesus. 15 Jesus said to her, "Woman, why are you
weeping? Whom do you seek?" Supposing him to be the gardener,
she said to him, "Sir, if you have carried him away, tell me where
you have laid him, and I will take him away." 16 Jesus said to her,
"Mary." She turned and said to him in Hebrew, "Răb-bō'nī!"
(which means Teacher). 17 Jesus said to her, "Do not hold me, for
I have not yet ascended to the Father; but go to my brethren and
say to them, I am ascending to my Father and your Father, to my
God and your God." 18 Mary Măg'dálēne went and said to the
disciples, "I have seen the Lord"; and she told them that he had
said these things to her.

Jesus appears to the ten in Jerusalem
(20.19–25; Lk 24.36–43)

19 On the evening of that day, the first day of the week, the

---

Margin references (left column):

19.42
ver 14,31,
20,41

20.1
Mt 27.60,66

20.2
Jn 13.23;
19.26;
21.7,20,24

20.3
Lk 24.12

20.5
Jn 19.40

20.8
ver 4

20.9
Mt 22.29;
Lk 24.26,46

*20.11
Mk 16.5;
ver 5

20.12
Mt 28.2,3;
Mk 16.5;
Lk 24.4

20.13
ver 2

20.14
Mt 28.9;
Jn 21.4

20.15
ver 13

20.17
Mt 28.10;
ver 27;
Jn 7.33

20.18
Lk 24.10,13

20.19
Lk 24.36–
39;
ver 21,26

20.11 The order of Christ's appearances
after the resurrection seems to be as follows:
(1) To Mary Magdalene and the other women
(Mt 28.9; Jn 20.11–18; Mk 16.9, 10); (2) to
the disciples on the Emmaus road (Lk 24.13-
15; Mk 16.12); (3) to Peter (Lk 24.34; 1 Cor
15.5); (4) to the ten in the upper room (20.19);
(5) to the eleven in the upper room with
Thomas present (20.26; Lk 24.36; Mk 16.14);
(6) to the disciples at the Sea of Tiberias
(21.1–24); (7) to the eleven on a mountain in
Galilee (Mt 28.16–20); (8) to the five hundred
brethren (1 Cor 15.6); (9) to James (1 Cor
15.7); (10) to all the apostles (1 Cor 15.7);
(11) to those who witnessed His ascension
(Lk 24.50, 51; Acts 1.3–12; Mk 16.19).

doors being shut where the disciples were, for fear of the Jews, Jesus came and stood among them and said to them, "Peace be with you." 20 When he had said this, he showed them his hands and his side. Then the disciples were glad when they saw the Lord. 21 Jesus said to them again, "Peace be with you. As the Father has sent me, even so I send you." 22And when he had said this, he breathed on them, and said to them, "Receive the Holy Spirit. 23 If you forgive the sins of any, they are forgiven; if you retain the sins of any, they are retained."

24 Now Thomas, one of the twelve, called the Twin, was not with them when Jesus came. 25 So the other disciples told him, "We have seen the Lord." But he said to them, "Unless I see in his hands the print of the nails, and place my finger in the mark of the nails, and place my hand in his side, I will not believe."

Jesus appears to Thomas and the ten (20.26–29)

26 Eight days later, his disciples were again in the house, and Thomas was with them. The doors were shut, but Jesus came and stood among them, and said, "Peace be with you." 27 Then he said to Thomas, "Put your finger here, and see my hands; and put out your hand, and place it in my side; do not be faithless, but believing." 28 Thomas answered him, "My Lord and my God!" 29 Jesus said to him, "Have you believed because you have seen me? Blessed are those who have not seen and yet believe."

The reason why John wrote his Gospel (20.30,31)

30 Now Jesus did many other signs in the presence of the disciples, which are not written in this book; 31 but these are written that you may believe that Jesus is the Christ, the Son of God, and that believing you may have life in his name.

Epilogue: (21.1–25)

1. Jesus appears to the disciples at the Sea of Tiberias (21.1–14)

21 After this Jesus revealed himself again to the disciples by the Sea of Tĭbër'ĭ-ăs; and he revealed himself in this way. 2 Simon Peter, Thomas called the Twin, Năthăn'ä-ĕl of Cānä in Găl'ĭleē, the sons of Zĕb'ĕdeē, and two others of his disciples were together. 3 Simon Peter said to them, "I am going fishing." They said to him, "We will go with you." They went out and got into the boat; but that night they caught nothing.

Cross references (right margin):

20.20 Lk 24.39, 40; Jn 16.20,22
20.21 Mt 28.19; Jn 17.18,19
*20.23 Mt 16.19; 18.18
20.24 Jn 11.16
20.25 ver 20
20.26 ver 21
20.27 ver 25; Lk 24.40
*20.28
20.29 I Pet 1.8
20.30 Jn 21.25
20.31 Jn 19.35; 3.15
*21.1 Jn 20.19, 26; 6.1
21.2 Jn 11.16; 1.45; Mt 4.21; Mk 1.19; Lk 5.10
21.3 Lk 5.5

20.23 See note to Mt 16.19 on the keys of the kingdom.

20.28 "Deity of Christ." The watershed of Christian theology is how one answers the question, "What do you think of Christ? Whose son is He?" The biblical evidences show conclusively that Christ is God. He is spoken of as eternally pre-existent (Isa 9.6; Jn 1.1, 2; Heb 13.8; Rev 22.13). He bore testimony to Himself that He was the only Son of God (10.30; 14.9; Mt 11.27; Mk 14.61, 62). In the New Testament letters He is sometimes referred to as God (Tit 2.13; 1 Jn 5.20). Attributes of deity are assigned to Him: (1) holiness (Heb 7.26; Jn 8.46; 2 Cor 5.21);

(2) omnipresence (Mt 18.20; 28.20); (3) omnipotence (Mt 28.18; Heb 1.3; Rev 1.8); (4) immutability (Heb 1.11, 12; 13.8); (5) creative activity (Col 1.16, 17; Jn 1.3; 1 Cor 8.6; Heb 1.8, 10); (6) His right to be worshiped (Mt 2.11; 28.9; 14.33; Heb 1.6; Phil 2.10); (7) His right to forgive sins (Mk 2.5, 7, 9, 10; Lk 24.47; Jn 1.29; Acts 10.43; 1 Jn 1.7). The deity of Christ is the foundation of the Christian faith. The denial of it invalidates the entire structure of Christian theology.

21.1 The Sea (or Lake) of Tiberias was also called Lake Gennesaret (Lk 5.1) and Sea of Galilee (Jn 6.1).

21.4
Jn 20.14
21.5
Lk 24.41
21.6
Lk 5.4,6,7
21.7
Jn 13.23;
20.2;
ver 20
21.9
ver 10,13
21.13
ver 9
21.14
Jn 20.19,26
*21.15
Jn 13.37;
Mt 26.33;
Mk 14.29
21.16
Mt 2.6;
Acts 20.28;
1 Pet 5.2;
Rev 7.17
21.17
Jn 16.30;
ver 16
21.19
2 Pet 1.14
21.20
ver 7;
Jn 13.25
21.22
Mt 16.27,
28; 25.31;
1 Cor 4.5;
11.26;
Rev 2.25;
3.11;
22.7,20
21.23
Acts 1.15

4 Just as day was breaking, Jesus stood on the beach; yet the disciples did not know that it was Jesus. 5 Jesus said to them, "Children, have you any fish?" They answered him, "No." 6 He said to them, "Cast the net on the right side of the boat, and you will find some." So they cast it, and now they were not able to haul it in, for the quantity of fish. 7 That disciple whom Jesus loved said to Peter, "It is the Lord!" When Simon Peter heard that it was the Lord, he put on his clothes, for he was stripped for work, and sprang into the sea. 8 But the other disciples came in the boat, dragging the net full of fish, for they were not far from the land, but about a hundred yards^m off.

9 When they got out on land, they saw a charcoal fire there, with fish lying on it, and bread. 10 Jesus said to them, "Bring some of the fish that you have just caught." 11 So Simon Peter went aboard and hauled the net ashore, full of large fish, a hundred and fifty-three of them; and although there were so many, the net was not torn. 12 Jesus said to them, "Come and have breakfast." Now none of the disciples dared ask him, "Who are you?" They knew it was the Lord. 13 Jesus came and took the bread and gave it to them, and so with the fish. 14 This was now the third time that Jesus was revealed to the disciples after he was raised from the dead.

2. Jesus questions Peter (21.15–23)

15 When they had finished breakfast, Jesus said to Simon Peter, "Simon, son of John, do you love me more than these?" He said to him, "Yes, Lord; you know that I love you." He said to him, "Feed my lambs." 16A second time he said to him, "Simon, son of John, do you love me?" He said to him, "Yes, Lord; you know that I love you." He said to him, "Tend my sheep." 17 He said to him the third time, "Simon, son of John, do you love me?" Peter was grieved because he said to him the third time, "Do you love me?" And he said to him, "Lord, you know everything; you know that I love you." Jesus said to him, "Feed my sheep. 18 Truly, truly, I say to you, when you were young, you girded yourself and walked where you would; but when you are old, you will stretch out your hands, and another will gird you and carry you where you do not wish to go." 19 (This he said to show by what death he was to glorify God.) And after this he said to him, "Follow me."

20 Peter turned and saw following them the disciple whom Jesus loved, who had lain close to his breast at the supper and had said, "Lord, who is it that is going to betray you?" 21 When Peter saw him, he said to Jesus, "Lord, what about this man?" 22 Jesus said to him, "If it is my will that he remain until I come, what is that to you? Follow me!" 23 The saying spread abroad among the brethren that this disciple was not to die; yet Jesus did not say to him

---

^{m} Greek two hundred cubits

21.15 The question, "Do you love me more than these?" is variously understood. Some believe that Jesus was asking, "Do you love me more than you love these other disciples"? Others take it to mean, "Do you love me more than these other disciples love me?" Still others, "Do you love me more than your boat, nets, and fishes?" It should also be noted that in ver 15–17, Jesus' first two uses of the word love is from the Greek agapaō, meaning "high, devoted love." His third use of love is translated from phileō, the humbler word for love (as love for a friend). Peter makes no claim to superior love.

that he was not to die, but, "If it is my will that he remain until I come, what is that to you?"

3. *The authentication (21.24, 25)*

24 This is the disciple who is bearing witness to these things, and who has written these things; and we know that his testimony is true.

25 But there are also many other things which Jesus did; were every one of them to be written, I suppose that the world itself could not contain the books that would be written.

21.24
Jn 15.27;
19.35

21.25
Jn 20.30

INTRODUCTION TO

THE

ACTS OF THE APOSTLES

Authorship and Background: As a companion volume to the Gospel of Luke (1.1–2 with Lk 1.1–4), Acts continues the story of the Christian movement from the ascension of Christ to Paul's arrival in Rome some thirty years later. The author (for which see the Introduction to Luke) is a participant in some of the events recorded, as seen by the use of "we" and "us" in some passages (16.10–17; 20.5—21.18; 27.1—28.16).

It is generally assumed that Acts was written soon after Luke, so that its date of composition is placed A.D. 60–70 by some, A.D. 80–90 by others.

Characteristics: The book traces the development and spread of the Christian church from the coming of the Holy Spirit at Pentecost, to Paul's preaching the gospel in Rome "openly and unhindered" (28.30) for two whole years.

The title "Acts of the Apostles" is in some ways inadequate, for the book tells of the acts of only two of the twelve apostles: Peter, who dominates the early part of the book (1.15—12.17), and John (3.1—4.22; 8.14–25). The only other apostle of whom anything specific is said is James, brother of John, who was put to death by Herod Agrippa I (12.2). The other great names in the book are not of the Twelve: Stephen (6.8—7.60) and Philip (8.4–13, 26–40; 21.8), two of the seven helpers chosen by the Jerusalem church; in addition there are Barnabas (4.36, 37; 9.27; 11.22–30; 12.25—15.39), and James, brother of the Lord and leader in the Jerusalem church (cf. 1.14; 15.13–21; 21.18). The dominant figure is Paul, born Saul of Tarsus, first seen at the martyrdom of Stephen (7.58; 8.1). His conversion is narrated in 9.1–30 (with two other recitals of the event in 22.3–16; 26.4–18), and early activities in 11.25–30 and 12.25. From chapter 13 the book becomes in fact "The Acts of Paul," as the author traces the activity of the great apostle to the Gentiles in preaching throughout the Roman Empire.

Many would call the book "The Acts of the Holy Spirit," since it is the Holy Spirit who empowers, directs, and confirms the work of the apostles and missionaries. Acts presents the thrilling account of the life of the early Church, the opposition faced and overcome, the problems met and solved; and above all, it is the story of divine grace in its redemptive power in the lives of early believers.

The development of the Christian movement is told in terms of people and places; the author was necessarily selective and did not trace all developments or describe how the gospel was first preached in all regions. For example, how or by whom the work was started in Damascus and Rome is not stated. With broad strokes of his pen the author shows how the Christian message was originally proclaimed in Jerusalem, and then in all Judea and Samaria, and so throughout the Empire to the capital city of Rome, in fulfilment of the Lord's command and promise (1.8). From this story the reader learns of early Christian worship and fellowship, of the bold witness of plain and simple laymen, and of

the opposition of the Jews and of the authorities. The author is careful to point out that the Christians were not enemies of the Empire: every time the missionaries were brought before Roman authorities they were absolved of all charges of sedition or insurrection.

Through all problems and opposition, by the power of the Holy Spirit in the lives of these early witnesses, "the word of God grew and multiplied" (12.24).

Contents:

THE
ACTS OF THE APOSTLES

I. *The Church Founded at Jerusalem 1.1–8.3*

A. *Introduction*

1. *Preface*

1.1
Lk 1.1–4
1.2
Mt 28.19
1.3
Mt 28.17;
Lk 24.34,
36;
1 Cor 15.5–
7
1.4
Lk 24.49;
Jn 14.16
1.5
Acts 11.16

1 In the first book, O Thë-ŏph'ịlŭs, I have dealt with all that Jesus began to do and teach, 2 until the day when he was taken up, after he had given commandment through the Holy Spirit to the apostles whom he had chosen. 3 To them he presented himself alive after his passion by many proofs, appearing to them during forty days, and speaking of the kingdom of God. 4And while staying *a* with them he charged them not to depart from Jerusalem, but to wait for the promise of the Father, which, he said, "you heard from me, 5 for John baptized with water, but before many days you shall be baptized with the Holy Spirit."

2. *The ascension*

1.6
Mt 24.3
1.7
Mt 24.36;
Mk 13.32
1.8
Acts 2.1–4;
Lk 24.48;
Jn 15.27
*1.9
Lk 24.51;
ver 2
1.10
Lk 24.4;
Jn 20.12
*1.11
Mt 24.30;
Mk 13.26;
Jn 14.3

6 So when they had come together, they asked him, "Lord, will you at this time restore the kingdom to Israel?" 7 He said to them, "It is not for you to know times or seasons which the Father has fixed by his own authority. 8 But you shall receive power when the Holy Spirit has come upon you; and you shall be my witnesses in Jerusalem and in all Judë'ȧ and Sàmạr'ïȧ and to the end of the earth." 9And when he had said this, as they were looking on, he was lifted up, and a cloud took him out of their sight. 10And while they were gazing into heaven as he went, behold, two men stood by them in white robes, 11 and said, "Men of Găl'ịleē, why do you stand looking into heaven? This Jesus, who was taken up from you into heaven, will come in the same way as you saw him go into heaven."

B. *The origin of the church*

1. *The disciples in prayer*

1.13
Acts 9.37,
39; 20.8;
Mt 10.2–4;
Mk 3.16–
19;
Lk 6.14–16
1.14
Acts 2.1,46;
Lk 23.49,
55;
Mt 12.46

12 Then they returned to Jerusalem from the mount called Ol'ịvĕt, which is near Jerusalem, a sabbath day's journey away; 13 and when they had entered, they went up to the upper room, where they were staying, Peter and John and James and Andrew, Philip and Thomas, Barthŏl'ȯmew and Matthew, James the son of Ȧlphaē'ŭs and Simon the Zealot and Judas the son of James. 14All these with one accord devoted themselves to prayer, together

a Or eating

1.9 Jesus left the earth forty days after the resurrection to ascend to the right hand of the Father. He was in the presence of the eleven disciples and two angels (or possibly two glorified men, such as Moses and Elijah, who had appeared on the Mount of Transfiguration). This episode took place on the Mount of Olives near Bethany (Lk 24.50). The disciples were assured that He would come back personally and physically. (See also Eph 4.8; Ps 68.18.)

1.11 Here we are told that Christ will return to earth in the same manner as He ascended into heaven. Elsewhere we learn that He will come: (1) in flaming fire (2 Thess 1.7, 8); (2) in His own heavenly glory (Mt 25.31); (3) with His saints (1 Thess 3.13); (4) as a thief in the night (1 Thess 5.2; 2 Pet 3.10; Rev 16.15); (5) with a cry of command and the archangel's call (1 Thess 4.16); (6) in company with the angels (2 Thess 1.7); (7) suddenly (Mk 13.36).

with the women and Mary the mother of Jesus, and with his brothers.

2. The replacement of Judas Iscariot

15 In those days Peter stood up among the brethren (the company of persons was in all about a hundred and twenty), and said, 16 "Brethren, the scripture had to be fulfilled, which the Holy Spirit spoke beforehand by the mouth of David, concerning Judas who was guide to those who arrested Jesus. 17 For he was numbered among us, and was allotted his share in this ministry. 18 (Now this man bought a field with the reward of his wickedness; and falling headlong[b] he burst open in the middle and all his bowels gushed out. 19And it became known to all the inhabitants of Jerusalem, so that the field was called in their language Ȧkĕl'dámá, that is, Field of Blood.) 20 For it is written in the book of Psalms,

'Let his habitation become desolate,
    and let there be no one to live in it';
and
'His office let another take.'

21 So one of the men who have accompanied us during all the time that the Lord Jesus went in and out among us, 22 beginning from the baptism of John until the day when he was taken up from us— one of these men must become with us a witness to his resurrection." 23And they put forward two, Joseph called Barsäb'bás, who was surnamed Jústús, and Mátthī'ás. 24And they prayed and said, "Lord, who knowest the hearts of all men, show which one of these two thou hast chosen 25 to take the place in this ministry and apostleship from which Judas turned aside, to go to his own place." 26And they cast lots for them, and the lot fell on Mátthī'ás; and he was enrolled with the eleven apostles.

C. The advent of the Holy Spirit

1. The gift of the Spirit

2 When the day of Pĕn'tĕcost had come, they were all together in one place. 2And suddenly a sound came from heaven like

b Or swelling up

Cross references

1.15
Jn 21.23;
Acts 6.3;
9.30

1.16
Jn 13.18

1.17
Jn 6.70,71;
ver 25;
Acts 20.24;
21.19

1.18
Mt 27.3–
10;26.14,15

1.20
Ps 69.25;
109.8

1.21
Lk 24.3

1.22
Mk 1.1;
ver 8;
Acts 2.32

1.24
1 Sam 16.7;
Jer 17.10;
Acts 15.8;
Rom 8.27

*1.26
Lev 16.8

*2.1
Lev 23.15;
Deut 16.9;
Acts 1.14

2.2
Acts 4.31

1.26 Matthias is chosen as an apostle to be, with the other apostles, *a witness to his* (Christ's) *resurrection.* The primary function of the apostolic office is stressed throughout the narrative of the apostles' ministry in the early chapters of Acts. The central element of the apostolic message was the Resurrection of Christ (cf. 2.32; 3.14, 15; 4.1, 2, 10, 33; 5.30–32; 10.39–41; 13.30, 31). As these passages show, the apostles preached Christ's resurrection not simply as the resuscitation of one who had been dead, but as the proof and evidence of the fact that God had exalted Jesus to Messiah and Lord: His resurrection was at the same time His exaltation and enthronement as Leader and Savior (see especially 2.36; 5.31).

2.1 The *day of Pentecost* marks the birthday of the Christian church of which the risen and exalted Christ is Head. Note: (1) it was an altogether supernatural event as evi-

denced by the suddenness of its occurrence; (2) the sound like that of a rushing mighty wind revealed the presence of the Holy Spirit; (3) the tongues as of fire proclaiming Christ's message in the many different languages were a token of the ultimate preaching of the gospel to the ends of the earth; (4) the symbol of fire itself typified the holy zeal and divinely empowered utterance of those who would speak forth the divine message.

Pentecost, from the Greek *pentekostē*, "fiftieth day," was celebrated on the sixth or seventh day of Sivan (May–June), fifty days after Passover. One of the three great annual feasts, it was called in Hebrew *the feast of weeks* (cf. Deut 16.10), and was referred to also as *the day of the first fruits* (Num 28.26), or *feast of harvest* (Ex 23.16). This was the Jewish feast of the wheat harvest. For details of its celebration see Lev 23.15–21. It is further referred to in 20.16 and 1 Cor 16.8.

2.4
Acts 4.8,31;
9.17; 13.9,
52;
1 Cor 12.10,
11; 14.21
2.5
Acts 8.2
2.7
ver 12;
Acts 1.11
2.9
1 Pet 1.1;
Acts 6.9;
16.6;
Rom 16.5;
1 Cor
16.19;
2 Cor 1.8
2.12
ver 7
2.13
1 Cor 14.23
2.15
1 Thess 5.7
2.17
Joel 2.28–
32;
Zech 12.10;
Jn 7.38;
Acts 10.45;
21.9
2.18
Acts 21.4,9,
10
2.20
Mt 24.29;
Mk 13.24;
Lk 21.25
2.21
Rom 10.13
2.22
Jn 3.2;
Acts 10.38;
Jn 4.48
2.23
Mt 26.24;
Lk 22.22;
Acts 3.18;
4.28; 3.13
2.24
Acts 3.15;
Rom 4.24;
2 Cor 4.14;
Eph 1.20;
Col 2.12;
Heb 13.20;
1 Pet 1.21
2.25
Ps 16.8–11
2.27
Mt 11.23;
Acts 13.35

the rush of a mighty wind, and it filled all the house where they were sitting. 3And there appeared to them tongues as of fire, distributed and resting on each one of them. 4And they were all filled with the Holy Spirit and began to speak in other tongues, as the Spirit gave them utterance.

5 Now there were dwelling in Jerusalem Jews, devout men from every nation under heaven. 6And at this sound the multitude came together, and they were bewildered, because each one heard them speaking in his own language. 7And they were amazed and wondered, saying, "Are not all these who are speaking Găl̆ilē′ăns? 8And how is it that we hear, each of us in his own native language? 9 Par′thĭăns and Mēdes and Ē′lămītes and residents of Mĕsŏpŏtā′-mĭă, Judē′ă and Căppădō′çĭă, Pŏntŭs and Asia, 10 Phrў̄ğ′ĭă and Pămphў̄l′ĭă, Egypt and the parts of Libya belonging to Çў̄rē′nĕ, and visitors from Rome, both Jews and proselytes, 11 Crētăns and Arabians, we hear them telling in our own tongues the mighty works of God." 12And all were amazed and perplexed, saying to one another, "What does this mean?" 13 But others mocking said, "They are filled with new wine."

2. Peter's Pentecostal sermon

14 But Peter, standing with the eleven, lifted up his voice and addressed them, "Men of Judē′ă and all who dwell in Jerusalem, let this be known to you, and give ear to my words. 15 For these men are not drunk, as you suppose, since it is only the third hour of the day; 16 but this is what was spoken by the prophet Jōĕl:
17 'And in the last days it shall be, God declares,
that I will pour out my Spirit upon all flesh,
and your sons and your daughters shall prophesy,
and your young men shall see visions,
and your old men shall dream dreams;
18 yea, and on my menservants and my maidservants in those days
I will pour out my Spirit; and they shall prophesy.
19 And I will show wonders in the heaven above
and signs on the earth beneath,
blood, and fire, and vapor of smoke;
20 the sun shall be turned into darkness
and the moon into blood,
before the day of the Lord comes,
the great and manifest day.
21 And it shall be that whoever calls on the name of the Lord shall
be saved.'

22 "Men of Israel, hear these words: Jesus of Năz′ărĕth, a man attested to you by God with mighty works and wonders and signs which God did through him in your midst, as you yourselves know—23 this Jesus, delivered up according to the definite plan and foreknowledge of God, you crucified and killed by the hands of lawless men. 24 But God raised him up, having loosed the pangs of death, because it was not possible for him to be held by it.
25 For David says concerning him,
'I saw the Lord always before me,
for he is at my right hand that I may not be shaken;
26 therefore my heart was glad, and my tongue rejoiced;
moreover my flesh will dwell in hope.
27 For thou wilt not abandon my soul to Hādēs,

nor let thy Holy One see corruption.

28 Thou hast made known to me the ways of life;
   thou wilt make me full of gladness with thy presence.'

29 "Brethren, I may say to you confidently of the patriarch David that he both died and was buried, and his tomb is with us to this day. 30 Being therefore a prophet, and knowing that God had sworn with an oath to him that he would set one of his descendants upon his throne, 31 he foresaw and spoke of the resurrection of the Christ, that he was not abandoned to Hādēs, nor did his flesh see corruption. 32 This Jesus God raised up, and of that we all are witnesses. 33 Being therefore exalted at the right hand of God, and having received from the Father the promise of the Holy Spirit, he has poured out this which you see and hear. 34 For David did not ascend into the heavens; but he himself says,

'The Lord said to my Lord, Sit at my right hand,
35 till I make thy enemies a stool for thy feet.'
36 Let all the house of Israel therefore know assuredly that God has made him both Lord and Christ, this Jesus whom you crucified."

3. *The first ingathering of souls*

37 Now when they heard this they were cut to the heart, and said to Peter and the rest of the apostles, "Brethren, what shall we do?" 38 And Peter said to them, "Repent, and be baptized every one of you in the name of Jesus Christ for the forgiveness of your sins; and you shall receive the gift of the Holy Spirit. 39 For the promise is to you and to your children and to all that are far off, every one whom the Lord our God calls to him." 40 And he testified with many other words and exhorted them, saying, "Save yourselves from this crooked generation." 41 So those who received his word were baptized, and there were added that day about three thousand souls. 42 And they devoted themselves to the apostles' teaching and fellowship, to the breaking of bread and the prayers.

4. *The brotherhood of believers*

43 And fear came upon every soul; and many wonders and signs were done through the apostles. 44 And all who believed were together and had all things in common; 45 and they sold their possessions and goods and distributed them to all, as any had need. 46 And day by day, attending the temple together and breaking bread in their homes, they partook of food with glad and generous hearts, 47 praising God and having favor with all the people. And the Lord added to their number day by day those who were being saved.

2.29
Acts 7.8,9;
13.36;
1 Ki 2.10;
Neh 3.16
2.30
2 Sam 7.12,
13;
Ps 132.11;
Rom 1.3
2.31
Ps 16.10
2.32
ver 24;
Acts 1.8
2.33
Acts 5.31;
1.4;
Jn 7.39;
14.26;
15.26;
Acts 10.45
2.34
Ps 110.1;
Mt 22.44
2.37
Lk 3.10;
Acts 9.6;
16.30
2.38
Lk 24.47;
Acts 3.19;
5.31;
8.12,16;
22.16
2.39
Isa 57.19;
Joel 2.32;
Acts 10.45;
Eph 2.13
2.43
Acts 5.12
2.44
Acts 4.32,
34
2.46
Acts 5.42;
20.7;
1 Cor 10.16
★2.47
Acts 4.33;
Rom 14.18;
Acts 5.14;
11.24

2.47 The church (Greek *ekklesia*, the "called-out-assembly," or "congregation") is composed of those who have been regenerated by the Spirit of God. The invisible church includes those who have already died in the faith, those believers who are yet alive (some also include among these their infant children), and those who are yet to become members of the body of Christ. A professing church may include both those who are members of the true church and those who are not. The New Testament uses the word *church* both for local assemblies of believers and for the church universal (e.g., 1 Cor 1.2; 2 Cor 1.1; Gal 1.2; Eph 1.22). Whether Israel in the Old Testament is to be equated with the church in the New Testament is a debatable question, although 7.38 speaks of the *congregation* (church) *in the wilderness*. Israel was a *true church*, but Eph 3.5 states that the Jewish-Gentile New Testament church was a mystery not clearly revealed in the Old Testament. In a sense, therefore, the church had its beginnings at Pentecost. Israel looked forward to Calvary, the church looks back at it, but both are redeemed by it.

D. The church at work in Jerusalem

1. Peter's second sermon: healing of the lame man

3 Now Peter and John were going up to the temple at the hour of prayer, the ninth hour. ²And a man lame from birth was being carried, whom they laid daily at that gate of the temple which is called Beautiful to ask alms of those who entered the temple. ³ Seeing Peter and John about to go into the temple, he asked for alms. ⁴And Peter directed his gaze at him, with John, and said, "Look at us." ⁵And he fixed his attention upon them, expecting to receive something from them. ⁶ But Peter said, "I have no silver and gold, but I give you what I have; in the name of Jesus Christ of Năz′ărĕth, walk." ⁷And he took him by the right hand and raised him up; and immediately his feet and ankles were made strong. ⁸And leaping up he stood and walked and entered the temple with them, walking and leaping and praising God. ⁹And all the people saw him walking and praising God, ¹⁰ and recognized him as the one who sat for alms at the Beautiful Gate of the temple; and they were filled with wonder and amazement at what had happened to him.

11 While he clung to Peter and John, all the people ran together to them in the portico called Solomon's, astounded. ¹²And when Peter saw it he addressed the people, "Men of Israel, why do you wonder at this, or why do you stare at us, as though by our own power or piety we had made him walk? ¹³ The God of Abraham and of Isaac and of Jacob, the God of our fathers, glorified his servant*c* Jesus, whom you delivered up and denied in the presence of Pilate, when he had decided to release him. ¹⁴ But you denied the Holy and Righteous One, and asked for a murderer to be granted to you, ¹⁵ and killed the Author of life, whom God raised from the dead. To this we are witnesses. ¹⁶And his name, by faith in his name, has made this man strong whom you see and know; and the faith which is through Jesus*d* has given the man this perfect health in the presence of you all.

17 "And now, brethren, I know that you acted in ignorance, as did also your rulers. ¹⁸ But what God foretold by the mouth of all the prophets, that his Christ should suffer, he thus fulfilled. ¹⁹ Repent therefore, and turn again, that your sins may be blotted out, that times of refreshing may come from the presence of the Lord, ²⁰ and that he may send the Christ appointed for you, Jesus, ²¹ whom heaven must receive until the time for establishing all that God spoke by the mouth of his holy prophets from of old. ²² Moses said, 'The Lord God will raise up for you a prophet from your brethren as he raised me up. You shall listen to him in whatever he tells you. ²³And it shall be that every soul that does not listen to that prophet shall be destroyed from the people.' ²⁴And all the prophets who have spoken, from Samuel and those who came afterwards, also proclaimed these days. ²⁵ You are the sons of the prophets and of the covenant which God gave to your fathers, saying to Abraham, 'And in your posterity shall all the families of the earth be blessed.' ²⁶ God, having raised up his servant,*c* sent him to you first, to bless you in turning every one of you from your wickedness."

c Or *child*   *d* Greek *him*

Marginal references:

3.1 Acts 2.46; Ps 55.17
3.2 Acts 14.8; Lk 16.20; ver 10
3.4 Acts 10.4
3.6 Acts 4.10
3.9 Acts 4.16, 21
3.10 Jn 9.8
3.11 Lk 22.8; Jn 10.23; Acts 5.12
3.13 Isa 52.13; Acts 5.30; Mt 27.2; Acts 2.23; Lk 23.4
3.14 Mk 1.24; Acts 4.27; 7.52; Mk 15.11; Lk 23.18–25
3.15 Acts 5.31; 2.24,32
3.17 Lk 23.34; Acts 13.27
3.18 Acts 2.23; Lk 24.27; Acts 17.3; 26.23
3.21 Acts 1.11; Mt 17.11; Lk 1.70
3.22 Deut 18.15; Acts 7.37
3.23 Deut 18.19
3.25 Acts 2.39; Rom 9.4,8; Gen 12.3; 28.14
3.26 Acts 13.46; 2.24; ver 22

2. The beginning of opposition
a. Peter and John arrested

4 And as they were speaking to the people, the priests and the
captain of the temple and the Săd′dúçeēs came upon them,
2 annoyed because they were teaching the people and proclaiming
in Jesus the resurrection from the dead. 3And they arrested them
and put them in custody until the morrow, for it was already
evening. 4 But many of those who heard the word believed; and
the number of the men came to about five thousand.

b. Peter's defense before the Sanhedrin

5 On the morrow their rulers and elders and scribes were gathered together in Jerusalem, 6 with Annas the high priest and Căi′-
áphás and John and Alexander, and all who were of the high-
priestly family. 7And when they had set them in the midst, they
inquired, "By what power or by what name did you do this?"
8 Then Peter, filled with the Holy Spirit, said to them, "Rulers
of the people and elders, 9 if we are being examined today concerning a good deed done to a cripple, by what means this man has
been healed, 10 be it known to you all, and to all the people of
Israel, that by the name of Jesus Christ of Năz′árėth, whom you
crucified, whom God raised from the dead, by him this man is
standing before you well. 11 This is the stone which was rejected
by you builders, but which has become the head of the corner.
12And there is salvation in no one else, for there is no other name
under heaven given among men by which we must be saved."

c. Peter and John set free

13 Now when they saw the boldness of Peter and John, and
perceived that they were uneducated, common men, they wondered; and they recognized that they had been with Jesus. 14 But
seeing the man that had been healed standing beside them, they
had nothing to say in opposition. 15 But when they had commanded
them to go aside out of the council, they conferred with one another, 16 saying, "What shall we do with these men? For that a
notable sign has been performed through them is manifest to all
the inhabitants of Jerusalem, and we cannot deny it. 17 But in order
that it may spread no further among the people, let us warn them
to speak no more to any one in this name." 18 So they called them
and charged them not to speak or teach at all in the name of Jesus.
19 But Peter and John answered them, "Whether it is right in the
sight of God to listen to you rather than to God, you must judge;
20 for we cannot but speak of what we have seen and heard."
21And when they had further threatened them, they let them go,
finding no way to punish them, because of the people; for all men
praised God for what had happened. 22 For the man on whom this
sign of healing was performed was more than forty years old.

d. The report to the church

23 When they were released they went to their friends and re-

4.1 Lk 22.4; Mt 3.7; Acts 6.12
4.2 Acts 17.18; 23.8
4.3 Acts 5.18
4.4 Acts 2.41
4.5 Lk 23.13
4.6 Lk 3.2; Mt 26.3
4.8 Acts 13.9; Lk 23.13; ver 5
4.10 Acts 3.6; 2.24
4.11 Ps 118.22; Isa 28.16; Mt 21.42
4.12 Mt 1.21; Acts 10.43; 1 Tim 2.5,6
*4.13 ver 31; Mt 11.25; 1 Cor 1.27
4.15 Mt 5.22
4.16 Jn 11.47; Acts 3.7–10
4.18 Acts 5.40
4.19 Acts 5.28, 29
4.20 Acts 1.8; 2.32
4.21 Acts 5.26; 3.7,8

4.13 The description of the apostles Peter and John as *uneducated*, *common men* reflects the point of view of the members of the Sanhedrin, the chief priests, elders, and scribes. The apostles were Galileans, and were not professional scholars (*agrammatoi*, "unlearned") or ordained teachers of religion (*idiōtai*, "laymen"), as were the members of the Sanhedrin. Their persuasive eloquence was, therefore, all the more astonishing.

ported what the chief priests and the elders had said to them. ²⁴And when they heard it, they lifted their voices together to God and said, "Sovereign Lord, who didst make the heaven and the earth and the sea and everything in them, 25 who by the mouth of our father David, thy servant,^c didst say by the Holy Spirit,

'Why did the Gentiles rage,
and the peoples imagine vain things?
²⁶ The kings of the earth set themselves in array,
and the rulers were gathered together,
against the Lord and against his Anointed'—^e

²⁷ for truly in this city there were gathered together against thy holy servant^c Jesus, whom thou didst anoint, both Hĕrŏd and Pŏnṭiùs Pīlàte, with the Gentiles and the peoples of Israel, 28 to do whatever thy hand and thy plan had predestined to take place. ²⁹And now, Lord, look upon their threats, and grant to thy servants^f to speak thy word with all boldness, 30 while thou stretchest out thy hand to heal, and signs and wonders are performed through the name of thy holy servant^c Jesus." ³¹And when they had prayed, the place in which they were gathered together was shaken; and they were all filled with the Holy Spirit and spoke the word of God with boldness.

32 Now the company of those who believed were of one heart and soul, and no one said that any of the things which he possessed was his own, but they had everything in common. ³³And with great power the apostles gave their testimony to the resurrection of the Lord Jesus, and great grace was upon them all. 34 There was not a needy person among them, for as many as were possessors of lands or houses sold them, and brought the proceeds of what was sold 35 and laid it at the apostles' feet; and distribution was made to each as any had need. 36 Thus Joseph who was surnamed by the apostles Bar'năbăs (which means, Son of encouragement), a Lēvīte, a native of Cyprus, 37 sold a field which belonged to him, and brought the money and laid it at the apostles' feet.

3. Discipline in the church
a. Ananias

5 But a man named Ănánī'ăs with his wife Sàpphī'rà sold a piece of property, 2 and with his wife's knowledge he kept back some of the proceeds, and brought only a part and laid it at the apostles' feet. 3 But Peter said, "Ănánī'ăs, why has Satan filled your heart to lie to the Holy Spirit and to keep back part of the proceeds of the land? 4 While it remained unsold, did it not remain your own?

^c Or child ^e Or Christ ^f Or slaves

Margin refs: 4.24 2 Ki 19.15; 4.25 Ps 2.1; Acts 1.16; 4.26 Heb 1.9; 4.27 ver 30; Lk 4.18; Jn 10.36; Mt 14.1; Lk 23.12; 4.28 Acts 2.23; 4.29 ver 13,31; Acts 9.27; 13.46; 28.31; 4.30 Acts 2.43; 5.12; 3.6,16; ver 27; 4.31 Acts 2.2,4; ver 29; *4.32 Acts 5.12; 2.44; 4.33 Acts 1.8; 1.22; 4.34 Acts 2.45; 4.35 ver 37; Acts 5.2; 2.45; 6.1; 4.37 ver 35; Acts 5.2; 5.2 Acts 4.37; *5.3 Deut 23.21; Lk 22.3; Jn 13.2,7; ver 9

4.32 A careful reading of 2.44, 45; 4.32–37 and 6.1 shows the nature, extent and purpose of the communal sharing in the early church in Jerusalem. It was a purely voluntary act, and no one was coerced into surrendering his property to the church. As Peter said to Ananias, the property belonged to him, and once he had sold it the money was his to do with as he pleased (5.4). The proceeds were distributed only to those in need, not to all members alike, and the distribution of the money was according to the needs of those being helped (2.45; 4.35). This was a genuine expression of Christian love and concern.

5.3 Scripture teaches that the Holy Spirit, the third person of the Trinity, is God and possesses the attributes of deity. In 5.3, 4 He is equated with God. In Mt 28.19 and 2 Cor 13.14 He is linked with the Father and the Son in such a way as to imply He is equal, and one, with them. These attributes of deity are ascribed to Him: (1) eternity (Heb 9.14); (2) omnipresence (Ps 139.7–13); (3) omnipotence (Rom 15.19; Lk 1.35); (4) omniscience (1 Cor 2.10). The Holy Spirit had a part in creation (Job 33.4). He was the divine author of Scripture (2 Pet 1.21). He had a part in man's redemption (Heb 9.14).

And after it was sold, was it not at your disposal? How is it that you have contrived this deed in your heart? You have not lied to men but to God." 5 When Ănănī′ăs heard these words, he fell down and died. And great fear came upon all who heard of it. 6 The young men rose and wrapped him up and carried him out and buried him.

5.5
ver 10,11
5.6
Jn 19.40

b. *Sapphira*

7 After an interval of about three hours his wife came in, not knowing what had happened. 8And Peter said to her, "Tell me whether you sold the land for so much." And she said, "Yes, for so much." 9 But Peter said to her, "How is it that you have agreed together to tempt the Spirit of the Lord? Hark, the feet of those that have buried your husband are at the door, and they will carry you out." 10 Immediately she fell down at his feet and died. When the young men came in they found her dead, and they carried her out and buried her beside her husband. 11And great fear came upon the whole church, and upon all who heard of these things.

5.8
ver 2
5.9
ver 3
5.10
ver 5
5.11
ver 5;
Acts 19.17

4. *The first persecution*
a. *Converts multiplied*

12 Now many signs and wonders were done among the people by the hands of the apostles. And they were all together in Solomon's Portico. 13 None of the rest dared join them, but the people held them in high honor. 14And more than ever believers were added to the Lord, multitudes both of men and women, 15 so that they even carried out the sick into the streets, and laid them on beds and pallets, that as Peter came by at least his shadow might fall on some of them. 16 The people also gathered from the towns around Jerusalem, bringing the sick and those afflicted with unclean spirits, and they were all healed.

5.12
Acts 2.43;
3.11; 4.32
5.13
Acts 2.47;
4.21
5.14
Acts 2.47;
11.24
5.15
Mt 9.21;
14.36;
Acts 19.12

b. *The apostles imprisoned*

17 But the high priest rose up and all who were with him, that is, the party of the Săd′dŭçēēs, and filled with jealousy 18 they arrested the apostles and put them in the common prison. 19 But at night an angel of the Lord opened the prison doors and brought them out and said, 20 "Go and stand in the temple and speak to the people all the words of this Life." 21And when they heard this, they entered the temple at daybreak and taught.

Now the high priest came and those who were with him and called together the council and all the senate of Israel, and sent to the prison to have them brought. 22 But when the officers came, they did not find them in the prison, and they returned and reported, 23 "We found the prison securely locked and the sentries standing at the doors, but when we opened it we found no one inside." 24 Now when the captain of the temple and the chief priests heard these words, they were much perplexed about them, wondering what this would come to. 25And some one came and told them, "The men whom you put in prison are standing in the temple and teaching the people." 26 Then the captain with the officers went and brought them, but without violence, for they were afraid of being stoned by the people.

27 And when they had brought them, they set them before the council. And the high priest questioned them, 28 saying, "We strictly charged you not to teach in this name, yet here you have

5.17
Acts 15.5;
4.1
5.18
Acts 4.3
5.19
Acts 12.7;
16.26
5.20
Jn 6.63,68
5.21
Acts 4.5,6;
ver 27,34,41
5.24
Acts 4.1
5.26
Acts 4.21
5.28
Acts 4.18;
2.33,36;
3.15; 7.52;
Mt 23.35;
27.25

filled Jerusalem with your teaching and you intend to bring this
man's blood upon us." 29 But Peter and the apostles answered,
"We must obey God rather than men. 30 The God of our fathers
raised Jesus whom you killed by hanging him on a tree. 31 God
exalted him at his right hand as Leader and Savior, to give repentance to Israel and forgiveness of sins. 32And we are witnesses
to these things, and so is the Holy Spirit whom God has given
to those who obey him."

c. The counsel of Gamaliel

33 When they heard this they were enraged and wanted to kill
them. 34 But a Pharisee in the council named Gamā'lĭ-ĕl, a
teacher of the law, held in honor by all the people, stood up and
ordered the men to be put outside for a while. 35And he said to
them, "Men of Israel, take care what you do with these men.
36 For before these days Theu'das arose, giving himself out to be
somebody, and a number of men, about four hundred, joined
him; but he was slain and all who followed him were dispersed
and came to nothing. 37After him Judas the Găḷḷē'án arose in the
days of the census and drew away some of the people after him;
he also perished, and all who followed him were scattered. 38 So
in the present case I tell you, keep away from these men and let
them alone; for if this plan or this undertaking is of men, it will
fail; 39 but if it is of God, you will not be able to overthrow them.
You might even be found opposing God!"

40 So they took his advice, and when they had called in the
apostles, they beat them and charged them not to speak in the
name of Jesus, and let them go. 41 Then they left the presence
of the council, rejoicing that they were counted worthy to suffer
dishonor for the name. 42And every day in the temple and at home
they did not cease teaching and preaching Jesus as the Christ.

5. The first deacons

6 Now in these days when the disciples were increasing in
number, the Hĕl'lĕnĭsts murmured against the Hebrews because their widows were neglected in the daily distribution. 2And
the twelve summoned the body of the disciples and said, "It is
not right that we should give up preaching the word of God to
serve tables. 3 Therefore, brethren, pick out from among you
seven men of good repute, full of the Spirit and of wisdom, whom
we may appoint to this duty. 4 But we will devote ourselves to

Marginal references: 5.29 Acts 4.19; 5.30 Acts 3.13, 15; 22.14; 10.39; 13.29; Gal 3.13; 1 Pet 2.24; 5.31 Acts 2.33; Heb 2.10; Acts 3.15; 5.32 Lk 24.48; Jn 15.26; Rom 8.16; 5.33 Acts 2.37; 7.54; *5.34; *5.36; *5.37; 5.38 Mt 15.13; 5.39 Acts 7.51; 9.5; 11.17; 5.40 Mt 10.17; Mk 13.9; 5.41 1 Pet 4.13, 16; Jn 15.21; 5.42 Acts 2.46; 8.35; 11.20; 17.18; Gal 1.16; *6.1 Acts 2.41, 47; 9.29; 11.20; 4.35; *6.3 Jn 21.23; Acts 1.15

5.34 This Gamaliel, an elder, was a respected rabbi among whose pupils was Saul of Tarsus (22.3). He belonged to the liberal group of Jewish teachers who followed the interpretations of Hillel, a venerated Jewish rabbi who lived shortly before the time of Jesus.
5.36 There is no other extant reference to a revolutionary leader called Theudas who led a revolt against the Roman authorities. Josephus, the Jewish historian, mentions a Theudas who led an ill-fated revolt in A.D. 44. The name was common, however, and there may have been two such revolutionaries with the same name.
5.37 According to Josephus, this Judas led a revolt against the census carried out by Quirinius in A.D. 6. Though he was defeated, his movement lived on in the Zealots, a revolutionary party dedicated to the overthrow of the Roman power by force.
6.1 It is commonly understood that Hellenists were Jews who spoke Greek and/or adopted some Greek customs, while Hebrews were more conservative Jews, perhaps largely natives of Jerusalem, who spoke Hebrew (or Aramaic) and abstained from Greek customs. Even in the early church a certain tension between the two groups was inevitable.
6.3 See note to 1 Tim 3.8 on the office of deacon.

prayer and to the ministry of the word." 5And what they said pleased the whole multitude, and they chose Stephen, a man full of faith and of the Holy Spirit, and Philip, and Prŏch'ŏrŭs, and Nĭcā'nŏr, and Tīmŏn, and Par'mĕnăs, and Nĭcŏlā'ŭs, a proselyte of Ăn'tĭŏch. 6 These they set before the apostles, and they prayed and laid their hands upon them.

7 And the word of God increased; and the number of the disciples multiplied greatly in Jerusalem, and a great many of the priests were obedient to the faith.

6. The first martyrdom
a. The arrest of Stephen

8 And Stephen, full of grace and power, did great wonders and signs among the people. 9 Then some of those who belonged to the synagogue of the Freedmen (as it was called), and of the Çȳrē'nĭăns, and of the Alexandrians, and of those from Çĭlĭ'çĭă and Asia, arose and disputed with Stephen. 10 But they could not withstand the wisdom and the Spirit with which he spoke. 11 Then they secretly instigated men, who said, "We have heard him speak blasphemous words against Moses and God." 12And they stirred up the people and the elders and the scribes, and they came upon him and seized him and brought him before the council, 13 and set up false witnesses who said, "This man never ceases to speak words against this holy place and the law; 14 for we have heard him say that this Jesus of Năz'ărĕth will destroy this place, and will change the customs which Moses delivered to us." 15And gazing at him, all who sat in the council saw that his face was like the face of an angel.

b. The defense of Stephen

7 And the high priest said, "Is this so?" 2And Stephen said: "Brethren and fathers, hear me. The God of glory appeared to our father Abraham, when he was in Mĕsŏpŏtā'mĭă, before he lived in Hāràn, 3 and said to him, 'Depart from your land and from your kindred and go into the land which I will show you.' 4 Then he departed from the land of the Chăldē'ăns, and lived in Hāràn. And after his father died, God removed him from there into this land in which you are now living; 5 yet he gave him no inheritance in it, not even a foot's length, but promised to give it to him in possession and to his posterity after him, though he had no child. 6And God spoke to this effect, that his posterity would be aliens in a land belonging to others, who would enslave them and ill-treat them four hundred years. 7 'But I will judge the nation which they serve,' said God, 'and after that they shall come out and worship me in this place.' 8And he gave him the covenant of circumcision. And so Abraham became the father of Isaac, and circumcised him on the eighth day; and Isaac became the father of Jacob, and Jacob of the twelve patriarchs.

9 "And the patriarchs, jealous of Joseph, sold him into Egypt; but God was with him, 10 and rescued him out of all his afflictions, and gave him favor and wisdom before Phăraōh, king of Egypt, who made him governor over Egypt and over all his household.

*6.5
Acts 11.19,
24; 8.5,26;
21.8

6.6
Acts 1.24;
8.17; 9.17;
13.3;
1 Tim 4.14;
5.22;
2 Tim 1.6

6.7
Acts 12.24;
19.20;
Acts 13.8;
14.22;
Gal 1.23;
6.10

6.10
Lk 21.15;
Acts 5.39
6.11
Mt 26.59,
60

6.13
Acts 7.58;
21.28
6.14
Mt 26.61;
15.1;
21.21;
26.3; 28.17

7.2
Acts 22.1;
Ps 29.3;
Gen 11.31;
15.7
7.3
Gen 12.1
7.4
Gen 12.5

7.5
Gen 12.7;
17.8; 26.3
7.6
Gen 15.13,
14;
Ex 12.40
7.7
Ex 3.12
7.8
Gen 17.9–
11; 21.2–4;
25.26;
29.31ff
7.9
Gen 37.4,
11,28;
39.2,21,23
7.10
Gen 41.37;
42.6

6.5 Nicolaus, one of the seven who were chosen to serve in the Jerusalem church, was a proselyte. He is the first Gentile Christian to be identified by name. Notice that on the day of Pentecost there were proselytes from Rome in Jerusalem who heard Peter's message (2,10).

11 Now there came a famine throughout all Egypt and Cānaàn, and great affliction, and our fathers could find no food. 12 But when Jacob heard that there was grain in Egypt, he sent forth our fathers the first time. 13And at the second visit Joseph made himself known to his brothers, and Joseph's family became known to Phạraōh. 14And Joseph sent and called to him Jacob his father and all his kindred, seventy-five souls; 15 and Jacob went down into Egypt. And he died, himself and our fathers, 16 and they were carried back to Shĕçhĕm and laid in the tomb that Abraham had bought for a sum of silver from the sons of Hāmor in Shechem.

17 "But as the time of the promise drew near, which God had granted to Abraham, the people grew and multiplied in Egypt 18 till there arose over Egypt another king who had not known Joseph. 19 He dealt craftily with our race and forced our fathers to expose their infants, that they might not be kept alive. 20At this time Moses was born, and was beautiful before God. And he was brought up for three months in his father's house; 21 and when he was exposed, Phạraōh'ṣ daughter adopted him and brought him up as her own son. 22And Moses was instructed in all the wisdom of the Egyptians, and he was mighty in his words and deeds.

23 "When he was forty years old, it came into his heart to visit his brethren, the sons of Israel. 24And seeing one of them being wronged, he defended the oppressed man and avenged him by striking the Egyptian. 25 He supposed that his brethren understood that God was giving them deliverance by his hand, but they did not understand. 26And on the following day he appeared to them as they were quarreling and would have reconciled them, saying, 'Men, you are brethren, why do you wrong each other?' 27 But the man who was wronging his neighbor thrust him aside, saying, 'Who made you a ruler and a judge over us? 28 Do you want to kill me as you killed the Egyptian yesterday?' 29At this retort Moses fled, and became an exile in the land of Mĭd′ĭàn, where he became the father of two sons.

30 "Now when forty years had passed, an angel appeared to him in the wilderness of Mount Sī′näï, in a flame of fire in a bush. 31 When Moses saw it he wondered at the sight; and as he drew near to look, the voice of the Lord came, 32 'I am the God of your fathers, the God of Abraham and of Isaac and of Jacob.' And Moses trembled and did not dare to look. 33And the Lord said to him, 'Take off the shoes from your feet, for the place where you are standing is holy ground. 34 I have surely seen the illtreatment of my people that are in Egypt and heard their groaning, and I have come down to deliver them. And now come, I will send you to Egypt.'

35 "This Moses whom they refused, saying, 'Who made you a ruler and a judge?' God sent as both ruler and deliverer by the hand of the angel that appeared to him in the bush. 36 He led them out, having performed wonders and signs in Egypt and at the Red Sea, and in the wilderness for forty years. 37 This is the Moses who said to the Israelites, 'God will raise up for you a prophet from your brethren as he raised me up.' 38 This is he who was in the congregation in the wilderness with the angel who spoke to him at Mount Sī′näï, and with our fathers; and he received living

---

7.14 See note to Gen 46.27.   **7.16** *a sum*, 400 shekels in Gen 23.16.

oracles to give to us. ³⁹ Our fathers refused to obey him, but thrust him aside, and in their hearts they turned to Egypt, ⁴⁰ saying to Aaron, 'Make for us gods to go before us; as for this Moses who led us out from the land of Egypt, we do not know what has become of him.' ⁴¹And they made a calf in those days, and offered a sacrifice to the idol and rejoiced in the works of their hands. ⁴² But God turned and gave them over to worship the host of heaven, as it is written in the book of the prophets:

'Did you offer to me slain beasts and sacrifices,
   forty years in the wilderness, O house of Israel?
⁴³ And you took up the tent of Mōlóch,
   and the star of the god Rēphán,
   the figures which you made to worship;
   and I will remove you beyond Babylon.'

44 "Our fathers had the tent of witness in the wilderness, even as he who spoke to Moses directed him to make it, according to the pattern that he had seen. ⁴⁵ Our fathers in turn brought it in with Joshua when they dispossessed the nations which God thrust out before our fathers. So it was until the days of David, ⁴⁶ who found favor in the sight of God and asked leave to find a habitation for the God of Jacob. ⁴⁷ But it was Solomon who built a house for him. ⁴⁸ Yet the Most High does not dwell in houses made with hands; as the prophet says,

⁴⁹ 'Heaven is my throne,
   and earth my footstool.
   What house will you build for me, says the Lord,
   or what is the place of my rest?
⁵⁰ Did not my hand make all these things?'

51 "You stiff-necked people, uncircumcised in heart and ears, you always resist the Holy Spirit. As your fathers did, so do you. ⁵² Which of the prophets did not your fathers persecute? And they killed those who announced beforehand the coming of the Righteous One, whom you have now betrayed and murdered, ⁵³ you who received the law as delivered by angels and did not keep it."

c. The stoning of Stephen

54 Now when they heard these things they were enraged, and they ground their teeth against him. ⁵⁵ But he, full of the Holy Spirit, gazed into heaven and saw the glory of God, and Jesus standing at the right hand of God; ⁵⁶ and he said, "Behold, I see the heavens opened, and the Son of man standing at the right hand of God." ⁵⁷ But they cried out with a loud voice and stopped their ears and rushed together upon him. ⁵⁸ Then they cast him out of the city and stoned him; and the witnesses laid down their garments at the feet of a young man named Saul. ⁵⁹And as they were stoning Stephen, he prayed, "Lord Jesus, receive my spirit." ⁶⁰And he knelt down and cried with a loud voice, "Lord, do not 8 hold this sin against them." And when he had said this, he fell asleep. ¹And Saul was consenting to his death.

Marginal references:

7.40 Ex 32.1,23
7.41 Ex 32.4,6; Ps 106.19
7.42 Ezek 20.25, 39; Amos 5.25, 26
★7.43
7.44 Ex 25.9,40
7.45 Josh 3.14–17; Ps 44.2
7.46 2 Sam 7.8–16; Ps 132.1–5
7.48 1 Ki 8.27; 2 Chr 2.6
7.49 Isa 66.1,2; Mt 5.34,35
7.51 Lev 26.41; Jer 6.10; 9.26
7.52 2 Chr 36.16; Mt 23.31, 37; Acts 3.14
7.53 Ex 20.1; Heb 2.2
7.55 Acts 6.5
7.56 Mt 3.16; Dan 7.13
7.58 Lk 4.29; Lev 24.16; Deut 13.9, 10
7.59 Acts 9.14
7.60 Acts 9.40
★8.1 Acts 7.58; 11.19

7.43 This quotation from Amos 5.25–27 employs the Greek form of the names of the two pagan deities, *Moloch* and *Rephan*, which in the Hebrew are called *Sakkuth* and *Kaiwan*. Moloch (or Molech) was the Canaanite deity to whom human sacrifices were offered. Rephan is the Greek name for the Hebrew Kaiwan (or Chiun), which is taken to refer to Repa, the Egyptian god of the planet Saturn. **8.1** *Saul* was the Hebrew name of Paul.

d. *The scattering of the church*

And on that day a great persecution arose against the church in Jerusalem; and they were all scattered throughout the region of Judē'ā and Sâmạr'ïä, except the apostles. 2 Devout men buried Stephen, and made great lamentation over him. 3 But Saul was ravaging the church, and entering house after house, he dragged off men and women and committed them to prison.

II. *Judea, Samaria, and on to Antioch of Syria 8.4–12.25*

A. *The ministry of Philip*

1. *Philip at Samaria*

4 Now those who were scattered went about preaching the word. 5 Philip went down to a city of Sâmạr'ïä, and proclaimed to them the Christ. 6And the multitudes with one accord gave heed to what was said by Philip, when they heard him and saw the signs which he did. 7 For unclean spirits came out of many who were possessed, crying with a loud voice; and many who were paralyzed or lame were healed. 8 So there was much joy in that city.

2. *Conversion of Simon the sorcerer*

9 But there was a man named Simon who had previously practiced magic in the city and amazed the nation of Sâmạr'ïä, saying that he himself was somebody great. 10 They all gave heed to him, from the least to the greatest, saying, "This man is that power of God which is called Great." 11And they gave heed to him, because for a long time he had amazed them with his magic. 12 But when they believed Philip as he preached good news about the kingdom of God and the name of Jesus Christ, they were baptized, both men and women. 13 Even Simon himself believed, and after being baptized he continued with Philip. And seeing signs and great miracles performed, he was amazed.

14 Now when the apostles at Jerusalem heard that Sâmạr'ïä had received the word of God, they sent to them Peter and John, 15 who came down and prayed for them that they might receive the Holy Spirit; 16 for it had not yet fallen on any of them, but they had only been baptized in the name of the Lord Jesus. 17 Then they laid their hands on them and they received the Holy Spirit. 18 Now when Simon saw that the Spirit was given through the laying on of the apostles' hands, he offered them money, 19 saying, "Give me also this power, that any one on whom I lay my hands may receive the Holy Spirit." 20 But Peter said to him, "Your silver perish with you, because you thought you could obtain the gift of God with money! 21 You have neither part nor

8.2
Gen 23.2;
50.10;
2 Sam 3.31

8.3
Acts 7.58;
22.4; 26.10,
11;
1 Cor 15.9;
Gal 1.13;
Phil 3.6;
1 Tim 1.13

8.4
ver 1;
Acts 15.35

8.5
Acts 6.5

8.7
Mt 4.24

8.9
Acts 13.6;
5.36

8.10
Acts 14.11;
28.6

8.12
Acts 1.3;
2.38

*8.13
ver 6;
Acts 19.11

8.14
ver 1

8.15
Acts 2.38

8.16
Acts 19.2;
Mt 28.19;
Acts 10.48;
19.5

8.17
Acts 6.6;
2.4

8.20
Acts 2.38;
Mt 10.8;
2 Ki 5.16

8.21
Ps 78.37

8.13 A miracle is commonly defined in the dictionaries as an effect in nature not attributable to any of the recognized operations of nature nor to the act of man, but indicative of superhuman power and serving as a sign or witness thereof; a wonderful work manifesting a power superior to the ordinary forces of nature. Whereas miracles were once regarded as an aid to faith, they now are stumbling blocks for a science-minded generation which has been taught to regard them as impossible. The Bible does not argue the case for miracles; it just assumes them. Efforts to explain away the miracles of Scripture or to discount them are most unsuccessful. They are part of the very warp and woof of the Bible and cannot be excised from the holy record without rendering much of the narrative implausible and unmotivated. The supreme miracle is the Incarnation of Jesus Christ who is the Word of God and by whom the miracle of salvation is wrought.

lot in this matter, for your heart is not right before God. 22 Repent therefore of this wickedness of yours, and pray to the Lord that, if possible, the intent of your heart may be forgiven you. 23 For I see that you are in the gall of bitterness and in the bond of iniquity." 24And Simon answered, "Pray for me to the Lord, that nothing of what you have said may come upon me."

8.23
Isa 58.6;
Heb 12.15

25 Now when they had testified and spoken the word of the Lord, they returned to Jerusalem, preaching the gospel to many villages of the Sămạr′ịtàns.

8.25
Lk 16.28;
ver 40

3. Conversion of the Ethiopian eunuch

26 But an angel of the Lord said to Philip, "Rise and go toward the southg to the road that goes down from Jerusalem to Gazà." This is a desert road. 27And he rose and went. And behold, an Ethiopian, a eunuch, a minister of the Cănda′çē, queen of the Ethiopians, in charge of all her treasure, had come to Jerusalem to worship 28 and was returning; seated in his chariot, he was reading the prophet Įsāi′áh. 29And the Spirit said to Philip, "Go up and join this chariot." 30 So Philip ran to him, and heard him reading Įsāi′áh the prophet, and asked, "Do you understand what you are reading?" 31And he said, "How can I, unless some one guides me?" And he invited Philip to come up and sit with him. 32 Now the passage of the scripture which he was reading was this:

8.26
Acts 5.19;
*8.27
Ps 68.31;
Zeph 3.10;
Jn 12.20

*8.29
Acts 10.19;
11.12;
13.2;
20.23;
21.11

8.32
Isa 53.7,8

"As a sheep led to the slaughter
    or a lamb before its shearer is dumb,
    so he opens not his mouth.
33 In his humiliation justice was denied him.
    Who can describe his generation?
    For his life is taken up from the earth."

34And the eunuch said to Philip, "About whom, pray, does the prophet say this, about himself or about some one else?" 35 Then Philip opened his mouth, and beginning with this scripture he told him the good news of Jesus. 36And as they went along the road they came to some water, and the eunuch said, "See, here is water! What is to prevent my being baptized?"h 38And he commanded the chariot to stop, and they both went down into the water, Philip and the eunuch, and he baptized him. 39And when they came up out of the water, the Spirit of the Lord caught up Philip; and the eunuch saw him no more, and went on his way rejoicing. 40 But Philip was found at Àzō′tùs, and passing on he preached the gospel to all the towns till he came to Çăĕsărē′à.

8.35
Mt 5.2;
Lk 24.27;
Acts 17.2;
18.28; 5.42
8.36
Acts 10.47

8.39
1 Ki 18.12;
2 Ki 2.16;
Ezek 3.12,
14

---

g Or at noon
h Other ancient authorities add all or most of verse 37, And Philip said, "If you believe with all your heart, you may." And he replied, "I believe that Jesus Christ is the Son of God."

8.27 As a Gentile convert to the Jewish faith, i.e., a proselyte, the Ethiopian eunuch had gone to Jerusalem to worship in the Temple, probably during one of the great feasts of the Jews. He is the second Gentile referred to specifically as a convert to the Christian faith (cf. note to 6.5 on Nicolaus).
8.29 (For the person of the Holy Spirit see notes to Jn 14.16 and Acts 5.3.) The Holy Spirit fulfils many offices, among which are: (1) directing God's servants where, when, and what to do or to preach (8.29; 10.19, 20;

16.6, 7; 1 Cor 2.13); (2) choosing and commissioning workers for Christ's service (13.2; 20.28); (3) teaching the church the truth of Christ (Jn 14.26; 1 Cor 12.3); (4) testifying to the Son and magnifying His glory (Jn 15.26; 16.14); (5) reproving sinners and convicting them of their guilt (Jn 16.8); (6) communicating the truths of Scripture to men (1.16; 2 Pet 1.21; 1 Pet 1.11, 12). The Holy Spirit may be resisted (7.51); He may be quenched (1 Thess 5.19); and He may be grieved (Eph 4.30).

B. The conversion of Saul (Paul)

1. His call on the Damascus road

9.1
Acts 8.3;
22.4–16;
26.9–18
*9.2

9.3
Acts 22.6;
26.12;
1 Cor 15.8

9.4
Acts 22.7;
26.14

9.7
Acts 22.9;
26.13,14

9.8
Acts 22.11;
Gal 1.17

9 But Saul, still breathing threats and murder against the disciples of the Lord, went to the high priest 2 and asked him for letters to the synagogues at Damascus, so that if he found any belonging to the Way, men or women, he might bring them bound to Jerusalem. 3 Now as he journeyed he approached Damascus, and suddenly a light from heaven flashed about him. 4And he fell to the ground and heard a voice saying to him, "Saul, Saul, why do you persecute me?" 5And he said, "Who are you, Lord?" And he said, "I am Jesus, whom you are persecuting; 6 but rise and enter the city, and you will be told what you are to do." 7 The men who were traveling with him stood speechless, hearing the voice but seeing no one. 8 Saul arose from the ground; and when his eyes were opened, he could see nothing; so they led him by the hand and brought him into Damascus. 9And for three days he was without sight, and neither ate nor drank.

2. His baptism by Ananias

9.10
Acts 22.12

9.11
Acts 21.39;
22.3

9.14
ver 21;
Acts 7.59;
1 Cor 1.2;
2 Tim 2.22

9.15
Acts 13.2;
Eph 3.7,8;
Gal 2.7,8;
Acts 25.22,
23; 26.1

*9.16
Acts 20.23;
21.11;
2 Cor 11.23

9.17
Acts 22.12,
13; 8.17;
2.4; 4.31

9.19
Acts 26.20

10 Now there was a disciple at Damascus named Ănăni′ás. The Lord said to him in a vision, "Ananias." And he said, "Here I am, Lord." 11And the Lord said to him, "Rise and go to the street called Straight, and inquire in the house of Judas for a man of Tarsús named Saul; for behold, he is praying, 12 and he has seen a man named Ănăni′ás come in and lay his hands on him so that he might regain his sight." 13 But Ănăni′ás answered, "Lord, I have heard from many about this man, how much evil he has done to thy saints at Jerusalem; 14 and here he has authority from the chief priests to bind all who call upon thy name." 15 But the Lord said to him, "Go, for he is a chosen instrument of mine to carry my name before the Gentiles and kings and the sons of Israel; 16 for I will show him how much he must suffer for the sake of my name." 17 So Ănăni′ás departed and entered the house. And laying his hands on him he said, "Brother Saul, the Lord Jesus who appeared to you on the road by which you came, has sent me that you may regain your sight and be filled with the Holy Spirit." 18And immediately something like scales fell from his eyes and he regained his sight. Then he rose and was baptized, 19 and took food and was strengthened.

3. His preaching at Damascus

9.21
Acts 8.3;
Gal 1.13,23

9.22
Acts 18.28

For several days he was with the disciples at Damascus. 20And in the synagogues immediately he proclaimed Jesus, saying, "He is the Son of God." 21And all who heard him were amazed, and said, "Is not this the man who made havoc in Jerusalem of those who called on this name? And he has come here for this purpose, to bring them bound before the chief priests." 22 But Saul increased all the more in strength, and confounded the Jews who lived in Damascus by proving that Jesus was the Christ.

9.2 *Way* is a name used in the book of Acts for the Christian faith (see also 19.9, 23; 24.14, 22). It is *the way of God* (18.26), *the way of salvation* (16.17). All these passages aptly describe the faith that rests on

Him who said, *I am the way* (Jn 14.6).
9.16 This prophecy was accurately fulfilled in the life of Paul who suffered greatly for the sake of Jesus. Those who follow Him do not necessarily live without suffering.

4. His escape from the Jews

23 When many days had passed, the Jews plotted to kill him, 24 but their plot became known to Saul. They were watching the gates day and night, to kill him; 25 but his disciples took him by night and let him down over the wall, lowering him in a basket.

9.23
Acts 23.12;
25.3
9.24
2 Cor 11.32,
33

5. His reception in Jerusalem

26 And when he had come to Jerusalem he attempted to join the disciples; and they were all afraid of him, for they did not believe that he was a disciple. 27 But Bar′nàbàs took him, and brought him to the apostles, and declared to them how on the road he had seen the Lord, who spoke to him, and how at Damascus he had preached boldly in the name of Jesus. 28 So he went in and out among them at Jerusalem, 29 preaching boldly in the name of the Lord. And he spoke and disputed against the Hĕl′lènists; but they were seeking to kill him. 30And when the brethren knew it, they brought him down to Çaĕsàrē′à, and sent him off to Tarsùs. 31 So the church throughout all Judē′à and Găl′ilee and Sàmạr′-ìà had peace and was built up; and walking in the fear of the Lord and in the comfort of the Holy Spirit it was multiplied.

*9.26
Acts 22.17;
Gal 1.17,18
9.27
Acts 4.36;
ver 20,22

9.29
Acts 6.1;
11.20;
2 Cor 11.26
9.31
Acts 8.1

C. The ministry of Peter

1. Aeneas healed

32 Now as Peter went here and there among them all, he came down also to the saints that lived at Lȳddà. 33 There he found a man named Aënē′às, who had been bedridden for eight years and was paralyzed. 34And Peter said to him, "Aënē′às, Jesus Christ heals you; rise and make your bed." And immediately he rose. 35And all the residents of Lȳddà and Shạròn saw him, and they turned to the Lord.

9.32
ver 13

*9.34
Acts 3.6,16;
4.10
9.35
1 Chr 5.16;
Acts 11.21

2. Tabitha raised from the dead

36 Now there was at Jŏppà a disciple named Tăb′ịthà, which means Dorcàs.ˣ She was full of good works and acts of charity. 37 In those days she fell sick and died; and when they had washed her, they laid her in an upper room. 38 Since Lȳddà was near Jŏppà, the disciples, hearing that Peter was there, sent two men to him entreating him, "Please come to us without delay." 39 So Peter rose and went with them. And when he had come, they took him to the upper room. All the widows stood beside him weeping, and showing tunics and other garments which Dorcàs màde while she was with them. 40 But Peter put them all outside and knelt down and prayed; then turning to the body he said, "Tăb′-ịthà, rise." And she opened her eyes, and when she saw Peter she sat up. 41And he gave her his hand and lifted her up. Then calling the saints and widows he presented her alive. 42And it became known throughout all Jŏppà, and many believed in the Lord. 43And he stayed in Jŏppà for many days with one Simon, a tanner.

9.36
Jon 1.3;
1 Tim 2.10;
Tit 3.8
9.37
Acts 1.13
9.38
Acts 11.26
9.39
Acts 6.1

9.40
Mt 9.25;
Acts 7.60;
Mk 5.41,42
9.41
ver 13

9.43
Acts 10.6

ˣ The name Tabitha in Aramaic and the name Dorcas in Greek mean *gazelle*

9.26 The Christians might well suspect that Paul's conversion was a trap to ensnare them.

9.34 This was another manifestation of the many signs and wonders which were part of the apostolic period. They subsequently decreased and were seldom repeated. The greater part of the miracles recorded in Scripture occurred within a relatively short space of time and they were connected with only a few names: Moses, Elijah, Elisha, Jesus, and the apostles.

3. *The conversion of Cornelius*
a. *Cornelius' vision*

10 At Çaĕsărĕ′á there was a man named Cornelius, a centurion of what was known as the Italian Cohort, 2 a devout man who feared God with all his household, gave alms liberally to the people, and prayed constantly to God. 3About the ninth hour of the day he saw clearly in a vision an angel of God coming in and saying to him, "Cornelius." 4And he stared at him in terror, and said, "What is it, Lord?" And he said to him, "Your prayers and your alms have ascended as a memorial before God. 5And now send men to Jŏppá, and bring one Simon who is called Peter; 6 he is lodging with Simon, a tanner, whose house is by the seaside." 7 When the angel who spoke to him had departed, he called two of his servants and a devout soldier from among those that waited on him, 8 and having related everything to them, he sent them to Jŏppá.

b. *Peter's vision*

9 The next day, as they were on their journey and coming near the city, Peter went up on the housetop to pray, about the sixth hour. 10And he became hungry and desired something to eat; but while they were preparing it, he fell into a trance 11 and saw the heaven opened, and something descending, like a great sheet, let down by four corners upon the earth. 12 In it were all kinds of animals and reptiles and birds of the air. 13And there came a voice to him, "Rise, Peter; kill and eat." 14 But Peter said, "No, Lord; for I have never eaten anything that is common or unclean." 15And the voice came to him again a second time, "What God has cleansed, you must not call common." 16 This happened three times, and the thing was taken up at once to heaven.

c. *The sending for Peter*

17 Now while Peter was inwardly perplexed as to what the vision which he had seen might mean, behold, the men that were sent by Cornelius, having made inquiry for Simon's house, stood before the gate 18 and called out to ask whether Simon who was called Peter was lodging there. 19And while Peter was pondering the vision, the Spirit said to him, "Behold, three men are looking for you. 20 Rise and go down, and accompany them without hesitation; for I have sent them." 21And Peter went down to the men and said, "I am the one you are looking for; what is the reason for your coming?" 22And they said, "Cornelius, a centurion, an upright and God-fearing man, who is well spoken of by the whole Jewish nation, was directed by a holy angel to send for you to come to his house, and to hear what you have to say." 23 So he called them in to be his guests.

d. *Peter's visit to Cornelius*

The next day he rose and went off with them, and some of the brethren from Jŏppá accompanied him. 24And on the following

Marginal references (left column):

*10.1
10.2
ver 22,35
10.3
Acts 9.10;
3.1; 5.19
10.4
Acts 3.4;
Rev 8.4;
Mt 26.13
10.6
Acts 9.43
10.9
Acts 11.5–
14;
Mt 24.17
10.10
Acts 22.17
10.11
Acts 7.56;
Rev 19.11
10.14
Acts 9.5;
Lev 11.4;
20.25;
Deut 14.3,
7;
Ezek 4.14
10.15
ver 28;
Mt 15.11;
Rom 14.14,
17,20;
1 Cor
10.25;
1 Tim 4.4;
Tit 1.15
10.17
ver 3
10.19
Acts 11.12
10.20
Acts 15.7
10.22
ver 2;
Acts 11.14
10.23
ver 45;
Acts 11.12*

10.1 Cornelius, the Roman centurion, is the third Gentile convert to be identified in the book of Acts (cf. notes on the Ethiopian eunuch, 8.27; Nicolaus the proselyte, 6.5). The descent of the Holy Spirit upon these Gentiles, Cornelius, his household, and friends (10.24, 44, 45) marks a new phase in the spread of the gospel (11.15–18). So Peter refers to it later (15.7–9). Note that he needed a vision before he would preach to a Gentile.

day they entered Çaĕsàrē′à. Cornelius was expecting them and had
called together his kinsmen and close friends. 25 When Peter
entered, Cornelius met him and fell down at his feet and worshiped him. 26 But Peter lifted him up, saying, "Stand up; I too
am a man." 27And as he talked with him, he went in and found
many persons gathered; 28 and he said to them, "You yourselves
know how unlawful it is for a Jew to associate with or to visit any
one of another nation; but God has shown me that I should not
call any man common or unclean. 29 So when I was sent for, I
came without objection. I ask then why you sent for me."

30 And Cornelius said, "Four days ago, about this hour, I was
keeping the ninth hour of prayer in my house; and behold, a man
stood before me in bright apparel, 31 saying, 'Cornelius, your prayer
has been heard and your alms have been remembered before
God. 32 Send therefore to Jŏppà and ask for Simon who is called
Peter; he is lodging in the house of Simon, a tanner, by the seaside.' 33 So I sent to you at once, and you have been kind enough
to come. Now therefore we are all here present in the sight of God,
to hear all that you have been commanded by the Lord."

e. *Peter's sermon to Cornelius*

34 And Peter opened his mouth and said: "Truly I perceive
that God shows no partiality, 35 but in every nation any one who
fears him and does what is right is acceptable to him. 36 You know
the word which he sent to Israel, preaching good news of peace by
Jesus Christ (he is Lord of all), 37 the word which was proclaimed
throughout all Judĕ′à, beginning from Găl′jleĕ after the baptism
which John preached: 38 how God anointed Jesus of Năz′àrĕth
with the Holy Spirit and with power; how he went about doing
good and healing all that were oppressed by the devil, for God was
with him. 39And we are witnesses to all that he did both in the
country of the Jews and in Jerusalem. They put him to death by
hanging him on a tree; 40 but God raised him on the third day and
made him manifest; 41 not to all the people but to us who were chosen by God as witnesses, who ate and drank with him after he rose
from the dead. 42And he commanded us to preach to the people,
and to testify that he is the one ordained by God to be judge of the
living and the dead. 43 To him all the prophets bear witness that
every one who believes in him receives forgiveness of sins through
his name."

f. *The baptism of Cornelius*

44 While Peter was still saying this, the Holy Spirit fell on all
who heard the word. 45And the believers from among the circumcised who came with Peter were amazed, because the gift of
the Holy Spirit had been poured out even on the Gentiles. 46 For
they heard them speaking in tongues and extolling God. Then
Peter declared, 47 "Can any one forbid water for baptizing these
people who have received the Holy Spirit just as we have?" 48And
he commanded them to be baptized in the name of Jesus Christ.
Then they asked him to remain for some days.

g. *Peter's defense of Gentile evangelization*

11 Now the apostles and the brethren who were in Judĕ′à
heard that the Gentiles also had received the word of God.

10.26
Acts 24.14,
15;
Rev 19.10
10.28
Jn 4.9;
18.28;
Acts 11.3;
15.8,9

10.30
Acts 1.10;
Mt 28.3;
Mk 16.5;
Lk 24.4

10.34
Deut 10.17;
Rom 2.11;
Eph 6.9;
Col 3.25;
I Pet 1.17
10.35
Acts 15.9
10.36
Isa 57.19;
Mt 28.18;
Rom 10.12;
Eph 1.20,22
10.38
Acts 2.22;
Jn 3.2
10.39
Lk 24.48;
Acts 5.30
10.40
Acts 2.24
10.41
Jn 14.17,22;
21.13
10.42
Mt 28.19,
20;
Rom 14.9;
2 Cor 5.10;
1 Pet 4.5
10.43
Isa 53.11;
Acts 26.22;
15.9;
Rom 10.11;
Gal 3.22
10.44
Acts 4.31;
8.15,16;
11.15; 15.8
10.45
ver 23;
Acts 11.18
10.47
Acts 8.36;
11.17
10.48
1 Cor 1.17;
Acts 2.38;
8.16; 19.5

★11.2
Acts 10.45
11.3
Acts 10.28;
Gal 2.12
11.4
Lk 1.3
11.5
Acts 10.9–
32

11.9
Acts 10.15

11.12
Acts 8.29;
15.9;
10.23
11.13
Acts 10.30
11.15
Acts 10.44;
2.4
11.16
Mt 3.11;
Jn 1.26,33;
Acts 1.5;
Joel 2.28;
3.18
11.17
Acts 10.45,
47
11.18
Rom 10.12,
13;
2 Cor 7.10

11.19
Acts 8.1,4
★11.20
Acts 4.36;
6.5; 13.1;
5.42
11.21
Lk 1.66;
Acts 2.47;
9.35
11.23
Acts 13.43;
14.22
11.24
Acts 6.5;
ver 21;
Acts 5.14
11.25
Acts
9.11,30
★11.26
Acts 26.28

2 So when Peter went up to Jerusalem, the circumcision party criticized him, 3 saying, "Why did you go to uncircumcised men and eat with them?" 4 But Peter began and explained to them in order: 5 "I was in the city of Jŏppá praying; and in a trance I saw a vision, something descending, like a great sheet, let down from heaven by four corners; and it came down to me. 6 Looking at it closely I observed animals and beasts of prey and reptiles and birds of the air. 7And I heard a voice saying to me, 'Rise, Peter; kill and eat.' 8 But I said, 'No, Lord; for nothing common or unclean has ever entered my mouth.' 9 But the voice answered a second time from heaven, 'What God has cleansed you must not call common.' 10 This happened three times, and all was drawn up again into heaven. 11At that very moment three men arrived at the house in which we were, sent to me from Çaĕsárĕ'á. 12And the Spirit told me to go with them, making no distinction. These six brethren also accompanied me, and we entered the man's house. 13And he told us how he had seen the angel standing in his house and saying, 'Send to Jŏppá and bring Simon called Peter; 14 he will declare to you a message by which you will be saved, you and all your household.' 15As I began to speak, the Holy Spirit fell on them just as on us at the beginning. 16And I remembered the word of the Lord, how he said, 'John baptized with water, but you shall be baptized with the Holy Spirit.' 17 If then God gave the same gift to them as he gave to us when we believed in the Lord Jesus Christ, who was I that I could withstand God?" 18 When they heard this they were silenced. And they glorified God, saying, "Then to the Gentiles also God has granted repentance unto life."

D. Barnabas at Antioch

19 Now those who were scattered because of the persecution that arose over Stephen traveled as far as Phoĕnĭ'ciá and Cyprus and Ăn'tĭŏch, speaking the word to none except Jews. 20 But there were some of them, men of Cyprus and Çȳrē'në, who on coming to Ăn'tĭŏch spoke to the Greeks *i* also, preaching the Lord Jesus. 21And the hand of the Lord was with them, and a great number that believed turned to the Lord. 22 News of this came to the ears of the church in Jerusalem, and they sent Bar'nábás to Ăn'tĭŏch. 23 When he came and saw the grace of God, he was glad; and he exhorted them all to remain faithful to the Lord with steadfast purpose; 24 for he was a good man, full of the Holy Spirit and of faith. And a large company was added to the Lord. 25 So Bar'nábás went to Tarsús to look for Saul; 26 and when he had found him, he brought him to Ăn'tĭŏch. For a whole year they met with *j* the church, and taught a large company of people; and in Antioch the disciples were for the first time called Christians.

i Other ancient authorities read *Hĕl'lĕnĭsts*   *j*Or *were guests of*

11.2 The early church was constantly vexed by the problem of legalism, particularly as it related to circumcision. Paul addressed himself to this question definitively in his letter to the Galatians.

11.20 ". . . spoke to the Greeks. . . ." The preaching of the gospel to the Greeks in Antioch by the Cypriot and Cyrenian evangelists, marks the first systematic attempt to evangelize the Gentiles as a whole. This initial campaign was followed by the far-spread missionary work of Paul in preaching throughout the whole Mediterranean world (cf. 14.27; 15.3).

11.26 It was in Antioch that the followers of Jesus were first called *Christians*, perhaps as a term of opprobrium. The word appears only two more times: 26.28 and 1 Pet 4.16.

27 Now in these days prophets came down from Jerusalem to Ăn′tĭŏçh. 28And one of them named Ăg′ăbŭs stood up and foretold by the Spirit that there would be a great famine over all the world; and this took place in the days of Claudius. 29And the disciples determined, every one according to his ability, to send relief to the brethren who lived in Jŭdē′a; 30 and they did so, sending it to the elders by the hand of Bar′năbăs and Saul.

E. Herod's persecution

1. Martyrdom of James; imprisonment of Peter

12 About that time Hĕrŏd the king laid violent hands upon some who belonged to the church. 2 He killed James the brother of John with the sword; 3 and when he saw that it pleased the Jews, he proceeded to arrest Peter also. This was during the days of Unleavened Bread. 4And when he had seized him, he put him in prison, and delivered him to four squads of soldiers to guard him, intending after the Passover to bring him out to the people. 5 So Peter was kept in prison; but earnest prayer for him was made to God by the church.

2. Deliverance of Peter

6 The very night when Hĕrŏd was about to bring him out, Peter was sleeping between two soldiers, bound with two chains, and sentries before the door were guarding the prison; 7 and behold, an angel of the Lord appeared, and a light shone in the cell; and he struck Peter on the side and woke him, saying, "Get up quickly." And the chains fell off his hands. 8And the angel said to him, "Dress yourself and put on your sandals." And he did so. And he said to him, "Wrap your mantle around you and follow me." 9And he went out and followed him; he did not know that what was done by the angel was real, but thought he was seeing a vision. 10 When they had passed the first and the second guard, they came to the iron gate leading into the city. It opened to them of its own accord, and they went out and passed on through one street; and immediately the angel left him. 11And Peter came to himself, and said, "Now I am sure that the Lord has sent his angel and rescued me from the hand of Hĕrŏd and from all that the Jewish people were expecting."

*11.27
Acts 18.22;
1 Cor 12.28
*11.28
Acts 21.10
11.29
Rom 15.26;
1 Cor 16.1;
2 Cor 9.1
*11.30
Acts 12.25;
14.23

*12.1

12.2
Mt 4.21;
20.23
12.3
Acts 24.27;
Ex 12.15;
23.15

12.5
Eph 6.18;
1 Thess
5.17

12.6
Acts 21.33

12.7
Acts 5.19;
16.26

12.9
Acts 9.10

12.10
Acts 16.26

12.11
Lk 15.17;
Dan 3.28;
6.22;
2 Cor 1.10;
2 Pet 2.9

11.27 Christian prophets are here mentioned for the first time. Both John the Baptist and Jesus are called prophets. Besides Agabus (see also 21.10), mention is made of the prophets in the church at Antioch (13.1); Judas and Silas are called prophets (15.32), and the four unmarried daughters of Philip the evangelist also prophesied (21.9). Elsewhere in the New Testament the prophets are referred to in 1 Cor 12.28, 29; 14.29, 37; Eph 4.11. It is not certain whether the prophets spoken of in Eph 2.20 and 3.5 are Christian or Old Testament prophets.

11.28 Claudius, emperor from A.D. 41–54, nephew of the emperor Tiberius, and grandson of Livia, the wife of Augustus. Agrippina, his last wife, was a niece. He adopted her son Nero.

11.30 This is the first mention in the New Testament of Christian church officers called elders (or presbyters). In Acts, the elders in the Jerusalem church are referred to further in 15.2–23; 16.4; 21.18. Other references to elders elsewhere in Acts are found in 14.23 and 20.17. Outside of Acts they are mentioned in 1 Tim 4.14; 5.17, 19; Tit 1.5; Jas 5.14; 1 Pet 5.1, 5; 2 Jn 1; 3 Jn 1. Nothing is said about the origin of church officers, but it is probable that the Christian elders were patterned in name and function after the Jewish elders of the synagogue. (See note to Tit 1.5.)

12.1 This is Herod Agrippa I, grandson of Herod the Great, born in 11 B.C. Reared in Rome, he was given the tetrarchies of Iturea, Trachonitis and Gaulinitis (cf. Lk 3.1) in A.D. 37 by the Roman emperor Gaius, who also conferred on him the title of king. Later he was also given rule over Galilee and Perea, and still later, under Claudius, his rule was extended to include Judea and Samaria.

3. The testimony of Peter

12 When he realized this, he went to the house of Mary, the mother of John whose other name was Mark, where many were gathered together and were praying. 13And when he knocked at the door of the gateway, a maid named Rhoda came to answer. 14 Recognizing Peter's voice, in her joy she did not open the gate but ran in and told that Peter was standing at the gate. 15 They said to her, "You are mad." But she insisted that it was so. They said, "It is his angel!" 16 But Peter continued knocking; and when they opened, they saw him and were amazed. 17 But motioning to them with his hand to be silent, he described to them how the Lord had brought him out of the prison. And he said, "Tell this to James and to the brethren." Then he departed and went to another place.

4. Herod's punishment of the guards

18 Now when day came, there was no small stir among the soldiers over what had become of Peter. 19And when Hĕrŏd had sought for him and could not find him, he examined the sentries and ordered that they should be put to death. Then he went down from Judē'à to Çaĕsàrē'à, and remained there.

5. Herod's death

20 Now Hĕrŏd was angry with the people of Tӯre and Sĭdŏn; and they came to him in a body, and having persuaded Blăstŭs, the king's chamberlain, they asked for peace, because their country depended on the king's country for food. 21 On an appointed day Hĕrŏd put on his royal robes, took his seat upon the throne, and made an oration to them. 22And the people shouted, "The voice of a god, and not of man!" 23 Immediately an angel of the Lord smote him, because he did not give God the glory; and he was eaten by worms and died.

24 But the word of God grew and multiplied.

25 And Bar'nàbàs and Saul returned from[k] Jerusalem when they had fulfilled their mission, bringing with them John whose other name was Mark.

III. Throughout the Roman Empire with Paul 13.1–28.31

A. First missionary tour

1. The call of Paul and Barnabas

13 Now in the church at Ăn'tĭŏçh there were prophets and teachers, Bar'nàbàs, Sĭmĕŏn who was called Nĭ́gĕr, Luçius of Çӯrē'nĕ, Mànà'-ĕn a member of the court of Hĕrŏd the tetrarch, and Saul. 2 While they were worshiping the Lord and fasting, the Holy Spirit said, "Set apart for me Bar'nàbàs and Saul for the work to which I have called them." 3 Then after fasting and praying they laid their hands on them and sent them off.

---

k Other ancient authorities read to

13.1 teachers, as a distinct group, are referred to here and in 1 Cor 12.28, 29; Eph 4.11; Heb 5.12; Jas 3.1. Paul's teaching ministry is often referred to (cf. Acts 11.26; 15.35; 18.11; 20.20; 28.31), and he calls himself a teacher in 1 Tim 2.7 and 2 Tim 1.11.

Margin references

12.12 Acts 15.37; ver 5
12.13 Jn 18.16,17
12.14 Lk 24.41
12.15 Gen 48.16; Mt 18.10
12.17 Acts 13.16; 19.33; 21.40
12.19 Acts 16.27; 27.42
12.20 Mt 11.21; 1 Ki 5.9,11; Ezek 27.17
12.23 1 Sam 25.38; 2 Sam 24.17
12.24 Acts 6.7; 19.20
12.25 Acts 13.5, 13; 15.37
*13.1 Acts 11.22–26
13.2 Acts 9.15; 22.21; 14.26
13.3 Acts 6.6; 14.26

2. Their ministry on Cyprus

4 So, being sent out by the Holy Spirit, they went down to Sëleu'çià; and from there they sailed to Cyprus. 5 When they arrived at Säl'àmìs, they proclaimed the word of God in the synagogues of the Jews. And they had John to assist them. 6 When they had gone through the whole island as far as Pāphŏs, they came upon a certain magician, a Jewish false prophet, named Bar-Jesus. 7 He was with the proconsul, Sèr'gĭüs Paulus, a man of intelligence, who summoned Bar'nàbàs and Saul and sought to hear the word of God. 8 But Ĕl'ymàs the magician (for that is the meaning of his name) withstood them, seeking to turn away the proconsul from the faith. 9 But Saul, who is also called Paul, filled with the Holy Spirit, looked intently at him 10 and said, "You son of the devil, you enemy of all righteousness, full of all deceit and villainy, will you not stop making crooked the straight paths of the Lord? 11And now, behold, the hand of the Lord is upon you, and you shall be blind and unable to see the sun for a time." Immediately mist and darkness fell upon him and he went about seeking people to lead him by the hand. 12 Then the proconsul believed, when he saw what had occurred, for he was astonished at the teaching of the Lord.

3. Their ministry to Perga and Antioch

13 Now Paul and his company set sail from Pāphŏs, and came to Pèrgà in Pămphy̆l'ĭà. And John left them and returned to Jerusalem; 14 but they passed on from Pèrgà and came to Ăn'tĭŏçh of Pĭsĭd'ĭà. And on the sabbath day they went into the synagogue and sat down. 15After the reading of the law and the prophets, the rulers of the synagogue sent to them, saying, "Brethren, if you have any word of exhortation for the people, say it." 16 So Paul stood up, and motioning with his hand said:

"Men of Israel, and you that fear God, listen. 17 The God of this people Israel chose our fathers and made the people great during their stay in the land of Egypt, and with uplifted arm he led them out of it. 18And for about forty years he bore with[m] them in the wilderness. 19And when he had destroyed seven nations in the land of Cānaàn, he gave them their land as an inheritance, for about four hundred and fifty years. 20And after that he gave them judges until Samuel the prophet. 21 Then they asked for a king; and God gave them Saul the son of Kish, a man of the tribe of Benjamin, for forty years. 22And when he had removed him, he raised up David to be their king; of whom he testified and said, 'I have found in David the son of Jĕssë a man after my heart, who will do all my will.' 23 Of this man's posterity God has brought

[m] Other ancient authorities read cared for (Deut. 1.31)

13.4	ver 2,3; Acts 4.36
*13.5	
13.5	Acts 9.20
13.6	Acts 8.9
13.7	ver 8,12
13.8	Acts 8.9; ver 7,12; Acts 6.7
13.9	Acts 4.8
13.10	Mt 13.38; Jn 8.44; Hos 14.9
13.11	Ex 9.3
13.12	ver 7,8; Acts 8.25
13.13	Acts 15.38
13.14	Acts 14.19, 21; 16.13
13.17	Deut 7.6-8
13.18	Ex 16.35; Deut 1.31
13.19	Deut 7.1; Josh 19.51
13.20	Judg 2.16; 1 Sam 3.20
13.21	1 Sam 8.5; 10.1
13.22	1 Sam 13.14; 15.23,26
13.23	Isa 11.1; Mt 1.21; Rom 11.26

13.5 The word synagogue comes from the Greek synagōgē—a place where people are brought together. The Old Testament does not make frequent reference to these places of worship. That they existed seems clear from Ps 74.8. Although there are no precise historical references as to the date and place of origin of the synagogues, it would appear that they originated among the Jews of the Dispersion, especially during the last century of the Persian rule (440–330 B.C.). The services in the synagogues consisted of prayer, reading the Old Testament Scriptures, expounding the Scriptures, and praise and thanksgiving to God (Mt 6.5; Acts 13.15; 15.21; Lk 4.16–21; Neh 9.5). Christ Himself attended, taught, and preached in synagogues, and performed miracles before their congregations (Lk 4.16; Mt 4.23; 12.9, 10; Lk 13.10–13). The apostles followed the practice of Christ in this respect (9.20; 13.5; 17.1, 17), though rejection of the gospel message often compelled them to preach their message elsewhere than in synagogues (18.8).

to Israel a Savior, Jesus, as he promised. 24 Before his coming John had preached a baptism of repentance to all the people of Israel. 25And as John was finishing his course, he said, 'What do you suppose that I am? I am not he. No, but after me one is coming, the sandals of whose feet I am not worthy to untie.'

26 "Brethren, sons of the family of Abraham, and those among you that fear God, to us has been sent the message of this salvation. 27 For those who live in Jerusalem and their rulers, because they did not recognize him nor understand the utterances of the prophets which are read every sabbath, fulfilled these by condemning him. 28 Though they could charge him with nothing deserving death, yet they asked Pilate to have him killed. 29And when they had fulfilled all that was written of him, they took him down from the tree, and laid him in a tomb. 30 But God raised him from the dead; 31 and for many days he appeared to those who came up with him from Găl'ilee to Jerusalem, who are now his witnesses to the people. 32And we bring you the good news that what God promised to the fathers, 33 this he has fulfilled to us their children by raising Jesus; as also it is written in the second psalm,

'Thou art my Son,
    today I have begotten thee.'

34And as for the fact that he raised him from the dead, no more to return to corruption, he spoke in this way,

'I will give you the holy and sure blessings of David.'

35 Therefore he says also in another psalm,

'Thou wilt not let thy Holy One see corruption.'

36 For David, after he had served the counsel of God in his own generation, fell asleep, and was laid with his fathers, and saw corruption; 37 but he whom God raised up saw no corruption. 38 Let it be known to you therefore, brethren, that through this man forgiveness of sins is proclaimed to you, 39 and by him every one that believes is freed from everything from which you could not be freed by the law of Moses. 40 Beware, therefore, lest there come upon you what is said in the prophets:

41 'Behold, you scoffers, and wonder, and perish;
    for I do a deed in your days,
    a deed you will never believe, if one declares it to you.'"

42 As they went out, the people begged that these things might be told them the next sabbath. 43And when the meeting of the synagogue broke up, many Jews and devout converts to Judaism followed Paul and Bar'nábás, who spoke to them and urged them to continue in the grace of God.

44 The next sabbath almost the whole city gathered together to hear the word of God. 45 But when the Jews saw the multitudes, they were filled with jealousy, and contradicted what was spoken by Paul, and reviled him. 46And Paul and Bar'nábás spoke out boldly, saying, "It was necessary that the word of God should be spoken first to you. Since you thrust it from you, and judge yourselves unworthy of eternal life, behold, we turn to the Gentiles. 47 For so the Lord has commanded us, saying,

'I have set you to be a light for the Gentiles,
    that you may bring salvation to the uttermost parts of the
    earth.'"

13.24 Mt 3.1; Lk 3.3
13.25 Mt 3.11; Lk 3.16
13.27 Lk 23.13; Acts 3.17; Lk 24.27
13.28 Mt 27.22
13.29 Lk 18.31; Mt 27.59
13.30 Mt 28.6
13.31 Mt 28.16; Lk 24.48
13.32 Gen 3.15; Rom 4.13
13.33 Ps 2.7
13.34 Isa 55.3
13.35 Ps 16.10; Acts 2.27
13.36 Acts 2.29; 1 Ki 2.10
13.38 Lk 24.47
★13.39 Rom 3.28; Acts 10.43
13.40 Jn 6.45
13.41 Hab 1.5
13.42 ver 14
13.43 Acts 11.23; 14.22
13.45 Acts 18.6; 1 Pet 4.4; Jude 10
13.46 ver 26; Acts 3.26; 18.6; 28.28
★13.47 Isa 49.6; Lk 2.32

13.39 See note to Hab 2.4 on justification.   **13.47** Reflects God's concern for all men.

48 And when the Gentiles heard this, they were glad and glorified the word of God; and as many as were ordained to eternal life believed. 49And the word of the Lord spread throughout all the region. 50 But the Jews incited the devout women of high standing and the leading men of the city, and stirred up persecution against Paul and Bar′nabas, and drove them out of their district. 51 But they shook off the dust from their feet against them, and went to Ĭcō′nǐum. 52And the disciples were filled with joy and with the Holy Spirit.

4. *Their ministry at Iconium*

14 Now at Ĭcō′nǐum they entered together into the Jewish synagogue, and so spoke that a great company believed, both of Jews and of Greeks. 2 But the unbelieving Jews stirred up the Gentiles and poisoned their minds against the brethren. 3 So they remained for a long time, speaking boldly for the Lord, who bore witness to the word of his grace, granting signs and wonders to be done by their hands. 4 But the people of the city were divided; some sided with the Jews, and some with the apostles. 5 When an attempt was made by both Gentiles and Jews, with their rulers, to molest them and to stone them, 6 they learned of it and fled to Lȳstra and Dĕrbē, cities of Lȳcaō′nǐa, and to the surrounding country; 7 and there they preached the gospel.

5. *Their ministry at Lystra*

8 Now at Lȳstra there was a man sitting, who could not use his feet; he was a cripple from birth, who had never walked. 9 He listened to Paul speaking; and Paul, looking intently at him and seeing that he had faith to be made well, 10 said in a loud voice, "Stand upright on your feet." And he sprang up and walked. 11And when the crowds saw what Paul had done, they lifted up their voices, saying in Lȳcaō′nǐan, "The gods have come down to us in the likeness of men!" 12 Bar′nabas they called Zeus, and Paul, because he was the chief speaker, they called Hĕr′mēs. 13And the priest of Zeus, whose temple was in front of the city, brought oxen and garlands to the gates and wanted to offer sacrifice with the people. 14 But when the apostles Bar′nabas and Paul heard of it, they tore their garments and rushed out among the multitude, crying, 15 "Men, why are you doing this? We also are men, of like nature with you, and bring you good news, that you should turn from these vain things to a living God who made the heaven and the earth and the sea and all that is in them. 16 In past generations he allowed all the nations to walk in their own ways; 17 yet he did not leave himself without witness, for he did good and gave you from heaven rains and fruitful seasons, satisfying your hearts with food and gladness." 18 With these words they scarcely restrained the people from offering sacrifice to them.

6. *Their return to Antioch*

19 But Jews came there from Ăn′tǐŏch and Ĭcō′nǐum; and having persuaded the people, they stoned Paul and dragged him out of the city, supposing that he was dead. 20 But when the disciples gathered about him, he rose up and entered the city; and on the next day he went on with Bar′nabas to Dĕrbē. 21 When they had preached the gospel to that city and had made many disciples, they

13.48
Acts 2.47;
Rom 8.28ff

13.51
Mt 10.14;
Mk 6.11;
Lk 9.5;
Acts 18.6
13.52
Acts 2.4

14.1
Acts 13.51;
13.5; 2.47;
18.4

14.3
Heb 2.4;
Jn 4.48

14.4
Acts 17.4,5;
ver 14

14.5
2 Tim 3.11
14.6
Mt 10.23

14.8
Acts 3.2
14.9
Acts 3.4;
10.4;
Mt 9.28,29

14.11
Acts 8.10;
28.6

14.15
Acts 10.26;
Jas 5.17;
1 Sam
12.21;
Jer 14.22;
1 Cor 8.4;
Gen 1.1;
Ps 146.6;
Rev 14.7
14.16
Ps 81.12;
Acts 17.30;
1 Pet 4.3
14.17
Acts 17.27;
Rom 1.20;
Deut 11.14;
Job 5.10;
Ps 65.10

14.19
Acts 13.45;
2 Cor
11.25;
2 Tim 3.11

14.20
ver 22,28

14.22 Acts 11.23; 13.43; Jn 16.33; 1 Thess 3.3; 2 Tim 3.12	returned to Lўstrá and to Īcō'nĭŭm and to Ăn'tĭŏçh, 22 strengthening the souls of the disciples, exhorting them to continue in the faith, and saying that through many tribulations we must enter the kingdom of God. 23And when they had appointed elders for
14.23 Tit 1.5; Acts 11.30; 13.3; 20.32	them in every church, with prayer and fasting, they committed them to the Lord in whom they believed.
14.26 Acts 11.19; 13.1,3; 15.40	24 Then they passed through Pĭsĭd'ĭá, and came to Pămphўl'ĭă. 25And when they had spoken the word in Pêrgà, they went down to Ăttálī'à; 26 and from there they sailed to Ăn'tĭŏçh, where they had been commended to the grace of God for the work which they
14.27 Acts 15.4, 12; 21.19; 1 Cor 16.9; 2 Cor 2.12; Col 4.3	had fulfilled. 27And when they arrived, they gathered the church together and declared all that God had done with them, and how he had opened a door of faith to the Gentiles. 28And they remained no little time with the disciples.

B. The Jerusalem conference

1. *The problem stated*

15.1 ver 24; Gal 2.12; ver 5; Gal 5.2; Acts 6.14	15 But some men came down from Judē'á and were teaching the brethren, "Unless you are circumcised according to the custom of Moses, you cannot be saved." 2And when Paul and Bar'nábàs had no small dissension and debate with them, Paul and
15.2 ver 7; Gal 2.2; Acts 11.30	Barnabas and some of the others were appointed to go up to Jerusalem to the apostles and the elders about this question. 3 So, being sent on their way by the church, they passed through both
★15.3 Acts 20.38; Rom 15.24; 1 Cor 16.6, 11; Acts 14.27	Phoèni'cià and Sàmạr'ĭá, reporting the conversion of the Gentiles, and they gave great joy to all the brethren. 4 When they came to Jerusalem, they were welcomed by the church and the apostles and the elders, and they declared all that God had done with them.
15.4 ver 12; Acts 14.27	5 But some believers who belonged to the party of the Phạr'ĭseẽs rose up, and said, "It is necessary to circumcise them, and to charge them to keep the law of Moses."

2. *The council deciding*

15.7 Acts 10.19, 20; 20.24	6 The apostles and the elders were gathered together to consider this matter. 7And after there had been much debate, Peter rose and said to them, "Brethren, you know that in the early days
15.8 Acts 1.24; 10.44,47	God made choice among you, that by my mouth the Gentiles should hear the word of the gospel and believe. 8And God who knows the heart bore witness to them, giving them the Holy
15.9 Acts 10.28, 34 43; 11.12	Spirit just as he did to us; 9 and he made no distinction between us and them, but cleansed their hearts by faith. 10 Now there-
15.10 Mt 23.4; Gal 5.1	fore why do you make trial of God by putting a yoke upon the neck of the disciples which neither our fathers nor we have been
15.11 Rom 3.24; Eph 2.5–8; Tit 2.11; 3.4,5	able to bear? 11 But we believe that we shall be saved through the grace of the Lord Jesus, just as they will."
★15.12 Jn 4.48; Acts 14.27	12 And all the assembly kept silence; and they listened to Bar'-

---

15.3 Conversion connotes a change *from* one condition or state *to* another condition or state. Turning *from* something involves repentance. Turning *to* something involves faith. Both elements are at work in the experience of conversion.

15.12 This is a very significant passage of Scripture (ver 12–18). From verse 12 it appears that the Jews felt there was no place for

Gentiles in the gospel economy. James proved, from the Old Testament Scriptures, that the Gentiles were spoken of by the prophets, and furthermore, Paul later argued cogently that the Gentile believers constitute the new Israel (see Gal 3 and Rom 9–11). Despite this, God still has a concern for Israel and Paul states that eventually *all Israel will be saved* (Rom 11.26).

nábás and Paul as they related what signs and wonders God had done through them among the Gentiles. [13]After they finished speaking, James replied, "Brethren, listen to me. [14] Sǐm´ē̇on has related how God first visited the Gentiles, to take out of them a people for his name. [15]And with this the words of the prophets agree, as it is written,

[16] 'After this I will return,
　　and I will rebuild the dwelling of David, which has fallen;
　I will rebuild its ruins,
　　and I will set it up,
[17] that the rest of men may seek the Lord,
　　and all the Gentiles who are called by my name,
[18] says the Lord, who has made these things known from of old.'
[19] Therefore my judgment is that we should not trouble those of the Gentiles who turn to God, [20] but should write to them to abstain from the pollutions of idols and from unchastity and from what is strangled[n] and from blood. [21] For from early generations Moses has had in every city those who preach him, for he is read every sabbath in the synagogues."

3. The decision communicated

22 Then it seemed good to the apostles and the elders, with the whole church, to choose men from among them and send them to Ǎn´tǐŏçh with Paul and Bar´nábás. They sent Judas called Barsǎb´bás, and Sǐlás, leading men among the brethren, [23] with the following letter: "The brethren, both the apostles and the elders, to the brethren who are of the Gentiles in Ǎn´tǐŏçh and Syria and Çǐlǐ´çǐá, greeting. [24] Since we have heard that some persons from us have troubled you with words, unsettling your minds, although we gave them no instructions, [25] it has seemed good to us, having come to one accord, to choose men and send them to you with our beloved Bar´nábás and Paul, [26] men who have risked their lives for the sake of our Lord Jesus Christ. [27] We have therefore sent Judas and Sǐlás, who themselves will tell you the same things by word of mouth. [28] For it has seemed good to the Holy Spirit and to us to lay upon you no greater burden than these necessary things: [29] that you abstain from what has been sacrificed to idols and from blood and from what is strangled[n] and from unchastity. If you keep yourselves from these, you will do well. Farewell."

30 So when they were sent off, they went down to Ǎn´tǐŏçh; and having gathered the congregation together, they delivered the letter. [31]And when they read it, they rejoiced at the exhortation. [32]And Judas and Sǐlás, who were themselves prophets, exhorted the brethren with many words and strengthened them. [33]And after they had spent some time, they were sent off in peace by the brethren to those who had sent them.[o] But Paul and Bar´nábás remained in Ǎn´tǐŏçh, teaching and preaching the word of the Lord, with many others also.

[n] Other early authorities omit and from what is strangled
[o] Other ancient authorities insert verse 34, But it seemed good to Sǐlás to remain there

15.13
Acts 12.17

15.15
Acts 13.40

15.16
Amos 9.11, 12;
Jer 12.15

15.20
ver 29;
1 Cor 8.7–13; 10.7, 8,14–28;
Rev 2.14, 20;
Gen 9.4;
Lev 3.17;
Deut 12.16, 23

15.21
Acts 13.15;
2 Cor 3.14, 15

15.22
Acts 11.20;
ver 27,32, 40

15.23
ver 1,41;
Acts 23.26;
Jas 1.1

15.24
ver 1;
Gal 1.7;
5.10

15.26
Acts 14.19;
1 Cor 15.30

*15.28

15.29
ver 20;
Acts 21.25;
Lev 17.14

15.33
Acts 16.36;
1 Cor 16.11;
Heb 11.31

15.28 At the first church council the apostles and elders rendered a decision based upon the guidance of the Holy Spirit. They were absolutely confident that He had revealed His will to them in arriving at this decision. But decisions made apart from the will and guidance of God are likely to prove wrong, and Scripture nowhere suggests that believers may safely rely upon self-determined decisions, no matter how sensible they may seem.

C. Second missionary tour

1. Asia Minor

a. Separation of Paul and Barnabas

★15.36ff
Acts 13.4,
13,14,51;
14.1,6,24,
25
15.37
Acts 12.12
15.38
Acts 13.13

15.41
Acts 16.5

16.1
Acts 14.6;
19.22;
Rom 16.21;
1 Cor 4.17;
2 Tim 1.2;
1.5
★16.3
Gal 2.3
16.4
Acts 15.28,
29; 15.2;
11.30
16.5
Acts 15.41
16.6
Acts 18.23;
2.9
16.7
ver 8;
Lk 24.49;
Rom 8.9;
Gal 4.6
16.8
ver 11;
2 Cor 2.12;
2 Tim 4.13
16.9
Acts 9.10;
18.5; 20.1,
3; 27.2

36 And after some days Paul said to Bar′nàbàs, "Come, let us return and visit the brethren in every city where we proclaimed the word of the Lord, and see how they are." 37And Bar′nàbàs wanted to take with them John called Mark. 38 But Paul thought best not to take with them one who had withdrawn from them in Pàmphŷl′ïà, and had not gone with them to the work. 39And there arose a sharp contention, so that they separated from each other; Bar′nàbàs took Mark with him and sailed away to Cyprus, 40 but Paul chose Sïlàs and departed, being commended by the brethren to the grace of the Lord. 41And he went through Syria and Çïlï′çïà, strengthening the churches.

b. Selection of Timothy

16 And he came also to Dèrbë and to Lŷstrà. A disciple was there, named Timothy, the son of a Jewish woman who was a believer; but his father was a Greek. 2 He was well spoken of by the brethren at Lŷstrà and Ïcō′nïüm. 3 Paul wanted Timothy to accompany him; and he took him and circumcised him because of the Jews that were in those places, for they all knew that his father was a Greek. 4As they went on their way through the cities, they delivered to them for observance the decisions which had been reached by the apostles and elders who were at Jerusalem. 5 So the churches were strengthened in the faith, and they increased in numbers daily.

c. The Macedonian call

6 And they went through the region of Phrŷ′gïà and Gàlā′tïà, having been forbidden by the Holy Spirit to speak the word in Asia. 7And when they had come opposite Mŷ′sïà, they attempted to go into Bïthŷn′ïà, but the Spirit of Jesus did not allow them; 8 so, passing by Mŷ′sïà, they went down to Trōàs. 9And a vision appeared to Paul in the night: a man of Màçèdō′nïà was standing beseeching him and saying, "Come over to Maçedonia and help

---

15.36ff Dissension existed between Paul and Barnabas over John Mark (see 15.39). The solution to their dissension lay in their decision to go their separate ways. It is not always possible, in this present life, for believers to work with everybody without dissension. While those who are in disagreement should go their own ways, it should be done without acrimony, recrimination, or hostility and bad feelings.

16.3 Paul circumcised Timothy despite his sturdy insistence that the rite was no longer necessary for salvation (Gal 2.3–5). Doctrinal principle did not require it, but strategic considerations made it desirable under the peculiar circumstances at that time. Scripture lays down the maxim that if an act is inherently wrong it is never to be performed no matter how expedient it may seem. (E.g., it appeared expedient to David to have Uriah the Hittite slain lest his adultery with Bathsheba be discovered. God reproved him both for the adultery *and* the sin of murder, which were forbidden (2 Sam 12.9). David did not slay Uriah himself, but was an accessory before the fact and thus charged with the crime by God.) But many acts are not inherently wrong and may be performed or not performed, depending on what will best promote the gospel. Paul argued that eating meat offered to idols was not sinful in itself, but he would eat no meat if by doing so his brother were offended. This is expediency (1 Cor 8.1–13). Paul's quotation, *All things are lawful* (1 Cor 6.12; 10.23) must be understood in the light of its context, for everywhere in Scripture it is recognized that there are acts which are always unlawful (e.g., the prohibitions expressed in the Ten Commandments which ever remain valid in principle). In the passage under consideration here, Paul had Timothy circumcised because it would enlarge the usefulness of his junior assistant for Christian evangelism to the Jews.

us." 10And when he had seen the vision, immediately we sought
to go on into Măçėdō'nĭä, concluding that God had called us to
preach the gospel to them.

2. The Macedonian ministry
a. At Philippi

11 Setting sail therefore from Trōäs, we made a direct voyage
to Săm'ŏthrāce, and the following day to Nĕ-ăp'ŏlĭs, 12 and from
there to Phĭl'ĭppī, which is the leading city of the district*x* of
Măçėdō'nĭä, and a Roman colony. We remained in this city some
days; 13 and on the sabbath day we went outside the gate to the
riverside, where we supposed there was a place of prayer; and we
sat down and spoke to the women who had come together. 14 One
who heard us was a woman named Lydia, from the city of Thÿătī'-
rä, a seller of purple goods, who was a worshiper of God. The
Lord opened her heart to give heed to what was said by Paul.
15And when she was baptized, with her household, she besought
us, saying, "If you have judged me to be faithful to the Lord, come
to my house and stay." And she prevailed upon us.

16 As we were going to the place of prayer, we were met by a
slave girl who had a spirit of divination and brought her owners
much gain by soothsaying. 17 She followed Paul and us, crying,
"These men are servants of the Most High God, who proclaim
to you the way of salvation." 18And this she did for many days.
But Paul was annoyed, and turned and said to the spirit, "I
charge you in the name of Jesus Christ to come out of her." And
it came out that very hour.

19 But when her owners saw that their hope of gain was gone,
they seized Paul and Sīlàs and dragged them into the market place
before the rulers; 20 and when they had brought them to the magistrates they said, "These men are Jews and they are disturbing
our city. 21 They advocate customs which it is not lawful for us Romans to accept or practice." 22 The crowd joined in attacking
them; and the magistrates tore the garments off them and gave
orders to beat them with rods. 23And when they had inflicted
many blows upon them, they threw them into prison, charging the
jailer to keep them safely. 24 Having received this charge, he put
them into the inner prison and fastened their feet in the stocks.

25 But about midnight Paul and Sīlàs were praying and singing
hymns to God, and the prisoners were listening to them, 26 and
suddenly there was a great earthquake, so that the foundations of
the prison were shaken; and immediately all the doors were
opened and every one's fetters were unfastened. 27 When the
jailer woke and saw that the prison doors were open, he drew
his sword and was about to kill himself, supposing that the prisoners had escaped. 28 But Paul cried with a loud voice, "Do not
harm yourself, for we are all here." 29And he called for lights and
rushed in, and trembling with fear he fell down before Paul and

x The Greek text is uncertain

*16.10
2 Cor 2.13

16.11
ver 8;
2 Tim 4.13
16.12
Phil 1.1;
Acts 18.5;
19.21,22,
29; 20.1,3;
27.2
16.13
Acts 13.14
16.14
Lk 24.45

16.15
Acts 11.14;
Lk 24.29

16.16
Deut 18.11;
1 Sam 28,3,
7
16.17
Mk 5.7

16.19
Acts 19.25,
26; 15.40;
17.6,7;
Jas 2.6
16.20
Acts 17.6
16.22
2 Cor 11.23,
25;
1 Thess 2.2
16.23
ver 27,36
16.24
Jer 20.2,3

16.25
Eph 5.19
16.26
Acts 4.31;
5.19;
12.7,10
16.27
Acts 12.19

16.10 For the first time the author of
Acts associates himself with the narrative
*we sought to go on into Macedonia, con-
cluding that God had called us to preach the
gospel to them.* This first so-called "we"
section begins here, and it appears that Luke
joined Paul and his group in Troas, went on
with them to Philippi, but did not accompany
them when they left Philippi (ver 40). The
other "we" section begins in Philippi, some
six or seven years later (20.5), and continues
to the end of the book.

Sīlás, 30 and brought them out and said, "Men, what must I do to be saved?" 31And they said, "Believe in the Lord Jesus, and you will be saved, you and your household." 32And they spoke the word of the Lord to him and to all that were in his house. 33And he took them the same hour of the night, and washed their wounds, and he was baptized at once, with all his family. 34 Then he brought them up into his house, and set food before them; and he rejoiced with all his household that he had believed in God.

35 But when it was day, the magistrates sent the police, saying, "Let those men go." 36And the jailer reported the words to Paul, saying, "The magistrates have sent to let you go; now therefore come out and go in peace." 37 But Paul said to them, "They have beaten us publicly, uncondemned, men who are Roman citizens, and have thrown us into prison; and do they now cast us out secretly? No! let them come themselves and take us out." 38 The police reported these words to the magistrates, and they were afraid when they heard that they were Roman citizens; 39 so they came and apologized to them. And they took them out and asked them to leave the city. 40 So they went out of the prison, and visited Lydia; and when they had seen the brethren, they exhorted them and departed.

b. At Thessalonica

17 Now when they had passed through Ămphĭp'olĭs and Ăp'ŏllō'nĭă, they came to Thěssălŏnī'cá, where there was a synagogue of the Jews. 2And Paul went in, as was his custom, and for three weeksᵖ he argued with them from the scriptures, 3 explaining and proving that it was necessary for the Christ to suffer and to rise from the dead, and saying, "This Jesus, whom I proclaim to you, is the Christ." 4And some of them were persuaded, and joined Paul and Sīlás; as did a great many of the devout Greeks and not a few of the leading women. 5 But the Jews were jealous, and taking some wicked fellows of the rabble, they gathered a crowd, set the city in an uproar, and attacked the house of Jāsón, seeking to bring them out to the people. 6And when they could not find them, they dragged Jāsón and some of the brethren before the city authorities, crying, "These men who have turned the world upside down have come here also, 7 and Jāsón has received them; and they are all acting against the decrees of Caesar, saying that there is another king, Jesus." 8And the people and the city authorities were disturbed when they heard this. 9And when they had taken security from Jāsón and the rest, they let them go.

c. At Beroea

10 The brethren immediately sent Paul and Sīlás away by night to Běroē'á; and when they arrived they went into the Jewish synagogue. 11 Now these Jews were more noble than those in Thěssălŏnī'cá, for they received the word with all eagerness, examining the scriptures daily to see if these things were so. 12 Many of them therefore believed, with not a few Greek women of high standing as well as men. 13 But when the Jews of Thěssălŏnī'cá learned that the word of God was proclaimed by Paul at Běroē'á also, they came there too, stirring up and inciting the crowds. 14 Then the brethren immediately sent Paul off on his way to the sea, but

ᵖ Or sabbaths

Sĭläs and Timothy remained there. ¹⁵ Those who conducted Paul brought him as far as Athens; and receiving a command for Sĭläs and Timothy to come to him as soon as possible, they departed.

17.15
Acts 15.3;
ver 16,
21,22;
Acts 18.5

3. The ministry in Greece
a. At Athens

16 Now while Paul was waiting for them at Athens, his spirit was provoked within him as he saw that the city was full of idols. ¹⁷ So he argued in the synagogue with the Jews and the devout persons, and in the market place every day with those who chanced to be there. ¹⁸ Some also of the Ĕpĭcūrē'ăn and Stŏĭc philosophers met him. And some said, "What would this babbler say?" Others said, "He seems to be a preacher of foreign divinities"—because he preached Jesus and the resurrection. ¹⁹And they took hold of him and brought him to the Ăr̆ĕ-ŏp'ăgŭs, saying, "May we know what this new teaching is which you present? ²⁰ For you bring some strange things to our ears; we wish to know therefore what these things mean." ²¹ Now all the Athenians and the foreigners who lived there spent their time in nothing except telling or hearing something new.

22 So Paul, standing in the middle of the Ăr̆ĕ-ŏp'ăgŭs, said: "Men of Athens, I perceive that in every way you are very religious. ²³ For as I passed along, and observed the objects of your worship, I found also an altar with this inscription, 'To an unknown god.' What therefore you worship as unknown, this I proclaim to you. ²⁴ The God who made the world and everything in it, being Lord of heaven and earth, does not live in shrines made by man, ²⁵ nor is he served by human hands, as though he needed anything, since he himself gives to all men life and breath and everything. ²⁶And he made from one every nation of men to live on all the face of the earth, having determined allotted periods and the boundaries of their habitation, ²⁷ that they should seek God, in the hope that they might feel after him and find him. Yet he is not far from each one of us, ²⁸ for

'In him we live and move and have our being';

as even some of your poets have said,

'For we are indeed his offspring.'

²⁹ Being then God's offspring, we ought not to think that the Deity is like gold, or silver, or stone, a representation by the art and imagination of man. ³⁰ The times of ignorance God over-

17.16
2 Pet 2.8

*17.18
1 Cor 4.10;
Acts 4.2

17.19
Acts 23.19;
ver 22

17.24
Isa 42.5;
Acts 14.15;
Mt 11.25;
Acts 7.48

17.25
Ps 50.10–
12;
Isa 42.5;
57.16;
Zech 12.1

17.26
Mal 2.10;
Deut 32.8

17.27
Rom 1.20;
Acts 14.17

17.28
Col 1.17;
Heb 1.3;
Epimenides;
Aratus,
Phaeno-
mena, 5

17.29
Isa 40.18ff

*17.30
ver 23;
Acts 14.16;
Rom 3.25;
Lk 24.47;
Tit 2.11,12;
1 Pet 1.14

17.18 The Epicureans derived their philosophic teachings from their founder Epicurus who was born 342 B.C. He lived in Athens during the later years of his life. He taught that the supreme good in life is pleasure or that which will bring man the greatest satisfaction. He argued that each man must consider the consequences of his actions and their effects on those who are related to him. The charge of the Stoics that his teaching led to sloth and sensuality was probably not justified. The Stoics also claimed that Epicurus was an atheist. The school of the Stoics was founded by Zeno (ca. 278 B.C.). The key concept of Stoicism was to possess the courage never to submit or yield. It was a philosophy of indifference to either pleasure or pain.

To both the Epicureans and the Stoics, the teaching of Paul was a novelty because it cut across the lines of their own teachings.

17.30 The doctrine of repentance is taught throughout the New Testament. No one can be regenerated without repentance. Repentance itself cannot confer salvation or merit it in any way, but it does bring a person to a place where the forgiving grace of God can meet him. There are five steps to genuine repentance: (1) a change of mind (Mt 21.28, 29; Lk 15.17, 18; Acts 2.38); (2) godly sorrow for sin (Ps 38.18; Lk 18.9–14; 10.13); (3) confession of sin (Lk 15.18; 18.13); (4) forsaking of sins (Jn 8.11 in RSV footnote; Prov 28.13; Isa 55.7); (5) turning to God as Savior and Lord (26.18; 1 Thess 1.9).

looked, but now he commands all men everywhere to repent, ³¹ because he has fixed a day on which he will judge the world in righteousness by a man whom he has appointed, and of this he has given assurance to all men by raising him from the dead."

32 Now when they heard of the resurrection of the dead, some mocked; but others said, "We will hear you again about this." ³³ So Paul went out from among them. ³⁴ But some men joined him and believed, among them Dīŏnўs'ĭŭs the Ar̄e-ŏp'ăġĭte and a woman named Dăm'ărĭs and others with them.

b. At Corinth

18 After this he left Athens and went to Corinth. ²And he found a Jew named Ăquĭ'lă, a native of Pŏntŭs, lately come from Italy with his wife Priscilla, because Claudius had commanded all the Jews to leave Rome. And he went to see them; ³ and because he was of the same trade he stayed with them, and they worked, for by trade they were tentmakers. ⁴And he argued in the synagogue every sabbath, and persuaded Jews and Greeks.

5 When Sīlăs and Timothy arrived from Măçĕdō'nĭă, Paul was occupied with preaching, testifying to the Jews that the Christ was Jesus. ⁶And when they opposed and reviled him, he shook out his garments and said to them, "Your blood be upon your heads! I am innocent. From now on I will go to the Gentiles." ⁷And he left there and went to the house of a man named Tĭţĭŭs^q Jŭstŭs, a worshiper of God; his house was next door to the synagogue. ⁸ Crĭspŭs, the ruler of the synagogue, believed in the Lord, together with all his household; and many of the Corinthians hearing Paul believed and were baptized. ⁹And the Lord said to Paul one night in a vision, "Do not be afraid, but speak and do not be silent; ¹⁰ for I am with you, and no man shall attack you to harm you; for I have many people in this city." ¹¹And he stayed a year and six months, teaching the word of God among them.

12 But when Găl'lĭŏ was proconsul of Ăchāi'ă, the Jews made a united attack upon Paul and brought him before the tribunal, ¹³ saying, "This man is persuading men to worship God contrary to the law." ¹⁴ But when Paul was about to open his mouth, Găl'lĭŏ said to the Jews, "If it were a matter of wrongdoing or vicious crime, I should have reason to bear with you, O Jews; ¹⁵ but since it is a matter of questions about words and names and your own law, see to it yourselves; I refuse to be a judge of these things." ¹⁶And he drove them from the tribunal. ¹⁷And they all seized Sŏs'thĕnēṣ, the ruler of the synagogue, and beat him in front of the tribunal. But Găl'lĭŏ paid no attention to this.

4. The return to Antioch

18 After this Paul stayed many days longer, and then took leave of the brethren and sailed for Syria, and with him Priscilla and

^q Other early authorities read Titus

17.34 Paul's ministry in Athens was evidently not too successful. It was one of the few places where no church was founded in connection with his preaching. He was discouraged, but when he came to Corinth God promised him fruit.
18.12 Achaia was the Roman province of

which Corinth was the capital. The proconsul Gallio, brother of the philosopher Seneca, and uncle of the poet Lucan, was appointed to his position by the emperor Claudius in July of A.D. 51.
18.18 For information on vows, see note to Num 6.2.

17.31 Mt 10.15; Acts 10.42; Lk 22.22; Acts 22.4
*17.34 ver 19,22
18.1 Acts 17.15; 1 Cor 1.2
18.2 Rom 16.3; 1 Cor 16.19; 2 Tim 4.19; Acts 11.28
18.3 Acts 20.34; 1 Cor 4.12; 1 Thess 2.9; 2 Thess 3.8
18.4 Acts 17.2
18.5 Acts 17.14, 15; 16.9; 20.21; ver 28; Acts 17.3
18.6 Acts 13.45, 51; 2 Sam 1.16; Ezek 18.13; Acts 20.26; 13.46
18.7 Acts 16.14
18.8 1 Cor 1.14
18.9 Acts 23.11
18.10 Mt 28.20
*18.12
18.14 Acts 23.29; 25.11,19
18.17 1 Cor 1.1
*18.18 Num 6.18; Acts 21.24; Rom 16.1

Aqui'la. At Çĕnҫhrē'-aĕ he cut his hair, for he had a vow. ¹⁹And
they came to Ēph'ĕsŭs, and he left them there; but he himself
went into the synagogue and argued with the Jews. ²⁰ When they
asked him to stay for a longer period, he declined; ²¹ but on taking
leave of them he said, "I will return to you if God wills," and he
set sail from Ēph'ĕsŭs.

*18.19

18.21
1 Cor 4.19

D. Third missionary tour

1. At Galatia and Phrygia

22 When he had landed at Çaĕsărē'ă, he went up and greeted
the church, and then went down to Ăn'tĭŏҫh. ²³After spending
some time there he departed and went from place to place through
the region of Gălā'tĭă and Phrŷg'ĭă, strengthening all the disciples.

18.22
Acts 11.19
18.23
Acts 16.6;
14.22;
15.32,41

2. At Ephesus
a. The preaching of Apollos

24 Now a Jew named Ăpŏl'lŏs, a native of Alexandria, came to
Ēph'ĕsŭs. He was an eloquent man, well versed in the scriptures.
²⁵ He had been instructed in the way of the Lord; and being
fervent in spirit, he spoke and taught accurately the things concerning Jesus, though he knew only the baptism of John. ²⁶ He
began to speak boldly in the synagogue; but when Priscilla and
Aqui'la heard him, they took him and expounded to him the way
of God more accurately. ²⁷And when he wished to cross to
Ăchāi'ă, the brethren encouraged him, and wrote to the disciples
to receive him. When he arrived, he greatly helped those who
through grace had believed, ²⁸ for he powerfully confuted the
Jews in public, showing by the scriptures that the Christ was
Jesus.

18.24
Acts 19.1;
1 Cor 1.12;
3.5,6; 4.6;
Tit 3.13
18.25
Rom 12.11;
Acts 19.3

18.27
ver 12,18

18.28
Acts 9.22;
17.3;
ver 5

b. Paul's and John's disciples

19 While Ăpŏl'lŏs was at Corinth, Paul passed through the
upper country and came to Ēph'ĕsŭs. There he found some
disciples. ²And he said to them, "Did you receive the Holy
Spirit when you believed?" And they said, "No, we have never
even heard that there is a Holy Spirit." ³And he said, "Into what
then were you baptized?" They said, "Into John's baptism."
⁴And Paul said, "John baptized with the baptism of repentance,
telling the people to believe in the one who was to come after him,
that is, Jesus." ⁵ On hearing this, they were baptized in the name
of the Lord Jesus. ⁶And when Paul had laid his hands upon them,
the Holy Spirit came on them; and they spoke with tongues and
prophesied. ⁷ There were about twelve of them in all.

19.1
1 Cor 1.12;
3.5,6;
Acts 18.1,
19–24
19.3
Acts 18.25
19.4
Mt 3.11;
Acts 13.24,
25
19.6
Acts 6.6;
8.17; 2.4;
10.46
19.8
Acts 17.2;
18.4; 1.3;
28.23

c. Paul in the synagogue and the hall of Tyrannus

8 And he entered the synagogue and for three months spoke

18.19 Paul, for the first time, entered this
city which was to become an important center in the early Christian work. At the beginning of his second missionary tour he
had been prevented by the Holy Spirit from
preaching in the Roman province of Asia, of
which Ephesus was the capital city (16.6).
Now, at the end of this tour, he stayed only a
few days, but returned to the city on his next

tour and stayed there for three years (19.1–
20.1; 20.31). On his return to Jerusalem he
avoided the city, since he was in a hurry to
reach Jerusalem by Pentecost (20.16), but at
Miletus he summoned the elders of the
church at Ephesus, addressed them in eloquent terms, and bade them farewell with the
sad prediction that they would not see him
again (20.17–38).

19.9
Acts 14.4;
2 Tim 1.15;
Acts 9.2;
ver 30
19.10
Acts 20.31;
ver 22,26,
27;
Acts 13.12

boldly, arguing and pleading about the kingdom of God; 9 but when some were stubborn and disbelieved, speaking evil of the Way before the congregation, he withdrew from them, taking the disciples with him, and argued daily in the hall of Tўrăn'nŭs.ʳ 10 This continued for two years, so that all the residents of Asia heard the word of the Lord, both Jews and Greeks.

d. *Miracles by Paul*

19.11
Acts 8.13
19.12
Acts 5.15
19.13
Mt 12.27;
Mk 9.38;
Lk 9.49

11 And God did extraordinary miracles by the hands of Paul, 12 so that handkerchiefs or aprons were carried away from his body to the sick, and diseases left them and the evil spirits came out of them. 13 Then some of the itinerant Jewish exorcists undertook to pronounce the name of the Lord Jesus over those who had evil spirits, saying, "I adjure you by the Jesus whom Paul preaches." 14 Seven sons of a Jewish high priest named Sçēvà were doing this. 15 But the evil spirit answered them, "Jesus I know, and Paul I know; but who are you?" 16And the man in whom the evil spirit was leaped on them, mastered all of them, and overpowered them, so that they fled out of that house naked and wounded. 17And this

19.17
Acts 2.43;
5.5,11

became known to all residents of Ēph'ėsŭs, both Jews and Greeks; and fear fell upon them all; and the name of the Lord Jesus was extolled. 18 Many also of those who were now believers came, confessing and divulging their practices. 19And a number of those who practiced magic arts brought their books together and burned them in the sight of all; and they counted the value of them and found it came to fifty thousand pieces of silver. 20 So the word of the Lord grew and prevailed mightily.

19.20
Acts 6.7;
12.24

e. *Paul's future plans*

19.21
Rom 15.24–
28
19.22
Acts 13.5;
Rom 16.23;
2 Tim 4.20;
ver 10

21 Now after these events Paul resolved in the Spirit to pass through Măçėdō'nĭă and Ȧçhāi'à and go to Jerusalem, saying, "After I have been there, I must also see Rome." 22And having sent into Măçėdō'nĭă two of his helpers, Timothy and Ĕrăs'tŭs, he himself stayed in Asia for a while.

f. *Demetrius and the riot at Ephesus*

19.23
ver 9
★19.24
Acts 16.16,
19

23 About that time there arose no little stir concerning the Way. 24 For a man named Dëmē'trĭŭs, a silversmith, who made silver shrines of Ar'tėmĭs, brought no little business to the craftsmen. 25 These he gathered together, with the workmen of like occupation, and said, "Men, you know that from this business we have

19.26
Ps 115.4;
Isa 44.10–
20;
Jer 10.3;
Acts 17.29

our wealth. 26And you see and hear that not only at Ēph'ėsŭs but almost throughout all Asia this Paul has persuaded and turned away a considerable company of people, saying that gods made with hands are not gods. 27And there is danger not only that this trade of ours may come into disrepute but also that the temple of the great goddess Ar'tėmĭs may count for nothing, and that she may even be deposed from her magnificence, she whom all Asia and the world worship."

19.28
Acts 18.19

28 When they heard this they were enraged, and cried out,

ʳ Other ancient authorities add *from the fifth hour to the tenth*

19.24 The Ephesian goddess Artemis is not to be identified with the Greek virgin goddess Artemis (Diana in Latin), but was the great goddess of fertility of Asia Minor, who was known by several names, and whose worship extended back to earliest times. The temple of Artemis at Ephesus was one of the seven great wonders of the ancient world.

"Great is Ar'tĕmĭs of the Ĕphē'ṣiănṣ!" 29 So the city was filled with the confusion; and they rushed together into the theater, dragging with them Gāiŭs and Aristar'chŭs, Măçĕdō'niănṣ who were Paul's companions in travel. 30 Paul wished to go in among the crowd, but the disciples would not let him; 31 some of the Ā'ṣĭ-archs also, who were friends of his, sent to him and begged him not to venture into the theater. 32 Now some cried one thing, some another; for the assembly was in confusion, and most of them did not know why they had come together. 33 Some of the crowd prompted Alexander, whom the Jews had put forward. And Alexander motioned with his hand, wishing to make a defense to the people. 34 But when they recognized that he was a Jew, for about two hours they all with one voice cried out, "Great is Ar'-tĕmĭs of the Ĕphē'ṣiănṣ!" 35And when the town clerk had quieted the crowd, he said, "Men of Ĕph'ĕsŭs, what man is there who does not know that the city of the Ĕphē'ṣiănṣ is temple keeper of the great Ar'tĕmĭs, and of the sacred stone that fell from the sky?ˢ 36 Seeing then that these things cannot be contradicted, you ought to be quiet and do nothing rash. 37 For you have brought these men here who are neither sacrilegious nor blasphemers of our goddess. 38 If therefore Dēmē'trĭŭs and the craftsmen with him have a complaint against any one, the courts are open, and there are proconsuls; let them bring charges against one another. 39 But if you seek anything further,ᵗ it shall be settled in the regular assembly. 40 For we are in danger of being charged with rioting today, there being no cause that we can give to justify this commotion." 41And when he had said this, he dismissed the assembly.

3. Paul's last visit to Macedonia and Achaia

20 After the uproar ceased, Paul sent for the disciples and having exhorted them took leave of them and departed for Măçĕdō'niă. 2 When he had gone through these parts and had given them much encouragement, he came to Greece. 3 There he spent three months, and when a plot was made against him by the Jews as he was about to set sail for Syria, he determined to return through Măçĕdō'niă. 4 Sō'pătĕr of Bĕroē'ă, the son of Py̆rrhŭs, accompanied him; and of the Thĕssălō'niănṣ, Aristar'chŭs and Sĕcŭn'dŭs; and Gāiŭs of Dĕrbĕ, and Timothy; and the Asians,

4. From Philippi to Miletus

Ty̆ch'ĭcŭs and Trŏph'ĭmŭs. 5 These went on and were waiting for us at Trōăs, 6 but we sailed away from Phĭl'ĭppī after the days of Unleavened Bread, and in five days we came to them at Trōăs, where we stayed for seven days.

7 On the first day of the week, when we were gathered together to break bread, Paul talked with them, intending to depart on the morrow; and he prolonged his speech until midnight. 8 There were many lights in the upper chamber where we were gathered. 9And a young man named Eū'ty̆chŭs was sitting in the window. He sank into a deep sleep as Paul talked still longer; and being

ˢ The meaning of the Greek is uncertain   ᵗ Other ancient authorities read *about other matters*

Marginal references:

19.29
Rom 16.23;
1 Cor 1.4;
Acts 20.4;
27.2;
Col 4.10;
Philem 24
*19.31
19.32
Acts 21.34
19.33
1 Tim 1.20;
2 Tim 4.14;
Acts 12.17
19.35
Acts 18.19
19.37
Rom 2.22
19.38
Acts 13.7
20.1
Acts 11.26;
1 Cor 16.5;
1 Tim 1.3
20.3
ver 19;
Acts 23.12;
25.3;
2 Cor 11.26
20.4
Acts 19.29;
27.2; 16.1;
Eph 6.21;
Col 4.7;
2 Tim 4.12;
Tit 3.12;
Acts 21.29;
2 Tim 4.20
20.6
Acts 16.8;
2 Cor 2.12;
2 Tim 4.13
20.7
1 Cor 16.2;
Rev 1.10
20.8
Acts 1.13

19.31 *Asiarchs* were provincial officials who had charge of the festival of emperor worship. Only one man bore the title at a time, and the plural "Asiarchs" was probably used of the actual Asiarch and his predecessors in office. They were civic benefactors.

20.10
1 Ki 17.21;
Mt 9.23,24

20.15
ver 17;
2 Tim 4.20
20.16
Acts 18.19;
21.4,12;
19.21; 2.1;
1 Cor 16.8
20.17
Acts 11.30
20.18
Acts 18.19;
19.1,10
20.20
ver 27
20.21
Acts 18.5;
2.38;
24.24;
26.18
20.22
ver 16
20.23
Acts 21.4,
11
20.24
Acts 21.13;
2 Cor 4.16;
Acts 1.17;
2 Cor 4.1;
Gal 1.1;
Tit 1.3
20.25
ver 38
20.26
Acts 18.6;
2 Cor 7.2
20.27
ver 20;
Acts 13.36
★20.28
1 Tim 4.16;
1 Pet 5.2;
1 Cor
12.28;
1 Pet 1.19;
20.29;
Mt 7.15
20.31
Acts 19.10
20.32
Acts 14.23;
9.31;
26.18;
Eph 1.18;
Col 1.12;
3.24;
1 Pet 1.4
20.33
1 Cor 9.12;
2 Cor 7.2;
11.9; 12.17

overcome by sleep, he fell down from the third story and was taken up dead. 10 But Paul went down and bent over him, and embracing him said, "Do not be alarmed, for his life is in him." 11And when Paul had gone up and had broken bread and eaten, he conversed with them a long while, until daybreak, and so departed. 12And they took the lad away alive, and were not a little comforted.

13 But going ahead to the ship, we set sail for Ăssŏs, intending to take Paul aboard there; for so he had arranged, intending himself to go by land. 14And when he met us at Ăssŏs, we took him on board and came to Mĭtўlē′nĕ. 15And sailing from there we came the following day opposite Çhĭŏs; the next day we touched at Sāmŏs; and u the day after that we came to Mĭlē′tŭs. 16 For Paul had decided to sail past Ĕph′ĕsŭs, so that he might not have to spend time in Asia; for he was hastening to be at Jerusalem, if possible, on the day of Pĕn′tĕcost.

5. *Paul's defense before the Ephesian elders*

17 And from Mĭlē′tŭs he sent to Ĕph′ĕsŭs and called to him the elders of the church. 18And when they came to him, he said to them:

"You yourselves know how I lived among you all the time from the first day that I set foot in Asia, 19 serving the Lord with all humility and with tears and with trials which befell me through the plots of the Jews; 20 how I did not shrink from declaring to you anything that was profitable, and teaching you in public and from house to house, 21 testifying both to Jews and to Greeks of repentance to God and of faith in our Lord Jesus Christ. 22And now, behold, I am going to Jerusalem, bound in the Spirit, not knowing what shall befall me there; 23 except that the Holy Spirit testifies to me in every city that imprisonment and afflictions await me. 24 But I do not account my life of any value nor as precious to myself, if only I may accomplish my course and the ministry which I received from the Lord Jesus, to testify to the gospel of the grace of God. 25And now, behold, I know that all you among whom I have gone preaching the kingdom will see my face no more. 26 Therefore I testify to you this day that I am innocent of the blood of all of you, 27 for I did not shrink from declaring to you the whole counsel of God. 28 Take heed to yourselves and to all the flock, in which the Holy Spirit has made you overseers, to care for the church of God*v* which he obtained with the blood of his own Son.*w* 29 I know that after my departure fierce wolves will come in among you, not sparing the flock; 30 and from among your own selves will arise men speaking perverse things, to draw away the disciples after them. 31 Therefore be alert, remembering that for three years I did not cease night or day to admonish every one with tears. 32And now I commend you to God and to the word of his grace, which is able to build you up and to give you the inheritance among all those who are sanctified. 33 I coveted no one's

u Other ancient authorities add *after remaining at Trōgўl′lĭŭm*
v Other ancient authorities read *of the Lord*
w Greek *with the blood of his Own* or *with his own blood*

20.28 Many different names are applied by the New Testament to the church of Jesus Christ. These names are often descriptive and reveal much concerning the nature of the church. Among these designations are: (1) his (Christ's) *body* (Eph 1.22, 23; Col 1.24); (2) *the flock of God* (1 Pet 5.2); (3) *God's field*, *God's building* (1 Cor 3.9); (4) the *temple of the living God* (2 Cor 6.16); (5) *the marriage of the Lamb* (Rev 19.7).

silver or gold or apparel. 34 You yourselves know that these hands ministered to my necessities, and to those who were with me. 35 In all things I have shown you that by so toiling one must help the weak, remembering the words of the Lord Jesus, how he said, 'It is more blessed to give than to receive.' "

36 And when he had spoken thus, he knelt down and prayed with them all. 37And they all wept and embraced Paul and kissed him, 38 sorrowing most of all because of the word he had spoken, that they should see his face no more. And they brought him to the ship.

6. Paul travels to Caesarea

21 And when we had parted from them and set sail, we came by a straight course to Cŏs, and the next day to Rhodes, and from there to Pătʹárȧ.ˣ 2And having found a ship crossing to Phoēniʹçíȧ, we went aboard, and set sail. 3 When we had come in sight of Cyprus, leaving it on the left we sailed to Syria, and landed at Tȳre; for there the ship was to unload its cargo. 4And having sought out the disciples, we stayed there for seven days. Through the Spirit they told Paul not to go on to Jerusalem. 5And when our days there were ended, we departed and went on our journey; and they all, with wives and children, brought us on our way till we were outside the city; and kneeling down on the beach we prayed and bade one another farewell. 6 Then we went on board the ship, and they returned home.

7 When we had finished the voyage from Tȳre, we arrived at Pţŏlĕmāʹïs; and we greeted the brethren and stayed with them for one day. 8 On the morrow we departed and came to Çaĕsárēʹȧ; and we entered the house of Philip the evangelist, who was one of the seven, and stayed with him. 9And he had four unmarried daughters, who prophesied. 10 While we were staying for some days, a prophet named Ăgʹábùs came down from Judēʹȧ. 11And coming to us he took Paul's girdle and bound his own feet and hands, and said, "Thus says the Holy Spirit, 'So shall the Jews at Jerusalem bind the man who owns this girdle and deliver him into the hands of the Gentiles.' " 12 When we heard this, we and the people there begged him not to go up to Jerusalem. 13 Then Paul answered, "What are you doing, weeping and breaking my heart? For I am ready not only to be imprisoned but even to die at Jerusalem for the name of the Lord Jesus." 14And when he would not be persuaded, we ceased and said, "The will of the Lord be done."

15 After these days we made ready and went up to Jerusalem. 16And some of the disciples from Çaĕsárēʹȧ went with us, bringing us to the house of Mņásòn of Cyprus, an early disciple, with whom we should lodge.

E. Paul a prisoner in Jerusalem, Caesarea, and Rome

1. Paul in Jerusalem

17 When we had come to Jerusalem, the brethren received us gladly. 18 On the following day Paul went in with us to James; and all the elders were present. 19After greeting them, he related one by one the things that God had done among the Gentiles through his ministry. 20And when they heard it, they glorified God. And

ˣ Other ancient authorities add and Mȳrȧ

20.34
Acts 18.3
20.35
Rom 15.1

20.36
Acts 9.40;
21.5
20.37
Gen 45.14
20.38
ver 25;
Acts 15.3

21.2
Acts 11.19

21.4
ver 11;
Acts 20.23
21.5
Acts 20.36

21.7
Acts 12.20;
1.15
21.8
Eph 4.11;
2 Tim 4.5;
Acts 6.5;
8.26,40
21.9
Acts 2.17;
Lk 2.36
21.10
Acts 11.28
21.11
ver 33;
Acts 20.23
21.13
Acts 20.24

21.14
Mt 26.42;
Lk 22.42

21.16
ver 3,4

21.17
Acts 15.4
21.18
Acts 12.17;
15.13
21.19
Acts 14.27;
1.17; 20.24
21.20
Acts 22.3;
Rom 10.2;
Gal 1.14

they said to him, "You see, brother, how many thousands there are among the Jews of those who have believed; they are all zealous for the law, 21 and they have been told about you that you teach all the Jews who are among the Gentiles to forsake Moses, telling them not to circumcise their children or observe the customs. 22 What then is to be done? They will certainly hear that you have come. 23 Do therefore what we tell you. We have four men who are under a vow; 24 take these men and purify yourself along with them and pay their expenses, so that they may shave their heads. Thus all will know that there is nothing in what they have been told about you but that you yourself live in observance of the law. 25 But as for the Gentiles who have believed, we have sent a letter with our judgment that they should abstain from what has been sacrificed to idols and from blood and from what is strangled^y and from unchastity." 26 Then Paul took the men, and the next day he purified himself with them and went into the temple, to give notice when the days of purification would be fulfilled and the offering presented for every one of them.

21.21
ver 28;
1 Cor 7.18,
19

*21.23
Acts 18.18
21.24
ver 26;
Acts 24.18

21.25
Acts 15.20,
29

21.26
Num 6.13;
Acts 24.18

21.27
Acts 24.18;
26.21
21.28
Acts 24.5,6

*21.29
Acts 20.4;
18.19

21.30
Acts 26.21;
16.19

21.32
Acts 23.27

21.33
Acts 20.23;
ver 11
21.34
Acts 19.32;
ver 37

21.36
Lk 23.18;
Jn 19.15;
Acts 22.22

21.37
ver 34

2. Paul's Imprisonment
a. His arrest

27 When the seven days were almost completed, the Jews from Asia, who had seen him in the temple, stirred up all the crowd, and laid hands on him, 28 crying out, "Men of Israel, help! This is the man who is teaching men everywhere against the people and the law and this place; moreover he also brought Greeks into the temple, and he has defiled this holy place." 29 For they had previously seen Tróph'ĭmŭs the Ĕphē'şĭăn with him in the city, and they supposed that Paul had brought him into the temple. 30 Then all the city was aroused, and the people ran together; they seized Paul and dragged him out of the temple, and at once the gates were shut. 31And as they were trying to kill him, word came to the tribune of the cohort that all Jerusalem was in confusion. 32 He at once took soldiers and centurions, and ran down to them; and when they saw the tribune and the soldiers, they stopped beating Paul. 33 Then the tribune came up and arrested him, and ordered him to be bound with two chains. He inquired who he was and what he had done. 34 Some in the crowd shouted one thing, some another; and as he could not learn the facts because of the uproar, he ordered him to be brought into the barracks. 35And when he came to the steps, he was actually carried by the soldiers because of the violence of the crowd; 36 for the mob of the people followed, crying, "Away with him!"

b. His defense

37 As Paul was about to be brought into the barracks, he said to the tribune, "May I say something to you?" And he said, "Do

^y Other early authorities omit *and from what is strangled*

21.23 See note to Num 6.2 on vows.
21.29 Trophimus was a Gentile Christian from Ephesus (20.4) who accompanied Paul to Jerusalem. Gentiles were allowed in the Temple area known as the Court of the Gentiles, but were forbidden, under pain of death, to go beyond the barrier that separated it from the inner courts of the Temple.

Notices in Greek and Latin were posted warning Gentiles to stay out. It was the report that Paul had taken a Gentile into the inner courts, where sacrifices were offered, that aroused the populace and caused the Temple gates to be closed (ver 30), since the Temple had presumably been defiled by the presence of a Gentile (ver 28).

you know Greek? 38Are you not the Egyptian, then, who recently stirred up a revolt and led the four thousand men of the Assassins out into the wilderness?" 39 Paul replied, "I am a Jew, from Tarsús in Çĭlĭ'çiá, a citizen of no mean city; I beg you, let me speak to the people." 40And when he had given him leave, Paul, standing on the steps, motioned with his hand to the people; and when there was a great hush, he spoke to them in the Hebrew language, saying:

22 "Brethren and fathers, hear the defense which I now make before you."

2 And when they heard that he addressed them in the Hebrew language, they were the more quiet. And he said:

3 "I am a Jew, born at Tarsús in Çĭlĭ'çiá, but brought up in this city at the feet of Gàmā'lǐ-él, educated according to the strict manner of the law of our fathers, being zealous for God as you all are this day. 4 I persecuted this Way to the death, binding and delivering to prison both men and women, 5 as the high priest and the whole council of elders bear me witness. From them I received letters to the brethren, and I journeyed to Damascus to take those also who were there and bring them in bonds to Jerusalem to be punished.

6 "As I made my journey and drew near to Damascus, about noon a great light from heaven suddenly shone about me. 7And I fell to the ground and heard a voice saying to me, 'Saul, Saul, why do you persecute me?' 8And I answered, 'Who are you, Lord?' And he said to me, 'I am Jesus of Năz'árĕth whom you are persecuting.' 9 Now those who were with me saw the light but did not hear the voice of the one who was speaking to me. 10And I said, 'What shall I do, Lord?' And the Lord said to me, 'Rise, and go into Damascus, and there you will be told all that is appointed for you to do.' 11And when I could not see because of the brightness of that light, I was led by the hand by those who were with me, and came into Damascus.

12 "And one Ănánĭ'ás, a devout man according to the law, well spoken of by all the Jews who lived there, 13 came to me, and standing by me said to me, 'Brother Saul, receive your sight.' And in that very hour I received my sight and saw him. 14And he said, 'The God of our fathers appointed you to know his will, to see the Just One and to hear a voice from his mouth; 15 for you will be a witness for him to all men of what you have seen and heard. 16And now why do you wait? Rise and be baptized, and wash away your sins, calling on his name.'

17 "When I had returned to Jerusalem and was praying in the temple, I fell into a trance 18 and saw him saying to me, 'Make haste and get quickly out of Jerusalem, because they will not accept your testimony about me.' 19And I said, 'Lord, they themselves know that in every synagogue I imprisoned and beat those who believed in thee. 20And when the blood of Stephen thy witness was shed, I also was standing by and approving, and keeping

*21.38
Acts 5.36;
Mt 24.26
21.39
Acts 9.11;
22.3
21.40
Acts 12.17;
22.2; 26.14
22.1
Acts 7.2
22.2
Acts 21.40
22.3
Acts 21.39;
20.4;
Lk 10.39;
Acts 26.5;
21.20
22.4
Acts 8.3;
26.9–11;
Phil 3.6;
1 Tim 1.13
22.5
Lk 22.66;
Acts 4.5;
9.2; 26.10,
12
22.6
Acts 9.3;
26.12,13
22.9
Acts 9.7;
26.13
22.10
Acts 16.30
22.11
Acts 9.8
22.12
Acts 9.17;
10.22
*22.14
Acts 3.13;
5.30; 9.15;
26.16;
1 Cor 9.1;
15.8;
Acts 7.52
22.15
Acts 23.11;
26.16
22.16
Acts 2.38;
Heb 10.22;
Acts 9.14;
Rom 10.13
22.17
Acts 9.26;
10.10
22.19
ver 4;
Acts 8.3;
26.11;
Mt 10.17
22.20
Lk 11.48;
Acts 8.1;
Rom 1.32

21.38 The Egyptian who led this ill-fated revolt is referred to by the Jewish historian Josephus, who reported that he had gathered his followers on the Mount of Olives about the year A.D. 54 to see the walls of Jerusalem fall. He was attacked and his forces routed by Felix, but he himself escaped unharmed.

22.14 The title *the Just One* (Greek *dikaios*) is used of Christ here; *the Righteous One* in 3.14; 7.52; *the righteous* in 1 Jn 2.1. Righteousness is one of the attributes of the Messiah (cf. Isa 32.1; 53.11), and it was natural that Christ should be called *the Righteous*.

22.21
Acts 9.15

*22.22
Acts 21.36;
25.24
22.23
Acts 7.58;
2 Sam 16.13
22.24
Acts 21.34
*22.25
Acts 16.37

22.29
ver 24,25

22.30
Acts 23.28;
21.33

23.1
Acts 22.30;
24.16;
2 Cor 1.12;
2 Tim 1.3
23.2
Jn 18.22
23.3
Mt 23.27;
Lev 19.35;
Deut
25.1,2;
Jn 7.51
23.5
Ex 22.28
*23.6
Acts 26.5;
Phil 3.5;
Acts 24.15,
16; 26.8

the garments of those who killed him.' 21And he said to me, 'Depart; for I will send you far away to the Gentiles.' "

22 Up to this word they listened to him; then they lifted up their voices and said, "Away with such a fellow from the earth! For he ought not to live." 23And as they cried out and waved their garments and threw dust into the air, 24 the tribune commanded him to be brought into the barracks, and ordered him to be examined by scourging, to find out why they shouted thus against him. 25 But when they had tied him up with the thongs, Paul said to the centurion who was standing by, "Is it lawful for you to scourge a man who is a Roman citizen, and uncondemned?" 26 When the centurion heard that, he went to the tribune and said to him, "What are you about to do? For this man is a Roman citizen." 27 So the tribune came and said to him, "Tell me, are you a Roman citizen?" And he said, "Yes." 28 The tribune answered, "I bought this citizenship for a large sum." Paul said, "But I was born a citizen." 29 So those who were about to examine him withdrew from him instantly; and the tribune also was afraid, for he realized that Paul was a Roman citizen and that he had bound him.

c. His trial before the Sanhedrin

30 But on the morrow, desiring to know the real reason why the Jews accused him, he unbound him, and commanded the chief priests and all the council to meet, and he brought Paul down and set him before them.

23 And Paul, looking intently at the council, said, "Brethren, I have lived before God in all good conscience up to this day." 2And the high priest Ānanī'ās commanded those who stood by him to strike him on the mouth. 3 Then Paul said to him, "God shall strike you, you whitewashed wall! Are you sitting to judge me according to the law, and yet contrary to the law you order me to be struck?" 4 Those who stood by said, "Would you revile God's high priest?" 5And Paul said, "I did not know, brethren, that he was the high priest; for it is written, 'You shall not speak evil of a ruler of your people.' "

6 But when Paul perceived that one part were Săd'ducees and the other Phar'isees, he cried out in the council, "Brethren, I am a Phar'isee, a son of Pharisees; with respect to the hope and the resurrection of the dead I am on trial." 7And when he had said this, a dissension arose between the Phar'isees and the Săd'-

---

22.22 The Jerusalem Jews listened carefully until Paul referred to the Gentiles, and then a riot broke out. In a similar way the Greeks in Athens listened attentively to Paul until he spoke of the resurrection of Christ; then the meeting broke up, for to the Greeks the idea of resurrection was nonsense (17.31, 32).

22.25 Paul here claimed Roman citizenship. In his day, one was automatically a Roman citizen if both parents were Roman citizens. However, if the woman in a marriage was not a Roman citizen, children born of such a marriage were not entitled to Roman citizenship either. Roman citizenship was also secured by manumission and by grant to individuals or districts as a reward for various

kinds of services rendered. The chief benefits accruing to those who held Roman citizenship were that they could not be scourged or put to death without the right to appeal to the emperor. Once an appeal was granted, the case was stopped until the emperor acted, but not all appeals to the emperor were granted. The accused, while waiting for his trial, might be kept in the common jail, housed in the home of a friend who vouched for his appearance, or placed either in the custody of a soldier to whom the accused was fastened with a chain or permitted to live in his own lodgings. Anyone falsely claiming Roman citizenship was guilty of a capital crime. In 25.11 Paul's appeal to Caesar was granted.

23.6 See notes to Mt 3.7.

dùçeēṣ; and the assembly was divided. 8 For the Săd'dùçeēṣ say that there is no resurrection, nor angel, nor spirit; but the Phar'-iṣeēṣ acknowledge them all. 9 Then a great clamor arose; and some of the scribes of the Phar'iṣeēṣ' party stood up and contended, "We find nothing wrong in this man. What if a spirit or an angel spoke to him?" 10And when the dissension became violent, the tribune, afraid that Paul would be torn in pieces by them, commanded the soldiers to go down and take him by force from among them and bring him into the barracks.

11 The following night the Lord stood by him and said, "Take courage, for as you have testified about me at Jerusalem, so you must bear witness also at Rome."

d. His removal to Caesarea

12 When it was day, the Jews made a plot and bound themselves by an oath neither to eat nor drink till they had killed Paul. 13 There were more than forty who made this conspiracy. 14And they went to the chief priests and elders, and said, "We have strictly bound ourselves by an oath to taste no food till we have killed Paul. 15 You therefore, along with the council, give notice now to the tribune to bring him down to you, as though you were going to determine his case more exactly. And we are ready to kill him before he comes near."

16 Now the son of Paul's sister heard of their ambush; so he went and entered the barracks and told Paul. 17And Paul called one of the centurions and said, "Take this young man to the tribune; for he has something to tell him." 18 So he took him and brought him to the tribune and said, "Paul the prisoner called me and asked me to bring this young man to you, as he has something to say to you." 19 The tribune took him by the hand, and going aside asked him privately, "What is it that you have to tell me?" 20And he said, "The Jews have agreed to ask you to bring Paul down to the council tomorrow, as though they were going to inquire somewhat more closely about him. 21 But do not yield to them; for more than forty of their men lie in ambush for him, having bound themselves by an oath neither to eat nor drink till they have killed him; and now they are ready, waiting for the promise from you." 22 So the tribune dismissed the young man, charging him, "Tell no one that you have informed me of this."

23 Then he called two of the centurions and said, "At the third hour of the night get ready two hundred soldiers with seventy horsemen and two hundred spearmen to go as far as Çaĕsàrē'à. 24Also provide mounts for Paul to ride, and bring him safely to Felix the governor." 25And he wrote a letter to this effect:

23.8
Mt 22.23;
Mk 12.18;
Lk 20.27
23.9
Acts 25.25;
26.31;
22.7,17,18
23.10
Acts 21.34

*23.11
Acts 18.9;
19.21;
28.23

23.12
ver 21,30;
Acts 25.3
23.14
ver 21

23.15
Acts 22.30

23.16
Acts 21.34;
ver 10

23.18
Eph 3.1

23.20
ver 14,15

23.21
ver 12,14

23.23
ver 33

*23.24
Acts 24.1,3,
10;25.14

23.11 The Lord appeared to Paul on the road to Damascus at his conversion (9.5; 22.8; 26.15); on his first visit to Jerusalem (22.17, 18); in Corinth (18.9, 10); and now on his last visit to Jerusalem.

23.24 Felix was the procurator of Judea, with both military and civil jurisdiction over his territory. His headquarters were in Caesarea, a seaport on the Mediterranean Sea. Felix was married to Drusilla, the youngest daughter of Herod Agrippa I, who deserted her husband Azizus, king of Emesa, for this Gentile (24.24). Felix's reputation was odious. He was of common origin and his appointment apparently was due to the friendship of Pallas, who was a favorite of Claudius Caesar. Nero, who followed Claudius, confirmed Felix's appointment. During Paul's stay there were serious riots which were quelled, but charges were leveled against Felix by the Jews and he was recalled to Rome. Pallas' influence protected him. Before departing for Rome Felix sought the favor of the Jews by leaving Paul in prison (24.27).

23.26
Acts 24.3;
15.23
23.27
Acts 21.32,
33; 22.25–
29
23.28
Acts 22.30
23.29
Acts 18.15;
25.19;
26.31
23.30
ver 20,21;
Acts 24.19;
25.16
23.32
ver 23
23.33
ver 23,24,26
23.34
Acts 21.39
★23.35
Acts 24.19;
25.16;
24.27

24.1
Acts 23.2,
30,35

24.3
Acts 23.26;
26.25
24.5
Acts 16.20;
17.6; 21.28
24.6
Acts 21.28

24.9
1 Thess 2.16

24.10
Acts 23.24
24.11
Acts 21.26
24.12
Acts 25.8;
28.17
24.13
Acts 25.7
24.14
Acts 9.2;
ver 5;
Acts 3.13;
26.22;
28.23

26 "Claudius Lўs´ĭăs to his Excellency the governor Felix, greeting. 27 This man was seized by the Jews, and was about to be killed by them, when I came upon them with the soldiers and rescued him, having learned that he was a Roman citizen. 28And desiring to know the charge on which they accused him, I brought him down to their council. 29 I found that he was accused about questions of their law, but charged with nothing deserving death or imprisonment. 30And when it was disclosed to me that there would be a plot against the man, I sent him to you at once, ordering his accusers also to state before you what they have against him."

31 So the soldiers, according to their instructions, took Paul and brought him by night to Ăntĭp´ătrĭs. 32And on the morrow they returned to the barracks, leaving the horsemen to go on with him. 33 When they came to Çaĕsărē´á and delivered the letter to the governor, they presented Paul also before him. 34 On reading the letter, he asked to what province he belonged. When he learned that he was from Çĭlĭ´çĭá 35 he said, "I will hear you when your accusers arrive." And he commanded him to be guarded in Hĕrŏd´ş praĕtor´ĭŭm.

e. Paul's defense at Caesarea
(1) PAUL BEFORE FELIX

24 And after five days the high priest Ănănĭ´ăs came down with some elders and a spokesman, one Tĕrtŭl´lŭs. They laid before the governor their case against Paul; 2 and when he was called, Tĕrtŭl´lŭs began to accuse him, saying:

"Since through you we enjoy much peace, and since by your provision, most excellent Felix, reforms are introduced on behalf of this nation, 3 in every way and everywhere we accept this with all gratitude. 4 But, to detain you no further, I beg you in your kindness to hear us briefly. 5 For we have found this man a pestilent fellow, an agitator among all the Jews throughout the world, and a ringleader of the sect of the Năz´ărēnĕş. 6 He even tried to profane the temple, but we seized him.ᶻ 8 By examining him yourself you will be able to learn from him about everything of which we accuse him."

9 The Jews also joined in the charge, affirming that all this was so.

10 And when the governor had motioned to him to speak, Paul replied:

"Realizing that for many years you have been judge over this nation, I cheerfully make my defense. 11As you may ascertain, it is not more than twelve days since I went up to worship at Jerusalem; 12 and they did not find me disputing with any one or stirring up a crowd, either in the temple or in the synagogues, or in the city. 13 Neither can they prove to you what they now bring up against me. 14 But this I admit to you, that according to the Way, which they call a sect, I worship the God of our fathers, believing everything laid down by the law or written in the prophets,

---

ᶻ Other ancient authorities add *and we would have judged him according to our law.* 7 *But the chief captain Lў´sĭăs came and with great violence took him out of our hands,* 8 *commanding his accusers to come before you.*

23.35 Herod's praetorium was the palace built by Herod the Great in Caesarea and used as a place of residence by the Roman procurators.

15 having a hope in God which these themselves accept, that there will be a resurrection of both the just and the unjust. 16 So I always take pains to have a clear conscience toward God and toward men. 17 Now after some years I came to bring to my nation alms and offerings. 18As I was doing this, they found me purified in the temple, without any crowd or tumult. But some Jews from Asia—19 they ought to be here before you and to make an accusation, if they have anything against me. 20 Or else let these men themselves say what wrongdoing they found when I stood before the council, 21 except this one thing which I cried out while standing among them, 'With respect to the resurrection of the dead I am on trial before you this day.'"

22 But Felix, having a rather accurate knowledge of the Way, put them off, saying, "When Lȳs'iȧs the tribune comes down, I will decide your case." 23 Then he gave orders to the centurion that he should be kept in custody but should have some liberty, and that none of his friends should be prevented from attending to his needs.

24 After some days Felix came with his wife Drusil'lȧ, who was a Jewess; and he sent for Paul and heard him speak upon faith in Christ Jesus. 25And as he argued about justice and self-control and future judgment, Felix was alarmed and said, "Go away for the present; when I have an opportunity I will summon you." 26At the same time he hoped that money would be given him by Paul. So he sent for him often and conversed with him. 27 But when two years had elapsed, Felix was succeeded by Porciùs Fěstùs; and desiring to do the Jews a favor, Felix left Paul in prison.

(2) PAUL BEFORE FESTUS

25 Now when Fěstùs had come into his province, after three days he went up to Jerusalem from Çaěsȧrē'ȧ. 2And the chief priests and the principal men of the Jews informed him against Paul; and they urged him, 3 asking as a favor to have the man sent to Jerusalem, planning an ambush to kill him on the way. 4 Fěstùs replied that Paul was being kept at Çaěsȧrē'ȧ, and that he himself intended to go there shortly. 5 "So," said he, "let the men of authority among you go down with me, and if there is anything wrong about the man, let them accuse him."

6 When he had stayed among them not more than eight or ten days, he went down to Çaěsȧrē'ȧ; and the next day he took his seat on the tribunal and ordered Paul to be brought. 7And when he had come, the Jews who had gone down from Jerusalem stood about him, bringing against him many serious charges which they could not prove. 8 Paul said in his defense, "Neither against the law of the Jews, nor against the temple, nor against Caesar have I offended at all." 9 But Fěstùs, wishing to do the Jews a favor, said to Paul, "Do you wish to go up to Jerusalem, and there be tried on these charges before me?" 10 But Paul said, "I am standing before Caesar's tribunal, where I ought to be tried; to the Jews I have done no wrong, as you know very well. 11 If then I am a wrongdoer, and have committed anything for which I deserve

24.15	Acts 23.6; 28.20; Dan 12.2; Jn 5.28,29
24.16	Acts 23.1
24.17	Acts 11.29, 30; Rom 15.25–28; 2 Cor 8.1–4; Gal 2.10
24.18	Acts 21.26, 27
24.19	Acts 23.30
24.21	Acts 23.6
24.23	Acts 23.35; 28.16; 23.16; 27.3
24.25	Gal 5.23; Acts 10.42
24.27	Acts 25.1,4, 9,14; 12.3; 23.35
*25.1	
25.2	Acts 24.1; ver 15
25.3	Acts 23.12, 15
25.4	Acts 24.23
25.7	Mk 15.3; Lk 23.2,10; Acts 24.5, 13
25.8	Acts 6.13; 24.12; 28.17
25.9	Acts 24.27; ver 20
25.11	ver 25; Acts 26.32; 28.19

25.1 Porcius Festus succeeded Felix in A.D. 60 as the procurator of Judea. Little is known of his family background. His suggestion to Paul that he stand trial in Jerusalem at the request of the Jews provoked Paul's appeal to Caesar. The appeal was allowed by Festus, since it was the inherent right of a Roman citizen to appeal to Caesar.

to die, I do not seek to escape death; but if there is nothing in their charges against me, no one can give me up to them. I appeal to Caesar." 12 Then Fĕstŭs, when he had conferred with his council, answered, "You have appealed to Caesar; to Caesar you shall go."

(3) FESTUS AND AGRIPPA

13 Now when some days had passed, Ȧgrĭp'pȧ the king and Bernice arrived at Çȧĕsȧrĕ'ȧ to welcome Fĕstŭs. 14And as they stayed there many days, Fĕstŭs laid Paul's case before the king, saying, "There is a man left prisoner by Felix; 15 and when I was at Jerusalem, the chief priests and the elders of the Jews gave information about him, asking for sentence against him. 16 I answered them that it was not the custom of the Romans to give up any one before the accused met the accusers face to face, and had opportunity to make his defense concerning the charge laid against him. 17 When therefore they came together here, I made no delay, but on the next day took my seat on the tribunal and ordered the man to be brought in. 18 When the accusers stood up, they brought no charge in his case of such evils as I supposed; 19 but they had certain points of dispute with him about their own superstition and about one Jesus, who was dead, but whom Paul asserted to be alive. 20 Being at a loss how to investigate these questions, I asked whether he wished to go to Jerusalem and be tried there regarding them. 21 But when Paul had appealed to be kept in custody for the decision of the emperor, I commanded him to be held until I could send him to Caesar." 22And Ȧgrĭp'pȧ said to Fĕstŭs, "I should like to hear the man myself." "Tomorrow," said he, "you shall hear him."

23 So on the morrow Ȧgrĭp'pȧ and Bernice came with great pomp, and they entered the audience hall with the military tribunes and the prominent men of the city. Then by command of Fĕstŭs Paul was brought in. 24And Fĕstŭs said, "King Ȧgrĭp'pȧ and all who are present with us, you see this man about whom the whole Jewish people petitioned me, both at Jerusalem and here, shouting that he ought not to live any longer. 25 But I found that he had done nothing deserving death; and as he himself appealed to the emperor, I decided to send him. 26 But I have nothing definite to write to my lord about him. Therefore I have brought him before you, and, especially before you, King Ȧgrĭp'pȧ, that, after we have examined him, I may have something to write. 27 For it seems to me unreasonable, in sending a prisoner, not to indicate the charges against him."

(4) PAUL BEFORE AGRIPPA

26 Ȧgrĭp'pȧ said to Paul, "You have permission to speak for yourself." Then Paul stretched out his hand and made his defense:

2 "I think myself fortunate that it is before you, King Ȧgrĭp'pȧ,

*25.13
25.14
Acts 24.27

25.15
Acts 24.1;
ver 2
25.16
ver 4,5

25.17
ver 6,10

25.19
Acts 18.15;
23.29
25.20
ver 9
25.21
ver 11,12
25.22
Acts 9.15

25.23
ver 13;
Acts 26.30

25.24
ver 2,3,7;
Acts 22.22

25.25
Acts 23.9,
29;26.31,32

26.1
Acts 9.15;
25.22

25.13 This Agrippa was Herod Agrippa II, the son of Herod Agrippa I. Paul appeared before him and his sister Bernice, of whom history has little good to report. Only seventeen at the time of his father's death, young Agrippa succeeded in building up a kingdom by degrees. He tried to reconcile Judaism and Hellenism without great success. His enigmatic statement of 26.28 translated, *In a short time you think to make me a Christian!* is open to various interpretations: (KJV, "Almost thou persuadest me to be a Christian"; Berkeley, "You are with a little effort convincing enough to make me a Christian").

I am to make my defense today against all the accusations of the Jews, 3 because you are especially familiar with all customs and controversies of the Jews; therefore I beg you to listen to me patiently.

4 "My manner of life from my youth, spent from the beginning among my own nation and at Jerusalem, is known by all the Jews. 5 They have known for a long time, if they are willing to testify, that according to the strictest party of our religion I have lived as a Phạr'ịseē. 6 And now I stand here on trial for hope in the promise made by God to our fathers, 7 to which our twelve tribes hope to attain, as they earnestly worship night and day. And for this hope I am accused by Jews, O king! 8 Why is it thought incredible by any of you that God raises the dead?

9 "I myself was convinced that I ought to do many things in opposing the name of Jesus of Năz'ạrěth. 10 And I did so in Jerusalem; I not only shut up many of the saints in prison, by authority from the chief priests, but when they were put to death I cast my vote against them. 11 And I punished them often in all the synagogues and tried to make them blaspheme; and in raging fury against them, I persecuted them even to foreign cities.

12 "Thus I journeyed to Damascus with the authority and commission of the chief priests. 13 At midday, O king, I saw on the way a light from heaven, brighter than the sun, shining round me and those who journeyed with me. 14 And when we had all fallen to the ground, I heard a voice saying to me in the Hebrew language, 'Saul, Saul, why do you persecute me? It hurts you to kick against the goads.' 15 And I said, 'Who are you, Lord?' And the Lord said, 'I am Jesus whom you are persecuting. 16 But rise and stand upon your feet; for I have appeared to you for this purpose, to appoint you to serve and bear witness to the things in which you have seen me and to those in which I will appear to you, 17 delivering you from the people and from the Gentiles—to whom I send you 18 to open their eyes, that they may turn from darkness to light and from the power of Satan to God, that they may receive forgiveness of sins and a place among those who are sanctified by faith in me.'

19 "Wherefore, O King Ạgrĭp'pá, I was not disobedient to the heavenly vision, 20 but declared first to those at Damascus, then at Jerusalem and throughout all the country of Judē'á, and also to the Gentiles, that they should repent and turn to God and perform deeds worthy of their repentance. 21 For this reason the Jews seized me in the temple and tried to kill me. 22 To this day I have had the help that comes from God, and so I stand here testifying both to small and great, saying nothing but what the prophets and Moses said would come to pass: 23 that the Christ must suffer, and that, by being the first to rise from the dead, he would proclaim light both to the people and to the Gentiles."

24 And as he thus made his defense, Fěstŭs said with a loud voice, "Paul, you are mad; your great learning is turning you mad." 25 But Paul said, "I am not mad, most excellent Fěstŭs, but I am speaking the sober truth. 26 For the king knows about these things, and to him I speak freely; for I am persuaded that none of these things has escaped his notice, for this was not done in a corner. 27 King Ạgrĭp'pá, do you believe the prophets? I know that you believe." 28 And Ạgrĭp'pá said to Paul, "In a short time you think to make me a Christian!" 29 And Paul said, "Whether short

26.3
Acts 6.14;
25.19;
ver 7
26.4
Gal 1.13,
14;
Phil 3.5
26.5
Acts 22.3;
23.6;
Phil 3.5
26.6
Acts 23.6;
13.32;
Rom 15.8;
Tit 2.13
26.7
Jas 1.1;
1 Thess
3.10;
1 Tim 5.5
26.9
Jn 16.2;
1 Tim 1.13;
Jn 15.21
26.10
Acts 8.3;
Gal 1.13;
Acts 9.14,21
26.12
Acts 9.3;
22.6
26.14
Acts 9.7;
21.40
26.16
Ezek 2.1;
Dan 10.11;
Acts 22.14,
15
26.17
Jer 1.8,19;
Acts 22.21
26.18
Isa 35.5;
42.7;
Eph 5.8;
Col 1.13;
1 Pet 2.9;
Lk 24.47;
Acts 2.38;
20.32
26.20
Acts 9.19–
29; 22.17–
20; 13.46;
9.15; 3.19;
Mt 3.8;
Lk 3.8
26.21
Acts 21.30,
31
26.22
Lk 24.27,
44;
Acts 24.14
26.23
Mt 26.24;
1 Cor 15.20;
Col 1.18;
Rev 1.5;
Lk 2.32
26.24
2 Ki 9.11;
Jn 10.20;
1 Cor 1.23
26.25
Acts 23.26;
24.3

or long, I would to God that not only you but also all who hear me this day might become such as I am—except for these chains."

26.30
Acts 25.33
26.31
Acts 23.29
26.32
Acts 28.18;
25.11

30 Then the king rose, and the governor and Bernice and those who were sitting with them; 31 and when they had withdrawn, they said to one another, "This man is doing nothing to deserve death or imprisonment." 32And Ágrĭp′pȧ said to Fĕstŭs, "This man could have been set free if he had not appealed to Caesar."

3. Paul sent to Rome
a. The embarkation and voyage

27.1
Acts 25.12,
25; 10.1
27.2
Acts 19.29;
16.9; 17.1
27.3
Acts 24.23;
28.16
27.4
ver 7
27.5
Acts 6.9;
13.13
27.6
Acts 28.11;
ver 1
27.7
ver 4,12,13

27 And when it was decided that we should sail for Italy, they delivered Paul and some other prisoners to a centurion of the Augŭs′tȧn Cohort, named Julius. 2And embarking in a ship of Ădrȧmȳt′tĭŭm, which was about to sail to the ports along the coast of Asia, we put to sea, accompanied by Arĭstar′chŭs, a Măçėdō′nĭȧn from Thĕssȧlŏnī′cȧ. 3 The next day we put in at Sīdŏn; and Julius treated Paul kindly, and gave him leave to go to his friends and be cared for. 4And putting to sea from there we sailed under the lee of Cyprus, because the winds were against us. 5And when we had sailed across the sea which is off Çĭlĭ′çiȧ and Pămphȳl′iȧ, we came to Mȳrȧ in Lȳç′iȧ. 6 There the centurion found a ship of Alexandria sailing for Italy, and put us on board. 7 We sailed slowly for a number of days, and arrived with difficulty off Cnī′dŭs, and as the wind did not allow us to go on, we sailed under the lee of Crēte off Săĺmō′në. 8 Coasting along it with difficulty, we came to a place called Fair Havens, near which was the city of Lăsē′ȧ.

★27.9
Lev 23.27–29
27.10
ver 21

9 As much time had been lost, and the voyage was already dangerous because the fast had already gone by, Paul advised them, 10 saying, "Sirs, I perceive that the voyage will be with injury and much loss, not only of the cargo and the ship, but also of our lives." 11 But the centurion paid more attention to the captain and to the owner of the ship than to what Paul said. 12And because the harbor was not suitable to winter in, the majority advised to put to sea from there, on the chance that somehow they could reach Phoēnĭx, a harbor of Crēte, looking northeast and southeast,a and winter there.

27.13
ver 7,12
27.14
Mk 4.37

13 And when the south wind blew gently, supposing that they had obtained their purpose, they weighed anchor and sailed along Crēte, close inshore. 14 But soon a tempestuous wind, called the northeaster, struck down from the land; 15 and when the ship was caught and could not face the wind, we gave way to it and were driven. 16And running under the lee of a small island called Caudȧ,b we managed with difficulty to secure the boat; 17 after hoisting it up, they took measuresc to undergird the ship; then, fearing that they should run on the Sȳr′tĭs, they lowered the gear, and so were driven. 18As we were violently storm-tossed, they began next day to throw the cargo overboard; 19 and the third day they cast out with their own hands the tackle of the ship. 20And when neither sun nor stars appeared for many a day, and no small

27.17
ver 26,29
27.18
Jon 1.5;
ver 38

a Or southwest and northwest   b Other ancient authorities read Claudȧ   c Greek helps

---

27.9 This is the one Jewish fast prescribed by Mosaic Law, the Day of Atonement (cf. Lev 16.29–34), on the 10th day of Tishri (Sep-tember–October). Assuming this incident took place in the year A.D. 59, the Day of Atonement was about October 5.

tempest lay on us, all hope of our being saved was at last abandoned.

21 As they had been long without food, Paul then came forward
among them and said, "Men, you should have listened to me, and
should not have set sail from Crēte and incurred this injury and
loss. 22 I now bid you take heart; for there will be no loss of life
among you, but only of the ship. 23 For this very night there stood
by me an angel of the God to whom I belong and whom I worship, 24 and he said, 'Do not be afraid, Paul; you must stand before
Caesar; and lo, God has granted you all those who sail with you.'
25 So take heart, men, for I have faith in God that it will be exactly
as I have been told. 26 But we shall have to run on some island."

b. *The shipwreck*

27 When the fourteenth night had come, as we were drifting
across the sea of Ā′driä, about midnight the sailors suspected that
they were nearing land. 28 So they sounded and found twenty
fathoms; a little farther on they sounded again and found fifteen
fathoms. 29And fearing that we might run on the rocks, they let
out four anchors from the stern, and prayed for day to come.
30And as the sailors were seeking to escape from the ship, and
had lowered the boat into the sea, under pretense of laying out
anchors from the bow, 31 Paul said to the centurion and the
soldiers, "Unless these men stay in the ship, you cannot be saved."
32 Then the soldiers cut away the ropes of the boat, and let it go.

33 As day was about to dawn, Paul urged them all to take some
food, saying, "Today is the fourteenth day that you have continued in suspense and without food, having taken nothing.
34 Therefore I urge you to take some food; it will give you strength,
since not a hair is to perish from the head of any of you." 35And
when he had said this, he took bread, and giving thanks to God in
the presence of all he broke it and began to eat. 36 Then they all
were encouraged and ate some food themselves. 37 (We were in all
two hundred and seventy-six[d] persons in the ship.) 38And when
they had eaten enough, they lightened the ship, throwing out the
wheat into the sea.

39 Now when it was day, they did not recognize the land, but
they noticed a bay with a beach, on which they planned if possible
to bring the ship ashore. 40 So they cast off the anchors and left
them in the sea, at the same time loosening the ropes that tied the
rudders; then hoisting the foresail to the wind they made for the
beach. 41 But striking a shoal[e] they ran the vessel aground; the
bow stuck and remained immovable, and the stern was broken
up by the surf. 42 The soldiers' plan was to kill the prisoners, lest
any should swim away and escape; 43 but the centurion, wishing
to save Paul, kept them from carrying out their purpose. He ordered those who could swim to throw themselves overboard first
and make for the land, 44 and the rest on planks or on pieces of the
ship. And so it was that all escaped to land.

c. *The stopover at Malta*

28 After we had escaped, we then learned that the island was
called Malta. 2And the natives showed us unusual kindness,

d Other ancient authorities read *seventy-six* or *about seventy-six*
e Greek *place of two seas*

27.21
ver 10,7,12,
13
27.22
ver 25,36
27.23
Acts 23.11;
5.19;
Rom 1.9
27.24
Acts 23.11;
ver 44
27.25
ver 22,36;
Rom 4.20,
21
27.26
Acts 28.1

27.30
ver 16

27.34
1 Ki 1.52;
Mt 10.30;
Lk 12.7;
21.18
27.35
1 Sam 9.13;
Mt 15.36;
Mk 8.6;
Jn 6.11;
1 Tim 4.3,4
27.36
ver 22,25
27.38
ver 18
27.39
Acts 28.1
27.40
ver 29
27.41
2 Cor 11.25
27.42
Acts 12.19
27.43
ver 3
27.44
ver 22,31
28.1
Acts 27.26,
39
28.2
Rom 1.14;
1 Cor
14.11;
Col 3.11

for they kindled a fire and welcomed us all, because it had begun
to rain and was cold. ³ Paul had gathered a bundle of sticks and
put them on the fire, when a viper came out because of the heat
and fastened on his hand. ⁴ When the natives saw the creature
hanging from his hand, they said to one another, "No doubt this
man is a murderer. Though he has escaped from the sea, justice
has not allowed him to live." ⁵ He, however, shook off the creature
into the fire and suffered no harm. ⁶ They waited, expecting him
to swell up or suddenly fall down dead; but when they had waited
a long time and saw no misfortune come to him, they changed their
minds and said that he was a god.

7 Now in the neighborhood of that place were lands belonging
to the chief man of the island, named Pùb'lĭŭs, who received us
and entertained us hospitably for three days. ⁸ It happened that
the father of Pùb'lĭŭs lay sick with fever and dysentery; and Paul
visited him and prayed, and putting his hands on him healed him.
⁹And when this had taken place, the rest of the people on the island
who had diseases also came and were cured. ¹⁰ They presented
many gifts to us;ᶠ and when we sailed, they put on board whatever
we needed.

11 After three months we set sail in a ship which had wintered
in the island, a ship of Alexandria, with the Twin Brothers as
figurehead. ¹² Putting in at Syracuse, we stayed there for three
days. ¹³And from there we made a circuit and arrived at Rhē'gĭŭm;
and after one day a south wind sprang up, and on the second day
we came to Pūtē̄ō'lĭ. ¹⁴ There we found brethren, and were invited to stay with them for seven days. And so we came to Rome.
¹⁵And the brethren there, when they heard of us, came as far as
the Forum of Ăp'pĭŭs and Three Taverns to meet us. On seeing
them Paul thanked God and took courage. ¹⁶And when we came
into Rome, Paul was allowed to stay by himself, with the soldier
that guarded him.

d. *The arrival at Rome*

17 After three days he called together the local leaders of the
Jews; and when they had gathered, he said to them, "Brethren,
though I had done nothing against the people or the customs of our
fathers, yet I was delivered prisoner from Jerusalem into the hands
of the Romans. ¹⁸ When they had examined me, they wished to
set me at liberty, because there was no reason for the death penalty
in my case. ¹⁹ But when the Jews objected, I was compelled to
appeal to Caesar—though I had no charge to bring against my
nation. ²⁰ For this reason therefore I have asked to see you and
speak with you, since it is because of the hope of Israel that I am
bound with this chain." ²¹And they said to him, "We have received
no letters from Jŭdē'ǎ about you, and none of the brethren coming
here has reported or spoken any evil about you. ²² But we desire
to hear from you what your views are; for with regard to this sect
we know that everywhere it is spoken against."

23 When they had appointed a day for him, they came to him
at his lodging in great numbers. And he expounded the matter to
them from morning till evening, testifying to the kingdom of God
and trying to convince them about Jesus both from the law of

28.4
Lk 13.2,4

28.5
Lk 10.19
28.6
Acts 14.11

28.8
Jas 5.14,15;
Mk 5.23

28.11
Acts 27.6

28.14
Acts 1.15

28.16
Acts 24.23;
27.3

28.17
Acts 13.50;
25.8; 6.14

28.18
Acts 22.24;
26.31,32;
23.29
28.19
Acts 25.11
28.20
Acts 26.6,7,
29;
Eph 3.1;
4.1; 6.20;
2 Tim 1.16
28.21
Acts 22.5
28.22
Acts 24.14;
1 Pet 2.12;
4.14
28.23
Acts 17.3;
19.8

ᶠ Or *honored us with many honors*

Moses and from the prophets. 24And some were convinced by
what he said, while others disbelieved. 25 So, as they disagreed
among themselves, they departed, after Paul had made one statement: "The Holy Spirit was right in saying to your fathers
through Iṣāi'áh the prophet:
26 'Go to this people, and say,
     You shall indeed hear but never understand,
     and you shall indeed see but never perceive.
27 For this people's heart has grown dull,
     and their ears are heavy of hearing,
     and their eyes they have closed;
     lest they should perceive with their eyes,
     and hear with their ears,
     and understand with their heart,
     and turn for me to heal them.'
28 Let it be known to you then that this salvation of God has been
sent to the Gentiles; they will listen."g

30 And he lived there two whole years at his own expense,h and
welcomed all who came to him, 31 preaching the kingdom of God
and teaching about the Lord Jesus Christ quite openly and unhindered.

g Other ancient authorities add verse 29, *And when he had said these words, the Jews departed,
  holding much dispute among themselves*   h Or *in his own hired dwelling*

28.24
Acts 14.4

28.26
Isa 6.9,10;
Mt 13.14,
15;
Rom 11.8

28.28
Mt 21.41,
43;
Acts 13.46,
47;
Rom 11.11

28.31
ver 23;
Eph 6.19;
2 Tim 2.9

INTRODUCTION TO

THE LETTER OF PAUL TO THE

ROMANS

Authorship and Background: Paul wrote to the Romans about A.D. 56. He was probably in Corinth during his three-month visit there (Acts 20.2, 3; cf. 1 Cor 16.5–7), at the end of his third missionary journey. Since he had never been in Rome, Paul expressed disappointment over his failure to visit them and spoke of his eagerness to see them (1.10–13; 15.22, 23; cf. Acts 19.21). First, however, he must go to Jerusalem with the relief offering raised by the churches in Macedonia and Achaia (15.25–27). Then after visiting Rome he planned to go to Spain, for which trip he hoped to enlist the approval and support of the Roman believers (15.24, 28).

The Roman church was already widely known (1.8), and Paul was eager to minister to the Christians there, for mutual strength and blessing (1.11–13). Since it was his policy not to carry on intensive work where the Gospel had been planted by others, Paul stated that he would see them in passing, so as not to trespass on another's field of work (15.20, 22, 28). His divine commission as an apostle to the Gentiles, however, made him anxious to preach the Gospel in Rome also (1.13–15). He wrote, therefore, to acquaint them with his message, thus preparing the way for his visit (15.14–17).

Characteristics: Paul sets forth in an orderly way his understanding of some of the fundamental principles of the Gospel. The letter is more formal and less personal in tone than his other letters (except for chapter 16, for which see note).

It is not known who planted the Gospel in Rome. On the day of Pentecost visitors from Rome were present in Jerusalem (Acts 2.10), and doubtlessly some of them carried the Christian message back to the imperial capital. Paul addressed himself both to Jews (2.17—4.25) and to Gentiles (1.13–15; 11.13). The proportion between the two in the Roman church nearly twenty-five years after Pentecost is unknown, but it would appear that the Gentiles outnumbered the Jews.

The theme is stated quite formally in 1.16, 17. This is followed by the development and exposition of the truth that "the gospel . . . is the power of God for salvation to every one who has faith." Indeed, for Paul the true doctrine of justification is the truth of all truths demanding attention because of the crisis in Galatia, Jewish unbelief, and pressing questions of ceremonialism. Justification is through faith alone: what this involves and what its consequences are in the lives of believers constitute the greater part of the letter. The apostle magnifies the grace of God in salvation with the corresponding responsibility of the believer who lives under grace, not law. He rises to heights of inspired eloquence

in chapter 8, which could be called "The Gospel of the Holy Spirit." Time and again the Spirit of God has used this letter to call God's people back to the foundational truths of the Christian faith.

Contents:

Note: Chapter 16 reads like a postscript and raises some questions, since in it Paul calls by name twenty-six people in a church he has never visited. Priscilla and Aquila (ver 3–5) shortly before this were in Ephesus (Acts 18.18, 19; 1 Cor 16.19) and later (2 Tim 4.19) they are not in Rome, but probably Ephesus. Epaenetus (ver 5) is the first convert of the province of Asia, whose capital was Ephesus. Paul spent over three years in Ephesus, and chapter 16 is more easily understood if it was addressed to Ephesus, not Rome.

In addition, the oldest manuscript has the benediction of 16.25–27 at the end of chapter 15. In other copies it occurs at the end of chapters 14 and 16.

These facts have led some scholars to conclude that a copy of the epistle with chapter 16 added was sent to Ephesus and it is this copy that has survived. This is simply a conjecture, of course, and in no way affects the content or destination of chapters 1—15. The fact that there is no single clear omission of chapter 16 in the manuscripts is strong evidence of its integrity.

THE LETTER OF PAUL TO THE
ROMANS

I. Introduction 1.1–17

A. Salutation

1 Paul, a servant^a of Jesus Christ, called to be an apostle, set apart for the gospel of God 2 which he promised beforehand through his prophets in the holy scriptures, 3 the gospel concerning his Son, who was descended from David according to the flesh 4 and designated Son of God in power according to the Spirit of holiness by his resurrection from the dead, Jesus Christ our Lord, 5 through whom we have received grace and apostleship to bring about the obedience of faith for the sake of his name among all the nations, 6 including yourselves who are called to belong to Jesus Christ;

7 To all God's beloved in Rome, who are called to be saints:

Grace to you and peace from God our Father and the Lord Jesus Christ.

B. Prayer of thanksgiving

8 First, I thank my God through Jesus Christ for all of you, because your faith is proclaimed in all the world. 9 For God is my witness, whom I serve with my spirit in the gospel of his Son, that without ceasing I mention you always in my prayers, 10 asking that somehow by God's will I may now at last succeed in coming to you. 11 For I long to see you, that I may impart to you some spiritual gift to strengthen you, 12 that is, that we may be mutually encouraged by each other's faith, both yours and mine. 13 I want you to know, brethren, that I have often intended to come to you (but thus far have been prevented), in order that I may reap some harvest among you as well as among the rest of the Gentiles. 14 I am under obligation both to Greeks and to barbarians, both to the wise and to the foolish: 15 so I am eager to preach the gospel to you also who are in Rome.

a Or slave

1.1 Believers are called *slaves* (Greek *douloi*) of Jesus Christ. The distinction between *hired servants* and *slaves* should be kept in mind. A hired servant (*misthios* or *diakonos*) had certain rights and privileges. He was not mere chattel as a slave was. Hired servants were engaged and paid for their labors, and when their terms of service expired they were free to go. The slave was not free but was the property of his master his life long. He had no rights or privileges. He was never free to go. Paul declares that true believers, for the sake of Christ, are also slaves to their fellow-believers (2 Cor 4.5).

1.7 *saints* is the Greek *hagioi*, from *hagios*, meaning "set apart," "separated unto God," "holy." This title is applied in the New Testament to those who have been regenerated by faith in Christ. It points to the position of the

believer as holy, and in sanctified possession of the Lord, indwelt by the Holy Spirit. Experientially, the sanctified believer becomes more and more filled with Jesus Christ and conformed to His character, even though he will not become perfectly like Him until he is with Him and sees Him as He is (1 Jn 3.2).

The Fatherhood of God may be understood in two senses: (1) God is the Father of all men in the sense that He is their creator (all men have been made by Him), just as a male parent is the father of all of his offspring. (2) God is especially the Father of those who believe. In this latter and special sense, God is not the Father of unbelievers at all (except as their creator). But He is the covenantal Father of all believers, for by the new birth they have become His children (1 Jn 3.2) and have been adopted into His family (Gal 4.5).

Marginal references:
*1.1 1 Cor 1.1; Acts 9.15; 2 Cor 11.7
1.2 Acts 26.6; Gal 3.8
1.3 Jn 1.14
1.4 Acts 13.33; Heb 9.14
1.5 Gal 1.16; Acts 6.7; 9.15
*1.7 1 Cor 1.2,3; Gal 1.3; Eph 1.2
1.8 Phil 1.3; Acts 16.19
1.9 Phil 1.8; Acts 24.14; Eph 1.16
1.10 Rom 15.32
1.11 Rom 15.23
1.13 Rom 15.22
1.14 1 Cor 9.16; Acts 28.2
1.15 Rom 12.18; 15.20

C. Theme

16 For I am not ashamed of the gospel: it is the power of God for salvation to every one who has faith, to the Jew first and also to the Greek. 17 For in it the righteousness of God is revealed through faith for faith; as it is written, "He who through faith is righteous shall live."*b*

II. The world's need of God 1.18–3.20

A. The Gentiles: guilty before God

18 For the wrath of God is revealed from heaven against all ungodliness and wickedness of men who by their wickedness suppress the truth. 19 For what can be known about God is plain to them, because God has shown it to them. 20 Ever since the creation of the world his invisible nature, namely, his eternal power and deity, has been clearly perceived in the things that have been made. So they are without excuse; 21 for although they knew God they did not honor him as God or give thanks to him, but they became futile in their thinking and their senseless minds were darkened. 22 Claiming to be wise, they became fools, 23 and exchanged the glory of the immortal God for images resembling mortal man or birds or animals or reptiles.

24 Therefore God gave them up in the lusts of their hearts to impurity, to the dishonoring of their bodies among themselves, 25 because they exchanged the truth about God for a lie and worshiped and served the creature rather than the Creator, who is blessed for ever! Amen.

26 For this reason God gave them up to dishonorable passions. Their women exchanged natural relations for unnatural, 27 and the men likewise gave up natural relations with women and were consumed with passion for one another, men committing shameless acts with men and receiving in their own persons the due penalty for their error.

28 And since they did not see fit to acknowledge God, God gave them up to a base mind and to improper conduct. 29 They were filled with all manner of wickedness, evil, covetousness, malice. Full of envy, murder, strife, deceit, malignity, they are gossips, 30 slanderers, haters of God, insolent, haughty, boastful, inventors of evil, disobedient to parents, 31 foolish, faithless, heartless, ruthless. 32 Though they know God's decree that those who do such things deserve to die, they not only do them but approve those who practice them.

b Or The righteous shall live by faith

Marginal references:

*1.16
2 Tim 1.8;
1 Cor 1.18;
Acts 3.26;
Rom 2.9
1.17
Rom 3.21;
Gal 3.11;
Heb 10.38

*1.18ff
Eph 5.6;
Col 3.6
1.19
Acts 14.17
1.20
Ps 19.1–6
1.21
Jer 2.5;
Eph 4.17,18
1.22
Jer 10.14
1.23
Ps 106.20;
Jer 2.11;
Acts 17.29
1.24
Eph 4.18,19;
1 Pet 4.3
1.25
Isa 44.20;
Jer 10.14;
Rom 9.5
1.26
Lev 18.22;
Eph 4.19;
1 Thess 4.5
1.27
Lev 18.22;
20.13
1.28
Eph 4.19
1.30
Ps 5.5;
2 Tim 3.2
1.31
2 Tim 3.3
1.32
Rom 6.21;
Acts 8.1;
22.20

1.16 The word *salvation* is derived from the Greek word *sōtēria*, meaning "safety" or "soundness." Comprehended under this term are such elements as "justification," "regeneration," "sanctification," "glorification," "redemption," "propitiation," "grace," and "forgiveness." Scripture states that salvation is: (1) of God (Ps 37.39); (2) by and through Christ (Acts 4.12; Heb 2.10; 5.9; Gal 1.4); (3) not of the works of men (11.6; Eph 2.9; 2 Tim 1.9; Tit 3.5). It has three aspects: past, present, and future; that is, the believer has already been redeemed from the guilt and penalty of sin; he is now being delivered from its power and will at last be delivered from its presence and be perfectly conformed to Christ's image.

1.18ff Instead of progression or evolution in religion, this account (ver 18–30) indicates that there is retrogression. Men turn from God to idols and from purity to gross sinfulness which they love and approve.

B. God's principles of judgment

2.1
Rom 1.20;
2 Sam
12.5–7;
Mt 7.1,2
2.4
Eph 1.7;
2.7;
Rom 11.22;
3.25;
Ex 34.6;
2 Pet 3.9
2.5
Deut 32.34;
Jude 6
2.6
Mt 16.27;
1 Cor 3.8;
2 Cor 5.10
2.8
Gal 5.20;
2 Thess 2.12
2.9
1 Pet 4.17
2.10
1 Pet 1.7;
ver 9
2.11
Deut 10.17;
Gal 2.6;
Eph 6.9
*2.12
Rom 3.19;
1 Cor 9.21
2.13
Jas 1.22,23,
25
*2.14ff
ver 15
*2.15
ver 14,27
2.16
Ecc 12.14;
1 Cor 4.5;
Acts 10.42;
1 Tim 1.11

2 Therefore you have no excuse, O man, whoever you are, when you judge another; for in passing judgment upon him you condemn yourself, because you, the judge, are doing the very same things. 2 We know that the judgment of God rightly falls upon those who do such things. 3 Do you suppose, O man, that when you judge those who do such things and yet do them yourself, you will escape the judgment of God? 4 Or do you presume upon the riches of his kindness and forbearance and patience? Do you not know that God's kindness is meant to lead you to repentance? 5 But by your hard and impenitent heart you are storing up wrath for yourself on the day of wrath when God's righteous judgment will be revealed. 6 For he will render to every man according to his works: 7 to those who by patience in well-doing seek for glory and honor and immortality, he will give eternal life; 8 but for those who are factious and do not obey the truth, but obey wickedness, there will be wrath and fury. 9 There will be tribulation and distress for every human being who does evil, the Jew first and also the Greek, 10 but glory and honor and peace for every one who does good, the Jew first and also the Greek. 11 For God shows no partiality.

12 All who have sinned without the law will also perish without the law, and all who have sinned under the law will be judged by the law. 13 For it is not the hearers of the law who are righteous before God, but the doers of the law who will be justified. 14 When Gentiles who have not the law do by nature what the law requires, they are a law to themselves, even though they do not have the law. 15 They show that what the law requires is written on their hearts, while their conscience also bears witness and their conflicting thoughts accuse or perhaps excuse them 16 on that day when, according to my gospel, God judges the secrets of men by Christ Jesus.

2.12 The condition of those who die without hearing of Christ presents a very serious problem. However, although nothing specific is said about those who die without hearing the gospel, it appears that Scripture assigns those who die without receiving Christ to everlasting punishment. Men are not judged for refusing to accept Christ if they have never heard of Him. They are then judged in the light of their own consciences, but as Romans here teaches us, no man really lives up to the light of his conscience. There is no Scripture which supports the idea of a second chance for the unevangelized heathen. The belief that men without Christ are lost has always been a motive for missionary outreach.

2.14–16 The law of God may be defined as the revealed will of God. It is found, imperfectly, in human conscience and perfectly in the Scriptures. The *moral law* of God is summarized in the Ten Commandments (Ex 20.2–17; Deut 5.6–21). The judicial and ceremonial laws of the Old Testament were transitory and adapted to the needs of a particular people for a particular time. The moral law is of permanent significance for all peoples and has the greatest relevance for Christians as a guide to pleasing their heavenly

Father. Even faith does not revoke this law.

2.15 God gave man a conscience beginning with Adam and Eve. In the Garden of Eden that conscience was uncorrupted. Subsequent to the fall, it was corrupted and depraved, but it was not totally erased. Conscience serves man as a witness to truth (2.15; Prov 20.27), but moral choice determines whether a man will obey what his conscience dictates (Josh 24.15). The conscience accuses men of sin (Gen 42.21; 2 Sam 24.10; Mt 27.3, 4) and its indictment will be confirmed in the last judgment when the books are opened. Every mouth will be stopped and His judgment will be seen to be according to righteousness (Rev 20.12–15). The spiritual Christian (1 Cor 3.1) has a conscience cleansed of guilt by faith in the atoning merits of Jesus Christ; he maintains a clear conscience by a sincere purpose of self-surrender to God (6.13; 12.1, 2) and immediate repentance and confession of any known sin (1 Cor 11.31). In this sense it is possible to have a conscience blameless and void of offense (Acts 24.16; Rom 9.1; 14.22). But conscience can be perfected and delivered from its bondage only through a genuine faith and trust in the atoning work of Christ (Heb 9.14; 10.2ff).

C. *The Jews: guilty before God*

17 But if you call yourself a Jew and rely upon the law and boast of your relation to God 18 and know his will and approve what is excellent, because you are instructed in the law, 19 and if you are sure that you are a guide to the blind, a light to those who are in darkness, 20 a corrector of the foolish, a teacher of children, having in the law the embodiment of knowledge and truth—21 you then who teach others, will you not teach yourself? While you preach against stealing, do you steal? 22 You who say that one must not commit adultery, do you commit adultery? You who abhor idols, do you rob temples? 23 You who boast in the law, do you dishonor God by breaking the law? 24 For, as it is written, "The name of God is blasphemed among the Gentiles because of you."

25 Circumcision indeed is of value if you obey the law; but if you break the law, your circumcision becomes uncircumcision. 26 So, if a man who is uncircumcised keeps the precepts of the law, will not his uncircumcision be regarded as circumcision? 27 Then those who are physically uncircumcised but keep the law will condemn you who have the written code and circumcision but break the law. 28 For he is not a real Jew who is one outwardly, nor is true circumcision something external and physical. 29 He is a Jew who is one inwardly, and real circumcision is a matter of the heart, spiritual and not literal. His praise is not from men but from God.

3 Then what advantage has the Jew? Or what is the value of circumcision? 2 Much in every way. To begin with, the Jews are entrusted with the oracles of God. 3 What if some were unfaithful? Does their faithlessness nullify the faithfulness of God? 4 By no means! Let God be true though every man be false, as it is written,

"That thou mayest be justified in thy words,
  and prevail when thou art judged."

5 But if our wickedness serves to show the justice of God, what shall we say? That God is unjust to inflict wrath on us? (I speak in a human way.) 6 By no means! For then how could God judge the world? 7 But if through my falsehood God's truthfulness abounds to his glory, why am I still being condemned as a sinner? 8And why not do evil that good may come?—as some people slanderously charge us with saying. Their condemnation is just.

D. *The world: guilty before God*

9 What then? Are we Jews any better off?c No, not at all; for Id have already charged that all men, both Jews and Greeks, are under the power of sin, 10 as it is written:
"None is righteous, no, not one;
11 no one understands, no one seeks for God.
12 All have turned aside, together they have gone wrong;
  no one does good, not even one."
13 "Their throat is an open grave,
  they use their tongues to deceive."
"The venom of asps is under their lips."
14 "Their mouth is full of curses and bitterness."
15 "Their feet are swift to shed blood,

c Or *at any disadvantage?*   d Greek *we*

2.17
ver 23;
Mic 3.11;
Rom 9.4
2.18
Phil 1.10
2.20
Rom 6.17;
2 Tim 1.13
2.21
Mt 23.3,4
2.22
Acts 19.37
2.23
ver 17
2.24
Isa 52.5
2.25
Gal 5.3
2.26
1 Cor 7.19;
Eph 2.11;
Rom 8.4
2.27
Mt 12.41
2.28
Mt 3.9;
Jn 8.39;
Rom 9.6;
Gal 6.15
2.29
Col 2.11;
2 Cor 10.18;
1 Pet 3.4
3.2
Deut 4.8;
Ps 147.19
3.3
Heb 4.2;
2 Tim 2.13
3.4
Jn 3.33;
Ps 116.11;
51.4
3.5
Rom 6.19;
Gal 3.15
3.6
Gen 18.25
3.7
ver 4
3.8
Rom 6.1

3.9
Gal 3.22

3.10
Ps 14.1–3

3.13
Ps 5.9
3.14
Ps 10.7;
140.3
3.15
Isa 59.7,8

3.18
Ps 36.1
3.19
Jn 10.34;
Rom 2.12
*3.20
Ps 143.2;
Acts 13.39;
Gal 2.16;
Rom 7.7
*3.21
Rom 1.17;
9.30; 1.2;
Acts 10.43
3.22
Rom 10.12;
Gal 3.28;
Col 3.11
*3.23
Gal 3.22
3.24
Rom 4.16;
Eph 1.7;
2.8;
Col 1.14;
Heb 9.12,15
*3.25
1 Jn 2.2;
Heb 9.14,
28;
1 Pet 1.19
3.27
Rom 2.17,
23; 4.2;
1 Cor 1.29–
31;
Eph 2.9

16 in their paths are ruin and misery,

17 and the way of peace they do not know."

18 "There is no fear of God before their eyes."

19 Now we know that whatever the law says it speaks to those who are under the law, so that every mouth may be stopped, and the whole world may be held accountable to God. 20 For no human being will be justified in his sight by works of the law, since through the law comes knowledge of sin.

III. Justification by faith alone 3.21–8.39

A. The means of salvation: faith

21 But now the righteousness of God has been manifested apart from law, although the law and the prophets bear witness to it, 22 the righteousness of God through faith in Jesus Christ for all who believe. For there is no distinction; 23 since all have sinned and fall short of the glory of God, 24 they are justified by his grace as a gift, through the redemption which is in Christ Jesus, 25 whom God put forward as an expiation by his blood, to be received by faith. This was to show God's righteousness, because in his divine forbearance he had passed over former sins; 26 it was to prove at the present time that he himself is righteous and that he justifies him who has faith in Jesus.

27 Then what becomes of our boasting? It is excluded. On what

---

3.20 The *moral law* serves four definite purposes: (1) it exhibits the moral perfection of God; (2) it reveals the inexcusable guilt of man and convicts him as a hopeless sinner; (3) it provides a standard by which human society is, at least imperfectly, governed; (4) it serves as a guide to believers as to how they may best please their redeeming God and do His will, which is to them the most important motive in life.

3.21 The word for *righteousness* (Greek *dikaiosynē*) is used in various ways in Scripture. At times it appears as an attribute of God, implying that He is faithful to what He is and to what He has promised. Or else it refers to His holy standard of moral purity in contrast to the sinfulness of man. God's reaction against sin is expressed in wrath or a holy displeasure toward all iniquity (1.18; Eph 5.6). When used of man, *righteousness* refers to a perfect conformity to God's will and moral standards. The Scripture teaches that no man has ever been truly righteous in this sense since all have sinned against God (3.10, 23). Yet the perfect righteousness of Jesus Christ is reckoned by grace to the justified believer, and the indwelling Holy Spirit imparts a power for godly living as an adopted child in God's holy family (3.21, 22; Phil 3.9). Thus the believer's imputed righteousness springs from God's righteousness, made possible on God's terms by faith in Christ. *Faith* is the *means* by which God's righteousness becomes man's righteousness; *justification* is the *act* of God which makes man righteous when he evidences faith in Christ; *righteousness* is the *result* of justification and is apprehended through faith.

3.23 Sin is basically a violation of the moral law of God which is revealed in the Word of God and through conscience. The failure to conform to the law of God is attended by the gravest penalities (Ezek 18.4, 20). The evil motive is essential, however, to constitute an action as sinful. For example, culpability is not implied when one is accidentally responsible for the death of another. But if one deliberately intends to commit murder that establishes the act as a grievous sin. Men cannot always read the hearts of others and so determine their true motives, but God always can (1 Chr 28.9; Heb 4.13). Sin already is present with a mere purpose or desire of evil, even before any overt offense is committed (Mt 5.28).

3.25 Theologians have argued whether there is a difference between *expiation* and *propitiation*. In this passage Paul uses the Greek word *hilastērion* which is also used in Heb 9.5 where it is translated *mercy seat*. Some interpreters see a distinction between expiation and propitiation in that the former refers to ritual satisfaction for sins committed, and the latter has to do with the person offended. Charles Hodge speaks of the two words as correlative terms, "The sinner, or his guilt, is expiated; God, or justice, is propitiated." SYSTEMATIC THEOLOGY (Wm. B. Eerdmans), Vol II, p. 478. John Knox says, "A price must be paid; a penalty must be suffered; a sacrifice must be offered . . . Paul . . . undoubtedly finds in the life and death of Christ the indispensable atoning sacrifice," THE INTERPRETER'S BIBLE (Abingdon Press) Vol 9, pp. 433, 434. In any event, man was reconciled to God by the death of Christ.

principle? On the principle of works? No, but on the principle of faith. 28 For we hold that a man is justified by faith apart from works of law. 29 Or is God the God of Jews only? Is he not the God of Gentiles also? Yes, of Gentiles also, 30 since God is one; and he will justify the circumcised on the ground of their faith and the uncircumcised through their faith. 31 Do we then overthrow the law by this faith? By no means! On the contrary, we uphold the law.

B. *The Old Testament proof: Abraham saved by faith*

4 What then shall we say about*e* Abraham, our forefather according to the flesh? 2 For if Abraham was justified by works, he has something to boast about, but not before God. 3 For what does the scripture say? "Abraham believed God, and it was reckoned to him as righteousness." 4 Now to one who works, his wages are not reckoned as a gift but as his due. 5And to one who does not work but trusts him who justifies the ungodly, his faith is reckoned as righteousness. 6 So also David pronounces a blessing upon the man to whom God reckons righteousness apart from works:

7 "Blessed are those whose iniquities are forgiven, and whose sins are covered;

8 blessed is the man against whom the LORD will not reckon his sin."

9 Is this blessing pronounced only upon the circumcised, or also upon the uncircumcised? We say that faith was reckoned to Abraham as righteousness. 10 How then was it reckoned to him? Was it before or after he had been circumcised? It was not after, but before he was circumcised. 11 He received circumcision as a sign or seal of the righteousness which he had by faith while he was still uncircumcised. The purpose was to make him the father of all who believe without being circumcised and who thus have righteousness reckoned to them, 12 and likewise the father of the circumcised who are not merely circumcised but also follow the example of the faith which our father Abraham had before he was circumcised.

13 The promise to Abraham and his descendants, that they should inherit the world, did not come through the law but through the righteousness of faith. 14 If it is the adherents of the law who are to be the heirs, faith is null and the promise is void. 15 For the law brings wrath, but where there is no law there is no transgression.

16 That is why it depends on faith, in order that the promise may rest on grace and be guaranteed to all his descendants—not only to the adherents of the law but also to those who share the faith of Abraham, for he is the father of us all, 17 as it is written, "I have made you the father of many nations"—in the presence of the God in whom he believed, who gives life to the dead and calls into existence the things that do not exist. 18 In hope he believed

e Other ancient authorities read *was gained by*

Marginal references

3.28 Acts 13.39; Eph 2.9
3.29 Rom 9.24; Acts 10.34, 35
3.30 Gal 3.8
4.2 1 Cor 1.31
4.3 Gen 15.6; Gal 3.6; Jas 2.23
4.4 Rom 11.6
★4.6
4.7 Ps 32.1,2
4.8 2 Cor 5.19
4.9 Rom 3.30; ver 3
4.11 Gen 17.10; Lk 19.9
4.13 Gen 17.4–6; Gal 3.29
4.14 Gal 3.18
4.15 Rom 3.20; 7.8,10,11; Gal 3.10
4.16 Rom 3.24; 9.8; 15.8
4.17 Gen 17.5; 1 Cor 1.28
4.18 Gen 15.5

4.6 God declares sinners righteous, not because they are intrinsically righteous or have anything righteous in themselves, but simply because of their faith, through which the righteousness of Jesus Christ is reckoned to their account. The guilt and punishment of the believer were borne by Christ (Isa 53.5, 11; Gal 3.13; 2 Cor 5.21) and the righteousness of Christ is reckoned to the believer's credit (1 Cor 1.30; 2 Cor 5.21; Phil 3.9). The believer's guilt is laid on Christ and Christ's merit is laid on the believer.

against hope, that he should become the father of many nations;
as he had been told, "So shall your descendants be." ¹⁹ He did not
weaken in faith when he considered his own body, which was as
good as dead because he was about a hundred years old, or when
he considered the barrenness of Sarah's womb. ²⁰ No distrust
made him waver concerning the promise of God, but he grew
strong in his faith as he gave glory to God, ²¹ fully convinced that
God was able to do what he had promised. ²² That is why his faith
was "reckoned to him as righteousness." ²³ But the words, "it was
reckoned to him," were written not for his sake alone, ²⁴ but for
ours also. It will be reckoned to us who believe in him that raised
from the dead Jesus our Lord, ²⁵ who was put to death for our
trespasses and raised for our justification.

C. The results of justification by faith

5 Therefore, since we are justified by faith, we*f* have peace with
God through our Lord Jesus Christ. ² Through him we have
obtained access*g* to this grace in which we stand, and we*h* rejoice
in our hope of sharing the glory of God. ³ More than that, we*h*
rejoice in our sufferings, knowing that suffering produces endurance, ⁴ and endurance produces character, and character produces
hope, ⁵ and hope does not disappoint us, because God's love has
been poured into our hearts through the Holy Spirit which has
been given to us.
  ⁶ While we were still weak, at the right time Christ died for
the ungodly. ⁷ Why, one will hardly die for a righteous man—
though perhaps for a good man one will dare even to die. ⁸ But
God shows his love for us in that while we were yet sinners Christ
died for us. ⁹ Since, therefore, we are now justified by his blood,
much more shall we be saved by him from the wrath of God. ¹⁰ For
if while we were enemies we were reconciled to God by the death
of his Son, much more, now that we are reconciled, shall we be
saved by his life. ¹¹ Not only so, but we also rejoice in God through
our Lord Jesus Christ, through whom we have now received our
reconciliation.

D. Christ the ground of our salvation

12 Therefore as sin came into the world through one man and

f Other ancient authorities read *let us* *g* Other ancient authorities add *by faith* *h* Or *let us*

4.19 Gen 17.17; Heb 11.11 **4.21** Gen 18.14; Heb 11.19 **4.23** Rom 15.4; 1 Cor 9.10; 10.11 **4.24** Rom 10.9; Acts 2.24 ***4.25** Isa 53.5,6; 2 Cor 5.21; 1 Cor 15.17 **5.1** Rom 3.28 **5.2** Eph 2.18; 1 Cor 15.1; Heb 3.6 **5.3** 2 Cor 12.10; Jas 1.2,3 **5.5** Phil 1.20; Eph 1.13 **5.6** Gal 4.4; Rom 4.25 **5.8** Jn 15.13; 1 Pet 3.18; 1 Jn 3.16 **5.9** Rom 3.5,25; Heb 9.14; 1 Thess 1.10 **5.10** Rom 11.28; Col 1.21,22; 2 Cor 5.18; Rom 8.34 ***5.12** Gen 2.17; 3.6,19; 1 Cor 15.21; Rom 6.23

4.25 *Dikaiōsis*, the Greek word for *justifica-tion*, occurs only twice in the New Testament, although the verb *dikaioō*, "justify," is quite frequently used. It refers to the believer's relationship to God by reason of the righteous-ness of Christ which is imputed to him (cf. note to 4.6). Through justification the penalty of sin is cancelled and the rewards promised to the obedient are declared to be the portion of the believer. No man can be justified by good works; no one is good enough to get to heaven (Gal 2.16; Phil 3.9; Gal 2.21; 3.10, 21; 5.3, 4; Rom 11.6; Eph 2.8, 9). Justifica-tion is more than a pardon. The demands of the law are not simply waived; they are fully satisfied. Thus the ground of justification is the atoning work of Christ on Calvary (3.24; 5.9, 19; 8.1; 10.4; 1 Cor 1.30; 2 Cor 5.21; Phil 3.9). Justification is made available to man by faith alone (Eph 2.8; Rom 5.1).

5.12 In this paragraph (5.12-21) Paul draws an analogy between Adam's sin and Christ's righteousness. Through Adam's dis-obedience, sin and death entered the world, and death spread to all men, because all sinned. Man is helpless to save himself from his lost condition, and death, as punishment for sin, is the lot of all. But in the righteous-ness (ver 18) or obedience (ver 19) of Jesus Christ, the situation is reversed, and instead of condemnation, man may have justification; instead of death, life (ver 16-18). The sinner

death through sin, and so death spread to all men because all men sinned—13 sin indeed was in the world before the law was given, but sin is not counted where there is no law. 14 Yet death reigned from Adam to Moses, even over those whose sins were not like the transgression of Adam, who was a type of the one who was to come.

15 But the free gift is not like the trespass. For if many died through one man's trespass, much more have the grace of God and the free gift in the grace of that one man Jesus Christ abounded for many. 16And the free gift is not like the effect of that one man's sin. For the judgment following one trespass brought condemnation, but the free gift following many trespasses brings justification. 17 If, because of one man's trespass, death reigned through that one man, much more will those who receive the abundance of grace and the free gift of righteousness reign in life through the one man Jesus Christ.

18 Then as one man's trespass led to condemnation for all men, so one man's act of righteousness leads to acquittal and life for all men. 19 For as by one man's disobedience many were made sinners, so by one man's obedience many will be made righteous. 20 Law came in, to increase the trespass; but where sin increased, grace abounded all the more, 21 so that, as sin reigned in death, grace also might reign through righteousness to eternal life through Jesus Christ our Lord.

E. The believer's life in Christ

1. United in his death

6 What shall we say then? Are we to continue in sin that grace may abound? 2 By no means! How can we who died to sin still live in it? 3 Do you not know that all of us who have been baptized into Christ Jesus were baptized into his death? 4 We were buried therefore with him by baptism into death, so that as Christ was raised from the dead by the glory of the Father, we too might walk in newness of life.

5 For if we have been united with him in a death like his, we shall certainly be united with him in a resurrection like his. 6 We know that our old self was crucified with him so that the sinful body might be destroyed, and we might no longer be enslaved to sin. 7 For he who has died is freed from sin. 8 But if we have died with Christ, we believe that we shall also live with him. 9 For we know that Christ being raised from the dead will never die again; death no longer has dominion over him. 10 The death he died he died to sin, once for all, but the life he lives he lives to God. 11 So you also must consider yourselves dead to sin and alive to God in Christ Jesus.

5.13
Rom 4.15
5.14
1 Cor 15.22, 45
5.15
ver 12,18, 19;
Isa 53.11;
Acts 15.11
5.17
2 Tim 2.12;
Rev 22.5
5.18
ver 12;
Rom 4.25
5.19
ver 12;
Rom 11.32;
Phil 2.8
5.20
Rom 7.7,8;
Gal 3.19;
1 Tim 1.14
5.21
ver 12,14;
Jn 1.17;
Rom 6.23
*6.1
Rom 3.5,8;
ver 15
6.2
Rom 7.4,6;
Gal 2.19;
Col 3.3;
1 Pet 2.24
6.3
Acts 2.38;
8.16; 19.5
6.4
Col 2.12;
Gal 6.15;
Eph 4.22–24;
Col 3.10
6.6
Eph 4.22;
Col 3.9;
Gal 2.20;
Rom 7.24
6.9
Rev 1.18
6.10
Heb 7.27
6.11
ver 2;
Gal 2.19

---

may now be declared righteous (ver 19), i.e., he may now be justified by God's free gift of righteousness. The analogy, as Paul makes clear (ver 15, 16, 20), is not precise: God's grace is much more than man's trespass and sin.

Verse 18 might appear to mean that all men will be saved. But read in close connection with 19, it is clear that Paul is stating that Christ's redemptive work is available and efficacious for all men: there is not one who cannot be justified by God's free grace in Jesus.

6.1 Some have supposed that the dispensation of the gospel releases man from any obligation to keep the law of God. This error is known as *antinomianism* (opposition to moral law), and in its extreme form has led to the notion that the more man sins the more the grace of God abounds. Here, and in 3.8; 6.15–23, Paul conclusively refutes this view and shows that salvation means deliverance from the power of sin and death, not a continued thralldom to it.

6.12
ver 14
6.13
Rom 7.5;
Col 3.5;
Rom 12.1
*6.14
Rom 8.2;
Gal 5.18

12 Let not sin therefore reign in your mortal bodies, to make you obey their passions. 13 Do not yield your members to sin as instruments of wickedness, but yield yourselves to God as men who have been brought from death to life, and your members to God as instruments of righteousness. 14 For sin will have no dominion over you, since you are not under law but under grace.

2. Slaves to righteousness

6.16
Rom 11.2;
Mt 6.24;
Jn 8.34;
2 Pet 2.19
6.17
Rom 1.8;
2 Tim 1.13
6.18
Jn 8.32;
Rom 8.2
6.19
Rom 3.5;
6.13; 12.1
6.20
Mt 6.24;
Jn 8.34
*6.21
Rom 7.5;
8.6,13,21
6.22
Jn 8.32;
1 Cor 7.22;
1 Pet 2.16
6.23
Rom 5.12;
5.21;
Gal 6.7,8

15 What then? Are we to sin because we are not under law but under grace? By no means! 16 Do you not know that if you yield yourselves to any one as obedient slaves, you are slaves of the one whom you obey, either of sin, which leads to death, or of obedience, which leads to righteousness? 17 But thanks be to God, that you who were once slaves of sin have become obedient from the heart to the standard of teaching to which you were committed, 18 and, having been set free from sin, have become slaves of righteousness. 19 I am speaking in human terms, because of your natural limitations. For just as you once yielded your members to impurity and to greater and greater iniquity, so now yield your members to righteousness for sanctification.

20 When you were slaves of sin, you were free in regard to righteousness. 21 But then what return did you get from the things of which you are now ashamed? The end of those things is death. 22 But now that you have been set free from sin and have become slaves of God, the return you get is sanctification and its end, eternal life. 23 For the wages of sin is death, but the free gift of God is eternal life in Christ Jesus our Lord.

3. Married to Christ

7.2
1 Cor 7.39

7.3
Mt 5.32

7.4
Rom 6.2,
11;
Gal 2.19;
Col 1.22
7.5
Rom 6.13,
21;
Gal 5.19;
Jas 1.15
7.6
Rom 2.29;
2 Cor 3.6

7 Do you not know, brethren—for I am speaking to those who know the law—that the law is binding on a person only during his life? 2 Thus a married woman is bound by law to her husband as long as he lives; but if her husband dies she is discharged from the law concerning the husband. 3 Accordingly, she will be called an adulteress if she lives with another man while her husband is alive. But if her husband dies she is free from that law, and if she marries another man she is not an adulteress.

4 Likewise, my brethren, you have died to the law through the body of Christ, so that you may belong to another, to him who has been raised from the dead in order that we may bear fruit for God. 5 While we were living in the flesh, our sinful passions, aroused by the law, were at work in our members to bear fruit for death. 6 But now we are discharged from the law, dead to that which held us captive, so that we serve not under the old written code but in the new life of the Spirit.

6.14 Paul's statements that *sin will have no dominion over you* (ver 14), *having been set free from sin* (ver 18), and *you have been set free from sin* (ver 22), show how dynamic a view he had of the salvation in Christ. Through God's grace, Christ truly delivers man from the slavery to sin, and makes him free under righteousness; instead of being an impotent and defeated subject under the dominion of sin, man is now set free and is able to obey God, to yield his life to God's demands, in a life of complete dedication (*sanctification*, ver 19, 22), to Him and look forward to eternal life. It is this boundless assurance of the reality of God's grace operating in a man's life that enables Paul to describe in such glowing terms the new life in Christ.

6.21 *return* (Greek *karpos*), i.e., fruit.

4. The Christian struggle

7 What then shall we say? That the law is sin? By no means! Yet, if it had not been for the law, I should not have known sin. I should not have known what it is to covet if the law had not said, "You shall not covet." 8 But sin, finding opportunity in the commandment, wrought in me all kinds of covetousness. Apart from the law sin lies dead. 9 I was once alive apart from the law, but when the commandment came, sin revived and I died; 10 the very commandment which promised life proved to be death to me. 11 For sin, finding opportunity in the commandment, deceived me and by it killed me. 12 So the law is holy, and the commandment is holy and just and good.

13 Did that which is good, then, bring death to me? By no means! It was sin, working death in me through what is good, in order that sin might be shown to be sin, and through the commandment might become sinful beyond measure. 14 We know that the law is spiritual; but I am carnal, sold under sin. 15 I do not understand my own actions. For I do not do what I want, but I do the very thing I hate. 16 Now if I do what I do not want, I agree that the law is good. 17 So then it is no longer I that do it, but sin which dwells within me. 18 For I know that nothing good dwells within me, that is, in my flesh. I can will what is right, but I cannot do it. 19 For I do not do the good I want, but the evil I do not want is what I do. 20 Now if I do what I do not want, it is no longer I that do it, but sin which dwells within me.

21 So I find it to be a law that when I want to do right, evil lies close at hand. 22 For I delight in the law of God, in my inmost self, 23 but I see in my members another law at war with the law of my mind and making me captive to the law of sin which dwells in my members. 24 Wretched man that I am! Who will deliver me from this body of death? 25 Thanks be to God through Jesus Christ our Lord! So then, I of myself serve the law of God with my mind, but with my flesh I serve the law of sin.

5. Life in the Spirit

a. Holiness a possibility

8 There is therefore now no condemnation for those who are in Christ Jesus. 2 For the law of the Spirit of life in Christ Jesus has set me free from the law of sin and death. 3 For God has done what the law, weakened by the flesh, could not do: sending his own

*7.7
Ex 20.17;
Deut 5.21;
Rom 3.20;
5.20
7.8
ver 11;
1 Cor 15.56
7.10
Lev 18.5;
Rom 10.5;
Gal 3.12
7.12
1 Tim 1.8
7.15
Gal 5.17
7.16
ver 12
7.17
ver 20
7.18
ver 25
7.19
ver 15
7.20
ver 17
7.21
ver 23,25
7.22
Ps 1.2;
2 Cor 4.16;
Eph 3.16
7.23
Gal 5.17
7.24
Rom 6.6;
8.2
7.25
1 Cor 15.57
8.1
Rom 5.16
8.2
1 Cor 15.45;
Rom 6.14,
18;
Jn 8.32,36
8.3
Acts 13.39;
Heb 7.18;
Phil 2.7;
Heb 2.14

7.7 This whole passage (7.7–25) dealing with Paul's experience with the law is one which is the subject of widely different interpretations. The principal question is whether Paul is speaking of his life before or after conversion. Perhaps the answer is not a sharp either/or but a both/and. Paul shows what God's law, itself holy, just, and good (ver 12), did for him. Before Paul was conscious of the law's demands he was unaware of his own sin and so, relatively speaking, he was then *alive* (ver 7, 9); but with the knowledge of the law came the awareness of his own sin and guilt. Thus sin sprang to life and "killed" Paul. Sin is powerless apart from the law; the law itself is good, but sin works through it to convict a man of his own sinfulness (ver 13).

Paul's description of the civil war raging within him (ver 15–24) is so intimate and vivid as to make it quite probable that he was talking of the paradox of the Christian life, stressing here the element of struggle, the recognition of one's own helplessness in attempting to live up to God's requirements. It is precisely the man who has experienced God's free grace and forgiveness who is the most acutely aware of his own sin and plight. The cry of despair, *Who will deliver me from this body of death?* (ver 24) is answered at once in the grateful assertion, *Thanks be to God through Jesus Christ our Lord!* (ver 25). God's grace is immeasurably greater than man's sin.

Son in the likeness of sinful flesh and for sin,[i] he condemned sin in the flesh, 4 in order that the just requirement of the law might be fulfilled in us, who walk not according to the flesh but according to the Spirit. 5 For those who live according to the flesh set their minds on the things of the flesh, but those who live according to the Spirit set their minds on the things of the Spirit. 6 To set the mind on the flesh is death, but to set the mind on the Spirit is life and peace. 7 For the mind that is set on the flesh is hostile to God; it does not submit to God's law, indeed it cannot; 8 and those who are in the flesh cannot please God.

9 But you are not in the flesh, you are in the Spirit, if in fact the Spirit of God dwells in you. Any one who does not have the Spirit of Christ does not belong to him. 10 But if Christ is in you, although your bodies are dead because of sin, your spirits are alive because of righteousness. 11 If the Spirit of him who raised Jesus from the dead dwells in you, he who raised Christ Jesus from the dead will give life to your mortal bodies also through his Spirit which dwells in you.

b. Holiness a duty

12 So then, brethren, we are debtors, not to the flesh, to live according to the flesh—13 for if you live according to the flesh you will die, but if by the Spirit you put to death the deeds of the body you will live. 14 For all who are led by the Spirit of God are sons of God. 15 For you did not receive the spirit of slavery to fall back into fear, but you have received the spirit of sonship. When we cry, "Abba! Father!" 16 it is the Spirit himself bearing witness with our spirit that we are children of God, 17 and if children, then heirs, heirs of God and fellow heirs with Christ, provided we suffer with him in order that we may also be glorified with him.

6. The future glory
a. A sure hope

18 I consider that the sufferings of this present time are not worth comparing with the glory that is to be revealed to us. 19 For the creation waits with eager longing for the revealing of the sons of God; 20 for the creation was subjected to futility, not of its own will but by the will of him who subjected it in hope; 21 because the creation itself will be set free from its bondage to decay and obtain the glorious liberty of the children of God. 22 We know that the whole creation has been groaning in travail together until now; 23 and not only the creation, but we ourselves, who have the first fruits of the Spirit, groan inwardly as we wait for adoption as sons, the redemption of our bodies. 24 For in this hope we were saved. Now hope that is seen is not hope. For who hopes for what he sees? 25 But if we hope for what we do not see, we wait for it with patience.

b. A sure help

26 Likewise the Spirit helps us in our weakness; for we do not

i Or and as a sin offering

Marginal references:

8.4 Gal 5.16,25
8.5 Gal 5.19–25
8.6 Rom 6.21; Gal 6.8
8.7 Jas 4.4
8.8 Rom 7.5
8.9 1 Cor 3.16; Gal 4.6; Phil 1.19; 1 Jn 4.13
8.10 Gal 2.20; Eph 3.17
8.11 Acts 2.24; Jn 5.21; 1 Cor 6.14
8.13 Gal 6.8; Col 3.5
8.14 Gal 5.18
8.15 2 Tim 1.7; Heb 2.15; Gal 4.5,6
*8.16 2 Cor 1.22; Eph 1.13
8.17 Gal 4.7; 2 Tim 2.12; 1 Pet 4.13
8.18 2 Cor 4.17; Col 3.4; 1 Pet 5.1
8.19 Col 3.4; 1 Pet 1.7,13; 1 Jn 3.2
8.20 Gen 3.17–19; Ecc 1.2
8.21 Acts 3.21; Rom 6.21; 2 Pet 3.13; Rev 21.1
8.23 2 Cor 1.22; 5.2,4; Gal 5.5
8.26 Mt 20.22; Eph 6.18

8.16 The Scripture defines the children of God as those who have received Christ as their Savior and are regenerated: *he gave power to become children of God* (Jn 1.12). There is no biblical basis for the common supposition that all men are by nature the children of God. By means of the new birth, sinners not only become saints; they are adopted into the family of God as His sons and daughters (Jn 1.13; 1 Jn 3.2).

know how to pray as we ought, but the Spirit himself intercedes for us with sighs too deep for words. 27And he who searches the hearts of men knows what is the mind of the Spirit, because*j* the Spirit intercedes for the saints according to the will of God.

28 We know that in everything God works for good*k* with those who love him,*l* who are called according to his purpose. 29 For those whom he foreknew he also predestined to be conformed to the image of his Son, in order that he might be the first-born among many brethren. 30And those whom he predestined he also called; and those whom he called he also justified; and those whom he justified he also glorified.

c. A certain salvation

31 What then shall we say to this? If God is for us, who is against us? 32 He who did not spare his own Son but gave him up for us all, will he not also give us all things with him? 33 Who shall bring any charge against God's elect? It is God who justifies; 34 who is to condemn? Is it Christ Jesus, who died, yes, who was raised from the dead, who is at the right hand of God, who indeed intercedes for us?*m* 35 Who shall separate us from the love of Christ? Shall tribulation, or distress, or persecution, or famine, or nakedness, or peril, or sword? 36As it is written,

"For thy sake we are being killed all the day long;
  we are regarded as sheep to be slaughtered."

37 No, in all these things we are more than conquerors through him who loved us. 38 For I am sure that neither death, nor life, nor angels, nor principalities, nor things present, nor things to come, nor powers, 39 nor height, nor depth, nor anything else in all creation, will be able to separate us from the love of God in Christ Jesus our Lord.

IV. Jew and Gentile in the plan of God 9.1–11.36

A. Paul's sorrow for Israel

9 I am speaking the truth in Christ, I am not lying; my con-
   science bears me witness in the Holy Spirit, 2 that I have great sorrow and unceasing anguish in my heart. 3 For I could wish that I myself were accursed and cut off from Christ for the sake of my brethren, my kinsmen by race. 4 They are Israelites, and to them belong the sonship, the glory, the covenants, the giving of the law, the worship, and the promises; 5 to them belong the patriarchs,

---

j Or that
k Other ancient authorities read in everything he works for good, or everything works for good
l Greek God   *m* Or It is Christ Jesus . . . for us

8.28 We know is the Christian's certainty.
8.29 Predestination or foreordination may be defined as that act of God by which the salvation of man is effected in accordance with the will of God. Some explain predestination as conditioned upon a foreknowledge by which God simply foresees what men are going to do, and then ordains that it shall come to pass as He foresaw it. This involves an interpretation of God's foreknowledge which is hard to reconcile with His absolute sovereignty. Perhaps it is better to conclude

that here we are confronted with a divine mystery in which God works out his sovereign will in such a way as to preserve inviolate that prerogative of free will which is implicit in the divine image (Gen 1.27) in which man was created. Thus man may act freely, i.e., he can accept or reject God's free offer of the gift of eternal life through Christ, though only the Holy Spirit can move him to accept it. At the same time his response to God's grace and truth are fully certain, foreknown, and fore-ordained in the mind and will of God.

Marginal references:

8.27 Ps 139.1,2; Lk 16.15; Rev 2.23
*8.28 ver 32
*8.29 Rom 11.2; 1 Pet 1.2,20; Eph 1.5,11; Phil 3.21; Heb 1.6
8.30 Eph 1.5,11; Rom 9.24; 1 Cor 6.11
8.31 Rom 4.1; Ps 118.6
8.32 Jn 3.16; Rom 5.8; 4.25
8.33 Lk 18.7; Isa 50.8,9
8.34 Col 3.1; Heb 1.3; 7.25; 9.24; 1 Jn 2.1
8.36 Ps 44.22; 2 Cor 4.11
8.37 1 Cor 15.57; Rev 1.5
8.38 Eph 1.21; 1 Pet 3.22
9.1 2 Cor 1.23; 11.10; 1 Tim 2.7
9.3 Ex 32.32
9.4 Acts 3.25; Ps 147.19; Heb 9.1
9.5 Col 1.16–19; Jn 1.1; Rom 1.25

and of their race, according to the flesh, is the Christ. God who is over all be blessed for ever.ⁿ Amen.

B. *The unbelief of the Jew not God's fault*

*9.6
Num 23.19;
Rom 2.28,
29;
Gal 6.16
9.7
Gal 4.23;
Heb 11.18
9.8
Rom 8.14;
Gal 3.29;
4.28
9.9
Gen 18.10
9.10
Gen 25.21
9.11
Rom 4.17;
8.28
9.12
Gen 25.23
9.13
Mal 1.2,3
9.14
2 Chr 19.7
9.15
Ex 33.19
9.16
Eph 2.8
9.17
Ex 9.16
9.19
2 Chr 20.6;
Job 23.13;
Dan 4.35
9.20
Isa 29.16;
64.8
*9.21
2 Tim 2.20
9.22
Rom 2.4
9.23
Eph 3.16;
Rom 8.29,
30
9.24
Rom 3.29
9.25
Hos 2.23;
1 Pet 2.10

6 But it is not as though the word of God had failed. For not all who are descended from Israel belong to Israel, 7 and not all are children of Abraham because they are his descendants; but "Through Isaac shall your descendants be named." 8 This means that it is not the children of the flesh who are the children of God, but the children of the promise are reckoned as descendants. 9 For this is what the promise said, "About this time I will return and Sarah shall have a son." 10 And not only so, but also when Rĕbĕc'cà had conceived children by one man, our forefather Isaac, 11 though they were not yet born and had done nothing either good or bad, in order that God's purpose of election might continue, not because of works but because of his call, 12 she was told, "The elder will serve the younger." 13 As it is written, "Jacob I loved, but Ēsau I hated."

14 What shall we say then? Is there injustice on God's part? By no means! 15 For he says to Moses, "I will have mercy on whom I have mercy, and I will have compassion on whom I have compassion." 16 So it depends not upon man's will or exertion, but upon God's mercy. 17 For the scripture says to Phäraōh, "I have raised you up for the very purpose of showing my power in you, so that my name may be proclaimed in all the earth." 18 So then he has mercy upon whomever he wills, and he hardens the heart of whomever he wills.

19 You will say to me then, "Why does he still find fault? For who can resist his will?" 20 But who are you, a man, to answer back to God? Will what is molded say to its molder, "Why have you made me thus?" 21 Has the potter no right over the clay, to make out of the same lump one vessel for beauty and another for menial use? 22 What if God, desiring to show his wrath and to make known his power, has endured with much patience the vessels of wrath made for destruction, 23 in order to make known the riches of his glory for the vessels of mercy, which he has prepared beforehand for glory, 24 even us whom he has called, not from the Jews only but also from the Gentiles? 25 As indeed he says in Hōsē'à,

"Those who were not my people
    I will call 'my people,'
and her who was not beloved
    I will call 'my beloved.' "

n Or *Christ, who is God over all, blessed for ever*

9.6 Paul distinguishes here between the physical and the spiritual descendants of Abraham: not all the former belong to the latter. The spiritual descendants are those who are children of promise, as was Isaac, who was born as a result of God's promise when it was impossible, humanly speaking, (cf. 4.19), for Isaac to have been conceived. So those who share Abraham's faith in God's promise, Jew or Gentile, are Abraham's real spiritual descendants.

9.21 Read in isolation from other passages this verse, and Paul's whole discussion of the subject here (ver 14–24), might appear to teach that man is merely an impotent vessel in God's hands, and therefore completely without responsibility for his own actions and ultimate destiny. But seen in the context of other teachings, it is clear that Paul here is emphasizing God's freedom in His mercy: man's redemption, finally, is not due to his own will but solely to God's mercy (ver 16).

26 "And in the very place where it was said to them, 'You are not my people,'
they will be called 'sons of the living God.' "

27 And Ĭṣāi'äh cries out concerning Israel: "Though the number of the sons of Israel be as the sand of the sea, only a remnant of them will be saved; 28 for the Lord will execute his sentence upon the earth with rigor and dispatch." 29And as Ĭṣāi'äh predicted,

"If the Lord of hosts had not left us children,
we would have fared like Sŏdŏm and been made like Gómor'-räh."

30 What shall we say, then? That Gentiles who did not pursue righteousness have attained it, that is, righteousness through faith; 31 but that Israel who pursued the righteousness which is based on law did not succeed in fulfilling that law. 32 Why? Because they did not pursue it through faith, but as if it were based on works. They have stumbled over the stumbling stone, 33 as it is written,

"Behold, I am laying in Zion a stone that will make men stumble,
a rock that will make them fall;
and he who believes in him will not be put to shame."

C. God's rejection the fault of the Jews

10 Brethren, my heart's desire and prayer to God for them is that they may be saved. 2 I bear them witness that they have a zeal for God, but it is not enlightened. 3 For, being ignorant of the righteousness that comes from God, and seeking to establish their own, they did not submit to God's righteousness. 4 For Christ is the end of the law, that every one who has faith may be justified.

5 Moses writes that the man who practices the righteousness which is based on the law shall live by it. 6 But the righteousness based on faith says, Do not say in your heart, "Who will ascend into heaven?" (that is, to bring Christ down) 7 or "Who will descend into the abyss?" (that is, to bring Christ up from the dead). 8 But what does it say? The word is near you, on your lips and in your heart (that is, the word of faith which we preach); 9 because, if you confess with your lips that Jesus is Lord and believe in your heart that God raised him from the dead, you will be saved. 10For man believes with his heart and so is justified, and he confesses with his lips and so is saved. 11 The scripture says, "No one who believes in him will be put to shame." 12 For there is no distinction between Jew and Greek; the same Lord is Lord of all and bestows his riches upon all who call upon him. 13 For, "every one who calls upon the name of the Lord will be saved."

14 But how are men to call upon him in whom they have not believed? And how are they to believe in him of whom they have never heard? And how are they to hear without a preacher? 15And how can men preach unless they are sent? As it is written, "How

---

Cross references (right column):

9.26 Hos 1.10
9.27 Isa 10.22, 23; Gen 22.17; Hos 1.10
9.29 Isa 1.4; 13.19; Jer 50.40
9.30 Rom 10.6; Gal 2.16; Heb 11.7
9.31 Rom 10.2, 3; Gal 5.4
9.32 1 Pet 2.6,8
9.33 Isa 28.16; Mt 21.42; Rom 10.11

10.2 Acts 21.20
*10.3 Rom 1.17; Phil 3.9
10.4 Gal 3.24; Rom 7.1–4
10.5 Neh 9.29; Ezek 20.11, 13,21; Rom 7.10
10.7 Heb 13.20
10.8 Deut 30.14
10.9 Mt 10.32; Lk 12.8; Acts 16.31
10.11 Isa 28.16; Rom 9.33
10.12 Rom 3.22, 29; Gal 3.28; Acts 10.36
10.13 Joel 2.32; Acts 2.21
10.15 Isa 52.7

10.3 Self-righteousness shuts out God's righteousness, which is bestowed through faith in Christ, and replaces it with a spurious righteousness of man which has no standing before God (Isa 64.6; Mk 10.18). It is based on the false supposition that man in himself is right with God or can make himself right by his own efforts. Rejecting God's righteousness and substituting for it man's pretended righteousness is sinful folly.

10.16
Heb 4.2;
Isa 53.1;
Jn 12.38

*10.17
Gal 3.2,5;
Col 3.16

10.18
Ps 19.4;
Col 1.6,23;
1 Thess 1.8

10.19
Deut 32.21;
Rom 11.11

10.20
Isa 65.1;
Rom 9.30

10.21
Isa 65.2

11.1
1 Sam
12.22;
Jer 31.37;
2 Cor
11.22;
Phil 3.5

11.2
Ps 94.19;
1 Ki 19.10;
Rom 8.29

11.4
1 Ki 19.18

11.5
2 Ki 19.4;
Rom 9.27

11.6
Rom 4.4

11.7
Rom 9.18,
31

11.8
Isa 29.10;
Deut 29.4;
Mt 13.13,
14

11.9
Ps 69.22,23

11.11
Acts 13.46;
Rom 10.19

11.12
ver 25

11.13
Acts 9.15;
Rom 15.16

beautiful are the feet of those who preach good news!" 16 But they have not all obeyed the gospel; for Iṣāi'äh says, "Lord, who has believed what he has heard from us?" 17 So faith comes from what is heard, and what is heard comes by the preaching of Christ.

18 But I ask, have they not heard? Indeed they have; for
"Their voice has gone out to all the earth,
and their words to the ends of the world."
19 Again I ask, did Israel not understand? First Moses says,
"I will make you jealous of those who are not a nation;
with a foolish nation I will make you angry."
20 Then Iṣāi'äh is so bold as to say,
"I have been found by those who did not seek me;
I have shown myself to those who did not ask for me."
21 But of Israel he says, "All day long I have held out my hands to a disobedient and contrary people."

D. Israel's rejection not final

1. The remnant

11 I ask, then, has God rejected his people? By no means! I myself am an Israelite, a descendant of Abraham, a member of the tribe of Benjamin. 2 God has not rejected his people whom he foreknew. Do you not know what the scripture says of Ēli'jäh, how he pleads with God against Israel? 3 "Lord, they have killed thy prophets, they have demolished thy altars, and I alone am left, and they seek my life." 4 But what is God's reply to him? "I have kept for myself seven thousand men who have not bowed the knee to Bā'ál." 5 So too at the present time there is a remnant, chosen by grace. 6 But if it is by grace, it is no longer on the basis of works; otherwise grace would no longer be grace.

7 What then? Israel failed to obtain what it sought. The elect obtained it, but the rest were hardened, 8 as it is written,
"God gave them a spirit of stupor,
eyes that should not see and ears that should not hear,
down to this very day."
9 And David says,
"Let their table become a snare and a trap,
a pitfall and a retribution for them;
10 let their eyes be darkened so that they cannot see,
and bend their backs for ever."

2. Israel's future salvation

11 So I ask, have they stumbled so as to fall? By no means! But through their trespass salvation has come to the Gentiles, so as to make Israel jealous. 12 Now if their trespass means riches for the world, and if their failure means riches for the Gentiles, how much more will their full inclusion mean!

13 Now I am speaking to you Gentiles. Inasmuch then as I am

10.17 A basic truth is taught here which bears on the missionary task of the church. Salvation is possible only when certain indispensable conditions are met. One must have faith (10.11), but faith is not possible unless the gospel is communicated, and the gospel can be communicated only by the preaching of the Word of God. Therefore the ultimate source from which salvation springs is necessarily the Word of God. This may be given to men in a variety of ways, such as by word of mouth or the printed page; but however it is conveyed, the Word of God is indispensable to salvation.

an apostle to the Gentiles, I magnify my ministry 14 in order to make my fellow Jews jealous, and thus save some of them. 15 For if their rejection means the reconciliation of the world, what will their acceptance mean but life from the dead? 16 If the dough offered as first fruits is holy, so is the whole lump; and if the root is holy, so are the branches.

17 But if some of the branches were broken off, and you, a wild olive shoot, were grafted in their place to share the richness*o* of the olive tree, 18 do not boast over the branches. If you do boast, remember it is not you that support the root, but the root that supports you. 19 You will say, "Branches were broken off so that I might be grafted in." 20 That is true. They were broken off because of their unbelief, but you stand fast only through faith. So do not become proud, but stand in awe. 21 For if God did not spare the natural branches, neither will he spare you. 22 Note then the kindness and the severity of God: severity toward those who have fallen, but God's kindness to you, provided you continue in his kindness; otherwise you too will be cut off. 23And even the others, if they do not persist in their unbelief, will be grafted in, for God has the power to graft them in again. 24 For if you have been cut from what is by nature a wild olive tree, and grafted, contrary to nature, into a cultivated olive tree, how much more will these natural branches be grafted back into their own olive tree.

25 Lest you be wise in your own conceits, I want you to understand this mystery, brethren: a hardening has come upon part of Israel, until the full number of the Gentiles come in, 26 and so all Israel will be saved; as it is written,
"The Deliverer will come from Zion,
   he will banish ungodliness from Jacob";
27 "and this will be my covenant with them
   when I take away their sins."
28As regards the gospel they are enemies of God, for your sake; but as regards election they are beloved for the sake of their forefathers. 29 For the gifts and the call of God are irrevocable. 30 Just as you were once disobedient to God but now have received mercy because of their disobedience, 31 so they have now been disobedient in order that by the mercy shown to you they also may*p* receive

11.14
Rom 10.19;
1 Cor 7.16;
9.22
11.15
Lk 15.24,32
11.16
Lev 23.10;
Num 15.18
*11.17
Jer 11.17;
Acts 2.39;
Eph 2.11,12

11.20
Rom 12.16;
2 Cor 1.24

11.22
1 Cor 15.2;
Heb 3.6;
Jn 15.2

11.23
2 Cor 3.16

*11.25
1 Cor 2.7–
10;
Eph 3.3–5,
9;
Rom 9.18
11.26
Isa 59.20,21

11.27
Isa 27.9

11.28
Deut 7.8;
10.15;
Rom 5.10;
9.5
11.29
Num 23.19
11.30
Eph 2.2

---

o Other ancient authorities read *rich root*   *p* Other ancient authorities add *now*

11.17 In his use of the figure of the olive tree, with some branches broken off and others grafted in, Paul constantly stresses the elements of unbelief and faith. It was through unbelief that the natural branches (Jews) were broken off (ver 20), and through faith that the branches of the wild olive tree (Gentiles) have been grafted in (ver 20). They will remain grafted in if they, the Gentiles, continue in God's kindness (ver 22), while the branches which have been broken off may be replaced in the tree if they abandon their unbelief (ver 23). All figures and analogies, whether that of a potter and his vessels (9.14–24), or of a gardener and his tree, are finally inadequate, of course, to carry the full meaning of the paradox of God's sovereignty and man's freedom; and the believer's proper response is that of thanksgiving and praise to God for His inscrutable ways (ver 33–36).

11.25 One of the fundamental tenets of the gospel is that a man is brought as an individual to God by His grace, irrespective of race; that God does not deal with national or racial blocs, as chosen or favored people; that no race has a privileged status with God; that there is only one way in which God deals with all individuals; that the new Israel is of all races and tongues. Yet at the same time Paul appears to be saying that God has not forgotten His people Israel: *a hardening has come upon part of Israel, until the full number of the Gentiles come in ... all Israel will be saved.* Certainly this is not to be understood to mean that every Israelite will be saved. But it cannot mean less than that substantial numbers of Israelites will turn to God in Christ before the end of the present age. The converts will be saved in exactly the same way and by the same means as anyone is being saved today.

11.32
Rom 3.9;
Gal 3.22,23

11.33
Eph 3.8;
Ps 92.5
11.34
Isa 40.13,
14;
1 Cor 2.16;
Job 36.22
11.36
1 Cor 8.6;
Heb 2.10;
Rom 16.27;
Heb 13.21

12.1
2 Cor 10.1,
2;
Rom 6.13,
16,19;
1 Pet 2.5
12.2
1 Pet 1.14;
1 Jn 2.15;
Eph 4.23;
5.10
12.3
Rom 15.15;
2 Cor 10.13;
Eph 4.7
12.4
1 Cor 12,12-
14;
Eph 4.4,16
12.6
1 Cor 7.7;
12.4,10;
1 Pet 4.10,
11
12.7
1 Cor 12.28;
14.26
12.8
Acts 15.32;
Mt 6.1-3;
1 Tim 5.17;
2 Cor 9.7
12.12
Heb 10.32,
36;
Acts 1.14
12.13
Rom 15.25;
Heb 13.2
12.14
Mt 5.44;
Lk 6.28
12.16
Rom 15.5;
11.25
12.17
Prov 20.22;
2 Cor 8.21
12.18
Mk 9.50;
Rom 14.19
12.19
Lev 19.18;
Heb 10.30

mercy. 32 For God has consigned all men to disobedience, that he may have mercy upon all.

3. Paul's concluding doxology

33 O the depth of the riches and wisdom and knowledge of God! How unsearchable are his judgments and how inscrutable his ways! 34 "For who has known the mind of the Lord,
    or who has been his counselor?"
35 "Or who has given a gift to him
    that he might be repaid?"
36 For from him and through him and to him are all things. To him be glory for ever. Amen.

V. Ethical teaching 12.1–15.13

A. The call to full surrender

12 I appeal to you therefore, brethren, by the mercies of God, to present your bodies as a living sacrifice, holy and acceptable to God, which is your spiritual worship. 2 Do not be conformed to this world*q* but be transformed by the renewal of your mind, that you may prove what is the will of God, what is good and acceptable and perfect.*r*

B. The use of God's gifts

3 For by the grace given to me I bid every one among you not to think of himself more highly than he ought to think, but to think with sober judgment, each according to the measure of faith which God has assigned him. 4 For as in one body we have many members, and all the members do not have the same function, 5 so we, though many, are one body in Christ, and individually members one of another. 6 Having gifts that differ according to the grace given to us, let us use them: if prophecy, in proportion to our faith; 7 if service, in our serving; he who teaches, in his teaching; 8 he who exhorts, in his exhortation; he who contributes, in liberality; he who gives aid, with zeal; he who does acts of mercy, with cheerfulness.

C. Christian conduct in personal relationships

9 Let love be genuine; hate what is evil, hold fast to what is good; 10 love one another with brotherly affection; outdo one another in showing honor. 11 Never flag in zeal, be aglow with the Spirit, serve the Lord. 12 Rejoice in your hope, be patient in tribulation, be constant in prayer. 13 Contribute to the needs of the saints, practice hospitality.

14 Bless those who persecute you; bless and do not curse them. 15 Rejoice with those who rejoice, weep with those who weep. 16 Live in harmony with one another; do not be haughty, but associate with the lowly;*s* never be conceited. 17 Repay no one evil for evil, but take thought for what is noble in the sight of all. 18 If possible, so far as it depends upon you, live peaceably with all. 19 Beloved, never avenge yourselves, but leave it*t* to the wrath of God; for it is written, "Vengeance is mine, I will repay, says the

q Greek age   *r* Or what is the good and acceptable and perfect will of God
s Or give yourselves to humble tasks   *t* Greek give place

Lord."20 No, "if your enemy is hungry, feed him; if he is thirsty, give him drink; for by so doing you will heap burning coals upon his head." 21 Do not be overcome by evil, but overcome evil with good.

12.20
Prov 25.21, 22;
Mt 5.44;
Lk 6.27

D. Christian conduct in relation to the state

13 Let every person be subject to the governing authorities. For there is no authority except from God, and those that exist have been instituted by God. 2 Therefore he who resists the authorities resists what God has appointed, and those who resist will incur judgment. 3 For rulers are not a terror to good conduct, but to bad. Would you have no fear of him who is in authority? Then do what is good, and you will receive his approval, 4 for he is God's servant for your good. But if you do wrong, be afraid, for he does not bear the sword in vain; he is the servant of God to execute his wrath on the wrongdoer. 5 Therefore one must be subject, not only to avoid God's wrath but also for the sake of conscience. 6 For the same reason you also pay taxes, for the authorities are ministers of God, attending to this very thing. 7 Pay all of them their dues, taxes to whom taxes are due, revenue to whom revenue is due, respect to whom respect is due, honor to whom honor is due.

★13.1
Tit 3.1;
1 Pet 2.13;
Jn 19.11;
Dan 2.21
13.2
Tit 3.1
13.3
1 Pet 2.14
13.4
1 Thess 4.6

13.5
Ecc 8.2;
1 Pet 2.19
13.7
Mt 22.21;
Mk 12.17;
Lk 20.25

E. The call to love

8 Owe no one anything, except to love one another; for he who loves his neighbor has fulfilled the law. 9 The commandments, "You shall not commit adultery, You shall not kill, You shall not steal, You shall not covet," and any other commandment, are summed up in this sentence, "You shall love your neighbor as yourself." 10 Love does no wrong to a neighbor; therefore love is the fulfilling of the law.

13.8
Gal 5.14;
Col 3.14;
Jas 2.8
★13.9
Ex 20.13, 14;
Mt 19.19
13.10
Mt 22.39,40
★13.11ff
1 Cor 7.29, 30; 15.34;
Eph 5.14;
1 Thess 5.5, 6

F. Hope, the Christian motivation

11 Besides this you know what hour it is, how it is full time now for you to wake from sleep. For salvation is nearer to us now than when we first believed; 12 the night is far gone, the day is at hand. Let us then cast off the works of darkness and put on the armor of light; 13 let us conduct ourselves becomingly as in the day, not in reveling and drunkenness, not in debauchery and licentiousness, not in quarreling and jealousy. 14 But put on the Lord Jesus Christ, and make no provision for the flesh, to gratify its desires.

13.12
1 Jn 2.8;
Eph 5.11;
1 Thess 5.8
13.13
1 Thess 4.12;
Gal 5.21;
Eph 5.18
13.14
Gal 3.27;
Eph 4.24;
Gal 5.16

13.1 Rulers or authorities are here said to be: (1) ordained by God (13.1); (2) a terror to evildoers (13.3); (3) bearers of the sword to execute vengeance (13.4); (4) entitled to be respected and obeyed (13.2); (5) entitled to gather taxes (13.6, 7). See also 1 Pet 2.13–17.

13.9 At least three statements of the believer's relationship to love as the governing principle of life may be found in the New Testament: (1) *You shall love your neighbor as yourself* (ver 9); (2) *Love does no wrong to a neighbor* (ver 10); (3) the Golden Rule of Mt 7.12. The proper use of these principles

in the relationships of men personally, nationally, and internationally would resolve most of our tensions and disputes. See also note to 1 Cor 10.23.

13.11ff Paul argues that the Christian should be motivated in his conduct by the prospect of the return of the Lord. In fact, some have argued that this passage indicates Paul believed in an imminent return of Christ and taught it as revealed truth. However, chapter 11 shows that he expected an extended future, or a long interval between the First and Second Coming.

G. The Christian and matters of conscience

1. Not to judge

14 As for the man who is weak in faith, welcome him, but not for disputes over opinions. 2 One believes he may eat anything, while the weak man eats only vegetables. 3 Let not him who eats despise him who abstains, and let not him who abstains pass judgment on him who eats; for God has welcomed him. 4 Who are you to pass judgment on the servant of another? It is before his own master that he stands or falls. And he will be upheld, for the Master is able to make him stand.

5 One man esteems one day as better than another, while another man esteems all days alike. Let every one be fully convinced in his own mind. 6 He who observes the day, observes it in honor of the Lord. He also who eats, eats in honor of the Lord, since he gives thanks to God; while he who abstains, abstains in honor of the Lord and gives thanks to God. 7 None of us lives to himself, and none of us dies to himself. 8 If we live, we live to the Lord, and if we die, we die to the Lord; so then, whether we live or whether we die, we are the Lord's. 9 For to this end Christ died and lived again, that he might be Lord both of the dead and of the living.

10 Why do you pass judgment on your brother? Or you, why do you despise your brother? For we shall all stand before the judgment seat of God; 11 for it is written,

"As I live, says the Lord, every knee shall bow to me,
   and every tongue shall give praise[u] to God."

12 So each of us shall give account of himself to God.

2. Not to be a stumbling block

13 Then let us no more pass judgment on one another, but rather decide never to put a stumbling block or hindrance in the way of a brother. 14 I know and am persuaded in the Lord Jesus that nothing is unclean in itself; but it is unclean for any one who thinks it unclean. 15 If your brother is being injured by what you eat, you are no longer walking in love. Do not let what you

u Or confess

14.8 The rules for Christian conduct may be determined in one of two ways: either by general principles laid down in Scripture, or else by specific biblical injunctions. Thus, by way of principle, the Christian is told to walk: (1) so as to command the respect of others (1 Thess 4.11, 12); (2) fully pleasing to God (Col 1.10); (3) in the Spirit (Gal 5.25); (4) in newness of life (6.4); (5) worthy of his calling (Eph 4.1). By way of specific injunction the believer is commanded: (1) to control his body (1 Cor 9.27); (2) to forgive those who wrong him (12.20); (3) to subdue anger (Eph 4.26; Jas 1.19); (4) to have no fellowship with sinners (Ps 1.1; 2 Thess 3.6); (5) to live peaceably with all men (12.18; Heb 12.14).

14.14 *nothing is unclean in itself* must not be taken as a general statement which includes all acts of conduct. Rather it is specifically related to the matter of foods, as the next

verse demonstrates. Some Christians in Rome thought they should, for religious reasons, abstain from certain kinds of food, particularly meat (ver 2). Paul calls them *weak* (perhaps "immature" is a better term), and warns them not to pass judgment on those who did not abide by their scruples (ver 3, 4, 10a), since those who ate did so with thanksgiving to God (ver 6). Those who were not bound by false scruples Paul called *strong* (15.1), and admonished them not to despise their weak brother (14.3, 10b). Furthermore, they had the added responsibility of not hurting their weak brother by their example, for if a man ate what he thought was impure he thus transgressed his own conscience and was thereby injured. All foods are clean (ver 20); none is in itself unclean (ver 14), a statement reminiscent of Jesus' teaching and the evangelist's comment: *Thus he declared all foods clean* (Mk 7.18, 19).

Marginal references:

14.1 — 1 Cor 8.9; 9.22
14.2 — 1 Tim 4.4; Tit 1.15
14.3 — Col 2.16
14.4 — Jas 4.12
14.5 — Gal 4.10
14.6 — 1 Cor 10.31; 1 Tim 4.3
14.7 — 2 Cor 5.15; Gal 2.20; Phil 1.20,21
*14.8 — Phil 1.20
14.9 — 2 Cor 5.15; Acts 10.36
14.10 — 2 Cor 5.10
14.11 — Isa 45.23; Phil 2.10,11
14.12 — Mt 12.36; 1 Pet 4.5
14.13 — Mt 7.1; 1 Cor 8.13
*14.14 — Acts 10.15; 1 Cor 8.7
14.15 — Eph 5.2; 1 Cor 8.11

eat cause the ruin of one for whom Christ died. 16 So do not let your good be spoken of as evil. 17 For the kingdom of God is not food and drink but righteousness and peace and joy in the Holy Spirit; 18 he who thus serves Christ is acceptable to God and approved by men. 19 Let us then pursue what makes for peace and for mutual upbuilding. 20 Do not, for the sake of food, destroy the work of God. Everything is indeed clean, but it is wrong for any one to make others fall by what he eats; 21 it is right not to eat meat or drink wine or do anything that makes your brother stumble.*v* 22 The faith that you have, keep between yourself and God; happy is he who has no reason to judge himself for what he approves. 23 But he who has doubts is condemned, if he eats, because he does not act from faith; for whatever does not proceed from faith is sin.*w*

3. To follow Christ's example

15 We who are strong ought to bear with the failings of the weak, and not to please ourselves; 2 let each of us please his neighbor for his good, to edify him. 3 For Christ did not please himself; but, as it is written, "The reproaches of those who reproached thee fell on me." 4 For whatever was written in former days was written for our instruction, that by steadfastness and by the encouragement of the scriptures we might have hope. 5 May the God of steadfastness and encouragement grant you to live in such harmony with one another, in accord with Christ Jesus, 6 that together you may with one voice glorify the God and Father of our Lord Jesus Christ.

7 Welcome one another, therefore, as Christ has welcomed you, for the glory of God. 8 For I tell you that Christ became a servant to the circumcised to show God's truthfulness, in order to confirm the promises given to the patriarchs, 9 and in order that the Gentiles might glorify God for his mercy. As it is written,

"Therefore I will praise thee among the Gentiles,
   and sing to thy name";
10 and again it is said,
"Rejoice, O Gentiles, with his people";
11 and again,
"Praise the Lord, all Gentiles,
   and let all the peoples praise him";
12 and further Īṣāi'áh says,
"The root of Jĕssë shall come,
   he who rises to rule the Gentiles;
   in him shall the Gentiles hope."
13 May the God of hope fill you with all joy and peace in believing, so that by the power of the Holy Spirit you may abound in hope.

VI. Conclusion and postscript 15.14–16.27

A. Paul's reasons for writing

14 I myself am satisfied about you, my brethren, that you yourselves are full of goodness, filled with all knowledge, and able to instruct one another. 15 But on some points I have written to you

v Other ancient authorities add *or be upset or be weakened*
w Other authorities, some ancient, insert here Ch 16.25-27

14.16
1 Cor 10.30
14.17
1 Cor 8.8;
Rom 15.13
14.18
2 Cor 8.21
14.19
Ps 34.14;
Heb 12.14;
Rom 15.2
14.20
ver 15;
1 Cor 8.9–
12
14.21
1 Cor 8.13
14.22
1 Jn 3.21

15.1
Rom 14.1;
Gal 6.1,2
15.2
1 Cor 10.33;
Rom 14.19
15.3
Ps 69.9;
2 Cor 8.9
15.4
Rom 4.23,
24;
2 Tim 3.16,
17
15.5
Rom 12.16;
1 Cor 1.10
15.6
Rev 1.6
15.7
Rom 14.1
15.8
Mt 15.24;
Acts 3.25,
26;
Rom 3.3;
2 Cor 1.20
15.9
Ps 18.49;
2 Sam 22.50
15.10
Deut 32.43
15.11
Ps 117.1
15.12
Isa 11.10;
Mt 12.21;
Rev 5.5;
22.16
15.13
Rom 14.17;
1 Thess 1.5

15.14
2 Pet 1.12;
1 Cor 8.1,7,
10
15.15
Rom 12.3;
Eph 3.7,8

very boldly by way of reminder, because of the grace given me by
God 16 to be a minister of Christ Jesus to the Gentiles in the
priestly service of the gospel of God, so that the offering of the
Gentiles may be acceptable, sanctified by the Holy Spirit. 17 In
Christ Jesus, then, I have reason to be proud of my work for God.
18 For I will not venture to speak of anything except what Christ
has wrought through me to win obedience from the Gentiles, by
word and deed, 19 by the power of signs and wonders, by the
power of the Holy Spirit, so that from Jerusalem and as far round
as Ĭllȳr´ĭcŭm I have fully preached the gospel of Christ, 20 thus
making it my ambition to preach the gospel, not where Christ has
already been named, lest I build on another man's foundation,
21 but as it is written,
"They shall see who have never been told of him,
and they shall understand who have never heard of him."

B. Paul's future plans

22 This is the reason why I have so often been hindered from
coming to you. 23 But now, since I no longer have any room for
work in these regions, and since I have longed for many years to
come to you, 24 I hope to see you in passing as I go to Spain, and to
be sped on my journey there by you, once I have enjoyed your company for a little. 25At present, however, I am going to Jerusalem
with aid for the saints. 26 For Măçėdō´nĭă and Ăchāi´ă have been
pleased to make some contribution for the poor among the saints
at Jerusalem; 27 they were pleased to do it, and indeed they are
in debt to them, for if the Gentiles have come to share in their
spiritual blessings, they ought also to be of service to them in
material blessings. 28 When therefore I have completed this, and
have delivered to them what has been raised,ˣ I shall go on by way
of you to Spain; 29 and I know that when I come to you I shall
come in the fulness of the blessingʸ of Christ.

30 I appeal to you, brethren, by our Lord Jesus Christ and by
the love of the Spirit, to strive together with me in your prayers
to God on my behalf, 31 that I may be delivered from the unbelievers in Judē´ä, and that my service for Jerusalem may be acceptable to the saints, 32 so that by God's will I may come to you
with joy and be refreshed in your company. 33 The God of
peace be with you all. Amen.

C. Commendations and greetings

16 I commend to you our sister Phoēbë, a deaconess of the
church at Çĕnçhrē´-aė, 2 that you may receive her in the Lord
as befits the saints, and help her in whatever she may require from
you, for she has been a helper of many and of myself as well.

3 Greet Prĭscă and Ăquĭ´lă, my fellow workers in Christ Jesus,
4 who risked their necks for my life, to whom not only I but also
all the churches of the Gentiles give thanks; 5 greet also the church
in their house. Greet my beloved Ĕpaē´nėtŭs, who was the first
convert in Asia for Christ. 6 Greet Mary, who has worked hard
among you. 7 Greet Ăndrŏn´ĭcŭs and Ju´nĭăs, my kinsmen and my

Cross-references

15.16
Acts 9.15;
Rom 11.13;
Phil 2.17

15.17
Phil 3.3;
Heb 2.17;
5.1

15.18
Acts 15.12;
21.19;
Rom 1.5;
16.26

15.19
Acts 19.11;
2 Cor 12.12

15.20
2 Cor 10.15,
16

15.21
Isa 52.15

15.22
Rom 1.13

15.23
Acts 19.21;
Rom 1.11

15.24
ver 28;
Acts 15.3

15.25
Acts 19.21;
24.27

15.26
2 Cor 8.1;
9.2;
1 Thess
1.7,8

15.27
1 Cor 9.11

15.30
Gal 5.22;
2 Cor 1.11;
Col 4.12

15.32
Rom 1.10;
Acts 18.21;
1 Cor 16.18

15.33
Rom 16.20;
2 Cor 13.11;
Phil 4.9;
Heb 13.20

16.1
Acts 18.18

16.2
Phil 2.29;
Rom 15.15,
31

16.3
Acts 18.2;
2 Tim 4.19

16.5
1 Cor 16.15,
19;
Col 4.15

ˣ Greek *sealed to them this fruit*   ʸ Other ancient authorities insert *of the gospel*

fellow prisoners; they are men of note among the apostles, and they were in Christ before me. 8 Greet Ampliā'tŭs, my beloved in the Lord. 9 Greet Ürbā'nŭs, our fellow worker in Christ, and my beloved StăchЎs. 10 Greet Ăpĕl'lĕs, who is approved in Christ. Greet those who belong to the family of Ărĭstŏb'ŭlŭs. 11 Greet my kinsman Hērō'dĭŏn. Greet those in the Lord who belong to the family of Narçĭs'sŭs. 12 Greet those workers in the Lord, TrЎ-phaē'nȧ and TrЎphō'sȧ. Greet the beloved Pĕrsĭs, who has worked hard in the Lord. 13 Greet Rufus, eminent in the Lord, also his mother and mine. 14 Greet ĂsЎn'crĭtŭs, Phlĕgŏn, Hĕrmēș, Pȧtrō'-bȧs, Hĕrmȧs, and the brethren who are with them. 15 Greet Phĭlŏl'ŏgŭs, Julia, Nēreus and his sister, and ŌlЎm'pȧs, and all the saints who are with them. 16 Greet one another with a holy kiss. All the churches of Christ greet you.

17 I appeal to you, brethren, to take note of those who create dissensions and difficulties, in opposition to the doctrine which you have been taught; avoid them. 18 For such persons do not serve our Lord Christ, but their own appetites,ᶻ and by fair and flattering words they deceive the hearts of the simple-minded. 19 For while your obedience is known to all, so that I rejoice over you, I would have you wise as to what is good and guileless as to what is evil; 20 then the God of peace will soon crush Satan under your feet. The grace of our Lord Jesus Christ be with you.ᵃ

21 Timothy, my fellow worker, greets you; so do Luçiŭs and Jāsón and Sōsĭp'ȧtĕr, my kinsmen.

22 I Tĕrţiŭs, the writer of this letter, greet you in the Lord.

23 Gāiŭs, who is host to me and to the whole church, greets you. Ĕrăs'tŭs, the city treasurer, and our brother Quartus, greet you.ᵇ

D. Doxology

25 Now to him who is able to strengthen you according to my gospel and the preaching of Jesus Christ, according to the revelation of the mystery which was kept secret for long ages 26 but is now disclosed and through the prophetic writings is made known to all nations, according to the command of the eternal God, to bring about the obedience of faith—27 to the only wise God be glory for evermore through Jesus Christ! Amen.

ᶻ Greek *their own belly* (Phil 3.19)   ᵃ Other ancient authorities omit this sentence
ᵇ Other ancient authorities insert verse 24, *The grace of our Lord Jesus Christ be with you all. Amen.*

16.9
2 Cor 5.17
16.10
2 Cor 5.17
16.11
ver 7,21;
1 Cor 1.11

16.15
ver 2,14
16.16
1 Cor 16.20;
2 Cor 13.12;
1 Thess 5.26
16.17
1 Tim 1.3;
6.3;
Gal 1.8,9;
2 Thess 3.6,
14;
2 Jn 10
16.18
Phil 3.19;
Col 2.4
16.19
Rom 1.8;
Mt 10.16;
1 Cor 14.20
16.20
Rom 15.33;
Gen 3.15;
1 Cor 16.23;
1 Thess 5.28
16.21
Acts 16.1;
13.1; 17.5;
20.4;
ver 7,11

INTRODUCTION TO
THE FIRST LETTER OF PAUL TO THE
CORINTHIANS

Authorship and Background: Before writing this letter Paul had already written to the Corinthians (5.9). This earlier letter has not survived, unless its contents have been preserved in 2 Cor 6.14—7.1, as some scholars believe. The Corinthian church then wrote to Paul about several matters (7.1) and sent the letter by a group which included Stephanas, Fortunatus, and Achaicus (16.17). It was in reply to this communication that Paul penned his second letter, known to us as 1 Corinthians. It appears to have been written in Ephesus, in A.D. 55, shortly before Pentecost, at the end of Paul's three-year stay there (16.8, 19). It was probably delivered to Corinth by Timothy (cf. 16.10–11).

Paul first came to Corinth from Athens on his second missionary tour (Acts 18.1). He arrived with some misgivings (2.3), but went to work in typical fashion, with the help of Aquila and Priscilla (Acts 18.2–4). He was joined eventually by Silas and Timothy, and spent eighteen months in intensive work (Acts 18.11). When Gallio was appointed proconsul of Achaia, in A.D. 51, Paul's enemies sought to have him jailed, but with no success (Acts 18.12–17). After spending some more time in Corinth, Paul went to the port city of Cenchreae, and on to Antioch (Acts 18.18–22). In all, he must have spent close to two years in Corinth (probably A.D. 49–51), establishing the work in the city and through-out the province of Achaia (cf. Rom 16.1 for Cenchreae, and "the whole of Achaia" in 2 Cor 1.1).

Characteristics: Corinth was a bustling metropolis, one of the largest centers of commerce and travel in the Roman Empire. Its reputation for immorality was so notorious that the verb "to corinthianize," meaning to live an immoral life, was coined. It is small wonder that even in the church there were problems of immorality (ch 5). Reports had also been brought by Chloe's family (or slaves) of factions in the church (1.11, 12), and the letter from the church itself raised several questions which Paul dealt with (7.1; see further "now concerning" in 7.1; 7.25; 8.1; 12.1; 16.1 which seem to refer to specific questions in the letter). In no other letter is there so vivid and realistic a portrait of the problems and difficulties confronting a church in a pagan and corrupt society. Here one may see the early Christians, "warts and all," their weakness serving to magnify the greatness of God's grace and power. In this letter are the earliest reports of the Lord's Supper (11.20–34), and the great hymn of love (ch 13), and the gospel of the resurrection (ch 15).

Contents:

and Christ had broken the unity of the church and made a mockery of the lordship of Christ. Such factions are intolerable: the apostles are fellow-servants, and it is God alone who supplies the life of the church (3.1–9) in which all are fellow members in the unity of Christ (3.21–23).

III.   Sexual morality. 5.1—7.40: Flagrant and unrepented immorality within the church has only one solution: the expulsion of the guilty from the Christian fellowship (5.1–13). All immorality is grievous sin against Christ: believers are His members and their bodies the temples of the Spirit (6.9–20). Christians should never appear in pagan courts in lawsuits against one another (6.1–8). Questions of marriage, celibacy, divorce, and remarriage are dealt with (7.1–40): sometimes Paul has a teaching from the Lord, at other times he gives his own judgment.

IV.   Christian liberty. 8.1—11.1: Christian life in a pagan society raised acute problems, especially that of table-fellowship with pagans, which involved eating meat offered in pagan temples; where no spiritual offense is involved (8.8) Christian love imposes voluntary restrictions on personal conduct (8.8–13; 9.19–23; 10.24, 31–33).

V.   Public worship. 11.2–14.40: Paul deals with women's dress (11.2–16), the Lord's Supper (11.17–34), spiritual gifts, their value and use (12.1—14.40). Love is the greatest of all gifts (13.1–13).

VI.   The resurrection. 15.1–58: The foundation of the Christian faith and message is the Resurrection of Christ, the guarantee of the believer's own resurrection.

VII.   Personal matters. 16.1–24: The offering for the Christians in Judea; future plans for Paul and his companions; final exhortations and benediction.

THE FIRST LETTER OF PAUL TO THE

CORINTHIANS

I. Introduction 1.1–9

A. Salutation

1.1
Rom 1.1;
2 Cor 1.1;
Eph 1.1;
Col 1.1;
Acts 18.17
1.2
Acts 18.1;
Rom 1.7;
Acts 7.59
1.3
Rom 1.7

1 Paul, called by the will of God to be an apostle of Christ Jesus, and our brother Sŏs'thĕnēṣ,
2 To the church of God which is at Corinth, to those sanctified in Christ Jesus, called to be saints together with all those who in every place call on the name of our Lord Jesus Christ, both their Lord and ours:
3 Grace to you and peace from God our Father and the Lord Jesus Christ.

B. Thanksgiving

1.4
Rom 1.8
1.5
2 Cor 9.11;
8.7
1.6
2 Tim 1.8;
Rev 1.2
1.7
Phil 3.20;
Tit 2.13;
2 Pet 3.12;
1.9
Isa 49.7;
1 Jn 1.3

4 I give thanks to God[a] always for you because of the grace of God which was given you in Christ Jesus, 5 that in every way you were enriched in him with all speech and all knowledge—6 even as the testimony to Christ was confirmed among you—7 so that you are not lacking in any spiritual gift, as you wait for the revealing of our Lord Jesus Christ; 8 who will sustain you to the end, guiltless in the day of our Lord Jesus Christ. 9 God is faithful, by whom you were called into the fellowship of his Son, Jesus Christ our Lord.

II. Factions 1.10–4.21

A. Exhortation to unity

*1.10
2 Cor 13.11;
Rom 12.16
1.13
2 Cor 11.4;
Mt 28.19;
Acts 2.38
1.14
Acts 18.8;
Rom 16.23
1.16
1 Cor 16.15
1.17
Jn 4.2;
Acts 10.48;
1 Cor 2.1,
4,13

10 I appeal to you, brethren, by the name of our Lord Jesus Christ, that all of you agree and that there be no dissensions among you, but that you be united in the same mind and the same judgment. 11 For it has been reported to me by Chlŏe'ṣ people that there is quarreling among you, my brethren. 12 What I mean is that each one of you says, "I belong to Paul," or "I belong to Ȧpŏl'lŏs," or "I belong to Çēphás," or "I belong to Christ." 13 Is Christ divided? Was Paul crucified for you? Or were you baptized in the name of Paul? 14 I am thankful[b] that I baptized none of you except Crĭspŭs and Gāiŭs; 15 lest any one should say that you were baptized in my name. 16 (I did baptize also the household of Stĕph'ănăs. Beyond that, I do not know whether I baptized any one else.) 17 For Christ did not send me to baptize but to preach

---

a Other ancient authorities read *my God*   b Other ancient authorities read *I thank God*

1.10 Schism is the rending of the body into warring parts. The Scripture here does not speak of separation caused by apostasy, but of divisions which arise about matters which are marginal to the gospel. Schism is condemned by God because it is destructive of the unity of His church and contrary to the will of Christ (1.13; 12.13; Jn 17.21–23). The existence of schism reveals carnality of spirit among the brethren (3.3). The great evil of schism is alluded to by Christ in Mt 12.25, where He describes the downfall of a house divided against itself. Believers are commanded to avoid fellowship with those who create dissension within the body of the church (Rom 16.17).

the gospel, and not with eloquent wisdom, lest the cross of Christ be emptied of its power.

B. *The wisdom of men and the "foolishness of God"*

18 For the word of the cross is folly to those who are perishing, but to us who are being saved it is the power of God. 19 For it is written,

"I will destroy the wisdom of the wise,
and the cleverness of the clever I will thwart."

20 Where is the wise man? Where is the scribe? Where is the debater of this age? Has not God made foolish the wisdom of the world? 21 For since, in the wisdom of God, the world did not know God through wisdom, it pleased God through the folly of what we preach to save those who believe. 22 For Jews demand signs and Greeks seek wisdom, 23 but we preach Christ crucified, a stumbling block to Jews and folly to Gentiles, 24 but to those who are called, both Jews and Greeks, Christ the power of God and the wisdom of God. 25 For the foolishness of God is wiser than men, and the weakness of God is stronger than men.

26 For consider your call, brethren; not many of you were wise according to worldly standards, not many were powerful, not many were of noble birth; 27 but God chose what is foolish in the world to shame the wise, God chose what is weak in the world to shame the strong, 28 God chose what is low and despised in the world, even things that are not, to bring to nothing things that are, 29 so that no human being might boast in the presence of God. 30 He is the source of your life in Christ Jesus, whom God made our wisdom, our righteousness and sanctification and redemption; 31 therefore, as it is written, "Let him who boasts, boast of the Lord."

2 When I came to you, brethren, I did not come proclaiming to you the testimony[c] of God in lofty words or wisdom. 2 For I decided to know nothing among you except Jesus Christ and him crucified. 3 And I was with you in weakness and in much fear and trembling; 4 and my speech and my message were not in plausible words of wisdom, but in demonstration of the Spirit and of power, 5 that your faith might not rest in the wisdom of men but in the power of God.

C. *True wisdom the gift of God*

6 Yet among the mature we do impart wisdom, although it is not a wisdom of this age or of the rulers of this age, who are doomed to pass away. 7 But we impart a secret and hidden wisdom of God, which God decreed before the ages for our glorification. 8 None of the rulers of this age understood this; for if they had, they would not have crucified the Lord of glory. 9 But, as it is written,

"What no eye has seen, nor ear heard,
nor the heart of man conceived,
what God has prepared for those who love him,"

10 God has revealed to us through the Spirit. For the Spirit searches everything, even the depths of God. 11 For what person

c Other ancient authorities read *mystery* (or *secret*)

1.18 Acts 17.18; 1 Cor 15.2; Rom 1.16
1.19 Isa 29.14
1.20 Isa 33.18; Rom 1.22
1.21 Gal 1.15; 1 Tim 4.16; Heb 7.25
1.22 Mt 12.38
1.23 Gal 5.11; 1 Cor 2.14
1.24 Rom 1.4; Col 2.3
1.26 Rom 11.29
1.27 Jas 2.5
1.29 Eph 2.9
1.30 1 Cor 6.11; 1 Thess 5.23; Eph 1.7,14; Rom 3.24
1.31 Jer 9.23,24; 2 Cor 10.17
2.1 1 Cor 1.17
2.2 Gal 6.14; 1 Cor 1.23
2.4 Rom 15.19; 1 Cor 4.20
2.5 2 Cor 4.7; 6.7
2.6 Eph 4.13; Phil 3.15; 1 Cor 1.20; 1.28
2.8 Acts 7.2; Jas 2.1
2.9 Isa 64.4; 65.17
2.10 Mt 16.17; Eph 3.3,5; Jn 14.26
2.11 Prov 20.27; Jer 17.9

knows a man's thoughts except the spirit of the man which is in him? So also no one comprehends the thoughts of God except the Spirit of God. 12 Now we have received not the spirit of the world, but the Spirit which is from God, that we might understand the gifts bestowed on us by God. 13And we impart this in words not taught by human wisdom but taught by the Spirit, interpreting spiritual truths to those who possess the Spirit.*d*

14 The unspiritual*e* man does not receive the gifts of the Spirit of God, for they are folly to him, and he is not able to understand them because they are spiritually discerned. 15 The spiritual man judges all things, but is himself to be judged by no one. 16 "For who has known the mind of the Lord so as to instruct him?" But we have the mind of Christ.

3 But I, brethren, could not address you as spiritual men, but as men of the flesh, as babes in Christ. 2 I fed you with milk, not solid food; for you were not ready for it; and even yet you are not ready, 3 for you are still of the flesh. For while there is jealousy and strife among you, are you not of the flesh, and behaving like ordinary men? 4 For when one says, "I belong to Paul," and another, "I belong to Ápŏl'lŏs," are you not merely men?

D. *The apostles: co-workers together*

5 What then is Ápŏl'lŏs? What is Paul? Servants through whom you believed, as the Lord assigned to each. 6 I planted, Ápŏl'lŏs watered, but God gave the growth. 7 So neither he who plants nor he who waters is anything, but only God who gives the growth. 8 He who plants and he who waters are equal, and each shall receive his wages according to his labor. 9 For we are God's fellow workers; you are God's field, God's building.

10 According to the grace of God given to me, like a skilled master builder I laid a foundation, and another man is building upon it. Let each man take care how he builds upon it. 11 For no other foundation can any one lay than that which is laid, which is Jesus Christ. 12 Now if any one builds on the foundation with gold, silver, precious stones, wood, hay, straw—13 each man's work will become manifest; for the Day will disclose it, because

d Or *interpreting spiritual truths in spiritual language;* or *comparing spiritual things with spiritual* *e* Or *natural*

2.14 The term here is *psychikos*, and designates the man who is dominated by his *psyche* or natural "soul" (that individuality or life-principle which man shares with animals, although his soul is possessed of a higher order of intelligence). The *psychikos* is the once-born man, the natural, fallen man, dead in trespasses and sins, without hope and without God (Eph 2.1, 12). The *natural* man is to be carefully distinguished from what the Bible calls the *carnal* man. The carnal (*sarkikos*) man is a Christian who is not fully surrendered to Christ and lives largely under the domination of his fleshly nature (see, e.g., 1 Cor 3.3). But the *natural* man is without spiritual discernment, blinded by the prince of this world (Jn 12.40; 2 Cor 4.4; 1 Jn 2.11).
3.1 Scripture distinguishes between two kinds of Christian walks. One walk is termed *carnal* and the other *spiritual*. The *carnal* believer is a converted believer whose life is fleshly (*sarkinos*) because he is under the domination of the *sarx* or self-relying, self-pleasing nature. Therefore he is not walking in full fellowship with the Lord Jesus nor is he wholly surrendered to the Spirit of God. He is not Spirit-filled although he should be (Eph 5.18); nor does his life reflect the fruit of the Spirit (Gal 5.22, 23). The *spiritual* Christian (*pneumatikos*) is one whose life is yielded to God and whose will is in subjection to the will of God. He is filled with the Spirit and men can see the evidences of spiritual vitality, for he produces the fruit of the Spirit in his life. An unbeliever is not spoken of as either *carnal* or *spiritual*. He is called a *natural* (*psychikos*) man. (See 2.14 where he is called the *unspiritual* man.)

*Marginal references: 2.12 Rom 8.15; 1 Cor 1.27; 2.13 1 Cor 1.17; *2.14 1 Cor 1.18; Jas 3.15; 2.16 Isa 40.13; Jn 15.15; *3.1 1 Cor 2.15; Rom 7.14; 1 Cor 2.14; Heb 5.13; 3.2 Heb 5.12, 13; 1 Pet 2.2; 3.3 1 Cor 1.11; Gal 5.20; Jas 3.16; 3.4 1 Cor 1.12; 3.8 Ps 62.12; Gal 6.4,5; 3.9 2 Cor 6.1; Isa 61.3; Eph 2.20-22; 1 Pet 2.5; 3.10 Rom 12.3; 15.20; 1 Cor 15.10; 3.11 Isa 28.6; Eph 2.20; 3.13 1 Cor 4.5; 2 Thess 1.7-10*

it will be revealed with fire, and the fire will test what sort of work each one has done. 14 If the work which any man has built on the foundation survives, he will receive a reward. 15 If any man's work is burned up, he will suffer loss, though he himself will be saved, but only as through fire.

16 Do you not know that you are God's temple and that God's Spirit dwells in you? 17 If any one destroys God's temple, God will destroy him. For God's temple is holy, and that temple you are.

18 Let no one deceive himself. If any one among you thinks that he is wise in this age, let him become a fool that he may become wise. 19 For the wisdom of this world is folly with God. For it is written, "He catches the wise in their craftiness," 20 and again, "The Lord knows that the thoughts of the wise are futile." 21 So let no one boast of men. For all things are yours, 22 whether Paul or Apŏl′lŏs or Çĕphás or the world or life or death or the present or the future, all are yours; 23 and you are Christ's; and Christ is God's.

E. The ministry judged by God

4 This is how one should regard us, as servants of Christ and stewards of the mysteries of God. 2 Moreover it is required of stewards that they be found trustworthy. 3 But with me it is a very small thing that I should be judged by you or by any human court. I do not even judge myself. 4 I am not aware of anything against myself, but I am not thereby acquitted. It is the Lord who judges me. 5 Therefore do not pronounce judgment before the time, before the Lord comes, who will bring to light the things now hidden in darkness and will disclose the purposes of the heart. Then every man will receive his commendation from God.

F. The humility of the apostles

6 I have applied all this to myself and Apŏl′lŏs for your benefit, brethren, that you may learn by us not to go beyond what is written, that none of you may be puffed up in favor of one against another. 7 For who sees anything different in you? What have you that you did not receive? If then you received it, why do you boast as if it were not a gift?

8 Already you are filled! Already you have become rich! Without us you have become kings! And would that you did reign, so

---

*3.14
1 Cor 4.5;
9.17
3.15
Job 23.10;
Jude 23
*3.16
1 Cor 6.19;
2 Cor 6.16

3.18
Isa 5.21;
1 Cor 8.2
3.19
Job 5.13;
1 Cor 1.20
3.20
Ps 94.11
3.21
1 Cor 4.6;
Rom 8.32
3.23
1 Cor
15.23;
2 Cor 10.7;
Gal 3.29

4.1
2 Cor 6.4;
1 Cor 9.17;
Rom 11.25;
16.25

4.4
2 Cor 1.12;
Rom 2.13
4.5
Rom 2.1;
2 Cor 10.18;
Rom 2.29

4.6
1 Cor 1.19,
31; 3.19,20;
1.12; 3.4

4.7
Rom 12.3,6

4.8
Rev 3.17,18

3.14 See also note to 2 Cor 5.10 on the judgment seat of Christ. Salvation is by grace through faith. Rewards are determined according to works performed subsequent to salvation. Scripture reveals that some will suffer *loss* entering heaven by the skin of their teeth and with the smell of smoke on their garments (3.15). While works constitute the basis of the reward, yet the reward is of grace and not merit since all of the believer's works are defective. God, however, judges the intent of the heart (1 Ki 8.17–19). It should be clearly understood that a self-seeking desire for heavenly rewards has no proper place in the Christian's motivation, since he lives no longer for himself, but for Him who died for

him (2 Cor 5.15). But the rewards have value only as a demonstration of the grace and righteousness of God. The Christian desires them only as a display of the glory of God.

3.16 Paul uses the Temple as a figure of the believer's body. Just as the Shekinah glory of God inhabited the Holy Place in the tabernacle and the Temple, so the Holy Spirit indwells the believer whose body becomes the temple of the Holy Spirit. Since the Holy Spirit indwells the believer, his body becomes holy and care must be exercised not to defile it in any manner. Certainly the most compelling reason to live a life of holiness unto the Lord is the fact that the Holy Spirit indwells the believer.

4.9
1 Cor 15.31;
2 Cor 11.23;
Rom 8.36;
Heb 10.33
4.10
1 Cor 1.18;
Acts 17.18;
1 Cor 3.18
4.11
Rom 8.35;
2 Cor 11.23–27
4.12
Acts 18.3;
1 Pet 3.9;
Jn 15.20;
Rom 8.35

that we might share the rule with you! 9 For I think that God has exhibited us apostles as last of all, like men sentenced to death; because we have become a spectacle to the world, to angels and to men. 10 We are fools for Christ's sake, but you are wise in Christ. We are weak, but you are strong. You are held in honor, but we in disrepute. 11 To the present hour we hunger and thirst, we are ill-clad and buffeted and homeless, 12 and we labor, working with our own hands. When reviled, we bless; when persecuted, we endure; 13 when slandered, we try to conciliate; we have become, and are now, as the refuse of the world, the offscouring of all things.

G. The appeal of Paul

4.14
1 Thess 2.11
4.15
1 Cor 1.30;
Philem 10
4.16
Phil 3.17;
1 Thess 1.6;
2 Thess 3.9
4.19
Acts 19.21;
2 Cor 1.15;
Rom 15.32
4.20
1 Thess 1.5
4.21
2 Cor 1.23;
13.10

14 I do not write this to make you ashamed, but to admonish you as my beloved children. 15 For though you have countless guides in Christ, you do not have many fathers. For I became your father in Christ Jesus through the gospel. 16 I urge you, then, be imitators of me. 17 Therefore I sent*g* to you Timothy, my beloved and faithful child in the Lord, to remind you of my ways in Christ, as I teach them everywhere in every church. 18 Some are arrogant, as though I were not coming to you. 19 But I will come to you soon, if the Lord wills, and I will find out not the talk of these arrogant people but their power. 20 For the kingdom of God does not consist in talk but in power. 21 What do you wish? Shall I come to you with a rod, or with love in a spirit of gentleness?

III. Sexual morality 5.1–7.40

A. Incest at Corinth

5.1
Lev 18.8;
Deut 22.30;
2 Cor 7.12
5.2
1 Cor 4.18;
2 Cor 7.7
5.3
Col 2.5
5.4
2 Thess 3.6;
2 Cor 2.10
5.5
1 Tim 1.20

5 It is actually reported that there is immorality among you, and of a kind that is not found even among pagans; for a man is living with his father's wife. 2 And you are arrogant! Ought you not rather to mourn? Let him who has done this be removed from among you.

3 For though absent in body I am present in spirit, and as if present, I have already pronounced judgment 4 in the name of the Lord Jesus on the man who has done such a thing. When you are assembled, and my spirit is present, with the power of our Lord Jesus, 5 you are to deliver this man to Satan for the destruction of the flesh, that his spirit may be saved in the day of the Lord Jesus.*h*

B. The duty to perform

5.6
Jas 4.16;
Gal 5.9
*5.7
1 Pet 1.19
5.8
Deut 16.3;
Mk 8.15

6 Your boasting is not good. Do you not know that a little leaven leavens the whole lump? 7 Cleanse out the old leaven that you may be a new lump, as you really are unleavened. For Christ, our paschal lamb, has been sacrificed. 8 Let us, therefore, celebrate the festival, not with the old leaven, the leaven of malice and evil, but with the unleavened bread of sincerity and truth.

g Or *am sending*   *h* Other ancient authorities omit *Jesus*

5.7 Christ is called the paschal or Passover lamb. This bespeaks the fulfilment of the Old Testament type of the sacrificial lamb which foreshadowed Christ and His atoning sacrifice. (Here read the note to Ex 12.11 on Passover.)

C. *The command to follow*

9 I wrote to you in my letter not to associate with immoral men; 10 not at all meaning the immoral of this world, or the greedy and robbers, or idolaters, since then you would need to go out of the world. 11 But rather I wrote[i] to you not to associate with any one who bears the name of brother if he is guilty of immorality or greed, or is an idolater, reviler, drunkard, or robber—not even to eat with such a one. 12 For what have I to do with judging outsiders? Is it not those inside the church whom you are to judge? 13 God judges those outside. "Drive out the wicked person from among you."

5.9
2 Cor 6.14;
Eph 5.11;
2 Thess 3.14
5.10
1 Cor 10.27
*5.11
2 Thess 3.6;
1 Cor 10.7,
14,20,21
5.12
Mk 4.11;
1 Cor 6.1–4
5.13
Deut 13.5;
21.21

D. *Lawsuits and the Christian*

6 When one of you has a grievance against a brother, does he dare go to law before the unrighteous instead of the saints? 2 Do you not know that the saints will judge the world? And if the world is to be judged by you, are you incompetent to try trivial cases? 3 Do you not know that we are to judge angels? How much more, matters pertaining to this life! 4 If then you have such cases, why do you lay them before those who are least esteemed by the church? 5 I say this to your shame. Can it be that there is no man among you wise enough to decide between members of the brotherhood, 6 but brother goes to law against brother, and that before unbelievers?

7 To have lawsuits at all with one another is defeat for you. Why not rather suffer wrong? Why not rather be defrauded? 8 But you yourselves wrong and defraud, and that even your own brethren.

6.1
Mt 18.17
6.2
Dan 7.22;
Mt 19.28;
Lk 22.30
6.4
1 Cor 5.12
6.5
1Cor 15.34;
Acts 1.15
6.6
2 Cor 6.14,
15
6.7
Mt 5.39,40;
Rom 12.17
6.8
1 Thess 4.6

E. *Kingdom standards*

9 Do you not know that the unrighteous will not inherit the kingdom of God? Do not be deceived; neither the immoral, nor idolators, nor adulterers, nor sexual perverts, 10 nor thieves, nor the greedy, nor drunkards, nor revilers, nor robbers will inherit the kingdom of God. 11 And such were some of you. But you were

6.9
Gal 5.21;
1 Tim 1.10;
Rev 22.15
*6.11
Eph 2.2;
Col 3.7;
Tit 3.3

i Or *now I write*

5.11 Scripture admonishes true believers to have no fellowship with the wicked works of darkness. Thus Paul lists here those sins which should cause believers to have no fellowship with so-called Christians who practice them. So strong is his warning against fellowship with them that he commands that they be driven from their midst (ver 13). Just as people having communicable diseases are isolated to keep them from infecting others, so Paul would protect believers by isolating these wicked persons from them.

6.11 There are two aspects to the biblical use of the term "sanctification" (*hagiasmos*, from *hagios*, or "holy"). The first aspect refers to that act of grace whereby a believer is at conversion *set apart* from the world (and from self-seeking) unto God as His sacred possession. In this sense we have already been perfectly sanctified in the sight of God (Heb 10.10). The second aspect refers to that process of spiritual growth by which the believer dies more and more to self and sin and lives more and more to Christ and righteousness. Justification and regeneration are "once for all" acts. Sanctification is progressive and continues to the end of one's earthly life. In justification God did something *for* us. In sanctification God does something *in* us. Justification has to do with our *standing* before God; sanctification concerns our *character* and *conduct*. Sanctification proceeds from Father, Son, and Holy Spirit (1 Thess 5.23; Heb 2.11; 13.12; 1 Cor 6.11; Rom 15.16). Negatively it implies the putting off of the old; positively it connotes the putting on of the new (Rom 6.11, 12; Col 3.5, 8, 12–17). The ultimate goal is to bring us into conformity to Jesus Christ (Rom 8.28, 29; 1 Thess 4.3) and to His sinless perfection. Either upon death or at the coming of Christ we shall be made perfect in holiness, for we shall see Him as He is (1 Jn 3.2).

washed, you were sanctified, you were justified in the name of the Lord Jesus Christ and in the Spirit of our God.

F. Chastity

12 "All things are lawful for me," but not all things are helpful. "All things are lawful for me," but I will not be enslaved by anything. 13 "Food is meant for the stomach and the stomach for food"—and God will destroy both one and the other. The body is not meant for immorality, but for the Lord, and the Lord for the body. 14 And God raised the Lord and will also raise us up by his power. 15 Do you not know that your bodies are members of Christ? Shall I therefore take the members of Christ and make them members of a prostitute? Never! 16 Do you not know that he who joins himself to a prostitute becomes one body with her? For, as it is written, "The two shall become one flesh." 17 But he who is united to the Lord becomes one spirit with him. 18 Shun immorality. Every other sin which a man commits is outside the body; but the immoral man sins against his own body. 19 Do you not know that your body is a temple of the Holy Spirit within you, which you have from God? You are not your own; 20 you were bought with a price. So glorify God in your body.

G. Marriage and celibacy

1. Principles of marriage

7 Now concerning the matters about which you wrote. It is well for a man not to touch a woman. 2 But because of the temptation to immorality, each man should have his own wife and each woman her own husband. 3 The husband should give to his wife her conjugal rights, and likewise the wife to her husband. 4 For the wife does not rule over her own body, but the husband does; likewise the husband does not rule over his own body, but the wife does. 5 Do not refuse one another except perhaps by agreement for a season, that you may devote yourselves to prayer; but then come together again, lest Satan tempt you through lack of self-control. 6 I say this by way of concession, not of command. 7 I wish that all were as I myself am. But each has his own special gift from God, one of one kind and one of another.

8 To the unmarried and the widows I say that it is well for them to remain single as I do. 9 But if they cannot exercise self-control, they should marry. For it is better to marry than to be aflame with passion.

2. The Christian and divorce

10 To the married I give charge, not I but the Lord, that the

6.12
1 Cor 10.23
6.13
Mt 15.17;
Eph 5.23
6.14
Rom 6.5,8;
8.11;
2 Cor 4.14;
Eph 1.19
6.15
Rom 12.5;
1 Cor 12.27
6.16
Gen 2.4;
Mt 19.5;
Eph 5.31
6.17
Jn 17.21–23;
Gal 2.20
6.18
Rom 6.12;
Heb 13.4;
1 Thess 4.4
6.19
Jn 2.21;
Rom 14.7,8
6.20
1 Cor 7.23;
1 Pet 1.18,19;
Rev 5.9
7.1
ver 8,26
★7.2
7.3
1 Pet 3.7
7.5
Ex 19.15;
1 Sam 21.4,5;
1 Thess 3.5
7.6
2 Cor 8.8
7.7
ver 8;
1 Cor 9.5;
12.11;
Mt 19.12
7.8
ver 1,26
7.9
1 Tim 5.14
7.10
Mal 2.14;
Mt 5.32;
19.3–9;
Mk 10.11;
Lk 16.18

7.2 Scripture states that a man should have one wife (Gen 2.24; Mk 10.6–8; 1 Cor 7.2–4). As head of the house, man is to have authority over his wife (Gen 3.16; 1 Cor 11.3; Eph 5.23). A husband has certain duties toward his wife other than the usual ones of support, protection, and care. They are: (1) to love her (Eph 5.25; Col 3.19); (2) to live considerately with her (1 Pet 3.7); (3) to be faithful to her (Mal 2.14, 15; Prov 5.19); (4) to live with her for life (Mt 19.3–9). A husband's duty to his wife precedes his obligations to parents and children; it is second only to his duty to God (Lk 14.26 and Mt 19.29).

wife should not separate from her husband 11(but if she does, let her remain single or else be reconciled to her husband)—and that the husband should not divorce his wife.

12 To the rest I say, not the Lord, that if any brother has a wife who is an unbeliever, and she consents to live with him, he should not divorce her. 13 If any woman has a husband who is an unbeliever, and he consents to live with her, she should not divorce him. 14 For the unbelieving husband is consecrated through his wife, and the unbelieving wife is consecrated through her husband. Otherwise, your children would be unclean, but as it is they are holy. 15 But if the unbelieving partner desires to separate, let it be so; in such a case the brother or sister is not bound. For God has called us*l* to peace. 16 Wife, how do you know whether you will save your husband? Husband, how do you know whether you will save your wife?

3. *The status quo*

17 Only, let every one lead the life which the Lord has assigned to him, and in which God has called him. This is my rule in all the churches.18 Was any one at the time of his call already circumcised? Let him not seek to remove the marks of circumcision. Was any one at the time of his call uncircumcised? Let him not seek circumcision. 19 For neither circumcision counts for anything nor uncircumcision, but keeping the commandments of God. 20 Every one should remain in the state in which he was called. 21 Were you a slave when called? Never mind. But if you can gain your freedom, avail yourself of the opportunity.*x* 22 For he who was called in the Lord as a slave is a freedman of the Lord. Likewise he who was free when called is a slave of Christ. 23 You were bought with a price; do not become slaves of men. 24 So, brethren, in whatever state each was called, there let him remain with God.

4. *Counsel to the unmarried*

25 Now concerning the unmarried,*y* I have no command of the Lord, but I give my opinion as one who by the Lord's mercy is trustworthy. 26 I think that in view of the present*m* distress it is well for a person to remain as he is. 27 Are you bound to a wife? Do not seek to be free. Are you free from a wife? Do not seek marriage. 28 But if you marry, you do not sin, and if a girl*z* marries she does not sin. Yet those who marry will have worldly troubles, and I would spare you that. 29 I mean, brethren, the appointed time has grown very short; from now on, let those who have wives live as though they had none, 30 and those who mourn as though

---

l Other ancient authorities read *you*   *x* Or *make use of your present condition instead*
m Or *impending*   *y* Greek *virgins*   *z* Greek *virgin*

7.15 See note to Deut 24.1 on divorce.

7.25 Paul did not belittle marriage. Indeed he entertained the very highest views of the marital estate (Eph 5.22–33). Nor did he suggest that to remain single was, in his judgment, best for all men at all times. By way of advice (not command) he urged remaining single at that time because of the *impending distress*. It was wise for those who had the gift of continence and a sincere purpose of devoting themselves to Christian service to refrain from marriage and its involvements. Presumably the *impending distress* (ver 26) referred to the terrible persecutions which were to come, when Christians might be put under undue pressures to forswear Christ in order to save their wives and children from brutal torture and death. Or it may have been a reference to the imminent end of the age (ver 28, 31b). In any case, this recommendation was not meant to be binding upon all Christians for all time.

7.12
ver 6;
2 Cor 11.17

7.14
Mal 2.15

*7.15
Rom 14.19;
1 Cor 14.33
7.16
1 Pet 3.1

7.17
Rom 12.3;
1 Cor 4.17;
14.33;
2 Cor 8.18;
11.28
7.18
Acts 15.1,2
7.19
Gal 5.6;
6.15;
Rom 2.25
7.20
ver 24
7.22
Jn 8.32,36;
Philem 16;
Eph 6.6
7.23
1 Cor 6.20

*7.25
2 Cor 8.8,
10;
1 Tim 1.13,
16
7.26
ver 1,8

7.29
Rom 13.11,
12;
ver 31

they were not mourning, and those who rejoice as though they were not rejoicing, and those who buy as though they had no goods, 31 and those who deal with the world as though they had no dealings with it. For the form of this world is passing away.

32 I want you to be free from anxieties. The unmarried man is anxious about the affairs of the Lord, how to please the Lord; 33 but the married man is anxious about worldly affairs, how to please his wife, 34 and his interests are divided. And the unmarried woman or girl[z] is anxious about the affairs of the Lord, how to be holy in body and spirit; but the married woman is anxious about worldly affairs, how to please her husband. 35 I say this for your own benefit, not to lay any restraint upon you, but to promote good order and to secure your undivided devotion to the Lord.

5. Asceticism and marriage

36 If any one thinks that he is not behaving properly toward his betrothed,[z] if his passions are strong, and it has to be, let him do as he wishes: let them marry—it is no sin. 37 But whoever is firmly established in his heart, being under no necessity but having his desire under control, and has determined this in his heart, to keep her as his betrothed,[z] he will do well. 38 So that he who marries his betrothed[z] does well; and he who refrains from marriage will do better.

6. Counsel to widows

39 A wife is bound to her husband as long as he lives. If the husband dies, she is free to be married to whom she wishes, only in the Lord. 40 But in my judgment she is happier if she remains as she is. And I think that I have the Spirit of God.

IV. Christian liberty 8.1—11.1

A. Food offered to idols

8 Now concerning food offered to idols: we know that "all of us possess knowledge." "Knowledge" puffs up, but love builds up. 2 If any one imagines that he knows something, he does not yet know as he ought to know. 3 But if one loves God, one is known by him.

4 Hence, as to the eating of food offered to idols, we know that "an idol has no real existence," and that "there is no God but one." 5 For although there may be so-called gods in heaven or on earth —as indeed there are many "gods" and many "lords"—6 yet for us there is one God, the Father, from whom are all things and for whom we exist, and one Lord, Jesus Christ, through whom are all things and through whom we exist.

7 However, not all possess this knowledge. But some, through

---

z Greek virgin

8.1 In the sacrifice of animals in heathen temples only a token part of the animal was burned in sacrifice, while the remainder was disposed of in meat markets for sale to the public (10.25). Some Corinthian Christians believed that the eating of such meat involved idolatry, since the animal had been offered in idol worship (ver 7). Paul again stresses the fact that food has no moral or spiritual value in itself. Those who were immature in the faith, however, had scruples about this, and it was the strong Christian's responsibility to abstain from what in itself was innocent in order not to hurt his weak brother.

being hitherto accustomed to idols, eat food as really offered to an idol; and their conscience, being weak, is defiled. 8 Food will not commend us to God. We are no worse off if we do not eat, and no better off if we do. 9 Only take care lest this liberty of yours somehow become a stumbling block to the weak. 10 For if any one sees you, a man of knowledge, at table in an idol's temple, might he not be encouraged, if his conscience is weak, to eat food offered to idols? 11And so by your knowledge this weak man is destroyed, the brother for whom Christ died. 12 Thus, sinning against your brethren and wounding their conscience when it is weak, you sin against Christ. 13 Therefore, if food is a cause of my brother's falling, I will never eat meat, lest I cause my brother to fall.

B. *The law of expediency*

1. *Christian rights acknowledged*

9 Am I not free? Am I not an apostle? Have I not seen Jesus our Lord? Are not you my workmanship in the Lord? 2 If to others I am not an apostle, at least I am to you; for you are the seal of my apostleship in the Lord.

3 This is my defense to those who would examine me. 4 Do we not have the right to our food and drink? 5 Do we not have the right to be accompanied by a wife,ⁿ as the other apostles and the brothers of the Lord and Çêphàs? 6 Or is it only Bar'nábàs and I who have no right to refrain from working for a living? 7 Who serves as a soldier at his own expense? Who plants a vineyard without eating any of its fruit? Who tends a flock without getting some of the milk?

8 Do I say this on human authority? Does not the law say the same? 9 For it is written in the law of Moses,"You shall not muzzle an ox when it is treading out the grain." Is it for oxen that God is concerned? 10 Does he not speak entirely for our sake? It was written for our sake, because the plowman should plow in hope and the thresher thresh in hope of a share in the crop. 11 If we have sown spiritual good among you, is it too much if we reap your material benefits? 12 If others share this rightful claim upon you, do not we still more?

Nevertheless, we have not made use of this right, but we endure anything rather than put an obstacle in the way of the gospel of Christ. 13 Do you not know that those who are employed in the temple service get their food from the temple, and those who serve at the altar share in the sacrificial offerings? 14 In the same way, the Lord commanded that those who proclaim the gospel should get their living by the gospel.

2. *Christian rights surrendered*

15 But I have made no use of any of these rights, nor am I

ⁿ Greek *a sister as wife*

8.8 Rom 14.17
*8.9 Gal 5.13; Rom 14.1, 13,20
8.10 1 Cor 10.28, 32
8.11 Rom 14.15, 20
8.13 Rom 14.21; 2 Cor 11.29
9.1 2 Cor 12.12; Acts 9.3,17; 18.9; 22.14, 18; 23.11; 1 Cor 3.6; 4.15
9.2 2 Cor 3.2,3
9.4 1 Thess 2.6; 2 Thess 3.8, 9
9.5 1 Cor 7.7,8; Mt 12.46; 8.14
9.6 Acts 4.36
9.7 2 Cor 10.4; 1 Tim 1.18; Deut 20.6; Prov 27.18
9.9 Deut 25.4; 1 Tim 5.18
9.11 Rom 15.27
9.12 2 Cor 6.3; 11.12
9.13 Lev 6.16; Deut 18.1
*9.14 Mt 10.10; Lk 10.7
9.15 Acts 18.3; 2 Cor 11.10

8.9 See note to Acts 16.3.
9.14 Paul was not paid for his ministerial labors. In order to avoid all possible accusation of mercenary motives in propagating this revolutionary new religion, Paul supported himself by plying his trade as a tentmaker. At the same time he insisted that as a matter of principle, both he and all other ministers of the gospel are entitled to wages for their labors. Some have mistakenly concluded that Paul's own example should be binding upon all Christian clergymen, but Paul's teaching itself refutes this position as unjustifiable. Gal 6.6 reiterates what is taught here.

9.16
Rom 1.14;
Acts 9.15
9.17
1 Cor 3.8,
14;
Gal 2.7;
Phil 1.16,
17;
Col 1.25
9.18
2 Cor 11.7;
12.13;
1 Cor 7.31
9.19
Gal 5.13;
Mt 18.15;
1 Pet 3.1
9.20
Acts 16.3;
21.23;
Rom 11.14;
Gal 2.19
9.21
Rom 2.12,
14;
Gal 3.2;
1 Cor 7.22
9.24
2 Tim 4.7;
Heb 12.1
9.25
Eph 6.12;
1 Tim 6.12
9.27
Rom 8.13;
Col 3.5;
Rom 6.18
10.1
Ex 13.21;
14.22,29;
Rom 1.13
10.3
Ex 16.4,35
10.4
Ex 17.6;
Num 20.11
10.5
Num 14.29,
30;
Heb 3.17
10.6
Num 11.4,
34;
Ps 106.14
10.7
Ex 32.4,6
10.8
Num 25.1ff
10.9
Num 21.5,6
*10.10
Num 16.41,
49;
Ex 12.23

writing this to secure any such provision. For I would rather die than have any one deprive me of my ground for boasting. 16 For if I preach the gospel, that gives me no ground for boasting. For necessity is laid upon me. Woe to me if I do not preach the gospel! 17 For if I do this of my own will, I have a reward; but if not of my own will, I am entrusted with a commission. 18 What then is my reward? Just this: that in my preaching I may make the gospel free of charge, not making full use of my right in the gospel.

19 For though I am free from all men, I have made myself a slave to all, that I might win the more. 20 To the Jews I became as a Jew, in order to win Jews; to those under the law I became as one under the law—though not being myself under the law—that I might win those under the law. 21 To those outside the law I became as one outside the law—not being without law toward God but under the law of Christ—that I might win those outside the law. 22 To the weak I became weak, that I might win the weak. I have become all things to all men, that I might by all means save some. 23 I do it all for the sake of the gospel, that I may share in its blessings.

3. *The true race*

24 Do you not know that in a race all the runners compete, but only one receives the prize? So run that you may obtain it. 25 Every athlete exercises self-control in all things. They do it to receive a perishable wreath, but we an imperishable. 26 Well, I do not run aimlessly, I do not box as one beating the air; 27 but I pommel my body and subdue it, lest after preaching to others I myself should be disqualified.

C. *The evil of self-indulgence illustrated*

10 I want you to know, brethren, that our fathers were all under the cloud, and all passed through the sea, 2 and all were baptized into Moses in the cloud and in the sea, 3 and all ate the same supernatural⁰ food 4 and all drank the same supernatural⁰ drink. For they drank from the supernatural⁰ Rock which followed them, and the Rock was Christ. 5 Nevertheless with most of them God was not pleased; for they were overthrown in the wilderness.

6 Now these things are warnings for us, not to desire evil as they did. 7 Do not be idolaters as some of them were; as it is written, "The people sat down to eat and drink and rose up to dance." 8 We must not indulge in immorality as some of them did, and twenty-three thousand fell in a single day. 9 We must not put the Lordᵖ to the test, as some of them did and were destroyed by serpents; 10 nor grumble, as some of them did and were destroyed

o Greek *spiritual*   *p* Other ancient authorities read *Christ*

10.10 Grumbling or complaining (KJV, "murmuring") is described by Scripture as a great sin against God. It involves rebelling bitterly against adverse circumstances whether they have been occasioned by sin, or sent by God for purposes of purification or testing. The wicked grumble (Jude 16); but saints are forbidden to do so (10.10; Phil 2.14). Complaining against God's dealings is unreasonable and indefensible (Lam 3.39), and God is justly provoked by it to measures of chastisement (Num 14.2, 11; Deut 9.8, 22). Grumblers are normally requited with punishment (Num 11.1; 14.27–29; 16.45, 46; Ps 106.25, 26; 1 Cor 10.9–11). Scripture abounds in warning illustrations dealing with this sin: e.g., Moses (Ex 5, 22, 23); Aaron (Num 12.1, 2, 8); Korah (Num 16.3); Jesus' disciples (Mk 14.4, 5); the Pharisees (Lk 15.2). Grumbling is basically sin against God.

by the Destroyer. 11 Now these things happened to them as a warning, but they were written down for our instruction, upon whom the end of the ages has come. 12 Therefore let any one who thinks that he stands take heed lest he fall. 13 No temptation has overtaken you that is not common to man. God is faithful, and he will not let you be tempted beyond your strength, but with the temptation will also provide the way of escape, that you may be able to endure it.

D. Participation in idol feasts prohibited

14 Therefore, my beloved, shun the worship of idols. 15 I speak as to sensible men; judge for yourselves what I say. 16 The cup of blessing which we bless, is it not a participation*q* in the blood of Christ? The bread which we break, is it not a participation*q* in the body of Christ? 17 Because there is one bread, we who are many are one body, for we all partake of the one bread. 18 Consider the people of Israel;*a* are not those who eat the sacrifices partners in the altar? 19 What do I imply then? That food offered to idols is anything, or that an idol is anything? 20 No, I imply that what pagans sacrifice they offer to demons and not to God. I do not want you to be partners with demons. 21 You cannot drink the cup of the Lord and the cup of demons. You cannot partake of the table of the Lord and the table of demons. 22 Shall we provoke the Lord to jealousy? Are we stronger than he?

E. The basic principles summed up

23 "All things are lawful," but not all things are helpful. "All things are lawful," but not all things build up. 24 Let no one seek his own good, but the good of his neighbor. 25 Eat whatever is sold in the meat market without raising any question on the ground of conscience. 26 For "the earth is the Lord's, and everything in it." 27 If one of the unbelievers invites you to dinner and you are disposed to go, eat whatever is set before you without raising any question on the ground of conscience. 28 (But if some one says to you, "This has been offered in sacrifice," then out of consideration for the man who informed you, and for conscience' sake—29 I mean his conscience, not yours—do not eat it.) For why should my liberty be determined by another man's scruples? 30 If I partake with thankfulness, why am I denounced because of that for which I give thanks?

31 So, whether you eat or drink, or whatever you do, do all to the glory of God. 32 Give no offense to Jews or to Greeks or to the church of God, 33 just as I try to please all men in everything I do, 11 not seeking my own advantage, but of that of many, that they may be saved. 1 Be imitators of me, as I am of Christ.

q Or communion
a Greek Israel according to the flesh

10.11
Rom 13.11;
Phil 4.5
10.12
Rom 11.20
10.13
2 Pet 2.9

10.14
2 Cor 6.17
10.16
Mt 26.26;
Acts 2.42
10.17
Rom 12.5;
1 Cor 12.27
10.18
Lev 7.6

10.20
Deut 32.17;
Ps 106.37;
Rev 9.20
10.21
2 Cor 6.15,
16
10.22
Deut 32.21;
Ecc 6.10;
Isa 45.9

★10.23
1 Cor 6.12;
Rom 14.19
10.24
ver 33;
Rom 15.1,
2;
Phil 2.4,21
10.25
1 Cor 8.7
10.26
Ps 24.1

10.29
Rom 14.16
10.30
Rom 14.6;
1 Tim 4.3,4
10.31
Col 3.17;
1 Pet 4.11
10.32
1 Cor 8.13
10.33
Rom 15.2;
1 Cor 9.22;
13.5
11.1
1 Cor 4.16

10.23 The law which governs all Christian conduct is the law of love—love toward God and toward one's fellow men. Practically, the believer follows this law with two considerations in mind, viz: (1) principle, by which anything which is expressly forbidden will be shunned by the Christian; (2) expediency, by which anything which is questionable, or may have an appearance of evil, or may cause a weaker brother to stumble, will be avoided. In the latter case a Christian often foregoes, out of love for God and his fellow believers, that which he does not think to be wrong in principle.

V. Public worship 11.2–14.40

A. The veiling of women

*11.2
1 Cor 4.17;
2 Thess 2.15
11.3
Eph 1.22;
4.15; 5.23;
1 Cor 3.23
11.4
Acts 13.1;
1 Thess 5.20
11.5
Acts 21.9;
Deut 21.12
11.7
Gen 1.26
11.8
Gen 2.21–
23
11.9
Gen 2.18
11.10
Gen 24.65
11.12
2 Cor 5.18;
Rom 11.36
11.13
Lk 12.57

11.16
1 Cor 7.17

2 I commend you because you remember me in everything and maintain the traditions even as I have delivered them to you. 3 But I want you to understand that the head of every man is Christ, the head of a woman is her husband, and the head of Christ is God. 4Any man who prays or prophesies with his head covered dishonors his head, 5 but any woman who prays or prophesies with her head unveiled dishonors her head—it is the same as if her head were shaven. 6 For if a woman will not veil herself, then she should cut off her hair; but if it is disgraceful for a woman to be shorn or shaven, let her wear a veil. 7 For a man ought not to cover his head, since he is the image and glory of God; but woman is the glory of man. 8 (For man was not made from woman, but woman from man. 9 Neither was man created for woman, but woman for man.) 10 That is why a woman ought to have a veil r on her head, because of the angels. 11 (Nevertheless, in the Lord woman is not independent of man nor man of woman; 12 for as woman was made from man, so man is now born of woman. And all things are from God.) 13 Judge for yourselves; is it proper for a woman to pray to God with her head uncovered? 14 Does not nature itself teach you that for a man to wear long hair is degrading to him, 15 but if a woman has long hair, it is her pride? For her hair is given to her for a covering. 16 If any one is disposed to be contentious, we recognize no other practice, nor do the churches of God.

B. The Lord's Supper

11.17
ver 2,22
11.18
1 Cor 1.10–
12
11.19
Mt 18.7;
Lk 17.1;
1 Tim 4.1;
Deut 13.3;
1 Jn 2.19
11.21
2 Pet 2.13;
Jude 12
11.22
1 Cor 10.32;
Jas 2.6
11.23
1 Cor 15.3;
Mt 26.26–
28;
Mk 14.22–
24;
Lk 22.17–20
11.25
2 Cor 3.6;
Lk 22.20

17 But in the following instructions I do not commend you, because when you come together it is not for the better but for the worse. 18 For, in the first place, when you assemble as a church, I hear that there are divisions among you; and I partly believe it, 19 for there must be factions among you in order that those who are genuine among you may be recognized. 20 When you meet together, it is not the Lord's supper that you eat. 21 For in eating, each one goes ahead with his own meal, and one is hungry and another is drunk. 22 What! Do you not have houses to eat and drink in? Or do you despise the church of God and humiliate those who have nothing? What shall I say to you? Shall I commend you in this? No, I will not.

23 For I received from the Lord what I also delivered to you, that the Lord Jesus on the night when he was betrayed took bread, 24 and when he had given thanks, he broke it, and said, "This is my body which is for s you. Do this in remembrance of me." 25 In

r Greek *authority* (the veil being a symbol of this)   s Other ancient authorities read *broken for*

11.2 The traditions Paul speaks of here refer to the records of Jesus' deeds and teachings which in the early years of the church were circulated and transmitted by word of mouth. Paul wrote this letter around the year A.D. 55, over twenty years after the Ascension of Christ and perhaps as much as ten years before the writing of the earliest gospel. What Christ had done and taught was transmitted by the apostles and early preachers and teachers, before the writing of the four Gospels. Note that in his instructions in chapter 7 Paul specifically quotes the Lord on divorce (ver 10, 11), while on other subjects, on which he does not have the Lord's teaching, he gives his own opinion (ver 8, 12, 25, 40). He makes further references to the traditions he has received and passed on to others in 2 Thess 2.15; 3.6.

the same way also the cup, after supper, saying,"This cup is the new covenant in my blood. Do this, as often as you drink it, in remembrance of me." 26 For as often as you eat this bread and drink the cup, you proclaim the Lord's death until he comes.

27 Whoever, therefore, eats the bread or drinks the cup of the Lord in an unworthy manner will be guilty of profaning the body and blood of the Lord. 28 Let a man examine himself, and so eat of the bread and drink of the cup. 29 For any one who eats and drinks without discerning the body eats and drinks judgment upon himself. 30 That is why many of you are weak and ill, and some have died.*t* 31 But if we judged ourselves truly, we should not be judged. 32 But when we are judged by the Lord, we are chastened*u* so that we may not be condemned along with the world.

33 So then, my brethren, when you come together to eat, wait for one another—34 if any one is hungry, let him eat at home—lest you come together to be condemned. About the other things I will give directions when I come.

C. The use of spiritual gifts

1. The gifts of the Spirit
a. The source of spiritual gifts

12 Now concerning spiritual gifts,*x* brethren, I do not want you to be uninformed. 2 You know that when you were heathen, you were led astray to dumb idols, however you may have been moved. 3 Therefore I want you to understand that no one speaking by the Spirit of God ever says "Jesus be cursed!" and no one can say "Jesus is Lord" except by the Holy Spirit.

b. Varieties of gifts

4 Now there are varieties of gifts, but the same Spirit; 5 and there are varieties of service, but the same Lord; 6 and there are varieties of working, but it is the same God who inspires them all in every one. 7 To each is given the manifestation of the Spirit for the common good. 8 To one is given through the Spirit the utterance of wisdom, and to another the utterance of knowledge according to the same Spirit, 9 to another faith by the same Spirit, to another gifts of healing by the one Spirit, 10 to another the working of miracles, to another prophecy, to another the ability to distinguish between spirits, to another various kinds of tongues, to another the interpretation of tongues. 11All these are inspired by one and the same Spirit, who apportions to each one individually as he wills.

c. Unity in diversity

12 For just as the body is one and has many members, and all the members of the body, though many, are one body, so it is with Christ. 13 For by one Spirit we were all baptized into one body—Jews or Greeks, slaves or free—and all were made to drink of one Spirit.

14 For the body does not consist of one member but of many.

---

t Greek *have fallen asleep* (as in 15.6, 20)
u Or *when we are judged we are being chastened by the Lord*
x Or *spiritual persons*

12.10 For a definition of prophecy see note to Isa 1.1.

12.12 See note to Jn 17.21 on the communion of saints.

Cross-references (side column)

11.26
1 Cor 4.5;
Jn 14.3;
Acts 1.11;
Rev 1.7

11.27
Heb 10.29

11.28
2 Cor 13.5

11.31
Ps 32.5;
1 Jn 1.9

11.32
Ps 94.12;
Heb 12.7–10;
1 Cor 1.20

11.34
ver 21,22;
1 Cor 4.19

12.1
1 Cor 14.1, 37;
Rom 1.13

12.2
Eph 2.11, 12;
1 Pet 4.3;
1 Thess 1.9;
Ps 115.5

12.3
1 Jn 4.2,3;
Rom 9.3;
10.9

12.4
Rom 12.4–7;
Heb 2.4

12.5
Eph 4.11

12.7
Eph 4.7

12.8
1 Cor 2.6,7;
Rom 15.4;
2 Cor 8.7

12.9
Mt 17.19, 20;
2 Cor 4.13;
ver 28,30

*12.10
Gal 3.5;
Rom 12.6;
1 Jn 4.1;
Acts 2.4;
1 Cor 13.1

12.11
2 Cor 10.13;
Heb 2.4

*12.12
Rom 12.4;
Gal 3.16

12.13
Eph 2.18;
Gal 3.28;
Col 3.11;
Jn 7.37-39

15 If the foot should say, "Because I am not a hand, I do not belong to the body," that would not make it any less a part of the body. 16And if the ear should say, "Because I am not an eye, I do not belong to the body," that would not make it any less a part of the body. 17 If the whole body were an eye, where would be the hearing? If the whole body were an ear, where would be the sense of smell? 18 But as it is, God arranged the organs in the body, each one of them, as he chose. 19 If all were a single organ, where would the body be? 20As it is, there are many parts, yet one body. 21 The eye cannot say to the hand, "I have no need of you," nor again the head to the feet, "I have no need of you." 22 On the contrary, the parts of the body which seem to be weaker are indispensable, 23 and those parts of the body which we think less honorable we invest with the greater honor, and our unpresentable parts are treated with greater modesty, 24 which our more presentable parts do not require. But God has so composed the body, giving the greater honor to the inferior part, 25 that there may be no discord in the body, but that the members may have the same care for one another. 26 If one member suffers, all suffer together; if one member is honored, all rejoice together.

d. Specific gifts

27 Now you are the body of Christ and individually members of it. 28And God has appointed in the church first apostles, second prophets, third teachers, then workers of miracles, then healers, helpers, administrators, speakers in various kinds of tongues. 29Are all apostles? Are all prophets? Are all teachers? Do all work miracles? 30 Do all possess gifts of healing? Do all speak with tongues? Do all interpret? 31 But earnestly desire the higher gifts.

And I will show you a still more excellent way.

2. The way of love
a. Love superior

13 If I speak in the tongues of men and of angels, but have not love, I am a noisy gong or a clanging cymbal. 2And if I have prophetic powers, and understand all mysteries and all knowledge, and if I have all faith, so as to remove mountains, but have not love, I am nothing. 3 If I give away all I have, and if I deliver

---

Margin references:

12.18
ver 28,11
12.20
ver 14
12.27
Eph 1.23;
4.12;
Col 1.18,24;
Eph 5.30;
Rom 12.5
*12.28
Eph 4.11;
2.30; 3.5;
Rom 12.6,
8;
ver 9.10
*12.30
ver 10
12.31
1 Cor 14.1,
39
13.2
Acts 13.1;
1 Cor 14.1;
Mt 7.22;
1 Cor 12.9;
Mt 17.20;
21.21
13.3
Mt 6.2

12.28 God calls men to specific offices in His church. This call includes the divine endowments which are given to men for their effectiveness in the work to which they have been called. Trinity is involved in the bestowal of these enablements. In Eph 4.11 the offices of the church (apostles, prophets, evangelists, pastors, teachers) are spoken of as gifts of Christ. Here in 12.28 they are called the gifts of God. In 12.8ff Paul designates the Spirit as the one who gives the gifts of healing, tongues, etc. Hence it follows that these gifts are from the Father and the Son through the agency of the Holy Spirit. A genuine call to the office must carry with it divine enablement to discharge its functions.

12.30 The gift of tongues is referred to several times in the New Testament. At Pentecost the disciples proclaimed the gospel message with other tongues. The gift came from the Holy Spirit *as the Spirit gave them utterance* (Acts 2.4). Here the gift was in known languages, or at least they were understood by the people who spoke these other languages. In 1 Corinthians the *tongues* are described as ecstatic utterances not corresponding to any known languages but giving direct expression to ineffable emotions and insights of the soul. Such tongues are not to be uttered in the church unless a Spirit-empowered interpreter is at hand to translate these utterances into intelligible discourse (14.28). Paul lists this gift as one of those bestowed by the Holy Spirit, but he classifies it as a lesser gift (12.7–11). Speaking in an unknown tongue cannot, as a matter of principle, be ruled out for the church age, but not all that goes by that name is genuine. Nor is speaking in tongues essential as an evidence of regeneration or sanctification.

my body to be burned,^{v} but have not love, I gain nothing.

b. *Love defined*

4 Love is patient and kind; love is not jealous or boastful; 5 it is
not arrogant or rude. Love does not insist on its own way; it is not
irritable or resentful; 6 it does not rejoice at wrong, but rejoices in
the right. 7 Love bears all things, believes all things, hopes all
things, endures all things.

c. *Love imperishable*

8 Love never ends; as for prophecies, they will pass away; as for
tongues, they will cease; as for knowledge, it will pass away. 9 For
our knowledge is imperfect and our prophecy is imperfect; 10 but
when the perfect comes, the imperfect will pass away. 11 When I
was a child, I spoke like a child, I thought like a child, I reasoned
like a child; when I became a man, I gave up childish ways. 12 For
now we see in a mirror dimly, but then face to face. Now I know
in part; then I shall understand fully, even as I have been fully
understood. 13 So faith, hope, love abide, these three; but the
greatest of these is love.

3. *The worth and use of spiritual gifts*
a. *Prophecy versus tongues*

14 Make love your aim, and earnestly desire the spiritual gifts,
especially that you may prophesy. 2 For one who speaks in
a tongue speaks not to men but to God; for no one understands
him, but he utters mysteries in the Spirit. 3 On the other hand, he
who prophesies speaks to men for their upbuilding and encouragement and consolation. 4 He who speaks in a tongue edifies
himself, but he who prophesies edifies the church. 5 Now I want
you all to speak in tongues, but even more to prophesy. He who
prophesies is greater than he who speaks in tongues, unless some
one interprets, so that the church may be edified.

6 Now, brethren, if I come to you speaking in tongues, how
shall I benefit you unless I bring you some revelation or knowledge
or prophecy or teaching? 7 If even lifeless instruments, such as the
flute or the harp, do not give distinct notes, how will any one know
what is played? 8 And if the bugle gives an indistinct sound, who
will get ready for battle? 9 So with yourselves; if you in a tongue
utter speech that is not intelligible, how will any one know what is
said? For you will be speaking into the air. 10 There are doubtless
many different languages in the world, and none is without meaning;
11 but if I do not know the meaning of the language, I shall be a
foreigner to the speaker and the speaker a foreigner to me. 12 So
with yourselves; since you are eager for manifestations of the Spirit,
strive to excel in building up the church.

13 Therefore, he who speaks in a tongue should pray for the
power to interpret. 14 For if I pray in a tongue, my spirit prays
but my mind is unfruitful. 15 What am I to do? I will pray with
the spirit and I will pray with the mind also; I will sing with the
spirit and I will sing with the mind also. 16 Otherwise, if you
bless^w with the spirit, how can any one in the position of an out-
sider^x say the "Amen" to your thanksgiving when he does not

13.4
Prov 10.12;
1 Pet 4.8
13.5
1 Cor 10.24;
2 Cor 5.19
13.6
2 Jn 4
13.7
Rom 15.1;
1 Cor 9.12
13.8
ver 1,2
13.9
1 Cor 8.2

13.12
2 Cor 5.7;
Phil 3.12;
1 Jn 3.2;
1 Cor 8.3
13.13
1 Cor 16.14

14.1
1 Cor 16.14;
12.31;
12.1; 13.2
14.2
Acts 10.46;
1 Cor 12.10,
28,30; 13.1
14.3
ver 5,12,17,
26;
Acts 4.36
14.5
Num 11.29
14.6
ver 26;
1 Cor 12.8;
Rom 6.17

14.8
Num 10.9
14.9
1 Cor 9.26

14.11
Acts 28.2
14.12
ver 4,5,17,26

14.15
Eph 5.19;
Col 3.16
14.16
1 Chr
16.36;
Ps 106.48;
Mt 15.36;
1 Cor 11.24

---

^{v} Other ancient authorities read *body that I may glory*
^{w} That is, *give thanks to God* ^{x} Or *him that is without gifts*

14.17
Rom 14.19

14.20
Eph 4.14;
Heb 5.12,
13;
Ps 131.2;
Rom 16.19;
1 Pet 2.2
14.21
Jn 10.34;
Isa 28.11,12
14.22
ver 1
14.23
Acts 2.13
14.25
Jn 4.19;
Lk 17.16;
Isa 45.14;
Zech 8.23

14.26
1 Cor 12.7–
10;
2 Cor 12.19;
Eph 4.12

14.29
1 Cor 12.10

14.32
1 Jn 4.1
14.33
ver 40;
1 Cor 4.17;
11.16
14.34
1 Tim 2.11,
12;
1 Pet 3.1;
Gen 3.16
14.37
2 Cor 10.7;
1 Jn 4.6
14.39
1 Cor 12.31
14.40
ver 33
15.1
Gal 1.11;
Rom 2.16;
5.2
15.2
Rom 1.16;
11.22;
Gal 3.4
15.3
1 Cor 11.23;
1 Pet 2.24;
Isa 53.5–12;
Lk 24.25–
27;
Acts 26.22,
23
15.4
Mt 16.21;
Ps 16.8–10;
Acts 2.24,
25

know what you are saying? 17 For you may give thanks well enough, but the other man is not edified. 18 I thank God that I speak in tongues more than you all; 19 nevertheless, in church I would rather speak five words with my mind, in order to instruct others, than ten thousand words in a tongue.

20 Brethren, do not be children in your thinking; be babes in evil, but in thinking be mature. 21 In the law it is written, "By men of strange tongues and by the lips of foreigners will I speak to this people, and even then they will not listen to me, says the Lord." 22 Thus, tongues are a sign not for believers but for unbelievers, while prophecy is not for unbelievers but for believers. 23 If, therefore, the whole church assembles and all speak in tongues, and outsiders or unbelievers enter, will they not say that you are mad? 24 But if all prophesy, and an unbeliever or outsider enters, he is convicted by all, he is called to account by all, 25 the secrets of his heart are disclosed; and so, falling on his face, he will worship God and declare that God is really among you.

b. *Rules regarding the use of spiritual gifts*

26 What then, brethren? When you come together, each one has a hymn, a lesson, a revelation, a tongue, or an interpretation. Let all things be done for edification. 27 If any speak in a tongue, let there be only two or at most three, and each in turn; and let one interpret. 28 But if there is no one to interpret, let each of them keep silence in church and speak to himself and to God. 29 Let two or three prophets speak, and let the others weigh what is said. 30 If a revelation is made to another sitting by, let the first be silent. 31 For you can all prophesy one by one, so that all may learn and all be encouraged; 32 and the spirits of prophets are subject to prophets. 33 For God is not a God of confusion but of peace.

As in all the churches of the saints, 34 the women should keep silence in the churches. For they are not permitted to speak, but should be subordinate, as even the law says. 35 If there is anything they desire to know, let them ask their husbands at home. For it is shameful for a woman to speak in church. 36 What! Did the word of God originate with you, or are you the only ones it has reached?

37 If any one thinks that he is a prophet, or spiritual, he should acknowledge that what I am writing to you is a command of the Lord. 38 If any one does not recognize this, he is not recognized. 39 So, my brethren, earnestly desire to prophesy, and do not forbid speaking in tongues; 40 but all things should be done decently and in order.

VI. *The Resurrection 15.1–58*

A. *The fact of the Resurrection*

15 Now I would remind you, brethren, in what terms I preached to you the gospel, which you received, in which you stand, 2 by which you are saved, if you hold it fast—unless you believed in vain.

3 For I delivered to you as of first importance what I also received, that Christ died for our sins in accordance with the scriptures, 4 that he was buried, that he was raised on the third day

in accordance with the scriptures, 5 and that he appeared to Çêphàs, then to the twelve. 6 Then he appeared to more than five hundred brethren at one time, most of whom are still alive, though some have fallen asleep. 7 Then he appeared to James, then to all the apostles. 8 Last of all, as to one untimely born, he appeared also to me. 9 For I am the least of the apostles, unfit to be called an apostle, because I persecuted the church of God. 10 But by the grace of God I am what I am, and his grace toward me was not in vain. On the contrary, I worked harder than any of them, though it was not I, but the grace of God which is with me. 11 Whether then it was I or they, so we preach and so you believed.

B. The necessity of the Resurrection

12 Now if Christ is preached as raised from the dead, how can some of you say that there is no resurrection of the dead? 13 But if there is no resurrection of the dead, then Christ has not been raised; 14 if Christ has not been raised, then our preaching is in vain and your faith is in vain. 15 We are even found to be misrepresenting God, because we testified of God that he raised Christ, whom he did not raise if it is true that the dead are not raised. 16 For if the dead are not raised, then Christ has not been raised. 17 If Christ has not been raised, your faith is futile and you are still in your sins. 18 Then those also who have fallen asleep in Christ have perished. 19 If for this life only we have hoped in Christ, we are of all men most to be pitied.

C. The assurance of the Resurrection

20 But in fact Christ has been raised from the dead, the first fruits of those who have fallen asleep. 21 For as by a man came death, by a man has come also the resurrection of the dead. 22 For as in Adam all die, so also in Christ shall all be made alive. 23 But each in his own order: Christ the first fruits, then at his coming those who belong to Christ. 24 Then comes the end, when he delivers the kingdom to God the Father after destroying every rule and every authority and power. 25 For he must reign until he has put all his enemies under his feet. 26 The last enemy to be destroyed is death. 27 "For God^z has put all things in subjection under his feet." But when it says, "All things are put in subjection under him," it is plain that he is excepted who put all things under him. 28 When all things are subjected to him, then the Son himself will also be subjected to him who put all things under him, that God may be everything to every one.

D. The logic of the Resurrection

29 Otherwise, what do people mean by being baptized on behalf

z Greek he

15.5 Lk 24.34; 1 Cor 1.12; Mt 28.17
15.7 Lk 24.33, 36,37; Acts 1.3,4
15.8 Acts 9.3–8; 1 Cor 9.1; Gal 1.16
15.9 Eph 3.8; 1 Tim 1.15; Acts 8.3
15.10 Eph 3.7,8; 2 Cor 11.23; 3.5; Gal 2.8; Phil 2.13
15.12 Acts 17.32; 23.8; 2 Tim 2.18
15.14 1 Thess 4.14
15.15 Acts 2.24
15.17 Rom 4.25
★15.18 1 Thess 4.16
15.19 2 Tim 3.12
15.20 1 Pet 1.3; ver 23; Acts 26.23; Rev 1.5
15.21 Rom 5.12
15.24 Dan 7.14,27
15.25 Ps 110.1
15.26 2 Tim 1.10; Rev 20.14
15.27 Ps 8.6; Mt 28.18; Heb 2.8
15.28 Phil 3.21; 1 Cor 3.23

15.18 Death for the Christian is spoken of as sleep so far as the bodily nature is concerned (see also 1 Thess 4.14). It is not something to be feared by believers but rather to be welcomed as a promotion to a higher estate. Paul speaks of it as a *gain* (Phil 1.21). John calls it *blessed* (Rev 14.13). Believers are at death ushered into Christ's presence (2 Cor 5.8; Phil 1.23) and exist in a state of blissful consciousness (Lk 16.19ff). In joyous fellowship with Him they await the resurrection, when they will live in their glorious resurrection bodies for all eternity (1 Thess 4.13ff; Rev 20.4–6).

of the dead? If the dead are not raised at all, why are people baptized on their behalf? 30 Why am I in peril every hour? 31 I protest, brethren, by my pride in you which I have in Christ Jesus our Lord, I die every day! 32 What do I gain if, humanly speaking, I fought with beasts at Ĕph'ĕsŭs? If the dead are not raised, "Let us eat and drink, for tomorrow we die." 33 Do not be deceived: "Bad company ruins good morals." 34 Come to your right mind, and sin no more. For some have no knowledge of God. I say this to your shame.

E. The nature of the resurrection body

35 But some one will ask, "How are the dead raised? With what kind of body do they come?" 36 You foolish man! What you sow does not come to life unless it dies. 37And what you sow is not the body which is to be, but a bare kernel, perhaps of wheat or of some other grain. 38 But God gives it a body as he has chosen, and to each kind of seed its own body. 39 For not all flesh is alike, but there is one kind for men, another for animals, another for birds, and another for fish. 40 There are celestial bodies and there are terrestrial bodies; but the glory of the celestial is one, and the glory of the terrestrial is another. 41 There is one glory of the sun, and another glory of the moon, and another glory of the stars; for star differs from star in glory.

42 So is it with the resurrection of the dead. What is sown is perishable, what is raised is imperishable. 43 It is sown in dishonor, it is raised in glory. It is sown in weakness, it is raised in power. 44 It is sown a physical body, it is raised a spiritual body. If there is a physical body, there is also a spiritual body. 45 Thus it is written, "The first man Adam became a living being"; the last Adam became a life-giving spirit. 46 But it is not the spiritual which is first but the physical, and then the spiritual. 47 The first man was from the earth, a man of dust; the second man is from heaven. 48As was the man of dust, so are those who are of the dust; and as is the man of heaven, so are those who are of heaven. 49Just as we have borne the image of the man of dust, we shall*a* also bear the image of the man of heaven. 50 I tell you this, brethren: flesh and blood cannot inherit the kingdom of God, nor does the perishable inherit the imperishable.

F. The Christian's confidence

51 Lo! I tell you a mystery. We shall not all sleep, but we shall

a Other ancient authorities read *let us*

15.42 The resurrection body has been the subject of much discussion. Scripture teaches that it is a body analogous in some respects to the earthly body, but with this major difference: the corruption and mortality attached to the mortal body as a consequence of sin will be removed. It will become an immortal, incorruptible, perfected body without any of the limitations imposed by the fall, and as far superior to the mortal body as the grown wheat plant is superior to the seed from which it has sprung.
15.45 The Edenic covenant between God

and Adam was conditioned upon Adam's perfect obedience. It was thus a covenant of works. Adam, as representative and ancestor of the whole human race, fell from a state of obedience and so broke the indispensable condition of the covenant. What the first Adam did not do, the second Adam did. Christ, as representative and spiritual forefather of the redeemed, obeyed God perfectly and kept the whole law of God. He came to fulfil the divine law (Isa 42.21; Rom 3.31), and His perfect obedience is contrasted with the disobedience of Adam (Rom 5.19).

all be changed, 52 in a moment, in the twinkling of an eye, at the last trumpet. For the trumpet will sound, and the dead will be raised imperishable, and we shall be changed. 53 For this perishable nature must put on the imperishable, and this mortal nature must put on immortality. 54 When the perishable puts on the imperishable, and the mortal puts on immortality, then shall come to pass the saying that is written:

"Death is swallowed up in victory."
55 "O death, where is thy victory?
O death, where is thy sting?"

56 The sting of death is sin, and the power of sin is the law. 57But thanks be to God, who gives us the victory through our Lord Jesus Christ.

58 Therefore, my beloved brethren, be steadfast, immovable, always abounding in the work of the Lord, knowing that in the Lord your labor is not in vain.

VII. *Personal matters 16.1–24*

A. *The contribution for the poor*

16 Now concerning the contribution for the saints: as I directed the churches of Gálãṭiả, so you also are to do. 2 On the first day of every week, each of you is to put something aside and store it up, as he may prosper, so that contributions need not be made when I come. 3And when I arrive, I will send those whom you accredit by letter to carry your gift to Jerusalem. 4 If it seems advisable that I should go also, they will accompany me.

B. *Paul's itinerary*

5 I will visit you after passing through Mắçĕdõ'nĭả, for I intend to pass through Macedonia, 6 and perhaps I will stay with you or even spend the winter, so that you may speed me on my journey, wherever I go. 7 For I do not want to see you now just in passing; I hope to spend some time with you, if the Lord permits. 8 But I will stay in Ĕph'ĕsŭs until Pĕn'tĕcost, 9 for a wide door for effective work has opened to me, and there are many adversaries.

10 When Timothy comes, see that you put him at ease among you, for he is doing the work of the Lord, as I am. 11 So let no one despise him. Speed him on his way in peace, that he may return to me; for I am expecting him with the brethren.

12 As for our brother Ắpŏl'lós, I strongly urged him to visit you with the other brethren, but it was not at all his will*b* to come now. He will come when he has opportunity.

C. *Concluding exhortations, greetings, and benediction*

13 Be watchful, stand firm in your faith, be courageous, be strong. 14 Let all that you do be done in love.

b Or *God's will for him*

15.52	Mt 24.31; Jn 5.25; 1 Thess 4.16
15.53	2 Cor 5.4
15.54	Isa 25.8; Heb 2.14; Rev 20.14
15.55	Hos 13.14
15.56	Rom 5.12; 4.15; 5.13
15.58	2 Pet 3.14; 1 Cor 16.10
16.1	Acts 24.17; 9.13; 16.6
★16.2	Acts 20.7; 2 Cor 9.4,5
16.3	2 Cor 8.18, 19
16.5	Acts 19.21
16.6	Acts 15.3
16.7	Acts 18.21
16.10	Acts 16.1; 19.22; 1 Cor 15.58
16.11	1 Tim 4.12; Acts 15.33
16.12	Acts 18.24; 1 Cor 1.12; 3.5,6
16.13	Phil 1.27; 2 Thess 2.15; Eph 6.10
16.14	1 Cor 14.1

16.2 Paul lays down the principles of Christian giving: (1) regular or periodic: on the first day of every week; (2) personal: each of you; (3) proportionate: as God prospers the giver; (4) preventive: so that collections need not be taken hurriedly.

16.15
Rom 16.5;
2 Cor 8.4;
Heb 6.10
16.16
Heb 13.1
16.17
2 Cor 7.6,7;
11.9
16.18
2 Cor 7.13;
Phil 2.29
16.19
Acts 16.6;
Rom 16.5

*16.22
Eph 6.24;
Rom 9.3
16.23
Rom 16.20

15 Now, brethren, you know that the household of Stĕph′ănăs were the first converts in Ăchāi′ă, and they have devoted themselves to the service of the saints; 16 I urge you to be subject to such men and to every fellow worker and laborer. 17 I rejoice at the coming of Stĕph′ănăs and Fortūnā′tŭs and Ăchā′ĭcus, because they have made up for your absence; 18 for they refreshed my spirit as well as yours. Give recognition to such men.

19 The churches of Asia send greetings. Ăquĭ′lă and Prĭscă, together with the church in their house, send you hearty greetings in the Lord. 20All the brethren send greetings. Greet one another with a holy kiss.

21 I, Paul, write this greeting with my own hand. 22 If any one has no love for the Lord, let him be accursed. Our Lord, come!*c* 23 The grace of the Lord Jesus be with you. 24 My love be with you all in Christ Jesus. Amen.

c Greek *Mărănăth′ă*

16.22 *Our Lord, come!* This is the English translation of the single word *Maranatha* (see RSV footnote), which is the Greek transliteration of the Aramaic *Marana tha*. This short prayer preserves the original language of worship and prayer of the early church, the language spoken by Jesus Himself. The word is found again in an ancient church book of teaching, THE DIDACHE (10.6), which was written perhaps in the first century of our era.

INTRODUCTION TO
THE SECOND LETTER OF PAUL TO THE
CORINTHIANS

Authorship and Background: Paul's letter to the Corinthians (known to us as 1 Corinthians) did not resolve the problems or reunite the factions. Although the story of the following events is not clearly spelled out, it can in part be reconstructed from 2 Corinthians. Instead of peace and harmony, the badly split church was plunged into greater controversy, and a full-fledged revolt was raised against Paul. Apparently some Jewish Christian leaders arrived, claiming to represent the Jerusalem apostles, and they detracted from Paul's apostolic commission and authority (11.4, 5, 12, 13, 20–23). There was one member of the church in Corinth who headed the revolt against Paul (2.5–8), and he evidently led the church, or a large part of it, to repudiate the apostle's leadership and authority.

Paul made a quick trip to Corinth, hoping to settle the controversy; he met with defeat, however, and returned to Ephesus. This seems clear from the references to a recent unhappy visit (2.1; 12.14; 13.1, 2). As a result of this painful and humiliating experience, Paul wrote to the church again—his third letter—in stern and severe terms. He referred to this letter in 2.3, 4, 9; 7.8, 12, and it is clear from what he said about it that he was not talking about 1 Corinthians. Has this "stern" letter survived? Some scholars feel that its contents have been preserved in 2 Cor 10—13, although this opinion is not unanimous.

Paul sent this stern letter to the church, probably by Titus (7.6–8), with instructions for him to return with news from Corinth. After Titus' departure Paul himself went on to Troas, hoping to meet him there; anxious and distressed at not finding him in Troas he went on to Macedonia (2.12, 13) where Titus met him (perhaps in Philippi) with good news: the crisis was past and the church was reconciled to Paul. With great joy and deep feeling Paul wrote the church the letter now known as 2 Corinthians, probably from Macedonia in A.D. 56.

A little later, maybe in the same year, Paul journeyed to Corinth, spending three months there (Acts 20.1–3), during which time he wrote to the Romans (cf. Introduction to Romans).

Characteristics: In no letter does Paul bare his feelings as he does in 2 Corinthians: he runs the whole gamut of emotion from hopeless despair to ecstatic joy, as he gives expression to his deep love and concern for his Corinthian brothers. The passionate defense of his apostolic commission and authority in chapters 10—13 is filled with sarcasm, denunciation, threats, and condemnation, and contrasts sharply with the joy and tenderness that overflow in chapters 1—9, a fact which lends some substance to the contention that chapters 10—13 are part of the "stern" letter. In any case, 2 Corinthians reflects a pastor's heart of love, as Paul attempts to guide his people into the paths of love and unity.

Introduction to 2 Corinthians

Contents:

THE SECOND LETTER OF PAUL TO THE

CORINTHIANS

I. Introduction 1.1–11

A. Salutation

1 Paul, an apostle of Christ Jesus by the will of God, and Timothy our brother.

To the church of God which is at Corinth, with all the saints who are in the whole of Áchāi'á:

2 Grace to you and peace from God our Father and the Lord Jesus Christ.

B. Thanksgiving

3 Blessed be the God and Father of our Lord Jesus Christ, the Father of mercies and God of all comfort, 4 who comforts us in all our affliction, so that we may be able to comfort those who are in any affliction, with the comfort with which we ourselves are comforted by God. 5 For as we share abundantly in Christ's sufferings, so through Christ we share abundantly in comfort too.[a] 6 If we are afflicted, it is for your comfort and salvation; and if we are comforted, it is for your comfort, which you experience when you patiently endure the same sufferings that we suffer. 7 Our hope for you is unshaken; for we know that as you share in our sufferings, you will also share in our comfort.

8 For we do not want you to be ignorant, brethren, of the affliction we experienced in Asia; for we were so utterly, unbearably crushed that we despaired of life itself. 9 Why, we felt that we had received the sentence of death; but that was to make us rely not on ourselves but on God who raises the dead; 10 he delivered us from so deadly a peril, and he will deliver us; on him we have set our hope that he will deliver us again. 11 You also must help us by prayer, so that many will give thanks on our behalf for the blessing granted us in answer to many prayers.

II. The defense of the ministry 1.12–7.16

A. Paul's change of plans

12 For our boast is this, the testimony of our conscience that we have behaved in the world, and still more toward you, with holiness and godly sincerity, not by earthly wisdom but by the grace of God. 13 For we write you nothing but what you can read and understand; I hope you will understand fully, 14 as you have understood in part, that you can be proud of us as we can be of you, on the day of the Lord Jesus.

15 Because I was sure of this, I wanted to come to you first, so that you might have a double pleasure;[b] 16 I wanted to visit you on my way to Mȧçėdō'niȧ, and to come back to you from Macedonia and have you send me on my way to Judē'ȧ. 17 Was I vacil-

Cross references (right margin):

1.1 Col 1.1; 1 Tim 1.1; 1 Cor 1.1
1.2 Rom 1.7; 1 Cor 1.3; Gal 1.3
1.3 Eph 1.3; 1 Pet 1.3; Rom 15.5
1.4 2 Cor 7.6,7, 13
1.5 2 Cor 4.10; Col 1.24
1.6 2 Cor 4.15
1.7 Rom 8.17; 2 Tim 2.12
1.8 Acts 19.23; 1 Cor 15.32
1.9 Jer 17.5,7
1.10 2 Pet 2.9
1.11 Rom 15.30; Phil 1.19; 2 Cor 4.15

1.12 2 Cor 2.17; 1 Cor 2.4,13
1.14 1 Cor 1.8
1.15 1 Cor 4.19; Rom 1.11; 15.29
1.16 1 Cor 16.5–7
1.17 2 Cor 10.2,3

---

a Or *For as the sufferings of Christ abound for us, so also our comfort abounds through Christ*
b Other ancient authorities read *favor*

lating when I wanted to do this? Do I make my plans like a worldly man, ready to say Yes and No at once? 18As surely as God is faithful, our word to you has not been Yes and No. 19 For the Son of God, Jesus Christ, whom we preached among you, Silvānús and Timothy and I, was not Yes and No; but in him it is always Yes. 20 For all the promises of God find their Yes in him. That is why we utter the Amen through him, to the glory of God. 21 But it is God who establishes us with you in Christ, and has commissioned us; 22 he has put his seal upon us and given us his Spirit in our hearts as a guarantee.

B. The reason for the change of plans

23 But I call God to witness against me—it was to spare you that I refrained from coming to Corinth. 24 Not that we lord it over your faith; we work with you for your joy, for you stand firm in your faith. 1 For I made up my mind not to make you another painful visit. 2 For if I cause you pain, who is there to make me glad but the one whom I have pained? 3And I wrote as I did, so that when I came I might not suffer pain from those who should have made me rejoice, for I felt sure of all of you, that my joy would be the joy of you all. 4 For I wrote you out of much affliction and anguish of heart and with many tears, not to cause you pain but to let you know the abundant love that I have for you.

C. Forgiveness of the penitent offender

5 But if any one has caused pain, he has caused it not to me, but in some measure—not to put it too severely—to you all. 6 For such a one this punishment by the majority is enough; 7 so you should rather turn to forgive and comfort him, or he may be overwhelmed by excessive sorrow. 8 So I beg you to reaffirm your love for him. 9 For this is why I wrote, that I might test you and know whether you are obedient in everything. 10Any one whom you forgive, I also forgive. What I have forgiven, if I have forgiven anything, has been for your sake in the presence of Christ, 11 to keep Satan from gaining the advantage over us; for we are not ignorant of his designs.

D. Paul's vindication of his ministry

1. A triumphant ministry

12 When I came to Trōäs to preach the gospel of Christ, a door was opened for me in the Lord; 13 but my mind could not rest because I did not find my brother Titùs there. So I took leave of them and went on to Măçèdō'nïă.

14 But thanks be to God, who in Christ always leads us in triumph, and through us spreads the fragrance of the knowledge of him everywhere. 15 For we are the aroma of Christ to God among those who are being saved and among those who are perishing, 16 to one a fragrance from death to death, to the other a fragrance from life to life. Who is sufficient for these things? 17 For we are not, like so many, peddlers of God's word; but as men of sincerity, as commissioned by God, in the sight of God we speak in Christ.

2. A commended ministry

3 Are we beginning to commend ourselves again? Or do we need, as some do, letters of recommendation to you, or from you? 2 You yourselves are our letter of recommendation, written on your^c hearts, to be known and read by all men; 3 and you show that you are a letter from Christ delivered by us, written not with ink but with the Spirit of the living God, not on tablets of stone but on tablets of human hearts.

3. A ministry of splendor

4 Such is the confidence that we have through Christ toward God. 5 Not that we are competent of ourselves to claim anything as coming from us; our competence is from God, 6 who has made us competent to be ministers of a new covenant, not in a written code but in the Spirit; for the written code kills, but the Spirit gives life.

7 Now if the dispensation of death, carved in letters on stone, came with such splendor that the Israelites could not look at Moses' face because of its brightness, fading as this was, 8 will not the dispensation of the Spirit be attended with greater splendor? 9 For if there was splendor in the dispensation of condemnation, the dispensation of righteousness must far exceed it in splendor. 10 Indeed, in this case, what once had splendor has come to have no splendor at all, because of the splendor that surpasses it. 11 For if what faded away came with splendor, what is permanent must have much more splendor.

12 Since we have such a hope, we are very bold, 13 not like Moses, who put a veil over his face so that the Israelites might not see the end of the fading splendor. 14 But their minds were hardened; for to this day, when they read the old covenant, that same veil remains unlifted, because only through Christ is it taken away. 15 Yes, to this day whenever Moses is read a veil lies over their minds; 16 but when a man turns to the Lord the veil is removed. 17 Now the Lord is the Spirit, and where the Spirit of the Lord is, there is freedom. 18 And we all, with unveiled face, beholding^d the glory of the Lord, are being changed into his likeness from one degree of glory to another; for this comes from the Lord who is the Spirit.

4. An honest ministry

4 Therefore, having this ministry by the mercy of God,^e we do not lose heart. 2 We have renounced disgraceful, underhanded ways; we refuse to practice cunning or to tamper with God's word, but by the open statement of the truth we would commend ourselves to every man's conscience in the sight of God. 3 And even if our gospel is veiled, it is veiled only to those who are perishing. 4 In their case the god of this world has blinded the minds of the unbelievers, to keep them from seeing the light of the gospel of the glory of Christ, who is the likeness of God. 5 For what we preach is not ourselves, but Jesus Christ as Lord, with ourselves as your servants^f for Jesus' sake. 6 For it is the God who said, "Let light shine out of darkness," who has shone in our hearts to give the light of the knowledge of the glory of God in the face of Christ.

c Other ancient authorities read our   d Or reflecting
e Greek as we have received mercy   f Or slaves

Cross references

3.1 2 Cor 5.12; 12.11; Acts 18.27
3.2 1 Cor 9.2
3.3 Jer 31.33; Ezek 11.19
3.4 Eph 3.12
3.5 2 Cor 2.16; 1 Cor 15.10
3.6 Heb 8.6,8; Gal 3.10; Jn 6.63
3.7 Ex 34.29–35
3.9 ver 7; Rom 1.17; 3.21
3.12 2 Cor 7.4; Eph 6.19
3.13 ver 7; Ex 34.33
3.14 Rom 11.7; Acts 13.15; ver 6
3.16 Rom 11.23
3.17 1 Cor 15.45; Isa 61.1,2; Jn 8.32
3.18 1 Cor 13.12; 2 Cor 4.4,6; Rom 8.29
4.1 2 Cor 3.6; 1 Cor 7.25
4.2 2 Cor 2.17
4.3 2 Cor 2.12; 3.14; 1 Cor 1.18
4.4 Jn 12.31; Col 1.15; Jn 1.18
4.5 1 Cor 1.13, 23; 9.19
4.6 Gen 1.3; 2 Pet 1.19

5. *A tried ministry*

4.7
2 Cor 5.1;
1 Cor 2.5
4.8
2 Cor 7.5;
6.12
4.9
Jn 15.20;
Heb 13.5;
Ps 37.24
4.10
Gal 6.17;
Rom 8.17
4.11
Rom 8.36
4.12
2 Cor 13.9
4.13
Ps 116.10
4.14
1 Thess
4.14
4.16
Rom 7.22;
Col 3.10
4.17
Rom 8.18;
1 Pet 1.6
4.18
Rom 8.24;
Heb 11.1

7 But we have this treasure in earthen vessels, to show that the transcendent power belongs to God and not to us. 8 We are afflicted in every way, but not crushed; perplexed, but not driven to despair; 9 persecuted, but not forsaken; struck down, but not destroyed; 10 always carrying in the body the death of Jesus, so that the life of Jesus may also be manifested in our bodies. 11 For while we live we are always being given up to death for Jesus' sake, so that the life of Jesus may be manifested in our mortal flesh. 12 So death is at work in us, but life in you.

13 Since we have the same spirit of faith as he had who wrote, "I believed, and so I spoke," we too believe, and so we speak, 14 knowing that he who raised the Lord Jesus will raise us also with Jesus and bring you into his presence. 15 For it is all for your sake, so that as grace extends to more and more people it may increase thanksgiving, to the glory of God.

16 So we do not lose heart. Though our outer nature is wasting away, our inner nature is being renewed every day. 17 For this slight momentary affliction is preparing for us an eternal weight of glory beyond all comparison, 18 because we look not to the things that are seen but to the things that are unseen; for the things that are seen are transient, but the things that are unseen are eternal.

6. *A courageous ministry*

5.1
2 Pet 1.13,
14
5.2
Rom 8.23;
ver 4
*5.3
5.4
1 Cor 15.53,
54
5.5
Rom 8.23;
2 Cor 1.22
5.6
Heb 11.13,
14
5.7
1 Cor 13.12
5.8
Phil 1.23
*5.10
Rom 14.10;
Eph 6.8
5.11
Heb 10.31;
Jude 23;
2 Cor 4.2

5 For we know that if the earthly tent we live in is destroyed, we have a building from God, a house not made with hands, eternal in the heavens. 2 Here indeed we groan, and long to put on our heavenly dwelling, 3 so that by putting it on we may not be found naked. 4 For while we are still in this tent, we sigh with anxiety; not that we would be unclothed, but that we would be further clothed, so that what is mortal may be swallowed up by life. 5 He who has prepared us for this very thing is God, who has given us the Spirit as a guarantee.

6 So we are always of good courage; we know that while we are at home in the body we are away from the Lord, 7 for we walk by faith, not by sight. 8 We are of good courage, and we would rather be away from the body and at home with the Lord. 9 So whether we are at home or away, we make it our aim to please him. 10 For we must all appear before the judgment seat of Christ, so that each one may receive good or evil, according to what he has done in the body.

7. *A dedicated and reconciling ministry*

11 Therefore, knowing the fear of the Lord, we persuade men;

5.3 Paul speaks here of the body as an *earthly tent* (ver 1), which is struck down at death; in its place the believer awaits the spiritual house, *eternal in the heavens*, which God has prepared for him (ver 1). It is Paul's deep desire to be clothed with the heavenly dwelling and thus escape the "nakedness" of the bodiless state at death. Notwithstanding his deep anxiety (ver 4), he knows that God will do all things well, for He has given the Spirit as pledge and security that man's mortality will be swallowed up by God's life.

5.10 There is a judgment appointed for believers, which takes place at the coming of the Lord (see also 1 Cor 4.5; 2 Tim 4.8; Rev 22.12). The works of all believers will be reviewed. Note that: (1) all believers must appear (Rom 14.12; 2 Cor 5.10); (2) each must render an account for himself (Rom 14.12); (3) both good deeds and bad must be reviewed (5.10); (4) rewards will be given according to what one has done (Rev 22.12); (5) some will receive no reward but will only be saved as by fire (1 Cor 3.12-15).

but what we are is known to God, and I hope it is known also to your conscience. 12 We are not commending ourselves to you again but giving you cause to be proud of us, so that you may be able to answer those who pride themselves on a man's position and not on his heart. 13 For if we are beside ourselves, it is for God; if we are in our right mind, it is for you. 14 For the love of Christ controls us, because we are convinced that one has died for all; therefore all have died. 15And he died for all, that those who live might live no longer for themselves but for him who for their sake died and was raised.

16 From now on, therefore, we regard no one from a human point of view; even though we once regarded Christ from a human point of view, we regard him thus no longer. 17 Therefore, if any one is in Christ, he is a new creation;g the old has passed away, behold, the new has come. 18All this is from God, who through Christ reconciled us to himself and gave us the ministry of reconciliation; 19 that is, in Christ God was reconcilingh the world to himself, not counting their trespasses against them, and entrusting to us the message of reconciliation. 20 So we are ambassadors for Christ, God making his appeal through us. We beseech you on behalf of Christ, be reconciled to God. 21 For our sake he made him to be sin who knew no sin, so that in him we might become the righteousness of God.

6 Working together with him, then, we entreat you not to accept the grace of God in vain. 2 For he says,
"At the acceptable time I have listened to you,
and helped you on the day of salvation."
Behold, now is the acceptable time; behold, now is the day of salvation. 3 We put no obstacle in any one's way, so that no fault may be found with our ministry, 4 but as servants of God we commend ourselves in every way: through great endurance, in afflictions, hardships, calamities, 5 beatings, imprisonments, tumults, labors, watching, hunger; 6 by purity, knowledge, forbearance, kindness, the Holy Spirit, genuine love, 7 truthful speech, and the power of God; with the weapons of righteousness for the right hand and for the left; 8 in honor and dishonor, in ill repute and good repute. We are treated as impostors, and yet are true; 9 as unknown, and yet well known; as dying, and behold we live; as punished, and yet not killed; 10 as sorrowful, yet always rejoicing; as poor, yet making many rich; as having nothing, and yet possessing everything.

8. An exhorting ministry
a. A call for sympathy

11 Our mouth is open to you, Corinthians; our heart is wide. 12 You are not restricted by us, but you are restricted in your own

5.12	2 Cor 3.1; 1.14
5.13	2 Cor 11.1, 16,17
5.14	Acts 18.5; Rom 5.15; Gal 2.20
5.15	Rom 14.7–9
5.16	2 Cor 11.18; Phil 3.4; Jn 8.15
5.17	Rom 16.7; Gal 5.6; Rev 21.4,5
*5.18	Col 1.20; Rom 5.10
5.20	2 Cor 3.6; Eph 6.20; 2 Cor 6.1
*5.21	1 Pet 2.22; 1 Jn 3.5; Gal 3.13
6.1	1 Cor 3.9; 2 Cor 5.20; Heb 12.15
6.2	Isa 49.8
6.3	Rom 14.13; 1 Cor 9.12; 10.32
6.5	2 Cor 11.23
*6.7	2 Cor 4.2; 10.4; Eph 6.11,13
6.9	Rom 8.36; 2 Cor 1.8–10; 4.10,11
6.10	Rom 8.32; 1 Cor 3.21
6.11	Ezek 33.22; 2 Cor 7.3; Isa 60.5

---

g Or creature h Or God was in Christ reconciling

5.18 Several times the New Testament says that we are reconciled to God: (1) through the death of His Son (Rom 5.10; Col 1.22); (2) through the blood of His cross (Col 1.20; Eph 2.16). Both in this Corinthian passage and in Romans 5, Paul uses reconciliation and justification as synonymous terms. Man cannot reconcile himself to God but must be reconciled through Christ whose work is appropriated by faith. Those who are reconciled have peace with God and access to Him as His children (Eph 2.16–18).

5.21 See note to 1 Pet 2.24 on substitution.

6.7 Paul speaks of the weapons of righteousness for the right hand and for the left. The weapon for offense, the sword, was carried in the right hand; that for defense, the shield, in the left hand. These, then, are weapons for offense and defense (see his description of the Christian's armor in Eph 6.11, 13–17).

affections. 13 In return—I speak as to children—widen your hearts also.

b. *A command to separation*

14 Do not be mismated with unbelievers. For what partnership have righteousness and iniquity? Or what fellowship has light with darkness? 15 What accord has Christ with Bē'li̇ăl?*i* Or what has a believer in common with an unbeliever? 16 What agreement has the temple of God with idols? For we are the temple of the living God; as God said,

"I will live in them and move among them,
and I will be their God,
and they shall be my people.

17 Therefore come out from them,
and be separate from them, says the Lord,
and touch nothing unclean;
then I will welcome you,

18 and I will be a father to you,
and you shall be my sons and daughters,
says the Lord Almighty."

7 Since we have these promises, beloved, let us cleanse ourselves from every defilement of body and spirit, and make holiness perfect in the fear of God.

c. *A plea for fellowship*

2 Open your hearts to us; we have wronged no one, we have corrupted no one, we have taken advantage of no one. 3 I do not say this to condemn you, for I said before that you are in our hearts, to die together and to live together. 4 I have great confidence in you; I have great pride in you; I am filled with comfort. With all our affliction, I am overjoyed.

d. *The joy of good news*

5 For even when we came into Măçĕdō'nĭă, our bodies had no rest but we were afflicted at every turn—fighting without and fear within. 6 But God, who comforts the downcast, comforted us by the coming of Tītŭs, 7 and not only by his coming but also by the comfort with which he was comforted in you, as he told us of your

i Greek *Bē'liăr*

Margin cross-references:

6.13 — 1 Cor 4.14

6.14 — Deut 7.2,3; 1 Cor 5.9, 10; Eph 5.7,11; 1 Jn 1.6

6.16 — 1 Cor 3.16; Jer 31.1; Ezek 37.27

*6.17 — Isa 52.11; Rev 18.4

6.18 — Hos 1.10; Isa 43.6

7.1 — 2 Cor 6.17, 18

7.2 — 2 Cor 6.12, 13

7.3 — 2 Cor 6.11, 12

7.4 — 2 Cor 1.4, 14; 3.12

7.5 — 2 Cor 2.13; 4.8; Deut 32.25

7.6 — 2 Cor 1.3,4; ver 13; 2 Cor 2.13

6.17 Separation from unbelievers and from the world is a policy enjoined by Scripture. Yet it has by some been misinterpreted and misunderstood. The believer is stated to be "in the world" but "not of the world." Separation, therefore, does not consist in leaving the world in a physical sense, whether by isolation, death, or monasticism. Christ Himself was "in the world" but He was "not of the world"; He was not defiled by His contacts with the world. Paul here states that believers are not to fellowship in a compromising relationship with unbelievers, for to do so is to be *mismated* (ver 14), or "unequally yoked" (KJV). This principle undoubtedly involves the following applications: (1) a believer should not marry an unbeliever; (2) he should not choose for his intimate companions those who are not believers; (3)

he should not be in cordial fellowship with those who are theologically apostate. (This, of course, does not preclude contacts such as a missionary might have with infidels for purposes of converting them to God.) This separation is not simply negative; it has its positive aspects also. One is not only to be separated *from* someone or something; he is also to be separated *unto* God. This separation unto God will often solve many practical problems. If separation is from people who are unbelievers it is also separation from attitudes and activities which belong to the world and to its system. Hence the Bible teaches that believers are to flee from *the lust of the flesh and the lust of the eyes and the pride of life* (1 Jn 2.15–17). The Christian must stay away from anything that is evil and cling to everything that is good.

longing, your mourning, your zeal for me, so that I rejoiced still more. 8 For even if I made you sorry with my letter, I do not regret it (though I did regret it), for I see that that letter grieved you, though only for a while. 9As it is, I rejoice, not because you were grieved, but because you were grieved into repenting; for you felt a godly grief, so that you suffered no loss through us. 10 For godly grief produces a repentance that leads to salvation and brings no regret, but worldly grief produces death. 11 For see what earnestness this godly grief has produced in you, what eagerness to clear yourselves, what indignation, what alarm, what longing, what zeal, what punishment! At every point you have proved yourselves guiltless in the matter. 12 So although I wrote to you, it was not on account of the one who did the wrong, nor on account of the one who suffered the wrong, but in order that your zeal for us might be revealed to you in the sight of God. 13 Therefore we are comforted.

And besides our own comfort we rejoiced still more at the joy of Titus, because his mind has been set at rest by you all. 14 For if I have expressed to him some pride in you, I was not put to shame; but just as everything we said to you was true, so our boasting before Titus has proved true. 15And his heart goes out all the more to you, as he remembers the obedience of you all, and the fear and trembling with which you received him. 16 I rejoice, because I have perfect confidence in you.

III. *The collection for the saints 8.1–9.15*

A. *The Macedonian example*

8 We want you to know, brethren, about the grace of God which has been shown in the churches of Măcĕdō′nĭä, 2 for in a severe test of affliction, their abundance of joy and their extreme poverty have overflowed in a wealth of liberality on their part. 3 For they gave according to their means, as I can testify, and beyond their means, of their own free will, 4 begging us earnestly for the favor of taking part in the relief of the saints—5 and this, not as we expected, but first they gave themselves to the Lord and to us by the will of God. 6Accordingly we have urged Titus that as he had already made a beginning, he should also complete among you this gracious work. 7 Now as you excel in everything —in faith, in utterance, in knowledge, in all earnestness, and in your love for us—see that you excel in this gracious work also.

B. *The example of Jesus*

8 I say this not as a command, but to prove by the earnestness of others that your love also is genuine. 9 For you know the grace of our Lord Jesus Christ, that though he was rich, yet for your sake he became poor, so that by his poverty you might become

7.8	2 Cor 2.2,4
7.10	Acts 11.18
7.11	2 Cor 2.6; Rom 3.5
7.12	ver 8; 2 Cor 2.3,9; 1 Cor 5.1,2
7.13	ver 6; 1 Cor 16.18
7.14	ver 4,6
7.15	2 Cor 2.9; Phil 2.12
7.16	2 Thess 3.4
*8.1	Acts 16.9
8.2	2 Cor 9.11
8.3	1 Cor 16.2
8.4	Acts 24.17; Rom 15.25, 26,31; 2 Cor 9.1
8.6	ver 17; 2 Cor 12.18; ver 16,23,10
8.7	2 Cor 9.8; 1 Cor 1.5; 12.13
8.8	1 Cor 7.6
8.9	2 Cor 13.14; Phil 2.6,7

8.1 Paul devotes a lengthy section of this letter to the offering he is carrying to the brethren in Jerusalem (8.1–9.15; see also 1 Cor 16.1–4). His careful plans, the appointment of trusted men to go with him, and the earnestness of his appeal to the Corinthians by referring to the generosity of the churches in Macedonia (ver 3), show that this offering was more than simply a relief mission. It would be, for the Jerusalem Christians, a demonstration of the oneness of the faith and love which united the Gentile and the Jewish churches into the fellowship of the one body of Christ. (Also see note to 1 Cor 16.2.)

rich. 10And in this matter I give my advice: it is best for you now to complete what a year ago you began not only to do but to desire, 11 so that your readiness in desiring it may be matched by your completing it out of what you have. 12 For if the readiness is there, it is acceptable according to what a man has, not according to what he has not. 13 I do not mean that others should be eased and you burdened, 14 but that as a matter of equality your abundance at the present time should supply their want, so that their abundance may supply your want, that there may be equality. 15As it is written, "He who gathered much had nothing over, and he who gathered little had no lack."

C. The coming of Titus and the messengers

16 But thanks be to God who puts the same earnest care for you into the heart of Titus. 17 For he not only accepted our appeal, but being himself very earnest he is going to you of his own accord. 18 With him we are sending the brother who is famous among all the churches for his preaching of the gospel; 19 and not only that, but he has been appointed by the churches to travel with us in this gracious work which we are carrying on, for the glory of the Lord and to show our good will. 20 We intend that no one should blame us about this liberal gift which we are administering, 21 for we aim at what is honorable not only in the Lord's sight but also in the sight of men. 22And with them we are sending our brother whom we have often tested and found earnest in many matters, but who is now more earnest than ever because of his great confidence in you. 23As for Titus, he is my partner and fellow worker in your service; and as for our brethren, they are messengers*j* of the churches, the glory of Christ. 24 So give proof, before the churches, of your love and of our boasting about you to these men.

D. Appeal to their liberality

9 Now it is superfluous for me to write to you about the offering for the saints, 2 for I know your readiness, of which I boast about you to the people of Măçĕdō′nĭa, saying that Açhāi′å has been ready since last year; and your zeal has stirred up most of them. 3 But I am sending the brethren so that our boasting about you may not prove vain in this case, so that you may be ready, as I said you would be; 4 lest if some Măçĕdō′nĭăns come with me and find that you are not ready, we be humiliated—to say nothing of you—for being so confident. 5So I thought it necessary to urge the brethren to go on to you before me, and arrange in advance for this gift you have promised, so that it may be ready not as an exaction but as a willing gift.

E. God's reward of the liberal giver

6 The point is this: he who sows sparingly will also reap sparingly, and he who sows bountifully will also reap bountifully. 7 Each one must do as he has made up his mind, not reluctantly or under compulsion, for God loves a cheerful giver. 8And God is able to provide you with every blessing in abundance, so that you may

j Greek apostles

always have enough of everything and may provide in abundance
for every good work. 9As it is written,
"He scatters abroad, he gives to the poor;
  his righteousness^k endures for ever."
10 He who supplies seed to the sower and bread for food will supply
and multiply your resources^l and increase the harvest of your
righteousness.^{k} 11 You will be enriched in every way for great
generosity, which through us will produce thanksgiving to God;
12 for the rendering of this service not only supplies the wants of
the saints but also overflows in many thanksgivings to God.
13 Under the test of this service, you^m will glorify God by your
obedience in acknowledging the gospel of Christ, and by the
generosity of your contribution for them and for all others; 14 while
they long for you and pray for you, because of the surpassing
grace of God in you. 15 Thanks be to God for his inexpressible gift!

IV. Paul's personal defense and appeal 10.1–13.10

A. Paul replies to the charge of weakness and cowardice

10 I, Paul, myself entreat you, by the meekness and gentleness
of Christ—I who am humble when face to face with you,
but bold to you when I am away!—2 I beg of you that when I am
present I may not have to show boldness with such confidence as
I count on showing against some who suspect us of acting in
worldly fashion. 3 For though we live in the world we are not
carrying on a worldly war, 4 for the weapons of our warfare are
not worldly but have divine power to destroy strongholds. 5 We
destroy arguments and every proud obstacle to the knowledge of
God, and take every thought captive to obey Christ, 6 being ready
to punish every disobedience, when your obedience is complete.

7 Look at what is before your eyes. If any one is confident that
he is Christ's, let him remind himself that as he is Christ's, so are
we. 8 For even if I boast a little too much of our authority, which
the Lord gave for building you up and not for destroying you, I
shall not be put to shame. 9 I would not seem to be frightening
you with letters. 10 For they say, "His letters are weighty and
strong, but his bodily presence is weak, and his speech of no
account." 11 Let such people understand that what we say by
letter when absent, we do when present. 12 Not that we venture
to class or compare ourselves with some of those who commend
themselves. But when they measure themselves by one another,
and compare themselves with one another, they are without understanding.

B. Paul stays within the limits of God's appointments

13 But we will not boast beyond limit, but will keep to the
limits God has apportioned us, to reach even to you. 14 For we
are not overextending ourselves, as though we did not reach you;
we were the first to come all the way to you with the gospel of
Christ. 15 We do not boast beyond limit, in other men's labors;
but our hope is that as your faith increases, our field among you

---

k Or benevolence l Greek sowing m Or they

9.9
Ps 112.9

9.10
Isa 55.10;
Hos 10.12
9.11
1 Cor 1.5,11
9.12
2 Cor 8.14
9.13
2 Cor 8.4;
Rom 15.31;
Mt 9.8;
2 Cor 2.12
9.15
2 Cor 2.14;
Rom 5.15,
16

10.1
Gal 5.2;
Rom 12.1
10.2
1 Cor 4.21;
2 Cor 13.2,
10
10.3
ver 2
10.4
1 Tim 1.18;
2 Tim 2.3;
Acts 7.22;
1 Cor 2.5;
Jer 1.10
10.5
1 Cor 1.19;
Isa 2.11,12;
2 Cor 9.13
10.6
2 Cor 2.9
10.7
Jn 7.24;
1 Cor 1.12;
14.37
10.8
2 Cor 7.4;
13.10
10.10
1 Cor 2.3;
Gal 4.13,
14;
1 Cor 1.17
10.12
2 Cor 3.1;
5.12

10.13
ver 15
10.14
2 Cor 2.12

10.15
Rom 15.20;
2 Thess 1.3

may be greatly enlarged, 16 so that we may preach the gospel in lands beyond you, without boasting of work already done in another's field. 17 "Let him who boasts, boast of the Lord." 18 For it is not the man who commends himself that is accepted, but the man whom the Lord commends.

C. *Paul's fear of false teachers*

11 I wish you would bear with me in a little foolishness. Do bear with me! 2 I feel a divine jealousy for you, for I betrothed you to Christ to present you as a pure bride to her one husband. 3 But I am afraid that as the serpent deceived Eve by his cunning, your thoughts will be led astray from a sincere and pure devotion to Christ. 4 For if some one comes and preaches another Jesus than the one we preached, or if you receive a different spirit from the one you received, or if you accept a different gospel from the one you accepted, you submit to it readily enough. 5 I think that I am not in the least inferior to these superlative apostles. 6 Even if I am unskilled in speaking, I am not in knowledge; in every way we have made this plain to you in all things.

D. *Paul's self-support*

7 Did I commit a sin in abasing myself so that you might be exalted, because I preached God's gospel without cost to you? 8 I robbed other churches by accepting support from them in order to serve you. 9 And when I was with you and was in want, I did not burden any one, for my needs were supplied by the brethren who came from Măçĕdō'nĭă. So I refrained and will refrain from burdening you in any way. 10 As the truth of Christ is in me, this boast of mine shall not be silenced in the regions of Açhāi'ă. 11 And why? Because I do not love you? God knows I do!

12 And what I do I will continue to do, in order to undermine the claim of those who would like to claim that in their boasted mission they work on the same terms as we do. 13 For such men are false apostles, deceitful workmen, disguising themselves as apostles of Christ. 14 And no wonder, for even Satan disguises himself as an angel of light. 15 So it is not strange if his servants also disguise themselves as servants of righteousness. Their end will correspond to their deeds.

E. *Paul's rightful boasting*

1. *The necessity for it*

16 I repeat, let no one think me foolish; but even if you do, accept me as a fool, so that I too may boast a little. 17 (What I am saying I say not with the Lord's authority but as a fool, in this boastful confidence; 18 since many boast of worldly things, I too will boast.) 19 For you gladly bear with fools, being wise yourselves! 20 For you bear it if a man makes slaves of you, or preys upon you, or takes advantage of you, or puts on airs, or strikes you in the face. 21 To my shame, I must say, we were too weak for that!

2. *The grounds for it*

But whatever any one dares to boast of—I am speaking as a fool—I also dare to boast of that. 22 Are they Hebrews? So am I. Are

---

10.17
Jer 9.24;
1 Cor 1.31
10.18
Rom 2.29;
1 Cor 4.5

11.1
ver 16,17,
21;
2 Cor 5.13
11.2
Hos 2.19;
Eph 5.26,
27;
2 Cor 4.14
11.3
Gen 3.4;
Jn 8.44
11.4
1 Cor 3.11;
Rom 8.15;
Gal 1.6–8
11.5
2 Cor
12.11;
Gal 2.6
11.6
1 Cor 1.17;
Eph 3.4;
2 Cor 4.2
11.7
2 Cor 12.13;
1 Cor 9.18
11.8
Phil 4.15,
18
11.9
2 Cor 12.13,
14
11.10
Rom 9.1;
1 Cor 9.15;
Acts 18.12
11.11
2 Cor 12.15
11.12
1 Cor 9.12
11.13
Gal 1.7;
2 Pet 2.1;
Phil 3.2
11.15
Phil 3.19
11.16
ver 1
11.17
1 Cor 7.6,
12,25;
Acts 9.24,
25
11.18
Phil 3.3,4
11.21
2 Cor 10.10;
Phil 3.4
11.22
Acts 6.1;
Phil 3.5;
Rom 9.4

they Israelites? So am I. Are they descendants of Abraham? So am I. 23Are they servants of Christ? I am a better one—I am talking like a madman—with far greater labors, far more imprisonments, with countless beatings, and often near death. 24 Five times I have received at the hands of the Jews the forty lashes less one. 25 Three times I have been beaten with rods; once I was stoned. Three times I have been shipwrecked; a night and a day I have been adrift at sea; 26 on frequent journeys, in danger from rivers, danger from robbers, danger from my own people, danger from Gentiles, danger in the city, danger in the wilderness, danger at sea, danger from false brethren; 27 in toil and hardship, through many a sleepless night, in hunger and thirst, often without food, in cold and exposure. 28And, apart from other things, there is the daily pressure upon me of my anxiety for all the churches. 29 Who is weak, and I am not weak? Who is made to fall, and I am not indignant?

30 If I must boast, I will boast of the things that show my weakness. 31 The God and Father of the Lord Jesus, he who is blessed for ever, knows that I do not lie. 32At Damascus, the governor under King Ar′etas guarded the city of Damascus in order to seize me, 33 but I was let down in a basket through a window in the wall, and escaped his hands.

12 I must boast; there is nothing to be gained by it, but I will go on to visions and revelations of the Lord. 2 I know a man in Christ who fourteen years ago was caught up to the third heaven—whether in the body or out of the body I do not know, God knows. 3And I know that this man was caught up into Paradise—whether in the body or out of the body I do not know, God knows—4 and he heard things that cannot be told, which man may not utter. 5 On behalf of this man I will boast, but on my own behalf I will not boast, except of my weaknesses. 6 Though if I wish to boast, I shall not be a fool, for I shall be speaking the truth. But I refrain from it, so that no one may think more of me than he sees in me or hears from me. 7And to keep me from being too elated by the abundance of revelations, a thorn was given me

11.23 1 Cor 15.10; Acts 16.23; 2 Cor 6.5
★11.24 Deut 25.3
11.25 Acts 16.22; 14.19
11.26 Acts 9.23; 14.5; 21.31; Gal 2.4
11.27 1 Thess 2.9; 1 Cor 4.11; 2 Cor 6.5
11.29 1 Cor 9.22
11.30 1 Cor 2.3
11.31 Gal 1.20; Rom 9.5
11.32 Acts 9.24,25
12.1 2 Cor 11.30; ver 7; Gal 1.12; 2.2
★12.2 Rom 16.7; Eph 4.10; 2 Cor 11.11
12.4 Lk 23.43
12.6 2 Cor 10.8; 11.16
★12.7

11.24 Paul speaks of having been whipped five times by the Jews with *forty lashes less one*. This refers to the beating administered in the synagogue to convicted Jewish offenders. This detail shows that Paul submitted himself to the synagogue discipline even after becoming a Christian: he was no less a Jew for having accepted and confessed Jesus of Nazareth as the promised Messiah and Lord.

The limit was forty lashes (Deut 25.1-3), but in order not to exceed the limit, only thirty-nine were given. According to the *Mishnah* (tractate "Makkoth"), the prisoner's garments were torn off and he was bound by his hands to two pillars, with arms outstretched. The minister of the synagogue administered the punishment with a triple-thonged whip: twenty-six lashes on the back and thirteen on the breast, while passages from the Old Testament were read. "And he that smites, smites with his one hand with all his might."

12.2 The word *heaven* is used in various senses in the Bible. Often it refers to the abode of God, the place from which Christ came

and to which He went at His ascension and from which He is coming again. It is also pictured as the place to which the saints go upon death. Of all the facts concerning heaven the following are of particular interest: (1) it is the place of God's throne (Isa 66.1); (2) Christ our Mediator has entered into heaven (Heb 6.20; 9.12, 24); (3) the angels are in heaven (Mt 18.10; 24.36); (4) the wicked are excluded from heaven (Gal 5.21; Rev 22.15); (5) the saints are rewarded in heaven (1 Pet 1.4); (6) here believers are to lay up treasure (Mt 6.20; Lk 12.33).

12.7 We do not know what Paul's thorn in the flesh was. One thing about it is plain enough: Paul regarded it as having come from Satan, yet he recognized God had permitted it to come into his life and intended to use it for His own glory. It was in the midst of the weakness resulting from this affliction that the power of God was able to manifest itself most conspicuously. It always has been so. Christians in every age find God's sustaining power greater than Satan's ability to afflict them and cast them down.

in the flesh, a messenger of Satan, to harass me, to keep me from
being too elated. 8 Three times I besought the Lord about this,
that it should leave me; 9 but he said to me, "My grace is sufficient
for you, for my power is made perfect in weakness." I will all the
more gladly boast of my weaknesses, that the power of Christ may
rest upon me. 10 For the sake of Christ, then, I am content
with weaknesses, insults, hardships, persecutions, and calamities;
for when I am weak, then I am strong.

F. The marks of a true apostle

11 I have been a fool! You forced me to it, for I ought to have
been commended by you. For I was not at all inferior to these
superlative apostles, even though I am nothing. 12 The signs of a
true apostle were performed among you in all patience, with signs
and wonders and mighty works. 13 For in what were you less
favored than the rest of the churches, except that I myself did
not burden you? Forgive me this wrong!

14 Here for the third time I am ready to come to you. And I
will not be a burden, for I seek not what is yours but you; for
children ought not to lay up for their parents, but parents for their
children. 15 I will most gladly spend and be spent for your souls.
If I love you the more, am I to be loved the less? 16 But granting
that I myself did not burden you, I was crafty, you say, and got
the better of you by guile. 17 Did I take advantage of you through
any of those whom I sent to you? 18 I urged Titus to go, and sent
the brother with him. Did Titus take advantage of you? Did we
not act in the same spirit? Did we not take the same steps?

G. The appeal for repentance

19 Have you been thinking all along that we have been defending ourselves before you? It is in the sight of God that we have
been speaking in Christ, and all for your upbuilding, beloved.
20 For I fear that perhaps I may come and find you not what I
wish, and that you may find me not what you wish; that perhaps
there may be quarreling, jealousy, anger, selfishness, slander,
gossip, conceit, and disorder. 21 I fear that when I come again my
God may humble me before you, and I may have to mourn over
many of those who sinned before and have not repented of the
impurity, immorality, and licentiousness which they have practiced.

13 This is the third time I am coming to you. Any charge must
be sustained by the evidence of two or three witnesses. 2 I
warned those who sinned before and all the others, and I warn
them now while absent, as I did when present on my second visit,
that if I come again I will not spare them—3 since you desire proof
that Christ is speaking in me. He is not weak in dealing with you,
but is powerful in you. 4 For he was crucified in weakness, but
lives by the power of God. For we are weak in him, but in dealing
with you we shall live with him by the power of God.

5 Examine yourselves, to see whether you are holding to your
faith. Test yourselves. Do you not realize that Jesus Christ is in
you?—unless indeed you fail to meet the test! 6 I hope you will
find out that we have not failed. 7 But we pray God that you may

12.8
Mt 26.44
12.9
Phil 4.13;
2 Cor 11.30;
1 Pet 4.14
12.10
Rom 5.3;
2 Cor 6.4;
2 Thess 1.4

12.11
2 Cor 11.1,5
12.12
Rom 15.18,
19
12.13
1 Cor 9.12,
18;
2 Cor 11.7
12.14
2 Cor 13.1;
1 Cor 10.24,
33; 4.14,
15;
Prov 19.14
12.15
Phil 2.17;
1 Thess 2.8

12.18
2 Cor 8.6,
16,18

12.19
Rom 9.1;
2 Cor 10.8

12.20
2 Cor 2.1–4;
1 Cor 1.11;
3.3
12.21
2 Cor 2.1,4;
13.2;
Gal 5.19

13.1
2 Cor 12.14;
Deut 19.15;
Mt 18.16
13.3
Mt 10.20;
1 Cor 5.4;
2 Cor 9.8;
10.4
13.4
Phil 2.7,8;
1 Pet 3.18;
Rom 6.4,8;
ver 9
13.5
Jn 6.6;
1 Cor 11.28;
9.27

not do wrong—not that we may appear to have met the test, but that you may do what is right, though we may seem to have failed. [8] For we cannot do anything against the truth, but only for the truth. [9] For we are glad when we are weak and you are strong. What we pray for is your improvement. [10] I write this while I am away from you, in order that when I come I may not have to be severe in my use of the authority which the Lord has given me for building up and not for tearing down.

13.9
2 Cor 11.30;
12.10

13.10
2 Cor 2.3;
Tit 1.13;
2 Cor 10.8

V. Conclusion 13.11–14

A. Exhortations and greetings

[11] Finally, brethren, farewell. Mend your ways, heed my appeal, agree with one another, live in peace, and the God of love and peace will be with you. [12] Greet one another with a holy kiss. [13] All the saints greet you.

13.11
Rom 15.33;
Eph 6.23

13.13
Phil 4.22

B. Benediction

[14] The grace of the Lord Jesus Christ and the love of God and the fellowship of[n] the Holy Spirit be with you all.

[n] Or *and participation in*

INTRODUCTION TO

THE LETTER OF PAUL TO THE

GALATIANS

Authorship and Background: The questions of the date and the destination of this letter of Paul cannot be answered decisively. As to the first, nothing in the letter itself, or in the book of Acts, determines whether Galatians was written before or soon after the Jerusalem Council in A.D. 49, or a few years later, about the same time Paul wrote to Corinth and Rome, A.D. 55–56. The date depends on whether the visit to Jerusalem described in 2.1–10 is to be identified with that mentioned in Acts 11.30, or in Acts 15.1–29. The "so quickly" in 1.6 seems to favor an earlier and not a later date for the letter.

Who were the Galatians? They were personal acquaintances, among whom Paul had worked (4.13–15). If Acts records Paul's ministry to these people, then they were the residents of the Roman province of Galatia, in the cities of Antioch (of Pisidia), Iconium, Lystra, and Derbe, visited during the first missionary tour (Acts 13.14—14.23). Most scholars believe that these were the Galatian churches (1.1) to whom Paul wrote; some, however, hold they were residents of northern Galatia, in and near the cities of Pessinus, Ancyra, and Tavium.

The letter was prompted by the inroads made into the churches by the Judaizers, Jewish Christians who insisted that Gentile converts to the Christian faith should submit to the Jewish rite of circumcision and respect certain ritual distinctions between pure and impure foods. They also attacked Paul personally, saying he was not a true apostle, and thus not on the same footing with the original Twelve, whose authority and prestige they claimed. Paul's gospel, in their eyes, was not the true gospel. Apparently their attempts met with considerable success: the inexperienced Galatians, impressed by their arguments and awed by their credentials, succumbed to their demands. Some, submitting themselves to Jewish legalism (4.21), began to observe Jewish religious feasts (4.10, 11) and accept circumcision (5.2–6).

Confronted with this grave danger to the spiritual welfare of the Galatian Christians, Paul wrote, warning, expounding, and pleading with them to resist the blandishments of the Judaizers.

Characteristics: The letter to the Galatians may rightly be called the *Magna Charta* of Christian liberty. Against all attempts to shackle Christian freedom with Jewish legalism, Paul stands firm: such an attempt is, in his thinking, nothing less than a complete perversion of the true gospel; a different, alien gospel (1.6–9). Those who follow this false gospel are apart from Christ and His grace (5.4). Paul's great theme is eloquently stated: the free and sovereign grace of God, by which man is justified, is through faith alone, not by works of the law (2.15, 16, 21). Christ's death meant that the law is not a means of salvation, and in sharing his death believers also die to the law; for were the law operative as a means of salvation, then Christ's death was useless (3.13, 14; 2.20, 21). Even

Abraham was justified by faith, not by works of law (3.6–9); and it was the prophet Habakkuk (Hab 2.4) who declared that life belongs to him who has been justified through faith (3.11). The law was never a means of justification: Abraham was justified by faith four hundred and thirty years before the law (3.16–19), and we are his spiritual descendants, sons and heirs (3.29–4.7). Christ gives us freedom: let us stand fast and not fall under the yoke of slavery (5.1)!

Contents:

GALATIANS

I. *Introduction 1.1–10*

A. *Salutation*

1.1
2 Cor 1.1;
ver 11,12;
Acts 9.6;
2.24

1 Paul an apostle—not from men nor through man, but through Jesus Christ and God the Father, who raised him from the dead—2 and all the brethren who are with me,

1.2
Phil 4.21;
1 Cor 16.1

To the churches of Gålå′tiå:

1.3
Rom 1.7

3 Grace to you and peace from God the Father and our Lord Jesus Christ, 4 who gave himself for our sins to deliver us from the present evil age, according to the will of our God and Father;

1.4
Rom 4.25;
Gal 2.20;
2 Cor 4.4

5 to whom be the glory for ever and ever. Amen.

1.5
Rom 16.27

B. *The occasion of the letter*

*1.6
Gal 5.8;
2 Cor 11.4

6 I am astonished that you are so quickly deserting him who called you in the grace of Christ and turning to a different gospel —7 not that there is another gospel, but there are some who trouble you and want to pervert the gospel of Christ. 8 But even if we, or an angel from heaven, should preach to you a gospel contrary to that which we preached to you, let him be accursed. 9As we have said before, so now I say again, If any one is preaching to you a gospel contrary to that which you received, let him be accursed.

1.7
Acts 15.24;
Gal 5.10

*1.8
2 Cor 11.4,
14;
Rom 9.3

1.9
Rom 16.17

1.10
1 Thess 2.4

10 Am I now seeking the favor of men, or of God? Or am I trying to please men? If I were still pleasing men, I should not be a servant*a* of Christ.

II. *Paul's apostolical authority 1.11–2.21*

A. *Of divine origin*

1.11
1 Cor 15.1

11 For I would have you know, brethren, that the gospel which was preached by me is not man's*b* gospel. 12 For I did not receive it from man, nor was I taught it, but it came through a revelation of Jesus Christ. 13 For you have heard of my former life in Judaism, how I persecuted the church of God violently and tried to destroy it; 14 and I advanced in Judaism beyond many of my own age among my people, so extremely zealous was I for the

1.12
ver 1,16;
Eph 3.3

1.13
Acts 8.3;
9.21

1.14
Acts 22.3;
Col 2.8

a Or *slave* *b* Greek *according to man*

1.6 Paul's feelings are evident. He writes in the white heat of an emotion compounded of sorrow, astonishment, and indignation, as he contemplates the possible defection of his beloved Galatians. His indignation is vividly stated in the anathema he calls down upon those who pervert the gospel (1.7–9), and in the surgery he recommends to those who are so eager to practice their doctrine of circumcision (5.12). His astonishment at the attitude of the Galatian converts runs through the whole letter (1.6; 3.1–5; 4.12–16), while

his deep love is expressed in tender terms (4.19). Paul's emotion is caused by his conviction that his readers were running the risk of deserting the gospel, defecting from Christ, and falling away from grace (1.6; 4.9; 5.4). This was no trifling question of doctrinal hairsplitting: it was a matter of life and death.

1.8 *accursed* is from the Greek word *anathema* now in the English language. Traditionally, an anathema was pronounced against an individual by ecclesiastical authority and it was accompanied by excommunication.

traditions of my fathers. 15 But when he who had set me apart before I was born, and had called me through his grace, 16 was pleased to reveal his Son to*c* me, in order that I might preach him among the Gentiles, I did not confer with flesh and blood, 17 nor did I go up to Jerusalem to those who were apostles before me, but I went away into Arabia; and again I returned to Damascus.

B. Independent of the apostles

18 Then after three years I went up to Jerusalem to visit Çēphås, and remained with him fifteen days. 19 But I saw none of the other apostles except James the Lord's brother. 20 (In what I am writing to you, before God, I do not lie!) 21 Then I went into the regions of Syria and Çīlı̆'çiå. 22And I was still not known by sight to the churches of Christ in Judē̆'å; 23 they only heard it said, "He who once persecuted us is now preaching the faith he once tried to destroy." 24And they glorified God because of me.

C. Accepted by the church

2 Then after fourteen years I went up again to Jerusalem with Bar'nåbås, taking Tītŭs along with me. 2 I went up by revelation; and I laid before them (but privately before those who were of repute) the gospel which I preach among the Gentiles, lest somehow I should be running or had run in vain. 3 But even Tītŭs, who was with me, was not compelled to be circumcised, though he was a Greek. 4 But because of false brethren secretly brought in, who slipped in to spy out our freedom which we have in Christ Jesus, that they might bring us into bondage—5 to them we did not yield submission even for a moment, that the truth of the gospel might be preserved for you. 6And from those who were reputed to be something (what they were makes no difference to me; God shows no partiality)—those, I say, who were of repute added nothing to me; 7 but on the contrary, when they saw that I had been entrusted with the gospel to the uncircumcised, just as Peter had been entrusted with the gospel to the circumcised 8 (for he who worked through Peter for the mission to the circumcised worked through me also for the Gentiles), 9 and when they perceived the grace that was given to me, James and Çēphås and John, who were reputed to be pillars, gave to me and Bar'nåbås the right hand of fellowship, that we should go to the Gentiles and they to the circumcised; 10 only they would have us remember the poor, which very thing I was eager to do.

D. Demonstrated in conflict with Peter

11 But when Çēphås came to Ăn'tĭŏçh I opposed him to his

c Greek *in*

1.15	Isa 49.1,5; Jer 1.5; Acts 9.15; Rom 1.1
1.16	Acts 9.20; Eph 6.12
★1.18	Acts 9.22, 23,26,27
1.19	Mt 13.55
1.21	Acts 9.30
1.22	1 Thess 2.14; Rom 16.7
2.1	Acts 15.2
2.2	Acts 15.12; Gal 1.6; Phil 2.16
2.3	2 Cor 2.13; Acts 16.3; 1 Cor 9.21
2.4	Acts 15.1; 2 Cor 11.26
2.5	ver 14; Col 1.5
2.6	Gal 6.3; Rom 2.11; 2 Cor 12.11
★2.7	1 Thess 2.4; Acts 13.46
2.9	Rom 12.3; Gal 1.16
2.10	Acts 11.29, 30; 24.17
★2.11	Acts 11.10

1.18 *Cephas* is the Aramaic form of the Greek name *Peter*, both of which mean "rock" (cf. Jn 1.42). The name Cephas is used of the apostle in Jn 1.42; 1 Cor 1.12; 3.22; 9.5; 15.5; Gal 1.18; 2.9, 11, 14.

2.7 *the gospel to the uncircumcised* entrusted to Paul and *the gospel to the circumcised*

entrusted to Peter are not two different gospels. The gospel is one and the same everywhere: Paul was given a special commission to proclaim it to the Gentiles; Peter to the Jews.

2.11 Paul did not rebuke Peter (Cephas) for entertaining heretical doctrine, but for his failure to practice consistently what he

2.12
Acts 11.2,3

2.13
ver 1
2.14
ver 5,9,11

2.15
Phil 3.4,5;
Mt 9.11
2.16
Acts 13.39;
Rom 1.17;
3.20
2.17
ver 15;
Gal 3.21

2.19
Rom 8.2;
6.14;
2 Cor 5.15;
1 Thess 5.10
2.20
1 Pet 4.2;
Eph 5.2;
Tit 2.14
2.21
Gal 3.21

3.1
Gal 1.2;
5.7;
1 Cor 1.23
3.2
Acts 2.38;
Rom 10.16,
17
3.3
Gal 4.9;
Heb 7.16
3.4
1 Cor 15.2
3.5
Phil 1.19;
1 Cor 12.10;
Rom 10.17
*3.6
Gen 15.6;
Rom 4.3;
Jas 2.23
3.7
ver 9
3.8
Gen 12.3;
Acts 3.25
3.9
Rom 4.16;
ver 7

face, because he stood condemned. 12 For before certain men came from James, he ate with the Gentiles; but when they came he drew back and separated himself, fearing the circumcision party. 13And with him the rest of the Jews acted insincerely, so that even Bar′nàbàs was carried away by their insincerity. 14 But when I saw that they were not straightforward about the truth of the gospel, I said to Çëphás before them all, "If you, though a Jew, live like a Gentile and not like a Jew, how can you compel the Gentiles to live like Jews?" 15 We ourselves, who are Jews by birth and not Gentile sinners, 16 yet who know that a man is not justified[d] by works of the law but through faith in Jesus Christ, even we have believed in Christ Jesus, in order to be justified by faith in Christ, and not by works of the law, because by works of the law shall no one be justified. 17 But if, in our endeavor to be justified in Christ, we ourselves were found to be sinners, is Christ then an agent of sin? Certainly not! 18 But if I build up again those things which I tore down, then I prove myself a transgressor. 19 For I through the law died to the law, that I might live to God. 20 I have been crucified with Christ; it is no longer I who live, but Christ who lives in me; and the life I now live in the flesh I live by faith in the Son of God, who loved me and gave himself for me. 21 I do not nullify the grace of God; for if justification[e] were through the law, then Christ died to no purpose.

III. Paul's doctrine of justification 3.1–4.31

A. The Galatians deceived

3 O foolish Gàlä′tiàns! Who has bewitched you, before whose eyes Jesus Christ was publicly portrayed as crucified? 2 Let me ask you only this: Did you receive the Spirit by works of the law, or by hearing with faith? 3Are you so foolish? Having begun with the Spirit, are you now ending with the flesh? 4 Did you experience so many things in vain?—if it really is in vain. 5 Does he who supplies the Spirit to you and works miracles among you do so by works of the law, or by hearing with faith?

B. The witness of Abraham

6 Thus Abraham "believed God, and it was reckoned to him as righteousness." 7 So you see that it is men of faith who are the sons of Abraham. 8And the scripture, foreseeing that God would justify the Gentiles by faith, preached the gospel beforehand to Abraham, saying, "In you shall all the nations be blessed." 9 So then, those who are men of faith are blessed with Abraham who had faith.

d Or reckoned righteous; and so elsewhere   e Or righteousness

---

believed. Nowhere did Peter teach that men could be saved by circumcision (see 2.14), but he withdrew himself from uncircumcised Gentiles because he was pressed to do so by circumcised Hebrew Christians. Presumably he was motivated by a desire to avoid offending prospective Jewish converts. But in this case his policy of expediency amounted to a surrender of basic principle: that salvation is

of grace, apart from obedience to the ritual Law of Moses. While Christians should be circumspect and concerned about the consciences of weaker brothers, there are times when conformity to their false scruples involves a betrayal of the gospel. This was one of those times.

3.6 See note to Gen 12.2 on the Abrahamic covenant.

C. Faith without works

10 For all who rely on works of the law are under a curse; for it is written, "Cursed be every one who does not abide by all things written in the book of the law, and do them." 11 Now it is evident that no man is justified before God by the law; for "He who through faith is righteous shall live";^f 12 but the law does not rest on faith, for "He who does them shall live by them." 13 Christ redeemed us from the curse of the law, having become a curse for us—for it is written, "Cursed be every one who hangs on a tree"— 14 that in Christ Jesus the blessing of Abraham might come upon the Gentiles, that we might receive the promise of the Spirit through faith.

D. The Abrahamic covenant

15 To give a human example, brethren: no one annuls even a man's will,^g or adds to it, once it has been ratified. 16 Now the promises were made to Abraham and to his offspring. It does not say, "And to offsprings," referring to many; but, referring to one, "And to your offspring," which is Christ. 17 This is what I mean: the law, which came four hundred and thirty years afterward, does not annul a covenant previously ratified by God, so as to make the promise void. 18 For if the inheritance is by the law, it is no longer by promise; but God gave it to Abraham by a promise.

E. The function of the law

19 Why then the law? It was added because of transgressions, till the offspring should come to whom the promise had been made; and it was ordained by angels through an intermediary. 20 Now an intermediary implies more than one; but God is one. 21 Is the law then against the promises of God? Certainly not; for if a law had been given which could make alive, then righteousness would indeed be by the law. 22 But the scripture consigned all things to sin, that what was promised to faith in Jesus Christ might be given to those who believe.

F. The superiority of faith over law

23 Now before faith came, we were confined under the law, kept under restraint until faith should be revealed. 24 So that the law was our custodian until Christ came, that we might be justified

---

f Or *the righteous shall live by faith*   g Or *covenant* (as in verse 17)

Cross references (margin):

*3.10 Deut 27.26
*3.11 Gal 2.16; Hab 2.4; Heb 10.38
3.12 Lev 18.5; Rom 10.5
3.13 Gal 4.5; Acts 5.30; Deut 21.23
3.14 Rom 4.9; Joel 2.28; Acts 2.33
3.15 Heb 9.17
3.16 Gen 12.3; 13.15; Acts 3.25
3.17 Ex 12.40; Rom 4.13
3.18 Rom 4.14; 8.17
3.19 Acts 7.53; Deut 5.5
3.20 Heb 8.6; 9.15; 12.24
3.21 Gal 2.17,21
3.22 Rom 3.9–19; 11.32
3.23 Rom 11.32
*3.24 Rom 10.4; 1 Cor 4.15; Gal 2.16

3.10 Man's inability to keep the law of God inevitably brings him under the curse of God, i.e., God's judgment upon sin. There is, therefore, no way for man to be saved by the law, for only through perfect obedience could man be saved under the system of law. It is through faith, and faith alone, that man is justified before God and attains unto life. The believer is redeemed from the curse of the law since Christ, in his Crucifixion, became a curse for us.

3.11 See note to Hab 2.4 on justification by faith alone.

3.24 The law is good and holy but it cannot save (Rom 7.12–14; 3.20). It is like the driver of a school bus who transports children to and from school, but is not the teacher of the children. The law performed this function until Christ came. But even so, the law enlightens but does not empower; it reveals what a man ought to do, but it does not give him the ability to do it. Salvation by law would mean salvation by works (an impossibility since Adam's fall), whereas salvation by grace is apart from justifying works of the law.

by faith. 25 But now that faith has come, we are no longer under a custodian; 26 for in Christ Jesus you are all sons of God, through faith. 27 For as many of you as were baptized into Christ have put on Christ. 28 There is neither Jew nor Greek, there is neither slave nor free, there is neither male nor female; for you are all one in Christ Jesus. 29And if you are Christ's, then you are Abraham's offspring, heirs according to promise.

4 I mean that the heir, as long as he is a child, is no better than a slave, though he is the owner of all the estate; 2 but he is under guardians and trustees until the date set by the father. 3 So with us; when we were children, we were slaves to the elemental spirits of the universe. 4 But when the time had fully come, God sent forth his Son, born of woman, born under the law, 5 to redeem those who were under the law, so that we might receive adoption as sons. 6And because you are sons, God has sent the Spirit of his Son into our hearts, crying, "Abba! Father!" 7 So through God you are no longer a slave but a son, and if a son then an heir.

G. Appeal against a return to bondage

8 Formerly, when you did not know God, you were in bondage to beings that by nature are no gods; 9 but now that you have come to know God, or rather to be known by God, how can you turn back again to the weak and beggarly elemental spirits, whose slaves you want to be once more? 10 You observe days, and months, and seasons, and years! 11 I am afraid I have labored over you in vain.

12 Brethren, I beseech you, become as I am, for I also have become as you are. You did me no wrong; 13 you know it was because of a bodily ailment that I preached the gospel to you at first; 14 and though my condition was a trial to you, you did not scorn or despise me, but received me as an angel of God, as Christ Jesus. 15 What has become of the satisfaction you felt? For I bear you witness that, if possible, you would have plucked out your eyes and given them to me. 16 Have I then become your enemy by telling you the truth?h 17 They make much of you, but for no good purpose; they want to shut you out, that you may make much of them. 18 For a good purpose it is always good to be made much of, and not only when I am present with you. 19 My little children, with whom I am again in travail until Christ be formed in you! 20 I could wish to be present with you now and to change my tone, for I am perplexed about you.

h Or by dealing truly with you

4.5 adoption (huiothesia, placing as a son) is a word used in the New Testament only by Paul, and designates the privilege of sonship (sons of God, and children of God) which God confers on His people. It is an adoptive sonship which the believer never possessed by natural birth but which springs from the new birth through the redemption of Christ. With this new position come the attendant rights and obligations of sonship. Believers are predestined to sonship (Rom 8.29; Eph 1.5-11), and while it is theirs now it extends to the transformation of their bodies only at the resurrection. Adopted children: (1) are objects of the Father's love (Jn 17.23; 1 Jn 4.7-11); (2) bear His image (Rom 8.29; 2 Pet 1.4); (3) are indwelt by His Spirit (4.6); (4) bear His name (1 Jn 3.1); (5) are dealt with and chastised as sons (Heb 12.5-11); (6) are heirs of God and joint heirs with Christ (Rom 8.17; 1 Pet 1.4).

4.13 It is not known for sure what Paul's bodily ailment was. No definite conclusion may be drawn from the little Paul says about it here and in 2 Cor 12.7-10. From Paul's words one may infer that it was chronic, recurring, and painful, repulsive to the spectator, and humiliating to Paul. Malaria, epilepsy, migraine, and ophthalmia are among the ailments most commonly suggested.

21 Tell me, you who desire to be under law, do you not hear the law? 22 For it is written that Abraham had two sons, one by a slave and one by a free woman. 23 But the son of the slave was born according to the flesh, the son of the free woman through promise. 24 Now this is an allegory: these women are two covenants. One is from Mount Sī′nāī, bearing children for slavery; she is Hāgar. 25 Now Hāgar is Mount Sī′nāī in Arabia;*i* she corresponds to the present Jerusalem, for she is in slavery with her children. 26 But the Jerusalem above is free, and she is our mother. 27 For it is written,

"Rejoice, O barren one who does not bear;
    break forth and shout, you who are not in travail;
for the children of the desolate one are many more
    than the children of her that is married."

28 Now we,*j* brethren, like Isaac, are children of promise. 29 But as at that time he who was born according to the flesh persecuted him who was born according to the Spirit, so it is now. 30 But what does the scripture say? "Cast out the slave and her son; for the son of the slave shall not inherit with the son of the free woman." 31 So, brethren, we are not children of the slave but of the free woman.

IV. *The effect of Christian liberty 5.1–6.10*

A. *Liberty threatened by legalism*

5 For freedom Christ has set us free; stand fast therefore, and do not submit again to a yoke of slavery.

2 Now I, Paul, say to you that if you receive circumcision, Christ will be of no advantage to you. 3 I testify again to every man who receives circumcision that he is bound to keep the whole law. 4 You are severed from Christ, you who would be justified by the law; you have fallen away from grace. 5 For through the Spirit, by faith, we wait for the hope of righteousness. 6 For in Christ Jesus neither circumcision nor uncircumcision is of any avail, but faith working*x* through love. 7 You were running well; who hindered you from obeying the truth? 8 This persuasion is not from him who calls you. 9 A little leaven leavens the whole lump. 10 I have confidence in the Lord that you will take no other view than mine; and he who is troubling you will bear his judgment, whoever he is. 11 But if I, brethren, still preach circumcision, why am I still persecuted? In that case the stumbling block of the cross has been removed. 12 I wish those who unsettle you would mutilate themselves!

i Other ancient authorities read *For Sinai is a mountain in Arabia*
j Other ancient authorities read *you*
x Or *made effective*

4.21	Lk 16.29
4.22	Gen 16.15; 21.2,9
4.23	Rom 9.7; Gen 18.10; Heb 11.11
4.24	Deut 33.2
4.26	Isa 2.2; Heb 12.22; Rev 3.12
4.27	Isa 54.1
4.28	Acts 3.25; Rom 9.8
4.29	Gen 21.9
4.30	Gen 21.10–12
*5.1	Jn 8.32; Acts 15.10
5.2	Acts 15.1
5.3	Gal 3.10
5.4	Heb 12.15; 2 Pet 3.17
5.5	Rom 8.23, 24; 2 Tim 4.8
5.6	1 Cor 7.19; Jas 2.18
5.7	1 Cor 9.24; Gal 3.1
5.8	Gal 1.6
5.9	1 Cor 5.6
5.10	2 Cor 2.3; Gal 1.7
5.11	Gal 4.29; 6.12; 1 Cor 1.23

5.1 Christian liberty is a consequence of salvation by grace, and is secured to the believer in and through Jesus Christ (Col 1.13; Gal 4.3–5). Liberty is freedom: (1) from the law (Rom 7.6; 8.2); (2) from the curse of the law (3.13); (3) from the fear of death (Heb 2.15); (4) from sin (Rom 6.7, 18); (5) from the yoke of Old Testament ritual ordinances (4.3; Col 2.20). But liberty must never be used as a cloak for sin; liberty must not become license. While the believer should resist any threat to his true liberty under the gospel, he must also remember that his very liberty has brought him into total subjection to Christ, whose servant he is and whom he must always obey (Rom 12.1). Paradoxically the Christian finds his greatest liberty when he is in bondage to Jesus Christ.

B. *Freedom defined*

5.13
1 Cor 8.9;
1 Pet 2.16;
1 Cor 9.19
5.14
Lev 19.18;
Mt 7.12;
22.39;
Rom 13.8

13 For you were called to freedom, brethren; only do not use your freedom as an opportunity for the flesh, but through love be servants of one another. 14 For the whole law is fulfilled in one word, "You shall love your neighbor as yourself." 15 But if you bite and devour one another take heed that you are not consumed by one another.

C. *Liberty in practice*

5.16
Rom 8.4;
ver 24,25;
Eph 2.3
5.17
Rom 7.15–
23
5.18
Rom 6.14
***5.19**
Eph 5.3;
Col 3.5
5.21
1 Cor 6.9
5.22
Eph 5.9;
Col 3.12–
15;
1 Cor 13.7
5.24
Rom 6.6

16 But I say, walk by the Spirit, and do not gratify the desires of the flesh. 17 For the desires of the flesh are against the Spirit, and the desires of the Spirit are against the flesh; for these are opposed to each other, to prevent you from doing what you would. 18 But if you are led by the Spirit you are not under the law. 19 Now the works of the flesh are plain: fornication, impurity, licentiousness, 20 idolatry, sorcery, enmity, strife, jealousy, anger, selfishness, dissension, party spirit, 21 envy,[k] drunkenness, carousing, and the like. I warn you, as I warned you before, that those who do such things shall not inherit the kingdom of God. 22 But the fruit of the Spirit is love, joy, peace, patience, kindness, goodness, faithfulness, 23 gentleness, self-control; against such there is no law. 24And those who belong to Christ Jesus have crucified the flesh with its passions and desires.

D. *Exhortations and warnings*

5.25
Rom 8.4
5.26
Phil 2.3
6.2
Rom 15.1;
Jas 2.8
6.3
Rom 12.3;
1 Cor 8.2;
2 Cor 3.5
6.4
1 Cor 11.28;
Phil 1.26
6.6
1 Cor 9.11
6.7
1 Cor 6.9;
Job 13.9
6.8
Hos 8.7;
Jas 3.18
6.9
1 Cor 15.58;
Heb 3.6;
Rev 2.10
6.10
Jn 9.4;
Tit 3.1;
Eph 2.19

25 If we live by the Spirit, let us also walk by the Spirit. 26 Let us have no self-conceit, no provoking of one another, no envy of one another.

6 Brethren, if a man is overtaken in any trespass, you who are spiritual should restore him in a spirit of gentleness. Look to yourself, lest you too be tempted. 2 Bear one another's burdens, and so fulfil the law of Christ. 3 For if any one thinks he is something, when he is nothing, he deceives himself. 4 But let each one test his own work, and then his reason to boast will be in himself alone and not in his neighbor. 5 For each man will have to bear his own load.

6 Let him who is taught the word share all good things with him who teaches.

7 Do not be deceived; God is not mocked, for whatever a man sows, that he will also reap. 8 For he who sows to his own flesh will from the flesh reap corruption; but he who sows to the Spirit will from the Spirit reap eternal life. 9And let us not grow weary in well-doing, for in due season we shall reap, if we do not lose heart. 10 So then, as we have opportunity, let us do good to all men, and especially to those who are of the household of faith.

k Other ancient authorities add *murder*

5.19 Paul uses the plural word *works* when speaking of the *works of the flesh* but in verse 22 when he speaks of the *fruit of the Spirit* he uses the singular word *fruit*. Thus it may be said that the redeemed life is an integrated whole or complete life, whereas the unregenerate life is fragmented and at odds with itself. The *fruit of the Spirit* may be likened to a diamond which has many facets. All of the facets together constitute the gem but each facet helps to reflect the true splendor of the one stone.

V. Conclusion 6.11–18

A. Liberty and the Cross

11 See with what large letters I am writing to you with my own hand. 12 It is those who want to make a good showing in the flesh that would compel you to be circumcised, and only in order that they may not be persecuted for the cross of Christ. 13 For even those who receive circumcision do not themselves keep the law, but they desire to have you circumcised that they may glory in your flesh. 14 But far be it from me to glory except in the cross of our Lord Jesus Christ, by which[1] the world has been crucified to me, and I to the world. 15 For neither circumcision counts for anything, nor uncircumcision, but a new creation. 16 Peace and mercy be upon all who walk by this rule, upon the Israel of God.

6.12
Mt 23.27, 28;
Acts 15.1;
Gal 5.11
6.13
Rom 2.25;
Phil 3.3
6.14
Gal 2.20;
Rom 6.2,6
6.15
2 Cor 5.17

B. The cost of liberty

17 Henceforth let no man trouble me; for I bear on my body the marks of Jesus.

6.17
2 Cor 1.5

C. The benediction

18 The grace of our Lord Jesus Christ be with your spirit, brethren. Amen.

[1] Or *through whom*

INTRODUCTION TO

THE LETTER OF PAUL TO THE

EPHESIANS

Authorship and Background: The determination of date, place of writing, and readers, presents problems in the Letter of Paul to the Ephesians. All three are intimately related, and the answer to one will help answer the others. As to the readers, the problem exists because the oldest and best Greek manuscripts omit the words "at Ephesus" in 1.1. The absence of any personal greetings and, particularly of specific matters of faith and conduct, make it probable, as many believe, that the letter to the Ephesians was not written to one church, but to several churches, as a general letter. The only person named is Tychicus (6.21, 22), who seems to have been the bearer of the letter. He is mentioned also in Col 4.7, 8, in identically the same terms (6.22 = Col 4.8). Paul refers to himself only as a prisoner (3.1; 4.1; 6.20).

Various conclusions have been drawn from these data: the most widely held, probably, is that Paul wrote this letter in Rome during his two-year imprisonment (A.D. 59–61), along with letters to the Philippians, Colossians, and Philemon. This letter to the Ephesians was sent to the various churches in the province of Asia, where Paul had worked for three years on his third missionary tour (Acts 19.1—20.1; 20.20). Some believe this was Paul's last letter; others think it was not written by Paul, but by an intimate disciple who, writing in the apostle's name, composed it as a covering letter for the published collection of Paul's epistles. It was not until the nineteenth century that the Pauline authorship was called into question despite the substantial evidence for regarding it as the product of the pen of the Apostle Paul. Conservative scholars have always accepted it as genuine, however.

Characteristics: Devoid of personal references and greetings, the letter is written in calm, deliberate fashion, free of polemics and reproof, dwelling profoundly upon the person of Christ and the church, the household of God, of which Christ is the cornerstone (2.20), and through which the manifold wisdom of God is manifest (3.10). The church is the body of Christ, who is its head (4.15, 16), and all believers are members of his body (1.23; 4.25; 5.23, 30). The relation of Christ to the church is like that of a husband to his wife (5.22–32). To God be glory in the church and in Jesus Christ for ever (3.21)!

Along with the exalted view of the church goes an equally high view of the unity of the faith (4.4–6), the greatness of God's plan of redemption (1.15–23), and his ultimate purpose to sum up all of creation in Christ (1.10). In a concept nowhere else developed in the New Testament, the apostle speaks of "the heavenly places" as the realm of redemption (1.3, 20; 2.6; 3.10; 6.12).

Upon such lofty theological affirmations, the apostle bases his practical exhortations to Christians in their daily lives, in relation to each other, to the world, and in the family (4.1—6.20).

Contents:

THE LETTER OF PAUL TO THE
EPHESIANS

I. Salutation 1.1,2

1.1
2 Cor 1.1;
1 Cor 1.1;
Phil 1.1;
Col 1.1,2
1.2
Rom 1.7

1 Paul, an apostle of Christ Jesus by the will of God,
To the saints who are also faithful*a* in Christ Jesus:
2 Grace to you and peace from God our Father and the Lord Jesus Christ.

II. Doctrinal affirmations 1.3–3.21

A. The origin of the church

★1.3
2 Cor 1.3;
Eph 2.6;
3.10; 6.12
★1.4
Eph 5.27;
Col 1.22;
Eph 4.2,15,
16
1.5
Rom 8.29f
1.7
Col 1.14
1.9
Rom 16.25
1.10
Gal 4.4;
Col 1.16,20
1.11
Eph 3.11;
Rom 9.11;
Heb 6.17
1.12
ver 6,14
★1.13
Col 1.5;
Eph 4.30

3 Blessed be the God and Father of our Lord Jesus Christ, who has blessed us in Christ with every spiritual blessing in the heavenly places, 4 even as he chose us in him before the foundation of the world, that we should be holy and blameless before him. 5 He destined us in love*b* to be his sons through Jesus Christ, according to the purpose of his will, 6 to the praise of his glorious grace which he freely bestowed on us in the Beloved. 7 In him we have redemption through his blood, the forgiveness of our trespasses, according to the riches of his grace 8 which he lavished upon us. 9 For he has made known to us in all wisdom and insight the mystery of his will, according to his purpose which he set forth in Christ 10 as a plan for the fulness of time, to unite all things in him, things in heaven and things on earth.

11 In him, according to the purpose of him who accomplishes all things according to the counsel of his will, 12 we who first hoped in Christ have been destined and appointed to live for the praise of his glory. 13 In him you also, who have heard the word of truth, the gospel of your salvation, and have believed in him, were sealed

a Other ancient authorities read *who are at Ĕph'ĕsŭs and faithful*
b Or *before him in love, having destined us*

1.3 *in the heavenly places* (or "heavenlies," Greek *hoi epouranioi*) is used in 1.3, 20; 2.6; 3.10; 6.12 in a sense quite different from its use elsewhere. It is the realm in which Christ now reigns by virtue of His Resurrection from the dead (1.20), which He shares with those who through God's grace have been raised with Christ from their trespasses (2.5, 6). In this realm believers enjoy every spiritual blessing (1.3), and here the Christian warfare is waged against the spiritual forces of evil (6.12). Here God's manifold wisdom is made known through the church to these spiritual principalities and powers (3.10).

1.4 "Election" is a sovereign outworking of God's power to effect that which is pleasing to Him according to His righteous and holy will. The New Testament uses the term "elect" (*eklektoi*) to include a variety of meanings. Thus every believer is elected or chosen: (1) to good works (2.10); (2) to conformity to the image of Christ (Rom 8.29); (3) to eternal glory (Rom 9.23); (4) to adoption as a son (1.5). But the aspect of election which

has given rise to dispute relates to salvation itself. It has been argued that if only those who are elected are saved, then the death of Christ was really intended only for them (limited atonement). Others insist that a "bona fide" offer to *all men everywhere to repent* (Acts 17.30) involves a divine intention for Christ's atonement to save all mankind (unlimited atonement). Scripture teaches that election is according to God's sovereign purpose (Rom 9.11; Eph 1.11) and that it is according to His foreknowledge (Rom 8.29; 1 Pet 1.2). But nowhere does the Bible make explicit what it is in God's foreknowledge that determines His elective choice. At all events, the Scriptures appear to teach clearly enough that men are free agents with moral responsibility, while at the same time God is sovereign and works out all things according to His own good pleasure.

1.13 Believers are saved by Christ and sealed by the Holy Spirit. Scripture states that Christ Himself was sealed as Messiah by God the Father (Jn 6.27). Paul says that God

with the promised Holy Spirit, 14 which is the guarantee of our inheritance until we acquire possession of it, to the praise of his glory.

B. Prayer for the Ephesians

15 For this reason, because I have heard of your faith in the Lord Jesus and your love[c] toward all the saints, 16 I do not cease to give thanks for you, remembering you in my prayers, 17 that the God of our Lord Jesus Christ, the Father of glory, may give you a spirit of wisdom and of revelation in the knowledge of him, 18 having the eyes of your hearts enlightened, that you may know what is the hope to which he has called you, what are the riches of his glorious inheritance in the saints, 19 and what is the immeasurable greatness of his power in us who believe, according to the working of his great might 20 which he accomplished in Christ when he raised him from the dead and made him sit at his right hand in the heavenly places, 21 far above all rule and authority and power and dominion, and above every name that is named, not only in this age but also in that which is to come; 22 and he has put all things under his feet and has made him the head over all things for the church, 23 which is his body, the fulness of him who fills all in all.

C. The building of the church

2 And you he made alive, when you were dead through the trespasses and sins 2 in which you once walked, following the course of this world, following the prince of the power of the air, the spirit that is now at work in the sons of disobedience. 3Among these we all once lived in the passions of our flesh, following the desires of body and mind, and so we were by nature children of wrath, like the rest of mankind. 4 But God, who is rich in mercy, out of the great love with which he loved us, 5 even when we were dead through our trespasses, made us alive together with Christ (by grace you have been saved), 6 and raised us up with him, and made us sit with him in the heavenly places in Christ Jesus, 7 that

c Other ancient authorities omit your love

1.14
2 Cor 1.22;
Acts 20.32
1.15
Col 1.4;
Eph 3.18
1.16
Rom 1.8,9;
Col 1.3,9
1.17
Jn 20.17;
Col 1.9
1.18
Acts 26.18;
Eph 4.4
1.19
Col 1.29;
Eph 6.10
1.20
Acts 2.24;
Heb 1.3
1.21
Phil 2.9,10
★1.22
Mt 28.18;
Eph 4.15;
5.23
1.23
Rom 12.5;
Col 2.17
2.1
ver 5;
Jn 5.24
2.2
Eph 6.12;
5.6
2.3
Gal 5.16,
17;
Rom 2.14;
5.10
2.4
Rom 10.12
2.5
ver 1,8
★2.6
Eph 1.20
2.7
Tit 3.4

has put his seal upon us and given us his Spirit in our hearts as a guarantee (2 Cor 1.22). The seal consists of the indwelling Holy Spirit Himself and this *guarantee is for the day of redemption* (4.30). Symbolically, this sealing implies: (1) an ownership or title to the believer which is vested in God (2 Tim 2.19); (2) the certainty of final salvation or redemption (4.30).
1.22 Christ is the Head of His church which He purchased with His blood (Acts 20.28) and which He has constituted as a spiritual organism (Rom 12.5; 1 Cor 10.17; 12.12; Gal 3.28). Believers are baptized into this one body by the Holy Spirit (1 Cor 12.13). To Him as Head of the body all members of that body are subject (Rom 7.4; Eph 5.24). Christ protects His church so that the powers of death will not prevail against it (Mt 16.18).
All true believers, regardless of denomina-

tional attachment, belong to this one true church of Christ. Thus there are people who may be members of visible churches who are not members of the true church of Christ. Likewise there may be those who are not members of any visible organization who are true members of the body of Christ. This body of Christ, by its very nature, possesses a spiritual unity which is independent of ecclesiastical organizations.
2.6 Believers are seated with Christ in the heavenly places by virtue of their union with Him. As such, they have a share in His royal status and authority; and through their intercessory prayers and evangelistic witness, Christ's kingdom is advanced. Moreover, they constitute a heavenly commonwealth (Phil 3.20); and while they are living in the world they are not of it. Spiritually also their life is *hid with Christ in God* (Col 3.3).

2.8
Gal 2.16;
ver 5
2.9
Rom 3.20,
28;
2 Tim 1.9
2.10
Eph 4.24;
Tit 2.14
2.11
Rom 2.28;
Col 2.11
2.12
1 Thess 4.5;
Gal 4.8
2.13
Acts 2.39;
Col 1.20
2.14
Col 3.15;
1 Cor 12.13
2.15
Col 1.21,22;
Gal 6.15
2.16
Col 1.20,22
2.17
Isa 57.19;
Ps 148.14
2.18
Eph 3.12;
1Cor12.13;
Col 1.12
2.19
Phil 3.20;
Gal 6.10
2.20
Mt 16.18;
Rev 21.14
2.21
1 Cor 3.16,
17
3.1
Acts 23.18;
Eph 4.1
3.2
Col 1.25;
1 Tim 1.4
3.3
Acts 22.17;
Gal 1.12;
Rom 16.25
3.4
1 Cor 4.1
3.5
Rom 16.26
3.6
Gal 3.29;
Eph 2.15,16
3.8
1 Cor 15.9;
Gal 1.16;
Col 1.27
3.9
Col 1.26,27

in the coming ages he might show the immeasurable riches of his grace in kindness toward us in Christ Jesus. 8 For by grace you have been saved through faith; and this is not your own doing, it is the gift of God—9 not because of works, lest any man should boast. 10 For we are his workmanship, created in Christ Jesus for good works, which God prepared beforehand, that we should walk in them.

11 Therefore remember that at one time you Gentiles in the flesh, called the uncircumcision by what is called the circumcision, which is made in the flesh by hands—12 remember that you were at that time separated from Christ, alienated from the commonwealth of Israel, and strangers to the covenants of promise, having no hope and without God in the world. 13 But now in Christ Jesus you who once were far off have been brought near in the blood of Christ. 14 For he is our peace, who has made us both one, and has broken down the dividing wall of hostility, 15 by abolishing in his flesh the law of commandments and ordinances, that he might create in himself one new man in place of the two, so making peace, 16 and might reconcile us both to God in one body through the cross, thereby bringing the hostility to an end. 17And he came and preached peace to you who were far off and peace to those who were near; 18 for through him we both have access in one Spirit to the Father. 19 So then you are no longer strangers and sojourners, but you are fellow citizens with the saints and members of the household of God, 20 built upon the foundation of the apostles and prophets, Christ Jesus himself being the cornerstone, 21 in whom the whole structure is joined together and grows into a holy temple in the Lord; 22 in whom you also are built into it for a dwelling place of God in the Spirit.

D. The function of the church

3 For this reason I, Paul, a prisoner for Christ Jesus on behalf of you Gentiles—2 assuming that you have heard of the stewardship of God's grace that was given to me for you, 3 how the mystery was made known to me by revelation, as I have written briefly. 4 When you read this you can perceive my insight into the mystery of Christ, 5 which was not made known to the sons of men in other generations as it has now been revealed to his holy apostles and prophets by the Spirit; 6 that is, how the Gentiles are fellow heirs, members of the same body, and partakers of the promise in Christ Jesus through the gospel.

7 Of this gospel I was made a minister according to the gift of God's grace which was given me by the working of his power. 8 To me, though I am the very least of all the saints, this grace was given, to preach to the Gentiles the unsearchable riches of Christ, 9 and to make all men see what is the plan of the mystery

2.8 Salvation is by grace through *faith* alone (*sola fide*). Saving faith involves: (1) knowledge of the gospel (Rom 10.14); (2) assent to the gospel—that is, one is intellectually convinced that the gospel message is true (Mk 1.24; Jas 2.19); (3) trust or personal appropriation of Christ and His promises. Knowing and assenting to truth, the believer receives the Lord Jesus as his own (Jn 1.12). It should be noted that (2) is not enough to satisfy the Scriptural definition of faith; (3) is most essential. While believers are saved through faith alone, saving faith is always attested by good works—because it is alive, it always finds expression through those works of righteousness which are its proper fruit. Biblical faith is a belief in the truth simply because God says so.

hidden for ages in^d God who created all things; 10 that through the church the manifold wisdom of God might now be made known to the principalities and powers in the heavenly places. 11 This was according to the eternal purpose which he has realized in Christ Jesus our Lord, 12 in whom we have boldness and confidence of access through our faith in him. 13 So I ask you not to^e lose heart over what I am suffering for you, which is your glory.

14 For this reason I bow my knees before the Father, 15 from whom every family in heaven and on earth is named, 16 that according to the riches of his glory he may grant you to be strengthened with might through his Spirit in the inner man, 17 and that Christ may dwell in your hearts through faith; that you, being rooted and grounded in love, 18 may have power to comprehend with all the saints what is the breadth and length and height and depth, 19 and to know the love of Christ which surpasses knowledge, that you may be filled with all the fulness of God.

20 Now to him who by the power at work within us is able to do far more abundantly than all that we ask or think, 21 to him be glory in the church and in Christ Jesus to all generations, for ever and ever. Amen.

III. Practical exhortations 4.1–6.20

A. The unity of the church

4 I therefore, a prisoner for the Lord, beg you to lead a life worthy of the calling to which you have been called, 2 with all lowliness and meekness, with patience, forbearing one another in love, 3 eager to maintain the unity of the Spirit in the bond of peace. 4 There is one body and one Spirit, just as you were called to the one hope that belongs to your call, 5 one Lord, one faith, one baptism, 6 one God and Father of us all, who is above all and through all and in all. 7 But grace was given to each of us according to the measure of Christ's gift. 8 Therefore it is said,

"When he ascended on high he led a host of captives,
    and he gave gifts to men."

9 (In saying, "He ascended," what does it mean but that he had also descended into the lower parts of the earth? 10 He who descended is he who also ascended far above all the heavens, that he might fill all things.) 11 And his gifts were that some should be apostles, some prophets, some evangelists, some pastors and teachers, 12 to equip the saints for the work of ministry, for building up the body of Christ, 13 until we all attain to the unity of the faith and of the knowledge of the Son of God, to mature manhood, to the measure of the stature of the fulness of Christ; 14 so that we may no longer be children, tossed to and fro, and carried about with every wind of doctrine, by the cunning of men, by their craftiness in deceitful wiles. 15 Rather, speaking the truth in love, we are to grow up in every way into him who is the head, into Christ, 16 from whom the whole body, joined and knit together by every joint with which it is supplied, when each part is working properly, makes bodily growth and upbuilds itself in love.

d Or by   e Or I ask that I may not

3.10
1 Pet 1.12;
1 Cor 2.7;
Eph 1.21

3.12
Heb 4.16;
Eph 2.18
3.13
2 Cor 4.1
3.14
Phil 2.10
3.16
Eph 1.18;
Col 1.11;
Rom 7.22
3.17
Jn 14.23;
Col 1.23
3.18
Eph 1.18;
Job 11.8,9
3.19
Col 2.10;
Eph 1.23
3.20
Rom 16.25
3.21
Rom 11.36

4.1
Eph 3.1;
Col 1.10
4.2
Col 3.12;
Eph 1.4
4.3
Col 3.14
4.4
1 Cor 12.12;
Eph 2.16;
1.18
4.6
Rom 11.36
4.7
Rom 12.3
4.8
Ps 68.18;
Judg 5.12;
Col 2.15
4.9
Jn 3.13
4.11
1 Cor 12.28
4.12
2 Cor 13.9;
Eph 1.23;
1 Cor 12.27
4.13
Col 2.2;
1 Cor 14.20;
Col 1.28
4.14
1 Cor 14.20;
Jas 1.6;
Eph 6.11
4.15
2 Cor 4.2;
Eph 1.22;
Col 1.18

B. The moral standards of the church

4.17
Col 3.7;
1 Pet 4.3;
Rom 1.21
4.18
Eph 2.1,12;
2 Cor 3.14
4.19
1 Tim 4.2;
Rom 1.24;
Col 3.5
4.22
1 Pet 2.1;
Rom 6.6
4.23
Col 3.10
4.24
Rom 6.4;
2 Cor 5.17
4.25
Zech 8.16;
Rom 12.5
4.26
Ps 37.8
4.27
2 Cor 2.10,
11
4.28
Acts 20.35;
Lk 3.11
*4.30
1 Thess
5.19;
Rom 8.23
4.31
Col 3.8;
Tit 3.3
4.32
2 Cor 2.10;
Mt 6.14,15
5.1
Lk 6.36
5.2
1 Thess 4.9;
Gal 1.4;
2 Cor 2.15
5.3
Rom 6.13;
Col 3.5;
1 Cor 5.1
5.5
1 Cor 6.9;
Col 3.5
5.6
Jer 29.8;
Rom 1.18
5.8
Jn 8.12;
Lk 16.8
5.9
Gal 5.22
5.11
1 Cor 5.9;
Rom 6.21
5.12
Rom 1.24
5.14
Isa 60.1;
Jn 5.25

17 Now this I affirm and testify in the Lord, that you must no longer live as the Gentiles do, in the futility of their minds; 18 they are darkened in their understanding, alienated from the life of God because of the ignorance that is in them, due to their hardness of heart; 19 they have become callous and have given themselves up to licentiousness, greedy to practice every kind of uncleanness. 20 You did not so learn Christ!—21 assuming that you have heard about him and were taught in him, as the truth is in Jesus. 22 Put off your old nature which belongs to your former manner of life and is corrupt through deceitful lusts, 23 and be renewed in the spirit of your minds, 24 and put on the new nature, created after the likeness of God in true righteousness and holiness.

25 Therefore, putting away falsehood, let every one speak the truth with his neighbor, for we are members one of another. 26 Be angry but do not sin; do not let the sun go down on your anger, 27 and give no opportunity to the devil. 28 Let the thief no longer steal, but rather let him labor, doing honest work with his hands, so that he may be able to give to those in need. 29 Let no evil talk come out of your mouths, but only such as is good for edifying, as fits the occasion, that it may impart grace to those who hear. 30 And do not grieve the Holy Spirit of God, in whom you were sealed for the day of redemption. 31 Let all bitterness and wrath and anger and clamor and slander be put away from you, with all malice, 32 and be kind to one another, tenderhearted, forgiving one another, as God in Christ forgave you.

5 Therefore be imitators of God, as beloved children. 2And walk in love, as Christ loved us and gave himself up for us, a fragrant offering and sacrifice to God.

3 But fornication and all impurity or covetousness must not even be named among you, as is fitting among saints. 4 Let there be no filthiness, nor silly talk, nor levity, which are not fitting; but instead let there be thanksgiving. 5 Be sure of this, that no fornicator or impure man, or one who is covetous (that is, an idolater), has any inheritance in the kingdom of Christ and of God. 6 Let no one deceive you with empty words, for it is because of these things that the wrath of God comes upon the sons of disobedience. 7 Therefore do not associate with them, 8 for once you were darkness, but now you are light in the Lord; walk as children of light 9 (for the fruit of light is found in all that is good and right and true), 10 and try to learn what is pleasing to the Lord. 11 Take no part in the unfruitful works of darkness, but instead expose them. 12 For it is a shame even to speak of the things that they do in secret; 13 but when anything is exposed by the light it becomes visible, for anything that becomes visible is light. 14 Therefore it is said,

"Awake, O sleeper, and arise from the dead,
    and Christ shall give you light."

4.30 To grieve the Holy Spirit is to go counter to the will of the Third Person of the Trinity who dwells within us. Since He is holy, loving, true, and peaceable, sins of unholiness, lack of love, untruthfulness, and harshness grieve Him and interrupt fellowship with God. To grieve the Holy Spirit disturbs communion with Christ and results in the loss of the Spirit's fulness and power. Elsewhere we are commanded: *Do not quench the Spirit* (1 Thess 5.19). Heb 10.29 says some have *outraged the Spirit of grace.*

15 Look carefully then how you walk, not as unwise men but as wise, 16 making the most of the time, because the days are evil. 17 Therefore do not be foolish, but understand what the will of the Lord is. 18And do not get drunk with wine, for that is debauchery; but be filled with the Spirit, 19 addressing one another in psalms and hymns and spiritual songs, singing and making melody to the Lord with all your heart, 20 always and for everything giving thanks in the name of our Lord Jesus Christ to God the Father.

C. The Christian household

21 Be subject to one another out of reverence for Christ. 22 Wives, be subject to your husbands, as to the Lord. 23 For the husband is the head of the wife as Christ is the head of the church, his body, and is himself its Savior. 24As the church is subject to Christ, so let wives also be subject in everything to their husbands. 25 Husbands, love your wives, as Christ loved the church and gave himself up for her, 26 that he might sanctify her, having cleansed her by the washing of water with the word, 27 that he might present the church to himself in splendor, without spot or wrinkle or any such thing, that she might be holy and without blemish. 28 Even so husbands should love their wives as their own bodies. He who loves his wife loves himself. 29 For no man ever hates his own flesh, but nourishes and cherishes it, as Christ does the church, 30 because we are members of his body. 31 "For this reason a man shall leave his father and mother and be joined to his wife, and the two shall become one flesh." 32 This mystery is a profound one, and I am saying that it refers to Christ and the church; 33 however, let each one of you love his wife as himself, and let the wife see that she respects her husband.

6 Children, obey your parents in the Lord, for this is right. 2 "Honor your father and mother" (this is the first commandment with a promise), 3 "that it may be well with you and that you may live long on the earth." 4 Fathers, do not provoke your children to anger, but bring them up in the discipline and instruction of the Lord.

5 Slaves, be obedient to those who are your earthly masters, with fear and trembling, in singleness of heart, as to Christ; 6 not

Cross references

5.16 Col 4.5; Eph 6.13
5.17 Rom 12.2; 1 Thess 4.3
*5.18 Prov 20.1; Lk 1.15
5.19 Col 3.16; Acts 16.25
5.20 Ps 34.1; Heb 13.15
*5.22 Gen 3.16; Eph 6.5
5.23 1 Cor 11.3; Col 1.18; Eph 1.23
5.24 Col 3.18
*5.25 Col 3.19
5.26 Tit 3.5
5.27 Col 1.22; Eph 1.4
5.28 ver 25
5.30 1 Cor 6.15; Eph 1.23
5.31 Gen 2.24; Mt 19.5; 1 Cor 6.16
5.32 Col 3.19; 1 Pet 3.6
6.1 Col 3.20
6.2 Deut 5.16
6.4 Col 3.21; Gen 18.19
6.5 Col 3.22; 1 Tim 6.1; Phil 2.12; 1 Chr 29.17

5.18 All believers are sealed by the Holy Spirit when they are regenerated (1.13, 14); however, not all believers are filled with the Spirit but some remain in a carnal state, leading a defeated life (1 Cor 3.1). (A *permanent* carnal state is evidence of an unsaved condition, according to Rom 8.6.) Yet the goal and ideal of the Christian life is always to be filled and controlled by the Spirit. This may be attained by: (1) being cleansed from all known sin—a prerequisite to being Spirit-filled (1 Jn 1.7–9; 2 Cor 7.1); (2) surrendering or yielding of self to the full control of God without any reservation (Rom 12.1; 6.13); (3) believing that God will fill with His Spirit those who confess their sins and surrender themselves to Him (see Rom 4.20–22); (4) embracing by faith the fact that they have already been filled by the Spirit and conduct-

ing themselves accordingly when these prior conditions have been met. Sin alone can destroy this kind of life in the Spirit.
5.22 See note to Tit 2.4 on duties of wives to husbands and children.
5.25 This is the clearest passage in Scripture which sets forth the character of the church as the bride of Christ. Yet the marriage relationship analogy appears elsewhere in Scripture as typical of God and His people. Hosea refers to this principle in a negative way, decrying the spiritual adultery of Israel. Likewise John, in the Revelation, speaks of the New Jerusalem coming down out of heaven like a *bride* adorned for her husband. Christ Himself used the figure of the bridegroom in His teachings (Mt 25.1–13; Lk 5.34, 35; Mt 9.15). Also see note to 1 Cor 7.2 on the subject of husbands.

6.7
Col 3.23

in the way of eyeservice, as men-pleasers, but as servants[f] of Christ, doing the will of God from the heart, 7 rendering service with a good will as to the Lord and not to men, 8 knowing that whatever good any one does, he will receive the same again from the Lord, whether he is a slave or free. 9 Masters, do the same to them, and forbear threatening, knowing that he who is both their Master and yours is in heaven, and that there is no partiality with him.

6.9
Lev 25.43;
Jn 13.13;
Col 3.25

D. The church's warfare

6.10
1 Cor 16.13;
Eph 1.19
6.11
1 Cor 16.21
6.12
1 Cor 9.25;
Rom 8.38
6.13
2 Cor 10.4;
Eph 5.16
6.14
Isa 11.5;
59.17
6.15
Isa 52.7
6.16
1 Jn 5.4
6.17
Isa 59.17;
Heb 4.12
6.18
Lk 18.1;
Mt 26.41;
Phil 1.4
6.19
Acts 4.29;
2 Cor 3.12
6.20
2 Cor 5.20;
Phil 1.20

10 Finally, be strong in the Lord and in the strength of his might. 11 Put on the whole armor of God, that you may be able to stand against the wiles of the devil. 12 For we are not contending against flesh and blood, but against the principalities, against the powers, against the world rulers of this present darkness, against the spiritual hosts of wickedness in the heavenly places. 13 Therefore take the whole armor of God, that you may be able to withstand in the evil day, and having done all, to stand. 14 Stand therefore, having girded your loins with truth, and having put on the breastplate of righteousness, 15 and having shod your feet with the equipment of the gospel of peace; 16 besides all these, taking the shield of faith, with which you can quench all the flaming darts of the evil one. 17 And take the helmet of salvation, and the sword of the Spirit, which is the word of God. 18 Pray at all times in the Spirit, with all prayer and supplication. To that end keep alert with all perseverance, making supplication for all the saints, 19 and also for me, that utterance may be given me in opening my mouth boldly to proclaim the mystery of the gospel, 20 for which I am an ambassador in chains; that I may declare it boldly, as I ought to speak.

IV. Conclusion 6.21–23

6.21
Acts 20.4

21 Now that you also may know how I am and what I am doing, Tých′icŭs the beloved brother and faithful minister in the Lord will tell you everything. 22 I have sent him to you for this very purpose, that you may know how we are, and that he may encourage your hearts.

6.23
1 Pet 5.14;
Gal 5.6

23 Peace be to the brethren, and love with faith, from God the Father and the Lord Jesus Christ. 24 Grace be with all who love our Lord Jesus Christ with love undying.

f Or slaves

INTRODUCTION TO
THE LETTER OF PAUL TO THE
PHILIPPIANS

Authorship and Background: Paul wrote this letter while in prison (1.12–14, 17), so that Philippians is grouped with Colossians, Philemon, and Ephesians as a "Prison Epistle." The most widely held view is that all four letters were written during the two-year imprisonment in Rome (Acts 28.30), A.D. 59–61. The references to the praetorian guard (1.13) and to Caesar's household (4.22) seem to support Rome as the place of imprisonment. This is not indisputable, however, and some scholars believe that Caesarea, where Paul was in prison for two years (Acts 24.27), was the place of writing; others hold it was Ephesus, although there is no reference to an imprisonment there, unless 1 Cor 15.32 is taken quite literally. On the whole, Rome seems to fulfil the requirements of the prison epistles better, assuming they were all written in the same place.

The church at Philippi had sent a gift to Paul by Epaphroditus, their messenger (4.18), who fell sick in Rome; the news of his illness had caused considerable alarm in Philippi and made him all the more eager to return home (2.25–30). Paul, therefore, wrote this letter to his dear friends in Philippi, expressing his gratitude for their love and help.

Characteristics: Paul's ministry in Philippi is one of the most thrilling chapters in all of Christian missions (Acts 16.12–40). He came to this Roman colony in the province of Macedonia in response to a divine call on his second missionary tour (Acts 16.8–10). Years later he returned to Macedonia after leaving Ephesus on his third missionary tour (Acts 20.1); and once again on his way back to Syria (Acts 20.3–6). Of all the churches Paul had founded, none was so near and dear to him as the church at Philippi. The letter to the Philippians breathes an atmosphere of perfect love and mutual confidence; these were friends who had often helped Paul with their gifts (4.15, 16) and had not forgotten him now that he was in prison. Love and gratitude are everywhere expressed in the pages of this Christian love letter. Fourteen times in this short letter the words "joy" and "rejoice" occur; this hymn of joy could have been written only by one who had found Christ to be all-sufficient.

There were perils to be watched: enemies of the gospel within (3.2, 3, 18, 19) and without (1.27, 28) who must be withstood and defeated. There was the danger of self-seeking and pride, which could lead to harmful divisions (2.2–4; 4.2, 3). With deep affection and from a pastor's heart, Paul wrote his beloved Philippians in terms at once simple, direct, and overflowing with love and thanksgiving. The strictly theological affirmations receive less proportionate space in this letter than personal and practical matters. Here, however, is the most sublime and profound statement of the meaning of the Incarnation (2.5–11). Paul's own philosophy of life is nowhere better expressed than in the words of 1.21: "For to me to live is Christ, and to die is gain."

Introduction to Philippians

Contents:

THE LETTER OF PAUL TO THE
PHILIPPIANS

I. *Introduction 1.1–11*

A. *Salutation*

1 Paul and Timothy, servants*a* of Christ Jesus,
To all the saints in Christ Jesus who are at Phil′ippī, with the
bishops*b* and deacons:

2 Grace to you and peace from God our Father and the Lord
Jesus Christ.

1.1
2 Cor 1.1;
Acts 16.1;
1 Cor 1.2
1.2
1 Pet 1.2

B. *Thanksgiving and prayer*

3 I thank my God in all my remembrance of you, 4 always in
every prayer of mine for you all making my prayer with joy,
5 thankful for your partnership in the gospel from the first day
until now. 6And I am sure that he who began a good work in you
will bring it to completion at the day of Jesus Christ. 7 It is right
for me to feel thus about you all, because I hold you in my heart,
for you are all partakers with me of grace, both in my imprisonment and in the defense and confirmation of the gospel. 8 For God
is my witness, how I yearn for you all with the affection of Christ
Jesus. 9And it is my prayer that your love may abound more and
more, with knowledge and all discernment, 10 so that you may
approve what is excellent, and may be pure and blameless for the
day of Christ, 11 filled with the fruits of righteousness which come
through Jesus Christ, to the glory and praise of God.

1.3
1 Cor 1.4
1.4
Rom 1.9
1.5
Acts 2.42;
16,17
1.6
ver 10
1.7
2 Pet 1.13;
2 Cor 7.3;
ver 13,14,17
1.8
Rom 1.9;
Gal 1.20
1.9
1 Thess
3.12;
Col 1.9

II. *Paul's personal circumstances 1.12–30*

12 I want you to know, brethren, that what has happened to me
has really served to advance the gospel, 13 so that it has become
known throughout the whole praetor′iăn guard*c* and to all the rest
that my imprisonment is for Christ; 14 and most of the brethren
have been made confident in the Lord because of my imprisonment, and are much more bold to speak the word of God without
fear.

*1.13
Phil 4.22
1.14
ver 7

15 Some indeed preach Christ from envy and rivalry, but others
from good will. 16 The latter do it out of love, knowing that I am
put here for the defense of the gospel; 17 the former proclaim
Christ out of partisanship, not sincerely but thinking to afflict me
in my imprisonment. 18 What then? Only that in every way,
whether in pretense or in truth, Christ is proclaimed; and in that
I rejoice.

1.15
Phil 2.3
1.16
1 Cor 9.17;
ver 12
1.17
Phil 2.3

a Or *slaves*   *b* Or *overseers*   *c* Greek *in the whole praetorium*

1.13 The praetorian guard was a picked
group of soldiers, organized by Augustus in
2 B.C. and composed originally of nine or ten
thousand men. These guards were attached to
the Emperor's palace in Rome and to the
palaces of the provincial governors and procurators. The word here translated *praetorian
guard* is *praitōriŏn* (from Latin *praetorium*),
used of Pilate's palace in Jerusalem (Mt 27.27;
Mk 15.16; Jn 18.28, 33; 19.9) and of the
governor's official residence in Caesarea (cf.
note to Acts 23.35).

1.19
2 Cor 1.11

1.20
Rom 8.19;
5.5;
Eph 6.19

1.23
2 Cor 5.8;
2 Tim 4.6

1.26
2 Cor 1.14;
5.12
1.28
2 Thess 1.5;
Rom 8.17

1.29
Mt 5.12;
Acts 14.22
1.30
1 Thess 2.2;
Col 2.1;
Acts 16.19
2.1
2 Cor 13.14;
Col 3.12
2.2
Jn 3.29;
Rom 12.16;
1 Pet 3.8
2.3
Gal 5.26;
Rom 12.10;
1 Pet 5.5
2.4
Rom 15.1,2
2.5
Mt 11.29;
1 Pet 2.21
2.6
Jn 1.1;
2 Cor 4.4;
Jn 5.18
*2.7
Jn 1.14;
Gal 4.4;
Heb 2.17
2.8
Mt 26.39;
Jn 10.18;
Heb 5.8
2.9
Acts 2.33;
Heb 2.9;
Eph 1.20,21
2.10
Mt 28.18;
Rom 14.11
2.11
Jn 13.13;
Acts 2.36

19 Yes, and I shall rejoice. For I know that through your prayers and the help of the Spirit of Jesus Christ this will turn out for my deliverance, 20 as it is my eager expectation and hope that I shall not be at all ashamed, but that with full courage now as always Christ will be honored in my body, whether by life or by death. 21 For to me to live is Christ, and to die is gain. 22 If it is to be life in the flesh, that means fruitful labor for me. Yet which I shall choose I cannot tell. 23 I am hard pressed between the two. My desire is to depart and be with Christ, for that is far better. 24 But to remain in the flesh is more necessary on your account. 25 Convinced of this, I know that I shall remain and continue with you all, for your progress and joy in the faith, 26 so that in me you may have ample cause to glory in Christ Jesus, because of my coming to you again.

27 Only let your manner of life be worthy of the gospel of Christ, so that whether I come and see you or am absent, I may hear of you that you stand firm in one spirit, with one mind striving side by side for the faith of the gospel, 28 and not frightened in anything by your opponents. This is a clear omen to them of their destruction, but of your salvation, and that from God. 29 For it has been granted to you that for the sake of Christ you should not only believe in him but also suffer for his sake, 30 engaged in the same conflict which you saw and now hear to be mine.

III. The Christian life 2.1–18

A. Christ our model

2 So if there is any encouragement in Christ, any incentive of love, any participation in the Spirit, any affection and sympathy, 2 complete my joy by being of the same mind, having the same love, being in full accord and of one mind. 3 Do nothing from selfishness or conceit, but in humility count others better than yourselves. 4 Let each of you look not only to his own interests, but also to the interests of others. 5 Have this mind among yourselves, which is yours in Christ Jesus, 6 who, though he was in the form of God, did not count equality with God a thing to be grasped, 7 but emptied himself, taking the form of a servant,[d] being born in the likeness of men. 8And being found in human form he humbled himself and became obedient unto death, even death on a cross. 9 Therefore God has highly exalted him and bestowed on him the name which is above every name, 10 that at the name of Jesus every knee should bow, in heaven and on earth and under the earth, 11 and every tongue confess that Jesus Christ is Lord, to the glory of God the Father.

d Or slave

2.7 "Kenosis" is the theological name often used in connection with Christ's incarnation. He "emptied himself" or "stripped himself" or "divested himself" of His divine powers and prerogatives as God the Son when He took upon Himself *the form of a servant*. He assumed the human limitations inherent in His becoming a true human being. It was a voluntary, self-imposed limitation. Christ in human form was both God and man—two distinct natures united in one person. Yet Scripture does not make clear the full implications of the kenosis. There are aspects of mystery connected with it which the minds of finite men are not able to fathom. (See also the following Scriptures associated with the kenosis: 2 Cor 8.9; Mt 27.46; Mk 13.32; Jn 17.4; Lk 2.40–52; Heb 4.15; 5.7, 8.)

B. Obligations of Christians

12 Therefore, my beloved, as you have always obeyed, so now, not only as in my presence but much more in my absence, work out your own salvation with fear and trembling; 13 for God is at work in you, both to will and to work for his good pleasure.

14 Do all things without grumbling or questioning, 15 that you may be blameless and innocent, children of God without blemish in the midst of a crooked and perverse generation, among whom you shine as lights in the world, 16 holding fast the word of life, so that in the day of Christ I may be proud that I did not run in vain or labor in vain. 17 Even if I am to be poured as a libation upon the sacrificial offering of your faith, I am glad and rejoice with you all. 18 Likewise you also should be glad and rejoice with me.

IV. The coming of Timothy and Epaphroditus 2.19–29

19 I hope in the Lord Jesus to send Timothy to you soon, so that I may be cheered by news of you. 20 I have no one like him, who will be genuinely anxious for your welfare. 21 They all look after their own interests, not those of Jesus Christ. 22 But Timothy's worth you know, how as a son with a father he has served with me in the gospel. 23 I hope therefore to send him just as soon as I see how it will go with me; 24 and I trust in the Lord that shortly I myself shall come also.

25 I have thought it necessary to send to you Ĕpăphrŏdī'tŭs my brother and fellow worker and fellow soldier, and your messenger and minister to my need, 26 for he has been longing for you all, and has been distressed because you heard that he was ill. 27 Indeed he was ill, near to death. But God had mercy on him, and not only on him but on me also, lest I should have sorrow upon sorrow. 28 I am the more eager to send him, therefore, that you may rejoice at seeing him again, and that I may be less anxious. 29 So receive him in the Lord with all joy; and honor such men, 30 for he nearly died for the work of Christ, risking his life to complete your service to me.

V. Exhortation and doctrine 3.1–4.9

A. The example of Paul

3 Finally, my brethren, rejoice in the Lord. To write the same things to you is not irksome to me, and is safe for you.

2 Look out for the dogs, look out for the evil-workers, look out for those who mutilate the flesh. 3 For we are the true circumcision, who worship God in spirit,*e* and glory in Christ Jesus, and

e Other ancient authorities read *worship by the Spirit of God*

*2.12f
Phil 1.5;
Eph 6.5
2.13
2 Cor 3.5
2.14
1 Cor 10.10;
Rom 14.1
2.15
Mt 5.45;
Eph 5.1;
5.8
2.16
2 Cor 1.14;
1 Thess 2.19
2.17
2 Tim 4.6;
Rom 15.16;
Col 1.24
2.19
Rom 16.21
2.20
1 Cor 16.10
2.21
1 Cor 10.24;
13.5
2.22
1 Cor 4.17;
1 Tim 1.2
2.24
Phil 1.25
2.25
Phil 4.18;
Philem 2
2.26
Phil 1.8
2.29
1 Cor 16.18;
1 Tim 5.17
2.30
1 Cor 16.17
3.1
Phil 4.4
3.2
Gal 5.15;
2 Cor 11.13
3.3
Rom 2.28,
29;
Gal 6.14,15

2.12, 13 Paul here stresses both the free agency of man and the absolute sovereignty of God. He urges the Philippians to work out their own salvation as though they were fully responsible and capable of good by their own exertions. In the next breath he adds, *for God is at work in you . . . for his good pleasure* as though the responsibility were all God's. Both man's free agency and God's unlimited sovereignty are firmly stressed, paradoxical though this may be. Actually, however, these two verses may be brought into harmony by recognizing that because God is at work in believers, and God's grace is available, believers are able to achieve the purposes for which God has saved them (cf. Eph 2.10).

put no confidence in the flesh. 4 Though I myself have reason for confidence in the flesh also. If any other man thinks he has reason for confidence in the flesh, I have more: 5 circumcised on the eighth day, of the people of Israel, of the tribe of Benjamin, a Hebrew born of Hebrews; as to the law a Phạr′iseē, 6 as to zeal a persecutor of the church, as to righteousness under the law blameless. 7 But whatever gain I had, I counted as loss for the sake of Christ. 8 Indeed I count everything as loss because of the surpassing worth of knowing Christ Jesus my Lord. For his sake I have suffered the loss of all things, and count them as refuse, in order that I may gain Christ 9 and be found in him, not having a righteousness of my own, based on law, but that which is through faith in Christ, the righteousness from God that depends on faith; 10 that I may know him and the power of his resurrection, and may share his sufferings, becoming like him in his death, 11 that if possible I may attain the resurrection from the dead.

12 Not that I have already obtained this or am already perfect; but I press on to make it my own, because Christ Jesus has made me his own. 13 Brethren, I do not consider that I have made it my own; but one thing I do, forgetting what lies behind and straining forward to what lies ahead, 14 I press on toward the goal for the prize of the upward call of God in Christ Jesus. 15 Let those of us who are mature be thus minded; and if in anything you are otherwise minded, God will reveal that also to you. 16 Only let us hold true to what we have attained.

B. Warning against antinomianism

17 Brethren, join in imitating me, and mark those who so live as you have an example in us. 18 For many, of whom I have often told you and now tell you even with tears, live as enemies of the cross of Christ. 19 Their end is destruction, their god is the belly, and they glory in their shame, with minds set on earthly things. 20 But our commonwealth is in heaven, and from it we await a Savior, the Lord Jesus Christ, 21 who will change our lowly body to be like his glorious body, by the power which enables him even to subject all things to himself.

C. Exhortation concluded

4 Therefore, my brethren, whom I love and long for, my joy and crown, stand firm thus in the Lord, my beloved.

2 I entreat Eū-ō′dĭă and I entreat Sўn′tўchë to agree in the Lord. 3 And I ask you also, true yokefellow, help these women, for they have labored side by side with me in the gospel together with Clement and the rest of my fellow workers, whose names are in the book of life.

3.5
Rom 11.1;
2 Cor 11.22
3.6
Acts 22.3;
Rom 10.5;
Lk 1.6
3.7
Mt 13.44;
Lk 14.33
3.8
Eph 4.13;
2 Pet 1.3
3.9
Rom 10.5;
9.30
3.10
Rom 6.3–5;
8.17
3.11
Acts 26.7
3.12
1 Tim 6.12;
1 Cor 13.10;
Acts 9.5,6
3.13
Lk 9.62;
1 Cor 9.24
3.14
Heb 6.1;
2 Tim 1.9
3.15
1 Cor 2.6;
Gal 5.10
3.16
Rom 12.16;
Gal 6.16
3.17
1 Cor 4.16;
1 Pet 5.3
3.18
Acts 20.31;
Gal 6.14
3.19
2 Cor 11.15;
Rom 16.18;
6.21; 8.5,6
★**3.20**
Eph 2.19;
Col 3.1;
1 Cor 1.7
3.21
1 Cor 15.43;
Col 3.4;
Eph 1.19
4.1
Phil 1.8;
1 Cor 16.13;
Phil 1.27
4.2
Phil 2.2
4.3
Rom 16.3;
Lk 10.20;
Rev 3.5

3.20 The true commonwealth or citizenship (*politeuma*) of the believer is in heaven. The world is not the believer's spiritual home, for it is impermanent and dominated by Satan, whereas heaven obeys the rule of God and endures forever. The normal attitude of the believer who is in this world but not of it, is to look for the coming of the Lord to celebrate His triumph over the powers of evil and perfect His work of redemption. The Christian rejoices in the prospect of living in the glory of Christ's presence, and of enjoying the bliss and delight of heaven's eternal home.

At the same time, one should neither overlook nor underestimate the present and effective Lordship of Christ over all things.

4 Rejoice in the Lord always; again I will say, Rejoice. 5 Let all men know your forbearance. The Lord is at hand. 6 Have no anxiety about anything, but in everything by prayer and supplication with thanksgiving let your requests be made known to God. 7And the peace of God, which passes all understanding, will keep your hearts and your minds in Christ Jesus.

8 Finally, brethren, whatever is true, whatever is honorable, whatever is just, whatever is pure, whatever is lovely, whatever is gracious, if there is any excellence, if there is anything worthy of praise, think about these things. 9 What you have learned and received and heard and seen in me, do; and the God of peace will be with you.

VI. *Acknowledgment of the Philippian gift 4.10–20*

10 I rejoice in the Lord greatly that now at length you have revived your concern for me; you were indeed concerned for me, but you had no opportunity. 11 Not that I complain of want; for I have learned, in whatever state I am, to be content. 12 I know how to be abased, and I know how to abound; in any and all circumstances I have learned the secret of facing plenty and hunger, abundance and want. 13 I can do all things in him who strengthens me.

14 Yet it was kind of you to share my trouble. 15And you Philíp'-piăns yourselves know that in the beginning of the gospel, when I left Măçĕdō'nĭă, no church entered into partnership with me in giving and receiving except you only; 16 for even in Thĕssălŏnī'că you sent me help*f* once and again. 17 Not that I seek the gift; but I seek the fruit which increases to your credit. 18 I have received full payment, and more; I am filled, having received from Ĕpăphrŏdī'tŭs the gifts you sent, a fragrant offering, a sacrifice acceptable and pleasing to God. 19And my God will supply every need of yours according to his riches in glory in Christ Jesus. 20 To our God and Father be glory for ever and ever. Amen.

VII. *Conclusion 4.21–23*

21 Greet every saint in Christ Jesus. The brethren who are with me greet you. 22All the saints greet you, especially those of Caesar's household.
23 The grace of the Lord Jesus Christ be with your spirit.

f Other ancient authorities read *money for my needs*

4.4
Rom 12.12;
Phil 3.1
4.5
Heb 10.37;
Jas 5.8,9
★**4.6**
Mt 6.25;
Eph 6.18
4.7
Jn 14.27;
Col 3.15;
1 Pet 1.5
4.8
1 Pet 2.12;
1 Thess 5.22
4.9
Phil 3.17;
Rom 15.33

4.11
1 Tim 6.6
4.12
1 Cor 4.11;
2 Cor 11.9
4.13
Jn 15.5;
2 Cor 12.9
4.14
Phil 1.7
4.15
2 Cor 11.8,9
4.16
Acts 17.1;
1 Thess 2.9
4.17
Tit 3.14
4.18
Phil 2.25;
2 Cor 2.14
4.19
Ps 23.1;
2 Cor 9.8;
Eph 1.7
4.20
Gal 1.4;
Rom 11.36

4.6 Believers are to pray with thanksgiving for the perfect answer they know God will give them in response to their petitions. Prayerlessness is sure to bring about growing anxiety and a sense of insecurity. To be anxious about nothing excludes everything. To pray about everything excludes nothing. But effective prayer must be accompanied by thanksgiving, which means that we thank God for the answer as soon as we have asked. This kind of prayer brings peace, a peace which passes natural human understanding because it is independent of circumstances and rests upon the perfection and love of God Himself.

INTRODUCTION TO
THE LETTER OF PAUL TO THE
COLOSSIANS

Authorship and Background: In writing to the Colossians, Paul addressed a group he did not know personally (2.1). Colossae was located in the Lycus valley, in the province of Asia, some one hundred miles east of the capital city of Ephesus; the city was close to Laodicea and Hierapolis, and the three were often associated together (4.13, 15, 16; 2.1). Colossae had at one time been the most important of the three cities but it had declined.

Paul was in prison (4.3, 18) and the personal references indicate that the letter was written at the same time as the letter to Philemon. These, with Philippians and Ephesians, are the four "Prison Epistles" composed in Rome, A.D. 59–61 (cf. the introductions to Ephesians and Philippians). The same names appear in Colossians and Philemon: Archippus (Col 4.17; Philem 2) and Onesimus (Col 4.9; Philem 10); Aristarchus, Mark, Epaphras, Luke, and Demas (Col 4.10, 12, 14; Philem 23–24). Timothy is associated with Paul in the writing of Philippians (1.1), Colossians (1.1), and Philemon (1).

Colossians was written to counteract some erroneous and dangerous teaching; doubtless, Paul heard of this from Epaphras, leader of the work in the three cities, who had come to see him (1.7, 8; 4.12, 13; cf. Philem 23). This teaching was related to some form of Gnosticism. Formulated in a Jewish framework, it deprived Jesus Christ of his unique status as the Son of God and Savior, and reduced Him to only one, albeit in an exalted place, of a series of created divine beings emanating in a graduated scale from the Godhead, through which creation and God were joined. Paul feared that asceticism, magical rites, and worship of heavenly bodies, all derived from the Gnostic dualism, would reduce Christianity to another religious philosophy, preliminary and inferior to the real "knowledge" of the Gnostic philosophy. The precise form of this Colossian heresy has long since passed away.

Characteristics: Paul met this dangerous heresy by proclaiming the uniqueness and complete sufficiency of Jesus Christ as the only Savior of all: He is the image of the invisible God, God's first-born who existed prior to all creation, and who was the agent in creation, through whom all created things, in heaven and on earth, came into being; He is the source, the controlling power, and the goal of all creation. In Him alone is the whole of the Godhead to be found—not dispersed through a series of divine and semi-divine beings. This being so, the Colossians are to reject any system that would belittle the person of Christ, and stand fast in the faith, holding to the hope contained in the gospel. They must reject fanciful teachings having to do with food, drink, festivals, and misplaced asceticism. In Christ they have been raised to newness of life, and in Him all grace and virtues are to be found. Hold fast to Him who is the source of life and spiritual growth!

Contents:

THE LETTER OF PAUL TO THE

COLOSSIANS

I. Introduction 1.1–14

A. Salutation

1.1
Eph 1.1

1 Paul, an apostle of Christ Jesus by the will of God, and Timothy our brother,

1.2
Rom 1.7

2 To the saints and faithful brethren in Christ at Cŏlŏs′saē: Grace to you and peace from God our Father.

B. Thanksgiving

1.3
Eph 1.16
1.4
Eph 1.15;
Gal 5.6
1.5
1 Thess 5.8;
1 Pet 1.4
1.6
Mt 24.14;
Jn 15.16
*1.7
Philem 23;
Col 4.7
1.8
Rom 15.30

3 We always thank God, the Father of our Lord Jesus Christ, when we pray for you, 4 because we have heard of your faith in Christ Jesus and of the love which you have for all the saints, 5 because of the hope laid up for you in heaven. Of this you have heard before in the word of the truth, the gospel 6 which has come to you, as indeed in the whole world it is bearing fruit and growing —so among yourselves, from the day you heard and understood the grace of God in truth, 7 as you learned it from Ĕp′áphrás our beloved fellow servant. He is a faithful minister of Christ on our[a] behalf 8 and has made known to us your love in the Spirit.

C. Apostolic prayer

1.9
Eph 1.15–
17;
Rom 12.2
1.10
Eph 4.1;
1 Thess 4.1;
Rom 1.13
1.11
Eph 3.16;
4.2;
Acts 5.41
1.12
Eph 5.20;
1.11
1.13
Eph 6.12;
2 Pet 1.11

9 And so, from the day we heard of it, we have not ceased to pray for you, asking that you may be filled with the knowledge of his will in all spiritual wisdom and understanding, 10 to lead a life worthy of the Lord, fully pleasing to him, bearing fruit in every good work and increasing in the knowledge of God. 11 May you be strengthened with all power, according to his glorious might, for all endurance and patience with joy, 12 giving thanks to the Father, who has qualified us[b] to share in the inheritance of the saints in light. 13 He has delivered us from the dominion of darkness and transferred us to the kingdom of his beloved Son, 14 in whom we have redemption, the forgiveness of sins.

II. Christian doctrine 1.15–3.4

A. The person and work of Christ

1.15
2 Cor 4.4;
Rev 3.14
1.16
Heb 1.2;
Eph 1.20,
21;
Heb 2.10

15 He is the image of the invisible God, the first-born of all creation; 16 for in him all things were created, in heaven and on earth, visible and invisible, whether thrones or dominions or principalities or authorities— all things were created through him

---

a Other ancient authorities read *your*   *b* Other ancient authorities read *you*

1.7 *Epaphras* is mentioned also in 4.12 and Philem 23. Like Timothy, he is called a *fellow servant* of Jesus Christ by Paul. (This term really means "bond-servant," from the Greek word *doulos*.) He seems to have been an evangelist and perhaps even the founder of the church of Colossae. He was with Paul during part of his first Roman imprisonment and may even have been imprisoned with him as a co-defendant. No higher tribute could be paid him than that expressed in the words of Paul here: *He is a faithful minister of Christ.*

and for him. 17 He is before all things, and in him all things hold together. 18 He is the head of the body, the church; he is the beginning, the first-born from the dead, that in everything he might be pre-eminent. 19 For in him all the fulness of God was pleased to dwell, 20 and through him to reconcile to himself all things, whether on earth or in heaven, making peace by the blood of his cross.

21 And you, who once were estranged and hostile in mind, doing evil deeds, 22 he has now reconciled in his body of flesh by his death, in order to present you holy and blameless and irreproachable before him, 23 provided that you continue in the faith, stable and steadfast, not shifting from the hope of the gospel which you heard, which has been preached to every creature under heaven, and of which I, Paul, became a minister.

B. The ministry of Paul

24 Now I rejoice in my sufferings for your sake, and in my flesh I complete what is lacking in Christ's afflictions for the sake of his body, that is, the church, 25 of which I became a minister according to the divine office which was given to me for you, to make the word of God fully known, 26 the mystery hidden for ages and generations[c] but now made manifest to his saints. 27 To them God chose to make known how great among the Gentiles are the riches of the glory of this mystery, which is Christ in you, the hope of glory. 28 Him we proclaim, warning every man and teaching every man in all wisdom, that we may present every man mature in Christ. 29 For this I toil, striving with all the energy which he mightily inspires within me.

C. Paul's concern for them

2 For I want you to know how greatly I strive for you, and for those at Lā'-ŏdĭçē'á, and for all who have not seen my face, 2 that their hearts may be encouraged as they are knit together in love, to have all the riches of assured understanding and the knowledge of God's mystery, of Christ, 3 in whom are hid all the treasures of wisdom and knowledge. 4 I say this in order that no one may delude you with beguiling speech. 5 For though I am absent in body, yet I am with you in spirit, rejoicing to see your good order and the firmness of your faith in Christ.

c Or from angels and men

1.17 Jn 1.1; 8.58
1.18 Eph 1.22, 23; Rev 1.5
1.19 Jn 1.16
1.20 2 Cor 5.18; Eph 2.13,14
1.21 Rom 5.10; Eph 2.3
★1.22 Rom 7.4; Eph 2.15; 5.27
1.23 Eph 3.17; Rom 10.18
1.25 Eph 3.2
1.26 Eph 3.3,4
★1.27 2 Cor 2.14; Rom 9.23; 1 Tim 1.1
1.28 Col 3.16; 1 Cor 2.6,7
1.29 1 Cor 15.10; Col 2.1; Eph 1.19
2.1 Col 1.29; 4.12
★2.2 Phil 3.8
2.3 Isa 45.3; Rom 11.33
2.5 1 Thess 2.17; 1 Cor 14.40; 1 Pet 5.9

1.22 Holiness is commanded by God (Lev 20.7) and has been made attainable by Him (Rom 6.22). It does not imply sinless perfection (1 Jn 1.8), but a condition wherein the believer is wholly yielded to God's will and set apart for His service. When the believer's conscience is kept clear before God by repentance and self-dedication, then his heart does not condemn him. Two erroneous notions are prevalent in relation to holiness. The first is that the believer *must* sin and the second that he *cannot* sin. The correct view is that the believer *can* sin but he *need not* do so.
1.27 Union with Christ is twofold: (1) it includes all believers who are partakers of the divine nature and members of His body through faith (Eph 3.17; Col 1.27), a union which is maintained by faith (Eph 3.17) as we feed on Him (Jn 6.56) and as His word abides in us (Jn 15.7); (2) it involves abiding in Him for the purpose of growth in grace and fruitfulness.
2.2 Christ is God's mystery. But Paul uses the term *mystery* here not in the sense of a continuing secret, but in the sense that that which was hidden has been disclosed; and it is God's intention for us to grasp, as fully as we are capable of grasping, all that He has revealed to us about the person and the work of Jesus Christ.

2.6
1 Thess 4.1
2.7
Eph 2.21

2.8
1 Cor 8.9;
1 Tim 6.20;
Gal 4.3
2.9
Jn 1.14;
Col 1.19
2.10
Eph 1.21,22
*2.11f
Rom 2.29;
Phil 3.3;
Rom 6.6;
Gal 5.24
2.12
Rom 6.4,5;
Acts 2.24
2.13
Eph 2.1
2.14
Eph 2.15
2.15
Gen 3.15;
Isa 53.12;
Eph 6.12

2.16
Rom 14.3;
14.17;14.5;
Gal 4.10,11
2.17
Heb 8.5
2.18
Phil 3.14;
ver 23
2.19
Eph 1.22;
4.16
*2.20
Rom 6.3,5;
Gal 4.3,9
2.22
1 Cor 6.13;
Isa 29.13;
Tit 1.14

6 As therefore you received Christ Jesus the Lord, so live in him, 7 rooted and built up in him and established in the faith, just as you were taught, abounding in thanksgiving.

D. The sufficiency of Christ

8 See to it that no one makes a prey of you by philosophy and empty deceit, according to human tradition, according to the elemental spirits of the universe, and not according to Christ. 9 For in him the whole fulness of deity dwells bodily, 10 and you have come to fulness of life in him, who is the head of all rule and authority. 11 In him also you were circumcised with a circumcision made without hands, by putting off the body of flesh in the circumcision of Christ; 12 and you were buried with him in baptism, in which you were also raised with him through faith in the working of God, who raised him from the dead. 13And you, who were dead in trespasses and the uncircumcision of your flesh, God made alive together with him, having forgiven us all our trespasses, 14 having canceled the bond which stood against us with its legal demands; this he set aside, nailing it to the cross. 15 He disarmed the principalities and powers and made a public example of them, triumphing over them in him.*d*

E. Asceticism and ritual condemned

16 Therefore let no one pass judgment on you in questions of food and drink or with regard to a festival or a new moon or a sabbath. 17 These are only a shadow of what is to come; but the substance belongs to Christ. 18 Let no one disqualify you, insisting on self-abasement and worship of angels, taking his stand on visions, puffed up without reason by his sensuous mind, 19 and not holding fast to the Head, from whom the whole body, nourished and knit together through its joints and ligaments, grows with a growth that is from God.

20 If with Christ you died to the elemental spirits of the universe, why do you live as if you still belonged to the world? Why do you submit to regulations, 21 "Do not handle, Do not taste, Do not touch" 22 (referring to things which all perish as they are

d Or *in it* (that is, the cross)

2.11, 12 These verses have assumed major importance in the discussion of infant-baptism. Paedobaptists understand them to signify that New Testament water baptism has replaced Old Testament circumcision as the sign and seal of admission into the covenant of grace. Therefore, since God ordained circumcision for the infant children of Israelites (Gen 17.12), baptism also is properly applied to the infants of New Testament believers. On the other hand, opponents of this view feel that the connection here made between circumcision and baptism is merely spiritual and should not be pressed to decide who are the proper subjects of baptism. They also take the phrase "buried in baptism" as indicating immersion to be the proper mode of administering the ordinance. Paedobaptists, however, understand this phrase as referring to the spiritual efficacy of baptism (since a believer by faith is united with Christ both in His death and in His Resurrection), and as having nothing to do with the mode.

2.20 This passage agrees with the Book of Hebrews in teaching that the ceremonial and ritual commandments of the Old Testament dispensation are no longer binding upon believers. The Mosaic code, with its minute prescriptions, replete with symbol and type, is referred to as mere *elements* (so translate *stoicheia* here, rather than the rendering *elemental spirits*) which were meant for the training of God's people in their immature stage before Christ's coming. But under the New Covenant, the laws of blood sacrifice, the dietary prohibitions, and so on, are to be followed no longer, since they were only shadows pointing forward to Jesus of Nazareth.

used), according to human precepts and doctrines? 23 These have indeed an appearance of wisdom in promoting rigor of devotion and self-abasement and severity to the body, but they are of no value in checking the indulgence of the flesh.*

F. The true locus of the Christian life

3 If then you have been raised with Christ, seek the things that are above, where Christ is, seated at the right hand of God. 2 Set your minds on things that are above, not on things that are on earth. 3 For you have died, and your life is hid with Christ in God. 4 When Christ who is our life appears, then you also will appear with him in glory.

III. The Christian life 3.5—4.6

A. The transformed walk

5 Put to death therefore what is earthly in you: fornication, impurity, passion, evil desire, and covetousness, which is idolatry. 6 On account of these the wrath of God is coming.ᶠ 7 In these you once walked, when you lived in them. 8 But now put them all away: anger, wrath, malice, slander, and foul talk from your mouth. 9 Do not lie to one another, seeing that you have put off the old nature with its practices 10 and have put on the new nature, which is being renewed in knowledge after the image of its creator. 11 Here there cannot be Greek and Jew, circumcised and uncircumcised, barbarian, Scỹth'ĭăn, slave, free man, but Christ is all, and in all.

12 Put on then, as God's chosen ones, holy and beloved, compassion, kindness, lowliness, meekness, and patience. 13 forbearing one another and, if one has a complaint against another, forgiving each other; as the Lord has forgiven you, so you also must forgive. 14 And above all these put on love, which binds everything together in perfect harmony. 15 And let the peace of Christ rule in your hearts, to which indeed you were called in the one body. And be thankful. 16 Let the word of Christ dwell in you richly, teach and admonish one another in all wisdom, and sing psalms and hymns and spiritual songs with thankfulness in your hearts to God. 17 And whatever you do, in word or deed, do everything in the name of the Lord Jesus, giving thanks to God the Father through him.

B. The Christian family

18 Wives, be subject to your husbands, as is fitting in the Lord. 19 Husbands, love your wives, and do not be harsh with them. 20 Children, obey your parents in everything, for this pleases the Lord. 21 Fathers, do not provoke your children, lest they become discouraged. 22 Slaves, obey in everything those who are your earthly masters, not with eyeservice, as men-pleasers, but in singleness of heart, fearing the Lord. 23 Whatever your task, work heartily, as serving the Lord and not men, 24 knowing that from

2.23	Rom 13.14; 1 Tim 4.8
3.1	Ps 110.1; Rom 8.34
3.2	Phil 3.19,20
3.3	Rom 6.2; 2 Cor 5.14
3.4	1 Jn 3.2; Jn 14.6
3.5	Rom 6.13; Eph 5.3,5
3.6	Rom 1.18; Eph 5.6
3.7	Eph 2.2
3.8	Eph 4.22,29
3.9	Eph 4.25; 4.22
3.10	Rom 12.2; Eph 4.23; 2.10
3.11	Gal 3.28; Eph 1.23
3.12	Gal 5.22,23; Phil 2.3; 2 Cor 6.6
3.13	Eph 4.2,32
3.14	Eph 4.3
3.15	Phil 4.7; 1 Cor 7.15; Eph 4.4
3.16	Eph 5.19
3.17	1 Cor 10.31; Eph 5.20
3.18	Eph 5.22– 6.9
3.19	Eph 5.25
3.20	Eph 6.1
3.21	Eph 6.4
3.22	Eph 6.5,6; Philem 16
3.24	Eph 6.8; 1 Cor 7.22

e Or are of no value, serving only to indulge the flesh
f Other ancient authorities add upon the sons of disobedience

the Lord you will receive the inheritance as your reward; you are
serving the Lord Christ. 25 For the wrongdoer will be paid back
for the wrong he has done, and there is no partiality.

4 Masters, treat your slaves justly and fairly, knowing that you
also have a Master in heaven.

C. Prayer

2 Continue steadfastly in prayer, being watchful in it with
thanksgiving; 3 and pray for us also, that God may open to us a
door for the word, to declare the mystery of Christ, on account of
which I am in prison, 4 that I may make it clear, as I ought to
speak.

D. Conduct

5 Conduct yourselves wisely toward outsiders, making the most
of the time. 6 Let your speech always be gracious, seasoned with
salt, so that you may know how you ought to answer every one.

IV. Conclusion 4.7–18

A. Regarding Tychicus and Onesimus

7 Tých′ĭcŭs will tell you all about my affairs; he is a beloved
brother and faithful minister and fellow servant in the Lord. 8 I
have sent him to you for this very purpose, that you may know
how we are and that he may encourage your hearts, 9 and with him
Onĕs′ĭmŭs, the faithful and beloved brother, who is one of yourselves. They will tell you of everything that has taken place here.

B. Greetings from friends and final instructions

10 Arĭstar′chŭs my fellow prisoner greets you, and Mark the
cousin of Bar′nàbàs (concerning whom you have received instructions—if he comes to you, receive him), 11 and Jesus who is called
Jŭstŭs. These are the only men of the circumcision among my
fellow workers for the kingdom of God, and they have been a
comfort to me. 12 Ĕp′áphràs, who is one of yourselves, a servantᵍ
of Christ Jesus, greets you, always remembering you earnestly in
his prayers, that you may stand mature and fully assured in all the
will of God. 13 For I bear him witness that he has worked hard for
you and for those in Lā′-ŏdĭçē′á and in Hī-ĕràp′ŏlĭs. 14 Luke the
beloved physician and Dēmàs greet you. 15 Give my greetings to
the brethren at Lā′-ŏdĭçē′á, and to Nŷmphà and the church in
her house. 16And when this letter has been read among you, have
it read also in the church of the Lā′-ŏdĭçē′àns; and see that you
read also the letter from Lā′-ŏdĭçē′á. 17And say to Arçhĭp′pŭs, "See
that you fulfil the ministry which you have received in the Lord."

18 I, Paul, write this greeting with my own hand. Remember
my fetters. Grace be with you.

g Or *slave*

3.25
Eph 6.8,9;
Acts 10.34
4.1
Lev 25.43,
53;
Eph 6.9

4.2
Rom 12.12;
Eph 6.18;
Phil 2.7
4.3
Eph 6.19;
1 Cor 16.9;
Eph 6.20

4.5
Eph 5.15,16
4.6
Eph 4.29;
Mk 9.50;
1 Pet 3.15

4.7
Eph 6.21,22

4.9
Philem 10

4.10
Acts 19.29;
15.37; 4.36
4.11
Acts 11.2;
Rom 16.3
4.12
Col 1.7;
Rom 15.30;
Phil 3.15
4.13
Col 2.1
4.14
2 Tim 4.10,
11;
Philem 24
4.15
Rom 16.5
4.17
Philem 2;
2 Tim 4.5
4.18
1 Cor 16.21;
Heb 13.3;
13.25

INTRODUCTION TO
THE FIRST LETTER OF PAUL TO THE
THESSALONIANS

Authorship and Background: Paul's two letters to the church at Thessalonica are, in the opinion of most scholars, among the earliest he wrote. Although the letters themselves afford no conclusive evidence as to place and time of writing, it would appear from Acts that they were written during the latter part of Paul's stay in Corinth (A.D. 49–51) on his second missionary tour. Paul arrived in Corinth alone (cf. Introduction to 1 Cor), after his ministry in Thessalonica, Beroea, and Athens (Acts 17.1—18.1). It seems that Timothy, at least, had joined Paul earlier in Athens and had been sent to Thessalonica (3.1, 2), although Acts does not mention this. In Corinth, then, Timothy and Silas joined Paul (Acts 18.5; 1 Thess 3.6); upon receipt of news from Thessalonica, Paul wrote the church there, associating both Silas and Timothy with himself in writing the letters (1.1; 2 Thess 1.1).

Thessalonica was the capital of the Roman province of Macedonia. It was a free city, ruled by its own magistrates, called "politarchs" (city authorities) (Acts 17.6, 8). Paul came to Thessalonica from Philippi on his second missionary tour (Acts 17.1–10). Acts speaks of a three-week ministry in the synagogue there (Acts 17.2), but it would seem from Paul's references to the Christians there as Gentiles (1.9; 2.14; cf. also "many of the devout Greeks" in Acts 17.4) and other references (cf. 2.9; 2 Thess 3.8; Phil 4.16), that the synagogue preaching was only the beginning of Paul's ministry in the city. How long he stayed is a matter of conjecture; perhaps for several months. The implacable hatred of the Thessalonian Jews and their persecutions (Acts 17.5) caused him to leave Thessalonica for Beroea (Acts 17.10), and then Athens (Acts 17.13–15). It would seem from the reference to Macedonia in Acts 20.1, 3 that Paul visited Thessalonica on his return to Jerusalem at the end of his third missionary tour in A.D. 56.

The following Christians from Thessalonica are known by name: Jason (Acts 17.5–9), Aristarchus (Acts 19.29; 20.4), Secundus (Acts 20.4; 27.2), and Gaius (Acts 19.29).

Characteristics: Timothy brought news to Paul about the Thessalonian church. The letter deals with special problems, particularly the Second Coming of Christ. Paul's love for the Christians at Thessalonica is evident from the personal references to their steadfast faith (1.3–10; 2.14; 3.6–9) and his lament at his inability to return (2.17–20). He shows concern for their spiritual welfare, warning them to order their lives worthy of Christians in relation to the immoral society in which they lived, and in Christian fellowship with one another (4.9–12; 5.5–22). He is especially concerned lest their misunderstanding about the Lord's return lead them to err in deed and doctrine (4.13—5.11).

Contents:

THE FIRST LETTER OF PAUL TO THE

THESSALONIANS

I. *Personal matters 1.1–3.13*

A. *Salutation*

1 Paul, Sïlvā′nŭs, and Timothy,
To the church of the Thĕssălō′nĭăns in God the Father and the Lord Jesus Christ:
Grace to you and peace.

*1.1
2 Thess 1.1;
2 Cor 1.19;
Acts 16.1;
17.1;
Rom 1.7

B. *Thanksgiving for them*

2 We give thanks to God always for you all, constantly mentioning you in our prayers, 3 remembering before our God and Father your work of faith and labor of love and steadfastness of hope in our Lord Jesus Christ. 4 For we know, brethren beloved by God, that he has chosen you; 5 for our gospel came to you not only in word, but also in power and in the Holy Spirit and with full conviction. You know what kind of men we proved to be among you for your sake. 6 And you became imitators of us and of the Lord, for you received the word in much affliction, with joy inspired by the Holy Spirit; 7 so that you became an example to all the believers in Măçĕdō′nĭă and in Ăchāi′á. 8 For not only has the word of the Lord sounded forth from you in Măçĕdō′nĭă and Ăchāi′á, but your faith in God has gone forth everywhere, so that we need not say anything. 9 For they themselves report concerning us what a welcome we had among you, and how you turned to God from idols, to serve a living and true God, 10 and to wait for his Son from heaven, whom he raised from the dead, Jesus who delivers us from the wrath to come.

1.2
2 Thess 1.3;
Rom 1.8,9
1.3
2 Thess
1.11; 1.3
1.5
2 Thess
2.14;
Col 2.2;
2 Thess 3.7
1.6
1 Cor 4.16;
11.1;
Acts 17.5–
10; 13.52
1.8
Rom 10.18;
1.8;
2 Thess 1.4
1.9
1 Cor 12.2;
Gal 4.8
1.10
2 Pet 3.12;
Acts 2.24;
Rom 5.9

C. *Paul's work among them*

2 For you yourselves know, brethren, that our visit to you was not in vain; 2 but though we had already suffered and been shamefully treated at Phĭl′ĭppĭ, as you know, we had courage in our God to declare to you the gospel of God in the face of great opposition. 3 For our appeal does not spring from error or uncleanness, nor is it made with guile; 4 but just as we have been approved by God to be entrusted with the gospel, so we speak, not to please men, but to please God who tests our hearts. 5 For we never used either words of flattery, as you know, or a cloak for greed, as God is witness; 6 nor did we seek glory from men, whether from you or from others, though we might have made demands as apostles of Christ. 7 But we were gentle[a] among you, like a nurse taking care of her children. 8 So, being affectionately desirous of you, we were ready to share with you not only the

2.1
1 Thess
1.5,9
2.2
Acts 16.22;
1 Thess 1.5;
Phil 1.30
2.3
2 Cor 7.2
2.4
2 Cor 2.17;
Gal 2.7;
1.10
2.5
Acts 20.33;
Rom 1.9
2.6
2 Cor 4.5;
1 Cor 9.1,2
2.7
ver 11;
Gal 4.19
2.8
2 Cor 12.15;
1 Jn 3.16

[a] Other ancient authorities read *babes*

1.1 *Silvanus* is the Latinized name of Paul's companion who in Acts is called *Silas* (Acts 15.22–18.5); in the Epistles he is always called Silvanus (2 Cor 1.19; 1 Thess 1.1; 2 Thess 1.1; 1 Pet 5.12). He was Paul's trusted companion on the second missionary tour.

gospel of God but also our own selves, because you had become very dear to us.

9 For you remember our labor and toil, brethren; we worked night and day, that we might not burden any of you, while we preached to you the gospel of God. 10 You are witnesses, and God also, how holy and righteous and blameless was our behavior to you believers; 11 for you know how, like a father with his children, we exhorted each one of you and encouraged you and charged you 12 to lead a life worthy of God, who calls you into his own kingdom and glory.

D. Paul's reception by them

13 And we also thank God constantly for this, that when you received the word of God which you heard from us, you accepted it not as the word of men but as what it really is, the word of God, which is at work in you believers. 14 For you, brethren, became imitators of the churches of God in Christ Jesus which are in Jude'ă; for you suffered the same things from your own countrymen as they did from the Jews, 15 who killed both the Lord Jesus and the prophets, and drove us out, and displease God and oppose all men 16 by hindering us from speaking to the Gentiles that they may be saved—so as always to fill up the measure of their sins. But God's wrath has come upon them at last!b

E. Timothy's mission among them

17 But since we were bereft of you, brethren, for a short time, in person not in heart, we endeavored the more eagerly and with great desire to see you face to face; 18 because we wanted to come to you—I, Paul, again and again—but Satan hindered us. 19 For what is our hope or joy or crown of boasting before our Lord Jesus at his coming? Is it not you? 20 For you are our glory and joy.

3 Therefore when we could bear it no longer, we were willing to be left behind at Athens alone, 2 and we sent Timothy, our brother and God's servant in the gospel of Christ, to establish you in your faith and to exhort you, 3 that no one be moved by these afflictions. You yourselves know that this is to be our lot. 4 For when we were with you, we told you beforehand that we were to suffer affliction; just as it has come to pass, and as you know. 5 For this reason, when I could bear it no longer, I sent that I might know your faith, for fear that somehow the tempter had tempted you and that our labor would be in vain.

F. The good news from them

6 But now that Timothy has come to us from you, and has brought us the good news of your faith and love and reported that you always remember us kindly and long to see us, as we long to see you—7 for this reason, brethren, in all our distress and

---

b Or completely, or for ever

2.9
Acts 20.34;
2 Thess 3.8;
2 Cor 12.13

2.10
1 Thess 1.5;
2 Cor 1.12

2.11
1 Cor 4.14;
ver 7

2.12
Eph 4.1;
1 Pet 5.10

★2.13
1 Thess 1.2;
Gal 4.14

2.14
Acts 17.5;
2 Thess 1.4

2.15
Acts 2.23;
7.52

2.16
Acts 9.23;
13.45,50ff;
Mt 23.32

2.17
1 Cor 5.3;
1 Thess 3.10

2.18
Rom 15.22;
1.13

2.19
2 Cor 1.14;
Phil 4.1;
1 Thess 3.13

2.20
2 Cor 1.14

3.1
ver 5;
Acts 17.15

3.2
2 Cor 1.1;
Col 1.1

3.3
Acts 9.16;
14.22

3.4
Acts 20.24;
1 Thess 2.14

3.5
1 Cor 11.3;
Gal 2.2

3.6
Acts 18.5;
1 Thess 1.3

3.7
2 Cor 1.4

2.13 See notes to 2 Tim 3.16 on inspiration and Ps 119.11 on proof of inspiration. Paul clearly distinguishes between the word of man and the Word of God.

affliction we have been comforted about you through your faith;
8 for now we live, if you stand fast in the Lord. 9 For what thanksgiving can we render to God for you, for all the joy which we feel for your sake before our God, 10 praying earnestly night and day that we may see you face to face and supply what is lacking in your faith?

3.8
Phil 4.1
3.9
1 Thess 1.2
3.10
2 Tim 1.3;
2 Cor 13.9

G. Paul's prayer for them

11 Now may our God and Father himself, and our Lord Jesus, direct our way to you; 12 and may the Lord make you increase and abound in love to one another and to all men, as we do to you, 13 so that he may establish your hearts unblamable in holiness before our God and Father, at the coming of our Lord Jesus with all his saints.

3.11
2 Thess 3.5
3.12
1 Thess 4.1,
10
3.13
1 Cor 1.8;
1 Thess
2.19; 4.17

II. Exhortation and instruction 4.1–5.28

A. Exhortation to purity

4 Finally, brethren, we beseech and exhort you in the Lord Jesus, that as you learned from us how you ought to live and to please God, just as you are doing, you do so more and more. 2 For you know what instructions we gave you through the Lord Jesus. 3 For this is the will of God, your sanctification: that you abstain from unchastity; 4 that each one of you know how to take a wife for himself[x] in holiness and honor, 5 not in the passion of lust like heathen who do not know God; 6 that no man transgress, and wrong his brother in this matter,[c] because the Lord is an avenger in all these things, as we solemnly forewarned you. 7 For God has not called us for uncleanness, but in holiness. 8 Therefore whoever disregards this, disregards not man but God, who gives his Holy Spirit to you.

4.1
Phil 1.27;
1 Thess
2.12;
Col 1.10
*4.3
1 Cor 6.18;
Col 3.5
4.4
1 Cor 7.2;
1 Pet 3.7
4.5
Col 3.5;
Eph 4.17;
1 Cor 15.34
4.6
1 Cor 6.8;
Heb 13.4
4.7
Lev 11.44;
1 Pet 1.15;
1 Thess 2.3
4.8
Rom 5.5

B. Exhortation to love and labor

9 But concerning love of the brethren you have no need to have any one write to you, for you yourselves have been taught by God to love one another; 10 and indeed you do love all the brethren throughout Măçĕdōʹnĭă. But we exhort you, brethren, to do so more and more, 11 to aspire to live quietly, to mind your own affairs, and to work with your hands, as we charged you; 12 so that you may command the respect of outsiders, and be dependent on nobody.

*4.9
Rom 12.10;
1 Thess 5.1
4.10
1 Thess 1.7;
3.12
4.11
Eph 4.28;
2 Thess
3.10–12
4.12
Rom 13.13

C. Comfort about the saved who sleep

13 But we would not have you ignorant, brethren, concerning those who are asleep, that you may not grieve as others do who have no hope. 14 For since we believe that Jesus died and rose again, even so, through Jesus, God will bring with him those who

4.13
Eph 2.12
4.14
1 Cor 15.13,
23

x Or *how to control his own body*
c Or *defraud his brother in business*

4.3 *sanctification*, see note to 1 Cor 6.11.   4.9 See note to Rom 13.9 concerning *love*.

have fallen asleep. 15 For this we declare to you by the word of the Lord, that we who are alive, who are left until the coming of the Lord, shall not precede those who have fallen asleep. 16 For the Lord himself will descend from heaven with a cry of command, with the archangel's call, and with the sound of the trumpet of God. And the dead in Christ will rise first; 17 then we who are alive, who are left, shall be caught up together with them in the clouds to meet the Lord in the air; and so we shall always be with the Lord. 18 Therefore comfort one another with these words.

D. The sudden coming of the Lord

5 But as to the times and the seasons, brethren, you have no need to have anything written to you. 2 For you yourselves know well that the day of the Lord will come like a thief in the night. 3 When people say, "There is peace and security," then sudden destruction will come upon them as travail comes upon a woman with child, and there will be no escape. 4 But you are not in darkness, brethren, for that day to surprise you like a thief. 5 For you are all sons of light and sons of the day; we are not of the night or of darkness. 6 So then let us not sleep, as others do, but let us keep awake and be sober. 7 For those who sleep sleep at night, and those who get drunk are drunk at night. 8 But, since we belong to the day, let us be sober, and put on the breastplate of faith and love, and for a helmet the hope of salvation. 9 For God has not destined us for wrath, but to obtain salvation through our Lord Jesus Christ, 10 who died for us so that whether we wake or sleep we might live with him. 11 Therefore encourage one another and build one another up, just as you are doing.

E. Practical exhortations

12 But we beseech you, brethren, to respect those who labor among you and are over you in the Lord and admonish you, 13 and to esteem them very highly in love because of their work. Be at peace among yourselves. 14 And we exhort you, brethren, admonish the idlers, encourage the fainthearted, help the weak, be patient with them all. 15 See that none of you repays evil for evil, but always seek to do good to one another and to all. 16 Rejoice always,

Cross references

*4.15
1 Ki 13.17;
20.35;
1 Cor 15.51,
52
4.16
Mt 24.31;
1 Cor 15.23;
2 Thess 2.1
4.17
1 Cor 15.52;
Acts 1.9;
Rev 11.12;
Jn 12.26

*5.1
Acts 1.7;
1 Thess 4.9
5.2
1 Cor 1.8;
2 Pet 3.10
5.3
Hos 13.13
5.4
Acts 26.18;
1 Jn 2.8
5.6
Rom 13.11;
1 Pet 1.13
5.7
Acts 2.15;
2 Pet 2.13
5.8
Eph 6.14,
23,17
5.9
2 Thess
2.13,14;
Rom 14.9
5.10
2 Cor 5.15
5.12
1 Tim 5.17;
Heb 13.17
5.14
2 Thess
3.11;
Rom 14.1
5.15
Rom 12.17;
1 Pet 3.9;
Gal 6.10;
2.13,14;
Rom 14.9
5.16
Phil 4.4

4.15 In this passage, verses 14–18, Paul deals with what has been termed by some the "rapture" or the "catching away" of the church. Certain truths appear here with great clarity: (1) the *coming of the Lord* (Greek the *parousia*) of verse 15, who will descend from heaven, shall occur; (2) the resurrection of all believers depends upon the Resurrection of Jesus (ver 14); (3) the dead in Christ will rise prior to other events connected with His coming (ver 16); (4) those who are then alive and in Christ along with the resurrected dead in Christ shall *together . . . meet the Lord in the air* (ver 16, 17), indicating that the Lord himself will remain in the air and call the saints to His side. The event itself shall be accompanied by: (1) the cry of command; (2) the archangel's call; (3) the sound of the trumpet of God. Some interpreters have seen

in this account evidence for the removal of the church for a period of time prior to the Second Advent. Both the pre-tribulationists and the mid-tribulationists so hold.

5.1 Here Paul warns his readers not to set any timetable for the eschatological events he writes about in 4.13–18. In words reminiscent of Christ's teaching (cf. Mt 24.42–44; Lk 12.39, 40), Paul tells the Thessalonians that Christ's coming will be totally unexpected, like that of a thief in the night. No one knows the times and seasons of the day of the Lord (cf. Mt 24.36; Mk 13.32; Acts 1.7), so it is necessary for believers always to be ready (1 Thess 5.6–8; Mt 24.42; 25.13; Mk 13.33–37; Lk 12.35–38), not in fear, but in hope and confidence, for *God has not destined us for wrath, but to obtain salvation through our Lord Jesus Christ* (ver 9).

¹⁷ pray constantly, ¹⁸ give thanks in all circumstances; for this is the will of God in Christ Jesus for you. ¹⁹ Do not quench the Spirit, ²⁰ do not despise prophesying, ²¹ but test everything; hold fast what is good, ²² abstain from every form of evil.

F. Conclusion

²³ May the God of peace himself sanctify you wholly; and may your spirit and soul and body be kept sound and blameless at the coming of our Lord Jesus Christ. ²⁴ He who calls you is faithful, and he will do it.

²⁵ Brethren, pray for us.

²⁶ Greet all the brethren with a holy kiss.

²⁷ I adjure you by the Lord that this letter be read to all the brethren.

²⁸ The grace of our Lord Jesus Christ be with you.

*5.19
Eph 4.30
5.21
1 Cor 14.29;
1 Jn 4.1

*5.23
Rom 15.33
5.24
1 Cor 1.9

5.25
Eph 6.19

5.27
Col 4.16

5.19 See note to Eph 4.30 on grieving the Spirit. Undoubtedly, Paul was not speaking of quenching the Spirit in the same sense that he spoke of grieving the Spirit. Here he was referring to the gifts of the Spirit which in his day included speaking in tongues, prophesying, and miraculous healings. Christians must beware of falling into two extremes, either being overly enthusiastic about such spiritual gifts or cold and indifferent to them. Paul says that we are not to dampen the fire of the Holy Spirit, but rather, in the employment of these special gifts by the Spirit, we are to use them: (1) for edifying (1 Cor 14.26); (2) decently and in order (4.12; 1 Cor 14.40).

5.23 Theologians disagree as to whether man is trichotomous (consisting of three parts) or dichotomous (consisting of two parts). Paul here speaks of man as possessing *spirit, soul,* and *body.* The Scriptural data are not so plain that an unqualified judgment can be rendered. Apparently the Hebrews looked upon man as a unit, neither dichotomous nor trichotomous. The Hebrew writers used the words "flesh," "heart," "soul" (*nephesh*), "spirit" (*ruach*), and so forth, without supposing that man is the sum of these different parts. However, Scripture does insist upon the continued real existence of man in a state of consciousness after physical death as evidenced by Lk 16.19ff, Phil 1.23, and Rev 7.14–17.

INTRODUCTION TO
THE SECOND LETTER OF PAUL TO THE
THESSALONIANS

Authorship and Background: 2 Thessalonians was probably written shortly after 1 Thessalonians, although opinions differ both as to the time and the place. It was designed to correct the widespread misunderstanding of Paul's teaching concerning the return of the Lord. The Thessalonians were disregarding what Paul had explicitly taught them in person (2.5, 15; 3.6–10), and what he had written in his previous letter (2.15). Apparently a letter had been received by the Thessalonians, ostensibly from the apostle (2.2), which had led them to conclude that the great eschatological drama had already begun; consequently many of them had ceased working, thinking the end of the world to be at hand. They were living in idleness, thus creating an embarrassing situation (3.6, 11). Paul wrote this letter to reprimand them sharply (3.6, 14, 15), and to command them to continue steadfastly in the true teaching, imitating his own example of work while he was with them (2.15; 3.7–10, 12), thus preparing themselves for the return of Jesus.

Characteristics: Less effusive than the first letter, 2 Thessalonians is marked by some severe warnings and commands, reminiscent of the letter to the Galatians. Paul dwells at length on the signs that will precede the Day of the Lord, and stresses the fact that the ultimate manifestation of "the lawless one," in a frenzy of apostasy and blasphemy, will occur before the appearing and coming of the Lord Jesus (2.3–12). He sharply reprimands the idlers, and instructs the church to withdraw fellowship from them, albeit in love, not hatred: "Do not look on him as an enemy, but warn him as a brother" (3.6, 14, 15).

Contents:

I. Salutation. 1.1, 2

II. Personal matters. 1.3–12: Paul's joy over the faithfulness of his readers, his assurance of their eventual vindication, and prayer for their continued spiritual welfare.

III. The Day of the Lord. 2.1–17: The Day of the Lord has not arrived: it is to be preceded by unmistakable appearance of apostasy, the revelation of "the man of lawlessness," "the son of perdition" (2.3), whom Christ will destroy with his appearing and his coming. Christians, therefore, are to stand firm in the truth of the gospel as proclaimed by Paul.

IV. Exhortations. 3.1–18: Pray for us; continue in the faith; discipline those in error, not as enemies but as brothers.

THE SECOND LETTER OF PAUL TO THE
THESSALONIANS

I. Salutation 1.1,2

1 Paul, Sīlvā′nŭs, and Timothy,
To the church of the Thĕssălō′nĭăns̩ in God our Father and the Lord Jesus Christ:
2 Grace to you and peace from God the Father and the Lord Jesus Christ.

1.1
1 Thess 1.1;
2 Cor 1.19;
Acts 16.1

1.2
Rom 1.7;
1 Cor 1.3

II. Personal matters 1.3–12

A. Thanksgiving

3 We are bound to give thanks to God always for you, brethren, as is fitting, because your faith is growing abundantly, and the love of every one of you for one another is increasing. 4 Therefore we ourselves boast of you in the churches of God for your steadfastness and faith in all your persecutions and in the afflictions which you are enduring.

1.3
1 Thess 1.2;
3.12
1.4
2 Cor 7.14;
1 Thess 1.3;
2.14

B. Encouragement to endure

5 This is evidence of the righteous judgment of God, that you may be made worthy of the kingdom of God, for which you are suffering—6 since indeed God deems it just to repay with affliction those who afflict you, 7 and to grant rest with us to you who are afflicted, when the Lord Jesus is revealed from heaven with his mighty angels in flaming fire, 8 inflicting vengeance upon those who do not know God and upon those who do not obey the gospel of our Lord Jesus. 9 They shall suffer the punishment of eternal destruction and exclusion from the presence of the Lord and from the glory of his might, 10 when he comes on that day to be glorified in his saints, and to be marveled at in all who have believed,

1.5
Phil 1.28;
1 Thess 2.14
1.6
Col 3.25;
Rev 6.10
1.7
1 Thess
4.16;
Jude 14
*1.8
Gal 4.8;
Rom 2.8
1.9
Phil 3.19;
2 Pet 3.7;
2 Thess 2.8

C. Prayer

because our testimony to you was believed. 11 To this end we always pray for you, that our God may make you worthy of his call, and may fulfil every good resolve and work of faith by his

1.10
Jn 17.10;
1 Cor 3.13;
1.6
1.11
ver 5;
1 Thess 1.3

1.8 The wrath of God may be thought of as the "zeal" with which God maintains His own holiness, honor, and righteousness. Wrath includes the just visitation of penal judgment on those who violate the law of God and thus oppose His holy nature. But this holy displeasure of God upon sin is to be understood as a reflex of His deep and abiding love for His creation. Just because God loves His moral universe so deeply, He cannot remain indifferent when He sees it attacked and violated by those who would trample on His moral law. And because He has a love for the fallen race of Adam, God has made the utmost possible sacrifice for man's redemption, in providing a mediator and sin-bearer in Jesus Christ, who bore the penalty of wrath on the cross. God's anger is said to be visited upon: (1) unbelief (Jn 3.36); (2) apostasy (Heb 10.26, 27); (3) idolatry (Deut 29.18, 20, 27, 28); (4) all wickedness (Rom 1.18). This wrath is averted from sinners only through the blood of Christ (Rom 5.9) by faith (Rom 3.25). God's justice is perfect and completely beyond man's questioning (Rom 9.20–23). In a cataclysmic way the wrath of God may be visited upon men and nations in time (thus the fall of Nineveh, Jerusalem, Rome, and other empires), or it may be delayed until its culminating phase in the "day of wrath" (Rev 6.17; 11.18; 19.15) at the end of the age.

1.12
Phil 2.9ff
power, 12 so that the name of our Lord Jesus may be glorified in you, and you in him, according to the grace of our God and the Lord Jesus Christ.

III. *The day of the Lord 2.1–17*

A. *Events preceding the day of the Lord*

2.1
1 Thess
4.15–17;
Mk 13.27
2.2
Eph 5.6;
2 Thess
3.17;
1 Cor 1.8
*2.3
Eph 5.6–8;
Dan 7.25;
8.25;11.36;
Rev 13.5ff;
Jn 17.12
2.4
1 Cor 8.5;
Isa 14.13,
14;
Ezek 28.2
*2.7
Rev 17.5,7
2.8
Dan 7.10;
Rev 19.15
2.9
Mt 24.24;
Jn 4.48
2.10
1 Cor 1.18
2.11
Rom 1.28;
Mt 24.5;
1 Tim 4.1
2.12
Rom 1.32

2 Now concerning the coming of our Lord Jesus Christ and our assembling to meet him, we beg you, brethren, 2 not to be quickly shaken in mind or excited, either by spirit or by word, or by letter purporting to be from us, to the effect that the day of the Lord has come. 3 Let no one deceive you in any way; for that day will not come, unless the rebellion comes first, and the man of lawlessness*a* is revealed, the son of perdition, 4 who opposes and exalts himself against every so-called god or object of worship, so that he takes his seat in the temple of God, proclaiming himself to be God. 5 Do you not remember that when I was still with you I told you this? 6And you know what is restraining him now so that he may be revealed in his time. 7 For the mystery of lawlessness is already at work; only he who now restrains it will do so until he is out of the way. 8And then the lawless one will be revealed, and the Lord Jesus will slay him with the breath of his mouth and destroy him by his appearing and his coming. 9 The coming of the lawless one by the activity of Satan will be with all power and with pretended signs and wonders, 10 and with all wicked deception for those who are to perish, because they refused to love the truth and so be saved. 11 Therefore God sends upon them a strong delusion, to make them believe what is false, 12 so that all may be condemned who did not believe the truth but had pleasure in unrighteousness.

B. *Thanksgiving and exhortation*

2.13
Eph 1.4;
1 Pet 1.2
2.14
1 Pet 5.10
2.15
1 Cor 16.13;
11.2

13 But we are bound to give thanks to God always for you, brethren beloved by the Lord, because God chose you from the beginning*b* to be saved, through sanctification by the Spirit*c* and belief in the truth. 14 To this he called you through our gospel, so that you may obtain the glory of our Lord Jesus Christ. 15 So then, brethren, stand firm and hold to the traditions which you were taught by us, either by word of mouth or by letter.

a Other ancient authorities read *sin*
b Other ancient authorities read *as the first converts*   *c* Or *of spirit*

2.3 Certain events must transpire before the Second Advent of Christ: (1) the gospel shall be preached unto all the world for a witness; (2) the great tribulation will precede the coming of Christ. During the tribulation period the man of lawlessness (sin) will rise to a short-lived supremacy. It will be a time of unparalleled misfortune for the human race and also of completely unrestrained wickedness. Prophetic references to this period include Dan 7.8ff; 9.27; Mt 24.15; Rev. 13.2–10.
2.7 This is a most difficult verse. Scripture does not plainly indicate the identity of the person or influence that is now restraining the lawlessness of our present age. Some have suggested that it is the Holy Spirit Himself who shall be removed from the world scene during the tribulation, but this is impossible to reconcile with the large number of conversions which will take place during those troubled years. (Apart from the Holy Spirit no man can be converted.) This much is plain, however—that the time will come when the restraint will be taken away, and the "mystery of iniquity," which now operates underhandedly in response to concealed Satanic influences, will be plainly unveiled before the eyes of men in all of its hatefulness.

16 Now may our Lord Jesus Christ himself, and God our Father, who loved us and gave us eternal comfort and good hope through grace, 17 comfort your hearts and establish them in every good work and word.

IV. Exhortations 3.1–18

A. To pray

3 Finally, brethren, pray for us, that the word of the Lord may speed on and triumph, as it did among you, 2 and that we may be delivered from wicked and evil men; for not all have faith. 3 But the Lord is faithful; he will strengthen you and guard you from evil.^d 4And we have confidence in the Lord about you, that you are doing and will do the things which we command. 5 May the Lord direct your hearts to the love of God and to the steadfastness of Christ.

B. To labor

6 Now we command you, brethren, in the name of our Lord Jesus Christ, that you keep away from any brother who is living in idleness and not in accord with the tradition that you received from us. 7 For you yourselves know how you ought to imitate us; we were not idle when we were with you, 8 we did not eat any one's bread without paying, but with toil and labor we worked night and day, that we might not burden any of you. 9 It was not because we have not that right, but to give you in our conduct an example to imitate. 10 For even when we were with you, we gave you this command: If any one will not work, let him not eat. 11 For we hear that some of you are living in idleness, mere busybodies, not doing any work. 12 Now such persons we command and exhort in the Lord Jesus Christ to do their work in quietness and to earn their own living. 13 Brethren, do not be weary in well-doing.

14 If any one refuses to obey what we say in this letter, note that man, and have nothing to do with him, that he may be ashamed. 15 Do not look on him as an enemy, but warn him as a brother.

C. Prayer, salutation, and benediction

16 Now may the Lord of peace himself give you peace at all times in all ways. The Lord be with you all.

17 I, Paul, write this greeting with my own hand. This is the mark in every letter of mine; it is the way I write. 18 The grace of our Lord Jesus Christ be with you all.

d Or the evil one

Cross references:
2.16 1 Thess 3.11; Jn 3.16
2.17 1 Thess 3.2; 2 Thess 3.3
3.1 1 Thess 4.1; 5.25; 1.8
3.2 Rom 15.31
3.3 1 Cor 1.9; 1 Thess 5.24; 2 Pet 2.9
3.4 2 Cor 2.3; Gal 5.10
3.5 1 Chr 29.18
3.6 1 Cor 5.4, 11; 2 Thess 2.15
3.7 1 Thess 1.6
3.8 1 Thess 2.9; Acts 18.3; Eph 4.28
3.9 1 Cor 9.4ff
3.10 1 Thess 4.11
3.11 1 Tim 5.13
3.12 1 Thess 4.1, 11; Eph 4.28
3.13 Gal 6.9
3.14 Mt 18.17
3.15 Gal 6.1; 1 Thess 5.14
3.16 Rom 15.33; Ruth 2.4
3.17 1 Cor 16.21
3.18 Rom 16.20; 1 Thess 5.28

INTRODUCTION TO
THE FIRST LETTER OF PAUL TO
TIMOTHY

Authorship and Background: The letters to Timothy and Titus are called "The Pastoral Epistles" since they deal with the qualifications and duties of church ministers.

Several factors have led some scholars to question whether the letters as they now stand were written personally by Paul: (1) Paul's travels described in the Pastorals do not fit into the account in Acts, which closes with Paul in prison, in Rome, for two years; the credibility of these travels rests on the assumption that they took place after the two-year imprisonment. This means that Paul was released, and after a period of freedom, rearrested and imprisoned again in Rome where he eventually suffered martyrdom. (2) There are significant differences in style, vocabulary, and point of view between the Pastoral and the other Pauline letters. (3) The condemned false doctrines seem to belong to a later period. (4) The church organization and the attitude toward the various ministries of the church seem also to belong to a later period.

These factors have led to different conclusions: some hold that Paul merely suggested the subject matter and left it to a scribe to develop and transcribe the letters; others believe that the letters contain some genuinely Pauline fragments, but were written after his death by some devoted disciple; and others conclude that the letters were written as late as the second century and preserve no firsthand information of Paul's ministry.

Scholars who accept the letters as Pauline explain the various factors as follows: (1) Paul was released from prison and traveled widely over the Roman Empire for two or three years, going perhaps as far west as Spain, before his last imprisonment and martyrdom. (2) The differences in style and vocabulary spring from the differences in circumstances, needs, and purposes of the letters, and/or the greater part played by an amanuensis in their composition. (3) The heresy combatted in the Pastorals was not unknown during Paul's lifetime, being in many respects similar to the errors attacked in the letter to the Colossians. (4) Nothing in the nature of the organization of the church requires a date after Paul's lifetime.

The arguments against Paul's authorship are largely inferential, of course, and it remains to be proved that Paul was not the author, as clearly stated in the three letters (1.1; 2 Tim 1.1; Tit 1.1).

Here in 1 Timothy Paul writes from an undetermined location, perhaps in Macedonia (1.3), while on his way to Nicopolis (cf. Tit 3.12). Timothy was in Ephesus (1.3), and Paul repeatedly states his desire and determination to visit Timothy (3.14, 15; 4.13), which shows that he was not in prison when he wrote the letter. Timothy had been assigned to a work which had serious problems and while the Apostle had every confidence in him he felt that Timothy needed guidance and help if he were to succeed in the oversight of the flock.

Characteristics: The letter concerns itself with the church and the qualifications and duties of various church officers. Timothy, who occupied a position of considerable influence and authority in the work in Ephesus, is carefully instructed in how to carry out his duties. Though no title is applied to him (he is called "minister"—servant—in 4.6), the tone of the instructions shows that he occupied a place of authority: he is to see that the teaching is true to the Gospel (1.3); he is to supervise the worship (2.1, 2, 8); he is to regulate the apparel and conduct of women (2.9–12); he is to instruct his fellow Christians (4.6), and carry out the prescribed functions of church service (4.13–15); he is to deal with old and young, both men and women (5.1, 2); he is told to enroll in the widows' group only those over sixty years of age who cannot otherwise be cared for (5.3–16); he is to rebuke elders who sin (5.20), and be an example in his personal conduct of purity and holiness in all things (4.12; 5.21, 22; 6.11–14).

Contents:

I.   Salutation. 1.1, 2

II.   Instructions for the church and church officers. 1.3—3.16: Warnings against false teachers, including Hymenaeus and Alexander; instructions for church life, prayers, apparel and conduct of women; qualifications of bishops, deacons, and their wives; proper conduct in the church of the living God, the pillar and bulwark of the truth.

III. Instructions to Timothy. 4.1—6.21: Warning against heretical teachings; instructions about Timothy's personal conduct; his relationship to the various groups in the church, particularly the widows; instructions to slaves, and to the rich. "Timothy, guard what has been entrusted to you" (6.20).

THE FIRST LETTER OF PAUL TO

TIMOTHY

I. Salutation 1.1,2

1.1
Acts 9.15;
Col 1.27
1.2
Acts 16.1;
2 Tim 1.2

1 Paul, an apostle of Christ Jesus by command of God our Savior and of Christ Jesus our hope,

2 To Timothy, my true child in the faith:

Grace, mercy, and peace from God the Father and Christ Jesus our Lord.

II. Instructions for the church and church officers 1.3–3.16

A. The problem at Ephesus: unsound doctrine

1.3
Acts 20.1;
Gal 1.6,7
*1.4
Tit 1.14;
1 Tim 6.4
1.5
2 Tim 2.22
1.6
Tit 1.10
1.7
Jas 3.1;
1 Tim 6.4

3 As I urged you when I was going to Măçĕdō'nĭă, remain at Ĕph'ĕsŭs that you may charge certain persons not to teach any different doctrine, 4 nor to occupy themselves with myths and endless genealogies which promote speculations rather than the divine training*a* that is in faith; 5 whereas the aim of our charge is love that issues from a pure heart and a good conscience and sincere faith. 6 Certain persons by swerving from these have wandered away into vain discussion, 7 desiring to be teachers of the law, without understanding either what they are saying or the things about which they make assertions.

1.8
Rom 7.12
1.9
Gal 3.19;
1 Pet 4.18
1.10
2 Tim 4.3;
Tit 1.9
1.11
Gal 2.7

8 Now we know that the law is good, if any one uses it lawfully, 9 understanding this, that the law is not laid down for the just but for the lawless and disobedient, for the ungodly and sinners, for the unholy and profane, for murderers of fathers and murderers of mothers, for manslayers, 10 immoral persons, sodomites, kidnapers, liars, perjurers, and whatever else is contrary to sound doctrine, 11 in accordance with the glorious gospel of the blessed God with which I have been entrusted.

B. The testimony of Paul

1.12
2 Cor 12.9;
Col 1.25
1.13
Acts 8.3
1.14
Rom 5.20;
2 Tim 1.13
1.15
2 Tim 2.11;
Tit 3.8

12 I thank him who has given me strength for this, Christ Jesus our Lord, because he judged me faithful by appointing me to his service, 13 though I formerly blasphemed and persecuted and insulted him; but I received mercy because I had acted ignorantly in unbelief, 14 and the grace of our Lord overflowed for me with the faith and love that are in Christ Jesus. 15 The saying is sure

a Or stewardship, or order

1.4 Myths were false teachings or invented tales which were being taught by the false teachers whose errors are dealt with in the Pastoral letters. Further references are made to these fanciful stories in 4.7, 2 Tim 4.4, and Titus 1.14. They are characterized as "godless and silly," the opposite of truth, and of Jewish origin.

Commentators are not agreed on the precise nature of the *endless genealogies* (see also Tit 3.9). Did they refer to Jewish stories and

legends about the patriarchs and their descendants, or to Gnostic teachings concerning the series of emanations or aeons which extended from God to creation? These emanations had less and less divine content as they progressed from God, and it was through them that creation came into being. Whatever the precise nature of these genealogies may be, they only bred costly controversy, and were to be avoided. If they were not dealt with, the church would be rent by dissension.

and worthy of full acceptance, that Christ Jesus came into the world to save sinners. And I am the foremost of sinners; 16 but I received mercy for this reason, that in me, as the foremost, Jesus Christ might display his perfect patience for an example to those who were to believe in him for eternal life. 17 To the King of ages, immortal, invisible, the only God, be honor and glory for ever and ever.*b* Amen.

1.16
ver 13;
Eph 2.7

1.17
Col 1.15;
Rom 11.36

C. The exhortation to Timothy

18 This charge I commit to you, Timothy, my son, in accordance with the prophetic utterances which pointed to you, that inspired by them you may wage the good warfare, 19 holding faith and a good conscience. By rejecting conscience, certain persons have made shipwreck of their faith, 20 among them Hȳmėnaē′ŭs and Alexander, whom I have delivered to Satan that they may learn not to blaspheme.

1.18
1 Tim 4.14;
2 Tim 2.2,3
1.19
1 Tim 6.12,
21
★1.20
2 Tim 2.17;
4.14

D. Public prayer

2 First of all, then, I urge that supplications, prayers, intercessions, and thanksgivings be made for all men, 2 for kings and all who are in high positions, that we may lead a quiet and peaceable life, godly and respectful in every way. 3 This is good, and it is acceptable in the sight of God our Savior, 4 who desires all men to be saved and to come to the knowledge of the truth. 5 For there is one God, and there is one mediator between God and men, the man Christ Jesus, 6 who gave himself as a ransom for all, the testimony to which was borne at the proper time. 7 For this I was appointed a preacher and apostle (I am telling the truth, I am not lying), a teacher of the Gentiles in faith and truth.

2.2
Ezra 6.10;
Rom 13.1
2.3
Rom 12.2;
1 Tim 4.10
2.4
Jn 3.16;
2 Tim 2.25
★2.5
Gal 3.20;
Heb 9.15
2.6
Mk 10.45;
1 Cor 1.6;
Gal 4.4
2.7
Eph 3.7,8;
Gal 1.16

E. The position of women

8 I desire then that in every place the men should pray, lifting holy hands without anger or quarreling; 9 also that women should adorn themselves modestly and sensibly in seemly apparel, not with braided hair or gold or pearls or costly attire 10 but by good deeds, as befits women who profess religion. 11 Let a woman learn in silence with all submissiveness. 12 I permit no woman to teach or to have authority over men; she is to keep silent. 13 For Adam was formed first, then Eve; 14 and Adam was not deceived, but the woman was deceived and became a transgressor. 15 Yet woman will be saved through bearing children,*c* if she continues*d* in faith and love and holiness, with modesty.

2.8
Ps 134.2
2.9
1 Pet 3.3

2.11
1 Cor 14.34
2.13
Gen 1.27;
1 Cor 11.8
2.14
Gen 3.6;
2 Cor 11.3
2.15
1 Tim 1.14

b Greek *to the ages of ages*   *c* Or *by the birth of the child*   *d* Greek *they continue*

1.20 The "delivering to Satan" here and in 1 Cor 5.5 seems to indicate remedial discipline, and probably refers to excommunication from the fellowship of the church.
2.5 A *mediator* is a "middleman," or one who stands between two opposing parties. Christ is pictured in Scripture as a mediator between God and guilty mankind. By His shed blood He has broken down the dividing wall of hostility between Jew and Gentile; between God and man (Eph 2.14). Through Him the redeemed have access to the Father (Rom 5.2; Eph 2.18; 3.12). Apart from Christ there is no mediator and no hope of eternal life (Acts 4.12). This passage rules out all other mediators, whether angels, saints, priests, or relatives of Jesus Himself. None of these has any validity before God.

F. The office of bishop

3.1
1 Tim 1.15;
Acts 20.28
3.2
Tit 1.6-8;
2 Tim 2.24
3.3
2 Tim 2.24;
1 Pet 5.2
3.4
Tit 1.6
3.5
ver 15
3.6
1 Tim 6.4
3.7
1 Cor 5.12;
2 Tim 2.26

3 The saying is sure: If any one aspires to the office of bishop, he desires a noble task. 2 Now a bishop must be above reproach, the husband of one wife, temperate, sensible, dignified, hospitable, an apt teacher, 3 no drunkard, not violent but gentle, not quarrelsome, and no lover of money. 4 He must manage his own household well, keeping his children submissive and respectful in every way; 5 for if a man does not know how to manage his own household, how can he care for God's church? 6 He must not be a recent convert, or he may be puffed up with conceit and fall into the condemnation of the devil;*f* 7 moreover he must be well thought of by outsiders, or he may fall into reproach and the snare of the devil.*f*

G. The office of deacon

***3.8**
Acts 6.3;
Tit 2.3
3.9
1 Tim 1.19
***3.11**
2 Tim 3.3;
Tit 2.3
3.13
Mt 25.21

8 Deacons likewise must be serious, not double-tongued, not addicted to much wine, not greedy for gain; 9 they must hold the mystery of the faith with a clear conscience. 10And let them also be tested first; then if they prove themselves blameless let them serve as deacons. 11 The women likewise must be serious, no slanderers, but temperate, faithful in all things. 12 Let deacons be the husband of one wife, and let them manage their children and their households well; 13 for those who serve well as deacons gain a good standing for themselves and also great confidence in the faith which is in Christ Jesus.

3.15
Eph 2.21;
ver 5;
1 Tim 4.10;
Gal 2.9
***3.16**
Jn 1.14;
1 Pet 3.18;
Acts 1.9

14 I hope to come to you soon, but I am writing these instructions to you so that, 15 if I am delayed, you may know how one ought to behave in the household of God, which is the church of the living God, the pillar and bulwark of the truth. 16 Great indeed, we confess, is the mystery of our religion:

He*h* was manifested in the flesh,
vindicated*i* in the Spirit,
    seen by angels,
preached among the nations,
believed on in the world,
    taken up in glory.

III. Instructions to Timothy 4.1—6.21

A. Of false doctrine

4.1
Jn 16.13;
2 Thess 2.3;
2 Tim 3.1;
3.13;
Rev 9.20

4 Now the Spirit expressly says that in later times some will depart from the faith by giving heed to deceitful spirits and

---

f Or *slanderer*
h Greek *Who;* other ancient authorities read *God;* others, *Which*   *i* Or *justified*

3.8 Two offices, those of *elder* or *bishop* and *deacon* are to be found in the organization of the New Testament church. (See note to Tit 1.5 on the offices of elder or bishop.) The office of deacon was created in Acts 6.1-6. Its purpose was to free the apostles for the business of preaching the word and for prayer, temporal affairs, such as caring for the poor, being entrusted to the deacons. The qualifications for this office are found both in Acts 6.3 and 1 Tim 3.8-13. Like elders and bishops,

deacons were ordained by the laying on of hands (Acts 6.6). The word *deacon* comes from the Greek *diakonos* and means "ministrant" (one who serves).

3.11 The women here referred to may be the wives of deacons, or deaconesses of the church. There is no way of determining which is meant. Phoebe (Rom 16.1) is the only deaconess mentioned in the New Testament.

3.16 See notes to Jn 1.14 on the incarnation, and Phil 2.7 on the kenosis.

doctrines of demons, 2 through the pretensions of liars whose consciences are seared, 3 who forbid marriage and enjoin abstinence from foods which God created to be received with thanksgiving by those who believe and know the truth. 4 For everything created by God is good, and nothing is to be rejected if it is received with thanksgiving; 5 for then it is consecrated by the word of God and prayer.

B. On godly living

6 If you put these instructions before the brethren, you will be a good minister of Christ Jesus, nourished on the words of the faith and of the good doctrine which you have followed. 7 Have nothing to do with godless and silly myths. Train yourself in godliness; 8 for while bodily training is of some value, godliness is of value in every way, as it holds promise for the present life and also for the life to come. 9 The saying is sure and worthy of full acceptance. 10 For to this end we toil and strive,*j* because we have our hope set on the living God, who is the Savior of all men, especially of those who believe.

C. On faithful service

11 Command and teach these things. 12 Let no one despise your youth, but set the believers an example in speech and conduct, in love, in faith, in purity. 13 Till I come, attend to the public reading of scripture, to preaching, to teaching. 14 Do not neglect the gift you have, which was given you by prophetic utterance when the council of elders laid their hands upon you. 15 Practice these duties, devote yourself to them, so that all may see your progress. 16 Take heed to yourself and to your teaching; hold to that, for by so doing you will save both yourself and your hearers.

D. On pastoral duties

1. Widows

5 Do not rebuke an older man but exhort him as you would a father; treat younger men like brothers, 2 older women like mothers, younger women like sisters, in all purity.

3 Honor widows who are real widows. 4 If a widow has children or grandchildren, let them first learn their religious duty to their own family and make some return to their parents; for this is acceptable in the sight of God. 5 She who is a real widow, and is left all alone, has set her hope on God and continues in supplications and prayers night and day; 6 whereas she who is self-indulgent is dead even while she lives. 7 Command this, so that they may be without reproach. 8 If any one does not provide for his

j Other ancient authorities read *suffer reproach*

5.3 The lengthy section on widows (5.3–16) shows how important a place they occupied in the organization of the early church. Ordinarily widows would be quite helpless unless they received adequate material support from children or grandchildren, so the churches made the necessary provisions for their welfare (cf. the same care provided by the church in Jerusalem, Acts 6.1). It was very important, however, that the churches provide only for those who were really in need and had no other recourse—hence the detailed instructions as to their enrollment in the widows' group.

relatives, and especially for his own family, he has disowned the faith and is worse than an unbeliever.

9 Let a widow be enrolled if she is not less than sixty years of age, having been the wife of one husband; 10 and she must be well attested for her good deeds, as one who has brought up children, shown hospitality, washed the feet of the saints, relieved the afflicted, and devoted herself to doing good in every way. 11 But refuse to enrol younger widows; for when they grow wanton against Christ they desire to marry, 12 and so they incur condemnation for having violated their first pledge. 13 Besides that, they learn to be idlers, gadding about from house to house, and not only idlers but gossips and busybodies, saying what they should not. 14 So I would have younger widows marry, bear children, rule their households, and give the enemy no occasion to revile us. 15 For some have already strayed after Satan. 16 If any believing woman*l* has relatives who are widows, let her assist them; let the church not be burdened, so that it may assist those who are real widows.

2. *Elders*

17 Let the elders who rule well be considered worthy of double honor, especially those who labor in preaching and teaching; 18 for the scripture says, "You shall not muzzle an ox when it is treading out the grain," and, "The laborer deserves his wages." 19 Never admit any charge against an elder except on the evidence of two or three witnesses. 20 As for those who persist in sin, rebuke them in the presence of all, so that the rest may stand in fear. 21 In the presence of God and of Christ Jesus and of the elect angels I charge you to keep these rules without favor, doing nothing from partiality. 22 Do not be hasty in the laying on of hands, nor participate in another man's sins; keep yourself pure.

23 No longer drink only water, but use a little wine for the sake of your stomach and your frequent ailments.

24 The sins of some men are conspicuous, pointing to judgment, but the sins of others appear later. 25 So also good deeds are conspicuous; and even when they are not, they cannot remain hidden.

3. *Servants*

6 Let all who are under the yoke of slavery regard their masters as worthy of all honor, so that the name of God and the teaching may not be defamed. 2 Those who have believing masters must not be disrespectful on the ground that they are brethren; rather they must serve all the better since those who benefit by their service are believers and beloved.

E. *Warning against false teachers*

Teach and urge these duties. 3 If any one teaches otherwise and does not agree with the sound words of our Lord Jesus Christ and the teaching which accords with godliness, 4 he is puffed up with conceit, he knows nothing; he has a morbid craving for controversy and for disputes about words, which produce envy, dissension, slander, base suspicions, 5 and wrangling among men who are

---

l Other ancient authorities read *man or woman;* others, simply *man*

5.10
Acts 16.15;
Heb 13.2;
Lk 7.44;
ver 16

5.13
2 Thess
3.11;
Tit 1.11

5.14
1 Cor 7.9;
Tit 2.5

5.16
ver 3,5

5.17
Phil 2.29;
Rom 12.8;
Acts 28.10

5.18
1 Cor 9.9;
Lev 19.13;
Deut 24.14,
15;
Mt 10.10

5.19
Deut 19.15

5.20
Tit 1.13;
Deut 13.11

5.21
1 Tim 6.13;
2 Tim 2.14

5.22
Acts 6.6;
2 Tim 1.6;
Eph 5.11

5.23
1 Tim 3.8

6.1
Tit 2.9;
1 Pet 2.18;
Tit 2.5,8

6.2
Gal 3.28;
Philem 16;
1 Tim 4.11

6.3
2 Tim 1.13;
Tit 1.1

6.4
1 Cor 8.2;
2 Tim 2.14

6.5
1 Cor 11.16;
Tit 1.11;
2 Pet 2.3

depraved in mind and bereft of the truth, imagining that godliness is a means of gain. 6 There is great gain in godliness with contentment; 7 for we brought nothing into the world, and*m* we cannot take anything out of the world; 8 but if we have food and clothing, with these we shall be content. 9 But those who desire to be rich fall into temptation, into a snare, into many senseless and hurtful desires that plunge men into ruin and destruction. 10 For the love of money is the root of all evils; it is through this craving that some have wandered away from the faith and pierced their hearts with many pangs.

F. Exhortation to Timothy

11 But as for you, man of God, shun all this; aim at righteousness, godliness, faith, love, steadfastness, gentleness. 12 Fight the good fight of the faith; take hold of the eternal life to which you were called when you made the good confession in the presence of many witnesses. 13 In the presence of God who gives life to all things, and of Christ Jesus who in his testimony before Pŏntiŭs Pĭlăte made the good confession, 14 I charge you to keep the commandment unstained and free from reproach until the appearing of our Lord Jesus Christ; 15 and this will be made manifest at the proper time by the blessed and only Sovereign, the King of kings and Lord of lords, 16 who alone has immortality and dwells in unapproachable light, whom no man has ever seen or can see. To him be honor and eternal dominion. Amen.

G. The use of wealth

17 As for the rich in this world, charge them not to be haughty, nor to set their hopes on uncertain riches but on God who richly furnishes us with everything to enjoy. 18 They are to do good, to be rich in good deeds, liberal and generous, 19 thus laying up for themselves a good foundation for the future, so that they may take hold of the life which is life indeed.

H. Final charge and benediction

20 O Timothy, guard what has been entrusted to you. Avoid the godless chatter and contradictions of what is falsely called knowledge, 21 for by professing it some have missed the mark as regards the faith.
Grace be with you.

m Other ancient authorities insert *it is certain that*

6.6 Phil 4.11; Heb 13.5
6.7 Job 1.21
6.8 Heb 13.5
6.9 1 Tim 3.7; 1.19
★6.10 1 Tim 3.3; Jas 5.19
6.12 1 Cor 9.25, 26; 1 Tim 1.18; Heb 13.23
6.13 1 Tim 5.21; Jn 18.37
6.14 Phil 1.6; 2 Thess 2.8
6.15 1 Tim 1.11, 17; Rev 17.14; 19.16
6.16 1 Tim 1.17; Jn 1.18; Eph 3.21
6.17 Lk 12.20, 21; 1 Tim 4.10; Acts 14.17
6.18 1 Tim 5.10; Rom 12.8, 13
6.20 2 Tim 1.14; 2.16

6.10 This verse does not teach that there is anything evil in money as such, or in the possession of wealth. But it does teach that the *love of money* is sinful. Men have been known to commit almost any crime for the sake of money. Hence, as Paul states, *the love of money is the root of all evils.* In verses 17 and 18 Christians are charged to trust in God and not in riches, but they are also admonished to be rich in good works.

INTRODUCTION TO
THE SECOND LETTER OF PAUL TO
TIMOTHY

Authorship and Background: See the Introduction to 1 Timothy. Paul wrote to Timothy as a prisoner (1.8, 16; 2.9) in Rome (1.17), with no hope of release (4.6–8), sensing that the end was near (4.6–8). Deserted by friends and companions (4.10, 11), he longed for Christian companionship, and thus wrote Timothy who was, presumably, in Ephesus (Onesiphorus was from Ephesus, 1.16–18; 4.19b; so were Prisca and Aquila, 4.19a; cf. 1 Tim 1.3). Lonely as Paul must have been in a human sense, he was not alone in his prison cell. With him were the saints and martyrs of all ages who suffered similar imprisonment and pain and who could also say, "I know whom I have believed."

It would seem that 2 Timothy, then, was written after 1 Timothy and Titus, and on the basis of this order of the letters, Paul's travels described in the Pastorals may be set forth as follows: after a visit to Crete, with Titus, whom he left there (Tit 1.5), Paul went to Ephesus (1 Tim 1.3), leaving Timothy there, and thence to Miletus (4.20), on to Troas, where he left his "books, and . . . parchments" (4.13); from there he went to Macedonia (1 Tim 1.3), where he probably wrote 1 Timothy and Titus. He then proceeded to Nicopolis, where he intended to spend the winter (Tit 3.12). He was arrested there and taken to Rome (1.16, 17) where he wrote 2 Timothy and soon thereafter died a martyr's death, according to tradition, on the Ostian way, west of the capital, during the reign of Nero.

Characteristics: The letter is intensely personal, and subdued in tone. Sensing that the end of his life is near, the apostle writes with some pathos of his condition, bereft of friends (1.15; 4.10). Luke alone is with him (4.11). Paul longs to see his friend Timothy (4.9), and asks that he bring Mark with him (4.11); winter is coming (4.21), so he asks for his cloak, as well as his books and parchments (4.13). He remembers his past persecutions and sufferings (3.10, 11), speaks bitterly of the failure of friends to stand by him in his first trial (4.16), and warns Timothy against men like Hymenaeus and Philetus (2.17, 18), and Alexander the coppersmith (4.14, 15).

His pastor's heart is burdened for the welfare of his beloved converts and the dangers they run from false teachings (2.14–19; 3.1–9; 4.3, 4). At the same time he counsels Timothy to keep aflame the gift of God which is in him (1.6), not to fear persecution and suffering (1.8; 2.3–7), to stay with the sound doctrine he has been taught (1.13, 14; 2.15, 22–26; 3.14–17), to preach the message with conviction and power (4.1–5).

In the midst of suffering and betrayals, persecution and bereavements, he knows the One whom he has believed (1.12; 2.11–13), and Who will reward him with the crown of righteousness on that Day (4.8). The letter ends on a note of triumph: "The Lord will rescue me from every evil and save me for his heavenly kingdom. To him be the glory for ever and ever" (4.18).

Introduction to 2 Timothy

Contents:

THE SECOND LETTER OF PAUL TO

TIMOTHY

I. Salutation 1.1,2

1 Paul, an apostle of Christ Jesus by the will of God according to the promise of the life which is in Christ Jesus,

2 To Timothy, my beloved child:

Grace, mercy, and peace from God the Father and Christ Jesus our Lord.

II. Appeal and exhortation to Timothy 1.3–2.13

3 I thank God whom I serve with a clear conscience, as did my fathers, when I remember you constantly in my prayers. 4 As I remember your tears, I long night and day to see you, that I may be filled with joy. 5 I am reminded of your sincere faith, a faith that dwelt first in your grandmother Lois and your mother Eunice and now, I am sure, dwells in you. 6 Hence I remind you to rekindle the gift of God that is within you through the laying on of my hands; 7 for God did not give us a spirit of timidity but a spirit of power and love and self-control.

8 Do not be ashamed then of testifying to our Lord, nor of me his prisoner, but share in suffering for the gospel in the power of God, 9 who saved us and called us with a holy calling, not in virtue of our works but in virtue of his own purpose and the grace which he gave us in Christ Jesus ages ago, 10 and now has manifested through the appearing of our Savior Christ Jesus, who abolished death and brought life and immortality to light through the gospel. 11 For this gospel I was appointed a preacher and apostle and teacher, 12 and therefore I suffer as I do. But I am not ashamed, for I know whom I have believed, and I am sure that he is able to guard until that Day what has been entrusted to me.*a* 13 Follow the pattern of the sound words which you have heard from me, in the faith and love which are in Christ Jesus; 14 guard the truth that has been entrusted to you by the Holy Spirit who dwells within us.

15 You are aware that all who are in Asia turned away from me, and among them Phȳġĕl'ŭs and Hĕrmŏġ'ĕnĕş. 16 May the Lord grant mercy to the household of Ōnĕsĭph'ŏrŭs, for he often refreshed me; he was not ashamed of my chains, 17 but when he arrived in Rome he searched for me eagerly and found me—18 may the Lord grant him to find mercy from the Lord on that Day—and you well know all the service he rendered at Ĕph'ĕsŭs.

a Or what I have entrusted to him

Cross references (margin):

1.1 2 Cor 1.1; Eph 3.6; Tit 1.2

1.2 1 Tim 1.2

1.3 Rom 1.8,9; 1 Thess 1.2, 21; Acts 20.37

1.4 2 Tim 4.9

*1.5 1 Tim 1.5; Acts 16.1

1.6 1 Tim 4.14

1.7 Rom 8.15; Jn 14.27

1.8 Rom 1.16; Eph 3.1; 2 Tim 2.3,9; 4.5

1.9 Heb 3.1; Rom 16.25

1.10 Eph 1.9; 1 Cor 15.54

1.11 1 Tim 2.7

1.12 Tit 3.8; 1 Tim 6.20

1.13 Tit 1.9; Rom 2.20; 1 Tim 1.14

1.14 Rom 8.9,11

*1.15 Acts 19.10; 2 Tim 4.10, 11,16

1.16 2 Tim 4.19

1.18 2 Thess 1.10; Heb 6.10

1.5 History does not afford us much information relative to Lois and Eunice, the grandmother and mother of Timothy. But Paul states that Timothy's faith is due in part to the influence of these godly women. Paul shows that faith can be communicated and that family religion is not to be sneered at. A godly home and background are a great blessing.

1.15 This is the only place where *Phygelus* and *Hermogenes* are mentioned. We know little concerning them, but their reputation is imperishably established in the biblical record occasioned by the disgrace attending their defection from the apostle. They are distinguished from the faithful Onesiphorus who was a devout believer.

2 You then, my son, be strong in the grace that is in Christ Jesus, 2 and what you have heard from me before many witnesses entrust to faithful men who will be able to teach others also. 3 Share in suffering as a good soldier of Christ Jesus. 4 No soldier on service gets entangled in civilian pursuits, since his aim is to satisfy the one who enlisted him. 5An athlete is not crowned unless he competes according to the rules. 6 It is the hard-working farmer who ought to have the first share of the crops. 7 Think over what I say, for the Lord will grant you understanding in everything.

8 Remember Jesus Christ, risen from the dead, descended from David, as preached in my gospel, 9 the gospel for which I am suffering and wearing fetters like a criminal. But the word of God is not fettered. 10 Therefore I endure everything for the sake of the elect, that they also may obtain salvation in Christ Jesus with its eternal glory.

11 The saying is sure:

If we have died with him, we shall also live with him;
12 if we endure, we shall also reign with him;
if we deny him, he also will deny us;
13 if we are faithless, he remains faithful—
for he cannot deny himself.

III. Sound doctrine, right conduct, and false teaching 2.14–4.8

A. Personal counsel to Timothy

14 Remind them of this, and charge them before the Lord[b] to avoid disputing about words, which does no good, but only ruins the hearers. 15 Do your best to present yourself to God as one approved, a workman who has no need to be ashamed, rightly handling the word of truth. 16Avoid such godless chatter, for it will lead people into more and more ungodliness, 17 and their talk will eat its way like gangrene. Among them are Hymenae′us and Phile′tus, 18 who have swerved from the truth by holding that the

b Other ancient authorities read God

Cross references (right margin):

2.1 2 Tim 1.2; Eph 6.10
2.2 2 Tim 1.13; 1 Tim 6.12; 1.18; 1.12
2.3 1 Tim 1.18
2.4 2 Pet 2.20
2.5 1 Cor 9.25
*2.8 Acts 2.24; Mt 1.1; Rom 2.16
2.9 Acts 9.16; Phil 1.7; Acts 28.31
2.10 Eph 3.13; 2 Cor 1.6
2.12 1 Pet 4.13; Mt 10.33
2.13 Rom 3.3; Num 23.19
2.14 1 Tim 5.21; 6.4
2.15 Jas 1.12
2.16 1 Tim 4.7
2.17 1 Tim 1.20
*2.18 1 Cor 15.12

2.8 See note to Lk 24.46.

2.18 Several kinds of error are distinguished in Scripture. Since all believers are imperfect and know only in part, it is impossible for any one individual to grasp all the truth or to be free from all error. There is an error which springs from honest ignorance (Acts 19.1–6). As an illustration of this, the Christian church has long been divided on questions of baptism, church government, and so forth. Obviously someone must be embracing error. Well-intentioned believers, however, willingly forsake their error when they are properly instructed, and they are not guilty of intentional sin, even though their error may be a grave one. But Paul is not speaking of the error of ignorance here. Rather he is denouncing those who by their peculiar views relative to the resurrection *are upsetting the faith of some.* Probably Paul does not mean to suggest here the idea of apostasy, which is something entirely different from errors of ignorance, or even of peculiar doctrinal views which, while incorrect, do not necessarily separate one from the household of faith. The Greek word for "apostasy" occurs in Acts 21.21 and 2 Thess 2.3, 4. To be an apostate is to enter into unbelief and to dissolve any union one might have had with God in Jesus Christ. The normal mark of a genuine apostate is his denial that Christ is very God or his repudiation of Christ's atoning work on the cross (Phil 3.18; 2 Pet 2.1; 1 Jn 4.1–3). Biblical descriptions of apostates may be found in 2 Pet 2.1–19 and in the Book of Jude. They should be dealt with in a forthright fashion (2 Jn 10; Rom 16.17, 18; 2 Tim 3.9). Apostates may be discovered when their doctrines are examined in the light of Scripture (1 Jn 4.1). There has always been apostasy in the church, but the end of this age will be characterized by widespread departure from the faith (3.1–13).

resurrection is past already. They are upsetting the faith of some. [19] But God's firm foundation stands, bearing this seal: "The Lord knows those who are his," and, "Let every one who names the name of the Lord depart from iniquity."

20 In a great house there are not only vessels of gold and silver but also of wood and earthenware, and some for noble use, some for ignoble. [21] If any one purifies himself from what is ignoble, then he will be a vessel for noble use, consecrated and useful to the master of the house, ready for any good work. [22] So shun youthful passions and aim at righteousness, faith, love, and peace, along with those who call upon the Lord from a pure heart. [23] Have nothing to do with stupid, senseless controversies; you know that they breed quarrels. [24]And the Lord's servant must not be quarrelsome but kindly to every one, an apt teacher, forbearing, [25] correcting his opponents with gentleness. God may perhaps grant that they will repent and come to know the truth, [26] and they may escape from the snare of the devil, after being captured by him to do his will.*c*

B. The coming of apostasy

3 But understand this, that in the last days there will come times of stress. [2] For men will be lovers of self, lovers of money, proud, arrogant, abusive, disobedient to their parents, ungrateful, unholy, [3] inhuman, implacable, slanderers, profligates, fierce, haters of good, [4] treacherous, reckless, swollen with conceit, lovers of pleasure rather than lovers of God, [5] holding the form of religion but denying the power of it. Avoid such people. [6] For among them are those who make their way into households and capture weak women, burdened with sins and swayed by various impulses, [7] who will listen to anybody and can never arrive at a knowledge of the truth. [8]As Jännës and Jämbrës opposed Moses, so these men also oppose the truth, men of corrupt mind and counterfeit faith; [9] but they will not get very far, for their folly will be plain to all, as was that of those two men.

C. The defense of the faith

10 Now you have observed my teaching, my conduct, my aim in life, my faith, my patience, my love, my steadfastness, [11] my persecutions, my sufferings, what befell me at Ăn′tĭŏçh, at Ĭcō′-nĭŭm, and at Lÿstră, what persecutions I endured; yet from them all the Lord rescued me. [12] Indeed all who desire to live a godly life in Christ Jesus will be persecuted, [13] while evil men and impostors will go on from bad to worse, deceivers and deceived. [14] But as for you, continue in what you have learned and have firmly believed, knowing from whom you learned it [15] and how from childhood you have been acquainted with the sacred writings which are able to instruct you for salvation through faith in Christ

2.19
Isa 28.16,
17;
1 Tim 3.15;
Jn 10.14;
1 Cor 1.2
2.20
Rom 9.21
2.21
Isa 52.11;
2 Tim 3.17
2.22
1 Tim 6.11;
1.14; 1.5
2.23
1 Tim 6.4;
Tit 3.9
2.24
1 Tim 3.3;
Tit 1.7;
1 Tim 3.2
2.25
Gal 6.1;
1 Pet 3.15
2.26
1 Tim 3.7

3.1
1 Tim 4.1
3.2
2 Pet 2.3;
Rom 1.30
3.3
Rom 1.31;
Tit 1.8
3.4
2 Pet 2.10;
Phil 3.19
3.5
2 Thess 3.6
3.6
Tit 1.11
3.7
2 Tim 2.25
*3.8
Ex 7.11;
Acts 13.8;
1 Tim 6.5
3.9
Ex 7.12
3.10
1 Tim 4.6;
Phil 2.22
3.11
Acts 13.45;
14.2,19
3.12
Ps 34.19;
Mt 16.24;
1 Thess 3.3
3.13
2 Tim 2.16;
Tit 3.3
3.14
2 Tim 1.13
3.15
2 Tim 1.5;
Jn 5.39

c Or *by him, to do his* (that is, God's) *will*

3.8 According to Jewish traditions Jannes and Jambres were the names of the Egyptian magicians who opposed Moses (Ex 7.11; 9.11). The names are found in ancient Jewish writings (perhaps as early as the first century A.D.), and in Christian apocryphal works.

Jesus. 16All scripture is inspired by God and *d* profitable for teaching, for reproof, for correction, and for training in righteousness, 17 that the man of God may be complete, equipped for every good work.

D. *The charge to preach sound doctrine*

4 I charge you in the presence of God and of Christ Jesus who is to judge the living and the dead, and by his appearing and his kingdom: 2 preach the word, be urgent in season and out of season, convince, rebuke, and exhort, be unfailing in patience and in teaching. 3 For the time is coming when people will not endure sound teaching, but having itching ears they will accumulate for themselves teachers to suit their own likings, 4 and will turn away from listening to the truth and wander into myths. 5As for you, always be steady, endure suffering, do the work of an evangelist, fulfil your ministry.

6 For I am already on the point of being sacrificed; the time of my departure has come. 7 I have fought the good fight, I have finished the race, I have kept the faith. 8 Henceforth there is laid up for me the crown of righteousness, which the Lord, the righteous judge, will award to me on that Day, and not only to me but also to all who have loved his appearing.

IV. *Conclusion: greetings and benediction 4.9–22*

9 Do your best to come to me soon. 10 For Dēmǎs, in love with this present world, has deserted me and gone to Thěssǎlǒnǐ′cǎ; Crěsçěns has gone to Gǎlā′țiǎ,*e* Tītǔs to Dǎlmā′tiǎ. 11 Luke alone is with me. Get Mark and bring him with you; for he is very useful in serving me. 12 Tўch′ícǔs I have sent to Ěph′ěsǔs. 13 When you come, bring the cloak that I left with Carpǔs at Trōǎs, also the books, and above all the parchments. 14Alexander the copper-

d Or *Every scripture inspired by God is also*   *e* Other ancient authorities read *Gaul*

★3.16
Rom 15.4; 2 Pet 1.20, 21
3.17
1 Tim 6.11; 2 Tim 2.21
4.1
1 Tim 5.21; Acts 10.42
4.2
1 Tim 5.20; Tit 1.13; 1 Tim 4.13
4.3
2 Tim 3.1,6; 1 Tim 1.10
4.5
Acts 21.8
4.6
Phil 2.17; 1.23
4.7
Phil 3.14; 1 Tim 6.12
★4.8
Jas 1.12; 1 Pet 5.4; 2 Tim 1.12
4.10
Col 4.14; 1 Jn 2.15
4.11
2 Tim 1.15; Col 4.14; Acts 12.12
4.14
Acts 19.33; Rom 12.19; Ps 119.98, 99

3.16 Jesus Christ is the Word of God incarnate. The Bible is the written Word of God. Paul here states that the written Word of God is *God-breathed* (Greek *theopneustos*), from which expression and from other Scripture is derived the concept of the *inspiration* of the Bible. Historically, the church has always agreed that the Bible is the inspired Word of God. But it has not always been in agreement as to what inspiration actually consists of. Some have assumed that inspiration came via mechanical dictation in which the writers were simply secretaries who merely recorded what they were told to write down. In this view, Scripture is verbally inspired and inerrant. Another view, which avoids mechanical dictation, holds to verbal inspiration and insists upon an inerrant Scripture but allows for the freedom of the writer to use his own style and manner while preserved from error through the superintending power of the Holy Spirit. Both views usually limit inerrancy to the original manuscripts (the autographa), recognizing that errors have crept into present-day manuscripts since God has not guaranteed infallibility in transmission. These views of inspiration are based upon what are believed to be biblically taught doctrines of inspiration derived from Scripture itself. Still others accept the Bible as inspired but do not regard its uniqueness as extending to freedom from error in all matters of science and history. Those who hold this view do not believe that the existence of minor historical and scientific errors, or minor alterations of any kind, damages the essential message of the Scriptures or destroys Christian faith.

4.8 The Scripture inculcates in believers an attitude of eager expectancy toward the Second Advent of Christ. Implicit in this attitude is the purpose: (1) to love His coming (4.8); (2) to look or wait for His coming (Phil 3.20; Tit 2.13; 1 Cor 1.7; 1 Thess 1.10); (3) to be ready for His coming (Mt 24.44; Lk 12.40); (4) to be patient until His coming (Jas 5.7, 8); (5) to pray for His coming (Rev 22.20).

smith did me great harm; the Lord will requite him for his deeds. 15 Beware of him yourself, for he strongly opposed our message. 16 At my first defense no one took my part; all deserted me. May it not be charged against them! 17 But the Lord stood by me and gave me strength to proclaim the message fully, that all the Gentiles might hear it. So I was rescued from the lion's mouth. 18 The Lord will rescue me from every evil and save me for his heavenly kingdom. To him be the glory for ever and ever. Amen.

19 Greet Prĭscă and Ȧquĭ′lȧ, and the household of Onĕsĭph′ŏrŭs. 20 Ërăs′tŭs remained at Corinth; Trŏph′ĭmŭs I left ill at Mĭlētŭs. 21 Do your best to come before winter. Eūbūlŭs sends greetings to you, as do Pūdĕnṣ and Līnŭs and Claudia and all the brethren. 22 The Lord be with your spirit. Grace be with you.

4.16
Acts 7.60
4.17
Acts 23.11;
2 Pet 2.9
4.18
Ps 121.7;
Rom 11.36
*4.19
Acts 18.2
*4.20
Acts 19.22
*4.21
ver 9
4.22
Gal 6.18;
Philem 25

4.19 *Prisca* (called Priscilla in Acts) was the wife of Aquila. Both fled from Rome when Claudius (A.D. 52) expelled the Jews. They went from Rome to Ephesus and returned to Rome later. Here (4.19) they are in Ephesus once again. Both were faithful followers of Christ and warm friends of the Apostle Paul.

4.20 *Erastus.* This name is also mentioned in Acts 19.22 and Rom 16.23. It is not known whether these are the same or different people, but the Erastus of Acts could be the same as the one in this verse. *Trophimus*, see note to Acts 21.29 for information on this Gentile-Christian.

4.21 *Eubulus.* Nothing is known of this character other than that he was a leading member of the Christian church in Rome who sent greetings to Timothy by the hand of Paul. *Pudens*, a Christian at Rome who sent greetings to Timothy. Beyond this fact nothing more is known about him. *Linus*, a Roman Christian who has been identified with one of the first bishops of Rome having the same name. *Claudia*, a Christian in Rome and friend of Paul who was sometimes thought to be the mother of Linus. She may have become the wife of Pudens.

INTRODUCTION TO
THE LETTER OF PAUL TO
TITUS

Authorship and Background: See the Introduction to 2 Timothy. The letter to Titus was probably written from Macedonia; Titus himself was on the island of Crete (1.5). Paul was on his way to Nicopolis, in Achaia, on the Adriatic Sea (3.12). Apparently he was arrested in Nicopolis and sent on to Rome.

There was much that needed to be done in Crete about the matters of church organization (1.5), false teaching (1.10, 11, 14–16), and immoral conduct. Paul quotes with approval what Epiminedes the Cretan poet of the sixth century B.C. had written of his fellow countrymen (1.12). All classes in the church needed instruction in Christian living (2.1–10); they are to respect authorities (3.1) and live at peace with all men (3.2). Controversies and senseless debates are to be avoided (3.9); dissenters who persist in their factiousness are to be banished (3.10, 11), and all are to do good deeds to discharge their Christian responsibilities (3.14).

The few personal references in the letter (1.5; 3.12–15) afford no sure indication of the exact time and place of writing. Tychicus may soon be sent to Crete (3.12; in 2 Tim 4.12 it is said he was sent to Ephesus; other references to Tychicus in Col 4.7, 8; Eph 6.21); Artemas (3.12) and Zenas the lawyer (3.13) are not mentioned elsewhere in the New Testament; Apollos (3.13) is probably the same as the one who appears in Acts (18.24–28) and 1 Corinthians.

Titus himself does not appear by name in the Book of Acts, and what information there is about him appears in Paul's letters.

Characteristics: This letter is much like 1 Timothy in its emphasis on church order and sound doctrine. Titus is charged with considerable responsibility on the island of Crete, with the authority to appoint elders in the various churches on the island (1.5), rebuke insubordinates (1.13; 3.10), teach sound doctrine (2.1), exhort and reprove with all authority (2.15; 3.8), and in general exercise spiritual and ecclesiastical oversight over the churches. "Let no one disregard you" (2.15) is the author's advice to him.

Contents:

THE LETTER OF PAUL TO

TITUS

I. Salutation 1.1–4

1.1
Rom 1.1;
2 Cor 1.1;
1 Tim 2.4;
6.3
1.2
2 Tim 1.1;
Rom 16.25
1.3
2 Tim 1.10;
1 Thess 2.4
1.4
2 Cor 2.13;
Eph 1.2;
1 Tim 1.2

1 Paul, a servant[a] of God and an apostle of Jesus Christ, to further the faith of God's elect and their knowledge of the truth which accords with godliness, 2 in hope of eternal life which God, who never lies, promised ages ago 3 and at the proper time manifested in his word through the preaching with which I have been entrusted by command of God our Savior;

4 To Titus, my true child in a common faith:

Grace and peace from God the Father and Christ Jesus our Savior.

II. Church organization 1.5–16

A. Qualifications for elders

*1.5
Acts 27.7;
14.23;
11.30
1.6
1 Tim 3.2–4
1.7
1 Cor 4.1;
Eph 5.18
1.8
1 Tim 3.2;
2 Tim 3.3
1.9
1 Tim 1.19;
1.10

5 This is why I left you in Crēte, that you might amend what was defective, and appoint elders in every town as I directed you, 6 if any man is blameless, the husband of one wife, and his children are believers and not open to the charge of being profligate or insubordinate. 7 For a bishop, as God's steward, must be blameless; he must not be arrogant or quick-tempered or a drunkard or violent or greedy for gain, 8 but hospitable, a lover of goodness, master of himself, upright, holy, and self-controlled; 9 he must hold firm to the sure word as taught, so that he may be able to give instruction in sound doctrine and also to confute those who contradict it.

B. Exposé of false teachers

1.10
1 Tim 1.6;
Acts 11.2
1.11
2 Tim 3.6;
1 Tim 6.5
1.12
Acts 17.28
1.13
2 Cor 13.10;
Tit 2.2
1.14
1 Tim 1.4;
Isa 29.13

10 For there are many insubordinate men, empty talkers and deceivers, especially the circumcision party; 11 they must be silenced, since they are upsetting whole families by teaching for base gain what they have no right to teach. 12 One of themselves, a prophet of their own, said, "Crētáns are always liars, evil beasts, lazy gluttons." 13 This testimony is true. Therefore rebuke them sharply, that they may be sound in the faith, 14 instead of giving

a Or *slave*

1.5 The terms for *bishop* (Greek *episkopos* "overseer") and *elder* (Greek *presbuteros*) are used interchangeably in the New Testament. Paul so uses the terms in 1.5, 7. The New Testament churches undoubtedly were governed by a plural eldership; there is no record of a single bishop or elder in a New Testament church although there are some references to single individuals, such as Diotrephes of 3 Jn 9, who seemed to have a controlling authority over the local church. The qualifications for the office of bishop are carefully laid down in Scripture (1 Tim 3.1–7; Tit 1.5–9). Of paramount importance is the call of the Holy Spirit or the divine appointment (Acts 20.28), but the divine call was to be ratified by the church and acknowledged by the laying on of hands by the other elders (Acts 14.23; Tit 1.5). The functions of the office included: (1) rulership (1 Tim 5.17); (2) preaching the gospel and preserving God's people from error (1.9); (3) watch-care of the flock as a shepherd over sheep (Acts 20.28; 1 Pet 5.2). The divine appointment was understood to include the divine endowment with the necessary gifts for the discharge of the functions of the office (1 Cor 12.28; Eph 4.11).

heed to Jewish myths or to commands of men who reject the truth.
15 To the pure all things are pure, but to the corrupt and unbelieving nothing is pure; their very minds and consciences are corrupted.
16 They profess to know God, but they deny him by their deeds;
they are detestable, disobedient, unfit for any good deed.

III. The Christian life 2.1–3.11

A. Among Christians

2 But as for you, teach what befits sound doctrine. 2 Bid the
older men be temperate, serious, sensible, sound in faith, in
love, and in steadfastness. 3 Bid the older women likewise to be
reverent in behavior, not to be slanderers or slaves to drink; they
are to teach what is good, 4 and so train the young women to love
their husbands and children, 5 to be sensible, chaste, domestic,
kind, and submissive to their husbands, that the word of God may
not be discredited. 6 Likewise urge the younger men to control
themselves. 7 Show yourself in all respects a model of good deeds,
and in your teaching show integrity, gravity, 8 and sound speech
that cannot be censured, so that an opponent may be put to shame,
having nothing evil to say of us. 9 Bid slaves to be submissive to
their masters and to give satisfaction in every respect; they are not
to be refractory, 10 nor to pilfer, but to show entire and true fidelity,
so that in everything they may adorn the doctrine of God our
Savior.

B. In the light of the blessed hope

11 For the grace of God has appeared for the salvation of all
men, 12 training us to renounce irreligion and worldly passions,
and to live sober, upright, and godly lives in this world, 13 awaiting
our blessed hope, the appearing of the glory of our great God and
Savior[c] Jesus Christ, 14 who gave himself for us to redeem us from
all iniquity and to purify for himself a people of his own who are
zealous for good deeds.

15 Declare these things; exhort and reprove with all authority.
Let no one disregard you.

C. Faith and works

3 Remind them to be submissive to rulers and authorities, to be
obedient, to be ready for any honest work, 2 to speak evil of no

c Or of the great God and our Savior

Cross references

1.15 Lk 11.39, 41; Rom 14.23
1.16 1 Jn 2.4; 2 Tim 3.5,8
2.1 Tit 1.9
2.2 Tit 1.13
2.3 1 Tim 3.8
*2.4
2.5 1 Cor 14.34; Eph 5.22; 1 Tim 6.1
2.7 1 Tim 4.12
2.8 1 Tim 6.3
2.9 Eph 6.5
2.10 Mt 5.16
2.11 Rom 5.15; 1 Tim 2.4
2.12 Tit 3.3; 2 Tim 3.12
*2.13 2 Thess 2.8; 2 Pet 1.1
2.14 1 Tim 2.6; Heb 9.14; Ex 19.5; Eph 2.10
3.1 Rom 13.1; 2 Tim 2.21
3.2 Eph 4.31; 2 Tim 2.24, 25

2.4 The New Testament teaches that the
duties of wives to their husbands are: (1) to
love them (2.4); (2) to live with them until death separates them (Rom 7.2, 3);
(3) to be submissive to them (1 Cor 14.34;
Tit 2.5); (4) to respect them (Eph 5.33);
(5) to perform the conjugal due (1 Cor 7.3–5).

2.13 The blessed hope of the Christian is
the Second Advent of Jesus Christ. The Greek
word epiphaneia was used by heathen authors
to refer to the theophanies or appearances of
their pagan gods. In the Bible it is used with

reference to the incarnation of Christ, the
first "epiphany" (2 Tim 1.10). But in the
present passage it can only refer to the Second
Coming of Christ (1 Tim 6.14; 2 Tim 4.1, 8),
the second "epiphany." But the term blessed
hope connotes more than simply the coming
of Christ. It includes also all the events
related to the end of the age, as described in
different parts of the New Testament. To
limit the blessed hope to the rapture of the
church can hardly be justified from its Scriptural usage.

one, to avoid quarreling, to be gentle, and to show perfect courtesy toward all men. ³ For we ourselves were once foolish, disobedient, led astray, slaves to various passions and pleasures, passing our days in malice and envy, hated by men and hating one another; ⁴ but when the goodness and loving kindness of God our Savior appeared, ⁵ he saved us, not because of deeds done by us in righteousness, but in virtue of his own mercy, by the washing of regeneration and renewal in the Holy Spirit, ⁶ which he poured out upon us richly through Jesus Christ our Savior, ⁷ so that we might be justified by his grace and become heirs in hope of eternal life. ⁸ The saying is sure.

I desire you to insist on these things, so that those who have believed in God may be careful to apply themselves to good deeds;ᵈ these are excellent and profitable to men. ⁹ But avoid stupid controversies, genealogies, dissensions, and quarrels over the law, for they are unprofitable and futile. ¹⁰As for a man who is factious, after admonishing him once or twice, have nothing more to do with him, ¹¹ knowing that such a person is perverted and sinful; he is self-condemned.

IV. *Personal matters and benediction 3.12–15*

12 When I send Ar′tĕmăs or Tўçh′ĭcŭs to you, do your best to come to me at Nĭcŏp′ŏlĭs, for I have decided to spend the winter there. 13 Do your best to speed Zēnăs the lawyer and Ȧpŏl′lŏs on their way; see that they lack nothing. ¹⁴And let our people learn to apply themselves to good deeds, ᵈ so as to help cases of urgent need, and not to be unfruitful.

15 All who are with me send greetings to you. Greet those who love us in the faith.

Grace be with you all.

ᵈ Or *enter honorable occupations*

Marginal references:

3.3 — 1 Cor 6.11; 1 Pet 4.3
3.4 — Tit 2.11; 1 Tim 2.3
3.5 — Rom 3.20; Eph 5.26; Rom 12.2
3.6 — Rom 5.5
3.7 — Rom 3.24; 8.17,24
3.8 — 1 Tim 1.15; Tit 2.14
3.9 — 1 Tim 1.4; 2 Tim 2.14
*3.10 — Rom 16.17
3.12 — Acts 20.4; 2 Tim 4.9,10
3.13 — Acts 18.24
3.14 — ver 8
3.15 — Col 4.18

3.10 *factious* is the translation of the Greek *hairetikos* (from which Greek word the English word "heretic" is derived). The word itself describes a man who refuses to abide by generally accepted teaching, and holds stubbornly to different ideas. In 2 Pet 2.1 the author condemns those who bring in *destructive heresies* (Greek *haireseis*). Paul's instruction on how to deal with the *factious* man implies that such a person has departed from the faith. Therefore: *have nothing more to do with him* (cf. note to 2 Tim 2.18).

INTRODUCTION TO
THE LETTER OF PAUL TO
PHILEMON

Authorship and Background: Along with Colossians, Philippians, and Ephesians, the letter to Philemon is classified as one of the "Prison Epistles" (cf. verses 9, 10, 13), written from Rome, A.D. 59–61 (cf. Introduction to Colossians). Onesimus, a slave, had fled from his master Philemon to Rome, where he was converted through Paul's ministry. Paul wanted the slave to return to his master Philemon and sent the letter along, perhaps by Tychicus, who was to accompany Onesimus (Col 4.7–9).

It should be noted that the letter is addressed not only to Philemon, the master of Onesimus, but also to Apphia (probably Philemon's wife), and Archippus, a fellow minister of the Gospel. Some have conjectured that he was the son of Philemon and Apphia. The church which met in Philemon's home is also included among the recipients, so that the letter is not strictly a private communication (notice the plurals "you" in verse 3, "your" and "you" in verse 22, and "your" in verse 25).

The letter itself does not indicate where Philemon lived. From Col 4.9 it appears that Onesimus ("who is one of yourselves") was from Colossae; in Col 4.17, however, Paul instructs the Colossians to give a message to Archippus (cf. Philem 2), which would be strange if Archippus, a church leader, were in Colossae. That he may have lived in Laodicea is possible, since the injunction to remind Archippus of his ministry comes with greetings to Laodicea and instructions concerning the letter to the Laodiceans (Col 4.15, 16).

There is the possibility, held by some, that the recipients of Philemon were in Laodicea, not Colossae. In any case, the three cities, Colossae, Laodicea, and Hierapolis, were quite close to each other, with Epaphras described as one who had worked in all three (Col 4.12, 13).

Paul had never visited Colossae (Col 2.1), so that he must have met Philemon elsewhere, perhaps in Ephesus, the capital of the province of Asia. It seems certain, from Paul's allusive remark in Philem 19, that Philemon was converted under his ministry. In returning Onesimus to his master, Paul promised to pay whatever Onesimus owed Philemon (ver 18, 19), the implication being that the slave had stolen some money or property when he ran away. As he sent Onesimus back home, Paul expressed the hope of being able to see his friends shortly (ver 22).

Characteristics: Of all Paul's letters, Philemon is the most personal in tone: artless, unpretentious, and direct, Paul writes his friend to receive Onesimus back, no longer merely as a slave, but above all as a brother in Christ (ver 16, 17). Now that he was a believer, Onesimus was really useful (ver 11)—a pun on the name Onesimus, which means "useful." Paul does not plead for Philemon to free the slave, but there is more than a broad hint to that effect in verse 16, 17,

"no longer as a slave but more than a slave . . . receive him as you would . . . me."
In verse 21, "knowing that you will do even more than I say" implies the same;
perhaps it also implies that Philemon should be kind enough to return Onesimus
to Paul so that he might continue to help the apostle (ver 13, 14).

In this brief letter, the shortest of all Paul's surviving correspondence, are to
be seen the best qualities of the Apostle Paul, ambassador in bonds.

Contents:

THE LETTER OF PAUL TO
PHILEMON

I. *Salutation 1–3*

1 Paul, a prisoner for Christ Jesus, and Timothy our brother,
To Phĭlē′mŏn our beloved fellow worker ² and Ăp′phĭă our
sister and Arçhĭp′pŭs our fellow soldier, and the church in your
house:
3 Grace to you and peace from God our Father and the Lord
Jesus Christ.

1
Eph 3.1;
2 Cor 1.1;
Phil 2.25
★2
Col 4.17;
Phil 2.25;
Rom 16.5

II. *Paul's love for Philemon 4–7*

4 I thank my God always when I remember you in my prayers,
⁵ because I hear of your love and of the faith which you have
toward the Lord Jesus and all the saints, ⁶ and I pray that the
sharing of your faith may promote the knowledge of all the good
that is ours in Christ. ⁷ For I have derived much joy and comfort
from your love, my brother, because the hearts of the saints have
been refreshed through you.

4
Rom 1.8,9
5
Eph 1.15;
Col 1.4
7
ver 20;
2 Cor 7.13

III. *Appeal for Onesimus 8–22*

8 Accordingly, though I am bold enough in Christ to command
you to do what is required, ⁹ yet for love's sake I prefer to appeal
to you—I, Paul, an ambassadorᵃ and now a prisoner also for Christ
Jesus—¹⁰ I appeal to you for my child, Ō̆nĕs′ĭmŭs, whose father
I have become in my imprisonment. ¹¹ (Formerly he was useless
to you, but now he is indeed usefulᵇ to you and to me.) ¹² I am
sending him back to you, sending my very heart. ¹³ I would have
been glad to keep him with me, in order that he might serve me
on your behalf during my imprisonment for the gospel; ¹⁴ but I
preferred to do nothing without your consent in order that your
goodness might not be by compulsion but of your own free will.
15 Perhaps this is why he was parted from you for a while, that
you might have him back for ever, ¹⁶ no longer as a slave but more
than a slave, as a beloved brother, especially to me but how much
more to you, both in the flesh and in the Lord. ¹⁷ So if you consider me your partner, receive him as you would receive me. ¹⁸ If
he has wronged you at all, or owes you anything, charge that to
my account. ¹⁹ I, Paul, write this with my own hand, I will repay
it—to say nothing of your owing me even your own self. ²⁰ Yes,
brother, I want some benefit from you in the Lord. Refresh my
heart in Christ.
21 Confident of your obedience, I write to you, knowing that
you will do even more than I say. ²²At the same time, prepare a
guest room for me, for I am hoping through your prayers to be
granted to you.

10
Col 4.9;
1 Cor 4.14,
15
13
Phil 1.7
14
1 Pet 5.2;
2 Cor 9.7
16
Mt 23.8;
1 Tim 6.2;
Col 3.22
17
2 Cor 8.23
21
2 Cor 2.3
22
Acts 28.23;
Phil 1.25;
2.24;
2 Cor 1.11

ᵃ Or *an old man*   ᵇ The name Onesimus means *useful* or (compare verse 20) *beneficial*

2 Philemon's house was a church which
had true religion. But the testimony of this
house did not affect Onesimus who remained
unconverted until after his contact with Paul.

IV. Greetings and benediction 23–25

23 Ĕp'áphrás, my fellow prisoner in Christ Jesus, sends greetings to you, 24 and so do Mark, Aristar'çhús, Dēmás, and Luke,
my fellow workers.

25 The grace of the Lord Jesus Christ be with your spirit.

---

23 *Epaphras*, see note to Col 1.7.
24 *Aristarchus*, a native of Thessalonica and
follower of the Apostle Paul. He may have
voluntarily participated in Paul's bonds, and
tradition has it that he was martyred in Rome
under Nero. *Demas*, of whom Paul speaks in

2 Tim 4.10 as having deserted him because
he was *in love with this present world*. Whether
his defection was temporary or final is not
known, although tradition has it that he was an
apostate from the true faith. After leaving Paul
he went to Thessalonica, probably his home.

INTRODUCTION TO
THE LETTER TO THE
HEBREWS

Authorship and Background: There is no sure indication of author, place of writing, date, and recipients of Hebrews. It seems almost certain that Paul was not the author; Luke, Apollos, or Barnabas are those most often suggested (if, in fact, the author's name appears in the New Testament). The title "To the Hebrews" is not original with the book but is a deduction from the general nature of the writing. Even its classification as a letter is not altogether irrefutable: the author called his writing a brief word of exhortation (13.22), and though there are personal greetings at the close (13.22–24) there are none at the beginning, and the whole reads more like a written sermon, or homily, than a letter as such.

The closing greetings afford no sure indication of the destination of the writing: "They of Italy" in 13.24 (KJV) is not explicit as to whether the people so named were in or out of Italy, although the most natural interpretation of the phrase would assume, as the RSV translates it, "Those who come from Italy," that they were not in Italy; this would lead to the further inference that the letter was addressed to people in Italy.

The author was personally acquainted with his readers (6.9–12; 10.32–34; 13.7); and expressed his hope to return to them (13.19–23). Timothy was a mutual friend (13.23). He and his readers seem to have been second generation believers, having received the gospel from those who had heard the Lord Jesus (2.3).

Various dates have been suggested for Hebrews, ranging from before A.D. 70 to the last decade of the first century A.D.

The occasion which gave rise to this "word of exhortation" (13.22) was the danger brought about by persecution which, while it had not yet reached the point of martyrdom (12.4), was severe (10.32–34). The readers seem to have been Jewish Christians who were in danger of abandoning their faith and lapsing back into Judaism; thus they were running the risk of apostasy, although the author felt that they had not yet reached this disastrous state of affairs (6.9–12). So he exhorts them to hold fast to their confession in Christ as Savior and Lord (4.14; 10.23).

Characteristics: This stirring challenge constitutes the earliest literary apology, or defense, of the Christian faith. The sufficiency and finality of Christ, and the consequent superiority of the Christian faith over Judaism, are developed in an orderly and impressive way, in dignified, stately, and eloquent literary style. The argument appears to use Neoplatonic philosophic terms, which contrast the real, which is heavenly and eternal, with the apparent, which is earthly and temporary. In all respects Christ is superior: He is superior to the prophets, to angels, to Moses, Joshua, and the Aaronic priesthood; His covenant is superior, His sacrifices and promises better.

Frequent homiletical devices lend support to the opinion that the major part of the writing was a sermon (cf. 5.11; 6.3; 9.5b; 11.32; 13.22). There are frequent exhortations (2.1; 3.1, 2; 4.11, 14; 10.19–25, 35; 12.1, 2, 12, 13; 13.13–15) and sharp warnings (2.2–4; 3.6, 12, 13; 3.16—4.1; 6.4–6; 10.26–31; 12.15–17, 25). The real humanity of the person of Christ is here emphasized as in no other book in the New Testament (2.9, 10; 2.14–18; 4.15; 5.7–9; 12.3; 13.12).

The great roll call of the heroes of the faith (11.1–40) and the challenging exhortation that follows (12.1, 2) have served Christians of all times and ages. On the bedrock truth of the all-sufficiency of Jesus Christ, "the same yesterday and today and for ever" (13.8), Christians of every clime and age have staked their faith and lives.

Contents:

THE LETTER TO THE
HEBREWS

I. *Introduction: Christ the final revelation of God 1.1–3*

1 In many and various ways God spoke of old to our fathers by the prophets; 2 but in these last days he has spoken to us by a Son, whom he appointed the heir of all things, through whom also he created the world. 3 He reflects the glory of God and bears the very stamp of his nature, upholding the universe by his word of power. When he had made purification for sins, he sat down at

II. *Christ: better than the angels 1.4–2.18*

A. *Christ the Son of God*

the right hand of the Majesty on high, 4 having become as much superior to angels as the name he has obtained is more excellent than theirs.

5 For to what angel did God ever say,
"Thou art my Son,
today I have begotten thee"?
Or again,
"I will be to him a father,
and he shall be to me a son"?
6 And again, when he brings the first-born into the world, he says,
"Let all God's angels worship him."
7 Of the angels he says,
"Who makes his angels winds,
and his servants flames of fire."
8 But of the Son he says,
"Thy throne, O God,^{a} is for ever and ever,
The righteous scepter is the scepter of thy^b kingdom.
9 Thou hast loved righteousness and hated lawlessness;
therefore God, thy God, has anointed thee
with the oil of gladness beyond thy comrades."
10 "And,
"Thou, Lord, didst found the earth in the beginning,
and the heavens are the work of thy hands;
11 they will perish, but thou remainest;
they will all grow old like a garment,
12 like a mantle thou wilt roll them up,
and they will be changed.^{c}
But thou art the same,
and thy years will never end."
13 But to what angel has he ever said,
"Sit at my right hand,
till I make thy enemies
a stool for thy feet"?
14 Are they not all ministering spirits sent forth to serve, for the sake of those who are to obtain salvation?

a Or *God is thy throne* *b* Other ancient authorities read *his*
c Other ancient authorities add *like a garment*

1.2
Gal 4.4;
Heb 2.3;
Ps 2.8;
Jn 1.3;
1 Cor 8.6
1.3
Jn 1.14;
Col 1.17;
Heb 7.27;
8.1

1.4
Eph 1.21;
Phil 2.9,10
1.5
Ps 2.7

1.6
Heb 10.5;
Deut 32.43
1.7
Ps 104.4

1.8
Ps 45.6,7

1.9
Phil 2.9;
Isa 61.1,3

1.10
Ps 102.25

1.11
Isa 34.4

1.12
Heb 13.8

1.13
Ps 110.1;
Heb 10.13

1.14
Ps 103.20;
Heb 5.9

B. Christ the son of man

1. Warning against rejecting God's revelation

2 Therefore we must pay the closer attention to what we have heard, lest we drift away from it. 2 For if the message declared by angels was valid and every transgression or disobedience received a just retribution, 3 how shall we escape if we neglect such a great salvation? It was declared at first by the Lord, and it was attested to us by those who heard him, 4 while God also bore witness by signs and wonders and various miracles and by gifts of the Holy Spirit distributed according to his own will.

2. The kingdom conferred on Christ

5 For it was not to angels that God subjected the world to come, of which we are speaking. 6 It has been testified somewhere,

"What is man that thou art mindful of him,
    or the son of man, that thou carest for him?
7 Thou didst make him for a little while lower than the angels,
    thou hast crowned him with glory and honor,[d]
8 putting everything in subjection under his feet."

Now in putting everything in subjection to him, he left nothing outside his control. As it is, we do not yet see everything in subjection to him. 9 But we see Jesus, who for a little while was made lower than the angels, crowned with glory and honor because of the suffering of death, so that by the grace of God he might taste death for every one.

3. Christ as true man

10 For it was fitting that he, for whom and by whom all things exist, in bringing many sons to glory, should make the pioneer of their salvation perfect through suffering. 11 For he who sanctifies and those who are sanctified have all one origin. That is why he is not ashamed to call them brethren, 12 saying,

"I will proclaim thy name to my brethren,
    in the midst of the congregation I will praise thee."
13And again,
"I will put my trust in him."
And again,
"Here am I, and the children God has given me."

4. Christ as man's true sacrifice

14 Since therefore the children share in flesh and blood, he himself likewise partook of the same nature, that through death he might destroy him who has the power of death, that is, the devil, 15 and deliver all those who through fear of death were subject to lifelong bondage. 16 For surely it is not with angels that

---

Side references (left margin):

*2.2
Heb 1.1;
Acts 7.53;
Heb 10.28,
35
2.3
Heb 10.29;
1.1;
Lk 1.2
2.4
Jn 4.48;
1 Cor 12.4;
Eph 1.5

2.5
Heb 6.5
2.6
Ps 8.4–6

*2.8
Mt 28.18;
1 Cor 15.27;
15.25
*2.9
Phil 2.7–9;
Acts 2.33;
Jn 3.16;
1 Jn 2.2

2.10
Lk 24.46;
Rom 11.36;
Acts 3.15;
5.31;
Lk 13.32
2.11
Heb 10.10;
Acts 17.26;
Jn 20.17
2.12
Ps 22.22
2.13
Isa 8.17,18;
Jn 10.29

2.14
Mt 16.17;
Jn 1.14;
1 Cor
15.54–57;
1 Jn 3.8
2.15
Rom 8.15;
2 Tim 1.7

---

d Other ancient authorities insert *and didst set him over the works of thy hands*

2.2 *the message declared by angels* refers to the giving of the Law to the Jewish people on Mt. Sinai. Old Testament references to angels at Sinai are found in Deut 33.2 (LXX "angels"), and Ps 68.17. The mediation of angels in the giving of the Law is further referred to in Acts 7.38, 53 and Gal 3.19.

2.8 *putting everything in subjection to him.* This is strong language. Christ's sovereignty extends to everything, *nothing* (is) *outside his control.*
2.9 *suffering of death.* This was a divine necessity in accord with the nature of God and the purpose of God to redeem men.

he is concerned but with the descendants of Abraham. 17 Therefore he had to be made like his brethren in every respect, so that he might become a merciful and faithful high priest in the service of God, to make expiation for the sins of the people. 18 For because he himself has suffered and been tempted, he is able to help those who are tempted.

*2.17
Phil 2.7;
Heb 4.15;
5.1,2;
1 Jn 2.2;
4.10
2.18
Heb 4.15

III. Christ: better than Moses and Joshua 3.1–4.13

A. Christ as Lord superior to Moses as servant

3 Therefore, holy brethren, who share in a heavenly call, consider Jesus, the apostle and high priest of our confession. 2 He was faithful to him who appointed him, just as Moses also was faithful in ᵉ God's house. 3 Yet Jesus has been counted worthy of as much more glory than Moses as the builder of a house has more honor than the house. 4 (For every house is built by some one, but the builder of all things is God.) 5 Now Moses was faithful in all God's house as a servant, to testify to the things that were to be spoken later, 6 but Christ was faithful over God's ᶠ house as a son. And we are his house if we hold fast our confidence and pride in our hope.ᵍ

3.1
Heb 2.11;
Phil 3.14;
Rom 15.8;
Heb 10.21
3.3
2 Cor 3.7–
11
3.4
Eph 2.10;
Heb 1.2
3.5
Num 12.7;
Ex 14.31;
Deut 18.18,
19
3.6
Heb 1.2;
1 Cor 3.16;
Rom 5.2;
Col 1.23

B. Christ's rest superior to that of Moses and Joshua

1. Introduction

7 Therefore, as the Holy Spirit says,
"Today, when you hear his voice,
8 do not harden your hearts as in the rebellion,
on the day of testing in the wilderness,
9 where your fathers put me to the test
and saw my works for forty years.
10 Therefore I was provoked with that generation,
and said, 'They always go astray in their hearts;
they have not known my ways.'
11 As I swore in my wrath,
'They shall never enter my rest.' "

3.7
Heb 9.8;
Ps 95.7

3.9
Acts 7.36

3.11
Heb 4.3,5

2. The necessity of persevering faith to enter Christ's rest

12 Take care, brethren, lest there be in any of you an evil, unbelieving heart, leading you to fall away from the living God. 13 But exhort one another every day, as long as it is called "today," that

3.12
Heb 12.25;
9.14
3.13
Heb 10.24,
25;
Eph 4.22

ᵉ Other ancient authorities insert all ᶠ Greek his
ᵍ Other ancient authorities insert firm to the end

2.17 The term *make expiation* represents the Greek *hilaskomai*, "to propitiate," "to make atonement." Christ accomplished His redemptive work on Calvary, where He atoned for the sins of mankind. Three elements are involved in the term "atonement": (1) the idea of *covering*—to put "under the blood" is to cover over, an idea which is emphasized by the Old Testament term *kipper*—"to cover over, or atone for"; (2) the idea of *reconciliation*, by which the broken relationship between sinners and God was restored through the death of Christ; (3) the idea of *substitution*, which requires that someone else actually stand in the sinner's place and bear the penalty due him (Isa 53.5). Old Testament illustrations of atonement are found in Ex 12.3–14 and Lev 16. Christ's atonement is founded upon the necessity of the shedding of blood for sin (Lev 17.11; Heb 9.22). It was a *once for all* sacrifice (9.26). Its benefits are secured to the believer by faith (Jn 1.12; 3.16; 5.24; 14.6; Eph 2.8). (See also note to Rom 3.25.)

3.14 ver 6	none of you may be hardened by the deceitfulness of sin. 14 For we share in Christ, if only we hold our first confidence firm to the
3.15 ver 7	end, 15 while it is said,

> "Today, when you hear his voice,
>   do not harden your hearts as in the rebellion."

3.16 Num 14.2	16 Who were they that heard and yet were rebellious? Was it not
3.17 Num 14.29; Ps 106.26	all those who left Egypt under the leadership of Moses? 17And with whom was he provoked forty years? Was it not with those who sinned, whose bodies fell in the wilderness? 18And to whom
3.18 Num 14.23; Heb 4.6	did he swear that they should never enter his rest, but to those who were disobedient? 19 So we see that they were unable to enter
3.19 Jn 3.36	because of unbelief.

3. *Warning against missing Christ's rest as typified*
by Canaan rest

4.1 Heb 12.15	**4** Therefore, while the promise of entering his rest remains, let us fear lest any of you be judged to have failed to reach it.
★4.2 1 Thess 2.13	2 For good news came to us just as to them; but the message which they heard did not benefit them, because it did not meet with faith
4.3 Ps 95.11; Heb 3.11	in the hearers.ʰ 3 For we who have believed enter that rest, as he has said,

> "As I swore in my wrath,
>   'They shall never enter my rest,'"

although his works were finished from the foundation of the world.

4.4 Gen 2.2; Ex 20.11	4 For he has somewhere spoken of the seventh day in this way, "And God rested on the seventh day from all his works." 5And
4.5 Ps 95.11; Heb 3.11	again in this place he said,

> "They shall never enter my rest."

4.6 Heb 3.18,19	6 Since therefore it remains for some to enter it, and those who formerly received the good news failed to enter because of dis-
4.7 Ps 95.7,8; Heb 3.7,8	obedience, 7 again he sets a certain day, "Today," saying through David so long afterward, in the words already quoted,

> "Today, when you hear his voice,
>   do not harden your hearts."

4.8 Josh 22.4; Heb 1.1	8 For if Joshua had given them rest, Godⁱ would not speak later of another day. 9 So then, there remains a sabbath rest for the
4.10 ver 4	people of God; 10 for whoever enters God's rest also ceases from his labors as God did from his.
4.11 Heb 3.18	11 Let us therefore strive to enter that rest, that no one fall by
4.12 Jer 23.29; Eph 6.17; 1 Cor 14.24, 25	the same sort of disobedience. 12 For the word of God is living and active, sharper than any two-edged sword, piercing to the division of soul and spirit, of joints and marrow, and discerning the
4.13 Ps 33.13– 15; Job 26.6	thoughts and intentions of the heart. 13And before him no creature is hidden, but all are open and laid bare to the eyes of him with whom we have to do.

ʰ Other manuscripts read *they were not united in faith with the hearers*   ⁱ Greek *he*

4.2 "Gospel" comes from the Greek word *euaggelion* meaning *good news, tidings, word.* Among the descriptive phrases occurring in the New Testament are: (1) *the gospel of peace* (Eph 6.15); (2) *the gospel of Christ* (1 Cor 9.12); (3) *the gospel of the grace of God* (Acts 20.24); (4) *the gospel of the kingdom* (Mt 24.14); (5) *an eternal gospel* (Rev 14.6). Some have argued for different gospels on the basis of these various titles. It appears, however, that such distinctions are quite forced and unwarrantable, especially in view of the solemn curse of Gal 1.8. Men in all ages have been saved by the gospel, either through a faith which looks forward to the sacrifice of Christ or by one which looks back upon it. Paul plainly declares that Abraham was saved by the gospel (Gal 3.8). The heart of the gospel is that the incarnate Son of God has died and risen again for man's justification.

IV. Christ: better than the Aaronic priesthood 4.14–7.28

A. Christ the way of approach to God

14 Since then we have a great high priest who has passed through the heavens, Jesus, the Son of God, let us hold fast our confession. 15 For we have not a high priest who is unable to sympathize with our weaknesses, but one who in every respect has been tempted as we are, yet without sin. 16 Let us then with confidence draw near to the throne of grace, that we may receive mercy and find grace to help in time of need.

4.14
Heb 3.1;
7.26; 10.23
★4.15
Heb 2.18;
2 Cor 5.21;
1 Pet 2.22
4.16
Eph 2.18

B. Christ, God's appointed high priest

5 For every high priest chosen from among men is appointed to act on behalf of men in relation to God, to offer gifts and sacrifices for sins. 2 He can deal gently with the ignorant and wayward, since he himself is beset with weakness. 3 Because of this he is bound to offer sacrifice for his own sins as well as for those of the people. 4And one does not take the honor upon himself, but he is called by God, just as Aaron was.

5.1
Heb 8.3,4;
7.27
5.2
Heb 2.18;
Jas 5.19;
Heb 7.28
5.3
Heb 7.27;
9.7
5.4
2 Chr 26.18;
Ex 28.1

5 So also Christ did not exalt himself to be made a high priest, but was appointed by him who said to him,
"Thou art my Son,
today I have begotten thee";
6 as he says also in another place,
"Thou art a priest for ever,
after the order of Mĕlchĭz'ĕdĕk."

5.5
Jn 8.54;
Ps 2.7;
Heb 1.1,5
5.6
Ps 110.4;
Heb 7.17

7 In the days of his flesh, Jesus[j] offered up prayers and supplications, with loud cries and tears, to him who was able to save him from death, and he was heard for his godly fear. 8Although he was a Son, he learned obedience through what he suffered; 9 and being made perfect he became the source of eternal salvation to all who obey him, 10 being designated by God a high priest after the order of Mĕlchĭz'ĕdĕk.

5.7
Mt 26.39,
53; 27.46;
Mk 14.36;
15.34
5.8
Heb 3.6;
Phil 2.8
5.9
Heb 2.10
★5.10
ver 5,6

C. Exhortation to lay hold of Christ and his redemption

1. The immature reproved

11 About this we have much to say which is hard to explain, since you have become dull of hearing. 12 For though by this time you ought to be teachers, you need some one to teach you again the first principles of God's word. You need milk, not solid food; 13 for every one who lives on milk is unskilled in the word of righteousness, for he is a child. 14 But solid food is for the mature,

5.12
Gal 4.3;
Heb 6.1;
Acts 7.38;
1 Cor 3.2
5.13
1 Cor 3.1
5.14
Isa 7.15

---

[j] Greek *he*

4.15 Sinlessness involves two elements. The first concerns the inward part of man or the motivation which governs his actions. The second has to do with the outward acts of man. Sinlessness implies that both one's inward motives and overt acts are perfect in God's sight. It is actual conformity to the good and the holy. That Jesus our Savior was sinless is the united testimony of the Bible. We have: (1) the warrant of Jesus' own words (Jn 8.46; see also Jn 8.29; 17.19); (2) the testimony of others (Jn 18.38; Mt 27.19; Lk 23.41; Mt 27.4); (3) the testimony of the apostles (2 Cor 5.21; Heb 4.15; 1 Pet 2.21, 22; Heb 7.26, 27; 1 Jn 3.5).

5.10 See notes to Gen 14.18 and Ps 110.1.

for those who have their faculties trained by practice to distinguish good from evil.

2. A warning advanced

6 Therefore let us leave the elementary doctrine of Christ and go on to maturity, not laying again a foundation of repentance from dead works and of faith toward God, 2 with instruction[k] about ablutions, the laying on of hands, the resurrection of the dead, and eternal judgment. 3And this we will do if God permits.[l] 4 For it is impossible to restore again to repentance those who have once been enlightened, who have tasted the heavenly gift, and have become partakers of the Holy Spirit, 5 and have tasted the goodness of the word of God and the powers of the age to come, 6 if they then commit apostasy, since they crucify the Son of God on their own account and hold him up to contempt. 7 For land which has drunk the rain that often falls upon it, and brings forth vegetation useful to those for whose sake it is cultivated, receives a blessing from God. 8 But if it bears thorns and thistles, it is worthless and near to being cursed; its end is to be burned.

3. True believers encouraged

9 Though we speak thus, yet in your case, beloved, we feel sure of better things that belong to salvation. 10 For God is not so unjust as to overlook your work and the love which you showed for his sake in serving the saints, as you still do. 11And we desire each one of you to show the same earnestness in realizing the full assurance of hope until the end, 12 so that you may not be sluggish, but imitators of those who through faith and patience inherit the promises.

4. God's covenant promise unchanging

13 For when God made a promise to Abraham, since he had no one greater by whom to swear, he swore by himself, 14 saying, "Surely I will bless you and multiply you." 15And thus Abraham,[m] having patiently endured, obtained the promise. 16 Men indeed swear by a greater than themselves, and in all their disputes an oath is final for confirmation. 17 So when God desired to show more convincingly to the heirs of the promise the unchangeable

---

Cross references (margin):

6.1 Phil 3.12–14; Heb 5.12; 9.14
6.2 Acts 19.3,4; 6.6; 17.31,32
6.3 Acts 18.21
*6.4ff Heb 10.26, 32; Eph 2.8; Gal 3.2,5
6.5 Heb 2.5
6.6 Heb 10.26–29
6.7 Ps 65.10
6.8 Gen 3.17,18
6.10 Mt 10.42; 25.40; 2 Thess 1.6, 7; 1 Thess 1.3; Rom 15.25
6.11 Heb 3.6,14; Col 2.2
6.12 Heb 10.36
6.13 Gen 22.16, 17; Lk 1.73
6.16 Gal 3.15; Ex 22.11
*6.17 Heb 11.9; Ps 110.4

---

k Other ancient manuscripts read *of instruction*
l Other ancient manuscripts read *let us do this if God permits*   *m* Greek *he*

6.4-6 For two thousand years Christians have disagreed about the answer to the question: Can a man who has truly been converted lose his salvation? The Arminians (followers of Jacob Arminius, a Dutch theologian who opposed the views of strict Calvinism) believe he can, and the Calvinists believe he cannot. Arminians believe that verses 4 and 5 contain a description of a truly regenerate man who subsequently falls away. Calvinists hold that the person described was not actually born again but was only on the threshold of salvation. This much is clear: verse 4 plainly teaches that *if* one does fall away after enjoying such knowledge, experience, and privilege, then it is impossible to restore him again to repentance. Whichever view we adopt of the apostate man prior to his apostasy, the outcome is virtually the same. That is to say, if a man openly rejects Jesus Christ, he is, in either view, to be regarded as an unregenerate, unsaved man, even though he had formerly appeared to human observers to be converted. The Arminian would say that he had lost his salvation; the Calvinist that he had never had it, but the result is identical.

6.17 God is immutable or unchangeable. The counsel of the Trinity (Father, Son, and Holy Spirit) stands sure from eternity to eternity. This divine immutability is the basis of the believer's faith and hope. Thus, whatever God has promised He will perform. Scripture here indicates that God has given two evidences on which we can build our faith: (1) His immutable promise; (2) His immutable oath which He swore by Himself.

character of his purpose, he interposed with an oath, 18 so that through two unchangeable things, in which it is impossible that God should prove false, we who have fled for refuge might have strong encouragement to seize the hope set before us. 19 We have this as a sure and steadfast anchor of the soul, a hope that enters into the inner shrine behind the curtain, 20 where Jesus has gone as a forerunner on our behalf, having become a high priest for ever after the order of Mĕlçhĭz'ĕdĕk.

6.18 Tit 1.2; Heb 7.19

6.19 Lev 16.2; Heb 9.7

6.20 Heb 4.14; 5.6

D. Christ's Melchizedek priesthood surpasses the Levitical

1. The priority of the Melchizedek priesthood

7 For this Mĕlçhĭz'ĕdĕk, king of Sālĕm, priest of the Most High God, met Abraham returning from the slaughter of the kings and blessed him; 2 and to him Abraham apportioned a tenth part of everything. He is first, by translation of his name, king of righteousness, and then he is also king of Sālĕm, that is, king of peace. 3 He is without father or mother or genealogy, and has neither beginning of days nor end of life, but resembling the Son of God he continues a priest for ever.

7.1 Gen 14.18-20

★7.3 ver 6,28

4 See how great he is! Abraham the patriarch gave him a tithe of the spoils. 5 And those descendants of Lĕvī who receive the priestly office have a commandment in the law to take tithes from the people, that is, from their brethren, though these also are descended from Abraham. 6 But this man who has not their genealogy received tithes from Abraham and blessed him who had the promises. 7 It is beyond dispute that the inferior is blessed by the superior. 8 Here tithes are received by mortal men; there, by one of whom it is testified that he lives. 9 One might even say that Lĕvī himself, who receives tithes, paid tithes through Abraham, 10 for he was still in the loins of his ancestor when Mĕlçhĭz'ĕdĕk met him.

7.4 Gen 14.20

7.5 Num 18.21, 26

7.6 Gen 14.19; Rom 4.13

7.8 Heb 5.6; 6.20

2. The transitory priesthood of Aaron versus the eternal priesthood of Christ

11 Now if perfection had been attainable through the Lĕvĭt'ĭcál priesthood (for under it the people received the law), what further need would there have been for another priest to arise after the order of Mĕlçhĭz'ĕdĕk, rather than one named after the order of Aaron? 12 For when there is a change in the priesthood, there is necessarily a change in the law as well. 13 For the one of whom these things are spoken belonged to another tribe, from which no one has ever served at the altar. 14 For it is evident that our Lord was descended from Judah, and in connection with that tribe Moses said nothing about priests.

7.11 ver 18,19; Heb 8.7; 10.1; ver 17

7.13 ver 14,11

7.14 Isa 11.1; Mt 1.3; Lk 3.33; Rom 1.3; Rev 5.5

15 This becomes even more evident when another priest arises in the likeness of Mĕlçhĭz'ĕdĕk, 16 who has become a priest, not according to a legal requirement concerning bodily descent but by the power of an indestructible life. 17 For it is witnessed of him,
"Thou art a priest for ever,
    after the order of Mĕlçhĭz'ĕdĕk."

7.16 Heb 9.10, 14

7.17 Ps 110.4; Heb 5.6; 6.20; ver 21

7.3 *without father or mother* means that there was no record of Melchizedek's parents: he appears in the narrative without any account of his father or mother (Gen 14.18-20). In like manner, *neither beginning of days nor end of life* does not mean that he experienced neither birth nor death, but simply that the Scriptures do not record them.

7.18
Rom 8.3;
Gal 4.9
7.19
Acts 13.39;
Rom 3.20;
Gal 2.16;
Heb 9.9;
6.18; 8.6;
4.16
*7.21
Ps 110.4

7.22
Heb 8.6;
9.15; 12.24
7.24
ver 28
7.25
ver 19;
Rom 8.34;
Heb 9.24

7.26
Heb 4.15;
8.1
7.27
Heb 5.1,3;
9.12;
Eph 5.2;
Heb 9.14,
28
7.28
Heb 5.2;
1.2; 2.10

8.1
Heb 2.17;
1.3
8.2
Heb 9.11,24
8.3
Heb 5.1;
9.14
8.4
Heb 5.1
8.5
Col 2.17;
Heb 9.23;
10.1;
Ex 25.40;
Heb 11.7;
12.25
8.6
1 Tim 2.5;
Heb 7.22
8.7
Heb 7.11,18

18 On the one hand, a former commandment is set aside because of its weakness and uselessness 19 (for the law made nothing perfect); on the other hand, a better hope is introduced, through which we draw near to God.

3. The superior efficacy of Christ's priesthood

20 And it was not without an oath. 21 Those who formerly became priests took their office without an oath, but this one was addressed with an oath,
"The Lord has sworn
and will not change his mind,
'Thou art a priest for ever.' "
22 This makes Jesus the surety of a better covenant.

23 The former priests were many in number, because they were prevented by death from continuing in office; 24 but he holds his priesthood permanently, because he continues for ever. 25 Consequently he is able for all time to save those who draw near to God through him, since he always lives to make intercession for them.

26 For it was fitting that we should have such a high priest, holy, blameless, unstained, separated from sinners, exalted above the heavens. 27 He has no need, like those high priests, to offer sacrifices daily, first for his own sins and then for those of the people; he did this once for all when he offered up himself. 28 Indeed, the law appoints men in their weakness as high priests, but the word of the oath, which came later than the law, appoints a Son who has been made perfect for ever.

V. Christ: his better covenant 8.1–10.18

A. The old and the new covenants

1. The new covenant better than the old

8 Now the point in what we are saying is this: we have such a high priest, one who is seated at the right hand of the throne of the Majesty in heaven, 2 a minister in the sanctuary and the true tent[n] which is set up not by man but by the Lord. 3 For every high priest is appointed to offer gifts and sacrifices; hence it is necessary for this priest also to have something to offer. 4 Now if he were on earth, he would not be a priest at all, since there are priests who offer gifts according to the law. 5 They serve a copy and shadow of the heavenly sanctuary; for when Moses was about to erect the tent,[n] he was instructed by God, saying, "See that you make everything according to the pattern which was shown you on the mountain." 6 But as it is, Christ[o] has obtained a ministry which is as much more excellent than the old as the covenant he mediates is better, since it is enacted on better promises. 7 For if that first covenant had been faultless, there would have been no occasion for a second.

n Or tabernacle   o Greek he

7.21 The Lord . . . will not change his mind. The new covenant is neither provisional nor temporary. It is permanent and it is effective.

The purposes of God will be fulfilled whereby men will be brought into fellowship with God and their sins forgiven.

2. The new covenant based on superior promises

8 For he finds fault with them when he says:
"The days will come, says the Lord,
when I will establish a new covenant with the house of Israel
and with the house of Judah;
9 not like the covenant that I made with their fathers
on the day when I took them by the hand
to lead them out of the land of Egypt;
for they did not continue in my covenant,
and so I paid no heed to them, says the Lord.
10 This is the covenant that I will make with the house of Israel
after those days, says the Lord:
I will put my laws into their minds,
and write them on their hearts,
and I will be their God,
and they shall be my people.
11 And they shall not teach every one his fellow
or every one his brother, saying, 'Know the Lord,'
for all shall know me,
from the least of them to the greatest.
12 For I will be merciful toward their iniquities,
and I will remember their sins no more."
13 In speaking of a new covenant he treats the first as obsolete. And what is becoming obsolete and growing old is ready to vanish away.

*8.8 Jer 31.31–34
8.9 Ex 19.5,6
8.10 Heb 10.16; 2 Cor 3.3; Zech 8.8
8.11 Isa 54.13; Jn 6.45; 1 Jn 2.27
8.12 Heb 10.17
8.13 2 Cor 5.17

B. Old and new covenant sacrifices compared

1. The temporary Levitical sacrifices

9 Now even the first covenant had regulations for worship and an earthly sanctuary. 2 For a tent[p] was prepared, the outer one, in which were the lampstand and the table and the bread of the Presence;[q] it is called the Holy Place. 3 Behind the second curtain stood a tent[p] called the Holy of Holies, 4 having the golden altar of incense and the ark of the covenant covered on all sides with gold, which contained a golden urn holding the manna, and Aaron's rod that budded, and the tables of the covenant; 5 above it were the cherubim of glory overshadowing the mercy seat. Of these things we cannot now speak in detail.

6 These preparations having thus been made, the priests go continually into the outer tent,[p] performing their ritual duties;

9.1 Ex 25.8
*9.2 Ex 25.8,9; 23–39
9.3 Ex 26.31–33
9.4 Ex 30.1–5; 25.10ff; 16.32,33; Num 17.10
9.5 Ex 25.17ff
9.6 Num 28.3

p Or tabernacle   q Greek the presentation of the loaves

8.8 The new covenant is superior to the old covenant. Under the old covenant the believer could repose his faith only in symbols and types of Christ, and the law was a standard placed before him for his guidance. But under the new covenant the believer puts his trust in the actual person of the Lord Jesus Himself and in His deed of atonement already accomplished on Calvary; moreover the law is now implanted in his heart by the indwelling Holy Spirit Himself, who permanently abides within him. In the Old Testament period Israel fell into a legalistic perversion of God's gracious law, attempting to use it as a means of self-justification and merit-earning. And yet, according to God's own intention, even in Old Testament times, salvation was not obtained by observing the law; it was then, as now, secured by the grace of God. The new covenant is based upon a better sacrifice: the once-for-all offering up of Christ Himself upon the altar. By this sacrifice our sins are not simply covered, but actually cleansed away (9.26). The single condition for securing the benefits of the new covenant is faith in Christ and total submission to His lordship (see Gal 3.13–29).

9.2 See note to Ex 25.9 on the tabernacle.

9.7
Lev
16.11ff;
Ex 30.10;
Heb 5.2,3
9.8
Heb 10.19,
20;
Jn 14.6
9.9
Heb 11.19;
5.1;
Gal 3.21
9.10
Lev 11.2ff;
Col 2.16;
Heb 7.16
*9.11ff
Heb 2.17;
10.1; 8.2
9.12
Heb 7.27;
10.4
9.13
Num 19.9,
17,18
9.14
1 Jn 1.7;
1 Pet 3.18;
Tit 2.14

7 but into the second only the high priest goes, and he but once a year, and not without taking blood which he offers for himself and for the errors of the people. 8 By this the Holy Spirit indicates that the way into the sanctuary is not yet opened as long as the outer tent[p] is still standing 9 (which is symbolic for the present age). According to this arrangement, gifts and sacrifices are offered which cannot perfect the conscience of the worshiper, 10 but deal only with food and drink and various ablutions, regulations for the body imposed until the time of reformation.

2. The eternal heavenly sacrifice of Christ

11 But when Christ appeared as a high priest of the good things that have come,[r] then through the greater and more perfect tent[p] (not made with hands, that is, not of this creation) 12 he entered once for all into the Holy Place, taking[s] not the blood of goats and calves but his own blood, thus securing an eternal redemption. 13 For if the sprinkling of defiled persons with the blood of goats and bulls and with the ashes of a heifer sanctifies for the purification of the flesh, 14 how much more shall the blood of Christ, who through the eternal Spirit offered himself without blemish to God, purify your[t] conscience from dead works to serve the living God.

3. The new covenant fulfilled in Christ's death
a. The covenant validated by the death of the testator

9.15
1 Tim 2.5;
Heb 3.1;
7.22

9.17
Gal 3.15

9.18
Ex 24.6
9.19
Ex 24.6ff;
Lev 14.4,7

9.20
Ex 24.8;
Mt 26.28
9.21
Lev 8.15
*9.22
Lev 17.11

15 Therefore he is the mediator of a new covenant, so that those who are called may receive the promised eternal inheritance, since a death has occurred which redeems them from the transgressions under the first covenant.[u] 16 For where a will[u] is involved, the death of the one who made it must be established. 17 For a will[u] takes effect only at death, since it is not in force as long as the one who made it is alive. 18 Hence even the first covenant was not ratified without blood. 19 For when every commandment of the law had been declared by Moses to all the people, he took the blood of calves and goats, with water and scarlet wool and hyssop, and sprinkled both the book itself and all the people, 20 saying, "This is the blood of the covenant which God commanded you." 21 And in the same way he sprinkled with the blood both the tent[p] and all the vessels used in worship. 22 Indeed, under the law almost everything is purified with blood, and without the shedding of blood there is no forgiveness of sins.

b. Christ the sufficient offering for sin

9.23
Heb 8.5

23 Thus it was necessary for the copies of the heavenly things to

---

p Or tabernacle   r Other manuscripts read good things to come   s Greek through
t Other manuscripts read our   u The Greek word here used means both covenant and will

---

9.11-15 Christ has become our priest as well as our prophet and king. The function of the Hebrew high priest was to minister at the altar, a function which he shared with his fellow priests. But he alone was permitted to enter into the Holy of Holies, and only on the Day of Atonement. Even then he could not enter without presenting a blood-sacrifice first for himself and then for the sins of the people. Salvation is impossible apart from the priestly work of Christ. Hebrews teaches that as our priest, Christ serves as intermediary between

man and God; He has once for all ministered at the altar with His own blood to make an efficacious atonement for the sins of men. Believers today still approach God through the one and only valid priest, Jesus Christ.
9.22 The blood of Christ shed on Calvary is the vital principle behind the atonement. God's forgiveness is possible only through Christ's sacrifice. Undoubtedly the writer here is referring to Christ's own words, this is my blood of the covenant, which is poured . . . for the forgiveness of sins (Mt 26.28).

be purified with these rites, but the heavenly things themselves with better sacrifices than these. 24 For Christ has entered, not into a sanctuary made with hands, a copy of the true one, but into heaven itself, now to appear in the presence of God on our behalf. 25 Nor was it to offer himself repeatedly, as the high priest enters the Holy Place yearly with blood not his own; 26 for then he would have had to suffer repeatedly since the foundation of the world. But as it is, he has appeared once for all at the end of the age to put away sin by the sacrifice of himself. 27And just as it is appointed for men to die once, and after that comes judgment, 28 so Christ, having been offered once to bear the sins of many, will appear a second time, not to deal with sin but to save those who are eagerly waiting for him.

4. The superiority and finality of the new covenant
a. Christ the once for all sacrifice

10 For since the law has but a shadow of the good things to come instead of the true form of these realities, it can never, by the same sacrifices which are continually offered year after year, make perfect those who draw near. 2 Otherwise, would they not have ceased to be offered? If the worshipers had once been cleansed, they would no longer have any consciousness of sin. 3 But in these sacrifices there is a reminder of sin year after year. 4 For it is impossible that the blood of bulls and goats should take away sins.

5 Consequently, when Christ*v* came into the world, he said,
"Sacrifices and offerings thou hast not desired,
but a body hast thou prepared for me;
6 in burnt offerings and sin offerings thou hast taken no pleasure.
7 Then I said, 'Lo, I have come to do thy will, O God,'
as it is written of me in the roll of the book."

8 When he said above, "Thou hast neither desired nor taken pleasure in sacrifices and offerings and burnt offerings and sin offerings" (these are offered according to the law), 9 then he added, "Lo, I have come to do thy will." He abolishes the first in order to establish the second. 10And by that will we have been sanctified through the offering of the body of Jesus Christ once for all.

b. The evidence of his finished work

11 And every priest stands daily at his service, offering repeatedly the same sacrifices, which can never take away sins. 12 But when Christ*w* had offered for all time a single sacrifice for sins, he

v Greek he   *w* Greek this one

margin references: 9.24 Heb 6.20; 8.2; 7.25; 1 Jn 2.1 | 9.25 ver 7; Heb 10.19 | 9.26 Heb 4.3; 7.27; 1.2 | 9.27 Gen 3.19; 2 Cor 5.10 | ⋆9.28 Rom 6.10; 1 Pet 2.24; Tit 2.13 | 10.1 Heb 9.9,11,23 | 10.3 Heb 9.7 | 10.4 Mic 6.6,7 | 10.5 Ps 40.6-8; Heb 1.6; 1 Pet 2.24 | 10.7 Jer 36.2 | 10.8 ver 5,6; Mk 12.33 | 10.9 ver 7 | 10.10 Jn 17.19; Heb 7.27; 1 Pet 2.24 | 10.11 Heb 5.1; ver 4 | ⋆10.12 Heb 1.3

9.28 The Second Advent of Christ is inextricably linked to the eternal purposes of God. His coming foreshadows: (1) the completion of the salvation of believers (9.28; 1 Pet 1.5); (2) His reign as absolute sovereign in heaven and earth (Rev 11.15); (3) the destruction of the power and reign of death (1 Cor 15.25, 26); (4) His being glorified in His saints and marveled at by all who have believed (2 Thess 1.10); (5) His bringing to light those things which are hidden in darkness (1 Cor 4.5); (6) His final judgment of the living and the dead (Jn 5.22; 2 Tim 4.1; Jude 15; Rev 20.11-13). The dead saints will rise first (1 Thess 4.16), and the living saints will be caught up together with them in the clouds (1 Thess 4.17). The man of sin will be destroyed at Christ's coming (2 Thess 2.8).

10.12 Here and in 1.3 the expression sat down is used of the finished work of Christ. In the tabernacle and in the Temple the priests performed their functions standing. The high priest who entered the Holy of Holies once a year also stood. The work of the Aaronic priesthood was an unfinished work. But when Christ accomplished His work of redemption he sat down at the right hand of the Majesty on high (1.3) or at the right hand of God (10.12), signifying a perfect and completed work.

10.13
Ps 110.1;
Heb 1.13
10.14
ver 1
10.15
Heb 3.7
10.16
Jer 31.33,34

10.17
Heb 8.12

sat down at the right hand of God, 13 then to wait until his enemies should be made a stool for his feet. 14 For by a single offering he has perfected for all time those who are sanctified. 15And the Holy Spirit also bears witness to us; for after saying,

16 "This is the covenant that I will make with them
after those days, says the Lord:
I will put my laws on their hearts,
and write them on their minds,"

17 then he adds,

"I will remember their sins and their misdeeds no more."

18 Where there is forgiveness of these, there is no longer any offering for sin.

VI. Faith: the better way 10.19–12.29

A. Exhortation to hold firm

1. Our access to God the ground of our hope

10.19
Eph 2.18;
Heb 9.8,12
10.20
Heb 9.8,3
10.21
Heb 2.17;
1 Tim 3.15
10.22
Heb 4.16;
Eph 3.12;
Heb 9.14;
Ezek 36.25
10.23
Heb 4.14;
1 Cor 1.9
10.24
Heb 13.1;
Tit 3.8
10.25
Acts 2.42;
Heb 3.13;
Phil 4.5

19 Therefore, brethren, since we have confidence to enter the sanctuary by the blood of Jesus, 20 by the new and living way which he opened for us through the curtain, that is, through his flesh, 21 and since we have a great priest over the house of God, 22 let us draw near with a true heart in full assurance of faith, with our hearts sprinkled clean from an evil conscience and our bodies washed with pure water. 23 Let us hold fast the confession of our hope without wavering, for he who promised is faithful; 24 and let us consider how to stir up one another to love and good works, 25 not neglecting to meet together, as is the habit of some, but encouraging one another, and all the more as you see the Day drawing near.

2. The judgment for failure to hold firm

10.26
Num 15.30;
2 Pet 2.20
10.27
Heb 9.27;
Isa 26.11
10.28
Deut 17.2–
6;
Heb 2.2
10.29
Heb 2.3;
6.6; 13.20;
Eph 4.30;
Heb 6.4
10.30
Deut 32.35,
36;
Rom 12.19

26 For if we sin deliberately after receiving the knowledge of the truth, there no longer remains a sacrifice for sins, 27 but a fearful prospect of judgment, and a fury of fire which will consume the adversaries. 28A man who has violated the law of Moses dies without mercy at the testimony of two or three witnesses. 29 How much worse punishment do you think will be deserved by the man who has spurned the Son of God, and profaned the blood of the covenant by which he was sanctified, and outraged the Spirit of grace? 30 For we know him who said, "Vengeance is mine, I will repay." And again, "The Lord will judge his people." 31 It is a fearful thing to fall into the hands of the living God.

3. Future reward for those who endure

10.32
Heb 6.4;
Phil 1.29,30
10.33
1 Cor 4.9;
1 Thess 2.14
10.34
Heb 9.15
10.35
Heb 2.2
10.36
Lk 21.19;
Col 3.24

32 But recall the former days when, after you were enlightened, you endured a hard struggle with sufferings, 33 sometimes being publicly exposed to abuse and affliction, and sometimes being partners with those so treated. 34 For you had compassion on the prisoners, and you joyfully accepted the plundering of your property, since you knew that you yourselves had a better possession and an abiding one. 35 Therefore do not throw away your confidence, which has a great reward. 36 For you have need of endurance, so that you may do the will of God and receive what is promised.

37 "For yet a little while,
   and the coming one shall come and shall not tarry;
38 but my righteous one shall live by faith,
   and if he shrinks back,
   my soul has no pleasure in him."
39 But we are not of those who shrink back and are destroyed, but of those who have faith and keep their souls.

B. Definition and illustration of faith

1. Faith defined

11 Now faith is the assurance of things hoped for, the conviction of things not seen. 2 For by it the men of old received divine approval. 3 By faith we understand that the world was created by the word of God, so that what is seen was made out of things which do not appear.

2. Faith of the early patriarchs

4 By faith Abel offered to God a more acceptable sacrifice than Cain, through which he received approval as righteous, God bearing witness by accepting his gifts; he died, but through his faith he is still speaking. 5 By faith Enoch was taken up so that he should not see death; and he was not found, because God had taken him. Now before he was taken he was attested as having pleased God. 6 And without faith it is impossible to please him. For whoever would draw near to God must believe that he exists and that he rewards those who seek him. 7 By faith Noah, being warned by God concerning events as yet unseen, took heed and constructed an ark for the saving of his household; by this he condemned the world and became an heir of the righteousness which comes by faith.

3. The faith of Abraham and his children

8 By faith Abraham obeyed when he was called to go out to a place which he was to receive as an inheritance; and he went out, not knowing where he was to go. 9 By faith he sojourned in the land of promise, as in a foreign land, living in tents with Isaac and Jacob, heirs with him of the same promise. 10 For he looked forward to the city which has foundations, whose builder and maker is God. 11 By faith Sarah herself received power to conceive, even when she was past the age, since she considered him faithful who had promised. 12 Therefore from one man, and him as good as dead, were born descendants as many as the stars of heaven and as the innumerable grains of sand by the seashore.

13 These all died in faith, not having received what was promised, but having seen it and greeted it from afar, and having acknowledged that they were strangers and exiles on the earth. 14 For people who speak thus make it clear that they are seeking a homeland. 15 If they had been thinking of that land from which they had gone out, they would have had opportunity to return. 16 But as it is, they desire a better country, that is, a heavenly one.

10.37 Hab 2.3,4; Lk 18.8
10.38 Rom 1.17; Gal 3.11
10.39 2 Pet 2.20; Acts 16.30
*11.1 Rom 8.24; 2 Cor 4.18; 5.7
11.2 ver 4,39
11.3 Gen 1.1; Jn 1.3; Heb 6.5
11.4 Gen 4.4,10; 1 Jn 3.12; Heb 12.24
*11.5 Gen 5.21–24
11.6 Heb 7.19
11.7 Gen 6.13–22
11.8 Gen 12.1–4; Acts 7.2–4
11.9 Gen 12.8; 18.1,9; Heb 6.17
11.10 Heb 12.22; 13.14; Rev 21.2
11.11 Gen 17.19; 18.11–14; 21.2
11.12 Rom 4.19; Gen 22.17; 32.12
11.13 Gen 23.4; Ps 39.12
11.16 Ex 3.6,15; Phil 3.20; Heb 13.14

11.1 For a definition of faith see note to Eph 2.8.

11.5 See note to Gen 5.24 on translation of Enoch.

Therefore God is not ashamed to be called their God, for he has prepared for them a city.

17 By faith Abraham, when he was tested, offered up Isaac, and he who had received the promises was ready to offer up his only son, 18 of whom it was said, "Through Isaac shall your descendants be named." 19 He considered that God was able to raise men even from the dead; hence, figuratively speaking, he did receive him back. 20 By faith Isaac invoked future blessings on Jacob and Ēsau. 21 By faith Jacob, when dying, blessed each of the sons of Joseph, bowing in worship over the head of his staff. 22 By faith Joseph, at the end of his life, made mention of the exodus of the Israelites and gave directions concerning his burial.ˣ

4. The faith of Moses the deliverer

23 By faith Moses, when he was born, was hid for three months by his parents, because they saw that the child was beautiful; and they were not afraid of the king's edict. 24 By faith Moses, when he was grown up, refused to be called the son of Pharaōh's daughter, 25 choosing rather to share ill-treatment with the people of God than to enjoy the fleeting pleasures of sin. 26 He considered abuse suffered for the Christ greater wealth than the treasures of Egypt, for he looked to the reward. 27 By faith he left Egypt, not being afraid of the anger of the king; for he endured as seeing him who is invisible. 28 By faith he kept the Passover and sprinkled the blood, so that the Destroyer of the first-born might not touch them.

5. The faith of the Israelites and Rahab

29 By faith the people crossed the Red Sea as if on dry land; but the Egyptians, when they attempted to do the same, were drowned. 30 By faith the walls of Jĕr'ĭchō fell down after they had been encircled for seven days. 31 By faith Rāhăb the harlot did not perish with those who were disobedient, because she had given friendly welcome to the spies.

6. The faith of the judges and prophets

32 And what more shall I say? For time would fail me to tell of Gideon, Bạràk, Săṁsȯn, Jĕphtháh, of David and Samuel and the prophets—33 who through faith conquered kingdoms, enforced justice, received promises, stopped the mouths of lions, 34 quenched raging fire, escaped the edge of the sword, won strength out of weakness, became mighty in war, put foreign armies to flight. 35 Women received their dead by resurrection. Some were tortured, refusing to accept release, that they might rise again to a better life. 36 Others suffered mocking and scourging, and even chains and imprisonment. 37 They were stoned, they were sawn in two,ʸ they were killed with the sword; they went about in skins

ˣ Greek *bones*   ʸ Other manuscripts add *they were tempted*

Marginal references:

11.17 Gen 22.1–10; Jas 2.21
11.18 Gen 21.12; Rom 9.7
11.19 Rom 4.21
11.21 Gen 48.5, 16,20
11.22 Gen 50.24, 25; Ex 13.19
11.23 Ex 2.2; 1.16
11.24 Ex 2.10
11.25 ver 37
11.26 Heb 13.13; 2.2
11.27 Ex 12.50, 51; ver 13
11.28 Ex 12.21
11.29 Ex 14.21–31
11.30 Josh 6.12–21
11.31 Josh 2.9ff; 6.23; Jas 2.25
*11.32
11.33 2 Sam 7.11; Judg 14.5; 1 Sam 17.34; Dan 6.22
11.34 2 Ki 20.7; Judg 15.8
11.35 1 Ki 17.22; Acts 22.25
11.36 Jer 20.2
11.37 1 Ki 21.13; Acts 7.58; 2 Ki 1.8

11.32 From verse 32 to verse 35 the writer describes the glorious deliverances which came to those who trusted God. But from the middle of verse 35 the tone changes as the writer mentions other multitudes who also had faith in God but who were not delivered. While faith in God is essential to the believer's life, it is not the determining factor by which deliverance from difficult circumstances may be secured. The determining factor is the will of God. Therefore, in days past, among people of like faith, some were delivered and others found their deliverance in suffering and martyrdom.

of sheep and goats, destitute, afflicted, ill-treated—38 of whom the world was not worthy—wandering over deserts and mountains, and in dens and caves of the earth.

39 And all these, though well attested by their faith, did not receive what was promised, 40 since God had foreseen something better for us, that apart from us they should not be made perfect.

C. Faith and the believer

1. Christ our example

12 Therefore, since we are surrounded by so great a cloud of witnesses, let us also lay aside every weight, and sin which clings so closely, and let us run with perseverance the race that is set before us, 2 looking to Jesus the pioneer and perfecter of our faith, who for the joy that was set before him endured the cross, despising the shame, and is seated at the right hand of the throne of God.

2. Chastening for spiritual development

3 Consider him who endured from sinners such hostility against himself, so that you may not grow weary or fainthearted. 4 In your struggle against sin you have not yet resisted to the point of shedding your blood. 5 And have you forgotten the exhortation which addresses you as sons?—

"My son, do not regard lightly the discipline of the Lord,
    nor lose courage when you are punished by him.
6 For the Lord disciplines him whom he loves,
    and chastises every son whom he receives."

7 It is for discipline that you have to endure. God is treating you as sons; for what son is there whom his father does not discipline? 8 If you are left without discipline, in which all have participated, then you are illegitimate children and not sons. 9 Besides this, we have had earthly fathers to discipline us and we respected them. Shall we not much more be subject to the Father of spirits and live? 10 For they disciplined us for a short time at their pleasure, but he disciplines us for our good, that we may share his holiness. 11 For the moment all discipline seems painful rather than pleasant; later it yields the peaceful fruit of righteousness to those who have been trained by it.

3. Exhortation to endurance

12 Therefore lift your drooping hands and strengthen your weak knees, 13 and make straight paths for your feet, so that what is lame may not be put out of joint but rather be healed. 14 Strive for peace with all men, and for the holiness without which no one will see the Lord. 15 See to it that no one fail to obtain the grace of God; that no "root of bitterness" spring up and cause trouble, and by it the many become defiled; 16 that no one be immoral or irreligious like Ēsau, who sold his birthright for a single meal. 17 For you know that afterward, when he desired to inherit the blessing, he was rejected, for he found no chance to repent, though he sought it with tears.

Cross-references (right margin)

11.38
1 Ki 18.4

11.40
Heb 5.9

*12.1
1 Cor 9.24;
Heb 10.36

12.2
Phil 2.8,9;
Heb 1.3,13;
1 Pet 3.22

12.3
Mt 10.24;
Gal 6.9
12.4
Heb 10.32–34;
1 Cor 10.13
12.5
Prov 3.11,12
12.6
Ps 94.12;
Jas 1.12
12.7
Deut 8.5
12.8
1 Pet 5.9
12.9
Lk 18.2;
Num 16.22;
Isa 38.16
12.10
2 Pet 1.4
12.11
1 Pet 1.6;
Jas 3.17,18

12.12
Isa 35.3
12.13
Prov 4.26;
Gal 6.1
12.14
Rom 14.19;
6.22;
Mt 5.8
12.15
Gal 5.4;
Deut 29.18;
Heb 3.12
*12.16
Gen 25.33
12.17
Gen 27.30–40

12.1 See note to Rom 14.8 on Christian walk.   12.16 See note to Gen 25.25 on Esau.

4. *Final warning against apostasy*

18 For you have not come to what may be touched, a blazing fire, and darkness, and gloom, and a tempest, 19 and the sound of a trumpet, and a voice whose words made the hearers entreat that no further messages be spoken to them. 20 For they could not endure the order that was given, "If even a beast touches the mountain, it shall be stoned." 21 Indeed, so terrifying was the sight that Moses said, "I tremble with fear." 22 But you have come to Mount Zion and to the city of the living God, the heavenly Jerusalem, and to innumerable angels in festal gathering, 23 and to the assembly[z] of the first-born who are enrolled in heaven, and to a judge who is God of all, and to the spirits of just men made perfect, 24 and to Jesus, the mediator of a new covenant, and to the sprinkled blood that speaks more graciously than the blood of Abel.

25 See that you do not refuse him who is speaking. For if they did not escape when they refused him who warned them on earth, much less shall we escape if we reject him who warns from heaven. 26 His voice then shook the earth; but now he has promised, "Yet once more I will shake not only the earth but also the heaven." 27 This phrase, "Yet once more," indicates the removal of what is shaken, as of what has been made, in order that what cannot be shaken may remain. 28 Therefore let us be grateful for receiving a kingdom that cannot be shaken, and thus let us offer to God acceptable worship, with reverence and awe; 29 for our God is a consuming fire.

VII. *Conclusion 13.1–25*

A. *Exhortations and warnings*

1. *General Christian obligations*

13 Let brotherly love continue. 2 Do not neglect to show hospitality to strangers, for thereby some have entertained angels unawares. 3 Remember those who are in prison, as though in prison with them; and those who are ill-treated, since you also are in the body. 4 Let marriage be held in honor among all, and let the marriage bed be undefiled; for God will judge the immoral and adulterous. 5 Keep your life free from love of money, and be content with what you have; for he has said, "I will never fail you nor forsake you." 6 Hence we can confidently say,

"The Lord is my helper,
  I will not be afraid;
  what can man do to me?"

2. *Warning against apostasy*

7 Remember your leaders, those who spoke to you the word of God; consider the outcome of their life, and imitate their faith. 8 Jesus Christ is the same yesterday and today and for ever. 9 Do not be led away by diverse and strange teachings; for it is well that the heart be strengthened by grace, not by foods, which have not

---

z *Or* angels, and to the festal gathering and assembly

13.4 See note to 1 Cor 7.25 on marriage.   **13.5** See note to 1 Tim 6.10.

Marginal references

12.18 Ex 19.12–22; Deut 4.11
12.19 Ex 20.19; Deut 5.5
12.20 Ex 19.12,13
12.21 Ex 19.16
12.22 Phil 3.20; Gal 4.26
12.23 Lk 10.20; Phil 3.12
12.24 1 Tim 2.5; Gen 4.10; Heb 11.4
12.25 Heb 2.2,3; 8.5; 11.7
12.26 Ex 19.18; Hag 2.6
12.27 1 Cor 7.31; 2 Pet 3.10
12.28 Dan 2.44; Heb 13.15
12.29 Deut 4.24
13.1 Rom 12.10; 1 Thess 4.9; 1 Pet 1.22
13.2 1 Pet 4.9; Gen 18.3
13.3 Mt 25.36; Col 4.18
*13.4 1 Cor 6.9; Rev 22.15
*13.5 Phil 4.11; Deut 31.6, 8; Josh 1.5
13.7 ver 17; Heb 6.12
13.8 Heb 1.12
13.9 Eph 4.14; Col 2.7,16

benefited their adherents. 10 We have an altar from which those who serve the tent*a* have no right to eat. 11 For the bodies of those animals whose blood is brought into the sanctuary by the high priest as a sacrifice for sin are burned outside the camp. 12 So Jesus also suffered outside the gate in order to sanctify the people through his own blood. 13 Therefore let us go forth to him outside the camp, and bear the abuse he endured. 14 For here we have no lasting city, but we seek the city which is to come. 15 Through him then let us continually offer up a sacrifice of praise to God, that is, the fruit of lips that acknowledge his name. 16 Do not neglect to do good and to share what you have, for such sacrifices are pleasing to God.

17 Obey your leaders and submit to them; for they are keeping watch over your souls, as men who will have to give account. Let them do this joyfully, and not sadly, for that would be of no advantage to you.

3. *Request for prayer*

18 Pray for us, for we are sure that we have a clear conscience, desiring to act honorably in all things. 19 I urge you the more earnestly to do this in order that I may be restored to you the sooner.

B. *Personal references and benedictions*

20 Now may the God of peace who brought again from the dead our Lord Jesus, the great shepherd of the sheep, by the blood of the eternal covenant, 21 equip you with everything good that you may do his will, working in you*b* that which is pleasing in his sight, through Jesus Christ; to whom be glory for ever and ever. Amen.

22 I appeal to you, brethren, bear with my word of exhortation, for I have written to you briefly. 23 You should understand that our brother Timothy has been released, with whom I shall see you if he comes soon. 24 Greet all your leaders and all the saints. Those who come from Italy send you greetings. 25 Grace be with all of you. Amen.

a Or *tabernacle* *b* Other ancient authorities read *us*

13.10
1 Cor 9.13;
10.18
13.11
Ex 29.14;
Lev 16.27
13.12
Jn 19.17
13.13
Heb 11.26
13.14
Phil 3.20;
Heb 10.34;
12.22
13.15
1 Pet 2.5;
Isa 57.9;
Hos 14.2
13.17
Isa 62.6;
Acts 20.28

13.18
1 Thess
5.25;
Acts 24.16
13.19
Philem 22

13.20
Rom 15.33;
Zech 9.11
13.21
1 Pet 5.10;
Phil 2.13

13.23
1 Thess 3.2;
1 Tim 6.12
13.24
ver 7
13.25
Col 4.18;
Tit 3.15

INTRODUCTION TO

THE LETTER OF

JAMES

Authorship and Background: The author of this letter is "James, a servant of God and of the Lord Jesus Christ" (1.1), traditionally identified as James, brother of the Lord (Mt 13.55; Mk 6.3). The brothers of Jesus did not believe in him during his ministry (cf. Mk 3.21, 31–35; Jn 7.3–9); after the ascension, however, the brothers of Jesus are found with the Jerusalem church (Acts 1.14), and Paul speaks of the appearance of the risen Lord to James (1 Cor 15.7), who became a leader in the Jerusalem church (Acts 12.17; 15.13; 21.18; Gal 1.19; 2.9, 12).

There is no personal information about the author in the letter itself, except that he calls himself a teacher (3.1). He counsels with authority, and addresses his readers throughout as "brethren" (4.11; 5.7, 9, 10), "my brethren" (1.2; 2.1, 14; 3.1, 10, 12; 5.12, 19), and "my beloved brethren" (1.16, 19; 2.5).

Nothing can be established as to the date of the letter. If the traditional identification of the author is correct, the letter must have been written before A.D. 62, the date of the martyrdom of James. Some hold it to be the first New Testament book to be written, around A.D. 45. Those who do not accept the traditional identification, date it much later, toward the end of the first century or beginning of the second century A.D.

The readers are identified simply as "the twelve tribes in the Dispersion" (1.1) by which, undoubtedly, Christians everywhere are meant. There are no references in the epistle which identify the readers with any particular locality, and the whole tone of the letter fully justifies the name of "general (or, catholic) epistle."

Characteristics: The letter is concerned mainly with the practical aspects of the Christian faith, consisting of maxims and counsel for everyday conduct, of the type known as wisdom, or sapiential, literature (like the Book of Proverbs in the Old Testament). There is very little reference to any of the central doctrines of the Christian faith, and the Lord Jesus Christ is mentioned but twice (1.1; 2.1).

Faith is manifested in works, and is not to be thought of simply in terms of belief (2.18, 19). Faith is shown to be alive and active by the work it brings forth: whoever claims to have faith without works is mistaken, for apart from works faith is barren and dead, and is not really saving faith (2.14–26). There is no contradiction between the teaching here and that of Paul concerning faith and works: Paul endeavored to show that the works of the law cannot bring salvation, but faith alone; James shows that saving faith must necessarily manifest itself in deeds, so that if there are no deeds there is no faith.

The teachings on curbing one's anger (1.19–21), charity and chastity (1.26, 27), taming the tongue (3.1–12), withholding censorious judgment (4.11, 12),

the vanity of material wealth (5.1–3), the prohibition of swearing (5.12), all contain echoes of the teaching of Jesus, particularly those included in the Sermon on the Mount.

At times flashes of indignation appear, as in the author's strictures against snobbery in preference to rich over poor (2.1–8), his condemnation of injurious talk (3.6–12), his objection to friendship with the world (4.1–4), and his warnings against the rich who trust in their wealth (5.1–6). This is no ivory tower philosophy: these are hard bits of practical advice delivered by one who knew the temptations to which all Christians are subject, and who was intensely concerned that in all things, in deed, word and thought, believers should be doers of the word, not merely hearers (1.22), always resisting the devil and drawing near to God (4.7, 8).

Contents:

THE LETTER OF

JAMES

I. Salutation 1.1

1.1
Acts 12.17;
Tit 1.1;
Acts 26.7;
Deut 32.26;
Jn 7.35;
1 Pet 1.1

1 James, a servant of God and of the Lord Jesus Christ,
To the twelve tribes in the Dispersion:
Greeting.

II. True religion 1.2–27

A. Evidenced by patience in temptation

*1.2
Mt 5.12;
Heb 10.34;
1 Pet 1.6
1.3
Rom 5.3
1.4
Col 4.12;
1 Thess 5.23
1.5
1 Ki 3.9;
Prov 2.3;
1 Jn 5.14
1.6
Mk 11.24
1.7
Jas 4.8
1.10
1 Cor 7.31;
1 Pet 1.24
1.11
Isa 40.6–8;
Ps 102.4,11
1.12
Heb 12.5;
Jas 2.5
*1.13
1.15
Job 15.35;
Ps 7.14;
Rom 6.21,
23
1.16
1 Cor 6.9;
ver 19
1.17
Jn 3.27;
Mal 3.6
1.18
Jn 1.13;
Eph 1.12;
Rev 14.4

2 Count it all joy, my brethren, when you meet various trials,
3 for you know that the testing of your faith produces steadfastness. 4And let steadfastness have its full effect, that you may be perfect and complete, lacking in nothing.

5 If any of you lacks wisdom, let him ask God, who gives to all men generously and without reproaching, and it will be given him. 6 But let him ask in faith, with no doubting, for he who doubts is like a wave of the sea that is driven and tossed by the wind. 7,8 For that person must not suppose that a double-minded man, unstable in all his ways, will receive anything from the Lord.

9 Let the lowly brother boast in his exaltation, 10 and the rich in his humiliation, because like the flower of the grass he will pass away. 11 For the sun rises with its scorching heat and withers the grass; its flower falls, and its beauty perishes. So will the rich man fade away in the midst of his pursuits.

12 Blessed is the man who endures trial, for when he has stood the test he will receive the crown of life which God has promised to those who love him. 13 Let no one say when he is tempted, "I am tempted by God"; for God cannot be tempted with evil and he himself tempts no one; 14 but each person is tempted when he is lured and enticed by his own desire. 15 Then desire when it has conceived gives birth to sin; and sin when it is full-grown brings forth death.

16 Do not be deceived, my beloved brethren. 17 Every good endowment and every perfect gift is from above, coming down from the Father of lights with whom there is no variation or shadow due to change.ᵃ 18 Of his own will he brought us forth by the word of truth that we should be a kind of first fruits of his creatures.

a Other ancient authorities read *variation due to a shadow of turning*

1.2 See note to Job 1.14 on testing of Job.
1.13 To *tempt* is to *test* (*peirazō*), with a view to revealing the quality of a person's character. This testing often involves applying pressure to induce a person to violate his own code of ethics and so lead him into sin. James states that God never takes the initiative in tempting a man to sin; this impulse comes rather from personal weakness in the face of some incitement or pressure. *Each person is tempted when he is lured and enticed by his own desire* (ver 14). But God does permit the Christian to undergo trials and testings for the purpose of perfecting his faith and purifying his heart. Verse 2 and 1 Pet 1.6 speak of trials and not temptations. When believers fall through temptation it often occurs because they walk into it themselves. They are so careless and ill-prepared for their spiritual warfare that they may fall into temptation unrestrained by God. For this reason we are constantly to pray: *Lead us not into temptation, but deliver us from evil* (Mt 6.13).

B. Evidenced by conduct

19 Know this, my beloved brethren. Let every man be quick to hear, slow to speak, slow to anger, 20 for the anger of man does not work the righteousness of God. 21 Therefore put away all filthiness and rank growth of wickedness and receive with meekness the implanted word, which is able to save your souls.

22 But be doers of the word, and not hearers only, deceiving yourselves. 23 For if any one is a hearer of the word and not a doer, he is like a man who observes his natural face in a mirror; 24 for he observes himself and goes away and at once forgets what he was like. 25 But he who looks into the perfect law, the law of liberty, and perseveres, being no hearer that forgets but a doer that acts, he shall be blessed in his doing.

26 If any one thinks he is religious, and does not bridle his tongue but deceives his heart, this man's religion is vain. 27 Religion that is pure and undefiled before God and the Father is this: to visit orphans and widows in their affliction, and to keep oneself unstained from the world.

III. True faith 2.1–3.12

A. Evidenced by impartiality

2 My brethren, show no partiality as you hold the faith of our Lord Jesus Christ, the Lord of glory. 2 For if a man with gold rings and in fine clothing comes into your assembly, and a poor man in shabby clothing also comes in, 3 and you pay attention to the one who wears the fine clothing and say, "Have a seat here, please," while you say to the poor man, "Stand there," or, "Sit at my feet," 4 have you not made distinctions among yourselves, and become judges with evil thoughts? 5 Listen, my beloved brethren. Has not God chosen those who are poor in the world to be rich in faith and heirs of the kingdom which he has promised to those who love him? 6 But you have dishonored the poor man. Is it not the rich who oppress you, is it not they who drag you into court? 7 Is it not they who blaspheme the honorable name which was invoked over you?

8 If you really fulfil the royal law, according to the scripture, "You shall love your neighbor as yourself," you do well. 9 But if you show partiality, you commit sin, and are convicted by the law as transgressors. 10 For whoever keeps the whole law but fails in one point has become guilty of all of it. 11 For he who said, "Do not commit adultery," said also, "Do not kill." If you do not commit adultery but do kill, you have become a transgressor of the law. 12 So speak and so act as those who are to be judged under the law of liberty. 13 For judgment is without mercy to one who has shown no mercy; yet mercy triumphs over judgment.

1.19 Prov 5.1,2; 10.19
1.21 Eph 4.22; 1 Pet 2.1; Eph 1.13; Tit 2.11
1.22 Mt 7.21; Rom 2.13; 1 Jn 3.7
1.23
1.24 Lk 6.47; 1 Cor 13.12
1.25 2 Cor 3.18; Jas 2.12; Jn 13.17
1.26 Ps 34.13; 1 Pet 3.10
1.27 Mt 25.36; Rom 12.2; 1 Jn 5.18

*2.1 Prov 24.23; Mt 22.16; 1 Cor 2.8
2.2 ver 3
2.3 ver 2
2.4 Jn 7.24
2.5 1 Cor 1.26–28; Lk 12.21; Jas 1.12
2.6 1 Cor 11.22; Acts 8.3
2.8 Lev 19.18; Mt 22.39
*2.10 Mt 5.19; Gal 3.10
2.11 Ex 20.13, 14; Deut 5.17, 18
2.12 Jas 1.25
2.13 Mt 5.7; 18.32–35

2.1 *show no partiality*. All men are one in Christ; there is neither Jew nor Gentile, bond nor free, male nor female. Position, power, wealth, race, or color distinctions find no support in Scripture. Those who allow for such distinctions are guilty of sin.
2.10 Scripture differentiates between quantitative and qualitative sins. Here James shows that one sin, be it large or small, makes a man a sinner and brings him under the condemnation of the whole law. Thus, while one may distinguish between greater and lesser sinners (quantitative), both *are* sinners (qualitative).

B. Evidenced by works

14 What does it profit, my brethren, if a man says he has faith but has not works? Can his faith save him? 15 If a brother or sister is ill-clad and in lack of daily food, 16 and one of you says to them, "Go in peace, be warmed and filled," without giving them the things needed for the body, what does it profit? 17 So faith by itself, if it has no works, is dead.

18 But some one will say, "You have faith and I have works." Show me your faith apart from your works, and I by my works will show you my faith. 19 You believe that God is one; you do well. Even the demons believe—and shudder. 20 Do you want to be shown, you shallow man, that faith apart from works is barren? 21 Was not Abraham our father justified by works, when he offered his son Isaac upon the altar? 22 You see that faith was active along with his works, and faith was completed by works. 23 and the scripture was fulfilled which says, "Abraham believed God, and it was reckoned to him as righteousness"; and he was called the friend of God. 24 You see that a man is justified by works and not by faith alone. 25And in the same way was not also Rāhăb the harlot justified by works when she received the messengers and sent them out another way? 26 For as the body apart from the spirit is dead, so faith apart from works is dead.

C. Evidenced by words

3 Let not many of you become teachers, my brethren, for you know that we who teach shall be judged with greater strictness. 2 For we all make many mistakes, and if any one makes no mistakes in what he says he is a perfect man, able to bridle the whole body also. 3 If we put bits into the mouths of horses that they may obey us, we guide their whole bodies. 4 Look at the ships also; though they are so great and are driven by strong winds, they are guided by a very small rudder wherever the will of the pilot directs. 5 So the tongue is a little member and boasts of great things. How great a forest is set ablaze by a small fire!

6 And the tongue is a fire. The tongue is an unrighteous world among our members, staining the whole body, setting on fire the cycle of nature,[b] and set on fire by hell.[c] 7 For every kind of beast and bird, of reptile and sea creature, can be tamed and has been tamed by humankind, 8 but no human being can tame the tongue —a restless evil, full of deadly poison. 9 With it we bless the Lord and Father, and with it we curse men, who are made in the likeness of God. 10 From the same mouth come blessing and cursing. My brethren, this ought not to be so. 11 Does a spring pour forth from the same opening fresh water and brackish? 12 Can a fig tree, my brethren, yield olives, or a grapevine figs? No more can salt water yield fresh.

b Or wheel of birth   c Greek Gĕhĕn'nà

2.14 James presents here the reverse side of the coin of faith. In effect, he argues strongly against the idea that a man can be saved by a faith which does not radically transform his life and conduct. Thus he makes plain the truth that there can be no true faith if there are no evidences to prove that faith. He does not argue that we are saved by works, but that works demonstrate the existence of genuine faith. This is consistent with Paul's teaching that the believer is a new creation (2 Cor 5.17), and as such will manifest a new kind of character and behavior which will reflect the life of the Lord Jesus.

IV. *True wisdom 3.13–5.18*

A. *True versus false wisdom*

13 Who is wise and understanding among you? By his good life
let him show his works in the meekness of wisdom. 14 But if you
have bitter jealousy and selfish ambition in your hearts, do not
boast and be false to the truth. 15 This wisdom is not such as comes
down from above, but is earthly, unspiritual, devilish. 16 For
where jealousy and selfish ambition exist, there will be disorder
and every vile practice. 17 But the wisdom from above is first pure,
then peaceable, gentle, open to reason, full of mercy and good
fruits, without uncertainty or insincerity. 18And the harvest of
righteousness is sown in peace by those who make peace.

B. *Worldly friendship*

4 What causes wars, and what causes fightings among you? Is
it not your passions that are at war in your members? 2 You
desire and do not have; so you kill. And you covet*d* and cannot
obtain; so you fight and wage war. You do not have, because you
do not ask. 3 You ask and do not receive, because you ask wrongly,
to spend it on your passions. 4 Unfaithful creatures! Do you not
know that friendship with the world is enmity with God? Therefore whoever wishes to be a friend of the world makes himself an
enemy of God. 5 Or do you suppose it is in vain that the scripture
says, "He yearns jealously over the spirit which he has made to
dwell in us"? 6 But he gives more grace; therefore it says, "God
opposes the proud, but gives grace to the humble." 7 Submit
yourselves therefore to God. Resist the devil and he will flee from
you. 8 Draw near to God and he will draw near to you. Cleanse
your hands, you sinners, and purify your hearts, you men of double
mind. 9 Be wretched and mourn and weep. Let your laughter be
turned to mourning and your joy to dejection. 10 Humble yourselves before the Lord and he will exalt you.

C. *Slander*

11 Do not speak evil against one another, brethren. He that
speaks evil against a brother or judges his brother, speaks evil
against the law and judges the law. But if you judge the law, you
are not a doer of the law but a judge. 12 There is one lawgiver and
judge, he who is able to save and to destroy. But who are you that
you judge your neighbor?

D. *False confidence*

13 Come now, you who say, "Today or tomorrow we will go
into such and such a town and spend a year there and trade and
get gain"; 14 whereas you do not know about tomorrow. What is
your life? For you are a mist that appears for a little time and then
vanishes. 15 Instead you ought to say, "If the Lord wills, we shall
live and we shall do this or that." 16As it is, you boast in your
arrogance. All such boasting is evil. 17 Whoever knows what is
right to do and fails to do it, for him it is sin.

d Or you kill and you covet

3.13 Gal 6.4; Jas 2.18
3.14 Rom 2.8; ver 16; 1 Tim 2.4; Jas 5.19
3.15 Jas 1.17; 1 Tim 4.1
3.16 Gal 5.20
3.17 1 Cor 2.6; Rom 12.9; 1 Pet 1.22
3.18 Prov 11.18; Isa 32.17
4.1 Tit 3.9; Rom 7.23
4.3 Ps 18.41; 1 Jn 3.22; 5.14
4.4 Jas 1.27; 1 Jn 2.15; Jn 15.19
4.5 Gen 6.5; Num 11.29
4.6 Ps 138.6; Prov 3.34
4.7 1 Pet 5.6–9
4.8 2 Chr 15.2; Isa 1.16; Jas 1.8
4.9 Lk 6.25
4.10 Mt 23.12
4.11 1 Pet 2.1
4.12 Mt 10.28; Rom 14.4
4.13 Prov 27.1
4.14 Job 7.7; Ps 102.3
4.15 Acts 18.21
4.16 1 Cor 5.6
4.17 Lk 12.47; Jn 9.41

E. The end of the oppressor

5 Come now, you rich, weep and howl for the miseries that are coming upon you. ² Your riches have rotted and your garments are moth-eaten. ³ Your gold and silver have rusted, and their rust will be evidence against you and will eat your flesh like fire. You have laid up treasure*ᵉ* for the last days. ⁴ Behold, the wages of the laborers who mowed your fields, which you kept back by fraud, cry out; and the cries of the harvesters have reached the ears of the Lord of hosts. ⁵ You have lived on the earth in luxury and in pleasure; you have fattened your hearts in a day of slaughter. ⁶ You have condemned, you have killed the righteous man; he does not resist you.

F. The patience of the saints

⁷ Be patient, therefore, brethren, until the coming of the Lord. Behold, the farmer waits for the precious fruit of the earth, being patient over it until it receives the early and the late rain. ⁸ You also be patient. Establish your hearts, for the coming of the Lord is at hand. ⁹ Do not grumble, brethren, against one another, that you may not be judged; behold, the Judge is standing at the doors. ¹⁰As an example of suffering and patience, brethren, take the prophets who spoke in the name of the Lord. ¹¹ Behold, we call those happy who were steadfast. You have heard of the steadfastness of Jōb, and you have seen the purpose of the Lord, how the Lord is compassionate and merciful.

G. The avoidance of oaths

¹² But above all, my brethren, do not swear, either by heaven or by earth or with any other oath, but let your yes be yes and your no be no, that you may not fall under condemnation.

H. Prayer for the sick and confession of sins

¹³ Is any one among you suffering? Let him pray. Is any cheerful? Let him sing praise. ¹⁴ Is any among you sick? Let him call for the elders of the church, and let them pray over him, anointing him with oil in the name of the Lord; ¹⁵ and the prayer of faith will save the sick man, and the Lord will raise him up; and if he has committed sins, he will be forgiven. ¹⁶ Therefore confess your sins to one another, and pray for one another, that you may be healed. The prayer of a righteous man has great power in its effects. ¹⁷ Ĕlī'jăh was a man of like nature with ourselves and he prayed fervently that it might not rain, and for three years and six months

ᵉ Or will eat your flesh, since you have stored up fire

Side references: 5.1 Lk 6.24; 5.2 Job 13.28; Mt 6.20; 5.3 ver 7,8; 5.4 Lev 19.13; Deut 24.15; Rom 9.29; 5.5 Amos 6.1; Jer 12.3; 25.34; 5.7 Deut 11.14; Jer 5.24; 5.8 1 Pet 4.7; 5.9 Jas 4.11,12; Mt 24.33; 5.10 Mt 5.12; 5.11 Mt 5.10; Job 1.21,22; 42.10; Num 14.18; 5.12 Mt 5.34-37; 5.13 ver 10; Ps 50.15; Col 3.16; 5.14 Mk 6.13; *5.15 5.16 Mt 3.6; 1 Pet 2.24; Jn 9.31; 5.17 Acts 14.15; 1 Ki 17.1; Lk 4.25

5.15 God does, upon occasion, heal the sick directly, apart from the skill of medical science. The evidences confirm this fact beyond question. James assures us that this healing may be granted in response to the prayer of faith. This makes it plain that believers may be able to pray the prayer of faith and should seek to do so. But it is not always possible to know whether it is the will of God to heal or not. So the believer must always pray, "If it be Thy will." Believers are admonished to pray for healing, but they also are to seek the will of God (1 Jn 5.14). (See also Paul's experience of praying earnestly for a healing which was not granted, 2 Cor 12.7-19.)

James 5.18–20

it did not rain on the earth. 18 Then he prayed again and the heaven gave rain, and the earth brought forth its fruit.

5.18
1 Ki 18.42,
45

V. Conclusion 5.19,20

19 My brethren, if any one among you wanders from the truth and some one brings him back, 20 let him know that whoever brings back a sinner from the error of his way will save his soul from death and will cover a multitude of sins.

*5.19
Mt 18.15
5.20
Rom 11.14;
1 Pet 4.8

5.19 James is not speaking here of one who has departed from theological truth or Christian belief, but of one who has departed from the practice of the faith in his daily life and conduct. A concern for one's bodily infirmities (ver 14) and prayer for deliverance is no more important than prayer for, and deliverance of, a brother who has a need for spiritual help. To aid in bringing back anyone to the right path is a necessary work for all believers, and in so doing they will *save his soul from death.*

INTRODUCTION TO
THE FIRST LETTER OF
PETER

Authorship and Background: "Peter, an apostle of Jesus Christ" (1.1) was the simple and unpretentious way in which the author introduced himself to his readers; he addressed the elders as "a fellow elder and a witness of the sufferings of Christ" (5.1). He wrote from "Babylon" (5.13), which was probably a pseudonym for Rome (as in Rev 14.8; 18.2, 10, 21). His scribe was Silvanus (5.12), probably the same as Silas in the Book of Acts (ch 15–18), who was called Silvanus in Paul's epistles (2 Cor 1.19; 1 Thess 1.1; 2 Thess 1.1). With him was Mark, whom he designated "my son" (5.13), probably the John Mark of the Book of Acts and Paul's epistles (Acts 12.25; 13.4–13; 15.37–39; Col 4.10; Philem 24; 2 Tim 4.11).

Peter wrote to Christians who lived in the Roman provinces of Pontus, Galatia, Cappadocia, Asia, and Bithynia (1.1), in the northern part of Asia Minor. It may be that he named the provinces in the order that conformed to the route the messenger would follow in taking the letter to the churches.

The letter reflects a time of suffering and trial; the readers have already undergone some persecution and further trials await them (1.6; 3.9, 13–17; 4.1, 2, 12–19; 5.9, 10). What was the nature of this "fiery ordeal" (4.12)? There is no record of widespread persecution of Christians by the Roman government before the time of Domitian, toward the end of the first century, and Nero's persecution in the sixties was confined to Rome and did not extend to the provinces. The sufferings referred to in this letter, therefore, were those which frequently arose as Christians lived their faith in a pagan and hostile society. The governing authorities are not blamed; on the contrary, the readers are exhorted to be subject to them, and to honor the emperor himself (2.13).

Since Peter died in A.D. 64 (or 67), this letter was probably written in the early sixties of the first century.

The readers are called "the exiles of the Dispersion" (1.1; cf. Jas 1.1), by which is meant that they, like Israel of old, were dispersed throughout the world. Most of them were probably Gentiles, not Jews, as seen from the references to their former way of life (1.14, 18; 2.9, 10; 4.3, 4).

Characteristics: The writer calls his letter a brief message of exhortation and testimony (5.12). This "epistle of grace and hope," as one modern writer calls it, is notable for its gentle tone of admonition and exhortation, which comes from a pastor who does not lord it over his flock but sets an example to them (5.2, 3). He exhorts (cf. 2.11; 5.1, 12) them to a life of purity and spirituality, abstaining from malice, envy, slander (2.1), and other carnal passions of heathen living (1.14; 2.11; 4.2, 3). They are God's chosen people, a royal priesthood, a holy nation, whose high calling it is to proclaim God's great deeds (2.9). They are to use their Christian freedom to live as befits God's servants (2.16), showing

sympathy, love (1.22; 4.8), humility (5.1–6), hospitality (4.9), and finally, "unity of spirit, sympathy, love of the brethren, a tender heart and a humble mind" (3.8). In suffering they are to follow Christ's example (2.20–25; 3.17, 18; 4.1, 12–19); the "living hope" which is theirs is ground for their indestructible confidence in God (1.3, 21). In all their afflictions and sufferings they are to trust in God, "for he cares about you" (5.6, 7).

No other New Testament book so reflects the real nature and effect of God's love in Christ as this short epistle.

Contents:

I. Salutation. 1.1, 2

II. The blessings of the redeemed. 1.3—2.10: A living hope, joy, freedom, confidence, are some of the blessings; therefore Christians are to live pure lives, abstain from all sins which destroy the Christian fellowship. They are now God's people and the objects of his mercy.

III. The duties of believers. 2.11—4.11: Live worthily of your calling, as free men: servants, wives, and husbands have their particular responsibilities. If suffering comes you are to follow Christ's example, each one employing his gift for the mutual welfare, that in everything God may be glorified through Jesus Christ.

IV. Constancy in trial. 4.12—5.11: Your coming trial is occasion for joy and witness; resist the enemy, for God cares for his own and will restore, establish, and strengthen you.

V. Conclusion and benediction. 5.12–14

THE FIRST LETTER OF
PETER

I. Salutation 1.1,2

1.1
2 Pet 2.1;
Acts 2.5,9
*1.2
2 Thess
2.13;
Heb 10.22;
2 Pet 1.2

1 Peter, an apostle of Jesus Christ,
To the exiles of the Dispersion in Pŏntŭs, Gălā'țiă, Căppă-
dō'çiă, Asia, and Bĭthўn'iă, 2 chosen and destined by God the
Father and sanctified by the Spirit for obedience to Jesus Christ
and for sprinkling with his blood:
May grace and peace be multiplied to you.

II. The blessings of the redeemed 1.3–2.10

A. The risen Christ

1.3
2 Cor 1.3;
Jas 1.18;
1 Cor 15.20
1.4
Col 3.24
1.5
Jn 10.28
1.6
Rom 5.2;
1 Pet 5.10;
Jas 1.2
1.7
Jas 1.3;
Ps 66.10;
Rom 2.7
1.8
1 Jn 4.20;
Jn 20.29
1.9
Rom 6.22

3 Blessed be the God and Father of our Lord Jesus Christ! By
his great mercy we have been born anew to a living hope through
the resurrection of Jesus Christ from the dead, 4 and to an inheritance which is imperishable, undefiled, and unfading, kept in
heaven for you, 5 who by God's power are guarded through faith
for a salvation ready to be revealed in the last time. 6 In this you
rejoice,[a] though now for a little while you may have to suffer
various trials, 7 so that the genuineness of your faith, more precious
than gold which though perishable is tested by fire, may redound
to praise and glory and honor at the revelation of Jesus Christ.
8 Without having seen[b] him you[c] love him; though you do not
now see him you[c] believe in him and rejoice with unutterable and
exalted joy. 9 As the outcome of your faith you obtain the salvation
of your souls.

B. The witness of the prophets

1.10
Mt 13.17;
26.24
1.11
2 Pet 1.21;
Isa ch 53
1.12
Dan 9.24;
Eph 3.10

10 The prophets who prophesied of the grace that was to be
yours searched and inquired about this salvation; 11 they inquired
what person or time was indicated by the Spirit of Christ within
them when predicting the sufferings of Christ and the subsequent
glory. 12 It was revealed to them that they were serving not themselves but you, in the things which have now been announced to
you by those who preached the good news to you through the
Holy Spirit sent from heaven, things into which angels long to
look.

a Or *Rejoice in this*   *b* Other ancient authorities read *known*   *c* Or omit *you*

1.2 Foreknowledge may be defined as that
attribute of God by which all things are
known by Him from the beginning. Thus,
God knew from eternity who would be converted. The problem is to relate *foreknowledge*
to the doctrine of *election*. (See note to Eph
1.4 on election and foreknowledge.)
Following the Old Testament pattern, the
blood was not only shed but it was also
sprinkled and applied to the altar or whatever
was to be cleansed. This sprinkling, then,
signified that believers had received the
benefit of the sacrifice of their innocent
substitute. The sprinkled blood of Christ
assures New Testament believers of four
benefits: (1) that they are justified (Rom 5.9);
(2) that they have the seal of God's covenant
promises to them (of which the Lord's
Supper is also a sign—Lk 22.20); (3) that
they are cleansed from all sin (1 Jn 1.7); (4)
that they are admitted into the citizenship of
heaven (Heb 10.19).

C. Exhortation to a holy life

13 Therefore gird up your minds, be sober, set your hope fully upon the grace that is coming to you at the revelation of Jesus Christ. 14 As obedient children, do not be conformed to the passions of your former ignorance, 15 but as he who called you is holy, be holy yourselves in all your conduct; 16 since it is written, "You shall be holy, for I am holy." 17 And if you invoke as Father him who judges each one impartially according to his deeds, conduct yourselves with fear throughout the time of your exile. 18 You know that you were ransomed from the futile ways inherited from your fathers, not with perishable things such as silver or gold, 19 but with the precious blood of Christ, like that of a lamb without blemish or spot. 20 He was destined before the foundation of the world but was made manifest at the end of the times for your sake. 21 Through him you have confidence in God, who raised him from the dead and gave him glory, so that your faith and hope are in God.[d]

22 Having purified your souls by your obedience to the truth for a sincere love of the brethren, love one another earnestly from the heart. 23 You have been born anew, not of perishable seed but of imperishable, through the living and abiding word of God; 24 for

"All flesh is like grass
and all its glory like the flower of grass.
The grass withers, and the flower falls,
25 but the word of the Lord abides for ever."

That word is the good news which was preached to you.

2 So put away all malice and all guile and insincerity and envy and all slander. 2 Like newborn babes, long for the pure spiritual milk, that by it you may grow up to salvation; 3 for you have tasted the kindness of the Lord.

D. Christ our cornerstone

4 Come to him, to that living stone, rejected by men but in God's sight chosen and precious; 5 and like living stones be yourselves built into a spiritual house, to be a holy priesthood, to offer

d Or so that your faith is hope in God

1.13 Eph 6.14; 1 Thess 5.6
1.14 Rom 12.2; Eph 4.18
1.15 2 Cor 7.1
1.16 Lev 11.44
1.17 Deut 10.17; Heb 12.28
*1.18 1 Cor 6.20; Ezek 20.18
1.19 Ex 12.5
1.20 Eph 1.4; Heb 9.26
1.22 Jas 4.8; Heb 13.1
*1.23 Jn 3.3; 1.13; Heb 4.12
1.24 Isa 40.6–9; Jas 1.10,11
1.25 Jn 1.1
2.1 Eph 4.22; Jas 1.21; 4.11
2.2 Mk 10.15; 1 Cor 3.2
2.3 Heb 6.5; Tit 3.4
2.4 ver 7
*2.5 Heb 13.15; Phil 4.18

1.18 The word here translated *ransomed* (*lutroō*) signifies "to buy back from bondage" or "to redeem." (This same verb is rendered *redeem* in Lk 24.21, and the noun *apolutrōsis* is translated "redemption.") The need for redemption arises from the sinner's bondage to sin and Satan (Rom 6.17; Jn 8.34; Rom 6.23). Redemption itself comes from God and is of free grace. It is made possible by Jesus Christ the Redeemer (1 Cor 1.30; Gal 3.13; 4.4, 5; Eph 1.7; Tit 2.14) on the basis of His shed blood. Redemption is both past and future. The price has been paid forever and believers are now redeemed, but they wait in hope for the final fulfilment of that which is already theirs by faith (Rom 8.23). The redeemed who once belonged to Satan now belong to God (1 Cor 6.20). Their chief end in life is to glorify the One who redeemed them (2.9).

1.23 See note to Jn 3.3 on the new birth.

2.5 Every believer, being united with Christ Himself by faith, is constituted a priest before the Lord. (See also 2.9; Rev 1.6.) In the Old Testament era, believers required a priest to mediate between them and God through his services at the altar. There was also a high priest who mediated for them in the Holy of Holies. But Christ has now become the believer's high priest (Heb 4.14; 5.10; 7.27; 9.11). Immediate access to God is possible through Him without any intermediary. The only priesthood of continuing validity spoken of in the New Testament is this priesthood of all believers, both laity and clergy. Never is the term "priest" (*hiereus*) applied to an apostle or ordained elder in the church, except as he partakes of this universal priesthood. A recovery of this New Testament truth furnished one of the great liberating impulses of the Reformation, from the time of Luther on.

2.6
Isa 28.16;
Eph 2.20
spiritual sacrifices acceptable to God through Jesus Christ. 6 For it stands in scripture:

"Behold, I am laying in Zion a stone, a cornerstone chosen and precious,
and he who believes in him will not be put to shame."

2.7
Ps 118.22;
Mt 21.42
7 To you therefore who believe, he is precious, but for those who do not believe,

"The very stone which the builders rejected
has become the head of the corner,"

2.8
Isa 8.14;
1 Cor 1.23;
Rom 9.22
8 and

"A stone that will make men stumble,
a rock that will make them fall";

for they stumble because they disobey the word, as they were destined to do.

2.9
Deut 10.15;
Acts 26.18
9 But you are a chosen race, a royal priesthood, a holy nation, God's own people,e that you may declare the wonderful deeds of him who called you out of darkness into his marvelous light.

2.10
Hos 1.9,10
10 Once you were no people but now you are God's people; once you had not received mercy but now you have received mercy.

III. The duties of believers 2.11–4.11

A. The Christian and unbelievers

2.11
Rom 12.1;
Ps 39.12;
Gal 5.16;
Jas 4.1
2.12
Phil 2.15;
1 Pet 3.16;
Mt 5.16
11 Beloved, I beseech you as aliens and exiles to abstain from the passions of the flesh that wage war against your soul. 12 Maintain good conduct among the Gentiles, so that in case they speak against you as wrongdoers, they may see your good deeds and glorify God on the day of visitation.

B. The Christian and the state

2.13
Rom 13.1
2.14
Rom 13.4,3
2.15
1 Pet 3.17;
Tit 2.8
2.16
Gal 5.1;
1 Cor 7.22
*2.17
Rom 12.10;
Heb 13.1
13 Be subject for the Lord's sake to every human institution,f whether it be to the emperor as supreme, 14 or to governors as sent by him to punish those who do wrong and to praise those who do right. 15 For it is God's will that by doing right you should put to silence the ignorance of foolish men. 16 Live as free men, yet without using your freedom as a pretext for evil; but live as servants of God. 17 Honor all men. Love the brotherhood. Fear God. Honor the emperor.

C. The servant and his master

2.18
Eph 6.5
2.19
Rom 13.5
18 Servants, be submissive to your masters with all respect, not only to the kind and gentle but also to the overbearing. 19 For one is approved if, mindful of God, he endures pain while suffering

e Greek *a people for his possession*   f Or *every institution ordained for men*

2.17 The concept of the brotherhood of man must be understood within the limitations imposed by Scripture. There is a sense in which all men are brothers in that they are descended from Adam as their common ancestor. But the Scripture nowhere speaks of this brotherhood (for Mal 2.10 is spoken only to Jews within the covenant bond). It does speak, however, of a brotherhood which springs from the new birth and the adoption of sons. By this new spiritual relationship believers are not only connected with God through Christ, but also with each other as children and heirs of God (1 Jn 3.2; Gal 3.26). Only those who have a Christian faith in the Lord are accounted as children of God in the biblical sense, and because of this they are brothers to all who own the same Lord.

unjustly. 20 For what credit is it, if when you do wrong and are
beaten for it you take it patiently? But if when you do right and
suffer for it you take it patiently, you have God's approval.

D. Christ our great example

21 For to this you have been called, because Christ also suffered
for you, leaving you an example, that you should follow in his
steps. 22 He committed no sin; no guile was found on his lips.
23 When he was reviled, he did not revile in return; when he
suffered, he did not threaten; but he trusted to him who judges
justly. 24 He himself bore our sins in his body on the tree,g that
we might die to sin and live to righteousness. By his wounds you
have been healed. 25 For you were straying like sheep, but have
now returned to the Shepherd and Guardian of your souls.

E. The husband and the wife

3 Likewise you wives, be submissive to your husbands, so that
some, though they do not obey the word, may be won without
a word by the behavior of their wives, 2 when they see your reverent and chaste behavior. 3 Let not yours be the outward adorning
with braiding of hair, decoration of gold, and wearing of fine
clothing, 4 but let it be the hidden person of the heart with the
imperishable jewel of a gentle and quiet spirit, which in God's
sight is very precious. 5 So once the holy women who hoped in
God used to adorn themselves and were submissive to their husbands, 6 as Sarah obeyed Abraham, calling him lord. And you are
now her children if you do right and let nothing terrify you.

7 Likewise you husbands, live considerately with your wives,
bestowing honor on the woman as the weaker sex, since you are
joint heirs of the grace of life, in order that your prayers may not
be hindered.

F. Christian conduct in review

8 Finally, all of you, have unity of spirit, sympathy, love of the

g Or carried up . . . to the tree

2.20	1 Pet 3.17
2.21	Mt 16.24; Acts 14.22
2.22	Isa 53.9
2.23	Isa 53.7; Heb 12.3; Lk 23.46
*2.24	Heb 9.28; Rom 6.2; Isa 53.5
2.25	Isa 53.6; 1 Pet 5.4
3.1	Eph 5.22; 1 Cor 7.16
*3.3	1 Tim 2.9; Isa 3.18–23
3.4	Rom 7.22
3.5	1 Tim 5.5
3.6	Gen 18.12
3.7	Eph 5.25; 1 Thess 4.4; Mt 5.23ff
3.8	Phil 2.3; 1 Pet 5.5

2.24 Christ died as a vicarious sacrifice for
sin. Three assumptions govern this doctrine:
(1) The sinner lies under the wrath of God
and is therefore lost and undone (Rom 1.18;
3.19; 6.23); (2) by the grace of God, provision
was made for Christ to offer Himself as a
sin-bearer (Isa 53.6; 2 Cor 5.21); (3) God
was willing to accept the atonement of Christ
so that the sinner himself secures the benefits
of forgiveness, peace, and fellowship with
God (Rom 5.1, 6, 8, 10). In the Old Testament the blood-sacrifices had to be repeated
because they could not take away sin once
and forever. When offered by faith, however,
these sacrifices looked toward the future death
of Christ and drew in advance upon the merit
of His atonement. Since His death there is
no need for further sacrifice in a holy communion which claims to repeat the sacrifice
of Calvary (Heb 10.4; 9.11–15).

3.3 Scripture does not prohibit the wearing
of adornments and jewelry as such, for that
interpretation of this verse would also require
a prohibition of wearing outer clothing of any
sort since this is the true meaning of the word
here translated robes. What is meant here
is that the true adornment of the Christian,
whether a man or a woman, consists in the
spiritual qualities of a gentle and peaceable
character. It may be fairly inferred also that
a certain modesty and circumspection in dress
should characterize Christian women. But
what is chiefly emphasized is the inward
attitude of the heart and a modesty in external
appearance and manner. Doubtless we may
assume that anyone who has crucified the
flesh with its passions and desires (Gal 5.24)
will avoid any mode of dress which is designed
to draw undue attention to one's own person.
(See also 1 Tim 2.9.)

brethren, a tender heart and a humble mind. 9 Do not return evil for evil or reviling for reviling; but on the contrary bless, for to this you have been called, that you may obtain a blessing. 10 For

"He that would love life
and see good days,
let him keep his tongue from evil
and his lips from speaking guile;
11 let him turn away from evil and do right;
let him seek peace and pursue it.
12 For the eyes of the Lord are upon the righteous,
and his ears are open to their prayer.
But the face of the Lord is against those that do evil."

G. *The Christian and persecution*

13 Now who is there to harm you if you are zealous for what is right? 14 But even if you do suffer for righteousness' sake, you will be blessed. Have no fear of them, nor be troubled, 15 but in your hearts reverence Christ as Lord. Always be prepared to make a defense to any one who calls you to account for the hope that is in you, yet do it with gentleness and reverence; 16 and keep your conscience clear, so that, when you are abused, those who revile your good behavior in Christ may be put to shame. 17 For it is better to suffer for doing right, if that should be God's will, than for doing wrong. 18 For Christ also died[h] for sins once for all, the righteous for the unrighteous, that he might bring us to God, being put to death in the flesh but made alive in the spirit; 19 in which he went and preached to the spirits in prison, 20 who formerly did not obey, when God's patience waited in the days of Noah, during the building of the ark, in which a few, that is, eight persons, were saved through water. 21 Baptism, which corresponds to this, now saves you, not as a removal of dirt from the body but as an appeal to God for a clear conscience, through the resurrection of Jesus Christ, 22 who has gone into heaven and is at the right hand of God, with angels, authorities, and powers subject to him.

H. *Exhortation to duty*

4 Since therefore Christ suffered in the flesh,[i] arm yourselves with the same thought, for whoever has suffered in the flesh has ceased from sin, 2 so as to live for the rest of the time in the flesh no longer by human passions but by the will of God. 3 Let the time that is past suffice for doing what the Gentiles like to do, living in licentiousness, passions, drunkenness, revels, carousing, and lawless idolatry. 4 They are surprised that you do not now join them in the same wild profligacy, and they abuse you; 5 but

---

Cross references (left margin):

3.9 Rom 12.17; Heb 6.14
3.10 Ps 34.12–16; Jas 1.26; 1 Pet 2.1,22
3.13 Prov 16.7
3.14 1 Pet 2.19ff; Isa 8.12,13
3.15 Col 4.6; 1 Pet 1.3; 1.17
3.16 Heb 13.18; 1 Pet 2.12, 15
3.17 1 Pet 2.20, 15
3.18 1 Pet 2.21; 2 Cor 13.4; Eph 3.12; 1 Pet 4.1,6
*3.19 1 Pet 4.6
3.20 Gen 6.3,5; Heb 11.7; Gen 8.18
*3.21 Tit 3.5; Heb 9.14; 1 Pet 1.3
3.22 Rom 8.34, 38
4.1 1 Pet 3.18; Gal 5.24
4.2 Gal 2.20; Rom 6.11
4.3 Eph 4.17
4.4 1 Pet 3.16
4.5 Acts 10.42; 2 Tim 4.1

---

h Other ancient authorities read *suffered*
i Other ancient authorities add *for us;* some *for you*

3.19 This verse has been much disputed. Some have interpreted it to mean that Christ, between His Crucifixion and Resurrection, preached to the lost in Hades (see note to Lk 10.15) so that they might have a second chance. This explanation, however, runs counter to other Scriptures which are quite explicit in precluding the possibility of a second chance (e.g., Lk 16.26; Heb 9.27). Others interpret this verse by reference to verse 20 and take it to mean that Christ was in Noah by the Holy Spirit when he preached to the doomed race of antediluvians.

3.21 See note to Mt 28.19*a* on baptism.

they will give account to him who is ready to judge the living and the dead. 6 For this is why the gospel was preached even to the dead, that though judged in the flesh like men, they might live in the spirit like God.

7 The end of all things is at hand; therefore keep sane and sober for your prayers. 8Above all hold unfailing your love for one another, since love covers a multitude of sins. 9 Practice hospitality ungrudgingly to one another. 10As each has received a gift, employ it for one another, as good stewards of God's varied grace: 11 whoever speaks, as one who utters oracles of God; whoever renders service, as one who renders it by the strength which God supplies; in order that in everything God may be glorified through Jesus Christ. To him belong glory and dominion for ever and ever. Amen.

IV. Constancy in trial 4.12–5.11

A. Exhortation to steadfastness

12 Beloved, do not be surprised at the fiery ordeal which comes upon you to prove you, as though something strange were happening to you. 13 But rejoice in so far as you share Christ's sufferings, that you may also rejoice and be glad when his glory is revealed. 14 If you are reproached for the name of Christ, you are blessed, because the spirit of glory[j] and of God rests upon you. 15 But let none of you suffer as a murderer, or a thief, or a wrongdoer, or a mischief-maker; 16 yet if one suffers as a Christian, let him not be ashamed, but under that name let him glorify God. 17 For the time has come for judgment to begin with the household of God; and if it begins with us, what will be the end of those who do not obey the gospel of God? 18And

"If the righteous man is scarcely saved,
  where will the impious and sinner appear?"

19 Therefore let those who suffer according to God's will do right and entrust their souls to a faithful Creator.

B. Exhortation to faithfulness

5 So I exhort the elders among you, as a fellow elder and a witness of the sufferings of Christ as well as a partaker in the glory that is to be revealed. 2 Tend the flock of God that is your charge,[k] not by constraint but willingly,[l] not for shameful gain but eagerly, 3 not as domineering over those in your charge but being examples to the flock. 4And when the chief Shepherd is manifested you will obtain the unfading crown of glory. 5 Likewise you that are younger be subject to the elders. Clothe yourselves, all of you, with humility toward one another, for "God opposes the proud, but gives grace to the humble."

6 Humble yourselves therefore under the mighty hand of God,

---

j Other ancient authorities insert *and of power*
k Other ancient authorities add *exercising the oversight*
l Other ancient authorities add *as God would have you*

5.1 See note to Tit 1.5 for information on the office of elder.

5.4 See note to Jn 10.11 on Christ, the good shepherd.

Marginal references

4.6 — 1 Pet 3.19
4.7 — Rom 13.11; 1 Pet 1.13
4.8 — Heb 13.1; 1 Cor 13.7
4.9 — Heb 13.2; 2 Cor 9.7
4.10 — Rom 12.6, 7; 1 Cor 4.1
4.11 — Eph 6.10; 5.20; 1 Tim 6.16
4.12 — 1 Pet 1.6,7
4.13 — Phil 3.10; Rom 8.17
4.14 — Mt 5.11
4.15 — 1 Thess 4.11
4.16 — Acts 5.41
4.17 — Jer 25.29; Mal 3.5
4.18 — Prov 11.31; Lk 23.31
4.19 — 2 Tim 1.12
*5.1 — Lk 24.48; 1 Pet 1.5,7; Rev 1.9
5.2 — Jn 21.16; 1 Cor 9.17; 1 Tim 3.3,8; Tit 1.7
5.3 — Ezek 34.4; Phil 3.17
*5.4 — Heb 13.20; 2 Tim 4.8
5.5 — Jas 4.6; Isa 57.15
5.6 — Jas 4.10

5.7
Ps 37.5;
Mt 6.25;
Heb 13.5
5.8
Lk 21.34;
Job 1.7
5.9
Jas 4.7;
Col 2.5;
Acts 14.22
5.10
Heb 13.21;
2 Thess 2.17

that in due time he may exalt you. 7 Cast all your anxieties on him, for he cares about you. 8 Be sober, be watchful. Your adversary the devil prowls around like a roaring lion, seeking some one to devour. 9 Resist him, firm in your faith, knowing that the same experience of suffering is required of your brotherhood throughout the world. 10And after you have suffered a little while, the God of all grace, who has called you to his eternal glory in Christ, will himself restore, establish, and strengthenᵐ you. 11 To him be the dominion for ever and ever. Amen.

V. Conclusion and benediction 5.12–14

5.12
2 Cor 1.19;
Heb 13.22
5.13
Acts 12.12
5.14
Rom 16.16;
Eph 6.23

12 By Sĭlvā′nŭs, a faithful brother as I regard him, I have written briefly to you, exhorting and declaring that this is the true grace of God; stand fast in it. 13 She who is at Babylon, who is likewise chosen, sends you greetings; and so does my son Mark. 14 Greet one another with the kiss of love.

Peace to all of you that are in Christ.

m Other ancient authorities read *restore, establish, strengthen and settle*

INTRODUCTION TO
THE SECOND LETTER OF
PETER

Authorship and Background: The author identifies himself as Simon Peter, "servant and apostle of Jesus Christ" (1.1). He speaks of his imminent death, in conformance with Christ's statement (1.13–15), which is probably a reference to Jn 21.18, 19. He also refers to the Transfiguration of Christ "on the holy mountain" (1.16–18). He speaks of a previous letter (3.1), and of the letters of Paul (3.15, 16).

The earliest references to this letter, in the writings of Origen, Eusebius, and Jerome, show that there were some who doubted the apostolic authorship of the letter, while others accepted it as apostolic. Eusebius, for example, did not say that the letter was spurious but at the same time he was not prepared to grant it equal footing with other books of the canon about which he had no question. Nor did Origen say that it was spurious, only that its authenticity was disputed. In the present time, many scholars believe that the letter is pseudonymous, written in the name of the apostle by an unknown Christian leader toward the middle of the second century. They base their position mainly on the difference in style and quality of Greek from 1 Peter; the description of the heresy being combatted; the reference to Paul's letters as Scriptures, and the time element implied in 3.4. Those who accept the apostolic authorship point to a similarity in the two letters in the use of certain words and phrases, the emphatic autobiographical references, and similarity in teaching. The date of the letter depends, of course, upon one's opinion of the authorship. Assuming Petrine authorship, as conservatives have always done, it was written shortly after 1 Peter.

The readers are not identified, but are addressed in general terms (1.1, 2). If the previous letter referred to in 3.1 is 1 Peter, then the readers are the same as those addressed in 1 Peter 1.1, 2.

Characteristics: The letter is a "reminder" (1.12; 3.1) of the truth of the Gospel, against the pernicious attacks of false teachers who were bringing in destructive heresies. Like Israel's false prophets, these false teachers were corrupt and immoral (2.2, 3, 10), indulging in revelries and carousals (2.13, 14), licentious, and defiled by the world and its passions (2.17–22). In their teaching they were scoffing at the belief in the Lord's return (3.3–10). The author, however, reminds his readers that the Lord will keep his promise (3.10–13); therefore, they are warned to keep themselves spotless and pure (3.14), and to grow in the grace and knowledge of our Lord and Savior Jesus Christ (3.18). God will punish the wicked (2.1, 3, 9, 10, 12, 17), even as he did the rebellious angels (2.4), the world of Noah's day (2.5), and Sodom and Gomorrah (2.6). He delays his punishment in order that men may repent; but the day will come when he will destroy the whole universe, and then there will be the new heavens and a new earth, in which righteousness dwells (3.8–13).

Introduction to 2 Peter

Contents:

THE SECOND LETTER OF

PETER

I. Salutation 1.1,2

1 Simeon[x] Peter, a servant and apostle of Jesus Christ,
To those who have obtained a faith of equal standing with
ours in the righteousness of our God and Savior Jesus Christ:[a]
2 May grace and peace be multiplied to you in the knowledge
of God and of Jesus our Lord.

II. True knowledge 1.3–21

A. The growth of true knowledge

3 His divine power has granted to us all things that pertain to
life and godliness, through the knowledge of him who called us
to[b] his own glory and excellence, 4 by which he has granted to us
his precious and very great promises, that through these you may
escape from the corruption that is in the world because of passion,
and become partakers of the divine nature. 5 For this very reason
make every effort to supplement your faith with virtue, and virtue
with knowledge, 6 and knowledge with self-control, and self-
control with steadfastness, and steadfastness with godliness, 7 and
godliness with brotherly affection, and brotherly affection with
love. 8 For if these things are yours and abound, they keep you
from being ineffective or unfruitful in the knowledge of our Lord
Jesus Christ. 9 For whoever lacks these things is blind and short-
sighted and has forgotten that he was cleansed from his old sins.
10 Therefore, brethren, be the more zealous to confirm your call
and election, for if you do this you will never fall; 11 so there will
be richly provided for you an entrance into the eternal kingdom
of our Lord and Savior Jesus Christ.

B. The ground of true knowledge

12 Therefore I intend always to remind you of these things,
though you know them and are established in the truth that you
have. 13 I think it right, as long as I am in this body,[c] to arouse you
by way of reminder, 14 since I know that the putting off of my
body[c] will be soon, as our Lord Jesus Christ showed me. 15 And I
will see to it that after my departure you may be able at any time
to recall these things.

16 For we did not follow cleverly devised myths when we made
known to you the power and coming of our Lord Jesus Christ,
but we were eyewitnesses of his majesty. 17 For when he received
honor and glory from God the Father and the voice was borne to
him by the Majestic Glory, "This is my beloved Son,[d] with whom
I am well pleased," 18 we heard this voice borne from heaven, for
we were with him on the holy mountain. 19 And we have the
prophetic word made more sure. You will do well to pay attention

1.1
Rom 1.1;
1 Pet 1.1;
Rom 1.12;
3.21–26;
Tit 2.13
1.2
1 Pet 1.2;
ver 3,8
1.3
1 Pet 1.5;
1 Thess 2.12
1.4
2 Cor 7.1;
Eph 4.24;
1 Jn 3.2;
2 Pet 2.18–
20
1.5
2 Pet 3.18;
Col 2.3
1.6
Acts 24.26;
Lk 21.19;
ver 3
1.7
1 Thess 3.12
1.8
Jn 15.2;
Tit 3.14
1.9
1 Jn 2.11;
Eph 5.26;
1 Jn 1.7
1.12
1 Jn 2.21
1.13
2 Cor 5.1
1.14
2 Tim 4.6;
Jn 21.18,19
1.16
1 Tim 1.4;
Mt 17.1;
Mk 9.2
1.17
Mt 3.17;
Lk 9.35
1.18
Mt 17.6
1.19
1 Pet 1.10,
11;
Ps 119.105;
Rev 22.16

x Other authorities read *Simon*
a Or *of our God and the Savior Jesus Christ*
b Or *by*   c Greek *tent*   d Or *my Son, my* (or *the*) *Beloved*

1841

to this as to a lamp shining in a dark place, until the day dawns and the morning star rises in your hearts. 20 First of all you must understand this, that no prophecy of scripture is a matter of one's own interpretation, 21 because no prophecy ever came by the impulse of man, but men moved by the Holy Spirit spoke from God.*e*

III. False teachers 2.1–22

A. The inroads of error

2 But false prophets also arose among the people, just as there will be false teachers among you, who will secretly bring in destructive heresies, even denying the Master who bought them, bringing upon themselves swift destruction. 2And many will follow their licentiousness, and because of them the way of truth will be reviled. 3And in their greed they will exploit you with false words; from of old their condemnation has not been idle, and their destruction has not been asleep.

B. Punishment of error

4 For if God did not spare the angels when they sinned, but cast them into hell*f* and committed them to pits of nether gloom to be kept until the judgment; 5 if he did not spare the ancient world, but preserved Noah, a herald of righteousness, with seven other persons, when he brought a flood upon the world of the ungodly; 6 if by turning the cities of Sŏdŏm and Gŏmor'răh to ashes he condemned them to extinction and made them an example to those who were to be ungodly; 7 and if he rescued righteous Lot, greatly distressed by the licentiousness of the wicked 8 (for by what that righteous man saw and heard as he lived among them, he was vexed in his righteous soul day after day with their lawless deeds), 9 then the Lord knows how to rescue the godly from trial, and to keep the unrighteous under punishment until the day of judgment, 10 and especially those who indulge in the lust of defiling passion and despise authority.

C. Character and conduct of deceivers

Bold and wilful, they are not afraid to revile the glorious ones, 11 whereas angels, though greater in might and power, do not pronounce a reviling judgment upon them before the Lord. 12 But these, like irrational animals, creatures of instinct, born to be caught and killed, reviling in matters of which they are ignorant, will be destroyed in the same destruction with them, 13 suffering wrong for their wrongdoing. They count it pleasure to revel in the daytime. They are blots and blemishes, reveling in their dissipa-tion,*g* carousing with you. 14 They have eyes full of adultery, insatiable for sin. They entice unsteady souls. They have hearts

e Other authorities read *moved by the Holy Spirit holy men of God spoke*
f Greek *Tar'tărŭs*   *g* Other ancient authorities read *love feasts*

1.20, 21 See note to 2 Tim 3.16 on inspira-tion. Also read verse 19.

2.1 See note to 2 Tim 2.18 on false doctrine and false teachers.

Margin references:
*1.20f Rom 12.6
1.21 2 Tim 3.16; 1 Pet 1.11; Acts 1.16
*2.1 1 Tim 4.1; Jude 18; 1 Cor 6.20
2.3 1 Tim 6.5; 2 Cor 2.17; Deut 32.35
2.4 Jude 6; Jn 8.44; Rev 20.1,2
2.5 Gen 7.1; Heb 11.7; 1 Pet 3.20
2.6 Gen 19.24; Jude 7; Num 26.10
2.7 Gen 19.16; 2 Pet 3.17
2.9 1 Cor 10.13; Jude 6
2.10 2 Pet 3.3; Jude 8; Tit 1.7
2.11 Jude 9
2.12 Jude 10
2.13 Rom 13.13; Jude 12; 1 Cor 11.20,21
2.14 ver 18; Jude 11; ver 3; Eph 2.3

trained in greed. Accursed children! 15 Forsaking the right way they have gone astray; they have followed the way of Bālaåm, the son of Bēor, who loved gain from wrongdoing, 16 but was rebuked for his own transgression; a dumb ass spoke with human voice and restrained the prophet's madness.

D. *Evil consequences of their deception*

17 These are waterless springs and mists driven by a storm; for them the nether gloom of darkness has been reserved. 18 For, uttering loud boasts of folly, they entice with licentious passions of the flesh men who have barely escaped from those who live in error. 19 They promise them freedom, but they themselves are slaves of corruption; for whatever overcomes a man, to that he is enslaved. 20 For if, after they have escaped the defilements of the world through the knowledge of our Lord and Savior Jesus Christ, they are again entangled in them and overpowered, the last state has become worse for them than the first. 21 For it would have been better for them never to have known the way of righteousness than after knowing it to turn back from the holy commandment delivered to them. 22 It has happened to them according to the true proverb, The dog turns back to his own vomit, and the sow is washed only to wallow in the mire.

IV. *The Second Advent of Christ 3.1–18*

A. *The promise of his coming*

3 This is now the second letter that I have written to you, beloved, and in both of them I have aroused your sincere mind by way of reminder; 2 that you should remember the predictions of the holy prophets and the commandment of the Lord and Savior through your apostles. 3 First of all you must understand this, that scoffers will come in the last days with scoffing, following their own passions 4 and saying, "Where is the promise of his coming? For ever since the fathers fell asleep, all things have continued as they were from the beginning of creation." 5 They deliberately ignore this fact, that by the word of God heavens existed long ago, and an earth formed out of water and by means of water, 6 through which the world that then existed was deluged with water and perished. 7 But by the same word the heavens and earth that now exist have been stored up for fire, being kept until the day of judgment and destruction of ungodly men.

B. *The time and circumstances*

8 But do not ignore this one fact, beloved, that with the Lord one day is as a thousand years, and a thousand years as one day. 9 The Lord is not slow about his promise as some count slowness, but is forbearing toward you,[h] not wishing that any should perish,

---

h Other ancient authorities read *on your account*

Marginal references:

*2.15
Num 22.5, 7;
Jude 11
2.16
Num 22.21, 23,28,30,31

2.17
Jude 12,13
2.18
Jude 16

*2.19f;
Jn 8.34;
Rom 6.16
2.20
Mt 12.45;
Lk 11.26;
2 Pet 1.2

2.21
Heb 6.4ff;
2 Pet 3.2;
Jude 3
2.22
Prov 26.11

3.3
1 Tim 4.1;
Jude 18;
2 Pet 2.10
3.4
Isa 5.9;
Jer 17.15;
Ezek 12.22;
Mt 24.48;
Acts 7.60;
Mt 10.6
3.5
Gen 1.6,9;
Heb 11.3;
Ps 24.2;
Col 1.17
3.6
Gen 7.21,22
3.7
ver 10;
2 Thess 1.7;
1 Cor 3.13
3.8
Ps 90.4
3.9
Heb 10.37;
Isa 30.18;
1 Pet 3.20;
Rom 2.4

2.15 The way of Balaam is the way of compromise. Balaam used his prophetic gift for personal gain. He sought to serve God and self-interest at the same time. False teachers like him will inevitably meet with divine condemnation. (See also notes to Num 22.19; Jude 11; Rev 2.14.)
2.19, 20 See note to Heb 6.4–6.

*3.10
Mt 24.43;
1 Thess 5.2;
Mt 24.35;
Rev 21.1

3.12
1 Cor 1.7;
Tit 2.13;
Ps 50.3;
Isa 34.4;
ver 10

3.13
Isa 65.17;
66.22;
Rev 21.1

3.14
2 Pet 1.10;
1 Cor 15.58;
Phil 2.15

3.15
ver 9;
1 Cor 3.10;
Eph 3.3

3.16
ver 14;
Heb 5.11;
2 Pet 2.14;
ver 2

3.17
1 Cor 10.12;
2 Pet 2.18;
Rev 2.5

but that all should reach repentance. 10 But the day of the Lord will come like a thief, and then the heavens will pass away with a loud noise, and the elements will be dissolved with fire, and the earth and the works that are upon it will be burned up.

11 Since all these things are thus to be dissolved, what sort of persons ought you to be in lives of holiness and godliness, 12 waiting for and hastening[i] the coming of the day of God, because of which the heavens will be kindled and dissolved, and the elements will melt with fire! 13 But according to his promise we wait for new heavens and a new earth in which righteousness dwells.

C. The concluding exhortation

14 Therefore, beloved, since you wait for these, be zealous to be found by him without spot or blemish, and at peace. 15And count the forbearance of our Lord as salvation. So also our beloved brother Paul wrote to you according to the wisdom given him, 16 speaking of this as he does in all his letters. There are some things in them hard to understand, which the ignorant and unstable twist to their own destruction, as they do the other scriptures. 17 You therefore, beloved, knowing this beforehand, beware lest you be carried away with the error of lawless men and lose your own stability. 18 But grow in the grace and knowledge of our Lord and Savior Jesus Christ. To him be the glory both now and to the day of eternity. Amen.

i Or earnestly desiring

3.10 *the day of the Lord.* This phrase appears also in Acts 2.20; 1 Thess 5.2, 4; 2 Thess 2.2; 1 Cor 5.5. Here, as is usual in the New Testament, the reference is to the Second Advent of Christ. Concerning that Advent, three deductions may be drawn from this Scripture and others related to it: (1) Christ's coming is certain: He will arrive in God's own time, not at a time predictable by man (Jn 14.3; Mk 13.32); (2) His coming will be sudden, i.e., unexpected and without warning (1 Thess 5.1–3); (3) it will be a day of solemn judgment (Acts 17.31). Here in 3.10 it is interesting to note that *the day of the Lord* is spoken of in relation to the dissolution of the material universe. It is this usage which, when co-ordinated with other eschatological passages in the New Testament, has led some to conclude that *the day of the Lord* is a period of time with at least a thousand years between its beginning and its ending.

INTRODUCTION TO
THE FIRST LETTER OF
JOHN

Authorship and Background: This general letter does not bear the author's name, nor does it identify its readers. From earliest times it was attributed to the Apostle John, and no other author was suggested. The author wrote as an eye-witness of the person and ministry of Jesus (1.1–3), in words strongly reminiscent of the Gospel of John (1.14; 19.35; 21.24). The tone of the letter, and especially his references to his readers as "little children" (2.1, 12, 28; 3.7, 18; 4.4; 5.21), imply that he was an old man.

Perhaps the author knew some of his readers, but the absence of personal references makes it likely that this was a general letter, addressed to Christians at large. Besides "children," the writer also called them "brethren" (3.13) and "beloved" (2.7; 3.2, 21; 4.1, 7, 11). His tone was warm and intimate as he wrote to them with obvious love and concern. Calmly and deliberately he recalled the fundamentals of the Christian faith, and assured them of the reality of their salvation, "that you may know that you have eternal life" (5.13).

He also wrote to warn his readers against a dangerous philosophy that would rob the Christian faith of its distinctive message concerning Jesus Christ. Based on the Greek moral distinction between matter and spirit, Gnostic philosophy regarded matter as inherently evil; for this reason one could not speak of a true incarnation of the Word of God, but only of an apparent one. The Son of God did not really become flesh but only seemed to do so—whence the name "Docetism" (from Greek *dokeō*, "to seem"). Others affirmed that the divine Christ had come upon the human Jesus at baptism and left him at the cross, since it was impossible that the divine Son of God should suffer and die.

On both counts, therefore, the Christian faith that the man Jesus was also the Christ, the Son of God, was effectively denied. The writer denounced these "antichrists" who denied the Son and, consequently, the Father as well (2.18–23); they were false prophets who did not confess that Jesus had come in the flesh (4.1–3); but Jesus Christ is he who came with the water and the blood (5.6–8). Both the real humanity and the real deity of Jesus Christ are emphasized (2.22; 4.2, 15; 5.1, 5).

The letter is usually dated around A.D. 90, written perhaps from Ephesus.

Characteristics: The book dwells on the great themes of the Christian faith and message in a way that recalls the Gospel of John. The writer contrasts light and darkness (1.6, 7; 2.8–11); love of the world versus love of God (2.15–17); the children of God and the children of the devil (3.4–10); love and hatred (3.11–18; 4.7–12; 16–21); the Spirit of God and the spirit of antichrist (4.1–3). He speaks of the forgiveness of sins (1.8—2.2; 2.12), of fellowship (1.3, 4), eternal life (2.25; 5.11–13, 20), and the Holy Spirit (2.27; 4.12, 13). Against the destructive Gnostic teaching that what is done in the flesh cannot affect the spirit,

the author stresses the need of obedience and purity of life (1.10; 2.15–17; 3.4–10; 5.18). The sum and substance may be thus summarized: "we should believe in the name of his Son Jesus Christ and love one another, just as he has commanded us" (3.23).

Contents:

I. Introduction. 1.1–4: The apostolic witness and authority asserted. The purpose of this letter.

II. Assurance and walking in the light. 1.5—2.29: Light and darkness; sin and forgiveness; confession and profession; love for the world and love of God; the false teachings of antichrists and the truth of the Spirit.

III. Assurance and abiding in love. 3.1—4.21: We are God's children; the power of sin is broken; love, the royal rule of life, is from God who manifested his love for us by sending his Son as the expiation for our sins. "We love, because he first loved us" (4.19).

IV. Faith and certainty. 5.1–12: To love God and keep his commandments is the whole duty of man. Faith that Jesus is the Son of God brings victory; in him alone is true life.

V. Conclusion. 5.13–21: We know: that God hears us when we ask according to his will; that the Son of God keeps God's children from the power of sin and evil; that we are of God; that the Son of God has come and brought us knowledge of the true God. Worship him and abjure all idols!

THE FIRST LETTER OF
JOHN

I. *Introduction 1.1–4*

1 That which was from the beginning, which we have heard, which we have seen with our eyes, which we have looked upon and touched with our hands, concerning the word of life—² the life was made manifest, and we saw it, and testify to it, and proclaim to you the eternal life which was with the Father and was made manifest to us—³ that which we have seen and heard we proclaim also to you, so that you may have fellowship with us; and our fellowship is with the Father and with his Son Jesus Christ. ⁴And we are writing this that our*ᵃ* joy may be complete.

II. *Assurance and walking in the light 1.5–2.29*

A. *The test of righteousness*

5 This is the message we have heard from him and proclaim to you, that God is light and in him is no darkness at all. ⁶ If we say we have fellowship with him while we walk in darkness, we lie and do not live according to the truth; ⁷ but if we walk in the light, as he is in the light, we have fellowship with one another, and the blood of Jesus his Son cleanses us from all sin. ⁸ If we say we have no sin, we deceive ourselves, and the truth is not in us. ⁹ If we confess our sins, he is faithful and just, and will forgive our sins and cleanse us from all unrighteousness. ¹⁰ If we say we have not sinned, we make him a liar, and his word is not in us.

2 My little children, I am writing this to you so that you may not sin; but if any one does sin, we have an advocate with the Father, Jesus Christ the righteous; ² and he is the expiation for our sins, and not for ours only but also for the sins of the whole world. ³And by this we may be sure that we know him, if we keep his commandments. ⁴ He who says "I know him" but disobeys his commandments is a liar, and the truth is not in him; ⁵ but whoever keeps his word, in him truly love for God is perfected. By this we may be sure that we are in him: ⁶ he who says he abides in him ought to walk in the same way in which he walked.

B. *The test of love*

7 Beloved, I am writing you no new commandment, but an old

ᵃ Other ancient authorities read *your*

1.1	Jn 1.1,14; 2 Pet 1.16; Jn 20.27
1.2	Jn 1.1–4; Rom 16.26; Jn 21.24
1.3	Acts 4.20; 1 Cor 1.9
1.4	1 Jn 2.1; Jn 3.29
1.5	1 Jn 3.11
1.6	2 Cor 6.14; Jn 8.55; 3.21
1.7	Heb 9.14; 1 Pet 1.19; Rev 1.5
1.8	Job 15.14; Prov 20.9; Jas 3.2; 1 Jn 2.4
★1.9	Ps 51.2
1.10	1 Jn 5.10; 2.14
★2.1	Rom 8.34; Heb 7.25
2.2	Rom 3.25; Jn 1.29
2.5	Jn 14.23; 1 Jn 4.12,13
2.6	Jn 15.4; 1 Pet 2.21
2.7	1 Jn 3.2; 2 Jn 5; 1 Jn 3.11

1.9 Following salvation, Christians are still capable of sin despite the radical change which has taken place in their lives, and they still need to be cleansed. 1 John deals with this practical problem. There are three aspects to this cleansing: (1) the means of cleansing— the blood of Christ (1.7); (2) the method of cleansing—confession of sin (1.9); (3) the measure of cleansing—from all unrighteousness (1.9).

2.1 Christ is our advocate. This is the same Greek word which is used for the Holy Spirit in Jn 16.7 (*parakletos*, "the one called alongside in order to help"). Children of God whose fellowship with God has been broken by sin have One whose finished work is sufficient to remove their guilt (after repentance and confession) and to bring them back into full fellowship with their Father in heaven.

commandment which you had from the beginning; the old commandment is the word which you have heard. 8 Yet I am writing you a new commandment, which is true in him and in you, because[b] the darkness is passing away and the true light is already shining. 9 He who says he is in the light and hates his brother is in the darkness still. 10 He who loves his brother abides in the light, and in it[c] there is no cause for stumbling. 11 But he who hates his brother is in the darkness and walks in the darkness, and does not know where he is going, because the darkness has blinded his eyes.

12 I am writing to you, little children, because your sins are forgiven for his sake. 13 I am writing to you, fathers, because you know him who is from the beginning. I am writing to you, young men, because you have overcome the evil one. I write to you, children, because you know the Father. 14 I write to you, fathers, because you know him who is from the beginning. I write to you, young men, because you are strong, and the word of God abides in you, and you have overcome the evil one.

15 Do not love the world or the things in the world. If any one loves the world, love for the Father is not in him. 16 For all that is in the world, the lust of the flesh and the lust of the eyes and the pride of life, is not of the Father but is of the world. 17And the world passes away, and the lust of it; but he who does the will of God abides for ever.

C. The test of true belief

18 Children, it is the last hour; and as you have heard that antichrist is coming, so now many antichrists have come; therefore we know that it is the last hour. 19 They went out from us, but they were not of us; for if they had been of us, they would have continued with us; but they went out, that it might be plain that they all are not of us. 20 But you have been anointed by the Holy One, and you all know.[d] 21 I write to you, not because you do not know the truth, but because you know it, and know that no lie is of the truth. 22 Who is the liar but he who denies that Jesus is the Christ? This is the antichrist, he who denies the Father and the Son. 23 No one who denies the Son has the Father. He who confesses the Son has the Father also. 24 Let what you heard from the beginning abide in you. If what you heard from the beginning abides in you, then you will abide in the Son and in the Father. 25And this is what he has promised us,[e] eternal life.

26 I write this to you about those who would deceive you; 27 but the anointing which you received from him abides in you, and you have no need that any one should teach you; as his anointing teaches you about everything, and is true, and is no lie, just as it has taught you, abide in him.

28 And now, little children, abide in him, so that when he

2.8
Eph 5.8;
1 Thess 5.5;
Jn 1.9

2.9
2 Pet 1.9

2.10
1 Jn 3.14;
ver 11

2.11
Jn 12.35

2.12
Lk 24.47

2.13
1 Jn 1.1;
ver 14

2.14
1 Jn 1.1;
Eph 6.10;
Jn 5.38

2.15
Rom 12.2;
Mt 6.24;
Jas 4.4

2.16
Rom 13.14;
Prov 27.20;
Jas 4.16

2.17
1 Cor 7.31

*2.18
1 Pet 4.7;
1 Jn 4.1,3

2.19
Acts 20.30;
Mt 24.24;
1 Cor 11.19

2.20
2 Cor 1.21;
Acts 3.14;
Jn 14.26

2.21
2 Pet 1.12;
1 Jn 3.19

2.23
Jn 14.7

2.24
2 Jn 6;
Jn 14.23

2.25
Jn 17.3

2.26
2 Jn 7

2.27
Jn 14.26,
17

2.28
1 Jn 3.2,
21; 4.17;
Mk 8.38;
1 Thess 2.19

---

b Or that   c Or him   d Other ancient authorities read you know everything
e Other ancient authorities read you

2.18 Scripture distinguishes *the antichrist* from *antichrists* and the *spirit of antichrist*. Here John speaks of those who are not *the antichrist* but who make common cause with him and whose malign spirit they emulate. Denying the cardinal truths of the gospel, they are called *antichrists*. (See also note to 4.3 for further discussion on antichrists.)

appears we may have confidence and not shrink from him in shame at his coming. 29 If you know that he is righteous, you may be sure that every one who does right is born of him.

III. *Assurance and abiding in love 3.1–4.21*

A. *Obedience in action*

3 See what love the Father has given us, that we should be called children of God; and so we are. The reason why the world does not know us is that it did not know him. 2 Beloved, we are God's children now; it does not yet appear what we shall be, but we know that when he appears we shall be like him, for we shall see him as he is. 3And every one who thus hopes in him purifies himself as he is pure.

4 Every one who commits sin is guilty of lawlessness; sin is lawlessness. 5 You know that he appeared to take away sins, and in him there is no sin. 6 No one who abides in him sins; no one who sins has either seen him or known him. 7 Little children, let no one deceive you. He who does right is righteous, as he is righteous. 8 He who commits sin is of the devil; for the devil has sinned from the beginning. The reason the Son of God appeared was to destroy the works of the devil. 9 No one born of God commits sin; for God's*f* nature abides in him, and he cannot sin because he is*g* born of God. 10 By this it may be seen who are the children of God, and who are the children of the devil: whoever does not do right is not of God, nor he who does not love his brother.

B. *Love in action*

11 For this is the message which you have heard from the beginning, that we should love one another, 12 and not be like Cain who was of the evil one and murdered his brother. And why did he murder him? Because his own deeds were evil and his brother's righteous. 13 Do not wonder, brethren, that the world hates you. 14 We know that we have passed out of death into life, because we love the brethren. He who does not love abides in death. 15Any one who hates his brother is a murderer, and you know that no murderer has eternal life abiding in him. 16 By this we know love, that he laid down his life for us; and we ought to lay down our lives for the brethren. 17 But if any one has the world's goods and sees his brother in need, yet closes his heart against him, how does God's love abide in him? 18 Little children, let us not love in word or speech but in deed and in truth.

f Greek *his*   *g* Or *for the offspring of God abide in him, and they cannot sin because they are*

2.29
1 Jn 3.7,9;
4.7

3.1
Jn 1.12;
16.3
3.2
Rom 8.15;
2 Cor 4.17;
Rom 8.29;
2 Pet 1.4;
2 Cor 3.18
3.4
Rom 4.15;
1 Jn 5.17
3.5
Isa 53.5,6;
2 Cor 5.21
★3.7
1 Jn 2.1,26,
29
3.8
Jn 8.44;
16.11;
Heb 2.14
★3.9
1 Jn 5.18;
1 Pet 1.23
3.10
1 Jn 2.29

3.11
1 Jn 1.5;
Jn 13.34,35;
2 Jn 5
3.13
Jn 15.18
3.14
Jn 5.24;
1 Jn 2.9,11
3.15
Mt 5.21,22;
Jn 8.44;
Gal 5.20,21
3.16
Jn 3.16;
13.1; 15.13
3.17
Deut 15.7;
1 Jn 4.20
3.18
Rom 12.9;
Jas 1.22

3.7 The claim to righteousness is most firmly established by the life the believer lives. This Scripture might be paraphrased, "He that performs righteousness is a righteous person." This is analogous to James' teaching that faith without works is dead (Jas 2.20–26).
3.9 This verse has been taken by some to mean that believers cannot sin. But 1.9 already reveals that believers do sin, and it outlines the method by which cleansing may

be obtained. From the Greek tenses used here in 3.9 the verse might well be paraphrased, "Whoever is born of God does not make sin the *practice* of his life." So while believers do sin, it is not their common custom nor are they confirmed in the direction of sin, for their nature is no longer the old, sinful nature, but one given by God. The thought is expressed further in 5.18: a child of God does not live a life of sin because the Son of God keeps him.

3.19
1 Jn 2.21
3.20
1 Cor 4.4
3.21
1 Jn 5.14
3.22
Mt 7.7;
21.22;
1 Jn 2.3
3.23
1 Jn 2.8
3.24
Rom 8.9;
1 Jn 4.13

19 By this we shall know that we are of the truth, and reassure our hearts before him 20 whenever our hearts condemn us; for God is greater than our hearts, and he knows everything. 21 Beloved, if our hearts do not condemn us, we have confidence before God; 22 and we receive from him whatever we ask, because we keep his commandments and do what pleases him. 23And this is his commandment, that we should believe in the name of his Son Jesus Christ and love one another, just as he has commanded us. 24All who keep his commandments abide in him, and he in them. And by this we know that he abides in us, by the Spirit which he has given us.

C. *Faith in action*

4.1
Mt 24.4;
2 Pet 2.1;
1 Jn 2.18
4.2
1 Cor 12.3;
1 Jn 2.23
*4.3
2 Jn 7;
1 Jn 2.22;
2 Thess 2.7
4.4
1 Jn 5.4
4.5
Jn 3.31;
15.19
4.6
Jn 8.47;
1 Cor 14.37;
Jn 14.17;
1 Tim 4.1
4.7
1 Jn 3.10,
11
4.8
ver 16

4 Beloved, do not believe every spirit, but test the spirits to see whether they are of God; for many false prophets have gone out into the world. 2 By this you know the Spirit of God: every spirit which confesses that Jesus Christ has come in the flesh is of God, 3 and every spirit which does not confess Jesus is not of God. This is the spirit of antichrist, of which you heard that it was coming, and now it is in the world already. 4 Little children, you are of God, and have overcome them; for he who is in you is greater than he who is in the world. 5 They are of the world, therefore what they say is of the world, and the world listens to them. 6 We are of God. Whoever knows God listens to us, and he who is not of God does not listen to us. By this we know the spirit of truth and the spirit of error.

D. *The source of love*

4.9
Jn 3.16;
1 Jn 5.11
4.10
Rom 5.8,
10;
1 Jn 2.2
4.11
Jn 3.16;
15.12
4.12
Jn 1.18;
1 Tim 6.16;
1 Jn 2.5
4.13
1 Jn 3.24
4.15
Rom 10.9
4.16
ver 8;
1 Jn 3.24
4.17
1 Jn 2.28
4.18
Rom 8.15;
ver 12

7 Beloved, let us love one another; for love is of God, and he who loves is born of God and knows God. 8 He who does not love does not know God; for God is love. 9 In this the love of God was made manifest among us, that God sent his only Son into the world, so that we might live through him. 10 In this is love, not that we loved God but that he loved us and sent his Son to be the expiation for our sins. 11 Beloved, if God so loved us, we also ought to love one another. 12 No man has ever seen God; if we love one another, God abides in us and his love is perfected in us. 13 By this we know that we abide in him and he in us, because he has given us of his own Spirit. 14And we have seen and testify that the Father has sent his Son as the Savior of the world. 15 Whoever confesses that Jesus is the Son of God, God abides in him, and he in God. 16 So we know and believe the love God has for us. God is love, and he who abides in love abides in God, and God abides in him. 17 In this is love perfected with us, that we may have confidence for the day of judgment, because as he is so are we in this world. 18 There is no fear in love, but perfect love casts

---

4.3 References to "antichrist(s)" in 2.18, 22; 4.3; 2 Jn 7 make it clear that their fundamental error was the denial of the reality of the incarnation. Some of them, at least (cf. 2.18, 19), had belonged to the Christian fellowship, but had forsaken it on account of their heresy. Their repudiation of the reality of the incarna- tion of the Son involved also a repudiation of the Father: to deny the Son is to deny the Father (2.22, 23). It would appear then, that their denial of the foundational belief of the gospel was a direct result of Gnostic teaching (cf. Introduction to 1 John). See also note to 1 Jn 2.18.

out fear. For fear has to do with punishment, and he who fears is not perfected in love. 19 We love, because he first loved us. 20 If any one says, "I love God," and hates his brother, he is a liar; for he who does not love his brother whom he has seen, cannot*ʰ* love God whom he has not seen. 21And this commandment we have from him, that he who loves God should love his brother also.

IV. *Faith and certainty 5.1–12*

A. *Victory through faith*

5 Every one who believes that Jesus is the Christ is a child of God, and every one who loves the parent loves the child. 2 By this we know that we love the children of God, when we love God and obey his commandments. 3 For this is the love of God, that we keep his commandments. And his commandments are not burdensome. 4 For whatever is born of God overcomes the world; and this is the victory that overcomes the world, our faith. 5 Who is it that overcomes the world but he who believes that Jesus is the Son of God?

B. *Faith through the Son*

6 This is he who came by water and blood, Jesus Christ, not with the water only but with the water and the blood. 7And the Spirit is the witness, because the Spirit is the truth. 8 There are three witnesses, the Spirit, the water, and the blood; and these three agree. 9 If we receive the testimony of men, the testimony of God is greater; for this is the testimony of God that he has borne witness to his Son. 10 He who believes in the Son of God has the testimony in himself. He who does not believe God has made him a liar, because he has not believed in the testimony that God has borne to his Son. 11And this is the testimony, that God gave us eternal life, and this life is in his Son. 12 He who has the Son has life; he who has not the Son of God has not life.

V. *Conclusion: the certainties of faith 5.13–21*

13 I write this to you who believe in the name of the Son of God, that you may know that you have eternal life. 14And this is the confidence which we have in him, that if we ask anything according to his will he hears us. 15And if we know that he hears us in whatever we ask, we know that we have obtained the requests made of him. 16 If anyone sees his brother committing what is not a mortal sin, he will ask, and God*ⁱ* will give him life for those whose sin is not mortal. There is sin which is mortal; I do not say that one is to pray for that. 17All wrongdoing is sin, but there is sin which is not mortal.

ʰ Other ancient authorities read *how can he*   *ⁱ* Greek *he*

4.19	ver 10
4.20	1 Jn 2.4; 1.6; 3.17
5.1	Jn 1.12; 1 Jn 2.22, 23; Jn 1.13; 8.42
5.2	1 Jn 2.5
5.3	Jn 14.15; 1 Jn 2.5; 2 Jn 6
5.4	Jn 16.33
5.5	1 Jn 4.15
*5.6	Jn 19.34
5.7	Jn 15.26
5.8	Mt 18.16
5.9	Jn 8.17,18; Mt 3.16,17
5.10	Rom 8.16; Gal 4.6; Jn 3.33
5.11	1 Jn 2.25; Jn 1.4
5.12	Jn 3.36
5.13	Jn 20.31; 1 Jn 1.1,2
5.14	1 Jn 3.21, 22; Mt 7.7
5.16	Jas 5.15; Heb 6.4,6
5.17	1 Jn 3.4

5.6 Jesus Christ came with the water and the blood. This is commonly interpreted to refer to the water of His baptism and the blood of His death, of which the Christian sacraments (ordinances) of baptism and the Lord's Supper are signs and symbols. In the context of this letter both emphasize the reality of the incarnation of Christ, whose saving ministry began in the waters of Jordan and was consummated on Calvary's Cross.

*5.18
1 Jn 3.9;
Jn 14.30
5.19
1 Jn 4.6;
Gal 1.4
5.20
Lk 24.45;
Jn 17.3;
Rev 3.7
*5.21
1 Cor 10.14

18 We know that any one born of God does not sin, but He who was born of God keeps him, and the evil one does not touch him.

19 We know that we are of God, and the whole world is in the power of the evil one.

20 And we know that the Son of God has come and has given us understanding, to know him who is true; and we are in him who is true, in his Son Jesus Christ. This is the true God and eternal life. 21 Little children, keep yourselves from idols.

5.18 *does not sin*. The intention of John here would be better understood by translating this verse, "any one born of God does not keep on sinning."

5.21 Idolatry was present everywhere, thus it was necessary for John to warn against this peril, and also to make it clear that there was need for effort on the part of those to whom he was writing. See also note to Ex 20.3 on idolatry.

INTRODUCTION TO
THE SECOND LETTER OF
JOHN

Authorship and Background: The writer of this short letter called himself "the elder" (1; also 3 Jn 1). Similarity in style and content argues strongly for common authorship of all three epistles, and the majority of scholars believe that the same man wrote all three, whether he was John the Apostle, or another John known as "the elder," or some other unnamed person. The time and place of writing of all three would be the same, perhaps around A.D. 90 in the city of Ephesus.

The letter was addressed to "the elect lady and her children" (1); some believe this referred to a woman, "the elect Kyria," and her children. But the reference to "some of your children" (4), the greetings from "the children of your elect sister" (13), and the whole tone of the letter seem conclusive that a church was addressed, not a family.

The elder wrote to emphasize the primacy of love in the Christian fellowship: to love means to obey God, and to obey is to love one another (5, 6). He also warned his readers against the heresy of those who denied the incarnation of the Son of God (7): such deceivers were the antichrist, claiming that theirs was a "superior" teaching, above the orthodox Christian message (9). Such false teachers should not even be received at home, for to entertain them meant to share in their wicked work (10, 11).

Characteristics: This short letter gives us an insight into church life in the latter part of the first century as responsible leaders do their best to counteract the ruinous effects of false teaching. False doctrine dilutes the Christian witness, and its effects are felt in the lives of the believers. Orthodox Christian theology is not simply a matter of theory: it is the very basis of the Christian message and mission. The elder's love of the truth and his concern for the spiritual welfare of his readers leads him to write this brief note to a church whose members are in real peril of abandoning the truth as it is in Jesus.

Contents:

I.   Salutation. 1–3

II.   Counsel and warnings. 4–11: The primacy of love in the Christian life; the reality of the incarnation of the Son of God. Take care that you are not deceived by false teachings and lose what you have worked for; shun all who carry strange doctrine.

III.   Conclusion. 12, 13

THE SECOND LETTER OF
JOHN

I. Salutation 1–3

1
3 Jn 1;
1 Jn 3.18;
Jn 8.32

2
2 Pet 1.12;
1 Jn 1.8

3
1 Tim 1.2

1 The elder to the elect lady and her children, whom I love in the truth, and not only I but also all who know the truth, 2 because of the truth which abides in us and will be with us for ever:

3 Grace, mercy, and peace will be with us, from God the Father and from Jesus Christ the Father's Son, in truth and love.

II. Counsel and warnings 4–11

4
3 Jn 3,4

5
1 Jn 2.7;
3.11

6
1 Jn 2.5;
2.24

7
1 Jn 4.1–3;
2.22

8
Mk 13.9;
1 Cor 3.8;
Heb 10.32

9
1 Jn 2.23

10
Rom 16.17

11
1 Tim 5.22

4 I rejoiced greatly to find some of your children following the truth, just as we have been commanded by the Father. 5And now I beg you, lady, not as though I were writing you a new commandment, but the one we have had from the beginning, that we love one another. 6And this is love, that we follow his commandments; this is the commandment, as you have heard from the beginning, that you follow love. 7 For many deceivers have gone out into the world, men who will not acknowledge the coming of Jesus Christ in the flesh; such a one is the deceiver and the antichrist. 8 Look to yourselves, that you may not lose what you*a* have worked for, but may win a full reward. 9Any one who goes ahead and does not abide in the doctrine of Christ does not have God; he who abides in the doctrine has both the Father and the Son. 10 If any one comes to you and does not bring this doctrine, do not receive him into the house or give him any greeting; 11 for he who greets him shares his wicked work.

III. Conclusion 12,13

12
3 Jn 13,14;
1 Jn 1.4

13
ver 1

12 Though I have much to write to you, I would rather not use paper and ink, but I hope to come to see you and talk with you face to face, so that our joy may be complete.

13 The children of your elect sister greet you.

a Other ancient authorities read *we*

INTRODUCTION TO

THE THIRD LETTER OF

JOHN

Authorship and Background: This letter was written also by "the elder," author of 2 John. It is a genuinely personal letter: all the second person pronouns are singular. It is addressed to Gaius, obviously a leader in a church; his position, however, is not specified. It may be that the previous letter written to the church, mentioned in verse 9, was 2 John. If so, the two letters were written to the same place, one to the church and the other to Gaius. It is impossible to determine whether this Gaius may be identified with any of the others with the same name in the New Testament (Acts 19.29; 20.4; Rom 16.23; 1 Cor 1.14).

The letter was written to solve problems relating to traveling Christian teachers, or prophets, whose ministry included several churches. Those who taught the true doctrine were to be entertained and helped in their travels. But Diotrephes, presumably the local leader, refused to receive these men, rejected the elder's authority and expelled the members of the church who welcomed the messengers. Therefore the elder wrote his good friend Gaius, urging him to help these itinerant preachers. Demetrius (12) may have taken the letter to Gaius, or he may have been a member of the church to which Gaius belonged.

Characteristics: The letter exhibits a degree of authority as the elder attacks Diotrephes' lack of cooperation. More may have been involved than the clash of two strong personalities: it is quite possible (especially if 2 John was written to this same church) that the elder feels that theological and doctrinal issues are also at stake (see 2 Jn 10, 11). In any case, the elder promises to visit the church and deal personally with the matter (10, 14).

Contents:

THE THIRD LETTER OF
JOHN

I. *Salutation 1–4*

1
2 Jn 1

3
2 Jn 4;
ver 5,10
4
1 Cor 4.15;
Philem 10

1 The elder to the beloved Gāïŭs, whom I love in the truth.

2 Beloved, I pray that all may go well with you and that you may be in health; I know that it is well with your soul. 3 For I greatly rejoiced when some of the brethren arrived and testified to the truth of your life, as indeed you do follow the truth. 4 No greater joy can I have than this, to hear that my children follow the truth.

II. *Encouragement for Gaius 5–8*

5
Rom 12.13;
Heb 13.2
6
Acts 15.3;
Tit 3.13
7
Acts 5.41;
20.33,35

5 Beloved, it is a loyal thing you do when you render any service to the brethren, especially to strangers, 6 who have testified to your love before the church. You will do well to send them on their journey as befits God's service. 7 For they have set out for his sake and have accepted nothing from the heathen. 8 So we ought to support such men, that we may be fellow workers in the truth.

III. *Reproof for Diotrephes 9,10*

9
2 Jn 9
10
2 Jn 12;
ver 5;
Jn 9.34

9 I have written something to the church; but Dīŏt'rĕphĕṣ, who likes to put himself first, does not acknowledge my authority. 10 So if I come, I will bring up what he is doing, prating against me with evil words. And not content with that, he refuses himself to welcome the brethren, and also stops those who want to welcome them and puts them out of the church.

IV. *Commendation for Demetrius 11,12*

11
Ps 37.27;
1 Jn 2.29;
3.6,9
12
1 Tim 3.7;
Jn 21.24

11 Beloved, do not imitate evil but imitate good. He who does good is of God; he who does evil has not seen God. 12 Dĕmē'trĭŭs has testimony from every one, and from the truth itself; I testify to him too, and you know my testimony is true.

V. *Conclusion 13–15*

13
2 Jn 12

15
1 Pet 5.14

13 I had much to write to you, but I would rather not write with pen and ink; 14 I hope to see you soon, and we will talk together face to face.

15 Peace be to you. The friends greet you. Greet the friends, every one of them.

INTRODUCTION TO
THE LETTER OF
JUDE

Authorship and Background: The writer identified himself as "Jude, a servant of Jesus Christ and brother of James" (1). This has been taken by conservatives to mean the brother of Jesus (cf. Mk 6.3; Mt 13.55); others think the author was another Jude, otherwise unknown; another opinion is that the letter is pseudonymous, written in the name of Jude, brother of Jesus.

This short letter did not gain immediate acceptance, and as late as the fourth century Eusebius of Caesarea reported that there were those who disputed its apostolic authorship. Nearly all of the contents of this letter are reproduced in 2 Peter, Jude having been written earlier. Some date this letter in the sixties of the first century, others around A.D. 150.

The readers are not identified. The letter was addressed to no particular locality, but to Christians in general (1). The author had intended to write about "our common salvation," but news of the destructive heresy that was being taught led him to write to them about the matter (3, 4).

False teachers had appeared, imbued with Gnostic philosophy, who perverted the grace of God into licentiousness and denied the lordship of Christ (4); defiling the flesh, rejecting authority, and reviling spiritual powers (8); these worldly people, devoid of the Spirit, were causing divisions in the church (19) with their flagrant immoralities and passions (10–13, 16). By denying that sins of the flesh could affect the welfare of the soul, they practiced and taught immoral behavior; it was urgently necessary that they be exposed and their evil teachings condemned.

Characteristics: The author condemns the heretics in no uncertain terms, using the strongest words in describing them (4, 8, 10, 16, 18, 19). He predicts their punishment and destruction (11–13), and urges his readers to continue growing in the faith and to keep themselves in the love of God and the mercy of Jesus Christ (20, 21), helping those who had been led astray by the false teachers (22, 23).

In warning his readers against the danger of apostasy, the author reminds them of God's judgment upon the faithless Israelites who were destroyed after having been freed from Egypt (5); of the fate of rebellious angels (6), and the destruction of the cities of Sodom and Gomorrah (7). Cain, Balaam, and Korah are other scriptural examples of the punishment meted out to the disobedient (11).

In verse 9 the author refers to the nonbiblical writing, "The Assumption of Moses," a Jewish work of the first century A.D., in citing the archangel Michael's dispute with the devil over the body of Moses; and in verses 14, 15 he quotes another nonbiblical writing, 1 Enoch, concerning the prophecy of "Enoch in the seventh generation from Adam" about the ultimate punishment of all the un-

godly. It was especially this use of 1 Enoch which caused problems in the early
church: some felt that 1 Enoch was an inspired writing since it was quoted in a
canonical book; others felt that since 1 Enoch was noncanonical, the Letter of
Jude was not inspired, a view not shared by the Christian church.

Finally, the author calls to mind the predictions of the apostles as to what
would happen "in the last time" (17–19). "Keep the faith!" is his urgent counsel.

Contents:

THE LETTER OF

JUDE

I. Introduction 1–4

1 Jude, a servant of Jesus Christ and brother of James,
To those who are called, beloved in God the Father and kept for Jesus Christ:
2 May mercy, peace, and love be multiplied to you.

3 Beloved, being very eager to write to you of our common salvation, I found it necessary to write appealing to you to contend for the faith which was once for all delivered to the saints. 4 For admission has been secretly gained by some who long ago were designated for this condemnation, ungodly persons who pervert the grace of our God into licentiousness and deny our only Master and Lord, Jesus Christ.*a*

II. Character and doom of false teachers 5–16

5 Now I desire to remind you, though you were once for all fully informed, that he*b* who saved a people out of the land of Egypt, afterward destroyed those who did not believe. 6And the angels that did not keep their own position but left their proper dwelling have been kept by him in eternal chains in the nether gloom until the judgment of the great day; 7 just as Sŏdŏm and Gŏmor'răh and the surrounding cities, which likewise acted immorally and indulged in unnatural lust, serve as an example by undergoing a punishment of eternal fire.

8 Yet in like manner these men in their dreamings defile the flesh, reject authority, and revile the glorious ones.*c* 9 But when the archangel Michael, contending with the devil, disputed about the body of Moses, he did not presume to pronounce a reviling judgment upon him, but said, "The Lord rebuke you." 10 But these men revile whatever they do not understand, and by those things that they know by instinct as irrational animals do, they are destroyed. 11 Woe to them! For they walk in the way of Cain, and abandon themselves for the sake of gain to Bălaăm'ş error, and perish in Kŏrăh'ş rebellion. 12 These are blemishes*d* on your

---

1
Acts 1.13;
1 Pet 1.5

2
1 Pet 1.2;
2 Pet 1.2

3
Tit 1.4;
1 Tim 6.12

4
Gal 2.4;
2 Pet 2.1;
Rom 9.22;
2 Pet 2.1

5
Num 14.29;
Ps 106.26

*6
Jn 8.44;
2 Pet 2.4;
Rev 20.10

7
2 Pet 2.6;
Gen 19.24

8
2 Pet 2.10

*9
Dan 10.13;
Zech 3.2

10
2 Pet 2.12;
Phil 3.19

*11
Gen 4.3–8;
1 Jn 3.12;
Num 22.7;
2 Pet 2.15;
Num 16.1–
3,31–35

12
2 Pet 2.13;
1 Cor
11.20ff;
Eph 4.14;
Mt 15.13

---

a Or *the only Master and our Lord Jesus Christ*
b Ancient authorities read *Jesus* or *the Lord* or *God*   *c* Greek *glories*   *d* Or *reefs*

---

6 The fact that these angels are spoken of as *fallen* obviously implies that at one time they were not fallen but enjoyed a heavenly status before God. They departed from righteousness, were expelled from heaven, and consigned to the lower regions, or *Tartarus* (2 Pet 2.4) to await their final punishment at the last judgment. At that time these angels will be cast with Satan into the lake of fire (Mt 25.41; Rev 20.7–15).

9 This controversy over the body of Moses is narrated in the Jewish apocryphal book, "The Assumption of Moses". According to accounts from some of the early church

Fathers, the devil tried to claim the body of Moses on two counts: (1) he, the devil, was the lord of matter, to which the angel replied that God is lord of all since He created all matter; (2) Moses was a murderer, and therefore his body belonged to the devil. At this accusation the angel replied, "*The Lord rebuke you*" (cf. Zech 3.2), at which the devil fled.

11 *Balaam's error* is to be understood in the light of *the way of Balaam* mentioned in 2 Pet 2.15. In both instances the element of greed and desire for personal gain is involved. It should, however, be distinguished from *the teaching of Balaam* (Rev. 2.14).

love feasts, as they boldly carouse together, looking after themselves; waterless clouds, carried along by winds; fruitless trees
in late autumn, twice dead, uprooted; 13 wild waves of the sea,
casting up the foam of their own shame; wandering stars for whom
the nether gloom of darkness has been reserved for ever.

14 It was of these also that Enoch in the seventh generation
from Adam prophesied, saying, "Behold, the Lord came with his
holy myriads, 15 to execute judgment on all, and to convict all the
ungodly of all their deeds of ungodliness which they have committed in such an ungodly way, and of all the harsh things which
ungodly sinners have spoken against him." 16 These are grumblers,
malcontents, following their own passions, loud-mouthed boasters,
flattering people to gain advantage.

III. *Admonition to hold the true faith 17–23*

17 But you must remember, beloved, the predictions of the
apostles of our Lord Jesus Christ; 18 they said to you, "In the last
time there will be scoffers, following their own ungodly passions."
19 It is these who set up divisions, worldly people, devoid of the
Spirit. 20 But you, beloved, build yourselves up on your most holy
faith; pray in the Holy Spirit; 21 keep yourselves in the love of
God; wait for the mercy of our Lord Jesus Christ unto eternal life.
22And convince some, who doubt; 23 save some, by snatching
them out of the fire; on some have mercy with fear, hating even
the garment spotted by the flesh.*e*

IV. *Benediction 24,25*

24 Now to him who is able to keep you from falling and to
present you without blemish before the presence of his glory with
rejoicing, 25 to the only God, our Savior through Jesus Christ our
Lord, be glory, majesty, dominion, and authority, before all time
and now and for ever. Amen.

e The Greek text in this sentence is uncertain at several points

---

13
Isa 57.20;
Phil 3.19;
2 Pet 2.17

*14
Gen 5.18;
Deut 33.2;
Dan 7.10

15
2 Pet 2.6ff;
1 Tim 1.9

16
2 Pet 2.18

17
2 Pet 3.2

18
1 Tim 4.1;
2 Pet 2.1

19
1 Cor 2.14,
15;
Jas 3.15

20
Col 2.7;
Eph 6.18

21
Tit 2.13;
2 Pet 3.12

23
Amos 4.11;
Zech 3.2–5

24
Rom 16.25;
Eph 3.20;
Col 1.22

25
1 Tim 1.17;
Rom 11.36

---

14 The noncanonical Book of Enoch
(parts of which are to be dated around the beginning of the Christian era) contains the following: "And behold! He cometh with ten
thousands of His holy ones to execute judgment upon all, and to destroy all the ungodly:
And to convict all flesh of all the works of
their ungodliness which they have ungodly
committed, and of all the hard things which
ungodly sinners have spoken against Him."
The phrase, *the seventh generation from Adam*
is from Enoch 60.8.

INTRODUCTION TO

THE

REVELATION TO JOHN

Authorship and Background: The author's name is John (1.1, 4, 9; 22.8), who called himself a servant of Christ and brother of the suffering Christians to whom he wrote (1.1, 9). He was in exile on the island of Patmos, off the west coast of Asia Minor, because of his steadfast witness to Jesus Christ (1.9), and he wrote of things he heard and saw in a revelation granted him by Jesus Christ (1.1, 2, 19; 22.8).

He is classified as a prophet (22.9; cf. also 10.11), and his book is a prophecy (1.3; 22.7). Nowhere does he indicate that he was an apostle, and in 21.14 he refers to the "twelve apostles of the Lamb" without specifying whether or not he belonged to the group. Traditionally this John has been identified with John the Apostle, son of Zebedee, from the earliest references to the book in the second century.

Although some date it earlier, before the destruction of Jerusalem in A.D. 70, the majority of scholars date the book in the latter years of the reign of the Emperor Domitian (A.D. 81–96), around the year A.D. 95.

The letter was written due to the persecution begun by the Emperor against Christians who were unwilling to engage in emperor worship. Calling himself "August," "Savior," "Lord," and even "God," the Emperor had statues built throughout the empire, and required citizens to offer sacrifices, as evidence of their allegiance to him. Christians, for whom there was only one God, and one Lord (1 Cor 8.6), refused to participate in this idolatry, and consequently suffered persecution in the form of arrest, loss of possessions, economic boycott, and in many cases, death.

To these persecuted and harried Christians in the churches of the Roman province of Asia, John addressed this strange and wonderful book, stressing the Lordship of Christ, the overruling sovereignty of God, and his eventual, final victory over the forces of sin and evil.

Characteristics: John describes the book as "the revelation of Jesus Christ, which God gave him to show to his servants what must soon take place" (1.1); this Jesus did by sending his angel to him (1.1; 22.16). The book is a prophecy (1.3; 22.7, 10, 18, 19), and is consciously written as inspired (1.10; 4.2; 17.3; 21.10); dire consequences are threatened against any who would either add to, or subtract from, the words of the book (22.18, 19). The author writes of "what is and what is to take place hereafter" (1.19): the latter involves the near advent of Jesus Christ who promises, "I am coming soon" (3.11; 22.7, 12, 20), to which the Spirit and the Bride answer, "Come!" (22.17). These future events are to take place soon (1.1; 22.6); the time is near (1.3; 22.10).

The book is a "revelation" (or apocalypse) (1.1). As such it employs symbols and figures common to apocalyptic literature: supernatural events, unearthly

creatures, metaphors, pseudonyms, and numbers. Perhaps not even the original readers of the book understood the precise meaning of all these strange symbols and metaphors; among modern commentators there is no agreement as to what they all mean.

There are four main schemes of interpretation of the book: (1) the preterit—everything has already been fulfilled; (2) the historical—the predictions are in the process of fulfilment; (3) the futurist—all predictions are in the future; and (4) the spiritual—the events described are only symbols of spiritual realities and struggles without any literal or historical application.

Whatever may be one's approach to, and interpretation of this book, two things should be kept in mind: (1) the practical purpose of the book was to strengthen the courage and faith of those early Christians; it was written primarily for them, and was meant to convey to them a message of hope and victory; (2) the author clearly and repeatedly stated that the time of these events was quite near (1.1, 3; 3.11; 22.6, 7, 10, 12, 20). The author anticipated that what he wrote about was to happen soon, either the whole series of events (if the coming of Christ and the end of the world are coincident), or else the first in the series of events (if the coming of Christ is to precede by a considerable length of time the final judgment and the new heaven and new earth). The fact that Christ has not yet returned does not destroy the sense of imminence.

The various interpretations of the thousand years in 20.1–10 have given rise to different eschatological schemes, usually known as pre-millennial, post-millennial, and a-millennial.

The literary development of the book follows a scheme of events in which the number seven often recurs: there are seven spirits of God (1.4; 4.5; 5.6); seven lampstands and seven stars (1.12–20); seven churches to which letters are sent (2.1—3.22); a book sealed with seven seals (5.1), opened one after the other (6.1–17; 8.1); seven angels who blow seven trumpets (8.2—9.21; 11.15–19); seven thunders (10.3, 4); seven angels with seven bowls (15.1, 5–8; 16.1–21); seven kings (17.10). The number three also occurs: three woes (9.12; 11.14), three angels (14.6–9), three foul spirits (16.13). The number twelve and its multiples are also used: twenty-four elders on thrones (4.4, 10–11); one hundred and forty-four thousand sealed, twelve thousand from each of the twelve tribes (7.4–8); the city with twelve gates and twelve foundations (21.10–21); the tree of life with twelve fruits (22.2). The most famous of all numbers, of course, is six hundred and sixty-six, the number of the beast (13.18).

There are symbolic and allegorical names: the Nicolaitans (2.6, 15), Jezebel (2.20–23), Abaddon, Apollyon (9.11), Sodom and Egypt (11.8), Armageddon (16.16), Babylon (17.5; 18.1–24), Gog and Magog (20.8).

It is the person of Christ, however, who dominates the book. He is both the Lamb, "as though it had been slain" (5.6), and the warrior who goes forth to conquer and rule, whose name is The Word of God (19.11–16).

Contents:

I. Introduction. 1.1–20: The author's commission to write; his vision of the resurrected and glorified Christ.

II. The messages to the seven churches. 2.1—3.22: Churches in the province of Asia: Ephesus, Smyrna, Pergamum, Thyatira, Sardis, Philadelphia, and Laodicea. "Behold, I stand at the door and knock. . . . He who has an ear, let him hear what the Spirit says to the churches" (3.20–22).

III.   The things which shall be. 4.1—22.5:

(1)   The heavenly worship. 4.1–11: God on his throne; four living creatures and twenty-four elders offer continuous worship to God.

(2)   Prelude to the seven seals. 5.1–14: the scroll opened and the Lamb adored.

(3)   The vision of the seven seals. 6.1—8.6: Interlude between the sixth and seventh seals (7.1–17).

(4)   The seven trumpets. 8.7—11.19: Interlude between the sixth and seventh trumpet; the prophet eats the little scroll in the angel's hand; he measures the temple of God; the two witnesses, their death, resurrection, and ascension into heaven.

(5)   The seven mystic figures. 12.1—14.20

(6)   The seven bowls of wrath. 15.1—16.21

(7)   The judgment of Babylon. 17.1—19.10

(8)   The defeat of the beast and the false prophet. 19.11–21

(9)   The binding of Satan. 20.1–3

(10) The millennial reign of Christ. 20.4–6

(11) The loosing of Satan. 20.7–10

(12) The great white throne judgment. 20.11–15

(13) The new heaven and the new earth. 21.1–8

(14) The new Jerusalem. 21.9—22.5

IV.   Epilogue. 22.6–21: The message authenticated, with warnings against any alteration; promise of reward and punishment. "'Surely I am coming soon.' Amen. Come, Lord Jesus!" (22.20)

THE
REVELATION TO JOHN

(The Apocalypse)

I. *Introduction 1.1–20*

A. *The source of the revelation*

*1.1
Jn 12.49;
Rev 22.16
1.2
1 Cor 1.6;
Rev 12.17
1.3
Lk 11.28;
Rev 22.10

1 The revelation of Jesus Christ, which God gave him to show to his servants what must soon take place; and he made it known by sending his angel to his servant John, 2 who bore witness to the word of God and to the testimony of Jesus Christ, even to all that he saw. 3 Blessed is he who reads aloud the words of the prophecy, and blessed are those who hear, and who keep what is written therein; for the time is near.

B. *The salutation*

1.4
Jn 1.1;
Rev 3.1; 4.5
1.5
Rev 3.14;
Col 1.18;
Ps 89.27;
Rev 17.14;
Jn 13.34;
Heb 9.14
1.6
1 Pet 2.5;
Rev 5.10;
Rom 11.36
1.7
Zech 12.10
1.8
Rev 21.6;
4.8; 16.7

4 John to the seven churches that are in Asia:

Grace to you and peace from him who is and who was and who is to come, and from the seven spirits who are before his throne, 5 and from Jesus Christ the faithful witness, the first-born of the dead, and the ruler of kings on earth.

To him who loves us and has freed us from our sins by his blood 6 and made us a kingdom, priests to his God and Father, to him be glory and dominion for ever and ever. Amen. 7 Behold, he is coming with the clouds, and every eye will see him, every one who pierced him; and all tribes of the earth will wail on account of him. Even so. Amen.

8 "I am the Alpha and the Ō·mē′gȧ," says the Lord God, who is and who was and who is to come, the Almighty.

C. *The voice and the vision*

1.9
Phil 4.14;
2 Tim 2.12
1.10
Rev 4.1,2
*1.11
ver 8,17

9 I John, your brother, who share with you in Jesus the tribulation and the kingdom and the patient endùrance, was on the island called Păt·mòs on account of the word of God and the testimony of Jesus. 10 I was in the Spirit on the Lord's day, and I heard behind me a loud voice like a trumpet 11 saying, "Write what you see in a book and send it to the seven churches, to Ĕph′ĕsùs and to

---

1.1 *revelation* is not the same as *inspiration. Revelation* means that disclosure of divine truth which is immediately given to holy men by the Holy Spirit. Some of the information in the Bible resulted from the investigation of the biblical writer himself (Lk 1.1–4). Some Scripture was undoubtedly copied from official records (as is implied by some statements in the Old Testament historical books— 2 Ki 1.18; 8.23; 10.34; 2 Chr 25.26; 27.7). Some Scripture has come from sources no longer to be identified but which may have included oral tradition (e.g., the events of the first eleven chapters of Genesis). Nevertheless conservative tradition has always held that the writers, in using information derived from possibly fallible records and oral tradition,

were preserved from error by the superintending power of the Holy Spirit. (The doctrine of inspiration does not involve the infallibility of the scribes who later made copies of the originals; yet while minor scribal errors may have crept into the text by transmission, there are no major doctrinal issues at stake in those few places.) Others hold that there are incidental errors in the original manuscripts.

1.11 The messages to the seven churches refer to: (1) actual, historical churches in existence in Asia Minor at the time John wrote; (2) conditions which existed not only in these churches but also in other churches of that time; (3) conditions which have arisen in the church of Jesus Christ in subsequent ages. A large and influential school of inter-

Smýrná and to Pėr'gàmùm and to Thýātï'rá and to Sardïs and to Philadelphia and to Lā'-ódïçē'à."

12 Then I turned to see the voice that was speaking to me, and on turning I saw seven golden lampstands, 13 and in the midst of the lampstands one like a son of man, clothed with a long robe and with a golden girdle round his breast; 14 his head and his hair were white as white wool, white as snow; his eyes were like a flame of fire, 15 his feet were like burnished bronze, refined as in a furnace, and his voice was like the sound of many waters; 16 in his right hand he held seven stars, from his mouth issued a sharp two-edged sword, and his face was like the sun shining in full strength.

17 When I saw him, I fell at his feet as though dead. But he laid his right hand upon me, saying, "Fear not, I am the first and the last, 18 and the living one; I died, and behold I am alive for evermore, and I have the keys of Death and Hādēṣ. 19 Now write what you see, what is and what is to take place hereafter. 20As for the mystery of the seven stars which you saw in my right hand, and the seven golden lampstands, the seven stars are the angels of the seven churches and the seven lampstands are the seven churches.

II. The messages to the seven churches 2.1–3.22

A. The message to Ephesus

2 "To the angel of the church in Ėph'ėsùs write: 'The words of him who holds the seven stars in his right hand, who walks among the seven golden lampstands.

2 " 'I know your works, your toil and your patient endurance, and now you cannot bear evil men but have tested those who call themselves apostles but are not, and found them to be false; 3 I know you are enduring patiently and bearing up for my name's sake, and you have not grown weary. 4 But I have this against you, that you have abandoned the love you had at first. 5 Remember then from what you have fallen, repent and do the works you did at first. If not, I will come to you and remove your lampstand from its place, unless you repent. 6 Yet this you have, you hate the works of the Nicŏlā'ïtànṣ, which I also hate. 7 He who has an ear, let him hear what the Spirit says to the churches. To him who conquers I will grant to eat of the tree of life, which is in the paradise of God.'

1.12
Ex 25.27;
Zech 4.2
1.13
Ezek 1.26;
Dan 7.13;
10.5
1.14
Dan 7.9;
10.6;
Rev 19.12
1.15
Dan 10.6;
Ezek 43.2
1.16
Rev 2.1;
3.1;
Heb 4.12;
Rev 2.12,16
1.17
Ezek 1.28;
Dan 8.18;
10.10;
Isa 41.4
1.18
Rom 6.9;
Rev 4.9;
20.1
1.20
Zech 4.2

2.1
Rev 1.16;
1.13
2.2
Rev 3.1,8;
1 Jn 4.1;
2 Cor 11.13
2.3
Jn 15.21
2.4
Mt 24.12
2.5
ver 16,22,2;
Rev 1.20
★2.6
ver 15
2.7
Mt 11.15;
Rev 3.6,13;
22.2,14;
Gen 2.9

---

pretation understands these seven churches as representing also seven successive epochs of the history of the Christian church as a whole between apostolic times and the end of the church age. As this scheme of interpretation has been worked out, however, it produces some remarkable incongruities, such as identifying the heroic period of the Protestant Reformation with Sardis and its unhappy state of being more dead than alive (3.1). It is therefore questionable whether these messages ought to be applied to particular periods in the history of the Christian church. And yet, in the opinion of many, at the end of the age there will be an intensifying of the evils described in the messages to the seven

churches and in particular the lukewarmness and empty self-conceit found in the Laodicean church (3.14–19).

2.6 The Nicolaitans were apparently a heretical sect whose doctrines were repudiated by the church at Ephesus but who were tolerated by the church at Pergamum (2.15). Very likely they were antinomians (see note to Rom 6.1) who abused Christian liberty under the guise of adherence to the doctrine of grace. Irenaeus, Clement, and Tertullian wrote of their indulgence in vice, adultery, eating of things offered to idols, and of their love of carnal pleasure. They also seem to have embraced errors about the person of Jesus Christ.

B. The message to Smyrna

2.8
Rev 1.11,
17,18
2.9
Rev 1.9;
Jas 2.5;
Rev 3.9
2.10
Rev 3.10;
Dan 1.12

2.11
Rev 20.14;
21.8

8 "And to the angel of the church in Smýrnà write: 'The words of the first and the last, who died and came to life.

9 " 'I know your tribulation and your poverty (but you are rich) and the slander of those who say that they are Jews and are not, but are a synagogue of Satan. 10 Do not fear what you are about to suffer. Behold, the devil is about to throw some of you into prison, that you may be tested, and for ten days you will have tribulation. Be faithful unto death, and I will give you the crown of life. 11 He who has an ear, let him hear what the Spirit says to the churches. He who conquers shall not be hurt by the second death.'

C. The message to Pergamum

2.12
Rev 1.11,16
2.13
Rev 14.12;
ver 9

*2.14
Num 24.14;
2 Pet 2.15;
Jude 11;
1 Cor 8.9;
10.19,20;
6.13
2.15
ver 6
2.16
2 Thess 2.8;
Rev 1.16
2.17
Jn 6.49,50;
Isa 62.2;
Rev 19.12

12 "And to the angel of the church in Pèr'gàmùm write: 'The words of him who has the sharp two-edged sword.

13 " 'I know where you dwell, where Satan's throne is; you hold fast my name and you did not deny my faith even in the days of Ãn'tìpàs my witness, my faithful one, who was killed among you, where Satan dwells. 14 But I have a few things against you: you have some there who hold the teaching of Bālaàm, who taught Bālàk to put a stumbling block before the sons of Israel, that they might eat food sacrificed to idols and practice immorality. 15 So you also have some who hold the teaching of the Nìcólā'ìtàns. 16 Repent then. If not, I will come to you soon and war against them with the sword of my mouth. 17 He who has an ear, let him hear what the Spirit says to the churches. To him who conquers I will give some of the hidden manna, and I will give him a white stone, with a new name written on the stone which no one knows except him who receives it.'

D. The message to Thyatira

2.18
Rev 1.11,
14,15
2.19
ver 2
*2.20
1 Ki 16.31;
21.25;
2 Ki 9.7;
Acts 15.20
2.21
Rom 2.4;
Rev 9.20
2.22
Rev 17.2;
18.9

18 "And to the angel of the church in Thȳàtì'rà write: 'The words of the Son of God, who has eyes like a flame of fire, and whose feet are like burnished bronze.

19 " 'I know your works, your love and faith and service and patient endurance, and that your latter works exceed the first. 20 But I have this against you, that you tolerate the woman Jèz'ébèl, who calls herself a prophetess and is teaching and beguiling my servants to practice immorality and to eat food sacrificed to idols. 21 I gave her time to repent, but she refuses to repent of her immorality. 22 Behold, I will throw her on a sickbed, and

---

2.14 the teaching of Balaam should be distinguished from the way of Balaam (2 Pet 2.15) and the error of Balaam (Jude 11, KJV). Balaam taught King Balak to subvert Israel by inviting them to worship his idols and unite in marriage or ritual prostitution with his people (Num 31.15, 16). Believers in all ages have been lost to the true faith when intermarriage with unbelievers has caused them to turn away from God to false human teachings. This sort of compromise inevitably leads to spiritual declension.

2.20 The teachings of Jezebel in Thyatira were the same as those of Balaam (ver 14), eat food sacrificed to idols, and practice immorality. In both instances it seems clear that the compound sin was that of idolatry and immorality. The two went together, for in many of the religions of that time, sexual indulgence was part of cult worship. It cannot be decided for certain whether Jezebel was the real name of the woman in question or simply a title for her, with obvious connotations (cf. 1 Ki 16.31; 2 Ki 9.22).

those who commit adultery with her I will throw into great tribulation, unless they repent of her doings; 23 and I will strike her children dead. And all the churches shall know that I am he who searches mind and heart, and I will give to each of you as your works deserve. 24 But to the rest of you in Thyắtī´rå, who do not hold this teaching, who have not learned what some call the deep things of Satan, to you I say, I do not lay upon you any other burden; 25 only hold fast what you have, until I come. 26 He who conquers and who keeps my works until the end, I will give him power over the nations, 27 and he shall rule them with a rod of iron, as when earthen pots are broken in pieces, even as I myself have received power from my Father; 28 and I will give him the morning star. 29 He who has an ear, let him hear what the Spirit says to the churches.'

2.23
Jer 11.20;
Acts 1.24;
Rom 8.27;
Ps 62.12
2.24
Acts 15.28

2.26
Heb 3.6;
Ps 2.8;
Rev 3.21
2.27
Rev 12.5;
Isa 30.14;
Jer 19.11
2.28
Rev 22.16

E. The message to Sardis

3 "And to the angel of the church in Sardïs write: 'The words of him who has the seven spirits of God and the seven stars.
" 'I know your works; you have the name of being alive, and you are dead. 2Awake, and strengthen what remains and is on the point of death, for I have not found your works perfect in the sight of my God. 3 Remember then what you received and heard; keep that, and repent. If you will not awake, I will come like a thief, and you will not know at what hour I will come upon you. 4 Yet you have still a few names in Sardïs, people who have not soiled their garments; and they shall walk with me in white, for they are worthy. 5 He who conquers shall be clad thus in white garments, and I will not blot his name out of the book of life; I will confess his name before my Father and before his angels. 6 He who has an ear, let him hear what the Spirit says to the churches.'

3.1
Rev 1.4,16;
2.2;
1 Tim 5.6

3.3
1 Thess 5.2,
6;
2 Pet 3.10
3.4
Acts 1.15;
Jude 23;
Rev 6.11;
7.9,13
3.5
Mt 10.32
3.6
Rev 2.7

F. The message to Philadelphia

7 "And to the angel of the church in Philadelphia write: 'The words of the holy one, the true one, who has the key of David, who opens and no one shall shut, who shuts and no one opens.
8 " 'I know your works. Behold, I have set before you an open door, which no one is able to shut; I know that you have but little power, and yet you have kept my word and have not denied my name. 9 Behold, I will make those of the synagogue of Satan who say that they are Jews and are not, but lie—behold, I will make them come and bow down before your feet, and learn that I have loved you. 10 Because you have kept my word of patient endurance, I will keep you from the hour of trial which is coming on the whole world, to try those who dwell upon the earth. 11 I am coming soon; hold fast what you have, so that no one may seize your crown. 12 He who conquers, I will make him a pillar in the temple of my God; never shall he go out of it, and I will write on him the name of my God, and the name of the city of my God, the new Jerusalem which comes down from my God out of heaven, and my own new name. 13 He who has an ear, let him hear what the Spirit says to the churches.'

3.7
Acts 3.14;
1 Jn 5.20;
Isa 22.22
3.8
Acts 14.27;
Rev 2.13
3.9
Rev 2.9;
Isa 49.23;
43.4
3.10
2 Pet 2.9;
Rev 16.14;
6.10; 17.8
3.11
Rev 22.7,
12,20;
2.25,10
3.12
Gal 2.9;
Rev 22.4;
21.2
3.13
ver 6

G. The message to Laodicea

14 "And to the angel of the church in Lā'-ŏdĭçē'á write: 'The words of the Amen, the faithful and true witness, the beginning of God's creation.

15 " 'I know your works: you are neither cold nor hot. Would that you were cold or hot! 16 So, because you are lukewarm, and neither cold nor hot, I will spew you out of my mouth. 17 For you say, I am rich, I have prospered, and I need nothing; not knowing that you are wretched, pitiable, poor, blind, and naked. 18 Therefore I counsel you to buy from me gold refined by fire, that you may be rich, and white garments to clothe you and to keep the shame of your nakedness from being seen, and salve to anoint your eyes, that you may see. 19 Those whom I love, I reprove and chasten; so be zealous and repent. 20 Behold, I stand at the door and knock; if any one hears my voice and opens the door, I will come in to him and eat with him, and he with me. 21 He who conquers, I will grant him to sit with me on my throne, as I myself conquered and sat down with my Father on his throne. 22 He who has an ear, let him hear what the Spirit says to the churches.' "

III. The things which shall be 4.1–22.5

A. The heavenly worship

4 After this I looked, and lo, in heaven an open door! And the first voice, which I had heard speaking to me like a trumpet, said, "Come up hither, and I will show you what must take place after this." 2 At once I was in the Spirit, and lo, a throne stood in heaven, with one seated on the throne! 3 And he who sat there appeared like jasper and carnelian, and round the throne was a rainbow that looked like an emerald. 4 Round the throne were twenty-four thrones, and seated on the thrones were twenty-four elders, clad in white garments, with golden crowns upon their heads. 5 From the throne issue flashes of lightning, and voices and peals of thunder, and before the throne burn seven torches of fire, which are the seven spirits of God; 6 and before the throne there is as it were a sea of glass, like crystal.

And round the throne, on each side of the throne, are four living creatures, full of eyes in front and behind: 7 the first living creature like a lion, the second living creature like an ox, the third living creature with the face of a man, and the fourth living creature like a flying eagle. 8 And the four living creatures, each of them with six wings, are full of eyes all round and within, and day and night they never cease to sing,

"Holy, holy, holy, is the Lord God Almighty,
who was and is and is to come!"

9 And whenever the living creatures give glory and honor and thanks to him who is seated on the throne, who lives for ever and ever, 10 the twenty-four elders fall down before him who is seated on the throne and worship him who lives for ever and ever; they cast their crowns before the throne, singing,

11 "Worthy art thou, our Lord and God,
to receive glory and honor and power,
for thou didst create all things,
and by thy will they existed and were created."

B. *Prelude to the seven seals:*
the scroll opened and the Lamb adored

5 And I saw in the right hand of him who was seated on the throne a scroll written within and on the back, sealed with seven seals; 2 and I saw a strong angel proclaiming with a loud voice, "Who is worthy to open the scroll and break its seals?" 3And no one in heaven or on earth or under the earth was able to open the scroll or to look into it, 4 and I wept much that no one was found worthy to open the scroll or to look into it. 5 Then one of the elders said to me, "Weep not; lo, the Lion of the tribe of Judah, the Root of David, has conquered, so that he can open the scroll and its seven seals."

6 And between the throne and the four living creatures and among the elders, I saw a Lamb standing, as though it had been slain, with seven horns and with seven eyes, which are the seven spirits of God sent out into all the earth; 7 and he went and took the scroll from the right hand of him who was seated on the throne. 8And when he had taken the scroll, the four living creatures and the twenty-four elders fell down before the Lamb, each holding a harp, and with golden bowls full of incense, which are the prayers of the saints; 9 and they sang a new song, saying,

"Worthy art thou to take the scroll and to open its seals,
   for thou wast slain and by thy blood didst ransom men for God
   from every tribe and tongue and people and nation,
10 and hast made them a kingdom and priests to our God,
   and they shall reign on earth."

11 Then I looked, and I heard around the throne and the living creatures and the elders the voice of many angels, numbering myriads of myriads and thousands of thousands, 12 saying with a loud voice, "Worthy is the Lamb who was slain, to receive power and wealth and wisdom and might and honor and glory and blessing!" 13And I heard every creature in heaven and on earth and under the earth and in the sea, and all therein, saying, "To him who sits upon the throne and to the Lamb be blessing and honor and glory and might for ever and ever!" 14And the four living creatures said, "Amen!" and the elders fell down and worshiped.

C. *The vision of the seven seals*

1. *The first seal: the white horse*

6 Now I saw when the Lamb opened one of the seven seals, and I heard one of the four living creatures say, as with a voice of thunder, "Come!" 2And I saw, and behold, a white horse, and its rider had a bow; and a crown was given to him, and he went out conquering and to conquer.

2. *The second seal: the red horse*

3 When he opened the second seal, I heard the second living creature say, "Come!" 4And out came another horse, bright red; its rider was permitted to take peace from the earth, so that men should slay one another; and he was given a great sword.

5.1
ver 7,13;
Ezek 2.9,10;
Isa 29.11;
Dan 12.4
5.2
Rev 10.1

*5.5
Gen 49.9;
Heb 7.14;
Isa 11.1,10;
Rom 15.12;
Rev 22.16
5.6
Rev 4.6;
Isa 53.7;
Rev 13.8;
Zech 3.9;
4.10;
Rev 4.5
5.7
ver 1
5.8
Rev 14.2;
Ps 141.2
5.9
Ps 40.3;
Rev 4.11;
1 Cor 6.20;
Heb 9.12

5.10
Ex 19.6;
Isa 61.6
5.11
Dan 7.10;
Heb 12.22
5.12
Rev 4.11

5.13
Phil 2.10;
ver 3;
1 Tim 6.16;
Rev 1.6;
6.16; 7.10
*5.14
Rev 19.4;
4.9,10

6.1
Rev 5.5–7,
1; 14.2;
19.6
6.2
Zech 6.3;
Rev 19.11;
Zech 6.11;
Rev 14.14
6.3
Rev 4.7
6.4
Zech 6.2

5.5 *Root of David,* i.e., the Messiah.   **5.14** The elders bowed in silent worship.

3. *The third seal: the black horse*

6.5
Rev 4.7;
Zech 6.2
*6.6
Rev 4.6,7;
9.4

5 When he opened the third seal, I heard the third living creature say, "Come!" And I saw, and behold, a black horse, and its rider had a balance in his hand; 6 and I heard what seemed to be a voice in the midst of the four living creatures saying, "A quart of wheat for a denarius,*a* and three quarts of barley for a denarius;*a* but do not harm oil and wine!"

4. *The fourth seal: the pale horse*

6.7
Rev 4.7
6.8
Zech 6.3;
Hos 13.14;
Ezek 5.12

7 When he opened the fourth seal, I heard the voice of the fourth living creature say, "Come!" 8And I saw, and behold, a pale horse, and its rider's name was Death, and Hādēs followed him; and they were given power over a fourth of the earth, to kill with sword and with famine and with pestilence and by wild beasts of the earth.

5. *The fifth seal: the martyrs*

6.9
Rev 14.18;
16.7; 20.4;
1.9; 12.17
6.10
Zech 1.12;
Ps 79.5;
Rev 3.7;
19.2
6.11
Rev 3.5;
7.9; 14.13;
Heb 11.40

9 When he opened the fifth seal, I saw under the altar the souls of those who had been slain for the word of God and for the witness they had borne; 10 they cried out with a loud voice, "O Sovereign Lord, holy and true, how long before thou wilt judge and avenge our blood on those who dwell upon the earth?" 11 Then they were each given a white robe and told to rest a little longer, until the number of their fellow servants and their brethren should be complete, who were to be killed as they themselves had been.

6. *The sixth seal: signs in the heavens*

6.12
Rev 16.18;
Mt 24.29;
Joel 2.31;
Acts 2.20
6.13
Rev 8.10;
9.1;
Isa 34.4
6.14
Isa 34.4;
Jer 3.23;
4.24;
Rev 16.10
6.15
Isa 2.10,19
6.16
Hos 10.8;
Lk 23.30;
Rev 9.6
6.17
Zeph 1.14;
Rev 16.14;
Ps 76.7

12 When he opened the sixth seal, I looked, and behold, there was a great earthquake; and the sun became black as sackcloth, the full moon became like blood, 13 and the stars of the sky fell to the earth as the fig tree sheds its winter fruit when shaken by a gale; 14 the sky vanished like a scroll that is rolled up, and every mountain and island was removed from its place. 15 Then the kings of the earth and the great men and the generals and the rich and the strong, and every one, slave and free, hid in the caves and among the rocks of the mountains, 16 calling to the mountains and rocks, "Fall on us and hide us from the face of him who is seated on the throne, and from the wrath of the Lamb; 17 for the great day of their wrath has come, and who can stand before it?"

7. *Interlude*
a. *The sealing of God's servants*

7.1
Rev 9.4

7 After this I saw four angels standing at the four corners of the earth, holding back the four winds of the earth, that no wind might blow on earth or sea or against any tree. 2 Then I saw another angel ascend from the rising of the sun, with the seal of the living God, and he called with a loud voice to the four angels who had been given power to harm earth and sea, 3 saying, "Do

7.3
Rev 6.6;
Ezek 9.4;
Rev 22.4

a The denarius was a day's wage for a laborer

6.6 The prices quoted for a quart of wheat and three quarts of barley indicate the scarcity of these staples. This means famine, when food becomes scarce, and the little available is sold at a very high price. A denarius was a day's wage.

not harm the earth or the sea or the trees, till we have sealed the
servants of our God upon their foreheads." ⁴And I heard the
number of the sealed, a hundred and forty-four thousand sealed,
out of every tribe of the sons of Israel, ⁵ twelve thousand sealed
out of the tribe of Judah, twelve thousand of the tribe of Reuben,
twelve thousand of the tribe of Găd, ⁶ twelve thousand of the tribe
of Ashĕr, twelve thousand of the tribe of Năph'tălī, twelve thousand of the tribe of Mănăs'sĕh, ⁷ twelve thousand of the tribe of
Sĭm'ëon, twelve thousand of the tribe of Lēvī, twelve thousand of
the tribe of Ĭs'săchar, ⁸ twelve thousand of the tribe of Zĕb'ŭlŭn,
twelve thousand of the tribe of Joseph, twelve thousand sealed out
of the tribe of Benjamin.

b. The white-robed tribulation saints

9 After this I looked, and behold, a great multitude which no
man could number, from every nation, from all tribes and peoples
and tongues, standing before the throne and before the Lamb,
clothed in white robes, with palm branches in their hands, ¹⁰ and
crying out with a loud voice, "Salvation belongs to our God who
sits upon the throne, and to the Lamb!" ¹¹And all the angels stood
round the throne and round the elders and the four living creatures, and they fell on their faces before the throne and worshiped
God, ¹² saying, "Amen! Blessing and glory and wisdom and thanksgiving and honor and power and might be to our God for ever and
ever! Amen."

13 Then one of the elders addressed me, saying, "Who are
these, clothed in white robes, and whence have they come?" ¹⁴ I
said to him, "Sir, you know." And he said to me, "These are they
who have come out of the great tribulation; they have washed their
robes and made them white in the blood of the Lamb.

¹⁵ Therefore are they before the throne of God,
     and serve him day and night within his temple;
     and he who sits upon the throne will shelter them with his
       presence.
¹⁶ They shall hunger no more, neither thirst any more;
     the sun shall not strike them, nor any scorching heat.
¹⁷ For the Lamb in the midst of the throne will be their shepherd,
     and he will guide them to springs of living water;
     and God will wipe away every tear from their eyes."

7.4-8 The tribe of Dan is not mentioned here among the twelve tribes. The tribe of Manasseh is substituted in its place although Ephraim, the brother of Manasseh (both of whom were sons of Joseph and grandsons of Jacob), is not mentioned either. It is very difficult to account for these two omissions, especially since Ephraim was historically one of the most important of the tribes. The *hundred and forty-four thousand* is hardly to be thought of as an exact number of converted Jews; some have taken it to imply that it represents the complete number of Jews who are the children of Abraham by faith, foreknown and chosen by God, who will turn to Christ during the closing days of the present age. The same number, *one hundred forty-four thousand*, occurs also in 14.1, 3.
7.14 The *great tribulation* is marked off in

Scripture as part of the closing years of our present age just prior to the return of Jesus Christ. Varying degrees of tribulation will come upon believers in all periods in church history, but the great tribulation is defined (Mt 24.21) as a time of unprecedented trial and affliction. According to many interpreters, during this time the people of God will be cruelly mistreated and many will have to seal their testimony with the blood of martyrdom. Some interpreters take 13.1–5 to refer to this period of intense persecution and suffering, consisting of three and one-half years just prior to the Second Advent of Christ. During that period Satan will give power to the *beast rising out of the sea* (13.1) and God will visit His wrath upon men in the judgment of the seven bowls described in chapter 16. See also note to Mt 24.3.

8. *The seventh seal: making ready the seven trumpets*

8 When the Lamb opened the seventh seal, there was silence in heaven for about half an hour. 2 Then I saw the seven angels who stand before God, and seven trumpets were given to them. 3And another angel came and stood at the altar with a golden censer; and he was given much incense to mingle with the prayers of all the saints upon the golden altar before the throne; 4 and the smoke of the incense rose with the prayers of the saints from the hand of the angel before God. 5 Then the angel took the censer and filled it with fire from the altar and threw it on the earth; and there were peals of thunder, voices, flashes of lightning, and an earthquake.

6 Now the seven angels who had the seven trumpets made ready to blow them.

D. *The seven trumpets*

1. *The first trumpet: hail, fire, and blood*

7 The first angel blew his trumpet, and there followed hail and fire, mixed with blood, which fell on the earth; and a third of the earth was burnt up, and a third of the trees were burnt up, and all green grass was burnt up.

2. *The second trumpet: the sea becomes blood*

8 The second angel blew his trumpet, and something like a great mountain, burning with fire, was thrown into the sea; 9 and a third of the sea became blood, a third of the living creatures in the sea died, and a third of the ships were destroyed.

3. *The third trumpet: the falling star*

10 The third angel blew his trumpet, and a great star fell from heaven, blazing like a torch, and it fell on a third of the rivers and on the fountains of water. 11 The name of the star is Wormwood. A third of the waters became wormwood, and many men died of the water, because it was made bitter.

4. *The fourth trumpet: the darkening of the sun, moon, and stars*

12 The fourth angel blew his trumpet, and a third of the sun was struck, and a third of the moon, and a third of the stars, so that a third of their light was darkened; a third of the day was kept from shining, and likewise a third of the night.

13 Then I looked, and I heard an eagle crying with a loud voice, as it flew in midheaven, "Woe, woe, woe to those who dwell on the earth, at the blasts of the other trumpets which the three angels are about to blow!"

5. *The fifth trumpet: the opening of the bottomless pit*

9 And the fifth angel blew his trumpet, and I saw a star fallen from heaven to earth, and he was given the key of the shaft of the bottomless pit; 2 he opened the shaft of the bottomless pit, and from the shaft rose smoke like the smoke of a great furnace, and the sun and the air were darkened with the smoke from the shaft. 3 Then from the smoke came locusts on the earth, and they were given power like the power of scorpions of the earth; 4 they were

Cross-references (margin)

8.1 Rev 6.1
8.2 1 Cor 15.52; 1 Thess 4.16
8.3 Rev 7.2; 5.8; Ex 30.1; Rev 6.9
8.4 Ps 141.2
8.5 Lev 16.12; Rev 4.5; 6.12
8.6 ver 2
8.7 Ezek 38.22; Rev 9.4
8.8 Jer 51.25; Rev 16.3
8.10 Isa 14.12; Rev 9.1; 16.4
8.11 Jer 9.15; 23.15
8.12 Rev 6.12,13
8.13 Rev 14.6; 19.17; 9.12; 11.14
9.1 Rev 8.10; Lk 8.31; Rev 17.8; 20.1
9.2 Gen 19.28; Ex 19.18; Joel 2.2,10
9.3 Ex 10.12–15; ver 10
9.4 Rev 6.6; 8.7; 7.2,3

told not to harm the grass of the earth or any green growth or any tree, but only those of mankind who have not the seal of God upon their foreheads; 5 they were allowed to torture them for five months, but not to kill them, and their torture was like the torture of a scorpion, when it stings a man. 6And in those days men will seek death and will not find it; they will long to die, and death will fly from them.

7 In appearance the locusts were like horses arrayed for battle; on their heads were what looked like crowns of gold; their faces were like human faces, 8 their hair like women's hair, and their teeth like lions' teeth; 9 they had scales like iron breastplates, and the noise of their wings was like the noise of many chariots with horses rushing into battle. 10 They have tails like scorpions, and stings, and their power of hurting men for five months lies in their tails. 11 They have as king over them the angel of the bottomless pit; his name in Hebrew is Abăd'dȯn, and in Greek he is called Apŏll'yȯn.*b*

12 The first woe has passed; behold, two woes are still to come.

6. *The sixth trumpet: the four angels released*

13 Then the sixth angel blew his trumpet, and I heard a voice from the four horns of the golden altar before God, 14 saying to the sixth angel who had the trumpet, "Release the four angels who are bound at the great river Eūphrā'tēs." 15 So the four angels were released, who had been held ready for the hour, the day, the month, and the year, to kill a third of mankind. 16 The number of the troops of cavalry was twice ten thousand times ten thousand; I heard their number. 17And this was how I saw the horses in my vision: the riders wore breastplates the color of fire and of sapphire*c* and of sulphur, and the heads of the horses were like lions' heads, and fire and smoke and sulphur issued from their mouths. 18 By these three plagues a third of mankind was killed, by the fire and smoke and sulphur issuing from their mouths. 19 For the power of the horses is in their mouths and in their tails; their tails are like serpents, with heads, and by means of them they wound.

20 The rest of mankind, who were not killed by these plagues, did not repent of the works of their hands nor give up worshiping demons and idols of gold and silver and bronze and stone and wood, which cannot either see or hear or walk; 21 nor did they repent of their murders or their sorceries or their immorality or their thefts.

7. *The second interlude*
a. *John eats the scroll*

10 Then I saw another mighty angel coming down from heaven, wrapped in a cloud, with a rainbow over his head, and his face was like the sun, and his legs like pillars of fire. 2 He had a little scroll open in his hand. And he set his right foot on the sea, and his left foot on the land, 3 and called out with a loud voice, like a lion roaring; when he called out, the seven thunders sounded. 4And

b Or *Destroyer*   *c* Greek *hyacinth*

9.5	ver 10,3
9.6	Job 3.21; Jer 8.3; Rev 6.16
9.7	Joel 2.4; Nah 3.17; Dan 7.8
9.8	Joel 1.6
9.9	Joel 2.5
9.10	ver 5,19
9.11	Eph 2.2; ver 1
9.12	Rev 8.13
9.13	Ex 30.1–3; Rev 8.3
9.14	Rev 16.12
9.15	ver 18
9.16	Rev 5.11; 7.4
9.17	ver 18; Rev 11.5
9.18	ver 15,17
9.20	Deut 31.29; 1 Cor 10.20; Ps 115.4; 135.15; Dan 5.23
*9.21	Rev 2.21; 18.23; 17.2,5
10.1	Rev 5.2; Mt 17.2; Rev 1.16,15
10.3	Isa 31.4; Rev 4.5
10.4	Dan 8.26; 12.4,9; Rev 22.10

9.21 One of the characteristic marks of the end of the age is the continued impenitence of the unconverted. Despite the fearful judgments which fall upon men and the warning conveyed by these judgments, they persist in their sins and in their refusal to repent.

when the seven thunders had sounded, I was about to write, but I heard a voice from heaven saying, "Seal up what the seven thunders have said, and do not write it down." 5And the angel whom I saw standing on sea and land lifted up his right hand to heaven 6 and swore by him who lives for ever and ever, who created heaven and what is in it, the earth and what is in it, and the sea and what is in it, that there should be no more delay, 7 but that in the days of the trumpet call to be sounded by the seventh angel, the mystery of God, as he announced to his servants the prophets, should be fulfilled.

8 Then the voice which I had heard from heaven spoke to me again, saying, "Go, take the scroll which is open in the hand of the angel who is standing on the sea and on the land." 9 So I went to the angel and told him to give me the little scroll; and he said to me, "Take it and eat; it will be bitter to your stomach, but sweet as honey in your mouth." 10And I took the little scroll from the hand of the angel and ate it; it was sweet as honey in my mouth, but when I had eaten it my stomach was made bitter. 11And I was told, "You must again prophesy about many peoples and nations and tongues and kings."

b. The two witnesses

11 Then I was given a measuring rod like a staff, and I was told: "Rise and measure the temple of God and the altar and those who worship there, 2 but do not measure the court outside the temple; leave that out, for it is given over to the nations, and they will trample over the holy city for forty-two months. 3And I will grant my two witnesses power to prophesy for one thousand two hundred and sixty days, clothed in sackcloth."

4 These are the two olive trees and the two lampstands which stand before the Lord of the earth. 5And if any one would harm them, fire pours from their mouth and consumes their foes; if any one would harm them, thus he is doomed to be killed. 6 They have power to shut the sky, that no rain may fall during the days of their prophesying, and they have power over the waters to turn them into blood, and to smite the earth with every plague, as often as they desire. 7And when they have finished their testimony, the beast that ascends from the bottomless pit will make war upon them and conquer them and kill them, 8 and their dead bodies will lie in the street of the great city which is allegorically*d* called Sŏdŏm and Egypt, where their Lord was crucified. 9 For three days and a half men from the peoples and tribes and tongues and nations gaze at their dead bodies and refuse to let them be placed in a tomb, 10 and those who dwell on the earth will rejoice over them and make merry and exchange presents, because these two prophets had been a torment to those who dwell on the earth. 11 But after the three and a half days a breath of life from God entered them, and they stood up on their feet, and great fear fell

Cross references (margin)

- **10.5** Ex 6.8; Dan 12.7
- **10.6** Rev 4.11; 14.7; 16.17
- **10.7** Rev 11.15; Rom 16.25
- **10.8** ver 4
- **10.9** Jer 15.16; Ezek 2.8
- **10.10** Ezek 3.3
- **10.11** Rev 11.1; Ezek 37.4,9
- **11.1** Ezek 40.3; Rev 21.15
- **11.2** Ezek 40.17; Lk 21.24; Rev 13.5
- ***11.3** Rev 19.10; 12.6
- **11.4** Ps 52.8; Jer 11.16; Zech 4.3; Mt 11.14
- **11.5** 2 Ki 1.10; Jer 5.14; Num 16.29
- **11.6** 1 Ki 17.1; Ex 7.17,19
- **11.7** Rev 13.1; 9.1,2; Dan 7.21
- **11.8** Rev 14.8; Isa 1.9; Heb 13.12
- **11.10** Rev 3.10; Est 9.19,22
- **11.11** Ezek 37.5, 9,10,14

d Greek *spiritually*

11.3 The two witnesses who prophesy for *one thousand two hundred sixty days* (or forty-two months, or three and a half years) are described in terms identified with Elijah and Moses. It was Elijah who for three and a half years shut the heavens so that it did not rain (cf. Lk 4.25; Jas 5.17), while Moses was given power to turn the waters into blood, as well as to call down the other plagues on the Egyptians. The two are paired in Mal 4.4, 5 and appeared at the Transfiguration of Christ (Mk 9.4 and parallels).

on those who saw them. 12 Then they heard a loud voice from heaven saying to them, "Come up hither!" And in the sight of their foes they went up to heaven in a cloud. 13And at that hour there was a great earthquake, and a tenth of the city fell; seven thousand people were killed in the earthquake, and the rest were terrified and gave glory to the God of heaven.

14 The second woe has passed; behold, the third woe is soon to come.

8. The seventh trumpet: the consummation

15 Then the seventh angel blew his trumpet, and there were loud voices in heaven, saying, "The kingdom of the world has become the kingdom of our Lord and of his Christ, and he shall reign for ever and ever." 16And the twenty-four elders who sit on their thrones before God fell on their faces and worshiped God,
17 saying,
"We give thanks to thee, Lord God Almighty, who art and who wast,
    that thou hast taken thy great power and begun to reign.
18 The nations raged, but thy wrath came,
    and the time for the dead to be judged,
for rewarding thy servants, the prophets and saints,
    and those who fear thy name, both small and great,
and for destroying the destroyers of the earth."

19 Then God's temple in heaven was opened, and the ark of his covenant was seen within his temple; and there were flashes of lightning, voices, peals of thunder, an earthquake, and heavy hail.

E. The seven mystic figures

1. The woman with child

12 And a great portent appeared in heaven, a woman clothed with the sun, with the moon under her feet, and on her head a crown of twelve stars; 2 she was with child and she cried out in her pangs of birth, in anguish for delivery. 3And another portent

2. The dragon

appeared in heaven; behold, a great red dragon, with seven heads and ten horns, and seven diadems upon his heads. 4 His tail swept down a third of the stars of heaven, and cast them to the earth. And the dragon stood before the woman who was about to bear a child, that he might devour her child when she brought it forth;

3. The male child

5 she brought forth a male child, one who is to rule all the nations with a rod of iron, but her child was caught up to God and to his throne, 6 and the woman fled into the wilderness, where she has

---

11.12
Rev 4.1;
2 Ki 2.11;
Acts 1.9

11.13
Rev 6.12;
14.7; 16.11

11.14
Rev 9.12

*11.15
Rev 10.7;
16.17; 19.1;
12.10;
Dan 2.44;
7.14,27

11.16
Rev 4.4;
5.8

11.17
Rev 1.8;
19.6

11.18
Ps 2.1;
Dan 7.9,10;
Rev 10.7;
19.5

11.19
Rev 15.5,8;
8.5; 16.21

12.2
Isa 66.7;
Gal 4.19

12.3
Rev 13.1;
Dan 7.7;
Rev 19.12

12.4
Rev 8.7,12;
Dan 8.10

12.5
Ps 2.9;
Rev 2.27;
2 Cor 12.2

12.6
Rev 11.3

11.15 Here is the fulfilment of *the mystery of God*, as promised in 10.7, namely, the proclamation of the joint kingship of God and Christ. *The kingdom of the world* is the sovereignty, or ruling power, over the world, and the loud voices in heaven proclaim the fact that the kingship over the world has become our Lord's and His Christ's *and he shall reign for ever and ever*. The words are reminiscent of the resurrected Christ saying to his disciples, *All authority in heaven and on earth has been given to me* (Mt 28.18).

a place prepared by God, in which to be nourished for one thousand two hundred and sixty days.

4. *The angel Michael*

7 Now war arose in heaven, Michael and his angels fighting against the dragon; and the dragon and his angels fought, 8 but they were defeated and there was no longer any place for them in heaven. 9And the great dragon was thrown down, that ancient serpent, who is called the Devil and Satan, the deceiver of the whole world—he was thrown down to the earth, and his angels were thrown down with him. 10And I heard a loud voice in heaven, saying, "Now the salvation and the power and the kingdom of our God and the authority of his Christ have come, for the accuser of our brethren has been thrown down, who accuses them day and night before our God. 11And they have conquered him by the blood of the Lamb and by the word of their testimony, for they loved not their lives even unto death. 12 Rejoice then, O heaven and you that dwell therein! But woe to you, O earth and sea, for the devil has come down to you in great wrath, because he knows that his time is short!"

13 And when the dragon saw that he had been thrown down to the earth, he pursued the woman who had borne the male child. 14 But the woman was given the two wings of the great eagle that she might fly from the serpent into the wilderness, to the place where she is to be nourished for a time, and times, and half a time. 15 The serpent poured water like a river out of his mouth after the woman, to sweep her away with the flood. 16 But the earth came to the help of the woman, and the earth opened its mouth and swallowed the river which the dragon had poured from his mouth. 17 Then the dragon was angry with the woman, and went off to make war on the rest of her offspring, on those who keep the commandments of God and bear testimony to Jesus. And he stood[e] on the sand of the sea.

5. *The beast from the sea*

13 And I saw a beast rising out of the sea, with ten horns and seven heads, with ten diadems upon its horns and a blasphemous name upon its heads. 2And the beast that I saw was like a leopard, its feet were like a bear's, and its mouth was like a lion's mouth. And to it the dragon gave his power and his throne and great authority. 3 One of its heads seemed to have a mortal wound, but its mortal wound was healed, and the whole earth followed the beast with wonder. 4 Men worshiped the dragon, for he had given his authority to the beast, and they worshiped the beast, saying, "Who is like the beast, and who can fight against it?"

5 And the beast was given a mouth uttering haughty and blasphemous words, and it was allowed to exercise authority for forty-two months; 6 it opened its mouth to utter blasphemies against God, blaspheming his name and his dwelling, that is, those who dwell in heaven. 7Also it was allowed to make war on the saints

e Other ancient authorities read And I stood, connecting the sentence with 13.1

12.9 The exact time when Satan is thrown down to earth out of heaven is not here stated. No more can be inferred than that in the struggle between God and Satan the latter will become a defeated foe whose end is sure through the victory of Christ (Jn 12.31).

Marginal references:

12.7
Dan 10.13;
Rev 20.2

*12.9
Gen 3.1,4;
Rev 20.2,
3,8,10;
Jn 12.31

12.10
Rev 11.15;
Job 1.9–11;
Zech 3.1

12.11
Rom 16.20;
Lk 14.26

12.12
Ps 96.11;
Isa 49.13;
Rev 18.20;
8.13; 10.6

12.13
ver 3,5

12.14
Ex 19.4;
Dan 7.25;
12.7

12.15
Isa 59.19

12.17
Gen 3.15;
Rev 11.7;
14.12; 1.2,
9

13.1
Dan 7.1–
6;
Rev 17.3

13.2
Rev 16.10

13.3
Rev 17.8

13.4
Rev 18.18

13.5
Dan 7.8,
11,25;
Rev 11.2

13.6
Rev 12.12

13.7
Dan 7.21;
Rev 11.7;
5.9

and to conquer them.*f* And authority was given it over every tribe and people and tongue and nation, 8 and all who dwell on earth will worship it, every one whose name has not been written before the foundation of the world in the book of life of the Lamb that was slain. 9 If any one has an ear, let him hear:
10 If any one is to be taken captive,
　　to captivity he goes;
　if any one slays with the sword,
　　with the sword must he be slain.
Here is a call for the endurance and faith of the saints.

6. The beast from the earth

11 Then I saw another beast which rose out of the earth; it had two horns like a lamb and it spoke like a dragon. 12 It exercises all the authority of the first beast in its presence, and makes the earth and its inhabitants worship the first beast, whose mortal wound was healed. 13 It works great signs, even making fire come down from heaven to earth in the sight of men; 14 and by the signs which it is allowed to work in the presence of the beast, it deceives those who dwell on earth, bidding them make an image for the beast which was wounded by the sword and yet lived; 15 and it was allowed to give breath to the image of the beast so that the image of the beast should even speak, and to cause those who would not worship the image of the beast to be slain. 16 Also it causes all, both small and great, both rich and poor, both free and slave, to be marked on the right hand or the forehead, 17 so that no one can buy or sell unless he has the mark, that is, the name of the beast or the number of its name. 18 This calls for wisdom: let him who has understanding reckon the number of the beast, for it is a human number, its number is six hundred and sixty-six.*g*

7. The Lamb on Mount Zion

14 Then I looked, and lo, on Mount Zion stood the Lamb, and with him a hundred and forty-four thousand who had his name and his Father's name written on their foreheads. 2 And I heard a voice from heaven like the sound of many waters and like the sound of loud thunder; the voice I heard was like the sound of harpers playing on their harps, 3 and they sing a new song before the throne and before the four living creatures and before the elders. No one could learn that song except the hundred and forty-four thousand who had been redeemed from the earth. 4 It is these who have not defiled themselves with women, for they are chaste;*h* it is these who follow the Lamb wherever he goes; these have been redeemed from mankind as first fruits for God and the Lamb, 5 and in their mouth no lie was found, for they are spotless.

8. Interlude: the angelic messages

6 Then I saw another angel flying in midheaven, with an eternal

---

13.8
Phil 4.3;
Rev 3.5;
17.8; 5.6
13.9
Mk 4.23;
Rev 2.7
13.10
Isa 33.1;
Mt 26.52;
Rev 14.12

13.11
Rev 11.7
13.12
ver 4,14;
Rev 14.9,
11; ver 3
★13.13
Mt 24.24;
Rev 16.14;
1 Ki 18.38;
Rev 20.9
13.14
Rev 12.9;
2 Thess 2.9,
10
13.15
Dan 3.5;
Rev 16.2
13.16
Rev 11.18;
19.5,18;
14.9
13.17
Rev 14.9,
11; 15.2
13.18
Rev 17.9;
15.2; 21.17

14.1
Rev 5.6;
Ps 2.6;
Rev 3.12;
7.3
14.2
Rev 1.15;
5.8
14.3
Rev 5.9;
ver 1
14.4
2 Cor 11.2;
Rev 3.4;
5.9;
Jas 1.18
14.5
Ps 32.2;
Zeph 3.13;
Eph 5.27

14.6
Rev 8.13;
3.10; 5.9

---

f Other ancient authorities omit this sentence
g Other ancient authorities read *six hundred and sixteen*　　*h* Greek *virgins*

13.13 *It works great signs.* The signs include *making fire come down from heaven* which is reminiscent of Elijah (1 Ki 18.38; 2 Ki 1.10). Jesus Christ told his disciples they would work great signs and miracles, but he also warned them against false prophets who would do the same (Mk 13.22). Here that warning is fulfilled.

gospel to proclaim to those who dwell on earth, to every nation and tribe and tongue and people; 7 and he said with a loud voice, "Fear God and give him glory, for the hour of his judgment has come; and worship him who made heaven and earth, the sea and the fountains of water."

8 Another angel, a second, followed, saying, "Fallen, fallen is Babylon the great, she who made all nations drink the wine of her impure passion."

9 And another angel, a third, followed them, saying with a loud voice, "If any one worships the beast and its image, and receives a mark on his forehead or on his hand, 10 he also shall drink the wine of God's wrath, poured unmixed into the cup of his anger, and he shall be tormented with fire and sulphur in the presence of the holy angels and in the presence of the Lamb. 11And the smoke of their torment goes up for ever and ever; and they have no rest, day or night, these worshipers of the beast and its image, and whoever receives the mark of its name."

12 Here is a call for the endurance of the saints, those who keep the commandments of God and the faith of Jesus.

13 And I heard a voice from heaven saying, "Write this: Blessed are the dead who die in the Lord henceforth." "Blessed indeed," says the Spirit, "that they may rest from their labors, for their deeds follow them!"

14 Then I looked, and lo, a white cloud, and seated on the cloud one like a son of man, with a golden crown on his head, and a sharp sickle in his hand. 15And another angel came out of the temple, calling with a loud voice to him who sat upon the cloud, "Put in your sickle, and reap, for the hour to reap has come, for the harvest of the earth is fully ripe." 16 So he who sat upon the cloud swung his sickle on the earth, and the earth was reaped.

17 And another angel came out of the temple in heaven, and he too had a sharp sickle. 18 Then another angel came out from the altar, the angel who has power over fire, and he called with a loud voice to him who had the sharp sickle, "Put in your sickle, and gather the clusters of the vine of the earth, for its grapes are ripe." 19 So the angel swung his sickle on the earth and gathered the vintage of the earth, and threw it into the great wine press of the wrath of God; 20 and the wine press was trodden outside the city, and blood flowed from the wine press, as high as a horse's bridle, for one thousand six hundred stadia.[i]

---

i About two hundred miles

Cross-references (left margin):

14.7 — Rev 15.4; 11.13; 4.11; 8.10

*14.8 — Isa 21.9; Jer 51.8; Rev 18.2; 17.5; 18.10

14.9 — Rev 13.14–16

14.10 — Isa 51.17; Jer 25.15; Rev 18.6; 20.10; 19.20

14.11 — Isa 34.10; Rev 19.3; 4.8; 13.17

14.12 — Rev 13.10; 12.17

14.13 — Rev 20.6; 1 Cor 15.18; 1 Thess 4.16

14.14 — Dan 7.13; Rev 1.13; 6.2

14.15 — Joel 3.13; Jer 51.33; Rev 13.12

14.18 — Rev 16.8; Joel 3.13

14.19 — Rev 19.15

14.20 — Isa 63.3; Heb 13.12; Rev 11.8

14.8 Read in this connection 16.17–21; 17.1—18.24 for further details on Babylon. The positive identification of Babylon in the Revelation with any known city or power is virtually impossible. Many different views have been proposed and sustained with learned argument, only to meet with equally learned dissent. Some have identified it with Babylon of the Old Testament. Some have insisted it to be Jerusalem. Some have thought it to be an ecclesiastical rather than a geographical symbol. In this view the Reformers thought it to be the Roman papacy while later writers have held it to be an apostate Christendom at the end of the age. Perhaps the strongest argument favors the identification of Babylon with Rome, the capital of Italy, where the emperor ruled over the civilized world of that time. In 17.4, 5 the woman arrayed in purple and scarlet is named *Babylon the great* and in 17.18 she is *the great city which has dominion over the kings of the earth*. In 16.17–21 John sees Babylon's impending destruction. In chapter 18 John sees it as fallen. It is apparent that Babylon, whatever its final identification, sheds the blood of Christians who remain faithful, seduces the peoples under her control, and shares the "wealth of her wantonness" with the merchants of the earth who shall suffer with her. At last *shall Babylon . . . be thrown down . . . and shall be found no more* (18.21).

F. The seven bowls of wrath

1. Preliminary vision in heaven

15 Then I saw another portent in heaven, great and wonderful, seven angels with seven plagues, which are the last, for with them the wrath of God is ended.

2 And I saw what appeared to be a sea of glass mingled with fire, and those who had conquered the beast and its image and the number of its name, standing beside the sea of glass with harps of God in their hands. 3And they sing the song of Moses, the servant of God, and the song of the Lamb, saying,

"Great and wonderful are thy deeds,
O Lord God the Almighty!
Just and true are thy ways,
O King of the ages!*j*
4 Who shall not fear and glorify thy name, O Lord?
For thou alone art holy.
All nations shall come and worship thee,
for thy judgments have been revealed."

5 After this I looked, and the temple of the tent of witness in heaven was opened, 6 and out of the temple came the seven angels with the seven plagues, robed in pure bright linen, and their breasts girded with golden girdles. 7And one of the four living creatures gave the seven angels seven golden bowls full of the wrath of God who lives for ever and ever; 8 and the temple was filled with smoke from the glory of God and from his power, and no one could enter the temple until the seven plagues of the seven angels were ended.

16 Then I heard a loud voice from the temple telling the seven angels, "Go and pour out on the earth the seven bowls of the wrath of God."

2. The first bowl: sores on men

2 So the first angel went and poured his bowl on the earth, and foul and evil sores came upon the men who bore the mark of the beast and worshiped its image.

3. The second bowl: the sea becomes like blood

3 The second angel poured his bowl into the sea, and it became like the blood of a dead man, and every living thing died that was in the sea.

4. The third bowl: rivers and fountains become blood

4 The third angel poured his bowl into the rivers and the fountains of water, and they became blood. 5And I heard the angel of water say,

"Just art thou in these thy judgments,
thou who art and wast, O Holy One.
6 For men have shed the blood of saints and prophets,
and thou hast given them blood to drink.
It is their due!"
7 And I heard the altar cry,
"Yea, Lord God the Almighty,
true and just are thy judgments!"

j Other ancient authorities read *the nations*

Marginal references

15.1 Rev 12.1,3; 16.1; Lev 26.21; Rev 14.10
15.2 Rev 4.6; 13.14,15; 5.8
15.3 Deut 32.3, 4; Ps 111.2; 145.17; Hos 14.9
15.4 Jer 10.7; Isa 66.23
15.5 Rev 11.19; Num 1.50
15.6 Rev 14.15; ver 1; Rev 1.13
15.7 Rev 4.6,9; 10.6
15.8 Ex 40.34; 1 Ki 8.10; Isa 6.4
16.1 Rev 15.1
16.2 Rev 8.7; Ex 9.9–11; Rev 13.15–17
16.3 Rev 8.8,9; Ex 17.17–21
16.4 Rev 8.10; Ex 7.17–21
16.5 Rev 15.3; 11.17; 15.4
16.6 Rev 17.6; 18.24; Isa 49.26
16.7 Rev 6.9; 14.18;15.3; 19.2

5. The fourth bowl: fierce heat of the sun

8 The fourth angel poured his bowl on the sun, and it was allowed to scorch men with fire; 9 men were scorched by the fierce heat, and they cursed the name of God who had power over these plagues, and they did not repent and give him glory.

6. The fifth bowl: darkness

10 The fifth angel poured his bowl on the throne of the beast, and its kingdom was in darkness; men gnawed their tongues in anguish 11 and cursed the God of heaven for their pain and sores, and did not repent of their deeds.

7. The sixth bowl: the foul spirits prepare for Armageddon

12 The sixth angel poured his bowl on the great river Eūphrā'-tēṣ, and its water was dried up, to prepare the way for the kings from the east. 13 And I saw, issuing from the mouth of the dragon and from the mouth of the beast and from the mouth of the false prophet, three foul spirits like frogs; 14 for they are demonic spirits, performing signs, who go abroad to the kings of the whole world, to assemble them for battle on the great day of God the Almighty. 15 ("Lo, I am coming like a thief! Blessed is he who is awake, keeping his garments that he may not go naked and be seen exposed!") 16 And they assembled them at the place which is called in Hebrew Armăgĕd'dŏn.

8. The seventh bowl: the earthquake

17 The seventh angel poured his bowl into the air, and a loud voice came out of the temple, from the throne, saying, "It is done!" 18 And there were flashes of lightning, voices, peals of thunder, and a great earthquake such as had never been since men were on the earth, so great was that earthquake. 19 The great city was split into three parts, and the cities of the nations fell, and God remembered great Babylon, to make her drain the cup of the fury of his wrath. 20 And every island fled away, and no mountains were to be found; 21 and great hailstones, heavy as a hundred-weight, dropped on men from heaven, till men cursed God for the plague of the hail, so fearful was that plague.

G. The judgment of Babylon

1. The great harlot

17 Then one of the seven angels who had the seven bowls came and said to me, "Come, I will show you the judgment of the great harlot who is seated upon many waters, 2 with whom the kings of the earth have committed fornication, and with the wine of whose fornication the dwellers on earth have become drunk." 3 And he carried me away in the Spirit into a wilderness, and I saw a woman sitting on a scarlet beast which was full of blasphemous names, and it had seven heads and ten horns. 4 The woman

---

Cross-references (left margin):

16.8
Rev 8.12;
14.18
16.9
Rev 2.21;
11.13

16.10
Rev 13.2;
9.2; 11.10
16.11
ver 9,21;
Rev 11.13;
2.21

16.12
Rev 9.14;
Isa 41.2
16.13
Rev 12.3;
13.1; 19.20
16.14
1 Tim 4.1;
Rev 13.3;
3.10; 17.14
16.15
1 Thess 5.2;
2 Cor 5.3
★16.16
Rev 19.19;
9.11;
2 Ki 23.29,
30

16.17
Eph 2.2;
Rev 11.15;
14.15; 21.6
16.18
Rev 4.5;
6.12;
Dan 12.1
16.19
Rev 17.18;
14.8; 18.5;
14.10
16.20
Rev 6.14
16.21
Rev 11.19;
Ex 9.23

17.1
Rev 21.9;
16.19; 19.2;
Jer 51.13
17.2
Rev 18.3;
14.8
17.3
Rev 12.3,6,
14
17.4
Jer 51.7;
Rev 18.16;
18.6

16.16 Armageddon is the name chosen by John to describe the final battle at the end of the age when the forces of good and evil clash. Evil will be defeated and destroyed. God will triumph. *A-millennialists* hold this to be the beginning of the end of history, for Christ will deliver the kingdom to His father. *Pre-millennialists* hold that Christ's triumph in this battle upon his Second Advent opens the period of his thousand year reign on earth (Read also 16.12–16 in this connection). (See note to 2 Chr 35.22 for location of Armageddon.)

was arrayed in purple and scarlet, and bedecked with gold and jewels and pearls, holding in her hand a golden cup full of abominations and the impurities of her fornication; 5 and on her forehead was written a name of mystery: "Babylon the great, mother of harlots and of earth's abominations." 6And I saw the woman, drunk with the blood of the saints and the blood of the martyrs of Jesus.

2. *The mystery of the harlot and the beast explained*

When I saw her I marveled greatly. 7 But the angel said to me, "Why marvel? I will tell you the mystery of the woman, and of the beast with seven heads and ten horns that carries her. 8 The beast that you saw was, and is not, and is to ascend from the bottomless pit and go to perdition; and the dwellers on earth whose names have not been written in the book of life from the foundation of the world, will marvel to behold the beast, because it was and is not and is to come. 9 This calls for a mind with wisdom: the seven heads are seven mountains on which the woman is seated; 10 they are also seven kings, five of whom have fallen, one is, the other has not yet come, and when he comes he must remain only a little while. 11As for the beast that was and is not, it is an eighth but it belongs to the seven, and it goes to perdition. 12And the ten horns that you saw are ten kings who have not yet received royal power, but they are to receive authority as kings for one hour, together with the beast. 13 These are of one mind and give over their power and authority to the beast; 14 they will make war on the Lamb, and the Lamb will conquer them, for he is Lord of lords and King of kings, and those with him are called and chosen and faithful."

15 And he said to me, "The waters that you saw, where the harlot is seated, are peoples and multitudes and nations and tongues. 16And the ten horns that you saw, they and the beast will hate the harlot; they will make her desolate and naked, and devour her flesh and burn her up with fire, 17 for God has put it into their hearts to carry out his purpose by being of one mind and giving over their royal power to the beast, until the words of God shall be fulfilled. 18And the woman that you saw is the great city which has dominion over the kings of the earth."

3. *The doom of Babylon announced*

18 After this I saw another angel coming down from heaven, having great authority; and the earth was made bright with his splendor. 2And he called out with a mighty voice, "Fallen, fallen is Babylon the great!
It has become a dwelling place of demons,
    a haunt of every foul spirit,
    a haunt of every foul and hateful bird;
3 for all nations have drunk*k* the wine of her impure passion,
    and the kings of the earth have committed fornication with her,
    and the merchants of the earth have grown rich with the wealth
        of her wantonness."

4. *The call to come out of Babylon*

4 Then I heard another voice from heaven saying,

k Other ancient authorities read *fallen by*

17.5
2 Thess 2.7;
Rev 14.8;
16.19; 18.9
17.6
Rev 18.24;
13.15; 12.11

17.7
ver 5,3,9

17.8
Rev 11.7;
13.10; 3.10;
13.3,8

17.9
Rev 13.18

17.11
ver 8
17.12
Dan 7.20;
Rev 13.1;
18.10,17,19
17.13
ver 17
17.14
Rev 16.14;
1 Tim 6.15;
Rev 19.16;
Mt 22.14
17.15
Isa 8.7;
Rev 5.9;
13.7
17.16
Rev 18.17,
19;
Ezek 16.37,
39;
Rev 19.18;
18.8
17.17
2 Thess
2.11;
Rev 10.7
17.18
Rev 16.19
18.1
Rev 17.1;
10.1;
Ezek 43.2
18.2
Rev 14.8;
Isa 13.21,
22;
Jer 50.39
18.3
Rev 14.8;
Jer 25.15,27

18.4
Isa 48.20;
Jer 50.8;
2 Cor 6.17

"Come out of her, my people,
 lest you take part in her sins,
 lest you share in her plagues;

18.5
Jer 51.9;
Rev 16.19
5 for her sins are heaped high as heaven,
 and God has remembered her iniquities.

18.6
Ps 137.8;
Jer 50.15;
Rev 14.10;
16.19
6 Render to her as she herself has rendered,
 and repay her double for her deeds;
 mix a double draught for her in the cup she mixed.

18.7
Ezek 28.2–
8;
Isa 47.7,8;
Zeph 2.15
7 As she glorified herself and played the wanton,
 so give her a like measure of torment and mourning.
Since in her heart she says, 'A queen I sit,
I am no widow, mourning I shall never see,'

18.8
Isa 47.9;
Rev 17.16;
Jer 50.34;
Rev 11.17
8 so shall her plagues come in a single day,
 pestilence and mourning and famine,
 and she shall be burned with fire;
for mighty is the Lord God who judges her."

5. *The lament of the world over Babylon*

18.9
Rev 17.2;
Jer 50.46;
ver 18;
Rev 19.3
9 And the kings of the earth, who committed fornication and were wanton with her, will weep and wail over her when they see the smoke of her burning; 10 they will stand far off, in fear of her torment, and say,

18.10
ver 15,17,16,
19
"Alas! alas! thou great city,
 thou mighty city, Babylon!
In one hour has thy judgment come."

18.11
ver 3;
Ezek 27.27
11 And the merchants of the earth weep and mourn for her, since no one buys their cargo any more, 12 cargo of gold, silver,

18.12
Rev 17.4
jewels and pearls, fine linen, purple, silk and scarlet, all kinds of scented wood, all articles of ivory, all articles of costly wood,

18.13
Ezek 27.13
bronze, iron and marble, 13 cinnamon, spice, incense, myrrh, frankincense, wine, oil, fine flour and wheat, cattle and sheep, horses and chariots, and slaves, that is, human souls.
14 "The fruit for which thy soul longed has gone from thee,
 and all thy dainties and thy splendor are lost to thee, never to
  be found again!"

18.15
Ezek 27.36,
31
15 The merchants of these wares, who gained wealth from her, will stand far off, in fear of her torment, weeping and mourning aloud,

18.16
Rev 17.4
16 "Alas, alas, for the great city
 that was clothed in fine linen, in purple and scarlet,
 bedecked with gold, with jewels, and with pearls!

18.17
Rev 17.16;
Isa 23.14;
Ezek 27.29
17 In one hour all this wealth has been laid waste."
And all shipmasters and seafaring men, sailors and all whose trade is on the sea, stood far off 18 and cried out as they saw the

18.18
Ezek 27.30;
Rev 13.4
smoke of her burning,
"What city was like the great city?"

18.19
Josh 7.6;
Job 2.12;
Ezek 27.30
19 And they threw dust on their heads, as they wept and mourned, crying out,
"Alas, alas, for the great city
 where all who had ships at sea grew rich by her wealth!
In one hour she has been laid waste.

6. *Heaven's rejoicing over Babylon's fall*

18.20
Isa 44.23;
Jer 51.48;
Rev 19.2
20 Rejoice over her, O heaven,

O saints and apostles and prophets,
for God has given judgment for you against her!"

7. Babylon's doom symbolically portrayed

21 Then a mighty angel took up a stone like a great millstone
and threw it into the sea, saying,

"So shall Babylon the great city be thrown down with violence,
and shall be found no more;

22 and the sound of harpers and minstrels, of flute players and
trumpeters,
shall be heard in thee no more;
and a craftsman of any craft
shall be found in thee no more;
and the sound of the millstone
shall be heard in thee no more;

23 and the light of a lamp
shall shine in thee no more;
and the voice of bridegroom and bride
shall be heard in thee no more;
for thy merchants were the great men of the earth,
and all nations were deceived by thy sorcery.

24 And in her was found the blood of prophets and of saints,
and of all who have been slain on earth."

8. Praise to God for judgment: the marriage supper of the Lamb

19 After this I heard what seemed to be the loud voice of a
great multitude in heaven, crying,

"Hallelujah! Salvation and glory and power belong to our God,
2 for his judgments are true and just;
he has judged the great harlot who corrupted the earth with her
fornication,
and he has avenged on her the blood of his servants."
3 Once more they cried,
"Hallelujah! The smoke from her goes up for ever and ever."
4 And the twenty-four elders and the four living creatures fell down
and worshiped God who is seated on the throne, saying, "Amen.
Hallelujah!" 5 And from the throne came a voice crying,
"Praise our God, all you his servants,
you who fear him, small and great."
6 Then I heard what seemed to be the voice of a great multitude,
like the sound of many waters and like the sound of mighty
thunderpeals, crying,
"Hallelujah! For the Lord our God the Almighty reigns.
7 Let us rejoice and exult and give him the glory,
for the marriage of the Lamb has come,
and his Bride has made herself ready;
8 it was granted her to be clothed with fine linen, bright and
pure"—
for the fine linen is the righteous deeds of the saints.

Cross references (right margin):

18.21 Jer 51.63; Rev 12.8
18.22 Isa 24.8; Ezek 26.13; Jer 25.10
18.23 Jer 25.10; 7.34; 16.9; Isa 23.8; Nah 3.4
18.24 Rev 17.6; Jer 51.49
19.1 Rev 11.15; 4.11; 7.10, 12; 12.10
19.2 Deut 32.43; Rev 6.10
19.3 Isa 34.10; Rev 14.11
19.4 Rev 4.4,6; 5.14
19.5 Ps 134.1; Rev 11.18; 20.12
19.6 Rev 11.15, 17; 14.2
*19.7 Mt 22.2; 25.10; 2 Cor 11.2; Eph 5.32; Rev 21.2,9
19.8 Rev 15.4

19.7 The marriage supper of the Lamb apparently precedes the Second Advent of Christ, since it is referred to first. In attendance at the supper are the *saints*, by which is meant the saved of all ages, i.e., those who were redeemed before and after Calvary and who have been declared righteous in Jesus Christ.

19.9
ver 10;
Rev 1.19;
Lk 14.15;
Rev 21.5
19.10
Rev 22.8;
Acts 10.26;
Rev 22.9;
12.17

9 And the angel said[l] to me, "Write this: Blessed are those who are invited to the marriage supper of the Lamb." And he said to me, "These are true words of God." 10 Then I fell down at his feet to worship him, but he said to me, "You must not do that! I am a fellow servant with you and your brethren who hold the testimony of Jesus. Worship God." For the testimony of Jesus is the spirit of prophecy.

H. *The defeat of the beast and the false prophet*

19.11
Rev 15.5;
6.2; 3.14;
Isa 11.4
19.12
Rev 1.14;
6.2; 2.17
19.13
Isa 63.2,3;
Jn 1.1
19.14
ver 8
19.15
Isa 11.4;
2 Thess 2.8;
Ps 2.9;
Rev 2.27;
14.19,20
19.16
Dan 2.47;
Rev 17.14
19.17
Rev 8.13;
Ezek 39.17
19.18
Ezek 39.18–
20;
Rev 11.18
19.19
Rev 11.7;
16.14,16
19.20
Rev 16.13;
13.12ff;
Dan 7.11;
Rev 20.10;
14.10; 21.8
19.21
ver 11,19,
15,17

11 Then I saw heaven opened, and behold, a white horse! He who sat upon it is called Faithful and True, and in righteousness he judges and makes war. 12 His eyes are like a flame of fire, and on his head are many diadems; and he has a name inscribed which no one knows but himself. 13 He is clad in a robe dipped in[m] blood, and the name by which he is called is The Word of God. 14And the armies of heaven, arrayed in fine linen, white and pure, followed him on white horses. 15 From his mouth issues a sharp sword with which to smite the nations, and he will rule them with a rod of iron; he will tread the wine press of the fury of the wrath of God the Almighty. 16 On his robe and on his thigh he has a name inscribed, King of kings and Lord of lords.

17 Then I saw an angel standing in the sun, and with a loud voice he called to all the birds that fly in midheaven, "Come, gather for the great supper of God, 18 to eat the flesh of kings, the flesh of captains, the flesh of mighty men, the flesh of horses and their riders, and the flesh of all men, both free and slave, both small and great." 19And I saw the beast and the kings of the earth with their armies gathered to make war against him who sits upon the horse and against his army. 20And the beast was captured, and with it the false prophet who in its presence had worked the signs by which he deceived those who had received the mark of the beast and those who worshiped its image. These two were thrown alive into the lake of fire that burns with sulphur. 21And the rest were slain by the sword of him who sits upon the horse, the sword that issues from his mouth; and all the birds were gorged with their flesh.

I. *The binding of Satan*

20.1
Rev 10.1;
1.18; 9.1
*20.2
2 Pet 2.4;
Jude 6;
Rev 12.9

20 Then I saw an angel coming down from heaven, holding in his hand the key of the bottomless pit and a great chain. 2And he seized the dragon, that ancient serpent, who is the Devil and

l Greek *he said*   *m* Other ancient authorities read *sprinkled with*

20.2 There are three general views of the millennium which find favor today: (1) The *post-millennialist* holds the millennium is a period of world history in which the reign of Christ has been established through His church which is destined to conquer the world with the gospel, and at the end of this golden age Christ will personally return to earth and inaugurate a new heaven and a new earth. (2) The *a-millennialist* denies that there will ever be a literal earth-rule of a thousand years, either before or after Christ's return. By some the *thousand* years are taken to be simply symbolic of eternity (although verse 5 poses a serious problem for this view), and the only reign spoken of in this passage is an eternal heavenly reign. Christ's return to earth will simply usher in the "new heaven and the new earth" and His only eschatological rule will be celestial, not in this world. By others the one thousand years of Christ's reign are taken to be the period between the

Satan, and bound him for a thousand years, 3 and threw him into the pit, and shut it and sealed it over him, that he should deceive the nations no more, till the thousand years were ended. After that he must be loosed for a little while.

20.3
Dan 6.17;
Rev 12.9

J. The millennial reign of Christ

4 Then I saw thrones, and seated on them were those to whom judgment was committed. Also I saw the souls of those who had been beheaded for their testimony to Jesus and for the word of God, and who had not worshiped the beast or its image and had not received its mark on their foreheads or their hands. They came to life, and reigned with Christ a thousand years. 5 The rest of the dead did not come to life until the thousand years were ended. This is the first resurrection. 6 Blessed and holy is he who shares in the first resurrection! Over such the second death has no power, but they shall be priests of God and of Christ, and they shall reign with him a thousand years.

20.4
Dan 7.9,22,
27;
Rev 6.9;
13.12,15,16

*20.5
Lk 14.14;
Phil 3.11;
1 Thess 4.16
20.6
Rev 14.13;
2.11;
21.8; 1.6

K. The loosing of Satan

7 And when the thousand years are ended, Satan will be loosed from his prison 8 and will come out to deceive the nations which are at the four corners of the earth, that is, Gŏg and Māgŏg, to gather them for battle; their number is like the sand of the sea. 9And they marched up over the broad earth and surrounded the camp of the saints and the beloved city; but fire came down from heaven[n] and consumed them, 10 and the devil who had deceived them was thrown into the lake of fire and sulphur where the

20.7
ver 2
20.8
Ezek 38.2;
39.1;
Rev 16.14;
Heb 11.12
20.9
Ezek 38.9,
22; 39.6
*20.10
ver 3,8

[n] Other ancient authorities read *from God, out of heaven,* or *out of heaven from God*

---

first and second comings of Christ. (3) The *pre-millennialist* looks for the return of Christ to earth at the beginning of a literal, thousand-year reign upon the earth when "the earth shall be filled with the knowledge of God as the waters cover the sea" and all the nations of mankind will be completely subservient to the Lord Jesus. At the end of this period Satan will be released again in order to stir up the secretly rebellious portion of mankind to a final open revolt against God (ver 7–9). After a second "Armageddon" the new heavens and the new earth will be ushered in.

Post-millennialism does not enjoy the favor it once did in Augustine's time and in the optimistic period of 1880–1910, for subsequent global conflicts have dimmed that optimism. As for *a-millennialism*, it divests 20.2, 7 of real significance and also the numerous Old Testament passages which speak of the ultimate regathering of the nation Israel to Palestine and a time of peace and prosperity for that nation. The issues at stake are not ones which should divide Christians since all three groups bow to the authority of Scripture, nor does a saving faith make mandatory the adoption of one view as against the others. It should perhaps be added that there is still another school of thought which does not regard any of these general views seriously, but looks upon Revelation as por-

traying an enduring spiritual struggle between the forces of good and evil in which the heavenly kingdom of God will finally triumph. To these interpreters none of the historical or geographical details have anything more than symbolic significance.

20.5 Here John speaks of *the first resurrection.* From this, many understand that the Scriptures teach us that there will be two resurrections at the end of the present age. The first is the resurrection of the righteous dead. Over them the second death has no power. Those who are so resurrected reign with Christ for a thousand years. After this comes the second resurrection. This distinction lends support to the *pre-millennial* view. Others hold that the first resurrection here referred to is for a single group of people, the martyrs of verse 4. These share Christ's reign for a thousand years. A general resurrection of the other dead follows.

20.10 Scripture does not answer every question which men raise about the person and work of Satan. His existence and malign influence cannot be denied, however, without denying the biblical evidences. Apparently Satan was one of God's holy angels who fell through sin and whose ultimate destiny is *the lake of fire.* Many hold that the serpent of Gen 3.1 was Satan. Jesus was tempted of the Devil (Mt 4.1; Lk 4.2). Paul

beast and the false prophet were, and they will be tormented day and night for ever and ever.

L. *The great white throne judgment*

*20.11f
Rev 4.2;
21.1;
Dan 2.35;
Rev 12.8
20.12
Mt 16.27;
Rev 2.3;
22.12
20.13
Rev 6.8;
Isa 26.19;
Rev 2.23
20.14
1 Cor 15.26;
Rev 6.8
21.1
Isa 65.17;
2 Pet 3.13;
Rev 20.11
*21.2
Heb 11.10;
12.22;
Rev 3.12
21.3
Ezek 37.27;
2 Cor 6.16;
Rev 7.15
21.4
Rev 7.17;
1 Cor 15.26;
Rev 20.14;
Isa 35.10;
65.19
21.5
Rev 4.9;
20.11;
Isa 43.19;
Rev 19.9
21.6
Rev 16.17;
1.8; 22.13;
Jn 4.10

11 Then I saw a great white throne and him who sat upon it; from his presence earth and sky fled away, and no place was found for them. 12And I saw the dead, great and small, standing before the throne, and books were opened. Also another book was opened, which is the book of life. And the dead were judged by what was written in the books, by what they had done. 13And the sea gave up the dead in it, Death and Hādēs gave up the dead in them, and all were judged by what they had done. 14 Then Death and Hādēs were thrown into the lake of fire. This is the second death, the lake of fire; 15 and if any one's name was not found written in the book of life, he was thrown into the lake of fire.

M. *The new heaven and the new earth*

21 Then I saw a new heaven and a new earth; for the first heaven and the first earth had passed away, and the sea was no more. 2And I saw the holy city, new Jerusalem, coming down out of heaven from God, prepared as a bride adorned for her husband; 3 and I heard a loud voice from the throne saying, "Behold, the dwelling of God is with men. He will dwell with them, and they shall be his people,*o* and God himself will be with them;*p* 4 he will wipe away every tear from their eyes, and death shall be no more, neither shall there be mourning nor crying nor pain any more, for the former things have passed away."

5 And he who sat upon the throne said, "Behold, I make all things new." Also he said, "Write this, for these words are trustworthy and true." 6And he said to me, "It is done! I am the Alpha

o Other ancient authorities read *peoples*   *p* Other ancient authorities add *and be their God*

speaks of him as *the prince of the power of the air* (Eph 2.2). Christ calls him *the ruler of this world* (Jn 12.31). Here in chapter 20 John speaks of Satan as *bound for a thousand years* (ver 2), and then *loosed from his prison* (ver 7), and then *thrown into the lake of fire and brimstone* (ver 10).

Some have challenged the Scriptural teaching of the eternal punishment of the wicked dead. They teach either a universalism in which all are ultimately saved, or annihilationism in which the wicked dead cease to exist in any form whatever. Yet the doctrine of eternal, conscious punishment is well established in Scripture. Compare the use of the following terms: (1) eternal fire (Mt 25.41); (2) unquenchable fire (Mk 9.48); (3) the lake that burns with fire and brimstone (21.8); (4) the fact that the same terms are used in the Greek both for the eternal existence and sovereignty of God as are used for endless death or separation from God. In each case the phrase is *eis tous aiōnas tōn aiōnōn* "unto the ages of ages" (cf. 1.18; 11.15; 14.11; 20.10).

20.11, 12 The last judgment will take place, so many believe, at the end of the thousand years when the resurrected wicked dead shall be judged at the great white throne of Jesus Christ. Many see in this passage a reference to three books, the book of life and two other books, which are thought to be the book of memory and the book of works. The absence of the names of the wicked dead from the book of life is reason for the sentence which is pronounced upon them. They are cast into the lake of fire. There is no appeal from His sentence. The fact that the works of the wicked are judged, indicates there are degrees of punishment for these malefactors (Lk 12.47, 48).

21.2 The new Jerusalem is the future abode of the people of God and becomes their eternal habitation after the judgment of the great white throne (Rev 20.11ff). There is to be *a new heaven and a new earth* (21.1); the Holy City will come down out of heaven from God. Its boundaries and its furniture and inhabitants are all described. That the description is written in poetic and symbolic language is obvious, but the new Jerusalem inhabitants may rest assured that its beauty and glory will far transcend their fondest imagination.

and the Ōmē′gȧ, the beginning and the end. To the thirsty I will give from the fountain of the water of life without payment. 7 He who conquers shall have this heritage, and I will be his God and he shall be my son. 8 But as for the cowardly, the faithless, the polluted, as for murderers, fornicators, sorcerers, idolaters, and all liars, their lot shall be in the lake that burns with fire and sulphur, which is the second death."

N. *The new Jerusalem*

1. *The city*

9 Then came one of the seven angels who had the seven bowls full of the seven last plagues, and spoke to me, saying, "Come, I will show you the Bride, the wife of the Lamb." 10 And in the Spirit he carried me away to a great, high mountain, and showed me the holy city Jerusalem coming down out of heaven from God, 11 having the glory of God, its radiance like a most rare jewel, like a jasper, clear as crystal. 12 It had a great, high wall, with twelve gates, and at the gates twelve angels, and on the gates the names of the twelve tribes of the sons of Israel were inscribed; 13 on the east three gates, on the north three gates, on the south three gates, and on the west three gates. 14 And the wall of the city had twelve foundations, and on them the twelve names of the twelve apostles of the Lamb.

2. *Its measurements*

15 And he who talked to me had a measuring rod of gold to measure the city and its gates and walls. 16 The city lies foursquare, its length the same as its breadth; and he measured the city with his rod, twelve thousand stadia;*q* its length and breadth and height are equal. 17 He also measured its wall, a hundred and forty-four cubits by a man's measure, that is, an angel's. 18 The wall was built of jasper, while the city was pure gold, clear as glass. 19 The foundations of the wall of the city were adorned with every jewel; the first was jasper, the second sapphire, the third agate, the fourth emerald, 20 the fifth onyx, the sixth carnelian, the seventh chrysolite, the eighth beryl, the ninth topaz, the tenth chrysoprase, the eleventh jacinth, the twelfth amethyst. 21 And the twelve gates were twelve pearls, each of the gates made of a single pearl, and the street of the city was pure gold, transparent as glass.

3. *Its light*

22 And I saw no temple in the city, for its temple is the Lord God the Almighty and the Lamb. 23 And the city has no need of sun or moon to shine upon it, for the glory of God is its light, and its lamp is the Lamb. 24 By its light shall the nations walk; and the kings of the earth shall bring their glory into it, 25 and its gates shall never be shut by day—and there shall be no night there; 26 they shall bring into it the glory and the honor of the nations. 27 But nothing unclean shall enter it, nor any one who practices abomination or falsehood, but only those who are written in the Lamb's book of life.

q About fifteen hundred miles

21.7
Rev 2.7;
ver 3
21.8
Heb 12.14;
Rev 22.15;
19.20; 2.11

21.9
Rev 15.1,6,
7; 20.14ff
21.10
Rev 1.10;
Ezek 40.2;
Rev 17.3
21.11
Rev 15.8;
22.5; 4.6
21.12
Ezek 48.31–
34

21.14
Mt 16.18;
Eph 2.20

21.15
Rev 11.1

21.18
ver 11,19,21;
Rev 4.6
21.19
Isa 54.11,
12;
ver 11,18;
Rev 4.3
21.20
Rev 4.3
21.21
ver 15,25,18

21.22
Jn 4.21,23;
Rev 1.8;
5.6
21.23
Isa 24.23;
60.19,20;
Rev 22.5
21.24
Isa 60.3,5
21.25
Isa 60.11;
Zech 14.7;
Rev 22.5
21.27
Isa 52.1;
Joel 3.17;
Rev 22.14;
3.5

4. Its blessings

22 Then he showed me the river of the water of life, bright as crystal, flowing from the throne of God and of the Lamb 2 through the middle of the street of the city; also, on either side of the river, the tree of life[r] with its twelve kinds of fruit, yielding its fruit each month; and the leaves of the tree were for the healing of the nations. 3 There shall no more be anything accursed, but the throne of God and of the Lamb shall be in it, and his servants shall worship him; 4 they shall see his face, and his name shall be on their foreheads. 5And night shall be no more; they need no light of lamp or sun, for the Lord God will be their light, and they shall reign for ever and ever.

IV. *Epilogue 22.6–21*

A. *Testimony to the truth of the revelation*

6 And he said to me, "These words are trustworthy and true. And the Lord, the God of the spirits of the prophets, has sent his angel to show his servants what must soon take place. 7And behold, I am coming soon."

Blessed is he who keeps the words of the prophecy of this book.

8 I John am he who heard and saw these things. And when I heard and saw them, I fell down to worship at the feet of the angel who showed them to me; 9 but he said to me, "You must not do that! I am a fellow servant with you and your brethren the prophets, and with those who keep the words of this book. Worship God."

B. *The distinction drawn*

10 And he said to me, "Do not seal up the words of the prophecy of this book, for the time is near. 11 Let the evildoer still do evil, and the filthy still be filthy, and the righteous still do right, and the holy still be holy."

12 "Behold, I am coming soon, bringing my recompense, to repay every one for what he has done. 13 I am the Alpha and the Ōmĕ′gă, the first and the last, the beginning and the end."

14 Blessed are those who wash their robes,[s] that they may have the right to the tree of life and that they may enter the city by the gates. 15 Outside are the dogs and sorcerers and fornicators and murderers and idolaters, and every one who loves and practices falsehood.

C. *The invitation given*

16 "I Jesus have sent my angel to you with this testimony for the churches. I am the root and the offspring of David, the bright morning star."

---

r Or *the Lamb. In the midst of the street of the city, and on either side of the river, was the tree of life,* etc.   s Other ancient authorities read *do his commandments*

22.11 *Let the evildoer still do evil, and the filthy still be filthy.* This phrase points up plainly the truth that the final condition of the wicked is one of hopelessness. There is no evidence here of universal salvation for all men. Rather, the door is shut forever, and those who remain outside shall never find entrance. But this dark picture must be weighed against the gracious and all embracing invitation of verse 17 which opens the doors of heaven to all who heed the voice of God and receive Jesus Christ as their sin-bearer and savior.

Marginal references:

22.1 Ezek 47.1; Zech 14.8; Rev 4.6
22.2 Gen 2.9; Rev 2.7; Ezek 47.12
22.3 Zech 14.11; Rev 7.15
22.4 Mt 5.8; Rev 14.1
22.5 Rev 21.25, 23; Dan 7.27
22.6 Rev 1.1; 19.19; 21.5
22.7 Rev 3.11; 1.3
22.8 Rev 1.1; 19.10
22.9 Rev 19.10; 1.1; ver 10,18,19; Rev 21.2
22.10 Dan 8.26; Rev 1.3
*22.11 Dan 12.10; Ezek 3.27
22.12 Isa 40.10; Jer 17.10; Rev 2.23
22.13 Rev 1.8,17; 21.6
22.15 Gal 5.19ff; Col 3.6; Phil 3.2
22.16 Rev 1.1; 5.5; Zech 6.12; 2 Pet 1.19; Rev 2.28

17 The Spirit and the Bride say, "Come." And let him who hears say, "Come." And let him who is thirsty come, let him who desires take the water of life without price.

18 I warn every one who hears the words of the prophecy of this book: if any one adds to them, God will add to him the plagues described in this book, 19 and if any one takes away from the words of the book of this prophecy, God will take away his share in the tree of life and in the holy city, which are described in this book.

20 He who testifies to these things says, "Surely I am coming soon." Amen. Come, Lord Jesus!

D. *The benediction*

21 The grace of the Lord Jesus be with all the saints.*ᵗ* Amen.

ᵗ Other ancient authorities omit *all*; others omit *the saints*

22.17
Rev 2.7;
21.2;
Isa 55.1;
Rev 21.6
22.18
Deut 4.2;
Prov 30.6;
Rev 15.6;
16.21
★**22.20**
Rev 1.2;
2 Tim 4.8;
Rom 16.20;
2 Thess 3.18

22.20 The Bible opens with man in the Garden of Eden in happiness and contentment. It ends with man in the new Jerusalem where he is again happy and contented. It is fitting that John should close the Book of the Revelation with a prayer in which he breathes out his fervent hope that Paradise restored will come about quickly.

Index to the Annotations

INDEX TO THE ANNOTATIONS

1892

Index to the Annotations

CONCORDANCE

TO THE

HOLY BIBLE

Revised Standard Version

INTRODUCTION

The concordance included in this Bible is the result of an extensive investigation of ways in which such helps to Bible study can be made truly reflective of Scripture content and fully useful to the average reader. In the preparation of this concordance, the first step was to examine carefully five different short concordances in order to determine the extent of agreement, the proportionate treatment of various books of the Bible, and the manner in which important biblical themes are handled. The short concordances were then compared with two exhaustive concordances in order to evaluate the objectivity and balance of content. This examination indicated that in order to avoid rather mechanical quotas for words and lines, and at the same time to guard against arbitrary selections or the accidental omission of certain important elements of the biblical message, several detailed procedures were necessary as a means of best guaranteeing relevance, balance, and objectivity. First, about three hundred key theological terms, for example, *grace*, *salvation*, *redemption*, *sin*, *justify*, *holy*, *love*, *faith*, and *hope*, were chosen in order that they might be given proportionately heavier treatment since they represent such significant themes in the biblical message. Second, lists of favorite passages and golden texts (including the last twenty-five years of the International Sunday School Lesson Series) were gleaned for important verses which people would most likely want to find. Third, in the selection of context lines, careful attention was paid to the location of a word within the passage. If the same word occurred more than once, special care was exercised to select that occurrence which was best known and the one with which there would be the most obvious associations. Fourth, since in the treatment of proper names it was obviously impossible to cite all the passages in which certain prominent individuals are mentioned in the Scriptures, short biographical summaries were prepared so as to provide a brief outline of the most important references to the events of these persons' lives. Fifth, in order that the words selected for any one passage might be those which the reader would most likely remember, attention was given to the "picturable quality" of the word in question. For example, in 1 Corinthians 13.1, words such as *speak*, *noisy*, and *clanging* are not as picturable as words such as *tongues*, *angels*, and *cymbal*, though of course the abstract word *love* is also listed in this verse, for it is the theme of the entire chapter.

Certain features of this concordance should be carefully noted in order that the reader may use it with the greatest facility and understanding:

1. Various grammatical forms of the same word (for example, the singular and plural of nouns and the various tense forms of the verbs) are included under the same key word, normally listed as such forms would be in a standard dictionary. When related forms of the same word differ radically, separate entries are employed.
2. In some instances, context lines are taken from material which is in a footnote to the text. Whenever this occurs, the letter *n* is placed immediately after the reference in order to indicate that this passage is to be found in the note and not in the text itself.
3. Wherever certain words have been omitted from the context line in order to include other words or phrases which are more meaningful, the omission is indicated by two dots.
4. The key word in any context line is represented by the first letter of the word in an italic font.
5. The punctuation of the context line is given exactly as in the text, including any initial or final marks of punctuation, since these signs often provide useful clues to the significance of the line in question.

The principal and immediate purpose of this concordance is not to provide a study guide for various biblical subjects, but rather to help the reader locate passages with which he is somewhat familiar. Nevertheless, because of the fact that many key theological themes, as reflected in a number of important words, are given proportionately heavier treatment, this concordance does have certain significant advantages over many others. A number of these words may be studied with at least some degree of completeness, not of course in the number of passages cited, but in the range of meaning which the selection of these passages reflects.

A limited concordance with multiple and practical purposes, designed to serve many different kinds of users, cannot be expected to meet all the needs of every reader. Nevertheless, in the extent of coverage, relevance of inclusion, and objectivity of selection, this concordance should prove to be a valuable tool for Bible reading, study, and comprehension.

—Eugene A. Nida, Ph.D.

CONCORDANCE

TO THE REVISED STANDARD VERSION
OF THE HOLY BIBLE

A

AARON
Brother of Moses, Ex 4.14; 7.1; commended for his eloquence, Ex 4.14; chosen to assist Moses, Ex 4.16, 27–28; co-leader with Moses, Ex 5.1; 8.25; supported Moses' arms, Ex 17.12; set apart as priest, Ex 28; Heb 5.4; made a golden calf, Ex 32; Acts 7.40–41; found fault with Moses, Num 12; his rod budded, Num 17; Heb 9.4; with Moses disobedient at Meribah, Num 20.10–13; died on Mount Hor, Num 20.26–29.

ABANDON — ED
The LORD will not *a* him	Ps 37.33
thou wilt not *a* my soul to	Acts 2.27
you have *a* the love you	Rev 2.4

ABASE
look on..proud and *a* him.	Job 40.11
a that which is high.	Ezek 21.26
walk in pride he is able to *a*.	Dan 4.37

ABEL
Now *A* was a keeper of sheep,	Gen 4.2
Cain said to *A* his brother,	4.8
another child instead of *A*,	4.25
from the blood of innocent *A*	Mt 23.35
By faith *A* offered to God	Heb 11.4
graciously than the blood of *A*.	12.24

ABHOR — RED
my intimate friends *a* me,	Job 19.19
They *a* me, they keep aloof	30.10
utterly *a* by his people	1Sam 27.12

ABIATHAR
A, escaped and fled after	1Sam 22.20
When *A*..fled to David	23.6
David said to *A* the priest,	30.7
Zadok and *A* carried the ark	2Sam 15.29
Zadok and *A* were priests;	20.25
when *A* was high priest,	Mk 2.26

ABIDE — S
spirit shall not *a*..for ever,	Gen 6.3
presence of the LORD, and *a*	1Sam 1.22
A in me, and I in you.	Jn 15.4
So faith, hope, love *a*,	1Cor 13.13
then you will *a* in the Son	1Jn 2.24
who *a* in..shadow of..Almighty,	Ps 91.1
My Spirit *a* among you; fear not.	Hag 2.5
No one who *a* in him sins;	1Jn 3.6
if we love one another, God *a*	4.12
because of the truth which *a*	2Jn 2

ABILITY
with *a* and intelligence,	Ex 31.3
according to the *a* of him	Lev 27.8
according to their *a* they	Ezra 2.69
to each according to his *a*.	Mt 25.15

ABIMELECH
And *A*..sent and took Sarah.	Gen 20.2

ABISHAI
Sought to kill Saul, 1Sam 26.5–9; pursued Abner, 2Sam 2.19,24; desired to kill

Shime-i, 2Sam 16.9–11; 19.21; one of David's key warriors, 2Sam 23.18–19; slew the Edomites, 1Chr 18.12.

ABLE
well *a* to overcome it."	Num 13.30
the LORD was not *a* to bring	14.16
no man..*a* to withstand you	Josh 23.9
"Who is *a* to stand before	1Sam 6.20
"The LORD is *a* to give you	2Chr 25.9
whom we serve is *a* to deliver	Dan 3.17
has your God,..been *a* to deliver	6.20
for I tell you, God is *a* from	Mt 3.9
"Do you believe that I am *a*	9.28
Are you *a* to drink the cup	20.22
not *a* to do as small a thing	Lk 12.26
no one is *a* to snatch them	Jn 10.29
God is *a* to provide you with	2Cor 9.8
is *a* to do far more abundantly	Eph 3.20
he is *a* to help those..tempted.	Heb 2.18

ABLUTIONS
with instruction about *a*,	Heb 6.2
deal only with food..various *a*,	9.10

ABNER
Captain of Saul's host, 1Sam 14.50; made Ish-bosheth king, 2Sam 2.8–11; fought David's forces, 2Sam 2.12–32; made a league with David, 2Sam 3.6–21; slain by Joab, 2Sam 3.22–30; mourned by David, 2Sam 3.31–39.

ABODE
mount..God desired for his *a*,	Ps. 68.16
blesses..*a* of the righteous.	Prov 3.33

ABOLISH — ED
I will *a*..war from the land;	Hos 2.18
Jesus,..*a* death..brought life	2Tim 1.10

ABOMINABLE
for every *a* thing which	Deut 12.31
corrupt, they do *a* deeds,	Ps 14.1

ABOMINATION — S
has not fins and scales,..an *a*	Lev 11.10
an *a* to the LORD your God.	Deut 17.1
seven which are an *a* to him:	Prov 6.16
A false balance is an *a* to	11.1
both alike an *a* to the LORD.	17.15
Diverse weights are an *a*	20.23
even his prayer is an *a*.	28.9
incense is an *a* to me.	Isa 1.13
the *a* that makes desolate.	Dan 11.31
a has been committed in Israel	Mal 2.11
"Go in, and see the vile *a*	Ezek 8.9
they will remove..all its *a*.	11.18
make known to Jerusalem her *a*,	16.2
upon the wing of *a* shall come	Dan 9.27
a golden cup full of *a* and	Rev 17.4

ABOUND — S — ED
and peace *a*, till the moon	Ps 72.7
faithful..*a* with blessings,	Prov 28.20
God's truthfulness *a* to his	Rom 3.7
where sin increased, grace *a*	5.20

ABRAHAM — 'S
Born, Gen 11.26; married Sarai, Gen

ABRAHAM — 'S (cont.)
11.29; migrated from Ur to Haran, Gen 11.31; called by God, Gen 12.1–5; Heb 11.8; went to Egypt, Gen 12.10–20; separated from Lot, Gen 13.7–11; rescued Lot, Gen 14.13–16; God's covenant with him, Gen 15.18; 17.1–21; Ishmael is born to him, Gen 16.15–16; entertained angels, Gen 18.1–21; interceded for Sodom, Gen 18.22–33; banished Hagar and Ishmael, Gen 21.9–21; offered up Isaac, Gen 22.1–14; buried Sarah, Gen 23; married Keturah, Gen 25.1; death and burial, Gen 25.8–10.

your name shall be *A*;   Gen 17.5
A journeyed toward..the Negeb,   20.1
God tested *A*, and said   22.1
'We have *A* as our father';   Mt 3.9
to you, before *A* was, I am."   Jn 8.58
By faith *A* obeyed when..called Heb 11.8
carried by..angels to *A* bosom. Lk 16.22

ABSALOM
Third son of David, 2Sam 3.3; avenged Tamar and fled, 2Sam 13.20–39; returned to Jerusalem, 2Sam 14.23–33; conspired against David, 2Sam 15.1–12; slain by Joab, 2Sam 18.9–17; mourned by David, 2Sam 18.33.

ABSENT
a in body..present in spirit,   1Cor 5.3
a in body..with you in spirit,   Col 2.5

ABSTAIN
write to them to *a* from   Acts 15.20
a from every form of evil. 1Thess 5.22

ABUNDANCE
than the *a* of many wicked.   Ps 37.16
gave..bread from heaven in *a*,   105.40
from the *a* of her glory."   Isa 66.11
out of the *a* of the heart   Mt 12.34
life does not consist in..*a*   Lk 12.15
their *a*, but she out of..poverty   21.4
their *a* of joy and..poverty   2Cor 8.2
with every blessing in *a*,   9.8

ABUNDANTLY
it has increased *a*;   Gen 30.30
may have life, and have it *a*.   Jn 10.10

ACCEPT — ED
a the work of his hands;   Deut 33.11
Was it a time to *a* money and   2Ki 5.26
I will *a* his prayer not to   Job 42.8
offering, I will not *a* them;   Jer 14.12
offerings; and I will *a* you,   Ezek 43.27
a that which is good and we   Hos 14.2
your..offerings, I will not *a*   Amos 5.22
will not *a* your testimony   Acts 22.18
will you not be *a*?   Gen 4.7

ACCEPTABLE
offering..*a* in the sight of   Lev 10.19
it will not be *a* for you.   22.20
proclaim..*a* year of the Lord." Lk 4.19
no prophet is *a* in his own   4.24
"At the *a* time I have listened 2Cor 6.2

ACCESS
Through him we have obtained *a* Rom 5.2
we both have *a* in one Spirit Eph 2.18
confidence of *a* through..faith   3.12

ACCOMPLISH — ED
works..Father..granted me to *a*, Jn 5.36

if only I may *a* my course   Acts 20.24
narrative of..things..*a* among us, Lk 1.1
having *a* the work which thou   Jn 17.4

ACCORD
and serve him with one *a*.   Zeph 3.9
one *a* gave heed to..Philip,   Acts 8.6
What *a* has Christ with Belial? 2Cor 6.15

ACCOUNT (v)
a for every careless word   Mt 12.36
I do not *a* my life of any   Acts 20.24

ACCOUNT — S (n)
Turn in..*a* of your stewardship, Lk 16.2
give *a* of himself to God.   Rom 14.12
anything, charge that to my *a*. Philem 18
king who wished to settle *a*   Mt 18.23

ACCURSED
a hanged man is *a* by God;   Deut 21.23
sinner a hundred years..be *a*. Isa 65.20
wish that I myself were *a*   Rom 9.3
no love..let him be *a*.   1Cor 16.22
gospel contrary..let him be *a*.   Gal 1.8

ACCUSATION
"What *a* do you bring against   Jn 18.29

ACCUSE — D
Yet let no one contend, and..*a*, Hos 4.4
at his right hand to *a* him.   Zech 3.1
so that they might *a* him.   Mt 12.10
has *a* his brother falsely,   Deut 19.18
Chaldeans..maliciously *a*..Jews. Dan 3.8
when he was *a* by the chief   Mt 27.12
the chief priests *a* him of   Mk 15.3
charge on which they *a* him, Acts 23.28

ACCUSER
Make friends with..your *a*,   Mt 5.25
As you go with your *a* before Lk 12.58

ACHAIA
Gallio was proconsul of *A*,   Acts 18.12
pass through Macedonia and *A*   19.21
Macedonia and *A* have been Rom 15.26
saying that *A* has been ready 2Cor 9.2
to all the believers..in *A*. 1Thess 1.7

ACKNOWLEDGE — S — D
turn again to thee, and *a* thy 1Ki 8.33
Then will I also *a* to you,   Job 40.14
In all your ways *a* him, and he Prov 3.6
Only *a* your guilt, that you   Jer 3.13
We *a* our wickedness, O LORD,   14.20
those who *a*..he shall magnify Dan 11.39
until they *a* their guilt   Hos 5.15
every one who *a* me before men, Mt 10.32
who *a* me before men, the Son Lk 12.8
I *a* my sin to thee, and I did Ps 32.5
having *a*..they were strangers Heb 11.13

ACQUIRE — D
The simple *a* folly, but the Prov 14.18
a great wisdom, surpassing all Ecc 1.16

ACQUIT — TED
who *a* the guilty for a bribe, Isa 5.23
but I am not thereby *a*.   1Cor 4.4

ACQUITTAL
may they have no *a* from thee. Ps 69.27
righteousness leads to *a* and Rom 5.18

ACT — S — ED — ING (v)
is time for the LORD to *a*, Ps 119.126
so *a* as those..to be judged Jas 2.12
prudent man *a* with knowledge Prov 13.16

ACT — S — ED — ING (v) (cont.)

I *a* for the sake of my name, Ezek 20.14
suspect us of *a* in worldly 2Cor 10.2

ACTION — S

God shall stand firm..take *a*. Dan 11.32
and by him *a* are weighed. 1Sam 2.3

ACTS (n)

made known..his *a* to..Israel Ps 103.7
a child..known by his *a*, Prov 20.11

ADAM

God made for *A*..garments Gen 3.21
book of the generations of *A*. 5.1
When *A* had lived a hundred 5.3
the son of *A*, the son of God. Lk 3.38
death reigned from *A* to Moses, Rom 5.14
as in *A* all die, so also 1Cor 15.22
first man *A* became a living 15.45
For *A* was formed first, then 1Tim 2.13

ADD — S

LORD *a* to me another son!" Gen 30.24
You shall not *a* to the word Deut 4.2
you shall not *a* to it 12.32
Do not *a* to his words, lest Prov 30.6
this book: if any one *a* to Rev 22.18

ADMONISH

to *a* every one with tears. Acts 20.31
but to *a* you as my beloved 1Cor 4.14
brethren, *a* the idle, 1Thess 5.14

ADMONITION

whose ear heeds wholesome *a* Prov 15.31

ADOPTION

as we wait for *a* as sons, Rom 8.23
we might receive *a* as sons. Gal 4.5

ADORN — ED

may *a* the doctrine of God Tit 2.10
as a bride *a* for her husband; Rev 21.2

ADULTERERS

They are all *a*; they are like Hos 7.4
the sorcerers, against the *a*, Mal 3.5

ADULTERESS

love a woman,who..is an *a*; Hos 3.1
a if she lives with another man Rom 7.3

ADULTERY — IES

"You shall not commit *a*. Ex 20.14
"If a man commits *a* Lev 20.10
" 'Neither..commit *a*. Deut 5.18
who commits *a* has no sense; Prov 6.32
I fed them..they committed *a* Jer 5.7
'You shall not commit *a*.' Mt 5.27
already committed *a* with her 5.28
marries another, commits *a*." 19.9
heart of men, come..murder, *a*, Mk 7.21
marries another, commits *a* 10.11
and marries another commits *a*, Lk 16.18
woman..had been caught in *a*, Jn 8.3n
They have eyes full of *a*, 2Pet 2.14
for all the *a* of..Israel, I had sent Jer 3.8
your abominations, your *a* 13.27

ADVANCE — D

served to *a* the gospel, Phil 1.12
and *a* her and her maids to Est 2.9

ADVANTAGE

you ask, 'What *a* have I? Job 35.3
man has no *a* over the beasts; Ecc 3.19
a king is an *a* to a land with 5.9
an *a* to those who see the sun. 7.11

Then what *a* has the Jew? Rom 3.1
not seeking my own *a*, but 1Cor 10.33
keep Satan from gaining the *a* 2Cor 2.11
Christ will be of no *a* to you. Gal 5.2

ADVERSARY — IES

a shall surround the land Amos 3.1
when the *a* of Judah and Ezra 4.1
Give me not up to..my *a*; Ps 27.12

ADVERSITY

He thinks..I shall not meet *a*." Ps 10.6
If you faint in..day of *a*, Prov 24.10

ADVICE

Listen to *a* and accept Prov 19.20
king, who..no longer take *a*, Ecc 4.13
in this matter I give my *a*; 2Cor 8.10

ADVOCATE

we have an *a* with the Father, 1Jn 2.1

AFFLICT — ED (v)

not *a* any widow or orphan. Ex 22.22
O LORD, and *a* thy heritage. Ps 94.5
you, I will *a* you no more. Nah 1.12
when the LORD has *a* me and Ruth 1.21
Before I was *a* I went astray; Ps 119.67
in faithfulness thou hast *a* 119.75
a,..he opened not his mouth; Isa 53.7
and gather..those whom I have *a*; Mic 4.6
If we are *a*, it is for your 2Cor 1.6
We are *a* in every way, but not 4.8

AFFLICTED (n)

he heard the cry of the *a*— Job 34.28
but gives the *a* their right. 36.6
not forget the cry of the *a*. Ps 9.12
The *a* shall eat and be satisfied; 22.26
let the *a* hear and be glad. 34.2
satisfy the desire of the *a*, Isa 58.10
bring good tidings to the *a*; 61.1

AFFLICTION — S

LORD..given heed to your *a*. Gen 16.11
LORD has looked upon my *a*; 29.32
God saw my *a* and the labor 31.42
"I have seen the *a* of my people Ex 3.7
the bread of *a*—for you came Deut 16.3
LORD will look upon my *a*, 2Sam 16.12
LORD saw that the *a* of Israel 2Ki 14.26
see the *a* of our fathers in Neh 9.9
days of *a* have taken hold Job 30.16
For he has not despised..the *a* Ps 22.24
thou didst lay *a* on our loins; 66.11
adversity and the water of *a* Isa 30.20
tried you in..furnace of *a*. 48.10
In..their *a* he was afflicted, 63.9
I am the man who has seen *a* Lam 3.1
to comfort those..in any *a*, 2Cor 1.4
I wrote you out of much *a* 2.4
With all our *a*, I am overjoyed. 7.4
that we were to suffer *a*; 1Thess 3.4
LORD will bring on you..*a*, Deut 28.59
Many..the *a* of the righteous; Ps 34.19
great endurance, in *a*, 2Cor 6.4
what is lacking in Christ's *a* Col 1.24

AFRAID

I was *a*, because I was naked; Gen 3.10
Then Jacob was greatly *a* 32.7
And the men were *a* 43.18
Then Moses was *a*, and thought, Ex 2.14
Moses..was *a* to look at God. 3.6
were you not *a* to speak Num 12.8
Saul was *a* of David, because 1Sam 18.12

AFRAID (cont.)

not *a* to put forth your hand 2Sam 1.14
not be *a*. .of the Chaldean 2Ki 25.24
David was *a* of God that day 1Chr 13.12
and made them *a* to build, Ezra 4.4
I am not *a* of ten thousands of Ps 3.6
my life; of whom shall I be *a*? 27.1
am *a*, I put my trust in thee. 56.3
I am *a* of thy judgments. 119.120
be not *a* of the Assyrians Isa 10.24
trust, and will not be *a*; 12.2
a, nor. .rend their garments.. Jer 36.24
and none shall make them *a*." Zeph 3.13
the crowds saw it, they were *a*, Mt 9.8
the angel said. ."Do not be *a*; 28.5
a as they entered the cloud. Lk 9.34
for I was *a* of you, because 19.21
neither let them be *a*. Jn 14.27
Pilate. .was the more *a*; 19.8
disciples;. .were all *a* of him, Acts 9.26
'Do not be *a*, Paul; you 27.24
not *a* of the king's edict. Heb 11.23

AGE — S

be at the close of the *a*. Mt 13.40
was about thirty years of *a*, Lk 3.23
A ago I was set up, at the Prov 8.23

AGED

Wisdom is with the *a*, Job 12.12
and the *a* are among us, 15.10
and the *a* rose and stood; 29.8

AGONY

Pangs and *a* will seize them; Isa 13.8
in. .*a* he prayed more earnestly; Lk 22.44

AGREE — D

if two of you *a* on earth Mt 18.19
not *a* with me for a denarius? 20.13
and their witness did not *a*. Mk 14.56
I *a* that the law is good. Rom 7.16
I entreat Syntyche to *a* in Phil 4.2
Abraham *a* with Ephron; Gen 23.16
So he *a*,. .to betray him to them Lk 22.6
you have *a* together to tempt Acts 5.9

AGREEMENT

with Sheol we have an *a*; Isa 28.15
What *a* has the temple of God 2Cor 6.16

AGRIPPA

A the king and Bernice Acts 25.13
A said to Paul, "You have 26.1
King *A*, do you believe the 26.27

AHAB

and *A* his son reigned in 1Ki 16.28
Elijah. .said to *A*, "As the LORD 17.1
When *A* saw Elijah, *A* said 18.17
after this *A* said to Naboth, 21.2
how *A* has humbled himself 21.29
make you like Zedekiah and *A*, Jer 29.22

AI

Bethel on the west and *A* Gen 12.8
between Bethel and *A*, 13.3
sent men from Jericho to *A*, Josh 7.2
and arise, go up to *A*; see, 8.1

AID

thou my help, hasten to my *a*! Ps 22.19
to Jerusalem with *a* for the Rom 15.25

AIM (v)

we *a* at what is honorable 2Cor 8.21
a at righteousness,. .faith, 1Tim 6.11

AIM (n)

Make love your *a*, and 1Cor 14.1
my conduct, my *a* in life, 2Tim 3.10

ALARM (n)

When you blow an *a*, Num 10.5
said in my *a*, "I am driven Ps 31.22

ALARMED (v)

the visions of my head *a* me. Dan 4.5
rumors of wars, do not be *a*; Mk 13.7

ALEXANDRIA

Apollos, a native of *A*, Acts 18.24
ship of *A* sailing for Italy, 27.6
a ship of *A*, with the Twin 28.11

ALIENS

desolate, as overthrown by *a*. Isa 1.7
a have come into. .holy places Jer 51.51
Beloved, I beseech you as *a* 1Pet 2.11

ALIVE

you who held fast. .are all *a* Deut 4.4
my son was dead, and is *a* Lk 15.24
whom Paul asserted to be *a*. Acts 25.19
and *a* to God in Christ Jesus. Rom 6.11
your spirits are *a* because 8.10
in Christ. .all be made *a*. 1Cor 15.22
he made *a*, when you were dead Eph 2.1
made us *a* together with Christ 2.5

ALL

For *a* things come from thee, 1Chr 29.14
If I give away *a* I have, 1Cor 13.3
able for *a* time to save those Heb 7.25

ALLEGORY — IES

riddle, and speak an *a* to Ezek 17.2
an *a* to the rebellious house 24.3
an *a*:. .women are two covenants. Gal 4.24
'Is he not a maker of *a*?' " Ezek 20.49

ALMIGHTY

"I am God *A*; walk before me, Gen 17.1
"God *A* appeared to me 48.3
as destruction from the *A* it Isa 13.6
Lord our God the *A* reigns. Rev 19.6

ALMOND — S

the *a* tree blossoms, the Ecc 12.5
I said, "I see a rod of *a*." Jer 1.11
and it bore ripe *a*. Num17.8

ALMS

when. .give *a*, sound no trumpet Mt 6.2
give for *a* those things which Lk 11.41
a. .ascended as a memorial Acts 10.4

ALONE

not good that the man. .*a*; Gen 2.18
nor let me *a* till I swallow Job 7.19
No one is good but God *a*. Lk 18.19
I am not *a*, for the Father Jn 16.32
by works and not by faith *a*. Jas 2.24

ALTAR — S

Then Noah built an *a* Gen 8.20
Abram. .built there an *a* 12.7
Abram. .built an *a* to. .LORD. 13.18
Abraham built an *a* there, 22.9
So he built an *a* there 26.25
There he erected an *a* 33.20
make there an *a* to the God 35.1
And Moses built an *a* Ex 17.15
make the *a* of acacia wood, 27.1
make an *a* to burn incense 30.1
He made the *a* of burnt offering 38.1
and the blood, on the *a* Deut 12.27

ALTAR — S (cont.)

build an *a* to the LORD your	Deut 27.5
built an *a* in Mount Ebal	Josh 8.30
built an *a* at the frontier	22.11
building an *a* to turn away	22.23
Saul built an *a* to the LORD;	1Sam 14.35
caught..horns of the *a*.	1Ki 1.50
repaired the *a* of the LORD	18.30
the *a* that was at Damascus.	2Ki 16.10
He made an *a* of bronze,	2Chr 4.1
I will go to the *a* of God,	Ps 43.4
coal..taken with tongs from..*a*.	Isa 6.6
an *a*..in the midst of..Egypt,	19.19
dimensions of..*a* by cubits	Ezek 43.13
LORD standing beside the *a*,	Amos 9.1
at the *a*, and there remember	Mt 5.23
an *a* with this inscription,	Acts 17.23
We have an *a* from which those	Heb 13.10
shall break down their *a*,	Deut 7.5
shall tear down their *a*,	12.3
he erected *a* for Baal, and	2Ki 21.3

AMALEK

Joshua mowed down *A* and his	Ex 17.13
"*A* was the first of the	Num 24.20
'I will punish what *A* did	1Sam 15.2

AMALEKITES

Agag the king of the *A*."	1Sam 15.32
destroyed the remnant of..*A*	1Chr 4.43

AMAZED

And they were *a* at him.	Mk 12.17
all were *a* and perplexed,	Acts 2.12
miracles performed, he was *a*.	8.13

AMAZEMENT

looked at one another in *a*.	Gen 43.33
And they were overcome with *a*.	Mk 5.42

AMBASSADOR — S

I am an *a* in chains; that I	Eph 6.20
which sends *a* by the Nile,	Isa 18.2
by sending *a* to Egypt,	Ezek 17.15
So we are *a* for Christ, God	2Cor 5.20

AMBUSH

they went to the place of *a*,	Josh 8.9
the LORD set an *a* against	2Chr 20.22

AMEN

everlasting to everlasting! *A*	Ps 41.13
can..outsider say the "*A*"	1Cor 14.16
'The words of the *A*, the	Rev 3.14

AMEND — S

A your ways and your doings,	Jer 7.3
Now therefore *a* your ways	26.13
deference..*a* for..offenses.	Ecc 10.4

AMMON

frontier of the sons of *A*,	Deut 2.19

AMMONITES

Ben-ammi..father of the *A*	Gen 19.38
cut down the *A* until the	1Sam 11.11
A paid tribute to Uzziah,	2Chr 26.8
and the *A* shall obey them.	Isa 11.14

AMOS

The words of *A*, who was	Amos 1.1
"*A* has conspired against you	7.10
A answered.."I am no prophet,	7.14
said, "*A*, what do you see?"	8.2

ANATHOTH

A with its pasture lands,	Josh 21.18
"Go to *A*, to your estate;	1Ki 2.26

Cry aloud,..Answer her, O *A*!	Isa 10.30
of the priests who were in *A*	Jer 1.1
why..not rebuked Jeremiah of *A*	29.27
'Buy my field which is at *A*,	32.7

ANDREW

Simon..Peter and *A* his brother,	Mt 4.18
Peter, and *A* his brother;	10.2
James and John and *A* asked him	Mk 13.3
One..who..followed him, was *A*,	Jn 1.40
A, Simon Peter's brother, said	6.8
Philip went and told *A*; *A* went	12.22
and John and James and *A*,	Acts 1.13

ANGEL — S

the *a* of God called to Hagar	Gen 21.17
he will send his *a* before you,	24.7
I send an *a* before you,	Ex 23.20
I will send an *a* before you,	33.2
sent an *a* and brought us	Num 20.16
my sight as an *a* of God;	1Sam 29.9
the king is like the *a*	2Sam 14.17
king is like the *a* of God;	19.27
an *a* spoke to me by the word	1Ki 13.18
an *a* touched him, and said	19.5
sent his *a* and delivered his	Dan 3.28
his *a*..shut the lions' mouths,	6.22
He strove with the *a* and	Hos 12.4
The *a* who talked with me said	Zech 1.9
the *a* said to her, "Do not be	Lk 1.30
appeared to him..*a* from heaven,	22.43
"An *a* has spoken to him."	Jn 12.29
was like the face of an *a*.	Acts 6.15
an *a* appeared in..Mount Sinai,	7.30
he saw..in a vision an *a* of God	10.3
no resurrection, nor *a*, nor spirit;	23.8
stood by me an *a* of the God	27.23
Satan disguises..as an *a*	2Cor 11.14
if we, or an *a* from heaven,	Gal 1.8
a of the church in Philadelphia	Rev 3.7
another mighty *a* coming down	10.1
a mighty *a* took up a stone	18.21
I saw an *a* standing in the sun,	19.17
"I Jesus have sent my *a* to you	22.16
The two *a* came to Sodom	Gen 19.1
the *a* urged Lot, saying,	19.15
the *a* of God were ascending	28.12
the *a* of God met him;	32.1
Man ate of the bread of the *a*;	Ps 78.25
will give his *a* charge of you	91.11
Bless the LORD, O you his *a*,	103.20
Praise him, all his *a*, praise	148.2
'He will give his *a* charge of you,'	Mt 4.6
devil left him, and behold,	4.11
and the reapers are *a*.	13.39
a..behold..face of the Father	18.10
he will send out his *a* with	24.31
and the *a* ministered to him.	Mk 1.13
'He will give his *a* charge	Lk 4.10
comes in his glory and..holy *a*.	9.26
will be denied before the *a*	12.9
joy before..*a*..over one sinner	15.10
and the *a* of God ascending	Jn 1.51
and she saw two *a* in white,	20.12
law..by and did not keep it."	Acts 7.53
death, nor life, nor *a*, nor	Rom 8.38
spectacle to the world, to *a*	1Cor 4.9
know that we are to judge *a*?	6.3
veil..because of the *a*.	11.10
the tongues of men and of *a*,	13.1
insisting on..worship of *a*,	Col 2.18
little while lower than the *a*,	Heb 2.7
into which *a* long to look.	1Pet 1.12

ANGEL — S (cont.)

if God did not spare the a	2Pet 2.4
the a that did not keep their	Jude 6
I saw four a standing at the	Rev 7.1
"Release the four a who are	9.14

ANGEL OF THE LORD

The a..found her by a spring	Gen 16.7
the a..called to him,.."Abraham,	22.11
a..appeared to him in a flame	Ex 3.2
ass saw..a..standing in the	Num 22.23
he saw the a..standing in..way,	22.31
a..came and sat..under..oak	Judg 6.11
the a..appeared to the woman	13.3
But the a..said to Elijah	2Ki 1.3
that night the a..went forth,	19.35
David..saw the a..standing	1Chr 21.16
The a..encamps around those	Ps 34.7
the a..went forth, and slew	Isa 37.36
a..appeared to him in a dream,	Mt 1.20
for an a..descended from heaven	28.2
there appeared to him an a..	Lk 1.11
And an a..appeared to them,	2.9
an a..went down..into the pool,	Jn 5.4n
an a..opened the prison doors	Acts 5.19
an a..said to Philip, "Rise	8.26
a..struck Peter on the side	12.7

ANGER — ED (v)

merciful..gracious, slow to a	Ps 103.8
He who is slow to a has	Prov 14.29
slow to a quiets contention.	15.18
who is slow to a is better	16.32
Be not quick to a, for a lodges	Ecc 7.9
The LORD is slow to a and	Nah 1.3
our fathers had a the God	Ezra 5.12
a him at..waters of Meribah,	Ps 106.32

ANGER (n)

until your brother's a turns	Gen 27.45
Jacob's a was kindled	30.2
let not your a burn against	44.18
the a of the LORD was kindled	Ex 4.14
dancing, Moses' a burned	32.19
when the LORD heard it, his a	Num 11.1
the a of the LORD was kindled	12.9
But God's a was kindled	22.22
the fierce a of the LORD	25.4
a of the LORD against Israel!	32.14
their a against him was abated	Judg 8.3
the a of the LORD was kindled	10.7
Then Saul's a was kindled	1Sam 20.30
the a of the LORD..kindled	2Sam 24.1
because of the a to which	1Ki 15.30
a of the LORD was kindled	1Chr 13.10
God will send his fierce a	Job 20.23
thy burning a overtake them.	Ps 69.24
the a of God rose against them	78.31
A gift in secret averts a;	Prov 21.14
the a of the LORD was kindled	Isa 5.25
his a is not turned away and	9.21
Ah, Assyria, the rod of my a,	10.5
upon him the heat of his a	42.25
for the fierce a of the LORD	Jer 4.8
a of the LORD will not turn	23.20
How the Lord in his a has set	Lam 2.1
the day of the a of the LORD	2.22
let thy a and thy wrath turn	Dan 9.16
Samaria. My a burns against	Hos 8.5
I will not execute my fierce a,	11.9
endure the heat of his a?	Nah 1.6
a,..at their hardness of heart,	Mk 3.5

ANGRY

And he was a with Eleazar	Lev 10.16
The LORD was a with me also	Deut 1.37
Why then are you a over	2Sam 19.42
Naaman was a, and went away,	2Ki 5.11
Asa was a with the seer,	2Chr 16.10
LORD was a with Amaziah	25.15
Be a, but sin not; commune with	Ps 4.4
thou hast been a; oh, restore	60.1
wicked man sees it and is a;	112.10
he with whom the LORD is a	Prov 22.14
backbiting tongue, a looks.	25.23
mother's sons were a with me,	Sol 1.6
will he be a for ever, will	Jer 3.5
"Do you do well to be a?"	Jonah 4.4
LORD was..a with your fathers.	Zech 1.2
one who is a with his brother	Mt 5.22
he was a and refused to go	Lk 15.28
nation I will make you a."	Rom 10.19
Be a but do not sin; do not	Eph 4.26

ANGUISH

and a have come upon me, but	Ps 119.143
a day of distress and a,	Zeph 1.15

ANNUL

not a a covenant previously	Gal 3.17

ANOINT — EST — ED (v)

shall a them and ordain them	Ex 28.41
you shall a with it the tent	30.26
shall a Aaron and his sons,	30.30
Wash..and a yourself, and put	Ruth 3.3
you shall a him to be prince	1Sam 9.16
you shall a for me him whom	16.3
"Arise, a him; for this is	16.12
I a you king over Israel.'	2Ki 9.3
and to a a most holy place.	Dan 9.24
that they might go and a him.	Mk 16.1
Jesus, whom thou didst a,	Acts 4.27
and salve to a your eyes,	Rev 3.18.
thou a my head with oil, my	Ps 23.5
Bethel, where you a a pillar	Gen 31.13
on Aaron's head, and a him,	Lev 8.12
the LORD a you to be burned	1Sam 10.1
a Solomon..blew the trumpet;	1Ki 1.39
proclaimed him king, and a	2Ki 11.12
heard that David had been a	1Chr 14.8
"Touch not my a ones, do my	16.22
they a him as prince for the LORD,	29.22
your God, has a you with the	Ps 45.7
with my holy oil I have a	89.20
saying, "Touch not my a ones,	105.15
a me to bring good tidings	Isa 61.1
With an a guardian cherub	Ezek 28.14
to the coming of an a one,	Dan 9.25
a with oil many that were sick	Mk 6.13
she has a my body..for burying.	14.8
because he has a me to preach	Lk 4.18
and a them with the ointment.	7.38
It was Mary who a the Lord	Jn 11.2
and a the feet of Jesus and	12.3
how God a Jesus of Nazareth	Acts 10.38
have been a by the Holy One,	1Jn 2.20

ANOINTED (n)

go in and out before my a	1Sam 2.35
LORD's a is before him."	16.6
for he is the LORD's a.'	24.10
hand against the LORD's a,	26.9
your lord, the LORD's a.	26.16
to destroy the LORD's a?	2Sam 1.14
steadfast love to his a,	22.51
against the LORD and his a,	Ps 2.2

ANOINTED (n) (cont.)

shows steadfast love to his *a*,	Ps 18.50
the saving refuge of his *a*.	28.8
look upon the face of thine *a*!	84.9
not turn away. .face of thy *a*	132.10
the LORD to his *a*, to Cyrus,	Isa 45.1
for the salvation of thy *a*.	Hab 3.13
the. .*a* who stand by the LORD	Zech 4.14

ANOINTING (n)

a which you received from him	1Jn 2.27

ANSWER — S — ED (v)

the LORD did not *a* him,	1Sam 28.6
king's command was, "Do not *a*	2Ki 18.36
How can I *a* him, choosing	Job 9.14
let the Almighty *a* me!)	31.35
'He will *a* none of my words'?	33.13
A me when I call, O God of my	Ps 4.1
The LORD *a* you in. .trouble!	20.1
be gracious to me and *a* me!	27.7
When he calls to me, I will *a*	91.15
call upon me,. .I will not *a*;	Prov 1.28
A not a fool according to	26.4
when he hears it, he will *a*	Isa 30.19
Before they call I will *a*,	65.24
I called you, you did not *a*,	Jer 7.13
Call to me and I will *a* you,	33.3
I will *a* the heavens and they	Hos 2.21
what have I wearied you? *A* me!	Mic 6.3
how or what you are to *a*	Lk 12.11
who *a* by fire, he is God."	1Ki 18.24
an altar to the God who *a*	Gen 35.3
Then the LORD *a* Job out of	Job 38.1
Then Job *a* the LORD: "I know	42.1,2
I *a* you in the secret place of	Ps 81.7

ANSWER (n)

give Pharaoh a favorable *a*."	Gen 41.16
angry. .they had found no *a*,	Job 32.3
an *a* for those who taunt me,	Ps 119.42
A soft *a* turns away wrath,	Prov 15.1
a of. .tongue is from the LORD.	16.1
If one gives *a* before he hears,	18.13
I called him, but he gave no *a*.	Sol 5.6
questioned. .but he made no *a*.	Lk 23.9

ANTICHRIST

have heard that *a* is coming,	1Jn 2.18
This is the *a*, he who denies	2.22
This is the spirit of *a*, of	4.3
is the deceiver and the *a*.	2Jn 7

ANTIOCH

Phoenicia and Cyprus and *A*,	Acts 11.19
in *A* the disciples were. .called	11.26
at *A* there were prophets	13.1
and came to *A* of Pisidia.	13.14
Jews came there from *A* and	14.19
from there they sailed to *A*,	14.26
Paul and Barnabas remained in *A*,	15.35
and then went down to *A*.	18.22
But when Cephas came to *A* I	Gal 2.11
what befell me at *A*, at	2Tim 3.11

ANXIETY — IES

A in a man's heart weighs	Prov 12.25
my *a* for all the churches.	2Cor 11.28
Have no *a* about anything,	Phil 4.6
Cast all your *a* on him, for	1Pet 5.7

ANXIOUS

my spirit within me was *a*,	Dan 7.15
do not be *a* about your life,	Mt 6.25
do not be *a* how. .to speak	10.19
Martha, you are *a* and troubled	Lk 10.41

do not be *a* how. .to answer	12.11
The unmarried man is *a* about	1Cor 7.32
genuinely *a* for your welfare.	Phil 2.20

APOLLOS

a Jew named *A*, a native of	Acts 18.24
While *A* was at Corinth, Paul	19.1
Paul," or "I belong to *A*,"	1Cor 1.12
another, "I belong to *A*,"	3.4
As for our brother *A*, I. .urged him	16.12
the lawyer and *A* on their way;	Tit 3.13

APOSTASY

and your *a* will reprove you.	Jer 2.19
if they then commit *a*,	Heb 6.6

APOSTLE — S

I am an *a* to the Gentiles,	Rom 11.13
called. .to be an *a* of Christ	1Cor 1.1
Am I not free? Am I not an *a*?	9.1
Paul an *a*—not from men nor	Gal 1.1
Paul, an *a* of Christ Jesus	1Tim 1.1
appointed a preacher and *a*	2Tim 1.11
a returned to Jesus, and told	Mk 6.30
the *a* told. .what they had done.	Lk 9.10
at table, and the *a* with him.	22.14
through the Holy Spirit to. .*a*	Acts 1.2
the *a* and. .brethren. .in Judea	11.1
appointed in the church. .*a*,	1Cor 12.28
inferior to these superlative *a*.	2Cor 11.5
been revealed to his holy *a*	Eph 3.5
that some should be *a*, some	4.11
commandment. .through your *a*.	2Pet 3.2
the predictions of the *a* of	Jude 17
call themselves *a* but are not,	Rev 2.2
names of the twelve *a* of the Lamb.	21.14

APOSTLESHIP

and *a* from which Judas turned	Acts 1.25
grace and *a* to bring about	Rom 1.5

APPALLED

and pulled hair. .and sat *a*.	Ezra 9.3
Upright men are *a* at this,	Job 17.8
be *a* because of their shame	Ps 40.15
I was *a*,. .no one to uphold;	Isa 63.5
but I was *a* by the vision	Dan 8.27

APPEAL (v)

that I cannot *a* to my Father,	Mt 26.53
to them. I *a* to Caesar."	Acts 25.11
I *a* to you therefore, brethren,	Rom 12.1
I *a* to you for my child,	Philem 10

APPEAL (n)

God making his *a* through us.	2Cor 5.20
Mend your ways, heed my *a*,	13.11
as an *a* to God for a clear	1Pet 3.21

APPEAR — ED — ING

your males *a* before the LORD	Ex 23.17
"When you come to *a* before me,	Isa 1.12
outwardly *a* righteous to men,	Mt 23.28
then will *a* the sign of the Son	24.30
kingdom. .was to *a* immediately.	Lk 19.11
all *a* before the judgment	2Cor 5.10
you. .will *a* with him in glory.	Col 3.4
to *a* in the presence of God	Heb 9.24
Christ,. .will *a* a second time	9.28
not yet *a* what we shall be,	1Jn 3.2
the LORD *a* to him by. .Mamre,	Gen 18.1
the LORD *a* to him, and said,	26.2
"God Almighty *a* to me	48.3
angel of the LORD *a* to him	Ex 3.2
the LORD *a* in the cloud.	16.10
glory of the LORD *a* to all	Num 16.19

APPEAR — ED — ING (cont.)

And the Lord *a* in the tent	Deut 31.15
angel of the Lord *a* to him	Judg 6.12
God *a* to Solomon, and said	2Chr 1.7
Lord *a* to Solomon in the night	7.12
the Lord *a* to him from afar.	Jer 31.3
he *a* first to Mary Magdalene,	Mk 16.9*n*
who *a* in glory and spoke of	Lk 9.31
God of glory *a* to our father	Acts 7.2
vision *a* to Paul in the night:	16.9
he has *a* once for all at the	Heb 9.26
until the *a* of our Lord	1Tim 6.14
to all who have loved his *a*.	2Tim 4.8

APPLE — S

kept. .as the *a* of his eye.	Deut 32.10
Keep me as the *a* of the eye;	Ps 17.8
keep my teachings as the *a* of	Prov 7.2
As an *a* tree among the trees	Sol 2.3
touches the *a* of his eye:	Zech 2.8
word fitly spoken is like *a*	Prov 25.11

APPLY

A your mind to instruction	Prov 23.12
careful to *a* themselves to good	Tit 3.8

APPOINT — ED

shall *a* Aaron. .to. .priesthood;	Num 3.10
I will *a* a place for my people	2Sam 7.10
he *a* his own priests for	2Chr 11.15
I was *a* to be their governor	Neh 5.14
to the house *a* for all	Job 30.23
my God; thou hast *a* a judgment.	Ps 7.6
the Lord *a* a great fish to	Jonah 1.17
Lord God *a* a plant, and made	4.6
God *a* a worm which attacked	4.7
he *a* twelve, to be with him,	Mk 3.14
After this the Lord *a* seventy	Lk 10.1
as my Father *a* a kingdom for me,	22.29
I chose you and *a* you that	Jn 15.16
the Christ *a* for you, Jesus,	Acts 3.20
God of our fathers *a* you	22.14
For this gospel I was *a* a	2Tim 1.11
Son, whom he *a* the heir of all	Heb 1.2

APPROACH

for who would dare. .to *a* me?	Jer 30.21
the priests who *a* the Lord	Ezek 42.13

APPROVAL

you will receive his *a*,	Rom 13.3
men of old received divine *a*.	Heb 11.2

APPROVE — D — ING

but *a* those who practice them.	Rom 1.32
and *a* what is excellent,	2.18
you may *a* what is excellent,	Phil 1.10
God has already *a* what you do.	Ecc 9.7
yourself to God as one *a*,	2Tim 2.15
also was standing by and *a*,	Acts 22.20

AQUILA

And he found a Jew named *A*,	Acts 18.2
with him Priscilla and *A*.	18.18
when Priscilla and *A* heard	18.26
Greet Prisca and *A*, my fellow	Rom 16.3
A and Prisca, together with	1Cor 16.19
Greet Prisca and *A*, and the	2Tim 4.19

ARABIA

and from all the kings of *A*	1Ki 10.15
thickets in *A* you will lodge,	Isa 21.13
but I went away into *A*; and	Gal 1.17
Hagar is Mount Sinai in *A*;	4.25

ARARAT

ark came. .the mountains of *A*.	Gen 8.4

ARCHANGEL — 'S

when the *a* Michael, contending	Jude 9
with the *a* call, and with	1Thess 4.16

ARGUE — S — D

desire to *a* my case with God.	Job 13.3
A your case with. .neighbor	Prov 25.9
who *a* with God,. .answer it."	Job 40.2
And they *a* with one another,	Mk 11.31
for three weeks he *a* with them	Acts 17.2
he *a* in the synagogue with. .Jews	17.17
he *a* in the synagogue every	18.4

ARGUMENT — S

If. .wise man has an *a* with	Prov 29.9
We destroy *a* and every proud	2Cor 10.5

ARIMATHEA

rich man from *A*, named Joseph,	Mt 27.57
After this Joseph of *A*, who	Jn 19.38

ARISE

A, walk through the length	Gen 13.17
Moses said, "*A*, O Lord,	Num 10.35
a, go over this Jordan,	Josh 1.2
A, O Lord! Let not man prevail;	Ps 9.19
A, O Lord! confront them,	17.13
Let God *a*, let his enemies be	68.1
a, O captive Jerusalem; loose	Isa 52.2
A, shine; for. .light has come,	60.1
trouble they say, '*A* and save	Jer 2.27
"Little girl, I say to you, *a*."	Mk 5.41
"Young man, I say to you, *a*."	Lk 7.14
called, saying, "Child, *a*."	8.54
sleeper, and *a* from the dead,	Eph 5.14

ARK

Make yourself an *a*	Gen 6.14
the *a* came to rest upon. .Ararat.	8.4
"They shall make an *a*	Ex 25.10
Bezalel made the *a* of acacia	37.1
the *a* of the covenant	Num 10.33
"When you see the *a* of the	Josh 3.3
a of the Lord to compass	6.11
(for the *a* of the covenant	Judg 20.27
Let us bring the *a* of the	1Sam 4.3
the *a* of God was captured;	4.11
Philistines took the *a* of God	5.2
saw the *a*, they rejoiced	6.13
looked into the *a* of the Lord;	6.19
"Bring hither the *a* of God."	14.18
up from there the *a* of God,	2Sam 6.2
Levites, bearing the *a*	15.24
let us bring again the *a* of	1Chr 13.3
they brought in the *a* of God,	16.1
to bring up the *a* of the	2Chr 5.2
no more say, "The *a* of the	Jer 3.16
and the *a* of the covenant	Heb 9.4
a of his covenant was seen	Rev 11.19

ARM — S

With him is an *a* of flesh;	2Chr 32.8
Have you an *a* like God,	Job 40.9
nor did their own *a* give them	Ps 44.3
His right hand and his holy *a*,	98.1
and his *a* rules for him;	Isa 40.10
to whom has the *a* of the Lord	Jn 12.38
are the everlasting *a*.	Deut 33.27
taking him in his *a*, he said	Mk 9.36
took them in his *a* and blessed	10.16

ARMAGEDDON

which is called in Hebrew *A*.	Rev 16.16

ARMOR

clothed David with his *a*;	1Sam 17.38
Put on the whole *a* of God,	Eph 6.11

ARMY 11 ASSEMBLE

ARMY — IES
as commander of the a of the   Josh 5.14
But the a of the Chaldeans   2Ki 25.5
great a, like an a of God.   1Chr 12.22
my great a, which I sent   Joel 2.25
hast not gone out with our a.   Ps 44.9

AROMA
we are the a of Christ to God   2Cor 2.15

AROUSE — D
to a you by way of reminder,   2Pet 1.13
This city has a my anger   Jer 32.31

ARRAY (n)
worship the LORD in holy a.   Ps 29.2
Worship the LORD in holy a;   96.9

ARRAYED (v)
was not a like one of these.   Mt 6.29
was not a like one of these.   Lk 12.27

ARRESTED
he heard that John had been a,   Mt 4.12
after John was a, Jesus came   Mk 1.14

ARROGANCE
Let not the foot of a come   Ps 36.11
you boast in your a.   Jas 4.16

ARROGANT
who is a is an abomination   Prov 16.5
we deem the a blessed;   Mal 3.15
Some are a, as though I   1Cor 4.18
And you are a! Ought you not   5.2

ARROW — S
"The LORD's a of victory,   2Ki 13.17
till an a pierces its entrails;   Prov 7.23
And I will shoot three a   1Sam 20.20
the a of the Almighty are in me.   Job 6.4
making his a fiery shafts.   Ps 7.13
he sent. .a, and scattered   18.14
thy a have sunk into me, and   38.2
Your a are sharp in the heart   45.5
a are sharp,. .their bows bent,   Isa 5.28
loose. .my deadly a of famine,   Ezek 5.16

ASCEND — ED — ING
Who. .shall a. .hill of the LORD? Ps 24.3
Thou didst a the high mount,   68.18
I a to heaven, thou art there!   139.8
a to heaven; above the stars   Isa 14.13
"Who will a into heaven?"   Rom 10.6
angel. .a in the flame of the   Judg 13.20
Who has a to heaven and come   Prov 30.4
No one has a into heaven but   Jn 3.13
I have not yet a to the Father;   20.17
"He a," what does it mean   Eph 4.9
were to see the Son of man a   Jn 6.62

ASHAMED
naked, and were not a.   Gen 2.25
"O my God, I am a and blush   Ezra 9.6
be a who are. .treacherous.   Ps 25.3
so your faces shall never be a.   34.5
were. .a when they committed   Jer 6.15
Were they a when they committed   8.12
shall be a of their harvests   12.13
whoever is a of me and of my   Mk 8.38
whoever is a of me and of my   Lk 9.26
I am not a of the gospel: Rom 1.16
not write this to make you a,   1Cor 4.14
Do not be a then of testifying   2Tim 1.8
But I am not a, for I know   1.12

ASHER
Leah. .called his name A.   Gen 30.13

from A, Pagiel. .son of Ochran; Num 1.13
And of A he said, "Blessed   Deut 33.24
A sat still at the coast   Judg 5.17

ASHES
I who am but dust and a.   Gen 18.27
maxims are proverbs of a.   Job 13.12
I have become like dust and a.   30.19

ASIA
Cappadocia, Pontus and A,   Acts 2.9
those from Cilicia and A, arose   6.9
forbidden. .to speak. .in A.   16.6
all the residents of A heard   19.10
she whom all A. .worship."   19.27
first convert in A for Christ.   Rom 16.5
The churches of A send   1Cor 16.19
Cappadocia, A, and Bithynia,   1Pet 1.1
seven churches that are in A: Rev 1.4

ASK — ED
that they a, every man of his   Ex 11.2
"A what I shall give you."   1Ki 3.5
"A what I shall give you."   2Chr 1.7
A of me, and I will make the   Ps 2.8
Two things I a of thee; deny   Prov 30.7
"A a sign of the LORD your   Isa 7.11
by those who did not a for me;   65.1
They shall a the way to Zion,   Jer 50.5
A rain from the LORD in the   Zech 10.1
knows what you need before you a Mt 6.8
"A, and it will be given you;   7.7
And whatever you a in prayer   21.22
king said to the girl, "A me   Mk 6.22
do for us whatever we a of you."   10.35
I tell you, A, and it will be   Lk 11.9
give. .Holy Spirit to those who a   11.13
Whatever you a in my name,   Jn 14.13
and my words abide in you, a   15.7
a, and you will receive,   16.24
than all that we a or think,   Eph 3.20
lacks wisdom, let him a God,   Jas 1.5
not have, because you do not a.   4.2
from him whatever we a,   1Jn 3.22
if we a anything according   5.14
not a mortal sin, he will a,   5.16
a of the Egyptians jewelry   Ex 12.35
"I have a him of the LORD."   1Sam 1.20
One thing have I a of the LORD, Ps 27.4
he gave them what they a, but   106.15
and a for the body of Jesus.   Mt 27.58
and a for the body of Jesus.   Lk 23.52

ASLEEP
or perhaps he is a and must   1Ki 18.27
by the waves; but he was a.   Mt 8.24
in the stern, a on the cushion;   Mk 4.38
come suddenly and find you a.   13.36
as they sailed he fell a.   Lk 8.23
when he. .said this, he fell a.   Acts 7.60
though some have fallen a.   1Cor 15.6
concerning those who are a,   1Thess 4.13

ASS — 'S
And the a saw the angel   Num 22.23
the a. .said to Balaam,   22.28
humble, and mounted on an a,   Mt 21.5
dumb a spoke with human voice 2Pet 2.16
coming, sitting on an a colt!"   Jn 12.15

ASSEMBLE — D
A and hear, O sons of Jacob,   Gen 49.2
a. .the congregation at the door Lev 8.3
"A yourselves and come, draw Isa 45.20
cry aloud. .'A, and let us go   Jer 4.5

ASSEMBLE — D (cont.)

a you out of the countries	Ezek 11.17
all beasts of the field, '*A*	39.17
they *a* the whole congregation	Num 1.18
Solomon *a* the elders of Israel	1Ki 8.1
Solomon *a* the elders of Israel	2Chr 5.2
people of Israel were *a* with	Neh 9.1
When you are *a*, and my spirit	1Cor 5.4

ASSEMBLY

to..LORD; it is a solemn *a*;	Lev 23.36
David said to all the *a*,	1Chr 29.20
the *a* made a covenant with	2Chr 23.3
Let the *a*..be gathered about	Ps 7.7
praise in..*a* of the faithful!	149.1
a fast; call a solemn *a*;	Joel 2.15
settled in the regular *a*.	Acts 19.39
to the *a* of the first-born	Heb 12.23
if a man..comes into your *a*,	Jas 2.2

ASSURANCE

he has given *a* to all men	Acts 17.31
realizing the full *a* of hope	Heb 6.11
faith..the *a* of things hoped for,	11.1

ASSYRIA

Hiddekel,..east of *A*.	Gen 2.14
king of *A* came and captured	2Ki 15.29
king of *A* I have heard.	19.20
bee which is in the land of *A*.	Isa 7.18
calling to Egypt, going to *A*.	Hos 7.11
A shall not save us, we will	14.3

ASTONISHED

every one passing..will be *a*,	2Chr 7.21
King Nebuchadnezzar was *a*	Dan 3.24
crowds were *a* at his teaching,	Mt 7.28
multitude..*a* at his teaching.	Mk 11.18
they were *a* at his teaching,	Lk 4.32

ASTRAY

The wicked go *a* from the womb,	Ps 58.3
Before..afflicted I went *a*;	119.67
those who lead this people..*a*,	Isa 9.16
spirit of harlotry..led..*a*,	Hos 4.12
and they will lead many *a*.	Mt 24.5
heed that no one leads you *a*.	Mk 13.5
heed that you are not led *a*;	Lk 21.8
he is leading the people *a*."	Jn 7.12
"Are you led *a*, you also?	7.47

ASUNDER

"Let us burst their bonds *a*,	Ps 2.3
together, let no man put *a*."	Mt 19.6

ATE

Saul *a* with Samuel that day.	1Sam 9.24
a them with the blood.	14.32
Thy words were found, and I *a*	Jer 15.16
and *a* grass like an ox, and	Dan 4.33
Those who *a* were four thousand	Mt 15.38
They *a*, they drank, they married	Lk 17.27
he took it and *a* before them.	24.43

ATHENS

brought him as far as *A*;	Acts 17.15
"Men of *A*, I perceive that	17.22
After this he left *A* and went	18.1
willing to be left..at *A*	1Thess 3.1

ATONE — D

evil..for which you cannot *a*;	Isa 47.11
to *a* for iniquity, to bring in	Dan 9.24
iniquity is *a* for, and	Prov 16.6

ATONEMENT

as a sin offering for *a*.	Ex 29.36

perhaps I can make *a* for..sin."	32.30
accepted for him to make *a*	Lev 1.4
consecrated..to make *a* for it.	8.15
people, and make *a* for them;	9.7
priest shall make *a* for him	14.18
that *a*..made for the people	16.34
it is the blood that makes *a*,	17.11
tenth day..is the day of *a*;	23.27
and make *a* for them;	Num 16.46
make *a* for ourselves before	31.50
to make *a* for all Israel.	2Chr 29.24
shall make *a* for the temple.	Ezek 45.20

ATTENTION

Gallio paid no *a* to this.	Acts 18.17
centurion paid more *a* to..captain	27.11
we must pay the closer *a* to	Heb 2.1

ATTENTIVE

Lord, let thy ear be *a* to	Neh 1.11
My son, be *a* to my words;	Prov 4.20
My son, be *a* to my wisdom,	5.1

ATTESTED

Jesus..*a* to you by God with	Acts 2.22
was *a* as having pleased God.	Heb 11.5

AUTHORITY — IES

commit your *a* to his hand;	Isa 22.21
he taught..as one who had *a*,	Mt 7.29
a man under *a*, with soldiers	8.9
the Son of man has *a*..to forgive	9.6
great men exercise *a* over them.	20.25
"By what *a* are you doing these	21.23
"All *a* in heaven and on earth	28.18
he taught..as one who had *a*,	Mk 1.22
Son of man has *a* on earth to	2.10
and have *a* to cast out demons:	3.15
their great men exercise *a*	10.42
"By what *a* are you doing these	11.28
"To you I will give all this *a*	Lk 4.6
with *a* and power he commands	4.36
the Son of man has *a* on earth	5.24
given..*a* to tread upon serpents	10.19
by what *a* you do these things,	20.2
given him *a* to execute judgment,	Jn 5.27
has *a* from the chief priests	Acts 9.14
there is no *a* except from God,	Rom 13.1
a little too much of our *a*,	2Cor 10.8
and the *a* of his Christ have	Rev 12.10
the dragon gave..great *a*.	13.2
be submissive to rulers and *a*,	Tit 3.1

AVENGE — D

that I may *a* on Jezebel the	2Ki 9.7
Jews were to be ready..to *a*	Est 8.13
I will..*a* myself on my foes.	Isa 1.24
I will *a* their blood, and I	Joel 3.21
never *a* yourselves, but leave	Rom 12.19
I swear I will be *a* upon you,	Judg 15.7
be *a* upon the Philistines	16.28
he has *a* on her the blood	Rev 19.2

AVENGER

refuge from the *a*, that	Num 35.12
the Lord is an *a* in all	1Thess 4.6

AVOID

path of the wicked,..*A* it;	Prov 4.15
may *a* the snares of death.	14.27
A such godless chatter, for	2Tim 2.16
to *a* quarreling, to be gentle,	Tit 3.2

AWAIT — ING

from it we *a* a Savior,	Phil 3.20
a our blessed hope, the	Tit 2.13

AWAKE — S — N

A, my soul! A, O harp and	Ps 57.8
a, put on your strength, O	Isa 52.1
master finds a when he comes;	Lk 12.37
I go to a him out of sleep."	Jn 11.11
Blessed is he who is a,	Rev 16.15
are like a dream when one a,	Ps 73.20
nor a love until it please.	Sol 8.4

AWE

held in a above all gods.	1Chr 16.25
the world stand in a of him!	Ps 33.8
stands in a of thy words.	119.161
they were filled with a,	Mt 27.54

AXE — S

his a head fell into the water;	2Ki 6.5
Shall the a vaunt itself over	Isa 10.15
now the a is laid to the root	Mt 3.10
the a is laid to the root of	Lk 3.9
labor with saws and. . a;	1Chr 20.3
hacked. . wooden trellis with a.	Ps 74.5

AZAZEL

LORD and the other lot for A.	Lev 16,8

B

BAAL — S

"Will you contend for B?	Judg 6.31
served B, and worshiped him.	1Ki 16.31
host of heaven, and served B.	2Ki 17.16
the prophets prophesied by B,	Jer 2.8
and gold which they used for B.	Hos 2.8
served the B and. . Ashtaroth.	Judg 2.13

BABE — S

the b leaped in her womb;	Lk 1.41
by the mouth of b and infants,	Ps 8.2
and b shall rule over them.	Isa 3.4
hidden. . revealed them to b;	Mt 11.25
'Out of the mouth of b and	21.16
and revealed them to b; yea,	Lk 10.21
men of. . flesh, as b in Christ.	1Cor 3.1

BABEL

its name was called B,	Gen 11.9

BABYLON

king. . brought people from B,	2Ki 17.24
Judah was taken into. . B	1Chr 9.1
By the waters of B,. .wept,	Ps 137.1
Go forth from B, flee from	Isa 48.20
time of the deportation to B.	Mt 1.11
She who is at B, who is	1Pet 5.13
fallen is B the great, she	Rev 14.8

BABYLONIA

up from B to Jerusalem.	Ezra 1.11

BACK — S

cast. . my sins behind thy b.	Isa 38.17
are these wounds on your b?'	Zech 13.6
make my enemies turn their b	Ps 18.40

BACKSLIDING — S

turned away in perpetual b?	Jer 8.5
b are many, we have sinned	14.7

BALAAM

sent messengers to B	Num 22.5
And B said to Balak, "Build	23.1
When B saw that it pleased	24.1
also slew B the son of Beor	31.8
what B the son of Beor answered	Mic 6.5
have followed the way of B,	2Pet 2.15
who hold the teaching of B,	Rev 2.14

BALANCE — S

A false b is an abomination	Prov 11.1
scales and the hills in a b?	Isa 40.12
rider had a b in his hand;	Rev 6.5
my calamity laid in the b!	Job 6.2
take b. . and divide the hair.	Ezek 5.1
TEKEL, you. . weighed in the b	Dan 5.27
in whose hands are false b,	Hos 12.7

BALDHEAD

saying, "Go up, you b! Go	2Ki 2.23

BANQUET — ING

a great b, and invited many;	Lk 14.16
He brought me to the b house,	Sol 2.4
queen,. .came into the b hall;	Dan 5.10

BAPTISM

The b of John, whence was it?	Mt 21.25
b with which I am baptized?"	Mk 10.38
Was the b of John from heaven	11.30
preaching a b of repentance	Lk 3.3
I have a b to be baptized	12.50
Was the b of John from heaven	20.4
one Lord, one faith, one b,	Eph 4.5
you were buried with him in b,	Col 2.12
B, which corresponds to this,	1Pet 3.21

BAPTIZE — D — ING

"I b. .with water for repentance,	Mt 3.11
"I b you with water; but he	Lk 3.16
"I b with water; but among you	Jn 1.26
Christ did not send me to b	1Cor 1.17
were b by him in the river	Mt 3.6
who believes and is b will	Mk 16.16n
justified God, having been b	Lk 7.29
shall be b with the. .Spirit."	Acts 1.5
were b, both men and women.	8.12
the eunuch, and he b him.	8.38
Then he rose and was b,	9.18
she was b, with her household,	16.15
Rise and be b, and wash away	22.16
who have been b into Christ	Rom 6.3
you b in the name of Paul?	1Cor 1.13
fathers. .were b into Moses	10.2
were all b into one body—	12.13
b on behalf of the dead?	15.29
For as many of you as were b	Gal 3.27
disciples of all nations, b	Mt 28.19
John also was b at Aenon	Jn 3.23
Jesus was making and b more	4.1

BAPTIZER

John the b appeared in the	Mk 1.4
"John the b. .raised from. .dead;	6.14

BARABBAS

for you?" And they said, "B."	Mt 27.21
there was a man called B.	Mk 15.7
release for them B instead.	15.11
released. . B; and. .scourged Jesus,	15.15
cried. . "Not this man, but B!"	Jn 18.40

BAREFOOT

David. . b and with his head	2Sam 15.30
Isaiah has walked naked and b	Isa 20.3

BAR-JONA

"Blessed are you, Simon B!	Mt 16.17

BARNABAS

Benevolent Acts 4.36–37; introduced Paul to the apostles, Acts 9.26–27; preached at Antioch, Acts 11.22–24; ministered with Paul at Antioch, Acts 11.25–26; took relief offerings to Judea, Acts 11.29–30; accompanied Paul on his first missionary journey,

BARNABAS (cont.)
Acts 13.1–14.28; attended the Council of Jerusalem, Acts 15.1–31; separated from Paul, Acts 15.36–41.

BARNS
then your *b* will be filled	Prov 3.10
sow nor reap nor gather into *b*,	Mt 6.26
my *b*, and build larger ones;	Lk 12.18

BARREN
Sarai was *b*; she had no child.	Gen 11.30
but Rachel was *b*.	29.31
Manoah; and his wife was *b*	Judg 13.2
He gives the *b* woman a home,	Ps 113.9
"Sing, O *b* one, who did not	Isa 54.1
had no child..Elizabeth was *b*,	Lk 1.7
"Rejoice, O *b* one that dost	Gal 4.27

BARTHOLOMEW
Philip and *B*; Thomas and	Mt 10.3
and John, and Philip, and *B*,	Lk 6.14
and Thomas, *B* and Matthew,	Acts 1.13

BARUCH
the deed of purchase to *B*	Jer 32.12
and *B* wrote upon a scroll	36.4
B answered them, "He dictated	36.18
but *B*..has set you against us,	43.3
Jeremiah the prophet spoke to *B*	45.1

BASKET — S
took..a *b* made of bulrushes,	Ex 2.3
behold, a *b* of summer fruit.	Amos 8.1
wall, lowering him in a *b*.	Acts 9.25
but I was let down in a *b*	2Cor 11.33
two *b* of figs placed before	Jer 24.1
they took up twelve *b* full	Mt 14.20
they took up seven *b* full of	15.37
how many *b*..of broken pieces	Mk 8.19

BATHE — D — ING
he shall *b* himself in water,	Deut 23.11
Then I *b* you with water and	Ezek 16.9
from the roof a woman *b*;	2Sam 11.2

BATHSHEBA
Taken by David, 2Sam 11.1–5; became the mother of Solomon, 2Sam 12.24; interceded for Solomon's succession on the throne, 1Ki 1.15–31; petitioned for Adonijah, 1Ki 2.12–25.

BATTLE
has come from the *b*; I fled	1Sam 4.16
"If thy people go out to *b*	1Ki 8.44
b is not yours but God's.	2Chr 20.15
who will get ready for *b*?	1Cor 14.8
to assemble them for *b* on	Rev 16.14

BEAR — S — ING (v)
greater than I can *b*.	Gen 4.13
then let me *b* the blame	43.9
then I shall *b* the blame	44.32
Aaron shall *b* their names	Ex 28.12
Aaron shall *b* the judgment	28.30
b iniquity..with the sanctuary	Num 18.1
not an enemy..then I could *b*	Ps 55.12
he shall *b* their iniquities.	Isa 53.11
LORD could no longer *b*..evil	Jer 44.22
does not *b* his own cross	Lk 14.27
b it if a man makes slaves	2Cor 11.20
as a man *b* his son, in all	Deut 1.31
the Lord, who daily *b* us up;	Ps 68.19
went out, *b* his own cross,	Jn 19.17
be saved through *b* children,	1Tim 2.15

BEAR (n)
there came a lion, or a *b*,	1Sam 17.34
beast, a second one, like a *b*.	Dan 7.5

BEAST — S
"Whoever lies with a *b*	Ex 22.19
Then I saw another *b* which	Rev 13.11
b that you saw was, and is not,	17.8
creeping things and *b*	Gen 1.24
you may eat among all the *b*	Lev 11.2
wild *b* grow too numerous	Deut 7.22
the *b*..at peace with you.	Job 5.23
ask the *b*, and they will teach	12.7
he is like the *b* that perish.	Ps 49.12
when all the *b*..creep forth.	104.20
show them..they are but *b*.	Ecc 3.18
dwelling shall be with the *b*	Dan 4.25
I fought with *b* at Ephesus?	1Cor 15.32

BEAUTIFUL
you are a woman *b* to behold;	Gen 12.11
and the woman was very *b*.	2Sam 11.2
the maiden was *b* and lovely,	Est 2.7
holy mountain, *b* in elevation,	Ps 48.2
He has made everything *b* in	Ecc 3.11
You are *b* as Tirzah, my love,	Sol 6.4
branch of the LORD shall be *b*	Isa 4.2
was given you, your *b* flock?	Jer 13.20
You grew exceedingly *b*, and	Ezek 16.13

BEAUTIFY
to *b* the house of the LORD	Ezra 7.27
In vain you *b* yourself	Jer 4.30

BEAUTY
to behold the *b* of the LORD,	Ps 27.4
the king will desire your *b*.	45.11
Do not desire her *b* in your	Prov 6.25
Charm is deceitful,..*b* is vain,	31.30
said, 'I am perfect in *b*.'	Ezek 27.3
proud because of your *b*;	28.17

BED — S
When I say, 'My *b* will comfort	Job 7.13
the *b* is too short to stretch	Isa 28.20
"Rise, take up your *b* and go	Mt 9.6
with his *b* through the tiles	Lk 5.19
Woe to those..upon *b* of ivory,	Amos 6.4

BEE — S
for the *b* which is in the land	Isa 7.18
Amorites..chased you as *b* do	Deut 1.44
b in the body of the lion,	Judg 14.8

BEELZEBUL
"It is only by *B*, the prince	Mt 12.24
"He is possessed by *B*, and	Mk 3.22

BEER-SHEBA
in the wilderness of *B*.	Gen 21.14
they made a covenant at *B*.	21.32
went together to *B*;	22.19
came to *B*, and offered	46.1
to *B* knew that Samuel was	1Sam 3.20
number Israel, from *B* to	1Chr 21.2
not enter..or cross over to *B*;	Amos 5.5

BEFITS
Rejoice..Praise *b* the upright.	Ps 33.1
teach what *b* sound doctrine.	Tit 2.1

BEGGAR
Bartimaeus, a blind *b*,	Mk 10.46
who had seen him before as a *b*,	Jn 9.8

BEGINNING
In the *b* God created	Gen 1.1
for you the *b* of months;	Ex 12.2

BEGINNING (cont.)
fear of the Lord is the *b* of Ps 111.10
fear of..Lord..*b* of knowledge; Prov 1.7
The *b* of wisdom..Get wisdom, 4.7
but the *b* of the sufferings, Mt 24.8
The *b* of the gospel of Jesus Mk 1.1
In the *b* was the Word, and Jn 1.1

BEGUILED
"The serpent *b* me, Gen 3.13

BEGUILING
no one..delude..with *b* speech Col 2.4
teaching and *b* my servants Rev 2.20

BEHAVE — D — ING
know how one ought to *b* in 1Tim 3.15
we have *b* in the world, and 2Cor 1.12
and *b* like ordinary men? 1Cor 3.3
he is not *b* properly toward his 7.36

BEHAVIOR
changed his *b* before them, 1Sam 21.13
revile your good *b* in Christ 1Pet 3.16

BEHEADED
and had John *b* in the prison, Mt 14.10
"John, whom I *b*, has been Mk 6.16

BEHEMOTH
"Behold, *B*, which I made as Job 40.15

BEHOLD — ING
I..*b* thy face in righteousness Ps 17.15
Come, *b* the works of the Lord, 46.8
all the peoples *b* his glory. 97.6
pleasant for..eyes to *b*..sun. Ecc 11.7
cities of Judah, "*B* your God!" 40.9
where I am, to *b* my glory Jn 17.24
with unveiled face, *b* the glory 2Cor 3.18

BELIEVE — S — D
for he did not *b* them. Gen 45.26
"that they may *b* that the Lord, Ex 4.5
"Because you did not *b* in me, Num 20.12
you did not *b* the Lord Deut 1.32
you..did not *b* him or obey 9.23
b his prophets, and you will 2Chr 20.20
not *b* that he was listening Job 9.16
I *b*..I shall see the goodness Ps 27.13
for I *b* in thy commandments. 119.66
speaks graciously, *b*..not, Prov 26.25
If you will not *b*, surely you Isa 7.9
that you may know and *b* me 43.10
b them not, though they speak Jer 12.6
a work..that you would not *b* Hab 1.5
"Do you *b*..I am able to do Mt 9.28
'Why then did you not *b* him?' 21.25
come down..and we will *b* in him. 27.42
repent, and *b* in the gospel." Mk 1.15
said.."Do not fear, only *b*." 5.36
ask in prayer, *b* that you receive it, 11.24
there he is!' do not *b* it. 13.21
seen by her, they would not *b* 16.11n
because you did not *b* my words, Lk 1.20
no root, they *b* for a while 8.13
only *b*, and she shall be well." 8.50
'Why did you not *b* him?' 20.5
"If I tell you, you will not *b*; 22.67
to *b* all that the prophets 24.25
that all might *b* through him. Jn 1.7
he who does not *b* is condemned 3.18
we *b*, for we have heard..ourselves 4.42
If you *b* Moses, you would *b* me, 5.46
his brothers did not *b* in him. 7.5
"Do you *b* in the Son of man?" 9.35

but you do not *b*, because 10.26
even though you do not *b* me, 10.38
I was not there, so..you may *b*. 11.15
yet they did not *b* in him; 12.37
b in God, *b* also in me. 14.1
also pray..for those who *b* 17.20
truth—that you also may *b*. 19.35
hand in his side, I will not *b*." 20.25
have not seen and yet *b*." 20.29
Philip said, "If you *b* with Acts 8.37n
we *b* that we shall be saved 15.11
"*B* in the Lord Jesus, and 16.31
Agrippa, do you *b* the prophets? 26.27
faith in..Christ for all who *b*. Rom 3.22
and *b* in your heart that God 10.9
preach to save those who *b*. 1Cor 1.21
not only *b*..but also suffer Phil 1.29
would draw near to God must *b* Heb 11.6
The simple *b* everything, but Prov 14.15
who *b* will not be in haste.' Isa 28.16
All..possible to him who *b*." Mk 9.23
who *b* and is baptized will 16.16n
whoever *b*..may have eternal Jn 3.15
who hears my word and *b* him 5.24
one who *b* in him receives Acts 10.43
he who *b*..not..put to shame." Rom 9.33
"No one who *b* in him will be put 10.11
Love bears all things, *b* all 1Cor 13.7
who *b* that Jesus is the Christ 1Jn 5.1
He who *b* in the Son of God has 5.10
And he *b* the Lord; Gen 15.6
And the people *b*; and when they Ex 4.31
they *b* in the Lord and 14.31
Then they *b* his words; they Ps 106.12
Who has *b* what we have heard? Isa 53.1
done for you as you have *b*." Mt 8.13
blessed is she who *b* that Lk 1.45
they *b* the scripture and the Jn 2.22
Samaritans from that city *b* 4.39
The man *b* the word..Jesus spoke 4.50
will live"; and he himself *b*, 4.53
we have *b*, and have come to know 6.69
Yet many of the people *b* in him; 7.31
Jews..had seen what he did, *b* 11.45
also went in, and he saw and *b*; 20.8
many who heard the word *b*; Acts 4.4
throughout all Joppa, and many *b* 9.42
great number that *b* turned 11.21
Then the proconsul *b*, when 13.12
that a great company *b*, both 14.1
Many of them therefore *b*, 17.12
and *b*, among them Dionysius 17.34
ruler of the synagogue, *b* 18.8
Abraham "*b* God, and it was Gal 3.6
so that those who have *b* in God Tit 3.8

BELIEVER — S
son of a Jewish woman..a *b*; Acts 16.1
more than ever *b* were added 5.14
word of God..at work in..*b*. 1Thess 2.13

BELLY
upon your *b* you shall go, Gen 3.14
out of..*b* of Sheol I cried, Jonah 2.2

BELONG — ED
for to thee *b* all the nations! Ps 82.8
b to..him who has been raised Rom 7.4
you live as if you still *b* to Col 2.20

BELOVED
"The *b* of the Lord,..dwells Deut 33.12
he was *b* by his God, and Neh 13.26
That thy *b* may be delivered, Ps 60.5

BELOVED (cont.)

he gives to his *b* in sleep.	Ps 127.2
My *b* is to me a cluster of	Sol 1.14
My *b* is mine and I am his,	2.16
What is your *b* more than another	5.9
I am my beloved's. .my *b* is mine;	6.3
coming up. .leaning upon her *b*?	8.5
Daniel,. .greatly *b*, give heed	Dan 10.11
"This is my *b* Son, with whom	Mt 3.17
"This is my *b* Son, with whom	17.5
"Thou art my *b* Son; with thee	Mk 1.11
"This is my *b* Son; listen to him."	9.7
a *b* son; finally he sent him	12.6
"Thou art my *b* Son; with thee	Lk 3.22
not *b* I will call 'my *b*.' "	Rom 9.25
b for. .sake of. .forefathers.	11.28
Greet Ampliatus, my *b* in the	16.8
freely bestowed on us in the *B*.	Eph 1.6
who benefit. .believers and *b*.	1Tim 6.2
"This is my *b* Son, with whom	2Pet 1.17
you, *b*, build yourselves up	Jude 20

BELT — S

looses the *b* of the strong.	Job 12.21
no bag, no money in their *b*;	Mk 6.8

BENEFIT — S

I say this for your own *b*,	1Cor 7.35
and forget not all his *b*,	Ps 103.2

BEN-HADAD I

King of Syria, 1Ki 15.18; made alliance with Asa, 1Ki 15.19; ravaged cities in northern Israel, 1Ki 15.20–21 (see also 2Chr 16.1–6).

BEN-HADAD II

King of Syria, 1Ki 20.1; besieged Samaria, 1Ki 20.1; defeated twice by Ahab, 1Ki 20.2–30; granted conditions of peace, 1Ki 20.31–34.

BEN-HADAD III

King of Syria, 2Ki 13.3,24; oppressed cities of Israel, 2Ki 13.3–13; defeated by Jehoahaz, king of Israel, 2Ki 13.22–25.

BENJAMIN (Son of Jacob)

Born, Gen 35.16–18; brought to Egypt, Gen 43; accused of theft but interceded for by Judah, Gen 44; blessed by Jacob, Gen 49.27.
Tribe of Benjamin: blessed by Moses, Deut 33.12; allotted its territory, Josh 18.11–28; decimated almost to extinction, Judg 20; rebuilt through new wives and families, Judg 21; Saul, the first king of Israel, and Paul, the apostle, from this tribe, 1Sam 9.1; Phil 3.5.

BEREAVE — D

b them till none is left.	Hos 9.12
"You have *b* me of. .children:	Gen 42.36
have *b* them, I have destroyed	Jer 15.7

BESEECH

"Remember now, O Lord, I *b*	2Ki 20.3
"We *b* thee, O Lord, let us	Jonah 1.14
We *b* you on behalf of Christ,	2Cor 5.20
Brethren, I *b* you, become as	Gal 4.12

BESET

They *b* me with words of hate,	Ps 109.3
Thou dost *b* me behind and	139.5

BESIDE

He leads me *b* still waters;	Ps 23.2
they said, "He is *b* himself."	Mk 3.21

BESIEGE — D

then you shall *b* it;	Deut 20.12
b you in all your towns,	28.52
if their enemies *b* them	2Chr 6.28
a great king came. .and *b* it,	Ecc 9.14
cucumber field, like a *b* city.	Isa 1.8
city. .*b* till the eleventh year	Jer 52.5

BESTIR

B thyself, and awake for my	Ps 35.23
Let. .nations *b* themselves,	Joel 3.12

BESTOWED

understand the gifts *b* on us	1Cor 2.12
grace which he freely *b* on us	Eph 1.6

BETHANY

went. .to *B* and lodged there.	Mt 21.17
at *B* in. .house of Simon the leper,	26.6
and *B*, at the mount. .Olivet,	Lk 19.29
led them out as far as *B*,	24.50
a. .man was ill, Lazarus of *B*,	Jn 11.1
Jesus came to *B*, where Lazarus	12.1

BETHEL

mountain on the east of *B*,	Gen 12.8
I am the God of *B*,	31.13
and lay between *B* and Ai,	Josh 8.9
circuit year by year to *B*,	1Sam 7.16
And he set one in *B*, and	1Ki 12.29
dwelt an old prophet in *B*.	13.11
The men of *B* and Ai, two	Ezra 2.28
"Come to *B*, and transgress;	Amos 4.4
Amaziah the priest of *B* sent	7.10
never again prophesy at *B*,	7.13

BETHLEHEM

way to Ephrath (that is, *B*),	Gen 35.19
on until they came to *B*.	Ruth 1.19
commanded, and came to *B*.	1Sam 16.4
his father's sheep at *B*.	17.15
water out of the well of *B*	2Sam 23.16
But you, O *B* Ephrathah, who	Mic 5.2
Now when Jesus was born in *B* of	Mt 2.1
you, O *B*, in the land of Judah,	2.6
city of David,. .called *B*,	Lk 2.4
from David, and comes from *B*,	Jn 7.42

BETH-SAIDA

woe to you, *B*! for if the	Mt 11.21
disciples. .go before him. .to *B*,	Mk 6.45
And they came to *B*. And some	8.22
withdrew. .to a city called *B*.	Lk 9.10

BETRAY — ED — ING

sought. .opportunity to *b* him.	Mt 26.16
he sought an opportunity to *b*	Mk 14.11
"Truly. .one of you will *b* me,	14.18
how he might *b* him to them.	Lk 22.4
he knew who was to *b* him;	Jn 13.11
by whom the Son of man is *b*!	Mt 26.24
Son of man is *b* into the hands	26.45
Judas Iscariot, who *b* him.	Mk 3.19
the Son of man is *b* into	14.41
Judas, who *b* him, also knew	Jn 18.2
when he was *b* took bread,	1Cor 11.23
"I have sinned in *b* innocent	Mt 27.4

BETROTH — ED

I will *b* you to me for ever;	Hos 2.19
seduces a virgin who is not *b*,	Ex 22.16
b a wife and has not taken	Deut 20.7
Mary had been *b* to Joseph,	Mt 1.18
to a virgin *b* to a man whose	Lk 1.27
to be enrolled with Mary, his *b*,	2.5
I *b* you to Christ to present	2Cor 11.2

BETTER
am I *b* off than if I..sinned?   Job 35.3
nothing *b*..than to be happy   Ecc 3.12
but in humility count others *b*   Phil 2.3
the covenant he mediates is *b*,   Heb 8.6
with *b* sacrifices than these.   9.23

BEWAILING
all were weeping and *b* her;   Lk 8.52

BEWARE
My son, *b* of anything beyond   Ecc 12.12
"*B* of false prophets, who come   Mt 7.15
b of the leaven of..Pharisees   16.6
"Take heed, *b* of the leaven of   Mk 8.15
"*B* of the scribes, who like   12.38

BID
do you want us to *b* fire come   Lk 9.54
I now *b* you take heart;   Acts 27.22

BIND — S
B them upon your heart   Prov 6.21
I will *b* up the crippled,   Ezek 34.16
whatever you *b* on earth shall   Mt 16.19
whatever you *b* on earth   18.18
He *b* up the waters in..clouds,   Job 26.8
He heals..*b* up their wounds.   Ps 147.3

BIRD — S — 'S
how can you say.."Flee like a *b*   Ps 11.1
I am like a lonely *b* on the   102.7
escaped as a *b* from the snare   124.7
a net..in the sight of any *b*;   Prov 1.17
like a speckled *b* of prey?   Jer 12.9
Does a *b* fall in a snare   Amos 3.5
let *b* fly above the earth   Gen 1.20
Like *b* hovering, so the LORD   Isa 31.5
and *b* of the air have nests;   Mt 8.20
b of the air come and make nests   13.32
so..*b* of the air can make nests   Mk 4.32
and *b* of the air have nests;   Lk 9.58
the *b* of the air made nests in   13.19
you..come upon a *b* nest,   Deut 22.6

BIRTH
forgot..God who gave you *b*.   Deut 32.18
Your origin and your *b* are of   Ezek 16.3
the *b* of Jesus..took place in   Mt 1.18

BIRTHRIGHT
"First sell me your *b*."   Gen 25.31
He took away my *b*;   27.36
according to his *b*   43.33

BISHOP — S
aspires to the office of *b*,   1Tim 3.1
a *b*, as God's steward, must   Tit 1.7
at Philippi, with the *b* and   Phil 1.1

BIT
will put my *b* in your mouth,   2Ki 19.28
and my *b* in your mouth,   Isa 37.29

BITTER
made life *b* for Isaac   Gen 26.35
is your doom, and it is *b*;   Jer 4.18
it will be *b* to your stomach,   Rev 10.9

BITTERNESS
shall have the water of *b*   Num 5.18
speak in the *b* of my soul.   Job 10.1
Another dies in *b* of soul,   21.25
The heart knows its own *b*,   Prov 14.10

BLADE
first the *b*, then the ear,   Mk 4.28

BLAME
then let me bear the *b*   Gen 43.9
then I shall bear the *b*   44.32
that no one should *b* us   2Cor 8.20

BLAMELESS
b in his generation; Noah   Gen 6.9
walk before me, and be *b*.   17.1
rest of you shall be *b*."   44.10
be *b* before the LORD   Deut 18.13
the heart of Asa was *b* all   2Chr 15.17
whose heart is *b* toward him.   16.9
Job..was *b* and upright,   Job 1.1
God will not reject a *b* man,   8.20
though I am *b*, he would prove   9.20
With the *b*..thou dost show..*b*; Ps 18.25
Mark the *b* man, and behold the   37.37
Blessed are those whose way is *b*,   119.1
May my heart be *b* in thy   119.80
You were *b* in your ways   Ezek 28.15
in..ordinances of the Lord *b*.   Lk 1.6
righteousness under..law *b*.   Phil 3.6

BLASPHEME — S — D — ING
and tried to make them *b*;   Acts 26.11
whoever *b* against the..Spirit   Mk 3.29
Israelite woman's son *b*   Lev 24.11
again your fathers *b* me,   Ezek 20.27
"The name of God is *b* among   Rom 2.24
I formerly *b* and persecuted   1Tim 1.13
to themselves, "This man is *b*."   Mt 9.3
b his name and his dwelling,   Rev 13.6

BLASPHEMOUS
b words against Moses and   Acts 6.11
and a *b* name upon its heads.   Rev 13.1

BLASPHEMY — IES
sin and *b* will be forgiven   Mt 12.31
"He has uttered *b*. Why do we   26.65
You have heard his *b*. What   Mk 14.64
for no good work but for *b*;   Jn 10.33
"Who is this that speaks *b*?   Lk 5.21

BLEMISH
None..who has a *b* may   Lev 21.17
in which there is no *b*,   Num 19.2
lambs a year old without *b*,   28.3
there was no *b* in him.   2Sam 14.25
youths without *b*, handsome   Dan 1.4

BLESS — ES — ED — ING (v)
and I will *b* you,   Gen 12.2
nations..shall *b* themselves by him? 18.18
I will indeed *b* you,   22.17
all..nations of the earth *b*   22.18
I may *b* you before I die."   27.4
not..go, unless you *b* me."   32.26
by God Almighty who will *b* you   49.25
The LORD *b* you and keep you: Num 6.24
will love you, *b* you,   Deut 7.13
stand upon Mount Gerizim to *b*   27.12
willingly, *b* the LORD!   Judg 5.2
answered, "The LORD *b* you."   Ruth 2.4
thou wouldst *b* me and enlarge 1Chr 4.10
please thee to *b* the house   17.27
"Stand up and *b* the LORD   Neh 9.5
LORD *b* his people with peace!   Ps 29.11
I will *b* the LORD at all times;   34.1
B our God, O peoples, let the   66.8
B the LORD, O my soul; and   103.1
From this day on I will *b* you." Hag 2.19
B those who persecute you;   Rom 12.14
When reviled, we *b*; when   1Cor 4.12
"Surely I will *b* you and   Heb 6.14

BLESS — ES — ED — ING (v) (cont.)

he who *b* himself in the land	Isa 65.16
And God *b* them, saying,	Gen 1.22
God *b* Noah and his sons,	9.1
LORD had *b* Abraham in all things.	24.1
said, "*B* be the LORD,	24.27
b be every one who blesses you!"	27.29
LORD *b* the Egyptian's house	39.5
and Jacob *b* Pharaoh.	47.7
the people, for they are *b*."	Num 22.12
b, and I cannot revoke it.	23.20
B be every one who blesses	24.9
Moses the man of God *b* the	Deut 33.1
since. .the LORD has *b* me?"	Josh 17.14
tent-dwelling women most *b*.	Judg 5.24
boy grew, and the LORD *b* him.	13.24
B be the man who took notice	Ruth 2.19
the LORD *b* Obededom and all	2Sam 6.11
"*B* be the LORD who has given	1Ki 8.56
b the household of Obededom	1Chr 13.14
B be the LORD, the God of	16.36
for there they *b* the LORD;	2Chr 20.26
b be the name of the LORD."	Job 1.21
LORD *b* the latter days of Job	42.12
B is the man who walks not in	Ps 1.1
B is he whose transgression is	32.1
B is he who considers the poor!	41.1
B is the man who fears. .LORD	Prov 28.14
children rise up and call her *b*;	31.28
b are all. .who wait for him.	Isa 30.18
people whom the LORD has *b*.	61.9
"*B* is the man who trusts in	Jer 17.7
Daniel *b* the God of heaven.	Dan 2.19
we deem the arrogant *b*;	Mal 3.15
"*B* are the poor in spirit,	Mt 5.3
b are your eyes, for they see,	13.16
he. .*b*, and broke. .the loaves	14.19
B is he who comes in the name	21.9
B is that servant whom his	24.46
and *b* them, laying his hands	Mk 10.16
"Hosanna! *B* is he who comes	11.9
"*B* are you among women, and *b*	Lk 1.42
"*B* be the Lord God of Israel,	1.68
him up in his arms and *b* God	2.28
"*B* are you poor, for yours is	6.20
"*B* are the eyes which see	10.23
"*B* is the womb that bore you,	11.27
awake. .*b* are those servants!	12.38
'*B* is he who comes in the name	13.35
"*B* is the King who comes in	19.38
lifting up his hands. .*b* them.	24.50
b are you if you do them.	Jn 13.17
B are those who have not seen	20.29
more *b* to give than to	Acts 20.35
God who is over all be *b* for	Rom 9.5
shall all the nations be *b*."	Gal 3.8
who has *b* us in Christ with	Eph 1.3
if you suffer. .you will be *b*.	1Pet 3.14
"Write this: *B* are the dead	Rev 14.13
B is he who keeps the words	22.7
B are those who wash their robes,	22.14
loosed, and he spoke, *b* God.	Lk 1.64
continually in the temple *b*	24.53
same mouth come *b* and cursing.	Jas 3.10

BLESSED (n)

'Come, O *b* of my Father, inherit	Mt 25.34
Christ, the Son of the *B*?"	Mk 14.61

BLESSING — S (n)

I will command my *b* upon you	Lev 25.21
before you this day a *b*	Deut 11.26
turned the curse into a *b*	23.5

words of the law, the *b*	Josh 8.34
b of the LORD makes rich,	Prov 10.22
By the *b* of the upright a	11.11
b in the midst of the earth,	Isa 19.24
they shall be showers of *b*.	Ezek 34.26
a *b* may rest on your house.	44.30
pour down. .an overflowing *b*.	Mal 3.10
fulness of the *b* of Christ.	Rom 15.29
The cup of *b* which we bless,	1Cor 10.16
all these *b* shall come	Deut 28.2
dost meet him with goodly *b*;	Ps 21.3
holy and sure *b* of David.'	Acts 13.34

BLIND — S — ED (v)

bribe to *b* my eyes with it?	1Sam 12.3
for a bribe *b* the eyes	Deut 16.19
god of this world has *b* the	2Cor 4.4
the darkness has *b* his eyes.	1Jn 2.11

BLIND (n)

as the *b* grope in darkness,	Deut 28.29
lame and the *b*, who are hated	2Sam 5.8
I was eyes to the *b*, and	Job 29.15
LORD opens the eyes of the *b*.	Ps 146.8
the eyes of the *b* shall see.	Isa 29.18
eyes of the *b* shall be opened,	35.5
I will lead the *b* in a way	42.16
grope for. .wall like the *b*,	59.10
the *b* receive their sight	Mt 11.5
the lame, the maimed, the *b*,	15.30
recovering of sight to the *b*,	Lk 4.18
invite the poor,. .the *b*,	14.13
demon open the eyes of the *b*?"	Jn 10.21
a guide to the *b*, a light	Rom 2.19

BLIND (adj)

to open the eyes that are *b*,	Isa 42.7
or *b* as the servant of the LORD?	42.19
people who are *b*, yet have eyes,	43.8
His watchmen are *b*, they	56.10
wandered, *b*, through. .streets,	Lam 4.14
offer *b* animals in sacrifice,	Mal 1.8
two *b* men followed him, crying	Mt 9.27
b and dumb demoniac. .brought	12.22
Let them alone; they are *b*	15.14
two *b* men. .by the roadside,	20.30
"Woe to you, *b* guides, who	23.16
people brought to him a *b* man,	Mk 8.22
And the *b* man said to him,	10.51
"Can a *b* man lead a *b* man?	Lk 6.39
on many. .*b* he bestowed sight.	7.21
b man. .sitting by the roadside	18.35
he saw a man *b* from his birth.	Jn 9.1
this. .our son. .was born *b*;	9.20
though I was *b*, now I see."	9.25
those who see may become *b*."	9.39
lacks these things is *b* and	2Pet 1.9
pitiable, poor, *b*, and naked.	Rev 3.17

BLINDNESS

struck with *b* the men	Gen 19.11
"Strike this people. .with *b*."	2Ki 6.18
strike every horse. .with *b*.	Zech 12.4

BLOOD

your brother's *b* is crying	Gen 4.10
not eat flesh with. .its *b*.	9.4
Whoever sheds the *b* of man,	9.6
a reckoning for his *b*."	42.22
Nile. .shall be turned to *b*,	Ex 7.17
took the *b* of the covenant	24.8
part of the *b* of the bull	29.12
some of the *b* of the bull,	Lev 16.14
the *b* that makes atonement,	17.11
you shall not eat the *b*;	Deut 12.16

BLOOD (cont.)

people ate them with the b.	1Sam 14.32
turned their waters into b,	Ps 105.29
his b I. . require at your hand.	Ezek 3.18
shedding. . b of the prophets.'	Mt 23.30
from the b of innocent Abel to	23.35
this is my b of the covenant,	26.28
"I am innocent of this man's b;	27.24
a flow of b for twelve years,	Mk 5.25
"This is my b of the covenant,	14.24
from the b of Abel to the b of	Lk 11.51
the new covenant in my b	22.20n
Son of man and drink his b,	Jn 6.53
was called. . Field of B.)	Acts 1.19
"Your b be upon your heads!	18.6
we are now justified by his b,	Rom 5.9
flesh and b cannot inherit	1Cor 15.50
have redemption through his b,	Eph 1.7
brought near in the b of Christ.	2.13
and not without taking b	Heb 9.7
but his own b, thus securing	9.12
enter. . sanctuary by. . b of Jesus	10.19
profaned the b of the covenant	10.29
with. . precious b of Christ,	1Pet 1.19
the b of Jesus his Son cleanses	1Jn 1.7
but with the water and the b.	5.6
white in the b of the Lamb.	Rev 7.14
waters to turn them into b,	11.6
conquered. . by the b of the Lamb	12.11
avenged on her the b of his	19.2

BLOODSHED

for justice, but behold, b;	Isa 5.7
keeps back his sword from b.	Jer 48.10

BLOT — S — TED

if not, b me,. . out of thy book	Ex 32.32
and b out their name from	Deut 9.14
b out the remembrance	25.19
Lord would b out his name	29.20
he would b out the name of	2Ki 14.27
mercy b out my transgressions.	Ps 51.1
b out their sin from. . sight.	Jer 18.23
who b out your transgressions	Isa 43.25
not. . sin of. . mother be b out!	Ps 109.14
that your sins may be b out,	Acts 3.19

BLOW

When you b an alarm,	Num 10.5
south wind! B upon my garden,	Sol 4.16

BOAST — S — ED (v)

we b of the name of the Lord	Ps 20.7
not rejoice over me, who b	38.16
Do not b about tomorrow,	Prov 27.1
and b of your relation to God	Rom 2.17
You who b in the law, do you	2.23
do not b over the branches.	11.18
So let no one b of men.	1Cor 3.21
I also dare to b of that.	2Cor 11.21
works, lest any man should b.	Eph 2.9
Let the lowly brother b in	Jas 1.9
the wicked b of the desires	Ps 10.3
buyer. . goes away, then he b.	Prov 20.14
b of a gift he does not give.	25.14
"Let him who b, b of. . Lord."	1Cor 1.31
"Let him who b, b of. . Lord."	2Cor 10.17
In God we have b continually,	Ps 44.8

BOAST — ING (n)

My soul makes its b in. . Lord;	Ps 34.2
this b of mine shall not	2Cor 11.10
Then what becomes of our b?	Rom 3.27
b before Titus. . proved true.	2Cor 7.14
proof. . of your love and of our b	8.24

BOAT

left the b and their father,	Mt 4.22
told his disciples to have a b	Mk 3.9
into a b with his disciples,	Lk 8.22
immediately the b was at. . land	Jn 6.21

BODILY

Spirit descended. . in b form,	Lk 3.22
it was because of a b ailment	Gal 4.13
fulness of deity dwells b,	Col 2.9

BODY — IES

took the b of Saul and the	1Sam 31.12
kill. . b but cannot kill. . soul;	Mt 10.28
Wherever the b is, there the eagles	24.28
"Take, eat; this is my b."	26.26
asked for the b of Jesus.	27.58
they came and took his b,	Mk 6.29
said, "Take; this is my b."	14.22
asked for the b of Jesus.	15.43
them, saying, "This is my b.	Lk 22.19
spoke of the temple of his b.	Jn 2.21
in one b we have many members,	Rom 12.4
b is not meant for immorality,	1Cor 6.13
your b is a temple of the. . Spirit	6.19
For just as the b is one	12.12
God has so adjusted the b,	12.24
Now you are the b of Christ	12.27
With what. . b do they come?"	15.35
on my b the marks of Jesus.	Gal 6.17
the church, which is his b,	Eph 1.23
There is one b and one Spirit,	4.4
the whole b, joined and knit	4.16
we are members of his b.	5.30
change our lowly b to be like	Phil 3.21
He is the head of the b,	Col 1.18
Head, from whom the whole b,	2.19
a b hast thou prepared for me;	Heb 10.5
the putting off of my b. . soon,	2Pet 1.14
disputed about the b of Moses,	Jude 9
nothing left. . but our b and	Gen 47.18
these were all dead b.	Isa 37.36
your b are members of Christ?	1Cor 6.15
dead b will lie in the street	Rev 11.8

BOG

He drew me. . out of the miry b,	Ps 40.2

BOIL — ED (v)

not b a kid in its mother's	Deut 14.21
we b my son, and ate him.	2Ki 6.29

BOILS (n)

dust. . become b breaking out	Ex 9.9
smite you with. . b of Egypt,	Deut 28.27

BOLD — NESS

wicked man puts on a b face,	Prov 21.29
such a hope, we are very b,	2Cor 3.12
are much more b to speak	Phil 1.14
saw the b of Peter and John,	Acts 4.13
speak thy word with all b,	4.29
Lord, in whom we have b and	Eph 3.12

BOND — S

the Spirit in the b of peace.	Eph 4.3
not despise his own. . in b.	Ps 69.33
loose the b of wickedness,	Isa 58.6

BONDAGE

out of the house of b.	Ex 20.2
out of the house of b.	Deut 5.6
were subject to lifelong b.	Heb 2.15

BONE — S

nor break a b of it;	Num 9.12
we are your b and flesh.	1Chr 11.1

BONE — S (cont.)
"Not a *b* of him. .be broken."   Jn 19.36
you shall carry up my *b*   Gen 50.25
Moses took the *b* of Joseph   Ex 13.19
The *b* of Joseph which the   Josh 24.32
man touched the *b* of Elisha,   2Ki 13.21
I can count all my *b*—they   Ps 22.17
He keeps all his *b*; not one   34.20
the *b* of the kings of Judah,   Jer 8.1
b came together, *b* to its *b*.   Ezek 37.7

BOOK — S
took the *b* of the covenant,   Ex 24.7
the *B* of the Wars of the Lord   Num 21.14
write for himself in a *b*   Deut 17.18
"Take this *b* of the law,   31.26
This *b* of the law shall not   Josh 1.8
the *b* of the law of Moses,   8.31
found the *b* of the law in the   2Ki 22.8
words of the *b* of the covenant   23.2
brought the *b* to the king,   2Chr 34.16
I found the *b* of the genealogy   Neh 7.5
bring the *b* of the law of Moses   8.1
were inscribed in a *b*!   Job 19.23
in thy *b* were written,. .days   Ps 139.16
words of a *b* that is sealed.   Isa 29.11
inscribe it in a *b*, that it   30.8
read from the *b* of the LORD: 34.16
everything written in this *b*,   Jer 25.13
Jeremiah wrote in a *b* all   51.60
inscribed in the *b* of truth: Dan 10.21
whose name. .written in the *b*.   12.1
a *b* of remembrance was written   Mal 3.16
The *b* of the genealogy of Jesus   Mt 1.1
The *b* of the prophet Isaiah.   Lk 4.17
signs. .not written in this *b*;   Jn 20.30
names are in the *b* of life.   Phil 4.3
sprinkled both the *b* itself   Heb 9.19
"Write what you see in a *b*   Rev 1.11
not blot his name out of the *b*   3.5
in the *b* of life of the Lamb   13.8
Also another *b* was opened,   20.12
in the Lamb's *b* of life.   21.27
Of making many *b*. .is no end,   Ecc 12.12
in judgment,. .*b* were opened.   Dan 7.10
in the *b* the number of years   9.2
could not contain the *b* that   Jn 21.25
brought their *b*. .and burned   Acts 19.19
also the *b*, and above all   2Tim 4.13

BOOTH — S
I will raise. .the *b* of David   Amos 9.11
made a *b* for himself there.   Jonah 4.5
Jacob. .made *b* for his cattle   Gen 33.17
the feast of *b* to the LORD.   Lev 23.34
dwell in *b* for seven days;   23.42
feast of *b* seven days,   Deut 16.13
Israel should dwell in *b*   Neh 8.14
I will make three *b* here, one   Mt 17.4
let us make three *b*, one for you   Mk 9.5
"Master,. .let us make three *b*,   Lk 9.33

BOOTY
b remaining of the spoil   Num 31.32
men of war had taken *b*,   31.53

BORE
many *b* false witness against   Mk 14.56
God also *b* witness by signs   Heb 2.4
He himself *b* our sins in   1Pet 2.24

BORN
be *b* to the house of David,   1Ki 13.2
Man. .*b* of woman. .of few days,   Job 14.1
who is *b* of woman be clean?   25.4

time to be *b*,. .a time to die;   Ecc 3.2
For to us a child is *b*, to us   Isa 9.6
before. .*b* I consecrated you;   Jer 1.5
Mary, of whom Jesus was *b*,   Mt 1.16
when Jesus was *b* in Bethlehem   2.1
among those *b* of women. .no one   11.11
child. .*b* will be called holy,   Lk 1.35
who were *b*, not of blood nor   Jn 1.13
unless one is *b* anew, he cannot   3.3
"You were *b* in utter sin,   9.34
for joy that a child is *b*   16.21
You have been *b* anew, not of   1Pet 1.23
No one *b* of God commits sin;   1Jn 3.9
one *b* of God does not sin,   5.18

BORROW — S
"Go outside, *b* vessels of all   2Ki 4.3
do not refuse him who would *b*   Mt 5.42
The wicked *b*, and cannot pay   Ps 37.21

BORROWER
b is. .slave of the lender.   Prov 22.7
the lender, so with the *b*;   Isa 24.2

BOSOM
Can a man carry fire in his *b*   Prov 6.27
he will carry them in his *b*,   Isa 40.11
Son. .in the *b* of the Father,   Jn 1.18

BOTHER — S
'Do not *b* me; the door is now   Lk 11.7
because this widow *b* me, I   18.5

BOTTLE
gathered. .waters of the sea in. .*b*;   Ps 3.7
put thou my tears in thy *b*!   56.8

BOUGH — S
Joseph is a fruitful *b*,   Gen 49.22
its *b* will be broken in   Ezek 31.12

BOUGHT
have *b* from the hand of Naomi   Ruth 4.9
I have *b* to be my wife,   4.10
have *b* back our Jewish brethren   Neh 5.8
I *b* her for fifteen shekels   Hos 3.2
you were *b* with a price.   1Cor 6.20
You were *b* with a price;   7.23
denying the Master who *b* them,   2Pet 2.1

BOUND (v)
his life is *b* up in the lad's   Gen 44.30
Are you *b* to a wife? Do not   1Cor 7.27
is *b* to keep the whole law.   Gal 5.3

BOUNDS (n)
he fixed the *b* of the peoples   Deut 32.8
fixed all the *b* of the earth.   Ps 74.17

BOUNTY
crownest the year with thy *b*;   Ps 65.11
LORD for all his *b* to me?   116.12

BOW — ED — ING (v)
father's sons shall *b*   Gen 49.8
not *b* down to their gods,   Ex 23.24
not *b* down to them or serve   Deut 5.9
not *b* down to a foreign god.   Ps 81.9
All the nations. .shall. .*b* down   86.9
b. .to the host of the heavens;   Zeph 1.5
of Jesus every knee should *b*,   Phil 2.10
and *b* down before your feet,   Rev 3.9
maids. .their children. .*b* down;   Gen 33.6
Joseph's brothers came,. .*b*   42.6
And they *b* their heads   43.28
that have not *b* to Baal,   1Ki 19.18
who is *b* down shall speedily   Isa 51.14
he *b* his head and gave up his   Jn 19.30
fell at his feet, *b* to the ground;   2Ki 4.37

BOW (n)

I set my *b* in the cloud,	Gen 9.13
an expert with the *b*.	21.20
For not in my *b* do I trust,	Ps 44.6
he breaks the *b*, and shatters	46.9
I will break the *b* of Israel	Hos 1.5

BOWL — S

new *b*, and put salt in it."	2Ki 2.20
seven *b* of the wrath of God."	Rev 16.1

BOY — S

Josiah..was yet a *b*, he began	2Chr 34.3
I will make *b* their princes,	Isa 3.4
city..of *b* and girls playing	Zech 8.5

BRANCH — ES

In that day the *b* of the LORD	Isa 4.2
a *b* shall grow..of his roots.	11.1
raise..for David a righteous *B*,	Jer 23.5
cause a righteous *B* to spring	33.15
I will bring my servant the *B*.	Zech 3.8
Every *b* of mine that bears no	Jn 15.2
and others spread leafy *b*	Mk 11.8
they took *b* of palm trees	Jn 12.13
do not boast over the *b*.	Rom 11.18

BREACH

"For every *b* of trust,	Ex 22.9
there was no *b* left in it	Neh 6.1
Moses,..stood in the *b*	Ps 106.23
stand in the *b* before me	Ezek 22.30

BREAD

I will rain *b* from heaven	Ex 16.4
man does not live by *b* alone,	Deut 8.3
but the *b* of the Presence,	1Sam 21.6
they eat the *b* of wickedness	Prov 4.17
blessed, for he shares his *b*	22.9
Cast your *b* upon the waters,	Ecc 11.1
taking away..whole stay of *b*,	Isa 3.1
loaf of *b* was given him daily	Jer 37.21
they may lack *b* and water,	Ezek 4.17
stones to become loaves of *b*."	Mt 4.3
he..ate the *b* of the Presence,	12.4
not fair to take..children's *b*	15.26
"Where are we to get *b* enough	15.33
Jesus took *b*, and blessed,	26.26
not right to take..children's *b*	Mk 7.27
can one feed these men with *b*	8.4
he took *b*, and blessed, and	14.22
command this stone to become *b*."	Lk 4.3
he took *b*, and when he had	22.19
he took the *b* and blessed,	24.30
not Moses who gave you the *b*	Jn 6.32
"I am the *b* of life; he who	6.35
Jesus came and took the *b*	21.13
when we..gathered..to break *b*,	Acts 20.7
The *b* which we break, is	1Cor 10.16
he was betrayed took *b*,	11.23

BREAK — ING

nor *b* a bone of it;	Num 9.12
shall *b* down their altars,	Deut 7.5
shall we *b* thy commandments	Ezra 9.14
So will I *b* this people and	Jer 19.11
If you can *b* my covenant	33.20
they did not *b* his legs.	Jn 19.33
have..code..but *b* the law.	Rom 2.27
weeping and *b* my heart?	Acts 21.13

BREASTPLATE

put on righteousness as a *b*,	Isa 59.17
put on the *b* of righteousness,	Eph 6.14
put on the *b* of faith and	1Thess 5.8

BREASTS

Your two *b* are like two fawns,	Sol 4.5
Beat upon your *b* for the	Isa 32.12

BREATH

the *b* of the Almighty, that	Job 32.8
LORD, at the blast of the *b* of	Ps 18.15
made,..by the *b* of his mouth.	33.6
Men of low estate are but a *b*,	62.9
thoughts of man,..are but a *b*.	94.11
Man is like a *b*, his days	144.4
b departs he returns to his earth;	146.4
They all have the same *b*,	Ecc 3.19
the *b* of his lips..shall slay	Isa 11.4
fades, when the *b* of the LORD	40.7
bones:..I..cause *b* to enter	Ezek 37.5
prophesy,..and say to the *b*,	37.9
b to the image of the beast	Rev 13.15

BREATHE — S — D — ING

and they *b* out violence.	Ps 27.12
Let everything that *b* praise	150.6
and *b* into his nostrils..life;	Gen 2.7
Saul, still *b* threats and	Acts 9.1

BRETHREN

my *b* who went up with me	Josh 14.8
to battle against our *b*	Judg 20.23
let us send abroad to our *b*	1Chr 13.2
or fight against your *b*.	2Chr 11.4
but you even sell your *b*	Neh 5.8
My *b* are treacherous as a	Job 6.15
put my *b* far from me,	19.13
will tell of thy name to my *b*;	Ps 22.22
become a stranger to my *b*,	69.8
one teacher, and you are all *b*.	Mt 23.8
these my *b*, you did to me.'	25.40
tell my *b* to go to Galilee,	28.10
The saying spread..among the *b*	Jn 21.23
you are *b*, why do you wrong	Acts 7.26
when..*b* knew..they sent him	9.30
send relief to..*b* in Judea;	11.29
gave great joy to all the *b*.	15.3
needs were supplied by the *b*	2Cor 11.9
not ashamed to call them *b*,	Heb 2.11
life, because we love the *b*.	1Jn 3.14

BRIBE — S

trustworthy and who hate a *b*;	Ex 18.21
a *b* blinds the officials,	23.8
you shall not take a *b*,	Deut 16.19
whose hand have I taken a *b*	1Sam 12.3
A *b* is like a magic stone	Prov 17.8
who take a *b*, and turn aside	Amos 5.12
give judgment for a *b*,	Mic 3.11
prince and..judge ask for a *b*,	7.3
took *b* and perverted justice.	1Sam 8.3
right hands are full of *b*.	Ps 26.10
he who hates *b* will live.	Prov 15.27

BRIBERY

fire consumes the tents of *b*.	Job 15.34

BRICK — S

a *b*..portray upon it a city,	Ezek 4.1
"Come, let us make *b*,	Gen 11.3
no longer give..straw to make *b*,	Ex 5.7
"The *b* have fallen, but we	Isa 9.10

BRIDE

You..ravished my heart,..my *b*,	Sol 4.9
a *b* adorns..with her jewels.	Isa 61.10
forget..a *b* her attire?	Jer 2.32
make to cease..voice of the *b*;	7.34
present you as a pure *b* to her	2Cor 11.2

BRIDE (cont.)

prepared as a *b* adorned for	Rev 21.2
I will show you the *B*, the wife	21.9

BRIDEGROOM

"You are a *b* of blood,"	Ex 4.26
which comes forth like a *b*	Ps 19.5
mourn as long as the *b* is with	Mt 9.15
wedding guests fast while the *b*	Mk 2.19
fast while the *b* is with them?	Lk 5.34
the friend of the *b*, who stands	Jn 3.29

BRIDLE (v)

I will *b* my mouth, so long as	Ps 39.1
and does not *b* his tongue	Jas 1.26
he is..able to *b* the whole body	3.2

BRIDLE (n)

must be curbed with bit and *b*,	Ps 32.9

BRIGHT — ER

I am..the *b* morning star."	Rev 22.16
your life will be *b* then	Job 11.17
from heaven, *b* than the sun,	Acts 26.13

BRIMSTONE

the LORD reigned on Sodom..*b*	Gen 19.24
fire and *b* rained from heaven	Lk 17.29
tormented with fire and *b*	Rev 14.10
lake of fire..burns with *b*.	19.20

BRING — S

I..will *b* you back	Gen 28.15
b your father, and come.	45.19
to *b*..his soul from the Pit,	Job 33.30
b your sons in their bosom,	Isa 49.22
anointed me to *b* good tidings	61.1
b them together into the midst	Jer 21.4
"Did you *b* to me sacrifices	Amos 5.25
B..tithes into the storehouse,	Mal 3.10
not..come to *b* peace on earth;	Mt 10.34
I *b* you good news of a great	Lk 2.10
when the LORD *b* you into	Ex 13.11
God *b* him out of Egypt;	Num 24.8
feet of him who *b* good tidings,	Isa 52.7
him who *b* good tidings,	Nah 1.15
and some one *b* him back,	Jas 5.19

BROKE — N

at ease, and he *b* me asunder;	Job 16.12
he has *b* my covenant."	Gen 17.14
my plans are *b* off, the	Job 17.11
bones; not one of them is *b*.	Ps 34.20
He has *b* my strength in	102.23
act, for thy law has been *b*.	119.126
a *b* spirit who can bear?	Prov 18.14
b my covenant, and transgressed	Hos 8.1
(and scripture cannot be *b*),	Jn 10.35

BROKENHEARTED

The LORD is near to the *b*,	Ps 34.18
sent me to bind up the *b*,	Isa 61.1

BRONZE

instruments of *b* and iron.	Gen 4.22
Moses made a *b* serpent,	Num 21.9
you..a fortified wall of *b*;	Jer 15.20
its belly and thighs of *b*,	Dan 2.32

BROOD

as a hen gathers her *b* under	Mt 23.37
"You *b* of vipers! Who warned you	Lk 3.7

BROOKS

I will make them walk by *b*	Jer 31.9
the water *b* are dried up,	Joel 1.20

BROTHER — S — 'S

Cain rose up against his *b*	Gen 4.8

given your *b* a thousand pieces	20.16
he is our *b*, our own flesh."	37.27
"I am your *b*, Joseph,	45.4
"If your *b* becomes poor,	Lev 25.25
"Thus says your *b* Israel:	Num 20.14
between a man and his *b*	Deut 1.16
his neighbor, his *b*, because	15.2
Edomite, for he is your *b*;	23.7
her husband's *b* shall go in	25.5
saying, "Alas, my *b*!"	1Ki 13.30
still live? He is my *b*."	20.32
a *b* is born for adversity.	Prov 17.17
A *b* helped is like a strong city	18.19
who sticks closer than a *b*.	18.24
near than a *b* who is far	27.10
and put no trust in any *b*;	Jer 9.4
say,..every one to his *b*,	23.35
devise evil against his *b*	Zech 7.10
"Is not Esau Jacob's *b*?"	Mal 1.2
every one..angry with his *b*	Mt 5.22
B will deliver up *b* to death,	10.21
my *b*, and sister, and mother."	12.50
"If your *b* sins against you,	18.15
how often shall my *b* sin	18.21
does the will of God is my *b*,	Mk 3.35
raise up children for his *b*.	12.19
And *b* will deliver up *b* to death,	13.12
if your *b* sins, rebuke him,	Lk 17.3
hands on him he said, "*B* Saul,	Acts 9.17
Why..pass judgment on your *b*?	Rom 14.10
that makes your *b* stumble.	14.21
who bears the name of *b* if	1Cor 5.11
b goes to law against *b*,	6.6
sending the *b* who is famous	2Cor 8.18
except James the Lord's *b*.	Gal 1.19
wrong his *b* in this matter,	1Thess 4.6
enemy, but warn him as a *b*.	2Thess 3.15
a beloved *b*, especially to me	Philem 16
he who hates his *b* is in the	1Jn 2.11
sees his *b* in need, yet closes	3.17
"I love God," and hates his *b*,	4.20
his *b* were jealous of him,	Gen 37.11
Judah, your *b* shall praise you;	49.8
at Ophrah, and slew his *b*	Judg 9.5
went and greeted his *b*.	1Sam 17.22
Judah became strong among..*b*	1Chr 5.2
pledges of your *b* for nothing,	Job 22.6
man who sows discord among *b*.	Prov 6.19
his mother and his *b* stood	Mt 12.46
are not his *b* James and Joseph	13.55
were indignant at the two *b*.	20.24
mother and..*b* are..outside,	Lk 8.20
his *b* did not believe in him.	Jn 7.5
made himself known to his *b*,	Acts 7.13
until your *b* anger turns	Gen 27.45
kingdom has..become my *b*,	1Ki 2.15
speck that is in your *b* eye,	Lk 6.41

BROUGHT

Moses *b* their case before	Num 27.5
Andrew..*b* him to Jesus..Simon	Jn 1.42

BRUISE — D

he shall *b* your head,	Gen 3.15
a *b* reed he will not break,	Isa 42.3

BUCKET

nations are..drop from a *b*,	Isa 40.15

BUILD — S — ING (v)

to *b* the house of the LORD.	1Ki 6.1
He shall *b* a house for me,	1Chr 17.12
Arise and *b* the sanctuary	22.19
who is able to *b* him a house,	2Chr 2.6

BUILD — S — ING (v) (cont.)

"Let us rise up and *b*." Neh 2.18
shall *b* up the ancient ruins, Isa 61.4
B houses and live in them; Jer 29.5
bring wood and *b* the house, Hag 1.8
"They may *b*,..I will tear down, Mal 1.4
on this rock I...*b* my church, Mt 16.18
began to *b*, and was not able Lk 14.30
which is able to *b* you up Acts 20.32
but not all things *b* up. 1Cor 10.23
b one another up, just 1Thess 5.11
beloved, *b* yourselves up on Jude 20
Unless the LORD *b* the house, Ps 127.1
Wisdom *b* her house, but folly Prov 14.1
Woe..who *b* a town with blood, Hab 2.12
like a man *b* a house, who dug Lk 6.48
excel in *b* up the church. 1Cor 14.12
the Lord gave for *b* you up 2Cor 10.8

BUILDERS

stone which the *b* rejected Ps 118.22
stone which the *b* rejected Lk 20.17

BUILDING — S (n)

you are God's field, God's *b*. 1Cor 3.9
stones and what wonderful *b*!" Mk 13.1

BUILT

So we *b* the wall; and all Neh 4.6
Wisdom has *b* her house, she Prov 9.1
By wisdom a house is *b*, and 24.3
b houses and planted vineyards Ecc 2.4
great Babylon, which I have *b* Dan 4.30
b upon the foundation of the Eph 2.20

BULRUSHES

she took..a basket made of *b*, Ex 2.3

BULWARK — S

thou hast founded a *b* because Ps 8.2
salvation as walls and *b*. Isa 26.1
her *b* have fallen, her walls Jer 50.15

BURDEN — ED — ING (v)

I myself did not *b* you? 2Cor 12.13
we might not *b* any of you. 2Thess 3.8
you have *b* me with your sins, Isa 43.24
not..others..eased and you *b*, 2Cor 8.13
I..will refrain from *b* you 11.9

BURDEN — S (n)

thou dost lay the *b* of all Num 11.11
the *b* is too heavy for me. 11.14
they weigh like a *b* too heavy Ps 38.4
Cast your *b* on the LORD, and 55.22
the yoke of his *b* and the staff Isa 9.4
in that day his *b* will depart 10.27
not bear a *b* on the sabbath Jer 17.21
'What is the *b* of the LORD?' 23.33
the *b* is..man's own word, 23.36
yoke is easy,..my *b* is light." Mt 11.30
equal to us who have..the *b* 20.12
no greater *b* than these Acts15.28
not lay upon you any other *b*; Rev 2.24
and looked on their *b*; Ex 2.11
They bind heavy *b*, hard to bear, Mt 23.4
load men with *b* hard to bear, Lk 11.46
Bear one another's *b*, Gal 6.2

BURN — ED — ING

urged..king not to *b*..scroll, Jer 36.25
"Did not our hearts *b* within Lk 24.32
the mountain *b* with fire Deut 4.11
and he *b* Hazor with fire. Josh 11.11
He even *b* his son as an 2Ki 16.3
mused, the fire *b*; then I spoke Ps 39.3

Chaldeans *b* the king's house Jer 39.8
he *b* the house of the LORD, 52.13
he has *b* like a flaming fire Lam 2.3
Gather the weeds..to be *b*, Mt 13.30
If any man's work is *b* up, 1Cor 3.15
deliver my body to be *b*, 13.3
books together and *b* them Acts 19.19
a *b* fire shut up in my bones, Jer 20.9
my loins are filled with *b*, Ps 38.7

BURNT OFFERING — S

where is the lamb for a *b*..?" Gen 22.7
it is a *b*..to the LORD; Ex 29.18
"If his offering is a *b*..from Lev 1.3
is on the fire; it is a *b*.., 1.17
This is the law of the *b*... 6.9
but if you make ready a *b*.., Judg 13.16
offered..whole *b*..to the LORD; 1Sam 7.9
myself, and offered the *b*..." 13.12
him for a *b*..upon the wall. 2Ki 3.27
B..and sin offering thou hast Ps 40.6
were I to give a *b*.., thou 51.16
the prince provides..a *b*..or Ezek 46.12
continual *b*..was taken away Dan 8.11
Noah..offered *b*..on the altar. Gen 8.20
LORD as great delight in *b*.. 1Sam 15.22
I will not offer *b*..to 2Sam 24.24
to offer *b*..to the LORD upon 1Chr 16.40
and presented *b*..and peace 21.26
offered the daily *b*..by number Ezra 3.4
your *b*..are continually before Ps 50.8
I have had enough..*b*..of rams Isa 1.11
"Add..*b*..to your sacrifices, Jer 7.21
Shall I come..with *b*.., with Mic 6.6

BURY — ING — IED

Do not *b* me in Egypt, Gen 47.29
"Lord, let me first go and *b* Mt 8.21
let me first go..*b* my father." Lk 9.59
she..anointed my body..for *b*. Mk 14.8
Abraham *b* Sarah his wife Gen 23.19
Esau and Jacob *b* him. 35.29
and he *b* him in the valley Deut 34.6
We were *b* therefore with him Rom 6.4
he was *b*,..he was raised 1Cor 15.4
you were *b* with him in baptism, Col 2.12

BUSH

out of the midst of a *b*; Ex 3.2
in the passage about the *b*, Lk 20.37
in a flame of fire in a *b*. Acts 7.30

BUSHEL

lamp and put it under a *b*, Mt 5.15
"Is a lamp..put under a *b*, Mk 4.21
a lamp..under a *b*, but Lk 11.33

BUSY

as your servant was *b* here 1Ki 20.40
to *b* myself with wicked deeds Ps 141.4

BUSYBODIES

mere *b*, not doing any work. 2Thess 3.11
but gossips and *b*, saying 1Tim 5.13

BUTLER

b told his dream to Joseph, Gen 40.9

BUY

When you *b* a Hebrew slave, Ex 21.2
but no man will *b* you." Deut 28.68
"No, but I will *b* it of you 2Sam 24.24
"No, but I will *b* it for 1Chr 21.24

BYWORD

a *b*, among all the peoples Deut 28.37
a proverb and a *b* among all 2Chr 7.20

BYWORD (cont.)

made me a *b* of the peoples, Job 17.6
made us a *b* among the nations, Ps 44.14

C

CAESAR — 'S

"Render therefore to *C* the Mt 22.21
a king sets himself against *C*." Jn 19.12
standing before *C* tribunal, Acts 25.10
the saints..of *C* household. Phil 4.22

CAESAREA

into..district of *C* Philippi, Mt 16.13
to the villages of *C* Philippi; Mk 8.27
preached..till he came to *C*. Acts 8.40
At *C* there was..Cornelius, 10.1
three men arrived..from *C*. 11.11
When he had landed at *C*, 18.22
came to *C* and delivered the 23.33
Paul was being kept at *C*, 25.4

CAIAPHAS

*High priest, Mt 26.3, 57; Lk 3.2; Jn 18.13;
"prophesied that Jesus should die," Jn
11.49–53; 18.14; took part in the trial of
Jesus, Mt 26.62–66 (Mk 14.60–64; Jn
18.19–24,28); present at examination of
Peter and John, Acts 4.6–21.*

CAIN

Eve..conceived and bore *C*, Gen 4.1
C brought..the LORD an offering 4.3
C rose up against his brother 4.8
C went away from..the LORD, 4.16
Abel, for *C* slew him." 4.25
more acceptable..than *C*, Heb 11.4
like *C* who was of the evil one 1Jn 3.12
they walk in the way of *C*, Jude 11

CAKE — S

"Let them take a *c* of figs, Isa 38.21
Ephraim is a *c* not turned. Hos 7.8
knead it, and make *c*." Gen 18.6

CALAMITY

Cannot my taste discern *c*? Job 6.30
They came upon me in..my *c*; Ps 18.18
I also will laugh at your *c*; Prov 1.26
c of Moab is near at hand Jer 48.16
the LORD has kept ready the *c* Dan 9.14
gloated..in the day of his *c*; Obad 1.13

CALEB

*Sent with the spies, Num 13.1–6; exhorted
the people, Num 13.30; 14.6–10; was
promised entrance into Canaan, Num
14.22–38 (32.10–12; Deut 1.34–36); Num
26.65; received Hebron as an inheritance,
Josh 14.6–15; 15.13–19; Judg 1.20.*

CALF — VES

took a *c*, tender and good, Gen 18.7
and made a molten *c*; Ex 32.4
there came out this *c*." 32.24
They made a *c* in Horeb and Ps 106.19
bring the fatted *c*..kill it. Lk 15.23
they made a *c* in those days, Acts 7.41
and made two *c* of gold. 1Ki 12.28
Sacrifice..Men kiss *c*! Hos 13.2

CALL — S — ED — ING (v)

c upon the name of the LORD. Gen 4.26
Then *c*, and I will answer; Job 13.22
Thou wouldest *c*, and I would 14.15
bread, and do not *c* upon God? Ps 53.4
But I *c* upon God; and the LORD 55.16
and we will *c* on thy name! 80.18

answer me..in the day..I *c*! 102.2
give thanks..*c* on his name, 105.1
c on him as long as I live. 116.2
the LORD is near to all who *c* 145.18
Does not wisdom *c*, does not Prov 8.1
and he shall *c* on my name; Isa 41.25
I *c* you by..name, I surname 45.4
c upon him while he is near; 55.6
Before they *c* I will answer, 65.24
I thought you would *c* me, My Jer 3.19
C to me and I will answer you, 33.3
a fast; *c* a solemn assembly; Joel 2.15
all who *c* upon the name of 2.32
bestows riches upon all who *c* Rom 10.12
how are men to *c* upon him 10.14
c upon the Lord from a pure 2Tim 2.22
He *c* to the heavens above and Ps 50.4
When he *c* to me, I will answer 91.15
no one that *c* upon thy name, Isa 64.7
he *c* together his friends Lk 15.6
where he *c* the Lord the God 20.37
he *c* his own sheep by name Jn 10.3
whoever *c* on..name of the Lord Acts 2.21
Abram..*c* on..name of the Gen 12.8
Abram *c* on..name of the LORD 13.4
Abraham *c* the name of..place 22.14
God *c* to him out of the bush, Ex 3.4
LORD *c* Moses to the top 19.20
Then Samson *c* to the LORD Judg 16.28
LORD *c*, "Samuel! Samuel!" 1Sam 3.4
c and you refused to listen, Prov 1.24
I *c* him, but he gave no answer. Sol 5.6
c from its farthest corners, Isa 41.9
I have *c* you in righteousness, 42.6
The LORD *c* me from the womb, 49.1
c..they have not answered." Jer 35.17
son; and he *c* his name Jesus. Mt 1.25
"Out of Egypt have I *c* my son." 2.15
And he *c*..his twelve disciples 10.1
went up into the hills, and *c* Mk 3.13
And he *c* to him the twelve, 6.7
be *c* the Son of the Most High; Lk 1.32
he *c* the twelve together and 9.1
first time *c* Christians. Acts 11.26
he *c* together the..leaders 28.17
who are *c* to belong to Jesus Rom 1.6
whom he predestined he also *c*; 8.30
who are *c*, both Jews and 1Cor 1.24
For God has *c* us to peace. 7.15
quickly deserting him who *c* you Gal 1.6
For you were *c* to freedom, 5.13
he is *c* by God, just as Aaron Heb 5.4
Abraham obeyed when he was *c* 11.8
he was *c* the friend of God. Jas 2.23
To those who are *c*, beloved in Jude 1
"Take heart; rise, he is *c* Mk 10.49
"Behold, he is *c* Elijah." 15.35

CALL (n)

the *c* of God are irrevocable. Rom 11.29
consider your *c*, brethren; 1Cor 1.26
confirm your *c* and election, 2Pet 1.10

CALM

sea; and there was a great *c*. Mt 8.26
and there was a great *c*. Mk 4.39
ceased, and there was a *c*. Lk 8.24

CAME

king *c* back to the Jordan; 2Sam 19.15
these presidents and satraps *c* Dan 6.6
he desired; and they *c* to him. Mk 3.13
Son of man..*c* not to be served 10.45
Lord *c* with his holy myriads, Jude 14

CAMEL — S — 'S

easier for a *c* to go through	Mt 19.24
out a gnat and swallowing a *c*!	23.24
easier for a *c* to go through	Mk 10.25
easier for a *c* to go through	Lk 18.25
took ten of his master's *c*	Gen 24.10
John wore a garment of *c* hair,	Mt 3.4

CAMP

When the *c* is to set out, Aaron	Num 4.5
put out of the *c* every leper,	5.2

CANA

a marriage at *C* in Galilee,	Jn 2.1
came again to *C* in Galilee,	4.46
Nathanael of *C* in Galilee,	21.2

CANAAN — ITE

Ham, the father of *C*, saw	Gen 9.22
"Cursed be *C*; a slave	9.25
to go into the land of *C*;	11.31
to go to the land of *C*.	12.5
famine..in the land of *C*.	42.5
give them the land of *C*,	Ex 6.4
view the land of *C*, which	Deut 32.49
sacrificed to the idols of *C*;	Ps 106.38
a *C* woman from that region	Mt 15.22

CAPERNAUM

he went and dwelt in *C* by the	Mt 4.13
As he entered *C*,..centurion came	8.5
you *C*, will you be exalted	11.23
they came to *C*, the collectors	17.24
he returned to *C* after some days,	Mk 2.1
of the people he entered *C*.	Lk 7.1
you *C*, will you be exalted	10.15
at *C* there was an official	Jn 4.46
synagogue, as he taught at *C*.	6.59

CAPTIVE — S

kinsmen had been taken *c*,	Gen 14.14
loose..bonds..O *c* daughter of	Isa 52.2
LORD's flock has been taken *c*.	Jer 13.17
shall carry them *c* to Babylon,	20.4
carried away *c* of the Jews	52.30
be led *c* among all nations;	Lk 21.24
making me *c* to the law of sin	Rom 7.23
take every thought *c* to obey	2Cor 10.5
If any one is to be taken *c*,	Rev 13.10
among the *c* a beautiful	Deut 21.11
mount, leading *c* in thy train,	Ps 68.18
Assyria lead..the Egyptians *c*	Isa 20.4
on high he led a host of *c*,	Eph 4.8

CAPTIVITY

who came up out of the *c*	Ezra 2.1
their idols..go into *c*.	Isa 46.2
those who are for *c*, to *c*." '	Jer 15.2
your lovers shall go into *c*;	22.22
Israel went into *c* for their	Ezek 39.23

CAPTORS

our *c* required of us songs,	Ps 137.3
will take captive..their *c*,	Isa 14.2

CARE — S — ST — D (v)

the son of man that thou dost *c*	Ps 8.4
shepherds over them who will *c*	Jer 23.4
do you not *c* if we perish?"	Mk 4.38
land..LORD your God *c* for;	Deut 11.12
no refuge..no man *c* for me.	Ps 142.4
Zion, for whom no one *c*!'	Jer 30.17
son of man, that thou *c* for him?	Heb 2.6
he *c* for him, he kept him	Deut 32.10

CARE — S (n)

to an inn, and took *c* of him.	Lk 10.34

take *c* how he builds upon it.	1Cor 3.10
members may have the same *c*	12.25
puts the same earnest *c* for	2Cor 8.16
c of the world, and..delight	Mk 4.19
choked by the *c* and riches	Lk 8.14
drunkenness and *c* of this life,	21.34

CAREFUL

You shall be *c* to do	Deut 5.32
if you will be *c* to do	11.22
"If you are not *c* to do	28.58
Jehu was not *c* to walk in	2Ki 10.31

CARELESS

a fool..restraint and is *c*.	Prov 14.16
account for every *c* word	Mt 12.36

CARMEL

king of Jokneam in *C*, one;	Josh 12.22
"Saul came to *C*, and..set	1Sam 15.12
"Go up to *C*, and go to Nabal,	25.5
Israel to me at Mount *C*,	1Ki 18.19
Your head crowns you like *C*,	Sol 7.5
the majesty of *C* and Sharon.	Isa 35.2

CARNAL

but I am *c*, sold under sin.	Rom 7.14

CARPENTER — 'S

The *c* stretches a line, he	Isa 44.13
Is not this the *c*, the son of	Mk 6.3
Is not this the *c* son? Is not	Mt 13.55

CARRY — ING — IED

you shall *c* up my bones	Gen 50.25
when he dies he will *c* nothing	Ps 49.17
take nothing..he may *c* away	Ecc 5.15
to gray hairs I will *c* you.	Isa 46.4
seize...*c* them to Babylon.	Jer 20.5
Simon..to *c* his cross.	Mk 15.21
to *c* out his purpose by being	Rev 17.17
always *c* in the body the	2Cor 4.10
He *c* away all Jerusalem, and	2Ki 24.14
also *c* part of the vessels	2Chr 36.7
he lifted them up and *c* them	Isa 63.9
and was *c* up into heaven	Lk 24.51*n*

CASE

Moses brought their *c* before	Num 27.5
"If any *c* arises requiring	Deut 17.8
I have prepared my *c*; I know	Job 13.18
I would lay my *c* before him	23.4
He who states his *c* first	Prov 18.17
Argue your *c* with..neighbor	25.9
Set forth your *c*, says..LORD;	Isa 41.21
Festus laid Paul's *c* before	Acts 25.14

CAST — S — ING

"*C* out this slave woman	Gen 21.10
I will *c* off the remnant	2Ki 21.14
Why are you *c* down, O my soul,	Ps 42.5
Why are you *c* down, O my soul,	43.5
C your burden on the LORD,	55.22
wicked are *c* down to ruin.	Prov 21.12
C your bread upon the waters,	Ecc 11.1
I will *c* you out of my sight,	Jer 7.15
have authority to *c* out demons:	Mk 3.15
"Why could we not *c* it out?"	9.28
they *c* him out of the vineyard	Lk 20.15
teach us?" And they *c* him out.	Jn 9.34
"*C* the net on the right side	21.6
by the prince of demons he *c*	Mk 3.22
"He *c* out demons by Beelzebul,	Lk 11.15
we saw a man *c* out demons in	9.49

CATCH — ES — ING

They set a trap; they *c* men.	Jer 5.26

CATCH — ES — ING (cont.)

"He c the wise in their 1Cor 3.19
henceforth you will be c men." Lk 5.10

CATTLE

c according to their kinds, Gen 1.25
Why are we counted as c? Job 18.3

CAUGHT

c up to the third heaven— 2Cor 12.2
be c up together with them 1Thess 4.17

CAUSE

to God would I commit my c; Job 5.8
without c they hid their net Ps 35.7
those who hate me without c; 69.4
Plead my c and redeem me; 119.154
maintains. .c of the afflicted, 140.12
plead their c against you. Prov 23.11
pleads the c of his people: Isa 51.22
judge not with justice the c Jer 5.28
'They hated me without a c.' Jn 15.25

CAVE — S

Lot. .dwelt in a c with his Gen 19.30
buried Sarah his wife in the c 23.19
buried him in the c of Mach-pelah ,25.9
with my fathers in the c 49.29
buried. .in the c. .Mach-pelah, 50.13
escaped to the c of Adullam; 1Sam 22.1
hid them by fifties in a c, 1Ki 18.4
he came to a c, and lodged 19.9
people hid themselves in c 1Sam 13.6
men shall enter. .c of. .rocks Isa 2.19

CEASE — S — D — ING

"Do not c to cry to the LORD 1Sam 7.8
force and power made them c. Ezra 4.23
the wicked c from troubling, Job 3.17
He makes wars c to the end Ps 46.9
quarreling and abuse will c. Prov 22.10
c to do evil, learn. .good; Isa 1.16
sacrifice and offering to c; Dan 9.27
and night they never c to sing, Rev 4.8
The. .love of the LORD never c, Lam 3.22
the sea c from its raging. Jonah 1.15
boat with them and the wind c. Mk 6.51
whoever. .suffered. .c from sin, 1Pet 4.1
sin. .by c to pray for you; 1Sam 12.23

CEDAR — S

the beams of our house are c, Sol 1.17
liken you to a c in Lebanon, Ezek 31.3
devour the c of Lebanon.' Judg 9.15
voice of the LORD breaks. .c, Ps 29.5
against all the c of Lebanon, Isa 2.13
we will put c in their place." 9.10

CENSUS

a c of all the congregation Num 26.2
Judas. .arose in. .days of the c Acts 5.37

CENTURION

he entered Capernaum, a c came Mt 8.5
When the c. .saw the earthquake 27.54
when the c, who stood facing Mk 15.39
a c had a slave who was dear Lk 7.2
when the c saw what had taken 23.47

CEPHAS

that he appeared to C, then 1Cor 15.5

CEREAL OFFERING

"When any one brings a c. .as an Lev 2.1
"And this is the law of the c.. 6.14

CHAFF

like c that the storm carries Job 21.18

wicked. .like c which the wind Ps 1.4
them be like c before the wind, 35.5
like c on the mountains Isa 17.13
the ruthless like passing c. 29.5
conceive c,. .bring forth stubble; 33.11
shall make the hills like c; 41.15
like the c of the. .threshing Dan 2.35
like the c that swirls from Hos 13.3
the c he will burn with. .fire." Mt 3.12
the c he will burn with. .fire." Lk 3.17

CHAIN — S

no one could bind him. .with a c; Mt 5.3
I am bound with this c." Acts 28.20
I am—except for these c." 26.29
he was not ashamed of my c, 2Tim 1.16

CHANGE — ST — D

purify yourselves, and c Gen 35.2
his own hurt and does not c; Ps 15.4
Can the Ethiopian c his skin Jer 13.23
I will c their glory into shame. Hos 4.7
"For I the LORD do not c; Mal 3.6
c our lowly body to be like Phil 3.21
"The Lord. .will not c his mind, Heb 7.21
Thou c them like raiment, Ps 102.26
you. .c my wages ten times. Gen 31.41
which had been c to a day Est 9.1
my people have c their glory Jer 2.11
his mind be c from a man's, Dan 4.16
but we shall all be c, 1Cor 15.51
being c into his likeness 2Cor 3.18

CHANNELS

He cuts out c in the rocks, Job 28.10
the c of the sea were seen, Ps 18.15

CHARACTER

endurance produces c, and c Rom 5.4
unchangeable c of his purpose, Heb 6.17

CHARGE — D (v)

But c Joshua, and encourage Deut 3.28
c certain persons not to teach 1Tim 1.3
c them not to be haughty, 6.17
Isaac called Jacob and. .c him Gen 28.1
he c Solomon his son, saying, 1Ki 2.1
he has c me to build. .a house Ezra 1.2
he sternly c him, and sent him Mk 1.43
he strictly c them that no one 5.43
he c them to tell no one what 9.9
he c them to tell no one what Lk 8.56
strictly c you not to teach Acts 5.28
for I have already c that all Rom 3.9

CHARGE — S (n)

will give his angels c of you Ps 91.11
will give his angels c of you,' Mt 4.6
over his head they put the c 27.37
puts his servants in c, each Mk 13.34
will give his angels c of you, Lk 4.10
brought no c in his case of Acts 25.18
any c against God's elect? Rom 8.33
To the married I give c, 1Cor 7.10
I brought c against the nobles Neh 5.7
against him many serious c Acts 25.7
not to indicate the c 25.27

CHARIOT — S

a c of fire and horses of 2Ki 2.11
horses, upon thy c of victory? Hab 3.8
Canaanites. .have c of iron, Josh 17.16
and c of fire round. .Elisha. 2Ki 6.17
Some boast of c, and some of Ps 20.7
trust. .c because they are many Isa 31.1
As with the rumbling of c, Joel 2.5

CHARIOT — S (cont.)

The c rage in the streets,	Nah 2.4
four c came out from between	Zech 6.1

CHARMER — S

there is no advantage in a c.	Ecc 10.11
it does not hear..voice of c	Ps 58.5

CHASE — D

you shall c your enemies,	Lev 26.7
Amorites..c you as bees do	Deut 1.44
therefore I c him from me.	Neh 13.28

CHASTE

your reverant and c behavior.	1Pet 3.2
with women, for they are c;	Rev 14.4

CHASTEN — S — ED (v)

anger, nor c me in thy wrath.	Ps 6.1
anger, nor c me in thy wrath!	38.1
When thou dost c man with	39.11
Blessed..whom thou dost c,	94.12
will c you in just measure,	Jer 30.11
I will c you in just measure,	46.28
whom I love, I reprove and c;	Rev 3.19
He who c the nations, does he	Ps 94.10
'Thou hast c me, and I was c,	Jer 31.18
we are c so that we may not	1Cor 11.32

CHASTENING (n)

despise not the c of the	Job 5.17
prayer when thy c was upon	Isa 26.16

CHASTISE — D

I will c you again sevenfold	Lev 26.18
and c you myself sevenfold	26.28
c them for their wicked deeds.	Hos 7.12
wayward people to c them;	10.10
therefore c him and release	Lk 23.16
My father c you with whips,	1Ki 12.11

CHASTISEMENT

upon him was the c that made	Isa 53.5
LORD..established them for c.	Hab 1.12

CHED-OR-LAOMER

the days of..C king of Elam,	Gen 14.1

CHEEK — S

struck Micaiah on the c,	1Ki 22.24
struck Micaiah on the c,	2Chr 18.23
give his c to the smiter,	Lam 3.30
strikes you on the right c,	Mt 5.39
Your c..comely with ornaments,	Sol 1.10
my c to those who pulled out	Isa 50.6

CHEER

I will..be of good c,'	Job 9.27
be of good c, I have overcome	Jn 16.33

CHEERFUL — NESS

A glad heart makes a c	Prov 15.13
A c heart is a good medicine,	17.22
for God loves a c giver.	2Cor 9.7
does acts of mercy, with c.	Rom 12.8

CHERISHED

If I had c iniquity in my	Ps 66.18
you c perpetual enmity,	Ezek 35.5

CHERUB

He rode on a c, and flew;	2Sam 22.11
With an anointed guardian c	Ezek 28.14

CHERUBIM

east..he placed the c,	Gen 3.24
you shall make two c of gold;	Ex 25.18
with c skilfully worked	26.1
he made two c of olivewood,	1Ki 6.23
art enthroned above the c,	Isa 37.16
glory..had gone up from the c	Ezek 9.3

c were standing on the south	10.3
above it were the c of glory	Heb 9.5

CHEW — S

does not c..cud is unclean	Lev 11.26
c the cud, among the animals,	Deut 14.6

CHILD — HOOD — LESS

and hurt a woman with c,	Ex 21.22
Naomi took the c and laid	Ruth 4.16
I am but a little c; I do not	1Ki 3.7
like the flesh of a little c,	2Ki 5.14
a c quieted at its mother's	Ps 131.2
a c makes himself known by	Prov 20.11
Train up a c in the way he	22.6
Folly..in the heart of a c,	22.15
a c left to himself brings	29.15
For to us a c is born, to us	Isa 9.6
a little c shall lead them.	11.6
c..die a hundred years old,	65.20
Israel was a c, I loved him,	Hos 11.1
with c of the Holy Spirit;	Mt 1.18
and search diligently for the c,	2.8
And calling to him a c, he put	18.2
alas for those who are with c	24.19
he took a c, and put him in	Mk 9.36
death, and the father his c,	13.12
"What then will this c be?"	Lk 1.66
you, c, will be called..prophet	1.76
the c grew and became strong	1.80
the c grew and became strong,	2.40
called, saying, "C, arise."	8.54
he took a c and put him by	9.47
I was a c, I spoke like a c,	1Cor 13.11
Timothy, my true c in..faith:	1Tim 1.2
To Timothy, my beloved c:	2Tim 1.2
who lives on milk..is a c.	Heb 5.13
who believes..is a c of God,	1Jn 5.1
she was with c and she cried	Rev 12.2
that he might devour her c	12.4
how from c you have been	2Tim 3.15
give me, for I continue c,	Gen 15.2

CHILDREN — 'S

he may charge his c	Gen 18.19
c..God has graciously given	33.5
when your c say to you,	Ex 12.26
iniquity of fathers upon c,	Num 14.18
your c, who this day have	Deut 1.39
they may teach their c so.'	4.10
with your c after you,	4.40
teach..diligently to your c,	6.7
not speaking to your c	11.2
with your c after you,	12.25
command them to your c,	32.46
you or your c, and do not keep	1Ki 9.6
c..death for the fathers;	2Ki 14.6
or the c be put to death for	2Chr 25.4
If your c have sinned against	Job 8.4
If his c forsake my law and	Ps 89.30
and his righteousness to..c,	103.17
your c..like olive shoots	128.3
Her c..call her blessed;	Prov 31.28
the c whom the LORD has given	Isa 8.18
c born in..your bereavement	49.20
c in sacrifice to..idols,	Ezek 23.39
Tell your c of it, and let	Joel 1.3
hearts of fathers to their c	Mal 4.6
sent and killed all the male c	Mt 2.16
able..to raise up c to Abraham.	3.9
give good gifts to your c,	7.11
Then c were brought to him	19.13
"Let the c come to me, and	19.14
c crying out in the temple,	21.15

CHILDREN — 'S (cont.)

said.."Let the c first be fed,	Mk 7.27
"Let the c come to me, do not	10.14
hearts of..fathers to the c,	Lk 1.17
from these stones to raise up c	3.8
like c sitting in the market	7.32
"Let the c come to me, and	18.16
gave power to become c of God;	Jn 1.12
"If you were Abraham's c,	8.39
Little c, yet a little while	13.33
promise is to you and..your c	Acts 2.39
witness..that we are c of God,	Rom 8.16
c of the promise are reckoned	9.8
your c would be unclean,	1Cor 7.14
do not be c in your thinking;	14.20
for c ought not to lay up	2Cor 12.14
like Isaac, are c of promise.	Gal 4.28
we were by nature c of wrath,	Eph 2.3
that we may no longer be c,	4.14
C, obey your parents in the Lord,	6.1
c of God without blemish	Phil 2.15
C, obey your parents in the	Col 3.20
As obedient c, do not be	1Pet 1.14
C, it is the last hour; and	1Jn 2.18
we should be called c of God;	3.1
your c following the truth,	2Jn 4
May you see your c children!	Ps 128.6
good man leaves..to his c	Prov 13.22
the c teeth are set on edge.'	Jer 31.29
the c teeth are set on edge'?	Ezek 18.2

CHOKE — D

delight in riches c the word,	Mt 13.22
cares..enter in and c the word,	Mk 4.19
the thorns grew up and c it,	4.7
thorns grew with it and c it.	Lk 8.7
they are c by the cares and riches	8.14

CHOOSE — S — ING

rod of the man whom I c	Num 17.5
c out of all your tribes	Deut 12.4
the LORD your God will c.	17.15
therefore c life, that you	30.19
c this day whom you will	Josh 24.15
C a man for yourselves, and	1Sam 17.8
Three things I offer you; c	2Sam 24.12
Three things I offer you; c	1Chr 21.10
who c another god multiply	Ps 16.4
instruct in the way..should c.	25.12
Blessed is he whom thou dost c	65.4
did not c..fear of the LORD,	Prov 1.29
refuse..evil and c the good.	Isa 7.15
Is such the fast that I c,	58.5
Zion and again c Jerusalem.' "	Zech 1.17
do what I c with what belongs	Mt 20.15
You did not c me, but I c you	Jn 15.16
to c men and send them to you	Acts 15.25
which I shall c I cannot tell.	Phil 1.22
man whom the LORD c shall	Num 16.7
c, to set his name there,	Deut 14.24
c..to share ill-treatment	Heb 11.25

CHORAZIN

"Woe to you, C! woe to you,	Mt 11.21
"Woe to you, C! woe to you,	Lk 10.13

CHOSE — N (v)

Lot c..the Jordan valley,	Gen 13.11
Moses c able men out of	Ex 18.25
and c their descendants	Deut 4.37
set his love upon you and c you,	7.7
I c him out of all the tribes	1Sam 2.28
He c our heritage for us, the	Ps 47.4
but he c the tribe of Judah,	78.68

the two families which he c'?	Jer 33.24
and c from them twelve, whom	Lk 6.13
how they c the places of honor,	14.7
they c Stephen, a man full of	Acts 6.5
God c what is foolish in	1Cor 1.27
arranged the organs..as he c.	12.18
he c us..before the foundation	Eph 1.4
God c you from..beginning	2Thess 2.13
No, for I have c him,	Gen 18.19
ones c from the congregation,	Num 1.16
your God has c him out	Deut 18.5
him whom the LORD has c?	1Sam 10.24
thy people whom thou hast c,	1Ki 3.8
Jerusalem which I have c."	11.13
which I have c, Jerusalem,	2Ki 23.27
sons of Jacob, his c ones!	1Chr 16.13
LORD has c you to build	28.10
for the LORD has c you to	2Chr 29.11
made a covenant with my c one,	Ps 89.3
led..his c ones with singing,	105.43
had not Moses, his c one,	106.23
c the way of faithfulness,	119.30
for I have c thy precepts.	119.173
good name is to be c rather	Prov 22.1
servant, Jacob, whom I have c,	Isa 41.8
my servant whom I have c,	43.10
because..the LORD,..has c you."	48.7
These have c their own ways,	66.3
signet ring; for I have c you,	Hag 2.23
my servant whom I have c,	Mt 12.18
many are called, but few..c."	22.14
I know whom I have c; it is	Jn 13.18
he is a c instrument of mine	Acts 9.15
Put on then, as God's c ones,	Col 3.12
by God, that he has c you;	1Thess 1.4
c and destined by God the	1Pet 1.2
you are a c race, a royal	2.9

CHOSEN (n)

my c, in whom..soul delights;	Isa 42.1
For the sake of..Israel my c,	45.4
my c shall inherit it, and my	65.9
my c shall long enjoy the work	65.22
"This is my Son, my C; listen	Lk 9.35

CHRIST

Jesus was born, who is called C.	Mt 1.16
"You are the C, the Son of..God."	16.16
God judges..secrets of men by C	Rom 2.16
the supernatural Rock..was C.	1Cor 10.4

CHRISTIAN — S

you think to make me a C!"	Acts 26.28
yet if one suffers as a C,	1Pet 4.16
the first time called C.	Acts 11.26

CHURCH — ES

on this rock I will build my c,	Mt 16.18
he refuses..tell it to the c;	18.17
the c throughout all Judea	Acts 9.31
came to the ears of the c	11.22
some who belonged to the c.	12.1
prayer..to God by the c.	12.5
to feed the c of the Lord	20.28
greet..the c in their house.	Rom 16.5
no offense..to the c of God,	1Cor 10.32
God has appointed in the c	12.28
he who prophesies edifies the c.	14.4
because I persecuted the c	15.9
head over all things for the c,	Eph 1.22
to him be glory in the c	3.21
As the c is subject to Christ,	5.24
how can he care for God's c?	1Tim 3.5
let the c not be burdened,	5.16

CHURCH — ES (cont.)
and the *c* in your house: Philem 2
and puts them out of the *c*. 3Jn 10
c were strengthened in..faith, Acts 16.5
shown in the *c* of Macedonia, 2Cor 8.1
John to the seven *c*..in Asia: Rev 1.4
all the *c* shall know that I 2.23

CIRCLE
he drew a *c* on the face of Prov 8.27
above the *c* of the earth, Isa 40.22

CIRCUMCISE — D
C therefore the foreskin Deut 10.16
God will *c* your heart 30.6
C yourselves to the LORD, Jer 4.4
you *c* a man upon the sabbath. Jn 7.22
Every male..shall be *c*. Gen 17.10
and every male was *c*, 34.24
and *c* the people of Israel Josh 5.3
"Unless you are *c* according Acts 15.1
was not compelled to be *c*, Gal 2.3
In him also you were *c* with Col 2.11

CIRCUMCISION
of blood," because of the *c*. Ex 4.26
the *c* party criticized him, Acts 11.2
his uncircumcision be..as *c*? Rom 2.26
He received *c* as a sign or seal 4.11
neither *c* counts for anything 1Cor 7.19
in Christ Jesus neither *c* nor Gal 5.6
by what is called the *c*, Eph 2.11

CISTERN — S
Drink water from your own *c*, Prov 5.15
and cast him into the *c* of Jer 38.6
hewed out a *c* for themselves, 2.13

CITY — IES
You shall march around the *c*, Josh 6.3
a breach was made in the *c*; 2Ki 25.4
streams make glad the *c* of God, Ps 46.4
praised in the *c* of our God! 48.1
wealth is his strong *c*; Prov 10.15
righteous, the *c* rejoices; 11.10
a little *c* with few men in it; Ecc 9.14
called the *c* of righteousness, Isa 1.26
a breach was made in the *c*. Jer 39.2
How lonely sits the *c* that Lam 1.1
said, "The *c* has fallen." Ezek 33.21
because thy *c* and thy people Dan 9.19
Jerusalem..the faithful *c*, Zech 8.3
c set on..hill cannot be hid. Mt 5.14
whole *c* was gathered together Mk 1.33
the *c* was full of idols. Acts 17.16
he looked forward to the *c* Heb 11.10
the name of the *c* of my God, Rev 3.12
the holy *c*, new Jerusalem, 21.2
to measure the *c* and its gates 21.15
shall be the six *c* of refuge, Num 35.6
set apart three *c* for you Deut 19.2
'Appoint the *c* of refuge, Josh 20.2
you are to be over five *c*.' Lk 19.19

CLAY
thou hast made me of *c*; and Job 10.9
your defenses are..of *c*. 13.12
was formed from a piece of *c*. 33.6
potter be regarded as the *c*; Isa 29.16
Does the *c* say to him who 45.9
we are the *c*..thou..our potter; 64.8
like..*c* in the potter's hand, Jer 18.6
made *c* of the spittle and Jn 9.6

CLEAN — NESS
seven pairs of all *c* animals, Gen 7.2

"You may eat all *c* birds. Deut 14.11
flesh was restored..he was *c*. 2Ki 5.14
Who can bring a *c* thing out Job 14.4
man, that he can be *c*? Or 15.14
he who is born of woman be *c*? 25.4
You say, 'I am *c*, without 33.9
the fear of the LORD is *c*, Ps 19.9
He who has *c* hands and a pure 24.4
in vain have I kept my heart *c* 73.13
Who can say,..my heart *c*; Prov 20.9
Wash..make yourselves *c*; Isa 1.16
How long..before you are..*c*?" Jer 13.27
if you will, you can make me *c*." Mt 8.2
you will, you can make me *c*." Mk 1.40
you will, you can make me *c*." Lk 5.12
everything is *c* for you. 11.41
You are..made *c* by the word Jn 15.3
Everything is indeed *c*, but Rom 14.20
according to the *c* of my hands Ps 18.20

CLEANSE — S — D
people of Israel, and *c* them. Num 8.6
and does not *c* himself, 19.13
house of the LORD to *c* it, 2Chr 29.16
and *c* my hands with lye, Job 9.30
iniquity, and *c* me from my sin! Ps 51.2
Blows that wound *c* away Prov 20.30
will *c* them from all the guilt Jer 33.8
from all your idols I will *c* Ezek 36.25
I will save..and..*c* them; 37.23
fall, to refine and to *c* them Dan 11.35
raise the dead, *c* lepers, Mt 10.8
you *c* the outside of the cup 23.25
let us *c* ourselves from every 2Cor 7.1
C your hands, you sinners, Jas 4.8
And the priest who *c* him Lev 14.11
c the bloodstains of Jerusalem Isa 4.4
a land that is not *c*, or Ezek 22.24
none of them was *c*, but..Naaman Lk 4.27
as they went they were *c*. 17.14
"What God has *c*, you must Acts 10.15
'What God has *c* you must not 11.9
having *c* her by the washing Eph 5.26

CLEAR
how can we *c* ourselves? Gen 44.16
C thou me from hidden faults. Ps 19.12
Thou didst *c* the ground for it; 80.9
to *c* his threshing floor, and Lk 3.17

CLEAVE — S — ING
shall *c* to the inheritance Num 36.7
to *c* to him, and to serve Josh 22.5
but *c* to the LORD your God 23.8
My bones *c* to my skin and Job 19.20
I *c* to thy testimonies, O LORD; Ps 119.31
a man..*c* to his wife, Gen 2.24
My soul *c* to the dust; revive Ps 119.25
obeying his voice, and *c* Deut 30.20

CLEVER — NESS
cleverness of the *c* I will 1Cor 1.19
c of the clever I will thwart." 1.19

CLOAK
let him have your *c* as well; Mt 5.40
bring the *c* that I left with 2Tim 4.13

CLOSE
sign..of the *c* of the age?" Mt 24.3
with you..to the *c* of the age." 28.20

CLOTH — S
unshrunk *c* on an old garment, Mt 9.16
wrapped him in swaddling *c*, Lk 2.7

CLOTHE — S — D (v)

will *c* him with your robe,	Isa 22.21
if God so *c*..grass of the field,	Mt 6.30
if God so *c* the grass which	Lk 12.28
God made for Adam..and *c*	Gen 3.21
with the spoil they *c* all	2Chr 28.15
righteousness, and it *c* me;	Job 29.14
clean turban on his head and *c*	Zech 3.5
demoniac sitting there, *c* and	Mk 5.15
they *c* him in a purple cloak,	15.17
c and in his right mind;	Lk 8.35

CLOTHING (n)

Your *c* did not wear out upon	Deut 8.4
if I have seen..lack of *c*,	Job 31.19
lambs will provide your *c*,	Prov 27.26
and the body more than *c*?	Mt 6.25
false prophets..in sheep's *c*	7.15
for my *c* they cast lots."	Jn 19.24

CLOUD

I set my bow in the *c*,	Gen 9.13
in a pillar of *c* to lead them	Ex 13.21
Then the *c* covered the tent	40.34
the *c* covered the tabernacle,	Num 9.15
LORD came down in a pillar of *c*,	12.5
the pillar of *c* stood by the	Deut 31.15
over her assemblies a *c* by day,	Isa 4.5
a bright *c* overshadowed them,	Mt 17.5
And a *c* overshadowed them,	Mk 9.7
c took him out of their sight.	Acts 1.9
baptized into Moses in the *c*	1Cor 10.2

CLOVEN-FOOTED

and is *c* and chews the cud,	Lev 11.3

COAL — S

having in his hand a burning *c*	Isa 6.6
c flamed forth from him.	Ps 18.8
Let burning *c* fall upon them!	140.10
heap of fire on his head,	Prov 25.22
heap burning *c* upon his head."	Rom 12.20

COAT — S

sue you and take your *c*, let	Mt 5.40
cloak do not withhold your *c*	Lk 6.29
two *c*, let him share with him	3.11

COCK

immediately the *c* crowed.	Mt 26.74
before the *c* crows twice,	Mk 14.30
gateway and the *c* crowed.	14.68*n*
Peter, the *c* will not crow	Lk 22.34
still speaking, the *c* crowed.	22.60
the *c* will not crow, till you	Jn 13.38

COIN — S

Bring me a *c*, and let me look	Mk 12.15
"Show me a *c*. Whose likeness	Lk 20.24
widow..put in two copper *c*,	Mk 12.42
poor widow put in two copper *c*.	Lk 21.2

COLD

most men's love will grow *c*.	Mt 24.12
you are..neither *c* nor hot,	Rev 3.16

COLLECTOR — S

a Pharisee and..a tax *c*.	Lk 18.10
Zacchaeus..was a chief tax *c*,	19.2
tax *c* and the harlots go into	Mt 21.31
tax *c* and sinners were sitting	Mk 2.15
Tax *c* also came to be baptized,	Lk 3.12
drink with tax *c* and sinners?"	5.30
and the tax *c* justified God,	7.29
friend of tax *c* and sinners!'	7.34

COLT

humble and riding..on a *c*	Zech 9.9
you will find a *c* tied, on	Mk 11.2
where..you will find a *c* tied,	Lk 19.30

COME — S — ING (v)

"*C* in, O blessed of the LORD;	Gen 24.31
c with us, and we will	Num 10.29
"Lo, I *c*;..it is written of me;	Ps 40.7
C and hear,..you who fear God,	66.16
C into his presence with singing!	100.2
none who go to her *c* back	Prov 2.19
better to be told, "*C*..here,"	25.7
C, my beloved, let us go forth	Sol 7.11
"*C*..let us reason together,	Isa 1.18
"*C*, let us go up to the mountain	2.3
c, let us walk in the light	2.5
C, my people, enter your	26.20
God. He will *c* and save you."	35.4
who thirsts, *c* to the waters;	55.1
"*C*, let us return to the LORD;	Hos 6.1
"*C*, let us go to the mountain	Mic 4.2
will suddenly *c* to his temple;	Mal 3.1
Thy kingdom *c*, Thy will be done,	Mt 6.10
I say..to another, '*C*,' and he *c*,	8.9
"Are you he who is to *c*, or	11.3
C to me, all who labor and	11.28
"If any man would *c* after me,	16.24
For many will *c* in my name,	24.5
"*C* away by yourselves..and rest	Mk 6.31
"If any man would *c* after me,	8.34
Many will *c* in my name, saying,	13.6
He said to them, "*C* and see."	Jn 1.39
"*C*, see a man who told me all	4.29
"You know me,..where I *c* from?	7.28
let him *c* to me and drink.	7.37
loud voice, "Lazarus, *c* out."	11.43
not..desolate; I will *c* to you.	14.18
Jesus,..will *c* in the same	Acts 1.11
"*C* over to Macedonia and help	16.9
longed for many years to *c*	Rom 15.23
be accursed. Our Lord, *c*!	1Cor 16.22
Do your best to *c* to me soon.	2Tim 4.9
But you have *c* to Mount Zion	Heb 12.22
"*C* out of her, my people,	Rev 18.4
Spirit and the Bride say, "*C*."	22.17
God *c*, he does not keep silence,	Ps 50.3
LORD..*c* to judge the earth.	96.13
Who is this that *c* from Edom,	Isa 63.1
day *c*, burning like an oven,	Mal 4.1
terrible day of the LORD *c*.	4.5
Blessed is he who *c* in the name	Mt 21.9
'Blessed be he who *c* in the name	23.39
"When the Son of man *c* in his	25.31
ashamed, when he *c* in the glory	Mk 8.38
who *c* in..name of the Lord!'"	Lk 13.35
who *c* to me shall not hunger,	Jn 6.35
who *c* to me I will not cast out.	6.37
Blessed..he who *c* in the name	1Cor 11.26
Lord's death until he *c*.	1Cor 11.26
a god *c* up out of..earth."	1Sam 28.13
on what day your Lord is *c*.	Mt 24.42
c on the clouds of heaven."	26.64
the Son of man *c* in clouds	Mk 13.26
c with the clouds of heaven."	14.62
Son of man is *c* at an hour	Lk 12.40
Son of man *c* in a cloud with	21.27
third time I am *c* to you.	2Cor 13.1
the *c* one shall..not tarry;	Heb 10.37
Behold, he is *c* with the clouds,	Rev 1.7
I am *c* soon; hold fast what	3.11
I am *c* soon, bringing my	22.12
says, "Surely I am *c* soon."	22.20

COMELY
I am..dark, but, c, O daughters   Sol 1.5
my love, c as Jerusalem, terrible   6.4

COMFORT — S — ED (v)
to condole with him and c   Job 2.11
you c me with empty nothings?   21.34
rod and thy staff, they c me.   Ps 23.4
thou wast angry..thou didst c   Isa 12.1
C, c my people, says your God.   40.1
For the LORD will c Zion;   51.3
he will c..her waste places,   51.3
our God; to c all who mourn;   61.2
his mother c, so I will c you;   66.13
she has none to c her; all   Lam 1.2
Therefore c one another   1Thess 4.18
I am he that c you; who are   Isa 51.12
So Isaac was c after   Gen 24.67
he refused to be c,   37.35
my soul refuses to be c.   Ps 77.2
LORD, hast helped me and c me.   86.17
the LORD has c his people,   Isa 49.13
for the LORD has c his people,   52.9
he is c..you are in anguish.   Lk 16.25
c us by the coming of Titus,   2Cor 7.6
Therefore we are c. And besides   7.13

COMFORT (n)
This is my c in my affliction   Ps 119.50
of mercies and God of all c,   2Cor 1.3
God..who..gave us eternal c   2Thess 2.16

COMFORTERS
miserable c are you all.   Job 16.2
and for c, but I found none.   Ps 69.20
whence shall I seek c for her?   Nah 3.7

COMING (n)
what will be the sign of your c   Mt 24.3
so will be the c of the Son   24.27
so..the c of the Son of man.   24.37
'My master is delayed in c.'   Lk 12.45
at his c those who belong   1Cor 15.23
before our Lord..at his c?   1Thess 2.19
at the c of our Lord Jesus   3.13
left until the c of the Lord,   4.15
blameless at the c of our Lord   5.23
concerning the c of our Lord   2Thess 2.1
patient,..until..c of the Lord.   Jas 5.7
the power and c of our Lord   2Pet 1.16
"Where is the promise of his c?   3.4
shrink..in shame at his c.   1Jn 2.28

COMMAND — S — ED (v)
speak all that I c you;   Ex 7.2
I will c my blessing upon you   Lev 25.21
LORD will c the blessing   Deut 28.8
whatever I c..you shall speak.   Jer 1.7
do all that I c you. So shall you   11.4
I c you to speak to them;   26.2
friends if you do what I c   Jn 15.14
he c even wind and water,   Lk 8.25
God c the man, saying,   Gen 2.16
Noah..did all that God c   6.22
all that the LORD had c Moses;   Ex 39.32
did all..the LORD c by Moses.   Lev 8.36
his covenant, which he c   Deut 4.13
Moses c us a law, as a possession   33.4
Have I not c you? Be strong   Josh 1.9
so Moses c..and so Joshua did;   11.15
he c, and it stood forth.   Ps 33.9
he c and they were created.   148.5
Jesus c them, "Tell no one   Mt 17.9
to observe all..I have c you;   28.20
Lord c..those who proclaim   1Cor 9.14

COMMAND (n)
At the c of the LORD   Num 9.18
you rebelled against my c   20.24
beyond the c of the LORD   22.18
The Lord gives the c; great is   Ps 68.11
Keep the king's c, and because   Ecc 8.2
what I am writing..is a c   1Cor 14.37

COMMANDER — S — 'S
Phicol the c of his army   Gen 21.22
as c of the army of the LORD   Josh 5.14
then c shall be appointed at   Deut 20.9
a c portion was reserved;   33.21

COMMANDMENT — S
who respects the c will be   Prov 13.13
A new c I give to you, that   Jn 13.34
and the c is holy and just   Rom 7.12
no new c, but an old c which   1Jn 2.7
not..writing you a new c, but   2Jn 5
the covenant, the ten c.   Ex 34.28
the c which..LORD commanded   Lev 27.34
keeping his statutes, his c   1Ki 2.3
break thy c..and intermarry   Ezra 9.14
and all thy c are true.   Ps 119.151
my words; keep my c, and live;   Prov 4.4
Fear God, and keep his c;   Ecc 12.13
enter life, keep the c."   Mt 19.17
love of God,..keep his c.   1Jn 5.3

COMMEND — S — ED
I c enjoyment, for man has no   Ecc 8.15
now I c you to God and to   Acts 20.32
I c to you our sister Phoebe,   Rom 16.1
beginning to c ourselves   2Cor 3.1
of those who c themselves.   10.12
the man whom the Lord c.   10.18
man is c according to his   Prov 12.8
master c the dishonest steward   Lk 16.8

COMMISSION (n)
According to the c of God given   1Cor 3.10
I am entrusted with a c.   9.17

COMMISSIONED (v)
in Christ, and has c us;   2Cor 1.21
as c by God, in the sight of God   2.17

COMMIT — TED
to God would I c my cause;   Job 5.8
Into thy hand I c my spirit;   Ps 31.5
C your way to the LORD; trust   37.5
C your work to the LORD,   Prov 16.3
into thy hands I c my spirit!"   Lk 23.46
have not c this treachery   Josh 22.31
to thee have I c my cause.   Jer 20.12
for the treason he has c   Ezek 17.20
the treachery..c against thee.   Dan 9.7

COMMON
and had all things in c;   Acts 2.44
they had everything in c.   4.32
cleansed,..you must not call c."   10.15
no temptation..not c to man.   1Cor 10.13
write..of our c salvation,   Jude 3

COMMONWEALTH
alienated from..c of Israel,   Eph 2.12
But our c is in heaven,   Phil 3.20

COMMUNE
c with your own hearts on your   Ps 4.4
I c with my heart in the night;   77.6

COMPANION — S
wife was given to his c,   Judg 14.20
a c of all who fear thee,   Ps 119.63
the c of fools will suffer   Prov 13.20

COMPANION — S (cont.)
c of gluttons shames his father. Prov 28.7
though she is your c and..wife Mal 2.14
c..listening for your voice; Sol 8.13

COMPANY — IES
you keep c with adulterers. Ps 50.18
in the c of the upright, in 111.1
adulterers, a c of treacherous Jer 9.2
sit in the c of merrymakers, 15.17
"Bad c ruins good morals." 1Cor 15.33
sit down by c upon the..grass. Mk 6.39

COMPARE — D
none can c with thee! Were I Ps 40.5
c me, that we may be alike? Isa 46.5
shall I c this generation? Mt 11.16
Not..to class or c ourselves 2Cor 10.12
who in the skies can be c to Ps 89.6

COMPASSION
c on you, and multiply you, Deut 13.17
Israel had c for Benjamin Judg 21.6
people had c on Benjamin 21.15
gracious to them and had c 2Ki 13.23
your children will find c 2Chr 30.9
he had c on his people 36.15
LORD..have c on his servants. Ps 135.14
The LORD will have c on Jacob Isa 14.1
with great c I will gather you. 54.7
I will again have c on them, Jer 12.15
God gave Daniel favor and c Dan 1.9
He will again have c upon us, Mic 7.19
pour out..a spirit of c Zech 12.10
When he saw..crowds, he had c Mt 9.36
he had c on them, and healed 14.14
said, "I have c on the crowd, 15.32
saw a great throng, and..had c Mk 6.34
"I have c on the crowd, because 8.2
he had c on her and said to Lk 7.13
when he saw him, he had c, 10.33
father saw him and had c, 15.20
you had c on the prisoners, Heb 10.34

COMPASSIONATE
I will hear, for I am c. Ex 22.27
he, being c, forgave their Ps 78.38
the Lord is c and merciful. Jas 5.11

COMPEL — LED
and c people to come in, Lk 14.23
how can you c the Gentiles Gal 2.14
they c to carry his cross. Mt 27.32
was not c to be circumcised, Gal 2.3

COMPETE
how will you c with horses? Jer 12.5
in a race all..runners c, 1Cor 9.24

COMPLAIN — ED
I will c in the bitterness Job 7.11
Abraham c to Abimelech Gen 21.25
people c in the hearing Num 11.1

COMPLAINT
"Today also my c is bitter, Job 23.2
and at noon I utter my c and Ps 55.17
I pour out my c before him, 142.2
ground for c against Daniel Dan 6.4
I will answer concerning my c. Hab 2.1

COMPLETE — D — ING
iniquity..not yet c." Gen 15.16
that you may be perfect and c, Jas 1.4
When therefore I have c this, Rom 15.28
and faith was c by works, Jas 2.22
matched by your c it out of 2Cor 8.11

COMPREHEND
things which we cannot c. Job 37.5
may have power to c with all Eph 3.18

CONCEAL — S — ED
glory of God to c things, Prov 25.2
prudent man c his knowledge, 12.23
He who c his transgressions 28.13
if I have c my transgressions Job 31.33

CONCEIT
any..wise in their own c." Job 37.24
he is puffed up with c, he 1Tim 6.4

CONCEIVE — D
they c words of deceit. Ps 35.20
Eve..c and bore Cain, Gen 4.1

CONCUBINE — S
his c became angry with him, Judg 19.2
Absalom..to his father's c 2Sam 16.22

CONDEMN — S — ED
When he is quiet, who can c? Job 34.29
c me that you may be justified? 40.8
and c the innocent to death. Ps 94.21
save him from those who c 109.31
and they will c him to death, Mt 20.18
they will c him to death, Mk 10.33
this generation and c it; Lk 11.32
not to c the world, but that Jn 3.17
who is to c? Is it Christ Rom 8.34
if our hearts do not c us, 1Jn 3.21
a man of evil devices he c. Prov 12.2
none..who take refuge..be c. Ps 34.22
let him be c when..to trial. 37.33
are they? Has no one c you?" Jn 8.10n
Cephas..because he stood c. Gal 2.11

CONDEMNATION
trespass led to c for all men, Rom 5.18
now no c for those..in Christ 8.1

CONDUCT — S (v)
let us c ourselves becomingly Rom 13.13
C yourselves wisely toward Col 4.5
who c..affairs with justice. Ps 112.5

CONDUCT (n)
wise c is a pleasure to a man Prov 10.23
good c among the Gentiles, 1Pet 2.12

CONDUIT
by the c of the upper pool, 2Ki 18.17
he made the pool and the c 20.20
he stood by the c of the..pool Isa 36.2

CONFESS — ES — ED — ING
c the sin he has committed, Lev 5.5
"But if they c their iniquity 26.40
c his sin..he has committed; Num 5.7
"I will c my transgressions Ps 32.5
one should c him to be Christ, Jn 9.22
if you c with your lips that Rom 10.9
every tongue c..Jesus..Lord, Phil 2.11
c your sins to one another, Jas 5.16
we c our sins, he is faithful 1Jn 1.9
I will c his name before my Rev 3.5
he who c and forsakes them Prov 28.13
c with his lips and..is saved. Rom 10.10
Whoever c that Jesus is the 1Jn 4.15
He c, he did not deny, but c, Jn 1.20
baptized by him..c their sins. Mt 3.6
baptized by him..c their sins. Mk 1.5
now believers came, c and Acts 19.18

CONFESSION
Ezra prayed and made c, Ezra 10.1

CONFESSION (cont.)
then make *c* to the LORD   Ezra 10.11
made *c*, saying, "O Lord, the   Dan 9.4
Jesus who. .made the good *c*,   1Tim 6.13
let us hold fast our *c*.   Heb 4.14

CONFIDENCE
On what do you rest this *c*   2Ki 18.19
people took *c* from the words   2Chr 32.8
for the LORD will be your *c*   Prov 3.26
On what do you rest this *c*   Isa 36.4
have no *c* in a friend; guard   Mic 7.5
I have great *c* in you;   2Cor 7.4
I have *c* in the Lord that   Gal 5.10
reason for *c* in the flesh,   Phil 3.4
we have *c* in the Lord about   2Thess 3.4
Through him you have *c* in God,   1Pet 1.21
c for the day of judgment,   1Jn 4.17
the *c* which we have in him,   5.14

CONFIDENT
though war. .yet I will be *c*.   Ps 27.3
is *c* that he is Christ's,   2Cor 10.7

CONFIRM — S — ED
c the word which the LORD   Deut 9.5
c the word of his servant,   Isa 44.26
sworn an oath and *c* it, to   Ps 119.106
every word. .*c* by the evidence   Mt 18.16
c the message by the signs   Mk 16.20*n*

CONFORMED
Do not be *c* to this world   Rom 12.2
do not be *c* to the passions   1Pet 1.14

CONFRONT
this song shall *c* them   Deut 31.21
Arise, O LORD! *c* them,   Ps 17.13

CONFUSION
and will throw into *c*   Ex 23.27
all Jerusalem was in *c*.   Acts 21.31
God is not a God of *c* but   1Cor 14.33

CONFUTE — D — ING
to *c* those who contradict it.   Tit 1.9
there was none that *c* Job,   Job 32.12
powerfully *c* the Jews in   Acts 18.28

CONGREGATION
"If the whole *c* of Israel   Lev 4.13
"Take a census of all the *c*   Num 1.2
the *c* shall judge between   35.24
in the. .*c* I will praise thee: Ps 22.22
in the great *c* I will bless   26.12
concealed. .from the great *c*.   40.10
Let them extol him in the *c*   107.32
in the *c* in the wilderness   Acts 7.38
midst of the *c* I will praise   Heb 2.12

CONQUER — S — ED — ING
the Lamb will *c* them, for   Rev 17.14
To him who *c* I will give. .manna   2.17
He who *c* shall be clad thus   3.5
who *c*, I will grant him to sit   3.21
who *c* shall have this heritage,   21.7
through faith *c* kingdoms,   Heb 11.33
Judah,. .Root of David, has *c*,   Rev 5.5
have *c* him by the blood of   12.11
those who had *c* the beast   15.2
he went out *c* and to conquer.   6.2

CONQUERORS
more than *c* through him who   Rom 8.37

CONSCIENCE
before God in all good *c*   Acts 23.1
take pains to have a clear *c*   24.16

their *c* also bears witness   Rom 2.15
not lying; my *c* bears me witness   9.1
but also for the sake of *c*.   13.5
encouraged if his *c* is weak,   1Cor 8.10
I mean his *c*, not yours—   10.29
holding faith and a good *c*.   1Tim 1.19
whom I serve with a clear *c*,   2Tim 1.3
perfect the *c* of the worshiper,   Heb 9.9
keep your *c* clear, so that,   1Pet 3.16
appeal to God for a clear *c*,   3.21

CONSECRATE — D — ING
"*C* to me all the first-born;   Ex 13.2
"Go to the people and *c* them   19.10
ordain them and *c* them,   28.41
you shall do to them to *c* them,   29.1
C yourselves therefore,   Lev 20.7
You shall *c* him, for he offers   21.8
you shall *c* to the LORD   Deut 15.19
anointed the tabernacle. .*c*   Lev 8.10
I *c* them for myself,   Num 8.17
before you were born I *c* you;   Jer 1.5
the unbelieving husband is *c*   1Cor 7.14
willingly, *c* himself today   1Chr 29.5

CONSENT — S — ING
if sinners entice. .do not *c*.   Prov 1.10
and she *c* to live with him,   1Cor 7.12
And Saul was *c* to his death.   Acts 8.1

CONSIDER — S — ED
c it, take counsel, and   Judg 19.30
for *c* what great things   1Sam 12.24
Job;. .*c* the wondrous works   Job 37.14
but I *c* thy testimonies.   Ps 119.95
Go to the ant, O sluggard; *c*   Prov 6.6
C how you have fared.   Hag 1.5
Pray now, *c* what will come   2.15
C the lilies of the field,   Mt 6.28
C the ravens: they neither sow   Lk 12.24
must *c* yourselves dead to sin   Rom 6.11
c Jesus, the apostle and high   Heb 3.1
let us *c* how to stir up one   10.24
C him who endured from sinners   12.3
Blessed is he who *c* the poor!   Ps 41.1
Who *c* the power of thy anger,   90.11
No one *c*, nor is. .knowledge   Isa 44.19
"Have you *c* my servant Job,   Job 1.8
Then I saw and *c* it; I looked   Prov 24.32
since she *c* him faithful   Heb 11.11
He *c* that God was able to raise   11.19

CONSIGNED
I am *c* to the gates of Sheol   Isa 38.10
c all men to disobedience,   Rom 11.32

CONSOLATION — S
and let this be your *c*.   Job 21.2
nor. .give him the cup of *c*   Jer 16.7
done, becoming a *c* to them.   Ezek 16.54
the dreamers. .give empty *c*.   Zech 10.2
looking for the *c* of Israel,   Lk 2.25
Are the *c* of God too small   Job 15.11

CONSOLE — D
come to Martha and Mary to *c*   Jn 11.19
you will be *c* for the evil   Ezek 14.22

CONSPIRACY
And the *c* grew strong,   2Sam 15.12
"Do not call *c* all that this   Isa 8.12
than forty who made this *c*.   Acts 23.13

CONSPIRE — D
Why do the nations *c*, and the   Ps 2.1
they *c* against him to kill   Gen 37.18

CONSPIRE — D (cont.)
his servant..c against him. 1Ki 16.9
"Amos has c against you in Amos 7.10

CONSTRAINED
but they c him, saying, "Stay Lk 24.29

CONSTRAINS
the spirit within me c me. Job 32.18

CONSULT — S — ED
when they say.."C the mediums Isa 8.19
do not look to..or c the Lord! 31.1
he c the teraphim, he looks Ezek 21.21
David c with the commanders 1Chr 13.1

CONSUME — S — D — ING
I may c them in a moment." Num 16.21
c them in wrath, c them till Ps 59.13
where neither moth nor rust c Mt 6.20
and the servants, and c them; Job 1.16
what is left in his tent will be c. 20.26
For we are c by thy anger; Ps 90.7
for our God is a c fire. Heb 12.29

CONTAIN
highest heaven cannot c thee; 1Ki 8.27
world..could not c the books Jn 21.25

CONTEMPT
looked with c on her mistress. Gen 16.4
with c upon their husbands, Est 1.17
there is c for misfortune; Job 12.5
into c the land of Zebulun Isa 9.1

CONTEND — ING
do not c with them; for I Deut 2.5
"Will you c for Baal? Or will Judg 6.31
why thou dost c against me. Job 10.2
Who..will c with me? 13.19
C, O Lord, with those who c Ps 35.1
Lord has taken his place to c, Isa 3.13
I will c with those who c 49.25
with your..children I will c. Jer 2.9
Yet let no one c, and..accuse, Hos 4.4
you to c for the faith which Jude 3
we are not c against flesh Eph 6.12

CONTENT
that we had been c to dwell Josh 7.7
and be c with your wages." Lk 3.14
I am c with weaknesses, 2Cor 12.10
whatever state I am, to be c. Phil 4.11
with these we shall be c. 1Tim 6.8

CONTENTIOUS
with a c and fretful woman. Prov 21.19
dripping..and a c woman are 27.15

CONTINUAL — LY
the c burnt offering was taken Dan 8.11
praise shall c be in my mouth. Ps 34.1

CONTINUE — D
O c thy steadfast love to Ps 36.10
"If you c in my word, you Jn 8.31
urged them to c in the grace Acts 13.43
c in sin that grace may abound? Rom 6.1
I shall remain and c with you Phil 1.25
c in what you have learned 2Tim 3.14
have c my faithfulness to you. Jer 31.3
they would have c with us; 1Jn 2.19

CONTRIBUTION — S
make some c for the poor Rom 15.26
concerning..c for the saints: 1Cor 16.1
by the generosity of your c 2Cor 9.13
faithfully brought in the c, 2Chr 31.12

CONTRITE
sacrifice acceptable..c heart, Ps 51.17
he..is humble and c in spirit Isa 66.2

CONTROL — S (v)
Joseph could not c himself Gen 45.1
the love of Christ c us, 2Cor 5.14

CONTROL (n)
having his desire under c, 1Cor 7.37
left nothing outside his c. Heb 2.8

CONTROVERSY
c with..inhabitants of the land. Hos 4.1
Hear, you mountains, the c of Mic 6.2

CONVERT — S
the first c in Asia for Christ. Rom 16.5
He must not be a recent c, 1Tim 3.6
the first c in Achaia, and 1Cor 16.15

CONVICT — S — ED
to c all the ungodly of Jude 15
Which of you c me of sin? Jn 8.46
outsider enters, he is c 1Cor 14.24

CONVINCE — D
he will c the world of sin Jn 16.8
And c some, who doubt; Jude 22
fully c that God was able Rom 4.21
Let every one be fully c in 14.5

CONVOCATION
sabbath of..rest, a holy c; Lev 23.3
you shall have a holy c; Num 28.26

COOL
God walking..in the c..day Gen 3.8
c spirit is..understanding. Prov 17.27

COPY
upon the stones a c of the law Josh 8.32
Mordecai also gave him a c Est 4.8
They serve a c and shadow of Heb 8.5

CORBAN
C' (that is, given to God)— Mk 7.11

CORD — S
A threefold c is not quickly Ecc 4.12
before..silver c is snapped, 12.6
The c of death encompassed me, Ps 18.4
Lord..cut the c of the wicked. 129.4
led them with c of compassion, Hos 11.4

CORINTH
left Athens and went to C. Acts 18.1
While Apollos was at C, Paul 19.1
church of God which is at C, 1Cor 1.2

CORNELIUS
man named C, a centurion Acts 10.1
an angel..saying to him, "C." 10.3
C was expecting them and 10.24
'C, your prayer has been heard 10.31

CORNER
this was not done in a c. Acts 26.26
become the head of the c," 1Pet 2.7

CORNERSTONE
Jesus himself being the c, Eph 2.20
in Zion a..c chosen..precious, 1Pet 2.6

CORRECT
seek justice, c oppression; Isa 1.17
C me,..but in just measure; Jer 10.24

CORRECTION
your children, they took no c; Jer 2.30
but they refused to take c. 5.3

CORRECTION (cont.)

to no voice, she accepts no c.	Zeph 3.2
fear me, she will accept c;	3.7

CORRUPT (adj)

earth was c in God's sight,	Gen 6.11
astray, they are all alike c;	Ps 14.3

CORRUPTED (v)

your people,..c themselves;	Ex 32.7
They have deeply c themselves	Hos 9.9
have c the covenant of Levi,	Mal 2.8

CORRUPTION

nor let thy Holy One see c.	Acts 2.27
not let thy Holy One see c.'	13.35

CORRUPTLY

c by making a graven image	Deut 4.16
They have dealt c with him,	32.5

COST (v)

offerings..c me nothing."	2Sam 24.24
offerings..c me nothing."	1Chr 21.24

COST (n)

let the c be paid from the	Ezra 6.4
sit down and count the c,	Lk 14.28
gospel without c to you?	2Cor 11.7

COUNCIL — S

you listened in the c of God?	Job 15.8
God has..place in the divine c;	Ps 82.1
feared in the c of the holy ones,	89.7
stood in the c of the LORD	Jer 23.18
He was a member of the c	Lk 23.50
they will deliver you..to c,	Mt 10.17

COUNSEL — S

I will give you c,	Ex 18.19
by the c of Balaam, to act	Num 31.16
the c which Ahithophel has	2Sam 17.7
But he forsook the c which	1Ki 12.8
forsook the c which the old	2Chr 10.8
The c of the wicked is far	Job 21.16
"Who is this that darkens c	38.2
walks not in the c of..wicked,	Ps 1.1
rulers take c together, against	2.2
c of the nations to nought;	33.10
c of the LORD stands for ever,	33.11
Thou dost guide me with thy c,	73.24
they did not wait for his c.	106.13
I have c and sound wisdom,	Prov 8.14
Without c plans go wrong,	15.22
the spirit of c and might,	Isa 11.2
LORD..he is wonderful in c,	28.29
performs..c of his messengers;	44.26
nor c from the wise, nor the	Jer 18.18
great in c and mighty in deed;	32.19
O king, let my c be acceptable	Dan 4.27
the Pharisees went and took c	Mt 22.15
elders of the people took c	27.1
declaring to you the whole c	Acts 20.27
according to..c of his will,	Eph 1.11
c of..wicked are treacherous.	Prov 12.5
but walked in their own c and	Jer 7.24

COUNSELOR — S

his c in doing wickedly.	2Chr 22.3
you a royal c? Stop! Why	25.16
the c and the skilful magician	Isa 3.3
name will be called "Wonderful C,	9.6
as his c has instructed him?	40.13
among these there is no c	41.28
Has your c perished, that pangs	Mic 4.9
he will give you another C,	Jn 14.16
when the C comes, whom I shall	15.26

the C will not come to you;	16.7
Thy testimonies..are my c.	Ps 119.24
your c as at the beginning.	Isa 1.26

COUNT — ED — ING

Who can c the dust of Jacob,	Num 23.10
c them,..more than the sand.	Ps 139.18
Indeed I c everything as loss	Phil 3.8
C it all joy, my brethren,	Jas 1.2
sin is not c where..no law.	Rom 5.13
not c their trespasses	2Cor 5.19

COUNTENANCE

Cain was..angry,..his c fell.	Gen 4.5
my c they did not cast down.	Job 29.24
Lift up the light of thy c upon	Ps 4.6
A glad heart..a cheerful c,	Prov 15.13

COUNTRY

and came to his own c; and his	Mk 6.1
they desire a better c,	Heb 11.16

COURAGE

Be strong and of good c;	Josh 1.6
Be strong and of good c;	1.9
be strong and of good c;	10.25
Take c, and acquit yourselves	1Sam 4.9
Be of good c, and let us	2Sam 10.12
Be of good c, and let us	1Chr 19.13
"Be strong and of good c,	28.20
Asa..took c, and put away	2Chr 15.8
and let your heart take c;	Ps 27.14
and let your heart take c,	31.24
Can your c endure, or can	Ezek 22.14
"Take c, for as you have	Acts 23.11
Paul thanked God and took c.	28.15
So we are always of good c;	2Cor 5.6

COURAGEOUS — LY

in your faith, be c, be strong.	1Cor 16.13
Deal c, and may the LORD be	2Chr 19.11

COURSE

strong man runs its c with joy.	Ps 19.5
only I may accomplish my c	Acts 20.24

COURT

make the c of the tabernacle.	Ex 27.9
judged by..any human c.	1Cor 4.3

COVENANT — S

I will establish my c	Gen 6.18
I establish my c with you	9.9
I will make my c between me and you,	17.2
and the two men made a c.	21.27
let us make a c with you,	26.28
Come now, let us make a c,	31.44
God remembered his c with	Ex 2.24
established my c with them,	6.4
make no c with them or..their	23.32
"Behold the blood of the c	24.8
the c, the ten commandments.	34.28
will confirm my c with you.	Lev 26.9
execute vengeance for the c;	26.25
remember..my c with Abraham,	26.42
give to him my c of peace;	Num 25.12
he will not..forget the c	Deut 4.31
did the LORD make this c,	5.3
you shall make no c with them,	7.2
faithful God who keeps c	7.9
God will keep with you the c	7.12
does..evil..in transgressing his c,	17.2
These are the words of the c	29.1
that you may enter into the sworn c	29.12
they forsook the c of the LORD,	29.25
thy word, and kept thy c.	33.9
so now make a c with us."	Josh 9.6

COVENANT — S (cont.)

So Joshua made a c..people	Josh 24.25
never break my c with you,	Judg 2.1
you shall make no c with the	2.2
Jonathan made..c with David,	1Sam 18.3
brought your servant into a sacred c	20.8
they may make a c with you,	2Sam 3.21
King David made a c with them	5.3
made with me an everlasting c,	23.5
keeping c and showing..love	1Ki 8.23
Israel have forsaken thy c,	19.10
Jehoiada..made a c with them	2Ki 11.4
Jehoiada made a c between the LORD	11.17
book of the c..had been found	23.2
the people joined in the c.	23.3
mindful of his c for ever,	1Chr 16.15
no God like thee,..keeping c	2Chr 6.14
a c to seek the LORD, the	15.12
of David, because of the c	21.7
made a c before the LORD,	34.31
let us make a c with our God	Ezra 10.3
for those who keep his c and	Ps 25.10
he makes known to them his c.	25.14
thee, or been false to thy c.	44.17
faithful ones, who made a c	50.5
against..friends, he violated his c.	55.20
Have regard for thy c; for	74.20
they were not true to his c.	78.37
against thee they make a c—	83.5
made a c with my chosen one,	89.3
to those who keep his c and	103.18
to Israel as an everlasting c,	105.10
remembered..his c,..and relented	106.45
If your sons keep my c and my	132.12
and forgets the c of her God;	Prov 2.17
your c with death..annulled,	Isa 28.18
given you as a c to the people,	42.6
this is my c with them, says	59.21
an everlasting c with them.	61.8
Israel..Judah have broken my c	Jer 11.10
do not break thy c with us.	14.21
"Because they forsook the c	22.9
I will make a new c with..Israel	31.31
with them an everlasting c,	32.40
then also my c with David	33.21
join..LORD in an everlasting c	50.5
yet I will remember my c	Ezek 16.60
with you an everlasting c,	16.60
by keeping his c it might stand.)	17.14
I will make a c of peace	37.26
he shall make a strong c with	Dan 9.27
heart..set against..holy c.	11.28
at Adam they transgressed the c;	Hos 6.7
that my c with Levi may hold,	Mal 2.4
companion and your wife by c.	2.14
this is my blood of the c,	Mt 26.28
"This is my blood of the c,	Mk 14.24
and to remember his holy c,	Lk 1.72
sons of..prophets and of..c	Acts 3.25
gave him..c of circumcision.	7.8
this will be my c with them	Rom 11.27
"This cup is the new c in	1Cor 11.25
to be ministers of a new c,	2Cor 3.6
when they read the old c,	3.14
annul a c previously ratified	Gal 3.17
Jesus the surety of a better c.	Heb 7.22
when I will establish a new c,	8.8
he is the mediator of a new c,	9.15
"This is the c that I will make	10.16
the ark of his c was seen	Rev 11.19
C are broken, witnesses are	Isa 33.8

with empty oaths they make c;	Hos 10.4
strangers to the c of promise,	Eph 2.12

COVER — S — ED — ING (v)

I will c you with my hand	Ex 33.22
thou dost c him with favor as	Ps 5.12
will c you with his pinions,	91.4
as the waters c the sea.	Isa 11.9
say to the mountains, C us,	Hos 10.8
say..to the hills, 'C us.'	Lk 23.30
but love c all offenses.	Prov 10.12
took her veil and c herself.	Gen 24.65
cloud c the tabernacle,	Num 9.15
behold, the cloud c it,	16.42
and with two he c his feet,	Isa 6.2
nothing is c that will not be	Mt 10.26
Nothing is c up that will not	Lk 12.2
prophesies with his head c	1Cor 11.4
waters..c them fifteen cubits	Gen 7.20

COVERING (n)

He made darkness his c around	Ps 18.11
the c too narrow to wrap	Isa 28.20

COVERT

In the c of thy presence thou	Ps 31.20

COVET — ED — ING

"You shall not c your	Ex 20.17
" 'Neither shall you c	Deut 5.21
They c fields, and seize them;	Mic 2.2
law..said, "You shall not c."	Rom 7.7
You shall not steal, You shall not c,"	13.9
fifty shekels, then I c them,	Josh 7.21
I c no one's silver or gold	Acts 20.33
c, wickedness, deceit,..envy,	Mk 7.22

COVETOUS — NESS

who is c (that is, an idolater),	Eph 5.5
Because of..iniquity of his c	Isa 57.17
Take heed,..beware of all c;	Lk 12.15
wickedness, evil, c, malice.	Rom 1.29
wrought in me all kinds of c.	7.8

CRAFT — INESS

against all the beautiful c.	Isa 2.16
takes the wise in their..c;	Job 5.13
catches the wise in their c,"	1Cor 3.19
by their c in deceitful wiles.	Eph 4.14

CRAFTSMAN — MEN

c encourages the goldsmith,	Isa 41.7
and the c are but men;	44.11

CRAFTY

frustrates..devices of the c,	Job 5.15
choose the tongue of the c.	15.5

CREATE — S — D

C in me a clean heart, O God,	Ps 51.10
LORD will c over..Mount Zion	Isa 4.5
I make weal and c woe, I am	45.7
I c new heavens and..earth;	65.17
for thou didst c all things,	Rev 4.11
and c the wind, and declares	Amos 4.13
God c the heavens..earth.	Gen 1.1
God c..sea monsters	1.21
God c man in his own image,	1.27
your father, who c you,	Deut 32.6
thy Spirit, they are c;	Ps 104.30
he commanded and they were c.	148.5
LORD c me at the beginning	Prov 8.22
high and see: who c these?	Isa 40.26
Holy One of Israel has c it.	41.20
the LORD, who c the heavens	42.5
whom I c for my glory, whom	43.7
the LORD, who c the heavens	45.18

CREATE — S — D (cont.)
the LORD has c a new thing	Jer 31.22
c in Christ Jesus for good	Eph 2.10
in him all things were c,	Col 1.16
everything c by God is good,	1Tim 4.4
who c heaven and what is in it,	Rev 10.6

CREATION
from the beginning of the c	Mk 13.19
the c itself will be set free	Rom 8.21
the whole c has been groaning	8.22
if..in Christ, he is a new c;	2Cor 5.17
uncircumcision, but a new c.	Gal 6.15
from the beginning of c."	2Pet 3.4

CREATOR
Remember..your C in the days	Ecc 12.1
C of the ends of the earth.	Isa 40.28
the C of Israel, your King."	43.15
creature rather than the C,	Rom 1.25

CREATURES
swarms of living c,	Gen 1.20
the spirit of the living c	Ezek 10.17
four living c, full of eyes	Rev 4.6

CREDITOR — S
"A certain c had two debtors;	Lk 7.41
which of my c is it to whom	Isa 50.1

CREEPING
cattle and c things and beasts	Gen 1.24

CRETE
Phoenix, a harbor of C,	Acts 27.12
This is why I left you in C,	Tit 1.5

CRIME — S
requited the c of Abimelech,	Judg 9.56
"I find no c in this man."	Lk 23.4
in him no c deserving death;	23.22
told them, "I find no c in him.	Jn 18.38
that I find no c in him."	19.4
for I find no c in him."	19.6
the land is full of bloody c	Ezek 7.23

CRINGE — ING
thy enemies c before thee.	Ps 66.3
obeyed me; foreigners came c	18.44

CRIPPLE — D
he was a c from birth, who	Acts 14.8
son of Jonathan; he is c	2Sam 9.3
had a son who was c in his feet.	4.4
I will bind up the c,	Ezek 34.16

CROOKED
men whose paths are c, and	Prov 2.15
c cannot be made straight,	Ecc 1.15
make straight what he..made c?	7.13
they have made their roads c,	Isa 59.8

CROPS
have nowhere to store my c?'	Lk 12.17
the first share of the c.	2Tim 2.6

CROSS
he who does not take his c and	Mt 10.38
take up his c and follow me..	16.24
man..compelled to carry his c.	27.32
deny himself and take up his c	Mk 8.34
compelled..Simon..to carry his c.	15.21
and come down from the c!"	15.30
take up his c daily and follow	Lk 9.23
does not bear his own c and	14.27
laid on him the c, to carry	23.26
went out, bearing his own c,	Jn 19.17
lest..c of Christ be emptied	1Cor 1.17
the stumbling block of the c	Gal 5.11

not be persecuted for the c	6.12
to glory except in the c of..Christ.	6.14
unto death, even death on a c.	Phil 2.8
enemies of the c of Christ,	3.18
aside, nailing it to the c.	Col 2.14
endured the c, despising the	Heb 12.2

CROWD — S
"I have compassion on the c,	Mk 8.2
And great c followed him	Mt 4.25

CROWN — EST (v)
dost c him with glory and honor.	Ps 8.5
Thou c the year with thy bounty;	65.11

CROWN (n)
king's son, and put the c	2Chr 23.11
thou dost set a c of fine gold	Ps 21.3
bestow on you a beautiful c."	Prov 4.9
wife is the c of her husband,	12.4
hoary head is a c of glory;	16.31
Woe to the proud c of the	Isa 28.1
LORD..will be a c of glory,	28.5
You shall be a c of beauty	62.3
c has fallen from our head;	Lam 5.16
beautiful c upon your head.	Ezek 16.12
make a c, and set it upon	Zech 6.11
for me the c of righteousness,	2Tim 4.8
that no one may seize your c.	Rev 3.11
son of man, with a golden c	14.14

CROWS
before the cock c twice,	Mk 14.30

CRUCIBLE
The c is for silver, and	Prov 17.3

CRUCIFY — IED
men..whom you will kill and c,	Mt 23.34
they cried out again, "C him."	Mk 15.13
they led him out to c him.	15.20
they shouted out, "C, c, him!"	Lk 23.21
they cried out, "C him, c him!"	Jn 19.6
power to release..and..c you?"	19.10
mocked and scourged and c,	Mt 20.19
They all said, "Let him be c."	27.22
And when they had c him,	27.35
I know..you seek Jesus who was c.	28.5
Jesus of Nazareth, who was c.	Mk 16.6
The Skull, there they c him,	Lk 23.33
There they c him, and with him	Jn 19.18
c and killed by..lawless men.	Acts 2.23
our old self was c with him	Rom 6.6
divided? Was Paul c for you?	1Cor 1.13
except Jesus Christ and him c.	2.2
they would not have c the Lord	2.8
For he was c in weakness,	2Cor 13.4
I have been c with Christ;	Gal 2.20
was publicly portrayed as c?	3.1
the world has been c to me,	6.14
Egypt, where their Lord was c.	Rev 11.8

CRUEL — LY
Thou hast turned c to me;	Job 30.21
but a c man hurts himself.	Prov 11.17
jealousy is c as the grave.	Sol 8.6
She deals c with her young,	Job 39.16

CRUMBS
yet even the dogs eat the c	Mt 15.27
dogs..eat the children's c."	Mk 7.28

CRUSE
the c of oil shall not fail,	1Ki 17.14

CRUSH — ED
by thee I can c a troop; and	Ps 18.29
assembly..to c my young men;	Lam 1.15

CRUSH — ED (cont.)

crowd, lest they should c him;   Mk 3.9
on any one it will c him."   Lk 20.18
God..will soon c Satan under Rom 16.20
has c and abandoned the poor, Job 20.19

CRY — ING — IED

I will surely hear their c;   Ex 22.23
and c, 'Unclean, unclean.'   Lev 13.45
I c out, 'Violence!' but   Job 19.7
Hearken to the sound of my c,   Ps 5.2
I c out in the night before thee.   88.1
LORD; let my c come to thee!   102.1
With my whole heart I c;   119.145
In my distress I c to the LORD,   120.1
Out of the depths I c to thee,   130.1
will not c or lift up his voice,   Isa 42.2
great city, and c against it;   Jonah 1.2
will not wrangle or c aloud,   Mt 12.19
very stones would c out."   Lk 19.40
your brother's blood is c   Gen 4.10
and lo, the babe was c.   Ex 2.6
words of his father, he c out   Gen 27.34
Samuel c to the LORD for   1Sam 7.9
Samuel was angry; and he c   15.11
to my God I c for help. From   Ps 18.6
They c to..LORD,..he answered   99.6
c to the LORD in their trouble,   107.28
blind men..c out, "Have mercy Mt 20.30

CUNNING

we refuse to practice c or   2Cor 4.2
carried about..by..c of men   Eph 4.14

CUP

and put my c, the silver c,   Gen 44.2
be the portion of their c.   Ps 11.6
LORD..chosen portion and my c;   16.5
head with oil, my c overflows.   23.5
hand of the LORD there is a c,   75.8
will lift up the c of salvation   116.13
drunk..the c of his wrath.   Isa 51.17
they refuse to accept the c   Jer 25.28
The c in the LORD's right hand   Hab 2.16
a c of cold water because he   Mt 10.42
able to drink the c that I am   20.22
cleanse the outside of the c   23.25
he took a c, and when he had   26.27
Father,..let this c pass from me;   26.39
a c of water to drink because   Mk 9.41
able to drink the c..I drink,   10.38
he took a c, and when he had   14.23
remove this c from me; yet   14.36
cleanse the outside of the c   Lk 11.39
he took a c, and when he had   22.17
willing, remove this c from me;   22.42
shall I not drink the c which   Jn 18.11
The c of blessing which we   1Cor 10.16
"This c is the new covenant   11.25
c of the fury of his wrath.   Rev 16.19

CURDS

he took c, and milk,   Gen 18.8
He shall eat c and honey when   Isa 7.15

CURED

In that hour he c many..diseases Lk 7.21
the rest..came and were c.   Acts 28.9

CURSE — S — D (v)

who curses you I will c;   Gen 12.3
Come..c this people for me,   Num 22.6
How can I c whom God has not   23.8
he will c thee to thy face."   Job 1.11
hold fast your integrity? C God,   2.9
loved to c; let curses come   Ps 109.17

Even in..thought, do not c   Ecc 10.20
bless those who c you, pray   Lk 6.28
"Whoever c his father or his   Ex 21.17
c his father or his mother,   Prov 20.20
c are you above all cattle,   Gen 3.14
you are c from the ground   4.11
C be their anger, for it is fierce;   49.7
"C before the LORD be the man Josh 6.26
"C be the man who eats   1Sam 14.24
as he came he c continually.   2Sam 16.5
"Naboth c God and the king." 1Ki 21.13
he c them in the name of the   2Ki 2.24
and c the day of his birth   Job 3.1
"C is..man who trusts in man Jer 17.5
C be the day..I was born!   20.14
"C is..work..with slackness;   48.10
fig tree..you c has withered."   Mk 11.21
ever says "Jesus be c!"   1Cor 12.3
"C be every one who hangs   Gal 3.13
they c the name of God who   Rev 16.9

CURSE — S — ING (n)

a blessing and a c: Deut 11.26
stand upon Mount Ebal for the c: 27.13
law, the blessing and the c,   Josh 8.34
The LORD's c is on the house   Prov 3.33
make them..a hissing and a c, Jer 25.18
c that goes out over the..land; Zech 5.3
then I will send the c upon you Mal 2.2
of the law are under a c;   Gal 3.10
"Their mouth is full of c   Rom 3.14
you have been a byword of c   Zech 8.13
mouth come blessing and c.   Jas 3.10

CURTAIN — S

the c of the temple was torn   Mt 27.51
the c of the temple was torn   Mk 15.38
the c of the temple was torn   Lk 23.45
Behind..second c stood a tent Heb 9.3
opened for us through the c,   10.20
the tabernacle with ten c   Ex 26.1

CUSH

flows around..land of C.   Gen 2.13

CUSTODIAN

law was our c until Christ   Gal 3.24
we are no longer under a c;   3.25

CUSTOM — S

impose tribute, c, or toll   Ezra 7.24
to the synagogue, as his c was, Lk 4.16
any of these abominable c   Lev 18.30
c of the peoples are false.   Jer 10.3

CUT

you shall not c yourselves   Deut 14.1
cried aloud, and c themselves 1Ki 18.28
c off..name and remnant,   Isa 14.22
anointed one shall be c off,   Dan 9.26
hand causes you to sin, c it off; Mk 9.43
they were c to the heart,   Acts 2.37

CYMBAL — S

noisy gong or a clanging c.   1Cor 13.1
Praise him with sounding c;   Ps 150.5

CYPRUS

Barnabas..a native of C,   Acts 4.36
as far as Phoenicia and C   11.19
from there they sailed to C.   13.4
Barnabas took Mark..to C,   15.39
sailed under the lee of C,   27.4

CYRUS

first year..C king of Persia,   Ezra 1.1
as King C..has commanded   4.3

CYRUS (cont.)
first year of *C* king of Babylon, Ezra 5.13
of *C*, 'He is my shepherd, Isa 44.28
LORD to his anointed, to *C*, 45.1
the first year of King *C*. Dan 1.21

D

DAILY
take up his cross *d* and follow Lk 9.23
Give us each day our *d* bread; 11.3

DAMASCUS
to Hobah, north of *D*. Gen 14.15
put garrisons in Aram of *D*; 2Sam 8.6
For the head of Syria is *D*, Isa 7.8
The word of the LORD..upon *D*. Zech 9.1
letters to..synagogues at *D*, Acts 9.2
'Rise, and go into *D*, and 22.10
At *D*, the governor under 2Cor 11.32
and again I returned to *D*. Gal 1.17

DAN (Son of Jacob)
Born, Gen 30.6; blessed by Jacob, Gen 49.16–17.
Tribe of Dan: blessed by Moses, Deut 33.22; allotted territory, Josh 19.40–48; migrated north, judg 18; became center of idolatry, 1Ki 12.28–30.

DAN (the City)
in pursuit as far as *D*. Gen 14.14
And they named the city *D*, Judg 9.29
Israel came out, from *D* to 20.1
from *D* to Beersheba knew 1Sam 3.20

DANCE — D (v)
daughters of Shiloh..to *d* Judg 21.21
'We piped..and you did not *d*; Mt 11.17
'We piped..and you did not *d*; Lk 7.32
David *d* before the LORD 2Sam 6.14
the daughter of Herodias *d* Mt 14.6
Herodias' daughter came..and *d*, Mk 6.22

DANCING (n)
saw..*d*, Moses' anger burned Ex 32.19
turned..my mourning into *d*; Ps 30.11
our *d*..turned to mourning. Lam 5.15

DANIEL (BELTESHAZZAR)
Trained in the king's palace, Dan 1.1–7; abstained from the king's food, Dan 1.8–16; interpreted Nebuchadnezzar's dreams, Dan 2; 4; interpreted the handwriting on the wall, Dan 5.10–29; delivered from the lion's den, Dan 6; visions and dreams, Dan 7—8; 10—12; prayed for his people, Dan 9.

DARE
good man will *d* even to die. Rom 5.7
brother, does he *d* go to law 1Cor 6.1

DARIUS
until the reign of *D* king Ezra 4.5
Then *D*..made a decree, and 6.1
D the Mede received..kingdom, Dan 5.31
prospered during..reign of *D* 6.28
In..second year of *D* the king, Hag 1.1
in the second year of *D*, Zech 1.1

DARK
In the *d* they dig through Job 24.16
I am very *d*, but comely, Sol 1.5
What I tell you in the *d*, utter Mt 10.27
a lamp shining in a *d* place, 2Pet 1.19

DARKEN — S — ED
d the earth in broad daylight. Amos 8.9
"Who is this that *d* counsel Job 38.2
stars..*d* and the clouds return Ecc 12.2
sun will be *d*, and the moon Mk 13.24

DARKNESS
great *d* fell upon him. Gen 15.12
d over the land of Egypt, Ex 10.21
land of gloom and deep *d*, Job 10.21
with the terrors of deep *d*. 24.17
and covered us with deep *d*. Ps 44.19
the *d* is not dark to thee, 139.12
but behold, distress and *d*, Isa 8.22
your God before he brings *d*, Jer 13.16
d and gloom, a day of clouds Joel 2.2
If..the light in you is *d*, Mt 6.23
cast him into the outer *d*; 22.13
cast..servant into the outer *d*; 25.30
there was *d* over all the land 27.45
there was *d* over the..land Mk 15.33
was *d* over the whole land Lk 23.44
out of *d* into his marvelous 1Pet 2.9

DAUGHTER — S
sister, the *d* of my father Gen 20.12
adopted her as his own *d*. Est 2.7
Shout aloud, O *d* of Jerusalem! Zech 9.9
"My *d* has just died; but come Mt 9.18
"Tell the *d* of Zion, Behold, 21.5
"My..*d* is at..point of death. Mk 5.23
the demon has left your *d*." 7.29
he had an only *d*, about twelve Lk 8.42
Pharaoh's *d* adopted him and Acts 7.21
the son of Pharaoh's *d*, Heb 11.24
Turn back, my *d*, go your way, Ruth 1.12
our *d* like corner pillars Ps 144.12
the heads of the *d* of Zion, Isa 3.17

DAVID
Anointed by Samuel, 1Sam 16.1–13; played the harp for Saul, 1Sam 16.14–23; killed Goliath, 1Sam 17; won Jonathan's friendship, 1Sam 18.1–4; incurred Saul's jealousy, 1Sam 18.5–9; married Michal, 1Sam 18.20–29; fled from Saul, 1Sam 19—22; fought the Philistines, 1Sam 23; spared Saul at En-gedi, 1Sam 24; David and Abigail, 1Sam 25; spared Saul at Ziph, 1Sam 26; lived among the Philistines, 1Sam 27.1—28.2; 29; defeated the Amalekites, 1Sam 30; made king over Judah, 2Sam 2.1–7; made king over Israel, 2Sam 5.1–16; brought the ark to Jerusalem, 2Sam 6; God's covenant with David, 2Sam 7; extended his kingdom, 2Sam 8; David and Bath-sheba, 2Sam 11:1—12.25; fled Absalom's revolt, 2Sam 15—16; returned to Jerusalem, 2Sam 19; David's song, 2Sam 22.1—23.7; numbered Israel and Judah, 2Sam 24; charged Solomon, 1Ki 2.1–9; died, 1Ki 2.10–12. (See also 1Chr 11—29.)

He chose *D* his servant, and Ps 78.70
raise up for *D* a righteous Jer 23.5
one shepherd, my servant *D*, Ezek 34.23
"Have you not read what *D* did, Mt 12.3
"Have..never read what *D* did, Mk 2.25
the throne of his father *D*, Lk 1.32
For *D* says concerning him, Acts 2.25
descended from *D* according to Rom 1.3
the Root of *D*, has conquered, Rev 5.5

DAWN
rise before d. .cry for help;   Ps 119.147
light break forth like the d,   Isa 58.8
toward the d of the first day   Mt 28.1
when the day shall d upon us   Lk 1.78

DAY — S
God called the light D,   Gen 1.5
God blessed the seventh d   2.3
There has been no d like it   Josh 10.14
This d is a d of good news;   2Ki 7.9
knows that a d of darkness   Job 15.23
D to d pours forth speech, and   Ps 19.2
By d the LORD commands. .love;   42.8
Thine is the d, thine also   74.16
This is the d. .LORD has made;   118.24
Every d I will bless thee,   145.2
LORD of hosts has a d against   Isa 2.12
In that d the root of Jesse   11.10
You will say in that d: "I will   12.1
Wail, for the d of the LORD   13.6
the LORD has a d of vengeance,   34.8
'This d is a d of distress,   37.3
d of the Lord GOD of hosts,   Jer 45.10
the d of the LORD is near;   Ezek 30.3
the d of the LORD is near,   Joel 1.15
the d of the LORD is great   2.11
Why. .have the d of the LORD? Amos 5.18
great d of the LORD is near,   Zeph 1.14
a d of the LORD is coming,   Zech 14.1
endure the d of his coming,   Mal 3.2
the d comes, burning like an oven,   4.1
trouble be sufficient for the d.   Mt 6.34
that d or. .hour no one knows,   Mk 13.32
when the d shall dawn upon us   Lk 1.78
rejoiced. .he was to see my d;   Jn 8.56
every d in the temple and at   Acts 5.42
becomingly as in the d, not   Rom 13.13
our Lord, I die every d!   1Cor 15.31
On the first d of every week,   16.2
on the d of the Lord Jesus.   2Cor 1.14
helped you on. .d of salvation."   6.2
completion at the d of Jesus   Phil 1.6
the d of the Lord will come   1Thess 5.2
you see the D drawing near.   Heb 10.25
the d of the Lord will come   2Pet 3.10
as your d, so shall your   Deut 33.25
So teach us to number our d   Ps 90.12
My d. .like an evening shadow;   102.11

DEACONS
with the bishops and d: Phil 1.1
D likewise must be serious,   1Tim 3.8

DEAD
your d bodies shall fall   Num 14.29
between the d and. .living;   16.48
behold, these were all d   2Ki 19.35
after that they go to the d.   Ecc 9.3
leave. .d to bury their own d."   Mt 8.22
girl is not d but sleeping."   9.24
deaf hear, and the d are raised   11.5
He is not God of the d, but   22.32
child is not d but sleeping."   Mk 5.39
wondered if he were already d;   15.44
"Your daughter is d; do not   Lk 8.49
"Leave the d to bury their. .d;   9.60
my son was d, and is alive   15.24
Paul. .supposing. .he was d.   Acts 14.19
fell down from the third story. .d   20.9
although your bodies are d   Rom 8.10
If the d are not raised   1Cor 15.29
you were d through. .trespasses   Eph 2.1
trees in late autumn, twice d,   Jude 12

name of being alive, and. .are d.   Rev 3.1
Blessed are the d who die in   14.13
I saw the d, great and small,   20.12

DEAF
You shall not curse the d   Lev 19.14
In that day the d shall hear   Isa 29.18
brought to him a man who was d Mk 7.32
the d hear and the dumb speak."   7.37

DEAL — T
not d. .according to our sins, Ps 103.10
he d well with Abram;   Gen 12.16
d thus with any other nation;   Ps 147.20

DEALINGS
Jews have no d with Samaritans. Jn 4.9

DEAR
consume like a moth what is d Ps 39.11
servants hold her stones d,   102.14
centurion had a slave who was d Lk 7.2

DEATH
die the d of the righteous,   Num 23.10
life and good, d and evil.   Deut 30.15
whether for d or for life,   2Sam 15.21
snares of d confronted me.   22.6
the gates of d been revealed   Job 38.17
the valley of the shadow of d,   Ps 23.4
snares of d encompassed me;   116.3
Precious is. .d of his saints,   116.15
its end is the way to d.   Prov 14.12
He will swallow up d for ever,   Isa 25.8
way of life and the way of d.   Jer 21.8
no pleasure in. .d of any one,   Ezek 18.32
O D, where are your plagues? Hos 13.14
powers of d shall not prevail   Mt 16.18
daughter is at the point of d.   Mk 5.23
against Jesus to put him to d;   14.55
those who sit. .in. .shadow of d, Lk 1.79
some here who will not taste d   9.27
seeking how to put him to d: 22.2
show by what d he was to die.   Jn 12.33
to show by what d he was to   21.19
d reigned from Adam to Moses, Rom 5.14
by the Spirit you put to d   8.13
I am sure that neither d,   8.38
"D. .swallowed up in victory." 1Cor 15.54
"O d, where is thy victory?   15.55
a fragrance from d to d,   2Cor 2.16
Put to d. .what is earthly   Col 3.5
Jesus, who abolished d and   2Tim 1.10
not be hurt by the second d.'   Rev 2.11

DEBORAH
Now D, a prophetess, the wife Judg 4.4
And D said to Barak, "Up!   4.14
Then sang D and Barak the son   5.1

DEBT — S
and every one who was in d,   1Sam 22.2
and the exaction of every d.   Neh 10.31
him and forgave him the d.   Mt 18.27
sell the oil and pay your d,   2Ki 4.7

DEBTORS
"A certain creditor had two d; Lk 7.41
summoning his master's d one   16.5
we are d, not to the flesh,   Rom 8.12

DECEIT
and their heart prepares d."   Job 15.35
my tongue will not utter d.   27.4
cursing and d and oppression; Ps 10.7
my prayer from lips free of d!   17.1
in whose spirit there is no d.   32.2

DECEIT (cont.)
and your lips from speaking *d.* Ps 34.13
and your tongue frames *d.*   50.19
D is in the heart of those   Prov 12.20
there was no *d* in his mouth.   Isa 53.9
and the *d* of their own minds.   Jer 14.14
wickedness, *d*, licentiousness,   Mk 7.22
murder, strife, *d*, malignity,   Rom 1.29

DECEITFUL — LY — NESS
LORD abhors bloodthirsty and *d*   Ps 5.6
words that devour, O *d* tongue.   52.4
Charm is *d*,..beauty is vain,   Prov 31.30
heart is *d* above all things,   Jer 17.9
false apostles, *d* workmen,   2Cor 11.13
their craftiness in *d* wiles.   Eph 4.14
deal *d* with false balances,   Amos 8.5
hardened by the *d* of sin.   Heb 3.13

DECEIVE — S — D — ING
"Why did you *d* us, saying,   Josh 9.22
Did I not say, Do not *d* me?"   2Ki 4.28
'Do not let Hezekiah *d* you,   18.29
Do not *d* yourselves, saying,   Jer 37.9
and flattering words they *d*   Rom 16.18
Let no one *d* you with empty   Eph 5.6
Let no one *d* you in any way;   2Thess 2.3
deceive him, as one *d* a man?   Job 13.9
who *d* his neighbor and says,   Prov 26.19
Every one *d* his neighbor,   Jer 9.5
Why then have you *d* me?"   Gen 29.25
"Why have you *d* me thus,   1Sam 19.17
d and the deceiver are his.   Job 12.16
GOD,..thou hast utterly *d*   Jer 4.10
O LORD, thou hast *d* me, and   20.7
called to my lovers but they *d*   Lam 1.19
Do not be *d*; neither..immoral,   1Cor 6.9
Do not be *d*: "Bad company   15.33
serpent *d* Eve by his cunning,   2Cor 11.3
Do not be *d*; God is not mocked,   Gal 6.7
Adam was not *d*, but the woman   1Tim 2.14
nations were *d* by thy sorcery.   Rev 18.23
against the LORD by *d* his   Lev 6.2

DECEIVER — S
is the *d* and the antichrist.   2Jn 7
Satan,..*d* of the whole world—   Rev 12.9
men, empty talkers and *d*,   Tit 1.10

DECENTLY
all things should be done *d*   1Cor 14.40

DECIDE — D
Now *d* what answer I shall   1Chr 21.12
and *d* with equity for the meek   Isa 11.4
He..shall *d* for strong nations   Mic 4.3
I *d* to know nothing among you   1Cor 2.2

DECISION — S
shall declare to you the *d.*   Deut 17.9
multitudes, in..valley of *d*!   Joel 3.14
Inspired *d* are on the lips   Prov 16.10
d..reached by the apostles   Acts 16.4

DECLARE — D
D his glory among..nations   1Chr 16.24
D his glory among the nations,   Ps 96.3
and I will *d* thy greatness.   145.6
d my glory among the nations.   Isa 66.19
And then will I *d* to them,   Mt 7.23
d to you the things..to come.   Jn 16.13
When I *d* not my sin, my body   Ps 32.3
"The former things I *d* of old,   Isa 48.3

DECREE — D (v)
Woe to those who *d* iniquitous   Isa 10.1
which God *d* before the ages   1Cor 2.7

heritage *d* for him by God."   Job 20.29
"Seventy weeks of years are *d*   Dan 9.24

DECREE — S (n)
I make a *d* regarding what   Ezra 6.8
I will tell of the *d* of the LORD: Ps 2.7
It is a *d* of the Most High,   Dan 4.24
a *d*, that in all my..dominion   6.26
d went out from Caesar Augustus   Lk 2.1
Thy *d* are very sure; holiness   Ps 93.5
against the *d* of Caesar,   Acts 17.7

DEDICATE — S — D
my God and *d* it to him for   2Chr 2.4
a man *d* his house to be holy   Lev 27.14
King David *d* to the LORD,   2Sam 8.11
which David his father had *d*,   1Ki 7.51
Israel *d* the house of the LORD.   8.63
From spoil won..they *d* gifts   1Chr 26.27

DEDICATION
the *d* of the altar on the day   Num 7.10
offered at the *d* of..house   Ezra 6.17
at the *d* of the wall of   Neh 12.27
come to the *d* of the image   Dan 3.2
feast of the *D* at Jerusalem;   Jn 10.22

DEED — S
bring every *d* into judgment,   Ecc 12.14
but in *d* and in truth.   1Jn 3.18
where are..his wonderful *d*   Judg 6.13
Praise him for his mighty *d*;   Ps 150.2
recompense..according to..*d*   Jer 25.14
they have made their *d* foul.   Mic 3.4
the due reward of our *d*; but   Lk 23.41
because their *d* were evil.   Jn 3.19
put to death the *d* of the body   Rom 8.13
to be rich in good *d*, liberal   1Tim 6.18
saved us, not because of *d*   Tit 3.5
for their *d* follow them!"   Rev 14.13

DEEP
find out the *d* things of God?   Job 11.7
D calls to *d* at the thunder   Ps 42.7
LORD! Thy thoughts are very *d*!   92.5
Thou didst cover it with the *d*   104.6
when..the fountains of the *d*,   Prov 8.28
he reveals *d* and mysterious   Dan 2.22
to Simon, "Put out into the *d*   Lk 5.4
call the *d* things of Satan,   Rev 2.24

DEFEAT
To have lawsuits..is *d* for you.   1Cor 6.7

DEFEND
I will *d* this city to save   2Ki 19.34
will *d* this city for my own   20.6
cause of truth and to *d* the   Ps 45.4
I will *d* this city to save   Isa 37.35

DEFENSE
his..*d* will be the fortresses   Isa 33.16
hear the *d* which I now make   Acts 22.1
my imprisonment and in the *d*   Phil 1.7

DEFENSELESS
I seek refuge; leave me not *d*!   Ps 141.8

DEFER — RED
"For my name's sake..*d*..anger,   Isa 48.9
Hope *d* makes the heart sick,   Prov 13.12

DEFILE — S — D — ING
"Do not *d* yourselves by   Lev 18.24
You shall not *d* the land   Num 35.34
you *d* yourselves with..idols   Ezek 20.31
They shall not *d* themselves   37.23
not *d* himself with the king's   Dan 1.8

DEFILE — S — D — ING (cont.)
which come out of a man..*d* Mk 7.15
does not cleanse himself, *d* Num 19.13
from the heart,..this *d* a man. Mt 15.18
comes out of a man is what *d* Mk 7.20
since he has *d* the sanctuary Num 19.20
they have *d* the priesthood Neh 13.29
they have *d* thy holy temple; Ps 79.1
when you came in you *d* my land, Jer 2.7
you have *d* my sanctuary with Ezek 5.11
they have *d* my sanctuary 23.38
They have *d* my holy name 43.8
played the harlot, Israel is *d*. Hos 5.3
conscience, being weak, is *d*. 1Cor 8.7
uncleanness..*d* my tabernacle Lev 15.31

DEFRAUDED
if I have *d* any one of anything Lk 19.8
wrong? Why not rather be *d*? 1Cor 6.7

DEFY
"I *d* the ranks of Israel 1Sam 17.10
men who maliciously *d* thee, Ps 139.20

DELIGHT — S — ED (v)
would the king *d* to honor Est 6.6
you will *d*..in the Almighty, Job 22.26
I *d* to do thy will, O my God; Ps 40.8
for thou didst *d* in them. 44.3
then..*d* in right sacrifices, 51.19
How long will scoffers *d* in Prov 1.22
I do not *d* in..blood of bulls, Isa 1.11
and *d* yourselves in fatness. 55.2
seek..and *d* to know my ways, 58.2
the messenger..in whom you *d*, Mal 3.1
I *d* in the law of God, in my Rom 7.22
If the LORD *d* in us, he will Num 14.8
whom the king *d* to honor." Est 6.11
not a God who *d* in wickedness; Ps 5.4
establishes..whose way he *d*. 37.23
greatly *d* in his commandments! 112.1
reproves..son in whom he *d*. Prov 3.12
for the LORD *d* in you, and Isa 62.4
because he *d* in steadfast love. Mic 7.18
Saul's son, *d* much in David. 1Sam 19.1
delivered me, because he *d* 2Sam 22.20
your God, who has *d* in you 1Ki 10.9

DELIGHT — S (n)
the tree was..a *d* to the eyes, Gen 3.6
as the LORD took *d* in..good Deut 28.63
again take *d* in prospering 30.9
"Has the LORD as great *d* 1Sam 15.22
he take *d* in the Almighty? Job 27.10
that he should take *d* in God.' 34.9
his *d* is in the law of the LORD, Ps 1.2
Take *d* in the LORD, and he will 37.4
thou hast no *d* in sacrifice; 51.16
live; for thy law is my *d*. 119.77
I was daily his *d*, rejoicing Prov 8.30
of blameless ways are his *d*. 11.20
prayer of..upright is his *d*. 15.8
Righteous lips are the *d* of 16.13
With..*d* I sat in his shadow, Sol 2.3
to take the *d* of your eyes Ezek 24.16
cares..and the *d* in riches, Mk 4.19
drink from the river of thy *d*. Ps 36.8

DELIVER — S — ED — ING
D me, I pray thee, from Gen 32.11
I have come down to *d* them Ex 3.8
d our lives from death." Josh 2.13
men that lapped I will *d* you, Judg 7.7
Say also: "*D* us, O God of 1Chr 16.35

Arise, O LORD! *D* me, O my God! Ps 3.7
O LORD, save my life; *d* me 6.4
that he may deliver their soul 33.19
D us for the sake of..love! 44.26
D me from my enemies, O my God, 59.1
nor will wickedness *d* those Ecc 8.8
saying, "The LORD will *d* us." Isa 36.18
none who can *d* from my hand; 43.13
"*D* me, for thou art my God!" 44.17
Or have I no power to *d*? 50.2
for I am with you to *d* you, Jer 1.8
I will *d* you on that day, 39.17
and gold are not able to *d* Ezek 7.19
able to *d* us from the burning Dan 3.17
Daniel, "May your God,..*d* you!" 6.16
and *d* him to the Gentiles; Mk 10.33
they will *d* you up to councils; 13.9
brother will *d* up brother 13.12
Who will *d* me from this body Rom 7.24
you are to *d* this man to Satan 1Cor 5.5
to *d* us from the present evil Gal 1.4
d..those..subject to..bondage. Heb 2.15
LORD helps them and *d* them; Ps 37.40
and thy right hand *d* me. 138.7
righteousness *d* from death. Prov 11.4
God..who has *d* your enemies Gen 14.20
"An Egyptian *d* us out of Ex 2.19
thou hast not *d* thy people 5.23
he had *d* them out of the hand 18.9
I *d* you from the hand of Judg 6.9
'My own hand has *d* me.' 7.2
LORD *d* Israel that day; 1Sam 14.23
"The king *d* us from the 2Sam 19.9
He *d* me from my strong enemy, 22.18
d me, because he delighted 22.20
because I *d* the poor who Job 29.12
He *d* me from my strong enemy, Ps 18.17
warrior is not *d* by..strength. 33.16
and *d* me from all my fears. 34.4
hast *d* me from every trouble, 54.7
and *d* them from the..enemy. 106.10
he *d* them from their distress; 107.6
he *d* them from their distress; 107.19
thou hast *d* my soul from death, 116.8
righteous is *d* from trouble, Prov 11.8
by his wisdom *d* the city. Yet Ecc 9.15
time your people shall be *d*, Dan 12.1
All things have been *d* to me Mt 11.27
Son of man is to be *d* into 17.22
the Son of man will be *d* to 20.18
Son of man will be *d* up to be 26.2
d him to Pilate the governor. 27.2
led him away..*d* him to Pilate. Mk 15.1
will be *d* to the Gentiles, Lk 18.32
will be *d* up even by parents 21.16
d them to what has been raised, Rom 15.28
d us from so deadly a peril, 2Cor 1.10
has *d* us from the dominion of Col 1.13
d you from the way of evil, Prov 2.12

DELIVERANCE
is hot, you shall have *d*.'" 1Sam 11.9
LORD has wrought *d* in Israel." 11.13
D belongs to the LORD; thy Ps 3.8
that..I may rejoice in thy *d*. 9.14
his *d* to a people yet unborn, 22.31
thou dost encompass me with *d*. 32.7
Say to my soul, "I am your *d*!" 35.3
d for Israel..come from Zion! 53.6
I bring near my *d*, it is not Isa 46.13
My *d* draws near speedily, 51.5
D belongs to the LORD!" Jonah 2.9
light; I shall behold his *d*. Mic 7.9

DELIVERANCE (cont.)
God was giving them *d* by his   Acts 7.25
this will turn out for my *d*,   Phil 1.19

DELIVERER
LORD raised up a *d* for the   Judg 3.9
and my fortress, and my *d*.   2Sam 22.2
my fortress, and my *d*, my God,   Ps 18.2
my strong *d*, thou hast covered   140.7

DELUDE — D
d you with beguiling speech.   Col 2.4
a *d* mind has led him astray,   Isa 44.20

DELUSION
Behold, they are all a *d*;   Isa 41.29
God sends..a strong *d*, to   2Thess 2.11

DEMON — S
daughter..possessed by a *d*."   Mt 15.22
and you say, 'He has a *d*.'   Lk 7.33
casting out a *d* that was dumb;   11.14
people answered, "You have a *d*!   Jn 7.20
diseases, and cast out many *d*;   Mk 1.34
by..prince of *d* he casts out..*d*."   3.22
casting out *d* in your name,   9.38
pagans sacrifice..to *d* and   1Cor 10.20
spirits and doctrines of *d*,   1Tim 4.1
the *d* believe—and shudder.   Jas 2.19
nor give up worshiping *d*   Rev 9.20
Babylon..dwelling place of *d*,   18.2

DEMONSTRATION
in *d* of the Spirit and power,   1Cor 2.4

DEN
a *d* of robbers in your eyes?   Jer 7.11
you make it a *d* of robbers."   Mt 21.13

DENY — ING — IES — IED
I also will *d* before my Father   Mt 10.33
let him *d* himself and take up   16.24
you will *d* me three times."   26.34
let him *d* himself and take up   Mk 8.34
you will *d* me three times."   14.30
three times *d* that you know   Lk 22.34
if we *d* him, he also will *d*   2Tim 2.12
they *d* him by their deeds.   Tit 1.16
you did not *d* my faith even   Rev 2.13
heresies, even *d* the Master   2Pet 2.1
who *d* me before men will be *d*   Lk 12.9
antichrist,..who *d* the Father   1Jn 2.22
Peter..*d* it before them all,   Mt 26.70
he *d* it, saying, "I neither know   Mk 14.68
But he *d* it, saying, "Woman,   Lk 22.57
one of his disciples?" He *d* it   Jn 18.25

DEPART — ED
said to God, '*D* from us,'   Job 22.17
D from evil, and do good;   Ps 34.14
d, go out thence, touch no   Isa 52.11
at his left hand, '*D* from me,   Mt 25.41
asked him to *d* from them;   Lk 8.37
Israel *d* to their tents.   1Ki 12.16
not wickedly *d* from my God.   Ps 18.21

DEPARTURE
in glory and spoke of his *d*,   Lk 9.31
after my *d* you may..recall   2Pet 1.15

DEPRAVED
They are all alike *d*; there   Ps 53.3
men who are *d* in mind and   1Tim 6.5

DEPRIVE
d the innocent of his right!   Isa 5.23
d..of my ground for boasting.   1Cor 9.15

DEPTHS
Out of the *d* I cry to thee,   Ps 130.1
Spirit searches..*d* of God.   1Cor 2.10

DERBE
fled to Lystra and *D*, cities   Acts 14.6
he came..to *D* and to Lystra.   16.1
Gaius of *D*, and Timothy;   20.4

DERIDED
who passed by *d* him, wagging   Mt 27.39
those who passed by *d* him,   Mk 15.29

DESCEND — ED
Lord himself will *d* from   1Thess 4.16
And the LORD *d* in the cloud   Ex 34.5
the Holy Spirit *d* upon him   Lk 3.22
our Lord was *d* from Judah,   Heb 7.14

DESCENDANTS
d I will give this land."   Gen 12.7
your *d* after you, the land   17.8
through Isaac shall your *d*   21.12
will give to your *d*..lands;   26.4
establish your *d* for ever,   Ps 89.4
told, "So shall your *d* be."   Rom 4.18
"Through Isaac shall your *d*   9.7

DESECRATED
they *d* the dwelling place of   Ps 74.7

DESERT (n)
Some wandered in *d* wastes,   Ps 107.4
break forth..streams in the *d*;   Isa 35.6
I will set in the *d* the cyprus,   41.19
d..cities lift up their voice,   42.11
d like the garden of the LORD;   51.3

DESERTED (v)
Demas,..has *d* me and gone   2Tim 4.10

DESERTING (v)
quickly *d* him who called you   Gal 1.6

DESERVE — S — ING
the man did not *d* to die,   Deut 19.6
for the laborer *d* his food.   Mt 10.10
They answered, "He *d* death."   26.66
"The laborer *d* his wages."   1Tim 5.18
condemned him as *d* death.   Mk 14.64

DESIGNATED
and *d* Son of God in power   Rom 1.4
being *d* by God a high priest   Heb 5.10

DESIGNS
favor the *d* of the wicked?   Job 10.3
we are not ignorant of his *d*.   2Cor 2.11

DESIRABLE
for whom is all that is *d* in   1Sam 9.20

DESIRE — S — ST — D (v)
We do not *d* the knowledge   Job 21.14
and offering thou dost not *d*;   Ps 40.6
the king will *d* your beauty.   45.11
nothing..I *d* besides thee.   73.25
Do not *d* her beauty in your   Prov 6.25
no beauty that we should *d*   Isa 53.2
days..coming when you will *d*   Lk 17.22
earnestly *d*..higher gifts.   1Cor 12.31
earnestly *d* to prophesy,   14.39
you who *d* to be under law,   Gal 4.21
soul of the wicked *d* evil;   Prov 21.10
thou *d* truth in..inward being;   Ps 51.6
of Sheba all that she *d*,   2Chr 9.12
orders..to do as every man *d*.   Est 1.8
More to be *d*..than gold, even   Ps 19.10
kings *d* to see what you see   Lk 10.24

DESIRE — S — ST — D (v) (cont.)
earnestly *d* to eat..passover Lk 22.15
Herod..had long *d* to see him, 23.8

DESIRE — S (n)
your *d*..for your husband, Gen 3.16
prosper all my help and..*d*? 2Sam 23.5
wilt hear the *d* of the meek; Ps 10.17
thou satisfiest the *d* of every 145.16
fulfils the *d* of all who fear 145.19
d of..righteous..be granted. Prov 10.24
The *d* of the righteous ends 11.23
d fulfilled is a tree of life. 13.12
d fulfilled is sweet to the soul; 13.19
The *d* of the sluggard kills 21.25
eyes than the wandering of *d*; Ecc 6.9
and *d* fails; because man goes 12.5
my beloved's,..*d* is for me. Sol 7.10
thy memorial name is the *d* Isa 26.8
Brethren, my heart's *d* and Rom 10.1
broken off,..*d* of my heart. Job 17.11
give you the *d* of your heart. Ps 37.4
Grant not, O LORD, the *d* of 140.8
the *d* of the flesh are against Gal 5.17
following the *d* of body and Eph 2.3

DESOLATE
God gives the *d* a home to dwell Ps 68.6
country lies *d*, your cities Isa 1.7
the LORD will..make it *d*, 24.1
your house is forsaken and *d*. Mt 23.38

DESOLATION
"The whole land shall be a *d*; Jer 4.27
know..its *d* has come near. Lk 21.20

DESPISE — S — D — ING
will this people *d* me? Num 14.11
therefore *d* not the chastening Job 5.17
Even young children *d* me; 19.18
therefore I *d* myself, and 42.6
fools *d* wisdom..instruction. Prov 1.7
do not *d* the LORD's discipline 3.11
"Because you *d* this word, Isa 30.12
Your lovers *d* you; they seek Jer 4.30
"I hate, I *d* your feasts, Amos 5.21
devoted to..one and *d* the other. Mt 6.24
do not *d* one of these little ones; 18.10
devoted to..one..*d* the other. Lk 16.13
Or do you *d* the church of 1Cor 11.22
let no one *d* him. Speed him 16.11
you did not scorn or *d* me, Gal 4.14
defiling passion..*d* authority. 2Pet 2.10
He who *d* the word brings Prov 13.13
Esau *d* his birthright. Ge. 25.34
he..*d* the word of the LORD, Num 15.31
these men have *d* the LORD." 16.30
she *d* him in her heart. 2Sam 6.16
They *d* his statutes, and 2Ki 17.15
we are *d*; turn back their taunt Neh 4.4
scorned by men, and *d* by the Ps 22.6
they *d* the pleasant land, 106.24
I am small and *d*, yet I do 119.141
they have *d* the Holy One of Isa 1.4
d the word of the Holy One 5.24
deeply *d*, abhorred by..nations, 49.7
all the day my name is *d*. 52.5
He was *d* and rejected by men; 53.3
I will make you..*d* among men. Jer 49.15
has *d* the day of small things Zech 4.10
were righteous and *d* others? Lk 18.9
God chose what is low and *d* 1Cor 1.28
of God, *d* his words, and 2Chr 36.16

DESPOIL — ED
you shall *d* the Egyptians." Ex 3.22
Thus they *d* the Egyptians. 12.36
"Because the poor are *d*, Ps 12.5

DESTINE — D
I will *d* you to the sword, Isa 65.12
He *d* us in love to be his sons Eph 1.5
God has not *d* us for wrath, 1Thess 5.9
was *d* before the foundation 1Pet 1.20

DESTITUTE
he will regard..prayer of..*d*, Ps 102.17
d, afflicted, ill-treated— Heb 11.37

DESTROY — S — ED
d all their figured stones, Num 33.52
d them from the camp, Deut 2.15
you must utterly *d* them; 7.2
you shall utterly *d* them, 20.17
Amalek, and utterly *d* all 1Sam 15.3
the LORD would not *d* Judah, 2Ki 8.19
d all the wicked in the land, Ps 101.8
they shall *d* with the sword." Jer 5.17
wilt thou *d* all that remains Ezek 9.8
'I am able to *d* the temple Mt 26.61
He will come and *d* the tenants, Mk 12.9
heard him say, 'I will *d* this 14.58
the people sought to *d* him; Lk 19.47
"*D* this temple, and in three Jn 2.19
through death he might *d* him Heb 2.14
complacence of fools *d* them; Prov 1.32
approaches and no moth *d*. Lk 12.33
If any one *d* God's temple, 1Cor 3.17
they should be utterly *d*, Josh 11.20
house of..wicked will be *d*, Prov 14.11
The Lord has *d* without mercy Lam 2.2
are *d* for lack of knowledge; Hos 4.6

DESTROYERS
I will prepare *d* against you, Jer 22.7
destroying..*d* of the earth." Rev 11.18

DESTRUCTION
end he shall come to *d*." Num 24.20
till the storms of *d* pass by. Ps 57.1
Pride goes before *d*, and a Prov 16.18
decree of *d* from the Lord Isa 28.22
grief because of the *d* of the Lam 2.11
for the *d* of the flesh, 1Cor 5.5
in the same *d* with them, 2Pet 2.12

DETERMINED
know that evil is *d* by him. 1Sam 20.7
God has *d* to destroy you, 2Chr 25.16
Haman..saw that evil was *d* Est 7.7
Since his days are *d*, and Job 14.5
for what is *d* shall be done. Dan 11.36
Son..goes as it has been *d*; Lk 22.22
having *d* allotted periods Acts 17.26
and has *d* this in his heart, 1Cor 7.37

DETESTABLE
Cast away the *d* things Ezek 20.7
d like the thing they loved. Hos 9.10

DEVIL
wilderness to be tempted by..*d*. Mt 4.1
enemy who sowed them is the *d*; 13.39
the *d* comes and takes away Lk 8.12
You are of your father the *d*, Jn 8.44
d..put it into the heart of Judas 13.2
give no opportunity to the *d*. Eph 4.27
Resist the *d* and he will flee Jas 4.7
Your adversary the *d* prowls 1Pet 5.8
d..sinned from the beginning. 1Jn 3.8

DEVIL (cont.)
the *d* is about to throw some	Rev 2.10
the *d* has come down to you	12.12
the *d* who had deceived them	20.10

DEVISE — D
for their minds *d* violence,	Prov 24.2
these are. .men who *d* iniquity	Ezek 11.2
Woe to those who *d* wickedness	Mic 2.1
son of Remaliah, has *d* evil	Isa 7.5

DEVOTE — D
d their gain to the LORD,	Mic 4.13
every *d* thing is most holy	Lev 27.28
Every *d* thing in Israel	Num 18.14
take any of the *d* things	Josh 6.18
in regard to the *d* things;	7.1
every *d* thing in Israel	Ezek 44.29

DEVOTION
because of my *d* to the house	1Chr 29.3
sincere. .pure *d* to Christ.	2Cor 11.3

DEVOUR — S — ED
"Shall the sword *d* for ever?	2Sam 2.26
all who *d* you shall be *d*,	Jer 30.16
and they *d* their rulers. All	Hos 7.7
for you *d* widows' houses and	Mt 23.14*n*
but a foolish man *d* it.	Prov 21.20
each *d* his neighbor's flesh,	Isa 9.20
you shall be *d* by the sword;	1.20

DEVOUT
Simeon,. .was righteous and *d*,	Lk 2.25
Jews, *d* men from every nation	Acts 2.5
a *d* man who feared God with	10.2
Ananias, a *d* man according	22.12

DEW
if there is *d* on the fleece	Judg 6.37
It is like the *d* of Hermon,	Ps 133.3
the clouds drop down the *d*.	Prov 3.20
but his favor is like *d*	19.12
like the *d* that goes early away,	Hos 6.4
the *d* that goes early away,	13.3
I will be as the *d* to Israel;	14.5

DIE — S — D
eat of it you shall *d*."	Gen 2.17
men *d* the common death	Num 16.29
shall *d* in the wilderness."	26.65
I must *d* in this land,	Deut 4.22
d on the mountain which	32.50
me *d* with the Philistines."	Judg 16.30
"Why did I not *d* at birth,	Job 3.11
and wisdom will *d* with you.	12.2
enemies say. ."When will he *d*,	Ps 41.5
I shall not *d*, but. .live,	118.17
fools *d* for lack of sense.	Prov 10.21
who despises the word will *d*.	19.16
why will you *d*, O house of	Ezek 33.11
"If I must *d* with you, I will	Mk 14.31
you will *d* in your sins unless	Jn 8.24
go, that we may *d* with him."	11.16
this disciple was not to *d*;	21.23
being raised. .never *d* again;	Rom 6.9
if we *d*, we *d* to the Lord;	14.8
our Lord, I *d* every day!	1Cor 15.31
is Christ, and to *d* is gain.	Phil 1.21
man *d*, and is laid low;	Job 14.10
One *d* in full prosperity,	21.23
wise man *d* just like the fool!	Ecc 2.16
if it *d*, it bears much fruit.	Jn 12.24
all flesh *d* that moved	Gen 7.21
Abraham. .*d* in a good old age,	25.8
Isaac,.*d* and was gathered	35.29

the king of Egypt *d*.	Ex 2.23
Moses. .servant of the LORD *d*	Deut 34.5
d, being a hundred and ten	Josh 24.29
Saul *d*, and his three sons,	1Sam 31.6
I had *d* instead of you, O	2Sam 18.33
So the king *d*, and was	1Ki 22.37
lap till noon, and then he *d*.	2Ki 4.20
Saul *d* for. .unfaithfulness;	1Chr 10.13
and at evening my wife *d*.	Ezek 24.18
a man who had *d* was being	Lk 7.12
Christ *d* for the ungodly.	Rom 5.6
who *d* to sin still live in it?	6.2
d to the law through. .Christ,	7.4
came, sin revived and I *d*;	7.9
brother for whom Christ *d*.	1Cor 8.11
and ill, and some have *d*.	11.30
that Christ *d* for our sins	15.3
convinced that one. .*d* for all;	2Cor 5.14
I through the law *d* to the law,	Gal 2.19
Christ also *d* for sins once	1Pet 3.18
every living thing *d*. .in. .sea.	Rev 16.3

DIFFERENCE
d between. .unclean and	Ezek 22.26
d between. .holy and. .common,	44.23

DIFFERENT
who sees anything *d* in you?	1Cor 4.7
and turning to a *d* gospel—	Gal 1.6

DIG — S
I am not strong enough to *d*,	Lk 16.3
who *d* a pit will fall into it;	Prov 26.27
who *d* a pit will fall into it;	Ecc 10.8

DILIGENT
The hand of the *d* will rule,	Prov 12.24
the soul of the *d* is richly	13.4
plans of. .*d* lead. .to abundance,	21.5

DIM
his eye was not *d*, nor his	Deut 34.7
My eyes grow *d* with waiting for	Ps 69.3

DINE
the men are to *d* with me	Gen 43.16
a Pharisee asked him to *d*	Lk 11.37

DINNER
a *d* of herbs where love is	Prov 15.17
I have made ready my *d*, my oxen	Mt 22.4
"When you give a *d* or. .banquet,	Lk 14.12

DIPPED
"He who has *d* his hand in	Mt 26.23
when he had *d* the morsel,	Jn 13.26

DIRECT — S — ED
d your heart to the LORD,	1Sam 7.3
and *d* their hearts toward	1Chr 29.18
d my steps by. .thy precepts;	Ps 119.128
but the LORD *d* his steps.	Prov 16.9
Who has *d* the Spirit of the	Isa 40.13
mountain to which Jesus had *d*	Mt 28.16
d by a holy angel to send	Acts 10.22

DIRECTION
did not ask *d* from the LORD.	Josh 9.14

DISAPPOINTED
the hope of man is *d*;	Job 41.9
they trusted, and were not *d*.	Ps 22.5

DISASTER
for *d*. .will rise suddenly,	Prov 24.22
nor. .desired the day of *d*,	Jer 17.16

DISCERN — EST — ED — ING
that I may *d* between good and	1Ki 3.9

DISCERN — EST — ED — ING (cont.)
thou *d* my thoughts from afar. Ps 139.2
they are spiritually *d*. 1Cor 2.14
drinks without *d* the body 11.29

DISCHARGED
husband dies she is *d* from. .law Rom 7.2
But now we are *d* from the law, 7.6

DISCIPLE — S
"A *d* is not above his teacher, Mt 10.24
A *d* is not above his teacher, Lk 6.40
does not renounce. .cannot be. .*d*. 14.33
his *d*, but we are *d* of Moses. Jn 9.28
saw his mother, and the *d* 19.26
Joseph of Arimathea, who was a *d* 19.38
to Simon Peter and the other *d*, 20.2
d at Damascus named Ananias. Acts 9.10
seal the teaching among my *d*. Isa 8.16
he called to him his twelve *d* Mt 10.1
the *d* gave them to the crowds. 14.19
your *d* transgress the tradition 15.2
your *d*,. .could not heal him." 17.16
Olives, then Jesus sent two *d*, 21.1
tell his *d* that he has risen 28.7
Go. .and make *d* of all nations, 28.19
withdrew with his *d* to the sea, Mk 3.7
he made his *d* get into the boat 6.45
to his *d* to set before the people; 8.6
teaching his *d*, saying to them, 9.31
and the *d* rebuked them. 10.13
John, calling. .two of his *d*, Lk 7.19
broke. .and gave them to the *d* 9.16
Olivet, he sent two of the *d*, 19.29
Olives; and the *d* followed 22.39
and his *d* believed in him. Jn 2.11
between John's *d* and a Jew 3.25
many of his *d* drew back and 6.66
my word, you are truly my *d*, 8.31
know that you are my *d*, if 13.35
fruit, and so prove to be my *d*. 15.8
doors. .shut where the *d* were 20.19
d did not know. .it was Jesus. 21.4

DISCIPLINE — S (v)
hear. .that he might *d* you; Deut 4.36
D your son while there is Prov 19.18
D your son, and he will give 29.17
had earthly fathers to *d* us Heb 12.9
that, as a man *d* his son, Deut 8.5

DISCIPLINE (n)
hate *d*, and you cast my words Ps 50.17
do not despise the LORD's *d* Prov 3.11
severe *d* for him who forsakes 15.10
Do not withhold *d* from a child; 23.13
do not regard lightly the *d* Heb 12.5
all *d* seems painful rather 12.11

DISCORD
who sows *d* among brothers. Prov 6.19
may be no *d* in the body, 1Cor 12.25

DISCOURAGE — D
Why will you *d* the heart Num 32.7
He will not fail or be *d* Isa 42.4

DISCOVER
would not God *d* this? For he Ps 44.21

DISCRETION
Blessed be your *d*, and 1Sam 25.33
may the LORD grant you *d* 1Chr 22.12
keep *d*, and. .guard knowledge. Prov 5.2

DISCUSS — ING
why. .*d* among yourselves the Mt 16.8
"What were you *d* on the way?" Mk 9.33

DISEASE — S — D
even in his *d*. .did not seek 2Chr 16.12
smote. .with an incurable *d*. 21.18
sent a wasting *d* among them. Ps 106.15
healing every *d* and. .infirmity Mt 4.23
felt. .she was healed of her *d*. Mk 5.29
I will put none of the *d* upon Ex 15.26
none of the evil *d* of Egypt, Deut 7.15
infirmities and bore our *d*." Mt 8.17
all who had *d* pressed upon him Mk 3.10
and to be healed of their *d*; Lk 6.17
age he was *d* in his feet. 1Ki 15.23

DISGRACE — FUL
a day of. .rebuke, and of *d*; 2Ki 19.3
I am filled with *d* and look Job 10.15
day long my *d* is before me, Ps 44.15
wise. .honor, but fools get *d*. Prov 3.35
and with dishonor comes *d*. 18.3
I bore the *d* of my youth.' Jer 31.19
is *d* for a woman to be shorn 1Cor 11.6
We have renounced *d*,. .ways; 2Cor 4.2

DISGUISE — D — ING
to his wife, "Arise, and *d* 1Ki 14.2
d myself and go into battle. 2Chr 18.29
Josiah. .*d* himself. .to fight 35.22
d himself with a bandage 1Ki 20.38
d themselves as apostles 2Cor 11.13

DISH
his hand in the *d* with me, Mt 26.23
cleanse the outside of the. .*d*, Lk 11.39

DISHONEST
eyes and heart. .for. .*d* gain, Jer 22.17
the *d* gain which you. .made, Ezek 22.13
master commended the *d* steward Lk 16.8

DISHONOR (v)
d all the honored of. .earth, Isa 23.9
do not *d* thy glorious throne; Jer 14.21

DISHONOR — ING (n)
accusers be clothed with *d*; Ps 109.29
and let our *d* cover us; for Jer 3.25
to the *d* of their bodies Rom 1.24

DISINHERIT
I will. .*d* them, and I will Num 14.12

DISMAYED
When I think of it I am *d*, Job 21.6
be not *d*, for I am your God; Isa 41.10
Daniel,. .was *d* for a moment, Dan 4.19
your mighty men shall be *d*, Obad 1.9

DISOBEDIENCE
by one man's *d* many were Rom 5.19
now at work in the sons of *d*. Eph 2.2

DISOBEDIENT
the *d* to. .wisdom of the just, Lk 1.17
King Agrippa, I was not *d* to Acts 26.19
held out my hands to a *d* Rom 10.21
For we. .were once foolish, *d*, Tit 3.3
but to those who were *d*? Heb 3.18

DISOBEY — ED
do not *d* either of them; Prov 24.21
'Because you have *d* the word 1Ki 13.21
"It is the man of God, who *d* 13.26
and I never *d* your command; Lk 15.29

DISOWNED
he *d* his brothers, and Deut 33.9
he has *d* the faith and is 1Tim 5.8

DISPERSE — D

d you through the countries,	Ezek 22.15
and gather the *d* of Judah	Isa 11.12
d through the countries;	Ezek 36.19

DISPERSION

to the *D* among the Greeks	Jn 7.35
To the exiles of the *D* in	1Pet 1.1

DISPLEASE — D — ING

d God and oppose all men	1Thess 2.15
head of Ephraim, it *d* him;	Gen 48.17
But the thing *d* Samuel when	1Sam 8.6
David had done *d* the LORD.	2Sam 11.27
had never..*d* him by asking,	1Ki 1.6
God was *d* with this thing,	1Chr 21.7
lest the LORD see..and be *d*,	Prov 24.18
The LORD saw it, and it *d* him	Isa 59.15
But it *d* Jonah exceedingly,	Jonah 4.1
was very *d* to Abraham	Gen 21.11
d in the sight of the LORD,	Gen 38.10

DISPLEASURE

and you shall know my *d*.'	Num 14.34
hot *d* which the LORD bore	Deut 9.19

DISPOSSESS — ED

go in to *d* nations greater and	Deut 9.1
with Joshua when they *d* the	Acts 7.45

DISPUTE — D (v)

not able to *d* with..stronger	Ecc 6.10
he..*d* against the Hellenists;	Acts 9.29

DISPUTE (n)

then both parties to the *d*	Deut 19.17
A *d* also arose among them,	Lk 22.24

DISQUALIFY — IED

Let no one *d* you, insisting	Col 2.18
lest..I myself should be *d*.	1Cor 9.27

DISREPUTE

this trade..may come into *d*	Acts 19.27
You..in honor, but we in *d*.	1Cor 4.10

DISSENSIONS

note of those who create *d*	Rom 16.17
there be no *d* among you,	1Cor 1.10
genealogies, *d*, and quarrels	Tit 3.9

DISSOLVED

elements will be *d* with fire,	2Pet 3.10
these things are thus to be *d*,	3.11

DISTANCE

while he was yet at a *d*,	Lk 15.20
Peter followed at a *d*;	22.54

DISTINCT

we are *d*, I and thy people,	Ex 33.16

DISTINCTION — S

the LORD makes a *d* between the	Ex 11.7
make a *d* between the unclean	Lev 11.47
make a *d* between the clean	20.25
he made no *d* between us	Acts 15.9
believe. For there is no *d*;	Rom 3.22
no *d* between Jew and Greek;	10.12
made *d* among yourselves, and	Jas 2.4

DISTINGUISH — ED

d between..holy and..common,	Lev 10.10
d..the unclean and..clean.	Ezek 44.23
d..the righteous and..wicked,	Mal 3.18
practice to *d* good from evil.	Heb 5.14
beloved..*d* among ten thousand.	Sol 5.10
Daniel became *d* above all the	Dan 6.3

DISTRESS (n)

therefore is this *d* come	Gen 42.21
in the time of your *d*."	Judg 10.14
And every one who was in *d*,	1Sam 22.2
when in their *d* they turned	2Chr 15.4
In..*d* he became..more faithless	28.22
in *d* he entreated the favor	33.12
Thou hast given me room..in *d*.	Ps 4.1
delivered them from their *d*;	107.6
I suffered *d* and anguish.	116.3
In my *d* I cry to the LORD,	120.1
d and anguish come upon you.	Prov 1.27
but behold, *d* and darkness,	Isa 8.22
LORD, in *d* they sought thee,	26.16
it is a time of *d* for Jacob;	Jer 30.7
to the LORD, out of my *d*,	Jonah 2.2
great *d* shall be upon..earth	Lk 21.23
in view of the impending *d*	1Cor 7.26

DISTRESSED (adj)

And now do not be *d*, or angry	Gen 45.5
She was deeply *d* and prayed	1Sam 1.10
Then the king,..was much *d*,	Dan 6.14
And they were greatly *d*.	Mt 17.23
Lot, greatly *d* by..wicked	2Pet 2.7

DISTRIBUTED

which Moses *d* in the plains	Josh 13.32
gifts of the Holy Spirit *d*	Heb 2.4

DISTURBED

"Why have you *d* me by	1Sam 28.15
authorities..*d* when they heard	Acts 17.8

DIVIDE — D — ING

d the booty into two parts,	Num 31.27
"*D* the living child in two,	1Ki 3.25
thou didst *d* the sea before	Neh 9.11
d the spoil with the strong;	Isa 53.12
"Teacher, bid my brother *d* the	Lk 12.13
"Take this, and *d* it among	22.17
and the waters were *d*.	Ex 14.21
in death they were not *d*;	2Sam 1.23
and no longer *d* into two	Ezek 37.22
kingdom *d* against itself is	Mt 12.25
kingdom is *d* against itself,	Mk 3.24
and *d* his garments among them.	15.24
every kingdom *d* against itself	Lk 11.17
will be *d*, father against son	12.53
Christ *d*? Was Paul crucified	1Cor 1.13
they finished *d* the land.	Josh 19.51

DIVINATION

learned by *d* that the LORD	Gen 30.27
fees for *d* in their hand;	Num 22.7
no more any..flattering *d*	Ezek 12.24
girl who had a spirit of *d*	Acts 16.16

DIVINE

according to the *d* office	Col 1.25
partakers of the *d* nature.	2Pet 1.4

DIVISION — S

d between my people and	Ex 8.23
No, I tell you, but rather *d*;	Lk 12.51
again a *d* among the Jews	Jn 10.19
piercing to the *d* of soul	Heb 4.12
The *d* of the sons of Aaron	1Chr 24.1
I hear that there are *d*	1Cor 11.18

DIVORCE (v)

"Moses allowed a man to..*d*,	Mk 10.4
her, she should not *d* him.	1Cor 7.13

DIVORCE (n)

he writes her a bill of *d*	Deut 24.1
Israel,..with a decree of *d*;	Jer 3.8
to give a certificate of *d*,	Mt 19.7

DO — DOES — DONE

God has..approved what you d. Ecc 9.7
Thus says the LORD: D justice Jer 22.3
humble..who d his commands; Zeph 2.3
wish that men would d to you, Mt 7.12
all that Jesus began to d Acts 1.1
hears my words and d them, Lk 6.47
which he had d in creation. Gen 2.3
God had d for the people; 2Chr 29.36
repay..man for what he has d. Mt 16.27
God had d among the Gentiles Acts 21.19
judged..by what they had d. Rev 20.12

DOCTRINE — S

you say, 'My d is pure, Job 11.4
carried..with every wind of d, Eph 4.14
not to teach any different d, 1Tim 1.3
give instruction in sound d Tit 1.9
adorn the d of God our Savior. 2.10
not abide in the d of Christ 2Jn 9
as d the precepts of men.' Mk 7.7

DOERS

the d of the law..justified. Rom 2.13
But be d of the word, and Jas 1.22

DOG — S

with his tongue, as a d laps, Judg 7.5
look upon a dead d such as 2Sam 9.8
your servant, who is but a d, 2Ki 8.13
takes a passing d by..ears. Prov 26.17
living d is better than a dead Ecc 9.4
The d turns back to his own 2Pet 2.22
shall d lick your..blood, 1Ki 21.19
they come back, howling like d Ps 59.6
they are all dumb d, they Isa 56.10
"Do not give d what is holy; Mt 7.6
bread and throw it to the d." 15.26
even the d under the table eat Mk 7.28
d came and licked his sores. Lk 16.21
Look out for the d, look out Phil 3.2

DOMINION

For d belongs to the LORD, Ps 22.28
May he have d from sea to sea, 72.8
Bless..in all places of his d. 103.22
break there the d of Egypt, Ezek 30.18
for his d is an everlasting d, Dan 4.34
his d shall be to the end. 6.26
his d shall be a great d. 11.5
his d shall be from sea to sea, Zech 9.10
death no longer has d over him. Rom 6.9

DOOR — S

Valley of Achor a d of hope. Hos 2.15
"Strive to enter..narrow d; Lk 13.24
knock at the d, saying, 'Lord, 13.25
I am the d of the sheep. Jn 10.7
I am the d; if any one enters 10.9
he had opened a d of faith Acts 14.27
a wide d for effective work 1Cor 16.9
open to us a d for the word, Col 4.3
have set before you an open d, Rev 3.8
I stand at the d and knock; 3.20
and lo, in heaven an open d! 4.1
and be lifted up, O ancient d! Ps 24.7
I will break in pieces the d Isa 45.2

DOORKEEPER

rather be a d in the house of Ps 84.10

DOORPOSTS

blood, and put it on..d and Ex 12.7

DORCAS

Tabitha, which means D or Acts 9.36
garments which D made while 9.39

DOT

not a d, will pass from the law Mt 5.18
one d of..law to become void. Lk 16.17

DOUBLE

they took d the money Gen 43.15
a d share of your spirit." 2Ki 2.9
flattering lips and a d heart Ps 12.2
received..d for all her sins. Isa 40.2
I will restore to you d. Zech 9.12

DOUBT (v)

if you have faith and never d, Mt 21.21
and does not d in his heart, Mk 11.23

DOUBT (n)

your life shall hang in d Deut 28.66
he who has d is condemned, Rom 14.23

DOVE — S

he sent forth a d from him, Gen 8.8
"O that I had wings like a d! Ps 55.6
Ephraim is like a d, silly and Hos 7.11
Spirit..descending like a d, Mt 3.16
Spirit..in bodily form, as a d, Lk 3.22
saw the Spirit descend as a d Jn 1.32
His eyes are like d beside Sol 5.12

DOWNFALL

righteous will look upon..d. Prov 29.16
tremble..on..day of your d. Ezek 32.10

DOWNTRODDEN

Let not the d be put to shame; Ps 74.21
The LORD lifts up the d, he 147.6

DRAGON

you are like a d in the seas; Ezek 32.2
behold, a great red d, with Rev 12.3

DRANK

to them, and they all d of it. Mk 14.23
d from the supernatural Rock 1Cor 10.4

DRAW — N

women go out to d water. Gen 24.11
"I will d for your camels 24.19
D near..me, redeem me, set me Ps 69.18
D me after you,..make haste. Sol 1.4
D near, O nations, to hear, Isa 34.1
d near with a true heart Heb 10.22
D near..God and he will d near Jas 4.8
O LORD, for thou hast d me up, Ps 30.1

DRAWERS

and d of water for all the Josh 9.21

DREAD

land..whose two kings you..d Isa 7.16
and do not fear..nor be in d. 8.12

DREAM — S — ED (v)

your old men shall d dreams, Acts 2.17
a hungry man d he is eating Isa 29.8
d that there was a ladder Gen 28.12
both d—the butler and..baker 40.5
I d a dream; and lo, a cake Judg 7.13

DREAM — S (n)

God came to Laban..in a d Gen 31.24
Joseph had a d, and..told 37.5
Pharaoh told them his d, 41.8
speak with him in a d. Num 12.6
appeared to Solomon in a d 1Ki 3.5
Let..prophet who has a d tell Jer 23.28
angel..appeared to him in a d, Mt 1.20
suffered..over him in a d." 27.19
Joseph remembered the d Gen 42.9
d increase, empty words grow Ecc 5.7

DREAM — S (n) (cont.)
Nebuchadnezzar had d; and his   Dan 2.1
your old men shall dream d,   Joel 2.28

DREAMER
"Here comes this d.   Gen 37.19
"If. .arises. .a d of dreams,   Deut 13.1

DRENCH
I d my couch with my weeping.   Ps 6.6
d the land. .with your. .blood; Ezek 32.6

DREW
he d me out of many waters.   Ps 18.16
time of the promise d near,   Acts 7.17

DRINK — S — ING (v)
make our father d wine,   Gen 19.32
'D, and I will water your camels'   24.14
"D no wine nor strong drink,   Lev 10.8
would give me water to d   2Sam 23.15
thou hast given us wine to d   Ps 60.3
He will d from the brook by   110.7
D water from your. .cistern.   Prov 5.15
thirsty, give him water to d;   25.21
and d: d deeply, O lovers!   Sol 5.1
made all the nations. .d it: Jer 25.17
answered, "We will d no wine,   35.6
neighbors d. .cup of his wrath, Hab 2.15
tasted it, he would not d it.   Mt 27.34
do not seek what. .to eat. .d,   Lk 12.29
So, whether you eat or d,   1Cor 10.31
and d the cup, you proclaim   11.26
made to d of one Spirit,   12.13
No longer d only water, but   1Tim 5.23
whoever d of the water that I   Jn 4.14
John. .neither eating nor d,   Mt 11.18
before the flood. .eating and d,   24.38
eating no bread and d no wine; Lk 7.33

DRINK (n)
givest them d from the river   Ps 36.8
strong d to him. .perishing,   Prov 31.6
drink no wine nor strong d,   Lk 1.15
said to her, "Give me a d."   Jn 4.7
not to be. .slaves to d; they   Tit 2.3

DRIVE — S — ING
Manasseh did not d out the   Judg 1.27
thou with thy own hand didst d Ps 44.2
Jehu. .for he d furiously."   2Ki 9.20
which the wind of the LORD d.   Isa 59.19
angel of the LORD d them on!   Ps 35.5

DROSS
the wicked. .dost count as d; Ps 119.119
Take away the d from. .silver, Prov 25.4
Your silver has become d,   Isa 1.22
and will smelt away your d   1.25

DROUGHT
a d upon the land and. .hills, Hag 1.11

DROVE
and he d away all his cattle,   Gen 31.18
the LORD d the sea back   Ex 14.21
Jesus. .d out all who sold and Mt 21.12

DROWNED
better. .to be d in the depth   Mt 18.6
the herd,. .were d in the sea. Mk 5.13
down. .into the lake. .were d. Lk 8.33

DRUNK
Noah. .became d,. .lay uncovered Gen 9.21
so that he made him d;   2Sam 11.13
Be d, but not with wine;   Isa 29.9

have d to the dregs the bowl   51.17
For these men are not d,   Acts 2.15

DRUNKARD — S
a glutton and a d, a friend   Mt 11.19
'Behold, a glutton and a d,   Lk 7.34
an idolater, reviler, d, or   1Cor 5.11
the d make songs about me.   Ps 69.12
crown of the d of Ephraim,   Isa 28.1

DRUNKEN — NESS
made Egypt stagger. .as a d   Isa 19.14
eats and drinks with the d,   Mt 24.49
for strength, and not for d!   Ecc 10.17
you will be filled with d   Ezek 23.33

DRY — IED (v)
I will d up your rivers';   Isa 44.27
the LORD d up the. .Red Sea   Josh 2.10

DRY (adj)
face of the ground was d.   Gen 8.13
priests. .stood on d ground   Josh 3.17

DUE
not. .a gift but as his d.   Rom 4.4
blood to drink. .is their d!"   Rev 16.6

DUG
he moved. .and d another well, Gen 26.22
one talent went and d in   Mt 25.18

DULL
people's heart has grown d, Acts 28.27
you have become d of hearing. Heb 5.11

DUMB
But I am like. .a d man who Ps 38.13
I was d and silent, I held my   39.2
d and unable to reprove them; Ezek 3.26
toward the ground and was d. Dan 10.15
d demoniac was brought to him. Mt 9.32
that the d man spoke and saw.   12.22
the maimed, the blind, the d,   15.30
deaf hear and the d speak." Mk 7.37
signs to them and remained d. Lk 1.22
d man spoke. .people marveled.   11.14

DUST
God formed man of d   Gen 2.7
and d you shall eat   3.14
you are d, and to d. .return."   3.19
descendants as the d   13.16
I who am but d and ashes.   18.27
and man would return to d. Job 34.15
when the d runs into a mass   38.38
turnest man back to the d,   Ps 90.3
he remembers that we are d.   103.14
die and return to their d.   104.29
from the d, and all turn to d   Ecc 3.20
and the d returns to. .earth   12.7
shake off the d from your feet Mt 10.14
d of your town. .we wipe off Lk 10.11

DUTY
the d of a husband's brother Deut 25.5
first learn their religious d   1Tim 5.4

DWELL — S — T
they could not d together,   Gen 13.6
And Moses was content to d Ex 2.21
I will d among the people   29.45
that you may d in the land Deut 30.20
Jebusites d with the people Josh 15.63
I d in a house of cedar,   2Sam 7.2
I will d among the children 1Ki 6.13
God indeed d on the earth?   8.27
will God d indeed with man 2Chr 6.18
let not wickedness d in your Job 11.14

DWELL — S — T (cont.)

shall *d* in..house of the LORD	Ps 23.6
I may *d* in the house of..LORD	27.4
Blessed..who *d* in thy house,	84.4
No..deceit shall *d* in my house;	101.7
there he lets the hungry *d*,	107.36
good..when brothers *d* in unity!	133.1
can *d* with..devouring fire?	Isa 33.14
Israel shall *d*..without king	Hos 3.4
return..*d* beneath my shadow,	14.7
again make you *d* in tents,	12.9
Christ may *d* in your hearts	Eph 3.17
spirit which he has made to *d*	Jas 4.5
He will *d* with them, and	Rev 21.3
d in..shelter of the Most High,	Ps 91.1
exalted, for he *d* on high;	Isa 33.5
the Father who *d* in me does	Jn 14.10
but sin which *d* within me.	Rom 7.17
that God's Spirit *d* in you?	1Cor 3.16
Abram *d* in..land of Canaan,	Gen 13.12
Lot..who *d* in Sodom,	14.12
Lot..*d* in a cave with his	19.30
Word became flesh and *d* among	Jn 1.14

DWELLING — S

d between his shoulders."	Deut 33.12
thy holy hill and to thy *d*!	Ps 43.3
He forsook his *d* at Shiloh,	78.60
in his own hired *d*	Acts 28.30*n*
the *d* of God is with men.	Rev 21.3
and his *d* shall be glorious.	Isa 11.10

DWELLING PLACE

The eternal God is your *d*..	Deut 33.27
How lovely is thy *d*.., O LORD	Ps 84.1
LORD, thou hast been our *d*..	90.1
a *d*..for the Mighty One	132.5
"Let us go to his *d*..; let us	132.7
d..shall be with them;	Ezek 37.27

DYING

as *d*, and behold we live;	2Cor 6.9

E

EAGER

I am *e* to preach the gospel	Rom 1.15

EAGLE — S

are an abomination: the *e*,	Lev 11.13
your command..the *e* mounts	Job 39.27
the way of an *e* in the sky,	Prov 30.19
the fourth the face of an *e*.	Ezek 10.14
A great *e* with great wings	17.2
mount up with wings like *e*,	Isa 40.31
"Where..body is, there the *e*	Lk 17.37

EAR — S

his master shall bore his *e*	Ex 21.6
heard of thee by..the *e*,	Job 42.5
thou hast given me an open *e*.	Ps 40.6
planted the *e*, does he not hear?	94.9
your *e* attentive to wisdom	Prov 2.2
the slave..and cut off his *e*.	Mt 26.51
the slave..and cut off his *e*.	Mk 14.47
and cut off his right *e*.	Lk 22.50
slave and cut off his right *e*.	Jn 18.10
no eye has seen, nor *e* heard,	1Cor 2.9
And if the *e* should say,	12.16
He who has an *e*, let him hear	Rev 2.29
and his *e* toward their cry.	Ps 34.15
have *e*, but they hear not,	135.17
people,..have *e*, but hear not.	Jer 5.21
have *e* to hear, but hear not;	Ezek 12.2
He who has *e*, let him hear."	Mt 13.9

"He who has *e* to hear, let him	Mk 4.9
If any man has *e* to hear,	4.23
He who has *e* to hear, let him	Lk 14.35

EARTH

God created the heavens..*e*.	Gen 1.1
God called the dry land *E*,	1.10
Lord of all the *e* is to pass	Josh 3.11
hangs the *e* upon nothing.	Job 26.7
The *e* is the LORD's and the	Ps 24.1
the *e* is full of the steadfast love	33.5
visitest the *e* and waterest it,	65.9
whole *e* is full of his glory."	Isa 6.3
e shall yield its increase,	Ezek 34.27
let all the *e* keep silence	Hab 2.20
didst bestride the *e* in fury,	3.12
all the *e* shall be consumed.	Zeph 3.8
the *e* shook, and the rocks	Mt 27.51
The *e* produces of itself,	Mk 4.28
For "the *e* is the Lord's,	1Cor 10.26
first man was from the *e*,	15.47
new *e* in which righteousness	2Pet 3.13
to take peace from the *e*,	Rev 6.4

EARTHLY

not by *e* wisdom but by..grace	2Cor 1.12
if..*e* tent we live in is destroyed,	5.1

EARTHQUAKE — S

and after the wind an *e*,	1Ki 19.11
thunder..*e* and great noise,	Isa 29.6
two years before the *e*.	Amos 1.1
great *e*; for..angel..descended	Mt 28.2
suddenly there was a great *e*,	Acts 16.26
e such as had never been	Rev 16.18
there will be *e* in various	Mk 13.8
there will be great *e*, and	Lk 21.11

EASE

I am not at *e*, nor am I quiet;	Job 3.26
are the wicked; always at *e*,	Ps 73.12
"Woe to those who are at *e*	Amos 6.1
take your *e*, eat, drink, be	Lk 12.19

EAST

we have seen his star in the *E*,	Mt 2.2
many will come from *e* and west	8.11
men will come from *e* and west,	Lk 13.29

EASY — IER

the way is *e*,..to destruction,	Mt 7.13
yoke is *e*,..burden is light."	11.30
which is *e*, to say, 'Your sins	9.5

EAT — S — EN — ING

tree of knowledge..not *e*,	Gen 2.17
the Egyptians might not *e*	43.32
shall *e* unleavened bread;	Ex 12.15
sat down to *e* and drink,	32.6
Moreover you shall *e* no blood	Lev 7.26
not *e*..flesh with the blood	19.26
you shall *e* before the LORD	Deut 12.7
evildoers who *e* up my people	Ps 14.4
When you..*e* with a ruler,	Prov 23.1
you shall *e*..good of the land;	Isa 1.19
"Let us *e* and drink, for	22.13
open..mouth, and *e* what I give	Ezek 2.8
e this scroll, and go, speak	3.1
"Why does your teacher *e* with	Mt 9.11
"Take, *e*; this is my body."	26.26
where I am to *e* the passover	Mk 14.14
"Why do you *e* and drink with	Lk 5.30
take your ease, *e*, drink, be	12.19
besought him.."Rabbi, *e*."	Jn 4.31
"Rise, Peter; kill and *e*."	Acts 10.13
'Rise, Peter; kill and *e*.'	11.7

EAT — S — EN — ING (cont.)

e whatever is set before you	1Cor 10.27
So, whether you e or drink,	10.31
"Let us e and drink, for	15.32
will not work, let. .not e.	2Thess 3.10
come in to him and e with him,	Rev 3.20
Let not him who e despise him	Rom 14.3
when they had e enough,	Acts 27.38
before the flood they were e	Mt 24.38

EBENEZER

Samuel took a stone. .name E;	1Sam 7.12

EDEN

God planted a garden in E,	Gen 2.8
make her wilderness like E,	Isa 51.3
You were in E, the garden	Ezek 28.13
land is like the garden of E	Joel 2.3

EDIFICATION

Let all things be done for e.	1Cor 14.26

EDOM — ITES

his name was called E.)	Gen 25.30
E refused to give Israel	Num 20.21
And he put garrisons in E;	2Sam 8.14
upon E I cast my shoe; over	Ps 108.9
Who is this that comes from E,	Isa 63.1
may possess the remnant of E	Amos 9.12
Esau the father of the E	Gen 36.9

EGYPT

Abram went down to E	Gen 12.10
they took Joseph to E.	37.28
set him over the land of E.	41.33
all my splendor in E,	45.13
I will lay my hand upon E	Ex 7.4
LORD brought us out of E,	13.14
alliance with Pharaoh. .of E;	1Ki 3.1
and out of E I called my son.	Hos 11.1
flee to E, and remain there	Mt 2.13
"Out of E have I called my son."	2.15
greater wealth than. .of E,	Heb 11.26

ELDER — S

e shall serve the younger."	Gen 25.23
e will serve the younger."	Rom 9.12
The e to the elect lady and	2Jn 1
The e to the beloved Gaius,	3Jn 1
the e of the congregation	Lev 4.15
seventy men. .the e of Israel	Num 11.16
ten men of the e of the city,	Ruth 4.2
Her husband. .sits among. .e	Prov 31.23
suffer many things from the e	Mt 16.21
sent to him a few of the Jews,	Lk 7.3
called. .the e of the church.	Acts 20.17
when the e laid their hands	1Tim 4.14
Let the e who rule well be	5.17
appoint e in every town as	Tit 1.5
sick? Let him call for the e	Jas 5.14
I exhort the e among you,	1Pet 5.1
on. .thrones were twenty-four e,	Rev 4.4
the twenty-four e and the four	19.4

ELECT

but for the sake of the e	Mt 24.22
gather his e from. .four winds,	24.31
but for the sake of the e,	Mk 13.20
gather his e from the four winds,	13.27
any charge against God's e?	Rom 8.33
The e obtained it, but the rest	11.7
endure. .for the sake of the e,	2Tim 2.10

ELECTION

God's purpose of e. .continue,	Rom 9.11
as regards e they are beloved	11.28
confirm your call and e,	2Pet 1.10

ELEMENTS

the e will be dissolved	2Pet 3.10
the e will melt with fire!	3.12

ELEVEN

Afterward he appeared to the e	Mk 16.14n
found the e gathered together	Lk 24.33

ELI

two sons of E. .were priets	1Sam 1.3
Hannah rose. Now E the priest	1.9
they brought the child to E.	1.25
presence of E the priest.	2.11
ministering to. .LORD under E.	3.1
two sons of E,. .were slain.	4.11
E was ninety-eight years old	4.15

ELIJAH

Predicted the drought, 1Ki 17.1; fed by ravens, 1Ki 17.2–7; fed by the widow of Zarephath, 1 Ki 17.8–16; revived the son of the widow, 1Ki 17.17–24; met Ahab, 1Ki 18.1–19; triumphed over the prophets of Baal, 1Ki 18.20–40; prayed for rain, 1Ki 18.41–46; fled to Mount Horeb, 1Ki 19.1–8; heard the still small voice, 1Ki 19.9–18; chose Elisha, 1Ki 19.19–21; reproved Ahab, 1Ki 21.17–29; called fire from heaven, 2Ki 1.3–16; taken up into heaven, 2Ki 2.1–11.

I will send you E the prophet	Mal 4.5
he is E who is to come.	Mt 11.14
appeared to them Moses and E,	17.3
I tell you that E has come,	Mk 9.13
"Behold, he is calling E."	15.35
in the spirit and power of E,	Lk 1.17
to bid fire come. .as E did?"	9.54n
"What then? Are you E?" He said	Jn 1.21
E was a man of like nature	Jas 5.17

ELISHA

Called, 1Ki 19.19–21; succeeded Elijah, 2Ki 2.1–15; purified the water, 2Ki 2.19–22; cursed the children, 2Ki 2.23–25; prophesied victory over the Moabites, 2Ki 3; increased the widow's oil, 2Ki 4.1–7; restored the life of the Shunammite's son, 2Ki 4.8–37; purified the pottage, 2Ki 4.38–41; fed a multitude, 2Ki 4.42–44; healed Naaman's leprosy, 2Ki 5; caused Syrians' blindness, 2Ki 6.8–23; promised food in time of famine 2Ki6.24—7.2; prophesied Hazael's cruelty, 2Ki 8.7–15; anointed Jehu, 2Ki 9.1–10; prophesied victory over Syria, 2Ki 13.14–19; death and burial, 2Ki 13.20; bones of Elisha, 2Ki 13.21.

ELIZABETH

a wife. .and her name was E.	Lk 1.5
wife E will bear you a son,	1.13
of Zechariah and greeted E.	1.40

ELOQUENT

my Lord, I am not e,	Ex 4.10
preach. .not with e wisdom,	1Cor 1.17

EMBRACED

Joseph. .kissed. .and e them.	Gen 48.10
and that his right hand e me!	Sol 2.6

EMMANU-EL

and his name shall be called E"	Mt 1.23

EMMAUS

going to a village named E,	Lk 24.13

EMPTY
God does not hear an *e* cry,   Job 35.13
praying do not heap up *e* phrases   Mt 6.7

ENCAMP — S
"The people of Israel shall *e*   Num 2.2
and *e* round about my tent.   Job 19.12
Though a host *e* against me,   Ps 27.3
I will *e* against you round   Isa 29.3
The angel of the LORD *e* around   Ps 34.7

ENCOURAGE — D
e him, for he shall cause   Deut 1.38
charge Joshua, and *e* and   3.28
that he may *e* your hearts.   Eph 6.22
and you have *e* the wicked,   Ezek 13.22
that their hearts may be *e* as   Col 2.2

ENCOURAGEMENT
(which means, Son of *e*),   Acts 4.36
if there is any *e* in Christ,   Phil 2.1

END — S (v)
thy years will never *e*."   Heb 1.12
Love never *e*; as for   1Cor 13.8

END — S (n)
make an *e* of all flesh;   Gen 6.13
their words to the *e* of..world.   Ps 19.4
"LORD, let me know my *e*, and   39.4
years come to an *e* like a sigh.   90.9
yet there is no *e* to..his toil,   Ecc 4.8
The *e* of the matter; all has   12.13
our *e* drew near; our days   Lam 4.18
The *e* has come upon the four   Ezek 7.2
come to his *e*,..none to help   Dan 11.45
"The *e* has come upon my people Amos 8.2
the vision..hastens to the *e*—   Hab 2.3
and then the *e* will come.   Mt 24.14
with the guards to see the *e*.   26.58
he loved them to the *e*.   Jn 13.1
and to the *e* of the earth."   Acts 1.8
Christ is the *e* of the law,   Rom 10.4
e of all things is at hand,   1Pet 4.7
what will be the *e* of those   4.17
e of the earth your possession.   Ps 2.8

ENDOWMENT
Every good *e* and every perfect   Jas 1.17

ENDURANCE
By..*e* you will gain your lives.   Lk 21.19
and *e* produces character,   Rom 5.4
great *e*, in afflictions,   2Cor 6.4
For you have need of *e*, so   Heb 10.36
call for the *e* of the saints,   Rev 14.12

ENDURE — S — D
can I *e* to see the calamity   Est 8.6
hold of it, but it does not *e*.   Job 8.15
May his name *e* for ever, his   Ps 72.17
They will perish,..thou..*e*;   102.26
Can your courage *e*, or can   Ezek 22.14
Who can *e*..heat of his anger?   Nah 1.6
who can *e* the day of his coming, Mal 3.2
have no root..but *e* for a while; Mk 4.17
that you may be able to *e*   1Cor 10.13
if we *e*, we shall also reign   2Tim 2.12
people will not *e* sound teaching,   4.3
his righteousness *e* for ever.   Ps 111.3
"His steadfast love *e* for ever."   118.2
his steadfast love *e* for ever.   136.2
who *e* to..end will be saved.   Mt 10.22
he who *e* to the end will be saved.   24.13
who *e* to the end will be saved.   Mk 13.13
food which *e* to eternal life,   Jn 6.27
Love..hopes all things, *e* all   1Cor 13.7

Blessed is the man who *e* trial,   Jas 1.12
for he *e* as seeing him who   Heb 11.27
e the cross, despising the shame,   12.2

ENEMY — IES
"Have you found me, O my *e*?" 1Ki 21.20
and count me as thy *e*?   Job 13.24
not rejoice when..*e* falls,   Prov 24.17
If your *e* is hungry, give him bread 25.21
neighbor and hate your *e*.'   Mt 5.43
"if your *e* is hungry, feed   Rom 12.20
last *e*..destroyed is death.   1Cor 15.26
become your *e* by telling you   Gal 4.16
your *e* who settle in it   Lev 26.32
be defeated before your *e*;   Deut 28.25
perish all thine *e*, O LORD!   Judg 5.31
Jews got relief from their *e*,   Est 9.22
him, and his *e* lick the dust!   Ps 72.9
thy *e*, O LORD,..shall perish;   92.9
makes..his *e* to be at peace.   Prov 16.7
I put thy *e* under thy feet"?   Mt 22.44
Love your *e*, do good to those   Lk 6.27
many..live as *e* of the cross   Phil 3.18

ENGRAVE
you *e* the two stones with   Ex 28.11
I will *e* its inscription,   Zech 3.9

ENJOY
my chosen..long *e* the work   Isa 65.22
than to *e*..fleeting pleasures   Heb 11.25

ENJOYMENT
and find *e* in his toil.   Ecc 2.24
fitting is to eat and..find *e*   5.18

ENLARGE — ST — D
E the place of your tent,   Isa 54.2
when thou *e* my understanding! Ps 119.32
among you may be greatly *e*, 2Cor 10.15

ENLIGHTENED
a zeal..but it is not *e*.   Rom 10.2
after you were *e*, you endured   Heb 10.32

ENLIGHTENING
commandment..pure, *e* the eyes; Ps 19.8

ENOCH
To *E* was born Irad;   Gen 4.18
Jared..became..father of *E*.   5.18
E walked with God after   5.22
E walked with God;..God took   5.24
son of *E*, the son of Jared,   Lk 3.37
By faith *E* was taken up so   Heb 11.5
It was of these also that *E*   Jude 14

ENRAGED
be *e* and will curse their king   Isa 8.21
LORD is *e* against all the nations,   34.2

ENRICH — ED
kills him, the king will *e*   1Sam 17.25
e in him with all speech   1Cor 1.5
You will be *e* in every way   2Cor 9.11

ENROLLED
all the world should be *e*.   Lk 2.1
the first-born..*e* in heaven,   Heb 12.23

ENSIGN — S
the root of Jesse..as an *e*   Isa 11.10
the *e* of their fathers' houses;   Num 2.2

ENSLAVED
might no longer be *e* to sin.   Rom 6.6
I will not be *e* by anything.   1Cor 6.12

ENTANGLED
the cords of Sheol *e* me,   2Sam 22.6
the cords of Sheol *e* me,   Ps 18.5

ENTER — S — ED

Moses..not able to e the tent   Ex 40.35
for he shall not e the land   Num 20.24
shall not e the assembly   Deut 23.1
may e into the sworn covenant   29.12
they should not e my rest.   Ps 95.11
E his gates with thanksgiving,   100.4
my people, e your chambers,   Isa 26.20
you will never e the kingdom   Mt 5.20
"E by the narrow gate; for   7.13
says.. 'Lord, Lord,' shall e   7.21
than for a rich man to e   19.24
no one can e a strong man's   Mk 3.27
who have riches to e the kingdom   10.23
you did not e yourselves,   Lk 11.52
he cannot e the kingdom of God.   Jn 3.5
Blessed..who e in the name of Ps 118.26
Noah and his sons..e the ark,   Gen 7.13

ENTHRONED

But the LORD sits e for ever,   Ps 9.7
who art e upon the cherubim,   80.1
O thou who art e in..heavens!   123.1

ENTICE — S — D

said to Samson's wife, "E   Judg 14.15
"E him, and see wherein his   16.5
LORD said, 'Who will e Ahab,   1Ki 22.20
he said, 'You are to e him,   2Chr 18.21
My son, if sinners e you,   Prov 1.10
man of violence e his neighbor   16.29
"If my heart has been e to   Job 31.9

ENTREAT — ED

"E the LORD to take away   Ex 8.8
"E me not to leave you or to   Ruth 1.16
to e the favor of the LORD,   Zech 7.2
we e you not to accept the   2Cor 6.1
I, Paul, myself e you, by   10.1
Then Manoah e the LORD, and Judg 13.8
not e thee for their good,   Jer 15.11
father came out and e him,   Lk 15.28

ENTREATY

how God received his e,   2Chr 33.19
and he listened to our e.   Ezra 8.23

ENTRUST — ED — ING

who will e to you..true riches? Lk 16.11
e to faithful men who will   2Tim 2.2
do right and e their souls   1Pet 4.19
he is e with all my house.   Num 12.7
the Jews are e with the oracles Rom 3.2
I am e with a commission.   1Cor 9.17
guard what has been e to you. 1Tim 6.20
guard..what has been e to me. 2Tim 1.12
and e to us the message of   2Cor 5.19

ENVIOUS

be not e of wrongdoers!   Ps 37.1
For I was e of the arrogant,   73.3
Be not e of evil men, nor   Prov 24.1

ENVOY — S

a faithful e brings healing.   Prov 13.17
e of the princes of Babylon,   2Chr 32.31
the e of peace weep bitterly.   Isa 33.7

ENVY — IED (v)

Do not e a man of violence   Prov 3.31
Let not your heart e sinners,   23.17
the Philistines e him.   Gen 26.14
no children, she e her sister;   30.1

ENVY (n)

out of e..they..delivered him Mt 27.18
out of e..the chief priests   Mk 15.10

EPHESUS

came to E, and he left them   Acts 18.19
Paul..came to E. There he found   19.1
decided to sail past E, so   20.16
I fought with beasts at E?   1Cor 15.32
remain at E that you may   1Tim 1.3
the angel of the church in E   Rev 2.1

EPHRAIM

the second he called E,   Gen 41.52
two sons, Manasseh and E.   48.1
the leader of the men of E: Num 7.48
And E did not drive out the   Judg 1.29
did not choose the tribe of E;   Ps 78.67
E is joined to idols, let him   Hos 4.17
E mixes himself with the peoples;   7.8
How can I give you up, O E!   11.8

EPILEPTIC — S

have mercy on my son,..an e   Mt 17.15
demoniacs, e, and paralytics,   4.24

EQUAL

making himself e with God.   Jn 5.18
faith of e standing with ours   2Pet 1.1

EQUITY

He will judge..peoples with e.   Ps 98.9
thou hast established e; thou   99.4

ERECT — ED

e no graven image or pillar,   Lev 26.1
There he e an altar   Gen 33.20

ERR — ED

"But if you e, and do not   Num 15.22
are a people who e in heart,   Ps 95.10
they not e that devise evil?   Prov. 14.22
me understand how I have e.   Job 6.24

ERROR — S

atonement for him for the e   Lev 5.18
because it was an e,   Num 15.25
my e remains with myself.   Job 19.4
e proceeding from the ruler: Ecc 10.5
the due penalty for their e.   Rom 1.27
our appeal..not..from e or   1Thess 2.3
But who can discern his e?   Ps 19.12
offers..for the e of the people. Heb 9.7

ESAU

Born, Gen 25.24–26; sold his birthright,
Gen 25.29–34; married Hittite women,
Gen 26.34; lost Isaac's blessing, Gen 27.30–
40; hated Jacob, Gen 27.41; married
Mahalath, Gen 28.9; reconciled with Jacob,
Gen 33.1–15.

ESCAPE — S — D (v)

palace you will e any more   Est 4.13
none..come to..Egypt shall e   Jer 44.14
there shall be those that e,   Obad 1.17
how shall we e if we neglect   Heb 2.3
he who pleases God e her, but   Ecc 7.26
e and fled after David.   1Sam 22.20
e as a bird from the snare   Ps 124.7
man who e from Jerusalem   Ezek 33.21
they have e the defilements   2Pet 2.20

ESCAPE (n)

also provide the way of e,   1Cor 10.13
and there will be no e.   1Thess 5.3

ESTABLISH — ED

I will e my covenant   Gen 17.7
e my covenant with Isaac,   17.21
LORD..e you as a people holy Deut 28.9
that he may e you this day   29.13

ESTABLISH — ED (cont.)

I will e his kingdom.	2Sam 7.12
I will e your royal throne	1Ki 9.5
e..work of our hands upon us,	Ps 90.17
and over his kingdom, to e it,	Isa 9.7
to e you in your faith and	1Thess 3.2
that he may e your hearts	3.13
God..will himself restore, e,	1Pet 5.10
who made you and e you?	Deut 32.6
Lord had e him king over	2Sam 5.12
his kingdom was firmly e.	1Ki 2.12
his throne shall be e for ever.	1Chr 17.14
and the stars which thou hast e;	Ps 8.3
thou hast e the luminaries	74.16
justice, thou hast e equity;	99.4
by understanding he the	Prov 3.19
e as the highest of..mountains,	Isa 2.2
will not believe,..shall not be e.' "	7.9
throne..e in steadfast love	16.5
e the world by his wisdom,	Jer 10.12
who..e the world by his wisdom,	51.15
it is God who e us with you	2Cor 1.21

ESTEEM — S — ED

e them very highly in love	1Thess 5.13
another man e all days alike.	Rom 14.5
before those who are least e	1Cor 6.4

ESTHER

is E, the daughter of his uncle,	Est 2.7
The command of Queen E fixed	9.32

ETERNAL

to be thrown into the e fire.	Mt 18.8
what..must I do, to have e life?"	19.16
receive..and inherit e life.	19.29
e fire prepared for the devil	25.41
but is guilty of an e sin"—	Mk 3.29
must I do to inherit e life?"	10.17
shall I do to inherit e life?"	Lk 10.25
receive you into..e habitations.	16.9
not perish but have e life.	Jn 3.16
will keep it for e life.	12.25
his commandment is e life.	12.50
to give e life to all whom thou	17.2
unworthy of e life, behold,	Acts 13.46
ordained to e life believed.	13.48
to those..he will give e life;	Rom 2.7
through righteousness to e life	5.21
things that are unseen are e.	2Cor 4.18
in hope of e life which God,	Tit 1.2
he has promised us, e life.	1Jn 2.25
know that you have e life.	5.13
This is the true God and e life.	5.20

ETERNITY

has put e into man's mind,	Ecc 3.11
lofty One who inhabits e,	Isa 57.15

ETHIOPIA — N

let E..stretch out her hands	Ps 68.31
E and Seba in exchange for	Isa 43.3
an E, a eunuch, a minister	Acts 8.27

EUNUCH — S

chief e, to bring some..people	Dan 1.3
an Ethiopian, a e, a minister	Acts 8.27
e who have been so from birth,	Mt 19.12

EUPHRATES

fourth river is the E.	Gen 2.14
Egypt to..the river E,	15.18
as far as the great river,..E,	Josh 1.4
lived of old beyond the E,	24.2
arise, go to the E, and hide	Jer 13.4
bowl on the great river E,	Rev 16.12

EVANGELIST — S

the house of Philip the e,	Acts 21.8
do the work of an e, fulfil	2Tim 4.5
some prophets, some e, some	Eph 4.11

EVE

called his wife's name E,	Gen 3.20
Adam knew E his wife,	4.1
as the serpent deceived E	2Cor 11.3
Adam..formed first, then E;	1Tim 2.13

EVENING

That e they brought to him many	Mt 8.16
That e,..they brought to him	Mk 1.32
e he came with the twelve.	14.17

EVERLASTING

remember the e covenant	Gen 9.16
an e covenant, to be God to you	17.7
name of the Lord, the E God.	21.33
and lead me in the way e!	Ps 139.24
Thy kingdom is an e kingdom,	145.13
Mighty God, E Father, Prince	Isa 9.6
the Lord God is an e rock.	26.4
Lord will be your e light,	60.19
with you an e covenant.	Ezek 16.60
shall awake, some to e life,	Dan 12.2
Art thou not from e, O Lord	Hab 1.12

EVIL — S

if it is e in thy sight,	Num 22.34
So you shall purge the e	Deut 13.5
Israel again did what was e	Judg 4.1
Israel again did what was e	10.6
that e is determined by him.	1Sam 20.7
Solomon did what was e in	1Ki 11.6
Omri did what was e in the	16.25
He did much e in the sight	2Chr 33.6
did more e than the nations	33.9
they did e again before thee,	Neh 9.28
he saw that e was determined	Est 7.7
the wicked man conceives e,	Ps 7.14
according to the e of their deeds;	28.4
Let them..who devise e against me!	35.4
no e shall befall you, no	91.10
let e hunt down the violent	140.11
do not walk in..way of e men.	Prov 4.14
feet that..haste to run to e,	6.18
preserve you from the e woman,	6.24
heart..is fully set to do e.	Ecc 8.11
Woe to those who call e good	Isa 5.20
for they proceed from e to e,	Jer 9.3
'Why..this great e against us?	16.10
bring upon them the day of e;	17.18
set my face against you for e,	44.11
turn back from your e ways;	Ezek 33.11
Does e befall a city, unless	Amos 3.6
plotted e against the Lord,	Nah 1.11
you shall fear e no more.	Zeph 3.15
If you..who are e,..give good	Mt 7.11
seven other spirits more e	12.45
separate the e from the righteous,	13.49
out of the heart come e thoughts,	15.19
"Why, what e has he done?"	27.23
"Why, what e has he done?"	Mk 15.14
who are e, know how to give	Lk 11.13
seven other spirits more e	11.26
I testify..that its works are e.	Jn 7.7
keep them from the e one.	17.15
'You shall not speak e of a ruler	Acts 23.5
distress for..human..who does e,	Rom 2.9
why not do e that good may come?	3.8
but the e I do not want..I do.	7.19
not..leaven of malice and e,	1Cor 5.8
Let no e talk come out of your	Eph 4.29

EVIL — S (cont.)

none of you repays *e* for *e*,	1Thess 5.15
to speak *e* of no one, to avoid	Tit 3.2
you have overcome the *e* one.	1Jn 2.13
money is the root of all *e*;	1Tim 6.10

EVILDOER — S

Let the *e* still do evil,	Rev 22.11
depart from me, you *e*.'	Mt 7.23

EXALT — S — ED — ING

I will begin to *e* you in the	Josh 3.7
Prize her. .she will *e* you;	Prov 4.8
e that which is low, and	Ezek 21.26
Righteousness *e* a nation,	Prov 14.34
he *e* himself to show mercy	Isa 30.18
who *e* himself will be humbled,	Lk 14.11
LORD *e* Joshua in the sight	Josh 4.14
the son of Haggith *e* himself,	1Ki 1.5
God is *e* in his power; who	Job 36.22
e be the God of my salvation,	Ps 18.46
God. .I am *e* in the earth!''	46.10
Be *e*, O God, above the heavens!	57.5
Be *e*, O God, above. .heavens!	108.5
e above everything thy name	138.2
for his name alone is *e*; his	148.13
the LORD alone. .*e* in that day.	Isa 2.11
and *e* those of low degree;	Lk 1.52
God *e* him at his right hand	Acts 5.31
Therefore God has highly *e* him	Phil 2.9
e yourself against my people,	Ex 9.17

EXAMINE — D — ING

sat down to *e* the matter;	Ezra 10.16
Let us test and *e* our ways,	Lam 3.40
defense to those who would *e*	1Cor 9.3
Let a man *e* himself, and so	11.28
E yourselves, to see whether	2Cor 13.5
find him, he *e* the sentries	Acts 12.19
ordered him. .*e* by scourging,	22.24
and after *e* him before you,	Lk 23.14
eagerness, the *e* scriptures	Acts 17.11

EXAMPLE — S

I have given you an *e*, that	Jn 13.15
you. .an *e* to all. .believers	1Thess 1.7
our conduct an *e* to imitate.	2Thess 3.9
his perfect patience for an *e*	1Tim 1.16
set. .believers an *e* in speech and	4.12
an *e*, . .follow in his steps.	1Pet 2.21
but being *e* to the flock.	5.3

EXCEED — S

latter works *e* the first.	Rev 2.19
unless your righteousness *e*	Mt 5.20

EXCELLENT

in counsel, and *e* in wisdom.	Isa 28.29
an *e* spirit, knowledge, and	Dan 5.12
show you a still more *e* way.	1Cor 12.31
you may approve what is *e*,	Phil 1.10

EXCHANGED

They *e*. .glory of God for	Ps 106.20
women *e* natural relations for	Rom 1.26

EXCUSE — S

made. So they are without *e*;	Rom 1.20
they have no *e* for their sin;	Jn 15.22
all alike began to make *e*.	Lk 14.18

EXECUTE

by fire will. .LORD *e* judgment,	Isa 66.16
e vengeance upon the nations	Mic 5.15

EXHORTATION

they rejoiced at the *e*.	Acts 15.31

he who exhorts, in his *e*;	Rom 12.8
bear with my word of *e*, for	Heb 13.22

EXILE (n)

into *e* for want of knowledge;	Isa 5.13
as men do who must go into *e*.	Ezek 12.4

EXILED (v)

Israel was *e* from their: .land	2Ki 17.23
captives. .being *e* to Babylon.	Jer 40.1

EXPECTATION

e of the wicked in wrath.	Prov 11.23
"Gone is. .my *e* from LORD."	Lam 3.18
were in *e*,. .concerning John,	Lk 3.15

EXPERIENCE

you *e* so many things in vain?—	Gal 3.4
same *e* of suffering is required	1Pet 5.9

EXPIATION

and makes *e* for the land	Deut 32.43
how shall I make *e*, that	2Sam 21.3
whom God put forward as an *e*	Rom 3.25
to make *e* for the sins. .people.	Heb 2.17
he is the *e* for our sins,	1Jn 2.2
Son to be the *e* for our sins.	4.10

EXPLAIN — ED

no one who could *e* it to me.''	Gen 41.24
Moses undertook to *e* this law,	Deut 1.5
to. .disciples he *e* everything.	Mk 4.34

EXPOSE — D

works of darkness,. .*e* them.	Eph 5.11
lest his deeds should be *e*.	Jn 3.20

EXPOUNDED

and *e* to him the way of God	Acts 18.26
he *e* the matter to them	28.23

EXTEND — S

the Lord will *e* his hand	Isa ·1.11
as grace *e* to more. .people	2Cor 4.15

EXTERNAL

nor is true circumcision. .*e*	Rom 2.28

EXTOL — LED

E the LORD our God; worship	Ps 99.5
e your love more than wine;	Sol 1.4
name of. .Lord Jesus was *e*.	Acts 19.17

EXULT

name is the LORD, *e* before him!	Ps 68.4
how long shall the wicked *e*?	94.3
your doom? Can you then *e*?	Jer 11.15
and *e* with all your heart,	Zeph 3.14
hearts shall *e* in the LORD.	Zech 10.7

EYE — S

e for *e*, tooth for tooth,	Ex 21.24
e for *e*, tooth for tooth;	Lev 24.20
e for *e*, tooth for tooth,	Deut 19.21
his *e* sees every precious	Job 28.10
but now my *e* sees thee;	42.5
My *e* wastes away. .of grief,	Ps 6.7
counsel you with my *e* upon you.	32.8
e of the LORD is on. .who fear	33.18
no *e* has seen a God besides	Isa 64.4
If. .right *e* causes you to sin,	Mt 5.29
'An *e* for an *e* and a tooth	5.38
if your *e* is sound, your whole	6.22
the speck. .in your brother's *e*,	7.3
if your *e* causes you to sin,	18.9
if your *e* causes you to sin,	Mk 9.47
e is the lamp of your body;	Lk 11.34
no *e* has seen, nor ear heard,	1Cor 2.9
Noah found favor in the *e*	Gen 6.8
you will serve as *e* for us.	Num 10.31

EYE — S (cont.)

the *e* of the LORD your God   Deut 11.12
is right in his own *e*;   12.8
or *e* to see, or ears to hear.   29.4
what was right in his own *e*.   Judg 17.6
was right in his own *e*.   21.25
the *e* of all Israel are upon you, 1Ki 1.20
that thy *e* may be open night   8.29
Asa did. . right in the *e* of   15.11
LORD opened the *e* of the   2Ki 6.17
that thy *e* may be open day   2Chr 6.20
the *e* of the LORD run to and fro   16.9
but our *e* are upon thee."   20.12
was righteous in his own *e*.   Job 32.1
his *e* behold, his eyelids   Ps 11.4
not speak; *e*, but do not see.   115.5
Open my *e* that I may behold   119.18
My *e* shed streams of tears,   119.136
I lift up my *e* to the hills.   121.1
To thee I lift up my *e*, O thou   123.1
have *e*, but they see not,   135.16
e behold my unformed substance; 139.16
The *e* of all look to thee,   145.15
your *e* look directly forward,   Prov 4.25
fool is right in his own *e*,   12.15
The *e* of the LORD are in every   15.3
The *e* of the LORD keep watch   22.12
who are pure in their own *e*   30.12
lest they see with their *e*,   Isa 6.10
the LORD. . has closed your *e*,   29.10
then the *e*. . will not be closed,   32.3
Your *e* will see the king in   33.17
open thy *e*, O LORD, and see;   37.17
Lift up your *e* round about   49.18
forgotten. . hid from my *e*.   65.16
people,. . have *e*, but see not,   Jer 5.21
and my *e* a fountain of tears,   9.1
set my *e* upon them for good,   24.6
e of the LORD. . upon the sinful Amos 9.8
of purer *e* than to behold evil   Hab 1.13
the *e* which see what you see!   Lk 10.23
their *e* were opened and they   24.31
e that should not see and   Rom 11.8
Look. . what is before your *e*.   2Cor 10.7
would have plucked out your *e*   Gal 4.15
laid bare to the *e* of him   Heb 4.13
the *e* of the Lord are upon   1Pet 3.12
and salve to anoint your *e*,   Rev 3.18

EYESERVICE

not. . *e*, as men-pleasers, but   Eph 6.6
Slaves, obey. . not with *e*,   Col 3.22

EYEWITNESSES

from the beginning were *e* and   Lk 1.2
we were *e* of his majesty.   2Pet 1.16

EZEKIEL

*Call: Ezek 2—3. Visions: cherubim, Ezek
1; 10; abominations in Jerusalem, Ezek
8—9; valley of dry bones, Ezek 37; the
temple, Ezek 40.1—47.12; division of land,
47.13—48.35. Prophecies: against Israel,
Ezek 4—7; 11—12; 14—24; 33; against
false prophets, Ezek 13; 34; against other
nations, Ezek 25—32; 35; 38—39; of
restoration, Ezek 11.14—20; 34; 36;
39.23—29.*

EZRA

E went up from Babylonia.   Ezra 7.6
For *E* had set his heart   7.10
While *E* prayed and made   10.1
told *E* the scribe to bring   Neh 8.1

F

FACE — S

LORD,. . speak to Moses *f* to *f*,   Ex 33.11
but my *f* shall not be seen."   33.23
the skin of his *f* shone   34.29
make his *f* to shine upon you,   Num 6.25
LORD spoke with you *f* to *f*   Deut 5.4
whom the LORD knew *f* to *f*,   34.10
look one another in the *f*."   2Ki 14.8
seek the *f* of the God of Jacob. Ps 24.6
"Thy *f*, LORD, do I seek."   27.8
Let thy *f* shine on thy servant;   31.16
The *f* of the LORD is against   34.16
make his *f* to shine upon us,   67.1
Make thy *f* shine upon thy   119.135
see your *f*,. . hear your voice,   Sol 2.14
could not look at Moses' *f*   2Cor 3.7
hypocrites,. . disfigure their *f*   Mt 6.16

FACTIONS

there must be *f* among you   1Cor 11.19

FAIL — ED

he will not *f* you or destroy   Deut 4.31
"Let no man's heart *f*   1Sam 17.32
not *f* you a man on the throne   1Ki 2.4
will not *f* or be discouraged   Isa 42.4
not one of them has *f*.   Josh 23.14
my close friends have *f* me;   Job 19.14

FAINT

and do not let your heart be *f*   Isa 7.4
He gives power to the *f*, and   40.29
he has left me. . *f* all the day   Lam 1.13
send. . away hungry, lest they *f* Mt 15.32
the crowd. . will *f* on the way;   Mk 8.3

FAIR — EST

a *f* garland for your head,   Prov 1.9
You are the *f* of the sons of men; Ps 45.2
If you. . O *f* among women,   Sol 1.8

FAITH

because you broke *f* with me   Deut 32.51
Israel broke *f* in regard to   Josh 7.1
because they had no *f* in God,   Ps 78.22
righteous shall live by his *f*.   Hab 2.4
not even in Israel. . such *f*.   Mt 8.10
afraid, O men of little *f*?"   8.26
"O woman, great is your *f*!   15.28
"Because of your little *f*.   17.20
if you have *f* and never doubt,   21.21
when Jesus saw their *f*, he said   Mk 2.5
are you afraid? Have you no *f*?"   4.40
your *f* has made you well;   5.34
Jesus answered them, "Have *f*   11.22
when he saw their *f* he said,   Lk 5.20
not even in Israel. . such *f*."   7.9
"Daughter, your *f*. . made you well; 8.48
clothe you, O men of little *f*?   12.28
to the Lord, "Increase our *f*!"   17.5
your *f* has made you well."   17.19
will he find *f* on earth?"   18.8
your *f* has made you well."   18.42
prayed for you that your *f*   22.32
he had *f* to be made well,   Acts 14.9
he had opened a door of *f*   14.27
and of *f* in our Lord Jesus   20.21
are sanctified by *f* in me.'   26.18
for I have *f* in God that   27.25
because your *f* is proclaimed   Rom 1.8
to every one who has *f*, to   1.16
overthrow the law by this *f*?   3.31
That is why it depends on *f*,   4.16

FAITH (cont.)

He did not weaken in *f* when	Rom 4.19
since we are justified by *f*,	5.1
according to the measure of *f*	12.3
the man who is weak in *f*,	14.1
not proceed from *f* is sin.	14.23
to another *f* by..same Spirit,	1Cor 12.9
we have the same spirit of *f*	2Cor 4.13
now preaching the *f* he once	Gal 1.23
justified by *f* in Christ,	2.16
but *f* working through love.	5.6
who are of the household of *f*.	6.10
I have heard of your *f* in the	Eph 1.15
you have been saved through *f*;	2.8
taking the shield of *f*, with	6.16
we have heard of your *f* in	Col 1.4
work of *f* and labor of love	1Thess 1.3
comforted..through your *f*;	3.7
great confidence in the *f*	1Tim 3.13
he has disowned the *f* and is	5.8
Fight the good fight of the *f*;	6.12
reminded of your sincere *f*,	2Tim 1.5
sharing of your *f* may promote	Philem 6
it did not meet with *f* in	Heb 4.2
my righteous one shall live by *f*,	10.38
Now *f* is the assurance of things	11.1
through *f* conquered kingdoms,	11.33
life, and imitate their *f*.	13.7
my works will show you my *f*.	Jas 2.18
You see that *f* was active	2.22
the genuineness of your *f*,	1Pet 1.7
you to contend for the *f*	Jude 3
who..keep..the *f* of Jesus.	Rev 14.12

FAITHFUL

raise up for myself a *f* priest,	1Sam 2.35
who..is so *f* as David,	22.14
and *f* before the LORD his	2Chr 31.20
more *f* and God-fearing man	Neh 7.2
thou didst find his heart *f*	9.8
The LORD preserves the *f*,	Ps 31.23
"Gather to me my *f* ones, who	50.5
whose spirit was not *f* to God.	78.8
will look with favor on the *f*	101.6
but a *f* man who can find?	Prov 20.6
F are the wounds of a friend;	27.6
f city has become a harlot,	Isa 1.21
formed of old, *f* and sure.	25.1
he was *f*, and no error or fault	Dan 6.4
Judah..is *f* to the Holy One.	Hos 11.12
"Who then is the *f* and wise	Mt 24.45
'Well done, good and *f* servant;	25.21
is the *f* and wise steward,	Lk 12.42
who is *f* in a very little is	16.10
you have been *f* in a very little,	19.17
to remain *f* to the Lord	Acts 11.23
God is *f*, by whom you were	1Cor 1.9
God is *f*, and he will not	10.13
Epaphras..a *f* minister of	Col 1.7
He who calls you is *f*,	1Thess 5.24
But the Lord is *f*; he will	2Thess 3.3
entrust to *f* men who will	2Tim 2.2
since she considered him *f*	Heb 11.11
Be *f* unto death, and I will	Rev 2.10
He..is called *F* and True,	19.11

FAITHFULNESS

heavens, thy *f* to the clouds.	Ps 36.5
I have spoken of thy *f* and	40.10
thy *f* to the clouds.	57.10
F will spring up from..ground,	85.11
declared..thy *f* in Abaddon?	88.11
thy *f* is firm as the heavens.	89.2

I will not..be false to my *f*.	89.33
to declare..thy *f* by night,	92.2
the *f* of the LORD endures	117.2
Thy *f* endures..generations;	119.90
thy testimonies..in all *f*.	119.138
In thy *f* answer me, in thy	143.1
I have continued my *f* to you.	Jer 31.3
every morning; great is thy *f*.	Lam 3.23
There is no *f* or kindness,	Hos 4.1

FAITHLESS — LY

way of the *f* is their ruin.	Prov 13.15
she did, that *f* one, Israel,	Jer 3.6
"O *f* and perverse generation,	Mt 17.17
"O *f* and perverse generation,	Lk 9.41
do not be *f*, but believing."	Jn 20.27
as for the cowardly, the *f*,	Rev 21.8
because they have acted *f*,	Ezek 15.8

FAITHLESSNESS

in this *f* the hand of the	Ezra 9.2
I will heal their *f*; I will	Hos 14.4
Does..*f* nullify..faithfulness	Rom 3.3

FALL — S — EN (v)

let none of his words *f* to	1Sam 3.19
he *f*,..not be cast headlong,	Ps 37.24
make them *f* in the wilderness,	106.26
Let the wicked..*f* into..nets,	141.10
say..to the hills, *F* upon us.	Hos 10.8
when I *f*, I shall rise; when	Mic 7.8
And then many will *f* away,	Mt 24.10
"You will all *f* away because	26.31
immediately they *f* away.	Mk 4.17
"You will all *f* away; for	14.27
they stumbled so as to *f*?	Rom 11.11
that no one *f* by..disobedience.	Heb 4.11
rock that will make them *f*";	1Pet 2.8
not rejoice when..enemy *f*,	Prov 24.17
"How are the mighty *f*	2Sam 1.25
"How you are *f* from heaven,	Isa 14.12
"*F*, *f* is Babylon; and all	Isa 21.9
Suddenly Babylon has *f* and	Jer 51.8
you have *f* away from grace.	Gal 5.4
"*F*, *f* is Babylon the great,	Rev 14.8

FALL — ING (n)

this child is set for the *f*	Lk 2.34
a cause of my brother's *f*,	1Cor 8.13

FALSE — LY

he was *f* to the LORD his	2Chr 26.16
I should have been *f* to God	Job 31.28
Put *f* ways.far from me; and	Ps 119.29
therefore I hate every *f* way.	119.104
for his images are *f*, and	Jer 51.17
Their heart is *f*; now they	Hos 10.2
"Beware of *f* prophets, who come	Mt 7.15
For *f* Christs and *f* prophets	24.24
God..true though..man be *f*,	Rom 3.4
make them believe what is *f*,	2Thess 2.11
you will not deal *f* with me	Gen 21.23

FALSEHOOD

left of your answers but *f*."	Job 21.34
They take pleasure in *f*. They	Ps 62.4
abhor *f*, but I love thy law.	119.163
Remove..from me *f* and lying;	Prov 30.8
draw iniquity with cords of *f*,	Isa 5.18
spoken *f* and divined a lie;	Ezek 13.6
putting away *f*, let every one	Eph 4.25

FAME

who..heard thy *f* will say,	Num 14.15
Herod..heard about..*f* of Jesus;	Mt 14.1
And at once his *f* spread	Mk 1.28

FAMILY — IES

taken away from his *f*,	Num 27.4
the *f* of the earth shall bless	Gen 12.3
makes their *f* like flocks.	Ps 107.41
God of all the *f* of Israel,	Jer 31.1
of all the *f* of the earth;	Amos 3.2

FAMINE

there was a *f* in the land.	Gen 12.10
arise seven years of *f*,	41.30
f was severe upon them.	47.20
judges ruled there was a	Ruth 1.1
a *f* in the days of David	2Sam 21.1
the *f* was severe in Samaria,	1Ki 18.2
was a great *f* in Samaria,	2Ki 6.25
the *f* was so severe in the	25.3
either three years of *f*;	1Chr 21.12
In *f* he will redeem you	Job 5.20
he summoned a *f* on the land,	Ps 105.16
'Sword and *f* shall not come	Jer 14.15
I will send sword, *f*, and	24.10
with the burning heat of *f*.	Lam 5.10
not a *f* of bread, nor..thirst	Amos 8.11
a great *f* over all the world;	Acts 11.28

FAST — ED — ING (v)

but your disciples do not *f*?"	Mt 9.14
but your disciples do not *f*?	Mk 2.18
"The disciples of John *f* often	Lk 5.33
before the LORD, and *f*	1Sam 7.6
we *f*, and thou seest it not?	Isa 58.3
was it for me that you *f*?	Zech 7.5
he *f* forty days and forty nights,	Mt 4.2
I continued *f* and praying	Neh 1.4

FAST — ING (n)

proclaimed a *f*..all Judah.	2Chr 20.3
I proclaimed a *f* there,	Ezra 8.21
hold a *f* on my behalf, and	Est 4.16
Nineveh..proclaimed a *f*,	Jon 3.5
and the *f* of the seventh,	Zech 8.19
Israel were assembled with *f*	Neh 9.1
mourning among the Jews, with *f*	Est 4.3
My knees are weak through *f*;	Ps 109.24
"return..with *f*, with weeping,	Joel 2.12
that their *f* may be seen by men.	Mt 6.16
out except by prayer and *f*"	17.21*n*
driven out by..prayer and *f*	Mk 9.29*n*

FATE

the *f* of the..men and..beasts	Ecc 3.19
since one *f* comes to all, to	9.2

FATHER — S — 'S

a man leaves his *f*	Gen 2.24
Adam..became the *f* of..Seth.	5.3
f of a multitude of nations.	17.5
go..and bury my *f*; then I	50.5
Is not he your *f*, who	Deut 32.6
to the voice of their *f*;	1Sam 2.25
"Pray let my *f* and my mother	22.3
I will be his *f*, and he	2Sam 7.14
His *f* had never at any time	1Ki 1.6
I will be his *f*, and he	1Chr 17.13
I was *f* to the poor, and	Job 29.16
"Has the rain a *f*, or who	38.28
f and my mother have forsaken	Ps 27.10
F of the fatherless and..is God	68.5
As a *f* pities his children,	103.13
A wise son makes a glad *f*,	Prov 10.1
the *f* of a fool has no joy.	17.21
Hearken to..*f* who begot you.	23.22
who robs his *f* or his mother	28.24
Yet, O LORD, thou art our *F*;	Isa 64.8
nor the *f* suffer for..son;	Ezek 18.20

Have we not all one *f*? Has	Mal 2.10
that you may be sons of your *F*	Mt 5.45
as your heavenly *F* is perfect.	5.48
Pray..Our *F* who art in heaven,	6.9
he who does the will of my *F*	7.21
I..will acknowledge before my *F*	10.32
loves *f* or mother more than me	10.37
a man shall leave his *f* and mother	19.5
call no man your *f* on earth,	23.9
'If a man tells his *f* or his	Mk 7.11
man shall leave..*f* and mother	10.7
let me first go and bury my *f*."	Lk 9.59
heavenly *F* give the Holy Spirit	11.13
be divided, *f* against son	12.53
and does not hate his own *f*	14.26
F who sent me has..given me	Jn 12.49
Abraham..*f* of all who believe	Rom 4.11
I became your *f* in Christ	1Cor 4.15
and I will be a *f* to you,	2Cor 6.18
He is without *f* or mother	Heb 7.3
coming down from the *F* of	Jas 1.17
put to death for the *f*;	Deut 24.16
the inheritance of my *f*."	1Ki 21.3
f..not be put to death for	2Ki 14.6
against the God of their *f*,	1Chr 5.25
our *f* have told us, what deeds	Ps 44.1
hearts of children to their *f*,	Mal 4.6
turn..the *f* to the children,	Lk 1.17
F, do not provoke your children	Eph 6.4
F, do not provoke..children,	Col 3.21
I am writing to you, *f*,	1Jn 2.13
Hear,..your *f* instruction,	Prov 1.8
I must be in my *F* house?"	Lk 2.49

FATHERLESS

executes justice for the *f*	Deut 10.18
the sojourner, the *f*, and	14.29
even cast lots over the *f*,	Job 6.27
arms of the *f* were crushed.	22.9
those who snatch the *f* child	24.9
the *f* who had none to help	29.12
hast been the helper of the *f*.	Ps 10.14
your *f* children, I will keep	Jer 49.11

FAULT

I have found no *f* in him	1Sam 29.3
no ground for complaint or..*f*,	Dan 6.4
"Why does he still find *f*?	Rom 9.19
so that no *f* may be found	2Cor 6.3
For he finds *f* with them when	Heb 8.8

FAVOR — ED

Noah found *f* in the eyes	Gen 6.8
if I have found *f* in your sight,	18.3
may find *f* in your sight.' "	32.5
find *f* in the sight of my lord."	33.8
And I will give this people *f*	Ex 3.21
LORD gave the people *f* in the	11.3
LORD had given the people *f*	12.36
also found *f* in my sight.'	33.12
if I find *f* in thy sight,	Num 11.15
I have found *f* with thee,	Judg 6.17
"Why have I found *f* in your	Ruth 2.10
I..found *f* in your sight,	2Sam 14.22
If I find *f* in the eyes of the LORD,	15.25
for a brief moment *f* has	Ezra 9.8
Esther found *f* in..eyes of all	Est 2.15
If I have found *f* in the	5.8
His children will seek the *f*	Job 20.10
Tyre will sue your *f* with	Ps 45.12
LORD God..bestow *f* and honor.	84.11
the *f* of the Lord..be upon us,	90.17
So you will find *f* and good	Prov 3.4
to the humble he shows *f*.	3.34

FAVOR — ED (cont.)

He who..seeks good seeks *f*, Prov 11.27
his *f* is like the clouds 16.15
and obtains *f* from the LORD. 18.22
words of a wise..win him *f*, Ecc 10.12
in my *f* I..had mercy on you. Isa 60.10
for I will show you no *f*. Jer 16.13
you have found *f* with God. Lk 1.30
the *f* of God was upon him. 2.40
and in *f* with God and man. 2.52
found *f* in the sight of God Acts 7.46
to do the Jews a *f*, Felix left Paul 24.27
O *f* one, the Lord is with you!" Lk 1.28

FAVORABLE

words of the prophets..are *f* 1Ki 22.13
LORD, thou wast *f* to thy land; Ps 85.1

FEAR — S — ED (v)

and you will live, for I *f* God: Gen 42.18
"F not, stand firm, Ex 14.13
people, such as *f* God, 18.21
LORD is with us; do not *f* Num 14.9
do not *f* or be dismayed.' Deut 1.21
to *f* me and to keep all my 5.29
you may *f* the LORD your God, 6.2
Israel shall hear, and *f*, 13.11
people shall hear, and *f*, 17.13
do not *f* or be dismayed." 31.8
said to Joshua, "Do not *f* Josh 8.1
therefore *f* the LORD, 24.14
says the LORD..'F not, 2Chr 20.15
friendship..for those who *f* Ps 25.14
not *f* though the earth..change, 46.2
nations..*f* the name of the LORD, 102.15
food for those who *f* him; 111.5
thy promise,..for those who *f* 119.38
f the LORD,..turn..from evil. Prov 3.7
son, *f* the LORD and the king, 24.21
dreams increase,..do you *f* God. Ecc 5.7
be well with those who *f* God, 8.12
F God,..keep..commandments; 12.13
f not, for I am with you, Isa 41.10
not say..'Let us *f* the LORD Jer 5.24
who shall hear..*f* and tremble 33.9
f not, O Jacob my servant, 46.27
f before the God of Daniel, Dan 6.26
F not..let..hands be strong." Zech 8.13
do not *f* to take Mary your wife Mt 1.20
F not,..you are of more value 10.31
his mercy is on those who *f* Lk 1.50
f him who..has power to cast 12.5
"F not, daughter of Zion; Jn 12.15
Who shall not *f* and glorify Rev 15.4
woman who *f* the LORD is Prov 31.30
Who among you *f* the LORD and Isa 50.10
But the midwives *f* God, Ex 1.17
he who *f* the word of the LORD 9.20
I *f* the people and obeyed 1Sam 15.24
they *f* the LORD but also 2Ki 17.33
Then Jehoshaphat *f*, and 2Chr 20.3
those who *f* the LORD spoke Mal 3.16
Herod..*f* the people, because Mt 14.5
Herod *f* John, knowing he was Mk 6.20
destroy him; for they *f* him, 11.18
this because they *f* the Jews, Jn 9.22
a devout man who *f* God with Acts 10.2

FEAR (n)

they were in great *f*. Ex 14.10
f of you upon the peoples Deut 2.25
f of God came on..kingdoms 2Chr 20.29
instructed him in the *f* of God; 26.5
the *f* of the Jews had fallen Est 8.17

f of the Lord,..is wisdom; Job 28.28
Serve the LORD with *f*, with Ps 2.11
the *f* of the LORD is clean, 19.9
no *f* of God before his eyes. 36.1
f of the LORD..the beginning Prov 1.7
f of the LORD is the beginning 9.10
f of the LORD is a fountain 14.27
f of the LORD leads to life; 19.23
The *f* of man lays a snare, 29.25
let him be your *f*, and..dread. Isa 8.13
And they cried out for *f*. Mt 14.26
heart, it is I; have no *f*." Mk 6.50
doors..shut..for *f* of..Jews, Jn 20.19
"There is no *f* of God before Rom 3.18
Would you have no *f* of him 13.3
and in much *f* and trembling; 1Cor 2.3
knowing the *f* of the Lord, 2Cor 5.11
fighting without and *f* within. 7.5
f..with which you received him. 7.15
he was heard for his godly *f*. Heb 5.7
There is no *f* in love, but 1Jn 4.18

FEAST — ED (v)

They *f* on the abundance of thy Ps 36.8
My soul is *f* as with marrow 63.5
Those who *f* on dainties perish Lam 4.5

FEAST — S — ING (n)

you shall keep a *f* to me. Ex 23.14
a *f* to the LORD seven days Lev 23.41
Solomon held the *f* at that 1Ki 8.65
for all peoples a *f* of fat Isa 25.6
King Belshazzar made a great *f* Dan 5.1
"Not during the *f*, lest there Mt 26.5
Now at the *f* the governor was 27.15
at the *f* he used to release Mk 15.6
every year at..*f* of..Passover. Lk 2.41
Levi made him..*f* in his house; 5.29
the *f* of Unleavened Bread 22.1
appointed *f* of the LORD Lev 23.2
LORD at your appointed *f*, Num 29.39
turn your *f* into mourning, Amos 8.10
and made that a day of *f* Est 9.17

FED

the bread with which I *f* you Ex 16.32
who *f* you in the wilderness Deut 8.16

FEEBLE

"What are these *f* Jews doing? Neh 4.2
Therefore all hands will be *f*, Isa 13.7

FEED

commanded a widow there to *f* 1Ki 17.9
The lips of the righteous *f* Prov 10.21
He will *f* his flock like a Isa 40.11
will *f* you with the heritage 58.14
Aliens..stand and *f* your flocks, 61.5
and he shall *f* on Carmel Jer 50.19
Should not shepherds *f* the Ezek 34.2
he shall stand and *f* his flock Mic 5.4
"How can one *f* these men with Mk 8.4
Jesus said to him, "F my sheep. Jn 21.17
to *f* the church of the Lord Acts 20.28

FEET

kiss his *f*, lest he be angry, Ps 2.12
hast put all things under his *f*, 8.6
turn my *f* to thy testimonies; 119.59
Thy word is a lamp to my *f* 119.105
How graceful are..*f* in sandals, Sol 7.1
the *f* of him who brings good Nah 1.15
put thy enemies under thy *f*"? Mt 22.44
hold of his *f* and worshiped 28.9
put thy enemies under thy *f*.' Mk 12.36

FEET (cont.)
to wet his *f* with her tears,   Lk 7.38
Mary, who sat at the Lord's *f*   10.39
See my hands and my *f*, that   24.39
and anointed the *f* of Jesus   Jn 12.3
began to wash the disciples' *f*,   13.5
f are swift to shed blood,   Rom 3.15
all his enemies under his *f*.   1Cor 15.25

FELL
Moses and Aaron *f* on their   Num 14.5
Moses heard it, he *f* on his face;   16.4
And they *f* on their faces,   16.22
they *f* on their faces.   16.45
Abigail..*f* before David on   1Sam 25.23
I *f* at his feet as though dead.   Rev 1.17

FELLOW
"This *f* came to sojourn,   Gen 19.9
"Why do you strike your *f*?"   Ex 2.13
fall, one will lift up his *f*;   Ecc 4.10
"Away with such a *f* from   Acts 22.22
how the Gentiles are *f* heirs,   Eph 3.6
my brother and *f* worker   Phil 2.25
f workers for..kingdom of God,   Col 4.11
be *f* workers in the truth.   3Jn 8

FELLOWSHIP
the apostles' teaching and *f*,   Acts 2.42
called into the *f* of his Son,   1Cor 1.9
and the *f* of the Holy Spirit   2Cor 13.14
Barnabas the right hand of *f*,   Gal 2.9
that you may have *f* with us;   1Jn 1,3

FEVER
Simon's mother-in-law..with *f*,   Mk 1.30
Simon's mother-in-law..high *f*,   Lk 4.38
seventh hour the *f* left him."   Jn 4.52
father of Publius lay..with *f*   Acts 28.8

FEW
therefore let your words be *f*.   Ecc 5.2
and those who find it are *f*.   Mt 7.14
will those who are saved be *f*?"   Lk 13.23

FIELD
who add *f* to *f*, until there   Isa 5.8
'Buy my *f*..at Anathoth, for   Jer 32.7
like treasure hidden in a *f*,   Mt 13.44
f was called..F of Blood.)   Acts 1.19
you are God's *f*, God's   1Cor 3.9

FIGHT — ING
The LORD will *f* for you,   Ex 14.14
God..will himself *f* for you,   Deut 1.30
the LORD..goes.. to *f* for you   20.4
shall not go up or *f* against   2Chr 11.4
come down to *f* upon Mount Zion Isa 31.4
fast only to quarrel and to *f*   58.4
They will *f* against you; but   Jer 1.19
I myself will *f* against you   21.5
Judah will *f*..Jerusalem.   Zech 14.14
my servants would *f*, that I   Jn 18.36
F the good *f* of the faith;   1Tim 6.12
f without and fear within.   2Cor 7.5

FIGS
nor *f* on the fig tree; even   Jer 8.13
two baskets of *f* placed before   24.1

FIG TREE — S
f..puts forth its figs,   Sol 2.13
like leaves falling from the *f*..   Isa 34.4
sit every man..under his *f*..,   Mic 4.4
Though the *f*..not blossom,   Hab 3.17
the *f*..withered at once.   Mt 21.19
And seeing..a *f*..in leaf,   Mk 11.13

"From the *f*..learn its lesson: 13.28
man had a *f*..planted..vineyard; Lk 13.6
parable: "Look at the *f*..,   21.29
under the *f*.., I saw you."   Jn 1.48
Can a *f*.., yield olives,   Jas 3.12
It has..and splintered my *f*..;   Joel 1.7

FILL — ED (v)
and *f* the waters in the seas,   Gen 1.22
f the earth and subdue it;   1.28
f the whole world with fruit.   Isa 27.6
said.."F the jars with water."   Jn 2.7
the glory of the LORD *f* the   Ex 40.35
be *f* with the glory of the   Num 14.21
come and eat and be *f*;   Deut 14.29
glory of the LORD *f* the house   1Ki 8.11
he *f* Jerusalem with innocent   2Ki 24.4
glory of the LORD *f* the   2Chr 5.14
glory of the LORD *f*..temple.   Ezek 43.5
glory of the LORD *f* the temple   44.4
earth..*f* with the knowledge   Hab 2.14
he has *f* the hungry with good   Lk 1.53
Every valley shall be *f*, and   3.5
all *f* with the Holy Spirit   Acts 2.4
you have *f* Jerusalem with   5.28
Already you are *f*! Already   1Cor 4.8
but be *f* with the Spirit,   Eph 5.18

FILL (n)
let us take our *f* of love   Prov 7.18
ate your *f* of the loaves.   Jn 6.26

FINAL
time of your *f* punishment,   Ezek 21.25
oath is *f* for confirmation.   Heb 6.16

FIND — S
your sin will *f* you out.   Num 32.23
seek the LORD..will *f* him,   Deut 4.29
where I might *f* him, that I   Job 23.3
understanding..*f* him out.   Prov 28.11
For he who *f* me *f* life and   8.35
who *f* a wife *f* a good thing,   18.22

FINGER
"This is the *f* of God."   Ex 8.19
written with the *f* of God.   31.18
written with the *f* of God;   Deut 9.10
not move them with their *f*.   Mt 23.4
if it is by the *f* of God   Lk 11.20
thy heavens, the work of thy *f*,   Ps 8.3
the *f* of a man's hand appeared Dan 5.5
burdens with one of your *f*.   Lk 11.46

FINISH — ED
to *f* the transgression, to   Dan 9.24
the third day I *f* my course.   Lk 13.32
heavens..earth were *f*,   Gen 2.1
built the house, and *f* it.   1Ki 6.14
house of the LORD is *f*.   1Chr 28.20
and this house was *f* on   Ezra 6.15
So the wall was *f* on the   Neh 6.15
he said, "It is *f*"; and..bowed Jn 19.30
I have *f* the race, I have kept   2Tim 4.7

FIRE
Gomorrah brimstone and *f*   Gen 19.24
And *f* came forth from before   Lev 9.24
f came forth from..the LORD   10.2
out of the midst of the *f*;   Deut 4.12
your God is a devouring *f*,   4.24
LORD spoke..out of the *f*,   5.4
haste to set the city on *f*.   Josh 8.19
smote..and set the city on *f*.   Judg 1.8
Then the *f* of the LORD fell,   1Ki 18.38
the LORD was not in the *f*;   19.12

FIRE (cont.)

and horses of *f* separated	2Ki 2.11
ended his prayer, *f* came	2Chr 7.1
we went through *f* and..water;	Ps 66.12
As *f* consumes the forest, as	83.14
For lack of wood the *f* goes	Prov 26.20
when you walk through *f* you	Isa 43.2
their *f* shall not be quenched,	66.24
burning *f* shut up in my bones,	Jer 20.9
Is not my word like *f*, says	23.29
scroll was consumed in the *f*	36.23
"From on high he sent *f*; into	Lam 1.13
four men..walking in the..*f*,	Dan 3.25
cut down and thrown into the *f*.	Mt 3.10
the Holy Spirit and with *f*.	3.11
eternal *f* prepared for the devil	25.41
the Holy Spirit and with *f*.	Lk 3.16
do you want us to bid *f* come	9.54
"I came to cast *f* upon..earth;	12.49
they saw a charcoal *f* there,	Jn 21.9
shook..creature into the *f*	Acts 28.5
the *f* will test what sort	1Cor 3.13
saved, but only as through *f*.	3.15
mighty angels in flaming *f*,	2Thess 1.7
for our God is a consuming *f*.	Heb 12.29
And the tongue is a *f*. The	Jas 3.6
a punishment of eternal *f*.	Jude 7
snatching them out of the *f*;	23
the lake that burns with *f*	Rev 21.8

FIRMAMENT

"Let there be a *f* in the midst	Gen 1.6
the *f* proclaims his handiwork.	Ps 19.1

FIRST

LORD, the *f*, and..the last;	Isa 41.4
But seek *f* his kingdom and	Mt 6.33
many that are *f* will be last,	19.30
"If any one would be *f*, he	Mk 9.35
let me *f* go..bury my father."	Lk 9.59
f convert in Asia for Christ.	Rom 16.5
The *f* man was from..earth,	1Cor 15.47
the *f* converts in Achaia,	16.15
but *f* they gave themselves	2Cor 8.5
Diotrephes,..to put himself *f*,	3Jn 9
"Fear not, I am the *f* and the	Rev 1.17
This is the *f* resurrection.	20.5

FIRST-BORN

all the *f* in the land of Egypt	Ex 11.5
Levites instead of all the *f*	Num 3.45
For all the *f* among the people	8.17
He smote all the *f* in Egypt,	Ps 78.51
make him the *f*, the highest	89.27
He is..the *f* of all creation;	Col 1.15

FIRSTLING

as a *f* belongs to the LORD,	Lev 27.26

FISH

dominion over the	Gen 1.26
the *f* in the Nile died;	Ex 7.21
LORD appointed a great *f*	Jonah 1.17
the LORD spoke to the *f*,	2.10
for a *f*, will give..a serpent?	Mt 7.10
five loaves here and two *f*."	14.17
"Seven, and a few small *f*."	15.34
take the first *f* that comes	17.27
they said, "Five, and two *f*."	Mk 6.38
And they had a few small *f*;	8.7
if his son asks for a *f*, will	Lk 11.11
five barley loaves and two *f*;	Jn 6.9
haul..in..the quantity of *f*.	21.6

FISHERMEN

The *f* will mourn and lament,	Isa 19.8
in the sea; for they were *f*.	Mk 1.16

FISHERS

I am sending for many *f*,	Jer 16.16
I will make you..*f* of men."	Mk 1.17

FIVE

Do you..remember the *f* loaves	Mt 16.9
they said, "*F*, and two fish."	Mk 6.38
ate the loaves were *f* thousand	6.44
"We have no more than *f* loaves	Lk 9.13
for you have had *f* husbands,	Jn 4.18

FIXED

eyes of all..were *f* on him.	Lk 4.20
because he has *f* a day on	Acts 17.31

FLAME

fire, and his Holy One a *f*;	Isa 10.17
the *f* shall not consume you.	43.2

FLASHES

jealousy..Its *f* are *f* of fire,	Sol 8.6
from the throne..*f* of lightning,	Rev 4.5

FLATTER — S — ING

For I do not know how to *f*,	Job 32.22
he *f* himself in his own eyes	Ps 36.2
he who *f* with his tongue.	Prov 28.23
who *f* his neighbor spreads	29.5
with *f* lips and a double heart	Ps 12.2
and a *f* mouth works ruin.	Prov 26.28

FLED

and she *f* from her.	Gen 16.6
But Moses *f* from Pharaoh,	Ex 2.15
"Joab *f* to the tent of	1Ki 2.29
I have *f* to thee for refuge!	Ps 143.9
as you *f* from the earthquake	Zech 14.5

FLEE

f to one of these cities	Deut 19.5
"Should such a man as I *f*?	Neh 6.11
how can you say to me, "*F*	Ps 11.1
wicked *f* when no one pursues,	Prov 28.1
F for safety, O people of	Jer 6.1
Jonah rose to *f* to Tarshish	Jonah 1.3
child and his mother, and *f* to	Mt 2.13
persecute you in one town, *f*	10.23
warned you to *f* from the wrath	Lk 3.7
let those who are in Judea *f*	21.21

FLEECE

I am laying a *f* of wool	Judg 6.37

FLEET (n)

King Solomon built a *f* of	1Ki 9.26
Moreover the *f* of Hiram, which	10.11

FLEETING (adj)

let me know how *f* my life is!	Ps 39.4
enjoy the *f* pleasures of sin.	Heb 11.25

FLESH

we are your bone and *f*.	1Chr 11.1
With him is an arm of *f*;	2Chr 32.8
without my *f* I shall see God,	Job 19.26
let all *f* bless his holy name	Ps 145.21
all *f* shall see it together,	Isa 40.5
All *f* is grass, and all its beauty	40.6
willing, but the *f* is weak."	Mt 26.41
willing, but the *f* is weak."	Mk 14.38
all *f* shall see the salvation	Lk 3.6
the Word became *f* and dwelt	Jn 1.14
life of the world is my *f*."	6.51
life, the *f* is of no avail;	6.63
nothing good dwells..in my *f*.	Rom 7.18

FLESH (cont.)

Son in the likeness of sinful *f*	Rom 8.3
To set..mind on the *f* is death,	8.6
But you are not in the *f,*	8.9
their race, according to the *f,*	9.5
but as men of the *f,* as babes	1Cor 3.1
for the destruction of the *f,*	5.5
For not all *f* is alike, but	15.39
f and blood cannot inherit	15.50
thorn was given me in the *f,*	2Cor 12.7
the Spirit are against the *f;*	Gal 5.17
reason for confidence in the *f,*	Phil 3.4

FLESHPOTS

when we sat by the *f* and ate	Ex 16.3

FLOAT — ED

a stick,..made the iron *f.*	2Ki 6.6
the ark *f* on..face of the waters.	Gen 7.18

FLOCK

stronger of the *f* were breeding	Gen 30.41
thy *f* found a dwelling in it;	Ps 68.10
lead thy people like a *f* by the hand	77.20
thy people, the *f.*.give thanks	79.13
He will feed his *f* like a	Isa 40.11
like the *f* at Jerusalem	Ezek 36.38
"Fear not little *f,* for it	Lk 12.32
Tend the *f* of God that is	1Pet 5.2

FLOOD — S

I will bring a *f* of waters	Gen 6.17
never again..*f* to destroy	9.11
LORD sits enthroned over..*f;*	Ps 29.10
the *f* came and destroyed them	Lk 17.27
the rain fell, and the *f* came,	Mt 7.27

FLOW — ING (v)

all the nations shall *f* to it,	Isa 2.2
f from the throne of God	Rev 22.1

FLOW (n)

a *f* of blood for twelve years.	Mk 5.25
a *f* of blood for twelve years	Lk 8.43

FLOWER — S

He comes forth like a *f,*	Job 14.2
grass withers, the *f* fades,	Isa 40.7
The *f* appear on the earth,	Sol 2.12

FLY — IES

LORD will whistle for the *f*	Isa 7.18
I will send swarms of *f*	Ex 8.21
Dead *f* make the perfumer's	Ecc 10.1

FOES

three months before your *f*	2Sam 24.13
O LORD, how many are my *f!*	Ps 3.1
God..will tread down our *f.*	108.13
man's *f* will be those of his	Mt 10.36

FOLD

they have forgotten their *f.*	Jer 50.6
other sheep,..not of this *f;*	Jn 10.16

FOLLOW — ED — ING

If the LORD is God, *f* him;	1Ki 18.21
adversaries because I *f*..good.	Ps 38.20
They shall *f* my ordinances	Ezek 37.24
"*F* me, and I will make you	Mt 4.19
"Teacher, I will *f* you wherever	8.19
"*F* me, and leave the dead to	8.22
Jesus..said to him, "*F* me."	9.9
and he said to him, "*F* me."	Mk 2.14
allowed no one to *f* him except	5.37
and he said to him, "*F* me."	Lk 5.27
take up his cross daily and *f*	9.23
because he does not *f* with us."	9.49

"I will *f* you wherever you go."	9.57
in heaven; and come, *f* me."	18.22
Philip and said to him, "*F* me."	Jn 1.43
sheep *f* him, for they know his	10.4
I know them, and they *f* me;	10.27
If any one serves me, he must *f*	12.26
"Lord, why cannot I *f* you	13.37
After this he said.."*F* me."	21.19
also *f*..example of the faith	Rom 4.12
they..wholly *f* the LORD.'	Num 32.12
yet I wholly *f* the LORD	Josh 14.8
they *f* the nations that were	2Ki 17.15
stubbornly *f* their own hearts	Jer 9.14
Peter *f* him at a distance,	Mt 26.58
they left their nets and *f* him.	Mk 1.18
we have left everything and *f*	10.28
Peter had *f* him at a distance,	14.54
women..*f* him and ministered	15.41
left our homes and *f* you."	Lk 18.28
Peter *f* at a distance;	22.54
heard John speak, and *f* him,	Jn 1.40
Simon Peter *f* Jesus, and so	18.15
your children *f* the truth,	2Jn 4

FOLLY — IES

she has wrought *f* in Israel	Deut 22.21
Nabal is his name, and *f*	1Sam 25.25
do not do this wanton *f.*	2Sam 13.12
The devising of *f* is sin,	Prov 24.9
a fool that repeats his *f.*	26.11
through..*f* of what we preach	1Cor 1.21
gifts of..Spirit..are *f* to him.	2.14
their hearts overflow with *f.*	Ps 73.7

FOOD — S

you shall have them for *f.*	Gen 1.29
tree was good for *f,*	3.6
there is no *f* and no water,	Num 21.5
children beg for *f,* but no one	Lam 4.4
For life is more than *f,*	Lk 12.23
"I have *f* to eat of which	Jn 4.32
"*F* is meant for the stomach	1 Cor 6.13
the right to our *f* and drink?	9.4
but if we have *f* and clothing,	1Tim 6.8
enjoin abstinence from *f*	4.3

FOOL — S

I have played the *f,* and	1Sam 26.21
Abner die as a *f* dies?	2Sam 3.33
Surely vexation kills the *f,*	Job 5.2
The *f* says.."There is no God."	Ps 14.1
f and the stupid alike must perish	49.10
The *f* says.."There is no God."	53.1
prating *f* will come to ruin.	Prov 10.8
but a *f* flaunts his folly.	13.16
Leave the presence of a *f,*	14.7
rather than a *f* in his folly.	17.12
Wisdom is too high for a *f;*	24.7
honor is not fitting for a *f.*	26.1
Answer a *f* according to his folly,	26.5
"What befalls the *f* will..me	Ecc 2.15
The *f* folds his hands, and eats	4.5
Be not wicked..neither..a *f;*	7.17
whoever says, 'You *f!*' shall	Mt 5.22
'*F!* This night your soul is	Lk 12.20
folly is the chastisement of *f.*	Prov 16.22
and *f* shall not err therein.	Isa 35.8
You *f!*..who made the outside	Lk 11.40
they became *f,* and exchanged	Rom 1.22
We are *f* for Christ's sake,	1Cor 4.10

FOOLISH

and makes their knowledge *f;*	Isa 44.25
"For my people are *f,* they	Jer 4.22

FOOLISH (cont.)
a *f* man who built his house   Mt 7.26
"O *f* men, and slow of heart   Lk 24.25

FOOT
He will not let your *f* be moved,   Ps 121.3
you have raced with men on *f*,   Jer 12.5
if your *f* causes you to sin,   Mk 9.45
If the *f* should say,   1Cor 12.15

FOOTSTOOL
till I make..enemies your *f*."   Ps 110.1
and the earth is my *f*;   Isa 66.1

FORBADE
in your name, and we *f* him,   Mk 9.38
in your name, and we *f* him,   Lk 9.49

FORBEARANCE
because in his divine *f* he   Rom 3.25
count the *f* of our Lord as   2Pet 3.15

FORBID — DEN
"My lord Moses, *f* them."   Num 11.28
not *f* speaking in tongues;   1Cor 14.39
f by the Holy Spirit to speak   Acts 16.6

FORCE (n)
men of violence take it by *f*.   Mt 11.12
take him by *f* to make him king,   Jn 6.15

FORCED (v)
I *f* myself, and offered   1Sam 13.12
slothful..be put to *f* labor.   Prov 12.24
I have been a fool! You *f* me   2Cor 12.11

FOREHEAD — S
a hard *f* and..stubborn heart.   Ezek 3.8
marked on the right hand or..*f*,   Rev 13.16
a mark upon the *f* of the men   Ezek 9.4

FOREIGN
and from the *f* wives."   Ezra 10.11
the LORD's song in a *f* land?   Ps 137.4

FOREIGNER — S
To a *f* you may lend upon   Deut 23.20
"Likewise when a *f*,..comes   1Ki 8.41
praise to God except this *f*?"   Lk 17.18
be a *f* to the speaker   1Cor 14.11
admitting *f*, uncircumcised   Ezek 44.7

FOREKNEW
whom he *f* he also predestined   Rom 8.29
God has not rejected..whom he *f*.   11.2

FOREKNOWLEDGE
definite plan and *f* of God,   Acts 2.23

FORFEIT — ED
gain..world and *f* his life?   Mk 8.36
yield be *f* to the sanctuary,   Deut 22.9

FORGAVE
f their iniquity, and did not   Ps 78.38
released..and *f* him the debt.   Mt 18.27
wicked servant! I *f* you all   18.32
When they could not pay, he *f*   Lk 7.42
as God in Christ *f* you.   Eph 4.32

FORGET — S — TING
he will not..*f* the covenant   Deut 4.31
take heed lest you *f* the LORD,   6.12
lest you *f* the LORD your God,   8.11
Why dost thou *f* our affliction   Ps 44.24
O daughter,..*f* your people   45.10
do not *f* the life of thy poor   74.19
and *f* not all his benefits,   103.2
I will not *f* thy word.   119.16
If I *f* you, O Jerusalem, let   137.5

My son, do not *f* my teaching,   Prov 3.1
drink and *f* their poverty,   31.7
who *f* my holy mountain,   Isa 65.11
to make my people *f* my name   Jer 23.27
Why dost thou *f* us for ever,   Lam 5.20
f the covenant of her God;   Prov 2.17
evil..*f* the LORD their God,   Judg 3.7
I do, *f* what lies behind   Phil 3.13

FORGIVE — S — N — ING
f the transgression of   Gen 50.17
if thou wilt *f* their sin—   Ex 32.32
and the LORD will *f* her.   Num 30.8
Pray *f* the trespass of   1Sam 25.28
and when thou hearest, *f*.   1Ki 8.30
and *f*, and act, and render   8.39
and when thou hearest, *f*.   2Chr 6.21
f their sin and heal their land.   7.14
not *f* your transgressions   Josh 24.19
Consider..and *f* all my sins.   Ps 25.18
deliver us, and *f* our sins,   79.9
f the iniquity of thy people;   85.2
for I will *f* their iniquity,   Jer 31.34
I will *f* all the guilt of their sin   33.8
f their iniquity and their sin."   36.3
men..brought low—*f* them not!   Isa 2.9
And *f* us our debts, As we also   Mt 6.12
neither will your Father *f*   6.15
if you do not *f* your brother   18.35
blasphemy! Who can *f* sins but God   Mk 2.7
whenever you stand praying, *f*,   11.25
f, and you will be forgiven;   Lk 6.37
and *f* us our sins, for we..*f*   11.4
and if he repents, *f* him;   17.3
Jesus said, "Father, *f* them;   23.34
If you *f* the sins of any,   Jn 20.23
you should rather turn to *f*   2Cor 2.7
he..will *f* our sins and cleanse   1Jn 1.9
who *f* all your iniquity, who   Ps 103.3
who *f* an offense seeks love,   Prov 17.9
atonement..they shall be *f*.   Lev 4.20
the sin..shall be *f* him.   19.22
they shall be *f*; because   Num 15.25
guilt of blood be *f* them.'   Deut 21.8
he whose transgression is *f*,   Ps 32.1
guilt is taken away,..sin *f*."   Isa 6.7
people..who dwell..will be *f*   33.24
rebelled, and thou hast not *f*.   Lam 3.42
my son; your sins are *f*."   Mt 9.2
sin and blasphemy will be *f*   12.31
paralytic,..your sins are *f*."   Mk 2.5
all sins will be *f*..men,   3.28
"Man, your sins are *f* you."   Lk 5.20
word against the Son..be *f*;   12.10
intent of your heart may be *f*   Acts 8.22
those whose iniquities are *f*,   Rom 4.7
having *f* us all our trespasses,   Col 2.13
your sins are *f* for his sake.   1Jn 2.12
f iniquity and transgression   Ex 34.7
steadfast love, *f* iniquity   Num 14.18
thou wast a *f* God to them, but   Ps 99.8

FORGIVENESS
But there is *f* with thee,   Ps 130.4
To..our God belong mercy and *f*;   Dan 9.9
baptized..for the *f* of..sins;   Acts 2.38
believes in him receives *f*   10.43
through this man *f* of sins   13.38
they may receive *f* of sins   26.18
redemption, the *f* of sins.   Col 1.14
without..shedding..blood..no *f*   Heb 9.22

FORGOT — TEN
chief butler..*f* him.   Gen 40.23

FORGOT — TEN (cont.)

they *f* the LORD their God;	1Sam 12.9
But they soon *f* his works;	Ps 106.13
in his heart, "God has *f*,	10.11
"Why hast thou *f* me? Why go I	42.9
though we have not *f* thee, or	44.17
Has God *f* to be gracious?	77.9
f the God of your salvation,	Isa 17.10
Israel, you will not be *f*	44.21
"The LORD has forsaken..*f* me."	49.14
have *f* the LORD, your Maker,	51.13
Yet my people have *f* me days	Jer 2.32
you have *f* me and trusted..lies.	13.25
But my people have *f* me, they	18.15
All your lovers have *f* you;	30.14
gone, they have *f* their fold.	50.6
you have *f* the law of your God,	Hos 4.6
they had *f* to bring bread;	Mk 8.14
not one of them..*f* before God.	Lk 12.6

FORK

have winnowed them with..*f*	Jer 15.7
winnowing *f* is in his hand,	Lk 3.17

FORM (n)

f of this world is passing	1Cor 7.31
though he was in the *f* of God,	Phil 2.6
holding the *f* of religion	2Tim 3.5

FORMED (v)

God *f* man of dust	Gen 2.7
out of the ground..God *f*	2.19
was *f* from a piece of clay.	Job 33.6
LORD..who created..who *f* you,	Isa 43.1
LORD..who *f* you from the womb	44.2
"Before I *f* you in the womb	Jer 1.5
until Christ be *f* in you!	Gal 4.19

FORMER

Tell us the *f* things, what	Isa 41.22
f things I declared of old.	48.3

FORMS (v)

he who *f* the mountains,	Amos 4.13

FORSAKE — N — ING

he will not fail you or *f* you;	Deut 31.8
I will not fail you or *f* you.	Josh 1.5
if you *f* him, he will cast	1Chr 28.9
if you turn aside and *f* my	2Chr 7.19
Cast me not off, *f* me not, O	Ps 27.9
he will not *f* his saints.	37.28
LORD will not *f* his people;	94.14
statutes; O *f* me not utterly!	119.8
Let not..faithfulness *f* you;	Prov 3.3
f not your mother's teaching.	6.20
those who *f*..shall be consumed.	Isa 1.28
let the wicked *f* his way,	55.7
because he has *f* me, and	1Ki 11.33
because you have *f* the	18.18
Because they have *f* me and	2Ki 22.17
our God, and we have not *f*	2Chr 13.10
hast not *f* those who seek thee.	Ps 9.10
my God, why hast thou *f* me?	22.1
have not seen the righteous *f*	37.25
"God has *f* him; pursue and	71.11
They have *f* the LORD, they	Isa 1.4
f me and served foreign gods	Jer 5.19
'Because your fathers have *f*	16.11
the LORD has *f* the land.' "	Ezek 8.12
virgin Israel; *f* on her land,	Amos 5.2
my God, why hast thou *f* me?"	Mt 27.46
my God, why hast thou *f* me?"	Mk 15.34
persecuted, but not *f*; struck	2Cor 4.9
f me and serving other gods,	1Sam 8.8

all their wickedness in *f* me;	Jer 1.16
by *f* the LORD..when he led you	2.17

FORSOOK

f the covenant of the LORD,	Deut 29.25
he *f* God who made him,	32.15
'Because they *f* the LORD	1Ki 9.9
Rehoboam..*f* the law of..LORD,	2Chr 12.1
For a brief moment I *f* you,	Isa 54.7
"Because they *f* the covenant	Jer 22.9
all the disciples *f* him, and	Mt 26.56
they all *f* him, and fled.	Mk 14.50

FORTRESS

Be thou..a strong *f* to save me!	Ps 31.2
thou art my rock and my *f*;	31.3
for thou, O God, art my *f*.	59.9
rock and my *f*, my stronghold	144.2
He shall honor the god of *f*	Dan 11.38

FORTUNES

God will restore your *f*,	Deut 30.3
LORD restored the *f* of Job,	Job 42.10
When the LORD restores the *f*	Ps 14.7
When God restores the *f* of his	53.6
thou didst restore the *f* of Jacob.	85.1
LORD restored the *f* of Zion,	126.1
when I restore their *f*: 'The	Jer 31.23
I will restore the *f* of Judah	33.7
restore the *f* of my people	Amos 9.14
mindful..and restore their *f*.	Zeph 2.7
when I restore your *f* before	3.20

FORTY

rain upon the earth *f* days	Gen 7.4
on the mountain *f* days	Ex 24.18
in the wilderness *f* years,	Num 14.33
these *f* years the LORD	Deut 2.7
at the end of *f* days and	9.11
F stripes may be given him,	25.3
I have led you *f* years	29.5

FOUND — ED

"He *f* him in a desert land,	Deut 32.10
evil shall not be *f* in you	1Sam 25.28
have *f* the book of the law	2Chr 34.15
they *f* it written in the law	Neh 8.14
'Deliver him..I..*f* a ransom;	Job 33.24
I *f* him whom my soul loves.	Sol 3.4
Thy words were *f*, and I ate	Jer 15.16
I will be *f* by you, says the LORD	29.14
'Rejoice with me, for I have *f*	Lk 15.9
my son..was lost, and is *f*.'	15.24
said.."We have *f* the Messiah"	Jn 1.41
"We have *f* him of whom Moses	1.45
and having *f* him he said,	9.35
not *f* written in the book of	Rev 20.15
he has *f* it upon the seas, and	Ps 24.2
LORD by wisdom *f* the earth;	Prov 3.19

FOUNDATION — S

But the *f* of the temple was	Ezra 3.6
because the *f* of the house	3.11
were you when I laid the *f*	Job 38.4
didst lay the *f* of the earth,	Ps 102.25
laying in Zion for a *f* a stone,	Isa 28.16
the *f* of the..temple was laid,	Hag 2.18
hidden since..*f* of the world."	Mt 13.35
I build on another man's *f*,	Rom 15.20
no other *f* can any one lay	1Cor 3.11
But God's firm *f* stands,	2Tim 2.19
if the *f* are destroyed, what	Ps 11.3
f..of the mountains trembled	18.7
the *f* of the earth tremble.	Isa 24.18
from the *f* of the earth?	40.21
lay your *f* with sapphires.	54.11

FOUNTAIN — S
with thee is the *f* of life; Ps 36.9
fear of the LORD is a *f* of Prov 14.27
Wisdom is a *f* of life to him 16.22
the *f* of wisdom is a gushing 18.4
muddied spring or a polluted *f* 25.26
pitcher is broken at the *f*, Ecc 12.6
a garden locked, a *f* sealed. Sol 4.12
they have forsaken me, the *f* Jer 2.13
and my eyes a *f* of tears, 9.1
LORD, the *f* of living water. 17.13
a *f* shall come forth from Joel 3.18
f opened for..house of David Zech 13.1
f of the water of life Rev 21.6
the *f* of the great deep burst Gen 7.11

FOX — ES
if a *f* goes up on it he will Neh 4.3
"Go and tell that *f*, 'Behold, Lk 13.32
and caught three hundred *f*, Judg 15.4
f, that spoil the vineyards, Sol 2.15
prophets have been like *f* Ezek 13.4
"*F* have holes, and birds of Mt 8.20
"*F* have holes, and birds of Lk 9.58

FRAGRANCE
The mandrakes give forth *f*, Sol 7.13
the *f* of the knowledge of him 2Cor 2.14

FRANKINCENSE
They shall bring gold and *f*, Isa 60.6
offered him gifts, gold and *f* Mt 2.11

FREE — LY
I will not go out *f*,' Ex 21.5
and be *f* of obligation to Num 32.22
And when you let him go *f* Deut 15.13
LORD sets the prisoners *f*; Ps 146.7
the souls that you hunt go *f* Ezek 13.20
the truth will make you *f*." Jn 8.32
So if the Son makes you *f*, 8.36
But the *f* gift is not like Rom 5.15
having been set *f* from sin, 6.18
the husband dies, she is *f* 1Cor 7.39
not *f*? Am I not an apostle? 9.1
there is neither slave nor *f*, Gal 3.28
"You may *f* eat of every tree Gen 2.16
will offer themselves *f* on Ps 110.3
gives *f*, yet grows..richer; Prov 11.24

FREED
he who has died is *f* from sin. Rom 6.7
not be *f* by..law of Moses. Acts 13.39
and has *f* us from our sins Rev 1.5

FREEDOM
if you can gain your *f*, 1Cor 7.21
Spirit of the Lord is,..is *f*. 2Cor 3.17
to spy out our *f* which we have Gal 2.4
For *f* Christ has set us free; 5.1
For you were called to *f*, 5.13
without using..*f* as a pretext 1Pet 2.16
They promise them *f*, but 2Pet 2.19

FREEWILL OFFERING — S
is a votive offering or a *f*.. Lev 7.16
with the tribute of a *f*.. Deut 16.10
f..for the house of God Ezra 1.4
made *f*..for the house of God, 2.68

FRIEND — S
as a man speaks to his *f*. Ex 33.11
descendants of Abraham thy *f*? 2Chr 20.7
withholds kindness from a *f* Job 6.14
and bargain over your *f*. 6.27
as though I grieved for my *f* Ps 35.14
Even my bosom *f* in whom I 41.9

But it is you,..my familiar *f*. 55.13
caused lover and *f* to shun me; 88.18
A *f* loves at all times, and Prov 17.17
every one is a *f* to a man 19.6
Faithful are..wounds of a *f*; 27.6
'My father,..the *f* of my youth— Jer 3.4
have no confidence in a *f*; Mic 7.5
f of tax collectors..sinners!' Mt 11.19
'*F*, I am doing you no wrong; 20.13
Jesus said.."*F*, why are you 26.50
a *f* of tax collectors and Lk 7.34
'*F*, lend me three loaves; 11.5
say to you, '*F*, go up higher'; 14.10
f Lazarus has fallen asleep, Jn 11.11
you are not Caesar's *f*; 19.12
he was called the *f* of God. Jas 2.23
But thy *f* be like the sun Judg 5.31
My *f* scorn me; my eye pours Job 16.20
and my close *f* have failed 19.14
Job,..had prayed for his *f*; 42.10
whisperer separates close *f*. Prov 16.28
There are *f* who pretend to be *f*, 18.24
Wealth brings many new *f*, 19.4
Make *f* quickly with..accuser, Mt 5.25
"Go home to your *f*, and tell Mk 5.19
my *f*, do not fear those who Lk 12.4
I tell you, make *f*..by mammon, 16.9
lay down his life for his *f*. Jn 15.13

FRIENDSHIP
the *f* of God was upon my tent; Job 29.4
The *f* of the LORD is for those Ps 25.14
f with a man given to anger, Prov 22.24
f with the world is enmity Jas 4.4

FRINGE
touched the *f* of his garment; Mt 9.20
touch the *f* of his garment; 14.36

FROGS
plague..your country with *f*; Ex 8.2
Their land swarmed with *f*, Ps 105.30

FRUIT — S
showed..the *f* of the land Num 13.26
in the *f* of your body, and Deut 30.9
like a tree..yields its *f* in Ps 1.3
shall eat the *f* of their way Prov 1.31
My *f* is better than gold, 8.19
f of the righteous is..life, 11.30
punish..the *f* of your doings, Jer 21.14
the *f* of my body for the sin Mic 6.7
nor *f* be on the vines, the Hab 3.17
to the tenants, to get his *f*; Mt 21.34
word and accept it and bear *f*, Mk 4.20
"May no one ever eat *f* from you 11.14
blessed is the *f* of your womb! Lk 1.42
not bear good *f* is cut down 3.9
no good tree bears bad *f*, 6.43
bring forth *f* with patience. 8.15
if it dies, it bears much *f*. Jn 12.24
he it is that bears much *f*, 15.5
the *f* of the Spirit is love, Gal 5.22
bearing *f* in every good work Col 1.10
peaceful *f* of righteousness Heb 12.11
f for which thy soul longed Rev 18.14
yielding its *f* each month; 22.2
the first *f* of your ground Ex 34.26
"On the day of the first *f*, Num 28.26
a cereal offering of first *f* Lev 2.14
the sheaf of the first *f* 23.10
first *f* of all your produce. Prov 3.9
orchard..with all choicest *f*, Sol 4.13
You will know them by their *f*. Mt 7.16

FRUIT — S (cont.)
kingdom of God..*f* of it."   Mt 21.43
dough offered as first *f* is   Rom 11.16
from the dead, the first *f*   1Cor 15.20
with the *f* of righteousness   Phil 1.11
we should be a kind of first *f*   Jas 1.18

FRUSTRATE — S
counselors against them to *f*   Ezra 4.5
He *f* the devices of the crafty, Job 5.12

FUGITIVE
you shall be a *f*..on..earth."   Gen 4.12
on that day a *f* will come   Ezek 24.26

FULFIL — S — LED — LING
I will *f* the oath..I swore   Gen 26.3
to *f* the word of the LORD   2Chr 36.21
the LORD *f* all your petitions!   Ps 20.5
LORD will *f* his purpose for me; 138.8
I will *f* the promise I made   Jer 33.14
it is fitting for us to *f* all   Mt 3.15
not to abolish..but to *f* them.   5.17
f what was spoken by..Isaiah,   8.17
took place to *f* what was spoken 21.4
This was to *f* the scripture.   Jn 19.24
He *f*..desire of all who fear   Ps 145.19
the LORD has *f* his promise   2Chr 6.10
the scriptures..might be *f*."   Mt 26.56
"The time is *f*, and the kingdom Mk 1.15
But let the scriptures be *f*."   14.49
scripture was *f* which says,   15.28*n*
"Today..scripture has been *f*   Lk 4.21
I shall not eat..until it is *f*, 22.16
and the psalms must be *f*."   24.44
that the scripture might be *f*.   Jn 17.12
they..*f* all..written of him,   Acts 13.29
who loves his neighbor has *f*   Rom 13.8
whole law is *f* in one word,   Gal 5.14
thus *f* the word of the LORD   1Ki 2.27
did not succeed in *f* that law.   Rom 9.31

FULL — Y
whole earth is *f* of his glory." Isa 6.3
this joy of mine is now *f*.   Jn 3.29
until..*f* number of..Gentiles   Rom 11.25
let steadfastness have..*f* effect, Jas 1.4
every one when he is *f* taught   Lk 6.40
But when the time had *f* come,   Gal 4.4

FULLER — S'
white as no *f*..could bleach   Mk 9.3
"For he is like..*f* soap;   Mal 3.2

FULNESS
earth is the LORD's and the *f*   Ps 24.1
from his *f* have we all received, Jn 1.16
come in the *f* of the blessing   Rom 15.29
filled with all the *f* of God.   Eph 3.19
in him the whole *f* of deity   Col 2.9
you have..*f* of life in him,   2.10

FURNACE
forth out of the iron *f*,   Deut 4.20
silver refined in a *f* on the   Ps 12.6
the *f* is for gold, and a man   Prov 27.21
LORD..whose *f* is in Jerusalem.   Isa 31.9
tried..in..*f* of affliction.   48.10
ordered..*f* heated seven times   Dan 3.19
throw them into the *f* of fire;   Mt 13.42

FURY
Haman was filled with *f*.   Est 3.5
The LORD..stirs up his *f*;   Isa 42.13
and I will satisfy my *f*;   Ezek 21.17
they were filled with *f* and   Lk 6.11

FUTILE
became *f* in their thinking   Rom 1.21
your faith is *f* and you   1Cor 15.17

FUTILITY
creation was subjected to *f*,   Rom 8.20
live..in the *f* of their minds;   Eph 4.17

G

GABRIEL
"*G*, make this man understand   Dan 8.16
in prayer, the man *G*,..came to me 9.21
"I am *G*, who stand in the   Lk 1.19
In the sixth month the angel *G*   1.26

GAD
Leah..called his name *G*.   Gen 30.11
The sons of *G*: Ziphion,   46.16
the leader of the men of *G*:   Num 7.42
to the sons of *G* and..Reuben   32.33

GAIN — S — ED (v)
What does man *g* by all the toil Ecc 1.3
Whoever seeks to *g* his life   Lk 17.33
in order that I may *g* Christ   Phil 3.8
if he *g* the whole world and   Mt 16.26
g the whole world and loses   Lk 9.25
nothing to be *g* under the sun.   Ecc 2.11
What you..*g*..is given to God,   Mt 15.5
what they had *g* by trading.   Lk 19.15
nothing to be *g* by it, but I   2Cor 12.1

GAIN (n)
Incline my heart..not to *g*!   Ps 119.36
for the *g* from it is better   Prov 3.14
what *g* has he that he toiled   Ecc 5.16
devote their *g* to the LORD,   Mic 4.13
Woe to him who gets evil *g*   Hab 2.9
is Christ, and to die is *g*.   Phil 1.21

GALATIA
the region of Phrygia and *G*,   Acts 16.6
region of *G* and Phrygia,   18.23
I directed the churches of *G*,   1Cor 16.1
with me, To the churches of *G*:   Gal 1.2
in Pontus, *G*, Cappadocia,   1Pet 1.1

GALILEAN
"You..were with Jesus the *G*."   Mt 26.69
one of them; for you are a *G*."   Mk 14.70
whether the man was a *G*.   Lk 23.6

GALILEE
they set apart Kedesh in *G*   Josh 20.7
glorious..*G* of the nations.   Isa 9.1
withdrew to the district of *G*.   Mt 2.22
arrested, he withdrew into *G*;   4.12
across the Jordan, *G* of the   4.15
great multitude from *G* followed; Mk 3.7
he is going before you to *G*;   16.7
Joseph also went up from *G*,   Lk 2.4
was a marriage at Cana in *G*,   Jn 2.1
Judea and departed again to *G*.   4.3
"Are you from *G* too? Search   7.52
"Men of *G*, why do you stand   Acts 1.11

GALLIO
G was proconsul of Achaia,   Acts 18.12
But *G* paid no attention to this. 18.17

GALLOWS
"Let a *g* fifty cubits high   Est 5.14

GAMALIEL
a Pharisee in the council..*G*,   Acts 5.34
brought up..at the feet of *G*,   22.3

GAME
go out..and hunt g for me,   Gen 27.3

GARDEN — ER
God planted a g in Eden,   Gen 2.8
like the g of the LORD,   13.10
A g locked is my sister, my   Sol 4.12
and like a g without water.   Isa 1.30
you were in Eden,..g of God; Ezek 28.13
The cedars in the g of God   31.8
become like the g of Eden;   36.35
The land is like the g of Eden Joel 2.3
was crucified there was a g,   Jn 19.41
Supposing him to be the g,   20.15

GARLIC
the onions, and the g;   Num 11.5

GARMENT — S
he..left his g in her hand,   Gen 39.13
man put on a woman's g;   Deut 22.5
like a g that is moth-eaten.   Job 13.28
Take a man's g when he has Prov 20.16
takes off a g on a cold day,   25.20
I had put off my g, how could Sol 5.3
deeds are like a polluted g.   Isa 64.6
a man who had no wedding g; Mt 22.11
unshrunk cloth on an old g;   Mk 2.21
the crowd and touched his   5.27
touch even the fringe of his g;   6.56
"No one tears..from a new g Lk 5.36
touched the fringe of his g;   8.44
God made for Adam..g   Gen 3.21
make holy g for Aaron your Ex 28.2
they divide my g among them, Ps 22.18
Let your g be always white;   Ecc 9.8
his g became white as light.   Mt 17.2
spread their g on the road,   21.8
they divided his g among them   27.35
spread their g on the road,   Mk 11.8
and divided his g among them,   15.24
spread their g on the road.   Lk 19.36
cast lots to divide his g.   23.34
from supper, laid aside his g, Jn 13.4
and g which Dorcas made   Acts 9.39
keeping the g of those who   22.20
awake, keeping his g that   Rev 16.15

GATE — S
Lot was sitting in the g   Gen 19.1
also suffered outside the g   Heb 13.12
its g which had been destroyed Neh 2.13
the g of death been revealed Job 38.17
Lift up your heads, O g! and Ps 24.7
within your g, O Jerusalem!   122.2
Open the g, that..righteous Isa 26.2
he is near, at the very g.   Mk 13.29

GATHER — S — ED — ING
let them g all the food   Gen 41.35
LORD has commanded: 'G of it, Ex 16.16
LORD your God will g you, Deut 30.4
g us from among the nations, Ps 106.47
'The dead bodies..none shall g Jer 9.22
I will g the remnant of my flock   23.3
g you from all the nations   29.14
who scattered Israel will g   31.10
g them from all the countries   32.37
I will g you into the midst Ezek 22.19
nations round about, g..there. Joel 3.11
save the lame..g the outcast, Zeph 3.19
does not g with me scatters. Mt 12.30
will g out of his kingdom   13.41
the angels, and g his elect Mk 13.27
he who does not g with me Lk 11.23

"G up the fragments left over, Jn 6.12
to g into one the children   11.52
son who g in summer..prudent, Prov 10.5
who g the outcasts of Israel, Isa 56.8
"Let the waters..be g   Gen 1.9
Joseph g up all the money   47.14
and g in from the lands, from Ps 107.3
I also g for myself silver   Ecc 2.8
that Israel might be g to him, Isa 49.5
the summer fruit has been g, Mic 7.1
two or three are g in my name, Mt 18.20
How often would I have g your Lk 13.34
man g sticks on the sabbath Num 15.32

GAVE
our God g him over to us; Deut 2.33
Solomon g to the queen of 2Chr 9.12
God g them into their hand.   13.16
the LORD g, and the LORD Job 1.21
spirit returns to God who g it. Ecc 12.7
who g himself for our sins Gal 1.4
loved me and g himself for me.   2.20

GAZA
Canaanites..as far as G, Gen 10.19
Judah also took G with its Judg 1.18
Samson went to G, and..saw   16.1
see it, and be afraid; G too, Zech 9.5
down from Jerusalem to G." Acts 8.26

GAZINGSTOCK
contempt, and make you a g.   Nah 3.6

GENEALOGY — IES
The book of the g of Jesus Mt 1.1
without father or mother or g, Heb 7.3
and endless g which promote 1Tim 1.4

GENERATION — S
A g goes, and a g comes, but Ecc 1.4
adulterous g seeks for a sign; Mt 12.39
of my words in this..sinful g, Mk 8.38
the g of the heavens..earth Gen 2.4
book of the g of Adam.   5.1
the g of the sons of Noah,   10.1
and his faithfulness to all g. Ps 100.5

GENEROUS — LY
food with glad and g hearts, Acts 2.46
good deeds, liberal and g, 1Tim 6.18
the man who deals g and lends, Ps 112.5

GENTILES
"Go nowhere among the G, and Mt 10.5
'Why did the G rage, and the Acts 4.25
the G also God has granted   11.18
would justify the G by faith, Gal 3.8

GENTLE — NESS
I am g and lowly in heart, Mt 11.29
we were g among you, like 1Thess 2.7
to avoid quarreling, to be g, Tit 3.2
jewel of a g and quiet spirit, 1Pet 3.4
or with love in a spirit of g? 1Cor 4.21
by the meekness and g of 2Cor 10.1
restore him in a spirit of g. Gal 6.1

GENUINENESS
the g of your faith, more 1Pet 1.7

GETHSEMANE
Jesus went with them to..G, Mt 26.36
a place which was called G; Mk 14.32

GHOST
terrified, saying, "It is a g!" Mt 14.26
they thought it was a g, and Mk 6.49

GIBEAH

but we will pass on to G."	Judg 19.12
went to his home at G,	1Sam 10.26
the watchmen of Saul in G	14.16
Ramah trembles, G..has fled.	Isa 10.29

GIDEON

son G was beating out wheat	Judg 6.11
(that is, G) and all the people	7.1
So G and the hundred men	7.19
And G came to the Jordan	8.4
G said.."I will not rule	8.23
G the son of Joash died	8.32
to tell of G, Barak, Samson,	Heb 11.32

GIFT — S

Accept, I pray you, my g	Gen 33.11
Levites as a g to Aaron	Num 8.19
A man's g makes room for him	Prov 18.16
A g in secret averts anger;	21.14
God's g to man..eat and drink	Ecc 3.13
receive the g of the..Spirit.	Acts 2.38
obtain..g of God with money!	8.20
If..God gave..same g to them	11.17
wages are not reckoned as a g	Rom 4.4
free g of God is eternal life	6.23
his own special g from God,	1Cor 7.7
to carry your g to Jerusalem.	16.3
God for his inexpressible g!	2Cor 9.15
the g of God's grace..given me	Eph 3.7
to the measure of Christ's g.	4.7
Not that I seek the g; but	Phil 4.17
Do not neglect the g you have,	1Tim 4.14
As each has received a g,	1Pet 4.10
people..sue your favor with g,	Ps 45.12
receiving g among men, even	68.18
Jerusalem kings bear g to thee.	68.29
of Sheba and Seba bring g!	72.10
loves a bribe..runs after g.	Isa 1.23
If you..know how to give good g	Mt 7.11
evil, know how to give good g	Lk 11.13
their g into the treasury;	21.1
Having g that differ according	Rom 12.6
there are varieties of g,	1Cor 12.4
earnestly desire..spiritual g,	14.1
and by g of the Holy Spirit	Heb 2.4

GILEAD

Jacob..fled..toward..G.	Gen 31.21
To Machir I gave G,	Deut 3.15
land, G as far as Dan,	34.1
boundary..is, half of G,	Josh 12.2
G is mine; Manasseh is mine;	Ps 60.7
Is there no balm in G? Is	Jer 8.22

GILGAL

encamped in G on the east	Josh 4.19
marched..all night from G.	10.9
by year to Bethel, G, and	1Sam 7.16
called out to join Saul at G.	13.4
to G,..multiply transgression;	Amos 4.4

GIRD — ED

and g him with the skilfully	Ex 29.5
For thou didst g me with	2Sam 22.40
G your sword upon your thigh,	Ps 45.3
thou hast..g me with gladness,	30.11

GIRDLE

Righteousness shall be the g	Isa 11.5
a leather g around his waist;	Mt 3.4
he took Paul's g and bound	Acts 21.11

GIRL — S — 'S

g is not dead but sleeping."	Mt 9.24
if a g marries..not sin.	1Cor 7.28

city..of boys and g playing	Zech 8.5
the g father made him stay,	Judg 19.4

GIVE — S — N — ING

land..I will g to you and	Gen 13.15
first-born..sons..g to me.	Ex 22.29
the poor shall not g less,	30.15
land which I swore to g	Deut 1.35
might g him into your hand,	2.30
and to Jacob, to g you,	6.10
LORD will g you there	28.65
"Pray, g loaves of bread	Judg 8.5
the LORD will g Israel also	1Sam 28.19
they would g the money that	2Ki 12.11
dost not g me up to Sheol,	Ps 16.10
"To you I will g..Canaan as	105.11
G me understanding, that I	119.34
My son, g me your heart,	Prov 23.26
How can I g you up, O Ephraim!	Hos 11.8
G us this day our daily bread;	Mt 6.11
you g them something to eat."	14.16
g you the keys of the kingdom	16.19
"You g them something to eat."	Mk 6.37
g, and it will be given to you;	Lk 6.38
said to her, "G me a drink."	Jn 4.7
"Lord, g us this bread always."	6.34
and I g them eternal life,	10.28
he will g you another Counselor,	14.16
more blessed to g than to	Acts 20.35
will he not..g us all things	Rom 8.32
husband should g to his wife	1Cor 7.3
may g you a spirit of wisdom	Eph 1.17
my Maker, who g songs in	Job 35.10
righteous is generous and g;	Ps 37.21
The Lord g the command; great	68.11
he who g food to all flesh,	136.25
For the LORD g wisdom; from	Prov 2.6
but the righteous g and	21.26
g to the poor will not want,	28.27
who pleases him God g wisdom	Ecc 2.26
"He scatters..g to the poor;	2Cor 9.9
I have g him into your hand,	Num 21.34
for I have g him and all	Deut 3.2
"Our god has g Samson..into	Judg 16.23
to him who has will more be g,	Mt 13.12
gained from me is g to God,	15.5
to him who has will more be g;	Mk 4.25
to him who has will more be g,	Lk 8.18
to whom much is g, of him	12.48
has g all judgment to the Son,	Jn 5.22
the Spirit had not been g,	7.39
the Spirit which he has g us.	1Jn 3.24
into partnership with me in g	Phil 5.15

GLAD — NESS

I will be g and exult in thee,	Ps 9.2
who seek thee rejoice and be g	40.16
a river whose streams make g	46.4
Egypt was g..they departed,	105.38
I was g when they said to me,	122.1
A g heart makes a cheerful	Prov 15.13
let us be g and rejoice in	Isa 25.9
be g and rejoice for ever	65.18
I am g and rejoice with you	Phil 2.17
the day of your g also,	Num 10.10
ate and drank..with great g.	1Chr 29.22
a day for g and feasting	Est 9.19
Serve the LORD with g! Come	Ps 100.2
joy and g are taken away from	Isa 16.10
oil of g instead of mourning,	61.3
of mirth and the voice of g,	Jer 7.34

GLORIFY — IED

deliver you, and you shall g	Ps 50.15

GLORIFY — IED (cont.)

I will *g* my glorious house.	Isa 60.7
Father, *g* thy name." Then	Jn 12.28
the hour has come; *g* thy Son	17.1
So *g* God in your body.	1Cor 6.20
Who shall not fear and *g* thy	Rev 15.4
Lord..will be *g* in Israel,	Isa 44.23
Israel, in whom I will be *g*."	49.3
Holy One..for he has *g* you.	55.5
they *g* God and were filled	Lk 5.26
they *g* God, saying, "A great	7.16
"Now is the Son of man *g*,	Jn 13.31
Father may be *g* in the Son;	14.13
Father is *g*, that you bear	15.8
silenced. And they *g* God,	Acts 11.18

GLORIOUS — LY

G things..spoken of you, O city	Ps 87.3
change..to be like his *g* body,	Phil 3.21
the Lord, for he has done *g*;	Isa 12.5

GLORY (v)

that we may..*g* in thy praise.	Ps 106.47
g in this, that..I am the Lord	Jer 9.24
they shall *g* in his name,"	Zech 10.12
far be it from me to *g* except	Gal 6.14

GLORY (n)

see the *g* of the Lord,	Ex 16.7
The *g* of the Lord settled on	24.16
the *g* of the Lord filled the	40.34
filled with the *g* of the Lord,	Num 14.21
the *g* of the Lord appeared	16.19
God has shown us his *g*	Deut 5.24
"The *g* has departed from	1Sam 4.21
the *G* of Israel will not lie	15.29
the *g* of the Lord filled	1Ki 8.11
Declare his *g* among..nations	1Chr 16.24
Thine, O Lord, is the..*g*,	29.11
the *g* of the Lord filled	2Chr 5.14
Thou whose *g* above..is chanted	Ps 8.1
heavens are telling the *g* of God;	19.1
His *g* is great through thy help;	21.5
ascribe to the Lord *g* and	29.1
all the peoples behold his *g*.	97.6
but to thy name give *g*, for	115.1
in the east give *g* to..Lord;	Isa 24.15
g of Lebanon shall be given	35.2
They shall see the *g* of the Lord,	35.2
the *g* of the Lord..revealed,	40.5
my *g* I give to no other, nor	42.8
this city..a *g* before all	Jer 33.9
likeness of the *g* of the Lord.	Ezek 1.28
as the *g* of the Lord arose	3.12
lo, the *g* of the Lord stood there,	3.23
the *g* of the God..had gone up	9.3
the *g* of the Lord went forth	10.18
manifest my *g* in the midst	28.22
set my *g* among the nations;	39.21
And behold, the *g* of the God	43.2
dominion and *g* and kingdom,	Dan 7.14
knowledge of the *g* of the Lord,	Hab 2.14
coming..with power and great *g*;	Mt 24.30
"*G* to God in the highest; and	Lk 2.14
I do not receive *g* from men.	Jn 5.41
own authority seeks his own *g*;	7.18
Yet I do not seek my own *g*;	8.50
"This illness is for the *g* of God,	11.4
with the *g* which I had with thee	17.5
my *g* which thou hast given me	17.24
exchanged the *g* of..God for	Rom 1.23
fall short of the *g* of God,	3.23
not worth comparing with the *g*	8.18
To him be *g* for ever. Amen.	11.36

in dishonor,..raised in *g*.	1Cor 15.43
Christ in you, the hope of *g*.	Col 1.27
from the *g* of his might,	2Thess 1.9
obtain the *g* of our Lord	2.14
him who called us to his own *g*	2Pet 1.3
saying, "Amen! Blessing and *g*	Rev 7.12
"Fear God and give him *g*,	14.7

GNASH — ED — ING

they hiss, they *g* their teeth,	Lam 2.16
men..weep and *g* their teeth.	Mt 24.51
he has *g* his teeth at me;	Job 16.9
g at me with their teeth.	Ps 35.16

GNAT — S

guides, straining out a *g*	Mt 23.24
g throughout all..Egypt.' "	Ex 8.16

GO

"*G* into the ark, you and	Gen 7.1
Rebekah..said, "I will *g*."	24.58
'Let my people *g*, that they may	Ex 5.1
"Let my people *g*, that they may	9.13
"Let us..*g* back to Egypt."	Num 14.4
"*G* and wash in the Jordan	2Ki 5.10
Teach me the way I should *g*,	Ps 143.8
g again, naked as he came,	Ecc 5.15
let us *g* up to the mountain	Isa 2.3
"*G*, and say to this people:	6.9
G forth from Babylon, flee	48.20
show us the way we should *g*,	Jer 42.3
They shall *g* after the Lord,	Hos 11.10
Lord said to me, '*G*, prophesy	Amos 7.15
let us *g* up to the mountain	Mic 4.2
when you pray, *g* into your room	Mt 6.6
Then *g*..and tell his disciples	28.7
G..and make disciples of all	28.19
"*G* home to your friends, and	Mk 5.19
But *g*, tell his disciples	16.7
"*G* into all the world and	16.15n
g and proclaim the kingdom	Lk 9.60
"Lord, to whom shall we *g*?	Jn 6.68

GOADS

sayings of the wise are like *g*,	Ecc 12.11
hurts..to kick against..*g*.'	Acts 26.14

GOD

G created the heavens..earth.	Gen 1.1
you will be like *G*, knowing	3.5
But *G* remembered Noah	8.1
"*G* will visit you, and	50.25
And *G* heard their groaning,	Ex 2.24
G did not lead them by way	13.17
The eternal *G* is your	Deut 33.27
Lord *G*..fought for Israel.	Josh 10.42
Israel,..*G* went to redeem	2Sam 7.23
my *G*, hearkening to the cry	1Ki 8.28
G also raised..an adversary	11.23
G..sent persistently to them	2Chr 36.15
mocking..messengers of *G*,	36.16
made him little less than *G*,	Ps 8.5
my *G*, why hast thou forsaken me?	22.1
the Lord *G* is my strength	Isa 12.2
Lord *G* is an everlasting rock.	26.4
comfort my people, says your *G*.	40.1
worked on the house of..*G*,	Hag 1.14
Will man rob *G*? Yet you are	Mal 3.8
"My *G*, my *G*, why hast thou	Mk 15.34
answered.."My Lord and my *G*!"	Jn 20.28
This Jesus *G* raised up, and	Acts 2.32
and said that he was a *g*.	28.6
G is not a *G* of confusion	1Cor 14.33
In their case the *g* of this	2Cor 4.4
But *G*, who is rich in mercy,	Eph 2.4

GOD

GOD (cont.)

doing, it is the gift of G—	Eph 2.8
created after the likeness of G	4.24
be imitators of G, as beloved	5.1
the grace of G has appeared	Tit 2.11
the glory of our great G	2.13
its temple is the Lord G	Rev 21.22
flowing from the throne of G	22.1

GODLESS

hope of. .g man shall perish.	Job 8.13
a g man shall not come before	13.16
joy of the g but for a moment?	20.5
what is the hope of the g when	27.8
"The g in heart cherish anger;	36.13
G men utterly deride me, but	Ps 119.51
Let the g be put to shame,	119.78
With his mouth the g man	Prov 11.9
every one. .g and an evildoer,	Isa 9.17
Against a g nation I send him,	10.6
trembling has seized the g:	33.14

GODLINESS

teaching which accords with g,	1Tim 6.3
imagining. .g is a means of gain.	6.5
g with brotherly affection,	2Pet 1.7

GODLY

the Lord has set apart the g	Ps 4.3
there is no longer any that is g;	12.1
or let thy g one see the Pit.	16.10
who is g offer prayer to thee;	32.6
of mischief done against the g?	52.1
who desire to live a g life	2Tim 3.12

GODS

Rachel stole. .household g.	Gen 31.19
why did you steal my g?"	31.30
Rachel had taken. .household g	31.34
forsaken me. .served other g;	Judg 10.13
"Their g are g of the hills,	1Ki 20.23
"You are g, sons of the Most	Ps 82.6
the fire; for they were no g,	Isa 37.19
served foreign g in your land,	Jer 5.19
Can man make for himself g?	16.20
fourth is like a son of the g."	Dan 3.25
in whom. .spirit of the holy g—	4.8
to Aaron, 'Make for us g to	Acts 7.40
there may be so-called g	1Cor 8.5

GOLD

Havilah, where there is g;	Gen 2.11
and all g of the offering	Num 31.52
if the Almighty is your g,	Job 22.25
"If I have made g my trust,	31.24
More to be desired. .than g,	Ps 19.10
knowledge rather than. .g;	Prov 8.10
A word. .like apples of g in	25.11
bring g and frankincense,	Isa 60.6
How the g has grown dim, how	Lam 4.1
head of this image was of. .g,	Dan 2.32
"I have no silver and g, but	Acts 3.6
while the city was pure g,	Rev 21.18

GOLGOTHA

they came to a place called G	Mt 27.33
brought. .to the place called G	Mk 15.22
which is called in Hebrew G.	Jn 19.17

GOLIATH

a champion named G,	1Sam 17.4
Philistine of Gath, G	17.23
sword of G the Philistine,	21.9

GOMORRAH

before the Lord destroyed. .G.	Gen 13.11
kings of Sodom and G fled,	14.10

Lord rained on. .G brimstone	19.24
like that of Sodom and G,	Deut 29.23
like Sodom, and become like G.	Isa 1.9
and G than for that town.	Mt 10.15
just as Sodom and G and the	Jude 7

GOOD — LY

God saw. .light was g;	Gen 1.4
God saw that it was g.	1.10
The thing seemed g to me,	Deut 1.23
for he never prophesies g	1Ki 22.8
may the Lord do what seems g	1Chr 19.13
Hear, and know it for your g."	Job 5.27
there is none that does g,	Ps 14.3
I have no g apart from thee."	16.2
G and upright is the Lord;	25.8
Depart from evil, and do g; so	37.27
g to give thanks to the Lord,	92.1
g and pleasant. .when brothers	133.1
Let a g man strike or rebuke	141.5
A g wife who can find? She	Prov 31.10
She does. .g, and not harm,	31.12
g name is better than precious	Ecc 7.1
who call evil g and g evil,	Isa 5.20
accept that which is g and	Hos 14.2
Hate evil, and love g, and	Amos 5.15
you. .hate the g and love. .evil,	Mic 3.2
how g and. .fair it shall be!	Zech 9.17
Other seeds fell on g soil	Mt 13.8
sorted the g into vessels but	13.48
'Well done, g and faithful	25.21
other seeds fell into g soil	Mk 4.8
No one is g but God alone.	10.18
on the sabbath to do g or. .harm	Lk 6.9
some fell into g soil and	8.8
"Can. .g come out of Nazareth?"	Jn 1.46
it seemed g to the apostles	Acts 15.22
why not do evil that g may come?	Rom 3.8
no one does g, not even one."	3.12
nothing g dwells within me,	7.18
God works for g with those who	8.28
do not let what is g to you	14.16
wise as to what is g and	16.19
g child, she hid. .three months.	Ex 2.2

GOODNESS

Surely g and mercy shall follow	Ps 23.6
O how abundant is thy g, which	31.19

GOSPEL

this g of the kingdom will be	Mt 24.14
wherever this g is preached	26.13
the g of Jesus Christ, the Son	Mk 1.1
into Galilee, preaching the g	1.14
the g must first be preached	13.10
wherever the g is preached	14.9
preach the g to the whole	16.15n
there they preached the g.	Acts 14.7
testify to the g of. .grace	20.24
set apart for the g of God	Rom 1.1
I am not ashamed of the g;	1.16
according to my g, God judges	2.16
have not all heeded the g;	10.16
strengthen you according to my g	16.25
I preached to you the g,	1Cor 15.1
acknowledging the g of Christ,	2Cor 9.13
to you with the g of Christ.	10.14
turning to a different g—	Gal 1.6
the g which was preached by me	1.11
the g to the uncircumcised,	2.7
the g of your salvation, and	Eph 1.13
equipment of the g of peace;	6.15
be worthy of the g of Christ,	Phil 1.27
not shifting from. .hope of. .g	Col 1.23

GOSPEL (cont.)

our *g* came to you not only	1Thess 1.5
glorious *g* of the blessed God	1Tim 1.11
share of suffering for the *g*	2Tim 1.8
g was preached..to the dead,	1Pet 4.6
angel..with an eternal *g* to	Rev 14.6

GOSSIPING (v)

who goes about *g* reveals	Prov 20.19

GOSSIPS (n)

malignity, they are *g*,	Rom 1.29
idlers but *g* and busybodies,	1Tim 5.13

GOVERN

who will *g* my people Israel.' "	Mt 2.6

GOVERNMENT

g will be upon his shoulder,	Isa 9.6

GOVERNOR — S

Joseph was *g* over the land;	Gen 42.6
I was appointed to be their *g*	Neh 5.14
appointed Gedaliah..*g* in the	Jer 40.7
no evil? Present that to your *g*;	Mal 1.8
made him *g* over Egypt and	Acts 7.10
you will stand before *g* and	Mk 13.9

GRACE — FUL

g is poured upon your lips;	Ps 45.2
found *g* in the wilderness;	Jer 31.2
amid shouts of '*G*, *g* to it!' "	Zech 4.7
among us, full of *g* and truth;	Jn 1.14
great *g* was upon them all.	Acts 4.33
to continue in the *g* of God.	13.43
witness to..word of his *g*,	14.3
commended to the *g* of God	14.26
commended..to..*g* of the Lord.	15.40
through whom we..received *g*	Rom 1.5
justified by his *g* as a gift,	3.24
that the promise may rest on *g*	4.16
access to..*g* in which we stand,	5.2
much more have the *g* of God	5.15
where sin increased, *g* abounded	5.20
continue in sin that *g* may abound?	6.1
because of the *g* given me by	15.15
by..*g* of God I am what I am,	1Cor 15.10
as *g* extends to more..people	2Cor 4.15
For you know the *g* of our Lord	8.9
"My *g* is sufficient for you,	12.9
The *g* of the Lord Jesus	13.14
him who called you in the *g* of	Gal 1.6
you have fallen away from *g*.	5.4
according to..riches of his *g*	Eph 1.7
immeasurable riches of his *g*	2.7
and good hope through *g*,	2Thess 2.16
the *g* of our Lord overflowed	1Tim 1.14
For the *g* of God has appeared	Tit 2.11
we might be justified by his *g*	3.7
draw near the throne of *g*,	Heb 4.16
heart be strengthened by *g*,	13.9
But he gives more *g*; therefore	Jas 4.6
stewards of God's varied *g*;	1Pet 4.10
but gives *g* to the humble."	5.5
God of all *g*,..has called you	5.10
grow in the *g* and knowledge	2Pet 3.18
who pervert the *g* of our God	Jude 4
How *g* are your feet in sandals,	Sol 7.1

GRACIOUS

The Lord..be *g* to you:	Num 6.25
the Lord was *g* to them and	2Ki 13.23
May God be *g* to us and bless	Ps 67.1
The Lord is merciful and *g*,	103.8
The Lord is *g* and merciful,	145.8
praises to our God;..he is *g*,	147.1

and whose speech is *g*, will	Prov 22.11
O Lord, be *g* to us; we wait	Isa 33.2
for he is *g* and merciful,	Joel 2.13
wondered at the *g* words which	Lk 4.22
Let your speech always be *g*,	Col 4.6

GRAIN

are no oxen, there is no *g*;	Prov 14.4
then the full *g* in the ear.	Mk 4.28
plucked and ate some ears of *g*,	Lk 6.1
that there was *g* in Egypt,	Acts 7.12
wheat or of some other *g*.	1Cor 15.37

GRAINFIELDS

through the *g* on the sabbath;	Mt 12.1

GRANT — ED

God of Israel *g* your petition	1Sam 1.17
desire of..righteous..be *g*.	Prov 10.24
all that the Lord has *g* us,	Isa 63.7
God has *g* you all those	Acts 27.24

GRAPES

with a single cluster of *g*,	Num 13.23
he looked for it to yield *g*,	Isa 5.2
fathers have eaten sour *g*,	Jer 31.29
fathers have eaten sour *g*,	Ezek 18.2
Like *g* in the wilderness, I	Hos 9.10
reaper and the treader of *g*	Amos 9.13

GRASS

they will soon fade like the *g*,	Ps 37.2
man, his days are like *g*;	103.15
as dry *g* sinks..in the flame,	Isa 5.24
All flesh is *g* and all its beauty	40.6
and ate *g* like an ox, and his	Dan 4.33
if God so clothes the *g* which	Lk 12.28
"All flesh is like *g* and all	1Pet 1.24
and all green *g* was burnt up.	Rev 8.7

GRASSHOPPERS

seemed to ourselves like *g*,	Num 13.33
its inhabitants are like *g*;	Isa 40.22
Your princes are like *g*,	Nah 3.17

GRAVE — S

straight to the *g*..descend,	Ps 49.14
her company..about her *g*;	Ezek 32.23
and raise you from your *g*,	37.12
like *g* which are not seen,	Lk 11.44

GREAT — ER — EST

thou art *g*, O Lord God;	2Sam 7.22
he is *g* in power and justice,	Job 37.23
say continually, "*G* is..Lord!"	Ps 40.16
say evermore, "God is *g*!"	70.4
So I became *g* and surpassed	Ecc 2.9
you seek *g* things for yourself?	Jer 45.5
the Lord has done *g* things!	Joel 2.21
you shall say, "*G* is the Lord,	Mal 1.5
teaches them shall be called *g*	Mt 5.19
"O woman, *g* is your faith!	15.28
he will be *g* before the Lord,	Lk 1.15
alas, for the *g* city that	Rev 18.10
And David became *g* and *g*,	2Sam 5.10
David became *g* and *g*, for	1Chr 11.9
something *g* than the temple	Mt 12.6
something *g* than Solomon is	12.42
"Who is the *g* in the kingdom	18.1
discussed..who was the *g*.	Mk 9.34
to be regarded as the *g*.	Lk 22.24
but the *g* of these is love.	1Cor 13.13

GREATNESS

show thy servant thy *g*	Deut 3.24
thou hast wrought all this *g*,	1Chr 17.19
and his *g* is unsearchable.	Ps 145.3

GREATNESS (cont.)

praise him according to..g!	Ps 150.2
"Whom are you like in your g?	Ezek 31.2
I..show my g and my holiness	38.23

GREECE

the he-goat is the king of G;	Dan 8.21
all against the kingdom of G.	11.2
O Zion, over your sons, O G,	Zech 9.13
encouragement, he came to G.	Acts 20.2

GREED — Y

His g is as wide as Sheol;	Hab 2.5
guilty of immorality or g,	1Cor 5.11
never used..a cloak for g,	1Thess 2.5
in their g they will exploit	2Pet 2.3
They have hearts trained in g.	2.14
with g eye at my sacrifices	1Sam 2.29
every one is g for unjust gain;	Jer 6.13
every one is g for unjust gain;	8.10
nor thieves, nor the g, nor	1Cor 6.10

GREEK — S

woman was a G, a Syrophoenician	Mk 7.26
in letters of G and Latin	Lk 23.38n
but his father was a G.	Acts 16.1
at the feast were some G.	Jn 12.20
believed, both..Jews and..G.	Acts 14.1
heard..both Jews and G.	19.10
testifying..to Jews and to G	20.21
obligation both to G and to	Rom 1.14
signs and G seek wisdom,	1Cor 1.22

GREET — ED (v)

G one another with a holy	Rom 16.16
seen it and g it from afar,	Heb 11.13

GREETING (n)

what sort of g this might be.	Lk 1.29
Elizabeth heard the g of Mary,	1.41
I, Paul, write this g with	1Cor 16.21

GREW

Samuel g in the presence	1Sam 2.21
Samuel g, and the LORD was	3.19
g up before him like a..plant,	Isa 53.2
the child g and became strong	Lk 1.80
the child g and became strong,	2.40
But the word of God g and	Acts 12.24
So the word of the Lord g	19.20

GRIEF

and the end of joy is g.	Prov 14.13
foolish son is a g to his father	17.25
godly g produces a repentance	2Cor 7.10

GRIEVE — D

long will you g over Saul,	1Sam 16.1
do not g the Holy Spirit of	Eph 4.30
you may not g as others	1Thess 4.13
it g him to his heart.	Gen 6.6
and g him in the desert!	Ps 78.40
rebelled and g his holy Spirit;	Isa 63.10
not g over the ruin of Joseph!	Amos 6.6
g at their hardness of heart,	Mk 3.5

GROAN — S — ING

wicked rule, the people g.	Prov 29.2
of Pharaoh, and he will g	Ezek 30.24
How the beasts g! The herds	Joel 1.18
the g of the prisoners come	Ps 79.11
in Egypt and heard their g,	Acts 7.34

GROPE

g at noonday as in the night.	Job 5.14
g in the dark without light;	12.25
g for the wall like the blind,	Isa 59.10

GROUND

and he g at the mill in	Judg 16.21
g their teeth against him.	Acts 7.54

GRUMBLE — ING

nor g, as some of them did	1Cor 10.10
Do all things without g or	Phil 2.14

GUARANTEE

Spirit in our hearts as a g.	2Cor 1.22
given us the Spirit as a g.	5.5
the g of our inheritance	Eph 1.14

GUARD — S — ED (v)

"He will g the feet of his	1Sam 2.9
angels..g..in all your ways.	Ps 91.11
G me, O LORD, from..wicked;	140.4
understanding will g you;	Prov 2.11
love her, and she will g you.	4.6
G your steps..to the house of	Ecc 5.1
g what has been entrusted	1Tim 6.20
He who g his mouth preserves	Prov 13.3
are g through faith for a	1Pet 1.5

GUARD (n)

and set a g as a protection	Neh 4.9
thou settest a g over me?	Job 7.12
Set a g over my mouth, O LORD,	Ps 141.3
hand you over to..judge, and..g,	Mt 5.25

GUARDIAN — S

Shepherd and G of your souls.	1Pet 2.25
Holy Spirit has made you g,	Acts 20.28
he is under g and trustees	Gal 4.2

GUEST — S

For I am thy passing g, a	Ps 39.12
Where is the g room, where	Lk 22.11
the LORD..consecrated his g.	Zeph 1.7
wedding hall..filled with g.	Mt 22.10

GUIDANCE

round and round by his g,	Job 37.12
Where..no g, a people falls;	Prov 11.14
by wise g you can wage..war,	24.6

GUIDE — D (v)

thy name's sake lead me and g	Ps 31.3
with equity and g the nations	67.4
dost g me with thy counsel,	73.24
in paths..not known I will g	Isa 42.16
LORD will g you continually,	58.11
Spirit of truth..will g you	Jn 16.13
and g them in the wilderness	Ps 78.52

GUIDE — S (n)

He will be our g for ever.	Ps 48.14
Judas who was g to those	Acts 1.16
you are a g to the blind,	Rom 2.19
have countless g in Christ,	1Cor 4.15

GUILE

hatred be covered with g,	Prov 26.26
Israelite..in whom is no g!"	Jn 1.47
got the better of you by g.	2Cor 12.16

GUILT — Y

Why should he bring g upon	1Chr 21.3
pardon my g, for it is great.	Ps 25.11
the g of your sister Sodom:	Ezek 16.49
he incurred g through Baal	Hos 13.1
remove the g of this land in	Zech 3.9
"In truth we are g	Gen 42.21
"When a ruler sins,..and is g,	Lev 4.22
he shall in any of these be g.	5.4
who walks in his g ways.	Ps 68.21
who acquit the g for a bribe,	Isa 5.23
who will declare me g? Behold,	50.9

GUILT — Y (cont.)
All who ate of it became g; Jer 2.3
become g by the blood..shed, Ezek 22.4
let not Judah become g. Hos 4.15
I did not find this man g of Lk 23.14
g of profaning the body and 1Cor 11.27

GUILTLESS
LORD will not hold him g Deut 5.11
for ever g before the LORD 2Sam 3.28
sustain you to the end, g 1Cor 1.8
you have proved yourselves g 2Cor 7.11

GUILT OFFERING
bring his g..to the LORD Lev 5.6
"This is the law of the g... 7.1

H

HABAKKUK
oracle of God which H..saw, Hab 1.1
A prayer of H the prophet, 3.1

HADES
in H, being in torment, he Lk 6.23
not abandon my soul to H, Acts 2.27
name was Death, and H followed Rev 6.8
Death and H were thrown into 20.14

HAGAR
maid whose name was H; Gen 16.1
And H bore Abram a son; 16.15
Sarah saw the son of H 21.9
water, and gave it to H, 21.14
children for slavery;..is H. Gal 4.24

HAGGAI
prophets, H and Zechariah Ezra 5.1
through the prophesying of H 6.14
word of the LORD came by H Hag 1.1
word of the LORD came by H 2.1

HAIL — STONES
I will cause very heavy h Ex 9.18
died because of the h Josh 10.11

HAIR — S
instead of well-set h, baldness; Isa 3.24
wiped them with the h of her Lk 7.38
long h, it is her pride? 1Cor 11.15
more than the h of my head; Ps 40.12
h of your head are numbered. Mt 10.30
h of your head are..numbered. Lk 12.7

HALLOW — ED
and h my sabbaths that they Ezek 20.20
blessed the seventh day..h it, Gen 2.3
I will be h among the people Lev 22.32
art in heaven, H be thy name. Mt 6.9
"Father, h be thy name. Thy Lk 11.2

HAMATH
out to the entrance of H, Num 34.8
from the entrance of H to 1Ki 8.65
Where are the gods of H and Isa 36.19
thence go to H the great; Amos 6.2

HAMMER
and took a h in her hand, Judg 4.21
neither h nor axe..was heard 1Ki 6.7
Is not my word like..a h Jer 23.29
the h of the whole earth is 50.23

HAND — S
into your h they are delivered. Gen 9.2
father laid his right h 48.17

compelled by a mighty h. Ex 3.19
"What is that in your h?" 4.2
stretch out thy right h, 15.12
lowered..h, Amalek prevailed 17.11
lay his h upon the head of Lev 4.24
"Is the LORD's h shortened? Num 11.23
given him into your h, 21.34
h of the LORD was against Deut 2.15
by war, by a mighty h 4.34
thence with a mighty h 5.15
out of Egypt with a mighty h 26.8
The h of the LORD was heavy 1Sam 5.6
then the h of the LORD will 12.15
"Let not my h be upon him, 18.17
strengthened his h in God. 23.16
the h of my servant David 2Sam 3.18
fall into the h of the LORD, 24.14
thy h might be with me, 1Chr 4.10
for the h of the LORD my Ezra 7.28
nor take the h of evildoers. Job 8.20
know that the h of the LORD 12.9
the h of God has touched me! 19.21
right h can give you victory. 40.14
My times are in thy h; deliver Ps 31.15
day and night thy h was heavy 32.4
keep thy right h in thy bosom? 74.11
when thou openest thy h, they 104.28
right h of..LORD is exalted, 118.16
their deeds are in..h of God; Ecc 9.1
Whatever your h finds to do, 9.10
his h is stretched out still. Isa 5.25
spoke..with his strong h upon me, 8.11
his h is stretched out still. 9.12
his h is stretched out still. 9.17
His h is stretched out, and 14.27
waters in the hollow of his h 40.12
the LORD's h is not shortened, 59.1
the h of the LORD..upon me; Ezek 3.14
h of the LORD was..upon me; 3.22
My h..against the prophets 13.9
mighty h and..outstretched arm, 20.33
my h against the Philistines, 25.16
h of the LORD had been upon me 33.22
The h of the LORD was upon me, 37.1
fingers of a man's h appeared Dan 5.5
His winnowing fork is in his h, Mt 3.12
if your right h causes you to sin, 5.30
know what your right h is doing, 6.3
if your h or your.foot causes 18.8
the man, "Stretch out your h." Mk 3.5
if your h causes you to sin, 9.43
whose right h was withered. Lk 6.6
he did so, and..h was restored. 6.10
and place my h in his side, Jn 20.25
h of the Lord was with them, Acts 11.21
the h of the Lord is upon you, 13.11
write..greeting with..own h. 2Thess 3.17
and he laid his h upon him, Num 27.23
Thy h fashioned and made me; Job 10.8
all the work of his h? 34.19
He who has clean h and a pure Ps 24.4
They have h, but do not feel; 115.7
reaches out her h to..needy. Prov 31.20
into the h of the Chaldeans Jer 32.28
unwashed h does not defile Mt 15.20
disciples ate with h defiled, Mk 7.2
See my h and my feet, that Lk 24.39
but also my h and my head!" Jn 13.9
showed them his h and..side. 20.20
"Unless I see in his h the print 20.25
I have held out my h to a Rom 10.21
a house not made with h, 2Cor 5.1
seen..and touched with our h, 1Jn 1.1

HANDMAID
let. . *h* speak in your ears, 1Sam 25.24
And your *h* had two sons, 2Sam 14.6
Mary said, "Behold, I am the *h* Lk 1.38

HANG — S — ED — ING
And the king said, "*H* him Est 7.10
and *h* the earth upon nothing. Job 26.7
a *h* man is accursed by God; Deut 21.23
his house in order, and *h* 2Sam 17.23
king about having Mordecai *h* Est 6.4
and he went and *h* himself. Mt 27.5
saw Absalom *h* in an oak." 2Sam 18.10
They put him to death by *h* Acts 10.39

HANNAH
the name of the one was *H*, 1Sam 1.2
H was speaking in her heart; 1.13
H also prayed and said, "My 2.1
visited *H*, and she conceived 2.21

HAPPY — IER
home one year, to be *h* with Deut 24.5
H are you, O Israel! Who is 33.29
H are your wives! *H* are 1Ki 10.8
H are your wives! *H* are 2Chr 9.7
h is the man. . God reproves; Job 5.17
H is the man who takes refuge Ps 34.8
H is the man. . his quiver full 127.5
H the people whose God is the 144.15
H is he whose help is. . God 146.5
H is the man. . finds wisdom, Prov 3.13
h. . those who keep my ways. 8.32
those *h* who were steadfast. Jas 5.11
h if she remains as she is. 1Cor 7.40

HARD — ER
anything too *h* for the LORD? Gen 18.14
Nothing is too *h* for thee, Jer 32.17
way is *h*, that leads to life, Mt 7.14
I knew you to be a *h* man, 25.24
in them *h* to understand, 2Pet 3.16
I worked *h* than any of them, 1Cor 15.10

HARDEN — S — ED — ING
but I will *h* his heart, Ex 4.21
I will *h* Pharaoh's heart, 7.3
you shall not *h* your heart Deut 15.7
LORD's doing to *h* their Josh 11.20
Why should you *h* your hearts 1Sam 6.6
H not your hearts, as at Ps 95.8
why dost thou. . *h* our heart, Isa 63.17
do not *h* your hearts as in Heb 3.8
he *h* the heart of whomever he Rom 9.18
But Pharaoh *h* his heart Ex 8.32
LORD your God *h* his spirit Deut 2.30
who has *h* himself against him, Job 9.4
spirit was *h* so that he dealt Dan 5.20
but their hearts were *h*. Mk 6.52
their eyes and *h* their heart, Jn 12.40
obtained it, but the rest were *h*, Rom 11.7
But their minds were *h*; for 2Cor 3.14
a *h*. . upon part of Israel, Rom 11.25

HARDNESS
"For. . *h* of heart Moses allowed Mt 19.8
grieved at their *h* of heart, Mk 3.5
"For your *h* of heart he wrote 10.5
unbelief and *h* of heart, 16.14*n*
due to their *h* of heart; Eph 4.18

HARLOT — S
Judah. . thought her. . a *h*, Gen 38.15
only Rahab the *h* and all Josh 6.17
Gaza, and there he saw a *h*, Judg 16.1
meets him, dressed as a *h*, Prov 7.10

For a *h* is a deep pit; an 23.27
You. . played the *h* with many Jer 3.1
You played the *h* also with Ezek 16.28
"Oholah played the *h* while 23.5
their mother has played the *h*; Hos 2.5
By faith Rahab the *h* did not Heb 11.31
Rahab the *h* justified by works Jas 2.25
"Babylon. . mother of *h* and of Rev 17.5

HARM
from me, and *h* befalls him, Gen 44.29
Then I will do you no *h*.' Jer 25.6
look after him well and do no *h*, 39.12
sabbath to do good or to do *h*, Lk 6.9
"Do not *h* yourself, for we Acts 16.28

HARMONY
grant you to live in such *h* Rom 15.5
love, . binds. . in perfect *h*. Col 3.14

HARP — S
Awake, O *h* and lyre! I will Ps 108.2
instruments, . flute and. . *h*, 1Cor 14.7
elders. . each holding a *h*, Rev 5.8
harpers playing on their *h*, 14.2

HARVEST — S
earth remains, . *h*. . not cease." Gen 8.22
reap its *h*, you shall bring Lev 23.10
snow in the time of *h* is a Prov 25.13
rejoice. . as with joy at the *h*, Isa 9.3
for upon your fruit and your *h* 16.9
They shall eat up your *h* and Jer 5.17
"The *h* is past, the summer 8.20
sickle, for the *h* is ripe. Joel 3.13
"The *h* is plentiful, but the Mt 9.37
both grow together until the *h*; 13.30
sickle, because. . *h* has come." Mk 4.29
send out laborers into his *h*. Lk 10.2
four months, then comes the *h*'? Jn 4.35
that I may reap. . *h* among you Rom 1.13
the *h* of your righteousness. 2Cor 9.10
the *h* of the earth is. . ripe." Rev 14.15
shall be ashamed of their *h* Jer 12.13

HASTE
Make *h*, escape there; Gen 19.22
Make *h* to help me, O Lord, Ps 38.22
O LORD, make *h* to help me! 70.1
O LORD; make *h* to me! Give 141.1
who makes *h* with his feet Prov 19.2
believes will not be in *h*.' Isa 28.16
went with *h*, and found Mary and Lk 2.16

HATE — S — D
I *h* the company of evildoers, Ps 26.5
let those who *h* him flee before 68.1
those who *h* me without cause; 69.4
I *h* the work of those who fall 101.3
I *h* doubled-minded men, but 119.113
poor man's brothers *h* him; Prov 19.7
this abominable thing. . I *h*!' Jer 44.4
H evil, and love good, and Amos 5.15
"Blessed are you when men *h* Lk 6.22
and does not *h* his own father 14.26
but I do the very thing I *h*, Rom 7.15
h what is evil, hold fast to 12.9
if any man *h* his neighbor, Deut 19.11
six things which the LORD *h*, Prov 6.16
"If the world *h* you, know that Jn 15.18
no man ever *h* his own flesh, Eph 5.29
says, "I love God," and *h* his 1Jn 4.20
Now Esau *h* Jacob Gen 27.41
Amnon *h* her with very great 2Sam 13.15
those who *h* them ruled them. Ps 106.41

HATE — S — D (cont.)
I *h* all my toil in which I | Ecc 2.18
I have loved Jacob but..*h* Esau; | Mal 1.3
you will be *h*..for my..sake. | Mt 10.22
h by all nations for my..sake. | 24.9
you will be *h* by all for my | Mk 13.13
you will be *h* by all for my | Lk 21.17
'They *h* me without a cause.' | Jn 15.25
and the world has *h* them | 17.14
"Jacob I loved, but Esau I *h*." | Rom 9.13
and *h* lawlessness; therefore | Heb 1.9

HATRED
if he stabbed him from *h*, | Num 35.20
with what violent *h* they hate | Ps 25.19
fear of..LORD is *h* of evil. | Prov 8.13

HAUGHTY
h eyes, a lying tongue, and | Prov 6.17
the daughters of Zion are *h* | Isa 3.16
eyes of the *h* are humbled. | 5.15
do not be *h*, but associate | Rom 12.16

HAWK
are an abomination:..the *h* | Lev 11.16
by your wisdom..the *h* soars, | Job 39.26

HEAD
put it under his *h* | Gen 28.11
and cut off his *h* with it. | 1Sam 17.51
to his father, "Oh, my *h*, | 2Ki 4.19
Your *h* crowns you like Carmel, | Sol 7.5
"Give me the *h* of John the | Mt 14.8
brought his *h* on a platter, | Mk 6.28
but also my hands and my *h*!" | Jn 13.9
the *h* of every man is Christ, | 1Cor 11.3
has made him the *h* over all | Eph 1.22
husband is the *h* of the wife | 5.23
He is the *h* of the body, | Col 1.18

HEAL — S — ED — ING (v)
"*H* her, O God, I beseech | Num 12.13
make alive; I wound and I *h*; | Deut 32.39
their sin and *h* their land. | 2Chr 7.14
h me, for I have sinned against | Ps 41.4
Peace,..and I will *h* him. | Isa 57.19
I will *h* your faithlessness." | Jer 3.22
H me, O LORD, and I shall be | 17.14
and your wounds I will *h*, | 30.17
I will *h* them and reveal to | 33.6
not able to..*h* your wound. | Hos 5.13
when I would *h* Israel, the | 7.1
I will *h* their faithlessness; | 14.4
H the sick, raise the dead, | Mt 10.8
and turn for me to *h* them.' | 13.15
disciples,..could not *h* him." | 17.16
'Physician, *h* yourself'; | Lk 4.23
to preach the kingdom..and to *h*. | 9.2
"Is it lawful to *h* on the sabbath, | 14.3
to come down and *h* his son, | Jn 4.47
who *h* all your diseases, | Ps 103.3
He *h* the brokenhearted, and | 147.3
and *h* the wounds inflicted | Isa 30.26
and God *h* Abimelech, | Gen 20.17
for help, and thou hast *h* me. | Ps 30.2
he sent forth his word, and *h* | 107.20
with his stripes we are *h*. | Isa 53.5
h the wound of my people lightly, | Jer 6.14
We would have *h* Babylon, but | 51.9
they did not know that I *h* them. | Hos 11.3
and *h* all who were sick. | Mt 8.16
followed him, and he *h* them | 12.15
had compassion..and *h* their sick. | 14.14
every one of them and *h* them. | Lk 4.40
to be *h* of their diseases; | 6.17

women who had been *h* of evil | 8.2
she had been immediately *h*. | 8.47
come on those days and be *h*, | 13.14
touched his ear and *h* him. | 22.51
man who had been *h* did not know | Jn 5.13
putting his hands on him *h* | Acts 28.8
By his wounds you have been *h*. | 1Pet 2.24
h every disease and..infirmity | Mt 4.23

HEALER — S
I am the LORD, your *h*." | Ex 15.26
h, helpers, administrators, | 1Cor 12.28

HEALING (n)
It will be *h* to your flesh | Prov 3.8
he will be broken beyond *h*. | 6.15
suddenly be broken beyond *h*. | 29.1
We looked..for a time of *h*, | Jer 8.15
so that there is no *h* for us? | 14.19
medicines;..no *h* for you. | 46.11
and their leaves for *h*." | Ezek 47.12
rise, with *h* in its wings. | Mal 4.2
to another gifts of *h* by | 1Cor 12.9
leaves..for..*h* of the nations. | Rev 22.2

HEALTH
no *h* in my bones because..sin. | Ps 38.3
the soul and *h* to the body. | Prov 16.24
For I will restore *h* to you, | Jer 30.17
given the man this perfect *h* | Acts 3.16
and that you may be in *h*; | 3Jn 2

HEAP — S (v)
he *h* up silver like dust, | Job 27.16
h coals of fire on his head, | Prov 25.22
man *h* up, and knows not who | Ps 39.6

HEAP (n)
it shall be a *h* for ever, | Deut 13.16
waters..stand in one *h*." | Josh 3.13
make Jerusalem a *h* of ruins, | Jer 9.11

HEAR — S — D (v)
let them *h* my words, | Deut 4.10
"*H*, O Israel, the statutes | 5.1
"*H*, O Israel: The LORD our | 6.4
that they may *h* and learn | 31.12
when you *h* the sound of | 2Sam 5.24
then *h* thou in heaven thy | 1Ki 8.39
LORD, and *h*; open thy eyes, | 2Ki 19.16
then *h* thou in heaven, | 2Chr 6.27
'*H*, and I will speak; I will | Job 42.4
H this, all peoples! Give ear, | Ps 49.1
H,..your father's instruction, | Prov 1.8
H, O heavens, and give ear, | Isa 1.2
'*H* and *h*, but do not understand; | 6.9
H, you who are far off, what | 33.13
I will let you *h* my words." | Jer 18.2
he that will *h*, let him *h*; | Ezek 3.27
who have ears to *h*, and *h* not: | 12.2
they *h*..but..will not do it; | 33.31
tell John what you *h* and see: | Mt 11.4
he said.."Take heed what you *h*; | Mk 4.24
came to *h* him and to be healed | Lk 6.17
sheep *h* his voice, and he calls | Jn 10.3
h, but never understand, | Acts 28.26
to *h* without a preacher? | Rom 10.14
Let every man be quick to *h*, | Jas 1.19
blessed are those who *h*, and | Rev 1.3
cry for help, and the LORD *h*, and | Ps 34.17
"He who *h* you *h* me, and he | Lk 10.16
who *h* my word and believes | Jn 5.24
If any one *h* my sayings and | 12.47
God *h* the voice of the lad; | Gen 21.17
And God *h* their groaning, | Ex 2.24
From his temple he *h* my | 2Sam 22.7

HEAR — S — D (v) (cont.)

"I have *h* your prayer, and	2Chr 7.12
and *h* his supplication and	33.13
wept when they *h* the words of	Neh 8.9
The LORD has *h* my supplication;	Ps 6.9
words of the wise *h* in quiet	Ecc 9.17
Have you not known?. .not *h*?	Isa 40.28
From of old no one has *h* or	64.4
Who has *h* such a thing? Who	66.8
I have *h* Ephraim bemoaning,	Jer 31.18
the LORD heeded and *h* them,	Mal 3.16
tell. .what you have seen and *h*:	Lk 7.22
what we have seen and *h*."	Acts 4.20
Spirit fell on all who *h*	10.44
all the residents of Asia *h*	19.10
who have never *h* of him."	Rom 15.21
we have *h*, which we have seen	1Jn 1.1

HEARING (n)

in the *h* of the Hittites,	Gen 23.10
the book of Moses in the *h*	Neh 13.1
eye, where would be the *h*?	1Cor 12.17

HEARKEN — ED

Give heed to him and *h*	Ex 23.21
you *h* to these ordinances,	Deut 7.12
they did not *h* to the voice	Josh 5.6
if you will not *h* to the	1Sam 12.15
If they *h* and serve him,	Job 36.11
H to. .father who begot you.	Prov 23.22
"*H* to me, you who pursue	Isa 51.1
h, O earth, and all that is	Mic 1.2
they *h* to the word of. .LORD,	2Chr 11.4
he *h* to them in this matter,	Dan 1.14

HEART — S

imagination. .man's *h* is evil	Gen 8.21
from every man whose *h*	Ex 25.2
upon his *h* before the LORD	28.30
whoever is of a generous *h*,	35.5
love. .God with all your *h*,	Deut 6.5
then your *h* be lifted up,	8.14
"Do not say in your *h*, after	9.4
God with all your *h* and with	10.12
yet the LORD set his *h*	10.15
shall not harden your *h*	15.7
lest his *h* turn away;	17.17
his *h* may not be lifted	17.20
LORD will give. .trembling *h*,	28.65
the *h* of your offspring,	30.6
mouth and in your *h*, so	30.14
crossed over, their *h* melted,	Josh 5.1
incline your *h* to the LORD,	24.23
direct your *h* to the LORD,	1Sam 7.3
God gave him another *h*;	10.9
a man after his own *h*;	13.14
the LORD looks on the *h*."	16.7
and his *h* died within him,	25.37
do all that is in your *h*;	2Sam 7.3
h is like the *h* of a lion,	17.10
David's *h* smote him after	24.10
uprightness of *h* toward thee;	1Ki 3.6
if they repent. .with all their *h*	8.48
his *h* had turned away from	11.9
the *h* of Asa was wholly true	15.14
your *h* has lifted you up,	2Ki 14.10
because your *h* was penitent,	22.19
to the LORD with all his *h*	23.25
"Do all that is in your *h*,	1Chr 17.2
in my *h* to build a house	28.2
serve him with a whole *h*	28.9
that thou triest the *h*,	29.17
in the *h* of David. .to build	2Chr 6.7

whose *h* is blameless toward	16.9
His *h* was courageous in the	17.6
your *h* has lifted you up in	25.19
his *h* was proud. Therefore	32.25
turned the *h* of the king	Ezra 6.22
Ezra had set his *h* to study	7.10
else but sadness of the *h*."	Neh 2.2
my *h* to do for Jerusalem.	2.12
"If you set your *h* aright,	Job 11.13
God has made my *h* faint;	23.16
"If my *h* has been enticed	31.9
godless in *h* cherish anger;	36.13
fool says in his *h*,. .no God."	Ps 14.1
are right, rejoicing the *h*;	19.8
has clean hands and a pure *h*,	24.4
he knows the secrets of the *h*.	44.21
My *h* overflows with a goodly	45.1
Create in me a clean *h*, O God,	51.10
fool says in his *h*,. .no God."	53.1
butter, yet war was in his *h*;	55.21
My *h* is steadfast, O God, my *h*	57.7
Insults have broken my *h*, so	69.20
commune with my *h* in the night;	77.6
They tested God in their *h*	78.18
will walk with integrity of *h*	101.2
My *h* is smitten like grass,	102.4
wine to gladden the *h* of man,	104.15
My *h* is steadfast, O God, my *h*	108.1
my *h* is stricken within me.	109.22
His *h* is steady, he will not	112.8
laid up thy word in my *h*,	119.11
my *h* within me is appalled.	143.4
wisdom will come into your *h*,	Prov 2.10
write them on. .tablet of your *h*.	3.3
Keep your *h* with all vigilance;	4.23
a *h* that devises wicked plans,	6.18
Before destruction a man's *h*	18.12
Who can say,. .my *h* clean;	20.9
king's *h* is a stream of water	21.1
My son, give me your *h*, and	23.26
smooth lips with an evil *h*.	26.23
nor let your *h* be hasty to	Ecc 5.2
wise man's *h* inclines. .right,	10.2
Set me as a seal upon your *h*,	Sol 8.6
sick, and the whole *h* faint.	Isa 1.5
Make the *h* of this people fat,	6.10
faithfulness with a whole *h*,	38.3
but he did not take it to *h*.	42.25
people in whose *h* is my law;	51.7
why dost thou. .harden our *h*,	63.17
Judah did not return. .whole *h*,	Jer 3.10
shepherds after my own *h*, who	3.15
Jerusalem, wash your *h* from	4.14
My *h* is beating wildly; I writhe	4.19
whose *h* turns away from. .LORD.	17.5
The *h* is deceitful above all	17.9
I will give them one *h* and	32.39
I will give them one *h*,	Ezek 11.19
"How lovesick is your *h*,	16.30
"Because your *h* is proud,	28.2
their *h* is set on their gain.	33.31
I will take out. .*h* of stone	36.26
uncircumcised in *h* and flesh,	44.7
you. .have not humbled your *h*,	Dan 5.22
Their *h* is false; now they	Hos 10.2
"return to me with all your *h*,	Joel 2.12
stout of *h* among the mighty	Amos 2.16
"Blessed are the pure in *h*,	Mt 5.8
adultery with her in his *h*.	5.28
treasure is, there will your *h*	6.21
said to the paralytic, "Take *h*,	9.2
this people's *h* has grown dull,	13.15
"Take *h*, it is I; have no fear."	14.27

HEART — S (cont.)

but their h is far from me;	Mt 15.8
out of the h come evil thoughts,	15.19
"Take h, it is I; have no fear."	Mk 6.50
but their h is far from me;	7.6
out of the h of man, come evil	7.21
"For your hardness of h he	10.5
love. . God with all your h,	12.30
unbelief and hardness of h,	16.14n
Mary. . pondering them in her h.	Lk 2.19
mother kept. . things in her h.	2.51
out of the good treasure of his h	6.45
'Out of his h shall flow	Jn 7.38
eyes and hardened their h,	12.40
therefore my h was glad,	Acts 2.26
were of one h and soul, and	4.32
into his h to visit his brother	7.23
uncircumcised in h and ears,	7.51
your h is not right before God.	8.21
David. . a man after my h,	13.22
God who knows the h bore witness	15.8
opened her h to give heed	16.14
weeping and breaking my h?	21.13
I now bid you take h; for	27.22
So take h, men, for I have	27.25
this people's h has grown dull,	28.27
and unceasing anguish in my h.	Rom 9.2
believe in your h that God	10.9
nor the h of man conceived,	1Cor 2.9
ministry. . we do not lose h.	2Cor 4.1
Corinthians; our h is wide.	6.11
his h goes out all the more	7.15
love that issues from a pure h	1Tim 1.5
discerning. . intentions of the h.	Heb 4.12
love one another. . from the h.	1Pet 1.22
yet closes his h against him,	1Jn 3.17
he who searches mind and h,	Rev 2.23
Absalom stole the h of the	2Sam 15.6
thou hast turned their h	1Ki 18.37
Harden not your h, as at	Ps 95.8
while their h are far from me,	Isa 29.13
I will write it upon their h;	Jer 31.33
made their h like adamant	Zech 7.12
he will turn the h of fathers	Mal 4.6
"Why. . question thus in your h?	Mk 2.8
but their h were hardened.	6.52
bread?. . Are your h hardened?	8.17
turn the h of the fathers to	Lk 1.17
"Did not our h burn within us	24.32
"Let not your h be troubled;	Jn 14.1
Let not your h be troubled,	14.27
"Lord, who knowest. . h of all	Acts 1.24
written on their h, while	Rom 2.15
he who searches the h of men	8.27
Lord direct your h to. . love	2Thess 3.5
do not harden your h as in	Heb 3.8
always go astray in their h;	3.10
voice, do not harden your h."	4.7
and write them on their h,	8.10
whenever our h condemn us;	1Jn 3.20

HEAVEN — S

God called the firmament H.	Gen 1.8
I will rain bread from h	Ex 16.4
I. . talked with you from h.	20.22
It is not in h, that you	Deut 30.12
Behold, h. . cannot contain thee	1Ki 8.27
should make windows in h,	2Ki 7.2
Behold, h. . cannot contain	2Chr 6.18
I ascend to h, thou art there!	Ps 139.8
"How you are fallen from h,	Isa 14.12
says the LORD: "H is my throne	66.1
till h and earth pass away,	Mt 5.18

Pray. . Our Father who art in h,	6.9
H and earth will pass away,	Mk 13.31
Jesus. . was taken up into h,	16.19n
H and earth will pass away,	Lk 21.33
a light from h flashed about	Acts 9.3
the image of the man of h.	1Cor 15.49
caught up to the third h—	2Cor 12.2
Christ, who has gone into h	1Pet 3.22
and lo, in h an open door!	Rev 4.1
great multitude in h, crying,	19.1
I saw a new h and a new earth;	21.1
The h are telling the glory of	Ps 19.1
h are high above the earth,	103.11
thy word is firmly fixed in. . h.	119.89
the h languish. . with the earth.	Isa 24.4
the h above. . withheld dew,	Hag 1.10
he saw the h opened and the	Mk 1.10
powers of the h. . be shaken.	Lk 21.26
by the word of God h existed	2Pet 3.5
we wait for new h and a new	3.13

HEAVENLY

believe if I tell you h things?	Jn 3.12
long to put on our h dwelling,	2Cor 5.2
spiritual blessing in h places,	Eph 1.3

HEAVY

charged with h tidings for	1Ki 14.6
day and night thy hand was h	Ps 32.4
evil which. . lies h upon men:	Ecc 6.1
all who labor and are h laden,	Mt 11.28
their ears are h of hearing,	13.15

HEBRON

Abram. . dwelt. . at H;	Gen 13.18
Canaanites who dwelt in H	Judg 1.10
David was king in H over	2Sam 2.11

HEED (v)

I should h his voice and let	Ex 5.2
to h all these words which	Deut 12.28
and thou dost not h me.	Job 30.20
Cursed. . man who does not h	Jer 11.3
to h the words of my. . prophets	26.5
and they will h my voice.	Jn 10.16

HEED (n)

you have not given h to	Judg 6.10
hast taken h of my adversities,	Ps 31.7
h. . the way that is blameless.	101.2
Give h to my reproof; behold,	Prov 1.23
Take h to. . path of your feet,	4.26
I have given h and listened,	Jer 8.6
O LORD, give h and act; delay	Dan 9.19
no h to the gods of his fathers,	11.37
stands take h lest he fall.	1Cor 10.12

HEEL

and you shall bruise his h."	Gen 3.15
taken hold of Esau's h;	25.26
has lifted his h against me.	Ps 41.9
took his brother by the h,	Hos 12.3

HEIFER

"Bring me a h three years old,	Gen 15.9
bring you a red h without	Num 19.2
had not plowed with my h,	Judg 14.18

HEIGHT

nor h, nor depth, nor anything	Rom 8.39

HEIR — S

a slave. . will be my h."	Gen 15.3
in the end find him his h.	Prov 29.21
Israel no sons? Has he no h?	Jer 49.1
the h; come, let us kill him	Mt 21.38
"This is the h; come, let us	Mk 12.7

HEIR — S (cont.)

'This is the *h*; let us kill | Lk 20.14
I mean that the *h*, as long as | Gal 4.1
h of..righteousness..by faith. | Heb 11.7
if children, then *h*, *h* of God | Rom 8.17
how the Gentiles are fellow *h*, | Eph 3.6

HELL

says, 'You fool!'..liable to..*h* | Mt 5.22
your whole body..thrown into *h*. | 5.29
be thrown into the *h* of fire. | 18.9
has power to cast into *h*; | Lk 12.5

HELLENISTS

H murmured against..Hebrews | Acts 6.1
and disputed against the *H*; | 9.29

HELMET

h of salvation upon his head; | Isa 59.17
take the *h* of salvation, and | Eph 6.17
for a *h*..hope of salvation. | 1Thess 5.8

HELP — S — ED (v)

shall be no one to *h* you. | Deut 28.31
there was none to *h* Israel. | 2Ki 14.26
there is none like thee to *h*, | 2Chr 14.11
h me when thou deliverest | Ps 106.4
fell down, with none to *h*. | 107.12
H me, O LORD my God! Save me | 109.26
O Israel; who can *h* you? | Hos 13.9
knelt..saying, "Lord, *h* me." | Mt 15.25
toiling one must *h* the weak, | Acts 20.35
the Lord GOD..therefore | Isa 50.7
Moses stood up and *h* them, | Ex 2.17
God *h* him against the | 2Chr 26.7
have *h* him who has no power! | Job 26.2
brother *h* is like a strong | Prov 18.19
in a day of salvation I have *h* | Isa 49.8

HELP (n)

and thy *h* made me great. | 2Sam 22.36
because I saw *h* in the gate; | Job 31.21
and thy *h* made me great. | Ps 18.35
I shall again praise him, my *h* | 42.5
I shall again praise him, my *h* | 42.11
Thou art my *h* and my deliverer; | 70.5
My *h* comes from the LORD, | 121.2
Egypt's *h* is worthless and | Isa 30.7
the *h* that comes from God, | Acts 26.22
in Thessalonica you sent me *h* | Phil 4.16

HELPER

I will make him a *h* | Gen 2.18
been the *h* of the fatherless. | Ps 10.14
Hear,..O LORD, be thou my *h*!" | 30.10
"The Lord is my *h*, I will | Heb 13.6

HELPFUL

but not all things are *h*. | 1Cor 6.12
but not all things are *h*. | 10.23

HELPLESS

I suffer thy terrors; I am *h*. | Ps 88.15
our hands fall *h*; anguish | Jer 6.24
While we were..*h*,..Christ died | Rom 5.6

HERITAGE

to be thy *h*, as thou didst | 1Ki 8.53
What..*h* from the Almighty | Job 31.2
I will make the nations your *h*, | Ps 2.8
yea, I have a goodly *h*. | 16.6
whom he has chosen as his *h*! | 33.12
LORD..will not abandon his *h*; | 94.14
house, I have abandoned my *h*; | Jer 12.7
loosen your hand from your *h* | 17.4
exult, O plunderers of my *h*, | 50.11

HERMON

valley of..Arnon to Mount *H* | Deut 3.8
Mount Sirion (that is, *H*), | 4.48
Lebanon below Mount *H*. | Josh 11.17
valley of..Arnon to Mount *H*, | 12.1
Tabor and *H* joyously praise | Ps 89.12
It is like the dew of *H*, which | 133.3
from the peak of Senir and *H*, | Sol 4.8

HEROD

born..in the days of *H* the king, | Mt 2.1
for *H* is about to search for | 2.13
Then *H*,..was in a furious rage, | 2.16
when *H* died, behold, an angel | 2.19
H the tetrarch heard about | 14.1
King *H* heard of it; for Jesus' | Mk 6.14
Pharisees and..leaven of *H*." | 8.15
and *H* being tetrarch of Galilee, | Lk 3.1
for *H* wants to kill you." | 13.31
he sent him over to *H*, who | 23.7
both *H* and Pontius Pilate, | Acts 4.27
H the king laid violent hands | 12.1
Now *H* was angry with..Tyre | 12.20
H put on his royal robes, | 12.21

HEZEKIAH

and *H* his son reigned in his | 2Ki 16.20
H received the letter from | 19.14
those days *H* became sick | 20.1
H sent to all Israel and | 2Chr 30.1
For *H* had prayed for them, | 30.18
H closed the upper outlet | 32.30
letters and a present to *H*, | Isa 39.1

HID — DEN

she *h* him three months. | Ex 2.2
man and his wife *h* themselves | 3.8
killed the Egyptian and *h* him | Ex 2.12
And Moses *h* his face, | 3.6
h him from Athaliah, so | 2Chr 22.11
I have not *h* thy saving help | Ps 40.10
"My way is *h* from the LORD, | Isa 40.27
in..shadow of his hand he *h* me; | 49.2
troubles..*h* from my eyes. | 65.16
and *h* it by the Euphrates, | Jer 13.5
prophet, but the LORD *h* them. | 36.26
city set on a hill cannot be *h*. | Mt 5.14
and *h* his master's money. | 25.18
nothing *h*, except to be made | Mk 4.22
nothing is *h* that shall not | Lk 8.17
taken the two men and *h* them; | Josh 2.4
he had *h* himself among the | 1Sam 10.22
Clear thou me from *h* faults. | Ps 19.12
trustworthy..keeps..thing *h*. | Prov 11.13
open rebuke than *h* love. | 27.5
h these things from the wise | Lk 10.21
before him no creature is *h*, | Heb 4.13

HIDE — ST — ING

"Shall I *h* from Abraham | Gen 18.17
Do not *h* it from me. May | 1Sam 3.17
h thyself in times of trouble? | Ps 10.1
How long wilt thou *h* thy face | 13.1
h me in the shadow of thy wings, | 17.8
he will *h* me in his shelter | 27.5
H not thy face from me. | 27.9
thou didst *h* thy face, I was | 30.7
h not..from my supplication! | 55.1
Wilt thou *h* thyself for ever? | 89.46
I will *h* my eyes from you; | Isa 1.15
and *h* in the dust from before | 2.10
I will not *h* my face any | Ezek 39.29
they *h* themselves on..Carmel, | Amos 9.3
When thou *h* thy face, they | Ps 104.29
thou art a God who *h* thyself, | Isa 45.15

HIDE — ST — ING (cont.)

Thou art my *h* place and my	Ps 119.114
like a *h* place from the wind,	Isa 32.2

HIGH — ER

folly is set in many *h* places,	Ecc 10.6
and make *h* the low tree,	Ezek 17.24
our iniquities have risen *h*	Ezra 9.6

HIGH PRIEST

when Abiathar was *h*..,and ate	Mk 2.26
they led Jesus to the *h*..;	14.53
h..then questioned Jesus	Jn 18.19
But the *h*..rose up and all	Acts 5.17
"Would you revile God's *h*..?"	23.4
faithful *h*..in the service	Heb 2.17
Jesus, the apostle and *h*..	3.1
then we have a great *h*..who	4.14
not exalt himself to be..a *h*..	5.5

HIGHWAY — S

will be a *h* from Assyria for	Isa 11.16
a *h* from Egypt to Assyria,	19.23
And a *h* shall be there, and	35.8
whose heart are the *h* to Zion.	Ps 84.5
my *h* shall be raised up.	Isa 49.11
'Go out to the *h* and hedges,	Lk 14.23

HILL — S

Who..ascend the *h* of the LORD?	Ps 24.3
gods of the *h*, and so they	1Ki 20.23
he went into the *h* to pray.	Mk 6.46
Jesus withdrew again to the *h*	Jn 6.15

HINDER

nothing can *h* the LORD from	1Sam 14.6
snatches away; who can *h* him?	Job 9.12

HINDRANCE

behind me, Satan! You are a *h*	Mt 16.23

HIRAM

And *H* king of Tyre sent	2Sam 5.11
Now *H* king of Tyre sent his	1Ki 5.1
Solomon sent and brought *H*	7.13
H also made the pots, the	7.40
when *H* came from Tyre to see	9.12
And *H* king of Tyre sent	1Chr 14.1

HIRE — D (n)

while no *h* was given to you;	Ezek 16.34
treat me as one of your *h*	Lk 15.19

HIRED (v)

they *h* against you Balaam	Deut 23.4
they *h* masons and carpenters	2Chr 24.12

HITTITE — S

Ephron the *H* answered	Gen 23.10
H, the Perizzites, the	15.20
Canaanites, the *H*, the Amorites,	Ex 3.8
the Amorites, and the *H*,	23.23
nations before you, the *H*,	Deut 7.1
left of the Amorites, the *H*,	1Ki 9.20
hired against us..the *H* and	2Ki 7.6
from the Canaanites, the *H*,	Ezra 9.1

HOLD

I *h* fast my righteousness,	Job 27.6
I *h* back my feet from..evil	Ps 119.101
to them; do not *h* back a word.	Jer 26.2
"Do not *h* me, for I have not	Jn 20.17
we *h*..man..justified by faith	Rom 3.28
h fast to what is good; love	12.9

HOLE — S

there was a *h* in the wall.	Ezek 8.7
wages to put..into a bag with *h*.	Hag 1.6

HOLINESS

O LORD,..majestic in *h*,	Ex 15.11
h befits thy house, O LORD,	Ps 93.5
manifest my *h* among you in	Ezek 20.41
vindicate the *h* of my..name,	36.23
O God, I vindicate my *h*	38.16
serve him..in *h*..righteousness	Lk 1.75
make *h* perfect in..fear of God.	2Cor 7.1
in true righteousness and *h*.	Eph 4.24
God has..called us..in *h*.	1Thess 4.7
for the *h* without which no	Heb 12.14

HOLLOW

touched the *h* of his thigh;	Gen 32.25
measured the waters in the *h*	Isa 40.12

HOLY

are standing is *h* ground."	Ex 3.5
priests and a *h* nation.	19.6
h place from the most *h*.	26.33
signet, '*H* to the LORD.'	28.36
inscription,.."*H* to the LORD."	39.30
said, 'I will show myself *h*	Lev 10.3
to distinguish between the *h*	10.10
and be *h*, for I am *h*.	11.44
Israel, You shall be *h*;	19.2
You shall be *h* to me; for I	20.26
They shall be *h* to their God,	21.6
keep away from the *h* things	22.2
not..look upon the *h* things	Num 4.20
he separates himself to..be *h*;	6.5
all the congregation are *h*,	16.3
sabbath day, to keep it *h*,	Deut 5.12
"For you are a people *h*	7.6
a people *h* to the LORD	14.2
your camp must be *h*,	23.14
"There is none *h* like..LORD,	1Sam 2.2
"You are *h* to the LORD, and	Ezra 8.28
to keep the sabbath day *h*.	Neh 13.22
of the *h* ones will you turn?	Job 5.1
thou art *h*, enthroned on the	Ps 22.3
and give thanks to his *h* name.	30.4
His *h* mountain, beautiful in	48.2
Worship the LORD in *h* array;	96.9
and terrible name! *H* is he!	99.3
Lift up..hands to the *h* place,	134.2
the *H* God shows himself *h* in	Isa 5.16
"*H*, *h*, *h* is the LORD of hosts;	6.3
him you shall regard as *h*;	8.13
it shall be called the *H* way;	35.8
shall be called The *h* people,	62.12
Israel was *h* to the LORD,	Jer 2.3
but keep the sabbath day *h*,	17.22
aliens..come into..*h* places	51.51
between the *h* and..common.	Ezek 42.20
not kept charge of my *h* things;	44.8
Then I heard a *h* one speaking;	Dan 8.13
shattering of the power of the *h*	12.7
all the *h* ones with him.	Zech 14.5
"Do not give dogs what is *h*;	Mt 7.6
the..sacrilege..in the *h* place	24.15
John,..a righteous and *h* man,	Mk 6.20
male that opens the womb..*h*	Lk 2.23
where you are standing is *h*	Acts 7.33
So the law is *h*, and the	Rom 7.12
as a living sacrifice, *h* and	12.1
how to be *h* in body and	1Cor 7.34
we should be *h* and blameless	Eph 1.4
church..*h* and without blemish.	5.27
a high priest, *h*, blameless,	Heb 7.26
as he..is *h*, be *h* yourselves	1Pet 1.15
Lord came with his myriads,	Jude 14
'The words of the *h* one,	Rev 3.7

HOLY (cont.)
"*H*, *h*, *h*, is the Lord God　　Rev 4.8
the *h* city, new Jerusalem,　　　21.2

HOLY ONE
knowledge of..*H*..is insight.　Prov 9.10
Redeemer is the *H*..of Israel.　Isa 41.14
Redeemer, the *H*..of Israel:　　　43.14
from everlasting,..my *H*..?　　Hab 1.12
that you are the *H*..of God."　　Jn 6.69
'Thou wilt not let thy *H*..see　Acts 13.35

HOLY SPIRIT
and take not thy *h*..from me.　Ps 51.11
to be with child of the *H*..;　　Mt 1.18
will baptize you with the *H*..."　Mk 1.8
men moved by the *H*..spoke　2Pet 1.21

HOME
God gives the desolate a *h*　　Ps 68.6
"Go *h* to your friends, and tell　Mk 5.19
he sent him away to his *h*,　　　8.26
"Return to your *h*, and declare　Lk 8.39
and make our *h* with him.　　Jn 14.23
disciple took her to his own *h*.　19.27
hungry, let him eat at *h*—　　1Cor 11.34
ask their husbands at *h*.　　　　14.35
while we are at *h* in the body　2Cor 5.6

HOMELAND
people who speak..seeking a *h*.　Heb 11.14

HONEST — Y
hold it fast in an *h* and good　Lk 8.15
So my *h* will answer for me　Gen 30.33

HONEY
land flowing with milk and *h*　Ex 3.8
like wafers made with *h*.　　　16.31
suck *h* out of the rock,　　Deut 32.13
tasted a little of this *h*.　　1Sam 14.29
gold; sweeter also than *h*　　Ps 19.10
with *h* from the rock..satisfy　81.16
thy words..sweeter than *h*　　119.103
son, eat *h*, for it is good,　Prov 24.13
h and milk..under your tongue; Sol 4.11
He shall eat curds and *h* when　Isa 7.15
scroll..was..as sweet as *h*.　Ezek 3.3
was sweet as *h* in my mouth,　Rev 10.10

HONOR — S — ED (v)
"*H* your father..your mother,　Ex 20.12
h the face of an old man,　Lev 19.32
" '*H* your father and..mother,　Deut 5.16
those who *h* me I will *h*,　1Sam 2.30
"I have sinned; yet *h* me　　　15.30
H the LORD with your substance Prov 3.9
h me with their lips, while　Isa 29.13
h it, not going your own ways,　58.13
shall *h* the god of fortresses　Dan 11.38
God commanded, '*H* your father Mt 15.4
H your father and mother,　　19.19
'*H* your father and..mother';　Mk 7.10
that all may *h* the Son, even　Jn 5.23
I *h* my Father, and you dishonor　8.49
"*H* your father and mother"　Eph 6.2
receive him..and *h* such men,　Phil 2.29
H widows who are real widows. 1Tim 5.3
thanksgiving..sacrifice *h* me;　Ps 50.23
"A son *h* his father, and a　Mal 1.6
people *h* me with their lips,　Mt 15.8
most *h* of all his family.　Gen 34.19
or *h* me with your sacrifices.　Isa 43.23
I will make them *h*, and they　Jer 30.19
h in the presence of all　　Lk 14.10
Christ will be *h* in my body,　Phil 1.20

HONOR (n)
surely do you great *h*,　　　Num 22.17
them I shall be held in *h*."　2Sam 6.22
not asked..wealth, *h*, or the　2Chr 1.11
"What *h*..bestowed on Mordecai Est 6,3
H and majesty are before him;　Ps 96.6
Thou art clothed with *h* and　　104.1
and humility goes before *h*.　Prov 15.33
lowly in spirit..obtain *h*.　　　29.23
gifts and rewards and great *h*.　Dan 2.6
"A prophet is not without *h*　Mt 13.57
prophet is not without *h*, except　Mk 6.4
how they chose..places of *h*,　Lk 14.7
who..seek for glory and *h* and　Rom 2.7
outdo one another in..*h*　　　12.10
due, *h* to whom *h* is due.　　13.7
You are held in *h*, but we　1Cor 4.10
in *h* and dishonor, in ill　　2Cor 6.8
To him be *h* and eternal　1Tim 6.16

HONORABLE
Jabez was more *h* than his　1Chr 4.9
we aim at what is *h* not only　2Cor 8.21
whatever is *h*, whatever..just,　Phil 4.8
they who blaspheme that *h* name Jas 2.7

HOPE — S — D (v)
upon us even as we *h* in thee.　Ps 33.22
H in God; for I shall again　　42.5
H in God; for I shall again　　43.5
But I will *h* continually, and　71.14
I *h* for thy salvation, O　119.166
in his name will..Gentiles *h*."　Mt 12.21
from whom you *h* to receive,　Lk 6.34
in him shall the Gentiles *h*."　Rom 15.12
For who *h* for what he sees?　8.24
who thus *h* in him purifies　1Jn 3:3
because I have *h* in thy word.　Ps 119.74
we had *h* that he was the one　Lk 24.21
we have *h* in Christ,　　1Cor 15.19
we who first *h* in Christ　Eph 1.12

HOPE (n)
now there is *h* for Israel　　Ezra 10.2
So the poor have *h*, and　　Job 5.16
he will slay me; I have no *h*;　13.15
thou destroyest the *h* of man.　14.19
where then is my *h*? Who　17.15
my *h* has he pulled up like　19.10
what is the *h* of the godless　27.8
on those who *h* in his..love,　33.18
art the *h* of all the ends of　65.5
they should set their *h* in God,　78.7
whose *h* is in the LORD his　146.5
The *h* of the righteous ends　Prov 10.28
H deferred makes the heart sick,　13.12
your son while there is *h*;　19.18
There is more *h* for a fool　29.20
because of Ethiopia their *h*　Isa 20.5
We set our *h* on thee, for　Jer 14.22
There is *h* for your future,　31.17
bones..dried up..*h* is lost;　Ezek 37.11
Valley of Achor a door of *h*.　Hos 2.15
because of the *h* of Israel　Acts 28.20
In *h* he believed against *h*,　Rom 4.18
Rejoice in your *h*, be patient　12.12
you may know what is the *h*　Eph 1.18
h laid up for you in heaven.　Col 1.5
not shifting from the *h* of　　1.23
Christ in you, the *h* of glory.　1.27
steadfastness of *h* in our Lord 1Thess 1.3
what is out *h*..joy or crown　2.19
awaiting our blessed *h*, the　Tit 2.13
to seize the *h* set before us.　Heb 6.18

HOPE (n) (cont.)
hold fast the confession of our *h* Heb 10.23
been born anew to a living *h* 1Pet 1.3

HORN — S
The *h* of Moab is cut off, Jer 48.25
cause a *h* to spring forth Ezek 29.21
hear the sound of the *h*, pipe, Dan 3.5
he. .raised up a *h* of salvation Lk 1.69
hold of the *h* of the altar. 1Ki 1.50
hold of the *h* of the altar. 2.28
a fourth beast,. .it had ten *h*. Dan 7.7
two *h*; and both *h* were high, 8.3
saw, and behold, four *h*! Zech 1.18
the ten *h* that you saw are Rev 17.12

HORSE — S
she laughs at the *h* and his Job 39.18
Be not like a *h* or a mule, Ps 32.9
The war *h* is a vain hope for 33.17
h is made ready for. .battle, Prov 21.31
A whip for the *h*, a bridle 26.3
a man riding upon a red *h*! Zech 1.8
multiply *h* for himself, Deut 17.16
hamstring their *h*, and burn Josh 11.6
Solomon's import of *h* was 1Ki 10.28
Solomon's import of *h* was 2Chr 1.16
four thousand stalls for *h* 9.25
Do *h* run upon rocks? Does Amos 6.12
The first chariot had red *h*, Zech 6.2
put bits into the mouths of *h* Jas 3.3

HOSANNAH
"*H* to the Son of David!" Mt 21.15
"*H*! Blessed is he who comes Mk 11.9

HOSEA
word of the LORD that came to *H* Hos 1.1
As indeed he says in *H*, Rom 9.25

HOSPITABLE
dignified, *h*, an apt teacher, 1Tim 3.2
but *h*, a lover of goodness, Tit 1.8

HOSPITALITY
needs of. .saints, practice *h*. Rom 12.13
Practice *h* ungrudgingly to 1Pet 4.9

HOST — S
finished,. .all the *h* of them. Gen 2.1
Though a *h* encamp against me, Ps 27.3
h under. .leadership of Moses Num 33.1
LORD of *h* is God over 2Sam 7.26
King of glory? The LORD of *h*, Ps 24.10
If the LORD of *h* had not left Isa 1.9

HOSTILE
eye be *h* to your. .brother, Deut 15.9
mind. .on the flesh is *h* to God; Rom 8.7
were estranged and *h* in mind, Col 1.21

HOUR
'These last worked only one *h*, Mt 20.12
know neither. .day nor the *h*. 25.13
that day or. .*h* no one knows, Mk 13.32
the *h* might pass from him. 14.35
the *h* has come; the Son of man 14.41
But this is your *h*, and the Lk 22.53
the *h* is coming when neither Jn 4.21
because his *h* had not yet come. 7.30
"The *h* has come for the Son 12.23
'Father, save me from this *h*'? 12.27
The *h* is coming, indeed it 16.32

HOUSE — S
h to be holy to the LORD, Lev 27.14
my *h*, we will serve. .LORD." Josh 24.15

LORD will make you a *h*. 2Sam 7.11
burned the *h* of the LORD, 2Ki 25.9
I have not dwelt in a *h* 1Chr 17.5
LORD will build you a *h*. 17.10
the *h* that is to be built 22.5
a *h* of rest for the ark 28.2
glory of the LORD filled. .*h* 2Chr 5.14
hid in the *h* of God, while 22.12
Joash. .restore the *h* of the LORD. 24.4
cleansed all the *h* of the LORD, 29.18
foundation of the *h* of. .LORD Ezra 3.11
this *h* was finished on 6.15
is the *h* of God forsaken?" Neh 13.11
procession to the *h* of God, Ps 42.4
olive tree in the *h* of God. 52.8
zeal for thy *h* has consumed me, 69.9
doorkeeper in the *h* of my God 84.10
planted in the *h* of the LORD, 92.13
"Let us go to the *h* of. .LORD!" 122.1
h shared with a contentious Prov 25.24
better to go to. .*h* of mourning Ecc 7.2
to the *h* of the God of Jacob; Isa 2.3
the *h* was filled with smoke. 6.4
weight of his father's *h*, 22.24
Set your *h* in order; for you 38.1
not enter the *h* of mourning, Jer 16.5
'This *h* shall be like Shiloh, 26.9
he burned the *h* of the LORD, 52.13
h was filled with the cloud, Ezek 10.4
fountain. .from the *h* of. .LORD Joel 3.18
while this *h* lies in ruins? Hag 1.4
my *h* that lies in ruins, while 1.9
'My *h*. .called a *h* of prayer'; Mt 21.13
h of. .ruler of the synagogue, Mk 5.38
enter a *h*, stay there until 6.10
'My *h*. .called a *h* of prayer 11.17
I must be in my Father's *h*?" Lk 2.49
like a man building a *h*, who 6.48
whatever *h* you enter, stay there 9.4
wages; do not go from *h* to *h*. 10.7
laid waste, and *h* falls upon *h*. 11.17
Behold, your *h* is forsaken. 13.35
'My *h* shall be a *h* of prayer'; 19.46
my Father's *h* a *h* of trade." Jn 2.16
in public and from *h* to *h*, Acts 20.20
with the church in their *h*, 1Cor 16.19
built goodly *h* and live in Deut 8.12
Most High does not dwell in *h* Acts 7.48

HOUSEHOLD — ER
her *h*. .clothed in scarlet. Prov 31.21
looks well to. .ways of her *h*, 31.27
foes. .those of his own *h*. Mt 10.36
believed, and all his *h*. Jn 4.53
be saved, you and your *h*." Acts 16.31
who are of the *h* of faith. Gal 6.10
the saints. .of Caesar's *h*. Phil 4.22
must manage his own *h* well, 1Tim 3.4
to behave in the *h* of God, 3.15
like a *h* who brings out of his Mt 13.52

HOUSETOP — S
live in a corner of the *h* Prov 21.9
who is on the *h* not go down Mt 24.17
let him. .on the *h* not go down, Mk 13.15
Peter went up on the *h* to Acts 10.9
whispered, proclaim upon the *h*. Mt 10.27
be proclaimed upon the *h*. Lk 12.3

HUMAN
stone. .cut out by no *h* hand, Dan 2.34
no *h* being will be justified Rom 3.20
not taught by *h* wisdom 1Cor 2.13
no *h*. .can tame the tongue— Jas 3.8

HUMBLE — S — D (v)
will you refuse to *h* yourself — Ex 10.3
that he might *h* you, testing — Deut 8.2
if my people..*h* themselves, — 2Chr 7.14
that we might *h* ourselves — Ezra 8.21
God will give ear, and *h* them, — Ps 55.19
my God may *h* me before you, — 2Cor 12.21
H yourselves before the Lord — Jas 4.10
H yourselves therefore under — 1Pet 5.6
Whoever *h* himself like..child, — Mt 18.4
whoever *h* himself will be — 23.12
who *h* himself will be exalted." — Lk 18.14
lay with her and *h* her. — Gen 34.2
uncircumcised heart is *h* — Lev 26.41
seen how Ahab has *h* himself — 1Ki 21.29
h yourself before the Lord, — 2Ki 22.19
and the king *h* themselves — 2Chr 12.6
few men of..Zebulun *h* — 30.11
But Hezekiah *h* himself for — 32.26
you *h* yourself before God — 34.27
eyes of the haughty are *h*. — Isa 5.15
They have not *h* themselves — Jer 44.10
you..Belshazzar, have not *h* — Dan 5.22
h yourself before your God, — 10.12
in human form he *h* himself — Phil 2.8

HUMBLE
Thou dost deliver a *h* — 2Sam 22.28
thou dost deliver a *h* people; — Ps 18.27
leads the *h* in what is right, — 25.9
he adorns the *h* with victory. — 149.4
of a contrite and *h* spirit, — Isa 57.15
Seek the Lord, all your *h* of — Zeph 2.3
leave..a people *h* and lowly. — 3.12
victorious is he, *h* and riding — Zech 9.9
your king is coming to you, *h*, — Mt 21.5
a tender heart and a *h* mind. — 1Pet 3.8

HUMILITY
and *h* goes before honor. — Prov 15.33
reward for *h* and fear of — 22.4
but in *h* count others better — Phil 2.3

HUNG
On..willows..*h* up our lyres. — Ps 137.2

HUNGER (v)
they shall not *h* or thirst, — Isa 49.10
h and thirst for righteousness, — Mt 5.6
"Blessed are you that *h* now, — Lk 6.21
who comes to me shall not *h*, — 6.35
To the present hour we *h* and — 1Cor 4.11
They shall *h* no more, neither — Rev 7.16

HUNGER (n)
young lions suffer want and *h*; — Ps 34.10
cistern; and he will die..of *h*, — Jer 38.9
your children, who faint for *h* — Lam 2.19
no more be consumed with *h* — Ezek 34.29
tumults, labors, watching, *h*; — 2Cor 6.5
in *h* and thirst, often — 11.27
of facing plenty and *h*, — Phil 4.12

HUNGRY
who were *h* have ceased to — 1Sam 2.5
"If I were *h*,..not tell you; — Ps 50.12
the *h* he fills with good — 107.9
if he steals..when he is *h*? — Prov 6.30
to one..*h*..bitter is sweet. — 27.7
greatly distressed and *h* and — Isa 8.21
returning to..city, he was *h*. — Mt 21.18
what David did, when he..*h*, — Mk 2.25
came from Bethany, he was *h*. — 11.12
filled the *h* with good things, — Lk 1.53
he became *h* and desired — Acts 10.10
is *h*, let him eat at home— — 1Cor 11.34

HUNT — ED
thou dost *h* me like a lion, — Job 10.16
let evil *h* down the violent — Ps 140.11
you *h* down souls belonging — Ezek 13.18
"Israel is a *h* sheep driven — Jer 50.17

HUNTER
Nimrod..mighty *h* before..Lord; — Gen 10.9
Esau was a skilful *h*, — 25.27

HURAM
Then *H* the king of Tyre — 2Chr 2.11

HURT
that it might not *h* me!" — 1Chr 4.10
man lords it over man to his *h*. — Ecc 8.9
They shall not *h* or destroy — Isa 11.9

HUSBAND — S — 'S
gave some to her *h*, and he ate. — Gen 3.6
and my *h* is old, shall I — 18.12
Her *h* is known in the gates, — Prov 31.23
For your Maker is your *h*, — Isa 54.5
broke, though I was their *h*, — Jer 31.32
father of Joseph the *h* of Mary, — Mt 1.16
"Go, call your *h*, and come — Jn 4.16
woman..bound by law to her *h* — Rom 7.2
and each woman her own *h*. — 1Cor 7.2
is consecrated through her *h*. — 7.14
affairs, how to please her *h*. — 7.34
see that she respects her *h*. — Eph 5.33
bishop..*h* of one wife, — 1Tim 3.2
with contempt upon their *h*, — Est 1.17
H, love your wives, as Christ — Eph 5.25
H, love your wives, and do — Col 3.19
you *h*, live considerately — 1Pet 3.7
h brother shall go in to her, — Deut 25.5

HYMN — S
And when they had sung a *h*, — Mt 26.30
And when they had sung a *h*, — Mk 14.26
each one has a *h*, a lesson, — 1Cor 14.26
one another in psalms and *h* — Eph 5.19
as you sing psalms and *h* — Col 3.16

HYPOCRISY
leaven of the Pharisees..is *h*. — Lk 12.1

HYPOCRITE — S
You *h*, first take the log out — Mt 7.5
no trumpet before you, as the *h* — 6.2
you must not be like the *h*; — 6.5
do not look dismal, like the *h*, — 6.16
You *h*! Well did Isaiah prophesy — 15.7
woe..scribes and Pharisees, *h*! — 23.13
"Woe..scribes and Pharisees, *h*! — 23.23
did Isaiah prophesy of you *h*, — Mk 7.6
"You *h*!..on the sabbath untie — Lk 13.15

HYSSOP
Take a bunch of *h* and dip it — Ex 12.22
Purge me with *h*, and I shall — Ps 51.7
sponge full of..vinegar on *h* — Jn 19.29

I

IDLE
But he said, "You are *i*, — Ex 5.17
he saw others standing *i* in — Mt 20.3

IDLENESS
brother who is living in *i* — 2Thess 3.6

IDOL — S
The *i*! a workman casts it, — Isa 40.19
lest you..say, 'My *i* did them, — 48.5
or that an *i* is anything? — 1Cor 10.19
shall make for yourselves no *i* — Lev 26.1

IDOL — S (cont.)

gods of the peoples are i;	1Chr 16.26
put away the abominable i	2Chr 15.8
those who pay regard to vain i;	Ps 31.6
sacrificed to the i of Canaan;	106.38
Their land is filled with i;	Isa 2.8
the i shall utterly pass away.	2.18
consult the i and..sorcerers,	19.3
All who make i are nothing,	44.9
and they are mad over i.	Jer 50.38
takes his i into his heart	Ezek 14.4
nor defile..with their i.	20.18
Ephraim is joined to i, let	Hos 4.17
made i for their own destruction.	8.4
all her i I will lay waste;	Mic 1.7
from the pollutions of i	Acts 15.20
the city was full of i.	17.16
sacrificed to i and from blood	21.25
concerning food offered to i:	1Cor 8.1
you turned to God from i,	1Thess 1.9
keep yourselves from i.	1Jn 5.21

IDOLATER — S

no..i), has any inheritance	Eph 5.5
nor i, nor adulterers, nor	1Cor 6.9

IGNORANCE

times of i God overlooked,	Acts 17.30
alienated..because of the i	Eph 4.18

IGNORANT

and i, I was like a beast	Ps 73.22
we do not want you to be i,	2Cor 1.8

ILL — NESS

"Lord, he whom you love is i."	Jn 11.3
why many..are weak and i,	1Cor 11.30
you heard that he was i.	Phil 2.26
in his i thou healest all his	Ps 41.3
"This i is not unto death;	Jn 11.4

ILL – TREATMENT

choosing rather to share i	Heb 11.25

IMAGE — S

"Let us make man in our i,	Gen 1.26
not make..yourself a graven i,	Ex 20.4
for yourself a graven i,	Deut 5.8
son, to make a graven i and	Judg 17.3
Danites set up the graven i	18.30
Michal took an i and laid	1Sam 19.13
O king, and behold, a great i.	Dan 2.31
since he is the i and glory	1Cor 11.7
the i of the invisible God,	Col 1.15
after the i of its creator.	3.10
destroy all their molten i,	Num 33.52
must make i of your tumors	1Sam 6.5
jealousy with their graven i.	Ps 78.58

IMAGINATION

every i..was only evil	Gen 6.5
the i of man's heart is evil	8.21

IMITATE — ING

Beloved, do not i evil but	3Jn 11
Brethren, join in i me, and	Phil 3.17

IMITATORS

I urge you, then, be i of me.	1Cor 4.16
Be i of me, as I am of Christ.	11.1
i of God, as beloved children.	Eph 5.1
you became i of us and of	1Thess 1.6
not..sluggish, but i of those	Heb 6.12

IMMANU-EL

and shall call his name I.	Isa 7.14
wings will fill..land, O I."	8.8

IMMORAL — ITY

neither the i, nor idolaters,	1Cor 6.9
reported..i among you,	5.1

IMMORTAL — ITY

exchanged the glory of..i God	Rom 1.23
mortal nature must put on i.	1Cor 15.53

IMPERISHABLE

sown..what is raised is i,	1Cor 15.42
to an inheritance which is i,	1Pet 1.4

IMPOSSIBLE

nothing..will now be i	Gen 11.6
with God nothing will be i."	Lk 1.37
it is i that..blood of bulls	Heb 10.4

IMPRISONED

enraged at Jeremiah,..i him	Jer 37.15
I i..those who believed	Acts 22.19

IMPRISONMENT — S

that i and afflictions await	Acts 20.23
that my i is for Christ;	Phil 1.13
Others suffered..chains and i.	Heb 11.36
beatings, i, tumults, labors,	2Cor 6.5
greater labors, far more i,	11.23

IMPULSE

no prophecy..by the i of man,	2Pet 1.21

IMPURITY

God gave them up..to i, to	Rom 1.24
have not repented of the i,	2Cor 12.21

IMPUTE — S

Let not the king i anything	1Sam 22.15
to whom the LORD i no iniquity,	Ps 32.2

INCENSE

make an altar to burn i upon;	Ex 30.1
make an i blended as by the	30.35
altar of i of acacia wood;	37.25
censer, and put i upon it,	Num 16.17
still sacrificed and burned i	2Ki 14.4
who burned i to Baal, to	23.5
to burn i on the altar of	2Chr 26.16
Let my prayer be counted as i	Ps 141.2
gods to whom they burn i,	Jer 11.12
smoke of..cloud of i went up.	Ezek 8.11
in every place i is offered	Mal 1.11
enter the temple..and burn i.	Lk 1.9

INCITED

and i David to number Israel.	1Chr 21.1
the Jews i the devout women	Acts 13.50

INCLINE — ING

that he may i our hearts	1Ki 8.58
I my heart to thy testimonies,	Ps 119.36
O my God, i thy ear and hear;	Dan 9.18
i your heart to understanding;	Prov 2.2

INCREASE — S — D (v)

Thou wilt i my honor, and	Ps 71.21
righteous man..i in learning.	Prov 9.9
When goods i, they i who eat	Ecc 5.11
He must i,..I must decrease."	Jn 3.30
may the Lord make you i	1Thess 3.12
speech i persuasiveness.	Prov 16.21
were fruitful and i greatly;	Ex 1.7
But thou hast i the nation,	Isa 26.15
Jesus i in wisdom and..stature,	Lk 2.52
they i in numbers daily.	Acts 16.5

INCREASE (n)

May the LORD give you i,	Ps 115.14
Of the i of his government	Isa 9.7
the earth shall yield its i,	Ezek 34.27

INCREDIBLE
Why is it thought *i* by any Acts 26.8
INDICATE — S
not to *i* the charges against Acts 25.27
By this the Holy Spirit *i* Heb 9.8
INDICTMENT
Oh, that I had the *i* written Job 31.35
LORD has an *i* against Judah, Hos 12.2
INDIGNANT
disciples saw it, they were *i*, Mt 26.8
when Jesus saw it he was *i*, Mk 10.14
to be *i* at James and John. 10.41
INDISPENSABLE
seem to be weaker are *i*, 1Cor 12.22
INDULGE
who *i* in the lust of defiling 2Pet 2.10
INFANTS
i will be dashed in pieces Isa 13.16
bringing even *i* to him that Lk 18.15
INFERIOR
I am not *i* to you. Who does Job 12.3
not..*i* to these..apostles, 2Cor 12.11
INFIRMITY — IES
you are freed from your *i*." Lk 13.12
in..illness thou healest all his *i*. Ps 41.3
INFORMED
things of which you have been *i*. Lk 1.4
Jews *i* him against Paul; Acts 25.2
you were once for all fully *i*, Jude 5
INHABITED
city shall be *i* for ever. Jer 17.25
INHABITS
lofty One who *i* eternity, Isa 57.15
INHERIT
'You shall *i* their land, Lev 20.24
You..*i* the land by lot Num 33.54
land..you shall *i* by lot, 34.13
the LORD will *i* Judah as his Zech 2.12
i the kingdom prepared for you Mt 25.34
must I do to *i* eternal life?" Mk 10.17
shall I do to *i* eternal life?" Lk 10.25
shall I do to *i* eternal life?" 18.18
that they should *i* the world, Rom 4.13
INHERITANCE
have no *i* in their land, Num 18.20
i to pass to his daughter. 27.8
gives..for an *i* to possess), Deut 15.4
Levi, shall have no..*i* with Israel; 18.1
cities..for an *i*, you shall save 20.16
possessions as an *i* to his sons, 21.16
are their *i*, as he said Josh 13.14
forbid that I..give you the *i* 1Ki 21.3
as your portion for an *i*." 1Chr 16.18
Canaan as your portion..an *i* Ps 105.11
A good man leaves an *i* to Prov 13.22
An *i* gotten hastily in the 20.21
Our *i* has been turned over to Lam 5.2
and this land..as your *i*. Ezek 47.14
thy people..the flock of thy *i*; Mic 7.14
and to give you the *i* among Acts 20.32
For if the *i* is by the law, Gal 3.18
the riches of his glorious *i* Eph 1.18
receive the *i* as your reward; Col 3.24
an *i* which is imperishable, 1Pet 1.4
INIQUITY — IES
visiting the *i* of the fathers Ex 34.7

house with you shall bear *i* Num 18.1
commits *i*, I will chasten 2Sam 7.14
if I have done *i*, I will do Job 34.32
If I had cherished *i* in my Ps 66.18
brought low through their *i*. Ps 106.43
laid on him the *i* of us all. Isa 53.6
into captivity for their *i*, Ezek 39.23
to redeem us from all *i* and Tit 2.14
for our *i* have risen higher Ezra 9.6
sins, and blot out all my *i*. Ps 51.9
The *i* of the wicked ensnare Prov 5.22
cleanse you from all your *i*, Ezek 36.33
INJUSTICE
do no *i* in judgment; Lev 19.15
sows *i* will reap calamity, Prov 22.8
and the city full of *i*; for Ezek 9.9
Is there *i* on God's part? Rom 9.14
INK
wrote..with *i* on the scroll." Jer 36.18
written not with *i* but with 2Cor 3.3
rather not use paper and *i*, 2Jn 12
INN
no place for them in the *i*. Lk 2.7
to an *i*, and took care of him. 10.34
INNOCENT — S
wilt thou slay an *i* people? Gen 20.4
purge the guilt of *i* blood Deut 19.13
acquitting the *i* and condemning 25.1
and lay not on us *i* blood; Jonah 1.14
filled Jerusalem with *i* blood, 2Ki 24.4
who that was *i* ever perished? Job 4.7
thou wilt not hold me *i*. 9.28
the *i* stirs himself up against 17.8
the *i* will divide the silver. 27.17
Job has said, 'I am *i*, and 34.5
I shall be blameless, and *i* of Ps 19.13
'I am *i*; surely his anger Jer 2.35
as serpents and *i* as doves. Mt 10.16
from the blood of *i* Abel to 23.35
"I am *i* of this man's blood; 27.24
"Certainly this man was *i*!" Lk 23.47
I am *i* of the blood of all Acts 20.26
filled..with the blood of *i*, Jer 19.4
INQUIRE — D
she went to *i* of the LORD. Gen 25.22
come to me to *i* of God; Ex 18.15
do not *i* about their gods, Deut 12.30
"Go, *i* of the LORD for me, 2Ki 22.13
"Go, *i* of the LORD for me 2Chr 34.21
"*I* of the LORD for us, for Jer 21.2
Is it to *i* of me that you come? Ezek 20.3
My people *i* of a thing of wood, Hos 4.12
and *i* of God, "Which of us Judg 20.18
And Saul *i* of God, "Shall I 1Sam 14.37
David *i* of the LORD, "Shall I go 23.2
David *i* of the LORD, "Shall I 2Sam 2.1
David *i* of the LORD, "Shall I 5.19
David *i* of God, "Shall I 1Chr 14.10
should I let myself be *i* of Ezek 14.3
INSCRIBED
Oh that they were *i* in a book! Job 19.23
hand was sent,..writing was *i*. Dan 5.24
is *i* in the book of truth: 10.21
INSCRIPTION
"Whose likeness and *i* is this?" Mt 22.20
"Whose likeness and *i* is this?" 12.16
the *i* of the charge against him 15.26
There was also an *i* over him, Lk 23.38

INSPIRED
All scripture is *i* by God   2Tim 3.16
INSPIRES
same God who *i* them all   1Cor 12.6
INSTRUCT — ED
Him will he *i* in the way that   Ps 25.12
I will *i* you and teach you   32.8
writings which are able to *i*   2Tim 3.15
who *i* him in the fear of God; 2Chr 26.5
Moses was *i* in all the wisdom Acts 7.22
Moses. .was *i* by God,   Heb 8.5
INSTRUCTION
He opens their ears to *i*,   Job 36.10
Take my *i* instead of silver,   Prov 8.10
those who murmur. .accept *i*." Isa 29.24
True *i* was in his mouth,   Mal 2.6
INSTRUMENT — S
he is a chosen *i* of mine to   Acts 9.15
play loudly on musical *i*,   1Chr 15.16
sing. .and invent. .*i* of music; Amos 6.5
INSULT — S (v)
brought. .a Hebrew to *i* us;   Gen 39.14
mocks the poor *i* his Maker;   Prov 17.5
INSULT — S (n)
the *i* of those who *i* thee have Ps 69.9
I have broken my heart, so   69.20
content with weaknesses, *i*,   2Cor 12.10
INTEGRITY
you still hold fast your *i*?   Job 2.9
and in your teaching show *i*,   Tit 2.7
INTERCEDE — S
man sins. .who can *i* for him?" 1Sam 2.25
let them *i* with the LORD   Jer 27.18
the Spirit himself *i* for us   Rom 8.26
INTERCESSION
made *i* for the transgressors. Isa 53.12
he always lives to make *i* for Heb 7.25
INTEREST
Take no *i* from him. .but fear Lev 25.36
Let us leave off this *i*.   Neh 5.10
not put out his money at *i*,   Ps 15.5
INTERMEDIARY
an *i* implies more than one;   Gal 3.20
INTERPRET — ED
i. .appearance of earth. .sky: Lk 12.56
each in turn; and let one *i*.   1Cor 14.27
he *i*. .concerning himself.   Lk 24.27
INTERPRETATION
dream, and we will show the *i*." Dan 2.4
we will tell the king its *i*.   2.36
O Belteshazzar, declare the *i*   4.18
Daniel. .he will show the *i*."   5.12
no prophecy. .one's own *i*,   2Pet 1.20
INTERPRETER
there was an *i* between them.   Gen 42.23
INVISIBLE
his *i* nature,. .his eternal   Rom 1.20
the image of the *i* God,   Col 1.15
King. .*i*, the only God,   1Tim 1.17
INVITED
Jesus also was *i* to. .marriage, Jn 2.2
who are *i* to the marriage   Rev 19.9
INVOKE — D
let the king *i* the LORD   2Sam 14.11
my name shall no more be *i* by Jer 44.26

IRON
Canaanites. .chariots of *i*,   Josh 17.16
a stick,. .made the *i* float.   2Ki 6.6
labor with saws and *i* picks   1Chr 20.3
his neck. .in a collar of *i*;   Ps 105.18
I sharpens *i*, and one man   Prov 27.17
in their place bars of *i*.   Jer 28.13
the *i*, the clay, the bronze,   Dan 2.35
IRONSMITH
The *i* fashions it and works   Isa 44.12
ISAAC
His birth foretold, Gen 18.1–15; born,
Gen 21.1–7; offered to God, Gen 22.1–19;
married Rebekah, Gen 24; father of twins,
Gen 25.19–26; dwelt in Gerar, Gen 26.1–
6; Isaac and Abimelech, Gen 26.7–33;
blessed Jacob, Gen 27.1–40; death and
burial, Gen 35.29.

son. .whom Sarah bore him, *I*. Gen 21.3
we,. .like *I*, are children of Gal 4.28
By faith *I* invoked future   Heb 11.20
ISAIAH
Called, Isa 6; father of two sons, Isa 7.3;
8.3; prophesied during the reign of Uzziah,
Jotham, Ahaz and Hezekiah, Isa 1.1;
counselled Ahaz, Isa 7; counselled Heze-
kiah, 2Ki 19—20 (Isa 37—39).

spoken of by the prophet *I*   Mt 3.3
Well did *I* prophesy of you,   15.7
the book of the prophet *I*.   Lk 4.17
he was reading the prophet *I*. Acts 8.28
ISHMAEL
you shall call his name *I*;   Gen 16.11
"O that *I* might live   17.18
the descendants of *I*,   25.12
ISRAEL
name. .no more. .Jacob, but *I*, Gen 32.28
sons of *I* who came to Egypt   Ex 1.1
I is my first-born son,   4.22
he pursued the people of *I*   14.8
after the people of *I* had gone 19.1
And the men of *I* did as Joshua Josh 4.8
Samuel judged the people of *I* 1Sam 7.6
Solomon was king over all *I*,   1Ki 4.1
So *I* has been in rebellion   12.19
"As the LORD. .God of *I* lives, 17.1
anointed king over all *I*,   1Chr 14.8
passover to the. .God of *I*.   2Chr 30.1
some of the people of *I*,   Ezra 7.7
Redeem *I*, O God, out of all   Ps 25.22
He made known. .his acts to. .*I*. 103.7
but *I* does not know, my people Isa 1.3
who will govern my people *I*.'" Mt 2.6
King of *I*; let him come down   27.42
for the consolation of *I*, and Lk 2.25
restore the kingdom to *I*?"   Acts 1.6
so all *I* will be saved; as   Rom 11.26
from the commonwealth of *I*,   Eph 2.12
new covenant with. .house of *I* Heb 8.8
tribes of the sons of *I* were   Rev 21.12
ISSACHAR
Leah. .called his name *I*.   Gen 30.18
I is a strong ass, crouching   49.14
The sons of *I* according   Num 26.23
thousand of the tribe of *I*,   Rev 7.7
IVORY
also made a great *i* throne,   1Ki 10.18

IVORY (cont.)

the *i* house which he built,	1Ki 22.39
From *i* palaces..instruments	Ps 45.8
the houses of *i* shall perish,	Amos 3.15
Woe to those..upon beds of *i*,	6.4

J

JABBOK

crossed the ford of the *J*.	Gen 32.22
far over as the river *J*,	Deut 3.16
the river *J*, the boundary of	Josh 12.2

JACOB (ISRAEL)

Born, Gen 25.19–26; obtained Esau's birthright, Gen 25.27–34; received Isaac's blessing, Gen 27.1–29; fled from Esau, Gen 27.41—28.5; dream at Bethel and his vow, Gen 28.10–22; served Laban for Rachel and Leah, Gen 29.1–30; dealings with Laban, Gen 30.25–43; departure from Paddan-aram, Gen 31; wrestled at Peniel, Gen 32.24–32; reconciled with Esau, Gen 33.1–16; blessed by God at Bethel, Gen 35.1–15; went down to Egypt, Gen 46—47; blessed Ephraim and Manasseh, Gen 48; blessed his own sons, Gen 49.1–27; death and burial, Gen 49.28—50.14.

star..come forth out of *J*,	Num 24.17
(*J* fled to the land of Aram,	Hos 12.12
and *J* in the kingdom of heaven,	Mt 8.11
written, "*J* I loved, but Esau	Rom 9.13
By faith *J*, when dying,	Heb 11.21
J well was there, and so Jesus	Jn 4.6

JAIRUS

one of..rulers of..synagogue, *J*	Mk 5.22
there came a man named *J*,	Lk 8.41

JAMES

he saw two other brothers, *J*	Mt 4.21
J the son of Alphaeus, and	10.3
Matthew, *J*..son of Alphaeus	Acts 1.13
Then he appeared to *J*, then	1Cor 15.7

JAPHETH

God enlarge *J*, and let	Gen 9.27

JAR — S

"The *j* of meal shall not be	1Ki 17.14
a man carrying a *j* of water	Mk 14.13
a man carrying a *j* of water	Lk 22.10
So the woman left her water *j*,	Jn 4.28
empty *j*, with torches inside	Judg 7.16

JAWBONE

found a fresh *j* of an ass,	Judg 15.15

JEALOUS

his brothers were *j* of him,	Gen 37.11
"Are you *j* for my sake?	Num 11.29
he was *j* for his God,	25.13
devouring fire, a *j* God.	Deut 4.24
I..your God am a *j* God,	5.9
Lord your God..is a *j* God;	6.15
he is a *j* God; he will not	Josh 24.19
Will..*j* wrath burn like fire?	Ps 79.5
When men..were *j* of Moses	106.16
I will be *j* for my holy name,	Ezek 39.25
Lord became *j* for his land,	Joel 2.18
Lord is a *j* God and avenging	Nah 1.2
j for Zion with great jealousy,	Zech 8.2
the patriarchs, *j* of Joseph,	Acts 7.9
Gentiles,..to make Israel *j*.	Rom 11.11
love is not *j* or boastful;	1Cor 13.4

JEALOUSY

if the spirit of *j* comes upon	Num 5.14
They have stirred me to *j*	Deut 32.21
provoked..to *j* with their sins	1Ki 14.22
For *j* makes a man furious,	Prov 6.34
j is cruel as the grave. Its	Sol 8.6
j of Ephraim shall depart,	Isa 11.13
I, the Lord,..spoken in my *j*,	Ezek 5.13
the seat of the image of *j*,	8.3
while there is *j* and strife	1Cor 3.3
I feel a divine *j* for you,	2Cor 11.2

JEHOSHAPHAT

and *J* his son reigned in his	1Ki 15.24
But *J* said, "Is there not	22.7
the Me-unites, came against *J*	2Chr 20.1
the realm of *J* was quiet,	20.30
J slept with his fathers,	21.1
down to the valley of *J*,	Joel 3.2

JEPHTHAH

J..was a mighty warrior	Judg 11.1
J made a vow to the Lord,	11.30
to *J*, "Why did you cross	12.1
Lord sent..*J*, and Samuel	1Sam 12.11
Samson, *J*, of David and	Heb 11.32

JEREMIAH

Called, Jer 1.1–10; vision of almond rod and boiling pot, Jer 1.11–19; sign of the waistcloth, Jer 13.1–11; sign of the potter's vessel, Jer 18; sign of the earthen flask, Jer 19; put in stocks, Jer 20.1–6; sign of the basket of figs, Jer 24; his life threatened, Jer 26; sign of purchase of field, Jer 32.6–44; prophesied to Rechabites, Jer 35; wrote prophecies, Jer 36; imprisoned, Jer 32.1–5; 37.11—38.28; released, Jer 39.11–14; 40.1–6; taken into Egypt, Jer 43.1–7.

others say Elijah,..others *J*	Mt 16.14

JERICHO

view the land, especially *J*."	Josh 2.1
I have given into your hand *J*,	6.2
Hiel of Bethel built *J*;	1Ki 16.34
leaving *J* with his disciples	Mk 10.46
By faith the walls of *J* fell	Heb 11.30

JEROBOAM

J..also lifted up his hand	1Ki 11.26
when *J* the son of Nebat heard	12.2
Then *J* built Shechem in the	12.25
J was standing by the altar	13.1
Abijah..son of *J* fell sick.	14.1
J reigned..twenty-two years;	14.20
war between Rehoboam and *J*	14.30
Nadab the son of *J* began to	15.25
walked in..way of *J* and in his sin	15.34
J the son of Joash, king of	2Ki 14.23
the rest of the acts of *J*,	14.28
J slept with his fathers,	14.29
in the days of *J* the son of	Hos 1.1
priest of Bethel sent to *J*	Amos 7.10

JERUSALEM

opposite Jebus (that is, *J*).	Judg 19.10
at *J* he reigned over all	2Sam 5.5
"In *J* will I put my name."	2Ki 21.4
to *J*, with harps and lyres	2Chr 20.28
broke down the wall of *J*,	36.19
build him a house at *J*,	36.23
in the second year..at *J*,	Ezra 3.8
pleasure; rebuild..walls of *J*,	Ps 51.18
Pray for the peace of *J*! "May	122.6

JERUSALEM (cont.)

If I forget you, O *J*, let my	Ps 137.5
LORD of hosts will protect *J*;	Isa 31.5
O *J*, herald of good tidings,	40.9
"O *J*, *J*, killing the prophets	Mt 23.37
witnesses in *J* and in..Judea	Acts 1.8
appointed to go up to *J* to	15.2
poor among the saints at *J*;	Rom 15.26
But the *J* above is free,	Gal 4.26
city of..God, the heavenly *J*,	Heb 12.22
new *J*, coming down out of	Rev 21.2

JESUS

His birth foretold, Lk 1.26–38; born, Mt 1.18–25; Lk 2.1–7; circumcised, Lk 2.21; presented in the temple, Lk 2.22–38; visited by the wise men, Mt 2.1–12; fled to Egypt, Mt 2.13–18; brought to Nazareth, Mt 2.19–23 (Lk 2.39); boyhood visit to Jerusalem, Lk 2.41–50; his brothers and sisters, Mt 13.55–56 (Mk 6.3); baptized, Mt 3.13–17 (Mk 1.9–11; Lk 3.21–22; Jn 1.31–34); tempted by the devil, Mt 4.1–11 (Mk 1.12–13; Lk 4.1–13); called his disciples, Mt 4.18–22 (Mk 1.16–20; Lk 5.1–11); Mt 9.9 (Mk 2.13–14; Lk 5.27–28); Jn 1.35–51; commissioned the twelve, Mt 10.1–4 (Mk 3.13–19; Lk 6.12–16); Sermon on the Mount, Mt 5—7 (Lk 6.17–49); sent out disciples, Mt 9.35—11.1 (Mk 6.7–13; Lk 9.1–6; 10.1–24); foretold his death and resurrection, Mt 16.21–28 (Mk 8.31–38; Lk 9.22–27); Mt 17.22–23 (Mk 9.30–32; Lk 9.43–45); Mt 20.17–28 (Mk 10.32–45; Lk 18.31–34); transfigured, Mt 17.1–8 (Mk 9.2–8; Lk 9.28–36); triumphal entry into Jerusalem, Mt 21.1–11 (Mk 11.1–11; Lk 19.29–44; Jn 12.12–19); instituted the Lord's supper, Mt 26.26–29 (Mk 14.22–25; Lk 22.17–20; 1Cor 11.23–26); betrayed, arrested, and forsaken, Mt 26.47–57 (Mk 14.43–53; Lk 22.47–54; Jn 18.2–13); crucified, Mt 27.31–56 (Mk 15.20–41; Lk 23.26–49; Jn 19.16–30); appeared after his resurrection, Mt 28.9–20 (Mk 16.9–18n; Lk 24.13–49; Jn 20.11–31); Acts 1.3–8; 1Cor 15.5–7; ascended to heaven, Lk 24.50–53 (Mk 16.19n); Acts 1.9–11.

JETHRO

flock of his father-in-law, *J*	Ex 3.1
Moses went back to *J*	4.18
J, the priest of Midian,	18.1
J, Moses' father-in-law,	18.12

JEW — S

there was a *J* in Susa the	Est 2.5
the *J* who came up from you	Ezra 4.12
asked them concerning the *J*	Neh 1.2
in the presence of all the *J*	Jer 32.12
and maliciously accused the *J*.	Dan 3.8
"Where is he..born king of..*J*?	Mt 2.2
"Are you the King of the *J*?"	27.11
Jesus the King of the *J*."	27.37
J were..seeking to stone you,	Jn 11.8
officers of the *J* seized Jesus	18.12
testifying to the *J* that	Acts 18.5
heard..both *J* and Greeks.	19.10
both *J* and Greeks, are under	Rom 3.9
called, not from the *J* only	9.24
For *J* demand signs and Greeks	1Cor 1.22

To the *J* I became a *J*,	9.20
Give no offense to *J* or to	10.32

JEWEL — S

the..*j* of a gentle..spirit,	1Pet 3.4
for wisdom is better than *j*,	Prov 8.11

JEWELRY

servant brought forth *j*	Gen 24.53
j of silver and of gold,	Ex 3.22

JEZREEL

Its territory included *J*,	Josh 19.18
vineyard in *J*, beside the	1Ki 21.1
punish..Jehu for..blood of *J*,	Hos 1.4
oil, and they shall answer *J*;	2.22

JOAB

Murdered Abner, 2Sam 3.22–30; set Uriah in the forefront, 2Sam 11.6–21; reconciled David and Absalom, 2Sam 14.28–33; killed Absalom, 2Sam 18.9–17; pursued Sheba and slew Amasa, 2Sam 20.4–22; put to death by Solomon, 1Ki 2.28–34.

JOB

whose name was *J*; and that	Job 1.1
you considered my servant *J*,	2.3
go to my servant *J*, and offer	42.8
LORD restored..fortunes of *J*,	42.10
And *J* died, an old man,	42.17
even if..Noah, Daniel, and *J*	Ezek 14.14
heard of..steadfastness of *J*,	Jas 5.11

JOEL

word of the LORD..came to *J*,	Joel 1.1
was spoken by the prophet *J*:	Acts 2.16

JOHN (the Apostle)

Called, Mt 4.21 (Mk 1.19; Lk 5.10); sent out with the twelve, Mt 10.2 (Mk 3.17); desire for revenge rebuked, Lk 9.51–56; selfish request rejected, Mt 20.20–24 (Mk 10.35–41); healed and preached in the temple, Acts 3.1—4.22.

JOHN (the Baptist)

Birth foretold, Lk 1.5–25; born, Lk 1.57–66; preached and baptized, Mt 3.1–12 (Mk 1.4–11; Lk 3.1–17; Jn 1.6–8, 19–28); imprisoned, Mt 14.3–4 (Mk 6.17–18; Lk 3.19–20); sent messengers to Jesus, Mt 11.1–6 (Lk 7.18–23); commended by Jesus, Mt 11.7–15 (Lk 7.24–35); beheaded and buried, Mt 14.6–12 (Mk 6.17–29).

JOIN — ED

many shall *j*..with flattery;	Dan 11.34
nations shall *j*..to the LORD	Zech 2.11
people *j* in the covenant.	2Ki 23.3
leave..and be *j* to his wife,	Mt 19.5
What..God has *j* together,	19.6
mother and be *j* to his wife,	Mk 10.7
What..God has *j* together,	10.9

JONAH

he spoke by his servant *J*	2Ki 14.25
word of the LORD came to *J*	Jonah 1.1
Then *J* prayed to the LORD	2.1
word of the LORD came to *J*	3.1
it displeased *J* exceedingly,	4.1
as *J* was three days and three	Mt 12.40
no sign..except the sign of *J*."	16.4
J became a sign to..Ninevah,	Lk 11.30
repented at the preaching of *J*,	11.32

JONATHAN (Son of Saul)

Smote the Philistine garrison, 1Sam 13.2–

JONATHAN (Son of Saul) (cont.)
4; 14.1–15; unknowingly transgressed Saul's oath, 1Sam 14.24–30; rescued by the people, 1Sam 14.36–46; made a covenant with David, 1Sam 18.1–5; friendship with David, 1Sam 20; killed by the Philistines, 1Sam 31.2; mourned by David, 2Sam 1.17–27; covenant with him remembered by David, 2Sam 9.

JOPPA
to you in rafts by sea to J,	2Chr 2.16
went..to J and found a ship	Jonah 1.3
at J a disciple..Tabitha,	Acts 9.36
send men to J, and bring	10.5

JORDAN
J valley was well watered	Gen 13.10
all Israel beyond the J	Deut 1.1
I should not cross the J,	4.21
finished passing over the J,	Josh 4.1
king came back to the J;	2Sam 19.15
wash in the J seven times,	2Ki 5.10
confident though J rushes	Job 40.23
from the land of J and of	Ps 42.6
Jesus came from Galilee to the J	Mt 3.1
they were baptized..in the..J,	3.6
region of Judea beyond the J;	19.1
who was with you beyond the J,	Jn 3.26
across the J to the place	10.40

JOSEPH (Husband of Mary, Jesus' mother)
Betrothed to Mary, Mk 1.18 (Lk 1.27); instructed by an angel, Mt 1.19–21; went to Bethlehem, Lk 2.4; fled into Egypt, Mt 2.13–15; returned to Nazareth, Mt 2.19–23.

JOSEPH (of Arimathea)
| man from Arimathea, named J, | Mt 27.57 |
| After this J of Arimathea, | Jn 19.38 |

JOSEPH (Son of Jacob)
Born, Gen 30.22–24; incurred jealousy by his dreams, Gen 37.5–11; sold into Egypt, Gen 37.12–28; refused Potiphar's wife, Gen 39.1–18; imprisoned, Gen 39.19–23; interpreted the prisoners' dreams, Gen 40; interpreted Pharaoh's dreams, Gen 41.1–36; made ruler over Egypt, Gen 41.37–49, 53–57; married, had two sons, Gen 41.50–52; met his brothers, Gen 42–43; made himself known to them, Gen 45; saw his father again, Gen 46.28–34; died, Gen 50.22–26; buried in Shechem, Josh 24.32.

And of J he said, "Blessed	Deut 33.13
sent a man ahead of them,	Ps 105.17
By faith J, at..end of his life,	Heb 11.22

JOSHUA (Priest, son of Jehozadak)
and to J the son of Jehozadak,	Hag 1.1
and to J the son of Jehozadak,	2.2
he showed me J the high priest	Zech 3.1
set it upon the head of J,	6.11

JOSHUA (Son of Nun)
Defeated the Amalekites, Ex 17.8–13; in charge of the place of worship, Ex 33.11; sent with the spies, Num 13.1–16; 14.6–9; chosen to succeed Moses, Num 27.18–23; Deut 3.28; commissioned by Moses, Deut 31.23; 34.9; encouraged by the LORD, Josh 1.1–9; sent spies to Jericho, Josh 2; passed over Jordan, Josh 3; captured Jericho, Josh 6; captured Ai, Josh 7—8; warred against the kings, Josh 10—12;

allotted the land, Josh 13.1—22.8; charged the people, Josh 23.1—24.24; made a covenant, Josh 24.25–27; death and burial, Josh 24.29–30.

JOSIAH
born to the house of David, J	1Ki 13.2
made J his son king in his	2Ki 21.24
J was eight years old when	22.1
year of King J this passover	23.23
J kept a passover to the	2Chr 35.1

JOY
to Jerusalem with j, for	2Chr 20.27
j of the LORD is:.strength."	Neh 8.10
Thou hast put more j in my	Ps 4.7
to God my exceeding j;..praise	43.4
Shout to God with..songs of j!	47.1
works of thy hands I sing for j.	92.4
let the hills sing for j	98.8
no stranger shares its j.	Prov 14.10
rejoice..with j at the harvest,	Isa 9.3
With j you will draw water	12.3
shall obtain j and gladness,	35.10
j and gladness..found in her,	51.3
"For you shall go out in j,	55.12
majestic..a j from age to age.	60.15
you will have j and gladness,	Lk 1.14
good news of a great j which	2.10
this j of mine is now full.	Jn 3.29
that my j may be in you, and	15.11
your sorrow will turn into j.	16.20
they may have my j fulfilled	17.13
there was much j in that city.	Acts 8.8
great j to all the brethren.	15.3
and j in the Holy Spirit;	Rom 14.17
j and peace in believing,	15.13
work with you for your j,	2Cor 1.24
rejoiced..at the j of Titus,	7.13
I have derived much j and	Philem 7
writing that our j may	1Jn 1.4

JUBILEE
| it shall be a j for you, | Lev 25.10 |
| when the j of..Israel comes, | Num 36.4 |

JUDAH (Son of Jacob)
Born, Gen 29.35; saved Joseph's life, Gen 37.26–28; Judah and Tamar, Gen 38; pleaded for Benjamin, Gen 44.14–34; blessed by Jacob, Gen 49.8–12.
Tribe of Judah: blessed by Moses, Deut 33.7.

And the LORD was with J,	Judg 1.19
Israel and J loved David;	1Sam 18.16
Israel and J thirty-three years.	2Sam 5.5
but he chose the tribe of J,	Ps 78.68
men of J, judge, I pray you,	Isa 5.3
fear not; say to the cities of J,	40.9
and her false sister J saw it.	Jer 3.7
year of Zedekiah king of J,	39.1
J has gone into exile because	Lam 1.3
I restore the fortunes of J	Joel 3.1

JUDAISM
| converts to J followed Paul | Acts 13.43 |
| head of my former life in J, | Gal 1.13 |

JUDAS (Brother of James)
| brother of James and Joses and J | Mk 6.3 |

JUDAS ISCARIOT
and J, who betrayed him.	Mt 10.4
J.., went to the chief priests	26.14
J, who betrayed him, said,	26.25
When J.. saw he was condemned,	27.3

JUDAS ISCARIOT (cont.)
and J.., who betrayed him.	Mk 3.19
Then Satan entered into J	Lk 22.3
"J, would you betray the Son	22.48
He spoke of J the son of Simon	Jn 6.71
But J.., one of his disciples	12.4
put it into the heart of J..,	13.2
concerning J who was guide	Acts 1.16

JUDE
J, a servant of Jesus Christ	Jude 1

JUDEA
Jesus was born in Bethlehem of J	Mt 2.1
preaching in the wilderness of J,	3.1
let those who are in J flee	Lk 21.21
"Men of J and all who dwell	Acts 2.14

JUDGE — S — ST — D (v)
God..j between us."	Gen 31.53
Moses sat to j the people,	Ex 18.13
congregation shall j between	Num 35.24
and j righteously between	Deut 1.16
The LORD will j the ends of	1Sam 2.10
May the LORD j between me	24.12
he comes to j the earth.	1Chr 16.33
for you j not for man but	2Chr 19.6
May he j..with righteousness,	Ps 72.2
set time..I will j with equity.	75.2
LORD..comes to j the earth.	96.13
He shall j between the nations,	Isa 2.4
with righteousness he shall j	11.4
j you according to your ways;	Ezek 7.3
"J not, that you be not j.	Mt 7.1
"J not, and you will not be j;	Lk 6.37
why..not j..what is right?	12.57
Do not j by appearances,	Jn 7.24
"Does our law j a man without	7.51
You j according to the flesh,	8.15
day on which he will j the	Acts 17.31
no excuse,..when you j another;	Rom 2.1
how could God j the world?	3.6
church whom you are to j?	1Cor 5.12
the saints will j the world?	6.2
know that we are to j angels?	6.3
ready to j..living and..dead.	1Pet 4.5
how long before thou wilt j	Rev 6.10
j the world with righteousness,	Ps 9.8
is a God who j on earth."	58.11
king j the poor with equity	Prov 29.14
when..God j the secrets of men	Rom 2.16
in righteousness he j and	Rev 19.11
O LORD..who j righteously,	Jer 11.20
conduct and their deeds I j	Ezek 36.19
small thing..I..j by you	1Cor 4.3
But if we j ourselves truly,	11.31
be j under the law of liberty.	Jas 2.12
dead. j by what was written	Rev 20.12

JUDGE — S (n)
Shall not the J of all	Gen 18.25
he would play the j!	19.9
you a prince and a j over us?	Ex 2.14
LORD, the J, decide this day	Judg 11.27
lest he drag you to the j,	Lk 12.58
a j who neither feared God	18.2
'Who made you..a j over us?	Acts 7.27
LORD raised up j for them,	Judg 2.18

JUDGMENT — S
I will bring j on the nation	Gen 15.14
my God; thou hast appointed a j.	Ps 7.6
but it is God who executes j,	75.7
God will bring you into j.	Ecc 11.9
the rash will have good j,	Isa 32.4

he is entering into j with	Jer 25.31
Thus far is the j on Moab.	48.47
my four sore acts of j,	Ezek 14.21
I entered into j with your fathers	20.36
and j was given for the saints	Dan 7.22
my j goes forth as the light.	Hos 6.5
I will enter into j with them	Joel 3.2
kills shall be liable to j.'	Mt 5.21
Nineveh will arise at the j	Lk 11.32
has given all j to the Son,	Jn 5.22
Now is the j of this world,	12.31
of righteousness and of j:	16.8
the j following one trespass	Rom 5.16
let not him who abstains pass j	14.3
all stand before the j seat	14.10
Why..pass j on your brother?	14.10
and drinks j upon himself.	1Cor 11.29
all appear before the j seat	2Cor 5.10
let no one pass j on you in	Col 2.16
to execute j on all, and to	Jude 15
God has given j for you	Rev 18.20
I will utter my j against them,	Jer 1.16
I execute j on you in anger	Ezek 5.15
Render true j, show kindness	Zech 7.9
How unsearchable are his j	Rom 11.33

JUST
You shall have j balances,	Lev 19.36
j weight you shall have,	Deut 25.15
j and right is he.	32.4
God of Israel, thou art j,	Ezra 9.15
Yet thou hast been j in all	Neh 9.33
can a man be j before God?	Job 9.2
A j balance and scales are	Prov 16.11
way of the Lord is not j.'	Ezek 18.25
"You shall have j balances,	45.10
husband Joseph, being a j man	Mt 1.19
rain on the j and on the unjust.	5.45
in order that the j requirement	Rom 8.4
law is not laid down for the j	1Tim 1.9
heard..angel..say, "J art thou	Rev 16.5

JUSTICE
Almighty will not pervert j.	Job 34.12
j to the weak and..fatherless;	Ps 82.3
receive instruction in..j,	Prov 1.3
in..place of j,..wickedness.	Ecc 3.16
Thus says the LORD: "Keep j,	Isa 56.1
look for j, but there is none;	59.11
let j roll down like waters,	Amos 5.24
and j never goes forth.	Hab 1.4
as he argued about j and	Acts 24.25
serves to show the j of God,	Rom 3.5

JUSTIFICATION
put to death..raised for our j.	Rom 4.25
if j were through the law,	Gal 2.21

JUSTIFY — IES — IED
desiring to j himself, said	Lk 10.29
He who j the wicked and he	Prov 17.15
he j him who has faith in	Rom 3.26
thou art j in thy sentence	Ps 51.4
by your words you will be j,	Mt 12.37
and the tax collectors j God,	Lk 7.29
this man..j rather than the other;	18.14
no human being will be j in	Rom 3.20
they are j by his grace as a gift,	3.24
For if Abraham was j by works,	4.2
you were j in the name of	1Cor 6.11
a man is not j by works of	Gal 2.16
that we might be j by faith.	3.24
that we might be j by his grace	Tit 3.7
Abraham our father j by works,	Jas 2.21

K

KADESH

Enmishpat (that is, K),   Gen 14.7
Moses sent messengers from K   Num 20.14
LORD shakes. . wilderness of K.   Ps 29.8

KADESH-BARNEA

sent. . from K to see the land.   Num 32.8
time from. . leaving K until   Deut 2.14
defeated them from K to   Josh 10.41

KEEP — S — ING

k alive for you many survivors.   Gen 45.7
you shall k this service   Ex 13.5
The LORD bless you and k you: Num 6.24
K them and do them; for that   Deut 4.6
and to k his commandments,   Josh 22.5
and k my commandments and   2Ki 17.13
"K the passover to the LORD   23.21
we k the charge of the LORD   2Chr 13.11
to k the passover to the LORD   30.1
for those who k his covenant   Ps 25.10
I remember. . and k thy law.   119.55
LORD will k you from all evil;   121.7
If your sons k my covenant   132.12
K your heart with. . vigilance.   Prov 4.23
eyes of the LORD k watch   22.12
For Zion's sake. . not k silent,   Isa 62.1
enter life, k. . commandments."   Mt 19.17
Father, k them in thy name,   Jn 17.11
uncircumcised but k the law   Rom 2.27
will k your hearts and. . minds   Phil 4.7
k yourselves in the love of God;   Jude 21
able to k you from falling   24
He who k his mouth and his   Prov 21.23
who k the law is a wise son,   28.7
blessed is he who k the law.   29.18
who k my works until the end,   Rev 2.26
k all the words of this law   Deut 17.19

KEEPER

am I my brother's k?"   Gen 4.9
I, the LORD, am its k; every   Isa 27.3

KEPT

And they k the passover   Num 9.5
the LORD has k me alive,   Josh 14.10
have you not k your oath   1Ki 2.43
our fathers have not k the   2Chr 34.21
precepts to be k diligently.   Ps 119.4
k. . and given you as a covenant   Isa 49.8
race, I have k the faith.   2Tim 4.7
and k for Jesus Christ: Jude 1
k by him in eternal chains   6
Because you have k my word   Rev 3.10

KEY — S

the k of the house of David;   Isa 22.22
taken away. . k of knowledge;   Lk 11.52
one, who has the k of David,   Rev 3.7
the k of the bottomless pit   20.1
give you the k of the kingdom   Mt 16.19
I have. . k of Death and Hades.   Rev 1.18

KILL — S — ED — ING

if. . a son, you shall k him;   Ex 1.16
Do you mean to k me as you   2.14
"You shall not k.   20.13
deal thus with me, k me   Num 11.15
Now therefore, k every male   31.17
" 'You shall not k.   Deut 5.17
k the body but cannot k the soul;   Mt 10.28
Jesus said, "You shall not k,   19.18
the heir; come, let us k him   21.38

and scourge him, and k him;   Mk 10.34
do not fear those who k the   Lk 12.4
Jews sought all the more to k   Jn 5.18
'Rise, Peter; k and eat.'   Acts 11.7
whoever k shall be liable to   Mt 5.21
Cain rose up. . and k him.   Gen 4.8
he k the Egyptian and hid   Ex 2.12
"Have you k, and also taken   1Ki 21.19
and be rejected. . and be k,   Mk 8.31
of the vineyard and k him.   Lk 20.15
k by the hands of lawless men.   Acts 2.23
Antipas. . was k among you,   Rev 2.13
"O. . Jerusalem, k the prophets   Mt 23.37

KIN

one of our nearest k."   Ruth 2.20
for you are next of k."   3.9
this day without next of k;   4.14

KIND — LY

who is k benefits himself,   Prov 11.17
happy. . who is k to the poor.   14.21
who is k to the poor lends   19.17
and be k to one another,   Eph 4.32
as I have dealt k with you,   Josh 2.12
not be quarrelsome but k   2Tim 2.24

KINDNESS

great k in saving my life;   Gen 19.19
made this last k greater   Ruth 3.10
him k for Jonathan's sake?"   2Sam 9.1
who withholds k from a friend   Job 6.4
show k and mercy each to his   Zech 7.9
God's k is meant to lead you   Rom 2.4
the k and. . severity of God: 11.22
goodness and loving k of God   Tit 3.4
tasted the k of the Lord.   1Pet 2.3

KING — S — 'S

the k of Egypt died.   Ex 2.23
'I will set a k over me,   Deut 17.14
there was no k in Israel;   Judg 18.1
there was no k in Israel!   21.25
will give strength to his k,   1Sam 2.10
appoint for us a k to govern   8.5
shouted, "Long live the k!"   10.24
they made Saul k before the LORD   11.15
LORD your God was your k.   12.12
you shall be k over Israel,   23.17
about bringing the k back?"   2Sam19.10
they proclaimed him k, and   2Ki 11.12
he is k over. . sons of pride."   Job 41.34
"I have set my k on Zion, my   Ps 2.6
Hearken. . sound of my cry, my K   5.2
The LORD is k for ever and   10.16
the K of glory may come in.   24.7
Thou art my K and my God, who   44.4
Give the k thy justice, O God,   72.1
let. . Zion rejoice in their K!   149.2
the word of the k is supreme,   Ecc 8.4
Woe. . when your k is a child,   10.16
k will reign in righteousness,   Isa 32.1
Creator of Israel, your K."   43.15
Who would not fear thee, O K   Jer 10.7
k who sits on. . throne of David,   29.16
David their k,. . I will raise up   30.9
sleep and not wake, says the K,   51.57
the Chaldeans said to the k,   Dan 2.4
You, O k, the k of k, to whom   2.37
their God, and David their k;   Hos 3.5
Their k will pass on before   Mic 2.13
Lo, your k comes to you;   Zech 9.9
a k who gave a marriage feast   Mt 22.2
the k will say to those at his   25.34
"Blessed is the K who comes   Lk 19.38

KING — S — 'S (cont.)

"Are you the *K* of the Jews?" Lk 23.3
You are the *K* of Israel!" Jn 1.49
to make him *k*, Jesus withdrew 6.15
Lord, even the *K* of Israel!" 12.13
"You say that I am a *k*. For 18.37
to the Jews, "Here is your *K*!" 19.14
k who had not known Joseph. Acts 7.18
there is another *k*, Jesus." 17.7
I am accused by Jews, O *k*! 26.7
To the *K* of ages, immortal, 1Tim 1.17
as *k*..the angel of the..pit; Rev 9.11
name inscribed, *K* of *k* and Lord 19.16
fear..*k* of..earth thy glory. Ps 102.15
By me *k* reign, and rulers Prov 8.15
It is not for *k*, O Lemuel, 31.4
four great beasts are four *k* Dan 7.17
Without us you have become *k*! 1Cor 4.8
for *k* and all who are in high 1Tim 2.2
way for the *k* from the east. Rev 16.12
he brought out the *k* son, 2Chr 23.11
The *k* heart is a stream of Prov 21.1

KINGDOM — S

you shall be to me a *k* of priests Ex 19.6
about the matter of the *k*, 1Sam 10.16
your *k* shall not continue; 13.14
I will establish his *k*. 2Sam 7.12
and I will establish his *k*. 1Chr 17.11
thine is the *k*, O Lord, 29.11
come to the *k* for such a time Est 4.14
glorious splendor of thy *k*. Ps 145.12
throne of David, and..his *k*, Isa 9.7
His *k* is an everlasting *k*, Dan 4.3
the Most High rules the *k* of 4.17
The *k* has departed from you, 4.31
the *k* and the dominion and 7.27
k shall be broken and divided 11.4
the *k* shall be the Lord's. Obad 1.21
the *k* of heaven is at hand." Mt 3.2
"Repent, for the *k* of heaven 4.17
preaching the gospel of the *k* 4.23
But seek first his *k* and his 6.33
and Jacob in the *k* of heaven, 8.11
'The *k* of heaven is at hand.' 10.7
never enter the *k* of heaven. 18.3
to such belongs the *k* of heaven." 19.14
k of God will be taken away 21.43
and *k* against *k* and there will 24.7
inherit the *k* prepared for you 25.34
with you in my Father's *k*." 26.29
k of God is at hand; repent, Mk 1.15
"The *k* of God is as if a man 4.26
before they see the *k* of God 9.1
Blessed is the *k* of our father 11.10
"You are not far from the *k* 12.34
nation, and *k* against *k*; 13.8
when I drink it new in the *k* 14.25
preach the good news of the *k* Lk 4.43
to know the secrets of the *k* 8.10
spoke to them of the *k* of God, 9.11
looks back is fit for the *k* 9.62
'The *k* of God has come near 10.9
"Every *k* divided against itself 11.17
seek his *k*, and these things 12.31
good news of the *k* of God 16.16
the *k* of God is in the midst 17.21
to such belongs the *k* of God. 18.16
for the sake of the *k* of God, 18.29
nation, and *k* against *k*; 21.10
know that the *k* of God is near. 21.31
as my Father appointed a *k* 22.29
he cannot enter the *k* of God. Jn 3.5

restore the *k* to Israel?" Acts 1.6
must enter the *k* of God. 14.22
pleading about the *k* of God; 19.8
testifying to the *k* of God 28.23
the *k* of God does not mean Rom 14.17
the *k* of God does not consist 1Cor 4.20
will inherit the *k* of God. 6.10
when he delivers the *k* to God 15.24
cannot inherit the *k* of God, 15.50
inheritance in the *k* of Christ Eph 5.5
worthy of the *k* of God, 2Thess 1.5
a *k* that cannot be shaken, Heb 12.28
entrance into the eternal *k* 2Pet 1.11
made us a *k*, priests to his God Rev 1.6
"The *k* of the world has become 11.15
four *k*..arise from his nation, Dan 8.22
overthrow the throne of *k*; Hag 2.22
showed him..the *k* of the world Mt 4.8
the devil..showed him all the *k* Lk 4.5

KINSMEN

no strife..for we are *k*. Gen 13.8
You are my *k*, you are my 2Sam 19.12
not go up..against your *k* 1Ki 12.24
and my *k* stand afar off. Ps 38.11

KISHON

The torrent *K* swept them Judg 5.21

KISS — ES — ED (v)

k his feet, lest he be angry, Ps 2.12
righteousness and peace will *k* 85.10
O that you would *k* me with Sol 1.2
Sacrifice..Men *k* calves! Hos 13.2
"The one I shall *k* is the man; Mt 26.48
"The one I shall *k* is the man; Mk 14.44
drew near to Jesus to *k* him; Lk 22.47
She seizes him and *k* him, Prov 7.13
a right answer *k* the lips. 24.26
Jacob *k* Rachel, and wept Gen 29.11
Esau ran..and *k* him, 33.4
he *k* all his brothers 45.15
Joseph..*k*..and embraced them. 48.10
Orpah *k* her mother-in-law, Ruth 1.14
and they *k* one another, 1Sam 20.41
and the king *k* Absalom. 2Sam 14.33
and embraced him and *k* him. Lk 15.20
embraced Paul and *k* him, Acts 20.37

KISS (n)

You gave me no *k*, but from Lk 7.45
Greet..with a holy *k*. Rom 16.16
one another with a holy *k*. 1Cor 16.20
Greet one another with the *k* 1Pet 5.14

KNEE — S

"To me every *k* shall bow, Isa 45.23
every *k* shall bow to me, Rom 14.11
the *k* that have not bowed 1Ki 19.18
fell upon my *k* and spread Ezra 9.5
upon his *k* three times a day Dan 6.10
Peter..fell down at Jesus' *k*, Lk 5.8

KNEEL — LT

he made the camels *k* down Gen 24.11
let us *k* before the Lord, our Ps 95.6
had *k* with hands outstretched 1Ki 8.54

KNEW

Thus Joseph *k* his brothers, Gen 42.8
until he *k* that..God rules Dan 5.21
I who *k* you in the wilderness, Hos 13.5
k..the word of the Lord. Zech 11.11
he himself *k* what was in man. Jn 2.25
for although they *k* God they Rom 1.21

KNIFE

Abraham..took..the k.	Gen 22.6
took the k to slay his son,	22.10
put a k to your throat if	Prov 23.2

KNOCK — ING

k, and it will be opened to you.	Mt 7.7
k, and it will be opened to you.	Lk 11.9
k at the door, saying, 'Lord,	13.25
I stand at the door and k;	Rev 3.20
But Peter continued k: and	Acts 12.16

KNOW — S — EST — N

king..who did not k Joseph.	Ex 1.8
Egyptians shall k that I am the LORD,	7.5
I k that the LORD is greater	18.11
k that I am the LORD their God,	29.46
you may k that I, the LORD	31.13
may k that I made the people	Lev 23.43
shown, that you might k	Deut 4.35
k therefore this day,	4.39
who did not k the LORD or the	Judg 2.10
all this assembly may k	1Sam 17.47
that all..may k thy name and	1Ki 8.43
may k that the LORD is God;	8.60
shall k that I am the LORD."	20.13
Solomon my son, k the God	1Chr 28.9
of yesterday, and k nothing,	Job 8.9
I k that my Redeemer lives,	19.25
they do not k the light.	24.16
I k..thou wilt bring..death,	30.23
Make me to k thy ways, O LORD;	Ps 25.4
still, and k that I am God.	46.10
This I k, that God is for me.	56.9
they say, "How can God k?	73.11
people who k the festal shout,	89.15
K that the LORD is God! It is	100.3
k that this is thy hand;	109.27
not k that want will come	Prov 28.22
I k..whatever God does endures	Ecc 3.14
wise man will k the time and..way.	8.5
Israel does not k, my people	Isa 1.3
kingdoms..may k..the LORD."	37.20
that men may see and k, may	41.20
all flesh shall k..your Savior,	49.26
my people shall k my name;	52.6
they shall k that..I..speak;	52.6
call nations that you k not,	55.5
my people k not the ordinance	Jer 8.7
a heart to k that I am the LORD.	24.7
no longer..saying, 'K the LORD,'	31.34
will k that I am the LORD."	Ezek 6.14
you shall k that I, the LORD,	17.21
will k that I am the LORD."	29.21
they will k that I am the LORD.	32.15
they shall k..I am the LORD,	34.27
k that I the LORD sanctify	37.28
shall k that I am the LORD,	39.7
Let us k, let us press on to k	Hos 6.3
they did not k..I healed them.	11.3
whoever is discerning, let him k	14.9
You shall k that I am in the	Joel 2.27
they do not k the thoughts	Mic 4.12
do not let your left hand k	Mt 6.3
that you may k that the Son of	9.6
and at an hour he does not k,	24.50
that you may k that the Son	Mk 2.10
you k neither the scriptures	12.24
you do not k when the master	13.35
I k who you are, the Holy One	Lk 4.34
that you may k..the Son of man	5.24
I do not k where you come from	13.27
"Teacher, we k that you speak	20.21

I k my own and my own k me,	Jn 10.14
By this all men will k that	13.35
eternal life, that they k thee	17.3
may k that thou hast sent me	17.23
they did not k the scripture,	20.9
"Jesus I k, and Paul I k;	Acts 19.15
Do you not k..you are God's	1Cor 3.16
I want you to k, brethren,	10.1
that you have come to k God,	Gal 4.9
you may k what is the hope	Eph 1.18
that I may k him and the	Phil 3.10
I k whom I have believed,	2Tim 1.12
shall not teach..'K the Lord,'	Heb 8.11
By this we k the spirit of truth	1Jn 4.6
k that you have eternal life.	5.13
We k that we are of God, and	5.19
" 'I k your works, your toil	Rev 2.2
he k the way that I take;	Job 23.10
LORD k the way of the righteous,	Ps 1.6
he k our frame; he remembers	103.14
the haughty he k from afar.	138.6
your Father k what you need	Mt 6.8
Father k that you need them	6.32
that day or..hour no one k,	Mk 13.32
God who k the heart bore	Acts 15.8
thou k thy servant, O Lord	2Sam 7.20
my spirit is faint, thou k my	Ps 142.3
But thou, O LORD, k me; thou	Jer 12.3
God is k, his name is great	Ps 76.1
make himself k to..Egyptians;	Isa 19.21
"You only have I k of all the	Amos 3.2
the tree is k by its fruit.	Mt 12.33
ordered them not to make him k.	Mk 3.12
the only Son,..has made him k.	Jn 1.18
family became k to Pharaoh.	Acts 7.13
king who had not k Joseph.	7.18
make the word of God fully k,	Col 1.25
better..never to have k the	2Pet 2.21
made it k by sending his angel	Rev 1.1

KNOWLEDGE

tree of the k of good and evil.	Gen 2.9
knows the k of the Most High,	Num 24.16
Such k..too wonderful for me;	Ps 139.6
k and discretion to..youth—	Prov 1.4
k of the Holy One is insight.	9.10
but k is easy for a man of	14.6
tongue of..wise dispenses k,	15.2
nor have I k of the Holy One.	30.3
go into exile for want of k;	Isa 5.13
full of the k of the LORD	11.9
fro, and k shall increase."	Dan 12.4
are destroyed for lack of k;	Hos 4.6
give k of salvation to his people	Lk 1.77
taken away the key of k;	11.52
with all speech and all k—	1Cor 1.5
"K" puffs up, but love builds	8.1
by your k this weak man is	8.11
by purity, k, forbearance,	2Cor 6.6
come to the k of the truth.	1Tim 2.4

KORAH — 'S

Now K the son of Izhar, son	Num 16.1
died in the affair of K.	16.49
and perish in K rebellion.	Jude 11

L

LABAN

brother whose name was L;	Gen 24.29
flee to L my brother	27.43
to L, the son of Bethuel	28.5
"Do you know L the son of	29.5

LABAN (cont.)
Jacob said to L, "Send me   Gen 30.25
L did not regard him   31.2
And Jacob outwitted L   31.20
L said, "This heap is a witness   31.48
L arose, and kissed   31.55

LABOR (v)
Six days you shall l,   Deut 5.13
those who build it l in vain.   Ps 127.1
for his hands refuse to l.   Prov 21.25
that peoples l only for fire,   Hab 2.13
Come to me, all who l and   Mt 11.28
Do not l for the food which   Jn 6.27

LABOR — S (n)
"Before she was in l she gave   Isa 66.7
your l is not in vain.   1Cor 15.58
you remember our l and toil,   1Thess 2.9
ceases from his l as God did   Heb 4.10

LABORER — S
Sweet is the sleep of a l,   Ecc 5.12
to hire l for his vineyard.   Mt 20.1
plentiful, but the l are few;   Lk 10.2
wages of the l who mowed your   Jas 5.4

LACK — S — ED
"You l one thing; go, sell   Mk 10.21
"One thing you still l. Sell   Lk 18.22
sandals, did you l anything?"   22.35
gathered little had no l."   2Cor 8.15
he l nothing..that he desires,   Ecc 6.2
you have l nothing.'   Deut 2.7

LAD — S
if the l is not with me?   Gen 44.34
I will send the l, saying,   1Sam 20.21
a l here who has five barley   Jn 6.9
bless the l; and in them   Gen 48.16

LAKE
into the l and were drowned.   Lk 8.33
thrown alive into the l of fire   Rev 19.20
thrown into the l of fire   20.10

LAMB — S
but where is the l   Gen 22.7
l shall be without blemish,   Ex 12.5
One l you shall offer in the   29.39
nothing but one little ewe l,   2Sam 12.3
like a l..to the slaughter,   Isa 53.7
The wolf and the l shall feed   65.25
But I was like a gentle l led   Jer 11.19
"Behold, the L of God, who   Jn 1.29
like that of a l without   1Pet 1.19
I saw a L standing, as though   Rev 5.6
"Worthy is the L who was slain,   5.12
and from the wrath of the L;   6.16
"Salvation belongs..to the L!"   7.10
on Mount Zion stood the L,   14.1
they will make war on the L,   17.14
marriage of the L has come,   19.7
the Bride, the wife of the L."   21.9
the twelve apostles of the L.   21.14
light, and its lamp is the L.   21.23
Go..as l in..midst of wolves.   Lk 10.3
He said to him, "Feed my l."   Jn 21.15

LAME
attack the l and the blind,   2Sam 5.8
then shall the l man leap   Isa 35.6
the l walking, and the blind   Mt 15.31
a man l from birth was being   Acts 3.2

LAMENT — ED
L like a virgin girded with   Joel 1.8

Israel l after the LORD.   1Sam 7.2
And David l..over Saul and   2Sam 1.17

LAMENTATION
most bitter l; for suddenly   Jer 6.26
man, raise a l over Tyre,   Ezek 27.2
Hear this..in l, O..Israel: Amos 5.1

LAMP — S
that a l may be set up   Ex 27.20
l of God had not..gone out,   1Sam 3.3
thou art my l, O LORD,   2Sam 22.29
always have a l before me   1Ki 11.36
God gave him a l in Jerusalem,   15.4
table, a chair, and a l, so   2Ki 4.10
since he promised to give a l   8.19
his l above him is put out.   Job 18.6
his l shone upon my head,   29.3
thou dost light my l; the LORD   Ps 18.28
Thy word is a l to my feet   119.105
For the commandment is a l   Prov 6.23
his l will be put out in   20.20
The spirit of man is the l   20.27
l of..wicked will be put out.   24.20
Her l does not go out at night.   31.18
Nor do men light a l and put   Mt 5.15
"The eye is the l of the body.   6.22
"Is a l..put under a bushel,   Mk 4.21
"No one after lighting a l   Lk 8.16
"No one after lighting a l   11.33
Your eye is the l of your body;   11.34
He was a burning and shining l,   Jn 5.35
and its l is the Lamb.   Rev 21.23
be girded and your l burning,   Lk 12.35

LAMPSTAND — S
make a l of pure gold.   Ex 25.31
also made the l of pure gold.   37.17
lamps in order upon the l   Lev 24.4
light in front of the l."   Num 8.2
behold, a l all of gold,   Zech 4.2
turning I saw seven golden l,   Rev 1.12

LAND — S
all the l which you see   Gen 13.15
l which I gave to Abraham   35.12
to the l which he swore   50.24
I will bring you into the l   Ex 6.8
and the l became defiled,   Lev 18.25
The l shall not be sold in   25.23
to the LORD part of the l   27.16
showed..the fruit of the l.   Num 13.26
let this l be given to your   32.5
this l shall be your possession   32.22
You..inherit the l by lot   33.54
You shall not defile the l   35.34
bringing you into a good l,   Deut 8.7
l..you are entering to take   11.10
the l..you are..to possess   11.11
LORD done thus to this l?   29.24
very much l to be possessed.   Josh 13.1
I gave you a l on which   24.13
went in and possessed the l,   Neh 9.24
LORD in the l of the living;   Isa 38.11
you defiled my l, and made   Jer 2.7
whole l shall be a desolation;   4.27
O l,..hear the word of the LORD!   22.29
these waste places in the l   Ezek 33.24
prophesy concerning the l of   36.6
the l as a holy district,   45.1
not remain in the l of the LORD; Hos 9.3
go into the l which I will show   Acts 7.3
Paul..intending..to go by l.   20.13
but our bodies and our l.   Gen 47.18
the gospel in l beyond you,   2Cor 10.16

LANDMARK — S
not remove..neighbor's *l*, Deut 19.14
Remove not the ancient *l* Prov 22.28
Do not remove an ancient *l* 23.10
Men remove *l*; they seize Job 24.2

LANGUAGE
the whole earth had one *l* Gen 11.1
not speak the *l* of Judah, Neh 13.24
nation whose *l* you do not Jer 5.15
foreign speech and a hard *l*, Ezek 3.5
heard..speaking in his own *l*. Acts 2.6

LANGUISH — ES — ING
they will *l* who spread nets Isa 19.8
My soul *l* for thy salvation; Ps 119.81
I am *l*; O LORD, heal me, for my 6.2

LASHES
received..the forty *l* less one. 2Cor 11.24

LAST
l state..worse than the first. Mt 12.45
many that are first will be *l*, 19.30
many that are first will be *l*, Mk 10.31
loud cry, and breathed his *l*. 15.37
some are *l* who will be first, Lk 13.30
in the *l* days there will come 2Tim 3.1
these *l* days he has spoken Heb 1.2
I am the first and the *l*, Rev 1.17

LAUGH — S — ED
and famine you shall *l*, Job 5.22
The righteous..shall *l* at him, Ps 52.6
thou, O LORD, dost *l* at them; 59.8
I..will *l* at your calamity; Prov 1.26
that weep now, for you shall *l*. Lk 6.21
he *l* at the rattle of javelins. Job 41.29
He who sits in the heavens *l*; Ps 2.4
the LORD *l* at the wicked, for 37.13
she *l* at the time to come. Prov 31.25
fell on his face and *l*, Gen 17.17
So Sarah *l* to herself, 18.12
but they *l* them to scorn, 2Chr 30.10
l at and held in derision, Ezek 23.32
but sleeping." And they *l* Mt 9.24
And they *l* at him. But he put Mk 5.40
they *l* at him, knowing that Lk 8.53

LAUGHTER
"God has made *l* for me; Gen 21.6
Even in *l* the heart is sad, Prov 14.13
I said of *l*, "It is mad," Ecc 2.2
Sorrow is better than *l*, for by 7.3

LAVER
also make a *l* of bronze, Ex 30.17
And he made the *l* of bronze 38.8

LAW — S
the *l* of the burnt offering. Lev 6.9
the *l* of the cereal offering. 6.14
the *l* of the sin offering. 6.25
the *l* of the guilt offering. 7.1
l of the sacrifice of peace 7.11
the *l* in cases of jealousy, Num 5.29
the *l* for the Nazirite, when 6.13
explain this *l*, saying, Deut 1.5
And Moses wrote this *l*, 31.9
read this *l* before all 31.11
"Take this book of the *l*, 31.26
This book of the *l* shall Josh 1.8
read all the words of the *l*, 8.34
Rehoboam..forsook the *l* of 2Chr 12.1
on his *l* he meditates day and Ps 1.2
The *l* of the LORD is perfect, 19.7

I will keep thy *l* continually, 119.44
people in whose heart is my *l*; Isa 51.7
my *l*, they have rejected it. Jer 6.19
I will put my *l* within them, 31.33
unless..with the *l* of his God." Dan 6.5
out of Zion shall go..the *l*, Mic 4.2
not..come to abolish the *l* Mt 5.17
the *l* prophesied until John; 11.13
and teachers of the *l* sitting Lk 5.17
one dot of the *l* to become void, 16.17
written about me in the *l* of 24.44
After the reading of the *l* Acts 13.15
who have sinned under the *l* Rom 2.12
For the *l* brings wrath, but 4.15
I delight in the *l* of God, 7.22
the *l* of the Spirit of life in Christ 8.2
Christ is the end of the *l*, 10.4
brother, does he dare go to *l* 1Cor 6.1
To those outside the *l* I became 9.21
book of the *l*, and do them." Gal 3.10
Why then the *l*? It was added 3.19
we were confined under the *l*, 3.23
Tell me,..do you not hear the *l*? 4.21
whole *l* is fulfilled in one word, 5.14
so fulfil the *l* of Christ. 6.2
we know that the *l* is good, 1Tim 1.8
the *l* made nothing perfect); Heb 7.19
who looks into the perfect *l*, Jas 1.25
convicted by..*l* as transgressors. 2.9
if you judge the *l*, you are 4.11
true *l*, good statutes and Neh 9.13

LAWFUL
not *l* to do on the sabbath." Mt 12.2
l to do good on the sabbath." 12.12
not *l* for you to have her." 14.4
to Herod, "It is not *l* for you Mk 6.18
Jews said.."It is not *l* for us Jn 18:31
"All things are *l* for me," 1Cor 6.12

LAWLESS — NESS
the *l* one will be revealed, 2Thess 2.8
the man of *l* is revealed, 2.3
commits sin is guilty of *l*; 1Jn 3.4

LAWYER — S
a *l* stood up to put him to Lk 10.25
he said, "Woe to you *l* also! Lk 11.46

LAY — ING
I *l* prostrate before the LORD Deut 9.18
Wise men *l* up knowledge, Prov 10.14
"Do not *l* up for yourselves Mt 6.19
Son of man has nowhere to *l* his 8.20
no other foundation can..*l* 1Cor 3.11
thus *l* up for themselves 1Tim 6.19

LAZARUS
at his gate lay a poor man..*L*, Lk 16.20
a..man was ill, *L* of Bethany, Jn 11.1
a loud voice, "*L*, come out." 11.43
L..whom Jesus had raised 12.1
priests planned to put *L* 12.10
with him when he called *L* 12.17

LEAD — S
I will *l* on slowly, Gen 33.14
the LORD alone did *l* him, Deut 32.12
Lead me,..in thy righteousness Ps 5.8
L me in thy truth, and teach 25.5
L thou me to the rock..higher 61.2
a little child shall *l* them. Isa 11.6
gently *l* those..with young. 40.11
So thou didst *l* thy people, 63.14
And *l* us not into temptation, Mt 6.13
"Can a blind man *l* a blind Lk 6.39

LEAD — S (cont.)

let every one *l* the life	1Cor 7.17
I..beg you to *l* a life worthy	Eph 4.1
l a life worthy of the Lord,	Col 1.10
to *l* a life worthy of God,	1Thess 2.12
He *l* me beside still waters;	Ps 23.2
l..in the way you should go.	Isa 48.17
if a blind man *l* a blind man,	Mt 15.14

LEAF — VES

Wilt thou frighten a driven *l*	Job 13.25
they sewed fig *l* together	Gen 3.7
Their *l* will not wither	Ezek 47.12
he found nothing but *l*, for	Mk 11.13
its branch..puts forth its *l*,	13.28

LEAGUE

a *l* between me and you, as	1Ki 15.19
For you shall be in *l* with	Job 5.23
"Syria is in *l* with Ephraim,"	Isa 7.2

LEAH

name of the older was L,	Gen 29.16
loved Rachel more than L,	29.30
When L saw..she had ceased	30.9
called Rachel and L into the field	31.4
The sons of L: Reuben	35.23
and L, who together built	Ruth 4.11

LEAP — ED — ING

by my God I can *l* over a	2Sam 22.30
babe *l* in her womb;..Elizabeth	Lk 1.41
And *l* up he stood and walked	Acts 3.8

LEARN — ED (v)

l to fear the Lord your God,	Deut 31.12
I *l* thy righteous ordinances.	Ps 119.7
afflicted that I might *l* thy	119.71
O simple ones, *l* prudence;	Prov 8.5
l to do good; seek justice,	Isa 1.17
the world *l* righteousness.	26.9
"L not the way of the nations,	Jer 10.2
Go and *l* what this means,	Mt 9.13
yoke upon you, and *l* from me;	11.29
No one could *l* that song	Rev 14.3
I have *l* by divination	Gen 30.27
What you have *l* and received	Phil 4.9
I have *l*, in whatever state I am,	4.11
you *l* from us how..to live	1Thess 4.1
he *l* obedience through what	Heb 5.8

LEARNING (n)

wise man..may..increase in *l*,	Prov 1.5
understanding *l*, and competent	Dan 1.4
four youths, God gave them *l*	1.17
"How is it that this man has *l*,	Jn 7.15
great *l* is turning you mad."	Acts 26.24

LEAST

I am the *l* in my family."	Judg 6.15
from the *l* of the tribes	1Sam 9.21
by no means *l* among the rulers	Mt 2.6
be called *l* in the kingdom	5.19
who is *l* in..kingdom of heaven	11.11
who is *l* in the kingdom of God	Lk 7.28
who is *l* among you..is..great,"	9.48
I am the *l* of the apostles,	1Cor 15.9
the very *l* of all the saints,	Eph 3.8

LEAVE

Elisha said,..I will not *l*	2Ki 2.2
as you..live, I will not *l*	4.30
L simpleness, and live, and	Prov 9.6
man shall *l*..father and mother	Mk 10.7

LEAVEN

you shall put away *l* out of	Ex 12.15

cereal offering..made with *l*;	Lev 2.11
kingdom of heaven is like *l*	Mt 13.33
beware of the *l* of..Pharisees	16.6
beware of..*l* of the Pharisees	Mk 8.15
"Beware of..*l* of the Pharisees,	Lk 12.1
like *l* which a woman took	13.21
a little *l* leavens the whole	1Cor 5.6
A little *l* leavens the whole	Gal 5.9

LEBANON

land of the Canaanites, and L,	Deut 1.7
devour the cedars of L.'	Judg 9.15
command that cedars of L be	1Ki 5.6
House of the Forest of L.	10.17
bring cedar trees from L	Ezra 3.7
Lord breaks the cedars of L.	Ps 29.5
His appearance is like L,	Sol 5.15
and L with its majestic trees	Isa 10.34
glory of L shall come to you,	60.13
Does the snow of L leave the	Jer 18.14

LED

the Lord has *l* me in the way	Gen 24.27
God *l* the people round by	Ex 13.18
and *l* him through..Canaan,	Josh 24.3
daytime he *l*..with a cloud,	Ps 78.14
he *l* them by a straight way,	107.7
to him who *l* his people	136.16
who *l* us in the wilderness,	Jer 2.6
I *l*..with cords of compassion,	Hos 11.4
Jesus was *l* up by the Spirit	Mt 4.1
l him to the brow of the hill	Lk 4.29
"As a sheep *l* to..slaughter	Acts 8.32
all who are *l* by the Spirit	Rom 8.14
if you are *l* by the Spirit	Gal 5.18

LEFT (v)

that the Lord had *l* him.	Judg 16.20
and I, even I only, am *l*;	1Ki 19.10
l alone, I fell upon my face,	Ezek 9.8
those who are *l* in Israel;	Zeph 3.13
l the boat and their father,	Mt 4.22
"Lo, we have *l* everything	19.27
they *l* their nets and followed	Mk 1.18
they *l* their father Zebedee	1.20
they *l* everything and followed	Lk 5.11

LEFT (n)

then I will go to the *l*."	Gen 13.9
do not let your *l* hand know	Mt 6.3
one at your right hand and..*l*,	20.21

LEGION — S

"My name is L; for we are many."	Mk 5.9
more than twelve *l* of angels?	Mt 26.53

LEGS

thighs..bronze, its *l*..iron,	Dan 2.33
they did not break his *l*.	Jn 19.33

LEHI

at L, and there came water	Judg 15.19
Philistines gathered..at L,	2Sam 23.11

LEND — S — ING

"If you *l* money to any	Ex 22.25
shall not *l* upon interest	Deut 23.19
shall *l* to many nations,	28.12
if you *l* to those from whom	Lk 6.34
who is kind..*l* to the Lord,	Prov 19.17
ever giving liberally and *l*,	Ps 37.26

LENGTH

l of..ark three hundred cubits,	Gen 6.15
the *l* of the measuring reed	Ezek 40.5
what is the breadth and *l*	Eph 3.18

LENT (v)
release what he has *l* to his — Deut 15.2
I have *l* him to the LORD; — 1Sam 1.28
I have not *l*, nor..borrowed, — Jer 15.10

LEOPARD
l shall lie down with the kid, — Isa 11.6
his skin or the *l* his spots? — Jer 13.23
like a *l*, with four wings — Dan 7.6

LEPER — S
"This shall be..law of the *l* — Lev 14.2
put out of the camp every *l*, — Num 5.2
man of valor, but he was a *l*. — 2Ki 5.1
king, so that he was a *l* — 15.5
a *l* came..and knelt before him, — Mt 8.2
in the house of Simon the *l*, — 26.6
a *l* came to him beseeching him, — Mk 1.40
in the house of Simon the *l*, — 14.3
four men who were *l* at the — 2Ki 7.3
the lame walk, *l* are cleansed — Mt 11.5
many *l* in Israel in the time — Lk 4.27
lame walk, *l* are cleansed, — 7.22
he was met by ten *l*, who stood — 17.12

LEPROUS — Y
behold, his hand was *l*, — Ex 4.6
and it turns into a *l* disease — Lev 13.2
I put a *l* disease in a house — 14.34
behold, Miriam was *l*, — Num 12.10
the *l* of Naaman shall cleave — 2Ki 5.27
became angry..*l* broke out — 2Chr 26.19
there came a man full of *l*; — Lk 5.12

LETTER — S
David wrote a *l* to Joab, — 2Sam 11.14
he brought the *l* to the king — 2Ki 5.6
a *l* came to him from Elijah — 2Chr 21.2
then answer be returned by *l* — Ezra 5.5
servant to me with an open *l* — Neh 6.5
Hezekiah received the *l* from — Isa 37.14
words of the *l* which Jeremiah — Jer 29.1
sent..with the following *l*: — Acts 15.23
together, they delivered the *l*. — 15.30
he wrote a *l* to this effect: — 23.25
delivered the *l* to the governor, — 23.33
are our *l* of recommendation, — 2Cor 3.2
when this *l* has been read — Col 4.16
l purporting to be from us, — 1Thess 2.2
the mark in every *l* of mine; — 2Thess 3.17
she wrote *l* in Ahab's name — 1Ki 21.8
wrote *l* also to Ephraim — 2Chr 30.1
l to..synagogues at Damascus, — Acts 9.2
I received *l* to the brethren, — 22.5
need..*l* of recommendation — 2Cor 3.1
not..frightening you with *l*. — 10.9
with what large *l* I am writing — Gal 6.11
as he does in all his *l*. — 2Pet 3.16

LEVI
his name was called L. — Gen 29.34
man from the house of L — Ex 2.1
L you shall not number, and — Num 1.49
set apart the tribe of L — Deut 10.8

LEVIATHAN
draw out L with a fishhook, — Job 41.1
strong sword will punish L — Isa 27.1

LEVITES
no portion..given to the L — Josh 14.4
service, the priests and..L, — 2Chr 31.2
which the L,..had collected — 34.9
And he said to the L who taught — 35.3

LIAR — S
I should be a *l* like you; — Jn 8.55

---

not believe..made him a *l*, — 1Jn 5.10
and all *l*, their lot shall be — Rev 21.8

LIBERTY
proclaim *l* throughout..land — Lev 25.10
and I shall walk at *l*, for — Ps 119.45
a proclamation of *l* to them, — Jer 34.8
gift..his to the year of *l*; — Ezek 46.17
glorious *l* of..children of God. — Rom 8.21
take care lest this *l* of yours — 1Cor 8.9
why should my *l* be determined — 10.29

LIE — S — D (v)
not man, that he should *l*, — Num 23.19
In peace I will both *l* down and — Ps 4.8
faithful witness does not *l*, — Prov 14.5
"Ananias, why..*l* to..Spirit — Acts 5.3
Do not *l* to one another, — Col 3.9
When he *l*, he speaks according — Jn 8.44
and drink water.'" But he *l* — 1Ki 13.18

LIE — S (n)
l which they are prophesying — Jer 27.10
the truth about God for a *l* — Rom 1.25
in their mouth no *l* was found, — Rev 14.5
godless besmear me with *l*, — Ps 119.69
we have made *l* our refuge, — Isa 28.15
your lips have spoken *l*, your — 59.3
bloody city, all full of *l* — Nah 3.1

LIFE — VES
everything that has..*l*, — Gen 1.30
tree of *l* also in the midst — 2.9
l of the flesh is in blood; — Lev 17.11
set before you this day *l* — Deut 30.15
for that means *l* to you and — 30.20
LORD kills and brings to *l*; — 1Sam 2.6
the *l* of my lord shall be — 25.29
whether for death or for *l*, — 2Sam 15.21
your *l* shall go for his *l*, — 1Ki 20.42
"Remember..my *l* is a breath; — Job 7.7
breath of..Almighty gives me *l*. — 33.4
he may see the light of *l*. — 33.30
dost show me the path of *l*; — Ps 16.11
What man is there who desires *l*, — 34.12
with thee is the fountain of *l*; — 36.9
steadfast love is better than *l*, — 63.3
Remember,..the measure of *l* — 89.47
against the *l* of the righteous, — 94.21
they will be *l* for your soul — Prov 3.22
they are *l* to him who finds — 4.22
he who finds me finds *l* and — 8.35
path of righteousness is *l*, — 12.28
fear of..LORD is a fountain of *l*, — 14.27
I hated *l*, because what is — Ecc 2.17
Enjoy *l* with..wife..you love, — 9.9
recorded for *l* in Jerusalem, — Isa 4.3
held back my *l* from the pit — 38.17
Death shall be preferred to *l* — Jer 8.3
I set before you the way of *l* — 21.8
let every man save his *l*! — 51.6
you will have saved your *l*." — Ezek 3.21
LORD, take my *l* from me, — Jonah 4.3
way is hard, that leads to *l*, — Mt 7.14
he who loses his *l* for my sake — 10.39
gains..world and forfeits his *l*? — 16.26
the righteous into eternal *l*." — 25.46
whoever would save his *l* will — Mk 8.35
whole world and forfeit his *l*? — 8.36
in the age to come eternal *l*. — 10.30
would save his *l* will lose it; — Lk 9.24
do not be anxious about your *l*, — 12.22
I do to inherit eternal *l*?" — 18.18
In him was *l*, and the *l* was — Jn 1.4
believes in the Son has eternal *l*; — 3.36

LIFE — VES (cont.)

water welling up to eternal *l*."	4.14
and believes..has eternal *l*;	5.24
you have the words of eternal *l*;	6.68
I came that they may have *l*,	10.10
lay down my *l* for the sheep.	10.15
and I give them eternal *l*,	10.28
"I am the resurrection and the *l*;	11.25
way and the truth, and the *l*;	14.6
eternal *l*, that they know thee	17.3
that believing you may have *l*	20.31
all the words of this *L*."	Acts 5.20
he himself gives to all men *l*	17.25
been brought from death to *l*,	Rom 6.13
free gift of God is eternal *l*	6.23
death, nor *l*, nor angels,	8.38
a fragrance from *l* to *l*.	2Cor 2.16
but the Spirit gives *l*.	3.6
so that the *l* of Jesus may	4.10
work in us, but *l* in you.	4.12
of my former *l* in Judaism,	Gal 1.13
the *l* I now live in the flesh	2.20
your *l*..hid with Christ in God.	Col 3.3
lead a quiet and peaceable *l*.	1Tim 2.2
power of an indestructible *l*.	Heb 7.16
Keep your *l* free from love of	13.5
What is your *l*? For you are	Jas 4.14
"He that would love *l* and	1Pet 3.10
passed out of death into *l*,	1Jn 3.14
he laid down his *l* for us;	3.16
grant to eat of the tree of *l*,	Rev 2.7
blot..name out of the book of *l*;	3.5
breath of *l* from God entered them,	11.11
in the book of *l* of the Lamb	13.8
They came to *l* again, and	20.4
fountain of the water of *l*.	21.6
in the Lamb's book of *l*.	21.27
the water of *l* without price.	22.17
lawlessness takes away *l*.	Prov 11.30
astray at the cost of your *l*.	Jer 42.20
endurance..will gain your *l*.	Lk 21.19
men who have risked their *l*	Acts 15.26
l of holiness and godliness	2Pet 3.11
they loved not their *l* even	Rev 12.11

LIFT — ED — ING

L up your heads, O gates!	Ps 24.7
To thee, O LORD, I *l* up my soul.	25.1
to thee,..do I *l* up my soul.	86.4
I *l* up my eyes to the hills.	121.1
L up your hands to the holy	134.2
LORD, my heart is not *l* up,	131.1
and *l* him out of the cistern.	Jer 38.13
must the Son of man be *l* up,	Jn 3.14
"When you have *l* up the Son	8.28
when I am *l* up from the earth,	12.32
not from the east..comes *l* up;	Ps 75.6

LIGHT — S

God said, "Let there be *l*";	Gen 1.3
people of Israel had *l*	Ex 10.23
that a *l* may be kept burning	Lev 24.2
dawns on them like the..*l*,	2Sam 23.4
they do not know the *l*.	Job 24.16
LORD is my *l* and my salvation;	Ps 27.1
your vindication as the *l*,	37.6
send out thy *l* and thy truth;	43.3
who will never more see the *l*.	49.19
L dawns for the righteous, and	97.11
Thy word..a *l* to my path.	119.105
unfolding..thy words gives *l*;	119.130
darkness is as *l* with thee.	139.12
path..righteous is like the *l*	Prov 4.18

l of the righteous rejoices,	13.9
L is sweet, and it is pleasant	Ecc 11.7
walk in the *l* of the LORD.	Isa 2.5
darkness for *l* and *l* for darkness,	5.20
given you as..a *l* to the nations,	42.6
I form *l* and create darkness,	45.7
give you as a *l* to the nations,	49.6
Then shall your *l* break forth	58.8
shine; for your *l* has come,	60.1
nations shall come to your *l*,	60.3
the LORD will be a *l* to me.	Mic 7.8
the people..have seen a great *l*,	Mt 4.16
it gives *l* to all in the house.	5.15
his garments became white as *l*.	17.2
l to those who sit in darkness	Lk 1.79
a *l* for revelation to the Gentiles,	2.32
dark shall be heard in the *l*,	12.3
The *l* shines in the darkness,	Jn 1.5
the *l* has come into the world,	3.19
"I am the *l* of the world;	8.12
I am the *l* of the world."	9.5
Walk while you have the *l*,	12.35
a *l* from heaven flashed about	Acts 9.3
to be a *l* for the Gentiles,	13.47
great *l* from heaven suddenly	22.6
on the way a *l* from heaven,	26.13
may turn from darkness to *l*	26.18
and put on the armor of *l*;	Rom 13.12
comes, who will bring to *l*	1Cor 4.5
from seeing..*l* of the gospel	2Cor 4.4
"Let *l* shine out of darkness,"	4.6
what fellowship has *l* with	6.14
now you are *l* in the Lord;	Eph 5.8
and Christ shall give you *l*."	5.14
darkness into his marvelous *l*.	1Pet 2.9
that God is *l* and in him is	1Jn 1.5
but if we walk in the *l*, as	1.7
the true *l* is already shining.	2.8
they need no *l* of lamp or sun,	Rev 22.5
let them be *l* in the firmament	Gen 1.15
coming..from the Father of *l*	Jas 1.17

LIGHTNING — S

as the *l* comes from the east	Mt 24.27
as the *l* flashes and lights	Lk 17.24
loud noises, flashes of *l*,	Rev 8.5
he flashed forth *l*, and routed	Ps 18.14

LIKE — NESS

that I should be *l* him? says	Isa 40.25
change our lowly body to be *l*	Phil 3.21
created man..in the *l* of God.	Gen 5.1
or what I compare with him?	Isa 40.18
"Whose *l* and inscription is	Mk 12.16
Whose *l* and inscription has	Lk 20.24
gods..in the *l* of men!"	Acts 14.11
Son in the *l* of sinful flesh	Rom 8.3
being born in the *l* of men.	Phil 2.7

LILY — IES

rose of Sharon,..*l* of..valleys.	Sol 2.1
l of the field, how they grow;	Mt 6.28
Consider the *l*, how they grow;	Lk 12.27

LINEN

wrapped him in the *l* shroud,	Mk 15.46
her to be clothed with fine *l*,	Rev 19.8

LION — S — 'S

and when there came a *l*,	1Sam 17.34
slew a *l* in a pit on a day	2Sam 23.20
a *l* met him on the road	1Ki 13.24
slew a *l* in a pit..when snow	1Chr 11.22
lest like a *l* they rend me,	Ps 7.2
Save me from the mouth of the *l*,	22.21

LION — S — 'S (cont.)
sluggard says, "There is a *l* Prov 26.13
My heritage..to me like a *l* Jer 12.8
like a *l* and had eagle's wings. Dan 7.4
young *l* to the house of Judah. Hos 5.14
as if a man fled from a *l*, Amos 5.19
devil..like a roaring *l*, 1Pet 5.8
the *L* of the tribe of Judah, Rev 5.5
young *l* roar for their prey, Ps 104.21
Daniel..cast into the den of *l*. Dan 6.16
stopped the mouths of *l*, Heb 11.33
I was rescued from..*l* mouth. 2Tim 4.17

LIPS
our *l* are with us; who is our Ps 12.4
Keep..*l* from speaking deceit. 34.13
Truthful *l* endure for ever, Prov 12.19
Righteous *l* are the delight 16.13
l of knowledge are..precious 20.15
Your *l*..like a scarlet thread, Sol 4.3
honor me with their *l*, while Isa 29.13
honors me with their *l*, but Mt 15.8
people honors me with their *l*, Mk 7.6
venom of asps..under their *l*." Rom 3.13
word is near you, on your *l* 10.8

LISTEN — S — ED — ING
shall not yield to him or *l* Deut 13.8
to *l* to the voice of Samuel; 1Sam 8.19
not *l*, and Manasseh seduced 2Ki 21.9
to *l* is better than..sacrifice Ecc 5.1
But if any nation will not *l*, Jer 12.17
if you *l* to me, says the LORD, 17.24
It may be they will *l*, and 26.3
my beloved Son; *l* to him." Mk 9.7
my Son, my Chosen; *l* to him!" Lk 9.35
who will *l* to anybody and 2Tim 3.7
a wise man *l* to advice. Prov 12.15
God *l* to..voice of Manoah, Judg 13.9
does evil..not *l* to my voice, Jer 18.10

LITTLE
Better..a *l*..the righteous has Ps 37.16
who gathers *l* by *l*..increase Prov 13.11
line, here a *l*, there a *l*." Isa 28.10
Bethlehem Ephrathah, who are *l* Mic 5.2
clothe you, O men of *l* faith? Mt 6.30
you afraid, O men of *l* faith?" 8.26
gives to one of these *l* ones 10.42
"O man of *l* faith, why..doubt?" 14.31
men of *l* faith, why do you discuss 16.8
whoever causes one of these *l* 18.6
who is forgiven *l*, loves *l*." Lk 7.47
cause one of these *l* ones to sin. 17.2
who gathered *l* had no lack." 2Cor 8.15

LIVE — S — ING (v)
let the male children *l*. Ex 1.17
let..*l*, to show you my power, 9.16
man shall not see me and *l*." 33.20
by doing which a man shall *l*: Lev 18.5
the bronze serpent and *l*. Num 21.9
that you may *l*, and go in Deut 4.1
with man and man still *l*. 5.24
that you may *l*, and that 5.33
that you may *l* and multiply, 8.1
man does not *l* by bread alone, 8.3
that you may *l* and inherit 16.20
shouted, "Long *l* the king!" 1Sam 10.24
say, 'Long *l* King Solomon!' 1Ki 1.34
If a man die, shall he *l* again? Job 14.14
I may *l* and observe thy word. Ps 119.17
give..understanding that I may *l*. 119.144
praise the LORD as long as I *l*; 146.2

keep my commandments, and *l*; Prov 4.4
Leave simpleness, and *l*, 9.6
It is better to *l* in a corner 21.9
Thy dead shall *l*, their bodies Isa 26.19
hear, that your soul may *l*; 55.3
serve him..his people, and *l*. Jer 27.12
If you..enter Egypt and go to *l* 42.15
said to you in your blood, 'L, Ezek 16.6
righteous, he shall surely *l*, 18.9
for..righteousness..he shall *l*. 18.22
by..observance man shall *l*. 20.11
and right, he shall *l* by it. 33.19
"Son of man, can these bones *l*?" 37.3
that we may *l* before him. Hos 6.2
and not evil, that you may *l*; Amos 5.14
'Man shall not *l* by bread alone, Mt 4.4
hand on her, and she will *l*." 9.18
not *l* according to the tradition Mk 7.5
'Man shall not *l* by bread alone.' Lk 4.4
do this, and you will *l*." 10.28
living; for all *l* to him." 20.38
who eats this bread will *l* Jn 6.58
because I *l*, you will *l* also. 14.19
for 'In him we *l* and move Acts 17.28
deeds of the body you will *l*. Rom 8.13
on the law shall *l* by it. 10.5
to *l* according to scripture, 1Cor 4.6
faith is righteous shall *l*"; Gal 3.11
If we *l* by the Spirit, let 5.25
no longer *l* as the Gentiles Eph 4.17
For to me to *l* is Christ, Phil 1.21
Jesus the Christ, so *l* in him, Col 2.6
we shall also *l* with him; 2Tim 2.11
to *l* sober, upright, and godly Tit 2.12
know that my Redeemer *l*, Job 19.25
None of us *l* to himself, Rom 14.7
man became a *l* being. Gen 2.7
the *l* God is among you, Josh 3.10
the armies of the *l* God." 1Sam 17.36
has sent to mock the *l* God, 2Ki 19.4
My soul thirsts..for the *l* God. Ps 42.2
l God and..everlasting King. Jer 10.10
that day *l* waters shall flow Zech 14.8
would have given you *l* water." Jn 4.10
I am the *l* bread which came 6.51
As the *l* Father sent me, 6.57
Adam became a *l* being"; 1Cor 15.45
to serve a *l* and true God, 1Thess 1.9
our hope set on the *l* God, 1Tim 4.10
fall away from the *l* God. Heb 3.12
Gentiles..*l* in licentiousness, 1Pet 4.3
the first..last, and the *l* one; Rev 1.18

LIVING (n)
between the dead and..*l*; Num 16.48
who has kept us among the *l*, Ps 66.9
blotted out of the book of the *l*; 69.28
dead more fortunate than the *l* Ecc 4.2
For the *l* know..they will die, 9.5
the dead on behalf of the *l*? Isa 8.19
The *l*, the *l*, he thanks thee, 38.19
not God of..dead, but of..*l*." Mt 22.32
not God of the dead, but..*l*; Mk 12.27
everything she had, her whole *l*." 12.44
he squandered..in loose *l*. Lk 15.13
seek the *l* among the dead? 24.5

LIZARD
l according to its kind, Lev 11.29
l you can take in..hands, Prov 30.28

LOAN
make your neighbor a *l* Deut 24.10
by this woman for the *l* 1Sam 2.20

LOATHE — D

we *l* this worthless food."   Num 21.5
"I *l* my life; I will give   Job 10.1
do I not *l* them that rise up   Ps 139.21
you will I. .your iniquities   Ezek 36.31
forty years I *l* that generation   Ps 95.10

LOAVES

"We have only five *l* here   Mt 14.17
Jesus said. . "How many *l* have you?" 15.34
"How many *l* have you? Go and   Mk 6.38
asked. . "How many *l* have you?"   8.5
no more than five *l* and two   Lk 9.13
'Friend, lend me three *l*;   11.5
has five barley *l* and two fish;   Jn 6.9
you ate your fill of the *l*.   6.26

LOCUST — S

of them you may eat: the *l*   Lev 11.22
the swarming *l* has eaten.   Joel 1.4
tomorrow I will bring *l*   Ex 10.4
coming like *l* for number;   Judg 6.5
He spoke, and the *l* came,   Ps 105.34
the *l* have no king, yet   Prov 30.27
behold, he was forming *l* in   Amos 7.1
his food was *l* and wild honey.   Mt 3.4
John. .ate *l* and wild honey.   Mk 1.6
from. .smoke came *l* on. .earth,   Rev 9.3

LODGE — D

father's house for us to *l* in?"   Gen 24.23
and where you *l* I will *l*;   Ruth 1.16
ark was *l* at Kiriath-jearim,   1Sam 7.2

LOFTY

stars, how *l* they are!   Job 22.12
l One who inhabits eternity,   Isa 57.15
not. .in *l* words or wisdom.   1Cor 2.1

LONELY

for I am *l* and afflicted.   Ps 25.16
Jesus. .withdrew. .to a *l* place   Mt 14.13
"Come away. .to a *l* place, and   Mk 6.31

LONG — S — ED (v)

who *l* for death, but it comes not, Job 3.21
Behold, I *l* for thy precepts;   Ps 119.40
As a hart *l* for flowing streams,   42.1
soul *l*, yea, faints for. .courts   84.2
king *l* to go. .to Absalom;   2Sam 13.39
righteous men *l* to see what   Mt 13.17
fruit for which thy soul *l*   Rev 18.14

LONGING (n)

My soul. . *l* for thy ordinances   Ps 119.20
creation waits with eager *l*   Rom 8.19

LOOK — S — ED — ING

l from the place where   Gen 13.14
"L toward heaven, and number   15.5
do not *l* back or stop   19.17
l at the bronze serpent   Num 21.9
L down from thy holy   Deut 26.15
"Do not *l* on his appearance   1Sam 16.7
When I *l* at thy heavens, the   Ps 8.3
God; *l* upon the face of thine   84.9
all *l* to thee, to give them   104.27
L on my affliction. .deliver   119.153
But you did not *l* to him who   Isa 22.11
L upon Zion, the city of our   33.20
Hear, you deaf; . . *l*, you blind,   42.18
l to the rock from which you   51.1
and *l* at the earth beneath;   51.6

l for justice, . .there is none;   59.11
as for me, I will *l* to the LORD,   Mic 7.7
and canst not *l* on wrong,   Hab 1.13
when you fast, do not *l* dismal,   Mt 6.16
I beg you to *l* upon my son,   Lk 9.38
begin to take place, *l* up   21.28
L at what is before your eyes. 2Cor 10.7
The LORD *l* down from heaven,   Ps 33.13
one who *l* at a woman lustfully   Mt 5.28
who *l* into the perfect law,   Jas 1.25
But Lot's wife. . *l* back,   Gen 19.26
Abraham. . *l*, and. .was a ram,   22.13
because they *l* into the ark   1Sam 6.19
They *l*, but there was none   2Sam 22.42
All men have *l* on it; man   Job 36.25
the LORD *l* at the earth,   Ps 102.19
he *l* for justice, but behold,   Isa 5.7
I *l*, . .there was no one to help.   63.5
I *l* for much, . .it came to little;   Hag 1.9
he *l* forward to the city   Heb 11.10
Joseph. . *l* for the kingdom   Mk 15.43
l for. .consolation of Israel,   Lk 2.25
he was *l* for the kingdom of God.   23.51
why. .stand *l* into heaven?   Acts 1.11
l to Jesus the pioneer and   Heb 12.2

LOOSE — S — D (v)

to *l* the bonds of wickedness,   Isa 58.6
whatever you *l* on earth shall   Mt 16.19
whatever you *l* on earth   18.18
and *l* the belt of the strong.   Job 12.21
LORD, . .Thou hast *l* my bonds. Ps 116.16
his tongue *l*, and he spoke,   Lk 1.64
Satan will be *l* from. .prison   Rev 20.7

LOOSE

the people had broken *l*   Ex 32.25
He let *l* on them his. .anger,   Ps 78.49
lips of a *l* woman drip honey,   Prov 5.3

LORD — S (n)

day that the L God made   Gen 2.4
favor in the eyes of the L.   6.8
Now the L said to Abram, "Go   12.1
by my name the L I did not   Ex 6.3
the L brought the people of   12.51
Israel sang this song to the L,   15.1
the L knew face to face,   Deut 34.10
"May my *l* King David live   1Ki 1.31
delight is in the law of the L,   Ps 1.2
thou alone, whose name is the L,   83.18
lovely. .thy dwelling place, O L   84.1
L has laid on him the iniquity   Isa 53.6
Son of man is *l* of the sabbath." Mt 12.8
Prepare the way of the L, make   Mk 1.3
"L, we do not know where you   Jn 14.5
answered. . "My L and my God!"   20.28
made him both L and Christ,   Acts 2.36
say "Jesus is L" except by   1Cor 12.3
confess that Jesus Christ is L,   Phil 2.11
"Thou, L, didst found. .earth   Heb 1.10
"Hallelujah! For the L our God Rev 19.6
many "gods" and many "*l*"—   1Cor 8.5

LORD JESUS

saved through. .grace of. .L. . Acts 15.11
"Believe in the L. ., and   16.31

LORD JESUS CHRIST

when we believed in the L. .,   Acts 11.17
peace with God through our L. .Rom 5.1
the victory through our L. .   1Cor 15.57
you know the grace of our L. ., 2Cor 8.9
power and coming of our L. ., 2Pet 1.16

LORD OF HOSTS
The *L.*.is with us; the God   Ps 46.7
the *L.*., him you shall regard   Isa 8.13

LORDS (v)
man *l* it over man to his hurt.   Ecc 8.9

LOSE — S
would save his life will *l* it,   Mt 16.25
l nothing of all..he has given   Jn 6.39
he who *l* his life for my sake   Mt 10.39
whoever *l* his life for my sake   Mk 8.35
whoever *l* his life for my sake,   Lk 9.24
l one coin, does not light..lamp   15.8
whoever *l* his life will preserve it.   17.33

LOST (v)
gone astray like a *l* sheep;   Ps 119.176
riches.. *l* in a bad venture;   Ecc 5.14
"Woe is me! For I am *l*; for   Isa 6.5
bones..dried up,..hope is *l*;   Ezek 37.11
go..to the *l* sheep of..Israel.   Mt 10.6
sent only to the *l* sheep of..Israel."   15.24
he was *l*, and is found.'   Lk 15.24
thou gavest me I *l* not one."   Jn 18.9

LOST (n)
seek the *l*, and..strayed,   Ezek 34.16
Son of man came to save the *l* Mt 18.11*n*
to seek and to save the *l*."   Lk 19.10

LOT
Accompanied Abram to Canaan, Gen 11.
31; 12.5; separated from Abram to live at
Sodom, Gen 13; rescued by Abram, Gen
14.1–16; sheltered angels, Gen 19.1–11;
fled to Zoar, Gen 19.15–23; Lot and his
daughters, Gen 19.30–38.

and *L* went with him. Abram   Gen 12.4
brought back his kinsman *L*   14.16
and *L* was sitting in the gate   19.1
in the days of *L*—they ate,   Lk 17.28
if he rescued righteous *L*,   2Pet 2.7

LOT — S
Then Saul said, "Cast the *l* 1Sam 14.42
throw in your *l* among us, we   Prov 1.14
The *l* is cast into the lap,   16.33
work, for that is his *l*;   Ecc 3.22
and the *l* fell upon Jonah.   Jonah 1.7
by *l* to enter the temple of   Lk 1.9
and the *l* fell on Matthias;   Acts 1.26
and Aaron shall cast *l* upon   Lev 16.8
for my raiment they cast *l*.   Ps 22.18
and cast *l* for Jerusalem,   Obad 1.11
among them by casting *l*;   Mt 27.35
cast *l* for it to see whose   Jn 19.24

LOVE — S — D (v)
those who *l* me and keep my   Ex 20.6
'I *l* my master, my wife,   21.5
l your neighbor as yourself: Lev 19.18
thousands of those who *l*   Deut 5.10
you shall *l* the LORD your God   6.5
he will *l* you, bless you,   7.13
to *l* him, to serve the LORD   10.12
L the sojourner therefore;   10.19
to know whether you *l* the LORD   13.3
so that you will *l* the LORD   30.6
to *l* the LORD your God.   Josh 23.11
l those who hate the LORD?   2Chr 19.2
with those who *l* him and keep   Neh 1.5
I *l* thee, O LORD, my strength.   Ps 18.1
L the LORD, all you his saints: 31.23
you *l* righteousness and hate   45.7

those who *l* thy salvation say   70.4
I *l* the LORD, because he has heard   116.1
Oh, how I *l* thy law! It is my   119.97
l her, and she will guard you.   Prov 4.6
I *l* those who *l* me, and those   8.17
L not sleep, lest you come   20.13
time to *l*, and a time to hate;   Ecc 3.8
life with the wife whom you *l*,   9.9
For I the LORD *l* justice,   Isa 61.8
l a woman who is..adulteress;   Hos 3.1
I will *l* them no more; all   9.15
I will *l* them freely, for   14.4
Hate evil, and *l* good, and   Amos 5.15
hate the good and *l* the evil,   Mic 3.2
to *l* kindness,..to walk humbly   6.8
'You shall *l* your neighbor   Mt 5.43
l your neighbor as yourself."   19.19
"You shall *l* the Lord your God   22.37
they *l* the place of honor   23.6
you shall *l* the Lord your God Mk 12.30
L your enemies, do good to   Lk 6.27
"If you *l* those who *l* you,   6.32
"You shall *l* the Lord your God   10.27
hate the one and *l* the other,   16.13
your Father, you would *l* me,   Jn 8.42
"Lord, he whom you *l* is ill."   11.3
that you also *l* one another.   13.34
"If you *l* me, you will keep   14.15
l one another as I have *l* you.   15.12
Lord; you know that I *l* you."   21.15
good with those who *l* him,   Rom 8.28
except to *l* one another;   13.8
prepared for those who *l* him," 1Cor 2.9
If I *l* you the more, am I   2Cor 12.15
Husbands, *l* your wives, as   Eph 5.25
Husbands, *l* your wives, and   Col 3.19
train the young women to *l*   Tit 2.4
promised to those who *l* him?   Jas 2.5
Without having seen him you *l* 1Pet 1.8
L the brotherhood. Fear God.   2.17
Do not *l* the world or the   1Jn 2.15
we should *l* one another,   3.11
let us *l* one another; for *l*   4.7
We *l*, because he first *l* us.   4.19
l God and obey his commandments.   5.2
Those whom I *l*, I reprove   Rev 3.19
and his father *l* him.'   Gen 44.20
because he *l* you and your   Deut 15.16
"Because the LORD *l* his   2Chr 2.11
Judah, Mount Zion, which he *l* Ps 78.68
LORD *l* those who hate evil;   97.10
LORD reproves him whom he *l*, Prov 3.12
l discipline *l* knowledge,   12.1
l him who pursues righteousness   15.9
A friend *l* at all times,   17.17
He who *l* transgression *l* strife;   17.19
He who *l* pleasure will be a poor   21.17
He who *l* purity of heart,   22.11
who *l* money will not be satisfied Ecc 5.10
I sought him whom my soul *l*;   Sol 3.1
LORD *l* him; he shall perform   Isa 48.14
who *l* father or mother more   Mt 10.37
he *l* our nation, and he built   Lk 7.5
For the Father *l* the Son,   Jn 5.20
For this reason the Father *l* me,   10.17
He who *l* his life loses it,   12.25
keeps them, he it is who *l* me;   14.21
for the Father himself *l* you,   16.27
one *l* God, one is known by him. 1Cor 8.3
for God *l* a cheerful giver.   2Cor 9.7
he who *l* his brother abides in   1Jn 2.10
To him who *l* us and has freed   Rev 1.5
he *l* her..Isaac was comforted Gen 24.67

LOVE — S — D (v) (cont.)

but Rebekah *l* Jacob.	25.28
Now Israel *l* Joseph more	37.3
because he *l* your fathers	Deut 4.37
the LORD your God *l* you.	23.5
he *l* his people; all those	33.3
and, although he *l* Hannah,	1Sam 1.5
And Saul *l* him greatly.	16.21
Jonathan *l* him as his own	18.1
Israel and Judah *l* David;	18.16
and that all Israel *l* him,	18.28
he *l* him as he *l* his own soul.	20.17
Solomon *l* the LORD, walking	1Ki 3.3
Because the LORD *l* Israel	10.9
Solomon *l* many foreign women:	11.1
l you with..everlasting love;	Jer 31.3
Israel was a child, I *l* him,	Hos 11.1
"I have *l* you," says the LORD.	Mal 1.2
Jesus looking upon him *l* him,	Mk 10.21
sins..forgiven, for she *l* much;	Lk 7.47
For God so *l* the world that	Jn 3.16
Jews said, "See how he *l* him!"	11.36
they *l* the praise of men more	12.43
world, he *l* them to the end.	13.1
As the Father has *l* me, so	15.9
thou hast sent me and..*l* them	17.23
disciple whom he *l* standing	19.26
"Jacob I *l*, but Esau I hated."	Rom 9.13
Son of God, who *l* me and gave	Gal 2.20
great love with which he *l* us,	Eph 2.4
Thou hast *l* righteousness	Heb 1.9
for they *l* not their lives	Rev 12.11

LOVE (n)

LORD set his *l* upon you	Deut 7.7
the loyal *l* of the LORD,	1Sam 20.14
not take my steadfast *l*	2Sam 7.15
Because he cleaves to me in *l*,	Ps 91.14
let us take our fill of *l*	Prov 7.18
but *l* covers all offenses.	10.12
dinner of herbs where *l* is	15.17
open rebuke than hidden *l*.	27.5
For your *l* is better than wine,	Sol 1.2
you are beautiful, my *l*;	1.15
Behold, you are beautiful, my *l*,	4.1
better is your *l* than wine,	4.10
seal..for *l* is strong as death,	8.6
Many waters cannot quench *l*,	8.7
l song concerning his vineyard:	Isa 5.1
in his *l* and..pity he redeemed	63.9
with..lips they show much *l*,	Ezek 33.31
Your *l* is like a morning cloud,	Hos 6.4
I led them with..bands of *l*,	11.4
most men's *l* will grow cold.	Mt 24.12
you..neglect justice and..*l*	Lk 11.42
Greater *l* has no man than this,	Jn 15.13
that the *l* with which thou	17.26
God's *l* has been poured	Rom 5.5
But God shows his *l* for us	5.8
separate us from the *l* of God	8.39
Let *l* be genuine; hate what	12.9
puffs up, but *l* builds up.	1Cor 8.1
but have not *l*, I am a noisy gong	13.1
the greatest of these is *l*.	13.13
the *l* of Christ controls us,	2Cor 5.14
by..the Holy Spirit, genuine *l*,	6.6
prove..that your *l*..is genuine.	8.8
of your *l* and of our boasting	8.24
Christ and the *l* of God and	13.14
but faith working through *l*.	Gal 5.6
through *l* be servants of one	5.13
your *l* toward all the saints,	Eph 1.15
to know the *l* of Christ	3.19

speaking the truth in *l*,	4.15
walk in *l*, as Christ loved us	5.2
prayer that your *l* may abound	Phil 1.9
The latter do it out of *l*,	1.16
the *l* which you have for all	Col 1.4
above all these put on *l*,	3.14
work of faith..labor of *l*	1Thess 1.3
concerning *l* of the brethren	4.9
Demas, in *l* with this present	2Tim 4.10
Let brotherly *l* continue.	Heb 13.1
since *l* covers a multitude	1Pet 4.8
See what *l* the Father has given	1Jn 3.1
By this we know *l*, that he	3.16
blemishes on your *l* feasts,	Jude 12
abandoned..*l* you had at first.	Rev 2.4

LOVELY

How *l* is thy dwelling place,	Ps 84.1
whatever is *l*, is gracious,	Phil 4.8

LOVERS

and drink: drink deeply, O *l*!	Sol 5.1
Your *l* despise you; they seek	Jer 4.30
l shall go into captivity;	22.22
All your *l* have forgotten you;	30.14
gifts to all your *l*, bribing	Ezek 16.33
rouse against you your *l*	23.22
alone; Ephraim has hired *l*.	Hos 8.9
For men will be *l* of self,	2Tim 3.2

LOW — EST

haughty looks..be brought *l*,	Isa 2.11
the lofty will be brought *l*.	10.33
He..lays it *l* to the ground,	26.5
with shame to take the *l* place.	Lk 14.9

LOWLY

proud, but he saves the *l*.	Job 22.29
better to be of a *l* spirit	Prov 16.19
l in spirit will obtain honor.	29.23
leave..a people humble and *l*.	Zeph 3.12

LOYAL — LY

"With the *l* thou dost show	2Sam 22.26
With the *l* thou dost show..*l*;	Ps 18.25
"I will deal *l* with Hanun	1Chr 19.2

LOYALTY

you showed this *l* to Saul	2Sam 2.5
desired in a man is *l*, and	Prov 19.22

LUKE

L the beloved physician and	Col 4.14
L alone is with me. Get Mark	2Tim 4.11
and *L*, my fellow workers.	Philem 24

LUKEWARM

So, because you are *l*, and	Rev 3.16

LUST — FULLY

the *l* of the flesh and the *l*	1Jn 2.16
looks at a woman *l* has already	Mt 5.28

LYING

Let the *l* lips be dumb, which	Ps 31.18
against me with *l* tongues.	109.2
haughty eyes, a *l* tongue, and	Prov 6.17

LYRE — S

father of all..who play the *l*	Gen 4.21
Praise the LORD with the *l*,	Ps 33.2
On the willows..we hung up our *l*.	137.2

LYSTRA

fled to *L* and Derbe, cities	Acts 14.6
they returned to *L* and to	14.21
came also to Derbe and to *L*.	16.1
and at *L*, what persecutions	2Tim 3.11

M

MACEDONIA
a man of *M*..beseeching him   Acts 16.9
and Timothy arrived from *M*,   18.5
sent into *M* two of his helpers,   19.22
For *M* and Achaia have been Rom 15.26
about you to the people of *M*,   2Cor 9.2
when I left *M*, no church   Phil 4.15
word of Lord sounded..in *M* 1Thess 1.8

MAD — NESS
driven *m* by the sight   Deut 28.34
feigned himself *m* in their   1Sam 21.13
"I am not *m*,..Festus, but   Acts 26.25
consider wisdom..*m* and folly; Ecc 2.12

MAGGOT
much less man, who is a *m*,   Job 25.6

MAGNIFICENCE
Artemis..deposed from her *m* Acts 19.27

MAGNIFICENT
house..must be exceedingly *m* 1Chr 22.5

MAGNIFY — IES — IED
O *m* the LORD with me, and let Ps 34.3
and dishonor who *m* themselves   35.26
or the saw *m* itself against   Isa 10.15
m his law..make it glorious.   42.21
to..Gentiles, I *m* my ministry Rom 11.13
Mary said, "My soul *m* the Lord, Lk 1.46
thy name will be *m* for ever,   2Sam 7.26
thy name will be..*m* for ever, 1Chr 17.24
It *m* itself,..up to the Prince   Dan 8.11

MAGOG
Gog, of the land of *M*, the   Ezek 38.2
Gog and *M*, to gather them   Rev 20.8

MAID
Sarai said..go in to my *m*;   Gen 16.2
little *m* from the land..Israel   2Ki 5.2
a *m* when she succeeds her   Prov 30.23
another *m* saw him, and..said Mt 26.71

MAIDEN — S
"Let a young *m* be sought for   1Ki 1.2
the way of a man with a *m*.   Prov 30.19
between..*m* playing timbrels: Ps 68.25
therefore the *m* love you.   Sol 1.3
kingdom..compared to ten *m*   Mt 25.1

MAINTAIN
m the right of..man with God, Job 16.21
m the rights of the poor   Prov 31.9

MAINTENANCE
gifts for the *m* of the house   1Chr 26.27

MAJESTIC
our Lord, how *m* is thy name in Ps 8.1
our Lord, how *m* is thy name in   8.9

MAJESTY
Will not his *m* terrify you,   Job 13.11
"Deck yourself with *m* and   40.10
there the LORD in *m* will be   Isa 33.21
Zion has departed all her *m*.   Lam 1.6
and for the glory of my *m*?"   Dan 4.30
my *m* and splendor returned   4.36
the *m* of the name of the LORD   Mic 5.4

MAKER
God..*m* of heaven and earth; Gen 14.19
none says, 'Where is..my *M*,   Job 35.10
kneel before the LORD, our *M*!   Ps 95.6
men will regard their *M*, and   Isa 17.7

"Woe..who strives with his *M*,   45.9
For your *M* is your husband,   54.5

MALACHI
word of the LORD to Israel by *M*. Mal 1.1

MALE
m and female he created   Gen 1.27
Every *m*..shall be circumcised.   17.10
there is neither *m* nor female; Gal 3.28

MALTA
the island was called *M*.   Acts 28.1

MAMMON
You cannot serve God and *m*.   Mt 6.24
make friends..of unrighteous *m*, Lk 16.9

MAN — 'S
make *m* in our image,   Gen 1.26
God formed *m* of dust   2.7
the *m* called every..creature,   2.19
m and his wife hid themselves   3.8
to David, "You are the *m*.   2Sam 12.7
a *m* be pure before his Maker? Job 4.17
but *m* is born to trouble   5.7
What is *m*, that thou dost   7.17
he is not a *m*, as I am,   9.32
"*M* that is born of a woman   14.1
But *m* dies, and is laid low;   14.10
What is *m*, that he can be   15.14
what is *m* that thou dost regard Ps 144.3
and one *m* sharpens another.   Prov 27.17
mind of *m* reflects the *m*.   27.19
way of *m* is not in himself,   Jer 10.23
declares to *m*..his thought;   Amos 4.13
what can a *m* give in return   Mk 8.37
no *m* to put me into the pool   Jn 5.7
"No *m* ever spoke like this *m*!"   7.46
as sin came..through one *m*   Rom 5.12
by your knowledge this weak *m* 1Cor 8.11
m was not made from woman,   11.8
create in himself one new *m*   Eph 2.15
"What is *m* that thou art   Heb 2.6
A *m* steps are ordered by   Prov 20.24

MANASSEH
Joseph called..first-born *M*,   Gen 41.51
two sons, *M* and Ephraim.   48.1
Of the people of *M*, their   Num 1.34
son of *M*, from the families   27.1
to the half-tribe of *M*.   Deut 3.13
my clan is the weakest in *M*,   Judg 6.15
M was twelve years old when   2Ki 21.1
M shed very much innocent   21.16
M slept with his fathers,   21.18
the altars which *M* had made   23.12
M was twelve years old when   2Chr 33.1
M knew that the LORD was   33.13
not..as *M* his father had   33.23

MANDRAKES
Reuben went and found *m*   Gen 30.14
The *m* give forth fragrance,   Sol 7.13

MANGER
and laid him in a *m*, because   Lk 2.7

MANIFEST — ED
Let thy work be *m* to thy   Ps 90.16
hid, except to be made *m*;   Mk 4.22
the life was made *m*, and we   1Jn 1.2
the love of God was made *m*   4.9
m thy might among the peoples. Ps 77.14

MANIFESTATION
until..day of his *m* to Israel.   Lk 1.80
given the *m* of the Spirit   1Cor 12.7

MANNA
Israel called its name *m*;	Ex 16.31
Israel ate the *m* forty years,	16.35
nothing at all but this *m*	Num 11.6
the *m* ceased on the morrow,	Josh 5.12
rained..upon them *m* to eat,	Ps 78.24
Our fathers ate *m* in..wilderness;	Jn 6.31
give some of the hidden *m*,	Rev 2.17

MAN OF GOD
told her husband, "A *m*..came	Judg 13.6
And there came a *m*..to Eli,	1Sam 2.27
there is a *m*..in this city,	9.6
a *m*..came out of Judah by	1Ki 13.1
m.., who disobeyed the word	13.26
I know that you are a *m*..,	17.24
a *m*..came near and said to	20.28
"If I am a *m*.., let fire come	2Ki 1.10
he died, as the *m*..had said	7.17
a *m*..came to him and said,	2Chr 25.7

MANTLE
he took up the *m* of Elijah	2Ki 2.13

MARK (JOHN MARK)
Cousin of Barnabas, Col 4.10; lived in Jerusalem, Acts 12.12; accompanied Barnabas and Paul to Antioch, Acts 12.25; began missionary work, Acts 13.5; deserted the group at Perga, Acts 13.13; subject of contention, Acts 15.37–38; went with Barnabas to Cyprus, Acts 15.39; ministered to Paul in Rome, Col 4.10; Philem 24; companion of Peter, 1Pet 5.13.

MARK — ED (v)
M the blameless man, and	Ps 37.37
"*M* this,..you who forget God,	50.22
If thou,..*m* iniquities, Lord,	130.3
to be *m* on the right hand	Rev 13.16

MARK — S (n)
LORD put a *m* on Cain,	Gen 4.15
put a *m* upon the foreheads	Ezek 9.4
receives a *m* on his forehead	Rev 14.9
received the *m* of the beast	19.20
on my body the *m* of Jesus.	Gal 6.17

MARKET — S
like children sitting in the *m*	Lk 7.32
love salutations in the *m*	20.46
and in the *m* place every day	Acts 17.17
Eat whatever..in the meat *m*	1Cor 10.25
coastlands were..special *m*,	Ezek 27.15

MARRIAGE — S
king who gave a *m* feast for	Mt 22.2
in with him to the *m* feast;	25.10
come home from the *m* feast,	Lk 12.36
forbid *m* and enjoin abstinence	1Tim 4.3
Let *m* be held in honor among	Heb 13.4
Make *m*..give your daughters	Gen 34.9
and make *m* with them,	Josh 23.12

MARRY — IES — IED
when they rise..they neither *m*	Mk 12.25
neither *m* nor are given in	Lk 20.35
m her, if then she finds	Deut 24.1
and whoever *m* a divorced woman	Mt 5.32
m another, commits adultery."	19.9
divorces..wife and *m* another,	Mk 10.11
who divorces his wife and *m*	Lk 16.18
Cushite woman whom he had *m*,	Num 12.1
m..daughter of a foreign god.	Mal 2.11
To the *m* I give charge,	1Cor 7.10
the *m* man is anxious about	7.33

MARTHA
M received him into her house.	Lk 10.38
village of Mary and..sister *M*.	Jn 11.1
M said to him, "I know that	11.24
they made a supper; *M* served,	12.2

MARTYRS
the blood of the *m* of Jesus.	Rev 17.6

MARVEL — ED
the angel said to me, "Why *m*?	Rev 17.7
When Jesus heard him, he *m*,	Mt 8.10
the men *m*,.."What sort of man	8.27
dumb man spoke;..the crowds *m*,	9.33
When they heard it, they *m*;	22.22
done for him; and all men *m*.	Mk 5.20
he *m* because of their unbelief.	6.6
When Jesus heard this he *m* at	Lk 7.9

MARVELOUS
m things without number:	Job 5.9
and *m* things without number.	9.10
the LORD's doing; it is *m*	Ps 118.23
do *m* things with this people,	Isa 29.14

MARY (Magdalene)
Healed of demons, Lk 8.2; stood by the cross, Mt 27.56 (Mk 15.40; Jn 19.25); watched Jesus' burial, Mt 27.61 (Mk 15.47); came early to the sepulchre, Mt 28.1 (Mk 16.1; Lk 24.10; Jn 20.1); saw the risen Lord, Mt 28.9 (Mk 16.9n; Jn 20.11–18).

MARY (Mother of Jesus)
Betrothed to Joseph, Mt 1.18 (Lk 1.27); Jesus' birth foretold to her, Lk 1.26–38; visited Elizabeth, Lk 1.39–45; "The Magnificat," Lk 1.46–55; went to Bethlehem, Lk 2.4–5; birth of Jesus, Mt 1.25 (Lk 2.7); found Jesus in the temple, Lk 2.41–51; attended the marriage at Cana, Jn 2.1–5; concerned over Jesus' ministry, Mk 3.31–35; at the cross, Jn 19.25–27; in the upper room, Acts 1.14.

MARY (of Bethany)
Listened to the Lord's teaching, Lk 10.38–42; present at the raising of Lazarus, Jn 11.1–45; anointed Jesus' feet, Jn 12.1–8.

MASTER — S
m saw..the LORD was with him,	Gen 39.3
'I love my *m*, my wife,	Ex 21.5
who guards his *m*..honored.	Prov 27.18
I am your *m*; I will take you,	Jer 3.14
who is both their *M* and yours	Eph 6.9
useful to the *m* of the house,	2Tim 2.21
"No one can serve two *m*; for	Mt 6.24
Neither be called *m*, for you	23.10
Those who have believing *m*	1Tim 6.2
be submissive to your *m* with	1Pet 2.18

MATTHEW
he saw a man called *M* sitting	Mt 9.9
Thomas and *M* the tax collector;	10.3
and *M*, and Thomas, and James	Mk 3.18
and *M*, and Thomas, and James	Lk 6.15
Thomas, Bartholomew and *M*,	Acts 1.13

MATURE
among..*m* we do impart wisdom,	1Cor 2.6
to *m* manhood, to the measure	Eph 4.13

MATURITY
go on to *m*, not laying again	Heb 6.1

MEASURE — D — ING (v)
"Rise and *m* the temple of God   Rev 11.1
a measuring rod of gold to *m*   21.15
has *m* the waters in..his hand   Isa 40.12
"If the heavens..can be *m*,   Jer 31.37
He stood and *m* the earth;   Hab 3.6
man with a *m* line in his hand! Zech 2.1

MEASURE (n)
what is the *m* of my days;   Ps 39.4
the *m* you give will be the *m* Mk 4.24
the *m* you give will be the *m* Lk 6.38

MEDE — S
by birth a *M*, who became king   Dan 9.1
and in the cities of the *M*.   2Ki 17.6
let it be written among..*M*   Est 1.19
The LORD has stirred up..*M*,   Jer 51.11
given to the *M* and Persians."   Dan 5.28
according to the law of the *M*   6.8

MEDIA
province of *M*, a scroll was   Ezra 6.2
of Persia and *M* and the nobles Est 1.3
Chronicles of the kings of *M*   10.2
ram..kings of *M* and Persia.   Dan 8.20

MEDIATOR
If there be for him..a *m*,   Job 33.23
one *m* between God and men,   1Tim 2.5
is the *m* of a new covenant,   Heb 9.15
Jesus,..*m* of a new covenant,   12.24

MEDITATE — S
Isaac went..to *m* in the field   Gen 24.63
m on it day and night,   Josh 1.8
and *m* on thee in the watches   Ps 63.6
I will *m* on all thy work, and   77.12
I will *m* on thy precepts, and   119.15
I will *m* on thy precepts.   119.78
I *m* on all that thou hast done;   143.5
on his law he *m* day and night.   1.2

MEDITATION
and hindering *m* before God,   Job 15.4
Let the words..and the *m* of my Ps 19.14
wisdom; the *m* of my heart   49.3
May my *m* be pleasing to him,   104.34
thy law!..is my *m* all the day.   119.97

MEEK — NESS
Moses was very *m*, more   Num 12.3
hear the desire of the *m*;   Ps 10.17
the *m* shall possess the land,   37.11
The *m* shall obtain fresh joy   Isa 29.19
"Blessed are the *m*, for they   Mt 5.5
by the *m* and gentleness of   2Cor 10.1
with all lowliness and *m*,   Eph 4.2
receive with *m* the implanted   Jas 1.21

MEET — ING
There I will *m* with you,   Ex 25.22
prepare to *m*..God, O Israel!"   Amos 4.12
the city came out to *m* Jesus;   Mt 8.34
in..clouds to *m* the Lord   1Thess 4.17
it did not *m* with faith in   Heb 4.2
not neglecting to *m* together,   10.25
burned all the *m* places of God Ps 74.8

MEGIDDO
the king of *M*, one;   Josh 12.21
of *M* and its villages;   17.11
M, and all Bethshean which   1Ki 4.12
he fled to *M*, and died there.   2Ki 9.27
Pharaoh Neco slew him at *M*,   23.29
mourning..in the plain of *M*.   Zech 12.11

MELCHIZEDEK
M king of Salem brought   Gen 14.18
priest..after the order of *M*." Ps 110.4
for ever, after the order of *M*." Heb 5.6
for ever after the order of *M*.   6.20
this *M*, king of Salem, priest   7.1
his ancestor when *M* met him.   7.10
priest..in the likeness of *M*,   7.15

MELT — S — ED
mountains *m* like wax before   Ps 97.5
sends forth his word, and *m*   147.18
inhabitants of Canaan..*m*   Ex 15.15
heard it, our hearts *m*,   Josh 2.11
crossed over, their heart *m*,   5.1
the hearts of the people *m*,   7.5
my heart is like wax; it is *m*   Ps 22.14
so you shall be *m* in..it;   Ezek 22.22

MEMBERS
Do not yield your *m* to sin   Rom 6.13
m do not have..same function,   12.4
Shall I..take the *m* of Christ   1Cor 6.15
because we are *m* of his body.   Eph 5.30

MEMORIAL
as a *m* between your eyes,   Ex 13.9
"Write this as a *m* in a book   17.14
these stones..a *m* for ever."   Josh 4.7
thy *m* name is the desire of   Isa 26.8
alms have ascended as a *m*   Acts 10.4

MEMORY
His *m* perishes from..earth   Job 18.17
his *m* be cut off from..earth!   Ps 109.15
The *m* of the righteous is a   Prov 10.7
but the *m* of them is lost.   Ecc 9.5
will be told in *m* of her."   Mt 26.13

MEN
and acquit yourselves like *m*,   1Sam 4.9
my transgressions from *m*,   Job 31.33
know that they are but men!   Ps 9.20
and behaving like ordinary *m*?   1Cor 3.3
So let no one boast of *m*.   3.21
Paul an apostle—not from *m*   Gal 1.1

MENE
inscribed: *M*, *M*, TEKEL, and   Dan 5.25

MEPHIBOSHETH
*Crippled by a fall, 2Sam 4.4; dined
continually at the royal table, 2Sam 9;
reported to David as a deserter, 2Sam
16.1–4; cleared himself before David,
2Sam 19.24–30.*

MERCHANT — S
kingdom..is like a *m* in search Mt 13.45
You increased your *m* more   Nah 3.16
the *m* of the earth have grown   Rev 18.3

MERCIFUL
LORD being *m* to him,   Gen 19.16
house of Israel are *m* kings;   1Ki 20.31
art a God *m* and gracious, slow Ps 86.15
thou art a gracious God and *m*, Jonah 4.2
"Blessed are the *m*, for they   Mt 5.7
Be *m*, even as your Father is *m*. Lk 6.36
m toward their iniquities,   Heb 8.12

MERCY — IES
God Almighty grant you *m*   Gen 43.14
show *m* on whom I will show *m*. Ex 33.19
and show no *m* to them.   Deut 7.2
for his *m* is very great;   1Chr 21.13
grant him *m* in the sight of   Neh 1.11

MERCY — IES (cont.)

Have *m* on me, O God,..love;	Ps 51.1
crowns you with..love and *m*,	103.4
I will surely have *m* on him,	Jer 31.20
I will grant you *m*, that he	42.12
told them to seek *m* of the God	Dan 2.18
known; in wrath remember *m*.	Hab 3.2
'I desire *m*, and not sacrifice.'	Mt 9.13
'I desire *m* and not sacrifice,'	12.7
"Have *m* on me, O Lord, Son of	15.22
"Have *m* on us, Son of David!"	20.30
law, justice and *m* and faith;	23.23
tell..how he has had *m* on you."	Mk 5.19
his *m* is on those who fear	Lk 1.50
to perform the *m* promised to	1.72
one who showed *m* on him."	10.37
'Father Abraham, have *m* upon me,	16.24
"Jesus, Son of David, have *m*	18.38
have *m* on whom I have *m*,	Rom 9.15
he has *m* upon whomever he wills,	9.18
glory for the vessels of *m*,	9.23
now have received *m* because	11.30
ministry by the *m* of God,	2Cor 4.1
But God had *m* on him, and	Phil 2.27
his *m* never come to an end;	Lam 3.22

MERCY SEAT

and from above the *m*..,	Ex 25.22
within..veil, before the *m*..	Lev 16.2

MEROM

at the waters of *M*, to fight	Josh 11.5
by the waters of *M*, and fell	11.7

MESSAGE

"I have a *m* from God for	Judg 3.20
Haggai,..with the Lord's *m*,	Hag 1.13
confirmed the *m* by the signs	Mk 16.20*n*
my *m*..not in plausible words	1Cor 2.4
This is the *m* we have heard	1Jn 1.5

MESSENGER — S

faithful *m* to those who send	Prov 25.13
a *m*..sent among the nations:	Jer 49.14
for he is the *m* of the Lord of	Mal 2.7
send my *m* to prepare the way	3.1
I send my *m* before thy face,	Mt 11.10
I send my *m* before thy face,	Mk 1.2
I send my *m* before thy face,	Lk 7.27
a *m* of Satan, to harass me,	2Cor 12.7
Jacob sent *m*..to Esau	Gen 32.3
sent..to them by his *m*,	2Chr 36.15
"On that day swift *m* shall go	Ezek 30.9
And he sent *m* ahead of him,	Lk 9.51

MESSIAH

said.."We have found the *M*"	Jn 1.41
"I know that *M* is coming	4.25

METHUSELAH

Thus all the days of *M*	Gen 5.27

MICAH

"*M* of Moresheth prophesied	Jer 26.18
word of the Lord that came to *M*	Mic 1.1

MICHAL

Married to David, 1Sam 18.20–30; helped David escape, 1Sam 19.12–17; restored to David, 2Sam 3.13–16; rebuked for despising David, 2Sam 6.12–23.

the name of the younger *M*;	1Sam 14.49
bring *M*, Saul's daughter,	2Sam 3.13
M..saw King David dancing	1Chr 15.29

MICHMASH

thousand were with Saul in *M*	1Sam 13.2

on the north in front of *M*,	14.5
at *M* he stores his baggage;	Isa 10.28

MIDIAN — ITE

M, Ishbak, and Shuah.	Gen 25.2
Moses..stayed in..land of *M*;	Ex 2.15
Lord said to Moses in *M*,	4.19
Jethro, the priest of *M*,	18.1
Moab said to the elders of *M*,	Num 22.4
into the hand of *M* seven years.	Judg 6.1
the camp of *M* was below him	7.8
They set out from *M* and	1Ki 11.18
Do to them as thou didst to *M*,	Ps 83.9
broken as on the day of *M*.	Isa 9.4
scourge, as when he smote *M*	10.26
Then *M* traders passed by;	Gen 37.28

MIDNIGHT

But Samson lay till *m*,	Judg 16.3
At *m* I rise to praise thee,	Ps 119.62
about *m* Paul and Silas were	Acts 16.25
prolonged his speech until *m*.	20.7

MIDWIVES

king..said to the Hebrew *m*,	Ex 1.15

MIGHT

"Go in this *m*..and deliver	Judg 6.14
not by *m* shall a man prevail.	1Sam 2.9
"Do you give the horse his *m*?	Job 39.19
But I will sing of thy *m*; I	Ps 59.16
to do, do it with your *m*; for	Ecc 9.10
men, whose own *m* is their god!	Hab 1.11
Not by *m*, nor by power, but by	Zech 4.6

MIGHTY — IER

"How are the *m* fallen	2Sam 1.25
the *m* men whom David had:	23.8
Why do the wicked..grow *m* in	Job 21.7
God is *m*, and does not despise	36.5
With the *m* deeds of the Lord	Ps 71.16
Lord..the *M* One of Israel:	Isa 1.24
"Wonderful Counselor, *M* God,	9.6
vindication, *m* to save."	63.1
who does a *m* work in my name	Mk 9.39
telling..the *m* works of God."	Acts 2.11
A wise..*m* than a strong man,	Prov 24.5
he who is *m* than I is coming,	Lk 3.16

MILE

if..one forces you to go one *m*,	Mt 5.41

MILK

he took curds, and *m*,	Gen 18.8
a land flowing with *m* and honey,	Ex 3.8
she opened a skin of *m*	Judg 4.19
thou not pour me out like *m*	Job 10.10
I fed you with *m*, not solid	1Cor 3.2
without getting some of the *m*?	9.7
You need *m*, not solid food;	Heb 5.12

MILLSTONE

woman threw an upper *m* upon	Judg 9.53
a..*m* fastened round his neck	Mt 18.6
better for him if a great *m*	Mk 9.42
better for him if a *m* were hung	Lk 17.2

MIND — S

father kept the saying in *m*.	Gen 37.11
a *m* to understand, or eyes	Deut 29.4
an understanding *m* to govern	1Ki 3.9
m of the king..was..troubled	2Ki 6.11
repent with all their *m* and	2Chr 6.38
the people had a *m* to work.	Neh 4.6
call to *m* the deeds of..Lord;	Ps 77.11
A tranquil *m* gives life to	Prov 14.30
A man's *m* plans his way,	16.9

MIND — S (cont.)
A man of crooked *m* does not	17.20
m of man reflects the man.	27.19
whose *m* is stayed on thee,	Isa 26.3
deluded *m* has led him astray,	44.20
his *m* be changed from a man's,	Dan 4.16
clothed and in his right *m*,	Mk 5.15
m..set on the flesh is hostile	Rom 8.7
who has known the *m* of the Lord,	11.34
we have the *m* of Christ.	1Cor 2.16
I will sing with the *m* also.	14.15
speak five words with my *m*,	14.19
do as he has made up his *m*,	2Cor 9.7
Have this *m* among yourselves,	Phil 2.5
speak visions of their own *m*,	Jer 23.16
a veil lies over their *m*;	2Cor 3.15
Set your *m* on things..above,	Col 3.2

MINDFUL
Be *m* of thy mercy, O Lord,	Ps 25.6
The Lord has been *m* of us;	115.12
their God will be *m* of them	Zeph 2.7
if, *m* of God, he endures pain	1Pet 2.19

MINISTER — ED — ING (v)
as they *m* at the tabernacle;	Num 3.7
m in the name of the Lord	Deut 18.7
join..the Lord, to *m* to him,	Isa 56.6
their kings shall *m* to you;	60.10
And the boy *m* to the Lord,	1Sam 2.11
went after Elijah, and *m* to	1Ki 19.21
They *m* with song before	1Chr 6.32
Samuel was *m* to the Lord	1Sam 3.1
women..followed..*m* to him;	Mt 27.55

MINISTER — S (n)
to be a *m* of Christ Jesus	Rom 15.16
of which I, Paul, became a *m*.	Col 1.23
Tychicus..faithful *m* and	4.7
makest..fire and flame thy *m*.	Ps 104.4
shall be *m* in my sanctuary,	Ezek 44.11

MINISTRY
and to the *m* of the word."	Acts 6.4
to..Gentiles, I magnify my *m*	Rom 11.13
the work of *m*, for building	Eph 4.12

MIRACLE — S
'Prove..by working a *m*,'	Ex 7.9
to another the working of *m*,	1Cor 12.10
he who..works *m* among you	Gal 3.5

MIRIAM
Song of Miriam, Ex 15.20–21; became leprous for criticizing Moses, Num 12.1–10; her leprosy healed, Num 12.11–16; died in Kadesh, Num 20.1.

MIRROR — S
skies, hard as a molten *m*?	Job 37.18
now we see in a *m* dimly,	1Cor 13.12
who observes his..face in a *m*,	Jas 1.23
the *m* of the ministering women	Ex 38.8

MISCHIEF
Philistines..I do them *m*."	Judg 15.3
wicked..is pregnant with *m*,	Ps 7.14
He plots *m* while on his bed;	36.4

MISCHIEF-MAKER
or a wrongdoer, or a *m*;	1Pet 4.15

MISERABLE
m comforters are you all.	Job 16.2

MISFORTUNE
M pursues sinners, but	Prov 13.21

MISS — ES — ED
sling a stone..and not *m*.	Judg 20.16
inspect..fold and *m* nothing.	Job 5.24
who *m* me injures himself;	Prov 8.36
you will be *m*, because your	1Sam 20.18

MIST
a *m* went up from the earth	Gen 2.6
You are a *m* that appears	Jas 4.14

MIZPAH
Laban..named..the pillar *M*,	Gen 31.49
words before the Lord at *M*.	Judg 11.11
"Gather all Israel at *M*,	1Sam 7.5
together to the Lord at *M*;	10.17
took captive..people..in *M*,	Jer 41.10

MOCK — S — ED — ING
sent to *m* the living God,	2Ki 19.4
and after I have spoken, *m* on.	Job 21.3
All who see me *m* at me, they	Ps 22.7
Assyria has sent to *m*..God,	Isa 37.4
those..far from you..*m* you,	Ezek 22.5
they will *m* him, and spit upon	Mk 10.34
who see it begin to *m* him,	Lk 14.29
m the poor insults his Maker;	Prov 17.5
all the day; every one *m* me.	Jer 20.7
you have *m* me, and told	Judg 16.10
at noon Elijah *m* them,	1Ki 18.27
"Whom have you *m* and reviled	2Ki 19.22
they *m* him, saying, "Hail,	Mt 27.29
also the chief priests *m* him	Mk 15.31
will be *m* and shamefully	Lk 18.32
The soldiers also *m* him,	23.36
some; but others said,	Acts 17.32
I shall seem to be *m* him,	Gen 27.12
kept *m* the messengers of	2Chr 36.16

MOLECH
devote them by fire to *M*,	Lev 18.21
daughter..an offering to *M*.	2Ki 23.10

MONEY
refund..*m* for his redemption.	Lev 25.52
redemption *m* from those who	Num 3.49
you shall turn it into *m*,	Deut 14.25
give the *m* that was weighed	2Ki 12.11
who loves *m*..not be satisfied	Ecc 5.10
wisdom is like the protection of *m*;	7.12
and *m* answers everything.	10.19
pieces of silver..are blood *m*."	Mt 27.6
gave a sum of *m* to the soldiers	28.12
Pharisees,..were lovers of *m*,	Lk 16.14
brought the *m* and laid it at	Acts 4.37
Simon saw..offered them *m*,	8.18
love of *m* is the root of all	1Tim 6.10
Keep..life free from love of *m*,	Heb 13.5

MONEY-CHANGERS
overturned the tables of the *m*	Mt 21.12
overturned the tables of the *m*	Mk 11.15
and the *m* at their business.	Jn 2.14

MOON
fair as the *m*, bright as..sun,	Sol 6.10
the *m* will not shed..light.	Isa 13.10
light of the *m*..as the sun,	30.26
and the fixed order of the *m*	Jer 31.35
m shall not give its light.	Ezek 32.7
the *m* will not give its light,	Mt 24.29
and the *m* into blood, before	Acts 2.20
another glory of the *m*,	1Cor 15.41

MORALS
"Bad company ruins good *m*."	1Cor 15.33

MORDECAI
Counseled Esther, Est 2.5–20; informed Esther of a conspiracy, Est 2.21–23; refused to reverence Haman, Est 3.2–6; arrayed in royal apparel, Est 6.1–11; promoted next to the king, Est 8.1–2; 10.3; reversed Haman's decree, Est 8.3—9.4; decreed feast of Purim, Est 9.20–31.

MORIAH
go to..M, and offer him there   Gen 22.2

MORNING
the *m* thou dost hear my voice;   Ps 5.3
but joy comes with the *m*.   30.5
The watchman says: "*M* comes,   Isa 21.12
in the *m*,..he rose and went out   Mk 1.35
I will give him the *m* star.   Rev 2.28
I am..the bright *m* star."   22.16

MORSEL
Better is a dry *m* with quiet   Prov 17.1
he to whom I shall give this *m*   Jn 13.26

MORTAL
m man..righteous before God?   Job 4.17
sin..reign in your *m* bodies,   Rom 6.12
this *m* nature must put on   1Cor 15.53
There is sin which is *m*;   1Jn 5.16

MOSES
Born, Ex 2.1–4; adopted by Pharaoh's daughter, Ex 2.5–10; trained at the Egyptian court, Acts 7.22; killed an Egyptian, Ex 2.11–12; fled to Midian, Ex 2.15–20; married Zipporah, Ex 2.21–22; called by God, Ex 3.1—4.17; returned to Egypt, Ex 4.18–31; interceded with Pharaoh, Ex 5—11; led the Israelites across the Red Sea, Ex 14; sang for triumph, Ex 15.1–18; appointed rulers, Ex 18.13–26; met God on Sinai, Ex 19.3–13; 24—31; enraged by Israel's idolatry, Ex 32; talked with the LORD, Ex 33—34; built the tabernacle, Ex 35—40; numbered the people, Num 1; vindicated before Aaron and Miriam, Num 12; sent twelve spies to Canaan, Num 13.1–20; consecrated Joshua as his successor, Num 27.18–23; Deut 31.23; recounted Israel's history, Deut 1—3; exhorted Israel to obedience, Deut 4.1–40; song of Moses, Deut 32.1–43; viewed Canaan, Deut 3.23–27; 32.48–52; 34.1–4; blessed the tribes, Deut 33; death and burial in Moab, Deut 34.5–7. (See also Acts 7.20–44.)

M, so I will be with you;   Josh 1.5
by the hand of *M* and Aaron.   Ps 77.20
He made known his ways to *M*,   103.7
would destroy them—had not *M*,   106.23
to go at the right hand of *M*,   Isa 63.12
M and Samuel stood before me,   Jer 15.1
appeared to them *M* and Elijah,   Mt 17.3
M allowed you to divorce..wives,   19.8
Abraham said, 'They have *M*   Lk 16.29
beginning with *M*..he interpreted   24.27
the law was given through *M*;   Jn 1.17
as *M* lifted up the serpent   3.14
If you believed *M*, you would   5.46
M said, 'The Lord God will   Acts 3.22
death reigned from Adam to *M*,   Rom 5.14
fathers..were baptized into *M*   1Cor 10.2
whenever *M* is read a veil   2Cor 3.15
Jannes and Jambres opposed *M*,   2Tim 3.8

just as *M* also was faithful   Heb 3.2
By faith *M*, when..born, was   11.23
disputed about the body of *M*,   Jude 9
they sing the song of *M*, the   Rev 15.3
could not look at *M* face   2Cor 3.7

MOTH
consume like a *m* what is dear   Ps 39.11
I am like a *m* to Ephraim,   Hos 5.12
treasures on earth, where *m*   Mt 6.19

MOTHER — S
she was the *m* of all living.   Gen 3.20
shall be a *m* of nations;   17.16
and called the child's *m*.   Ex 2.8
arose as a *m* in Israel.   Judg 5.7
his *m* used to make for him   1Sam 2.19
slay it; she is its *m*."   1Ki 3.27
his *m*, King Asa removed   2Chr 15.16
making her the joyous *m* of   Ps 113.9
only one in the sight of my *m*,   Prov 4.3
As one whom his *m* comforts,   Isa 66.13
"Who..my *m*, and..brothers?"   Mt 12.48
my brother, and sister, and *m*."   12.50
a man shall leave..father and *m*   19.5
"Who are my *m* and brothers?"   Mk 3.33
'Honor your father and your *m*';   7.10
disciple, "Behold, your *m*!"   Jn 19.27
is free, and she is our *m*.   Gal 4.26
Lois and your *m* Eunice and   2Tim 1.5
treat..older women like *m*,   1Tim 5.2

MOTHER-IN-LAW
Naomi her *m* said to her,   Ruth 3.1
Simon's *m* lay sick with..fever,   Mk 1.30

MOUNTAIN — S
long enough at this *m*;   Deut 1.6
going about this *m* country   2.3
O mighty *m*, *m* of Bashan; O   Ps 68.15
the *m* of the house of the LORD   Isa 2.2
or destroy in all my holy *m*;   11.9
On this *m* the LORD of hosts   25.6
to go to the *m* of the LORD,   30.29
on my holy *m*, the *m* height   Ezek 20.40
the stone..became a great *m*   Dan 2.35
have drunk upon my holy *m*,   Obad 1.16
the *m* of the LORD of hosts,   Zech 8.3
devil took him to a..high *m*,   Mt 4.8
he went up on the *m*, and when   5.1
led them up a high *m* apart.   17.1
says to this *m*, 'Be taken up   Mk 11.23
went up on the *m* to pray.   Lk 9.28
Thy righteousness is like the *m*   Ps 36.6
not fear..though the *m* shake   46.2
go before you and level the *m*,   Isa 45.2
You *m* of Israel, hear the word   Ezek 6.3
And the *m* will melt under him   Mic 1.4
as the highest of the *m*,   4.1
Hear, you *m*, the controversy   6.2
on the *m* the feet of him   Nah 1.15
those..in Judea flee to the *m*;   Mk 13.14
faith, so as to remove *m*,   1Cor 13.2

MOUNT OF OLIVES
feet shall stand on the *M*..   Zech 14.4
to the *M*.., then Jesus sent   Mt 21.1
on the *M*.., the disciples came   24.3
they went out to the *M*...   26.30
but Jesus went to the *M*...   Jn 8.1*n*

MOURN — ED — ING (v)
m for him, as..an only child,   Zech 12.10
"Blessed are those who *m*, for   Mt 5.4
who *m* as though they were not   1Cor 7.30
Jacob..*m*..his son many days.   Gen 37.34

MOURN — ED — ING (v) (cont.)
they *m* and wept and fasted	2Sam 1.12
David *m* for his son day	13.37
Why go I *m*..the oppression of	Ps 43.2
Daniel, was *m* for three weeks.	Dan 10.2

MOURNING (n)
shall call the farmers to *m*	Amos 5.16
like the *m* for an only son,	8.10
neither shall there be *m*	Rev 21.4

MOUTH — S
out of the *m* of the LORD.	Deut 8.3
the child, putting his *m* upon	2Ki 4.34
I lay my hand on my *m*.	Job 40.4
praise..continually be in my *m*.	Ps 34.1
My *m* is filled with thy praise,	71.8
Set a guard over my *m*, O LORD,	141.3
put your hand on your *m*.	Prov 30.32
And he touched my *m*, and said:	Isa 6.7
True instruction was in his *m*,	Mal 2.6
"Their *m* is full of curses	Rom 3.14
that every *m* may be stopped,	3.19
deceitful *m* are..against me,	Ps 109.2
have *m*, but they speak not,	135.16

MOVE — D — ING
for 'In him we live and *m*	Acts 17.28
live in them and *m* among	2Cor 6.16
places where I have *m* with	1Chr 17.6
right hand, I shall not be *m*.	Ps 16.8
the Most High..shall not be *m*.	21.7
God is..she shall not be *m*;	46.5
He will not let your foot be *m*,	121.3
Jesus, deeply *m* again came to	Jn 11.38
men *m* by the Holy Spirit	2Pet 1.21
Spirit..was *m* over..the waters	Gen 1.2
I have been *m* about in a tent	2Sam 7.6

MULTIPLY — IED
let birds *m* on the earth."	Gen 1.22
God..bless you and..*m* you,	28.3
be fruitful and *m*; a nation	35.11
bless you, and *m* you;	Deut 7.13
Thou hast *m* the nation, thou	Isa 9.3

MULTITUDE — S
led them..a *m* keeping festival.	Ps 42.4
love covers a *m* of sins.	1Pet 4.8
behold, a great *m* which no man	Rev 7.9
m, in the valley of decision!	Joel 3.14

MURDER
evil thoughts, *m*, adultery,	Mt 15.19
who had committed *m* in the	Mk 15.7
thrown into prison..for *m*.	Lk 23.19

MURDERER
He was a *m* from the beginning,	Jn 8.44
asked for a *m* to be granted	Acts 3.14

MURMUR — ED
wicked congregation *m*	Num 14.27
what is Aaron that you *m*	16.11
people of Israel *m* against Moses	Ex 16.2
the people *m* against Moses,	17.3
m against Moses and Aaron;	Num 14.2
Israel *m* against Moses	16.41
and you *m* in your tents,	Deut 1.27
m against the leaders.	Josh 9.18
They *m* in their tents, and	Ps 106.25
The Jews then *m* at him,	Jn 6.41
Hellenists *m* against..Hebrews	Acts 6.1

MUSTARD
kingdom..is like a grain of *m*	Mt 13.31
faith as a grain of *m* seed,	17.20

It is like a grain of *m* seed,	Mk 4.31
It is like a grain of *m* seed	Lk 13.19
faith as a grain of *m* seed,	17.6

MYRRH
robes are all fragrant with *m*	Ps 45.8
gold and frankincense and *m*.	Mt 2.11
offered..wine mingled with *m*;	Mk 15.23

MYRTLE
instead of the brier..the *m*;	Isa 55.13
He was standing among the *m*	Zech 1.8

MYSTERY — IES
seek mercy..concerning this *m*,	Dan 2.18
you to understand this *m*,	Rom 11.25
to the revelation of the *m*	16.25
Lo! I tell you a *m*. We shall	1Cor 15.51
made known..the *m* of his will,	Eph 1.9
insight into the *m* of Christ,	3.4
This is a great *m*, and I take	5.32
proclaim the *m* of the gospel,	6.19
the *m* hidden for ages and	Col 1.26
the knowledge of God's *m*,	2.2
m of lawlessness is..at work;	2Thess 2.7
hold the *m* of the faith with	1Tim 3.9
Great..the *m* of our religion:	3.16
the *m* of God, as he announced	Rev 10.7
written a name of *m*: "Babylon	17.5
stewards of the *m* of God.	1Cor 4.1
and understand all *m* and	13.2

MYTHS
to occupy themselves with *m*	1Tim 1.4
giving heed to Jewish *m*	Tit 1.14
not follow cleverly devised *m*	2Pet 1.16

N

NAAMAN
N, commander of the army of	2Ki 5.1
cleansed,..only *N* the Syrian."	Lk 4.27

NAHUM,
The book of the vision of *N*	Nah 1.1

NAILING (v)
set aside, *n* it to the cross.	Col 2.14

NAILS (n)
like *n* firmly fixed..sayings	Ecc 12.11
in..hands the print of the *n*,	Jn 20.25

NAKED — NESS
"*N* I came from my mother's	Job 1.21
They go about *n*, without	24.10
shall go again, *n* as he came,	Ecc 5.15
Isaiah..walked *n* and barefoot	Isa 20.3
when you see the *n*, to cover	58.7
and leave you *n* and bare.	Ezek 16.39
linen cloth and ran away *n*.	Mk 14.52
You shall not uncover the *n* of	Lev 18.7
Your *n* shall be uncovered,	Isa 47.3

NAME — S
Abram..called on the *n*..LORD.	Gen 12.8
"Tell me, I pray, your *n*."	32.29
ask..his *n*?' what shall I say	Ex 3.13
by my *n* the LORD I did not	6.3
my *n* may be declared throughout	9.16
the LORD is his *n*.	15.3
shall not take the *n* of the LORD	20.7
proclaimed the *n* of the LORD.	34.5
woman's son blasphemed the *N*,	Lev 24.11
not take the *n* of the LORD	Deut 5.11
by the *n* of the LORD:	28.10
this glorious and awful *n*	28.58

NAME — S (cont.)

I will proclaim the *n* of the LORD.	32.3
wilt..do for thy great *n*?"	Josh 7.9
"What is your *n*, so that	Judg 13.17
and it be called by my *n*."	2Sam 12.28
and put my *n* there for ever;	1Ki 9.3
blessed..in the *n* of the LORD,	1Chr 16.2
I will make for you a *n*,	17.8
and praise thy glorious *n*.	29.13
Lord, how majestic is thy *n* in	Ps 8.9
know thy *n* put their trust in	9.10
May his *n* endure for ever,	72.17
n endures to all generations;	102.12
enters in the *n* of the LORD!	118.26
exalted above everything thy *n*	138.2
n of the LORD is a strong	Prov 18.10
A good *n* is to be chosen	22.1
good *n* is better than precious	Ecc 7.1
n of..LORD comes from far,	Isa 30.27
brings out their host..by *n*;	40.26
surname..by the *n* of Israel."	44.5
all the day my *n* is despised.	52.5
give them an everlasting *n*	56.5
you shall be called by a new *n*	62.2
this house,..called by my *n*,	Jer 7.11
and thy *n* is great in might.	10.6
are prophesying lies in my *n*;	14.14
had concern for my holy *n*,	Ezek 36.21
be jealous for my holy *n*.	39.25
of hosts, the LORD is his *n*:	Hos 12.5
all who call upon the *n* of	Joel 2.32
not mention..*n* of the LORD."	Amos 6.10
the nations..called by my *n*,"	9.12
did we not prophesy in your *n*,	Mt 7.22
baptizing..in the *n* of the Father	28.19
casting out demons in your *n*,	Mk 9.38
Many will come in my *n*, saying,	13.6
you shall call his *n* Jesus.	Lk 1.31
casting out demons in your *n*,	9.49
"Father, hallowed be thy *n*.	11.2
I have come in my Father's *n*,	Jn 5.43
Father, glorify thy *n*." Then	12.28
will give it to you in my *n*.	16.23
his *n*, by faith in his *n*,	Acts 3.16
by the *n* of Jesus Christ of	4.10
no other *n* under heaven	4.12
performed through the *n* of	4.30
preached..about..the *n* of Jesus	8.12
carry my *n* before the Gentiles	9.15
the *n* of..Lord..was extolled.	19.17
to die..for the *n* of the Lord	21.13
"The *n* of God is blasphemed	Rom 2.24
that my *n* may be proclaimed	9.17
bestowed..the *n*..above every *n*,	Phil 2.9
in the *n* of the Lord Jesus,	Col 3.17
who names the *n* of the Lord	2Tim 2.19
n..more excellent than theirs.	Heb 1.4
blaspheme that honorable *n*	Jas 2.7
If..reproached for the *n*	1Pet 4.14
a white stone, with a new *n*	Rev 2.17
fear and glorify thy *n*, O Lord?	15.4
man gave *n* to all cattle,	Gen 2.20
engrave on them the *n*	Ex 28.9
The *n* of the twelve apostles	Mt 10.2
rejoice that your *n* are written	Lk 10.20
whose *n* are in the book of life.	Phil 4.3

NAPHTALI

Rachel..called his name *N*.	Gen 30.8
N is a hind let loose,	49.21
families of *N* according	Num 26.50
And of *N* he said,..possess	Deut 33.23
N did not drive out the	Judg 1.33

of Zebulun, the princes of *N*.	Ps 68.27
Zebulun and the land of *N*,	Isa 9.1
territory of Zebulun and *N*,	Mt 4.13

NARROW

"Enter by the *n* gate; for the	Mt 7.13
"Strive to enter by ..*n* door;	Lk 13.24

NATHAN

Counseled David about the people, 2Sam 7.2–17 (1Chr 17.1–15); rebuked David, 2Sam 12.1–23; anointed Solomon as king, 1Ki 1.8–45.

NATHANAEL

Philip found *N*, and said to him,	Jn 1.45

NATION — S

I will make of you a great *n*,	Gen 12.2
become a great and mighty *n*,	18.18
will make of you a great *n*.	46.3
For what great *n* is there	Deut 4.7
take a *n* for himself from	4.34
and there he became a *n*,	26.5
LORD will bring a *n* against you	28.49
What other *n* on earth is	2Sam 7.23
rejoice in..gladness of thy *n*,	Ps 106.5
Righteousness exalts a *n*,	Prov 14.34
n..not lift up sword against *n*,	Isa 2.4
Thou hast multiplied the *n*,	9.3
n that did not obey the voice	Jer 7.28
cease from being a *n* before me	31.36
make them one *n* in the land,	Ezek 37.22
to a *n* producing the fruits	Mt 21.43
in every *n*..who fears him	Acts 10.35
sons of Japheth..in their *n*.	Gen 10.5
father of a multitude of *n*.	17.5
all of the *n* of the earth bless	22.18
all the *n* of the earth shall bless	26.4
slaves from among the *n* that	Lev 25.44
govern us like all the *n*."	1Sam 8.5
his glory among the *n*, his	1Chr 16.24
save us from among the *n*,	16.35
make me the head of the *n*.	Ps 18.43
counsel of the *n* to nought;	33.10
Let the *n* be glad and sing	67.4
Pour out thy anger on the *n*	79.6
Declare his glory among the *n*,	96.3
execute judgment among the *n*,	110.6
then they said among the *n*,	126.2
all the *n* shall flow to it,	Isa 2.2
the *n* are like a drop from	40.15
give you as a light to the *n*,	49.6
n shall come to your light,	60.3
I am coming to gather all *n*	66.18
declare my glory among the *n*.	66.19
then *n* shall bless themselves	Jer 4.2
All the *n* shall serve him	27.7
worst..*n* to take possession	Ezek 7.24
removed them..among the *n*,	11.16
n will know..I am the LORD,	36.23
set my glory among the *n*;	39.21
a byword among the *n*. Why	Joel 2.17
I will gather all..*n* and bring	3.2
Let the *n* bestir themselves,	3.12
upon the *n* that did not obey.	Mic 5.15
Look among the *n*, and see;	Hab 1.5
all the *n* against Jerusalem	Zech 14.2
my name is great among the *n*,	Mal 1.11
all *n* will call you blessed,	3.12
hated by all *n* for my..sake.	Mt 24.9
house of prayer for all..*n*'?	Mk 11.17
preached in his name to all *n*,	Lk 24.47
The *n* raged, but thy wrath	Rev 11.18

NATION — S (cont.)

n. . deceived by thy sorcery.	18.23
By its light shall the n walk.	21.24

NATURE

men, of like n with you,	Acts 14.15
do by n what the law requires,	Rom 2.14
by n a wild olive tree, and	11.24
Elijah was a man of like n	Jas 5.17
for God's n abides in him,	1Jn 3.9

NAZARETH

he. . dwelt in a city called N,	Mt 2.23
leaving N he. . dwelt in Capernaum	4.13
Jesus from N of Galilee."	21.11
"This man was with Jesus of N."	26.71
you seek Jesus of N, who was	Mk 16.6
prophets wrote, Jesus of N,	Jn 1.45
Jesus of N, a man attested	Acts 2.22
how God anointed Jesus of N	10.38
'I am Jesus of N whom you	22.8

NAZIRITE

the vow of a N, to separate	Num 6.2
the boy shall be a N to God	Judg 13.5

NEBO

Moses went up. . to Mount N,	Deut 34.1

NEBUCHADNEZZAR
(NEBUCHADREZZAR)

Won the battle of Carchemish, 2Ki 24.1–7; Jer 46.2; conquered Judah, 2Ki 24.10– 25.10 (2Chr 36.6–19; Jer 39.1–8; 52.1–14); deported the people, 2Ki 24.14–16; 25.11– 21 (2Chr 36.20–21; Jer 39.9–10; 52.15– 30); favored Jeremiah, Jer 39.11–14; his dreams revealed, Dan 2.1–13; 4.4–18; set up the golden image, Dan 3.1–7; punished for boasting, Dan 4.31–33; his reason returned, Dan 4.34–37.

NECK — S

Your n is like. . tower of David,	Sol 4.4
break the yoke. . off their n,	Jer 30.8
put your feet upon the n of	Josh 10.24
risked their n for my life,	Rom 16.4

NEED — S (v)

Father knows that you n them	Mt 6.32
and give him whatever he n.	Lk 11.8

NEED — S (n)

we have no n to answer you	Dan 3.16
say, 'The Lord has n of them,'	Mt 21.3
'The Lord has n of it and will	Mk 11.3
'The Lord has n of it.' "	Lk 19.31
made to each as any had n.	Acts 4.35
Contribute to. . n of. . saints,	Rom 12.13

NEEDFUL

one thing is n. Mary has	Lk 10.42

NEEDLE

through the eye of a n than	Lk 18.25

NEEDY

to bring down the poor and n,	Ps 37.14
I am poor and n; but the LORD	40.17
raises up the n out of affliction,	107.41
kind to the n honors him,	Prov 14.31
reaches out her hands to the n.	31.20
the n lie down in safety;	Isa 14.30
the n for a pair of shoes—	Amos 2.6
not a n person among them,	Acts 4.34

NEGLECT — ED — ING

not n the house of our God.	Neh 10.39
how shall we escape if we n	Heb 2.3

you. . n the weightier matters	Mt 23.23
done, without n the others.	Lk 11.42

NEHEMIAH

The words of N the son of	Neh 1.1
After him N the son of Azbuk,	3.16
in the days of N the governor	12.26

NEIGHBOR — S — 'S

love your n as yourself:	Lev 19.18
kills his n unintentionally,	Deut 4.42
kills his n unintentionally	19.4
if any man hates his n,	19.11
a reproach against his n;	Ps 15.3
Him who slanders his n secretly	101.5
not plan evil against your n	Prov 3.29
if. . become surety for your n,	6.1
godless man would destroy. . n,	11.9
despises his n is a sinner,	14.21
Better is a n who is near	27.10
each speaks peaceably to his n,	Jer 9.8
proclaiming liberty,. . to his n;	34.17
love your n and hate. . enemy.'	Mt 5.43
love your n as yourself.	22.39
love your n as yourself.'	Mk 12.31
to Jesus, "And who is my n?"	Lk 10.29
love your n as yourself."	Rom 13.9
love your n as yourself."	Gal 5.14
love your n as yourself,"	Jas 2.8
that they were their n,	Josh 9.16
speak peace with their n, while	Ps 28.3
I am. . a horror to my n, an	31.11
n drink. . the cup of his wrath,	Hab 2.15
who goes in to his n wife;	Prov 6.29
be seldom in your n house,	25.17

NEPHILIM

The N were on the earth	Gen 6.4
And there we saw the N	Num 13.33

NET — S

seizes the poor. . into his n.	Ps 10.9
take me out of the n which is	31.4
For in vain is a n spread	Prov 1.17
I will spread my n over him,	Ezek 17.20
kingdom of heaven is like a n	Mt 13.47
brother of Simon casting a n	Mk 1.16
who spread n upon the water.	Isa 19.8
in their boat mending the n.	Mk 1.19

NEW — NESS

LORD creates something n,	Num 16.30
He put a n song in my mouth,	Ps 40.3
O sing to the LORD a n song;	96.1
Sing to the LORD a n song,	149.1
"See, this is n"? It has been	Ecc 1.10
and n things I now declare;	Isa 42.9
Behold, I am doing a n thing;	43.19
I make you hear n things,	48.6
you shall be called by a n name	62.2
the n heavens and a n earth	66.22
when I will make a n covenant	Jer 31.31
his mercies. . n every morning	Lam 3.23
A n heart I will give you,	Ezek 36.26
in the n world, when the Son	Mt 19.28
my blood of the n covenant,	Mk 14.24n
tears a piece from a n garment	Lk 5.36
A n commandment I give to you,	Jn 13.34
or hearing something n.	Acts 17.21
in the n life of the Spirit.	Rom 7.6
"This cup is the n covenant	1Cor 11.25
ministers of a n covenant,	2Cor 3.6
in Christ, he is a n creation;	5.17
they sang a n song, saying,	Rev 5.9
saw a n heaven and a n earth;	21.1

NEW — NESS (cont.)
"Behold, I make all things *n.*"   21.5
we too might walk in *n* of life.   Rom 6.4

NICODEMUS
named *N*, a ruler of the Jews.   Jn 3.1
N, who had gone to him before,   7.50
N also, who had at first come   19.39

NIGHT
darkness he called *N.*   Gen 1.5
that *n* God appeared to Solomon 2Chr 1.7
n to *n* declares knowledge.   Ps 19.2
at *n* his song is with me, a   42.8
makest darkness, and it is *n*,   104.20
the time of *n* and darkness.   Prov 7.9
toiled all *n* and took nothing!   Lk 5.5
This *n* your soul is required   12.20
This man came to Jesus by *n*   Jn 3.2
while it is day; *n* comes,   9.4
walks in the *n*, he stumbles,   11.10
he. .went out; and it was *n.*   13.30
there shall be no *n* there;   Rev 21.25

NILE
the *N* shall become foul,   Ex 7.18
'My *N* is my own; I made it.'   Ezek 29.3

NIMROD
Cush became. .father of *N*;   Gen 10.8

NINEVEH
into Assyria, and built *N*,   Gen 10.11
"Arise, go to *N*, that great   Jonah 1.2
And should not I pity *N*,   4.11
N is like a pool whose waters   Nah 2.8
N will arise at the judgment   Mt 12.41
Jonah. .a sign to the men of *N*, Lk 11.30
men of *N* will arise at. .judgment 11.32

NOAH
Born, Gen 5.29; walked with God, Gen 6.9;
built the ark, Gen 6.11–22; preserved
through the flood, Gen 7.1—8.19; built an
altar, Gen 8.20–22; covenant with God,
Gen 9.8–17; his drunkenness, Gen 9.20–21;
prophesied concerning his sons, Gen 9.22–
27; died, Gen 9.28–29.

NOBLE
Hear, for I will speak *n* things,   Prov 8.6
these Jews were more *n* than   Acts 17.11
not many were of *n* birth;   1Cor 1.26
for *n* use, some for ignoble,   2Tim 2.20

NOISE
Make a joyful *n* to God, all   Ps 66.1
Make a joyful *n* to the LORD,   100.1

NORTH
He stretches out the *n* over   Job 26.7
I stirred up one from the *n*,   Isa 41.25
I will say to the *n*, Give up,   43.6

NOTHING
Is it not in your sight as *n*?   Hag 2.3
have not love, I gain *n.*   1Cor 13.3

NOUGHT
"Does Job fear God for *n*?   Job 1.9
every vision comes to *n*'?   Ezek 12.22

NUMBER —ED (v)
stars, if you are able to *n*   Gen 15.5
"Go, *n* Israel and Judah."   2Sam 24.1
"Go, *n* Israel, from Beer-sheba 1Chr 21.2
thou wouldest *n* my steps,   Job 14.16
So teach us to *n* our days   Ps 90.12
So he *n* them in the wilderness Num 1.19

the people of Israel as *n* by   2.32
was *n* with the transgressors;   Isa 53.12

NUMBER (n)
I will let you go in by *n.*   Ezek 20.37
the Lord added to their *n*   Acts 2.47
beast, for it is a human *n*,   Rev 13.18

O

OAK — S
like an *o*, whose leaf withers,   Isa 1.30
or an *o*, whose stump remained   6.13
be called *o* of righteousness,   61.3

OATH
will be free from this *o*   Gen 24.8
you will be free from my *o.*   24.41
shall make her take an *o*,   Num 5.19
an *o* to walk in God's law   Neh 10.29
love no false *o*, for all   Zech 8.17
o which he swore to our father   Lk 1.73
o neither to eat nor drink   Acts 23.21
And it was not without an *o.*   Heb 7.20

OBADIAH
The vision of *O.* Thus says   Obad 1.1

OBEDIENCE
to him shall be the *o*   Gen 49.10
to bring about *o* of the faith   Rom 1.5
while your *o* is known to all,   16.19
sanctified. .for *o* to Jesus   1Pet 1.2

OBEDIENT
If you are willing and *o*,   Isa 1.19
came to Nazareth,. .was *o* to   Lk 2.51
many of the priests were *o*   Acts 6.7
and became *o* unto death,   Phil 2.8

OBEY — ED — ING
son; only *o* my word, and go, Gen 27.13
my son, *o* my voice;   27.43
if you will *o* my voice   Ex 19.5
your God and *o* his voice;   Deut 4.30
commandments and *o* his voice,   13.4
son. .will not *o* our voice;   21.20
if you *o* the commandments   28.13
you did not *o* the voice   28.45
and *o* his voice in all that   30.2
shall again *o* the voice   30.8
obeyed Moses. .we will *o* you;   Josh 1.17
not *o* the voice of the LORD? 1Sam 15.19
Behold, to *o* is better than   15.22
because they did not *o* the   2Ki 18.12
they refused to *o*, and were   Neh 9.17
command I gave. .,'*O* my voice, Jer 7.23
nation. .did not *o* the voice   7.28
and *o* the voice of the LORD   26.13
But they did not *o* thy voice   32.23
O now the voice of the LORD   38.20
will *o* the voice of the LORD   42.6
did not *o* the voice of the LORD,   43.4
dominions shall serve and *o*   Dan 7.27
diligently *o* the voice of   Zech 6.15
that even winds and sea *o* him?" Mt 8.27
even the unclean spirits,. .*o*   Mk 1.27
even wind and sea *o* him?"   4.41
wind and water, and they *o*   Lk 8.25
"We must *o* God rather than   Acts 5.29
and do not *o* the truth, but   Rom 2.8
every thought captive to *o*   2Cor 10.5
refuses to *o* what we say   2Thess 3.14
salvation to all who *o* him,   Heb 5.9
O your leaders and submit   13.17

OBEY — ED — ING (cont.)

who do not *o* the gospel of	1Pet 4.17
because you have *o* my voice."	Gen 22.18
because Abraham *o* my voice	26.5
the people of Israel *o* him,	Deut 34.9
that you have not *o* my voice,	Jer 3.13
We have *o* the voice of Jonadab	35.8
o the voice of the LORD their	Hag 1.12
By faith Abraham *o* when he	Heb 11.8
as Sarah *o* Abraham, calling	1Pet 3.6
by not *o* the priest who	Deut 17.12
who hindered you from *o* the	Gal 5.7

OBSERVE — S — ING

o the feast of unleavened	Ex 12.17
his statutes, and *o* his laws.	Ps 105.45
Blessed are they who *o* justice,	106.3
and *o* it with my whole heart.	119.34
teaching them to *o* all that I	Mt 28.20
You *o* days, and months, and	Gal 4.10
all, and *o* all their deeds.	Ps 33.15
who *o* the wind will not sow;	Ecc 11.4
keep the sabbath, *o*	Ex 31.16

OCCUPATION

and says, 'What is your *o*?'	Gen 46.33
What is your *o*? And whence	Jonah 1.8
with the workmen of like *o*,	Acts 19.25

OFFENDED

baker *o*..the king of Egypt.	Gen 40.1
the Pharisees were *o* when they	Mt 15.12
nor against Caesar have I *o*	Acts 25.8

OFFENSE

who forgives an *o* seeks love,	Prov 17.9
a sanctuary, and a stone of *o*,	Isa 8.14
blessed is he who takes no *o*	Mt 11.6
the carpenter,..And they took *o*	Mk 6.3
blessed is he who takes no *o*	Lk 7.23
said.."Do you take *o* at this?	Jn 6.61
Give no *o* to Jews or..Greeks	1Cor 10.32

OFFER — ED (v)

go to..Moriah, and *o* him there	Gen 22.2
"You shall not *o* the blood	Ex 34.25
not *o* anything that has	Lev 22.20
the king take and *o* up	2Sam 24.22
O right sacrifices, and put	Ps 4.5
I will *o* in his tent sacrifices	27.6
O..sacrifice of thanksgiving,	50.14
reconciled..and then come and *o*	Mt 5.24
'Did you *o* to me slain beasts	Acts 7.42
o to God acceptable worship,	Heb 12.28
Israel..*o* sacrifices to..God	Gen 46.1
and *o* unholy fire before the	Lev 10.1
who *o* his offering the first	Num 7.12
who *o* themselves willingly	Judg 5.9
had *o* freely to the LORD;	1Chr 29.9
Solomon *o* up burnt offerings	2Chr 8.12
have freely *o* to the God of	Ezra 7.15
o to live in Jerusalem.	Neh 11.2
they *o* a sacrifice to..LORD	Jonah 1.16
eating of food *o* to idols,	1Cor 8.4
By faith Abel *o* to God a more	Heb 11.4
he was tested, *o* up Isaac,	11.17

OFFERING — S (n)

Take from among you an *o*	Ex 35.5
bring an *o*, and come before	1Chr 16.29
brethren..an *o* to the LORD,	Isa 66.20
o..shall belong to..priests;	Ezek 44.30
the *o* of Judah and Jerusalem	Mal 3.4
that the *o* of the Gentiles	Rom 15.16
May he remember all your *o*,	Ps 20.3

OFFICER — S

chief *o* in..house of the LORD,	Jer 20.1
o answered, "No man ever spoke	Jn 7.46

OFFSPRING

your *o* as the grass of the	Job 5.25
what does he desire? Godly *o*.	Mal 2.15
'For we are indeed his *o*.'	Acts 17.28

OIL

sacred anointing *o* blended	Ex 30.25
the house, except a jar of *o*."	2Ki 4.2
thou anointest my head with *o*,	Ps 23.5
anointed..with..*o* of gladness	45.7
they are not..softened with *o*.	Isa 1.6
but the wise took flasks of *o*	Mt 25.4
and anointed with *o* many..sick	Mk 6.13

OINTMENT — S

Dead flies make..perfumer's *o*	Ecc 10.1
expensive *o*, and she poured it	Mt 26.7
jar of *o* of pure nard, very	Mk 14.3
and prepared spices and *o*.	Lk 23.56

OLD

now *o* and well advanced	Josh 23.2
counsel which the *o* men gave	2Chr 10.8
unshrunk cloth on an *o* garment,	Mt 9.16
unshrunk cloth on an *o* garment;	Mk 2.21
things known from of *o*.'	Acts 15.18
when they read the *o* covenant,	2Cor 3.14

OLIVE

a freshly plucked *o* leaf;	Gen 8.11
your children..like *o* shoots	Ps 128.3
his beauty shall be like the *o*,	Hos 14.6
you, a wild *o* shoot,..grafted	Rom 11.17

OLIVET

lodged on the mount called *O*.	Lk 21.37
returned..from..mount..*O*,	Acts 1.12

OLIVE TREES

When you beat your *o*..,	Deut 24.20
And there are two *o*..by it,	Zech 4.3
These are the two *o*..and the	Rev 11.4

ONE

they become *o* flesh.	Gen 2.24
since *o* fate comes to all, to	Ecc 9.2
and the two shall become *o*.'	Mk 10.8
made from *o* every nation	Acts 17.26
and *o* Lord, Jesus Christ,	1Cor 8.6
and the two shall become *o*."	Eph 5.31

ONESIMUS

with him *O*, the faithful and	Col 4.9
I appeal..for my child, *O*,	Philem 10

OPEN — S — EST — ED

o thou my lips, and my mouth	Ps 51.15
O my eyes that I may behold	119.18
o your eyes, and you will	Prov 20.13
"*O* to me, my sister, my love,	Sol 5.2
he shall *o*, and none..shut;	Isa 22.22
O the gates, that the righteous	26.2
gates shall be *o* continually;	60.11
o thy eyes and behold our	Dan 9.18
upon..Judah I will *o* my eyes,	Zech 12.4
"I will *o* my mouth in parables,	Mt 13.35
to *o* their eyes, that they	Acts 26.18
have set before you an *o* door,	Rev 3.8
he *o* the ears of men, and	Job 33.16
She *o* her mouth with wisdom,	Prov 31.26
when thou *o* thy hand, they	Ps 104.28
your eyes will be *o*,	Gen 3.5
the eyes of both were *o*,	3.7
LORD *o* the mouth of the ass,	Num 22.28

OPEN — S — EST — ED (cont.)
I have *o* my mouth to the Judg 11.35
LORD *o* the eyes of the young 2Ki 6.17
I *o*..but my beloved had..gone. Sol 5.6
The Lord GOD has *o* my ear, Isa 50.5
So I *o* my mouth, and he gave Ezek 3.2
the heavens were *o* and he saw Mt 3.16
blind..And their eyes were *o*. 9.30
the tombs also were *o*, and 27.52
the heavens *o* and the Spirit Mk 1.10
He *o* the book and found the Lk 4.17
their eyes were *o* and they 24.31
he *o* their minds to understand 24.45
Jesus made..clay and *o* his eyes. Jn 9.14
he had *o* a door of faith Acts 14.27
The Lord *o* her heart to..heed 16.14
effective work has *o* to me, 1Cor 16.9
door was *o* for me in the Lord; 2Cor 2.12
the Lamb *o* one of the..seals, Rev 6.1

OPENLY
could no longer *o* enter..town, Mk 1.45
Yet..no one spoke *o* of him. Jn 7.13
teaching about the Lord..*o* Acts 28.31

OPPORTUNITY
an *o* I will summon you." Acts 24.25
concerned..but you had no *o*. Phil 4.10

OPPOSE — S — D — ING
these men also *o* the truth, 2Tim 3.8
son of perdition, who *o* 2Thess 2.4
"God *o* the proud, but gives 1Pet 5.5
Cephas..I *o* him to his face, Gal 2.11
might even be found *o* God!" Acts 5.39

OPPRESS — ES — ED (v)
"You shall not *o* a stranger; Ex 23.9
not *o* your neighbor or rob Lev 19.13
shall not *o* a hired servant Deut 24.14
if you do not *o* the alien, Jer 7.6
false balances, he loves to *o*. Hos 12.7
o the poor,..crush the needy, Amos 4.1
they *o* a man and his house, Mic 2.2
o the widow, the fatherless, Zech 7.10
who *o* the hireling in..wages, Mal 3.5
who *o* a poor man insults his Prov 14.31
who *o* the poor to increase 22.16
A poor man who *o* the poor 28.3
who..*o* the poor and needy, Ezek 18.12
be *o* for four hundred years; Gen 15.13
or if he has *o* his neighbor Lev 6.2

OPPRESSED (n)
Let the *o* see it and be glad; Ps 69.32
save all the *o* of the earth. 76.9
by showing mercy to the *o*, Dan 4.27

OPPRESSION — S
Why go I mourning..the *o* of Ps 42.9
o and fraud do not depart 55.11
o makes the wise man foolish, Ecc 7.7
seek justice, correct *o*; Isa 1.17
trust in *o* and perverseness, 30.12
By *o* and judgment he was taken 53.8
practicing *o* and violence." Jer 22.17
the *o* that are practiced Ecc 4.1

OPPRESSOR
to the needy, and crush the *o*! Ps 72.4
"How the *o* has ceased, the Isa 14.4
where is the fury of the *o*? 51.13
no *o* shall again overrun them, Zech 9.8

ORACLE — S
The *o* concerning Babylon Isa 13.1
An *o* concerning Damascus. 17.1

An *o* concerning Egypt. Behold, 19.1
o concerning..wilderness of..sea. 21.1
The *o* concerning Arabia. In 21.13
The *o* concerning Tyre. Waii, 23.1
An *o* concerning Nineveh. Nah 1.1
o of God which Habakkuk..saw Hab 1.1
An *O* The word of the LORD Zech 9.1
An *O* The word of the LORD 12.1
The *o* of the word of the LORD Mal 1.1
Jews are entrusted with the *o* Rom 3.2

ORDAIN — ED
anoint them and *o* them Ex 28.41
O LORD, thou wilt *o* peace Isa 26.12
"Today you have *o* yourselves Ex 32.29
the LORD had *o* to defeat 2Sam 17.14
unless the Lord has *o* it? Lam 3.37
hast *o* them as a judgment; Hab 1.12
the one *o* by God to be judge Acts 10.42
as many as were *o* to eternal 13.48
it was *o* by angels through Gal 3.19

ORDER
priest for ever after the *o* of Ps 110.4
empty, swept, and put in *o*. Mt 12.44
be done decently and in *o*. 1Cor 14.40

ORDINANCES
passover..its statutes and..*o* Num 9.3
has..*o* so righteous as all Deut 4.8
know the *o* of the heavens? Job 38.33

ORGANIZED
David *o* them according to 1Chr 24.3
Levites whom David had *o* 2Chr 23.18

OVEN
will make them as a blazing *o* Ps 21.9
tomorrow is thrown into the *o*, Lk 12.28

OVERCOME — S
cheer, I have *o* the world." Jn 16.33
evil, but *o* evil with good. Rom 12.21
you are of God, and have *o* them; 1Jn 4.4
one stronger..*o* him, he takes Lk 11.22
the victory that *o* the world, 1Jn 5.4

OVERFLOW — S — ED — ING
their hearts *o* with follies. Ps 73.7
also *o* in many thanksgivings 2Cor 9.12
grace of our Lord *o* for me 1Tim 1.14
pour down..an *o* blessing. Mal 3.10

OVERLOOK — ED
God is not so unjust as to *o* Heb 6.10
times of ignorance God *o*, Acts 17.30

OVERTHROW
to destroy and to *o*, to build Jer 1.10
to *o* the throne of kingdoms; Hag 2.22
Do we..*o* law by this faith? Rom 3.31

OVERWHELM — S — ED
dost *o* me with all thy waves. Ps 88.7
come upon me, and horror *o* me. 55.5
I sat there *o* among them Ezek 3.15
may be *o* by excessive sorrow. 2Cor 2.7

OWE — D
O no one anything, except Rom 13.8
who *o*..ten thousand talents, Mt 18.24

OWN — ER
plant them on thy *o* mountain, Ex 15.17
Jesus has made me his *o*. Phil 3.12
The ox knows its *o*, Isa 1.3

OX
"When an *o* gores a man Ex 21.28

OX (cont.)

as the *o* licks up the grass	Num 22.4
not muzzle an *o* when it	Deut 25.4
he follows her, as an *o* goes	Prov 7.22
The *o* knows its owner, and	Isa 1.3
o that has fallen into a well,	Lk 14.5
shall not muzzle an *o* when	1Cor 9.9
shall not muzzle an *o* when	1Tim 5.18

P

PAIN

multiply. .*p* in childbearing;	Gen 3.16
feels only the *p* of his own	Job 14.22
all his days are full of *p*,	Ecc 2.23
put away *p* from your body;	11.10
Your *p* is incurable. Because	Jer 30.15
For if I cause you *p*, who	2Cor 2.2

PAINTED

Jezebel. .*p* her eyes, and	2Ki 9.30
you bathed. .*p* your eyes, and	Ezek 23.40

PALACE — S

enter the *p* of the king.	Ps 45.15
fully armed, guards his own *p*,	Lk 11.21
From ivory *p*. .instruments	Ps 45.8

PALM

righteous flourish like the *p*	Ps 92.12
I will climb the *p* tree and	Sol 7.8
they took branches of *p* trees	Jn 12.13

PANGS

Many. .the *p* of the wicked;	Ps 32.10
Will not *p* take hold of you,	Jer 13.21
The *p* of childbirth come from	Hos 13.13

PARABLE — S

I will open my mouth in a *p*;	Ps 78.2
kingdom. .what *p* shall we use	Mk 4.30
not speak to them without a *p*,	4.34
p. .The seed is the word of God.	Lk 8.11
he told them many things in *p*,	Mt 13.3

PARADISE

you will be with me in *P*."	Lk 23.43
man was caught up into *P*—	2Cor 12.3

PARALYTIC — S

they brought. .a *p*,. .on his bed.	Mt 9.2
they came, bringing to him a *p*	Mk 2.3
and *p*, and he healed them.	Mt 4.24

PARALYZED

"Lord, my servant is lying *p*	Mt 8.6
on a bed a man who was *p*,	Lk 5.18
Aeneas,. .bedridden. .and was *p*.	Acts 9.33

PARDON — ED — ING

p our iniquity and our sin,	Ex 34.9
P the iniquity of this	Num 14.19
Lord would not *p* him,	Deut 29.20
I pray, *p* my sin, and return	1Sam 15.25
may the Lord *p* your servant:	2Ki 5.18
and the Lord would not *p*.	24.4
"The good Lord *p* every one	2Chr 30.18
Why. .not *p* my transgression	Job 7.21
p my guilt, for it is great.	Ps 25.11
God, for he will abundantly *p*.	Isa 55.7
seeks truth; that I may *p* her.	Jer 5.1
"How can I *p* you? Your children	5.7
I will *p* those whom I leave	50.20
that her iniquity is *p*, that	Isa 40.2
Who is a God like thee, *p*	Mic 7.18

PARENTS

children will rise against *p*	Mt 10.21

his *p* went to Jerusalem every	Lk 2.41
who sinned, this man or his *p*,	Jn 9.2
they called the *p* of the man	9.18
but *p* for their children.	2Cor 12.14
obey your *p* in the Lord, for	Eph 6.1
disobedient to their *p*,	2Tim 3.2

PARTAKE

not to *p* of the. .holy food,	Ezra 2.63
not to *p* of the. .holy food,	Neh 7.65
we all *p* of the one bread.	1Cor 10.17

PARTED

the water was *p* to the. .side	2Ki 2.8
p my garments among them,	Jn 19.24

PARTIAL

you shall not be *p* to. .poor	Lev 19.15
shall not be *p* in judgment;	Deut 1.17
terrible God, who is not *p*	10.17
not good to be *p* to a wicked	Prov 18.5

PARTIALITY

you shall not show *p*;	Deut 16.19
perversion of justice. .or *p*,	2Chr 19.7
P in judging is not good.	Prov 24.23
To show *p* is not good; but	28.21
I perceive. .God shows no *p*,	Acts 10.34
For God shows no *p*.	Rom 2.11
God shows no *p*)—those, I say,	Gal 2.6
that there is no *p* with him.	Eph 5.9
favor, doing nothing from *p*.	1Tim 5.21
show no *p* as you hold the faith	Jas 2.1

PARTICIPATION

a *p* in the body of Christ?	1Cor 10.16
if. .any *p* in the Spirit, any	Phil 2.1

PARTNER — S

p of a thief hates. .life;	Prov 29.24
if you consider me your *p*,	Philem 17
to their *p* in the other boat	Lk 5.7
not want you. .*p* with demons.	1Cor 10.20

PARTNERSHIP

what *p* have righteousness	2Cor 6.14
thankful for your *p* in the	Phil 1.5
no church entered into *p* with me	4.15

PARTRIDGE

like one who hunts a *p*	1Sam 26.20
the *p* that gathers a brood	Jer 17.11

PASCHAL

For Christ, our *p* lamb, has	1Cor 5.7

PASS — ES — ED — ING

Lord will *p* over the door,	Ex 12.23
calling to those who *p* by,	Prov 9.15
When you *p* through the waters	Isa 43.2
nothing to you, all you who *p*	Lam 1.12
Heaven and earth will *p* away,	Mt 24.35
Heaven and earth will *p* away,	Mk 13.31
knowledge, it will *p* away.	1Cor 13.8
life,. .he *p* like a shadow?	Ecc 6.12
have not *p* this way before.	Josh 3.4
I have *p* out of mind like one	Ps 31.12
he *p* by on the other side.	Lk 10.31
we. .*p* out of death into life,	1Jn 3.14
finished *p* over the Jordan.	Josh 3.17
p along by the Sea of Galilee,	Mk 1.16

PASSION — S

but *p* makes the bones rot.	Prov 14.30
men. .with *p* for one another,	Rom 1.27
if his *p* are strong, and	1Cor 7.36
we. .lived in the *p* of our flesh,	Eph 2.3
your *p*. .at war in your members?	Jas 4.1

PASSOVER
eat..in haste..the LORD's *p*.	Ex 12.11
evening, is the LORD's *p*.	Lev 23.5
kept the *p* in the first month,	Num 9.5
first month is the LORD's *p*,	28.16
and keep the *p* to the LORD	Deut 16.1
on the morrow after the *p*,	Josh 5.11
"Keep the *p* to the LORD	2Ki 23.21
to keep the *p* to the LORD	2Chr 30.1
who were present kept the *p*	35.17
returned exiles kept the *p*.	Ezra 6.19
after two days the *P* is coming,	Mt 26.2
It was..two days before the *P*	Mk 14.1
room, where I am to eat the *p*	14.14
on which the *p* lamb had to be	Lk 22.7
before the feast of the *P*,	Jn 13.1
release one man..at the *P*;	18.39
By faith he kept the *P* and	Heb 11.28

PASTORS
some evangelists, some *p* and	Eph 4.11

PASTURE — S
will restore Israel to his *p*,	Jer 50.19
makes me lie down in green *p*.	Ps 23.2

PATH — S
Lead me in the *p* of thy	Ps 119.35
Thy word..a light to my *p*.	119.105
p of the righteous is like	Prov 4.18
wise man's *p* leads upward	15.24
taught him the *p* of justice,	Isa 40.14
make them walk..a straight *p*	Jer 31.9
some seeds fell along the *p*,	Mt 13.4
some seed fell along the *p*,	Mk 4.4
the *p* of all who forget God;	Job 8.13
passes along the *p* of the sea.	Ps 8.8
held fast to thy *p*, my feet	17.5
in *p* that they have not known	Isa 42.16

PATIENCE
'Have *p* with me,..I will pay	Mt 18.29
and bring forth fruit with *p*.	Lk 8.15
we wait for it with *p*.	Rom 8.25
God,..has endured with much *p*	9.22
lowliness, meekness, and *p*,	Col 3.12
example of suffering and *p*,	Jas 5.10

PATIENT — LY
p in tribulation, be constant	Rom 12.12
Love is *p* and kind; love	1Cor 13.4
be *p*. Establish your hearts,	Jas 5.8
your toil and your *p* endurance,	Rev 2.2
faith..service and *p* endurance,	2.19
suffer for it you take it *p*,	1Pet 2.20

PATMOS
was on the island called *P*	Rev 1.9

PAUL
Born in Tarsus, Acts 22.3; educated under Gamaliel, Acts 22.3; consented to Stephen's death, Acts 7.58; 8.1 (22.20); persecuted the church, Acts 8.3; 9.1–2 (22.4–5; 26.10–11; 1Cor 15.9; Gal 1.13; Phil 3.6); went into Arabia, Gal 1.17; preached in Damascus, Gal 1.17; went up to Jerusalem, Acts 9.26–28; Gal 1.18–19; name changed to Paul, Acts 13.9; missionary work, Acts 13—14; 15.36—18.22; 18.23—21.17; attended the Council of Jerusalem, Acts 15.1–29; Gal. 2.1–10; arrested in Jerusalem, Acts 21.27–40; imprisoned in Caesarea, Acts 23.23–35; defended himself before Felix, Acts 24; appealed to Caesar, Acts 25.10–12;
defended himself before Agrippa, Acts 26; journeyed to Rome, Acts 27.1—28.16; preached during imprisonment, Acts 28.17–31.

divided? Was *P* crucified for	1Cor 1.13
one says, "I belong to *P*,"	3.4
our beloved brother *P* wrote	2Pet 3.15

PAY — ING
Joseph will hate us and *p*	Gen 50.15
then I will *p* for it;	Num 20.19
I will *p* thee my vows,	Ps 66.13
I will *p* my vows to the LORD	116.18
You received without *p*, give	Mt 10.8
P all of them their dues,	Rom 13.7
you *p* me back for something?	Joel 3.4

PEACE
I will give *p* in the land,	Lev 26.6
The LORD..give you *p*.	Num 6.26
offer terms of *p* to it.	Deut 20.10
"*P* be to you; do not fear,	Judg 6.23
present. But he held his *p*.	1Sam 10.27
shall be *p* from the LORD	1Ki 2.33
"Why not, if there will be *p*	2Ki 20.19
son of Jesse! *P*, *p* to you,	1Chr 12.18
they made *p* with David,	19.19
give *p* and quiet to Israel	22.9
for the LORD gave him *p*.	2Chr 14.6
beasts..be at *p* with you.	Job 5.23
For they do not speak *p*, but	Ps 35.20
righteousness and *p* will kiss	85.10
Great *p*..who love thy law;	119.165
I am for *p*; but when I speak,	120.7
Pray for the *p* of Jerusalem!	122.6
and all her paths are *p*.	Prov 3.17
in his eyes..one who brings *p*.	Sol 8.10
of *p* there will be no end,	Isa 9.7
dost keep him in perfect *p*,	26.3
O LORD, thou wilt ordain *p*	26.12
let them make *p* with me, let	27.5
effect of righteousness..*p*,	32.17
king of Assyria: Make your *p*	36.16
be *p* and security in my days."	39.8
Then your *p*..like a river,	48.18
no *p*,".."for the wicked."	48.22
publishes *p*,..brings good tidings	52.7
my covenant of *p* shall not	54.10
joy, and be led forth in *p*;	55.12
P, *p*, to the far and..near,	57.19
I will make your overseers *p*	60.17
'*P*, *p*,' when there is no *p*.	Jer 6.14
'*P*, *p*,' when there is no *p*.	8.11
We looked for *p*,..no good came;	14.19
seek *p*,..there shall be none.	Ezek 7.25
misled my people, saying, '*P*,'	13.10
the prophets saw..visions of *p*	13.16
"I will make..a covenant of *p*	34.25
I will make a covenant of *p*	37.26
cry "*P*" when they have..to eat,	Mic 3.5
And..*p*, when the Assyrian comes	5.5
tidings, who proclaims *p*!	Nah 1.15
shall command *p* to..nations;	Zech 9.10
I have not come to bring *p*,	Mt 10.34
to the sea, "*P*! Be still!"	Mk 4.39
be at *p* with one another."	9.50
our feet into the way of *p*."	Lk 1.79
on earth *p* among men with whom	2.14
faith has saved you; go in *p*."	7.50
faith..made you well; go in *p*."	8.48
say, '*P* be to this house!'	10.5
come to give *p* on earth? No,	12.51
said to them, "*P* to you!"	24.36*n*

PEACE (cont.)

P I leave with you; my *p* I	Jn 14.27
that in me you may have *p*.	16.33
said to them, "*P* be with you."	20.19
said..again, "*P* be with you.	20.21
preaching good news of *p*	Acts 10.36
we have *p* with God through our	Rom 5.1
pursue what makes for *p* and	14.19
God of *p* will soon crush	16.20
Grace to you and *p* from God	2Cor 1.2
For he is our *p*, who has made	Eph 2.14
place of the two, so making *p*,	2.15
he came and preached *p* to you	2.17
the *p* of God, which passes all	Phil 4.7
God of *p* will be with you.	4.9
p by the blood of his cross.	Col 1.20
let the *p* of Christ rule in	3.15
may the God of *p* who brought	Heb 13.20
let him seek *p* and pursue it.	1Pet 3.11
rider was permitted to take *p*	Rev 6.4

PEACEABLY

could not speak *p* to him.	Gen 37.4
she said, "Do you come *p*?"	1Ki 2.13
If possible,..live *p* with all.	Rom 12.18

PEACEMAKERS

"Blessed are the *p*, for they	Mt 5.9

PEACE OFFERING — S

offering is a sacrifice of *p*..,	Lev 3.1
people..Israel from their *p*..;	Ex 29.28
law of the sacrifice of *p*..	Lev 7.11

PEARLS

do not throw your *p* before swine,	Mt 7.6
merchant in search of fine *p*,	13.45

PEN

Oh that with an iron *p* and	Job 19.24
my tongue is like the *p* of a	Ps 45.1
the false *p* of the scribes	Jer 8.8
written with a *p* of iron;	17.1
rather not write with *p* and	3Jn 13

PENNY

two sparrows sold for a *p*?	Mt 10.29
put in two copper coins,..a *p*.	Mk 12.42

PENTECOST

When the day of *P* had come,	Acts 2.1
stay in Ephesus until *P*,	1Cor 16.8

PEOPLE — S

beating a Hebrew, one of his *p*.	Ex 2.11
I will take you for my *p*,	6.7
"Let my *p* go, that they may serve	7.16
till the *p* pass by whom	15.16
burn hot against thy *p*,	32.11
that this nation is thy *p*."	33.13
your God,..you shall be my *p*.	Lev 26.12
art in the midst of this *p*;	Num 14.14
stubbornness of this *p*,	Deut 9.27
chosen you to be a *p* for his	14.2
p for his own possession,	26.18
establish you..as his *p*,	29.13
LORD's portion is his *p*,	32.9
the *p* served the LORD all the	Judg 2.7
visited his *p* and given them	Ruth 1.6
your *p* shall be my *p*, and	1.16
abhorred by his *p* Israel;	1Sam 27.12
I will save my *p* Israel	2Sam 3.18
Israel to be thy *p* for ever;	7.24
'Since..I brought my *p* Israel	1Ki 8.16
my *p* as your *p*, my horses	22.4
I am as you are, my *p* as your	2Ki 3.7

---

they should be the LORD's *p*;	11.17
a place for my *p* Israel,	1Chr 17.9
What..nation..is like thy *p*	17.21
make thy *p* Israel to be thy *p*	17.22
if my *p* who are called by	2Chr 7.14
had compassion on his *p*	36.15
he led forth his *p* like sheep,	Ps 78.52
we are his *p*, and the sheep	100.3
anger..kindled against his *p*,	106.40
Your *p* will offer themselves	110.3
LORD is round about his *p*,	125.2
Happy the *p* whose God is the	144.15
raised up a horn for his *p*,	148.14
LORD takes pleasure in his *p*;	149.4
For thou hast rejected thy *p*,	Isa 2.6
My *p*—children are..oppressors,	3.12
my *p* go into exile for want	5.13
The *p* who walked in darkness	9.2
angry with my *p*, I profaned my	47.6
declare to..*p* their transgression,	58.1
he said, Surely they are my *p*,	63.8
rejoice..and be glad in my *p*;	65.19
my *p* have committed two evils:	Jer 2.13
God, and you shall be my *p*;	7.23
for me a *p*, a name, a praise,	13.11
But my *p* have forgotten me,	18.15
they shall be my *p* and I will	24.7
And you shall be my *p*, and	30.22
And they shall be my *p*, and	32.38
they..my *p*, and I..their God.	Ezek 11.20
that they may be my *p* and	14.11
you..my *p*, and I..your God.	36.28
to them, "You are not my *p*,"	Hos 1.10
say to Not my *p*, 'You are my *p*';	2.23
the LORD had pity on his *p*.	Joel 2.18
like the Ethiopians..O *p* of	Amos 9.7
LORD has a controversy with his *p*,	Mic 6.2
have many *p* in this city."	Acts 18.10
not my *p* I will call 'my *p*,'	Rom 9.25
Once..no *p* but now..God's *p*;	1Pet 2.10
that all the *p* of the earth	1Ki 8.60
Let the *p* praise thee, O God;	Ps 67.5
hills; and *p* shall flow to it,	Mic 4.1

PERCEIVE — D

shall indeed see but never *p*.	Mt 13.14
may indeed see but not *p*,	Mk 4.12
no bread? Do you not yet *p*	8.17
I *p*..God shows no partiality,	Acts 10.34
Gideon *p*..he was the angel	Judg 6.22
sanctuary..then I *p* their end.	Ps 73.17
no one has heard or *p* by..ear,	Isa 64.4
he *p* that it was out of envy	Mk 15.10
they *p* that he had told this	Lk 20.19
and deity, has been clearly *p*	Rom 1.20

PERFECT — ED

which cannot *p* the conscience	Heb 9.9
in him truly love for God is *p*.	1Jn 2.5

PERFECT — LY

This God—his way is *p*;	2Sam 22.31
one who is *p* in knowledge	Job 36.4
This God—his way is *p*;	Ps 18.30
My dove, my *p* one, is only one,	Sol 6.9
Thou dost keep him in *p* peace,	Isa 26.3
You, therefore must be *p*, as	Mt 5.48
"If you would be *p*, go, sell	19.21
thou hast brought *p* praise'?"	21.16
but when the *p* comes, the	1Cor 13.10
Not that I..am already *p*;	Phil 3.12
make the pioneer..salvation *p*	Heb 2.10
being made *p* he became the	5.9
Son who has been made *p* for ever.	7.28

PERFECT — LY (cont.)
every *p* gift is from above,   Jas 1.17
that they may become *p* one,   Jn 17.23

PERFECTION
Out of Zion, the *p* of beauty,   Ps 50.2
have seen a like to all *p*,   119.96
Now if *p* had been attainable   Heb 7.11

PERFORM — ED
to *p* the words of. .covenant   2Ki 23.3
your vows to. .God, and *p* them; Ps 76.11
I will speak the word and *p*   Ezek 12.25
to *p* the mercy promised to our Lk 1.72
Who has *p* and done this,   Isa 41.4

PERIL
bread at the *p* of our lives,   Lam 5.9
Why am I in *p* every hour? 1Cor 15.30

PERISH — ES — ED — ING
shall *p* among the nations,   Lev 26.38
you will soon utterly *p*   Deut 4.26
that you shall surely *p*.   8.19
you shall *p* quickly from   Josh 23.16
"So *p* all thine enemies,   Judg 5.31
go to the king,. .if I *p*, I *p*."   Est 4.16
he will *p* for ever like his   Job 20.7
But the wicked *p*; the enemies Ps 37.20
who are far from thee shall *p*;   73.27
They will *p*, but thou. .endure; 102.26
they *p*,. .righteous increase. Prov 28.28
our God has doomed us to *p*,   Jer 8.14
repent. .so that we *p* not?"   Jonah 3.9
one of. .little ones should *p*.   Mt 18.14
who take the sword will *p* by   26.52
unless you repent you will. .*p*. Lk 13.3
they *p*,. .thou remainest;   Heb 1.11
the wicked dies, his hope *p*,   Prov 11.7
they stumbled and *p* before thee. Ps 9.3
veiled. .to those who are *p*.   2Cor 4.3

PERISHABLE
do it to receive a *p* wreath,   1Cor 9.25
What is sown is *p*, what is   15.42
ransomed. .not with *p* things 1Pet 1.18

PERMITS
with you, if the Lord p.   1Cor 16.7
this we will do if God p.   Heb 6.3

PERPLEXED
but the city of Susa was *p*.   Est 3.15
Herod. .was *p*, because it was   Lk 9.7
While they were *p* about this,   24.4
p, but not driven to despair;   2Cor 4.8

PERSECUTE — D
those. .put to shame who *p* me, Jer 17.18
When they *p* you in one town,   Mt 10.23
whom they will kill and *p*,'   Lk 11.49
and *p* you, delivering you up   21.12
If they *p* me, they will *p* you; Jn 15.20
did not your fathers *p*? And   Acts 7.52
Saul, why do you *p* me?"   9.4
Saul, why do you *p* me?'   22.7
Bless those who *p* you; bless Rom 12.14
who are *p* for righteousness'   Mt 5.10
this was why the Jews *p* Jesus, Jn 5.16
I *p* this Way to the death,   Acts 22.4
I *p* them even to foreign cities.   26.11
bless; when *p*, we endure;   1Cor 4.12
because I *p* the church of God.   15.9
p, but not forsaken; struck   2Cor 4.9
how I *p* the church of God   Gal 1.13
p him. .born according to. .Spirit,   4.29

not. .*p* for the cross of Christ.   6.12
in Christ Jesus will be *p*,   2Tim 3.12

PERSECUTION — S
when tribulation or *p* arises   Mt 13.21
p arose against the church   Acts 8.1
scattered because of the *p*   11.19
children and lands, with *p*,   Mk 10.30
and faith in all your *p* and   2Thess 1.4
at Lystra, what *p* I endured;   2Tim 3.11

PERSIA
first year of Cyrus king of P,   Ezra 1.1
wrote to Artaxerxes king of P;   4.7
reign of Darius king of P.   4.24
banquet for. .army chiefs of P   Est 1.3
prince of the kingdom of P   Dan 10.13

PERSUADE — D — ING
fear of the Lord, we *p* men;   2Cor 5.11
some. .were *p*, and joined Paul Acts 17.4
and *p* Jews and Greeks.   18.4
Paul has *p* and turned away   19.26
man is *p* men to worship God   18.13

PERVERT — ED — ING
does the Almighty *p* the right?   Job 8.3
Almighty will not *p* justice.   34.12
you *p* the words of. .God,   Jer 23.36
abhor justice and *p* all equity, Mic 3.9
because they have *p* their way, Jer 3.21
found this man *p* our nation,   Lk 23.2

PESTILENCE
The LORD will make the *p*   Deut 28.21
three days' *p* in your land?   2Sam 24.13
p that stalks in darkness,   Ps 91.6
on them sword, famine, and *p*, Jer 29.17

PETER (CEPHAS, SIMON, SYMEON)
*Called to be a fisher of men, Mt 4.18–20
(Mk 1.16–18; Lk 5.1–11); also named
Cephas, which means "rock", Jn 1.42n;
sent out with the twelve, Mt 10.2 (Mk
3.16); walked on the sea, Mt 14.28–33;
confessed Jesus as the Christ, Mt 16.13–20
(Mk 8.27–30; Lk 9.18–22); interceded for
by the Lord, Lk 22.31–32; cut off the
servant's ear, Jn 18.10–11; denied Jesus
three times, Mt 26.69–75 (Mk 14.66–72;
Lk 22.54–62; Jn 18.15–18, 25–27); "Feed
my sheep," Jn 21.15–19; addressed the
disciples, Acts 1.15–26; preached at
Pentecost, Acts 2.14–42; healed the lame
man, Acts 3.1–10; witnessed in Solomon's
portico, Acts 3.11–26; preached to the
Council, Acts 4.1–12; imprisoned and
released, Acts 5.17–42; denounced Simon
Magus, Acts 8.14–24; visited Cornelius
after the vision, Acts 10; reported to the
Jerusalem Church, Acts 11.1–18; imprisoned and delivered, Acts 12.1–19; at
the Council of Jerusalem, Acts 15.6–12;
visited by Paul, Gal 1.18; blamed by Paul,
Gal 2.11–14; Peter's wife's mother, Mt
8.14 (Mk 1.30; Lk 4.38); his wife, 1Cor
9.5.*

PETITION — S
whoever makes *p* to. .god or man Dan 6.7
the LORD fulfil all your *p*!   Ps 20.5

PHARISEES
when he saw many of the P and   Mt 3.7
exceeds. .the scribes and P,   5.20
when the P saw this, they said,   9.11
But when the P saw it, they   12.2

PHARISEES (cont.)
P went out and took counsel — Mt 12.14
beware of the leaven of the *P* — 16.6
And *P* came up. .and tested him — 19.3
the *P* went and took counsel — 22.15
and the *P* sit on Moses' seat; — 23.2
priests and the *P* gathered — 27.62
man of the *P*, named Nicodemus, Jn 3.1
and the *P* brought a woman — 8.3*n*
the *P* rose up, and said, — Acts 15.5
Sadducees and the other *P*, — 23.6

PHILEMON
To *P* our beloved fellow — Philem 1

PHILIP
P and Bartholomew; Thomas — Mt 10.3
Jesus. .found *P* and said to him, Jn 1.43
Jesus said to *P*, "How are we — 6.5
Greeks. .came to *P*, who was — 12.21
P said to him, "Lord, show us — 14.8
and Andrew, *P* and Thomas, — Acts 1.13
P went. .to a city of Samaria, — 8.5
But *P* was found at Azotus, — 8.40
we entered the house of *P* — 21.8

PHILIPPI
voyage. .from there to *P*, — Acts 16.12
we sailed away from *P* after — 20.6
in Christ Jesus who are at *P*, — Phil 1.1
shamefully treated at *P*, — 1Thess 2.2

PHILISTIA
on the inhabitants of *P*. — Ex 15.14
"Rejoice not, O *P*, all of — Isa 14.29
"What are you to me, O. .*P*? — Joel 3.4
make an end of the pride of *P*. Zech 9.6

PHILISTINES
Abimelech king of the *P*. — Gen 26.1
the *P* seized him and gouged Judg 16.21
out to battle against the *P*; — 1Sam 4.1
When the *P* captured the ark of God, 5.1
out of the hand of the *P*." — 7.3
the *P* fought against Israel; — 31.1
David defeated the *P* and — 2Sam 8.1
and of soothsayers like the *P*, — Isa 2.6
P from Caphtor and the Syrians Amos 9.7

PHILOSOPHERS
Epicurean and Stoic *p* met — Acts 17.18

PHILOSOPHY
makes a prey of you by *p* and — Col 2.8

PHYSICAL
If there is a *p* body, there — 1Cor 15.44

PHYSICIAN — S
Gilead? Is there no *p* there? — Jer 8.22
well have no need of a *p*, — Mt 9.12
well have no need of a *p*, — Mk 2.17
proverb, '*P*, heal yourself; — Lk 4.23
well have no need of a *p*, — 5.31
Luke the beloved *p* and Demas Col 4.14
p to embalm his father. — Gen 50.2
worthless *p* are you all. — Job 13.4
suffered much under many *p*, — Mk 5.26
spent all her living upon *p* — Lk 8.43*n*

PIECES
twelve baskets full of broken *p* Mk 6.43
broken *p* did you take up?" — 8.19
twelve baskets of broken *p*. — Lk 9.17

PIERCE — D
sword will *p* through your. .soul Lk 2.35
they have *p* my hands and — Ps 22.16
look on him whom they. .*p*, — Zech 12.10

one of. .soldiers *p* his side — Jn 19.34
see him, every one who *p* him; — Rev 1.7

PIETY
"Beware of practicing your *p* — Mt 6.1
by our own power or *p* we — Acts 3.12

PIGEON — S
"Bring me. .a young *p*." — Gen 15.9
bring his offering. .of young *p*. Lev 1.14

PILATE (PONTIUS)
Governor of Judea, Lk 3.1; killed some Galileans, Lk 13.1; sentenced Jesus to be crucified, Mt 27.1–25 (Mk 15.1–15; Lk 23.1–26; Jn 18.28—19.22); Jesus "suffered under Pontius Pilate," Acts 3.13; 13.28; 1Tim 6.13.

PILLAR — S
she became a *p* of salt. — Gen 19.26
stone. .set it up for a *p* — 28.18
in a *p* of cloud to lead them — Ex 13.21
set up for himself the *p* — 2Sam 18.18
p. .of Baal, and burned it. — 2Ki 10.26
by a *p* of fire in the night — Neh 9.12
"Let me feel the *p* on which Judg 16.26
who were reputed to be *p*, — Gal 2.9

PIONEER
make the *p* of their salvation — Heb 2.10
Jesus the *p* and perfecter — 12.2

PIT
or let thy godly. .see the *P*. — Ps 16.10
thrust you down into the *P*, — Ezek 28.8
bring up my life from the *P*, — Jonah 2.6

PITY — IES — IED (v)
your eye shall not *p* them; — Deut 7.16
LORD said, "You *p* the plant, Jonah 4.10
As a father *p* his children, — Ps 103.13
No eye *p*. .out of compassion Ezek 16.5
of all men most to be *p*. — 1Cor 15.19

PITY (n)
She took *p* on him and said, — Ex 2.6
have *p* on me, O. .my friends, Job 19.21
It hurls at him without *p*; — 27.22
He has *p* on the weak and — Ps 72.13
he who has *p*. .will lead them, Isa 49.10
will not spare. .nor. .have *p*; Ezek 7.4
not spare, nor will I have *p*; — 8.18
have *p* on the house of Judah, Hos 1.7
LORD. .had *p* on his people. — Joel 2.18
For I will no longer have *p* — Zech 11.6
out of *p*. .the lord. .released Mt 18.27
Jesus in *p* touched their eyes, — 20.34
with *p*, he stretched out his — Mk 1.41
have *p* on us and help us." — 9.22

PLACE
the dove found no *p* to set — Gen 8.9
till all these things take *p*. — Mt 24.34
was no *p* for them in the inn. — Lk 2.7

PLAGUE — S
severe *p* upon your cattle — Ex 9.3
"Yet one *p* more I will bring — 11.1
smote. .with a very great *p*. Num 11.33
died by *p* before the LORD — 14.37
p had already begun among — 16.47
those that died by the *p* — 25.9
that the *p* may be averted — 1Chr 21.22
Phinehas. .the *p* was stayed. Ps 106.30
p. .will smite. .the peoples Zech 14.12
great *p* because of Sarai, — Gen 12.17

PLAN — S

God had frustrated their *p*,   Neh 4.15
carry out a *p*, but not mine;   Isa 30.1
and devising a *p* against you.   Jer 18.11
according to the definite *p*   Acts 2.23
if this *p*..is of men, it will   5.38
a *p* for the fulness of time,   Eph 1.10
the *p* of the mystery hidden   3.9
past, my *p* are broken off,   Job 17.11
crafty *p* against thy people;   Ps 83.3
Many are the *p* in the mind   Prov 19.21
P are established by counsel;   20.18
I know the *p* I have for you,   Jer 29.11

PLANT — S — ED (v)

bring them in, and *p* them   Ex 15.17
Israel, and will *p* them,   1Chr 17.9
nations; but them thou didst *p*;   Ps 44.2
I will *p* them in this land   Jer 32.41
I will *p* them upon their land,   Amos 9.15
Who *p*..vineyard without eating   1Cor 9.7
stock which thy right hand *p*.   Ps 80.15
Yet I *p* you a choice vine,   Jer 2.21
plant..my..Father has not *p*   Mt 15.13
I *p*, Apollos watered, but God   1Cor 3.6

PLANT — S (n)

when no *p*..yet in the earth   Gen 2.5
God appointed a *p*, and made   Jonah 4.6
"Let the earth put forth..*p*   Gen 1.11
the *p*..they will teach you;   Job 12.8

PLATTER

head of John..Baptist on a *p*."   Mk 6.25

PLAY — ING

and drink, and rose up to *p*.   Ex 32.6
child shall *p* over the hole   Isa 11.8
son of Hagar..*p* with..Isaac.   Gen 21.9

PLEAD — S

stand still, that I may *p*   1Sam 12.7
P my cause and redeem me;   Ps 119.154
the LORD will *p* their cause   Prov 22.23
"*P* with your mother, *p*—   Hos 2.2
God..*p*..cause of his people: Isa 51.22

PLEASANT — NESS

made to grow every tree..*p*   Gen 2.9
lines have fallen..in *p* places;   Ps 16.6
they despised the *p* land,   106.24
p it is when brothers dwell   133.1
knowledge will be *p* to your   Prov 2.10
bread eaten in secret is *p*."   9.17
Her ways are ways of *p*, and   3.17

PLEASE — S — D — ING

may it *p* thee to bless   2Sam 7.29
may it *p* thee to bless the   1Chr 17.27
that it would *p* God to crush   Job 6.9
When a man's ways *p* the LORD,   Prov 16.7
nor awaken love until it *p*.   Sol 2.7
nor awaken love until it *p*.   3.5
nor awaken love until it *p*.   8.4
in the flesh cannot *p* God.   Rom 8.8
weak, and not to *p* ourselves;   15.1
unmarried..how to *p* the Lord;   1Cor 7.32
just as I try to *p* all men   10.33
make it our aim to *p* him.   2Cor 5.9
Or am I trying to *p* men? If   Gal 1.10
not to *p* men, but to *p* God   1Thess 2.4
"Get her..for she *p* me well."   Judg 14.3
maiden who *p* the king be queen   Est 2.4
Whatever the LORD *p* he does,   Ps 135.6
he who *p* God escapes her, but   Ecc 7.26
for he does whatever he *p*.   8.3

because we..do what *p* him.   1Jn 3.22
Manassites spoke, it *p* them   Josh 22.30
it has *p* the LORD to make   1Sam 12.22
it *p* David well to be the king's   18.26
that the king did *p* all   2Sam 3.36
And the advice *p* Absalom   17.4
It *p* the Lord that Solomon   1Ki 3.10
it *p* the king to send me;   Neh 2.6
p, for..righteousness' sake,   Isa 42.21
Will the LORD be *p* with..rams,   Mic 6.7
p with you or show you favor?   Mal 1.8
Son, with whom I am well *p*."   Mt 3.17
Son, with whom I am well *p*;   17.5
Son; with whom I am well *p*."   Mk 1.11
Son; with thee I am well *p*."   Lk 3.22
with most..God was not *p*;   1Cor 10.5
was *p* to reveal his Son to me,   Gal 1.16
fulness of God was *p* to dwell,   Col 1.19
attested as having *p* God.   Heb 11.5
words of the pure are *p* to   Prov 15.26
Preacher sought..*p* words,   Ecc 12.10
I always do what is *p* to him."   Jn 8.29
learn what is *p* to the Lord.   Eph 5.10
sacrifice acceptable and *p*   Phil 4.18
worthy of the Lord, fully *p*   Col 1.10
such sacrifices are *p* to God.   Heb 13.16

PLEASURE — S

any *p* to the Almighty if you   Job 22.3
takes *p* in those who fear   Ps 147.11
LORD takes *p* in his people;   149.4
who loves *p* will be a poor   Prov 21.17
I will make a test of *p*; enjoy   Ecc 2.1
I kept my heart from no *p*,   2.10
for he has no *p* in fools. Pay   5.4
Have I any *p* in the death   Ezek 18.23
no *p* in the death of the wicked,   33.11
the house, that I may take *p* in   Hag 1.8
I have no *p* in you, says..LORD   Mal 1.10
your Father's good *p* to give   Lk 12.32
you might have a double *p*;   2Cor 1.15
and to work for his good *p*.   Phil 2.13
had *p* in unrighteousness.   2Thess 2.12
in..offerings thou has..no *p*.   Heb 10.6
You..lived..in luxury and..*p*;   Jas 5.5
in thy right hand are *p* for   Ps 16.11
choked by..riches and *p* of life,   Lk 8.11
than to enjoy the fleeting *p*   Heb 11.25

PLEDGE

garment in *p*,..restore it   Ex 22.26
or an upper millstone in *p*;   Deut 24.6
shall not sleep in his *p*;   24.12
hold him in *p* when he gives   Prov 20.16
hold him in *p* when he gives   27.13
the wicked restores the *p*,   Ezek 33.15
lay..upon garments taken in *p*;   Amos 2.8

PLENTY

seven years of great *p*   Gen 41.29
tills his land will have *p*   Prov 12.11
the secret of facing *p* and   Phil 4.12

PLOT — S

do you *p* against the LORD?   Nah 1.9
A worthless man *p* evil, and   Prov 16.27

PLOW — S — ED (v)

not *p* with an ox and an ass   Deut 22.10
those who *p* iniquity..reap   Job 4.8
The sluggard does not *p* in   Prov 20.4
the plowman should *p* in hope   1Cor 9.10
Does he who *p* for sowing plow   Isa 28.24
The plowers *p* upon my back;   Ps 129.3
Zion shall be *p* as a field;   Jer 26.18

PLOW — S — ED (v) (cont.)
You have p iniquity, you   Hos 10.13
Zion shall be p as a field;   Mic 3.12

PLOW (n)
hand to the p and looks back   Lk 9.62

PLOWSHARES
Beat your p into swords,   Joel 3.10
shall beat their swords into p,   Mic 4.3

PLUCK — ED
will p up the house of Judah   Jer 12.14
eye causes you to sin, p it out,   Mt 5.29
you would have p out your eyes   Gal 4.15

PLUMB LINE
beside..wall built with a p..,   Amos 7.7

PLUNDER — ED — ING
the lot of those who p us.   Isa 17.14
enter..house and p his goods,   Mt 12.29
p the city, because their sister   Gen 34.27
and p the camp of the Syrians.   2Ki 7.16
Because you have p many nations,   Hab 2.8
accepted..p of your property,   Heb 10.34

POMP
Man cannot abide in his p,   Ps 49.12
Your p is brought..to Sheol,   Isa 14.11

PONDERING
Mary kept all these things, p   Lk 2.19
Peter was p the vision,   Acts 10.19

POOL — S
Jerusalem by the Sheep Gate a p,   Jn 5.2
"Go, wash in the p of Siloam"   9.7
islands, and dry up the p.   Isa 42.15

POOR — EST
the p of your people may eat;   Ex 23.11
the p shall not give less,   30.15
leave them for the p and for   Lev 19.10
gleanings..leave..for the p   23.22
"If your brother becomes p,   25.25
"If..is among you a p man,   Deut 15.7
For the p will never cease   15.11
raises up the p from..dust;   1Sam 2.8
the p man had nothing but   2Sam 12.3
So the p have hope, and   Job 5.16
crushed and abandoned the p,   20.19
thrust the p off the road;   24.4
because I delivered the p   29.12
withheld anything that the p   31.16
hope of the p shall not perish   Ps 9.18
the wicked hotly pursue the p;   10.2
This p man cried,..LORD heard   34.6
I am p and needy; but the LORD   40.17
Blessed..who considers the p!   41.1
May he defend..cause of the p   72.4
answer me, for I am p and needy.   86.1
For I am p and needy, and   109.22
raises the p from the dust,   113.7
poverty of..p is their ruin.   Prov 10.15
p man who walks in..integrity   19.1
a p man's brothers hate him;   19.7
The rich and the p meet   22.2
king judges..p with equity   29.14
spoil of..p is in your houses.   Isa 3.14
with righteousness..judge the p,   11.4
thou..a stronghold to the p,   25.4
who oppress the p, who crush   Amos 4.1
because you trample upon the p   5.11
we may buy the p for silver   8.6
"Blessed are the p in spirit,   Mt 5.3
the p have good news preached   11.5

give to the p, and you will   19.21
you always have the p with you,   26.11
go, sell..and give to the p,   Mk 10.21
sold..and given to the p."   14.5
to preach good news to the p.   Lk 4.18
"Blessed are you p, for yours   6.20
give a feast, invite the p,   14.13
at..gate lay a p man..Lazarus,   16.20
Sell..and distribute to the p,   18.22
half of my goods I give to the p; 19.8
not sold..and given to the p?"   Jn 12.5
The p you always have with you,   12.8
as p, yet making many rich;   2Cor 6.10
for your sake he became p,   8.9
"He scatters..gives to the p;   9.9
have us remember the p,   Gal 2.10
God chosen those who are p   Jas 2.5
you are wretched, pitiable, p,   Rev 3.17
p of..land to be vinedressers   2Ki 25.12

PORTENT — S
I have been as a p to many;   Ps 71.7
a great p appeared in heaven,   Rev 12.1
I saw another p in heaven,   15.1
I will give p in the heavens   Joel 2.30

PORTION — S
LORD's p is his people,   Deut 32.9
would give Hannah only one p,   1Sam 1.5
"We have no p in David,   2Sam 20.1
"What p have we in David?   1Ki 12.16
the wicked man's p from God,   Job 20.29
The LORD is my chosen p and   Ps 16.5
The LORD is my p; I promise   119.57
Thou art my refuge, my p in   142.5
he who is the p of Jacob,   Jer 10.16
LORD is my p," says my soul.   Lam 3.24
send p to him for whom nothing   Neh 8.10

POSSESS — ED — ING
his descendants shall p it.   Num 14.24
p the inheritance of his fathers. 36.8
give it, and they shall p it.   Deut 1.39
given you this land to p;   3.18
p the lake and the south."   33.23
Will you not p what Chemosh   Judg 11.24
enter in and p the land.   18.9
tell them to go in to p the   Neh 9.15
his children shall p the land.   Ps 25.13
who wait for the LORD shall p   37.9
house of Israel will p them   Isa 14.2
they shall p it for ever,   34.17
descendants will p the nations   54.3
they shall p the land for ever,   60.21
shall you then p the land?   Ezek 33.26
and they shall p you, and   36.12
and p the kingdom for ever,   Dan 7.18
Jacob shall p their own   Obad 1.17
remnant of this people to p   Zech 8.12
my daughter is..p by a demon."   Mt 15.22
nothing,..yet p everything.   2Cor 6.10

POSSESSION — S
Canaan, for an everlasting p;   Gen 17.8
this land for an everlasting p.'   48.4
you shall be my own p   Ex 19.5
that is their perpetual p.   Lev 25.34
this land shall be your p   Num 32.22
go in and take p of the land   Deut 1.8
to be a people of his own p,   4.20
take p of the good land   6.18
a people for his own p,   14.2
a people for his own p,   26.18
take p of the land which   Josh 1.11
go in..take p of the land,   18.3

POSSESSION — S (cont.)

to drive us out of thy *p*,	2Chr 20.11
he apportioned them for a *p*	Ps 78.55
himself, Israel as his own *p*.	135.4
they entered and took *p* of it.	Jer 32.23
no *p* in Israel; I am their *p*.	Ezek 44.28
my special *p* on the day when	Mal 3.17
until we acquire *p* of it,	Eph 1.14
I had also great *p* of herds	Ecc 2.7
sorrowful; for he had great *p*.	Mt 19.22
will set him over all his *p*.	24.47
not..abundance of his *p*."	Lk 12.15

POSSIBLE

with God all things are *p*."	Mt 19.26
All..*p* to him who believes."	Mk 9.23
all things are *p* with God."	10.27
if it were *p*, the hour might	14.35
with men is *p* with God."	Lk 18.27

POSTERITY

P shall serve him; men shall	Ps 22.30
May his *p* be cut off; may	109.13

POT — S

there is death in the *p*!"	2Ki 4.40
"I see a boiling *p*,	Jer 1.13
as when earthen *p* are broken	Rev 2.27

POTTER — 'S

trample..as the *p* treads clay.	Isa 41.25
an earthen vessel with the *p*!	45.9
Has the *p* no right over the	Rom 9.21
dash..in pieces like a *p* vessel."	Ps 2.9
breaking is like..a *p* vessel	Isa 30.14
go down to the *p* house, and	Jer 18.2
like the clay in the *p* hand,	18.6
"Go, buy a *p* earthen flask,	19.1
earthen pots, the work of a *p*	Lam 4.2
bought with them the *p* field,	Mt 27.7

POUR — ED — ING

remember, as I *p* out my soul:	Ps 42.4
p water on the thirsty land,	Isa 44.3
wrath of the LORD;.."*P* it out	Jer 6.11
P out..wrath upon the nations	10.25
soon *p* out my wrath upon you,	Ezek 7.8
I..*p* out my wrath like water.	Hos 5.10
p out my spirit on all flesh;	Joel 2.28
p out..spirit of compassion	Zech 12.10
I will *p* out my Spirit upon	Acts 2.17
drew water and *p* it out	1Sam 7.6
he *p* it out to the LORD,	2Sam 23.16
he *p* it out to the LORD,	1Chr 11.18
until the Spirit is *p* upon us	Isa 32.15
and my wrath will be *p* out	Jer 7.20
ointment,..she *p*..on his head,	Mt 26.7
she broke the jar and *p* it	Mk 14.3
God's love..*p* into our hearts	Rom 5.5
I have been *p* out my soul	1Sam 1.15

POVERTY

p will come..like a vagabond,	Prov 6.11
P and disgrace come to him	13.18
and *p* will come upon you	24.34
worthless..have plenty of *p*.	28.19
but she out of her *p* has put	Mk 12.44
joy and..*p* have overflowed	2Cor 8.2
and your *p* (but you are rich)	Rev 2.9

POWER

no *p* to stand before..enemies.	Lev 26.37
and the *p*, and the glory,	1Chr 29.11
God has *p* to help or to	2Chr 25.8
contend with me in..his *p*?	Job 23.6
his *p* who can understand?"	26.14

We will sing and praise thy *p*.	Ps 21.13
my soul from the *p* of Sheol,	49.15
So great is thy *p* that thy	66.3
thy saving *p* among all nations.	67.2
Ascribe *p* to God, whose	68.34
delivered them from the *p* of	106.10
kingdom, and tell of thy *p*,	145.11
when it is in your *p* to do it.	Prov 3.27
not give him *p* to enjoy them,	Ecc 6.2
No man has *p* to retain..spirit,	8.8
because he is strong in *p* not	Isa 40.26
He gives *p* to the faint, and	40.29
I will make them know my *p*	Jer 16.21
and the earth by thy great *p*	32.17
His *p* shall be great, and	Dan 8.24
as for me, I am filled with *p*,	Mic 3.8
nor by *p*, but by my Spirit,	Zech 4.6
the *p* and the glory, forever.	Mt 6.13*n*
scriptures nor the *p* of God.	22.29
perceiving in himself that *p*	Mk 5.30
kingdom of God come with *p*."	9.1
scriptures nor the *p* of God?	12.24
Son..at the right hand of *P*,	14.62
the *p* of the Most High will	Lk 1.35
the *p* of the Lord was with him	5.17
touch him, for *p* came forth	6.19
that *p* has gone forth from me."	8.46
far country to receive kingly *p*	19.12
coming in a cloud with *p*	21.27
hour, and the *p* of darkness."	22.53
right hand of the *p* of God."	22.69
until you are clothed with *p*	24.49
I have *p* to lay it down,	Jn 10.18
I have *p* to release you,	19.10
receive *p* when the Holy Spirit	Acts 1.8
as though by our own *p* or	3.12
with great *p* the apostles	4.33
Stephen, full of grace and *p*,	6.8
that *p* of God..called Great."	8.10
from the *p* of Satan to God,	26.18
the *p* of God for salvation	Rom 1.16
by the *p* of the Holy Spirit	15.13
by the *p* of the Holy Spirit,	15.19
saved it is the *p* of God.	1Cor 1.18
demonstration of..Spirit and *p*,	2.4
not..in..men but in the *p* of God.	2.5
assembled..with the *p* of our Lord	5.4
and every authority and *p*.	15.24
weakness, it is raised in *p*.	15.43
speech, and the *p* of God;	2Cor 6.7
p of Christ may rest upon me.	12.9
my *p*..made perfect in weakness."	12.9
but lives by the *p* of God.	13.4
greatness of his *p* in us who	Eph 1.19
by the *p* at work within us	3.20
the *p* of his resurrection,	Phil 3.10
not only in word, but..in *p*	1Thess 1.5
him who has the *p* of death,	Heb 2.14
who by God's *p* are guarded	1Pet 1.5
His divine *p* has granted to us	2Pet 1.3
give him *p* over the nations,	Rev 2.26
thou hast taken thy great *p*	11.17
give over their *p*..to the beast;	17.13

PRAISE — D (v)

thank thee, our God, and *p*	1Chr 29.13
P the LORD with the lyre,	Ps 33.2
also *p* thee with the harp for	71.22
wrath of men shall *p* thee;	76.10
servants of the LORD, *p* the name	113.1
At midnight I rise to *p* thee,	119.62
P the LORD, O Jerusalem!	147.12
P him, all his angels, *p* him,	148.2

PRAISE — D (v) (cont.)

Let everything that breathes *p*   Ps 150.6
Let another *p* you, and not   Prov 27.2
death cannot *p* thee; those   Isa 38.18
I will *p* thee among. .Gentiles,   Rom 15.9
"*P* the Lord, all Gentiles;   15.11
Lord, and greatly to be *p*,   1Chr 16.25
I blessed the Most High, and *p*   Dan 4.34

PRAISE — S (n)

He is your *p*; he is your God   Deut 10.21
render *p* to him; and tell   Josh 7.19
thy *p* reaches to the ends of   Ps 48.10
P is due to thee, O God, in   65.1
My mouth is filled with thy *p*,   71.8
Accept my offerings of *p*, O   119.108
Jerusalem. .a *p* in the earth.   Isa 62.7
loved the *p* of men more than   Jn 12.43
every tongue shall give *p*   Rom 14.11
any cheerful? Let him sing *p*.   Jas 5.13
Sing *p* to God, sing *p*! Sing   Ps 47.6
So will I ever sing *p* to thy name,   61.8

PRAY — S — ED — ING

Let me go over, I *p*, and see   Deut 3.25
"*P* for your servants to   1Sam 12.19
by ceasing to *p* for you;   12.23
has found courage to *p*   2Sam 7.27
David said, "O Lord, I *p*   15.31
hand, I *p* thee, be against me   24.17
acknowledge thy name, and *p*   1Ki 8.33
found courage to *p* before   1Chr 17.25
Job shall *p* for you, for I   Job 42.8
P for the peace of Jerusalem!   Ps 122.6
comes to his sanctuary to *p*,   Isa 16.12
do not *p* for this people,   Jer 7.16
do not *p* for this people, or   11.14
Then you will. .*p* to me, and   29.12
"*P* for us to the Lord our God."   37.3
Love your enemies and *p* for   Mt 5.44
they love to stand and *p* in   6.5
P then like this: Our Father   6.9
p. .the Lord of the harvest   9.38
into the hills by himself to *p*.   14.23
lay his hands on them and *p*.   19.13
P that your flight may not be   24.20
"Sit here, while I go. .and *p*."   26.36
Watch and *p* that you may not   26.41
he went into the hills to *p*.   Mk 6.46
P that it. .not happen in winter.   13.18
Take heed, watch and *p*;   13.33*n*
he said. ."Sit here, while I *p*."   14.32
Watch and *p* that you may not   14.38
he went out into the hills to *p*;   Lk 6.12
p for those who abuse you.   6.28
went up on the mountain to *p*.   9.28
laborers are few; *p* therefore   10.2
"Lord, teach us to *p*, as John   11.1
that they ought always to *p*   18.1
And I will *p* the Father,   Jn 14.16
I do not *p* that thou. .take them   17.15
"I do not *p* for these only,   17.20
Simon answered, "*P* for me   Acts 8.24
we do not know how to *p* as   Rom 8.26
p. .with her head uncovered?   1Cor 11.13
I will *p* with the mind also;   14.15
we *p* God that you may not   2Cor 13.7
P at all times in the Spirit,   Eph 6.18
have not ceased to *p* for you,   Col 1.9
p constantly, give thanks   1Thess 5.17
we always *p* for you, that   2Thess 1.11
every place the men should *p*,   1Tim 2.8
P for us, for we are sure   Heb 13.18

Is any. .suffering? Let him *p*.   Jas 5.13
beloved,. .*p* in the Holy Spirit;   Jude 20
man *p* to God, and he accepts   Job 33.26
Then Abraham *p* to God;   Gen 20.17
and Moses *p* to the Lord,   Num 11.2
and I *p* for Aaron also at   Deut 9.20
And I *p* to the Lord, 'O Lord   9.26
deeply distressed and *p*   1Sam 1.10
For this child I *p*; and the   1.27
And Samuel *p* to the Lord.   8.6
two of them,. .*p* to the Lord.   2Ki 4.33
Elisha *p*, and said, "O Lord,   6.17
Hezekiah *p* before the Lord,   19.15
his face to the wall, and *p*   20.2
Hezekiah. .*p* because of this   2Chr 32.20
He *p* to him, and God   33.13
we *p* to our God, and set a   Neh 4.9
Job,. .had *p* for his friends;   Job 42.10
when they were sick—. .I *p*   Ps 35.13
And Hezekiah *p* to the Lord: Isa 37.15
turned. .face to the wall, and *p*   38.2
p and gave thanks before. .God,   Dan 6.10
Jonah *p* to the Lord his God   Jonah 2.1
he. .*p* for the third time,   Mt 26.44
lonely place, and there he *p*.   Mk 1.35
to the wilderness and *p*.   Lk 5.16
The Pharisee stood and *p* thus   18.11
he. .knelt down and *p*,   22.41
they *p* and said, "Lord,. .show   Acts 1.24
when they had *p*, the place   4.31
who came down and *p* for them   8.15
But Peter. .knelt down and *p*;   9.40
on the beach we *p* and bade   21.5
and Paul visited him and *p*,   28.8
I continued fasting and *p*   Neh 1.4
p to a god that cannot save.   Isa 45.20
people. .*p* outside at the hour   Lk 1.10
when Jesus. .was *p*, the heaven   3.21
as he was *p* alone the disciples   9.18
I am *p* for them; I am not *p*   Jn 17.9
Saul; for behold, he is *p*,   Acts 9.11
gathered together and were *p*.   12.12
after fasting and *p* they laid   13.3
Paul and Silas were *p* and   16.25
p earnestly night and day   1Thess 3.10

PRAYER — S

granted his *p*, and Rebekah   Gen 25.21
have regard to the *p* of thy   2Chr 6.19
their *p* came to his holy   30.27
heard. .the Lord accepts my *p*.   Ps 6.9
Give ear to my *p* from lips free   17.1
godly offer *p* to thee;   32.6
night his song is with me, a *p*   42.8
O thou who hearest *p*! To thee   65.2
May *p* be made for him. .and   72.15
regard the *p* of the destitute,   102.17
accuse me, even as I make *p*   109.4
Let my *p* be counted as incense   141.2
p of. .upright is his delight.   Prov 15.8
hears. .*p* of the righteous.   15.29
a *p* when thy chastening was   Isa 26.16
your *p* for the remnant that   37.4
a house of *p* for all peoples.   56.7
I call and. .he shuts out my *p*;   Lam 3.8
so that no *p* can pass through.   3.44
Lord God, seeking him by *p*   Dan 9.3
never comes out except by *p*   Mt 17.21*n*
shall be called a house of *p*";   21.13
And whatever you ask in *p*, you   21.22
driven out by anything but *p*."   Mk 9.29
called a house of *p* for all   11.17
whatever you ask in *p*, believe   11.24

PRAYER — S (cont.)

Zechariah, for your *p* is heard,	Lk 1.13
house shall be a house of *p*';	19.46
devoted themselves to *p*,	Acts 1.14
the hour of *p*, the ninth hour.	3.1
we will devote ourselves to *p*	6.4
ninth hour of *p* in my house;	10.30
Peter. .in prison; but earnest *p*	12.5
appointed. .with *p* and fasting,	14.23
there was a place of *p*;	16.13
tribulation, be constant in *p*.	Rom 12.12
may devote yourselves to *p*;	1Cor 7.5
You also must help us by *p*,	2Cor 1.11
in every *p* of mine for you	Phil 1.4
by *p* and supplication with	4.6
Continue steadfastly in *p*,	Col 4.2
The *p* of a righteous man	Jas 5.16
a pretense you make long *p*;	Mt 23.14*n*
for a pretense make long *p*	Mk 12.40
disciples. .fast. .and offer *p*,	Lk 5.33
for a pretense make long *p*.	20.47
"Your *p* and your alms have	Acts 10.4
mention you always in my *p*,	Rom 1.9
together with me in your *p*	15.30
remembering you. .in his *p*,	Col 4.12
I urge that supplications, *p*,	1Tim 2.1
continues in. .*p* night and day;	5.5
when I remember you. .in my *p*.	2Tim 1.3
Jesus offered up *p* and	Heb 5.7
your *p* may not be hindered.	1Pet 3.7
sane and sober for your *p*.	4.7
which are the *p* of the saints;	Rev 5.8

PREACH — ED — ING

"Do not *p*"—thus they *p*—	Mic 2.6
twelve,. .to be sent out to *p*	Mk 3.14
p. .gospel to. .whole creation.	16.15*n*
to *p* good news to the poor.	Lk 4.18
p the good news of the kingdom	4.43
he sent them out to *p* the kingdom	9.2
God had called us to *p* the	Acts 16.10
While you *p* against stealing,	Rom 2.21
men *p* unless they are sent?	10.15
my ambition to *p* the gospel,	15.20
not. .to baptize but to *p* the	1Cor 1.17
what we *p* is not ourselves,	2Cor 4.5
Some. .*p* Christ from envy and	Phil 1.15
p the word,. .urgent in season	2Tim 4.2
wherever this gospel is *p*	Mt 26.13
he *p*,. . "After me comes he who	Mk 1.7
and *p* that men should repent.	6.12
the gospel must first be *p*	13.10
forgiveness of sins. .be *p*	Lk 24.47
that I *p* the gospel to you	Gal 4.13
while we *p* to you the gospel	1Thess 2.9
p to the spirits in prison,	1Pet 3.19
came John. .*p* in the wilderness	Mt 3.1
p the gospel of the kingdom,	9.35
and he was *p* the word to them.	Mk 2.2
about the Jordan, *p* a baptism	Lk 3.3
those. .scattered went about *p*	Acts 8.4
Paul was occupied with *p*,	18.5
p the kingdom of God and	28.31
what is heard comes by the *p*	Rom 10.17
once persecuted us is now *p*	Gal 1.23
who labor in *p* and teaching;	1Tim 5.17

PREACHER

The words of the *P*, the son	Ecc 1.1
be the *p* for this people!	Mic 2.11
they to hear without a *p*?	Rom 10.14
For this I was appointed a *p*	1Tim 2.7

PRECEPT — S

For it is *p* upon *p*, *p* upon *p*,	Isa 28.10
the *p* of the LORD are right,	Ps 19.8
all his *p* are trustworthy,	111.7
companion of all. .keep thy *p*.	119.63
I will never forget thy *p*;	119.93
for I give you good *p*; do not	Prov 4.2

PRECIOUS

his eye sees every *p* thing.	Job 28.10
How *p* is thy steadfast love,	Ps 36.7
p is their blood in his sight.	72.14
P in the sight of the LORD is	116.15
like the *p* oil upon the head,	133.2
How *p* to me are thy thoughts,	139.17
She is more *p* than jewels.	Prov 3.15
lips of knowledge. .a *p* jewel.	20.15
wife. .more *p* than jewels.	31.10
Because you are *p* in my eyes,	Isa 43.4
nor as *p* to myself, if only	Acts 20.24
your faith, more *p* than gold	1Pet 1.7
a cornerstone chosen and *p*,	2.6

PREDESTINED

thy plan had *p* to take place.	Acts 4.28
those whom he *p* he also called;	Rom 8.30

PREDICTED

man of God. .*p* these things	2Ki 23.17
as Isaiah *p*, "If the Lord	Rom 9.29

PREDICTING

p the sufferings of Christ	1Pet 1.11

PREPARATION

since it was the day of *P*,	Mk 15.42
It was the day of *P*, and	Lk 23.54

PREPARE — S — D

P yourselves according to	2Chr 35.4
"In the wilderness *p* the way	Isa 40.3
go through the gates, *p* the way	62.10
p to meet your God, O Israel"	Amos 4.12
"Where will you have us *p*	Mt 26.17
P the way of the Lord, make	Mk 1.3
p for you to eat the passover?"	14.12
before the Lord to *p* his ways,	Lk 1.76
P the way of the Lord, make	3.4
who shall *p* thy way before thee."	7.27
when I go and *p* a place for you,	Jn 14.3
p a guest room for me, for I	Philem 22
he *p* rain for the earth, he	Ps 147.8
to him for whom nothing is *p*;	Neh 8.10
I. .*p* a lamp for my anointed.	Ps 132.17
a burning place has. .been *p*;	Isa 30.33
the LORD has *p* a sacrifice	Zeph 1.7
it has been *p* by my Father."	Mt 20.23
those for whom it has been *p*."	Mk 10.40
ready for the Lord a people *p*."	Lk 1.17
thou hast *p* in the presence	2.31
he has *p* beforehand for glory,	Rom 9.23
God has *p* for those who love	1Cor 2.9
a body hast thou *p* for me;	Heb 10.5

PRESENCE

Cain went away from the *p*	Gen 4.16
"If thy *p* will not go with me,	Ex 33.15
in thy *p* there is fulness of joy,	Ps 16.11
Tremble,. .at the *p* of the LORD,	114.7
fleeing. .the *p* of the LORD,	Jonah 1.10
Gabriel, who stand. .*p* of God;	Lk 1.19
to appear in the *p* of God	Heb 9.24
without blemish before the *p*	Jude 24

PRESENT — ED

to Jerusalem to *p* him to the	Lk 2.22
here *p* in the sight of God,	Acts 10.33

PRESENT — ED (cont.)

to *p* your bodies as a living	Rom 12.1
p you as a pure bride to her	2Cor 11.2
he might *p*..church to himself	Eph 5.27
to *p* you holy and blameless	Col 1.22
that we may *p* every man mature	1.28
to *p* you without blemish	Jude 1.24
and *p* them to Pharaoh.	Gen 47.2
They *p* many gifts to us;	Acts 28.10

PRESENT (n)

a *p* for his brother Esau,	Gen 32.13
"Give me a *p*; since you	Josh 15.19
a *p* to the king of Assyria.	2Ki 16.8
allowance of food and a *p*,	Jer 40.5

PRESERVE — S — ST — D — ING

sent me before you to *p* life.	Gen 45.5
P me, O God, for in thee I	Ps 16.1
integrity and uprightness *p* me,	25.21
thy faithfulness ever *p* me!	40.11
p my life from dread of..enemy,	64.1
in thy justice *p* my life.	119.149
trouble, thou dost *p* my life;	138.7
and faithfulness *p* the king,	Prov 20.28
he *p* the lives of his saints;	Ps 97.10
The LORD *p* the simple; when	116.6
The LORD *p* all who love him;	145.20
guards his way *p* his life.	Prov 16.17
thou *p* me from trouble; thou	Ps 32.7
and *p* us in all the way	Josh 24.17
he has *p* us and given into	1Sam 30.23
and *p* the way of his saints.	Prov 2.8

PRESS — ED

let us *p* on to know the LORD;	Hos 6.3
I *p* on toward the goal for	Phil 3.14
she *p* him hard with..words	Judg 16.16
I am hard *p* between the two.	Phil 1.23

PRESUMPTUOUS

thy servant also from *p* sins;	Ps 19.13

PRETENSE

for a *p* you make long prayers;	Mt 23.14*n*
for a *p* make long prayers.	Mk 12.40
whether in *p* or in truth,	Phil 1.18

PREVAIL — ED

When our transgressions *p* over	Ps 65.3
striven with God and..*p*."	Gen 32.28
held up his hand, Israel *p*;	Ex 17.11
strove with the angel and *p*,	Hos 12.4

PREVENT — ED

What..*p* my being baptized?"	Acts 8.37
John would have *p* him, saying,	Mt 3.14

PRICE

give the *p* of the field;	Gen 23.13
without money and without *p*.	Isa 55.1
you were bought with a *p*.	1Cor 6.20
You were bought with a *p*;	7.23

PRIDE

Reuben..pre-eminent in *p*	Gen 49.3
and cut off *p* from man;	Job 33.17
king over all the sons of *p*."	41.34
P and arrogance and the way	Prov 8.13
When *p* comes, then..disgrace;	11.2
P goes before destruction,	16.18
the inhabitants..who say in *p*	Isa 9.9
We..heard of the *p* of Moab—	Jer 48.29
has blossomed, *p* has budded.	Ezek 7.10
The *p* of Israel testifies to	Hos 5.5
p of your heart has deceived	Obad 1.3

lot in return for their *p*,	Zeph 2.10
envy, slander, *p*, foolishness.	Mk 7.22

PRIEST — S

Melchizedek..was *p* of God	Gen 14.18
for myself a faithful *p*,	1Sam 2.35
"You are a *p* for ever after	Ps 110.4
the people, so with the *p*;	Isa 24.2
shall be a *p* by his throne,	Zech 6.13
while..serving as *p* before God	Lk 1.8
"Go and show yourself to the *p*,	5.14
since we have a great *p* over	Heb 10.21
land of the *p* alone did not	Gen 47.26
to me a kingdom of *p*	Ex 19.6
let the *p* who come near	19.22
kill the *p* of the LORD;	1Sam 22.17
he deposed the idolatrous *p*	2Ki 23.5
his own *p* for..high places,	2Chr 11.15
not driven out the *p* of the LORD,	13.9
called the *p* of the LORD,	Isa 61.6
and the iniquities of her *p*,	Lam 4.13
Levitical *p*,..sons of Zadok,	Ezek 44.15
sackcloth and lament, O *p*,	Joel 1.13
you, O *p*, who despise my name.	Mal 1.6
for any but the *p* to eat,	Lk 6.4
many of the *p* were obedient	Acts 6.7
made us a kingdom, *p* to his God	Rev 1.6
made them a kingdom and *p*	5.10

PRIESTHOOD

would you seek the *p* also?	Num 16.10
you shall attend to your *p*	18.7
through the Levitical *p*	Heb 7.11
he holds his *p* permanently,	7.24
a holy *p*, to offer spiritual	1Pet 2.5

PRINCE — S

is *p* among his brothers.	Deut 33.16
appointed you *p* over Israel,	1Sam 25.30
that you should be *p* over	2Sam 7.8
Everlasting Father, *P* of Peace."	Isa 9.6
say to the *p* of Tyre, Thus	Ezek 28.2
rise up against the *P* of *p*;	Dan 8.25
p and..judge ask for a bribe,	Mic 7.3
Your *p* are rebels..companions	Isa 1.23
When the *p* of Judah heard	Jer 26.10

PRISON

master..put him into the *p*,	Gen 39.20
while you remain in *p*,	42.16
freed..king of Judah from *p*;	2Ki 25.27
Bring me out of *p*, that I may	Ps 142.7
had gone from *p* to the throne	Ecc 4.14
Zedekiah,..in *p* till..death.	Jer 52.11
guard, and you be put in *p*;	Mt 5.25
seized John and..put him in *p*,	14.3
in *p* till he..pay the debt.	18.30
I was in *p* and you came to me.'	25.36
seized John, and bound him in *p*	Mk 6.17
Herod..shut up John in *p*.	Lk 3.20
So Peter was kept in *p*; but	Acts 12.5
they threw them into *p*,	16.23
out of the *p*, and visited Lydia;	16.40
many of the saints in *p*,	26.10
preached to the spirits in *p*,	1Pet 3.19
throw some of you into *p*,	Rev 2.10

PRISONER — S

notorious *p*, called Barabbas.	Mt 27.16
release for them one *p* whom	Mk 15.6
I, Paul, a *p* for Christ Jesus	Eph 3.1
I..a *p* for the Lord, beg you	4.1
Paul, a *p* for Christ Jesus,	Philem 1
Let the groans of the *p* come	Ps 79.11
to hear the groans of the *p*,	102.20

PRISONER — S (cont.)

p in affliction and in irons,	107.10
The LORD sets the p free;	146.7
to bring..p from the dungeon,	Isa 42.7
your stronghold, O p of hope;	Zech 9.12
The..plan was to kill the p,	Acts 27.42
you had compassion on the p,	Heb 10.34

PROCLAIM — S — ED — ING

p liberty throughout the land	Lev 25.10
p the name of the LORD.	Deut 32.3
and p his deliverance to a	Ps 22.31
Go, and p these words toward	Jer 3.12
"Stand..and p there this word,	7.2
"Sing..p, give praise,..say,	31.7
P this among the nations:	Joel 3.9
go to Nineveh,..and p to it	Jonah 3.2
what you hear whispered, p	Mt 10.27
he..began to p in the Decapolis	Mk 5.20
worship as unknown, this I p	Acts 17.23
who p the gospel should get	1Cor 9.14
you p the Lord's death until	11.26
p Christ out of partisanship,	Phil 1.17
Many a man p his own loyalty,	Prov 20.6
p to the end of the earth:	Isa 62.11
immediately he p Jesus,	Acts 9.20
at Salamis, they p the word	13.5
p..how much Jesus had done	Lk 8.39
p in Jesus the resurrection	Acts 4.2

PROCLAMATION

Cyrus..made a p throughout	2Chr 36.22
Cyrus..made a p throughout	Ezra 1.1

PROFANE — S — D

Molech, and so p the name	Lev 18.21
"Do not p your daughter by	19.29
appear and p the temple and	Dan 11.31
every one who p it shall	Ex 31.14
so that I am p among them.	Ezek 22.26
in..trade..p your sanctuaries;	28.18
I will not let my..name be p	39.7

PROFIT — S (v)

people that cannot p them,	Isa 30.5
God, who teaches you to p,	48.17
what will it p a man, if he	Mt 16.26
what does it p a man, to gain	Mk 8.36
What does it p, my brethren,	Jas 2.14
'It p a man nothing that he	Job 34.9

PROFIT (n)

"What p is..in my death, if	Ps 30.9
In all toil there is p, but	Prov 14.23
What p is an idol when its	Hab 2.18

PROMISE — D (v)

I will bring..good that I p	Jer 32.42
They p them freedom, but	2Pet 2.19
bless you, as he has p you!	Deut 1.11
territory, as he has p	12.20
the land which he p to give	19.8
as the LORD your God p	Josh 23.5
thou hast p this good thing	2Sam 7.28
gave Solomon wisdom, as he p	1Ki 5.12
according to all that he p;	8.56
throne of Israel, as..LORD p,	2Chr 6.10
but p to give it to him in	Acts 7.5
what God p to the fathers,	13.32
which he p beforehand through	Rom 1.2
God..able to do what he..p.	4.21
God, who never lies, p ages ago	Tit 1.2
the p eternal inheritance,	Heb 9.15
of God and receive what is p.	10.36
did not receive what was p,	11.39
God has p to those who love	Jas 1.12

PROMISE — S (n)

God, let thy p to David	2Chr 1.9
having no faith in his p.	Ps 106.24
eyes fail..watching for thy p;	119.82
I send the p of my Father	Lk 24.49
wait for the p of the Father,	Acts 1.4
p is to you and..your children	2.39
the time of the p drew near,	7.17
on trial for hope in the p	26.6
The p to Abraham and his	Rom 4.13
that the p may rest on grace	4.16
children of the p are reckoned	9.8
son of..free woman through p.	Gal 4.23
like Isaac, are children of p.	4.28
partakers of the p in Christ	Eph 3.6
the p of entering his rest	Heb 4.1
"Where is the p of his coming?	2Pet 3.4
Lord is not slow about his p	3.9
his p at an end for all time?	Ps 77.8
the p given to the patriarchs,	Rom 15.8
all the p of God find their	2Cor 1.20
Since we have these p, beloved,	7.1
the p were made to Abraham	Gal 3.16
law then against the p of God?	3.21
and patience inherit the p.	Heb 6.12
it is enacted on better p.	8.6
his precious and very great p,	2Pet 1.4

PROOF — S

put the LORD to the p	Ex 17.7
put me to the p..ten times	Num 14.22
your fathers..put me to the p,	Ps 95.9
gift..for a p to the people."	Mt 8.4
what Moses commanded, for a p	Mk 1.44
as Moses commanded, for a p	Lk 5.14
give p, before the churches,	2Cor 8.24
p that Christ is speaking in me.	13.3
presented..alive..by many p,	Acts 1.3

PROPHECY

Where there is no p the	Prov 29.18
miracles, to another p,	1Cor 12.10
and our p is imperfect;	13.9
words of the p of this book.	Rev 22.7

PROPHESY — ING — IES — IED

who should p with lyres,	1Chr 25.1
smooth things, p illusions,	Isa 30.10
the prophets p falsely, and	Jer 5.31
"Do not p..or you will die	11.21
the LORD had sent him to p,	19.14
against those who p lying	23.32
"You,..p against them all	25.30
"Why do you p and say, 'Thus	32.3
you shall p against the city.	Ezek 4.7
Therefore p against them, p,	11.4
p against..prophets of Israel,	13.2
p against the land of Israel	21.2
p to the mountains of Israel,	36.1
"P to these bones, and say	37.4
son of man, p, and say to Gog,	38.14
saying, 'You shall not p.'	Amos 2.12
eat bread there, and p there;	7.12
did we not p in your name,	Mt 7.22
saying, "P to us, you Christ!	26.68
strike him, saying..,"P!"	Mk 14.65
"P! Who is it that struck you?"	Lk 22.64
sons and..daughters shall p,	Acts 2.17
p, in proportion to our faith;	Rom 12.6
I want you..even more to p.	1Cor 14.5
I was told, "You must again p	Rev 10.11
prophets p lies in my name;	Jer 14.14
a lie which they are p to you	29.9
never p good concerning me,	1Ki 22.8

PROPHESY — ING — IES — IED (cont.)
never *p* good concerning me, 2Chr 18.7
spirit..upon them, they *p*. Num 11.25
they *p* by Baal and led..astray. Jer 23.13
I did not speak..yet they *p*. 23.21
"Micah of Moresheth *p* in the 26.18
And his father Zechariah..*p*, Lk 1.67
spoke with tongues and *p*. Acts 19.6
Enoch..*p*, saying, "Behold, Jude 14

PROPHET — S
restore..wife; for he is a *p*, Gen 20.7
your brother shall be your *p*. Ex 7.1
If there is a *p* among you, Num 12.6
"If a *p* arises among you, Deut 13.1
will raise up for you a *p* 18.15
not arisen a *p* since in Israel 34.10
a *p* to the people of Israel; Judg 6.8
Samuel..as a *p* of the LORD. 1Sam 3.20
dwelt an old *p* in Bethel. 1Ki 13.11
"Is there not here another *p* 22.7
he may know that there is a *p* 2Ki 5.8
not here another *p*..of whom 2Chr 18.6
a *p* of the LORD was there, 28.9
before Jeremiah the *p*, 36.12
there is no longer any *p*, Ps 74.9
and the *p* who teaches lies is Isa 9.15
p to priest..deals falsely. Jer 8.10
know that there has been a *p* Ezek 2.5
I, the LORD, have deceived that *p*, 14.9
know..a *p* has been among them." 33.33
The *p* is a fool, the man of Hos 9.7
By a *p* the LORD brought Israel 12.13
Amos answered..,"I am no *p*, Amos 7.14
receives a *p* because he is a *p* Mt 10.41
"A *p* is not without honor except 13.57
fulfil what was spoken by the *p*, 21.4
"This is the *p* Jesus from 21.11
"A *p* is not without honor, Mk 6.4
all held that John was a..*p*. 11.32
no *p* is acceptable in his Lk 4.24
"A great *p* has arisen among us:" 7.16
convinced that John was a *p*." 20.6
they asked.."Are you the *p*?" Jn 1.21
I perceive that you are a *p*. 4.19
said, "This is really the *p*." 7.40
will raise up for you a *p* Acts 7.37
a *p* of their own, said, Tit 1.12
and with it the false *p* who Rev 19.20
all the LORD's people..*p*, Num 11.29
you will meet a band of *p* 1Sam 10.5
Is Saul also among the *p*?" 10.11
"Is Saul also among the *p*?" 19.24
spoke by his servants the *p*. 2Ki 24.2
believe his *p*, and you will 2Chr 20.20
warn..by thy Spirit through..*p*; Neh 9.30
appalled and the *p* astounded." Jer 4.9
The *p* will become wind; the 5.13
sent all my servants the *p* 7.25
So do not listen to your *p*, 27.9
I sent..my servants the *p*, 44.4
p have seen..false..visions; Lam 2.14
This was for the sins of her *p* 4.13
Her *p* are wanton, faithless Zeph 3.4
"O..Jerusalem, killing the *p* Mt 23.37
Christs and false *p* will arise 24.24
and others one of the *p*." Mk 8.28
fathers did to the false *p*. Lk 6.26
one of the old *p* has risen." 9.19
p and kings desired to see 10.24
Jerusalem, killing the *p* and 13.34
the *p* and the psalms must be 24.44
reading of..law and the *p*, Acts 13.15
"Lord, they have killed thy *p*, Rom 11.3
first apostles, second *p*, 1Cor 12.28
the spirits of *p* are subject 14.32
should be apostles, some *p*, Eph 4.11
p who prophesied of..grace 1Pet 1.10
false *p*..arose among..people, 2Pet 2.1
announced to..servants the *p*, Rev 10.7

PROPHETESS
Deborah, a *p*, the wife of Josh 4.4
p,.conceived and bore a son. Isa 8.3

PROPHETIC
And if I have *p* powers, and 1Cor 13.2
the *p* word made more sure 2Pet 1.19

PROSELYTE
and land to make a single *p*, Mt 23.15

PROSPER — S — ED
send..angel..and *p* your way; Gen 24.40
the LORD made it *p*. 39.23
that you may *p* in all that 1Ki 2.3
he sought..God made him *p*. 2Chr 26.5
"May they *p* who love you! Ps 122.6
He who conceals..will not *p*, Prov 28.13
and he will *p* in his way. Isa 48.15
will of..LORD shall *p* in his hand; 53.10
no weapon..against you shall *p*, 54.10
p in..things for which I sent it. 55.11
and you will not *p* by them. Jer 2.37
does the way of the wicked *p*? 12.1
store it up, as he may *p*, 1Cor 16.2
and *p* in their hands. Ezra 5.8
In all that he does, he *p*. Ps 1.3
fret not..over him who *p* in 37.7
wherever he turns he *p*. Prov 17.8
whether the LORD had *p* Gen 24.21
wherever he went forth, he *p*. 2Ki 18.7
with all his heart, and *p*. 2Chr 31.21
Daniel *p* during the reign of Dan 6.28

PROSPERITY
One who dies in full *p*, being Job 21.23
He himself shall abide in *p*, Ps 25.13
I said in my *p*, "I shall never 30.6
the meek..in abundant *p*. 37.11
In the day of *p* be joyful Ecc 7.14
extend *p* to her like a river, Isa 66.12
in this place I will give *p*, Hag 2.9

PROSPEROUS
you shall make your way *p*, Josh 1.8

PROTECT — S
name of the God of Jacob *p* you! Ps 20.1
God, *p* me from those who rise 59.1
so the LORD..will *p* Jerusalem; Isa 31.5
LORD of hosts will *p* them, Zech 9.15
the LORD *p* him and keeps him Ps 41.2
new thing..a woman *p* a man." Jer 31.22

PROUD
he was strong, he grew *p*, 2Chr 26.16
one that is *p*, and abase him. Job 40.11
ease, the contempt of the *p*. Ps 123.4
Haughty eyes and a *p* heart, Prov 21.4
Hear and give ear; be not *p*, Jer 13.15
he has scattered the *p* in Lk 1.51
"God opposes the *p*, but gives Jas 4.6

PROVE — D — ING
P me, O LORD, and try me; test Ps 26.2
Neither can they *p* to you Acts 24.13
which they could not *p*. 25.7
p what is the will of God, Rom 12.2
p..that your love..is genuine. 2Cor 8.8

PROVE — D — ING (cont.)

and there he *p* them,   Ex 15.25
Saul..*p* that Jesus was the   Acts 9.22
explaining and *p* that it was   17.3

PROVERB — S

shall become a horror, a *p*,   Deut 28.37
became a *p*, "Is Saul also   1Sam 10.12
Israel will become a *p* and   1Ki 9.7
I will incline my ear to a *p*;   Ps 49.4
to understand a *p*..a figure,   Prov 1.6
a *p* in the mouth of fools   26.9
"Son of man, what is this *p*   Ezek 12.22
p about you, 'Like mother,   16.44
p, 'Physician, heal yourself';   Lk 4.23
uttered three thousand *p*;   1Ki 4.32

PROVIDE — S — D

"God will *p*..the lamb   Gen 22.8
there I will *p* for you,   45.11
Who *p* for the raven its prey,   Job 38.41
and *p* food for her household   Prov 31.15
And Joseph *p* his father,   Gen 47.12
I have *p* for the house of   1Chr 22.14
I have *p* for the house of my God.   29.2

PROVISION — S

p for..father on..journey.   Gen 45.23
Solomon's *p* for one day was   1Ki 4.22
make no *p* for the flesh,   Rom 13.14
and went and made ready *p*,   Josh 9.4

PROVOKE — D — ING

And her rival used to *p* her   1Sam 1.6
why should you *p* trouble   2Ki 14.10
why should you *p* trouble   2Chr 25.19
people who *p* me to my face   Isa 65.3
I whom they *p*? says the LORD.   Jer 7.19
Why do you *p* me to anger with   44.8
p him to speak of many things,   Lk 11.53
we *p* the Lord to jealousy?   1Cor 10.22
Fathers, do not *p* your children   Eph 6.4
you *p* the LORD to wrath.   Deut 9.22
p me with their idols.   32.21
they *p* the LORD to anger.   Judg 2.12
they *p* him to jealousy with   1Ki 14.22
and *p* the LORD, the God of   22.53
and *p* the Holy One of Israel.   Ps 78.41
p him..with their high places;   78.58
I was *p* with that generation,   Heb 3.10
the Lord, *p* him to anger.   2Ki 17.17
to other gods, *p* to anger   2Chr 28.25

PRUDENT

a *p* wife is from the LORD.   Prov 19.14
he who is *p* will keep silent   Amos 5.13

PSALMIST

David,..the sweet *p* of   2Sam 23.1

PSALMS

prophets and the *p* must be   Lk 24.44
addressing one another in *p*   Eph 5.19
as you sing *p* and hymns   Col 3.16

PUBLISH — ED

p it not in the streets   2Sam 1.20
he made a proclamation and *p*   Jonah 3.7

PUFFED

that none of you may be *p* up   1Cor 4.6

PUFFS

"Knowledge" *p* up, but love   1Cor 8.1

PULPIT

Ezra the scribe stood on a..*p*   Neh 8.4

PUNISH — ED

Awake to *p* all the nations;   Ps 59.5
then I will *p*..with the rod   89.32
he will *p*..arrogant boasting   Isa 10.12
p the world for its evil,   13.11
On that day the LORD will *p*   24.21
Shall I not *p* them for these   Jer 5.9
Shall I not *p* them for these   9.9
p..those who are circumcised   9.25
p..according to your..doings,   21.14
will *p* the images of Babylon;   51.47
I will *p* her for the feast days   Hos 2.13
iniquity, and *p* their sins;   8.13
iniquity, he will *p* their sins.   9.9
p Jacob according to his ways,   12.2
on the day I *p* Israel for   Amos 3.14
as *p*, and yet not killed;   2Cor 6.9

PUNISHMENT

p is greater than I can bear.   Gen 4.13
will you do on the day of *p*,   Isa 10.3
greater than the *p* of Sodom,   Lam 4.6
so long shall you bear the *p*   Ezek 4.5
they shall bear their *p*—   14.10
The days of *p* have come, the   Hos 9.7
p by the majority is enough   2Cor 2.6
p of eternal destruction   2Thess 1.9

PURCHASE — ED

gave the deed of *p* to Baruch   Jer 32.12
the field which Abraham *p*   Gen 25.10
pass by whom thou hast *p*.   Ex 15.16

PURE — R

with the *p* thou dost show   2Sam 22.27
a man be *p* before his Maker?   Job 4.17
if you are *p* and upright,   8.6
you say, 'My doctrine is *p*,   11.4
promises of the LORD..are *p*,   Ps 12.6
with the *p* thou dost show..*p*;   18.26
commandment of the LORD is *p*,   19.8
clean hands and a *p* heart,   24.4
good..to those who are *p* in   73.1
can a young man keep..way *p*?   119.9
words of the *p* are pleasing   Prov 15.26
ways of a man are *p* in his   16.2
who are *p* in their own eyes   30.12
"Blessed are the *p* in heart,   Mt 5.8
led astray from..*p* devotion   2Cor 11.3
man's sins; keep yourself *p*.   1Tim 5.22
To the *p* all things are *p*,   Tit 1.15
of *p* eyes than to behold evil   Hab 1.13

PURGE — D

P me with hyssop, and I shall   Ps 51.7
I will *p* out the rebels from   Ezek 20.38
and *p* Judah and Jerusalem.   2Chr 34.5

PURIFICATION

when the time came for their *p*   Lk 2.22
When he had made *p* for sins,   Heb 1.3

PURIFY — ING — IES — IED

You shall *p* every garment,   Num 31.20
p yourselves, you who bear   Isa 52.11
Many shall *p* themselves,   Dan 12.10
he will *p* the sons of Levi   Mal 3.3
p your conscience from dead   Heb 9.14
disciples and a Jew over *p*.   Jn 3.25
hopes in him *p* himself as   1Jn 3.3
and the Levites *p* themselves;   Neh 12.30
Paul..*p* himself with them   Acts 21.26
everything is *p* with blood,   Heb 9.22
Having *p*..souls by..obedience   1Pet 1.22

PURPOSE — D (v)

I p to build a house for	1Ki 5.5
Solomon p to build a temple	2Chr 2.1

PURPOSE — S (n)

to frustrate their p, all the	Ezra 4.5
p in a man's mind is like	Prov 20.5
let the p of the Holy One	Isa 5.19
p..concerning the whole earth;	14.26
will fear because of the p	19.17
I will accomplish all my p,'	46.10
lawyers rejected the p of God	Lk 7.30
the Lord with steadfast p;	Acts 11.23
p which he set forth in Christ	Eph 1.9
p of him who accomplishes all	1.11
according to the eternal p	3.11
but in virtue of his own p	2Tim 1.9
unchangeable character of..p,	Heb 6.17
carry out his p by being of	Rev 17.17
the LORD's p against Babylon	Jer 51.29

PURSUE — S — D

Why do you, like God, p me?	Job 19.22
thou p them with thy tempest	Ps 83.15
I will p them with sword,	Jer 29.18
p..in anger and destroy them	Lam 3.66
then p what makes for peace	Rom 14.19
p righteousness and kindness	Prov 21.21
he p the people of Israel	Ex 14.8
but p the poor and needy	Ps 109.16
p his brother with the sword,	Amos 1.11

PUT

But p on the Lord Jesus	Rom 13.14
to p on our heavenly dwelling,	2Cor 5.2
P off your old nature which	Eph 4.22
and p on the new nature,	4.24
P on then, as God's chosen	Col 3.12

Q

QUARREL — ING

quit before the q breaks	Prov 17.14
a wife's q is a continual	19.13
that there is a q among you,	1Cor 1.11
perhaps there may be q,	2Cor 12.20
holy hands without anger or q;	1Tim 2.8

QUEEN

made her q instead of Vashti.	Est 2.17
at your right hand stands the q	Ps 45.9
The q of the South will arise	Mt 12.42
The q of the South will arise	Lk 11.31

QUENCH — ED

Many waters cannot q love,	Sol 8.7
burn together, with none to q	Isa 1.31
burning wick he will not q;	42.3
or q a smoldering wick, till	Mt 12.20
Do not q the Spirit,	1Thess 5.19
die, and the fire is not q.	Mk 9.48

QUESTION — ED (v)

you q me about my children,	Isa 45.11
"Why..q thus in your heart?	Mk 2.8
men q..concerning John,	Lk 3.15

QUESTIONS (n)

to test him with hard q.	1Ki 10.1
to test him with hard q,	2Chr 9.1

QUIET — LY

he is q, who can condemn?	Job 34.29
resolved to divorce her q.	Mt 1.19
to aspire to live q,	1Thess 4.11

QUIETNESS

Better is a handful of q than	Ecc 4.6
result of righteousness, q	Isa 32.17

QUIVER

Happy is the man..his q full	Ps 127.5

R

RACE

the r is not to the swift,	Ecc 9.11
in a r all the runners	1Cor 9.24
the r that is set before us,	Heb 12.1

RACHEL

and see, R his daughter	Gen 29.6
name of the younger was R.	29.16
Jacob loved R; and he said,	29.18
loved R more than Leah,	29.30
Then God remembered R,	30.22
R had taken..household gods	31.34
R died, and she was buried	35.19
like R and Leah, who..built	Ruth 4.11
R weeping for her children;	Mt 2.18

RADIANT

Look to him, and be r;	Ps 34.5
Then you shall see and be r,	Isa 60.5
r over..goodness of..LORD,	Jer 31.12

RAFTS

make it into r to go by sea	1Ki 5.9
bring it to you in r by sea	2Chr 2.16

RAGE — S — D — ING

nations r, the kingdoms totter;	Ps 46.6
his heart r against the LORD.	Prov 19.3
The nations r, but thy wrath	Rev 11.18
'I know..your r against me.	Isa 37.28

RAIN (v)

God had not caused it to r	Gen 2.5
R in abundance, O God, thou	Ps 68.9
skies r down righteousness;	Isa 45.8

RAIN — S (n)

seven days I will send r	Gen 7.4
give the r for your land	Deut 11.14
give the r of your land	28.12
there is no r because they	1Ki 8.35
nor r these years, except by	17.1
sound of the rushing of r."	18.41
he gives r upon the earth	Job 5.10
"Has the r a father, or	38.28
plants a cedar..r nourishes	Isa 44.14
"For as the r and the snow	55.10
God,..gives..r in its season,	Jer 5.24
the early and the latter r,	Joel 2.23
I also withheld the r from you	Amos 4.7
Ask r from the LORD in the	Zech 10.1
there will be no r upon them.	14.17
sends r on..just and..unjust.	Mt 5.45
r fell, and the floods came,	7.25
that no r may fall during	Rev 11.6
give..your r in their season,	Lev 26.4
gave you from heaven r and	Acts 14.17

RAINBOW

and round the throne was a r	Rev 4.3

RAISE — S — D

r me up, that I may requite	Ps 41.10
look up and r your heads,	Lk 21.28
but r it up at the last day.	Jn 6.39
and the Lord will r him up;	Jas 5.15
as the Father r the dead	Jn 5.21
thought incredible..God r	Acts 26.8

RAISE — S — D (cont.)

He has *r* up a horn for his	Ps 148.14
the Baptist,. .*r* from the dead;	Mt 14.2
and on the third day be *r*.	16.21
until the Son of man is *r*	17.9
he will be *r* on the third day."	20.19
But after I am *r* up, I will go	26.32
"John the baptizer has been *r*	Mk 6.14
after I am *r* up, I will go	14.28
that John had been *r* from. .dead	Lk 9.7
God *r* the Lord and will. .*r* us	1Cor 6.14
he was *r* on the third day	15.4
then Christ has not been *r*;	15.13
he who *r* the Lord. .will *r* us	2Cor 4.14
Author of life, whom God *r*	Acts 3.15
God *r* him on the third day	10.40
God *r* him from the dead;	13.30
to Pharaoh, "I have *r* you up	Rom 9.17
when he *r* him from the dead	Eph 1.20
r us up with him, and made us	2.6
If. .you have been *r* with Christ,	Col 3.1
confidence in God, who *r* him	1Pet 1.21

RAM

Bring. .a *r* three years old,	Gen 15.9
a *r*, caught in a thicket	22.13

RAMAH

at *R*. And Elkanah knew	1Sam 1.19
Then Elkanah went home to *R*.	2.11
elders. .came to Samuel at *R*,	8.4
and he came to Samuel at *R*,	19.18
Israel. .buried him in *R*,	28.3
against Judah, and built *R*,	2Chr 16.1
R trembles, Gibeah. .has fled.	Isa 10.29
"A voice is heard in *R*,	Jer 31.15
voice was heard in *R*, wailing	Mt 2.18

RAMOTH-GILEAD

go to battle against *R*, or	1Ki 22.6
oil in your hand, and go to *R*.	2Ki 9.1

RAN

they. .*r* to tell his disciples.	Mt 28.8
both *r*, but the other disciple	Jn 20.4

RANSOM — ED (v)

Or, '*R* me from the hand of	Job 6.23
Truly no man can *r* himself,	Ps 49.7
Shall I *r* them from. .Sheol?	Hos 13.14
thy blood didst *r* men for God	Rev 5.9
So the people *r* Jonathan,	1Sam 14.45
You know that you were *r*	1Pet 1.18

RANSOM (n)

each. .give a *r* for himself	Ex 30.12
'Deliver him. .I. .found a *r*;	Job 33.24
greatness of the *r* turn you	36.18
the *r* of his life is costly,	Ps 49.8
The wicked is a *r* for the	Prov 21.18
I give Egypt as your *r*,	Isa 43.3
his life as a *r* for many."	Mt 20.28
give his life. .a *r* for many."	Mk 10.45
who gave himself as a *r* for	1Tim 2.6

RARE

word. .was *r* in those days;	1Sam 3.1
make men more *r* than. .gold,	Isa 13.12

RASH

therefore my words have been *r*.	Job 6.3
Be not *r* with your mouth, nor	Ecc 5.2

RAVEN — S

Noah. .sent forth a *r*;	Gen 8.7
Who provides for the *r* its	Job 38.41

commanded the *r* to feed you	1Ki 17.4
the *r*:. .neither sow nor reap,	Lk 12.24

RAVISH — ED

R them and do. .what seems	Judg 19.24
You have *r* my heart, my sister,	Sol 4.9

RAZOR

no *r* shall come upon his head;	Num 6.5
Your tongue is like a sharp *r*,	Ps 52.2
the Lord will shave with a *r*	Isa 7.20
sword; use it as a barber's *r*	Ezek 5.1

READ — S — ING

he shall *r* in it all the days	Deut 17.19
r this law before all	31.11
he *r* in their hearing all	2Ki 23.2
he *r* from it facing the square	Neh 8.3
they *r* from the book of Moses	13.1
"*R* this," he says, "I cannot,	Isa 29.11
r from the book of the Lord:	34.16
you shall *r* the words of. .Lord	Jer 36.6
and Jehudi *r* it to the king	36.21
I will *r* the writing to the king	Dan 5.17
"Have you. .*r* in. .scriptures:	Mt 21.42
Have you not *r* this scripture:	Mk 12.10
not *r* in the book of Moses,	12.26
"Have you not *r* what David did	Lk 6.3
to be known and *r* by all	2Cor 3.2
"Whoever *r* this writing, and	Dan 5.7
so he may run who *r* it.	Hab 2.2
Blessed is he who *r* aloud	Rev 1.3
he was *r* the prophet Isaiah.	Acts 8.28

READY

I have made *r* my dinner,	Mt 22.4
Then he said. .'The wedding is *r*,	22.8
Therefore you also must be *r*;	24.44
who were *r* went in with him	25.10
but did not make *r* or act	Lk 12.47
who will get *r* for battle?	1Cor 14.8
saying that Achaia has been *r*	2Cor 9.2

REAP — S

you shall not *r* your field	Lev 19.9
"And when you *r* the harvest	23.22
and sow trouble *r* the same.	Job 4.8
who sow in tears *r* with. .joy!	Ps 126.5
sows injustice. .*r* calamity	Prov 22.8
regards the clouds will not *r*.	Ecc 11.4
You shall sow, but not *r*;	Mic 6.15
the birds. .neither sow nor *r*	Mt 6.26
we *r* your material benefits?	1Cor 9.11
man sows, that he will also *r*.	Gal 6.7
r, for. .hour to *r* has come,	Rev 14.15
He who *r* receives wages,	Jn 4.36

REBEKAH (REBECCA)

became the father of *R*.	Gen 22.23
behold, *R*, who was born	24.15
So they sent away *R*	24.59
Then Isaac. .took *R*,	24.67
but *R* loved Jacob.	25.28
R was listening when	27.5
they buried Isaac and *R*	49.31
when *R* had conceived children	Rom 9.10

REBEL — LED — LING (v)

do not *r* against the Lord;	Num 14.9
who *r* against the light,	Job 24.13
But if you refuse and *r*, you	Isa 1.20
you *r* against my command	Num 20.24
you *r* against my word	27.14
but *r* against the command	Deut 1.26
you *r* against the command	1.43
Moab *r* against the king of	2Ki 3.5

REBEL — LED — LING (v) (cont.)

for they have r against thee. Ps 5.10
How often they r against him 78.40
r against the words of God, 107.11
but they have r against me. Isa 1.2
now. .that you have r against me? 36.5
r and grieved his holy Spirit; 63.10
because she has r against me, Jer 4.17
rebels, who have r against me; Ezek 2.3
Israel r against me in the 20.13
she has r against her God; Hos 13.16
Are you r against the king?" Neh 2.19
r against the Most High in the Ps 78.17

REBEL — S (n)

from birth you were called a r. Isa 48.8
"Hear now, you r; Num 20.10
Your princes are r. .companions Isa 1.23
r. .sinners. .destroyed together, 1.28

REBELLION

an altar this day in r Josh 22.16
r is as. .sin of divination, 1Sam 15.23
Israel has been in r against 1Ki 12.19
So Israel has been in r; 2Chr 10.19
For he adds r to his sin; Job 34.37
talked r against the LORD.' " Jer 29.32

REBELLIOUS

and r son, who will not obey Deut 21.18
a r city, hurtful to kings Ezra 4.15
"Woe to the r children," says Isa 30.1
"Say now to the r house, Ezek 17.12

REBUILD

r the house of the LORD, Ezra 1.3
If he tears down, none can r; Job 12.14
r the walls of Jerusalem, Ps 51.18

REBUKE — D (v)

surely r you if in secret Job 13.10
O LORD, r me not in thy anger, Ps 6.1
LORD, r me not in thy anger, 38.1
Thou dost r the insolent, 119.21
those who r the wicked will Prov 24.25
"The LORD r you, O Satan! Zech 3.2
Peter took him and began to r Mt 16.22
Peter took him, and began to r Mk 8.32
Do not r an older man but 1Tim 5.1
but said, "The Lord r you." Jude 9
God saw my. .labor. .and r Gen 31.42
his father r him, and said 37.10
he r kings on their account, 1Chr 16.21
he r kings on their account, Ps 105.14
r the Red Sea; . .it became dry; 106.9
why have you not r Jeremiah Jer 29.27
Jesus r him,. .demon came out Mt 17.18
Jesus. .r the unclean spirit, Mk 9.25
Jesus r him,. . "Be silent, and Lk 4.35
Jesus r the unclean spirit, 9.42
But he turned and r them. 9.55

REBUKE (n)

and are astounded at his r. Job 26.11
At thy r, O God of Jacob, both Ps 76.6
At thy r they fled; at the sound 104.7
A r goes deeper into a man Prov 17.10
Better is open r than hidden love. 27.5

RECEIVE — S — D — ING

and shall we not r evil?" Job 2.10
R instruction from his mouth, 22.22
heritage which oppressors r 27.13
what does he r from your hand? 35.7
will r blessing from the LORD, Ps 24.5

from. .Sheol, for he will r me. 49.15
thou wilt r me to glory. 73.24
r instruction in wise dealing, Prov 1.3
if you r my words and treasure 2.1
He who is able to r this, Mt 19.12
they thought they would r more; 20.10
you will r, if you have faith." 21.22
immediately r it with joy; Mk 4.16
if any place will not r you 6.11
r the kingdom. .like a child 10.15
who will not r a hundredfold 10.30
"Master, let me r my sight." 10.51
sinners lend to sinners, to r Lk 6.34
wherever they do not r you, 9.5
the people would not r him, 9.53
town and they do not r you, 10.10
who will not r manifold more 18.30
"R your sight; your faith 18.42
"No one can r anything except Jn 3.27
his own name, him you will r. 5.43
to them, "R the Holy Spirit. 20.22
"Did you r the Holy Spirit Acts 19.2
that you may r her in the Lord Rom 16.2
unspiritual man does not r 1Cor 2.14
Did you r the Spirit by works Gal 3.2
r the promise of the Spirit 3.14
we might r adoption as sons. 4.5
For every one who asks r, Mt 7.8
"He who r you r me, and he 10.40
"Whoever r one such child in my 18.5
"Whoever r one such child Mk 9.37
"Whoever r this child in my name Lk 9.48
every one who asks r, and he 11.10
he who r any one whom I send Jn 13.20
he has r him safe and sound.' Lk 15.27
came down, and r him joyfully. 19.6
But to all who r him, who Jn 1.12
who r his word were baptized, Acts 2.41
For I r from the Lord what 1Cor 11.23
what I also r, that Christ 15.3
but r me as an angel of God, Gal 4.14
As. .you r Christ. .the Lord, Col 2.6
r the word in. .affliction, 1Thess 1.6
we are r the due reward of Lk 23.41

RECKON — ED — ING

r with him who bought him Lev 25.50
God r righteousness apart Rom 4.6
he r it. .as righteousness. Gen 15.6
r to him as righteousness Ps 106.31
r with the transgressors" Mk 15.28n
he was r with transgressors'; Lk 22.37
believed God, and it was r Rom 4.3
We say. .faith was r to Abraham 4.9
faith was "r. .as righteousness." 4.22
comes a r for his blood." Gen 42.22
like one who is inwardly r. Prov 23.7
When he began the r, one was Mt 18.24

RECOMPENSE — D (v)

Let him r it to themselves, Job 21.19
will doubly r their iniquity Jer 16.18
r. .according to their deeds 25.14
LORD has r me according to 2Sam 22.25
Therefore the LORD has r me Ps 18.24

RECONCILE — D

might r us both to God in one Eph 2.16
through him to r. .all things, Col 1.20
first be r to your brother, Mt 5.24
much more, now that we are r, Rom 5.10
else be r to her husband)— 1Cor 7.11
who through Christ r us to 2Cor 5.18

RECONCILIATION
we have now received our *r.*   Rom 5.11
if their rejection means..*r*   11.15

RECOUNT — S
I shall live, and *r* the deeds   Ps 118.17
I will *r* the steadfast love   Isa 63.7
He *r* to men his salvation,   Job 33.26

RECOVER
'Shall I *r* from this sickness?'   2Ki 8.8
second time to *r* the remnant   Isa 11.11

REDEEM — S — ED (v)
r you with an outstretched arm   Ex 6.6
the first-born..you shall *r*   34.20
But if he wishes to *r* it,   Lev 27.13
the first-born..you shall *r,*   Num 18.15
If you will *r* it, *r* it;   Ruth 4.4
to *r* to be his people,   2Sam 7.23
God went to *r* to be his   1Chr 17.21
In famine he will *r* you   Job 5.20
R Israel, O God, out of all   Ps 25.22
r me, and be gracious to me.   26.11
Draw near to me, *r* me, set me   69.18
with thy arm *r* thy people,   77.15
and *r* you from the grasp of   Jer 15.21
I would *r* them, but they speak   Hos 7.13
he was the one to *r* Israel.   Lk 24.21
to *r* those..under the law,   Gal 4.5
gave himself for us to *r* us   Tit 2.14
the LORD *r* the life of his   Ps 34.22
who *r* your life from the Pit,   103.4
the angel who has *r* me from   Gen 48.16
the people whom thou hast *r,*   Ex 15.13
then he shall let her be *r;*   21.8
and *r* you from the house of   Deut 7.8
r through thy greatness,   9.26
LORD lives, who has *r* my life   2Sam 4.9
LORD lives, who has *r* my soul   1Ki 1.29
thy people, whom thou hast *r*   Neh 1.10
He has *r* me, O LORD, faithful   Job 33.28
hast *r* me, O LORD, faithful   Ps 31.5
Zion shall be *r* by justice,   Isa 1.27
"Fear not, for I have *r* you;   43.1
LORD has *r* his servant Jacob!"   48.20
you shall be *r* without money.   52.3
r you from..house of bondage;   Mic 6.4
for I have *r* them, and they   Zech 10.8
Lord..visited and *r* his people,   Lk 1.68
Christ *r* us from the curse   Gal 3.13

REDEEMED (n)
Let the *r* of the LORD say so,   Ps 107.2
but the *r* shall walk there.   Isa 35.9
a way for the *r* to pass over?   51.10
holy people, The *r* of the LORD;   62.12

REDEEMER
For I know that my *R* lives,   Job 19.25
O LORD, my rock and my *r.*   Ps 19.14
the Most High God their *r.*   78.35
For their *R* is strong; he   Prov 23.11
your *R* is the Holy One of   Isa 41.14
King of Israel and his *R,*   44.6
Our *R*—the LORD of hosts is   47.4
compassion on you, says..your *R.*   54.8
he will come to Zion as *R,*   59.20
Their *R* is strong; the LORD   Jer 50.34

REDEMPTION
give for the *r* of his life   Ex 21.30
shall grant a *r* of the land.   Lev 25.24
exercise his right of *r,*   25.33
refund the money for his *r.*   25.52

So Moses took the *r* money   Num 3.49
Take my right of *r* yourself,   Ruth 4.6
He sent *r* to his people; he   Ps 111.9
and with him is plenteous *r.*   130.7
a poor man has no means of *r.*   Prov 13.8
for the right of *r*..is yours.'   Jer 32.7
looking for the *r* of Jerusalem.   Lk 2.38
your *r* is drawing near."   21.28
r which is in Christ Jesus.   Rom 3.24
Jesus, whom God made our..*r;*   1Cor 1.30
we have *r* through his blood,   Eph 1.7
were sealed for the day of *r.*   4.30
thus securing an eternal *r.*   Heb 9.12

RED SEA
and drove them into the *R*..;   Ex 10.19
officers are sunk in the *R*...   15.4
led Israel onward from the *R*..,   15.22
LORD your God did to the *R*..,   Josh 4.23
the *R*..,and it became dry;   Ps 106.9
in Egypt and at the *R*..,   Acts 7.36
By faith..crossed the *R*..   Heb 11.29

REED
Egypt, that broken *r* of a   2Ki 18.21
a bruised *r* he will not break,   Isa 42.3
a measuring *r* in his hand;   Ezek 40.3
A *r* shaken by the wind?   Mt 11.7
he will not break a bruised *r*   12.20
A *r* shaken by the wind?   Lk 7.24

REFINE — D
I will *r* them and test them,   Jer 9.7
r them as one refines silver,   Zech 13.9
r you, but not like silver;   Isa 48.10
buy from me gold *r* by fire,   Rev 3.18

REFLECTS
the mind of man *r* the man.   Prov 27.19
He *r* the glory of God and bears   Heb 1.3

REFRESH — ES — ED
that you may *r* yourselves,   Gen 18.5
r me with apples; for I am sick   Sol 2.5
r the spirit of his masters.   Prov 25.13
and the alien, may be *r.*   Ex 23.12
and be *r* in your company.   Rom 15.32
they *r* my spirit as well as   1Cor 16.18
Onesiphorus,..often *r* me;   2Tim 1.16
the saints..*r* through you.   Philem 7

REFUGE
six cities of *r,* where   Num 35.6
be cities of *r* for you,   35.11
rock in which they took *r,*   Deut 32.37
'Appoint the cities of *r,*   Josh 20.2
you have come to take *r!"*   Ruth 2.12
Blessed..all who take *r* in him.   Ps 2.12
my God, in thee do I take *r;*   7.1
poor, but the LORD is his *r.*   14.6
O God, for in thee I take *r.*   16.1
In thee, O LORD, do I seek *r;*   31.1
God is our *r* and strength,   46.1
of thy wings I will take *r,*   57.1
thou art my *r,* a strong tower   61.3
In thee, O LORD, do I take *r;*   71.1
but thou art my strong *r.*   71.7
GOD my *r,* that I may tell of   73.28
say to the LORD, "My *r* and my   91.2
better to take *r* in the LORD   118.8
no *r* remains..,no man cares   142.4
finds *r* through..integrity.   Prov 14.32
shield to those who take *r*   30.5
r and a shelter from the storm   Isa 4.6
for we have made lies our *r,*   28.15

REFUGE (cont.)

he who takes r..shall possess	Isa 57.13
my r in the day of trouble,	Jer 16.19
my r in the day of evil.	17.17
LORD is a r to his people,	Joel 3.16
he knows those who take r	Nah 1.7
seek r in..name of the LORD,	Zeph 3.12

REFUSE — D

r the evil and choose..good.	Isa 7.15
they r to know me, says..LORD.	Jer 9.6
evil people, who r to hear my	13.10
Do not r one another except	1Cor 7.5
See that you do not r him	Heb 12.25
he r..his master's wife,	Gen 39.8
Thus Edom r to give Israel	Num 20.21
the people r to listen to	1Sam 8.19
they r to obey, and were not	Neh 9.17
But Queen Vashti r to come	Est 1.12
r to walk according to..law.	Ps 78.10
called and you r to listen,	Prov 1.24
they r to take correction.	Jer 5.3
they have r to return to me.	Hos 11.5
But they r to hearken, and	Zech 7.11
they r to love the truth	2Thess 2.10
r to be called the son of	Heb 11.24

REGARD — S — ED (v)

not r any..wise in..conceit."	Job 37.24
men will r their Maker, and	Isa 17.7
I will r as good the exiles	Jer 24.5
you do not r..position of men,	Mk 12.14
nor r the rich more than	Job 34.19
he r their distress, when	Ps 106.44
for he has r the low estate	Lk 1.48

REGARD (n)

the LORD had r for Abel	Gen 4.4
And I will have r for you	Lev 26.9
Yet have r to the prayer	1Ki 8.28
and see; have r for this vine,	Ps 80.14

REHOBOAM

and R his son reigned in his	1Ki 11.43
R went to Shechem, for all	12.1
Now R the son of Solomon	14.21
war between R and Jeroboam	15.6
and Solomon the father of R,	Mt 1.7

REIGN — S — ED

"Are you indeed to r over us?	Gen 37.8
The LORD will r for ever	Ex 15.18
'Shall Saul r over us?'	1Sam 11.12
a godless man should not r,	Job 34.30
The LORD will r for ever,	Ps 146.10
By me kings r, and rulers	Prov 8.15
LORD..will r on Mount Zion	Isa 24.23
king will r in righteousness,	32.1
r as king and deal wisely,	Jer 23.5
thou, O LORD, dost r for ever;	Lam 5.19
will r over them in Mount Zion	Mic 4.7
will r over the house of Jacob	Lk 1.33
"We do not want this man to r	19.14
grace also might r through	Rom 5.21
Let not sin..r in your..bodies,	6.12
must r until he has put all	1Cor 15.25
he shall r for ever and ever."	Rev 11.15
let them say.."The LORD r!"	1Chr 16.31
God r over the nations; God	Ps 47.8
The LORD r;..robed in majesty;	93.1
LORD r; let the earth rejoice;	97.1
Lord our God the Almighty r.	Rev 19.6
time that David r over Israel	1Ki 2.11
r with Christ a thousand years.	Rev 20.4

REJECT — S — ED — ING

I r you from being a priest	Hos 4.6
who r reproof goes astray.	Prov 10.17
who r me r him who sent me."	Lk 10.16
who r me and does not receive	Jn 12.48
you have r the LORD who	Num 11.20
have r me from being king	1Sam 8.7
this day r your God, who	10.19
stone which the builders r	Ps 118.22
For thou has r thy people,	Isa 2.6
LORD..r those..whom you trust,	Jer 2.37
as for my law, they have r it.	6.19
for the LORD has r them."	6.30
the LORD has r and forsaken	7.29
Or hast thou utterly r us?	Lam 5.22
because they have r the law	Amos 2.4
stone which the builders r	Mt 21.42
stone which the builders r	Mk 12.10
r by..elders and chief priests	Lk 9.22
and be r by this generation.	17.25
stone which the builders r	20.17
then, has God r his people?	Rom 11.1
r my ordinances and..statutes.	Ezek 5.6
fine way of r the commandment	Mk 7.9

REJOICE — S — D — ING

you shall r before the LORD	Lev 23.40
shall r before the LORD	Deut 16.11
those who seek the LORD r!	1Chr 16.10
all who take refuge in thee r,	Ps 5.11
R in the LORD, O you righteous!	33.1
my soul shall r in the LORD,	35.9
righteous will r when he sees	58.10
that thy people may r in thee?	85.6
let us r and be glad in it.	118.24
sons of Zion r in their King!	149.2
r in the wife of your youth,	Prov 5.18
in authority, the people r;	29.2
desert shall r and blossom;	Isa 35.1
you shall r in the LORD; in	41.16
I will greatly r in the LORD,	61.10
so shall your God r over you.	62.5
"R with Jerusalem, and be glad	66.10
the maidens r in the dance,	Jer 31.13
made the enemy r over you,	Lam 2.17
Let not the buyer r, nor	Ezek 7.12
sons of Zion,..r in the LORD,	Joel 2.23
yet I will r in the LORD,	Hab 3.18
R greatly, O daughter of Zion!	Zech 9.9
R and be glad, for your reward	Mt 5.12
R in that day,..leap for joy,	Lk 6.23
do not r..that the spirits are	10.20
began to r and praise God	19.37
we r in our hope of sharing	Rom 5.2
we..r in God through..Christ,	5.11
R with those who r, weep with	12.15
"R, O Gentiles, with his people";	15.10
who r as though they were not	1Cor 7.30
Love..does not r at wrong,	13.6
proclaimed; and in that I r.	Phil 1.18
brethren, r in the Lord.	3.1
R in the Lord always; again	4.4
R always, pray constantly,	1Thess 5.16
you believe in him and r	1Pet 1.8
But r in so far as you share	4.13
the righteous, the city r;	Prov 11.10
The light of the eyes r the heart,	15.30
he r over it more than over	Mt 18.13
my spirit r in God my Savior,	Lk 1.47
the ark, they r to see it.	1Sam 6.13
people r because these had	1Chr 29.9
city of Susa shouted and r.	Est 8.15
When they saw the star, they r	Mt 2.10

REJOICE — S — D — ING (cont.)
people *r* at all the..things..   Lk 13.17
Abraham *r* that he was to see   Jn 8.56
loved me, you would have *r*,   14.28
he *r* with all his household   Acts 16.34
precepts..right, *r* the heart;   Ps 19.8
lays it on his shoulders, *r*.   Lk 15.5

REKINDLE
to *r* the gift of God..within you 2Tim 1.6

RELEASE — D (v)
to *r* for them one prisoner   Mk 15.6
chastise him and *r* him."   Lk 23.16
have me *r*..King of the Jews?"   Jn 18.39
Pilate..*r* for them Barabbas;   Mk 15.15

RELEASE (n)
years you shall grant a *r*.   Deut 15.1
time of the year of *r*,   31.10
I would wait, till my *r*   Job 14.14

RELIEF
Noah..shall bring us *r*   Gen 5.29
speak, that I may find *r*;   Job 32.20
to send *r* to the brethren   Acts 11.29

RELIGION
strictest party of our *r* I   Acts 26.5
Great..the mystery of our *r*:   1Tim 3.16
form of *r*..denying the power   2Tim 3.5
R that is pure and undefiled   Jas 1.27

RELIGIOUS
in every way you are very *r*.   Acts 17.22
If any one thinks he is *r*,   Jas 1.26

RELY — ING
make you to *r* on the LORD   2Ki 18.30
God, for we *r* on thee, and   2Chr 14.11
not *r* on the LORD your God,   16.7
they *r* on empty pleas, they   Isa 59.4
to make us *r* not on ourselves   2Cor 1.9
you are *r* now on Egypt,   2Ki 18.21

REMAIN — S — ED
r every man of you in his   Ex 16.29
ark..must not *r* with us;   1Sam 5.7
If you will *r* in this land,   Jer 42.10
to death; *r* here, and watch."   Mk 14.34
And *r* in the same house,   Lk 10.7
my will that he *r* until I come,   Jn 21.22
in whatever state..let him *r*   1Cor 7.24
there *r* yet very much land   Josh 13.1
but the earth *r* for ever.   Ecc 1.4
yet his bow *r* unmoved,   Gen 49.24

REMEMBER — S — ED — ING
I will *r* my covenant   Gen 9.15
butler said to Pharaoh, "I *r*   41.9
"*R* this day, in which   Ex 13.3
R Abraham, Isaac, and   32.13
r my covenant with Jacob,   Lev 26.42
We *r* the fish we ate in Egypt   Num 11.5
tassel to look upon and *r*   15.39
r what the LORD your God did   Deut 7.18
R..how you provoked the LORD   9.7
r that you were a slave   15.15
r that you were a slave   16.12
r that you were a slave   24.18
R the days of old, consider   32.7
Israel did not *r* the LORD   Judg 8.34
"O Lord God, *r* me, I pray   16.28
thy maidservant, and *r* me,   1Sam 1.11
"*R* now, O LORD,..how I have   2Ki 20.3
R the wonderful works that   1Chr 16.12
R thy steadfast love for   2Chr 6.42

Joash..did not *r* the kindness   24.22
R the word which thou didst   Neh 1.8
R the Lord, who is great and   4.14
R for my good, O my God, all   5.19
R Tobiah and Sanballat, O my   6.14
R me, O my God, concerning   13.14
therefore I *r* thee from the   Ps 42.6
R thy congregation, which thou   74.2
Do not *r* against us..iniquities   79.8
R, O Lord,..the measure of life   89.47
R the wonderful works that   105.5
R, O LORD, against the Edomites   137.7
and *r* their misery no more.   Prov 31.7
r that the days of darkness   Ecc 11.8
R..your Creator in the days   12.1
"*R* now, O LORD, I beseech   Isa 38.3
"*R* not the former things,   43.18
and I will not *r* your sins.   43.25
"*R* this and consider, recall it   46.8
I *r* the devotion of your youth,   Jer 2.2
R how I stood before thee   18.20
not *r*..days of your youth,   Ezek 16.22
there you shall *r* your ways   20.43
Then you will *r* your evil ways,   36.31
that I *r* all their evil works.   Hos 7.2
Tyre..did not *r* the covenant   Amos 1.9
people, *r* what Balak..devised,   Mic 6.5
known; in wrath *r* mercy.   Hab 3.2
far countries..shall *r* me,   Zech 10.9
"*R* the law of my servant Moses,   Mal 4.4
there *r*..something against you,   Mt 5.23
Abraham said, 'Son, *r* that   Lk 16.25
R Lot's wife.   17.32
"Jesus, *r* me when you come   23.42
R the word that I said to you,   Jn 15.20
they would have us *r* the poor,   Gal 2.10
Therefore *r* that at one time   Eph 2.11
R Jesus Christ, risen from   2Tim 2.8
I will *r* their sins no more."   Heb 8.12
R those who are in prison,   13.3
r, beloved, the predictions   Jude 17
R then what you received and   Rev 3.3
Jerusalem *r* in..her affliction   Lam 1.7
God *r* Noah and all the beasts   Gen 8.1
God *r* Abraham, and sent Lot   19.29
Then God *r* Rachel,   30.22
And Joseph *r* the dreams   42.9
God *r* his covenant with   Ex 2.24
thus I am to be *r* throughout   3.15
I have *r* my covenant.   6.5
cause my name to be *r*   20.24
may be *r* before the LORD   Num 10.9
these days should be *r* and   Est 9.28
They *r*..God was their rock,   Ps 78.35
He has *r* his steadfast love   98.3
righteous..will be *r* for ever.   112.6
who *r* us in our low estate,   136.23
former things shall not be *r*   Isa 65.17
I *r* the LORD; and my prayer   Jonah 2.7
Peter *r* the saying of Jesus,   Mt 26.75
And they *r* his words,   Lk 24.8
God has *r* her iniquities.   Rev 18.5
increased her harlotry, *r*   Ezek 23.19
r you earnestly in his prayers,   Col 4.12

REMEMBRANCE
bear their names..for *r*.   Ex 28.12
to be stones of *r* for the sons   39.7
bring the people of Israel to *r*   30.16
they shall serve you for *r*   Num 10.10
make the *r* of them cease   Deut 32.26
my sin to *r*, and to cause   1Ki 17.18
in death there is no *r* of thee;   Ps 6.5

REMEMBRANCE (cont.)

is no *r* of former things,	Ecc 1.11
You who put the LORD in *r*,	Isa 62.6
a book of *r* was written before	Mal 3.16
for you. Do this in *r* of me."	Lk 22.19n
Do this in *r* of me."	1Cor 11.24

REMNANT

surviving *r*..of Judah shall	2Ki 19.30
cast off..*r* of my heritage,	21.14
may turn again to the *r* of	2Chr 30.6
our God, to leave us a *r*,	Ezra 9.8
that day the *r* of Israel and	Isa 10.20
your prayer for the *r* that	37.4
surviving *r* of..house of Judah	37.31
the *r* of the house of Israel,	46.3
I will gather..*r* of my flock	Jer 23.3
LORD..saved his people, the *r*	31.7
king..had left a *r* in Judah	40.11
gracious to the *r* of Joseph.	Amos 5.15
they may possess the *r* of Edom	9.12
I will gather the *r* of Israel;	Mic 2.12
the lame I will make the *r*;	4.7
r of Jacob..among the nations,	5.8
for the *r* of his inheritance?	7.18
marvelous in..sight of the *r*	Zech 8.6
r of this people to possess	8.12
only a *r* of them will be saved;	Rom 9.27
there is a *r*, chosen by grace.	11.5

REMOVE — D

shall not *r* your neighbor's	Deut 19.14
LORD said, "I will *r* Judah	2Ki 23.27
so far..*r* our transgressions	Ps 103.12
R not the ancient landmark	Prov 22.28
R vexation from your mind,	Ecc 11.10
I will *r* the guilt of this land	Zech 3.9
hills..*r*, but..love shall not	Isa 54.10

RENDER — ED

r them their due reward.	Ps 28.4
What shall I *r* to the LORD	116.12
to..coastlands..*r* requital.	Isa 59.18
"*R* therefore to Caesar the	Mt 22.21
Jesus said.."*R* to Caesar the	Mk 12.17
"Then *r* to Caesar the things	Lk 20.25
r to..man according to..works:	Rom 2.6
to her as she herself has *r*,	Rev 18.6

RENEW — ED

and there *r* the kingdom."	1Sam 11.14
LORD shall *r* their strength,	Isa 40.31
O LORD,..*R* our days as of old!	Lam 5.21
the midst of the years *r* it;	Hab 3.2
he will *r* you in his love;	Zeph 3.17
youth is *r* like the eagle's.	Ps 103.5
being *r* in knowledge after	Col 3.10

RENOUNCE — S

whoever of you does not *r* all	Lk 14.33
the man greedy..*r* the LORD.	Ps 10.3

RENOWN

These were..mighty men..of *r*.	Gen 6.4
thy *r*, O LORD, throughout all	Ps 135.13

REPAIR — ED — ING

let the priests..*r* the house	2Ki 12.5
he *r* the altar of the LORD	1Ki 18.30
And next to them Meremoth..*r*.	Neh 3.4
to the workmen who were *r*	2Ki 12.14
at the house of the LORD, *r*	22.5

REPENT — S — ED

"Lest the people *r* when	Ex 13.17
r of this evil against thy people.	32.12
not man,..that he should *r*.	Num 23.19
"I *r* that I have made Saul	1Sam 15.11
been carried captive, and *r*,	1Ki 8.47
if they *r* with all their mind	2Chr 6.38
despise myself, and *r* in dust	Job 42.6
who *r*, by righteousness.	Isa 1.27
turns from its evil, I will *r*	Jer 18.8
the LORD will *r* of the evil	26.13
did not the LORD *r* of the evil	26.19
Thus says the Lord GOD: *R*	Ezek 14.6
R and turn away from all	18.30
God may yet *r* and turn from	Jonah 3.9
"*R*, for the kingdom of heaven	Mt 3.2
"*R*, for the kingdom of heaven	4.17
done, because they did not *r*.	11.20
they..preached..men should *r*.	Mk 6.12
unless you *r* you will..perish."	Lk 13.3
from the dead they will *r*.'	16.30
Peter said to them, "*R*, and	Acts 2.38
R therefore, and turn again,	3.19
he commands all men..to *r*,	17.30
grant that they will *r* and	2Tim 2.25
for he found no chance to *r*,	Heb 12.17
r and do the works you did	Rev 2.5
R then. If not, I will come	2.16
I gave her time to *r*, but	2.21
mankind..did not *r* of the works	9.20
they did not *r* and give him	16.9
no man *r* of his wickedness,	Jer 8.6
LORD *r* that he had made	1Sam 15.35
the LORD *r* of the evil,	2Sam 24.16
the LORD saw, and he *r* of	1Chr 21.15
The LORD *r* concerning this;	Amos 7.3
r at the preaching of Jonah,	Mt 12.41
but afterward he *r* and went.	21.29
he *r* and brought back..silver	27.3
they would have *r* long ago,	Lk 10.13
they *r* at the preaching of Jonah,	11.32

REPENTANCE

Bear fruit that befits *r*,	Mt 3.8
preaching a baptism of *r* for	Mk 1.4
preaching a baptism of *r* for	Lk 3.3
Bear fruits that befit *r*,	3.8
come to call..sinners to *r*."	5.32
than..persons who need no *r*.	15.7
that *r* and forgiveness of sins	24.47
to give *r* to Israel and	Acts 5.31
Gentiles also God has granted *r*	11.18
to Jews and to Greeks of *r*	20.21
perform deeds worthy of their *r*.	26.20
is meant to lead you to *r*?	Rom 2.4
godly grief produces a *r*	2Cor 7.10
to restore again to *r* those	Heb 6.4
but that all should reach *r*.	2Pet 3.9

REPORT

r was heard in Pharaoh's	Gen 45.16
an evil *r* of the land	Num 13.32
we have heard a *r* of him,	Josh 9.9
be not fearful at the *r* heard	Jer 51.46
a *r* concerning him went out	Lk 4.14
r went abroad concerning him;	5.15

REPROACH — ES — ED (v)

sheaves, and do not *r* her.	Ruth 2.15
in saying this you *r* us also."	Lk 11.45
I may answer him who *r* me.	Prov 27.11
ointment..And they *r* her.	Mk 14.5
If you are *r* for the name of	1Pet 4.14

REPROACH — ES (n)

"God has taken away my *r*";	Gen 30.23
I have rolled away..*r* of Egypt	Josh 5.9
word of the LORD..for me a *r*	Jer 20.8

REPROACH — ES (n) (cont.)

You shall be a *r* and a taunt,   Ezek 5.15
made you a *r* to the nations,   22.4
no more. . a *r* among. . nations.   Joel 2.19
to take away my *r* among men." Lk 1.25
a bishop must be above *r*,   1Tim 3.2
turn back upon him his *r*.   Hos 12.14
"The *r* of. . thee fell on me."   Rom 15.3

REPROOF

Give heed to my *r*; behold,   Prov 1.23
and my heart despised *r*!   5.12
he who heeds *r* is honored.   13.18
The rod and *r* give wisdom,   29.15

REPROVE — D

not *r* you for your sacrifices;   Ps 50.8
r a man of understanding,   Prov 19.25
and your apostasy will *r* you.   Jer 2.19
who is often *r*, yet stiffens   Prov 29.1

REPUTE

a poor man and of no *r*?"   1Sam 18.23
LORD gave Solomon great *r*   1Chr 29.25

REQUEST

Queen Esther? What is your *r*?   Est 5.3
and my people at my *r*.   7.3
"O that I might have my *r*,   Job 6.8
not withheld the *r* of his lips.   Ps 21.2
Daniel made *r* of the king,   Dan 2.49

REQUIRE — S — D

God *r* of you, but to fear   Deut 10.12
his blood. . *r* at your hand.   Ezek 3.18
blood I. . *r* at. . watchman's hand.   33.6
what does the LORD *r* of you   Mic 6.8
who *r* of you this trampling   Isa 1.12
whatever else is *r* for. . house   Ezra 7.20
the blood. . may be *r* of this   Lk 11.50
This night your soul is *r* of you;   12.20
given, of him will much be *r*;   12.48

REQUITE — S — D

work of a man he will *r* him,   Job 34.11
They *r* me evil for good; my   Ps 35.12
dost *r* a man according to his   62.12
nor *r* us according to our   103.10
R her according to her deeds,   Jer 50.29
"Thou wilt *r* them, O LORD,   Lam 3.64
but I will *r* their deeds   Ezek 9.10
and *r* them for their deeds.   Hos 4.9
Lord will *r* him for his deeds.   2Tim 4.14
Happy shall he be who *r* you   Ps 137.8
your lewdness shall be *r*   Ezek 23.49

RESCUE — D

congregation shall *r* the   Num 35.25
LORD, wilt thou look on? *R* me   Ps 35.17
r me from sinking in the mire;   69.14
In thy righteousness. . *r* me;   71.2
R those who are being taken   Prov 24.11
r my sheep from their mouths, Ezek 34.10
no one. . could *r* from his power; Dan 8.4
Lord. . *r* me from every evil   2Tim 4.18
David *r* his two wives.   1Sam 30.18
my soul also,. . thou hast *r*.   Ps 71.23
and *r* us from our foes, for   136.24
sent his angel and *r* me   Acts 12.11
and if he *r* righteous Lot,   2Pet 2.7

RESIST

R the devil and he will flee   Jas 4.7
R him, firm in your faith,   1Pet 5.9

RESOLVED

Daniel *r* that he would not   Dan 1.8

RESPECT — S

saying, 'They will *r* my son.'   Mt 21.37
saying, 'They will *r* my son.'   Mk 12.6
it may be they will *r* him.'   Lk 20.13
see that she *r* her husband.   Eph 5.33

REST — S — ED (v)

r yourselves under the tree,   Gen 18.4
seventh day you shall *r*;   Ex 23.12
land shall *r*, and enjoy its   Lev 26.34
the man will not *r*, but will   Ruth 3.18
the night his mind does not *r*.   Ecc 2.23
Spirit of. . LORD. . *r* upon him,   Isa 11.2
you shall *r*, and shall stand   Dan 12.13
they may *r* from their labors,   Rev 14.13
spirit of Elijah *r* on Elisha."   2Ki 2.15
he *r* on the seventh day   Gen 2.2
God *r* on the seventh day from   Heb 4.4

REST (n)

a sabbath of solemn *r* to you,   Lev 16.31
sabbath of solemn *r* for the land,   25.4
until the LORD gives *r*   Deut 3.20
r from all your enemies   12.10
God has given you *r* from   25.19
until the LORD gives *r* to   Josh 1.15
the land had *r* from war.   11.23
LORD had given *r* to Israel   23.1
the land had *r* for forty years.   Judg 3.11
land had *r* for forty years.   5.31
LORD had given him *r* from   2Sam 7.1
with the *r* of the multitude,   2Ki 25.11
to build a house of *r* for   1Chr 28.2
after they had *r* they did evil   Neh 9.28
there the weary are at *r*.   Job 3.17
and take your *r* in safety.   11.18
they should not enter my *r*.   Ps 95.11
Return, O my soul, to your *r*;   116.7
"In returning and *r* you   Isa 30.15
what is the place of my *r*?   66.1
the *r* of his brethren. . return   Mic 5.3
Come. . and I will give you *r*.   Mt 11.28
still sleeping and taking. . *r*?   Mk 14.41
waterless places seeking *r*;   Lk 11.24
Macedonia, our bodies had no *r* 2Cor 7.5
'They shall never enter my *r*.' "   Heb 3.11
there remains a sabbath *r*   4.9
and the *r* were terrified   Rev 11.13

RESTORE — S — D

then *r* the man's wife;   Gen 20.7
you shall *r* it to him.   Deut 22.2
Joash. . *r* the house of the   2Chr 24.4
R us, O LORD God of hosts! let Ps 80.19
R us. ., O God of our salvation,   85.4
r your judges as at the first,   Isa 1.26
For I will *r* their fortunes,   Jer 33.26
R us to thyself, O LORD, that   Lam 5.21
word to *r* and build Jerusalem   Dan 9.25
I will *r* to you the years   Joel 2.25
"Elijah does come,. . he is to *r*   Mt 17.11
at this time *r* the kingdom to   Acts 1.6
spiritual should *r* him in a   Gal 6.1
it is impossible to *r* again   Heb 6.4
still waters; he *r* my soul.   Ps 23.3
to the woman whose son he had *r* 2Ki 8.1
He also *r* the altar of the   2Chr 33.16
health of. . people not been *r*?   Jer 8.22
the sanctuary shall be *r* to   Dan 8.14
was *r*, whole like the other.   Mt 12.13
he did so, and his hand was *r*.   Lk 6.10

RESTRAIN — S — ED — ING

and he did not *r* them.   1Sam 3.13
I will not *r* my mouth; I will   Job 7.11

RESTRAIN — S — ED — ING (cont.)

r thyself at these things,	Isa 64.12
r his words has knowledge,	Prov 17.27
people were *r* from bringing;	Ex 36.6
you know what is *r* him now	2Thess 2.6

RESTRAINT

but a fool throws off *r* and	Prov 14.16
no prophecy..people cast off *r*,	29.18
not to lay any *r* upon you,	1Cor 7.35

RESURRECTION

who say that there is no *r*;	Mt 22.23
who say that there is no *r*;	Mk 12.18
repaid at the *r* of the just."	Lk 14.14
who say that there is no *r*,	20.27
done good, to the *r* of life,	Jn 5.29
"I am the *r* and the life;	11.25
became..a witness to his *r*."	Acts 1.22
foresaw and spoke of the *r*	2.31
he preached Jesus and the *r*.	17.18
respect to..hope and the *r*	23.6
that there will be a *r* of	24.15
united with him in a *r* like his.	Rom 6.5
there is no *r* of the dead?	1Cor 15.12
holding that the *r* is past	2Tim 2.18
received their dead by *r*.	Heb 11.35
living hope through the *r* of	1Pet 1.3
This is the first *r*.	Rev 20.5

RETURN — S — ED — ING

"*R* to your mistress,	Gen 16.9
the LORD said to Jacob, "*R*	31.3
LORD who didst say to me, '*R*	32.9
"*R*, O LORD, to the ten	Num 10.36
you will *r* to the LORD	Deut 4.30
and *r* to the LORD your God,	30.2
I go whence I shall not *r*,	Job 10.21
If you *r* to the Almighty	22.23
and sinners will *r* to thee.	Ps 51.13
R, O my soul, to your rest;	116.7
R, *r*, O Shulammite, *r*, *r*, that	Sol 6.13
ransomed of the LORD shall *r*,	Isa 35.10
r to me, for I have redeemed	44.22
ransomed of the LORD shall *r*,	51.11
it shall not *r* to me empty,	55.11
lovers; and would you *r* to me?	Jer 3.1
'*R*, faithless Israel, says	3.12
"If you *r*, O Israel, says the	4.1
"If you *r*, I will restore	15.19
r to me with their whole heart.	24.7
Jacob shall *r* and have quiet	30.10
'I will..*r* to my first husband,	Hos 2.7
"Come, let us *r* to the LORD;	6.1
R, O Israel, to the LORD	14.1
yet you did not *r* to me,"	Amos 4.8
R to me, says..LORD of hosts,	Zech 1.3
R to me, and I will *r* to you,	Mal 3.7
"*R* to your home, and declare	Lk 8.39
'I will *r* to my house from	11.24
Was no one found to *r* and give	17.18
'After this I will *r*, and	Acts 15.16
spirit *r* to God who gave it.	Ecc 12.7
'Why have you *r* evil for good?	Gen 44.4
Joseph *r* to Egypt with his	50.14
half-tribe of Manasseh *r*	Josh 22.9
"If you are *r* to the LORD	1Sam 7.3

REUBEN (Son of Jacob)

Born, Gen 29.32; found mandrakes for Leah, Gen 30.14; rescued Joseph, Gen 37.21–22; blessed by Jacob, Gen 49.3–4. Tribe of Reuben: blessed by Moses, Deut 33.6

REVEAL — S — ED — ING

the Son chooses to *r* him.	Mt 11.27
the Son chooses to *r* him."	Lk 10.22
pleased to *r* his Son to me,	Gal 1.16
who goes about gossiping *r*	Prov 20.19
God in heaven *r* mysteries,	Dan 2.28
things that are *r* belong	Deut 29.29
had not yet been *r* to him.	1Sam 3.7
LORD *r* himself to Samuel	3.21
the LORD had *r* to Samuel:	9.15
he has *r* his vindication in	Ps 98.2
LORD of hosts has *r* himself	Isa 22.14
the arm of the LORD been *r*?	53.1
come, and my deliverance be *r*.	56.1
the mystery was *r* to Daniel	Dan 2.19
covered that will not be *r*,	Mt 10.26
hidden..and *r* them to babes;	11.25
flesh and blood has not *r* this	16.17
r to him by the Holy Spirit	Lk 2.26
thoughts of many hearts..*r*."	2.35
hidden..and *r* them to babes;	10.21
covered up that will not be *r*,	12.2
when the Son of man is *r*.	17.30
that he might be *r* to Israel."	Jn 1.31
the arm of the Lord been *r*?"	12.38
the righteousness of God is *r*	Rom 1.17
God has *r* to us through the	1Cor 2.10
it will be *r* with fire,	3.13
when the Lord Jesus is *r*	2Thess 1.7
It was *r* to them that they	1Pet 1.12
be glad when his glory is *r*.	4.13
nothing, without *r* his secret	Amos 3.7
the *r* of the sons of God;	Rom 8.19
you wait for the *r* of our Lord	1Cor 1.7

REVELATION

according to the *r* of the	Rom 16.25
through a *r* of Jesus Christ.	Gal 1.12
I went up by *r*; and I laid	2.2
was made known to me by *r*,	Eph 3.3
at the *r* of Jesus Christ.	1Pet 1.13

REVENGE

not spare when he takes *r*.	Prov 6.34
and take our *r* on him."	Jer 20.10

REVENUE

royal *r* will be impaired.	Ezra 4.13
your *r* was..grain of Shihor,	Isa 23.3
Pay..*r* to whom *r* is due,	Rom 13.7

REVERENCE

and *r* my sanctuary: I am	Lev 19.30
sabbaths and *r* my sanctuary:	26.2
in your hearts *r* Christ as	1Pet 3.15

REVERENT

older women likewise to be *r*	Tit 2.3
they see your *r*..behavior.	1Pet 3.2

REVILE — D

"You shall not *r* God,	Ex 22.28
Is the enemy to *r* thy name	Ps 74.10
"Blessed are you when men *r* you	Mt 5.11
you *r* God's high priest?"	Acts 23.4
not afraid to *r* the glorious	2Pet 2.10
have you mocked and *r*?	2Ki 19.22
and *r* me upon the hills, I	Isa 65.7
When *r*, we bless; when	1Cor 4.12

REVIVE — D — ING

Will they *r* the stones out	Neh 4.2
Wilt thou not *r* us again, that	Ps 85.6
r me according to thy word!	119.25
to *r*..spirit of the humble,	Isa 57.15
for food to *r* their strength.	Lam 1.11

REVIVE — D — ING (cont.)

After two days he will *r* us;	Hos 6.2
their father Jacob *r*;	Gen 45.27
spirit returned, and he *r*.	Judg 15.19
into him again, and he *r*.	1Ki 17.22
the bones of Elisha, he *r*,	2Ki 13.21
have *r* your concern for me;	Phil 4.10
law of the LORD..*r* the soul;	Ps 19.7

REWARD (v)

may..LORD *r* you with good	1Sam 24.19
So they *r* me evil for good,	Ps 109.5
who sees in secret will *r* you.	Mt 6.6

REWARD (n)

your *r* shall be very great."	Gen 15.1
in keeping them there is..*r*.	Ps 19.11
there is a *r* for the righteous;	58.11
behold, his *r* is with him,	Isa 40.10
for your *r* is great in heaven,	Mt 5.12
who love you, what *r* have you?	5.46
shall receive a prophet's *r*,	10.41
will by no means lose his *r*.	Mk 9.41
expecting nothing..*r*..great,	Lk 6.35
What then is my *r*? Just this:	1Cor 9.18

RIBS

God..took one of his *r*	Gen 2.21

RICH — ER

Now Abram was very *r*	Gen 13.2
'I have made Abram *r*.'	14.23
The *r* shall not give more,	Ex 30.15
The *r* man had..many flocks	2Sam 12.2
he will not be *r*, and his	Job 15.29
blessing of..LORD makes *r*,	Prov 10.22
but the *r* has many friends.	14.20
The *r* and the poor meet	22.2
hard for a *r* man to enter	Mt 19.23
came a *r* man from Arimathea,	27.57
than for a *r* man to enter the	Mk 10.25
the *r* he has sent empty away.	Lk 1.53
"But woe to you that are *r*,	6.24
land of a *r* man brought forth	12.16
a *r* man who had a steward,	16.1
r man,..was clothed in purple	16.19
became sad, for he was very *r*.	18.23
Already you have become *r*!	1Cor 4.8
who desire to be *r* fall into	1Tim 6.9
for the *r* in this world,	6.17
the *r* in his humiliation,	Jas 1.10
you *r*, weep and howl for the	5.1
your poverty (but you are *r*)	Rev 2.9
For you say, I am *r*, I have	3.17
grown *r* with..her wantonness."	18.3
gives freely, yet grows..*r*;	Prov 11.24

RICHES

Solomon excelled..in *r* and	1Ki 10.23
swallows down *r* and vomits	Job 20.15
I delight as much as in..*r*.	Ps 119.14
R do not profit in the day	Prov 11.4
and violent men get *r*.	11.16
He who trusts in his *r* will	11.28
for *r* do not last for ever;	27.24
who gets *r* but not by right;	Jer 17.11
r they gained have perished.	48.36
delight in *r* choke the word,	Mt 13.22
cares..and the delight in *r*,	Mk 4.19
hard..for those who have *r*	10.23
presume upon the *r* of his	Rom 2.4
if their trespass means *r* for	11.12
O the depth of the *r* and	11.33
the unsearchable *r* of Christ,	Eph 3.8

according to..*r* of his glory	3.16
according to his *r* in glory	Phil 4.19

RIDDLE

"Let me now put a *r* to you;	Judg 14.12
those who had told the *r*.	14.19

RIGHT — S

then I will go to the *r*;	Gen 13.9
man doing whatever is *r*	Deut 12.8
what was *r* in his own eyes.	Judg 17.6
what was *r* in his own eyes.	21.25
Joash did what was *r* in	2Chr 24.2
you are not *r*. I will answer	Job 33.12
Do you say, 'It is my *r* before	35.2
gives the afflicted their *r*.	36.6
not spoken of me what is *r*,	42.7
Let thy eyes see the *r*!	Ps 17.2
decree what is *r*, you gods? Do	58.1
that you may be proved *r*.	Isa 43.26
"The LORD is in the *r*, for I	Lam 1.18
for all his works are *r* and	Dan 4.37
one at your *r* hand..one at	Mt 20.21
sat down at..*r* hand of God.	Mk 16.19*n*
exalted at the *r* hand of God,	Acts 2.33
Jesus standing at the *r* hand	7.55
does what is *r* is acceptable	10.35
use of my *r* in the gospel.	1Cor 9.18
Love..rejoices in the *r*.	13.6
if we are in our *r* mind,	2Cor 5.13
made him sit at his *r* hand	Eph 1.20
Whoever knows what is *r* to do	Jas 4.17
who does *r* is born of him.	1Jn 2.29
righteous man knows the *r* of	Prov 29.7
maintain the *r* of the poor	31.9
not defend the *r* of the needy.	Jer 5.28

RIGHTEOUS

Noah was a *r* man,	Gen 6.9
spare it for the fifty *r*	18.24
"She is more *r* than I,	38.26
die the death of the *r*,	Num 23.10
so *r* as all this law	Deut 4.8
"You are more *r* than I;	1Sam 24.17
and vindicating the *r* by	1Ki 8.32
mortal man be *r* before God?	Job 4.17
Yet the *r* holds to his way,	17.9
can a man be *r* before God?	25.4
Job..was *r* in his own eyes.	32.1
the LORD knows the way of the *r*,	Ps 1.6
God is a *r* judge, and a God who	7.11
destroyed, what can the *r* do"?	11.3
with the generation of the *r*.	14.5
The *r* shall possess the land,	37.29
Let the *r* rejoice in the LORD,	64.10
But let the *r* be joyful; let	68.3
My mouth will tell of thy *r* acts,	71.15
The *r* flourish like..palm tree,	92.12
Light dawns for the *r*, and joy	97.11
R art thou, O LORD, and	119.137
no man living is *r* before thee.	143.2
path of the *r* is like..light	Prov 4.18
memory of the *r*..a blessing,	10.7
wage of the *r* leads to life,	10.16
hope of the *r* ends in gladness,	10.28
the *r* escapes from trouble.	12.13
r man turns away from evil,	12.26
In the house of the *r* there	15.6
tower; the *r* man runs into it	18.10
r man who walks in..integrity—	20.7
justice..is a joy to the *r*,	21.15
a *r* man..before the wicked.	25.26
the *r* are bold as a lion.	28.1
they perish, the *r* increase.	28.28

RIGHTEOUS (cont.)

God will judge the *r* and the	Ecc 3.17
not a *r* man on earth who does	7.20
r men to whom it happens	8.14
one fate comes to all, to the *r*	9.2
Tell the *r*. .it shall be well	Isa 3.10
that the *r* nation. .may enter	26.2
make many to be accounted *r*;	53.11
The *r* man perishes, and no one	57.1
r deeds. .like a polluted garment.	64.6
cause a *r* Branch to spring	Jer 33.15
if you warn the *r*. .not to sin,	Ezek 3.21
"If a man is *r* and does	18.5
But when a *r* man turns away	18.24
When a *r* man turns away	18.26
the *r* shall live by his faith.	Hab 2.4
The LORD within her is *r*,	Zeph 3.5
the *r* will shine like the sun	Mt 13.43
separate the evil from the *r*,	13.49
Then the *r* will answer him,	25.37
nothing to do with that *r* man,	27.19
feared John,. .a *r* and holy man,	Mk 6.20
they were both *r* before God,	Lk 1.6
Simeon, and this man was *r*	2.25
were *r* and despised others:	18.9
who through faith is *r* shall	Rom 1.17
"None is *r*, no, not one;	3.10
to prove. .that he himself is *r*	3.26
one will hardly die for a *r*	5.7
by one. .many will be made *r*.	5.19
"He who through faith is *r*	Gal 3.11
my *r* one shall live by faith,	Heb 10.38
you have killed the *r* man;	Jas 5.6
the *r* for the unrighteous,	1Pet 3.18
the *r* man is scarcely saved,	4.18
if he rescued *r* Lot, greatly	2Pet 2.7
by what that *r* man saw and heard	2.8
fine linen is the *r* deeds of	Rev 19.8

RIGHTEOUSNESS

reckoned it to him as *r*.	Gen 15.6
by doing *r* and justice;	18.19
in *r*. .judge your neighbor.	Lev 19.15
it will be *r* for us, if we	Deut 6.25
"It is because of my *r* that the	9.4
r to you before the LORD	24.13
rewards every man for his *r*	1Sam 26.23
I hold fast my *r*, and will	Job 27.6
I put on *r*, and it clothed me;	29.14
and ascribe *r* to my Maker.	36.3
r he will not violate.	37.23
He loves *r* and justice; the	Ps 33.5
Thy *r* is like the mountains	36.6
you love *r* and hate wickedness.	45.7
The heavens declare his *r*,	50.6
thy power and thy *r*, O God,	71.19
R and justice are the foundation	89.14
who exult. .and extol thy *r*.	89.16
will judge the world with *r*,	96.13
been reckoned to him as *r*	106.31
and his *r* endures for ever.	112.3
Thy *r* is righteous for ever,	119.142
Then you will understand *r*	Prov 2.9
but *r* delivers from death.	10.2
steadfast in *r* will live,	11.19
In the path of *r* is life,	12.28
R exalts a nation, but sin	14.34
throne is established by *r*.	16.12
who pursues *r* and kindness	21.21
man who perishes in his *r*,	Ecc 7.15
for *r*, but behold, a cry!	Isa 5.7
with *r* he shall judge the poor,	11.4
r abide in the fruitful field.	32.16

fill Zion with justice and *r*;	33.5
in. .LORD,. .are *r* and strength;	45.24
In *r* you shall be established;	54.14
tell of your *r* and. .doings,	57.12
as if. .a nation that did *r*	58.2
put on *r* as a breastplate,	59.17
they may be called oaks of *r*,	61.3
covered me with the robe of *r*,	61.10
Do justice and *r*, and deliver	Jer 22.3
called: 'The LORD is our *r*.'	23.6
their own lives by their *r*,	Ezek 14.14
for the *r* which he has done	18.22
r. .shall not deliver him when	33.12
break off your sins by. .*r*,	Dan 4.27
To thee, O Lord, belongs *r*	9.7
not. .on the ground of our *r*,	9.18
Sow for yourselves *r*, reap	Hos 10.12
r like an everflowing stream.	Amos 5.24
fitting for us to fulfil all *r*."	Mt 3.15
unless your *r* exceeds. .scribes	5.20
John came. .in the way of *r*,	21.32
in holiness and *r* before him	Lk 1.75
of sin. .of *r* and of judgment:	Jn 16.8
he will judge the world in *r*	Acts 17.31
the *r* of God is revealed	Rom 1.17
the *r* of God has been manifested	3.21
was reckoned to him as *r*."	4.3
God reckons *r* apart from works:	4.6
one man's act of *r* leads to	5.18
yield your members to *r* for	6.19
Gentiles who did not pursue *r*	9.30
ignorant of the *r* that comes	10.3
Jesus, whom God made our. .*r*	1Cor 1.30
dispensation of *r* must. .exceed	2Cor 3.9
we might become the *r* of God.	5.21
it was reckoned to him as *r*."	Gal 3.6
r would indeed be by the law.	3.21
in true *r* and holiness.	Eph 4.24
the *r*. .that depends on faith;	Phil 3.9
aim at *r*, godliness, faith,	1Tim 6.11
and for training in *r*,	2Tim 3.16
an heir of the *r* which comes	Heb 11.7
anger. .not work the *r* of God.	Jas 1.20
harvest of *r* is sown in peace	3.18

RING — S

the king took his signet *r*	Est 3.10
and put a *r* on his hand,	Lk 15.22
r that were in their ears;	Gen 35.4
"Take off the *r* of gold	Ex 32.2

RISE — S — N — ING

R up, take your journey,	Deut 2.24
R up, come to our help!	Ps 44.26
your light *r* in the darkness	Isa 58.10
to the paralytic—"*R*, take up	Mt 9.6
r, take up your pallet and go	Mk 2.11
and after three days *r* again.	8.31
after three days he will *r*."	9.31
r, take up your bed and go	Lk 5.24
and on the third day *r*."	24.7
"*R*, take up your pallet, and	Jn 5.8
"Your brother will *r* again."	11.23
to Philip, "*R* and go toward	Acts 8.26
but *r* and enter the city,	9.6
"*R*, Peter; kill and eat."	10.13
by being the first to *r*	26.23
dead in Christ will *r* first;	1Thess 4.16
falls seven times, and *r*	Prov 24.16
tell the people, 'He has *r*	Mt 27.64
He is not here; for he has *r*,	28.6
until the Son of man. .*r* from	Mk 9.9
He has *r*, he is not here;	16.6

RISE — S — N — ING (cont.)
He is not here, but has *r*   Lk 24.5*n*
"The Lord has *r* indeed, and   24.34
Remember Jesus Christ, *r*   2Tim 2.8
From the *r* of the sun to its   Ps 113.3
fall and *r* of many in Israel,   Lk 2.34

RIVER — S
A *r* flowed out of Eden   Gen 2.10
a *r* whose streams make glad   Ps 46.4
razor. . hired beyond the *R*—   Isa 7.20
peace would have been like a *r*,   48.18
prosperity to her like a *r*,   66.12
the *r* of the water of life,   Rev 22.1
He turns *r* into a desert,   Ps 107.33
place of broad *r* and streams,   Isa 33.21
open *r* on the bare heights,   41.18
my eyes flow with *r* of tears   Lam 3.48

ROADSIDE
blind beggar,. . by the *r*.   Mk 10.46

ROAR — S
Let the sea *r*, and all   1Chr 16.32
let the sea *r*, and all that   Ps 96.11
LORD, he will *r* like a lion;   Hos 11.10
Does a lion *r* in the forest,   Amos 3.4
"The LORD *r* from Zion, and   1.2

ROB — S — BED
Do not *r* the poor, because   Prov 22.22
Will man *r* God? Yet you are   Mal 3.8
r his father or his mother   28.24
r other churches by accepting   2Cor 11.8

ROBBER — S
you come out as against a *r*,   Mk 14.48
Now Barabbas was a *r*.   Jn 18.40
this house,. . become a den of *r*   Jer 7.11
you have made it a den of *r*."   Mk 11.17
with him they crucified two *r*,   15.27
he fell among *r*, who stripped   Lk 10.30
from rivers, danger from *r*,   2Cor 11.26

ROBE — S
a long *r* with sleeves.   Gen 37.3
stripped him of his *r*,   37.23
took Joseph's *r*, and killed   37.31
also made the *r* of the ephod   Ex 39.22
will clothe him with your *r*,   Isa 22.21
with the *r* of righteousness,   61.10
'Bring quickly the best *r*,   Lk 15.22
crown of thorns and. . purple *r*.   Jn 19.5
they were each given a white *r*   Rev 6.11
your *r* are all fragrant with   Ps 45.8
princess. . with gold-woven *r*;   45.13
of gold, and wearing of *r*,   1Pet 3.3

ROCK
strike the *r*, and water shall   Ex 17.6
tell the *r*. . to yield. . water   Num 20.8
R, his work is perfect;   Deut 32.4
their *r* is not as our *R*,   32.31
there is no *r* like our God.   1Sam 2.2
"The LORD is my *r*, and my   2Sam 22.2
The LORD is my *r*, and my   Ps 18.2
who is a *r*, except our God?—   18.31
he will set me high upon a *r*.   27.5
To thee, O LORD, I call; my *r*,   28.1
bog, and set my feet upon a *r*,   40.2
the *r* that is higher than I;   61.2
He only is my *r* and. . salvation,   62.6
Thou art my *r* and my fortress.   71.3
made streams come out of. . *r*,   78.16
and the *R* of my salvation.'   89.26
LORD is upright; he is my *r*,   92.15

He opened the *r*, and water   105.41
who turns the *r* into a pool   114.8
not remembered. . *R* of. . refuge;   Isa 17.10
shade of a great *r* in a weary land.   32.2
the *r* from which you were hewn,   51.1
like a hammer. . breaks the *r*   Jer 23.29
built his house upon the *r*;   Mt 7.24
Peter, and on this *r* I will build   16.18
laid the foundation upon *r*;   Lk 6.48
supernatural *R*. . was Christ.   1Cor 10.4

ROD
in your hand?" He said, "A *r*."   Ex 4.2
Moses took the *r* of God.   4.20
Aaron's name upon. . *r* of Levi.   Num 17.3
break them with a *r* of iron,   Ps 2.9
spares the *r* hates his son,   Prov 13.24
the *r* of discipline drives it far   22.15
If you beat him with a *r*,   23.14
a *r* for the back of fools.   26.3
Assyria, the *r* of my anger,   Isa 10.5
Shall I come to you with a *r*,   1Cor 4.21

ROLL (v)
"Who will *r* away the stone   Mk 16.3
like a mantle. . *r* them up,   Heb 1.12

ROLL (n)
in the *r* of the book. . written   Ps 40.7
of me in the *r* of the book."   Heb 10.7

ROMAN — S
scourge a man who is a *R*   Acts 22.25
the *R* will come and destroy   Jn 11.48
not lawful for. . *R* to accept   Acts 16.21
not the custom of the *R* to   25.16

ROME
Cyrene, and visitors from *R*,   Acts 2.10
commanded. . Jews to leave *R*.   18.2
bear witness also at *R*."   23.11
when we came into *R*, Paul   28.16
To all God's beloved in *R*,   Rom 1.7
preach to you. . who are in *R*.   1.15
he arrived in *R* he searched   2Tim 1.17

ROOF
Make a *r* for the ark,   Gen 6.16
they removed the *r* above him;   Mk 2.4

ROOM — S
Thou hast given me *r* when I was   Ps 4.1
A man's gift makes *r* for him   Prov 18.16
when you pray, go into your *r*   Mt 6.6
done, and still there is *r*.'   Lk 14.22
will show you a large upper *r*   22.12
they went up to the upper *r*,   Acts 1.13
prepare a guest *r* for me,   Philem 22
whispered in private *r* shall   Lk 12.3
In my Father's house are many *r*;   Jn 14.2

ROOT — ED (v)
and *r* up Israel out of this   1Ki 14.15
gathering the weeds you *r* up   Mt 13.29
the treacherous will be *r* out   Prov 2.22
"Every plant. . will be *r* up.   Mt 15.13
being *r* and grounded in love,   Eph 3.17
r and built up in him and   Col 2.7

ROOT (n)
but the *r* of the righteous   Prov 12.3
the *r* of Jesse shall stand as   Isa 11.10
Judah shall again take *r*   37.31
scarcely has their stem taken *r*   40.24
axe is laid to. . *r* of the trees;   Mt 3.10
"The *r* of Jesse shall come,   Rom 15.12
love of money is the *r* of   1Tim 6.10
I am the *r* and the offspring   Rev 22.16

ROPE — S
she let them down by a *r*	Josh 2.15
they drew Jeremiah up with *r*	Jer 38.12

ROSE
I am a *r* of Sharon, a lily of	Sol 2.1

ROUTED
the LORD *r* the Egyptians	Ex 14.27
And the LORD *r* Sisera and all	Judg 4.15

RUDE
love. .is not arrogant or *r*.	1Cor 13.5

RUIN — S
Let *r* come upon them unawares!	Ps 35.8
folly brings his way to *r*,	Prov 19.3
the fortified city a *r*; the	Isa 25.2
This whole land. .become a *r*	Jer 25.11
Memphis shall become a. .*r*,	46.19
A *r*, *r*, *r* I will make it;	Ezek 21.27
not grieved over. .*r* of Joseph!	Amos 6.6
laid his strongholds in *r*.	Ps 89.40

RULE — S — D (v)
lesser light to *r* the night;	Gen 1.16
husband. .shall *r* over you."	3.16
shall *r* over many nations,	Deut 15.6
the LORD will *r* over you."	Judg 8.23
who can *r* this thy people,	2Chr 1.10
dost *r* the raging of the sea;	Ps 89.9
R in the midst of your foes!	110.2
much less for a slave to *r*	Prov 19.10
and babes shall *r* over them.	Isa 3.4
who shall *r* with great dominion	Dan 11.3
supposed to *r* over. .Gentiles	Mk 10.42
he shall *r* them with a rod	Rev 2.27
male child, one who is to *r*	12.5
he will *r* them with a rod	19.15
and he *r* over the nations.	Ps 22.28
who *r* his spirit than he who	Prov 16.32
and his arm *r* for him;	Isa 40.10
the Most High *r* the kingdom	Dan 4.17
the Most High *r* the kingdom	4.25
learned that the Most High *r*	4.32
Solomon *r* over all. .kingdoms	1Ki 4.21
he *r* over all the kings	2Chr 9.26
who hated them *r* over them.	Ps 106.41
lords besides thee have *r*	Isa 26.13
with. .harshness you. .*r* them.	Ezek 34.4

RULE (n)
my *r* in all the churches.	1Cor 7.17
after destroying every *r*	15.24
upon all who walk by this *r*,	Gal 6.16
far above all *r* and authority	Eph 1.21

RULER — S
r over all the land of Egypt.	Gen 45.8
Joseph is. .*r* over. .Egypt."	45.26
"When a *r* sins,. .unwittingly	Lev 4.22
Without having any. .*r*, she	Prov 6.7
When you. .eat with a *r*,	23.1
If a *r* listens to falsehood,	29.12
our judge, the LORD is our *r*,	Isa 33.22
one who is to be *r* in Israel,	Mic 5.2
r came in and knelt before him,	Mt 9.18
Jairus,. .*r* of the synagogue;	Lk 8.41
r of the synagogue, indignant	13.14
now shall the *r* of this world	Jn 12.31
the *r* of this world is judged.	16.11
seized Sosthenes, the *r* of	Acts 18.17
and the *r* of kings on earth.	Rev 1.5
be warned, O *r* of the earth.	Ps 2.10
makes the *r*. .as nothing.	Isa 40.23
the *r* transgressed against me;	Jer 2.8

Peter. .said. ."*R* of the people	Acts 4.8
For *r* are not a terror to good	Rom 13.3
None of the *r* of this age	1Cor 2.8

RUMOR — S
he shall hear a *r* and return	2Ki 19.7
so that he shall hear a *r*,	Isa 37.7
a *r*! Behold, it comes!—	Jer 10.22
hear of wars and *r* of wars;	Mt 24.6

RUN — S — NING
I will *r* in the way of thy	Ps 119.32
R to and fro through the streets	Jer 5.1
Many shall *r* to and fro, and	Dan 12.4
so he may *r* who reads it.	Hab 2.2
let us *r* with perseverance	Heb 12.1
to the earth; his word *r*	Ps 147.15
be *r* or had run in vain.	Gal 2.2
You were *r* well; who hindered you	5.7

RUNNER — S
"My days are swifter than a *r*;	Job 9.25
all the *r* compete, but only	1Cor 9.24

RUTH
and the name of the other *R*.	Ruth 1.4
R the Moabitess said to Naomi,	2.2
"I am *R*, your maidservant;	3.9
Boaz took *R* and she became	4.13
Boaz the father of Obed by *R*,	Mt 1.5

S

SABBATH — S
a *s*, there will be none."	Ex 16.26
"Remember the *s* day, to keep	20.8
observing the *s* throughout	31.16
a *s* of solemn rest to you,	Lev 16.31
s of solemn rest for the land,	25.4
gathering sticks on the *s*	Num 15.32
" 'Observe the *s* day, to keep	Deut 5.12
doing, profaning the *s* day?	Neh 13.17
Blessed. .who keeps the *s*,	Isa 56.2
"If you turn back. .from the *s*,	58.13
s to *s*, all flesh shall. .worship	66.23
not bear a burden on the *s*	Jer 17.21
went through. .grainfields on. .*s*;	Mt 12.1
flight may not be. .on a *s*.	24.20
after the *s*, toward the dawn	28.1
One *s*. .through the grainfields;	Mk 2.23
he would heal him on the *s*,	3.2
And when the *s* was past, Mary	16.1
on the *s*. .he stood up to read;	Lk 4.16
a *s*,. .through the grainfields,	6.1
Jesus had healed on the *s*,	13.14
One *s* when he went to dine	14.1
"It is the *s*, it is not lawful	Jn 5.10
If on the *s* a man receives	7.23
s day when Jesus made the clay	9.14
the *s* day we went outside	Acts 16.13
keep my *s* and reverence my	Lev 19.30
keep my *s* and reverence my	26.2
my *s*, as a sign between me	Ezek 20.12
they shall keep my *s* holy.	44.24

SACKCLOTH
they girded *s* on their loins,	1Ki 20.32
and put *s* upon his flesh,	21.27
covered himself with *s*, and	2Ki 19.1
Mordecai. .put on *s* and ashes,	Est 4.1
when they were sick—I wore *s*,	Ps 35.13
When I made *s* my clothing, I	69.11
loose the *s* from your loins,	Isa 20.2
covered himself with *s*, and	37.1

SACKCLOTH (cont.)
proclaimed a fast,..put on *s*, Jonah 3.5
ago, sitting in *s* and ashes. Lk 10.13

SACRED
Artemis, and of the *s* stone Acts 19.35
acquainted with..*s* writings 2Tim 3.15

SACRIFICE — S — D (v)
wilderness, that we may *s* Ex 3.18
you shall not *s* it to the Deut 15.21
he shall *s* upon you..priests 1Ki 13.2
S and offering thou dost not Ps 40.6
a freewill offering I will *s* 54.6
they *s* flesh and eat it; Hos 8.13
I with..thanksgiving will *s* Jonah 2.9
what pagans *s* they offer to 1Cor 10.20
one fate..to him who *s* and Ecc 9.2
our paschal lamb, has been *s*. 1Cor 5.7

SACRIFICE — S (n)
to obey is better than *s*, 1Sam 15.22
in the morning I prepare a *s* Ps 5.3
thou hast no delight in *s*; 51.16
s of the wicked..abomination Prov 15.8
is more acceptable..than *s*. 21.3
The *s* of the wicked is an 21.27
to offer the *s* of fools; Ecc 5.1
cause *s* and offering to cease; Dan 9.27
steadfast love and not *s*. Hos 6.6
you offer blind animals in *s*, Mal 1.8
'I desire mercy, and not *s*.' Mt 9.13
'I desire mercy, and not *s*,' 12.7
to offer a *s* according to..law Lk 2.24
your bodies as a living *s*, Rom 12.1
fragrant offering and *s* to God. Eph 5.2
a *s* acceptable and pleasing Phil 4.18
to put away sin by the *s* of Heb 9.26
for all time a single *s* for sins, 10.12
performed *s* to the LORD, 1Chr 29.21
is the multitude of your *s*? Isa 1.11
nor your *s* pleasing to me. Jer 6.20
bring your *s* every morning, Amos 4.4
love..is much more than..*s*." Mk 12.33

SACRILEGE
when you see the desolating *s* Mt 24.15
when you see the desolating *s* Mk 13.14

SACRILEGIOUS
men here who are neither *s* Acts 19.37

SADDUCEES
and *S* coming for baptism, he Mt 3.7
And the Pharisees and *S* came, 16.1
leaven of..Pharisees and *S*." 16.6
The same day *S* came to him, 22.23
and the *S* came upon them, Acts 4.1
the *S*,..filled with jealousy 5.17
one part were *S* and the other 23.6

SAFE — LY
strength, and made my way *s*. Ps 18.32
Oh to be *s* under the shelter of 61.4
Hold me up, that I may be *s* 119.117
bring him *s* to Felix the Acts 23.24

SAFETY
O LORD, makest me dwell in *s*. Ps 4.8
"I will place him in the *s* 12.5
the needy lie down in *s*; Isa 14.30

SAIL — ED
that we should *s* for Italy, Acts 27.1
from there they *s* to Cyprus. 13.4
Paul..*s* for Syria, and with 18.18

SAINTS
the *s* in the land, they are Ps 16.3
you his *s*, and give thanks 30.4
O fear the LORD, you his *s*, 34.9
he will not forsake his *s*. 37.28
flesh of thy *s* to the beasts 79.2
Precious..is the death of his *s*. 116.15
preserving the way of his *s*. Prov 2.8
But the *s* of the Most High Dan 7.18
given to the people of the *s* 7.27
destroy..the people of the *s*. 8.24
bodies of the *s*..were raised, Mt 27.52
evil he has done to thy *s* Acts 9.13
I..shut up many of the *s* in 26.10
contribute to..needs of..*s*, Rom 12.13
Jerusalem with aid for the *s*. 15.25
called to be *s* together with 1Cor 1.2
the *s* will judge the world? 6.2
about the offering for the *s*, 2Cor 9.1
you, as is fitting among *s*. Eph 5.3
now made manifest to his *s*. Col 1.26
washed the feet of the *s*, 1Tim 5.10
the *s* have been refreshed Philem 7
with the prayers of all the *s* Rev 8.3
allowed to make war on the *s* 13.7
for the endurance of the *s*, 14.12
men have shed the blood of *s* 16.6
surrounded the camp of the *s* 20.9

SALT — ED
she became a pillar of *s*. Gen 19.26
"You are the *s* of the earth; Mt 5.13
"S is good; but if *s* has lost Lk 14.34
every one will be *s* with fire. Mk 9.49

SALUTATIONS
and *s* in the market places, Mt 23.7
have *s* in the market places Mk 12.38
you love..*s* in the market Lk 11.43

SALVATION
I wait for thy *s*, O LORD. Gen 49.18
see the *s* of the LORD, Ex 14.13
and he has become my *s*; 15.2
because I rejoice in thy *s*. 1Sam 2.1
my shield..the horn of my *s*, 2Sam 22.3
Tell of his *s* from day to 1Chr 16.23
given me the shield of thy *s*, 22.36
my heart shall rejoice in thy *s*. Ps 13.5
The LORD is my light and my *s*; 27.1
The *s*..is from the LORD; he is 37.39
him..I will show the *s* of God!" 50.23
Restore to me the joy of thy *s*, 51.12
silence; from him comes my *s*. 62.1
May those who love thy *s* say 70.4
With long life..show him my *s*. 91.16
I will lift up the cup of *s* 116.13
my song; he has become my *s*. 118.14
eyes fail..watching for..*s*, 119.123
our *s* in the time of trouble. 33.2
God is my *s*; I will trust, and Isa 12.2
earth open, that *s* may sprout 45.8
saved..with everlasting *s*; 45.17
but my *s* will be for ever, 51.6
publishes *s*, who says to Zion, 52.7
for soon my *s* will come, 56.1
you shall call your walls *S*, 60.18
in..God is the *s* of Israel. Jer 3.23
wait quietly for..*s* of..LORD. Lam 3.26
I will wait for the God of my *s*; Mic 7.7
Thou wentest forth for the *s* Hab 3.13
I will joy in the God of my *s*. 3.18
raised up a horn of *s* for us Lk 1.69
give knowledge of *s* to his people 1.77

SALVATION (cont.)

mine eyes have seen thy *s*	Lk 2.30
all flesh shall see the *s* of God."	3.6
"Today *s* has come to this house,	19.9
know, for *s* is from the Jews.	Jn 4.22
there is *s* in no one else,	Acts 4.12
bring *s* to the uttermost parts	13.47
this *s* of God has been sent	28.28
it is the power of God for *s*	Rom 1.16
For *s* is nearer to us now	13.11
behold, now is the day of *s*.	2Cor 6.2
heard..the gospel of your *s*,	Eph 1.13
their destruction,..your *s*,	Phil 1.28
work out your own *s* with fear	2.12
to obtain *s* through our Lord	1Thess 5.9
those who are to obtain *s*?	Heb 1.14
obtain the *s* of your souls.	1Pet 1.9
forbearance of our Lord as *s*.	2Pet 3.15
write to you of our common *s*,	Jude 3
"*S* belongs to our God who	Rev 7.10
"Now the *s* and the power and	12.10
"Hallelujah! *S* and glory	19.1

SAMARIA

He bought the hill of *S*	1Ki 16.24
Ahab..reigned over Israel in *S*	16.29
king of Assyria captured *S*,	2Ki 17.6
the head of *S* is the son of	Isa 7.9
And your elder sister is *S*,	Ezek 16.46
I have spurned your calf, O *S*.	Hos 8.5
make *S* a heap in the..country,	Mic 1.6
along between *S* and Galilee.	Lk 17.11
He had to pass through *S*.	Jn 4.4
a woman of *S* to draw water.	4.7
my witnesses in..Judea and *S*	Acts 1.8
Philip went..to a city of *S*,	8.5

SAMARITANS

and enter no town of the *S*,	Mt 10.5
to many villages of the *S*.	Acts 8.25

SAMSON

and called his name *S*;	Judg 13.24
S went down to Timnah,	14.1
S went to visit his wife	15.1
S went to Gaza, and there	16.1
S said, "Let me die with	16.30
to tell of Gideon, Barak, *S*,	Heb 11.32

SAMUEL

Born, 1Sam 1.19–20; dedicated to God, 1Sam 1.21–28; ministered before God, 1Sam 2.11, 18–21; called, 1Sam 3.1–18; judged Israel, 1Sam 7.3–17; warned Israel for requesting a king, 1Sam 8.10–18; anointed Saul king, 1Sam 10.1–8; reasoned with Israel, 1Sam 12; reproved Saul, 1Sam 13.8–15; 15.10–23; hewed Agag in pieces, 1Sam 15.33; anointed David, 1Sam 16.1–13; died, 1Sam 25.1; 28.3.

Moses and *S* stood before me,	Jer 15.1
prophets who have spoken,..*S*	Acts 3.24
he gave them judges until *S*	13.20

SANCTIFICATION

Jesus, whom God made our..*s*	1Cor 1.30
this is..will of God, your *s*:	1Thess 4.3

SANCTIFY — IES — IED

"*S* yourselves; for tomorrow	Josh 3.5
Up, *s* the people, and say,	7.13
Levites! Now *s* yourselves,	2Chr 29.5
they will *s* the Holy One of	Isa 29.23
that I the LORD *s* them.	Ezek 20.12

S a fast, call a solemn	Joel 1.14
S them in the truth; thy word	Jn 17.17
s her, having cleansed her by	Eph 5.26
God of peace himself *s* you	1Thess 5.23
to *s* the people through his	Heb 13.12
he who *s* and those who are *s*	2.11
with the ashes of a heifer *s*	9.13
shall be *s* by my glory;	Ex 29.43
and the Levites *s* themselves	1Chr 15.14
place among those who are *s*	Acts 26.18
to those *s* in Christ Jesus,	1Cor 1.2
you were washed, you were *s*,	6.11
we have been *s* through the	Heb 10.10
for all time those who are *s*.	10.14

SANCTUARY

let them make me a *s*,	Ex 25.8
in the construction of the *s*	36.1
nor come into the *s*, until	Lev 12.4
nor profane the *s* of his God;	21.12
build the *s* of the LORD God,	1Chr 22.19
build a house for the *s*;	28.10
Go out of the *s*; for you	2Chr 26.18
May he send..help from the *s*,	Ps 20.2
have looked upon thee in the *s*,	63.2
until I went into the *s* of God;	73.17
They set thy *s* on fire; to the	74.7
Judah became his *s*, Israel his	114.2
And he will become a *s*, and	Isa 8.14
comes to his *s* to pray,	16.12
drink it in..courts of my *s*."	62.9
throne..the place of our *s*,	Jer 17.12
seen the nations invade her *s*,	Lam 1.10
scorned..altar, disowned his *s*;	2.7
you have defiled my *s* with	Ezek 5.11
yet I have been a *s* to them	11.16
they have defiled my *s* on	23.38
Behold, I will profane my *s*,	24.21
the *s* in the midst of it.	48.8
then the *s* shall be restored	Dan 8.14
thy face to shine upon thy *s*,	9.17
Bethel,..is the king's *s*,	Amos 7.13
Judah has profaned the *s* of	Mal 2.11
for worship and an earthly *s*.	Heb 9.1
way into the *s* is not..opened	9.8
to enter the *s* by the blood	10.19

SAND

multiply..descendants as..*s*	Gen 22.17
your descendants as the *s*	32.12
stone is heavy;..*s* is weighty,	Prov 27.3
Israel..as the *s* of the sea,	Isa 10.22
of Israel shall be like the *s*	Hos 1.10
who built his house upon the *s*;	Mt 7.26
sons of Israel be as the *s*	Rom 9.27
innumerable grains of *s* by	Heb 11.12

SANDAL — S

pull his *s* off his foot,	Deut 25.9
drew off his *s* and gave it to	Ruth 4.7
whose *s* I am not worthy to	Mk 1.7
wear *s* and not put on two tunics.	6.9
thong of whose *s* I am not	Lk 3.16
s..I am not worthy to untie.'	Acts 13.25

SARAH (SARAI)

Wife of Abraham, Gen 11.29; barren, Gen 11.30; Sarai and Hagar, Gen 16.1–6; represented as Abraham's sister, Gen 12.10–20; 20.1–18; name changed to Sarah, Gen 17.15; laughed at the LORD's promise, Gen 18.9–15; bore Isaac, Gen 21.1–8; jealous of Ishmael, Gen 21.9–11; died at Hebron, Gen 23.2; buried in Machpelah, Gen 23.19.

SARAH (SARAI) (cont.)
S. .barren; she had no child.   Gen 11.30
S, Abram's wife, bore. .no children. 16.1
"Where is S your wife?"   18.9
LORD did to S as he had promised. 21.1
By faith S herself received   Heb 11.11
as S obeyed Abraham, calling   1Pet 3.6
the barrenness of S womb.   Rom 4.19

SAT
Bethel, and s there till evening Judg 21.2
river Chebar. And I s there   Ezek 3.15
colt. .on which no one. .ever s; Mk 11.2
and s down at the right hand   16.19n
he s down at the right hand   Heb 1.3
he s down at the right hand   10.12

SATAN
S stood up against Israel,   1Chr 21.1
and S also came among them.   Job 1.6
and S also came among them   2.1
S standing at his right hand   Zech 3.1
Jesus said to him, "Begone, S! Mt 4.10
if S casts out S, he is divided   12.26
to Peter, "Get behind me, S!   16.23
"I saw S fall like lightning   Lk 10.18
"Ananias, why has S filled   Acts 5.3
to keep S from gaining the   2Cor 2.11
S disguises. .as an angel of light. 11.14
but are a synagogue of S.   Rev 2.9
serpent. .called the Devil and S, 12.9
dragon,. .who is the Devil and S, 20.2

SATISFY — IES — IED
S us. .with thy steadfast love, Ps 90.14
I will s her poor with bread.   132.15
labor for that which does not s? Isa 55.2
and s your desire with good   58.11
For I will s the weary soul,   Jer 31.25
they cannot s their hunger   Ezek 7.19
governor's ears, we will s him Mt 28.14
to s the one who enlisted him. 2Tim 2.4
For he s him who is thirsty,   Ps 107.9
afflicted shall eat and be s;   22.26
s with the goodness of thy house, 65.4
earth is s with. .fruit of thy work. 104.13
never s are the eyes of man.   Prov 27.20
Three things are never s;   30.15
the eye is not s with seeing,   Ecc 1.8
who loves money will not be s   5.10
travail of his soul and be s;   Isa 53.11
people. .s with my goodness,   Jer 31.14
You shall eat, but not be s,   Mic 6.14
the Father, and we shall be s." Jn 14.8

SATYR — S
s shall cry to his fellow;   Isa 34.14
slay their sacrifices for s   Lev 17.7
for. .high places, and. .s,   2Chr 11.15

SAUL (King of Israel)
Son of Kish, 1Sam 9.1–2; met Samuel,
1Sam 9.5–24; anointed by Samuel, 1Sam
10.1–8; prophesied with the prophets,
1Sam 10.9–13; chosen king at Mizpah,
1Sam 10.20–24; defeated the Ammonites,
1Sam 11.5–11; made king in Gilgal, 1Sam
11.12–15; reproved for his burnt offering,
1Sam 13.8–15; built an altar, 1Sam 14.35;
rejected as king, 1Sam 15.11–30; refreshed
by David's harp playing, 1Sam 16.14–23;
became jealous of David, 1Sam 18.6–30;
sought to kill David, 1Sam 19.1–17; killed
the priests of Nob, 1Sam 22.11–19; spared
by David, 1Sam 24.1–7; 26.1–12; con-
sulted the woman of Endor, 1Sam 28.3–25;
died and buried, 1Sam 31.

king; and God gave them S   Acts 13.21

SAUL (PAUL)
S, who is also called Paul,   Acts 13.9

SAVE — S — D — ING
God walks in the midst. .to s Deut 23.14
may come among us and s us   1Sam 4.3
our God, s us, I beseech   2Ki 19.19
I will defend this city to s it,   19.34
gather and s us from among   1Chr 16.35
and thou wilt hear and s.'   2Chr 20.9
O s thy people, and bless thy   Ps 28.9
God will s Zion and rebuild   69.35
judgment to s all the oppressed   76.9
s thy servant who trusts in thee.   86.2
I beseech thee, s my life!"   116.4
s yourself like a gazelle   Prov 6.5
s his life from Sheol.   23.14
waited. .that he might s us.   Isa 25.9
our God, s us from his hand,   37.20
there is no one to s you.   47.15
vindication, mighty to s."   63.1
for I am with you to s you   Jer 15.20
s me, and I shall be saved;   17.14
I will s you from afar, and   30.10
I will s you from afar, and   46.27
let every man s his life!   51.6
speak to warn. .to s his life, Ezek 3.18
I will s my flock, they   34.22
Where now is your king, to s   Hos 13.10
Assyria shall not s us, we   14.3
nor. .the mighty s his life;   Amos 2.14
s the lame and. .the outcast,   Zeph 3.19
his name Jesus, for he will s   Mt 1.21
"S, Lord; we are perishing."   8.25
Peter. .cried out, "Lord, s me." 14.30
whoever would s his life will   16.25
Son of man came to s the lost   18.11n
it in three days, s yourself!   27.40
whoever would s his life will   Mk 8.35
s yourself, and come down   15.30
whoever would s his life will   Lk 9.24
men's lives but to s them"   9.55n
you will s your husband?   1Cor 7.16
might by all means s some.   9.22
into the world to s sinners.   1Tim 1.15
s. .yourself and your hearers.   4.16
able. .to s those who draw near Heb 7.25
but to s those who are eagerly   9.28
will s his soul from death   Jas 5.20
s some, by snatching them   Jude 23
the LORD s not with sword   1Sam 17.47
But he s the fatherless   Job 5.15
Thus the LORD s Israel   Ex 14.30
be s from your enemies.   Num 10.9
a people s by the LORD,   Deut 33.29
Rahab. .Joshua s alive;   Josh 6.25
he s them from the hand of   Judg 2.18
I am s from my enemies.   2Sam 22.4
warn him, so that he s himself 2Ki 6.10
So the LORD s Hezekiah and   2Chr 32.22
and I am s from my enemies.   Ps 18.3
LORD heard him, and s him out   34.6
face shine, that we may be s!   80.3
he s them for his name's sake,   106.8
and rest you shall be s;   Isa 30.15
long time, and shall we be s?   64.5
summer. .ended,. .we are not s." Jer 8.20
In his days Judah will be s,   23.6
yet he shall be s out of it.   30.7

SAVE — S — D — ING (cont.)

In those days Judah will be *s*	Jer 33.16
you will have *s* your life.	Ezek 3.19
saying, "Who then can be *s*?"	Mt 19.25
endures to the end will be *s*.	24.13
to him, "Then who can be *s*?"	Mk 10.26
the woman, "Your faith has *s*	Lk 7.50
will those who are *s* be few?"	13.23
said, "Then who can be *s*?"	18.26
"He *s* others; let him save	23.35
say this that you may be *s*.	Jn 5.34
calls on. . Lord shall be *s*.'	Acts 2.21
by which you will be *s*,	11.14
of Moses, you cannot be *s*."	15.1
we shall be *s* through. . grace	15.11
what must I do to be *s*?"	16.30
the ship, you cannot be *s*."	27.31
be *s* by him from the wrath of	Rom 5.9
For in this hope we were *s*.	8.24
prayer. . that they may be *s*.	10.1
and believe. . you will be *s*.	10.9
and so all Israel will be *s*;	11.26
but to us who are being *s*	1Cor 1.18
though he himself will be *s*,	3.15
that his spirit may be *s* in the day	5.5
of many, that they may be *s*.	10.33
gospel, . . by which you are *s*,	15.2
Gentiles that they. . be *s*—	1Thess 2.16
God chose you. . to be *s*,	2Thess 2.13
who desires all men to be *s*	1Tim 2.4
who *s* us and called us with	2Tim 1.9
he *s* us, not because of deeds	Tit 3.5
eight persons, were *s* through	1Pet 3.20
righteous man is scarcely *s*,	4.18
he who *s* a people out of the land	Jude 5
can hinder the LORD from *s*	1Sam 14.6
know the *s* acts of the LORD."	Mic 6.5

SAVIOR — S

a *s*, so that they escaped	2Ki 13.5
They forgot God, their *S*,	Ps 106.21
he will send them a *s*, and	Isa 19.20
Holy One of Israel, your *S*.	43.3
and besides me there is no *s*.	43.11
a righteous God and a *S*;	45.21
that I, the LORD, am your *S*	60.16
thou hope of Israel, its *s*	Jer 14.8
besides me there is no *s*.	Hos 13.4
my spirit rejoices in God my *S*,	Lk 1.47
born in the city of David a *S*,	2.11
has brought to Israel a *S*,	Acts 13.23
in the sight of God our *S*,	1Tim 2.3
who is the *S* of all men,	4.10
Son as the *S* of the world.	1Jn 4.14
only God, our *S* through Jesus	Jude 25
S shall go up to Mount Zion	Obad 1.21

SAYING — S

The *s* is sure and worthy of	1Tim 1.15
The *s* is sure and worthy of	4.9
hears my *s* and does not keep	Jn 12.37

SCALES

A just balance and *s* are	Prov 16.11
and false *s* are not good.	20.23
acquit the man with wicked *s*	Mic 6.11

SCARLET

bind. . *s* cord in the window	Josh 2.18
though your sins are like *s*,	Isa 1.18
and put a *s* robe upon him,	Mt 27.28

SCATTER — S — ED

and *s* them in Israel.	Gen 49.7
I will *s* you among. . nations,	Lev 26.33

And the LORD will *s* you	Deut 4.27
the LORD will *s* you among	28.64
I will *s* them among the nations	Jer 9.16
I will *s* you like chaff driven	13.24
Like the east wind I will *s*	18.17
I swore. . that I would *s* them	Ezek 20.23
the wolf snatches them and *s*	Jn 10.12
and all their flock is *s*.	Jer 10.21
s them among the countries,	Ezek 11.16
the horns which *s* Judah,	Zech 1.21
I *s* them with a whirlwind	7.14
I *s* them among the nations,	10.9
hour. . come, when you will be *s*,	Jn 16.32
who were *s* went. . preaching	Acts 8.4

SCEPTER

The *s* shall not depart	Gen 49.10
s and with their staves."	Num 21.18
s shall rise out of Israel;	24.17
Your royal *s* is a *s* of equity;	Ps 45.6
Ephraim. . my helmet; Judah is my *s*.	60.7

SCOFFED

s at. . Rock of his salvation.	Deut 32.15
heard. . this, and. . *s* at him.	Lk 16.14

SCOFFER — S

s does not listen to rebuke.	Prov 13.1
A *s* seeks wisdom in vain,	14.6
A *s* does not like to be reproved;	15.12
Strike a *s*, and the simple	19.25
the *s* cease, and all who	Isa 29.20
nor sits in the seat of *s*;	Ps 1.1
How long will *s* delight in	Prov 1.22
'Behold, you *s*, and wonder,	Acts 13.41

SCORCH — ED

allowed to *s* men with fire;	Rev 16.8
inhabitants of. . earth are *s*,	Isa 24.6
when the sun rose they were *s*;	Mt 13.6

SCORN — S — ED (v)

you did not *s* or despise me,	Gal 4.14
God's the wicked, but the	Prov 14.9
have utterly *s* the LORD,	2Sam 12.14

SCORN (n)

they laughed them to *s*,	2Chr 30.10
I am the *s* of. . my adversaries,	Ps 31.11
become the *s* of his neighbors.	89.41
word of the LORD. . object of *s*,	Jer 6.10
bear the *s* of the peoples."	Mic 6.16

SCOURGE — D (v)

they will *s* him and kill him,	Lk 18.33
mocked and *s* and crucified,	Mt 20.19
having *s* Jesus, delivered him	27.26
Pilate took Jesus and *s* him.	Jn 19.1

SCOURGE — ING (n)

hid from the *s* of the tongue,	Job 5.21
will wield against them a *s*,	Isa 10.26
him to be examined by *s*,	Acts 22.24

SCRIBE — S

the *s* of the law of the God	Ezra 7.12
a *s* came up and said to him,	Mt 8.19
every *s* who has been trained	13.52
Where is the *s*? Where is	1Cor 1.20
"The *s* and the Pharisees sit	Mt 23.2
s who came down from Jerusalem	Mk 3.22
crowd. . and *s* arguing with them.	9.14
"Beware of the *s*, who like	12.38

SCRIPTURE — S

Have you not read this *s*:	Mk 12.10
the *s* was fulfilled which says,	15.28n
"Today. . *s* has been fulfilled	Lk 4.21

SCRIPTURE — S (cont.)

they believed the *s* and the	Jn 2.22
(and *s* cannot be broken),	10.35
that the *s* may be fulfilled,	13.18
that the *s* might be fulfilled.	17.12
This was to fulfil the *s*.	19.24
(to fulfil the *s*), "I thirst."	19.28
s says, "They shall look on him	19.37
Philip..beginning with this *s*	Acts 8.35
man, well versed in the *s*.	18.24
For the *s* says to Pharaoh,	Rom 9.17
the *s*, foreseeing that God	Gal 3.8
the *s* consigned all things	3.22
the *s* say? "Cast out the slave	4.30
royal law, according to the *s*,	Jas 2.8
the *s* was fulfilled which says,	2.23
that the *s* says, "He yearns	4.5
no prophecy of *s*..one's own	2Pet 1.20
"Have you never read in the *s*:	Mt 21.42
know neither the *s* nor..power	22.29
how..should the *s* be fulfilled,	26.54
you know neither the *s* nor	Mk 12.24
But let the *s* be fulfilled."	14.49
while he opened to us the *s*?"	Lk 24.32
minds to understand the *s*,	24.45
You search the *s*, because	Jn 5.39
argued with them from the *s*,	Acts 17.2
examining the *s* daily to see	17.11
the *s* we might have hope.	Rom 15.4
died..in accordance with..*s*,	1Cor 15.3
twist as they do the other *s*.	2Pet 3.16

SCROLL

the skies roll up like a *s*.	Isa 34.4
"Take a *s* and write on it	Jer 36.2
wrote them with ink on the *s*."	36.18
s was consumed in the fire	36.23
Then Jeremiah took another *s*	36.32
lo, a written *s* was in it;	Ezek 2.9
saw, and behold, a flying *s*!	Zech 5.1
s written within and on..back,	Rev 5.1
the sky vanished like a *s*	6.14
He had a little *s* open in his hand.	10.2
told him to give me the little *s*;	10.9

SEA — S

LORD drove the *s* back	Ex 14.21
in rafts by *s* to Joppa,	2Chr 2.16
thou didst divide the *s*	Neh 9.11
but the *s* is not full; to the	Ecc 1.7
arose a great storm on the *s*,	Mt 8.24
came to them, walking on the *s*.	Mk 6.48
they saw Jesus walking on the *s*	Jn 6.19
in the cloud and in the *s*,	1Cor 10.2
standing beside the *s* of glass	Rev 15.2
waters..he called S.	Gen 1.10

SEAL — ED (v)

and *s* it with the king's ring;	Est 8.8
to *s* both vision and prophet,	Dan 9.24
s the book, until..the end.	12.4
"*S* up what the seven thunders	Rev 10.4
"Do not *s* up the words of	22.10
my transgression would be *s*	Job 14.17
words of a book that is *s*.	Isa 29.11
the words are shut up and *s*	Dan 12.9
s with the promised..Spirit,	Eph 1.13
God, in whom you were *s* for	4.30
a scroll..*s* with seven seals;	Rev 5.1
till we have *s* the servants	7.3

SEAL — S — ING (n)

his testimony sets his *s* to	Jn 3.33
on him God the Father set his *s*."	6.27
circumcision as a sign or *s*	Rom 4.11

the *s* of my apostleship in	1Cor 9.2
he has put his *s* upon us	2Cor 1.22
the Lamb opened the seventh *s*,	Rev 8.1
those..who have not the *s* of God	9.4
Lamb opened one of the seven *s*,	6.1
sepulchre secure by *s* the stone	Mt 27.66

SEA OF GALILEE

by the S..he saw two brothers,	Mt 4.18
Jesus..passed along the S..	15.29
to the other side of the S..,	Jn 6.1

SEARCH — ES — ED — ING (v)

S me, O God, and know my	Ps 139.23
"I the LORD *s* the mind and	Jer 17.10
I will *s* out and take them;	Amos 9.3
I will *s* Jerusalem with lamps,	Zeph 1.12
"Go..*s* diligently for the child,	Mt 2.8
You *s* the scriptures, because	Jn 5.39
S and you will see..no prophet	7.52
who *s* the hearts of men knows	Rom 8.27
For the Spirit *s* everything,	1Cor 2.10
I am he who *s* mind and heart,	Rev 2.23
this we have *s* out; it is	Job 5.27
thou hast *s* me and known me!	Ps 139.1
"Every one is *s* for you."	Mk 1.37

SEARCH (n)

go in *s* of the one..astray?	Mt 18.12

SEASON (v)

lost..saltness, how will you *s*	Mk 9.50

SEASON — S (n)

For everything there is a *s*,	Ecc 3.1
lights..for signs and for *s*	Gen 1.14

SEAT

gave him a *s* above the seats	2Ki 25.28
I might come even to his *s*!	Job 23.3
prepared my *s* in the square,	29.7
for you love the best *s* in	Lk 11.43

SECRET — S

"The *s* things belong to	Deut 29.29
Absalom sent *s* messengers	2Sam 15.10
our *s* sins in the light of thy	Ps 90.8
into judgment, with every *s*	Ecc 12.14
I did not speak in *s*, in a	Isa 45.19
I have not spoken in *s*, from	48.16
Can a man hide himself in *s*	Jer 23.24
nothing, without revealing..*s*	Amos 3.7
so that your alms may be *s*;	Mt 6.4
given the *s* of the kingdom	Mk 4.11
s, except to come to light.	4.22
we impart..*s* and hidden wisdom	1Cor 2.7
he knows the *s* of the heart.	Ps 44.21
a talebearer reveals *s*, but	Prov 11.13
to know the *s* of the kingdom	Mt 13.11
when..God judges the *s* of men	Rom 2.16
s of his heart are disclosed;	1Cor 14.25

SECRETLY

Why..flee *s*, and cheat me,	Gen 31.27
Israel did *s* against the LORD	2Ki 17.9
The king questioned him *s*	Jer 37.17
Herod summoned the wise men *s*	Mt 2.7

SECT

of the *s* of the Nazarenes.	Acts 24.5
with regard to this *s* we know	28.22

SECURITY

in a matter of deposit or *s*,	Lev 6.2
saw..how they dwelt in *s*,	Judg 18.7
He gives them *s*, and they	Job 24.23
I am oppressed; be thou my *s*!	Isa 38.14

SEE — S — N — ING

go and *s* him before I die."	Gen 45.28

SEE — S — N — ING (cont.)

I have let you s it with your	Deut 34.4
without my flesh. .s God,	Job 19.26
or s the work of his hands.	Isa 5.12
eyes, so that they cannot s,	44.18
earth shall s the salvation	52.10
he shall s his offspring,	53.10
pure in heart,. .shall s God.	Mt 5.8
tell John what you hear and s:	11.4
indeed s but never perceive.	13.14
risen,. .Come, s. .where he lay.	28.6
may indeed s but not perceive,	Mk 4.12
all flesh shall s the salvation	Lk 3.6
s how the fields are. .white	Jn 4.35
keeps my word,. .will never s death."	8.51
though I was blind, now I s."	9.25
that those who do not s may s,	9.39
"Sir, we wish to s Jesus."	12.21
a little while, and you will s me."	16.16
"Unless I s in his hands the	20.25
indeed s but never perceive.	Acts 28.26
now we s in a mirror dimly,	1Cor 13.12
But we s Jesus, who for a	Heb 2.9
for we shall s him as he is.	1Jn 3.2
and every eye will s him,	Rev 1.7
for the LORD s not as man s;	1Sam 16.7
prudent man s danger and	Prov 27.12
who say, "Who s us? Who	Isa 29.15
I have s the affliction of	1Sam 9.16
people. .have s a great light,	Mt 4.16
practicing. .piety. .to be s by them;	6.1
"Go. .tell John what you have s	Lk 7.22
light, that it may be clearly s	Jn 3.21
what we have s and heard."	Acts 4.20
on the road he had s the Lord,	9.27
have heard, which we have s	1Jn 1.1
"Thou art a God of s";	Gen 16.13
keep them from s the light	2Cor 4.4

SEED

every plant yielding s	Gen 1.29
enmity. .between your s	3.15
goes. .weeping, bearing the s	Ps 126.6
In the morning sow your s,	Ecc 11.6
who sowed good s in his field;	Mt 13.24
good s means. .sons of. .kingdom;	13.38
as if a man should scatter s	Mk 4.26

SEEK — S — ING

to s out a resting place for	Num 10.33
there you will s the LORD	Deut 4.29
S the LORD and his strength,	1Chr 16.11
If you s him, he will be found	28.9
and pray and s my face,	2Chr 7.14
commanded Judah to s the LORD,	14.4
in his disease he did not s	16.12
set your heart to s God."	19.3
not forsaken those who s thee.	Ps 9.10
if there are any. .that s after God.	14.2
who s the face of the God of	24.6
Thou hast said, "S ye my face."	27.8
may all who s thee rejoice	40.16
are wise, that s after God.	53.2
ruthless men s my life; they	54.3
God, I s thee, my soul thirsts	63.1
who s God, let. .hearts revive,	69.3
those who s the LORD rejoice!	105.3
s him with their whole heart,	119.2
For. .God, I will s your good.	122.9
They will s me diligently but	Prov 1.28
he will s at harvest and	20.4
I applied my mind to s and	Ecc 1.13
people did not. .s the LORD of	Isa 9.13

S and read from the book of	34.16
I did not say. .'S me in chaos.'	45.19
"S. .LORD while he may be found,	55.6
You will s me and find me;	Jer 29.13
you s great things for yourself?	45.5
s peace,. .there shall be none.	Ezek 7.25
so will I s out my sheep;	34.12
shall return and s the LORD	Hos 3.5
their guilt and s my face,	5.15
Israel: "S me and live;	Amos 5.4
S good, and not evil, that	5.14
S the LORD, all you humble	Zeph 2.3
nations. .come to s the LORD	Zech 8.22
But s first his kingdom and	Mt 6.33
s, and you will find; knock,	7.7
s, and you will find; knock,	Lk 11.9
Instead, s his kingdom, and	12.31
Son of man came to s and to	19.10
"Why do you s the living among	24.5
I s not my own will but the	Jn 5.30
you s me, not because you saw	6.26
you will s me and. .not find me;	7.34
you will s me and die in your sin;	8.21
Yet I do not s my own glory;	8.50
said to them, "Whom do you s?"	18.4
you weeping? Whom do you s?"	20.15
rest of men may s the Lord,	Acts 15.17
that they should s God, in	17.27
am left, and they s my life."	Rom 11.3
I s not what is yours but	2Cor 12.14
s the things that are above,	Col 3.1
he that s my life s your	1Sam 22.23
God s what has been driven away.	Ecc 3.15
spirit within me earnestly s	Isa 26.9
good. .to the soul that s him.	Lam 3.25
evil generation; it s a sign,	Lk 11.29
such the Father s to worship	Jn 4.23
understands, no one s for God.	Rom 3.11
s his God, he did with all	2Chr 31.21
Lord God, s him by prayer and	Dan 9.3
come s fruit on this fig tree,	Lk 13.7

SEER — S

prophet was. .called a s.)	1Sam 9.9
who say to the s, "See not";	Isa 30.10
the s shall be disgraced,	Mic 3.7

SELF-CONTROL

man without s is like a city	Prov 25.28
argued about justice and s	Acts 24.25
if they cannot exercise s,	1Cor 7.9
Every athlete exercises s	9.25

SELFISHNESS

anger, s, slander, gossip,	2Cor 12.20
Do nothing from s or conceit,	Phil 2.3

SELL — S

"First s me your birthright."	Gen 25.31
because they s the righteous	Amos 2.6
S your possessions, and give	Lk 12.33
in his joy he goes and s all	Mt 13.44

SEND — S

Come, I will s you to Pharaoh	Ex 3.10
Oh s out thy light and. .truth;	Ps 43.3
He will s from heaven and save	57.3
I said, "Here am I! S me."	Isa 6.8
I s my messenger to prepare	Mal 3.1
s. .laborers into his harvest."	Mt 9.38
Son of man will s his angels,	13.41
I s my messenger before thy face,	Mk 1.2
begged him, "S us to the swine,	5.12
believed that thou didst s me.	Jn 17.8
thou didst s me into the world,	17.18

SEND — S (cont.)

sent me, even so I s you."	Jn 20.21
did not s me to baptize but	1Cor 1.17
He s forth his command to	Ps 147.15

SENNACHERIB

S king of Assyria came up	2Ki 18.13
hear the words of S, which	19.16
S king of Assyria departed,	19.36
S..came and invaded Judah	2Chr 32.1
hear all the words of S,	Isa 37.17
S king of Assyria departed,	37.37

SENT

God s me before you	Gen 45.5
"The LORD s me to prophesy	Jer 26.12
These twelve Jesus s out,	Mt 10.5
me receives him who s me.	10.40
John..s word by his disciples	11.2
he s two of his disciples	Mk 11.1
he s two of the disciples,	Lk 19.29
As the living Father s me,	Jn 6.57
God s forth his Son, born of	Gal 4.4
God has s the Spirit of his Son	4.6
God s his only Son into the	1Jn 4.9

SEPARATE — D

lights to s..day from..night;	Gen 1.14
brow of him who was s	49.26
s for you the holy place	Ex 26.33
Israel s from..uncleanness	Lev 15.31
For thou didst s them from	1Ki 8.53
do his will; s yourselves	Ezra 10.11
he will s..one from another	Mt 25.32
Who shall s us from the love	Rom 8.35
able to s us from the love	8.39
unbelieving partner..to s,	1Cor 7.15
be s from them, says the Lord,	2Cor 6.17
God s the light from..darkness	Gen 1.4
they s from each other.	13.11
have s you from the peoples.	Lev 20.24
have not s themselves from	Ezra 9.1
they s from Israel all those	Neh 13.3
Cephas..s himself, fearing the	Gal 2.12

SEPARATION

his s to God is upon his head.	Num 6.7
your iniquities have made a s	Isa 59.2
make a s between the holy	Ezek 42.20

SERAPHIM

Above him stood the s; each	Isa 6.2

SERPENT — S

the s was more subtle	Gen 3.1
became a s; and Moses fled	Ex 4.3
his rod..became a s.	7.10
"Make a fiery s, and set	Num 21.8
broke in pieces the bronze s	2Ki 18.4
At..last it bites like a s,	Prov 23.32
punish Leviathan the fleeing s,	Isa 27.1
as Moses lifted up the s in	Jn 3.14
s deceived Eve by..cunning,	2Cor 11.3
the dragon, that ancient s,	Rev 20.2
LORD sent fiery s among	Num 21.6
I am sending among you s,	Jer 8.17
You s, you brood of vipers,	Mt 23.33
they will pick up s, and	Mk 16.18n
tread upon s and scorpions,	Lk 10.19

SERVANT — S

Not so with my s Moses;	Num 12.7
you were a s in the land	Deut 5.15
"If you will be a s to this people	1Ki 12.7
"Have you considered my s Job,	Job 2.3
my s Job shall pray for you,	42.8
Keep back thy s..from..sins;	Ps 19.13

He chose David his s, and	78.70
give thy strength to thy s,	86.16
shame; may thy s be glad!	109.28
adversaries, for I am thy s.	143.12
Do not slander a s to his	Prov 30.10
But you, Israel, my s, Jacob,	Isa 41.8
Behold my s, whom I uphold,	42.1
Who is blind but my s, or	42.19
"and my s whom I have chosen,	43.10
"But now hear, O Jacob my s,	44.1
my s shall prosper, he shall	52.13
the king of Babylon, my s,	Jer 25.9
fear not, O Jacob my s, says	30.10
one shepherd, my s David,	Ezek 34.23
Daniel, s of the living God,	Dan 6.20
I will bring my s the Branch.	Zech 3.8
greatest among you..be your s;	Mt 23.11
'Well done, good and faithful s;	25.23
he must be last..and s of all."	Mk 9.35
would be great..be your s,	10.43
he sent a s to the tenants,	12.2
He has helped his s Israel,	Lk 1.54
now lettest thou thy s depart	2.29
Does he thank the s because	17.9
'Well done, good s! Because	19.17
he sent a s to the tenants,	20.10
s..not greater than his master;	Jn 13.16
God, having raised up his s,	Acts 3.26
David, thy s, didst say by	4.25
against thy holy s Jesus,	4.27
Paul, a s of Jesus Christ,	Rom 1.1
he is God's s for your good.	13.4
the Lord's s must not be	2Tim 2.24
a s to testify to the things	Heb 3.5
For they are my s, whom I	Lev 25.42
my s whom I brought forth	25.55
spoke by his s the prophets.	2Ki 24.2
hand of..LORD is with his s,	Isa 66.14
sent all my s the prophets	Jer 7.25
to you all his s the prophets,	25.4
he sent his s to the tenants,	Mt 21.34
called his s and entrusted	25.14
treat me as one of your..s." '	Lk 15.19
No longer do I call you s,	Jn 15.15
with ourselves as your s	2Cor 4.5
Are they of Christ? I am	11.23
S, be submissive to..masters	1Pet 2.18
sealed the s of our God upon	Rev 7.3
and his s shall worship him;	22.3

SERVE — S — D — ING

elder shall s the younger."	Gen 25.23
s God upon this mountain."	Ex 3.12
let us s the Egyptians'?	14.12
not bow down to..or s them;	20.5
to s me as priests—Aaron	28.1
fear..God; you shall s him,	Deut 6.13
all the people..shall s you.	20.11
you shall s other gods,	28.36
to s him with all your heart	Josh 22.5
my house, we will s the LORD."	24.15
yoke upon us, and we will s	1Ki 12.4
and s the king of Babylon,	2Ki 25.24
and s him with a whole heart	1Chr 28.9
Almighty,..we should s him?	Job 21.15
S the LORD with fear, with	Ps 2.11
will not s you shall perish;	Isa 60.12
shall s the king of Babylon	Jer 25.11
All the nations shall s him	27.7
But they shall s the LORD	30.9
we will not s your gods or	Dan 3.18
said, 'It is vain to s God.	Mal 3.14
the Son of man came..to s,	Mt 20.28

SERVE — S — D — ING (cont.)

No servant can s two masters;	Lk 16.13
appoint you to s and bear	Acts 26.16
we s not under the old written	Rom 7.6
do not s our Lord Christ,	16.18
ministering spirits sent..to s,	Heb 1.14
God, and s him day and night	Rev 7.15
the leader as one who s.	Lk 22.26
If any..s me, he must follow	Jn 12.26
and they s other gods.	Josh 24.2
the people s the LORD all the	Judg 2.7
and they s their gods.	3.6
forsaken me..s other gods;	10.13
and they s the LORD only.	1Sam 7.4
whom I had not known s me	2Sam 22.44
and they s idols, of which	2Ki 17.12
They s their idols,..a snare	Ps 106.36
a thousand thousands s him,	Dan 7.10
fever left..she rose and s him.	Mt 8.15
fever left her; and she s them.	Mk 1.31
immediately she rose and s	Lk 4.39
has s with me in the gospel.	Phil 2.22
Martha was distracted with..s;	Lk 10.40
for his sake in s the saints,	Heb 6.10

SERVICE

lives bitter with hard s,	Ex 1.14
all who can enter the s, to do	Num 4.3
"Has not man a hard s upon	Job 7.1
think he is offering s to God.	Jn 16.2
if s, in our serving; he who	Rom 12.7
those..employed in..temple s	1Cor 9.13
devoted..to the s of the saints;	16.15

SETH

and called his name S,	Gen 4.25
his image, and named him S.	5.3
son of S, the son of Adam,	Lk 3.38

SEVEN

march around the city s times,	Josh 6.4
S times a day I praise thee	Ps 119.164
s loaves of the four thousand,	Mt 16.10
forgive..As many as s times?"	18.21
there were s brothers among us;	22.25
Now there were s brothers;	Lk 20.29
who has the s spirits of God	Rev 3.1

SEVENFOLD

If Cain is avenged s,	Gen 4.24
chastise..s for your sins,	Lev 26.18
if..caught, he will pay s;	Prov 6.31

SEVENTH

s day God finished his work	Gen 2.2
the s day is a sabbath	Ex 20.10
God rested on the s day from	Heb 4.4

SEVENTY

shall serve..Babylon s years.	Jer 25.11
When s years are completed	29.10
of Jerusalem, namely, s years.	Dan 9.2
"S weeks of years are decreed	9.24
the Lord appointed s others,	Lk 10.1

SEVERE

famine was s in the land.	Gen 12.10
I may not have to be s in	2Cor 13.10

SEX

the woman as the weaker s,	1Pet 3.7

SHADOW

let the s go back ten steps."	2Ki 20.10
our days..are like a s,	1Chr 29.15
he flees like a s, and	Job 14.2
My days..like an evening s;	Ps 102.11

life,..he passes like a s?	Ecc 6.12
With..delight I sat in his s,	Sol 2.3
at least his s..fall on some	Acts 5.15
only a s of what is to come;	Col 2.17
since the law has but a s of	Heb 10.1

SHADRACH

Hananiah he called S, Mishael	Dan 1.7
and he appointed S, Meshach,	2.49
you..appointed..S, Meshach, and	3.12
S, Meshach, and Abednego, fell	3.23
Then the king promoted S,	3.30

SHAKE — S — N

go out..and s myself free."	Judg 16.20
and s the house of Israel	Amos 9.9
I will s the heavens and..earth	Hag 2.6
s off the dust from your feet	Mt 10.14
I will s not only the earth	Heb 12.26
voice of..LORD s..wilderness,	Ps 29.8
at..hand that I may not be s;	Acts 2.25
the place..was s; and they	4.31

SHAME

covered with s the faces	2Sam 19.5
he returned with s of face	2Chr 32.21
how long..my honor suffer s?	Ps 4.2
let me never be put to s;	31.1
Let me not be put to s, O LORD,	31.17
to s, for God has rejected them.	53.5
be wrapped in their own s as	109.29
Then I shall not be put to s,	119.6
when..neighbor puts you to s?	Prov 25.8
protection of Pharaoh..your s	Isa 30.3
you shall not be put to s	45.17
shall not be put to s."	49.23
I hid not my face from s and	50.6
forget the s of your youth,	54.4
Instead of..s..a double portion,	61.7
Bel is put to s, Merodach is	Jer 50.2
s is upon all faces, and	Ezek 7.18
will change their glory into s.	Hos 4.7
Ephraim shall be put to s,	10.6
never again be put to s.	Joel 2.26
and unwilling to put her to s,	Mt 1.19
his adversaries were put to s;	Lk 13.17
I say this to your s. Can it	1Cor 6.5
I say this to your s.	15.34
not shrink from him in s at	1Jn 2.28

SHARE

Gentiles have come to s in	Rom 15.27
who serve at the altar s in	1Cor 9.13
as you s in our sufferings,	2Cor 1.7
who is taught the word s all	Gal 6.6
and may s his sufferings,	Phil 3.10
s in..inheritance of..saints	Col 1.12
children s in flesh and blood,	Heb 2.14
do good and..s what you have,	13.16
as you s Christ's sufferings,	1Pet 4.13

SHARP

Your arrows are s in the heart	Ps 45.5
their tongue s as a serpent's,	140.3

SHATTER — S — ED — ING

God will s the heads..enemies	Ps 68.21
iron breaks to pieces and s	Dan 2.40
"We are s but we will rebuild	Mal 1.4
the s of the power of the holy	Dan 12.7

SHAVE — D

the Lord will s with a razor	Isa 7.20
They shall not s their heads	Ezek 44.20
that they may s their heads.	Acts 21.24
and s off half the beard	2Sam 10.4

SHEAVES
joy, bringing his *s* with him.   Ps 126.6

SHEBA
queen of *S* heard of the fame   1Ki 10.1
the kings of *S*..bring gifts!   Ps 72.10
frankincense..to me from *S*,   Jer 6.20

SHECHEM
their father's flock near *S*.   Gen 37.12
they could not live on at *S*.   Judg 9.41
they were carried back to *S*   Acts 7.16

SHED
hands did not *s* this blood,   Deut 21.7
Manasseh *s*..much innocent   2Ki 21.16

SHEEP
s which have no shepherd."   Num 27.17
David..who is with the *s*."   1Sam 16.19
took..from following the *s*,   2Sam 7.8
these *s*, what have they done?   24.17
as *s* that have no shepherd;   1Ki 22.17
s, what have they done?   1Chr 21.17
as *s* that have no shepherd;   2Chr 18.16
made us like *s* for slaughter,   Ps 44.11
accounted as *s* for..slaughter.   44.22
Like *s*..appointed for Sheol;   49.14
Why..anger smoke against the *s*   74.1
led forth his people like *s*,   78.52
pasture, and the *s* of his hand.   95.7
we are his people, and the *s*   100.3
gone astray like a lost *s*;   119.176
we like *s* have gone astray;   Isa 53.6
Pull them out like *s* for the   Jer 12.3
scatter the *s* of my pasture!"   23.1
"My people have been lost *s*;   50.6
my *s*, the *s* of my pasture,   Ezek 34.31
like *s* without a shepherd.   Mt 9.36
lost *s* of the house of Israel.   10.6
one *s* and it falls into a pit   12.11
as a shepherd separates the *s*   25.32
the *s*..will be scattered.'   26.31
and the *s* will be scattered.'   Mk 14.27
hundred *s*, if he has lost one   Lk 15.4
I lay down my life for the *s*.   Jn 10.15
My *s* hear my voice, and I know   10.27
He said to him, "Tend my *s*."   21.16
"As a *s* led to the slaughter   Acts 8.32
we are regarded as *s* to be   Rom 8.36
you were straying like *s*,   1Pet 2.25

SHEEPFOLD — S
who does not enter the *s* by   Jn 10.1
He chose David..from the *s*;   Ps 78.70

SHEET
descending, like a great *s*,   Acts 10.11

SHEKEL
according to the *s* of the   Ex 30.13
its mouth you will find a *s*;   Mt 17.27

SHELTER
For he will hide me in his *s*   Ps 27.5
who dwells in..*s* of..Most High,   91.1
s from the storm and a shade   Isa 25.4

SHEM
"Blessed by..God be *S*;   Gen 9.26

SHEOL
S is naked before God, and   Job 26.6
The wicked shall depart to *S*,   Ps 9.17
thou dost not give me up to *S*,   16.10
If I make my bed in *S*, thou   139.8
her steps follow..path to *S*;   Prov 5.5
Her house is the way to *S*,   7.27

S and Abaddon lie open   15.11
S has enlarged its appetite   Isa 5.14
S..is stirred up to meet you   14.9
with *S* we have an agreement;   28.15
and sent down even to *S*.   57.9
speak..out of..midst of *S*;   Ezek 32.21
S, where is your destruction?   Hos 13.14

SHEPHERD — S
as sheep which have no *s*."   Num 27.17
be *s* of my people Israel,   2Sam 5.2
LORD is my *s*, I shall not want;   Ps 23.1
Give ear, O *S* of Israel, thou   80.1
He will feed his flock like a *s*,   Isa 40.11
says of Cyrus, 'He is my *s*,   44.28
break..the *s* and his flock;   Jer 51.23
I will set up over them one *s*,   Ezek 34.23
S thy people with thy staff,   Mic 7.14
afflicted for want of a *s*.   Zech 10.2
I became the *s*..doomed to be slain   11.7
a *s* who does not care for   11.16
"Strike the *s*, that the sheep   13.7
helpless,..sheep without a *s*.   Mt 9.36
'I will strike the *s*, and   26.31
were like sheep without a *s*;   Mk 6.34
written, 'I will strike the *s*,   14.27
who enters by the door is the *s*   Jn 10.2
I am the good *s*. The good *s*   10.11
Jesus, the great *s* of the   Heb 13.20
the chief *S* is manifested   1Pet 5.4
the Lamb..will be their *s*,   Rev 7.17
and the men are *s*,   Gen 46.23
your children shall be *s*   Num 14.33
s also have no understanding;   Isa 56.11
brought..out of the sea the *s*   63.11
For the *s* are stupid, and do   Jer 10.21
Woe to the *s* who destroy and   23.1
"Wail, you *s*, and cry, and   25.34
prophesy against the *s* of   Ezek 34.2
s, hear the word of the LORD: 34.7
Amos, who was among the *s* of   Amos 1.1
Your *s* are asleep, O king   Nah 3.18
there were *s* out in the field,   Lk 2.8
the *s* returned, glorifying..God   2.20

SHIBBOLETH
"Then say *S*," and he said   Judg 12.6

SHIELD
my *s* and the horn of my   2Sam 22.3
thou, O LORD, art a *s* about me,   Ps 3.3
cover..with favor as with a *s*.   5.12
My *s* is with God, who saves   7.10
my *s*, and the horn of my   18.2
a *s* for all..who take refuge   18.30
given me the *s* of..salvation,   18.35
LORD is my strength and my *s*;   28.7
Take hold of *s* and buckler,   35.2
the LORD God is a sun and *s*;   84.11
For our *s* belongs to the LORD,   89.18
his faithfulness is a *s* and   91.4
He is their help and their *s*.   115.9
he is a *s* to those who walk   Prov 2.7
put a *s* about..Jerusalem   Zech 12.8
taking the *s* of faith, with   Eph 6.16

SHILOH
before the LORD in *S*."   Josh 18.8
to the LORD of hosts at *S*,   1Sam 1.3
in *S*, wearing an ephod.   14.3
He forsook his dwelling at *S*,   Ps 78.60
I will make this house like *S*,   Jer 26.6

SHINE — D
make his face to *s* upon you,   Num 6.25

SHINE — D (cont.)

light will *s* on your ways.   Job 22.28
man's wisdom makes his face *s*,   Ecc 8.1
those who are wise shall *s*   Dan 12.3
they shall *s* on his land.   Zech 9.16
Let your light so *s* before men,   Mt 5.16
righteous will *s* like the sun   13.43
you *s* as lights in the world,   Phil 2.15
darkness, on them has light *s*.   Isa 9.2

SHIP — S

way of a *s* on the high seas,   Prov 30.19
Jehoshaphat made *s* of   1Ki 22.48
There are the *s*, and Leviathan   Ps 104.26
went down to the sea in *s*,   107.23
shall go forth in *s*   Ezek 30.9*n*

SHIPWRECK — ED

have made *s* of their faith,   1Tim 1.19
Three times I have been *s*;   2Cor 11.25

SHOES

put off your *s* from your feet,   Ex 3.5
"Put off your *s* from your   Josh 5.15
his hand, and *s* on his feet;   Lk 15.22
'Take off the *s* from your   Acts 7.33

SHORTENED

hand *s*, that it cannot redeem?   Isa 50.2
if those days had not been *s*,   Mt 24.22
if the Lord had not *s* the days,   Mk 13.20

SHOUT — S

"*S*; for the Lord has given   Josh 6.16
S, and sing for joy, O..Zion,   Isa 12.6
The Lord..cries out, he *s*   42.13

SHOW — S — ED — N

"I pray thee, *s* me thy glory."   Ex 33.18
I will *s* them marvelous things.   Mic 7.15
go, *s* yourself to the priest,   Mt 8.4
"Lord, *s* us the Father, and   Jn 14.8
to *s* by what death he was to   21.19
to *s* God's righteousness,   Rom 3.25
But God *s* his love for us   5.8
God *s* no partiality)—those,   Gal 2.6
Lord *s* him all the land,   Deut 34.1
He..*s* you, O man, what is good;   Mic 6.8
he *s* them his hands and his   Lk 24.40*n*
but God has *s* me that I   Acts 10.28

SHOWERS

the *s* have been withheld, and   Jer 3.3
they shall be *s* of blessing.   Ezek 34.26
he will come to us as the *s*,   Hos 6.3
dew from the Lord, like *s*   Mic 5.7

SHUN

S immorality. Every other sin   1Cor 6.18
s the worship of idols.   10.14
you, man of God, *s* all this;   1Tim 6.11

SHUT

the Lord *s* him in.   Gen 7.16
he shall open, and none..*s*;   Isa 22.22
s the kingdom..against men;   Mt 23.13

SICK

Hezekiah became *s* and was   2Ki 20.1
were *s* through their sinful   Ps 107.17
Hope deferred..heart *s*,   Prov 13.12
tell him I am *s* with love.   Sol 5.8
The whole head is *s*, and the   Isa 1.5
my heart is *s* within me.   Jer 8.18
his mother-in-law lying *s*   Mt 8.14
physician, but those who are *s*.   9.12
any..*s* with various diseases   Lk 4.40
physician, but those who are *s*;   5.31

slave..*s*..at the point of death.   7.2
they even carried out the *s*   Acts 5.15
Is any among you *s*? Let him   Jas 5.14

SICKLE

shall not put a *s* to your   Deut 23.25
Put in the *s*, for the harvest   Joel 3.13
"Put in your *s*, and reap,   Rev 14.15

SICKNESS

take away from you all *s*;   Deut 7.15
'Shall I recover from this *s*?'   2Ki 8.8
vexation and *s* and resentment?   Ecc 5.17
wasting *s* among..warriors,   Isa 10.16
When Ephraim saw his *s*, and   Hos 5.13

SIDE

the Lord who was on our *s*,   Ps 124.1
one of..soldiers pierced his *s*   Jn 19.34

SIDON

father of *S*, his first-born,   Gen 10.15
had been done in Tyre and *S*,   Mt 11.21
to the district of Tyre and *S*.   15.21
Tyre and *S* a great multitude,   Mk 3.8
Elijah..sent to..the land of *S*,   Lk 4.26
The next day we put in at *S*;   Acts 27.3

SIDONIANS

the *S* call Hermon Sirion,   Deut 3.9
how they were far from the *S*   Judg 18.7
how to cut timber like the *S*."   1Ki 5.6
the abomination of the *S*,   2Ki 23.13

SIGH — ING

years come to an end like a *s*.   Ps 90.9
sorrow, and my years with *s*;   31.10

SIGHT

good in the *s* of all..people   1Sam 18.5
Better is the *s* of the eyes   Ecc 6.9
not only in the Lord's *s* but   2Cor 8.21

SIGN — S

"This is the *s* of the covenant   Gen 9.12
"or heed the first *s*,   Ex 4.8
a *s* between me and you   31.13
shall be a *s* to the people   Num 16.38
this may be a *s* among you,   Josh 4.6
show me a sign..who speakest   Judg 6.17
shall be the sign to you: 1Sam 2.34
the *s* that the Lord has   1Ki 13.3
"Ask a *s* of the Lord your God,   Isa 7.11
Lord himself will give you a *s*.   7.14
this shall be the *s* for you: 37.30
the *s* to you from the Lord,   38.7
a memorial,..an everlasting *s*   55.13
This shall be the *s* to you,   Jer 44.29
a *s* for the house of Israel.   Ezek 4.3
for I have made you a *s* for   12.6
make him a *s* and a byword   14.8
shall Ezekiel be to you a *s*;   24.24
no *s* shall be given..except   Mt 12.39
show them a *s* from heaven.   16.1
what will be the *s* of your coming   24.3
betrayer had given them a *s*,   26.48
Pharisees..seeking from him a *s*   Mk 8.11
what will be the *s* when these   13.4
betrayer had given them a *s*,   14.44
this will be a *s* for you: Lk 2.12
for a *s* that is spoken against   2.34
sought..a *s* from heaven.   11.16
it seeks a *s*, but no *s* shall   11.29
the *s* when this is about to   21.7
to see some *s* done by him.   23.8
"What *s* have you to show us   Jn 2.18
"John did no *s*, but everything   10.41

SIGN   151   SIN

SIGN — S (cont.)
notable *s* has been performed   Acts 4.16
circumcision as a *s* or seal   Rom 4.11
tongues. .a *s*. .for unbelievers,   1Cor 14.22
lights. .for *s* and for seasons   Gen 1.14
I and the children. .are *s* and   Isa 8.18
dismayed at. .*s* of the heavens   Jer 10.2
How great are his *s*, how mighty   Dan 4.3
interpret the *s* of the times.   Mt 16.3
false prophets will. .show *s*   Mk 13.22
these *s* will accompany those   16.17*n*
first of his *s*, Jesus did   Jn 2.11
believed. .when they saw the *s*   2.23
"Unless you see *s* and wonders   4.48
because they saw the *s* which   6.2
Now Jesus did many other *s*   20.30
many *s* and wonders were done   Acts 5.12
s and wonders God had done   15.12
Jews demand *s* and Greeks   1Cor 1.22
great *s*,. .making fire come   Rev 13.13
by the *s*. .it deceives those   13.14
demonic spirits, performing *s*,   16.14

SIGNAL
He will raise a *s* for a nation   Isa 5.26
On a bare hill raise a *s*,   13.2
a *s* is raised on the mountains,   18.3
"I will *s*. .and gather them in,   Zech 10.8

SIGNET
the *s* ring on my right hand,   Jer 22.24
king sealed it with his own *s*   Dan 6.17

SILAS
They sent Judas. .and *S*,   Acts 15.22
Paul chose *S* and departed,   15.40
they seized Paul and *S* and   16.19
persuaded,. .joined Paul and *S*;   17.4
When *S* and Timothy arrived   18.5

SILENCE
if you keep *s* at such a time   Est 4.14
O God, do not keep *s*; do not   Ps 83.1
all the earth keep *s* before him.   Hab 2.20
no one to interpret,. .keep *s*   1Cor 14.28
women. .keep *s* in the churches.   14.34
Let a woman learn in *s* with   1Tim 2.11
there was *s* in heaven for about   Rev 8.1

SILENT
But the people were *s* and   2Ki 18.36
commune. .on your beds, and be *s*.   Ps 4.4
I was dumb and *s*,. .to no avail;   39.2
a fool who keeps *s* is. .wise;   Prov 17.28
Be *s* before the Lord GOD!   Zeph 1.7
Be *s*, all flesh, before the   Zech 2.13
But Jesus was *s*. And the high   Mt 26.63
"Be *s*, and come out of him!"   Mk 1.25
you will be *s* and unable to   Lk 1.20

SILOAM
upon whom the tower in *S* fell   Lk 13.4
"Go, wash in the pool of *S*"   Jn 9.7

SILVANUS
preached among you, *S* and   2Cor 1.19
Paul, *S* and Timothy, To the   1Thess 1.1
By *S*, a faithful brother as   1Pet 5.12

SILVER
promises. .pure, *s* refined in   Ps 12.6
and my yield than choice *s*.   Prov 8.19
Your *s* has become dross, your   Isa 1.22
Refuse *s* they are called, for   Jer 6.30
The *s* is mine, and the gold   Hag 2.8
paid him thirty pieces of *s*;   Mt 26.15
brought back the. .pieces of *s*   27.3

ten *s* coins, if she loses one   Lk 15.8
Peter said, "I have no *s* and   Acts 3.6

SILVERSMITH
s,. .made it. .a graven image   Judg 17.4
Demetrius, a *s*, who made   Acts 19.24

SIMEON (Son of Jacob)
Born, Gen 29.33; detained as a hostage, Gen 42.24; his future predicted, Gen 49.5–7.

SIMEON (the Prophet)
name was *S*, and this man was   Lk 2.25
and *S* blessed them and said   2.34

SIMON
S the Cananaean, and Judas   Mt 10.4
Thaddaeus, and *S* the Cananaean,   Mk 3.18
and *S* the Zealot and Judas   Acts 1.13

SIMPLE
testimony. .making wise the *s*;   Ps 19.7
The LORD preserves the *s*;   116.6
imparts understanding to the *s*.   119.130
"How long, O *s* ones, will you   Prov 1.22
"Whoever is *s*,. .turn in here!"   9.4

SIN — S — NED — NING (v)
and so to *s* against the LORD   Deut 20.18
should *s* against the LORD   1Sam 12.23
"Let not the king *s* against   19.4
no man who does not *s*—   1Ki 8.46
"If they *s* against thee—   2Chr 6.36
If I *s*, what do I do to thee,   Job 7.20
If I *s*, thou dost mark me,   10.14
I might not *s* against thee.   Ps 119.11
If. .right eye causes you to *s*,   Mt 5.29
or your foot causes you to *s*,   18.8
causes. .who believe in me to *s*,   Mk 9.42
if your hand causes you to *s*,   9.43
cause one of. .little ones to *s*.   Lk 17.2
"See, you are well! *S* no more,   Jn 5.14
weak, you *s* against Christ.   1Cor 8.12
if we *s* deliberately after   Heb 10.26
writing. .that you may not *s*;   1Jn 2.1
If any one *s* unwittingly in   Lev 4.2
if a man *s* against the LORD,   1Sam 2.25
a righteous man. .who. .never *s*.   Ecc 7.20
"If your brother *s* against you,   Mt 18.15
if your brother *s*, rebuke him,   Lk 17.3
immoral man *s* against his own   1Cor 6.18
no one who *s* has either seen   1Jn 3.6
Pharaoh. .said. ."I have *s* this   Ex 9.27
"You have *s* a great sin.   32.30
done foolishly and have *s*.   Num 12.11
promised; for we have *s*."   14.40
"I have *s*, for I did not know   22.34
'We have *s* against the LORD;   Deut 1.41
you had *s* against the LORD   9.16
Israel has *s*; they have   Josh 7.11
"We have *s* against thee,   Judg 10.10
"We have *s* against the LORD."   1Sam 7.6
said to Samuel, "I have *s*;   15.24
I have not *s* against you,   24.11
"I have *s* against the LORD."   2Sam 12.13
David said. ."I have *s* greatly   24.10
Jeroboam. .*s* and. .made Israel   1Ki 14.16
Israel had *s* against the LORD   2Ki 17.7
David said to God, "I have *s*   1Chr 21.8
which we have *s* against thee.   Neh 1.6
'I *s*, and perverted what   Job 33.27
If you have *s*, what do you   35.6
they still *s*; despite. .wonders   Ps 78.32
LORD, against whom we have *s*,   Isa 42.24

SIN — S — NED — NING (v) (cont.)

because we. .s against the LORD. Jer 8.14
many, we have s against thee. 14.7
Jerusalem s grievously, Lam 1.8
Our fathers s, and are no more; 5.7
we have s and done wrong and Dan 9.5
you have s, O Israel; there Hos 10.9
because I have s against him, Mic 7.9
"I have s in betraying innocent Mt 27.4
"Father, I have s against. .you; Lk 15.18
who s, this man or his parents, Jn 9.2
All who have s without the law Rom 2.12
all have s and fall short 3.23
are s against the LORD, 1Sam 14.33

SIN — S — NING (n)

s is couching at the door; Gen 4.7
What is my s, that you 31.36
wickedness,. .s against God?" 39.9
Whoever curses his God. .s. Lev 24.15
your s will find you out. Num 32.23
put to death for his own s. Deut 24.16
the s of the young men was 1Sam 2.17
forgive the s of. .Israel, 1Ki 8.36
bring my s to remembrance, 17.18
besides the s. .he made Judah 2Ki 21.16
forgive the s of thy people 2Chr 6.25
shall die for his own s." 25.4
iniquity and search for my s, Job 10.6
Make me know. .and my s, 13.23
I acknowledged my s to thee, Ps 32.5
I confess. .I am sorry for my s. 38.18
caught in the toils of his s. Prov 5.22
say,. .I am pure from my s"? 20.9
The devising of folly is s, 24.9
Let not. .mouth lead you into s, Ecc 5.6
who draw s as with cart ropes, Isa 5.18
that they may add s to s; 30.1
"The s of Judah is written Jer 17.1
fruit of my body for the s of Mic 6.7
every s and blasphemy will be Mt 12.31
gather out. .all causes of s 13.41
takes away the s of the world! Jn 1.29
"Let him who is without s 8.7n
will seek me and die in your s; 8.21
Which of you convicts me of s? 8.46
they have no excuse for their s. 15.22
he will convince the world of s 16.8
do not hold this s against Acts 7.60
are under the power of s, Rom 3.9
as s came into the world 5.12
s will have no dominion over you, 6.14
the wages of s is death, 6.23
law, I should not have known s. 7.7
It was s, working death in me 7.13
not proceed from faith is s. 14.23
he made him. .who knew no s, 2Cor 5.21
consigned all things to s, Gal 3.22
As for those who persist in s, 1Tim 5.20
by the deceitfulness of s. Heb 3.13
In your struggle against s 12.4
He committed no s; no guile 1Pet 2.22
If we say we have no s, we 1Jn 1.8
and in him there is no s. 3.5
No one born of God commits s; 3.9
not a mortal s, he will ask, 5.16
plagues. .as many as your s. Lev 26.21
or woman commits any of. .s Num 5.6
they did not depart from the s 2Ki 13.6
Have you not s of your own 2Chr 28.10
Remember not. .s of my youth, Ps 25.7
deliver us, and forgive our s, 79.9
not deal. .according to our s, 103.10

cast. .my s behind thy back. Isa 38.17
you. .burdened me with your s, 43.24
to the house of Jacob their s. 58.1
was for the s of her prophets Lam 4.13
break off your s by practicing Dan 4.27
and how great are your s— Amos 5.12
save his people from their s." Mt 1.21
paralytic,. .your s are forgiven." Mk 2.5
all s will be forgiven. .men, 3.28
"Man, your s are forgiven Lk 5.20
If you forgive the s of any, Jn 20.23
wash away your s, calling Acts 22.16
you are still in your s. 1Cor 15.17
who gave himself for our s Gal 1.4
dead through. .trespasses and s Eph 2.1
remember their s. .no more." Heb 10.17
bore our s in his body on 1Pet 2.24
Christ also died for s once 3.18
tempted as we. .yet without s. Heb 4.15

SINAI

into the wilderness of S. Ex 19.1
LORD came down upon Mount S, 19.20
Moses came down from Mount S, 34.29
"The LORD came from S, and Deut 33.2
S quaked at. .presence of God, Ps 68.8
from Mount S, bearing children Gal 4.24

SINFUL

Ah, s nation, a people laden Isa 1.4
for I am a s man, O Lord." Lk 5.8

SING — S — ING

"Spring up, O well!—S Num 21.17
S to him, s praises to him, 1Chr 16.9
appointed those. .to s to 2Chr 20.21
caused the widow's heart to s Job 29.13
But I will s of thy might; Ps 59.16
s praises to the God of Jacob. 75.9
S aloud to God our strength; 81.1
I will s of thy steadfast love, 89.1
O come, let us s to the LORD; 95.1
S to the LORD, bless his name; 96.2
I will s and make melody! 108.1
"S praises to the LORD, for Isa 12.5
in the dust, awake and s for joy! 26.19
tongue of the dumb s for joy. 35.6
s to stringed instruments 38.20
S to the LORD a new song, 42.10
S, O heavens, for the LORD 44.23
together they s for joy; for 52.8
"S, O barren one, who did not 54.1
my servants. .s for gladness 65.14
S to the LORD; praise the Jer 20.13
S and rejoice, O daughter of Zech 2.10
Gentiles, and s to thy name"; Rom 15.9
I will s with the mind also. 1Cor 14.15
they s a new song before the Rev 14.3
righteous man s and rejoices. Prov 29.6
the time of s has come, and Sol 2.12
they break forth into s. Isa 14.7
exult over you with loud s Zeph 3.17
praying and s hymns to God, Acts 16.25

SINNER — S

to the s he gives the work Ecc 2.26
woman of the city, who was a s, Lk 7.37
more joy in heaven over one s 15.7
guest of a man who is a s." 19.7
can a man who is a s do such Jn 9.16
we know that this man is a s." 9.24
still being condemned as a s? Rom 3.7
whoever brings back a s from Jas 5.20
he instructs s in the way. Ps 25.8

SINNER — S (cont.)

s be consumed from the earth,	Ps 104.35	
Misfortune pursues s, but	Prov 13.21	
and to destroy its s from it.	Isa 13.9	
many tax collectors and s came	Mt 9.10	
not to call..righteous, but s."	9.13	
collectors and s were sitting	Mk 2.15	
not to call..righteous, but s."	2.17	
betrayed into the hands of s.	14.41	
For even s love those who love	Lk 6.32	
Even s lend to s, to receive	6.34	
these Galileans were worse s	13.2	
"This man receives s and eats	15.2	
by one..many were made s,	Rom 5.19	
ourselves were found to be s,	Gal 2.17	
but for the ungodly and s,	1Tim 1.9	

SIN OFFERING

fire outside the camp;..a s..	Ex 29.14	
bull without blemish..for a s..	Lev 4.3	
This is the law of the s...	6.25	

SISTER — S

Say you are my s,	Gen 12.13	
said of..his wife, "She is my s."	20.2	
about his wife.."She is my s";	26.7	
And his s stood at a distance,	Ex 2.4	
Say to wisdom, "You are my s,"	Prov 7.4	
You..ravished my heart, my s,	Sol 4.9	
a little s,..has no breasts.	8.8	
your s Sodom and..daughters	Ezek 16.48	
my brother, and s, and mother."	Mk 3.35	
the son of Paul's s heard	Acts 23.16	
accompanied by a s as wife,	1Cor 9.5n	
children of your elect s greet	2Jn 13	
treat..younger women like s,	1Tim 5.2	

SIT — TING

"S at my right hand, till I	Ps 110.1	
s in..company of merrymakers,	Jer 15.17	
s every man under his vine	Mic 4.4	
"Grant us to s, one at your	Mk 10.37	
said to my Lord, S at my right	12.36	
said to my Lord, S at my right	Lk 20.42	
my Lord, S at my right hand,	Acts 2.34	
I saw the Lord s upon a throne,	Isa 6.1	
Son of man s at the right hand	Mk 14.62	
like children s in the market	Lk 7.32	

SIXTH

from the s hour..was darkness	Mt 27.45	
In..s month the angel Gabriel	Lk 1.26	
to pray, about the s hour.	Acts 10.9	

SKILFUL

s in playing the lyre;	1Sam 16.16	
guided them with a s hand.	Ps 78.72	
see a man s in his work?	Prov 22.29	

SKIN — S

took bread and a s of water,	Gen 21.14	
"S for s! all..he will give for	Job 2.4	
my s hardens, then breaks out	7.5	
escaped by the s of my teeth.	19.20	
Can..Ethiopian change his s	Jer 13.23	
God made..garments of s,	Gen 3.21	
the wine will burst the s,	Mk 2.22	

SKIRT

spread your s over your	Ruth 3.9	
Saul laid hold upon the s	1Sam 15.27	
cut off the s of Saul's robe.	24.4	
and I spread my s over you,	Ezek 16.8	

SKULL

(..means the place of a s),	Mt 27.33	
(which means the place of a s).	Mk 15.22	

The S, there they crucified	Lk 23.33	
called the place of a s,	Jn 19.17	

SKY — IES

righteousness..from the s.	Ps 85.11	
interpret the..earth and s;	Lk 12.56	
the s vanished like a scroll	Rev 6.14	
the s roll up like a scroll.	Isa 34.4	

SLAIN

Nay, for thy sake we are s	Ps 44.22	
who had been s for the word	Rev 6.9	
book..of the Lamb that was s.	13.8	

SLANDER — S — ED

who does not s with his tongue,	Ps 15.3	
you s your own mother's son.	50.20	
Do not s a servant to his	Prov 30.10	
who s his neighbor secretly	Ps 101.5	
when s, we try to conciliate;	1Cor 4.13	

SLANDERER

not go up and down as a s	Lev 19.16	
s, haters of God, insolent,	Rom 1.30	

SLAUGHTER — ED

accounted as sheep for the s.	Ps 44.22	
gentle lamb led to the s.	Jer 11.19	
regarded as sheep to be s."	Rom 8.36	

SLAVE — S

"Cursed be Canaan; a s	Gen 9.25	
son of this s woman shall	21.10	
shall not treat her as a s,	Deut 21.14	
much less for a s to rule	Prov 19.10	
"Is Israel a s?..a homeborn	Jer 2.14	
first among you must be your s;	Mt 20.27	
first among you must be s	Mk 10.44	
struck the s of the high priest	14.47	
struck the s of the high priest	Lk 22.50	
who commits sin is a s to sin.	Jn 8.34	
Were you a s when called?	1Cor 7.21	
there is neither s nor free,	Gal 3.28	
child, is no better than a s,	4.1	
no longer as a s but more	Philem 16	
'We were Pharaoh's s in	Deut 6.21	
some of you shall always be s,	Josh 9.23	
I have seen s on horses, and	Ecc 10.7	
took back..s they had set free,	Jer 34.11	
S rule over us; there is none	Lam 5.8	
to any one as obedient s,	Rom 6.16	
we were s to the elemental spirits	Gal 4.3	
S, be obedient to..masters,	Eph 6.5	
S, obey..your earthly masters,	Col 3.22	
Bid s..be submissive to..masters	Tit 2.9	
they..are s of corruption;	2Pet 2.19	

SLAVERY

not receive..spirit of s to	Rom 8.15	
submit again to a yoke of s.	Gal 5.1	

SLAY

thou s an innocent people?	Gen 20.4	
"My father, shall I s them?	2Ki 6.21	
he will s me; I have no hope;	Job 13.15	
the Lord Jesus will s him	2Thess 2.8	

SLEEP — ING (v)

I lie down and s;..LORD sustains	Ps 3.5	
lighten my eyes, lest I s the s	13.3	
he..will neither slumber nor s.	121.4	
who s in the dust of the earth	Dan 12.2	
let us not s, as others do,	1Thess 5.6	
the girl is not dead but s."	Mt 9.24	
disciples and found them s;	26.40	
The child is not dead but s."	Mk 5.39	
And he came and found them s,	14.37	

SLEEP — ING (v) (cont.)
again he came and found them s, Mk 14.40
he..found them s for sorrow, Lk 22.45

SLEEP (n)
God caused a deep s Gen 2.21
deep s from the LORD had 1Sam 26.12
he gives to his beloved in s. Ps 127.2
I will not give s to my eyes 132.4
lie down,..s will be sweet. Prov 3.24
Give your eyes no s and your 6.4
little s, a little slumber, 24.33
Sweet is the s of a laborer, Ecc 5.12
upon you a spirit of deep s, Isa 29.10
swoon..and s a perpetual s Jer 51.39
I fell on my face in a deep s Dan 10.9
I go to awake him out of s." Jn 11.11

SLEPT
I s, but my heart was awake. Sol 5.2

SLIP — S — PED
when their foot shall s; Deut 32.35
Thou..and my feet did not s. Ps 18.36
his heart; his steps do not s. 37.31
who boast..when my foot s!" 38.16
thy paths, my feet have not s. 17.5

SLIPPERY
Let their way be dark and s, Ps 35.6
dost set them in s places; 73.18

SLOW
who is s to anger is better Prov 16.32
sense makes a man s to anger, 19.11

SLUGGARD
Go to the ant, O s; consider Prov 6.6
s craves, and gets nothing, 13.4
desire of the s kills him 21.25
The s says, "There is a lion 22.13
s buries his hand in the dish; 26.15
s is wiser in his own eyes 26.16

SLUMBER — S
he who keeps you will not s. Ps 121.3
A little sleep, a little s, Prov 6.10
none stumbles,..s or sleeps, Isa 5.27

SMALL — EST
I am of s account; what shall Job 40.4
mustard..is the s of all seeds, Mt 13.32

SMELLED
he s..his garments, Gen 27.27

SMELT
and will s away your dross Isa 1.25

SMITE
I will s all the first-born Ex 12.12
LORD..s you with the boils Deut 28.27
sun shall not s you by day, Ps 121.6

SMITH
no s to be found throughout 1Sam 13.19
I..created the s who blows Isa 54.16

SMITTEN
You have s Uriah the Hittite 2Sam 12.9
My heart is s like grass, and Ps 102.4
Why will you still be s, that Isa 1.5
yet we esteemed him..s by God, 53.4
Thou hast s them, but they felt Jer 5.3

SMOKE
the s of the land went up Gen 19.28
As s is driven away, so drive Ps 68.2
teeth, and s to the eyes, Prov 10.26
filled with s from the glory Rev 15.8

SMOOTH
adventuress with her s words, Prov 2.16
speak to us s things, prophesy Isa 30.10
rough ways shall be made s; Lk 3.5

SMOTE
LORD s all the first-born Ex 12.29
David's heart s him, because 1Sam 24.5
David's heart s him after 2Sam 24.10
as he s those who s them? Isa 27.7
I s you and all the products Hag 2.17

SNARE — S
will surely be a s to you." Ex 23.33
that would be a s to you. Deut 7.16
and their gods shall be a s Judg 2.3
and it became a s to Gideon 8.27
she may be a s for him, 1Sam 18.21
table before them become a s; Ps 69.22
his lips are a s to himself. Prov 18.7
entangle yourself in a s. 22.25
The fear of man lays a s, 29.25
I set a s for you..O Babylon, Jer 50.24
he shall be taken in my s; Ezek 12.13
upon you suddenly like a s; Lk 21.34
fall into..the s of the devil. 1Tim 3.7
Therefore s are round..you, Job 22.10
who seek my life lay their s, Ps 38.12
they talk of laying s secretly, 64.5
they..laid s for my feet. Jer 18.22

SNATCH — ING
those who s the fatherless Job 24.9
no one shall s them out of Jn 10.28
save some, by s them out of Jude 23

SNOW
slew a lion..when s had fallen. 2Sam 23.20
If I wash myself with s, Job 9.30
the storehouses of the s, 38.22
wash me,..I..be whiter than s. Ps 51.7
He gives s like wool; he 147.16
cold of s in the..harvest Prov 25.13
Like s in summer or rain in 26.1
She is not afraid of s for 31.21
they shall be as white as s; Isa 1.18
Does the s of Lebanon leave Jer 18.14
Her princes were purer than s, Lam 4.7
and his raiment white as s. Mt 28.3

SOBER
let us keep awake and be s. 1Thess 5.6
be s, set your hope fully 1Pet 1.13

SODOM
in the direction of S, Gen 10.19
men of S were wicked, 13.13
Lot..who dwelt in S, 14.12
LORD rained on S..brimstone 19.24
overthrew S and Gomorrah Jer 50.40
the land of S and Gomorrah Mt 10.15
the mighty works..done in S, 11.23
when Lot went out from S Lk 17.29
city..allegorically called S Rev 11.8

SOFT
A s answer turns away wrath, Prov 15.1
To see a man clothed in s Mt 11.8

SOILED
who have not s their garments; Rev 3.4

SOJOURN — S — ED
Abram went..to Egypt to s Gen 12.10
"This fellow came to s, 19.9
LORD, who shall s in thy tent? Ps 15.1
"When a stranger s with you Lev 19.33

SOJOURN — S — ED (cont.)
And if a stranger *s* among you, Num 9.14
Jacob *s* in the land of Ham.   Ps 105.23
By faith he *s* in the land   Heb 11.9

SOJOURNER — S
for the poor and for the *s*:   Lev 19.10
law for the *s* and for the native;   24.22
loves the *s*, giving him   Deut 10.18
Love the *s* therefore;   10.19
the justice due to the *s*   24.17
s has not lodged in the street; Job 31.32
I am thy passing guest, a *s*,   Ps 39.12
I am a *s* on earth; hide not   119.19
oppress. . the *s*, or the poor; Zech 7.10
The LORD watches over the *s*,   Ps 146.9

SOLD
For he has *s* us,   Gen 31.15
and *s* him to the Ishmaelites   37.28
Joseph. .*s* to the Egyptians,   41.56
Joseph, whom you *s* into Egypt.   45.4
not be *s* in perpetuity,   Lev 25.23
shall be *s* or redeemed;   27.28
he *s* them into the power of   Judg 2.14
none who *s* himself to do   1Ki 21.25
and *s* themselves to do evil   2Ki 17.17
For we are *s*, I and my people, Est 7.4
s thy people for a trifle,   Ps 44.12
Joseph, who was *s* as a slave   105.17
of lands or houses *s* them,   Acts 4.34
jealous of Joseph, *s* him into   7.9
I am carnal, *s* under sin.   Rom 7.14

SOLDIER — S
as a *s* at his own expense?   1Cor 9.7
gave a sum of money to the *s*   Mt 28.12
S. .asked. .what shall we do?" Lk 3.14
with *s* under me: and I say to   7.8
When the *s* had crucified Jesus Jn 19.23

SOLE
Every place on which the *s*   Deut 11.24
place that the *s* of your foot Josh 1.3

SOLID
fed. .with milk, not *s* food;   1Cor 3.2
You need milk, not *s* food;   Heb 5.12

SOLOMON — 'S
Born, 2Sam 12.24; anointed king, 1Ki
1.32–40; established his kingdom, 1Ki
2.12–46; married Pharaoh's daughter,
1Ki 3.1; asked for wisdom, 1Ki 3.5–15;
judged wisely, 1Ki 3.16–28; conferred with
Hiram, 1Ki 5; 7.13–14; built the temple,
1Ki 6; 7.15–51; built his own house,
1Ki 7.1–12; dedicated the temple, 1Ki 8;
the LORD's covenant with Solomon, 1Ki
9.1–9; visited by the queen of Sheba,
1Ki 10.1–13; turned from the LORD, 1Ki
11.1–40; died, 1Ki 11.41–43. (See also
2Chr 1–9.)

proverbs of *S*, son of David,   Prov 1.1
even *S* in all his glory was not Mt 6.29
came. .to hear the wisdom of *S*, Lk 11.31
something greater than *S* is here.   11.31
temple, in the portico of *S*.   Jn 10.23
The Song of Songs, which is *S*. Sol 1.1
in the portico called *S*,   Acts 3.11

SON — S
your wife shall have a *s*."   Gen 18.10
"Take your *s*, your only *s*   22.2

stubborn and rebellious *s*,   Deut 21.18
and he shall be my *s*.   2Sam 7.14
of you, O Absalom, my *s*,   18.33
no *s*, and her husband is old." 2Ki 4.14
when. .you shall embrace a *s*."   4.16
woman whose *s* he had restored   8.1
and he shall be my *s*;   1Chr 17.13
He said to me, "You are my *s*, Ps 2.7
My *s*, if you receive my words Prov 2.1
LORD reproves. .as a father the *s*   3.12
A wise *s* makes a glad father,   10.1
spares the rod hates his *s*,   13.24
A foolish *s* is a grief to his father 17.25
He. .is a *s* who causes shame   19.26
Hear, my *s*, and be wise,   23.19
My *s*, give me your heart,   23.26
Be wise, my *s*, and make my   27.11
Discipline your *s*, and he   29.17
and bear a *s*,. .Immanu-el.   Isa 7.14
to us a child is born,. .a *s* is given;   9.6
Is Ephraim my dear *s*? Is he   Jer 31.20
The *s* shall not suffer for   Ezek 18.20
no prophet, nor a prophet's *s*; Amos 7.14
s treats. .father with contempt, Mic 7.6
if his *s* asks him for bread,   Mt 7.9
"Have mercy on us, *S* of David."   9.27
"Can this be the *S* of David?"   12.23
Is not this the carpenter's *s*?   13.55
'They will respect my *s*.'   21.37
gave a marriage feast for his *s*,   22.2
said to him, "The *s* of David." 22.42
"Thou art my beloved *S*; with   Mk 1.11
my beloved *S*; listen to him."   9.7
"Teacher, I brought my *s* to you,   9.17
a beloved *s*;. .he sent them to them, 12.6
Christ, the *S* of the Blessed?"   14.61
bear a *s*, and you shall call   Lk 1.31
Elizabeth. .gave birth to a *s*.   1.57
his mother said to him, "*S*, why   2.48
being carried out, the only *s*   7.12
I beg you to look upon my *s*,   9.38
if his *s* asks for a fish, will   11.11
be divided, father against *s*   12.53
the *s* said to him, 'Father,   15.21
he also is a *s* of Abraham.   19.9
I will send my beloved *s*;   20.13
Lord; so how is he his *s*?"   20.44
glory as of the only *S* from   Jn 1.14
that he gave his only *S*,   3.16
to come down and heal his *s*,   4.47
So if the *S* makes you free,   8.36
this. .our *s*. .was born blind;   9.20
lost but the *s* of perdition,   17.12
"Woman, behold, your *s*!"   19.26
"You *s* of the devil, you   Acts 13.10
'Thou art my *S*, today I   13.33
pleased to reveal his *S* to me, Gal 1.16
God sent forth his *S*, born of   4.4
a *s*, and if a *s* then an heir.   4.7
the kingdom of his beloved *S*, Col 1.13
he has spoken to us by a *S*,   Heb 1.2
faithful over God's house as a *s*.   3.6
"Thou art my *S*, today I have   5.5
ready to offer up his only *s*,   11.17
"My *s*, do not regard lightly   12.5
and with his *S* Jesus Christ.   1Jn 1.3
No one who denies the *S* has   2.23
God sent his only *S* into the world, 4.9
sent his *S* as the Savior of   4.14
He who has the *S* has life;   5.12
the *s* of God saw. .daughters   Gen 6.2
if only your *s* take heed   2Chr 6.16
s are a heritage from the LORD, Ps 127.3

SON — S (cont.)

If your *s* keep my covenant	Ps 132.12
May our *s* in their youth be	144.12
Hear, O *s*,..instruction, and	Prov 4.1
delighting in the *s* of men.	8.31
"*S*..I reared and brought up,	Isa 1.2
a rebellious people, lying *s*,	30.9
your *s*..taught by the LORD,	54.13
Zion..brought forth her *s*.	66.8
wife, nor shall you have *s* or	Jer 16.2
s shall eat their fathers;	Ezek 5.10
them, "S of the living God."	Hos 1.10
peacemakers,..called *s* of God.	Mt 5.9
Jesus said..the *s* are free.	17.26
A man had two *s*; and he went	21.28
you will be *s* of the Most High;	Lk 6.35
wiser..than the *s* of light.	16.8
you may become *s* of light."	Jn 12.36
led by the Spirit..*s* of God.	Rom 8.14
men of faith..*s* of Abraham.	Gal 3.7
to be his *s* through Jesus	Eph 1.5
upon the *s* of disobedience.	Col 3.6n
you are all *s* of light and	1Thess 5.5

SONG — S

LORD is my strength and my *s*,	Ex 15.2
therefore write this *s*,	Deut 31.19
now I have become their *s*,	Job 30.9
with my *s* I give thanks to him.	Ps 28.7
Sing to him a new *s*, play	33.3
He put a new *s* in my mouth,	40.3
Raise a *s*, sound the timbrel,	81.2
LORD is my strength and my *s*;	118.14
sing a new *s* to thee, O God;	144.9
Sing to the LORD a new *s*, his	149.1
love *s* concerning his vineyard:	Isa 5.1
GOD is my strength and my *s*,	12.2
In that day this *s* will be sung	26.1
You shall have a *s* as in..night	30.29
they shall take up a taunt *s*	Mic 2.4
a new *s*, saying, "Worthy art	Rev 5.9
they sing the *s* of Moses,	15.3
my Maker, who gives *s* in	Job 35.10
the drunkards make *s* about me.	Ps 69.12
noise to him with *s* of praise!	95.2
Thy statutes have been my *s*	119.54
our captors required of us *s*,	137.3
who sings *s* to a heavy heart	Prov 25.20
I am the burden of their *s*.	Lam 3.63
like one who sings love *s*	Ezek 33.32

SON OF GOD

"If you are the *S*.., command	Mt 4.3
have you to do with us, O *S*..?	8.29
"Truly you are the *S*..."	14.33
tell us if you are..the *S*..."	26.63
If you are the *S*.., come down	27.40
said, "Truly this was the *S*...!	27.54
"Truly this man was the *S*..!"	Mk 15.39
will be called holy, the *S*...	Lk 1.35
witness that this is the *S*..."	Jn 1.34
not believed in..the only *S*...	3.18
because I said, 'I am the *S*..'?	10.36
he has made himself the *S*..."	19.7
saying, "He is the *S*..."	Acts 9.20
and designated *S*..in power	Rom 1.4
attain..knowledge of the *S*..,	Eph 4.13
high priest..Jesus, the *S*..,	Heb 4.14
since they crucify the *S*..on their	6.6
man who has spurned the *S*..,	10.29
confesses..Jesus the *S*..,	1Jn 4.15
words of the *S*.., who has eyes	Rev 2.18

SON OF MAN

s..that thou dost care for him?	Ps 8.4
"*S*.., stand upon your feet,	Ezek 2.1
"*S*.., I have made you a watchman	3.17
"*S*.., speak to..elders of Israel,	20.3
"*S*.., I have broken the arm	30.21
there came one like a *s*..,	Dan 7.13
but the *S*..has nowhere to lay	Mt 8.20
the *S*..has authority on earth	9.6
Israel, before the *S*..comes.	10.23
the *S*..is lord of the sabbath."	12.8
word against the *S*..forgiven;	12.32
sows the good seed is the *S*..	13.37
S..is to come with his angels	16.27
"The *S*..is to be delivered	17.22
so will be the coming of the *S*...	24.27
the sign of the *S*..in heaven,	24.30
"When the *S*..comes in his glory,	25.31
and the *S*..will be delivered up	26.2
The *S*..goes as it is written	26.24
hereafter you will see the *S*..	26.64
S..has authority..to forgive	Mk 2.10
"The *S*..will be delivered into	9.31
the *S*..goes as it is written	14.21
you will see the *S*..sitting	14.62
"The *S*..is lord of the sabbath."	Lk 6.5
"The *S*..must suffer many things,	9.22
S..delivered into the hands of	9.44
the *S*..seated at the right hand	22.69
descended from heaven, the *S*...	Jn 3.13
so must the *S*..be lifted up,	3.14
heavens opened, and the *S*..	Acts 7.56
..midst of..lampstands..a *s*..	Rev 1.13
on the cloud one like a *s*..,	14.14

SONSHIP

received the spirit of *s*.	Rom 8.15
Israelites,..to them belong the *s*,	9.4

SONS OF GOD

when the *s*..came to present	Job 1.6
all the *s*..shouted for joy?	38.7
you are all *s*..,through faith.	Gal 3.26

SORCERESS

not permit a *s* to live.	Ex 22.18

SORROW — S

How long must I..have *s* in my	Ps 13.2
For my life is spent with *s*,	31.10
My soul melts away for *s*;	119.28
knowledge increases *s*	Ecc 1.18
S is better than laughter,	7.3
and *s* and sighing shall flee	Isa 35.10
and *s* and sighing shall flee	51.11
from..womb to see toil and *s*,	Jer 20.18
LORD has added *s* to my pain;	45.3
if there is any *s* like my *s*	Lam 1.12
with drunkenness and *s*.	Ezek 23.33
you, *s* has filled your hearts.	Jn 16.6
your *s* will turn into joy.	16.20
I have great *s* and unceasing	Rom 9.2
overwhelmed by excessive *s*.	2Cor 2.7
another god multiply their *s*;	Ps 16.4
man of *s*,..acquainted with grief;	Isa 53.3

SORROWFUL

s; for he had great possessions.	Mk 10.22
"My soul is very *s*, even to death;	14.34
as *s*, yet always rejoicing;	2Cor 6.10

SORRY

LORD was *s*..he had made man	Gen 6.6
I confess..I am *s* for my sin.	Ps 38.18
And the king was *s*; but because	Mt 14.9

SOSTHENES
S,..ruler of the synagogue,   Acts 18.17
Paul,..and our brother *S*,   1Cor 1.1

SOUGHT
Preacher *s*..pleasing words,   Ecc 12.10
I *s* him whom my soul loves;   Sol 3.1
they have *s* and worshiped;   Jer 8.2
I *s* for a man among them   Ezek 22.30

SOUL — S
idols;..my *s* will abhor you.   Lev 26.30
keep your *s* diligently,   Deut 4.9
the *s* of Jonathan was knit   1Sam 18.1
in the bitterness of my *s*.   Job 7.11
my *s* is poured out within me;   30.16
still waters; he restores my *s*.   Ps 23.3
Why are you cast down, O my *s*,   42.11
delivered my *s* from death,   56.13
Bless the LORD, O my *s*; and   103.1
The *s* of the wicked desires   Prov 21.10
the *s* is torn by trouble.   27.9
Tell me, you whom my *s* loves,   Sol 1.7
appointed feasts my *s* hates;   Isa 1.14
my *s* will weep in secret for   Jer 13.17
I will satisfy the weary *s*,   31.25
the *s* that sins shall die.   Ezek 18.4
body for the sin of my *s*?"   Mic 6.7
he whose *s* is not upright in   Hab 2.4
body but cannot kill the *s*;   Mt 10.28
heart, and with all your *s*,   22.37
heart, and with all your *s*,   Mk 12.30
"My *s* is very sorrowful, even   14.34
Mary said, "My *s* magnifies   Lk 1.46
S, you have ample goods laid up   12.19
thou wilt not abandon my *s*   Acts 2.27
that it is well with your *s*.   3Jn 2
fruit for which thy *s* longed   Rev 18.14
you hunt down *s* belonging   Ezek 13.18
Having purified your *s* by   1Pet 1.22
slaves, that is, human *s*.   Rev 18.13
I saw the *s* of those..beheaded   20.4

SOUND — NESS
they heard the *s* of the LORD   Gen 3.8
wings like the *s* of..waters,   Ezek 1.24
the *s* of the day of the LORD   Zeph 1.14
when your eye is *s*, your..body   Lk 11.34
Follow..pattern of..*s* words   2Tim 1.13
sensible, *s* in faith, in love,   Tit 2.2
s speech that cannot be censured,   2.8
There is no *s* in my flesh   Ps 38.3
to the head, there is no *s*   Isa 1.6

SOW — S — ED — N
you shall *s* the land.   Gen 47.23
s fields,..plant vineyards,   Ps 107.37
who *s* in tears reap with..joy!   126.5
observes the wind will not *s*;   Ecc 11.4
you who *s* beside all waters,   Isa 32.20
ground, and *s* not among thorns.   Jer 4.3
I will *s* the house of Israel   31.27
For they *s* the wind, and..reap   Hos 8.7
S for yourselves righteousness,   10.12
You shall *s*, but not reap;   Mic 6.15
birds..neither *s* nor reap nor   Mt 6.26
'Sir, did you not *s* good seed   13.27
"Listen! A sower went out to *s*.   Mk 4.3
ravens: they neither *s* nor reap,   Lk 12.24
What you *s* does not come to   1Cor 15.36
who *s* discord among brothers.   Prov 6.19
He who *s* injustice..reap calamity   22.8
true, 'One *s* and another reaps."   Jn 4.37
he who *s* sparingly will..reap   2Cor 9.6

whatever a man *s*,..also reap.   Gal 6.7
Isaac *s* in that land,   Gen 26.12
I reap where I have not *s*,   Mt 25.26
have *s* wheat..reaped thorns,   Jer 12.13
if we have *s* spiritual good   1Cor 9.11

SOWER
saying: "A *s* went out to sow.   Mt 13.3
"Hear..the parable of the *s*.   13.18
The *s* sows the word.   Mk 4.14
"A *s* went out to sow his seed;   Lk 8.5

SPAIN
as I go to *S*, and to be sped   Rom 15.24
go on by way of you to *S*;   15.28

SPAN
add one cubit to his *s* of life?   Mt 6.27
can add..to his *s* of life?   Lk 12.25

SPARE — S — D
your power; only *s* his life."   Job 2.6
thy steadfast love *s* my life,   Ps 119.88
not *s* when he takes revenge.   Prov 6.34
He who did not *s* his own Son   Rom 8.32
who *s* the rod hates his son,   Prov 13.24
Saul and the people *s* Agag,   1Sam 15.9
some bade me kill you, but I *s*   24.10
king *s* Mephibosheth, the son   2Sam 21.7
that the wicked man is *s* in   Job 21.30

SPARROW — S
Even the *s* finds a home, and   Ps 84.3
Are not two *s* for a penny?   Mt 10.29
five *s* sold for two pennies?   Lk 12.6

SPAT
they *s* in his face and struck   Mt 26.67
he *s* and touched his tongue;   Mk 7.33
they struck..and *s* upon him,   15.19

SPEAK — S — ING
let not God *s* to us, lest we die."   Ex 20.19
I will *s* with you of all that   25.22
the LORD would *s* with Moses.   33.9
went into..to *s* with the LORD,   Num 7.89
With him I *s* mouth to mouth,   12.8
we have this day seen God *s*   Deut 5.24
'*S*, LORD, for thy servant   1Sam 3.9
says to me, that I will *s*."   1Ki 22.14
God says, that I will *s*."   2Chr 18.13
he will *s* peace to his people,   Ps 85.8
keep silence, and a time to *s*;   Ecc 3.7
S tenderly to Jerusalem, and   Isa 40.2
I do not know how to *s*, for   Jer 1.6
wilderness,...*s* tenderly to her.   Hos 2.14
he..would not allow them to *s*,   Lk 4.41
began to *s* in other tongues,   Acts 2.4
not to *s* in the name of Jesus,   5.40
For God *s* in one way, and   Job 33.14
LORD, and summons the earth   Ps 50.1
who *s* a word against the Son   Lk 12.10
that *s* evil against a brother   Jas 4.11
through his faith he is still *s*.   Heb 11.4

SPEAR — S
with one stroke of the *s*,   1Sam 26.8
pierced his side with a *s*,   Jn 19.34
their *s* into pruning hooks;   Isa 2.4

SPECK
see the *s*..in your brother's eye,   Mt 7.3
s that is in your brother's eye,   Lk 6.41

SPEECH
but I am slow of *s* and   Ex 4.10
Day to day pours forth *s*, and   Ps 19.2
Fine *s*..not becoming to a fool;   Prov 17.7

SPEECH (cont.)

not. .to a people of foreign s	Ezek 3.5
change the s. .to a pure s,	Zeph 3.9
enriched in him with all s	1Cor 1.5
and his s of no account."	2Cor 10.10
Let your s always be gracious,	Col 4.6

SPEECHLESS

wedding garment?'. .he was s.	Mt 22.12
The men. .with him stood s,	Acts 9.7

SPEND — T

we will s. .night in. .street."	Gen 19.2
our money is all s;	47.18
I am utterly s and crushed; I	Ps 38.8

SPEW

I will s you out of my mouth.	Rev 3.16

SPICE — S

fragrance of. .oils than. .s!	Sol 4.10
in linen cloths with the s,	Jn 19.40

SPIES (n)

took us to be s of the land.	Gen 42.30
secretly from Shittim as s,	Josh 2.1
men who had been s went in,	6.23
And the s saw a man coming	Judg 1.24

SPIRIT — S

"My s shall not abide. .for ever,	Gen 6.3
some of the s which is upon	Num 11.17
put his s upon them!"	11.29
a man in whom is the s,	27.18
God sent an evil s between	Judg 9.23
an evil s from the LORD came	1Sam 19.9
"Divine for me by a s, and	28.8
a s came forward and stood	1Ki 22.21
"The s of Elijah rests on	2Ki 2.15
with you in s when the man	5.26
gavest thy good S to instruct	Neh 9.20
you turn your s against God,	Job 15.13
But it is the s in a man,	32.8
and saves the crushed in s.	Ps 34.18
I meditate, and my s faints.	77.3
s was not faithful to God.	78.8
When thou sendest forth thy S,	104.30
for they made his s bitter,	106.33
Whither shall I go from thy S?	139.7
my s is faint, thou knowest	142.3
thy good s lead me on a level	143.10
but the LORD weighs the s.	Prov 16.2
downcast s dries up the bones.	17.22
A man's s will endure. .but	18.14
The s of man is the lamp	20.27
Who knows whether the s of man	Ecc 3.21
No man has power to retain. .s,	8.8
do not know how the s comes	11.5
and the s returns to God who	12.7
a s of judgment and. .burning.	Isa 4.4
until the S is poured upon us	32.15
I have put my S upon him,	42.1
my S upon your descendants,	44.3
wherever the s would go, they	Ezek 1.12
the s. .was in the wheels.	1.20
S lifted me up between earth	8.3
the s of the living creatures	10.17
I will put my s within you,	36.27
I will put my S within you,	37.14
in whom is the s of. .holy gods –	Dan 4.8
in whom is the s of the holy gods.	5.11
pour out my s on all flesh;	Joel 2.28
S abides among you; fear not.	Hag 2.5
nor by power, but by my S,	Zech 4.6
formed the s of man within him:	12.1

Jesus was led up by the S into	Mt 4.1
"Blessed are the poor in s,	5.3
the S of your Father speaking	10.20
I will put my S upon him,	12.18
s. .is willing,. .flesh is weak."	26.41
voice and yielded up his s.	27.50
a man with an unclean s;	Mk 1.23
the s indeed is willing, but	14.38
my s rejoices in God my Savior,	Lk 1.47
And Jesus. .was led by the S	4.1
supposed that they saw a s.	24.37
which is born of the S is s.	Jn 3.6
not by measure. .he gives the S;	3.34
words. .I have spoken. .are s	6.63
I will pour out my S upon all	Acts 2.17
to Jerusalem, bound in the S,	20.22
according to the S of holiness	Rom 1.4
law of the S of life in Christ	8.2
not. .flesh but according to the S.	8.4
who live according to the S	8.5
to set the mind on S is life	8.6
by the power of the Holy S,	15.19
revealed to us through the S.	1Cor 2.10
that God's S dwells in you?	3.16
by one S we were all baptized	12.13
given us his S in our hearts	2Cor 1.22
God has sent the S of his Son	Gal 4.6
who sows to the S will from	6.8
sealed with the promised. .S,	Eph 1.13
but be filled with the S,	5.18
who worship God in s, and	Phil 3.3
Do not quench the S,	1Thess 5.19
did not give us a s of timidity	2Tim 1.7
through the eternal S offered	Heb 9.14
body apart from the s is dead,	Jas 2.26
yearns jealously over the s	4.5
by the S which he has given us.	1Jn 3.24
the S, the water, and the blood;	5.8
let him hear what the S says	Rev 2.7
The S and the Bride say,	22.17
he commands the unclean s,	Lk 4.36
Are they not all ministering s	Heb 1.14
him who has the seven s of God	Rev 3.1
fire, which are the seven s of God;	4.5

SPIRIT OF GOD

S. .was moving over. .the waters	Gen 1.2
man. .in whom is the S. .?"	41.38
filled him with the S..,	Ex 31.3
And the S.. .came upon him,	Num 24.2
s. .came mightily upon Saul	1Sam 11.6
S. .came upon the messengers	19.20
The S. .came upon Azariah	2Chr 15.1
the S. .took possession of	24.20
the s. .is in my nostrils;	Job 27.3
The s. .has made me, and	33.4
all. .led by the S. .are sons	Rom 8.14
By this you know the S..	1Jn 4.2

SPIRIT OF THE LORD

The S. .came upon him, and he	Judg 3.10
the S. .took possession of Gideon;	6.34
the S. .came upon Jephthah,	11.29
the S. .began to stir him	13.25
the S. .came mightily upon him	15.14
the S. .came mightily upon	1Sam 16.13
the S. .will carry you whither	1Ki 18.12
"How did the S. .go from me	22.24
the S. .came upon Jahaziel	2Chr 20.14
the S. .shall rest upon him,	Isa 11.2
Who has directed the S..,	40.13
And the S. .fell upon me, and	Ezek 11.5
Is the S. .impatient? Are these	Mic 2.7

SPIRIT OF THE LORD (cont.)
"The *S.* .is upon me, because he   Lk 4.18
together to tempt the *S.* .?   Acts 5.9
where the *S.* .is,. .is freedom.   2Cor 3.17

SPIRITUAL
circumcison is. .*s.* .not literal.   Rom 2.29
We know that the law is *s*;   7.14
Spirit, interpreting *s* truths   1Cor 2.13
I. .could not address you as *s*   3.1
concerning *s* gifts, brethren,   12.1
there is also a *s* body.   15.44
who are *s* should restore him   Gal 6.1

SPIT
and *s* in his face;. .and say   Deut 25.9
some began to *s* on him, and   Mk 14.65

SPLENDOR
your beauty. .through the *s*   Ezek 16.14
The latter *s* of this house   Hag 2.9
permanent must have. .more *s.*   2Cor 3.11

SPOIL — S
and our enemies have gotten *s.*   Ps 44.10
like one who finds great *s.*   119.162
they got no *s* of silver.   Judg 5.19

SPOKE — N
God *s* all these words,   Ex 20.1
in the cloud and *s* to him,   Num 11.25
LORD *s* with you face to face   Deut 5.4
Jesus *s* to him first, saying,   Mt 17.25
"No man ever *s* like this man!"   Jn 7.46
Glorious things are *s* of. .city   Ps 87.3

SPOKESMAN
elders and a *s*,. .Tertullus.   Acts 24.1

SPREAD — S
Philistines had come and *s*   2Sam 5.18
letter. .*s* it before the LORD.   2Ki 19.14
I *s* out my hands to thee.   Ps 88.9
I *s* out my hands all the day   Isa 65.2
and I *s* my skirt over you,   Ezek 16.8
crowd *s*. .garments on the road.   Mt 21.8
many *s*. .garments on the road,   Mk 11.8
they *s*. .garments on the road.   Lk 19.36
flatters his neighbor *s* a net   Prov 29.5

SPRING — S
his *s* shall be parched; it   Hos 13.15
Does a *s* pour forth. .fresh   Jas 3.11
give me also *s* of water."   Josh 15.19
Thou makest *s* gush forth in   Ps 104.10
These are waterless *s* and   2Pet 2.17

SPROUT
the rod of the man. .shall *s*;   Num 17.5
the wicked *s* like grass   Ps 92.7

SPURN — S — ED
if you *s* my statutes, and if   Lev 26.15
is not good; he *s* not evil.   Ps 36.4
who has *s* the Son of God,   Heb 10.29

SPY — IED (v)
"Send men to *s* out the land   Num 13.2
to *s* out the land of Canaan,   13.17
to overthrow and to *s* out   1Chr 19.3
s out our freedom which we have   Gal 2.4
and *s* out the land from. .Zin   Num 13.21

SQUANDERED
he *s* his property in loose   Lk 15.13

SQUANDERS
with harlots *s* his substance.   Prov 29.3

STABILITY
a king gives *s* to the land,   Prov 29.4
he will be. .*s* of your times,   Isa 33.6

STAFF
who bear the marshal's *s*;   Judg 5.14
lay my *s* upon the face of   2Ki 4.29
nothing for. .journey except a *s*;   Mk 6.8

STAGGER — ED
makes them *s* like a drunken   Job 12.25
and *s* like drunken men, and   Ps 107.27

STALLS
four thousand *s* for horses   2Chr 9.25

STAMMERING
s in a tongue. .you cannot   Isa 33.19

STAND — S — ING
able to *s* against you,   Deut 7.24
s before the LORD to minister   10.8
"You *s* this day all of you   29.10
made all. .present. .*s* to it.   2Chr 34.32
none can *s* before thee   Ezra 9.15
boastful may not *s* before thy   Ps 5.5
mark iniquities,. .who could *s*?   130.3
you that *s* in. .house of. .LORD,   135.2
I. .purposed, so shall it *s*,   Isa 14.24
"*S* by the roads, and look,   Jer 6.16
"Son of man, *s* upon your feet,   Ezek 2.1
to *s* before the Son of man."   Lk 21.36
Be watchful, *s* firm in your   1Cor 16.13
set us free; *s* fast therefore,   Gal 5.1
S therefore, having girded   Eph 6.14
s firm thus in the Lord,   Phil 4.1
if you *s* fast in the Lord.   1Thess 3.8
grace of God; *s* fast in it.   1Pet 5.12
who thinks that he *s*. .heed   1Cor 10.12
But God's firm foundation *s*,   2Tim 2.19
Son of man *s* at the right   Acts 7.56

STANDARD
shall encamp each by his own *s*,   Num 2.2
The *s* of the camp of the men   10.14
his officers desert the *s*   Isa 31.9
Raise a *s* toward Zion, flee   Jer 4.6

STAR — S
a *s* shall come forth out of   Num 24.17
fallen from heaven, O Day *S*,   Isa 14.12
we have seen his *s* in the East,   Mt 2.2
the morning *s* rises in your   2Pet 1.19
a great *s* fell from heaven,   Rev 8.10
I am. .the bright morning *s*."   22.16
he made the *s* also.   Gen 1.16
Look. .and number the *s*,   15.5
multiply. .descendants as the *s*   22.17
s of heaven for multitude.   Deut 1.10
has made you as the *s*   10.22
Whereas you were as the *s*   28.62
From heaven fought the *s*,   Judg 5.20
Israel as many as the *s* of   1Chr 27.23
we labored. .till the *s* came   Neh 4.21
the morning *s* sang together,   Job 38.7
He determines. .number of. .*s*,   Ps 147.4
host of the *s* it cast down   Dan 8.10
shine. .like the *s* for ever   12.3
descendants as many as the *s*   Heb 11.12
right hand he held seven *s*,   Rev 1.16

STATE
last *s*. .worse than the first.   Mt 12.45
last *s* of. .man becomes worse   Lk 11.26
should remain in the *s* in   1Cor 7.20

STATURE
increased in wisdom and in *s*,   Lk 2.52

STATUTE — S
for a *s* and ordinance to you Num 35.29
therefore keep my *s* and my Lev 18.5
I will meditate on thy *s*. Ps 119.48
and not walking in my *s*. Ezek 5.6

STAY — ING
and *s* themselves on the God Isa 48.2
s with him until you depart. Mt 10.11
I must *s* at your house today." Lk 19.5
Teacher), where are you *s*?" Jn 1.38
while *s* with them he charged Acts 1.4

STEADFAST — NESS
My heart is *s*, O God, my heart Ps 57.7
brethren, be *s*, immovable, 1Cor 15.58
for our instruction, that by *s* Rom 15.4
love of God and..*s* of Christ. 2Thess 3.5
testing of..faith produces *s*. Jas 1.3
and self-control with *s*, and 2Pet 1.6

STEADFAST LOVE
show *s*..to my master Abraham Gen 24.12
I am not worthy of..all the *s*.. 32.10
the LORD..showed him *s*.., 39.21
LORD..keeping *s*..for thousands, Ex 34.7
for his *s*..endures for ever! 1Chr 16.34
for his *s*..endures for ever." 2Chr 7.3
who extended to me his *s*.. Ezra 7.28
Wondrously show thy *s*.., Ps 17.7
mercy, O LORD, and of thy *s*.., 25.6
according to thy *s*..remember me, 25.7
For thy *s*..is before my eyes, 26.3
How precious is thy *s*.., O God! 36.7
I have not concealed thy *s*.. 40.10
thy *s*..is better than life, 63.3
Answer me..for thy *s*..is good; 69.16
Has his *s*..for ever ceased? 77.8
S..and faithfulness will meet; 85.10
thy *s*..was established for ever, 89.2
declare thy *s*..in the morning, 92.2
his *s*..endures for ever. 100.5
s..of the LORD is..everlasting 103.17
thank the LORD for his *s*.., 107.8
consider the *s*..of the LORD. 107.43
his *s*..endures for ever. 118.1
in thy *s*..spare my life, 119.88
for his *s*..endures for ever. 136.1
recount the *s*..of the LORD, Isa 63.7
taken away..my *s*..and mercy. Jer 16.5
s..of the LORD never ceases, Lam 3.22
I desire *s*..and not sacrifice, Hos 6.6

STEAL — S
why did you *s* my gods?" Gen 31.30
"You shall not *s*. Ex 20.15
" 'Neither shall you *s*. Deut 5.19
Will you *s*, murder, commit Jer 7.9
thieves do not break in and *s*. Mt 6.20
You shall not *s*, You shall not 19.18
Let the thief no longer *s*, Eph 4.28
"If a man *s* an ox or a sheep, Ex 22.1
he *s* to satisfy his appetite Prov 6.30

STEEP
herd rushed down the *s* bank Mt 8.32

STEP — S
a *s* between me and death." 1Sam 20.3
shadow..or go back ten *s*?" 2Ki 20.9
thou wouldest number my *s*, Job 14.16
His strong *s* are shortened 18.7
ways and number all my *s*? 31.4
wide place for my *s* under me, Ps 18.36
The *s* of a man..from the LORD, 37.23
nor have our *s* departed from 44.18

my *s* had well nigh slipped. 73.2
Keep steady my *s* according 119.133
but the LORD directs his *s*. Prov 16.9
man's *s* are ordered by the LORD; 20.24
dial of Ahaz turn back ten *s*." Isa 38.7
not in man..to direct his *s*. Jer 10.23
Men dogged our *s* so that we Lam 4.18
Did we not take the same *s*? 2Cor 12.18

STEPHEN
they chose *S*, a man full of Acts 6.5
arose and disputed with *S*. 6.9
as they were stoning *S*, he 7.59
Devout men buried *S*, and made 8.2
persecution..arose over *S* 11.19
the blood of *S* thy witness 22.20

STEWARD — S
of the vineyard said to his *s*, Mt 20.8
is the faithful and wise *s*, Lk 12.42
a rich man who had a *s*, 16.1
and *s* of the mysteries of God. 1Cor 4.1

STEWARDSHIP
Turn in the account of your *s*, Lk 16.2
s of God's grace that was given Eph 3.2

STICK — S
take a *s* and write on it, Ezek 37.16
gathering *s* on the sabbath Num 15.32
there is a friend who *s* closer Prov 18.24

STIFF-NECKED
for you are a *s* people." Ex 33.3
Do not now be *s* as your 2Chr 30.8
"You *s* people, uncircumcised Acts 7.51

STILL
And the sun stood *s*, and Josh 10.13
after the fire a *s* small voice. 1Ki 19.12
Be *s* before the LORD, and wait Ps 37.7
"Be *s*, and know that I am God. 46.10
he made the storm be *s*, and 107.29

STING — S
O death, where is thy *s*?" 1Cor 15.55
tails like scorpions, and *s*, Rev 9.10

STIR — S — RED
s up one another to love and Heb 10.24
A greedy man *s* up strife, Prov 28.25
"He *s* up the people, teaching Lk 23.5
every one whose heart *s* him, Ex 35.21
LORD *s* up..spirit of Cyrus 2Chr 36.22
the LORD *s* up the spirit of Hag 1.14
they *s* up the people and the Acts 6.12
your zeal..*s* up most of them. 2Cor 9.2

STOCKS
puttest my feet in the *s*, Job 13.27
prophet, and put him in the *s* Jer 20.2
fastened their feet in the *s*. Acts 16.24

STOLE — N
Absalom *s* the hearts of the 2Sam 15.6
have men of Judah *s* you away, 19.41

STOMACH
into..mouth passes into..*s*, Mt 15.17
enters, not his heart but..*s*, Mk 7.19
for the *s* and the *s* for food" 1Cor 6.13
wine for the sake of your *s* 1Tim 5.23

STONE — D — ING (v)
let all the congregation *s* Lev 24.14
congregation said to *s* them Num 14.10
You shall *s* him to death Deut 13.10
city shall *s* him to death, 21.21
Moses commanded us to *s* such. Jn 8.5*n*

STONE — D — ING (v) (cont.)

Jews took up stones again to s | Jn 10.31
congregation..s him to death | Num 15.36
And all Israel s him with | Josh 7.25
out of the city and s him; | Acts 7.58
with rods; once I was s. | 2Cor 11.25
killing the prophets and s | Mt 23.37

STONE — S — ING (n)

wrote..upon two tables of s, | Deut 5.22
'Hew two tables of s like the first, | 10.1
he took a great s, and set | Josh 24.26
The great s, beside which | 1Sam 6.18
Samuel took a s and set it up | 7.12
him, and he became as a s. | 25.37
The s..the builders rejected | Ps 118.22
s is heavy,..sand is weighty, | Prov 27.3
a foundation a s, a tested s, | Isa 28.16
to a s, 'You gave me birth.' | Jer 2.27
the s that struck the image | Dan 2.35
s will cry out from the well, | Hab 2.11
for bread, will give him a s? | Mt 7.9
s which the builders rejected | 21.42
who falls on this s will be | 21.44n
not be left here one s upon | 24.2
sealing the s and setting a guard. | 27.66
s which the builders rejected | Mk 12.10
will not be left here one s | 13.2
saw that the s was rolled back; | 16.4
command this s to become bread." | Lk 4.3
a loaf, will give him a s; | 11.11n
s which the builders rejected | 20.17
shall not be left here one s | 21.6
they found the s rolled away | 24.2
Jesus said, "Take away the s." | Jn 11.39
saw that the s had been taken | 20.1
is the s which was rejected | Acts 4.11
not on tablets of s but on | 2Cor 3.3
Behold, I am laying in Zion a s, | 1Pet 2.6
you engrave the two s with | Ex 28.11
'What do those s mean to you?' | Josh 4.6
and chose five smooth s | 1Sam 17.40
able from these s to raise up | Lk 3.8
the very s would cry out." | 19.40
So they took up s to throw | Jn 8.59
the people spoke of s him, | 1Sam 30.6

STONY

I will take the s heart out | Ezek 11.19

STOOD

still s before the LORD. | Gen 18.22
And he s between the dead | Num 16.48
And the sun s still, and | Josh 10.13
he opened it all the people s. | Neh 8.5

STOOL

till I make thy enemies a s | Lk 20.43
make thy enemies a s for thy | Acts 2.35
enemies should be made a s | Heb 10.13

STOPPED

the mouths of liars will be s. | Ps 63.11
that every mouth may be s, | Rom 3.19

STORED

And Joseph s up grain | Gen 41.49
heavens..earth..s up for fire, | 2Pet 3.7

STOREHOUSE — S

Bring..tithes into the s, | Mal 3.10
Joseph opened all the s, | Gen 41.56
entered the s of the snow, | Job 38.22
bottle; he put the deeps in s. | Ps 33.7
all that was found in his s. | Isa 39.2
brings..the wind from his s. | Jer 10.13

STORK

are an abomination:..the s | Lev 11.19
the s in the heavens knows | Jer 8.7

STORM

he made the s be still, and | Ps 107.29
the s of the LORD! Wrath has | Jer 23.19
arose a great s on the sea, | Mt 8.24
And a great s of wind arose, | Mk 4.37

STRAIGHT

and he will make s your paths. | Prov 3.6
blameless keeps his way s, | 11.5
make s what he..made crooked | Ecc. 7.13
I will make s all his ways; | Isa 45.13
go to the street called S, | Acts 9.11

STRAIGHTFORWARD

not s about the truth of the | Gal 2.14

STRAINING

blind guides, s out a gnat | Mt 23.34
s forward to what lies ahead, | Phil 3.13

STRANGE

forth our hands to a s god, | Ps 44.20
s lips..with an alien tongue | Isa 28.11

STRANGER — S

"I am a s and a sojourner | Gen 23.4
"You shall not oppress a s; | Ex 23.9
The s who sojourns with you | Lev 19.34
gleanings..leave..for the s: | 23.22
one law..for you and..the s | Num 15.16
become a s to my brethren, | Ps 69.8
why shouldst thou be like a s | Jer 14.8
I was a s and you welcomed me, | Mt 25.35
we are s before thee, and | 1Chr 29.15
inheritance..turned over to s, | Lam 5.2
s..never again pass through | Joel 3.17
s to the covenants of promise, | Eph 2.12

STRAW

no longer give the people s | Ex 5.7
That they are like s before | Job 21.18
has s in common with wheat? | Jer 23.28

STREAMS

like a tree planted by s of water, | Ps 1.3
As a hart longs for flowing s, | 42.1
My eyes shed s of tears, | 119.136
s of water in a dry place, | Isa 32.2
break forth..s in the desert; | 35.6

STREET — S

go to the s called Straight, | Acts 9.11
cast..out like..mire of the s. | Ps 18.42

STRENGTH

The LORD is my s and my song, | Ex 15.2
but now our s is dried up, | Num 11.6
days, so shall your s be. | Deut 33.25
wherein your great s lies, | Judg 16.6
thou didst gird me with s | 2Sam 22.40
What is my s, that I should | Job 6.11
contest of s, behold him! | 9.19
His s is hunger-bitten, | 18.12
God who girded me with s, | Ps 18.32
In thy s the king rejoices, O | 21.1
ascribe to the LORD glory and s. | 29.1
May the LORD give s to his | 29.11
show thy s, O God, thou who | 68.28
God is the s of my heart and | 73.26
Sing aloud to God our s; shout | 81.1
Blessed..whose s is in thee, | 84.5
s and beauty..in his sanctuary. | 96.6
broken my s in mid-course; | 102.23
Seek the LORD and his s, | 105.4

STRENGTH (cont.)

LORD is my s and my song;	Ps 118.14
Wisdom gives s to the wise	Ecc 7.19
feast at the proper time, for s,	10.17
"By the s of my hand I have	Isa 10.13
in trust shall be your s."	30.15
lift up your voice with s,	40.9
my God has become my s—	49.5
put on s, O arm of the LORD;	51.9
awake, put on your s, O Zion;	52.1
LORD, my s and my stronghold,	Jer 16.19
GOD, the Lord, is my s;	Hab 3.19
He has shown s with his arm,	Lk 1.51
praying that you may have s	21.36
not. .tempted beyond your s,	1Cor 10.13
and in the s of his might.	Eph 5.10
by the s which God supplies;	1Pet 4.11

STRENGTHEN — S — ED — ING

I could s you with my mouth,	Job 16.5
my arm also shall s him.	Ps 89.21
S the weak hands,. .make firm	Isa 35.3
I will s you, I will help you,	41.10
lengthen. .cords and s. .stakes.	54.2
and I will s the weak, and	Ezek 34.16
"I will s the house of Judah,	Zech 10.6
to him who is able to s you	Rom 16.25
restore, establish, and s you.	1Pet 5.10
Awake, and s what remains	Rev 3.2
all things in him who s me.	Phil 4.13
and s his hand in God.	1Sam 23.16
David s himself in the LORD	30.6
they s their hands for the	Neh 2.18
you have s the weak hands.	Job 4.3
a man touched me and s me.	Dan 10.18
that. .he may grant you to be s	Eph 3.16
May you be s with all power,	Col 1.11
Cilicia, s the churches.	Acts 15.41
s all the disciples.	18.23

STRETCH — ES — ED

let Ethiopia. .s out her hands	Ps 68.31
to the man, "S out your hand."	Mt 12.13
Zion s out her hands, but	Lam 1.17
he s himself upon the child	1Ki 17.21
who alone s out the heavens,	Job 9.8
s out the heavens like a tent,	Ps 104.2

STRIFE

s between the herdsmen	Gen 13.7
see violence and s in the city.	Ps 55.9
the heedless make s, but	Prov 13.10
house full of feasting with s.	17.1
The beginning of s is like	17.14
A fool's lips bring s, and	18.6
A greedy man stirs up s,	28.25
A man of wrath stirs up s,	29.22
pressing anger produces s.	30.33
jealousy and s among you,	1Cor 3.3

STRIKE — S

Let a good man s or rebuke me	Ps 141.5
'I will s the shepherd, and	Mk 14.27
or puts on airs, or s you	2Cor 11.20

STRIP — PED

not s your vineyard bare,	Lev 19.10
Moses s Aaron of. .garments,	Num 20.28
He has s from me my glory,	Job 19.9
for plunderers have s them	Nah 2.2

STRIVE — N — ING

who keep the law s against	Prov 28.4
those who s. .shall perish.	Isa 41.11
"S to enter by. .narrow door;	Lk 13.24

s to excel in building up	1Cor 14.12
how greatly I s for you,	Col 2.1
S for peace with all men,	Heb 12.14
name. .Israel, for you have s	Gen 32.28
with one mind s side by side	Phil 1.27

STRONG — ER

Out of the s came. .sweet."	Judg 14.14
though Judah became s among	1Chr 5.2
"Be s and of good courage,	28.20
he was s, he grew proud,	2Chr 26.16
Wait for the LORD; be s,	Ps 27.14
my s deliverer,. .covered my	140.7
nor the battle to the s, nor	Ecc 9.11
can one enter a s man's house	Mt 12.29
When a s man,. .guards his	Lk 11.21
s ought to bear with. .weak,	Rom 15.1
God chose. .to shame the s,	1Cor 1.27
Finally, be s in the Lord	Eph 5.10
my son, be s in the grace	2Tim 2.1
young men, because you are s,	1Jn 2.14
and David grew s and s,	2Sam 3.1
not able to dispute with one s	Ecc 6.10
weakness of God is s than men.	1Cor 1.25

STRONGHOLD

LORD is a s for the oppressed,	Ps 9.9
horn of my salvation, my s.	18.2
The LORD is the s of my life;	27.1
the LORD has become my s,	94.22
thou hast been a s to. .poor,	Isa 25.4
a s to the people of Israel.	Joel 3.16
a s in the day of trouble;	Nah 1.7

STRUCK

and s the rock with his rod	Num 20.11
And the LORD s the child	2Sam 12.15
"They s me," you will say,	Prov 23.35
s the slave of the high priest	Lk 22.50
officers standing by s Jesus	Jn 18.22

STRUGGLE

In your s against sin you	Heb 12.4

STUBBLE

Egypt, to gather s for straw.	Ex 5.12
like s, the fire consumes	Isa 47.14
and all evildoers will be s;	Mal 4.1
stones, wood, hay, s—	1Cor 3.12

STUBBORN — NESS

for you are a s people.	Deut 9.6
practices or their s ways.	Judg 2.19
would not listen, but were s,	2Ki 17.14
gave them over to. .s hearts,	Ps 81.12
Israel are. .of a s heart.	Ezek 3.7
I walk in the s of my heart.'	Deut 29.19
s. .as iniquity and idolatry.	1Sam 15.23

STUDY

s is a weariness of the flesh.	Ecc 12.12

STUMBLE — D

and your foot will not s.	Prov 3.23
not know over what they s.	4.19
feet s on. .twilight mountains,	Jer 13.16
my persecutors will s, they	20.11
The proud one shall s and fall,	50.32
walks in the day, he does not s,	Jn 11.9
that makes your brother s.	Rom 14.21
For Jerusalem has s, and Judah	Isa 3.8
s over the stumbling stone,	Rom 9.32
have they s so as to fall?	11.11

STUMBLING BLOCK — S

decide never to put a s. .or	Rom 14.13
Christ crucified, a s. .to Jews	1Cor 1.23

STUMBLING BLOCK — S (cont.)
become a s..to the weak.   1Cor 8.9
the s..of the cross has been   Gal 5.11
who taught Balak to put a s..   Rev 2.14
lay before this people s..   Jer 6.21

SUBDUE — D
fill the earth and s it;   Gen 1.28
I would soon s their enemies,   Ps 81.14
no one had..strength to s him.   Mk 5.4
He s peoples under us, and   Ps 47.3

SUBJECT — ED
Israel, and became s to   2Sam 10.19
David, and became s to him.   1Chr 19.19
demons..s to us in your name!"   Lk 10.17
s to..governing authorities.   Rom 13.1
spirits of prophets are s   1Cor 14.32
Wives, be s to your husbands,   Eph 5.22
Wives, be s to your husbands,   Col 3.18
Be s for the Lord's sake to   1Pet 2.13
Son himself will also be s   1Cor 15.28

SUBMISSIVE
Bid slaves to be s to..masters   Tit 2.9
Remind them to be s to rulers   3.1
wives, be s to your husbands,   1Pet 3.1

SUBORDINATE
women..should be s, as even 1Cor 14.34

SUBSTANCE
Honor the Lord with your s   Prov 3.9

SUCCEED — ED
do many things and will s   1Sam 26.25
you may s in building the   1Chr 22.11
none of his offspring shall s   Jer 22.30
fight..you shall not s'?"   32.5
a large army. Will he s?   Ezek 17.15
himself against him, and s?—   Job 9.4

SUCCESS — FUL
then you shall have good s.   Josh 1.8
David had more s than all   1Sam 18.30
Joseph,..became a s man;   Gen 39.2

SUFFER — S — ED — ING (v)
I s from those who hate me,   Ps 9.13
simple go on, and s for it.   Prov 27.12
So also the Son of man will s   Mt 17.12
that the Son of man must s   Mk 8.31
Son of man must s many things, Lk 9.22
first he must s many things   17.25
necessary that the Christ..s   24.26
written, that..Christ should s   24.46
that his Christ should s,   Acts 3.18
counted worthy to s dishonor   5.41
that the Christ must s, and   26.23
heirs..provided we s with him Rom 8.17
one member suffers, all s   1Cor 12.26
but also s for his sake,   Phil 1.29
none of you s as a murderer,   1Pet 4.15
epileptic and he s terribly;   Mt 17.15
I have s much over him today   27.19
For his sake I have s the loss   Phil 3.8
but though we had already s   1Thess 2.2
he..has s and been tempted,   Heb 2.18
because Christ also s for you,   1Pet 2.21
he s, he did not threaten;   2.23
Christ s in the flesh, arm   4.1
over what I am s for you,   Eph 3.13

SUFFERING — S (n)
knowing..s produces endurance Rom 5.3

s as a good soldier of Christ   2Tim 2.3
taskmasters; I know their s,   Ex 3.7
I rejoice in my s for your sake, Col 1.24

SUFFICIENT
Let the day's own trouble be s   Mt 6.34
Not..s of ourselves to claim   2Cor 3.5
"My grace is s for you, for   12.9

SUMMER
earth remains,..s..not cease."   Gen 8.22
Like snow in s or rain in   Prov 26.1
s is ended, and we are not   Jer 8.20

SUN
"S, stand thou still at   Josh 10.12
he has set a tent for the s,   Ps 19.4
Lord God is a s and shield;   84.11
From the rising of the s to   113.3
is nothing new under the s.   Ecc 1.9
the s will be dark at..rising   Isa 13.10
Lord,..gives the s for light   Jer 31.35
cover the s with a cloud,   Ezek 32.7
s shall be turned to darkness,   Joel 2.31
make the s go down at noon,   Amos 8.9
The s and moon stood still   Hab 3.11
s of righteousness shall rise,   Mal 4.2
his s rise on..evil and..good   Mt 5.45
the s will be darkened, and   24.29
the s..turned into darkness   Acts 2.20
There is one glory of the s,   1Cor 15.41
do not let the s go down on   Eph 4.26

SUPERNATURAL
all ate the same s food   1Cor 10.3

SUPPER
likewise the cup after s,   Lk 22.20n
during the s, when the devil   Jn 13.2
it is not the Lord's s that   1Cor 11.20

SUPPLICATION — S
If you will seek God and make s Job 8.5
Hear the voice of my s, as I   Ps 28.2
They will make s to you,   Isa 45.14
"Let our s come before you,   Jer 42.2
Lord heeded s for the land,   2Sam 24.25
he has heard the voice of my s.   Ps 28.6

SUPPLY
their abundance..s your want, 2Cor 8.14
my God will s every need of   Phil 4.19

SUPPORT
land could not s both of them   Gen 13.6
Those who s Egypt shall fall,   Ezek 30.6
by accepting s from them   2Cor 11.8
So we ought to s such men,   3Jn 8

SURE
I am s that neither death,   Rom 8.38
I am s that he who began   Phil 1.6
we feel s of better things   Heb 6.9
we may be s that we know him, 1Jn 2.3

SURROUND — ED
"Master, the multitudes s you   Lk 8.45
all the people..s the house;   Gen 19.4
They s me, s me on every   Ps 118.11
since we are s by so great   Heb 12.1

SURVIVORS
"The s..who escaped exile   Neh 1.3
among the s shall be those   Joel 2.32

SUSA
I was in S the capital,   Neh 1.1
royal throne in S the capital,   Est 1.2

SUSA (cont.)

a Jew in S the capital whose	Est 2.5
the city of S shouted and	8.15
the Jews who were in S	9.18

SUSPENSE

"How long will you keep us in s?	Jn 10.24

SUSTAIN

s them in the wilderness,	Neh 9.21
the LORD, and he will s you;	Ps 55.22
Christ;. .will s you to the end,	1Cor 1.8

SWADDLING

wrapped him in s cloths, and	Lk 2.7

SWALLOW — S — ED (v)

He will s up death for ever,	Isa 25.8
a great fish to s up Jonah;	Jonah 1.17
and s them up, with all	Num 16.30
not say, "We have s him up."	Ps 35.25
"Death is s up in victory."	1Cor 15.54
what is mortal may be s up	2Cor 5.4

SWALLOW (n)

Like a s or a crane I clamor,	Isa 38.14
the turtledove, s, and crane	Jer 8.7

SWARMING (adj)

"Every s thing. .abomination;	Lev 11.41

SWARMS (n)

"Let the waters bring forth s	Gen 1.20
I will send s of flies on you	Ex 8.21

SWEAR — S

make you s by the LORD,	Gen 24.3
any. .rash oath that men s,	Lev 5.4
not s by my name falsely,	19.12
who s by the name of the LORD,	Isa 48.1
if you s, 'As the LORD lives,'	Jer 4.2
I s by myself, says the LORD,	22.5
Do not s at all, either by	Mt 5.34
do not s, either by heaven	Jas 5.12
who s to his own hurt and	Ps 15.4
every one who s falsely shall	Zech 5.3
s by the gold of the temple,	Mt 23.16

SWEAT

in the s of your face	Gen 3.19
his s became like great drops	Lk 22.44

SWEET·

strong came something s."	Judg 14.14
David,. .the s psalmist of	2Sam 23.1
How s are thy words to my	Ps 119.103

SWEPT

I have s away your. .sins like	Isa 44.22
empty, s, and put in order.	Mt 12.44

SWIFT

the race is not to the s, nor	Ecc 9.11

SWINE — 'S

s, because it parts the hoof	Lev 11.7
send us. .into the herd of s."	Mt 8.31
"Send us to the s, let us enter	Mk 5.12
herd of s was feeding there	Lk 8.32
into his fields to feed s.	15.15
a gold ring in a s snout	Prov 11.22

SWORD — S

flaming s which turned	Gen 3.24
the s of Gideon the son of	Judg 7.14
"A s for the LORD and for	7.20
king said, "Bring me a s."	1Ki 3.24
He made my mouth like a. .s,	Isa 49.2
I will send the s after them,	Jer 9.16

because of. .s of the oppressor,	25.38
a s is sharpened and. .polished,	Ezek 21.9
O s, against my shepherd,	Zech 13.7
not. .to bring peace, but a s.	Mt 10.34
drew his s, and struck the slave	26.51
his s, and struck the slave	Mk 14.47
a s will pierce through your	Lk 2.35
and the s of the Spirit,	Eph 6.17
sharper than any two-edged s,	Heb 4.12
issued a sharp two-edged s,	Rev 1.16
his mouth issues a sharp s	19.15
beat their s into plowshares,	Isa 2.4
Beat your plowshares into s,	Joel 3.10
beat their s into plowshares,	Mic 4.3

SWORE — N

which he s to your fathers,	Deut 6.10
LORD has s and will not change	Ps 110.4
LORD has s by his right hand	Isa 62.8
I have s by my great name,	Jer 44.26
GOD has s by his holiness	Amos 4.2
to the Lord what you have s.'	Mt 5.33

SYCAMORE

and a dresser of s trees,	Amos 7.14
climbed up into a s tree to see	Lk 19.4

SYCHAR

a city of Samaria, called S,	Jn 4.5

SYMPATHY

showed. .s and comforted him	Job 42.11
all of you have unity of spirit, s,	1Pet 3.8

SYNAGOGUE

house of the ruler of the s,	Mk 5.38
he began to teach in the s;	6.2
nation, and he built us our s."	Lk 7.5
Jairus. .a ruler of the s;	8.41
he argued in the s every	Acts 18.4
And he entered the s and	19.8

SYRIA

commander of the army of. .S,	2Ki 5.1
For the head of S is Damascus,	Isa 7.8
fame spread throughout all S,	Mt 4.24
Quirinius was governor of S.	Lk 2.2
went through S and Cilicia,	Acts 15.41

SYRIANS

the S came no more on raids	2Ki 6.23
Caphtor and the S from Kir?	Amos 9.7

T

TABERNACLE — S

pattern of. .t, and. .furniture,	Ex 25.9
erect the t according to the plan	26.30
erect the t of the tent of meeting	40.2
Jews' feast of T was at hand.	Jn 7.2

TABLE — S

make a t of acacia wood;	Ex 25.23
made the t of acacia wood;	37.10
put there for him a bed, a t,	2Ki 4.10
Thou preparest a t before me	Ps 23.5
their own t. .become a snare;	69.22
"Can God spread a t in the	78.19
that the LORD's t is polluted,	Mal 1.12
partake of the t of the Lord	1Cor 10.21
two t of the testimony,	Ex 31.18
"Cut two t of stone like	34.1
two t of stone written	Deut 9.10
give up preaching. .to serve t.	Acts 6.2

TABLET — S
"Take a large *t* and write upon   Isa 8.1
he asked for a writing *t*, and   Lk 1.63
but on *t* of human hearts.   2Cor 3.3

TAKE — S — N
that they *t* for me an offering;   Ex 25.2
T my instruction instead of   Prov 8.10
"*T*, eat; this is my body."   Mt 26.26
said, "*T*; this is my body."   Mk 14.22
glad to *t* him into the boat,   Jn 6.21
I will come again and will *t* you   14.3
lawlessness *t* away lives.   Prov 11.30
any one *t* away from the words Rev 22.19
"Thou hast *t* up my cause, O   Lam 3.58
found, because God had *t* him. Heb 11.5

TALE
seemed to them an idle *t*,   Lk 24.11

TALEBEARER
a *t* reveals secrets, but   Prov 11.13

TALENTS
who owed him ten thousand *t*,   Mt 18.24
to one he gave five *t*,   25.15

TALK — ED — ING (v)
my tongue will *t* of thy..help   Ps 71.24
began to *t* freely about it,   Mk 1.45
the angel who *t* with me said   Zech 1.14
Paul *t* with them, intending   Acts 20.7
While they were *t*..Jesus   Lk 24.15

TALK (n)
man full of *t* be vindicated?   Job 11.2
"Should he argue in unprofitable *t*,   15.3
put devious *t* far from you.   Prov 4.24

TAME
no human being can *t* the tongue Jas 3.8

TAMPER
or to *t* with God's word,   2Cor 4.2

TARSHISH
The sons of Javan:..*T*,   Gen 10.4
the king's ships went to *T*   2Chr 9.21
building ships to go to *T*,   20.36
didst shatter the ships of *T*.   Ps 48.7
kings of *T*..render him tribute,   72.10
Wail, O ships of *T*, for your   Isa 23.14
Jonah rose to flee to *T*   Jonah 1.3

TARSUS
for a man of *T* named Saul;   Acts 9.11
went to *T* to look for Saul;   11.25
"I am a Jew, from *T* in Cilicia,   21.39

TASKMASTERS
t over them to afflict them   Ex 1.11
Pharaoh commanded the *t*   5.6

TASTE — D (v)
O *t* and see..the LORD is good! Ps 34.8
not *t* death before they see   Mt 16.28
not *t* death before they see   Mk 9.1
some..who will not *t* death   Lk 9.27
to *t* no food till we have   Acts 23.14
Do not *t*, Do not touch"   Col 2.21
he might *t* death for every one. Heb 2.9
who have *t* the heavenly gift,   6.4
t the kindness of the Lord   1Pet 2.3

TASTE (n)
is there any *t* in the slime   Job 6.6
but if salt has lost its *t*,   Mt 5.13

TAUGHT
Behold, I have *t* you statutes   Deut 4.5
they *t* in Judah, having   2Chr 17.9
I have *t* you..of wisdom;   Prov 4.11
tongue of those who are *t*,   Isa 50.4
I have *t* them persistently   Jer 32.33
he *t*..as one who had authority, Mt 7.29
he *t* them in their synagogue,   13.54
he *t*..as one who had authority, Mk 1.22
t them many things in parables,   4.2
he *t* in their synagogues,   Lk 4.15
they shall all be *t* by God.'   Jn 6.45
he spoke and *t* accurately   Acts 18.25
Let him who is *t* the word share Gal 6.6
about him and were *t* in him,   Eph 4.21

TAUNT (v)
my adversaries *t* me,.."Where   Ps 42.10
All the day my enemies *t* me,   102.8

TAUNT (n)
Thou hast made us the *t* of   Ps 44.13
t against the king of Babylon: Isa 14.4
take up their *t* against him,   Hab 2.6

TAX — ES
Matthew sitting at the *t* office;   Mt 9.9
"Does..your teacher pay the *t*?"   17.24
Levi..sitting at the *t* office,   Mk 2.14
Levi, sitting at the *t* office;   Lk 5.27
Is it lawful to pay *t* to Caesar, Mt 22.17
lawful to pay *t* to Caesar,   Mk 12.14
same reason you also pay *t*,   Rom 13.6

TEACH — ES — ING (v)
t you what you shall speak."   Ex 4.12
you shall *t* them the statutes   18.20
you..*t* the people of Israel   Lev 10.11
ordinances which I *t* you,   Deut 4.1
may *t* their children so.'   4.10
which you shall *t* them,   5.31
you shall *t* them diligently   6.7
t them to your children,   11.19
that they may not *t* you   20.18
write this song, and *t* it   31.19
t Jacob thy ordinances,   33.10
come again to us, and *t* us   Judg 13.8
and to *t* his statutes and   Ezra 7.10
ask the beasts,..they will *t*   Job 12.7
Will any *t* God knowledge,   21.22
ways. O LORD; *t* me thy paths. Ps 25.4
T me thy way, O LORD; and lead 27.11
I will *t* you the fear of the LORD. 34.11
T me thy way, O LORD, that I   86.11
So *t* us to number our days   90.12
O LORD; *t* me thy statutes!   119.12
T me,..the way of thy statutes; 119.33
T me to do thy will, for thou   143.10
t a righteous man and he will Prov 9.9
that he may *t* us his ways   Isa 2.3
"Whom will he *t* knowledge,   28.9
no longer shall each man *t*   Jer 31.34
t my people the difference   Ezek 44.23
t them the letters and language Dan 1.4
its priests *t* for hire,   Mic 3.11
that he may *t* us his ways   4.2
on the sabbath he began to *t*   Mk 6.2
to *t* them that the Son of man   8.31
"Lord, *t* us to pray, as John   Lk 11.1
the Holy Spirit will *t* you   12.12
Holy Spirit,..will *t* you all   Jn 14.26
that Jesus began to do and *t*,   Acts 1.1
not to speak or *t* at all in   4.18
will you not *t* yourself?   Rom 2.21
as you *t* and admonish one   Col 3.16

TEACH — ES — ING (v) (cont.)

I permit no woman to t or	1Tim 2.12
they shall not t every one	Heb 8.11
He who t men knowledge, the	Ps 94.10
If any one t otherwise and	1Tim 6.3
as his anointing t you about	1Jn 2.27
and without a t priest,	2Chr 15.3
he went about all Galilee, t	Mt 4.23
he was t his disciples, saying	Mk 9.31
I was with you in the temple t,	14.49
he was t them on the sabbath;	Lk 4.31
men..you put in prison are..t	Acts 5.25
in Antioch, t and preaching	15.35
This is the man who is t	21.28

TEACHER — S

God..who is a t like him?	Job 36.22
your eyes shall see your T.	Isa 30.20
disciple is not above his t,	Mt 10.24
"Does not your t pay the tax?"	17.24
not..rabbi, for you have one t,	23.8
'The T says, My time is at hand;	26.18
Why trouble the T any further?"	Mk 5.35
A disciple is not above his t,	Lk 6.40
"The T is here and is calling	Jn 11.28
"Rabboni!" (which means T).	20.16
more understanding than..t,	Ps 119.99
Pharisees and t of the law	Lk 5.17
some pastors and t,	Eph 4.11
desiring to be t of the law,	1Tim 1.7

TEACHING (n)

May my t drop as the rain,	Deut 32.2
reject not your mother's t;	Prov 1.8
The t of the wise is a fountain	13.14
beware of..t of the Pharisees	Mt 16.12
they were astonished at his t,	Lk 4.32
"My t is not mine, but his	Jn 7.16
about his disciples and his t.	18.19
devoted..to the apostles' t	Acts 2.42
filled Jerusalem with your t	5.28
they did not cease t and	5.42
"May we know what this new t is	17.19
obedient..to the standard of t	Rom 6.17
attend..to preaching, to t,	1Tim 4.13
who labor in preaching and t;	5.17
t which accords with godliness,	6.3
Now you have observed my t,	2Tim 3.10
profitable for t, for reproof,	3.16

TEAR — S

God will wipe away every t	Rev 7.17
he will wipe away every t	21.4
My t have been my food day	Ps 42.3
put thou my t in thy bottle!	56.8
Lord GOD will wipe away t	Isa 25.8
heard your prayer,..seen your t;	38.5
I wrote you..with many t,	2Cor 2.4

TEETH

escaped by the skin of my t.	Job 19.20
Your t..like a flock of ewes	Sol 4.2
children's t are set on edge'?	Ezek 18.2

TEKOA

Joab sent to T, and fetched	2Sam 14.2
into the wilderness of T;	2Chr 20.20
Blow the trumpet in T, and	Jer 6.1
among the shepherds of T,	Amos 1.1

TELL

t the rock..to yield..water	Num 20.8
T it not in Gath, publish it	2Sam 1.20
t of all his wonderful works!	Ps 105.2

T us the former things, what	Isa 41.22
will t you great and hidden	Jer 33.3
Jeremiah said.."If I t you,	38.15
go quickly and t his disciples	Mt 28.7
go, t his disciples and Peter	Mk 16.7

TEMPER

quick t acts foolishly,	Prov 14.17

TEMPEST

the t passes, the wicked is	Prov 10.25
great t has come upon you."	Jonah 1.12

TEMPESTUOUS

For the sea grew more..t.	Jonah 1.11
soon a t wind, called the	Acts 27.14

TEMPLE

The LORD is in his holy t,	Ps 11.4
in his t all cry, "Glory!"	29.9
God, in the midst of thy t.	48.9
be satisfied with..thy holy t!	65.4
they have defiled thy holy t;	79.1
of the t, 'Your foundation	Isa 44.28
deceptive words:..t of the LORD,	Jer 7.4
glory of the LORD filled..t.	Ezek 43.5
portray the t,..arrangement,	43.11
appear and profane the t and	Dan 11.31
the LORD is in his holy t;	Hab 2.20
build the t of the LORD.	Zech 6.12
set him on..pinnacle of the t,	Mt 4.5
Jesus entered the t of God	21.12
point out..buildings of the t.	24.1
able to destroy the t of God,	26.61
"You who would destroy the t	27.40
he entered the t and began to	Mk 11.15
carry anything through the t.	11.16
say, 'I will destroy this t	14.58
You who would destroy the t	15.29
they found him in the t,	Lk 2.46
set him on..pinnacle of the t,	4.9
"Two men went up into the t	18.10
entered..t and began to drive	19.45
In the t he found those who	Jn 2.14
"Destroy this t, and in three	2.19
even tried to profane the t,	Acts 24.6
know that you are God's t	1Cor 3.16
your body is a t of the Holy	6.19
we are the t of..living God;	2Cor 6.16
grows into a holy t in..Lord;	Eph 2.21
"Rise and measure the t of God	Rev 11.1
God's t in heaven was opened,	11.19
the t was filled with smoke	15.8
its t is the Lord God the	21.22

TEMPT — ED

'You shall not t the Lord	Mt 4.7
'You shall not t the Lord	Lk 4.12
to t the Spirit of the Lord?	Acts 5.9
lest Satan t you through lack	1Cor 7.5
forty days, t by Satan; and	Mk 1.13
in the wilderness, t by..devil.	Lk 4.2
able to help those who are t.	Heb 2.18
t as we are, yet without sinning.	4.15
Let no one say when he is t,	Jas 1.13

TEMPTATION — S

And lead us not into t, but	Mt 6.13
that you may not enter into t;	26.41
that you may not enter into t;	Mk 14.38
and in time of t fall away.	Lk 8.13
and lead us not into t."	11.4
No t has overtaken you that	1Cor 10.13
"T to sin are sure to come;	Lk 17.1

TEMPTER
And the *t* came and said to him,   Mt 4.3
fear that..the *t* had tempted   1Thess 3.5

TEN
Suppose *t* are found there."   Gen 18.32
that is, the *t* commandments   Deut 4.13
he was met by *t* lepers,   Lk 17.12

TENANTS
vineyard,..let it out to *t*,   Mt 21.33
tower, and let it out to *t*,   Mk 12.1
come and destroy those *t*,   Lk 20.16

TEND — ED
T the flock of God that is   1Pet 5.2
With upright heart he *t* them,   Ps 78.72

TENT — S
Bethel, and pitched his *t*,   Gen 12.8
place where his *t* had been   13.3
consecrate the *t* of meeting   Ex 29.44
called it the *t* of meeting.   33.7
spoke..from the *t* of meeting,   Lev 1.1
the *t* of meeting there;   Josh 18.1
ark of God dwells in a *t*."   2Sam 7.2
but the ark..is under a *t*."   1Chr 17.1
friendship of God..upon my *t*;   Job 29.4
who shall sojourn in thy *t*?   Ps 15.1
he has set a *t* for the sun,   19.4
t of the upright..flourish.   Prov 14.11
Jerusalem,..an immovable *t*,   Isa 33.20
spreads..like a *t* to dwell in;   40.22
My *t* is destroyed, and all   Jer 10.20
fathers had the *t* of witness   Acts 7.44
if the earthly *t* we live in   2Cor 5.1
Moses was about to erect the *t*,   Heb 8.5
temple of the *t* of witness   Rev 15.5
father of those who dwell in *t*   Gen 4.20

TENTH
And Abram gave him a *t*   Gen 14.20
I will give the *t* to thee."   28.22
every *t* animal..holy to..LORD   Lev 27.32
And though a *t* remain in it,   Isa 6.13
to him Abraham apportioned a *t*   Heb 7.2

TENT-MAKERS
for by trade they were *t*.   Acts 18.3

TERRIFY — IED
distress and anguish *t* him;   Job 15.24
and *t* them in his fury, saying,   Ps 2.5
the Almighty has *t* me;   Job 23.16
t, saying, "It is a ghost!"   Mt 14.26

TERROR
appoint over you sudden *t*,   Lev 26.16
not fear the *t* of the night,   Ps 91.5
from before the *t* of the LORD,   Isa 2.19
At evening time, behold, *t*!   17.14
for..healing, but behold, *t*.   Jer 8.15
will make you a *t* to yourself   20.4
He who flees..the *t* shall fall   48.44

TEST — S — ED — ING (v)
by them I may *t* Israel,   Judg 2.22
she came to *t* him with hard   1Ki 10.1
Let us *t* and examine our ways,   Lam 3.40
"*T* your servants for ten days;   Dan 1.12
sign from heaven, to *t* him.   Mk 8.11
to *t* him, sought from him a   Lk 11.16
This he said to *t* him, for   Jn 6.6
This they said to *t* him,   8.6n
T yourselves. Do you not   2Cor 13.5
let each one *t* his own work,   Gal 6.4

t everything; hold fast   1Thess 5.21
but *t* the spirits to see   1Jn 4.1
The LORD *t* the righteous and   Ps 11.5
God *t* Abraham, and said   Gen 22.1
By this you shall be *t*:   42.15
For thou, O God, hast *t* us;   Ps 66.10
They *t* God in their heart   78.18
t and rebelled against..God,   78.56
I *t* you at the waters of Meribah.   81.7
when your fathers *t* me, and   95.9
the word of the LORD *t* him   105.19
Pharisees came up..and *t* him   Mt 19.3
humble you, *t* you to know   Deut 8.2
LORD your God is *t* you, to know   13.3

TEST — ING (n)
not put the LORD..to the *t*,   Deut 6.16
put God to *t* in the desert;   Ps 106.14
not put the LORD to the *t*."   Isa 7.12
put me to the *t*, says the LORD   Mal 3.10
but when they put God to the *t*   3.15
"Why put me to the *t*, you   Mt 22.18
"Why put me to the *t*? Bring   Mk 12.15
not put the Lord to the *t*,   1Cor 10.9
in a severe *t* of affliction,   2Cor 8.2
the *t* of your faith produces   Jas 1.3

TESTIFY — ING — IES — IED
Here I am; *t* against me   1Sam 12.3
you own lips *t* against you.   Job 15.6
O Israel, I will *t* against you.   Ps 50.7
and our sins *t* against us;   Isa 59.12
our iniquities *t* against us,   Jer 14.7
things they *t* against you?"   Mt 27.13
I *t*..that its works are evil.   Jn 7.7
I affirm and *t* in the Lord,   Eph 4.17
we have seen and *t* that the   1Jn 4.14
Demetrius..I *t* to him too,   3Jn 12
t both to Jews and to Greeks   Acts 20.21
pride of Israel *t* to his face;   Hos 5.5
who *t* to these things says,   Rev 22.20
when they had *t* and spoken   Acts 8.25
and *t* to the truth of your life.   3Jn 3

TESTIMONY — IES
put into the ark the *t*   Ex 25.16
the *t* of the LORD is sure,   Ps 19.7
He established a *t* in Jacob,   78.5
Bind..the *t*, seal the teaching   Isa 8.16
preached..as..*t* to all nations;   Mt 24.14
whole council sought false *t*   26.59
shake off the dust..for a *t*   Mk 6.11
for my sake, to bear *t* before them.   13.9
council sought *t* against Jesus   14.55
dust from your feet as a *t*   Lk 9.5
a time for you to bear *t*.   21.13
"What further *t* do we need?   22.71
He came for *t*, to bear witness   Jn 1.7
believed..because of..woman's *t*,   4.39
said..your *t* is not true."   8.13
the *t* of two men is true;   8.17
the *t* to Christ was confirmed   1Cor 1.6
not..*t* of God in lofty words   2.1
the *t* of our conscience   2Cor 1.12
If we receive the *t* of men,   1Jn 5.9
on those who..bear *t* to Jesus.   Rev 12.17
the *t* of Jesus is the spirit   19.10
with this *t* for the churches.   22.16
they kept his *t*, and..statutes   Ps 99.7

THADDAEUS
the son of Alphaeus, and *T*;   Mt 10.3
T, and Simon the Cananaean,   Mk 3.18

THANK — ED (v)

Let them *t* the LORD for his	Ps 107.21
For Sheol cannot *t* thee,	Isa 38.18
Jesus declared, "I *t* thee,	Mt 11.25
"I *t* thee, Father, Lord of	Lk 10.21
Does he *t* the servant because	17.9
"Father, I *t* thee that thou	Jn 11.41
First, I *t* my God through Jesus	Rom 1.8
I *t*..God in all my remembrance	Phil 1.3
we also *t* God constantly	1Thess 2.13
seeing them Paul *t* God and	Acts 28.15

THANK OFFERING — S

offer with the *t*..unleavened	Lev 7.12
bring sacrifices and *t*..to	2Chr 29.31
I will render *t*..to thee.	Ps 56.12
bringing *t*..to the house of	Jer 17.26

THANKS (n)

and gave *t* to the LORD,	2Chr 7.3
who gave *t* stood in the house	Neh 12.40
give to the LORD the *t* due	Ps 7.17
I will give *t* to thee for ever.	30.12
We give *t* to thee, O God; we	75.1
It is good to give *t* to the LORD,	92.1
Give *t* to him, bless his name!	100.4
O give *t* to the LORD, for he	107.1
I give thee *t*, O LORD, with	138.1
"I will give *t* to thee, O	Isa 12.1
I give *t* and praise, for thou	Dan 2.23
having given *t* he broke them	Mt 15.36
at Jesus' feet, giving him *t*.	Lk 17.16
giving *t* to God in the	Acts 27.35
honor..God or give *t* to him,	Rom 1.21
But *t* be to God, that you	6.17
T be to God through Jesus	7.25
abstains..and gives *t* to God.	14.6
you may give *t* well enough,	1Cor 14.17
But *t* be to God, who gives	15.57
t be to God, who in Christ	2Cor 2.14
But *t* be to God who puts	8.16
not cease to give *t* for you,	Eph 1.16
giving *t* in the name of our LORD	5.20
giving *t* to God the Father	Col 3.17
give *t* in all circumstances;	1Thess 5.18
to give *t* to God always for	2Thess 1.3

THANKSGIVING

sacrifice of *t* to the LORD,	Lev 22.29
appointed that *t* be sung	1Chr 16.7
singing aloud a song of *t*,	Ps 26.7
Offer to God a sacrifice of *t*,	50.14
He who brings *t* as his sacrifice	50.23
I will magnify him with *t*.	69.30
to thee the sacrifice of *t*	116.17
t and the voice of song.	Isa 51.3
out of them..come songs of *t*,	Jer 30.19
offer a sacrifice of *t* of	Amos 4.5
what *t* can we render to God	1Thess 3.9
if it is received with *t*;	1Tim 4.4
glory and wisdom and *t* and	Rev 7.12

THESSALONICA

they came to *T*, where there	Acts 17.1
more noble than those in *T*,	17.11
Aristarchus..Macedonian from *T*.	27.2
even in *T* you sent me help	Phil 4.16
deserted me and gone to *T*;	2Tim 4.10

THICKET

a ram, caught in a *t*	Gen 22.13

THIEF — VES

then that *t* shall die;	Deut 24.7
see a *t*, you are a friend	Ps 50.18
Do not despise a *t* if he	Prov 6.30
partner of a *t* hates..life;	29.24
"As a *t* is shamed when caught,	Jer 2.26
the night the *t* was coming,	Mt 24.43
known at what hour the *t* was	Lk 12.39
but because he was a *t*,	Jn 12.6
the day..will come like a *t*,	2Pet 3.10
I will come like a *t*, and	Rev 3.3
where *t* break in and steal,	Mt 6.19

THIGH

"Put your hand under my *t*,	Gen 24.2
touched the hollow of his *t*;	32.25

THINK — S

when I *t* of thee upon my bed,	Ps 63.6
and his mind does not so *t*;	Isa 10.7
"*T* not that I have come to	Mt 5.17
"What do you *t* of the Christ?	22.42
not to *t* of himself more	Rom 12.3
that no one may *t* more of me	2Cor 12.6
than all that we ask or *t*,	Eph 3.20
T over what I say, for the	2Tim 2.7
one *t* that he is a prophet,	1Cor 14.37
if any one *t* he is something,	Gal 6.3

THIRD

he will be raised on..*t* day."	Mt 17.23
he..prayed for the *t* time,	26.44
only the *t* hour of the day;	Acts 2.15

THIRST — S — ED (v)

hunger and *t* for righteousness,	Mt 5.6
"If any one *t*, let him come	Jn 7.37
fulfil the scripture), "I *t*."	19.28
hunger no more, neither *t*	Rev 7.16
My soul *t* for God, for the	Ps 42.2
my soul *t* for thee; my flesh	63.1
my soul *t* for thee like a	143.6
"Ho, every one who *t*, come	Isa 55.1
They *t* not when he led them	48.21

THIRST (n)

for my *t* they gave me vinegar	Ps 69.21
tongue is parched with *t*,	Isa 41.17
young men shall faint for *t*.	Amos 8.13
in hunger and *t*, often	2Cor 11.27

THIRSTY

cold water to a *t* soul, so	Prov 25.25
a *t* man dreams he is drinking	Isa 29.8
to deprive the *t* of drink.	32.6
the *t* ground springs of water;	35.7
drink, but you shall be *t*;	65.13
I was *t* and you gave me drink,	Mt 25.35
if he is *t*, give him drink;	Rom 12.20
let him who is *t* come, let	Rev 22.17

THIRTY

wages *t* shekels of silver.	Zech 11.12
paid him *t* pieces of silver.	Mt 26.15
brought back the *t* pieces of silver	27.3

THOMAS

Bartholomew; *T* and Matthew	Mt 10.3
Matthew, and *T*, and James	Mk 3.18
T, called the Twin, said	Jn 11.16
T said to him, "Lord, we do	14.5
to *T*, "Put your finger here,	20.27
Simon Peter, *T* called the Twin,	21.2

THONG

the *t* of whose sandals I am not	Mk 1.7

THORN — S

t was given me in the flesh,	2Cor 12.7

THORN — S (cont.)

t and thistles..bring forth	Gen 3.18
and *t* in your sides,	Num 33.55
briers and *t* shall grow up;	Isa 5.6
Other seeds fell upon *t*, and	Mt 13.7
a crown of *t*..on his head,	27.29
Other seed fell among *t* and	Mk 4.7
a crown of *t* they put it on	15.17
figs are not gathered from *t*,	Lk 6.44
And some fell among *t*; and	8.7
wearing the crown of *t* and	Jn 19.5
if it bears *t* and thistles,	Heb 6.8

THOUGHT — S

but the LORD takes *t* for me.	Ps 40.17
We have *t* on they steadfast love,	48.9
and declares to man..his *t*;	Amos 4.13
take every *t* captive to obey	2Cor 10.5
"Behold, I know your *t*, and	Job 21.27
his *t* are, "There is no God."	Ps 10.4
multiplied,..thy *t* toward us;	40.5
their *t* are against me for evil.	56.5
O LORD! Thy *t* are very deep!	92.5
the LORD, knows the *t* of man,	94.11
precious to me are thy *t*, O	139.17
I will pour out my *t* to you;	Prov 1.23
t of the righteous are just;	12.5
The *t* of the wicked are an	15.26
For my *t* are not your *t*,	Isa 55.8
their *t* are *t* of iniquity,	59.7
know their works and their *t*,	66.18
may know the *t* of your mind.	Dan 2.30
they do not know the *t* of	Mic 4.12
Jesus, knowing their *t*, said	Mt 9.4
out of the heart come evil *t*,	15.19
But he knew their *t*, and he said	Lk 6.8
But he, knowing their *t*, said	11.17
no one comprehends the *t* of	1Cor 2.11
t of the wise are futile."	3.20
discerning..*t* and intentions	Heb 4.12

THOUSAND — S

mine, the cattle on a *t* hills.	Ps 50.10
day in thy courts..better than a *t*	84.10
One man among a *t* I found,	Ecc 7.28
distinguished among ten *t*.	Sol 5.10
and a *t* years as one day.	2Pet 3.8
bound him for a *t* years,	Rev 20.2
"Saul has slain his *t*, And	1Sam 18.7
With..*t* upon *t*, the LORD came	Ps 68.17

THREE

his petition *t* times a day."	Dan 6.13
I will make *t* booths here,	Mt 17.4
There are *t* witnesses, the Spirit,	1Jn 5.8

THRESH — ED — ING

you shall *t* the mountains	Isa 41.15
heifer that loved to *t*,	Hos 10.11
because they have *t* Gilead	Amos 1.3
tonight at the *t* floor.	Ruth 3.2
Babylon is like a *t* floor	Jer 51.33

THRESHER

t thresh in hope of a share	1Cor 9.10

THROAT

seizing him by the *t* he said,	Mt 18.28
"Their *t* is an open grave,	Rom 3.13

THRONE — S

he shall sit upon my *t*"?	1Ki 1.13
Solomon, and make his *t*	1.37
your royal *t* over Israel for	9.5
also made a great ivory *t*,	10.18

I will establish his *t* for	1Chr 17.12
thou hast sat on the *t* giving	Ps 9.4
Your divine *t* endures for ever	45.6
thy *t*..established from of old;	93.2
LORD has..*t* in the heavens,	103.19
"One of the sons..on your *t*.	132.11
for the *t* is established by	Prov 16.12
and his *t* will be established	25.5
had gone from prison to the *t*	Ecc 4.14
I saw the Lord sitting upon a *t*,	Isa 6.1
t..established in steadfast love	16.5
"Heaven is my *t* and the earth	66.1
Jerusalem..the *t* of the LORD,	Jer 3.17
A glorious *t* set on high from	17.12
set his *t* above these stones	43.10
thy *t* endures to..generations.	Lam 5.19
the *t* of his father David,	Lk 1.32
'Heaven is my *t*, and earth	Acts 7.49
took his seat upon the *t*,	12.21
"Thy *t*, O God, is for ever	Heb 1.8
draw near the *t* of grace,	4.16
at the right hand of the *t* of	8.1
and lo, a *t* stood in heaven,	Rev 4.2
I saw a great white *t* and	20.11
flowing from the *t* of God	22.1
As I looked, *t* were placed	Dan 7.9
you..will also sit on twelve *t*,	Mt 19.28
twenty-four *t*, and seated on	Rev 4.4
I saw *t*, and seated on them	20.4

THRONG

praise him in..midst of..*t*.	Ps 109.30
the great *t* heard him gladly.	Mk 12.37

THROW — N

and *t* you like a ball into	Isa 22.18
Son of God, *t* yourself down;	Mt 4.6
and *t* them into the furnace	13.42
sons of the kingdom will be *t*	8.12

THUMMIN

put the Urim and the *T*,	Ex 28.30
he put the Urim and the *T*.	Lev 8.8

THUNDER — S — ED

LORD, that he may send *t*	1Sam 12.17
Boanerges, that is, sons of *t*;	Mk 3.17
God of glory *t*,..upon..waters.	Ps 29.3
The LORD *t* from heaven,	2Sam 22.14
LORD also *t* in the heavens,	Ps 18.13

TIDINGS

charged with heavy *t* for you.	1Ki 14.6
host of those who bore the *t*:	Ps 68.11
O Zion, herald of good *t*;	Isa 40.9
Jerusalem a herald of good *t*.	41.27
t from the east...alarm him,	Dan 11.44

TIGLATH-PILESER (PUL)

Received tribute from Menahem, 2Ki 15. 19–20; carried the people captive to Assyria, 2Ki 15.29; paid homage by Ahaz, 2Ki 16.7–10 (2Chr 28.20–21); deported some of the tribes of Israel, 1Chr 5.26.

TIGRIS

name of the third river is *T*,	Gen 2.14
great river, that is, the *T*,	Dan 10.4

TILL

there was no man to *t*	Gen 2.5
God sent him..to *t* the ground	3.23

TILLER

Noah was the first *t*	Gen 9.20
I am a *t* of the soil;	Zech 13.5

TIME — S

t of which God had spoken	Gen 21.2
t that the people of Israel	Ex 12.40
Was it a *t* to accept money	2Ki 5.26
to the kingdom for such a *t*	Est 4.14
It is *t* for the LORD to act,	Ps 119.126
and a *t* for every matter under	Ecc 3.1
every matter has its *t* and way,	8.6
t and chance happen to. .all.	9.11
a day of clouds, a *t* of doom	Ezek 30.3
still the vision awaits its *t*;	Hab 2.3
people say. .*t* has not yet come	Hag 1.2
to torment us before the *t*?"	Mt 8.29
Teacher says, My *t* is at hand;	26.18
"My *t* has not yet come, but	Jn 7.6
appointed *t* has grown. .short;	1Cor 7.29
making the most of the *t*,	Eph 5.16
making the most of the *t*.	Col 4.5
therein; for the *t* is near.	Rev 1.3
she is to be nourished for a *t*,	12.14
My *t* are in thy hand; deliver	Ps 31.15
I will bless the LORD at all *t*;	34.1
he prophesies of *t* far off.'	Ezek 12.27

TIMOTHY

Paul's son in the Lord, 1Cor 4.17; 1Tim 1.2, 18; 2Tim 1.2; son of a Greek father and a Jewish mother, Acts 16.1; brought up in a devout home, 2Tim 1.5; 3.14–15; lived in Lystra (or Derbe), Acts 16.1; circumcised, Acts 16.3; accompanied Paul in the second missionary journey, Acts 16.1–4; 17.14–15; 18.5; 1Thess 3.2–6; ordained, 1Tim 4.14; 2Tim 1.6; sent to the church in Corinth, 1Cor 4.17; 16.10; accompanied Paul in the third missionary journey, Acts 20.4; in charge of the church in Ephesus, 1Tim 1.3; 4.12; urged by Paul to visit him in prison, 2Tim 4.9, 13; imprisoned and released, Heb 13.23.

Therefore I sent to you *T*,	1Cor 4.17
When *T* comes, see that you	16.10

TITHE (v)

t all the yield of your seed,	Deut 14.22
you *t* mint. .dill and cummin,	Mt 23.23
Pharisees! for you *t* mint	Lk 11.42

TITHE — S (n)

redeem any of his *t*, he shall	Lev 27.31
Levites I have given. .*t*	Num 18.21
t of the people of Israel	18.24
finished paying all the *t*	Deut 26.12
to bring to the Levites the *t*	Neh 10.37
robbing thee?' In your *t* and	Mal 3.8
t, paid *t* through Abraham,	Heb 7.9

TITLE

Pilate also wrote a *t* and put	Jn 19.19

TITUS

not find my brother *T* there.	2Cor 2.13
comforted us by. .coming of *T*,	7.6
Accordingly we have urged *T*	8.6
As for *T*, he is my partner	8.23
Did *T* take advantage of you?	12.18
with Barnabas, taking *T* along	Gal 2.1
to Galatia, *T* to Dalmatia.	2Tim 4.10
To *T*, my true child in. .faith:	Tit 1.4

TODAY

O that *t* you would hearken to	Ps 95.7
t you will be with me in	Lk 23.43
"*T*, when you hear his voice,	Heb 3.15

TOGETHER

went both of them *t*.	Gen 22.8
they were all *t* in one place.	Acts 2.1
attending the temple *t* and	2.46
in him all things hold *t*.	Col 1.17

TOIL — ED (v)

Do not *t* to acquire wealth;	Prov 23.4
they neither *t* nor spin;	Lk 12.27
For this I *t*, striving with	Col 1.29
"Master, we *t* all night and took	Lk 5.5

TOIL (n)

In all *t* there is profit,	Prov 14.23
What does a man gain by.. *t*	Ecc 1.3
take pleasure in all his *t*.	3.13
all *t* and all skill in work	4.4
quietness than two hands. .of *t*	4.6
yet there is no end to. .his *t*,	4.8
and find enjoyment in his *t*—	5.19
the *t* of man is for his mouth,	6.7
The *t* of a fool wearies him,	10.15
in *t* and hardship, through	2Cor 11.27
" 'I know your works, your *t*	Rev 2.2

TOLD

land which thou hadst *t* their	Neh 9.23
t the glad news of deliverance	Ps 40.9
The herdsmen fled, and *t* it	Mk 5.14
Philip. .*t* him the good news	Acts 8.35
things that cannot be *t*,	2Cor 12.4

TOLL

they will not pay. .*t*,	Ezra 4.13
not lawful to impose. .*t* upon	7.24
From whom do kings. .take *t*	Mt 17.25

TOMB — S

a *t*. .hewn out of the rock;	Mt 15.46
stone to the door of the *t*,	27.60
his body, and laid it in a *t*.	Mk 6.29
went to the *t*, taking. .spices	Lk 24.1
going to the *t* to weep there.	Jn 11.31
in the garden a new *t* where	19.41
went into the *t*; he saw the linen	20.6
you are like whitewashed *t*,	Mt 23.27
and he lived. .among the *t*.	Lk 8.27
build the *t* of the prophets	11.47
all. .in the *t* will hear his voice	Jn 5.28

TOMORROW

Do not boast about *t*, for	Prov 27.1
eat and drink, for *t* we die."	Isa 22.13
today is alive and *t* is thrown	Mt 6.30
and drink, for *t* we die."	1Cor 15.32
you do not know about *t*.	Jas 4.14

TONGUE — S

hid from the scourge of the *t*,	Job 5.21
they flatter with their *t*.	Ps 5.9
Keep your *t* from evil, and	34.13
Then my *t* shall tell of thy	35.28
that I may not sin with my *t*;	39.1
my *t* is like the pen of a. .scribe.	45.1
Your *t* is like a sharp razor;	52.2
t of. .righteous is. .silver;	Prov 10.20
perverse *t* will be cut off.	10.31
t of the wise brings healing.	12.18
are in the power of the *t*,	18.21
soft *t* will break a bone.	25.15
bow, every *t* shall swear.'	Isa 45.23
you shall confute every *t*	54.17
taught their *t* to speak lies;	Jer 9.5
Their *t* is a deadly arrow; it	9.8
t was released, and he spoke	Mk 7.35

TONGUE — S (cont.)

one who speaks in a *t* speaks — 1Cor 14.2
and does not bridle his *t* — Jas 1.26
So the *t* is a little member — 3.5
shelter from the strife of *t*. — Ps 31.20
who whet their *t* like swords, — 64.3
they will speak in new *t*; — Mk 16.17*n*
appeared to them *t* as of fire, — Acts 2.3
spoke with *t* and prophesied. — 19.6
to another various. . *t*, — 1Cor 12.10
If I speak in the *t* of men — 13.1
written, "By men of strange *t* — 14.21
t are a sign. . for unbelievers, — 14.22

TOOTH

eye for eye, *t* for *t*, — Ex 21.24
eye for eye, *t* for *t*, — Deut 19.21
bad *t* or a foot that slips. — Prov 25.19

TORCH — ES

t passed between. . pieces. — Gen 15.17
empty jars, with *t* inside — Judg 7.16
before the throne burn seven *t* — Rev 4.5

TORMENT — ED (v)

"How long will you *t* me, — Job 19.2
Have you come here to *t* us — Mt 8.29
adjure you by God, do not *t* me." — Mk 5.7
I beseech you, do not *t* me." — Lk 8.28
they will be *t* day and night — Rev 20.10

TORMENT (n)

you shall lie down in *t*. — Isa 50.11
in Hades,. . in *t*, he lifted up — Lk 16.23

TORN

The LORD has *t* the kingdom — 1Sam 15.28
curtain of the temple was *t* — Mk 15.38

TOSSING

I am full of *t* till the dawn. — Job 7.4
wicked are like the *t* sea; — Isa 57.20

TOUCH — ES — ED

fruit. . neither shall you *t* it, — Gen 3.3
there shall no evil *t* you. — Job 5.19
saying, "*T* not my anointed — Ps 105.15
"If I only *t* his garment, I — Mt 9.21
only *t*. . fringe of his garment — 14.36
"If I *t* even his garments, I — Mk 5.28
they might *t* even the fringe — 6.56
for a man not to *t* a woman. — 1Cor 7.1
and *t* nothing unclean; then — 2Cor 6.17
the evil one does not *t* him. — 1Jn 5.18
it *t* you, and you are dismayed. — Job 4.5
who *t*. . the apple of his eye: — Zech 2.8
whose hearts God had *t*. — 1Sam 10.26
forth his hand and *t* my mouth; — Jer 1.9
stretched out his hand and *t* him, — Mt 8.3
he *t* her hand, and the fever — 8.15
Then he *t* their eyes, saying, — 9.29
Jesus in pity *t* their eyes, — 20.34
said, "Who was it that *t* me?" — Lk 8.45

TOWEL

and girded himself with a *t*. — Jn 13.4

TOWER — S

let us build. . a city, and a *t* — Gen 11.4
and station myself on the *t*, — Hab 2.1
upon whom the *t* in Siloam fell — Lk 13.4
build a *t*,. . count the cost, — 14.28

TRADED

land of Israel *t* with you; — Ezek 27.17
five talents. . and *t* with them; — Mt 25.16

TRADITION — S

transgress the *t* of the elders? — Mt 15.2
not live according to the *t* — Mk 7.5
and hold fast the *t* of men." — 7.8
stand firm. . hold to the *t* — 2Thess 2.15

TRAIN — S — ED — ING

T up a child in the way he — Prov 22.6
so *t* the young women to love — Tit 2.4
who *t* my hands for war, and — Ps 144.1
Abram. . led forth his *t* men, — Gen 14.14
divine *t* that is in faith; — 1Tim 1.4
bodily *t* is of some value, — 4.8
t us to renounce irreligion — Tit 2.12

TRAITOR

Judas Iscariot, who became a *t*. — Lk 6.16

TRAMPLE — D

Be gracious. . men *t* upon me; — Ps 56.1
didst *t* the sea with. . horses, — Hab 3.15
and *t* the waves of the sea; — Job 9.8

TRANSFER — RED

to *t* the kingdom from. . Saul, — 2Sam 3.10
and *t* us to the kingdom of — Col 1.13

TRANSFIGURED

t before them,. . his face shone — Mt 17.2
and he was *t* before them, — Mk 9.2

TRANSFORMED

t by the renewal of your mind, — Rom 12.2

TRANSGRESS — ES — ED

if you *t* the covenant — Josh 23.16
my mouth does not *t*. — Ps 17.3
"Come to Bethel, and *t*; to — Amos 4.4
When a land *t* it has many — Prov 28.2
I have not *t* any of thy — Deut 26.13
people have *t* my covenant — Judg 2.20
but *t* his covenant, even — 2Ki 18.12
But they *t* against the God — 1Chr 5.25
the men who *t* my covenant — Jer 34.18
"We have *t* and rebelled, and — Lam 3.42
at Adam they *t* the covenant; — Hos 6.7

TRANSGRESSION — S

Forgive, I pray you, the *t* — Gen 50.17
Blessed is he. . *t* is forgiven, — Ps 32.1
punish their *t* with the rod — 89.32
When words are many, *t* is — Prov 10.19
Are you not children of *t*, — Isa 57.4
All this is for the *t* of Jacob — Mic 1.5
sins. . not like the *t* of Adam, — Rom 5.14
and because of their *t*, — Lev 16.16
if I have concealed my *t* — Job 31.33
Deliver me from all my *t*. — Ps 39.8
For I know my *t*, and my sin — 51.3
who conceals his *t* will not — Prov 28.13
t are multiplied before thee, — Isa 59.12
t are many,. . apostasies. . great. — Jer 5.6
None of the *t* which he has — Ezek 18.22
their uncleanness and their *t*, — 39.24
"For three *t* of Damascus, — Amos 1.3
on the day I punish Israel for his *t*, — 3.14

TRANSGRESSOR — S

then I prove myself a *t*. — Gal 2.18
"He was reckoned with the *t*" — Mk 15.28*n*
he was reckoned with *t*"; — Lk 22.37

TRANSIENT

things that are seen are *t*, — 2Cor 4.18

TRAVAIL (n)

anguish as of a woman in *t*. — Ps 48.6

TRAVAIL (n) (cont.)

like..pangs of a woman in *t*;	Isa 21.3
fruit of the *t* of his soul	53.11
pain as of a woman in *t*.	Jer 6.24
When a woman is in *t* she	Jn 16.21
whole creation groaning in *t*	Rom 8.22
with whom I am again in *t*	Gal 4.19
as *t* comes upon a woman	1Thess 5.3

TRAVEL — ED

| appointed by..churches to *t* | 2Cor 8.19 |
| ships of Tarshish *t* for you | Ezek 27.25 |

TREACHEROUS

My brethren are *t* as a	Job 6.15
crookedness of the *t* destroys	Prov 11.3
the *t* deal..treacherously,	Isa 24.16
men will be..*t*, reckless	2Tim 3.4

TREACHERY

confess their..*t*..against me,	Lev 26.40
'What is this *t* which you	Josh 22.16
fled, saying to Ahaziah, "*T*,	2Ki 9.23
their houses are full of *t*;	Jer 5.27

TREAD — S — ING

through thy name we *t* down	Ps 44.5
t on the lion and the adder,	91.13
t our iniquities under foot.	Mic 7.19
makes me *t* upon..high places.	Hab 3.19
you shall *t* down the wicked,	Mal 4.3
the sole of your foot *t*	Deut 11.24
ox when it is *t* out the grain."	1Cor 9.9

TREASON

| Athaliah..and cried, "*T*! *t*!" | 2Ki 11.14 |
| Athaliah..and cried, "*T*! | 2Chr 23.13 |

TREASURE — D (v)

| receive my words and *t* up my | Prov 2.1 |
| have *t* in my bosom the words | Job 23.12 |

TREASURE — S (n)

put *t* in your sacks for you;	Gen 43.23
showed them all his *t* house,	2Ki 20.13
In the..righteous..is much *t*,	Prov 15.6
great *t* and trouble with it.	15.16
Precious *t* remains in a wise	21.20
silver and gold and the *t* of	Ecc 2.8
the fear of the Lord is his *t*.	Isa 33.6
out of his good *t* brings..good,	Mt 12.35
kingdom..is like *t* hidden in	13.44
out of his *t* what is new and	13.52
out of the good *t* of his heart	Lk 6.45
who lays up *t* for himself,	12.21
where your *t* is, there will	12.34
we have this *t* in earthen	2Cor 4.7
he took away the *t* of the	1Ki 14.26
search for it as..hidden *t*;	Prov 2.4
give you the *t* of darkness,	Isa 45.3
your *t* I will give as spoil,	Jer 15.13
the *t* of the kings of Judah	20.5
Can I forget..*t* of wickedness	Mic 6.10
t of all nations shall come in,	Hag 2.7
opening their *t*, they offered	Mt 2.11
"Do not lay up for yourselves *t*	6.19
in whom are hid all the *t* of	Col 2.3

TREASURY

go into the *t* of the Lord."	Josh 6.19
"Cast it into the *t*"—	Zech 11.13
putting money into the *t*.	Mk 12.41
These words he spoke in the *t*,	Jn 8.20

TREE — S

| the *t* of life also in the midst | Gen 2.9 |

Lord showed him a *t*, and he	Ex 15.25
shall not plant any *t* as an	Deut 16.21
and you hang him on a *t*,	21.22
sat down under a broom *t*;	1Ki 19.4
hope for a *t*, if it be cut	Job 14.7
I am like a green olive *t* in	Ps 52.8
gentle tongue is a *t* of life,	Prov 15.4
like a *t* planted by water,	Jer 17.8
no *t* in the garden of God	Ezek 31.8
a *t* in the midst of the earth;	Dan 4.10
sit every man..under his fig *t*,	Mic 4.4
every sound *t* bears good fruit,	Mt 7.17
the *t* is known by its fruit;	12.33
no good *t* bears bad fruit,	Lk 6.43
into a sycamore *t* to see him,	19.4
took him down from the *t*,	Acts 13.29
every one who hangs on a *t*"—	Gal 3.13
He..bore our sins..on the *t*,	1Pet 2.24
grant to eat of the *t* of life,	Rev 2.7
the *t* of life with its twelve	22.2
have..right to the *t* of life	22.14
shall not destroy its *t*	Deut 20.19
The *t*..watered abundantly,	Ps 104.16
I saw upon the bank..many *t*	Ezek 47.7

TREMBLE (v)

Lord reigns; let the peoples *t*!	Ps 99.1
I will make the heavens *t*,	Isa 13.13
the man who made the earth *t*,	14.16
foundations of the earth *t*.	24.18
T, you women who are at ease,	32.11
nations..*t* at thy presence!	64.2
Lord, you who *t* at his word:	66.5
Shall not the land *t* on this	Amos 8.8

TREMBLING (n)

| woman,..came in fear and *t* | Mk 5.33 |
| for *t* and astonishment had come | 16.8 |

TRESPASS — ES

the *t* of your handmaid;	1Sam 25.28
man is overtaken in any *t*,	Gal 6.1
For if you forgive men their *t*,	Mt 6.14
Father..may forgive..your *t*."	Mk 11.26
put to death for our *t* and	Rom 4.25
not counting..*t* against them,	2Cor 5.19
having forgiven us all our *t*,	Col 2.13

TRIAL — S

let me make *t* only this once	Judg 6.39
why do you make *t* of God	Acts 15.10
to rescue the godly from *t*,	2Pet 2.9
keep you from the hour of *t*	Rev 3.10
continued with me in my *t*;	Lk 22.28
and with tears and with *t*	Acts 20.19

TRIBE — S

"One *t* is cut off from Israel	Judg 21.6
and Israel is the *t* of his	Jer 51.19
sealed, out of every *t* of the	Rev 7.4
t go up, the *t* of the Lord,	Ps 122.4

TRIBULATION — S

When you are in *t* and	Deut 4.30
besieged..with bitterness and *t*;	Lam 3.5
when *t* or persecution arises	Mt 13.21
then there will be great *t*,	24.21
after the *t* of those days	24.29
such *t* as has not been from	Mk 13.19
after that *t*, the sun will	13.24
In the world you have *t*; but	Jn 16.33
There will be *t* and distress	Rom 2.9
Shall *t*, or distress, or persecution,	8.35
be patient in *t*, be constant	12.12

TRIBULATION — S (cont.)

share with you in Jesus the *t*	Rev 1.9
" 'I know your *t* and. .poverty	2.9
I will throw into great *t*,	2.22
have come out of the great *t*;	7.14
through many *t* we must enter	Acts 14.22

TRIBUTE

the LORD's *t* of sheep was	Num 31.37
Israel sent *t*. .to Eglon	Judg 3.15
Is it lawful for us to give *t*	Lk 20.22

TRIUMPH — ED — ING (v)

When the righteous *t*, there	Prov 28.12
offspring of Israel shall *t*	Isa 45.25
"Sing to the LORD,. .he has *t*	Ex 15.21
in that my enemy has not *t*	Ps 41.11
t over them in him.	Col 2.15

TRIUMPH — S (n)

God,. .always leads us in *t*,	2Cor 2.14
repeat the *t* of the LORD,	Judg 5.11
Great *t* he gives to his	2Sam 22.51
Great *t* he gives to his king,	Ps 18.50

TROAS

Mysia, they went down to *T*.	Acts 16.8
were waiting for us at *T*,	20.5
When I came to *T* to preach	2Cor 2.12
that I left with Carpus at *T*,	2Tim 4.13

TROUBLE — D (v)

shall *t* you in the land	Num 33.55
t the hearts of many peoples,	Ezek 32.9
"Why do you *t* the woman?	Mt 26.10
why do you *t* her? She has done	Mk 14.6
dead; do not *t* the Teacher	Lk 8.49
but there are some who *t* you	Gal 1.7
let no man *t* me; for I bear	6.17
the king heard this, he was *t*,	Mt 2.3
greatly distressed and *t*.	Mk 14.33
Martha, you are anxious and *t*	Lk 10.41
"Why are you *t*, and why do	24.38
the pool, and *t* the water:	Jn 5.4*n*
the pool when the water is *t*,	5.7
"Now is my soul *t*. And what	12.27
Jesus. .was *t* in spirit, and	13.21
"Let not your hearts be *t*;	14.1

TROUBLE — S (n)

"Why did you bring *t* on us?	Josh 7.25
now when you are in *t*?"	Judg 11.7
see how this man is seeking *t*;	1Ki 20.7
have no rest; but *t* comes."	Job 3.26
man is born to *t* as the sparks	5.7
of few days, and full of *t*.	14.1
his shelter in the day of *t*;	Ps 27.5
refuge in the time of *t*.	37.39
a very present help in *t*.	46.1
call upon me in the day of *t*;	50.15
promised when I was in *t*.	66.14
not in *t* as other men are;	73.5
their span is but toil and *t*;	90.10
great treasure and *t* with it.	Prov 15.16
but the soul is torn by *t*.	27.9
there shall be a time of *t*,	Dan 12.1
stronghold in the day of *t*;	Nah 1.7
will deliver you from six *t*;	Job 5.19
saved him out of all his *t*.	Ps 34.6
who marry. .have worldly *t*,	1Cor 7.28

TRUE

his heart was not wholly *t*	1Ki 11.4
the words. .prophesied come *t*,	Jer 28.6
"I am the *t* vine, and my Father	Jn 15.1

Let God be *t* though every man	Rom 3.4
brethren, whatever is *t*,	Phil 4.8
This testimony is *t*.	Tit 1.13

TRUMPET — S

and a very loud *t* blast,	Ex 19.16
blew the *t*, and proclaimed,	2Ki 9.13
that day a great *t* will be	Isa 27.13
heard the sound of the *t*,	Ezek 33.5
Blow the *t* in Zion; sound	Joel 2.1
Is a *t* blown in a city, and	Amos 3.6
Lord GOD will sound the *t*,	Zech 9.14
give alms, sound no *t* before you,	Mt 6.2
t will sound, and the dead	1Cor 15.52
the sound of the *t* of God.	1Thess 4.16
proclaimed with blast of *t*,	Lev 23.24
"Make two silver *t*;	Num 10.2
three companies, and put *t*	Judg 7.16
With *t*. .make a joyful noise	Ps 98.6

TRUST — S — ED — ING (v)

O my God, in thee I *t*, let me	Ps 25.2
But I *t* in thee, O LORD, I	31.14
because we *t* in his holy name.	33.21
T in the LORD, and do good;	37.3
men who *t* in their wealth	49.6
days. But I will *t* in thee.	55.23
T in him at all times, O people;	62.8
fortress; my God, in whom I *t*."	91.2
like them;. .all who *t* in them.	115.8
Those who *t*. .are like Mount Zion,	125.1
T in the LORD with all your	Prov 3.5
T in a faithless man in time	25.19
T in the LORD for ever, for	Isa 31.1
Woe to those. .who *t* in chariots	31.1
to shame, who *t* in. .images,	42.17
not *t* in these deceptive words:	Jer 7.4
Shemaiah. .made you *t* in a lie,	29.31
for those who *t* in riches	Mk 10.24*n*
Jesus did not *t* himself to them,	Jn 2.24
For the king *t* in the LORD;	Ps 21.7
blessed is. .man who *t* in thee!	84.12
He who *t* in his riches will	Prov 11.28
happy is he who *t* in the LORD.	16.20
he who *t*. .will be enriched.	28.25
t in the name of the LORD	Isa 50.10
"Cursed is. .man who *t* in man	Jer 17.5
t him who justifies the ungodly,	Rom 4.5
walls, in which you *t*,	Deut 28.52
He *t* in the LORD the God	2Ki 18.5
from the tent in which he *t*,	Job 18.14
have *t* in thy steadfast love;	Ps 13.5
but *t* in the abundance of his	52.7
forgotten me and *t* in lies.	Jer 13.25
because you *t* in. .strongholds	48.7
because he had *t* in his God.	Dan 6.23
you have *t* in your chariots	Hos 10.13
heart is firm, *t* in the LORD.	Ps 112.7

TRUST (n)

his *t* is a spider's web.	Job 8.14
"If I have made gold my *t*,	31.24
Blessed. .who makes. .LORD his *t*,	Ps 40.4
Put not your *t* in princes,	146.3
your *t* may be in the LORD,	Prov 22.19
quietness and *t* for ever.	Isa 32.17
the man. .whose *t* is in the LORD.	Jer 17.7
Put no *t* in a neighbor, have	Mic 7.5
"I will put my *t* in him."	Heb 2.13

TRUSTWORTHY

all his precepts are *t*,	Ps 111.7
required of stewards. .*t*.	1Cor 4.2
these words are *t* and true."	Rev 21.5

TRUTH

and speaks *t* from his heart;	Ps 15.2
speaks the *t* gives honest	Prov 12.17
Buy *t*, and do not sell it;	23.23
I the LORD speak the *t*, I	Isa 45.19
confess. . not in *t* or right.	48.1
t was cast down to the ground,	Dan 8.12
that you may know the *t*	Lk 1.4
and you will know the *t*,	Jn 8.32
"I am the way, and the *t*,	14.6
Pilate said. . "What is *t*?"	18.38
exchanged the *t* about God for	Rom 1.25
unleavened bread of. . and *t*.	1Cor 5.8
the *t*, but only for the *t*.	2Cor 13.8
in him, as the *t* is in Jesus.	Eph 4.21
whether in pretense or in *t*,	Phil 1.18
and the *t* is not in him;	1Jn 2.4

TRUTHFUL

T lips endure for ever.	Prov 12.19
A *t* witness saves lives,	14.25

TRY — IES — IEST — IED

Does not the ear *t* words	Job 12.11
Prove me, O LORD, and *t* me;	Ps 26.2
T me and know my thoughts!	139.23
"I the LORD. . *t* the heart,	Jer 17.10
gold, and the LORD *t* hearts.	Prov 17.3
thou who *t* the minds and hearts,	Ps 7.9
If thou *t* my heart, if thou	17.3
and *t* my mind toward thee.	Jer 12.3
O LORD. . who *t* the righteous,	20.12
when he has *t* me, 1. . as gold.	Job 23.10
Would like Job were *t* to the end,	34.36
Thy promise is well *t*, and	Ps 119.140

TUMULT

a day of *t* and trampling and	Isa 22.5
the *t* of war shall arise	Hos 10.14
lest. . a *t* among the people."	Mt 26.5
lest there be a *t* of. . people."	Mk 14.2

TUNICS

sandals and not put on two *t*.	Mk 6.9
money; and do not have two *t*.	Lk 9.3

TURMOIL

My heart is in *t*, and is	Job 30.27
for nought are they in *t*; man	Ps 39.6

TURN — S — ED

every seer, saying, "*T* from	2Ki 17.13
T, O LORD, save my life;	Ps 6.4
who does not *t* to the proud,	40.4
"*T* back, O children of men!"	90.3
I do not *t* away from thy law.	119.51
t your foot away from evil.	Prov 4.27
T away from man. . for of what	Isa 2.22
understand. . *t* and be healed."	6.10
"*T* to me and be saved, all	45.22
they did not *t* from their ways.	Jer 15.7
'*T* now, every one. . from. . evil	25.5
I will *t*. . mourning into joy,	31.13
saying, '*T*. . from his evil way,	35.15
and *t* away from your idols;	Ezek 14.6
t back from your evil ways;	33.11
right cheek, *t* to him the other	Mt 5.39
and *t* for me to heal them.'	13.15
t and become like children,	18.3
lest they should *t* again,	Mk 4.12
he will *t* many of the sons	Lk 1.16
t from these vain things	Acts 14.15
and *t* for me to heal them.'	28.27
righteous man *t*. . from evil,	Prov 12.26
that nation,. . *t* from its evil,	Jer 18.8

your God *t* the curse into	Deut 23.5
no king like him,. . *t* to. . LORD	2Ki 23.25
had *t* the heart of the king	Ezra 6.22
I *t* my mind to know and to	Ecc 7.25
we. . *t* every one to his own way;	Isa 53.6
abundance. . shall be *t* to you,	60.5
they have *t* aside and gone	Jer 5.23
and when you have *t* again,	Lk 22.32
who have *t* the world upside	Acts 17.6
how you *t* to God from idols,	1Thess 1.9

TURTLEDOVE — S

"Bring me. . a *t* and a young	Gen 15.9
the voice of the *t* is heard	Sol 2.12
bring his offering of *t* or of	Lev 1.14
law of the Lord, "a pair of *t*,	Lk 2.24

TWELVE

and tore it into *t* pieces.	1Ki 11.30
names of the *t* apostles are	Mt 10.2
appointed *t*, to be with him,	Mk 3.14
And he called to him the *t*,	6.7
evening he came with the *t*.	14.17
when he was *t* years old,	Lk 2.42
and chose from them *t*, whom	6.13
an only daughter, about *t* years	8.42
Jesus said to the *t*, "Will you	Jn 6.67

TWINKLING

in the *t* of an eye, at the	1Cor 15.52

TWINS

there were *t* in her womb.	Gen 25.24
there were *t* in her womb.	38.27

TWO

bring *t* of every sort	Gen 6.19
T are better than one, because	Ecc 4.9
and with *t* he covered his feet,	Isa 6.2
"No one can serve *t* masters;	Mt 6.24
where *t* or three are gathered	18.20
A man had *t* sons; and he went	21.28
t men will be in the field;	24.40
"Which of the *t* do you want	27.21
That very day *t* of them were	Lk 24.13
"The *t* shall become one."	1Cor 6.16

TYPE

a *t* of. . one who was to come.	Rom 5.14

TYRE

the fortified city of *T*;	Josh 19.29
king of *T* sent his servants	1Ki 5.1
Hiram king of *T* had supplied	9.11
his father was a man of *T*.	2Chr 2.14
people of *T* will sue. . favor	Ps 45.12
The oracle concerning *T*. Wail,	Isa 23.1
T and Sidon a great multitude,	Mk 3.8
if the mighty works. . done in *T*	Lk 10.13
to Syria, and landed at *T*;	Acts 21.3

U

UNBELIEF

did not. . because of their *u*.	Mt 13.58
he marveled because of their *u*.	Mk 6.6
said, "I believe; help my *u*!"	9.24
broken off because of. . *u*,	Rom 11.20

UNBELIEVERS

against brother,. . before *u*?	1Cor 6.6
and outsiders or *u* enter,	14.23
Do not be mismated with *u*.	2Cor 6.14

UNBELIEVING

the *u* husband is consecrated	1Cor 7.14
To the. . *u* nothing is pure;	Tit 1.15

UNCHASTITY
except on the ground of *u*,   Mt 5.32
write..to abstain from..*u*   Acts 15.20

UNCIRCUMCISED
no *u* person shall eat of it.   Ex 12.48
wife from the *u* Philistines?"   Judg 14.3
the *u* because of their faith.   Rom 3.30
at the time of his call *u*?   1Cor 7.18

UNCLEAN
he shall pronounce him *u*.   Lev 13.3
cover..lip and cry, '*U*, *u*.!   13.45
shall be *u* seven days;   Num 19.11
for I am a man of *u* lips, and   Isa 6.5
no more..uncircumcised and..*u*.   52.1
become like one who is *u*,   64.6
what they offer there is *u*.   Hag 2.14
"When the *u* spirit has gone   Mt 12.43
met him. man with an *u* spirit,   Mk 5.2
was possessed by an *u* spirit,   7.25
had the spirit of an *u* demon;   Lk 4.33
Jesus rebuked the *u* spirit,   9.42
"When the *u* spirit has gone   11.24
never eaten..common or *u*."   Acts 10.14
should not call any man..*u*.   10.28
your children would be *u*,   1Cor 7.14

UNCLEANNESS
Or if he touches human *u*,   Lev 5.3
end to end with their *u*.   Ezra 9.11
cleanse them from sin and *u*.   Zech 13.1
to practice every kind of *u*.   Eph 4.19
appeal..not..from error or *u*,   1Thess 2.3

UNCONDEMNED
beaten us publicly, *u*, men   Acts 16.37
is a Roman citizen, and *u*?"   22.25

UNDERSTAND (v)
not *u* one another's speech."   Gen 11.7
Aramaic language, for we *u*   2Ki 18.26
of his power who can *u*?"   Job 26.14
uttered what I did not *u*,   42.3
I *u* more than the aged, for   Ps 119.100
Evil men do not *u* justice,   Prov 28.5
speak..in Aramaic,..we *u* it;   Isa 36.11
have not heard they shall *u*.   52.15
so wise that he can *u* this?   Jer 9.12
In the latter days you will *u*   23.20
"*U*, O son of man,..the vision   Dan 8.17
shall indeed hear but never *u*,   Mt 13.14
they did not *u* about the loaves,   Mk 6.52
you *u* what you are reading?"   Acts 8.30
and *u* with their heart,   28.27
I want you to *u* this mystery,   Rom 11.25

UNDERSTANDING (n)
there is no *u* in them.   Deut 32.28
hast closed their minds to *u*,   Job 17.4
who by *u* made the heavens,   Ps 136.5
his *u* is beyond measure.   147.5
discretion..*u* will guard you.   Prov 2.11
who heeds admonition gains *u*.   15.32
fool takes no pleasure in *u*,   18.2
who formed it, "He has no *u*?"   Isa 29.16
showed him the way of *u*?   40.14
by his *u* stretched out the   Jer 10.12
people without *u*..come to ruin.   Hos 4.14
"Are you also still without *u*?   Mt 15.16
"Then are you also without *u*?   Mk 7.18
to love him..with all the *u*,   12.33
all..amazed at his *u* and answers.   Lk 2.47

UNDERSTOOD
that the people *u* the reading.   Neh 8.8

"Have you *u* all this?" They   Mt 13.51
as you have *u* in part, that   2Cor 1.14

UNDYING
love our Lord..with love *u*.   Eph 6.24

UNFAITHFUL — NESS
punish..put him with the *u*.   Lk 12.46
U creatures! Do you not know   Jas 4.4
So Saul died for his *u*;   1Chr 10.13

UNFRUITFUL
choke the word,..it proves *u*.   Mt 13.22
spirit prays but..mind is *u*.   1Cor 14.14
to help..and not to be *u*.   Tit 3.14

UNGODLY
God gives me up to the *u*,   Job 16.11
are the dwellings of the *u*,   18.21
my cause against *u* people;   Ps 43.1
time Christ died for the *u*.   Rom 5.6

UNINTENTIONALLY
any one kills his neighbor *u*   Deut 19.4

UNITE — D
to *u* all things in him,   Eph 1.10
against the city, *u* as one   Judg 20.11
who is *u* to the Lord becomes   1Cor 6.17

UNITY
good..when brothers dwell in *u*!   Ps 133.1
maintain the *u* of the Spirit   Eph 4.3
attain to the *u* of the faith   4.13

UNJUST — LY
from the grasp of the *u* and   Ps 71.4
hates *u* gain will prolong   Prov 28.16
An *u* man is an abomination   29.27
but the *u* knows no shame.   Zeph 3.5
rain on the just and on the *u*.   Mt 5.45
"How long will you judge *u* and   Ps 82.2

UNKNOWN
inscription, 'To an *u* god.'   Acts 17.23
as *u*, and yet well known;   2Cor 6.9

UNLEAVENED
feast of *u* bread to the LORD;   Lev 23.6
you shall eat *u* bread;   Deut 16.8
kept the feast of *u* bread   2Chr 30.21

UNMARRIED
To the *u* and the widows I say   1Cor 7.8

UNRIGHTEOUS — NESS
not..faithful in the *u* mammon,   Lk 16.11
who builds his house by *u*,   Jer 22.13

UNSEARCHABLE
who does great things and *u*,   Job 5.9
the LORD,..his greatness is *u*.   Ps 145.3
so the mind of kings is *u*.   Prov 25.3
How *u* are his judgments and   Rom 11.33
to the Gentiles the *u* riches   Eph 3.8

UNSKILLED
Even if I am *u* in speaking,   2Cor 11.6
u in..word of righteousness,   Heb 5.13

UNSTAINED
u and free from reproach   1Tim 6.14
u, separated from sinners,   Heb 7.26
keep oneself *u* from the world.   Jas 1.27

UNTIE
not worthy to stoop down and *u*.   Mk 1.7
u it and bring it here.   Lk 19.30

UNVEILED
prophesies with her head *u*   1Cor 11.5
u face, beholding the glory   2Cor 3.18

UNWASHED
hands defiled, that is, *u.* Mk 7.2

UNWITTINGLY
If any one sins *u* in any Lev 4.2
done *u* without the knowledge Num 15.24

UNWORTHY
you. .say, 'We are *u* servants; Lk 17.10
the cup of the Lord in an *u* 1Cor 11.27

UPBUILDING
speaks to men for their *u* 1Cor 14.3
and all for your *u*, beloved. 2Cor 12.19

UPHOLD — S
There is none to *u* your cause, Jer 30.13
but the LORD *u* the righteous. Ps 37.17
thy right hand *u* me. 63.8

UPPER
will show you a large *u* room Lk 22.12
they went up to the *u* room, Acts 1.13

UPRIGHT — NESS
for the Levites were more *u* 2Chr 29.34
where were the *u* cut off? Job 4.7
God, who saves the *u* in heart. Ps 7.10
the *u* shall behold his face. 11.7
shout for joy, all you *u* in heart! 32.11
The *u* see it and are glad; 107.42
the *u* will inhabit the land, Prov 2.21
the *u* are in his confidence. 3.32
God made man *u*, but they have Ecc 7.29
he whose soul is not *u* in him Hab 2.4
who walks in *u* fears. .LORD, Prov 14.2

UR
Haran died. .in the land. .*U* Gen 11.28
went forth together from *U* 11.31
LORD who brought you from *U* 15.7
Abram and bring him. .out of *U* Neh 9.7

URGE — D
I *u* you, then, be imitators 1Cor 4.16
necessary to *u* the brethren 2Cor 9.5
woman lived, who *u* him to eat 2Ki 4.8
accept two talents.'' And he *u* 5.23

URIM
put the *U* and the Thummim, Ex 28.30
in. .breastpiece he put the *U* Lev 8.8
dreams. .*U*, or by prophets. 1Sam 28.6

USEFUL
he is very *u* in serving me. 2Tim 4.11
now he is indeed *u* to you Philem 11

UZ
The sons of Aram: *U*, Gen 10.23
a man in the land of *U*, Job 1.1
the kings of the land of *U* Jer 25.20
dweller in the land of *U*; Lam 4.21

UZZIAH
people of Judah took *U*, 2Chr 26.1
Moreover *U* had an army 26.11
not for you, *U*, to burn 26.18
King *U* was a leper to the 26.21
all that. .*U* had done—only 27.2
Jerusalem in the days of *U*, Isa 1.1
In the year that King *U* died 6.1
and Joram the father of *U*, Mt 1.8

V

VAIN
for *v* is the help of man! Ps 60.11
"Men are all a *v* hope." 116.11
those who build it labor in *v*. 127.1
beauty is *v*, but a woman who Prov 31.30
Bring no more *v* offerings; Isa 1.13
"But they say, 'That is in *v*! Jer 18.12
turn from these *v* things Acts 14.15
then our preaching is in *v* 1Cor 15.14

VALLEY — S
the *v* of the shadow of death, Ps 23.4
concerning the *v* of vision. Isa 22.1
Every *v* shall be lifted up, 40.4
called. .the *V* of Slaughter. Jer 19.6
the *v*; it was full of bones. Ezek 37.1
in the *v* of decision! For Joel 3.14
Every *v* shall be filled, and Lk 3.5
he is not a god of the *v*," 1Ki 20.28

VALUE
finding one pearl of great *v*, Mt 13.46
you are of more *v* than many Lk 12.7
bodily training is of some *v*, 1Tim 4.8

VANISH — ED
their days *v* like a breath Ps 78.33
the angel. .*v* from his sight. Judg 6.21
you have *v* from the seas, Ezek 26.17
and he *v* out of their sight. Lk 24.31
the sky *v* like a scroll Rev 6.14

VANITY
V of vanities, says the Preacher, Ecc 1.2
also is *v* and a great evil. 2.21
V of vanities, says the Preacher; 12.8

VARIETIES
there are *v* of gifts, but 1Cor 12.4
there are *v* of service, but 12.5

VEIL — ED
took her *v* and covered Gen 24.65
the *v* shall separate for you Ex 26.33
he put a *v* on his face; 34.33
made the *v* of blue and purple 36.35
holy place within the *v*, Lev 16.2
same *v* remains unlifted, 2Cor 3.14
gospel is *v*, it is *v* only to 4.3

VENGEANCE
If any one slays Cain, *v* Gen 4.15
not take *v* or bear any grudge Lev 19.18
V is mine, and recompense, Deut 32.35
rejoice when he sees the *v*; Ps 58.10
O LORD, thou God of *v*,. .shine 94.1
day of *v* was in my heart, Isa 63.4
visit me, and take *v* for me Jer 15.15
this is the *v* of the LORD: 50.15
LORD takes *v* on. .adversaries Nah 1.2
"*V* is mine, I will repay, Rom 12.19
"*V* is mine, I will repay." Heb 10.30

VERSED
were *v* in law and judgment, Est 1.13
well *v* in the scriptures. Acts 18.24

VESSEL — S
I have become like a broken *v*. Ps 31.12
glaze covering an earthen *v* Prov 26.23
the *v* he was making of clay Jer 18.4
as one breaks a potter's *v*, 19.11
Coniah. .a *v* no one cares for? 22.28
among the nations. .a useless *v*. Hos 8.8

VESSEL — S (cont.)

one *v* for beauty and another	Rom 9.21
empty *v* and not too few.	2Ki 4.3
who bear the *v* of the LORD.	Isa 52.11
sorted the good into *v* but	Mt 13.48
this treasure in earthen *v*,	2Cor 4.7
there are not only *v* of gold	2Tim 2.20

VICTORIOUS

uphold you with my *v*..hand.	Isa 41.10
v is he, humble and riding	Zech 9.9

VICTORY

the LORD..to give you the *v*.'	Deut 20.4
has wrought this great *v*	1Sam 14.45
the LORD gave *v* to David	2Sam 8.6
v..was turned into mourning	19.2
the arrow of *v* over Syria!	2Ki 13.17
the LORD gave *v* to David	1Chr 18.6
stand still, and see the *v*	2Chr 20.17
right hand can give you *v*.	Job 40.14
we shout for joy over your *v*,	Ps 20.5
nor did..own arm give them *v*;	44.3
who givest *v* to kings, who	144.10
the *v* belongs to the LORD.	Prov 21.31
whom *v* meets at every step?	Isa 41.2
so my own arm brought me *v*,	63.5
midst, a warrior who gives *v*;	Zeph 3.17
LORD will give *v* to..Judah	Zech 12.7
till he brings justice to *v*;	Mt 12.20
"Death..swallowed up in *v*."	1Cor 15.54
the *v* that overcomes the world,	1Jn 5.4

VIGILANCE

Keep your heart with all *v*;	Prov 4.23

VINDICATE — S — ING

LORD will *v* his people	Deut 32.36
V me, O God, and defend my	Ps 43.1
the LORD will *v* his people,	135.14
'*V* me against my adversary.'	Lk 18.3
he who *v* me is near. Who will	Isa 50.8
v the righteous by rewarding	1Ki 8.32
v the righteous by rewarding	2Chr 6.23

VINDICATION

v from..God of his salvation.	Ps 24.5
revealed his *v* in the sight of	98.2
The LORD works *v* and justice	103.6

VINE — S

every man under his *v*	1Ki 4.25
didst bring a *v* out of Egypt;	Ps 80.8
see; have regard for this *v*,	80.14
Your mother was like a *v*	Ezek 19.10
Israel is a luxuriant *v* that	Hos 10.1
sit every man under his *v*	Mic 4.4
not drink,..this fruit of the *v*	Mt 26.29
fruit of the *v* until that day	Mk 14.25
"I am the true *v*, and my Father	Jn 15.1
and planted it with choice *v*;	Isa 5.2
It has laid waste my *v*, and	Joel 1.7

VINEGAR

for my thirst they gave me *v*	Ps 69.21
Like *v* to the teeth, and	Prov 10.26

VINEYARD — S

Noah..planted a *v*;	Gen 9.20
planted a *v* and..not enjoyed	Deut 20.6
sow your *v* with two kinds of seed,	22.9
Naboth..had a *v* in Jezreel,	1Ki 21.1
but, my own *v* I have not kept!	Sol 1.6
My beloved had a *v* on a very	Isa 5.1
"A pleasant *v*, sing of it!	27.2

to hire laborers for his *v*.	Mt 20.1
'Son, go and work in the *v*	21.28
a *v*, and set a hedge around it,	21.33
parables. "A man planted a *v*,	Mk 12.1
"A man planted a *v*, and let	Lk 20.9
for our *v* are in blossom."	Sol 2.15

VINTAGE

the *v* will fail, the fruit	Isa 32.10
upon your..*v* the destroyer	Jer 48.32
gathered the *v* of the earth,	Rev 14.19

VIOLATE — D

righteousness he will not *v*.	Job 37.23
A man who has *v* the law of	Heb 10.28

VIOLENCE

deliver me from men of *v*.	2Sam 22.49
although there is no *v* in my	Job 16.17
cry out, '*V*!' but I am not	19.7
on his own pate his *v* descends.	Ps 7.16
v covers them as a garment.	73.6
gain by *v*;..takes away..life	Prov 1.19
do no wrong or *v* to the alien,	Jer 22.3
destruction and *v*..before me;	Hab 1.3
covering one's garment with *v*,	Mal 2.16
kingdom of heaven..suffered *v*,	Mt 11.12
"Rob no one by *v* or by false	Lk 3.14

VIPER — S

tongue of a *v* will kill him.	Job 20.16
a *v* came out because of	Acts 28.3
"You brood of *v*! Who warned you	Mt 3.7
brood of *v*! how can you speak	12.34

VIRGIN — S

fair to look upon, a *v*,	Gen 24.16
shall take to wife a *v* of his	Lev 21.14
king, with her *v* companions,	Ps 45.14
as a young man marries a *v*,	Isa 62.5
the *v* daughter of my people	Jer 14.17
may comfort you, O *v* daughter	Lam 2.13
Lament like a *v* girded with	Joel 1.8
"Fallen,..is the *v* Israel;	Amos 5.2
v shall conceive and bear a son,	Mt 1.23
to a *v* betrothed to a man	Lk 1.27
four hundred young *v* who	Judg 21.12

VIRGINITY

in her the tokens of *v*,'	Deut 22.14
broken out..tokens of her *v*	22.15
bewailed her *v* upon the	Judg 11.38

VIRTUE

supplement your faith with *v*,	2Pet 1.5

VISION — S

in a *v*, "Fear not, Abram,	Gen 15.1
known to him in a *v*,	Num 12.6
there was no frequent *v*.	1Sam 3.1
v of Isaiah the son of Amoz,	Isa 1.1
concerning the valley of *v*.	22.1
v of..this has become..sealed.	29.11
prophesying to you a lying *v*,	Jer 14.14
her prophets obtain no *v*	Lam 2.9
seek a *v* from the prophet,	Ezek 7.26
the Spirit..brought me in the *v*	11.24
and every *v* comes to nought'?	12.22
seen a delusive *v*, and uttered	13.7
Daniel said, "I saw in my *v*	Dan 7.2
Daniel, alone saw the *v*, for	10.7
The *v* of Obadiah. Thus says	Obad 1.1
LORD answered.."Write the *v*;	Hab 2.2
prophet..ashamed of his *v*	Zech 13.4
had even seen a *v* of angels,	Lk 24.23
and in a trance I saw a *v*,	Acts 11.5

VISION — S (cont.)

a *v* appeared to Paul in..night: Acts 16.9
Lord said to Paul one night in a *v*, 18.9
not disobedient to the..*v*, 26.19
Amid thoughts..*v* of the night, Job 4.13
and terrify me with *v*, 7.14
they speak *v* of their own Jer 23.16
opened, and I saw *v* of God. Ezek 1.1
brought me in the *v* of God 40.2
Daniel..understanding in all *v* Dan 1.17
it was I who multiplied *v*, Hos 12.10
your young men shall see *v*, Acts 2.17
but I will go on to *v* and 2Cor 12.1

VISIT — EST — ED

"God will *v* you; then you Ex 13.19
I will *v* their sin upon them." 32.34
dost *v* him every morning, Job 7.18
seventy years..I will *v* you, Jer 29.10
Thou *v* the earth and waterest it Ps 65.9
The Lord *v* Sarah as he Gen 21.1
the Lord had *v* his people Ruth 1.6
God first *v* the Gentiles, Acts 15.14

VOICE — S

"The *v* is Jacob's voice, Gen 27.22
v speaking to him from above Num 7.89
saw no form;..only a *v*. Deut 4.12
ever hear the *v* of a god 4.33
would not obey the *v* of..Lord 8.20
you did not obey the *v* 28.45
lips moved,..*v* was not heard; 1Sam 1.13
after the fire a still small *v*. 1Ki 19.12
v of the Lord..upon the waters. Ps 29.3
sends forth his *v*,..mighty *v*. 68.33
I hear a *v* I had not known: 81.5
you would hearken to his *v*! 95.7
The *v* of my beloved! Behold, Sol 2.8
I heard the *v* of the Lord Isa 6.8
his majestic *v* to be heard 30.30
A *v* says, "Cry!" And I said, 40.6
The *v* of the Lord, rendering 66.6
mirth and the *v* of gladness, Jer 7.34
make to cease..*v* of mirth and 16.9
will obey the *v* of the Lord 42.6
The Lord utters his *v* before Joel 2.11
v of..Lord cries to the city— Mic 6.9
"The *v*..crying in the wilderness: Mt 3.3
lo, a *v* from heaven, saying, 3.17
and a *v* from the cloud said, 17.5
and a *v* came from heaven, Mk 1.11
a *v* came out of the cloud, 9.7
"The *v* of one crying in the Lk 3.4
a *v* came out of the cloud, 9.35
"I am the *v* of one crying in Jn 1.23
dead will hear the *v* of the Son 5.25
His *v* you have never heard, 5.37
and they will heed my *v*. 10.16
the *v* of the Lord came, Acts 7.31
"The *v* of a god,..not of man!" 12.22
I heard a *v* saying to me 26.14
"Their *v* has gone out to all Rom 10.18
this *v* borne from heaven, 2Pet 1.18
I heard a *v* from heaven like Rev 14.2
lifted their *v* together to God Acts 4.24

VOID

earth..without form and *v*, Gen 1.2
earth,..it was waste and *v*; Jer 4.23
I will make *v* the plans of Judah 19.7

VOMIT — S — ED (v)

be sated with it and *v* it. Prov 25.16
swallows down riches and *v* Job 20.15

land *v* out its inhabitants. Lev 18.25
the fish, and it *v* out Jonah Jonah 2.10

VOMIT (n)

dog that returns to his *v* Prov 26.11
dog turns back to his own *v*, 2Pet 2.22

VOW — S — ED (v)

you *v* a *v* to God, do not delay Ecc 5.4
When a man *v*..to the Lord, Num 30.2
Israel *v* a vow to the Lord, 21.2

VOW — S (n)

Then Jacob made a *v*, Gen 28.20
Bethel, where you..made a *v* 31.13
offering,..in payment of a *v* Lev 22.18
makes a special *v* of persons 27.2
special *v*,..of a Nazirite, Num 6.2
"When you make a *v* to Deut 23.21
Jephthah made a *v* to the Judg 11.30
vowed a *v* and said, "O Lord 1Sam 1.11
cut his hair,..he had a *v*. Acts 18.18
my *v* I will pay before those Ps 22.25
My *v* to thee I must perform, 56.12
to thee shall *v* be performed, 65.1
I will pay my *v* to the Lord 116.18

VOYAGE

the *v* will be with injury Acts 27.10

W

WAGES

name your *w*, and I will Gen 30.28
changed my *w* ten times, 31.7
I will give you your *w*." Ex 2.9
and does not give him his *w*; Jer 22.13
earns *w* to put them into a bag Hag 1.6
and be content with your *w*." Lk 3.14
the *w* of sin is death, but Rom 6.23
his *w* according to his labor. 1Cor 3.8

WAIT — S — ING

none that *w* for thee..to shame; Ps 25.3
for thee I *w* all the day long. 25.5
W for the Lord; be strong, 27.14
Be still before the Lord, and *w* 37.7
W for the Lord, and keep to 37.34
I *w* for the Lord, my soul 130.5
repay evil"; *w* for the Lord, Prov 20.22
I will *w* for the Lord, who Isa 8.17
O Lord, we *w* for thee; thy 26.8
who *w* for the Lord shall renew 40.31
the coastlands *w* for his law. 42.4
those who *w*..not..put to shame." 49.23
the coastlands shall *w* for me, 60.9
God..who works for those who *w* 64.4
good that one should *w* quietly Lam 3.26
w continually for your God." Hos 12.6
w for the God of my salvation; Mic 7.7
w for me," says the Lord, Zeph 3.8
as we *w* for adoption as sons, Rom 8.23
as you *w* for the revealing 1Cor 1.7
to eat, *w* for one another— 11.33
by faith, we *w* for the hope Gal 5.5
w for his Son from heaven, 1Thess 1.10
For God..my soul *w* in silence; Ps 62.1
Lord *w* to be gracious to you, Isa 30.18
Blessed is he who *w* and comes Dan 12.12
I *w* patiently for the Lord; Ps 40.1
As they have *w* for my life, 56.6
My eyes grow dim..*w* for my God. 69.3
they were all *w* for him. Lk 8.40

WAIT — S — ING (cont.)

men who are *w* for their master Lk 12.36
w for and hastening the 2Pet 3.12

WAKE — NS

for you to *w* from sleep. Rom 13.11
Morning by morning he *w*, he Isa 50.4

WALK — S — ED — ING

Arise, *w* through the..land, Gen 13.17
"I am God Almighty; *w* before me, 17.1
Lord, before whom I *w*, 24.40
shall not *w* in the customs Lev 20.23
"If you *w* in my statutes and 26.3
And I will *w* among you, and 26.12
"Then if you *w* contrary 26.21
not hearken..but *w* contrary 26.27
w in all the way which Deut 5.33
to *w* in all his ways, 10.12
You shall *w* after the Lord 13.4
and to *w* in all his ways, Josh 22.5
sons did not *w* in his ways, 1Sam 8.3
if you will *w* in my ways, 1Ki 3.14
if you..*w* before me, as David 9.4
Jehu was not careful to *w* in 2Ki 10.31
did not *w* in the way of the Lord. 21.22
love to thy servants who *w* 2Chr 6.14
if you *w* before me, as David 7.17
Ought you not to *w* in..fear Neh 5.9
an oath to *w* in God's law 10.29
W about Zion, go round about Ps 48.12
may *w* before God in the light 56.13
refused to *w* according to..law. 78.10
that Israel would *w* in my ways! 81.13
they *w* about in darkness; all 82.5
who *w*, O Lord, in the light of 89.15
will *w* with integrity of heart 101.2
I *w* before the Lord 116.9
who *w* in the law of the Lord! 119.1
Though I *w* in..trouble, thou 138.7
my son, do not *w* in the way Prov 1.15
you will *w* in the way of good 2.20
I *w* in the way of righteousness, 8.20
w in the ways of your heart Ecc 11.9
that we may *w* in his paths." Isa 2.3
warned me not to *w* in the way 8.11
"This is the way, *w* in it," 30.21
they shall *w* and not faint. 40.31
spirit to those who *w* in it: 42.5
in whose ways they would not *w*, 42.24
who *w* in their uprightness. 57.2
rebellious people,..*w* in a way 65.2
the good way is; and *w* in it, Jer 6.16
I will make them *w* by brooks 31.9
they may *w* in my statutes Ezek 11.20
your God; *w* in my statutes, 20.19
"Do two *w* together, unless Amos 3.3
w each in the name of its god, Mic 4.5
to *w* humbly with your God? 6.8
If you will *w* in my ways Zech 3.7
or to say, 'Rise and *w*'? Mt 9.5
take up your pallet, and *w*." Jn 5.8
W while you have the light, 12.35
in the name of Jesus..*w*." Acts 3.6
we..might *w* in newness of life. Rom 6.4
who *w* not according to..flesh 8.4
But I say, *w* by the Spirit, Gal 5.16
let us also *w* by the Spirit. 5.25
that we should *w* in them. Eph 2.10
w in love, as Christ loved us- 5.2
Lord; *w* as children of light 5.8
ought to *w* in the same way 1Jn 2.6
they shall *w* with me in white, Rev 3.4
God *w* in the midst of..camp Deut 23.14

he *w* on the vault of heaven.' Job 22.14
Blessed..who *w* in his ways! Ps 128.1
who *w* in integrity *w* securely, Prov 10.9
poor who *w* in his integrity 28.6
He who *w* in integrity will 28.18
but the fool *w* in darkness; Ecc 2.14
He who *w* righteously and Isa 33.15
not in man who *w* to direct Jer 10.23
If any one *w* in the day, Jn 11.9
Enoch *w* with God after Gen 5.22
Noah *w* with God. 6.9
I have *w* before you from my 1Sam 12.2
because he *w* before thee in 1Ki 3.6
he *w* in all the sins which 15.3
he *w* in..way of Jeroboam 16.26
to sin, but *w* in them; 2Ki 13.6
he *w* in the way of the kings 16.3
and *w* in the customs of the 17.8
but *w* in the customs which 17.19
with Jehoshaphat,..he *w* in 2Chr 17.3
you have not *w* in the ways 21.12
for I have *w* in my integrity, Ps 26.1
God's house we *w* in fellowship. 55.14
The people who *w* in darkness Isa 9.2
have not *w* in my statutes, Ezek 11.12
you have *w* in their counsels; Mic 6.16
Peter..*w* on the water and came Mt 14.29
and sins in which you once *w*, Eph 2.2
heard..God *w* in the garden Gen 3.8
by *w* in his ways, and Deut 30.16
I see four men..*w* in..fire, Dan 3.25
w..in mourning before the Lord Mal 3.14
came to them, *w* on the sea. Mt 14.25
he came to them, *w* on the sea. Mk 6.48
but they look like trees, *w*." 8.24
w in all the commandments Lk 1.6
they saw Jesus *w* on the sea and Jn 6.19
and *w* in the fear of the Lord Acts 9.31
you are no longer *w* in love. Rom 14.15

WALL — S

waters being a *w* to them Ex 14.22
they were a *w*..both by night 1Sam 25.16
inspected the *w*; and I turned Neh 2.15
So the *w* was finished on 6.15
at the dedication of the *w* 12.27
by my God I can leap over a *w*. Ps 18.29
like..high *w* protecting him. Prov 18.11
man's hand..wrote on..the *w* Dan 5.5
I will build a *w* against her, Hos 2.6
I will be to her a *w* of fire Zech 2.5
let him down over the *w*, Acts 9.25
strike you, you white-washed *w*! 23.3
broken down the dividing *w* Eph 2.14
cities fortified with..*w*, Deut 3.5
salvation as *w* and bulwarks. Isa 26.1
an iron pillar, and bronze *w*, Jer 1.18
By faith the *w* of Jericho Heb 11.30

WANDER — S — ED — ING

w in the wilderness forty Num 32.13
May his children *w* about and Ps 109.10
"They have loved to *w* thus, Jer 14.10
w from..way of understanding Prov 21.16
if any..*w* from the truth Jas 5.19
Some *w* in desert wastes, Ps 107.4
w, blind, through the streets, Lam 4.14
Better..than the *w* of desire; Ecc 6.9
'A *w* Aramean was my father; Deut 26.5

WANDERER — S

shall be a fugitive and a *w* Gen 4.12
shall be *w* among the nations. Hos 9.17

WANT

my shepherd, I shall not *w*;	Ps 23.1
those who fear him have no *w*!	34.9
Not that I complain of *w*;	Phil 4.11

WAR — RED (v)

those who *w*..shall be..nothing	Isa 41.12
They *w* against Midian,	Num 31.7

WAR — S (n)

w with Bera king of Sodom,	Gen 14.2
He trains my hands for *w*, so	Ps 18.34
though *w* arise against me, yet	27.3
who trains my hands for *w*,	144.1
neither shall they learn *w*	Isa 2.4
to Jerusalem to wage *w* against it,	7.1
in *w*, will not sit down first	Lk 14.31
not carrying on a worldly *w*,	2Cor 10.4
Now *w* arose in heaven, Michael	Rev 12.7
dragon..went off to make *w*	12.17
He makes *w* cease to the end	Ps 46.9
you will hear of *w* and rumors	Mt 24.6
when you hear of *w* and rumors	Mk 13.7
when you hear of *w* and tumults,	Lk 21.9
What causes *w*, and what causes	Jas 4.1

WARFARE

cry to her that..*w* is ended,	Isa 40.2
weapons of..*w*..not worldly	2Cor 10.4
you may wage the good *w*.	1Tim 1.19

WARMING

with the guards, and *w* himself	Mk 14.54
Peter..standing and *w* himself.	Jn 18.18

WARN — ED (v)

I solemnly *w* you this day	Deut 8.19
Thus he used to *w* him, so	2Ki 6.10
w them, lest they..come into	Lk 16.28
w them to speak no more	Acts 4.17
"The man solemnly *w* us,	Gen 43.3
the LORD *w* Israel and Judah	2Ki 17.13
I *w* them on the day when	Neh 13.15
by them is thy servant *w*;	Ps 19.11
I solemnly *w* your fathers	Jer 11.7
w in a dream not to return	Mt 2.12
vipers! Who *w* you to flee	3.7
By faith Noah, being *w* by God	Heb 11.7

WARNING — S (n)

and they became a *w*.	Num 26.10
you shall give them *w* from me	Ezek 3.17
trumpet, and did not take *w*;	33.5
happened to them as a *w*,	1Cor 10.11
these things are *w* for us,	10.6

WARRIOR

Jephthah..was a mighty *w*,	Judg 11.1
he runs upon me like a *w*.	Job 16.14
midst, a *w* who gives victory;	Zeph 3.17

WASH — ED

and *w* them with water.	Ex 29.4
w them off into the water	Num 5.23
elders..shall *w* their hands	Deut 21.6
w in the Jordan seven times,	2Ki 5.10
If I *w* myself with snow,	Job 9.30
I *w* my hands in innocence, and	Ps 26.6
W me..from my iniquity, and	51.2
W..make yourselves clean;	Isa 1.16
Though you *w* yourself with lye	Jer 2.22
Jerusalem, *w* your heart from	4.14
fast, anoint your head and *w*	Mt 6.17
did not first *w* before dinner.	Lk 11.38
"Go, *w* in the pool of Siloam"	Jn 9.7

began to *w* the disciples' feet,	13.5
w away your sins, calling	Acts 22.16
and *w* my hands in innocence.	Ps 73.13
the Lord..*w* away the filth	Isa 4.4
took water and *w* his hands	Mt 27.24
But you were *w*,..sanctified,	1Cor 6.11

WASTE

the LORD will lay *w* the earth	Isa 24.1
to generation it shall lie *w*;	34.10
land a *w*; your cities..ruins	Jer 4.7
indignant, saying, "Why this *w*?	Mt 26.8
But Saul laid *w* the church,	Acts 8.3

WATCH — ES — ED — ING (v)

"The LORD *w* between you	Gen 31.49
I will take my stand to *w*,	Hab 2.1
W..for you do not know on	Mt 24.42
W..for you know neither the day	25.13
remain here, and *w* with me."	26.38
W and pray that you may not	26.41
heed, *w*; for you do not know	Mk 13.33
death; remain here, and *w*."	14.34
But *w* at all times, praying	Lk 21.36
the LORD,..*w* all his paths.	Prov 5.21
days when God *w* over me;	Job 29.2
w over my word to perform it."	Jer 1.12
friends, *w* for my fall.	20.10
traffickers..who were *w* me,	Zech 11.11

WATCH (n)

keeping *w* on the evil and	Prov 15.3
they..kept *w* over him there.	Mt 27.36

WATCHFUL

Be *w*, stand firm in..faith,	1Cor 16.13
in prayer, being *w* in it with	Col 4.2

WATCHMAN — MEN

the *w* called out and told	2Sam 18.25
"*W*, what of the night? *W*,	Isa 21.11
have made you..*w* for..Israel	Ezek 3.17
But if the *w* sees the sword	33.6
prophet is the *w* of Ephraim,	Hos 9.8
my soul waits..more than *w*	Ps 130.6
O Jerusalem, I have set *w*;	Isa 62.6
I set *w* over you, saying,	Jer 6.17
when *w* will call in..Ephraim:	31.6

WATER — S — ED (v)

keeper; every moment I *w* it.	Isa 27.3
one who *w* will himself be *w*.	Prov 11.25
mist went up..and *w*..ground—	Gen 2.6
Jordan valley was well *w*	13.10
Jacob..*w* the flock of Laban	29.10
I planted, Apollos, but God	1Cor 3.6

WATER — S (n)

there was no *w* for the people	Ex 17.1
shall have..*w* of bitterness	Num 5.18
no *w* for the congregation	20.2
w out of the flinty rock,	Deut 8.15
"Fill four jars with *w*, and	1Ki 18.33
struck the *w*, saying, "Where	2Ki 2.14
cold *w* to a thirsty soul,	Prov 25.25
w from the wells of salvation.	Isa 12.3
his bread..his *w* will be sure.	33.16
pour *w* on the thirsty land,	44.3
they find no *w*, they return	Jer 14.3
He is like a tree planted by *w*,	17.8
LORD,..fountain of living *w*.	17.13
sprinkle clean *w* upon you,	Ezek 36.25
w was issuing from below	47.1
baptize..with *w* for repentance,	Mt 3.11
w because he is a disciple,	10.42

WATER — S (n) (cont.)

took w and washed his hands	Mt 27.24
w to drink because you bear	Mk 9.41
"I baptize you with w; but he	Lk 3.16
his finger in w and cool my	16.24
"I baptize with w; but among	Jn 1.26
said.."Fill the jars with w."	2.7
born of w and the Spirit,	3.5
the w that I shall give him	4.14
waiting for..moving of the w;	5.3n
flow rivers of living w.' "	7.38
eunuch said, "See, here is w!	Acts 8.36
"Can any one forbid w for	10.47
Christ, not with the w only	1Jn 5.6
who desires take..w of life	Rev 22.17
the w of Gihon and directed	2Chr 32.30
he drew me out of many w,	Ps 18.16
the w have come up to my neck.	69.1
By the w of Babylon,..wept,	137.1
Many w cannot quench love,	Sol 8.7
When you pass through the w I	Isa 43.2
a spring..whose w fail not.	58.11
O that my head were w, and	Jer 9.1
let justice roll down like w,	Amos 5.24
as the w cover the sea.	Hab 2.14
living w shall flow out from	Zech 14.8

WAVE — S

he who doubts is like a w of	Jas 1.6
all thy w..have gone over me.	Ps 42.7
overwhelm me with all thy w.	88.7
all thy w and thy billows	Jonah 2.3
boat..was..beaten by the w;	Mt 14.24
and the w beat into the boat,	Mk 4.37

WAVE OFFERING

for a w..before the LORD.	Ex 29.24
brought the sheaf of the w..;	Lev 23.15
Levites..a w..from the people	Num 8.11

WAVERING

trusted in the LORD without w.	Ps 26.1
of our hope without w, for	Heb 10.23

WAY — S

guard the w to the tree	Gen 3.24
LORD has prospered my w;	24.56
became impatient on the w.	Num 21.4
to walk in the w of the LORD	Judg 2.22
of God, to tell us our w."	1Sam 9.8
This God—his w is perfect;	2Sam 22.31
walked in..w of Jeroboam	1Ki 16.26
the w..I shall not return.	Job 16.22
He has walled up my w, so	19.8
he knows the w that I take;	23.10
Man does not know the w to	28.13
"God understands the w to it,	28.23
w to the dwelling of light,	38.19
LORD knows..w of the righteous,	Ps 1.6
make thy w straight before me.	5.8
This God—his w is perfect;	18.30
and teaches the humble his w.	25.9
Commit your w to the LORD;	37.5
him in whose w he delights;	37.23
Wait..and keep to his w, and	37.34
that thy w may be known upon	67.2
Thy w, O God, is holy. What	77.13
walks in the w that is blameless	101.6
can a young man keep..w pure?	119.9
lead me in the w everlasting!	139.24
preserving..w of his saints.	Prov 2.8
Her house is the w to Sheol,	7.27
walk in..w of righteousness,	8.20

to him whose w is upright,	10.29
but the w of the faithless	13.15
w which seems right to a man,	14.12
The w of the wicked is an	15.9
w of a sluggard is overgrown	15.19
w which seems right to a man,	16.25
can man understand his w?	20.24
Train up a child in the w he	22.6
"This is the w, walk in it,"	Isa 30.21
prepare the w of the LORD,	40.3
"My w is hid from the LORD,	40.27
who makes a w in the sea,	43.16
turned every one to his own w;	53.6
Remove..from my people's w."	57.14
The w of peace they know not,	59.8
do not know the w of the LORD,	Jer 5.4
w of man is not in himself,	10.23
I set before you the w of life	21.8
their w shall be..slippery	23.12
w of the Lord is not just.'	Ezek 18.25
the wicked turn from his w	33.11
w of the Lord is not just';	33.17
His w is in whirlwind and	Nah 1.3
their own country by another w.	Mt 2.12
Prepare the w of the Lord,	3.3
who shall prepare thy w before	11.10
teach the w of God truthfully,	22.16
messenger..shall prepare thy w;	Mk 1.2
but truly teach the w of God.	12.14
Prepare the w of the Lord,	Lk 3.4
who shall prepare thy w before	7.27
"I am the w, and the truth,	Jn 14.6
found any belonging to the W,	Acts 9.2
to you the w of salvation."	16.17
expounded to him the w of God	18.26
no little stir concerning the W.	19.23
I persecuted this W to the death,	22.4
the W..they call a sect,	24.14
w of peace they do not know."	Rom 3.17
the w into the sanctuary	Heb 9.8
by the new and living w	10.20
known the w of righteousness	2Pet 2.21
prepare the w for the kings	Rev 16.12
kept the w of the LORD,	2Sam 22.22
your God, walking in his w	1Ki 2.3
if you will walk in my w.	3.14
walked in the w of the kings	2Chr 28.2
the knowledge of thy w.	Job 21.14
his eyes are upon their w.	24.23
Does not he see my w, and	31.4
I have kept the w of the LORD,	Ps 18.21
and they do not regard my w."	95.10
He made known his w to Moses,	103.7
man's w are before..the LORD,	Prov 5.21
All the w of a man are pure	16.2
She looks well to the w of	31.27
that he may teach us his w	Isa 2.3
will make straight all his w;	45.13
so are my w higher than your w	55.9
Your w and your doings have	Jer 4.18
my eyes are upon all their w;	16.17
every man according to his w,	17.10
judge you according to your w;	Ezek 7.3
works are right..w are just;	Dan 4.37
that he may teach us his w	Mic 4.2
sank low. His w were as of old.	Hab 3.6
and how inscrutable his w!	Rom 11.33
Just and true are thy w, O	Rev 15.3

WAYFARER

saw the w in the open square	Judg 19.17
opened my doors to the w);	Job 31.32
a w who turns aside to tarry	Jer 14.8

WEAK

and all knees w as water.	Ezek 7.17
The w..have not strengthened,	34.4
help the w, remembering	Acts 20.35
the man who is w in faith,	Rom 14.1
bear with..failings of the w,	15.1
God chose what is w in the	1Cor 1.27
We are w, but you are strong.	4.10
conscience, being w, is defiled.	8.7
To the w I became w, that	9.22
Who is w, and I am not w?	2Cor 11.29
when I am w, then I am strong.	12.10
help the w, be patient with	1Thess 5.14
w women, burdened with sins	2Tim 3.6

WEAKNESS — ES

the w of God is stronger	1Cor 1.25
I was with you in w and in	2.3
For he was crucified in w,	2Cor 13.4
to sympathize with our w,	Heb 4.15

WEALTH

have gotten me this w.'	Deut 8.17
if I..rejoiced because my w	Job 31.25
men who trust in their w	Ps 49.6
W and riches are in his house;	112.3
diligent man will get..w.	Prov 12.27
pretends to be poor, yet has..w.	13.7
W hastily gotten will dwindle,	13.11
the sinner's w is laid up	13.22
Do not toil to acquire w; be	23.4
to whom God has given w and	Ecc 5.19
offered for love all the w of	Sol 8.7
eat the w of the nations,	Isa 61.6
become proud in your w—	Ezek 28.5
w of liberality on their part.	2Cor 8.2
abuse..for..Christ great w	Heb 11.26
this w has been laid waste."	Rev 18.17

WEAPON — S

"You are my hammer and w of	Jer 51.20
Wisdom..better than w of war,	Ecc 9.18
with the w of righteousness	2Cor 6.7
for the w of our warfare	10.4

WEAR

"A woman shall not w	Deut 22.5
or she will w me out by her	Lk 18.5

WEARINESS

All things are full of w;	Ecc 1.8
much study is a w of the flesh.	12.12

WEARY — IES — IED (v)

w men, that you w my God also?	Isa 7.13
The toil of a fool w him, so	Ecc 10.15
w me with your iniquities.	Isa 43.24
w with your many counsels;	47.13
w with the length of your way,	57.10
In what have I w you? Answer	Mic 6.3
w the Lord with your words.	Mal 2.17

WEARY

there the w are at rest.	Job 3.17
fought..and David grew w.	2Sam 21.15
feasts.I am w of bearing them.	Isa 1.14
None is w, none stumbles,	5.27
have been w of me, O Israel!	43.22
you;—I am w of relenting.	Jer 15.6
let us not grow w in well-doing	Gal 6.9
do not be w in well-doing.	2Thess 3.13

WEATHER

you say, 'It will be fair w;	Mt 16.2

WEAVER — 'S

like a w..rolled up my life;	Isa 38.12
swifter than a w shuttle,	Job 7.6

WEB

his trust is a spider's w.	Job 8.14

WEDDING

Then he said..'The w is ready,	Mt 22.8

WEEDS

his enemy came and sowed w	Mt 13.25

WEEKS

keep the feast of w	Deut 16.10
"Seventy w of years..decreed	Dan 9.24

WEEP — ING

had no more strength to w.	1Sam 30.4
time to w,..a time to laugh;	Ecc 3.4
gone..to the high places to w;	Isa 15.2
my soul will w in secret for	Jer 13.17
W not for him who is dead,	22.10
"For these things I w; my eyes	Lam 1.16
they w over you in bitterness	Ezek 27.31
the ministers of the Lord, w	Joel 2.17
Tell it not in Gath, w not	Mic 1.10
there men will w and gnash	Mt 8.12
men..w and gnash their teeth.	24.51
"Blessed are you that w now,	Lk 6.21
"Do not w; for she is not dead	8.52
do not w for me, but w for	23.28
going to the tomb to w there.	Jn 11.31
rejoice, w with those who w.	Rom 12.15
will w and wail over her	Rev 18.9
My face is red with w, and	Job 16.16
I drench my couch with my w.	Ps 6.6
for the Lord has heard..my w.	6.8
W may tarry for the night, but	30.5
Rachel is w for her children;	Jer 31.15
My eyes are spent with w;	Lam 2.11
there sat women w for Tammuz.	Ezek 8.14
Rachel w for her children;	Mt 2.18
Mary stood w outside the tomb,	Jn 20.11
"Woman, why are you w? Whom	20.15
"What are you doing, w and	Acts 21.13

WEIGH — S — ED

let..others w what is said.	1Cor 14.29
but the Lord w the spirit.	Prov 16.2
but the Lord w the heart.	21.2
who w the heart perceive it?	24.12
and by him actions are w.	1Sam 2.3
"O that my vexation were w,	Job 6.2
(Let me be w in a just balance,	31.6
and w the mountains in scales	Isa 40.12
and w the money on scales.	Jer 32.10
TEKEL, you have been w in	Dan 5.27
And they w out as my wages	Zech 11.12

WEIGHTS

in your bag two kinds of w,	Deut 25.13
Diverse w..an abomination	Prov 20.10

WELCOME — D

W one another, therefore,	Rom 15.7
Jesus returned, the crowd w	Lk 8.40
he w them and spoke to them	9.11
and w all who came to him,	Acts 28.30

WELFARE

inquired about their w,	Gen 43.27
come to seek the w of..Israel.	Neh 2.10
who delights in the w of his	Ps 35.27
abundant w will they give you.	Prov 3.2
in its w you will find your w.	Jer 29.7
not seeking the w of his people,	38.4

WELL — S (n)

she saw a *w* of water;	Gen 21.19
Abimelech about a *w* of water	21.25
outside the city by the *w*	24.11
moved..and dug another *w*,	26.22
"Spring up, O *w*!—Sing	Num 21.17
from the *w* of Bethlehem	2Sam 23.15
a *w* of living water,	Sol 4.15
As a *w* keeps its water fresh,	Jer 6.7
ox that has fallen into a *w*,	Lk 14.5
Jacob's *w* was there, and so	Jn 4.6
from the *w* of salvation.	Isa 12.3

WELL (adv)

"Is it *w* with the young	2Sam 18.29
your faith has made you *w*."	Mt 9.22
she may be made *w*, and live."	Mk 5.23
many as touched it were made *w*.	6.56
it is *w* that we are here;	Lk 9.33
he had faith to be made *w*,	Acts 14.9

WEPT

Esau lifted..his voice and *w*.	Gen 27.38
turned away from them and *w*;	42.24
Joseph..entered..and *w* there	43.30
he *w* aloud, so..the Egyptians	45.2
Joseph..*w* on his neck	46.29
and *w* before the LORD until	Judg 20.23
had seen the first house, *w*	Ezra 3.12
and *w*, and mourned for days;	Neh 1.4
the people *w* when they heard	8.9
w, when we remembered Zion.	Ps 137.1
he went out and *w* bitterly.	Mt 26.75
Peter..broke down and *w*.	Mk 14.72
saw the city he *w* over it,	Lk 19.41
he went out and *w* bitterly.	22.62
Jesus *w*.	Jn 11.35
I *w* much that no one was found	Rev 5.4

WEST

far as the east is from the *w*,	Ps 103.12
many will come from east and *w*	Mt 8.11
men will come from east and *w*,	Lk 13.29

WHALE

in the belly of the *w*, so will	Mt 12.40

WHEAT

Gideon was beating out *w*	Judg 6.11
has straw in common with *w*?	Jer 23.28
sowed weeds among the *w*,	Mt 13.25
the weeds you root up the *w*	13.29
gather the *w* into his granary,	Lk 3.17
unless a grain of *w* falls	Jn 12.24

WHEEL

there he was working at his *w*.	Jer 18.3
as it were a *w* within a *w*.	Ezek 1.16
as if a *w* were within a *w*.	10.10

WHIP

A *w* for the horse, a bridle	Prov 26.3
making a *w* of cords, he drove	Jn 2.15

WHIRLWIND

Elijah went up by a *w* into	2Ki 2.11
and their wheels like the *w*.	Isa 5.28
sow..and they shall reap the *w*.	Hos 8.7

WHISPER

All who hate me *w* together	Ps 41.7
speech shall *w* out of..dust.	Isa 29.4

WHISPERER

a *w* separates close friends.	Prov 16.28
words of a *w* are like delicious	17.8
words of a *w* are like delicious	26.22

WHITE

Let your garments be always *w*;	Ecc 9.8
garments became..intensely *w*,	Mk 9.3
two men stood..in *w* robes,	Acts 1.10
his head and his hair were *w*	Rev 1.14

WHITEWASH — ED

As for you, you *w* with lies;	Job 13.4
for you are like *w* tombs,	Mt 23.27
shall strike you, you *w* wall!	Acts 23.3

WHOLESOME

I have made this water *w*;	2Ki 2.21
ear heeds *w* admonition	Prov 15.31

WICK

burning *w* he will not quench;	Isa 42.3
or quench a smoldering *w*, till	Mt 12.20

WICKED — LY

men of Sodom were *w*,	Gen 13.13
"Should you help the *w* and	2Chr 19.2
given into the hand of the *w*;	Job 9.24
the eyes of the *w* will fail;	11.20
The *w* man writhes in pain	15.20
that the *w* man is spared in	21.30
portion of a *w* man with God,	27.13
Break thou the arm of the *w*	Ps 10.15
and the *w* will be no more;	37.10
seen a *w* man overbearing,	37.35
how long shall the *w* exult?	94.3
The *w* man sees it and is angry;	112.10
indignation..because of the *w*,	119.53
that thou wouldst slay the *w*,	139.19
my prayer..against their *w*	141.5
the *w*..cut off from the land,	Prov 2.22
the mouth of the *w* conceals	10.6
w will not dwell in the land.	10.30
but sin overthrows the *w*.	13.6
God scorns the *w*, but the	14.9
the *w* for the day of trouble.	16.4
w flee when no one pursues,	28.1
If favor is shown to the *w*,	Isa 26.10
they made his grave with the *w*	53.9
does the way of the *w* prosper?	Jer 12.1
when a *w* man turns away	Ezek 18.27
if the *w* restores the pledge,	33.15
but the *w* shall do wickedly;	Dan 12.10
'You *w* servant! I forgave you	Mt 18.32
'You *w* and slothful servant!	25.26
"Drive out the *w* person from	1Cor 5.13
brethren, do not act so *w*;	Judg 19.23
have sinned and done very *w*.	1Chr 21.17
and we have acted *w*;	Neh 9.33

WICKEDNESS

LORD saw..*w* of man was great	Gen 6.5
was this *w* brought to pass?"	Judg 20.3
wicked comes forth *w*';	1Sam 24.13
"Though *w* is sweet in his	Job 20.12
w is..abomination to my lips.	Prov 8.7
For *w* burns like a fire, it	Isa 9.18
fast..to loose the bonds of *w*,	58.6
so she keeps fresh her *w*;	Jer 6.7
before your *w* was uncovered?	Ezek 16.57
in turning..you from your *w*."	Acts 3.26
by their *w* suppress the truth.	Rom 1.18
filled with all manner of *w*,	1.29

WIDOW — S

fatherless, and the *w*,	Deut 14.29
fatherless, and his wife a *w*!	Ps 109.9
fatherless, plead for the *w*.	Isa 1.17
How like a *w* has she become,	Lam 1.1
poor *w*..put in two..coins,	Mk 12.42

WIDOW — S (cont.)

the only son..she was a *w*;   Lk 7.12
poor *w* put in two copper coins.   21.2
You have sent *w* away empty,   Job 22.9
that *w* may be their spoil,   Isa 10.2
and let your *w* trust in me."   Jer 49.11
many *w* in Israel in the days   Lk 4.25
their *w* were neglected in   Acts 6.1
Honor *w* who are real *w*.   1Tim 5.3
take a *w* garment in pledge;   Deut 24.17
I caused the *w* heart to sing   Job 29.13
maintains the *w* boundaries.   Prov 15.25
for you devour *w* houses and   Mt 23.14*n*
scribes..who devour *w* houses   Mk 12.40

WIFE — 'S

his *w*'; then they will kill   Gen 12.12
If any man's *w* goes astray   Num 5.12
Ruth and she became his *w*;   Ruth 4.13
Abigail, to make her his *w*.   1Sam 25.39
then let my *w* grind for   Job 31.10
Your *w* will be..fruitful vine   Ps 128.3
rejoice in..*w* of your youth,   Prov 5.18
goes in to his neighbor's *w*;   6.29
who finds a *w* finds a good   18.22
prudent *w* is from the Lord.   19.14
A good *w* who can find? She   31.10
Enjoy life with..*w*..you love,   Ecc 9.9
"If a man divorces his *w* and   Jer 3.1
as a faithless *w* leaves her   3.20
and at evening my *w* died.   Ezek 24.18
"Go, take..a *w* of harlotry   Hos 1.2
Israel did service for a *w*,   12.12
she is your..*w* by covenant.   Mal 2.14
took his *w*, but knew her not   Mt 1.24
'Whoever divorces his *w*, let   5.31
leave..and be joined to his *w*,   19.5
his *w* sent word to him,   27.19
lawful..man to divorce his *w*?"   Mk 10.2
take the *w*, and raise up children   12.19
'I have married a *w*, and   Lk 14.20
Remember Lot's *w*.   17.32
his *w* came in, not knowing   Acts 5.7
the *w* does not rule over her   1Cor 7.4
Are you bound to a *w*? Do not   7.27
A *w* is bound to her husband   7.39
right to be accompanied by a *w*,   9.5
man shall..be joined to his *w*,   Eph 5.31
you know how to take a *w*   1Thess 4.4
w quarreling is a continual   Prov 19.13

WILDERNESS

"They shall die in the *w*."   Num 26.65
the great and terrible *w*,   Deut 8.15
the strongholds in the *w*,   1Sam 23.14
What is..coming up from the *w*,   Sol 3.6
w and..dry land shall be glad,   Isa 35.1
make the *w* a pool of water,   41.18
holy cities have become a *w*,   64.10
brought them into the *w*.   Ezek 20.10
he was in the *w* forty days,   Mk 1.13
for forty days in the *w*, tempted   Lk 4.2
go out into the *w* to behold?   7.24

WILL — S (v)

touched him, saying, 'I *w*; be   Mt 8.3
"If you *w*,..make me clean."   Mk 1.40
not what I *w*, but what thou *w*."   14.36
to *w* and to work for his good   Phil 2.13
ought to say, "If the Lord *w*,   Jas 4.15

WILL (n)

according to the *w* of your   Ezra 7.18
I delight to do thy *w*, O my   Ps 40.8

w of the Lord to bruise him;   Isa 53.10
Thy *w* be done, On earth as it   Mt 6.10
whoever does..*w* of my Father   12.50
it is not the *w* of my Father   18.14
unless I drink it, thy *w* be done."   26.42
does..*w* of God is my brother,   Mk 3.35
"My food is to do the *w* of him   Jn 4.34
but the *w* of him who sent me.   5.30
but the *w* of him who sent me;   6.38
if any man's *w* is to do his *w*,   7.17
"The *w* of the Lord be done." Acts 21.14
by God's *w* I may..succeed   Rom 1.10
know his *w* and approve what   2.18
it depends not upon man's *w*   9.16
prove what is the *w* of God,   12.2
if I do this of my own *w*,   1Cor 9.17
and to us by the *w* of God.   2Cor 8.5
according to the *w* of our God   Gal 1.4
what the *w* of the Lord is.   Eph 5.17
assured in all the *w* of God.   Col 4.12
For this is the *w* of God,   1Thess 4.3
I have come to do thy *w*, O   Heb 10.7
God's *w* that by doing right   1Pet 2.15
if that should be God's *w*,   3.17
passions but by the *w* of God.   4.2
who does the *w* of God abides   1Jn 2.17
by thy *w* they existed and   Rev 4.11

WILLING — LY

"Father, if thou art *w*, remove   Lk 22.42
Who then will offer *w*,   1Chr 29.5

WILLOWS

boughs..and *w* of the brook;   Lev 23.40
On the *w*..we hung..our lyres.   Ps 137.2

WIN

slave to all, that I might *w*   1Cor 9.19
not lose..but..*w* a full reward.   2Jn 8

WIND

strong *w* rent the mountains,   1Ki 19.11
By his *w*..heavens..made fair;   Job 26.13
from the raging *w* and tempest."   Ps 55.8
a stormy *w* came out of..north,   Ezek 1.4
For they sow the *w*, and..reap   Hos 8.7
Ephraim..pursues the east *w*   12.1
east *w*, the *w* of the Lord,   13.15
like the rush of a mighty *w*,   Acts 2.2
he awoke and rebuked the *w*   Lk 8.24
The *w* blows where it wills,   Jn 3.8

WINDOW — S

in a basket through a *w* in   2Cor 11.33
w of the heavens..opened   Gen 7.11
"If the Lord..make *w* in   2Ki 7.2
he had *w* in his upper chamber   Dan 6.10

WINE

Noah awoke from his *w*   Gen 9.24
made their father drink *w*   19.35
"Drink no *w* nor strong drink   Lev 10.8
shall separate himself from *w*   Num 6.3
drink no *w* or strong drink,   Judg 13.4
heart is merry with *w*,   2Sam 13.28
the king was merry with *w*,   Est 1.10
W is a mocker, strong drink   Prov 20.1
Those who tarry long over *w*,   23.30
how to cheer my body with *w*—   Ecc 2.3
For your love is better than *w*, Sol 1.2
tarry..till *w* inflames them!   Isa 5.11
who are heroes at drinking *w*,   5.22
an outcry..for lack of *w*;   24.11
they say, "let us get *w*,   56.12
answered, "We will drink no *w*,   Jer 35.6
No priest shall drink *w*,   Ezek 44.21

WINE (cont.)
drank *w*, and praised the gods Dan 5.4
W and new *w* take away the Hos 4.11
who drink *w* in bowls, and Amos 6.6
Moreover, *w* is treacherous; Hab 2.5
they offered him *w* to drink, Mt 27.34
puts new *w* into old wineskins; Mk 2.22
offered..*w* mingled with myrrh; 15.23
no one puts new *w* into old Lk 5.37
tasted the water now become *w*, Jn 2.9
"They are filled with new *w*." Acts 2.13
And do not get drunk with *w*, Eph 5.18
use a little *w* for the sake 1Tim 5.23

WINE PRESS
beating out wheat in the *w*.., Judg 6.11
"I have trodden the *w*..alone, Isa 63.3
threw it into the great *w*.. Rev 14.19

WINESKINS
new wine put into old *w*; if Mt 9.17
no one puts new wine into old *w*; Lk 5.37

WINGS
I bore you on eagles' *w* Ex 19.4
under those *w* you have come Ruth 2.12
hide me in..shadow of thy *w*, Ps 17.8
came..upon the *w* of the wind. 18.10
refuge in the shadow of thy *w*. 36.7
"O that I had *w* like a dove! 55.6
safe under the shelter of thy *w*! 61.4
takes..*w*, flying like..eagle Prov 23.5
the seraphim; each had six *w*: Isa 6.2

WINKS
w with his eyes, scrapes with Prov 6.13
He who *w*..eye causes trouble, 10.10

WINNOW
You shall *w* them and the wind Isa 41.16
Babylon..and they shall *w* her, Jer 51.2

WINTER
earth remains,..*w*..not cease." Gen 8.22
w is past, the rain is over Sol 2.11
harbor was not suitable to *w* Acts 27.12
or even spend the *w*, so that 1Cor 16.6
Do your best..come before it. 2Tim 4.21
decided to spend the *w* there. Tit 3.12

WISDOM
that will be your *w* and your Deut 4.6
my lord has *w* like the *w* 2Sam 14.20
And God gave Solomon *w* and 1Ki 4.29
he was full of *w*, understanding, 7.14
seen all the *w* of Solomon, 10.4
Solomon excelled..and in *w*. 10.23
Give me now *w* and knowledge 2Chr 1.10
greatness of your *w* was not told 9.6
and *w* will die with you. Job 12.2
"But where shall *w* be found? 28.12
Who has put *w* in the clouds, 38.36
mouth of..righteous utters *w*, Ps 37.30
My mouth shall speak *w*; the 49.2
fear of..LORD..beginning of *w*; 111.10
That men may know *w* and Prov 1.2
W cries aloud in the street; 1.20
w will come into your heart, 2.10
for *w* is better than jewels, 8.11
W builds her house, but folly 14.1
To get *w* is better than gold; 16.16
He who gets *w* loves himself; 19.8
No *w*, no understanding, no 21.30
By a house is built, and 24.3
She opens her mouth with *w*, 31.26
search..by *w* all that is done Ecc 1.13

protection of *w* is like the 7.12
the poor man's *w* is despised, 9.16
spirit of *w* and understanding, Isa 11.2
prudent? Has their *w* vanished? Jer 49.7
established the world by his *w*, 51.1
And in every matter of *w* and Dan 1.20
and *w*, like the *w* of the gods, 5.11
I have..come out to give you *w* 9.22
w is justified by her deeds." Mt 11.19
to hear the *w* of Solomon, 12.42
"Where did this man get this *w* 13.54
Jesus increased in *w* and in Lk 2.52
w is justified by..her children." 7.35
to hear the *w* of Solomon, 11.31
will give you a mouth and *w*, 21.15
Moses was instructed in..*w* Acts 7.22
w and knowledge of God! Rom 11.33
and not with eloquent *w*, 1Cor 1.17
the power..and the *w* of God. 1.24
Jesus, whom God made our *w*, 1.30
among the mature we do impart *w*, 2.6
the *w* of this world is folly 3.19
To one..the utterance of *w*, 12.8
may give you a spirit of *w* Eph 1.17
w of God might..be made known 3.10
If any of you lacks *w*, let him Jas 1.5
w from above is first pure, 3.17
according to the *w* given him, 2Pet 3.15

WISE
If they were *w*, they would Deut 32.29
I give you a *w* and..mind, 1Ki 3.12
the *w* in their own craftiness; Job 5.13
see that even the *w* die, Ps 49.10
The *w* of heart will heed Prov 10.8
A *w* son hears his father's 13.1
and a *w* man will appease it. 16.14
hear the words of the *w*, and 22.17
who are *w* in their own eyes, Isa 5.21
Where then are your *w* men? 19.12
"How can you say, 'We are *w*, Jer 8.8
commanded that all the *w* men Dan 2.12
those who are *w* shall shine 12.3
is *w*, let him understand Hos 14.9
w men from the East came to Mt 2.1
does them will be like a *w* man 7.24
be *w* as serpents and innocent 10.16
hidden these things from the *w* 11.25
the faithful and *w* servant, 24.45
Where is the *w* man? Where 1Cor 1.20
bear with fools, being *w* 2Cor 11.19
not as unwise men but as *w*, Eph 5.15
Who is *w* and understanding Jas 3.13

WISER
thy commandment makes me *w* Ps 119.98
you are indeed *w* than Daniel; Ezek 28.3
are *w* in their own generation Lk 16.8

WITHER — S — ED
and *w* like the green herb. Ps 37.2
Their leaves will not *w* nor Ezek 47.12
The grass *w*, the flower fades, Isa 40.7
the trees of the field are *w*; Joel 1.12
there was a man with a *w* hand. Mt 12.10
And the fig tree *w* at once. 21.19
man was there who had a *w* hand. Mk 3.1
since it had no root it *w* away. 4.6
tree which you cursed has *w*." 11.21
man..whose right hand was *w*. Lk 6.6

WITHHELD
you have not *w* your son, Gen 22.12
"If I have *w*..that the poor Job 31.16

WITHHELD (cont.)

not *w* the request of his lips.   Ps 21.2
I also *w* the rain from you   Amos 4.7

WITHHOLD

No good thing does the LORD *w*   Ps 84.11
Do not *w* good from those to   Prov 3.27
do not *w* your coat as well.   Lk 6.29

WITNESS — ES (v)

call heaven and earth to *w*   Deut 4.26
call heaven and earth to *w*   30.19
Thus you *w* against yourselves,   Mt 23.31
w that this is the Son of God.''   Jn 1.34
The pride of Israel *w* against   Hos 7.10

WITNESS — ES (n)

you may be a *w* for me   Gen 21.30
God is *w* between you and me.''   31.50
''You shall not bear false *w*   Ex 20.16
the testimony of one *w*.   Num 35.30
'' 'Neither. .bear false *w*   Deut 5.20
that this song may be a *w* for me   31.19
be a *w* between us and you,   Josh 22.27
LORD will be *w* between us;   Judg 11.10
behold, my *w* is in heaven,   Job 16.19
A faithful *w* does not lie,   Prov 14.5
A truthful *w* saves lives,   14.25
false *w* will not go unpunished,   19.5
Be not a *w* against. .neighbor   24.28
A man who bears false *w*   25.18
made him a *w* to the peoples,   Isa 55.4
and I am *w*, says the LORD.' ''   Jer 29.23
true and faithful *w* against us   42.5
let the Lord GOD be a *w* against   Mic 1.2
the LORD was *w* to the covenant   Mal 2.14
swift *w* against the sorcerers,   3.5
bear *w* to what we have seen;   Jn 3.11
to whom you bore *w*, here he is,   3.26
bears *w* to what he has seen   3.32
If I bear *w* to myself, my   5.31
Father. .himself borne *w* to me.   5.37
it is they that bear *w* to me;   5.39
Spirit. .will bear *w* to me;   15.26
bear *w* to the wrong; but if   18.23
bearing *w* to these things,   21.24
Lord, who bore *w* to the word   Acts 14.3
not leave himself without *w*,   14.17
you will be a *w* for him to all   22.15
blood of Stephen thy *w* was   22.20
you must bear *w* also at Rome.''   23.11
and bear *w* to the things   26.16
For God is my *w*, whom I serve   Rom 1.9
the prophets bear *w* to it,   3.21
Spirit. .bearing *w* with our spirit   8.16
who bore *w* to the word of God   Rev 1.5
Jesus Christ the faithful *w*,   1.5
the faithful and true *w*, the   3.14
slain. .for the *w* they had borne;   6.9
On the evidence of two *w*   Deut 17.6
And they said, ''We are *w*.''   Josh 24.22
''We are *w*. May the LORD make   Ruth 4.11
''You are my *w*,'' says. .LORD,   Isa 43.10
declared it? And you are my *w*!   44.8
I signed the deed,. .got *w*,   Jer 32.10
evidence of two or three *w*.   Mt 18.16
''Why do we still need *w*?   Mk 14.63
You are *w* of these things.   Lk 24.48
you also are *w*, because   Jn 15.27
shall be my *w* in Jerusalem   Acts 1.8
and of that we all are *w*.   2.32
we are *w* to these things,   5.32
we are *w* to all that he did   10.39
evidence of two or three *w*.   2Cor 13.1

You are *w*, and God also,   1Thess 2.10
by so great a cloud of *w*,   Heb 12.1
three *w*, the Spirit, the water,   1Jn 5.8
I will grant my two *w* power   Rev 11.3

WIVES

W, be subject to. .husbands,   Eph 5.22
W, be subject to. .husbands,   Col 3.18
w, be submissive to. .husbands,   1Pet 3.1

WOE

If I am wicked, *w* to me!   Job 10.15
W to those who join house to   Isa 5.8
W to those who rise early in   5.11
''*W* is me! For I am lost; for   6.5
I make weal and create *w*, I   45.7
w to that man by whom the Son   Mk 14.21
W to me if I do not preach   1Cor 9.16
as it flew in midheaven, ''*W*,   Rev 8.13

WOLF — VES

w shall dwell with the lamb,   Isa 11.6
The *w* and the lamb shall feed   65.25
after my departure fierce *w*   Acts 20.29

WOMAN

she shall be called *W*,   Gen 2.23
''The *w* whom thou gavest   3.12
A foolish *w* is noisy; she is   Prov 9.13
a *w* who fears the LORD is   31.30
the *w* whose heart is snares   Ecc 7.26
a young *w* shall conceive and   Isa 7.14
a *w* who had. .a hemorrhage   Mt 9.20
w of the city, who was a sinner,   Lk 7.37
w. .had a spirit of infirmity   13.11
''O *w*, what have you to do with   Jn 2.4
a *w*. .caught in adultery,   8.3n
When a *w* is in travail she   16.21
for a man not to touch a *w*.   1Cor 7.1
created for *w*, but *w* for man.)   11.9
sent forth his Son, born of *w*,   Gal 4.4
a *w* clothed with the sun,   Rev 12.1
the *w* fled into the wilderness,   12.6
a *w* sitting on a scarlet beast   17.3

WOMB

how the spirit comes. .in the *w*   Ecc 11.5
''Blessed is the *w* that bore   Lk 11.27
second time into his mother's *w*   Jn 3.4

WOMEN

Solomon loved many foreign *w*:   1Ki 11.1
seven *w*. .take hold of one man   Isa 4.1
you *w* who are at ease, hear   32.9
also *w* looking on from afar,   Mk 15.40
be two *w* grinding together;   Lk 17.35
and the *w* who had followed   23.49
natural relations with *w*   Rom 1.27
the *w* should keep silence   1Cor 14.34
that *w* should adorn. .modestly   1Tim 2.9
W received their dead by   Heb 11.35

WONDER — ED (v)

why do you *w* at this, or why   Acts 3.12
no. .answer, so that Pilate *w*.   Mk 15.5
all who heard it *w* at what   Lk 2.18
they *w*; and they recognized   Acts 4.13

WONDERFUL

my name, seeing it is *w*?''   Judg 13.18
your love to me was *w*,   2Sam 1.26
not understand, things too *w*   Job 42.3
Thy testimonies are *w*;   Ps 119.129
Such knowledge. .too *w* for me;   139.6
W are thy works! Thou knowest   139.14
Three things are too *w* for   Prov 30.18
will be called ''*W* Counselor,   Isa 9.6

WONDERFUL (cont.)

for thou hast done *w* things,　Isa 25.1
"Great and *w* are thy deeds,　Rev 15.3

WONDERS (n)

smite Egypt with all the *w*　Ex 3.20
glorious deeds, doing *w*?　15.11
has done, the *w* he wrought　1Chr 16.12
Dost thou work *w* for the dead? Ps 88.10
him who alone does great *w*,　136.4
I will show *w* in the heaven　Acts 2.19

WONDROUS

and telling all thy *w* deeds.　Ps 26.7
who alone does *w* things.　72.18
behold *w* things out of thy law.　119.18

WOOL

mingled stuff, *w* and linen　Deut 22.11
She seeks *w* and flax, and　Prov 31.13
they shall become like *w*.　Isa 1.18

WORD — S

whether my *w* will come true　Num 11.23
But the *w* is very near you;　Deut 30.14
"If one ventures a *w* with you,　Job 4.2
and my *w* dropped upon them.　29.22
In God, whose *w* I praise,　Ps 56.10
he sent forth his *w*, and healed　107.20
guarding it according to thy *w*.　119.9
laid up thy *w* in my heart,　119.11
thy *w* is firmly fixed in the　119.89
to the earth; his *w* runs swiftly.　147.15
a good *w* makes him glad.　Prov 12.25
w in season, how good it is!　15.23
w fitly spoken is like apples　25.11
w of. .God will stand for ever.　Isa 40.8
a *w* that shall not return:　45.23
so shall my *w* be that goes　55.11
let him. .speak my *w* faithfully. Jer 23.28
shall know whose *w* will stand,　44.28
not. .bread alone, but by every *w* Mt 4.4
say the *w*, and my servant will　8.8
account for every careless *w*　12.36
he was preaching the *w* to them. Mk 2.2
The sower sows the *w*.　4.14
and ministers of the *w*,　Lk 1.2
in peace, according to thy *w*;　2.29
for his *w* was with authority.　4.32
at your *w* I will let down the nets."　5.5
say the *w*, and let my servant　7.7
with God, and the *W* was God.　Jn 1.1
who hears my *w* and believes　5.24
do not have his *w* abiding in you,　5.38
"If you continue in my *w*, you　8.31
because my *w* finds no place　8.37
already made clean by the *w*　15.3
and they have kept thy *w*.　17.6
Sanctify them. .thy *w* is truth.　17.17
fell on all who heard the *w*.　Acts 10.44
Gentiles should hear the *w*　15.7
received the *w* with. .eagerness,　17.11
and to the *w* of his grace,　20.32
not as though the *w*. .failed.　Rom 9.6
w is near you, on your lips　10.8
from the Gentiles, by *w* and　15.18
not,. .peddlers of God's *w*;　2Cor 2.17
Let him who is taught the *w*　Gal 6.6
washing of water with the *w*,　Eph 5.26
holding fast the *w* of life,　Phil 2.16
Let. .*w* of Christ dwell in you　Col 3.16
received. .*w* in. .affliction,　1Thess 1.6
rightly handling. .*w* of truth.　2Tim 2.15
preach the *w*, be urgent in　4.2

must hold firm to the sure *w*　Tit 1.9
first principles of God's *w*.　Heb 5.12
but the *w* of the oath, which　7.28
with meekness the implanted *w*,　Jas 1.21
may be won without a *w* by　1Pet 3.1
the prophetic *w* made sure　2Pet 1.19
concerning the *w* of life—　1Jn 1.1
liar, and his *w* is not in us.　1.10
whoever keeps his *w*, in him　2.5
and yet you have kept my *w*　Rev 3.8
earth had one language. .few *w*. Gen 11.1
let them hear my *w*,　Deut 4.10
lay up these *w* of mine　11.18
put my *w* in his mouth,　18.18
tells the king of Israel the *w*　2Ki 6.12
not denied the *w* of the Holy　Job 6.10
think that you can reprove *w*,　6.26
or in *w*. .can do no good?　15.3
"How long will you hunt for *w*?　18.2
lay up his *w* in your heart.　22.22
treasured in my bosom the *w*　23.12
is no speech, nor are there *w*;　Ps 19.3
Let the *w* of my mouth and　19.14
see a man. .hasty in his *w*?　Prov 29.20
The *w* of Agur son of Jakeh　30.1
therefore let your *w* be few.　Ecc 5.2
The *w* of a wise man's mouth　10.12
Thy *w* were found, and I ate　Jer 15.16
let us not heed any of his *w*."　18.18
but my *w* will not pass away.　Mt 24.35
but my *w* will not pass away.　Mk 13.31
but my *w* will not pass away.　Lk 21.33
You have the *w* of eternal life; Jn 6.68
The *w* that I say to you I　14.10
speak to the people all the *w*　Acts 5.20
speak five *w* with my mind,　1Cor 14.19

WORD OF GOD

make known to you the *w*. ." 1Sam 9.27
the *w*. .came to Shemaiah the　1Ki 12.22
Every *w*. .proves true; he　Prov 30.5
you have made void the *w*. . .　Mt 15.6
making void the *w*. .through　Mk 7.13
the *w*. .came to John the son　Lk 3.2
people pressed. .to hear the *w*. .,　5.1
parable. .The seed is the *w*. .　8.11
who hear the *w*. .and do it."　8.21
who hear the *w*. .and keep it!"　11.28
give up. .preaching the *w*. .　Acts 6.7
And the *w*. .increased;　6.7
Samaria had received the *w*. .,　8.14
Gentiles also. .received the *w*. .　11.1
the *w*. .grew and multiplied.　12.24
It was necessary that the *w*. .　13.46
sword of the Spirit. .is the *w*. . . Eph 6.17
much more bold to speak the *w*. . Phil 1.14
accepted it. .as. .the *w*. .,　1Thess 2.13
consecrated by. .*w*. .and prayer. 1Tim 4.5
But the *w*. .is not fettered.　2Tim 2.9
that the *w*. .not be discredited.　Tit 2.5
the *w*. .is living and active,　Heb 4.12
tasted the goodness of the *w*. .　6.5
the living and abiding *w*. .;　1Pet 1.23
by the *w*. .heavens existed　2Pet 3.5
and the *w*. .abides in you,　1Jn 2.14
who bore witness to the *w*. .　Rev 1.2
those. .slain for the *w*. .　6.9
name. .is called. .The *W*. . .　19.13
had been beheaded for. .the *w*. .　20.4

WORD — S OF THE LORD

w. .came to Abram in a vision, Gen 15.1
Then he who feared the *w*. .　Ex 9.20

WORD — S OF THE LORD (cont.)

go beyond..w.., to do..good   Num 24.13
to declare to you the w..;   Deut 5.5
the w..was rare in those days;   1Sam 3.1
the w..came to Nathan,   2Sam 7.4
according to the w..,which   1Ki 14.18
"This is the w..,which he   2Ki 9.36
Hezekiah to Isaiah, "The w..   20.19
defiled it, according to the w..   23.16
the w..came to Nathan,   1Chr 17.3
For the w..is upright; and all   Ps 33.4
By the w..heavens were made,   33.6
came to pass the w..tested him   105.19
law, and the w..from Jerusalem.   Isa 2.3
Then the w..came to Isaiah: 38.4
w..you have spoken is good."   39.8
Hear the w.., you who tremble   66.5
w..came in the days of Josiah   Jer 1.2
the w..is..an object of scorn,   6.10
they have rejected the w..,   8.9
w..has become..a reproach   20.8
The w..that came to Hosea the   Hos 1.1
The w..that came to Joel,   Joel 1.1
the w..came to Jonah the son   Jonah 1.1
the w..which came to Zephaniah   Zeph 1.1
w..grew and prevailed mightily   Acts 12.20
they spoke the w..to him   16.32
that the w..may speed on   2Thess 3.1
therefore hearken to the w...   1Sam 15.1
read the w..from the scroll   Jer 36.6
famine..of hearing the w..,   Amos 8.11

WORK — S — ED — ING (v)

the people had a mind to w.   Neh 4.6
w, for I am with you, says   Hag 2.4
We must w the works of him   Jn 9.4
one who does not w but trusts   Rom 4.5
w out your own salvation   Phil 2.12
If any one will not w, let   2Thess 3.10
and w with willing hands.   Prov 31.13
God w for good with those who   Rom 8.28
'These last w only one hour,   Mt 20.12
while the Lord w with them   Mk 16.20n
w through me..for..Gentiles),   Gal 2.8
there he was w at his wheel.   Jer 18.3
working still, and I am w."   Jn 5.17
W together with him, then,   2Cor 6.1

WORK — S (n)

rested..from all his w   Gen 2.2
your w, but on the seventh   Ex 23.12
seen all the great w of the   Deut 11.7
necks to the w of their Lord.   Neh 3.5
to despise the w of thy hands   Job 10.3
according to the w of a man   34.11
do not regard..w of his hands,   Ps 28.5
heavens are the w of thy hands.   102.25
Man goes forth to his w and   104.23
the w..comes back to him.   Prov 12.14
Commit your w to the Lord,   16.3
I saw all the w of God, that   Ecc 8.17
I am doing a w in your days   Hab 1.5
thy w, O Lord, do I fear.   3.2
having accomplished the w   Jn 17.4
each man's w will become   1Cor 3.13
nearly died for..w of Christ,   Phil 2.30
esteem..because of their w.   1Thess 5.13
establish..in every good w   2Thess 2.17
equipped for every good w.   2Tim 3.17
heavens are the w of thy hands;   Heb 1.10
tell of all his wonderful w!   1Chr 16.9
consider the wondrous w of   Job 37.14
Lord, how manifold are thy w!   Ps 104.24

All thy w shall give thanks   145.10
w praise her in the gates.   Prov 31.31
I know their w and..thoughts,   Isa 66.18
w which the Father..granted me   Jn 5.36
the w of God..manifest in him.   9.3
The w that I do in my Father's   10.25
Dorcas..was full of good w   Acts 9.36
justified in his sight by w   Rom 3.20
not because of w but..of..call,   9.11
no longer on the basis of w;   11.6
receive..Spirit by w of the law, Gal 3.2
the w of the flesh are plain: 5.19
not because of w, lest any man   Eph 2.9
faith..if it has no w, is dead.   Jas 2.17
Abraham..justified by w,   2.21

WORKERS

A w appetite works for him;   Prov 16.26
depart..you w of iniquity!'   Lk 13.27
we are fellow w for God;   1Cor 3.9
may be fellow w in the truth.   3Jn 8

WORKMAN — SHIP

as one approved, a w who   2Tim 2.15
Are not you my w in the Lord?   1Cor 9.1
For we are his w, created   Eph 2.10

WORLD — LY

their words to the end of..w.   Ps 19.4
the field is the w, and the   Mt 13.38
"Go into all the w and preach   Mk 16.15n
gains the whole w and loses   Lk 9.25
you are of this w, I am not   Jn 8.23
"For judgment I came into..w,   9.39
the w has gone after him."   12.19
In the w you have tribulation;   16.33
even as I am not of the w.   17.14
the w may believe that thou   17.21
turned the w upside down   Acts 17.6
as sin came into the w through   Rom 5.12
spectacle to the w, to angels,   1Cor 4.9
For though we live in the w   2Cor 10.3
the w was created by the word   Heb 11.3
of whom the w was not worthy—   11.38
Do not love the w or the   1Jn 2.15
Do not wonder..w hates you.   3.13
They are of the w, therefore   4.5
weapons..not w but have divine   2Cor 10.4

WORM — S

But I am a w, and no man;   Ps 22.6
Fear not, you w Jacob, you   Isa 41.14
where their w does not die,   Mk 9.48
he was eaten by w and died.   Acts 12.23

WORSE

no avail; my distress grew w,   Ps 39.2
last state..w than the first.   Mt 12.45
from bad to w, deceivers   2Tim 3.13

WORSHIP — S — ED — ING

lad will go yonder and w.   Gen 22.5
elders of Israel, and w afar   Ex 24.1
(for you shall w no other god,   34.14
w before the Lord your God;   Deut 26.10
by year from his city to w   1Sam 1.3
W the Lord in holy array;   1Chr 16.29
I will w toward thy holy temple   Ps 5.7
nations shall w before him.   22.27
w the Lord in holy array.   29.2
come, let us w and bow down,   95.6
W the Lord in holy array;   96.9
let us w at his footstool!"   132.7
their idols..they made..to w,   Isa 2.20
will come and w the Lord   27.13

WORSHIP — S — ED — ING (cont.)

"You shall *w* before this altar"?	Isa 36.7
who enter these gates to *w*	Jer 7.2
and *w* any god except their own	Dan 3.28
year after year to *w*. .King,	Zech 14.16
East, and have come to *w* him."	Mt 2.2
if you will fall down and *w* me."	4.9
'You shall *w* the Lord your God	4.10
If you, then, will *w* me, it	Lk 4.7
nor in Jerusalem will you *w*	Jn 4.21
must *w* in spirit and truth."	4.24
among those who went up to *w*	12.20
over to *w* the host of heaven,	Acts 7.42
to *w* God contrary to the law."	18.13
she whom. .Asia and. .world *w*."	19.27
he will *w* God and declare	1Cor 14.25
true circumcision, who *w* God	Phil 3.3
"Let all God's angels *w* him."	Heb 1.6
who dwell on earth will *w* it,	Rev 13.8
and *w* him who made heaven	14.7
I fell down at his feet to *w*	19.10
I fell down to *w* at the feet	22.8
All the earth *w* thee; they sing	Ps 66.4
also he makes a god and *w* it,	Isa 44.15
man bowed his head and *w*	Gen 24.26
bowed their heads and *w*.	Ex 4.31
bowed their heads and *w*.	12.27
served other gods and *w*	Deut 17.3
rose. .and *w* before the LORD;	1Sam 1.19
house of the LORD, and *w*;	2Sam 12.20
summit, where God was *w*,	15.32
bowed their heads, and *w*	1Chr 29.20
fell upon the ground, and *w*.	Job 1.20
they fell down and *w* him.	Mt 2.11
And those in the boat *w* him,	14.33
hold of his feet and *w* him.	28.9
they *w* him, and returned	Lk 24.52*n*
I believe"; and he *w* him.	Jn 9.38
Cornelius met him. .and *w*	Acts 10.25
the elders fell down and *w*.	Rev 5.14
Men *w* the dragon, for he had	13.4
Jerusalem fell down. .*w* the	2Chr 20.18
w with fasting and prayer	Lk 2.37

WORSHIPER — S

if any one is a *w* of God	Jn 9.31
all the *w* of Baal came, so	2Ki 10.21

WORTH

that you are a woman of *w*.	Ruth 3.11
you are *w* ten thousand of	2Sam 18.3
sufferings. .not *w* comparing	Rom 8.18
But Timothy's *w* you know,	Phil 2.22

WORTHY

not *w* of the least of all	Gen 32.10
sandals I am not *w* to carry;	Mt 3.11
"Lord, I am not *w* to have you	8.8
mother more than me is not *w*	10.37
sandals I am not *w* to. .untie.	Mk 1.7
"He is *w* to have you do this	Lk 7.4
I am not *w* to have you come	7.6
I am no longer *w* to be called	15.21
sandal I am not *w* to untie."	Jn 1.27
counted *w* to suffer dishonor	Acts 5.41
sandals. .I am not *w* to untie.'	13.25
that our God may make you *w*	2Thess 1.11
Jesus. .*w* of as much more glory	Heb 3.3
of whom the world was not *w*—	11.38
in white, for they are *w*.	Rev 3.4
"*W* art thou, our Lord and God,	4.11
"Who is *w* to open the scroll	5.2
"*W* art thou to take the scroll	5.9

WOUND — ED — ING (v)

make alive; I *w* and I heal;	Deut 32.39
"Turn about,. .for I am *w*."	1Ki 22.34
"Turn about,. .for I am *w*."	2Chr 18.33
was *w* for our transgressions,	Isa 53.5
For the wound. .is my heart *w*,	Jer 8.21
another servant, and they *w* him	Mk 12.4
this one they *w* and cast out.	Lk 20.12
and *w* their conscience when	1Cor 8.12

WOUND — S (n)

my hurt! My *w* is grievous.	Jer 10.19
Why is. .my *w* incurable,	15.18
and your *w* is grievous.	30.12
For her *w* is incurable; and	Mic 1.9
hurt, your *w* is grievous.	Nah 3.19
but its mortal *w* was healed,	Rev 13.3
My *w* grow foul and fester	Ps 38.5
Who has *w* without cause?	Prov 23.29
Faithful are. .*w* of a friend;	27.6
and sores and bleeding *w*;	Isa 1.6
are these *w* on your back?'	Zech 13.6
bound up his *w*, pouring on oil	Lk 10.34

WRAPPED

hast *w* thyself with a cloud	Lam 3.44
w him in the linen shroud,	Mk 15.46
and *w* him in swaddling cloths,	Lk 2.7

WRATH

great is the *w* of the LORD	2Ki 22.13
till the fierce *w* of our God	Ezra 10.14
He has torn me in his *w*,	Job 16.9
the *w* of men shall praise	Ps 76.10
king's *w* is like. .growling	Prov 19.12
dread *w* of a king is like	20.2
I. .pour out my *w* like water.	Hos 5.10
known; in *w* remember mercy.	Hab 3.2
Was thy *w* against the rivers,	3.8
the day of the *w* of the LORD.	Zeph 2.2
to flee from the *w* to come?	Mt 3.7
not see life, but the *w* of God	Jn 3.36
w for yourself on the day of *w*	Rom 2.5
God. .unjust to inflict *w* on us?	3.5
For the law brings *w*, but	4,15
account of these the *w* of God	Col 3.6
who delivers us from the *w*	1Thess 1.10
and from the *w* of the Lamb;	Rev 6.16
wine press of the *w* of God;	14.19

WREATH — S

to receive a perishable *w*,	1Cor 9.25
nets. .with *w* of chain work	1Ki 7.17

WRESTLED

I have *w* with my sister,	Gen 30.8
a man *w* with him until	32.24

WRETCHED — NESS

W man that I am! Who will	Rom 7.24
that I may not see my *w*."	Num 11.15

WRITE — ING (v)

"*W* this as a memorial in a	Ex 17.14
I will *w* upon the tables	34.1
w them on the doorposts	Deut 6.9
w them upon the doorposts	11.20
w for himself in a book	17.18
w upon them all the words	27.3
w them on. .tablet of. .heart.	Prov 7.3
W in a book all the words	Jer 30.2
"Take a scroll and *w* on it	36.2
Were I to *w* for him my laws	Hos 8.12
LORD answered. ."*W* the vision;	Hab 2.2
and *w* them on their hearts,	Heb 8.10
and *w* them on their minds,"	10.16

WRITE — ING (v) (cont.)

I w this to you who believe	1Jn 5.13
Now w what you see, what is	Rev 1.19
w on him the name of my God,	3.12
man..in linen, with a w case	Ezek 9.2
he asked for a w tablet, and	Lk 1.63

WRITING — S (n)

the w was the w of God,	Ex 32.16
sacred w which are able to	2Tim 3.15

WRITTEN

w with the finger of God.	Ex 31.18
it is w in the law of Moses,	2Chr 23.18
as it is w in the law.	Neh 10.34
in the roll of the book it is w	Ps 40.7
Have I not w for you thirty	Prov 22.20
"The sin of Judah is w with	Jer 17.1
whose name shall be found w	Dan 12.1
how is it w of the Son of man,	Mk 9.12
your names are w in heaven."	Lk 10.20
"What I have w I have w."	Jn 19.22
signs..not w in this book;	20.30
is w in the second psalm,	Acts 13.33
whatever was w in former days	Rom 15.4
for the w code kills, but	2Cor 3.6

WRONG — ED (v)

You shall not w one another,	Lev 25.17
we have w..corrupted no one,	2Cor 7.2
If he has w you at all, or	Philem 18

WRONG — S (n)

man that did the w, "Why	Ex 2.13
full restitution for his w,	Num 5.7
Saul said, "I have done w;	1Sam 26.21
"I have done w; withdraw	2Ki 18.14
declared Job to be in the w.	Job 32.3
if there is w in my hands,	Ps 7.3
says, "I have done no w."	Prov 30.20
Jeremiah also said.."What w	Jer 37.18
"Is not this why you are w,	Mk 12.24
this man has done nothing w."	Lk 23.41
the Jews I have done no w,	Acts 25.10
Why not rather suffer w?	1Cor 6.7
you? Forgive me this w!	2Cor 12.13
in your hearts you devise w;	Ps 58.2

WROTE

Moses w all the words of	Ex 24.4
Moses w this law, and gave	Deut 31.9
questioned him; and he w	Judg 8.14
Preacher..w words of truth.	Ecc 12.10
I w..with ink on the scroll."	Jer 36.18
Jesus bent down and w with	Jn 8.6n
our beloved brother Paul w	2Pet 3.15

WROUGHT

said 'What has God w!'	Num 23.23
tell what God has w, and ponder	Ps 64.9

Y

YEAR — S

atonement..once in the y	Lev 16.34
proclaim..y of..Lord's favor,	Isa 61.2
my y of redemption has come.	63.4
his to the y of liberty;	Ezek 46.17
same, and thy y have no end.	Ps 102.27
y of..wicked will be short.	Prov 10.27
reign with him a thousand y.	Rev 20.6

YES

say..simply 'Y' or 'No';	Mt 5.37

to say Y and No at once?	2Cor 1.17
promises of God find their Y	1.20

YESTERDAY

for we are but of y, and	Job 8.9
same y..today and for ever.	Heb 13.8

YIELD — ED

but y yourselves to the Lord,	2Chr 30.8
now y..to righteousness for	Rom 6.19
voice and y up his spirit.	Mt 27.50

YOKE

broken the bars of your y	Lev 26.13
father made our y heavy.	1Ki 12.4
father made our y heavy.	2Chr 10.4
For the y of his burden, and	Isa 9.4
y..destroyed from your neck."	10.27
his y shall depart from them,	14.25
to undo the thongs of the y,	58.6
the y of the king of Babylon.	Jer 28.2
"My transgressions..into a y;	Lam 1.14
who eases the y on their jaws,	Hos 11.4
I will break his y from..you	Nah 1.13
Take my y upon you, and learn	Mt 11.29
putting a y upon the neck	Acts 15.10

YOKEFELLOW

true y, help these women,	Phil 4.3

YOUNG

"Solomon my son,..is y and	1Chr 29.1
She deals cruelly with her y,	Job 39.16
Rejoice, O y man, in..youth,	Ecc 11.9
The y man said to him, "All	Mt 19.20
a y man followed him, with	Mk 14.51
entering..tomb,..saw a y man	16.5
when you were y, you girded	Jn 21.18
this y man to the tribune;	Acts 23.17
I am writing to you, y men,	1Jn 2.13

YOUNGER

make sport of me, men..y	Job 30.1
y of them said to his father,	Lk 15.12
"The elder will serve the y."	Rom 9.12
urge the y men to control	Tit 2.6

YOUTH — S

man's heart is evil from..y;	Gen 8.21
for you are but a y, and he	1Sam 17.33
Remember not the sins of my y,	Ps 25.7
y is renewed like the eagle's.	103.5
like dew your y will come	110.3
given..discretion to the y—	Prov 1.4
Remember..Creator in..your y,	Ecc 12.1
to speak, for I am only a y."	Jer 1.6
been your way from your y,	22.21
you and the wife of your y,	Mal 2.14
I have observed from my y."	Mk 10.20
I have observed from my y."	Lk 18.21
manner of life from my y,	Acts 26.4
Let no one despise your y,	1Tim 4.12
y without blemish, handsome	Dan 1.4

Z

ZACCHAEUS

Z..was a chief tax collector,	Lk 19.2
"Z, make haste and come down;	19.5
Z stood and said to the Lord,	19.8

ZEAL

and see my z for the Lord."	2Ki 10.16
The z of the Lord will do	19.31

ZEAL (cont.)

z for thy house. . consumed me,	Ps 69.9
My z consumes me, because	119.139
z of the LORD. . will do this.	Isa 9.7
see thy z for thy people, and	26.11
z of the LORD will accomplish	37.32
Where are thy z and. . might?	63.15
"Z for thy house will consume	Jn 2.17
they have a z for God, but	Rom 10.2
he told us of. . your z for me,	2Cor 7.7
that your z for us might be	7.12
your z has stirred up most	9.2
as to z a persecutor of the	Phil 3.6

ZEALOUS

they are all z for the law,	Acts 21.20
being z for God as you all are	22.3
so extremely z was I for the	Gal 1.14
be z to be found by him	2Pet 3.14

ZEBULUN

Leah. . called his name Z.	Gen 30.20
Z shall dwell at the shore	49.13
The sons of Z, according	Num 26.26
And of Z he said, "Rejoice,	Deut 33.18
the princes of Z, the princes	Ps 68.27
the land of Z and. . Naphtali,	Isa 9.1

territory of Z and Naphtali,	Mt 4.13
thousand of the tribe of Z,	Rev 7.8

ZECHARIAH

the prophets, Haggai and Z	Ezra 5.1
Haggai the prophet and Z	6.14
word of the LORD came to Z	Zech 1.1
the word of the LORD came to Z	7.1

ZEPHANIAH

word of the LORD. . came to Z	Zeph 1.1

ZERUBBABEL

They came with Z, Jeshua,	Ezra 2.2
they approached Z and the	4.2
Then Z the son of Shealtiel	5.2
They came with Z, Jeshua,	Neh 7.7
the word. . came by Haggai. . to Z	Hag 1.1
"Speak now to Z the son of	2.2
word. . to Z: Not by might,	Zech 4.6

ZION

set my king on Z, my holy hill."	Ps 2.6
Mount Z, in the far north,	48.2
Out of Z, the perfection of	50.2
daughter of Z is. . like a booth	Isa 1.8
out of Z shall go forth the law,	2.3
you have come to Mount Z	Heb 12.22

The Exodus

BASHAN

The Great Sea
(Mediterranean Sea)

Megiddo

Jordan

AMMON

Joppa

Ai
Jericho
Heshbon

CANAAN

Jahaz
Salt
Sea
Gaza
Dibon

Arad
MOAB
Hormah
Kir-moab
Zoar
Iye-abarim

Raamses
Baal-zephon
Zilu
Oboth
Goshen
Punon
Wilderness
of Zin

Succoth
Wilderness
Petra
Pithom
of Shur
Kadesh-barnea

Bitter
EDOM
Lakes
On
(Heliopolis)
Wilderness
of Paran

Noph
(Memphis)
Ezion-geber
Marah?
SINAI
Elim?
Wilderness
of Sin

Nile
Dophkah?
Hazeroth?

Kibroth-hattaavah?

Rephidim
Mt. Sinai
MIDIAN

EGYPT

Gulf of Suez
Gulf of Aqaba

Red Sea

Probable route of Exodus ———▶
Trade routes ————

© 1976 by The Zondervan Corporation

Black S

HITTITE K[

Lake Tuz

TAURUS MTS.

RHODES

CAPHTOR
(CRETE)

KITTIM
(CYPRUS)

The Great Sea
(Mediterranean Sea)

Me

She

He

Ge

Tanis

Zoan

On

Noph

EGYPTIAN KINGDON

SINA

Nile

World of the Patriarchs

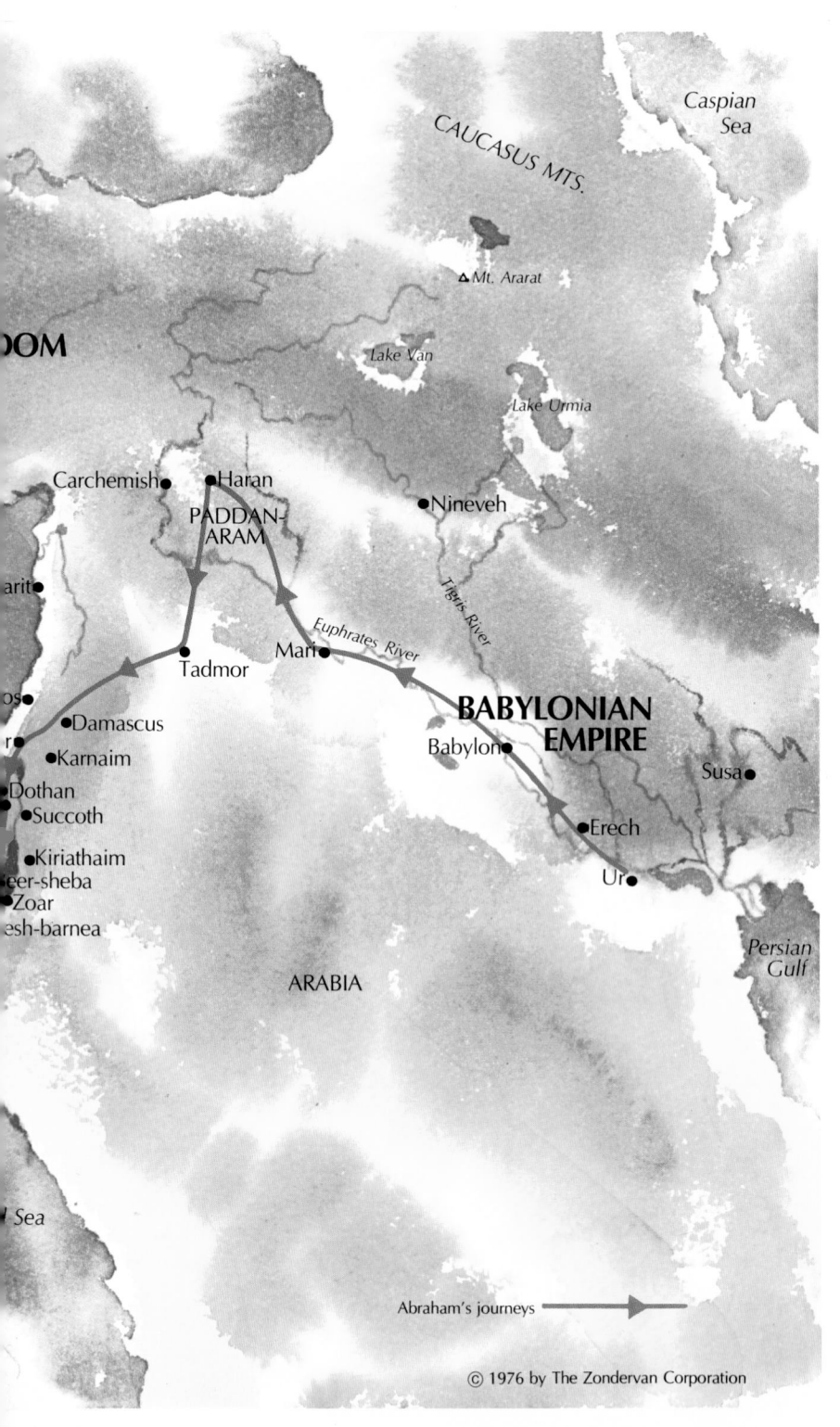

Caspian
Sea

CAUCASUS MTS.

△ Mt. Ararat

Lake Van

Lake Urmia

OOM

Carchemish•   •Haran

PADDAN-
ARAM

•Nineveh

Tigris River

Euphrates River

arit•

Tadmor

Mari•

BABYLONIAN
EMPIRE

os•

•Damascus

Babylon•

Susa•

r•

•Karnaim

Dothan•

•Succoth

•Erech

Ur•

•Kiriathaim

eer-sheba

•Zoar

esh-barnea

Persian
Gulf

ARABIA

Sea

Abraham's journeys ⟶

© 1976 by The Zondervan Corporation

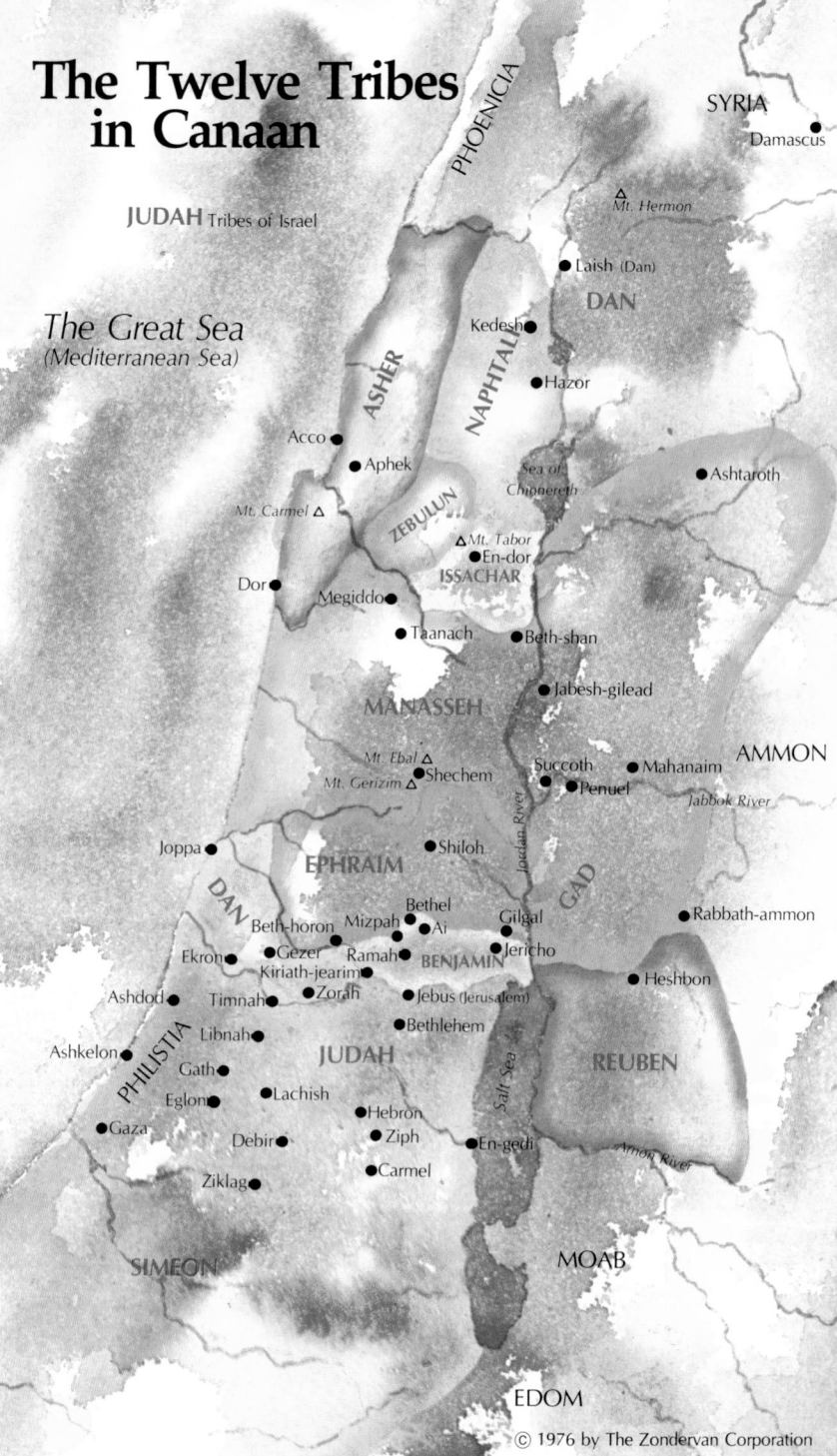

The Twelve Tribes in Canaan

SYRIA
Damascus

JUDAH Tribes of Israel

△ Mt. Hermon

The Great Sea
(Mediterranean Sea)

Laish (Dan)

DAN

Kedesh

ASHER

NAPHTALI

Hazor

Acco

Aphek

Sea of Chinnereth

Ashtaroth

△ Mt. Carmel

ZEBULUN

△ Mt. Tabor
En-dor

ISSACHAR

Dor

Megiddo

Taanach

Beth-shan

Jabesh-gilead

MANASSEH

AMMON

Mt. Ebal △
Mt. Gerizim △ Shechem

Succoth
Penuel

Mahanaim

Jabbok River

Joppa

EPHRAIM

Shiloh

Jordan River

GAD

Bethel

Beth-horon   Mizpah
Ekron   Ai   Gilgal
        Gezer   Ramah   Jericho
    Kiriath-jearim BENJAMIN

Rabbath-ammon

Ashdod   Timnah   Zorah
                              Jebus (Jerusalem)

Heshbon

Libnah

Ashkelon

Bethlehem

PHILISTIA

Gath

JUDAH

REUBEN

Eglon   Lachish
Gaza   Hebron
        Debir   Ziph

Salt Sea

En-gedi

Arnon River

Ziklag   Carmel

SIMEON

MOAB

EDON

© 1976 by The Zondervan Corporation

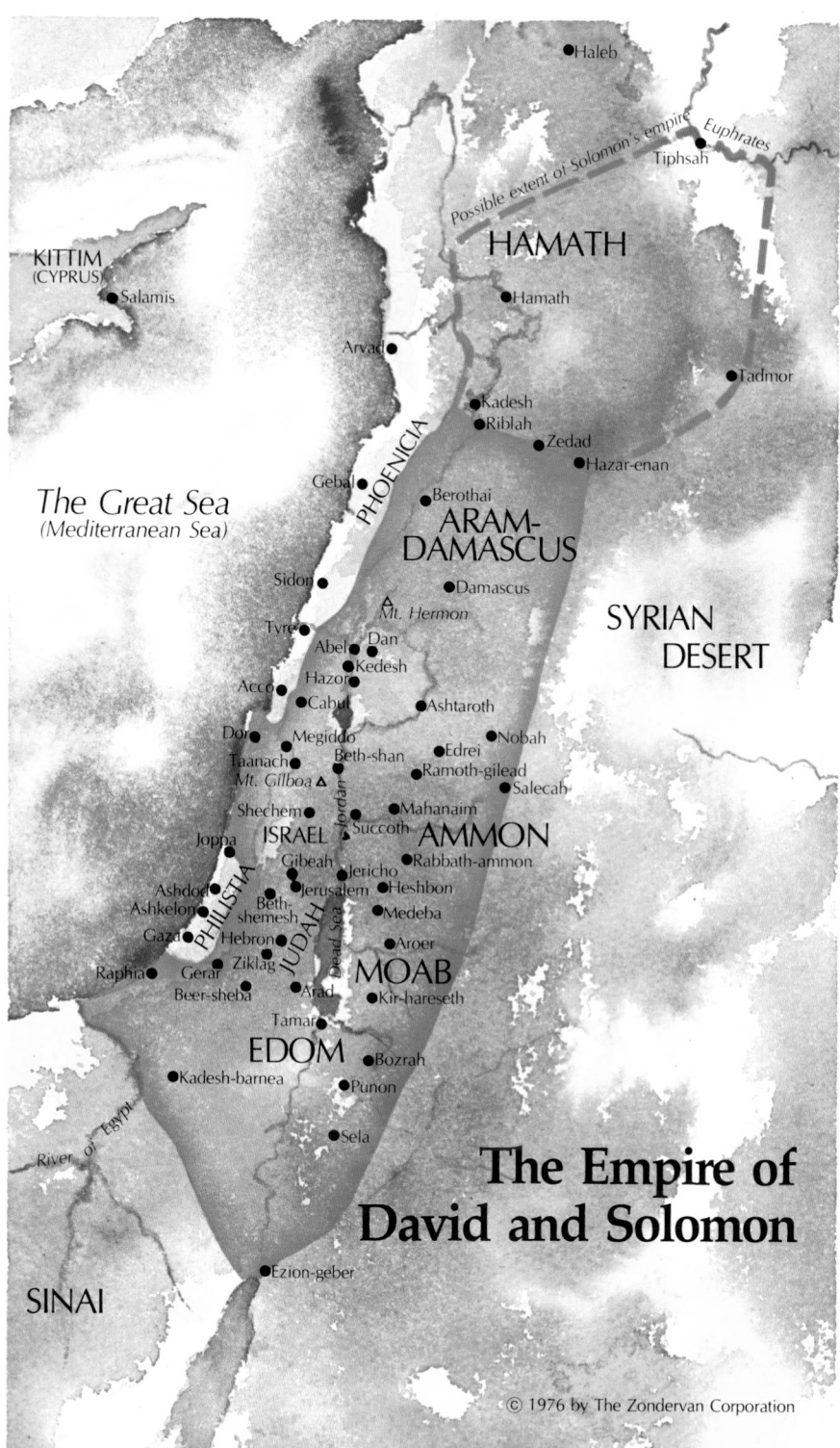

The Empire of David and Solomon

Jerusalem in David's Time

Temple

Palace?

Kidron Valley

Valley Gate

Gihon Spring

Present city walls

Expansion by Solomon

City of David

Valley of Hinnom

© 1976 by The Zondervan Corporation

Solomon's Temple

Storerooms

Pillar

Ark

Holy
of
Holies

Holy Place

Porch

Lampstands

Storerooms

Pillar

© 1976 by The Zondervan Corporation

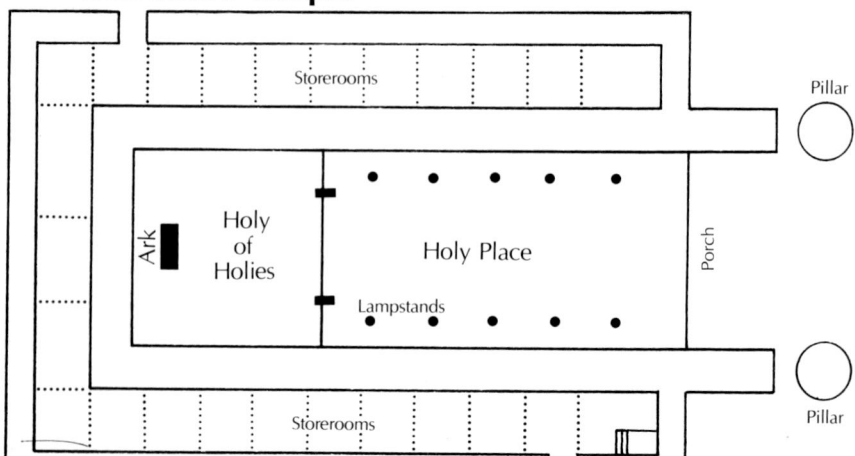

Sidon

PHOENICIA

Damascus

SYRIA

Tyre

Dan

The Great Sea
(Mediterranean Sea)

Hazor

Acco

Ashtaroth

Dor

Megiddo

Ramoth-gilead

Beth-shan

ISRAEL

Samaria
Shechem

Penuel

Jordan River

Rabbath-ammon

Joppa

AMMON

Gezer

PHILISTIA

Heshbon

Ashdod

Jerusalem

Ashkelon

Hebron

Salt Sea

Dibon

Gaza

JUDAH

Raphia

Arad

MOAB

Beer-sheba

Kir-moab

Tamar

EDOM

Kadesh-barnea

Bozrah

The Divided Kingdom

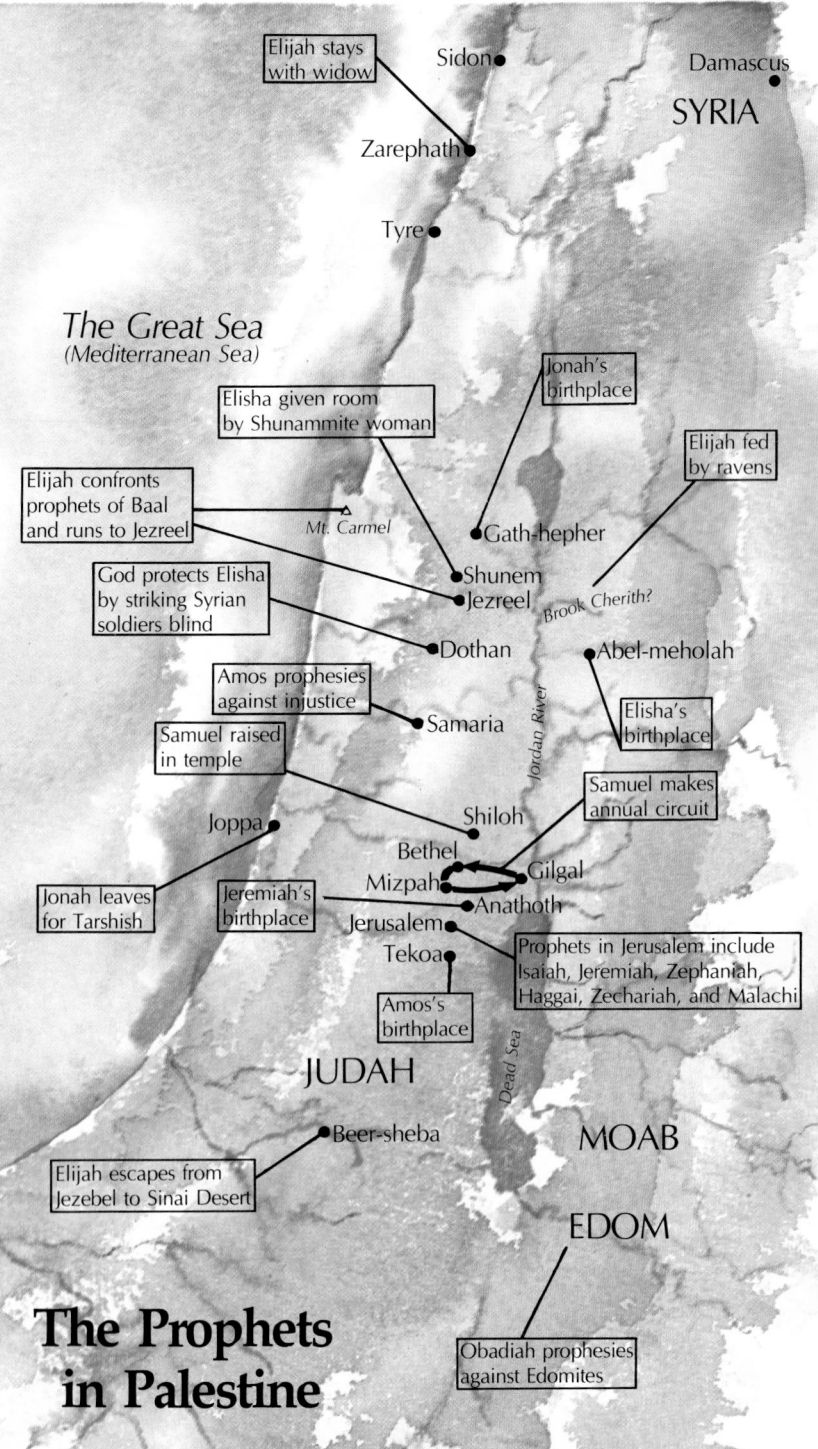

Sidon

Damascus

SYRIA

Elijah stays
with widow

Zarephath

Tyre

The Great Sea
(Mediterranean Sea)

Jonah's
birthplace

Elisha given room
by Shunammite woman

Elijah fed
by ravens

Elijah confronts
prophets of Baal
and runs to Jezreel

Mt. Carmel

Gath-hepher

God protects Elisha
by striking Syrian
soldiers blind

Shunem

Jezreel

Brook Cherith?

Abel-meholah

Amos prophesies
against injustice

Dothan

Elisha's
birthplace

Samuel raised
in temple

Samaria

Jordan River

Samuel makes
annual circuit

Shiloh

Joppa

Bethel

Gilgal

Jonah leaves
for Tarshish

Mizpah

Anathoth

Jeremiah's
birthplace

Jerusalem

Prophets in Jerusalem include
Isaiah, Jeremiah, Zephaniah,
Haggai, Zechariah, and Malachi

Tekoa

Amos's
birthplace

JUDAH

Dead Sea

Beer-sheba

MOAB

Elijah escapes from
Jezebel to Sinai Desert

EDOM

The Prophets
in Palestine

Obadiah prophesies
against Edomites

© 1976 by The Zondervan Corporation

The Route of the Exile

Deportation of Judah (586 B.C.)

Return from Exile under Shesh-bazzar (538 B.C.)

Return from Exile under Ezra and Nehemiah (457-445 B.C.)

© 1976 by The Zondervan Corporation

Susa

Nippur

Chebar River

Babylon

Tigris River

Arbela

Asshur

Euphrates River

Haran

Rezeph

Tadmor

Carchemish

Aleppo

Orontes River

Hamath

Riblah

Damascus

Samaria

Mizpah

Jerusalem

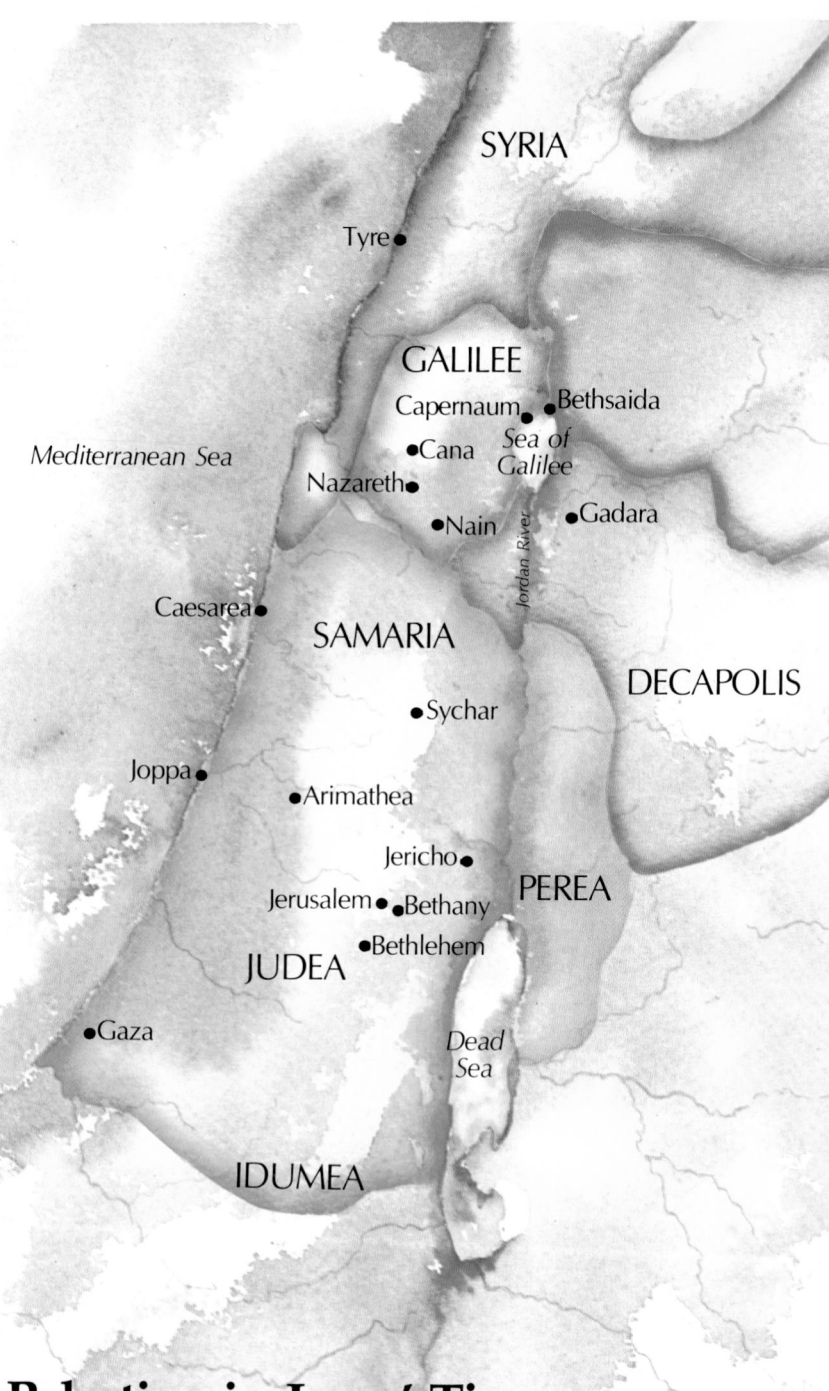

Palestine in Jesus' Time

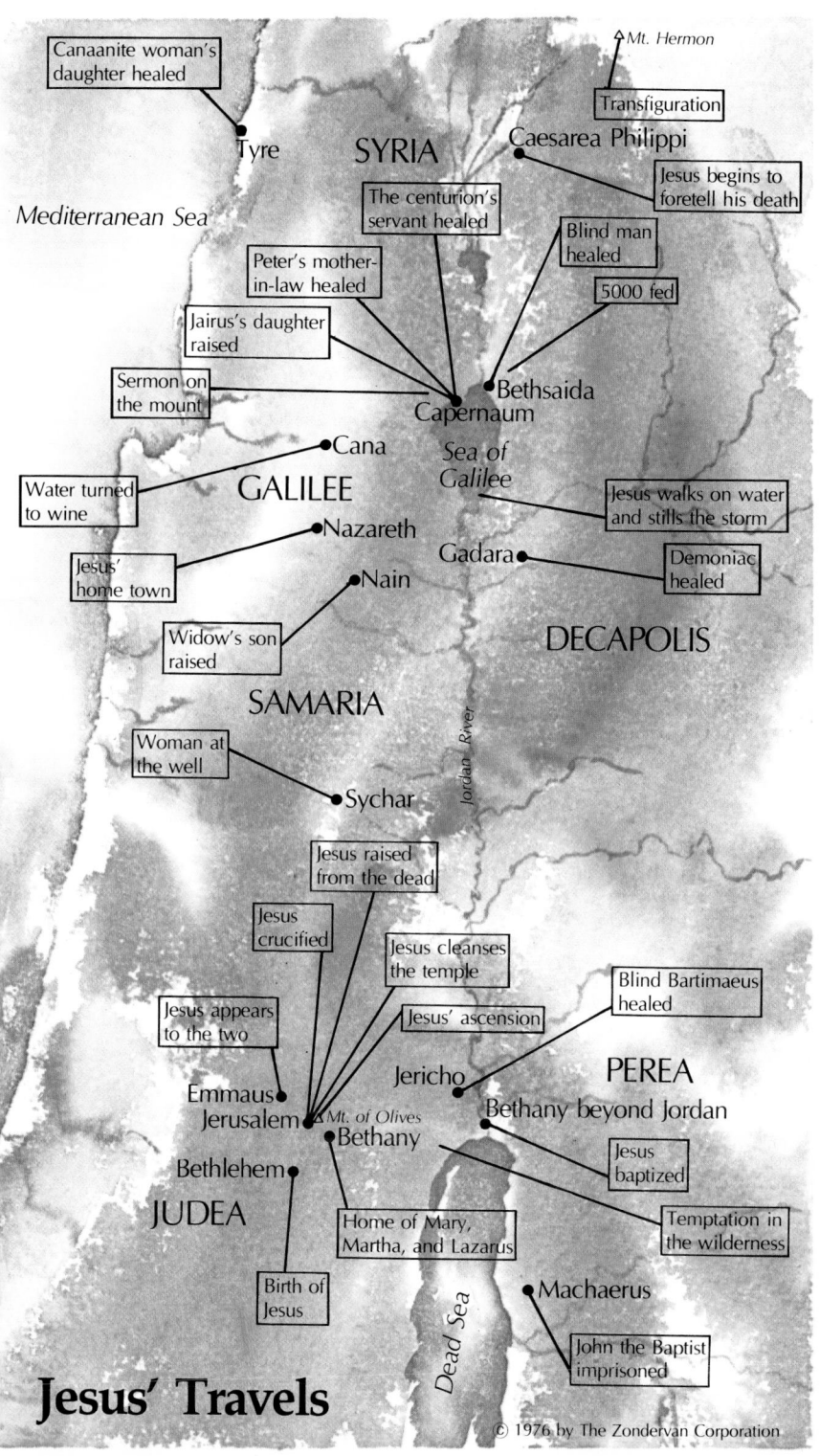

Canaanite woman's daughter healed

Mt. Hermon

Transfiguration

Caesarea Philippi

Jesus begins to foretell his death

Tyre

SYRIA

Mediterranean Sea

The centurion's servant healed

Blind man healed

5000 fed

Peter's mother-in-law healed

Jairus's daughter raised

Sermon on the mount

Bethsaida

Capernaum

Cana

Sea of Galilee

Water turned to wine

GALILEE

Jesus walks on water and stills the storm

Nazareth

Gadara

Demoniac healed

Jesus' home town

Nain

DECAPOLIS

Widow's son raised

SAMARIA

Jordan River

Woman at the well

Sychar

Jesus raised from the dead

Jesus crucified

Jesus cleanses the temple

Blind Bartimaeus healed

Jesus appears to the two

Jesus' ascension

Emmaus

Jericho

PEREA

Jerusalem

Mt. of Olives

Bethany beyond Jordan

Bethany

Bethlehem

Jesus baptized

JUDEA

Home of Mary, Martha, and Lazarus

Temptation in the wilderness

Birth of Jesus

Machaerus

Dead Sea

John the Baptist imprisoned

Jesus' Travels

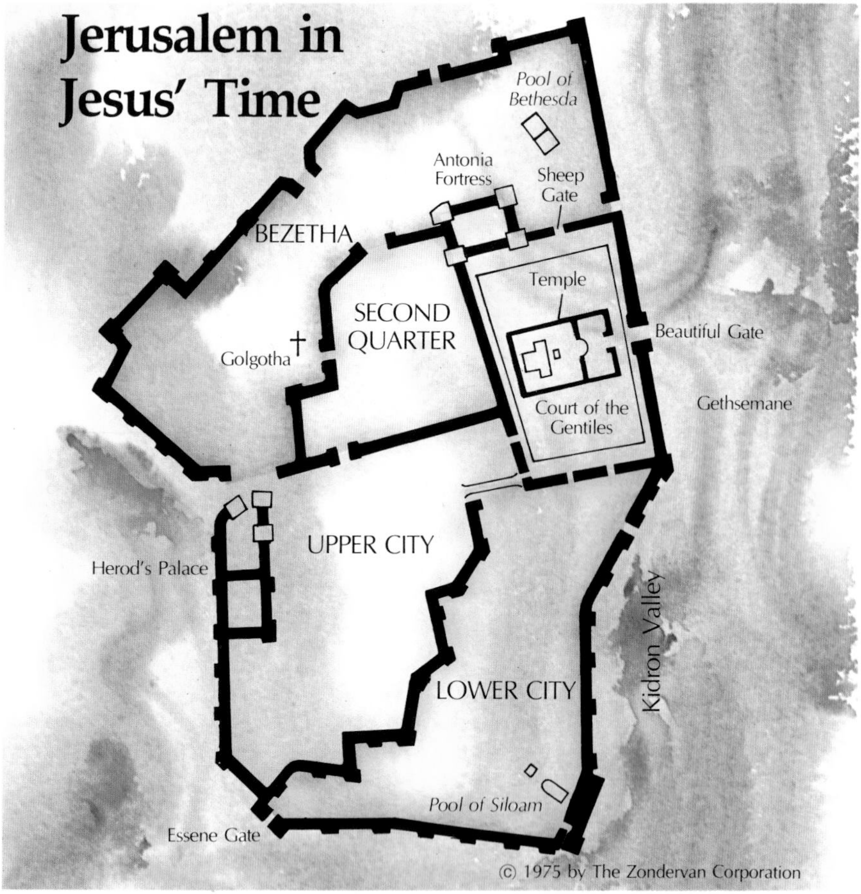

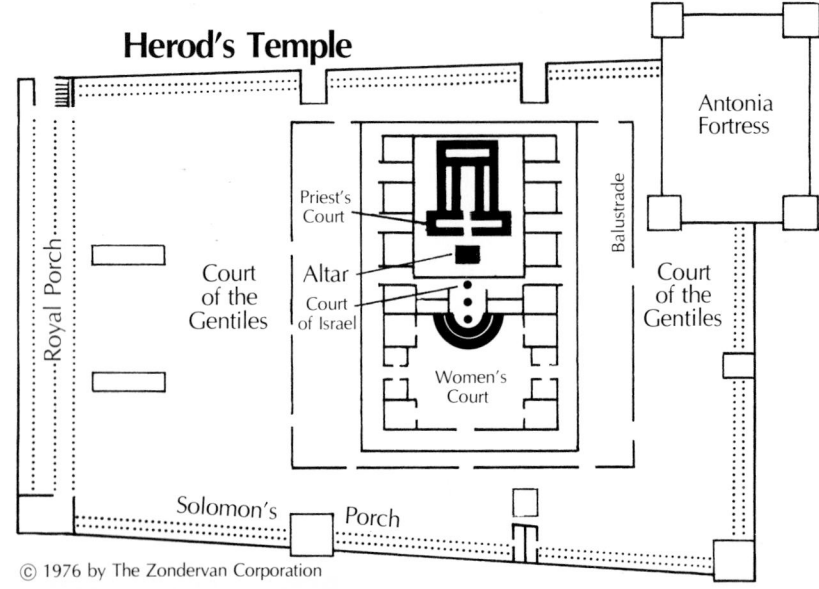

Jerusalem in Jesus' Time

Pool of Bethesda

Antonia Fortress

Sheep Gate

BEZETHA

Temple

Beautiful Gate

Golgotha

SECOND QUARTER

Court of the Gentiles

Gethsemane

Herod's Palace

UPPER CITY

Kidron Valley

LOWER CITY

Pool of Siloam

Essene Gate

© 1975 by The Zondervan Corporation

Herod's Temple

Antonia Fortress

Royal Porch

Court of the Gentiles

Priest's Court

Altar

Court of Israel

Women's Court

Balustrade

Court of the Gentiles

Solomon's Porch

© 1976 by The Zondervan Corporation

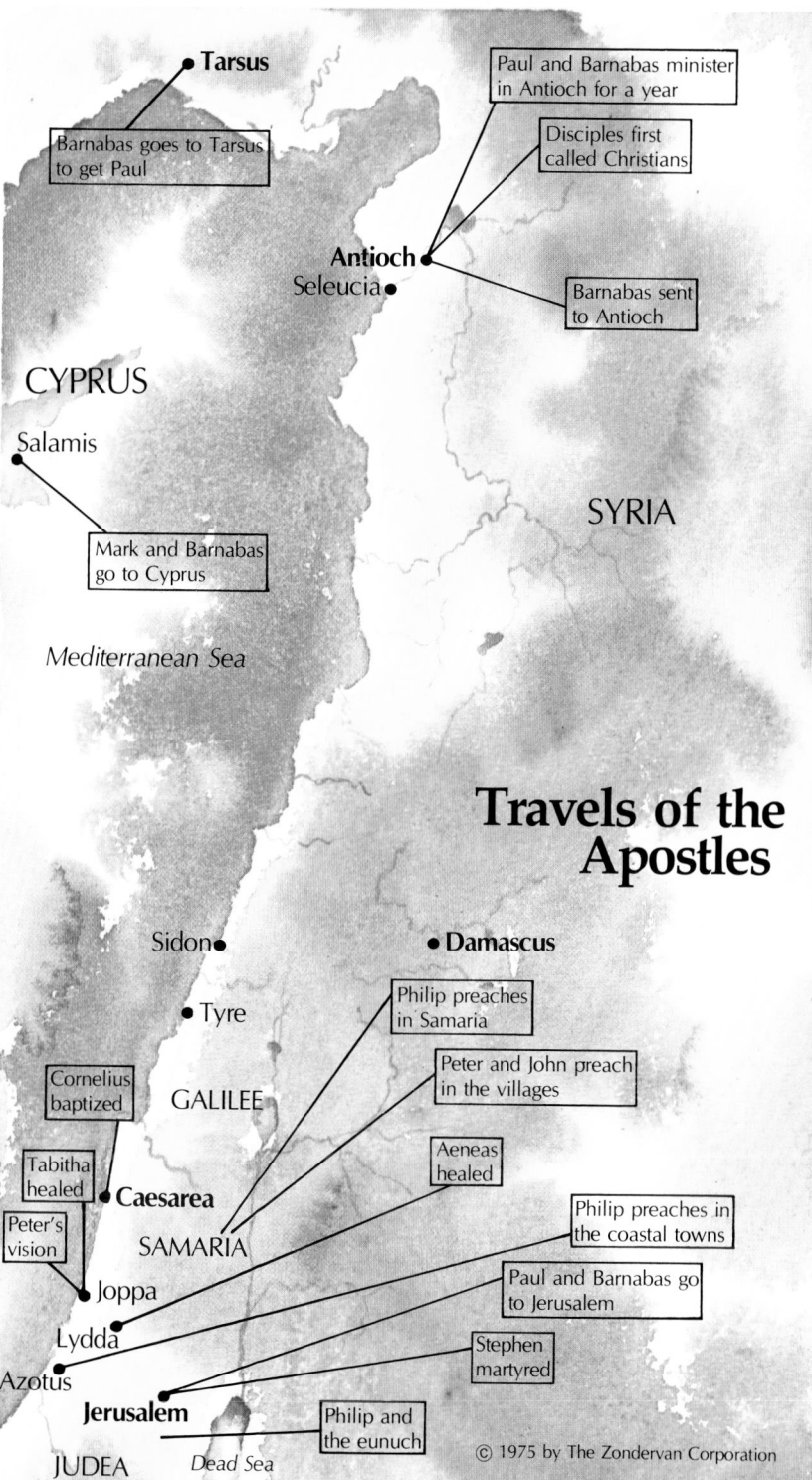

Tarsus

Barnabas goes to Tarsus to get Paul

Paul and Barnabas minister in Antioch for a year

Disciples first called Christians

Antioch
Seleucia

Barnabas sent to Antioch

CYPRUS

Salamis

Mark and Barnabas go to Cyprus

Mediterranean Sea

SYRIA

Travels of the Apostles

Sidon

Damascus

Tyre

Philip preaches in Samaria

Peter and John preach in the villages

Cornelius baptized

GALILEE

Aeneas healed

Tabitha healed

Caesarea

SAMARIA

Philip preaches in the coastal towns

Peter's vision

Joppa

Paul and Barnabas go to Jerusalem

Lydda

Stephen martyred

Azotus

Jerusalem

Philip and the eunuch

JUDEA   *Dead Sea*

© 1975 by The Zondervan Corporation

Paul's Missionary Journeys

Paul's first missionary journey
Paul's second missionary journey
Paul's third missionary journey
Paul's journey to Rome

Black Sea

Mediterranean Sea

Mysia

GALATIA

CAPPADOCIA

Troas

Mitylene

ASIA

Lydia

Phrygia

Antioch

Iconium

Lystra

Derbe

Antioch

Ephesus

Colosse

Miletus

Perga

Attalia

Seleucia

COS

Cnidus

Patara

Myra

CYPRUS

Salamis

RHODES

Paphos

Sidon

Tyre

Ptolemais

Caesarea

Jerusalem

Judea

EGYPT

polis

lis

THRACE

CHIOS

© 1975 by The Zondervan Corporation

The Roman Empire

BRITAIN

GERMANY

GAUL

Atlantic Ocean

SPAIN

ITALY

Rome•

MAURETANIA

ILLYRICUM

MACEDONIA

ACHAIA

AFRICA

Mediterranean Sea

DACIA

THRACE

Black Sea

ASIA

CAPPADOCIA

ARMENIA

MACEDONIA

SYRIA

MESOPOTAMIA

PARTHIA

ARABIA

•Jerusalem

•Alexandria

EGYPT

Red Sea

9014